REFERENCE ENCYCLOPEDIA OF THE AMERICAN INDIAN

REFERENCE ENCYCLOPEDIA

OF THE
AMERICAN INDIAN

7th Edition

BARRY T. KLEIN

Published by:
Todd Publications
P.O. Box 301
West Nyack, NY 10994
(914) 358-6213

REFERENCE ENCYCLOPEDIA OF THE AMERICAN INDIAN

7th Edition

Copyright © 1995

TODD PUBLICATIONS

ISBN 0-915344-45-9 (hardcover)
ISBN 0-915344-46-7 (softcover)

Contents

Contents (CONT'D)

Section Two
Canadian Section

Section Three
Bibliography

Section Four
Biographies

Introduction

According to figures released by the U.S. Census Bureau, there are approximately 2,000,000 American Indians, Eskimos and Aleuts in the United States. The most populous states in terms of Indians is California with approximately 250,000, Oklahoma, 200,000, Arizona, 200,000, and New Mexico, 150,000; Alaska has more than 75,000 Eskimos and Aleuts. Population figures have been increasing at a rate of more than 70% per decade since 1960. There is no one Federal or tribal definition that establishes a person's identity as Indian. Government Agencies use different criteria for determining who is an Indian. Similarly, tribal groups have varying requirements for determining tribal membership.

There are approximately 300 Federal Indian reservations and 500 federally recognized tribes in the United States including about 200 Alaska Native village groups. An Indian reservation is an area of land reserved for Indian use. The name comes from the early days of Indian-white relations when Indian tribes relinquished land through treaties, reserving a portion for their own use. Congressional acts, Executive orders, and agreements have also created reservations. Many reservations today, however, have some non-Indian residents and non-Indian landowners. Tribe among the North American Indians originally meant a body of persons bound together by blood ties who were socially, politically, and religiously organized, and who lived together, occupying a definite territory and speaking a common language or dialect. With the relegation of Indians to reservations, the word tribe developed a number of different meanings. Today, it can be a distinct group within an Indian village or community, a large number of communities, several different groups or villages speaking different languages but sharing a common government, or a widely scattered number of villages with a common language but no common government. According to a 1990 estimate of the Bureau of Indian Affairs, about 800,000 Indians live on or adjacent to reservations. The remaining 1,200,000 American Indians reside in cities and suburbs across the country.

A special U.S. Senate committee charged with investigating fraud and mismanagement in the Bureau of Indian Affairs has recommended adoption of what it calls *"A New Federalism,"* in which the federal government would abolish the BIA and transfer annual federal appropriations directly to tribal governments. The committee said new agreements are needed between the federal governments and the tribes "that both allow American Indians to run their own affairs and pledge permanent federal support for tribal governments." These new agreements would not affect any existing treaty rights or alter the legal status of tribal governments. An Office of Federal-Tribal Relations (OFTR) would be created within the executive office of the President. The OFTR would be responsible for negotiating and overseeing implementation of formal agreements with federally recognized Indian tribes. "The agreements will allow any tribe that so chooses to exit the current bureaucracy of federal Indian programs and to receive and use at its own discretion a proportional share of the federal Indian budget." The committee proposes that funding be allocated to tribal governments based solely on population figures. The special committee also recommended that each House of Congress create a permanent full committee on Indian affairs, with additional staff specifically assigned to perform oversight and investigations.

The U.S., upon ratification of an agreement by both a tribe and the federal government, would provide the tribe with an annual Tribal Self-Governance Grant (TSGG), equalling its fair share of the current federal Indian budget. The size of the grant would be proportional to the population base of the tribe. Each grant would be supplemented by an annual cost-of-living allowance. Equally important, there would be a transfer from the BIA and Indian Health Service and any other federal agency with Indian-related programs to the contracting tribes, such assets as necessary for the tribe to carry out their new responsibilities under the agreement.

This 7th Edition of *Reference Encyclopedia of the American Indian* is divided into four main sections. The *first section* contains source listings. Three new chapters have been added to this section: Indian Education Programs in the public schools, Casinos & Bingo Halls (tribally owned), and Native American Events (powwows, Indian Days, etc.). Each listing gives address, phone number, chief personnel and, in most cases, a brief description of activities and pertinent information. Listings are arranged either alphabetically or alpha-geographically . At the beginning of each section there is an explanatory note detailing the type of sources listed and the manner in which they are arranged. The length of each listing reflects the amount of material received from each source. Material has been researched directly from questionnaires or has been gathered from other reliable sources. For further information on any listed source, it is suggested that the reader write to the address or call the number given in the listing. The *second section* is solely Canadian listings; the *third section* of the book is a bibliography of approximately 4,500 in-print books. Listed alphabetically, each book gives basic bibliographic information. The alphabetical section is broken down into a subject categories section with corresponding titles listed for each category. A publishers index is provided at the end giving the publishers' addresses and phone numbers. The *fourth section* contains approximately 2,500 biographical sketches of prominent Native Americans prominent in Indian Affairs, business, the arts and professions, as well as non-Indians active in Indian affairs, history, art, anthropology, archaeology, etc., and the many fields to which the subject of the American Indian is related.

Barry Klein
Compiler & Editor

P.S.   All changes and additions to the listings in this book should be directed to me at the address given at the bottom of the title page.

REFERENCE ENCYCLOPEDIA OF THE AMERICAN INDIAN

Listed in this section are reservation tribal councils, organizations, and governing bodies, which handle tribal and/or reservation affairs and which represent the tribes and create policy on land, enrollment, etc. Listings are arranged alphabetically within states.

Approximately 520 Indian communities are officially recognized by the U.S. government. These communities are entitled to U.S. legal protections of tribal self-government and rights to tribally owned land. There are also about 150 non-recognized Indian communities who have not signed treaties or have not had regular legal relations with the U.S. government.

The U.S. Dept. of the Interior, Bureau of Indian Affairs (BIA) is the agency that identifies and recognizes Indian tribal entities for establishing and maintaining federal government to government relations with Indians. Those tribes, bands and groups that have been recognized by the BIA are listed below, with the agency or area office (of the BIA) of jurisdiction indicated for each listing.

ALABAMA

MOWA BAND OF CHOCTAW INDIANS
Route 1, Box 330-A, Reservation Rd.
Mt. Vernon, AL 36560
(205) 829-5500 Fax 829-5580
Framon Weaver, Chief
Tribe: Choctaw. *In Residence*: 3,715. *Acreage*: 300. *Geographic Boundaries*: North Mobile County & South Washington County. *Special programs*: Pow wows; Mowa Choctaw Dancers; operates two Indian schools. *Tribal Council*: Framon Weaver, Verma Reed, Kesler Weaver, Prentiss Taylor, Sebron Weaver, Natalie Bruner, Duggar Lofton, Johnny Weaver, Darren Snow, George Snow. *Reservation served*: Choctaw Indian Reservation. *Population served*: 3,715. Choctaw Agency.

POARCH BAND OF CREEK INDIANS
HCR69A, Box 85-B, Atmore, AL 36502
(205) 368-9136 Fax 368-4502
Eddie Tullis, Chairperson
Tribe served: Creek. Choctaw Agency.

ALASKA

NATIVE VILLAGE OF AFOGNAK
P.O. Box 1277, Kodiak, AK 99615

NATIVE VILLAGE OF AKHIOK
P.O. Box 5030, Akhiok, AK 99615
(907) 836-2229
Nick Peterson, Sr., President
Tribe: Eskimo. *In residence*: 90.
Anchorage Agency.

AKIACHAK NATIVE COMMUNITY
P.O. Box 70, Akiachak, AK 99551
(907) 825-4626 Fax 825-4029
Willie Kasayulie, President
Phillip K. Peter, Sr., Vice Chairperson
Fritz George, Secretary/Treasurer
Tribe: Yup'ik Eskimo. *In residence*: 500. *Area*: 115,600 acres. Cooperatively manage community library with the school district. Bethel Agency.

AKIAK NATIVE COMMUNITY
P.O. Box 52165, Akiak, AK 99552
(907) 765-7112/7426
Owen Ivan, President
Tribe: Eskimo. *In residence*: 225. Bethel Agency.

NATIVE VILLAGE OF AKUTAN
P.O. Box 89, Akutan, AK 99553
(907) 698-2301
Jacob Stepetin, President
Anchorage Agency.

VILLAGE OF ALAKANUK
P.O. Box 167, Alakanuk, AK 99554
(907) 238-3313
Raymond D. Oney, President
Bethel Agency.

ALATNA VILLAGE
General Delivery, Alatna, AK 99720
(907) 968-2241
Gerald Sam, Chief
Fairbanks Agency.

NATIVE VILLAGE OF ALEKNAGIK
P.O. Box 115, Aleknagik, AK 99555
(907) 842-2229
Raymond Conquest, President
Tribe: Athapascan. *In residence*: 175.
Anchorage Agency.

NATIVE VILLAGE OF ALGAACIQ
P.O. Box 48, St. Mary's, AK 99658
(907) 438-2932
Moses Paukan, Sr., President
Tribe: Eskimo. *In residence*: 125. Bethel Agency.

ALLAKAKET COMMUNITY
P.O. Box 30, Allakaket, AK 99720
(907) 968-2241
Gilbert Vent, First Chief
Tribe: Athapascan. *In residence*: 120.
Fairbanks Agency.

NATIVE VILLAGE OF AMBLER
P.O. Box 47, Ambler, AK 99786
(907) 445-2181
Louie Commack, Jr., President
Nome Agency.

VILLAGE OF ANAKTUVUK PASS
General Delivery, Anaktuvuk Pass, AK 99721
(907) 661-3113
Raymond Paneak, President
Tribe: Eskimo. *In residence*: 100.
Fairbanks Agency.

ANDREAFSKI TRIBAL COUNCIL
P.O. Box 368, St. Mary's, AK 99658
(907) 438-2312 Fax 438-2512
George Beans, Sr., President
John Elia, Jr., Vice Chief
Tribe: Andreafski. *Membership*:150. *Publication*: Andreafsky Tribal Newsletter. *Activities*: Monthly meetings. Bethel Agency.

ANGOON COMMUNITY ASSOCIATION
P.O. Box 188, Angoon, AK 99820
(907) 788-3441/3994
Wally Frank, President
Juneau Area Office.

VILLAGE OF ANIAK
P.O. Box 176, Aniak, AK 99557
(907) 675-4349
Ruth B. Vaska, President
Tribe: Eskimo. *In residence*: 150. Bethel Agency.

ANVIK VILLAGE
General Delivery, Anvik, AK 99558
(907) 663-6335
Ken Chase, Chief
Tribe: Eskimo. *In residence*: 150. Bethel Agency.

VILLAGE ARCTIC VILLAGE
P.O. Box 22050, Arctic Village, AK 99722
(907) 587-5320
Tribble Gilbert, Chief
Tribe: Athapascan. Fairbanks Agency.

NATIVE VILLAGE OF ATKA
P.O. Box 47030, Atka, AK 99574
(907) 767-8001
Raymond Goldoff, President
Anchorage Agency.

VILLAGE OF ATMAUTLUAK
P.O. Box ATT, Atmautluak, AK 99559
(907) 553-5610
Oscar Nick, President
Bethel Agency.

ATQASUK VILLAGE
General Delivery, Atkasuk, AK 99723
Jimmy Nayukok, President
Fairbanks Agency.

AUKQUAN TRADITIONAL COUNCIL
9296 Stephen Richards Memorial Dr.
Juneau, AK 99801
(907) 465-4120
Albert Wallace, Chief
Juneau Area Office.

NATIVE VILLAGE OF BARROW
P.O. Box 1139, Barrow, AK 99723
(907) 852-4411/2293/2611
Arnold J. Brower, Jr., President
Tribe: Eskimo. *In residence*: 3,000.
Fairbanks Agency.

BEAVER VILLAGE
P.O. Box 24029, Beaver, AK 99724
(907) 628-6126
Arlene Pitka, Chief
Tribes: Eskimo, Athapascan, Indian.
In residence: 150. Fairbanks Agency.

NATIVE VILLAGE OF BELKOFSKY
P.O. Box 57, King Cove, AK 99612
(907) 497-2304
Simeon Kuzchikin, President
Tribe: Aleut. *In residence*: 200. Anchorage Agency.

NATIVE VILLAGE OF BILL MOORE'S SLOUGH
P.O. Box 20037, Kotlik, AK 99620
(907) 899-4712
Mark Okitkun, Tribal Chairperson
Bethel Agency.

BIRCH CREEK VILLAGE COUNCIL
P.O. Box KBC, Fort Yukon, AK 99740
(907) 221-9133
Randall Baalam, First Chief
Fairbanks Agency.

NATIVE VILLAGE OF BREVIG MISSION
General Delivery, Brevig Mission, AK 99785
(907) 642-3851
Elmer Seetot, President
Nome Agency.

NATIVE VILLAGE OF BUCKLAND
P.O. Box 67, Buckland, AK 99727
(907) 494-2171

Percy Ballot, President
Nome Agency.

NATIVE VILLAGE OF CANTWELL
P.O. Box 94, Cantwell, AK 99729
 (907) 768-2151
 David Nicklie, President
Tribe: Athapascan. Anchorage Agency.

**CENTRAL COUNCIL OF THE TLINGIT
& HAIDA INDIAN TRIBES OF ALASKA**
320 W. Willoughby Ave. # 300
Juneau, AK 99801
 (907) 586-1432
 Edward K. Thomas, President
Fairbanks Agency.

CHALKYITSIK VILLAGE
P.O. Box 57, Chalkyitsik, AK 99788
 (907) 848-8893
 James Nathaniel, Sr., First Chief
Fairbanks Agency.

NATIVE VILLAGE OF CHANEGA
P.O. Box 8079, Chenega Bay, AK 99574
 (907) 573-5132
 Larry Evanoff, President
Anchorage Agency.

VILLAGE OF CHEFORNAK
P.O. Box 29, Chefornak, AK 99561
 (907) 867-8850 Fax 867-8429
 Steven Billy, President
Tribe: Eskimo. *In residence*: 175.
Bethel Agency.

CHEVAK NATIVE VILLAGE
P.O. Box 5514, Chevak, AK 99563
 (907) 858-7428/7711 Fax 858-7812
 James Ayuluk, President
Tribe: Eskimo. *In residence*: 400.
Bethel Agency.

NATIVE VILLAGE OF CHICKALOON
P.O. Box 1105, Chickaloon, AK 99674
 (907) 746-0505
 Alan Larson, President
 David Harrison, Tribal Administrator
Maintains school. *Publication*: "Traditional Stories
About Values" by Katherine Wade. Anchorage
Agency.

NATIVE VILLAGE OF CHIGNIK
P.O. Box 11, Chignik Lake, AK 99563
 (907) 749-2285
 George Tinker, President
Tribe: Eskimo. *In residence*: 385.
Anchorage Agency.

NATIVE VILLAGE OF CHIGNIK LAGOON
P.O. Box 57, Chignik Lagoon, AK 99565
 (907) 840-2206
 Rodney Anderson, President
Tribe: Eskimo. Anchorage Agency.

NATIVE VILLAGE OF CHIGNIK LAKE
P.O. Box 33, Chignik Lake, AK 99548
 (907) 845-2212
 John Lina, President
Tribe: Eskimo. Anchorage Agency.

CHILKAT INDIAN VILLAGE OF KLUKWAN
P.O. Box 210, Haines, AK 99827
 (907) 767-5505 Fax 767-5515
 Joe Hotch, President
Juneau Area Office.

CHILKOOT INDIAN ASSOCIATION OF HAINES
P.O. Box 490, Haines, AK 99827
 (907) 766-2310/2299
 Charles Paddock, President
Tribe: Chilkoot. Juneau Area Office.

CHINIK ESKIMO COMMUNITY (aka Golovin)
P.O. Box 62020, Golovin, AK 99762
 (907) 779-3521 Fax 779-3261
 Tonsashay Esparza, President
Tribe: Eskimo. *In residence*: 140.
Nome Agency.

NATIVE VILLAGE OF CHISTOCHINA
P.O. Box 241, Gakona, AK 99586
 (907) 822-3503
 Karen Eskilida, President
Tribe: Athapascan. Anchorage Agency.

NATIVE VILLAGE OF CHITINA
P.O. Box 31, Chitina, AK 99566
 (907) 563-6643
 Harry Billum, President
Anchorage Agency.

NATIVE VILLAGE OF CHUATHBALUK
P.O. Box 31, Chuathbaluk, AK 99557
 (907) 467-4313
 Sophie Sakar, Chief
Bethel Agency.

NATIVE VILLAGE OF CHULOONAWICK
General Delivery, Chuloonawick, AK 99581
 (907) 949-1147
 Russ Akers, President
Bethel Agency.

CIRCLE NATIVE COMMUNITY
General Delivery, Circle, AK 99733
 (907) 733-5498
 Allen John, Chief
Tribe: Athapascan. *In residence*: 115.
Fairbanks Agency.

NATIVE VILLAGE OF CLARK'S POINT
P.O. Box 16, Clark's Point, AK 99569
 (907) 236-1221
 Joseph Clark, President
Anchorage Agency.

COOK INLET TRIBAL COUNCIL
670 W. Fireweed Lane, Anchorage, AK 99503
 (907) 276-3343
 Lisa Dolchok, Director
Head Start Program.

CRAIG COMMUNITY ASSOCIATION
P.O. Box 828, Craig, AK 99821
 (907) 826-3321 Fax 826-3980
 Ralph Mackie, Vice President
Juneau Area Office.

NATIVE VILLAGE OF CROOKED CREEK
P.O. Box 69, Crooked Creek, AK 99575
 (907) 432-2227
 Johnnie John, Jr., President
Tribe: Athapascan. Bethel Agency.

NATIVE VILLAGE OF DEERING
P.O. Box 89, Deering, AK 99736
 (907) 363-2145
 Wilbur Karmun, Sr., President
Tribe: Eskimo. *In residence*: 250. Nome Agency.

DILLINGHAM VILLAGE COUNCIL
P.O. Box 216, Dillingham, AK 99576
 (907) 842-2384

Ida Roehl, President
Tribes: Athapascan and Indian. *In residence*: 450.
Anchorage Agency.

NATIVE VILLAGE OF DIOMEDE (aka Inalik)
P.O. Box 7099, Diomede, AK 99762
 (907) 686-3021 Fax 686-2181
 Orville Ahkinga, President
Nome Agency.

VILLAGE OF DOT LAKE
P.O. Box 2272, Dot Lake, AK 99737
 (907) 882-2669 Fax 882-2112
 William Miller, President
Fairbanks Agency.

DOUGLAS INDIAN ASSOCIATION
P.O. Box 020478, Juneau, AK 99802
 (907) 586-1798
 Amos Wallace, President
Juneau Area Office.

VILLAGE OF EAGLE
P.O. Box 19, Eagle, AK 99738
 (907) 547-2271
 David Howard, First Chief
Tribes: Eskimo & Indian. Fairbanks Agency.

NATIVE VILLAGE OF EEK
P.O. Box 87, Eek, AK 99578
 (907) 536-5426
 Fritz Willie, President
Tribe: Eskimo. *In residence*: 190.
Bethel Agency.

EGEGIK VILLAGE COUNCIL
P.O. Box 29, Egegik, AK 99579
 (907) 233-2211
 Richard Deigh, President
Tribes: Eskimo & Indian. *In residence*: 140.
Anchorage Agency.

EKLUTNA NATIVE VILLAGE
26339 Eklutna Village Rd.,
Chugiak, AK 99567
 (907) 688-6020 Fax 688-6021
 George Ondola, President
Tribe: Athapascan. Anchorage Agency.

NATIVE VILLAGE OF EKUK
P.O. Box 1409, Ekuk, AK 99576
 (907) 842-1053
 Robert Heyano, President
Anchorage Agency.

EKWOK VILLAGE COUNCIL
P.O. Box 70, Ekwok, AK 99580
 (907) 464-3311
 Peter Walcott, Sr., President
Anchorage Agency.

NATIVE VILLAGE OF ELIM
P.O. Box 39070, Elim, AK 99739
 (907) 890-3741 Fax 890-3072
 Luther Nagaruk, President
Tribe: Eskimo. *In residence*: 225.
Nome Agency.

EMMONAK VILLAGE
General Delivery, Emmonak, AK 99581
 (907) 949-1720 Fax 949-1926
 Billy A. Charles, President
Bethel Agency.

EVANSVILLE VILLAGE
P.O. Box 26025, Evansville, AK 99726
 (907) 692-5467

Rhonda Musser, Clerk
Tribes: Eskimo and Indian. *In residence:* 65.
Fairbanks Agency.

NATIVE VILLAGE OF EYAK
P.O. Box 1388, Cordova, AK 99574
(907) 424-3622/7739
Ruth Hansen, President
Anchorage Agency.

NATIVE VILLAGE OF FALSE PASS
P.O. Box 29, False Pass, AK 99583
(907) 548-2227 Fax 548-2214
Gilda Shellikoff, Vice President
Anchorage Agency.

NATIVE VILLAGE OF FORT YUKON
P.O. Box 126, Fort Yukon, AK 99740
(907) 662-2581 Fax 662-2222
Clarence L. Alexander, Chief
Tribes: Athapascan & Indian. *In residence:* 600.
Fairbanks Agency.

NATIVE VILLAGE OF GAKONA
P.O. Box 124, Gakona, AK 99586
(907) 822-3497
David Gene, President
Anchorage Agency.

GALENA VILLAGE
P.O. Box 182, Galena, AK 99741
(907) 656-1666
Paddy Nollner, Chief
Tribe: Athapascan. *In residence:* 175.
Fairbanks Agency.

NATIVE VILLAGE OF GAMBELL
P.O. Box 99, Gambell, AK 99742
(907) 985-5346 Fax 985-5520
Gerrard Koonooka, President
Nome Agency.

NATIVE VILLAGE OF GEORGETOWN
General Delivery, Georgetown, AK
Glen Fredericks, President
Bethel Agency.

NATIVE VILLAGE OF GOODNEWS BAY
P.O. Box 3, Goodnews Bay, AK 99589
(907) 697-8629
James M. Smith, President
Bethel Agency.

ORGANIZED VILLAGE OF GRAYLING
(aka HOLIKACHU)
General Delivery, Grayling, AK 99590
(907) 967-8929
Henry Deacon, President
Fairbanks Agency.

GULKANA VILLAGE COUNCIL
P.O. Box 254, Gakona, AK 99586
(907) 822-3746
Eileen L. Ewan, President
Tribe: Athapascan. Anchorage Agency.

NATIVE VILLAGE OF HAMILTON
P.O. Box 20130, Koatlik, AK 99620
(907) 899-4313 Fax 899-4826
Willie Kamkoff, President
Bethel Agency.

HEALY LAKE VILLAGE
P.O. Box 667, Delta Junction, AK 99737
(907) 452-7915
Fred Kirsteatter, President
Fairbanks Agency.

HOLY CROSS VILLAGE
P.O. Box 203, Holy Cross, AK 99602
(907) 476-7134
Stan Peters, Chief
Tribes: Eskimo and Athapascan. *In residence:* 220.
Fairbanks Agency.

HOONAH INDIAN ASSOCIATION
P.O. Box 602, Hoonah, AK 99829
(907) 945-3220 Fax 945-3445
Kenneth Grant, President
Juneau Area Office.

NATIVE VILLAGE OF HOOPER BAY
P.O. Box 2193, Hooper Bay, AK 99604
(907) 758-4915 Fax 758-4815
Joseph Smart, President
Tribe: Eskimo. *In residence:* 450.
Bethel Agency.

HUGHES VILLAGE
P.O. Box 45010, Hughes, AK 99745
(907) 899-2206
Gerald Oldman, Chief
Tribe: Athapascan. Fairbanks Agency.

HUSLIA VILLAGE COUNCIL
P.O. Box 32, Huslia, AK 99746
(907) 829-2202 Fax 829-2214
Warner Vent, Sr., Chief
Tribe served: Huslia Athabascan. *Activities:* Owns
and operates Athabasca Cultural Journeys, tourism project located at P.O. Box 10, Huslia, AK
99746 (800) 423-0094 Fax (907) 452-8148.
Fairbanks Agency.

HYDABURG COOPERATIVE ASSOCIATION
P.O. Box 323, Hydaburg, AK 99922
(907) 285-3666 Fax 285-3944
Viola Burgess, President
Juneau Area Office.

IGIUGIG VILLAGE CENTER
P.O. Box 4008, Iguigig, AK 99613
(907) 533-3211
Trefim Andrew, President
Anchorage Agency.

NATIVE VILLAGE OF ILIAMNA
P.O. Box 286, Iliamna, AK 99606
(907) 571-1246
Harvey Anelon, President
Tribes: Athapascan and Indian.
Anchorage Agency.

INUPIAT COMMUNITY OF THE ARCTIC SLOPE
P.O. Box 1232, Barrow, AK 99723
(907) 825-6907
George Edwardson, President
Fairbanks Agency.

IVANOFF BAY VILLAGE
P.O. Box K1B, Ivanoff Bay, AK 99502
(907) 699-2204
Archie Kalmakoff, President
Anchorage Agency.

ORGANIZED VILLAGE OF KAKE
P.O. Box 316, Kake, AK 99830
(907) 785-6471 Fax 785-4902
Henrich Kadake, President
Juneau Area Office.

KAKTOVIK VILLAGE
P.O. Box 8, Kaktovik, AK 99747
Archie Brower, President
Fairbanks Agency.

NATIVE VILLAGE OF KALSKAG
General Delivery, Kalskag, AK 99607
(907) 471-2248
Annie Lou Williams, President
Tribe: Eskimo. *In residence:* 225.
Bethel Agency.

NATIVE VILLAGE OF KALTAG
P.O. Box 9, Kaltag, AK 99748
(907) 534-2230
Franklin Madros, Sr., Chief
Nome Agency.

NATIVE VILLAGE OF KANATAK
P.O. Box 693, Dillingham, AK 99576
(907) 842-4004 Fax 274-3721
Mariane Shanigan, CEO
Tribe: Kanatak. *Goal:* To improve living conditions
of tribal members and to protect and preserve our
culture. Anchorage Agency.

NATIVE VILLAGE OF KARLUK
P.O. Box 22, Karluk, AK 99608
(907) 241-2218 Fax 241-2203
Alicia Reft, President
Tribe: Aleut. *In resdidence:* 225.
Anchorage Agency.

ORGANIZED VILLAGE OF KASAAN
General Delivery, Kasaan, AK 99924
(907) 542-2214 Fax 542-2215
Louis Thompson, President
Juneau Area Office.

NATIVE VILLAGE OF KASIGLUK
P.O. Box 19, Kasigluk, AK 99609
(907) 477-6927
Yanko Brink, President
Tribe: Eskimo. *In residence:* 175.
Bethel Agency.

KENAITZE INDIAN TRIBE
P.O. Box 988, Kenai, AK 99611
(907) 283-3633
Clara Swan, Tribal Chairperson
Anchorage Agency.

KETCHIKAN INDIAN CORPORATION
429 Deermount Ave., Ketchikan, AK 99901
(907) 225-5158 Fax 247-0429
Christine Collison, President
Juneau Area Office.

NATIVE VILLAGE OF KIANA
P.O. Box 69, Kiana, AK 99749
(907) 475-2109
Ben Atoruk, President
Tribe: Eskimo. *In residence:* 220.
Nome Agency.

AGDAAGUX TRIBE OF KING COVE
P.O. Box 18, King Cove, AK 99612
(907) 497-2648 Fax 497-2444
Della Trimble, President
Anchorage Agency.

KING ISLAND NATIVE COMMUNITY
P.O. Box 992, Nome, AK 99762
(907) 443-5494/5487
Marilyn Koezlina-Irelan, Chief
Nome Agency.

NATIVE VILLAGE OF KIPNUK
P.O. Box 57, Kipnuk, AK 99614
(907) 896-5515 Fax 896-5240
Johnnie Paul, President
Bethel Agency.

NATIVE VILLAGE OF KIVALINA
Kivalina IRA Council
P.O. Box 50051, Kivalina, AK 99750
　(907) 645-2153
　Joseph Swan, Sr., President; David Swan, VP
Tribe: Inupiat of Kivalina. *In residence*: 360. *Council members*: Fred Swan and Oscar Sage, Sr. *Activities*: New Years Day traditional activities celebration; cultural enrichment Summer Youth Camp. Nome Agency.

KLAWOCK COOPERATIVE ASSOCIATION
P.O. Box 112, Klawock, AK 99925
　(907) 755-2265 Fax 755-8800
　Roseann Demmert, President
Juneau Area Office.

NATIVE VILLAGE OF KLUTI-KAAH
(aka COPPER CENTER)
P.O. Box 68, Copper Center, AK 99573
　(907) 822-5541
　Sam George, President
Tribe: Athapascan. *In residence*: 115.
Anchorage Agency.

KNIK VILLAGE COUNCIL
P.O. Box 872130, Wasilla, AK 99687
　(907) 376-2845
　Paul B. Theodore, President
Anchorage Agency.

NATIVE VILLAGE OF KOBUK
Kobuk, AK 99751
　(907) 948-2214
Tribe: Eskimo. Nome Agency.

KOKHANOK VILLAGE
P.O. Box 1007, Iliamna, AK 99606
　(907) 282-2202
　John Nelson, President
Tribe: Aleut. Anchorage Agency.

NEW KOLIGANEK VILLAGE
New Koliganek Village Council
P.O. Box 5057, Koliganek, AK 99576
　(907) 596-3434 Fax 596-3462
　Herman Nelson, President; Robert Larson, VP
Tribes: Athapascan and Indian. *In residence*: 205. *Council members*: Gust Tunguing, Sr., Gust Tunguing, Jr., Blunka Ishnook, Jr., Betty Lee, and Edward Kapatak. Anchorage Agency.

KONGIGANAK NATIVE VILLAGE
P.O. Box 5069, Kongiganak, AK 99559
　(907) 557-5226 Fax 557-5611
　Martina Azean, President
Bethel Agency.

NATIVE VILLAGE OF KOTLIK
P.O. Box 20096, Kotlik, AK 99620
　(907) 899-4326
　Michael Hunt, President
Tribe: Eskimo. Bethel Agency.

NATIVE VILLAGE OF KOTZEBUE
Kotzebue IRA Council
P.O. Box 296, Kotzebue, AK 99752
　(907) 442-3467 Fax 442-2162
　Peter Schaeffer, Chairperson
Tribe: Eskimo. *In residence*: 1,900. *Activities*: N.W. Alaska Native Trade Fair. Nome Agency.

NATIVE VILLAGE OF KOYUK
P.O. Box 30, Koyuk, AK 99753
　(907) 984-6414 Fax 984-3442
　Roy Otton, President
Tribe: Eskimo. *In residence*: 190. Nome Agency.

KOYUKUK NATIVE VILLAGE
P.O. Box 49, Koyukuk, AK 99754
　(907) 927-2214
　Leo Lolnitz, Chief
Tribe: Athapascan. *In residence*: 115.
Fairbanks Agency.

KWETHLUK VILLAGE
P.O. Box 84, Kwethluk, AK 99621
　(907) 757-6714 Fax 757-6328
　Joseph Guy, President
Tribe: Eskimo. *In residence*: 350. Bethel Agency.

KWIGILLINGOK NATIVE VILLAGE
P.O. Box 49, Kwigillingok, AK 99622
　(907) 588-8114 Fax 588-8429
　Willie Atti, President
Tribe: Eskimo. *In residence*: 350. Bethel Agency.

NATIVE VILLAGE OF KWINHAGAK
Quinhagak I.R.A. Council
Quinhagak, AK 99655
　(907) 556-8449 (phone & fax)
　Wassillie Bavilla, President
Tribe: Yup'ik Eskimo. *In residence*: 600. *Total acreage*: 120,000. *Council members*: Marie Smith, Grace Friendly, Paul Beebe, Willard Church, Annie Cleveland, and Charles Evans. Bethel Agency.

NATIVE VILLAGE OF LARSEN BAY
P.O. Box 35, Larsen Bay, AK 99624
　(907) 847-2207
　Roy Jones, Jr., President
Tribe: Eskimo. Anchorage Agency.

LEVELOCK VILLAGE
P.O. Box 70, Levelock, AK 99625
　(907) 287-3030
　Christopher Apokedak, President
Tribe: Aleut. Anchorage Agency.

LIME VILLAGE
Lime Village, AK 99627
　(907) 526-5126
　Phillip Bobby, President
Bethel Agency.

LOWER KALSKAG VILLAGE
P.O. Box 27, Lower Kalskag, AK 99626
　(907) 471-2307
　George Sam, President
Tribe: Eskimo. *In residence*: 175. Bethel Agency.

MANLEY HOT SPRINGS VILLAGE
Manley Hot Springs, AK 99756
　(907) 672-3331
　Dixie Dayo, President
Fairbanks Agency.

MANOKOTAK VILLAGE
P.O. Box 169, Manokotak, AK 99628
　(907) 289-2067
　Wassillie Tugatuk, Sr., President
Tribes: Eskimo and Indian. *In residence*: 190.
Anchorage Agency.

NATIVE VILLAGE OF MARSHALL
(aka FORTUNA LEDGE)
P.O. Box 10, Fortuna Ledge, AK 99585
　(907) 679-6215 Fax 679-6220
　Alvin Owletuck, Sr., President
Tribe: Eskimo. *In residence*: 115. Bethel Agency.

NATIVE VILLAGE OF MARY'S IGLOO
P.O. Box 572, Teller, AK 99778
　(907) 642-3731
　Dan Topkok, President
Nome Agency.

McGRATH NATIVE VILLAGE
P.O. Box 134, McGrath, AK 99627
　(907) 524-3024
　Lewis Vanderpool, Chief
Tribes: Athapascan, Indian &Eskimo.
In residence: 125. Bethel Agency.

MEKORYUK NATIVE VILLAGE
P.O. Box 66, Mekoryuk, AK 99630
　(907) 827-8828 Fax 827-8215
　Solomon Williams, President
Tribe: Eskimo. *In residence*: 220. Bethel Agency.

MENTASTA LAKE VILLAGE
Mentasta Lake, AK 99780
　(907) 291-2319
　Norman Ewan, First Chief
Anchorage Agency.

METLAKATLA INDIAN COMMUNITY COUNCIL
P.O. Box 8, Metlakatla, AK 99926
　(907) 886-4441 Fax 886-7997
　Jim Scudero, Mayor
Portland Area Office. Head Start Program.

NATIVE VILLAGE OF MINTO
P.O. Box 26, Minto, AK 99758
　(907) 798-7112
　Berkman Silas, Chief
Tribes: Athapascan and Indian. *In residence*: 225.
Fairbanks Agency.

NATIVE VILLAGE OF MOUNTAIN VILLAGE
P.O. Box 32249, Mountain Village, AK 99632
　(907) 591-2048 Fax 591-2234
　Elmer T. Beans, Sr., President
Tribe: Eskimo. *In residence*: 275. Bethel Agency.

NAKNEK NATIVE VILLAGE
P.O. Box 106, Naknek, AK 99633
　(907) 246-4210
　Norman Anderson, President
Tribes: Aleut & Indian. Anchorage Agency.

NANWALEK VILLAGE (aka ENGLISH BAY)
Homer, AK 99603
　(907) 281-9219
　Vincent Kvasnikoff, President
Tribe: Eskimo. *In residence*: 115.
Anchorage Agency.

NAPAKIAK NATIVE VILLAGE
General Delivery, Napakiak, AK 99634
　(907) 589-2227
　Albert Kernak, President
Tribe: Eskimo. *In residence*: 200. Bethel Agency.

NATIVE VILLAGE OF NAPAIMUTE
P.O. Box 96, Aniak, AK 99557
　Agnes E. Charles, President
Bethel Agency.

NAPASKIAK VILLAGE COUNCIL
P.O. Box 6109, Napaskiak, AK 99559
　(907) 737-7626
　Peter Williams, Sr., President
Tribe: Eskimo. *In residence*: 175. Bethel Agency.

NATIVE VILLAGE OF NELSON LAGOON
P.O. Box 13 - NLG, Nelson Lagoon, AK 99571
　(907) 989-2204 Fax 989-2234
　Paul Gunderson, President
Anchorage Agency.

NENANA NATIVE ASSOCIATION
P.O. Box 356, Nenana, AK 99760
　(907) 832-5662

Moses Paul, Chief
Tribes: Athapascan & Indian. *In residence*: 175.
Fairbanks Agency.

NEW STUYAHOK VILLAGE
P.O. Box 49, New Stuyahok, AK 99636
(907) 693-3173
Natalia Wassiliey, President
Tribe: Athapascan. *In residence*: 140.
Anchorage Agency.

NEWHALEN VILLAGE COUNCIL
P.O. Box 165, Iliamna, AK 99606
(907) 571-1410
Gusty Wassillie, President
Tribes: Aleut & Indian. Anchorage Agency.

NEWTOK VILLAGE COUNCIL
P.O. Box WWT, Newtok, AK 99559
(907) 237-2314
Larry Charles, President
Bethel Agency.

NATIVE VILLAGE OF NIGHTMUTE
Nightmute, AK 99690
(907) 647-6213
Dick Anthony, Vice President
Tribe: Eskimo. Bethel Agency.

NIKOLAI VILLAGE
Rural Branch, Nikolai, AK 99691
(907) 293-2226
Ignatti Petruaka, Chief
Tribes: Athapscans & Indian. *In residence*: 145.
Fairbanks Agency.

NATIVE VILLAGE OF NIKOLSKI
General Delivery, Nikolski, AK 99638
(907) 576-2225 Fax 576-2205
Leonte Ermeloff, President
Anchorage Agency.

**NINILCHIK VILLATE
TRADITIONAL COUNCIL**
P.O. Box 39070, Ninilchik, AK 99639
(907) 567-3313 Fax 567-3308
Gassim Oskolkoff, President
Tribe: Kenaitse. *In residence*: 120.
Anchorage Agency.

NATIVE VILLAGE OF NOATAK
P.O. Box 89, Noatak, AK 99761
(907) 485-2173
Rickie Ashby, President
Tribes: Eskimo & Indian. *In residence*: 550.
Nome Agency.

NOME ESKIMO COMMUNITY
P.O. Box 1090, Nome, AK 99762
(907) 443-2246 Fax 443-3539
Andrew Miller, Jr., President
Tribes: Eskimo & Indian. *In residence*: 1,750.
Nome Agency.

NONDALTON VILLAGE COUNCIL
P.O. Box 49, Nondalton, AK 99640
(907) 294-2254
William Trefon, Sr., President
Tribe: Athapascan. *In residence*: 175.
Anchorage Agency.

NOORVIK NATIVE COMMUNITY
P.O. Box 71, Noorvik, AK 99763
(907) 636-2144
Gordon Newlin, President
Tribe: Eskimo. *In residence*: 450. Nome Agency.

NORTHWAY VILLAGE
P.O. Box 516, Northway, AK 99764
(907) 778-2271
Lee Titus, President
Tribe: Athapascan. *In residence*: 150.
Fairbanks Agency.

NATIVE VILLAGE OF NUIQSUT
Nuiqsut, AK 99723
(907) 480-6714
Maggie Kavalsky, Mayor
Tribe: Athapascan. *In residence*: 125.
Fairbanks Agency.

NULATO VILLAGE COUNCIL
Nulato, AK 99765
(907) 898-2231
Victor Nickolas, President
Tribe: Athapascan. *In residence*: 250.
Fairbanks Agency.

NATIVE VILLAGE OF NUNAPITCHUK
P.O. Box 130, Nunapitchuk, AK 99641
(907) 527-5705
Chuck Chaliak, President
Tribe: Eskimo. *In residence*: 200. Bethel Agency.

NATIVE VILLAGE OF OHOGAMIUT
General Delivery, Fortuna Ledge, AK 99585
(907) 679-6740
Nick Isaac, President
Bethel Agency.

NATIVE VILLAGE OF OLD HARBOR
P.O. Box 62, Old Harbor, AK 99643
(907) 286-2215
Tony Azuyak, President
Tribe: Eskimo. *In residence*: 200. Anchorage
Agency.

**ORUTSARARMUIT NATIVE COUNCIL
(aka BETHEL)**
P.O. Box 927, Bethel, AK 99559
(907) 543-2608 Fax 543-2639
Thadeus Tikiun, Jr., Chairperson
Roy Hall, Vice-Chairperson
Henry Hunter, Secretary/Treasurer
Population served: Bethel Native Corporation
Shareholders. *Programs*: Social Services; Voca-
tional Training; Higher Education grants; Energy
Assistance; Housing Improvement. Bethel Agency.

OSCARVILLE TRADITIONAL COUNCIL
P.O. Box 1554, Oscarville, AK 99559
(907) 737-7321
Ignati Jacob, President
Tribes: Indian and Eskimo. Bethel Agency.

VILLLAGE OF OUZINKIE
P.O. Box 130, Ouzinkie, AK 99644
(907) 680-2259
Joe Lianos, President
Anchorage Agency.

PEDRO BAY VILLAGE
P.O. Box 4720, Pedro Bay, AK 99647
(907) 850-2225
Carl Jensen, President
Tribe: Athapascan. Anchorage Agency.

PERRYVILLE VILLAGE
P.O. Box 101, Perryville, AK 99648
(907) 853-2203
Harry W. Kosbruk, President
Tribe: Eskimo. *In residence*: 175.
Anchorage Agency.

PETERSBURG INDIAN ASSOCIATION
P.O. Box 1418, Petersburg, AK 99833
(907) 772-3636 Fax 772-3637
Leilani N. Kito, President
Juneau Area Office.

NATIVE VILLAGE OF PIAMUIT
Hooper Bay, AK 99604
(907) 758-4420
FranklinNapoleon, President
Bethel Agency.

NATIVE VILLAGE OF PILOT POINT
P.O. Box 449, Pilot Point, AK 99649
(907) 797-2208
James Shannigan, President
Anchorage Agency.

PILOT STATION TRADITIONAL COUNCIL
P.O. Box 5040, Pilot Station, AK 99650
(907) 549-3512
Nicky Myer, Acting President
Tribe: Eskimo. Bethel Agency.

NATIVE VILLAGE OF PITKA'S POINT
P.O. Box 127, St. Mary's, AK 99658
(907) 438-2833
William John, President
Tribe: Eskimo. Bethel Agency.

PLATINUM VILLAGE COUNCIL
Platinum, AK 99651
(907) 979-8126
James T. Kasayulie, President
Tribe: Eskimo. Bethel Agency.

POINT HOPE VILLAGE COUNCIL
P.O. Box 91, Point Hope, AK 99766
(907) 368-2453
Ernie Frankson, President
Tribe: Eskimo. *In residence*: 385.
Nome Agency.

POINT LAY NATIVE VILLAGE
P.O. Box 101, Point Lay, AK 99759
(907) 833-2428
Annie Martin, Village Coordinator
Tribe: Eskimo. *In residence*: 125.
Fairbanks Agency.

PORT GRAHAM VILLAGE
P.O. Box PGM, Port Graham, AK 99603
(907) 284-2227
Eleanor McMullen, President
Tribe: Eskimo. *In residence*: 115.
Anchorage Agency.

NATIVE VILLAGE OF PORT HEIDEN
P.O. Box 49007, Port Heiden, AK 99549
(907) 284-2218
Robert Christiansen, President
Anchorage Agency.

NATIVE VILLAGE OF PORT LIONS
P.O. Box 69, Port Lions, AK 99550
(907) 454-2234
Robert J. Nelson, President
Anchorage Agency.

PORTAGE CREEK VILLAGE
P.O. Box 1031, Portage Creek, AK 99576
(907) 842-5218
Charlie Johnson, President
Anchorage Agency.

RAMPART VILLAGE COUNCIL
P.O. Box 67029, Rampart, AK 99767

(907) 358-3312
Sheila Woods, Chief
Tribe: Athapascan. *In residence*: 140.
Fairbanks Agency.

RED DEVIL VILLAGE
P.O. Box 49, Red Devil, AK 99656
(907) 447-9901
Glenn Morgan, Sr., President
Bethel Agency.

NATIVE VILLAGE OF RUBY
General Delivery, Ruby, AK 99768
(907) 468-4406
Donald Honea, Sr., President
Tribe: Athapascan. *In residence*: 150.
Fairbanks Agency.

IQURMUIT TRIBE (RUSSIAN MISSION)
P.O. Box 9, Russian Mission, AK 99657
(907) 584-5511
Mary Belkoff, President
Tribe: Iqurmuit (Eskimo). Bethel Agency.

SALAMANTOF, VILLAGE OFAK
P.O. Box 2682, Kenai, AK 99611
(907) 283-7864
James Sequra, President
Anchorage Agency.

NATIVE VILLAGE OF SAND POINT
P.O. Box 447, Sand Point, AK 99661
(907) 383-3525 Fax 383-3535
Glenn Gardner, Jr., President
Tribe: Qagun Tayagungin (Aleut).
Anchorage Agency.

NATIVE VILLAGE OF SAVOONGA
P.O. Box 129, Savoonga, AK 99769
(907) 984-6414 Fax 984-6027
Kenneth Kingeekuk, President
Tribe: Eskimo. *In residence*: 330. Nome Agency.

ORGANIZED VILLAGE OF SAXMAN
Route 2, Box 2, Ketchikan, AK 99901
(907) 225-5163
Joyce Frank, President
Juneau Area Office.

NATIVE VILLAGE OF SCAMMON BAY
P.O. Box 126, Scammon Bay, AK 99662
(907) 558-5113 Fax 558-5626
Timothy Kaganak, President
Bethel Agency.

NATIVE VILLAGE OF SELAWIK
P.O. Box 59, Selawik, AK 99770
(907) 484-2225 Fax 484-2226
Allan Ticket, Sr., President
Nome Agency.

SELDOVIA VILLAGE TRIBE
P.O. Drawer L, Seldovia, AK 99663
(907) 234-7625
Fred H. Elvasaas, President
Bethel Agency.

SHAGELUK NATIVE VILLAGE
General Delivery, Shageluk, AK 99665
(907) 473-8239
Hamilton Hamilton, Sr., Chief
Tribe: Athapascan. *In residence*: 150.
Bethel Agency.

SHAKTOOLIK NATIVE VILLAGE
P.O. Box 100, Shaktoolik, AK 99771
(907) 955-3701 Fax 955-3151

Edgar Jackson, President
Nome Agency.

NATIVE VILLAGE OF SHELDON'S POINT
General Delivery, Sheldon's Point, AK 99666
(907) 498-4226
Edward J. Adams, Sr., President
Bethel Agency.

NATIVE VILLAGE OF SHISHMAREF
P.O. Box 72110, Shishmaref, AK 99772
(907) 649-3821 Fax 649-3013
Stella Weyiouanna, President
Tribe: Eskimo. *In residence*: 200.
Nome Agency.

SHOONAQ TRIBE OF KODIAK
P.O. Box 1974, Kodiak, AK 99615
(907) 486-4449
Margaret Roberts, President

NATIVE VILLAGE OF SHUNGNAK
P.O. Box 63, Shungnak, AK 99773
(907) 437-2163
Ernest Berry, President
Tribe: Eskimo. *In residence*: 200.
Nome Agency.

SITKA TRIBE OF ALASKA
456 Katlian St., Sitka, AK 99835
(907) 747-3207 Fax 747-4915
Lawrence Widmark, Jr., President
Tribe: Sitka. Juneau Area Office.

SKAGWAY VILLAGE
P.O. Box 399, Skagway, AK 99840
(907) 983-2885
Minnie Stevens, President
Juneau Area Office.

NATIVE VILLAGE OF SLEETMUTE
P.O. Box 21, Sleetmute, AK 99668
(907) 449-9901
Jane Zaukar, President
Tribes: Athapascan and Indian. *In residence*: 175.
Bethel Agency.

NATIVE VILLAGE OF SOLOMON
P.O. Box 243, Solomon, AK 99762
(907) 443-2844 Fax 443-5098
Rose Ann Timbers, President
Nome Agency.

SOUTH NAKNEK VILLAGE
P.O. Box 70106, South Naknek, AK 99670
(907) 246-6566
Donald F. Nielsen, President
Anchorage Agency.

ST. GEORGE ISLAND
P.O. Box 940, St. George Island, AK 99660
(907) 859-2205
Gilbert G. Kashevarof, President
Anchorage Agency.

NATIVE VILLAGE OF ST. MICHAEL
General Delivery, St. Michael, AK 99659
(907) 923-3222 Fax 923-3142
Pius Washington, President
Nome Agency.

ALEUT COMMUNITY OF ST. PAUL ISLAND
P.O. Box 86, St. Paul Island, AK 99660
(907) 546-2211 Fax 546-2407
Rena J. Kudrin, President
Tribe: Aleut. Anchorage Agency.

STEBBINS COMMUNITY ASSOCIATION
P.O. Box 2, Stebbins, AK 99671
(907) 934-3561 Fax 934-3560
Fred Pete, Sr., President
Tribe: Eskimo. *In residence*: 175. Nome Agency.

NATIVE VILLAGE OF STEVENS
General Delivery, Stevens Village, AK 99774
(907) 478-9226
Horace Smoke, First Chief
Tribe: Athapascan. *In residence*: 125.
Fairbanks Agency.

NATIVE VILLAGE OF STONEY RIVER
P.O. Box SRV, Stoney River, AK 99557
(907) 537-3214
Nattie Donhauser, President
Bethel Agency.

TAKOTNA VILLAGE
P.O. Box TYC, Takotna, AK 99675
(907) 298-2212
David Miller, First Chief
Tribes: Eskimo & Indian. Bethel Agency.

NATIVE VILLAGE OF TANACROSS
P.O. Box 77130, Tanacross, AK 99776
(907) 366-7160
Eileen Kozevnikoff, Executive Director
Tribe: Athapascan. *In residence*: 150.
Fairbanks Agency.

NATIVE VILLAGE OF TANANA
P.O. Box 77093, Tanana, AK 99777
(907) 366-7160 Fax 366-7195
Dennis Charley, President
Tribes: Athapascan & Indian. In *residence*: 225.
Fairbanks Agency.

NATIVE VILLAGE OF TATITLEK
P.O. Box 171, Tatitlek, AK 99677
(907) 325-2311
Gary Kompkoff, President
Tribe: Aleut. *In residence*: 150. Anchorage Agency.

NATIVE VILLAGE OF TAZLINA
P.O. Box 188, Glenallen, AK 99588
(907) 822-5965
Robert Marshall, President
Anchorage Agency.

TELIDA VILLAGE
General Delivery, Telida, AK 99629
Steve Eluska, Chief
(907) 843-8115
Fairbanks Agency.

TELLER VILLAGE COUNCIL
P.O. Box 509, Teller, AK 99778
(907) 642-3381 Fax 642-4014
Chuck Okpealuk, President
Tribe: Eskimo. *In residence*: 200. Nome Agency.

TETLIN VILLAGE COUNCIL
P.O. Box 520, Tetlin, AK 99780
(907) 883-2321
Donald Joe, Vice President
Tribe: Athapascan. *In residence*: 125.
Fairbanks Agency.

TRADITIONAL VILLAGE OF TOGIAK
P.O. Box 209, Togiak, AK 99678
(907) 493-5920
Jack Hyexikok, Sr., President
Tribe: Eskimo. *In residence*: 175.
Anchorage Agency.

NATIVE VILLAGE OF TOKSOOK BAY
Nelson Island, Toksook Bay, AK 99637
(907) 427-7114 Fax 427-7714
Joseph Asuluk, Sr., President
Bethel Agency.

TSIMSHIAN TRIBAL COUNCIL
1067B Woodland Ave., Ketchika, AK 99901
(907) 225-2961
Juneau Area Office.

TULUKSAK NATIVE COMMUNITY
P.O. Box 156, Tuluksak, AK 99679
(907) 695-6828
John Napoka, Sr., President
Tribe: Eskimo. *In residence*: 200.
Bethel Agency.

NATIVE VILLAGE OF TUNTUTULIAK
P.O. Box 77, Tuntutuliak, AK 99680
(907) 256-2128
Peter Pavilla, President
Tribe: Eskimo. *In residence*: 120.
Bethel Agency.

TUNUNAK NATIVE VILLAGE
P.O. Box 77, Tununak, AK 99681
(907) 652-6527 Fax 652-6011
John J. Oscar, President
Bethel Agency.

TWIN HILLS TRIBAL
P.O. Box TWA, Twin Hills, AK 99576
(907) 525-4820
Arthur Sharp, President
Anchorage Agency.

NATIVE VILLAGE OF TYONEK
P.O. Box 82009, Tyonek, AK 99682
(907) 583-2201
Donald Standifer, President
Tribe: Athapascan. *In residence*: 200.
Anchorage Agency.

UGASHIK VILLAGE
P.O. Box 651, King Salmon, AK 99613
(907) 842-4004
Roy S. Matsuno, President
Tribes: Eskimo and Indian. Anchorage Agency.

UMKUMIUT VILLAGE COUNCIL
General Delivery, Nightmute, AK 99690
(907) 647-6213
Simon Agnus, President
Bethel Agency.

NATIVE VILLAGE OF UNALAKLEET
P.O. Box 270, Unalakleet, AK 99684
(907) 624-3622 Fax 624-3402
Stanton Katchatag, President
Fred Katchatag, Vice Presdient
Tribes: Eskimo and Indian. *In residence*: 840. *Total acreage*: 258. *Council members*: Paul Katchatag, Ruth Blatchford, and Eleanor Bahr. *Activities*: Operates a clinic. Nome Agency.

UNALASKA VILLAGE (QUALINGIN)
P.O. Box 334, Unalaska, AK 99685
(907) 581-2290 Fax 581-3644
Harriet Berikoff, President
Anchorage Agency.

NATIVE VILLAGE OF UNGA
P.O. Box 508, Sand Point, AK 99661
(907) 383-5215
Bjorne Lee, President
Anchorage Agency.

VALDEZ NATIVE ASSOCIATION
P.O. Box 1108, Valdez, AK 99686
(907) 835-4951

VENETIE VILLAGE COUNCIL
P.O. Box 99, Arctic Village, AK 99781
(907) 849-8212
Eddie Frank, First Chief
Tribe: Athapascan. *In residence*: 125.
Fairbanks Agency.

NATIVE VILLAGE OF WAINWRIGHT
P.O. Box 184, Wainwright, AK 99782
(907) 763-2726
George Agnassaga, President
Tribe: Eskimo. *In residence*: 335.
Fairbanks Agency.

NATIVE VILLAGE OF WALES
P.O. Box 549, Wales, AK 99783
(907) 664-3511 Fax 664-3641
Luther Komonaseak, President
Tribe: Eskimo. *In residence*: 225. Nome Agency.

NATIVE VILLAGE OF WHITE MOUNTAIN
P.O. Box 84082, White Mountain, AK 99784
(907) 638-3651 Fax 638-3421
Lincoln Simon, President
Tribes: Eskimo & Indian. *In residence*: 200.
Nome Agency.

WRANGELL COOPERATIVE ASSOCIATION
P.O. Box 868, Wrangell, AK 99929
(907) 874-3747
Margaret Sturtevant, President
Juneau Area Office.

NATIVE VILLAGE OF YAKUTAT
P.O. Box 418, Yakutat, AK 99689
(907) 784-3932 Fax 784-3595
Bert Adams, Sr., President
Tribes: Tlingit & Haida. Juneau Area Office.

ARIZONA

CAMERON RESERVATION
Cameron, AZ 86020
Tribe: Navajo. Western Navajo Agency.

CAMP VERDE RESERVATION
YAVAPAI-APACHE COMMUNITY COUNCIL
P.O. Box 1188, Camp Verde, AZ 86322
(602) 567-3649 Fax 567-3994
Theodore Smith, Sr., President
Tribe served: Yavapai-Apache. *In residence*: 600.
Area: 500 acres. Truxton Canon Agency.

CHILCHINBETO RESERVATION
c/o Western Navajo Agency
Tribe: Navajo. Located in Arizona and Utah.
See listing under Utah.

CHINLE RESERVATION
Tribe: Navajo. Chinle Agency.

COALMINE RESERVATION
Tribe: Navajo. Western Navajo Agency.

COCOPAH RESERVATION
Cocopah Tribal Council
P.O. Bin G, Somerton, AZ 85350
(602) 627-2102 Fax 627-3173
Peter Soto, Chairperson
Tribe served: Cocopah. *In residence*: 550.
Head Start Program. Fort Yuma Agency.

COLORADO RIVER INDIAN
TRIBES RESERVATION
CRIT Tribal Council
Route 1, Box 23-B, Parker, AZ 85344
(602) 669-9211 Fax 669-5675
Daniel Eddy, Jr., Chairperson
Russell Welsh, Vice Chair
LaWanda Laffoon, Secretary
Eldred Enas, Treasurer
Tribes served: Mohave, Chemehuevi, Hopi, and Navajo. *Tribal enrollment*: 3,100. *Area*: 286,691 acres (226,000 acres in Arizona, and 42,700 acres in California). *Council members*: Herman Laffoon, Jr., Conner Byestewa, Jr., Fernando Flores, Sr., Dennis Patch, and Rayford Patch. *Tribal services*: Tribal police, courts, museum and library; also, departments: fish and game, education, health and social services, recreation, manpower, building and zoning, fire, housing. *Local attractions*: Colorado River; Old Mohave Presbyterian Church, National Historic Site; archaeological excavations and ruins of La Paz, a former gold mining town; Tribal Museum and Library. *Activities*: National Indian Day, Mohave Day, All-Indian Rodeo, 4th of July Celebration; Annual Thanksgiving and Christmas Program. *Facilities*: Lodging, and camping. *Publication*: CRIT Newsletter, quarterly. Head Start Program. Colorado River Agency.

COPPER MINE RESERVATION
Tribe: Navajo. Western Navajo Agency.

CORNFIELDS RESERVATION
Tribe: Navajo. Fort Defiance Agency.

COYOTE CANYON RESERVATION
Tribe: Navajo. Fort Defiance Agency.

CRYSTAL RESERVATION
Tribe: Navajo. Fort Defiance Agency. Located in AZ & NM. See listing under New Mexico.

DENNEHOTSO RESERVATION
Dennehotso, AZ 86535
Tribe: Navajo. Western Navajo Agency.

DILKON COMMUNITY
Winslow, AZ 86047
Tribe: Navajo. *In residence*: 1,000.
Western Navajo Agency.

FOREST LAKE RESERVATION
Heber, AZ 85928
Tribe: Navajo. Chinle Agency.

FORT APACHE INDIAN RESERVATION
White Mountain Apache Tribal Council
P.O. Box 700, Whiteriver, AZ 85941
(602) 338-4346 Fax 338-4778
Ronnie Lupe, Chairperson
Tribe: White Mountain Apache. *In residence*: 8,500. *Area*: 1,664,872 acres. *Local attraction*: Apache Cultural Center and Museum. Head Start Program. Fort Apache Agency.

FORT DEFIANCE RESERVATION
Tribe: Navajo. Fort Defiance Agency.
Located in Arizona and New Mexico.
See listing under New Mexico.

FORT McDOWELL RESERVATION
Mohave-Apache Tribal Council
P.O. Box 17779, Fountain Hills, AZ 85268
(602) 837-5121 Fax 837-1630
Clinton Pattea, President
Tribes: Mohave-Apache. *In residence*: 550. *Area*: 24,680 acres; located 20 miles northeast of Phoe-

nix on the Verde River. *Local attractions*: Roosevelt Dam and Reservoir; Bartlett Reservoir. Salt River Agency.

FORT MOHAVE RESERVATION
Fort Mohave, AZ 86427
Tribe: Mohave. Located in Arizona, California and Nevada. See listings in California and Nevada. Colorado River Agency.

FORT YUMA RESERVATION
Quechan Tribal Council
P.O. Box 11352, Yuma, AZ 85364
(619) 572-0213 Fax 572-2102
Fritz Brown, President
Tribe: Quechan. Located in AZ & CA. Fort Yuma Agency.

GANADO RESERVATION
P.O. Box 188, Ganado, AZ 86505
Tribe: Navajo. Fort Defiance Agency.

GILA BEND RESERVATION
Gila Bend, AZ 85337
Tribe: Papago. *In residence*: 300. *Area*: 10,000 acres. Located four miles north of Gila Bend. *Local attractions*: Kitt Peak National Observatory on San Xavier Reservation. Papago Agency.

GILA RIVER RESERVATION
Gila River Indian Community Council
P.O. Box 97, Sacaton, AZ 85247
(602) 562-3311 Fax 562-3422
Mary V. Thomas, Governor
Tribes: Pima-Maricopa. *In residence*: 9,750. *Area*: 370,000 acres. *Activities*: Operates a casino. Head Start Program. Pima Agency.

GREASEWOOD RESERVATION
Greasewood, AZ 86505
Tribe: Navajo. Fort Defiance Agency.

HAVASUPAI RESERVATION
Havasupai Tribal Council
P.O. Box 10, Supai, AZ 86435
(602) 448-2961 Fax 448-2551
Rex Tilousi, Chairperson
Tribe: Havasupai. *In residence*: 500. *Area*: 3,058 acres. Located in Cataract Canyon, within the Grand Canyon. *Facilities*: Tribal lodge. Head Start Program. Truxton Canon Agency.

HOPI RESERVATION
Hopi Tribal Council
P.O. Box 123, Kykotsmovi, AZ 86039
(602) 734-2441 Fax 734-6665
Ferrell Secakuku, Chairperson
Wayne Taylor, Vice-Chairperson
Tribes: Hopi & Tewa. *In residence*: 8,500. *Area*: 1,565,376 acres. *Facilities*: Hopi Cultural Center; arts and crafts shops; tribal museum; motels and restaurants. Head Start Program. Hopi Agency.

HOUCK RESERVATION
Houck, AZ 86506
Tribe: Navajo. Fort Defiance Agency.

HUALAPAI RESERVATION
Hualapai Tribal Council
P.O. Box 179, Peach Springs, AZ 86434
(602) 769-2216 Fax 769-2343
Delbert Havatone, Chairperson
Tribe: Hualapai. *In residence*: 1,200. *Area*: 995,000 acres. Head Start Program. Truxton Canon Agency.

INSCRIPTION HOUSE RESERVATION
Tribe: Navajo. Western Navajo Agency.

JEDDITO RESERVATION
Tribe: Navajo. Fort Defiance Agency.

KAIBAB RESERVATION
Kaibab Paiute Tribal Council
HC65, Box 2, Fredonia, AZ 86022
(602) 643-7245 Fax 643-7260
Gloria Bulletts-Benson, Chairperson
Tribe: Paiute. *In residence*: 250. Located in AZ & UT. Southern Paiute Field Station.

KAIBITO RESERVATION
Kaibito, AZ 86053
Tribe: Navajo. Western Navajo Agency.

KAYENTA RESERVATION
Kayenta, AZ 86033
Tribe: Navajo. Western Navajo Agency.

KINLICHEE RESERVATION
Tribe: Navajo. Fort Defiance Agency

KLAGETOH RESERVATION
Tribe: Navajo. Fort Defiance Agency

LECHEE RESERVATION
Tribe: Navajo. Western Navajo Agency

LEUPP RESERVATION
Leupp, AZ 86035
Tribe: Navajo. Western Navajo Agency.

LOW MOUNTAIN RESERVATION
Tribe: Navajo. Fort Defiance Agency

LUKACHUKAI RESERVATION
Lukachukai, AZ 86507
Tribe: Navajo. Chinle Agency.

LUPTON RESERVATION
Lupton, AZ 86508
Tribe: Navajo. Fort Defiance Agency.

MANY FARMS RESERVATION
Many Farms, AZ 86538
Tribe: Navajo. Chinle Agency.

MARICOPA RESERVATION
Ak Chin Indian Community Council
42507 N. Peters & Nall Rd.
Maricopa, AZ 85239
(602) 568-2227 Fax 254-6133
Martin Antone, Sr., Chairperson
Tribes: Papago and Pima. *In residence*: 450. *Area*: 21,500 acres. *Activities*: Operates a casino. Pima Agency.

MEXICAN SPRINGS RESERVATION
Tribe: Navajo. Fort Defiance Agency

MEXICAN WATERS RESERVATION
Tribe: Navajo. Located in Arizona, New Mexico and Utah. See listings under New Mexico and Utah. Shiprock Agency

NASCHITTI RESERVATION
Tribe: Navajo. Fort Defiance Agency

NAVAJO MOUNTAIN RESERVATION
Tribe: Navajo. Located in Arizona & Utah. See listing in Utah. Western Navajo Agency

NAVAJO NATION
P.O. Box 9000, Window Rock, AZ 86515
(602) 871-6352 Fax 871-4025
Albert Hale, President
Tribe served: Navajo of Arizona, New Mexico & Utah. *In residence*: 185,000. *Area*: 16 million acres. Located in northern Arizona, northwest New Mexico, and southern Utah. *Local attractions*: Navajo Nation Fair (September); summer & winter ceremonials (each week); Office of Navajo Veterans Affairs:P.O. Box 430; (602) 871-6597 Ext. 6598. Museum and library. He*ad Start Program*: Division of Child Development, Drawer 260, Fort Defiance, Az 86505 (602) 729-5360. Tribal council. Navajo Area Office.

NAZLINI RESERVATION
Tribe: Navajo. Chinle Agency

OAK SPRINGS RESERVATION
Tribe: Navajo. Fort Defiance Agency

OLJATOH RESERVATION
Tribe: Navajo. Located in Arizona and Utah. Western Navajo Agency. See listing under Utah.

PASCUA-YAQUI INDIAN COMMUNITY
Pascua-Yaqui Tribal Council
7474 S. Camino De Oeste, Tucson, AZ 85746
(602) 883-2838 Fax 883-7770
Arcadio Gastelum, Chairperson
Tribe served: Pascua-Yaqui. Head Start Program. Salt River Agency.

PINON RESERVATION
Pinon, AZ86510
Tribe: Navajo. Chinle Agency.

RED LAKE RESERVATION
Tribe: Navajo. Fort Defiance Agency

RED LAKE RSERVATION
Tribe: Navajo. Western Navajo Agency

RED MESA RESERVATION
Tribe: Navajo. Located in Arizona, New Mexico and Utah. Shiprock Agency. See listings in New Mexico and Utah.

RED ROCK RESERVATION
Tribe: Navajo. Located in Arizona and New Mexico. See listing under New Mexico. Shiprock Agency

ROUGH ROCK RESERVATION
Tribe: Navajo. Chinle Agency

ROUND ROCK RESERVATION
Tribe: Navajo. Chinle Agency

ST. MICHAELS RESERVATION
Tribe: Navajo. Fort Defiance Agency

SALT RIVER RESERVATION
Salt River Pima-Maricopa Indian Community Council
Route 1, Box 216, Scottsdale, AZ 85256
(602) 941-7277 Fax 949-2909
Ivan Makil, President
Tribes: Pima-Maricopa. *In residence*: 3,500. *Area*: 46,619 acres. Located in Salt River Valley, adjacent to Phoenix. Head Start Program. Salt River Agency.

SAN CARLOS APACHE RESERVATION
San Carlos Tribal Council
P.O. Box 0, San Carlos, AZ 85550

(602) 475-2361 Fax 475-2567
  Harrison Talgo, Sr., Chairperson
Tribe: Apache. *In residence*: 6,000. *Area*:
1,877,216 acres. *Local attractions*: Coolidge Dam;
San Carlos Reservoir; Tonto National Forest.
Activities: Apache Tribal Fair (October); Indian
Round-up (May and November). Head Start Program. San Carlos Agency.

SAN JUAN SOUTHERN PAIUTE COUNCIL
P.O. Box 2663, Tuba City, AZ 86045
  (602) 283-4583 Fax 283-5761
  Evelyn James, President
Tribes served: Paiute-Navajo. *Population served*:
300. Federally recognized in March 1990 with a
sub-agency in Tuba City. *Tribal Officials*: Jack Owl,
Ezra Owl, Clyde Whiskers, Grace Lehi, Mabel
Lehi, and Mary Tillman. *Publications*: Sands to the
Mountains; The Paiute Indians of North America.
Southern Paiute Field Station.

SELLS RESERVATION
Tohono O'Odham Council
P.O. Box 837, Sells, AZ 85634
  (602) 383-2221 Fax 383-3379
  Sylvester Listo, Chairperson
Tribe: Papago. *In residence*: 7,700. *Reservations
served*: Sells, San Xavier, and Gila Bend. *Area*:
2,774,000 acres. Located 25 miles west of Tucson. Papago Agency.

SAN XAVIER RESERVATION
San Xavier, AZ 85640
Tribe: Papago. *In residence*: 1,000. *Area*: 71,000
acres. Papago Agency.

SANOTSEE RESERVATION
Tribe: Navajo. Located in Arizona and New Mexico.
Shiprock Agency. See listing under New Mexico.

SAWMILL RESERVATION
Tribe: Navajo. Fort Defiance Agency

SHONTO RESERVATION
Shonto, AZ 86054
Tribe: Navajo. Located in Arizona and Utah.
Western Navajo Agency. See listing in Utah.

STEAMBOAT RESERVATION
Tribe: Navajo. Fort Defiance Agency

TEECNOSPOS RESERVATION
Tribe: Navajo. Located in Arizona, New Mexico
and Utah. Shiprock Agency. See listings in New
Mexico & Utah.

TEESTO RESERVATION
Tribe: Navajo. Fort Defiance Agency

TOHATCHI RESERVATION
Tribe: Navajo. Fort Defiance Agency

TOLANI LAKE RESERVATION
Tribe: Navajo. Western Navajo Agency

TONTO APACHE RESERVATION
Tonto Apache Tribal Council
#30 Tonto Reservation, Payson, AZ 85541
  (602) 474-5000 Fax 474-9125
  Jeri Johnson, Chairperson
Tribe served: Tonto Apache.
Truxton Canon Agency.

TSAILE-WHEATFIELDS RESERVATION
Tsaile, AZ 86556
Tribe: Navajo. Located in Arizona and New Mexico.
Chinle Agency. See listing in New Mexico.

TSELANI RESERVATION
Tribe: Navajo. Chinle Agency

TUBA CITY RESERVATION
Tuba City, AZ 86045
Tribe: Navajo. Western Navajo Agency.

TWIN LAKES RESERVATION
Tribe: Navajo. Fort Defiance Agency

WHITE CONE RESERVATION
Tribe: Navajo. Fort Defiance Agency

WIDE RUINS RESERVATION
Wide Ruins, AZ 86502
Tribe: Navajo. Fort Defiance Agency.

YAVAPAI-PRESCOTT RESERVATION
Yavapai-Prescott Board of Directors
530 E. Merritt St., Prescott, AZ 86301
  (602) 445-8790 Fax 778-9445
  Stan Rice, President
Tribe: Yavapai. In r*esidence*: 175. *Area*: 1,402
acres. *Special program*: Pow-wow; 10-K. *Publication*: Viola Jimulla, The Indian Chieftess. Library.
Truxton Canon Agency.

CALIFORNIA

AGUA CALIENTE RESERVATION
Agua Caliente Tribal Council
960 E. Tahquitz Way #106
Palm Springs, CA 92262
  (619) 325-5673 Fax 325-0593
  Richard Milanovich, Chairperson
Tribe: Cahuilla. *In residence*: 220. *Area*: 2,600
acres. Palm Springs Field Office.

ALTURAS RANCHERIA
P.O. Box 1035, Alturas, CA 96101
  Fax (916) 233-3055
  Paul Del Rosa, Chairperson
Tribe served: Pit River. *In residence*: 15.
Area: 20 acres. Northern California Agency.

AUGUSTINE RESERVATION
Thermal, CA 92274
Tribe: Cahuilla. Unoccupied. *Area*: 500 acres.
Southern California Agency.

BARONA RESERVATION
Barona General Business Council
1095 Barona Rd., Lakeside, CA 92040
  (619) 433-6612/3
  Clifford M. LaChappa, Sr., Chairperson
Tribe: Diegueno (Barona Band of Mission Indians).
In residence: 330. *Area*: 5,000 acres.
Southern California Agency.

BECLABITO RESERVATION
Tribe: Navajo. Located in Arizona and New Mexico.
Shiprock Agency. See listing under New Mexico.

BENTON PAIUTE RESERVATION
Utu Utu Gwaitu Paiute Tribal Council
Star Route 4, Box 56-A, Benton, CA 93512
  (619) 933-2321 (recording)
  Rose Marie Bahe, Chairperson
Tribe: Utu Utu Gwaitu Paiute. *In residence*: 70.
Area: 160 acres. Located in Mono County, in Blind
Springs Valley about three miles from Benton Hot
Springs. Activity: Annual Meeting. Central California Agency.

BERRY CREEK RANCHERIA
1779 Mitchell Ave., Oroville, CA 95966
  (916) 534-3895
  Albert Martin, Chairperson
  Kathy Frazier, Vice-Chairperson
Tribe: Tyme Maidu. *In residence*: 275. *Area*: 66
acres. *Publication*: Monthly tribal newsletter. Tribal
Council. Central California Agency.

BIG LAGOON RANCHERIA
P.O. Box Drawer 3060, Trinidad, CA 95570
  (707) 826-2079 Fax 826-1737
  Virgil Moorehead, Chairperson
Tribes: Yurok & Tolowa. *In residence*: 12. *Area*: 9
acres. General council. Northern California
Agency.

BIG PINE RESERVATION
P.O. Box 700, Big Pine, CA 93513
  (619) 938-2003 Fax 938-2942
  Cheryl Andreas, Chairperson
Tribes: Paiute & Shoshone. *In residence*: 110.
Population served: 450. *Area*: 280 acres. General
council. Central California Agency.

BIG SANDY RANCHERIA
P.O. Box 337, Auberry, CA 93602
  (209) 855-4003
  Jeannette Sample, Chairperson
Tribe: Mono. *In residence*: 55. *Area*: 8 acres.
Tribal council. Central California Agency.

BIG VALLEY RANCHERIA
P.O. Box 955, Lakeport, CA 95453
  (707) 262-0629
  Valentino Jack, Chairperson
Central California Agency.

BIRD SPRINGS RESERVATION
Tribe: Navajo. Western Navajo Agency

BISHOP INDIAN TRIBAL COUNCIL
P.O. Box 548, Bishop, CA 93514
  (619) 873-3584 Fax 873-4143
  Allen Summers, Chairperson
Tribes: Paiute & Shoshone. *In residence*: 1,075.
Area: 877 acres. *Facilities*: Culture Center. *Activities*: Toiyabe Indian health project; career development; education center; child care; elders program; culture center; maintains museum. Central
California Agency.

BLUE GAP RESERVATION
Tribe: Navajo. Chinle Agency

BLUE LAKE RANCHERIA
P.O. Box 428, Blue Lake, CA 95525
  (707) 668-5101 Fax 668-4272
  Claudia Brundin, Chairperson
Tribes served: Wiyot, Yurok, Cherokee, Warm
Springs, Black Foot, Towala. *In residence*: 35.
Area: 31 acres. Business council. Northern California Agency.

BRIDGEPORT INDIAN COLONY
P.O. Box 37, Bridgeport, CA 93517
  (619) 932-7083 Fax 932-7846
  Herb Glazier, Chairperson
Tribe: Paiute. *In residence*: 100. General council.
Central California Agency.

BROADWAY RESERVATION
Tribe: Navajo. Western Navajo Agency

BUENA VISTA RANCHERIA
4650 Coalmine Rd., Ione, CA 95640
  (209) 455-7652

Donna Marie Potts, Spokesperson
Tribe served: Mewuk. Central California Agency.

CABAZON BAND OF MISSION INDIANS
Cabazon General Council
84-245 Indio Spring Dr., Indio, CA 92203
(619) 342-2593 Fax 347-7880
John A. James, Chairperson
Brenda Soulliere, 1st Vice Chair;
Charles Welmas, 2nd Vice Chair
Tribe served: Cabazon Band of Mission Indians.
In residence: 38. *Total acreage*: 1,700 acres located in Coachella Valley, Riverside County. *Activities*: Pow-wows (Spring & Thanksgiving); operates Cahuilla Child Development Center; Cabazon Cultural Museum; and Cabazon Tribal Reference Library. *Publications*: Cabazon Circle Newsletter; Code of Cabazon Band of Mission Indians, and Return of the Buffalo-The Explosion of Indian Gaming. Southern California Agency.

CAHUILLA BAND OF MISSION INDIANS
P.O. Box 391760, Anza, CA 92539
(714) 763-5549 Fax 763-2808
Michelle Delgado, Spokesperson
Tribe: Cahuilla. *In residence*: 175. *Area*: 18,270
acres. General council. So. California Agency.

CAMPO BAND OF MISSION INDIANS
1779 Campo Truck Trail, Campo, CA 92006
(619) 478-9046 Fax 478-5818
Ralph Goff, Chairperson
Tribe: Diegueno (Campo Band of Mission Indians).
In residence: 225. *Area*: 15,000 acres.
General council. Southern California Agency.

CAPITAN GRANDE RESERVATION
Lakeside, CA 92040
Tribe: Diegueno (Capitan Grande Band of
Mission Indians). Southern California Agency.

CEDARVILLE RANCHERIA
P.O. Box 126, Cedarville. CA 96104
Fax (916) 233-2439
Tribe: Paiute. In residence: 22. Area: 17 acres.
Community council. Northern California Agency.

CHEMEHUEVI RESERVATION
P.O. Box 1780, Havasu Lake, CA 92363
(619) 858-4219
Matthew Leivas, Sr., Chairperson
Tribe: Chemehuevi. *In residence*: 135. Tribal council. Located in CA & AZ. Colorado River Agency.

CHICKEN RANCH RANCHERIA
P.O. Box 1699, Jamestown, CA 95327
(209) 984-3057
Lloyd Mathieson, Chairperson
Central California Agency.

CHICO RANCHERIA
3006 Esplanade St., Chico, CA 95926
(916) 899-8922 Fax 899-8517
Delores McHenry, Chairperson
Central California Agency.

CLOVERDALE RANCHERIA COUNCIL
4555 Redwood Hwy., S., Petaluma, CA 94952
(707) 766-9758
Central California Agency.

COLD SPRINGS RANCHERIA
P.O. Box 209, Tollhouse, CA 93667
(209) 855-8187 Fax 855-8359
Jennifer Fred, Acting Chairperson
Tribe: Mono. *In residence*: 235. *Area*: 98 acres.
Tribal council. Central California Agency.

COLORADO RIVER RESERVATION
Route 1, Box 23-B, Parker, AZ 85344
(602) 669-9211 Fax 669-5675
Daniel Eddy, Jr., Chairperson
Tribes: Mohave, Chemehuevi, Hopi, and Navajo.
In residence: 2,400. *Area*: 28,691 acres. Tribal council. Colorado River Agency (See listing in Arizona.) Located along the Colorado River in southwest California.

COLUSA RANCHERIA
P.O. Box 8, Colusa, CA 95932
(916) 458-8231 Fax 787-4006
Delbert Benjamin, Chairperson
Tribe: Cachil DeHe Band of Wintun Indians. *In residence*: 55. *Area* 300 acres. Community council.
Central California Agency.

CORTINA RANCHERIA
P.O. Box 7470, Citrus Heights, CA 95621
(916) 726-7118 Fax 726-3608
Mary Norton, Chairperson
Tribe: Wintun. *In residence*: 90. *Area*: 640 acres.
General council. Central California Agency.

COYOTE VALLEY RESERVATION
P.O. Box 39, 7901 Hwy. 101 N.
Redwood Valley, CA 95470
(707) 485-8723 Fax 468-1247
Doris Renick, Chairperson
Tribe served: Pomo. Central California Agency.

CUYAPAIPE GENERAL COUNCIL
2271 Alpine Blvd. #D, Alpine, CA 91901
(619) 478-5289
Tony J. Pinto, Chairperson
Tribe: Diegueno (Campo Band of Mission Indians).
In residence: 30. *Area*: 4,100 acres.
General council. Southern California Agency.

DEATH VALLEY INDIAN COMMUNITY
P.O. Box 206, Death Valley, CA 92325
(619) 786-2374
Pauline Esteves, Chairperson
Tribe served: Timbi-Sha Shoshone.
Southern California Agency.

DRY CREEK RANCHERIA
P.O. Box 607, Geyserville, CA 95441
(707) 857-3842
Amy Martin, Chairperson
Tribe served: Pomo. *Population served*: 135.
Area: 75 acres. General council. Central
California Agency.

ELK VALLEY RANCHERIA
P.O. Box 1042, Crescent City, CA 95531
(707) 464-4680 Fax 464-4519
John Green, Vice-Chairperson
Northern California Agency.

FORT BIDWELL RESERVATION
Fort Bidwell Community Council
P.O. Box 127, Fort Bidwell, CA 96112
(916) 279-6310 Fax 279-2233
Ralph DeGarmo, Chairperson
Tribe: Paiute. *In residence*: 200. *Area*: 3,330 acres.
Activity: Pow Wows. Tribal council. Northern California Agency.

FORT INDEPENDENCE RESERVATION
P.O. Box 67, Independence, CA 93526
(619) 878-2126 Fax 878-2311
Richard Wilder, Chairperson
Tribes: Paiute and Shoshone. *In residence*: 110.
Area: 356 acres. Central California Agency.

FORT MOJAVE RESERVATION
Fort Mojave Tribal Council
500 Merriman Ave., Needles, CA 92363
(619) 326-4591 Fax 326-2468
Patricia Madueno, Chairperson
Tribe served: Mojave. *Population served*: 600.
Located in California, Arizona, and Nevada. Colorado River Agency. *Activities*: Operates a casino.

FORT YUMA RESERVATION
Located in Arizona & California. Fort Yuma Agency.
See listing in Arizona.

GREENVILLE RANCHERIA
645 Antelope Blvd. #15, Red Bluff, CA 96080
(916) 528-9000 Fax 529-9002
Douglas Mullen, Chairperson
Community council. Central California Agency.

GRINDSTONE RANCHERIA
P.O. Box 63, Elk Creek, CA 95939
(916) 968-5116 Fax 968-5366
Daryl F. Burrows, Chairperson
Tribe served: Wintun. *Population served*: 185.
Area: 80 acres. General council. Central California Agency.

GUIDIVILLE RANCHERIA
P.O. Box 339, Talmadge, CA 95481
(707) 462-3682 Fax 462-9183
Keith R. Pike, Chairperson
Tribe served: Pomo. *Population served*: 100.
Northern California Agency.

HOOPA EXTENSION RESERVATION
Weitchpec, CA 95546
Tribe: Yurok. In residence: 300. *Area*: 6,800 acres.
Northern California Agency.

HOOPA VALLEY INDIAN RESERVATION
P.O. Box 1348, Hoopa, CA 95546
(916) 625-4211 Fax 625-4594
Dale Risling, Chairperson
Tribe served: Hoopa. *In residence*: 2,200. *Area*:
86,042 acres. Located along Trinity River, 35 miles
northeast of Eureka, California. Business council.
Head Start Program. Northern California Agency.

HOPLAND RESERVATION
P.O. Box 610, Hopland, CA 95449
(707) 744-1647 Fax 744-1506
Hale P. Knight, Chairperson
Tribe: Hopland Band of Pomo Indians.
In residence: 150. *Area*: 2,070 acres.
Tribal council. Central California Agency.

INAJA & COSMIT BAND OF MISSION INDIANS
P.O. Box 491, Santa Ysabel, CA 92070
(714) 276-6624
Rebecca Maxcy, Spokesperson
Tribe: Diegueno. *In residence*: 15. *Area*: 880 acres.
Southern California Agency.

JACKSON RANCHERIA
P.O. Box 429
Jackson, CA 95642
(209) 223-1935 Fax 223-5366
Margaret Dalton, Chairperson
Tribe: Me-Wuk (Miwok). *Area*: 330 acres.
Interim council. Central California Agency.

JAMUL BAND OF MISSION INDIANS
P.O. Box 612, Jamul, CA 91935
(619) 669-4785 Fax 669-4817
Raymond Hunter, Chairperson
Tribe: Diegueno. Southern California Agency.

KARUK TRIBE OF CALIFORNIA
P.O. Box 1016, Happy Camp, CA 96039
(916) 493-5305 Fax 493-5322
Alvis Johnson, Chairperson
Tribe: Karuk. Interim committee.
Northern California Agency.

KASHIA BUSINESS COMMITTEE
Stewarts Point Rancheria
P.O. Box 3854, Stewarts Point, CA 95480
(707) 725-0721
Calvin H. Smith, Sr., Chairperson
Tribe served: Kashia Pomo. Population
served: 215. Central California Agency.

LA JOLLA BAND OF MISSION INDIANS
Star Route, Box 158, Valley Center, CA 92082
(619) 742-3771 Fax 742-3772
Geneva Fitzsimmons, Chairperson
Tribe served: Luiseno. Population served: 235.
General council. Sacramento Area Office.

LA POSTA BAND OF MISSION INDIANS
1064 Barona Rd., Lakeside, CA 92040
(619) 561-2924
Gwendolyn Parada, Chairperson
Tribe: Diegueno (La Posta Band of Mission Indians). Unoccupied. Area: 3,600 acres. General council. Southern California Agency.

LAYTONVILLE RANCHERIA
P.O. Box 1239, Laytonville, CA 95454
(707) 984-6197
Carmen Ochoa, Chairperson
Tribe: Cahto-Pomo. In residence: 150. Area: 200
acres. General council. Central California Agency.

LONE PINE RESERVATION
P.O. Box 747, Lone Pine, CA 93545
(619) 876-5414
Sandra Jefferson Yonge, Chairperson
Tribe served: Paiute-Shoshone. Population
served: 225. Area: 237 acres. Tribal council. Central California Agency.

LOOKOUT RANCHERIA COUNCIL
P.O. Drawer 1570, Burney, CA 96013
(916) 335-5421
Laura Craig, Chairperson
Tribe served: Pit River. Northern California Agency.

LOS COYOTES BAND OF MISSION INDIANS
P.O. Box 249, Warner Springs, CA 92086
(619) 782-3269
Banning Taylor, Sr., Spokesperson
Tribe: Luiseno. In residence: 195. Area: 25,000
acres. General council. So. California Agency.

LYTTON RANCHERIA
P.O. Box 7882, Santa Rosa, CA 95407
(707) 537-1655 Fax 537-1705
Eleanor Lopez, Chairperson
Tribe served: Yurok. Population served: 100.
Central California Agency.

MANCHESTER/PORT ARENA RANCHERIA
P.O. Box 623, Point Arena, CA 95468
(707) 882-2788 Fax 882-4142
Darnell White, Interim Chairperson
Tribe served: Pomo. Population served: 100.
Area: 364 acres. Community council. Central
California Agency.

MANZANITA GENERAL COUNCIL
P.O. Box 1302, Boulevard, CA 92005
(619) 766-4930
Frances Shaw, Chairperson

Tribe served: Diegueno. Population served: 20.
In residence: 22. Area: 3,579 acres. Activities:
Economic Development Project. General council.
Southern California Agency.

MESA GRANDE BAND OF MISSION INDIANS
P.O. Box 270, Santa Ysabel, CA 92070
(619) 282-9650 Fax 282-7838
Carlos Guaffac, Chairperson
Tribe served: Diegueno (Mesa Grande Band of
Mission Indians). In residence: 70. Area: 3,500
acres. Tribal library. General Council. Southern
California Agency.

MIDDLETOWN RANCHERIA
P.O. Box 292, Middletown, CA 95461
Lucas Simon, Chairperson
Tribe served: Pomo. Population served: 65. Area:
109 acres. Interim council. Central California
Agency.

MOORETOWN RANCHERIA
P.O. Box 1842, Oroville, CA 95965
(916) 533-3625 Fax 533-3680
Darlene Cummings, Chairperson
Tribes served: Concow, Maidu. General council.
Central California Agency.

MORONGO BAND OF MISSION INDIANS
11581 Potrero Rd., Banning, CA 92220
(909) 849-4697/8 Fax 849-4425
Rodney Mathews, Vice-Chairperson
Tribe: Cahuilla. In residence: 375. Population
served: 750. Area: 32,250 acres. General Council. Southern California Agency.

NORTH FORK RANCHERIA
P.O. Box 120, 3027 Clement #2
San Francisco, CA 94121
(415) 752-9085
Delores Roberts, Spokesperson
Tribe served: Mono. Central California Agency.

PALA BAND OF MISSION INDIANS
P.O. Box 43, Pala, CA 92059
(619) 742-3784 Fax 742-141 1
Robert Smith, Chairperson
Tribe served: Cupa. In residence: 395. Population served: 580. Area: 11,000 acres. Activities:
Cupa Day (May); Museum. Publication: Pala
Mumalki, newsletter. Southern California Agency.

PAUMA BAND OF MISSION INDIANS
P.O. Box 86, Pauma Valley, CA 92061
(619) 742-1289 Fax 742-3422
Maurice J. Magante, Chairperson
Tribe served: Luiseno (Pauma Band of Mission
Indians.) Reservation served: Pauma & Yuima
Reservation. Population served: 35. Area: 5,750
acres. Activities: education center; memorial celebration. Tribal Council. So. California Agency.

PECHANGA BAND OF MISSION INDIANS
P.O. Box 1477, Temecula, CA 92593
(909) 676-2768 Fax 699-6983
Jennie Miranda, Spokesperson
Tribe served: Luiseno. Population served: 450.
Tribal Council. Southern California Agency.

PICAYUNE RANCHERIA
P.O. Box 269
Coarsegold, CA 93614
(209) 683-6633 Fax 683-0599
Gilbert Cordero, Chairperson
Tribe served: Chuckchansi. In residence: 65. Area:
78 acres, located from the San Joaquin River to
the south to Yosemite National Park to the north,

North Fork to the east to Chowchilla to the west.
Elected officials: Armanda Ramirez, Treasurer;
Nancy Ayala, Secretary; Holly Wyatt & Louie
Ramirez, Jr. Special activity: Pow-Wow. Library.
Tribal council. Central California Agency.

PINOLEVILLE RANCHERIA
367 N. State St. #204, Ukiah, CA 95482
(707) 463-1454
Leona Williams, Chairperson
Central California Agency.

PIT RIVER TRIBAL COUNCIL
P.O. Drawer 1570, Burney, CA 96013
(916) 335-5421 Fax 335-5241
Loomis Jackson, Chairperson
Tribe served: Pit River of XL Ranch. Area: 9,242
acres. Tribal Council. Northern California Agency.

POTTER VALLEY RANCHERIA
755 El Rio St. #B, Ukiah, CA 95482
(707) 468-7494 Fax 468-0874
Shirley Laiwa, Representative
Tribe served: Pomo. Central California Agency.

QUARTZ VALLEY INDIAN RESERVATION
P.O. Box 737, Etna, CA 96032
(916) 467-3307 Fax 467-3466
Fred A. Chase, Chairperson
Lester Alford, Vice Chair
Tribes served: Karuk & Shasta. Membership: 250.
Area: Legal boundaries encompass 640 acres in
Quartz Valley - all tribal land was lost to termination process. Facility: Library. Publication: Quartz
Valley Indian News, newsletter. Northern California Agency.

RAMONA BAND OF CAHUILLA INDIANS
3940 Cary Rd., Anza, CA 92539
(909) 763-0371
Manuel Hamilton, Representative
Tribe: Cahuilla. Southern California Agency.

REDDING RANCHERIA
2000 Rancheria Rd., Redding, CA 96001
(916) 241-8979 Fax 241-1879
Edward R. Foreman, Chairperson
Tribes served: Pit River, Wintun, Yana.
Northern California Agency.

REDWOOD VALLEY RANCHERIA
P.O. Box 499, Redwood Valley, CA 95470
(707) 485-0361
Rita Hoel, Chairperson
Tribe served: Pomo. Central California Agency.

RESIGHINI RANCHERIA
Coast Indian Community Council
P.O. Box 529, Klamath, CA 95548
(707) 482-2431 Fax 482-3425
Donald McCovey, President
Tribe served: Yurok. Population served: 110.
Area: 230 acres. Northern California Agency.

RINCON BAND OF MISSION INDIANS
P.O. Box 68, Valley Center, CA 92082
(619) 749-1051 Fax 749-8901
Robert Calac, Chairperson
Tribe served: Luiseno. Population served: 275.
In residence: 150. Business Committee.
Southern California Agency.

ROBINSON RANCHERIA
P.O. Box 1119, Nice, CA 95464
(707) 275-0527/0227 Fax 275-0235
Douglas Duncan, Chairperson
Tribe served: Pomo. Central California Agency.

**BEAR RIVER BAND OF
ROHNERVILLE RANCHERIA**
P.O. Box 108, Eureka, CA 95502
(707) 443-6150 Fax 442-6403
Brenda Bowie, Chairperson
Tribe served: Wiyot-Mattole.
Northern California Agency.

ROUND VALLEY RESERVATION
Covelo Indian Community Council
P.O. Box 448, Hwy. 162, Covelo, CA 95428
(707) 983-6126 Fax 983-6128
Joseph A. Russ, Sr., President
Tribes: Wailaki, Yuki, Nomlacki, Pomo, Concow,
Pit River, Little Lake. *In residence*: 1,300. *Area*:
33,000 acres one mile north of Covelo. *Activities*:
Operates health center, career center, education
center, senior center, and tribal library; California
Indian Days, annually, 3rd weekend in Septem-
ber; All Indian Rodeo Spring & Fall Festivals. *Pub-
lication*: Poekan Tribal Newsletter/Newspaper.
Central California Agency.

RUMSEY RANCHERIA
P.O. Box 18, Brooks, CA 95606
(916) 796-3400 Fax 796-2143
Paula Lorenzo, Chairperson
Tribe: Wintun. *Population served*: 50. *Area*: 67
acres. Community Council. Central California
Agency.

SAN MANUEL BAND OF MISSION INDIANS
P.O. Box 266, Patton, CA 92369
(909) 864-8933
Lynn R. LeRoy, Chairperson
Tribe served: Serrano (San Manuel Band of
Serrano Mission Indians). *In residence*: 55. *Popu-
lation served*: 90. *Area*: 650 acres. General Coun-
cil. Southern California Agency.

SAN PASQUAL GENERAL COUNCIL
P.O. Box 365, Valley Center, CA 92082
(619) 749-3200
Ray Natividad, Chairperson
Tribe served: Diegueno (San Pasqual Band of
Mission Indians.) *Population served*: 350. *Area*:
1,380 acres. Tribal Council. Southern California
Agency.

SANTA ROSA RANCHERIA
P.O. Box 8, Lemoore, CA 93245
(209) 924-1278 Fax 924-3583
Clarence Atwell, Jr., Chairperson
Tribe served: Tache, Yokut. *In residence*: 135.
Population served: 275. *Area*: 170 acres. General
Council. Central California Agency.

SANTA ROSA RESERVATION
325 N. Western St., Hemet, CA 92343
(909) 849-4761
Anthony Largo, Spokesperson
Tribe served: Cahuilla. *In residence*: 110. *Area*: 11,000
acres. General Council. So. California Agency.

SANTA YNEZ BAND OF MISSION INDIANS
P.O. Box 517, Santa Ynez, CA 93460
(805) 688-7997 Fax 688-8005
David Dominguez, Chairperson
Tribe: Chumash (Santa Ynez Band of Chumash
Mission Indians). *In residence*: 100. *Population
served*: 200. *Area*: 100 acres. General Council.
Southern California Agency.

SANTA YSABEL BAND OF MISSION INDIANS
P.O. Box 130, Santa Ysabel, CA 92070
(619) 765-0845 Fax 765-0320
Ben Scerato, Chairperson

Tribe: Diegueno (Santa Ysabel Band of Mission
Indians). *In residence*: 325. *Population served*:
900. *Area*: 15,500 acres. General Council. Southern California Agency.

SCOTTS VALLEY BAND OF POMO INDIANS
149 N. Main #200, Lakeport, CA 95453
(707) 263-4771 Fax 263-4773
Leslie Miller, Chairperson
Tribe served: Pomo. *Population served*: 100.
General Council. Central California Agency.

SHERWOOD VALLEY RANCHERIA
190 Sherwood Hill Dr., Willits, CA 95490
(707) 459-9690 Fax 459-6936
Mike Knight, Chairperson
Tribe served: Pomo. *Population served*: 175.
General Council. Central California Agency.

SHINGLE SPRINGS RANCHERIA
P.O. Box 1340, Shingle Springs, CA 95682
(619) 676-8010 phone & fax
W. David Murry & Elsie Shilin, Co-Chairs
Tribe served: Me-Wuk. Unoccupied.
Area: 160 acres. Central California Agency.

SMITH RIVER RANCHERIA
Smith River Rancheria Tribal Council
P.O. Box 239, Smith River, CA 95567
(707) 487-9255 Fax 487-0930
Loren J. Bommelyn, Chairperson
Tribe served: Tolowa. *In residence*: 175.
Area: 161 acres. Northern California Agency.

SOBOBA BAND OF POMO INDIANS
P.O. Box 487, San Jacinto, CA 92383
(909) 654-2765 Fax 654-4198
Ernest Salgado, Jr., Chairperson
Tribe served: Luiseno (Soboba Band of Mission
Indians.) *Population served*: 450. *Area*: 5,000
acres. Southern California Agency.

STEWARTS POINT RANCHERIA
P.O. Box 38, Stewarts Point, CA 95480
(707) 528-4267
Calvin H. Smith, Sr., Chairperson
Tribe: Kashia Pomo. *In residence*: 100. *Area*: 40
acres. Committee. Central California Agency.

SULPHUR BANK RANCHERIA
ELEM INDIAN COLONY OF POMO INDIANS
Elem General Council
P.O. Box 618, Clearlake Oaks, CA 95423
(707) 998-2549
Thomas Brown, Chairperson
Tribe served: Pomo. *In residence*: 55.*Population
served*: 165. Central California Agency.

SUSANVILLE RANCHERIA
P.O. Drawer U, Susanville, CA 96130
(916) 257-6264 Fax 257-6983
Nicolas J. Padilla, Chairperson
Tribes: Paiute, Maidu, and Pit River. *In residence*:
350. *Area*: 140 acres. Business Council. Central
California Agency.

SYCUAN RESERVATION
5459 Dehesa Rd., El Cajon, CA 92021
(619) 445-2613 Fax 445-1927
Daniel Tucker, Spokesperson
Tribe: Diegueno (Sycuan Band of Mission Indians).
In residence: 70. *Area*: 640 acres. Business Committee. Southern California Agency.

TABLE BLUFF RANCHERIA
P.O. Box 519, Loleta, CA 95551
(707) 733-5055 Fax 733-5601

Albert E. James, Chairperson
Tribe served: Wiyot. *In residence*: 218.
Area: 102 acres. Northern California Agency.

TABLE MOUNTAIN RANCHERIA
P.O. Box 243, Friant, CA 93626
(209) 822-2587 Fax 822-2693
Vernon Castro & Lewis Barnes, Co-Chairpersons
Tribe served: Yokut. Central California Agency.

TIMBISHA SHOSHONE TRIBE
P.O. Box 206, Death Valley, CA 92328
(619) 786-2374 Fax 786-2375
Roy Kennedy, Chairperson
Tribe: Timbisha Shoshone. *In residence*: 45.
Publication: "Nangkawittu," newsletter.
Central California Agency.

**TORRES-MARTINEZ
BAND OF MISSION INDIANS**
66-725 Martinez Rd., Thermal, CA 92274
(619) 397-8144 Fax 397-0300
Mary E. Belardo, Chairperson
Tribe: Cahuilla. *In residence*: 90. *Area*: 25,000
acres. Business Committee. Southern California
Agency.

TRINIDAD RANCHERIA
P.O. Box 630, Trinidad, CA 95570
(707) 677-0211 Fax 677-3921
Marian Crutchfield, Chairperson
Tribe served: Yurok. *Population served*: 70.
Community Council. Northern California Agency.

TULE RIVER RESERVATION
P.O. Box 589, Porterville, CA 93258
(209) 781-4271 Fax 781-4610
Irma Hunter, Chairperson
Tribe served: Yokut. *In residence*: 550.
Area: 54,000 acres. Tribal Council. Central
California Agency.

TUOLUMNE ME-WUK RANCHERIA
P.O. Box 699, Tuolumne, CA 95379
(209) 928-3475 Fax 928-1295
Sonny Hendricks, Chairperson
Tribe: Me-Wuk (Miwok). *Population served*: 285.
Area: 325 acres. Community Council. Central
California Agency.

**TWENTY NINE PALMS
BAND OF MISSION INDIANS**
555 Sunrise Hwy. #200
Palm Springs, CA 92264
(619) 320-8168
June Mike, Chairperson
Tribe: Luiseno (Twenty-Nine Palms Band of Mission Indians). Unoccupied. *Area*: 160 acres. Southern California Agency.

UNITED LUMBEE NATION OF N.C. & AMERICA
P.O. Box 512, Fall River Mills, CA 96028
(916) 336-6701
Eva Silver Star Reed, Chief
Elnora Bailey, Vice Chief
Elmer "Shorty" Gray, Secretary
Billy Reed, Treasurer
Tribe served: United Lumbee Nation. *Council El-
ders*: Morning Hawk Lawson, Momma Quail
Potvin, Paul Savage, and Helyn Taylor. Pow-wow.
Publications: United Lumbee Nation Times, quar-
terly newspaper; "United Lumbee Ceremonies,"
1982, "Over the Cooking Fires," 1982, and "United
Lumbee's Deer Clan Cook Book," 1988, all by
Princess Silver Star Reed; and "A Message to Our
People," by Frank Chilcote & Princess Silver Star
Reed. Northern California Agency.

UPPER LAKE RANCHERIA
P.O. Box 245272, Sacramento, CA 95820
(916) 371-2576
Phyllis Harden, Vice-Chairperson
Tribe served: Pomo. Central California Agency.

VIEJAS (BARON LONG) RESERVATION
Viejas Tribal Council
P.O. Box 908, Alpine, CA 92001
(619) 445-3810 Fax 445-5337
Anthony Pico, Chairperson
Tribe: Diegueno (Viejas Baron Long Capitan Grande Band of Mission Indians). *In residence*: 195. *Area*: 1,600 acres. Tribal Committee. Southern California Agency.

WINNEMUCCA INDIAN COLONY
420 Pardee, Susanville, CA 96130
(916) 257-7093
Glenn Wasson, Chairperson
Tribe: Paiute. *In residence*: 110. *Area*: 340 acres. Tribal Council. Western Nevada Agency.

WOODFORDS COMMUNITY COUNCIL
96 Washoe Blvd., Markleeville, CA 96120
(916) 694-2170
M. Kevin Jones, Chairperson
Tribe served: Component Band of the Washoe Tribe. Western Nevada Agency.

YUROK INDIAN RESERVATION
517 Third St., Suite 21, Eureka, CA 95501
(800) 848-8765; (707) 444-0433 Fax 444-0437
Susie L. Long, Chairperson
Tribe served: Yurok. Tribal council. Northern California Agency.

COLORADO

SOUTHERN UTE TRIBE
P.O. Box 737, Ignacio, CO 81137
(303) 563-0100 Fax 563-0396
Leonard C. Burch, Chairperson
Tom Shipps, Tribal Attorney
Tribe served: Southern Ute. *In residence*: 1,200. *Area*: 307,000 acres located along the Colorado-New Mexico border. *Activities*: Sun Dance, Bear Dance, and Ute Fair. *Publication*: Ute Drum, newspaper. Library. *Head Start Program*: P.O. Box 400 (303) 563-4566. Cheryl Clay, Director - provides comprehensive early childhood development services to 95 children and their families in the reservation area. Tribal council. Southern Ute Agency.

UTE MOUNTAIN RESERVATION
Ute Mountain Ute Tribal Council
P.O. Box 52, Towaoc, CO 81334
(303) 565-3751 Fax 565-7412
Judy Knight-Frank, Chairperson
Tribe: Ute Mountain Ute. *In residence*: 1,600. *Area*: 590,000 acres. Located in Colorado, New Mexico, and Utah. Ute Mountain Agency.

CONNECTICUT

EASTERN PEQUOT RESERVATION
North Stonington, CT 06359
Roy Sebastian (Chief Hockeo), Chairperson
Tribe: Pequot. *Area*: 220 acres. Eastern Area Office.

GOLDEN HILL INDIAN RESERVATION
Golden Hill Paugussett 3 Chief
Traditional Government
95 Stanavage Rd., Trumbull, CT 06415
(203) 537-0390
Moonface Bear, Leader
Chief Big Eagle (Aurelius H. Piper, Sr.)
Chief Quiet Hawk (Aurelius H. Piper, Jr.)
Tribe served: Paugussett Pequot and Mohegan. *In residence*: 5. *Population served*: 80. *Area*: 1/4 acre, 1 house. *Program*: Sweatlodge; White Buffalo Society. *Publications*: Quarter Acre of Heartache, and Red Man in Red Square. Eastern Area Office.

MASHANTUCKET PEQUOT TRIBAL NATION
P.O. Box 3060, Ledyard, CT 06339
(203) 536-2681 Fax 572-0421
Richard A. (Skip) Hayward, Chairperson
Kenneth M. Reels, Vice-Chairperson
Gary Carter, Secreaty/Treasurer
Terry Bell, Director-PR & Cultural Resources
Charlene Jones, Tribal Librarian
Bruce MacDonald, Pequot Times Editor
Nation federally recognized in 1983. *Tribe served*: Mashantucket Pequot. *Area*: 184 acres. *Tribal council members*: Barbara Hartwell, Pedro Johnson, Michael Thomas, Juanita H. Montey. *Activity*: Foxwoods Resort & Casino; Library; Museum & Cultural Center being being planned and will open around January 1, 1998. *Publications*: The Pequot Times, monthly tribal newspaper; and sells the book, "The Pequots in Southern New England: The Fall and Rise of an American Indian Nation." Eastern Area Office.

MOHEGAN TRIBAL COUNCIL
47 N. Main St., West Hartford, CT 06107
(203) 527-5216
Ralph W. Sturges, Chief
Recognized as a tribe by the Federal Government in March of 1994. Has bought about 700 acres for a reservation including 244 acres on the Thames River in Montville where the tribe plans to convert a closed-down factory into a casino. The state is also giving the tribe the 116-acre Fort Shantok State Park, overlooking the river, which is the site of the Mohegans' only active burial ground. Once the casino is operating, however, the tribe would pay $3 million for the park out of its revenue. Eastern Area Office.

PAUCATUCK EASTERN PEQUOT TRIBE
935 Lantern Hill Rd., Ledyard, CT 06339
Roy Sebastian (Chief Hockeo), Chairperson
Eastern Area Office.
Tribe served: Paucatuck Eastern Pequot.

SCHAGHTICOKE TRIBAL NATION OF KENT
Schaghticoke Rd., Kent, OH 06757
Schaghticoke Tribal Council
605 Main St., Monroe, CT 06468
(203) 459-2531 Fax 459-2535
Richard Velky, Chairperson
Paulette S. Crone-Morange, Vice Chair
Tribe: Schaghticoke. *In residence*: 300. *Area*: 400 acres. Located in Kent, CT. Eastern Area Office.

FLORIDA

BIG CYPRESS RESERVATION
c/o Seminole Agency, 6075 Stirling Rd.
Hollywood, FL 33024
Tribe: Miccosukee Seminole. *In residence*: 450. *Area*: 42,700. Located in southern Florida.

BRIGHTON RESERVATION
c/o Seminole Agency
6075 Stirling Rd., Hollywood, FL 33024
Tribe: Cow Creek. *In residence*: 440. *Area*: 35,800 acres located in south-central Florida.

MICCOSUKEE RESERVATION
Miccosukee Business Committee
Box 440021, Tamiami Sta., Miami, FL 33144
(305) 223-8380/3 Fax 223-101 1
Billy Cypress, Chairman
Tribe served: Miccosukee-Creek. *Tribe*: Creek. In residence: 495. *Area*: 333 acres located on Tamiami Trail, 40 miles west of Miami. Business Committee. Head Start Program. Eastern Area Office.

SEMINOLE RESERVATION
6073 Stirling Rd., Hollywood, FL 33024
(305) 583-7112 Fax 581-8917
James Billie, Chairperson
Tribe: Seminole. *In residence*: 500. *Population served*: 1,450. *Area*: 480 acres. Located on U.S. 441, in the Fort Lauderdale-Miami area. *Local attractions*: Seminole Indian Village featuring typical village life and customs, native arts & crafts, native animal exhibits. *Activities*: Indian ceremonials held in mid-July. Museum and Library. Tribal council. Head Start Program. Seminole Agency.

IDAHO

COEUR D'ALENE RESERVATION
Coeur D'Alene Tribal Council
Route 1, Plummer, ID 83851
(208) 686-1800 Fax 686-1 182
Ernest Stensgar, Chairperson
Tribe: Coeur D'Alene (Skitswish). *In residence*: 850. *Area*: 69,435 acres located 35 miles south of Coeur D'Alene, Idaho. Tribal Council. Northern Idaho Agency.

DUCK VALLEY RESERVATION
Duck Valley Shoshone Paiute Tribal Council
P.O. Box 219, Owyhee, NV 89832
(702) 757-3161
Tribes: Shoshone and Paiute.
Located in Idaho and Nevada.

FORT HALL RESERVATION
Fort Hall Business Council
P.O. Box 306, Fort Hall, ID 83203
(208) 238-3700 Fax 237-0796
Marvin Osborne, Chairperson
Tribes: Shoshone-Bannock. *In residence*: 4,000. *Area*: 523,917 acres. Located near Pocatello, Idaho, east and south of the Snake River. *Local attractions*: Annual Shoshone-Bannock Indian Festival; Trading Post; Museum & Library; Fishing & Hunting in the "Bottoms area of Reservation; High Stakes Bingo; American Falls. Head Start Program. Fort Hall Agency.

KOOTENAI RESERVATION
Kootenai Tribal Council
P.O. Box 1269, Bonners Ferry, ID 83805
(208) 267-3519 Fax 267-2762
Velma Bahe, Chairperson
Tribe: Kootenai. *In residence*: 150. *Area*: 2,680 acres. Located in Boundary County, near Mirror Lake and the Canadian border. Tribal Council. Northern Idaho Agency.

NEZ PERCE RESERVATION
Nez Perce Tribal Executive Committee
P.O. Box 305, Lapwai, ID 83540
  (208) 843-2253 Fax 843-7354
  Charles H. "Pete" Hayes, Chairperson
Tribe: Nez Perce. *In residence*: 2,200. *Area*:
92,685 acres located a few miles from the city of
Lewiston in Nez Perce, Lewis, Clearwater and
Idaho Counties. Tribal Council. Head Start Program. Northern Idaho Agency.

NORTHWESTERN BAND
OF SHOSHONI NATION
P.O. Box 637, Blackfoot, ID 83221
  (208) 785-7401 Fax 785-2206
  George Worley, Chairperson
Tribe served: Shoshoni. Located in Iowa & Utah.
Tribal council. Fort Hall Agency.

INDIANA

INDIANA MIAMI COUNCIL
641 Buchanan St., Huntington, IN 46750
Not yet federally recognized.

MIAMI NATION OF INDIANS
OF INDIANA COUNCIL
P.O. Box 41, Peru, IN 46970
  (317) 473-9631
Not yet federally recognized.

UPPER KISPOKO BAND
OF THE SHAWNEE NATION
Kokomo, IN 46901
  (317) 457-5376
Not yet federally recognized.

IOWA

OMAHA RESERVATION
Omaha Tribal Council
P.O. Box 368, Macy, NE 68039
  (402) 837-5391 Fax 878-2943
  Doran L. Morris, Sr., Chairperson
Tribe: Omaha. Located in Iowa and Nebraska.
Winnebago Agency. See listing under Nebraska.

SAC AND FOX RESERVATION
Sac and Fox Tribal Council
3137 F Ave., Tama, IA 52339
  (515) 484-4678/5358 Fax 484-5424
  Gailey Wanatee, Chief
Tribe served: Sac and Fox. *Population served*:
700. *Area*: 10 acres. Sac & Fox Area Field Office.

WINNEBAGO RESERVATION
Winnebago Tribal Council
Winnebago, NE 68071
  (402) 878-2272 Fax 878-2963
  John Blackhawk, Chairperson
Tribe: Winnebago. Located in Nebraska and Iowa
(off-reservation lands in Iowa.) Winnebago Agency.
See listing under Nebraska.

KANSAS

IOWA RESERVATION
Iowa of Kansas Executive Committee
Rt. 1, Box 58A, White Cloud, KS 66094
  (913) 595-3258 Fax 595-6610

  Leon Campbell, Chairperson
Tribe: Iowa. *In residence*: 310. Located in Kansas
and Nebraska. Tribal Council. (See listing under
Nebraska.) Horton Agency.

KICKAPOO RESERVATION
Kickapoo of Kansas Tribal Council
P.O. Box 271, Horton, KS 66439
  (913) 486-2131 Fax 486-2801
  Emery Negonsott, Chairperson
Tribe served: Kickapoo. *Population served*: 600.
Head Start Program. Anadarko Area Office.

PRAIRIE POTAWATOMI RESERVATION
Prairie Band Potawatomi Tribal Council
14880 K. Road, Mayetta, KS 66509
  (913) 966-2255 Fax 966-2144
  Gary E. Mitchell, Chairperson
Tribe served: Prairie Brand Potawatomi.
Population served: 1,350. Horton Agency.

SAC & FOX TRIBE OF MISSOURI TRIBE
Sac & Fox of Missouri Tribal Council
Route 1, Box 60, Reserve, KS 66434
  (913) 742-7471 Fax 742-3785
  Joan Rebar, Chairperson
Tribe served: Sac & Fox of Kansas & Nebraska.
Horton Agency. See listing under Nebraska.

LOUISIANA

CHITIMACHA RESERVATION
Chitimacha Tribal Council
P.O. Box 661, Charenton, LA 70523
  (318) 923-7215 Fax 923-7791
  Ralph Darden, Chairperson
Tribe: Chitimacha. *In residence*: 310. *Area*: 283
acres. *Activities*: Chitimacha Tribal Fair (Fourth of
July Weekend). *Publication*: The Chitimacha
People, by Herbert T. Hoover (part of the tribal
series.) Museum and library. Eastern Area Office.

COUSHATTA RESERVATION
Coushatta Tribal Council
P.O. Box 818, Elton, LA 70532
  (318) 584-2261 Fax 584-2998
  Lovelin Poncho, Chairperson
Tribe: Coushatta. *In residence*: 295.
Choctaw Agency.

HOUMA INDIAN COMMUNITIES
Tribe: Houma. *In residence*: 2,750 (six communities.) Located in southeast Louisiana, Terrebonne
and Lafourche parishes. No coporate land base.

TUNICA-BILOXI INDIAN TRIBE
P.O. Box 311, Mansura, LA 71351
  (318) 253-9767 Fax 253-9791
  Earl Barbry, Sr., Chairperson
Tribe served: Tunica-Biloxi. Eastern Area Office.

MAINE

AROOSTOOK BAND OF MICMAC INDIANS
P.O. Box 772, Presque Island, ME 04769
  (207) 764-1972 Fax 764-7667
  Roger Pictou, President
Tribe served: Micmac. *Population served*: 485. The
total Micmac population is about 15,000, most of
whom live in Canada. Between 550 and 700
Micmacs live in Maine and are the most traditional
Indians in the eastern U.S. Eastern Area Office.

HOULTON BAND OF MALISEET INDIANS
Route 3, Box 450, Houlton, ME 04730
  (207) 532-4273 Fax 532-2660
  Mr. Clair Sabattis, Chairperson
Tribe served: Maliseet. *Population served*: 300.
Eastern Area Office.

INDIAN TOWNSHIP RESERVATION
Indian Township Passamaquoddy Tribe
P.O. Box 301, Princeton, ME 04668
  (207) 796-2301 Fax 796-5256
  John Stevens, Tribal Governor
Tribe: Passamaquoddy. *In residence*: 395. *Area*:
18,000 acres. Indian communities at Peter Dana
Point and The Strip. Eastern Area Office.

PENOBSCOT RESERVATION
Penobscot Tribal Council
PENOBSCOT TRIBAL COUNCIL
Community Bldg. - Indian Island
Old Town, ME 04468
  (207) 827-7776 Fax 827-6042
  Jerry Pardilla, Tribal Governor
Tribe: Penobscot. *In residence*: 1,150. *Area*: 4,400
acres on Indian Island. Eastern Area Office.

PLEASANT POINT RESERVATION
Pleasant Point Passamaquoddy Tribe
P.O. Box 343
Perry, ME 04667
  (207) 853-2551 Fax 853-6039
  Cliv Dore, Tribal Governor
Tribe served: Passamaquoddy. *In residence*: 800.
Area: 212 acres. *Council Members*: Gerald
Barnes, Maxwell Barnes, Ralph Dana, Frederick
Francis, John Francis, and Shirley Mitchell. *Activities*: Annual Indian Day Ceremoies-2nd weekend in August; operates Beatrice Rafferty School
and Waponahki Museum & Resource Center.
Publications. Eastern Area Office.

MASSACHUSETTS

WAMPANOAG RESERVATION
Wampanoag Tribal Council of Gay Head
(a.k.a. Aquinnah)
State Rd., RR 1 Box 137,
Gay Head, MA 02535
  (508) 645-9265 Fax 645-3790
  Beverly Wright, Chairperson
Tribe: Wampanoag. *In residence*: 550.
Area: 475 acres. Eastern Area Office.

MICHIGAN

BAY MILLS RESERVATION
Bay Mills Executive Council
Route 1, Box 313, Brimley, MI 49715
  (906) 248-3241 Fax 248-3283
  Jeff Parker, Chairperson
Tribe: Chippewa (Bay Mills and Sault Ste Marie
Bands.) *In residence*: 475. *Area*: 2,200 acres.
Executive Council. Michigan Agency.

GRAND TRAVERSE RESERVATION
Grand Traverse Band Tribal Council
Peshawbestown Community Center
2605 N.W. Bayshore Dr., P.O. Box 118
Suttons Bay, MI 49682
  (616) 271-3538 Fax 271-4861
  Joseph C. Raphael, Chairperson
Tribe served: Chippewa. Michigan Agency.

HANNAHVILLE INDIAN COMMUNITY
N14911 Hannahville Blvd. Rd., Wilson, MI 49896
(906) 466-2342 Fax 466-2933
Kenneth Meshiguad, Chairperson
Tribe served: Potawatomi. *In residence*: 375. *Area*: 2,850 acres. Tribal Council. Michigan Agency.

ISABELLA RESERVATION
Saginaw-Chippewa Tribal Council
7070 E. Broadway Rd., Mt. Pleasant, MI 48858
(517) 772-5700 Fax 772-3508
Gail George, Chief
Tribe: Saginaw-Chippewa. *In residence*: 450. *Area*: 1,125 acres. Michigan Agency.

L'ANSE RESERVATION
Keweenah Bay Tribal Council
Route 1, Box 45, Baraga, MI 49908
(906) 353-6623 Fax 353-7540
Frederick Dakota, Chairperson
Tribe: Chippewa (Keewenah Bay, L'Anse, and Ontonagan Bands.) *In residence*: 950. *Area*: 10,000 acres. Michigan Agency.

LAC VIEUX DESERT BAND OF LAKE SUPERIOR CHIPPEWA INDIANS
P.O. Box 249, Choate Rd., Watersmeet, MI 49969
(906) 358-4577/8/9 Fax 358-4785
John C. McGeshick, Chairperson
Tribe: Chippewa (Lac Vieux Desert Band.) Michigan Agency.

SAULT STE. MARIE TRIBE OF CHIPPEWA INDIANS RESERVATION
Sault Ste. Marie Chippewa Tribal Council
2218 Shunk Rd., Sault Ste. Marie, MI 49783
(906) 635-6050 Fax 635-0741
Bernard Bouschor, Chairperson
Tribe served: Sault Ste. marie Chippewa. *Reservations served*: St. Ignace, Manistique, Munising, Michigan. *In residence*: 2,500. *Area*: 242 acres. *Activities*: Tribal pow-wows (two each summer, July 4th (Sault Ste. Marie), and first week in August (St. Ignace.) *Publication*: Nisasotowen, Tribal newspaper. Michigan Agency.

MINNESOTA

FOND DU LAC RESERVATION
Business Committee
105 University Rd., Cloquet, MN 55720
(218) 879-4593 Fax 879-4164
Robert "Sonny" Peacock, Chairperson
Peter J. Defoe, Secretary-Treasurer
Tribe: Chippewa. *In residence*: 1,750. *Area*: 100,000 acres. *Activities*: Ni-mi-win pow wow; Mash-ka-wisen pow wow. Operates Fond du Lac Ojibway School (Library); operates Big Bucks Casino & Bingo Hall, and Fond De Luth Casino & Bingo Hall. Head Start Program. Component reservation of Minnesota Chippewa Tribe. Minnesota Agency.

GRAND PORTAGE RESERVATION
Business Committee
P.O. Box 428, Grand Portage, MN 55605
(218) 475-2279/7 Fax 475-2284
Norman DesChampe, Chairperson
Tribe: Chippewa. *In residence*: 325. *Area*: 43,836 acres located near Lake Superior, adjacent to the Canadian border. *Activities*: Operates hotel, bingo & casino facility. Head Start Program. Component reservation of Minnesota Chippewa Tribe. Minnesota Agency.

LEECH LAKE RESERVATION
Business Tribal Council
Route 3, Box 100, Cass Lake, MN 56633
(218) 335-8200 Fax 335-8309
Alfred "Tig" Pemberton, Chairperson
James D. Michaud, Secretary-Treasurer
Tribe served: Chippewa (Mississippi & Pillanger Bands.) *In residence*: 5,200. *Area*: 27,760 acres. *Tribal representatives*: Alfred Fairbanks, Jr., District I; Jack H. Seelye, District II; Myron F. Ellis, District III. *Activities*: Five annual pow-wows: Spring, Fourth of July, Labor Day, Veterans Day, and Winter; operates Chief Bug-O-Nay-Ge-Shig School & Leech Lake Tribal College; operates The Palace Bingo & Casino, and Northern Lights Casino & Bingo Hall. Head Start Program. *Publication*: Leech Lake Reservation Fact Sheet. Component reservation of Minnesota Chippewa Tribe. Minnesota Agency.

LOWER SIOUX INDIAN COMMUNITY
Lower Sioux Indian Community Council
RR 1, Box 308, Morton, MN 56270
(507) 697-6185 Fax 697-6110
Joseph Goodthunder, President
Tribe served: Mdewakanton Sioux. *In residence*: 230. *Area*: 1,750 acres. Minneapolis Area Office.

MILLE LACS RESERVATION
Business Committee
HCR 67 Box 194, Onamia, MN 56359
(612) 532-4181 Fax 532-4209
Marjorie Anderson, Chairperson
Tribe served: Chippewa. *In residence*: 950. *Area*: 3,600 acres. *Activities*: Operates Grand Casino Hinckley & Bingo Hall. Head Start Program. Component reservation of Minnesota Chippewa Tribe. Minnesota Agency.

MINNESOTA CHIPPEWA TRIBE
Tribal Executive Committee
P.O. Box 217, Cass Lake, MN 56633
(218) 335-8581 Fax 335-6562
Darrell Wadena, President
Tribe served: Chippewa. *Reservations served*: Nett Lake, Fond du Lac, Grand Portage, Leech Lake, Mill Lac, White Earth. Minnesota Agency.

NETT LAKE RESERVATION
Bois Forte Tribal Business Committee
P.O. Box 16, Nett Lake, MN 55772
(218) 757-3261 Fax 757-3312
Gary Donald, Chairperson
Tribe served: Chippewa (Deer Creek). *In residence*: 1,250. *Area*: 41,750 acres. Head Start Program. Component reservation of Minnesota Chippewa Tribe. Minnesota Agency.

PRAIRIE ISLAND RESERVATION
Prairie Island Community Council
1158 Island Blvd., Welch, MN 55089
(612) 388-2554 Fax 388-1576
Curtis Campbell, Sr., President
Tribe served: Mdewakanton Sioux. *In residence*: 135. *Area*: 534 acres. *Activities*: Operates Treasure Island Casino & Bingo Hall. Minneapolis Area Office.

RED LAKE RESERVTION
Red Lake Tribal Council
P.O. Box 550, Red Lake, MN 56671
(218) 679-3341 Fax 679-3378
Bobby Whitefeather, Chairperson
Tribe served: Chippewa. *In residence*: 4,850. *Area*: 564,364 acres along lower Red Lake, 30 miles north of Bemidji, MN. *Activities*: Operates three casinos. Head Start Program. Red Lake Agency.

SHAKOPEE SIOUX COMMUNITY
Shakopee Sioux Community Council
2330 Sioux Trail, NW, Prior Lake, MN 55372
(612) 445-8900 Fax 445-8906
Stanley Crooks, Chairperson
Tribe served: Mdewakanton Sioux. *In residence*: 110. *Activity*: Operates Mystic Lake Casino & Bingo Hall. Minneapolis Area Office.

UPPER SIOUX INDIAN COMMUNITY
Upper Sioux Board of Trustees
P.O. Box 147, Granite Falls, MN 56241
(612) 564-2360 Fax 564-3264
Lorraine Gouge, Chairperson
Tribe served: Santee Sioux. *In residence*: 150. *Area*: 750 acres. *Activities*: Operates Fire Fly Creek Casino. Minneapolis Area Office.

WHITE EARTH RESERVATION
Business Committee
Hwy. 224, Box 418, White Earth, MN 56591
(218) 983-3285 Fax 983-3641
Darrell Wadena, Chairperson
Tribe served: Chippewa. *In residence*: 3,500. *Area*: 27,560 acres. *Activities*: Operates Shooting Star Casino & Bingo in Mahnomen, Minnesota. Head Start Program. Component reservation of Minnesota Chippewa Tribe. Minnesota Agency.

MISSISSIPPI

MISSISSIPPI CHOCTAW RESERVATION
Tribal Council of the Mississippi Band of Choctaws
Box 6010 - Choctaw Branch,
Philadelphia, MS 39350
(601) 656-5251 Fax 656-1992
Phillip Martin, Tribal Chief
Tribe served: Mississippi Band of Choctaws. *Membership*: 6,000. *In residence*: 5,500. *Area*: 21,000 acres located in nine east-central Mississippi counties centering on eight distinct Indian communities. *Tribal services*: Education - operates six grammar schools, a middle school, and a high school; Adult Education Program; Health Care - tribe manages a 43 bed hospital; Choctaw Housing Authority - manages over 500 housing units. *Economic Activities and Resources*: Chahta Enterprise; Choctaw Electronics Enterprise; Choctaw manufacturing Enterprise; Choctaw Greetings Enterprise; First American Printing and Dirct Mail Enterprise; Choctaw Residential Center Enterprise; Choctaw Shopping Enterprise; Choctaw-Creek Technologies; Chata Development Co.; Choctaw Transit Authority; and Operates Choctaw Resort & Casino. Tribal enterprises employ 1,700 workers and generates over $60 million in annual sales. *Communication*: tribe operates local station WHTV. *Activities*: Annual Choctaw Indian Fair (July). Museum. Library. *Publications*: Choctaw Community News, monthly newspaper. Head Start Program. Choctaw Agency.

MISSOURI

EASTERN SHAWNEE TRIBE OF OKLAHOMA
Eastern Shawnee Tribal Council
P.O. Box 350, Seneca, MO 64865
(918) 666-2435 Fax 666-3325
George J. (Buck) Captain, Chief
Tribe: Eastern Shawnee. *In residence*: 395. *Area*: 210 acres. *Special activity*: Traditional Indian head-

ing classes. *Publication*: Shooting Star, Tribal newsletter. Library. Tribal Council. Miami Agency.

MONTANA

BLACKFEET RESERVATION
Blackfeet Tribal Business Council
P.O. Box 850, Browning, MT 59417
(406) 338-7521 Fax 338-7530
Earl Old Person, Chairperson
Tribe served: Blackfeet. In residence: 7,000. Area: 955,241 acres. Located west of Glacier National Park, south of the Canadian border. Local attraction: Museum of the Plains Indians. Activities: Annual Blackfeet Medicine Lodge Ceremonial and Sun Dance (July.) Owns the Blackfeet National Bank. Head Start Program. Blackfeet Agency.

CROW INDIAN RESERVATION
Crow Tribal Council
P.O. Box 159, Crow Agency, MT 59022
(406) 638-2601 Fax 638-7283
Clara Nomee, Chairperson
Joseph Pickett, Vice Chair
Tribe: Crow. *In residence*: 9,000 (enrolled). *Total acreage*: 2.1 million acres located in south eastern Montana within Big Horn County, 15 miles southeast of Hardin, Montana. Occupies a total of 408,444 acres of trust land. *Activities*: Annual Crow Fair and Rodeo Celebration, 3rd week-end in August; pow-wow at New Years; operates tribal college and library, "Little Bighorn College. *Local attraction*: Custer Battlefield National Monument and Museum. *Publication*: The Crow Briefs, monthly tribal newsbrief. *Head Start Program*: Crow Central Education Commission, P.O. Box 249 (406) 638-2697. Crow Agency.

FLATHEAD RESERVATION
Confederated Salish & Kootenai Tribe
P.O. Box 278, Pablo, MT 59855
(406) 675-2700 Fax 675-2806
Michael T. Pablo, Chairperson
Tribe served: Salish & Kootenai. *In residence*: 3,500. *Area*: 140,000 acres. Head Start Program. Flathead Agency.

FORT BELKNAP RESERVATION
Fort Belknap Community Council
RR 1, Box 66, Harlem, MT 59526
(406) 353-2205 Fax 353-2797
Harlan K. Mount, President
Tribes: Gros Ventre and Assiniboine-Sioux. *In residence*: 2,500. *Area*: 622,644 acres. Located 50 miles east of Havre, Montana. Head Start Program. Fort Belknap Agency.

FORT PECK RESERVATION
Fort Peck Tribal Executive Board
P.O. Box 1027, Poplar, MT 59255
(406) 768-5155 Fax 768-5478
Caleb Shields, Chairperson
Tribe: Assiniboine-Sioux. *In residence*: 5,500. *Area*: 981,144 acres. Loctaed 20 miles south of the Canadian border. Head Start Program. Fort Peck Agency.

NORTHERN CHEYENNE RESERVATION
Northern Cheyenee Tribal Council
P.O. Box 128, Lame Deer, MT 59043
(406) 477-8284 Fax 477-6210
Lievando Fisher, President
Tribe served: Northern Cheyenne. *In residence*: 3,300. *Area*: 425,000 acres. Head Start Program. Northern Cheyenne Agency.

ROCKY BOY'S RESERVATION
Chippewa-Cree Business Committee
Rocky Boy Route, Box 544, Box Elder, MT 59521
(406) 395-4282 Fax 395-4497
John SunChild, Chairperson
Tribes served: Chippewa & Cree. *Reservation served*: Rocky Boy's Reservation. *Population served*: 1,950. *Area*: 107,532 acres located in Bear Paw Mountains, north-central Montana. Head Start Program. Rocky Boy's Agency.

NEBRASKA

IOWA RESERVATION
Tribe: Iowa. Located in Kansas & Nebraska. See listing under Kansas.

OMAHA RESERVATION
Omaha Tribal Council
P.O. Box 368, Macy, NE 68039
(402) 837-5391 Fax 878-2943
Dr. Rudi L. Mitchell, Chairperson
Tribe: Omaha. *In residence*: 1,500. *Area*: 27,700 acres. Located in Nebraska and Iowa. Head Start Program. Winnebago Agency.

PINE RIDGE RESERVATION
Tribe: Oglala Sioux. Located 60 miles east of the Black Hills, extending into Nebraska. See listing under South Dakota.

PONCA TRIBE OF NEBRASKA
P.O. Box 288, Niobrara, NE 68760
(402) 857-3391
Ms. Deb Wright, Chairperson
Located in Nebraska and South Dakota. Yankton Agency.

SAC & FOX TRIBE OF KANSAS & NEBRASKA TRIBE
Located in Nebraska and Kansas. See listing under Kansas.

SANTEE SIOUX RESERVATION
Santee Sioux Tribal Council
Route 2, Niobrara, NE 68760
(402) 857-3302 Fax 857-2307
Richard Kitto, Chairperson
Tribe served: Santee Sioux. *In residence*: 425. *Area*: 3,600 acres. Head Start Program. Winnebago Agency.

WINNEBAGO RESERVATION
Winnebago Tribal Council
Hwy. 75, Box 687, Winnebago, NE 68071
(402) 878-2272 Fax 878-2963
John Blackhawk, Chairperson
Tribe served: Winnebago. *In residence*: 1,100. *Area*: 27,000 acres located in Nebraska and Iowa (off-reservation lands in Iowa.) Head Start Program. Winnebago Agency.

NEVADA

BATTLE MOUNTAIN RESERVATION
Battle Mountain Band Council
35 Mountain View Dr. #138-13
Battle Mountain, NV 89820
(702) 635-2004 Fax 635-8016
Paul Snooks, Chairperson
Tribe: Te-Moak Band of Western Shoshone. A constituent band of the Te-Moak Tribe of Western Shoshone Indians. *Area*: 700 acres. Eastern Nevada Agency.

CARSON INDIAN COLONY
Carson Colony Community Council
P.O. Box 3269, Carson City, NV 89702
(702) 883-6431
Sherri Johnson, Chairperson
Tribe: Washoe. A component band of the Washoe Tribe. *Area*: 150 acres. Western Nevada Agency.

DRESSLERVILLE INDIAN COLONY
Dresslerville Community Council
1585 Watasheamu Rd., Gardnerville, NV 89410
(702) 265-5845
Romaine Smokey, Jr., Chairperson
Tribe: Washoe. A component band of the Washoe Tribe. *Area*: 40 acres. Western Nevada Agency.

DUCK VALLEY RESERVATION
Shoshone Paiute Business Council
P.O. Box 219, Owyhee, NV 89832
(702) 757-3161 Fax 757-2219
Lindsey Manning, Chairperson
Tribes: Shoshone-Paiute. *In residence*: 1,100. *Area*: 145,000 acres. Located in Nevada and Idaho. Eastern Nevada Agency.

DUCKWATER RESERVATION
Duckwater Shoshone Tribal Council
P.O. Box 140068, Duckwater, NV 89314
(702) 738-0569 Fax 738-4710
Boyd Graham, Chairperson
Tribe: Shoshone. *In residence*: 150. *Area*: 800 acres. Eastern Nevada Agency.

ELKO INDIAN COLONY
Elko Band Council
P.O. Box 748, Elko, NV 89801
(702) 738-8889 Fax 753-5439
Davis Gonzales, Chairperson
Tribe: Te-Moak Band of Western Shoshone. A constituent band of the Te-Moak Tribe of Western Shoshone Indians. *Area*: 200 acres. Eastern Nevada Agency.

ELY INDIAN COLONY
Ely Colony Council
16 Shoshone Circle, Ely, NV 89301
(702) 289-3013 Fax 289-3156
Jerry Charles, Chairperson
Tribe: Shoshone. *Population served*: 250. *Area*: 111 acres. Eastern Nevada Agency.

FALLON RESERVATION & COLONY
Fallon Business Council
8955 Mission Rd., Fallon, NV 89406
(702) 423-6075 Fax 423-5202
Thomas C. Burton, Chairperson
Tribes: Paiute & Shoshone. *In residence*: 700. *Area*: 5,500 acres. Tribal Council. Western Nevada Agency.

FORT McDERMITT RESERVATION
Fort McDermitt Tribal Council
P.O. Box 457, McDermitt, NV 89421
(702) 532-8259 Phone & Fax
William Crutcher, Chairperson
Tribes: Shoshone and Paiute. *In residence*: 710. *Area*: 16,400 acres located in Nevada and Oregon. Western Nevada Agency.

FORT MOHAVE RESERVATION
Tribe: Mohave. Located in Arizona, California & Nevada. See listing under Arizona.

LAS VEGAS INDIAN COLONY
Las Vegas Colony Council
One Paiute Dr., Las Vegas, NV 89106
(702) 386-3926 Fax 383-4019
Kenny Anderson, Chairperson
Tribe: Paiute. *In residence*: 125. *Area*: 10 acres.
Southern Paiute Field Station.

LOVELOCK INDIAN COLONY
Lovelock Tribal Council
P.O. Box 878, Lovelock, NV 89419
(702) 273-7861 Fax 273-7861
Harry B. Summerfield, Jr., Chairperson
Tribe: Paiute. *In residence*: 175. *Area*: 20 acres.
Western Nevada Agency.

MOAPA RIVER INDIAN RESERVATION
Moapa Business Council
P.O. Box 340, Las Vegas, NV 89025
(702) 865-2787 Fax 865-2875
Rosalyn Mike, Chairperson
Tribe: Moapa Band of Paiute Indians (Southern
Paiute). *In residence*: 295. *Area*: 73,258 acres.
Southern Paiute Field Station.

PYRAMID LAKE RESERVATION
Pyramid Lake Paiute Tribal Council
P.O. Box 256, Nixon, NV 89424
(702) 574-1000 Fax 574-1008
Alvin R. James, Chairperson
Tribe: Paiute. *In residence*: 850. *Area*: 1,195,000
acres. Western Nevada Agency.

RENO-SPARKS INDIAN COLONY
Reno-Sparks Tribal Council
98 Colony Rd., Reno, NV 89502
(702) 329-2936 Fax 359-8716
Arian Melendez, Chairperson
Tribes: Washoe & Paiute. *Population served*: 625.
Western Nevada Agency.

RUBY VALLEY (TE-MOAK) RESERVATION
**Tribal Council of the Te-Moak Western
Shoshone Indians of Nevada**
525 Sunset St., Elko, NV 89801
(702) 738-9251 Fax 738-2345
Dale S. Malotte, Chairperson
Tribe: Te-Moak Band of Western Shoshone.
Area: 15,000 acres. Business Council.
Eastern Nevada Agency.

SOUTH FORK INDIAN COLONY
South Fork Band Council
Box B-13, Lee, NV 89829
(702) 744-4273
Stillman Knight, Jr., Chairperson
Tribe: Te-Moak Band of Western Shoshone. A
constituent band of the Te-Moak Tribe of Western
Shoshone Indians. *Area*: 15,000 acres. Eastern
Nevada Agency.

STEWART INDIAN COLONY
Stewart Indian Community Council
5300 Snyder Ave., Carson City, NV 89701
(702) 883-7767
Jacqueline Steele, Chairperson
Tribe: Washoe. A component band of the
Washoe Tribe. Western Nevada Agency.

SUMMIT LAKE RESERVATION
Summit Lake Paiute Council
665 Anderson St., Winnemucca, NV 89445
(702) 623-5151 Fax 623-0558
Robert Sam, Chairperson
Tribe: Paiute. *Area*: 10,500 acres.
Western Nevada Agency.

WALKER RIVER RESERVATION
Walker River Paiute Tribal Council
P.O. Box 220, Schurz, NV 89427
(702) 773-2306 Fax 773-2585
Irwin Miller, Chairperson
Tribe: Paiute. In residence: 1,100. Area: 320,000
acres. Western Nevada Agency.

WASHOE TRIBE OF NEVADA & CALIFORNIA
Washoe Tribal Council
919 U.S. Hwy. 395 S., Gardnerville, NV 89410
(702) 265-4191 Fax 265-6240
A. Brian Wallace, Chairperson
Lenora Kizer, Vice Chair
Tribe served: Washoe. *In residence*: 1,380. *Area*:
4,300 acres; plus over 60,000 acres of ten
noncontiguous parcels and numerous public do-
main allotments. *Colonies served*: Dresslerville,
Woodfords, Carson Colony, and Stewart Colony.
Activities: Annual Tribal Picnic. Library and Ar-
chives being established at Stewart Colony;
Washoe Cultural Center in progress at Lake
Tahoe. *Publication*: Washoe Newsletter. Western
Nevada Agency.

WELLS INDIAN COLONY
Wells Indian Colony Band Council
P.O. Box 809, Wells, NV 89835
(702) 752-3045
Bruce Stevens, Chairperson
Tribe: Te-Moak Tribe of Western Shoshone. A
constituent band of the Te-Moak Tribe of Western
Shoshone Indians. Eastern Nevada Agency.

WINNEMUCCA INDIAN COLONY
P.O. Box 1075, Winnemucca, NV 89445
(702) 623-6918
Glenn Wasson, Chairperson
Western Nevada Agency.

YERRINGTON INDIAN COLONY
Yerington Paiute Tribal Council
171 Campbell Lane, Yerington, NV 89447
(702) 463-3301; 463-2416
Stacy L. Stahl, Chairperson
Tribe: Yerrington Paiute. *In residence*: 430. *Area*:
1,160 acres. *Council Members*: Linda Howard,
Lawrence Conway, Raynese Salas, Cecelia Emm,
and Victor Sam. Western Nevada Agency.

YOMBA RESERVATION
Yomba Tribal Council
HC61, Box 6275, Austin, NV 89310
(702) 964-2463 Fax 964-2443
James Birchum, Chairperson
Tribe: Shoshone. *In residence*: 135. *Area*: 4,700
acres. Western Nevada Agency.

NEW MEXICO

ACOMA PUEBLO
Acoma Pueblo Council
P.O. Box 309, Acomita, NM 87034
(505) 552-6604 Fax 552-6600
Reginald Pasqual, Governor
Tribe: Pueblo. *In residence*: 3,100. *Area*: 25,000
acres located 50 miles west of Albuquerque. Head
Start Program. Southern Pueblos Agency.

ANETH RESERVATION
Tribe: Navajo. Shiprock Agency.

BACA RESERVATION
Tribe: Navajo. Eastern Navajo Agency.

BECENTI RESERVATION
Tribe: Navajo. Eastern Navajo Agency.

BECLABITO RESERVATION
Tribe: Navajo. Shiprock Agency.

BREAD SPRINGS RESERVATION
Tribe: Navajo. Eastern Navajo Agency.

BURNHAM RESERVATION
Tribe: Navajo. Shiprock Agency.

CANONCITO RESERVATION
Tribe: Navajo. Eastern Navajo Agency.

CASAMERO LAKE RESERVATION
Tribe: Navajo. Eastern Navajo Agency.

CHEECHILGEETHO RESERVATION
Tribe: Navajo. Eastern Navajo Agency.

CHURCH ROCK RESERVATION
Tribe: Navajo. Eastern Navajo Agency.

COCHITI PUEBLO
Cochiti Pueblo Council
P.O. Box 70, Cochiti, NM 87072
(505) 465-2244 Fax 465-2245
Andrew Quintana, Governor
Tribe: Pueblo. *In residence*: 975. *Area*: 28,000
acres located in Sandoval County near U.S. 85 on
the west bank of the Rio Grande River. Southern
Pueblos Agency.

CROWNPOINT RESERVATION
Tribe: Navajo. Eastern Navajo Agency.

CRYSTAL RIVER RESERVATION
Tribe: Navajo. Located in Arizona and New Mexico.
(See listing under Arizona.)

DALTON PASS RESERVATION
Tribe: Navajo. Eastern Navajo Agency.

FORT DEFIANCE RESERVATION
Tribe: Navajo. Located in Arizona and New Mexico.
See listing under Arizona.

HUERFANO RESERVATION
Tribe: Navajo. Eastern Navajo Agency.

ISLETA PUEBLO
Isleta Pueblo Council
P.O. Box 1270, Isleta, NM 87022
(505) 869-31 11/6333 Fax 869-4236
Alvino Lucero, Governor
Tribe: Pueblo. *In residence*: 3,500. *Area*: 209,000
acres. Head Start Program. Southern Pueblos
Agency.

JEMEZ PUEBLO
Jemez Pueblo Council
P.O. Box 100, Jemez, NM 87024
(505) 834-7359 Fax 834-7331
Jose L. Pecos, Governor
Tribe: Pueblo. *In residence*: 2,000. *Area*: 88,500
acres located 44 miles north of Albuquerque.
Southern Pueblos Agency.

IYANBIT RESERVATION
Tribe: Navajo. Eastern Navajo Agency.

JICARILLA APACHE RESERVATION
Jicarilla Apache Tribal Council
P.O. Box 507, Dulce, NM 87528
(505) 759-3242 Fax 759-3005
Leonard Atole, President

Tribe: Jicarilla Apache. *In residence*: 2,600. *Area*: 742,303 acres located about two miles northwest of Albuquerque. Jicarilla Agency.

LAGUNA PUEBLO
Laguna Pueblo Council
P.O. Box 194, Laguna, NM 87026
(505) 552-6654 Fax 552-6941
  Harry D. Early, Governor
Tribe: Pueblo. *In residence*: 4,250. *Area*: 420,000 acres located 40 miles west of Albuquerque, on U.S. 66. Head Start Program. Laguna Agency.

LAKE VALLEY RESERVATION
Tribe: Navajo. Eastern Navajo Agency.

LITTLE WATER RESERVATION
Tribe: Navajo. Eastern Navajo Agency.

MANUELITO RESERVATION
Tribe: Navajo. Eastern Navajo Agency.

MARIANO RESERVATION
Tribe: Navajo. Eastern Navajo Agency.

MESCALERO APACHE RESERVATION
Mescalero Apache Tribal Council
P.O. Box 176, Mescalero, NM 88340
(505) 671-4495
  Wendell Chino, President
Tribe: Mescalero Apache. *In residence*: 2,750. *Area*: 460,173 acres located 30 miles northeast of Alamagordo, New Mexico. Head Start Program. Mescalero Agency.

MEXICAN WATER RESERVATION
Tribe: Navajo. Located in Arizona & Utah. Shiprock Agency.

NAGEEZI RESERVATION
Tribe: Navajo. Eastern Navajo Agency.

NAMBE PUEBLO
Nambe Pueblo Council
Route 1, Box 117-BB, Santa Fe, NM 87501
(505) 455-2036/7 Fax 455-2038
  Herbert Yates, Governor
Tribe: Pueblo. *In residence*: 400. *Area*: 19,000 acres located five miles east of Pojoaque, New Mexico, on Hwy. 285. Northern Pueblos Agency.

NENAHNEZAD RESERVATION
Tribe: Navajo. Shiprock Agency.

OJO ENCINO RESERVATION
Tribe: Navajo. Eastern Navajo Agency.

PICURIS PUEBLO
Picuris Pueblo Council
P.O. Box 127, Penasco, NM 87553
(505) 587-2519 Fax 587-1071
  Reyes Martinez, Governor
Tribe: Pueblo. *In residence*: 200. *Area*: 1,500 acres located east of the Rio Grande River, 20 miles south of Taos, NM.. Northern Pueblos Agency.

PINEDALE RESERVATION
Tribe: Navajo. Eastern Navajo Agency.

POJOAQUE PUEBLO
Pojoaque Pueblo Council
Rte. 11, Box 71, Santa Fe, NM 87501
(505) 455-2278/9 Fax 455-2950
  Jacob Viarrial, Governor
Tribe: Pueblo. *In residence*: 175. *Area*: 11,500 acres. *Activities*: Annual Feast Day (December). Northern Pueblos Agency.

PUEBLO PLAINTADO RESERVATION
Tribe: Navajo. Eastern Navajo Agency.

PUERTOCITO (ALAMO) RESERVATION
Tribe: Navajo. Eastern Navajo Agency.

RAMAH NAVAJO RESERVATION
Ramah Navajo Chapter Council
Rte. 2, Box 13, Ramah, NM 87321
(505) 775-3342 Fax 775-3538
  Curley Biggs, President
Tribe: Navajo. Ramah-Navajo Agency.

RED LAKE RESERVATION
Tribe: Navajo. Located in Arizona & New Mexico. Western Navajo Agency

RED MESA RESERVATION
Tribe: Navajo. Located in New Mexico, Arizona and Utah. Shiprock Agency.

RED ROCK RESERVATION
Tribe: Navajo. Located in Arizona &New Mexico. Shiprock Agency.

ROCK POINT RESERVATION
Tribe: Navajo. Shiprock Agency.

ROCK SPRINGS RESERVATION
Tribe: Navajo. Eastern Navajo Agency.

SAN FELIPE PUEBLO
San Felipe Pueblo Council
P.O. Box A, San Felipe, NM 87001
(505) 867-3381 Fax 867-3383
  Joseph Sanchez, Governor
Tribe: Pueblo. *In residence*: 2,200. *Area*: 49,000 acres located ten miles north of Bernalillo, off U.S. 85. Head Start Program. Southern Pueblos Agency.

SAN ILDEFONSO PUEBLO
San Ildefonso Tribal Council
Rte. 5, Box 315-A, Santa Fe, NM 87501
(505) 455-2273 Fax 455-7351
  Elmer C. Torres, Governor
  Randy Sanchez & Gary Roybal, Lt. Governors
Tribe: San Ildefonso Tewa. *In residence*: 600. *Area*: 26,000 acres located 20 miles northwest of Santa Fe, off Highway 285. *Activities*: Annual Feast Day (January 23). Operates small museum and library. Northern Pueblos Agency.

SAN JUAN PUEBLO
San Juan Pueblo Council
P.O. Box 1099, San Juan Pueblo, NM 87566
(505) 852-4400/4210 Fax 852-4820
  Simon Cata, Governor
Tribe: Pueblo. *In residence*: 1,500. *Area*: 12,000 acres located five miles north of Espanola, near Highway 64. Northern Pueblos Agency.

SANDIA PUEBLO
Sandia Tribal Council
P.O. Box 6008, Bernalillo, NM 87004
(505) 867-3317 Fax 867-9235
  Joe M. Lujan, Governor
Tribe: Pueblo. *In residence*: 320. *Area*: 23,000 acres located 14 miles north of Albuquerque, on U.S. 85. Southern Pueblos Agency.

SANOSTEE RESERVATION
Tribe: Navajo. Shiprock Agency.

SANTA ANA PUEBLO
Santa Ana Pueblo Council
2 Dove Rd., Bernalillo, NM 87004

(505) 867-3301 Fax 867-3395
  Andrew Gallegos, Governor
Tribe: Pueblo. *In residence*: 550. *Area*: 4,200 acres located near Jemez Creek, eight miles from Bernalillo. Southern Pueblos Agency.

SANTA CLARA PUEBLO
Santa Clara Pueblo Council
P.O. Box 580, Espanola, NM 87532
(505) 753-7326 Fax 753-8988
  Walter Dasheno, Governor
  Stanley Tafoya, Lt. Gov.
Tribe: Santa Clara Pueblo. *In residence*: 1,350. *Area*: 45,744 acres located 25 miles northwest of Santa Fe. *Activities*: Annual Feasts, June & August. Operates small library. *Publication*: Monthly newsletter. Northern Pueblos Agency.

SANTO DOMINGO PUEBLO
Santo Domingo Pueblo Council
P.O. Box 99
Santo Domingo, NM 87052
(505) 465-2214 Fax 465-2688
  Ernie Lovato, Governor
Tribe: Pueblo. *In residence*: 2,750. *Area*: 70,000 acres located in Sandoval County, ten miles east of the Rio Grande River. Head Start Program. Southern Pueblos Agency.

SHEEP SPRINGS RESERVATION
Tribe: Navajo. Shiprock Agency.

SHIPROCK RESERVATION
Tribe: Navajo. c/o Shiprock Agency.

SMITH LAKE RESERVATION
Tribe: Navajo. Eastern Navajo Agency.

STANDING ROCK RESERVATION
Tribe: Navajo. Eastern Navajo Agency.

SWEETWATER RESERVATION
Tribe: Navajo. Shiprock Agency.

TAOS PUEBLO
Taos Pueblo Council
P.O. Box 1846, Taos, NM 87571
(505) 758-9593 Fax 758-4604
  Carl Concha, Governor
Tribe: Pueblo. *In residence*: 1,750. *Area*: 75,000 acres. Northern Pueblos Agency.

TEECNOSPOS RESERVATION
Tribe: Navajo. Located in Arizona, Utah & New Mexico. Shiprock Agency.

TESUQUE PUEBLO
Tesuque Pueblo Council
Route 11, Box 1, Santa Fe, NM 87501
(505) 983-2667 Fax 983-2331
  Paul Swazo, Governor
Tribe: Pueblo. *In residence*: 325. *Area*: 17,000 acres located ten miles north of Santa Fe. Tribal Council. Northern Pueblos Agency.

THOREAU RESERVATION
Tribe: Navajo. Eastern Navajo Agency.

TORREON & STAR LAKE RESERVATION
Tribe: Navajo. Eastern Navajo Agency.

TSAYATOH RESERVATION
Tribe: Navajo. Eastern Navajo Agency.

TSAILE-WHEATFIELDS RESERVATION
Tribe: Navajo. Located in Arizona & New Mexico. See listing under Arizona.

TWO GREY HILLS RESERVATION
Tribe: Navajo. Shiprock Agency.

UPPER FRUITLAND RESERVATION
Tribe: Navajo. Shiprock Agency.

UTE MOUNTAIN RESERVATION
Tribe: Ute. Located in Colorado, Utah and New Mexico. (See listing in Colorado.)

WHITE ROCK RESERVATION
Tribe: Navajo. Eastern Navajo Agency.

WHITEHORSE LAKE RESERVATION
Tribe: Navajo. Eastern Navajo Agency.

ZIA PUEBLO
Zia Pueblo Tribal Council
135 Capitol Square Dr., Zia Pueblo, NM 87053
(505) 867-3304 Fax 867-3308
Henry Shije, Governor
Tribe: Pueblo. *In residence*: 650. *Area*: 112,000 acres located 16 miles northwest of Bernalillo. Cultural Center/Library. Southern Pueblos Agency.

ZUNI RESERVATION
Zuni Pueblo Tribal Council
P.O. Box 339, Zuni, NM 87327
(505) 782-4481 Fax 782-2700
Robert Lewis, Governor
Tribe: Zuni Pueblo. *In residence*: 7,450. *Area*: 407,247 acres located 40 miles south of Gallup, New Mexico, on the Arizona border. *Population served*: 7,100. Head Start Program. Zuni Agency.

NEW YORK

ALLEGHENY RESERVATION
P.O. Box 31, Salamanca, New York 14779
(716) 945-1790
Tribes: Seneca. *In residence*: 750. *Area*: 30,469 acres located along the Allegheny River on Route 17. Museum & Library. New York Field Office.

CATTARAUGUS RESERVATION
Seneca Nation Tribal Council
1490 Rt. 438, Irving, NY 14081
(716) 532-4900 Fax 532-9132
Dennis Bowen, President
Tribe served: Seneca. *Reservations served*: Allegany & Cattaraugus. *In residence*: 3,500. *Area*: 21,680 acres located along Route 438. *Activities*: Seneca Fall Festival (2nd weekend in September; Allegany Indian Fair (late August); Spring and Christmas Bazaars. Operates Seneca-Iroquois National Museum in Salamanca; Seneca Nation Library (branches for both Allegany & Cattaraugus Reservation); Seneca Nation Bingo at Irving; and Seneca Sports Arena located at the Cattaraugus Reservation. *Publication*: Tribal Newsletter. Head Start Program. N.Y. Liaison Office.

CAYUGA INDIAN NATION
Cayuga Nation Tribal Council
P.O. Box 11, Versailles, NY 14168
(716) 532-4847 Fax 532-5417
Vernon Isaac, Chief
Tribe: Cayuga. *In residence*: 110. Tribal Council. New York Liaison Office.

OIL SPRING RESERVATION
Cuba Lake, New York 14727
Tribe: Seneca. *Area*: 640 acres. Located near Cuba Lake in Allegheny Co., N.Y. Liaison Office.

ONEIDA INDIAN NATION OF NEW YORK
P.O. Box 1, West Rd., Oneida, NY 13421
Council address: P.O. Box 1, Vernon, NY 13476
(315) 829-3090 Fax 829-3141
Ray Halbritter, Nation Representative
Tribe: (Six Nations) Oneida. *In residence*: 1,100. *Area*: 32 acres. Located three miles south of the city of Oneida in Madison County in Central New York. *Programs*: Health Center; educational scholarship incentives; youth corps; elderly meals program; housing development. *Activities*: Operates the Turning Stone Casino in Verona, NY; Bingo Hall; Lacrosse Box; Pool/Recreation Center; Traditional ceremonies held in Council House. Museum-Shako:wi Cultural Center located on territory open Tues-Sunday 9 am - 5 pm. Developing library. *Publication*: Oneida Nation Newsletter. New York Liaison Office.

ONONDAGA RESERVATION
Onondaga Nation Tribal Council
RR 1, Box 270A, Nedrow, NY 13120
(716) 469-8507
Leon Shenandoah, Sr., Head Chief
Irving Powless, Jr., Secretary of Council of Chiefs
Tribes: Onondaga, Oneida and Cayuga. *In residence*: 1,500. *Area*: 7,300 acres. Located near Nedrow, six miles south of Syracuse. Tribal Council. New York Liaison Office.

POOSPATUCK RESERVATION
P.O. Box 86, Mastic, NY 11950
(516) 281-6464
Tribe: Unkechauge Nation (Poospatuck). *In residence*: 100. *Area*: 60 acres. Located on Mastic River near Brookhaven, L.I., NY. Eastern Area Office.

ST. REGIS MOHAWK INDIAN RESERVATION
St. Regis Mohawk Council Chiefs
RR 1, Box 14 C, Hogansburg, NY 13655
(518) 358-2272 Fax 358-3203
John Loran, Head Chief
Tribe: St. Regis Mohawk. *In residence*: 6,500. *Area*: 14,640 acres located in Franklin County on Route 37. Straddles the Canadian border; portion lies within Quebec and Ontario. *Activities*: Operates museum & library; and operates the St. Regis Casino, a 40,000 sq. ft. facility. *Publication*: Kariwenhawi, monthly newsletter. New York Liaison Office.

TONAWANDA RESERVATION
Tonawanda Band of Senecas Council of Chiefs
7027 Meadville Rd., Basom, NY 14013
(716) 542-4244 Fax 542-9692
Bernie Parker, Chief
Tribe: Tonawanda Band of Seneca Indians. *In residence*: 675. *Area*: 7,550 acres. Located on Route 267, near Batavia, NY. Council of Chiefs. New York Liaison Office.

TUSCARORA RESERVATION
Tuscarora Tribal Business Council
5616 Walmore Rd., Lewiston, NY 14092
(716) 297-4990
Arnold Hewitt, Head Chief
Joseph Anderson & Kenneth Patterson, Chiefs
Tribe: Tuscarora. *In residence*: 775. *Area*: 5,700 acres. Located in Niagara County near Sanborn and Lewiston on Upper Mountain Rd. New York Liaison Office.

NORTH CAROLINA

CHEROKEE RESERVATION
Eastern Band of Cherokee Tribal Council
P.O. Box 455, Cherokee, NC 28719
(704) 497-2771 Fax 497-2952
Jonathan L. Taylor, Principal Chief
Tribe: Eastern Band of Cherokee. *In residence*: 8,800. *Area*: 56,572 acres located 50 miles west of Asheville, North Carolina. *Activities*: Operates school and hospital. *Local attractions*: Replica of an Oconaluftee Indian Village; Museum of the Cherokee; Qualla Arts and Crafts Cooperative. *Special activity*: Annual Cherokee Fall Festival. Tribal Council. Cherokee Agency.

NORTH DAKOTA

DEVIL'S LAKE SIOUX RESERVATION
Devil's Lake Sioux Tribal Council
Sioux Community Center, Fort Totten, ND 58335
(701) 766-4221 Fax 766-4854
Peter Belgarde, Jr., Chairperson
Tribe: Sisseton-Wahpeton Sioux. *In residence*: 3,500. *Area*: 185,045 acres located along the Cheyenne River. *Activities*: Annual Fort Totten Days Pow-Wow (July). Tribal Council. Fort Totten Agency.

FORT BERTHOLD RESERVATION
Three Affiliated Tribes Business Council
P.O. Box 220, Tribal Administration Bldg.
New Town, ND 58763
(701) 627-4781 Fax 627-3805
Russell Mason, Sr., Chairperson
Tribes: Thre Affiliated Tribes - Mandan, Hidatsa and Arikara. *In residence*: 4,000. *Area*: 980,000 acres. Located above Garrison Dam on the Missouri River, southwest of Minot, North Dakota. *Special activity*: Community Pow-Wows through the summer months. Operates schools at Mandaree, White Shield and Twin Buttes, ND; Museum at 4-Bears complex new New Town, ND; and Library at Fort Berthold Community College. *Publication*: Mandan, Hidatsa & Arikara Times, tribal newspaper. Head Start Program. Fort Berthold Agency.

OJIBWA OF THE RED RIVER
Tribe: Ojibwa (Chippewa). *In residence*: 850. Located in northeast North Dakota.

STANDING ROCK RESERVATION
Standing Rock Sioux Tribal Council
P.O. Box E, Fort Yates, ND 58538
(701) 854-7231 Fax 854-7299
Jesse Taken Alive, Chairperson
Tribe: Sioux. *In residence*: 9,500 (4,500 Yankton Sioux in North Dakota, and 5,000 Teton Sioux in South Dakota.) *Area*: 306,000 acres (ND); 540,000 acres (SD). Located 60 miles south of Bismarck, N.D., in North and South Dakota. Head Start Program. Standing Rock Agency.

TURTLE MOUNTAIN RESERVATION
Turtle Mountain Tribal Council
P.O. Box 900, Belcourt, ND 58316
(701) 477-6451 Fax 477-6836
Richard "Jiggers" LaFromboise, Chairperson
Tribe: Chippewa. *In residence*: 8,950. *Area*: 34,528 acres. Located west of the Canadian border. Head Start Program. Turtle Mountain Agency.

OKLAHOMA

NOTE: There are no reservations in Oklahoma. Rather, there are land holdings by the various Oklahoma Indian tribes.

ABSENTEE-SHAWNEE TRIBE
Absentee-Shawnee Executive Committee
2025 S. Gordon Cooper Dr., Shawnee, OK 74801
(405) 275-4030 Fax 275-5637
Larry Nuckolls, Governor
Tribe: Absentee-Shawnee. *Population served*: 1,500. Shawnee Agency.

ALABAMA-QUASSARTE TRIBAL TOWN
P.O. Box 537, Henryetta, OK 74437
(918) 652-8708
Duke Harjo, Chief
Tribe: Creek. Okmulgee Agency.

APACHE TRIBE OF OKLAHOMA
Apache Business Committee
P.O. Box 1220, Anadarko, OK 73005
(405) 247-9493 Fax 247-9232
Henry Kostzuta, Chairperson
Amos Pewenofkit, Sr., Vice-Chairperson
Tribe: Apache & Kiowa. *Population served*: 550. Anadarko Agency.

CADDO INDIAN TRIBE
Caddo Tribal Council
P.O. Box 487, Binger, OK 73009
(405) 656-2344 Fax 247-2005
Elmo Clark, Chairperson
Tribe: Caddo. *Population served*: 1,250. Anadarko Agency.

CHEROKEE NATION OF OKLAHOMA
P.O. Box 948, Tahlequah, OK 74465
(918) 456-0671 Fax 456-6485
John Ketcher, Deputy Chief
Tribe: Cherokee of Oklahoma. *Population served*: 45,000. Head Start Program. Muskogee Area Office.

CHEYENNE-ARAPAHO TRIBE
Cheyenee-Arapaho Business Committee
P.O. Box 38, Concho, OK 73022
(405) 262-0345 Fax 262-0745
Viola Hatch, Chairperson
Tribes: Cheyenne and Arapaho.
Population served: 7,500. Concho Agency.

THE CHICKASAW NATION
P.O. Box 1548, Ada, OK 74820
The Chickasaw Tribal Legislature
P.O. Box 2669, Ada, OK 74821
(405) 436-1460 Fax 436-4287
Bill Anoatubby, Governor
Tribe: Chickasaw. *Population served*: @ 25,000 in U.S.; 12,000+ in residence. *Area*: 7,648 square miles inside boundary; 1,600 owned by Chickasaw Nation. *Special activitiy*: Chickasaw Festival in Tishomingo, OK in September/October. Operates Carter Seminary. Chickasaw Council House Museum in Tishomingo; and tribal museum and Library in Ada. *Publications*: Chickasaw Times, monthly tribal newspaper; Chickasaw Dictionary. Head Start Program. Chickasaw Agency.

CHOCTAW NATION OF OKLAHOMA
P.O. Drawer 1210, 16th & Locust Sts.
Durant, OK 74701
(405) 924-8280 Fax 924-1150
Hollis E. Roberts, Chief
Tribe: Choctaw. *Population served*: 22,000. Geographic boundaries include 10 1/2 counties in southeastern Oklahoma. *Activities*: Annual commemorative "Trail of Tears" Walk, Skullyville, OK; annual Labor Day Festival, Tuskahoma, OK. Maintains museum. *Publication*: Bishinik, monthly newspaper. Head Start Program. Talihina Agency.

CITIZEN BAND POTAWATOMI TRIBE
Citizen Band Potawatomi
Business Committee
1901 S. Gordon Cooper Dr.,
Shawnee, OK 74801
(405) 275-3121 Fax 275-0198
John A. Barrett, Chairperson
Tribe: Citizen Band Potawatomi. *Population served*: 4,500 in Oklahoma; 12,500 nationwide. Acts on behalf of the tribe on all matters except claims & treaties. *Area*: 300 acres (in trust). *Facilities*: Tribal Museum & Trading Post. *Publications*: HowNikan, tribal newsletter; Grandfather , Tell Me A Story, oral history book. Shawnee Agency.

COMANCHE INDIAN TRIBE OF OKLAHOMA
Comanche Tribal Business Committee
HC 32 Box 1720, Lawton, OK 73502
(405) 492-4988 Fax 492-4981
Wallace E. Coffey, Chairperson
Tribe: Comanche. *Population served*: 4,000. Anadarko Agency.

CREEK NATION OF OKLAHOMA
P.O. Box 580, Okmulgee, OK 74447
(918) 756-8700 Fax 756-2911
Bill S. Fife, Principal Chief
Tribe served: Muscogee Creek. *Population served*: 30,000. *Area*: 6,000 acres located in an eight county area in northeastern Oklahoma–bounded on the north at Admiral St. in the city of Tulsa, and on the south by the Canadian River. Activities: Green Corn, Creek Festival, and Creek Rodeo. Museum. Library. Head Start Program. Okmulgee Agency.

DELAWARE TRIBE OF WESTERN OKLAHOMA
Delaware Executive Committee
P.O. Box 825, Anadarko, OK 73005
(405) 247-2448 Fax 247-2005
Lawrence F. Snake, President
Tribe: Delaware. *Population served*: 950. *Area*: 2,400 acres held jointly with the Wichita and Caddo Tribes.*Publications*: Cooley's Traditional Stories of the Delaware, and Turtle Tales: Oral Traditions of the Delaware of Western Oklahoma, both edited by Duane Hale. Library. Anadarko Agency.

EASTERN SHAWNEE TRIBE OF OKLAHOMA
P.O. Box 350, Seneca, MO 64865
Tribe: Eastern Shawnee. Miami Agency.
See listing under Missouri.

FORT SILL APACHE TRIBE OF OKLAHOMA
Fort Sill Apache Business Committee
Route 2, Box 121, Apache, OK 73006
(405) 588-2298 Fax 588-3133
Mildred Cleghorn, Chairperson
Tribe: Fort Sill Apache. *Population served*: 375. Anadarko Agency.

IOWA TRIBE OF OKLAHOMA
Iowa Tribe Business Committee
Rt. 1, Box 721, Perkins, OK 74059
(405) 547-2403 Fax 547-5294
Wallace Murray, Chairperson
Tribe: Iowa. All tribes living within jurisdiction. *Population served*: 6,000. *Programs*: Social Services; Higher Education; Law Enforcement; Direct Employment Assistance; Substance Abuse. Small reference library. Shawnee Agency.

KAW TRIBE OF OKLAHOMA
Kaw Business Committee
Drawer 50, Kaw City, OK 74641
(405) 269-2552 Fax 269-2301
Wanda Stone, Chairperson
Tribe: Kaw. *Population served*: 1,200. Located at the northeast section of Kay County, Oklahoma. *Activities*: Tribal Pow-Wow (2nd Thursday of August). Pawnee Agency.

KIALEGEE TRIBAL TOWN
318 S. Washila, Box 332, Wetumka, OK74883
(405) 452-3413
Tony Martin, Tribal Town King
Tribe: Creek. Okmulgee Agency.

KICKAPOO TRIBE OF OKLAHOMA
Kickapoo of Oklahoma Business Committee
P.O. Box 70, McLoud, OK 74851
(405) 964-2075 Fax 964-2745
Kendall Scott, Chairperson
Tribe: Kickapoo. *Population served*: 800. Head Start Program. Shawnee Agency.

KIOWA TRIBE OF OKLAHOMA
Kiowa Business Committee
P.O. Box 369, Carnegie, OK 73015
(405) 654-2300 Fax 654-2188
Billy Evans Horse, Chairperson
Tribe: Kiowa. *Membership*: 10,000. Operates Kiowa Tribal Museum which exhibits the new Kiowa Murals.*Publication*: Kiowa Indian News. Head Start Program. Anadarko Agency.

MIAMI TRIBE OF OKLAHOMA
Miami Business Committee
P.O. Box 1326, Miami, OK 74355
(918) 542-1445 Fax 542-7260
Floyd Leonard, Chief; Jim Estes, Manager
Tamra Big, Program Administrator
Tribe: Miami. *Membership*: 1,450. Library. Miami Agency.

MODOC TRIBE OF OKLAHOMA
P.O. Box 939, Miami, OK 74354
(918) 542-1190 Fax 542-7202
Bill G. Follis, Chief
Tribe: Modoc. Miami Agency.

OSAGE TRIBE OF OKLAHOMA
P.O. Box 178, Tribal Administration Bldg.
Pawhuska, OK 74056
(918) 287-2495Fax 287-2257
George E. Tallchief, President
Dudley P. Whitehorn, V.P.
Charles Tillman, Mineral Council Chief
Shannon Love Edwards, Supreme Court Judge
Tribe: Osage. *Population served*: 6,000. Head Start Program. Osage Agency.

OTOE-MISSOURIA TRIBE OF OKLAHOMA
Otoe-Missouria Tribal Council
Rt. 1, Box 62, Red Rock, OK 74651
(405) 723-4434 Fax 723-4273
Kenneth E. Black, Chairperson
Tribe: Otoe-Missouria. *Population served*: 1,250. Pawnee Agency.

OTTAWA TRIBE OF OKLAHOMA
P.O. Box 110, Miami, OK 74355
(918) 540-1536 Fax 542-3214
Charles Dawes, Chief
Tribe: Ottawa. Miami Agency.

PAWNEE INDIAN TRIBE OF OKLAHOMA
Pawnee Business Committee
P.O. Box 470, Pawnee, OK 74058

(918) 762-3624 Fax 762-2389
Alex Matthews, Chairperson
Tribe: Pawnee. *Population served* : 2,500.
Pawnee Agency.

PEORIA INDIAN TRIBE OF OKLAHOMA
P.O. Box 1527, Miami, OK 74355
 (918) 540-2535 Fax 540-2528
 Donald E. Giles, Chief
Tribe: Peoria. Miami Agency.

PONCA TRIBE OF OKLAHOMA
Ponca Business Committee
P.O. Box 2, White Eagle
Ponca City, OK 74601
 (405) 762-8104 Fax 762-7436
 Genevieve Pollak, Chairperson
Tribe: Ponca. *Population served* : 2,500.
Pawnee Agency.

QUAPAW TRIBE OF OKLAHOMA
Quapaw Tribal Business Committee
P.O. Box 765, Quapaw, OK 74363
 (918) 542-1853 Fax 542-4594
 Grace Goodeagle, Chairperson
Tribe: Quapaw. *Population served* : 1,450.
Miami Agency.

SAC & FOX NATION
Sac & Fox Business Committee
Route 2, Box 246, Stroud, OK 74079
 (918) 968-3526 Fax 968-3887
 Elmer Manatowa, Jr., Principal Chief
 Merle Boyd, Second Chief
Tribe: Sac and Fox. Membership: 2,300. Total
acreage: 800 acres. *Activities*: Pow-wow. Library.
Publications : Sac and Fox News, monthly news-
paper; Sac and Fox Nation Welcomes You to
Capitol (historical & tourism brochure); Sac and
Fox Court: Justice for a Nation (court brochure).
Pawnee Agency.

SEMINOLE NATION OF OKLAHOMA
P.O. Box 1498, Wewoka, OK 74884
 (405) 257-6287 Fax 257-5017
 Jerry G. Haney, Principal Chief
Tribe: Seminole. *Population served* : 4,500.
Program: Head Start. Wewoka Agency.

SENECA-CAYUGA TRIBE OF OKLAHOMA
Seneca-Cayuga Business Committee
P.O. Box 1283, Miami, OK 74355
 (918) 542-6609 Fax 542-3684
 Terry L. Whitetree, Chief
Tribes: Seneca & Cayuga. *Population served* : 750.
Miami Agency.

THLOPTHLOCCO TRIBAL TOWN
P.O. Box 706, Okemah, OK 74859
 (918) 623-2620 Fax 623-2404
 Charley McGertt, Town King
Tribe: Creek. Tribal Town Council.
Okmulgee Agency.

TONKAWA TRIBE OF OKLAHOMA
Tonkawa Business Committee
P.O. Box 70, Tonkawa, OK 74653
 (405) 628-2561 Fax 628-3375
 Virginia Combrink, President
Tribe: Tonkawa. *Population served* : 1,500.
Pawnee Agency.

UNITED KEETOOWAH BAND OF CHEROKEE
United Keetoowah band Tribal Council
2450 S. Muskogee Ave., P.O. Box 746
Tahlequah, OK 74465
 (918) 456-5491 Fax 456-9601

John Ross, Chief; Jim Henson, Ass't Chief
Tribe: United Keetoowah Band of Cherokee. *Mem-
bership*: 7,700. *Council members* : Emma Sue
Holland, Allogan Slagle, Adalene Smith, Jim Proc-
tor, Richard Manus, Roberta Smoke, Charlie Bird,
Susan Adair, and Mose Killer . *Activities*: Annual
Tribal Celebration (1st Saturday in Oct.). Library .
Muskogee Area Office.

WICHITA TRIBE OF OKLAHOMA
Wichita Executive Committee
P.O. Box 729
Anadarko, OK 73005
 (405) 247-2425 Fax 247-2005
 Gary McAdams, Acting President
Tribe: Wichita. *Population served* : 700.
Anadarko Agency.

WYANDOTTE TRIBE OF OKLAHOMA
Wyandotte Business Committee
P.O. Box 250, Wyandotte, OK 74370
 (918) 678-2297/8 Fax 678-2944
 Leaford Bearskin, Chief
Tribe: Wyandotte. *Population served* : 500.
Miami Agency.

OREGON

BURNS PAIUTE INDIAN COLONY
Burns Paiute General Council
HC 71, 100 Pa Si Go St., Burns, OR 97720
 (503) 573-2088 Fax 573-2323
 Herbert W. Hawley, Chairperson
Tribe: Paiute. *In residence*: 220. *Area*: 11,944 acres
located in Harney Basin, Harney County . Tribal
Council. Warm Springs Agency.

CONFEDERATED TRIBES OF COOS
LOWER UMPQUA & SUISLAW INDIANS
455 South 4th St., Coos Bay , OR 97420
 (503) 267-5454 Fax 269-1647
 Gregory A. Norton, Chairperson
Tribes: Umpqua & Suislaw . Siletz Agency.

GRANDE RONDE INDIAN COMMUNITY
Conferdated Tribes of the
Grande Ronde Tribal Council
9615 Grand Ronde Rd.
Grande Ronde, OR 97347
 (503) 879-5215 Fax 879-5964
 Mark Mercier, Chairperson
Tribes: Confederated Tribes. *In residence* : 640.
Located in northwest Oregon. Tribal Council. Siletz
Agency.

CONFEDERATED TRIBES OF THE
WARM SPRINGS RESERVATION
P.O. Box C, 1233 Veteran St.
Warm Springs, OR 97761
 (503) 553-1161 Fax 553-1924
 Raymond Calica, Sr., Chairperson
Tribes: Warm Springs, Wasco, Paiute, Walla Walla,
and Waco. *In residence* : 2,750. *Area*: 563,916
acres. Located in Jefferson & Wasco Counties,
east of the Cascade Mountains. Tribal Council.
Head Start Program. Warm Springs Agency.

COQUILLE INDIAN TRIBE
P.O. Box 1435, Coos Bay, OR 97420
 (503) 276-4587 Fax 269-2573
 Ed Metcalf, Chairperson
Tribes: Upper & Lower Coquilles. *Population
served*: 630. *Area*: 6 acres (planning stages of land
acquisition for economic and community development) located on the southern coast of Oregon,

primarily in Coos County . *Activity*: Annual Restoration Celebration and Salmon Bake, last weekend in June. Tribe restored 1989. Siletz Agency.

COW CREEK BAND OF UMPQUA INDIANS
Community Council
2400 Stewart Parkway #300
Roseburg, OR 97470
 (503) 672-9405 Fax 673-0432
 Sue M. Shaffer, Chairperson
Tribe: Umpqua. Siletz Agency.

FORT McDERMITT RESERVATION
Tribes: Paiute and Shoshone. Located in
Oregon & Nevada. See listing in Nevada.

KLAMATH RESERVATION
Klamath General Council
P.O. Box 436, Chiloquin, OR 97624
 (503) 783-2219 Fax 783-2029
 Marvin Garcia, Chairperson
Tribe: Klamath. Warm Springs Agency.

SILETZ RESERVATION
Siletz Tribal Council
P.O. Box 549, Siletz, OR 97380
 (503) 444-2513/32 Fax 444-2307
 Delores Pigsley, Chairperson
Tribes: Confederated Tribes. *In residence*: 800.
Located on northwest Oregon coast. *Population
served*: 1,800. *Activities*: Memorial Day and Res-
toration Day Celebrations in May and November
respectively; pow wow in August. Museum/Archive
currently being established. Siletz Agency. Head
Start Program.

UMATILLA RESERVATION
Umatilla Board of Trustees
P.O. Box 638, Pendleton, OR, 97801
 (503) 276-3165 Fax 276-9060
 Donald Sampson, Chairperson
Tribes: Umatilla, Cayuse, and Walla Walla. *In resi-
dence*: 1,750. *Population served* : 1,500. *Area*:
95,273 acres. Located in Umatilla County , adja-
cent to Pendleton and west of Umatilla National
Forest. Umatilla Agency.

PUERTO RICO

TAINO NATION
Box 1126, Trujillo Alto, PR 00977
 (809) 760-6218
New York address: P.O. Box 883
New York, NY 10025 (212) 866-4573
Governed by Council of Chiefs. *Goal*: Reclaim right
to aboriginal identity , restore tribal government,
acquire lands at home for tribal purposes, restore
culture, language, customs, traditions and heritage. *Activities*: Impart conferences at colleges,
universities and educational institutions of all levels; promote knowledge of aboriginal music, song
and dance through Taino musical group. *Publication*: Bi-monthly newsletter .

RHODE ISLAND

NARRAGANSETT INDIAN RESERVATION
Narragansett Indian Tribal Council
P.O. Box 268, Charleston, RI 02813
 (401) 364-1100 Fax 364-1104
 George H. Hopkins, Chief Sachem
Tribe: Narragansett. Eastern Area Office.

SOUTH CAROLINA

CATAWBA INDIAN NATION
P.O. Box 11106, Rock Hill, SC 29731
(803) 366-4792 Fax 366-9150
Gilbert Blue, Chairperson
Tribe: Catawba. Eastern Area Office.

SOUTH DAKOTA

CHEYENNE RIVER RESERVATION
Cheyenne River Sioux Tribal Council
P.O. Box 590, Eagle Butte, SD 57625
(605) 964-4155 Fax 964-4151
Gregg Bouland, Chairperson
Tribe: Cheyenne River Sioux. *In residence*: 5,500.
Area: 2,811,480 acres. Located in Dewey and
Zeibach Counties. Head Start Program. Cheyenne
River Agency.

CROW CREEK RESERVATION
Crow Creek Sioux Tribal Council
P.O. Box 50, Fort Thompson, SD 57339
(605) 245-2221/2 Fax 245-2216
Duane Big Eagle, Chairperson
Tribe: Crow Creek Sioux. *In residence*: 2,500.
Area: 125,000 acres. Head Start Program.
Crow Creek Agency.

FLANDREAU SANTEE SIOUX RESERVATION
Flandreau Santee-Sioux Executive Committee
Flandreau Field Office
P.O. Box 283, Flandreau, SD 57028
(605) 997-3891 Fax 997-3878
Bill Schumacher, Chairperson
Tribe: Santee Sioux. *In residence*: 440. *Area*: 2,180
acres. *Activities*: Runs Royal River Casino. Aber-
deen Area Office.

LOWER BRULE RESERVATION
Lower Brule Sioux Tribal Council
Lower Brule, SD 57548
(605) 473-5561 Fax 473-5491
Michael Jandreau, Chairperson
Tribe: Lower Brule Sioux. *In residence*: 1,100.
Area: 114,500 acres. Head Start Program.
Lower Brule Agency.

PINE RIDGE RESERVATION
Oglala Lakotah Tribal Council
P.O. Box H, #468, Pine Ridge, SD 57770
(605) 867-5821 Fax 867-5582
Wilbur Between Lodges, President
Mel Lone Hill, Vice-President
Crystal Eagle Elk, Treasurer
Tribe: Oglala Sioux. *In residence*: 14,500. *Area*:
1,560,196 acres (SD) and 90,000 acres (Nebraska), located 60 miles east of the Black Hills,
extending into Nebraska. *Activities*: Plans to open
a casino in the near future. The Lakota Fund, P.O.
Box 340, Kyle, SD 57750 (605) 455-2500, Elsie
Meeks, Executive Director - formed to help build
a private sector economy on the Reservation by
providing loans and technical assistance & business training; and arts & crafts marketing assistance tribal members. *Local attractions*: Wounded
Knee Battlefield (15 miles northeast of Pine Ridge);
Badlands National Monument. *Activities*: Annual
Oglala Sioux Sun Dance (August). Head Start
Program. Pine Ridge Agency.

PONCA TRIBE OF NEBRASKA
Located in NE & SD. See listing in Nebraska.

ROSEBUD RESERVATION
Rosebud Sioux Tribal Council
P.O. Box 430, Rosebud, SD 57570
(605) 747-2381 Fax 2243
William Kindle, President
Tribe: Rosebud Sioux. *In residence*: 9,900. *Area*:
964,778 acres located in south-central South Dakota, adjoining the Nebraska State line. *Local attraction*: Crazy Horse Canyon Park (tribe-oper-
ated); St. Francis Mission; Sioux Indian Museum.
Head Start Program. Rosebud Agency.

SISSETON-WAHPETON RESERVATION
Sisseton-Wahpeton Dakota Tribal Council
Route 2 - Agency Village, Sisseton, SD 57262
(605) 698-3911 Fax 698-3708
Russell Hawkins, Chairperson
Tribe: Sisseton-Wahpeton Sioux. *In residence*:
4,000. *Area*: 105,000 acres located in North and
South Dakota (only a minor portion in North Da-
kota.) Tribal Council. Sisseton Agency.

STANDING ROCK RESERVATION
Tribes: Teton Sioux (SD) & Yankton Sioux (ND).
Located in North & South Dakota.
See listing in North Dakota.

YANKTON SIOUX RESERVATION
Yankton Sioux Tribal Business Committee
P.O. Box 248, Marty, SD 57361
(605) 384-3804 Fax 384-5687
Darrell Drapeau, Chairperson
Tribe: Yankton Sioux. *In residence*: 2,600.
Area: 35,000 acres. Yankton Agency.

TEXAS

ALABAMA-COUSHATTA TRIBE
Alabama-Coushatta Tribal Council
Route 3, Box 659, Livingston, TX 77351
(409) 563-4391 Fax 563-4397
Frances Battise, Perry Williams, Chairs
Tribe: Alabama-Coushatta of Texas.
Shawnee Agency.

KICKAPOO TRADITIONAL TRIBE OF TEXAS
P.O. Box 972, Eagle Pass, TX 78853
(512) 773-2105 Fax 757-9228
Raul Garza, Chairperson
Tribe served: Kickapoo. Shawnee Agency.

YSLETA DEL SUR PUEBLO
Ysleta Del Sur Pueblo Council
P.O. Box 17579, Ysleta Sta.,
El Paso, TX 79917
(915) 859-7913/4/8 Fax 859-2988
Elias Torres, Governor
Tribe served: Tigua. Southern Pueblos Agency.

UTAH

CHILCHINBETO RESERVATION
Tribe: Navajo. Located in Utah & Arizona.
See listing under Arizona.

DENNEHOTSO RESERVATION
Tribe: Navajo. Located in Utah & Arizona.
See listing under Arizona.

GOSHUTE RESERVATION
Goshute Business Council
P.O. Box 6104, Ibapah, UT 84034
(801) 234-1136 Fax 234-1162
Harlen Pete, Chairperson
Tribe: Goshute. *In residence*: 200. *Population
served*: 380. *Area*: 113,000 acres. Located in Utah
and Nevada. Eastern Nevada Agency.

KAYENTA RESERVATION
Tribe: Navajo. Located in Utah and Arizona.
See listing under Arizona.

MEXICAN WATER RESERVATION
Tribe: Navajo. Located in Utah and Arizona.
See listing under New Mexico.

NAVAJO MOUNTAIN RESERVATION
Tribe: Navajo. Located in Utah and Arizona.
See listing under Arizona.

OLJATOH RESERVATION
Tribe: Navajo. Located in Utah & Arizona.
See listing under Arizona.

PAIUTE INDIAN TRIBE OF UTAH
Tribal Council of Paiute Indian Tribe of Utah
600 N. 100 E. Paiute Dr., Cedar City, UT 84720
(801) 586-1121 Fax 586-7388
Alex Shepherd, Chairperson
Tribe: Paiute (Cedar Band, Indian Peaks Band,
Kanosh Band, Koosharem Band, and Shivwits
Band). *In residence*: 600. *Area*: Southwestern
Utah. *Special activity*: Paiute Restoration Gather-
ing & Pow Wow in June. So. Paiute Field Station.

RED MESA RESERVATION
Tribe: Navajo. Located in Utah & Arizona.
(See listing under New Mexico.)

SHONTO RESERVATION
Tribe: Navajo. Located in Utah & Arizona.
(See listing under Arizona.)

SKULL VALLEY INDIAN COMMUNITY
Skull Valleu General Council
c/o Uintah & Ouray Agency, BIA
P.O. Box 130, Fort Duchesne, UT 84026
(801) 722-2406 Fax 722-2406
Lawrence Bear, Chairperson
Tribe: Skull Valley Band of Goshute.
In residence: 85. Uintah & Ouray Agency.

TEECNOSPOS RESERVATION
Tribe: Navajo. Located in Utah, Arizona &
New Mexico. See listing under New Mexico.

UINTAH & OURAY RESERVATION
Uintah & Ouray Tribal Business Council
P.O. Box 190, Fort Duchesne, UT 84026
(801) 722-5141 Fax 722-2374
Stewart Pike, Chairperson
Tribe: Ute. *In residence*: 2,000. *Area*: 852,411.
Located in the Uintah Basin in northeast Utah.
Head Start Program. Uintah & Ouray Agency.

UTE MOUNTAIN RESERVATION
Tribe: Ute. Located in Utah, New Mexico
& Colorado. See listing under Colorado.

WASHAKIE RESERVATION
Tribe: Northwest Band of Shoshone of Utah.
Located in Utah. See listing under Idaho.

VIRGINIA

CHEROKEE TRIBE OF VIRGINIA
Cherokee of Virginia Tribal Council
Route 1, Box 499, Rapidan, V A 22733
(703) 672-4841
 Samuel W. Beeler, Sr., Principal Chief
 Samuel W. Beeler, Jr., Vice Principal Chief
Tribe: Cherokee Tribe of Virginia. *Population served*: 150. Samuel W. Beeler, III, Treasurer. *Council Members*: Helen A. Beeler, Samad Beller, Romena, Beeler, Emma Beeler, Sandra Beller, Joe Beeler, Edwin C. Estrella, Jr., Oliver B. Warren, Jr., Kay Lindsey and David Lindsey. *Activities*: Traditional Cherokee holidays, festivals, and ceremonies. Library. Eastern Area Office.

PAMUNKEY INDIAN RESERVATION
Pamunkey Tribal Council
Rt. 1, Box 2220, King William, VA 23086
(804) 843-3526
 William P. Miles, Chief
Tribe: Pamunkey. *In residence*: 90. *Area*: 1,250 acres. *Council*: Raymond Bosh, Walter Hill, Robert Grey, Tom Dennis, William P. Miles. Museum.

WASHINGTON

CHEHALIS RESERVATION
Chehalis Community Council
P.O. Box 536, Oakville, W A 98568
(206) 273-5911 Fax 273-5914
 Magdelena "Mena" Medina, Chairperson
Tribe: Chehalis. *In residence*: 750. *Area*: 4,250 acres located in Grays Harbor County. Head Start Program. Olympic Peninsula Agency.

COLVILLE RESERVATION
Colville Business Committee
P.O. Box 150, Nespelem, W A 99155
(509) 634-4711 Fax 634-4116
 Eddie Palmanteer, Jr., Chairperson
Tribes: Confederated Tribes (Colville, Okanogan, Lakes, San Poil, Methow, Nespelem, Entiat, Wenatchee, Moses, Nez Perce, Palouse.) *In residence*: 3,750 (Tribal rolls: 6,200). *Area*: 1,087,271 acres located in Okanogan & Ferry Counties. *Local attractions*: Grand Coulee Dam; Old Fort Okanogan; burial place of Nez Perce, Chief Joseph. *Activities*: Operates a Casino. Head Start. Colville Agency.

HOH RESERVATION
Hoh Tribal Business Committee
HC 80, Box 917, Forks, W A 98331
(206) 374-6582 Fax 374-6549
 Vivian Lee, Vice-Chairperson
Tribe: Hoh. *In residence*: 75. *Area*: 443 acres located at Cape Flattery in Jefferson County. Olympic Peninsula Agency.

JAMESTOWN S'KLALLAM RESERVATION
Jamestown S'Klallem Tribal Council
1033 Old Blyn Hwy., Sequim, WA 98382
(206) 683-1109 Fax 683-4366
 William Ron Allen, Chairperson
Tribe: Jamestown Band of S'Klallem Indians. *In residence*: 250. *Area*: 18 acres in Clallam County. *Tribal Officers*: Sandy Ehrhom, Vice Chairperson; Ann Balch, Secretary; Jerry Allen, Treasurer. *Programs*: Childrens Cultural Program; and annual gathering called, "S'Klallam Qwen Seyu." Library. Olympic Peninsula Agency.

KALISPEL RESERVATION
Kalispel Business Committee
P.O. Box 39, Usk, WA 99180
(509) 445-1147 Fax 455-1705
 Glen Nenema, Chairperson
Tribe: Kalispel. *In residence*: 250. Located in Pend Oreille County. Spokane Agency.

ELWHA S'KLALLAM RESERVATION
Elwha S'Klallam Business Council
2851 Lower Elwha Rd., Port Angeles, WA 98362
(206) 452-8471 Fax 452-4848
 Francis G. Charles, Chairperson
Tribe served: Elwha Band of S'Klallam Indians (main membership). *In residence*: 470. *Area*: 430 acres located in Clallam County. *Activities*: Substance abuse program; health clinic; housing department; hatchery-fisheries department; higher adult-vocational education department. Olympic Peninsula Agency.

LUMMI RESERVATION
Lummi Business Council
2616 Kwina Rd., Bellingham, W A 98226
(206) 734-8180 Fax 384-5521
 Henry Cagey, Chairperson
Tribe: Lummi. *In residence*: 3,300. *Area*: 12 acres (tribally-owned); 7,073 acres (allotted). Located in Whatcom County *Activities*: Lummi Water Stommish Festival. Operates middle school, high school, and community college. *Publication*: Bi-weekly community newsletter. Puget Sound Agency. Head Start Program.

MAKAH RESERVATION
Makah Tribal Council
P.O. Box 115, Neah Bay, WA 98357
(206) 645-2201 Ext. 36 Fax 645-2323
 Hubert Markishtum, Chairperson
Tribe: Makah. *In residence*: 1,250. *Area*: 27,012 acres located on the Pacific Ocean & Straits of Juan De Fuca in Clallam County. Head Start Program. Olympic Peninsula Agency.

MUCKLESHOOT RESERVATION
Muckleshoot Tribal Council
39015 172nd St., SE, Auburn, WA 98002
(206) 939-3311 Fax 939-5311
 Virginia Cross, Chairperson
Tribe: Muckleshoot. *In residence*: 2,500. *Area*: 1,959 acres located in King County. Head Start Program. Puget Sound Agency.

NISQUALLY INDIAN COMMUNITY
Nisqually Indian Community Council
4820 She-Nah-Num Dr., SE, Olympia, WA 98503
(206) 456-5221 Fax 456-5280
 Dorian Sanchez, Chairperson
Tribe: Nisqually. *In residence*: 1,400. *Area*: 941 acres located in Thurston County. Head Start Program. Puget Sound Agency.

NOOKSACK RESERVATION
Nooksack Tribal Council
P.O. Box 157, Deming, W A 98244
(206) 592-5176 Fax 592-5721
 Joe Johnson, Chairperson
Tribe: Nooksack. *In residence*: 750. *Area*: 2,906 acres located in Whatcom County. Head Start Program. Puget Sound Agency.

PORT GAMBLE INDIAN COMMUNITY
Port Gamble S'Klallam Tribal Council
31912 Little Boston Rd., NE, Kingston, W A 98346
(206) 297-2646 Fax 297-7097
 Gerald J. Jones, Chairperson
Tribe: Port Gamble Band of S'Klallam Indians. *In*

residence: 450. *Area*: 1,301 acres located in Kitsap County. Head Start Program. Puget Sound Agency.

PORT MADISON RESERVATION
Suquamish Tribal Council
P.O. Box 498, Suquamish, W A 98392
(206) 598-3311 Fax 598-6295
 Lyle Emerson George, Chairperson
Tribe: Suquamish. *In residence*: 480. *Area*: 8,000 acres located in Kitsap County. *Population served*: 650. *Activities*: Chief Seattle Day (annual traditional tribal celebration, held in August). *Local attractions*: Totem Poles throughout the Reservation; Suquamish Museum; Photographic Archives and Oral History Collection. *Publications*: Dsub'Wub'Siatsub (Suquamish News), tribal newsletter; A Guide to Oral History in the Native American Community; Suquamish Tribal *Photographic Archives Project*: A Case Study; Suquamish Today; and The Eyes of Chief Seattle (exhibit catalog.) Library. Puget Sound Agency.

PUYALLUP RESERVATION
Puyallup Tribal Council
2002 East 28th St., Tacoma, WA 98404
(206) 597-6200 Fax 272-9514
 Roberta M. Young, Chairperson
Tribes: Puyallup, Nisqually, Muckleshoot, Skwawksnamish, and Steilacoom. *Population served*: 6,500. *Area*: 33 acres located in Pierce County. Tribal Council. Puget Sound Agency.

QUILEUTE RESERVATION
Quileute Tribal Council
P.O. Box 279, LaPush, W A 98350
(206) 374-6163 Fax 374-6311
 Douglas Woodruff, Chairperson
Tribe: Quileute. *Population served*: 300. *Area*: 1 square mile located on the Pacific Ocean in Clallam County. *Program*: Head Start. *Activities*: Quileute Days (July); Elders Week Celebration (May); Operate Tribal School serving K-8. *Publication*: Quileute Indian News, monthly; The Quileute of La Push, book. Olympic Peninsula Agency.

QUINAULT RESERVATION
Quinault Business Committee
P.O. Box 189, Taholah, WA 98587
(206) 276-8211 Fax 276-4191
 Pearl Capoeman-Baller, President
Tribe: Quinault. *In residence*: 2,200. *Area*: 136,456 acres located 40 miles north of Hoguiam, on the Pacific Ocean in Grays Harbor County. *Activities*: Annual celebration in July. *Local attraction*: Indian village. Head Start Program. Olympic Peninsula Agency.

SAUK-SUIATTLE INDIAN RESERVATION
Sauk-Suiattle Tribal Council
5318 Chief Brown Lane, Darrington, W A 98241
(206) 436-0131 Fax 436-1511
 J. Lawrence Joseph, Chairperson
Tribe: Sauk-Suiattle. *In residence*: 215. *Area*: 23 acres located in Skagit County. *Activities*: Annual Huckleberry Festival (September); Annual Yo-Buch Days (July). Library. Tribal Council. Puget Sound Agency.

SHOALWATER BAY RESERVATION
Shoalwater Bay Tribal Council
P.O. Box 130, Tokeland, WA 98590
(206) 267-6766 Fax 267-6778
 Herbert "Ike" Whitish, Chairperson
 James Anderson, Vice-Chairperson
Tribe: Shoalwater. *In residence*: 100. *Area*: 335

acres located in Pacific County, near Tokeland. Olympic Peninsula Agency.

SKOKOMISH INDIAN RESERVATION
Skokomish Tribal Council
N. 80 Tribal Center Rd., Shelton, WA 98584
　(206) 426-4232 Fax 877-5148
　Francis Twiddy, Chairperson
Tribe: Skokomish. *In residence*: 350. *Population served*: 1,000. *Area*: 6,300 acres located in Mason County. *Council members*: Pat and Denise Laclair. *Activities*: 1st Plant Ceremony (April); 1st Salmon Ceremony (August); 1st Elk Ceremony (October). Small museum and library. *Publication*: Portrait of a Tribe: An Intro to the Skokomish. Head Start Program. Olympic Peninsula Agency.

SPOKANE RESERVATION
Spokane Business Council
P.O. Box 100, Wellpinit, WA 99040
　(509) 258-4581 Fax 258-9243
　Bruce Wynne, Chairperson
Tribe: Spokane. *In residence*: 1,200 (tribal roll, 2,500). *Area*: 138,750 acres located in the southwest corner of Stevens County. *Local attractions*: Old Fort Spokane; Tsimshian Mission (1838). Spokane Agency.

SQUAXIN ISLAND RESERVATION
Squaxin Island Tribal Council
SE 70, Squaxin Lane, Shelton, WA 98584
　(206) 426-9781 Fax 426-6577
　David Lopeman, Chairman
Tribes: Squaxin Island, Nisqually, Steilacoom, and others. *In residence*: 1,000. *Location*: Mason County. Olympic Peninsula Agency.

STILLAGUAMISH RESERVATION
Stillaquamish Board of Directors
P.O. Box 277, Arlington, WA 98223
　(206) 652-7362 Fax 435-2204
　Gail Greger, Chairperson
Tribe served: Stillaguamish. *Location*: Snohomish County. Puget Sound Agency.

SWINOMISH INDIAN TRIBAL COMMUNITY
Swinomish Indian Senate
P.O. Box 817, LaConnor, WA 98257
　(206) 466-3163 Fax 466-5309
　Robert Joe, Sr., Chairperson
Tribes: Swinomish, Suiattle, Skagit, and Kikiallus. *In residence*: 750. *Area*: 1,000 acres located in Skagit County. Puget Sound Agency.

TULALIP RESERVATION
Tulalip Board of Directors
6700 Totem Beach Rd., Marysville, WA 98270
　(206) 653-4585 Fax 653-0255
　Stanley Jones, Sr., Chairperson
Tribe: Tulalip (Snohomish, Snoqualmie, Skagit, Suiattle, Samish, and allied bands). *In residence*: 950. *Area*: 22,000 acres located in Snohomish County.*Activities*: Operates Tulalip Casino. Puget Sound Agency.

UPPER SKAGIT INDIAN RESERVATION
Upper Skagit Tribal Council
2284 Community Plaza, Sedro Wooley, WA 98284
　(206) 856-5501 Fax 856-3175
　Floyd Williams, Chairperson
Tribe: Upper Skagit. *In residence*: 200. *Area*: 99 acres located in Skagit County. Puget Sound Agency.

YAKAMA RESERVATION
Yakama Tribal Council
P.O. Box 151, Toppenish, WA 98948

(509) 865-5121 Fax 865-5528
　Jerry Meninick, Chairperson
Tribe: Yakama. *In residence*: 9,000. *Area*: 1,134,830 acres located in Yakama & Klickitat Counties. *Activities*: All-Indian Rodeo (June); Annual Pow-Wow (July); Huckleberry Feast (August). Head Start Program. Yakama Agency.

WISCONSIN

BAD RIVER RESERVATION
Bad River Tribal Council
P.O. Box 39, Odanah, WI 54861
　(715) 682-7111 Fax 682-7118
　Elizabeth Drake, Chairperson
Tribe: Bad River Band of Lake Superior Band of (Ojibwe) Chippewa. *In residence*: 1,550. *Area*: 125,000 acres. Located on Lake Superior, southeast of Duluth, Minnesota. *Special activity*: Annual Minomin Wild Rice Powwow in August. *Council members*: Robert Bender, Charles Wiggins, and Matt O'Claire. Library. Head Start. Great Lakes Agency.

FOREST COUNTY POTAWATOMI COMMUNITY
Forest County Potawatomi Executive Council
P.O. Box 340, Crandon, WI 54520
　(715) 478-2903 Fax 478-5280
　Hartford Shegonee, Chairperson
Tribe: Forest County Potawatomi. *In residence*: 450. *Area*: 10,000 acres. Great Lakes Agency.

HO CHUNK(WINNEBAGO) RESERVATION
Wisconsin Ho Chunk Business Committee
P.O. Box 667, Black River Falls, WI 54615
　(715) 284-9343 Fax 284-1760
　Gordon Thunder, Chairperson
Tribe: Wisconsin Ho Chunk. *In residence*: 1350. *Population served*: 1,850. *Area*: 4,100 acres. *Activity*: Casino. Head Start Program. Great Lakes Agency.

LAC COURTE OREILLES RESERVATION
Lac Courte Oreilles Tribal Governing Board
Route 2, Box 2700, Hayward, WI 54843
　(715) 634-8934 Fax 634-4797
　Gaiashkibos, Chairperson
Tribe served: Lac Courte Oreilles Band of Chippewa. *In residence*: 2,000. *Area*: 70,000 acres. Located within Sawyer County. *Program*: Head Start - Cathy Barber, Program Director. *Goals*: To provide comprehensive child development services to 94 LCO children and their families. *Publication*: LCO Ojibwe Early Childhood Curriculum. Library. Great Lakes Agency.

LAC DU FLAMBEAU RESERVATION
Lac du Flambeau Tribal Council
P.O. Box 67, Lac du Flambeau, WI 54538
　(715) 588-3303 Fax 588-7930
　Thomas Maulson, President
Tribe: Lake Superior Chippewa. *In residence*: 2,400. *Area*: 144 square miles. *Activities*: Annual Bear River Pow Wow; Museum & Cultural Center; Library. Head Start. Great Lakes Agency.

MENOMINEE RESERVATION
Menominee Tribal Legislature
P.O. Box 910, Keshena, WI 54135
　(715) 799-5100 Fax 799-3373
　Glenn Miller, Chairperson
Tribe: Menominee. *In residence*: 3,750. *Area*: 233,800 acres. *Council members*: Louis Dixon, Leslie 'Easter' Penass, and John Teller. *Activities*:

Annual Pow-wow, 1st weekend in August; Restoration Day, Dec. 22nd. Operates Menominee Tribal School in Neopit, WI; and College of the Menominee Nation in Keshena, WI. Head Start Program (awarded grant for family literacy). Minneapolis Area Office.

ONEIDA RESERVATION
Oneida Tribal Council
P.O. Box 365, Oneida, WI 54155
　(414) 869-2214 Fax 869-2194
　Deborah Doxtator, Chairperson
Tribe: Oneida. *In residence*: 2,700 (tribal roll: 3,800). *Area*: 2,600 acres. *Activities*: Owns & operates the Oneida Bingo & Casino and the Oneida Radisson Inn in Green Bay, WI. Head Start Program. Great Lakes Agency.

RED CLIFF RESERVATION
Red Cliff Tribal Council
P.O. Box 529, Bayfield, WI 54814
　(715) 779-3701 Fax 779-3704
　Rose Gurnoe, Chairperson
Tribe: Red Cliff Band of Chippewa. *In residence*: 1,500. *Area*: 7,311 acres. Extends over Lake Superior, approximately 25 miles northwest of Ashland, Wisconsin. Great Lakes Agency.

ST. CROIX RESERVATION
St. Croix Council
P.O. Box 287, Hertel, WI 54845
　(715) 349-2195 Fax 349-5768
　Lewis Taylor, Chairperson
Tribe: St. Croix Chippewa. *In residence*: 1,100. *Area*: 2,230 acres. Great Lakes Agency.

SOKAOGON CHIPPEWA COMMUNITY
Sokaogon Chippewa Tribal Council
Route 1, Box 625, Crandon, WI 54520
　(715) 478-2604 Fax 478-5275
　Arlyn Ackley, Chairperson
Tribe: Mole Lake Chippewa. *In residence*: 275. *Area*: 1,700 acres. Great Lakes Agency.

STOCKBRIDGE-MUNSEE COMMUNITY
Stockbridge-Munsee Tribal Council
8476 Moh He Con Nuck Rd., Bowler, WI 54416
　(715) 793-4111 Fax 793-4299
　Laura Coyhis, Chairperson
Tribe: Stockbridge-Munsee Mohican Indians of Wisconsin. *In residence*: 850 (tribal roll: 1,600). *Area*: 16,000 acres. *Activity*: North Star Casino. Head Start Program. Great Lakes Agency.

WYOMING

WIND RIVER RESERVATION
Shoshone & Arapahoe Joint Tribal Business Council
P.O. Box 217, Fort Washakie, WY 82514
　(307) 332-3532 Fax 332-3055 (Shoshone)
　(307) 332-6120 Fax 332-7543 (Arapahoe)
　Darwin St. Clair, Chairperson (Shoshone)
　Harvey Spoonhunter, Chairperson (Arapahoe)
Tribe served: Wind River Shoshone & Arapaho. *In residence*: 5,500. *Population served*: 8,000. *Area*: 1,887,372 acres. Located in east-central Wyoming. *Program*: Head Start - Karen King, Director. *Goals*: To provide comprehensive child care services to low-income children and families in the areas of education, health, nutrition, social services and parent involvement. *Publications*: Social Service Directory, handbooks and pamphlets. Library. Wind River Agency.

This section lists Indian tribes, groups, and bands who represent the interests of their members, They are, in most cases, landless, recognized by the various states, but not yet federally recognized.

ALABAMA

CHEROKEES OF JACKSON CITY
P.O. Box 41, Higdon, AL 35979

CHEROKEES OF NORTHEAST ALABAMA
3912 Cahaba Rd., Birmingham, AL 34243

CHEROKEES OF SOUTHEAST ALABAMA
Dothan, Alabama 36301

ECHOTA CHEROKEE TRIBE OF ALABAMA
Route 1, Box 122-A, Maylene, AL 35114

**MACHIS LOWER ALABAMA
CREEK INDIAN TRIBE**
708 South John St., New Brockton, AL 36351

**PRINCIPAL CREEK INDIAN NATION
EAST OF THE MISSISSIPPI**
Florala, AL 36442

**STAR CLAN OF MUSKOGEE CREEK
TRIBE OF PIKE COUNTY**
P.O. Box 126, Goshen, AL 36035

UNITED CHEROKEE TRIBE OF ALABAMA
Route 1, Box 8, Daleville, AL 36322

ARIZONA

BARRIO PASCUA
San Ignacio Yaqui Council, Inc.
2256 North Calle Central, Tucson, AZ 85705

GUADALUPE ORGANIZATIONS
8810 South 56th St., Guadalupe, AZ 85705

SAN IGNACIO YAQUI COUNCIL
Tucson, AZ 85705

SAN JUAN NORTHERN PAIUTE
P.O. Box 2656, Tuba City, AZ 86045

ARKANSAS

**OUACHITA INDIANS OF
ARKANSAS & AMERICA**
P.O. Box 34, Story, AR 71970
 (501) 867-4252
High Council of Ouchita Indians
2156 Higdon Ferry Rd.,
Hot Springs, AR 71913
 (501) 525-9927
 Lone Elk (John Woodall), Grand Head Chief
 Great Eagle, Grand Head Vice Chief
Tribe: Ouachita Indians of Arkansas. *Programs*:
Education in Indian traditions and customs; environmental concerns of Mother Earth. *Activities*:
Pow-wows and craft fairs; personal appearances
of Chief Lone Elk and members for school children and organizations. Museum

CALIFORNIA

**AMERICAN INDIAN COUNCIL OF
MARIPOSA COUNTY (a.k.a. YOSEMITE)**
P.O. Box 1200, Mariposa, CA 95338
 (209) 966-4296

**AMAH BAND OF OHLONE/
COSTANOAN INDIANS**
789 Canada Rd., Woodside, CA 94062
 (415) 851-7489

ANTELOPE VALLEY INDIAN COMMUNITY
P.O. Box 168, Coleville, CA 96107

**ATAHUN SHOSHONES OF
SAN JUAN CAPISTRANO**
2352 Bahia Dr., La Jolla, CA 92037

BIG MEADOWS LODGE TRIBE
P.O. Box 362, Chester, CA 96020

**CALAVERAS COUNTY BAND
OF MEWUK INDIANS**
Star Route 1, West Point, CA 92555

CHOINUMNI TRIBE
2548 Cedar South, Fresno, CA 93725

COASTAL BAND OF CHUMASH INDIANS
Santa Barbara Urban Indian Health
610 Del Monte Ave., Santa Barbara, CA 93101

**COSTANOAN BAND OF
CARMEL MISSION INDIANS**
P.O. Box 1657, Monroavia, CA 91016

DUNLAP BAND OF MONO INDIANS
P.O. Box 126, Dunlap, CA 93621

HOWNONQUET COMMUNITY ASSOCIATION
P.O. Box 179, Smith River, CA 95567

**INDIAN CANYON BAND OF COSTANOAN/
MUTSUN INDIANS OF CALIFORNIA**
General Delivery, Hollister, CA 95024

JAMUL BAND
P.O. Box 353, Jamul, CA 92035

JUANENO BAND OF MISSION INDIANS
31742 Via Belardes,
San Juan Capistrano, CA 92675
 (714) 493-4933

KERN VALLEY INDIAN COMMUNITY
P.O. Bin DD, Kernville, CA 93238
 (619) 376-3761

LIKELY RANCHERIA
P.O. Drawer 1570, Burney, CA 96013
 (916) 335-5421
Tribe served: Pit River.

MAIDU NATION
P.O. Box 204, Susanville, CA 96130

MELOCHUNDUM BAND OF TOLOWA INDIANS
P.O. Box 388, Fort Dick, CA 95538

MONO LAKE INDIAN COMMUNITY
P.O. Box 237, Lee Vining, CA 93541

MONO TRIBAL COUNCIL OF DUNLAP
P.O. Box 344, Dunlap, CA 93621
 (209) 338-2329
Tribe served: Mono.

MONTGOMERY CREEK RANCHERIA
P.O. Drawer 1570, Burney, CA 96013
 (619) 335-5421
Tribe served: Pit River.

**NOR-EL-MUK WINTU INDIANS
OF NORTH CALIFORNIA**
P.O. Box 673, Hayfork, CA 96041
 (916) 628-5175

NORTHERN MAIDU TRIBE
P.O. Box 217, Greenville, CA 95947

OHLONE/COSTANOAN MUWEKMA TRIBE
1845 The Alameda, San Jose, CA 95126
 (408) 293-9956

ROARING CREEK RANCHERIA
Montgomery Creek, Shasta, CA 96065
Tribe: Pit River

SALINAN NATION
P.O. Box 610546, San Jose, CA 95161

SAN LUIS REY BAND OF MISSION INDIANS
Mission Indian Bands Paralegal Consortium
360 N. Midway, Suite 301, Escondido, CA 92027

SHASTA NATION
P.O. Box 1054, Yreka, CA 96097
 (916) 842-5654

SHEEP RANCH RANCHERIA
Sheep Ranch, CA 95250
Tribe served: Me-Wuk.

**SONOMA COUNTY
AMERICAN INDIAN COUNCIL**
930 Piner Rd., Santa Rosa, CA 95401

TEHATCHAPI TRIBE
219 East H St., Tehatchapi, CA 95401

TOLOWA NATION
P.O. Box 213, Fort Dick, CA 95538
 (707) 464-7332

TOLOWA-TUTUTNI TRIBE OF INDIANS
P.O. Box 388, Fort Dick, CA 95538

WASHOE/PAIUTE OF ANTELOPE VALLEY
Coleville, CA 96107

WINTU INDIAN TRIBAL COUNCIL
P.O. Box 1036, Project City, CA 96079

**WINTUN TRIBE-RUMSEY
RANCHERIA COUNCIL**
P.O. Box 18
Brooks, CA 95606
 (916) 796-3400

WUKCHUMNI COUNCIL
36787 Rd. 197, Woodlake, CA 93286
 (916) 335-5421

YOKAYO POMO RANCHERIA
1114 Helen Ave., Unkiah, CA 95482

COLORDO

**MUNSEE THAMES RIVER DELAWARE
TRIBAL COUNCIL**
Manitou Springs, CO

CONNECTICUT

GOLDEN HILL PAUGUSSETT TRIBE
Reservation - Stanavage Rd.
Colchester, CT 06415

PAUCATUCK PEQUOT TRIBE
939 Lantern Hill Rd., Ledyard, CT 06339

DELAWARE

NANTICOKE INDIAN ASSOCIATION
Rte. 4, Box 107-A, Millsboro, DE 19966
(302) 945-3400

FLORIDA

CREEKS EAST OF THE MISSISSIPPI
c/o Thomley, 7701 Ennon School Rd.
Walnut Hill, FL 32568
(904) 587-2116

**FLORIDA TRIBE OF
EASTERN CREEK INDIANS**
P.O. Box 3028
Bruce, FL 32455
(904) 835-2078 (phone & fax)
John C.B. Thomas, Chairperson
Kenneth McKenzie, Vice-Chairperson
Chief Andrew Ramsey
Ceremonies: Pine Arbor Tribal Town; Berry, Green
Corn, Little Green Corn, Harvest. The Museum
(Blountstown, FL); Library. *Publication*: The Florida
Muskogee (Creek) News.

**NORTH BAY CLAN OF LOWER
CREEK MUSCOGEE TRIBE**
P.O. Box 687, Lynn Haven, FL 32444
(904) 265-3345
Lonzo Woods, Chief

OKLEWAHA BAND OF SEMINOLE INDIANS
P.O. Box 521, Orange Springs, FL 32182
(904) 546-1386

TOPACHULA TRIBAL COUNCIL
Pine Arbor Tribal Town
602 Gunther St., Tallahassee, FL 32308

**TUSCOLA UNITED CHEROKEE TRIBE
OF FLORIDA & ALABAMA**
P.O. Box 49, Geneva, FL 32732

GEORGIA

**CANE BREAK BAND OF EASTERN
CHEROKEES TRIBAL COUNCIL**
Rte. 3, Box 750, Dahlonega, GA 30533
(706) 864-6010

**CHEROKEE INDIANS OF
GEORGIA TRIBAL COUNCIL**
Columbus, GA

**GEORGIA TRIBE OF EASTERN
CHEROKEES TRIBAL COUNCIL**
P.O. Box 993, Dahlonega, GA 30533
(706) 864-3805

**LOWER MUSKOGEE CREEK TRIBE-
EAST OF THE MISSISSIPPI**
Tama Reservation, Cairo, GA 31728

**SOUTHEASTERN CHEROKEE
CONFEDERACY**
120 Will Hatcher Rd., Albany, GA 31705-9430

**TENNESSEE RIVER BAND
OF CHICKAMAUGA CHEROKEE**
P.O. Box 291, Flintstone, GA 30725
(615) 855-2909
David Q. Brown, Raven, Chairperson
Robert T. Murray, Chief
Tribes served: Metis Cherokee of TN, GA, and
AL. *Publication*: Voices of the Council Fire, news-
letter.

IDAHO

DELAWARES OF IDAHO TRIBAL COUNCIL
3677 N. Maple Grove Rd., Boise, ID 83704

INDIANA

**INDIANA MIAMI INDIAN
ORGANIZATIONAL COUNCIL**
641 Buchanan St., Huntington, IN 46750

KANSAS

DELAWARE-MUNCIE TRIBAL COUNCIL
P.O. Box 274, Pomona, KS 66076

**KAWEAH INDIAN NATION OF WESTERN USA
& MEXICO**
P.O. Box 3121, Hutchinson, KS 67504
(316) 665-3614
Chief Thunderbird Webber, Grand Chief
Publication: Itza Voice.

SWAN CREEK & BLACK RIVER CHIPPEWAS
519 Willow St., Ottawa, KS 66067

LOUISIANA

**CHOCTAW-APACHE COMMUNITY OF EBARB
Choctaw-Apache Tribal Council**
P.O. Box 858, Zwolle, LA 71486
(318) 645-2744
Tommy Bolton, Chief
Victor Sepulvado, Vice Chief
Sheli Lafitte, Treasurer
Tribe: Choctaw and Lipan Apache. *In residence*:
900. *Location*: West Central Sabine Parish. *Ac-
tivities*: Annual Pow-wow, last weekend in May.
Maintains school - only officially recognized "In-
dian School" in the state of Louisiana.

**CLIFTON CHOCTAW INDIANS
TRIBAL COUNCIL**
P.O. Box 32, Gardner, LA 71431
(318) 793-8796

HOUMA NATION TRIBAL COUNCIL
Star Rte., Box 95-A
Golden Meadow, LA 70357
(504) 475-6640

JENA BAND OF CHOCTAWS
P.O. Box 14, Jena, LA 71342

MARYLAND

PISCATAWAY INDIAN NATION COUNCIL
P.O. Box 312, Port Tobacco, MD 20677
(301) 932-0808

MASSACHUSETTS

GAY HEAD WAMPANOAG TRIBE
State Rd., RFD Box 137
Gay Head, MA 02535

MASHPEE-WAMPANOAG INDIAN TRIBE
Route 1048, Mashpee, MA 02649
(617) 477-0208

**NEW ENGLAND COASTAL SCHAGTICOKE
INDIAN ASSOCIATION**
P.O. Box 551, Avon, MA 02322
(617) 961-1346
Laurence "Swift Tide" Shanks, Chief

NIPMUC TRIBAL COUNCIL
Box 3, 22 Front St., Worcester, MA 01614
(508) 753-0440

MICHIGAN

**BURT LAKE BAND OF OTTAWA
& CHIPPEWA INDIANS COUNCIL**
P.O. Box 206, Brutus, MI 49716
(616) 529-6113
State recognized.

**GRAND RIVER BAND OF THE
OTTAWA NATION COUNCIL**
268 Irvin St., Muskegon, MI 49442
(616) 726-2567

HURON POTAWATOMI INDIAN COUNCIL
2221 1.5 Mile Rd., Fulton, MI 49052
(616) 729-5151
State recognized.

**LAC VIEUX DESERT BAND OF LAKE
SUPERIOR CHIPPEWA INDIAN TRIBE**
P.O. Box 446, Watersmeet, MI 49969

**LAKE SUPERIOR CHIPPEWA
OF MARQUETTE TRIBAL COUNCIL**
P.O. Box 1071, Marquette, MI 49855
(906) 249-3969

**LITTLE RIVER BAND OF
OTTAWA INDIANS COUNCIL**
409 Water St., Manistee, MI 49660
(616) 723-8288

**LITTLE TRAVERSE BAY BAND
OF ODAWA INDIANS COUNCIL**
P.O. Box 4009, Petoskey, MI 49770
(616) 348-3410

NORTHERN MICHIGAN OTTAWA TRIBE
1391 Terrace St., Muskegon, MI 49441

**POKAGAN BAND OF POTAWATOMI
INDIANS COUNCIL**
53237 Town Hall Rd., Dowagiac, MI 49047
(616) 782-6323

**POTAWATOMI INDIAN TRIBE
OF INDIANA & MICHIGAN**
Route 6, Box 526, Dowagiac, MI 49047

MISSOURI

**NORTHERN CHEROKEE NATION OF
THE OLD LOUISIANA TERRITORY**
1502 E. Broadway #201, Columbia, MO 65201

MONTANA

**LITTLE SHELL TRIBE OF CHIPPEWA
INDIANS OF MONTANA**
P.O. Box 347, Havre, MT 59501
(406) 265-2741

SWAN CREEK & BLACK RIVER CHIPPEWA
Dixon, MT 59831

NEVADA

PAHRUMP BAND OF PAIUTE INDIANS
P.O. Box 73, Pahrump, NV 89041
(702) 486-5211

NEW JERSEY

NANTICOKE LENNI-LENAPE INDIANS OF NJ
18 E. Commerce St., Bridgeton, NJ 08302
(609) 455-8210/6910
Mark M. Gould, Chairperson
Programs: Cultural Center - job training/employment, drug/alcohol/cigarette abuse program; AIDS education program;elders program; referral service; cultural-dancing, singing & drumming; annual pow-wow. Maintains museum and library.

NATIVE DELAWARE INDIANS
c/o New Jersey Indian Office
300 Main St., Suite 3F, Orange, NJ 07050
(201) 675-0694

**POWHATTAN RENAPE NATION
RANKOKUS RESERVATION**
P.O. Box 225, Rancocas, NJ 08073
(609) 261-4747
Chief Nemattanew (Roy Crazy Horse)
Description: Located near Mt. Holly, NJ, the reservation consists of the Powhatan ancestral village with a conference center, heritage museum and art gallery, library, gift shop, and nature trails.
Special programs: Crafts - Indian artists demon-

strate their skills; cultural programs; audio-visual presentations; & classes & meetings in Powhatan language and traditions are held. Annual Arts Festival.

RAMAPOUGH MOUNTAIN INDIANS
19 Mountain Rd., Mahwah, NJ 07430
(201) 529-5750
Ronald Redbone Van Dunk, Chief

NEW MEXICO

**PUEBLO OF SAN JUAN DE GUADALUPE
Piro/Manso/Tiwa Indian Tribal Council**
P.O. Box 16243, Las Cruces, NM 88004
(800) 527-1699; (505) 527-1699
Fax (505) 521-1449
Louis Roybal, President
Frank Sanchez, Vice President
Andrew Roybal, Project Coordinator
Tribes served: Piro, Manso and Tiwa. *Population served*: 350. *Project*: Establishing a tribal cultural center. *Activities*: Tribal ceremonies and feast days occur four times a year in March, June, September and December. State recognized. Federal recognition is pending.

TIWA INDIAN TRIBE
4028 San Ysidro Rd., San Ysidro, NM 88005
a.k.a. San Juan de Guadalupe Tiwa

NEW YORK

ABENAKI INDIAN VILLAGE
Lake George, New York 12845

MONTAUK INDIAN TRIBE
Hempstead Dr., Sag Harbor, NY 11963

POOSPATUCK TRIBE
Poospetuck Reservation
198 Poospetuck Lane, Mastic, NY 11950
(516) 399-3843
Howard E. Treadwell, Chief

SHINNECOCK TRIBE
P.O. Box 59, Southampton, NY 11968
(516) 283-1643
Brad Smith, Kevin Eleazer, James Eleazer, Jr.,
Trustees
Tribe: Shinnecock. In residence: 375. *Area*: 400 acres. Located in Suffolk County, NY, near Southampton. Eastern Area Office.

UNKECHAUGE NATION COUNCIL
Poospatuck Reservation
P.O. Box 86, Mastic, NY 11950
(516) 281-6464

NORTH CAROLINA

CHEROKEE INDIANS OF HOKE CITY
Rt. 1, Box 129-C, Lumber Bridge, NC 28357

**CHEROKEE INDIANS OF ROBESON
& ADJOINING COUNTIES**
Rte. 2, P.O. Box 272-A, Red Springs, NC 28377

**CHEROKEE-POWHATTAN
INDIAN ASSOCIATION**
P.O. Box 3265, Roxboro, NC 27573

COHAIRIE INDIAN TRIBE
Rte. 3, Box 356-B, Clinton, NC 28328
(919) 564-6909

DROWNING CREEK RESERVATION
Rte. 2, Box 108, Maxton, NC 28364
(919) 844-3827
Tribe: Tuscarora.

FAIRCLOTH INDIAN TRIBE
P.O. Box 161, Atlantic, NC 28511

HALIWA-SAPONI TRIBE
P.O. Box 99, Hollister, NC 27844
(919) 586-4017 Fax 586-3918
Joseph Richardson, Chairperson
Michael Mills, Vice Chair
W.R. Richardson, Chief;
Barry Richardson, Administrator
Tribe: Haliva-Saponi. Activities: Pow-wow (3rd Saturday in April). Small museum and library serving the community.

HATTADARE INDIAN TRIBE
Rte. 1, Box 85-6, Bunnlevel, NC 28323
(919) 893-2512

**HATTERAS TUSCARORA INDIAN
TRIBAL FOUNDATION**
Rte. I, Box 385, Maxton, NC 28364
(919) 844-5857

KAWEAH INDIAN NATION, INC.
Oriental, NC 28571

**LUMBEE REGIONAL DEVELOPMENT
ASSOCIATION, INC.**
East Main St., Box 68, Pembroke, NC 28372
(919) 521-8602

MEHERRIN INDIAN TRIBE
P.O. Box 508, Winton, NC 27986
(919) 358-4375
George Earl Pierce, Chief
Calvin Hall, Chairperson
Council: Ira Mitchell, Wayne Brown, Argustus Chavis, Tracy Watford, Lise Hall, and Marion Brewington. *Activity*: Annual Pow-Wow. *Publication*: Monthly newsletter for tribal members.

PERSON COUNTY INDIANS
Rte. 6, Box 104, Roxboro, NC 27573

TUSCARORA INDIAN TRIBE
Drowning Creek Reservation
Route 2, Box 108, Maxton, NC 28364
(919) 844-3827
Chief Wise Owl

WACCAMAW SIOUAN TRIBE
P.O. Box 221, Bolton, NC 28423

NORTH DAKOTA

CHRISTIAN PEMBINA CHIPPEWA INDIANS
P.O. Box 727, Dunseith, ND 58329

LITTLE SHELL BAND OF CHIPPEWA
Dunseith, ND 58329

OHIO

AMERICAN INDIAN MISSION
2501 Mahoning Rd. NE
Alleghenny Tribal Council
2111 16th St. NE, Canton, OH 44705
 (216) 453-6224 Fax 453-2867
 Sakim, Chief (lifetime)
Tribe: Alleghenny Lenape. *Membership*: 17,000 (nationwide). *Activities*: Annual Festival in June; crafts, dancing and medicine ceremonies.

**NORTH EASTERN U.S. MIAMI
INTER-TRIBAL COUNCIL**
1535 Florencedale, Youngstown, OH 44505
 (216) 746-4956

*PIQUA SECT OF OHIO SHAWNEE INDIANS
Bancohio Bldg., Suite 828
4 W. Main St., Springfield, OH 45502
 (513) 325-7621

SHAWNEE NATION UNITED REMNANT BAND
P.O. Box 162, Dayton, OH 45401

OKLAHOMA

**CHICKAMAUGA CHEROKEE INDIAN
NATION OF ARKANSAS & MISSOURI**
133 J St., N.W., Miami, OK 74354
 (918) 540-1492 Fax 540-1630

YUCHI TRIBAL ORGANIZATION
P.O. Box 1990, Sapulpa, OK 74067
 (918) 227-3898

OREGON

CHETCO TRIBE
564 Fern St., Brookings, OR 97415

CHINOOK TRIBE
5621 Altamont Dr., Klamath Falls, OR 97603

**CONFEDERATED TRIBES OF COOS,
LOWER UMPQUAH & SIUSLAW INDIANS**
533 Buchanan, Coos Bay, OR 97420

COQUILLE INDIAN TRIBE
250 Hull St., Coos Bay, OR 97420

KLAMATH TRIBE
P.O. Box 436, Chiloquin, OR 97624

**NORTHWEST CHEROKEE WOLF BAND
OF THE SOUTHEASTERN CHEROKEE
CONFEDERACY**
P.O. Box 592, Talent, OR 97540

TCHINOUK INDIANS (CHINOOK)
5621 Altamont Dr., Klamath Falls, OR 97601

SOUTH CAROLINA

FOUR HOLE INDIAN ORGANIZATION
Edisto Tribal Council, Ridgeville, SC 29472
 (803) 871-2126

PEE DEE INDIAN ASSOCIATION
P.O. Box 6068, Clio, SC 29525

SANTEE TRIBE
White Oak Indian Community
Route 1, Box 34-M, Holly Hill, SC 29059

**WACCAMAW-SIOUAN INDIAN
ASSOCIATION OF SOUTH CAROLINA**
2217 Hwy. 501 W, Galivant's Ferry, SC 29544
 (803) 248-9843
 Robert Wolf Eagle, Principal Chief
 Vince Michel, Second Chief
 Michael Myler, Tribal Chairman
Tribe: Waccamaw. Organized in 1992 under the laws of the state of South Carolina. Purpose: To perpetuate the cultural heritage of the W accamaw Indian people as well as all other indigenous peoples of South Carolina; to act as an international bridge between Indians and non-Indians. *Facility*: The Education and Cultural Center. *Activities*: Offers programs in traditional crafts, spirituality, traditional medicines, and foods, as well as children's programs; Sweat Lodges. Goals: To develop the South Carolina Museum and Library of Native American History.

TENNESSEE

ETOWAH CHEROKEE NATION
P.O. Box 5454, Cleveland, TN 37320
 Hugh Gibbs, Chief
Tribes served: Upper towns, Cherokee and descendants. *In residence*: 150. *Total acreage*: 1.5 Historic-Council grounds area. Historic home range - Upper towns-Ohio River Valley to Tennessee River Valley; contemporary home range - Tennessee and tributaries River Valleys. *Activities*: School/public presentations; 7 Cherokee ceremonials. Museum & Library specializing in Upper towns material. *Publications*: My People The Cherokee by Hu Gibbs.

**RED CLAY INTER-TRIBAL INDIAN BAND
OF SOUTHEASTERN CHEROKEE CONFED-
ERACY**
7703 Georgetown Rd., Ooltewah, TN 37363

TEXAS

ALABAMA-COUSHATTA TRIBES OF TEXAS
Alabama-Coushatta Reservation
Route 3, Box 640, Livingston, TX 77351

TIGUA (TIWA) TRIBE
P.O. Box 17579, Ysleta Station
El Paso, TX 79917

UTAH

**NORTHEASTERN BAND
OF SHOSHONE INDIANS**
660 South 200 West
Brigham City, UT 84302

WHITE MESA UTE COUNCIL
P.O. Box 340, Blanding, UT 84511
 (801) 678-3397

VERMONT

ABENAKI TRIBAL COUNCIL
P.O. Box 276, Swanton, VT 05488
 (802) 868-7146
 Homer St. Francis, Chief
Tribe: St. Francis/Sokoki Band of Abenakis of Vermont.

VIRGINIA

CHICKAHOMINY INDIAN TRIBE
RFD 1, Box 299, Providence Forge, VA 23140
 (804) 829-2186
 A. Leonard Adkins, Chief

EASTERN CHICKAHOMINY INDIAN TRIBE
Route 2, Box 90, Providence Forge, V A 23140
 (804) 745-6508 (work); (804) 966-2719 (home)
 Marvin Bradby, Chief

MATTAPONI TRIBE
Rte. 2, Box 255, West Point, VA 23181
 (804) 769-2194
 Webster Custalow, Chief
Tribe: Mattaponi. Operates a museum
& trading post.

**MONACAN INDIAN TRIBE
Monacan Indian Tribal Council**
P.O. Box 1136, Madison Heights, VA 24572
 (804) 929-6911/7571
 Ronnie Branham, Chief
Tribe: Monacan. *In residence*: 400-1,000. *Total acreage*: 110 acres located on near Bear Mountain, 10 miles northwest of Lynchburg, VA. *Activities*: Annual Pow-wow, Homecoming Festival, Monacan Auction (scholarship fund). Museum in planning stages. *Speakers Bureau*: George Whitewolf, Sue Elliot, Kenneth Branham, Roy & Buddy Johns. Received state recognition in 1989.

NANSEMOND INDIAN TRIBAL ASSOCIATION
P.O. Box 9293, 3429 Galberry Rd. (Chief)
3316 Fietz Dr.(Asst. Chief)
Chesapeake, VA 23321
 (804) 487-5116
 Earl Running Deer Bass, Chief
 William K. Langston (Strong Bear), Asst. Chief
Councilmen: Alvin L. Bond; Kenneth P. Bass, Sr. (Iron Horse); Barry W. Bass (Big Buck); Charles T. Bond; Gary F. Bond (Red Hawk).

PAMUNKEY TRIBAL GOVERNMENT
Rte. 1, Box 987, King William, VA 23086
 (804) 843-2851
 William P. Miles, Chief
Tribe: Pamunkey. Operates a museum. *Council Members*: Raymond Bosh, Walter Hill, Robert Grey, Tom Dennis, William P. Miles, Ivy Bradley. Museum.

UNITED RAPPAHANNOCK TRIBE
Indian Neck, VA 23077
 (804) 769-3128
 Captain Nelson, Chief

UPPER MATTAPONI INDIAN TRIBE
P.O. Box 182, King William, VA 23086
 (804) 769-0041
 Ray Adams, Chief

WASHINGTON

CHINOOK INDIAN TRIBE
P.O. Box 228, Chinook, WA 98614
(206) 777-8303
Donald Mechals, Chairperson
Located in Pacific County. As of March, 1992, this tribe did not yet have a permanent reservation.

COWLITZ INDIAN TRIBE
P.O. Box 2547, Longview, WA 98632
(206) 577-8140
Ronald C. Aalvik, Chairperson
Located in Cowlitz County.

DUWAMISH TRIBAL COUNCIL
212 Wells Ave. S. #C, Renton, WA 98055
(206) 244-0606 Fax 431-8645
Cecile Maxwell Hanson, Chairperson
Tribe served: Duwamish. Membership: 460. Located in King County. *Council members*: Cindy Williams, Secretary/Treasurer; James Rasmussen, Jolene Williams, Manny Oliver, Edie Nelson, Virginia Nelson, and Robert Eley. *Activities*: Annual meeting in June. *Publication*: Washington's "Landless" Tribes: Our Quest for Federal Tribal Recognition.

KIKIALLUS INDIAN NATION
3933 Bagley Ave. N., Seattle, WA 98103
Paul Lavan, Chief
Located in King County

MARIETTA BAND OF NOOKSACK TRIBE
1827 Marine Dr., Bellingham, WA 98226
Robert Davis, Jr., Chairperson

MITCHELL BAY BAND
P.O. Box 4444, Friday Harbor, WA 98250

NOO-WHA-HA BAND
1120 Huff Rd., Burlington, WA 98233

SAMISH TRIBE
P.O. Box 217, Anacortes, WA 98221
(206) 293-6404
Margaret Green, Chairperson
Located in Skagit County.

SNOHOMISH TRIBE
1422 Rosario Rd., Anacortes, WA 98221
(206) 293-7716
Alfred B. Cooper, Chairperson
Jack M. Kidder, Financial Secretary
Located in Skagit County.

SNOQUALMIE TRIBE
P.O. Box 280, Carnation, WA 98014
(206) 333-6551 Fax 333-6553
Andy de los Angeles, Chairperson
Located in Kings County.

SNOQUALMOO TRIBE
P.O. Box 463, Couperville, WA 98239
(206) 221-8301
Lon J. Posenjak, Chairperson
Located in Island County.

STEILACOOM INDIAN TRIBE
P.O. Box 419, Steilacoom, WA 98388
(206) 584-6308
Joan K. Ortez, Chairperson
Located in Pierce County. As of May 1994, this tribe did not yet have a permanent reservation. *Tribal membership*: approximately 650.

WISCONSIN

BROTHERTON INDIANS OF WISCONSIN
AV2848 Witches Lake Rd., Woodruff, WI 54568
(715) 542-3913
June Ezold, Chairperson
Phyllis Mattern, Vice President
Leo Tousey, Treasurer Mary Hoey, Secretary
Tribe: Brotherton. *Council members*: Bernard Sampson, Irene Shady, Cyrus Welch, Platt Welch, Renee Sheppard, and George Wentz. *Activities*: Annual Picnic in July, and Annual Homecoming in October. Archives held at Marian College, Fond du Lac, WI. *Publication*: The Brotherton Indian Nation of Wisconsin: A Brief History, brochure.

WYOMING

NORTHWESTERN BAND OF SHOSHONE NATION
Rock Springs, WY 82901
(307) 382-3943

ALASKAN NATIVES
Aleuts, Eskimos, and Indians (Athapascans)

APACHE
Apache Tribe of Oklahoma
Camp Verde Reservation, Arizona
Fort Apache Reservation (White Mountain), AZ
Fort Sill Apache Tribe of Oklahoma
Fort McDowell Reservation, Arizona
Jicarilla Apache Reservation, New Mexico
Mescalero Apache Reservation, New Mexico
San Carlos Reservation, Arizona
Tonto Apache Tribe of Arizona

ARAPAHOE
Arapahoe Tribe of Oklahoma
Wind River Reservation, Wyoming

ASSINIBOINE-SIOUX
Fort Belknap Reservation, Montana
Fort Peck Reservation, Montana

BANNOCK (SHOSHONE-BANNOCK)
Fort Hall Reservation, Idaho

BLACKFEET
Blackfeet Reservation, Montana

CADDO
Caddo Indian Tribe of Oklahoma

CAHUILLA
Agua Calienta Reservation, Palm Springs
Augustine Reservation, California
Cabazon Reservation, California
Cahuilla Reservation, California
Los Coyotes Reservation, California
Morongo Reservation, California
Ramona Reservation, California
Santa Rosa Reservation, California
Torres Martinez Reservation, California

CAYUGA
Cayuga Nation of New York
Cayuga Tribe of Oklahoma

CHEHALIS
Confederated Tribes of the Chehalis
Reservation, Washington

CHEMEHUEVI
Chemehuevi Reservation, California

CHEROKEE
Cherokee Nation of Oklahoma
Eastern Band of Cherokee, North Carolina
United Keetoowah Band of Cherokee, OK

CHEYENNE
Cheyenne Tribe of Oklahoma
Northern Cheyenne Tribe of Montana

CHICKASAW
Chickasaw Nation of Oklahoma

CHIPPEWA
Bay Mills Reservation (Sault Ste. Marie Band),
Michigan
raverse Band of Chippewa, Michigan
Isabella Reservation (Saginaw Chippewa),
Michigan
L'Anse Reservation, Michigan
Lake Superior Band of Chippewa:
Bad River Reservation, Wisconsin
Lac Courte Oreilles Reservation, Wisconsin
Lac du Flambeau Reservation, Wisconsin
Red Cliff Reservation, Wisconsin

Minnesota Chippewa Tribe (six reservations):
Nett Lake (Boise Forte) Reservation
Fond du Lac Reservation
Grand Portage Reservation
Leech Lake Reservation
Mill Lac Reservation
White Earth Reservation
Red Lake Reservation, Minnesota
Rocky Boy's Reservation, Montana
Sault Ste. Marie Reservation, Michigan
St. Croix Reservation, Wisconsin
Sokoagon Chippewa Community
(Mole Lake Band), Wisconsin
Turtle Mountain Reservation, North Dakota

CHITIMACHA
Chitimacha Tribe of Louisiana

CHOCTAW
Choctaw Nation of Oklahoma
Mississippi Band of Choctaw, Mississippi

CHUMASH (MISSION INDIANS)
Santa Ynez Reservation, California

COCOPAH
Cocopah Tribe of Arizona

COEUR D' ALENE
Coeur D' Alene Reservation, Idaho

COLORADO RIVER
Colorado River Reservation, AZ & CA

COLVILLE
Confederated Tribes of the Colville Reservation,
Washington

COMANCHE
Comanche Indian Tribe of Oklahoma

COUSHATTA
Coushatta Tribe of Louisiana

CREE
Cree Indians of Rocky Boy's Reservation, MT

CREEK NATION OF OKLAHOMA
Alabama-Quassarte Tribal Town
Kialegee Tribal Town of the Creek Nation
Thlopthlocco Tribal Town of the Creek Nation

CROW
Crow Tribe of Montana

DELAWARE
Delaware Tribes of Western Oklahoma

DIEGUENO (MISSION INDIANS)
Barona Reservation, California
Campo Reservation, California
Capitan Grande Reservation, California
Cuyapaipe Reservation, California
Inaga and Cosmit Reservations, California
LaPosta Reservation, California
Manzanita Reservation, California
Mesa Grande Reservation, California
San Pasqual Reservation, California
Santa Ysabel, Reservation, California
Sycuan Reservation, California
Viejas Reservtion, California

GOSHUTE
Confederated Tribes of the Goshute
Reservation, Nevada and Utah
Skull Valley Band of the Goshute Indians of Utah

GROS VENTRE
Fort Belknap Reservation, Montana

HAVASUPAI
Havasupai Tribe of Arizona

HO CHUNK (WINNEBAGO)
Ho Chunk (Winnebago) Tribe of Nebraska
Ho Chink (Winnebago) Tribe of Wisconsin

HOH
Hoh Reservation, Washington

HOOPA
Hoopa Valley Reservation, California

HOPI
Hopi Tribe of Arizona

HUALAPAI
Hualapai Reservation, Arizona

IOWA
Iowa Tribe of Oklahoma
Iowa Reservation, Nebraska and Kansas

KALISPEL
Kalispel Reservation, Washington

KAROK
Karok Tribe of California

KAW
Kaw Indian Tribe of Oklahoma

KICKAPOO
Kickapoo Reservation, Kansas
Kickapoo Tribe of Oklahoma

KIOWA
Kiowa Tribe of Oklahoma

KLALLAM (WASHINGTON)
Jamestown Band of Klallam Indians
Lower Elwha Reservation
Port Gamble Reservation

KOOTENAI
Kootenai Tribe of Idaho

LUISENO (MISSION INDIANS)
La Jolla Reservation, California
Pala Reservation, California
Pauma and Yuima Reservation, California
Pechanga Reservation, California
Rincon Reservation, California
Soboba Reservation, California
Twenty-Nine Palms Reservation, California

LUMMI
Lummi Reservation, Washington

MAIDU
Berry Creek Rancheria, California
Enterprise Rancheria, California
Round Valley Reservation (Covelo Indian
Community), California
Susanville Indian Rancheria, California

MAKAH
Makah Reservation, Washington

MARICOPA
Gila River Reservation, Arizona
Salt River Reservation, Arizona

ME-WUK (MIWOK)
Jackson Rancheria, California
Sheep Ranch Rancheria, California
Shingle Springs Band of Me-Wuk Indians of CA
Trinidad Rancheria
Tuolumne Band of Me-Wuk Indians of California

MENOMINEE
Menominee Reservation, Wisconsin

MIAMI
Miami Tribe of Oklahoma
Table Bluff Rancheria of California

MICCOSUKEE
Miccosukkee Tribe of Florida

MODOC
Modoc Tribe of Oklahoma

MOHAVE
Fort McDowell Reservation, Arizona

MOHAWK
St. Regis Band of Mohawk, New York

MONO
Cold Springs Rancheria, California

MUCKLESHOOT
Muckleshoot Reservation, Washington

NAVAJO
Navajo Reservation, AZ, NM & UT

NEZ PERCE
Nez Perce Reservation, Idaho

NISQUALLY
Nisqually Reservation, Washington

NOOKSACK
Nooksack Indian Tribe of Washington

OMAHA
Omaha Tribe of Nebraska

ONEIDA
Oneida Nation of New York
Oneida Tribe of Wisconsin

ONONDAGA
Onondaga Nation of New York

OSAGE
Osage Tribe of Oklahoma

OTOE-MISSOURIA
Otoe-Missouria of Oklahoma
OTTAWA
Grande Traverse Band, Michigan
Ottawa Tribe of Oklahoma

PAIUTE
Benton (Utu Utu Gwaitu) Paiute Reservation,CA
Big Pine Reservation, California
Bishop Colony, California
Bridgeport Indian Colony, California
Burns Paiute Indian Colony, Oregon
Cedarville Rancheria, California
Duck Valley Reservation, Nevada
Fallon Reservation and Colony, Nevada
Fort Bidwell Reservation, California
Fort Independence Reservation, California

Fort McDermitt Reservation, Nevada
Kaibab Reservation, Arizona
Las Vegas Indian Colony, Nevada
Lone Pine Reservation, California
Lovelock Indian Colony, Nevada
Moapa River Reservation, Nevada
Pyramid Lake Reservation, Nevada
Reno-Sparks Indian Colony, Nevada
Summit Lake Reservation, Nevada
Utah: Cedar City, Indian Peaks, Kanosh,
  Koosharen and Shivwite
Walker River Reservation, Nevada
Winnemucca Indian Colony, Nevada
Yerington Colony and Campbell Ranch, Nevada

PASQUA YAQUI
Pascua Yaqui Tribe of Arizona

PASSAMAQUODDY
Passamaquoddy Tribe of Maine

PAWNEE
Pawnee Indian Tribe of Oklahoma

PENOBSCOT
Penobscot Tribe of Maine

PEORIA
Peoria Tribe of Oklahoma

PIMA
Gila River Reservation, Arizona
Salt River Reservation, Arizona

PIT RIVER
Alturas Indian Rancheria, California
Big Bend Rancheria, California
Lookout Rancheria, California
Montgomery Creek Rancheria, California
Roaring Creek Rancheria, California
Susanville Indian Rancheria, California
X-L Ranch Reservation, California

POMO (CALIFORNIA)
Coyote Valley Band
Dry Creek Rancheria
Hopland Rancheria (Hopland Band)
Laytonville Rancheria (Cahto Indian Tribe)
Manchester--Point Arena Rancheria
  (Manchester Band)
Middletown Rancheria
Robinson Rancheria
Sherwood Valley Rancheria
Stewarts Point Rancheria (Kashia Band)
Sulphur Bank Rancheria (Elem Indian Colony)
Upper Lake Band

PONCA
Ponca Tribe of Nebraska
Ponca Tribe of Oklahoma

POTAWATOMI
Citizen Band Potawatomi Indians of Oklahoma
Forest County Potawatomi Community of WI
Hannahville Indian Community of Michigan
Prairie Band of Potawatomi of Kansas

PUEBLO (NEW MEXICO)
Pueblo of Acoma
Pueblo of Cochiti
Pueblo of Jemez
Pueblo of Ildefonso
Pueblo of Isleta
Pueblo of Laguna

Pueblo of Nambe
Pueblo of Picuris
Pueblo of Pojoaque
Pueblo of San Felipe
Pueblo of San Juan
Pueblo of Sandia
Pueblo of Santa Ana
Pueblo of Santa Clara
Pueblo of Santo Domingo
Pueblo of Taos
Pueblo of Tesuque
Pueblo of Zia
Zuni Reservation (Zuni Tribe)

PUYALLUP
Puyallup Reservation, Washington

QUAPAW
Quapaw Tribe of Oklahoma

QUECHAN
Fort Yuma Reservation (Yuma), California

QUILEUTE
Quileute Reservation, Washington

QUINAULT
Quinault Reservation, Washington

SAC & FOX
Sac & Fox Reservation (Sac & Fox of the
  Missouri), Kansas and Nebraska
Sac & Fox Tribe of the Mississippi, Iowa
Sac & Fox Tribe of Oklahoma

SALISH & KOOTENAI
Flathead Reservation (Confederated Tribes),
  Montana

SAUK-SUIATTLE
Sauk-Suiattle Tribe of Washington

SEMINOLE
Seminole Nation of Oklahoma
Seminole Tribe of Florida

SENECA
Seneca-Cayuga Tribe of Oklahoma
Seneca Nation of New York
Tonawanda Band, New York

SERRANO
San Manual (Band) Reservation, California

SHAWNEE
Absentee Shawnee of Oklahoma
Eastern Shawnee Tribe of Oklahoma

SHOALWATER
Shoalwater Bay Reservation, Washington

SHOSHONE
Battle Mountain Colony (Te-Moak Band), Nevada
Big Pines Band (Owens Valley), California
Duck Valley Reservation, Nevada
Duckwater Reservation, Nevada
Elko Colony (Te-Moak Band), Nevada
Ely Indian Colony, Nevada
Fallon Reservation and Colony, Nevada
Fort McDermitt Reservation, Nevada
Lone Pine Reservation, California
Northwestern Band, Utah
South Fork Colony, Nevada
Wind River Reservation, Wyoming
Yomba Shoshone Tribe of Nevada

SILETZ
Confederated Tribes of the Siletz Reservation, Oregon

SIOUX
Cheyenne River Reservation, South Dakota
Crow Creek Reservation, South Dakota
Devils Lake Reservation, North Dakota
Flandreau Santee Sioux Reservation, SD
Fort Peck Reservation (Assiniboine & Sioux), South Dakota
Lower Brule Sioux Reservation, South Dakota
Lower Sioux Community (Mdewakanton), MN
Pine Ridge Reservation (Oglala), South Dakota
Prairie Island Reservation (Mdewakanton), MN
Rosebud Reservation, South Dakota
Santee Sioux Reservation, Nebraksa
Shakopee Mdewakanton Sioux Community, MN
Sisseton-Wahpeton Sioux Reservation, SD
Standing Rock Reservation, North/South Dakota
Upper Sioux Reservation, Minnesota
Yankton Sioux Tribe of South Dakota

SKAGIT
Upper Skagit Indian Tribe of Washington

SKOKOMISH
Skokomish Reservation, Washington

SMITH RIVER
Big Lagoon Rancheria, California

SPOKANE
Spokane Tribe of Washington

SQUAXIN ISLAND
Squaxin Island Reservation, Washington

STILLAGUAMISH
Stillaguamish Tribe of Washington

STOCKBRIDGE-MUNSEE
Stockbridge-Munsee Community of Mohican Indians, Wisconsin

SWINOMISH
Swinomish Reservation, Washington

SUQUAMISH
Port Madison Reservation, Washington

TACHE
Santa Rosa Rancheria, California

**THREE AFFILIATED TRIBES
(GROSS VENTRE, HIDATSA, MANDAN)**
Three Affiliated Tribes of Fort Berthold, ND

TOHONO O'ODHAM (PAPAGO)
Maricopa (Ak Chin) Reservation, Arizona
Gila Bend Reservation, Arizona
San Xavier Reservation, Arizona
Sells Reservation, Arizona

TOLOWA
Cher-Ae Heights Community, Trinidad Rancheria, California

TONKAWA
Tonkawa Tribe of Oklahoma

TULALIP
Tule River Reservation, California

TUSCARORA
Tuscarora Nation of New York

UMATILLA
Confederated Tribes of the Umatilla Reservation, Oregon

UTE
Southern Ute Reservation, Colorado
Uintah and Ouray Reservation, Utah
Ute Mountain Reservation, Colorado, Utah and New Mexico

WYANDOTTE
Wyandotte Tribe of Oklahoma

WARM SPRINGS
Confederated Tribes of the Warm Springs Reservation (Walla Walla and Cayuga), Oregon

WASHOE
Carson Colony, Nevada
Dresslerville Rancheria, Nevada
Reno-Sparks Indian Colony, Nevada
Susanville Indian Rancheria, California
Washoe Rancheria, Nevada

WICHITA
Wichita Tribe of Oklahoma

WINTUN
Colusa Rancheria (Cachil DeHe Band), CA
Cortina Indian Rancheria, California
Grindstone Indian Rancheria (Wintun-Wailaki), California
Rumsey Indian Rancheria, California

YAKIMA
Yakima Reservation (Confederated Tribes), WA

YAVAPAI
Camp Verde Reservation, Arizona
Yavapai-Prescott Tribe of Arizona

YOKUT (CALIFORNIA)
Santa Rosa Rancheria
Table Mountain Rancheria

YUROK(CALIFORNIA)
Berry Creek Reservation
Hoopa Valley Reservation
Resighini Rancheria
Trinidad Rancheria (Cher-Ae Heights)

This section is an alpha-geographical listing of government agencies--regional and state, mainly--concerned in various ways with the American Indian and his affairs. The principal federal agency in this area is the Bureau of Indian Affairs of the U.S. Department of the Interior. The following is a description of the activities of the Bureau, with a directory of its Central (Washington, DC) Office. The geographical listings follow.

BUREAU OF INDIAN AFFAIRS
1849 C St., NW - MS 4140-MIB
WASHINGTON, DC 20240-0001
Ada Deer, Assistant Secretary (202) 208-7163
Walter Mills, Deputy Commissioner 208-51 16
Joe Kahklen, Alaska Liaison Officer 208-5819
Carl Shaw, Director-Public Affairs 219-4150

Description: Established in 1824, the Bureau of Indian Affairs is an agency of the U.S. Department of the Interior. Its original function was the trusteeship of Indian lands--which now number some fifty-three million acres of land held in trust by the U.S. for various Indian tribes and individuals. Though most trust land is reservation land, all reservation land is not trust land. The Secretary of the Interior functions on behalf of the U.S. as the trustee, with many of the more routine responsibilities delegated to the Bureau of Indian Affairs officials. The Bureau's mission is to enhance the quality of life, to promote economic opportunity, and to carry out the responsibility to protect & improve the trust assets of American Indian tribes & Alaska Natives. This will be accomplished through the delivery of quality services, maintaining government-to-government relationships within the spirit of Indian self-determination.

Budget – The Bureau receives approximately 1.8 billion dollars per year for its programs & projects. The budget includes money for education, Indian services which include law enforcement, social service programs and other local governmental programs; economic development and employment programs; natural resources development; trust responsibilities; facilities management; general administration; construction; for Indian loan guarantees and insurance fund; the BIA receives additional money for reservation road construction through the Dept. of Transportation, under provisions of the Highway Improvement Act of 1982.

In accordance with the policy of Indian Self-Determination, the Bureau encourages tribes to operate their own reservation programs under contract with the Bureau. More than one third of the total BIA budget was transmitted directly to tribal governments for the operation of such contracted programs.

Appropriations for other federal Indian Agencies: Indian Health Service, and Administration for Native Americans, Department of Health and Human Services); Indian Education Office in the Department of Education; and the Navajo-Hopi Relocation Commission. Other federal agencies, such as Agriculture, Commerce and HUD, also receive funding specifically designated for Indian programs.

Education -- There are approximately 250,000 Indian children of school age, two-thirds of whom are enrolled in public schools. Legislation: In recent years, two major laws have resulted in a restructuring of the entire Bureau education program. In 1975, the passage of P.L. 93-638, The Indian Self Determination & Education Assistance Act, greatly facilitated contracting for the operation of education programs by tribal groups. The passage of P.L. 95-561, The Indian Education Act, in 1978, mandated a major change in the operation of both Bureau-operated and tribally contracted schools. The implementation of P.L. 95-561 resulted in decision-making powers for Indian school boards, local hiring of teachers and staff, direct funding to the schools, and increased authority for the Director of Indian Education Programs within the Bureau.

Federal Schools: In 1994, the B.I.A. will fund a total of 184 school facilities, 84 of which are contracted out and operated directly by Indian tribes. These include day schools, on-reservation boarding schools, off-reservation boarding schools, tribally contracted schools, and dormitories. Dormitories are operated by the Bureau to facilitate public school attendance for Indian students.

Indian Children in Federal Schools: About 12% of the Indian children (43,000) attend BIA-funded schools. The remaining 88% (335,000) attend public or private schools.

Public School Assistance (Johnson O'Malley Program): The B.I.A. provides funds under the Johnson-O'Malley Act of 1934 to meet the special needs of Indian students in public schools. These funds, which are largely administered through contracts with tribal organizations, public school districts and state departments of education, enable the contractors to provide supplemental programs for Indian students. Approximately 200,000 Indian students in 26 states receive assistance from JOM funds. The Bureau has JOM contracts for administration and development of programs with about 230 tribal organizations, 76 public schools and six state departments of education. There are more than 800 Indian parent committees working with these contractors.

Indians in College: In 1993-94, there were approximately 33,000 Indian students on BIA, IHS, and ED scholarships and fellowships. In 1993, more than 2,000 Indian students at the graduate and undergraduate levels earned degrees. About 500 students receiving BIA assistance are in law school and other graduate programs. Total appropriations provided through the BIA for Indian higher education were about $30 million in 1993.

Tribally Controlled Colleges: The BIA provides grants for the operation of 23 tribally controlled community colleges. There are approximately 15,000 Indian students (half of them part time) enrolled in these community colleges. Tribal colleges must pass a stringent feasibility study in order to be eligible for grants under the Tribally Controlled Community College Assistance Act of 1978.

B.I.A. Post-Secondary Schools: The B.I.A. operates three post-secondary schools. They are Haskell Indian Junior College in Lawrence, Kansas with an enrollment of about 750 students; Institute of American Indian Arts at Santa Fe, New Mexico with about 200 students; and Southwestern Indian Polytechnic Institute at Albuquerque, New Mexico with about 500 students.

Handicapped Children's Program: Under the Handicapped Children's Act, P.L. 94-142, the Bureau provides financial support for the educational costs of handicapped Indian children. An average of 200 children are served annually in about 25 different facilities.

Substance/Alcohol Abuse Education Programs: The objective of B.I.A. educational programs in substance and alcohol abuse is to provide Bureau-funded schools with curriculum materials and technical assistance in developing and implementing alcohol and substance abuse programs in areas of identification, assessment, prevention, and crisis intervention through the use of referrals and additional counselors at the schools.

Health – Indian Health Service: An agency of the Department of Health & Human Services and the primary federal health resource for approximately one million eligible American Indians and Alaskan Natives.

Housing – In cooperation with the Department of Housing and Urban Development (HUD) tribes are treated as local government units with authority to establish local housing authorities, the instruments through which Indians may obtain low-income housing from the Federal Government. More than 200 tribes have established such housing authorities.

Water Rights – The Office of Indian Water Rights, established in 1972, is designed to protect the water rights of reservation Indians. Since its formation, water allocation studies have been made on many reservations, and legal suits have been filed to protect Indian water.

Forestry -- Established in 1910 to bring about order in the management of Indian owned forest property. Some objectives of management are to preserve the property in perpetuity by providing effective protection services, by applying sound economic principles to the harvesting of forest crops, and by making adequate provisions for the continuity in growth of forest crops.

Employment with the B.I.A. -- The Bureau employs approximately 13,000 people. Native Americans make up more than 75% of that work force. Only about 425 work in the Washington central office. (Preference in employment with the B.I.A. has been granted for some years to Indians who are members of Federally recognized tribes or are one-half or more degree Indian blood.) Native Americans hold most of the top management positions in the Bureau's Central and Area offices and constitutes most of the positions in the Bureau's federally operated schools of which many are teachers, teacher's aides, administrators and workmen.

*   *   *

The following is a directory of the Central (Washington, DC) Office (zip code 20245) of the Bureau of Indian Affairs and its various offices & divisions. Listings of B.I.A. area & field offices & agencies may be found under specific states in the geographical part of this section which follows Independent Agencies.

Office of the Assistant Secretary for Indian Affairs: Ada Deer, Assistant Secretary (202) 208-7163; Gordon T. Delorimiere, Administrative Assistant Secretary (208-5649); Lydia Beckford & Les Ramirez, Special Assistants (208-7163).

Deputy Commissioner of Indian Affairs: Hilda Manual (208-51 16)

Alaska Liaison Officer: Joe Kahklen (208-5819); Sandra Todd, Secretary

Office of Indian Education Programs: Provides quality education opportunities from early childhood through life for enrolled members of federally recognized Indian tribes and Alaska Natives. *Personnel*: Dr. John W. Tippeconnic, Director (MS 3530-MIB; 208-6123); William Mehojah, Deputy Director (208-6175); C.L. Henson, Chief-Division of Administration (208-4234); Joy Martin, Chief - Branch of Administrative Services (208-4555); Jim Womack, Chief, Branch of Management Information Services (208-71 11); Dr. Dennis Fox, Chief-Division of Education Programs (208-7388); Charles Geboe, Chief - Branch of Elementary & Secondary Education (208-1 129); Reginald Rodriquez, Chief-Branch of Post Secondary Education (208-4871); Lena Mills, Acting Chief-Branch of Exceptional Education (208-6675); Sharon Lynn, Chief - Branch of Supplemental Support Services (208) 6364); Dr. James Martin, Director - Planning, Oversight and Evaluation (208-3550); Sandra Fox, Chief-Branch of Monitoring & Evaluation (219-3817); Keener Cobb, Chief-Branch of Planning (219-1 131); John Reimer, Chief, Branch of Research & Policy Analysis (208) 3562). Albuquerque Field Office - Dr. Kenneth Ross, Rodney Young, Dr. Benjamin Atencio and Cecilia Baca (505) 766-3850

Office of Tribal Services: Works directly with tribal governments and in partnership with them, provides for housing, social services, tribal enrollment, judicial systems, and police protection. *Personnel*: Deborah Maddox, Acting Director (MS 4603-MIB; 208-3463); Harry Rainbolt, Jr., Budget & Program Officer; Judy Baggett, Child Protection Coordinator (208-6858); Jerry Cordova, Acting Chief-Division of Tribal Government Services (208-7446); Lathal Duffield, Chief - Branch of Tribal Enrollment (208-3702); Holly Reckford, Chief - Branch of Acknowledgement and Research (208-3592); Lathal Duffield, Acting Chief - Branch of Tribal Relations (208-7445); Bettie Rushing, Chief - Branch of Judicial Services (208-4400); V acant, Chief - Division of Housing Services (208-3671); David Hickman, Chief-Division of Social Services (208-2721); James Thomas, Chief-Division of Self-Determination Services (208-5727

Office of Management & Administration: Responsible for the recommendation and formulation of policy to the Deputy Commissioner. Functions include personnel management, contracts and grants administration, property management, data systems, and the Equal Employment Opportunity office. *Personnel*: Carol Bacon, Director (MS 4657-MIB; 208-4174); Cora Jones, Deputy Director (208-4174); Anthony Howard, Chief - Division of Contracts & Grants (208-2825); Peter S. Markey, Chief - Contracting & Grants Operations (208-2809); Robyn York, Chief - Branch of Planning & Support (208-2825); Kimberly Romine, Chief - Branch of Stabndards, Compliance & Info Systems (208-2825); Quanah Crossland-Stamps, Chief - Branch of Acquisition Review (208-2825); Martin Johnson, Chief - Branch of Employee Relations; Bob Andres, Labor Relations Specialist (208-2540); Mercedes Lewis, Chief - Branch of Staffing & Manpower (208-2506); Frank Carroll, Chief - Branch of Position Management & Classification (208-2613); Domenick Parrella, Chief - Branch of Employee Development (T raining) (208-2691); Allan Young, Chief - Division of Personnel Services (208-7581); Kay Hayes, Supervisor - Personnel Staffing Specialist (208-2706); Bernice Orndoff, Supervisor - Employee/Labor Relations Specialist (208-2531); John C. Nicholas, Director of Equal Opportunity Programs (703-235-5866)

Office of Trust Responsibilities : Provides administrative direction, policy development, planning and management of renewable natural resources of Indian owned land on Federal reservations including wildlife and parks, water resources, agriculture, range, irrigation, and forestry . *Personnel*: Patrick Hayes, Director (MS 4513-MIB 208-5831); Frank Keel, Deputy Director (208-3600); Glenda Brokeshoulder, Supervisor - Program Analysis Officer & Staff Coordinator(208-7216); George R. Farris, Chief - Branch of Environmental Services (208-4791); Samuel M. Miller , Chief - Division of W ater & Land Resources (208-4004); Larry R. Morrin, Chief - Division of Real Estate Services (208-7737); James Howe, Chief - Division of Forestry (208-6067); Richard B. Geiger, Chief - Division of Transportation (208-4359); Neil N. Rouseau, Chief - Branch of Program Operations (Albuquerque, NM - (505) 766-2672); William J. Bonner , Chief - Branch of Geographic Information Systems (303) 231-5100; Don Aubertin, Chief - Division of Energy & Minerals (303) 231-5070

Office of Economic Development : Enhances reservation economies and services to Indians & Alaska Native people by developing and recommending policies, standards and procedures to assist Bureau management and Indian tribes and individuals in the development and implementation of economic development projects. *Personnel*: Nancy L. Jemison, Director (MS 4060-MIB; 208-5326); Ruby DeCorah, Program Analyst (208-5324);Lynn Forcia, Vocational Development Specialist (208-2570); John Jollie, Minority Business Enterrprise Coordinator; Dean Poleahla, Program Specialist; Jerry Folsom, Financial Assistance (208-5324)

Office of Financial Management : Linda Richardson, Assistant Director (208-6342); Mitchell Chouteau, Chief - Division of Accounting Management; Fred Dorsey, Central Office Accounting Liaison (208-4807); Gary Ceccucci, Chief - Division of Program Development & Implementation (208-6181); Mike Reed, Chief - Branch of Planning & Budget Formulation (208-3640); Stella Delaware, Chief - Branch of Formulation & Presentation (208-3580); Joyce Matherly , Chief - Branch of Budget Execution (208-6582); Michael L. Hackett, Chief - Branch of Property & Supply Operations (208-2591); Charles Jaynes, Chief - Division of Safety Management, Albuquerque Branch (505) 766-2863

Office of Public Affairs : Carl Shaw, Director (219-4150); Evelyn Pickett, General Inquiries (208-3711)

Office of American Indian Trust : Tom Bond, Director (208-3338); Marshall Cutsforth, Sr . Trust Resources Officer; Thomas Bond, Program Analyst; Debra Purvis, Environmental Specialist (208-4791); James Berch, Realty Specialist; Eric Wilson, Program Analyst

Office of Audit & Evaluation : Ronal Eden, Director (208-1916); Daphne Berwald, Administrative Officer (208-1916)

Office of Self-Governance : William G. Lavell, Director (219-0240)

Office of Congressional & Legislative Affairs : Franklin Keel, Acting Director (208-5706); Marge Wilkins, Legislative Coordinator; Tammy Harris & Rae Wynn, Legislative Specialists.

Office of Indian Gaming Management Staff : Nancy Pierskella, Director (219-4068)

Division of Law Enforcement : Ted Quasula, Director (208-5786); Harry DeLashmutt, Law Enforcement & Security Coord.; Debra Feathers, Administrative Officer; Mark Mullins, Augustine Abeita & David Nicholas, Criminal Investigators

Office of Alcohol & Substance Abuse Prevention: Velma Mason, Director (208-6179); Beverly Harmer, Program Specialist; Ella Lankford, Indian Youth Program Specialist

Office of Data Systems : James Getter, Acting Director (208-2813) Catherine A. Barrows, Chief - Technical Coordination Staf f; June Henkel, Chief - Division of ADP Central Management (208-2988); Gordon Babby , Chief - Requirements Evaluation & Special Projects Branch (208-2796); Jim Roubidoux, Chief-National Technical Support Center, Albuquerque, NM (505) 766-3627

Indian Arts & Crafts Board: Geoffrey Stamm, Acting General Manager (Rm. 4004) (202) 208-3773

Office of Trust Fund Management : Responsible for implementing, operating and controlling accounting systems which properly record and report on all funds collected, disbursed, invested and held in trust for Indian tribes and individuals. It makes recommendations on investments of trust funds to realize the benefits associated with cash concentration and economies of scale. *Personnel*: Jim Parris, Director, 505 Marquette St., NW , Albuquerque, NM 87102 (505) 766-3230

Office of Facilities Management (Albuquerque, NM): Ralph Esquerra, Director (505) 766-2825

* * *

The following are federal of fices that direct special programs for Indians and related other federal and congressional of fices.

EXECUTIVE BRANCH

The White House
1600 Pennsylvania Ave., NW
Washington, DC 20500
Personnel: Loretta Avent, Special Assistant to the President for Intergovernment Affairs, Old Executive Office Bldg., Room 122, 17th and Pennsylvania Ave., NW, Washington, DC 20503 (202) 456-2896. Staff specialists: New Executive Office Bldg., Washington, DC 20503 - Indian Affairs (202) 395-4993; Indian Education (202) 395-5880; Indian Health Service (202) 395-4926

U.S. Department of Agriculture
14th and Independence Ave., SW
Washington, DC 20250
Personnel: Mike Espy, Secretary; Elwood H. "Woody" Patawa, Director of Native American Programs - Office of Intergovernmental Affairs, Room 102-A, Administration Bldg. (202) 720-3805; Ronald P. Andrade, Equal Opportunity Specialist, Indian Affairs, Room 2305, Auditor's Bldg. (202) 720-7370; Douglas V. Sellars, Liaison for Indian Assistance, Rural Development Staf f, Soil Conservation Service, Room 6103, South Bldg., P.O. Box 2890, Washington, DC 20013 (202) 720-7690.

U.S. Department of Commerce
U.S. Small Business Administration
Office of Native American Affairs
409 3rd St., SW
Washington, DC 20416
(202) 205-6421
Personnel: Pete Homer, Jr., Director

Bureau of the Census
Federal Center, Suitland, MD 20233
Personnel: Edna Paisano, Liaison for American Indians and Alaska Natives (301) 763-2607 Fax 763-3862

U.S. Department of Education
Office of Indian Education
Rm. 2177, Federal Office Bldg. 6
400 Maryland Ave., SW
Washington, DC 20202
(202) 401-1887
Dr. Aaron Shedd, Director
Programs: Educational Personnel Development Program; Educational Services Program; Formula Grant Program; Indian-Controlled Schools Enrichment Program; Indian Fellowship Program (202) 401-1916; Indian Gifted and Talented Pilot Program (202) 401-1916; and Planning, Pilot, and Demonstration Program. Office of the Assistant Secretary for Elementary and Secondary Education (202) 401-1342 - Native Hawaiian Model Curriculum Development, and School Improvement Program-Native Hawaiian Gifted and Talented; and Native Hawaiian Family-Based Education Centers. Office of the Assistant Secretary for Vocational and Adult Education, Division of National Programs, Vocational Education - Indian and Hawaiian Natives. Office of Special Education and Rehabilitative Services, Native Hawaiians Special Education, 330 C St., SW, Rm. 4072, Switzer Bldg., Washington, DC 20202 (202) 732-1353, Fax (202) 732-3897

Funds six regional Indian Education Technical Assistance Centers (IETACs) which serves educators of Native students within specific geographical regions (see Indian Education Section). Also funds ten Regional Educational Laboratories which have joined together to form the Native American Education Initiative whose purpose is to improve the access of educators serving Native students to the many resources available through the various laboratories (see Indian Education Section).

U.S. Department of Energy
Denver Support Office
2801 Youngfield, Suite 380
Golden, CO 80401
(303) 231-5750
Program: Indian Energy Resource Development.

U.S. Department of Health & Human Services
Humphrey Bldg., 200 Independence Ave., SW
Washington, DC 20201
Personnel: Donna Shalala, Secretary, Room 615 F (202) 690-7000 Fax 245-3380; Gary Niles Kimble, Commissioner - Administration for Native Americans (202) 690-7776 (Established to provide economic and social self-sufficiency among American Indians, Native Hawaiians, and Alaskan Natives. Provides grants to achieve goals); Sharon McCully, Executive Director - Intra-Departmental Council on Indian Affairs (202) 690-6546; Fred Luhmann, Associate Commissioner - American Indian, Alaskan Native & Native Hawaiian Programs, 330 Independence Ave., SW, Washington, DC 20201 (202) 619-2957 or 619-0641; Dr. Michael H. Trujillo, M.D., Director - Indian Health Service, Room 5A-55, Parklawn Bldg., 5600 Fishers Lane, Rockville, MD 20857 (301) 443-1083; Head Start Bureau, American Indian Program, Administration for Children and Families, P.O. Box 1182, Washington, DC 20013 (202) 254-0437.

Department of Housing & Urban Development (HUD)
451 7th St., SW
Washington, DC 20410
(202) 708-0417 Fax 755-0299
Personnel: Henry G. Cisneros, Secretary; Vacant, Special Assistant to the Secretary for Indian and Alaska Native Programs, Room 10222 (202) 708-0420; Assistant Secretary for Public and Indian Housing, Room 4100 (202) 708-0950; Office of Indian Housing, Room 4232 (202) 708-1015.

Department of the Interior
1849 C St., NW
Washington, DC 20240
(202) 208-7351 Fax 208-6956
Personnel: Bruce Babbitt, Secretary; Ada Deer, Assistant Secretary for Indian Affairs, Room 4160 (202) 208-7163; Geoffrey Stamm, Acting General Manager - Indian Arts & Crafts Board, Room 4004 (202) 208-3773.

Department of Justice
10th & Constitution Ave., NW
Washington, DC 20530
(202) 514-2001
Personnel: Janet Reno, Attorney General; James Brookshire, Chief - Indian Claims Section, Land and Natural Resources Division, Room 648, 550 11th St., N.W., Washington, D.C. 20530 (202) 724-7375; Hank Meshorer, Chief - Indian Resources Section, Land and Natural Resources Division, Room 624 (202) 724-7156.

Department of Labor
200 Constitution Ave., NW
Washington, DC 20210
(202) 219-8271
Personnel: Robert Reich, Secretary; Division of Indian and Native American Programs, Employment & Training Administration (202) 219-6827

Department of Transportation
400 7th St., SW
Washington, DC 20590
(202) 366-1111
Regional Office (Fort Worth, Texas), Director - American Indian Nations, National Highway Traffic Safety Administration, (817) 334-4300.

LEGISLATIVE BRANCH-CONGRESS

SENATE

Senate Select Committee on Indian Affairs
838 Hart Senate Office Bldg.
Washington, DC 20510
(202) 224-2251 Fax 224-2309
John McCain (R-AZ), Chairperson
Daniel Inouye (D-HI), Vice-Chairperson
Has full jurisdiction over all proposed legislation and other matters relating to Indian affairs, including Indian education at all levels. Committee members: Dennis DeConcini (D-AZ), Thomas Daschle (D-SD), Kent Conrad (D-ND), Harry Reid (D-NV), Paul Simon (D-IL), Daniel Akaka (D-HI), Paul Wellstone (D-MN), Byron L. Dorgan (D-ND), Ben Nighthorse Campbell (D-CO), Frank Murkowski (R-AK), Thad Cochran (R-MS), Slade Gorton (R-WA), Pete Domenici (R-NM), Nancy Kassebaum (R-KS), Don Nichels (R-OK), Mark O. Hatfield (R-OR). Pete Taylor, General Counsel and Alan Parker, Staff Director.

HOUSE OF REPRESENTATIVES

House Committee on Interior & Insular Affairs
Subcommittee on Native American Affairs
1522 Longworth House Office Bldg.
New Jersey & Independence Ave., SE
Washington, DC 20515
(202) 226-7736 Fax 226-0522
Rep. Bill Richardson, Chairperson
Tadd Johnson, Majority Staff Director
Has legislative and oversight jurisdiction over measures related to the care and management of Indians and the federal government's management of Indian programs.

BUREAU OF INDIAN AFFAIRS AREA OFFICES

ABERDEEN AREA OFFICE
Bureau of Indian Affairs
Federal Bldg., 115 4th Ave., SE
ABERDEEN, SD 57401
  (605) 226-7343 Fax 226-7446
  Dr. Jerry L. Jaeger, Area Director
Administers BIA programs for regions of North and South Dakota, and Nebraska. *Responsible for the following agencies and schools*: Cheyenne River Agency, Crow Creek Agency, Flandreau Indian School, Fort Berthold Agency, Fort Totten Agency, Lower Brule Agency, Pine Ridge Agency, Rosebud Agency, Sisseton Agency, Standing Rock Agency, Turtle Mountain Agency, Wahpeton Indian School, Winnebago Agency, and Yankton Agency.

ALBUQUERQUE AREA OFFICE
Bureau of Indian Affairs
P.O. Box 26567
ALBUQUERQUE, NM 87125
  (505) 766-3170 Fax 766-1964
  Joseph D. Little, Area Director
Administers BIA programs for regions of Colorado and New Mexico. *Responsible for the following agencies*: Jicarilla, Laguna, Mescalero, Northern Pueblos, Ramah-Navajo, Southern Pueblo, Southern Ute, Ute Mountain Ute, and Zuni. *Programs*: Full range of BIA land and human resource programs. *Total population served*: 55,000.

ANADARKO AREA OFFICE
Bureau of Indian Affairs
P.O. Box 368
ANADARKO 73005
  (405) 247-6673 Fax 247-2242
  L.W. (Bill) Collier, Jr., Area Director
Administers BIA programs for regions of OK, KS, MO & TX. *Tribes served*: 24 Oklahoma tribes - Apache, Caddo, Comanche, Delaware, Ft. Sill Apache, Kiowa, Wichita and Affiliated, Cheyenne-Arapaho, Kaw, Otoe-Missouria, Pawnee, Ponca, Tonkawa, Absentee-Shawnee, Citizen Band Potawatomi, Iowa, Kickapoo, Sac & Fox; Kansas tribes - Iowa, Kickapoo, Prairie Band Potawatomi, Sac & Fox of Missouri; Texas tribes - Alabama-Coushatta, and Kickapoo Traditional. *Population served*: 36,310. *Programs*: Provides services to support tribal governments and protect Indian land.

BILLINGS AREA OFFICE
Bureau of Indian Affairs
316 North 26th St.
BILLINGS, MT 59101
  (406) 657-6315 Fax 657-6559
  Richard Whitesell, Area Director
Administers BIA programs for the region of Montana and Wyoming. *Responsible for the following agencies*: Blackfeet, Crow, Fort Belknap, Fort Peck, Northern Cheyenne, Rocky Boy's, and Wind River. *Tribes served*: Blackfeet, Crow, Gros-Ventre and Assiniboine, Sioux and Assiniboine, Northern Cheyenne, Chippewa Cree, and Shoshone and Arapahoe. *Total population served*: 48,000.

EASTERN AREA OFFICE
Bureau of Indian Affairs
3701 N. Fairfax Dr., MS #260
ARLINGTON, VA 22203
  (703) 235-3006 Fax 235-8610
  Bill D. Ott, Area Director
Administers BIA programs through the following agencies: Cherokee, Choctaw, Miccosukee, Seminole, and New York Liaison Office.

JUNEAU AREA OFFICE
Bureau of Indian Affairs
9109 Mendenhall, Suite 5
P.O. Box 25520
JUNEAU, AK 99802
  (907) 586-7177 Fax 586-7169
  Niles Cesar, Area Director
Administers all BIA services within the State of Alaska. *Responsible for the following agencies*: Anchorage, Bethel, Fairbanks, Nome, Southeast, and the Seattle Support Center. *Tribes served*: Eskimo, Aleut, and Alaska Indians. *Total population served*: 70,000.

MINNEAPOLIS AREA OFFICE
Bureau of Indian Affairs
331 Second Ave. S.
MINNEAPOLIS, MN 55401
  (612) 373-1000 Fax 373-1186
  Denise Homer, Acting Area Director
Administers BIA programs in the State of Iowa, Michigan, Minnesota, and Wisconsin. *Responsible for the following agencies and field offices*: Great Lakes, Michigan, Minnesota, Tribal Operations-Menominee Area Representative Office, Tribal Operations-Minnesota Sioux Field Representative Office, Red Lake, and Sac and Fox Area Field Office. *Total population served*: 22,000.

MUSKOGEE AREA OFFICE
Bureau of Indian Affairs
101 N. 5th St.
MUSKOGEE, OK 74401
  (918) 687-2296 Fax 687-2571
  Merritt Youngdeer, Area Director
Administers BIA programs for regions of Oklahoma. *Responsible for the following agencies*: Ardmore, Okmulgee, Osage, Miami, Tahlequah, Talihina, and Wewoka. *Tribes served*: Cherokee, Chickasaw, Choctaw, Creek, Seminole, Osage, Seneca-Cayuga, Keetowah, Eastern Shawnee, Quapaw, Wyandotte, Miami, Peoria, Ottawa, Cherokee-Shawnee, and Modoc. *Total population served*: 75,000.

NAVAJO AREA OFFICE
Bureau of Indian Affairs
P.O. Box 1060
GALLUP, NM 87301
  (505) 863-8314 Fax 863-8245
  Wilson Barber, Jr., Area Director
Tribe served: Navajo (in Arizona, New Mexico and Utah.) *Total population served*: 200,000. *Programs*: Natural Resources; Forestry; Roads Construction & Maintenance; Irrigation Project. Museum. *Responsible for the following agencies*: Navajo Area Office (Administration), Chinle, Eastern Navajo, Fort Defiance, Navajo Irrigation Project, Shiprock, and Western Navajo.

PHOENIX AREA OFFICE
Bureau of Indian Affairs
P.O. Box 10
PHOENIX, AZ 85001
  (602) 379-6600 Fax 379-4413
  Walter Mills, Area Director
Administers BIA programs for regions of Arizona, California, Nevada and Utah. *Responsible for the following agencies*: Colorado River, Eastern Nevada, Fort Apache, Fort Yuma, Hopi, Papago, Pima, Salt River, San Carlos, San Carlos Irrigation Project, Southern Paiute Field Station, Truxton Canon, Uintah and Ouray, and Western Nevada.

PORTLAND AREA OFFICE
Bureau of Indian Affairs
911 NE 11th Ave.
PORTLAND, OR 97232
  (503) 231-6702 Fax 231-2201
  Stanley M. Speaks, Area Director
Administers BIA programs for regions of Oregon, Washington, and Idaho. *Responsible for the following agencies, projects and stations*: Chiloquin Sub-Agency, Colville Agency, Fort Hall Agency, Flathead Agency, Division of Flathead Irrigation, Metlakatla Field Station, Northern Idaho Agency, Spokane Agency, Umatilla Agency, Wapato Irrigation Project, Olympic Peninsula Agency, Siletz Agency, Warm Springs Agency, Puget Sound Agency, and Yakima Agency.

SACRAMENTO AREA OFFICE
Bureau of Indian Affairs
2800 Cottage Way
SACRAMENTO, CA 95825
  (916) 978-4691 Fax 978-4695
  Ronald M. Jaeger, Area Director
Administers BIA programs through the following agencies: Central California Agency, Northern California Agency, Southern California Agency, and Palm Springs Field Agency. *Total population served*: 45,000.

BIA AGENCY OFFICES

ALASKA

ANCHORAGE AGENCY
Bureau of Indian Affairs
1675 C St.
ANCHORAGE 99501
  (907) 271-4088 Fax 271-4083
  Albert Kahklen, Supt.
Responsible for six Indian regional cooperative schools, and the maintenance of plant facilities for an additional 21 schools; active in numerous other projects and functions related to regional problems. *Tribes served*: Eskimo, Athapascan, Aleut. *Total population served*: 20,000. Under jurisdiction of Juneau Area Office.

BETHEL AGENCY
Bureau of Indian Affairs
P.O. Box 347
BETHEL 99559
  (907) 543-2727 Fax 543-3574
  David Hendrickson, Supt.
Area served: Southwestern Alaska--Calista Region. *Tribe served*: Yup'ik Eskimo. *Total population served*: 20,000. *Programs*: All BIA programs--grants, natural resources, realty, social services, housing, etc. Under jurisdiction of Juneau Area Office.

FAIRBANKS AGENCY
Bureau of Indian Affairs
Federal Bldg. & Courthouse
101 12th Ave., Box 16
FAIRBANKS 99701
  (800) 822-3596; (907) 456-0222 Fax 456-0225
  Samuel S. Demientieff, Supt.
Reservations served: Arctic Village, Venetie and Tetlin. *Tribes served*: Eskimo, Athapascan. *Total population served*: 12,000. *Programs*: HIP Housing; Natural Resources; Realty; 638 Contracts & Grants; Adult Vocational Training/Direct Employment; Social Services and Tribal Operations. Under jurisdiction of Juneau Area Office.

METLAKATLA FIELD STATION
Bureau of Indian Affairs
P.O. Box 450
METLAKATLA 99926
 (907) 886-3791 Fax 886-7738
 Henry C. Alameda, Sr., Supt.
Under jurisdiction of Portland Area Office.

NOME AGENCY
Bureau of Indian Affairs
P.O. Box 1108
NOME 99762
 (907) 443-2284 Fax 443-2317
 Dennis Tiepelman, Supt.
Under jurisdiction of Juneau Area Office.

ARIZONA

CHINLE AGENCY
Bureau of Indian Affairs
P.O. Box 7H
CHINLE 86503
 (602) 674-5201 ext. 101 Fax ext. 105
 Rosie Wilkerson, Acting Supt.
Tribe served: Navajo. Under jurisdiction of Navajo
Area Office.

SAN CARLOS IRRIGATION PROJECT
Bureau of Indian Affairs
P.O. Box 209
COOLIDGE 85228
 (602) 723-5439
 Henry Dodge, Supt.
Under jurisdiction of Phoenix Area Office.

FORT DEFIANCE AGENCY
Bureau of Indian Affairs
P.O. Box 619
FORT DEFIANCE 86504
 (602) 729-7221 Fax 729-7225
 Roy Dan, Acting Supt.
Tribe served: Navajo. Under jurisdiction
of Navajo Area Office.

HOPI AGENCY
Bureau of Indian Affairs
P.O. Box 158
KEAMS CANYON 86034
 (602) 738-2228 Fax 738-5522
 Robert Carolin, Supt.
Tribes served: Hopi & Paiute. *Total population
served*: 7,500. Under jurisdiction of Phoenix Area
Office.

COLORADO RIVER AGENCY
Bureau of Indian Affairs
Route 1, Box 9-C
PARKER 85344
 (602) 669-7111 Fax 669-7187
 Allen Anspach, Supt.
Tribes served: Chemehuevi, Colorado River (in
Arizona and California), Mohave (in Arizona, Cali-
fornia and Nevada.) *Total population served*:
6,500. Under jurisdiction of Phoenix Area Office.

PIMA AGENCY
Bureau of Indian Affairs
P.O. Box 8
SACATON 85247
 (602) 562-3326 Fax 562-3543
 Paul Smith, Supt.
Tribes served: Papago, Pima, and Maricopa. *To-
tal population served*: 10,000. Under jurisdiction of
Phoenix Area Office.

SAN CARLOS AGENCY
Bureau of Indian Affairs
P.O. Box 209
SAN CARLOS 85550
 (602) 475-2321 Fax 475-2783
 Nina Innis, Supt.
Tribe served: San Carlos Apache. *Population
served*: 10,500. *Programs*: Administrative/Tribal
Operations; Employment Assistance; Law En-
forcement & Social Services; Indian Self-Deter-
mination Services; Natural Resources; Facilities
& Fire Management; Soil & Moisture; Real Estate
Services; Credit & Finance; Roads. Under juris-
diction of Phoenix Area Office.

SALT RIVER AGENCY
Bureau of Indian Affairs
10000 E. McDowell Rd.
SCOTTSDALE 85256
 (602) 640-2842 Fax 640-2809
 Veronica Murdock, Supt.
Tribes served: Pima, Maricopa, Mohave, and
Apache. *Population served*: 3,500. Under jurisdic-
tion of Phoenix Area Office.

PAPAGO AGENCY
Bureau of Indian Affairs
P.O. Box 578
SELLS 85634
 (602) 383-3286 Fax 383-2087
 Nina Sisqueros, Supt.
Tribe served: Tohono O'odham. *Population served*:
17,500. Under jurisdiction of Phoenix Area Office.

WESTERN NAVAJO AGENCY
Bureau of Indian Affairs
P.O. Box 127
TUBA CITY 86045
 (602) 283-4531 Fax 283-4259
 Wilfred Brown, Supt.
Tribe served: Navajo. Under jurisdiction
of Navajo Area Office.

TRUXTON CANON AGENCY
Bureau of Indian Affairs
P.O. Box 37
VALENTINE 86437
 (602) 769-2286 Fax 769-2444
 Danny Breuninger, Supt.
Tribes served: Hualapai, Havasupai, Yavapai-
Apache, Yavapai-Prescott, and Payson Tonto-
Apache. *Total population served*: 3,000. Under ju-
risdiction of Phoenix Area Office.

FORT APACHE AGENCY
Bureau of Indian Affairs
P.O. Box 560
WHITERIVER 85941
 (602) 338-5353 Fax 338-5383
 Benjamin H. Nuvamsa, Supt.
Tribe served: Apache. *Total population served*:
7,000. Under jurisdiction of Phoenix Area Office.

FORT YUMA AGENCY
Bureau of Indian Affairs
P.O. Box 1591
YUMA 85364
 (619) 572-0248 Fax 572-0895
 Felix J. Montague, Supt.
Tribes served: Cocopah, and Quechan (in Cali-
fornia and Arizona.) *Total population served*: 1,800.
Under jurisdiction of Phoenix Area Office.

CALIFORNIA

PALM SPRINGS FIELD AGENCY
Bureau of Indian Affairs
P.O. Box 2245
PALM SPRINGS 92262
 (619) 322-3086 Fax 322-322-2031
 Terry Beckwith, Supt.
Under jurisdiction of Sacramento Area Office.

NORTHERN CALIFORNIA AGENCY
Bureau of Indian Affairs
P.O. Box 494879
REDDING 96049
 (916) 246-5141 Fax 246-5167
 Dr. Virgil Akins, Supt.
Under jurisdiction of Sacramento Area Office.

SOUTHERN CALIFORNIA AGENCY
Bureau of Indian Affairs
3600 Lime St., Suite 722
RIVERSIDE 92501
 (714) 276-6624 Fax 276-6641
 Virgil Townsend, Supt.
Serves the Mission area in southern California.
Under jurisdiction of Sacramento Area Office.

CENTRAL CALIFORNIA AGENCY
Bureau of Indian Affairs
1824 Tribute Rd., Suite J
SACRAMENTO 95815
 (916) 978-4337 Fax 978-5589
 Harold Bradford ,Supt.
Under jurisdiction of Sacramento Area Office.

COLORADO

SOUTHERN UTE AGENCY
Bureau of Indian Affairs
P.O. Box 315
IGNACIO 81137
 (303) 563-4511 Fax 563-9321
 Ralph R. Pensoneau, Supt.
Tribe served: Ute. *Total population served*: 1,000.
Under jurisdiction of Albuquerque Area Office.

UTE MOUNTAIN UTE AGENCY
Bureau of Indian Affairs
General Delivery
TOWAOC 81334
 (303) 565-8471 Fax 565-8906
 Arthur L. Blazer, Supt.
Tribe served: Ute. *Total population served*: 1,750.
Under jurisdiction of Albuquerque Area Office.

DISTRICT OF COLUMBIA

BUREAU OF INDIAN AFFAIRS
1951 Constitution Ave., N.W.
WASHINGTON 20245
See Central Office listing at the beginning
of this section.

INDIAN ARTS & CRAFTS BOARD
U.S. Dept. of the Interior
Room 4004, Main Interior Bldg.
WASHINGTON 20240-0001
 (202) 208-3773
 Geoffrey Stamm, Acting General Manager
Purpose: To promote the development of Indian

and Alaskan Native arts and handicrafts. *Activities*: Provides business and personal professional advice, information, and promotion to artists & craftsmen & their organizations; operates the Museum of the Plains Indian, Browning, MT; Sioux Indian Museum, Rapid City, SD; and Southern Plains Indian Museum, Anadarko, OK. *Publication*: Source Directory: Indian, Eskimo, Aleut Owned and Operated Arts & Crafts Businesses. Established 1935.

FLORIDA

SEMINOLE AGENCY
Bureau of Indian Affairs
6075 Stirling Rd.
HOLLYWOOD 33024
 (305) 581-7050 Fax 792-7340
 Leland D. Keel, Supt.
Tribe served: Seminole. *Total population served*: 1,750. Under jurisdiction of Eastern Area Office.

MICCOSUKEE AGENCY
Bureau of Indian Affairs
P.O. Box 44021
TAMIAMI STATION 33144
 (305) 323-8380
 Buffalo Tiger, Superintendent
Tribe served: Miccosukee-Creek. *Total population served*: 600. Under jurisdiction of Eastern Area Office.

IDAHO

FORT HALL AGENCY
Bureau of Indian Affairs
P.O. Box 220
FORT HALL 83203
 (208) 238-2301 Fax 237-0466
 Dennis T. Whiteman, Supt.
Tribes served: Shoshone & Bannock. *Total population served*: 4,000. Under jurisdiction of Portland Area Office.

NORTHERN IDAHO AGENCY
Bureau of Indian Affairs
P.O. Box 227
LAPWAI 83540
 (208) 843-2300 Fax 834-7142
 Karole D. Overberg, Supt.
Tribes served:: Coeur d'Alene, Kootenai, and Nez Perce. *Total population served*: 2,200. Programs: Law Enforcement & Social Services; Real Estate Services; Finance & Economic Development; Education; Aid to Tribal Governments. Under jurisdiction of Portland Area Office.

PLUMMER FIELD OFFICE
Agency Rd.
PLUMMER 83851
 (208) 686-1277
 Michael A. Morigeau, Field Rep.
Under jurisdiction of Portland Area Office.

IOWA

SAC & FOX AREA FIELD OFFICE
Bureau of Indian Affairs
1657 320th St.
TAMA 52339

 (515) 484-4041 Fax 484-6518
 James Fenelon, Director
Tribe served: Sac & Fox. *Total population served*: 850. Under jurisdiction of Minneapolis Area Off..

KANSAS

HORTON AGENCY
Bureau of Indian Affairs
P.O. Box 31
HORTON 66439
 (913) 486-2161 Fax 486-2515
 Linda Saunders, Supt.
Tribes served:: Iowa, Kickapoo of Kansas, Sac and Fox of Missouri, and Prairie Band Potawatomi of Kansas. *Total population served*: 1,500. Under jurisdiction of Anadarko Area Office.

HASKELL INDIAN JUNIOR COLLEGE
Bureau of Indian Affairs
LAWRENCE 66044
 (405) 841-2000
 Gerald Gipp, Supt.
Under jurisdiction of Anadarko Area Office.

MICHIGAN

MICHIGAN AGENCY
Bureau of Indian Affairs
Federal Square Office Plaza
2901.5 I-75 Business Spur
SAULT STE. MARIE 49783
 (906) 632-6809 Fax 632-0689
 Anne E. Bolton, Supt.
Tribes served: Bay Mills, Grand Traverse, Hannahville, Keweenaw Bay, Lac Vieux Desert, Saginaw Chippewa, and Sault Ste. Marie. Under jurisdiction of Minneapolis Area Office.

MINNESOTA

MINNESOTA AGENCY
Bureau of Indian Affairs
Route 3, Box 112
CASS LAKE 56633
 (218) 335-6913 Fax 335-2819
 Franklin Annette, Supt.
Tribes served: Chippewa and Sioux. *Total population served*: 12,000. Under jurisdiction of Minneapolis Area Office.

TRIBAL OPERATIONS
MENOMINEE AREA REPRESENTATIVE
Minneapolis Area Office
Bureau of Indian Affairs
331 Second Ave., South
MINNEAPOLIS 55401-2241
 (612) 373-1000
 Nancy Pierskalla, Area Rep.
Under jurisdiction of Minneapolis Area Office.

TRIBAL OPERATIONS
MINNESOTA SIOUX FIELD REPRESENTATIVE
Minneapolis Area Office
Bureau of Indian Affairs
331 Second Ave., South, 6th Floor
MINNEAPOLIS 55402
 (612) 349-3382
 Don Murdock, Field Rep.
Under jurisdiction of Minneapolis Area Office.

RED LAKE AGENCY
Bureau of Indian Affairs
RED LAKE 56671
 (218) 679-3361
 Francis Brun, Supt.
Tribe served: Chippewa (Red Lake Band.) *Population served*: 4,500. Contracted by Tribe.

MISSISSIPPI

CHOCTAW INDIAN AGENCY
Bureau of Indian Affairs
421 Powell
PHILADELPHIA 39350
 (601) 656-1521 Fax 656-2350
 Robert C. Benn, Supt.
Tribe served: Mississippi Band of Choctaw. *Population served*: 5,500. Museum. Library. Publications: Choctaw Community News; Choctaw Drummer. Under jurisdiction of Eastern Area Office.

MONTANA

ROCKY BOY'S AGENCY
Bureau of Indian Affairs
BOX ELDER 59521
 (406) 395-4476 Fax 395-4382
 Duane Bird Bear, Supt.
Tribe served: Chippewa Cree. *Total population served*: 1,750. Under jurisdiction of Billings Area Office.

BLACKFEET AGENCY
Bureau of Indian Affairs
P.O. Box 880
BROWNING 59417
 (406) 338-7544 Fax 338-7716
 Eric LaPointe Supt.
Tribe served: Blackfeet. *Total population served*: 7,000. Under jurisdiction of Billings Area Office.

CROW AGENCY
Bureau of Indian Affairs
CROW AGENCY 59022
 (406) 638-2672 Fax 638-2380
 John J.V. Pereau, Supt.
Tribe served: Crow. *Total population served*: 5,000. Under jurisdiction of Billings Area Office.

FORT BELKNAP AGENCY
Bureau of Indian Affairs
P.O. Box 98
HARLEM 59526
 (406) 353-2901 Ext 23 Fax 353-2886
 Edith Adams, Supt.
Tribes served:: Assiniboine & Gros Ventre. *Total population served*: 2,200. Under jurisdiction of Billings Area Office.

NORTHERN CHEYENNE AGENCY
Bureau of Indian Affairs
P.O. Box 40
LAME DEER 59043
 (406) 477-8242 Fax 477-6636
 Kenneth W. Davis, Supt.
Tribe served: Northern Cheyenne. *Total population served*: 5,800. Programs: Tribal Operations; Law Enforcement; Administrative Services; Forestry; among others. Under jurisdiction of Billings Area Office.

FORT PECK AGENCY
Bureau of Indian Affairs
P.O. Box 637
POPLAR 59255
(406) 768-5312 Fax 768-3405
Wyman Babby, Supt.
Tribes served: Sioux and Assiniboine. *Total population served*: 5,000. Under jurisdiction of Billings Area Office.

FLATHEAD AGENCY
Bureau of Indian Affairs
P.O. Box A
PABLO 59855
(406) 675-2700 Fax 675-2805
Ernest Moran, Sr., Supt.
Tribes served: Salish & Kootenai. *Total population served*: 6,000. Under jurisdiction of Portland Area Office.

DIVISION OF FLATHEAD IRRIGATION
Bureau of Indian Affairs
P.O. Box 666
ST. IGNATIUS 59865
(406) 745-2661 Fax 745-2303
Chane Salois, Manager
Reservation served: Flathead. *Activities*: Deliver irrigation water to 127,600 acres of land. Under jurisdiction of Portland Area Office

NEBRASKA

WINNEBAGO AGENCY
Bureau of Indian Affairs
Route 1, Box 18
WINNEBAGO 68071
(402) 878-2502 Fax 878-2943
Russell Bradley, Supt.
Tribes served: Omaha, Winnebago, and Santee Sioux of Nebraska. *Total population served*: 5,100; total Indians enrolled, 10,000. *Programs*: Adminiustrative Services; Tribal Government; Social Services; Law Enforcement; Forestry & Land Operations; among others. Under jurisdiction of Aberdeen Area Office.

NEVADA

WESTERN NEVADA AGENCY
Bureau of Indian Affairs
1677 Hot Springs Rd.
CARSON CITY 89706
(702) 887-3500 Fax 702-3531
Robert L. Hunter, Supt.
Tribes served: Shoshone, Paiute, Washoe, and Goshute. *Total population served*: 6,500. Under jurisdiction of Phoenix Area Office.

EASTERN NEVADA AGENCY
Bureau of Indian Affairs
P.O. Box 5400
ELKO 89802
(702) 738-0569 Fax 738-4710
Steven Tibbetts, Supt.
Reservations served: Duck Valley, Te-Moak Bands--Western Shoshone, Battle Mountain Colony, Elko Colony, South Fork, Ruby Valley Allotments, Odgers Ranch, Goshute, Ely Colony, and Duck Water. *Total population served*: 3,500. Under jurisdiction of Phoenix Area Office.

NEW MEXICO

EMPLOYEE DATA & COMPENSATION
Bureau of Indian Affairs
P.O. Box 2026
ALBUQUERQUE 87103
(505) 766-2336
Chuck Roe, Supt.

NATIONAL TECHNICAL SUPPORT CENTER
Bureau of Indian Affairs
P.O. Box 888
ALBUQUERQUE 87103
(505) 766-3627
James Roubidoux, Supt.

OFFICE OF FACILITIES MANAGEMENT
Bureau of Indian Affairs
P.O. Box 1248
500 Gold Ave., SW, 8th Floor
ALBUQUERQUE 87103
(505) 766-2825
Virgil Pochop, Supt.

SOUTHERN PUEBLOS AGENCY
Bureau of Indian Affairs
P.O. Box 1667
ALBUQUERQUE 87103
(505) 766-3020 Fax 766-3023
Fred R. Lujan, Supt.
Tribe served: Pueblo. *Total population served*: 17,500. Under jurisdiction of Albuquerque Area Office.

EASTERN NAVAJO AGENCY
Bureau of Indian Affairs
P.O. Box 328
CROWNPOINT 87313
(505) 786-6100 Fax 786-6112
Theodore Namingha, Acting Supt.
Tribe served: Navajo (in Arizona, New Mexico & Utah.) Under jurisdiction of Navajo Area Office.

JICARILLA AGENCY
Bureau of Indian Affairs
P.O. Box 167
DULCE 87528
(505) 759-3951 Fax 759-3948
Sherryl J. Vigil, Supt.
Tribe served: Jicarilla Apache. *Total population served*: 2,500. Under jurisdiction of Albuquerque Area Office.

NORTHERN PUEBLOS AGENCY
Bureau of Indian Affairs
P.O. Box 4269, Fairview Station
ESPANOLA 87533
(505) 753-1400 Fax 753-1404
Florine L. Gutierrez, Acting Supt.
Tribes served: Nambe Pueblo, Picuris Pueblo, Pojoaque Pueblo, San Ildefonso Pueblo, San Juan Pueblo, Santa Clara Pueblo, Taos & Tesuque Pueblo. *Programs*: All BIA programs; adult education & social services. *Total population served*: 6,500. Under jurisdiction of Albuquerque Area Office.

NAVAJO IRRIGATION PROJECT
Bureau of Indian Affairs
New Energy Bldg., Room 103
FARMINGTON 87401
(505) 325-1864
Leo Soukup, Supt.
Under jurisdiction of Navajo Area Office.

NAVAJO AREA OFFICE
Bureau of Indian Affairs
P.O. Box 1060
GALLUP 87305
(505) 863-8314 Fax 863-8324
Wilson Barber, Jr., Area Director
Tribe served: Navajo. *Population served*: 200,000. *Programs*: Administration; Navajo Irrigation Project; Tribal Operations and Contracts; Technical Services & Resource Protection; Law Enforcement & Social Services; Real Estate Services; Housing; Agriculture; Adult Education & Training. *Has jurisdiction over five field agencies*: Eastern & Western Navajo Agencies, Shiprock, Ft. Defiance, and Chinle.

LAGUNA AGENCY
Bureau of Indian Affairs
P.O. Box 1448
LAGUNA 87026
(505) 552-6001 Fax 552-7497
Freda F. Wabnum, Supt.
Tribe served: Pueblo of Laguna. *Population served*: 4,000 on reservation; 3,000 off reservation. *Programs*: Administrative Services, Property & Supply; Natural Resources; Roads, Real Estate Services; Law Enforcement & Social Services. Under jurisdiction of Albuquerque Area Office.

MESCALERO AGENCY
Bureau of Indian Affairs
P.O. Box 189
MESCALERO 88340
(505) 671-4423 Fax 671-4601
Tribe served: Mescalero Apache. *Population served*: 3,600. *Programs*: BIA programs; Rehab Center; Wildlife Conservation; Tribal Court; Elementary School. Under jurisdiction of Albuquerque Area Office.

RAMAH-NAVAJO AGENCY
Bureau of Indian Affairs
RAMAH 87321
(505) 775-3235 Fax 775-3387
Lori Dieguez, Acting Supt.
Tribe served: Navajo (in Arizona, New Mexico & Utah.) *Population served*: 1,750. Under jurisdiction of Albuquerque Area Office.

SHIPROCK AGENCY
Bureau of Indian Affairs
P.O. Box 966
SHIPROCK 87420
(505) 368-4301 Fax 368-4321
Alyce Rouwalk, Supt.
Tribe served: Navajo (in Arizona, New Mexico & Utah.) Under jurisdiction of Navajo Area Office.

ZUNI AGENCY
Bureau of Indian Affairs
P.O. Box 369
ZUNI 87327
(505) 782-5591 Fax 782-5715
Michael Hackett, Supt.
Tribe served: Zuni. *Total population served*: 6,000. Under jurisdiction of Albuquerque Area Office.

NEW YORK

NEW YORK FIELD OFFICE
Bureau of Indian Affairs
P.O. Box 7366, 100 S. Clinton St., #523
SYRACUSE 13261
(315) 423-5476 Fax 423-5577

Dean A. White, Field Rep.
Tribes served: Seneca Reservations (Allegany, Cattaraugus, Oil Springs), Cayuga, St. Regis Mohawk, Onondaga, Poosepatuck, Oneida, Tuscarora, Tonawanda Seneca. *Total population served:* 15,000. *Activities:* Administers BIA programs for reservations & tribes in New York State. Under jurisdiction of Eastern Area Office.

NORTH CAROLINA

CHEROKEE AGENCY
Bureau of Indian Affairs
CHEROKEE 28719
(704) 497-9131 Fax 497-6715
Wilbur Paul, Supt.
Tribe served: Cherokee. *Total population served:* 6,000. Under jurisdiction of Eastern Area Office.

NORTH DAKOTA

TURTLE MOUNTAIN AGENCY
Bureau of Indian Affairs
P.O. Box 60
BELCOURT 58316
(701) 477-3191 Fax 477-6628
Doreen Bruce, Supt.
Tribe served: Chippewa. *Total population served:* 9,000. Under jurisdiction of Aberdeen Area Office.

FORT TOTTEN AGENCY
Bureau of Indian Affairs
P.O. Box 270
FORT TOTTEN 58335
(701) 766-4545 Fax 766-4854
James Charles, Supt.
Tribe served: Devils Lake Sioux. *Population served:* 3,500. *Programs:* Law Enforcement & Social Services; Property/Procurement; Agriculture; Realty; Road Maintenance and Facilty Management. Under jurisdiction of Aberdeen Area Office.

STANDING ROCK AGENCY
Bureau of Indian Affairs
P.O. Box E
FORT YATES 58538
(701) 854-3433 Fax 854-7541
Russell Bradley, Supt.
Tribe served: Sioux (in North and South Dakota.) *Total population served:* 6,000. Under jurisdiction of Aberdeen Area Office.

FORT BERTHOLD AGENCY
Bureau of Indian Affairs
P.O. BOX 370
NEW TOWN 58763
(701) 627-4707 Fax 627-3601
Terrance C. Walters, Supt.
Tribes served:: Arikara, Mandan, and Hidatsa. *Total population served:* 8,500. Under jurisdiction of Aberdeen Area Office.

WAHPETON INDIAN SCHOOL
Bureau of Indian Affairs
WAHPETON 58075
(701) 642-3796
Leroy W. Chief, Principal
Under jurisdiction of Aberdeen Area Office.

OKLAHOMA

ANADARKO AGENCY
Bureau of Indian Affairs
P.O. Box 309
ANADARKO 73005
(405) 247-6673 Fax 247-9232
James DeHaas, Supt.
Tribes served:: Apache, Kiowa, Comanche, Caddo, Delaware, and Wichita. *Population served* : 22,000. Under jurisdiction of Anadarko Area Office.

CHICKASAW AGENCY
Bureau of Indian Affairs
P.O. Box 2240
ADA 74821
(405) 436-0784 Fax 436-3215
Robert Impson, Supt.
Tribe served: Chickasaw. *Total population served:* 7,000. Under jurisdiction of Muskogee Area Office.

CONCHO AGENCY
Bureau of Indian Affairs
P.O. Box 68
EL RENO 73036
(405) 262-7481 Fax 262-3140
Galila Mattwaoshshe, Supt.
Tribes served: Cheyenne-Arapaho of Oklahoma. *Total population served:* 7,000. Under jurisdiction of Anadarko Area Office.

MIAMI AGENCY
Bureau of Indian Affairs
P.O. Box 391
MIAMI 74355
(918) 542-3396 Fax 542-7202
Jack C. Naylor, Supt.
Tribes served: Shawnee, Miami, Seneca-Cayuga, and Quapaw. Under jurisdiction of Muskogee Area Office.

OKMULGEE AGENCY
Bureau of Indian Affairs
P.O. Box 370
OKMULGEE 74447
(918) 756-3950 Fax 756-9626
Jimmy Gibson, Supt.
Tribe served: Creek. *Total population served:* 16,000. Under jurisdiction of Muskogee Area Office.

OSAGE AGENCY
Bureau of Indian Affairs
P.O. Box 1539
PAWHUSKA 74056
(918) 287-1032 Fax 287-4320
Gordon Jackson, Supt.
Tribe served: Osage. *Total population served:* 13,000. *Programs:* Tribal Social Services; Tribal Court; Law Enforcement; Finance & Administration. Under jurisdiction of Muskogee Area Office.

PAWNEE AGENCY
Bureau of Indian Affairs
P.O. Box 440
PAWNEE 74058
(918) 762-2585 Fax 762-3201
Julia M. Langan, Supt.
Tribes served: Kaw, Pawnee, Ponca, Otoe-Missouria, and Tonkawa. Under jurisdiction of Anadarko Area Office.

SHAWNEE AGENCY
Bureau of Indian Affairs
624 W. Independence, Suite 114
SHAWNEE 74801
(405) 273-0317 Fax 273-0072
Robert Jones, Supt.
Tribes served: Iowa, Kickapoo of Oklahoma and Texas, Iowa Tribe of Oklahoma, Citizen Band Potawatomi, Sac and Fox, and Absentee Shawnee. *Total population served:* 15,000. Under jurisdiction of Anadarko Area Office. *Programs:* Tribal Government, Social Services, Higher Education, Law Enforcement and Realty.

TAHLEQUAH AGENCY
Bureau of Indian Affairs
P.O. Box 828
TAHLEQUAH 74465
(918) 456-6146
Dennis Wickliffe, Supt.
Tribe served: Cherokee. *Population served:* 14,000. Contracted by tribe.

TALIHINA AGENCY
Bureau of Indian Affairs
P.O. Drawer H
TALIHINA 74571
(918) 567-2207 Fax 567-2061
Larry W. Mings, Acting Supt.
Tribe served: Choctaw. *Total population served:* 12,000. Under jurisdiction of Muskogee Area Office.

WEWOKA AGENCY
Bureau of Indian Affairs
P.O. Box 1060
WEWOKA 74884
(405) 257-6257 Fax 257-6748
James Fields, Supt.
Tribe served: Seminole. *Total population served:* 6,500. Under jurisdiction of Muskogee Area Office.

OREGON

CHILOQUIN SUB-AGENCY
Bureau of Indian Affairs
P.O. Box 360
CHILOQUIN 97624
(503) 783-2189 Fax 783-2946
Greg Lafrance, Field Rep.
Under jurisdiction of Portland Area Office.

UMATILLA AGENCY
Bureau of Indian Affairs
P.O. Box 520
PENDLETON 97801
(503) 278-3786 Fax 278-3791
Philip Sanchez, Supt.
Tribes served: Cayuse, Umatilla, and Walla Walla. *Total population served:* 2,000. Under jurisdiction of Portland Area Office.

SILETZ AGENCY
Bureau of Indian Affairs
P.O. Box 569
SILETZ 97380
(503) 444-2679 Fax 444-2513
T.L. Traversie, Supt.
Under the jurisdiction of Portland Area Office.

Government Agencies

41

WARM SPRINGS AGENCY
Bureau of Indian Affairs
P.O. Box 1239
WARM SPRINGS 97761
(503) 553-2411 Fax 553-2426
Gordon Cannon, Supt.
Tribes served: Paiute, Walla Walla, Chinook, Cayuse, and Wasco. T*otal population served*: 2,750. Under jurisdiction of Portland Area Office.

SOUTH DAKOTA

CHEYENNE RIVER AGENCY
Bureau of Indian Affairs
P.O. Box 325
EAGLE BUTTE 57625
(605) 964-6611 Fax 964-4060
Russell McClure, Supt.
Tribe served: Sioux. *Total population served*: 5,000. Under jurisdiction of Aberdeen Area Office.

CROW CREEK AGENCY
Bureau of Indian Affairs
P.O. Box 139
FORT THOMPSON 57339
(605) 245-2311 Fax 245-2343
Frank A. Joseph, Supt.
Tribe served: Crow Creek Sioux. *Total population served*: 2,900. *Programs*: Social services; Land Operations; Law Enforcement; Facilities Management, Realty, Property & Supply. Library. Under jurisdiction of Aberdeen Area Office.

LOWER BRULE AGENCY
Bureau of Indian Affairs
P.O. Box 190
LOWER BRULE 57548
(605) 473-5512 Fax 473-5491
Noble LaCroix, Supt.
Tribe served: Sioux. *Total population served*: 1,200. Under jurisdiction of Aberdeen Area Office.

PINE RIDGE AGENCY
Bureau of Indian Affairs
P.O. Box 1203
PINE RIDGE 57770
(605) 867-5125 Fax 867-1141
Delbert Brewer, Supt.
Tribe served: Oglala Sioux (in South Dakota and Nebraska. *Total population served*: 13,500. Under jurisdiction of Aberdeen Area Office.

ROSEBUD AGENCY
Bureau of Indian Affairs
P.O. Box 550
ROSEBUD 57570
(605) 747-2224 Fax 747-2805
Alonzo Spang, Sr., Supt.
Tribe served: Rosebud Sioux. *Total population served*: 12,000. Under jurisdiction of Aberdeen Area Office.

SISSETON AGENCY
Bureau of Indian Affairs
P.O. Box 688
AGENCY VILLAGE 57262
(605) 698-7676 Fax 698-7784
Vacant, Supt.
Tribe served: Sisseton-Wahpeton Sioux (in North & South Dakota.) *Reservation served*: Lake Traverse. *Total population served*: 9,000. Under jurisdiction of Aberdeen Area Office.

YANKTON AGENCY
Bureau of Indian Affairs
P.O. Box 577
MARTY 57361
(605) 384-3651 Fax 384-5706
Timothy Lake, Supt.
Tribe served: Sioux. *Total population served*: 1,250. Under jurisdiction of Aberdeen Area Office.

UTAH

UINTAH & OURAY AGENCY
Bureau of Indian Affairs
P.O. Box 130
FORT DUCHESNE 84026
(801) 722-2406 Fax 722-2406 ext. 61
Perry J. Baker, Supt.
Tribes served: Ute and Goshute. *Total population served*: 2,000. P*ublication*: Ute Bulletin. Under jurisdiction of Phoenix Area Office.

SOUTHERN PAIUTE FIELD STATION
Bureau of Indian Affairs
P.O. Box 720
ST. GEORGE 84771
(801) 674-9720 Fax 674-9714
Flossie I. Girty, Field Rep.
Tribes served: Paiute Indian Tribe of Utah, Kaibab Paiute Tribe, Moapa Band of Paiute Indians, San Juan Southern Paiute Tribe, and Las Vegas Paiute Indian Tribe. Under jurisdiction of Phoenix Area Office.

WASHINGTON

PUGET SOUND AGENCY
Bureau of Indian Affairs
3006 Colby Ave., Federal Bldg.
EVERETT 98201
(206) 258-2651 ext. 232 Fax 258-1254
William A. Black, Supt.
Tribes served: Lummi, Muckleshoot, Nisqually, Nooksack, Port Gamble, Puyallup, Sauk-Suiattle, Stillaguamish, Suquamish, Swinomish, Tulalip, Upper Skagit, and Snoqualmie. *Population served*: 15,500. *Programs*: Tribal Administration/Operation; Contracts & Grants; Social Services, Realty; Law Enforcement; Education. Under jurisdiction of Portland Area Office.

OLYMPIC PENINSULA AGENCY
Bureau of Indian Affairs
P.O. Box 120, Office Bldg.
HOQUIAM 98550
(206) 533-9100 Fax 533-9141
Raymond Maldonado, Supt.
Under jurisdiction of Portland Area Office.

MAKAH AGENCY
Bureau of Indian Affairs
P.O. Box 116
NEAH BAY 98357
(206) 645-2229 Fax 645-2164
Under jurisdiction of Portland Area Office.

COLVILLE AGENCY
Bureau of Indian Affairs
P.O. Box 111
NESPELEM 99155
(509) 634-4901 Fax 634-8751

Gene Nicholson, Supt.
Tribes served: Columbia, Colville, Lakes, Nespelem, and Nez Perce. *Total population served*: 3,500. Under jurisdiction of Portland Area Office.

SEATTLE SUPPORT CENTER
Bureau of Indian Affairs
P.O. Box 80947
SEATTLE 98104
(206) 764-3328
Gerald W. Taylor, Supt.
Under jurisdiction of Juneau Area Office.

YAKIMA AGENCY
Bureau of Indian Affairs
P.O. Box 632
TOPPENISH 98948
(509) 865-2255 Fax (700) 446-8198
Ambrose Jack, Acting Supt.
Tribe served: Yakima. *Total population served*: 9,000. Under jurisdiction of Portland Area Office.

WAPATO IRRIGATION PROJECT
Bureau of Indian Affairs
P.O. Box 220
WAPATO 98951
(509) 877-3155
Louis Hilderbrand, Supt.
Under jurisdiction of Portland Area Office.

SPOKANE AGENCY
Bureau of Indian Affairs
P.O. Box 389
WELLPINIT 99040
(509) 258-4561 Fax 258-7542
Duane Bird Bear, Supt.
Tribe served: Spokane. *Total population served*: 900. Under jurisdiction of Portland Area Office.

WISCONSIN

GREAT LAKES AGENCY
Bureau of Indian Affairs
615 Main St. West
ASHLAND 54806
(715) 682-4527 Fax 682-8897
Robert Jaeger, Supt.
Tribes served: Chippewa, Oneida, Forest Potawatomi, Stockbridge-Munsee, Winnebago (in Minnesota and Wisconsin.) *Total population served*: 9,000. Under jurisdiction of Minneapolis Area Office.

WYOMING

WIND RIVER AGENCY
Bureau of Indian Affairs
FORT WASHAKIE 82514
(307) 332-7810 Fax 332-4578
David Allison, Supt.
Tribes served:: Arapaho & Shoshone. *Total population served*: 5,500. Under jurisdiction of Billings Area Office.

This section lists national associations, societies, and organizations active in Indian affairs; also, religious, charitable, and philanthropic associations. Listings are arranged alphabetically.

AMERICAN ACADEMY OF PEDIATRICS
Committee on Indian Health
Box 927, 141 N.W. Point Rd.
Elk Grove Village, IL 60007
(312) 228-5005
M. Harry Jennison, M.D., Executive Director
Purpose: To provide leadership in the review and development of methods and procedures that will improve pediatric services to Indians and Alaskan natives. *Activities*: Provides advisory pediatric service to Indian and Alaskan natives through the Division of Indian Health, U.S. Public Health Service. Founded 1965.

AMERICAN ANTHROPOLOGICAL ASSOCIATION
1703 New Hampshire Ave., NW
Washington, DC 20009
(202) 232-8800 Fax 667-5345
Eugene L. Sterud, Executive Director
Membership: 10,000. Professional society of anthropologists, educators, students and others interested in the biological and cultural origin and development of mankind. *Activities*: Sponsors visiting lecturers, congressional fellowship, and departmental services programs. Maintains speaker's bureau, consultants' bureau, and placement service. Sponsors competitions; bestows awards; conducts research programs and compiles statistics. *Full-time staff*: David Givens, PhD (Director of Information Services, Editor, Anthropology Newsletter; and Judith Lisansky, PhD (Director, External Affairs). *Publications*: Special Publications, periodic monograph series; American Anthropologist, quarterly journal; Anthropology and Education Quarterly journal; Anthropology Newsletter, 9x/year; Cultural Anthropology, quarterly journal; Guide to Departments of Anthropology, annual. Founded 1902.

AMERICAN ANTIQUARIAN SOCIETY
185 Salisbury St.
Worcester, MA 01609
(617) 755-5221
Ellen S. Dunlap, President
Nancy H. Burkett, Librarian
Membership: 560. *Purpose*: To collect, preserve and encourage serious study of the materials of American history and life through 1876. Library. Newsletter. Founded 1812.

AMERICAN ETHNOLOGICAL SOCIETY
c/o Nancy McDowell, Ph.D., Sec.
Dept. of Anthropology
Franklin and Marshall College
Lancaster, PA 17604
(717) 291-4193
Membership: 2,500. A division of American Anthropological Association. Includes anthropologists and others interested in the field of ethnology and social anthropology. *Activities*: Conducts symposia. *Publications*: American Ethnologist, quarterly journal; Monograph Series, periodic; Unit News in Anthropology Newsletter, monthly; Proceedings, The Development of Political Organization in Native North America. Annual conference in conjunction with AAA. Founded 1942.

AMERICAN FRIENDS SERVICE COMMITTEE
Native American Affairs
1501 Cherry St.
Philadelphia, PA 19102
(215) 241-7000
Asia A. Bennett, Executive Secretary
Description: One of the corporate expressions of Quaker faith and practice. *Purpose*: To conduct programs with U.S. communities on the problem of minority groups--housing, employment and denial of legal rights. Founded 1917.

AMERICAN HISTORICAL ASSOCIATION
400 A St., S.E.
Washington, D.C. 20003
(202) 544-2422
Samuel R. Gamnon, Executive Director
Membership: 13,000. Professional historians, educators, and others interested in promoting historical studies and collecting and preserving historical manuscripts. *Publications*: American Historical Review, 5/yr. Library. Founded 1884.

AMERICAN INDIAN ADOPTION RESOURCE EXCHANGE
Council of Three Rivers
American Indian Center, Inc.
200 Charles St.
Pittsburgh, PA 15238
(412) 782-4457
Description: This organization maintains registers of prospective Indian adoption homes and Indian children who are available for placement. Although not an adoption agency, the exchange provides information on the adoption of Indian children.

AMERICAN INDIAN ANTI-DEFAMATION COUNCIL
215 W. Fifth Ave.
Denver, CO 80204
(303) 892-7011
Russell Means, Chair
Purpose: To combat racism by countering negative images of Native Americans in academia, the arts, film, and literature. *Activities*: Engages in public education, direct action, and selective litigation. Membership: Open to all, $25/year. Organization announcements and updates.

AMERICAN INDIAN ARBITRATION ASSN.
Minneapolis, MN (**Address Unknown**)
Michael Haney, Consultant

AMERICAN INDIAN ARCHAEOLOGICAL INSTITUTE
Curtis Rd., Box 1260
Washington, CT 06793
(203) 868-0518
Susan F. Payne, Director
Purpose: To discover, preserve, and interpret information about the lifeways of the first peoples of the Northeast Woodlands area of the U.S., and to enhance appreciation for their cultures and achievements. *Activities*: Conducts archaeological surveys and excavations; provides indoor and outdoor exhibits; sponsors archaeological training sessions, teacher workshops, craft workshops, summer youth programs-educational programs to school groups. *Publication*: Artifacts, quarterly magazine; annual research report; bibliography and educational resource pamphlets. Annual conference, with symposium - always November, Lowell, MA.. Museum. Library. Established in 1971.

AMERICAN INDIAN COLLEGE FUND
21 W. 68th St., Suite 1F
New York, NY 10023
(800) 776-3863
(212) 787-6312
Ronald S. McNeil, President
Barbara Bratone, Executive Director
Purpose: To raise funds to support the 29 member colleges of the American Indian Higher Education Consortium that are located in the U.S. *Activities*: Disbursements made directly to member colleges. *Publication*: Annual report. Established in 1989.

AMERICAN INDIAN CONTEMPORARY ARTS
685 Market St., Suite 250, Monadnock Bldg.
San Francisco, CA 94105
(415) 495-7600
Janeen Antoine, Executive Director
Description: Serves as an educational, advocacy, and economic development organization for today's Indian artists who are trying to bridge the gap between the traditional and the contemporary, and between Native and non-native peoples. A non-profit independent center dedicated to presenting the finest art of Indian America today. Provides numerous avenues for living Indian artists to share their creative vision with the world. Through a comprehensive program of exhibition, educational outreach, promotion and sales, lectures, and workshops, AICA has been instrumental in helping shape the dominant culture's understanding of contemporary American Indian art. Maintains a slide registry storing over 2,500 slides representing the work of more than 150 artists.

AMERICAN INDIAN COUNCIL OF ARCHITECTS & ENGINEERS
P.O. Box 15096
Portland, OR 97215
(503) 235-4402 Fax 228-2058

AMERICAN INDIAN CULTURE RESEARCH CENTER
Blue Cloud Abbey
P.O. Box 98
Marvin, SD 57251
(605) 432-5528
Rev. Stanislaus Maudlin, Executive Director
Purpose: To support Indian leaders, and educators in their ambitions for rebuilding the Indian community; aids in teaching the non-Indian public of the culture & philosophy of the Indian. *Programs*: Compiled oral history & photographic collection; distributes films, records, and tapes; conducts workshops & seminars; maintains speakers bureau. Library. Established 1967.

AMERICAN INDIAN DANCE THEATRE
223 East 61st St.
New York, NY 10021
Barb Schwei, Founder
Hanay Geiogamah, Director
The group has 20 dancers, representing various tribes across the country, including Zuni, Ute, Apache, Cheyenne & Creek. They perform dances of different tribes touring the U.S. and Europe. Founded 1987.

AMERICAN INDIAN DEFENSE OF AMERICAS
P.O. Box 3121
Hutchinson, KS 67501
(316) 665-3614
Chief Thunderbird Webber, National Chair
Chief Red Eagle Steorts, Co-National Chair
Chef Stewart Rodda, National Director

Purpose: To deal with Indian problems in North & South America. Has an international membership. Membership, $10 (life). Pu blication: American Defense news. Established 1974.

AMERICAN INDIAN DEVELOPMENT FOUNDATION
American Indian Science & Engineering Soc.
1630 30th St., Suite 301
Boulder, CO 80301-1014
(303) 492-8658
Purpose: To encourage Native American Indian students to pursue their educational goals. Scholarships available.

AMERICAN INDIAN DISABILITY LEGISLATION: TOWARD THE DEVELOPMENT OF A PROCESS THAT RESPECTS SOVEREIGNTY & CULTURAL DIVERSITY
52 Corbin Hall, University of Montana
Missoula, MT 59801
(406) 243-5467
Julie Clay, Coordinator
Description: New project funded by the Of fice of Special Education and Rehabilitation, of the Dept. of Education. *Goal*: To develop and test methods for fostering the adoption of disability legislation by American Indian tribes that is consistent with principles established within the American With Disabilities Act and are respectful of tribal sovereignty and cultural diversity .

AMERICAN INDIAN EDUCATION ADVISORY COUNCIL
900 Grant St., Room 400
Denver, CO 80203
(303) 764-3579
Phyl Ogden, Contact

AMERICAN INDIAN EDUCATION POLICY CENTER
Pennsylvania State University
320 Rackley Bldg.
University Park, P A 16803
(814) 865-1489
Dr. L.A. Napier, Director
Program: American Indian Leadership Program. Goal: To train qualified leaders for service to Indian nations by providing graduate degrees in educational administration and certification credentials in principal ship and superintendency. Fellowships. Library . Founded 1970.

AMERICAN INDIAN FILM INSTITUTE
333 Valencia St., Suite 322
San Francisco, CA 94103
(415) 554-0525 Fax 554-0542
Mike Smith, Director
Activities: Annual Silver Star Pow W ow & Indian Market

AMERICAN INDIAN GRADUATE CENTER
4520 Montgomery Blvd., N.E., Suite 1-B
Albuquerque, NM 87109
(505) 881-4584
Lorraine P. Edmo, Director
Activities: Provides scholarship and fellowship assistance for Indian students from federally recognized tribes at the graduate and professional school levels. *Publication*: American Indian Graduate Record, semiannual. Semiannual board meeting. Founded 1969. Formerly American Indian Scholarships.

AMERICAN INDIAN HEALTH CARE ASSN.
245 East 6th St., Suite 499
St. Paul, MN 55101

(612) 293-0233
Michael Arfsten, Executive Director
Joan Myrick, AIDS Education Coordinator
Membership: Approximately 40 Indian health programs and 50 staf f and support persons. *Purpose*: A national organization that provides technical assistance and training to urban Indian health program clinics funded by Indian Health Service. Technical assistance includes administration, financial and clinical development. Bestows awards and recognition for Indian health care achievements. *Publications*: Newsbriefs, quarterly newsletter; AIDS Briefs, quarterly newsletter; Summary Program Publication, annual; Diabetes Surveillance Survey , periodic; directory of programs and W orld Health Day materials which are Indian specific; AIDS education comic books (aimed at 5-16 year olds). Annual Urban Indian Health Care Management Conference. Founded 1975.

AMERICAN INDIAN HERITAGE FOUNDATION
6051 Arlington Blvd.
Falls Church, V A 22044
(703) 237-7500
Princess Pale Moon, President
Dr. Wil Rose, Chief Executive Of ficer
Membership: 250,000+. Tribal members and individual donors. *Purpose*: To inform and educate non-Indians concerning the culture and heritage of the American Indian; to be responsive to the felt needs of Indian people both at the tribal and urban levels; to introduce a positive Indian presence into every strata of society where it is appropriate; and to initiate creative programs to actively share the diverse Indian culture in many creative ways. *Activities/Programs*: Meets emergency needs, distributes gifts-in-kind; promotes an Outstanding Achievement Youth Role Model Program; sponsors the National Miss Indian USA Pageant, the National PowWow and Arts and Crafts Festival on the Washington Monument grounds, the Annual National Children's Thanksgiving Concert, and promotes the National American Indian Heritage Month. *Publication*: Monthly project letter; Pathfinder, periodic newsletter; Tsa-La-Gi Columns, quarterly newsletter . Museum and Library (limited-but major expansion is anticipated). Annual national festival and pow-wow on July 4th in Washington, DC. Founded 1973.

AMERICAN INDIAN HIGHER EDUCATION CONSORTIUM (AIHEC)
513 Capitol Court, NE, Suite 100
WASHINGTON, DC 20002
(202) 544-9289
Georgiana Tiger, Director
Purpose: To represent 29 tribally-controlled colleges in the U.S. to the Congress, federal agencies, and other national organizations, in an effort to acquire funds, support programs, and growth; to build a satellite network linking the 29 tribal colleges

AMERICAN INDIAN HORSE REGISTR Y
Route 3, Box 64
Lockhart, TX 78644
(512) 398-6642
Nanci Falley, President
Membership: 1,200. Persons who own or desire to own American Indian horses. *Purpose*: To collect, record, and preserve the pedigrees of American Indian horses. *Activities*: National Indian Horse Show each June; awards programs for members. Maintains Indian Horse Hall of Fame Museum. *Publications*: American In-

dian Horse Studbook, annual; quarterly newsletter. Library. Founded 1961.

AMERICAN INDIAN INSTITUTE
555 Constitution Ave.
Norman, OK 73037
(405) 325-4127
Anita Chisholm
Description: A non-profit Indian service, training, and research organization promoting education, training and career development opportunities for Indian people; to foster and facilitate economic development; and an advocate of the perpetuation of Native American culture and tradition. A department within Public Responsibility and Community Affairs at the University of Oklahoma.

AMERICAN INDIAN LA W CENTER
P.O. Box 4456, Station A
1117 Stanford, N.E.
Albuquerque, NM 87196
(505) 277-5462
Philip S. Deloria, Executive Director
Description: Staff of 12 Indian law graduates and attorneys; located at the University of New Mexico, School of Law . *Purpose*: To render services, primarily research and training, of a broad legal and governmental nature; and, to assist tribes in making legal decisions when assistance is necessary. *Programs*: Helped found and currently provides staf f support to the Commission on State-T ribal Relations; provides individualized training for tribal judges and tribal prosecutors; administers the Special Scholarship Program in Law for American Indians through which students receive admission advice, financial assistance, tutorial aid, and job placement services; provides assistance to Alaskan natives; sponsors conferences and seminars. *Publications*: American Indian Law Newsletter , bimonthly; manuals for tribal judges and prosecutors, and on Indian criminal court procedures. Library. Founded 1967.

AMERICAN INDIAN LAW & POLICY CENTER
University of Oklahoma College of Law
300 Timberdell Rd.
Norman, OK 73019
(405) 325-4676
Prof. Rennard Strickland, Director
Jan Young, Secretary

AMERICAN INDIAN LA WYER TRAINING PROGRAM, INC.
American Indian Resource Institute
319 MacArthur Blvd.
Oakland, CA 94610
(510) 834-9333 Fax 834-3836

AMERICAN INDIAN LIBERA TION CRUSADE
4009 S. Halldale Ave.
Los Angeles, CA 90062
(213) 299-1810
Dr. Henry E. Hedrick, President
Membership: 4,000. A missionary outreach to Native Americans on their reservation. *Purpose*: To act as an information center , making known the needs of the American Indian; to help the Indians, both spiritually and materially . *Programs*: The American Indian Hour--the radio voice of the American Indian Liberation Crusade--broadcasts on 17 radio stations across the country. Located at P .O. Box 4187, Inglewood, California 90309-4187; relief ministry to Indian families on several major reservations; sending Indian children to summer Bible

Camp; building Indian churches; supporting native pastors and missionaries. *Publication*: Indian Crusader, quarterly. Founded 1952.

AMERICAN INDIAN LIBRARY ASSOCIATION (AILA)
American Library Association
Office of Library Outreach Services (OLOS)
50 East Huron St.
Chicago, IL 60611
(312) 944-6780
Naomi Caldwell-Wood, President (AILA)
Lotsee Patterson, Vice President
John Aubrey, Chairperson, Library Services for American Indian People
Purpose: To promote the development, maintenance, & improvement of libraries, library systems, and cultural & information services on reservations and in communities of Native Americans & Native Alaskans. *Publication*: American Indian Libraries Newsletter. Founded 1979.

AMERICAN INDIAN LORE ASSOCIATION
960 Walhonding Ave.
Logan, OH 43138
(614) 385-7136
Leland L. Conner, Chief
Description: Students and patrons of the Indian arts, crafts and history. *Purpose*: To study, interpret, and perpetuate the lore of the historical American Indian. *Award*: Catlin Peace Pipe Award, annual. *Publication*: The Evanpaha, bimonthly. Museum. Library. Founded 1957.

AMERICAN INDIAN MOVEMENT
Minneapolis, MN (Address unknown)
Dennis Banks, Clyde Bellecourt et al, Founding members
Membership: 5,000. Primary objective is to encourage self-determination among American Indians and to establish international recognition of American Indian treaty rights. Founded Heart of the Earth Survival School which enrolls 600 students from preschool to adult programs. Maintains historical archives and speakers' bureau; conducts research. *Publication*: Survival News, quarterly. Annual meeting. Founded 1968.

AMERICAN INDIAN PROFESSIONAL TRAINING PROGRAM IN SPEECH-LANGUAGE PATHOLOGY & AUDIOLOGY
University of Arizona
Dept. of Speech & Hearing Sciences
Tucson, AZ 85721
(602) 621-1969/1644
Dr. Theodore Glattke, Director
Betty D. Nunnery, Program Coordinator
Pamela Wood, Clinical Supervisor, Audiologist
Objectives: To recruit, retain, and provide education to American Indian men and women in the fields of speech-language pathology or audiology. *Goals*: To qualify students for a Master's degree in speech-language pathology or audiology; to integrate the study of Indian languages and cultures into the training program; to develop therapy programs sensitive to Indian cultural needs; to establish a professional work force to serve American Indians who have communication disorders both on and off reservations. *Activities/Programs*: Speech & hearing clinics operated on two reservation sites. Scholarship recipients receive a tuition waiver and a stipend. *Publications*: Directory of Native Americans in Speech-Language Pathology & Audiology; newsletter, Desert Connections, a network publication for Native American speech-lan-

guage pathologists & audiologists. Library. Established 1978.

AMERICAN INDIAN RADIO ON SATELLITE
P.O. Box 83111
Lincoln, NE 68501
(800) 571-6885; (402) 472-9333 Fax 472-8675
Susan Braine, Manager
Goal: To distribute programs that address political, social, economic, health, artistic, and spiritual concerns and issues of Native American communities. *Activity*: To inventory Native American content radio programs for the public radio system.

AMERICAN INDIAN RELIEF COUNCIL
P.O. Box 6200, 317 E. St. Patrick St.
Rapid City, SD 57709
(605) 399-9905 Fax 399-9908
Brian J. Brown, President
Description: A non-profit organization which develops self-help programs and emergency relief services for Native Americans, including: emergency food distribution to over 2,000 Indian families every month; emergency shelter for the homeless; computer learning lab; scholarships for Indian youth; free health care; jobs & training program; free distribution of new and used clothing; voter education and registration drive.

AMERICAN INDIAN RESEARCH & DEVELOPMENT
2424 Springer Dr., Suite 200
Norman, OK 73069
(405) 364-0656 Fax 364-5464
Stuart A. Tonemah, President
Description: Educational service organization which seeks to improve the quality of education for gifted and talented Native American students. *Activities*: Provides training and technical assistance to local and state education agencies, tribes, and other Native American organizations; offers summer and weekend programs; leadership enrichment programs for gifted and talented American and Alaska Native students; conducts research; develops curriculum and teaching materials; maintains speaker's bureau; sponsors competitions; and compiles statistics. *Publications*: American Indian Gifted and Talented Assessment Model; and Elementary American Indian Gifted and Talented Assessment Model. Founded 1982.

AMERICAN INDIAN RESOURCE & EDUCATION COALITION (A.I.R.E.C.)
P.O. Box 3585
Austin, TX 78764
(512) 648-7023
Ardena Rodriguez, Executive Director
Purpose: To identify resources and advocate concerns of reservation and urban American Indians. Our mission is to establish a statewide central information and referral center dedicated to educational goals, youth advocacy, urban Indian issues, health and welfare, preservation of heritage and promotion of InterTribal unity. Library. Established 1990.

AMERICAN INDIAN RESOURCES INSTITUTE
319 MacArthur Blvd.
Oakland, CA 94610
(510) 834-9333
Purpose: To design and implement programs to promote tribal sovereignty and self-determination through provision of training resources to Indian attorneys, law students, and advocates

committed to serving the legal needs of Indian people. *Program*: American Indian Lawyer Training Program. Founded 1973.

AMERICAN INDIAN RITUAL OBJECT REPATRIATION FOUNDATION
463 East 57th St.
New York, NY 10022
(212) 980-9441
Elizabeth Sackler, Founder/President
Rose Garvin-Jackson & Kate Morris, Outreach Coordinators
Purpose: Committed to the return of sacred objects to American Indian Nations. *Activities*: Sponsors conferences & seminars addressing the significance of sacred material culture to the American Indian; a resource to American Indian Nations preparing to receive sacred objects; a liaison, assisting museums in locating & contacting American Indian individuals needed to authenticate and/or escort home sacred objects identified for repatriation; an information center to provide collectors who currently possess sacred ritual objects with information about their cultural & spiritual significance.

AMERICAN INDIAN SCIENCE & ENGINEERING SOCIETY (AISES)
1630 30th St., Suite 301
Boulder, CO 80303
(303) 492-8658 Fax 492-7090
Norbert S. Hill, Jr., Executive Director
Membership: 1,500. American Indian and non-Indian students and professionals in science, technology, and engineering fields. *Purpose*: To increase the number of American Indian scientists and engineers in the nation; seeks to motivate and encourage students to pursue graduate studies in science, engineering and technology; and the ultimate goal is to serve as a catalyst for the advancement of American Indians to become more self-reliant members of society. *Activities*: American Indian Science and Education Center - provides training and educational opportunities to American Indian college students and tribal leaders; teacher-training programs; sponsors internships nationwide & specially designed workshops; curriculum materials development; conducts research and community-affiliated programs; sponsors scholarship; bestows awards; maintains speakers bureau and job placement service. AISES Environmental Institute - camp for about 35 kids, ages 11-17, for 1-2 week sessions to experience nature and to put together the best of modern science with traditional American Indian values and teachings. Located in Pike Mountain National Forest, about 50 miles southwest of Denver. *Publications*: Journal, biennial; Winds of Change, quarterly magazine; Science Education Newsletter, quarterly; Annual Report. Annual conference. Library. Founded 1977.

AMERICAN INDIAN STUDIES RESEARCH INSTITUTE
Indiana University
BLOOMINGTON 47405
(812) 855-1203
Raymond J. De Mallie, Director

AMERICAN INDIAN VETERANS ASSN.
P.O. Box 543
Isleta, NM 87022
(505) 869-9284
Description: Organized for the benevolence of American Indian veterans of the Armed Forces of the U.S. Established 1977.

AMERICAN INDIANS IN FILM
65 N. Allen Ave., Suite 105
Pasadena, CA 91106
(818) 578-0344
Sonny Skyhawk, Executive Director

AMERICAN NATIVE PRESS
ARCHIVES & RESEARCH ASSOCIATION
American Indian and Alaska Native Periodicals
Research Clearinghouse
502 Stabler Hall, University of Arkansas
33rd & University Ave.
Little Rock, AR 72204
(501) 569-3160
Johnye E. Strickland, Sec.-Treas.
Purpose: To promote and foster academic research concerning the American native press, those involved in it, and American native periodical literature as a whole; disseminate research results; refine methodolcgies. Annual Meeting. Founded 1984.

AMERICAN SOCIETY FOR
CONSERVATION ARCHAEOLOGY
Museum of New Mexico
P.O. Box 2087
Santa Fe, NM 87503
(505) 827-8941
Curtis F. Schaafsma, President
Membership: 500. Promotes and coordinates activities, including public education which aid in the preservation and protection of historic and prehistoric archaeological resources. *Publications*: Bi-monthly report; directory; scholarly articles. Founded 1974.

AMERICAN SOCIETY FOR ETHNOHISTORY
P.O. Box 917
Goshen, IN 46527
(219) 875-7237
William O. Autry, Sec/Treas.
Membership: 1,300. Anthropologists, historians, geographers, etc. *Purpose*: To promote the educational and scientific study of world societies and cultures, cultural change, and history; and to foster the study of ethnohistory worldwide. *Awards*: Robert F. Heizer Award, annual for best article concerning ethnohistory; and Erminie Wheeler-Voegel Award, annual for best book-length work in ethnohistory . Library of copies of Ethnohistory and Society's archives. *Publication*: Ethnohistory, quarterly journal) by Duke University Press. Annual Meeting. Founded 1954.

AMERICAN STUDIES ASSOCIATION
307 College Hall/CO
University of Pennsylvania
Philadelphia, PA 19104
(215) 898-5408
John F. Stephens, Executive Director
Membership: 2,200. Persons concerned with American culture. *Purpose*: To promote the interdisciplinary study of American culture. *Publication*: American Quarterly; ASA Newsletter; American Studies: An Annotated Bibliography. Founded 1951.

AMERICANS FOR INDIAN OPPORTUNITY
681 Juniper Hill Rd.
Bernalillo, NM 87004
(505) 867-0278
LaDonna Harris, Founder/President
Description: Created to serve as a catalyst for new concepts & opportunities for Indian people. Creates coalitions among tribes & between Indians and non-Indians to enhance the cultural,

social, political, and economic self-suf ficiency of tribes. Strives to increase the role & participation of tribal governments within the social & political fabric of the U.S. *Purpose*: To help American Indians, Eskimos and Aleuts establish self-help programs at the local level; to improve communications among Native-Americans and with non-Indians; and to educate the public on the achievements and needs of Native-Americans today . *Activities*: The Ambassador Program - a Native American Leadership Training Program, Indian operated computer civic network - INDIANnet, clearing house; supports Indian action projects in education, health, housing, job development, and training and opportunities for Indian young people; conducts research; bestows awards; holds seminars and weekly meetings for Indian interest groups. *Publication*: Red Alert, irregular; You Don't Have to Be Poor to Be Indian; Messing With Mother Nature; Core Cultural Valves. Founded 1970.

THE AMERIND FOUNDATION, INC.
P.O. Box 248
Dragoon, AZ 85609
(602) 586-3666 Fax 586-3667
Anne I. Woosley, Ph.D., Director
Description: A nonprofit archaeological research institution and museum specializing in the Native American cultures of the Americas. *Activities*: Archaeological field research in Greater Southwest; advanced seminar programs and internships; research library; anthropology museum and art gallery . Publishes monograph series on archaeology of the Southwest and Northern Mexico. Museum. Library . Semiannual meeting in May & November . Founded 1937.

ANTHROPOLOGY FILM
CENTER FOUNDATION
P.O. Box 493
Santa Fe, NM 87594
(505) 983-4127
Joan S. Williams, Director
Purpose: To further scholarship, research and practice in visual anthropology through consultation and research services, seminars, publications, teaching, equipment outfitting and specialized facilities. *Program*: Intensive 9 month filmmaking program stressing cultural factors in documentary film production. American Indian graduates: Larry Littlebird, Rain Parrish, George Burdeau, and Ron Sarracino, and others. *Publication*: Filmography for American Indian Education. Library-Archives. Founded 1971.

ANTHROPOLOGY RESOURCE CENTER
608 Highland Ave.
Falls Church, VA 22041
(703) 237-5376
Dr. Shelton H. Davis, Director
Membership: 8,000. Serves as a documentation & information center on land and economic issues involving Native-Americans and other indigenous peoples. *Publication*: Global Reporter, quarterly journal; books. Founded 1975.

ANTI-YUN WIYA SOCIETY
3601 Wenatchee Ave.
Bakersfield, CA 93306
(805) 871-2977
Dick Hutchinson, Contact
Purpose: To enlighten the public about American Indian af fairs, by providing information about the uniqueness of the dif ferent tribes and their cultures, and genealogical research; holding pow wows.

ARCHAEOLOGICAL CONSERVANCY
415 Orchard Dr.
Santa Fe, NM 87501
(505) 982-3278
Mark Michel, President
Membership: 7,500. People interested in preserving prehistoric and historic sites for interpretive or research purposes. *Purpose*: To acquire for permanent preservation the ruins of past American cultures, primarily those of American Indians. *Publication*: The Archaeological Conservancy NEW, quarterly newsletter. Founded 1979.

ARCHAEOLOGICAL
INSTITUTE OF AMERICA
675 Commonwealth Ave.
Boston, MA 02215
(617) 353-9361
Mark Meister, Executive Director
Membership: 11,000. Educational and scientific society of archaeologists and others interested in archaeological study and research. *Publication*: Archaeology, bimonthly; American Journal of Archaeology, quarterly; Archaeological Fieldwork Opportunities Bulletin, annual. Annual meeting. Founded 1879.

ARROW, INC.(AMERICANS FOR THE RES-
TITUTION AND RIGHTING OF OLD WRONGS)
1000 Connecticut Ave., N.W., Suite 1206
Washington, D.C. 20036
(202) 296-0685
Robert-LaFollette Bennett, President
Tom Colosimo, Executive Director
Membership: 2,200. *Purpose*: The betterment of American Indian health, education and justice. *Activities*: Undertakes constructive ef forts at the reservation level embracing direct aid, education, health and training; programs on alcohol, drug and child abuse; recruits physicians and RN's from the private sector to help fill shortages at Indian hospitals; conducts training for Indian court and law enforcement personnel; and of fers direct aid and scholarships. *Committees*: American Indian Court System Improvement; and, National American Indian Youth. *Publications*: Americans for the Restitution and Righting of Old Wrongs, annual; American Indian Courtline, periodic (in conjunction with National American Indian Court Clerks Association) includes Directory of Indian Court Clerks and Administrators. Also publishes Adolescence- A Tough Time for Indian Youth and Protecting Youth from Alcohol and Substance Abuse: What Can We Do? Annual meeting. Founded 1949.

ASSOCIATED COMMITTEE OF
FRIENDS ON INDIAN AFFAIRS
P.O. Box 2326
Richmond, IN 47375
(317) 962-9169
Harold Smuck, Director
Description: Missionary project of the Religious Society of Friends (Quakers.) Work is concentrated in Indian Centers in Oklahoma and Alabama. *Publication*: Indian Progress, 3/yr . Founded 1869.

ASSOCIATION FOR THE STUDY OF
AMERICAN INDIAN LITERATURES
Box 112, University of Richmond
Richmond, VA 23173
(804) 289-8311 Fax 289-8313
Robert M. Nelson, Contact
Membership: Primarily academic, and those in-

volved one way or another with the study of or creation of Native American literatures (oral as well as print, old time as well as contemporary . *Publication*: Studies in American Indian Literatures, quarterly scholarly journal focusing exclusively on American Indian literature.

ASSOCIATION OF AMERICAN INDIAN & ALASKA NATIVE SOCIAL WORKERS
1220 South Third Ave.
Portland, OR 97204
(503) 231-2641
Membership: Indian social workers concerned with the social welfare of Indian people. *Purpose*: To meet the unique needs of Indians according to their customs, traditions, life style and values. Founded 1970.

ASSOCIATION OF AMERICAN INDIAN LAW SCHOOLS
Center for the Study of
American Indian Law &Policy
University of Oklahoma-College of Law
300 W. Timberdell Rd.
Norman, OK 73019
(405) 325-4699
Prof. Rennard Strickland, President

ASSOCIATION OF AMERICAN INDIAN PHYSICIANS
1235 Sovereign Row, Suite C-7
Oklahoma City, OK 73108
(405) 946-7072 Fax 946-7651
Matthew Kauley, Executive Director
Membership: 235. Physicians (M.D. or D.O.) of 1/8 American Indian descent or more. *Purpose*: To encourage and recruit American Indians into the health professions; to provide a forum for the interchange of ideas and information of mutual interest between physicians; to make recommendations to government agencies regarding the health of American Indians and Alaska Natives; to enter into contracts with these agencies to provide consultation and other expert opinions regarding health care of American Indians and Alaska Natives. *Activities*: Seeks scholarship funds for Indian professional students; conducts seminars for students interested in health careers. *Publications*: Quarterly newsletter; American Indian Health Careers Handbook. Annual conference. Founded 1971.

ASSOCIATION OF NATIVE AMERICAN MEDICAL STUDENTS
1235 Sovereign Row, Suite C7
Oklahoma City, OK 73159
(913) 677-1468
Laurie McLemore, MD, Director
Publication: AIDS Regional Directory: Resources in Indian Country.

ASSOCIATION ON AMERICAN INDIAN AFFAIRS, INC.
245 Fifth Ave., Suite 1801
New York, NY 10016
(212) 689-8720 Fax 685-4692
Joy J. Hanley, President
Vacant, Executive Director
Pauline Pierro, Director of Development
Membership: 50,000. *Purpose*: To assist Native Americans and Alaska Native Communities in their efforts to achieve full economic, social, and civil equality, and to defend their rights. *Programs*: Conducts programs in Indian community development, health, education, legal defense, Indian Child Welfare, Religious Freedom, and public education. Aids Indian tribes in mo-

bilizing all available resources--federal, state and private--for a coordinated attack on the problems of poverty and injustice, and protects the constitutional and treaty rights of Native peoples, as well as their special aboriginal rights; the Adolph Van Pelt Special Fund for Indian Scholarships offers scholarships to undergraduate and graduate students in amounts ranging from $500 to $800; the Sequoyah Graduate Fellowship Program provides a one-year $1,500 unrestricted stipend paid in two equal installments; the Emergency Aid Scholarship Program provides grants of $50 to $300 to American Indian & Alaska Native students. Pu *blications*: Indian Affairs, quarterly newsletter; Tribal Bond Handbook; Arts & Crafts Resource Guide; Economic & Community Development Resource Guide for Native Americans; Sacred Lands & Religious Freedom; Proceedings of the National Sacred Sites Caucus. Founded 1922.

ATLATL
2303 N. Central Ave., Suite 104
Phoenix, AZ 85004
(602) 253-2731 Fax 256-6385
Margaret Wood, Executive Director
Description: A non-profit Native American arts service organization founded as a national advocate for Native American art. *Goals*: To heighten awareness of indigenous aesthetics and modes of expression; to create an informational network between Native American artists and arts; and provide training opportunities and economic development for Native American artists. *Activities*: Traveling Exhibit Service; technical assistance and consulting services; maintains resource files; slide packets of Native American arts; distributes audio-visual materials by and about Native Americans. Sponsors annual workshops; hosts a national conference for Native artists and administrators (Native Arts Network) ; and maintains resource files on Native artists and art organizations. *Publications*: Native Arts Update, quarterly newsletter; Directory of Native American Performing Artists; periodic special reports (Survey of State Arts Agency Support of Native Arts Programs); exhibit catalogs. Founded 1977.

BEAR TRIBE MEDICINE SOCIETY
P.O. Box 9167
Spokane, WA 99209
(509) 326-6561
Sun Bear, Founder
Wabun James, Executive Director
Description: An educational organization. *Purpose*: To teach people respect for the earth as the giver and sustainer of life. It uses the Native American ways of viewing the earth to help people find their connection with the earth so that people will begin to think about the ef fects of their actions on the earth. *Activities*: Educational workshops, lectures, tours, survival camps, visitor programs; operates a bookstore/ mail order business; of fers a barter or trade system for people who want to take their programs but cannot af ford them--they of fer their skills in return for the programs. *Publications*: The Path of Power; The Medicine Wheel Book; Buf falo Hearts; The Self-Reliance Book. Founded 1971.

BUFFALO BILL MEMORIAL ASSOCIATION
Buffalo Bill Historical Center
P.O. Box 1000
Cody, WY 82414
(307) 587-4771; (800) 533-3838
Peter H. Hassrick, Director

Purpose: The preservation and exhibition of Western Americana pertaining to Rocky Mountain and Northern Plains region. *Activities*: Operates the Buffalo Bill Museum, Whitney Gallery of Western Art, Cody Firearms Museum, and Plains Indian Museum. *Publication*: Quarterly newsletter. Library. Founded 1917.

BUREAU OF CATHOLIC INDIAN MISSIONS
2021 H St., N.W.
Washington, DC 20006
(202) 331-8542
Msgr. Paul A. Lenz, Executive Director
Purpose: The support of Catholic Indian missions, parishes, schools, centers, and activities; the advocacy for national legislation for the benefit of all American Indian tribes, pueblos, nations. *Activities*: Participation in the Tekakwitha Conference; testimony to congressional committees on legislation af fecting Indian groups; presentations on Indian issues to organizations; grants to Catholic Indian organizations through the diocese in which they are located. *Publication*: Monthly newsletter . Archives--located in the library at Marquette University , Milwaukee, Wisconsin. Founded 1874.

CENTER FOR AMERICAN ARCHAEOLOGY
P.O. Box 366
Kampsville, IL 62053
(618) 653-4316
Jane E. Buikstra, Director & President
Membership: 500. Institutions, professional and amateur archaeologists, students and others interested in archaeology in the U.S. *Activities*: Conducts archaeological research and disseminates the results; excavates, analyzes, and conserves archaeological sites and artifacts; sponsors tours, lectures, and educational and outreach programs; conducts teachers workshops; maintains speaker's bureau and library; and operated Kampsville Archaeological Museum. *Publications*: Quarterly newsletter; research series and technical reports; monographs; annual report. Founded 1958.

CENTER FOR INDIGENOUS STUDIES IN THE AMERICAS
1121 North 2nd St.
Phoenix, AZ 85004
(602) 253-4938
Cory Dale Breternitz, President
Established to promote archaeological and anthropological research of indigenous peoples and national history of the Americas. *Goal*: To contribute to a better and fuller knowledge of the archaeology, ethnology, and arts of the Native American. The focus of the organization is the anthropology of Native Americans. *Staff*: Michael S. Foster , Douglas R. Mitchell, Christine K. Robinson, Adrian S. White. *Activities*: Archaeological tours; research facilities (of fice and lab); publications. Library .

CENTER FOR THE STUDY OF AMERICAN INDIAN LAW & POLICY
University of Oklahoma-College of Law
300 W. Timberdell Rd.
Norman, OK 73072
(405) 325-4699
Prof. Rennard Strickland, Director
Publication: Handbook of Federal Indian Law .

CENTER FOR THE STUDY OF THE FIRST AMERICANS
Oregon State University
Corvallis, OR 97331

National Associations

47

(503) 737-4515
Robson Bonnichsen, PhD, Director

CENTER FOR SUPPORT & PROTECTION OF INDIAN RELIGIONS & INDIGENOUS TRADITIONS
National Congress of American Indians
900 Pennsylvania Ave., SE
Washington, DC 20003
(202) 546-9404 Fax 546-3741
John Lavelle, Director

CENTER OF AMERICAN INDIAN & MINORITY HEALTH
School of Medicine
10 University Dr.
Duluth, MN 55812-2487
(218) 726-7235 Fax 726-6235
Dr. Gerald Hill, Director
Purpose: To offer today's American Indian students a pathway to achieve a successful career in health or science related careers.

COALITION FOR INDIAN EDUCATION
8200 Mountain Rd., NE, Suite 203
Albuquerque, NM 871 10
(505) 262-2351
Loretta Metoxen, President
Dr. Lester Sandoval, V.P.
Dr. Dean Chavers, Editor
Membership: 600. Native Americans and others working to ensure that education, health, and other social welfare programs for Native Americans are funded adequately by the U.S. government. Conducts advocacy activities. *Publication*: Newsletter, 3/year. Annual conference. Founded 1987.

COMMISSION FOR MULTICULTURAL MINISTRIES OF ELCA
Native American Program
8765 W. Higgens Rd.
Chicago, IL 60631
(302) 380-2700
Rose Robinson, Director
Description: Consists of a nine member board of American Indians and Alaskan natives. A program of the Evangelical Lutheran Church in America. Acts as an advocate and consultant to Lutheran churches on behalf of the needs of Indian communities. Supports American Indian and Alaskan native rights. Supersedes the National Indian Lutheran Board (founded 1970). Biennial conference. Founded 1987.

CONCERNED AMERICAN INDIAN PARENTS
CUHCC Clinic
2016 16th Ave. S.
Minneapolis, MN 55404
(612) 627-4774
Fred Veileux, Contact
Description: Serves as a network for American Indian parents and others interested in abolishing symbols that are degrading to American Indians, such as the Redskins, Braves, Indians, etc. logos adopted by sports teams in the U.S. Seeks to make the future easier for native American children by educating the public about racial messages inherent in such symbols. Founded 1987.

CONTINENTAL CONFEDERATION OF ADOPTED INDIANS
960 Walhonding Ave.
Logan, OH 43138
(614) 385-7136
Leland L. Conner, Chief

Membership: 150. *Description*: Non-Indians who have been presented with honorary tribal chieftainship, an official Indian name, or recipients of any other Indian-oriented awards. Membership also open to blooded Indians. *Activities*: Maintains Indian Lore Hall of Fame; maintains speakers bureau; bestows annual National Catlin Peace Pipe Achievement Award. *Publication*: Sunlodge Buffalo Tales, quarterly newsletter. Research Library. Founded 1950.

CORPORATE RESOURCE CONSULTANTS
6233 Harrison, Box 22583
Kansas City, MO 64113
(816) 361-2059 Fax 361-21 15
Phyllis A. Meiners, President
Description: A full service consulting firm specializing in private sector fundraising consultation for Indian agencies and charities. *Activities*: Sponsors the Corporate Resource Center library which houses thousands of grant maker research profiles for sale to the public; private sector fundraising seminars & grant writing services designed for Native American tribes and organizations are also available; *Publications*: The National Directory of Philanthropy for Native Americans; Corporate & Foundation Fundraising Manual for Native Americans; and Church Philanthropy for Native Americans & Other Minorities.

COUNCIL FOR INDIAN EDUCATION
P.O. Box 31215
Billings, MT 59107
(406) 252-7451
Dr. Hap Gilliland, President
Membership: 100. *Purpose*: To improve and secure higher standards of education for American Indian children. *Activities*: Promotes quality children's literature on Indian culture; publishes books about American Indian life; conducts in-service education of teachers working on Indian reservations. Founded 1970.

COUNCIL FOR NATIVE AMERICAN INDIANS
280 Broadway, Suite 316
New York, NY 10007
(212) 732-0485
Walter S. James, Jr., Executive Director
Membership: 850. Individuals interested in the holistic philosophies and teachings of the earlier indigenous groups of North and Central America. Conducts research between the indigenous groups and the 16th century settlers in New York City and Long Island, NY. *Publications*: Newsletter, [periodic; Earth Walk and Four Directions for Peace and Medicine Lodge, both newsletters. Annual meeting. Founded 1974.

COUNCIL FOR TRIBAL EMPLOYMENT RIGHTS (CTER)
19655 1st Ave. S. #206
Seattle, WA 98148
(800) 631-9951; (206) 878-3000
(Southwest Regional Office)
301 W. Indian School Rd., Suite 126
Phoenix, Arizona 85013
(602) 234-1871
Purpose: To provide training and technical assistance to Indian tribes, national Indian organizations, Government agencies and private sector employers.

COUNCIL OF ENERGY RESOURCE TRIBES (CERT)
1999 Broadway, Suite 2600
Denver, CO 80202

(303) 297-2378 Fax 296-5690
A. David Lester, Executive Director
Membership: 57. American Indian Tribes owning energy resources. *Purpose*: To promote the general welfare of members through the protection, conservation, control and prudent management of their oil, coal, natural gas, uranium, and other resources. *Activities*: Provides on-site, technical assistance to Tribes in energy resource management; conducts programs to enhance Tribal planning and management capacities; sponsors workshops. Founded 1975.

COUNCIL ON TRIBAL EMPLOYMENT
918 16th St., NW, Suite 503
Washington, DC 20006

CRAZY HORSE MEMORIAL FOUNDATION
The Black Hills
Avenue of the Chiefs
Crazy Horse, SD 57730
(605) 673-4681
Ruth Ziolkowski, Chairperson
Anne Ziolkowski, Director
Purpose: To carve a mountain (Thunderhead Mountain) into the memorial statue of the Sioux Chief Crazy Horse, astride his pony, pointing to the lands of his people (563' high and 641' long.) Carved from Thunderhead Mountains in South Dakota by sculptor Korczak Ziolkowski, 1908-1982; and to build and maintain a university, museum, and medical center for Native Americans. *Activities*: Operates the Indian Museum of North America and Crazy Horse Memorial; offers scholarships to Native Americans. *Publications*: Crazy Horse Progress, quarterly newsletter; Korczak: Storyteller in Stone (biography); Crazy Horse and Korczak; and Korczak, Saga of Sitting Bull's Bones and Crazy Horse Memorial 40th Anniversary Booklet. Library. Annual meeting. Founded 1948.

CULTURAL SURVIVAL, INC.
215 First St.
Cambridge, MA 02142
(617) 621-3818 Fax 621-3814
Purpose: To defend the rights of indigenous people and ethnic minorities in the face of encounters with industrial society. *Publication*: Cultural Survival Quarterly; monthly bulletin. *Membership*: $45 donation receive Quarterly; $25, bulletin. Founded 1972.

DAKOTA WOMEN OF ALL RED NATIONS
c/o Lorelei DeCora, Chairperson
P.O. Box 423
Rosebud, SD 57570
Description: Grass roots organization of American Indian women seeking to advance the Native American movement. *Activities*: Establishes local chapters to work on issues of concern such as women's health, adoption and foster-care abuse, community education, legal and juvenile justice problems; supports leadership roles for American Indian women. Publishes reports on health problems of American Indian women. Annual conference. Founded 1978.
Formerly Women of All Red Nations.

EAGLE VISION EDUCATIONAL NETWORK
8657 Bronson Dr.
Granite Bay, CA 95746
(916) 791-7910
Cathy White Eagle, Director
Purpose: To present in an accurate manner the history, philosophy and concept of "Earth Stewardship of the American Indian Nations" for the

general public. *Activities*: Community cultural powwow; interactive presentations for elementary schools; lecture series; cultural scholarships and youth camps for American Indian children. Museum. Library. *Publications*: Quarterly newsletter; Matter of Fact Educational Sheets for the classroom; teacher in-service workbooks on accurate history and current issues. Founded 1992.

EARLY SITES RESEARCH SOCIETY
c/o James Whittall
Long Hill
Rowley, MA 01969
(508) 948-2410
　James P. Whittall, Director
Membership: 220. *Purpose*: To research and record unknown stonework, petroglyphs, artifacts, and other unexplained antiquities in the U.S. Activities: Archaeological Field School; research awards, and art/archaeological grant; video material. *Publications*: Newsletter; bulletin; other occasional publications. Museum. Library. Founded 1973.

THE EDUCATION FOR PARENTS OF INDIAN CHILDREN WITH SPECIAL NEEDS (EPICS) PROJECT
Southwest Communication Resources, Inc.
P.O. Box 788
Bernalillo, NM 87004
(800) 765-7320; (505) 867-3396
　Norman Segel, Executive Director
Purpose: To provide services to parents of children with special needs and professionals who serve them. EPICS conducts workshops and provides individual assistance to parents. The staff provides input to state and national advisory boards on issues affecting Indian families that have children with special needs. Library . Established 1985.

THE EDUCATIONAL FOUNDATION OF AMERICA
35 Church Lane
Westport, CT 06880
(203) 226-6498
　Diane M. Allison, Executive Director
Goal: The availability of quality education to all. *Activities*: Provides educational grants--aid for Native Americans. Ettinger Scholarships.

ERIC/CRESS CLEARINGHOUSE ON RURAL EDUCATION & SMALL SCHOOLS
Appalachia Educational Laboratory
P.O. Box 1348
Charleston, WV 25325
(800) 624-9120
　Craig B. Howley, Director
Purpose: To provide information about education to all who request it and to build a bibliographic database on the education of American Indians, Alaskan Natives, Mexican-Americans & migrants, and on rural education, outdoor education and small schools. *Activities*: Build database, provide free searches, publish free research summaries; develop ERIC microfiche collection. Library. Publication: ERIC/CRESS Bulletin; ERIC Digests; monographs. Founded 1966

THE FALMOUTH INSTITUTE, INC.
3918 Prosperity Ave., Suite 302
Fairfax, VA 22031
(703) 641-9100
　Richard Phelps, Director
Purpose: To provide quality training, technical assistance, and consulting to the American Indian and Alaska native communities. *Activities/programs*: Training programs - quarterly brochure. Scholarships: Awarded to an American Indian who is a member of a federally recognized tribe and is a high school senior accepted to an accredited college. *Publications*: American Indian Report, monthly subscription newsletter; Native American Law Digest, monthly; Indian Gaming Handbook; various course manuals. Library. Founded 1985.

FEDERAL BAR ASSOCIATION
1815 H St., NW, Suite 408
Washington, DC 20006
(202) 638-0252 Fax 775-0295
　Lawrence R. Baca, Chairperson
　John G. Blanche, III, Executive Staff Director Indian Law Section. Committees include: Indian Law Development, Public Education, Tribal Justice, and Legislation. *Purpose*: To participate as amicus in important Indian law cases, comment on developing Indian legislation, and offer expertise and advice to developing tribal court systems. *Activities*: Annual Indian Law Conference. The Conference is an aggregate of lawyers, law students, law professors, and federal, state, and tribal personnel - Indians and non-Indians - serving as speakers and listeners. It focuses on putting in perspective the court decisions and legislative action and analyzing how they impact the exercise of tribal sovereignty and other Indian rights. Also, offers a limited number of partial scholarships to individuals from law schools, public interest and other organizations unable to allocate funds for the full Conference registration fee. Library . Publications. Indian Law Section established in 1990.

FIRST AMERICANS NETWORK
Native American Television, Inc.
P.O. Box 8120
Minneapolis, MN 55408
(612) 825-9525
　Lynne C. Gray, President
Purpose: To serve the informational needs of Native communities and their neighbors. Activities: Produce weekly television programs: "First Americans Journal," "Indian News Network," "Sovereignty On Our Own Terms," "Native American Forum." Library & programs produced Archive. Founded 1990.

FIRST NATIONS ARTS
The Stores Bldg., 11917 Main St.
Fredericksburg, VA 22408
(703) 371-5615 Fax 371-3505
　Dennis R. Fox, Jr., Ass't Director
An organization which offers marketing assistance to all Native American artists within the U.S. Wholesale, mail order . Brochure and catalog available.

FIRST NATIONS DEVELOPMENT INSTITUTE
The Stores Bldg., 11917 Main St.
Fredericksburg, VA 22408
(703) 371-5615 Fax 371-3505
　B. Thomas Vigil, Chairperson
　Rebecca Adamson, President
　Sherry Salway Black, Vice President
　Michael E. Roberts, Director
Purpose: To assist American Indian tribes and communities obtain economic self-sufficiency; promote economic development and commercial enterprises of reservation-based Indian tribes through technical assistance and workshops. *Programs*: Six primary program components: The Eagle Staff which encapsulates the Field, Policy and Research components; The Oweesta Program, which re-lends capital to reservation-based micro-enterprise loan funds and revolving loan funds; The Tribal Commerce and Enterprise Management Program; and First Nations Arts, a national arts marketing program. Provides economic research and demographic data. The Eagle Staff Fund grants money for reservation-based economic development projects. Offers scholarships to American Indian students. *Publications*: The Business Alert, bimonthly newsletter; The Indian Giver, quarterly newsletter on Native American Philanthropy; and Bear Tracks, quarterly newsletter on Indian arts & crafts marketing. Annual board meeting. Founded 1980.

FOURTH WORLD CENTER FOR THE STUDY OF INDIGENOUS LAW & POLITICS
University of Colorado, Dept. of Political Science
Campus Box 190, P.O. Box 173364
Denver, CO 80217
(303) 556-2850
　Glenn T. Morris, Executive Director
Purpose: Seeks to promote peaceful change through dissemination of information and ideas. *Activities*: Develops academic courses, compiles and publishes literature and documentation, and presents a public forum and arbitration in the political arena.

FRIENDS COMMITTEE ON NATIONAL LEGISLATION
245 Second St., NE
Washington, DC 20010
(202) 547-6000
　Joe E. Volk, Executive Director
Description: A Quaker lobbying organization seeking to impact public policy and the Congress on issues of concern, among which are Native American rights including the upholding of treaty rights, the self-determination of Indian communities, and the Federal trusteeship responsibility. FCNL has specifically advocated, along with tribes and Indian organizations, on land and water rights. Federal Indian programs, health care, education, economic development, fishing rights, and self-determination. *Publication*: Indian Report, quarterly newsletter . Founded 1943.

FUTURES FOR CHILDREN
805 Tijeras, N.W.
Albuquerque, NM 87102
(505) 247-4700
　Ruth T. Frazier, President
Purpose: To promote American Indian community development through self-reliance. *Programs*: Community Self-Help Programs for Indian people. Currently working among Southwest American Indian tribes; maintains speakers bureau and children's services. Financial assistance to sponsored students from nine tribes in the Southwest. *Publication*: Semiannual newsletter. Library. Founded 1961.

GATHERING OF NATIONS
P.O. Box 75102, Station 14
Albuquerque, NM 87120-1269
(505) 836-2810
　Derek Mathews, Director
Purpose: To promote the traditions and culture of the American Indian, in the most positive manor possible; to dispel stereotypes created about the American Indian; to provide Indian people the opportunity to participate, practice,

teach, and exchange tribal traditions and costumes among all the tribes; and to enlighten the non-Indian about the history and culture of America's first inhabitants. *Activities*: Academic support for Indian students in college; development instructional materials on Indian history and culture for elementary and secondary schools; sponsors periodic song, dance, and Miss Indian World competitions; bestows awards. Annual Pow-Wow (North America's biggest powwow, the largest annual gathering of Native Americans in the world). *Publications*: Video Lesson Plans - Elementary & Secondary Schools. Founded 1984.

GENERAL COMMISSION
ON RELIGION & RACE
110 Maryland Ave., NE #48
Washington, DC 20002
(202) 547-4828
Ken Deere

GREAT COUNCIL OF U.S.
IMPROVED ORDER OF RED MEN
P.O. Box 683
Waco, TX 76703
(817) 756-1221
Robert E. Davis, National Secretary
Membership: 54,000. Goals: Freedom, friendship and charity. *Activities*: sponsors the education of approximately 200 American Indian children through Save the Children Federation; active in A.I.D., American Indians for Development. The Degree of Pocahontas--a degree of the Great Council for Red Men and their female relatives and friends. *Publications*: Red Men Magazine, 4/yr.; History of Improved Order of Red Men. Founded 1765.

GREENFIELD REVIEW PRESS
Two Middle Grove Rd., Box 308
Greenfield Center, NY 12833
(518) 584-1728
James Bruchac, Owner
Publishes books of folklore & multicultural literature, especially Native American works. Conducts various projects aimed at education and continuation of Native American culture. The North American Native Authors Project - a free 50-page catalog of books and cassettes by native American writers and performers. The NDAKINNA Wilderness Project - teaching of wilderness and cultural understanding from a Native American perspective, servicing northeastern U.S. & southeastern Canada. The Abenaki Heritage Day Tape - live recording of the 1993 Heritage Day performance. The Dawn Land Singers - a combination of traditional and contemporary music in both Abenaki and English, all with Native American themes.

GEORGE BIRD GRINNELL AMERICAN
INDIAN CHILDREN'S EDUCATION
FOUNDATION
Box 47H, RD #1
Dover Plains, NY 12522
Patricia Trudell Gordon, President
Schuyler M. Meyers, Jr., Secretary/Treasurer
Purpose: To support and assist organizations whose efforts improve educational opportunities and enhance the quality of life for American Indian children and their families.

HONOR, INC. (HONOR OUR
NEIGHBORS ORIGINS & RIGHTS)
2647 N. Stowell Ave.
Milwaukee, WI 53211

(414) 963-1324 Fax 963-0137
Dianne Wyss (Washington, DC satellite office)
Description: A treaty support group consisting of a coalition of church, citizen and Native American groups focusing on Native American issues. *Purpose*: To seek justice on critical concerns facing Native Americans today. *Activities*: Efforts include advocacy, action, education, and communication; operates Indian Nation Network (INN) and Electronic Bulletin Board (EBB), devoted entirely to issues affecting and relating to Indian country (through satellite office in Washington, DC (Dianne Wyss (202) 338-7851). Founded 1988.

INDIAN ARTS & CRAFTS ASSOCIATION
122 La Veta Dr., NE, Suite B
Albuquerque, NM 87108
(505) 265-9149
Helen Skredergard, Executive Director
Membership: 700. Indian crafts people and artists, museums, retailer and wholesalers, and collectors. *Purpose*: To promote, preserve, and protect the handmade creations of the Native American Indian. *Activities*: Semi-annual wholesale markets for retailers only; marketing information; Artist of the Year Prints. *Award*: Artist of the Year Award, annually, $1,500. *Publications*: Monthly newsletter; annual directory; brochures for point-of-purchase distribution. Semiannual wholesale trade shows. Small library. Founded 1974.

INDIAN ARTS & CRAFTS BOARD
Room 4004, U.S. Dept. of the Interior
Washington, D.C. 20240
(202) 343-2773
Geoffrey Stamm, Acting General Manager
Purpose: To promote the development of Indian arts and crafts. *Activities*: Provides business and personal professional advice, information, and promotion to Native-American artists and craftsmen and their organizations; operates three regional museums: Museum of the Plains Indian and Crafts Center, Browning, Montana; Sioux Indian Museum and Cultural Center, Rapid City, South Dakota; and, Southern Plains Indian Museum and Cultural Center, Anadarko, Oklahoma. *Publication*: Indian, Eskimo, Aleut Owned and Operated Arts Businesses Source Directory. Founded 1936.

INDIAN CHOIR
Bacone College
Muskogee, OK 74401
(918) 683-4581
Dr. Marlene Smith
Description: Music sung in several Indian languages as well as English. Tours around country.

INDIAN HEALTH SERVICE
U.S. Dept. of Health & Human Services
5600 Fishers Lane, Parklawn Bldg.
Rockville, MD 20857
(301) 443-1083
Michael H. Trujillo, M.D., Director
Goals: To raise the status of health of American Indians to the highest levels possible. *Programs*: Provides a full range of curative, preventive, and rehabilitative services for approximately 1.4 million eligible American Indians and Alaskan Natives. *Publication*: Trends in Indian Health, annual. Established 1955. See Indian Health Service section for names and locations of facilities across the U.S.

INDIAN HERITAGE COUNCIL
Henry St., Box 2302
Morristown, TN 37816
(615) 581-5714
Louis Hooban, CEO
Purpose: To promote and support Indian endeavors. Seeks a deeper understanding between Indians and non-Indians of the cultural, educational, spiritual, and historical aspects of Native Americans. *Activities*: Conducts research and educational programs; cultural events; sponsors charitable events; operates speaker's bureau; and sponsors the Annual National Pow Wow in October, in Townsend, Tennessee; monthly conference. *Publication*: quarterly newsletter. Library. Founded 1987.

INDIAN LAW RESOURCE CENTER
508 Stuart St., 3rd Floor
Helena MT 59601
(406) 449-2006 Fax 449-2031
Robert T. Coulter, Executive Director
District Office: 601 E St., S.E.
Washington, D.C. 20003
(202) 547-2800 Fax 547-2803
Curtis Berkey, Director
Purpose: To provide a legal, educational and research service for American Indians and other Indian tribes and nations and other indigenous peoples in the Western Hemisphere; seeks to enable Indian people to survive as distinct peoples with unique living cultures; to combat discrimination and injustice in the law; and protection of the environment. *Activities*: Engages in human rights advocacy on behalf of Indians at the U.N.; and offers free legal help to tribes. *Publications*: Indian Rights-Human Rights, quarterly newsletter; articles, reports, and reprints. Founded 1978.

INDIAN LIFE MINISTRIES
Intertribal Christian Communications
P.O. Box 32
Pembina, ND 58271
(204) 661-9333 Fax 661-3982
Tim Nielsen, General Director
Publication: Indian Life: Christian Media for Native North Americans.

INDIAN RIGHTS ASSOCIATION
c/o Janney Montgomery
1601 Market St.
Philadelphia, PA 19103
(215) 665-4523
Janney Montgomery, Executive Officer
Membership: 1,000. Individuals interested in protection of the legal and human rights of American Indians and promotion of their welfare. Maintains first-hand knowledge of conditions in Indian communities; keeps in touch with governmental Indian affairs; acts as a clearinghouse for appeals of all sorts for aid to Indians and for information on all aspects of Indian affairs. Sponsors prominent artists and speakers in programs introducing local communities to Native American cultures. Maintains archives and library. *Publications*: Indian Truth, bimonthly newsletter; also publishes pamphlets and American Indian Lands and Communities (map). Annual Meeting. Founded 1882.

INDIAN YOUTH OF AMERICA
P.O. Box 2786
609 Badgerow Bldg., 4th & Jackson
Sioux City, IA 51106
(800) 828-4492; (712) 276-0794
Patricia Trudell Gordon, Executive Director

Purpose: To improve the lives of Indian children; to inform families, social service agencies, and courts on the rights of Indian people under the Indian Child Welfare Act. *Program*: The American Indian Child Service Program--attempts to prevent the distressful effects brought on by the breakup of Indian families. *Facility*: Resource Center. *Publications*: Newsletter and brochures. 3/year Meetings; holds annual Substance Abuse and Indian Child Welfare Act Workshops. Founded 1978.

INDIANS FOR UNITED SOCIAL ACTION
3575 South Fox
Englewood, CO 80110
 (303) 762-6579
 Dr. Gregory W. Frazier, Executive Director
Purpose: To provide a viable vehicle for American Indian and Alaska Native communities and people; to carry out projects and programs designed to reduce unemployment in our communities; to serve as a catalyst to improve the social and economic condition of American Indian and Alaska Native communities; to create bridges through communication between the Native American community and other minority communities to the community at large; to discharge and distribute information to the community at large; to engage in projects for the betterment of Indian communities; and to provide information to the general public through the publication and distribution of printed materials. *Activities*: National Indian Writers Project; National Indian Business Information Center; Indian Consultant Provider; Speakers' Bureau; Indian/Alaska Technical Assistance Center assistance. Founded 1989.

INDIANS INTO MEDICINE
University of North Dakota School of Medicine
501 N. Columbia Rd.
Grand Forks, ND 58201
 (701) 777-3037 Fax 777-3277
 Gary D. Farris, Director
Purpose: To assist American Indian students preparing for health careers; provide summer academic enrichment sessions at the junior high, high school, college and pre-medical levels; provide academic year support for college and professional students; to increase the awareness of and interest in health care professions among young American Indians. *Services*: Referral and counseling services; tutoring; financial aid; minority medical education program (for college students); and Med Prep (for students preparing for medical school). The INMED director is a coordinator for Indian Health Service scholarships; provides short term emergency loans to participating students. *Publications*: Indians Into Medicine (recruitment book); Healthy Games and Teasers (activity book); Good Medicine for Our People (coloring book); Serpent, Staff and Drum (quarterly newsletter). Library-The INMED Learning Resource Center includes a variety of books and journals to assist students in their courses and in preparing for health careers entrance exams; distributes recruitment publications. Periodic educational conferences. Founded 1973.

INDIGENOUS COMMUNICATIONS ASSOCIATION
P.O. Box 748
Hogansburg, NY 13655
 (518) 358-4185
 Ray Cook, Executive Director
Description: Native American owned and/or operated radio stations in the U.S. *Purpose*: To help develop the Native American Public Radio Satellite Network in conjunction the Native American Public Broadcasting Consortium to provide programming to Native-controlled public radio stations.

INDIGENOUS ENVIRONMENTAL NETWORK
P.O. Box 485
Bemidji, MN 56601
 (218) 679-3959
 Tom Goldtooth

INDIGENOUS PEOPLE'S NETWORK
226 Blackman Hill Rd.
Berkshire, NY 13736
 (607) 657-8413
 John Mohawk, Co-Director
Membership: 75. Indigenous, human rights and energy-conscious organizations. *Purpose*: To provide communications services and information to people in remote areas that have little access to public media; to disseminate information on threats to the existence of indigenous people; seeks to raise the consciousness of people in North America and Western Europe. *Activities*: Documentation missions; indigenous refugee project; Radio Network which features taped interviews with indigenous leaders and community elders; maintains speakers bureau. *Publications*: Congressional Indian Report, weekly; IPN Weekly Report; Federal Register and Environmental Report, weekly; and Native Peoples in Struggle (book); emergency bulletins. Founded 1983.

INDIGENOUS WOMEN'S NETWORK
P.O. Box 174
Lake Elmo, MN 55042
 (612) 770-3861
 Winona LaDuke, President
Description: An activist organization formed to help grass roots Indian women in developing economic, social and political programs to address their needs. *Publication*: Indigenous Woman, semiannual.

INSTITUTE FOR THE DEVELOPMENT OF INDIAN LAW
Oklahoma City University-School of Law
2501 N. Blackwelder
Oklahoma City, OK 73106
 (405) 521-5188
 K. Kirke Kickingbird, Executive Director
Description: A research training center on federal Indian law, with special emphasis on Indian sovereignty, self-confidence and self-government, and clarification of historical and legal foundations of modern Indian rights. *Activities*: Research and analysis; training and technical assistance; dissemination of educational materials relating to federal Indian law, Indian Treaties, curriculum and community development. Conducts educational programs; holds seminars. *Publications*: American Indian Journal, quarterly; Publications and Materials List, semiannual; Annual Publications Catalog; The Indians and U.S. Constitution (book, brochure and videotape); distributed films, videotapes and filmstrips. Library. Founded 1971.

INSTITUTE FOR NATIVE AMERICAN DEVELOPMENT (INAD)
Native American Studies Dept.
1812 Las Lomas Dr., NE
University of New Mexico
Albuquerque, NM 87131
 (505) 277-3917
 Ted Jojola, Director
 Alison Freese, Information Specialist
Purpose: To advocate and develop research for and with Native Americans and their communities. *Activities*: Varies from year-to-year; sponsors lecture series, specialized seminars and conferences; regular course of offerings. Publications. Library. Founded in 1980.

INSTITUTE FOR NATIVE AMERICAN NEWS AND TV
P.O. Box 77
Fairfax, CA 94930
 (414) 459-0321; 721-3801
 Woableza La Batte, Director
Purpose: To network with regional media organizations and to train Native Americans to develop and produce their own tribal or community news programming for major TV networks. *Programs*: Career TV jobs bank; 2-4 week TV production and writing seminars. *Financial aid*: Will provide only tuition scholarships initially with plans to develop travel and accommodation scholarship funds. Library: will be coordinating with College of Marin's Media/Broadcast libraries and San Francisco State University's Communications/Broadcast libraries. Founded 1992.

INSTITUTE FOR THE STUDY OF NATURAL SYSTEMS
P.O. Box 637
Mill Valley, CA 94942
 (415) 383-5064
 James A. Swan, Ph.D., President
Purpose: To promote solutions to environmental problems from a cross-cultural perspective. *Activities*: Coordinates fundraising activities for Native Americans working to restore buffalo herds. The Buffalo Tour-a series of concerts to support bison restoration on Indian reservations-will begin in 1992 and will culminate in the first annual Buffalo Festival, which will be held in late July 1993, in the LaCrosse, Wisconsin area in cooperation with the first International Bison Conference; sponsors symposia; conducts research, charitable, and educational programs. *Publication*: In Harmony, bi-annual newsletter; books, Sacred Places, The Power of Place, and Nature As Teacher and Healer, all by James Swan. Founded 1987.

INSTITUTE FOR THE STUDY OF TRADITIONAL AMERICAN INDIAN ARTS
P.O. Box 66124
Portland, OR 97266
 (503) 233-8131
 John M. Gogol, President
Purpose: To promote traditional Native American arts through publications, lectures, and seminars. Conducts research. *Publication*: American Indian Basketry and Other Native Arts, quarterly magazine. Founded 1982.

INSTITUTE OF ALASKA NATIVE ARTS
P.O. Box 70769
Fairbanks, AK 99707
 (907) 456-7491/7406
Purpose: To provide opportunities for the advancement of the visual, literary, and performing arts of the Aleut, Indian, and Eskimo people of Alaska. *Activities*: Programs and services to assist Alaska Native artists achieve their artistic potential and encourage the study, interest, and understanding of Alaska Native art: exhibitions; workshops, symposia, and residences; festivals; scholarships, fellowships, and intern-

ships; produces resource materials; operates Information Center; and of fers technical assistance. Pub*lication*: Journal of Alaska Native Arts. bi-monthly. Founded 1976.

INSTITUTE OF AMERICAN INDIAN ARTS
P.O. Box 20007
Santa Fe, NM 87504
 (505) 988-6463 Fax 988-6446
 Kathryn Harris Tijerina, President
Description: A federally chartered private institution of fering learning opportunities in the arts and crafts to Native American youth (Indian, Eskimo and Aleut.) Emphasis is placed upon Indian traditions as the basis for creative expression in the fine arts. *Activities*: Sponsors Indian arts-oriented Junior College of fering Associate of Fine Arts degrees in various fields as well as seminars, and exhibition program, and traveling exhibits; maintains extensive library , museum, and biographical archives. *Publications*: Coyote on the Turtle's Back, annual; Faculty & Student Handbooks and School Catalog, annual; Spawning the Medicine River , annual. Founded 1962.

INSTITUTE OF EARLY AMERICAN HISTORY & CULTURE
P.O. Box 8781
Williamsburg, V A 23187
 (804) 221-1110
 Ronald Hof fman, Director
Purpose: To encourage study and research in American history before 1820, especially but not exclusively, through book and periodical publications, conferences, etc. *Programs*: Do not deal exclusively with American Indian history , but has been significantly represented in its recent activities; book publishing in conjunction with UNC Press. *Award*: Two-Year Postdoctoral Fellowships, annually--research topics on American Indian history , 1500-1820 are eligible. *Publications*: The William & Mary Quarterly . Library. Founded 1943.

INSTITUTE OF THE GREA T PLAINS
Museum of the Great Plains
P.O. Box 68
601 Ferris, Elmer Thomas Park
Lawton, OK 73502
 (405) 353-5675
 Steve Wilson, Director
Membership: 825. *Purpose*: To further the study and understanding of the history , ecology, anthropology, archaeology, and sociology of the Great Plains of North America. *Activities*: Conducts research; maintains the Museum of the Great Plains, the Great Plains Archives, and Library. *Publications*: Great Plains Journal, annual; irregular newsletter; books for sale. Founded 1961.

INTER-AMERICAN INDIAN INSTITUTE
Av. Insurgentes Sur 1690
Col. Florida
Mexico D.F. 01030 MEXICO
 (905) 660-0007/660-0132
 Dr. Oscar Arze Quintanilla, Director
Activities: Conducts development programs for Indian communities in the Americas; trains technical personnel; investigates culture of extinct Indian groups; provides information services. *Publications*: America Indigena; quarterly journal; books. Library. Founded 1940.

INTER-TRIBAL INDIAN CEREMONIAL ASSN.
P.O. Box 1
Church Rock, NM 87311
 (505) 863-3896
 Laurance D. Linford, Executive Director
Membership: 350. *Description*: Indian people, businessmen, dealers in Indian arts and crafts, and other individuals interested in the annual Inter-Tribal Indian Ceremonial. *Goals*: The preservation and promotion of American Indian culture, with an emphasis on the handmade arts and crafts. *Activities*: Annual Inter-Tribal Indian Ceremonial, a four day Indian exposition of dances, sports, crafts, rituals and a rodeo, held each August in Gallup, New Mexico; Summer Indian Dance Program; the Indian Country Guide Service; bestows awards; conducts specialized educational and children's services; maintains biographical archives; plans a Hall of Fame; publishes educational materials on Indian crafts for teachers; color slides of Indian ceremonials available. Closely associated with the Red Rock Museum, which houses the majority of Association's collections. *Scholarships*: Indian art scholarships to accredited colleges and universities beginning in 1995. *Publications*: Inter-Tribal America Magazine, quarterly newsletter; A Measure of Excellence, annual; "So You Want to Buy A Navajo Rug?", information pamphlet. Library. Annual meeting in Gallup, NM in November. Founded 1922.

INTERNATIONAL INDIAN TREATY COUNCIL
123 Townsend St. #575
San Francisco, CA 94107
 (415) 566-0251
 William A. Means, Executive Director
Description: Organization of 98 traditional Indian governments formed to draw attention to Indian problems and Indian rights, largely through the efforts of the American Indian Movement. Makes regular presentations to the U.N. Commission on Human Rights. Maintains a research and documentation center in South Dakota and an Information Center in New York City. *Publication*: Treaty Council News, quarterly . Annual conference. Founded 1974.

INTERNATIONAL NATIVE AMERICAN PERFORMERS
119-30 199th St.,
St. Albans, NY 11412
 (718) 276-5764
 Adolph Allwood, Executive Director

INTERTRIBAL AGRICULTURAL COUNCIL
100 North 27th St., Suite 500
Billings, MT 59101
 (406) 259-3525
 Greg Smitman, Executive Director
Purpose: To pursue and promote the conservation, development and use of Indian resources for the betterment of Indian people. *Activities*: Annual Indian Agriculture Symposium. *Publications*: National Indian Agriculture Profile; Indian Borrowers Guide to Agriculture Lending Programs of the FmHA and BIA; Indian Guide to Farmer Programs of the Soil Conservation Service, USDA. Established 1987.

INTERTRIBAL BISON COOPERA TIVE
520 Kansas City St., Suite 209
Rapid City, SD 57701
 (605) 394-9730 Fax 394-7742
 Fred DuBray, President
 Mark Heckert, Executive Director

Description: A consortium of 27 tribes. *Purpose*: To re-establish buf falo herds on Indian lands in a manner that promotes economic development, cultural enhancement, ecological restoration, and spiritual revitalization. *Member tribes*: Blackfeet, MT; Cheyenne River Sioux, SD; Choctaw Nation, OK; Confederated Salish & Kootenai, MT; Crow, MT; Crow Creek Sioux, SD; Ft. Sill Apache, OK; Gros V entre & Assiniboine, MT; Kalispel, W A; Lower Brule Sioux, SD; Modoc of OK; Nez Perce, ID; Northern Cheyenne, MT; Oglala Sioux, SD; Oneida of WI; Picuris Pueblo, NM; Round V alley, CA; Santee Sioux, NE; Shoshone-Bannock, ID; Sisseton-Wahpeton Dakota Nation, SD; Southern Ute, CO; Standing Rock Sioux, ND; Taos Pueblo, NM; Ute, UT; Winnebago of NE; WI W innebago; Yankton Sioux, SD. *Activities*: Education & training; Native American Bison Refuge; Yellowstone Project; Elementary Buf falo Curriculum; Public Education; Tribal Advocacy. Library. *Publications*: Quarterly newsletter; Annual Report. Established 1992.

INTERTRIBAL COUNCIL OF AMERICAN INDIANS, INC.
1765 Woodchuck Ave.
Pensacola, FL 32504
 (904) 484-9292
 William Irontail McCay , Executive Director
Purpose: To preserve the heritage, culture and crafts of all Indian people regardless of their original nation; to develop community health, educational and economic programs. *Activities*: Pow wows, corn roasts, lecture, multi-media events, scholarships, health programs. Museum. Library. Founded 1991.

INTERTRIBAL TIMBER COUNCIL
4370 NE Halsey St.
Portland, OR 97213
 (503) 282-4296
Purpose: To promote the conservation and development of tribal timber resources for the benefit of tribal members. Founded 1977.

THE JACOBSON FOUNDATION
609 Chautauqua
Norman, OK 73071
 (405) 329-3012
 Linda Sexton, Administrative Assistant
Description: A non-profit educational foundation concerned with the understanding and preservation of Native American arts and culture. The Jacobson House is a resource center for Native Americans and the study of Native American art and culture, as a gallery and hospitality center hosting varied events. Library .

KROEBER ANTHROPOLOGICAL SOCIETY
c/o University of California
Dept. of Anthropology
232 Kroeber Hall
Berkeley, CA 94720
 (415) 642-6932
Description: Professional anthropologists, students, interested laymen and institutional members (200 major universities and anthropological institutions. *Publications*: Papers, annual. Annual conference. Founded 1949.

LEONARD PELTIER DEFENSE COMMITTEE
P.O. Box 583
Lawrence, KS 66044
 (913) 842-5774
 Leonard Peltier , Director
 Lisa A. Faruolo, Co-Manager

Purpose: To obtain justice for Leonard Peltier and all political prisoners; equality under the law; sovereignty; economic, health care, and educational reform. *Activities*: Prisoner art program; pilot program with Dr. Jeffrey Timmons (Harvard) on economic reform on Pine Ridge; Dr. Stuart Selkin (NY) on health care reform on Rosebud; year round food and clothing drive. *Publication*: Spirit of Crazy Horse, bimonthly newspaper.

MARQUETTE LEAGUE FOR CATHOLIC INDIAN MISSIONS
1011 First Ave.
New York, NY 10022
(212) 371-1000
Rev. Thomas A. Modugno, Director
Purpose: To provide financial support for the material welfare of Catholic Indian Missions in the U.S. Founded 1904.

D'ARCY McNICKLE CENTER FOR THE HISTORY OF THE AMERICAN INDIAN
Newberry Library
60 West Walton St.
Chicago, IL 60610
(312) 943-9090
Frederick E. Hoxie, Director
Description: A research and education center on Indian history. See Library section for further information.

MIGIZI COMMUNICATIONS, INC.
3123 E. Lake St., Suite 200
Minneapolis, MN 55406
(612) 721-6631
Lori Mollenhof f, President
Laura Wittstock, Director
Purpose: To provide a national Indian news service. Goals: To provide the best balanced coverage of Indian news and information to the American Indian and general public, and to train Indian journalists. *Programs*: Radio production- - First Person Radio, Jackie Dionne, Producer- -half-hour program of American Indian news, information and public af fairs programming--the only weekly, nationally distributed American Indian radio program in the U.S.--goes out to over 50 stations in 23 states; produces the weekly local television public af fairs program, Madagimo, for WUSA-TV, Gary D. Fife, Producer/Host; produces live radio programs, video documentaries, and publications; also produces public af fairs announcements for Indian organizations and the City of Minneapolis. *Projects*: American Indian Women into Media, Gertrude Buckanaga, Director -- trains high school girls and women in journalism, radio engineering, computer literacy and other skills; Achievement Through Communications, W. Roger Buffalohead, Director -- after-school program for Indian high school students that introduces students to the expanding communications field; Media Access Project, Lesley Lilligren, Director -- encourages more Indian people to enter media careers; Media Curriculum Project, Laura Waterman Wittstock, Director -- to increase the reading skills of elementary students. *Publication*: Communicator. Library. Founded 1977.

MORNING STAR INSTITUTE
403 10th St., SE
Washington, DC 20003
(202) 547-5531 Fax 546-6724
Suzan Shown Harjo, Pres./Exec. Director
Purpose: To secure statutory protections for Native peoples' sacred sites and religious free-

dom. *Activities*: Conducts programs for environmental and youth concerns promoting Native images and voices in popular culture; provides small grants to support cultural work of others. Founded 1984.

MORRISON'S INDIAN RESEARCH
P.O. Box 41
Boaz, AL 35957
(205) 593-7336
Robert Morrison, President
Purpose: Provides individual and family heritage charts for Cherokees nationally, and some research is done for Choctaws, Chickasaws and Seminoles. The charge is $10 a name or $20 for family charts.

NATIONAL ADVISORY COUNCIL ON INDIAN EDUCATION (NACIE)
330 C St., SW, Room 4072
Washington, DC 20202
(202) 205-8353 Fax 205-8897
Purpose: To assist the Secretary of Education in carrying out responsibilities under Section 441(a) of the Indian Education Act (Title IV of P.L. 92-318), through advising Congress, the Secretary of Education, the Under Secretary of Education, and the Assistant Secretary of Elementary and Secondary Education with regard to education programs benefiting Indian children and adults. *Activities*: Full Council/Subcommittee meetings in the field on or near Indian reservations to receive public testimony regarding Title IV monies. *Publications*: Newsletters and annual reports. Library. Founded 1972.

NATIONAL AMERICAN INDIAN CATTLEMAN'S ASSOCIATION
c/o Tim Foster, President
1541 Foster Rd.
Toppenish, WA 98948
(509) 854-1329
Description: Indian cattle producers. *Purpose*: To carry on all activities necessary for the betterment of the Indian cattle industry; and to serve as clearinghouse for the accumulation and dissemination of information. *Publication*: Monthly newsletter; Yearbook. Founded 1974.

NATIONAL AMERICAN INDIAN COURT JUDGES ASSOCIATION
1000 Connecticut Ave., NW, Suite 1206
Washington, DC 20036
(202) 296-0685
Judge Elbridge Coochise, President
Membership: 360. Indian court judges. *Purpose*: To improve the American Indian court system throughout the U.S. by furthering knowledge and understanding of it, and maintaining its integrity in providing equal protection to all persons. *Activities*: Offers periodic training sessions on criminal law and family law/child welfare; conducts research and continuing education programs; annual meeting. *Publication*: Indian Courts Newsletter, quarterly. Annual meeting. Founded 1968.

NATIONAL AMERICAN INDIAN HOUSING COUNCIL
900 2nd St., NE, Suite 220
Washington, DC 20002
(202) 789-1754
Jacqueline L. Johnson, Chairperson
Ruth A. Jaure, Executive Director
Description: Nonprofit organization contracted by the U.S. Dept. of Housing & Urban Develop-

ment (HUD) to make recommendations for Indian housing and development. *Activities*: Conducts technical assistance and training programs for Indian housing authorities; conducts advocacy on behalf of Native Americans desiring better living conditions; convenes annual meeting. Facilities: Maintains Indian Housing Resource Center, the only one of its kind in the U.S. *Publications*: Quarterly newsletter, NAIHC Pathway News; and legislative updates, NAIHC Washington Update, published periodically; NAIHC Annual Report. Founded 1974.

NATIONAL ASSOCIATION FOR NATIVE AMERICAN CHILDREN OF ALCOHOLICS
1402 3rd Ave. #1110
Seattle, WA 98101
(206) 322-5601
Anna Whiting-Sorrell, President
Membership: 1,450. *Purpose*: To promote awareness of the needs of Native American children of alcoholics. *Activities*: Develops educational and support programs for Native American communities; conducts programs to educate local and national policy makers. *Publication*: Healing Our Hearts, quarterly newsletter. Annual conference. Founded 1988.

NATIONAL ASSOCIATION OF INDIAN LEGAL SERVICES
510 16th St., Suite 301
Oakland, CA 94612
(510) 835-0284
Michael Pfeffer, Executive Director
Mary Trimble Norris, Deputy Director

NATIONAL ASSOCIATION OF NATIVE AMERICAN DEAF
c/o Frank Bagley
1130 S.W. 43rd St.
Oklahoma City, OK 73109

NATIONAL CENTER FOR AMERICAN INDIAN & ALASKA NATIVE MENTAL HEALTH RESEARCH
Dept. of Psychiatry, UCHSC, C249
Denver, CO 80262
(303) 270-4600
Spero M. Manson, Director
Purpose: To increase knowledge and understanding of psychological dysfunction and psychotic illness among American Indian and Alaska natives. *Activities*: Research, training, information dissemination, and limited technical assistance. *Publications*: Special reports and annual journal.

NATIONAL CENTER FOR AMERICAN INDIAN ENTERPRISE DEVELOPMENT
953 E. Juanita Ave.
Mesa, AZ 85204
(800) 462-2433; (602) 831-7524
Steven L.A. Stallings, President
Purpose: To promote business and economic development among American Indians and tribes. Business consulting firm which provides management services and technical assistance; sponsors Management Institute-- training for Indian managers; workshops and seminars. *Publication*: Reporter, quarterly voice of American Indian business; Directory of American Indian Businesses, annual. Annual Indian Progress in Business Conference; annual awards banquet and periodic Reservation Economic Summit. Founded 1970. Formerly the United Indian Development Association.

NATIONAL CENTER FOR AMERICAN INDIAN MENTAL HEALTH RESEARCH
University of South Dakota
Julian Hall, Room 341
Vermillion, SD 57069

NATIONAL CONGRESS OF AMERICAN INDIANS
900 Pennsylvania Ave., SE
Washington, DC 20003
(202) 546-9404 Fax 546-3741
Gaiashkibos, President
JoAnne Chase, Executive Director
Mary Ann Antone, Treasurer
Membership: 2,200. Consists of individuals and 155 tribes representing 650,000 Native-Americans. *Purpose*: To protect Native American traditional cultural and religious rights; to conserve and develop Indian natural and human resources; to serve legislative interests of Indian tribes; to improve the health, education, and economic conditions of Native-Americans. *Activities*: Through its committees, the NCAI involves Executive Council and delegates in formulating positions in a wide variety of issues; conducts research on Indian problems as service to Indian tribes; bestows congressional awards; administers NCAI fund for educational and charitable purposes; legal aid program; maintains speakers bureau. *Committee*: Religious Rights Committee, Ray Apodaca, Chairperson. *Publications*: Sentinel, quarterly newsletter; bulletin, NCAI News; Tribal Government Textbook; annual conference report. Annual Congress. Founded 1944.

NATIONAL COUNCIL OF BUREAU OF INDIAN AFFAIRS EDUCATORS
8009 Mountain Rd. Place NE
Albuquerque, NM 871 10
(505) 266-6638
Fannie Bahe, Executive Of ficer
Membership: 150 professional educators employed in federal schools operated by the Bureau of Indian Affairs. *Purpose*: To meet the unique needs and interests of teachers within the BIA's Office of Indian Education Programs. Supports programs and projects that will improve the entire educational program in BIA schools. Maintains speakers' bureau. *Publication*: Smoke Signals, newsletter. Library. Annual meeting. Founded 1967.

NATIONAL COUNCIL FOR INDIAN BUSINESS
National Urban Indian Council
Box 100134, University Park Station
Denver, CO 80210

NATIONAL GEOGRAPHIC SOCIETY
17th & M Sts., N.W.
Washington, D.C. 20036
(202) 857-7000
Gilbert M. Grosvenor, President
Membership: 10,500,000. *Activities*: Sponsors expeditions and research in geography , archaeology, and ethnology of American Indians; disseminates knowledge through its magazine, maps, books, films, filmstrips, and information services for press, radio and network programs; maintains Explorer's Hall; produces Audiovisual materials for schools; awards gold medals for outstanding achievement. *Publications*: National Geographic, monthly magazine; National Geographic World, monthly; National Geographic Research, quarterly; National Geographic Traveler, quarterly. Library. Founded 1888.

NATIONAL INDIAN ATHLETIC ASSN.
Cass lake, MN 56633
(218) 335-8289
Henry S. Harper , Contact

NATIONAL INDIAN BILINGUAL CENTER
Community Service Bldg.
Arizona State University
Tempe, AZ 85287
(602) 965-5688
Provides training and support services to American Indian Title VII projects and limited English proficient students. There are four satellite centers located in Arizona, Oklahoma, New Mexico, and South Dakota.

NATIONAL INDIAN BUSINESS ASSN.
P.O. Box 8716, Station C
Albuquerque, NM 87108
(505) 299-9317

NATIONAL INDIAN BUSINESS COUNCIL
3575 South Fox
Englewood, CO 801 10
(303) 762-6579
Dr. Gregory W. Frazier, Executive Director
Purpose: To promote the development of American Indian and Alaska Native owned and operated businesses on and of f reservations. *Activities*: Market research; assists in mergers and acquisitions; training; management and technical assistance; information dissemination; job marketing and placement assistance; fund-raising; holds workshops and seminars; maintains a national computerized list of Indian businesses. *Publications*: Smoke Signals, newsletter; Directory of Indian/Alaska Native Owned and Operated Businesses, $75.00.

NATIONAL INDIAN CHILD WELFARE ASSN.
3611 SW Hood St., Suite 201
Portland, OR 97201
(503) 222-4044 Fax 222-4007
Gary W. Peterson, Board President
Terry L. Cross, Executive Director
Staff: Iona Hansel, Administrative Assistant; Masha Azure, Training Coordinator; Evelyn Bolme, Development Coordinator; David Simmons, Program Specialist. *Purpose*: To preserve and protect Indian children by promoting, safety, health, and a positive sense of Indian heritage. *Activities*: Maintains clearinghouse of over 3,000 articles, books, periodicals on Indian child welfare, mental health, and social work issues *Publications*: National Indian Child W el-fare Institute Directory (biennial); Heritage and Helping; Positive Indian Parenting; Cross Culture Skills; and Honoring the Children. Founded 1987.

NATIONAL INDIAN COUNCIL ON AGING
City Centre, Suite #510-W
6400 Uptown Blvd., NE
Albuquerque, NM 871 10
(505) 888-3302
Dave Baldridge, Executive Director
Eva Gardipe, Executive Secretary
Frieda Clark, DOL/SCSEP Program Director
Laura Graham, SSI Project Director
Membership: 300. *Goal*: To bring about improved comprehensive services to American Indian and Alaskan Native elders. *Purpose*: To act as a focal point for the articulation of the needs of Indian elderly; to provide meaningful part-time employment experience in community services; and to enroll elders into the SSI entitlement program. *Activities*: disseminates in-

formation on Indian aging programs; provides technical assistance and training to tribal governments and organizations in the development of their programs; conducts research on needs of Indian elderly . *Publication*: Elder Voices, monthly newsletter . Biennial conference. Founded 1976.

NATIONAL INDIAN COUNSELORS ASSN.
Washington State University
Wilson Hall, Room 104
Pullman, WA 99164
(509) 335-8676
Dora K. Thompson, President
Membership: 100. *Description*: Native American counselors concerned with improving the counseling of Native Americans. Promotes educational and counseling growth and leadership. *Activities*: Conducts networking among Native American counselors, and workshops related to counseling Native Americans. Maintains database. Founded 1980.

NATIONAL INDIAN EDUCATION ASSN.
1819 H St., N.W., Suite 800
Washington, DC 20006
(202) 835-3001
Lorena Zah-Bahe, President
Lorraine Edmo, Executive Director
Membership: 2,000. Advocates educational programs to improve the social and economic well-being of American Indians and Alaskan Native people. *Purpose*: To evaluate and improve the delivery of state and local educational services; and to intercede and establish liaison with state and federal agencies. *Activities*: Conducts an annual National Conference on American Indian Education and holds workshops in conjunction with the conferences; assesses and coordinates existing technical assistance sources. *Scholarship*: John Rouillard Scholarship. *Publications*: Indian Education Newsletter - 6/year); Contemporary Issues of the American Indian; and guides for establishing Indian libraries. Library . Founded 1970.

NATIONAL INDIAN GAMING ASSN.
904 Pennsylvania Ave., SE
Washington, DC 20003
(202) 546-7711
Rick Hill, Chairperson
S. Timothy Wapato, Executive Director
Activities: Holds Indian Gaming Enterprise and Management Law Seminars; and Annual Convention and Trade Show. Professional training for tribal casino management, staf f, and for tribal start up operations.

NATIONAL INDIAN GAMING & HOSPITALITY INSTITUTE
Menominee Indian Tribe of Wisconsin
P.O. Box 1210
Keshena, WI 54135
(715) 799-5600 Fax 799-1308
Dr. Verna Fowler , Contact
Purpose: To explore and address economic, social and cultural issues related to the development of gaming enterprises on American Indian reservations; to provide certificate and associate degree education programs designed to expand the trained workforce with expertise in Indian gaming nationally; to establish a central clearinghouse and library; and a new gaming product development center .

NATIONAL INDIAN HEALTH BOARD
P.O. Box 6940
Denver, CO 80206
(303) 270-5598
Linda Yardley, Contact
Purpose: To elevate the health status of American Indians and Alaska Natives equal to that of the rest of the U.S. population; to secure maximum tribal and consumer participation in the delivery of health services to Indian people; and, to enhance and promote education of Indian health issues. *Activities*: Provides technical assistance to members and Indian organizations; bestows awards; and sponsors annual health conference. *Publications*: NIHB Health Reporter, newsletter; health conference report. Library. Annual conference. Founded 1972.

NATIONAL INDIAN HOUSING IMPROVEMENT ASSOCIATION
P.O. Box 3481
Carson City, NV 89702
(702) 882-4448

NATIONAL INDIAN JUSTICE CENTER
#7 Fourth St., Suite 46
Petaluma, CA 94952
(707) 762-8113 Fax 762-7681
Joe Myers, Executive Director

NATIONAL INDIAN POLICY CENTER
The George Washington University
2101 F St., NW
Washington, DC 20052
(202) 994-1446 Fax 994-4404
Dr. Ronald Trosper, Director
Orna Weinroth, Information Specialist
Description: Established by congressional initiative to provide information services on a wide range of policy issues to over 500 U.S. American Indian tribes & Alaska Native villages. Operates under the direction of a planning committee comprised of tribal leaders, representatives of major Indian organizations and Indian policy experts. The center has seven task forces conducting research projects. *Purpose*: To commission Native American research and policy analysis; to serve as information clearinghouse for Native Americans;to sponsor seminars & conferences on issues of concern to American Indians & Alaska Natives. *Activities*: Commissions reports & projects; conducts seminars & conferences; provides internships. Library, online clearinghouse. *Publication*: Bibliography of Demonstration Research and Policy Papers.

NATIONAL INDIAN SOCIAL WORKERS ASSN
P.O. Box 27463
Albuquerque, NM 87125
Mary Kihega, Sec.-Treas.
Membership: 200. *Purpose*: To develop, support, and promote social service programs which adequately meet the needs of American Indian people and that are consistent with the desires, customs, and lifestyle and traditions of Indians. *Activities*: Provides training and technical assistance to tribal and nontribal organizations; holds seminars on Indian child welfare; conducts survey research; sponsors competitions; maintains speakers' bureau. Annual conference; regional organizations. *Publication*: Quarterly newsletter. Founded 1970.

NATIONAL INDIAN TRAINING & RESEARCH CENTER
2121 S. Mill Ave., Suite 216
Tempe, AZ 85282

(602) 967-9484
Francis McKinley, Executive Director
Purpose: To involve American Indians in leadership and professional roles in training and research projects for the social and economic betterment of Indian people; to orient and train professionals working with American Indians. *Activities*: Conduct training programs to educate; sponsors research and development to increase information and knowledge about American Indians. *Publication*: Introducing Public School Finance to Native Americans; Indian Education Update, newsletter. Library. Founded 1969.

NATIONAL INDIAN YOUTH COUNCIL
318 Elm St., S.E.
Albuquerque, NM 87102
(505) 247-2251 Fax 247-4251
Norman Ration, President-Board
Kenneth Tsosie, Executive Director
Jim Anaya, Staff Attorney
Membership: 45,000. *Purpose*: To provide young Indian people with a working knowledge of serving and understanding their tribal communities and to implement educational resources through research, training and planning on local, regional and national levels. *Activities*: Operates Indian health, education, and employment programs; annual meeting. *Publication*: Americans Before Columbus, bimonthly tabloid; Indian Voter Survey Reports, periodic describing political attitudes of Native Americans living on reservations. Annual meeting in June. Founded 1961.

NATIONAL LAWYERS GUILD
55 Ave. of the Americas, 3rd Floor
New York, NY 10013
(212) 260-1360
Barbara Dudley, Executive Director
Purpose: Dedicated to seeking economic justice, social equality, and the right to political dissent. Committee on Native American Struggles. *Publication*: Monthly Bulletin; Referral Directory, biennial. Annual meeting.

NATIONAL LEGAL AID & DEFENDER ASSN.
1625 K St., NW 8th Floor
Washington, DC 20006
(202) 452-0620
Clinton Lyons, Executive Director
Membership: 2,750. *Purpose*: To provide technical and management assistance to local organizations offering services to poor persons in civil or criminal cases. *Activities*: Clearinghouse for information; sponsors research and educational training programs; presents awards. *Committee*: Native American Committee. *Publications*: Cornerstone, 10/yr.; Directory of Legal Aid and Defender Offices in the U.S., semiannual. Founded 1911.

NATIONAL MARROW DONOR PROGRAM
7910 Woodmont Ave.
Bethesda, MD 20814
(800) 627-7693
Carol Field, Director-
Native American Recruitment
Purpose: To interest Native American people in joining the National Registry of Marrow Donors so that Native American patients with Leukemia can locate a matching marrow donor for a life saving marrow transfusion. *Activities*: Offers simple, free blood test to Native people interested in joining the National Registry. Founded 1987.

NATIONAL NATIVE AMERICAN AIDS PREVENTION CENTER
3515 Grand Ave. #100
Oakland, CA 941600
(510) 444-2051 Fax 444-1593
Ronald Rowell, MPH, Director
Dana Ridling, Chairperson
Purpose: To stop the spread of HIV and related diseases among American Indians, Alaska Natives, and Native Hawaiians by improving their health status through empowerment and self determination. *Special programs*: Conduct outreach to Native organizations and communities; trains community-based HIV educators; and provides technical assistance in community organizing. *Activities*: Operates a toll-free Native American AIDS Information Hot Line: (800) 283-2437 (Alaska AIDS Hot Line (800) 478-2437); operates a national clearinghouse for Native-specific HIV/AIDS information; provides ongoing information services; and develops curricula for target populations. Division of Client Services, 205 West 8th St., Suite 103, Lawrence, KS 66044 (913) 865-4297 Fax 842-0145; National Indian AIDS Media Consortium (Native-owned newspapers, radio stations, and television programs), 1433 E. Franklin Ave., Suite 3A, Minneapolis, MN 55404 (612) 872-8860 Fax 872-8864; Ahalaya HIV Case Management Project, 1200 N. Walker, Suite 605, Oklahoma City, OK 73101 (405) 235-3701 Fax 235-1801. *Publications*: Seasons, quarterly magazine; Raven's Guide, resource guide; Policy Guidelines; Speaker's directory; books and videos. Library. Established 1987.

NATIONAL NATIVE AMERICAN AIDS TASK FORCE
c/o Indian Health Council
P.O. Box 406
Pauma Valley, CA 92061
(619) 749-1410
Tom Lidot, Executive Director

NATIONAL NATIVE AMERICAN ANCESTRAL RELIGION
Route 2, Box 108
Maxton, NC 28364
(919) 844-3827

NATIONAL NATIVE AMERICAN CHAMBER OF COMMERCE
225 Valencia St.
San Francisco, CA 94103
Chockie Cottier, Contact
Purpose: To support the development of regional and local chambers of commerce for Native Americans. *Activities*: Promotes business related education for Native American youth and businesspeople. Founded 1985.

NATIONAL NATIVE AMERICAN CO-OP & INDIAN INFORMATION & TRADE CENTER
P.O. Box 1000
San Carlos, AZ 85550
(602) 622-4900
Fred Synder, Director-Consultant
Carole J. Garcia, International Rep.
Membership: 2,700+ American Indian artisans representing over 300 tribes. *Purpose*: the preservation of Native American contemporary and traditional crafts, culture, and education through involvement in Indian cultural programs, including dance, traditional food, fashion shows, and performers. *Activities*: Multi-faceted marketing, barter and trade; information and consultant services; sponsors crafts and cultural demon-

strations; conducts powwows, cultural festivals, information services; developing North American Indian Trade and Information Center; operated speaker's bureau; American Indian Crafts Cooperative; American Indian Chamber of Commerce. *Traveling Exhibits* : Basketry, beadwork/ quillwork; Indian doll collection; maintains museum, biographical archives, and 30,000 volume library. *Scholarships* : Travel expenses to artists exhibiting at events, pow wows, and celebrations. *Publication* : Native American Directory -- Alaska, Canada, U.S.; Pow W ow on the Red Road; quarterly Calendar of Events. Library . Founded 1969.

NATIONAL NATIVE AMERICAN LAW STUDENTS ASSOCIATION
American Indian Law Center
P.O. Box 4456, Station A
1117 Stanford, N.E.
Albuquerque, NM 87196
(505) 277-5462
Sally Hernandez

NATIONAL NATIVE AMERICAN PURCHASING ASSOCIATION
P.O. Box 309
Willamina, OR 97396
(503) 876-3307 Fax 876-2123
Sharon Jacox, Executive Director

NATIONAL TRIBAL CHAIRMAN'S ASSN.
Washington, DC 20006
(202) 293-0031
Raymond Field, Executive Director
Membership : 190. *Description* : Consists of federally recognized tribes and their leaders. *Purpose* : To provide a united front for elected Indian leaders to consult with government of ficials; to assist Indian groups in obtaining full rights from federal agencies; to monitor federal programs that af fect Indians. *Publication* : List of Tribes and Tribal Leaders, quarterly; Newsbrief, periodic. Founded 1971.

NATIONAL TRIBAL COURT CLERKS ASSN.
1000 Connecticut Ave., NW, Suite 1206
Washington, DC 20036
(202) 296-0685
Janet Waupoose, President
Margaret Houten & Eliza Martinez, V .P.s
Tom Colosimo, Treasurer; Diana Muniz, Sec.
Membership : 300. *Description* : Consists of American Indian court clerks and administrators. *Purpose* : To improve the ef ficiency and provide for the upgrading of the American Indian court system; to provide support services for all court officers at a professional level; and to improve the integrity and capability of the court system; and to elevate the status of court clerks and administrators. *Programs* : Training and continuing education programs. *Publication* : Courtline, semiannual newsletter; reports, training materials for in-house programs. Founded 1980.

NATIONAL TRIBAL ENVIRONMENTAL OFFICE
Eastern Band of Cherokee Indians
P.O. Box 455
Cherokee, NC 28719
(800) 451-2764; (704) 497-3814 Fax 497-3615
Activities : Sponsors the National Tribal Conference on Environmental Management held in Cherokee, NC in May .

NATIONAL URBAN INDIAN COUNCIL
100068 University Park Station
Denver, CO 80210
(303) 750-2695
Doris R. Nye, President
Membership : 500. *Purpose* : To promote the social and economic self-suf ficiency of off-reservation American Indians and Alaska Natives. *Activities* : Community economic development; housing, employment and training; health, education, and advocacy for of f-reservation Indian people. *Publications* : quarterly, American Indian Review; monthly bulletin; and Source Document of Urban American Indians and Alaska Natives. Annual conference. Library . Founded 1975.

NATIONS MINISTRIES
P.O. Box 70
Honobia, OK 74549
(918) 755-4570
Riley Donica, Director
Description : Consists of individuals and churches conducting evangelical Christian ministry on American Indian reservations in the U.S. *Activities* : Bestows awards; maintains speaker's bureau; Chaplains service - Indian Hospital, Talihina, OK; adult and youth camps; academic scholarships. *Publication* : The Nations News, bimonthly. Annual meeting. Founded 1983.

NATIVE AMERICAN BAR ASSOCIATION
Native American Legal Resource Center
Oklahoma City University Law School
2501 N. Blackwelder
Oklahoma City, OK 73106
(405) 521-5277
Connie Hart, President

NATIVE AMERICAN CENTER FOR THE LIVING ARTS
25 Rainbow Blvd. S.
Niagara Falls, NY 14303
(716) 284-2427
Elwood Green, Director
Purpose : Committed to the self-determination and cultural survival of the Native American people. *Programs* : Arts, culture, education and social awareness. Internship programs. *Publication* : Turtle Quarterly magazine. Founded 1970.

NATIVE AMERICAN CENTER OF EXCELLENCE CONSORTIUM
College of Medicine, P .O. Box 26901
Oklahoma City, OK 73190
(405) 271-2316
Philip A. McHale, PhD
Purpose: To recruit and retain Native Americans to medical and dental school; recruit Native American faculty in medicine and dentistry; stimulate research on Native American health issues. Activities: MCAT Preparation; enrichment programs; faculty development programs; tutoring programs; extensive recruitment. Library. Founded 1992.

NATIVE AMERICAN COMMUNITY BOARD
P.O. Box 572
Lake Andes, SD 57356
(605) 487-7072 Fax 487-7964
Charon Asetoyer, Director
Description : A non-membership organization that works toward the educational, social, and economic advancement of American Indians. *Purpose* : Concerned with treaty and environmental issues involving Native Americans. Ac-

tivities: Maintains Native American Women Health Education Resource Center , which provides self-help programs and workshops on issues such as fetal alcohol syndrome, AIDS awareness, family planning, child & domestic abuse. Conducts adult education classes, employment services; scholarship program; conducts charitable programs; of fers children's services; maintains speaker's bureau and placement service. *Publication* : Wicozanni-W owapi, quarterly newsletter; also publishes brochures and pamphlets. Founded 1984.

NATIVE AMERICAN CONSULTANTS
725 2nd St., NE
Washington, DC 20002
Louis R. Bruce, President

NATIVE AMERICAN DANCE TROOPS
Chickahominy Red Men Dancers
P.O. Box 473
Providence Forge, V A 23140
(804) 829-2152
Preston Adkins, Coordinator

NATIVE AMERICAN FISH & WILDLIFE SOCIETY
750 Burbank St.
Boulder, CO 80020
(303) 466-1725
Patricia K. Manor , Administrator
Special program : Indian Youth Practicum - to encourage Indian youth to pursue careers in the fish and wildlife fields.

NATIVE AMERICAN INDIAN MEDIA CORP.
P.O. Box 59
Strawberry Plains, TN 37871
(615) 933-6246
Frank Eastes, Jr., Executive Director
Purpose : To develop American Indian art and artists, and to develop Indian involvement in the media. *Programs* : Provides low-cost access to professional quality film and video equipment to independent filmmakers; provides equipment access grants; develops and sponsors Indian art projects. Maintains film, video and audio archives. Founded 1981.

NATIVE AMERICAN INDIANS IN MEDIA
P.O. Box 16115, UT Station
Knoxville, TN 37916
Dr. MaCaki Peshewa, Director

NATIVE AMERICAN INTERNATIONAL CAUCUS
United Methodist Church
3821 Madison Ave.
Fayetteville, NC 28304
(919) 424-0894
Dr. Sam Wynn, Executive Director
Purpose : To provide a liaison between the Church and about 150 Native American congregations.

NATIVE AMERICAN JOURNALISTS ASSN.
1433 E. Franklin Ave., Suite 11
Minneapolis, MN 55404-2135
(612) 874-8833 Fax 874-9007
Karen Lincoln Michel, President
Gordon Regguinti, Executive Director
Theresa Lumbar & Robyn Dudley , Staff
Purpose : To support and increase the involvement of Native Americans in the media. *Programs* : Provides educational and training for 350 plus Native communicators at its annual con-

ference; recruits more Native Americans into the field of journalism through its summer high school workshops, college scholarships, career days and job referral service. Scholarships available for qualified American Indian journalist students. *Publication*: Medium Rare, bi-monthly newsletter. Established 1984.

NATIVE AMERICAN LANGUAGE INSTITUTE
P.O. Box 963
Choctaw, OK 73020
(405) 769-4650/6125
Patricia Locke, Director

NATIVE AMERICAN LAW STUDENTS ASSN.
American Indian Law Center
P.O. Box 4456, Station A
1117 Stanford, N.E.
Albuquerque, NM 87196
(505) 277-5462
Ronald Eagleye Johnny, President
Indian Law Clinic
University of Montana Law School
Missoula, MT 59806
(406) 243-6480
Magel Bird, President
Membership: 160. American Indian and Native Alaskan law students. *Purpose*: To promote unity, communication and cooperation among Indian law students. *Programs*: Financial aid, and summer employment opportunities; research projects and curriculum development in Indian law; maintains speakers bureau of students in the field of Indian law. *Publication*: Newsletter. Annual meeting. Founded 1970.

NATIVE AMERICAN LEGAL RESOURCE CENTER
Oklahoma City University-School of Law
2501 Blackwelder
Oklahoma City, OK 73106
(405) 521-5188
Kirke Kickingbird, Director

NATIVE AMERICAN POLICY NETWORK
Barry University
11300 2nd Ave., N.E.
Miami, FL 33161
(305) 899-3473
Michael E. Melody, Director
Membership: 400. Consists of social scientists, policy makers and Native American leaders. *Purpose*: To facilitate and to increase research in all areas of Native American policy as well as the policy-making process. Organizes panels and seminars at the annual conventions of the American Political Science Association and Western Social Science Association. *Publications*: Newsletter, 3/year; periodic Directory. Annual meeting. Founded 1980.

NATIVE AMERICAN PUBLIC BROADCASTING CONSORTIUM
P.O. Box 83111
Lincoln, NE 68501
(402) 472-3522 Fax 472-1785
Frank Blythe, Executive Director
Membership: 70. *Purpose*: To encourage the creation, production, promotion and distribution of quality programming by, for and about Native-Americans. *Activities*: New programs are screened and cataloged on a continuous basis from all available sources; bestows awards; makes available a job reference file listing qualified Native Americans in the media; sponsors workshops. Developed the Native American Public Radio Satellite Network in conjunction

with the Indigenous Communications Association. *Publications*: Newsletter, bimonthly; Library Catalog (all programs); Native American Ascertainment, three reports on serving Native American broadcast needs. Library of videotapes, films and radio programs. Founded 1977.

NATIVE AMERICAN RELIGIOUS & HERITAGE SOCIETY
P.O. Box 4000 Complex 'B' Chapel
California State Prison - Solano
Vacaville, CA 95696-4000

NATIVE AMERICAN RESEARCH INFORMATION SERVICE
American Indian Institute
555 Constitution Ave.
Norman, OK 73037
(405) 325-4127

NATIVE AMERICAN RIGHTS FUND
1506 Broadway
Boulder, CO 80302
(303) 447-8760 Fax 443-7776
Richard Hayward, Chairperson
John E. Echohawk, Executive Director
Offices: 1712 N St., NW, Washington, DC 20036 (202) 785-4166; 310 K St., Suite 708, Anchorage, Alaska 99501 (907) 276-0680. *Purpose*: The protection of Indian rights; the preservation of tribal existence; the protection of tribal natural resources; the promotion of human rights; the accountability of governments to Native-Americans; and the development of Indian law. *Activities*: Serves as National Indian Law Support Center; maintains the National Indian Law Library. *Publications*: NARF Legal Review, quarterly; Indian Law Support Center Reporter, monthly; monthly newsletter; National Indian Law Library Catalogue, supplemented quarterly; indexes to Indian Claims Commission Decisions; annual report. Semiannual board of directors' meeting in May and November. Founded 1970.

NATIVE AMERICAN SCHOLARSHIP FUND
8200 Mountain Rd. NE Suite 203
Albuquerque, NM 871 10
(505) 262-2351
Dr. Dean Chavers, President
Purpose: To raise funds to provide Native American students with merit scholarships for university study at the undergraduate and graduate levels. *Activities*: Conducts educational programs. *Publication*: Brochures. Library. Founded 1987.

NATIVE AMERICAN TELEVISION, INC.
P.O. Box 455
St. Cloud, MN 56302-0455
(800) 848-41 17; (612) 252-4190
Martha Crow, President; Lynn C. Gray, V.P.
Description: Dedicated to the design, production, and broadcast of television programming for and about Native Americans. Produces a weekly, half-hour news and information television program called "First Americans Update," Tom Beaver, Host, Lynn C. Gray, Producer.

NATIVE AMERICANS FOR A CLEAN ENVIRONMENT
P.O. Box 1671
Tahlequah, OK 74465
(918) 458-4322 Fax 458-0322
Lance Hughes, Director
Membership: 500. *Description*: Individuals devoted to halting contamination of the environ-

ment by nuclear waste. *Purpose*: To promote forms of energy production that are safer than nuclear power; to educate the public. *Activities*: Speakers for lectures on the nuclear industry, food irradiation, and uranium mining. *Publications*: NACE News, quarterly newsletter; also publishes Raffinate (brochure). Founded 1985.

NATIVE COMMUNICATIONS GROUP
P.O. Box 83111
Lincoln, NE 68501
(402) 472-3522
Frank Blythe & Laverne Sheppard, Co-Chairs
Members include: Native American Public Broadcasting Consortium, Native American Journalists Association, Migizi Communications, Native Hawaiian/Pacific Island Media Group, Indigenous Communications Association, Alaskan Public Radio Network, Institute of American Indian Art, and the Educational Native American Network. *Purpose*: To propose policy; provide effective influence and advocacy through a unified effort by Native communication groups; orient and educate Native communities to the value of effective communications; coordinate training and educational capabilities; identify resources and methodologies; and promote Native ownership and development of communications industries.

NATIVE CULTURE & ECOLOGY FOUNDATION
c/o Mr. Alderson
R.R. 1, Box 31 17
Havana, FL 32333-9801

NATIVE YOUTH ALLIANCE
Washington Peace Center
1832 Park Rd., NW
Washington, DC 20010
(202) 328-9060
Nathan Phillips, Executive Director
Purpose: To help Native children whose parents are in the prison system.

NAVAJO ARTS & CRAFTS GUILD
Drawer A
Window Rock, AZ 86515
Purpose: The rehabilitation and better utilization of the resources of the Navajo and Hopi Tribes and reservations as (they) relate to the members of the Navajo Tribe. *Activities*: Maintains retail outlets; operates a mail order business and a wholesale business; crafts exhibit held at the Heard Museum. Founded 1941.

NORTH AMERICAN INDIAN ASSOCIATION
22720 Plymouth Rd.
Detroit, MI 48239
(313) 535-2966
Irene Lowry, Director
Membership: 300. At least one-quarter North American Indian blood. *Purpose*: To promote economic development and self-sufficiency for American Indian people through human services. *Activities*: Employment and educational services; senior center offers nutrition, social and educational services; Indian child welfare provides protective services for Indian children and families; Arts and Crafts Gallery business. Operates Native American Gallery; speaker's bureau. Russ Wright Scholarship Fund--assists students with the expense of educational supplies. *Publication*: Native Sun, monthly newsletter. Library. Annual meeting and powwow. Founded 1940.

NORTH AMERICAN INDIAN MISSION (NAIM) MINISTRIES
P.O. Box 151
Point Roberts, WA 98281
 (604) 946-1227
 William Lottis, General Director
Membership: 110. *Purpose*: To establish indigenous Native American churches in urban centers and on reservations. *Activities/Programs*: 8 week summer program for college students who live on reserve during the program; Wilderness Trails program, similar to Outward Bound; conducts economic, educational, social, and rehabilitation programs; offers alcohol treatment, sexual abuse and AIDS seminars, and cross-cultural communication seminars. *Publications*: Dear Team, monthly; Intercessor, bimonthly; Infocus, quarterly. Library. Annual meeting. Founded 1949.

NORTH AMERICAN INDIAN TRADE & INFORMATION CENTER
2830 S. Thrasher
Tucson, AZ 85713
 (602) 622-4900
A division of National Native American Cooperative in San Carlos, AZ.

NORTH AMERICAN INDIAN WOMEN'S ASSOCIATION
P.O. Box 805
Eagle Butte, SD 57625
 (605) 964-2136
 Marcella LeBau, President
Membership: Women 18 years old and over who are members of federally recognized tribes. *Purpose*: To promote inter-tribal communications, awareness of the Native American culture, betterment of family life, health and education. Brochure. Annual meeting. Founded 1970.

ORBIS ASSOCIATES
1411 K St., NW, Suite 700
Washington, DC 20005
 (202) 628-4444
 Gwen Shunatona, Executive Director
Description: An American Indian controlled and managed non-profit corporation. *Purpose*: To provide expertise in training and consulting for education, research, program administration and evaluation. *Activities*: Training and technical assistance in a variety of management, evaluation and education related areas; needs assessment design and implementation; data collection and analysis; classroom instructional strategies; youth development; holistic counseling; and primary prevention; culture-based curriculum development; research and data analysis of community needs and services. Library - contains culture-based curriculum materials for Grades K-12. Founded 1982.

ORDER OF THE INDIAN WARS
P.O. Box 7401
Little Rock, AR 72217
 (501) 225-3996
 Jerry L. Russell, National Chairman
Membership: 600. Professionals and informal historians interested in the study of the frontier conflicts between the Indians and the white man, and among Indian tribes during the early settlement of the U.S. *Purpose*: Seeks to protect and preserve historic sites related to those wars. *Publications*: Journal of the Order of the Indian Wars, quarterly; Communique, monthly. Founded 1979.

ORGANIZATION OF NORTH AMERICAN INDIAN STUDENTS
Box 26, University Center
Northern Michigan University
Marquette, MI 49855
 (906) 227-2138
 Ted DeVerney, Executive Officer
Membership: 45. University students of American Indian ancestry and other interested students. *Purpose*: To encourage pride and identity in Indian culture and tradition; to establish communications among the native communities; to promote scholarships among Indian students attending institutes of higher learning. *Activities*: Sponsors basket weaving seminars; annual Indian Awareness Week. Library. Founded 1971.

PALEO-INDIAN INSTITUTE
Eastern New Mexico University
P.O. Box 2154
Portales, NM 88130

PAN-AMERICAN INDIAN ASSOCIATION
P.O. Box 244
Nocatee, FL 33864
 (813) 494-6930
 Chief Piercing Eyes, Executive Director
Purpose: To help find perspective in the Indian Revival amidst claims of authenticity, ancient traditions, etc. To examine historical actualities, mainly aimed at the 65 million persons of Indian blood who are denied access to their own culture. *Programs*: Ceremonies and lectures; scouting program. *Publication*: 16-page Indian tabloid newspaper. Library. Established 1984.

R.A.I.N. RIGHTS FOR ALL INDIGENOUS NATIONS, INC.
R.D. 1, Box 308A
Petersburg, NY 12138
 (518) 658-3055
 Hank Hazelton
Description: A non-profit educational and action organization dedicated to the survival of Indigenous Nations worldwide.

SACRED RUN FOUNDATION, INC.
P.O. Box 315
Newport, KY 41071
 (606) 581-9456
 Dennis J. Banks, Director
 Alice Lambert-Banks, Executive Director
Purpose: Dedicated to promoting Native American culture through spiritual running and special events. *Activities*: Local, national and international multi-cultural spiritual runs - sobriety New Years Eve Powwow; craft weekends; drum performances. *Publication*: Sacred Run Newsletter. Founded 1978; Incorporated in 1990.

SAVE THE CHILDREN FEDERATION
54 Wilton Rd.
Westport, CT 06880
 (203) 226-7271
 David L. Guyer, President
Purpose: To assist children, families and communities in the U.S. and abroad to achieve social and economic stability through community development and family self-help projects; and to aid victims of disaster. *Activities*: Conducts child sponsorship programs and community development projects, with emphasis on community self-help through grass roots organization as well as training and technical assistance; conducts programs on Indian reservations. *Scholarship*: Ruth Bronson Memorial Scholarship for American Indian Graduate Students.

Publications: Lifeline Magazine, quarterly; annual reports, and papers on development issues. Library. Founded 1932.

SEVENTH GENERATION FUND FOR INDIAN DEVELOPMENT, INC.
P.O. Box 10
Forestville, CA 95436
 (707) 887-1559
 John Mohawk, Chairman
 Chris Peters, Executive Director
Purpose: Committed to giving pragmatic political and economic reality to the concept of sovereignty. *Activities*: Provides private funding and technical assistance directly to local Indian communities for efforts to deal with their own problems; assists projects to generate and manage funds on their own behalf. *Program*: Operating Program in Economic Development--to develop new approaches to reservation economic development. *Grants*: Makes small seed grants averaging $3,000. *Publications*: Native Self-Sufficiency, quarterly newspaper; Native Americans and Energy Development II (book), in cooperation with the Akbar Fund, American Indian Directions, newsletter on Indian issues for the philanthropic community; Field Notes on the Work of Native Women. Library. Founded 1977.

S.H.A.R.E. (SACRED HOOP OF AMERICAN RESOURCE EXCHANGE)
114 Cat Rock Rd.
Cos Cob, CT 06807
 (203) 622-6525
 Tek Nickerson, National Director
Purpose/Goals: To build bridges of understanding and mutual support between the American Indian community & the North American community at large; to restore traditional values to Native youth; to help balance non-Native lives; to help balance Native communities. *Activities/Programs*: Cultural Camp; Sacred Sites Conservancy; Native Oral History Program; SHARE the Warmth Blanket Program; Native American awareness weeks & speaker's bureau; continual networking of employment opportunities; training staff to manage SHARE programs and then spin them off for independent, wholly owned & operated Native operations. Founded 1984.

SMOKI PEOPLE
P.O. Box 123
Prescott, AZ 86302
 (602) 445-1230
 Michael E. Kennelly, Chief
Membership: 1,600. Local business and professional people (non-Indian.) *Purpose*: To perpetuate by authentic artistic reproduction of the age-old ceremonials and dances of Indian tribes of North and South America. *Publication*: Smoki Ceremonials and Snake Dance, annual. Museum. Library. Annual meeting. Founded 1921.

SOCIETY FOR ADVANCEMENT OF CHICANOS & NATIVE AMERICANS IN SCIENCE
Sinsheimer Labs, University of California
Santa Cruz, CA 95064
 (408) 459-4272
 Dr. Frank Talamantes, Executive Officer
Membership: 500. *Description*: College professors, professionals, and students. *Purpose*: To increase the participation of Chicanos & native American students in the sciences. *Activities*: Workshops & technical symposia; bestows awards; operates speaker's bureau. *Publication*: SACNAS, quarterly newsletter. Founded 1973.

SOCIETY FOR ETHNOMUSICOLOGY
Indiana University, Morrison Hall 005
Bloomington, IN 47405
 (812) 855-6672
Membership: 2,000. Ethnomusicologists, anthropologists, musicologists, and laymen interested in music as an aspect of culture. *Purpose*: Seeks to integrate the study of manifold facets of non-Western music with Western folk and art music. *Awards*: Seeger Prize and Jaap Kunst Prize. *Publications*: Ethnomusicology, 3/yr.; Directory, 3/yr.; Newsletter, 3/yr.; publishes monographs, bibliographies and pamphlets. Annual Conference. Founded 1955.

SOCIETY FOR HISTORICAL ARCHAEOLOGY
P.O. Box 30446
Tucson, AZ 85751
 (602) 886-8006
 Leland G. Ferguson, President
Membership: 2,000. *Purpose*: Concerned with the archaeology of the modern world (A.D. 1400-present), with the main focus the era since the beginning of European settlement and the effects on Native American peoples. *Activities*: Promotes scholarly research and the dissemination of knowledge concerning historical archaeology. *Publications*: Historical Archaeology, quarterly journal; quarterly newsletter; special publication series. Annual meeting. Founded 1967.

THE SUNDANCE INSTITUTE
c/o S.P.E.
10202 W. Washington Blvd.
Culver City, CA 90232
 (310) 204-2091 Fax 204-3901
 Michelle Satter, Dir. of Feature Film Prog.
 Jeff Gilmore, Director of Film Festival

SURVIVAL INTERNATIONAL, U.S.A.
Washington, DC 20008
 (202) 265-1077
 Mary George Hardman, Executive Director
Membership: 1,200. *Description*: Individuals concerned with the rights of tribal peoples. *Purpose*: To support tribal groups in their efforts towards self-determination. *Publication*: Survival International News, semiannual; pamphlets and documents. Founded 1979.

SURVIVAL OF AMERICAN INDIAN ASSNS.
7803-A Samurai Dr., SE
Olympia, WA 98503
 (206) 459-2679
 Hank Adams, National Director
Membership: 500. *Activities*: Provides public education on Indian rights and tribal government reform action; supports independent Indian educational institutions; speakers bureau. *Publication*: The Renegade: A Strategy Journal of Indian Opinion, annual. Founded 1964.

TCI, INC.
2126 Connecticut Ave., NW #52
Washington, D.C. 20008
 (202) 333-6350
 Corrine L. Levy
Publishes newsletters: LINKAGES - American Indian child welfare and family services; Indians Against Alcohol and Drug Abuse (IAADA); Alternative Health Therapies; and Faculty Advocate - opportunities for health professionals in the Indian Health Service.

TEKAKWITHA CONFERENCE NATIONAL CENTER
P.O. Box 6759
Great Falls, MT 59406
 (406) 727-0147
 Fr. Gilbert F. Hemauer, O.F.M., Cap. Executive Director
Membership: 12,000. Catholic missionaries among American Indians; Eskimo and American Indian deacons and lay persons involved in ministry. *Purpose*: To develop Catholic evangelization in the areas of Native American Ministry, catechesis, liturgy, family life, spirituality, and theology. Provides a forum for the exchange of ideas among Catholic Native Americans, Eskimos, and missionaries. Encourages development of Native American ministry by Indian people. *Publications*: Special Bulletin, quarterly; quarterly newsletter; annual proceedings. Library. Annual conference. Founded 1939.

THUNDERBIRD AMERICAN INDIAN DANCERS
c/o Louis Mofsie
McBurney YMCA
215 West 23rd St.
New York, NY 10011
 (201) 587-9633
 Louis Mofsie, Director
Membership: 30. Indians and non-Indians who raise money for the Thunderbird Indian Scholarship Fund for Indian students. *Activities*: Offers cultural classes in crafts, singing, dancing, and language; sponsors Indian studies programs for Indian youth; monthly pow-wows in New York City--open to public. Founded 1956.

TIPI PRESS
St. Joseph's Indian School
P.O. Box 89
Chamberlain, SD 57325
 (605) 734-6021
 Rev. Tom Westhoven
Purpose: To promote better understanding of Siouan culture, and better understanding of Catholic/Christian evangelization among Plains Indian Tribes, and appreciation for Siouan art and artists through prints, calendars, and note cards.

UNITED NATIONAL INDIAN TRIBAL YOUTH, INC. (UNITY)
4010 Lincoln Blvd., Suite 202
P.O. Box 25042
Oklahoma City, OK 73125
 (405) 424-3010 Fax 424018
 J.R. Cook, Executive Director
 George Thomas, Deputy Director
Purpose: To empower American Indian and Alaska Native youth with the spiritual, mental, physical, and social qualities necessary to strengthen their lives and communities. *Purpose*: To establish a National Leadership Training Center for American Indian/Alaska Native Youth through the development of a national UNITY council annual national leadership development conferences, development of tribal, village, and community youth councils, motivational seminars, coordination of American Indian/Alaska Native Youth Day on the last Wednesday of September each year. *Publications*: UNITY News, quarterly. Founded 1976.

UNITED NATIVE AMERICANS
2434 Faria Ave.
Pinole, CA 94564
 (415) 758-8160
 Lehman L. Brightman, Director
Membership: 12,000. *Purpose*: To promote the general welfare of Native Americans; to establish educational scholarships; provide legal aid, housing and counseling for Indians. Maintains speakers' bureau. *Publication*: Warpath, monthly. Sells historical posters of Native American life. Annual meeting. Founded 1968.

UNITED SOUTH & EASTERN TRIBES, INC.
711 Stewarts Ferry Pike #100
Nashville, TN 37214
 (615) 361-8700
 Lionel John, Executive Director
Description: Alliance of Indian tribes: Cherokees (NC), Choctaws (MS), Seminoles and Miccosukees (FL), Senecas (NY), Chitimacha and Coushatta (LA), St. Regis Mohawks (NY), Penobscot, Passamaquoddy & Maliseits (ME), Mashantucket Pequot (CT), Poarch Band of Creek (AL), Narrangansett (RI). *Activities*: Arranges & sponsors courses of special interest to Indian people; job training and placement; community development services and training; Indian Health Service. *Publication*: The Calumet, bimonthly newsletter. Semiannual meeting. Founded 1968.

VIETNAM ERA VETERANS INTER-TRIBAL ASSOCIATION
805 Rosa
Shawnee, OK 74801
 (405) 382-3128
 Randall Herrod, National Commander
 Bill Haney, Assistant Commander
Membership: 1,000. American Indian veterans representing 200 tribes who served in Vietnam or who served in the armed forces during the Vietnam era. 1964-1975. *Purpose*: To promote a positive image of the Indian Vietnam veteran; to remember fellow servicemen who died in the ward and in the years following; to foster exchange of information on problems related to Vietnam. *Publications*: Redsmoke Indian News, quarterly newsletter; Souvenir Pow-Wow Program, annual; Membership List, periodic; Veteran Small Business Directory; papers. Annual National Pow-Wow. Founded 1981.

VIOLA WHITE WATER FOUNDATION
4225 Concord St.,
Harrisburg, PA 17109
 (717) 652-2040
 Sandy Gutshall, President
 Jimmy Little Turtle, Sec./Treas.
Description: Non-profit organization dedicated to helping Native Americans live and educate their children in the traditional ways. "Main goal now is Mohawk Valley settlement in Fonda, NY." *Activities*: Funding of Akwesasne Freedom School, and Mohawk Valley settlement in Fonda, NY. Grants are made to individuals, schools and colleges. *Publication*: quarterly newsletter.

WENNER-GREN FOUNDATION
220 Fifth Ave., 16th Floor
New York, NY 10001
 (212) 683-5000
 Dr. Sydel Silverman, President
Activities: Provides grants-in-aid to scholars for research and preparation of publications in all

branches of anthropology and in related disciplines. *Activities*: Awards qualified scholars grants to aid basic research, doctoral dissertation research, conference grants, and grants for write-up of research results for publication. *Publications*: Current Anthropology, bimonthly journal; Annual Report; issues V iking Fund Publications in Anthropology. Periodic conferences. Founded 1941.

WESTERN AMERICA INSTITUTE FOR EXPLORATION, INC.
1821 East 9th St.
The Dalles, OR 97058
(503) 296-9414
Jay Ellis Ransom, Executive Director
Purpose: To assist and further expeditions in archaeology and anthropology toward developing original researches in ethnology and native linguistics, as well as exploring paleo-Indian ethnological and cosmological belief systems that are reflected in 20th century tribal societies as commonalties out of ancient times. *Activities*: Collect, arrange, and preserve data, records, and materials; to make such data available for scientific use; to encourage dissemination of ideas, data, and other forms of knowledge. *Publications*: Archaeolinguistics & Paleoethnography of Ancient Rock Structures in W estern North America; anthropological papers. Founded 1954.

WINGS OF AMERICA
53 Old Santa Fe Trail
Santa Fe, NM 87501
(505) 982-6761
Will Channing, President
Margie Kamine, Administrative Director
Purpose: "To promote alternative and self-reliance among American Indian youth to ef fect change in themselves and their communities, and to take pride in cultural identities." *Activities*: takes 65 high school runners to USA Track & Field National Cross Country Championships every year; holds mini-running camps for Indian youth ages 6-14. *Publication*: The W ind Messenger, newsletter.

WOMEN OF ALL RED NATIONS
P.O. Box 2508
Rapid City, SD 57709
Madonna Thunderhawk, Field Coordinator
Description: A grass roots organization of American Indian women seeking to advance the Native-American movement. *Activities*: Establish local chapters to work on issues like sterilization abuse and women's health, adoption and foster care abuse, community education, and problems caused by energy resource development; publishes reports on health problems of American Indian women. Founded 1978.

WORLD INDIGENOUS GAMES
Route 3, Suite 181F
Jaspa, GA 30143
(404) 735-6275 Fax 735-6272
Chipa W olf, Executive Director
Description: The first Olympic-style international event to be held in the summer of 1996 in various locations across the northern part of the state of Georgia. Provides athletic competition featuring the traditional games played by Native Americans. Also, other sports and games played by native populations from other regions of the world, and displays of food, dance, costume, and art, all representing the cultures of indigenous people throughout the world.

WORLD VISION INTERNATIONAL
919 W. Huntington Dr.
Monrovia, CA 91016
(818) 303-8811
Betty Lou Williams, Contact
Publication: Native American Christian Community: A directory of Indian, Aleut, and Eskimo Churches, Missions, Advanced Research and Communication Centers (2,500 Indian religious groups, churches, missions, colleges, etc.).

NATIVE AMERICAN FINANCIAL INSTITUTIONS
(OWNED & OPERATED)

BANKS

BLACKFEET NATIONAL BANK
P.O. Box 730
Browning, MT 59417
(406) 338-7000
Eloise Cobell, Contact

FIRST OKLAHOMA BANK OF SHAWNEE
P.O. Box 68
Shawnee, OK 74802
(405) 275-8830

FIRST STATE BANK OF OKLAHOMA
P.O. Box 459
Hulbert, OK 74441
(918) 772-2572
J.D. Colbert, Contact

LUMBEE GUARANTEE BANK
P.O. Box 908
Pembroke, NC 28372
(919) 521-9707

CREDIT UNIONS

FIRST AMERICAN CREDIT UNION
1001 N. Pinal Ave.
Casa Grande, AZ 85222
(602) 871-4767

SISSETON-WAHPETON FEDERAL CREDIT UNION
P.O. Box 627
Sisseton, SD 57262
(605) 698-3462

FIRST AMERICAN CAPITAL MANAGEMENT GROUP, INC.
2330 Sioux Trail, NW, Suite 114
Prior Lake, MN 55372
(612) 445-5332 Fax 445-2821
John R. Herrera, President
Purpose: To provide consultation and equipment leasing services to a client base of Native American tribes. *Activities*: Reservation development assistance; tax and tax exempt bond placement advisory services; Government program evaluation/feasibility studies; certified vendor through the Bureau of Indian Affairs.

RESERVATION-BASED LOAN FUNDS

THE ADAH COMMUNITY LOAN ASSOCIATION, INC.
P.O. Box 2986
Shiprock, NM 87420
(505) 368-4906
David McKenzie, Contact

CHEROKEE INITIATIVE
1106 S. Muskogee Ave., Suite A
Tahlequah, OK 74464
(918) 456-0765
Warren Hawk, Executive Director

THE LAKOTA FUND
P.O. Box 340
Kyle, SD 57752
(605) 455-2500
Elsie Meeks, Executive Director
Purpose: Formed to help build a private sector economy on the Pine Ridge Reservation by providing loans, technical assistance & business training; and arts & crafts marketing assistance tribal members. *Activities*: Loans for small business and microenterprises. *Publication*: The Lakota Fund newsletter.

NEE-SHOCH-HA-CHEE
P.O. Box 748
Winnebago, NE 68071
(402) 878-2972
John Vandell, Contact

SICANGU ENTERPRISE CENTER
P.O. Box 205
Mission, SD 57555
(605) 856-2955
Eileen Lunderman, Contact

THE TINAA CORPORATION
320 W. Willoughby, Suite 210
Juneau, AK 99801
(907) 463-7123
Dawn Dinwoodie, Contact

(Includes Urban Indian Centers)

This section is an alpha-geographical listing of state and regional agencies and organizations concerned mainly with Native-American affairs in their particular state and/or region of the U.S.

ALABAMA

ALABAMA DEPARTMENT OF EDUCATION
Coordinator of Indian Education
Gordon Persons Bldg.
50 N. Ripley St.
MONTGOMERY, AL 36130
(205) 242-8199 Fax 242-8024
Marsha Johnson, Contact
Serves as the liaison for the State Dept. of Education with the Indian Affairs Section of the U.S. Dept. of Education, the Indian Education Technical Assistance Center, the Alabama Commission on Indian Affairs, and local Indian education coordinators.

ALABAMA INDIAN AFFAIRS COMMISSION
669 S. Lawrence St.
MONTGOMERY, AL 36104
(205) 261-2831
Jane L. Weeks, Executive Director

ALASKA

The Alaska Native Claims Settlement Act of December 18, 1971, established regional village corporations and associations, both profit and non-profit. Listings are arranged alphabetically.

ALASKA FEDERATION OF NATIVES
3201 C St. #608
ANCHORAGE, AK 99503
(907) 274-3611
Julia E. Kitka, President
Membership: 77,000. Alaskan Natives (Aleut, Eskimo, and Indian); regional profit and non-profit corporations. *Purpose*: To act as lobbyist and advocate on behalf of statewide Native community and to provide technical assistance to these groups. Publications: Monthly newsletter; annual report. Maintains biographical archives and library of government reports and economic material. Annual meeting in October. Founded 1966.

ALASKA LEGAL SERVICES CORP.
1016 W. Sixth Ave., Suite 200
ANCHORAGE, AK 99501
(907) 276-6282

ALASKA NATIVE COALITION
P.O. Box 200908
ANCHORAGE, AK 99520
(907) 258-6917
Purpose: Seeks to protect Native ancestral lands, strengthen tribal governments, and protect the subsistence way of life. It has also organized to monitor the 1991 legislative effort, in response to ANCSA provisions, which the Coalition believes threaten Native communities and their ancestral lands. Founded 1986.

ALASKA NATIVE EDUCATION COUNCIL
P.O. Box 200923
ANCHORAGE, AK 99520

(907) 272-3399
Luanne Pelagio, Contact

ALASKA STATE COUNCIL ON THE ARTS
411 W. 4th Ave., Suite 1E
ANCHORAGE, AK 99501
(907) 297-1558 Fax 279-4330
Purpose: To provide grants to support Native Alaskan art and crafts.

ALEUTIAN PRIBILOFF ISLAND ASSN.
401 E. Fireweed Lane #201
ANCHORAGE, AK 99503
(907) 276-2700
Native non-profit association.
Serves as a health clinic.

ASSOCIATION OF ALASKA NATIVE CONTRACTORS
700 W. 58th, Unit F
ANCHORAGE, AK 99518
(907) 562-1866 Fax 561-3006
Linda J.E. Henerickson, President

CALISTA CORPORATION
601 W. 5th Ave., Suite 200
ANCHORAGE, AK 99501
(907) 279-5516 Fax 272-5060
Johnny T. Hawk, Executive Director
Felix P. Hess, Chairperson
Native for-profit regional corporation with 13,306 shareholders (Yup'ik Eskimos of Southwestern Alaska).

CHUGACH NATIVES, INCORPORATED
Anchorage, AK 99503
(907) 276-1080
Native for-profit regional corporation.

COOK INLET NATIVE ASSOCIATION
ANCHORAGE, AK 99503
(907) 278-4641
Franklin L. Berry, Executive Director
Native non-profit association of about 1,500 Alaskan Natives & American Indians dedicated to nurturing pride in the heritage and traditions of Alaska Natives, and preserving the customs, folklore, and art of the people. Operates a health clinic, Alaska Native Community Center. *Publication*: Trail Blazer, quarterly newsletter.

COOK INLET REGION, INC.
P.O. Drawer 4-N
ANCHORAGE, AK 99509
(907) 274-8638
Native for-profit regional corporation.

INUIT CIRCUMPOLAR CONFERENCE
Alaska Federation of Natives
3201 C St. #608
ANCHORAGE AK 99503
(907) 258-6917
An international organization of Inuit (Eskimo) from Alaska, Canada and Greenland holding non-governmental organizations status with the United Nations. The ICC is committed to upholding and advancing the cultural, economic, political, and civil rights of indigenous people across the Arctic rim countries and worldwide.

NATIVE AMERICAN RIGHTS FUND
310 K St., Suite 708
ANCHORAGE, AK 99501
(907) 276-0680
Branch office headquartered in Boulder, CO. See listing in National Associations section.

NATIVE SPIRITUAL CULTURE COUNCILS, INC.
3212 W. 29th Ave.
ANCHORAGE, AK 99503
(907) 243-0135
Non-profit organization comprised of Alaskan Native Aleut, Eskimo, Indian and Native Americans formed for bringing about spiritual rebirth and reawakening of the native people.

NORTH PACIFIC RIM NATIVE ASSN.
4201 Tudor Centre Dr., Suite 210
ANCHORAGE, AK 99508
(907) 276-2121
Native non-profit association.
Operates a health clinic.

ORRE DRUMRITE WALKING HERITAGE
P.O. Box 221689
ANCHORAGE, AK 99522-1689
(907) 243-2421
Elizabeth A. Wells, Executive Director
Purpose: To unite all tribes to pray our street Indians back to responsible lives; to teach traditional heritage. *Programs*: Parade of the Spirits; World Drum: Secrets of Life, a peace crusade. *Publication*: Dancing Prayers. Established 1990.

ARCTIC VILLAGE TRADITIONAL COUNCIL
P.O. Box 22050
ARCTIC VILLAGE, AK 99722
(907) 587-5320
Trimble Gilbert, Chief
(907) 587-5226
Lincoln Tritt, 2nd Chief
Tribe: Gwitch'in Athapascan. *Elected officials*: Sarah James, Rose Lee, Louie John, Steve Lee, Jim Christian. Fairbanks Agency.

ARCTIC SLOPE NATIVE ASSOCIATION
P.O. Box 566
BARROW, AK 99723
Native non-profit association.

ARCTIC SLOPE REGIONAL CORP.
P.O. Box 129
BARROW, AK 99723
(907) 852-8633/8533
Native for-profit regional corporation.

NORTH SLOPE BOROUGH HEALTH CORP.
P.O. Box 69
BARROW, AK 99723
(907) 852-3999
Health Clinic.

ASSOCIATION OF VILLAGE COUNCIL PRESIDENTS, INC.
P.O. Box 219
BETHEL, AK 99559
(907) 543-3521
Myron P. Naneng, President
Purpose: To provide human development, social services, and other culturally relevant programs for the people; to promote self-determination protection and enhancement of our culture and traditions through a working partnership with member villages of the Yukon-Kuskokwim Delta. *Activities*: Childcare Development services; economic development; education, employment & training; family justice; housing improvement; social services; tribal operations; financial aid-higher education scholarships; operates Yup'ik Cultural Center & Museum; Head Start Program. Founded 1964.

YUKON-KUSKOKWIM HEALTH CORP.
P.O. Box 528
BETHEL, AK 99559
(907) 543-3321

COPPER RIVER HEALTH AUTHORITY
P.O. Drawer H
COPPER CENTER, AK 99573
(907) 822-3521
Health clinic of the Copper River Native
Association.

COPPER RIVER NATIVE ASSOCIATION
P.O. Drawer G
COPPER RIVER, AK 99573
(907) 822-5241
Native non-profit association.

BRISTOL BAY AREA HEALTH CORP.
P.O. Box 10235
DILLINGHAM, AK 99576
(907) 842-5266/7; 842-5201 (hospital)
Health clinic affiliated with Bristol Bay Native
Association.

BRISTOL BAY NATIVE ASSOCIATION
P.O. Box 179
DILLINGHAM, AK 99576
(907) 842-5257/5258
Native non-profit assn. Head Start Program.

BRISTOL BAY NATIVE CORPORATION
P.O. Box 198
DILLINGHAM, AK 99576
(907) 842-5261
Native for-profit regional corporation.

DOYON LIMITED
201 1st Ave.
FAIRBANKS, AK 99701
(907) 452-4755
Native for-profit regional corporation.

FAIRBANKS NATIVE ASSOCIATION
201 1st Ave., 2nd Floor
FAIRBANKS, AK 99701
(907) 452-1648
Samuel S. Demientief f, Executive Director
Purpose: To provide professional, quality human
services to membership and Fairbanks community; to preserve Native culture and improve the
quality of life for the community . *Programs*: Elders program; Public Assistance and Family
Counseling; Employment, Education (small
scholarships), Treatment Center for Alcohol and
Drug Abuse; Substance Abuse Counselor Training; Head Start Program. *Publication*: Monthly
newsletter. Library. Founded 1960.

INSTITUTE OF ALASKA NATIVE ARTS
P.O. Box 70769, 455 Third Ave. #117
FAIRBANKS, AK 99707
(907) 456-7491 Fax 451-7268
Susie Bevins-Ericsen, President
Patricia J. Petrivelli, Executive Director
Jan Steinbright, Program Director
Tammy Young, Office Administrator
Purpose: "To foster the continuation of Alaska
Native traditions into contemporary expressions
of the highest quality ." *Activities*: Programs and
services to enhance the artistic, professional and
economic status of Alaska Native artists and to
heighten awareness of Alaska Native aesthetics and traditions through exhibitions, workshops, scholarships, publications and technical
assistance. Operates Information Center consisting of an artists registry of hard copy files

and slides; photographic files; and resource library with over 600 titles and audio and video
tapes. Offers scholarships for academic study .
Publication: Journal of Alaska Native Arts, quarterly; exhibit catalogs and resource materials on
Alaska Native arts. Founded 1976.

TANANA CHIEFS CONFERENCE, INC.
122 1st Ave.
FAIRBANKS, AK 99701
(907) 452-8251
Sarah Kuenzil, Director
Regional non-profit corporation. Maintains
a health clinic. Head Start Program.

AHTNA, INC.
P.O. Box 649
GLENNALLEN, AK 99588
(907) 822-3476
Wilson Justin, President
A native for-profit regional corporation. *Activi-
ties*: Construction, real estate; student loans and
scholarships, and loans to shareholders for busi-
ness ventures. *Publications*: Annual reports;
Shareholder's Handbook. Library .

KLUKWAN HERITAGE FOUNDATION
P.O. Box 972
HAINES, AK 99827
Janice Hill, President

**ALASKA DEPT. OF COMMUNITY
& REGIONAL AFFAIRS**
P.O. Box 112100
JUNEAU, AK 99811
(907) 465-4700
Edgar P. Blatchford, Commissioner

ALASKA DEPT. OF EDUCATION
Rural Native & Education Programs
P.O. Box F
JUNEAU, AK 99811
(907) 465-8716 Fax 465-3396

ALASKA OFFICE OF THE GOVERNOR
P.O. Box A
JUNEAU, AK 99811
(907) 465-3500
Mike Irwin, Special Staf f Assistant

ASSISTANT FOR ALASKA NATIVE AFFAIRS
Office of the Governor
Pouch A
JUNEAU, AK 99811

**CENTRAL COUNCIL OF THE TLINGIT
& HAIDA INDIAN TRIBES OF ALASKA**
320 W. Willoughby Ave., Suite 300
JUNEAU, AK 99801
(907) 585-1432
Edward Thomas, President
Under jurisdiction of Southeast Agency of the
Bureau of Indian Affairs.

SEALASKA CORPORATION
One Sealaska Plaza, Suite 400
JUNEAU, AK 99801
(907) 586-1512
Byron I. Mallott, Chief Executive Of ficer
Description: A regional native for-profit corpo-
ration, established by Congress under the
Alaska Native Claims Settlement Act of 1971.
Activities: Owns a forest products company , a
seafood products company , and a building prod-
ucts company; conducts workshops for share-
holders; political action committee, SEAP AC;
Sealaska Heritage Foundation--an af filiate--pre-

serves and promotes the cultural traditions of
the Tlingit, Haida and Tsimpshian people; provides scholarships, and maintains archives.
Publications: The Sealaska Shareholder , bimonthly newspaper; annual reports.

SEALASKA HERITAGE FOUNDATION
1 Sealaska Plaza, Suite 201
JUNEAU, AK 99801
(907) 463-4844
David G. Katzeek, Executive Director
Timothy Wilson, Development Director
Encourages & promotes the preservation of the
arts & culture of the Tlingit, Haida, and Tsimshian
people of Southeast Alaska through programs
in language and cultural studies, traditional celebrations, scholarship-heritage studies, tribal
archives, and Naa Kahidi theatre. *Publication*:
Naa Kaani, a quarterly newsletter .

**SOUTHEAST ALASKA
REGIONAL HEALTH CORP.**
3245 Hospital Dr .
JUNEAU, AK 99801
(907) 463-4040 Fax 463-4012
TLINGIT/HAIDA CENTRAL COUNCIL
320 West Willoughby Ave., Suite 300
JUNEAU, AK 99801
(907) 585-1432
Edward K. Thomas, President

**KENAITZE INDIAN TRIBE EXECUTIVE
COMMITTEE/TRIBAL COUNCIL**
Box 988
KENAI, AK 99611
(907) 283-3633
Ms. Claire Swan, Chairperson
Serve more than 1,750 Alaska Natives on the
Kenai Peninsula. After three years of litigation,
the Kenaitze Tribe recently won a land-mark
Federal Court decision restoring the Kenaitze
Indian Tribal members the right to enjoy their
traditional and customary subsistence fishing
rights on the Kenai Peninsula. Those rights had
been denied for 40 years by the State of Alaska.

KODIAK AREA NATIVE ASSOCIATION
KODIAK, AK 99615
(907) 486-5725
Gordon L. Pullar , President
Description: A native non-profit association promoting pride on the part of the natives of Alaska
in their heritage and traditions; promotes the
physical, economic, and social well-being of the
natives of Alaska. *Activities*: Over 40 programs
administered under the Department of Health;
education and family services; community and
economic development; health clinic. *Scholarships*: Higher education and adult vocational
training scholarships funded by the Bureau of
Indian Affairs; education and social work scholarships funded by the Department of Health and
Human Services; Skip Eaton Scholarship, an
independent local award. Library .

MANIILAQ ASSOCIATION
P.O. Box 256
KOTZEBUE, AK 99752
(800) 478-3312; (907) 442-331 1 Fax 442-2381
Marie N. Greene, President
Description: A native non-profit association serving 11 Alaskan Eskimo villages ranging from 100
to 3,000 in population. *Activities*: Promotes the
public health and social welfare in the Northwest Arctic Borough region of Alaska; attempts
to preserve and promote the Eskimo customs,
arts and language, and advance education in

all forms. Operates a health corporation serving a population of 6,500. *Publications*: Northwest Arctic Nuna, monthly newsletter; Nuna Regional Strategy Plan, and Nana Coastal Zone Management Plan. Founded 1966.

NANA REGIONAL CORPORATION
P.O. Box 49
KOTZEBUE, AK 99752
(907) 442-3301
A native for-profit regional corporation.

METLAKATLA INDIAN COMMUNITY COUNCIL
P.O. Box 8
METLAKATLA, AK 99926
(907) 886-4441 Fax 886-7997
Casey Nelson, Mayor

BERING STRAITS NATIVE CORPORATION
P.O. Box 1008
NOME, AK 99762
(907) 443-5252
A native for-profit regional corporation.

KAWERAK, INC.
P.O. Box 948
NOME, AK 99762
(907) 443-5231
Loretta Bullard, President
Eileen Norbert, Deputy Director
Description: A native non-profit association organized to promote the social and economic welfare of the Kawerak, the Native people of the Bering Straits Region, and those Native people enrolled to Native Corporations under ANCSA, and those villages in the region. *Activities*: Adult education; child care; community and economic development; housing and social services; JTPA Jobs; Tribal Employment Rights; Eskimo Heritage Project. *Publication*: Joint newsletter with Norton Sound Health Corp. Head Start Program.

NORTON SOUND HEALTH CORPORATION
P.O. Box 966
NOME, AK 99762
(907) 443-3311
Carolyn Michels, President
Description: A health care organization formed to improve the mental and physical health of the people of the region to the highest possible levels through education, preventive programs and high quality health care; and assist in creating a healthy and economically positive environment. *Publication*: Newsletter, jointly with Kawerak, Inc. Medical Library. Established 1970.

SOVEREIGNTY NETWORK
HC04 Box 9880
PALMER, AK 99645

SOUTHEAST ALASKA INDIAN CULTURAL CENTER
106 Metlakatla St.
SITKA, AK 99835
(907) 747-8061
Ellen Hays, Executive Director
Purpose: To displays native arts produced in the Center over the past 20 years, including wood carving, silverwork, costumes, and robes. *Activities*: Audiovisual programs; provides demonstrations of traditional native arts such as woodcarving, costume design, and metalworking that are representative of the Tlingit people and Southeast Alaska. Established 1968.

ARIZONA

NATIVE AMERICAN BUSINESS COALITION
6025 N. Smokerise
FLAGSTAFF, AZ 86004
(602) 526-0035 Fax 526-2383
Bruce Yazzie, President

NATIVE AMERICANS FOR COMMUNITY ACTION, INC.
Flagstaff Indian Center
2717 N. Steves Blvd., Suite 1 1
FLAGSTAFF, AZ 86004
(602) 526-2968 Fax 526-0708
Rick Tewa, Jr., Executive Director
Willard S. Gilbert, Board President
Purpose: A community based organization to meet the needs of Native Americans residing off reservation in Flagstaf f. *Programs*: Family health center; substance abuse counseling; child & family counseling; training assistance & employment; adult education; social services; youth & elders programs; and economic development. Established 1971.

INDIAN CHILDREN'S PROGRAM
Good Shepard Mission
P.O. Box 920
FORT DEFIANCE, AZ 86504
(602) 729-5986
Ela M. Yazzie-King, Coordinator
Purpose: To perform diagnostic services for children with special needs; to assist in health and education problems for Native American children in Arizona, Utah and New Mexico. *Activities*: Provides assessments in occupational, physical therapy, speech and language, psychological and vocational, and training for parents and agencies. Library. Founded 1991.

NATIVE AMERICAN FINANCE OFFICERS ASSOCIATION
P.O. Box 170
FORT DEFIANCE, AZ 86504
(602) 729-6218 Fax 729-2135
Marlene Lynch, President

NAVAJO NATION BUSINESS ASSOCIATION
P.O. Box 1217
KAYENTA, AZ 86033
(602) 697-3534 Fax 697-3464
Richard Mike, President

ARIZONA INDIAN BUSINESS DEVELOPMENT CENTER
953 E. Juanita St.
MESA,, AZ 85204
(602) 831-7524

ARIZONA COMMISSION ON INDIAN AFFAIRS
1645 W. Jefferson, Suite 127
PHOENIX, AZ 85007
(602) 542-3123
Tony Machukay, Executive Director

ARIZONA DEPARTMENT OF EDUCATION
Indian Education Unit
1535 W. Jefferson St.
PHOENIX, AZ 85007
(602) 542-4391 Fax 542-3099
Kathryn Stevens, Director

ARIZONA INDIAN AFFAIRS COMMISSION
1645 W. Jefferson, Room 127
PHOENIX, AZ 85007
(602) 542-3123

ARIZONA INDIAN CENTERS, INC.
1515 E. Osborn Rd., Annex
PHOENIX, AZ 85014
(602) 279-0618 Fax 279-0699
Joy Hanley, Executive Director
Purposes: A statewide representative, identifying and addressing urban issues; as a system of support, through training and technical assistance for urban Indian centers, organizations and communities; as an information center gathering and disseminating information relevant to the needs of urban Indian centers and organizations.

INTER-TRIBAL COUNCIL OF ARIZONA
4205 N. 7th Ave., Suite 200
PHOENIX, AZ 85013
(602) 248-0071 Fax 248-0080
John Lewis, Executive Director

PHOENIX INDIAN CENTER
2601 North 3rd St., Suite 160
PHOENIX, AZ 85004
(602) 263-1017 F AX 263-7822
William Thorne, Jr., Executive Director
Purpose: To promote the social and economic self sufficiency of the American Indian population in Maricopa County. *Programs*: Employment & Training; Case Management; Behavioral; Child Welfare and Aging. *Publication*: Eagle Free Press, newspaper. Library. Established 1947.

URBAN INDIAN HEALTH PROJECT
1427 N. 3rd St., Suite 100
PHOENIX, AZ 85004
(602) 263-8094
Erma Mundy, Executive Director

FOUR RIVERS INDIAN LEGAL SERVICES
P.O. Box 68
SACATON, AZ 85247
(602) 562-3369
La Nita Plummer & Roger Sigal, Contacts

INDIAN LAW SECTION OF ARIZONA BAR ASSOCIATION
P.O. Box 400
SACATON, AZ 85247
(602) 562-3611
Rod Lewis, Chairperson

APACHES FOR CULTURAL PRESERVATION
San Carlos Apache Reservation
P.O. Box 249
SAN CARLOS, AZ 85550
(602) 475-2494
Wendsler Nosie, Sr., Co-Chairperson

ARIZONA INDIAN BUSINESS DEVELOPMENT CENTER
2070 E. Southern Ave.
TEMPE, AZ 85282
(602) 945-2635

APACHE SURVIVAL COALITION
P.O. Box 1237
SAN CARLOS,AZ 85550
(602) 475-2543, or 294-1863
Ola Cassadore Davis, Chairperson

ARIZONA ARCHAEOLOGICAL & HISTORICAL SOCIETY
Arizona State Museum, University of Arizona
TUCSON, AZ 85721
(602) 621-4011
Ronald H. Towner, Director
Purpose: To encourage scholarly pursuits in

areas of history and anthropology of the southwestern U.S. and Northern Mexico; to encourage the preservation of archaeological and historical sites; to publish the results of archaeological, historical, and ethnographic investigations; and to provide educational opportunities through lectures, field trips, and other activities. Provides scholarship, research and travel grants. *Publication*: Kiva: The Journal of Southwestern Anthropology and History. Founded 1916.

SOUTHWEST PARKS & MONUMENTS ASSN.
221 N. Court Ave.
TUCSON, AZ 85701
 (602) 622-1999
 T.J. Priehs, Executive Director
Purpose: To aid in the preservation and interpretation of Southwestern features of outstanding national interests. *Activities*: Sponsors research projects; publishes authoritative literature, and books on Indians, archaeological ruins, and history. Founded 1937.

TRADITIONAL INDIAN ALLIANCE
2925 South 12th Ave.
Tucson, AZ 85713
 (602) 882-0555 Fax 623-6529

TUCSON INDIAN CENTER
131 E. Broadway, P.O. Box 2307
TUCSON, AZ 85702
 (602) 884-7131 Fax 884-0240
 William Quiroga, Executive Director
Purpose: To provide services to the urban Indian population of Pima County. *Activities/programs*: Employment & Training Services (vocational training); Housing Assistance for emergency shelter; also Counseling & Prevention activities to youth at risk for drug & gang involvement, crisis intervention; and referrals to other resources. Established 1963.

HOPI LEGAL SERVICES
P.O. Box 558
WINDOW ROCK, AZ 86515
 (602) 738-2251

WINSLOW INDIAN CENTER
407 E. 3rd St.
WINSLOW, AZ 86047
 (602) 289-4525
 Cheryl Sorrell, Executive Director
Alcoholism Project.

ARKANSAS

AMERICAN INDIAN CENTER OF ARKANSAS
235 N. Greenwood
FORT SMITH, AR 72901
 (501) 785-5149
See listing below.

AMERICAN INDIAN CENTER OF ARKANSAS
2 Van Circle, Suite 2
LITTLE ROCK, AR 72207
 (501) 666-9032
 Paul S. Austin, Director
Purpose: To advance the social, cultural and economic well-being of Indian people residing in Arkansas through job training. *Program*: Indian Manpower Program offers employment assistance, training and counseling. Established 1977.

ARKANSAS DEPARTMENT OF EDUCATION
Federal Programs
34 Capitol Mall, Room 205-B
LITTLE ROCK, AR 72201
 (501) 682-4268
 Clarence Lovell, Contact

CALIFORNIA

CENTER FOR INDIAN COMMUNITY DEVELOPMENT
Humboldt University, Brero House 93
ARCATA, CA 95521
 (707) 826-3711
 Lois Risling, Director
Activities: Works with tribes, organizations and Indian communities to develop educational, economic and social programs to help gain self-determination.

AMERICAN INDIAN CENTER OF CENTRAL CALIFORNIA
P.O. Box 607, 32980 Auberry Rd.
AUBERRY, CA 93602
 (209) 855-2695/2705
 David Works, Chairperson
 Orie Medicinebull, Executive Director
Description: Educational entity seeking academic and social advancement for American Indian students. *Activities*: Pre-school to high school to college emphasis including: Indian education; California Indian Education Center; American Indian Women's Association; videotapes with handbook, produced and directed by Orie Medicinebull, "Colliding Worlds," "Visions of Youth," "Success for American Indian Children." Library. Founded 1989.

AMERICAN INDIAN FREE CLINIC
9500 Artesia Blvd.
BELLFLOWER, CA 90706
 (310) 920-7227 Fax 920-5677
 Joan Freeman, Executive Director

INYO CHILD CARE SERVICES, INC.
Route 3, Box B-75
BISHOP, CA 93514
 (619) 872-3911
Head Start Program.

CALIFORNIA INDIAN LEGAL SERVICES
819 N. Barlow Lane
BISHOP, CA 93514
 (619) 873-3582 Fax 873-8788
 Dorothy Alther & Lawrence Stidham,
 Staff Attorneys
See Oakland (main office) listing. *Counties served*: Alpine, Inyo, Kern, Mono, and Tuolumne.

PIT RIVER HEALTH SERVICES, INC.
P.O. Box 2720
BURNEY, CA 96013
 (916) 335-5090

SOUTHERN CALIFORNIA INDIAN CENTER
500 E. Carson Plaza Dr. #101
CARSON, CA 90746
 (213) 329-9595
Purpose: To promote social and economic self-sufficiency for American Indian people (Los Angeles & Orange counties) by establishing and maintaining educational, cultural, economic and

recreational programs. *Goal*: To assist individuals in finding employment; & supportive services.

SOUTHERN CALIFORNIA INDIAN CENTER
5900 S. Eastern Ave. #104
COMMERCE, CA 90040
 (213) 728-8844
Purpose: To promote social and economic self-sufficiency for American Indian people (Los Angeles & Orange counties) by establishing and maintaining educational, cultural, economic and recreational programs. *Goal*: To assist individuals in finding employment; other programs include: Tutorial Services, Cultural & Traditional Arts Education, Enrichment Trips and Activities, Advocacy, Career & Higher Education Guidance, Parent Development Workshops. Resource library.

AMERICAN INDIAN FREE CLINIC, INC.
1330 South Long Beach Blvd.
COMPTON, CA 90221
 (213) 537-0103
 Joan Freeman, Executive Director
Supplies quality low-cost medical, psychological, dental, social and related services to American Indians and others in Los Angeles county.

TECUMSEH CENTER
University of California
DAVIS, CA 95616
 (916) 752-3237
 Dave Risling, Coordinator

CHAPA-DE INDIAN EDUCATION CENTER
6240 Main St., P.O. Box 847
ELDORADO, CA 85623
 (916) 626-3284
 Florence Thomas, Director

CALIFORNIA INDIAN LEGAL SERVICES
120 W. Grand Ave., Suite 204
ESCONDIDO, CA 92025
 (619) 746-8941 Fax 746-1815
 James E. Cohen, Directing Attorney
 Nancy Rank & Cynthia Kiersnowski,
 Staff Attorneys
See Oakland (main office) listing. *Counties served*: Imperial, Los Angeles, Orange, Riverside, San Bernardino, San Diego, Santa Barbara, and Ventura.

CALIFORNIA INDIAN LEGAL SERVICES
324 F St., Suite A
EUREKA, CA 95501
 (707) 443-8397 Fax 443-8913
 Marilyn Miles & Mary Risling, Staff Attorneys
See Oakland (main office) listing. *Counties served*: Del Norte, Humboldt, Lassen, Modoc, Shasta, Siskiyou, Tehama, and Trinity.

INDIAN ACTION COUNCIL OF NORTHWESTERN CALIFORNIA
P.O. Box 1287, 2725 Myrtle Ave.
EUREKA, CA 95502-1287
 (707) 443-8401
 June Chilton, Director

NORTHERN CALIFORNIA INDIAN DEVELOPMENT CENTER
241 F St.
EUREKA, CA 95501
 (707) 445-8451
 Douglas Risling, Director
Description: A social service agency providing education and employment services through the Job Training and Partnership Act.

**YA-KA-AMA INDIAN EDUCATION
& DEVELOPMENT, INC.**
6215 Eastside Rd.
Forestville, CA 95436
  (707) 887-1541
  Luwana Quitiquit, Executive Director
Purpose: Provide programs for five-county Native American population to advance their educational, economic, social and cultural opportunities necessary to the attainment of sovereignty and self-determination. *Special programs:* Vocational training in horticulture, business and merchandising. Operates Native plant nursery and organic produce; Native Arts Gallery and Native crafts store; Library. Publication: Quarterly newsletter. Founded 1972.

CALIFORNIA INDIAN EDUCATION ASSN.
5108 E. Clinton Way, Suite 108
FRESNO, CA 93727
  (209) 456-9195
  Virginia Grieco, Executive Director
Purpose: To create a better understanding of the history, culture, and contributions of California Indians; to stimulate and promote research and study of the earl American Indians; to support the preservation of California's Native cultural heritage; and to encourage Indian parents to become involved in improving their children's education.

SOUTHERN CALIFORNIA INDIAN CENTER
12755 Brookhurst St., P.O. Box 2550
GARDEN GROVE, CA 92642-2550
  (714) 530-0225
  John Castillo, Executive Director
Purpose: To promote social and economic self-sufficiency for American Indian people (Los Angeles & Orange counties) by establishing and maintaining educational, cultural, economic and recreational programs. *Special programs:* Senior citizens center, tutoring, annual pow-wow and job fair. *Publication:* SCIC News, monthly newsletter. Library. Established 1968.

MENDOCINO COUNTY INDIAN CENTER
Native-American Education Center
P.O. Box 495, Hwy. 101 S.
HOPLAND, CA 95449

INDIAN FREE CLINIC
7300 South Santa Fe Ave.
HUNTINGTON PARK, CA 90225

**LOS ANGELES AMERICAN INDIAN
LIAISON TO THE MAYOR**
200 N. Spring St.
LOS ANGELES, CA 90012
  (213) 485-8881
  Roxanne Burgess, Liaison

**LOS ANGELES CITY/COUNTY NATIVE
AMERICAN INDIAN COMMISSION**
500 W. Temple St., Room 780
LOS ANGELES, CA 90012
  (213) 974-7554 Fax 626-7034
  Fr. Paul Ojibway, Commissioner
  Glenda Ahhitty, Director
Purpose: To promote the general welfare, public interest, and well being of the Los Angeles Indian community, the largest urban Indian population in the U.S.

**LOS ANGELES COUNTY
DEPT. OF HEALTH SERVICES**
313 N. Figueroa
LOS ANGELES, CA 90012

  (213) 974-7741
  Colleen Colson, American Indian
  Community Liaison

SOUTHERN CALIFORNIA INDIAN CENTER
2500 Wilshire Blvd. #750
LOS ANGELES, CA 90057
  (213) 387-5772
Purpose: To promote social and economic self-sufficiency for American Indian people (Los Angeles & Orange counties) by establishing and maintaining educational, cultural, economic and recreational programs. *Goal:* To assist individuals in finding employment; Maintains Indian Child and Family Services section.

UNITED AMERICAN INDIAN INVOLVEMENT
118 Winston St.
LOS ANGELES, CA 90013
  (213) 625-2565
  David L. Rambeau, Executive Director
Purpose: To provide assistance to the American Indian population within the Los Angeles County area suffering from the disease of alcoholism and other drugs. Emphasis targeted are skid row Los Angeles City. *Special programs:* Counseling; nutrition; personal hygiene; housing assistance; youth diversion programs, family activities; day sleep facilities; sober living; limited detox and other crisis assistance as needed. Established 1974.

CALIFORNIA INDIAN LEGAL SERVICES
510 16th St., Suite 301
OAKLAND, CA 94612
  (510) 835-0284 Fax 835-8045
  Michael S. Pfeffer, Executive Director
Description: A statewide nonprofit corporation organized to provide legal representation to low-income Native Americans for legal problems unique to Native American people. This is the main office which houses the program administration and also serves as a field office. *Counties served:* Alameda, Amador, Calaveras, Contra Costa, El Dorado, Fresno, Kings, Madera, Marin, Mariposa, Merced, Monterey, Placer, Sacramento, San Benito, San Francisco, San Joaquin, San Luis Obispo, San Mateo, Santa Clara, Santa Cruz, Solano, Stanislaus, Tulare, and Yolo. Services are provided by each office in the counties included within its service area. Each office has 2-3 attorneys and paralegals on staff. Other offices located in Bishop, Escondido, Eureka, and Ukiah, CA. Indian Law Library. Founded 1967.

INTERTRIBAL FRIENDSHIP HOUSE
523 East 14th St.
OAKLAND, CA 94606
  (510) 452-1235
  Jim Lamenti, Executive Director
  Loretta VanWinkle, Executive Secretary
  Sharon Bennett, Social Worker
  Susan Lobo, Community History Proj. Coord.
Purpose: To promote and maintain the well-being of American Indian life in the modern and traditional way. *Programs:* Cultural; social services; senior program; community history project. Gift Shop. Artifacts exhibit, visual arts and writing, tapes (video and music), historical records. Book currently being written. Established 1955.

**NATIVE AMERICAN ALCOHOLISM
& DRUG ABUSE PROGRAM**
1815 39th Ave. No. A
OAKLAND, CA 94601

URBAN INDIAN CHILD RESOURCE CENTER
OAKLAND, CA 94610
  (510) 832-2386
  Carol Marquez-Baines, MPH, Director
Serves the American Indian people residing in the San Francisco Bay area. *Programs:* Indian Child Welfare Act Advocacy; Mental Health Services; Foster Care Recruitment and Certification; Social Services; Cultural Awareness; Treatment Seminars; In-Service Training to public and private agencies; continuing education. Library.

**CHRISTIAN HOPE INDIAN-
ESKIMO FELLOWSHIP (CHIEF)**
P.O. Box 2600
ORANGE, CA 92669

AMERICAN INDIAN EDUCATION CENTER
P.O. Box 40
PALA, CA 92059
  (619) 742-1121

CALIFORNIA DEPARTMENT OF EDUCATION
American Indian Education Office
P.O. Box 944272
SACRAMENTO, CA 94244
  (916) 657-3696 Fax 657-3859
  Jane Holzmann, Consultant
Purpose: To provide statewide coordination and technical assistance. *Activity:* Has reissued *The American Indian: Yesterday, Today and Tomorrow: A Handbook for Educators*.

**CALIFORNIA NATIVE AMERICAN
HERITAGE COMMISSION**
915 Capitol Mall, Room 288
SACRAMENTO, CA 95814
  (916) 322-7791
  Loretta Allen, Chair
Description: Composed of California tribal members. *Purpose:* To protect historical remains uncovered through construction, and to ensure the return of remains to the appropriate tribe for reburial. Responsible for implementing California's strong state repatriation laws.

**NATIVE AMERICAN
HERITAGE COMMISSION**
915 Capitol Mall, Room 364
SACRAMENTO, CA 95814
  (916) 653-4082
  Larry Myers, Executive Secretary

SACRAMENTO INDIAN CENTER
Alcoholism Awareness Program
2729 P St.
SACRAMENTO, CA 95816

**SACRAMENTO URBAN
INDIAN HEALTH PROJECT**
801 Broadway, Suite B
SACRAMENTO, CA 95818
  (916) 441-0918

AMERICAN INDIAN MEDICAL CLINIC
2561 First Ave.
SAN DIEGO, CA 92103
  (714) 234-2158

AMERICAN INDIAN FRIENDSHIP HOUSE
80 Julian Ave.
SAN FRANCISCO, CA 94103

NATIVE AMERICAN HEALTH CENTER
56 Julian Ave.
SAN FRANCISCO,,CA 94103
  (415) 621-8051

Regional, State & Local Organizations

65

**AMERICAN INDIAN CENTER
OF SANTA CLARA VALLEY**
919 The Alameda
SAN JOSE, CA 95126
(408) 971-9622
Nolan Grayson, Acting Director
Purpose: To promote the social, educational and economic welfare, and to secure justice and equal opportunities for persons of American Indian descent. Personnel: Jennifer Patel, JTP A Coordinator; Cheryl Valdo, Library worker; Mark Coyote & Juanita Montgomery, I&R workers. *Programs*: Job Training Partnership Act; Four Winds Lodge; cultural dance group; mini gallery; food program. *Publication*: Monthly newsletter. Library. Founded 1970.

URBAN INDIAN HEALTH PROJECT
610 Del Monte Ave.
SANTA BARBARA, CA 93101
(805) 965-0718

**SONOMA COUNTY PEOPLE
FOR ECONOMIC OPPORTUNITY**
555 Sebastopol Rd. #A
SANTA ROSA, CA 95407-6867

**ANTELOPE INDIAN CIRCLE
RELIGIOUS GROUP**
P.O. Box 790
SUSANVILLE,, CA 96130
(916) 257-2181 Ext. 468
Craig Pearce, Chairperson
Michael Gabuil, Vice Chairperson
Donald Selder & Walt Strait, Sponsors
Goals: To provide suitable opportunity, such as self-improvement development within the Indian community, with emphasis on communication and inter-personal relationships; to preserve and protect cultural values, historical monuments, spiritual beliefs, religions, and sacred artifacts. *Special programs/activities*: Resident placement, employment, and job training for Indians. Founded 1974.

CALIFORNIA INDIAN LEGAL SERVICES
Box 488, 200 W. Henry St.
UKIAH, CA 95482
(707) 462-3825 Fax 462-4235
Maureen Geary, Contact
See Oakland (main office) listing. *Counties served*: Butte, Colusa, Glenn, Lake, Mendocino, Napa, Nevada, Plumas, Sierra, Sonoma, Sutter, and Yuba.

MENDOCINO COUNTY INDIAN CENTER
1621 Talmadge Rd.
UKIAH, CA 95482

AMERICAN INDIAN CULTURAL GROUP
P.O. Box 2000
VACAVILLE, CA 95688

SOUTHERN CALIFORNIA INDIAN CENTER
6309 Van Nuys Blvd., Suite 104
VAN NUYS, CA 91401
(818) 782-1191
Purpose: To promote social and economic self-sufficiency for American Indian people (Los Angeles & Orange counties) by establishing and maintaining educational, cultural, economic and recreational programs. *Goal*: To assist individuals in finding employment; other programs include: child & family services; education component & supportive services.

COLORADO

COLORADO INDIAN BAR ASSOCIATION
Native American Rights Fund
1506 Broadway
BOULDER, CO 80302
(303) 447-8760
Melody McCoy, President;
L. Robert Muray, V.P.
Patrice Kunesh, Secretary/Treasurer

**FREDERICKS, PELCYGER,
HESTER & WHITE**
Canyon Center, 1881 9th St. #216
BOULDER, CO 80302
(303) 443-1683 Fax 443-6490
Thomas W. Fredericks, Sr. Partner
Description: Law firm which specializes in Indian law.

**COLORADO COMMISSION
OF INDIAN AFFAIRS**
Room 130, State Capitol
DENVER, CO 80203
(303) 866-3027
Mary Jo Dennis, Executive Secretary
Purpose: To improve the government to government relationship of the Indian people of Colorado, primarily the two Ute tribes located in southwest Colorado.

**COLORADO INDIAN EMPLOYMENT
ASSISTANCE CENTER**
Box 10134, University Park Station
DENVER, CO 80210
Purpose: To provide research/job training and direct placement of Indians and Alaska Natives in job market. *Activities*: Various publications and research projects. Library (private).

DENVER INDIAN HEALTH BOARD
2035 East 18th St., Suite 8
DENVER, CO 80206
(303) 320-3974

DENVER NATIVE AMERICANS UNITED, INC.
Denver Indian Center
4407 Morrison Rd.
DENVER, CO 80219
(303) 937-0401
Lisa Harjo, Director
Program: The Circle of Learning program embodies a cultural approach to teaching in a preschool setting. Indian culture is interwoven into all classroom activities. Developed a multicultural preschool curriculum model called *The Circle Never Ends*.

**EAGLE LODGE--AMERICAN INDIAN
ALCOHOLISM REHABILITATION PROGRAM**
1264 Race St.
DENVER, CO 80206

SOUTHERN UTE CULTURAL CENTER
P.O. Box 737
IGNACIO, CO 81137
(303) 563-9583
Helen Hoskins, Director
Purpose: To locate and preserve Ute Indian artifacts and educate about Ute culture. *Activities*: Workshops, tours. *Publications*: The Ute Legacy, education packet with Ute history books, videotape and study guide. Museum. Library. Founded 1972.

CONNECTICUT

CONNECTICUT INDIAN AFFAIRS COUNCIL
Department of Environmental Protection
165 Capitol Ave., Rm. 245
HARTFORD, CT 06106
(203) 566-5193
Ed Sarabia, Indian Affairs Coordinator

AMERICAN INDIANS FOR DEVELOPMENT
P.O. Box 117, 236 West Main St.
MERIDEN, CT 06450
(203) 238-4009
Kenneth Attocknie, Executive Director
Purpose: To assist the native American population in Connecticut through development of education and employment opportunities, and to act as a clearinghouse for social service programs. *Activities*: Emergency food bank; pow-wows and social events; educational material. *Publication*: Bimonthly newsletter.

AMERICAN INDIAN STUDIES INSTITUTE
Curtis Rd., Box 1260
WASHINGTON, CT 06793
(203) 868-0518
Susan F. Payne, Director
Purpose: To discover, preserve, and interpret information about the lifeways of the first peoples of the Northeast Woodlands area of the U.S., and to enhance appreciation for their cultures and achievements. *Activities*: Conducts archaeological surveys and excavations; provides indoor and outdoor exhibits; sponsors archaeological training sessions, teacher workshops, craft workshops, summer youth programs-educational programs to school groups. *Publication*: Artifacts, quarterly magazine; annual research report; bibliography and educational resource pamphlets. Annual conference, with symposium - always November, Lowell, MA.. Museum. Library. Founded 1971.

DELAWARE

NANTICOKE INDIAN ASSOCIATION
Route 4, Box 107-A
MILLSBORO, DE 19966
(302) 945-7022
Kenneth Clark, Director

DELAWARE HUMAN RELATIONS DIVISION
820 N. French, 4th Floor
WILMINGTON, DE 19801
(302) 571-3716
Andrew Turner, Jr., Director

DISTRICT OF COLUMBIA

**AMERICAN INDIAN SOCIETY
OF WASHINGTON, DC**
P.O. Box 6431
FALLS CHURCH, VA 22040
(804) 448-3707
Jay Hill, President
See listing under Virginia.

FLORIDA

FLORIDA GOVERNOR'S COUNCIL ON INDIAN AFFAIRS, INC.
1020 E. Lafayette St., Suite 102
TALLAHASSEE, FL 32301
(904) 488-0730
Joe A. Quetone, Executive Director

GEORGIA

OGLE WANAGI GALLERY & CENTER
842 b. N. Highland Ave.
ATLANTA 30306
(404) 872-4213
Tom Perkins & Vickie Dunken, Owners
Purpose: To act as a networking facility for Indian needs, as an educational center , and as a meeting place for Indian and other groups. *Activities*: AA programs; arts & crafts gallery . Library. Founded 1990.

GEORGIA CHEROKEE HERITAGE SOCIETY
Rt. 3 Box 750
DAHLONEGA, GA 30533
(706) 864-6010
Mel Hawkins, Contact

THE NATIVE AMERICAN CENTER OF GEORGIA, INC. (NACOG)
110 S. Main St., Suite 203, P .O. Box 2249
WOODSTOCK, GA 30188
(404) 924-3738
Warren Genett, Chairperson
Purpose: A non-profit organization promoting the unity and success of·Native Americans in Georgia through community-based services that combine traditional Native American values with contemporary life and thereby strengthen our identity as a community .

HAWAII

CONGRESS OF THE HAWAIIAN PEOPLE
98-1364 Akaaka St.
ALEA, HI 96701
(808) 488-6905
John Agare, President
Purpose: A coalition of Hawaiian organizations and individuals who seek to preserve the cultural heritage and improve the social, economic, and educational welfare of Native Hawaiians and their communities.

HALE NAUA III SOCIETY OF NATIVE HAWAIIAN ARTS
99-919 Kalawina Pl.
ALEA, HI 96701
(808) 487-6949
Rocky Jensen, Director
Purpose: To serve Hawaiian artists of native descent, by providing exhibits, lectures, workshops, and historical tours.

HUI MALAMA OLA NA 'OIWI
Kona Office, P.O. Box 447
CAPTAIN COOK, HI 96704
(808) 323-3618 Fax 323-3096

HUI NO KE OLA PONO
Hana Office, 4293-A Hana Hwy.
HANA, HI 96713
(808) 248-7502

QUEEN LILIUOKALANI CHILDREN'S CENTER
Windward Oahu Office
53-516 Kamehameha Hwy .
HAUULA, HI 96717
(808) 293-8577 Fax 293-5182

ALU LIKE, INC.
Hawaii Island Center
32 Kinoole St., Suite 218
HILO, HI 96720
(808) 961-2625

CENTER FOR GIFTED & TALENTED NATIVE HAWAIIAN CHILDREN
University of Hawaii at Hilo
HILO, HI 96720
(808) 933-3678
David Sing, Director
Purpose: To increase opportunities for Native Hawaiian children to participate in educational enrichment activities. One of five federally funded projects designed to raise the educational status of Native Hawaiians.

HAWAI'I ISLAND COUNCIL/HUI NA'AUAO
193 Kino'ole St., Suite 5
HILO, HI 96720
(808) 935-8191 Fax 935-8296

HUI MALAMA OLA NA 'OIWI
305 Wailuku Dr., Suite 3
HILO, HI 96720
(808) 969-9220 Fax 961-4794
Anuhea Reimann Geiger , President
Purpose: To provide health care services to Native Hawaiian residents of the island of Hawai'i. Operates three local clinics in Captain Cook, Waimea, and Pahoa.

ABIGAIL K. KAWANANAKOA TRUST
420 Kekau Place
HONOLULU, HI 96817
(808) 533-7370
Abigail Kawananakoa, President
Purpose: To fund a Halau and offers instruction in the Hawaiian art of Hula.

ALU LIKE, INC.
1624 Mapunapuna St.
HONOLULU, HI 96819
(808) 836-8940
Haunani Apoliona, President
Purpose: To assist Native Hawaiians in their efforts to achieve social and economic excellence. *Programs*: Employment and Training Program; Substance Abuse Prevention Project; Vocational Education Program; Native Hawaiian Library Project. *Activities*: Operates five Island centers. *Publication*: Monthly newsletter . Founded 1974.

ALU LIKE, INC.
Business Development Center
1120 Mauna Kea St., Suite 273
HONOLULU, HI 96817
(808) 524-1225 Fax 522-5314
James Mi'ikeha, Director
Purpose: Offers professional and technical services to small business owners through the Business Services Center . *Programs*: Operates the Entrepreneurship Training Program, and the

Management and Technical Assistance Program for individuals of Hawaiian descent.

ALU LIKE, INC.
Ohau Island Center
1505 Dillingham Blvd., Suite 218
HONOLULU, HI 96817
(808) 847-3868

AMERICAN INDIAN CENTER OF HONOLULU
810 N. Vineyard Blvd.
HONOLULU, HI 96817
(808) 847-3544
John H. Ide, Contact
Purpose: To provide a meeting place for and services to American Indians and Native Alaskans in Hawaii. *Programs*: American Indian Service Corporation; alcoholism counseling and referral service; Hawaii Council of American Indian Nations; American Indian Pow-W ow Association; social and cultural programs; Indian education programs. *Publication*: Honolulu Drum Newsletter . Library.

AMERICAN INDIAN SERVICE CORP.
1007 Dillingham St. #102
HONOLULU, HI 96817
(808) 847-2511
Antoinette Vatter, Director

DAUGHTERS OF HAWAII
2913 Pali Hwy.
HONOLULU, HI 96817
(808) 595-6291 Fax 595-4395
Ellen Vasconcellos, Regent
Purpose: Works to perpetuate the memory and spirit of old Hawaii and preserve the Hawaiian language. *Activities*: Meetings and classes.

DEPT. OF HAWAIIAN HOME LANDS
P.O. Box 1879
HONOLULU, HI 96805
(808) 548-6450
George K. Kaeo, Contact

E OLA MAU
1374 Nu'uanu Ave., Suite 201
HONOLULU, HI 96817
(808) 531-1628 Fax 521-2967
Nanette K. Judd, MPH, President
Purpose: Native Hawaiian health care providers working to achieve good health among Native Hawaiians. Founded 1986.

HAWAII CULTURAL RESEARCH FOUNDATION
P.O. Box 4590
HONOLULU, HI 96813
(808) 524-0884
Hanakaulani A. Ferreria, Contact
Purpose: Offers grants supporting research in Hawaiian arts and philosophy .

HAWAII DEPT. OF EDUCATION SPECIAL PROGRAMS
3430 Leahi Ave., Bldg. E
HONOLULU, HI 96815
(808) 735-9024
Stafford Natani, Contact

HAWAII CULTURE & THE ARTS FOUNDATION
335 Merchant St., Rm. 202
HONOLULU, HI 96813
(808) 548-4145
Wendell Silva, Contact

HAWAII STITCHERY & FIBRE ART GUILD
P.O. Box 61364
HONOLULU, HI 96839
(808) 737-0002
Rebecca Kendro, President
Purpose: To conduct classes, lectures, and
workshops that encourage the development of
Hawaiian stitchery and related fiber arts.

HAWAIIAN CANOE RACING ASSOCIATION
169 S. Kukui St.
HONOLULU, HI 96813
(808) 526-1969 Fax 524-4028
Michael Tongg, President
Purpose: To promote and perpetuate the tradition of Hawaiian canoe racing and Hawaiian
canoes.

HAWAIIAN HOME LANDS DEPARTMENT
P.O. Box 1879
HONOLULU, HI 96805
(808) 548-6450 Fax 586-3835
Ilima A. Pilanaia, Director

HEALTH RESOURCES ADMINISTRATION
Hawaii Health Dept.-Office of Hawaiian Health
1250 Punchbowl St.
HONOLULU, HI 96813
(808) 548-8816 Fax 548-3263

HISTORIC HAWAII FOUNDATIONS
P.O. Box 1658
HONOLULU, HI 96806
(808) 537-9564 Fax 526-3989
Phyllis G. Fox, President
Purpose: To preserve historic buildings, objects,
and sites in Hawaii.

HUI NA-AUAO
3415 Ka'ochiani Dr.
HONOLULU, HI 96817
(808) 595-6647 Fax 595-8105
Elizabeth Pa Martin, President
Purpose: Coalition of over 50 organizations that
seek to promote awareness of Native Hawaiian
sovereignty and self-determination.

**KALIHI-PALAMA
CULTURE & ART SOCIETY**
357 N. King St.
HONOLULU, HI 96817
(808) 521-6905
Hazel Naone, President
Purpose: Sponsors ongoing culture and arts
workshops, hula competitions, annual art exhibits and conference on traditional Hawaiian poetry, chants, and hula.

KE OLA MAMO
1374 Nu'uanu Ave., Suite 200
HONOLULU, HI 96802
(808) 599-5200 Fax 523-9983
Claire Hughes, President
Purpose: To provide health care services to the
Native Hawaiian residents of the island of O'ahu.

NATIVE HAWAIIAN ADVISORY COUNCIL
1088 Bishop St., Suite 1204
HONOLULU, HI 96813
(808) 523-1445 Fax 599-4380
Elizabeth Pa Martin, Executive Director
Purpose: To protect the rights and entitlements
of people of Native Hawaiian ancestry. *Programs*: Water Resources Control Project; conducts workshops. *Publication*: KE KIA'I, monthly
newsletter.

NATIVE HAWAIIAN LIBRARY PROJECT
2810 Pa'a St., Suite 1-A
HONOLULU, HI 96819
(808) 839-7784
Mahealani Merryman, Administrator
Purpose: To establish library programs and services for Native Hawaiians; to increase availability of library resources, and to encourage
parent and child reading programs. Administered by Alu Like, Inc.

**NATIVE HAWAIIAN VOCATIONAL
EDUCATION PROGRAM**
2879 Pa'a St., Suite 201
HONOLULU, HI 96819
(808) 839-7922
Robert Allen, Administrator
Purpose: To improve the academic & employment skills of Native Hawaiian high school students, by helping them enter community college
vocational education programs; & establishing
vocational educational services to assist Native
hawaiian adults in becoming productive members of the labor force. Administered by Alu Like.

OFFICE OF HAWAIIAN AFFAIRS
State of Hawaii
711 Kapiolani Blvd., 5th Floor
HONOLULU, HI 96805
(808) 586-3777 Fax 586-4745
Clayton Hee, Chair

PACIFIC REGION EDUCATIONAL LAB
828 Fort Street Mall #500
HONOLULU, HI 96813
Rita Hocog Inos, Contact

PAPA OLA LOKAHI
Kawaiaha'o Plaza
567 S. King St., Suite 102
HONOLULU, HI 96813
(808) 536-9453 Fax 545-1783
Larry Miike, MD, JD, Executive Director
Purpose: To provide statewide planning and
support to the five Native Hawaiian health care
service providers.

**QUEEN LILIUOKALANI
CHILDREN'S CENTER**
1300 Halona St.
HONOLULU, HI 96817
(808) 847-1302
Purpose: To provide child welfare services
to orphaned Native Hawaiian children.

ROYAL HAWAIIAN BAND
2805 Monsarrat Ave.
HONOLULU, HI 96815
(808) 922-5331 Fax 924-2841
Aaron Mahi, Director
Activities: Performs Native Hawaiian music.

STATE COUNCIL ON HAWAIIAN HERITAGE
P.O. Box 3022
HONOLULU, HI 96807
(808) 586-0335 Phone & Fax
Keahi Allen, Director
Activities: Conducts seminars in dance and presents the annual King Kamehameha Hula Competition. Also sponsors conferences and seminars on storytelling, legends, etc.

KE OLA MAMO
Ko'olaulao Office
601 Haole Camp Rd.
KAHUKU, HI 96731
(808) 203-5414

HALAU MOHALA ILIMA
1110 Aalapapa Dr.
KALLUA, HI 96734
(808) 261-0689
Activities: Provides instruction in
hula and Hawaiian culture.

KE OLA MAMO
Waimanalo Office
1051 Keolu Dr., Suite 240
KALLUA, HI 96734

ALU LIKE, INC.
Hawaii Island Center
Kailua-Kona Annex
74-5622 Alapa St., 2nd Floor
KALLUA-KONA, HI 96740
(808) 885-4700

HO'OLA LAHUI HAWAI'I 1
Kapa'a Office
P.O. Box 29
KAPA'A, HI 96746
(808) 822-2058 Fax 822-3694

KA IMI NAAUAO O HAWAII NEI
P.O. Box 218
KAUMAKANI, HI 96747
(808) 335-3628
Roselle F.K. Bailey, President
Activities: Offers instruction in hula
dancing and Hawaiian culture.

ALU LIKE, INC.
Molokai Island Center
P.O. Box 392
KAUNAKAI, HI 96748
(808) 553-5393

NA PU'UWAI
P.O. Box 130
KAUNAKAI, HI 96748
(808) 567-6831 Fax 567-9004
Emmett Aluli, MD, President
Purpose: To provide health care services to the
Native Hawaiian residents of the island of
Molokai, Kalaupapa, and Lana'i.

LAHAINA ARTS SOCIETY
649 Wharf St.
LAHAINA, HI 96761
(808) 661-0111
Daniel Schroyer, Director
Description: Nonprofit organization that conducts classes, operates galleries, and awards
scholarships to promote art and culture.

ALU LIKE, INC.
Kauai Island Center
4334 Rice St., Suite 204-C
LIHUE, HI 96766
(808) 245-8545

HUI MALAMA OLA NA 'OIWI
Puna Office, P.O. Box 1455
PAHOA, HI 96778

KALANI HONUA
P.O. Box 4500
PAHOA, HI 96778
(808) 965-7828 Fax 965-9443
Richard Koob, Founder
Description: Intercultural conference and retreat
center that includes the site of an ancient Hawaiian school. Accomodations and workshop
facilities for about 100 participants; seminars
and an artist-in-residence program.

HALAU HULA O MILILANI
85-711 Kaupuni Place
WALANAU, HI 96792
(808) 696-2145
Mililani Allen, Director
Description: Hula school that also provides instruction in traditional Hawaiian crafts, languages, and culture.

HALE OLA HO'OPAKOLEA, INC.
89-137 Nanakuli Ave.
WALANAE, HI 96792
(808) 668-2361
Description: Provides outpatient alcohol and drug abuse treatment to Native Hawaiians.

**QUEEN LILIUOKALANI
CHILDREN'S CENTER**
Leeward Oahu Office
87-1876 Farrington Hwy.
WALANAE, HI 96792
(808) 293-8577 Fax 668-881 1

**WAIANAE COAST
CULTURE & ARTS SOCIETY**
89-188 Farrington Hwy.
WALANAE, HI 96792
(808) 668-1549
Agnes Cope, Director
Description: Works for community participation in traditional artistic heritages of ethno-culture through activities in cultural workshops and presentations of dance, music, and craft.

ALU LIKE, INC.
Maui Island Center
400 Hookahi St., Suite 209
WALLUKU, HI 96793
(808) 242-9774

HUI NO KE OLA PONO
P.O. Box 894
WALLUKU, Hi 96793
(808) 244-4647 Fax 242-6676
Joseph Kamaka, MD, President
Purpose: To provide health care services to the Native Hawaiian residents of the island of Maui.

OHANA COUNCIL
41-275 Nakini St.
WALMANALO, HI 96765

HO'OLA LAHUI HAWAI'I
Waimea Medical Clinic
P.O. Box 909
WALMEA, HI 96796
(808) 338-0031 Fax 338-1845
Wayne Fukino, MD, President
Purpose: To provide health care services to the Native hawaiian residents of the islands of Kaua'i and Ni'ihau.

HUI MALAMA OLA NA 'OIWI
Waimea Office
P.O. Box 6288
WALMEA, HI 96743
(808) 885-0489

IDAHO

HUMAN RIGHTS COMMISSION
450 W. State St.
BOISE, ID 83720
(208) 334-2873

Marilyn Shuler, Director
IDAHO DEPT. OF EDUCATION
Adult Education & Indian Education
Jordan Bldg., 650 W. State St.
BOISE, ID 83720
(208) 334-2186 Fax 334-2228
Shirley Spencer, Contact

ILLINOIS

AMERICAN INDIAN CENTER
1630 West Wilson
CHICAGO, IL 60640
(312) 275-5871/561-8183
Samson Keahna, Director

AMERICAN INDIAN HEALTH SERVICE
838 West Irving Park Rd.
CHICAGO, IL 60613
(312) 883-9100

ILLINOIS BOARD OF EDUCATION
Adult and Ethnic Education
100 W. Randolph St.
CHICAGO, IL 60601
(312) 814-3606 Fax 814-2282
Joseph Frattaroli, Contact

ST. AUGUSTINE'S CENTER
4512 North Sheridan Rd.
CHICAGO, IL 60640
(312) 784-1050
Elmira McClure, Director

**QUAD CITY LEAGUE
OF NATIVE AMERICANS**
418 19th St.
ROCK ISLAND, IL 61201
Regina M. Mahieu

INDIANA

**CIVIL RIGHTS COMMISSION
ON INDIAN AFFAIRS**
Indiana Government Center North
100 N. Senate Ave., Room N103
INDIANAPOLIS, IN 46204
(317) 232-2600

MINNETRISTA CULTURAL CENTER
P.O. Box 1527, 1200 N. Minnetrista Pkwy.
MUNCIE, IN 47303
(317) 282-4848 Fax 288-5520
Thomas A. Sargent, PhD, Chairperson
Nicholas L. Clark, President & CEO
Owen R. Glendening, Vice President
Description: The parent organization of and headquarters for the Minnetrista Council for Great Lakes Native American Studies, the largest consortium of Woodland Tribes in America. *Personnel*: Pamela Conrad, Director of Operations; Karen Vincent, Director of Collections. *Activities*: The 23 allied tribes sponsor workshops, pow wows, exhibits, cultural activities and serve as a network for information concerning Woodland culture; maintains lists of tribal artists and tradition bearers for use by those seeking access to Woodland Tribes. Museum collections emphasizing the history, art and sciences of east cenbtral Indiana from pre-history to modern times. Library of public archives of written and video materials. *Publication*:

Minnetrista Columns, monthly newsletter.
Founded 1988.

INDIAN AWARENESS CENTER
Fulton County Historical Society
37 E 375 N
ROCHESTER, IN 46975
(219) 223-4436
Bobbie Bear, President
Judy Cecrle, V.P.; Shirley Willard, Sec/Treas.
Description: Organization of Potawatomi and Miami Indians with roots in Indiana, and people interested in Indians. *Special projects*: Establishing Trail of Death Regional Historic Trail with historical markers from Indiana to Kansas, commemorating forced removal in 1838 of Potawatomi from N. Indiana to Kansas; sponsors Trail of Death Commemorative Caravan every five years (next one planned for 1998); produces Trail of Courage Living History Festival (3rd weekend in September); sponsors Woodland Indian Village at Festival, and Potawatomi Memorial Village; helps with Indian dances. *Publication*: Quarterly newsletter.

IOWA

IOWA GOVERNOR'S LIAISON
1405 Truman Place, State Capitol
AMES, IA 50010
(515) 232-5320

IOWA DEPT. OF HUMAN SERVICES
Hoover State Office Bldg.
DES MOINES, IA 50319
(515) 281-5452
Charles M. Palmer, Director

IOWA CIVIL RIGHTS COMMISSION
c/o Grimes State Office Bldg.
211 E. Maple St., 2nd Floor
DES MOINES, IA 50319
(515) 281-4121

NATIVE AMERICAN CULTURAL CENTER
216 S. 8th St.
FORT DODGE, IA 50501
(515) 576-3867
Jim L. Palmer, Founder/Director
Description: A non-profit organization involved in providing social services & educational activities to area Native Americans.

**NATIVE AMERICAN ALCOHOLISM
TREATMENT PROGRAM**
P.O. Box 790-A
2720 Larpenteau Ave., Bldg. 544
Sargeant Bluff, IA 51054

INDIAN YOUTH OF AMERICA
P.O. Box 2786
SIOUX CITY, IA 51106

SIOUX CITY AMERICAN INDIAN CENTER
619 6th St.
SIOUX CITY, IA 51102
(712) 255-8957
Ernest Ricehill, Executive Director
Purpose: To promote Indian culture and social economic conditions of the community by providing social service programs in health, employment, food, etc.

KANSAS

LAWRENCE INDIAN CENTER
1423 Haskell Ave.
LAWRENCE, KS 66044
 (913) 841-7202
 Charmain Billy, Executive Director
Purpose: To provide community services, such as: emergency food, utility and shelter assistance, housing, job board, craft workshops. Operates Tall Grass Giftshop and Share/Care garden. *Personnel:* Dan Spurgin and Nicole Jay. Library.

KANSAS ASSOCIATION FOR NATIVE AMERICAN EDUCATION
Haskell Indian Jr. College
P.O. Box H-1304
LAWRENCE, KS 66044
 (913) 749-8468
 Marilyn Bread, Contact

MID-AMERICAN ALL-INDIAN CENTER
650 N. Seneca
WICHITA, KS 67203
 (316) 262-5221
 Jerry L. Aday, Executive Director
 Denny Zimmerman, Fiscal Officer
 Jerry Martin, Museum Director
Purpose: To promote awareness of Native American culture in the community; to offer emergency social services for members of the Native American community and transients. *Programs/Activities:* Job Training Program Assistance; pow wows; kiva rental. Museum and Library. Established 1969.

WICHITA INDIAN HEALTH CENTER
2318 East Central
WICHITA, KS 67214
 (316) 262-2415

LOUISIANA

LOUISIANA DEPT. OF EDUCATION
Office of Migrant & Indian Education Programs
P.O. Box 44064
BATON ROUGE, LA 70804
 (504) 342-3517
 Nedra Ourso Loftin, Contact

GOVERNOR'S COMMISSION ON INDIAN AFFAIRS
1885 Wooddale Blvd., Suite 111
BATON ROUGE, LA 70806
 (504) 925-4509
 Diana S. Williamson, Executive Director

MAINE

MAINE INDIAN AFFAIRS COMMISSION
State House Station, #38
AUGUSTA, ME 04333
 (207) 287-5800 Fax 287-5900
 Leo Martin, Contact

MAINE INDIAN TRIBAL STATE COMMISSION
P.O. Box 87
HALLOWELL, ME 04347
 (207) 622-4815
 Diana C. Scully, Executive Director

MAINE TRIBAL/STATE RELATIONS OFFICE
6 River Rd.
INDIAN HEAD, ME 04468
 (202) 827-7776
 Priscilla A. Attean, Contact

TRIBAL GOVERNORS
93 Maine St.
ORONO, ME 04473

MARYLAND

BALTIMORE AMERICAN INDIAN CENTER
113 South Broadway
BALTIMORE 21231
 (301) 675-3535
 Barry Richardson, Executive Director
Purpose: To help American Indians with their cultural, social, economic, housing and educational needs. *Programs:* BAIC Scholarship Fund; Rev. James Dial Memorial Fund; housing; business development; job placement; community services; alcoholism; youth program; Brantley Blue Awards; Annual Pow-Wow. *Publication:* Smoke Signals, newsletter.

MARYLAND DEPARTMENT OF EDUCATION
Liaison to Indian Education
200 W. Baltimore St.
BALTIMORE, MD 21201
 (410) 333-2234 Fax 333-2226
 Jill S. Christianson

MARYLAND COMMISSION ON INDIAN AFFAIRS
100 Community Place
CROWNSVILLE, MD 21032
 (410) 514-7651
 Patricia L. King, Director
Consists of nine members appointed by the Governor for three-year terms. *Purpose:* To support, initiate, coordinate and implement educational, social and economic projects which affect the diverse Indian communities in Maryland; and to increase public awareness and appreciation of the contributions that Indians have made to life in Maryland. *Publication:* Directory of American Indian Organizations in Maryland. Established 1976.

MARYLAND INDIAN HERITAGE SOCIETY
P.O. Box 905
WALDORF 20601
 (301) 888-1566
 Hugh Proctor, President

MASSACHUSETTS

MASSACHUSETTS CENTER FOR NATIVE AMERICAN AWARENESS, INC.
P.O. Box 5885
BOSTON, MA 02114
 (617) 884-4227
 Burne Stanley, Director
Purpose: To serve the cultural, spiritual, and social needs of the Native American peoples residing in Massachusetts. Also, to promote and preserve the cultural and traditional ways of the Native Americans of the land. *Programs:* Legal Assistance Fund; Scholarship Fund; Emergency Needs Fund. *Activities:* Adult lecture series (Spring & Fall); children's workshops (mid-Winter & Spring); monthly festivals/pow wows and socials. Scholarship: The Chief Red Blanket Scholarship Fund. *Publication:* Turtletalk, quarterly newsletter. Established 1989.

MASSACHUSETTS COMMISSION ON INDIAN AFFAIRS
1 Ashburton Place, Room 1004
BOSTON, MA 02108
 (617) 727-6394/6966
 John A. Peters (Slow Turtle), Exec. Director
Consists of seven members of American Indian descent representing the major tribes of the Commonwealth of Massachusetts. *Purpose:* To assist Native American residents of Massachusetts with any problem common to them: social services, legal assistance, housing, employment, civil rights, treaty rights, etc. *Programs:* Reinternment Program; Scholarship Program. Established 1976.

BOSTON INDIAN COUNCIL
105 S. Huntington
JAMAICA PLAIN, MA 02130
 (617) 232-0343
 Jimmy L. Sam, Executive Director
A multi-service social delivery system for the American Indian community of the Greater Boston area, and provides a mechanism for cultural activities. *Programs:* Employment and training; adult education; Head Start; day care; elderly; crafts; Indian Health Service; battered women; housing assistance; alcoholic treatment with halfway house; and speakers bureau. *Publication:* The Circle, monthly newsletter. Library.

MASSACHUSETTS INDIAN ASSOCIATION
245 Rockland Rd.
WALPOLE, MA 01741
 (508) 369-1235
 Marjorie M. Findlay, Director
Purpose: To help Native Americans go to college. *Scholarship Fund:* Financial assistance to Native Americans who live in Massachusetts and are interested in pursuing postsecondary education. Stipends range up to $500 for undergraduates and $1,000 for graduate students

MICHIGAN

AMERICAN INDIANS UNLIMITED
515 East Jefferson
ANN ARBOR, MI 48104

ABORIGINAL RESEARCH CLUB
Dearborn Historical Museum
915 Brady Rd.
DEARBORN, MI 48124
 (313) 565-3000
 Jerry Atkinson, President
Membership: Professional and amateur archaeologists, historians and ethnologists interested in the archaeology of Michigan, Great Lakes region, and Indians of the area. Library. Bimonthly meeting. Founded 1940.

NORTH AMERICAN INDIAN ASSOCIATION OF DETROIT, INC.
22720 Plymouth Rd.
DETROIT, MI 48239
 (313) 535-2966
 Irene Lowry, Director
Membership: 450. *Purpose:* To promote economic development and self-sufficiency for American Indian people through human ser-

vices. *Programs*: Employment and educational services; senior center of fers nutrition, social and educational services; Indian child welfare provides protective services for Indian children and families; Arts and Crafts Gallery business. Russ Wright Scholarship Fund--assists students with the expense of educational supplies. *Publication*: Native Sun, monthly newsletter. Library. Annual meeting and powwow. Founded 1940.

URBAN INDIAN AFFAIRS
1200 - 6th Ave., 8th Floor
DETROIT, MI 48052
(313) 256-1633
Thelma Henry-Shipman

GENESSEE INDIAN CENTER
609 W. Court St.
FLINT, MI 48503
(313) 239-6621
Sam Fisher, Chairperson
Purpose: To provide social and economic development opportunities to the 6,000 Native-Americans living in the following Michigan Counties: Genesee, Lapeer, Shiawassee, Huron, Sanilac and Tuscola. *Programs*: Outreach services (housing, education, health, etc.); cultural and recreational activities; craft classes; Native-American art shows; Indian crafts store. *Publication*: GVIA Grapevine, monthly newsletter. Museum. Library.

GRAND RAPIDS INTER-TRIBAL COUNCIL
45 Lexington N.W.
GRAND RAPIDS, MI 49504
(616) 774-8331

MICHIGAN INDIAN PRESS
45 Lexington NW
GRAND RAPIDS, MI 49504
(616) 774-8331
J. Wagner Wheeler, Executive Director
Purpose: To offer the unique perspective of Native Amerian peoples - striving for cultural accuracy in all publications. *Programs*: Publishes textbooks by and about Native Americans. *Publications*: People of the Three Fires, by James Clifton, George Cornell & James McClurken; Aobe NaBing, by M.T. Bussey, and Research & Writing Tribal Histories, by Dr. Duane Hale.

LANSING INDIAN CENTER
1235 Center St.
LANSING, MI 48906

MICHIGAN COMMISSION ON INDIAN AFFAIRS
Dept. of Management & Budget
Box 30026, 611 W. Ottawa St., 3rd Floor
LANSING, MI 48909
(517) 373-0654
Betty Klenitz, Director
Provides financial assistance to Native American high school graduates of Michigan who are interested in attending college in Michigan. Amount of awards vary.

MICHIGAN DEPT. OF EDUCATION
Native American Programs Unit
P.O. Box 30008
LANSING, MI 48909
(517) 373-6059 Fax (612) 297-7895
Pam Martell, Coordinator

OAKLAND CO. DEPT. OF SOCIAL SERVICES
196 Oakland Ave.
PONTIAC, MI 48342
(810) 858-1837
Booker T. Denis, Indian Outreach Worker
Purpose: To provide services to the Indian community in Okalnad County. Work as Liaison for Indian residents and all human service agencies.

SAGINAW INTER-TRIBAL ASSN.
3239 Christy Way
SAGINAW, MI 48603
(517) 792-4610
Victoria G. Miller, Executive Director
Services the socio-economic needs of American Indians in the Saginaw-Bay area. *Programs*: Cultural enrichment and awareness classes; community health and health referrals; substance abuse referrals; genealogy referrals; information. *Publication*: Bear Talk, monthly newsletter. Exhibits artifacts. Library.

INTER-TRIBAL COUNCIL OF MICHIGAN
405 E. Easterday Ave.
SAULT STE. MARIE, MI 49783
(906) 632-6896
Sharon L. Teeple, Executive Director
Established to plan and carry out programs which will improve the economy, education and quality of life for Michigan Indian people. *Programs*: Families First Program; Commodity Food Program; Head Start and Parent Child Center Programs; Low Income Energy Assistance; Single Parent Program; Mental Health Program. Founded 1968.

MICHIGAN INDIAN CHILD WELFARE AGENCY
405 E. Easterday Ave.
SAULT STE. MARIE, MI 49783
(906) 635-9400
LeAnne E. Silvey, Executive Director
Purpose: To provide foster care and adoption/placement agency for Native American children, founded to facilitate P.L. 95-608 (The Indian Child Welfare Act) of 1978. Provides social services, foster care placement, foster home licensing, adoption placement and home studies. *Program*: Family Friend Program. *Publications*: Family Friend Training Manual; Model Tribal Adoption Code. Founded 1978.

MICHIGAN INDIAN LEGAL SERVICES
160 E. State St.
TRAVERSE CITY, MI 49684
(616) 947-0122

SOUTH EASTERN MICHIGAN INDIANS, INC.
P.O. Box 861
WARREN, MI 48090
(313) 756-1350
Nancy Ragsdale, Contact
Purpose: To provide services to the Native American Indian of the metro tri-county areas including: job placement, employment raining referrals, transportation, emergency food and clothing, and the preservation of Indian culture. *Publication*: Talking Peace Pipes, monthly newspaper. Founded 1975.

MINNESOTA

MINNESOTA STATE DEPT. OF EDUCATION
State Services Center
1819 Bemidji Ave.
BEMIDJI, MN 56601
(218) 755-2926
Indian Scholarship Program: Financial assistance to Native American high school graduatess in Minnesota who are interested in pursuing postsecondary education. Scholarships range from $500 to $2,000. The average award is $1,200.

MINNESOTA INDIAN AFFAIRS COUNCIL
1819 Bemidji Ave.
BEMIDJI, MN 56601
(218) 755-3825
Joseph Day, Executive Director
Purpose: The official liaison between state and tribal governments and advisor to the state on urban Indian issues and concerns: health, education, welfare and other public support, housing economic development, protection of the environment, and protection of tribal rights. The council is governed by the elected tribal chair of the 11 reservations throughout the state, and two at large members from other states. The council has an Urban Indian Advisory Committee. Minnesota has an American Indian population of about 52,000. Branch office located in St. Paul, MN.

ANISHINABE LEGAL SERVICES
P.O. Box 157
CASS LAKE, MN 56633
(218) 335-2223

INDIAN LEGAL ASSISTANCE PROGRAM
217 N. 4th Ave., W.
DULUTH, MN 55806
(218) 727-2881

JUNIOR ACHIEVEMENT'S URBAN AMERICAN INDIAN PROGRAM
3939 W. 69th St.
EDINA, MN 55435
(612) 927-8354
Ron Cody, Contact
Purpose: To target the problems of urban Native American Youth. Programs: 20 Native American students 14-19 years old, who will develop and run their own business (developed with the American Indian Opportunities Industrialization Center); Native American Economic Initiative - provides Native American K-12 students at the Mille Lacs Reservation in-class economic education including work force readiness skills. Publication: Native Models for Business Success.

INDIAN CENTER
5633 Regent Ave. North
MINNEAPOLIS, MN 55440

INDIAN FAMILY SERVICES, INC.
1305 E. 24th St.
MINNEAPOLIS, MN 55404
(612) 348-5788
Doreen Day, Director
Helps the Indian elderly and disabled become more independent through social and recreational activities.

INDIAN HEALTH BOARD OF MINNEAPOLIS
1315 East 24th St.
MINNEAPOLIS, MN 55404
(612) 721-7425
Noreen Smith, Director of Indian
Family Services.

MINNEAPOLIS AMERICAN INDIAN CENTER
1530 East Franklin Ave.
MINNEAPOLIS, MN 55404
(612) 871-4555
Frances Fairbanks, Executive Director
Goals: To foster the social and economic development of the Indian community of Minneapolis. Provides a variety of social, educational, cultural and economic programs and services, including: Indian Child Welfare; Chemical Dependency Counseling and Prevention Education; Adult Basic Education; JTPA Employment and Training; Youth Intervention; Recreation; and Senior Citizens. Operates Two Rivers Gallery art museum, First People's Gallery, and Circle Cafe. Publication: The Circle, monthly newspaper. Founded 1974.

MINNESOTA AMERICAN INDIAN BAR ASSN.
Suite 840, Midland Square Bldg.
MINNEAPOLIS, MN 55401
(612) 540-3728
Jeffrey Crawford, President; Shirley Cain, V.P.
Robert Blaeser, Secretary/Treasurer

MINNESOTA DEPT. OF INDIAN WORK
3045 Park Ave.
MINNEAPOLIS, MN 55407

MINNESOTA INDIAN EDUCATION ASSN.
Metropolitan State University
730 Hennepin Ave.
MINNEAPOLIS, MN 56603
(612) 729-7397
Flo Wiger, Contact

**MINNESOTA INDIAN WOMEN'S
RESOURCE CENTER**
2300 15th Ave. S.
MINNEAPOLIS, MN 55404
(612) 728-2000 Fax 728-2039
Margaret Peake Raymond, Exec. Director
Purpose: To provide charitable services to American Indian women and their children in the following areas: housing, chemical dependency treatment, family reunification/crisis intervention, children's day care, and training. Activities: Staff training, community lectures and program technical assistance services; and parenting education training. Library. Established 1974.

**UPPER MIDWEST
AMERICAN INDIAN CENTER**
1113 West Broadway
MINNEAPOLIS, MN 55411
(612) 522-4436
Dennis Morrison, Executive Director

LAKOTA CULTURAL EDUCATION SERVICE
806 S. Water St.
NORTH FIELD, MN 55057
(507) 663-1090

AMERICAN INDIAN CENTER
St. Cloud State University
720 4th Ave. S.
ST. CLOUD, MN 56301

AMERICAN INDIAN HEALTH CARE ASSN.
245 East Sixth St., Suite 815
ST. PAUL, MN 55101
(612) 293-0233

IRA HAYES FRIENDSHIP HOUSE
1671 Summit Ave.
ST. PAUL, MN 55105

MINNESOTA DEPT. OF EDUCATION
550 Cedar St.
ST. PAUL, MN 55101
(612) 296-6458 Fax 297-7895
Will Antell, Contact
Purpose: To administer several programs designed to assist Indian learners in public, tribal and Indian controlled schools of Minnesota.

MINNESOTA DEPT. OF HUMAN SERVICES
Chemical Dependency Program Division
444 Lafayette Rd.
ST. PAUL, MN 55155-3823

MINNESOTA HISTORICAL SOCIETY
690 Cedar St.
ST. PAUL, MN 55101

MINNESOTA INDIAN AFFAIRS COUNCIL
1450 Energy Park Dr. #140
ST. PAUL, MN 55108
(612) 643-3032
See listing of main office in Bemidji, MN.

TWIN CITIES CHIPPEWA COUNCIL
1592 Hoyt Ave. East
ST. PAUL, MN 55105

MISSOURI

HEART OF AMERICA INDIAN CENTER
1340 East Admiral Blvd.
KANSAS CITY, MO 64124
(816) 421-7608

AMERICAN INDIAN CENTER
4115 Connecticut
ST. LOUIS, MO 63116
Publication: Eyapaha, newsletter.

SOUTHWEST MISSOURI INDIAN CENTER
2422 West Division
SPRINGFIELD, MO 65802
(417) 869-9550
Mike Fields, Executive Director
Purpose: Established to alleviate the problems of low-income Native American Indians in the urban setting. To provide understanding between Indian people and the white dominated community. To provide cultural presentations to assist in the learning process. Activities: Social services, counseling, emergency services, referral, alcohol & drug abuse prevention program. Publication: "Rising Sun Newsletter, monthly newsletter.

MONTANA

**ANACONDA INDIAN ALLIANCE
HEALTH PROGRAM**
P.O. Box 1108, 506 East Park
ANACONDA, MT 59711
(406) 563-3459

BILLINGS AMERICAN INDIAN COUNCIL
P.O. Box 853
BILLINGS, MT 59103
(406) 248-1648
Publication: Newsletter.

INDIAN HEALTH BOARD OF BILLINGS
P.O. Box 203, 721 North 29th
BILLINGS, MT 59101

MONTANA INTER-TRIBAL POLICY BOARD
c/o Roland Kennedy
P.O. Box 850
BROWNING, MT 59417
(406) 652-3113
Merle R. Lucas, Executive Director
Organized to represent, develop, protect, and advance the economic, cultural, social, and political well-being of Indian people in the State of Montana. Provides training and technical assistance to seven Indian reservations in the areas of social services, economic development, law and order, natural resource development, and personnel management.

NORTHERN PLAINS INDIAN CRAFTS ASSN.
P.O. Box E
BROWNING, MT 59417
(406) 338-5661
Description: An independent business owned by Native American craftsmen from the Northern Plains region. Objectives: To provide a sales outlet for the finest contemporary Native American arts and crafts products; and to help promote the careers of outstanding Native American artists and craftsmen. Products include paintings, Indian dance accessories, jewelry, dolls, Indian pipes, quill-work items, beadwork items, etc. Museum shop located in the Northern Plains Museum. Established 1942.

NORTH AMERICAN INDIAN ALLIANCE
P.O. Box 286, 12 East Galena
BUTTE, MT 59701
(406) 723-4361

GREAT FALLS INDIAN EDUCATION CENTER
P.O. Box 2531
GREAT FALLS, MT 59403
(406) 761-3165

**NATIVE AMERICAN CENTER
HEALTH PROGRAM**
P.O. Box 2612, 700 Tenth St. South
GREAT FALLS, MT 59403

MONTANA INDIAN EDUCATION ASSN.
P.O. Box 547
HARLEM, MT 59526
(406) 353-2205
Marge Perez, Contact
Activities: Sponsors and annual conference.
Publication: The Buckskin Journal, bimonthly newsletter. Established in 1979.

GOVERNOR'S OFFICE OF INDIAN AFFAIRS
State Coordinator of Indian Affairs
Rm. 202, State Capitol Bldg.
HELENA, MT 59620
(406) 444-3702
Kathleen M. Fleury, Coordinator
Purpose: To provide a greater understanding between Montana's Indian population and local, state and federal government agencies; to seek ways and means of communicating their opinions and needs to agencies of responsibility and actively assist them in organizing their efforts;

and to act as representative for organized bodies of Indians.

HELENA INDIAN ALLIANCE
Leo Pocha Memorial Health Clinic
436 North Jackson
HELENA, MT 59601
 (406) 442-9334

MONTANA COMMERCE DEPT.
Indian Affairs
1424 9th Ave.
HELENA, MT 59260
 (406) 444-3702
 Kathleen Fleury, Coordinator

**MONTANA STATE OFFICE
OF PUBLIC INSTRUCTION**
Indian Education Specialist
State Capitol - Room 106
HELENA, MT 59620
 (406) 444-3031 Fax 444-3924
 Robert Parsley, Contact
Purpose: To provide technical assistance and materials in the area of Indian education. *Activities*: Training for teaching Indian children is provided for parents, school boards & teachers.

MONTANA UNITED INDIAN ASSOCIATION
436 N. Last Chance Gulch, No. 2
HELENA, MT 59601

**INDIAN DEVELOPMENT
& EDUCATION ALLIANCE**
P.O. Box 726
MILES CITY, MT 59301
 (406) 232-6112

MISSOULA INDIAN CENTER
Native American Services Agency
2300 Regent St. #A
MISSOULA, MT 59801
 (406) 329-3373
 Bill Walls, Executive Director
 Joann Youngbear, Health Coordinator
 Debbie Tatsey, Health Outreach Worker
 Joe Whitehawk, Cultural Specialist
Purpose: To provide for the general welfare of the Missoula Urban Indian community through provision of health and human services. *Special programs*: Youth Indian Cultural Enrichment Programs; Health Intervention & Prevention; AIDS/STD Awareness; Mental Health Program; Alcohol/Substance Abuse Program. *Publication*: Buffalo Grass Newsletter. Established 1970.

NEBRASKA

LINCOLN INDIAN CENTER
1100 Military Rd.
LINCOLN, NE 68508
 (402) 474-5231
 Charlene Flood-Johnson, Director
Publication: Lincoln Indian Journal.

**NEBRASKA STATE COMMISSION
ON INDIAN AFFAIRS**
Box 94981, State Capitol, 6th Floor East
LINCOLN, NE 68509
 (402) 471-3475
 John Blackhawk, Executive Director

AMERICAN NATIVE CORPORATION
2451 St. Mary's St.
OMAHA, NE 68102

(402) 341-8471
 Violet M. Fickel, Executive Director

**NEBRASKA INDIAN INTER-TRIBAL
DEVELOPMENT CORPORATION**
Route 1, Box 66A
WINNEBAGO, NE 68071
 (402) 878-2242
 Frank Dean La Mere, Director
Purpose: To aid in the social and economic development of the Omaha, Winnebago and Santee Sioux Tribes of Nebraska. *Programs*: Job Traiing Partnership Act; Indian Food Distribution Program; Economic & Community Development Programs; et al. Founded 1969.

NEVADA

NATIVE AMERICAN ELDERS UNITED
808 Ivy St.
CARSON CITY, NV 89701

NEVADA URBAN INDIANS
675 Fairview Dr., Suite 222
CARSON CITY, NV 89701
 (702) 883-4439
See Sparks listing.

LAS VEGAS INDIAN CENTER
2300 W. Bonanza Rd.
LAS VEGAS, NV 89106
 (702) 647-5842
 Richard W. Arnold, Executive Director
 Anna Johnson, Associate Director
Promotes the social and economic self-suf ficiency of American Indians through the provision of education and employment. *Special programs*: Social services, adult education, career education, employment and training assistance, cultural activities, alcoholics anonymous, energy assistance, and special interest workshops and seminars. Founded 1972.

INTER-TRIBAL COUNCIL OF NEVADA
P.O. Box 7440
RENO, NV 89510
 (702) 355-0600
Head Start Program.

NEVADA INDIAN COMMISSION
4600 Kietzke Lane #B-1 16
RENO, NV 89503
 (702) 789-0347
 Leslie L. Blossom, Director
Purpose: To study matters af fecting the social and economic welfare and well-being of American Indians residing in Nevada; to improve cooperation between agencies and Indian groups; to enhance a general understanding of Indian law; and to assist tribes in acquiring or reacquiring federal land, identifying and researching problems to find solutions. *Publications*: Directory; Supplement to directory; Guide to Nevada Indian-Owned Businesses; and Population Profile. Established 1965.

NEVADA URBAN INDIANS
2100 Capurro W ay, Suite A
SPARKS, NV 89431
 (702) 356-81 11
 Jeffrey Richardson, Executive Director
Purpose: To provide quality health care to the area's urban Indian population by providing a variety of social and health services using a

blend of traditional and modern medicine. *Activities*: Community health care, health promotion and disease prevention, alcohol and drug abuse prevention and treatment program, mental health services. *Publications*: Reno Talking Leaf, quarterly newsletter; brochures on available services. Established 1975.

NEW HAMPSHIRE

**NEW ENGLAND ANTIQUITIES
RESEARCH ASSOCIATION**
305 Academy Rd.
PEMBROKE, NH 03275
 (603) 485-5655
 Daniel J. Leary, President
Purpose: To explore the origins of enigmatic stone structures throughout the Northeastern U.S.; to form a better understanding of our historic and prehistoric past. *Publications*: NEARA Journal, Semiannual; NEARA Transit Newsletter Semiannual. Library. Founded 1964.

NEW JERSEY

**AMERICAN INDIAN COUNCIL
OF NEW JERSEY**
P.O. Box 553, 18A East Commerce St.
BRIDGETON, NJ 08302
 (609) 455-6910

INTER-TRIBAL INDIANS OF NEW JERSEY
21 Village Rd.
MORGANVILLE, NJ 07751
 (908) 591-8335/390-1642
 Marvin Davis, President
Purpose: To support needs of members by providing programs and projects which reflect the Native American Indian culture and heritage; to promote well-being and self-esteem of members through cultural activities; to collect information and serve as a resource on American Indian cultures and services available to Native Americans. *Council members*: Brenda & Marvin Davis, Lelaruth Greco, Monica Paul, Helen Rende, Dabid Shanks, and Bob W eiler. *Activities*: Language (Mohawk) and crafts classes; educational programs for self and community . Library. *Publication*: Quarterly newsletter .

NEW JERSEY INDIAN OFFICE
300 Main St., Suite 3F
ORNAGE, NJ 07050
 (201) 675-0694
 James Lone Bear Revey , Chairperson
Description: Headquarters for the Delaware or Lenape Indians of New Jersey who can trace back to colonial times. *Programs*: Maintains library of historical documents, genealogies; craft and ceremonial items; costume parts, etc. Publications on the Delaware or Lenape Indian are available.

NEW JERSEY GOVERNOR'S OFFICE
Ethnic Advisory Council
State House CN001, 125 W . State St.
TRENTON, NJ 08625
 (609) 292-6000; 261-4747
 Roy Crazy Horse, Chief
 Kathryn Schneberk-King, Attorney

NEW MEXICO

TEN SOUTHERN PUEBLOS COUNCIL
Pueblo of Acoma
P.O. Box 309
ACOMITA, NM 87034

**ALBUQUERQUE URBAN INDIAN
HEALTH-HUMAN SERVICES**
4100 Silver Ave., SE #B
ALBUQUERQUE, NM 87108

ALL INDIAN PUEBLO COUNCIL
3939 San Pedro NE, Suite D
P.O. Box 3256 (87190)
ALBUQUERQUE, NM 87196
(505) 881-1992
James S. Hena, Chairman
Membership: 19. *Purpose*: To serve as advocate on behalf of 19 Pueblo Indian tribes on
education, health, social and economic issues.
Activities: Operates boarding school, Indian
Pueblo Cultural Center Museum, and theatre in
Albuquerque. Maintains business development
center, and library and archival collection.
Projects: Indian Business Development Corporation; Social Economic Development Strategies. *Publication*: Governors 19 Indian Pueblos,
annual directory; pamphlets and brochures. Library. Founded 1598.

**FARMINGTON INTERTRIBAL
INDIAN ORGANIZATION**
P.O. Box 2322, 100 West Elm
ALBUQUERQUE, NM 87401
(505) 327-6296

INDIAN ADVISORY COMMISSION
P.O. Box 1667
ALBUQUERQUE, NM 87107

**INDIAN LAW SECTION OF NEW MEXICO
BAR ASSOCIATION**
c/o Gover Stetson & Williams
2501 Rio Grand Blvd., NW
ALBUQUERQUE, NM 87104
(505) 842-6961 Fax 842-6208
Jana Walker, Chairperson

INDIAN YOUTH COUNCIL
P.O. Box 892
ALBUQUERQUE, NM 87301

KIVA CLUB
University of New Mexico
Mesa Vista Hall #1 117-A
ALBUQUERQUE, NM 87131-2066
(505) 277-8259
Lucille Stillwell, Executive Director
Rick Cate, President; Shawn Secatero, V.P.
Description: A social group that focuses on Native Amerian cultures and heritage and retention among Native American students. *Special
programs*: Counseling; career planning and
placement; Anizhone Week in April that features
Native Amerian speakers, films, and contemporary singers, and ends with an on-campus powwow. Established 1952.

NEW MEXICO INDIAN BAR ASSOCIATION
P.O. Box 2122
ALBUQUERQUE, NM 87125
Peggy Bird, Esq., President
(505) 368-4377 Fax 368-4557

NEW MEXICO INDIAN BUSINESS ASSN.
P.O. Box 2247
ALBUQUERQUE, NM 87103
(505) 255-4537

**NEW MEXICO INDIAN BUSINESS
DEVELOPMENT CENTER**
P.O. Box 3256
ALBUQUERQUE, NM 87910
(505) 889-9092
Theodore M. Pedro, Project Director
Business consulting.

**NEW MEXICO STATE TRIBAL
RELATIONS COMMITTEE**
P.O. Box 4456, Station A
ALBUQUERQUE, NM 87196
(505) 277-5462
SIPI ALCOHOLISM PROGRAM
P.O. Box 10146, 9169 Coors Rd., NW
ALBUQUERQUE, NM 87114

SOUTH WEST INDIAN STUDENT COALITION
1812 Los Lomas
ALBUQUERQUE, NM 87131
(503) 277-6065
Robert E. Cline, President
Carol Nez, Secretary; Jackie Callen, Treasurer
Purpose: To highlight contemporary realities of
Native American students and their people
within western culture. *Programs*: Cultural/po-
litical Forums, workshops, poetry readings, drum
groups, and education programs - "Rediscov-
ering the History of the Americas 1492-1992."
Publication: The People Before Columbus, annual journal.

STATE TRIBAL RELATIONS COMMITTEE
P.O. Box 4456, Station A
ALBUQUERQUE, NM 87196
(505) 277-5462

**URBAN INDIAN HEALTH
& HUMAN SERVICES, INC.**
4100 Silver, SE, Suite B
ALBUQUERQUE, NM 87108
(505) 262-2481
Charles J. Ederer, Executive Director
Purpose: To serve the Native American popula-
tion of Albuquerque with programs and services
designed to elevate the standard of health,
socio-economic standing, and educational level.
Programs: Primary Care Clinic; WIC Nutrition;
Alcohol and Substance Abuse; Community
Health and Health Education; Emergency As-
sistance; Information & Referral. Founded 1985.

WATER INFORMATION NETWORK
P.O. Box 4524
ALBUQUERQUE, NM 87106
(505) 255-4072 Fax 262-1864
Lila Bird, Contact

FIVE SANDOVAL INDIAN PUEBLOS, INC.
P.O Box 580
BERNALILLO, NM 87004
(505) 867-3351
William F. Weahkee, Executive Director
Purpose: To serve pueblos (Sandia, Santa Ana,
Jemez, Cochiti and Zia) as a consortium with
various human services and needs. *Programs*:
Health & Human Services; Employment & Train-
ing; Head Start, Women, Infant & Children pro-
grams; Economic & Social Development pro-
gram. Small reference library. Founded 1966.

UNITED INDIAN PUEBLO LAWYERS ASSN.
P.O. Box 402
ISLETA PUEBLO, NM 87022
(505) 869-3421
Christine Zuni, Contact

EIGHT NORTHERN PUEBLOS, INC.
P.O. Box 969
SAN JUAN PUEBLO, NM 87566
(505) 852-4265
Head Start Program.

HISTORICAL SOCIETY OF NEW MEXICO
Palace of the Governors
SANTA FE, NM 87501

NEW MEXICO INDIAN EDUCATION ASSN.
P.O. Box 16356
SANTA FE, NM 87506
(505) 989-5569
Julia Nathanson/Catherine Coulter, Contacts
Purpose: To foster the self-sufficiency of Native
Americans through the identification, develop-
ment and dissemination of quality educational
projects. *Publications*: The NMIEA Newsletter;
three historical documents for teachers.

NEW MEXICO OFFICE ON INDIAN AFFAIRS
La Villa Rivera Bldg., 228 E. Palace Ave.
SANTA FE, NM 87501
(505) 827-6440 Fax 827-6445
Regis Pecos, Executive Director

**NEW MEXICO SENATE STANDING
COMMITTEE ON INDIAN AFFAIRS**
State Capitol
SANTA FE, NM 87503
(505) 986-4314
John Pinto, Contact

NEW MEXICO STATE DEPT. OF EDUCATION
Division of Indian Education
Education Bldg., 300 Don Gaspar
SANTA FE, NM 87501
(505) 827-6679 Fax 827-6696
Nancy Martine Alonzo, Contact
Purpose: Responsible for promoting quality edu-
cation for Indian students in New Mexico. *Ac-
tivities*: Assists schools in preparing curricula for
Indian students; disseminates information, plans
sessions with tribal entities, and developes work-
shops.

**SOUTHWESTERN ASSOCIATION
FOR INDIAN AFFAIRS, INC.**
509 Camino de los Marquez, Suite 1
SANTA FE, NM 87501
(505) 983-5220 Fax 983-7647
Don Owen, Executive Director
Produces the Santa Fe Indian Market - over 550
booths and more than 1,000 Indian artists - in
August each year. Also, runs many educational
programs which benefit the artists.

NEW YORK

**TONAWANDA INDIAN
COMMUNITY LIBRARY**
P.O. Box 326, 372 Bloomingdale Rd.
AKRON, NY 14001
(716) 542-5618
Ramona Charles, Director

NY STATE DEPT. OF INDIAN AFFAIRS
40 N. Pearl St.
ALBANY, NY 12243

NY STATE EDUCATION DEPT.
Native Americans Program
543 Education Bldg. Annex
Washington Ave.
ALBANY, NY 12234
  (518) 474-0537 Fax 473-2912
  Minerva White, Coordinator

AMERICAN INDIAN INFORMATION CENTER
139-11 87th Ave.
BRIARWOOD, NY 11435
  (718) 291-7732
  Mifaunwy Shuntona Hines, Director
NEW YORK STATE DEPT.
OF SOCIAL SERVICES
Bureau of Indian Affairs
General Donovan State Office Bldg.
125 Main St., Room 471
BUFFALO, NY 14203
  (716) 847-3123 Fax 847-3464
  Kim M. Thomas, Indian Affairs Specialist
Purpose: To provide social services to Native Americans; to maintain liaison with Native American nations and other Native Americans organizations. *Activities*: provides consultative and information and referral services; searches and reviews historical files to assist Native Americans to research their ancestry. *Special programs*: provides special training programs to local departments; teenage pregnancy programs, housing programs; crisis intervention and counseling; preventive and child welfare development services; parenting. Educational and counseling services rendered by the Buffalo North American Indian Cultural Center. *Publication*: A Proud Heritage - Native American Services in New York State.

NORTHEASTERN NATIVE AMERICAN ASSN.
P.O. Box 230266
HOLLIS, NY 11423
  (718) 978-7057
  William "Wassaja" Gibson, President
Purpose: To honor, respect and keep alive the traditions & spirituality of our Native American ancestors. To acquaint our members with the current needs of our people. *Activities*: Oppose the desecration and commercialization of the graves & sacred places of all natives. *Publication*: Smoke Signals, newsletter. Founded 1990.

AMERICAN INDIAN COMMUNITY HOUSE
404 Lafayette St., 2nd Floor
NEW YORK, NY 10003
  (212) 598-0100 Fax 598-4909
  Rosemary Richmond, Executive Director
Purpose: To further the status of the American Indian through education, social services, media promotion, and business sponsorships. *Programs*: Job training and placement; alcoholism and substance abuse; health and social services; legal services; community development; art gallery, and theatre ensemble; Native American Council for New York City for 1992. *Publication*: AICH Bulletin, quarterly newsletter.

AMERICAN INDIAN LAW ALLIANCE
404 Lafayette St., 2nd Floor
NEW YORK, NY 10003
  (212) 598-0100 x 257
  Tonya Gonnella Frichner, Esq., Director
Purpose: To advocate for the survival of Native cultures, individuals and nations with the em-

phasis of our advocacy in the law. *Activities/Programs*: Research and technical support for traditional original Native governments on national and international levels; legal services project for individuals in New York City with specific legal problems. Founded 1987.

INTERCULTURAL RESOURCE CENTER
Columbia University
523 West 113th St.
NEW YORK, NY 10025
  Diane Blackman, Coordinator

AMERICAN INDIAN CLUB OF ROCHESTER
P.O. Box 272
ROCHESTER, NY 14601
  (716) 244-7353
NORTHEASTERN NATIVE AMERICAN ASSN.
198-04 120th Ave.
ST. ALBANS, NY 11412
  Chief William (Wasaja) Gibson

SHINNECOCK NATIVE AMERICAN
CULTURAL COALITION
P.O. Box 59
SOUTHAMPTON, NY 11968
  (516) 283-6143

NORTH AMERICAN INDIAN CLUB
P.O. Box 851
SYRACUSE, NY 13201
  (315) 476-7425
  Carol Moses, Manager
Operates retail arts and crafts shop.

NORTH CAROLINA

CHEROKEE HISTORICAL ASSOCIATION
P.O. Box 398
CHEROKEE, NC 28719
  (704) 497-2111
  Dr. Ed Hanson, Executive Director
  Barry Hipps, General Manager
Purpose: To preserve and perpetuate history and culture of the Eastern Band of Cherokee Indians. *Exhibits*: Unto These Hills, an outdoor drama which portrays history of the Cherokee Indians from 1540 to their removal to Oklahoma in 1838 (Mid-June thru late August); the Oconaluftee Indian Village, a replica of a Cherokee community of the 1750 period (Mid-May thru late October); and the Cherokee Cyclorama Wax Museum (April-November). *Publication*: Annual souvenir booklet, $4.00. Founded 1948.

QUALLA INDIAN BOUNDARY
P.O. Box 1310
CHEROKEE, NC 28719
  (704) 497-9416
Head Start Program.

NATIVE AMERICAN HERITAGE
P.O. Box 3029
DURHAM, NC 27715
Provides Native American Heritage cards. Founded 1994.

CUMBERLAND COUNTY
ASSOCIATION OF INDIAN PEOPLE
102 Indian Dr.
FAYETTEVILLE, NC 28301

GUILFORD NATIVE AMERICAN ASSN.
P.O. Box 5623
GREENSBORO, NC 27403

(919) 273-8686
Financial assistance programs.

NORTH CAROLINA ADVISORY
COUNCIL ON INDIAN EDUCATION
c/o Hope County Schools
P.O. Box 468
HALIFAX, NC 27839
  (919) 583-5111
  Ralph Evans, Chairperson

NORTH CAROLINA ADVISORY
COUNCIL ON INDIAN EDUCATION
NC Dept. of Public Instruction
c/o Pembroke State University
PEMBROKE, NC 28372
  Gerald Maynor, Contact
Purpose: To advise the State Board of Education on ways to meet more effectively the education needs of Indian students.

NORTH CAROLINA CONSORTIUM
ON INDIAN EDUCATION
P.O. Box 666
PEMBROKE, NC 28372
  (919) 422-3467
  Agnes H. Chavis, Director
Description: Statewide nonprofit organization chartered by the State of North Caolina. Consists of parents and guardians of Indian students who have served or currently serve on Title V. *Purpose*: To serve as an advocacy role on state and national issues related to Indian education and networks with more than 300 individuals, agencies, organizations, and projects involved in Indian education.

NORTH CAROLINA COMMISSION
ON INDIAN AFFAIRS
North Carolina Dept. of Administration
325 N. Salisbury St., Suite 579
RALEIGH, NC 27603
  (919) 733-5998
  A. Bruce Jones, Executive Director
North Carolina Amerian Indian Student Legislative Grant: Financial assistance to American Indians in North Carolina who are interested in postsecondary education in an approved North Carolina school. Up to $500 per year. Deadlines vary with each school.

NORTH CAROLINA STATE
DEPT. OF PUBLIC INSTRUCTION
Division of Indian Education
301 N. Wilmington St.
RALEIGH, NC 27601
  (919) 715-1000
  Betty Oxendine Mangum, Director

TRIANGLE NATIVE AMERICAN SOCIETY
P.O. Box 26841
RALEIGH, NC 27611
Mark Ulmer Native American Scholarship: Financial assistance to Native Americans in North Carolina who are interested in contiuing their college education. The stipend is $500 per year. *Deadline*: April.

NORTH DAKOTA

NORTH DAKOTA DEPT.
OF PUBLIC INSTRUCTION
Indian Education Office
600 E. Blvd., 9th Floor
BISMARCK, ND 58505

(701) 224-2250
Cheryl M. Kulas, Director
Purpose: To increase the capacity of the state and school districts to more effectively develop and conduct educational programs for American Indian learners; to provide technical assistance in developing awareness and understanding of Indian learner needs. *Activities*: Maintains networking/liaison efforts in support of Indian education. Small library. *Publications*: Centennial Curriculum of North Dakota Native Americans; 1994 North Dakota Tribal Curriculum; Bibliography of Resource Materials for Educators. Founded 1982.

NORTH DAKOTA INDIAN AFFAIRS COMMISSION
600 E. Blvd., 1st Floor-Judicial Wing
BISMARCK, ND 58505
(701) 224-2428
Deborah A. Painte, Executive Director
Purpose: A liaison/referral agency established to facilitate tribal/state relations. *Programs*: Indian Youth Alcohol and Other Drug Prevention Programs. *Publications*: Update, quarterly newsletter; Directory of Statewide Indian Programs. Established 1947.

NATIVE AMERICAN COALITION OF PROGRAMS
P.O. Box 1914
FARGO, ND 58107
(701) 235-3124
Beverly Olson, Native American Outreach
Renee Perala, Title V Coordinator
Lynette Seminole, N.A. Ecumenical Ministry
Purpose: To be a resource and referral service for Native Americans; to provide support and networking within the community; and to advocate for health care needs of Native Americans.

NORTH DAKOTA INDIAN EDUCATION ASSN.
P.O. Box 199
FORT TOTTEN, ND 58335
(701) 766-4161
Patricia Walking Eagle, Contact

DAKOTA WOMEN OF ALL RED NATIONS
P.O. Box 69
FORT YATES, ND 58538
(701) 854-7592
Mabel Ann Phillips, Chairperson
Advocacy for Native American treaty rights. *Program*: Health Education Program. Newsletter.

OHIO

NORTH AMERICAN INDIAN CULTURAL CENTERS
1062 Triplett Blvd.
AKRON, OH 44306
(216) 724-1280 Fax 724-9298
H. Clark Hosick, Executive Director

CLEVELAND AMERICAN INDIAN CENTER
5500-02 Loraine Ave.
CLEVELAND, OH 44102
(216) 961-3490

NATIVE AMERICAN INDIAN CENTER
P.O. Box 07705
COLUMBUS, OH 43207
(614) 443-6120

OHIO CENTER FOR NATIVE AMERICAN AFFAIRS
203 E. Broad St.
COLUMBUS, OH 43215
(614) 228-0460
Kenneth D. Irwin, Chairperson
Purpose: To provide a means through which issues of concern to the Native community may be forcefully considered; seeks to enhance and strengthen Native American cultures in Ohio and to inform all citizens of issues concerning the Native American community. *Activities*: Clearinghouse for Indian information; speaker's bureau; cultural programs, powwows and workshops. Library. Founded 1991.

OHIO INDIAN CENTER
c/o R. Smith, 3949 Dryden Dr.
N. OLMSTED, OH 44070

FRIENDS OF THE SERPENT MOUND AND THE OHIO BRUSH CREEK
c/o Tom Johnson
18240 SR 41
WEST UNION, OH 45693

OKLAHOMA

FIVE CIVILIZED TRIBES FOUNDATION
c/o Chickasaw Nation
P.O. Box 1548
ADA, OK 74820
(405) 436-2603
Overton James, Chairman
Comprised of the Cherokee, Choctaw, Chickasaw, Creek, and Seminole Nations of Oklahoma. *Purpose*: To provide coordination to tribal activities and programs including social programs, industrial development, and administrative activities; and provides representation for the tribes at the national level. Founded 1974.

FOUR TRIBES CONSORTIUM OF OKLAHOMA
P.O. Box 1193
ANADARKO, OK 73005
(405) 247-9711/2021
Jeff Foster, Executive Director
Purpose: To assist skilled men and women with employment and training; to educate Native American people of their civil rights, and assists in mediating discrimination toward the Native American. *Publication*: Program pamphlet. Founded 1987.

OKLAHOMA INDIAN ARTS & CRAFTS COOPERATIVE
P.O. Box 966
ANADARKO, OK 73005
(405) 247-3486
Nettie Standing, Manager
Purpose: To promote the careers of contemporary Oklahoma Indian artists and craftsmen by providing a sales outlet for their works. *Products include*: beadwork, featherwork, jewelry, fashion accessories, leatherwork, dance costumes and accessories, dolls, musical instruments, as well as orginal paintings by Native American artists. Mail order price list available. Established 1955.

OKLAHOMA NATIVE AMERICAN LANGUAGE DEVELOPMENT INSTITUTE
P.O. Box 963
CHOCTAW, OK 73020

(405) 454-2158
Carl Downing, Contact
Purpose: To promote successful native language acquisition, maintenance, and perpetuation. *Objectives*: To train teachers and teacher assistants for Indian bilingual programs, and to provide assistance that will help tribal people be more effective teachers of native languages.

INTER-TRIBAL COUNCIL OF NORTHEAST OKLAHOMA
P.O. Box 1308
MIAMI, OK 74354

OKLAHOMA ANTHROPOLOGICAL SOCIETY
1000 Horn St.
MUSKOGEE, OK 74403
(405) 364-2279
Alicia Jones Hughes, President
Encourages scientific collection, preservation, classification and study of American Indian ethnological and archaeological materials. Newsletter; annual bulletin. Library (members only.)

INDIAN EDUCATION TECHNICAL ASSISTANCE CENTER
2424 Springer Dr., Suite 200
NORMAN, OK 73069
(800) 451-2191; (800) 422-0966 (in OK)
(405) 360-1163 Fax 364-5464
Mary Ann Brittan, Contact
Serves schools in the following states: OK, TX.
Activities: Sponsors an annual conference in September; co-sponsors Oklahoma Exposition in April. *Publication*: OCIE Newsletter

OKLAHOMANS FOR INDIAN OPPORTUNITY
555 E. Constitution
NORMAN, OK 73069
(405) 329-3737
Purpose: To improve opportunities for Oklahoma Indians and draw them more fully into the Oklahoma economy and culture. *Programs*: Indian education; job opportunity and training; housing; health. *Publication*: OIO News - provides information on Indian business development and similar issues.

AMERICAN INDIAN CENTER
1608 N.W. 35th
OKLAHOMA CITY, OK 73117

THE OKLAHOMA CITY INDIAN CLINIC
1214 N. Hudson
OKLAHOMA CITY, OK 73103
(405) 232-1526
Mary Helen Deer Smith, Contact
Purpose: To provide outpatient primary medical care; general medical and dental services; drug and alcohol abuse treatment; health education; seminars; prevention and outreach.

OKLAHOMA DEPT. OF EDUCATION
Indian Education Section
2500 N. Lincoln Blvd.
OKLAHOMA CITY, OK 73105
(405) 521-3311 Fax 521-6205
Mary Reid, Director

OKLAHOMA HISTORICAL SOCIETY
Wiley Post Bldg., 2100 N. Lincoln
OKLAHOMA CITY, OK 73105
(405) 521-2491
C. Earle Metcalf
Purpose: The preservation microfilming of documents relating to the Indian tribes of Oklahoma. *Programs*: An archives and Manuscripts Divi-

sion acts as a repository of a large body of U.S. Government Indian records and papers of missionaries to the tribes of Oklahoma. *Publication*: Chronicles of Oklahoma, quarterly . Library and museum.

OKLAHOMA INDIAN AFFAIRS COMMISSION
4545 N. Lincoln Blvd., Suite 282
OKLAHOMA CITY, OK 73105
 (405) 521-3828
 Barbara Warner, Executive Director

OKLAHOMA INDIAN LEGAL SERVICES
3033 N. Walnut Ave., Suite 103-W
OKLAHOMA CITY, OK 73105
 (405) 528-5500

OKLAHOMA INDIAN BAR ASSOCIATION
P.O. Box 1062
OKLAHOMA CITY, OK 73101
 (405) 879-5924
 Arvo Mikkanen, President; M. Allen Core, V.P. Formed to provide a forum for Indian law practitioners to communicate with one another , exchange ideas on the issues involving the tribal sovereignty of Indian nations within the state.

OKLAHOMA INDIAN LEGAL SERVICES, INC.
Founders Tower, 5900 Mosteller Dr . #610
OKLAHOMA CITY, OK 73112
 (800) 658-1497; (405) 840-5255 Fax 840-7060
 Michael C. Snyder , Executive Director
Purpose: To provide legal services to low income Native Americans by direct representation on status related issues of significance; legal training. *Activities*: Sponsors and provides speakers to conference addressing Indian Child W elfare, Indian Housing, Tribal Sovereignty , Natural Resources, and Individual Rights; also sponsors Indian Law Legal Intern Program. Maintains Indian law library . *Publications*: Handbook on the Indian Child W elfare Act; brochures. Founded 1982.

RED EARTH INDIAN CENTER
2100 NE 52 St.
OKLAHOMA CITY, OK 73111
 (405) 427-4228
 Barbara Jobe, Executive Director
 Christi Alcox, Festival Coordinator
 Scott Tigert, Curator
 Micki Pratt, Special Projects
Purpose: To give tangible expression to American Indian cultures, and to increase appreciation of them through information exchange and cultural activities, such as the Red Earth Festival (second weekend in June) "world's largest Native American cultural festival; and annual Native American Fair (February); museum exhibits. Library. Founded 1976.

CREEK INDIAN MEMORIAL ASSOCIATION
Creek Council House Museum, Town Square
OKMULGEE, OK 74447
 (918) 756-2324
 James L. Milroy , President
 Tommy A. Steinsiek, Curator
Membership: 115. *Purpose*: Established to collect and exhibit artifacts and documents pertaining to the Muscogee Creek Tribe. *Activities*: Operates Museum of Creek Indian Culture; sponsors annual Muscogee Creek Masters Exhibit every December; sponsors Oklahoma Indian Art Market every October. Publishes booklets and leaflets on Creek history and legend. Monthly meetings. Founded 1923.

NATIVE AMERICANS IN BIOLOGICAL SCIENCES
307 Life Science East, O.S.U.
STILLWATER, OK 74078
 (405) 744-6802
 Myra Alexander, Manager-Counseling
Description: A four-week summer camp for Native American junior and senior high school students who are interested in further study in the bioloigcal sciences. Five scholarships available to OK tribal students who are enrolled members of the Otoe-Missouria, Pawnee and Ponca tribes, in the Frontier, Pawnee and Ponca City School Districts. Applicants must demonstrate activity in tribal/school programs & submit a 500 word essay describing their lifetime goals.

CHEROKEE NATIONAL HISTORICAL SOCIETY
P.O. Box 515
TAHLEQUAH, OK 74465
 (918) 456-6007
 Myrna Moss, Executive Director
Purpose: To preserve the history and traditions of the Cherokee Nation, and provide educational and social services to members of the Cherokee Indian tribe. *Activities*: Operates the Cherokee Heritage Center , which includes the Cherokee National Museum & Cherokee National Archives. Maintains a "living" Indian V illage; sponsors annual Trail of Tears Indian art show; conducts a lecture series on Cherokee history and culture. Maintains Cherokee Hall of Fame. Also maintains the Ho-Chee-Nee Trail of Tears Memorial Chapel. *Publication*: The Columns, newsletter; Trail of Tears Drama Program, annual. Color prints available. Founded 1963.

INDIAN HEALTH CARE RESOURCE CENTER
Box 184, 915 S. Cincinnati
TULSA, OK 74119
 (918) 582-7225

NATIVE AMERICAN COALITION OF TULSA
1740 West 41st St.
TULSA, OK 74107
 (918) 446-8432
 John McClelland, Chairman
 Pam Chibitty, Executive Director
Purpose: To serve more than 100 tribes and 38,000 Native-Americans. *Programs*: Transportation service for the elderly; nutrition; Headstart; clothing and food donations for families; referrals. *Publication*: Semiannual paper .

CENTRAL TRIBES OF SHAWNEE
Route 5, Box 148-B
SHAWNEE, OK 74801
 (405) 275-0663
 Head Start Program.

OREGON

MOTHER EARTH'S CHILDREN
9140 Cape Arago Hwy.
COOS BAY, OR 97420
 (503) 888-4584
Purpose: To promote positive Indian education, economic and social benefits through the development of innovative programs. *Activities*: An American Indian Repertory Theater, presents traditional Indian stories in a visual manner; The Anne C. Thornton Memorial Fund Scholarship, annual awards of $500 to four American Indian/Alaskan Native students who live in Oregon.

OREGON INDIAN EDUCATION ASSN.
720 Nantucket
EUGENE, OR 97204
 (503) 687-3489
 Twila Souers, President
Purpose: A liaison for information specific to educational programs, procedures, and opportunities for American Indian people in Oregon, and disseminates that information to all members and interested parties. *Activities*: Sponsors annual conference and co-sponsors special statewide events relevant to Indian education.

NANITCH SAHALLIE
Confederated Tribes of Grand Ronde
5119 River Rd. N.
KEIZER, OR 97303
 (800) 552-0939; (503) 390-5904
 Fax (503) 390-6973
Description: A youth residential treatment program; a 44 bed facility for the treatment of Native American chemical dependent adolescents between the ages of 12 and 18 who reside in the Portland Area of the Indian Health Service.

ORGANIZATION OF THE FORGOTTEN AMERICAN
P.O. Box 1257
KLAMATH FALLS, OR 97601
 (503) 882-4441/2
 Leonard Norris, Director
Purpose: To enhance the future of the Native American population. *Activities*: Administers the Job Training Partnership Act program for 22 counties; Employment and trainign services for eligible Native Americans. Branch offices in Astoria, Coos Bay, Medford, Pendleton, Roseburg, and The Dalles, Oregon.

NORTHWEST INDIAN FISHERIES COMMISSION
6730 Martin W ay E.
OLYMPIA, WA 98506
 (206) 438-1180

AFFILIATED TRIBES OF THE NORTHWEST INDIANS
825 NE 20th Ave., Suite 310
PORTLAND, OR 97232
 (503) 230-0293 Fax 230-0580
Purpose: To bring together tribal delegates from the Pacific Northwest Tribes. Tribal Government leaders meet three times per year , fall, winter, and mid-year, to confer on issues affecting Indian country.

AMERICAN INDIAN ASSN. OF PORTLAND
1827 NE 44th Ave., Suite 225
PORTLAND, OR 97213
 (503) 249-0296

COLUMBIA RIVER INTER-TRIBAL FISH COMMISSION (CRITFC)
729 N.E. Oregon, Suite 200
PORTLAND, OR 97232
 (503) 238-0667 Fax 235-4228
 Tim Wapato, Executive Director
 Carol Craig, Media Specialist
Purpose: To ensure a unified voice in the overall management of the fishery resources; to protect reserved treaty rights through exercise of inherent sovereign powers of the tribes: Yakima, Nez Perce, Umatilla and W arm Springs. *Publication*: Wana Chinook Tymoo (Columbia River Salmon Stories), quarterly magazine.

CONCERNED INDIAN COMMITTEE
6008 N. Syracuse
PORTLAND, OR 97203
(503) 285-4474

NATIVE AMERICAN ART COUNCIL
Portland Art Museum
1219 SW Park Ave.
PORTLAND, OR 97205
(503) 226-2811
Description: An educational group organizaed to support the Portland Art Museum's collection of Native American art. *Activities*: Sponsors educational programs: guest speakers, films, demonstration and field trips. Founded 1985.

NATIVE AMERICAN BUSINESS ALLIANCE
8435 SE 17th Ave.
PORTLAND, OR 97202
(503) 233-4841
Description: Non-profit organiztion organizaed to promote economic development for all Indians through the formation of an alliance of profit-oriented Indian businesses. *Activities*: Conduct quarterly meetings in Oregon and W ashington. *Publication*: Indian Business Review , quarterly .

**NATIVE AMERICAN PROGRAM
LEGAL SERVICE**
Oregon Legal Services Corp.
917 SW Oak, Suite 410
PORTLAND, OR 07205
(503) 223-9483 Fax 294-1429
Purpose: To provide legal representation to Oregon's Indian community . Case load includes: economic development, protection of archaelogical, sacred and burial sites, worship, Indian health services, Indian Child W elfare Act and protection of Tribal-Federal relationship, treaty rights, federal Indian law training tribal sovereignty. Founded 1979.

**NATIVE AMERICAN REHABILITATION
ASSOCIATION OF THE NORTHWEST**
1438 S.E. Division
PORTLAND, OR 97218
(503) 231-2641
Purpose: To Operate an outpatient clinic and two residential treatment centers, Totem Lodge--men and women and W omen's Support Center--women and children, for the treatment of alcoholism and alcohol/drug abuse in the Native-American community with a specialist treatment approach which embodies Indian cultural awareness and the philosophy of Alcoholics Anonymous.

**NORTHWEST PORTLAND
AREA INDIAN HEALTH BOARD**
520 SW Harrison, Suite 440
PORTLAND, OR 97266
(503) 228-4185
Description: A federally-funded, non-profit advisory board which represents the 40 Federally recognized Tribes in Oregon, W ashington, and Idaho on health related issues. The board is composed of delegates representing each tribe. *Purpose*: To serve as liaison between tribes and the Indian Health Service; to provide training for tribal reps and tribal staf f on various health issues; to conduct research and evaluation projects; to serve as a regional center for statistics for Northwest Tribes.

**NORTHWEST TRIBAL
RECRUITMENT PROJECT**
520 SW Harrison, Suite 335
PORTLAND, OR 97201
(503) 228-4185
Purpose: To recruit health professionals for the 40 dif ferent American Indian tribes located in Washington, Oregon, and Idaho.

OREGON INDIAN EDUCATION ASSN.
2125 N. Flint
PORTLAND, OR 97227
(503) 275-9600
Purpose: To promote Indian education in schools and Indian communities, and to inform association members of state and federal laws af fecting Indian education. *Activities*: Textbook review projects; to communicate concerns of Indian educators to the U.S. Of fice of Education; and administers AIDS Education and Prevention Program.

**RESEARCH & DEVELOPMENT
PROGRAM FOR INDIAN EDUCATION**
Northwest Regional Educational Laboratory
101 SW Main St., Suite 500
PORTLAND, OR 97204
(503) 275-9500 Fax 275-9489
Purpose: To provide in-service training on school improvement to schools serving Indian children in the Northwest. *Activities*: Annual, one week, "Institute of Excellence in American Indian Education. *Publications*: Effective Practices in Indian Education: Teacher Curriculum, Administrator Monographs, an Administrator's Guide; & Teachers Do Make A Difference: What Indian Graduates Say About Their School Experience.

SACRED EARTH COALITION
7003 N.E. Everett St.
PORTLAND, OR 97213
(503) 221-0162
Sohar O'Mohundro

**CHEMAWA ALCOHOLISM
EDUCATION CENTER**
3760 Chemawa Rd., NE
SALEM, OR 97305
(503) 399-5942
Description: An alcohol and drug abuse intervention project designed especially for Indian students in attendance at Chemawa Indian High School.

INIPI O'YATE'KI - INDIAN CULTURE CLUB
Oregon State Correctional Institution
3405 Deer Park Dr., SE
SALEM, OR 97310
(503) 373-0174
Description: A social organization within the walls of the correctional institution. Focuses on activities traditional to the Indian culture.

LAKOTA OYATE-KI - INDIAN CULTURE CLUB
Oregon State Penitentiary
2605 State St.
SALEM, OR 97310
(503) 378-2289
Description: Indian organization wiothin the walls of the penitentiary . Membership involved in cultural, traditional and religious activities.

NORTHWEST PAINT CLAN, INC.
585 Lorida Ave. S.
SALEM, OR 97302
(503) 399-8781

Purpose: To preserve American Indian heritage and provide cultural learning opportunities for members and the public.

**OREGON INDIAN COALITION ON
POST SECONDARY EDUCATION**
2708 Shelly Ann Way, NE
SALEM, OR 97305
Morrie Jimenez, Chairperson

**OREGON COMMISSION
ON INDIAN SERVICES**
454 State Capitol
SALEM, OR 97310
(503) 986-1067
Douglas W. Hutchinson, Director
Purpose: To develop and sponsor programs to make needs of Oregon Indians known to the public and private agencies which serve them; to recommend new or improved methods of meeting these needs; and to compile and disseminate information about services for Indians in Oregon. *Publication*: Oregon Directory of American Indian Resources.

OREGON DEPT. OF EDUCATION
Indian Education and Race Equity
700 Pringle Parkway SE
SALEM, OR 97310
(503) 378-3606 Fax 373-7968
Robin A. Butterfield, Coordinator

**SISTER'S OF THE FOUR WINDS-
OWCC INDIAN CLUB**
Oregon Women's Correctional Center
2809 State St.
SALEM, OR 97310
(503) 378-2667
Purpose: To enhance the self-image of American Indian inmates and bring a better understanding of Indian ways to others.

TAHANA WHITECROW FOUNDATION
P.O. Box 18181
SALEM, OR 97305
(503) 585-0564
(508) 585-0564
Melanie Smith, Director
Purpose: To pormote and provide multi approaches to urban Indian issues and to serve single point-of-contact multi-service center . *Activities*: Outpatient, ancillary mental health, emergency food, youth assistance (of fenders), crim evictim support, community referral and advocacy, conmservatorium. *Publication*: Oyate Wo-wapi, quarterly newsletter; Circle of Reflections, bi-annual poetry anthology . Library. Established 1987.

ART MITCHELL SINGERS
P.O. Box 124
WARM SPRINGS, OR 97761
(503) 553-1 161
A Native American singing group who regularly provide drumming and singing for pow-wows, tribal celebrations and various cultural events on the Warm Springs Reservation. The group also performs for other reservations, communities, schools and universities, and coventions.

**OREGON NATIVE AMERICAN BUSINESS
& ENTREPRENEURIAL NETWORK**
P.O. Box 1359
WARM SPRINGS, OR 97761
Wes Patterson, President

PENNSYLVANIA

COUNCIL OF THREE RIVERS
AMERICAN INDIAN CENTER, INC.
200 Charles St.
DORSEYVILLE, PA 15238
(412) 782-4457
Russell Sims, Executive Director
Purpose: Addresses the needs and secures
services for the Native-American community .
Programs: Indian manpower employment and
training; Native-American elders program; Native-American cultural programs; Native-American family and child services; Native-American
Adoption Resource Exchange, and Indian Adoption Awareness Project (national); Singing
Winds Head Start; Rainbow Project--adoption
agency for western Pennsylvania. Financial
assistance for education and training is provided
through the Job Training Partnership Act Program. *Publication*: The Singing W inds Newsletter, monthly; Pow-W ow Booklet, annual. Library .

ERIE COUNTY COALITION
FOR INDIAN AFFAIRS, INC.
2324 East 26th St.
ERIE, PA 16510
Edward Livingston, Contact

NATIVE AMERICAN INDIAN COMMUNITY
Rd. 2 Box 247A
KITTANNING, PA 16201
(412) 548-7335
Brandy Weeasayha\Myers, Director
Purpose: To educate all people about American
Indians. *Activities*: Support programs dealing
with Native people; educational program for
schools and counseling for prison inmates. *Publications*: Spiritwalker Newsletter; educational
material on Native people; cookbook.

SUSQUEHANNA VALLEY
NATIVE AMERICAN EAGLE
Box 99, W alnut Valley Farm
LOGANVILLE, PA 17342
(717) 428-1440
Rick Edmund & Jerry Dietz, Co-Editors
Purpose: To provide a positive communication
of Native American culture-past and present in
the mid-Atlantic region. *Activities*: Sometimes
personal speaking engagements can be arranged. Small library . *Publication*: Bi-monthly
newsletter. Founded 1987.

NATIVE AMERICAN CULTURAL
CENTER OF DELAWARE VALLEY
927 No. 6th St.
PHILADELPHIA, PA 19123
(215) 627-7304
Charles H. Juancito, Executive Director
Purpose: To provide programs in health, edu-
cation and welfare for the Powhatan Renape
Nation. Library . *Publication*: Catalog.

UNITED AMERICAN INDIANS
OF THE DELAWARE VALLEY
225 Chestnut St.
PHILADELPHIA, PA 19106
(215) 574-9020/2/3/4
Susan Heide, Executive Director
Personnel: Yvonne Bernardino, Of ice Manager;
John Albrecht, Vocational Counselor , Miriam
Cathcart, Outreach Specialist; and Janice Ritt,
Receptionist. *Purpose*: To be recognized and
accepted as a community-based, social service
organization assisting all American Indians re-

siding within Philadelphia metropolitan area to
enhance their standard of living and improve
their social-economic self-suf ficiency. *Special
programs*: Cultural, educational, employment,
housing, and public relations. *Special activities*:
Annual Pow-W ow, 1st weekend in August; annual Fall Festival, 2nd weekend in October .
Trading Post.

RHODE ISLAND

RHODE ISLAND INDIAN COUNCIL
444 Friendship St.
PROVIDENCE, RI 02907

SOUTH CAROLINA

ASSISTANT TO THE GOVERNOR
P.O. Box 11450
COLUMBIA, SC 2921 1

SOUTH CAROLINA COUNCIL
ON NATIVE AMERICANS
P.O. Box 219221
COLUMBIA, SC 29221

SOUTH CAROLINA STATE
DEPT. OF EDUCATION
Multicultural/Equity Issues
1429 Senate St., 808 Rutledge Bldg.
COLUMBIA, SC 29201
(803) 734-8366 Fax 734-8624

FOUR HOLES INDIAN ORGANIZA TION
113 Tee Pee Dr.
RIDGEVILLE, SC 29472
(803) 871-2126/6740
Matthew Creel, Chief
Purpose: To better Indian people in Ridgeville
& the surrounding community . "Our goal is to
be recognized as Indians by the Federal Government." Established 1969.

SOUTH DAKOTA

HAN-PA-O-YE
P.O. Box 624, Northern State College
ABERDEEN, SD 57401

SOUTH DAKOTA INDIAN EDUCATION ASSN.
P.O. Box 62
BATESLAND, SD 57716
(605) 867-5633
Chris Bordeaux, President
Activity: Sponsors annual conference in Oct.

ST. JOSEPH'S LAKOTA
DEVELOPMENT COUNCIL
St. Joseph's Indian School
CHAMBERLAIN, SD 57326
(605) 734-6021
A non-profit organization which sells products
(kachina dolls, leatherwork, beadwork, quilts,
etc.) through mail order and wholesale-retail.

THE LAKOTA FUND
P.O. Box 340
KYLE, SD 57750
(605) 455-2500
Elsie Meeks, Executive Director

Purpose: To build a private sector economy on
the Pine Ridge Indian Reservation by providing
loans and technical assistance to Oglala Sioux
tribal members. *Activities*: Small business loans;
microenterprise loans; technical assistance &
business training; and arts and crafts marketing assistance. *Publication*: The Lakota Fund
newsletter. Established 1986.

NATIVE AMERICAN WOMEN'S HEAL TH
EDUCATION RESOURCE CENTER
Native American Community Board
P.O. Box 572
LAKE ANDRES, SD 57356
(605) 487-7072 Fax 487-7964
Charon Asetoyer, Executive Director

SOUTH DAKOTA STATE DEPT. OF
EDUCATION & CULTURAL AFFAIRS
Indian Education Program
700 Governors Dr .
PIERRE, SD 57501
(605) 773-4670 Fax 773-6139
Don Schanadore, Contact

SOUTH DAKOTA HISTORICAL SOCIETY
Memorial Bldg.
PIERRE, SD 57501

SOUTH DAKOTA INDIAN AFFAIRS OFFICE
Public Safety Bldg., 1 18 W. Capitol, Rm. 300
PIERRE, SD 57501
(605) 773-3415
Francis WhiteBird, Coordinator

AMERICAN INDIAN RELIEF COUNCIL
P.O. Box 6200
RAPID CITY, SD 57709
Brian J. Brown, President

SIOUX SAN ALCOHOLISM PROGRAM
3200 Canyon Lake Dr .
RAPID CITY, SD 57701

MINNEHAHA INDIAN CLUB
1413 Thompson Dr.
SIOUX FALLS, SD 57105

LAKOTA AOMICIYE
Black Hills State College
SPEAFISH, SD 57783

TENNESSEE

CHATTANOOGA INTERTRIBAL ASSN.
P.O. Box 71585
CHATTANOOGA, TN 37407
(615) 266-6551 or 892-6346
John Anderson, President; Alva Crowe, V.P.
Purpose: To provide representation for concerned Native Americans on a local, state and
federal level; to increase awareness of historical Native Amefican contributions in the State
of Tennessee; to of fer and support educational,
employment, and social opportunities for all Indian citizens; and to perserve Native American
cultural heritage and local burial grounds.

TENNESSEE COMMISSION
ON INDIAN AFFAIRS
112 Cynthia Lane, Apt. C
KNOXVILLE, TN 37922
John Martin, Chairperson

INDIAN HERITAGE COUNCIL
Box 2302, Henry St.
MORRISTOWN, TN 37816
(615) 581-5714
Louis Hooban, C.E.O.
Purpose: To promote understanding, culture and ideas of the Native population. Activities: Sponsors the annual National Pow-wow in Townsend, Tennessee; newsletter and cultural events. Library. Established 1987.

NATIVE AMERICAN INDIAN ASSOCIATION OF TENNESSEE
401 Stahlman Bldg., 211 Union St.
Nashville, TN 37201
(615) 726-0806
Don Yahola, Contact

TENNESSEE COMMISSION ON INDIAN AFFAIRS
401 Church St., L&C Towers, 10th Floor
NASHVILLE, TN 37243
(615) 532-0745
Luvenia H. Butler, Executive Director

TEXAS

TEXAS INDIAN COMMISSION
P.O. Box 2960
AUSTIN, TX 78768-2960
(512) 458-1203
Raymond D. Apodaca, Executive Director
Purpose: To assist the Alabama-Coushatta Indian Tribe and the Tigua Tribe of Texas in the development of the human and economic resources of their respective Reservations; to assist the Texas Band of Kickapoo Indians in improving its health, educational, agricultural, business, and industrial capacities; to romote unity and understanding among the American Indian people of Texas, and promote and enhance increased understanding of American Indian and Texas Indian culture and history by the general public. Approximate Indian population is 65,000. Publications: Americans Indians in Texas, 1984; Texas Indian Commission Profile and History, 20 page report.

DALLAS INTER-TRIBAL CENTER
209 E. Jefferson
DALLAS, TX 75203
(214) 941-1050 (Community/Healtf)
(214) 941-6535 (Employment/Training)
Richard Lucero, Executive Director
Purpose: To provide health care and other social services to Indian families residing in the Dallas/Fort Worth area. Programs: Community services such as: emergency food assistance, transportation, crisis intervention services, information and referral; Indian child welfare; medical-dental clinic; WIC Program; nutrition education services; health education; screening. Publication: DIC Smoke Signals, monthly newsletter.

AMERICAN INDIAN CENTER
818 E. Davis
GRAND PRAIRIE, TX 75050
(214) 262-1349
Hilton G. Queton, Executive Director
Richard E. Bloomfield, President
Purpose: To promote, assist, and further the social, educational, and cultural development of American Indians in present day societies.

Activities: Provides information services, cultural training, education service, employment service, drug and alcoohol treatment, child care and family assistance. Special Programs: Residential Treatment Program; annual Cultural Awareness conference in April. Founded 1969.

FIRST AMERICAN BAR ASSN. OF TEXAS
144-B E. San Antonio St.
SAN MARCOS, TX 78666
(512) 392-3708
Tricia Tingle, President

UTAH

UTAH NAVAJO DEVELOPMENT COUNCIL
P.O. Box 129
BIUFF, UT 84512
(801) 678-2285
Herbert Clah, Executive Director
Purpose: To help the Navajos on the Utah Portion of the Navajo Reservation provide services in health, education, natural resources, and housing. Programs: Operates clinics for medical services; adult education; vocational education; home rehabilitation; and construction. Scholarships. Artifacts exhibited.

UTAH BOARD OF INDIAN AFFAIRS
144 N. Pinewood Cir.
LAYTON, UT 84041
(801) 626-6818
Marcia Galli, Chairperson

RAINDANCER YOUTH SERVICE, INC.
P.O. Box 2499
ST. GEORGE, UT 84770
(801) 673-6474
Kevin J. Van Gilder, Administrative Director

INDIAN ALCOHOLISM COUNSELING & RECOVERY HOUSE PROGRAM
P.O. Box 1500, 538 South West
SALT LAKE CITY, UT 84101

UTAH DIVISION OF INDIAN AFFAIRS
324 S. State St., Suite 103
SALT LAKE CITY, UT 84111
(801) 538-8808 Fax 538-8888
Wil Numkena, Executive Director
Purpose: To assist tribes and Native-American organizations in Utah in solving problems, and serve as a liaison between the State and all tribes and Indian organizations. Activities: Annual Conference in April.

UTAH STATE OFFICE OF EDUCATION
Special Assistant for Indian Education
250 E 500 S
SALT LAKE CITY, UT 84111
(801) 538-7645
Shirley Weights, Contact

VERMONT

THE GOVERNOR'S ADVISORY COMMISSION ON NATIVE AMERICAN AFFAIRS
Pavilion Office Bldg, 109 State St.
MONTPELIER 05609
(802) 828-3333
Jeff Benay

ABENAKI SELF-HELP ASSOCIATION
P.O. Box 276
SWANTON 05488

VIRGINIA

RISING WATERS DANCERS
Route 2, Box 107-B
BRUINGTON, VA 23023
Nokomis Lemons, Coordinator

AMERICAN INDIAN SOCIETY OF WASHINGTON, DC
P.O. Box 6431
FALLS CHURCH, VA 22040
(703) 914-0548
Jay Hill, President
Bob Tenequer & Willie Chism, V.P.'s
Karen Collins, Secretary
Barbara Davis, Treasurer
Purpose: To promote and preserve Indian tradition; provide scholarship assistance for young Indian people. Special program: American Indian Inaugural Ball. Publications: Monthly newsletter; American Indian Society Cookbook, $6.00. Established 1966.

NATIVE AMERICAN PROGRAMS, FOREST SERVICE
500 W. Westmorland Rd.
FALLS CHURCH, VA 22046
Robert Tippeconnie, Manager

MATTAPONI-PAMUNKEY-MONACAN JTPA CONSORTIUM
P.O. Box 360
KING WILLIAM, VA 23086
(804) 769-4767
Warren Cook, Director

VIRGINIA NATIVE AMERICAN CULTURAL CENTER
c/o Kay Ensing
1119 Mill Dr.
MANQUIN, VA 23106

VIRGINIA COUNCIL ON INDIANS
P.O. Box 1475
RICHMOND, VA 23219
(804) 786-7765
Gary Flowers, Director

RAPPAHANNOCK-MATTAPONI DANCERS
Route 1, Box 522
TAPPAHANNOCK, VA 23023
(804) 769-4205
Judy Fortune, Coordinator

WASHINGTON

FIRST NATIONS FINANCIAL PROJECT
2016 NE 3rd Ave.
CAMAS, WA 98607
(206) 834-7716
Chris Swenson, Contact

NORTHWEST INDIAN BAR ASSOCIATION
220 8Th Ave. N.
EDMONDS, WA 98020
(206) 774-5808 (Fax)
Mary Pearson, President

INDIGENOUS TRIBES ASSOCIATION
1030 S. 317th St.
FEDERAL WAY, WA 98003
(206) 839-5635
Fred Tidewaters Raven, Contact

4 DIRECTIONS FOUNDATION
23431 130th Ave. SE
KENT, WA 98031
(206) 854-1611
Sheilah Hardwick, Director
Description: A nonprofit Native American training and human development organization offering self-esteem and leadership workshops; also alcohol and addiction recovery programs. Established 1991.

POINT NO POINT TREATY COUNCIL
7999 NE Salish Lane
KINGSTON, WA 98346

**TULALIP TRIBES
ENTERTAINMENT CENTER**
MARYSVILLE WA 98270
(206) 653-5551

**WASHINGTON STATE INDIAN
EDUCATION ASSOCIATION**
c/o Colville Conferedated Tribes
P.O. Box 150
NESPELEM, WA 99155
(509) 634-4711 Fax 634-8799
Gloria Adkins, Contact
Activities: Sponsors annual conference and publishes newsletter, Washington State Indian Education Update.

GOVERNOR'S OFFICE OF INDIAN AFFAIRS
1515 S. Cherry St., Box 40909
OLYMPIA, WA 98504
(206) 753-2411
Michelle PenOziequah Aguilar, Exec. Director
Purpose: To act as a liaison office between the State of Washington and the 26 federally recognized tribes, the 10 non-federally recognized tribes, and various Indian organizations; to educate; to work with Indian tribes; to establish a relationship involving tribal, local, state, and federal governments that will improve communications and joint problem-solving efforts. The office also seeks to enhance the government-to-government relationship between the state and tribes. *Programs*: Conducts "State-Tribal Relations Training," twice a month - this two-day class covers federal legislation and policy, tribal governments, cultural identity, spirituality, reservation economies. Small resource library. Established in 1980.

**WASHINGTON STATE DEPT.
OF PUBLIC INSTRUCTION**
Indian Education Office
Old Capitol Bldg., P.O. Box 47200
OLYMPIA, WA 98504
(206) 753-3635 Fax 753-6754
Patricia L. Martin, Supervisor
Purpose: To administer 20 Johnson O'Malley Indian education programs, funded by the Bureau of Indian Affairs. *Activities*:Provides technical assistance to schools, communities, organizations, etc. in matters pertaining to Indian education.

SEATTLE INDIAN ALCOHOLISM PROGRAM
1912 Minor Ave.
SEATTLE, WA 98101

SEATTLE INDIAN HEALTH BOARD
611-12th Ave. So., Suite 200
SEATTLE, WA 98144
(206) 324-9360
Ralph Forquera, Executive Director
Rebecca Gonzales, Assistant Director
Goal: "To raise to the highest level possible, the physical, mental, spiritual, and social health of American Indian and Alaskan Natives in the Greater Seattle area by providing programs for alcoholism, medical, dental, and mental health." Library. Established 1970.

BERNIE WHITEBEAR
P.O. Box 99100
SEATTLE, WA 98199
(206) 285-4425
Bernie Whitebear, Director
Purpose: To provide social services to the Native American community in the Seattle area. *Programs*: Academic educational programs; employment assistance; headstart and ECEAP program; elder nutrition program. *Publications*: Daybreak Star Press - Native American curriculum materials for schools; Daybreak Star Reader, monthly magazine.

WAKINIKONA HAWAIIAN CLUB
c/o Tukwila Sr. Center
SEATTLE, WA 98168
(206) 776-9420
Doug Kaapana, President
Purpose: To promote traditional Native hawaiian culture and history. *Activities*: Performs ancient Hawaiian music and dance. Sponsors the Hawaiian Summer Festival in Seattle.

KITSAP COUNTY INDIAN CENTER
3337 N.W. Byron St.
SILVERDALE, WA 98383
(206) 692-7460
Larry Dixon, Director

**SPOKANE URBAN INDIAN
HEALTH SERVICES**
East 905 Third Ave.
SPOKANE, WA 99202
(509) 535-0868 Fax 535-3230
Leonard Hendrickx, Exeutive Director
Debra Beeson, MD, Medical Director
Ted Carman & Carolyn Norman, Coordinators
Dean Matt, Project Specialist
Purpose: To provide primary health care services for the Native American community and for residents of the area with no health insurance or access to health care. *Special programs*: Women, Infant Children Nutrition Program; Native American Addictions Program; Pathfinder Program - 135 S. Scott St., Spokane, WA 99202 (509) 534-8334/0848 - incorporates "holistic approaches to preventing and abating substance abuse" and addresses intervention, treatment, reentry, community support, and relapse prevention for Native Americann individuals and families; Low Income Sattelite Clinic.

**SMALL TRIBES ORGANIZATION
OF WESTERN WASHINGTON**
P.O. Box 578
SUMMER, WA 98390
(206) 840-4746 (phone & fax)
Purpose: To secure federal recognition for Washington's aboriginal Indian population in western Washington. Approximately 20% (6,600) of Washington's aboriginal population

are currently enrolled members of Washington's petitioning tribes. The Chinook, Cowlitz, Duwamish, Samish, Snohomish, Snoqualmie and Syeilacoom Tribes of Washington State, along with approximately 100 other U.S. tribes are seeking the federal acknowledgement of the U.S. Government. Each of these tribes has filed a petition with the Bureau of Indian Affairs. *Publication*: Washington's "Landless" Tribes: Our Quest for Federal Tribal Recognition.

NORTHWEST INDIAN WOMEN'S CIRCLE
P.O. Box 8279
TACOMA, WA 98408
(206) 458-7610
Janet McCloud, Contact
Purpose: To provide information about Indian women, their communities, and their struggle. *Publication*: Moccasin Line, newsletter.

THE 13TH REGIONAL CORPORATION
The First Place Plaza
13215-C8 Mill Plain, Suite 393
VANCOUVER, WA 98684
(206) 254-0688 Fax 230-7703

WEST VIRGINIA

**WEST VIRGINIA DIVISION
OF CULTURE & HISTORY**
The Cultural Center, Capitol Complex
CHARLESTON, WV 25305
(304) 348-0220

WISCONSIN

**WISCONSIN NATIVE AMERICAN
DOMESTIC ABUSE SHELTER**
Outreach advocates available in Bad River, LCO, Mole Lake, and Red Cliff
(800) 236-7660 - 24-hour confidential hotline
Benase Equay Wakaigan

CITIZENS FOR TREATY RIGHTS
5013 Sundstein Rd.
EAGLE RIVER, WI 54521

UNITED AMERINDIAN HEALTH CENTER
P.O. Box 2248
GREEN BAY, WI 54306
(414) 435-6773

WISCONSIN INDIAN EDUCATION ASSN.
Menominee Indian Tribe
P.O. Box 910
KESHENA, WI 54135
(715) 799-5110 Fax 799-4525
Virginia Nuske, Contact
Purpose: To promote educational opportunities for Indian people of Wisconsin through a united effort of Indian and non-Indian members interested in social and economic advancement of Indian people. *Programs*: Educational scholarships, awards, and grants for Indin students residing in Wisconsin. *Publication*: Wisconsin Indian Education Resource Directory.

GREAT LAKES INTER-TRIBAL COUNCIL
P.O. Box 9
LAC DU FLAMBEAU, WI 54538
(715) 588-3324
Joseph N. Bresette, Executive Director

**MADISON TREATY RIGHTS
SUPPORT GROUP**
731 State St.
MADISON, WI 53703

**WISCONSIN DEPT. OF
HEALTH & SOCIAL SERVICES**
DCS/DES Tribal Programs
P.O. Box 7935
MADISON, WI 53707
(608) 266-5862
Nancie Young, Director

WISCONSIN GOVERNOR'S INDIAN DESK
P.O. Box 7863
MADISON, WI 53701

**AMERICAN INDIAN
CHAMBER OF COMMERCE**
1228 W. Mitchell
MILWAUKEE, WI 53204
(414) 383-7531
Sharilynne Denning, Chairperson

**AMERICAN INDIAN COUNCIL
ON ALCOHOLISM**
2240 West National Ave.
MILWAUKEE, WI 53204

MILWAUKEE INDIAN HEALTH CENTER
930 North 27th St.
MILWAUKEE, WI 53208
(414) 931-8111
Sharilynne Denning, Director
Satelite: 1225 W. Mitchell, Milwaukee,
WI 53204 (383-9526

**AMERICAN INDIAN
COUNCIL ON ALCOHOLISM**
2451 W. North Ave.
MILWAUKEE, WI 53205

GREAT LAKES NATIVE DIABETES PROJECT
2318 W. Merrill St.
MILWAUKEE, WI 53204
Laura Bearskin, Project Coordinator

**GREAT LAKES INDIAN
FISH & WILDLIFE COMMISSION**
P.O. Box 9
ODANAH, WI 54861
(715) 682-6619 Fax 682-9294
James H. Schlender, Executive Director
13 Chippewa tribes concerned with wildlife conservation in the Great Lakes region. *Purpose*: To coordinate effective management of the resources and implement the exercise of treaty rights in an environmentally safe and meaningful manner. Promotes tribal self-government, and encourages ecosystem protection. *Publications*: Masinaigan, monthly newspaper; Chippewa Treaty Rights; Moving Beyong Argument; resource manuals; brochures; video tapes; and annual report. Annual conference. Founded 1983.

WISCONSIN INDIAN LAWYERS LEAGUE
P.O. Box 365
ONEIDA, WI 54155
(414) 869-2345
Gerald L. Hill, Contact

ONEIDA RIDERS ASSOCIATION
N6935 Hwy. 55
SEYMOUR, WI 54165
(414) 833-2323
Jacqueline Johnson, Executive Director
Purpose: To educate members on the horse and its role in Native American culture. *Activities*: Conducts parades, trail rides, speakers, educational clinics, arts & crafts; compiles information on how the horse was used, stories and legends, regalia of horse and rider, training, symbols, etc. Founded 1994.

WISCONSIN NATIVE AMERICAN ARTISTS
John Michael Kohler Arts Center
P.O. Box 489
SHEBOYGAN, WI 53082

NATIVE AMERICAN CENTER
012 Old Main, UW-Stevens Point
STEVENS POINT, WI 54481
(715) 346-2004
Ben Raniirez-Shlwegnaabi, Director

WYOMING

GOVERNOR'S INDIAN COMMISSION
U.S. West Bldg., Room 259B
6101 Yellowstone
CHEYENNE, WY 82002
(307) 777-6779
Gary Maier, Commissioner

WYOMING INDIAN EDUCATION ASSN.
P.O. Box 248
FORT WASHAKIE, WY 82514
(307) 332-2681
Larry Murry, President
Purpose: To promote education of the Shoshone and Arapaho youth on the W ind River Indian Reservation and is supported by both tribes.

Indian children attend Federal, public, private and mission schools. There are approximately 250,000 Indian students, age 5 to 18 years inclusive, enrolled in these schools in the U.S. Education of Indian children residing in the States of California, Idaho, Michigan, Minnesota, Nebraska, Oregon, Texas, Washington, and Wisconsin is the responsibility of the State concerned.

U.S. DEPT. OF THE INTERIOR - BUREAU OF INDIAN AFFAIRS

Listed here are elementary and high schools operated by the Bureau of Indian Affairs, as well as other Indian schools; arranged by type of school (i.e., day and boarding schools), and by geographic location.

Listed first are Bureau of Indian Affairs' agencies and area offices with education program administrators, superintendents, and chairpersons; with telephone and telefax numbers.

OFFICE OF INDIAN EDUCATION PROGRAMS
Bureau of Indian Affairs
1849 C St., N.W.
WASHINGTON, DC 20240-0001
 (202) 208-Extension
 Dr. John Tippeconnic, Director (6123 Fax 3312)
 William Mehojah, Dep. Director (6175 Fax 3312)
Staff: C.L. Henson, Chief, Division of Administration (208-4234 Fax 208-3271); Joy Martin, Chief, Branch of Administrative Services (208-3519 Fax 208-3271); Jim Womack, Chief, Branch of Management & Information Services (208-7111 Fax 208-5599); Dr. Dennis Fox, Chief, Div. of Education (208-7388 Fax 208-3200); Charles Globe, Chief, Branch of Elem. & Sec. Ed. (219-1129 Fax 219-9583); Reggie Rodriguez, Chief, Branch of Post Secondary Education (208-4871); Keener Cobb, Chief, Branch of Exceptional Education (208-6675 Fax 208-5993); Sharon Lynn, Chief, Branch of Supplemental Services (208-6364); Dr. James Martin, Chief, Branch of Planning, Oversight & Evaluation (208-3550 Fax 219-0221); Dr. Sandra Fox, Chief, Branch of Monitoring & Evaluation (208-3550 Fax 219-0221); Dixie Owen, Chief, Branch of Planning (219-1131 Fax 219-0221); John Reimer, Chief, Branch of Research & Planning Analysis (208-3562).

ABERDEEN AREA INSTRUCTIONAL COORDINATOR
Bureau of Indian Affairs
115 4th Ave., SE, Federal Bldg.
ABERDEEN, SD 57401
 (605) 226-7431 Fax 226-7434
 Sandra Carlsgaard, Special Ed. Coordinator

ALBUQUERQUE EDUCATION FIELD OFFICE
Bureau of Indian Affairs
P.O. Box 26567
ALBUQUERQUE, NM 87125
 (505) 766-3850
 Dr. Kenneth Ross; Rodney Young,
 Dr. Benjamin Atencio, Cecilia Baca

ANCHORAGE EDUCATION FIELD OFFICE
Bureau of Indian Affairs
1675 C St.
ANCHORAGE, AK 99501
 (907) 271-4115/6 Fax 271-3678
 Robert Pringle, Ed. Programs Administrator

BILLINGS AREA OFFICE
Bureau of Indian Affairs
316 North 26th St.
BILLINGS, MT 59101
 (406) 657-6375 Fax 657-6466
 Larry Parker, Education Programs Administrator
Responsible for the following schools : Blackfeet Dormitory; Busby School; St. Stephens Indian School.

CHEYENNE RIVER AGENCY
Bureau of Indian Affairs
P.O. Box 2020
EAGLE BUTTE, SD 57625
 (605) 964-8722 Fax 964-1155
 Dr. Cherie Farlee, Supt. for Education
Responsible for the following schools : Takini School; Promise Day School; Swift Bird Day School; White Horse Day School; Cheyenne-Eagle Butte School; Pierre Indian Learning Center

CHINLE AGENCY
Bureau of Indian Affairs
P.O. Box 6003
CHINLE, AZ 86503
 (602) 674-5201 Ext. 201
 Andrew Tah, Supt. for Education
 Marvin Chee, Chairperson
Responsible for the following schools : Cottonwood Day School; Low Mountain Boarding School; Lukachukai Boarding School; Nazlini Boarding School; Pinon Dormitory; Rock Point Community School; Rough Rock Demonstration School; Chinle Boarding School; Many Farms High School; Black Mesa Community School

CHOCTAW FIELD OFFICE
Bureau of Indian Affairs
421 Powell ST.
PHILADELPHIA, MS 39350
 (601) 656-1521/2 Fax 656-2350
 Bonnie Martin, Education Specialist
Responsible for the following schools : Red Water Elementary School; Standing Pine Elementary School; Tucker Elementary School; Boque Chitto Elementary School; Conehatta Elementary School; Choctaw Central High School & Middle School

CROW CREEK/LOWER BRULE AGENCY
Bureau of Indian Affairs
P.O. Box 139
FORT THOMPSON, SD 57339
 (605) 245-2398; 473-5531 Fax 245-2399
 Dan Schroyer, Supt. for Education
 Silas Blaine (Crow) & Ben Jaris (Lower Brule), Chairpersons
Responsible for the following schools : Fort Thompson Elementary School; Crow Creek Reservation High School; Lower Brule Day School.

EASTERN NAVAJO AGENCY
Bureau of Indian Affairs
P.O. Box 328
CROWNPOINT, NM 87313
 (505) 786-6150/1/2 Fax 786-6112
 Larry D. Holman, Supt. for Education
 Raymond Morgan, Chairperson
Responsible for the following schools : Baca Community School; Dibe Yazhi Habitiin Olta (Borrego Pass School); Bread Springs Day School; Chi-Ch'll-Tah/Jones Ranch Community School; Huerfano Dormitory; Lake Valley Navajo School; Mariano Lake Community School; Ojo Encino Day School; Pueblo Pintado Community School; Standing Rock Community School; Dlo'ay Azhi Community School; Na'Neelzhiin Ji'Olta (Torreon); Wingate Elementary School; Wingate High School; Crownpoint Community School; Dzilth-Na-O-Dith-Hle Community School; To-Hajiilee-He (Canoncito); Alamo Navajo School

EASTERN STATES AGENCY
Bureau of Indian Affairs
3701 N. Fairfax Dr., Suite 260/Mailroom
ARLINGTON, VA 22203
 (703) 235-3233/3180 Fax 235-3351
 Lena F. Mills, Education Administrator
Responsible for the following schools : Chitimacha Day School; Cherokee Central School; Ahfachkee Day School; Miccosukee Indian School; Indian Township School; Beatrice Rafferty School; Indian Island School.

FORT APACHE AGENCY
Bureau of Indian Affairs
P.O. Box 560
WHITE RIVER, AZ 85941
 (602) 338-4647/4665 Fax 338-1944
 Vacant, Supt. for Education
 Judy DeHose, Chairperson
Responsible for the following schools : Cibecue Community School; John F. Kennedy Day School; Theodore Roosevelt School

FORT DEFIANCE AGENCY
Bureau of Indian Affairs
P.O. Box 110
FORT DEFIANCE, AZ 86504
 (602) 729-5041 Ext. 255 Fax 729-5041
 Charles E. Johnson, Supt. for Education
 Wallace Tsosie, Chairperson
Responsible for the following schools : Chuska/Tohatchi Consolidated School; Crystal Boarding School; Dilcon Boarding School; Greasewood/Toyei Consolidated School; Holbrook Dormitory; Hunters Point Boarding School; Kinlichee Boarding School; Pine Springs Boarding School; Seba Dalkai Boarding School; Wide Ruins Boarding School; Winslow Dormitory

HOPI AGENCY
Bureau of Indian Affairs
P.O. Box 568
KEAMS CANYON, AZ 86034
 (602) 738-2262/3/4 Fax 738-5139
 John D. Wahnee, Supt. for Education
 Brant Hopahnis, Chairperson
Responsible for the following schools : Polacca Day School; Second Mesa Day School; Hopi Day School; Hotevilla Bacavi Community School; Moencopi Day School; Keams Canyon Boarding School; Hopi High School; Havasupai School

LAGUNA AGENCY
Bureau of Indian Affairs
P.O. Box 298
OLD LAGUNA, NM 87026
 (505) 552-6653 Fax 552-7294
 Phillip Belone, Supt. for Education
 Josephine Tsosie, Chairperson
Responsible for the following schools : Laguna Elementary School; Laguna Middle School

MINNEAPOLIS AREA OFFICE
Bureau of Indian Affairs
331 Second Ave., South
MINNEAPOLIS, MN 55401
 (612) 373-1090 Fax 373-1186
 Betty Walker, Ed. Programs Administrator
Responsible for the following schools : Sac & Fox Settlement School; Chief Bug-O-Nay-Ge Shig School; Circle of Life Survival School; Fond du

Lac Ojibway School; Nay Ah Shing School; Lac Courte Oreeilles Ojibwa School; Oneida Tribal School; Menominee Tribal School; Hannahville Indian School; Flandreau Indian School; Wahpeton Indian Boarding School

NORTHERN PUEBLOS AGENCY
Bureau of Indian Affairs
P.O. Box 4269, Fairview Station
ESPANOLA, NM 87533
(505) 753-1465/9 Fax 753-1475
Dr. Juanita O. Cata, Supt. for Education
Charlie Dorame, Chairperson
Responsible for the following schools : San Ildefonso Day School; San Juan Day School; Santa Clara Day School; Taos Day School; Tesuque Day School; Santa Fe Indian School; Jicarilla Dormitory

OKLAHOMA EDUCATION OFFICE
Bureau of Indian Affairs
4149 Highline Blvd., Suite 380
OKLAHOMA CITY, OK 73180
(405) 945-6051/2/3/4 Fax 945-6057
Jimmy Baker, Education Program Administrator
Responsible for the following schools : Riverside Indian School; Carter Seminary; Kickapoo Nation School; Eufaula Dormitory; Sequoyah High School; Jones Academy.

PAPAGO AGENCY
Bureau of Indian Affairs
P.O. Box 38
SELLS, AZ 85634
(602) 383-3292/3/4 Fax 383-2399
George Scott, Supt. for Education
Mark Miguel, Chairperson
Responsible for the following schools : Santa Rosa Ranch School; Santa Rosa Boarding School; San Simon School; Tohono O'Odham High School.

PIMA AGENCY
Bureau of Indian Affairs
P.O. Box 8
SACATON, AZ 85247
(602) 562-3557, 963-6907 Fax 963-9749
Beverly Mestes, Supt. for Education
Drake Lewis, Chairperson
Responsible for the following schools : Blackwater Community School; Casa Blanca Day School; Gila Crossing Day School; Salt River Day School

PINE RIDGE AGENCY
Bureau of Indian Affairs
P.O. Box 333
PINE RIDGE, SD 57770
(605) 867-1306 Fax 867-5610
Basil Brave Heart, Supt. for Education
Shirley Plume, Chairperson
Responsible for the following schools : American Horse School; Little Wound Day School; Wounded Knee School District; Loneman Day School; Pine Ridge School; Porcupine Day School; Crazy Horse School.

PORTLAND AREA OFFICE
Bureau of Indian Affairs
911 N.E. 11th Ave.
PORTLAND, OR 97232
(503) 230-5682 Fax 231-6219
Van Peters, Education Programs Administrator
Responsible for the following schools : Chemawa Indian School; Paschal Sherman Indian School; Sho-Ban School District No. 512; Coeur D'Alene Tribal School; Quileute Tribal School; Wa He Lut Indian School; Lummi Tribal School System;

Lummi High School; Chief Leschi School System; Muckleshoot Tribal School; Yakima Tribal School; Two Eagle River School

ROSEBUD AGENCY
Bureau of Indian Affairs
P.O. Box 669
MISSION, SD 57555
(605) 856-4478 Fax 856-4487
Neva Sherwood, Supt. for Education
Responsible for the following schools : St. Francis Indian School; Rosebud Dormitories; Marty Indian School.

SACRAMENTO AREA OFFICE
Bureau of Indian Affairs
2800 Cottage Way
SACRAMENTO, CA 95825
(916) 978-4680 Fax 978-4695
Fayetta Babby, Ed. Programs Administrator
Responsible for the following schools : Sherman Indian High School; Pyramid Lake High School; Duckwater Shoshone Elementary School.

SHIPROCK AGENCY
Bureau of Indian Affairs
P.O. Box 3239
SHIPROCK, NM 87420
(505) 368-4427 Ext. 360 Fax 368-4427
Lester Hudson, Supt. for Education
Harry Tome, Chairperson
Responsible for the following schools : Aneth Community School; Aztec Dormitory; Beclabito Day School; Cove Day School; Nenahnezad Boarding School; Red Rock Day School; Sanostee Day School; Teecnospos Boarding School; Toadlena Boarding School; Shiprock Reservation Dormitory; Shiprock Alternative Kindergarten; Shiprock Alternative High School; Navajo Prepatory School

SISSETON AGENCY
Bureau of Indian Affairs
205 East Oak
SISSETON, SD 57262
(605) 698-7676 Fax 698-3375
Dr. Blossom Keeble, Supt. for Education
Responsible for the following schools : Enemy Swim Day School; Tiospa Zina Tribal School; Four Winds Community School.

SOUTHERN PUEBLOS AGENCY
Bureau of Indian Affairs
1000 Indian School Rd., N.W.
P.O. Box 1667
ALBUQUERQUE, NM 87103
(505) 766-3034/5/6 Fax 766-2179
Val Cordova, Supt. for Education
Roger Madalena, Chairperson
Responsible for the following schools : Sky City Community School; Isleta Elementary School; Jemez Day School; San Felipe Day School; Zia Day School; Pine Hill Schools; Mescalero Elementary School

STANDING ROCK AGENCY
P.O. Box E
Bureau of Indian Affairs
FORT YATES, ND 58538
(701) 854-3497/8 Fax 854-3842
Bobby Thompson, Supt. for Education
Charles Red Bear, Chairperson
Responsible for the following schools : Rock Creek Day School; Littel Eagle Day School; Standing Rock Community School; Theodore Jamerson Elementary School.

TURTLE MOUNTAIN AGENCY
Bureau of Indian Affairs
P.O. Box 30
BELCOURT, ND 58316
(701) 477-6471 Ext. 21 1 Fax 477-5944
Dr. James L. Davis, Supt. for Education
Responsible for the following schools : Dunseith Day School; Ojibwa Indian School; Turtle Mountain Elementary & Middle School; Turtle Mountain High School; Mandaree Day School; Twin Buttes Day School; White Shield School

WESTERN NAVAJO AGENCY
Bureau of Indian Affairs
P.O. Box 746
TUBA CITY, AZ 86045
(602) 283-4531
Beverly Crawford, Supt. for Education
Shonie C. Keith, Chairperson
Responsible for the following schools : Chilchinbeto Day School; Dennehotso Boarding School; Flagstaff Dormitory; Kaibeto Boarding School; Kayenta Boarding School; Leupp Boarding School; Navajo Mountain Boarding School; Red Lake Day School; Richfield Dormitory; Rocky Ridge Boarding School; Shonto Boarding School; Tuba City Boarding School; Greyhills High School; Little Singer Community School

ALABAMA

REEDS CHAPEL ELEMENTARY & CALCEDEAVER SCHOOLS
Choctaw Indian Reservation
Rt. 1, Box 330-A, Reservation Rd.
MT. VERNON 36560
(205) 829-5500 Fax 829-5580

ALASKA

AKIACHAK IRA CONTRACT SCHOOL
General Delivery
AKIACHAK 99551
(907) 825-4428
Gil Gutierrez, Principal
Willie Kasayulie, Chair
Day School; Grades K-8. Under jurisdiction of Anchorage Education Field Office.

ARLICAQ SCHOOL
Yupiit School District
P.O. Box 227
AKIAK 99552
(907) 765-7212/5
Larry Ctibor, Principal
Day School; Grades K-12. *Enrollment*: 76. *Instructors*: Debbie Jackson, Elizabeth Lake, Ida Jasper, Lena Williams. *Special programs* : Bilingual Bicultural Education Program (Abbey Augustine, Coordinator); Yupiit Reading Project; Cultural Heritage Program. Library. Under jurisdiction of Anchorage Education Field Office.

CHEFORNAK IRA CONTRACT SCHOOL
General Delivery
CHEFORNAK 99561
(907) 867-8707
Jerry Twitchell, Principal
Peter Panruk, Chair
Day School; Grades K-8. Under jurisdiction of Anchorage Education Field Office.

CHEVAK IRA CONTRACT SCHOOL
CHEVAK 99563
 (907) 858-7713
 Alex Tatem, Principal
 Xiver Atcherian, Chair
Day School; Grades K-12. Under jurisdiction
of Anchorage Education Field Office.

KASIGLUK DAY SCHOOL
KASIGLUK 99609
 (907) 477-6714
 Karen A. Rhoades, Principal
 Yeako Slim, Chair
Day School; Grades K-8. Under jurisdiction
of Anchorage Education Field Office.

KIPNUK DAY SCHOOL
KIPNUK 99614
 (907) 896-5513
 Leslie Smith, Principal/Teacher
 Peter J. Paul, Chair
Day School; Grades K-8. Under jurisdiction
of Anchorage Education Field Office.

NEWTOK DAY SCHOOL
General Delivery
NEWTOK 99559
 (907) 237-2328
 Rodney Sehorn, Principal
 Joseph Tommy, Chair
Day School; Grades 1-8. Under jurisdiction
of Anchorage Education Field Office.

NUNAPITCHUK DAY SCHOOL
NUNAPITCHUK 99641
 (907) 527-5711
 Karen K. Waters, Principal/Teacher
 Jimmy Stevens, Chair
Day School; Grades K-8. Under jurisdiction
of Anchorage Education Field Office.

MT. EDGECUMBE HIGH SCHOOL
1332 Seward
SITKA 99835
 (907) 966-2201
 Bill Denkinger, Principal
 Larrae Rocheleau, Superintendent
Boarding School; Grades 9-12; *Enrollment*: 300.
Special courses: Pacific Rim Cultures; Alaska
Native History.

TOKSOOK BAY DAY SCHOOL
TOKSOOK 99637
 (907) 543-2746
 Wilma M. Moore, Principal/Teacher
 Joseph Henry, Chair
Day School; Grades 1-6. Under jurisdiction
of Anchorage Education Field Office.

TULUKSAK IRA CONTRACT SCHOOL
TULUKSAK 99679
 (907) 695-6212
 Howard Diamond, Principal
 Andrew Alexie, Chair
Day School; Grades K-8. Under jurisdiction
of Anchorage Education Field Office.

ARIZONA

CASA BLANCA DAY SCHOOL
P.O. Box 940
BAPCHULE 85221
 (602) 315-3489/10/11 Fax 315-1199
 Alfred G. Martinez, Principal

 Arnold Charles, Chairperson
Day School; Grades K-4.
Under jurisdiction of Pima Agency.

WIDE RUINS BOARDING SCHOOL
P.O. Box 309
CHAMBERS 86502
 (602) 652-3251 Fax 652-3252
 Lawrence G. Wright, Principal
 Ernest Hubbell, Chairperson
Boarding School; Grades K-5. Under
jurisdiction of Fort Defiance Agency.

BLACK MESA COMMUNITY SCHOOL
RRDS, Box 215
CHINLE 86503
 (602) 674-3632 Fax 674-3632
 George Cukro, Director
 Jones Begay, Chairperson
Day School; Grades K-8. Under jurisdiction
of Chinle Agency.

COTTONWOOD DAY SCHOOL
CHINLE 86503
 (602) 725-3256/3235 Fax 674-5201
 Carol Green, Principal
 Ethelou Yazzie, Chairperson
Day School; Grades K-8. Under jurisdiction
of Chinle Agency.

LOW MOUNTAIN BOARDING SCHOOL
CHINLE 86503
 (602) 725-3308 Fax 674-5201
 Joe Hardy, Principal
 Frances Kanuho, Chairperson
Boarding School; Grades K-4.
Under jurisdiction of Chinle Agency.

ROUGH ROCK DEMONSTRATION SCHOOL
RRDS, Box 217
CHINLE 86503
 (602) 728-3311/6 Fax 728-3215
 Carl Levi, Director/Supt.
 Ernest W. Dick, Chairperson
Day School; Grades K-12. Under jurisdiction
of Chinle Agency.

CIBECUE COMMUNITY SCHOOL
P.O. Box 68
CIBECUE 85911
 (602) 332-2444/2480 Fax 332-2586
 Bill Walters, Principal
 Judy DeHose, Chairperson
Day School; Grades K-12; *Enr ollment*: 350. *Special courses*: Bilingual (Apache). *Instructors*:
Bonnie Luis, Bilingual; Joyce Kruger, Gifted; Fay
Fernando, Chapter I Coordinator; Eric Carlson,
Special Ed. Coordinator; Margaret Burnette, Indian Club. Special programs: American Indian Day
Pageant, in Sept.; Arts and Crafts Fair/Pow-Wow,
in May; Indian Club (children learn and perform
Native American dances and music). Library Media Center with about 7,500 resources. *Publication*: Biweekly newsletter. Under jurisdiction of Fort
Apache Agency.

BLACKWATER COMMUNITY SCHOOL
Route 1, Box 95
COOLIDGE 85228
 (602) 215-5859
 S. Jo Lewis, Principal
Day School. Grades K-2. Under jurisdiction
of Pima Agency.

DENNEHOTSO BOARDING SCHOOL
P.O. Box LL
DENNEHOTSO 86535

 (602) 658-3201/2 Fax 658-3221
 Velma Eisenberger, Principal
 Allen Gray, Chairperson
Boarding School; Grades K-8. Under
jurisdiction of Western Navajo Agency.

FLAGSTAFF DORMITORY
P.O. Box 609
FLAGSTAFF 86002
 (602) 774-5270
 James Kimery, Director/Counselor
 Chester Claw, Chairperson
Dormitory School; Grades 9-12. Under
jurisdiction of Western Navajo Agency.

THEODORE ROOSEVELT SCHOOL
P.O. Box 567
FORT APACHE 85926
 (602) 338-4464 Fax 338-1009
 Bill Hastings, Principal
 Robert Lupe, Chairperson
Day and Boarding School; Grades 4-12; 9-12
(Boarding only). Under jurisdiction of Fort Apache
Agency.

**GREASEWOOD/TOYEI CONSOLIDATED
BOARDING SCHOOL**
GANADO 86505
 (602) 654-3331/2 Fax 654-3384
 Catherine T. Begay, Principal
 Ronald Gishey, Sr., Chairperson
Boarding School; Grades K-8. Under
jurisdiction of Fort Defiance Agency.

KINLICHEE BOARDING SCHOOL
GANADO 86505
 (602) 755-3430/9
 Elsie Belone, Principal
Boarding School; Grades K-6. *Enrollment*: 110.
Instructors: T. Piechewski, R. Venn, S. Litson, T.
Cline, J. Lemler, H. Parkhurst. 95% of students
are Navajo Indians. Library. Under jurisdiction of
Fort Defiance Agency.

NAZLINI BOARDING SCHOOL
GANADO 86505
 (602) 755-6125 Fax 674-5201
 William H. Draper, Principal
 Arthur Tracey, Chairperson
Boarding School; Grades K-6.
Under jurisdiction of Chinle Agency.

HOLBROOK DORMITORY
1100 W. Buffalo, P.O. Box 758
HOLBROOK 86025
 (602) 524-6222/3 Fax 524-2231
 Gary E. Joka, Principal
 Edward D. Yazzie, Chairperson
Dormitory School; Grades 9-12. Under
jurisdiction of Fort Defiance Agency.

HOTEVILLA BACAVI COMMUNITY SCHOOL
P.O. Box 48
HOTEVILLA 86030
 (602) 734-2462 Fax 734-2227
 Leroy Shingoitewa, Chief Administrator
 Philbert Dennis, Chairperson
Day School; Grades K-6. *Enrollment*: 122. *Special programs*: Bilingual computer program; special education. Community library. *Publication*:
Tales in Hopi Language (published by students).
Under jurisdiction of Hopi Agency.

PINE SPRINGS BOARDING SCHOOL
P.O. Box 198
HOUCK 86506
 (602) 871-4311

Charles W. Riley, II, Principal
Charles Morrison, Chairperson
Boarding School; Grades K-6. *Enrollment*: 62.
Under jurisdiction of Fort Defiance Agency.

KAIBETO BOARDING SCHOOL
KAIBETO 86053
(602) 673-3480
Patrick Suriano Principal
Kelsey Begaye, Chairperson
Boarding School; Grades K-8. Under
jurisdiction of Western Navajo Agency.

CHILCHINBETO DAY SCHOOL
P.O. Box 547
KAYENTA 86033
(602) 697-3448
Wanda Sorenson, Principal
Shonie Keith, Chairperson
Day School; Grades K-8. Under
jurisdiction of Western Navajo Agency.

KAYENTA BOARDING SCHOOL
P.O. Box 188
KAYENTA 86033
(602) 697-3439 Fax 697-3490
Loren Joseph, Principal
Willie Begay, Sr., Chairperson
Boarding School; Grades K-8. Under
jurisdiction of Western Navajo Agency.

HOPI HIGH SCHOOL
P.O. Box 337
KEAMS CANYON 86034
(602) 738-5111/2/3 Fax 738-5266
Gerald L. Clayton Principal
Leon Nuvayestewa, Chairperson
Day School; Grades 7-12. Under
jurisdiction of Hopi Agency.

KEAMS CANYON BOARDING SCHOOL
P.O. Box 397
KEAMS CANYON 86034
(602) 738-2385 Fax 738-5139
Douglas R. Philbrick, Principal
Boarding School; Grades K-6.
Under jurisdiction of Hopi Agency.

HOPI DAY SCHOOL
P.O. Box 42
KYKOTSMOVI 86039
(602) 734-2468 Fax 738-5139
Edward Vermillion, Principal
Phyllis Norton, Chairperson
Day School; Grades K-6. Under
jurisdiction of Hopi Agency.

ROCKY RIDGE BOARDING SCHOOL
P.O. Box 299
KYKOTSMOVI 86039
(602) 725-3415
Frederick M. Johnson, Principal
Lorenzo Yazzie, Chairperson
Boarding School; Grades K-8. Under
jurisdiction of Western Navajo Agency.

GILA CROSSING DAY SCHOOL
P.O. Box 10
LAVEEN 85339
(602) 237-4834/77
Mary Jo Walter, Principal
Marian Miles, Chairperson
Day School; Grades K-6. Under jurisdiction
of Pima Agency.

LUKACHUKAI BOARDING SCHOOL
LUKACHUKAI 86507
(602) 787-2301 Fax 674-5201
Leo Gishie, Principal
Leon Harvey, Chairperson
Boarding School; Grades K-8.
Under jurisdiction of Chinle Agency.

CHINLE BOARDING SCHOOL
P.O. Box 70
MANY FARMS 86538
(602) 781-6221/2 Fax 674-5201
Lorraine Boyiddle, Principal
Marvin Chee, Chairperson
Boarding School; Grades K-8.
Under jurisdiction of Chinle Agency.

MANY FARMS HIGH SCHOOL
P.O. Box 307
MANY FARMS 86538
(602) 781-6226/7 Fax 674-5201
Harold King, Principal
Eddie Arthur, Chairperson
Boarding School; Grades 9-12.
Under jurisdiction of Chinle Agency.

PHOENIX INDIAN SCHOOL
P.O. Box 10
PHOENIX 85001
(602) 241-2126
Fred Wilson, Principal
Boarding School; Grades 9-12.
Under jurisdiction of Phoenix Area Office.

PINON DORMITORY
P.O. Box 159
PINON 86510
(602) 725-3250/3234 Fax 725-3232
Phyllis Bedonie, Director
Alice Labahe, Chairperson
Boarding School; Grades K-5.
Under jurisdiction of Chinle Agency.

POLACCA DAY SCHOOL
P.O. Box 750
POLACCA 86042
(602) 737-2581 Fax 738-5139
Glenn C. WhiteEagle, Principal
Clark Tenakhongua, Chairperson
Day School; Grades K-6.
Under jurisdiction of Hopi Agency.

RED ROCK DAY SCHOOL
P.O. Drawer 10
RED VALLEY 86544
(602) 653-4456
Eva M. Benally, Principal
Harry Tome, Chairperson
Day School; Grades K-8. Under
jurisdiction of Shiprock Agency.

ROCK POINT COMMUNITY SCHOOL
ROCK POINT 86545
(602) 659-4221/4 Fax 659-4235
Jimmy C. Begay, Director
James M. Begay, Chairperson
Day School; Grades K-12. Under
jurisdiction of Chinle Agency.

HUNTERS POINT BOARDING SCHOOL
P.O. Box 99
ST. MICHAELS 86511
(602) 871-4439/4793
Winifred C. Peters, Principal
Katherine Keeto, Chairperson
Boarding School; Grades K-5. Under
jurisdiction of Fort Defiance Agency.

SALT RIVER DAY SCHOOL
Route 1, Box 117
SCOTTSDALE 85256
(602) 640-2810 Fax 640-2809
Austin Buckles, Principal
Maria Chavez, Chairperson
Day School; Grades K-6.
Under jurisdiction of Pima Agency.

SECOND MESA DAY SCHOOL
P.O. Box 98
SECOND MESA 86043
(602) 737-2571 Fax 737-2565
Betty Paymella, Principal
Michael Day, Chairperson
Day School; Grades K-6. Under
jurisdiction of Hopi Agency.

SAN SIMON SCHOOL
Star Route 1, Box 92
SELLS 85634
(602) 362-2331/2232 Fax 362-2405
Della R. Williams, Principal
Fern Salcido, Chairperson
Boarding School; Grades K-8.
Under jurisdiction of Papago Agency.

SANTA ROSA BOARDING SCHOOL
SELLS 85634
(602) 361-2331/2276 Fax 361-2511
John Leffue, Principal
Rose Martin, Chairperson
Boarding School; Grades K-8.
Under jurisdiction of Papago Agency.

TOHONO O'ODHAM HIGH SCHOOL
P.O. Box 513
SELLS 85634
(602) 362-2400/2401 Fax 362-2256
Karen Dawson, Principal
Marjorie Juan, Chairperson
Day School; Grades 9-12. Under
jurisdiction of Papago Agency.

SHONTO BOARDING SCHOOL
SHONTO 86054
(602) 672-2652 (Phone & Fax)
Roland E. Smith, Principal
Stanley Yazzie, Chairperson
Boarding School; Grades K-8. Under
jurisdiction of Western Navajo Agency.

HAVASUPAI SCHOOL
P.O. Box 40
SUPAI 86435
(602) 448-2901/2071 Fax 448-2551
Harry Doten, Principal
Daley Manakaja, Chairperson
Day School; Grades K-8.
Under jurisdiction of Hopi Agency.

TEECNOSPOS BOARDING SCHOOL
TEECNOSPOS 86514
(602) 656-3451/3252 Fax 656-3486
Alice Tynes, Principal
May Howard, Chairperson
Boarding School; Grades K-8. Under
jurisdiction of Shiprock Agency.

NAVAJO MOUNTAIN BOARDING SCHOOL
P.O. Box 10010
TONALEA 86044
(602) 672-2851 Fax 672-2335
Herbert C. Black, Principal
Jamie Holgate, Chairperson
Boarding School; Grades K-8. Under
jurisdiction of Western Navajo Agency.

RED LAKE DAY SCHOOL
P.O. Box 39
TONALEA 86044
(602) 283-6325
Harlan Hornbacher, Principal
Wilson Gray, Chairperson
Day School; Grades K-8. Under
jurisdiction of Western Navajo Agency.

MOENCOPI DAY SCHOOL
P.O. Box 185
TUBA CITY 86045
(602) 283-5361 Fax 738-5139
Dr. John L. Thomas, Principal
Brant Honahnie, Chairperson
Day School; Grades K-6. Under
jurisdiction of Hopi Agency.

TUBA CITY BOARDING SCHOOL
P.O. Box 187
TUBA CITY 86045
(602) 283-4531 ext. 336 Fax 283-4531
Jerry E. Diebel, Principal
Mary Maloney, Chairperson
Boarding School; Grades K-8. Under
jurisdiction of Western Navajo Agency.

GREYHILLS HIGH SCHOOL
P.O. Box 160
TUBA CITY 86045
(602) 283-6271 (phone & fax)
Dr. Harold Begay, Director
Emmett Tso, Chairperson
Boarding School; Grades 9-12. *Enrollment*: 450.
An Academy High School with a uniquely Native
American thrust in education. In partnership with
Northern Arizona University and Uiversity of Ha-
waii in developing a curriculum based on a Labo-
ratory school approach. Library. Under jurisdiction
of Western Navajo Agency.

SANTA ROSA RANCH SCHOOL
HC04 #7570
TUCSON 85735
(602) 383-2359
Louis Barajas, Principal
Mark Miguel, Chairperson
Boarding School; Grades K-8.
Under jurisdiction of Papago Agency.

JOHN F. KENNEDY DAY SCHOOL
P.O. Box 130
WHITE RIVER 85941
(602) 338-4593
Patricia Allen, Principal
Thurman Susan, Chairperson
Day School; Grades K-8. Under
jurisdiction of Fort Apache Agency.

DILCON BOARDING SCHOOL
Star Route
WINSLOW 86047
(602) 657-3211/2 Fax 657-3370
Dottie Hobson, Principal
James Paddock, Chairperson
Boarding School; Grades K-8. Under
jurisdiction of Fort Defiance Agency.

LEUPP BOARDING SCHOOL
P.O. Box HC-61
WINSLOW 86047
(602) 686-6211/6270 Fax 686-6216
Donald Harvey, Director
Jonathan R. Dover, Chairperson
Boarding School; Grades K-12. *Enrollment*: 375.
Special course: Entrepreneurship. *Instructor*: Jim

Store. *Publication*: Today at Leupp. Library. Under jurisdiction of Western Navajo Agency.

LITTLE SINGER COMMUNITY SCHOOL
HC 61, Box 239
WINSLOW 86047
(602) 526-6680 (Phone Fax)
Mark Sorenson, Director
Hoover Schultz, Chairperson
Boarding School; Grades K-6. Under
jurisdiction of Western Navajo Agency.

SEBA DALKAI BOARDING SCHOOL
Star Route #1
WINSLOW 86047
(602) 657-3208/9 Fax 657-3224
Holly D. Butler, Principal
Lulu Mae Stago, Chairperson
Boarding School; Grades K-6. *Enrollment*: 183.
Special programs: Special Education, Gifted and
Talented; Intensive Residential Guidance Pro-
gram; & Substance Abuse. Bilingual Education.
Under jurisdiction of Fort Defiance Agency.

WINSLOW DORMITORY
600 N. Alfred Ave.
WINSLOW 86047
(602) 289-4483/8
Helen C. Higdon, Principal
Elmer Clark, Chairperson
Dormitory School; Grades 7-12. Under
jurisdiction of Fort Defiance Agency.

CALIFORNIA

SHERMAN INDIAN HIGH SCHOOL
9010 Magnolia Ave.
RIVERSIDE 92503
(714) 276-6334 Fax 276-6336
Ken Taylor, Acting Principal
Daniel Troe, Chairperson
Boarding School; Grades 9-12. Under
jurisdiction of Sacramento Area Office.

FLORIDA

AHFACHKEE DAY SCHOOL
Star Route, Box 40
CLEWISTON 33440
(813) 983-6348 Fax 983-6535
Martin Coyle, Principal
James E. Billy, Chairperson
Day School; Grades K-6. Under
jurisdiction of Eastern States Agency.

MICCOSUKEE INDIAN SCHOOL
Box 440021, Tamiami Station
MIAMI 33144
(305) 223-8380 Fax 223-1011
Bruce Hoffman, Principal
Lois Billie, Jr., Chairperson
Day School; Grades K-12. Library. Under
jurisdiction of Eastern States Agency.

IDAHO

COEUR D'ALENE TRIBAL SCHOOL
P.O. Box 338
DeSMET 83824

(208) 274-6921 Fax 274-2114
John H. Ruegamer, Supt.
Alfred Nomee, Chairperson
Day School; Grades Pre K-8. Under
jurisdiction of Portland Area Office.

SHO'BAN SCHOOL DISTRICT #512
P.O. Box 306
FORT HALL 83203
(208) 238-3975 Fax 237-0797
Pete A. Lipovac, Supt.
Velda Auck, Chairperson
Day School; Grades 7-12. Under
jurisdiction of Portland Area Office.

IOWA

SAC & FOX SETTLEMENT SCHOOL
1657 320th St.
TAMA 52339
(515) 484-4990 Fax 484-3264
Dr. Beth Silhanek, Administrator
Deron Ward, Chairperson
Day School; Grades Pre-K-8. Under
jurisdiction of Minneapolis Area Office.

KANSAS

HASKELL INDIAN JUNIOR COLLEGE
P.O. Box H1305
LAWRENCE 66044
(913) 749-8472
Dr. Gerald E. Gipp, President
Administered by the Bureau of Indian Affairs,
under the jurisdiction of the Horton Agency.

KICKAPOO NATION SCHOOL
P.O. Box 106
POWHATTAN 66527
(913) 474-3550/3364 Fax 474-3530
Joseph Fast Horse, Supt.
Steve Cadue, Chairperson
Day School; Grades K-12. Under
jurisdiction of Oklahoma Education Office.

LOUISIANA

CHITIMACHA DAY SCHOOL
Route 2, Box 222
JEANERETTE 70544
(318) 923-4921 Fax 923-7791
Leonard Sudduth, Principal
Terry Martin, Chairperson
Day School; Grades K-8. Under
jursidiction of Eastern Area Office.

**CHOCTAW-APACHE
OF EBARB INDIAN SCHOOL**
P.O. Box 858
ZWOLLE 71486
(318) 645-2744
Day School. Grades: K-12. Enrollment: 285. Only
officially recognized "Indian School" in the state
of Louisiana.

MAINE

INDIAN ISLAND SCHOOL
P.O. Box 566, 1 River Rd.
OLD TOWN 04468
(207) 827-4285 Fax 827-3599
Sr. Janet Campbell, Principal
Kenneth Paul, Chairperson
Day School; Grades Pre K-8. *Enrollment*: 120.
Special courses: Penobscot Culture. *Instructor*:
Barry Dana. Under jurisdiction of Eastern States
Agency.

BEATRICE RAFFERTY SCHOOL
Pleasant Point Reservation
PERRY 04667
(207) 853-6085 FAX 853-6210
Sr. Maureen Wallace, Principal
Susan Newell, Chairperson
Day School; Grades K-8. Under
jurisdiction of Eastern States Agency.

INDIAN TOWNSHIP SCHOOL
Peter Dana Point
PRINCETON 04668
(207) 796-2362 Fax 796-2726
Linda Leotsakos, Principal
Glenna Levesque, Chairperson
Day School; Grades Pre K-8; *Enrollment*: 100.
Special course: Passamaquoddy Language/Culture. *Instructor*: Karen Sabbattus. Under jurisdiction of Eastern States Agency.

MICHIGAN

HANNAHVILLE INDIAN SCHOOL
N14911 Hannahville B1 Rd.
WILSON 49896
(906) 466-2556/9933 Fax 466-2418
Thomas G. Miller, Administrator
Elaine Meshingaud, Chairperson
Day School; Grades K-12. Under
jurisdiction of Minneapolis Area Office.

MINNESOTA

CHIEF BUG-O-NAY-GE SHIG SCHOOL
Route 3, Box 100
CASS LAKE 56633
(218) 665-2282/3 Fax 665-2285
Patricia Cornelius, Supt.
Alfred Pemberton, Chairperson
Day School; Grades K-12. Under
jurisdiction of Minneapolis Area Office.

FOND DU LAC OJIBWAY SCHOOL
105 University Rd.
CLOQUET 55720
(218) 879-0241/4593 Fax 879-0007
Dr. Thomas D. Peacock, Supt.
Sandi Savage, Chairperson
Day School; Grades: K-12. *Enrollment*: 270. *Special courses*: Gifted & Talented; Ojibwe Language,
Culture & History. *Publications*: newsletter; newspaper. Library. Under jurisdiction of Minneapolis
Area Office.

NAY AH SHING SCHOOL
HC 67, Box 242
ONAMIA 56359
(612) 532-4181 Fax 532-4209

Mushkooub, Commissioner of Education
Frances Boswell, Chairperson
Day School; Grades 7-12. *Enrollment*: 35. *Special courses*: Native American Studies; Cultural
Crafts; Reservation History Curriculum; Native
Ojibwe Language Curriculum; basic core curriculum. *Instructors*: Millie Benjamin, Lynn Fischer,
Kathy Morrow, Natalie Weyaus, and Jade Racelo.
Publications: Mille Lacs Nay Ah Shing School
Newsletter; Broken Windows (book of poetry,
1980.) Under jurisdiction of Minneapolis Area Office.

MOUNDS PARK ALL-NATIONS MAGNET SCHOOL
1075 E. 3rd St.
SAINT PAUL 55106
(612) 293-5938
Dr. Cornel Pewewardy, Principal
Day School; Grades K-8. *Enrollment*: 400.
Special program: Circle Time. Library.

CIRCLE OF LIFE SURVIVAL SCHOOL
P.O. Box 447
WHITE EARTH 56591
(218) 983-3285 ext. 269 Fax 983-3641
William Wessels, School Administrator
Doris Weaver, Chairperson
Day School; Grades K-12. Under
jurisdiction of Minneapolis Area Office.

MISSISSIPPI

RED WATER ELEMENTARY SCHOOL
Route 4, Box 30
CARTHAGE 39051
(601) 267-8500 Fax 267-5193
Marcella B. Vaughn, Principal
Day School; Grades K-8. Under
jurisdiction of Choctaw Field Office.

CONEHATTA ELEMENTARYSCHOOL
Route 1, Box 343
CONEHATTA 39057
(601) 775-8254 Fax 775-9229
William P. Williamson, Principal
Day School; Grades K-8. Under
jurisdiction of Choctaw Field Office.

BOGUE CHITTO ELEMENTARY SCHOOL
Route 2, Box 274
PHILADELPHIA 39350
(601) 656-8611 Fax 656-8648
William E. Bruner, Principal
Day School; Grades K-8. Under
jurisdiction of Choctaw Field Office.

CHOCTAW CENTRAL HIGH SCHOOL
Route 7, Box 72
PHILADELPHIA 39350
(601) 656-8870/8990/9
James Pair, Principal
Day School; Grades 9-12. Under
jurisdiction of Choctaw Field Office.

CHOCTAW CENTRAL MIDDLE SCHOOL
Route 7, Box 23
PHILADELPHIA 39350
(601) 656-8938
Terry A. Ben, Principal
Day School; Grades 7-8. Under
jurisdiction of Choctaw Field Office.

PEARL RIVER ELEMENTARY SCHOOL
Route 7, Box 19-H
PHILADELPHIA 39350
(601) 656-9051/2/4
Billy M. Wilbanks, Principal
Day School; Grades K-6. Under jurisdiction
of Choctaw Field Office.

TUCKER ELEMENTARY SCHOOL
Route 4, Box 351
PHILADELPHIA 39350
(601) 656-8775/4991
Pamela L. Dalme, Principal
Day School; Grades K-8. Under jurisdiction
of Choctaw Field Office.

STANDING PINE ELEMENTARY SCHOOL
Route 2, Box 236
WALNUT GROVE 39189
(601) 267-9225 Fax 267-9129
Jackie Harpole, Principal
Day School; Grades K-6. Under
jurisdiction of Choctaw Field Office.

MONTANA

LABRE INDIAN SCHOOL
P.O. Box 406
ASHLAND 59003
(406) 784-2347
William D. Walker, Supt.
Day School; Grades K-12. Under
jurisdiction of Billings Area Office.

ROCKY BOY TRIBAL HIGH SCHOOL
Box 620, Rocky Boy Route
BOX ELDER 59521
(406) 395-4291 Fax 395-4829
Sandra Murie, Acting Supt.
Day School; Grades 9-12. Under
jurisdiction of Billings Area Office.

BLACKFEET DORMITORY
Blackfeet Agency
P.O. Box 820
BROWNING 59417
(406) 338-7441 Fax 338-5725
Leonard L. Guardipee, Home Living Specialist
Alice DeRoche, Chairperson
Dormitory School; Grades 1-12. Under
jurisdiction of Billings Area Office.

BUSBY SCHOOL
P.O. Box 38
BUSBY 59016
(406) 592-3646 Fax 592-3645
Ted Rowland Supt.
Delbert Little Bird, Chairperson
Day School; Grades K-12. Under
jurisdiction of Billings Area Office.

TWO EAGLE RIVER SCHOOL
P.O. Box 362
PABLO 59855
(406) 675-0292 (Phone & Fax)
Larry Anderson, Supt./Principal
Virginia Hunter, Chairperson
Day School; Grades 9-12. Under
jurisdiction of Portland Area Office.

NEVADA

DUCKWATER SHOSHONE ELEMENTARY SCHOOL
P.O. Box 140038
DUCKWATER 89314
(702) 863-0242 Fax 863-0301
Laura Weaver, Administrator
Anita Davis, Chairperson
Day School; Grades K-8. Under jurisdiction of Sacramento Area Office.

PYRAMID LAKE HIGH SCHOOL
P.O. Box 256
NIXON 89424
(702) 574-1016/7 Fax 574-1037
Harold Sayler, Principal
Tim Wadsworth, Chairperson
Day School; Grades 9-12. Under jurisdiction of Sacramento Area Office.

NEW MEXICO

SKY CITY COMMUNITY SCHOOL
P.O. Box 349
ACOMA 87034
(505) 552-6671 Fax 552-6672
Charlotte Garcia, Principal
Marvin Garcia, Chairperson
Day School; Grades K-8. *Enrollment*: 250. *Special courses*: Gifted & Talented; Computer Laboratory. *Instructors*: Elizabeth Coon (Gifted & Talented), and Irwin Witzel (Computer Laboratory). Library. Under jurisdiction of Southern Pueblos Agency.

AZTEC DORMITORY
1600 Lydia Rippey Rd.
AZTEC 87410
(505) 334-6565
John Nolan, Supvr. Home Living Specialist
William Tso, Chairperson
Dormitory School; Grades 9-12. Under jurisdiction of Shiprock Agency.

DZILTH-NA-O-DITH-HLE COMMUNITY SCHOOL
Star Route 4, Box 5003
BLOOMFIELD 87413
(505) 632-1697
D. Duane Robinson, Principal
Evelyn Bekes, Chairperson
Day School: K-8; Boarding School: Grades 9-12. Under jurisdiction of Eastern Navajo Agency.

HUERFANO DORMITORY
P.O. Box 639
BLOOMFIELD 87413
(505) 786-3411
Darvin E. Homer, Principal
Pauline Platero, Chairperson
Dormitory School; Grades 1-12; K on day basis. Under jurisdiction of Eastern Navajo Agency.

CROWNPOINT COMMUNITY SCHOOL
P.O. Box 178
CROWNPOINT 87313
(505) 786-6160/1
Laura V. Garcia, Principal
Charles Long, Chairperson
Boarding School; Grades K-8. Under jurisdiction of Eastern Navajo Agency.

DIBE YAZHI HABITIIN OLTA, INC.
Borrego Pass School
P.O. Drawer A
CROWNPOINT 87313
(505) 786-5237
William Poe, Principal
Thomas Barbone, Chairperson
Boarding School; Grades K-8. Under jurisdiction of Eastern Navajo Agency.

LAKE VALLEY NAVAJO SCHOOL
P.O. Drawer 748
CROWNPOINT 87313
(505) 786-5392
David J. Atanasoff, Principal
Milton Chee, Chairperson
Boarding School; Grades K-8. Under jurisdiction of Eastern Navajo Agency.

MARIANO LAKE COMMUNITY SCHOOL
P.O. Box 498
CROWNPOINT 87313
(505) 786-5265
Douglas V. Simmons, Principal
Young Jeff Tom, Chairperson
Boarding School; Grades K-5. Under jurisdiction of Eastern Navajo Agency.

STANDING ROCK COMMUNITY SCHOOL
Drawer 828
CROWNPOINT 87313
(505) 786-5389
Sherry Woodside, Principal
Chee Bobby Thompson, Chairperson
Boarding School; Grades K-3. Under jurisdiction of Eastern Navajo Agency.

NA'NEELZHIIN JI' OLTA' (TORREON)
HCR 79, Box 9
CUBA 87013
(505) 731-2272/3 Fax 731-2252
Harvey Dale Allison, Principal
Harry Jackson, Chairperson
Boarding School; Grades K-8. Under jurisdiction of Eastern Navajo Agency.

OJO ENCINO DAY SCHOOL
HCR 79, Box 7
CUBA 87013
(505) 731-2333
Cyrus J. Chino, Principal
Jeanette Vice, Chairperson
Day School; Grades K-8. Under jurisdiction of Eastern Navajo Agency.

PUEBLO PINTADO COMMUNITY SCHOOL
HCR 79, Box 80
CUBA 87013
(505) 655-3341
Clyde David Kannon, Principal
Nelson Sandoval, Chairperson
Boarding School; Grades K-8. Under jurisdiction of Eastern Navajo Agency.

JICARILLA DORMITORY
P.O. Box 1009
DULCE 87528
(505) 759-3101 Fax 759-3948
Emilio Cordova, Principal
Sharon Julian, Chairperson
Dormitory School; Grades 1-12. Under jurisdiction of Northern Pueblos Agency.

SANTA CLARA DAY SCHOOL
P.O. Box HHH
ESPANOLA 87532

(505) 753-4406 Fax 753-8866
Solomon Padilla, Jr., Principal
Robert Jenkins, Chairperson
Day School; Grades K-6. Under jurisdiction of Northern Pueblos Agency.

NAVAJO PREPARATORY SCHOOL
1200 West Apache
FARMINGTON 87401
(505) 326-6571 Fax 326-2155
Betty O'jay, Director
William Tso, Chairperson
Boarding School; Grades 9-12. Under jurisdiction of Shiprock Agency.

WINGATE ELEMENTARY SCHOOL
P.O. Box 1
FORT WINGATE 87316
(505) 488-6470/1 Fax 488-6478
David L. Braswell, Principal
Walter Hudson, Chairperson
Boarding School; Grades 1-8. *Enrollment*: 400. Library. Under jurisdiction of Eastern Navajo Agency.

WINGATE HIGH SCHOOL
P.O. Box 2
FORT WINGATE 87316
(505) 488-6400 Fax 488-6444
Jay Bruce Hoover, Principal
Lawrence Morgan, Chairperson
Boarding School; Grades 9-12. Under jurisdiction of Eastern Navajo Agency.

NENAHNEZAD BOARDING SCHOOL
P.O. Box 337
FRUITLAND 87416
(505) 598-6922/9277 Fax 598-0970
Rena L. Teller, Principal
Delphine Mason, Chairperson
Boarding School; Grades K-6. *Enrollment*: 445. *Special courses*: Navajo Language and Culture; Writing Labs in Navajo and English. *Instructor*: Rosalyn Junes, Writing Lab. *Special program*: Navajo Language programs for all grades. Under jurisdiction of Shiprock Agency.

BREAD SPRINGS DAY SCHOOL
P.O. Box 1117
GALLUP 87305
(505) 778-5665
Richard Toledo, Principal
Jimmie Yazzie, Chairperson
Day School; Grades K-3. *Enrollment*: 130. Under jurisdiction of Eastern Navajo Agency.

ISLETA ELEMENTARY SCHOOL
P.O. Box 550
ISLETA 87022
(505) 869-2321/2 Fax 869-1625
Dr. Michael Schoenfeld, Principal
Frances Cherino, Chairperson
Day School; Grades K-6. *Enrollment*: 254. *Instructors*: Joyce Flournoy, Sofia Sanchez, Ethel Trujillo, Pauline Gallegos, and Mike Jojola. *Publication*: Isleta Eagle Pride, newspaper. Under jurisdiction of Southern Pueblos Agency.

JEMEZ DAY SCHOOL
P.O. Box 139
JEMEZ PUEBLO 87024
(505) 834-7304
Joseph V. Green, Principal
Randy Padilla, Chairperson
Day School; Grades K-6. Enrollment: 190. Under jurisdiction of Southern Pueblos Agency.

LAGUNA ELEMENTARY SCHOOL
P.O. Box 191
LAGUNA 87026
  (505) 552-9200/6255 Fax 552-7294
  Mary Ann Apodaca, Principal
  LuAnn Johnson, Chairperson
Day School; Grades K-6. Laguna Agency.

LAGUNA MIDDLE SCHOOL
P.O. Box 268
LAGUNA 87026
  (505) 552-9091 Fax 552-6398
  Nicholas Cheromiah, Principal
  Richard Smith, Chairperson
Day School; Grades 6-8. Under jurisdiction
of Laguna Agency.

TO'HAJIILEE-HE (CANONCITO)
P.O. Box 438
LAGUNA 87026
  (505) 831-6426 Fax 836-4914
  Jim Byrnes, Principal
  Margaret Platero, Chairperson
Boarding School; Grades K-12.
Eastern Navajo Agency.

ALAMO NAVAJO SCHOOL
P.O. Box 907
MAGDALENA 87825
  (505) 854-2543/2635 Fax 854-2545
  Marcel Kerkman, Principal
  George Apachito, Chairperson
Day School; Grades K-12. Under
jurisdiction of Eastern Navajo Agency.

MESCALERO ELEMENTARY SCHOOL
P.O. Box 230
MESCALERO 88340
  (505) 671-4431 Fax 671-4822
  William Butler, Supt.
  Freddie Peso, Chairperson
Day School; Grades K-6. Under jurisdiction
of Southern Pueblos Agency.

CRYSTAL BOARDING SCHOOL
NAVAJO 87328
  (505) 777-2385/6
  Lena R. Wilson, Principal
  Mary Stevens, Chairperson
Boarding School; Grades K-6. Under
jurisdiction of Fort Defiance Agency.

TOADLENA BOARDING SCHOOL
P.O. Box 857
NEWCOMB 87455
  (505) 789-3201/5
  Ollie Gelpin, Principal
  Bennie Joe, Chairperson
Boarding School; Grades K-8.
Under jurisdiction of Shiprock Agency.

PINE HILL SCHOOLS
CPO Drawer H
PINE HILL 87357
  (505) 775-3242/4 Fax 775-3240
  William Reese, Director of Education
  Frank E. Paul, Chairperson
Boarding School; Grades K-12. Under
jurisdiction of Southern Pueblos Agency.

BACA COMMUNITY SCHOOL
P.O. Box 509
PREWITT 87045
  (505) 876-2769
  Beatrice L. Woodward, Principal
  Kenneth Peterson, Chairperson

Boarding School; Grades K-4. Under jurisdiction
of Eastern Navajo Agency.

SAN FELIPE DAY SCHOOL
P.O. Box E
SAN FELIPE PUEBLO 87001
  (505) 867-3364
  Richard Torralba, Principal
  Jimmie Cimarron, Chairperson
Day School; Grades K-6. Under jurisdiction
of Southern Pueblos Agency.

SKY CITY COMMUNITY SCHOOL
P.O. Box 40
SAN FIDEL 87049
  (505) 552-6671
  Cyrus J. Chino, Principal
Day School; Grades K-8. Under jurisdiction
of Southern Pueblos Agency.

SAN JUAN DAY SCHOOL
P.O. Box 1077
SAN JUAN PUEBLO 87566
  (505) 852-2154/2801
  Mary J. Shoemaker, Principal
  Joe Garcia, Chairperson
Day School; Grades K-6. Under jurisdiction
of Northern Pueblos Agency.

ZIA DAY SCHOOL
SAN YSIDRO 87053
  (505) 867-3553/5079
  Michael J. LeCam, Principal
  Lawrence Pino, Chairperson
Day School; Grades K-6. Under jurisdiction
of Southern Pueblos Agency.

SANOSTEE DAY SCHOOL
P.O. Box 159
SANOSTEE 87461
  (505) 723-2476
  Jeanne Haskie, Principal
  Harrison Barber, Chairperson
Day School; Grades K-2. Under
jurisdiction of Shiprock Agency.

SAN ILDEFONSO DAY SCHOOL
Route 5, Box 308
SANTA FE 87501
  (505) 455-2366/7194
  Mary L. Naranjo, Principal/Teacher
  Raymond Gonzales, Chairperson
Day School; Grades K-6. Under
jurisdiction of Northern Pueblos Agency.

SANTA FE INDIAN SCHOOL
1501 Cerrillos Rd.
SANTA FE 87501
  (505) 989-6300/10 Fax 989-6317
  Joseph Abeyta, Jr., Supt.
  Regis Pecos, Chairperson
Boarding School; Grades 7-12. Under
jurisdiction of Northern Pueblos Agency.

TESUQUE DAY SCHOOL
Route 11, Box 2
SANTA FE 87501
  (505) 982-1516
  Marjorie Maestas, Principal
  Charlie Dorame, Chairperson
Day School; Grades K-6. Under jurisdiction
of Northern Pueblos Agency.

BECLABITO DAY SCHOOL
P.O. Box 1146
SHIPROCK 87420

  (602) 656-3555/6 Fax 656-3557
  Daniel Sosnowski, Principal
  Bruce Billy, Chairperson
Day School; Grades K-4. Under jurisdiction
of Shiprock Agency.

COVE DAY SCHOOL
P.O. Box 3537
SHIPROCK 87420
  (602) 653-4457
  Paul J. Yazzie, Principal
  Jessie J. Harrison, Chairperson
Day School; Grades K-6. Under jurisdiction
of Shiprock Agency.

SHIPROCK ALTERNATIVE SCHOOLS
P.O. Box 1799
SHIPROCK 87420
  (505) 368-5144 (9-12) 5170 (K)
  Fax (505) 368-5102 (9-12)
  Karen Dixon Bates, Director
  Frank John, Sr., Chairperson (K)
  William Tso, Chairperson (9-12)
Boarding School; Grades 9-12; and Day School,
K. Under jurisdiction of Shiprock Agency.

SHIPROCK RESERVATION DORMITORY
SHIPROCK 87420
  (505) 368-5070 Fax 368-5113
  Larry Tsosie, Sr., Director
  Virgil Kirk, Chairperson
Dormitory School; Grades 9-12.
Under jurisdiction of Shiprock Agency.

TAOS DAY SCHOOL
P.O. Drawer X
TAOS 87571
  (505) 758-3652/1566
  Robert C. Martinez, Principal
  Karel Mirabel, Chairperson
Day School; Grades K-6. Under
jurisdiction of Northern Pueblos Agency.

DLO'AY AZHI COMMUNITY SCHOOL
P.O. Box 789
THOREAU 87323
  (505) 862-7525
  Amy W. Mathis, Principal
  Kenneth Peterson, Chairperson
Boarding School; Grades K-6. Under
jurisdiction of Eastern Navajo Agency.

**CHUSKA/TOHATCHI
CONSOLIDATED SCHOOL**
P.O. Box 321
TOHATCHI 87325
  (505) 733-2280/2296 Fax 733-2222
  Dr. Helen Zongolowicz, Principal
  Fern Detsoi, Chairperson
Boarding School; Grades K-8. Under
jurisdiction of Fort Defiance Agency.

**CHI-CH'IL-TAH/JONES RANCH
COMMUNITY SCHOOL**
P.O. Box 278
VANDERWAGEN 87326
  (505) 778-5573/4
  John L. Taylor, Principal
  Roselyn John, Chairperson
Day School; Grades K-8. Under
jurisdiction of Eastern Navajo Agency.

NEW YORK

AKWESASNE FREEDOM SCHOOL
P.O. Box 290
ROOSEVELTOWN 13683
 Daniel Benedict, Director

NORTH CAROLINA

CHEROKEE CENTRAL SCHOOL
P.O. Box 134
CHEROKEE 28719
 (704) 497-6370 Fax 497-4373
 Joyce Dugan, Supt.
 Joan Henry, Chairperson
Day School; Grades K-6 & 7-12. Enrollment: Approximately 1,500. *Program*: Cherokee Boys Club, Ray Kinsland, Director. Under jurisdiction of Eastern Area Office.

NORTH DAKOTA

OJIBWA INDIAN SCHOOL
P.O. Box 600
BELCOURT 58316
 (701) 477-3108
 Mary Beth Reed, Principal
 Shirley Allery, Chairperson
Boarding School; Grades K-8. *Enrollment*: 360. Under jurisdiction of Turtle Mountain Agency.

**TURTLE MOUNTAIN
ELEMENTARY & MIDDLE SCHOOL**
P.O. Box 440
BELCOURT 58316
 (701) 477-6471 ext. 270
 Roman Marcellais, Elementary Principal
 Louis Douphinais, Middle School Principal
 James Parisien, Chairperson
Day School; Grades K-8. Under jurisdiction of Turtle Mountain Agency.

TURTLE MOUNTAIN HIGH SCHOOL
P.O. Box 440
BELCOURT 58316
 (701) 477-6471 ext. 222 Fax 477-6470
 Rosemary Jaros, Principal
 Allen Malaterre, Chairperson
Day School; Grades 9-12. Enrollment: 405. *Special courses*: Vocational (building, welding, health, distributive education); special education (speech and emotionally disturbed.) *Instructors*: Verlin Allery, Robert Marion, Marilyn Dionne, Frank Bercier, Tilmer Ruff, Louise Fraser, Marie Hanson, Kristi Ammerman, Sharon Rance, Mary Glover, and Tom Glover. Library. Under jurisdiction of Turtle Mountain Agency.

**THEODORE JAMERSON
ELEMENTARY SCHOOL**
3315 University Dr.
BISMARCK 58504
 (701) 255-3285 Ext. 304/5
 Sam Azure, Principal
 Pam Carlascio, Chairperson
 Amanda Bird Bear, Business Manager
Boarding School; Grades K-8, plus pre school and nursery. *Enrollment*: 95. Special courses: Math/Reading; Special Education; Gifted & Talented. Instructors: Judy Dasovick, Linda Heck, Terry Moericke, Marilyn McClelland, Dorvin Froseth,

among others. Media Centrer-Library. Under jurisdiction of Standing Rock Agency.

DUNSEITH DAY SCHOOL
P.O. Box 759
DUNSEITH 58371
 (701) 263-4636
 Karen Gillis, Principal
 Claudette Counts, Chairperson
Day School; Grades K-8. Under jurisdiction of Turtle Mountain Agency.

FOUR WINDS COMMUNITY SCHOOL
P.O. Box 199
FORT TOTTEN 58335
 (701) 766-4161 Fax 766-4766
 Judy Ami, Principal
 Lorraine Greybear, Chairperson
Day School; Grades K-8. Under jurisdiction of Sisseton Agency.

STANDING ROCK COMMUNITY SCHOOL
P.O. Box 377
FORT YATES 58538
 (701) 854-3865 (K-6); 854-3461 (7-12)
 Fax (701) 854-3842
 Linda Lawrence, Elementary Principal
 Roman Weiler, High School Principal
 Mike Faith, Chairperson
Boarding School; Grades K-12. Enrollment: approximately 800. Standing Rock Agency.

TWIN BUTTES DAY SCHOOL
Route 1, Box 65
HALLIDAY 58636
 (701) 938-4396
 Elaine Incoguito, Administrator
 Arby Little Soldier, Chairperson
Day School; Grades K-8. Under jurisdiction of Turtle Mountain Agency.

MANDAREE DAY SCHOOL
P.O. Box 488
MANDAREE 58757
 (701) 759-3311 Fax 759-3493
 Frank Taylor, Supt.
 Gilbert White Owl, Chairperson
 Tex G. Hall, Principal (Secondary)
 Patsy Hammeren, Principal (Elementary)
Day School; Grades K-12. *Enrollment*: 275. *Special courses*: Hidatsa Language; Tribal History & Government; Special Education, Cultural. *Instructors*: JoAnn White Owl, Bilingual; and Damon Brady, Tribal History, Social Studies. *Special programs*: Indian Club and Rodeo Club; Alternative Education; Gifted & Talented Programs. Under jurisdiction of Fort Berthold Agency.

WHITE SHIELD SCHOOL
HC 1, Box 45
ROSEGLEN 58775
 (701) 743-4355 Fax 743-4501
 Gene LaFromboise, Supt.
 Wesley Fox, Chairperson
Day School; Grades K-12. Under jurisdiction of Turtle Mountain Agency.

WAHPETON INDIAN SCHOOL
832 8th St. North
WAHPETON 58075
 (701) 642-3796/6631 Fax 642-5880
 Robert Hall, Administrator
 Allen English, Chairperson
Boarding School; Grades 4-8. *Enrollment*: 250. *Special programs*: Intense Residential Guidance Program. Library (small museu). Under jurisdiction of Minneapolis Area Office.

OKLAHOMA

RIVERSIDE INDIAN SCHOOL
Route 1
ANADARKO 73005
 (405) 247-6673 ext. 340 Fax 247-5529
 Joe Frazier, Principal
 Cleta Adair, Chairperson
Boarding School; Grades 2-12. Under jurisdiction of Oklahoma Education Office.

CARTER SEMINARY
2400 Chickasaw Blvd.
ARDMORE 73401
 (405) 223-8547 Fax 223-6325
 Jeff Frazier, Director
 Jeanie Lunsford, Chairperson
Dormitory School; Grades 1-12. Under jurisdiction of Oklahoma Education Office.

EUFAULA DORMITORY
Swadley Dr.
EUFAULA 74432
 (918) 689-2522/3181 Fax 297-2364
 Greg Anderson, Administrator
 Abe McIntosh, Chairperson
Dormitory School; Grades 1-12. Under jurisdiction of Oklahoma Education Office.

JONES ACADEMY
Route 1, Box 102-5
HARTSHORNE 74547
 (918) 297-2518 Fax 297-2364
 Mike Bailey, Administrator
 Alma Mason, Chairperson
Dormitory School; Grades 1-12. Under jurisdiction of Oklahoma Education Office.

SEQUOYAH HIGH SCHOOL
P.O. Box 948
TAHLEQUAH 74464
 (918) 456-0631 Fax 456-0634
 Delton Cox, Supt.; Amon Baker, Chairperson
Boarding School; Grades 9-12. Under jurisdiction of Oklahoma Education Office.

OREGON

CHEMAWA INDIAN SCHOOL
3700 Chemawa Rd., N.E.
SALEM 97305
 (503) 399-5721 Fax 399-5870
 Gerald J. Gray, Principal
 Virgil James, Chairperson
Boarding School; Grades 9-12. Under jurisdiction of Portland Area Office.

SOUTH DAKOTA

TIOSPA ZINA TRIBAL SCHOOL
P.O. Box 719
AGENCY VILLAGE 57262
 (605) 698-3953/4 Fax 698-7686
 Roger Bordeaux, Supt.
 Gilbert Robertson, Chairperson
Day School; Grades K-12. Under jurisdiction of Sisseton Agency.

AMERICAN HORSE SCHOOL
P.O. Box 660
ALLEN 57714

(605) 455-2480 Fax 867-1141
Don Standing Elk, Principal
Francis X. BigCrowm Chairperson
Day School; Grades K-8. Under jurisdiction
of Pine Ridge Agency.

ROCK CREEK DAY SCHOOL
BULLHEAD 57621
(605) 823-4971
Emmet White Temple, Principal
Charles Red Bear, Chairperson
Day School; Grades K-8. Under jurisdiction
of Standing Rock Agency.

CHERRY CREEK DAY SCHOOL
CHERRY CREEK 57622
(605) 538-4238
Faye Longbrake, Principal
Day School; Grades K-6. Under jurisdiction
of Cheyenne River Agency.

CHEYENNE-EAGLE BUTTE SCHOOL
P.O. Box 672
EAGLE BUTTE 57625
(605) 964-8744/77 Fax 964-1155
Lyman Morin, Principal
Mike Rousseau, Chairperson
Boarding School; Grades K-12. Enrollment: 900.
Under jurisdiction of Cheyenne River Agency.

FLANDREAU INDIAN SCHOOL
1000 N. Crescent
FLANDREAU 57028
(605) 997-2724 Fax 997-2601
Jack Belkham, Chief School Administrator
Cynthia Kipp, Chairperson
Boarding School; Grades 9-12. Enrollment: 750.
Under jurisdiction of Minneapolis Area Office.

FORT THOMPSON ELEMENTARY SCHOOL
P.O. Box 139
FORT THOMPSON 57339
(605) 245-2372 Fax 245-2399
Douglas L. Daughters, Principal
Silas Blaine, Chairperson
Day School; Grades K-6. Enrollment: 200. Under
jurisdiction of Crow Creek/Lower Brule Agency.

SWIFT BIRD DAY SCHOOL
HCR 3, Box 119
GETTYSBURG 57442
(605) 733-2143
George Schreiber, Principal/Teacher
Duke Dupree, Chairperson
Day School; Grades K-8. Under jurisdiction
of Cheyenne River Agency.

BRIDGER DAY SCHOOL
HOWES 57748
(605) 538-4313
Faye Longbrake, Principal
Day School; Grades 1-6. Under jurisdiction
of Cheyenne River Agency.

RED SCAFFOLD SCHOOL
P.O. Box 168
HOWES 57748
(605) 538-4317
Larry Mendoza, Director
Day School; Grades K-12. Under jurisdiction
of Cheyenne River Agency.

TAKINI SCHOOL
HC 77, Box 537
HOWES 57748
(605) 538-4399 Fax 538-4315
Dr. Ken Englehardt, Supt.
Emmett Hollow Horn, Chairperson

Day School; Grades Pre K-12. Enrolment: 250+.
Instructors: Stephanie Charging Eagle, Culture
Center; Mike Jetty, Social Science Dept. Special
courses: Tribal Government, Lakota Drum and
Singing Group. Special programs: Annual Pow
Wow and Wacipi in Spring for fund raising and
honoring people. Library. Publications: Biweekly
newsletter; yearbook. Under jurisdiction of Cheyenne River Agency.

LITTLE WOUND DAY SCHOOL
P.O. Box 500
KYLE 57752
(605) 455-2461
Dr. Lynda Earring, Supt. for Education
Everett Janis, Chairperson
Day School; Grades K-12. Enrollment: 500.
Under jurisdiction of Pine Ridge Agency.

LITTLE EAGLE DAY SCHOOL
P.O. Box 26
LITTLE EAGLE 57639
(605) 823-4235
Adele F. Little Dog, Principal
Magdelina Red Legs, Chairperson
Day School; Grades K-8. Enrollment: 100.
Under jurisdiction of Standing Rock Agency.

LOWER BRULE DAY SCHOOL
P.O. Box 245
LOWER BRULE 57548
(605) 473-5382(Elementary)
(605) 473-5510 (Secondary)
Fax (605) 473-9217
Vacant, Elementary Principal
Neil Russell, Secondary Principal
Ben Janis, Chairperson
Day School; Grades K-12. Enrollment: 225. Un-
der jurisdiction of Crow Creek/Lower Brule Agency.

WOUNDED KNEE SCHOOL DISTRICT
P.O. Box 350
MANDERSON 57756
(605) 867-5433/5156
Shirley Garnette, Principal
C.J. Clifford, Chairperson
Day School; Grades K-8. Enrollment: 225.
Under jurisdiction of Pine Ridge Agency.

MARTY INDIAN SCHOOL
P.O. Box 187
MARTY 57361
(605) 384-5431 Fax 384-5933
Dennis Schutt, Supt. for Education
Robert Cournoyer, Chairperson
Boarding School; Grades K-12.
Under jurisdiction of Rosebud Agency.

ROSEBUD DORMITORIES
P.O. Box 669
MISSION 57555
(605) 856-4486 Fax 856-4487
Eustace Night Shield, Home Living Specialist
Sandy Murray Wilcox, Chairperson
Dormitory School; Grades 1-12. Enrollment: 250.
Under jurisdiction of Rosebud Agency.

PROMISE DAY SCHOOL
HCR 30, Box 10
MOBRIDGE 57601
(605) 733-2148
Tina Farmer, Head Teach; Angie LeBeau,
Chairpersons
Day School; Grades K-8. Under jurisdiction
of Cheyenne River Agency.

LONEMAN DAY SCHOOL
P.O. Box 50
OGLALA 57764
(605) 867-5633 Fax 867-5109
Raymond Howe, Principal
Day School; Grades K-8. Under
jurisdiction of Pine Ridge Agency.

PIERRE INDIAN LEARNING CENTER
HC 31, Box 148
PIERRE 57501
(605) 224-8661 Fax 224-8465
Darrell Jeanotte, Supt. of Education
Gilbert Robertson, Chairperson
Boarding School; Grades 1-8. Enrollment: 100.
Special courses: Special education school for chil-
dren with learning disabilities or emotional prob-
lems. Contract school serving 15 reservations in
North and South Dakota, and Nebraska. Under
the jurisdiction of the Cheyenne River Agency.

PINE RIDGE SCHOOL
P.O. Box 1202
PINE RIDGE 57770
(605) 867-5198 Fax 867-5482
Imogene Horse, Principal
Anthony Whirlwind Horse, Chairperson
Boarding School; Grades K-12. Enrollment: 1,000.
Under jurisdiction of Pine Ridge Agency.

RED CLOUD INDIAN SCHOOL
Holy Rosary Mission
PINE RIDGE 57770
(605) 867-5491
Rev. E.J. Kurth, S.J., Supt.
Boarding School; Grades K-12. Special program:
Montessori pre-school (ages 3 and up, including
some first graders.)

PORCUPINE DAY SCHOOL
P.O. Box 180
PORCUPINE 57772
(605) 867-5336 Fax 867-5480
Andrew Rendon, Principal
Charles Bettelyoun, Chairperson
Day School; Grades K-8. Under
jurisdiction of Pine Ridge Agency.

ST. FRANCIS INDIAN SCHOOL
P.O. Box 379
ST. FRANCIS 57572
(605) 747-2299 Fax 747-2379
Ted Bogda, Supt. for Education
Bob Gednalski, Elementary Principal
Tom White, High School Principal
Teresa Archambault, Chairperson
Boarding School; Grades K-12.
Under jurisdiction of Rosebud Agency.

CROW CREEK HIGH SCHOOL
P.O. Box 12
STEPHAN 57346
(605) 852-2455
William Shroll, Principal/Supt.
Duane Big Eagle, Chairperson
Day School; Grades 7-12. Enrollment: 225. Spe-
cial programs: Special Education; Intensive Resi-
dential Counseling; Career Counseling; Substance
Abuse Counseling. Under jurisdiction of Crow
Creek/Lower Brule Agency.

CRAZY HORSE SCHOOL
P.O. Box 260
WANBLEE 57577
(605) 462-6511 Fax 462-6510
Thomas Raymond, Management Team
Francis Red Willow, Chairperson

Day School; Grades K-12. Under
jurisdiction of Pine Ridge Agency.

ENEMY SWIM DAY SCHOOL
RR 1, Box 87
WAUBAY 57273
  (605) 947-4605 (Phone & Fax)
  Edna Greenhagen, Principal
  Ellen M. Fisher, Chairperson
Day School; Grades K-3. Under
jurisdiction of Sisseton Agency.

WHITE HORSE DAY SCHOOL
P.O. Box 7
WHITE HORSE 57661
  (605) 733-2183
  Barbara Longcrow, Principal/Teacher
Day School; Grades K-8. Under jurisdiction
of Cheyenne River Agency.

UTAH

ANETH COMMUNITY SCHOOL
P.O. Box 600
MONTEZUMA CREEK 84534
  (801) 651-3271 Fax 651-3272
  Johnny C. Begay, Principal
  Nora Manybeads, Chairperson
Boarding School; Grades K-6.
Under jurisdiction of Shiprock Agency.

RICHFIELD DORMITORY
P.O. Box 638
RICHFIELD 84701
  (801) 896-5101 Fax 896-6157
  Kevin Skenandore, Director
  Stanley Yazzie, Chairperson
Dormitory School; Grades 9-12. Under
jurisdiction of Western Navajo Agency.

WASHINGTON

MUCKLESHOOT TRIBAL SCHOOL
39015 172nd Ave., SE
AUBURN 98002
  (206) 939-6709 Fax 939-531 1
  Teresa Boone, Principal
  Leo LaClair, Chairperson
Day School; Grades K-3. *Enrollment*: 50. *Special
program*: Writing multi-media curriculum for tribal
language and culture, using computers, video and
books, crossing all curriculum areas. Under jurisdiction of Portland Area Office.

LUMMI HIGH SCHOOL
2522 Kwina Rd.
BELLINGHAM 98226
  (206) 676-2772 Ext 133 Fax 733-3385
  Paul Avery, Principal
  Bernie Thomas, Chairperson
Day School; Grades 9-12. Under
jurisdiction of Portland Area Office.

LUMMI TRIBAL SCHOOL SYSTEM
2530 Kwina Rd..
BELLINGHAM 98225
  (206) 647-6251 Fax 384-4737
  William Stogsdill, Director
  Bernie Thomas, Chairperson
Day School; Grades K-8. *Enrollment*: 125. Library.
Under jurisdiction of Portland Area Office.

QUILEUTE TRIBAL SCHOOL
P.O. Box 39
La PUSH 98350
  (206) 374-2061/6163 Fax 374-9608
  Franklin S. Hanson, Supt.
  Roger Jackson, Sr., Chairperson
Day School; Grades K-8. Under jurisdiction
of Portland Area Office.

WA HE LUT SCHOOL
11110 Conine Ave., SE
OLYMPIA 98503
  (206) 456-1311 Fax 456-1319
  Larry Pierce, Principal
  Alison Gottfriedson, Chairperson
Day School; Grades Pre K-8. *Enrollment*: 50.
Course emphasis on Native American culture. In-
structors: Teresa Shattuck, Marilyn Clements, Sue
Schumacher, Linda Dittmar, Rob Brainerd. *Spe-
cial program*: Special Education (Marylynn Twohy);
Chapter One (Annie Schlipphacke); Talented/
Gifted (Judy Fitzpatrick); Art (Vivian Kendall);
Speech (Sherri Nemec); and Ocuupational
Therapy (Jan Harrison). Library. Under jurisdic-
tion of Portland Area Office.

PASCHAL SHERMAN INDIAN SCHOOL
Omak Lake Rd.
OMAK 98841
  (509) 826-2097 Fax 826-3855
  Jack Fry, Principal
  Jude C. Stensgor, Chairperson
Boarding School; Grades Pre K-8.
Under jurisdiction of Portland Area Office.

AMERICAN INDIAN HERITAGE SCHOOL
1330 N. 90th St.
SEATTLE 98103
  (206) 298-7895
  Robert Eaglestaf f, Principal
Day School; Grades 6-12. *Enrollment*: 120. All
academic classes are taught with an enrichment
from the Indian culture. Cultural classes in art,
sewing, singing, dancing, drama, and computers.
Instructors: Mary Lee Colby, R. Marina Sabbas,
Courage Benally, Turk Markishtum, Marc Strash,
and Bonnie Harding. *Special courses*: Native
American Literature, History and Government.
Special programs: American Indian Heritage Pupil Services Program - enrollment of 1,436 - provides, on a referral basis district wide, Indian cultural enrichment and awareness activities in various subjects and levels; Culture Night every
Wednesday; 2 major Pow W ows. Library. *Publication*: Pathways, monthly newspaper.

CHIEF LESCHI SCHOOL SYSTEM
2002 East 28th St.
TACOMA 98404
  (206) 593-0218 Fax 593-0143
  Linda Rudolph, Supt.
  Connie McCloud, Chairperson
Day School; Grades Pre K-12. *Enrollment*: 350+.
Library. Under jurisdiction of Portland Area Office.

YAKAMA TRIBAL SCHOOL
P.O. Box 151
TOPPENISH 98948
  (509) 865-5121 Fax 865-6092
  Anita L. Swan, Supt.
  Wilfred Yallup, Chairperson
Day School; Grades 7-12. *Enrollment*: 105. *Spe-
cial course*: Yakama Language. Under jurisdiction
of Portland Area Office.

WISCONSIN

LAC COURTE OREILLES OJIBWA SCHOOL
Route 2, Box 2800
HAYWARD 54843
  (715) 634-8924 Fax 634-6058
  Don Wiesen, School Administrator
  Gaiashkibos, Chairperson
Day School; Grades K-12. Under
jurisdiction of Minneapolis Area Office.

INDIAN COMMUNITY SCHOOL
3126 W. Kilbourn Ave.
MILWAUKEE 53208

MENOMINEE TRIBAL SCHOOL
P.O. Box 39
NEOPIT 54150
  (715) 756-2354 Fax 756-2364
  Dr. Verna Fowler, Supt.
  Lynette Miller, Chairperson
Day School; Grades K-8. *Enrollment*: 240. *Spe-
cial courses*: Menominee Cultural Couses. Library.
Under jurisdiction of Minneapolis Area Office.

ONEIDA TRIBAL SCHOOL
P.O. Box 365, c/o Oneida Tribe
ONEIDA 54155
  (414) 869-2795 Fax 869-2194
  Sharon A. Mousseau, Administrator
  Leland Danforth, Chairperson
Day School; Grades K-8. Under
jurisdiction of Minneapolis Area Office.

WYOMING

WYOMING INDIAN HIGH SCHOOL
ETHETE 82520

ST. STEPHENS INDIAN SCHOOL
P.O. Box 345
ST. STEPHEN 82524
  (307) 856-4147 Fax 856-3742
  Margaret J. Puebla, Supt.
  Margaret St. Clair, Chairperson
Boarding School; Grades Pre K-12.
Under jurisdiction of Billings Area Office.

NATIVE HAWAIIAN SCHOOLS

HALE KAKO'O PUNANA LEO/HILO
1744 Kino'ole St.
Hilo, HI 96720
  (808) 959-4979
  Namaka Rawlins, Contact
Hawaiian Imersion schools support center.

KEAUKAHA SCHOOL
240 Desha Ave.
Hilo, HI 96720
  (808) 935-1959
  Kathe W ebster, Principal
Grades: K-6. Enrollment: 400. *Special program*:
Hawaiian Language Immersion Program. Library.

PUNANA LEO O HILO
1744 Kino'ole St.
Hilo, HI 96720
  (808) 959-4700
  Leina'ala Poepoe, Director
Hawaiian Imersion preschool.

HALE KAKO'O PUNANA LEO/HONOLULU
2002-L Hunnewell St.
Honolulu, HI 96822
 (808) 941-0584
 Lilinoe Andrews, Contact
Hawaiian Imersion schools support
and materials development center.

**KAMEHAMEHA SCHOOLS/BERNICE
PAUAHI BISHOP ESTATE**
Education Group, Program Services Div.
Kapalama Heights
Honolulu, HI 96817
 (808) 842-8881 Fax 842-8875
Description: Offers a variety of educational ser-
vices, and gives preference to children of Hawai-
ian ancestry. *Activities*: Hawaiian Studies Institute.
Operates the KS Press which publshers educa-
tional materials with a focus on Hawaiian studies.
Programs: Natuive Hawaiian Higher Education
Program; Scholarship and Counseling Program;
Health Professions Scholarship Program; Native
Hawaiian Drug-Free Schools and Communities
Program.

PUNANA LEO O KONA
73-1385 Ihumoe St.
Kailua-Kona, HI 96740
 Rayann Godden, Contact
Hawaiian Immersion preschool.

PU'OHALA ELEMENTARY SCHOOL
45-233 Kulauli St.
Kane'ohe. HI 96744
 (808) 235-1361
 Malia Souki, Contact
Hawaiian Immersion school. Grades 1-8.

KAPA'A ELEMENTARY SCHOOL
4886 Kawaihau Rd.
Kapa'a, HI 96746
 (808) 822-4141
 Puanani Wilhelm, Contact
Hawaiian Immersion school; grades 1-8.

KUALAPU'U ELEMENTARY SCHOOL
Kualapu'u, HI 96757
 (808) 567-6126
 Manuwai Peters, Contact
Hawaiian Immersion school; grades 1-8.

WAIAU ELEMENTARY SCHOOL
98-450 Ho'okanike St.
Pearl City, HI 96782
 (808) 456-9222
 Kalani Akana, Contact
Hawaiian Immersion school; grades 1-8.

PA'IA ELEMENTARY SCHOOL
955 Baldwin Ave.
Pa'ia, HI 96779
 (808) 579-9967
 Kaiki Kawai'ae'a, Contact
Hawaiian Immersion school; grades 1-8.

INDIAN EDUCATION TECHNICAL ASSISTANCE CENTERS (IETAC)

Listed here are six regional Indian Education Technical Assistance Centers (IETACs) funded by the
U.S. Department of Education, Office of Indian
Education to serve educators of Native students
within specific geographical regions.

U.S. DEPT. OF EDUCATION
Office of Indian Education
Rm. 2177, 400 Maryland Ave., SW
WASHINGTON, DC 20202-6335
 (202) 401-1887
 Elizabeth Whitehorn
Disseminates information, provide training and
technical assistance to grantees and prospective
grantees in program planning, developing, man-
agement and evaluation.

REGIONAL EDUCATIONAL LABORATORIES

Funded by the U.S. Department of Education,
these ten Regional Educational Laboratories each
serve a designated geographical region. Their
purpose is to link the communities of research and
practice. Thus they offer training, technical assistance, and publications based on research that
address the practical concerns of educators and
policymakers. The laboratories have joined together to form the Native Education Initiative - the
purpose is to improve the access of educators
serving Native students to the many resources
available through the various laboratories.

**APPALACHIA EDUCATIONAL
LABORATORY, INC. (AEL)**
P.O. Box 1348
Charleston, WV 25325-1348
 (800) 624-9120; Fax (304) 347-0487
 Pat Chahape, Contact
Serves Native students, state, tribal and local
agencies and K-12 schools in the following states:
KY, TN, VA, WV. Houses ERIC Clearinghouse on
Rural Education and Small Schools (CRESS),
which specializes in American Indian and Alaska
Native education.

**FAR WEST LABORATORY FOR EDUCA-
TIONAL RESEARCH & DEVELOPMENT**
Rural Schools Assistance Program
730 Harrison St.
San Francisco, CA 94107-1242
 (415) 565-3040 Fax 565-3012
 Elsie Trumbull Estrin, Contact
Serves Native students, state, tribal and local
agencies and K-12 schools in the following states:
AZ, CA, NV, UT.

**MID-CONTINENT REGIONAL
EDUCATIONAL LABORATORY (McREL)**
2550 S. Parker Rd., Suite 500
Aurora, CO 80014
 (303) 337-0990 ext. 3012 Fax 337-3005
 Joann Sebastian Morris, Contact
Serves Native students, state, tribal and local
agencies and K-12 schools in the following states:
CO, KS, MO, NE, ND, SD, WY.

**NORTH CENTRAL REGIONAL
EDUCATIONAL LABORATORY (NCREL)**
1900 Spring Brook Rd., Suite 300
Oak Brook, IL 60521-1480

 (800) 252-0283; (708) 571-4700 Fax 571-4716
 Beverly J. Walker, Contact
Serves Native students, state, tribal and local
agencies and K-12 schools in the following states:
IL, IN, IA, OH, MI, MN, WI.

**NORTHWEST REGIONAL EDUCATIONAL
LABORATORY (NWREL)**
Research & Development for Indian Education
101 SW Main St., Suite 500
Portland, OR 97204
 (503) 275-9500 Fax 275-9489
 Anita Tsinnajinnie, Contact
Serves Native students, state, tribal and local
agencies and K-12 schools in the following states:
AK, ID, MT, OR, WA. *Activities*: Conducts studies
of issues and qualities of Indian education. *Publi-
cations*: Effective Practices in Indian Education,
teacher's curriculum monograph; newsletter,
Northwest Report.

**PACIFIC REGIONAL EDUCATIONAL
LABORATORY (PREL)**
1164 Bishop St., Suite 1409
Honolulu, HI 96813
 (808) 532-1900 Fax 532-1922
 Rita Hocog Inos, Contact
Serves Native students, state, tribal and local
agencies and K-12 schools in the following states:
HI, Guam, American Somoa.

**REGIONAL LABORATORY FOR EDUCA-
TIONAL IMPROVEMENT OF THE NORTHEAST
& VIRGIN ISLANDS/THE NETWORK, INC.**
300 Brickstone Square, Suite 900
Andover, MA 01810
 (800) 347-4200; (508) 470-0098 ext. 246
 Fax 475-9220
 Cinnamon Noley, Contact
Serves Native students, state, tribal and local
agencies and K-12 schools in the following states:
CT, ME, MA, NH, NY, ,PR, RI, VT, VI (Virgin Is-
lands).

RESEARCH FOR BETTER SCHOOLS, INC.
Native Education Project
444 N. 3rd St.
Philadelphia, PA 19123-4107
 (215) 574-9300 ext. 230 Fax 574-0133
 Margaret Lion, Contact
Serves Native students, state, tribal and local
agencies and K-12 schools in the following states:
DE, DC, MD, NJ, PA.

**SOUTH EASTERN REGIONAL
VISION FOR EDUCATION (SERVE)**
345 S. Magnolia Dr. D-23
Tallahassee, FL 32301
 (800) 352-6001; (904) 922-2300 Fax 352-6001
Serves Native students, state, tribal and local
agencies and K-12 schools in the following states:
AL, FL, GA, MS, NC, SC. *Activities*: Provides outreach, information and assistance to Native American communities in the Southeast regarding early
childhood education, parent involvement and education, and substance abuse prevention.

**SOUTHWEST EDUCATIONAL
DEVELOPMENT LABORATORY (SEDL)**
211 E. 7th St.
Austin, TX 78701
 (512) 476-6861 Fax 476-2286
 Nancy Fuentes, Contact
Serves Native students, state, tribal and local
agencies and K-12 schools in the following states:
AR, LA, NM, OK, TX.

INDIAN EDUCATION PROGRAMS

Listed, are Indian Education Programs in public schools throughout the U.S. Arranged alpha-geographically. First listed are the five regional Technical Assistance Centers.

IETAC I - ORBIS
1411 K St., NW, Suite 700
Washington, DC 20005
  (800) 621-2998; (202) 628-4444 Fax 628-2241
  Gwen Shunatona, Contact
Serves schools in the following states: AL, AR, CT, DE, FL, GA, IL, IN, KY, LA, ME, MD, MA, MI, MO, MS, NH, NJ, NY, NC, OH, PA, RI, SC, TN, VT, VA, WV, DC.

**IETAC II - UNITED TRIBES
TECHNICAL COLLEGE**
3315 University Dr.
Bismarck, ND 58504
  (800) 437-8054; (701) 258-0437 Fax 258-0454
  Phil Baird, Contact
Serves schools in the following states:
IA, KS, MN, NE, ND, SD, WI.

IETAC III - GONZAGA UNIVERSITY
School of Education
302 E. Sharp
Spokane, WA 99258
  (800) 533-2554; (509) 328-4220 ext. 2812
  Fax 484-6965
  Raymond Reyes, Contact
Serves schools in the following states:
CO, ID, MT, OR, UT, WA, WY.

**IETAC IV - NATIONAL INDIAN
TRAINING & RESEARCH CENTER**
2121 S. Mill Ave., Suite 216
Tempe, AZ 85282
  (800) 528-6425; (602) 967-9428 Fax 921-1015
  Shirley Hendricks, Contact
Serves schools in the following states:
AZ, CA, HI, NM, NV.

**IETAC V - AMERICAN INDIAN
RESEARCH & DEVELOPMENT, INC.**
2424 Springer Dr., Suite 200
Norman, OK 73069
  (800) 422-0966 (in OK)
  (800) 451-2191 (national)
  (405) 360-1163 Fax 364-5464
  Mary Ann Brittan, Contact
Serves schools in the following states: OK, TX.

IETAC VI - COOK INLET TRIBAL COUNCIL
670 Fireweed Lane
Anchorage, AK 99503
  (800) 478-0014; (907) 272-7529 Fax 277-9071
  Ramona Suetopka-Duerre, Contact
Serves schools in Alaska Native villages and Native organizations, institutions, and parent committees involved in the education of Alaska Native and Native American students.

ALABAMA

Escambia County Middle School
Indian Education Program
P.O. Drawer 1236
Atmore, AL 36504
  (205) 368-9105 Fax 368-0674
  David Nolin, Director
Grades K-8. *Description*: Provides tutoring ser-

vices and cultural enrichment programs. *Instructors*: Hazel Rolin, Mary Boytte, Joyce Pilyaw.

Poarch Band of Creeks
Indian Education Program
Route 3, Box 243-A
Atmore, AL 36502
  Gloria Fowler, Contact

Washington County Schools
Indian Education Program
P.O. Drawer L
Chatom, AL 36518
  Vivian Dearman, Contact

Coffee County School System
Indian Education Program
400 Reddoch Hill Rd.
Elba, AL 36323
  (205) 897-5016 Fax 897-6207
  Laura June Brown, Director
Grades K-12. *Description*: Provides culturally related academic activities and computer instruction for Indian students enrolled in the Coffee County School System. *Instructors*: Vicki Chamblee, Pam Flowers, Bonnie Campbell.

DeKalb County Schools
Indian Education Program
Box 777, 209 Grand Ave. S.
Fort Payne, AL 35967
  Maurice McGee, Contact

Fort Payne City Schools
Indian Education Program
P.O. Box 1029
Fort Payne, AL 35967
  Bill Rupil, Contact

Madison County Schools
Indian Education Program
P.O. Box 226
Huntsville, AL 35804
  (205) 852-7073 Fax 852-6708
  Melvina Phillips, Director
Grades K-12. *Description*: Designed to meet the academic and cultural needs of Indian students; works with high school students to get scholarships, participation in academic camps, etc. *Instructor*: Linda Williams. *Special project*: Develop cultural software

Washington County Schools
Indian Education Program
P.O. Box 209
McIntosh, AL 36553
  Gallasnead Weaver, Contact

Mobile County Schools
Indian Education Program
P.O. Box 1327
Mobile, AL 36633
  Henrietta Powell, Contact

Monroe County Schools
Indian Education Program
P.O. Box 967
Monroeville, AL 36461
  Dr. Brooks Steele, Contact

Lawrence County Schools
Indian Education Program
Box 365, 129 College St.
Moulton, AL 35650
  (205) 905-2494
  Rickey Butch Walker, Director
Grades K-12. *Description*: Provides a cultural heri-

tage and tutoring program; sponsors a local Indian museum and annual Indian Festival in May. *Instructors*: Cindy Compton, Cynthia Early, Jan McEleya, Michelle Latham, Becky Dutton, Rhonda Hood, Rena Woodruff, Marie Jeffreys, Lisa Stone, Leisa Turner, Tangela Orr, Cynthia Gold.

Mobile County Schools
Indian Education Program
20185 Richard Weaver Rd.
Mt. Vernon, AL 36560
  Johnny Weaver, Jr., Contact

Scottsboro City Schools
Indian Education Program
906 S. Scott St.
Scottsboro, AL 35971
  Sue DeWitt, Contact

Pike County Schools
Indian Education Program
109 E. Church St.
Troy, AL 36081
  Manell Langford, Contact

ARKANSAS

Cedarville School District
Indian Education Program
P.O. Box 97
Cedarville, AR 72932
Dr. Melvin Landers

Fort Smith School District
Indian Education Program
P.O. Box 1948
Fort Smith, AR 72902
  Cheryl Takawana, Contact

Gravette Public Schools
Indian Education Program
P.O. Box 480
Gravette, AR 72736
  Larry Ben, Contact

ARIZONA

Ajo Unified School District
Indian Education Program
P.O. Box 68
Ajo, AZ 85321
  Siana Chalrey, Contact

Casa Blanca Day School
Indian Education Program
P.O. Box 940
Bapchule, AZ 85221
  Betty Sanchez, Contact

Colorado River Unified HS Dist.
Indian Education Program
2251 Highway 95
Bullhead City, AZ 86442
  Nancy Doss, Contact

Casa Grande Elementary School
Indian Education Program
1460 N. Pinal Ave.
Casa Grande, AZ 85222
  Gene Moffett, Contact

Casa Grande Union High School
Indian Education Program
420 E. Florence Blvd.
Casa Grande, AZ 85222
 Orlenda F. Roberts, Contact

Wide Ruins Boarding School
Indian Education Program
P.O. Box 309
Chambers, AZ 86502
 Ernestine Reeder, Contact

Chandler Unified School District
Indian Education Program
500 W. Galveston St.
Chandler, AZ 85224
 Lucinda Williams, Contact

Black Mesa Community School
Indian Education Program
Star Rt. 1, Box 215-RRDS
Chinle, AZ 86503
 George Cukro, Contact

Chinle Unified School District
Indian Education Program
P.O. Box 587
Chinle, AZ 86503
 Dinah Todacheeny, Contact

Cottonwood Day School
Indian Education Program
Chinle, AZ 86503
 Carol Greene, Contact

Low Mountain Boarding School
Indian Education Program
Chinle, AZ 86503
 Joe Hardy, Contact

Rock Point Commuity School
Indian Education Program
General Delivery
Chinle, AZ 86503
 Jimmie C. Begay, Contact

Rough Rock Demonstration School
Indian Education Program
RRDS-P.O. Box 217
Chinle, AZ 86503
 Mary Benally, Contact

Cibecue Community School
Indian Education Program
Cibecue, AZ 85911
 Raymond Bierner, Contact

Blackwater Community School
Indian Education Program
Route 1, Box 95
Coolidge, AZ 85228
 S. Jo Lewis, Contact

Coolidge Unified School District
Indian Education Program
P.O. Box 1499
Coolidge, AZ 85228
 Pam Thompson, Contact

Dennehotso Boarding School
Indian Education Program
P.O. Box LL
Dennehotso, AZ 86535
 Velma Eisenberger

Flagstaff Unified School District
Indian Education Program
3285 E. Sparrow Ave.
Flagstaff, AZ 86004
 Jane Wilson, Contact

Window Rock Unified School District
Indian Education Program
P.O. Box 559
Fort Defiance, AZ 86504
 Tim Clashin, Contact

Ft. Thomas Unified School District
Indian Education Program
P.O. Box 28
Fort Thomas, AZ 85536
 Eldon Woodall, Contact

Fountain Hills Unified School District
Indian Education Program
14605 North Del Cambre
Fountain Hills, AZ 85268
 Walter Dunne, Contact

Fredonia-Moccasin Unified School District
Indian Education Program
P.O. Box 247
Fredonia, AZ 86022
 Charles Eberhard, Contact

Ganado Unified School District
Indian Education Program
P.O. Box 1757
Ganado, AZ 86505
 Evelyn Begay, Contact

Greasewood/Toyei School
Indian Education Program
Ganado, AZ 86505
 Janet Lope, Contact

Kinlichee Boarding School
Indian Education Program
Ganado, AZ 86505
 Patricia Rigby, Contact

Nazlini Boarding School
Indian Education Program
Ganado, AZ 86505
 William H. Draper, Contact

Gila Bend Unified School Dist. #24
Indian Education Program
P.O. Box V
Gila Bend, AZ 85337
 Dr. Charles Landis, Contact

Glendale Unified School District
Indian Education Program
4508 W. Northern Ave.
Glendale, AZ 85302
 Toni Munoz, Contact

Globe Unified School District
Indian Education Program
501 Ash St.
Globe, AZ 85501
 Dr. James Hazzard, Contact

Grand Canyon Unified School District
Indian Education Program
P.O. Box 519
Grand Canyon, AZ 86023
 Shana Henry, Contact

Holbrook Unified School District
Indian Education Program
P.O. Box 640
Holbrook, AZ 86025
 Esther Stant, Contact

Hotevilla Bocavi Community School
Indian Education Program
P.O. Box 48
Hotevilla, AZ 86030
 Jeanette Cole, Contact

Pine Springs Boarding School
Indian Education Program
P.O. Box 198
Houck, AZ 86506
 Charles Riley, Contact

Kaibeto Boarding School
Indian Education Program
Kaibeto, AZ 86053
 Charlotte Webb, Contact

Chilchinbeto Day School
Indian Education Program
P.O. Box 547
Kayenta, AZ 86033
 Gerald Fields, Contact

Kayenta Boarding School
Indian Education Program
Box 188
Kayenta, AZ 86033
 Charlene Nez, Contact

Kayenta Unified School District
Indian Education Program
Box 337
Kayenta, AZ 86033
 Dan McLaughlin, Contact

Cedar Unified School District #25
Indian Education Program
P.O. Box 367
Keams Canyon, AZ 86034
 Bob Breton, Contact

Hopi Jr./Sr. High School
Indian Education Program
P.O. Box 337
Keams Canyon, AZ 86034
Bruce Steele

Keams Canyon Boarding School
Indian Education Program
P.O. Box 397
Keams Canyon, AZ 86034
 Sam Billison, Contact

Hopi Day School
Indian Education Program
P.O. Box 42
Kykotsmovi, AZ 86039
 Ed Vermillion, Contact

Rocky Ridge Boarding School
Indian Education Program
P.O. Box 299
Kykotsmovi, AZ 86039
 Fred M. Johnson, Contact

Gila Crossing Day School
Indian Education Program
P.O. Box 10
Laveen, AZ 85339
 Mary Jo Walter, Contact

Laveen Elementary School District
Indian Education Program
P.O. Box 29
Laveen, AZ 85339
  Donna Boe, Contact

Lukachukai Boarding School
Indian Education Program
Lukachukai, AZ 86507
  Leo Gishie, Contact

Chinle Boarding School
Indian Education Program
P.O. Box 70
Many Farms, AZ 86538
  Dr. F. Anderson, Contact

Many Farms High School
Indian Education Program
P.O. Box 307
Many Farms, AZ 86538
  S. Norman Rodgers, Contact

Marana Unified School Dist. #6
Indian Education Program
11279 W. Grier Rd.
Marana, AZ 85653
  Fredrica Powell, Contact

Maricopa Unified School Dist. #20
Indian Education Program
P.O. Box 310
Maricopa, AZ 85239
  Alma Farrow, Contact

McNary Elementary School District
Indian Education Program
P.O. Box 598
McNary, AZ 85930
  Lizzie Shumate, Contact

Mesa Unified School District
Indian Education Program
1025 N. Country Club
Mesa, AZ 85201
  Theresa Price, Contact

Mohave Valley Elem. School Dist.
Indian Education Program
P.O. Box 5070
Mohave Valley, AZ 86440
  Lee Robinson, Contact

Page Unified School District
Indian Education Program
500 S. Navajo, Box 1927
Page, AZ 86040
  Kathy Hannemann, Contact

Parker Unified School District
Indian Education Program
P.O. Box 1089
Parker, AZ 85344
  Judy Holmes, Contact

Peach Springs Elem. USD
Indian Education Program
P.O. Box 360
Peach Springs, AZ 86434
  Lucille Watahomogie, Contact

Alhambra Elementary School District #68
Indian Education Program
4510 N. 37th Ave.
Phoenix, AZ 85019
  (602) 336-2944 Fax 336-2271

James Rice, Title V Coordinator
Grades K-8. *Description*: Provides tutoring services and promotes parental involvement through communications, parent workshops, meetings and family activities. 435 Native American students, representing more than 20 tribes, have been identified an d attend schools in Alhambra District. *Instructors*: Shirley Maves, Lois Lindsay.

Balsz School District
Indian Education Program
4309 E. Bellview
Phoenix, AZ 85008
  Janet Glass, Contact

Creighton School District #14
Indian Education Program
2702 E. Flower St.
Phoenix, AZ 85016
  Pamela Burkhart, Contact

Isaac School District
Indian Education Program
3801 W. Roanoke
Phoenix, AZ 85009
  Patti Cobos, Contact

Madison Elementary School Dist. #38
Indian Education Program
5601 N. 16th St.
Phoenix, AZ 85016
  Mike Melton, Contact

Murphy Elementary School District
Indian Education Program
2615 W. Buckeye Rd.
Phoenix, AZ 85009
  Rosemary Ruiz, Contact

Osborn School District #8
Indian Education Program
1226 W. Osborn Rd.
Phoenix, AZ 85013
  Alice Zimmerman, Contact

Paradise Valley Unified School District
Indian Education Program
15002 North 32nd St.
Phoenix, AZ 85032
  Don Skowski, Contact

Phoenix Elem. School District #1
Indian Education Program
1817 North 7th St.
Phoenix, AZ 85006
  Alvis Robertson, Contact

Phoenix Union High School District
Indian Education Program
4502 N. Central Ave., CES 3rd Floor
Phoenix, AZ 85017
  Sam Mackey, Contact

Scottsdale Unified School District #48
Indian Education Program
3811 N. 44th St.
Phoenix, AZ 85018
  Rosa Muna, Contact

Washington Elementary School District
Indian Education Program
8610 N. 19th Ave.
Phoenix, AZ 85201
  Jesus Escarcego, Contact

Pinon Community School
Indian Education Program
P.O. Box 159
Pinon, AZ 86510
  Phyllis Badoni, Contact

Pinon Unified School District #4
Indian Education Program
P.O. Box 839
Pinon, AZ 86510
  Margaret Etsitty, Contact

Polacca Day School
Indian Education Program
P.O. Box 750
Polacca, AZ 86042
  Glenn White Eagle, Contact

Prescott Unified School District
Indian Education Program
146 S. Granite St.
Prescott, AZ 86303
  Gordon Meredith, Contact

Red Rock Day School
Indian Education Program
P.O. Drawer 10
Red Valley, AZ 86544
  Hazel Dayish, Contact

Sacaton Public Schools #18
Indian Education Program
P.O. Box 98
Sacaton, AZ 85247
  Scott Goodson, Contact

Hunter's Point Boarding School
Indian Education Program
P.O. Box 99
St. Michaels, AZ 86511
  Winnifred Peters, Contact

San Carlos School District
Indian Education Program
P.O. Box 207
San Carlos, AZ 85550
  Catherine Steele, Contact

Sanders Unified School District
Indian Education Program
P.O. Box 250
Sanders, AZ 86515
  Doug McIntyre, Contact

Salt River Day School
Indian Education Program
Route 1, Box 117
Scottsdale, AZ 85256
  Austin Buckles, Contact

Second Mesa Day School
Indian Education Program
P.O. Box 98
Second Mesa, AZ 86043
  Allen Doering, Contact

Indian Oasis Baboquivari USD #40
Indian Education Program
P.O. Box 248
Sells, AZ 85634
  Mike Ryan, Contact

San Simon School
Indian Education Program
Star Route 1, Box 92
Sells, AZ 85634
  Della R. Williams, Contact

Santa Rosa Boarding School
Indian Education Program
Sells, AZ 85634
  John Leffue, Contact

Theodore Roosevelt Boarding School
Indian Education Program
P.O. Box 513
Sells, AZ 85634
  Mark Wilkerson, Contact

Tohono O'Odham High School
Indian Education Program
P.O. Box 513
Sells, AZ 85634
  Karen Dawson, Contact

Shonto Boarding School
Indian Education Program
Shonto, AZ 86054
  Arnold Studebaker, Contact

Snowflake Unified School District
Indian Education Program
P.O. Box 1100
Snowflake, AZ 85937
  Pearl Evans, Contact

Stanfield Elem. School District
Indian Education Program
P.O Box 578
Stanfield, AZ 85272
  Bryant Ridgeway, Contact

Havasupai Elementary School
Indian Education Program
P.O. Box 40
Supai, AZ 86435
  Harry Doten, Contact

Red Mesa Unified School District
Indian Education Program
HCR 6100, Box 40
Teec Nos Pos, AZ 86514
  Sarah Begay, Contact

Teec Nos Pos Boarding School
Indian Education Program
Teec Nos Pos, AZ 86514
  K. Holiday, Contact

Kyrene Elementary School Dist. #28
Indian Education Program
8700 S. Kyrene Rd.
Tempe, AZ 85284
  Rita Van Loenen, Contact

Tempe Elementary School District
Indian Education Program
P.O. Box 27708
Tempe, AZ 85282
  Michael Walsh, Contact

Tempe Union High School District
Indian Education Program
500 W. Guadalupe Rd.
Tempe, AZ 85283
  Jean Paisley, Contact

Union Elementary School District
Indian Education Program
3834 S. 91st Ave.
Tolleson, AZ 85353
  Lee Kemper, Contact

Tolleson Union High School District
Indian Education Program
9419 W. Van Buren
Tolleson, AZ 85353
  Gene Hernandez, Contact

Navajo Mountain Boarding School
Indian Education Program
P.O. Box 10010
Tonalea, AZ 86044
  Julie Richardson, Contact

Red Lake Day School
Indian Education Program
P.O. Box 39
Tonalea, AZ 86044
  Perrell Whitey, Contact

Moencopi Day School
Indian Education Program
P.O. Box 185
Tuba City, AZ 86045
  John Thomas, Contact

Tuba City Boarding School
Indian Education Program
P.O. Box 187
Tuba City, AZ 86045
  Roxanne Brown, Contact

Tuba City High School Board
Indian Education Program
Box 160
Tuba City, AZ 86045
  Kyril Calsoyas, Contact

Amphitheater School District
Indian Education Program
701 West Wetmore
Tucson, AZ 85705
  Anna Chana, Contact

Santa Rosa Ranch School
Indian Education Program
HCO4 #7570
Tucson, AZ 85735
  Louis Barajas, Contact

Sunnyside Unified School District
Indian Education Program
2238 E. Ginter Rd.
Tucson, AZ 85706
  Erwin Rope, Contact

Tucson Unified School District
Indian Education Program
P.O. Box 40400
Tucson, AZ 85717
  Alberta Plannery, Contact

Tuba City Unified School District
Indian Education Program
Box 67
Tuba City, AZ 86045
  Chee Benally, Contact

Horse Mesa School District
Indian Education Program
11 Coolidge St.
Wafb, AZ 85225
  Connie Gibbons, Contact

John F. Kennedy Day School
Indian Education Program
P.O Box 130
White River, AZ 85941
  Patricia Allen, Contact

Whiteriver Unified School Dist. #20
Indian Education Program
P.O. Box 190
Whiteriver, AZ 85941
  Brian Patrick, Contact

Dilcon Boarding School
Indian Education Program
Star Route
Winslow, AZ 86047
  Steve Summers, Contact

Leupp Boarding School
Indian Education Program
HC61
Winslow, AZ 86047
  Victoria Sorrell, Contact

Little Singer Community School
Indian Education Program
HC-61, Box 239
Winslow, AZ 86047
  Mark Sorenson, Contact

Seba Dalkai Boarding School
Indian Education Program
Winslow, AZ 86047
  Deborah Kent, Contact

Winslow Unified School District
Indian Education Program
P.O. Box 580
Winslow, AZ 86047
  Sr. Michael Wilson, Contact

Yuma Unified School District
Indian Education Program
450 West 6th St.
Yuma, AZ 85364
  Dr. McCraley, Contact

CALIFORNIA

Alpine Union School District
Indian Education Program
1323 Administration Way
Alpine, CA 92001
  Barbara Miller, Contact

Modoc Joint Unified School District
Indian Education Program
906 West 4th St.
Alturas, CA 96101
  Ray Curtis, Contact

Anderson Union High School
Indian Education Program
1471 Perry St.
Anderson, CA 96007
  Vickie McMasters, Contact

Cascade Union Elementary District
Indian Education Program
1645 W. Mill St.
Anderson, CA 96007
  Tom Worthen, Contact

Happy Valley Union School District
Indian Education Program
7480 Palm Ave.
Anderson, CA 96007
  Robert Ferrera, Contact

Auberry Union Elem. School District
Indian Education Program
33367 N. Auberry Rd.
Auberry, CA 93602
  Madeline Elliott, Contact

Golden Hills School District
Indian Education Program
33367 N. Auberry
Auberry, CA 93602
  Joyce Harper, Contact

Auburn Union School District
Indian Education Program
471 Maidu Dr.
Auburn, CA 95603
  Mary Jane Mace, Contact

Placer Union High School District
Indian Education Program
P.O. Box 5048
Auburn, CA 95603
  Patti Stone, Contact

Kern Union High School District
Indian Education Program
2000 24th St.
Bakersfield, CA 93301
  Diane Fletcher, Contact

Banning Unified School District
Indian Education Program
161 W. Williams
Banning, CA 92220
  Olivia Hershey, Contact

Barstow Unified School District
Indian Education Program
551 S. Avenue H
Barstow, CA 92311
  Dennis Wilson, Contact

Big Pine Unified School District
Indian Education Program
500 S. Main St.
Big Pine, CA 93513
  Dave Manship, Contact

Bishop Union High School District
Indian Education Program
301 N. Fowler St.
Bishop, CA 93514
  Dollie Manuelito, Contact

Bonsall Union School District
Indian Education Program
P.O. Box 3
Bonsall, CA 92003
  Barbara Rohrer, Contact

San Juan Unified School District
Indian Education Program
3738 Walnut Ave.
Carmichael, CA 95608
  (916) 971-5206
  Isabel Johnson, Contact
Grades K-12. Indian cultural curriculum.

Fall River Joint USD
Indian Education Program
P.O. Box 89
Cassell, CA 96016
  William Cummings, Contact

Surprise Valley Joint USD
Indian Education Program
P.O. Box 28-F
Cedarville, CA 96104
  Richard Cunnison, Contact

Gateway Unified School District
Indian Education Program
P.O. Box 818
Central Valley, CA 96019

Shasta Lake Union Elem. School Dist.
Indian Education Program
P.O. Box 818
Central Valley, CA 96019
  Robert Stathem, Contact

Ceres Unified School District
Indian Education Program
P.O. Box 307
Ceres, CA 95307
  Lillie Fiskin, Contact

ABC Unified School District
Indian Education Program
16700 Norwalk Blvd.
Cerritos, CA 90701
  Mary Sieu Anderson, Contact

Konocti School District
Indian Education Program
P.O. Box 577
Clearlake Oaks, CA 95422
  Nancy Todd, Contact

Clovis Unified School District
Indian Education Program
55 West Shaw, Suite 218
Clovis, CA 93612
  Joan Short, Contact

Colfax Elementary School District
Indian Education Program
P.O. Box 699
Colfax, CA 95713
  Jewell Delapp, Contact

Colusa County School Districts
Native American Education Program
345-5th St., Suite C
Colusa, CA 95932
  (916) 458-0305 Fax 458-2376
  Joan Saltzen, Director
Grades K-12. *Description*: Promotes cultural awareness activities, and parental involvement; monitors Native American students grades and attendance; and acts as a resource center for the general public. *Instructor*: Serena Morrow, Resource Specialist.

Round Valley USD
Indian Education Program
P.O. Box 276
Covelo, CA 95428
  Howard Chavez, Contact

Del Norte Co. Unified School Dist.
Indian Education Program
301 W. Washington Blvd.
Crescent City, CA 95531
  Robert Appel, Contact

Butte Co. Office of Education
Indian Education Program
5 A County Center Dr.
Oroville, CA 95965
  Terri Tozier, Contact

Jefferson School District
Indian Education Program
101 Lincoln Way
Daly City, CA 94015
  James Cannon, Contact

Elk Grove Unified School District
Indian Education Program
8820 Elk Grove Blvd.
Elk Grove, CA 95624
  Michelle Meagher, Contact

Escondido Union High School Dist.
Indian Education Program
240 S. Maple St.
Escondido, CA 92025
  Marsha Mooradian, Contact

Eureka City Schools
Indian Education Program
3200 Walford Ave.
Eureka, CA 95501
  (707) 441-2454 Fax 445-1956
  Sandra Burton, Director
Grades K-12. *Description*: Provides tutoring services and cultural enrichment programs.

Fairfield-Suisun Unified School District
Indian Education Program
1125 Missouri St.
Fairfield, CA 94533
  Aracella Cantu-Tong, Contact

Fallbrook Union High School Dist.
Indian Education Program
P.O. Box 368
Fallbrook, CA 92028
  Ken Brower, Contact

Farmersville Elem. School District
Indian Education Program
281 S. Farmersville Blvd.
Farmersville, CA 93223
  Ronald Garcia, Contact

Fontana Unified School District
Indian Education Program
9453 Citrus Ave.
Fontana, CA 92335
  Linda Donaldson, Contact

Foresthill Union School District
Indian Education Program
P.O. Box 609
Foresthill, CA 95613
  Rebecca Miller, Contact

Fortuna Union High School District
Indian Education Program
379 12th St.
Fortuna, CA 95540
  Sheri Johnson, Contact

Fremont Unified School District
Indian Education Program
2650 Bruce Dr.
Fremont, CA 94539
  Linda Santillon, Contact

Fresno Unified School District
Indian Education Program
3132 E. Fairmont St.
Fresno, CA 93726
  Mike Giovannetti, Contact

Southern Humboldt USD
Indian Education Program
P.O. Box 129
Garberville, CA 95440
  Cynthia Grover, Contact

Garden Grove Unified School District
Indian Education Program
10331 Stanford Ave.
Garden Grove, CA 92640
  Eileen Dibb, Contact

Siskiyou Union H.S. District
Indian Education Program
P.O. Box 437
Happy Camp, CA 96039
  Jay Clark, Contact

Hemet Unified School District
Indian Education Program
2350 W. Latham Ave.
Hemet, CA 92343
  Sid Cottrell, Contact

Klamath-Trinity Joint USD
Indian Education Program
P.O. Box 1308
Hoopa, CA 95546
  (916) 625-4412 Fax 625-4133
  Sarah Supahan, Director
Grades K-12. *Description*: Develops locally produced curriculum integrating Indian culture into all academic areas; tutoring and career guidance. *Instructors*: Jolene Gates, Erma Marshall, Joyce Tracy, Addrian Gilkison, Sunny Aguiar, and Socorro Valdez. *Videos produced*: The Theft of Fire; How Panther Got Tear Marks; Karuk Basketmakers-A Way of Life; Why Coyote Has the Best Eyes.

Huntington Beach Union H.S. District
Indian Education Program
10251 Yorktown Ave.
Huntington Beach, CA 92646
  Alma Rail, Contact

Oceanview Elementary School District
Indian Education Program
16940 B St.
Huntington Beach, CA 92647
  Monica Ortez, Contact

Desert Sands Unified School District
Indian Education Program
82-879 Highway 111
Indio, CA 92201
  Shirley Durham, Contact

Lake Co. Office of Ed.
Indian Education Program
1152 S. Main St.
Lakeport, CA 95453
  Richard Gage, Contact

Lakeside Union School District
Indian Education Program
P.O. Box 578
Lakeside, CA 92040
  Dan Nasman, Contact

Laytonville Unified School District
Indian Education Program
P.O. Box 868
Laytonville, CA 95454
  Mark Iacuaniello, Contact

Lemoore Union H.S. District
Indian Education Program
101 E. Bush St.
Lemoore, CA 93245
  David Ross, Contact

Livermore Valley Joint Union School Dist.
Indian Education Program
685 E. Jack London Blvd.
Livermore, CA 94550
  Mary Puthoff, Contact

Long Beach Uified School District
Indian Education Program
701 Locust Ave.
Long Beach, CA 90813
  Eva Northrup, Contact

Los Angeles Unified School District
Indian Education Program
450 N. Grand Ave., Room H243
Los Angeles, CA 90012
  (213) 625-6760 Fax 687-7482
  Tim Faulkner, Director
Grades K-12. *Description*: Provides cultural & academic enrichment programs for American Indian and Native Alaskan students.

Lone Pine Unified School District
Indian Education Program
Box 159
Lone Pine, CA 93545
  William Schmidt, Contact

Mariposa Co. Unified School District
Indian Education Program
P.O. Box 127
Mariposa, CA 95338
  Lynette Carpenter, Contact

Marysville Joint Unified School District

Indian Education Program
1919 B St.
Marysville, CA 95901
  Jim Graham, Contact

McKinleyville High School
Indian Education Program
1300 Murray Rd.
McKinleyville, CA 95521
  Kenny Richard, Contact

Placer Hills Union School District
Indian Education Program
P.O. Box 68
Meadow Vista, CA 95722
  April Moore, Contact

**Milpitas/Berryessa/Oak Grove
School Districts**
Indian Education Program
1331 E. Calaveras Blvd.
Milpitas, CA 95035
  (408) 945-2387
  Nicholas V. Comella, Title V Liaison
Grades K-12. Provides referral services, tutorial services, cultural classes, student advocacy, and parent training.

Mountain Union School District
Indian Education Program
Box 368
Montgomery Creek, CA 96065
  Stan Caspary, Contact

Napa Valley Unified School District
Indian Education Program
2425 Jefferson St.
Napa, CA 94558
  Evelyn Agnew, Contact

Needles Unified School District
Indian Education Program
1900 Erin Dr.
Needles, CA 92363
  Terry Brace, Contact

Newcastle Elementary School District
Indian Education Program
Valley View Dr.
Newcastle, CA 95658
  Dr. Edward F. Gilligan, Contact

Chawanakee Joint School District
Indian Education Program
P.O. Box 707
North Fork, CA 93643
  Mary George, Contact

Twin Ridges Elem. School District
Indian Education Program
P.O. Box 529
North San Juan, CA 95960
  Donna Hajuk, Contact

Bass lake School District
Indian Education Program
P.O. Box 395
Oakhurst, CA 93644

Oakland Unified School District
Indian Education Program
1025 Second Ave.
Oakland, CA 94606
  Evelyn Lamenti, Contact

Ontario-Montclair School District
Indian Education Program
P.O. Box 313
Ontario, CA 91761
Jeanette Troesh, Contact

Orange Unified School District
Indian Education Program
370 North Glassell
Orange, CA 92666
  Thomas Saenz, Contact

Oroville Union High School District
Indian Education Program
2211 Washington Ave.
Oroville, CA 95966
  Judith Wilmarth, Contact

Palermo Union Elem. School District
Indian Education Program
7350 Bulldog Way
Palermo, CA 95968
  Bill Linebarger, Contact

Palm Springs Unifie School Dist.
Indian Education Program
333 S. Farrell Dr.
Palm Springs, CA 92262
  Sandia Williams, Contact

Pauma Valley USD
Indian Education Program
P.O. Box 409
Pauma Valley, CA 92016
  Suzan Cooke, Contact

Penryn Elem. School District
Indian Education Program
P.O. Box 349
Penryn, CA 95663
Mary L. Roche, Contact

Pittsburg Unified School District
Indian Education Program
2000 Railroad Ave.
Pittsburg, CA 94565
Wayne Miller, Contact

El Dorado Co. Office of Education
Indian Education Program
6767 Green Valley Rd.
Placerville, CA 95667
James Marquez, Contact

Porterville Public Schools
Indian Education Program
589 W. Vine
Porterville, CA 93257
Jim Edwards, Contact

Plumas Unified School District
Indian Education Program
P.O. Box 2080
Portola, CA 96122
Donna Waller, Contact

Ramona Unified School District
Indian Education Program
415 8th St.
Ramona, CA 92065
(619) 788-5010
Pauline Parker, Title V Director
Grades K-12. Provides tutorial, career guidance,
financial aid information, and cultural awareness
programs.

Kings Canyon USD
Indian Education Program
P.O. Box 552
Reedly, CA 93654
Dr. Marvin L. Sohns, Contact

Richmond Unified School District
Indian Education Program
P.O. Box 4014
Richmond, CA 94802
Pat Lasarte, Contact

Sherman Indian High School
Indian Education Program
9010 Magnolia Ave.
Riverside, CA 92503

Sacramento City USD
Indian Education Program
4701 Joaquin Way
Sacramento, CA 95822
Paulette Kelly, Contact

San Bernardino City USD
Indian Education Program
777 North F St.
San Bernardino, CA 92410
Betsy Manzano, Contact

San Diego Unified School District
Indian Education Program
6880 Mohawk St., Room 3
San Diego, CA 92115

San Francisco USD
Indian Education Program
1950 Mission St., Rm. 12
San Francisco, CA 94103
Carolyn Silverman, Contact

San Jacinto USD
Indian Education Program
600 E. Main St.
San Jacinto, CA 92383
Hank Richardson, Contact

Alum Rock Union Elem. School District
Indian Education Program
2930 Gay Ave.
San Jose, CA 95127
Gloria Lundine, Contact

East Side Union High School District
Indian Education Program
830 N. Capital Ave.
San Jose, CA 95133
John Amon, Contact

Oak Grove Elem. School District
Indian Education Program
6578 Santa Teresa Blvd.
San Jose, CA 95119
Charles Loyd, Contact

Santa Clara Co. Ed. Deveeopment Center
Indian Education Program
100 Skyport Dr.
San Jose, CA 95115
Gerald Casimere, Contact

Capistrano Unified School District
Indian Education Program
32972 Calle Perfecto
San Juan Capistrano, CA 92675
Joe D. Wilson, Contact

San Lorenzo USD
Indian Education Program
15510 Usher St.
San Lorenzo, CA 94580
Deanna Espina, Contact

San Marcos Jr. High School
Indian Education Program
650 W. Mission Rd.
San Marcos, CA 92069

Santa Clara USD
Indian Education Program
P.O. Box 397
Santa Clara, CA 95052
Gwen Stierer, Contact

Mark West Union School District
Indian Education Program
5187 Old Redwood Hwy.
Santa Rosa, CA 95401
Ida Victorson, Contact

Roseland School District
Indian Education Program
950 Sebastopol Rd.
Santa Rosa, CA 95407
Jane Clayton, Contact

Santa Rosa City School District
Indian Education Program
P.O. Box 940
Santa Rosa, CA 95402
Marcie Becerra, Contact

Sebastopol Union Schools
Indian Education Program
7905 Valentine Ave.
Sebastopol, CA 95472
James Pascoe, Contact

Sonora Union High School
Indian Education Program
251 S. Baretta St.
Sonora, CA 95370
Edmund B. Duggan, Jr., Contact

San Mateo Co. Office of Education
Indian Education Program
227 Arroyo Dr.
S. San Francisco, CA 94080
Lonni Sopko, Contact

Stockton Unified School District
Indian Education Program
701 N. Madison
Stockton, CA 95202
Dr. Mary Gonzales, Contact

Fremont Union High School District
Indian Education Program
P.O. Box F
Sunnyvale, CA 94087
Mary Stone, Contact

Lassen Union H.S. District
Indian Education Program
1110 Main St.
Susanville, CA 96130
Nancy Ash, Contact

Susanville Elem. School District
Indian Education Program
2005 4th St.
Susanville, CA 96130
David Burriel, Contact

Coachella Valley Unified School District
Indian Education Program
P.O. Box 847
Thermal, CA 92274
Joe Gallegos, Contact

Sierra Joint Union H.S. District
Indian Education Program
33326 N. Lodge Rd.
Tollhouse, CA 93667
John Ginet, Contact

Tracy Public Schools
Indian Education Program
315 E. 11th St.
Tracy, CA 95376
Alda Brothers, Contact

Summerville Elementary School District
Indian Education Program
18451 Carter St.
Tuolumne, CA 95379
Karen Bretz, Contact

Summerville Union H.S.
Indian Education Program
17555 Tuolumne Rd.
Tuolumne, CA 95379
Richard Thorsted, Contact

Ukiah Unified School District
Indian Education Program
925 N. State St.
Ukiah, CA 95482
Damon Dickenson, Contact

Vacaville Unified School District
Indian Education Program
751 School St.
Vacaville, CA 95688
Judith Cook, Contact

Ventura Unified School District
Indian Education Program
120 E. Santa Clara St.
Ventura, CA 93001
Floyd O. Beller, Contact

Visalia Unified School District
Indian Education Program
315 E. Acequia St.
Visalia, CA 93291
Juan Lopez, Contact

Warner School District
Indian Education Program
Box 8
Warner Springs, CA 92086
Wayne Taylor, Contact

Washington Unified School District
Indian Education Program
930 West Acres Rd., Room 17
West Sacramento, CA 95691
(916) 371-9300 ext. 70 Fax 371-8319
Sarah Taylor, Director
Grades 5-9. *Description*: Provides academic, cultural and advisory services for approximately 150 Indian students enrolled in the program. *Instructor*: Lori L. Rigney.

Westminster School District
Indian Education Program
14121 Cedarwood Ave.
Westminster, CA 92683
Marilyn Moniz, Contact

Windsor Union School District
Indian Education Program
7650 Bell Rd.
Windsor, CA 95492
Linda Chase, Contact

San Pasqual Valley USD
Indian Education Program
Rte. 1, 676 Baseline Rd.
Winterhaven, CA 92283
Herbert Jagow, Contact

Yreka Union School District
Indian Education Program
405 Jackson St.
Yreka, CA 96097
Pat Spillers, Contact

COLORADO

Adams-Arapahoe Joint School Dist.
Indian Education Program
15700 East 1st Ave.
Aurora, CO 80011
David Wood, Joyce Vigil, Contacts

MCREL
Indian Education Program
2550 S. Parker Rd., Suite 500
Aurora, CO 80014
J. Morris

Boulder Valley School District
Indian Education Program
P.O. Box 9011
Boulder, CO 80301
Teressa Halsey, Contact

Montezuma Cortez District RE-1
Indian Education Program
P.O. Drawer R
Cortez   CO 81321
George Schumpelt, Contact

Colorado Dept. of Education
Indian Education Program
201 E. Colfax Ave.
Denver, CO 80203
Vicente Z. Serrano, Contact

Denver Public School District
Indian Education Program
900 Grant St., Room 604
Denver, CO 80203
D. Echohawk, Contact

Mapleton Public Schools
Indian Education Program
501 E. 80th Ave.
Denver, CO 80229
Frieda Diaz, Contact

Cherry Creek School District
Indian Education Program
4700 S. Yosemite St.
Englewood, CO 80111
A. Clyburn, Contact

Jefferson Co. P.S., Div. of Hum.
Indian Education Program
1829 Denver West Dr., Bldg. 27
Golden, CO 80401
Dr. Patsy James, Contact

Ignacio United School District
Indian Education Program
P.O. Box 460
Ignacio, CO 81137
Bryce Fauble, B. Chevarillo, Contacts

St. Vrain Valley School District
Indian Education Program
395 S. Pratt Parkway
Longmont, CO 80501
Lu Munoz, Elaine Worrell, Contacts

CONNECTICUT

Bridgeport Board of Education
Indian Education Program
45 Lyon Ter., Rm. 318
Bridgeport, CT 06604
Michael Kelly, Contact

FLORIDA

Hendry Co. School District
Indian Education Program
475 E. Osceola St.
Clewiston, FL 33440
Sylvester Humphrey, Contact

Seminole Tribe of Florida
Ahfachkee School
Star Route, Box 40
Clewiston, FL 33440
Martin Coyle, Principal

Broward Co. School District
Indian Education Program
701 N. 31st Ave.
Ft. Lauderdale, FL 33311
Tina Van Vleet, Contact

Seminole Tribe of Florida
Indian Education Program
6075 Stirling Rd.
Hollywood, FL 33024
Pat Jagiel, Contact

Miccosukee Corp.
Indian Education Program
Tamiami Station, Box 440021
Miami, FL 33144
Delores Billie, Contact

Collier Co. Public Schools
Indian Education Program
3710 Estey Ave.
Naples, FL 33942
Dr. John Visosky, Contact

Okeechobee Co. School District
Brighton Reservation
100 SW 5th Ave.
Okeechobee, FL 34974
Nancy Billy, Zella Kirk, Contact

IDAHO

American Falls School District #381
Indian Education Program
827 Fort Hall Ave.
American Falls, ID 83211
J. Brulotte, Contact

Blackfoot School District #55
Indian Education Program
270 E. Bridge
Blackfoot, ID 83221
S. Norton, Contact

Idaho Dept. of Education
Indian Education Program
650 W. State St.
Boise, ID 83720
Shirley Spencer, Contact

Boundary Co. School District #101
Indian Education Program
P.O. Box 899
Bonners Ferry, ID 83805
R. Singleton, Contact

Coeur d'Alene Tribal School
Indian Education Program
P.O. Box 338
Desmet, ID 83824
D. Beach, Contact

Shoshone Bannock Tribes
Indian Education Program
Box 306
Fort Hall, ID 83203
Maxine Edmo, Contact

Tribal High School
Indian Education Program
P.O. Box 306
Fort Hall, ID 83203
 Leona Jim, Contact

Kamiah School District #304
Indian Education Program
P.O. Box 877
Kamiah, ID 83536
 H. Yates, Contact

Lapwai School District #341
Indian Education Program
P.O. Box 247
Lapwai, ID 83540
 R. Sobotta, Doug Wells, Contacts

Independent School Dist. #1
Indian Education Program
3317 12th St.
Lewiston, ID 83501
 C.M. Hibbard, Dawn Leighton, Contacts

W. Benawah School District #42
Indian Education Program
P.O. Box 130
Plummer, ID 83851
 K. Browning, Contact

Bannock Co. School District #25
Indian Education Program
P.O. Box 1390
Pocatello, ID 83204
 G. Von Houten, Contact

Idaho State University
Indian Education Program
Campus Box 8054
Pocatello, ID 83209
 Donna Ellsworth, Contact

Worley School District #275
Indian Education Program
P.O. Box 98
Worley, ID 83876
 J. Brock, Contact

ILLINOIS

Audubon School
Indian Education Program
3500 N. Hoyne
Chicago, IL 60618
 Renee de la Cruz, Contact

Chicago Board of Ed.
Indian Education Program
P.O. Box 699005
Chicago, IL 60609
 Preston Bryant, Contact

Chicago Public Schools
Audubon School
3500 N. Hoyne
Chicago, IL 60618
 Juris Graudins, Contact

Chicago Public Schools
Indian Education Program
1819 W. Pershing Rd.
Chicago, IL 60609
 Fernando Martinez,
 Dr. James Somday, Contacts

INDIANA

South Bend Community Schools
Indian Education Program
635 S. Main St.
South Bend, IN 46635
 Edward Myers, Contact

IOWA

Davenport Community School District
Federal Program Coordinator
1002 W. Kimberly Rd.
Davenport, IA 52806
 (319) 386-0404
 Denise Jensen, Title V Liaison

Sioux City Commuity Schools
Indian Education Program
1221 Pierce St.
Sioux City, IA 51105
 Lynn Huenemann

Sac & Fox Settlement School
Title V Director
RR #2, Box 56C
Tama, IA 52339
 Wayne Pushetonequa, Contact

South Tama Co. Community Schools
Title V Director
1702 Harding St.
Tama, IA 52339
 Billie Jean Snyder, Contact

KANSAS

Arkansas City Schools - USD #470
Indian Education Program
420 South 5th
Arkansas City, KS 67005
 (316) 441-2000 Fax 441-2009
 Glenn Clarkson, Director
Grades K-12. Provides school-home liaison.

Coffeyville Public School
Indian Education Program
7th and Ellis
Coffeyville, KS 67337
 Larry Thomas, Contact

Horton/S. Brown Co. USD #430
Indian Education Program
114 West 8th St.
Horton, KS 66439
 Jean Becker, Contact

Lawrence Public Schools
Indian Education Program
3705 Clinton Pkwy.
Lawrence, KS 66047
 Dr. Al Szinger, Contact

Lawrence Public Schools
Indian Education Program
1919 Delware St.
Lawrence, KS 66046
 Theresa Rogers, Contact

Royal Valley U.S.D. #337
Indian Education Program
P.O. Box 155
Mayetta, KS 66509
 (913) 966-2251 Fax 966-2253
 Laverne F. Hale, Director
Grades K-12. Description: Provides tutoring services, cultural enrichment programs, and guidance counseling. Instructors: Rose Masquat, Terri Greemore.

U.S.D. #321 Kaw Valley Special Services
P.O. Box 578 - 303 E. Hwy. 24
Rossville, KS 66533
 (913) 584-6731 Fax 584-6720
 Dorothy Rockefeller, PhD, Director
Grades K-12. Description: Provides tutoring in academic areas, cultural enrichment with related activities, and developing a plan for employment or education after graduation. About 30 identified Native Americans in the district enrollment.

Kaw Valley USD
P.O. Box 160
St. Mary's, KS 66536
 George Brown, Contact

Topeka Public Schools
Dir. of Curriculum
624 West 24th St.
Topeka, KS 66611
 Phyllis Chase, Contact

Wichita Public School
Indian Studies
217 N. Water
Wichita, KS 67202
 Dr. Tulio Tablada, Contact

LOUISIANA

Rapides Parish School District
Indian Education Program
P.O. Box 1230
Alexandria, LA 71309
 Karyn Richardson, Contact

Chitimacha Tribe of LA
Indian Education Program
P.O. Box 661
Charenton, LA 70523
 Alton LeBlanc, Jr., Contact

Lafourche Parish School District
Indian Education Program
2617 Alcide St.
Golden Meadow, LA 70357
 Brenda Pitre, Contact

Jefferson Parish School District
Indian Education Program
501 Manhattan Blvd.
Harvey, LA 70058
 John Alexander, Contact

Terrebonne Parish School District
Indian Education Program
301 Academy St., Box 5097
Houma, LA 70360
 Diane Boudreaux, Contact

Chitimacha Day School
Indian Education Program
Route 2, Box 222
Jeanerette, LA 70544
Leonard Sudduth

LaSalle Parish School District
Indian Education Program
P.O. Drawer 90
Jena, LA 71342
Lee A. McDowell, Contact

Sabine Parish School District
Indian Education Program
P.O. Box 1079
Many, LA 71449
 Lambert Peterson, Contact

Allen Parish School District
Indian Education Program
P.O. Drawer C
Oberlin, LA 70655
 Linda Sylestine, Contact

Terrebonne Parish School
Indian Education Program
2247 Brady Rd.
Theriot, LA 70397
 Janie Luster, Contact

Lafourche Parish School Board
Indian Education Program
P.O. Box 879
Thibodeaux, LA 70302
 Lorene Watkins, Contact

MAINE

Indian Township School
Indian Education Program
River Rd., Box 412
Calais, ME 04619
Linda Leotsakos, Principal

Maine Indian Education
P.O. Box 412
Calais, ME 04619
 Brian Smith, Supt.

Maine School Admin. Dist. 29
Indian Education Program
P.O. Box 190
Houlton, ME 04730
 William E. McDonnell, Contact

Indian Island School Comm.
Indian Education Program
P.O. Box 566
Old Town, ME 04468
 Sr. Janet Campbell, Principal

Beatrice Rafferty School
Indian Education Program
Box 412, River Rd.
Perry, ME 04667
 Sr. Maureen Wallace, Contact

MARYLAND

Baltimore City Schools
Hampstead Hill Middle School
101 S. Ellwood Ave.
Baltimore, MD 21224
 Jeanette Walker, Contact

Baltimore City Public Schools
Indian Education Program
200 E. North Ave.
Baltimore, MD 21202
 Art Pierce, Contact

Baltimore City Schools
Office of Adult & Alt. Ed.
200 E. North Ave., Rm. 105-M2
Baltimore, MD 21202
 Irene Williams, Contact

Charles Co. Board of Ed.
Indian Education Program
Box D
LaPlata, MD 20646
 Mervin Savoy, Contact

P.G. Co. Public Schools
Oxon Hill Staff Dev. Center
7711 Livingstone
Oxon Hill, MD 20745
 Betty C. Proctor, Contact

Montgomery Co. Public Schools
Indian Education Program
850 Hungerford Dr., Rm. 232
Rockville, MD 20850
 Mary Gabarde, Contact

Montgomery Co. Public Schools
Indian Education Program
4910 Macon Rd.
Rockville, MD 20852
 Madeline McElveen, Contact

P.G. Co. Public Schools
Indian Education Program
14201 School Lane, Sasser Bldg.
Upper Marlboro, MD 20772
 Robert T. Coombs, Contact

MASSACHUSETTS

Boston Public Schools
Indian Education Program
26 Court St.
Boston, MA 02108
 Josephine Brooks, Contact

Martha's Vineyard Schools
Indian Education Program
RR 1, Box 161B
Gayhead, MA 02535
 Adriana Ignacio, Contact

Mashpee School District
Indian Education Program
150 Old Barnstable Rd.
Mashpee, MA 02649
 Joan Tavares, Contact

Martha's Vineyard Schools
Indian Education Program
Regional HS, Edgartown Rd.
Oak Bluffs, MA 02557
 Gregory Scotten, Contact

MICHIGAN

Avondale School District
Indian Education Program
2950 Waukegan
Auburn Hills, MI 48326
 Eva Young, Contact

Bay City Public School District
Indian Education Program
1001 Marsac
Bay City, MI 48708
 Gregory Marciniak, Contact

Bay City Public School District
Indian Education Program
1201 4th St.
Bay City, MI 48708
 Dr. Jose Valderes

Brighton Area Schools
Indian Education Program
4740 Bauer Rd.
Brighton, MI 481 16
 Dr. Sally Bell, Contact

Brighton Area Schools
Indian Education Program
125 S. Church St.
Brighton, MI 481 16
 Teresa Lysz, Contact

Brimley Area Schools
Indian Education Program
P.O. Box 156
Brimley, MI 49715
 Kaye A. Clarke, Contact

Les Cheneaux Community Schools
Indian Education Program
P.O. Box 366
Cedarville, MI 49719
 John Causley, Jr., Contact

Center Line Public Schools
Indian Education Program
6775 E. Ten Mile Rd.
Center Line, MI 48015
 Thomas Laskowski, Contact

Big Bay de Noc School District
Indian Education Program
County Rd., M-193
Cooks, MI 49817
 Sally Gerometta, Contact

Davison Community School Dist.
Indian Education Program
615 East Clark St.
Davison, MI 48423
 Daniel Root, Contact

Detroit School District
Pelham Middle School, Rm. 105
2001 Martin Luther King
Detroit, MI 48208
 Judith Mays, Contact

Detroit Public Schools
Indian Education Program
5057 Woodward Ave.
Detroit, MI 48202
  Barbara Shorts, Contact

East Jordan Public Schools
Indian Education Program
P.O. Box 399
East Jordan, MI 49727
  Lori Gee, Contact

Mason Consolidated School Dist.
Indian Education Program
2400 Lakeside Rd.
Erie, MI 48133
  Mary Weglian, Contact

Escanaba Area Public Schools
Indian Education Program
111 N. 5th St.
Escanaba, MI 49829
  Tom Smith, Contact

Escanaba P.S.-Kennedy School
Indian Education Program
1919 14th Ave., North
Escanaba, MI 49829
  Phyllis Eastman, Contact

Algonac Community Schools
Indian Education Program
A361 Broad Bridge, FH Elem. School
Fair Haven, MI 48023
  John Clyne, Contact

Hazel Park Schools
Indian Education Program
1700 Shevlin, Edison School
Ferndale, MI 48220
  Cathy Pappas, Contact

Carman-Ainsworth Schools
Indian Education Program
G-3475 W. Court St.
Flint, MI 48532
  Carol Lantz, Contact

Beecher Commuity School District
Indian Education Program
1020 W. Coldwater Rd.
Flint, MI 48505
  Burnestyne Allen, Contact

Carman-Ainsworth Schools
Indian Education Program
1181 W. Scottwood Ave.
Flint, MI 48507
  Jean Keen, Contact

Flint City School District
Indian Education Program
2421 Corunna Rd.
Flint, MI 48506
  Veda Balla, Contact

Flint City School District
Indian Education Program
923 E. Kearsley St.
Flint, MI 48502
  Eugene Grice, Contact

Fowlerville Community Schools
Indian Education Program
P.O. Box 769
Fowlerville, MI 48836
  David Peden, Diana W oods, Contacts

Gladstone School District
Indian Education Program
400 S. 10th St.
Gladstone, MI 49837
  Jessie Sargent, Contact

Grand Haven School District
Indian Education Program
1415 Beech Tree St.
Grand Haven, MI, 49417
  Christine Baker, Contact

Grand Rapids Public Schools
Indian Education Program
143 Bostwick, NE
Grand Rapids, MI 49503
  Jose Florez, Contact

Grand Rapids Public Schools
Indian Education Program
615 Turner NW
Grand Rapids, MI 49504
  Sherri Mamagona, Contact

Harbor Springs Schools
Indian Education Program
327 E. Bluff Dr.
Harbor Springs, MI 49740
  Michael Breen, Contact

Bark River-Harris School District
Indian Education Program
Highway U.S. 2 & 41
Harris, MI 49801
  (616) 466-5321 Fax 466-2925
  Gerald Sundquist, Principal
Grades K-12. *Description*: Provides tutoring services and cultural activities. *Instructor*: Mrs. Gebhardt.

Hart Public Schools
Indian Education Program
300 Johnson St.
Hart, MI 49420
  Jane Thocher, Contact

Hazel Park City School Dist.
Indian Education Program
23136 Hughes
Hazel Park, MI 48030
  Ann Bachynski, Contact

Huron Valley Public Schools
Indian Education Program
5061 Duck Lake Rd.
Highland, MI 48356
  Charlotte McKeough, Contact

Howell Public Schools
Indian Education Program
415 N. Barnard St.
Howell, MI 48843
  Gail Luebke, Contact

Howell Public Schools
Indian Education Program
511 N. Highlander W ay
Howell, MI 48843
  Audrey Dunlap, Contact

Wilson School
Indian Education Program
100 Helen St.
Inkster, MI 48141
  Barbara Skone, Contact

Kalamazoo City Schools
Indian Education Program
403 Portage St.
Kalamazoo, MI 49007
  Dianne Spencer, Contact

Kalamazoo City Schools
Indian Education Program
604 W. Vine St.
Kalamazoo, MI 49008
  Jodie Palmer, Contact

L'Anse Township Schools
Indian Education Program
201 N. Fourth
L'Anse, MI 49946
  Lynn Ketola, Contact

Lansing School District
Indian Education Program
519 W. Kalamazoo
Lansing, MI 48933
  Linda Kent, Contact

Mackinac Island Schools
Indian Education Program
Box 340, Lake Shore Dr.
Mackinac Island, MI 49757
  Dan Seeley, Contact

Manistique Area Schools
Indian Education Program
100 N. Cedar St.
Manistique, MI 49854
  (906) 341-2195 ext. 142
  Janet Krueger, Coordinator
Grades K-12. *Description*: Provides tutoring and cultural awareness program.

Marquette Public Schools
Indian Education Program
1201 W. Fair Ave.
Marquette, MI 49855
  Char Shelafoe & Pat Bawden, Contacts

Clintondale School District
Indian Education Program
35300 Little Mack
Mt. Clemens, MI 48043
  Regina Zapinski, Contact

Mt. Morris Cons. Schools
Indian Education Program
1000 Genesee St.
Mt. Morris, MI 48458
  Rita Green, Contact

Mt. Morris Cons. Schools
Indian Education Program
12356 Walter St.
Mt. Morris, MI 48458
  Burton Jones, Contact

Mt. Pleasant Public Schools
Indian Education Program
7070 E. Broadway
Mt. Pleasant, MI 48858
  Bonnie Eckdahl, Contact

Mt. Pleasant Public Schools
Indian Education Program
201 S. University
Mt. Pleasant, MI 48858
  Judith Schaftenaar, Contact

Mt. Pleasant Public Schools
Saginaw Chippewa Ed. Dept.
7070 E. Broadway
Mt. Pleasant, MI 48858
 Carla Sinaway, Contact

Munising Public School District
Indian Education Program
P.O. Box 70
Munising, MI 49862
 Kim Swanberg, Contact

Muskegon Hts. School District
Indian Education Program
2603 Leahy St.
Muskegon, MI 49444
 Malcom Stevens, Contact

Muskegon Public Schools
Indian Education Program
1580 Park St.
Muskegon, MI 49440
 Carol Wimpee, Contact

Anchor Bay School District
Indian Education Program
33700 Hooker Rd.
New Baltimore, MI 48047
 Karen Gorman, Contact

Tahquamenon Area Schools
Indian Education Program
700 Newberry Ave.
Newberry, MI 49868
 William Peltier

Northport Public Schools
Indian Education Program
104 Wing St., Box 88
Northport, MI 49670
 Sheri Hough, Contact

Pellston Public Schools
Indian Education Program
4644 Tower Rd.
Pellston, MI 49769
 Sally Scheier, Contact

Petoskey Public Schools
Indian Education Program
1500 Hill St.
Petoskey, MI 49770
 Kathy McCann, Contact

Pontiac City School District
Indian Education Program
350 E. Wide Track Dr.
Pontiac, MI 48058
 Maria Y. Etienne, Contact

Port Huron Area School District
Data Svcs. & Fed. Prog.
2720 Riverside Dr.
Port Huron, MI 48060
 Charles Kempf, Contact

Port Huron Area School District
Indian Education Program
1925 Lapeer Ave., Box 5013
Port Huron, MI 48061
 (810) 984-3101 Fax 984-6606
 Sharon L. Kota, Director
Grades K-12. *Description*: Provides academic, cultural enrichment and tutoring services for American Indian children residing in the district. *Instructors*: American Indian artists, elders and scholars.

Rapid River Schools
Indian Education Program
P.O. Box 68
Rapid River, MI 49878
 Diane Kuchan, Contact

Chippewa Hill Schools
Indian Education Program
3226 Arthur Rd., Rt. 2
Remus, MI 49340
 Marvin Lett, Contact

Rudyard Public Schools
Indian Education Program
Second & Williams
Rudyard, MI 49780
 Debra Crozier, Contact

Sault Ste. Marie Schools
Indian Education Program
460 W. Spruce
Sault Ste. Marie, MI 49783
 Adel Easterday, Contact

Lake Shore Public Schools
Indian Education Program
30401 Taylor
St. Clair Shores, MI 48082
 Jane Erickson, Contact

St. Ignace Area Schools
Indian Education Program
840 Portage Rd.
St. Ignace, MI 49781
 Don Gustafson, Contact

Airport Community Schools
Indian Education Program
5650 Carleton Rockwood
S. Rockwood, MI 48179
 Louanna Czaikolski, Contact

Suttons Bay Public Schools
Indian Education Program
P.O. Box 367
Suttons Bay, MI 49682
 Fred Elmore, Contact

Swartz Creek Community Schools
Indian Education Program
8354 Cappy Lane
Swartz Creek, MI 48473
 Cheryl Spaniola, Contact

Taylor School District
Indian Education Program
11010 Janet
Taylor, MI 48180
 Vicky Horth, Contact

Taylor School District
Indian Education Program
9601 Westlake
Taylor, MI 48180
 Dr. Gary Ford, Contact

Traverse City Public Schools
Indian Education Program
P.O. Box 32
Traverse, MI 49685
 Cherie Domine, Contact

Walled Lake Cons. Schools
Indian Education Program
615 N. Pontiac Trail
Walled Lake, MI 48390
 Sally Banks, Contact

Warren Consolidated Schools
Indian Education Program
29500 Cosgrove
Warren, MI 48089
 Alfred Snider, Contact

Warren Consolidated Schools
Indian Education Program
2460 Arden
Warren, MI 48092
 Shirley Zapinski, Contact

Watersmeet Township School District
Indian Education Program
C Ave., Box 217
Watersmeet, MI 49969
 J.E. Vesitch, Contact

Wayne-Westland Community Schools
Indian Education Program
1225 S. Wildwood
Westland, MI 48185
 Dorothy Tufnell, Contact

Grand Traverse Band
Education Dept.
7741 M-72 E.
Williamsburg, MI 49690
 Joyce Wilson, Contact

Hannahville Indian School (Nah T ah Wahsh)
Indian Education Program
N14911 Hannahville B-1 Rd.
Wilson, MI 49896
 (906) 466-2952
 Tom Miller, Director
Grades K-12. *Description*: Culture program revolves around Ojibwa language instruction. *Instructors*: Larry Matrious, Vicki Dowd.

Hannahville Indian School
Indian Education Program
Route 1
Wilson, MI 49896
 Bill Boda, Contact

MINNESOTA

Bagley Public Schools ISD
Indian Education Program
308 N. Bagley Ave.
Bagley, MN 56621
 Cleve Goodwin, Contact

Bemidji ISD
Title V Director
201-l5th St., NW
Bemidji, MN 56601
 Vince Beyl, Contact

Bloomfield Municipal Schools
Indian Education Program
325 N. Bergin Lane
Bloomfield, MN 87413
 Irma Arrellano, Contact

Browns Valley Public School
HS Principal
P.O. Box N
Browns Valley, MN 56219
 Todd Cameron, Contact

Carlton ISD #93
Indian Home-School Coord.
Box 310
Carlton, MN 55718
  Sandra Shabiash, Contact

Cass Lake-Bena Public Schools
Indian Education
Rt 3, Box 4
Cass Lake, MN 56633
  Judy Hanks, Contact

Chief Bug O Nay Ge Shig School
Rt. 3, Box 100
Cass Lake, MN 56633
  Patt Cornelius, Contact

Chisholm ISD
Indian Education Program
300 SW 3rd Ave.
Chisholm, MN 55719
  Barbara Paradis, Contact

Centennial School District
Indian Education Program
4707 North Rd.
Circle Pines, MN 55014
  Clifford Holman, Contact

Cloquet ISD #94
509 Carlton Ave.
Cloquet, MN 55720
  Mary Bassett, Contact

Fond du Lac Ojibwe School
Indian Education Program
105 University Rd.
Cloquet, MN 55720
  (218) 879-4593/0241 Fax 879-0007
  Michael Rabideaux, Director
Early Childhood-Grade 12. *Mission Statement*: "In order to survive both as a people and a culture, we must return full circle to our traditional manner of education. Traditional Anishinabe society was outcome based and results oriented. Our society was community focused; it was so in order to survive." *Returning Full Circle*: "A conceptual model for implementing a results oriented tribal-operated community learning center which focuses upon life long learning."

Coleraine/Mashwauk ISD
Indian Education Program
P.O. Box 195
Coleraine, MN 55722
  Bruce Baird, Contact

Anoka-Hennepin ISD
Indian Education
11299 Hanson Blvd. NW
Coon Rapids, MN 55433
  Jerry Staples, Contact

Deer River ISD #317
Title V Director
P.O. Box 307
Deer River, MN 56636
  Warren Goggleye, Contact

Detroit Lakes ISD #22
Director of Special Education
702 Lake Ave.
Detroit Lakes, MN 56501
  James Kjelstrup, Contact

Duluth ISD #709
Indian Education Program
Lake Ave. & Second St.
Duluth, MN 55802
  Geraldine Kozlowski, Contact

East Grand Forks PS Dist.
1420 4th Ave., Box 151
East Grand Forks, MN 56721
  John Roche, Contact

Elk River ISD #728
Indian Education Program
400 School St.
Elk River, MN 55330
  Dr. Gretchen Grewe, Contact

Ely ISD #696
Indian Education Program
600 E. Harvey St.
Ely, MN 55731
  (218) 365-6196
  Dawn Gerzin, Director
Grades K-12. *Description*: Provides cultural activities and tutoring.

Eveleth ISD #697
Indian Ed. Coord.
801 Jones St.
Eveleth, MN 55734
  Sue Emery, Contact

Fosston Public Schools
Title V Director
301 East 1st St.
Fosston, MN 56542
  Diane Sonstelie, Contact

Frazee/Vergas Public Schools
Indian Ed. Coord.
Box 186
Frazee, MN 56544
  Renee Christofferson, Contact

Cook Co. ISD #166
Title V Director
Box F
Grand Marais, MN 55604
  Sue Smith, Contact

Grand Rapids ISD #318
Indian Education Program
303 SE 1st St.
Grand Rapids, MN 55744
  Caroline Stangel, Contact

Granite Falls Public School
Project Director
450 Ninth Ave.
Granite Falls, MN 56241
  Patricia Kubly, Contact

Hibbing ISD #701
Title V Director
8th Ave. E. & 21st St.
Hibbing, MN 55746
  Jean Tye, Contact

Hinckley/Finlayson Public Schools
P.O. Box 308
Hinkley, MN 55037
  O.W Pat Ostrand, Contact

International Falls Public School
Indian Education Program
900 5th St.
International Falls, MN 56649
  Beth Parmeter, Contact

Isle School District ISD #473
Title V Director
Box 25
Isle, MN 56342
  Sarah Gravel, Contact

Kelliher School District #36
Indian Education Program
P.O. Box 259
Kelliher, MN 56650
  James Gednalske, Contact

Mahnomen ISD #432
Indian Education Program
P.O. Box 319
Mahnomen, MN 56557
  Brent Gish, Contact

Osseo ISD #279
Cultural Prog. Sp.
11200 93rd Ave. N.
Maple Grove, MN 55369
  Jerry Buckanaga, Contact

McGregor ISD #4
Indian Education Program
P.O. Box 160
McGregor, MN 55760
  Antoinette F. Johns, Contact

Four Winds School
Indian Education Program
2300 Chicago Ave. S.
Minneapolis, MN 55404
  Dale Weston, Contact

Minneapolis Public Schools
Indian Education Program
807 NE Broadway
Minneapolis, MN 55413
  Dr. Robert Ferrera, Jan Witthuhn, Contacts

Robbinsdale ISD #281
Multicultural Coordinator
4148 Winnetka Ave. North
Minneapolis, MN 55427
  Jacqueline Fraedrich, Contact

South West High School
3419 W. 47th St.
Minneapolis, MN 55410
  Michelle Thompson Tuttle, Contact

Moorhead Public School
1330 8th Ave. N.
Moorhead, MN 56560
  Mary Jo Schmid, Contact

Morton Public School
Box 69
Morton, MN 56270
  Jan Dallenback, Contact

Mt. Iron/Buhl High School
5820 Mineral Ave.
Mt. Iron, MN 55768
  (218) 735-8216
  Renee M. Koski, Title V Director
Description: Offers services to Indian children K-12. includes resources of books, films, literature, as well as counseling, and tutorial services.

Nett Lake ISD #707
13090 Westley Dr.
Nett Lake, MN 55772
Ray Toutloff, Contact

Onamia ISD #480
RR 2, Box 22
Onamia, MN 56359
Kent Baldry, Contact

May Ah Shing/Mille Lacs School
Indian Education Program
HC 67, Box 242
Onamia, MN 56359
George Weber, Contact

Park Rapids ISD #309
Indian Education Dept.
P.O. Box 591
Park Rapids, MN 56470
Sharon Fisher, Contact

Pine City Public School
Indian Education Program
1400 S. 6th St.
Pine City, MN 55063
Emmaline Dunkley, Contact

Pine Poit SD #25
Indian Education Program
P.O. Box 61
Ponsford, MN 56575
Dr. James Noonan, Contact

Red Lake ISD #38
Indian Education Program
Red Lake Indian Reservation
Red Lake, MN 56671
E.D. Kroenke, Contact

Red Lake ISD #38
Title V Director
P.O. Box 280
Red Lake, MN 56671
Delores Cloud, Contact

Red Wing ISD #256
Dir. of Spec. Ed.
444 6th St.
Red Wing, MN 55066
Stanley Nerhaugen, Contact

Remer ISD #118
Indian Education Program
Route 1, Box A
Remer, MN 56672
Cecelia McKeig, Contact

Rochester ISD #535
Indian Education Program
615 SW 7th St.
Rochester, MN 55902
Patricia Mohn, Contact

St. Louis Co. School ISD #706
Indian Education
P.O. Box 128
Saginaw, MN 55779
Robert Malander, Contact

Virginia ISD #706
Indian Education Program
Tech Bldg./5th Ave. South
St. Louis, MN 55792
Darlene Johnson, Contact

Mounds View School Dist. #621
Indian Education Program
2959 Hamline Ave.
St. Paul, MN 55113
Leanne Peterson, Contact

St. Paul Public Schools
Indian Education Program
1028 Van Slyke
St. Paul, MN 55103
Loretta Gagnon, Contact

Sandstone Public Schools
Indian Education Program
Court Ave. at 5th St.
Sandstone, MN 55072
Harold Berg, Contact

Shakopee ISD #720
Dir. of Admin. Svcs.
505 S. Holmes St.
Shakopee, MN 55379
Ronald Ward, Contact

Victoria St. Center
4665 N. Victoria St.
Shoreview, MN 55126
Leanne Peterson-Burnette, Contact

Stillwater ISD #834
Indian Education Program
1875 S. Greeley St.
Stillwater, MN 55082
David Wettergren, Contact

Stilwater ISD #834
Coord. Gifted/Talented
1875 S. Greeley St.
Stillwater, MN 55082
Nancy Hof, Contact

Thief River Falls ID #564
Title V Director
808 S. Crocker
Thief River Falls, MN 56701
Julie Rambeck, Contact

Tower ISD #708
Home-School Coord.
Box 469
Tower, MN 55790
Barbara Babcock, Contact

Walker-Hackensack-Akeley ISD #113
Indian Ed. Coord.
P.O. Box 4000
Walker, MN 56484
Sharon Simpson, Contact

Warroad Public Schools - ISD #690
Indian Education Dept.
510 Cedar Ave.
Warroad, MN 56763
(218) 386-1472 Fax 386-1909
Henry C. Boucha, Coordinator
Grades K-12. *Description*: Provides tutorial assistance, information and referral services, post-secondary financial aid information, home/school liaison services, and Indian advocates. *Instructor*: Daphne Johnson.

Waubun-Ogema ISD #435
Title V Director
Box 98
Waubun, MN 56589
John Clark, Contact

Circle of Life School
P.O. Box 447
White Earth, MN 56591
William Wessels, Contact

MISSOURI

Independence School District
Indian Education Program
1231 S. Windsor
Independence, MO 64055
Marcia Haskin, Contact

N. Kansas City School District
Indian Education Program
2000 N.E. 46th St.
Kansas City, MO 64116
Larry Keisker, Contact

Neosho R-5 School District
Indian Education Program
511 Neosho Blvd.
Neosho, MO 64850
Roy B. Shaver, Contact

Seneca R7 School District
Indian Education Program
P.O. Box 469
Seneca, MO 64865
Mary Rule, Contact

School District of Springfield
Indian Education Program
940 N. Jefferson St.
Springfield, MO 65802
Dr. Paul Hagerty, Contact

MISSISSIPPI

Newton Co. School District
Indian Education Program
P.O. Box 97
Decatur, MS 39327
Dr. Ken Evans, Contact

Louisville Municipal School Dist.
Indian Education Program
200 Ivy Ave.
Louisville, MS 39339
Gladys Taylor, Contact

Mississippi Band of Choctaws
Indian Education Program
P.O. Box 6010
Philadelphia, MS 39350
Douglas Weaver

Jones Co. School District
Indian Education Program
P.O. Drawer E
Sandersville, MS 39477
Mary Ann Stevens, Contact

MONTANA

Arlee Elem. & H.S. District 8J
Indian Education Program
P.O. Box 37
Arlee, MT 59821
L. LaCounte, Contact

Billings Public Schools
Indian Education Program
415 North 30th St.
Billings, MT 59102
 N. Laird, Contact

Eastern Montana College
Indian Education Program
1500 North 30th St.
Billings, MT 59101
J. Reyhner, Contact

Title V Parent Committee
Indian Education Program
2240 Dallas Dr.
Billings, MT 59102
 M.E. Matt, Contact

Charlo School District #7
Indian Education Program
P.O. Box 5
Charlo, MT 59824
 Steve Gaub, Contact

Box Elder Public Schools
Indian Education Program
P.O. Box 205
Box Elder, MT 59521
 R. Hughes, Contact

Rocky Boy Elem. S.D. #87-J
Indian Education Program
P.O. Box 620
Box Elder, MT 59521
 S. Murie, Contact

Brockton Public S.D. #55-55F
Indian Education Program
P.O. Box 198
Brockton, MT 59213
 Dr. James Hall, Contact

Browning Elem./HS Dist. #9
Indian Education Program
P.O. Box 610
Browning, MT 59417
 Ivan Small, Contact

Busby School
Indian Education Program
P.O. Box 38
Busby, MT 59016

Butte School District #1
Indian Education Program
111 N. Montana St.
Butte, MT 59701
 Daniel Ferriter, Contact

Culbertson Public School 17J/C
Indian Education Program
P.O. Box 615
Culbertson, MT 59218
 R. Stuber, Contact

Cut Bank School District #15
Indian Education Program
101 3rd Ave. SE
Cut Bank, MT 59427
 B. Parker, Contact

Dixon Elem. School District #9
Indian Education Program
P.O. Box 10
Dixon, MT 59831
 Keith Cable, Contact

Dodson Elem. School District 2A
Indian Education Program
P.O. Box 278
Dodson, MT 59524
 N. Sherman, Contact

Frazer School District 2-2B
Indian Education Program
P.O. Box 488
Frazer, MT 59225
 J. Marlett, Contact

Great Falls Public School
Indian Education Program
P.O. Box 2429
Great Falls, MT 59403
 D. Parisian, Contact

Hardin School District 17-H and 1
Indian Education Program
P.O. Box 310
Hardin, MT 59034
 R. Svee, Contact

Harlem P.S. District #12
Indian Education Program
P.O. Box 339
Harlem, MT 59526
 D. Wetzel, L. Brockie, Contacts

Havre Public School
Indian Education Program
P.O. Box 7791
Havre, MT 59501
 J. Erickson, L. Larson, Contacts

Hays/Lodge Pole Schools
Indian Education Program
P.O. Box 110
Hays, MT 59527
 R. Dahl, Contact

Hays/Lodge Pole Public S.D. #150
Indian Education Program
P.O. Box 880
Hays, MT 59527
 M. Allen, Contact

Heart Butte School District #1
Indian Education Program
P.O. Box 259
Heart Butte, MT 59448
 Jack Edmo, Dale Shupe, Contacts

Helena School District #1
Indian Education Program
P.O. Box 5417
Helena, MT 59604
 Ervin Winslow, Aaron Stansberry, Contacts

State Office of Public Instruction
Indian Education Program
State Capitol, Room 106
Helena, MT 59620
 R. Parsley, Contact

Lame Deer School
Indian Education Program
P.O. Box 96
Lame Deer, MT 59043
 C. Baker, B. Charette, Contacts

Northern Cheyenne Tribal Ed. Dept.
Indian Education Program
P.O. Box 307
Lame Deer, MT 59043
 Norma Bixby, Contact

Lodge Grass School District 2 & 27
Indian Education Program
Drawer AF
Lodge Grass, MT 59050
 R. Heppner, Contact

Missoula School District #1
Indian Education Program
215 S. 6th West
Missoula, MT 59801
 J. Block, Contact

Two Eagle River School
Flathead Indian Reservation
P.O. Box 362
Pablo, MT 59855
 (406) 675-0292 (phone & fax)
 Larry Anderson, Supt.
Grades 9-12. *Description*: Alternative school, tribally operated, serving 100 students focusing on academic improvement, cultural integration and parent involvement.

Polson School District #23
Indian Education Program
111 4th Ave. E
Polson, MT 59860
 A. Vies, Contact

Poplar Public School
Indian Education Program
P.O. Box 458
Poplar, MT 59255
 D. Sullivan, Contact

Pryor Public S.D. 2 & 3
Indian Education Program
P.O. Box 229
Pryor, MT 59066
 J. Tietema, Contact

Ronan School District #30
Indian Education Program
130 3rd Ave. N.W.
Ronan, MT 59864
 B. Halgren, Contact

St. Ignatius School District #28
Indian Education Program
P.O. Box 400
St. Ignatius, MT 59865
 S. Pasquale, Contact

Valier High/Elem. School
Indian Education Program
Box 528
Valier, MT 59486
 J. Brott, Contact

Wolf Point Public S.D. #45-45A
Indian Education Program
220 4th Ave. South
Wolf Point, MT 59201
 R. Kinna, Contact

Wyola School District #29
Indian Education Program
P.O. Box 66
Wyola, MT 59089
 TurnPlenty, Contact

NEBRASKA

Alliance City Schools
Indian Ed. Program
1604 Sweetwater
Alliance, NE 69301
Martin Petersen, Contact

Alliance Middle School
Indian Ed. Program
1115 Laramie St.
Alliance, NE 69301
Jim Bovee, Contact

Chadron Public Schools
Indian Ed. Program
Brooks Hall, 245 E. 10th
Chadron, NE 69337
Stephen Sexton, Contact

Lincoln Public Schools
Home-School Coord.
P.O. Box 82889
Lincoln, NE 68501
James Lapointe, Contact

Lincoln Public Schools
Indian Ed. Program
P.O. Box 82889
Lincoln, NE 68501
Dr. Deila Stiener, Contact

Macy Public School
Title V Director
P.O. Box 280
Macy, NE 68039
Mitchell Sheridan, Contact

Omaha Public Schools
Indian Ed. Program
3215 Cuming St.
Omaha, NE 68131
Sandra Mehojah, Contact

Rushville Public Schools
Indian Ed. Program
P.O. Box 590
Rushville, NE 69360
Dr. John Cruzeiro, Contact

Santee Public School
Indian Ed. Program
Route 2, Box 207
Santee, NE 68760
Jim Berryman, Contact

Scottsbluff/Gering Public Schools
Indian Ed. Program
2601 Broadway
Scottsbluff, NE 69361
Ronald Sylvester, Contact

Winnebago Public School
Title V Director
P.O. Box KK
Winnebago, NE 68071
Jeff Pope, Contact

Walthill Public School
Title V Director
Little & Main St., Box 3C
Walthill, NE 68067
Diane Bockman, Contact

Gordon Public Schools
Title V Director
P.O. Box 530
Gordon, NE 69343
Catherine Cole, Contact

NEW JERSEY

Fairfield Twp. Board of Education
Indian Education Program
RD #4, Ramah Rd., Box 337
Bridgeton, NJ 08302
Vivian Noblett, Contact

Mahwah Twp. Public Schools
Indian Education Program
Admin. Center, Ridge Rd.
Mahwah, NJ 07430
Barrent M. Henry, Marcella Perrano, Contacts

Ringwood Borough Schools
Indian Education Program
121 Carletondale Rd.
Ringwood, NJ 07456
Rudolph Selliti, Contact

Ringwood Borough Schools
Indian Education Program
EG Hewitt School, Sloatsburg Rd.
Ringwood, NJ 07456
Frank Van Dunk, Contact

NEVADA

Lander County School District
Indian Education Program
P.O. Box 1300
Battle Mountain, NV 89820
Steve Larsgaard, Contact

Carsen City School District
Indian Education Program
P.O. Box 603
Carson City, NV 89702
James Parry, Contact

Duckwater Shoshone Elementary School
P.O. Box 140038
Duckwater, NV 89314
(702) 863-0242 Fax 863-0301
Laurel Weaver, Education Administrator
Grades K-8. Duckwater Shoshone tribal school.
Instructors: Keith Honaker, grades 5-8; Lynn
Lawrence, grades K-3. Shelly Lupe

Elko County School District
Indian Education Program
Box 1012
Elko, NV 89801
Gretchen Greiner, Contact

Churchill County School District
Indian Education Program
545 E. Richards St.
Fallon, NV 89406
Dr. Bonnie Carter, Contact

Douglas County School District
Indian Education Program
P.O. Box 157
Gardnerville, NV 89410
Sherry Smokey, Contact

Mineral County School District
Indian Education Program
P.O. Box 1540
Hawthorne, NV 89415
Ihsan Qureshi, Contact

Clark County School District
Indian Education Program
600 North 9th St.
Las Vegas, NV 89101
Mary Willson, Contact

Pyramid Lake High School
Indian Education Program
P.O. Box 256
Nixon, NV 89424
Hal Saylor, Contact

Washoe County School District
Indian Education Program
1401 Old Virginia Rd.
Reno, NV 89511
Randy Malendez, Contact

Humboldt County School District
Indian Education Program
P.O. Box 1070
Winnemucca, NV 89445
Gerald H. Lugert, Contact

Lyon County School District
Indian Education Program
25 E. Goldfield Ave.
Yerington, NV 89447
Dr. J. Higginbotham, Contact

NEW MEXICO

Sky City Community School
Indian Education Program
P.O. Box 349
Acoma, NM 87034
Fred Vallo, Contact

Albuquerque Public Schools
Indian Education Program
3315 Louisiana Blvd. NE
Albuquerque, NM 871 10
Gus Keene, Contact

Bernalillo Public SchOols
Indian Education Program
Box 640
Bernalillo, NM 87004
Barbara Jiron-Sanchez, Contact

Huerfano School
Indian Education Program
Star Route 4, Box 5003
Bloomfield, NM 87413
Tom Nagahiro, Contact

Borrego Pass School
Indian Education Program
P.O. Drawer A
Crownpoint, NM 87313
William Poe, Contact

Crownpoint Community School
Indian Education Program
PO. Box 178
Crownpoint, NM 87313
Laura Garcia, Contact

Lake Valley Navajo School
Indian Education Program
P.O. Drawer E
Crownpoint, NM 87313
 Frances Vitali, Contact

Mariano Lake Community School
Indian Education Program
P.O. Box 498
Crownpoint, NM 87313
 Stanton D. Curtis, Contact

Standing Rock Community School
Indian Education Program
P.O. Drawer H
Crownpoint, NM 87313
 Sherry Woodside, Contact

Cuba Independent Schools
Indian Education Program
Box 70
Cuba, NM 87013
 Anita Tsinnijinnie, Contact

Torreon Day School
Indian Education Program
Star Route
Cuba, NM 87013
 Johnny Abeyta, Contact

Ojo Encino Day School
Indian Education Program
P.O. Box 57
Cuba, NM 87013
 Olsen Juan, Contact

Pueblo Pintado Community School
Indian Education Program
HCR 79, Box 80
Cuba, NM 87013
 Mike Craig, Contact

Dulce Independent Schools
Indian Education Program
P.O. Box 547
Dulce, NM 87528
 Gloria Bissmeyer, Contact

Espanola Municipal Schools
Indian Education Program
P.O. Box 249
Espanola, NM 87532
 Ursula Bowie, Contact

Santa Clara Day School
Indian Education Program
P.O. Box HHH
Espanola, NM 87532
 Solomon Padilla, Contact

Farmington Municipal School #5
Indian Education Program
P.O. Box 5850
Farmington, NM   87499
 Arlene Kirstine, Contact

Navajo Preparatory School
Indian Education Program
1200 W. Apache St.
Farmington, NM 87401
 Dr. Henry Schmitt, Contact

Wingate Elementary School
Indian Education Program
P.O. Box 1
Fort Wingate, NM 87316
 Diane Owens, Contact

Wingate Board of Education
Indian Education Program
P.O. Box 2
Fort Wingate, NM 87316
 Frank A. Shepard, Contact

Nenahnezad Boarding School
Indian Education Program
P.O. Box 337
Fruitland, NM 87416
 Rena Teller, Contact

Jemez Mountain School District 53
Indian Education Program
Box 121
Gallina, NM 87017
 Mary Robinson, Contact

Gallup-McKinley County Schools
Indian Education Program
P.O. Box 1318
Gallup, NM 87301
 Boyd Hogner, Contact

Grants-Cibola County Schools
Indian Education Program
P.O. Box 8
Grants, NM 87020
 Wilfred Toya, Contact

Bread Springs Day School
Indian Education Program
P.O. Box 1117
Gallup, NM 87313
 Richard Toledo, Contact

Isleta Elementary School
Indian Education Program
PO. Box 550
Isleta, NM 87022
 Joseph Green, Contact

Jemez Day School
Indian Education Program
P.O. Box 139
Jemez Pueblo, NM 87024
 Jonnito Complo, Contact

Jemez Valley Public Schools
Indian Education Program
Canyon Rt. Box 4A
Jemez Pueblo, NM 87024
 Paul Tosa, Contact

Canoncito Community School
Indian Education Program
P.O. Box 438
Laguna, NM 87026
Jim Byrnes

Laguna Elementary School
Indian Education Program
P.O. Box 191
Laguna, NM 87026
 Dale Hunt, Contact

Los Lunas Schools
Indian Education Program
Drawer 1300
Los Lunas, NM 87031
 Rebecca Garcia Lutz, Contact

Alamo Navajo School Board
Indian Education Program
P.O. Box 907
Magdalena, NM 87825
 Herman James, Contact

Magdalena Municipal School
Indian Education Program
P.O. Box 24
Magdalena, NM 87825
 Peggy Summers, Contact

Mescalero Apache Elementary School
Indian Education Program
P.O. Box 230
Mescalero, NM 88340
 Bill Butler, Contact

Crystal Boarding School
Indian Education Program
Navajo, NM 87328
 Lena R. Wilson, Contact

Penasco Independent School
Indian Education Program
P.O. Box 520
Penasco, NM 87553
 Michael Garcia, Contact

Ramah Navajo School Board
Indian Education Program
CPO Drawer H
Pine Hill, NM 87321
 Mary Cohoe, Contact

Baca Community School
Indian Education Program
P.O. Box 509
Prewitt, NM 87045
 Beatrice Woodward, Contact

Ruidoso Municipal Schools
Indian Education Program
200 Horton Cr.
Ruidoso, NM 88345
 Paul Wirth, Contact

San Felipe School
Indian Education Program
P.O. Box E
San Felipe Pueblo, NM 87001
 Edward Doler, Contact

San Juan Day School
Indian Education Program
P.O. Box 1077
San Juan Pueblo, NM 87566
 Mary Shoemaker, Contact

Zia Day School
Indian Education Program
San Ysidro, NM 87053
 Gilbert Lucero, Contact

Sanostee Day School
Indian Education Program
P.O. Box 159
Sanostee, NM 87461
 Jeanne Haskie, Contact

Pojoaque Valley School
Indian Education Program
P.O. Box 3468
Santa Fe, NM 87501
 Arthur Blea, Contact

San Ildefonso Day School
Indian Education Program
Route 5, Box 308
Santa Fe, NM 87501
 Mary Naranjo, Contact

Santa Fe Public Schools
Indian Education Program
610 Alta Vista St.
Santa Fe, NM 87501
  Wilson Romero, Contact

Santa Fe Indian School
Indian Education Program
P.O. Box 5335
Santa Fe, NM 87501
  Glenda Moffit, Contact

Tesuque Day School
Indian Education Program
Route 11, Box 2
Santa Fe, NM 87501
  Dolly Smith, Contact

Beclabito Day School
Indian Education Program
P.O. Box 1146
Shiprock, NM 87420
  Daniel Sosnowski, Contact

Central Consolidated Schools
Indian Education Program
P.O. Box 6002 T-4
Shiprock, NM 87420
  Herbert Frazier, Contact

Cove Day School
Indian Education Program
P.O. Box 3537
Shiprock, NM 87420
  Paul Yazzie, Contact

Shiprock Alt. High School
Indian Education Program
P.O. Box 1799
Shiprock, NM 87420
  Karen Bates, Contact

Taos Day School
Indian Education Program
P.O. Drawer X
Taos, NM 87571
  Robert Martinez, Contact

Taos Municipal Schools
Indian Education Program
213 Paseo Del Canon
Taos, NM 87571
  Robert Gonzalez, Contact

Dlo Ay Azhi Community School
Indian Education Program
P.O. Box 789
Thoreau, NM 87323
  David Braswell, Contact

Toadlena Boarding School
Indian Education Program
P.O. Box 857
Toadlena, NM 87324
  Evangeline Yazzie, Contact

Chuska Boarding School
Indian Education Program
P.O. Box 321
Tohatchi, NM 87325
  Bruce Fredericks, Contact

Tularosa Municipal Schools
Indian Education Program
504 First St.
Tularosa, NM 88352
  Michael Dorame, Contact

Chichiltah-Jones Ranch School
Indian Education Program
P.O. Box 365
Vanderwagon, NM 87236
  John Lewis Taylor, Contact

Zuni Public School District
Indian Education Program
P.O. Drawer A
Zuni, NM 87327
  Hayes Lewis, Contact

NEW YORK

Akron Central Schools
Indian Education Program
47 Bloomingdale Ave.
Akron, NY 14001
  Linda LaPress, Contact

Buffalo School District - School #19
Indian Education Program
97 W. Delavan
Buffalo, NY 14213
  Dr. Lloyd Elm, Contact

Center Moriches USD
Indian Education Program
511 Main St.
Center Moriches, NY 11934
  Arlene Crandall, Contact

N. Syracuse School District
Indian Education Program
CNS High Norstar Dr., Rt. 3
Cicero, NY 13039
  Ellie M. Peavey, Contact

E. Bloomfield Central School
Indian Education Program
Oakmount Ave.
East Bloomfield, NY 14443
  Pat Cowley, Contact

Salmon River Central Schools
Indian Education Program
Akwesasne Mohawk Project
Fort Covington, NY 12937
William Perkins, Principal
  Ann Marie FitzRandolph, Director

St. Regis Mohawk Reservation
Gowanda Central School District
Indian Education Program
Gowanda Elem. School, Rm. 107
Gowanda, NY 14070
  Carrine Martin, Contact

Rush-Henrietta Central School District
Indian Education Project
2034 Lehigh Station Rd.
Henrietta, NY 14467
(716) 359-5047
  Barbara Bethmann-Mahooty, Director
Grades K-12. *Description*: Teaches culture, history, arts & crafts; provides field trips for children; brings in speakers; teaches traditional dancing, singing, modified Mohawk language; provides workshops for teachers, and presentations on Native American culture. *Instructor*: Jeanette Miller.

Gowanda Central School District
Indian Education Program
Prospect St.
Irving, NY 14070

New York City Public Schools
Indian Education Program
234 W. 109th St., Rm. 507
New York, NY 10025
  Wanda Hunter, Contact

Niagara Falls City Schools
Indian Education Program
P.O. Box 399, 561 Portage Rd.
Niagara Falls, NY 14302
  C. Bianco/Loretta Hill, Contacts

Rochester City School District
Native American Resource Center
200 University Ave.
Rochester, NY 14605
  (716) 262-8970 Fax 262-8963
  Barbara Smoke, Director
Grades K-6. *Description*: Designed to meet the educational and cultural-related academic needs of Native American students in the District; teach students their cultural heritage through traditional arts & crafts & history. *Instructor*: Gloria Gearhart.

Salamanca City Schools
Indian Education Program
50 Iroquois Dr.
Salamanca, NY 14779
  Brian Mohr, Contact

Silver Creek Central School
Indian Education Program
Box 270, Dickinson St.
Silver Creek, NY 14136
  Audrey Thompson, Contact

Southampton Schools
Indian Education Program
P.O. Box 59, 70 Leland Lane
Southampton, NY 11968
  Sherry Smith, Contact

Syracuse City Schools
Indian Education Program
725 Harrison St.
Syracuse, NY 13210
  Jacob Thompson, Contact

N. Syracuse Central School District
Indian Education Program
5355 W. Taft Rd. N.
Syracuse, NY 13212
  Dr. William DeLucia, Contact

NORTH CAROLINA

Swain County Schools
Indian Education Program
Whittier School, P.O. Box U
Bryson City, NC 28713
  Sue Carpenter, Contact

Charlotte/Mecklenburg Schools
Indian Education Program
Euclid Center, 1501 Euclid Ave.
Charlotte, NC 28203
  Rosa Winfree, Contact

Cherokee Central School System
Indian Education Program
P.O. Box 134
Cherokee, NC 28719
(704) 497-6370
  Joyce Dugan, Director
Grades K-12. *Description*: Offers "state of the art"

curriculum with modern computer labs; alternative approach classrooms with integrated subjects.

Clinton City Schools
Indian Education Program
P.O. Box 646
Clinton, NC 28328
Farrell Carter, Contact

Sampson County Schools
Indian Education Program
Route 1, Box 107-B
Clinton, NC 28328
Joyce Locklear, Contact

Cabarrus County Schools
Indian Education Program
Box 388, 505 Hwy. 495
Concord, NC 28025
Robin R. Odell, Contact

Halifax County Schools
Indian Education Program
Box 143-A, Route 2
Enfield, NC 27823
Angela Richardson, Contact

Cumberland County Schools
Indian Education Program
P.O. Box 2357
Fayetteville, NC 28302
Trudy Locklear, Contact

Greensboro City Schools
Indian Education Program
712 N. Eugene, Drawer V
Greensboro, NC 27401
Derek Lowry, Contact

Halifax County Schools
Indian Education Program
P.O. Box 468
Halifax, NC 27839
Joseph Ray, Contact

Richmond County Schools
Indian Education Program
P.O. Box 1259
Hamlet, NC 28345
Trent Strickland, Contact

Scotland County Schools
Indian Education Program
233 E. Church St.
Laurinburg, NC 28352
Vicki Jones/Rose McNeil, Contacts

Harnett County Schools
Indian Education Program
P.O. Box 1029
Lillington, NC 27546
Dr. Sue Arnold, Contact

Robeson County School District
Indian Education Program
P.O. Box 2909
Lumberton, NC 28359
Maybelle Elk, Contact

Hoke County School System
Indian Education Program
P.O. Box 370
Raeford, NC 28376
Jerry Oxendine, Contact

Graham County Schools
Indian Education Program
P.O. Box 605
Robbinsville, NC 28771
Chip Carringer, Contact

Person County Schools
Indian Education Program
P.O. Drawer 1078
Roxboro, NC 27573
Leon Hanlin, Contact

Smokey Mountain High School
Indian Education Program
505 E. Main St.
Sylva, NC 28779
(704) 586-2311 Fax 586-5450
Nancy Sherrill, Coordinator
Grades 9-12. *Description*: Works directly with Indian students on attendance, academics, and special programs; parental involvement on health issues, rules and regulations, scholarships and special programs. *Social worker*: Vangie Stephens.

Warren County School District
Indian Education Program
P.O. Box 110
Warrenton, NC 27589
Ogletree Richardson, Contact

Columbus County Schools
Indian Education Program
P.O. Box 279
Whiteville, NC 28472
Kenwood Royal, Contact

Smokey Mountain Elementary School
Indian Education Program
Rte. 1, Box 242
Whittier, NC 28789
(704) 586-2334 Fax 586-5450
Clarence Hubbell, Director
Grades K-8. *Description*: Provides tutoring services, and cultural enrichment programs. *Instructors*: Rose Long & Barbara Gilbert.

Hertford Co. Board of Ed.
Indian Education Program
P.O. Box 158
Winton, NC 27986
Arthur Brown, Contact

NORTH DAKOTA

Belcourt School District
Title V Director
P.O. Box 440
Belcourt, ND 58316
Mike Vann, Contact

Ojibwa Indian School
Title V Director
P.O. Box 600
Belcourt, ND 58316
Cathie Lafountaine, Contact

Bismarck Public School District
Title V Director
400 Avenue E East
Bismarck, ND 58501
Sue Kramer, Contact

Theodore Jamerson Elementary School
Indian Education Program
3315 University Dr.
Bismarck, ND 58504
Sam Azure, Contact

Devils Lake Public School
Title V Director
325 7th St.
Devils Lake, ND 58301
Robert Gibson, Contact

Dunseith Indian Day School
P.O. Box 759
Dunseith, ND 58329
Karen Gillis, Contact

Dunseith Public School District
Indian Education Program
P.O. Box 789
Dunseith, ND 58329
Myron Haugse, Contact

Fargo Public Schools
Title V Director
1104 2nd Ave. South
Fargo, ND 58103
Renee Perala, Contact

Fort Totten Public School
Title V Director
P.O. Box 239
Fort Totten, ND 58335
Adelaine Trottier, Contact

Tate Topa Tribal School
Title V Director
P.O. Box 199
Fort Totten, ND 58335
Evelyn Cavenvagh, Contact

Fort Yates Public School
Home/School Coord.
P.O. Box 428
Fort Yates, ND 58538
Della No Heart, Contact

Standing Rock Community School
Title V Director
P.O. Box 377
Fort Yates, ND 58538
Sherman Laubach, Contact

Garrison Public School District
Title V Director
Box 249
Garrison, ND 58540
Hy Schlieve, Contact

Grand Forks Public Schools
Title V Director
P.O. Box 6000
Grand Forks, ND 58201
Glenn Gilbraigh, Contact

Lake Agassiz Elem. School
Indian Education Program
605 Stanford Rd.
Grand Forks, ND 58203
Sheri Baker, Contact

Twin Buttes Public School
Title V Director
RR 1, Box 65
Halliday, ND 58636
Eugene Holen, Contact

Hazen Public School
Title V Director
Hazen, ND 58545
  Jerry Enget, Contact

Mandaree Public School
Home School Liaison
P.O. Box 488
Mandaree, ND 58757
  Wayne White Eagle, Contact

New Town Public School District
Title V Director
P.O. Box 700
New Town, ND 58767
  Marc Bluestone, Contact

Parshall School District
Title V Director
P.O. Box 158
Parshall, ND 58770
  Henry Friedt, Contact

Rolette Public School District
Title V Director
P.O. Box 97
Rolette, ND 58366
  Merrill Krueger, Contact

Mt. Pleasant School District
Indian Education Program
RR 1, Box 93
Rolla, ND 58367
  Norman Baumgarn

White Shield School District
Title V Director
HC 1, Box 45
Roseglen, ND 58775
  Clyde Bearstail, Contact

St. John School District
Title V Director
P.O. Box 200
St. John, ND 58369
  Donald Davis, Contact

Selfridge School District
School Consultant
P.O. Box 45
Selfridge, ND 58568
  Charles Fields, Contact

Sheyenne Public School
Indian Education Program
P.O. Box 67
Sheyenne, ND 58374
  Myron Jury, Contact

Solen School District
Title V Director
P.O. Box 128
Solen, ND 58570
  Bruce Houck, Contact

Eight Mile School District
Title V Director
P.O. Box 239
Trenton, ND 58853
  Lincoln Napton, Contact

Wahpeton Indian School
Title V Director
832 8th St. N.
Wahpeton, ND 58075
  Bob Hall, Contact

Warwick Public School District
Indian Education Program
P.O. Box 7
Warwick, ND 58381
  Rocklyn Cofer, Contact

Williston Public School
Title V Director
P.O. Box 1407
Williston, ND 58801
  Valli Helstad, Contact

Warwick Public School District
Title V Director
P.O. Box 7
Warwick, ND 58381
  Kelly Gannon, Contact

OHIO

Columbus Public Schools
Indian Education Program
873 Walcutt Ave.
Columbus, OH 43219
  Richard Snide, Contact

Lorain Public Schools
Indian Education Program
1020 Seventh St.
Lorain, OH 44052
  Gerald Kordelski, Contact

OKLAHOMA

Achille Public Schools
Indian Education/Title V
P.O. Box 820
Achille, OK 74720

Vanoss Public School
Indian Education/Title V
Rt. 5, Box 119
Ada, OK 74820

Ada City Schools, I.S.D. #19
Indian Education/Title V
P.O. Box 1359
Ada, OK 74820

Byng School I-16
Indian Education/Title V
Rt. 3
Ada, OK 74820

Latta Public School
Indian Education/Title V
Rt. 8, Box 811
Ada, OK 74820

Pickett-Center School
Indian Education/Title V
P.O. Box 1363
Ada, OK 74820

Adair Public Schools
Indian Education/Title V
P.O. Box 197
Adair, OK 74330

Afton Public School
Indian Education/Title V
P.O. Box 100
Afton, OK 74331

Agra Public School I-134
Indian Education/Title V
P.O. Box 279
Agra, OK 74824

Albion Grade School
Indian Education/Title V
P.O. Box 189
Albion, OK 74521

Alex Public Schools
Indian Education/Title V
P.O. Box 188
Alex, OK 73002

Allen Public School
Indian Education/Title V
Box 430
Allen, OK 74852

Anadarko School District
Indian Education/Title V
1400 S. Mission
Anadarko, OK 73005

Riverside Indian School
Indian Education/Title V
Route 1
Anadarko, OK 73005

Antlers Public Schools
Indian Education/Title V
P.O Drawer 627
Antlers, OK 74523

Boone/Apache Public Schools
Indian Education/Title V
Rt. 2, Box 177
Apache, OK 73006

Ardmore City Schools
Indian Education/Title V
P.O. Box 1709
Ardmore, OK 73402

Dickson ISD #77
Indian Education/Title V
Rt. 4, Box 122
Ardmore, OK 73401

Plainview Public Schools
Indian Education/Title V
1140 S. Plainview Rd.
Ardmore, OK 73401

Arkoma Public School
Indian Education/Title V
P.O. Box 349
Arkoma, OK 74901

Tushka Public Schools
Indian Education/Title V
Rt. 4, Box T 2630
Atoka, OK 74525

Atoka Public Schools
Indian Education/Title V
P.O. Box 720
Atoka, OK 74525

Harmony School
Indian Education/Title V
Route 2, Box 2215
Atoka, OK 74525

Schools

Barnsdale Public School District I-29
Indian Education/Title V
P.O. Box 629
Barnsdale, OK 74002

Bartlesville School District I-30
Indian Education/Title V
P.O. Box 1357
Bartlesville, OK 74005

Tri-County Area Voc-Tech
Indian Education/Title V
6101 Nowata Rd.
Bartlesville, OK 74006

Battiest Public School I-71
Indian Education/Title V
P.O. Box 199
Battiest, OK 74722

Bennington ISD
Indian Education/Title V
P.O. Box 10
Bennington, OK 74723

Binger/Olney ISD #15
Indian Education/Title V
P.O. Box 280
Binger, OK 73009

Blackwell Public Schools I-45
Indian Education/Title V
934 South First
Blackwell, OK 74631

Blanchard Public Schools
Indian Education/Title V
P.O. Box 2620
Blanchard, OK 73010

Rock Creek I.S.D.
Indian Education/Title V
P.O. Box 208
Bokchito, OK 74849

Bokoshe Public Schools I-26
Indian Education/Title V
P.O. Box 158
Bokoshe, OK 74930

Boswell School I-1
Indian Education/Title V
Box 839
Boswell, OK 74727

Bowlegs Public School
Indian Education/Title V
P.O. Box 88
Bowlegs, OK 74830

Boynton Public School
Indian Education/Title V
P.O. Box 97
Boynton, OK 74422

Braggs Public Schools
Indian Education/Title V
P.O. Box 59
Braggs, OK 74423

Braman School
Indian Education/Title V
P.O. Box 130
Braman, OK 74632

Bristow Schools
Indian Education/Title V
134 West 9th
Bristow, OK 74010

Broken Bow ISD #74
Indian Education/Title V
108 W. Fifth St.
Broken Bow, OK 74728

Lukfata School District #9
Indian Education/Title V
P.O. Box 940
Broken Bow, OK 74728

Cache Public School
Indian Education/Title V
P.O. Box 418
Cache, OK 73527

Caddo Public School
Indian Education/Title V
P.O. Box 128
Caddo, OK 74729

Calera Public School
Indian Education/Title V
P.O. Box 386
Calera, OK 74730

Calumet School
Indian Education/Title V
P.O. Box 10
Calumet, OK 73014

Calvin Public School ISD #48
Indian Education/Title V
P.O. Box 127
Calvin, OK 74531

Cameron School Grades 1-12
Indian Education/Title V
P.O. Box 190
Cameron, OK 74932

Caney Public School
Indian Education/Title V
P.O. Box 368
Caney, OK 74533

Canton/Longdale Public School I-105
Indian Education/Title V
P.O. Box 639
Canton, OK 73724

Carnegie ISD 33
Indian Education/Title V
P.O. Box 159
Carnegie, OK 73015

Catoosa ISD #2
Indian Education/Title V
2000 S. Cherokee
Catoosa, OK 74015

Checotah ISD 19
Indian Education/Title V
310 Southwest Second
Checotah, OK 74426

Chelsea ISD #3
Indian Education/Title V
306 West 6th St.
Chelsea, OK 74016

Choctaw/Nicoma Park P.S.
Indian Education/Title V
12880 N.E. 10th
Choctaw, OK 73020

Tiawah School
Indian Education/Title V
Rt. 7, Box 257
Claremore, OK 74017

Verdigris School I-8
Indian Education/Title V
6101 S.W. Verdigris Rd.
Claremore, OK 74017

Sequoyah Public Schools
Indian Education/Title V
Rt. 3, Box 200
Claremore, OK 74017

Claremore Public Schools
Indian Education/Title V
P.O. Box 907
Claremore, OK 74018
 (918) 341-5270 Fax 341-8447
 Pam Leuthen, Counselor
Grades 1-12. Provides tutorial program,
and counseling for grades 9-12.

Justus Public School District 0
Indian Education/Title V
P.O. Box 864
Claremore, OK 74018

Clayton Public School District I-10
Indian Education/Title V
P.O. Box 190
Clayton, OK 74536

Clinton Public Schools
Indian Education/Title V
P.O. Box 729
Clinton, OK 73601

Coalgate Public Schools I-1
Indian Education Program
P.O Box 1368
Coalgate, OK 74538

Cottonwood School
Indian Education/Title V
P.O. Box 347
Coalgate, OK 74538

Colbert Public Schools
Indian Education/Title V
Colbert, OK 74733

Colcord Public Schools
Indian Education/Title V
P.O. Box 188
Colcord, OK 74338

Mosseley Public School
Indian Education/Title V
Rt. 4, Box 88
Colcord, OK 74338

Commerce Public School District I-18
Indian Education/Title V
420 D St.
Commerce, OK 74339

Collinsville Public School I-6
Indian Education/Title V
2400 W. Broadway
Collinsville, OK 74021

Coweta Public School I-17
Indian Education/Title V
P.O. Box 550
Coweta, OK 74429

Butner Schools
Indian Education/Title V
Box 157
Cromwell, OK 74837

Crowder Public Schools
Indian Education/Title V
P.O. Box B
Crowder, OK 74430

Cushing Public Schools
Indian Education/Title V
P.O Drawer 1609
Cushing, OK 74023

Custer Public School
Indian Education/Title V
P.O. Box 200
Custer City, OK 73639

Davis Public School
Indian Education/Title V
400 East Atlanta
Davis, OK 73030

Delaware Public School I-30
Indian Education/Title V
P.O. Box 69
Delaware, OK 74027

Leach School District 14
Indian Education/Title V
Box 211
Delaware, OK 74368

Depew School District
Indian Education/Title V
Box 257
Depew, OK 74028

Gypsy School D-12
Indian Education/Title V
Route 1, Box 400
Depew, OK 74028

Dewar Public Schools
Indian Education/Title V
P.O. Box 790
Dewar, OK 74431

Dibble Public Schools I-002
Indian Education/Title V
P.O. Box 9
Dibble, OK 73031

Olive Independent S.D. I-17
Indian Education/Title V
Rt. 1, Box 337
Drumright, OK 74030

Durant Public Schools I-72
Indian Education/Title V
118 North 7th
Durant, OK 74701

Silo School
Indian Education Program
HC-62, Box 227
Durant, OK 74701
 (405) 924-7000 Fax 924-7045
 Sue Hopkins, Director

Grades K-12. *Description*: Provides tutorial services, arts & crafts and music programs. *Instructors*: Thelma Andrew, Michael Payne, Dolores Whiye, Sue Hopkins.

Dustin Public Schools
Indian Education/Title V
P.O. Box 660
Dustin, OK 74893

Edmond Public School District I-12
Indian Education/Title V
215 North Blvd.
Edmond, OK 73034

Elgin Public Schools I-16
Indian Education/Title V
P.O. Box 369
Elgin, OK 73583

Stony Point School #124
Indian Education/Title V
Rt. 1, Box 2200
Elgin, OK 73538

Elmore City Public Schools
Indian Education/Title V
P.O. Box 99
Elmore City, OK 73035

Darlington School
Indian Education/Title V
Box 145-A Rt. 3
El Reno, OK 73036

El Reno ISD #34
Indian Education/Title V
P.O. Box 580
El Reno, OK 73036

Enid Public Schools
Indian Education Program
831 E. Oklahoma
Enid, OK 73701
 (405) 242-7185 Fax 249-3565
 Margie E. Marney, Director
Grades K-12. *Description*: Provides tutoring services, cultural activities and education of Indian customs and heritage. *Instructors*: Marsha Booth, Veryl Mills, Lisa Pritchard, Chris Smith.

Eufaula Public Schools I-1
Indian Education/Title V
P.O. Box 609
Eufaula, OK 74432

Woodland Public Schools
Indian Education/Title V
P.O. Box 487
Fairfax, OK 74637

Fairland Public Schools I-31
Indian Education/Title V
P.O. Box 689
Fairland, OK 74343

Fanshawe School District #39
Indian Education/Title V
P.O. Box 55
Fanshawe, OK 74935

McLish Public Schools
Indian Education/Title V
I-22, Box 29
Fittstown, OK 74842

Ft. Cobb/Broxton Public S.D. I-17
Indian Education/Title V
P.O. Box 130
Ft. Cobb, OK 73038

Fort Gibson Public Schools
Indian Education/Title V
P.O. Box 280
Fort Gibson, OK 74434

Ft. Towson Schools
Indian Education Program
P.O. Box 39
Ft. Towson, OK 74735
 (405) 873-2712
 James Gibbs, Supt.
Grades K-12. *Description*: Home liaison/curriculum aide to improve knowledge of Indian history and culture and home/school communications.

Foyil Public Schools
Indian Education/Title V
P.O. Box 49
Foyil, OK 74031

Fox Public Schools
Indian Education/Title V
P.O. Box 248
Fox, OK 73435

Frederick Public Schools
Indian Education/Title V
P.O. Box 370
Frederick, OK 73542

Gans Public School
Indian Education/Title V
P.O. Box 52
Gans, OK 74936

Geary School District I-80
Indian Education/Title V
P.O. Box 188
Geary, OK 73040

Glenpool Public Schools
Indian Education/Title V
P.O. Box 1149
Glenpool, OK 74033

Gore Public School
Indian Education/Title V
P.O. Box 580
Gore, OK 74435

Gum Springs School D-69
Indian Education/Title V
Rt. 1, Box 129-T
Gore, OK 74435

Grandfield Public Schools
Indian Education/Title V
Box 639
Grandfield, OK 73546

Grove Public Schools
Indian Education/Title V
P.O. Box 789
Grove, OK 74344

Guthrie Public School
Indian Education/Title V
802 East Vilas
Guthrie, OK 73044

Schools

Haileyville Public Schools
Indian Education/Title V
P.O. Box 29
Haileyville, OK 74546

Hammon Public School I-66
Indian Education/Title V
P.O. Box 279
Hammon, OK 73650

Hanna Public Schools
Indian Education/Title V
P.O. Box "H"
Hanna, OK 74845

Harrah Public School District ISD-1007
Indian Education Program
20670 Walker St.
Harrah, OK 73045
 (405) 454-6244 Fax 454-6844
 Vernon L. Pierce, Assistant Supt.
Grades K-12. *Description*: Provides tutorial services, classroom/activity supplies, and a Native American Heritage Program. *Instructors*: Connie Norris, Cecillia Ann Fujii, Frances Benson, Laura Roberts.

Hartshorne Public School Dist. I-1
Indian Education/Title V
520 S. Fifth St.
Hartshorne, OK 74547

Healdton Public School
Indian Education/Title V
432 West Texas
Healdton, OK 73438

Haskell ISD #2
Indian Education/Title V
P.O. Box 278
Haskell, OK 74436

Haworth Public School
Indian Education/Title V
Box 99
Haworth, OK 74740

Heavener Public School
Indian Education/Title V
Box 698
Heavener, OK 74937

Wilson School I-7
Indian Education/Title V
Rt. 1, Box 274
Henryetta, OK 74437

Henryetta Public Schools
Indian Education/Title V
618 W. Main
Henryetta, OK 74437

Ryal School
Indian Education/Title V
Route 2
Henryetta, OK 74437

Hodgen Public School
Indian Education/Title V
P.O. Box 69
Hodgen, OK 74939

Holdenville Public School
Indian Education/Title V
P.O. Box 977
Holdenville, OK 74848

Moss Public School I-01
Indian Education/Title V
Rt. 2, Box 57
Holdenville, OK 74848

Hominy ISD #38
Indian Education/Title V
P.O. Box 400
Hominy, OK 74035

Howe Public Schools
Indian Education/Title V
P.O. Box 259
Howe, OK 74940

Hugo City Public Schools
Indian Education/Title V
208 N. 2nd St.
Hugo, OK 74743

Hulbert Public School ISD #16
Indian Education/Title V
P.O. Box 125
Hulbert, OK 74441

Lost City Public School
Indian Education/Title V
Route 3
Hulbert, OK 74441

Norwood School
Indian Education/Title V
Rt. 1, Box 537
Hulbert OK 74441

Shady Grove School
Indian Education/Title V
Rt. 2, Box 438
Hulbert, OK 74441

Idabel ISD #5
Indian Education/Title V
P.O. Box 29
Idabel, OK 74745

McCurtain Co. Title V
Indian Education/Title V
Court Plaza Bldg.
Idabel, OK 74745

Indiahoma Public School
Indian Education/Title V
P.O. Box 8
Indiahoma, OK 73552

Inola Public School
Indian Education/Title V
P.O. Box 1149
Inola, OK 74036

Jay Public Schools ISD #1
Indian Education/Title V
P.O. Box C-1
Jay, OK 74346

Jenks Public Schools
Indian Education Program
205 East "B" St.
Jenks, OK 74037
 (918) 299-4411 ext. 213 Fax 299-9197
 Sharon Pyeatte, Director
Grades K-12. *Description*: Provides academic enhancement and advancement through tutoring, evening and/or summer school programs. Cultural enrichment through community and school assemblies, classes, and activities.

Jennings Public School
Indian Education/Title V
Drawer 439
Jennings, OK 74038

Jones Public School
Indian Education/Title V
P.O. Box 790
Jones, OK 73049

Kansas Public School
Indian Education/Title V
P.O. Box 196
Kansas, OK 74347

Kellyville Public Schools
Indian Education/Title V
P.O. Box 99
Kellyville, OK 74039

Keota Public Schools
Indian Education/Title V
P.O. Box 160
Keota, OK 74941

Ketchum Public Schools
Indian Education/Title V
P.O. Box 720
Ketchum, OK 74349

Kingston Public School
Indian Education/Title V
P.O. Box 370
Kingston, OK 73439

Kinta Public Schools
Indian Education/Title V
Box 219
Kinta, OK 74552

Kiowa Public Schools
Indian Education/Title V
P.O. Box 6
Kiowa, OK 74553

Konawa Public Schools
Indian Education/Title V
Rt. 1, Box 3
Konawa, OK 74849

Lane School
Indian Education/Title V
P.O. Box 39
Lane, OK 74555

Lawton Public Schools
Indian Education/Title V
753 Fort Sill Blvd.
Lawton, OK 73501
 (405) 357-6900 Fax 355-0789
 Dr. Carolyn D. Mayes, Program Director
Grades 1-12. *Description*: Tutoring services in reading and math for students in grades 1-7, and support services for students in grades 7-12. *Instructors*: Carla Whiteman, Ardith McGee, Shirley Kaulaity, Tammy Chasenah, Vera Hudson, and Sandra Mithlo.

Leflore School Board
Indian Education/Title V
P.O. Box 147
Leflore, OK 74942

Leon Public Schools
Indian Education/Title V
P.O. Box 506
Leon, OK 73441

Lexington Public Schools
Indian Education/Title V
420 NE 4th
Lexington, OK 73051

Locust Grove Public S.D. #17
Indian Education/Title V
P.O. Box 399
Locust Grove, OK 74352

Lone Grove School
Indian Education/Title V
Box 1330
Lone Grove, OK 73443

Lookeba-Sickley Public School
Indian Education/Title V
P.O. Box 34
Lookeba, OK 73053

Macomb Public School
Indian Education/Title V
P.O. Box 10
Macomb, OK 74852

Madill ISD #2
Indian Education/Title V
601 W. McArthur
Madill, OK 73446

Mannford Public Schools
Indian Education/Title V
P.O. Box 100
Mannford, OK 74044

Marble City School District 35
Indian Education/Title V
P.O. Box 1
Marble City, OK 74945

Marietta School District I-016
Indian Education/Title V
P.O. Box 289
Marietta, OK 73448

Mason School District I-2
Indian Education/Title V
Rt. 1, Box 143B
Mason, OK 74859

Maud ISD #117
Indian Education/Title V
Box 130
Maud, OK 74854

Maysville Public Schools I-7
Indian Education/Title V
Box 780
Maysville, OK 73057

McAlester Public Schools
Indian Education/Title V
P.O. Box 1027
McAlester, OK 74502

McLoud Public Schools
Indian Education/Title V
P.O. Box 40
McLoud, OK 74851

Meeker Public School
Indian Education/Title V
P.O. Box 68
Meeker, OK 74855

Sparks Schools
Indian Education/Title V
P.O. Box 68
Meeker, OK 74855

Milburn Public School
Indian Education Program
P.O. Box 276, 8th & Grande
Milburn, OK 73450
 (405) 443-5522 Fax 443-5303
 Richard McKee, Supt.
Instructor: Debbie Speers.

Mill Creek Public Schools
Indian Education/Title V
Box 105
Mill Creek, OK 74856

Moffett Elementary School
Indian Education/Title V
P.O. Box 180
Moffett, OK 74946

Monroe Elementary School
Indian Education/Title V
P.O. Box 10
Monroe, OK 74947

Moore Public School District I-02
Indian Education/Title V
2009 N. Janeway
Moore, OK 73160

Morris Public Schools
Indian Education/Title V
P.O. Box 80
Morris, OK 74445

Liberty Public Schools I-14
Indian Education/Title V
Rt. 1, Box 354
Mounds, OK 74047

Mounds Public Schools
Indian Education Program
P.O. Box 189
Mounds, OK 74047
 (918) 827-6758 Fax 827-3704
 Yvette Britt, Director
Grades K-12. *Description*: Provides tutorial services, Indian cultural awareness programs, and career counseling to Indian students in the Mounds Public Schools.

Mountain View/Gotebo Public School
Indian Education/Title V
P.O. Box B
Mountain View, OK 73062

Moyers Public School
Indian Education/Title V
P.O. Box 88
Moyer, OK 74557

Belfonte School District 50
Indian Education/Title V
Rt. 3, Box 282
Muldrow, OK 74948

Liberty School
Indian Education/Title V
Rt. 3, Box 143-2
Muldrow, OK 74948

Muldrow Public Schools
Indian Education/Title V
P.O. Box 660
Muldrow, OK 74948

Hilldale Public Schools, I-29
Indian Education/Title V
Rt. 8, Box 141
Muskogee, OK 74401

Muskogee City Schools
Indian Education/Title V
570 North 6th St.
Muskogee, OK 74401

Nashoba Public Schools
Indian Education/Title V
P.O. Box 17
Nashoba, OK 74558

Newcastle Public Schools I-1
Indian Education Program
101 N. Main St.
Newcastle, OK 73065
 (405) 387-4304 Fax 387-2891
 Sharon Giles, Director
Grades K-12. *Description*: Provides academic tutoring and cultural heritage programs. *Instructors*: Deana Sykes, Georgia Small, Julie Wickersham.

Noble Public School I-40
Indian Education/Title V
P.O. Box 499
Noble, OK 73068

Norman Public Schools
Indian Education/Title V
1133 W. Main
Norman, OK 73069

Little Axe Schools
Indian Education/Title V
Rt. 2, Box 266
Norman, OK 73071

Nowata Public School
Indian Education/Title V
707 West Osage
Nowata, OK 74048

Oaks Mission Public Schools
Indian Education/Title V
P.O. Box 160
Oaks, OK 74359

Okay Public School
Indian Education/Title V
P.O. Box 188
Okay, OK 74446

Okemah Public Schools
Indian Education/Title V
Second & Date Sts.
Okemah, OK 74859

Oklahoma City Public Schools
Indian Education/Title V
900 N. Klein
Oklahoma City, OK 73106

Putman City Independent School
Indian Education/Title V
5700 NW 40th
Oklahoma City, OK 73122

Western Heights P.S. I-51
Indian Education/Title V
8401 SW 44th St.
Oklahoma City, OK 73179

Nuyaka School
Indian Education/Title V
Rt. 4, Box 140
Okmulgee, OK 74447

Okmulgee Public Schools District I-1
Indian Education/Title V
P.O. Box 1346
Okmulgee, OK 74447

Oktaha Public Schools
Indian Education/Title V
P.O. Box 9
Oktaha, OK 74437

Oologah-Talala Public School
Indian Education/Title V
P.O. Box 189
Oologah, OK 74053

Paden Schools
Indian Education/Title V
Box 370
Paden, OK 74860

Panama Public Schools
Indian Education/Title V
P.O. Box 550
Panama, OK 74951

Keys Elementary School
Indian Education Program
HC 69, Box 151
Park Hill, OK 74451
  (918) 456-4501 Fax 456-7559
  Charles A. Gourd, PhD, Director
Grades K-6. *Description*: Provides transitional bilingual education. *Instructors*: Norma Fourkiller, Kelly Porter, Kathy Roark.

Pauls Valley School I-18
Indian Education/Title V
P.O. Box 780
Pauls Valley, OK 73075

Whitebread School
Indian Education/Title V
Rt. 3, Box 214
Pauls Valley, OK 73975

Pawhuska School District I-2
Indian Education/Title V
1505 N. Lynn Ave.
Pawhuska, OK 74056

Pawnee Public Schools
Indian Education/Title V
Box 615
Pawnee, OK 74059

Peggs School
Indian Education/Title V
P.O. Box 49
Peggs, OK 74452

Pittsburg Public School
Indian Education/Title V
General Delivery
Pittsburg, OK 74560

Pocola Public Schools
Indian Education/Title V
P.O. Box 640
Pocola, OK 74902

Ponca City Public S.D. I-71
Indian Education/Title V
P.O. Drawer 271
Ponca City, OK 74602

Porter Consolidated District I-365
Indian Education/Title V
P.O. Box 120
Porter, OK 74454

Porum Public Schools
Indian Education/Title V
P.O. Box 189
Porum, OK 74455

Poteau Public S.D. I-29
Indian Education/Title V
307 Mockingbird Lane
Poteau, OK 74953

Prue Public Schools
Indian Education/Title V
P.O. Box 130
Prue, OK 74060

Quapaw Public Schools
Indian Education/Title V
P.O. Box 130
Prue, OK 74060

Osage Elementary
Indian Education/Title V
P.O. Box 579
Pryor, OK 74362

Purcell Public School K-12
Indian Education/Title V
919 N. Ninth St.
Purcell, OK 73080

Quinton Public S.D. I-17
Indian Education/Title V
P.O. Box 670
Quinton, OK 74561

Rattan Public School
Indian Education/Title V
P.O. Box 44
Rattan, OK 74562

Red Oak School I-2
Indian Education/Title V
P.O. Box 310
Red Oak, OK 74563

Frontier Public Schools I-4
Indian Education/Title V
P.O. Box 130
Red Rock, OK 73651

Ringling Public Schools
Indian Education/Title V
P.O. Box 1010
Ringling, OK 73456

Ripley Public School Dist. I-3
Indian Education/Title V
P.O. Box 97
Ripley, OK 74062

Kenwood School
Indian Education/Title V
Rt. 1, Box 179
Salina, OK 74365

Salina Public S.D. I-16
Indian Education/Title V
PO. Box 98
Salina, OK 74365

Wickliffe Public School
Indian Education/Title V
Rt. 1, Box 130
Salina, OK 74365

Brushy School District D-36
Indian Education/Title V
P.O. Box 507
Sallisaw, OK 74955

Central Public Schools
Indian Education/Title V
Rt. 1, Box 36
Sallisaw, OK 74955

Sallisaw Public School I-1
Indian Education/Title V
604 E. Cherokee
Sallisaw, OK 74955

Anderson Elementary School
Indian Education/Title V
Rt. 5, Box 161
Sand Springs, OK 74063

Sand Springs Public Schools
Indian Education Program
P.O. Box 970
Sand Springs, OK 74063
  (918) 245-1088
  Mrs. Jerre Brokaw, Director
Grades K-12. *Description*: Provides tutoring, cultural programs, and college/vocational assistance. Staff is of Indian descent.

Sapupla Public School ISD #33
Indian Education/Title V
1 S. Mission
Sapulpa, OK 74066

Lone Star School
Indian Education/Title V
P.O. Box 1170
Sapulpa, OK 74067

Sasakwa I.S.D. I-10
Indian Education/Title V
PO. Box 323
Sasakwa, OK 74867

Savanna Public Schools
Indian Education/Title V
P.O. Box 266
Savanna, OK 74565

Schulter Public Schools
Indian Education/Title V
P.O. Box 203
Schulter, OK 74460

Seiling Public School
Indian Education/Title V
P.O. Box 780
Seiling, OK 73668

Pleasant Grove S.D. I-5
Indian Education/Title V
Rt. 1, Box 247
Seminole, OK 74868

Seminole I.S.D. #1
Indian Education/Title V
P.O. Box 1031
Seminole, OK 74868

Strother Public School
Indian Education/Title V
Rt. 3, Box 265
Seminole, OK 74868

Varnum School
Indian Education/Title V
Rt. 4, Box 148
Seminole, OK 74868

Shady Point Elementary
Indian Education/Title V
P.O. Drawer C
Shady Point, OK 74956

Bethel Public School ISD #3
Indian Education/Title V
36000 Clear Pond Dr.
Shawnee, OK 74801

North Rock Creek S.D. 10
Indian Education/Title V
42400 Garretts Lake Rd.
Shawnee, OK 74801

Pleasant Grove School
Indian Education/Title V
1927 E. Walnut
Shawnee, OK 74801

Shawnee Public School I-93
Indian Education/Title V
326 N. Union St.
Shawnee, OK 74801

Skiatook Public Schools
Indian Education/Title V
710 S. Osage
Skiatook, OK 74070

Smithville Public School I-14
Indian Education/Title V
P.O. Box 8
Smithville, OK 74957

Soper Public School
Indian Education/Title V
P.O. Box 149
Soper, OK 74759

Spavinaw School
Indian Education/Title V
Box 108
Spavinaw, OK 74336

Sperry Public Schools
Indian Education/Title V
P.O. Box 610
Sperry, OK 74073

Spiro Schools
Indian Education/Title V
600 W. Broadway
Spiro, OK 74959

Springer Public Schools
Indian Education/Title V
P.O Box 249
Springer, OK 73458

Sterling Public Schools
Indian Education/Title V
P.O. Box 158
Sterling, OK 73567

Stidham Public School D-16
Indian Education/Title V
General Delivery
Stidham, OK 74461

Stigler Public Schools
Indian Education/Title V
302 N.W. E St.
Stigler, OK 74462

Stillwater Independent School
Indian Education/Title V
314 S. Lewis
Stillwater, OK 74074

Bell Elementary School
Indian Education/Title V
P.O. Box 346
Stilwell, OK 74960

Cave Springs Public Schools
Indian Education/Title V
Rt. 1, Box 300
Stilwell, OK 74960

Dahlonegah Elem. School District #29
Indian Education/Title V
Rt. 1, Box 351
Stilwell, OK 74960

Greasy Public School
Indian Education/Title V
P.O. Box 467
Stilwell, OK 74960

Maryetta Public School District 22
Indian Education/Title V
Rt. 4, Box 413
Stilwell, OK 74960

Peavine S.D. #19
Indian Education/Title V
P.O. Box 389
Stilwell, OK 74960

Rocky Mountain S.D. 24
Indian Education/Title V
Rt. 1, Box 665
Stilwell, OK 74960

Stilwell Public School
Indian Education/Title V
Highway 100 West
Stilwell, OK 74960

Zion School
Indian Education/Title V
P.O. Box 347
Stilwell, OK 74960

Stonewall Schools
Indian Education/Title V
Rt. 2, Box 1-A
Stonewall, OK 74871

Stratford Public S.D. I-2
Indian Education/Title V
241 N. Oak St., Box 589
Stratford, OK 74872

Stringtown ISD #7
Indian Education/Title V
P.O. Box 130
Stringtown, OK 74569

Stroud Independent S.D. 54
Indian Education/Title V
212 W. 7th, Box 410
Stroud, OK 74079

Sulphur Public Schools
Indian Education/Title V
1021 West 9th St.
Sulphur, OK 73086

Swink Elementary School
Indian Education/Title V
P.O. Box 73
Swink, OK 74761

Woodall School
Indian Education/Title V
Rt. 5, Box 226
Tahlequah, OK 74464

Briggs Elementary School
Indian Education Program
Rt. 3, Box 656
Tahlequah, OK 74464
  (18) 456-4221 Fax 456-4049
  Mrs. Jessie Craig, Director
Grades K-8. *Description*: Organizes cultural trips and programs; Sponsors Indian Club; teaches Cherokee language.

Grand View School
Indian Education/Title V
Rt. 4, Box 195
Tahlequah, OK 74464

Lowrey School D-10
Indian Education/Title V
HC-11, Box 190-1
Tahlequah, OK 74464

Tahlequah Public S.D. I-35
Indian Education/Title V
P.O. Box 517
Tahlequah, OK 74465

Sequoyah High School
Indian Education/Title V
P.O. Box 948
Tahlequah, OK 74465

Buffalo Valley Public School I-3
Indian Education/Title V
Rt. 2, Box 3505
Talihina, OK 74571

Talihina Public School
Indian Education/Title V
P.O. Box 38
Talihina, OK 74571

Tecumseh Public Schools
Indian Education/Title V
302 S. 9th
Tecumseh, OK 74873

Temple Public Schools
Indian Education/Title V
206 School Rd.
Temple, OK 73568

Thomas I-6 Public School
Indian Education/Title V
P.O. Box 190
Thomas, OK 73669

Tuskahoma Public School
Indian Education/Title V
P.O. Box 97
Tiskahoma, OK 74574

Tonkawa Public Schools
Indian Education/Title V
P.O Box 10
Tonkawa, OK 74653

Berryhill Public School I-10
Indian Education/Title V
3128 South 63 West Ave.
Tulsa, OK 74107

Tulsa Independent S.D. #1
Indian Education/Title V
3909 E. 5th Place
Tulsa, OK 74112

Tupelo Public Schools
Indian Education/Title V
Box 310
Tupelo, OK 74572

Valliant Public Schools
Indian Education/Title V
Box 777
Valliant, OK 74764

Vian Public School I-2
Indian Education/Title V
P.O. Box 434
Vian, OK 74962

Vinita Public Schools I-65
Indian Education/Title V
P.O. Box 408
Vinita, OK 74301

White Oak Public Schools
Indian Education/Title V
Rt. 4, Box 274
Vinita, OK 74301

Wagoner Public School Dist. I-19
Indian Education/Title V
204 Casaver
Wagoner, OK 74467

Walter Independent S.D. I-00
Indian Education/Title V
418 S. Broadway
Walter, OK 73572

Wanette Public School
Indian Education/Title V
P.O. Box 161
Wanette, OK 74878

Wapanucka Public School
Indian Education/Title V
P.O. Box 88
Wapanucka, OK 73461

Warner Public School
Indian Education/Title V
Rt. 1, Box 1240
Warner, OK 74469

Washington Public School
Indian Education/Title V
P.O. Box 98
Washington, OK 73093

Watonga Public School Dist. I-42
Indian Education/Title V
P.O. Box 310
Watonga, OK 73772

Watts Public School Dist. I-4
Indian Education/Title V
P.O. Box 10
Watts, OK 74964

Skelly School District I
Indian Education/Title V
Rt. 1, Box 918
Watts, OK 74964

Wayne Public School
Indian Education/Title V
P.O. Box 40
Wayne, OK 73095

Weatherford Public Schools
Indian Education/Title V
516 N. Broadway
Weatherford, OK 73096

Webbers Falls Public Schools
Indian Education/Title V
P.O. Box 300
Webber Falls, OK 74470

Welch School District I-17
Indian Education/Title V
P.O. Box 189
Welch, OK 74369

Weleetka Public Schools I-31
Indian Education/Title V
P.O. Box 278
Weleetka, OK 74880

Graham Public School
Indian Education/Title V
Route 1
Weleetka, OK 74880

Tenkiller Public Schools
Indian Education/Title V
Rt. 1, Box 750
Welling, OK 74653

Westville Public Schools
Indian Education/Title V
P.O. Box 410
Westville, OK 74965

Wetumka Public School I-005
Indian Education/Title V
P.O. Box 8
Wetumka, OK 74883

Justice School District 54
Indian Education/Title V
Rt. 1, Box 246
Wewoka, OK 74884

Wewoka Public Schools
Indian Education/Title V
P.O. Box 870
Wewoka, OK 74884

New Lima ISD 6
Indian Education/Title V
Rt. 1, Box 96
Wewoka, OK 74884

Whitefield Elementary School
Indian Education/Title V
P.O. Box 188
Whitefield, OK 74472

Whitesboro Public Schools I-65
Indian Education/Title V
P.O. Box 150
Whitesboro, OK 74577

Wilburton Public S.D. I-1
Indian Education/Title V
1201 W. Blair St.
Wilburton, OK 74578

Wilson Public School
Indian Education/Title V
P.O. Drawer 730
Wilson, OK 73463

Wister Public School
Indian Education/Title V
P.O. Box 489
Wister, OK 74966

Wright City Public Schools
Indian Education/Title V
P.O. Box 329
Wright, OK 74766

Wyandotte P.S. Dist. I-1
Indian Education/Title V
P.O. Box 360
Wyandotte, OK 74370

Joy Public School
Indian Education/Title V
Rt. 1, Box 57
Wynnewood, OK 73098

Osage Co. Coop Wynona School
Indian Education/Title V
P.O. Box 700
Wynona, OK 74084

OREGON

Bandon School District #54
Indian Education Program
455 Ninth St., SW
Bandon, OR 97411
Jackie Beacher, Contact

Interface Ed. Network-Title V
Indian Ed. Prog.
4800 SW Griffith Dr. #202
Beaverton, OR 97005
E. Puentes/J. Brown, Contact

Brookings Harbor S.D. 17C
Indian Education Program
564 Fern St.
Brookings Harbor, OR 97415
Linda Timeus, Contact

Burns Paiute Reservation
Indian Education Program
HC-71, 100 PaSiGo St.
Burns, OR 97720
  J. Holbrook, Contact

Harney Co. School District
Indian Education Program
458 E. Washington St.
Burns, OR 97720
  N. Eddy, Contact

Coos Bay School District #9
Indian Education Program
P.O. Box 509
Coos Bay, OR 97420
  Jim Thornton, Gloria Reeves, Contacts

Coquille School District #8
Indian Education Program
140 E. Tenth
Coquille, OR 97423
  C. Crawford, Contact

London School
Indian Education Program
73288 London Rd.
Cottage Grove, OR 97424
  Mary Nisewander, Contact

Eugene School District 4-J
Indian Education Program
3411-A Willamette
Eugene, OR 97405
  Twila Souers, Contact

Grand Ronde Grade School
Indian Education Program
P.O. Box 7
Grand Ronde, OR 97347
M. Kimsey, Contact

Klamath Co. School District
Indian Education Program
10501 Washburn Way
Klamath Falls, OR 97603
  Lynn Corwin, Contact

Klamath Falls Dist. #1
Indian Education Program
475 S. Alameda Ave.
Klamath Falls, OR 97603
  C. Fries, Contact

K.U.H.S.
Indian Education Program
Mon Claire St.
Klamath Falls, OR 97601
  H. Smith, Contact

Jefferson Co. School District 509-J
Indian Education Program
1355 Buff St.
Madras, OR 97741
  P. Riley, Contact

S. Umpqua School District #19
Indian Education Program
558 SW Chadwick Lane
Myrtle Creek, OR 97457
  M. Bengston, Contact

Small Fires Hawk
Indian Education Program
247 16th St.
Myrtle Point, OR 97458
  Coordinator

Myrtle Point School District #41
Indian Education Program
212 Spruce St.
Myrtle Point, OR 97458
  C. Leibelt, Contact

Lincoln Co. School District
Indian Education Program
P.O. Box 1110
Newport, OR 97365
  M. Darcy, Contact

North Bend School District #13
Indian Education Program
1313 Airport Lane
North Bend, OR 97459
  D. Caldwell, Contact

Oregon City School District
Indian Education Program
P.O. Box 591
Oregon City, OR 97045
  Ruth Jensen, Contact

Umatilla School District
Indian Education Program
2001 SW Rye
Pendleton, OR 97801
  V. Lyles, Contact

American Indian Assn. of Portland
Indian Education Program
1438 SE Division St. #B
Portland, OR 97202
  R. Soto Rank, Contact

Indian Education Program
3558 SE Harold Ct.
Portland, OR 97202
  Norine S. Smith, Contact

Northwest Reg. Ed. Lab
Indian Education Program
101 SW Main St., Suite 500
Portland, OR 97204
  Joe Coburn, Contact

Portland School District #1
Indian Education Program
P.O. Box 3107
Portland, OR 97208
  M. Caba, Contact

Portland Schools
Indian Education Program
8020 N.E. Tillamook
Portland, OR 97213
  Robie Clark, Contact

Powers School District #1
Indian Education Program
P.O. Box 479
Portland, OR 97466
  S. Stallard, Contact

Chemawa Indian School
Indian Education Program
3700 Chemawa Rd. NE
Salem, OR 97305
  G. Gray, Contact

Salem-Keizer P.S. #24J
Indian Education Program
2575 Commecial St. SE
Salem, OR 97302, Contact
  G. Hammond

State Dept. of Education
Indian Education Program
700 Pringle Park S.E.
Salem, OR 97310
  Robin Butterfield, Contact

Springfield Public Schools
Indian Education Program
525 Mill St.
Springfield, OR 97477
  (503) 726-3430 Fax 726-9555
  Laurie Brown-Godfrey, Director
Grades K-12. *Description*: Educational & cultural
services to students enrolled in the program.

Indian Education Program
1521 E. 15th
The Dalles, OR 97058
  Nancy Plant, Contact

WASCO School District
Indian Education Program
422 E. 3rd St.
The Dalles, OR 97058
  K. Krauss, Contact

Indian Education Program
P.O. Box 849
Warm Springs, OR 97761
  R. Danzuha, Contact

Columbia School District 5-J
Indian Education Program
Westport, OR 97016
  R. Theis, Contact

Willamina School District 30-J
Indian Education Program
324 SE Adams
Willamina, OR 97396
  K. Shelly, Contact

RHODE ISLAND

Narragansett Indian Tribe
Indian Education Program
P.O. Box 268
Charleston, RI 02813

Charijo School District
Indian Education Program
Switch Rd.
Wood River Junction, RI 02894
  Robert Andreotti, Contact

SOUTH DAKOTA

Aberdeen Public Schools
Title V Director
203 Third Ave., SE
Aberdeen, SD 57401
  Georgine Tyon-Pourier, Contact

Tiospa Zina Tribal School
P.O. Box 719
Agency Village, SD 57262
  Dr. Roger Bordeaux, Contact

Tiospa Zina Tribal School
Box 719
Agency Village, SD 57262
  Dick Thompson, Contact

American Horse School Principal
P.O. Box 660
Allen, SD 57714
  Donald Standing Elk, Contact

Shannon Co. School District
Title V Director
P.O. Box 109
Batesland, SD 57716
  Maurice Twiss, Contact

Bonesteel-Fairfax School District
P.O. Box 410
Bonesteel, SD 57317
  Richard W. Parry, Contact

Rock Creek Day School
P.O. Box 127
Bullhead, SD 57621
  Emmett White Temple, Contact

Dupree School District
P.O. Box 10
Dupree, SD 57623
  Bruce Carrier, Contact

Eagle Butte School District
Title V Director
P.O. Box 260
Eagle Butte, SD 57625
  Jean Bowman, Contact

Flandreau Indian School
Title V Director
1000 N. Crescent
Flandreau, SD 57028
  Bernie Wells, Jack Belkham, Contacts

Flandreau Public School
600 1st Ave. West
Flandreau, SD 57028
  Troy Garrett/Cindy Jones, Contacts

Fort Thompson Elem. School
P.O. Box 139
Fort Thompson, SD 57339
  Douglas Daughters, Contact

Swift Bird Day School
HCR #3, Box 121
Gettysburg, SD 57442

Hot Springs Public Schools
Indian Education Program
1609 University Ave.
Hot Springs, SD 57747
  (605) 745-4145 Fax 745-4178
  Ronald J. Bergen, Director
Grades K-12. *Description*: Tutoring services and career education. *Instructors*: Barbara Blosser, Arlene Chavez.

Takini School
Title V Director
P.O. Box 168
Howes, SD 57748
  Dr. Loretta Engelhardt, Contact

Isabel School District 20-2
P.O. Box 134
Isabel, SD 57633
  Charles Begeman, Contact

Little Wound School
P.O. Box 500
Kyle, SD 57752
  Dr. Lynda Earring, Gerald Bettelyoun, Contacts

Andes Central School
P.O. Box 40
Lake Andes, SD 57356
  Clifford Bernie, Janet Varejcka, Contacts

Little Eagle Day School
P.O. Box 26
Little Eagle, SD 57639
  Adele Little Dog, Contact

Lower Brule School
Title V Director
P.O. Box 245
Lower Brule, SD 57548
  Cody Russell, Contact

Wounded Knee School District
P.O. Box 350
Manderson, SD 57756
  Shirley Garnette, Contact

Bennett Co. School District
P.O. Box 580
Martin, SD 57551
  Wade R. Olson, Contact

Marty Indian School
P.O. Box 187
Marty, SD 57361
  Vince Two Eagle, Contact

McIntosh School District
Principal
Box 80
McIntosh, SD 57641
  Olaus Njas, Contact

McLaughlin School District
P.O. Box 880
McLaughlin, SD 57642
  Harlan Krein, Contact

Todd Co. School District
Title V Director
P.O. Box 87
Mission, SD 57555
  Richard Bordeaux,
  Lydia Whirlwind Soldier, Contacts

Mitchell School District
Native Am. H/S Coord.
P.O. Box 7760
Mitchell, SD 57301
  Bette Masheck, Contact

Mobridge District Schools
Title V Director
114 East 10th
Mobridge, SD 57601
  Dixie Silva, Contact

Promise Day School
HCR 30, Box 10
Mobridge, SD 57601
  Rick Pagels, Contact

Loneman School
P.O. Box 50
Oglala, SD 57764
  Saunie Wilson, Goldie Starr, Contacts

Pierre Indian Learning Center
HC 31, Box 148
Pierre, SD 57501
  Darrell Jeanotte, Contact

Pierre Jr. High School
Indian Education Program
120 S. Highland
Pierre, SD 57501
  Joanne Beare, Contact

Pierre School District
Indian Education Program
302 E. Dakota
Pierre, SD 57501
  Thomas W. Sogaard, Contact

Pine Ridge School
P.O. Box 1202
Pine Ridge, SD 57770
  Imogene Horse, Basil Brave Heart, Contacts

Rapid City School District
Indian Education Program
300 Sixth St.
Rapid City, SD 57701
  (605) 394-4071 Fax 394-1816
Grades K-12. *Description*: Provides instructional assistance, and supplemental special educational and culturally related needs to Indian students.

St. Francis Indian School
P.O. Box 379
St. Francis, SD 57572
  Mark Bordeaux, Contact

Sioux Falls School District
Supvr.-Indian Ed.
201 East 38th St.
Sioux Falls, SD 57117
  Marilyn Charging, Contact

Sisseton Public School District
Title V Director
302 E. Maple St.
Sisseton, SD 57262
  Delphine Wanna, Contact

Crow Creek High School
P.O. Box 12
Stephan, SD 57346
  Gary Spawn, Contact

Timber Lake School District
P.O. Box 1000
Timber Lake, SD 57656
  Frank Seiler, Contact

Vermillion School District
Title V Director
17 Prospect St.
Vermillion, SD 57069
  Kathy Prasek, Contact

Wagner Community Schools
Title V Director
P.O. Box 310
Wagner, SD 57380
  Dana Sanderson, Contact

Smee School District
P.O. Box 8
Wakpala, SD 57658
  Greg East, Contact

Crazy Horse School
Title V Director
P.O. Box 260
Wanblee, SD 57577
  Lamoine Pulliam

Schools

123

Enemy Swim Day School
RR 1, Box 87
Waubay, SD 57273
Edna Greenhagen, Contact

Waubay School District
RR 1, Box 11
Waubay, SD 57273
Dennis Nelson, Contact

White Horse School District
Box 7
White Horse, SD 57661
Barbara Longcrow, Contact

White River School District
P.O. Box 273
White River, SD 57579
Dr. Don Barnhart, Contact

Wilmot School District 54-7
Indian Education Program
P.O. Box 100
Wilmot, SD 57279
(605) 938-4272
Jerry T. Martinson, Director
Grades K-12. *Description*: Provides tutoring services, and cultural enrichment programs. *Instructors*: Tammy Redwing, Lynette Williams.

Winner School District
P.O. Box 231
Winner, SD 57580
Keith Gebhart, Contact

Yankton School District
Dir-Student Svcs.
1900 Ferdig Ave.
Yankton, SD 57078
Joyce Wentworth, Contact

TENNESSEE

Lauderdale Board of Education
Indian Education Program
402 S. Washington
Ripley, TN 38063
Robert Webb, Contact

TEXAS

Dallas I.S.D.
Indian Education/Title V
3700 Ross Ave.
Dallas, TX 75204

Eagle Pass I.S.D.
Indian Education/Title V
P.O. Box 1409
Eagle Pass, TX 78853

Ysleta I.S.D.
Indian Education/Title V
9600 Sims
El Paso, TX 79925

Grand Prairie I.S.D.
Indian Education/Title V
202 West College
Grand Prairie, TX 75050

UTAH

Alpine School District
Indian Education Program
50 N. Center
American Forks, UT 84003
Vicki Anderson, Contact

Iron Co. School District
Indian Education Program
P.O. Box 879
Cedar City, UT 84720

Neola Elementary School
Indian Education Program
P.O. Box 446
Duchesne, UT 84021

Davis Co. School District
Indian Education Program
45 E. State St.
Farmington, UT 84025
Susan Ross, Contact

Ute Tribe Adult Education
Indian Education Program
P.O. Box 146
Ft. Duchesne, UT 84026
Jean Noble, Contact

Aneth Commuity School
Indian Education Program
P.O. Box 600
Montezuma Creek, UT 84534
Eva Benally, Contact

Division of Indian Affairs
Indian Education Program
324 S. State St., Suite 103
Salt Lake City, UT 84111
Wil Numkena, Contact

Granite S.D. Multicultural Ctr.
Indian Education Program
340 E. 3545 South
Salt Lake City, UT 84115

State Office of Education
Indian Education Program
250 East 500 South
Salt Lake City, UT 84111
Jay Taggart, Contact

Jordan School District
Indian Education Program
9361 South 300 East
Sandy, UT 84070

VERMONT

Franklin NW Supv. USD
Indian Education Program
17 Grand Ave.
Swanton, VT 05488
Jeff Benay, Contact

VIRGINIA

Charles City Co. Public Schools
Indian Education Program
10910 Court House Rd.
Charles City, VA 22030
Melvin Robertson, Contact

King William Co. School Board
Indian Education Program
P.O. Box 185
King William, VA 23086
Miles A. Reid, Contact

WASHINGTON

Aberdeen School District #5
Indian Education Program
216 No. G St.
Aberdeen, WA 98520
L. Rhoden, Contact

Arlington School District
Indian Education Program
600 E. First St.
Arlington, WA 98223
S. Case, Contact

Auburn School District
Indian Education Program
915 Fourth St. NE
Auburn, WA 98002
V. Cross, Contact

Muckleshoot School District
Indian Education Program
39015 172nd Ave. SE
Auburn, WA 98002
Jim Kallesar, Contact

Bellingham High School
Indian Education Program
2020 Cornwall Ave.
Bellingham, WA 98225
Janice Smith, Contact

Bellingham School District #501
Indian Education Program
P.O Box 878
Bellingham, WA 98227
M. Montague, Contact

Lummi Tribal School
Indian Education Program
2530 Dwina Rd.
Bellingham, WA 98226
C. Wilson, Contact

Bremerton School District #100
Indian Education Program
300 N. Montgomery
Bremerton, WA 98312
L. Owen, Contact

Puget Sound Educational Service District
Indian Education Program
400 S.W. 152nd St.
Burien, WA 98166
(206) 439-3636 Fax 439-3961
Carol DittBenner, Director
Grades K-12. *Description*: Provides personalized

services to Native American students attending public schools in the district. Services include tutoring, and career/vocational counseling. *Instructors*: David Norman, Myrna Gonzalez, Alice Thoreson, Phyllis Covington, Galen Williams.

Grand Coulee Dam School District
Indian Education Program
Stevens and Grant
Coulee Dam, WA 99116
E. Moses, Contact

Cusick School District #59
Indian Education Program
305 Monumental Way, Box 270
Cusick, WA 99119
C. Crickman, Contact

Darrington School District #330
Indian Education Program
P.O. Box 27
Darrington, WA 98241
B. Mmauldin, Contact

Nooksack Parent Ed. Comm.
Indian Education Program
P.O. Box 34
Deming, WA 98244
Sandra Joseph, Contact

Mt. Baker School District
Indian Education Program
P.O. Box 45
Deming, WA 98244
Pam Terhorst, P. Bieber, Contacts

Nooksack Indian Tribe
Indian Education Program
5048 Mt. Baker Hwy.
Deming, WA 98244
E. Tom, Contact

Elma School District
Indian Education Program
30 Elma Monte Rd.
Elma, WA 98541
L. Burbridge, Contact

Federal Way School District #210
Indian Education Program
31405 18th Ave. S.
Federal Way, WA 98003
D. Salyers, Contact

Ferndale School District #502
Indian Education Program
P.O. Box 428
Ferndale, WA 98248
Tracy Parker, L. Lane-Oreiro, Contacts

Queets-Clearwater S.D. #20
Indian Education Program
HC-80, Box 1750
Forks, WA 98331
F. Hansen, Contact

Quillayute Valley S.D. #402
Indian Education Program
P.O. Box 60
Forks, WA 98331
R. Harmon, Contact

Glenwood School District #401
Indian Education Program
P.O. Box 12, 320 Bunnell St.
Glenwood, WA 98619
(509) 364-3438 Fax 364-3689

Chris Anderson, Director
Grades K-12. *Description*: Provides support for students to attend youth conference; cultural activities and awareness education; and summer school, athletic and academic camps. *Instructor*: Emma Jane LaVallie.

Granger School District #204
Indian Education Program
P.O. Box 400
Granger, WA 98932
K. Heggens, Contact

Central Valley S.D. #356
Indian Education Program
E. 19307 Cataldo
Greenacres, WA 99016
Dan Iyall, Contact

Hoquiam School District
Indian Education Program
312 Simpson
Hoquiam, WA 98550
E. Rusi, Contact

Columbia School District #206
Indian Education Program
P.O. Box 7
Hunters, WA 99137
K. Anderson, Contact

Ocean Beach School District #101
Indian Education Program
P.O. Box 860
Ilwaco, WA 98624
T. Akerlund, Contact

Inchelium School District #70
Indian Education Program
P.O. Box 285
Inchelium, WA 99138
N. Kirby, Jim Perkins, Contacts

WA State Indian Education
Indian Education Program
P.O. Box 259
Indianola, WA 98342
M. Boushie, Contact

Crescent School District #313
Indian Education Program
P.O. Box 2
Joyce, WA 98343
R. Wilson, Contact

Kelso School District #453
Indian Education Program
404 Long Ave.
Kelso, WA 98626
D. Taylor, Contact

Kent School District
Indian Education Program
12033 SE 256th St.
Kent, WA 98031
J. Brownell, Contact

Lake Washington School District
Indian Education Program
P.O. Box 2909
Kirkland, WA 98083
R. Watt, Contact

La Conner School District
Indian Education Program
P.O. Box D
La Conner, WA 98257
N. Hoffman, Contact

Indian Education Program
P.O. Box 33
La Push, WA 98350
Roger Jackson, Contact

Quileute Tribal School
Indian Education Program
P.O. Box 39
La Push, WA 98350
T. Tavenner, Contact

North Thurston School District
Indian Education Program
305 College St., NE
Lacey, WA 98506
R. Kelly, Contact

Lake Stevens School District
Indian Education Program
12708 20th St., NE
Lake Stevens, WA 98258
K. Musser, Contact

Longview School District
Indian Education Program
28th & Lilac
Longview, WA 98632
C. Jenkins, Contact

Lyle School District #406
Indian Education Program
P.O. Box 368
Lyle, WA 98635
D. Oldenberg, Contact

Edmonds School District #15
Indian Education Program
20420 68th Ave. W
Lynwood, WA 98036
S. Fink, Contact

Marysville School District
Indian Education Program
4220 80th NE
Marysville, WA 98270
Roberta Basch, Contact

Monroe School District
Indian Education Program
P.O. Box 687
Monroe, WA 98272
Harold Bakken, Contact

Indian Education Program
P.O. Box 127
Nespelem, WA 99155
Valorie Smith, Contact

Indian Heritage Association
Makah Cultural Center
P.O. Box 160
Neah Bay, WA 98357
A. Renker, Contact

Nespelem School District #014
Indian Education Program
P.O. Box 291
Nespelem, WA 99155
E. Hyde

Nooksack Valley School District
Indian Education Program
P.O. Box 307
Nooksack, WA 98276
  D. Newell, Contact

North Kitsap School District
Indian Education Program
18360 Caldart NE
North Kitsap, WA 98370
  Coordinator

Oakville School District #400
Indian Education Program
P.O. Box H
Oakville, WA 98568
  L. Eliason, Contact

Okanogan School District #105
Indian Education Program
P.O. Box 592
Okanogan, WA 98840
  Mr. Spearing, Contact

Nisqually Indian Tribe
Indian Education Program
4820 She-Nah-Num Dr. SE
Olympia, WA 98503
  Y. Scott/A. Frazier, Contact

Olympia School District #1 11
Indian Education Program
1113 E. Legion Way
Olympia, WA 98501
E. Allen, Contact

Wa He Lut Indian Day
Indian Education Program
1111 Conine Ave. SE
Olympia, WA 98503
  B. Przusnyski, Contact

North Beach School District #64
Indian Education Program
P.O. Box 159
Ocean Shores, WA 98569
  R. Torrens, Contact

Indian Education Office
Indian Education Program
State Dept. of Public Instruction
Olympia, WA 98504
  Patsy Martin, Contact

Colville Confederated Tribes
Indian Education Program
Rt. 1, Box 66-A
Omak, WA 98841
  K. St. Paul, Contact

Omak School District #19
Indian Education Program
P.O. Box 833
Omak, WA 98841
  M.V. Power, Contact

Port Angeles School District #121
Indian Education Program
216 E. Fourth St.
Port Angeles, WA 98362
  R. Carr, Contact

South Kitsap School District #402
Indian Education Program
1962 Hoover SE
Port Orchard, WA 98366
  S. Blanchard, Contact

North Kitsap School District
Indian Education Program
18360 Caldart NE
Poulsbo, WA 98370
  J. Schiersch, Contact

Parent Committee
Indian Education Program
7415 56th St. E
Puyallup, WA 98371
  Helen Gray-Teo, Contact

Puyallup School District
Indian Education Program
214 W. Main St.
Puyallup, WA 98371
  N. Polich, Contact

Renton School District #403
Indian Education Program
435 Main Ave. S
Renton, WA 98056
  C. Rekdal, Contact

ACE Project
Indian Education Program
9010 13th Ave. NW
Seattle, WA 98117
  N. George, Contact

Highline Public S.D. #401
Indian Education Program
15675 Ambaum Blvd. SW
Seattle   WA 98166
  J. Hopkins, Contact

Indian Center Education Clinic
Indian Education Program
611 12th Ave. S, Suite 300
Seattle, WA 98144
  B. Gutierrez, Contact

Indian Education Program
9600 College Way N.
Seattle, WA 98103
  Willard Bill, Contact

Seattle Public School District
Indian Education Program
1330 N. 90th Bldg. 500
Seattle, WA 98103
  Dick Basch, Contact

Seattle Indian Center
Indian Education Program
611 12th Ave. S.
Seattle, WA 98144
  J. Shelton, Contact

Seattle Public School District 1
Indian Education Program
815 Fourth Ave.
Seattle, WA 98109
  J. Iman, Contact

Title V Parent Committee
Indian Education Program
6702 Earl St.
Seattle, WA 98117
  Cissy Leask, Contact

United Indians of All Tribes
Indian Education Program
P.O. Box 99100
Seattle, WA 98199
  G. Boots, Contact

University of Washington
Indian Education Program
375 Schmitz Hall, PC45
Seattle, WA 98195
  R. Haines, Contact

Washington Research Institute
Indian Education Program
180 Nickerson St., Suite 103
Seattle, WA 98109
  Mary Maddox, Contact

Sedro-Woolley S.D. #101
Indian Education Program
2079 Cook Rd.
Sedro-Woolley, WA 98284
  D. Handy, Contact

Upper Skagit Indian Tribe
Indian Education Program
2284 Commecial Plaza
Sedro-Woolley, WA 98282
  Archy Cavanaugh, Contact

Cape Flattery S.D. #401
Indian Education Program
P.O. Box 109
Sekiu, WA, 98381
  D. Hunter, Contact

Hood Canal S.D. #404
Indian Education Program
N. 111 Hwy. 106
Shelton, WA 98584
  Dr. R. Weir, Contact

Skokomish Indian Tribe
Indian Education Program
N. 80 Tribal Center Rd.
Shelton, WA 98584
  Roberta Peterson, Contact

South Bend School District
Indian Education Program
P.O. Box 437
South Bend, WA 98586
  P. Pearson, Contact

Native Project
Indian Education Program
W 1803 Maxwell
Spokane, WA 99201
  F. Spotted Eagle, Contact

Spokane Public School District
Indian Education Program
Ad Bldg. N. 200 Bernard St.
Spokane, WA 99201
  Don Barlow, Contact

Mary Walker School District #207
Indian Education Program
P.O. Box 159
Springdale, WA 99173
  F. Jones, Contact

Clover Park School District #400
Indian Education Program
10903 Gravelly Lake Dr. SW
Tacoma, WA 98499
  K. Lemmer, Contact

Indian Education Program
1329 E. 55th St.
Tacoma, WA 98404
  Virginia Bill, Contact

Indian Education Program
6316 South C St.
Tacoma, WA 98408
  Jack Shepard, Contact

Puyallup Tribal School
Indian Education Program
2002 E. 28th
Tacoma, WA 98404
  N. Dorpat, Contact

Tacoma School District #10
Indian Education Program
P.O. Box 1357
Tacoma, WA 98401
  J. Egawa, Contact

Taholah School District #77
Indian Education Program
P.O. Box 249
Taholah, WA 98587
  R. Anthony, Contact

Toppenish School District #202
Indian Education Program
106 Franklin Ave.
Toppenish, WA 98948
  Irene Sumner, J. Torres, Contacts

Yakima Tribal Ed. Center
Indian Education Program
P.O. Box 151
Toppenish, WA 98948
  Alvin Schuster, Contact

Yakima School District
Indian Education Program
P.O. Box 151
Toppenish, WA 98948
  P. Martin, H. Umtuck, Contacts

Vancouver School District #37
Indian Education Program
605 N. Devine Rd.
Vancouver, WA 98668
  J. Tangeman, Contact

Weelpinit School District #49
Indian Education Program
P.O. Box 390
Wellpinit, WA 99040
  J. Cruzen, Contact

Wapato School District #207
Indian Education Program
P.O. Box 38
Wapato, WA 98951
  R. Foss, Contact

Indian Education Program
Box 324
Wellpinit, WA 99040
  Teresa Payne, Contact

Mt. Adams School District #209
Indian Education Program
P.O. Box 578
White Swan, WA 98952
  R.J. Hoptowit, Contact

Educational Service District #105
Indian Education Program
33 S. Second Ave.
Yakima, WA 98902
  Marsha Pastrana, Contact

Yakima School District
Indian Education Program
104 N. Fourth Ave.
Yakima, WA 98902
  N. Le Cuyer, Contact

Yelm School District
Indian Education Program
P.O. Box 476
Yelmm, WA 98597
  M. Zodrow, Contact

WISCONSIN

Appleton Area School District
Home School Coord.
P.O. Box 2019
Appleton, WI 54913
  Debra Torbeck, Contact

Houdini Elementary School
Principal
2305 W. Capitol Rd.
Appleton, WI 54915
  Alan Schroeder, Contact

Ashland School District
Dir. of Curriculum
1900 Beaser Ave.
Ashland, WI 54806
  Timothy Foley, Contact

Unity School
Home-School Coord.
P.O. Box 307
Balsam Lake, WI 54810
  Jeanie Buck, Contact

Baraboo School District
Deputy Supt.
101 Second St.
Baraboo, WI 53913
  Anthony Kujawa, Contact

Fairfield Center
Home School Liaison
E-12654 County Hiway T
Baraboo, WI 53913
  Dianne Littlegeorge, Contact

Bayfield School District-Supt.
P.O. Box 5001
Bayfield, WI 54814
  Guy Habeck, Contact

Black River Falls School
Business Admin.
301 N. 4th St.
Black River Falls, WI 54615
  Ted Kozlowski, Contact

Bowler Public Schools
500 S. Almon Rd.
Bowler, WI 54416
(414) 793-4101
  Donna Miller, Director
Grades Pre K-12. *Description*: Tutorial assistance,
cultural activities & Native American information.

Crandon School District
Home-School Coord.
P.O. Box 310
Crandon, WI 54520
Tim Laabs, Contact

Cumberland School District
P.O. Box 67
Cumberland, WI 54829
  Merwin Moen, Contact

West De Pere School District
1155 Westwood St.
De Pere, WI 541 15
  James Lamal, Contact

Eau Claire School District
Indian Education Program
500 Main St.
Eau Claire, WI 54701
(715) 833-3491
  Patti Gardner, Director
Grades K-12. *Description*: Designed to meet the
special educational needs of American Indian children in the Eau Claire School District.

Freedom Area School District
Title V Coordinator
P.O. Box 1008
Freedom, WI 54131
  Tonie Anderson, Contact

Green Bay Area Public School Dist.
Title V Director
P.O. Box 23387
Green Bay, WI 54305
  Adam Webster, Contact

Howard-Suamico School District
Title V Director
1935 Cardinal Lane
Green Bay, WI 54313
  Cecilia Turriff, Contact

Hayward Community Schools
Curriculum Coord.
P.O. Box 860
Hayward, WI 54843
  Virginia Metzdorf, Contact

Lac Courte Oreilles Ojibwe School
Route 2, Box 2800
Hayward, WI 54843
  School Administrator

Menominee Indian School District
Dir. of Instruction
P.O. Box 399
Keshena, WI 54135
  Mark Smits, Contact

Madison Metro. School District
Indian Education Program
545 W. Dayton St.
Madison, WI 53703
  Kenneth White Horse, Contact

Menominee Indian School District
P.O. Box 399
Keshena, WI 54135
  Joseph Vigil, Contact

Menominee Tribal School
Administrator
P.O. Box 910
Keshena, WI 54135
  Kenneth Lehman, Contact

La Crosse School District
Supvr. Humanities
807 East Ave. South
La Crosse, WI 54601
  Karen Murray, Contact

Lac du Flambeau Public School
510 Old Abe Rd.
Lac du Flambeau, WI 54538
 Dr. Lauren Villagomez, Contact

Milwaukee Public Schools
Indian Education Program
P.O. Drawer 10-K
Milwaukee, WI 53201
 John Clifford, Contact

Lakeland Union High School
Ass't. Principal
8669 Old Hwy. 70 West
Minocqua, WI 54548
 Renee Tennant, Contact

Nekoosa Public Schools
310 1st St.
Nekoosa, WI 54457
 Peter Pavioski, Contact

Oneida Tribal School
Title V Director
P.O. Box 365
Oneida, WI 54155
 Grace Wills, Sharon Mousseau, Contacts

Osseo-Fairchild School District-Supt.
P.O. Box 130
Osseo, WI 54758
 Gerald Nelson, Contact

Pulaski Community School
Title V Director
P.O. Box 36
Pulaski, WI 54162
 Judy Kasper, Contact

Seymour Community School District
Title V Director
10 Circle Dr.
Seymour, WI 54165
 Thomas Hughes, Contact

Shawano-Gresham School District
Title V Coordinator
210 S. Franklin
Shawano, WI 54166
 William Matthias, Contact

Siren School District
Title V Director
P.O. Box 29
Siren, WI 54872
 Francis Decorah, Contact

Stevens Point Public School
 Curriculum Admin.
1900 Polk St.
Stevens Point, WI 54481
 Mike Bubla, Contact

Superior School District
Indian Ed. Coord.
3025 Tower Ave.
Superior, WI 54880
 Carol Stevens, Contact

Tomah Area School District
Dir. of Instruction
901 Lincoln Ave.
Tomah, WI 54660
 Pamela Knorr, Contact

Wabeno School District
Title V Coord.
4343 Mill Lane
Wabeno, WI 54566
 Debra Tucker Kruger, Contact

Washburn School District
305 W. 4th St.
Washburn, WI 54891
 Clyde Sukanen

Wausau School District
Instructional Services
415 Seymour St.
Wausau, WI 54401
 Berland Meyer, Contact

Webster School District
Title V Director
26428 Lakeland Ave.
Webster, WI 54893
 Jery Olson, Contact

Winter Community Schools
JTPA Coord.
P.O. Box 7
Winter, WI 54896
 Richard C. Olson, Contact

Wisconsin Dells School District
Director of Curriculum
300 Vine St.
Wisconsin Dells, WI 53965
 Scott Herrmann, Contact

Wisconsin Rapids Public Schools
Native American Coord.
510 Peach St.
Wisconsin Rapids, WI 54494
 Bonnie Smith, Contact

Wittenberg-Birnamwood School
P.O. Box 269
Wittenberg, WI 54499
 Richard Roth, Contact

WYOMING

Fremont Co. School District #38
Indian Education Program
P.O. Box 211
Arapahoe, WY 82510
Bob Gutierrez, Contact

Wyoming Indian School #14
Indian Education Program
Lander Route, Box 340
Ethete, WY 82520
 Coordinator

Ft. Washakie School District #21
Indian Education Program
Box 110 Ethete Rd.
Fort Washakie, WY 82512
 George Zerga, Contact

Wyoming Indian Education Office
Indian Education Program
P.O. Box 886
Fort Washakie, WY 82514
 Nola McLeod, Contact

Fremont Co. School District #1
Indian Education Program
Baldwin Creek Rd.
Lander, WY 82520
 Jim Robeson, Contact

Wyoming Indian Education Assn.
Indian Education Program
360 Main St.
Lander, WY 82520
 Larry Murray, Contact

Fremont Co. School District #25
Indian Education Program
2001 West Sunset
Riverton, WY 82501
B. Weldon Shelley, Contact

St. Stephans Indian School
Indian Education Program
P.O. Box 345
St. Stephans, WY 82524
 George Moss, Contact

This section, alpha-geographically arranged, lists departments and personnel of various institutions of higher learning which of fer courses on the American Indian. Includes both Indian colleges, and universities with Native Studies Departments, departments of anthropology , and other departments offering related courses.

ALABAMA

AUBURN UNIVERSITY
Department of Sociology & Anthropology
6090 Haley Center
AUBURN 36849
(205) 844-2818
Instructors: John Cottier, PhD, James Gundlach, PhD. *Facilities*: Library-study collections. *Publications*: Archaeological monograph series.

UNIVERSITY OF ALABAMA
Department of Anthropology
19 Ten Hoor Hall, Box 870210
TUSCALOOSA 35487
(205) 348-5947
Graduate program emphasizes the anthropology of health & complex societies of Native Americans.

ALASKA

UNIVERSITY OF ALASKA
Department of Anthropology
3211 Providence Dr.
ANCHORAGE 99508
(907) 786-1344
Instructors: Douglas W. Veltre, PhD, Chairperson, William B. Workman, PhD, Robert A. Mack, Charles E. Holmes (Northern Athabascan ethnoarchaeology). Institute of Social and Economic Research.

UNIVERSITY OF ALASKA
Department of Alaskan Native Studies
Department of Anthropology
310 Eielson Bldg.
FAIRBANKS 99775
(907) 474-7288; 474-6243
W. Rogers Powers, Dept. Head
Courses: Native Cultures of North America, South America, and Alaska; Arctic and New World Prehistory; Biology of Arctic Peoples; seminars on specialized aspects of Eskimo, Aleut, and Athapaskan groups. Regular instruction in Inupiaq, Yup'ik, and Athabaskan offered by the Alaska Native Language Center . *Instructors*: Lydia T. Black, PhD, Phyllis Morrow , PhD, Joseph J. Gross, PhD, W. Rogers Powers, PhD, G. Richard Scott, PhD William S. Schneider , PhD. *Programs*: Graduate and faculty research is primarily directed to the study of Eskimo-Aleuts and North American Indians (their prehistory , cultural variability , and human biology); teaching assistantships to graduate students. *Affiliated facilities* : University of Alaska Museum; Alaska Native Language Center. *Publications* : Anthropological Papers of the University of Alaska.

UNIVERSITY OF ALASKA
Northwest College Campus
Pouch 400
NOME 99762
(907) 443-2201
Barbara Oleson, Contact

A rural site of the Rural College of the University of Alaska, Fairbanks providing post-secondary education to the Seward Peninsula region.

SHELDON JACKSON COLLEGE
SITKA 99835
Native Studies Program.

ARIZONA

NORTHERN ARIZONA UNIVERSITY
Graduate College
Consortium for Graduate Opportunities
for American Indians
P.O. Box 4085
FLAGSTAFF 86011
Description: A consortium of institutions cooperating in the recruitment of American Indian students to academic graduate programs. *Activities*: Identifies a pool of qualified Indian undergraduate students at participating institutions; organizes faculty networks; provides inforamtion on financial aid. *Publication*: Newsletter .

NORTHERN ARIZONA UNIVERSITY
Department of Anthropology
P.O. Box 15200
FLAGSTAFF 86011
(602) 523-3180
Special Program : Native American Indian Studies. *Courses*: Native American Indian History; Contemporary U.S. Indians; Southwest Ethnology: Pueblo and non-Pueblo; Tribal Law and Government; Financing Tribal Government and Administration; Tribal Planning and Management; Current Issues in Tribal Administration. *Instructors*: Reed D. Riner, PhD (Advisor to Program); Joanne W . Kealiinohomoku, PhD, P . David Seaman, PhD, David R. Wilcox, PhD (Curator, Museum of Northern Arizona), Ross L. Wooduff, PhD. *Special program*: Native American United Club. *Affiliated facilities*: Department participates in the Museum of Northern Arizona Joint Scholar in Residence Program; a cooperative program with the Navajo Nation Archaeology Dept.; and has cooperative agreements with Grand Canyon National Park, Glen Canyon National Recreation Area, and Wupatki National Monument; Native Americans for Community Action, Flagstaf f. *Publications*: Anthropological Papers; Technical Report Series.

NORTHERN ARIZONA UNIVERSITY
Native American Forestry Program
School of Forestry
FLAGSTAFF 86011
(602) 523-6653 Fax 523-6143
Purpose: To develop educational and research activities that support Native American tribes in achieving self-determination in the management of their natural resources. *Goal*: To increase the retention and graduation of Native Americans at the School of Forestry .

NORTHERN ARIZONA UNIVERSITY
Navajo Nation Archaeology Dept.
P.O. Box 6013
FLAGSTAFF 86011
(602) 523-7428
Anthony L. Klesert, PhD, Director
Miranda Warburton, Manager
Established to enable Navajos who are interested in a career in anthropology and gaining practical experience and training in cultural resource management.

SCOTTSDALE COMMUNITY COLLEGE
Native American Studies Program
9000 E. Chaparral St.
SCOTTSDALE 85256
(602) 423-6139
John Silvester, Contact

ARIZONA STATE UNIVERSITY
Department of Anthropology
Box 872402
TEMPE 85287
(602) 965-6213
Division: Indian Education; American Indian Linguistics; and Center for Indian Affairs. *Instructors (partial)* : Elizabeth A. Brandt, Ph.D. (North American Indian languages); Robert Bruenig, Ph.D.; Robert C. Euler , Ph.D.; Scott C. Russell, Ph.D. (Native American Studies); Peter W elsh, Ph.D.; Kathleen M. Sands, Ph.D. (American Indian literatures, Dept. of English). *Facilities* : Heard Museum; Pueblo Grande Museum; A.A. Dahlberg Memorial Collection of 9,000 Pima Indian dental casts and genealogies.

ARIZONA STATE UNIVERSITY
College of Education
Center for Indian Education
TEMPE 85287
(602) 965-6292

ARIZONA STATE UNIVERSITY
College of Law
Indian Legal Program
Box 877906
TEMPE 85287
(602) 965-6204
Siera Russell, Director

COOK COLLEGE & THEOLOGICAL SCHOOL
708 S. Lindon Lane
TEMPE 85281
(602) 968-9354 Fax 968-9357
Eunice Robbins, Contact
The residency program of fers foundational studies and an AA Degree in Pastoral Studies. Member of the Native American Theological Education Consortium in the U.S.

EASTERN ARIZONA COLLEGE
626 Church St.
THATCHER 85552

NAVAJO COMMUNITY COLLEGE
P.O. Box 218
TSAILE 86556
(602) 724-3311 Fax 724-3327
Tom Lewis, Jr., President
Fully accredited and chartered by the Navajo Nation Council. Enrolls an average of 1,800 students. *Degrees*: Associate of Arts, Associate of Applied Science; Preprofessional programs; Certification programs. Navajo history , language and culture are integrated into the traditional academic subjects of all College curriculum to enhance students' respect for the Navajo heritage. *Navajo and Indian Studies Program* : Offers many courses in the broad area of Navajo studies; some are directly related to the Navajo, and others are related to Indians in general. *Courses (partial)* : Navajo History and Culture; Navajo Language; American Indian Economic Development; The Urban Indians; Navajo Crafts courses. *Instructors (partial)* : Wilson Aronilth, Jr., Lorraine C. Begay , Anna Lee Walters. *Programs*: Special Services Program for academically unprepared students; Learning Center provides tutorial services for students. *Scholarships*: For information, contact the Financial Aide

Office, ext. 223/224. *Facility*: College Library houses the Moses Donner Indian Collection; Hatathli Gallery - products include jewelry , paintings, rugs, sand paintings and other art items. *Branch*: Shiprock Branch, P.O. Box 580, Shiprock 87420.

UNIVERSITY OF ARIZONA
Dept. of Speech & Hearing Sciences
American Indian Professional Training Program
in Speech-Language Pathology & Audiology
TUCSON 85721
 (602) 621-1969
 Dr. Ted Glatke, Director
 Betty Nunnery, Program Coordinator
Objectives: To recruit, retain, and provide education to American Indian men and women in the fields of speech-language pathology or audiology . *Goals*: To qualify students for a Master's degree in speech-language pathology or audiology; to integrate the study of Indian languages and cultures into the training program; to develop therapy programs sensitive to Indian cultural needs; to establish a professional work force to serve American Indians who have communication disorders both on and off reservations. *Activities/Programs*: Speech & hearing clinics operated on two reservation sites. Scholarship recipients receive a tuition waiver and a stipend. Library . *Publications*: Directory of Native Americans in Speech-Language Pathology & Audiology; newsletter , Desert Connections, a network publication for Native American speech-language pathologists & audiologists.

UNIVERSITY OF ARIZONA
American Indian Studies Program
Harvill Bldg. Room 430
TUCSON 85721
 (602) 621-7108
 Joseph H. Stauss, Contact
Departments: Anthropology; Linguistics--special programs in American Indian languages; Bureau of Applied Research in Anthropology. The Inter-Tribal Graduate Council provides graduate programs offering opportunities for advanced study in American Indian law and policy , American Indian societies and culture, and American Indian languages and literatures. *Instructors*: Jane E. Hill, Ph.D. (sociolinguistics of Native American languages); Willem J. de Reuse, Ph.D. (Native American languages-Eskimo-Aleut, Siouan and Quechua); Jerrold E. Levy , Ph.D.; James E. Officer, Ph.D.; Susan U. Philips, Ph.D.; Daniel S. Matson, MA; Clara Lee Tanner, MA (Southwestern U.S. Indian arts and crafts); Keith H. Basso, PhD (Apachean languages and cultures); Raymond H. Thompson, PhD, Director of Arizona State Museum; Jan Bell, Curator of Collections at Arizona State Museum; Gordon V . Krutz (Coordinator of IndianPrograms); Teresa L. McCarty, PhD (bilingual/American Indian education); Thomas R. McGuire, PhD; Anne L. Wright, PhD (Navajo); Emory Sekaquaptewa, JD (Hopi language and culture). *SpecialPrograms*: Archaeological Field School; Native American Research and Training Center (602) 621-5075; Native American Speech and Hearing Program (602) 621-1969. *Financial Aid*: Graduate Student support. *Facilities*: Native American Resource Center (602) 621-3835; W estern Archaeological Center; Arizona State Museum. *Publication*: Anthropological Papers of the University of Arizona.

UNIVERSITY OF ARIZONA
American Indian Graduate Student Center
Office of Indian Programs
TUCSON 85721
 (602) 621-2794
 Glenn Johnson, Director
Responsible for providing financial support, publication opportunities, academic counseling and cultural support to the 80 Native American graduate students at the University . It is the only graduate center of its kind in the nation.

UNIVERSITY OF ARIZONA
Native American Research & Training Center
TUCSON 85721
 Carol Locust, Contact
Project: American Indian Disability Legislation: Toward the Development of a Process that Respects Soveriegnty and Cultural Diversity .

ARKANSAS

UNIVERSITY OF ARKANSAS
Dept. of Anthropology
Old Main 330
FAYETTEVILLE 72701
 (501) 575-2508 Fax 575-2642
Courses: Indians of North America; Indians of Arkansas and the South; American Indians Today; North American Prehistory; Peoples of the Arctic. *Instructors*: Michael P. Hoffman, PhD; Marvin Kay , PhD; and Allen McCartney , PhD. *Special Programs*: Summer Archaeological Field School. *Scholarships*: Arkansas residency for tuition purposes to tribes which once lived in the State (Caddo, Cherokee, Choctaw , Creek, Kickapoo, Osage, Quapaw , Shawnee and Tunica). S.C. Dellinger Award for promising anthropology students; minority graduate fellowships. *Facility*: University of Arkansas Museum. *Publications*: Plains Anthropologist; Arctic Anthropology; publications of the Arkansas Archaeological Survey.

CALIFORNIA

HUMBOLDT STATE UNIVERSITY
The Center for Community Development
ARCATA 95521
 (707) 826-3711
 Victor Golla, Director
American Indian Languages and Literature Program: The program first adapted an internationally acknowledged, easy-to-learn, uniphonetic alphabet to write Indian languages precisely , and then schooled fluent local speakers in its use and dissemination. The program has enabled four northwestern California tribes to salvage their venerable literatures; publish them in tribally compiled textbooks; document their (pre-) history; and, record and compile their traditional music. The Program has produced five internationally acclaimed documentary films explicating this complex cultural regenerative process; and organize these elements into curricula for use in preschool, elementary and secondary schools, and in college and unversity classrooms. A scholarly curriculum was created in an intertribal network of American Indian community development projects. The California Department of Education recognized the program, and the most eminent (generally elderly) Indian graduates were given

credentials to teach in the public schools and colleges. *Special program* : Special project/lectureship stipends and bilingual teacher training internships. *Publications*. Library (primarily own publications, such as Indian language and literature texts, and American Indian bilingual teacher training instructional materials.)

HUMBOLDT STATE UNIVERSITY
Dept. of Sociology, Anthropology & Social W ork
ARCATA 95521
 (707) 826-3139
Instructors: Llyn Smith, PhC (Religion), Pat Wenger, PhD (Linguistics), Allan Bramlette (Native American Studies), V ictor Golla, PhD (Native American Studies; Director , Center for Community Development).

HUMBOLDT STATE UNIVERSITY
Indian Natural Resource -
Science & Engineering Program
McMahan House 80
ARCATA 95521
 (707) 826-4994
 Russell Boham, Director
Description: Support program for Native American students pursuing a degree in Natural Resources, Science, or Engineering. Courtses pertinent to Native American natural resources (e.g. Native American water law, tribal government, abd tribal perspectives toward natural resources.

HUMBOLDT STATE UNIVERSITY
Indian Teacher and Education Personnel Program
Spidell House 85
ARCATA 95521
 (707) 826-3672
 Andrew Andreoli, Director
Description: A support program (the oldest in the nation) which recruits and trains American Indians to become educators and ancillary education personnel. Offers courses and field work.

UNIVERSITY OF CALIFORNIA
Native American Studies
Dwinelle Hall, Suite 3415
BERKELEY 94720
 (510) 642-6717
Instructors (partial): Robert A. Black, PhD; Terry P. Wilson, PhD; Jean Molesky , MA, Gerald Vizenor, MA, Clara Sue Kidwell, PhD, Karen Biestman, LLD, and Louana Ross, PhD.

UNIVERSITY OF CALIFORNIA
American Indian Graduate Program
School of Public Health
140 Earl Warren Hall
BERKELEY 94720
 (510) 642-3228
 Felicia Hodge, Contact
Description: Recruitment and retention program for American Indians and Alaska Natives interested in graduate education in public health, social welfare, ethnic studies, law , and other fields.

D-Q (DEGANAWIDA QUETZECOATL) UNIVERSITY
Native American Studies Program
P.O. Box 409
DAVIS 95617
 (916) 758-0470 Fax 758-4891
 Carlos Cordero, President
Description: A two-year community college, tribally owned and controlled, dedicated to the progress of the Native-American & Chicano people. The student body is 70% Native Amerian

(with an upward of 60 tribal afiliations from across the country represented). *Purpose*: To educate indigenous people, while fering the traditional programs as well as specialized majors in indigenous studies. *Programs*: Provides educational and community services to Indian tribes and their people. The curriculum leads to an A.A. or A.S. degree in 9 academic majors. Financial aid available.

UNIVERSITY OF CALIFORNIA
College of Letters and Science
Native American Studies Dept.
2401 Hart Hall
DAVIS 95616
 (916) 752-3237 Fax 752-7097
 Jack D. Forbes, PhD, Dept. Head
Description: Interdisciplinary in its approach, the department focuses upon the indigenous people of the Americas - the peoples, nations, and tribes who have lived in North, Central, and South America for thousands of years. Of fers undergraduate and graduate degrees in Native American Studies *Instructors*: Jack D. Forbes, PhD; Steven Crum, PhD; Ines Hernandez, PhD; Sarah Hutchison, MA, Emeritus; George C. Longfish, PhD; Martha Macri, PhD; Annette Reed-Crum, MA; David Risling, Jr., MA, Emeritus; Stefano Varese, PhD; Wilbor Wilson, PhD. *Services/Programs*: Native American Organized Research Program (Director, Dr. Stefano Varese); EOP Outreach Services; Counseling; workshops, educational programs, lectures, and conferences. *Financial Aid*:Various awards; Mentorships & Internships. *Facilities*: The C.N. Gorman Museum and Art Gallery - maintains a permanent collection and shows works by Indian and Chicano artists as well as staff and students. *Publications*: American Words...Native Words Used in English; A Model of Grassroots Community Development: The DQU Native American Language Project; History of Tecumseh Center; Racism, Scholarship & Pluralism in Higher Education; Religious Freedom & the Protection of Native American Places of Worship; The Papago-Apache Treaty of 1853: Property Rights & Religious Liberties.

COLLEGE OF THE REDWOODS
Native American Studies Progam
EUREKA 95501
 (800) 458-5300; (707) 445-6761
 Jim Harrington, Dean of Student Services

CALIFORNIA STATE UNIVERSITY
Department of Anthropology
HAYWARD 94542
 (415) 881-3168
Instructor: Lowell J. Bean, Ph.D. (Director, Smith Museum of Anthropology). *Special Facility*: Clarence E. Smith Museum of Anthropology.

CALIFORNIA STATE UNIVERSITY
Department of Ethnic Studies
HAYWARD 94542
 (415) 881-3181
 Michael Clark, Chairperson
Instructor: Roxanne Dunbar Ortiz,
Native American Studies.

UNIVERSITY OF CALIFORNIA, IRVINE
School of Social Sciences
Program in Comparative Culture
IRVINE 92717
 (714) 856-4074
Instructor: Joseph G. Jorgensen, Ph.D.
(Native American language and culture).

UNIVERSITY OF CALIFORNIA, IRVINE
Native American Preparatory School
School of Social Ecology
IRVINE 92717
 (714) 856-7698
 Randal Ray, Admissions
Summer program. A five-week residential learning experience open too gifted and talented Native Ameican students entering 8th or 9th grade.

CALIFORNIA STATE UNIVERSITY
Department of Anthropology
1250 Bellflower Blvd.
LONG BEACH 90840
 (213) 498-5171
 Pamela A. Bunte, Chair
Special program: Certificates in American Indian Studies. *Instructors* (partial): Pamela A. Bunte, PhD, and Keith Dixon, PhD.

UNIVERSITY OF CALIFORNIA, LOS ANGELES
American Indian Studies Center
3220 Campbell Hall, 405 Hilgard Ave.
LOS ANGELES 90024
 (310) 206-7508 Fax 206-7060
 Duane Champagne, Director
 Paul Kroskrity, Chair (MA Program)
 Leslie Logan, Graduate Advisor
Description: Coordinates educational, research, and action-oriented programs designed to meet the needs of American Indian students at UCLA and the American Indian communities in general. *Activities*: Encourages the development of new courses; promotes hiring of Native American faculty; sponsors research on American Indians; publishes journals, books, monographs, and other media reflecting contemporary Indian research and issues. *Staff*: Dr. Anthony D. Brown, Assistant Director; Marie Shepherd, Administrative Assistant; Donna Kuyiyesva, Secretary; Judy Takata, Conference Coordinator; Earl Dean Sisto, Coordinator of Student/Community Relations; Velma Salabiye, Librarian; William Oandasan, Coordinator of Publications; Dr. Lenore A. Stiffarm-Noriega, Coordinator of Research Development and Extramural Funding. *Program*: Administers an Interdepartmental Master's Program in American Indian Studies. *Instructors*: Duane Champagne (Sociology); Jennie Joe (Anthropology); Charlotte Heth (Music). *Fellowships*: Postdoctoral Fellowships in American Indian Studies. *Facilities*: The Museum of Cultural History; Library.

UNIVERSITY OF CALIFORNIA, LOS ANGELES
Department of Anthropology
LOS ANGELES 90024
 (310) 825-2055
Faculty: Gail E. Kennedy, PhD; Paul V. Kroskrity, PhD (American Indian languages); James N. Hill, PhD.

CALIFORNIA STATE UNIVERSITY
Department of Anthropology
18111 Nordhoff St.
NORTHRIDGE 91330
 (818) 885-3331
Program: American Indian Studies Program.
 Instructors: Beatrice Medicine, PhD;
Charles Muzny, PhD.

UNIVERSITY OF CALIFORNIA, RIVERSIDE
Ethnic Studies Dept.
University Office Bldg., Rm. 101
RIVERSIDE 92521
 (909) 787-4577
 Clifford Trafzer, Chairperson

Program: Native American Studies. *Instructors*: Clifford Trafzer (History, Literature, Religion); Rebecca Kugel (History, Families); Cheryl Duren (Bibliography, Special Collections). *Special program*: Chancellor's Native American Community Committee. *Publications*: Native American Studies: University of California, Riverside, by Cliford Trafzer, 1991; Dear Christopher, Letters by Contemporary Native Americans to Christopher Columbus, by Darryl Wilson and Barry Joyce, 1992.

SONOMA STATE UNIVERSITY
Native American Studies Program
1801 East Cotati Ave.
ROHNERT PARK 94928
 (707) 664-2450
 Edward D. Castillo, Ph.D., Director
Provides a minor featuring a multi-disciplinary approach to Indian ethnography, history, sociology, and humanities. *Cour ses*: Indians of California, North America, and Southwest; Native American Philosophic Systems; Archaeology of California; Seminar of California Indian Communities. *Instructors*: Priscilla Rios, David A. Frederickson, PhD, Shirley K. Silver, PhD, Albert L. Wahrhaftig, PhD, and David W. Peri. *Special activity*: Spring Indian Fair. *Scholarships*: E.O.P. Scholarships; Sonoma State University Native American Student ScholarshipFacilities: Archaeology and ethnography labs and archives. Planning to publish Occasional Papers of Native American Studies.

CALIFORNIA STATE UNIVERSITY
Department of Anthropology
6000 Jay St.
SACRAMENTO 95819
 (916) 278-6452
Special program: California Indian Studies. *Instructors*: Dorothea J. Theodoratus, PhD, and Valerie Wheeler, PhD.

CALIFORNIA STATE UNIVERSITY
Native American Studies Program
6000 Jay St.
SACRAMENTO 95819
 (916) 278-3901
 Larry Glasmire, Contact

SAN DIEGO STATE UNIVERSITY
American Indian Studies Department
College Ave.
SAN DIEGO 92182-0387
 (619) 594-6991
 Dr. Clifford E. Trafzer, Professor & Chair
 Donna Boggs, Administrative Coordinator
Description: Offers a minor in American Indian studies offering courses on a variety of subjects from Indian heritage to contemporary society, literature, music, and history. *Instructors*: Dr. Linda S. Parker, Dr. Jay Stauss, David Whitehorse, Ralph Forquera, Patricia Dixon, Richard Carrico. *Special programs*: American Indian Storytellings; annual American Indian Pow Wow. Student Organization: The North American Indian Student Alliance. American Indian Culture Week each spring. Library: Golsh Collection - consists of rare documents and books. *Publications*: Publications in American Indian Studies; American Indian Identity, edited by C.E. Trafzer; Strangers in a Stolen Land, by Carrico; The Quechens; Gods Among Us, by Coates.

SAN DIEGO STATE UNIVERSITY
Department of Anthropology
SAN DIEGO 92182
 (619) 594-5527

Special facilities: The linguistics laboratory of fers facilities for experience with local Indian dialects; Athabaskan. *Instructor*: Philip J. Greenfield, PhD (Linguistics).

CALIFORNIA INSTITUTE OF INTEGRAL STUDIES
Traditional Knowledge Program
765 Ashbury St.
SAN FRANCISCO 941 17
(415) 753-6100 ext. 229 Fax 753-1 169
Patricia Perrine, Program Coordinator
Edyne Decker, Residency Coordinator
Description: The mission of the Traditional Knowledge PhD program is to train practitioners of traditional or indigenous life and mind, to maintain and strengthen the integrity of traditional lifeways, and to use indigenous scientific knowledge to reverse the destruction of the planet. *Faculty*: Pamela Colorado, PhD, Jurgen Kremer, PhD. Facility: The Center for Traditional Knowledge supports the program with a limited number of scholarships.

SAN FRANCISCO STATE UNIVERSITY
American Indian Studies Department
1600 Holloway Ave.
SAN FRANCISCO 94132
(415) 469-2046
Departments: American Indian Studies; Anthropology. *Instructors*: John Adair, PhD, Luis S. Kemnitzer, PhD, and Mary Shepardson, PhD. *Program*: On-going research project in physical anthropology of California Indians. *Facility*: The Adan E. Treganza Anthropology Museum.

CALIFORNIA POLYTECHNIC STATE UNIVERSITY
Ethnic Studies Program
SAN LUIS OBISPO 93401
(805) 756-1707
Robert F. Gish, Chairperson
Program offers a minor in Ethnic Studies with concentration in American Indian Studies. *Instructor*: Robert Gish. Courses: American Cultural Images: American Indians; Ethnic American Literature: American Indians. *Publication*: SIYO; A Journal of New Writers.

PALOMAR COMMUNITY COLLEGE
American Indian Studies Program
1140 W. Mission Rd.
SAN MARCOS 92069
(619) 744-1 150 Fax 744-8123
Steven J. Crouthamel, Chairperson
Description: Certification Program in American Indian Studies. *Courses*: History of Native American Arts; California Indian Arts, American Indian Literature; American Indian Philosophy & Religion; American Indian W omen; History of the Plains and Southwest Indians; American Indian Education; among others. *Faculty*: Steven Crouthamel, Patricia Dixon, Linda Locklear; instructors - Flora Howe, Michael Lewis, James Barker, Christopher Sullivan, Juana Majel Dixon. Financial aid available.

SANTA BARBARA CITY COLLEGE
Native American Studies Program
SANTA BARBARA 93109
(805) 965-0581
Jane G. Craven

STANFORD UNIVERSITY
American Indian Program
P.O. Box 2990
STANFORD 94305
(415) 725-6944
Jim Larimore, Director
Description: The American Indian Program Of fice and the Stanford American Indian Organization work together to provide advising, coordinating and support of cultural activities. The University has a Native American Cultural Center to serve as a meeting place for groups such as: Stanford Pow-wow Committee, American Indian Science and Engineering Society, Organization of North American Indian College Students, Stanford American Indian medical and law students, Native American graduate students, Alaskan Native Student Association, et al. There is also an American Indian Summer Institute for incoming freshman.

COLORADO

ADAMS STATE COLLEGE
ALAMOSA 81102

UNIVERSITY OF COLORADO
American Indian Studies Program
Dept. of Anthropology, Campus Box 233
BOULDER 80309
(303) 492-7947 Fax 492-1871
Ward Churchill, Director
Instructors: Ward Churchill, PhD; Olivia Arrieta, PhD; Frank W. Eddy, PhD; Gottfried O. Lang, PhD; Deward F. Walker, Jr, PhD.

COLORADO COLLEGE
Department of Anthropology
14 E. Cache la Poudre
COLORADO SPRINGS 80903
(719) 389-6362
Instructors: Paul Kutsche, PhD (Cherokee); Marianne L. Stoller, PhD (Social Anthropology); Laurel J. Watkins, PhD (Linguistics), H. Marie Wormington, PhD (Cultures); and V ictoria L. Levine, PhD (Music); David H. Snow (Archaeology); and Beatrice Medicine (V isiting Professor). *Facility*: Alice Bemis Taylor Museum.

UNIVERSITY OF DENVER
University College
American Indian Studies Program
2211 S. Josephine St.
DENVER 80208
(303) 871-3155 ext. 254
Jan Steinhauser, Contact
Offers courses leading to a Certificate of Advanced Study in American Indian Studies, as well as a Master of Liberal Arts with a concentration in American Indian Studies. Also offers an interdisciplinary look at the American Indian community and the current vitality and continuous development of the Indian people.

FORT LEWIS COLLEGE
Division of Intercultural Studies
120 Miller Student Center
DURANGO 81301
Mary Jean Mosely, Director
Courses: Native American and Southwest Studies. *Activities*: Hozhoni Days–a celebration sponsored by the Indian Club for sharing Native-American culture with students and faculty on campus. *Scholarships*: Tuition waiver for Native-American students certified by their respective tribes. *Facility*: The Center for Southwest Studies–a research oriented center holding collections of documents focused on various regional topics including the American Indian. *Publication*: Wamidiota Newsletter.

COLORADO STATE UNIVERSITY
Native American Student Services
312 Student Services Bldg.
FORT COLLINS 80523
(303) 491-1332
Carolyn K. Fiscus, Director
Purpose: Provides support services for Native-American students of Colorado State University; to educate the university and Fort Collins communities about Native American culture and history. *Programs*: Recruiting; orientation; skill development workshops; tutorial assistance; employment opportunity advisement; financial aid assistance; peer counseling; social & cultural activities.

CONNECTICUT

WESLEYAN UNIVERSITY
Department of Anthropology
MIDDLETOWN 06457
(203) 347-9411
Courses: Ethnography of Southeastern, Southwestern and Northeastern U.S.; Native American Music. *Instructors*: Willard Walker, PhD, and David McAllester, PhD (Music).

UNIVERSITY OF CONNECTICUT
Department of Anthropology
U Box 158, 344 Mansfield Rd.
STORRS 06269
(203) 486-4865
Amy DenOuden, Coordinator
Program: Developing a program for undergraduate and graduate students of fering course work in Native cultures, histories, and contemporary political issues, as well as courses that would directly serve the particular economic needs and concerns of Native communities in New England and surrounding areas.

DISTRICT OF COLUMBIA

THE AMERICAN UNIVERSITY
Department of Anthropology
4400 Massachusetts Ave., NW
WASHINGTON 20016
(202) 885-1830
Courses: North American Indians; Bilingual Eduction (heavy Indian emphasis); American Indian Languages. A graduate (MA) degree in applied anthropology, emphasizing language and education, cultural resource management, and the process of rural community development is available throughout the department. Doctoral students often concentrate on American Indian related cultural and/or linguistic questions. *Instructors*: John J. Bodine, PhD, W illiam L. Leap, PhD, and L ynne S. Robins, PhD. *Special program*: Summer training program operated on Northern Ute reservation providing instruction in language analysis, language awareness, curriculum development, and language instruction techniques to teachers of Uto-Aztecan languages and cultures in public and tribally controlled schools. *Financial assistance*: Students of American Indian background are eligible for special opportunity funds from several sources. *Facilities*: Library of Congress and Smithsonian Institution (among others.)

AMERICAN UNIVERSITY
Native American National Intern Program
4400 Massachusetts Ave., NW
WASHINGTON 20016
(202) 885-5951
David Harrison, Director
Description: University plays host to 50 Native American and Alaska Native college students from June 4 to August 15. Designed to give the students a Washington based education, experience, and training that they can use to help their tribal communities. Program consists of three phases. The first year - a ten week internship at the White House, U.S. Congress, Dept. of HH, or other government agency and studying government at American University; the second year - an inter-tribal work-study program; and the third phase - for Native American graduate students to work and study on a reservation while writing their graduate thesis.

GEORGE WASHINGTON UNIVERSITY
Center for Native American Studies
& Indian Policy Development
2136 Pennsylvania Ave., N.W.
Washington, DC 20052
(202) 676-4401

HAWAII

UNIVERSITY OF HAWAII AT HILO
Hawaiian Studies Program
523 W. Lanikaula St.
HILO 96720
(808) 933-3414
Winifred Tatsuta, Director of Admissions

UNIVERSITY OF HAWAII AT MANOA
Hawaiian Studies Program
HONOLULU 96822
(808) 948-8975
Donald R. Fukuda, Director of Admissions

UNIVERSITY OF HAWAII
School of Public Health
American Indian & Alaska Native Program
1890 East West Rd., Moore Hall 405
HONOLULU 96822
(800) 927-3297 Fax (808) 956-6230
Rick Haverkate, MPH, Director
Special program: Educational Opportunities Program recruits Native Americans into the School as part IHS emphasis to increase numbers of Native Americans with Master's Degrees. *Instructors*: Gigliola Baruf fi, MD, MPH; Kathryn L. Braun, MPH, DrPH; John Casken, RN, MPH, PhD; Alan R. Katz, MD, MPH; W alter K. Partick, MPH; and Barbara Z. Siegel, PhD.

IDAHO

IDAHO STATE UNIVERSITY
Dept. of Sociology, Anthropology, Social Work
Indian Studies Program
P.O. Box 8005
POCATELLO 83209
(208) 236-2170
Instructors: Christopher Loether , PhD, Director (Linguistics, Language); Teri-Christine Ruan Hall, PhD, Assoc. Director (Health-Nutrition); Earnest Lohse, PhD (Native American Material Culture).

ILLINOIS

NAES COLLEGE (NATIVE AMERICAN EDUCATIONAL SERVICES)
Tribal Research Center
2838 W. Peterson Ave.
CHICAGO 60659
(312) 761-5000 Fax 761-3808
Faith Smith, President (NAES)
David R.M. Beck, Center Director
Description: An educational program accredited by the Commission on Institutions of Higher Education of the North Central Association of Colleges & Schools. Offers a B.A. degree in community studies for persons employed in American Indian programs in four communities: Chicago, Mineapolis-St. Paul; Fort Peck Reservation, MT ; and Menominee Reservation, WI. *Courses & Instructors*: Public Policy, Government & Law , Traditional and Customary Law , Advanced Studies (Robert V. Dumont, Jr.); History, Advanced Studies (David Beck); Adjunct faculty are brought in for Tribal Research seminars. For example: Basil Johnston, Darrell Kipp, Michael Tsosie and Leo Schelbert. *Special programs*: The Tribal Research Center runs the Advanced Studies program of fering courses in issues germane to tribal commuties. Week-long seminar courses in Tribal Language, History, Child and Family Issues, and research couses such as Indian Archival Research in Washington, DC and in Chicago. Students may earn an Advanced Studies Certificate in Tribal Research. In addition, the Tribal Research Center creates and disseminates bibliographies in areas relevant to the college curriculum, and provides research services to Indian communities by contract. *Facilities*: Library and Resource Center; Archives. *Publications*: College catalog directory (biennial); Indians of the Chicago Area. Monthly newsletter , TRC News; In-progress: "Public Policy Issues for American Indian Families and Children"; "Demographic Study of Children and Families in Chicago American Indian Community ." Financial aid is available through the NAES College Financial Aid Office. Library.

UNIVERSITY OF CHICAGO
American Institute of Indian Studies
Foster Hall
CHICAGO 60637
(312) 702-8638

SOUTHERN ILLINOIS UNIVERSITY
Department of Anthropology
P.O. Box 1451
EDWARDSVILLE 62026
(618) 692-2744
Instructors: Charlotte J. Frisbie, PhD, Theodore R. Frisbie, PhD, Ernest L. Schusky , PhD, Fred W. Voget, PhD (Prof. Emeritus), Margaret K. Brown, PhD (Site Director, Cahokia Mounds Interpretive Center, Collinsville, IL).

INDIANA

INDIANA UNIVERSITY
Department of Anthropology
Rawles Hall 108
BLOOMINGTON 47405
(812) 855-1203
Instructors: Della Collins Cook, PhD; Loretta Fowler, PhD (contemporary Native Americans);

Martha Kendall, PhD (ethnography & linguistics); Douglas R. Parks, PhD (linguistics). *Special Resources and Facilities*: American Indian Studies Research Institute.

BALL STATE UNIVERSITY
Department of Anthropology
MUNCIE 47306
(317) 285-1575
Native American Studies Minor . Instructor: James L. Coffin, PhD. *Special program*: An Interdisciplinary Native American Studies Program. *Facility*: Archaeology Laboratory .

INDIANA STATE UNIVERSITY
Department of Anthropology
TERRE HAUTE 47809
(812) 237-3990
Courses: Indians of North America; Native American Art and Cultures; Peoples of Middle and South America; Archaelogical Field School (excavation of Wabash Valley sites); Cultural Resource Management Practicum in lab and field procedures. *Instructors*: Hilda Delgado Pang, PhD; C. Russell Stafford, PhD; *Facility*: Archaeology Laboratory . *Scholarship*: Robert E. Pace Memorial Scholarship.

PURDUE UNIVERSITY
Dept. of Sociology & Anthropology
WEST LAFAYETTE 47907
(317) 494-4672
Courses: Indians of North America; Indians of the Greater Southwest and Great Basin; Archaeology of North America; Native American Religions and World Views; Peoples of Middle America. *Instructors*: Richard E. Blanton, PhD & Jack O. W addell, PhD.

IOWA

IOWA STATE UNIVERSITY
Department of Anthropology
319 Curtis Hall
AMES 50011
(515) 294-7139
Special Program: North American Minority Groups. *Instructors*: Benjamin R. Kracht, PhD; Helen H. Schuster, PhD (Research); R. Dale Terry (Nutritional Anthropology).

UNIVERSITY OF IOWA
American Indian & Native Studies Program
113 Macbride Hall
IOWA CITY 52242
(319) 335-0539 Fax 335-0653
June Helm, Director
A number of courses from the departments of American Studies, Anthropology, Art History, English, History, and Law are approved courses leading to a certificate or minor in the undergraduate program.

UNIVERSITY OF IOWA
College of Law
276 Boyd Law Bldg.
IOWA CITY 52242
(319) 335-9071
James Thomas & John Gates, Contacts
Offers one of the strongest Native American law programs in the country . *Faculty*: Indian law specialists - Profs. Robert Clinton & S. James Anaya. *Activities*: The Native American Law Student As-

sociation and the University of Iowa College of Law have established the Iowa Indian Defense Network, a computer bulletin board dedicated to the exchange of information, views, assistance, and rights, to Indian policy , tribal government, tribal news, and other Indian af fairs questions.

MORNINGSIDE COLLEGE
Indian Studies Department
1503 Morningside Ave.
SIOUX CITY 51106
(712) 274-5147
Dennis J. Smith, Dept. Head
Lenore Snake, Administrative Assistant
Robert J. Conley , PhD, Director, Indian Studies Program.
Courses: Dakota Languages; The Indian in American History; Native American Arts and Crafts; Literature, North American Indian Cultures, Federal Indian Law; Indian Education; Contemporary Issues; American Indian Religions; Federal Indian Law. *Programs*: Major in Indian Studies and Tribal Management; Minor in Indian Studies. *Activities*: Annual Indian Awareness Days. *Facility*: College Library with special Indian studies collection.

KANSAS

HASKELL INDIAN NATIONS UNIVERSITY
155 Indian Ave. #1305, Box I I-1304
LAWRENCE 66044
(913) 749-8403/4 Fax 749-841 1
Robert G. Martin, President
Raymond Morgan, Chairperson
Purpose: To prepare Native American students to enter colleges and universities as a first semester junior. *Programs*: Natural and Social Sciences, Humanities, Health and Physical Education, Business, Teacher Education. Operated by the Bureau of Indian Affairs.

UNIVERSITY OF KANSAS
Department of Anthropology
622 Fraser Hall
LAWRENCE 66045
(913) 864-4103
Courses: North American Indians; Contemporary North American Indians; North Americn Archaeology; Archaeology of the Great Plains; Ancient American Civilizations; Indians of South America; Physical Anthropology of American Indians; North American Indian Languages. *Instructors*: Jack L. Hofman, PhD, Alfred E. Johnson, PhD, Donald D. Stull, PhD, Robert J. Squier , PhD, Michael J. Crawford, PhD, Akira Y. Yamamoto, PhD, Robert J. Smith, PhD, and W illiam S. L yon. *Special programs*: Dr. Yamamoto works closely with the Hualapai; Dr. Stull works closely with the Kansas Kickapoo; Dr. Lyon does independent research on Native American medicine people, Plains culture. Research, technical assistance, and employment opportunities are available in the areas of applied linguistics, applied anthropology , planning and development, tribal studies, and curriculum development. *Scholarships*: Graduate fellowships and teaching and research assistantships. *Facility*: Museum of Anthropology .

KANSAS STATE UNIVERSITY
Dept. of Sociology, Anthropology, & Social W ork
204 Waters Hall
MANHATTAN 66506
(913) 532-6865 Fax 532-7004
Dr. Martin Ottenheimer , Dept. Head

Instructors: Harald Prins, PhD (Indigenous Peoples and Cultures, Native Rights Issues, Indians of Kansas); Patricia J. O'Brien, PhD (American Indian Archaeology, Precolumbian Civilizations); Walter R. AdamsPhD (Indians of Mexico and Central America); Harriet Ottenheimer , PhD, Director, American Ethnic Studies Program. *Special program*: Kansas Archaeological Field School during summer with the University of Kansas. *Financial Aid*: Educational Opportunity Fund; Minority Leadership Scholarship. *Publication*: Plains Anthropologist.

KENTUCKY

NORTHERN KENTUCKY UNIVERSITY
Department of Anthropology
Nunn Drive
HIGHLAND HEIGHTS 41099
(606) 572-5259
James F. Hopgood, Chairperson
Courses: North American Indians; Modern American Indians; North American Archaeology; Mesoamericn Archaeology. *Instructors*: James F. Hopgood, PhD, Timothy D. Murphy , PhD, Sharlotte Neely, PhD, and Barbara Thiel, PhD. *Facility*: Museum of Anthropology.

MASSACHUSETTS

HAMPSHIRE COLLEGE
Native American Studies Program
AMHERST 01002
(413) 549-4600
Olga Euben, Contact

UNIVERSITY OF MASSACHUSETTS
Harbor Campus-Dept. of Anthropology
BOSTON 02125
(617) 929-8150/8151
Courses: North American Indians; Cultures and History of Native New England; Language in Culture; Anthropology of Religion; New W orld Archaeology; Myths in Cultural Context: North America; Prehistory of Eastern North America; Meso-America: Peoples and Cultures, Prehistory and Ethnohistory. *Instructors*: Thomas Buckley, PhD, Barbara E. Luedtke, PhD, Lucy Kaplan, R. Timothy Sieber, PhD, Michiko Takaki, PhD, and Alan Harwood, PhD. *Special programs*: Field seminar in archaeology; Independent Research in Native-American Cultures and History; programs in urban anthropology and in contemporary ethnicity in the U.S.; Native American Support Group (student organization.) *Facilities*: Boston Museum of Fine Arts; Boston Library Consortium.

HARVARD UNIVERSITY
Harvard Native American Program
Graduate School of Education
Read House, Appian Way
CAMBRIDGE 02138
(617) 495-4923 Fax 495-0540
Jeffrey Hamley, Director
Purpose: To prepare American Indians to fill positions of leadership in schools and school systems serving American Indians. The Council of Native American Students is a university-wide umbrella organization comprised of Native American student organizations of the various schools of Harvard. Programs: Master's & doctorate degrees in education.

MICHIGAN

BAY MILLS COMMUNITY COLLEGE
Roue 1, Box 315A
BRIMLEY 49715
(906) 248-3354 Fax 248-3351
Martha A. McLeod, President
Description: A 2-year college providing career-oriented degree programs promoting the preservation of the customs and beliefs of Native Americans. Offers extension classes on every reservation in Michigan and many neighboring communities. *Degree programs*: Associate of Arts in Great Lakes Native American studies-Ojibway language and tribal history and literature; Associate of Applied Science in computer infomation systems, office technology and tribal administration; and Certificate programs in general business, and retailing. Instructors: Donald Abel (Ojibwe Language), Richard Jacobson, Susan Johnson-Cox, Mary McGarvey, Christine Miller, Barbara Ogston, Steven Pietrangelo, Patricia Ewing, Shirley Smart, Judy Webb, and David W illiams. Special program: Inter-Active Television Program. Facility: James Keene Cultural Heritage Center . Financial aid available.

LAKE SUPERIOR STATE UNIVERSITY
Native American Center
1000 College Dr .
Sault Stc. Maric 49783
(906) 635-2223/2195
John F. Kibble, Director

MINNESOTA

BEMIDJI STATE UNIVERSITY
Native American Studies Dept.
BEMIDJI 56601
(218) 755-2032
Dr. John Quistgaard, Contact

LEECH LAKE TRIBAL COLLEGE
Route 3, Box 100
CASS LAKE 56633

FOND DU LAC COMMUNITY COLLEGE
2101 14th St.
CLOQUET 55720
(218) 879-0880 Fax 879-0296
Lester Jack Briggs, President
Description: Tribally owned and operated 2-year college offering associate and certificate degree programs including Ojibwe language and culture, human services and student support services. *Special Program*: The Ojibwe Specialist Program is designed to meet the needs of of the Ojibwe Indian people in Minnesota, as well as reservations in the adjoining states and Canadian provinces.

ANOKA RAMSEY COMMUNITY COLLEGE
American Indian Student Services
11200 Mississippi Blvd., N.W .
COON RAPIDS 55433
(612) 422-3470 Fax 422-3341
Sharon Romano, Director

COLLEGE OF ST. SCHOLASTICA
Native American Studies Dept.
DULUTH 55811
(218) 723-6046
Nancy J. Ferreira, Contact

UNIVERSITY OF MINNESOTA, DULUTH
American Indian Learning Resource Center
114 Cina Hall, 10 University Dr.
DULUTH 55812
(218) 726-6379 Fax 726-6331
Rick J. Smith, Director
Provides campus-wide student support services to American Indian students. The goals are the recruitment and retention of American Indians, and the enhancement of their educational experience. *Services*: Academic, personal and financial aid counseling; recruitment; tutorial services; culturally oriented library; computer access; also consulting services to tribal governments & organizations; coordinates forums, seminars, & speakers.

UNIVERSITY OF MINNESOTA, DULUTH
American Indian Studies Program
American Indian Teacher Training Program
114 Cina Hall, 10 University Dr.
DULUTH 55812
(218) 726-1339
Works to prepare American Indian students for careers in professional fields including teaching, medicine, social work, and business administration. *Special program*: Master of Social Work program with a special focus on American Indian communities. *Facilities*: American Indian Learning Resource Center; Center of American Indian and Minority Health; Center of Excellence for American Indian Medical Education.

SOUTHWEST STATE UNIVERSITY
1501 State St.
MARSHALL 56258
(507) 537-6169
Bruce Carter, Contact
Provides courses in Native American history, anthropology and language.

AUGSBURG COLLEGE
American Indian Support Program
MINNEAPOLIS 55455
(612) 330-1138
Bonnie Wallace, Director
Cindy Peterson, Education Assistant
Programs: Direct assistance; counseling; advocacy. An Amerian Indian Studies minor is being proposed. The Program is connected to many community and tribal agencies. We interface with the Minneapolis American Indian Center, the Indiann Health Board, the Minnesota Indian Women's Resource Center, the Division of Indian Work, as well as India support programs in other institutions of higher education throughout the State. Also work closely with tribal education offices and departments of Indian education for Minneapolis, St. Paul and the State of Minnesota. Founded 1978.

MINNESOTA COMMUNITY COLLEGE
Dept. of Social Sciences/American Indian
1501 Hennepin Ave.
MINNEAPOLIS 55403

UNIVERSITY OF MINNESOTA
American Indian Studies Dept.
230 Williamson Hall
231 Pillsbury Dr. SE
MINNEAPOLIS 55455
(612) 625-9565; (800) 752-1000
Thomas King, Chairperson
Leo D. Abbott, Director of Administration
Offers a committment to the education of American Indian students through the following resources: American Indian Learning Resource Center, American Indian Student Cultural Center,

OMSSA Summer Institute, five American Indian student organizations, and 300 American Indian students. Ojibwe and Dakota languages of fered. Financial aid available.

MOORHEAD STATE UNIVERSITY
Department of Indian Studies
11th St. South
MOORHEAD 56560

ST. CLOUD STATE UNIVERSITY
720 4th Ave. S.
ST. CLOUD, MN 56301

MESABI COMMUNITY COLLEGE
9th & W. Chestnut St.
VIRGINIA 55792
(218) 749-7727
Jean Bakka, Director of Indian Services and Ojibwe Language & Cultural Studies Program.

MISSOURI

UNIVERSITY OF MISSOURI
Department of Anthropology
210 Switzler Hall
COLUMBIA 65211
(314) 882-4731
Courses: Cultures of Native America; Ancient American Civilization; North American Archaeology; North American Indian Culture. *Instructors*: Louanna Furbee, PhD, H. Clyde W ilson, PhD, W. Raymond Wood, PhD, and Robert F.G. Spier, PhD, and Harold W. Marshall, Director-Missouri Cultural Heritage Center–provides research opportunities in historical archaeology, history and ethnography of Missouri and surrounding states.

WASHINGTON UNIVERSITY
Center for American Indian Studies
in Social Services
Campus Box 1196
ST. LOUIS 63130
(314) 889-6288
Dana Wilson Kar, MSW, JD, Director
Established to promote the higher education of Native Americans and prepare educational and social work practitioner leaders to serve American Indians. A scholarship is of fered to Native American students intending to teach or practice social work with Indian people.

MONTANA

EASTERN MONTANA COLLEGE
Native American Studies Dept.
1500 North 30th St.
BILLINGS 59101

STONE CHILD COMMUNITY COLLEGE
Rocky Boy Route, Box 1082
BOX ELDER 59521
(406) 395-4313 Fax 395-4829
Peggy Nagel, President
A tribally-controlled (2-year) college of the Chippewa-Cree Tribe.

MONTANA STATE UNIVERSITY
Center for Native American Studies
2-152 Wilson Hall
BOZEMAN 59717
(406) 994-3881

Dr. Wayne Stein, Dept. Chair
Instructors: Walter Fleming (Native American Literature, Montana Indians); Dr. Dan Voyich (Native Amerian Education); Dr. Nancy Tucker (Native American Religion & Art, Policy & Law); Nate St. Pierre (Introduction to Native American Studies); Dr. Wayne Stein (Contemporary Issues). Special programs: Of fice of Tribal Services; American Indians Into Mathematics; Graduate Programs in Education and Political Science. Financial aid available. *Publication*: WinterCount, Bi-annual newsletter.

BLACKFEET COMMUNITY COLLEGE
P.O. Box 819
BROWNING 59417
(406) 338-5441 Fax 338-7808
Carol Tatsey-Murray, President

LITTLE BIG HORN COLLEGE
P.O. Box 370
CROW AGENCY 59022
(406) 638-2228 Fax 638-7213
Janine Pease-W indy Boy, President

FORT BELKNAP COLLEGE
P.O. Box 547
HARLEM 59526
(406) 353-2578 Fax 353-2797
Margaret C. Perez, President
Tribally controlled community college providing quality post-secondary educational opportunities for Indian residents (Assiniboine and Gros V entre Tribes) of the Fort Belknap communities. *Programs*: Vocational education, cooperative education, academic, cultural, community interest programs, courses and activities. *Services*: Assistance to tribal institutions, depts. in staf f preparation, planning research & evaluation services. Library. Financial aid available. Established 1984.

FLATHEAD VALLEY COMMUNITY COLLEGE
777 Grandview Dr.
KALISPEL 59901
(406) 755-5222

DULL KNIFE MEMORIAL COLLEGE
P.O. Box 98
LAME DEER 59043
(406) 477-6215 Fax 477-6219
Dr. Arthur MacDonald, President
Native American Studies Program

UNIVERSITY OF MONTANA
Department of Anthropology
MISSOULA 59812
(406) 243-2693
Courses: North American Indian Linguistics; Indians of North America; Indians and Indian Agents in the American West; Indians of Montana; Indians of the Southwestern U.S.; Modern Indian Problems; Archaeology of Montana-North America-Southwestern U.S.; Race and Minorities. Instructors: Carling I. Malouf, PhD, Anthony Mattina, PhD, Charlene G. Smith, PhD, Gregory R. Campbell, PhD, and Katherine M. W eist, PhD. Special resources: Extensive study collections of northwest plains ethnological and archaeological materials; Northern Plains Ethnohistory Project; Salish Linguistic Studies. *Special program*: Ethnological and archaeological field courses. *Publications*: Papers in anthropology and linguistics.

UNIVERSITY OF MONTANA
SCHOOL OF LAW
Indian Law Clinic
MISSOULA 59812
 (406) 243-4311

SALISH KOOTENAI COLLEGE
P.O. Box 117
PABLO 59855
 (406) 675-4800 Fax 675-4801
 Dr. Joseph McDonald, President
Established in 1977 by the Salish & Kootenai Tribal Council and is designed to serve the post-secondary needs of the Flathead Reservation as well as other Native Americans. *Degrees*: Offers a four-year Bachelor Degree in Human Services & several Associate Degrees and Certificates. Provides instruction in a wide variety of Native American culture programs.

FORT PECK COMMUNITY COLLEGE
P.O. Box 398
POPLAR 59255
 (406) 768-5551 Fax 768-5478
 Dr. James Shanley, President
 Anita Scheetz, Director-Library
Fully accredited two-year associates degree program. *Programs*: Native American Studies Program; and General Studies Program (business, computers, electronics, etc.). Financial aid available. Library.

NEBRASKA

UNIVERSITY OF NEBRASKA
Department of Anthropology
Bessey Hall
LINCOLN 68588
 (402) 472-2411
Program: Native American Studies Program. *Instructors*: Warren W. Caldwell, PhD, James A. Gibson, PhD, Elizabeth S. Grobsmith, PhD, Raymond Hames, PhD.

AMERICAN INDIAN SATELLITE
COMMUNITY COLLEGE
801 E. Benjamin Ave.
NORFOLK 68701
Established 1973.

NEBRASKA INDIAN COMMUNITY COLLEGE
P.O. Box 752
WINNEBAGO 68071
 (402) 878-2414 Fax 878-2522
 Thelma Thomas, President
 David Beaver, Development Officer
Description: A co-educational liberal arts and vocational education institution chartered by the Omaha, Santee Sioux and Winnebago Tribes of Nebraska. *Program*: Native American Studies.

NEVADA

UNIVERSITY OF NEVADA, LAS VEGAS
Dept. of Anthropology & Ethnic Studies
4505 Maryland Parkway
LAS VEGAS 89154
 (702) 895-3590 Fax 895-3850
Courses: Peoples & Cultures of Native North America; Contemporary Native Americans; Indians of the Southwest: Indians of Nevada & Utah (Martha C. Knack, PhD); American Indian Myth &

Religion (Palmer). *Publication*: University of Nevada Papers in Anthropology, annual.

NEW HAMPSHIRE

UNIVERSITY OF NEW HAMPSHIRE
Deptartment of Sociology & Anthropology
Horton Social Science Center
DURHAM 03824
 (603) 862-1864
Instructors: Les Field, PhD, & Robert Goodby, MA.

DARTMOUTH COLLEGE
Native American Studies Department
306-307 Bartlett Hall, Hinman Box 6152
HANOVER 03755-3530
 (603) 646-3530 Fax 646-3115
 Sergei Kan, PhD, Chair
 Linda M. Welch, Academic Assistant
Instructors: Melissa L. Meyer, PhD (North American Native History, Pre-Contact to 1830; North American Native History, 1830 to Present, Biography & Autobiography of American Indians); Elaine A. Jahner, PhD (Native American Language & Literature); Sergei Kan, PhD (Peoples and Cultures of Native North America, Contemporary Native American Society, Early Christian Missionaries Among Indian Tribes); Deborah Nichols, PhD (Ancient Native Americans); Russell G. Thornton, PhD (American Indian Population History, American Indian Revitalization Movements, Methods and Research in Native American History); Christopher Jocks, Native American Pre-Doctoral Fellow (American Indian Religion, The Iroquois and the Longhouse Religion); Michael Hanitchak, Instructor (American Indians in Film and Video); Colin G. Calloway, Visiting PhD (The New England Indians, American Indians and American Wars); Bruce Duthu, PhD (American Indian Law & Policy); and Michael A. Dorris, M.Phil. (Adjunct Professor). *Special programs*: Native American Program Student Support System and NAD (Native Americans at Dartmouth), Leisha Conners, Director; Native American Recruiting, John Sirois, Admissions Officer. *Activities*: Annual Dartmouth College Native American Pow-Wow (usually held the Saturday before Mother's Day each Spring). *Facilities*: Native American Studies Library & Research Center; Native American House; and Hood Museum of Art.

NEW JERSEY

UPSALA COLLEGE
Dept. of Sociology, Anthropology & Social Work
EAST ORANGE 07019
 (201) 266-7282
Instructor: Sylvia MacColl Rudy, PhD, Chair. *Special facilities*: North American Indian Library collection; ethnographic film collection.

RAMAPO COLLEGE
School of Intercultural Studies
Anthropology Program
P.O. Box 542
MAHWAH 07430

RUTGERS UNIVERSITY
Department of Anthropology
Douglass College, Box 270
NEW BRUNSWICK 08903
 (908) 932-9886

Special program: Native American Indian studies. Faculty: Anne-Marie Cantwell, PhD, Marla N. Powers, PhD, William K. Powers, PhD.

SETON HALL UNIVERSITY
Department of Sociology & Anthropology
FAHY Hall
SOUTH ORANGE 07070
 (201) 761-9170
Faculty: Herbert Kraft, DHL, and Maria Powers, PhD. *Special program*: Summer Lakota Field School at the Pine Ridge Reservation, Pine Ridge, South Dakota. *Special resources*: University Museum and Archaelogical Research Center maintains extensive collections of mnaterial culture of New Jersey Indian; and archaeological and ethnographical materials.

NEW MEXICO

SOUTHWESTERN INDIAN
POLYTECHNIC INSTITUTE
P.O. Box 10146, 9169 Coors Rd., NW
ALBUQUERQUE 87184
 (505) 897-5347 Fax 897-5343
 Dr. Carol Elgin, President
 Duane Yazzie, Chairperson
Administered by the Bureau of Indian Affairs, under the jurisdiction of Albuquerque Area Office. SIPI is dedicated to training American Indian adults for jobs in the technical-vocational fields. *Special Student Services*: Program offers special assistance and support services to students and staff in the understanding and treatment of alcohol and drug abuse. Sponsors health promotion education class, support groups, sweatlodge, peer counseling training, and substance abuse education classes. Library. Publishes numerous pamphlets related to substance abuse. Established in 1974.

UNIVERSITY OF NEW MEXICO
American Indian Graduate Center
4520 Montgomery Blvd. NE, Suite 1-B
ALBUQUERQUE 87131
 (505) 881-4584
Provides fellowship grants to Indian graduate students. Assists about 600 students from 130 tribes at over 200 colleges throughout the U.S.

UNIVERSITY OIF NEW MEXICO
SCHOOL OF LAW
American Indian Law Center
1117 Stanford Dr. N.E.
ALBUQUERQUE 87131

UNIVERSITY OF NEW MEXICO
Department of Anthropology
ALBUQUERQUE 87131
 (505) 277-4524
Instructors: Louise A. Lamphere, PhD, Alfonso A. Ortiz, PhD, Keith H. Basso, PhD, Ali Mohammed Ali Elmak, MA (Research), David R. Risser, PhD (Research). *Facility*: Maxwell Museum of Anthropology. *Publication*: Journal of Anthropological Research. Library.

UNIVERSITY OF NEW MEXICO
Native American Studies Dept.
1812 Las Lomas Dr., NE
ALBUQUERQUE 87131
 (505) 277-3917
 Theodore Jojola, PhD, Chairperson
 Alison Freese, PhD, Information Specialist
 Jimmy Shendo, Student Resource Specialist

Description: Develops and promotes regional studies of Native Americans, their concerns and their communities. *Special programs*: Native American Inervention and Retention Project; Information and Materials Resource Collection. *Activities*: Sponsors lecture series, specialized seminars and conferences; regular course of ferings. Library. *Facilities*: Institute for Native American Development. *Financial aid*: Various scholarships available. *Publications*: NAS Newsline, monthly newsletter; Pathways Off the Rez, a student handbook.

CROWNPOINT INSTITUTE OF TECHNOLOGY
P.O. Box 849
CROWNPOINT 87313
  (505) 786-5851 Fax 786-5644
  Robert M. Dorak, President
Description: Tribally owned and controlled education institution chartered by the Navajo Nation. *Programs*: Training; adult basic education; academic remediation; income tax preparation; and young entrpreneurship training.

NEW MEXICO UNIVERSITY
Department of Sociology & Anthropology.
Box 30001, Dept. 3BV
LAS CRUCES 88003
  (505) 646-3821
Instructors: Bradley A. Blake, PhD, Michelle Hegman, PhD, Fred Plog, PhD, E. Scott Rushforth, PhD. *Special program*: Cultural Resources Management Division--specializing in New Mexico; summer field school in archaeology (Mogollon), Southwest studies. Facilities: University Museum; laboratories for research.

NEW MEXICO UNIVERSITY
Indian Resource Development
Box 3000, Dept. 3IRD
LAS CRUCES 88003
  (505) 646-1347 Fax 646-5975
  Lance Lujan, Director
Purpose: To encourage American Indian students to attend the university of their choice and major in natural resouce related fields. *Publications*: Indian Country Student News; Sources of Financial Aid Available to American Indian Students (booklet). Established in 1977.

NEW MEXICO HIGHLANDS UNIVERSITY
Native American Studies Department
LAS VEGAS 87701
  (505) 425-7511
Description: Provides an opportunity for Indians and non-Indians to study Indian cultures and their significant contributions to contemporary U.S. culture. It is a compenent of the Behavioral Sciences Department and has the concentration of study in sociology/anthropology; provided in combination with courses containing Indian content of fered in other University divisions. *Instructors*: Margaret Vasquez-Geffroy, PhD (anthropolgy), Michael L. Olsen, PhD (history), William Lux, PhD (history), and Wallace Johnson (art.) *Special program*: Kat-Zi-Ma-To-Wah--Native American students club. Scholarships available.

EASTERN NEW MEXICO UNIVERSITY
Dept. of Social and Behavioral Sciences
PORTALES 88130
  (505) 562-2438/2583
  Dr. Phillip H. Shelley, Dept. Head
Instructors: George Agogino, PhD, William Hawk, PhD, Phillip Shelley, PhD, Joanne Dickenson, MA, and John L. Montgomery, PhD. Financial Aid: Graduate Assistantships, work study, Blackwater Draw Undergraduate Museum Fellowships. *Spe-*

cial facilities: Peleo-Indian Institute and Museum; ceramic and lithic anaylsis laboratories; University Library.

INSTITUTE OF AMERICAN INDIAN ARTS
P.O. Box 20007
SANTA FE 87504
  (505) 988-6463 Fax 988-6446
  Dr. Perry G. Horse, President
  Robert H. Ames Piestewa (Hopi),
  Wiley T. Buchanan III, David Lester (Creek),
  and William S. Johnson, Board of Trustees
Description: Federally chartered private institution. The only accredited fine arts college devoted solely to the study of American Indian and Alaska Native art. Offers learning opportunities in the arts and crafts to Native American youth (Indian, Eskimo and Aleut.) Emphasis is placed upon Indian traditions as the basis for creative expression in the fine arts. *Activities*: Maintains the Center for Research and Cultural Exchanges, Reuben A. Snake, Dean. Sponsors Indian arts-oriented Junior College offering Associate of Fine Arts degrees in various fields as well as seminars, and exhibition program, and traveling exhibits; maintains extensive library, museum, and biographical archives. *Publications*: Coyote on the Turtle's Back, annual; Faculty & Student Handbooks and School Catalog, annual; Spawning the Medicine River, annual. Founded 1962.

SCHOOL OF AMERICAN RESEARCH
Indian Arts Research Center
P.O. Box 2188
SANTA FE 87504
  (505) 982-3584 Fax 989-9809
  Douglas W. Schwartz, PhD, President
  Duane Anderson, PhD, VP Operations
Courses: American Indian art and archaeology; Southwest archaeology and anthropology; Pueblo pottery. *Instructors*: Lynn Brittner-Hutton (Curator of Collections), Christy S. Hof fman (Associate Collections Manager); Michael J. Hering (Director of Indian Arts Research Center), Jane Kepp (Publications Director), Douglas W. Schwartz, PhD, Cecile Stein (Academic Program Coordinator), Debra Martin, PhD (Resident Scholar, Prehistoric American Indian Health). *Special programs*: Resident Scholar Programs; Anthropology Program; Fellowships in Native American Art and Education Program; lectures and exhibitions. *Special resources*: collection of 9,000+ objects of Southwestern American Indian art and anthropology; archaeology laboratory. *Fellowships*: Katrin H. Lamon Resident Scholar and Artist Fellowships for Native Americans. *Publications*: Advanced Seminar Series; American Indian Art Series; Grand Canyon Archaeology Series; Arroyo Hondo Archaeological Series. Library.

NAVAJO COMMUNITY COLLEGE
P.O. Box 580
SHIPROCK 87420
  (505) 368-5291
See Navajo Community College (T saile, Arizona)

ZUNI ARCHAEOLOGY PROGRAM
Pueblo of Zuni, P.O. Box 339
ZUNI 87327
  (505) 782-4814
  Roger Anyon, Director
Staff: Roger Anyon, Ramona Avallone, Craig Birrell, Carol Brandt, Edward Kotyk, Kaer Morris, Jeanette Quintero, Patricia Ruppe, Mark Sant, Elizabeth Skinner, Jeffrey Waseta, Robert Waterworth, Rose W yaco, Jerome Zunie. *Research Facilities*: Collections; large amounts of

unpublished data and historical photos for Zuni Indian Reservation. Library. *Publications*: Report Series.

NEW YORK

STATE UNIVERSITY OF NEW YORK, ALBANY
Department of Anthropology
1400 Washington Ave.
ALBANY 12222
  (518) 442-4700 Fax 442-5710
  Richard G. Wilkinson, Chairperson
Faculty: Richard Wilkinson, PhD; Liliana R. Goldin, PhD; Gary H. Gosen, PhD; Robert W. Jarvenpa, PhD; Gail H. Landsman, PhD; Lawrence M. Schell, PhD; Gary A. Wright, PhD; G. Aaron Broadwell, PhD; Hetty Jo Brumbach, PhD; Louise Burkhart, PhD; James Collins, PhD; John Justeson, PhD; Michael Smith, PhD; Dean Snow, PhD; and Robert M. Carmack, PhD. Special programs/facilities: Teaching laboratories in archaeology and physical anthropology; field schools in archaeology and ethnology, U.S. and Mesoamerica. Financial aid available. *Publications*: Northeast Anthropology; Institute for Mesoamerican Studies publications; Institute for Archaeological Studies publications; Departmental Guide for Graduate Studies.

BUFFALO STATE COLLEGE
Native American Student Services
1300 Elmwood Ave.
BUFFALO 14222
  (716) 878-4631 Fax 878-6600

STATE UNIVERSITY OF NEW YORK, BUFFALO
Dept. of Anthropology
4242 Ridge Lea Rd.
BUFFALO 14261
  (716) 636-2414
Programs: Linguistics; American Studies. *Instructors*: Frederick Gearing, PhD, Ann P. McElroy, PhD, Ben A. Nelson, PhD, Ezra B. W. Zubrow, PhD, William Engelbrecht, PhD, Charles M. Keil, PhD, Dennis Tedlock, PhD, and Madeleine Mathiot, PhD. *Special program*: Contemporary North American Indians and Eskimos; Northeast U.S. prehistory. Museum. Library.

STATE UNIVERSITY OF NEW YORK, BUFFALO
Native American Studies Programs
Hayes Annex A, Main St. Campus
BUFFALO 14214
  (716) 831-2111

STATE UNIVERSITY OF NEW YORK, GENESEO
Dept. of Anthropology
GENESEO 14454
  (716) 245-5277
Instructors: Russell Judkins (Iroquois, Catawba); Sue N. Roark-Calnek (Native American ethnicity, Algonquin & W oodlands ethnology).

COLGATE UNIVERSITY
Dept. of Sociology & Anthropology
HAMILTON 13346
  (315) 824-7543
Instructors: Gary Urton, PhD, Chairperson; and Anthony F. Aveni, PhD. *Special program*: Interdisciplinary topical concentration in Amerindian Studies, embracing the fields of Native-American religion, astronomy, art, and archaeology. *Special facility*: Longyear Museum of Anthropology/ laboratory–features collections of local Oneida Iroquois & Mesoamerican archaeological materials.

FRIENDS WORLD COLLEGE
Native American Studies Program
HUNTINGTON 11743
(516) 549-1102

CORNELL UNIVERSITY
American Indian Program
300 Caldwell Hall
ITHACA 14853
(607) 255-4308
Ron LaFrance, Director
Debbie Bannister, Admin. Aide
Robert Venables, Faculty
Purpose: To extend Cornell resources to Indian communities; to create public and published forums to examine Indian issues, and to encourage opportunities for faculty members in all disciplines to incorporate Indian content in their courses. The American Indian Program is a multi-disciplinary, intercollege program, coordinating activities in academics, student support, extension, university residence life, and publications.

STATE UNIVERSITY OF NEW YORK
Department of Anthropology
Anthropology House
NEW PALTZ 12561
(914) 257-2990 Fax 257-3009
B.E. Pierce, PhD, Chair
Programs: Nati ve American Studies Minor. Instructors: Karin Andriolo (Ancient MesoAmerica); Joseph Diamond (Archaeology); Giselle Hendel-Sebastye (Indians of North America). *Special programs*: Archeology Field School (summers); excavations in the Hudson Valley.

STATE UNIVERSITY OF NEW YORK
Department of Anthropology
ONEONTA 13820
(607) 431-3345
Instructors: William A. Starna, PhD; and Jack Campisi, PhD (part-time). Eastern W oodlands, Iroquoians, Algonquians.

STATE UNIVERSITY OF NEW YORK
Department of Anthropology & Sociology
OSWEGO 13126
(315) 341-4190
Program: Native American Studies. *Instructors*: Charles A. Bishop, PhD, M. Estellie Smith, PhD.

STATE UNIVERSITY OF NEW YORK
Dept. of Anthropology
POTSDAM 13676
(315) 267-2053
Program: Native American Studies minor.

NORTH CAROLINA

PEMBROKE STATE UNIVERSITY
Native American Resource Center
Native American Studies Program
PEMBROKE 28372
(919) 521-4214
Juanita O. Locklear, Director

NORTH DAKOTA

TURTLE MOUNTAIN COMMUNITY COLLEGE
P.O. Box 340
BELCOURT 58316
(701) 477-5605 Fax 477-5028

Gerald Monette, President
Dr. Larry Belgarde, Academic Dean
Description: Functions as an autonomous Indian controlled college on the reservation focusing on general studies and vocational education programs. Seeks to establish an administration, faculty and student body involved in community affairs. *Courses and Faculty*: Social Sciences (R. Kekahbah, L. Peltier, E. Wilkie); Computer Science (M. Belgarde); Business (Julie Desjarlais and R. Gustafson); Wildlife Studies (Jef f Desjarlais); Humanities (I. Mikkelson); Building Trades (R. Parisien); among others. *Special program*: Indian Entrepreneurship Program. Financial aid available. *Publications*: The Michif Dictionary; Chippewa/Cree Language; The Cree Dictionary.

UNITED TRIBES TECHNICAL COLLEGE
3315 University Dr.
BISMARCK 58501
(701) 255-3285 Ext. 293 Fax 255-1844
David M. Gipp, President
Publication: Indian Recipe Book, $5.00.

LITTLE HOOP COMMUNITY COLEGE
P.O. Box 269
FORT TOTTEN 58335
(701) 766-4415 Fax 766-4389
Dr. Merril Berg, President
Head Start Program.

STANDING ROCK COLLEGE
HC 1, Box 4
FORT YATES 58538
(701) 854-3861 Fax 854-3403
Offers A.A., A.A.S. & A.S. two year degrees. *Special programs*: B.A. degree through Minot State University; offer Irrigation Farm Management program. Scholarships. *Affiliation*: American Indian Higher Education Consortium.

UNIVERSITY OF NORTH DAKOTA
Dept. of Indian Studies
GRAND FORKS 58202
(701) 777-4314
John L. Salter, Jr., Ph.D., Chair
Courses: Introductory Law, Contemporary Problems; Plains Indian W omen, Art; Literature, Philosophy, Religion. *Instructors*: John Salter, Ph.D., Mary Jane Schneider, PhD, Joseph DeFlyer, PhD; Janet G. Ahler, PhD (Center for Teaching and Learning); John Crawford, PhD (English); Fred Schneider, Ph.D. & Stanley A. Ahler, PhD (Anthropology). *Special programs*: Specializes in the archaeology and anthropology of the Northern Plains; summer Field School in Archaeology; Archaeology programs at Knife River Indian V illages and Knife River Flint Quarries.

UNIVERSITY OF NORTH DAKOTA
School of Medicine
Indians Into Medicine Program
501 N. Columbia Rd., Box 9001
GRAND FORKS 58203
(701) 777-3037
Gary Farris, Director
Program: Offers assistance to students who are preparing to study or are currently studying to become physicians, nurses and other health professionals. *Publication*: Serpent, Staf f and Drum, a quarterly newsletter.

UNIVERSITY OF NORTH DAKOTA
College of Nursing
P.O. Box 9025
GRAND FORKS 58203
(701) 777-3224 Fax 777-4558

Chris Burd, RN, Director
Deb Wilson, MS, Coordinator
Program: Quentin N. Burdick Indians Into Nursing (RAIN Program - The Recruitment/Retention of American Indians Into Nursing (RAIN) Project is a support program for American Indians pursuing their bachelors or master's degrees in nursing at the University of North Dakota. *Financial aid*: Scholarships are based on availability of funds. *Publication*: RAIN Notes, newsletter.

FORT BERTHOLD COMMUNITY COLLEGE
P.O. Box 490
NEW TOWN 58763
(701) 627-3665 Fax 627-3805
Lynn Dockter-Pinnick, President
Description: Located near the scenic Lake Sakakawea area of Fort Berthold Reservation. Tribally owned & controlled. The curriculum is founded in liberal arts, which integrates successfully with most professional and paraprofessional career pursuits.

OHIO

UNION INSTITUTE
Native American Studies Program
CINCINNATI 45202
(513) 621-6400

OKLAHOMA

UNIVERSITY OF SCIENCE & ARTS OF OK
Dept. of American Indian Studies
CHICKASHA 73018
(405) 224-3140 Fax 521-6244
Howard Meredith, Chairperson
Courses: Cross-Cultural Communication; Oklahoma Indian Tradition & History; Contemporary American Indian Issues; American Indian Literature, Education, Economics, History and Arts; Tribal Government & Law. *Faculty*: Rose Marie Smith, Sarah W ebb; lecturers - Nathan Hart, John Thompson, V anessa Morgan. *Special program*: Internships with regional tribes and organziations. Financial aid available.

ROGERS STATE COLLEGE
Native American Studies Program
CLAREMORE 74017
(918) 341-7510
Betty F. Scott, Contact

ROSE STATE COLLEGE
Native American Studies Program
MIDWEST CITY 73110
(405) 733-7308
Joe Johnson, Contact

BACONE COLLEGE
2299 Old Bacone Rd.
MUSKOGEE 74403
(918) 683-4581
Louie Jackson, Counselor
David Comsilk, Contact
Description: 115 year-old, one-room schoolhouse at Cherokee Baptist Mission in Tahlequah (Indian Territory), Oklahoma's oldest continuing center of higher education, and the only church-related college in the country with an educational mission to American Indians. *Progams*: Offers AA degrees.

UNIVERSITY OF OKLAHOMA
Dept. of Anthropology
455 W. Lindsey
NORMAN 73019
 (405) 325-3261/2519
Instructors: Paul E. Minnis, PhD, John H. Moore, Ph.D., Susan C. Vehik, PhD, Morris E. Opler , PhD, Joseph Whitecotton, PhD, Patricia A. Gilman, PhD, Richard A. Pailes, PhD, Morris Foster , Ph.D., Robert Fields (Plains Indian Culture), Henry F . Dobyns, PhD (Adjunct Professor), John A. Dunn, PhD (Linguistic Dept.), Rain V ehik, PhD (Director-Archaeology Research and Management Center), and Don G. Wyckoff, PhD (Director-Oklahoma Archaeological Survey.) The Department specializes in the study of the American Indian with emphasis on the Indians of OK, the Plains, Southwestern U.S. and Mexico. *Financial aids* : Graduate Teaching Assistantships, Minority Graduate Fellowships. *Facilities* : Western History Collection; OK Museum of Natural History; within easy access to representatives of more than 60 Indian tribes; the presence of an active Salvage archaeology program for the State of OK; resources of the Stovall Museum, and an extensive library collection on the American Indian of fer special opportunities for the study of the archaeology , linguistics, ethnohistory and ethnology of the American Indian.

UNIVERSITY OF OKLAHOMA
Native American Studies Program
Dept. of Anthropology
455 W. Lindsey, Rm. 804
NORMAN 73019
 (405) 325-2312 Fax 325-0535
 Barbara Hopson, PhD, Interim Director
Courses & Instructors : Native Peoples of Oklahoma & North America (Bill Anderson & Martha McCollough); Contemporary Indian Problems; Inrtermediate American Indian Languages (Laura Anderson, Jack Schultz, Pam Innes, Marcia Haag); Oklahoma Prehistory (Robert Brooks); Ethnology of the Greater Southwest & Desert Cultures of North America (Richard Pailes); Anthropology of the Caddoan People (Don W yckoff); Native Peoples of the Southeastern U.S. (Morris Foster); Native American Intercultural Communication & The Indian in American Popular Culture (Phil Lujan); American Indian Literature & Native American Communication Research (Geary Hobson); Prehistoric American Indian Aesthetics & 20th Century American Indian Aesthetics (Mary Jo Watson); Native American Music (Mary Jo Ruggles); Cultural Geography of Indigenous Native America (Bob Rundstrom).

UNIVERSITY OF OKLAHOMA
COLLEGE OF LAW
Center for the Study of
American Indian Law & Policy
300 W. Timberdell Rd.
NORMAN 73019
 (405) 325-4699
 Prof. Rennard Strickland, Director

UNVERSITY OF OKLAHOMA
HEALTH SCIENCES CENTER
Headlands Indian Health Careers
P.O. Box 26901
Oklahoma City 73190
 (405) 271-2250
Description : Provides a science & mathematics enrichment and reinforcement program, consisting of courses in biology , chemistry, physics and mathematics. 8 weeks during the summer . Grants to Native American students who are interested in preparing for careers as health professionals.

UNIVERSITY OF OKLAHOMA
COLLEGE OF MEDICINE
Native American Center of Excellence
P.O. Box 26901
OKLAHOMA CITY 73190
 (405) 271-2316
 Philip A. McHale, Contact
A federally-funded collaborative program whose ultimate goal is to increase the number of Native American physicians practicing medicine in the U.S. Jointly sponsored by the Center for Tribal Studies, Northeastern State University (T ahlequah, OK) and the University of Oklahoma College of Medicine.

NORTHEASTERN STATE UNIVERSITY
Native American Center of Excellence
Center for Tribal Studies
TAHLEQUAH 74464
 (918) 456-5511 ext. 3690 Fax 458-2193
 Dr. Neil Morton, Director
Description : A federally-funded collaborative program whose ultimate aim is to increase the number of Native American physicians practicing medicine in the U.S. It is jointly sponsored by the Center for Tribal Studies at Northeastern State University and The University of Oklahoma College of Medicine.

UNIVERSITY OF TULSA COLLEGE OF LAW
American Indian Law Certification Program
3120 E. 4th Place
TULSA 74104
 (918) 631-2439
 Gloria Valencia-W eber, Contact
Prepares students for legal work on critical issues that concern American Indians and Native Alaskans. Studies include course work, research, and practical experience in externships and tribal entities. The American Indian Law Student Organization at the University of Tulsa College of Law is devoted to meeting the social, cultural and educational needs of it membership. Students completing the program receive the J.D. degree and certification in the Indian law specialty .

OREGON

OREGON STATE UNIVERSITY
Department of Anthropology
Waldo Hall 238
CORVALLIS 97331
 (503) 737-4515
Special program : Devotes special emphasis and coordination to programs in cultural resources, applied anthropology , cooperative studies with American Indians, historical archaeology , and ethnohistory. *Instructors* : David R. Brauner, PhD, Richard E. Ross, PhD.

UNIVERSITY OF OREGON
 Department of Anthropology
EUGENE 97403
 (503) 346-5102
Instructors : C. Melvin Aikens, PhD, Madonna L. Moss, PhD, Ann Gibson Simonds, PhD; Richard D. Cheatham, PhD and Thomas J. Connolly (Archaeology-Museum of Anthropology).

EASTERN OREGON STATE COLLEGE
Native American Program
1410 "L" Ave.
LA GRANDE, OR 97850
 (503) 962-3741

Goal : To assist in the development of student potential so that they may achieve educational and personal goals. Assists American Indian and Alaskan Native students in financial aid planning, academic and career counsleing and personal guidance. *Activities* : Speel-Ya Indian Student Organization - a cultural and social support group on campus working to educate the campus and community of La Grande on traditional and contemporary Native American life.

BLUE MOUNTAIN COMMUNITY COLLEGE
Indian Education Coordinator
P.O. Box 100, 2411 NW Carden
PENDLETON 97801
 (503) 276-1260 ext. 289
Special program : Provides assistance for Native American students in securing financial aid, academic and social counseling & general assistance.

PORTLAND STATE UIVERSITY
Dept. of Anthropology
P.O. Box 751
PORTLAND 97207
 (503) 725-3914
Instructors : Thomas Biolsi, PhD, Joe E. Pierce (Professor Emeritus), Fred W . Voget, PhD (Adjunct Professor).

PENNSYLVANIA

GETTYSBURG COLLEGE
Department of Sociology & Anthropology
P.O. Box 412
GETTYSBURG 17325
 (717) 337-6191
Instructors : Franklin Loveland, PhD; Amelia M. Trevelyan, PhD (Native American art, symbolic anthropology). *Special Resources* : Harcourt Library holdings on Native Americans; The Herman Finkelstein Primitive Mask Collection.

GETTYSBURG COLLEGE
American Indian Research & Resource Institute
Gettysburg 17325
 (717) 337-6265
 Dr. Frank W. Porter, III, Director
Purpose : To study the history and culture of American Indians, with emphasis on tribes residing in the eastern U.S.; to provide technical assistance to non-recognized tribes seeking Federal acknowledgment from the B.I.A. *Facilities* : Harcourt Library maintains a special collection on Native Americans; also the Herman Finkelstein Primitive Mask Collection. Founded 1983.

PENNSYLVANIA STATE UNIVERSITY
American Indian Leadership Program (AILP)
320 Rackley Bldg.
UNIVERSITY PARK 16802
 (814) 865-1489
 Linda Warner, PhD, Director
Description: "AILP is the oldest on-going graduate program for Native Americans in the country . The training of qualified leaders for service to Indian nations is the central aim of the program." Provides advanced degrees of fered are MBA, MEd, MS, DEd, and PhD. *Activities* : American Indian Seminar; Native American Indian Student Association; Research Projects; National Conferences; Field Trips. Fianncial aid available in the form of fellowships and graduate asistantships. Publications. Library . Established 1970.

College Courses & Programs

PENNSYLVANIA STATE UNIVERSITY

American Indian Special Education
Teacher Training Program
226B Moore Bldg.
UNIVERSITY PARK 16802
(814) 863-2284
Dr. Anna H. Gajar, Director

Description: Designed to prepare highly trained professionals for careers in the field. The program integrates a behavioral approach to special educatin in the areas of autism, mental retardation, severe emotional disorders, mild learning and behavioral disabilities, and early childhood disabilities. Issues in American Indian special and regular education are emphasized in seminars and coursework. Graduates receive a master's or a doctoral degree in special education. Financial aid available. Established 1983

SOUTH DAKOTA

CHEYENNE RIVER COMMUNITY COLLEGE

P.O. Box 220, N. Elm St.
EAGLE BUTTE 57625
(605) 964-8635 Fax 964-1000
Joe Lends His Horse, President

Description: Located on the Cheyenne River Sioux Reservation serving the higher education needs of over 10,000 area residents & approximately 5,500 enrolled tribal members.

OGLALA LAKOTA COLLEGE

P.O. Box 490
KYLE 57752
(605) 455-2321 Fax 867-1 141
Dr. Elgin Bad W ound, President

Programs: Native American Studies Program; Native American Studies Graduate Program.

SINTE GLESKA COLLEGE

Lakota Studies/Creative W riting Program
P.O. Box 8
MISSION 57555
Victor Douville, Dept. Head

Instructors: Charlene Lowry and Simon J. Ortiz.
Special activities: Annual creative writing and storytelling festival; poetry reading series and residences, & performances and lectures by writers, scholars, and oral tradition masters; awards for creative writing (fiction and poetry .) *Publication*: Wanbli Ho Journal, by creative writing program.

DAKOTA WESLEYAN UNIVERSITY

Native American Studies Program
MITCHELL 57301
(605) 995-2650

OGLALA SIOUX COMMUNITY COLLEGE

PINE RIDGE 57770

SINTE GLESKA COLLEGE

P.O. Box 490
ROSEBUD 57570
(605) 747-2263 Fax 747-2098
Lionel Bordeaux, President;
Cheryl Crazybull, V.P.
Lavina Mile, East Reservation Branch Coord.
Established to provide postsecondary education on the Rosebud Sioux Reservation. *Departments & Faculty*: General Studies: Godfrey Loudner & Diana Torson (Co-Chair), Curt Yehnert and Don Krug; Lakota Studies: V ictor Douville (Chair), Duane Hollow Horn Bear , Doris Leader Charge,

Leland Little Dog, Stanley Red Bird, and Albert White Hat; Education: Archie Beauvais & Cheryl Medearis (Co-Chair) and Trudy Knowles; Secondary Education: Leland Bordeaux (Director), Joe Gill, Mark Ward and David W iesser; Applied Science (Vocational Education): James Poignee (Director/Chair), Arlene Brandis, Rod Bordeaux, Vernon Kuper , Trent Teegerstrom, and Benjamin Whiting; Human Services: Sheryl Klein (Chair), Bill Akard, Burdette Clif ford and Rodger Hornby; Student Support Services: Fred Leader Charge (Chair), Irene Garrett, Scot Harrison, Jerry Lester and Dwayne Stenstrom; Special Education: Wendy Murray; Art Institute: Margaret MacKichan and Paul Koehler; Business Administration & Management: Nora Antoine (Chair), Craig Anderson and Ron Hutchinson. *Special program*: A Health Careers Opportunity Program (Oyate Kin Zanipi Ktelo-Health for the People) designed to increase the number of American Indians entering health professions—health careers financial aid information is available directly from the Health Careers Program. *Financial Aid*: Available through the College's Financial Aid Office. *Special facility*: Lakota Archives and Historical Center .

SIOUX FALLS COLLEGE

Dept. of Native American Studies
1501 South Prairie Ave.
SIOUX FALLS 57101

SISSETON-WAHPETON COMMUNITY COLLEGE

Agency Village CPO, Box 689
SISSETON 57262
(605) 698-3966 Fax 698-3132
Gwen Hill, President

A 2-year tribal college of fering Associate of Arts degrees. *Special programs*: Community education; Dakota Studies Department. Scholarship: $500 for graduating high schoo senior at attend SWCC. *Facilities*: Tribal Archives Development. *Publication*: Dakota Language Text (3 texts for learning the Dakota Language. Established 1974.

BLACK HILLS STATE UNIVERSITY

Native American Studies Program
SPEARFISH 57783
(605) 642-6343

UNIVERSITY OF SOUTH DAKOTA

Institute of American Indian Studies
414 East Clark St.
VERMILLION 57069-2390
(605) 677-5209
Leonard R. Bruguier , Director

Serves as the focal point for American Indian related projects, activities, and programs involving the University of South Dakota. *Activities*: Organizes campus programs to promote education and awareness of American Indian culture, issues, and problems; assisting University ef forts to recruit and retain Amerian Indian students and faculty; encouraging increased levels of research on American Indian life; and stregthening relations with tribes, tribal colleges, and other appropriate American Indian organizations in the state and region. University sponsored graduate/research assistantship for school year . *Publications*: Who's Who Among the Sioux, $15.00; reports, papers, conference proceedings. Library .

YANKTON COLLEGE

221 W. 3rd St.
YANKTON 57078-4322

TEXAS

UNIVERSITY OF TEXAS

Department of Anthropology
AUSTIN 78712
(512) 471-4206

Instructors: Thomas N. Campbell, PhD, E. Mott Davis, PhD, James A. Neely, PhD, Joel Sherzer, PhD, Brian M. Stross, PhD, Greg P . Urban, PhD, Darrell G. Creel, PhD, Anthony C. Woodbury (Linguistics Dept.) *Special programs*: MA & PhD in Folklore. *Special facility*: TX Archaeological Research Laboratory; TX Memorial Museum; Linguistic Research Center; A.A. Hill Linguistics Library .

TEXAS TECH UNIVERSITY

Ethnic Studies Program
Department of Anthropology
LUBBOCK 79409
(806) 742-2228
James A. Goss, PhD, Director.

INCARNATE WORD COLLEGE

Native American Studies Program
Department of Anthropology
4301 Broadway
SAN ANTONIO 78209
(512) 828-1261 ext. 247

Instructors: Donald L. McKain, PhD, and Eloise Stoker. *Special program*: Interdisciplinary Program in Native American Studies.

UTAH

UTAH STATE UNIVERSITY

Native American Studies Program
LOGAN 84322
(801) 750-1106

BRIGHAM YOUNG UNIVERSITY

Indian Education Program
Department of Anthropology
PROVO 84602
(801) 378-3058

Education Instructors: Willis M. Banks, Owen C. Bennion, Hall L. Black, Janice White Clemmer , Arturo DeHoyos, William Fox, Frederick R. Gowans, Rondo S. Harmon, Kenneth Rush Sumpter, Victor R. Westover, Darlene Herndon, Charlotte D. Lofgreen, John R. Maestas, V ergus C. Osborn, and W . Dean Rigby. *Anthropology Instructors*: Dale L. Berge, PhD, Donald W . Forsyth, PhD, Ray T. Matheny, PhD, Joel C. Janetski, PhD, James D. Wilde, PhD (Museum of Peoples and Cultures). *Special programs*: Field Schools, historic and prehistoric site, Utah; Nancy Patterson Village Project, southeastern Utah. *Special facilities*: Museum of Peoples and Cultures; archaeological laboratories; Gates Collection on Middle American Languages. Library .

UNIVERSITY OF UTAH

Center for Ethnic Student Affairs (CESA)
318 Union Bldg.
SALT LAKE CITY 84112
(801) 581-8151
Beverly Sutteer

VERMONT

GODDARD COLLEGE
Native American Studies Program
PLAINFIELD 05667
(802) 454-8311

VIRGINIA

HAMPTON UNIVERSITY
American Indian Ed. Opportunities Program
The Graduate College
HAMPTON 23668
(804) 727-5454
Dr. Paulette Molin, Director

WASHINGTON

NORTHWEST INDIAN COLLEGE
2522 Kwina Rd.
BELLINGHAM 98226
(206) 676-2772 Fax 384-4737
Dr. Robert J. Lorence, President
Purpose: To provide postsecondary opportunities for Indian people. Includes academic and vocational education. Provides in-service training, planning, research, & evaluation services to tribal institutions and departments. A tribally-controlled insitution chartered by the Lummi Indian Business Council.

WESTERN WASHINGTON UNIVERSITY
Department of Anthropology, MS-9083
BELLINGHAM 98225
(206) 650-3620 Fax 650-7295
Robert C. Marshall, Chairperson
Courses: Native Peoples of North America, Indians of the Northwest Coast; Ethnohistory, Prehistory of North America, Archaeology of Northwestern North America. *Instructors*: Daniel L. Boxberger, PhD, Sarah Campbell, PhD, and James Louchy, PhD; and adjunct faculty: Lynn A. Robbins, PhD & Leslie Conton, PhD. *Special program*: Archaeological and Ethnohistory Field Schools. *Special facilities*: Archaeological laboratory; Northwest Ethnohistory Archives (research on culture change and American Indian ethnohistory.) The Dept. of American Cultural Studies offers: The Native American Experience.

EASTERN WASHINGTON UNIVERSITY
Native American Studies Dept.
CHENEY 99004
(509) 359-2433

EVERGREEN STATE COLLEGE
Native American Studies Program
OLYMPIA 98505
(206) 866-6000

WASHINGTON STATE UNIVERSITY
Comparative American Studies
Department of Anthropology
PULLMAN 99164-4910
(509) 335-3441
Courses: Native Peoples of North America, Conntemporary Native Peoples of the Americas, America Before Columbus. *Instructors*: Robert E. Ackerman, PhD, John H. Bodley, PhD (Chair), Mark S. Fleisher, PhD, Timothy A. Kohler, PhD, William D. Lipe, PhD, Peter J. Mehringer, Jr., PhD,

Kenneth L. Petersen, PhD (Adjunct Prof.) Allan H. Smith, PhD (Prof. Emeritus), Lillian A. Ackerman, PhD (Researcher), Geofrey L. Gamble, PhD (Linguistics), and William Willard, PhD (Comparative American Studies.) *Special programs*: Archaeology and ethnography of the western U.S., with emphasis on American Indian, Pacific and Asian cultural, anthropology, linguistics and archaeology. *Special facilities*: Research laboratories; Museum; extensive research and reference collections in western U.S. archaeology, botany, and ethnographic basketry.

UNIVERSITY OF WASHINGTON
American Indian Studies Center
Department of Anthropology
SEATTLE 98195
(206) 543-5240
James D. Nason, PhD, Director
Special program: The principal areal interests represented by the faculty include Native North America; the American Indian Studies Center, which offers some instruction in North American Indian languages, is an integral part of the Department. *Full-time Faculty*: Marilyn G. Bentz, PhD, Carol M. Eastman, PhD, Donald K. Grayson, PhD, Eugene S. Hunn, PhD, Tsianina Lomawaima, PhD, Eric Alden Smith, PhD, Julie K. Stein, PhD, Gary J. Witherspoon, PhD; *Part-time Faculty*: Tracy J. Andrews, PhD, Bill Holm, MFA (Prof. Emeritus), Kenneth M.T. Jackson, PhD (Adjunct Prof.), Barbara Lane, PhD, James D. Nason, PhD, Marshall T. Newman, PhD, George I. Quimby, M.A., Kathryn Shanley, PhD, and Gail Thompson, PhD. *Special facilities*: Specialized library collection on the American Indian; Thomas Burke Memorial Museum (extensive collections of Northwest Coast Indians and Eskimos artifacts.)

WISCONSIN

NORTHLAND COLLEGE
Native American Studies Program
P.O. Box 165
ASHLAND 54806
(715) 682-1240

UNIVERSITY OF WISCONSIN-EAU CLAIRE
American Ethnic Coordinating Office
American Indian Program
EAU CLAIRE, WI 54701
(715) 836-3367; (715) 836-2721
Erik Hill Phelps, Library 2044 (Undergraduate)
Ronald Satz, 201 Schofield Hall (Graduate)

LAC COURTE OREILLES
OJIBWA COMMUNITY COLLEGE
RR 2, Box 2357
HAYWARD 54843
(715) 634-4790 Fax 634-4979
Dr. Jasjit Minhas, President

COLLEGE OF THE MENOMINEE NATION
P.O. Box 1179, State Hwy. 47/55
KESHENA 54135
(715) 799-5118
Dr. Verna Fowler, Contact
Offers Associate of Arts and Associate of Science degrees in College Academics, Natural Resources, Health/Nursing, Early Childhood Education, and one in Hospitality Industry and Gaming Management from the National Indian Gaming and Hospitality Institute at the College. Credits are transferable to University of Wisconsin colleges and technical colleges.

MOUNT SENARIO COLLEGE
Native American Studies Program
1500 College Ave.
LADYSMITH, WI 54848
(715) 532-5511 Fax 532-7690
Carol A. Trebian, MS Ed., Director
Instructors: Gladyce Nahbenayash, Joseph Corbine, John Anderson, and Carol Trebian (American Indian Studies); Marie Butler (Indian Tribal Law). Financial aid available.

MADISON AREA TECHNICAL COLLEGE
3550 Anderson St., Room 171
MADISON 53704
(608) 246-6109
Larry J. White Feather, Counselor
Two year degree programs.

UNIVERSITY OF WISCONSIN
American Indian Studies Program
1188 Educational Sciences
1025 W. Johnson St.
MADISON 53706
(608) 263-5501 Fax 263-6448
C. Matthew Snipp, Director
Beth Ketterer, Program Assistant
Jeanne Lacourt & Darlene St. Clair,
Graduate Project Assistant
Description: Recruits Indian faculty and develop courses that deal in depth with American Indians. Assists and encourages Indian students to pursue advanced and professional degrees. Provides information and assistance to individuals and groups interested in American Indians. *Faculty*: Ada E. Deer (senior lecturer-on leave-now serving as Secretary of Interior for Indian Affairs in Washington, DC); Teresa D. LaFromboise (Counseling Psychology & Education); Richard A. Monette (Law); Peter Nabokov and James B. Stoltman (Anthropology); Catherine Price (History); Gary D. Sandefur (Sociology); C. Matthews Snipp, Thomas A. Heberlein, and Gene Summers (Rural Sociology); Jefrey Steele and Roberta Hill Whiteman (English). *Special programs*: Brown Bag Lecture Series; Resource Center; Student Organization, "Wunk Sheek"; Indigenous Law Student Association; Council of American Indian Graduate and Professional Students; branch of American Indian Science & Engineering Society. *Publication*: Newsletter.

MARQUETTE UNIVERSITY
Dept. of Social & Cultural Sciences
MILWAUKEE 53233
(414)288-6838 Fax 288-3300
Donald Metz, Ph.D., Chair
Instructor: Alice B. Kehoe, PhD. *Special program*: American Indian Counselor; sponsors a Pow-wow each year organized by the American Indian counselor. Financial aid available. University library houses archives of Catholic Board of Indian Missions (Mark Thiel, Archivist).

UNIVERSITY OF WISCONSIN
Native American Studies Program
College of Letters & Sciences
P.O. Box 413
MILWAUKEE 53201
John Boatman, PhD, Coordinator
Courses: Great Lakes American Indian ethnobotany; anthropology (courses on American Indians of Northeast, Wisconsin, general American Indian societies and cultures, religions, and the southwest); ethnic studies (western Great Lakes American Indian community life of the past); history (courses on American Indian history); philosophy (Great Lakes American Indian philosophy);

dreams and visions in American Indian metaphysics. *Instructors*: John Boatman, PhD; Jo Allyn Archambault, PhD; Keewaydinoquay , and Fixico. Special programs: American Indian Art Festival; Wisconsin Woodland American Indian Summer Field Institute. *Financial aid* : Minority Achievement Scholarship for high school seniors; Undergraduate Minority Retention Grant for 2nd, 3rd and 4th year college students; Bureau of Indian Affairs and Wisconsin Indian grants. *Special facility*: Milwaukee Public Museum.

UNIVERSITY OF WISCONSIN-OSHKOSH
Minority Studies Program
Department of Anthropology
OSHKOSH 54901
 (414) 424-4406
Instructor: Kathleen A. Dahl, PhD.

UNIVERSITY OF WISCONSIN-STEVENS POINT
Weekend College Program for Native Americans
122 Collins Classroom Center
STEVENS POINT 54481
 (715) 346-2044
 Beth Rose Hanson, Coordinator
Associates Degree program for Native Americans designed to accomodate the employment and family obligations of the individual.

WYOMING

UNIVERSITY OF WYOMING
American Indian Studies Program
Room 109A, Anthropology Bldg.
LARAMIE 82701
 (307) 766-6521
 Dr. Judith A. Antell, PhD, Director
Faculty members : Colin Collaway , PhD, History; Silvester Brito, PhD, English; Judith Antell, PhD, Sociology; and Michael Harkin, PhD, Anthropology. *Description*: Offers an 18 credit hour academic minor. Examines Native North American culture and social life. Both historical and contemporary perspectives on American Indian experiences are included. *Programs*: American Indians in Geology - provides a variety of opportunities and services to American Indian students pursuing earth science education; Outreach - actively developing strategies to address the concerns of the American Indian communities in W yoming. The Summer Institute for the Ef fective Teaching of American Indian Students and the Wind River Initiatives - projects that involve staf f and faculty in outreach efforts; American Indian Alumni Association; Honoring of American Indian Graduates. *Events*: Fall Forum each November and American Indian W eek in March. Financial Aid: The Frank and Cynthia McCarthy Scholarship.

UNIVERSITY OF WYOMING
College of Arts and Sciences
Indian Education Of fice
P.O. Box 3254
LARAMIE 82071
 (307) 766-6520
Provides support services to American Indian students who attend the University of W yoming.

AMERICAN INDIAN COLLEGE FUND MEMBER COLLEGES

Bay Mills Community College, Brimley , MI
Blackfeet Community College, Browning, MT
Cheyenne River Community College,
 Eagle Butte, SD
College of the Menominee Nation, Keshena, WI
Crownpoint Institute of Technology,
 Crownpoint, NM
D-Q University, Davis, CA
Dull Knife Memorial College, Lame Deer , MT
Fond du Lac Community College, Cloquet, MN
Fort Belknap Community College, Harlem, MT
Fort Berthold Community College, New Town, ND
Fort Peck Community College, Poplar , MT
Haskell Indian Nations University , Lawrence, KS
Institute of American Indian Arts, Santa Fe, NM
Lac Courte Oreilles Ojibwa Community College,
 Hayward, WI
Leech Lake Tribal College, Cass Lake, MN
Little Big Horn College, Crow Agency, MT
Little Hoop Community College, Fort Totten, ND
Navajo Community College, Tsaile, AZ
Nebraska Indian Community College,
 Winnebago, NE
Northwest Indian College, Bellingham, W A
Oglala Lakota College, Kyle, SD
Salish Kootenai College, Pablo, MT
Sinte Gleska University , Rosebud, SD
Sisseton Wahpeton Community College,
 Sisseton, SD
Southwest Indian Polytechnic Institute,
 Albuquerque, NM
Standing Rock College, Fort Yates, ND
Stone Child Community College, Box Elder , MT
Turtle Mountain Community College, Belcourt, ND
United Tribes Technical College, Bismarck, ND

DIRECTORIES & REFERENCE BOOKS

CHURCH PHILANTHROPY FOR NATIVE AMERICANS & OTHER MINORITIES
Phyllis A. Meiners, Editor
Profiles over 50 grant programs & more than 25 loan programs from church & religious institutions for Native American, Hispanic, and other minority groups. Eleven denominations are included. with contact persons, special interests, sample grants, application deadlines & procedures, etc. CRC Publishing, 1994. $1 18.95.

CORPORATE & FOUNDATION FUNDRAISING MANUAL FOR NATIVE AMERICANS
A step-by-step guide to securing private sector grants, outlining basic fundraising and research procedures. Helps Native American planners diversify their funding base with private sector dollars. CRC Publishing, 1993. $129.95.

EDUCATION ASSISTANCE FOR AMERICAN INDIANS & ALASKA NATIVES
MPH Program for American Indians
School of Public Health, 1994. No charge.

FEDERAL PROGRAMS OF ASSISTANCE TO AMERICAN INDIANS: A REPORT PREPARED FOR THE SENATE SELECT COMMITTEE ON INDIAN AFFAIRS OF THE U.S. SENATE
Roger Walke, Editor
335 pp. U.S. Government Printing Of fice, Dec. 1991. No charge.

NATIONAL DIRECTORY OF PHILANTHROPY FOR NATIVE AMERICANS
Phyllis A. Meiners, Editor
Profiles 39 private sector grant makers (24 foundations, 12 corporations, and 3 religious institutions), prominent funders of Native American programs. 140 pp. CRC Publishing, 1993. $69.95.

SOURCES OF FINANCIAL AID AVAILABLE TO AMERICAN INDIAN STUDENTS
Leslie A. Kedelty, Editor
Major sources of financial aid for Native American students; and admissions & financial aid information. Includes program reps, BIA area offices, and job opportunities. 78 pp. Annual. Paper. Indian Resource Development (IRD), $5.

FOUNDATION GRANT MAKERS

ACADEMY OF APPLIED SCIENCES
1 Maple St.
Concord, NH 03301
(603) 225-2072
Research and Engineering Apprenticeship Program (REAP) for High School Students. $1,250 stipend. *Deadline*: February.

ALASKA STATE COUNCIL ON THE ARTS
Anchorage, AK 99501
(907) 279-1558
Traditional Native Arts Apprenticeships: Grants of $2,000 each for the maintenance and development of the traditional arts of Alaska's native people. *Deadline*: February, May, August & November.

ALL INDIAN PUEBLO COUNCIL SCHOLARSHIP PROGRAM
P.O. Box 3256
Albuquerque, NM 87190
(505) 884-3820
Ray H. Trujillo, Director
Grants for eligible unergraduate students from Cochiti, Sandia, and Santa Ana Pueblos. *Deadlines*: March 1 & November 1.

AMERICAN ASSOCIATION OF UNIVERSITY WOMEN EDUCATIONAL FOUNDATION
1111 16th St., NW
Washington, DC 20036
(202) 728-7603
Focus Professions Fellowships: Financial assistance to underrepresented minority women who are interested in entering designated fields with traditionally low female participation. The stipends range from $5,000 to $9,500 for full-time study. *Deadline*: December. Harris Fellowship: To minority women postdoctorates who have achieved distinction or promise of distinction. The stipend is $20,000. *Deadline*: November. *Postdoctoral Fellowships*: The stipend ranges from $20,000 to $25,000. *Deadline*: November.

AMERICAN BAR FOUNDATION
750 N. Lake Shore Dr.
Chicago, IL 60611
(312) 988-600
Law and Social Science Summer Research Fellowships for Minorities: To provide work experience to underrepresented minority undergraduates who might be considering a legal career. Participants receive $300 per week for ten weeks during the summer. *Deadline*: May.

AMERICAN FUND FOR DENTAL HEALTH
ADA Endowment & Assistance Fund, Inc.
211 East Chicago Ave., Suite 820
Chicago, IL 60611
(312) 440-2567 Fax 440-2822
Marsha Mountz, Contact
Dental Scholarships for Minority Students: To recruit more minority Americans into the field of dentistry. $2,000 per year. *Deadline*: July 1. *Dental Laboratory Technology Scholarship*. $1,000 per year. Deadline: August 15. *Requirements*: Must be a member of a minority group, including Native Americans; must have at least a 2.5 GP A.

AMERICAN GEOLOGICAL INSTITUTE
4220 King St.
Alexandria, VA 22302
(703) 379-2480 Fax 379-7563
AGI Minority Geoscience Scholarships: To minority undergraduate or graduate students interestd in pursuing degrees in the geosciences. Up to $10,000 per year. *AGI Fellowships for Ethnic Minorities*: Up to $4,000 per year. *Deadline*: February 1st.

AMERICAN INDIAN GRADUATE CENTER
4520 Montgomery Blvd. NE, Suite 1-B
Albuquerque, NM 87109
(505) 881-4584
Provides fellowship grants to American Indian and Alaska Native graduate students. In 1994 the Center assisted about 600 students from 130 tribes who were working on graduate degrees at over 200 colleges throughout the U.S. *Deadline*: May 1st.

AMERICAN INDIAN HERITAGE FOUNDATION
6051 Arlington Blvd.
Falls Church, VA 22044
(703) 237-7500
Scholarship: To Native American youth interested in pursuing postsecondary education. Amount awarded varies. *Miss Indian USA*: To recognize and reward the most beautiful and talented Native American women. A full scholarship to a college or university-up to $15,000 per year. *Outstanding Indian Youth Program*: Financial assistance to Native American youth interested in pursuing postsecondary education.

AMERICAN INDIAN LAW CENTER
P.O. Box 4456, Station A
Albuquerque, NM 87196
(505) 277-5462
Prelaw Summer Institutes for American Indians and Alaska Natives: To prepare Native Amerians to be successful law students and lawyers. Students receive funding to cover tuition, textbooks, personal expenses, and some travel. *Deadline*: March.

AMERICAN INDIAN MENTAL HEALTH RESEARCH & DEVELOPMENT CENTER
Minority Research Resources Branch
National Institutes of Mental Health
Parklawn Bldg., Room 1895
5600 Fishers Lane
Rockville, MD 20857
(301) 443-3724
Grants: To provide funding for American Indian mental health research and development centers. The amount varies, depending upon the nature of the proposed program. Recipient organizations must agree to serve as a resource for the training of both new and established American Indian mental health researchers. *Deadline*: dates vary each year. Check the Federal Register for current schedule.

AMERICAN INDIAN SCHOLARSHIP FUND/TRY, INC.
c/o American Indian Studies Center
University of California, Los Angeles
405 Hilgard Ave.
Los Angeles, CA 90024
(213) 825-0893
Earl Dean Sisto, Contact
American Indian Loan Program: To Native American college students on an emergency basis. Up to $500 per application. No deadlines.

AMERICAN INDIAN SCHOLARSHIPS, INC.
4520 Montgomery Blvd., N.E., Suite 1-B
Albuquerque, NM 87109
(505) 881-4584
Graduate Fellowships for American Indians: Financial assistance to Native American students who wish to pursue graduate education. From $250 to $10,000 per year based on need. *Deadline*: April - summer session; May - fall session.

AMERICAN INDIAN SCIENCE & ENGINEERING SOCIETY
1630 30th St., Suite 301
Boulder, Colorado 80301
(303) 492-8658 Fax 492-7090
Norbert S. Hill, Jr., Executive Director
A.T. Anderson Memorial Scholarship Program: To aid Native American (at least 25% descent) science and engineering students. Must attend an

accredited college, be a member of the Society , and major in science, engineering, or a related discipline. Average scholarship is $1,000 per year , renewable. *Deadline* : June 30th - August 1st. *CERT Schoalrships* : Administered for the Council of Energy Resource Tribes (CERT) with requirements and amounts same as the T.S. Anderson Memorial scholarships, except the award is continuous, the student enters as a freshman after attending the TRIBES program administered by CERT, and the student must major in a field related to energy resource management. *Conference Grants* : Financial assistance for members of the society who wish to attend the society's annual conference. Pays conference fees, room and board. 200 awarded each year . *Santa Fe Pacific Foundation Grant* : Financial assistance to outstanding Native American high school seniors interested in pursuing postsecondary education. Amount ranges from $1,000 to $2,500 per year . *Deadline* : March. *Polingaysi Qoyawayma Scholarship* : Continued teacher education in science and math. Graduate study . *Deadline* : June.

AMERICAN INDIAN STUDIES CENTER
University of California, Los Angeles
3220 Campbell Hall
Los Angeles, CA 90024
(213) 825-7315
Postdoctoral and V isiting Scholar Award : Financial assistance to Native Americans who wish to pursue their research at UCLA's American Indian Studies Center. Postdoctoral fellows receive from $20,000 to 25,000 per year . *Deadline* : December.

AMERICAN INDIAN TEACHER TRAINING PROGRAM
2424 Springer Dr ., Suite 200
Norman, OK 73069
(405) 364-0656
  Stuart A. Tonemah, Contact
Requirements : Must be American Indian or Alaska Native; undergraduate degree with 3.0 GP A; must be an American Indian teacher or teacher of American Indian/Alaska Natives. Selected paricipants will study for a Masters of Education degree at Oklahoma City University. *Amount* : Full tuition, living stipend, and dependence allowance.

AMERICAN LEGION AUXILIARY
1718 Statz St.
North Las Vegas, NV 89030
Silver Eagle Indian Scholarship : Financial assistance for postsecondary education to the dependents of American Indian veterans. The stipend is $200.

AMERICAN PHILOSOPHICAL SOCIETY
Attn: Library, 105 S. Fifth St.
Philadelphia, P A 19106
(215) 440-3400 Fax 440-3436
  Dr. Edward C. Carter , Librarian
Phillips Fund Grants for Research in American Indian Linguistics and Ethnohistory . Prefers supporting the work of younger scholars, including graduate students. From $1,000 to 1,500 per year . *Deadline* : March 15th.

AMERICAN PHYSICAL SOCIETY
American Center for Physics
1 Physics Ellipse
College Park, MD 20740
(212) 682-7341
  Arlene F. Modeste, Contact
Corporate Sponsored Scholarships for Minority Undergraduate Students in Physics . $2,000

awarded to the student for tuition, room and board, and $500 awarded to the host department. *Deadline* : Feb. 14.

AMERICAN PLANNING ASSOCIATION
1776 Massachusetts Ave., N.W.
Washington, D.C. 20036
(202) 872-0611 Fax 872-0643
  C. Vlaskamp, Contact
Planning Fellowships : For minority students enroled in a master's degree program at recognized planning schools. From $2,000 to $5,000 per year. *Deadline* : May. *The Planning and the Black Commuity Division - Undergraduate Minority Scholarship Program* : Available to minority students seeking an undergraduate planning degree. *Deadline* : May 15th.

AMERICAN SOCIETY FOR MICROBIOLOGY
1325 Massachusetts Ave., NW
Washington, DC 20005
(202) 737-3600 Ext. 295
Predoctoral Minority Fellowship Program : Financial assistance to minority predoctoral graduate students in microbiology . A stipend of up to $5,000 and an additional amount of up to $4,250 to cover tuition and fees. Funded by the Proctor & Gamble Co. and the Foundation for Microbiology . *Deadline* : April.

ARIZONA BOARD OF REGENTS
2020 N. Central Ave. #230
Phoenix, AZ 85004-4503
(602) 255-4082
Arizona Indian Tuition Remission : To Native Americns in Arizona who wish to pursue postsecondary education. *Deadline* : Applications are to be submitted to the student aid of fices at the campuses where the students are accepted.

ASSOCIATION OF AMERICAN INDIAN PHYSICIANS
1235 Sovereign Row , Suite C-7
Oklahoma City, OK 73108
(405) 946-7072 Fax 946-7651
  Matthew Kauley , Executive Director
Pew Memorial Trust Scholarship : Financial assistance for Native American students interested in the medical sciences. Amount varies. *Deadline* : July. *Whitecloud Scholarship Fund* : Financial aid to Native American medical students in need of emergency assistance. Up to $250.

ASSOCIATION ON AMERICAN INDIAN AFFAIRS, INC.
245 Fifth Ave., Suite 1801
New York, NY 10016
(212) 689-8720 Fax 685-4692
  Harriet Skye, Scholarship Coordinator
Emergency Aid and Health Professions Scholarships : to provide emergency financial aid, from $50 to $300 to American Indian and Alaskan Native students pursuing college-level education; *Sequoyah Graduate Fellowship* : Provides a one-year, $1,500 unrestricted stipend paid in two equal installments. *Adolph V an Pelt Special Fund for Indian Scholarships* : to undergraduate and graduate students in amounts ranging from $500 to $800. *Displaced Homemaker Scholarship* : $1,500 unrestricted stipend. One year . *Requirements* : Must be an enrolled member of an American Indian tribe or Alaska Native corporation with a certificate of degree of Indian blood. *Deadline* : Applications accepted from July 1 to September 13th.

BACONE COLLEGE
Muskogee, OK 74403
(918) 683-4581
  Sarah Morgan, Contact
Miss Louie LeFlore Scholarship and Mr . Grant Foreman Centennial Award . Must be a member of one of the Five Civilized Tribes of Oklahoma and be at least 1/4 Indian blood. Preference is given to students in nursing or health related fields. From $100 to $300. *Deadline* : July 1.

BAY AREA URBAN LEAGUE
Attn: Education Committee
344 20th St., Suite 21 1
Oakland, CA 94612
(415) 839-8011
Scholarhip Awards : Financial assistance to Native Americans who live in northern California and are interested in pursuing postsecondary education. Minimum 3.0 grade point average. The stipends, $1,000 each. *Deadline* : May of each year .

BERGER MEMORIAL SCHOLARSHIP
Center for Native American Studies
2-152 Wilson Hall - Montana State University
Bozeman, MT 59717
(406) 994-3881
  Dr. Stein, Contact
Requirements : Must be a Native American attending MSU and maintain the required GP A. Amount: $1,000 per year per student. *Deadline* : March1.

BHP-MINERALS SCHOLARSHIP
Attn: Human Resources
P.O Box 155
Fruitland, NM 87416
(505) 598-5861
  Raymond O. Tsosie, Contact
Scholarship for enrolled member of Navajo or Ute Mountain Ute Indian. One year , renewable contingent on eligibility until attainment of Bachelor's Degree. Minimum 3.0 grade point average. Minimum individual awards - $500. *Deadline* . Aug. 1.

BLACK (JAMES B.) SCHOLARSHIPS
Pacific Gas & Electric Co. Scholarship Program
77 Beale St., Room 2825F
San Francisco, CA 94106
(415) 973-1338
  Carol Thomas, Contact
Scholarships for a high school senior who lives or attends school in PG&E's service area and who plans on studying engineering, computer science, math, marketing, business, or economics. Twelve $4,000 scholarships and twelve $2,000 scholarships are awarded each year . *Deadline* : Nov. 15th.

BREMER (OTTO) FOUNDATION
445 Minnesota St., Suite 2000
St. Paul, MN 55101
(612) 227-8036 Fax 227-2522
  Charlotte S. Johnson, Contact
Grants awarded to promote cooperation that makes people self-reliant. Programs which focus on racism and rural poverty are of high priority . Also specific priorities include: community af fairs, education, health, human services, and religion. *Geographic Interest* : Minnesota, North Dakota, and Wisconsin.

BROWN UNIVERSITY
John Carter Brown Library
P.O. Box 1894
Providence, RI 02912
(401) 863-2725
John Carter Brown Library Long-T erm & Short-

Term Research Fellowships : To support scholars interested in conducting reseach at the library , renowned for its collection of historical sources pertaining to the exploration, settlement, and development of the New W orld (especially those relating to Native American populations and development.) Long-Term - stipends for 6-month fellowships are $13,750; stipends for 12-month fellowships are $27,500; Short-T erm - $800 per month. *Deadline* : January .

BUDER SCHOLARSHIP FOR AMERICAN INDIAN LAW STUDENTS
Washington University School of Law
Campus Box 1120
St. Louis, MO 63130
(314) 935-4525
Kip Darcy, Contact
Requirements : Must be enrolled in a federally recognized Indian tribe or possessing one-eighth degree of Indian blood; appllicant must be accepted into any School of Law . *Amount* : Full tuition or partial tuition for three years. *Deadline* : March 1.

BUSH FOUNDATION
E-900 First National Bank Bldg.
332 Minnesota
St. Paul, MN 55101
(612) 227-0891
Humphrey Doermann, President
170 grants awarded in the following special interest areas: education, culture, arts, social services, health, scholarships, minorities, women, historic preservation, medicine

BUSINESS & PROFESSIONAL WOMEN'S FOUNDATION
2012 Massachusetts Ave., N.W.
Washington, D.C. 20036
(202) 293-1200
Linda Sayer & Jean Findeis, Contacts

JOHN CARTER BROWN LIBRARY
Brown University
P.O. Box 1894
Providence, RI 02912
(401) 863-2725
Long-Term and Short-Term Research Fellowships : For scholars interested in doing research at the Library. Applicant must hold a doctorate. Long-Term - $13,750 (6 months) and $27,500 (one year.); Short-Term -$800 per month (1-4 months). *Deadline* : February.

CALIFORNIA DEPARTMENT OF EDUCATION
c/o American Indian Education Of fice
P.O. Box 944272
Sacramento, CA 94244
(916) 322-9744
Maple Creek W illie Scholarship Fund : For educational purposes to high school graduate California Indians. Up to $1,250 per year .

CARMINE FELICA D'ONOFRIO SCHOLARSHIP
Georgia Tech University
Atlanta, GA 30332
(404) 894-3354
Dr. Lytia Howard
Scholarship open to any Native American who will attend Georgia Institute of Technology in the disciplines of engineering or computer science. Must be a member of a Federal or State recognized tribe. $3,000 per year . Deadline: flexible.

CARNEGIE CORPORATION OF NEW YORK
437 Madison Ave.
New York, NY 10022
(212) 371-3200
David A. Hamburg, President
Special interests include : public af fairs, education, health, children, youth, minorities, world peace, drug abuse, nonprofit management, scholarships. Grants to schools, colleges, universities, and organizations.

CITIZEN'S SCHOLARSHIP FOUNDATION OF AMERICA, INC.
P.O. Box 297
St. Peter, MN 56082
(507) 931-1682
Fluor Daniel Engineering Scholarship Program for Minorities and Women . Applicants are limited to a small number of major universities. Amount awarded varies but is generally at least $1,000 each year. *Deadline* : February of each year .

CLARK (EDNA McCONNELL) FOUNDA TION
250 Park Ave., Room 900
New York, NY 10177
(212) 986-7050
Peter D. Bell, President
Special interests" children, disadvantaged, youth, homelessness, families, justice, research, education. The foundation's mission is to improve conditions of people who are poorly served by existing social institutions. The foundation has in recent years made several grants to American Indian projects.

COLLEGE SCHOLARSHIP SERVICE OF THE COLLEGE BOARD
45 Columbus Ave.
New York, NY 10019
(212) 713-8000
Business Administration & Engineering Scholar - ship Programs for Minority Community College Graduates . Sponsored by the General Electric Foundation. Amounts awarded depends upon financial needs. *Deadline* : December of each year .

CONSORTIUM FOR GRADUA TE STUDY IN MANAGEMENT
Box 1132, One Brookings Dr .
St. Louis, MO 63130
(314) 889-6353
Dr. Wallace L. Jones, Executive Director
Graduate Fellowships in Business Administration for Minorities : Tuition and $3,000 stipend (first year) and $2,000 (second year). *Deadline* : January.

CONTINENTAL SOCIETY, DAUGHTERS OF INDIAN WARS
2876 Faraday Court
Decatur, GA 30033
Denise G. Rice, Contact
Scholarship to a certified tribal member of a Federally recognized tribe who plan to work in the field of education or social services on a reservation. *Amount* : $500. One year renewable. *Deadline* : March 1.

COUNCIL OF ENERGY RESOURCE TRIBES (CERT)
1999 Broadway , Suite 2600
Denver, CO 80202
(303) 297-2378
Lesley Jackson, Contact
Scholarship : To Native American college students who are interested in pursuing postsecondary education in the areas of engineering, sciences,

or business, and have at least a 2.5 GP A. $1,000 per year. *Deadline* : March 1 (Internship); June 1 (Graduate); August 1 (Undergraduate).

CROWE MEMORIAL SCHOLARSHIP FUND
P.O. Box 892
Cherokee, NC 28719
Amy Walker, President
Doris Hipps, V.P.

DANFORTH FOUNDATION
231 S. Bemiston Ave.
St. Louis, MO 63105-1903
(314) 862-6200
Dorothy Danforth Compton Minority Fellowships : To minority graduate students who wish to be college teachers and who attend one of 10 universities supported by Danforth Foundation grants: Brown, Chicago, Columbia, Howard, Stanford, Texas at Austin, UCLA, V anderbilt, W ashington and Yale. Contact universities for application and information.

D'ARCY McNICKLE CENTER FOR THE HISTORY OF THE AMERICAN INDIAN
Newberry Library
60 W. Walton St.
Chicago, IL 60610
(312) 943-9090
Margaret Curtis, Contact
Predoctoral Fellowships : To support doctoral research in residence at the Newberry Library's D'Arcy McNickel Center. $9,000 per year . *Deadline* : January. *Memorial Fellowships* : Short-term fellowships for Native Americans interested in writing their tribal histories, or graduate research. $300 per each week of residency . *Deadline* : January & July. *Frances C. Allen Fellowships* : To promote Native American women college graduates. Amount varies. *Dealine* : January & July. *Rockefeller Foundation Junior & Senior Postdoctoral Fellowships for Indian History* : To support research in residence at the Center for scholars interested in Indian-white relations and Western Americana. Junior - $17,000 per year; Senior - $27,500 per year . *Deadline* : January. *Summer Institute in American Indian History Fellowships* : Financial assistance to secondary school teachers and administrators interested in attending the Summer Institute at the Newberry Library. $2,200 per year . *Deadline* : March. *Documentary Fellowships* : To college and university faculty who have participated in the center's Documentary Workshop. $800 per month. *Deadline* : February or July.

DAUGHTERS OF THE AMERICAN REVOLUTION
American Indian Committee
5414 Richinbacher , Apt. 101
Alexandria, VA 22304
Velma Musick, Contact
American Indian Scholarship for undergraduate students. $250 per term. *Deadlines* : December 1 for Spring, August 1 for Fall.

EDMONDS EDUCATIONAL FOUNDATION
P.O. Box 2518
Houston, TX 77252-2518
(713) 652-6533
Elizabeth A. Calved, Contact

THE EDUCATIONAL FOUNDATION OF AMERICA
23161 V entura Blvd., Suite 201
Woodland Hills, CA 91364

(818) 999-0921
Richard W. Hansen, Executive Director
Ettinger Scholarships provides educational grants--aid for Native Americans. Has supported a variety of projects for American Indian educational institutions.

FLORIDA DEPARTMENT OF EDUCATION
Office of Student Financial Assistance
Knott Bldg.
Tallahassee, FL 32399
(904) 488-6181
Seminole - Miccosukee Indian Scholarship Program: For Florida's Seminole and Miccosukee Indian students who wish to pursue postsecondary education in a Florida college or university . Up to $2,000 per year. *Deadline*: August.

FORD FOUNDATION
320 E. 43rd St.
New York, NY 10017
(212) 573-5000
Franklin A. Thomas, President
Promotes cultural diversity, strengthening nonprofit management, and a policy of collaborating with other grant makers. Cultural/ethnic/gender diversity is particularly important. *Special interests*: disadvantaged, community & economic development, social services, minorities, education, health, etc.

GENERAL SERVICE FOUNDATION
P.O. Box 4650
Boulder, CO 80306
(303) 447-9541 Fax 447-0593
Robert W. Musser, President/Director
More than 50 grants are given in special interests of: natural resources, environment, health, economic development, human rights, nonprofit management. Emphasis is placed on improving the management and quality f water , particularly west of the Mississippi.

GOLDEN STATE MINORITY FOUNDATION
1999 W. Adams Blvd.
Los Angeles, CA 90018
(213) 731-7771
Ivan A. Houston, Contact
Scholarship of $2,000 per year for ethnic minority with at least a 3.0 GP A and attending any accredited 4-year college of university in California, Michigan, or Houston, Texas in business administration, economics, or related field.

GOUGH (HELEN) SCHOLARSHIP FOUNDATION
P.O. Box 69-Courthouse
Stanley, ND 58784
(701) 628-2955 Fax 628-3706
Karen Colbenson, Chairperson
Financial assistance for educational purposes to members of the Three Affiliated Tribes of the Fort Berthold Reservation in North Dakota. Up to $500 per year, renewable. *Deadline*: June 1.

GOULD (CHARLES P.) AWARD
Financial Aid Office
University of California, Davis
Davis, CA 95616
(916) 752-2390
Felicia Miller, Contact
Awards to UCD American Indian students only , with students from Arizona tribes receiving first priority. *Amount*: $200-$3,000 as determined by financial need.

GOULD (EDWIN) FOUNDATION FOR CHILDREN
23 Gramacy Park South
New York, NY 10003
Helen Alessi, Contact
Student mentor scholarship program for needy children, including those in the foster care system.

GRINNELL (GEORGE BIRD) AMERICAN INDIAN CHILDREN'S EDUCATION FOUNDATION
Box 47H, Rd. #1
Dover Plains, NY 12522
(914) 877-6425
Schuyler M. Meyer, Jr., Secretary/Treasurer
The Al Qoyawayma Award for Excellence in Science, Engineering, and the Arts. $2,000, annually to a Native American undergraduate college student majoring either in science or engineering, and who has a documented knowledge of American Indian culture and religion.

GROTTO FOUNDATION, INC.
West - 2090 First National Bank Bldg.
St. Paul, MN 55101
(612) 224-9431
A.A. Heckman, Executive Director
Provides grants for special projects relating to American Indians.

GUILFORD NATIVE AMERICAN ASSOCIATION
P.O. Box 5623
Greensboro, NC 27403
(919) 273-8686
Scholarship: To native-Americans who are planning to attend college. Native-American high school seniors in the Guilford, Alamance, Forsyth and other adjacent counties in North Carolina. Stipends range from $250 to $1,000 per year . *Deadline*: February.

HAHN (PHILIP Y.) FOUNDATION
c/o California First Bank
P.O. Box B
Rancho Santa Fe, CA 92067
(714) 294-4592
c/o Gilbert L. Brown, Jr., Manager
Alcala Park, San Diego, CA 92110
Provides financial aid for needy American Indian children in the Southwest.

HARVARD GRADUATE PRIZE FELLOWSHIP
Harvard - GSAS
8 Garden St.
Cambridge, MA 02138
Requirement: Must be a member of a minority group, including Native Americans; must enroll at Harvard GSAS. Any Native American who is admitted to the GSAS will receive this fellowship. *Amount*: Tuition + $10,500 stipend. *Deadline*. January 2md.

HEADLANDS INDIAN HEALTH CAREERS
P.O. Box 26901
Oklahoma City, OK 73190
(405) 271-2250
Grants: For Native American students who are interested in preparing for careers as health professionals. The Headlands program is held at the Headlands Conference Center near Mackinaw City, Michigan. The program is sponsored by the University of Oklahoma's Health Sciences Center. *Deadline*: March.

HEARST FOUNDATION
90 New Montgomery St., Suite 1212
San Francisco, CA 94105

(415) 543-0400
Thomas Eastham, V.P.
Awards more than 270 grants in educationm arts, culture, social services, children, youth, mental health, religion, and historic preservation. Support for Indian organizations tend to fall under the category of education

HOWARD SIMONS FUND FOR AMERICAN INDIAN JOURNALISTS
403 Tenth St., SE
Washington, DC 20003
(202) 547-5531 Fax 546-6724
Suzan Harjo or Margaret Engel (301) 986-5342
Short-term fellowships for Native American journalists.

INDIANA UNIVERSITY
Kirkwood Hall 1 14
Bloomington, IN 47405
(800) 457-4420 in IN (812) 855-0822
CIC Minorities Fellowships Program : To increase the number of undrepresented minority group members among Ph.D. degree recipients in the humanities, social sciences, sciences, mathematics and engineering. Full tuition plus a stipend of at least $9,000 for graduate study at a CIC-af filiated university. *Deadline*: January. Minority Faculty Recruitment Fellowship Program: Includes a salary equivalent to that ordinarily paid to an Indiana University faculty, plus a $3,000 stipend for research and living expenses. *Deadline*: Sept.

INDUSTRIAL RELATIONS COUNCIL ON GOALS
Box 4363
E. Lansing, MI 48826-4363
(800) 344-6257 (517) 351-6122
Graduate Fellowship Program for Minorities in Labor and Industrial Relations : To provide funding for minority students who are interested in obtaining a master's degree in labor/industrial relations at a participating school. Pays tuition, fees, and a stipend of $7,800 per year .

INROADS, INC.
1221 Locust
St. Louis, MO 63108
(314) 241-7488
INROADS/College Internship : Places minority youth interns in local companies in various cities. *Deadline*: January.

INSTITUTE FOR THE STUDY OF WORLD POLITICS
1775 Massachusetts Ave., N.W., Suite 500
Washington, D.C. 20036
(202) 797-0882
Dorothy Danforth Compton Fellowships for Minority-Group Students on World Affairs: Amount of award varies. *Deadline*: February.

INSTITUTE OF ALASKA NATIVE ARTS
P.O. Box 70769, 455 Third Ave. #117
FAIRBANKS, AK 99707
(907) 456-7491
Susie Bevins-Ericsen, President
Patricia Petrivelli, Executive Director
Scholarships for academic study , up to $2,000; and for short-term study , $500.

INTER-TRIBAL COUNCIL OF THE FIVE CIVILIZED TRIBES
c/o Financial Aid Office
Bacone College
Muskogee, OK 74403
(918) 683-4581

Grant Foreman Scholarships: Assistance to male Native American high school graduates who are interested in postsecondary education. *Louie Leflore Scholarship*: Financial assistance to female Native American high school graduates. $100 to $300 per year. Applicants must be members of one of the Five Civilized Tribes of Oklahoma. Deadline: June.

INTERTRIBAL INDIAN CEREMONIAL ASSN.
P.O. Box 1
Church Rock, NM 87311
(505) 863-3896
 Laurence D. Linford, Executive Director
Indian art scholarships to accredited colleges and universities.

INTERNATIONAL ORDER OF THE KING'S DAUGHTERS & SONS
North American Indian Scholarship Program
P.O. Box 1017
Chautauqua, NY 14722
(716) 357-1951
Indian Scholarship Program: To provide supplemental aid to Native American students interested in pursuing secondary and postsecondary education in the health fields or Christian studies. Up to $500 per year. *Deadline*: April in even-numbered years, June in odd-numbered years.

JOHNSON (ROBERT WOOD) FOUNDATION
P.O. Box 2316
Princeton, NJ 08543
(609) 452-8701
 Edward H. Robbins, Proposal Manager
Serving populations where services are not available is a traditional foundation focus. Improving the health of Native Americans is a priority. *Minority Medical Faculty Development Program*: For minority physicians who are interested in academic medicine. Stipend is $50,000 per year, plus a $25,000 annual research allowance. *Deadline*: April.

JOYCE FOUNDATION
135 S. LaSalle St., Suite 4010
Chicago, IL 60603
(312) 782-2464 Fax 782-4160
Joel D. Gretzendanner, V.P. Programs
Special interests: economic development, disadvantaged, conservation, environment, education, arts, culture, public affairs. Focuses on "the Strength of Diversity."

KELLOGG (W.K.) FOUNDATION
400 North Ave.
Battle Creek, MI 49016
(616) 968-1611
 Norman A. Brown, President
Specific priorities: youth, leadership, community-based, problem-focused health services, higher education, and food systems. Supports educational and service projects with an emphasis on the application of new knowledge to human needs. *Geographic interest*: national, especially Michigan.

KEMPER (JAMES S.) FOUNDATION
Long Grove, IL 60049
Kemper Grantee Program Scholarships. $1,000-3,500 per year. *Deadline*: Varies at each participating institution.

LILLY ENDOWMENT, INC.
2801 N. Meridian, Box 88068
Indianapolis, IN 46208
(317) 924-5471 Fax 926-4431
 John M. Mutz, President

Special interests: religion, education, community development, children/youth, and nonprofit management. *Geographic interest*: national, especially Indiana.

MAINE INDIAN SCHOLARSHIP COMMITTEE
153 Illinois Ave.
Bangor, ME 04401
Scholarships: To provide financial assistance for postsecondary education to members of the Passamaquoddy or Penobscot tribes.

MALKI MUSEUMS, INC.
11-795 Fields Rd.
Morongo Indian Reservation
Banning, CA 92220
(714) 849-7289
Scholarships: For enrolled members of southern California Indian reservations as members of their tribe interested in pursuing postsecondary education in California. $150 to $300 per quarter or semester.

MASSACHUSETTS INDIAN ASSOCIATION
c/o Mrs. Warren G. Hunt
180 Main St.
Walpole, MA 02081-4033
(617) 326-8945
Scholarship Fund: For Massachusetts Indians who are interested in pursuing postsecondary education. Up to $500 per year for undergraduates; up to $1,000 for graduate students. *Deadlines*: January and September.

McCARTHUR (JOHN D. & CATHERINE T.) FOUNDATION
140 S. Dearborn St.
Chicago, IL 60603
(312) 726-8000
 Adele Simmons, President
The foundation has demonstrated an interest in native rights and the self development of Native peoples. *Special interests*: education, resources, economic development, health, and environment. *Geographic interest*: national, especially Florida.

McKNIGHT FOUNDATION
TCF Tower, 121 S. 8th St. #600
Minneapolis, MN 55402
(612) 333-4220
 Cynthia Binger Boynton, President
Special interests: human services, economic development, health, education, and environment. *Geographic interest*: national, especially Minnesota.

MEYER MEMORIAL TRUST
1515 W. Fifth Ave., Suite 500
Portland, OR 97201
(503) 228-5512
 Charles S. Rooks, Executive Director
Special interests: children/youth, arts & humanities, health, education, social welfare. *Geographic interest*: national groups; Alaska, Idaho, Montana; Oregon (especially Portland), Washington.

MICHIGAN COMMISSION ON INDIAN AFFAIRS
Department of Management and Budget
P.O. Box 30026
611 W. Ottawa, North Tower, 3rd Floor
Lansing, MI 48909
(517) 373-0654
Michigan Indian Awards: To Native American high school graduates who are interested in attending college in Michigan. Applicant must be a legal resident of Michigan for at least one year. Free tuition at any Michigan public 2-4 college or university.

MINNESOTA STATE DEPT. OF EDUCATION
State Services Center
1819 Bemidji Ave.
Bemidji, MN 5601
(218) 755-2926
Minnesota Indian Scholarship Program: For Native American high school graduates in Minnesota who wish to pursue postsecondary education. From $500 to $2,000. The average award is $1,200.

MONTANA BOARD OF REGENTS
Attn: Project Coordinator, Talent Search
33 S. Last Chance Gulch
Helena, MT 59620
Montana Indian Fee-Waiver Program: Financial assistance for Montana Indian students interested in pursuing postsecondary education. Tuition is waved for recipients at a select number of Montana schools.

MOTT (CHARLES STEWART) FOUNDATION
500 Mott Bldg.
Flint, MI 48502
(313) 238-5651
 Jim L. Krause, Director
Special interests: education, environment, community & economic development, arts, health. *Geographical interest*: national groups, especially Michigan.

MR. COGITO
c/o John M. Gogol, Editor
P.O. Box 66124
Portland, OR 97266
American Indian Poetry Prize: To recognize and reward outstanding poetry on the topic of the American Indian. $50 and publication in Mr. Cogito magazine. *Deadline*: May.

MURDOCK (M.J.) CHARITABLE TRUST
P.O. Box 1618
Vancouver, WA 98668
(206) 694-8415 Fax (503) 285-4086
 Ford A. Anderson, Executive Director
Special interests: education, community & economic development, health, arts & culture, social services, religion. *Geographic interest*: national groups; Alaska, Idaho, Montana, Oregon, Washington (especially Greater Vancouver).

MUSKOGEE TRIBE
Old Federal Bldg.
Muskogee, OK 74401
(918) 687-2306
Tribal Scholarship Grant: Financial assistance for postsecondary education to undergraduates and graduate students who belong to the Muskogee Tribe. Up to $2,000 per year.

NATIONAL ACTION COUNCIL FOR MINORITIES IN ENGINEERING
3 West 35th St.
New York, NY 10001
(212) 279-2626
Incentive Grant Program: financial support to minority students in engineering. Colleges and universities with engineering curricula may submit requests for scholarship funds. Grants to participating schools range from $5,000 to $40,000. *Summer Engineering Employment Project (SEEP)*: Internships in NACME donor corporations for minority engineering students. $3,600 for the summer. For scholarships please contact the financial aid office at your school.

NATIONAL ASSOCIATION FOR BILINGUAL EDUCATION
Maricopa Community College
3910 E. Washington St.
Phoenix, AZ 85034
 (602) 392-2233
Outstanding Dissertations Competition : To recognize and reward dissertations in bilingual education field. Semifinalists receive certificates of recognition and finalists receive travel & lodging expenses to the annual convention. *Deadline* : November.

NATIONAL ASSOCIATION FOR THE ADVANCEMENT OF COLORED PEOPLE
4805 Mt. Hope Dr.
Baltimore, MD 21215
 (301) 358-8900
NAACP Honeywell Engineering Scholarship : Financial assistance to underrepresented minority students interested in majoring in engineering in college. Up to $4,000 per year and opportunity to work summers prior to graduation at a Honeywell division. *Deadline* : April.

NATIONAL CENTER FOR GRADUATE EDUCATION FOR MINORITIES (GEM)
P.O. Box 537
Notre Dame, IN 46556
 (219) 287-1097
 Dr. Howard G. Adams, Contact
Master's Fellowship Program : For minority students entering graduate engineering studies. Tuition, fees, and a stipend of $6,000 for one year and a summer internship; *Ph.D. Engineering & Science Fellowship Program* : To provide opportunities for minority students to obtain a Ph.D. in engineering and the natural sciences. Tuition, fees and a stipend of $12,000 per year . Recipients must participate in the GEM summer internship. *Deadline* : December 1.

NATIONAL FEDERATION OF STATE POETRY SOCIETIES
c/o Pat Stodghill
1424 Highland Rd.
Dallas, TX 75218
Our American Indian Heritage Poetry Contest : To recognize and reward outstanding poems written about American Indians. $25 first place, $15 second place, $10 third place. *Deadline* : March.

NATIONAL GALLERY OF ART
Attn: Academic Programs
Washington, D.C. 20565
 (202) 842-6182
Minority Internships : To provide work experience to underrepresented minority undergraduates who might be considering a museum career . The stipend is $14,000. *Deadline* : March.

NATIONAL INDIAN CHILD CONFERENCE
129 Jackson, N.E.
Albuquerque, NM 87108
Ruth Muskrat Bronson Memorial Scholarship : To assist American Indian and Alaskan Native graduate students in meeting the costs of a graduate education. Amount awarded varies. *Deadline* : November and March.

NATIONAL MEDICAL FELLOWSHIPS, INC.
254 West 31st St., 7th Floor
New York, NY 10001
 (212) 714-0933 Fax 239-9718
Franklin C. McLean Award : For senior medical school minority students. $3,000. *Deadline* : June.
Hugh H. Anderson Memorial Scholarships : For minority students attending Minnesota medical schools. $2,500 to $4,000 per year . *Deadline* : August. *Irving Graef Memorial Scholarship* : Third-year minority medical school students' achievements. $2,000. *Deadline* : July. *William and Charlotte Cadbury Award* : Minority school students' achievements. $2,000. *Deadline* : June. *Henry J. Kaiser Family Foundation Merit Awards Programs* : For contributions to medicine on the part of graduating medical students. $3,000, average award. *Baxter Foundation Scholarship* : Open to second-year minority medical students who received NMF financial assistance during their first year . $2,500. *Deadline* : July. *The Commonwealth Fund Medical Fellowship* : To minority students attending accredited U.S. medical schools. Preference is given to third-year students. $5,000. *Deadline* : October. Glaxo, Inc. *Fellowship Program in Aids Research* : To second and third-year minority students for research into academic medicine or health education and policy. The stipend is $5,000. Nominations requested in August. *William T. Grant Behavior Development Research Fellowships* : For minority students who show promise for careers in child psychiatry, behavior development research or mental health policy . $3,500. *Deadline* : September. *AT&T Foundation Fellowship Program in Aids Education and Public Policy* . The stipend is $5,000. Nominations requested in August. *Metropolitan Life Foundation Awards for Academic Excellence in Medicine* : $2,500 per year . *Deadline* : August. *W.K. Kellogg Foundation Fellowship Program in Community Medicine* : To underrepresented minority medical students who wish to work in community-based health centers. The stipend is $5,000. *Deadline* : October. Syntex Corporation Award for Postgraduate Medical Research and Training. $2,000.

NATIONAL NATIVE AMERICAN COOPERATIVE
P.O. Box 1000
San Carlos, AZ 85550
 (602) 230-3399
Purpose : To assist in the continuation of traditional or contemporary American Indian culture. Applicant must be a Native American artist. Raw craft materials are presented to the artist.

NATIONAL RESEARCH COUNCIL
The Fellowship Office
2101 Constitution Ave.
Washington, D.C. 20418
 (202) 334-2872/2860
 Gretchen Redmond, Program Specialist
To increase minority presence in the arts and sciences on college and university faculties. Financial assistance for master's and doctoral degree minority students. Awards will be made in the behavioral and social sciences, humanities, engineering, math, physical sciences, and biological sciences. *NSF Incentives for Excellence Scholarship Prizes* : For outstanding minority undergraduate students who are preparing for careers in engineering or science. Up to $1,000. Awards each Spring. *Ford Foundation Dissertation Fellowship Program for Minorities* : $18,000 per year . *Deadline* : November. *Ford Foundation Predoctoral Fellowship Program for Minorities* . $11,000 per year . *Deadline* : November. *Ford Foundation Postdoctoral Fellowships for Minorities* . $25,000 per year . *Deadline* : January. *National Science Foundation Graduate Fellowships & Minority Graduate Fellowships* : $12,900 per year each. *Deadline* : October. *Minority Women in Engineering* : Fellows receive about $13,000 and a $1,000 research travel allowance. Fellowship institutions,

on behalf of each fellow , a cost-of-education allowance of $6,000 to cover all tuition costs and fees. *Deadline* : November.

NATIONAL SCIENCE FOUNDATION
1800 G St., Room 321
Washington, D.C. 20550
 (202) 357-7474
Comprehensive Regional Centers for Minorities Projects :Financial assistance to centers designed to increase minority presence in science and engineering. *Deadline* : December. *Directorate for Engineering Supplemental Funding for Support of Women, Minority, and Handicapped Engineering Research Assistants. Minority Research Initiation Planning Grants* . Up to $10,000. *Deadline* : February & June. *Minority Research Initiation Program Grants* . From $25,000 to $90,000 per year . *Research Improvement in Minority Institutions* : To foster research activities of predominantly minority colleges and universities in the U.S. by supporting research. Up to $300,000. *Deadline* : November. *BBS/DCB Minority Postdoctoral Fellowships* : To prepare minority scientists for positions of scientific research in the disciplines covered by the Biological, Behavioral and Social Sciences Directorate (BBS) of the NSF at U.S. research institutes. Fellows receive $28,000 per year , plus $4,600 for research-related costs or health insurance and $24,000 per year for an institutional allowance. Also, up to $3,000 for travel expense. *Deadline* : October.

NATIONAL SCIENCE FOUNDATION - MINORITY GRADUATE FELLOWSHIPS
Oak Ridge Associated Universities
P.O. Box 3010
Oak Ridge, TN 37831
 (615) 483-3344
Requirements : U.S. citizen and member of minority group, including American Indian and Native Alaskan-Eskimo or Aleut. Awarded for study and research leading to master's or doctoral degrees in the mathematical, physical, biological, engineering, behavioral and social sciences. *Amount* : stipend of $14,000 per year and $7,500 cost-of-education allowance.

NATIONAL SOCIETY OF THE DAUGHTERS OF THE AMERICAN REVOLUTION
American Indian Scholarship Committee
11001 Elon Dr.
Mitchellville, MD 20720
 (301) 262-6654
 Suzanne W. O'Malley, Contact
Requirements : Must be Native American undergraduate student with at least a 2.75 GP A and show financial need. Amount: $500 renewable. *Deadlines* : December 1 and August 1.

NATIONAL SOCIETY OF PROFESSIONAL ENGINEERS EDUCATIONAL FOUNDATION
1420 King St.
Alexandria, VA 22314
 (703) 684-2800
NSPE Minority Scholarships : Financial assistance to high school seniors from underrepresented minority groups who have a genuine interest in a career in engineering. $1,000 per year . *Deadline* : December.

NATIONAL WILDLIFE FEDERATION
1412 Sixteenth St.
Washington, D.C. 20036
 (703) 790-4267
 Maurice N. LeFranc, Jr ., Contact
Environmental Conservation Fellowship Program :

For graduate research in environmental studies, natural resources, etc. Up to $10,000 per year . *Deadline* : July 15 for upcoming academic year .

NATIONS MINISTRIES
P.O. Box 70
Honobia, OK 74549
(918) 755-4570
Riley Donica, Editor
Academic scholarships.

NATIVE AMERICAN JOURNALISTS ASSN.
University of Colorado School of Journalism
Campus Box 287
Boulder, CO 80309
(303) 492-7397
Laverne Sheppard, Executive Director
Scholarships for qualified American Indian journalist students.

NATIVE AMERICAN PUBLIC BROADCASTING CONSORTIUM
P.O. Box 83111
Lincoln, NE 68501
(402) 472-3522
National Indian Communications Scholarships : Travel expenses to Native American college students who wish to attend the annual National Indian Communications conference.

NATIVE AMERICAN MINISTRIES
The Presbyterian Center
100 Whitherspoon St.
Louisville, KY 40202-1396
Native American Education Grants : For needy Native American students to continue their college education. From $200 to $1,500. *Deadline* : June 1. *Native American Seminary Scholarships* : For students interested in preparing for church occupations. Amount varies.

NATIVE AMERICAN SCHOLARSHIP FUND
3620 Wyoming Blvd., N.E., Suite 208-C
Albuquerque, NM 871 11
(505) 275-9788
MESBEC Program : Financial assistance to Native American students interested in pursuing postsecondary education. Amount varies but is generally about $500 per year . *Native American Leadership in Education (NALE)* : Financial assistance to American Indian paraprofessionals in the education field who wish to return to school. From $500 and up.

NATIVE AMERICAN SCHOLARSHIP PROGREAM
Santa Fe Pacific Foundation
1700 E. Golf Rd.
Schaumburg, IL 60173
Requirements : Open to high school seniors who are at least 1/4 Native American. *Amount* : Up to $2,500 per year , 4-year renewable, depending on need. *Deadline* : March 31st.

NEEDMOR FUND
1730 15th St.
Boulder, CO 80302
(303) 449-5801
Dinny Stranaham, Coordinator
Special interests : community & economic development, family, disadvantaged. Geographic interest: national, especially Ohio (T oledo).

NEVADA INTER-TRIBAL COUNCIL
806 Holman W ay
Sparks, NV 89431
(702) 355-0600

Health Occupations Indian Scholarship Program : To Indian students in Nevada interested in careers in the health fields. *John H. Dressler Memorial Scholarship* : Emergency financial assistance to Native American college students who are residents of Nevada. $200. *Deadline* : August.

NEW MEXICO EDUCATIONAL ASSISTANCE FOUNDATION
3900 Osuna Rd., NE, P .O. Box 27020
Albuquerque, NM 87125-7020
(505) 345-3371 ext. 315
Fax (505) 345-3371 ext. 400
New Mexico Minority Doctoral Fellowship/Loan Program : Minority students graduating from a school in New Mexico and who wish to pursue a doctoral degree in mathematics, engineering, or the physical or life sciences in the state. The stipend is $25,000 per year . *Deadline* : January.

NEW WORLD FOUNDATION
100 E. 85th St.
New York, NY 10028
(212) 249-1023
Colin Greer , President
Special interests : equal rights & opportunities, disadvantaged, health, environment, education, community & economic development.

NEW YORK STATE EDUCATION DEPT.
State and Federal Scholarship and Fellowship Unit
Cultural Education Center , Room 5C64
Albany, NY 12230
(518) 474-1201
Regents Professional Opportunity Scholarships : From $1,000 to $5,000 per year for Native Americans and other minority students interested in pursuing professional careers. Recipients must enroll in approved programs in New York state. *Deadline* : April. *Regents Health Care Scholarships* : Financial assistance to minority students enrolled in an approved program in medicine or dentistry. From $1,000 to $5,000 per year . *Deadline* : April.

NEW YORK STATE EDUCATION DEPT.
Native American Indian Education Unit
485 Education Bldg. Annex
Albany, NY 12234
(518) 473-2912
Deborah H. Cunningham, Contact
State Aid for Native Americans at Postsecondary Institutions in the State of New York . Applicants must be residents of New York state and be accepted by an approved accredited postsecondary institution. $1,350 per year for full-time study . *Deadline* : May for Summer term, July for Fall term, and December for Spring term.

NEW YORK UNIVERSITY
Institute of Afro-American Affairs
269 Mercer St., Roopm 601
New York, NY 10003
(212) 598-7095
AEJ/NYU Summer Internship Program for Minorities in Journalism : To provide work experience in the communications industry for minority group members who are interested in journalism. $200 per week and housing accommodations at NYU. *Deadline* : December.

NORTH AMERICAN INDIAN SCHOLARSHIP PROGRAM
The International Order of the King's, Daughters & Sons, Inc.
1916 Rosedale Dr .
Indianapolis, IN 46227

(317) 784-5163
Mrs. Vernon Parish
Requirement : Must be a Native American undergraduate student with proof of Indian blood. Scholarships are awarded for vocational, technical and college training.

NORTH CAROLINA COMMISSION OF INDIAN AFFAIRS
North Carolina Dept. of Administration
325 N. Salisbury St.
Raleigh, NC 27603-5940
(919) 733-5998
United Tribes of North Carolina Scholarship Award : Financial assistance to Native Americans in North Carolina who are interested in continuing their college education. Amount of award varies. *Deadline* : March. *American Indian Student Legislative Grant* : To needy NC Indian students who are interested in pursuing postsecondary education. Applicants must be admitted to or attending to enroll in one of the constituent institutions of the University of North Carolina. $500 per year . *American Indian Doctoral Fellowship* : Financial assistance to American Indians who wish to pursue doctoral degrees in one of four institutions of the University of NC system. $4,000 per year .

NORTH DAKOTA INDIAN AFFAIRS COMMISSION
State Capitol Bldg., 1st Floor
Bismarck, ND 58505
(701) 224-2428
Jillian D. Nodland, Contact
Scholarship Program : To provide financial assistance to undergraduate and graduate Native American students in North Dakota colleges and universities. From $200 to $2,000 per year . Average award is $700. *Deadline* : June.

NORTHWEST AREA FOUNDATION
West 975 National Bank Bldg.
332 Minnesota
St. Paul, MN 55101
(612) 224-9635
Terry T. Saario, President
Special interests : economic development, health, natural resources, social & legal services. *Geographic interests* : national groups; Idaho, Iowa, Minnesota, North & South Dakota, Oregon, and Washington.

OAK RIDGE ASSOCIATED UNIVERSITIES
P.O. Box 117
Oak Ridge, TN 37831-0117
(615) 576-1090
Minority Institution Research T ravel Program : Financial assistance for energy-related research at minority academic institutions. All approved travel expenses are covered. Applications must be received at least 30 days prior to the planned departure date from home campus.

PEW CHARITABLE TRUSTS
One Commerce Square
2005 Market St., Suite 1700
Philadelphia, P A 19103
(215) 575-4700 Fax 575-4939
Thomas W . Langfitt, M.D., President
Specific poriorities : religion, health & human services, health care, education, culture, and environment.

PUBLIC LIBRARY ASSOCIATION
American Library Association
50 E. Huron St.
Chicago, IL 60611

(800) 545-2433 (312) 944-6780
Fax (312) 440-9374
Leonard Wertheimer Multilingual Award: To recognize and reward work that enhances and promotes multilingual public library service. $1,000 and a certificate. *Deadline*: November.

PUBLIC WELFARE FOUNDATION
2600 Virginia Ave., NW, Suite 505
Washington, DC 20037
(202) 965-1800
Veronica Keating, Director
Special interests: disadvantaged, environment, community development, education, health, social services.

RED CLOUD INDIAN ART SHOW
Heritage Center, Inc.
Box 100
Pine Ridge, SD 57770
Thunderbird Foundation Scholarship: Financial assistance for the education of Native American artists. Native American tribal members (18 years of age or older) who submit artistic works to the Indian Art Show are considered for this award. $5,000 in art scholarships is awarded. *Deadline*: May. *Edward S. Curtis Purchase Awards*: To recognize and reward young Native American artists at the show. $2,000. *Red Cloud Indian Art Show Awards*: To recognize and reward Native American artists who submit works to the Show. $300 each. Also, *Allan & Joyce Niederman Award & Aplan Award*: To recognize and reward the best traditional art work submitted at the art show. $100 each. *Bonnie Erickson Award*: To recognize and reward the best art work representing children. $100. *M.L. Woodard Award, Tony Begay Memorial Award & Pepion Family Award*. $50 each. *Powers Award*: To recognize and reward artists whose works at the Show depict Indian women. $100. *Bill and Sue Hensler Award*: To recognize and reward Native American sculptors. $50. Awards presented annually in May. *Barkley Art Center Award*: To recognize and reward the most innovative art work at the show. $100. *Rich Decker Award*: For the best artistic representation of American Indian heritage submitted to show. $200.

ROCK (HOWARD) FOUNDATION
Scholarship Program
1577 C St., Suite 304
Anchorage, AK 99501
(907) 274-5400; (800) 478-2332 (within Alaska)
Irmtraud Wieghel, Contact
Requirements: Must be a member of a Community Enterprise Development Corporation of Alaska membership organization; must be majoring in fields of study that promote the economic well-being of life for residents of rural Alaska; must be a full-time student and must be able to prove financial need. *Amount*: $2,500 (undergraduate); and $5,000 (graduate).

SCHOOL OF AMERICAN RESEARCH
P.O. Box 2188
Santa Fe, NM 87504-2188
(505) 982-2919
Katrin H. Lamon Resident Scholar Program for Native Americans: Funding for Native American scholars who would benefit from a residency at the School. Scholars in the areas of anthropology, the humanities, the social sciences, or the arts. Participants receive room, board, medical insurance, and a stipend of up to $28,000. *Deadline*: November.

SEVENTH GENERATION FUND
P.O. Box 10
Forestville, CA 95436
(707) 887-7256
Seed Grants: To support Native American efforts to restore their culture and promote their well-being. Average of $3,000 per year. Applications may be submited at any time.

SIMPLOT (J.R.) COMPANY
Minerals and Chemcials Division
P.O. Box 912
Pocatello, ID 83204
(208) 232-6620
Simplot Company Indian Scholarships: Financial assistance for educational purposes to members of the Shoshone-Bannock Tribes who live on the Fort Hall Indian Reservation. Amount varies.

SKAGGS (L.J. & MARY C.) FOUNDATION
1221 Broadway, 21st Floor
Oakland, CA 94612
(510) 451-3300 Fax 451-1527
David Knight, Program Director
Special interests: arts, culture, historic preservation, environment, education, medicine. *Geographic interest*: national groups, especially California (Oakland).

SMITHSONIAN INSTITUTION
Office of Fellowships and Grants
955 L'Enfant Plaza, Room 7000
Washington, DC 20560
(202) 287-3271
Native American Community Scholar Fellowship: Subsistance and travel expenses to Native Americans to pursue projects related to Native American topics at the Smithsonian. *Native American Museum Program*: To provide educational training opportunities to staff who work in museums and cultural centers that house Native American collections. *Deadline*: February, June & October. *Native American Student Internship Program*: Financial assistance for Native Americans to pursue projects related to Native American topics at the Smithsonian. $300 per week for graduates, and $250 per week for undergraduates. *Deadline*: April, May & September.

SNOW (JOHN BEN) MEMORIAL TRUST
P.O. Box 378
Pulaski, NY 13142
(315) 298-6401
Vernon F. Snow, Contact
Special interests: arts, culture, education, religion, community development, health care, social services. *Geographic interest*: national groups, especially New York (Pulaski) Nevada.

SOCIAL SCIENCE RESEARCH COUNCIL
605 Third Ave.
New York, NY 10158
(212) 661-0280
Undergraduate Research Assistantships: To provide funding to faculty members for the support and training of talented undergraduate students (at least one half of whom must be minorities) while contributing to an understanding. Up to $4,000 per year. Deadline: January. *Urban Underclass Dissertation Fellowships*: To minority graduate stduents working on a dissertation dealing with the urban underclass. The stipend is $1,000 per month. In addition, there is a $4,000 allowance to cover research expenses incurred during the fellowship period. *Deadline*: January.

SOCIETY FOR ADVANCEMENT OF CHICANOS & NATIVE AMERICANS IN SCIENCE
Thiman Labs-University of California
Santa Cruz, CA 95064
SACNAS Conference Grants: Funds for conference attendance costs of Chicano and Native American students and faculty who are eligible.

SOCIETY OF WOMEN ENGINEERS SCHOLARSHIPS
United Engineering Center, Room 305
345 East 47th St.
New York, NY 10017
(212) 705-7855

SOUTH DAKOTA BOARD OF REGENTS
207 E. Capitol Ave.
Pierre, SD 57501
(605) 773-3455 Fax 773-5320
Ardell Bjugstad Memorial Scholarship: Undergraduate scholarship for a North or South Dakota resident and member of a federally recognized tribe whose reservation is located in the Dakotas. For a freshman with a agricutlural major. $500.

SOUTHWEST ASSOCIATION ON INDIAN AFFAIRS
P.O. Box 1964
Santa Fe, NM 87504
(505) 983-5220
Scholarship Program: Financial assistance to American Indian students who wish to pursue a college education. Amount varies. Indian Craftsmen Fellowships: To contribute to the growth and development of Native American art. From $1,000 to $2,500. *Deadline*: April. *Annual Indian Market and Competition*: To recognize and reward outstanding Indian fiber-textile and basketry work submitted at the Indian Market each August. $1,000 Best of Show award. Up to $300 in special awards; and up to $500 in prizes.

STANFORD HUMANITIES CENTER
Stanford University - Mariposa Hall
Stanford, CA 94305-8630
(415) 723-3052
Stanford External Faculty Fellowships: For minority scholars interested in humanistic issues research. *Deadline*: November.

TRIANGLE NATIVE AMERICAN SOCIETY
P.O. Box 26841
Raleigh, NC 27611
Mark Ulmer Native American Scholarship: Financial assistance to Native Americans in North Carolina who are interested in continuing their college education. The stipend is $500 per year. *Deadline*: April.

UNITED SOUTH & EASTERN TRIBES
1101 Kermit Dr., Suite 302
Nashville, TN 37217
(615) 361-8700
Christine Garduno, Contact
Scholarship Fund: To provide financial assistance to Native Americans in the United South and Eastern Tribes service area who wish to pursue postsecondary education. $500 per year. *Deadline*: April 1.

UNIVERSITY OF CALIFORNIA
American Indian Graduate Program
140 Earl Warren Program
Berkeley, CA 94720
(415) 642-3228 collect

Rick St. Germaine, Ph.D., Contact
Fellowship/Graduate Minority Scholarship : For graduate study at the University of California, Berkeley. Tuition and fees plus stipend. *Deadline*: January 5.

UNIVERSITY OF CALIFORNIA
Office of the President
300 Lakeside Dr., 18th Floor
Oakland, CA 94612-3550
(415) 987-9500
President's Fellowship Program : For minorities and women in pursuit of careers in university teaching and research. Stipend of from $25,000 to $29,000 per year plus benefits and research expenses. *Deadline*: December.

UNIVERSITY OF ILLINOIS AT URBANA-CHAMPAIGN
Attn: Associate Dean, Graduate College
202 Coble Hall, 801 S. Wright St.
Champaign, IL 61820
(217) 333-4860
Illinois Minority Graduate Incentive Program : To increase the number of underrepresented minority students pursuing doctoral degrees in the natural sciences at graduate schools in Illinois. Full tuition and fees and an annual stipend of $12,500 and annual allowance for books, travel, etc. of $1,500. *Deadline*: February.

UNIVERSITY OF ILLINOIS AT URBANA-CHAMPAIGN
Associate Vice Chancellor for Academic Affairs
Swanlund Administration Bldg.
601 East John St.
Champaign, IL 61802
(217) 333-0885
Chancellor's Minority Fellow Program : To assist underrepresented faculty interested in research careers. The stipends range from $25,000 to $30,000 per year. Health coverage and funds for research-related expenses (up to $1,800 per year.) *Deadline*: November.

UNIVERSITY OF NEW MEXICO
American Indian Graduate Center
4520 Montgomery Blvd. NE, Suite 1-B
ALBUQUERQUE 87131
(505) 881-4584
Provides fellowship grants to Indian graduate students. Assists about 600 students from 130 tribes at over 200 colleges throughout the U.S. *Deadline*: April 30th.

UNIVERSITY OF NEW MEXICO
College of Engineering, Student Programs Office
Farris Engineering Center, Room 157
Albuquerque, NM 87131
(505) 277-4354
Gail Ward, Contact
UNM College of Engineering Freshman Scholarship Program. *Deadline*: April 1.

UNIVERSITY OF NEW MEXICO SCHOLARSHIP PROGRAM
Minority Engineering Programs
UNM College of Engineering
Engineering Annex Room 209
Albuquerque, NM 87131
(505) 277-8795
Ricardo Maestas, Contact
Requirements: Must be a Native American (or another minority), and attend UNM full time in enginnering or computer science.

UNIVERSITY OF WYOMING
American Indian Studies Program
Room 109, Anthropology Bldg.
Laramie, WY 82071
(307) 766-6521
Dr. Judith A. Antell, Director
The Frank and Cynthia McCarthy Scholarship : Each year four American Indian students can receive a McCarthy Scholarship in the amount of $500 each. Selection is based on academic achievement and record of university service.

UNTO THESE HILLS EDUCATIONAL FUND
P.O. Box 398
Cherokee, NC 28719
(704) 497-2111
Scholarship: Financial assistance to Eastern Band of Cherokee Indians who wish to pursue postsecondary education at the undergraduate level. $500 per year. *Deadline*: April.

VAN PELT (ADOLPH) FOUNDATION, INC.
c/o Association on American Indian Affairs
245 Fifth Ave., Suite 1801
New York, NY 10016-8728
(212) 689-8720
Scholarships: To Native American students interested in postsecondary eduction. Applicants must be Native American students under 30 years of age. Amount awarded varies. *Deadline*: April.

VANGUARD PUBLIC FOUNDATION
14 Precita Ave.
San Francisco, CA 94110
(415) 285-2005
Grants to support grassroots, social change-organizing projects in the San Francisco Bay area with priotiy given to proposals submitted by groups working for the rights of Native Americans. Up to $10,000 per grant. Average grant is $5,000. Emergency grants up to $500 are also available. *Deadlines*: March, June, September & December.

VIRGINIA CENTER FOR THE HUMANITIES
Virginia Foundation for the Humanities
1939 Ivy Rd.
Charlottesville, VA 22903-1171
(804) 924-3296
Residencies Fellowships : To offer funding for research, writing, or programming at the Center. The stipend varies, up to $3,000 per month. *Deadline*: March or October.

WASHINGTON CENTER SCHOLARSHIPS
The Washington Center for Internships and Academic Seminars
750 First St., NE, Suite 650
Washington, DC 20002
(202) 336-1593
Arleen R. Borysiewicz, Contact
Minority scholarship available.

WENNER-GREN FOUNDATION
220 Fifth Ave., 16th Floor
New York, NY 10001
(212) 683-5000
Dr. Sydel Silverman, President
Activities: Provides grants-in-aid to scholars for research and preparation of publications in all branches of anthropology and in related disciplines. *Activities*: Awards up to $12,000 to qualified scholars to aid basic research, doctoral dissertation research, and write-up of research results for publications. Conference grants up to $10,000. Includes a limited number of Richard

Carley Hunt Postdoctoral Fellowships. *Publications*: Current Anthropology, bimonthly journal; Annual Report; issues Viking Fund Publications in Anthropology. Periodic conferences. Founded 1941.

WHATCOM MUSEUM
Jacobs Research Funds
121 Prospect St.
Bellingham, WA 98225
(206) 676-6981
Gladys Fullford, Contact
Kathrine S. French, PhD, Chairperson
Provides small grants (maximum $1,200) for research in the field of social and cultural anthropology among living North American native peoples: Indians, Eskimos, Inuits, and Aleuts. Preference is given to the Pacific Northwest as an area of study, but other regions of North America are considered. Cultural expressive systems - music, language, dance, mythology, world view, plastic and graphic arts, intellectual life, religion - are appropriate topics. *Deadline*: February 15.

WISCONSIN HIGHER EDUCATIONAL AIDS BOARD
P.O. Box 7885
Madison, WI 53707
(608) 267-2206
Wisconsin Native American Grants: Financial aid for higher education to Native Americans in Wisconsin. Up to $1,800 per year. Additional funds are available on a matching basis from the Bureau of Indian Affairs.

WOODROW WILSON NATIONAL FELLOWSHIP FOUNDATION
Box 642
Princeton, NJ 08540
(609) 924-4758
Minority Advancement Program (MAP): Financial assistance to underpresented minority students who are interested in careers in public service and international affairs. Junior & Senior year summer institute undergraduate students receive room, board, and a living allowance. Fellowships given to graduate students cover tuition, fees, and living expenses. *Deadline*: March. Administrative Fellows Program in Higher Education Administration. Relocation expenses and partial salary subsidy of from $22,000 to $32,000 per year to interns who qualify. *Deadline*: January.

ZONTA INTERNATIONAL FOUNDATION
557 W. Randolph St.
Chicago, IL 60606
(312) 930-5848
Lorelei Marshall, Contact
Zonta Amelia Earhart Fellowship : For women pursuing graduate study in aerosapce science or engineering. $6,000 per year. *Deadline*: December 1.

U.S. GOVERNMENT FINANCIAL AID

BUREAU OF INDIAN AFFAIRS
Department of the Interior
Deputy to the Assistant Secretary/Indian Affairs
(Trust & Economic Development)
18th & C Sts., NW
Washington, DC 20245
(202) 343-3657
Indian Loans - Claims Assistance: To Indian tribes or groups of Indians without available funds to obtain assistance in preparing and processing claims pending before the U.S. Court of Claims. From $500 to $250,000. *Economic Development (Indian Business Development Program)*: To Indians, tribes and organizations to help promote the economic development of reservations. From $20,000 to $250,000.

BUREAU OF INDIAN AFFAIRS
Department of the Interior
Office of Indian Education Programs
1951 Constitution Ave., NW
Washington, DC 20245
(202) 343-4871
B.I.A. Higher Education Program: Must be a member of an Indian tribe recognized by the Bureau. There are three funding programs available: Educational scholarships - administered by the following B.I.A. area offices:

Anchorage Area Office, Office of Indian Ed. ,1675 C St., Anchorage, AK 99501 (907) 371-41 15 Robert J. Pringle, Contact; **Billings Area Office**, 316 North 26th St., Billings, MT 59101 (406) 657-6375 Larry Parker, Contact; **Eastern Area Office**, MS 711 Broyhill - Education, 1951 Constitution Ave. NW, Washington, DC 20245 (703) 235-3351; Glen White-Eagle, Contact; **Juneau Area Office**, P.O. Box 25520, Juneau, AK 99802 (907) 586-7183 Richard E. See, Contact; **Minneapolis Area Office**, 331 South 2nd Ave., Minneapolis, MN 55401 (612) 373-1090 Betty W alker, Contact; **Navajo Area Office**, Higher Education Of fice, P.O. Drawer S, Window Rock, AZ 86515 (800) 223-7133 (in AZ); (800) 243-2956 (in NM, UT & CO) Regis Clauschee, Contact; **Portland Area Office**, 911 NE 11th Ave., Portland, OR 97232 (503) 230-5682 Marlin Reimer, Contact; **Sacramento Area Office**, Office of Indian Education, 2800 Cottage W ay, Sacramento, CA 95825 (916) 978-4680; Fayette Babby, Contact

Fellowhsips are available from Bureau's contractor, American Indian Scholarships, 4520 Montgomery Blvd., NE, Albuquerque, NM 87109; and educational loans are administered from the Revolving Loan Fund. Applications for these loans must be made through either the Tribal Credit Association or the bureau's agency of fices. Amount awarded varies depending upon the program's funding and the recipient's needs. *Deadlines*: March for Fall, April for Summer, and October for Winter semesters.

Indian Education-Colleges and Universities: Financial aid to eligible Indian students (recognized by the Bureau as members of an Indian tribe, and have at least 25% Indian blood. Amount depends upon financial need. Awards range from $200 to $7,000 per year. *Deadline*: April, June & October.

BUREAU OF INDIAN AFFAIRS
Dept. of the Interior
Division of Social Services
Office of Indian Services
1951 Constitution Ave., NW, Room 310-S
Washington, DC 20245
(202) 343-6434
Indian Housing Assistance: Grants for repairs, temporary and emergency housing, down payments, and new housing. Child W elfare Assistance; For foster home care and other institutional care for Indian children residing on or near reservations. From $100 to $1,000 monthly . *Indian Child Welfare Act - Title II Grants*: Financial assistance for child-related facilities-day care centers, after-school care programs, foster care, family assistance centers. From $15,000 to $300,000. *General Assistance*: Financial assistance to needy Indians living on or near reservations. *Deadline*: Generally applications are due in February .

BUREAU OF INDIAN AFFAIRS
Department of the Interior
Office of Indian Services
Code 480, Division of Self-Determination Services
1951 Constitution Ave., NW
Washington, DC 20240
(202) 343-4045
Self Determination Grants-Indian T ribal Governments: Funds for improving governing capabilities of the tribes. *Training and Technical Assistance-Indian T ribal Governments*: Funds to tribal governments to develop skills needed to improve capabilities of tribal management. Amount varies.

BUREAU OF INDIAN AFFAIRS
Division of Financial Assistance
1849 C St., NW
Washington, DC 20240
(202) 343-8427
Indian Loan Guaranty Fund: To finance Indian-owned, commercial, industrial, agricultural, or business activity organized for profit, provided that eligible Indian ownership constitutes not less than 51 percent of the business. No limits on the amount available for tribes or organizations, but there is a $500,000 limitation on guaranteed loans to individuals. Up to 30-year loans available. Requested must benefit the economy of an Indian reservation. Indian Revolving Loan Fund: Direct loans to Indian tribes, organizations and individuals for financing of economic enterprises that will contribute to the economy of an Indian reservation. *Indian Business Development Grants*: Matching grants to Native American individuals and public and private entities for the development, construction, improvement, and operation of business enterprises that will improve economies on Indian reservations or in Alaskan native villages. Up to $100,000 for individuals, and $250,000 for tribes and villages.

BUREAU OF INDIAN AFFAIRS
Dept. of the Interior
Division of Housing Assistance
Office of Tribal Services
18th & C Sts., N.W., Room 316S
Washington, D.C. 20245
(202) 343-8427
Indian Housing Assistance: Grants for home improvements, for housing construction in isolated areas, and for technical assistance in establishing housing plans and in obtaining other federal funds. Grants include a maximum of $20,000 per recipient for repairs; $2,500 for temporary and emergency housing; $5,000 for a down payment to obtain a housing loan; and $45,000 for new standard housing ($55,000 in Alaska only.)

BUREAU OF INDIAN AFFAIRS
Dept. of the Interior
Division of Job Placement and Training
Office of Tribal Services
18th and C Sts., N.W., Room 1350 MIB
Washington, D.C. 20245
(202) 343-3668
Indian Employment Assistance Grants: To provide vocational training and job placement for Native Americans. From $800 to $6,500 per year . The average award is $5,000.

BUREAU OF INDIAN AFFAIRS
Department of the Interior
General Manager, Indian Arts & Crafts Board
18th & C Sts., NW, Room 4004M
Washington, D.C. 20245
(202) 343-2773
Program planning assistance toward the encouragement and promotion of the development of American Indian arts & crafts.

INDIAN HEALTH EMPLOYEES SCHOLARSHIP FUND, INC.
Federal Bldg., Room 215
115 Fourth Ave. SE
Aberdeen, SD 57401
(605) 226-7451
Scholarship: Postsecondary education, particularly in health fields. Stipends are usually in the $200 to $300 range. *Deadlines*: May, September, and December.

INDIAN HEALTH SERVICE
12300 Twinbrook Pkwy.
Twinbrook Metro Plaza, Suite 100
Rockville, MD 20852
(301) 443-6197
IHS Area Coordinator, Contact
3 Scholarship Programs: Health Professions Preparatory; Health Professionals Pregraduate ; and Health Professions. Applicants must be American Indian or Alaska Native, high school graduate or equivalent with at least a 2.5 GP A, and intend to serve Indian people upon completion of program. Up to 4 years support available. *Deadline*: Mid-April.

U.S. DEPT. OF AGRICULTURE
Farmers Home Administration
South Agricultural Bldg., Room 6304
Washington, D.C. 20250
(202) 382-1490
Indian Tribal Land Acquisition Loans: To enable tribes and tribal corporations to mortgage lands as secutiry for loans from the Farmers Home Administration to buy additional land within the reservation. Amount varies depending upon project costs. Each loan must be adequately secured.

U.S. DEPT. OF COMMERCE
Office of Program Development
Minority Business Agency-American Indian Prog.
14th & Constitution Ave., N.W., Rm. 5096
Washington, D.C. 20230
(202) 377-5770
Competetive grant awards to six Indian Business Development Centers and one American Indian Business Consultant, to provide management and technical assistance of all types to new or existing American Indian businesses. *Amount*: From $165,000 to $300,000.

U.S. DEPT. OF EDUCATION
Division of Innovation & Development
400 Maryland Ave., SW
Washington, DC 20202
  (202) 732-2379/80
Vocational Education-Indian and Hawaiian Natives Grants and Contracts . *Amount* : From $50,000 to $2+ million.

U.S. DEPT. OF EDUCATION
Office of Bilingual Education
& Minority Languages Affairs
400 Maryland Ave., SW
Washington, DC 20202
  (202) 245-2595, 732-1840 & 732-2369
Fellowships Grants : Financial assistance to bilingual education programs and activities that meet special bilingual needs of children 3 to 18 years of age who have limited English language ability and who come from families where primary language is not English. From $25,000 to $1.5 million. *Deadline* : July. *Development of Instructional Materials in Bilingual Education Grants* . Up to $250,000 per year. *Deadline* : June. Educational Personnel Training Program Grants. $4 million per year is available for distribution. *Deadline* : June. *Special Populations Program Grants* : Financial support for bilingual education programs designed for special education for preschool children. Up to $2.5 million is available for distribution each year . *Deadline* : June. *Bilingual Vocational Instructional Materials, Methods, and Techniques Grants and Contracts*. Average $250,000. Bilingual V ocational Instructor Training Grants. From $125,000 to $225,000. *Deadline* : January. *Bilingual Vocational Training Grants* . From $100,000 to $350,000. *Family English Literacy Program Grants* . $250,000. *Deadline* : June. *Transitional Bilingual Education Grants* . To support structured English-language instruction and native language instruction. *Deadline* : June.

U.S. DEPT. OF EDUCATION
Office of Indian Education
400 Maryland Ave., S.W., Rm. 2177, MS: 6335
Washington, DC 20202
  (202) 401-1902/1916
  Bruce Stacey, Contact
Indian Fellowship Program : financial assistance to graduate students and selected undergraduate students who are Native Americans interested in preparing for various professional careers. Awards range from $2,500 to $13,000 per year; $6,000 average. *Deadline* : January 21. *Adult Indian Education Grants* : support of programs for adult Indian education. From $30,000 to $250,000. *Deadline* : December. *Johnson-O'Malley Educational Assistance Program* : assistance to schools - reimburse schools that provide supplementary educational programs to eligible Indian students. *Formula Grants to Local Educational Agencies and Tribal Schools* : financial assistance to agencies or tribal schools for programs designed to meet the special and culturally-related educational needs of Indian children. From $2,000 to over $1 million. *Deadline* : January. *Grants to Indian Controlled Schools* . From $37,000 to $300,000. *Deadline* : December. *Special Programs and Projects Grants* : To provide financial assistance in improving educational opportunities for Indian children. From $20,000 to $300,000. *Deadline* : December.

DOE/INDUSTRY NATIVE AMERICAN SCHOLARSHIP PROGRAM
National Advisory Council on Indian Education
330 C St., SW, Room 4072
Washington, DC 20202

  (202) 205-8353 Fax 205-8897
  Robert K. Chiago, Executive Director
The Dept. of Energy scholarship program is intended to encourage Native Americans to pursue math and science degrees within the Nation's community college system. Focused primarily towards students enrolled at two-year community colleges.

U.S. DEPT. OF HEALTH & HUMAN SERVICES
Administration for Native Americans
Director, Planning and Support Division
200 Independence Ave., S.W., Room 344F
Washington, D.C. 20201
  (202) 245-7776
Financial Assistance Grants . to promote self-sufficiency among Native Americans; for business starts for Indian-owned companies, improved Indian housing management, development of tribal health care systems, and local control of social services. From $40,000 to $2 Million; awards average $125,000 for tribal grants and $100,000 for urban grants. *Deadline* : June. *Research, Demonstration, and Evaluation Grants* : financial assistance for new methods of promoting social and economic self-suf ficiency. From $46,000 to $250,000; awards average $130,000. *Training and Technical Assistance Grants* : for the planning and management of community-based social and economic programs. From $8,000 to $80,000; awards average $15,000.

U.S. DEPT. OF HEALTH & HUMAN SERVICES
Office for American Indian, Alaskan Natives and Native Hawaiian Programs
330 Independence Ave., S.W., Room 4752
Washington, D.C. 20201
  (202) 245-2957
Grants to Native Americans for Aging Services : Financial assistance to Indian tribes to provide nutritional and supportive services to older Native Americans. The average grant is $50,000. Check Federal Register for schedule of deadline dates.

U.S. DEPT. OF HEALTH & HUMAN SERVICES
Division of Research and Demonstrations
Office of Policy Development
200 Independence Ave., S.W.
Washington, D.C. 20201
  (202) 245-6233
Social Services Research & Demonstration : Funds for new social service concepts. From $100,000 to $250,000.

U.S. DEPT. OF HEALTH & HUMAN SERVICES
Indian Health Service
5600 Fishers Lane, Room 6A05
Rockville, MD 20857
  (301) 443-1104
  Larry Thomas, Branch Chief
Health Professional Pregraduate Scholarship Program : To American Indian or Alaska Native students interested in pursuing postsecondary education in the health professions; *Health Professions Preparatory Scholarship Program for Indians* : To students who need compensatory preprofessional education to qualify for enrollemnt or reenrollment in a health professions school. From $5,000 to $12,000 per year; *Health Professions Program* : Financial assistance to Native Americans who are interested in completing health professional degrees. From $7,000 to $12,000 per year. *Deadline* : April. *Management Development Program* : For projects that help encourage Indians to pursue a career in the health professions. From $40,000 to over $250,000 per year . *Indian Health Care Improvement Grants* . Average $80,000 per grant.

U.S. DEPT. OF HEALTH & HUMAN SERVICES
Indian Health Service, Manpower Support Branch
12300 Twinbrook Pkwy., Suite 100
Rockville, MD 20852
  (301) 443-4242
IHS Loan Repayment Program : Provides financial assistance to Native Americans who are studying a health-related curriculum in graduate school and would be willing to work at an Indian Health Service (IHS) facility upon graduation. From $3,000 to $75,000.

U.S. DEPT. OF HUD
Community Planning & Development
451 7th St., S.W.
Washington, D.C. 20410
  (202) 755-6092
Indian Community Development Block Grant Program : From $10,000 to $600,000 to improve housing, community facilities, and expand job opportunities for Indian tribes and Alaskan Native villages. The average award is about $300,000. Deadlines may be found in the Federal Register .

U.S. DEPT. OF LABOR
Division of Indian and Native American Programs
Employment and Training Administration
601 D St., N.W.
Washington, D.C. 20213
  (202) 376-6102
Employment & T raining Grants : To reduce the economic disadvantages and advance the economic and social development of Indians and others of Native American descent. From 50,000 to over $7 million per year . Notice of intent to apply due by March of each year .

U.S. FISH & WILDLIFE SER VICE
Cooperative Research Units Center
Department of the Interior
Washington, D.C. 20240
Cooperative Education Agreement : Tuition and up to $11,000 per year for part-time employment in turn for graduate education and work assignments at the service facilities. Contact your local Cooperative and Wildlife Research Unit. No deadline.

U.S. JUSTICE DEPT.
Main Justice Bldg.
10th St. & Constitution Ave.
Washington, D.C. 20530
  (202) 633-2007
Aleut Reparations : To compensate Aleuts taken to internment camps during W orld War II. Each eligible Aleut receives $12,000. Of th original 881 Aleuts taken to the camps and the children born there, about 400 are still alive and eligible for this payment.

U.S. NATIONAL INSTITUTES OF HEAL TH
Division of Research Grants
Westwood Bldg., Room A27
Bethesda, MD 20892
  (301) 496-7221
Short-Term Training Students in Health Professional Schools Grants : Financial assistance to attract qualified minority professional students into biomedical and behavioral research careers. The current stipend is about $550 per month with up to $125 per month to defray other costs. *Deadline* : January.

TRIBAL SCHOLARSHIPS

PUEBLO OF ACOMA HIGHER EDUCATION PROGRAM
P.O. Box 307
Pueblo of Acoma, NM 87034
(505) 552-6621/2
Lloyd Tortalita, Director
Carleen Salvador , Higher Ed. Coordinator
Tribal scholarships. *Deadlines* : June 1 & Oct. 1.

ALL INDIAN PUEBLO COUNCIL, INC.
3939 San Pedro NE, #D, Box 3256
Albuquerque, NM 87190
(505) 884-3820 Ext. 202
Ray H. Trujillo, Contact
Scholarship Grant Program : Financial assistance for postsecondary education to Pueblo Indians. Amount awarded varies. *Deadline* : Februrary for Summer or Fall terms, and Oct. for Spring term.

BLACKFEET TRIBAL EDUCATION DEPT.
P.O. Box 850
Browning, MT 59417
(406) 338-7538
Graduation Grant : To recognize and reward Blackfeet Indians who complete their high school requirements. The ward is $50. *Education Grant* : For undergraduate or graduate education to members of the Blackfeet Tribe. The amount awarded varies depending upon the recipient's educational requirements and financial needs. *Deadlines* : Feb. for Spring; June for Fall; and Nov . for Winter.

CHEROKEE NATION OF OKLAHOMA
Higher Education Foundation
P.O. Box 948
Tahlequah, OK 74465
(800) 722-4325; (918) 456-0671
Wauneta Sanders, Coordinator
Tribal Scholarship Grant : To members of the tribe for postsecondary education. Amount awarded varies. *Deadline* : March for Summer & Fall terms, and November for Spring term. *Trail of Tears Scholarship* : Must be a Cherokee college junior or senior with a 3.0 GP A. *Deadline* : April 1. *Graduate Scholarship Award* : Financial assistance to college graduates who belong to the Cherokee Nation of Oklahoma who wish to pursue a graduate education. Amount awarded varies depending upon the educational requirements and the financial needs of the recipient. *Deadline* : June for Fall term, and October for Spring term.

CHEYENNE-ARAPAHO TRIBE
Department of Education
P.O. Box 38
Concho, OK 73022
(405) 262-0345 Fax 262-0745
Higher Education Assistance Program Grant : To tribal members who are interested in pursuing postsecondary education. $100 and up. *Deadline* : March for Summer, May for Fall, and October for Spring.

CHICKASAW NATION EDUCATION FOUNDATION
Dept. of Education
P.O. Box 1548
Ada, OK 74820
(405) 436-2603 Fax 436-4287
Roland Barrick, Director
Scholarship grant of $200-$350 per semester . Applicants must have proof of Chickasaw ancestry, and at least a 2.5 GP A. *Deadline* : May 1.

CHOCTAW NATION
P.O. Drawer 1210
Durant, OK 74702
(405) 924-8280
Higher Education Program : Financial assistance to Choctaw Indians who are interested in pursuing postsecondary education. Applicants must be at least 25% Choctaw/Indian blood. Up to $1,600 per year for single students and $2,000 for married students. *Deadline* : December of each year .

CREEK NATION HIGHER EDUCATION
P.O. Box 580
Okmulgee, OK 74447
(918) 756-8700
Scholarship Program : Provides educational grants to aid Creek undergraduate or graduate students who are interested in pursuing postsecondary studies. Up to $2,000 per year . *Deadline* : May for Fall semester; October for Spring. *Tribal Funds Grant* : Grants to aid enrolled citizens of the Muskogee (Creek) Nation attending an accredited college or university . $400 per year to full-time students, $200 per year to part-time students. *Tribal Incentive Grant Program* : Financial assistance to enrolled citizens of the Muskogee (Creek) Nation attending an accredited college or university. $300 per semester for full-time students; $150 per semester for part-time students. *Deadline* : June for Fall semester , November for Spring semester.

EIGHT NORTHERN INDIAN PUEBLOS COUNCIL, INC.
P.O. Box 969
San Juan Pueblo, NM 87566
(505) 753-1808 Fax 735-8988
Francis Tafoya, Director
Higher education scholarships. Must be an enrolled member of one of the Eight Northern Pueblos. *Deadlines* : March 1 & November 1.

HOPI DEPARTMENT OF EDUCATION
c/o Grants Manager
P.O. Box 123
Kykotsmovi, Arizona 86039
(602) 734-2445
Tribal Grants and Scholarship Program : To provide financial assistance to Hopi Indians who are interested in attending college. Amount awarded varies. *Deadline* : May.

HUALAPAI TRIBAL COUNCIL
P.O. Box 168
Peach Springs, AZ 86434
(602) 769-2216
Tribal Scholarships : Financial assistance for members of the Hualapai Tribe who are interested in pursuing undergraduate education. Up to $1,500 per year . *Vocational Training Program* : For tribal members who have graduated high schoo or earned the GED. Amount varies. Applications must be submitted at least 2 weeks before each term begins.

JEMEZ SCHOLARSHIP PROGRAM
Pueblo of Jemez
P.O. Box 9
Jemez Pueblo, NM 87024
(505) 834-9171 Fax 834-7331
Dr. Nilla Vallo, Education Director
Tribal Scholarships . *Deadlines* : June 30 & October 30.

JICARILLA HIGHER EDUCATION PROGRAM
Jicarilla Apache Tribe
P.O. Box 507
Dulce, NM 87528
(505) 759-3615
Josephine Lefthand, Director
Rhonda Riley, Counselor
FredVigil, Counselor
Chester E. Faris Higher Education Fund : Financial assistance for undergraduate or graduate education to members of the Jicarilla Apache tribe. Up to $1,800 per year . *Deadlines* : March 1 & October 1.

LAGUNA SCHOLARSHIP PROGRAM
Laguna Pueblo
P.O. Box 194
Old Laguna, NM 87026
(505) 552-6654 Ext. 33/66
Vivian Brewster, Director
Gloria Mariano, Counselor
Tribal scholarships. *Deadlines* : May 1 for Fall semester; October 1 for Spring semester; and April 15 for Summer semester .

MENOMINEE INDIAN TRIBE OF WISCONSIN
P.O. Box 397
Keshena, WI 54135
(715) 799-3341
Scholarships : For Menominee Indians who are interested in pursuing postsecondary studies. *Adult Vocational Training Program* : Financial assistance to Menominee Indians who are interested in obtaining a diploma or certificate an associates of arts at a vocational/technical/junior college. Up to $1,800 per year . *Deadline* : February.

MESCALERO APACHE TRIBAL SCHOLARSHIP
Mescalero Tribal Education
P.O. Box 176
Mescalero, NM 88340
(505) 671-4494
Clarence Buurma, Director
Naomi Saenz, Career Counselor
Tribal scholarships. *Amount* : maximum of $6,00 per year. *Deadline* : July 1 & November 1.

MINNESOTA CHIPPEWA TRIBE SCHOLARSHIP
P.O. Box 217
Cass Lake, MN 56633
(218) 335-8584
Richard Tanner, Contact
Critical Professions Program : For Minnesota Chippewa Indian students with at least a 2.0 GP A, who wish to pursue an undergraduate or graduate degree in critical professions (business, natural resources-forestry, computer programming, urban and rural planning, or teaching.) Award varies; graduate students receive $650 per month and undergraduate students receive $450 per month (plus $90 per dependent) . *Scholarship Program* : For Tribal high school graduates who wish to pursue postsecondary education. $3,000 per year, based on need. *Deadline* : June 1.

NAVAJO NATION
P.O. Box 508
Window Rock, AZ 86515
(602) 871-4941 Ext. 1627
Miss Navajo Contest : to recognize and reward outstanding young Navajo women. The winner is selected at the annual Navajo Tribal Fair. Tribal position - $15,000 per year .

NAVAJO NATION HIGHER EDUCATION
P.O. Box Drawer S
Window Rock, AZ 86515
(602) 871-7435/6; (800) 223-7133 (in AZ)
(800) 243-2956 (outside AZ)
Regis Clauschee, Program Manager
Fred Tahe, Management Analyst
Grace Fourkiller, Head Counselor
Scholarship Assistance Program: provides financial assistance to members of the Navajo Nation who are interested in pursuing undergraduate education. Amount of award varies. *Deadlines*: June 30 (Fall), Nov. 30 (Spring) & April 30 (Summ.)

NAVAJO VETERAN AFFAIRS OFFICE
P.O. Box 430
Window Rock, AZ 86515
(602) 871-6597 Ext. 6598
Navajo Nation Veterans Fund: Emergency aid ($450 or more) to Navajo veterans waiting for assistance from the Veterans Administration.

NORTHERN ARAPAHOE TRIBE
Sky People Higher Education
P.O. Box HH
Ethete, WY 82520
(307) 332-5286
Tribal Scholarship: Financial assistance to members of the Northern Arapahoe Tribe who are high school graduates or seniors about to graduate and are interested in postsecondary education. Up to $2,000 per year. *Deadline*: June.

NORTHERN CHEYENNE TRIBE
P.O. Box 307
Lame Deer, MT 59043
(406) 477-6467
Northern Cheyenne Adult Vocational Training Program: Financial assistance to tribal members who are interested in pursuing voctional training. *Career Development Scholarships*: Financial assistance to members of the Northern Cheyenne Tribe who are high school graduates or seniors about to graduate and are interested in postsecondary education in the state of Montana. *Deadline*: Feb.

MAE LASLEY/OSAGE SCHOLARSHIP FUND
P.O. Box 2009
Tulsa, OK 74101
(918) 587-3115
Marilyn Connor
Tribal Scholarship Grant: Financial assistance to eligible tribal members for postsecondary education. *Requirements*: Proof of Osage Indian descent, and must show financial need. Amount: $1,000 per year, renewable. *Deadline*: June 15.

MARY TINKER SCHOLARSHIP
Osage Agency
Pawhuska, OK 74056
(918) 287-1032
Marion Cass, Contact
Scholarships are awarded for college/university training. Must have at least a 2.0 GPA. Amount: $20-$50 per semester; up to eight semesters.

OSAGE TRIBAL EDUCATION COMMITTEE SCHOLARSHIP
c/o Oklahoma Area Indian Education Office
4149 Highline, Suite 380
Oklahoma City, OK 73108
Requirements: Proof of Osage descent; verification of school enrollment. Must have at least a 2.0 GPA. Scholarships are awarded for vocational, technical and college/university training. *Amount*: $200-$500 per semester. *Deadlines*: July 1 & Dec. 31.

SANTO DOMINGO SCHOLARSHIP PROGRAM
P.O. Box 99
Santo Domingo Pueblo, NM 87052
(505) 465-2214 ext. 25
Guadalupe Mina Sr., Director
Tribal scholarships. *Deadlines*: March 1 & November 1.

SENECA NATION OF INDIANS EDUCATIONAL FOUNDATION
P.O. Box 231, Jimerson Town Rd.
Salamanca, NY 14779
(716) 945-1790
Education Grants: Financial assistance to Seneca Nation members who are interested in pursuing postsecondary education. Up to $4,000 per year.

SHOSHONE TRIBE
Community Development Office
Wind River Indian Agency
Fort Washakie, WY 82514
Tribal Scholarships: Financial assistance to members of the Wind River Shoshone Tribe who are high school graduates or seniors about to graduate and are interested in postsecondary education. Up to $2,000 per year. *Deadline*: June.

WIND RIVER INDIAN AGENCY
Community Development Office
Fort Washakie, WY 82514
Northern Arapahoe Tribal Scholarship: For enrolled members of the tribe who are interested in postsecondary education (any public institution in Wyoming.) Up to $2,00 per year. *Shoshone Tribal Scholarship*: For Wind River Shoshone Indian students who are interested in pursuing post-secondary education. Up to $2,00 per year.

YAKIMA INDIAN NATION
Higher Education Programs
Dept. of Human Services
P.O. Box 151
Toppenish, WA 98948
(800) 543-2802
(509) 865-5121 Ext. 530 or 534
Scholarship: Financial assistance to Yakima tribe members who wish to pursue postsecondary education. $1,000 per year for undergraduate students; $2,000 per year for graduate students. *Deadline*: February, May, July and November. *Yakima College Student Assistance Program*: For Yakima Indians who wish to pursue postsecondary education. Amount varies according to need. *Deadline*: January, April, June and October. *Yakima Incentive Awards Program*: To recognize and reward outstanding academic achievement of Yakima Indians. *Vocational Training for Adults Program*: To Yakima Indians who are interested in acquiring technical training by attending an accredited vocational school, college, or trade institute. *Direct Employment Assistance for Adults*: To eligible Yakima Indians who are searching for a permanent job.

ZUNI SCHOLARSHIP PROGRAM
P.O. Box 339
Zuni, NM 87327
(505) 782-4481 Ext. 482, 489
Ray H. Trujillo, Scholarship Officer
Tribal scholarships. *Deadlines*: June 30 for Fall semester; October 30 for Spring semester; April 30 for Summer semester.

CORPORATE GRANT MAKERS

ALCOA FOUNDATION
1501 Alcoa Bldg.
Pittsburgh, PA 15219
(412) 553-4694
F. Worth Hobbs, Director
Places a high priority on serving populations in areas where the company has facilities. *Special interests*: education, health & welfare, cultural, covic & community, youth.

AMOCO FOUNDATION
200 E. Randolph Dr.
Chicago, IL 60601
(312) 856-6306
Pamela J. Barbara, Executive Director
Special interests: education, community service, environment & civic, culture & art, neighborhood economies.

ARCO FOUNDATION
515 So. Flower St.
Los Angeles, CA 90071
(213) 486-3342
Eugene R. Wilson, Director
Special interests: education, arts & humanities, community development, environment, and public information (media).

AT&T BELL LABORATORIES
Special Programs Administrator
Crawfords Corner Rd., Room 1E-219
Holmdel, NJ 07733-1988
(908) 949-4301
Dual Degree Scholarship Program; Engineering Scholarship Program; Summer Employment Programs; and AT&T Graduate Research Fellowship Program for Women: To develop scientists and engineers among minority group members, and to provide work experience at AT&T Bell Labs. Annual award of $1,500. *Deadline*: January 15th.

DAYTON HUDSON FOUNDATION
Dayton Hudson Corp.
777 Nicollet Mall
Minneapolis, MN 55402
(612) 370-6553
Vivian K. Stuck, Administrative Officer
Special interests: community & economic development, social services, arts & cultural. Twins Cities Program and National Program.

EXXON EDUCATION FOUNDATION
225 E. John W. Carpenter Freeway
Irving, TX 75062
(214) 444-1104
Edward F. Ahnert, Executive Director
Special interests: education, community & economic development, health, arts.

FREEDOM FORUM
Gannett Company
1101 Wilson Blvd
Arlington, VA 22209
(703) 284-2802
Brian Buchanan, Staff
Special interests: media, public affairs, education, social services, youth, community development.

GENERAL MILLS FOUNDATION
9200 Wayzata Blvd., Box 1113
Minneapolis, MN 55440
(612) 540-4662 Fax 540-4925
Dr. Reatha Clark King, Executive Director

Special interests : education, social services, health, arts & culture, civic af fairs.

HUGHES AIRCRAFT COMPANY
Corporate Fellowship & Rotation Programs
Technical Education Center
P.O. Box 80028
Los Angeles, CA 90080
 (310) 568-6736
 Peggy Heathscote, Contact
Master of Science Fellowship, Howard Hughes Doctoral Fellowship and Engineer Degree Fellowship are awarded on a competetive basis to qualified individuals in engineering, computer sciences, physics and mathematics. *Amount* : Tuition, books, stipend ($25,000-$50,000).

IBM (INTERNATIONAL BUSINESS MACHINES CORPORA TION)
Manager, University and Scientific Relations
Thomas J. Watson Research Center
P.O. Box 218
Yorktown Heights, NY 10598
IBM Miority/Women's Fellowship Program : For graduate research in engineering and the sciences. $10,000 stipend and tuition. *Deadline* : February 15.

METROPOLITAN LIFE FOUNDATION
One Madison Ave.
New York, NY 10010
 (212) 578-6272
 Sibyl Jacobson, President
Special interests : health, education, culture, civic affairs, and community & economic development.

MOBIL FOUNDATION, INC.
150 E. 42nd St.
New York, NY 10017
 (212) 883-2174
 Richard G. Mund, Executive Director
Special interests : education, social services, arts & culture, civic af fairs, and health.

PACIFIC GAS & ELECTRIC CO.
245 Market St., Room 1300
San Francisco, CA 94106
 (415) 973-1338
James B. Black College Scholarships : Financial assistance for postsecondary education to Black, Hispanic and Native American students in California. Up to $4,000. *Deadline* : November.

PRUDENTIAL FOUNDATION
751 Broad St., 15th Floor
Newark, NJ 07103
 (201) 877-7354/5
 Elisa D. Puzzuoli, Programs
Special interests : education, health & human services, economic & community development, arts & culture, disadvantaged, environment.

SANTA FE SOUTHERN PACIFIC FOUNDATION
224 S. Michigan Ave.
Chicago, IL 60604-2401
 (312) 786-6204
 R.L. Holden, Contact
Native American Scholarship Program : Open to high school seniors who are at least 1/4 Native American Indian. Up to $2,500 per year , depending on need. *Deadline* : March 15th.

TEXACO FOUNDATION
2000 Westchester Ave.
White Plains, NY 10650
 (914) 253-4150
 Maria Mike-Mayer , Director
Special interests : education, environment, arts & culture, economic & community development, health & human services, natural resources, historic preservation, research.

U.S. WEST FOUNDATION
78000 E. Orchard Rd., Suite 300
Englewood, CO 801 11
 (303) 793-6578
 Jane Prancan, Executive Director
Special interests : education, economic & community development, arts & culture, health & human services, children/youth.

WELLS FARGO BANK
343 Sansom St., 3rd Floor
San Francisco, CA 94163
 (415) 396-0109
Richard & Jessie Barrington Educational Fund : Financial assistance for postsecondary education to enrolled members of the W ashoe Tribe who reside in California or Nevada. Up to $5,000 per year. Contact the Washoe Tribe of Nevada & California Education Department, 919 Highway 395 South, Gardnerville, NV 89410 (702) 265-4191.

RELIGIOUS INSTITUTION GRANT MAKERS

NORTH SHORE UNITARIAN UNIVERSALIST VEATCH PROGRAM
Plandome Rd.
Plandome, NY 11030
 (516) 627-6576
 Barbara Dudley, Executive Director
Special interests : social & economic justice, civil & constitutional rights, religion, environmental.

PRESBYTERIAN CHURCH U.A.S.
Presbyterian Committee on the
Self Development of People
100 Witherspoon St.
Louisville, KY 40202
 (502) 569-5760/5776/5735
 Maria Alvarez, Contact
Special interests : disadvantaged, social services, human rights, religion, community & economic development. *Native American Education Grants* : To provide Indian, Eskimo and Aleut students financial assistance to continue their college education. *Requirements* : Preference is given to Presbyterian students at an undergraduate level who can confirm at least a 1/4 Native American ancestry. Stipends range from $200 to $1,500 per year , renewable. *Deadline* : June 1. *Native American Seminary Scholarships* : Financial assistance to Native American students interested in preparing for church occupations. From $1,000-$3,000/ year .

UNITED METHODIST CHURCH
The General Commission on Religion & Race
110 Maryland Ave., NE #48
Washington, DC 20002
 (202) 547-4828
 Bishop Joseph B. Behem, Chair
Purpose : To promote empowerment, self determination, justice, power and liberation for minorities, including Native Americans.

UNITED METHODIST CHURCH
Board of Higher Education & Ministry
P.O. Box 871
Nashville, TN 37202-0871
 (615) 340-7344
 Diane DeForest, Contact
HANA Scholars Program : Financial assistance to outstanding United Methodist Native American undergraduate and graduate full-time college students. Applicants must be a member of the Church for at least one year . Stipend is $1,000 for undergraduates and $3,000 for graduate students. *Deadline* : April 1. *Ethnic Minority Scholarships* : Must be an active member of the Church. From $100 to $1,000. *Deadline* : May 1.

Since 1955, the U.S. Public Health Service (PHS), through its Indian Health Service (IHS), an agency of the Department of Health and Human Services, is the primary federal health resource for more than one million American Indians and Alaskan Natives. The mission of the IHS is to ensure the equity, availability and accessibility of a comprehensive high quality health care delivery system providing maximum involvement of American Indians and Alaska Natives in defining their health needs, setting priorities for their local areas, and managing and controlling their health program. This section lists hospitals, medical and health centers under the jurisdiction of the Indian Health Service. Listings arranged alpha-geographically.

(OUTBOUND BUILDING ADDRESS)
12300 Twinbrook Parkway
Rockville, MD 20857

(HEADQUARTERS)
Parklawn Bldg., 5600 Fishers Lane
Rockville, MD 20857
 (301) 443-1083 Fax 443-4794
 IHS Hotline Number (301)443-0658

Office of the Director:
Room 6-05 (301) 443-1083
 Dr. Michael Trujillo, Director
 Michel E. Lincoln, Deputy Director
 Luana L. Reyes, Acting Director of
  Headquarters Operations
 Cynthia A. Smith, Senior Advisor to the Director
 Milburn H. Roach, Exec. Ass't. to the Director
 Phyllis Eddy, Special Assistant to the Director
  Headquarters Op., Rm. 6-22 (443-7261)
 Patricia A. DeAsis, Director of Communications,
  Room 6-35 (443-3593)

Office of Administration & Management:
Room 6-25 (301) 443-7493
 George Buzzard, Associate Director
 Jack Markowitz, Acting Deputy Associate Dir.
 John Richardson, Special Assistant to the
  Associate Director
 Aaron Poolaw, Program Integrity Officer,
  Rm. 4B-05 (443-4137)
 James P. Dunnick, Jr., Director, Div. of Resource
  Management, Room 5A-54 (443-1270)
 Sam Elrod, Director, Div. of Administrative
  Services, Room 4B-42 (443-0815)

Office of Tribal Activities:
Room 6A-05 (301) 443-1104
 Douglas Black, Associate Director
 Athena Schoening, Deputy Associate Director
 Beulah Bowman, Director, Div. of Community
  Services (443-6840)
 Mitchell Parks, Director, Div. of Self-
  Determination Services (443-1044)
 Hickory Starr, Jr., Director, Div. of Tribal
  Information Services (443-6958)

Office of Planning, Evaluation & Legislation:
TMP, Suite 450 (301) 443-4245
 Edward Simermeyer, Acting Associate Director
 Leo J. Nolan, Director, Div. of Program
  Evaluation (443-4700)
 Richard McCloskey, Director, Div. of Legislation/
  Regulations (443-1116)
 Anthony J. D'Angelo, Director, Div. of Program
  Statistics (443-1180)
 Patricia Logan, Director, Div. of Health Services
  Planning (443-4724)

Office of Information Resources Management:
Room 5A-21 (301) 443-0750
 Richard M. Church, Associate Director
 James Garvie, Dep. Assoc. Director (443-1064)

Office of Environmental Health & Engineering:
TMP, Suite 600A (301) 443-1247
 James Waskiewicz, Associate Director
 Gary Radtke, Director, Div. of Facilities Planning,
  Suite 600C (443-1850)
 Gary Hartz, Director, Div. of Environmental
  Health, Suite 610 (443-1043)
 Alan L. Petersen, Director, Div. of Facilities
  Management, Suite 600B (443-3121)

Office of Health Programs:
Room 6A-55 (301) 443-3024
 Phillip L. Smith, MD, Associate Director
 Mary Beth Skupien, Deputy Associate Director
 Carl Harper, Executive Officer
 Stephen Permison, MD, Director,
  Health Care Policy
 Richard Olson, MD, Director, Patient Care
  Professional Affairs
 W. Craig Vanderwagen, MD, Director, Division
  of Clinical Services, Rm. 6A-54 (443-4644)

Office of Human Resources:
Room 6-49 (301) 443-6290
 Robert G. McSwain, Acting Associate Director
 Kenneth D. Cannon, Executive Officer

Nursing Education Center for Indians
5600 Fishers Lane, Rockville, MD 20857
 (301) 443-1840
 Louise Kiger, RN, Director

Clinical Support Center, IHS
1616 East Indian School Rd.
Aztec Square, Suite 375
Phoenix, AZ 85016 (602) 640-2140
 Wesley J. Picciotti, Director
Staff: Thomas J. Ambrose, Office of Program Support; Edward Y. Hopper, MD, Office of Continuing Education; Cyril Rosseau, Office of Emergency Medical Services Training; Wilma Morgan, IHS Primary Care Provider.

(HEADQUARTERS WEST)
5300 Homestead Rd., NE
Albuquerque, NM 87110
(505) 837-4101 Fax 837-4115

Office of the Director:
 Eleanor Robertson, Acting Program Manager
 Evelyn C. Trujillo, Administrative Officer
 Bernadette L. Callahan, Administrative Services
  Chief (837-4108)
 Emmett Chase, MD, AIDS Coord. (837-4116)
 Charlene Hill, Coord., FAS Project (837-4228)
 Carmelita Sorrelman, Coordinator -
  Headstart Project (837-4231)
 Gene Gerber, Liaison Services (837-4239)
 Dorothy Gohdes, MD, Director -
  Diabetes Program (837-4182)
 Eva Marie Smith, Chief - Alcohol & Substance
  Abuse Program (837-4121)
 Joseph G. Trujillo, Chief - Property
  Management, (837-4266)
 Scott H. Nelson, MD, Chief - Mental Health
  Programs (837-4245)
 Nathaniel Cobb, Director - Cancer Prevention
  & Control Program (837-4132)
 William Freeman, Director - Research
  Development Program (837-4141)
 Anthony P. Ortega, Director - Traditional Cultural
  Advocacy Program (837-4237)

Dental Field Support & Program Development
(505) 837-4175 Fax 837-4181
 William J. Niendorff, DDS, Director -
  Dental Information Standards
 Horace Whitt, DDS, Director - Dental
  Information Systems Development
 Scott Bingham, Director - Dental Staff Develop.

Office of Information Resource Management
(505) 837-4189 Fax 837-4199
 James McArthur, Director - Systems Develop.
 Bruce E. Parker, Director - Data Processing
 Myron Taylor, Director - Systems Management

Nutrition & Dietetics Training Branch
P.O. Box 5558, 1700 Cerillos Rd., Bldg. #5
Santa Fe, NM 87502 (505) 988-6518
 Joanne Proulx, Chief

IHS AREA OFFICES
(Alphabetically Arranged)

ABERDEEN IHS AREA OFFICE
Federal Bldg., 115 Fourth Ave., SE
Aberdeen, SD 57401
 (605) 226 + Ext.; Fax 226-7670
States served: North & South Dakota & Iowa.
 Donald Bad Moccasin, Director (7581)
 Tony Peterson, Executive Officer (7581)
 Esther Anderson, MD, Chief Medical (7581)

Hospitals & Clincs Program
 Jerome DeWolfe, Management Officer (7501)
 Richard Figenshow, Audiology Service (7456)
 Bill Savage, DDS, Dental Services
 Andrew Qualm, OD, Optometry Services (7501)
 Verna Schad, Nursing Services (7501)
 Esther Anderson, MD, Medical Care
  Evaluation Program (7306)
 Jerome DeWolf, Planning & Legislation (7535)
 Letha Leader Charge, Community Health
  Representative (7584)
 Rick Sorenson, Program Management Officer
  (7584)
 Reba Walker, Planning & Legislation (7535)
 Webster Two Hawk, Tribal Health Management
  Program (Pierre) (605) 224-8454
 Chris Krough, MD, Maternal & Child Health
  Services (Rapid City) (605) 348-1900

Tribal Projects Specialists: Dennis Renvilles (Bismarck) (701) 222-3540; Priscilla Lee (Pierre) (605) 224-8544 Roger Condon (Aberdeen) (605) 226-7584; and Pat Giroux Rapid City (605) 348-1900

Has jurisdiction over the following Indian hospitals : Eagle Butte (SD); Winnebago (NE) ; Pine Ridge (SD); Rapid City (SD); Rosebud (SD); Sisseton (SD); Fort Yates (ND); Belcourt (ND) ; Wagner (SD); and the following health centers: Fort Berthold (New Town, ND); Fort Totten (ND); Carl T. Curtis Health Center (Macy, NE); Sac & Fox Tribe of the Mississippi in Iowa (Tama, IA); Fort Thompson (SD); Lower Brule (SD); and McLaughlin (SD).

ALASKA AREA NATIVE HEALTH SERVICES
250 Gambell St., Third & Gambell St.
Anchorage, AK 99501
 (907) 257 + Ext.; Fax 257-1168
State served: Alaska.
 G.H. Ivey, Director (1153)
 David J. Schraer, MD, Deputy Director &
  Chief Medical Officer (1154)
 Richard D. Frost, Executive Officer (1155)

Jim Sozoff, EEO Officer (1105)
James E. Berner, MD, Office of Community
  Health Services (1309)
Sandra L. Haldane, RN, Office of Patient
  Care Standards (1 156)
Jim Armbrust, Office of Regional & Contract
  Health Care (1368)
Robert Olver, Office of Personnel & Training
  (1157)
Deborah D. Segelhorst, Office of Awards &
  Administrative Services (1 172)
Floyd Laverdure, Financial Management (1350)
Jim Crum, Environmental Health & Engineering
  228 W. 8th Ave. #65, Anchorage, AK 99513
  (907) 271-4700 ext. 1 11

Has jurisdiction over the following Indian hospi-
tals in Alaska: Anchorage; Barrow; Bethel (Y ukon-
Kuskokwim Delta); Bristol Bay Area (Dillingham);
Kotzebue; Mt. Edgecumbe (Sitka); Norton Sound
(Nome); and the following health centers:
Metlakatla; Fairbanks; Juneau; and Ketchikan.

ALBUQUERQUE AREA IHS
505 Marquette Ave., N.W., Suite 1502
Albuquerque, NM 87102-2163
  (505) 766 + Ext.; Fax 766-2157
  Josephine T. Waconda, Director (2151)
  Judith A. Kitzes, MD, Deputy Director &
    Chief Medical Officer (2151)
  Dorothy Dupree, Office of Administration &
    Management (2151)
  Richie K. Grinnell, Office of Environmental
    Health (2139)
  Roger Golub, MD, Office of Hospital/Ambulatory
    Care (5507)
  Georgia Pedro, Office of Planning, Evaluation,
    Information (2147)
  Michael E. Bird, Office of Preventive Health
    Programs (5546)
  Christine Antonio, Office of Tribal Activities (2287)

States served: New Mexico & Colorado. Has jurisdiction over the following Indian hospitals :
Acomita-Canoncita-Laguna (San Fidel); Albuquerque; Mescalero; Santa Fe; and Zuni (all in NM);
and the following health centers: Alamo (Magdalena); Dulce; Santa Clara (Espanola); Taos;
Ramah; and in CO: Ignacio and Towaoc.

BEMIDJI AREA IHS
127 Federal Bldg.
Bemidji, MN 56601 (800) 892-3079
  (218) 759 + Ext.; Fax 759-351 1
  Kathleen Annette, MD, Director (3412)
  Charlene Molash, Executive Officer (3413)
  Ron Wahlberg, MD, Chief Medical Of ficer (3414)
  Janet Greendeer, Scholarship Coord. (3415)
  James Bredon, Chief, Program Planning (3447)
  Norm Landsem, Health Programs (3351)
  Richard Perrault, Information Systems Coord.
  Douglas Jackson, Director of Environmental
    Health Progams (3363)
  Marvin Edevold, Office of Tribal Activities (3424)

Field Offices

Rhinelander Field Office
P.O. Box 537
Rhinelander, WI 54501
  (715) 362-5145
  James E. Pete, Director

Ashland OEH Field Office
2800 Lake Shore Dr . East
Ashland, WI 54806

Field Health Office/MITC
312 Water Tower Dr.
Kincheloe, MI 49788
  (906) 495-2289
  Char Hewitt, Director

States served: Minnesota, Michigan & Wisconsin.
Has jurisdiction over the following Indian hospi-
tals: Cass Lake and Red Lake (in MN); and the
following Indian health centers : Min-No-A ya-Win
Clinic (Cloquet, MN); White Earth (MN); Eastern
Michigan (Kincheloe, MI); Stockbridge-Munsee
Community Clinic (Bowler , WI); Lac Courte
Oreilles (Hayward, WI); Keshena (WI); Chippewa
Health Center (Lac du Flambeau, WI); Oneida
(WI); and IHS Field Office (Rhinelander, WI).

BILLINGS AREA IHS
P.O. Box 2143, 711 Central Ave.
Billings, MT 59103
  (406) 657 + Ext.; Fax 657-6333
  Duane L. Jeanotte, Director (6403)
  Joseph P. Plumage, Deputy Area Director (6403)
  Cynthia Tiger, Health Systems
    Administrator Ext. 6184
  Garfield Little Light, Office of Administrative
    Support (6403)
  Kermit Smith, DO, MPH, Office of Health
    Care (6941)
  George Allen, Environmental Health (6451)
  Cecil P. Conway, Office of Tribal Programs (6007)
  Thomas M. Danielson, Planning, Information
    & Evaluation Branch (6403)

States served: Montana & W yoming. Has juris-
diction over the following Indian hospitals : Brown-
ing; Crow Agency; and Harlem; and the following
Indian health centers: Lodge Grass; St. Ignatius;
Poplar; Wolf Point; Lame Deer; Box Elder; and
Fort Washakie and Arapaho (in WY).

CALIFORNIA AREA IHS
1825 Bell St., Suite 200
Sacramento, CA 95825
  (916) 978-4202; Fax 978-4216
  Thomas J. Harwood, Director
  J. Paul Redeagle, Deputy Director
  John Yao, MD, Chief Medical Of ficer
  Edwin Fluette, Office of Environmental Health
    & Engineering
  Debrah Baldy, Chief, Office of Admin. Services
  Dennis Heffington, Office of Tribal Activities
  LaMerle Fridley, Office of Health Programs

State served: California. Has jurisdiction over the
following Indian health programs in California :
Chapa-De Indian Health Progam (Auburn); Cen-
tral Valley Indian Health Project (Clovis); Consoli-
dated Tribal Health Project (Ukiah); Hoopa V alley
Tribal Council (Hoopa); Indian Health Council
(Pauma Valley); Karuk Tribal Health Program
(Happy Camp); Lake County Tribal Health Con-
sortium (Lakeport); Lassen Indian Health Program
(Susanville) Modoc Indian Health Project (Alturas);
Northern Valley Indian Health (Oroville); Pit River
Health Services; W arner Mountain Health Station;
Redding Rancheria Indian Health Services; Riv-
erside/San Bernardino County Indian Health (Ban-
ning); Round V alley Indian Health Program
(Covelo); Santa Ynez Tribal Health Program
(Santa Ynez); Sonoma County Indian Health Pro-
gram (Santa Rosa); Southern Indian Health Coun-
cil (Al Pine); Sycuan Tribal Health Program;

Toiyabe Indian Health Program (Bishop); Tule
River Indian Health Center (Porterville); Tuolumne
Rural Indian Health Program (T uolumne); United
Indian Health Services (T rinidad).

NASHVILLE AREA IHS
711 Stewarts Ferry Pike
Nashville, TN 37214
  (615) 736-Ext.; Fax 736-2391
  James C. Meredith, Director (2400)
  Michael D. Tiger, Deputy Director (2400)
  Shirley A. Dreadfulwater, Operations
    Services Specialist (2400)
  Franklin Dreadfulwater , Executive Officer (2407)
  Edwin McLemore, Office of Extramural
    Awards & Agreement (241 1)
  Timothy G. Amstutz, Div. of Information
    Resources Management (2441)
  Peggy Akers, Div. of Property Mgmt. (2465)
  William K. Dew, Office of Tribal Activities (2478)
  Beth Drabant, MD, Health Programs (2487)
  Keith Enders, Environmental Health &
    Engineering (2503)
  Harding Brewster, Alcohol/Drug Abuse
    Program Specialist (497-5030)

States served: Eastern states. Has jurisdiction over
Cherokee Indian Hospital, Cherokee, NC; and
Choctaw Health Center , Philadelphia, MS.

NAVAJO AREA IHS
P.O. Box 9020
Window Rock, AZ 86515
  (602) 871-Ext.; Fax 871-5896
States served: Northeast Arizona, Northwest
New Mexico, Southern Utah.
  John Hubbard, Jr., Director (581 1)
  Douglas G. Peter , MD, Chief Medical (5813)
  Ron C. Wood, Executive Officer (5812)
  Brenda Gabbard, RN, MPH, Director of
    Nursing Services (5842)
  Gary S. Malone, Div. of Administrative
    Services (5861)
  Charles O. Dowell, Office of Environmental
    Health & Engineering (5851)
  Jenny L. Notah, Office of Program
    Planning & Evaluation (5821)

Has jurisdiction over the following Indian hospitals: Chinle; Fort Defiance; Tuba City; Crownpoint,
(NM); Gallup (NM); Shiprock (NM); and the following Indian health centers: Kayenta; Winslow;
and Dzilth-Na-O-Dith-Hle (Bloomfield, NM).

OKLAHOMA CITY AREA IHS
Five Corporate Plaza, 3625 NW 56th St.
Oklahoma City, OK 73112
  (405) 945+ Ext.; Fax 945-6870
  Robert H. Harry, DDS, Director (6820)
  Randy Grinnell, Deputy Area Director (6820)
  Clark Marquart, MD, Chief Medical Of ficer (6820)
  Karen Begay, Quality Improvement Officer (6820)
  Franklin Dale Keel, Health Program
    Services(6875)
  Luke McIntosh, Office of Administration &
    Management (6820)
  Ranell Harry, Div. of Planning (6890)
  Randy Grinnell, Office of Environmental
    Health (6800)
  Max Tahsuda, Tribal Development (6825)

States served: Oklahoma & Kansas. Has jurisdiction over the following Indian hospitals : Carl Albert
(Ada); Clinton; Lawton; W .W. Hastings (Tahlequah); Choctaw (Talihina); and the following Indian health centers: Cherokee Nation (Sallisaw
and Stilwell), Eufaula (Creek Nation); Chickasaw

Nation (Ardmore and Tishomingo); Choctaw Nation (Broken Bow); Hugo; McAlester; W ewoka; Claremore; Delaware District (Jay); Miami; Okemah; Sapulpa; Salina; Shawnee; Concho; Watonga; Anadarko; Carnegie; Pawnee; Pawhuska; White Eagle (Ponca City); and Haskell (Lawrence, KS) and Holton (KS).

PHOENIX AREA IHS
3738 N. 16th St., Suite A
Phoenix, AZ 85016
  (602) 640 + Ext.; Fax 640-2557
  Don J. Davis, Area Director (2052)
  Mary Lou Stanton, Deputy Director (2052)
  Theodore Redding, MD, Chief Medical Of ficer (2052)
  Gary P. Breshears, Executive Of ficer (2054)
  Mary Campbell, Of fice of Administration (2070)
  Keith Longie, Planning & Evaluation (2061)
  Alan Croft, Of fice of Environmental Health (2046)
  Michael Joseph, Tribal Activities Ext. 2106
  E. Paul Hornyak, Health Programs (5664)
  Richard C. Gwilt, IHS Medical Imaging Program (2543)
  Gary Waubaunsee, Of fice of Third-Party Health Resource Management (2120)

Phoenix/Tucson Area Adolescent Regional Treatment Center
P.O. Box 458, 198 S. Skill Center Rd.
Sacaton, AZ 85247
  (602) 562-3801
  Annie Brayboy , Director

Has jurisdiction over the following Indian hospitals: Parker; Fort Yuma;Keams Canyon; Phoenix Indian Medical Center; Sacaton; San Carlos; Whiteriver; and Owyhee and Schurz (in NV); and the following Indian health center: Peach Springs; Second Mesa; Cibicue; Riverside (CA); Stewart (NV); Reno-Sparks (NV); and Fort Duchesne (Roosevelt, UT).

Consists of one medical center , eight hospitals, four health centers, and two school health clinics. *States served*: Arizona, Nevada & Utah. *Tribes served*: (47 separate tribes-Papago, Apache, Pima, Maricopa, Hopi, Paiute, Navajo, Ute, Goshute, Shoshone, W ashoe, Hualapai, Havasupai, Mojave, Cocopah, Quechan, and urban tribes in the metropolitan area.) *Number of professionals on staff*: 772. *Number of beds*: 424. *Numbers served annually*: In-patient, 15,000; Out-patient, 450,000. *Services*: All primary medical services are provided. Programs: Accredited residency programs in obstetrics, pediatrics, family practice, dental, general practice, and public health nursing; continuing education; research (sponsored by the National Institutes of Health) at several facilities; Health Education Program--comprised of 15 professional staf f who provide a co-ordinated program of health education throughout the Phoenix area; Indian Health Service Training Committee; instrumental in implementing the Health Emphasis Campaign, a seven year program to develop disease prevention and health promotion practices among Indian community residents. Scholarships: Participates in the National Health Service Corps and the Indian Health Care Improvement Scholarship Programs. Library .

PORTLAND AREA IHS
Federal Building, Room 476
1220 S.W. Third Ave.
Portland, OR 97204
  (503) 326 + Ext.; Fax 326-7280
  James R. Floyd, Director (2020)

  Daniel C. Madrano, Executive Of ficer (2024)
  Timothy R. Webster, Office of Environmental Health & Engineering (2001)
  Cheryl A. Bittle, Health Programs (3288)
  J. Michael W ood, Office of Planning, Evaluation & Information (2009)
  Thomas L. Austin, Tribal Operations (4123)

States served: Idaho, Oregon, W ashington. Has jurisdiction over the following Indian health centers: Yellowhawk (Pendleton, OR); W arm Springs (OR); Chemawa Indian School (Salem, OR); Klamath Service Unit (Chiloquin, OR); Colville (Nespelem, W A); Neah Bay (WA); Northwest Washington (Bellingham, W A); Puget Sound (Seattle, WA); Taholah (WA); Wellpinit (WA); Yakima (Toppenish, W A); Fort Hall (ID); and Northern Idaho (Lapwai, ID).

IHS OFFICE OF HEAL TH PROGRAM RESEARCH & DEVELOPMENT
7900 South "J" Stock Rd.
Tucson, AZ 85746
  (602) 295 + Ext.; Fax 295-2602
  Eleanor A. Robertson, Director (2406)
  Charles J. Erickson, Deputy Associate Director (2406)
  John B. Narcho, Executive Of ficer (2406)
  John Kittredge, MD, Chief Medical Of ficer (2406)
  John P. Carney, Div. of Health Services Systems (2498)
  George H. Lomayesva, Div .of Human Resource Systems (2478)
  William Freeman, MD, Director of Medical Systems R&D (2500)

State served: Arizona. *Has jurisdiction over the following Indian hospital and health centers* : Sells Indian Hospital, Sells, AZ; Santa Rosa Indian Health Center , Sells, AZ; and San Xavier Indian Health Center , Tucson, AZ.

ALASKA

ALASKA NATIVE MEDICAL CENTER
255 Gambell St.
Anchorage, AK 99501
  (907) 279-6661; Fax 257-1781
  Richard Mandsager , MD, Director
  Frank Williams, Director of Support Services
  David Barrett, MD, Medical Director
Number of Beds : 170. Affiliated with Alaska Area Native Health Service.

ALEUTIAN/PRIBILOF ISLANDS ASSOCIATION
401 E. Fireweed Lane, Suite 201
Anchorage, AK 99503
  (907) 276-2700; Fax 279-4351
  Demitri Philemonof, Executive Director
  Hedy Lestenkof, Health Director
Affiliated with Alaska Area Native Health Service. Tribally operated.

CHUGACHMIUT
4201 Tudor Centre, Suite 210
Anchorage, AK 99508
  (907) 562-4155; Fax 563-2891
  Derenty Tabios, Executive Director
  Joan Domnick, Clinical Director
Affiliated with Alaska Area Native Health Service. Tribally operated.

SOUTHCENTRAL FOUNDATION
670 W. Fireweed Lane, Suite 123
Anchorage, AK 99503

  (907) 276-3343; Fax 258-5212
  Katherine Grosdidier , Executive Director
  David Thundereagle, Special Assistant
Affiliated with Alaska Area Native Health Service. Tribally operated.

BARROW PHS ALASKA NATIVE HOSPITAL
Barrow, AK 99723
  (907) 852-4611; Fax 852-2016
  Carolyn McClintock, Director
  George Attatayuk, Administrative Of ficer
  James C. Kussy, MD, Clinical Director
Number of Beds : 14. Affiliated with Alaska Area Native Health Service.

NORTH SLOPE BOROUGH DEPT. OF HEAL TH & SOCIAL SERVICES
P.O. Box 69
Barrow, AK 99723
  (907) 852-0260; Fax 852-0268
  Irene MacIntosh, Health Director
  Caroline Jessup, Administrative Assistant
Affiliated with Alaska Area Native Health Service. Tribally operated.

YUKON-KUSKOKWIM HEALTH CORP.
P.O. Box 528
Bethel, AK 99559
  (907) 543-3321; Fax 543-5277
  Gene Peltola, President/CEO
  Orie Williams, Executive VP
  Donald Kruse, MD, Medical Director
Affiliated with Alaska Area Native Health Service. Tribally operated.

YUKON-KUSKOKWIM HOSPIT AL
Pouch 3000
Bethel, AK 99559
  (907) 543-3711; Fax 543-5285
  Ed Hansen, VP Hospital Operations
  Shawn Stitham, MD, Clinical Director
Number of Beds: 50. Affiliated with Alaska Area Native Health Service.

COPPER RIVER NA TIVE ASSOCIATION
Drawer H
Copper Center, AK 99573
  (907) 822-5241; Fax 822-5247
  Ken Johns, Executive Director
  Valerie Naquin, Health Director
Affiliated with Alaska Area Native Health Service. Tribally operated.

BRISTOL BAY AREA HEALTH CORP.
P.O. Box 130
Dillingham, AK 99576
  (907) 842-5201; Fax 842-9354
  Robert Clark, Chief Executive Of ficer
  Darrel Richardson, Chief Operations Of ficer
  Timothy Slavens, MD, Clinical Director
Number of Beds : 28. Affiliated with Alaska Area Native Health Service. Tribally operated.

CHIEF ANDREW ISAAC HEAL TH CENTER
1638 Cowles St.
Fairbanks, AK 99701
  (907) 451-6682; Fax 451-1002
  Marilyn Harasick, Director
Affiliated with Alaska Area Native Health Service. Tribally operated.

TANANA CHIEFS CONFERENCE, INC. HEALTH CENTER
122 First Ave.
Fairbanks, AK 99701
  (907) 452-8251; Fax 451-8936
  Will Mayo, President

Eileen Kozevnikof f, Health Service Director
Affiliated with Alaska Area Native Health Service.
Tribally operated.

SEARHC JUNEAU MEDICAL CENTER
3245 Hospital Dr.
Juneau, AK 99801
 (907) 463-4000 Fax 463-4012
 Joe Cladouhos, Administrator
 Mark Peterson, MD, Clinical Director
Affiliated with Alaska Native Health Service.
Serves 19 communities and villages in Southeast
Alaska.

SOUTHEAST ALASKA
REGIONAL HEALTH CORP.
3245 Hospital Dr.
Juneau, AK 99801
 (907) 463-4000; Fax 463-4075
 Ethel Lund, President
 Sara Paddock, Administrative Assistant
Affiliated with Alaska Area Native Health Service.
Tribally operated.

KENAITZE INDIAN TRIBE HEAL TH CENTER
P.O. Box 988
Kenai, AK 99611
 (907) 283-3633; Fax 283-3052
 Rita Smagge, Executive Director
 Berry Campbell, MD, Administrator
Affiliated with Alaska Area Native Health Service.
Tribally operated.

SEARHC HEALTH CENTER
3289 Tongass Ave.
Ketchikan, AK 99901
 (907) 225-4156; Fax 225-4339
 Bill Burton, Health Systems Administrator
 Carol Alley, MD, Clinical Director
Affiliated with Alaska Area Native Health Service.

KODIAK AREA NATIVE ASSOCIATION
HEALTH CENTER
402 Center Ave.
Kodiak, AK 99615
 (907) 486-5725 Fax 486-2763
 Kelly Simeonof f, Jr., President
Affiliated with Alaska Area Native Health Service.
Tribally operated.

MANIILAQ ASSOCIATION MEDICAL CENTER
P.O. Box 43
Kotzebue, AK 99752
 (907) 442-3321; Fax 442-2022
 Joseph A. Ballot, President
 Paul Hansen, Administrator
 Janet Shackles, MD, Clinical Director
Affiliated with Alaska Area Native Health Service.
Tribally operated.

ANNETTE ISLAND SER VICE UNIT
Metlakatla Indian Community
P.O. Box 439
Metlakatla, AK 99926
 (907) 886-4741; F AX 886-6976
 Harris Atkinson, Mayor
 Ken Whitehair, Service Unit Director
 Sam Hunkler, MD, Clinical Director
Affiliated with Alaska Area Native Health Service.

NINILCHIK TRADITIONAL
COUNCIL HEALTH CLINIC
P.O. Box 39070
Ninilchik, AK 99639
 (907) 567-3313; Fax 567-3308
 D.L. Oskolkoff, Executive Director
 Pat Oskolkoff, Health Director

Affiliated with Alaska Area Native Health Service.
Tribally operated.

NORTON SOUND HEALTH CORP.
P.O. Box 966
Nome, AK 99762
 (907) 443-3311 Fax 443-3139
 Carolyn Michels, President
 Maurice Ninham, VP Operations
 David Head, MD, Clinical Director
 Randy Wirick, VP Hospital Services
Tribes served: 20 Federally recognized tribes in
Bering Straits Region. *Professionals on staff*: 7
physicians. *Services*: Inpatient, Outpatient, Emer-
gency, Mental Health and Substance Abuse. *Pro-
grams*: Staff Education; Community Health Edu-
cation. Scholarships provided to Natives of region
who are interested in pursuing health careers. Li-
brary. Affiliated with Alaska Native Health Service.
Tribally owned & operated.

SEARHC MT. EDGECUMBE HOSPITAL
222 Tongass Dr.
Sitka, AK 99801
 (907) 966-2411; Fax 986-8300
 Arthur Willman, VP Operations
 Frank Sutton, Director of Hospital Services
 Susan Carlson, MD, Clinical Director
Number of Beds: 78. Serves 19 communities and
villages in Southeast Alaska. Affiliated with Alaska
Area Native Health Service. Tribally operated.

TANANA IRA NATIVE COUNCIL
HEALTH CENTER
P.O. Box 93
Tanana, AK 99777
 (907) 366-7222/7160; Fax 366-7195
 Carla K. Bonney, Director
 Susan Hensel Henry, F.N.P., Supvry. Clinician
Affiliated with Alaska Area Native Health Service.
Tribally operated.

ARIZONA

CHINLE COMPREHENSIVE
HEALTH CARE FACILITY
P.O. Drawer PH
Chinle, AZ 86503
 (602) 674-5282
 Ronald Tso, Director
 Kevin Rand, MD, Clinical Director
Number of Beds: 52. Affiliated with Navajo
Area Indian Health Service.

CIBECUE PHS INDIAN HEAL TH CENTER
Cibecue, AZ 85941
 (602) 332-2560
 Nina Desbien, Director
Affiliated with Phoenix Area Indian Health Service.

FT. DEFIANCE PHS INDIAN HOSPITAL
P.O. Box 649
Ft. Defiance, AZ 86504
 (602) 729-5741
 Franklin Freeland, EdD, Director
 Paula Damon, Administrative Of ficer
 David Meehan, MD, Clinical Director
Number of Beds: 68. Affiliated with Navajo
Area Indian Health Service.

INSCRIPTION HOUSE PHS
INDIAN HEALTH CENTER
Inscription House, AZ 86054
 (602) 672-2611

Darlene Walker, Director
 James Thomas, Jr., MD, Clinical Director
Affiliated with Navajo Area Indian Health Service.

KAYENTA PHS INDIAN HEALTH CENTER
P.O. Box 368
Kayenta, AZ 86033
 (602) 697-3211
 Linda R. White, R.P ., Director
 Steven Konicek, MD, Clinical Director
Affiliated with Navajo Area Indian Health Service.

KEAMS CANYON PHS INDIAN HOSPITAL
P.O. Box 98
Keams Canyon, AZ 86034
 (602) 738-2211
 Taylor Satala, Director
 David Daniels, MD, Clinical Director
Number of Beds: 26. Affiliated with Phoenix
Area Indian Health Service.

SECOND MESA PHS INDIAN HEALTH CENTER
P.O. Box 98
Keams Canyon, AZ 86034
 (602) 738-2297
 Taylor Satala, Director
 David Daniels, MD, Clinical Director
*Tribes served: Hopi, Kaibab-Paiute, Navajo. Num-
ber of professionals on staff*: 71. *Number of Beds*:
24. *Numbers served annually*: 950; outpatient:
33,000. *Community health education programs*:
Substance abuse, health education, et al. Affili-
ated with Phoenix Area Indian Health Service.

PARKER PHS INDIAN HOSPITAL
Route 1, Box 12
Parker, AZ 85344
 (602) 669-2137
 Dave Morgan, Director
 Gus Meier, MD, Clinical Director
Number of Beds: 20. Affiliated with Phoenix
Area Indian Health Service.

PEACH SPRINGS PHS
INDIAN HEALTH CENTER
P.O. Box 190
Peach Springs, AZ 86434
 (602) 769-2204
 Robert W. Pipe, Director
 Sue Ellen McGee, MD, Clinical Director
Tribes served: Hualapai, Havasupai. *Profession-
als on staff*: 6. *Services*: General outpatient medi-
cal care; dental. *Program*: Community Health
Education. Affiliated with Phoenix Area Indian
Health Service.

PHOENIX INDIAN MEDICAL CENTER
4212 North 16th St.
Phoenix, AZ 85016
 (602) 263-1200
 Anna Albert, Service Unit Director
 Richard M. Bryan, MD, Hospital Services
 Vincent Berkley, D.O., Clinical Services
Tribes served: Navajo, Hopi, Apache, Hualapai,
Pima, Papago, Mohave, Yavapai, Havasupai,
Cocopah, Paiute, and Pascua-Y aqui. *Profession-
als on staff*: 70 physicians, 400 nurses. *Number
of Beds*: 150. *Services*: Primary Care/Family Prac-
tice, Pediatrics, Dental, OB-GYN, Surgery, Emer-
gency Medicine, Mental Health, Ophthalmology,
Pharmacy, Physical Therapy, Podiatry, Radiology.
Programs: Staff Education, Training and Re-
search; Community Health Education. Library.
Publication: The IHS Primary Care Provider. Affiliated with Phoenix Area Indian Health Service.

HUHUKAM MEMORIAL HOSPITAL
P.O. Box 38
Sacaton, AZ 85247
(602) 562-3321
Viola Johnson, Director
Kelly Moore, MD, Clinical Director
Affiliated with Phoenix Area Indian Health Service.

BYLAS HEALTH CENTER
P.O. Box 208
San Carlos, AZ 85550
(602) 485-2686
Arlie Beeson, Director
Affiliated with Phoenix Area Indian Health Service.

SAN CARLOS PHS INDIAN HOSPITAL
P.O. Box 208
San Carlos, AZ 85550
(602) 475-2371
Frederick L. Hubbard, Unit Director
Yvette Roubideaux, MD, Clinical Director
Number of Beds: 28. Affiliated with Phoenix
Area Indian Health Service.

SCOTTSDALE SALT RIVER CLINIC
Route 1, Box 215
Scottsdale, AZ 85256
(602) 379-4281
Dan Brown, MD, Clinical Director
Affiliated with Phoenix Area Indian Health Service.

SANTA ROSA PHS INDIAN HEALTH CENTER
Star Route, Box 71
Sells, AZ 85634
(602) 383-2261
Evelyn Torn, RN, Director
Affiliated with Tucson Office of Health Programs
Research & Development.

SELLS PHS INDIAN HOSPITAL
P.O. Box 548
Sells, AZ 85634
(602) 383-7251
Donald Benchof f, Director
Theresa Cullen, MD, Clinical Director
Number of Beds: 40. Affiliated with Tucson Office
of Health Programs Research and Development.

HAVASUPAI INDIAN HEALTH STATION
Supai, AZ 86435
(602) 448-2641
Tribe served: Havasupai. Staff: 1. Primary medical services: Provides 7 day a week 24 hours a
day outpatient medical services to 4,200 patients,
annually, at isolated site at bottom of the Grand
Canyon. Affiliated with Phoenix Area Indian Health
Service. Special programs: Prenatal education,
diabetic education, substance abuse program,
weight reduction/exercise programs.

TSAILE PHS INDIAN HEALTH CENTER
P.O. Box 467
Tsaile, AZ 86556
(602) 724-3391
Lillie M. Haskie, Health Administrator
David Long, MD, Medical Director
Tribe served: Navajo, mainly. Professional on staff:
17. Services: Family Medicine, Ambulatory Care.
Program: Community Health Education. Affiliated
with Navajo Area Indian Health Service.

TUBA CITY INDIAN MEDICAL CENTER
P.O. Box 600
Tuba City, AZ 86045
(602) 283-6211
Rosalyn Curtis, Director
Dudley Beck MD, Clinical Director

Number of Beds: 101. Affiliated with Navajo Area
Indian Health Service.

SAN XAVIER PHS INDIAN HEALTH CENTER
7900 S.J. Stock Rd.
Tucson, AZ 85746
(602) 295-2550
Frank Saenz, Acting Director
Affiliated with Tucson Office of Health Programs
Research and Development.

WHITERIVER PHS INDIAN HOSPITAL
P.O. Box 860
Whiteriver, AZ 85941
(602) 338-4911
Carla Alchesay-Nachu, Director
David Yost, MD, Clinical Director
Number of Beds: 44. Affiliated with Phoenix
Area Indian Health Service.

WINSLOW PHS INDIAN HEALTH CENTER
P.O. Drawer 40
Winslow, AZ 86047
(602) 289-4646
Vida Khow, Director
Carenda Little, Administrative Officer
Jerod Scott, MD, Clinical Director
Affiliated with Navajo Area Indian Health Service.

FORT YUMA PHS INDIAN HOSPITAL
P.O. Box 1368
Yuma, AZ 85364
(602) 572-0217
Ken Hernasy, Director
David Hoovestol, MD, Clinical Director
Number of Beds: 17. Affiliated with Phoenix
Area Indian Health Service.

CALIFORNIA

SOUTHERN INDIAN HEALTH COUNCIL
P.O. Box 2128
Alpine, CA 91903
(619) 445-1188 Fax 445-4131
Joe Bulfer, Director
Affiliated with California Program Of fice.
Tribally operated.

MODOC COUNTY INDIAN HEALTH PROGRAM
P.O. Box 251
Alturas, CA 96101
(916) 233-4591 Fax 233-3055
Erin Forrest, Director
Affiliated with California Program Of fice.
Tribally operated.

**CHAPA-DE (AUBURN)
INDIAN HEALTH PROGRAM**
11670 Atwood Rd.
Auburn, CA 95603
(916) 885-3757
Carol Ervin, Director
Affiliated with California Program Of fice.
Tribally operated.

**AMERICAN INDIAN COUNCIL
OF CENTRAL CALIFORNIA**
2210 Chester Ave., Suite A
Bakersfield, CA 93301
(805) 327-2207 Fax 327-4533
Colleen Alvary, Director
Tribes served: 87 different tribes - mostly Paiutes,
Shoshones, Yokuts, Apaches, Cherokees,
Choctaws, and Chumash. Profesionals on staff:

3. Services: Outpatient primary medical services.
Programs: Staff Education, Training and Research; Community Health Education; Grants. Library. Affiliated with California Program Of fice.

**RIVERSIDE/SAN BERNADINO
INDIAN HEALTH PROGRAM**
11555 1/2 Potrero Rd.
Banning, CA 92220
(714) 849-4761 Fax 849-5612
Curtis Hesse, Director
Affiliated with California Program Of fice.
Tribally operated.

AMERICAN INDIAN FREE CLINIC, INC.
9500 E. Artesia Blvd.
Bellflower, CA 90708
(310) 920-7272 Fax 920-5677
Rick Bouchard, Director
Affiliated with California Program Of fice.

TOIYABE INDIAN HEALTH COUNCIL
P.O. Box 1296
Bishop, CA 93515
(619) 873-8464 Fax 873-3935
David Lent, Director
Affiliated with California Program Of fice.
Tribally operated.

PIT RIVER INDIAN HEALTH CENTER
P.O. Box 2720
Burney, CA 96013
(916) 335-5091 Fax 335-5241
Janie Butterfield, Director
Affiliated with California Program Of fice.
Tribally operated.

**CENTRAL VALLEY INDIAN
HEALTH PROGRAM**
20 North Dewitt
Clovis, CA 93612
(209) 299-2578 Fax 299-0245
Chuck Fowler, Director
Affiliated with California Program Of fice.
Tribally operated.

**ROUND VALLEY INDIAN
HEALTH PROGRAM**
P.O. Box 247
Covelo, CA 95428
(707) 983-6181 Fax 983-6842
Arthur Acoya, Director
Affiliated with California Program Of fice.
Tribally operated.

SYCUAN MEDICAL/DENTAL CENTER
5442 Dehesa Rd.
El Cajon, CA 92019
(619) 445-0707 Fax 445-0988
Diane Parr, Administrator
Affiliated with California Program Of fice.

WARNER MOUNTAIN INDIAN HEALTH
P.O. Box 127
Fort Bidwell, CA 96112
(918) 279-6194 Fax 279-2233
Cindy Lamebull, Clinic Director
Affiliated with California Program Of fice.

FRESNO INDIAN HEALTH ASSOCIATION
4991 E. McKinley, Suite 109
Fresno, CA 93727
(209) 255-0261
Scott Pesulch, Director
Affiliated with California Program Of fice.

GREENVILLE RANCHERIA TRIBAL HEALTH
P.O. Box 279
Greenville, CA 95947
 (916) 284-6135 Fax 284-7135
 Leslie Hall, Director
Affiliated with California Program Office.

KARUK TRIBAL HEALTH PROGRAM
P.O. Box 1016
Happy Camp, CA 96039
 (916) 493-5305 Fax 493-5322
 Alvis Johnson, Director
Affiliated with California Program Office.
Tribally operated.

HOOPA HEALTH ASSOCIATION
P.O. Box 1288
Hoopa, CA 95546
 (916) 625-4261 Fax 625-4781
 Richard Conti, Director
Affiliated with California Program Office.
Tribally operated.

LAKE COUNTY TRIBAL HEALTH
5124 Hill Rd. E.
Lakeport, CA 95453
 (707) 263-8382 Fax 263-0329
Tribe served: Pomo. *Services*: Outpatient. Affiliated with California Program Office. Tribally operated.

URBAN INDIAN HEALTH BOARD
3124 E. 14th St.
Oakland, CA 94601
 (510) 261-0524 Fax 261-6438
 Martin Waukazoo, Director
Affiliated with California Program Office.
Tribally operated.

FEATHER RIVER INDIAN HEALTH
2167 Montgomery St.
Oroville, CA 95965
 (916) 534-6135 Fax 534-3820
 Dorothy Chapin, Director
Affiliated with California Program Office.

INDIAN HEALTH COUNCIL, INC.
P.O. Box 406
Pauma Valley, CA 92061
 (619) 749-1410 Fax 749-1564
 Dennis Magee, Director
Tribes served: Luiseno, Digueno, Cahuilla and Cupeno, Bands of California Mission Indians in San Diego County. *Professionals on staff*: 12. *Population served*: 7,500, annually. *Services*: Medical and dental outpatient care including social services, public health nursing, counseling, etc. Affiliated with California Program Office. Tribally operated.

TULE RIVER INDIAN HEALTH PROGRAM
P.O. Box 768
Porterville, CA 93257
 (209) 784-2316 Fax 781-6514
 Sajjan Bajwa, Director
Affiliated with California Program Office.
Tribally operated.

REDDING RANCHERIA HEALTH CENTER
3184 Churn Creek Rd.
Redding, CA 96002
 (916) 224-2700 Fax 224-2738
 Arvada Paul, Director
Affiliated with California Program Office.
Tribally operated.

SHERMAN SCHOOL HEALTH CENTER
8934 Magnolia
Riverside, CA 92503
 (714) 276-6321
Affiliated with Phoenix Area Indian Health Service.

SACRAMENTO URBAN INDIAN HEALTH
801 Broadway, Suite B
Sacramento, CA 95819
 (916) 441-0918 Fax 441-1261
 Beth Ninke, Director
Affiliated with California Program Office.
Tribally operated.

SAN DIEGO AMERICAN INDIAN HEALTH
2561 First Ave.
San Diego, CA 92103
 (619) 234-2158 Fax 234-0206
 William Poff, Director
Affiliated with California Program Office.

NATIVE AMERICAN HEALTH CLINIC
56 Julian Ave.
San Francisco, CA 94103
 (415) 621-8051 Fax 621-3985
 Martin Waukazoo, Director
Affiliated with California Program Office.

**INDIAN HEALTH CENTER
OF SANTA CLARA VALLEY**
1333 Meridian Ave.
San Jose, CA 95125
 (408) 294-7553 Fax 294-6452
 Nick Fay, Director
Tribes served: All American Indian Tribes, Eskimo & Aleut. Professionals on staff: 10. *Population served*: 4,500 outpatients. Primary medical services: Pre-natal & peri-natal; diabetes case management; substance abuse counseling; nutrition; mental health outreach & referral; AIDS/HIV testing & counseling; and community health education programs. Library. Affiliated with California Program Office.

**SONOMA COUNTY INDIAN
HEALTH PROGRAM**
P.O. Box 7308
Santa Rosa, CA 95407
 (707) 544-4056 Fax 526-1015
 William Holman, Director
Affiliated with California Program Office.
Tribally operated.

SANTA YNEZ INDIAN HEALTH PROGRAM
P.O. Box 539
Santa Ynez, CA 93460
 (805) 688-4886 Fax 688-2060
 Rosa Pace, Administrator
Affiliated with California Program Office.
Tribally operated.

LASSEN INDIAN HEALTH CENTER
745 Joaquin St.
Susanville, CA 96130
 (916) 257-2542 Fax 257-6983
 Leah Exendine, Director
Affiliated with California Program Office.

**TUOLUMNE RIVER INDIAN
HEALTH PROGRAM**
P.O. Box 577
Tuolumne, CA 95379
 (209) 928-4277 Fax 928-1295
 Sonny Hendricks, Director
Affiliated with California Program Office.
Tribally operated.

UNITED INDIAN HEALTH SERVICES
P.O. Box Box 420
Trinidad, CA 95570
 (707) 677-3693 Fax 677-3170
 Jerome J. Simone, Director
Tribes served: All American Indians with verification. Professionals on staff: 8. *Population served*: 20,000 patients served annually. Primary Medical Services: Complete family practice including obstetrics. Awards to local American Indians who are pursuing health careers. Medical and dental libraries. Affiliated with California Program Office. Tribally operated.

CONSOLIDATED TRIBAL HEALTH PROJECT
564 S. Dora St., Suite D
Ukiah, CA 95482
 (707) 468-5341 Fax 468-8610
 Maria Anaya, MPH, Director
Tribe served: Pomo Tribes - Coyote Valley, Hopland Band, Guidiville Reservation, Laytonville Vahto Tribe, Pinoleville Indian Community, Potter Valley Rancheria, Redwood Valley Rancheria, Sherwood Valley Rancheria. *Professionals on staff*: 30-35. *Services*: Outpatient; Family Practice-Perinatal Program; Dental. *Programs*: Staff Education, Training and Research; Community Health Education. Affiliated with California Program Office. Tribally operated.

SHASTA-TRINITY INDIAN HEALTH PROGRAM
P.O. Box 1603
Weaverville, CA 96093
 (916) 365-0125
 Ray Tickner, Director
Affiliated with California Program Office.
Tribally operated.

**NORTHERN VALLEY
INDIAN HEALTH PROGRAM**
827-A S. Tehama St.
Willows, CA 95988
 (916) 934-9293 Fax 534-6140
 Carol Ervin, Director
Affiliated with California Program Office.
Tribally operated.

COLORADO

SOUTHERN COLORADO UTE SERVICE UNIT
P.O. Box 778
Ignacio, CO 81137
 (303) 563-9447 (phone & fax)
 Walter L. Poolheco, Director
 George H. Maxted, MD, Clinical Director
Affiliated with Albuquerque Area Indian
Health Service. Tribally operated

IGNACIO PHS INDIAN HEALTH CENTER
P.O. Box 889
Ignacio, CO 81137
 (303) 563-4581
 Michael N. Mericle, Director
 George H. Maxted, MD, Clinical Director
Affiliated with Albuquerque Area Indian
Health Service.

TOWAOC PHS INDIAN HEALTH CENTER
General Delivery
Towaoc, CO 81334
 (303) 565-4441 Fax 565-4945
 Ronald D. Thomas, Director
 George H. Maxted, MD, Clinical Director
Affiliated with Albuquerque Area Indian
Health Service.

IDAHO

**NOT-TSOO GAH-NEE
INDIAN HEALTH CENTER**
P.O. Box 717
Fort Hall, ID 83203
(208) 238-2400
Bernadine R. Ricker, Administrative Officer
Roger H. Applegate, MD, Clinical Director
Affiliated with Portland Area Indian Health Service.

**NORTHERN IDAHO PHS
INDIAN HEALTH CENTER**
P.O. Drawer 367
Lapwai, ID 83540
(208) 843-2271
Joseph Moquino, Director
June Pinkham, Administrative Officer
Kent Locklear, MD, Clinical Director
Affiliated with Portland Area Indian Health Service.

IOWA

**SAC & FOX TRIBE OF THE MISSISSIPPI
IN IOWA INDIAN HEALTH CENTER**
Tama, IA 52339
(515) 484-4094
Affiliated with Aberdeen Area Indian Health
Service. Tribally operated.

KANSAS

HOLTON PHS INDIAN HEALTH CENTER
100 West 6th St.
Holton, KS 66436
(913) 364-2177 Fax 364-3691
Patrick J. Halton, Acting Director
Greg Abbott, DO, Clinical Director
Tribes served: Kickapoo of Kansas, Potawatomi,
Sac & Fox of Kansas & Nebraska, and Iowa Tribe.
Profesionals on staff: 8. *Services*: General outpa-
tient medical care, with laboratory & pharmacy.
Library. Affiliated with Oklahoma City Area Indian
Health Service.

KICKAPOO HEALTH CENTER
Kickapoo Tribe of Kansas
P.O. Box 271
Horton, KS 66439
(913) 486-2822
Affiliated with Oklahoma City Area Indian
Health Service. Tribally operated.

HASKELL PHS INDIAN HEALTH CENTER
2415 Massachusetts Ave.
Lawrence, KS 66044
(913) 843-3750 Fax 843-8815
JoAnn Skaggs, Director
Bonnie Abram, Administrative Officer
Rick Caldwell, MD, Clinical Director
*Tribes served: Students attending Haskell Indian
Junior College - representing over 135 different
tribes; Indians residing in Northeast Kansas. Professionals on staff*: 20. *Numbers served*: 15,600
outpatients served annually. *Primary Medical Services*: Family practice, alcohol/drug abuse, dental. *Programs*: Staff education; community health
education. Library. Affiliated with Oklahoma City
Area Indian Health Service.

HUNTER HEALTH CENTER
2318 E. Central
Wichita, KS 67214
(316) 262-3611 Fax 262-0741
Robert Beauvais, Acting Executive Director

MICHIGAN

**KEWEENAW BAY INDIAN
COMMUNITY HEALTH CLINIC**
Route 1
Baraga, MI 49908
(906) 353-6671
John Seppanen, Director
Geoffrey Coleman, MD, Clinical Director
Affiliated with Bemidji Area Office.
Tribally operated.

**BAY MILLS INDIAN COMMUNITY
HEALTH CLINIC**
Route 1, Box 313
Brimley, MI 49715
(906) 248-3204
Laurel Keenan, Director
Vicki Newland, Clinical Director
Affiliated with Bemidji Area Office.
Tribally operated.

SAULT STE. MARIE TRIBAL CLINIC
Wilson Rd., Bldg. 312
Kincheloe, MI 49788
(906) 495-5615
Russell Vizina, Director
David Vogt, D.O., Clinical Director
Affiliated with Bemidji Area Office.
Tribally operated.

NIMKEE MEMORIAL WELLNESS CENTER
2591 S. Leaton Rd.
Mt. Pleasant, MI 48858
(517) 773-9887
Audrey Falcon, Health Administrator
Deborah Eisenmann, MD, Clinical Director
Tribes served: Saginaw Chippewa Indian Tribe of
Michigan, and other federally recognized tribes.
Professionals on staff: 25. *Services*: Primary
pateint care; dental, nursing, psychological, sub-
stance abuse counseling, and health education
and fitness. *Programs*: Staff Education, Training
and Research; Community Health Education.
Scholarships. Affiliated with Bemidji Area Office.
Tribally operated.

**GRAND TRAVERSE OTTAWA/CHIPPEWA
HEALTH CLINIC**
Route 1, Box 135
Suttons Bay, MI 49682
(616) 271-3882
Ruth Bussey, Director
Affiliated with Bemidji Area Office.
Tribally operated.

LAC VIEUX DESERT BAND HEALTH CLINIC
P.O. Box 446
Watersmeet, MI 49969
(906) 358-4457
Beatrice Kelley, Health Administrator
Affiliated with Bemidji Area Office.
Tribally operated.

**HANNAHVILLE INDIAN
COMMUNITY HEALTH CLINIC**
N14911 Hannahville B1 Rd.
Wilson, MI 49896

(906) 466-2782
Jeff Pecotte, Director
Cynthia Lack, MD, Clinical Director
Affiliated with Bemidji Area Office.
Tribally operated.

MINNESOTA

LEECH LAKE BAND HEALTH CLINIC
Route 3 - Box 100
Cass Lake, MN 56633
(218) 335-8851
Eli Hunt, Health Director
Affiliated with Bemidji Area Office.

PHS INDIAN HOSPITAL
P.O. Box 60
Cass Lake, MN 56633
(218) 335-2293
Luella Brown, RN, Director
Paulo Guimares, MD, Clinical Director
Number of Beds: 22. Affiliated with Bemidji
Area Office.

**MIN NO AYA WIN
HUMAN SERVICES CENTER**
927 Trettel Lane
Cloquet, MN 55720
(218) 879-1227
Phil Norrgard, Director
Harlen Whitling, R.N., Medical Coordinator
Charles Vergona, MD, Medical Staff
Tribe served: Fond du Lac Reservation. 17 professionals on staff. 3,700 outpatients and 400 inpatients annually. *Primary services*: Outpatient
medical and dental services; public health nursing; social services Professional staff education,
training and research programs. Community
health education programs. Library. Affiliated with
Bemidji Area Office. Tribally operated.

GRAND PORTAGE BAND
P.O. Box 428
Grand Portage, MN 55605
(218) 475-2235
Mark Abrahamson, Health Director
Affiliated with Bemidji Area Office.
Tribally operated.

UPPER SIOUX BOARD OF TRUSTEES
P.O. Box 147
Granite Falls, MN 56241
(612) 564-2360
Laurie Gardner, Health Administrator
Affiliated with Bemidji Area Office.
Tribally operated.

LOWER SIOUX COMMUNITY COUNCIL
P.O. Box 308, Route 1
Morton, MN 56270
(507) 697-6185
Teri Schemmel, Health Director
Affiliated with Bemidji Area Office.
Tribally operated.

BOIS FORT TRIBAL CLINIC
P.O. Box 16
Nett Lake, MN 55772
(218) 757-3296
Jeneal Goggleye, Health Director
Ray Hawk, Clinical Director
Affiliated with Bemidji Area Office.
Tribally operated.

MILL LACS NE-IA-SHING CLINIC
HCR 67, Box 241
Onamia, MN 56359
  (615) 532-4163
  Dan Milbridge, Commissioner
    Health/Human Services
Believed to be the first clinic in the nation built with casino profits. Affiliated with Bemidji Area Office. Tribally operated.

SHAKOPEE MDEWAKANTON HEALTH COUNCIL
2320 Sioux Trail, NW
Prior Lake, MN 55372
  (612) 445-8900
  Joe Flemming, Health Director
Affiliated with Bemidji Area Office. Tribally operated.

RED LAKE COMPREHENSIVE HEALTH SERVICE
Red Lake, MN 56671
  (218) 679-3316 Fax 679-3390
  Oran Beaulieu, Project Director
Affiliated with Bemidji Area Office.

RED LAKE PHS INDIAN HOSPITAL
Red Lake, MN 56671
  (218) 679-3912
  Essimae Stevens, Director
  Paul Ditmanson, MD, Clinical Director
Number of Beds: 23. Affiliated with Bemidji Area Office.

PRAIRIE ISLAND COMMUNITY COUNCIL
1158 Island Blvd.
Welch, MN 55089
  (612) 385-2554
  Terri Buck, Health Director
  Mike Anderson, MD, Medical Director
Affiliated with Bemidji Area Office. Tribally operated.

WHITE EARTH BAND CLINIC
P.O. Box 418
White Earth, MN 56591
  (218) 983-3285
  JoEllen Anywaush, Health Director
Affiliated with Bemidji Area Office.

WHITE EARTH PHS INDIAN HEALTH CENTER
White Earth, MN 56591
  (218) 983-3221
  Franklin Heisler, Director
  Howard Hayes, MD, Clinical Director
Affiliated with Bemidji Area Office.

MISSISSIPPI

CHOCTAW HEALTH CENTER
Route 7, Box R-50
Philadelphia, MS 39350
  (601) 656-2211
  Marianna Hane, Director
  Nolan Fulton, M.D., Chief of Staff
Hospital. *Number of Beds*: 40. Affiliated with Nashville Area Office. Tribally operated.

MONTANA

ROCKY BOY'S PHS INDIAN HEALTH CENTER
Rocky Boy Rt., P.O. Box 664
Box Elder, MT 59521
  (406) 395-4489
  Curt W. Smith, Director
  Ernestine Belcourt, Administrative Officer
  John Fox, M.D., Clinical Director
Tribes served: Chippewa/Cree. *Professionals on staff*: 20; (total, 44). *Services*: Primary patient care. *Programs*: Staff Education, Training and Research; Community Health Education. Affiliated with Billings Area Indian Health Service.

BLACKFEET PHS INDIAN HOSPITAL
Browning, MT 59417
  (406) 338-6153 (Admin.); 338-6100 (Clinic)
  Mary Ellen LaFromboise, Director
  Reis Fisher, Administrative Officer
  Randy Rottenbiller, MD, Clinical Director
Number of Beds: 34. Affiliated with Billings Area Indian Health Service.

CROW AGENCY PHS INDIAN HOSPITAL
Crow Agency, MT 59022
  (406) 638-2624 (Admin.); 638-2626 (Clinic)
  Tenneyson Doney, Director
  Leonard Bends, Administrative Officer
  James Upchurch, Clinical Director
Number of Beds: 34. Affiliated with Billings Area Indian Health Service.

FORT BELKNAP PHS INDIAN HOSPITAL
Harlem, MT 59526
  (406) 353-2651
  Charles J. Plumage, Director
  Patricia Quisno, Administrative Officer
  Craig Nicholson, Clinical Director
Number of Beds: 18. Affiliated with Billings Area Indian Health Service.

NORTHERN CHEYENNE PHS INDIAN HEALTH CENTER
P.O. Box 70
Lame Deer, MT 59043
  (406) 477-6201
  David Means, Director
  Bill Mason, Administrative Officer
  Jon Hauxwell, MD, Clinical Director
Affiliated with Billings Area Indian Health Service.

LODGE GRASS PHS INDIAN HEALTH CENTER
Lodge Grass, MT 59050
  (406) 639-2317
  Dan Gun Shows, Administrative Officer
  Mark Schulein, MD, Medical Officer
Affiliated with Billings Area Indian Health Service.

FORT PECK PHS INDIAN HEALTH CENTER
Poplar, MT 59255
  (406) 768-3491
  Kenneth Smoker, Jr., Director
  Edna Wetsit, Administrative Officer
  Bob Camper, Clinical Director
Affiliated with Billings Area Indian Health Service.

FLATHEAD PHS INDIAN HEALTH CENTER
P.O. Box 280
St. Ignatius, MT 59865

  (406) 745-2411
  Greg Dumontier, Administrator
  Janet Barce, Health Services Coordinator
  Michael Dempsey, MD, Medical Advisor
Tribes served: Confederated Salish and Kootenai Tribes-Flathead Reservation. 10 professionals on staff. Outpatient clinics with main focus on Women's Clinics. *Special Program*: Narcotic Treatment Program, Sherry Saddler, Director. Community health education programs. Affiliated with Billings Area Indian Health Service.

FORT PECK PHS INDIAN HEALTH CENTER
Wolf Point, MT 59201
  (406) 653-1641
  Eden Wells, MD, Medical Officer
Affiliated with Billings Area Indian Health Service.

NEBRASKA

CARL T. CURTIS HEALTH CENTER
Macy, NE 68039
  (402) 837-5381 Fax 837-5303
  Matthew Sheridan, Sr., Project Officer
Tribes served: Omaha & Winnebago or any other Native American on the reservation needing medical care. *Professionals on staff*: 2. *Services*: Ambulatory Care, Family Practice, OB/GYN, Well Child, WIC, and Community Health. *Programs*: Staff Education, Training and Research, Community Health Education. Library. Affiliated with Aberdeen Area Indian Health Service. Tribally operated.

WINNEBAGO PHS INDIAN HOSPITAL
Winnebago, NE 68071
  (402) 878-2231 Fax 878-2535
  Wehonna St. Cyr, Director
  Vivian Snow, Administrative Officer
  James Vandelden, MD, Clinical Director
Tribes served: Omaha & Winnebago. *Number of Beds*: 38. Affiliated with Aberdeen Area Indian Health Service.

NEVADA

ELKO SOUTHERN BAND CLINIC
515 Shoshone Circle
Elko, NV 89801
  (702) 738-2252
  Dennis Vettese, Director
Affiliated with Phoenix Area Indian Health Service.

FALLON COMMUNITY HEALTH SERVICE
P.O. Box 1980
Fallon, NV 89406
  (702) 423-3634
  Bryan Elkins, Director
Affiliated with Phoenix Area Indian Health Service. Tribally operated.

WASHOE TRIBAL HEALTH CENTER
950 Hwy. 395 S.
Gardnerville, NV 89410
  (702) 883-4137
  John Ketcher, Director
Affiliated with Phoenix Area Indian Health Service. Tribally operated.

McDERMITT TRIBAL HEALTH CENTER
P.O. Box 457
McDermitt, NV 89421
(702) 532-8259
Cheryl Barney, Director
Tribes served: Paiute/Shoshone. *Number of professionals on staff*: 6. General medical services provided. Affiliated with Phoenix Area Indian Health Service. Tribally operated.

PYRAMID LAKE HEALTH DEPT.
P.O Box 227
Nixon, NV 89424
(702) 574-1018
Genevieve John, Director
Tribe served: Pyramid Lake Paiute. *Professionals on staff*: 4. *Services*: General outpatient medical care. *Program*: Community Health Education. Affiliated with Phoenix Area Indian Health Service. Tribally operated.

OWYHEE PHS INDIAN HOSPITAL
P.O. Box 364
Owyhee, NV 89832
(702) 757-2415
Wally Paisano, Director
Tribes served: Northeastern Nevada Tribes of Western Shoshone. 57 professionals on staff. Number of *Beds*: 15. Outpatient medical services. Community health education programs. Affiliated with Phoenix Area Indian Health Service.

RENO TRIBAL HEALTH STATION
34 Reservation Rd.
Reno, NV 89502
(702) 329-5162
Tom Dressler, Director
Affiliated with Phoenix Area Indian Health Service. Tribally operated.

SCHURZ INDIAN HEALTH CENTER
P.O. Drawer A
Schurz, NV 89427
(702) 773-2345
Elvin Willie, Director
John Friedrich, MD, Clinical Director
Number of Beds: 14. Affiliated with Phoenix Area Indian Health Service.

WALKER RIVER PAIUTE TRIBAL HEALTH CENTER
P.O. Drawer C
Schurz, NV 89427
(702) 773-2005
Kenneth Richardson, Director
Affiliated with Phoenix Area Indian Health Service.

YERINGTON HEALTH DEPT.
171 Campbell Lane
Yerington, NV 89447
(702) 463-3301
Linda Sheldon, Director
Affiliated with Phoenix Area Indian Health Service.

NEW MEXICO

ALBUQUERQUE PHS INDIAN HOSPITAL
801 Vassar Dr., NE
Albuquerque, NM 87106
(505) 254-4000 Fax 256-4088
Raymond Rodgers, Director
Bautisto Sangre, Administrative Officer
Charles North, MD, Clinical Director
Number of Beds: 54. Affiliated with Albuquerque Area Indian Health Service.

IHS SENSORY DISABILITIES PROGRAM
2401 12th St., NW
Albuquerque, NM 87102
(505) 766-1232
Joseph L. Stewart, Ph.D., Director
Provides oversight and evaluation of national program for detection and amelioration of ear disease and hearing loss. *Primary services*: Audiological and otolaryngolic.

SOUTHWESTERN INDIAN POLYTECHNIC INSTITUTE
Dental Training Center
Box 25927, 9168 Coors Rd., NW
Albuquerque, NM 87125
(505) 897-5306 Fax 897-5311
Darlene Sorrell, DDS, Chief, Dental Program
Affiliated with Albuquerque Area Indian Health Service.

DZILTH-NA-O-DITH-HLE PHS INDIAN HEALTH CENTER
Star Route 4, Box 5400
Bloomfield, NM 87413
(505) 632-1801
Leroy S. Dick, Director
Jim Couch, MD, Medical Director
Tribe served: 85% Navajo. *Professionals on staff*: 7. *Population served*: 26,000 people per year. *Services*: Complete diagnostic medical treatment services are provided: medical outpatient clinic, dental service, counseling service, community health nursing service. Affiliated with Navajo Area Indian Health Service.

CROWNPOINT COMPREHENSIVE HEALTH CARE FACILITY
P.O. Box 358
Crownpoint, NM 87313
(505) 786-5291
Anita Muneta, Director
Ronald C. Begay, Administrative Officer
Arnold Loera, MD, Clinical Director
Number of Beds: 28. Affiliated with Navajo Area Indian Health Service.

DULCE PHS INDIAN HEALTH CENTER
P.O. Box 187
Dulce, NM 87528
(505) 759-3291 Fax 759-3532
Joe Hussion, Director
Affiliated with Albuquerque Area Indian Health Service.

SANTA CLARA PHS INDIAN HEALTH CENTER
P.O. Box 446
Espanola, NM 87532
(505) 753-9421 Fax 753-5039
Laura Carver, Director
Affiliated with Albuquerque Area Indian Health Service.

FORT WINGATE INDIAN SCHOOL HEALTH CENTER
Gallup, NM 87301
(505) 488-5481
Affiliated with Navajo Area Indian Health Service.

GALLUP INDIAN MEDICAL CENTER
P.O. Box 1337
Gallup, NM 87305
(505) 722-1000
Timothy Flemming, MD, Director
Thomas Todacheeney, Administrative Officer
Gary Escudero, MD, Clinical Director
Number of Beds: 116. Affiliated with Navajo Area Indian Health Service.

ALAMO NAVAJO HEALTH STATION
P.O. Box 907
Magdalena, NM 87825
(505) 854-2626 Fax 854-2545
Mary Helen Creamer, Director
Affiliated with Albuquerque Area Indian Health Service. Tribally operated.

MESCALERO PHS INDIAN HOSPITAL
P.O. Box 210
Mescalero, NM 88340
(505) 671-4441 Fax 671-4422
David Civic, MD, Clinical Director
Affiliated with Albuquerque Area Native Health Service. Tribally operated.

PINE HILL PHS INDIAN HEALTH CENTER
P.O. Box 310
Pine Hill, NM 87357
(505) 775-3271 Fax 775-3240
Robert Newcombe, Director
Steven J. Drilling, MD, Clinical Director
Affiliated with Albuquerque Area Indian Health Service. Tribally operated.

ACOMA-CANONCITO LAGUNA PHS INDIAN HOSPITAL
P.O. Box 130
San Fidel, NM 87049
(505) 552-6634 Fax 552-7363
Pete Little, Administrative Officer
Michael Landen, MD, Clinical Director
Affiliated with Albuquerque Area Indian Health Service.

NEW SUNRISE REGIONAL TREATMENT CENTER
P.O. Box 219
San Fidel, NM 87049
(505) 552-6091 Fax 552-6527
Richanda A. Bears Ghost, Administrative Officer
Joe Neidhardt, Clinical Director
Affiliated with Albuquerque Area Indian Health Service.

SANTA FE PHS INDIAN HOSPITAL
1700 Cerrillos Rd.
Santa Fe, NM 87501
(505) 988-9821 Fax 983-6243
Lawrence Jordan, Director
Joseph L. Montoya, Administrative Officer
Ben Whitehall, MD, Clinical Director
Number of Beds: 55. Affiliated with Albuquerque Area Indian Health Service.

SHIPROCK PHS INDIAN HOSPITAL
P.O. Box 160
Shiprock, NM 87420
(505) 368-4971
Daalbaaleh Hutchison, Director
Fanessa Comer, Administrative Officer
Allen S. Craig, MD, Clinical Director
Affiliated with Navajo Area Indian Health Service.

TAOS PHS INDIAN HEALTH CENTER
P.O. Box 1956
Taos, NM 87571
(505) 758-4224 Fax 758-1822
Kay Tsouhlarakis, Director
Affiliated with Albuquerque Area Indian Health Service.

TOHATCHI PHS INDIAN HEALTH CENTER
P.O. Box 142
Tohatchi, NM 87325
(505) 733-2244
Affiliated with Navajo Area Indian Health Service.

ZUNI PHS INDIAN HOSPITAL
P.O. Box 467
Zuni, NM 87327
(505) 782-4431 Fax 782-5723
Jean Othole, Director
Clyde Yatsattie, Administrative Officer
David Kessler, MD, Clinical Director
Number of Beds: 45. Affiliated with Albuquerque Area Indian Health Service.

NORTH CAROLINA

CHEROKEE PHS INDIAN HOSPITAL
Cherokee, NC 28719
(704) 497-9163 Fax 497-9163 Ext. 225
Jim Smith, Health Systems Administrator
Peggy Jenks, Administrative Officer
George Granning, MD, Clinical Director
Number of Beds: 35. Affiliated with Nashville Area Indian Health Service.

CHEROKEE TECHNICAL SUPPORT CENTER
P.O. Box 429, Butler Bldg.
Rt. 1, Sequoyah Trail
Cherokee, NC 28719
(704) 497-5030 Fax 497-5104
Mary G. Wachacha, Health Education Coord.
Affiliated with Nashville Area Indian Health Service.

UNITED REGIONAL YOUTH TREATMENT CENTER
P.O. Box C-201, 441 N. Sequoyah Trail Dr.
Cherokee, NC 28719
(704) 497-3958 Fax 497-6826
Mary Anne Farrell, MD, Director
Affiliated with Nashville Area Indian Health Service.

NORTH DAKOTA

BELCOURT PHS INDIAN HOSPITAL
P.O. Box 160
Belcourt, ND 58316
(701) 477-6112
Clarence Frederick, Director
Lynn Davis, Administrative Officer
James Blain, MD, Clinical Director
Tribe served: Turtle Mountain Sioux. *Number of Beds*: 46. Affiliated with Aberdeen Area Indian Health Service.

FORT TOTTEN PHS INDIAN HEALTH CENTER
P.O. Box 200
Fort Totten, ND 58335
(701) 766-4291 Fax 766-4295
John Gobert, Director
Lillie Owl boy, Administrative Officer
William Kingree, MD, Clinical Director
Tribe served: Devils Lake Sioux Tribe. *Professionals on staff*: 11. *Services*: Family Practice. *Programs*: Staff Education, Training and Research; Community Health Education. Medical Library. Affiliated with Aberdeen Area Indian Health Service.

FORT YATES PHS INDIAN HOSPITAL
P.o. Box J
Fort Yates, ND 58538
(701) 854-3831 Fax 854-7399
Terry Pouier, Director
Sonja Keener, Administrative Officer

Eduardo Lago, M.D., Clinical Director
Number of Beds: 32. Affiliated with Aberdeen Area Indian Health Service.

FORT BERTHOLD PHS INDIAN HEALTH CENTER
P.O. Box 400
New Town, ND 58763
(701) 627-4701 Fax 627-3902
Fred Baker, Director
Ronald Ilvedson, MD, Clinical Director
Affiliated with Aberdeen Area Indian Health Service.

TRENTON-WILLISTON INDIAN SERVICE AREA
P.O. Box 210
Trenton, ND 58853
(701) 774-0461 Fax 572-0124
Ron Falcon, Tribal Health Director
Bhanat K. Patel, MD, Medical Officer
Affiliated with Aberdeen Area Indian Health Service. Tribally operated.

OKLAHOMA

CARL ALBERT INDIAN HOSPITAL
1001 N. Country Club Dr.
Ada, OK 74820
(405) 436-3980 Fax 332-1421
Tom Bear, Acting Director
Delores Little, Administrative Officer
Sara Dye, MD, Clinical Director
Professionals on staff: 4. *Number of Beds*: 53. *Services*: Offers general out-patient medical services; workshops and in-service training. Affiliated with Oklahoma City Area Indian Health Service.

ANADARKO PHS INDIAN HEALTH CENTER
P.O. Box 828
Anadarko, OK 73005
(405) 247-2458 Fax 247-7052
Gary Cody, Director
Affiliated with Oklahoma City Area Indian Health Service.

ARDMORE CHICKASAW HEALTH CLINIC
2510 Chickasaw Blvd.
Ardmore, OK 73401
(405) 226-8181
Madeline Johnson, Director
Tribe served: Chickasaw. *Professionals on staff*: 7. *Numbers served*: 5,400 annually. *Services*: Offers general out-patient medical services; workshops and in-service training. Library. Affiliated with Oklahoma City Area Indian Health Service. Tribally operated.

CHOCTAW NATION HEALTH CLINIC
205 E. 3rd St.
Broken Bow, OK 74728
(405) 584-2740 Fax 584-2073
Shannon McDaniel, Director
Affiliated with Oklahoma City Area Indian Health Service. Tribally operated.

CARNEGIE PHS INDIAN HEALTH CENTER
P.O. Box 1120
Carnegie, OK 73105
(405) 654-1100
Ralph Kauley, Jr., Director
Affiliated with Oklahoma City Area Indian Health Service.

CLAREMORE PHS INDIAN HOSPITAL
W. Will Rogers & Moore
Claremore, OK 74017
(918) 342-6200 Fax 342-6585
John Daugherty, Director
Carl Ellison, MD, Clinical Director
Number of Beds: 60. Affiliated with Oklahoma City Area Indian Health Service.

CLINTON PHS INDIAN HOSPITAL
P.O. Box 279
Clinton, OK 73601
(405) 323-2884 Fax 323-2884 Ext. 211
Thedis Mitchell, Director
William McKee, Administrative Officer
Louise Yates, MD, Clinical Director
Number of Beds: 14. Affiliated with Oklahoma City Area Indian Health Service.

EL RENO PHS INDIAN HEALTH CLINIC
1631A E. Highway 66
El Reno, OK 73036
(405) 262-7631 Fax 262-8099
Wayne Parrish, Director
Affiliated with Oklahoma City Area Indian Health Service.

EUFAULA INDIAN HEALTH CLINIC
800 Forest Ave.
Eufaula, OK 74432
(918) 689-2547
Linda Lowe, Administrator
Tribes served: Mostly Creek, but all tribes within area. *Professionals on staff*: 21. *Services*: General outpatient medical care; dental, laboratory, counseling, nursing. *Program*: Community Health Education. Affiliated with Oklahoma City Area Indian Health Service. Tribally operated.

HUGO HEALTH CENTER
P.O. Box 340
Hugo, OK 74743
(405) 326-7561
Roy Lyles, Director
Affiliated with Oklahoma City Area Indian Health Service. Tribally operated.

SAM HIDER JAY COMMUNITY CLINIC
P.O. Box 350
Jay, OK 74346
(918) 253-4271 Fax 434-5397
Rick Richards, Director
Affiliated with Oklahoma City Area Indian Health Service. Tribally operated.

LAWTON PHS INDIAN CENTER
Lawton, OK 73501
(405) 353-0350 Fax 353-0350 Ext. 206
George Howell, Director
Wallace Boyd, Administrative Officer
Angel Rivera, MD, Clinical Director
Number of Beds: 52. Affiliated with Oklahoma City Area Indian Health Service.

McALLESTER HEALTH CENTER
903 E. Monroe
McAlester 74501
(918) 423-8440
Dave Galloway, Director
Tribes served: All tribes in this area, predominantly Choctaw. *Number of professionals on staff*: 9. *Numbers served*: 11,000, annually. *Medical services*: Family practice. *Programs*: Diabetic and prenatal classes; CPR training; immunization program; home health care. Affiliated with Oklahoma City Area Indian Health Service. Tribally operated.

MIAMI PHS INDIAN HEALTH CENTER
P.O. Box 1498
Miami, OK 74355
 (918) 542-1655 Fax 540-1685
 Marion Ted Bearden, Director
Tribes served: Seneca-Cayuga, Eastern
Shawnee, Miami, Modoc, Ottawa, Quapaw, Peoria, Wyandott and Cherokee. *Professionals on staff*: 15; *Numbers served*: Out-patients, 35,000 annually. *Medical services*: Medical, pharmacy, dental, optometry, mental health, public health nursing and laboratory. *Community programs*: Educational activities in the schools and tribal communities. Small medical library.

NOWATA INDIAN HEALTH CLINIC
Cherokee Nation of Oklahoma
507 E. Redwood
Nowata, OK 74048
 (918) 273-0192
 Gordon Watkins, Director
Affiliated with Oklahoma City Area
Indian Health Service. Tribally operated.

CREEK NATION COMMUNITY HOSPITAL
Creek Nation of Oklahoma
P.O. Box 228
Okemah, OK 74859
 (918) 623-1424
 Alan Harjo, Director
Affiliated with Oklahoma City Area
Indian Health Service. Tribally operated.

OKEMAH INDIAN HEALTH CENTER
P.O. Box 429
Okemah, OK 74859
 (918) 623-0555
 Geneva Harris, Health Systems Administrator
Affiliated with Oklahoma City Area
Indian Health Service. Tribally operated.

OKLAHOMA CITY URBAN HEALTH CLINIC
Central OK American Indian Health Council
1214 N. Hudson
Oklahoma City, OK 73103
 (405) 235-5877
 Terry Hunter, Executive Director

PAWHUSKA PHS INDIAN HEALTH CENTER
715 Grandview
Pawhuska, OK 74056
 (918) 287-4491
 John W. Williams, Director
Affiliated with Oklahoma City Area
Indian Health Service.

PAWNEE PHS INDIAN HEALTH CENTER
RR 2, Box 1
Pawnee, OK 74058
 (918) 762-2517 Fax 762-2517 Ext. 200
 Gary Davis, Director
 Anita RedEagle, Administrative Officer
 Steve Sanders, DO, Clinical Director
Affiliated with Oklahoma City Area
Indian Health Service.

**WHITE EAGLE PHS
INDIAN HEALTH CENTER**
P.O. Box 2071
Ponca City, OK 74601
 (405) 765-2501 Fax 765-6348
 Gwen Pickering, Director
Affiliated with Oklahoma City Area
Indian Health Service.

SALINA COMMUNITY CLINIC
P.O. Box 936
Salina, OK 74365
 (918) 434-5397
 Robert Park, Director
Affiliated with Oklahoma City Area Indian
Health Service. Tribally operated.

REDBIRD SMITH HEALTH CENTER
301 JT Stitkes Ave.
Sallisaw, OK 74955
 (918) 775-9159 Fax 775-4778
 Jerry Chuculate, Director
Affiliated with Oklahoma City Area
Indian Health Service. Tribally operated.

SAPULPA HEALTH CENTER
Creek Nation of Oklahoma
1125 East Cleveland
Sapulpa, OK 74066
 (918) 224-9310
 Sherry Baker, Director
Affiliated with Oklahoma City Area
Indian Health Service. Tribally operated.

SHAWNEE PHS INDIAN HEALTH CENTER
2001 S. Gordon Cooper Dr.
Shawnee, OK 74801
 (405) 275-4270 Fax 275-4270 Ext. 268
 James Cussen, Director
 Jerry Levi, Administrative Officer
 Ronald Fried, DO, Clinical Director
Serves patients from various tribes. *Professionals on staff*: 30. *Numbers served*: 45,000 outpatients, annually. *Primary service*: Family practice.
Programs: Staff education and training; community health education. Scholarships available. Library. Affiliated with Oklahoma City Area IHS.

CHEROKEE NATION HEALTH CENTER
1311 W. Locust St.
Stilwell, OK 74960
 (918) 696-6911
 Beverly Stone, Director
Affiliated with Oklahoma City Area
Indian Health Service. Tribally operated.

BLACK HAWK HEALTH CENTER
Sac & Fox Nation of Oklahoma
Rte. 2, Box 246
Stroud, OK 73079
 (918) 968-9531
 Cindy Schoenecke, Director
Affiliated with Oklahoma City Area Indian Health
Service. Tribally operated.

W.W. HASTINGS INDIAN HOSPITAL
100 S. Bliss
Tahlequah, OK 74464
 (918) 458-3100 Fax 458-3262
 Delbert Nutter, Director
 Leonard Thompson, Administrative Officer
 Gayle Harris, MD, Clinical Director
Number of Beds: 60. Affiliated with Oklahoma
City Area Indian Health Service.

CHOCTAW NATION INDIAN HOSPITAL
Rt. 2, Box 1725
Talihina, OK 74571
 (918) 567-2211 Fax 567-2211 Ext. 319
 Roy Lyles, Acting Administrator
 Patrick Mason, Clinical Director
Tribes served: Choctaw and others. *Professionals on staff*: 77. *Number of Beds*: 52. *Numbers served*: 1,300 inpatients and 32,000 outpatients, annually. *Programs*: Staff Education and Training Programs; Community Health Education Pro-

grams. Affiliated with Oklahoma City Area Indian
Health Service. Tribally operated.

TISHOMINGO CHICKASAW HEALTH CENTER
815 E. 6th St.
Tishomingo, OK 73460
 (405) 371-2392 Fax 371-9323
 Joseph Bennett, Director
Tribe served: Chickasaw. *Professionals on staff*: 8. *Numbers served*: 8,000 annually. Library. Affiliated with Oklahoma City Area Indian Health Service. Tribally operated.

TULSA URBAN HEALTH CLINIC
Indian Health Care Resource Center of Tulsa, Inc.
915 S. Cincinnati
Tulsa, OK 74119
 (918) 582-7230 Fax 582-6405
 Carmelita Skeeter, Executive Director

WATONGA PHS INDIAN HEALTH CENTER
P.O. Box 878
Watonga, OK 73772
 (405) 623-4991 Fax 623-5490
 Larry Scott, Director
Tribes served: Primarily Cheyenne and Arapaho; members of all local tribes. *Professionals on staff*: 10. *Numbers served annually*: Out-patient, 1,200 plus. *Medical services*: General out-patient medical and dental services. *Community programs*: Weekly diabetic and prenatal clinics; headstart dental prevention and nursing bottle caries prevention. Small medical library. Affiliated with Oklahoma City Area Indian Health Service.

WEWOKA PHS INDIAN HEALTH CENTER
P.O. Box 1475
Wewoka, OK 74884
 (405) 257-6281 Fax 257-2696
 Jayme Longbrake, Acting Director
 Rena BlueEyes, Administrative Officer
 Imelda Buendia, MD, Clinical Director
Affiliated with Oklahoma City Area
Indian Health Service.

OREGON

YELLOWHAWK PHS INDIAN HEALTH CENTER
P.O. Box 160
Pendleton, OR 97801
 (503) 278-3870
 Doris W. Thompson, Director
 Allan Jio, Pharm., Clinical Director
Services provided: Contract health, dental care, environmental health, health education, Lab/X-ray, mental health, outpatient clinic, pharmacy, public health nursing, and wellness programs. Affiliated with Portland Area Indian Health Service.

CHEMAWA INDIAN HEALTH CENTER
3750 Chemawa Rd., NE
Salem, OR 97305
 (503) 399-5937
 James E. Edge, MPH, Director
 Lorraine A. Hesketh, Administrative Officer
 Mark J. Nurre, MD, Clinical Director
Tribes served: Confederated Tribes of Siletz; Confederated Tribes of Grand Ronde; Cow Creek Band of Umpqua Tribe; Confederated Tribes of Coos, Lower Umpqua, Siuslaw; Coquille Tribe. *Number of professionals on staff*: 30. *Numbers served*: 15,000, Outpatient. *Services provided*: Outpatient medical, dental, mental health, nutrition, public health nursing. Affiliated with Portland Area Indian Health Service.

CONFEDERATED TRIBES OF SILETZ COMMUNITY HEALTH CLINIC
107 SE Swan Ave., P.O. Box 320
Siletz, OR 97380
 (800) 648-0449; Fax (503) 444-1278
Provides comprehensive health care to federally recognized American Indians.

WARM SPRINGS PHS INDIAN HEALTH CENTER
P.O. Box 1209
Warm Springs, OR 97761
 (503) 553-1196
 Russ Alger, Director
 Roberta Queahpama, Administrative Officer
 Thomas J. Creelman, MD, Clinical Director
Services provided: Out-patient clinical; dental care; contract health; nutrition; and public health nursing. Affiliated with Portland Area Indian Health Service.

SOUTH DAKOTA

EAGLE BUTTE PHS INDIAN HOSPITAL
P.O. Box 1012
Eagle Butte, SD 57625
 (605) 964-7030 FAX 964-1110
 Orville Night Pipe, Director
 Don Annis, Administrative Officer
 Jeff Henderon, MD, Clinical Director
Tribe served: Cheyenne River Sioux. *Professionals on staff*: 6. *Number of Beds*. 26. 680 inpatients anmd 3,600 outpatients, annually. *Primary services*: Acute medicine; OB/GYN' Pediatrics. Community Health Education Programs. Affiliated with Aberdeen Area Indian Health Service.

FORT THOMPSON PHS INDIAN HEALTH CENTER
P.O. Box 200
Fort Thompson, SD 57339
 (605) 245-2285 Fax 245-2399
 Nancy Miller, Director
 Theo Matheny, MD, Clinical Director
Affiliated with Aberdeen Area Indian Health Service.

KYLE PHS HEALTH CENTER
P.O. Box 540
Kyle, SD 57752
 (605) 455-2451 Fax 455-2808
 Joseph Smith, Director
 Georgia Amiotte, Administrative Officer
Affiliated with Aberdeen Area Indian Health Service.

LOWER BRULE PHS INDIAN HEALTH CENTER
P.O. Box 248
Lower Brule, SD 57548
 (605) 473-5544
 Patricia Howell, Director
 Clarenda Menzie, Administrative Officer
 Peter Magnus, MD, Clinical Director
Affiliated with Aberdeen Area Indian Health Service.

McLAUGHLIN PHS INDIAN HEALTH CENTER
P.O. Box 879
McLaughlin, SD 57642
 (605) 823-4459 Fax 823-4755
 James Foote, Director
 Daisy LeCompte, Administrative Assistant

Tribes served: Standing Rock Sioux, Cheyenne River Sioux, Rosebud Sioux, Fort Totten Sioux, Fort Thompson Crow Creek Sioux, and Yankton Sioux. *Professionals on staff*: 8. 9,500 outpatients, annually. *Primary services*: Outpatient and dental services. Library. Affiliated with Aberdeen Area Indian Health Service.

PINE RIDGE PHS INDIAN HOSPITAL
Pine Ridge, SD 57770
 (605) 867-5131 Fax 867-1018
 Leonard Little Finger, Director
 Bill Pourier, Administrative Officer
 Gene Biever, MD, Clinical Director
Number of Beds: 58. Affiliated with Aberdeen Area Indian Health Service.

RAPID CITY PHS INDIAN HEALTH HOSPITAL
3200 Canyon Lake Dr.
Rapid City, SD 57702
 (605) 348-1900 Fax 348-7150
 James Cournoyer, Director
 Midge Breen, Administrative Officer
 Rodney Larson, MD, Clinical Director
Number of Beds: 39. Affiliated with Aberdeen Area Indian Health Service.

ROSEBUD PHS INDIAN HOSPITAL
Rosebud, SD 57570
 (605) 747-2231 Fax 747-2216
 Gayla Twiss, Director
 Sophie Two Hawk, MD, Clinical Director
Number of Beds: 29. Affiliated with Aberdeen Area Indian Health Service.

SISSETON PHS INDIAN HOSPITAL
P.O. Box 189
Sisseton, SD 57262
 (605) 698-7606 Fax 698-4270
 Richard Huff, Director
 Ramona Saul, Administrative Officer
 Jeannie Griffith, MD, Clinical Director
Number of Beds: 20. Affiliated with Aberdeen Area Indian Health Service.

WAGNER PHS INDIAN HOSPITAL
110 Washington St.
Wagner, SD 57380
 (605) 384-3621 Fax 384-5229
 Vern Donnell, Director
 Darlene Williamson, Administrative Officer
 Ramon Rodriguez, MD, Clinical Director
Tribes served: Yankton Sioux and Santee Sioux. *Professionals on staff*: 30; Number of Beds: 26. *Medical services*: In-patient; medical and surgical. Library. Affiliated with Aberdeen Area Indian Health Service.

TEXAS

DALLAS INTER-TRIBAL COUNCIL HEALTH CENTER
209 E. Jefferson
Dallas, TX 75203
 (214) 941-1050 Fax 941-6537
 Ernest Sickey, Executive Director

YSLETA DEL SUR SERVICE UNIT
119 S. Old Pueblo Rd., Box 17579
El Paso, TX 79907
 (915) 859-7913 Fax 859-2988
 Joe Salas, Director

UTAH

FORT DUCHESNE PHS INDIAN HEALTH CENTER
P.O. Box 160
Roosevelt, UT 84026
 (801) 722-5122
 Tom Gann, Director
 Paul Ebbert, MD, Clinical Director
Tribes served: Northern Ute; Paiute Tribe of Utah; and Skull Valley Goshute. *Professionals on staff*: 47. Community health education. Affiliated with Phoenix Area Indian Health Service.

WASHINGTON

LUMMI PHS INDIANHEALTH CENTER
2592 Kwina Rd.
Bellingham, WA 98226
 (206) 676-8373
 Marilyn M. Scott, Director
 Adam Kartman, MD, Clinical Director
Affiliated with Portland Area Indian Health Service.

SOPHIE TRETTEVICK INDIAN HEALTH CENTER
P.O. Box 410
Neah Bay, WA 98357
 (206) 645-2233
 John R. Heinz, Director
 Shirley M. Johnson, Administrative Officer
 Elizabeth Koch, MD, Clinical Director
Affiliated with Portland Area Indian Health Service.

COLVILLE PHS INDIAN HEALTH CENTER
P.O. Box 71, Agency Campus
Nespelem, WA 99155
 (509) 634-4771
 Mel Tonasket, Director
 Janice Matt, Administrative Officer
 Paul Phillips, DMD, Clinical Director
Affiliated with Portland Area Indian Health Service.

PUGET SOUND PHS INDIAN HEALTH STATION
2201 Sixth Ave., Room 300
Seattle, WA 98121
 (206) 615-2781
 Ernest H. Kimball, Director
Affiliated with Portland Area Indian Health Service.

TAHOLAH PHS INDIAN HEALTH CENTER
P.O. Box 219
Taholah, WA 98587
 (206) 276-4405
 Dorothy L. DeLaCruz, Director
 Carl Schilling, Clinical Director
Affiliated with Portland Area Indian Health Service.

YAKIMA PHS INDIAN HEALTH CENTER
401 Buster Rd.
Toppenish, WA 98948
 (509) 865-2102
 William H. Picotee, Director
 Carl Olden, MD, Clinical Director
Affiliated with Portland Area Indian Health Service.

DAVID C. WYNECOOP MEMORIAL CLINIC
P.O. Box 357
Wellpinit, WA 99040
 (509) 258-4517
 Virgil L. Gunn, Director
 Paul Willard, MD, Clinical Director
Affiliated with Portland Area Indian Health Service.

WISCONSIN

RED CLIFF HEALTH SERVICES
P.O. Box 529
Bayfield, WI 54814
 (715) 779-3707
 Joan Slack, Director
Affiliated with Bemidji Area Office.
Tribally operated.

WISCONSIN WINNEBAGO HEALTH DEPT.
P.O. Box 636
Black River Falls, WI 54615
 (715) 284-7548/7830
 Jeremy Rockman, Health Director
Affiliated with Bemidji Area Office.
Tribally operated.

STOCKBRIDGE-MUNSEE HEALTH CENTER
P.O. Box 86-N8705 Moh He Con Nuk Rd.
Bowler, WI 54416
 (715) 793-4144
 Lu Ann Tousey, Director
 Richard Dalve, MD, Clinical Director
Affiliated with Bemidji Area Office.
Tribally operated.

FOREST CO. POTAWATOMI COMMUNITY CLINIC
P.O. Box 346
Crandon, WI 54520
 (715) 478-3431
 Dori Shewano, Health Administrator
Affiliated with Bemidji Area Office.
Tribally operated.

SOKAOGAN CHIPPEWA COMMUNITY CLINIC
P.O. Box 616
Crandon, WI 54520
 (715) 478-5180
 Peter McGeshick, Jr., Health Administrator
Affiliated with Bemidji Area Office.
Tribally operated.

LAC COURTE OREILLES TRIBAL CLINIC
Route #2, Box 2750
Hayward, WI 54843
 (715) 634-4153/4795
 Don Smith, Director
 Modesto Ferrar, MD, Clinical Director
Affiliated with Bemidji Area Office.
Tribally operated.

ST. CROIX HEALTH SERVICES
P.O. Box 287
Hertel, WI 54845
 (715) 349-2195
 Phyllis Lowe, Director
 Bill Marx, Clinical Director
Affiliated with Bemidji Area Office.
Tribally operated.

MENOMINEE TRIBAL CLINIC
P.O. Box 970
Keshena, WI 54135
 (715) 799-5482
 Jerry L. Waukau, Health Administrator
 Geoffrey Coleman, MD, Clinical Director
Tribe served: Menominee. *Professionals on staff*: 80. Consists of four full-time physicians with staff privileges at the Shawano Community Hospital. *Services*: The Community Health Nursing Service consists of a staff of eight that provides a number of outreach services to the community; the Human Resource Center provides outpatient mental health services; Emergency Medical Services. *Programs*: Staff education, training and research; community health education; environmental health program. Library. Affiliated with Bemidji Area Office. Tribally operated.

PETER CHRISTENSEN HEALTH CENTER
450 Old Abe Rd.
Lac du Flambeau, WI 54538
 (715) 588-3371
 Glen Safford, Health Administrator
Affiliated with Bemidji Area Office.
Tribally operated.

BAD RIVER HEALTH SERVICES
P.O Box 39
Odanah, WI 54861
 (715) 682-7137
 Mary Bigboy, Health Director
Affiliated with Bemidji Area Office.
Tribally operated.

ONEIDA COMMUNITY HEALTH CENTER
P.O. Box 365
Oneida, WI 54155
 (414) 869-2711
 Judy Skenandore, Director
 Tammy Fox, PA, Clinical Director
Affiliated with Bemidji Area Office.
Tribally operated.

WYOMING

ARAPAHO PHS INDIAN HEALTH CENTER
Arapaho, WY 82510
 (307) 856-9281
 John Oberly, Administrative Officer
 Margaret Cooper, Clinical Director
Affiliated with Billings Area Indian Health Service.

WIND RIVER PHS INDIAN HEALTH CENTER
Fort Washakie, WY 82514
 (307) 332-9416/8
 Ken Nicholson, Director
 John Oberly, Administrative Officer
 Robert McKnight, MD, Clinical Director
Affiliated with Billings Area Indian Health Service.

This section is an alpha-geographical listing of museums, monuments and parks maintaining permanent exhibits or collections related to the Native-American. Where no annotation follows a listing, the museum failed to answer our questionnaire, but is known, from other sources, to display Indian artifacts.

NATIONAL MUSEUM OF THE AMERICAN INDIAN

Washington D.C. (planning stages)
Now under construction, the National Museum of the American Indian as a living memorial dedicated to the collection, preservation, study and exhibition of American Indian languages, literature, history, art and culture. The centerpiece of the new museum will be the priceless collection of more than 1 million artifacts in the Museum of the American Indian, Heye Foundation, in New York City. This collection which includes a library, photo archives and other resource materials, will be transferred to the Smithsonian Institution.

The second exhibition site, called the George Gustav Heye Center of the National Museum of the American Indian, is located in the Old U.S. Customs House in lower Manhattan, New York City. A storage, research and conservation facility will be built at the Smithsonian's Museum Support Center in Suitland, MD. The law also provides for the loan of exhibits and artifacts to American Indian museums, cultural centers, educational institutions and libraries.

There is a 25-member (three-year) governing board of trustees. At least seven members of the initial board will be American Indians. A partial list includes: Fred Hoxie, Chicago; Jennie Joe (Navajo), Tucson, AZ; Alfonso Ortiz (San Juan Pueblo), Albuquerque, NM; Janine Pease-W indy Boy (Crow), Crow Agency, MT; Helen Sheirbeck (Lumbee), Pembroke, NC; David Hurst Thomas, New York, NY; Arturo Warman, Mexico City; Rosita Worl (Tlingit), Juneau, AK. The remaining 17 are the secretary of the Smithsonian, an assistant secretary, and 15 current members of the board of trustees of the Museum of the American Indian. At least 12 of these members will be American Indian. When the three-year term expires, the new trustees will be appointed by the Smithsonian board of regents from a list of nominees recommended by the trustees. At least 12 of those members will be American Indians.

ALABAMA

POARCH CREEK INDIAN HERITAGE CENTER
HCR 69A, Box 85B
ATMORE 36502
(205) 368-9136
Patricia L. Brewer, Executive Director
Sandra L. Ridley, Curator
Museum under construction. Collections will pertain to Creek Indians of the Southeast. Library. Established 1990.

RUSSELL CAVE NATIONAL MONUMENT
Route 1, Box 175
BRIDGEPORT 35740
(205) 495-2672
Farrell Saunders, Superintendent
Larry N. Beane, Curator
Description: An excavated, 310-acre archaeological site which shows the life of the people Russell Cave sheltered for 8,000 years. From archaic man to Indians--Woodlands and Cherokee. Museum contains artifacts from the Archaic, Woodland, and Mississippian periods. Special program: Indian Day - April, includes demonstrations of prehistoric techniques, arts and crafts. Publication: Investigations in Russell Cave. Library. Founded 1961.

INDIAN MOUND & MUSEUM
S. Court St.
FLORENCE 35630
(205) 760-6427
Description: The pre-Columbian Indian mound is one of the largest domiciliary Indian mounds in the Tennessee Valley. The museum contains Indian artifacts.

ALABAMA STATE ARCHIVES & HISTORY MUSEUM
624 Washington Ave.
MONTGOMERY 36130
(205) 242-4363
Descritpion: Collections include artifacts that trace the culture of five American Indian tribes that lived in Alabama.

MOUNDVILLE ARCHAEOLOGICAL PARK
Alabama Museum of Natural History
P.O. Box 66
MOUNDVILLE 35474
(205) 371-2572
Dr. Douglas E. Jones, Director
Eugene Futato, Curator
Description: A park and museum located on the Black Warrior River, preserves 317 acres of what was once a large and powerful Southeastern Indian community of about 3,000 @ 1500 A.D. The site of 20 preserved mounds and the building of the wooden palisade that once defended the site. An Archaeological Museum holds one of the largest and most important collections of Native American artifacts and related materials for scientific research anywhere in the Southeast; also maintains a reconstructed Indian temple atop the tallest mound. Activities: Moundville Native American Festival featuring Southeastern Native American crafts, food, storytelling, musicians and dancers; other special programs with Native Americans from Choctaw, Creek, Cherokee, and Seminole tribes. Publications: NatureSouth, Bulletin, Nature Notebooks, Ephemera series. Established 1939.

FORT TOULOUSE-JACKSON PARK
Route 6, Box 6
WETUMPKA 36092
(205) 567-3002
Ned Jenkins, Site Manager
Description: A 165 acre National Historic Landmark situated at the junction of the Coos and Tallapoosa Rivers where they form the Alabama River. Occupied by the moundbuilder Alabama Indians, who were part of the Creek Confederacy. Like the other moundbuilders in the area, these Indians were the first farmers-corn, beans and squash. When DeSoto passed through in 1540 this area was probably a part of the chiefdom of Talise.

ALASKA

SIMON PANEAK MEMORIAL MUSEUM
P.O. Box 21085
ANAKTUVUK PASS 99721
(907) 661-3413 Fax 661-3414
Grant Spearman, Curator
Description: Local history and culture museum pertaining to the "Nunamiut" or inland Eskimos of Alaska's Central Brooks Range. Collections represent a combination of archaeological and ethnographic objects as well as extensive oral history, photographic and archival materials. Special Education Program: Work in conjunction with the North Slope Borough School District and the Borough's Inupiaq History, Language and Culture Commission to research and produce educational mat3erials based on oral history research with Nunamiut elders about traditional tools, implements, practices and values. Library. Gift Shop.

ANCHORAGE MUSEUM OF HISTORY & ART
121 W. 7th Ave.
ANCHORAGE 99501
(907) 343-4326 Fax 343-6149
Patricia B. Wolf, Director
Description: Permanent exhibits on Alaskan art and artifacts of all periods. Eskimo, Aleut, Tlingit and Athapaskan crafts. 8,000 ethnographic pieces. Special programs: Annual Native Heritage Festival (March) which features 10-20 contemporary Alaskan Native craftsmen and artists; Summer Native dance series provided by Cook Inlet Tribal Council. Publications: An Introduction to the Native Art of Alaska; monthly newsletter. Library. Museum shop. Established in 1968.

ANGOON CULTURAL CENTER MUSEUM
ANGOON 99820

INUPIAT UNIVERSITY OF THE ARCTIC MUSEUM
P.O. Box 429
BARROW 99723

YUPIIT PICIRYARAIT CULTURAL CENTER & MUSEUM
Association of Village Council Presidents
P.O. Box 219
BETHEL 99559
(907) 543-3521
Mary Stachelrodt, Director
Description: Exhibits Yup'ik Eskimo artifacts of southwest Alaska, such as baskets, clothing, utensils, ceremonial regalia, masks, and other items of historical value. Programs: Elder Mentor Program; Community Educational Programming Outreach; Interactive Exhibitions & Seasonal Yup'ik Ceremonies & Festivals.

UNIVERSITY OF ALASKA MUSEUM
Box 95351, 907 Yukon Dr.
COLLEGE 99708
(907) 474-7505
Basil C. Hedrick, Director
Description: Collection of Eskimo artifacts by Otto Geist. Tlingit, Athapascan and Aleut material on exhibit.

SAMUEL K. FOX MUSEUM
P.O. Box 273, Seward & D Sts.
DILLINGHAM 99576
(907) 842-2322 Fax 842-5691
Lynn M. Fox, Director/Curator
Phil Pryse, Curator
Description: Located in the Dillingham Public Library Building, the museum houses southwest Yup'ik Eskimo arts and crafts, and Siberian Yup'ik and Inupiak Eskimo artifacts. Also a collection of art from the late Eskimo artist Sam Fox.

DILLINGHAM HERITAGE MUSEUM
Pouch 202
DILLINGHAM 99576
 (907) 842-5601/5221
 Irma O'Brien, Coordinator
 Norma Adkison, Chairwoman
Description: Alaskan Indian museum with south-west Yup'ik Eskimo arts and crafts, and Siberian Yup'ik and Inupiak Eskimo artifacts.

ALASKA NATIVE VILLAGE MUSEUM
P.O. Box 80583, Alaskaland Park
FAIRBANKS 99708

ALASKA INDIAN ARTS, INC.
P.O. Box 271, 23 Fort Seward Dr.
HAINES 99827
 (907) 766-2160
 Carl W. Heinmiller, Executive Director
Description: Indian Living Village Museum, collection of Tlingit Indian costumes and art; Chilkat Indian dancing. Small reference library.

SHELDON MUSEUM & CULTURAL CENTER
P.O. Box 269
HAINES 99827
 (907) 766-2366
 Lynette Jentoft-Nilsen, Director
 Cynthia L. Jones, Curator
Description: Historical and Tlingit art museum, depicting the Tlingit Indian culture and history of the Upper Lynn Canal (northern part of Southeast Alaska). Tlingit artifacts, including blankets, baskets, costumes, and implements. *Special programs*: Movies/slide shows; Haines Mission (Indian school/orphanage); travelling & special exhibits-often including native artists; school programs; Tlingit Indian Week. *Publications*: A Personal Look at the Sheldon Museum; Haines: The First Century; The Tlingit Indian; Journey to the Tlingits; historical monographs about local history and Tlingit culture. *Publication*: Journey to the Tlingits. Library. Founded 1975 (public).

ALASKA STATE MUSEUM
Pouch FM, 395 Whittier St.
JUNEAU 99811
 (907) 465-2901
Description: Maintains a collection of more than 10,000 objects relating to the Eskimo, Tlingit, Northwest Coast, Athapascan, Aleut, and Haida. *Publications*: Newsletter; Northern Notebook Series; classroom materials for learning kits.

SEALASKA GALLERY CULTURAL MUSEUM
Sealaska Plaza Bldg.
JUNEAU 99801

KENAI HISTORICAL SOCIETY & MUSEUM
P.O. Box 1348
KENAI 99611

KETCHIKAN INDIAN MUSEUM
P.O. Box 5454
KETCHIKAN 99901

TONGASS HISTORICAL MUSEUM
629 Dock St.
KETCHIKAN 99901
 (907) 225-5600
 Virginia McGillvray, Director
Description: Collections on Indian artifacts, objects and photos relating to the Tlingit, Haida and Tsimshian cultures. Totem Heritage Center-totem poles and fragments from Tlingit Villages of Village Island and Tongass Island, and from Haida

Village. *Publications*: Growth in Southeast Alaska Natives Look to the Future; quarterly newsletter. Library.

TOTEM HERITAGE CENTER
629 Dock St.
KETCHIKAN 99901
 (907) 225-5600 Fax 225-5075
 Roxanna Adams, Museum Director
Description: City of Ketchikan's museum department and archives holdings include photographs on all Alaska villages with totem poles; index to all Alaska totem poles; vertical file on Northwest Coast Indian art and culture. Covers Tlingit, Haida and Tsimshian tribes - art, anthjropology, totem poles. *Programs*: Art and crafts slides available for use; lecture series on traditional Alaska Native arts and culture.

BARANOV MUSEUM
Erskine House, 101 Marine Way
KODIAK 99615
 (907) 486-5920
 Peggy Dyson, President
Description: Collections include items from the Kodiak and Aleutian Islands and Eskimo artifacts.

KOTZEBUE MUSEUM, INC.
P.O. Box 46
KOTZEBUE 99752
 (907) 442-3401 Fax 442-3742
 Gene Moore, Manager
Description: Contains Eskimo artifacts, arts and crafts, costumes, and Indian artifacts.

NANA MUSEUM OF THE ARCTIC
P.O. Box 49
KOTZEBUE 99752
 (907) 442-3301 Fax 442-2866
 Phyllis Short, Director
Description: Inupiat Museum of the Arctic houses land and sea mammal exhibits, arts & crafts, technical diorama & slide presentations. *Activities*: Eskimo dancers and a traditional Eskimo Blanket Toss. *Program*: Maintains a multi-media interpretive program explaining traditional Inupiat skills and culture. Founded 1980.

DUNCAN COTTAGE MUSEUM
P.O. Box 282, Duncan St.
Annette Island Reserve
METLAKATLA 99926
 LaVerne Welcome, Director/Curator
Description: Historic House, 1894--home of Father William Duncan, missionary teacher of the Tsimshian Indian people of Metlakatla.

BRISTOL BAY REGIONAL MUSEUM
P.O. Box 152
NAKNEK 99633

KUZHGIE CULTURAL CENTER MUSEUM
P.O. Box 949
NOME 99762

CARRIE McLAIN MUSEUM
P.O. Box 53
NOME 99762
 (907) 443-2566
 Marlene Carpenter, Director
Description: Old Eskimo artifacts. Library.

CLAUSEN MEMORIAL MUSEUM
203 Fram St., Box 708
PETERSBURG 99833
 (907) 772-3598

Michale Edgington, Director
Description: Collections contain material on Tlingit Indians, including canoes and tools.

SELDOVIA NATIVE ASSOCIATION
Fine Arts and Cultural Center Museum
P.O. Box 201
SELDOVIA 99663

SHELDON JACKSON MUSEUM
104 College Dr.
SITKA 99835
 (907) 747-8981 Fax 747-3004
 Karen R. Crane, Director
 Bruce Kato & Peter Corey, Curators
Description: Museum is the oldest museum in the state of Alaska and is housed in the first concrete building erected in Alaska. Features Alaskan Eskimo, Aleut, Athapascan, Tlingit, Haida and Tsimshian artifacts and Alaskan history collections (period 1888-1930). *Special collections*: Argillite carvings; 400 Eskimo dance masks. *Publications*: Spruce Root Basketry of the Alaska Tlingit; Tlingit Women's Root Basket; Faces, Voices & Dreams: Centennial of the Sheldon Jackson Museum; Tlingit Ways of Long Ago; Tlingit Legends. Library. Museum Shop. Established in 1887.

SOUTHEAST ALASKA INDIAN CULTURAL CENTER
106 Metlakatla St.
SITKA 99835
 (907) 747-8061
 Ellen Hays, Executive Director
Description: Displays native arts produced in the Center over the past 20 years, including wood carving, silverwork, costumes, and robes. *Activities*: Audiovisual programs; Provides demonstrations of traditional native arts such as woodcarving, costume design, and metalworking that are representative of the Tlingit people and Southeast Alaska. Established 1968.

SITKA NATIONAL HISTORICAL PARK
106 Metlakatla, P.O. Box 738
SITKA 99835
 (907) 747-6281
 Michele M. Hellickson, Supt.
 Sue Thorsen, Curator
Description: A collection of more than 4,000 artifacts; totem poles and Chilkat Robes; traditional native arts such as woodcarving, costume design, and metalworking. *Publication*: Carved History: A Guide to the Totem Poles of Sitka National Historical Park. Library.

SHAKES ISLAND TRIBAL HOUSE OF THE BEAR
P.O. Box 868
WRANGELL 99929
 (907) 874-3747
 Margaret Sturtevant, Curator
Description: Indian Museum housed in Tribal House with exhibits of costumes, Tlingit totem poles, ancient wood carving. *Publication*: Guide to Shakes Island.

WRANGELL MUSEUM
Box 2050, 1126 Second St.
WRANGELL 99929
 (907) 874-3770
 Pat Green, Director/Curator
Description: Displays Tlingit totem poles and artifacts; photo collection. *Publication*: The History of Chief Shakes and His Clan; newsletter.

ARIZONA

BISBEE MINING & HISTORICAL MUSEUM
5 Cooper Queen Plaza, Box 12
BISBEE 85603
 (602) 432-7071

**MONTEZUMA CASTLE
NATIONAL MONUMENT**
P.O. Box 219
CAMP VERDE 86322
 (602) 567-3322
 Glen E. Henderson, Supt.
Description: Prehistoric Pueblo Indian ruins. *Museum*: Indian artifacts obtained from the Monument excavations. Library.

**YAVAPAI-APACHE
VISITOR ACTIVITY CENTER**
P.O. Box 219
CAMP VERDE 86322
 (602) 567-5276
Description: Exhibits depict historic and contemporary Indian lifestyles. *Programs*: A slide presentation of area's prhistoric Indian cultures and a film on the Yavapai-Apache tribe.

CANYON DE CHELLY NATIONAL MONUMENT
P.O. Box 588
CHINLE 86503
 (602) 674-5436 Fax 674-3439
 Roger Siglin, Supt.
Description: Displays Anasazi and Navajo Indian artifacts from the area. A National Historic Landmark. Library. Bookstore.

TUZIGOOT NATIONAL MONUMENT
P.O. Box 68
CLARKDALE 86324
 (602) 634-5564
 Glen E. Henderson, Supt.
Description: Remnants of prehistoric town built by the Sinagua Indians who farmed Arizona's Verde Valley between 1125-1400 A.D. Museum: Exhibits artifacts found during excavations. Library.

**CASA GRANDE RUINS
NATIONAL MONUMENT**
1100 N. Ruins Dr.
COOLIDGE 85228
 (602) 723-3172 Fax 723-7209
 Sam R. Henderson, Supt.
Museum: Located on the Hohokam village site of 500-1450 A.D.; contains pre-Columbian Pueblo and Hohokam Indian artifacts; ethnological material of the Pima and Papago Indians—basketry and pottery. A National Historic Landmark. Library.

THE AMERIND FOUNDATION
P.O. Box 248
DRAGOON 85609
 (602) 586-3666
 Dr. Anne I. Woosley, Director
 Allan J. McIntyre, Curator
Archaeology and Ethnology Museum: Maintains collections of archaeological specimens from the Southwest and northern Mexico; ethnological material from the Southwest, Pacific Northwest, Great Plains, Eastern Woodlands, California, and the Arctic; includes Hopi ceremonial kachina art. *Programs*: Archaeological field work, seminars, docent training, museum interpretation, and artifact preservation. Publishes the results of its research jointly with the University of New Mexico. Library. Founded 1937.

ARIZONA HISTORICAL SOCIETY
2340 N. Fort Valley Rd.
FLAGSTAFF 86001
 (602) 774-6272
Description: Maintains museum and library with collections on Native American history & culture.

MUSEUM OF NORTHERN ARIZONA
Route 4, Box 720
FLAGSTAFF 86001
 (602) 774-5211
 Philip M. Thompson, Director
Description: Exhibits the arts and artifacts of the Indians of Northern Arizona, with specific reference to the Hopi and Navajo. Annual art show. Book store. *Publication*: Plateau, quarterly journal; bimonthly newsletter; Archaeological Research Papers; bulletins. Library.

MALMUT CANYON NATIONAL MONUMENT
Route 1, Box 25
FLAGSTAFF 86001
 (602) 526-3367
 T. Dwayne Collier, Supt.
Description: Located on the site of approximately 400 prehistoric Indian ruins of the Sinagua Indians dating back to 1100-1270 A.D. Displays artifacts excavated from the site. Library.

WALNUT CANYON NATIONAL MONUMENT
Walnut Canyon Rd.
FLAGSTAFF 86004
 (602) 526-3367
 Sam Henderson, Supt.
Description: A park museum located onthe site of prehistoric ruins of the Sinagua Indian culture.

**WUPATKI & SUNSET CRATER
NATIONAL MONUMENT**
HC 33, Box 444A
FLAGSTAFF 86001
 (602) 527-7152 Fax 556-7154
 Henry L. Jones, Supt.
 Anna Fender, Chief Ranger
Description: Exhibits four sets of ruins: Lomaki, Nalakihu-Citadel, Wuwoki, and Wupatki. Displays artifacts excavated from the ruins. Library.

FORT APACHE CULTURAL CENTER
P.O. Box 507
FORT APACHE 85926

**HUBBELL TRADING POST
NATIONAL HISTORIC SITE**
P.O. Box 150
GANADO 86505
 (602) 755-3475
 Charles D. Wyatt, Supt.
 Shirley Harding, Curator
Description: The oldest continually operating Indian trading post (1878) maintains artifacts related to Lorenzo Hubbell - his historic 1902 home and furnishings are part of the collection. Extensive collections of Native American and Southwest art on display. *Special programs*: Navajo rug weaving and silversmithing demonstrations; tours; buying and selling Navajo, Hopi, Pueblo, Zuni and other tribal crafts. Library. Established 1967.

GILA COUNTY HISTORICAL MUSEUM
Box 2891, 1330 N. Broad St.
GLOBE 85502
 (602) 425-7385
 Rayna Barela, Director
Description: Maintains prehistoric Salado Indian artifacts (1125-1400 A.D.) Library.

TUSAYAN RUIN AND MUSEUM
Grand Canyon National Park
P.O. Box 129
GRAND CANYON 86023
 (602) 638-7701
 Robert S. Chandler, Supt.
 Carolyn Richard, Curator
Description: Exhibits artifacts from the Tusayan prehistoric ruins; over 200,000 objects in six areas: archaeology, history, geology, ethnography, biology and paleontology Library. A National Historic Landmark. Established 1919.

MOHAVE MUSEUM OF HISTORY & ARTS
400 W. Beale St.
KINGMAN 86401
 (602) 753-3195
 Robert R. Yost, Director
 Karin Goudy, Photographs
 Mona Cochran, Library & Archives
Description: The Walapai Room: Houses a life size Indian wickieup and figures, Hopi kachinas; also Hualapai, Mohave basketry and pottery. Mohave Miniature: A miniature rendition of a typical Mohave Indian Village. *Publication*: The History of Mohave County to 1912; monthly newsletter, Mohave Epic. Research Library. Established 1960.

**AK-CHIN INDIAN HIM-DAK
MUSEUM/ARCHIVES**
P.O. Box 897
MARICOPA 85239
 (602) 568-9480
 Elaine F. Peters, Director
Description: Maintains 8,000 square feet of Ak-Chin artifacts - over 700 boxes of artifacts on exhibit and storage. *Archives*: Ak-Chin Tribal Records from early 1900's to present. *Special program*: Language programs. Tribal newsletter. Library. Established 1990.

COLORADO RIVER INDIAN TRIBES MUSEUM
Route 1, Box 23-B
PARKER 85344
 (602) 669-9211 Ext. 335 Fax 669-5675
 Betty L. Cornelius, Executive Director
Description: Indian Museum displaying Mohave, Chemehuevi, Navajo and Hopi artifacts, including pottery, baskets, silver, wool rugs, fine arts, Kachinas, beadwork; also prehistoric Mogollon, Anasazi, Hohokam and Patayan collections. *Special collections/exhibits*: Chemehuevi Basket Collection; Mohave Pottery; historical information; Old Presbyterian Indian Church; Mohave and Chemehuevi Archives. Library. Established 1966

HUALAPAI TRIBAL MUSEUM
P.O. Box 179
PEACH SPRINGS 86434

THE HEARD MUSEUM
22 E. Monte Vista Rd.
PHOENIX 85004-1480
 (602) 252-8840 Fax 252-9757
 Herbert Bool, President
 Martin Sullivan, Ph.D., Director
 Diana Pardue, Curator of Collections
 Margaret Archuleta, Curator of Fine Arts
 Gloria Lomahaftewa, Assistant Curatorr
 Mario Nick Klimiades, Librarian/Archivist
Description: Anthropology and art museum exhibiting works by American Indians; Paintings, prints, sculpture, and the finest in contemporary craft arts are regularly on exhibit, as well as an extensive exhibit of historic materials from the Southwest. Southwestern archaeological and ethnological

collection of more than 30,000 objects, and includes artifacts from North American Indian tribes, as well as native cultures of South America, Asia, and Africa. The Museum staf f has developed social studies instructional materials. *Special collections*: Hopi Kachina dolls, and Navajo rugs and blankets. *Special programs*: Guided tours; lectures; workshops; annual Indian Fair and Market; Speakers Bureau; films; traveling exhibitions-Artist & Performers on the Road. *Publication*: Earth Song, Museum membership newsletter; variety of catalogues accompanying exhibitions. Library . Established 1929.

**PUEBLO GRANDE MUSEUM
& CULTURAL PARK**
4619 E. Washington St.
PHOENIX 85034-1909
(602) 495-0901
Roger W. Lidman, Director
Barbara Moulard & Holly Young, Curators
Description: Archaeological site museum containing exhibits of prehistoric Hohokam cultural material, circa A.D. 500 to A.D. 1450. Ethnographic material from the Indians of the Greater Southwest. *Special programs*: Annual Indian market; how-to workshops taught by Native-Americans. *Publications*: Volume I, Pueblo Grande Museum Anthropology Papers; museum brochures and catalogs. Library. Established 1929.

SMOKI MUSEUM
N. Arizona Ave., Box 10224
PRESCOTT 86301
(602) 445-1230
Description: Indian Museum featuring artifacts of the Tuzigoot, King and Fitzmaurice ruins. Paintings. Annual Indian ceremonials.

TONTO NATIONAL MONUMENT
Hwy. 88, P.O. Box 707
ROOSEVELT 85545
(602) 467-2241 Fax 467-2225
Carol Kruse, Supt.
Description: Prehistoric Salado Indian Clif f Dwellings in Sonoran Desert setting. *Museum*: Collection of prehistoric Salado Indian artifacts--pottery , cloth, tools, etc. Library .

GILA RIVER ARTS & CRAFTS MUSEUM
P.O. Box 457
SACATON 85247
(602) 963-3981
Description: Contains a park with reconstructed Indian villages that depict more than 2,000 years of Native American life in the Gila River Basin. The Hohokum, Papago, and Apache cultures are represented. A museum and craft center adjoin the park.

HOPI CULTURAL CENTER MUSEUM
P.O. Box 7
SECOND MESA 86043
(602) 734-6650

MUSEUM OF ANTHROPOLOGY
Eastern Arizona College
626 Church St.
THATCHER 85552
(602) 428-1133
Betty Graham Lee, Director
Description: Displays artifacts from Mogollon, Anasazi and Hohokam material culture; ethnographics in Apache, Navajo & Hopi. Library .

NAVAJO NATIONAL MONUMENT
HC 71, Box 3
TONALEA 86044
(602) 672-2366 Fax 672-2345
Stephen Miller , Supt.
Description: Exhibits materials of the Kayenta, Anasazi and Navajo cultures. On the site of three prehistoric Clif f Villages. Library . Arts and crafts for sale.

THE NED A. HATATCHLI CENTER MUSEUM
Navajo Community College
TSAILE 86556

ARIZONA STATE MUSEUM
University of Arizona
TUCSON 85721
(602) 621-6281
Dr. Raymond H. Thompson, Director
Jan Bell, Curator of Collections
Dr. R.G. Vivian & Dr. Paul Fish,
Curators of Archaeology
Dr. Nancy J. Parezo, Curator of Ethnology
Description: Permanent exhibits on the prehistoric and contemporary American Indian cultures of the Southwest - about 22,000 specimens of U.S. Southwestern and northwest Mexican ethnographic items; approximately 150,000 archaeological items, notably Hohokam items, artifacts of the Anasazi and Mogollon cultures; about 225,000 photographic items. *Publication*: The Kiva; Museum Archaeological Series; informational pamphlets and popular booklets. Library . Established1893.

MISSION SAN XAVIER DEL BAC
Route 11, Box 645
TUCSON 85706
(602) 294-2624
Father Kieran McCarthy , Rector
Description: Historic building and site of the Spanish-Colonial Indian Mission of 1783. Library .

**WESTERN ARCHAEOLOGICAL
& CONSERVATION CENTER**
Box 41058, 1415 N. Sixth Ave.
TUCSON 85717
(602) 792-6501
Carol A. Martin, Chief
Description: Displays Southwestern prehistoric and ethnographic artifacts. Publications. Library .

COCHISE VISITOR CENTER & MUSEUM
c/o Willcox Chamber of Commerce
1500 N. Circle I Rd.
WILLCOX 85643
(602) 384-2272
Description: Collections include Apache Indian artifacts.

NAVAJO TRIBAL MUSEUM
P.O. Box 308, Hwy . 264
WINDOW ROCK 86515
(602) 871-6673
Russell P. Hartman, Director/Curator
Description: Exhibits approximately 4,500 objects relating to the history and culture of the Navajo Indians and the prehistory and natural history of the Four-Corners area. Photo archive of about 35,000 negatives and prints, mostly from 1930-1960, relating to the Navajos. *Special programs*: Art exhibits/sales; Navajo information service; school and group tours. Publications.

ARKANSAS

THE UNIVERSITY MUSEUM
338 Hotz Hall
University of Arkansas
FAYETTEVILLE 72701
Johnnie L. Gentry , Jr., Director
Description: Exhibits material relative to Arkansas Indians. Publications. Library .

HOT SPRINGS NATIONAL PARK
P.O. Box 1860
HOT SPRINGS 71901
Description: Interpretive programs about the life of the Caddo Indians and their predecessors and explains the use of the thermal springs by the Indians. *Museum*: Exhibits Indian artifacts. *Publications*: Indians of Tonico; The Valley of the Vapors.

MUSEUM OF SCIENCE & HISTORY
MacArthur Park
LITTLE ROCK 72202
Description: Exhibits include material relating to Arkansas Mound Builders, American Plains Indians, and Southwestern Indians. Library .

KA-DO-HA INDIAN VILLAGE
P.O. Box 669, Route 1
MURFREESBORO 71958
(501) 285-3736
Sam Johnson, Director
Description: Prehistoric Caddo Indian (Mound Builders) grounds with museum housing artifacts from the excavation of the site. Publications for sale. Library.

TOLTEC MOUNDS STATE PARK
490 Toltec Mounds Rd.
SCOTT 72141
(501) 961-9442
Jack Pratt, Supt.
Jama Best & Hollie Holmes, Interpreters
Description: Situated in the modern farmlands of the Arkansas River Valley, 16 miles southeast of North Little Rock, of f US Hwy. 165, are the remains of a large group of ancient Indian earthworks known as Toltec Mounds. Maintains a collection of prehistoric artifacts of the Plum Bayou Indian culture. Designated a National Historic Landmark in 1978, Toltec contained 16 mounds a century ago. Today, several mounds and a remnant of the embankment are visible. *Activities*: Archaeological research and interpretive programs. *Publication*: Emerging Patterns of the Plum Bayou Culture. Established 1975.

ARKANSAS STATE UNIVERSITY MUSEUM
P.O. Box 490
STATE UNIVERSITY 72467
(501) 972-2074
Charlott A. Jones, Ph.D., Director
Description: Displays Native-American artifacts including Arkansas--Quapaw, Caddo, Osage, Cherokee, Choctaw and Chickasaw; Southwestern-- Navajo, Hopi, Pueblo and Apache; and an exhibit of Indian baskets and Indian dolls. Newsletter. Library.

CALIFORNIA

MALKI MUSEUM, INC.
11-795 Fields Rd.
Morongo Indian Reservation
BANNING 92220
(714) 849-7289
Katherine Siva Saubel, President
Matt Pablo, Director/Curator
Description: Adobe museum building housing Southern California Indian artifacts of the Cahuilla, Serrano, Luiseno, and other tribal groups; large collection of Indian basketry. *Programs*: College scholarship program for Southern California Indian students; research on California Indians; Annual Malki Museum fiesta on Sunday of Labor Day weekend. *Publications*: Journal of California and Great Basin Anthropology, twice annually; brochures on the Cahuilla, Serrano, Chemehuevi and Chumash; Malki Museum Press publishes books on the California Indians. Library. Established 1964.

ROBERT H. LOWIE MUSEUM OF ANTHROPOLOGY
103 Kroeber Hall, University of California
BERKELEY 94720
(415) 642-3681
James J. Deetz, Curator
Description: Research and study collections include California archaeological and ethnographical items, majority of which are basketry items representing practically every tribe in California; also Eskimo and Aleut material, and Plains Indian artifacts; large collections of baskets and carvings from Northwest Coast tribes, especially Haida, Tlingit and Tsimshean. Also an extensive collection of recorded materials. Library.

OWENS VALLEY PAIUTE-SHOSHONE INDIAN CULTURAL CENTER MUSEUM
P.O. Box 1281
BISHOP 93514

BEARCLOUD GALLERY & MIWOK HERITAGE MUSEUM
Box 308, 11175 Damin Rd.
COLUMBIA 95310
(209) 532-5869
Tom White Eagle, Director/Curator
Description: Artifacts and photos from local area Rancherias. Small library of books on Miwok culture and surrounding tribes. Established in 1989.

CARL NELSON GORMAN MUSEUM
2401 Hart Hall, Native American Studies
University of California
DAVIS 95616
(916) 752-6567
George Longfish, Director
Theresa Horlan, Curator
Description: Maintains a permanent collection of California basketry, Navajo weavings, and contemporary American Indian art, and shows works by Indian and Chicano artists as well as staff and students. *Special program*: Changing exhibitions program - 4 each year with speciific focus on American Indian issues. *Publications*: Artist monographs for each exhibition with interviews with the artists.

CABOT'S OLD INDIAN PUEBLO MUSEUM CALIFORNIA INDIAN MONUMENT
67-616 E. Desert View Ave., Box 1267
DESERT HOT SPRINGS 92240

(619) 329-7610 Fax 329-1956
Colbert H. Eyraud, President & Chief Curator
Description: A four story Hopi Indian style Pueblo built by Cabot Yerxa as a tribute to the Indian cultures; Peter Toth sculpture–monument 43' high, 20 tons from a Sequoia redwood; Pueblo Art Gallery. *Exhibits*: Inuit collection; and Sioux collection from the Battle of the Little Big Horn; Chumash and Pueblo culture collections. *Special programs*: Slide and lecture presentations to schools and organizations; sculpting for the handicapped; single artist exhibitions; arts interview radio show. *Publication*: Musings From the Pueblo. Trading Post. Library. Established 1968.

HOOPA TRIBAL MUSEUM
P.O. Box 1348
HOOPA 95546
(916) 625-4110
David E. Hostler, Curator
Description: A living museum which maintains a collection of baskets from the Hupa, Yurok and Karuk tribes; also jewlery, artifacts, and Indian dance regailia with feathers used in the dances. Special programs: Ceremonial displays, cultural shows and village tours. Publications: Museum brochures; Hoopa history books and pamphlets. Established 1972.

EASTERN CALIFORNIA MUSEUM
155 N. Grant St., Box 206
INDEPENDENCE 93526
(619) 878-2411 Ext. 2258
William H. Michael, Director
Description: Collections of Inyo County Paiute, Shoshone, Washoe and Yokut Indian artifacts, including basketry, beadwork and lithics. *Publication*: Quarterly newsletter; book - Mountains to Desert: Selected Inyo Readings. Library. Established 1928.

CABAZON CULTURAL MUSEUM
Cabazon Band of Mission Indians
84-245 Indio Springs Dr.
INDIO 92203
(619) 342-2593 Fax 347-7880

END OF THE TRAIL MUSEUM-TREES OF MYSTERY
15500 Highway 101 North
KLAMATH 95548
(707) 482-2251
John Thompson, Gen. Mgr. (Trees of Mystery)
Coleen Kelley Marks & Marylee Smith, Curators
Description: Private museum permanently exhibiting the collection of Marylee Smith (over 2,000 objects. Extensive collection of Indian baskets, clothing, tools, kachinas, Navajo rugs, Northwest Coast carvings, pottery, masks. *Special collection*: extensive collection of baby baskets and cradles from entire North American Continent. Research library. Established in 1983.

ANTELOPE VALLEY INDIAN MUSEUM
1051 Avenue M #201
LANCASTER 93535
(805) 942-0662

THE LOMPOC MUSEUM
200 South H St.
LOMPOC 93436
(805) 736-3888
Debra D. Argel, Director & Curator of Anthro.
Carol Fisher, Education
Donna Whitney, Admin. Asst.
Description: Holds a large collection of archaeo-

logical and ethnographic specimens, mostly from northern Santa Barbara County. Other areas include northern California and Oregon. *Special collection*: Clarence Ruth Collection: Chumash and western Alaskan Indian artifacts. *Publication*: Galleries, bi-monthly newsletter. Library. Established 1969.

GENE AUTRY WESTERN HERITAGE MUSEUM
4700 Western Heritage Way
LOS ANGELES 90027
(213) 667-2000

NATURAL HISTORY MUSEUM OF LOS ANGELES
900 Exposition Blvd.
LOS ANGELES 90007
(213) 744-3414

SOUTHWEST MUSEUM
234 Museum Dr., Box 41558
LOS ANGELES 90041
(213) 221-2164 Fax 224-8223
Dr. Kathleen Whitaker, Chief Curator
Description: Collections focus on native people of the Americas including 250,000 artifacts pertaining to the American Indian, Eskimo, and Aleut from prehistoric, historic and modern times; 150,000 photographs; archival materials; paintings, and prints. Special collections on the Plains, California, Southwest, and Northwest Indians. *Special program*: Intertribal Marketplace (over 200 artisans) in November; Urban American Indian Art Competition & Exhibition, in May. *Publication*: The Masterkey, quarterly journal. Library. Museum shop.

MARIPOSA MUSEUM & HISTORY CENTER
5119 Jessie St.
MARIPOSA 95338
(209) 966-2924
Muriel Powers, Curator
Description: Located on the museum grounds is an Indian Village and its bark houses and sweat house, constructed by local Indians. Publication: Quaterly newsletter. Library.

MONTEREY STATE HISTORICAL PARK
20 Custom House Plaza
MONTEREY 93940
(408) 649-2836
Mary Wright, Director; Kris Quist, Curator
Description: Holman Exhibit of American Indian Artifacts. Primarily California and Western North America basketry and weavings.

SIERRA MONO MUSEUM
P.O. Box 275
NORTH FORK 93643

MARIN MIWOK MUSEUM
P.O. Box 864, 2200 Novato Blvd.
NOVATO 94947
(510) 897-4064
Mary Hilderman Smith, Executive Director
Dawn Carlson, Chairperson
Description: Collections oriented to Native-American cultures of western North America, with particular emphasis on Indian cultures of California, especially local Coast Miwok people of Marin and southern Sonoma Counties. The Kettenhofen Collection of Edward Curtis Photogravures. Includes archival materials from Alaska. *Special program*: Educational classes, lectures, and instruction. *Publication*: Surface Scatter, quarterly newsletter. Library. Founded 1973.

THE OAKLAND MUSEUM
1000 Oak St.
OAKLAND 94607
(510) 834-2413
Description: Exhibits present native Californians in pre-contact times.

WILL ROGERS STATE HISTORIC PARK
PACIFIC PALISADES 90272
(213) 454-8212
  Pam Raffetto, Curator
Description: Ranch belonged to the American humorist, Will Rogers (of Cherokee Indian descent), containing original buildings and furnishings; Indian artifacts, rugs and blankets. *Publication*: Monthly newsletter. Library. Founded 1944.

CUPA CULTURAL CENTER
Temecula Rd., Box 1
PALA 92059
Description: Located on the Pala Indian Reservation in San Diego County, the Cultural Center maintains a museum, library and work areas for crafts, and classroom space.

**MUSEUM OF MISSION
SAN ANTONIO DE PALA**
P.O. Box 70
PALA 92059
  (619) 742-3317
Description: Historic Mission Building (Pala Indians.) Exhibits Indian artifacts--basketry, stone carvings, pottery and jewelry. *Activities*: Dance festivals.

PALM SPRINGS DESERT MUSEUM
101 Museum Dr.
PALM SPRINGS 92263
(619) 325-7168

REDDING MUSEUM OF ART & HISTORY
P.O. Box 990427
REDDING 96099
(916) 225-4155
  Patricia Leach, Director
Description: California contemporary art collection; history collection; large textile and clothing collection; Native American basketry (approximately 1,100 pieces) and artifacts; also pre-Columbian artifacts; North American ethnographic materials Special programs: tours; outreach to schools; Spring Lawn Festival for children; Fall Art & Craft Fair; regional artists. Reference Library. Publications: Monthly newsletter; occasional papers. Established 1963.

SAN BERNARDINO COUNTY MUSEUM
2024 Orange Tree Lane
REDLANDS 92374
(714) 798-8570
  Dr. Allan Griesemer, Director
  Carol Rector, Curator of Anthropology
Description: Displays various artifacts and lithic tools of Indian occupation of San Bernardino County; history and artifacts of local bands--Serrano, Cahuilla, Mojave, Chemehuevi, and others are being preserved. *Publication*: Bi-monthly newsletter; quarterly journal. Library. Established in 1956.

SHERMAN INDIAN MUSEUM
Sherman Institute
9010 Magnolia Ave.
RIVERSIDE 92503

**CALIFORNIA STATE INDIAN MUSEUM
2618 K St.**
SACRAMENTO 95816
(916) 324-0971
  Mike Tucker, Area Manager
Description: Collections pertain to the cultures of the Indians of California. Pomo feather baskets; artifacts from Ishi; north coast redwood dugout. Emphasis is on lifestyle, spiritual and the continuing culture.

SAN DIEGO MUSEUM OF MAN
1350 El Prado, Balboa Park
SAN DIEGO 92101
Description: Exhibits on Indians of three Americas--collections of material culture, Indian habitats. Library.

AMERICAN INDIAN HISTORICAL SOCIETY
1451 Masonic Ave.
SAN FRANCISCO 94117
  Jeanette Henry Costo, Director
Description: Maintains a library and museum of Indian Arts. In the process of establishing the Rupert Costo Hall of American Indians at the University of California.

**JESSE PETER NATIVE AMERICAN
ART MUSEUM**
1501 Mendocino Ave.
SANTA ROSA 95401
(707) 527-4479
  Foley C. Benson, Director/Curator
  Lynn Fox, Exhibit Coordinator
Description: Collections of traditional Native-American art, including California basketry, Southwest pottery and basketry; Navajo textiles and jewelry; Plains, Plateau and Great Lakes beadwork; Eskimo and Arctic stone carvings and regalia; Living wall - photographic essay of Native Americans of today from several cultures; Pomo Roundhouse and baskets. Special program: Self-guided tours for elementary, secondary and college classes. *Publications*: Hopitu – A Collection of Kachina Dolls of the Hopi Indians; Straw Into Gold (North American Basketry) by Foley Benson. Small reference library. Established in 1932.

STANFORD UNIVERSITY MUSEUM OF ART
Lomita Dr.
STANFORD 94305
(415) 725-0462
  Thomas K. Seligman, Director
  Ruth W. Franklin, Curator
Description: Collection of Native American works, especially basketry of the Yurok, Karuk, and Hupa tribes of California; and a group of Haida argilites. Publication: Museum Journal, biennial. The main museum building is closed for repairs due to earthquake damage. Will reopen in 1997.

THE HAGGIN MUSEUM
1201 N. Pershing Ave.
STOCKTON 95203
(209) 462-4116
  Tod Ruhstaller, Director; Barry J. Ward, Archivist
Description: Fine art and regional history collections, including significnt displays on Native Americans of the area. Library. Publications. Established in 1931.

LAVA BEDS NATIONAL MONUMENT
P.O. Box 867
TULELAKE 96134
(916) 667-2282
  Gary Hathaway, Curator

Description: Site of the Modoc Indian War (November 1872 to June 1873.) *Museum*: Modoc Indian artifacts; Indian rock art and pictographs on walls of caves.

RINCON TRIBAL EDUCATION CENTER
P.O. Box 1147
VALLEY CENTER 92082

YOSEMITE MUSEUM
P.O. Box 577
YOSEMITE NATIONAL PARK 95389
(209) 372-0282
  David M. Forgang, Curator
  Craig D. Bates, Cuirator of Ethnography
Description: Collection of over 4,000 Sierra Miwok, Mono Lake Paiute and other ethnographic materials; over 20,000 archaeological specimens. A reconstructed Miwok/Paiute village depicts the traditional culture of the Miwok and Paiute people of the Yosemite region, from pre-contact times through present day. *Special Programs*: Annual summer Kaluga dance celebration; demonstrations of native crafts. *Publication*: Tradition and Innovation: A Basket History of the Indians of the Yosemite - Mono Lake Area. Library. Established in 1915.

SISKIYOU COUNTY MUSEUM
910 S. Main St.
YREKA 96097
(916) 842-3836
  Michael Hendryx, Director
Description: Contains displays on Indians of Siskiyou County--Modoc, Shasta, and Karuk. Maintains an extensive basket collection of the Karuk and Shasta tribes. *Special programs*: School program for 3rd graders; interpretive programs; field trips. Library. *Publications*: The Siskiyou Pioneer, 1947-1994; occasional paper series; technical leaflets - "Walking the Medicine Path," and "Plants & the People - Ethnobotany of the Karuk Tribe. Established in 1950.

COLORADO

ADAMS STATE COLLEGE MUSEUM
Richardson Hall
ALAMOSA 81102
(719) 589-7121 Fax 589-7522
  Dr. Joseph Hesbrook, Curator
Description: Exhibits Pueblo Indian cultural artifacts, primarily pottery; Navajo weaving.

SAND CREEK MASSACRE MONUMENT
Hwy. 96
CHIVINGTON 81031
Description: A monument to the over 500 Cheyenne Indians who were massacred in November 1864 by the U.S. Army led by Major John Chivington.

**THE TAYLOR MUSEUM FOR
SOUTHWESTERN STUDIES**
Colorado Springs Fine Arts Center
30 West Dale St.
COLORADO SPRINGS 80903
(719) 634-5581 Fax 634-0570
  Cathy L. Wright, Curator & Director
Description: Collections of Native-American arts of the Southwest, Pacific Northwest, Great Plains, Great Basin, and California, including: Navajo textiles and jewelry, Pueblo textiles, baskets and pottery, kachinas, and jewelry. *Special collection*: John

Frederick Huckel Collection of Navajo sandpainting reproductions. *Publications*: Navajo Sandpainting: The Huckel Collection; Arroyo Hondo: The Folk Art of a New Mexican Village; Pottery of the Pueblos of New Mexico, 1700-1940. Library .

COLORADO STATE MUSEUM
Colorado Historical Society
1300 Broadway
DENVER 80203
 (303) 866-3682
 Barbara Sudler , President
Description: Extensive ethnological and photographic collections of Plains and Southwest Indians; source materials on the Indian Wars; materials from the Rosebud Indian Agency, 1885 to 1890. *Publication*: The Colorado Magazine. Library .

DENVER ART MUSEUM
100 W. 14th Ave. Pkwy.
DENVER 80204
 (303) 575-2256
 Dr. Lewis Sharp, Director
 Richard Conn & Nancy Blomberg, Curators
Description: Collection of North American Indian art; also, an ethnographic collection of Indian women's costumes, Navajo and Pueblo pottery , Hopi kachina dolls, Blackfoot ceremonial equipment, and wood carvings of the Northwest Coast. *Special programs*: Lectures; programs for children; annual Pow-wow; and classes. *Publications*: Membership newsletter; exhibition and collection catalogues. Library .

DENVER MUSEUM OF NATURAL HISTORY
City Park
DENVER 80205
 (303) 370-6357
 Joyce L. Herold, Curator
Description: Hall of Prehistoric People of the Americas: Exhibits on early man, and collections of Paleo-Indian specimens. *Special collection*: Crane Collection of American Indian Materials.

ANASAZI HERITAGE CENTER
27501 Hwy. 184
DOLORES 81323
 (303) 882-4811
Description: Preserved sites of two late Anasazi communities. Exhibits of Anasazi farming, food preparation, crafts, and trade. Videos. Traveling exhibits.

HISTORICAL MUSEUM & INSTITUTE OF WESTERN COLORADO
4th and Ute
GRAND JUNCTION 81501
Special collections: Ute Indian Collection and Teller Indian School Collection: Basketry , artifacts, manuscripts and photographs of the Ute Indians. Library .

SOUTHERN UTE MUSEUM
Indian Cultural Center
Box 737, Hwy. 172
IGNACIO 81137
 (303) 563-9583 Fax 563-4033
 Lillian Selbel, Chairperson
Description: Located on the Southern Ute Indian reservation an d maintains photo and artifact collections pertaining to Ute Indians and other Native American tribes. *Activities*: It sponsors art festivals, Native American dance recitals, hobby workshops, and lectures. Gift Shop.

KOSHARE INDIAN MUSEUM
P.O. Box 580, 115 W. 18th
LA JUNTA 81050
 (719) 384-4411
 David Bailey, CEO
 J.F. Burshears, Executive Director
Description: Indian arts and crafts museum. *Publication*: Koshare News. Library . Indian arts and crafts for sale.

MANITOU CLIFF DWELLINGS MUSEUM
U.S. Hwy 24, Box 272
MANITOU 80829
 (719) 685-5242
Description: Depicts the lives and architectural achievements of the Indians of the Southwest during the Great Pueblo Period A,D, 1100-1300).

MESA VERDE NATIONAL PARK MUSEUM
MESA VERDE 81330
 (303) 529-4475 Fax 529-4465
 Donald C. Fiero, Chief of Interpretation
Description: A prehistoric Pueblo Indian community – pithouses, cliff dwellings, etc. Museum preserves Anasazi archaeological remains dating from 500-1330 A.D. Library.

UTE INDIAN MUSEUM- OURAY MEMORIAL PARK
17253 Chipeta Dr ., P.O. Box 1736
MONTROSE 81402
 (303) 249-3098
 Glen Gross, Director
Description: Indian History Museum located on the site of Chief Ouray's 400 acre farm. Depicts the history of the Utes through use of dioramas and objects which the Utes made and used; photographs and maps; portraits of some Ute leaders. *Activities*: Exhibits artifacts; maintains botanical gardens of plants used by the Native American Culture; vhanging exhibit gallery; lectures; and cultural fair in the Fall. *Publication*: Colorado History News. Established 1956.

UTE MOUNTAIN TRIBAL PARK
General Delivery
TOWAOC 81334

CONNECTICUT

CONNECTICUT HISTORICAL SOCIETY MUSEUM
1 Elizabeth St.
HARTFORD 06105
 (203) 236-5621
 Christopher P. Bickford, Executive Director
 Elizabeth Pratt Fox, Curator
Description: Collections of more than 100,000 artifacts, including Native American baskets, tools, and lithic materials. *Special collection*: Bates Collection of Native American baskets, tools, and implements. Library . *Publications*: Notes & News, newsletter; Bulletin, quarterly scholarly journal; numerous books relating to Connecticut. Established in 1825.

MUSEUM OF CONNECTICUT HISTORY
Connecticut State Library
231 Capitol Ave.
HARTFORD 06115
Special collection: George Mitchelson Collection: Contains pottery , tools, arrowheads, and other artifacts of Native-American culture of Connecticut. Library.

MASHANTUCKET PEQUOT MUSEUM & CULTURAL RESEARCH CENTER
P.O. Box 3060, Indiantown Rd.
LEDYARD 06339
 (203) 536-7200
 Terry Bell, Director
Description: A museum and cultural research center is in the planning stages and is scheduled to open around January 1, 1998. A 308,000 square-foot building located within the 350-year-old Pequot Village. There will be three main exhibits: the era up to European contact; th era of increasing aggression by the English, leading up to the Pequot Massacre of 1637; and what life at Mashantuckt has been like in the 350 years since. *Exhibits*: Dioramas of paleo or prehistoric era up to European contact; Clash of Cultures; The Mashantucket Pequots Today; photos, sculptures and craftwork, diaries and other documents, and tribal voices all will be used to personalize the museum. *Facilities*: Maintains a recreated Pequot village of 350 years ago; a circular theater which seats 100 people; research library; research laboratories; and herbarium; photo/technical rooms; a 300-seat auditorium; and gift shops.

EELS-STOW HOUSE
Milford Historical Society
34 High St., Box 337
MILFORD 06460
 (203) 874-2664
 Virginia Hoagland, President
Special collection: Claude C. Coffin Indian Collection: Indian relics and artifacts primarily from the Milford-Stratford area of southern Connecticut. Library.

TANTAQUIDGEON INDIAN MUSEUM
Rte. 32, 1819 Norwich-New London Rd.
UNCASVILLE 06382
 (203) 848-9145
 Gladys Tantaquidgeon, Owner/Curator
Description: Built in 1931 by the late John Tantaquidgeon and his son, Harold, direct descendents of Uncas, Chief of the once powerful Mohegan Nation. To preserve and perpetuate the history and traditions of the Mohegan and other Indian tribes. Displays objects of stone, bone, and wood made by Mohegan and other New England Indian artists and craftsmen, past and present. Established in 1931.

THE INSTITUTE FOR AMERICAN INDIAN STUDIES
38 Curtis Rd., P.O. Box 1260
WASHINGTON 06793-0260
 (203) 868-0518 Fax 868-1649
 Alberto C. Meloni, Director
 Lynne Williamson, Curator
Description: A research and education museum dedicated to discovering and interpreting our 10,000 year-old American Indian heritage—the history of Native-American people of the Northeast Woodlands. Algonkian Village-3 wigwams, a longhouse, a rock shelter and a garden. *Special Programs*: Educational services - Field Trips/Assemblies; craft workshops; lectures; training sessions; exhibitions. *Publications*: Artifacts, magazine; research reports; books: A Key Into the Language of Woodsplint Baskets; Native Harvests; and exhibition pamphlets. Library . Formerly The American Indian Archaeological Institute. Established in 1975.

**HISTORICAL MUSEUM OF THE
GUNN MEMORIAL LIBRARY**
Wykeham Rd. at the Green
WASHINGTON 06793
Description: Senator Orville Platt Memorial Indian
Room: Contains Indian artifacts--including more
than 100 baskets from many W estern tribes.

DELAWARE

NANTICOKE INDIAN MUSEUM
Route 4, Box 170A
MILLSBORO 19966
 (302) 945-7022
 Odette Wright, Curator
Description: Collection contains Native American
artifacts - clothing, baskets, pottery , etc. Special
programs for school groups. Annual Nanticoke
Pow-wow. Library. Established in 1984.

DISTRICT OF COLUMBIA

**INDIAN ARTS & CRAFTS BOARD
U.S. DEPT. OF INTERIOR ART MUSEUM**
Room 4004-MIB, U.S. Dept. of the Interior
18th & C Sts., NW
WASHINGTON 20240
 (202) 208-3773 Fax 208-6950
 Geoffrey E. Stamm, Acting General Manager
 Rosemary Ellison, Chief Curator
Description: Maintains collections of Native-Ameri-
can arts of the U.S. The Board's mission is to
promote the development of the creative work of
American Indians and Alaska Natives so that they
benefit economically from the demand for their
work. The Board operates three museums: Mu-
seum of the Plains Indian, Browning, Mont.; Sioux
Indian Museum, Rapid City , SD; and Southern
Plains Indian Museum, Anadarko, OK. *Publications*: Source Directory: American Indian and
Alaska Native Owned and Operated Arts and
Crafts Businesses; Native American Art Series;
bibliography. Established 1935.

NATIONAL ANTHROPOLOGICAL ARCHIVES
Smithsonian Institution
WASHINGTON 20560
 (202) 357-1976
 James R. Glenn, Director
Records and Manuscript Collections : Includes
vocabularies, grammatical data, and texts relating to Native-Americans; also, ethnographic and
archaeological field notes and drafts of reports,
and transcripts of oral history and of music. *Photographs Collection* : A general file of black and
white prints relating to the North American Indians. *Publication*: Monthly magazine. Library .

NATIONAL MUSEUM OF AMERICAN HISTORY
American Indian Program
Room 5119, Smithsonian Institution
WASHINGTON 20560
 (202) 357-1534
 Rayna Green, Program Manager
Description: Established in 1984 to of fer technical
assistance and cooperative support to American
Indian tribes and communities, as well as to other
educational and cultural institutions; produce exhibitions, publications, and educational and scholarly materials; sponsor research and training; develop collections, public programs, and collaborative initiatives on American Indians. *Special ac-*

tivities: Plans a major exhibition for the
"Quincentenary Program," that will focus on the
initial period of meeting between the Indian and
the European worlds.

**NATIONAL MUSEUM OF
THE AMERICAN INDIAN**
Smithsonian Institution - National Campaign
P.O. Box 65303
1130 Connecticut Ave., NW
WASHINGTON 20036
 (202) 357-3164
 W. Richard West, Jr., Director
 Doug Evelyn, Deputy Director
 Dan Agent, Public Affairs Specialist
 Pablita Abeyta, Cong. Liaison Of ficer
 Diane Gunn, Facilities Planning & Development
 Karen Fort, Exhibitions Project Manager
 Clara Sue Kidwell, Ass't Director for Curatorial

**NATIONAL MUSEUM OF NA TURAL HISTORY
NATIONAL MUSEUM OF MAN**
NHB 112, Smithsonian Institution
WASHINGTON 20560
 (202) 357-4760
 JoAllyn Archambault, Director
Description: Established in 1986 to serve as an
outreach program to Native American reservations
and communities; to make the Smithsonian more
accessible to Indian people; and to encourage
collection, research, exhibitions, and public programming by and about Indian peoples. Collection includes about 62,000 ethnological objects
representing historic Indian groups from all parts
of North America, and 250,000 archaeological
specimens; film and video materials of Native
Americans are part of the museum's Human Studies Film Archives and include historic film from the
early 20th century, as well as more recent ethnographic footage. In the Department of Anthropology are eight curators with research specialties in
North American Indian/Inuit ethnology , archaeology, linguistics, and ethnohistory . Supervised internships and research fellowships are available
through the Native American Awards Program.
Special activities: Planning a major exhibition for
the "Quincentenary Program," tentatively titled
"Seeds of Change," which will focus on the exchange of plants, animals, and diseases that occurred as a result of contact between the Old and
New Worlds/

SMITHSONIAN INSTITUTION
American Indian Museums Studies Program
Office of Museum Programs
Arts & Industries Bldg., Room 2235
WASHINGTON 20560
 (202) 357-3101
 Karen Cooper , Curriculum Projects Manager
Description: Provides information services, edu-
cational opportunities, and access to resources
to Native Americans and others who work closely
with the study and preservation of indigenous cul-
tures in the U.S. and abroad. *Special program* :
Quincentenary Programs - V arious activities and
programs relating to the 500th anniversary of the
Columbus voyages to the New W orld.

U.S. DEPT. OF THE INTERIOR MUSEUM
1849 C St., NW, MS 5412-MIB
WASHINGTON 20240
 (202) 208-4743
 Debra Berke, Director/Curator
Description: Exhibits include dioramas, scientific
specimens, and paintings. A collection of Native
American pottery , baskets, carvings, beadwork

and other artifacts such as kachinas and weavings.
Library. Established 1938.

FLORIDA

LOWE ART MUSEUM
University of Miami
1301 Miller Dr .
CORAL GABLES 33146
Description: Gallery's Barton Wing (Collection)
contains 4,000 items – blankets, Pueblo pottery ,
Plains Indian baskets, kachina dolls, jewelry , costumes and ceramics, largely of Southwestern origin. Publications. Library .

ST. LUCIE COUNTY HISTORICAL MUSEUM
414 Seaway Dr .
FORT PIERCE 33450
Description: Features Seminole Indian pictures,
artifacts and records from the Brighton Seminole
Indian Reservation. Sells Indian-made handicrafts.

INDIAN TEMPLE MOUND MUSEUM
Box 4009, 139 Miracle Strip Parkway
FORT WALTON BEACH 32549
 (904) 243-6521
 Steve Tuthill, Director
Description: Exhibits prehistoric Indian artifacts
found within a 40 mile radius of the museum are
displayed interpreting 10,000 years of Gulf Coast
living. The Temple Mound, a National Historic
Landmark, is the largest Mississippian Temple
Mound on the Gulf Coast. *Special programs* : Edu-
cational programs; guided tours. *Publications* : In-
dians of the Florida Panhandle; Pottery of the Fort
Walton Period; The Buck Burial Mound. Library .
Museum Shop.

JACKSONVILLE CHILDREN'S MUSEUM
1025 Gulf Life Dr .
JACKSONVILLE 32207
Description: Displays artifacts of the Florida Indians of the past and present, including the Seminole and Micosukee tribes. Research library .

**HISTORICAL MUSEUM
OF SOUTHERN FLORIDA**
101 W. Flagler St.
MIAMI 33130
 (305) 375-1492
 Randy Nimnicht, Executive Director
Description: A depository of maps, manuscripts,
and published materials of Southern Florida and
the Caribbean. Permanent and temporary exhibitions, 28,600 artifacts, including Seminole-
Miccosukee objects. *Programs* : Folklife programs,
research, off-site programs for all ages; annual
Harvest Festival. Publications. Library . Established
1940.

MICCOUSUKEE CUL TURAL CENTER
P.O. Box 44021, Tamiami Station
MIAMI 33144
 (305) 223-8380

PENSACOLA HISTORICAL MUSEUM
405 S. Adams St.
PENSACOLA 32501
Description: A collection of local Indian artifacts
from the prehistoric period through the late 19th-
century. A large collection relating to George
Medhurst Wratten, interpreter for Geronimo and
Apaches, and the Apaches as prisoners of war in
Florida and Alabama (manuscript form.) Library .

**SAN LUIS ARCHAEOLOGICAL
& HISTORIC SITE**
2020 W. Mission Rd.
TALAHASSEE 32399
(904) 487-3711/3655
Bonnie G. McEwan, Director
Description: An active dig that was on the site of a 17th century Apalachee Indian village and a Spanish mission. Maintains trails with interpretive displays describing the excavations and history of the site. The 50-acre outdoor museum of fers exhibits across the site, a visitor center and a history shop. Collection consists primarily of archaeological remains from the Apalachee and Spanish residents of the mission community. *Publications*: Apalachee: The Land Between the Rivers, by John Hann; and The Spanish Missions of La Florida, edited by Bonnie McEwan (University Press of Florida). Established in 1983.

SOUTHEAST ARCHAEOLOGICAL CENTER
P.O. Box 2416
TALLAHASSEE 32316
(904) 222-1167
Richard D. Faust, Chief

TALLAHASSEE JUNIOR MUSEUM, INC.
3945 Museum Dr.
TALLAHASSEE 32304
Special collection: Gundrum Collection: Displays reproductions of pre-Columbian Florida Indian pottery and weapons; Apalachee Indian Farm (Reconstructed.) *Publication*: Apalachee Indian Farm Guide.

SEMINOLE TRIBAL MUSEUM
5221 Orient Rd.
TAMPA 33610

GEORGIA

**KOLOMOKI MOUNDS
STATE PARK & HISTORIC SITE**
Route 1, Box 114
BLAKELY 31723
(912) 723-5296; 723-3398 (museum)
Lawrence Blankenship, Jr., Park Manager
Billy Adams, Interpretive Ranger
Description: Historic site--13th-century Indian burial mound and village--artifacts from the excavations are on display. About 1,300 acres located six mile north of Blakely of f Hwy. 27. Museum - exhibits artifacts and interprets the mounds and Indian culture. *Publication*: Report of the Excavations at Kolomoki. Established 1938.

NEW ECHOTA HISTORIC SITE
1211 Chatsworth Hwy. N.E.
CALHOUN 30701
(404) 629-8151
Frankie Mewborn, Supt.
Jeff Stancil, Curator
Description: A Preservation Project -- 1825 Capitol town of the Cherokee Nation. Museum and five historical buildings housing archaeological materials used by the Cherokees at New Echota in the early 1800's. *Research*: Cherokee genealogy; Trail of Tears. *Publication*: Early Georgia Spring 1954 - New Echota edition. Library. Established 1961.

ETOWAH INDIAN MOUNDS HISTORIC SITE
813 Indian Mounds Rd., S.W.
CARTERSVILLE 30120
(404) 387-3747

Libby Forehand Bell, Manager
Description: A National Historic Landmark. Large Indian site with seven mounds surrounded by a moat partially filled. Materials recovered from the excavations are on display. The Etowah Indians occupied the Valley between A.D. 700 and 1650. Several thousand Indians lived in this fortified town. Established 1953.

INDIAN SPRINGS MUSEUM
Indian Springs State Park
Route 1, Box 439, 678 Lake Clark Rd.
FLOVILLA 30216
(404) 775-7241
Don Coleman, Park Manager
Description: Traces the history of Indian Springs--items that reflect stages of Indian civilizations.. Includes the treaties signed, Chief McIntosh's Assassination; and exhibits Creek Indian artifacts. *Research*: Creek Indians in Georgia. *Special programs*: Indian sign language, hunting techniques, pottery, basket making, etc. Founded 1825.

OCMULGEE NATIONAL MONUMENT
1207 Emery Highway
MACON 31201
(912) 752-8257
Mark Corey, Supt.
Sylvia Flowers, Cultural Resource Specialist
Sam Lawson, Park Ranger/Interp. Specialist
Description: Site of seven mounds constructed by a group of farming Indians one thousand years ago. Located on the eastern edge of Macon, GA, along U.S. 80. An estimated 2,000 people lived here at one time. Archaeology Museum: Collections explain the culture of the Indians who constructed the area mounds, and of five other Indian groups that have inhabited the area since. Publications. Creek Indian Trading Post. Library. A National Historic Landmark. Established in 1936.

CHIEFTAINS MUSEUM
501 Riverside Pkwy.
ROME 30162
(404) 291-9494
Josephine Ransom, Director
Description: History museum housed in a 1794 log cabin, and an 1820 plantation house belonging to Cherokee leader Major Ridge. Contains items from archaic Indian occupation to the present. Artifacts reflect life style of a rapidly changing Indian society; story of removal to the west. Maintains rotating art and history exhibits, local history. *Special programs*: Lecture series; educational programs. *Publication*: Quarterly membership newsletter. Library. Established 1970.

THE CHIEF JOHN ROSS HOUSE
P.O. Box 863
ROSSVILLE 30741
(706) 861-3954
Frances Jackson, President
Description: Historic house of 1797 with displays of artifacts; Cherokee alphabet.

HAWAII

**LYMAN MISSION HOUSE
MEMORIAL MUSEUM**
276 Haili St.
HILO 996720
(808) 935-5021 Fax 969-7685
Richard Henderson, President
Description: 19th a d early 20th century Hawaiian

Artists' Gallery, Hawaiian cultural relics, and ethnic displays of seven national groups living in Hawaii.

BERNICE PAUAHI BISHOP MUSEUM
P.O. Box 19000-A
HONOLULU 96817
(808) 847-3511 Fax 841-8968
Siegfried S. Kagawa, President
Description: State museum of cultural and natural history with exhibits relating to Hawaii and the Pacific, including a collection of Hawaiian royal artifacts. *Activities*: Research Hawaiian archaeology, language, art, culture and ethnic groups. *Publications*: Bulletin; annual papers, anthropology reports.

HAWAII CHILDREN'S MUSEUM
650 Iwilei Rd.
HONOLULU 96817
(808) 522-0040 Fax 545-7961
Description: Exhibits relating to Hawaiian and other cultures.

IOLANI PALACE
P.O. Box 259
HONOLULU 96804
(808) 522-0822 Fax 532-1051
Alice F. Guild, Director
Description: Artifacts of the Hawaiian monarch, 1882-93.

MISSION HOUSE MUSEUM
553 S. King St.
HONOLULU 96813
(808) 531-0481
Deborah Pope, CEO
Description: Hawaiian language material.

MOANALUA GARDENS FOUNDATION
1352 Pineapple Place
HONOLULU 96819
(808) 839-5334
Paulie K. Jennings, Executive Director
Description: Collections include items relating to Hawaiian cultural history.

**PU'UHONUA O HONAUNAU
NATIONAL HISTORICAL PARK**
P.O. Box 129
HONAUNAU 96726
(808) 328-2326 Fax 328-9485
Jerry Y. Shimoda, Supt.
Description: Collection of Hawaiian artifacts and burial remains.

HULIHEE PALACE
75-5718 Alii Dr.
KAILUA-KONA 96740
(808) 329-1877
Julia L. Soehren, CEO
Description: Collections include ancient Hawaiian artifacts.

KAMUELA MUSEUM
KAMUELA 96743
(808) 885-4724
Description: Includes a large Hawaiian cultural collection, including royal artifacts.

KAUAI MUSEUM
P.O. Box 248
LIHUE 96766
(808) 245-6931
Dan Dahl, Director
Description: Maintains Hawaiian collection, and ethnic and heritage displays.

BAILEY HOUSE MUSEUM
2375A Main St.
WAILUKU 96793
(808) 244-3326 Fax 242-4378
John Cooper, Executive Director
Description: Collections include Native Hawaiian artifacts. Activities: Conducts research on local history and archaeology of Maui County.

IDAHO

IDAHO STATE HISTORICAL MUSEUM
610 N. Julia Davis Dr.
BOISE 83702
(208) 334-2120
Description: A collection of prehistoric and historic artifacts of the Shoshone, Nez Perce, Northern Paiute, with general Plains Indian material represented; a large collection of Northwest Coast and Alaskan material collected in the early 1900's. Publications: Idaho Yesterdays, quarterly magazine; newsletter. Library.

SHOSHONE-BANNOCK TRIBAL MUSEUM
P.O. Box 793
FORT HALL 83203
(208) 237-9791
Joyce Ballard, Director
Description: Views prehistoric and contemporary lifestyles of the Shoshone-Bannock Tribes. Several exhibits display artifacts, photographs and contemporary fine art of tribal members. Special programs: Hosts a Spring and Fall Art Show for local artists; special tours to view tribes buf falo herd and a monument marking the original Fort Hall site in the "Bottoms" area (an important fish and wildlife habitat on the Snake River) of the Reservation. Library. Publication: Sho-Ban News, weekly newspaper. Established in 1984.

NEZ PERCE NATIONAL HISTORICAL PARK & MUSEUM
P.O. Box 93, Hwy. 95
SPALDING 83551
(208) 843-2261
Franklin C. Walker, Supt.
Susan J. Buchel, Curator
Description: 24 sites which illustrate the history and culture of the Nez Perce Indians, and historic events which affected them. Museum houses exhibits of Nez Perce ethnological material; 4,000 photos of Nez Perce Indians. Research: Nez Perce Indians. Publications: Sapat'gayn: 20th-Century Nez Perce Artists, 72 page book; Nez Perce Country - 220 page book. Library.

HERRETT MUSEUM
College of Southern Idaho
315 Falls Ave., Box 1238
TWIN FALLS 83303
(208) 733-9554 Fax 734-2362
James C. Woods, Director
Description: Maintains collections on American Indians, archaeology, and ethnology.

IDAHO HERITAGE MUSEUM
2390 Hwy. 93 S.
TWIN FALLS 83303
(208) 655-4444
Description: Maintains collections of Indian artifacts.

ILLINOIS

SCHLINGOETHE CENTER FOR NATIVE AMERICAN CULTURES
Aurora University
347 S. Gladstone, Dunham Hall
AURORA 60506
(708) 844-5402
Marcia Lautanen-Raleigh, Director
Description: Contemporary Native American art and ethnographic materials, including beadwork, pottery, clothing, textiles, basketry, some prehistoric stone tools. Special collections: Southwestern pottery and kachinas. Special program: Annual Native American Festival and Pow-Wow in May. Publication: Spreading Wings, quarterly member newsletter. Library. Established in 1990.

FIELD MUSEUM OF NATURAL HISTORY
Roosevelt Rd. at Lake Shore Dr.
CHICAGO 60605
(312) 922-9410
Dr. William Boyd, President
Dr. Bennett Bronson, Chairman-Anthropology
Description: Seven exhibit halls devoted to the American Indian. Collections cover prehistoric and living Indians and Eskimos from Alaska to Cape Horn. Publications: Field Museum Bulletin; catalogs, handbooks, leaflets. Library. Founded 1893.

CAHOKIA MOUNDS STATE HISTORIC SITE & MUSEUM
Box 681 (Site); Box 382 (Museum)
COLLINSVILLE 62234
(618) 346-5160 (Site); 344-9221 (Museum)
Dr. Margaret Brown, Site Superintendent
Description: Contains over 30 exhibits, including authentic and replica artifacts from site and region; dioramas, graphics, mostly dealing with prehistoric Cahokia Mounds site. Outdoor reconstruction of Late Woodland pithouses and Mississippian wall trench house, stockade, garden; Woodhenge reconstruction. Special programs: Slide/tape presentations; guided tours; Native-American craft classes; lecture series. Publication: Cahokia, newsletter; publishes books. Museum shop. Library. A National Historic Landmark.

MADISON COUNTY HISTORICAL MUSEUM
715 N. Main St.
EDWARDSVILLE 62025
(618) 656-7562
Anna Symanski, Director
Special collection: John R. Sutter and Raymond P. Smith Collections--Contains more than 3,000 American Indian artifacts of local and south central Illinois, as well as some from Southwest tribes. Library. Publication: Museum newsletter.

SCHOOL OF NATIONS MUSEUM
Principia College
ELSAH 62028
(618) 374-2131 ext. 312
Bonnie Gibbs, Director
Description: Maintains a collection of American Indian crafts--baskets, clothing, dolls, pottery, textiles, etc. Library.

THE MITCHELL INDIAN MUSEUM
Kendall College
2408 Orrington Ave.
EVANSTON 60201
(708) 866-1395 Fax 866-1320
Dr. Thomas Kerr, CEO
Description: Contains North American Indian art

and artifacts, Eskimo art, and objects from cultures of the Plains, Woodlands, Southwest, and Northwest coast. Library.

DICKSON MOUNDS MUSEUM
LEWISTON 61542
(309) 547-3721 Fax 547-3189
Judith A. Franke, Director
Description: Exhibits archaeological material from west central Illinois, Mississippian and Middle Woodland sites on grounds--Paleo-Indian to Mississippian cultures.

HAUBERG INDIAN MUSEUM
Black Hawk State Park
1510 46th Ave.
ROCK ISLAND 61201
(309) 788-9536
Elizabeth A. Carvey, Director
Neil Rangen, Supt.
Description: Located on the site of the main villages of the Sauk and Fox Indian Nations. Contains artifacts on permanent display are of Sauk and Mesquakie origin; also other Eastern Woodland artifacts; includes many articles of Plains origin; large basket collection of the Northwest, West and Southwest; four dioramas depicting the daily life of the Sauk and Mesquakie about 1800. Publication: Two Nations, One Land: A Cultural Summation of the Sauk and Mesquakie in Illinois.

ILLINOIS STATE MUSEUM
Corner Spring & Edwards
SPRINGFIELD 62706
(217) 782-6695
R. Bruce McMillan, Director
Description: Midwestern archaeological collections; North American ethnographic materials especially western basketry; Dickson Mounds skeletal collection. Library.

MUSEUM OF NATURAL HISTORY
University of Illinois
URBANA 61801
Description: Maintains prehistoric and historic exhibits of Indians of North America, with emphasis on the prehistory of Illinois, the Navajo and Pueblo Indians, and the Eskimo of Greenland.

STARVED ROCK STATE PARK
P.O. Box 116
UTICA 61373
(815) 667-4726 Fax 667-5353
Jon Blume, Complex Supt.
Description: Located on the site of former Indian village of Illinois Indians, later occupied by Ottawa and Potawatomi Indians, 1673-1760.

INDIANA

INDIANA UNIVERSITY MUSEUM
Student Bldg.
BLOOMINGTON 47401
Description: Exhibits approximately 100,000 archaeological and ethnological specimens on American Indians from many areas of the New World. Special collection: Wanamaker Collection of American Indian Photographs, taken by Joseph Dixon--includes about 15,000 items. Library.

WILLIAM HAMMOND MATHERS MUSEUM
601 East Eighth St.
BLOOMINGTON 47405
(812) 855-6873

Geoffrey W. Conrad, Director
Description: Over 30,000 ethnographic artifacts from North, Central and South America. *Special Collection*: Wanamaker Collection of Native American Photographs - features over 8,000 images (primarily portraits) of American Indians taken between 1908 & 1922 by Dr. Joseph Dixon. Established 1963.

ANGEL MOUNDS STATE HISTORIC SITE
8215 Pollack Ave.
EVANSVILLE 47715
 (812) 853-3956
 Rebecca Means Harris, Director
 Kate Jones, Curator
Description: A 103 acre prehistoric Mississippian Indian archaeological site. Ten mounds, 1250-1450, inhabiting 1000 people; reconstructed structures: portion of a stockade house, and the temple. *Special programs*: Monthly lecture series on archaeology and nature; Native American Days Festival, annual in August. *Publication*: Smoke Signals, quarterly newsletter; Ancient Treasure of the Americas: A Pre-Columbian Exhibition, exhibit catalogue. Library. Founded 1939.

THE POTAWATOMI MUSEUM
P.O. Box 631
FREMONT 46737
Description: Exhibits over 5,000 material cultural items of prehistoric and historic periods. Library.

CHILDREN'S MUSEUM OF INDIANAPOLIS
3010 N. Meridian St.
INDIANAPOLIS 46208
Description: Collections consist of over 2,000 objects representing the tribes of Woodlands, Southeast, Plains, Plateau, Southwest, Northwest Coast, California and Canadian Indians. *Publication*: Newsletter. Library.

EITELJORG MUSEUM OF AMERICAN INDIANS & WESTERN ART
500 W. Washington St.
INDIANAPOLIS 46204
 (317) 636-9378 Fax 264-1427
 Philip Thompson, President/CEO
 Victoria Copenhaver, Robert Tucker,
 Jennifer Complo & Marla Dankert, Curators
Description: The American Western collection spans the early 19th century to the present and includes paintings, drawings, graphics, and sculpture - works by members of the original Taos art colony, such as Joseph Henry Sharp, E.I. Couse, Ernest Blumenschein, and Victor Higgins, as well as Western American artists, including Albert Bierstadt, Frederic Remington, Charles Russell, and Georgia O'Keeffe; the Native American collection consists of art and artifacts from throughout North America, and includes pottery, basketry, woodcarvings, and clothing. *Special programs*: Conducts research on Native American culture; lectures, film series, workshops, and craft demonstrations; special programs for school children; Western Festival (June); Annual Indian Market (August); Artists-in-Residence - Fall & Spring. Small library. *Publication*: Eiteljorg Museum Newsletter, quarterly; exhibition catalogues. Museum Shop. Established 1989.

MUSEUM OF INDIAN HERITAGE
500 W. Washington St.
INDIANAPOLIS 46204
 (317) 293-4488
 Vicki Cummings, Director
Description: Maintains a Native-American archaeological and ethnographic collection, prima-

rily from North America, with emphasis on the culture areas of the Northeast Woodlands, the Great Plains, and the Southwest. *Publication*: Quarterly newsletter. Library.

NORTHERN INDIANA HISTORICAL SOCIETY MUSEUM
808 W. Washington St.
SOUTH BEND 46601
Description: Exhibits on prehistoric Indians, the Mound Builders in Indiana; an historic Indian exhibit on the lifestyle of the Potawatomis and Miamis of northern Indiana. *Publication*: The Old Courthouse News, quarterly magazine.

SONOTABAC PREHISTORIC INDIAN MOUND & MUSEUM
P.O. Box 941, 2401 Wabash Ave.
VINCENNES 47591
 (812) 885-4330/7679
 John A. Ward, President
Description: Indian Museum & Historic Site located at the foot of the largest Ceremonial Mound in Indiana, containing exhibits covering 10,000 B.C. to the present. *Publication*: Monthly newsletter

IOWA

UNIVERSITY OF NORTHERN IOWA MUSEUM
31st and Hudson Rd.
CEDAR FALLS 50613
Description: Maintains a collection of approximately 8,000 Indian artifacts.

DAVENPORT MUSEUM
1717 W. 12th St.
DAVENPORT 52804
Description: Maintains collections of prehistoric Indian artifacts from Mounds in central Mississippi River Valley; Southwestern basketry and pottery; and ethnological items from various tribes, primarily from the upper Great Lakes region and Plains. Library.

IOWA STATE HISTORICAL MUSEUM
East 12th and Grand Ave.
DES MOINES 50319
 (515) 281-5111
 Adrien D. Anderson, Director
Description: Displays Indian beadwork; historic and prehistoric artifacts, photos, and relative written material. Publication: The Annals of Iowa, quarterly magazine. Library.

MISSISSIPPI RIVER MUSEUM
400 East 3rd St., Box 266
DUBUQUE 52004
 (319) 557-9545
 Jerome A. Enzler, Director
Description: History of the Mississippi River from prehistoric times to present. Collections include Indian-made circa 1860 dugout canoe, two birchbarks made in Chippewa tradition, several prehistoric stone artifacts from the Upper Mississippi, and historic trade material from EuroAmerican contact period - Winnebago, Mesquakie, Crow, and Cheyenne. The museum houses a small collection of baskets and pottery (Zuni and Navajo). Publications: Museum monographs. Library. Established in 1964.

AUDUBON COUNTY HISTORICAL SOCIETY
c/o Jerry Finnerty
P.O. Box 155
EXIRA 50076

 (712) 563-3984
Description: Indian Museum maintaining collections of Indian artifacts.

EFFIGY MOUNDS NATIONAL MONUMENT
RR 1, Box 25A, 151 Hwy. 76
HARPERS FERRY 52146
 (319) 873-3491 Fax 873-3743
 Thomas A. Munson, Supt.
 Don Wollenhaupt, Chief Ranger
Description: A 1,500 acre park with visitor center, the collection contains archaeological and archival material from prehistoric (500 B.C. - 1300 A.D.) and historic period (1673-present). Consists of 200 prehistoric Woodland Indian burial mounds with an archaeological museum exhibiting artifacts excavated from the mounds area. Special collection: Ellison Orr collection. Special programs: Education programs - guided walks, moonlight hikes, winter film festival. Library. Publications: The Effigy Mounds Mystique, annual newsletter; Junior Ranger work booklet - Mounds Mystique 3; educational handbook. A National Historic Landmark. Established 1949.

SIOUX CITY PUBLIC MUSEUM
2901 Jackson St.
SIOUX CITY 51104
Description: Exhibits artifacts of the Plains and Eastern Woodlands Indians. Library.

MUSEUM OF HISTORY AND SCIENCE
503 South St.
WATERLOO 50701
Description: Contains six exhibit cases of Indian artifacts and beadwork, and a rare book collection (53 volumes) of Indian history and lore.

KANSAS

KAW INDIAN MISSION
500 North Mission
COUNCIL GROVE 66846
 (316) 767-5410
 Ron Parks, Director
Description: Mission school opened by the Methodist Episcopal Church in 1851 for the Kaw (Kansa) Indians. An historic house and museum featuring Kaw Indian relics. *Special program*: Wah Shun Gah Days, summer.

IOWA, SAC & FOX PRESBYTERIAN MISSION
Rte. 1, Box 152C, E. Mission Rd.
HIGHLAND 66035
 (913) 442-3304
 Mark A. Hunt, Director
 Andrew Clements, Curator
Description: A three story stone house serving as a mission to the Iowa, and Sac and Fox Indians. Displays Iowa, and Sac and Fox Indian artifacts.

MUSEUM OF ANTHROPOLOGY
University of Kansas
LAWRENCE 66045
 (913) 864-4245
 Alfred E. Johnson, Ph.D., Director
 Anta Montet-White, Doct., Curator
 Robert J. Smith, Ph.D., Curator
Description: Maintains a collection of over 100,000 prehistoric American Indian artifacts, mainly from the Midwestern U.S.; about 4,000 North American Indian ethnographic items from the Plains, Southwest, and Northwest Coast; and an extensive skeletal collection. *Special collection*: Con-

temporary American Indian art displayed in the Lawrence, Kansas Indian Art Show. *Publication*: Quarterly newsletter. Library. Founded 1979.

CORONADO-QUIVIRA MUSEUM
221 E Ave. South
LYONS 67554
 (316) 257-3941
 Clyde Ernst, Director/Curator
Description: Exhibits Coronado and Quivira Indian artifacts, and Papago Indian baskets, pre-1934.

RILEY COUNTY HISTORICAL MUSEUM
Memorial Auditorium Bldg.
2309 Claflin Rd.
MANHATTAN 66502
Special collection: The Walter Collection--900 Indian relics & artifacts of northeast Kansas & southwest Nebraska. *Publication*: Newsletter. Library.

LAST INDIAN RAID MUSEUM
258 S. Penn Ave.
OBERLIN 67749
 (913) 475-2712
 Fonda Farr, Director
Description: Historical museum located near the sites of the 1878 Last Indian Raid on Kansas soil with the Northern Cheyenne Indians. One room dedicated to the Native American artifacts and the story of the Last Indian Raid. *Publication*: Quarterly newsletter. Established in 1958.

OLD DEPOT MUSEUM
Tecumseh and Main
OTTAWA 66067
Special collection: Indians of Franklin County, and Early Indian Clothing. Displays scrolls of membership in the Chippewa Tribe, and maps locating tribal lands.

PAWNEE INDIAN VILLAGE MUSEUM STATE HISTORICAL SITE
Box 475, Rt. 1
REPUBLIC 66964
 (913) 361-2255
 Richard Gould, Director
Description: Archaeology museum located on the best preserved Pawnee earth lodge site on the Plains. Displays describe Pawnee life on the Great Plains. *Special program*: Pawnee Days Celebration, in Fall. Main feature-Pawnee Indian dancers and singers as well as a large mountain man encampment. Brochure. Library. Established 1901.

EL QUARTELEJO KIVA INDIAN MUSEUM
c/o News Chronicle Printing Co., Inc.
P.O. Box 218
SCOTT CITY 67871
Description: Displays Cheyenne and Pueblo artifacts, especially Taos; Indian War material.

SHAWNEE METHODIST MISSION
3403 West 53rd
SHAWNEE MISSION 66205
 (913) 262-0867
 Mark A. Hunt, Director
 Lee Wright, Curator
Description: Re-creation of Indian Manual Labor School, operated 1830-1862, for Shawnee children and other emigrant tribes. *Special program*: Slide show of the history of the Mission.

KANSAS MUSEUM OF HISTORY
Kansas State Historical Society
6425 SW 6th St.
TOPEKA 66615-1099

 Mark A. Hunt, Director
 Diane Good, Curator
Description: Collection features Indian relics--tools, utensils & clothing of Kansas Indian tribes. Library. Founded 1876.

MID-AMERICA ALL-INDIAN CENTER MUSEUM
650 N. Seneca
WICHITA 67203
 (316) 262-5221
 Jerry Aday, Executive Director
 Jerry Martin, Museum Director
Description: Located on the site of old Indian Council grounds. Maintains collections of Native American art and artifacts. *Research*: Native American life, art, and religion. *Publication*: Gallery Notes, quarterly newsletter. Library. Established 1968.

KENTUCKY

MUSEUM OF ANTHROPOLOGY
Northern Kentucky University
200 Landrum Academic Center
HIGHLAND HEIGHTS 41099
 (606) 572-5259
 James F. Hopgood, Director
Description: Collections focus on contemporary Native American arts of the Southeast and Southwest U.S. Library.

MUSEUM OF ANTHROPOLOGY
University of Kentucky
LEXINGTON 40506
 (602) 258-4219
 Dr. Lathel F. Duffield, Director
Description: Exhibits archaeological material from sites excavated in Kentucky, including Navajo and Eskimo artifacts.

J.B. SPEED ART MUSEUM
2035 S. Third St., P.O. Box 2600
LOUISVILLE 40201
 (502) 636-2893 Fax 636-2899
 Peter Morrin, Director; Ruth Cloudman, Curator
Description: Maintains ethnological and archaeological exhibits illustrating Indian life of 19th and early 20th century Plains groups. *Special collection*: The Charles and Charlotte Price Gallery for Native Amerian Art consists primarily of works from the Plains region. Objects from many tribes including Dakota or Sioux, the Cheyenne, the Arapaho, the Kiowa, and the Crow are represented. Frederick Weygold Collection--Work in flint, stone and bone from prehistoric Kentucky and southern Indiana. *Publication*: Quarterly Program Guide; J.B. Speed Art Museum Handbook; catalog for various Native American exhibits. Library. Established 1927.

WICKLIFFE MOUNDS RESEARCH CENTER
P.O. Box 155
WICKLIFFE 42087
 (502) 335-3681
 Kit W. Wesler, Director; Lisa M. Engen, Curator
Description: Museum is based on archaeological site of the Mississippi period, dated ca. A.D. 1100-1350. Displays artifacts from the excavations of the Mound Builders. Small research library. *Publication*: Wickliffe Mounds Research Center Reports Series.

LOUISIANA

LOUISIANA ARTS & SCIENCE CENTER
100 S. River Rd.
BATON ROUGE 70801
Description: Exhibits Eskimo soapstone carvings, artifacts and lithographs; North American Indian crafts, contemporary pottery and weaving.

LAFAYETTE NATURAL HISTORY MUSEUM
637 Girard Park Dr.
LAFAYETTE 70503
Special collection: Contemporary Baskets of Chitimacha and Koasati Indians of Louisiana--Baskets and weaving of the Acadian culture and Louisiana Indian cultures. Publications. Library.

MAINE

ROBERT ABBE MUSEUM
P.O. Box 286
BAR HARBOR 04609
 (207) 288-3519
 Diane R. Kopec, Director
 Rebecca Cole-Will & Bette Swanton, Curators
 Anne Stocking, Museum Educator
Description: Displays Native-American prehistoric and ethnographic materials with emphasis on Maine and the Maritime provinces. Includes baskets, quillwork, and birchbark of Passamaquoddy Penobscot, Micmac and Malicite artists ca. 1800 - contemporary. *Special collection*: Mary C. Wheelwright Collections of ethnographic northeastern baskets of ash, birchbark and quill; archival photos and documents. *Special programs*: Workshops, demonstrations, and children's programs throughout the summer. School programs year around. Lecture series for specific exhibits. *Publications*: Bulletin series on Native American arts and crafts and archaeological research. Library. Open mid-May to mid-October. Established 1923.

THE PEARY-MacMILLAN ARCTIC MUSEUM
Bowdoin College
Hubbard Hall
BRUNSWICK 04011
 (207) 725-3416
 Dr. Susan A. Kaplan, Director
 Dr. Gerald F. Bigelow, Curator
Description: An exhibition of Peary and MacMillan Arctic explorations -- Labrador, Baffin and Greenland Inuit and Indian cultures; photographic archives. Collections include historic artifacts, photographs and Inuit art, clothing and equipment. *Special programs*: Lecture series; tours. *Publication*: Newsletter. Library.

WILSON MUSEUM
Perkins St., P.O. Box 196
CASTINE 04421
 (207) 326-8753
 E.W. Doudiet, Director
 P.L. Hutchins, Curator
Description: North American and some South American Indian stone artifacts, pottery and baskets, most obtained between 1880 and 1920. *Publications*: Triannual newsletter; pamphlets and book on local history. Open May 27th thru September 30th, 2-5 PM, except Monday. Established 1921.

NOWETAH'S AMERICAN INDIAN MUSEUM
Route 27, Box 40
NEW PORTLAND 04954
  (207) 628-4981
  Nowetah Timmerman, Owner/Operator
Description: Displays American Indian art and crafts, including over 300 old Maine Indian baskets and bark containers. *Special program*: Educational program, visits and classes available for schools and scout groups. Gift Store. Established 1969.

**WAPONAHKI MUSEUM
& RESOURCE CENTER**
Pleasant Point Reservation
P.O. Box 343
PERRY 04667
  (207) 853-4001
A collection of artifacts of the Passamaquoddy Indians.

MAINE TRIBAL UNITY MUSEUM
Quaker Hill Rd.
UNITY 04988
  (207) 948-3131
  Christopher Marshall, Director
Description: Indian Museum housed in 1880 Old Unity Town House, maintaining a collection of Northeast Indian basketry and artifacts. *Research*: Basket-making techniques. Library.

MARYLAND

**NATIONAL COLONIAL FARM
OF THE ACCOKEEK FOUNDATION**
3400 Bryan Point Rd.
ACCOKEEK 20607
  (301) 283-2113 Fax 283-2049
  Robert Ware Staus, President
Description: Collections include Indian artifacts.

MASSACHUSETTS

**ROBERT S. PEABODY
MUSEUM OF ARCHAEOLOGY**
Phillips Academy
ANDOVER 01810
  (508) 749-4490
  James W. Bradley, Director
  Malinda Blustain, Collections Manager
Description: One of the nation's major repositories of Native American archaeological collections, representing nearly every culture area in North America. Collections are especially strong in the Northeast, Southeast, Midwest, Southwest, Mexico, and the Arctic, in many areas from Paleo-Indian (11,500 years ago) to European contact. Material includes stone and bone tools, pottery, and carved shell and copper artifacts. Ethnographic collection, from the last 150 years, includes baskets, textiles, and other objects. *Special collections*: Kidder collection from Pecos Pueblo; pre-contact Southeastern ceramics; West Coast baskets (19th century); Tehuacan Valley collection; artifacts of the Northeast. *Special programs*: Outreach; hosts meetings, special classes, and visiting speakers. Research library - 5,000 volumes and a large collection of historical photographs. Publications. Established in 1901.

TRUSTEES OF RESERVATIONS
572 Essex St.
BEVERLY 01915
  (508) 921-1944 Fax 921-1948
  Herbert W. Vaughan, Chairperson
Description: An open space and historic preservation project maintainting and protecting about 75 properties in Massachusetts.

CHILDREN'S MUSEUM
Museum Wharf, 300 Congress St.
BOSTON 02210
  (617) 426-6500
  Pat Stewart, Acting Director
  Joan Lester, Native American Curator
Description: Collection includes Penobscot, Passamaquoddy, Iroquois, Chippewa, Wampanoag and Narragansett materials from both past and present traditions. *Special exhibit*: We're Still Here—American Indians in New England Long Ago and Today. *Programs*: Workshops/courses. Museum Shop. Library. Open to public by appointment only to specially interested visitors, and classes studying Eastern cultures in depth (fee charged.)

**PEABODY MUSEUM OF
ARCHAEOLOGY & ETHNOLOGY**
Harvard University
11 Divinity Ave.
CAMBRIDGE 02138
  (617) 495-2248
  C.C. Lamberg-Karlowsky, Director
  Dr. Ian Brown, Curator
Description: Contains large collections of archaeological, ethnological and somatological artifacts of North America. *Special exhibit*: North American Indian: Change and Continuity; deals with the last 500 years of interaction between Indians & Whites. It's focus is on the creative aspects of this dynamic relationship. *Publication*: Newsletter. Library.

INDIAN HOUSE MEMORIAL
Box 121, Main St.
DEERFIELD 01342
  (413) 772-0845
  John Abercrombie, President
Description: Collections of Native American artifacts, decorative arts, pottery, weaving, and looms.

LONGHOUSE MUSEUM
Hassanamisco Reservation
GRAFTON 01519
Description: Memorial to the Eastern Native-American: Artifacts of the Nipmuc Tribe (central Massachusetts); beadwork, utensils, baskets, paintings, and rugs. Publications. Library.

FRUITLANDS MUSEUMS
102 Prospect Hill Rd.
HARVARD 01451
  (508) 456-3924
  Robert Farwell, Director; Maggie Stier, Curator
Description: American Indian museum contains Dioramas of local Indian scenes and specimens of historic Indian arts and industries. Special exhibits and educational programs; tours for school groups. Library. Founded 1913.

HOLYOKE MUSEUM–WISTARIAHURST
238 Cabot St.
HOLYOKE 01041
Description: Maintains a collection of Northeast Indian artifacts--Iroquois masks and rattles; pottery of the Southeast and Southwest; basketry of the Southwest, Plains and Northwest Coast; Iroquois and Plains Indian beadwork.

PLIMOTH PLANTATION
Wampanoag Indian Program
P.O. Box 1620
PLYMOUTH 02360
  (617) 746-1622
  Nanepashemet, Program Manager
Description: An outdoor living history museum which displays Native-American artifacts from the colonial period, and recreates the life and times of a Wampanoag family which lived at Plymouth in the 1620's. Researches and depicts 17th-century Native history and culture. Staff demonstrations and discussions. *Publication*: Almanack, membership newsletter. Library. Established 1947.

MICHIGAN

MUSEUM OF ANTHROPOLOGY
University of Michigan
ANN ARBOR 48109-1079
  (313) 764-0485
  Dr. Jeffrey R. Parsons, Director
Description: Contains extensive holdings in North American archaeology and ethnography. *Special collections*: Hinsdale Collection–Great Lakes Basketry; Greenland Eskimo Collection; Seri and Tarahumara Indian Collection. *Publications*: Papers, memoirs, and technical reports. Library.

CRANBROOK INSTITUTE OF SCIENCE
500 Lone Pine Rd., Box 801
BLOOMFIELD HILLS 48303-0801
  (313) 645-3260
Description: Exhibits cover all major culture areas of North America, especially Woodlands and Plains. *Activities*: School group program. *Publications*: Bimonthly newsletter and brochure; bulletin series; annual report. Selective government depository. Library. Founded 1930.

CHILDREN'S MUSEUM
Detroit Public Schools
67 East Kirby
DETROIT 48202
Special collection: American Indian Collection--basketry, costumes, crafts, dolls, textiles, musical instruments, tools and weapons for various cultural areas of American Indians. Reference Library.

DETROIT INSTITUTE OF THE ARTS
5200 Woodward Ave.
DETROIT 48202
  (313) 833-7900
  David Penney, Contact
Special collection: The Chandler-Pohrt Collection - 19th-century Native American objects from tribes of the North American woodlands, prairies, and plains. It is notable for being focused on the artistic quality of Indian material at a time when it was not considered art. It includes clothing, pipes, drums, shields, drawings, etc.

MUSEUM OF ANTHROPOLOGY
Wayne State University
6001 Cass Ave.
DETROIT 48202
  (313) 577-2598/3056
  Arnold Pilling, Ph.D., Director
Description: Maintains a collection of Indian artifacts. Research Library.

MICHIGAN STATE UNIVERSITY MUSEUM
Division of Anthropology
EAST LANSING 48824

(517) 353-7861
 Charles E. Cleland, Ph.D., Curator-Anthropology
Special collection: Indians of the Great Lakes--Contains 30 displays relating to the history , technology, religion, and social organization of the Indians of the Great Lakes area.

GRAND RAPIDS PUBLIC MUSEUM
54 Jefferson
GRAND RAPIDS 49503
 (616) 456-3977
 Weldon D. Frankforter , Director
Description: Exhibits Hopewell archaeological material; artifacts from the Historic Site--Norton Indian Mounds (Hopewell.)

BLACKBIRD MUSEUM
P.O. Box 192
HARBOR SPRINGS 49740
(616) 526-2104
 Stephen B. Graham, Chairman
Description: Indian Museum. 1855 Andrew J. Blackbird House displaying Indian artifacts and clothing of American Indians.

MICHIGAN HISTORICAL MUSEUM
Michigan History Div.-Dept. of State
505 N. Washington Ave.
LANSING 48918
Description: Maintains Indian exhibits related to the history of Michigan and the old Northwest Territory.

MACKINAC ISLAND STATE PARK MUSEUM
P.O. Box 370
MACKINAC ISLAND 49757
Description: Features Indian material from the upper Great Lakes; Chippewa Indian costumes. Publications. Library .

TEYSEN'S WOODLAND INDIAN MUSEUM
P.O. Box 399
415 W. Huron Ave.
MACKINAW CITY 49701
(616) 436-7011
 Kenneth Teysen, CEO
Description: Collections include Indian artifacts from the Great Lakes area, including tools, weapons, clothing, food, and trade items.

**MARQUETTE COUNTY
HISTORICAL SOCIETY MUSEUM**
213 N. Front St.
MARQUETTE 49855
 (906) 226-3571
 Joseph Bertucci, Director; Kaye Hiebel, Curator
Description: Displays Indian archaeological and historical material of the upper peninsula of Michigan, with main focus on the Chippewa. Dioramas depicting a Chippewa family group. Includes baskets, beadwork, medicine bags, calumets, moccasins, canoes. *Publications*: Indians of Gitche Gumee; Harlow's Wooden Man, quarterly magazine; books for sale. Library .Established 1918.

FORT ST. JOSEPH MUSEUM
508 East Main St.
NILES 49120
 (616) 683-4702
 Melissa Olson, Director
Special collections : Collection of Sioux Indian artifacts; 12 drawings by Sitting Bull; large pictograph tapestry by Rain-in-the-Face; Potawatomi and early Native American objects (projectile points, stone tools). Established 1932.

CROOKED TREE ARTS COUNCIL
461 E. Mitchell St.
PETOSKEY 49770
 (616) 347-4337 Fax 347-3429
 Sean Ley, Director
Description: Maintains a fine arts collection with emphasis on Indians of the Great Lakes area. Research: Art of Ojibway, Odawa, and Nishnawbe Indians.

**FATHER MARQUETTE NATIONAL
MEMORIAL & MUSEUM**
Father Marquette State Park
720 Church St.
SAINT IGNACE 49781
 (906) 643-8620
Description: Displays artifacts, including an Indian longhouse and canoe, and maintains exhibits of early French and Indian cultures.

FORT DE BUADE MUSEUM, INC.
Mail: 701 N. Logan, Lansing, MI 48915
334 N. State St.
SAINT IGNACE 49781
 (906) 643-8686
 Donald E. Benson, Director
Description: Indian Museum located on the site of 1681, Fort de Buade, built by the French. Displays artifacts, beadwork, photos, lithos, and oils of Woodland Indians.

MUSEUM OF OJIBWA CULTURE
500 N. State St.
SAINT IGNACE 49781
 (906) 643-9161
Description: Displays artifacts and reproductions relating to Ojibwa culture.

**LUCKHARD'S MUSEUM-
THE INDIAN MISSION**
821 E. Bay St.
SEBEWAING 48759
Description: Using 17th century archaeological items, the museum interprets the Ojibwa who lived in the area prior to contact, and the Huron and Ojibwa refugees who came. The French fur trader and Jesuits and their impact on Native culture. Exhibits Indian artifacts and pioneer relics of the 19th-century, housed in original Indian mission of the Chippewa Indians (1845.) *Special program* : A video presentation on the Ojibwa family - the importance of every member , the interdependence. *Publications*: "The Story of Wafted Across," and "Southern Feather's Story ," by Margaret Peacock, short stories about an Ojibwa family (fiction).

SEBEWAING INDIAN MUSEUM
612 E. Bay St.
SEBEWAING 48759
 (517) 883-3730
 Jim Bunke, CEO
Description: An 1849 mission home, with collections of Native American canoes, arrowheads, and headress.

INDIAN DRUM LODGE MUSEUM
Mail: 2308 North U.S. 31
Camp Greilick, 4754 Scout Camp Rd.
TRAVERSE CITY 49684
 Martin A. Melkild, Curator
Description: Indian Museum housed in 1850, Chief Peter Ringnose's log cabin, maintaining ceremonial artifacts, clothing, and wood crafts.

MINNESOTA HISTORY CENTER
Grand Mound History Center
Rte. 7, Box 453
INTERNATIONAL FALLS 56649
 (218) 279-3332
 Nina Archabal, CEO
Description: A prehistoric Native American mounds and habitation area. *Research*: On middle and late Woodland, Laurel, and Blackduck Indian cultures.

TWO RIVERS GALLERY
Minneapolis American Indian Center
1530 Franklin Ave. East
MINNEAPOLIS 55404
 (612) 871-9421
 Sammy Watso, Director
Description: Ongoing visual arts exhibitions of both contemporary and more traditional artforms. *Programs*: School tours; special lectures. *Publication*: The Dragonfly, biannual newsletter.

PLAINS ART MUSEUM
Box 37, 521 Main Ave.
MOOREHEAD 56560
 (218) 236-7171
 Carol Rice, Curator
Description: Exhibits North American Indian art and Eskimo sculpture.

LOWER SIOUX AGENCY HISTORIC SITE
RR 1, Box 125
MORTON 56270
 (507) 697-6321
 Thomas R. Ellig, Manager
Description: 260 acre site of beginning of U.S.-Dakota War of 1862. Site includes History Center and a 15 minute video of Dakota history from late 18th century through early 20th century. *Special programs*: Focus on various aspects of Native and Euro-American history and culture, during the summer season. Library.*Publications*: Minnesota Historical Society publications and others pertaining to Dakota and Plains Indians history; also books and sales items of Indian culture (pottery, pipestone, beadwork, etc.) Museum Store. Established 1972.

MILLE LACS INDIAN MUSEUM
SR, Box 195
ONAMIA 56359
 (612) 532-3632
Description: This trading post and museum portrays Ojibwe culture. Exhibits include life-size dioramas showing typical scenes of Ojibwe life for each season.

PIPESTONE COUNTY MUSEUM
113 S. Hiawatha
PIPESTONE 56164
 (507) 825-2563
 Dave Rambow, Director; Joe Ager, Curator
Description: Contains artifacts from the Dakota and Ojibwa Tribes--Plains Indian saddle, and ceremonial pipes. Library. *Publication*: Quarterly journal. Established in 1880.

PIPESTONE NATIONAL MONUMENT
P.O. Box 727
PIPESTONE 56164
 (507) 825-5464
 Vincent J. Halvorson, Supt.
Description: Original pipestone (catlinite, named for noted painter of Indians, George Catlin) quarry

from which the Dakota Sioux fashioned their ceremonial pipes. *Local History Museum and Upper Midwest Indian Cultural Center* : Exhibits Indian ceremonial pipes and pipestone objects; pipestone quarries. *Special program* : Cultural demonstration programs-April - October-pipecarving, beadwork, quillwork, etc. *Publications* : Pipes on the Plains, Pipestone: A History; and Circle Trail booklet. Library. Established 1937.

MINNESOTA HISTORICAL SOCIETY MUSEUM

345 Kellogg Blvd. W.
ST. PAUL 55102
(612) 297-7913 Fax 296-1004
Timothy C. Glines, Administrative Officer
Description : Exhibits depicting prehistoric and contemporary Indian life in Minnesota. Major collecting areas include Dakota and Ojibwa material; photo collection. Maintains Grand Mound History Center. *Publication* : Minnesota History , quarterly magazine; Historic Sites Travel Guide brochure; publications from the Minnesota Historical Society Press. Library.

MINNESOTA MUSEUM OF ART

75 W. Fifth St.
ST. PAUL 55102
(612) 292-4355
Katherine Van Tassell, Curator
Description : American art 1850 to the present. Small collection of Native American artifacts (half Southwestern, half Northwest Coast). *Special programs* : Occasional shows of Native American artists. Publications: Newsletter; occasional catalogs. Established 1927.

WALKER WILDLIFE & INDIAN ARTIFACTS MUSEUM

St. Hwy. 200, Box 336
WALKER 56484
(218) 547-1257
Renee Geving, Manager
Description : Collections include Ojibway and Chippewa Indian handicraft and artifacts from 1892-1962.

WINNEBAGO AREA MUSEUM

WINNEBAGO 56098
(506) 893-3692
Marion Muir, President
Description : An archaeological museum exhibiting Oneonta (900-1500 A.D.) artifacts, Woodland (1000-8000 B.C.) artifacts; beadwork of the Chippewa and Sioux. Library .

MISSISSIPPI

WINTERVILLE INDIAN MOUNDS STATE PARK

Route 3, Box 600
GREENVILLE 38701
Description : Maintains museum with a collection of Indian artifacts, excavated from the Mounds area. Library .

JP MUSEUM OF INDIAN ARTIFACTS

Mail: Rt. 1, Box 715, Saucier , MS 39574
Highway 49
LYMAN 39574
John and Patricia Wright, Owner/Directors
Description : Archaeology and Indian Museum housed in a World War II barrack, containing more than 8,000 Indian artifacts from 14 States. *Research* : Indian artifacts and genealogy . Library .

COBB INSTITUTE OF ARCHAEOLOGY

Drawer AR
MISSISSIPPI STATE UNIVERSITY 39762
(601) 325-3826
E.J. Vardaman, Director
Description : Exhibits Indian materials of Mississippi culture. *Publication* : Indians of Mississippi. Library.

GRAND VILLAGE OF THE NATCHEZ INDIANS

400 Jefferson Davis Blvd.
NATCHEZ 39120
(601) 446-6502 Fax 359-6905
James F. Barnett, Jr., Director
Description : A 128 acre National Historic Landmark site is the location of the ceremonial mound center for the Natchez tribe during the French colonization of the area (ca. 1682-1730.) *Museum* : Contains Indian and European artifacts gathered from the excavations and interpreted exhibits on the Natchez and Southeastern Indians. *Special programs* : Educational programs; slide lectures and guided tours. Library .

OLD SPANISH FORT & MUSEUM

4602 Fort St.
PASCAGOULA 39567
Description : Features Indian artifacts, tools and implements; and maps showing Indian settlements prior to 1700. Library .

THE CHOCTAW MUSEUM OF THE SOUTHERN INDIAN

Mississippi Band of Choctaw Indians
P.O. Box 6010
PHILADELPHIA 39350
(601) 656-5251

MISSOURI

MUSEUM OF ANTHROPOLOGY
University of Missouri

104 Swallow Hall
COLUMBIA 65211
(314) 882-3764
Dr. Michael J. O'Brien, Director
Molly K. O'Donnell, Associate Curator
Description : Displays of Native American material, Missouri archaeology , and Missouri history . Maintains collections of ethnographic material from the Plains and Southwest Indians; Eskimo and Mexican materials. *Special collection* : The Grayson Collection of archery and archery-related material; Museum Curation Center . *Special programs* : Tours; Outreach. Gift Shop. Established in 1939.

TOWOSAHGY STATE HISTORIC SITE

Big Oak Tree State Park
P.O. Box 35
EAST PRAIRIE 63845
Ken Cole, Archaeologist
Description : Exhibits Indian artifacts excavated from the site (1000-1400 A.D. Mississippian Culture Civic Ceremonial Center .)

MISSOURI STATE MUSEUM

State Capitol
JEFFERSON CITY 65101
Description : Collections include Musquakie ceremonial material, Missouri pottery , Kema Cave artifacts, Indian burial mound material, stone artifacts and archaic Indian artifacts.

OSAGE VILLAGE HISTORIC SITE

P.O. Box 176
JEFFERSON CITY 65102
(314) 751-8363 Fax 751-8656
Larry Grantham, Contact
Description : Houses collections of excavated materials and conducts research on Osage Indians.

KANSAS CITY MUSEUM

3218 Gladstone Blvd.
KANSAS CITY 64123
(816) 483-8300
Dr. David Ucko, President
Denise Morrison, Archivist
Description : The American Indian collections number about 2,500 pieces, most of which were collected by Col. Daniel Dyer and Ida Dyer during his tenure as Indian Agent at Fort Reno, Oklahoma in 1884-85, includes clothing and textiles, rocks and minerals, tools and technology , and archival documents. Also, other collections include artifacts from Southern and Central Plains, Eastern Woodlands, the Southwest and Northwest Coast Indian cultures. Two notable objects in the collection are the First Greenville Treaty Peace Medal and the Second Greenville Treaty Peace Pipe. The Peace Medal dates to 1795, when it was presented by a representative of George Washington to Chief White Swan of the Wea tribe. The Pipe is one of three presented to Wyandotte, Delaware and Shawnee Tribes by a representative of President James Madison at the Second Treaty of Greenville, Ohio in 1814. *Publication* : Quarterly newsletter . Reference Library . Established 1939.

WILLIAM ROCKHILL NELSON GALLERY & ATKINS MUSEUM OF FINE ARTS

4525 Oak St.
KANSAS CITY 64111
Description : Exhibits Native arts of the Americas, with emphasis on the Southwest, Mesoamerica, and South America. Publications. Library .

THE ST. LOUIS ART MUSEUM

Forest Park
ST. LOUIS 63110
(314) 721-0067
James Burke, Supt.
John Nunley & Jackie Lewis Harris, Curators
Description : Maintains a collection of artifacts, pottery, carvings, basketry and clothing of the Pueblo, Pueblo Mimbres, Plains, West Coast, and Mound Builder Indians. Bulletin. Library . Established 1904.

MONTANA

MUSEUM OF THE ROCKIES

Montana State University
BOZEMAN 59717
(406) 994-2251
Arthur H. Wolf, Director
Special collections : 1,500-piece Ethnology Collection, primarily an exhibit collection, represents Native Americans of the Plains, Northern Rockies and Plateau culture areas; and The Prehistoric Archaeology Collection - 100,000 artifacts of stone, bone and antler . Staff: Leslie B. Davis, PhD; Michael C. Wilson.

MUSEUM OF THE PLAINS INDIAN
P.O. Box 400, Highway 89
BROWNING 59417
(406) 338-2230
Loretta F. Pepion, Curator
Description: Administered by the Indian Arts and Crafts Board. Presents historic arts created by the tribal peoples of the Northern Plains, including the Blackfeet, Crow, Northern Cheyenne, Sioux, Assiniboine, Arapaho, Shoshone, Nez Perce, Flathead, Chippewa, and Cree. Displays the varied traditional costumes of Northern Plains men, women and children in complete detail on life-size figures. Special programs: North American Indian Days - annual public event presented in July on the Blackfeet Tribal Fairgrounds, adjacent to the museum. A four-day program of Indian dancing, games and sports events, and parades; film, "Winds of Change"--about the evolution of Indian cultures on the Northern Plains, narrated by Vincent Price; series of one-person exhibitions; painted tipis on the grounds during summer; demonstrations of Native-American arts and crafts techniques; tours. Publications: Illustrated catalogs and brochures. Established 1941.

LITTLE BIGHORN BATTLEFIELD NATIONAL MONUMENT
P.O. Box 39
CROW AGENCY 59022
(406) 638-2621/2
Gerard Baker, Superintendent
Kitty Belle Deernose, Curator
Description: Historic site of the Battle of the Little Big Horn, June 25-26, 1876. Arapaho, Sioux, and Cheyenne Indians fought and defeated Lt. Col. George Armstrong Custer and his troops of the 7th U.S. Cavalry Arikara and Crow Indians scouted for military. Museum: Educational and interpretive exhibits and a permanent collection of 24,000 objects, includes historical documents authored by or associated with George A. Custer, the Battle of the Little Big Horn, and other events and persons associated with the Indian W ars on the Northern Plains (1865-1891.) Military and ethnographic specimens relating to the conflict, including items associated with the Sioux, Crow, and Northern Cheyenne Tribes. Special programs: Talks on the Battle; 30 minute documentary film, "Red Sunday" on battle available on request to schools and organizations; archaeological slide shows; tours. Publications: Battklefield Dispatch, quarterly newsletter; and The Greasy Grass, annual magazine; publications of Custer Battlefield Historical and Museum Association. Library: 2,050 volumes. Established in 1952.

CROW TRIBE HISTORICAL & CULTURAL COMMISSION
P.O. Box 173
CROW AGENCY 59022
(406) 638-2328

H. EARLE CLACK MUSEUM
P.O. Box 1675
HAVRE 59501
(406) 265-9641
Duane Nabor, Director
Mrs. Louis Clack, Curator
Exhibit includes historic artifacts from the Chippewa and Cree Indians, excavated from site area; dioramas.

MONTANA HISTORICAL SOCIETY MUSEUM
225 No. Roberts
HELENA 59620
(406) 444-2394

Lawrence Sommer, Director
Susan R. Near, Curator
Description: Collection contains approximately 3,500 pieces of ethnographic artifacts primarily of tribes of the region, mostly Blackfeet and Sioux. The Photographic Archives contains over 2,000 photo prints and negatives that depict Indians, primarily of the Blackfeet, Sioux, Crow and Flathead. Special collection: Towe Ford Collection--Features the chronological story of Montana's frontier through dioramas and other displays. C.M. Russell Gallery of W estern Art. Publication: Montana: The Magazine of W estern History, quarterly. Library. Established 1865.

NORTHERN CHEYENNE TRIBAL MUSEUM
P.O. Box 128
LAME DEER 59043

CENTRAL MONTANA MUSEUM
P.O. Box 818, 408 NE Main St.
LEWISTON 59457
(406) 538-5436
Frank Machler, Curator
Description: Collection of Native American artifacts

MONTANA STATE UNIVERSITY MUSEUM
Fine Arts Bldg.
MISSOULA 59801
Description: Displays Indian art & artifacts of Mont.

FORT PECK TRIBAL MUSEUM
P.O. Box 115
POPLAR 59255

CHIEF PLENTY COUPS STATE PARK & MUSEUM
P.O. Box 100
PRYOR 59066
(406) 252-1287
Rich Pittsley, Director
Description: Memorial museum to Chief Plenty Coups - last chief of the Crow - includes personal collection of medicine bundles, clothing, weapons, pictures, documents; Crow Indian artifacts; ethnographic material of the Crow people; paintings, drawings; prehistoric artifacts. Special program: Native American interpreter. Established in 1972.

FLATHEAD INDIAN MUSEUM
Flathead Indian Reservation
#1 Museum Lane
ST. IGNATIUS 59865
(406) 745-2951
Jeanine Allard, Director
Col. Doug Allard, Curator
Description: Indian artifacts from the Flathead Tribe and other W estern tribes. Special collection: Flathead Photo Collection. Established in 1975.

BIG HOLE NATIONAL BATTLEFIELD
P.O. Box 237
WISDOM 59761
(406) 689-3155
Anthony J. Schetzsle, Supt.
Bob Chenoweth, Curator
Description: A 655 acre battlefield which preserves the scene of a battle between Nez Perce Indians and the Seventh U.S. Infantry, fought on August 9 and 10, 1877. The Heritage Center is located in the historic old school building constructed in 1888 by Jesuit priests. Museum: Exhibits detailing Nez Perce culture and soldier life of the 1870's; Native American art, including paintings, graphics, and sculptures; artifacts from battle participants, including beadwork. Special programs: Audiovisual program; self guiding trails; presentations by rang-

ers. Library. Gift Shop. Publications: Information packets; brochure.

NEBRASKA

MUSEUM OF THE FUR TRADE
HC 74, Box 18, 6321 Hwy. 20
CHADRON 69337
(308) 432-3843
Charles E. Hanson, Jr., Director
Brenda Olsen, Curator
Description: Maintains a collection of material illustrating the cultures of North American Indians, and the influence of the fur trade on those cultures. Restored and outfitted 1833 Indian trading post and warehouse. Indian garden for crops obtained from Mandan, Dakota, Assiniboine, Arikara, Hidatsa and Omaha Indians. Publication: Quarterly magazine. Library. Established 1955.

FORT ROBINSON MUSEUM
Nebraska State Historical Society
P.O. Box 304
CRAWFORD 69339
(308) 665-2852
Thomas R. Buecker, Curator
Description: Interpretive exhibits housed in 1905 Post Headquarters with displays of artifacts from Fort Robinson (1874 to 1948.) Crazy Horse, the great Oglala warrior, met his death there in 1877. Microfilm records of Red Cloud and Spotted Tail Indian Agencies. Guided tours.

HASTINGS MUSEUM
P.O. Box 1286
HASTINGS 68902
Description: A collection of Indian artifacts; Sioux Indian habitat group. Indian film. Publications.

FORT KEARNEY MUSEUM
311 South Central Ave.
KEARNEY 68847
Description: Displays Indian art from the Rosebud Indian Reservation.

MUSEUM OF NEBRASKA HISTORY
Nebraska State Historical Society
P.O. Box 82554, 15th & P Sts.
LINCOLN 68501
(402) 471-4757
Lawrence Sommer, Director
Gail DeBuse Potter, Curator
Description: A 5,000 square foot exhibit "The First Nebraskans," Plains Indian archaeology, and historic artifacts primarily from the 19th & 20th centuries. Period settings include a Pawnee earthlodge, and a Winnebago Reservation house. Special collection: Photo collection - Indians of Nebraska and the Great Plains. Library. Publications: Nebraska History, quarterly; Historical Newsletter; monographs on Nebraska history and anthropology; educational materials. Museum Shop. Established 1878.

NEBRASKA STATE MUSEUM
University of Nebraska
14th & U Sts.
LINCOLN 68508
(402) 472-3779
Hugh H. Genoways, Director
Description: Native American ethnographic collections on Plains & Southwest. Includes costumes & artifacts of Indians of NE. Special exhibit: "Nomads of the Plains" Gallery. Publication: "Magic in Clay," and Birth and Rebirth of the Omaha."

HERITAGE HOUSE MUSEUM
107 Clinton
WEEPING WATER 68463
(402) 267-4765
Deborah Freeman, President
Description: Maintains a prehistoric Indian artifact collection with items that date back 20,000 years.

NEVADA

NEVADA STATE MUSEUM
600 N. Carson St.
CARSON CITY 89710
(702) 687-4810
Scott Miller, Director
Judy Hendrix, Ass't. Director
Donald Tuohy, Curator of Anthropology
Description: Maintains study collections of Nevada Indian artifacts; large basket collection. Publications. Library. Established 1939.

STEWART INDIAN MUSEUM ASSOCIATION
5366 Snyder Ave.
CARSON CITY 89701

NORTHEASTERN NEVADA MUSEUM
1515 Idaho St.
ELKO 89801
(702) 738-3418
Howard Hickson, Executive Director
Shawn Hall, Assistant Director
Description: Contains ten local Shoshone Indian exhibits. *Special programs*: Talks on Native American culture and customs; contiuous art exhibit featuring 2 different artists each month. *Publication*: Quarterly historical journal. Library. Established 1969.

NEVADA STATE LOST CITY MUSEUM OF ARCHAEOLOGY
721 S. Moapa Valley Blvd., P.O. Box 753
OVERTON 89040
(702) 397-2193
Kathryn Olson, Curator
Description: Collections include prehistoric, protohistoric, and historic Native American material culture, including: lithics, basketry, fiber arts, articles of adronment, historic hotos, etc. Housed in Adobe facility constructed in 1935. Puebloan artifacts excavated from Pueblo Grande de Nevada, Lost City, Paiute Indian artifacts, and southwestern Indian crafts. Special collection: Photographs of 1920-30 Los City Excavations and local history. Library.

NEW JERSEY

THE MONTCLAIR ART MUSEUM
3 S. Mountain Ave.
MONTCLAIR 07042
(201) 746-5555
Robert J. Koenig, Director
Description: Exhibits feature costumes, jewelry, and artifacts of Eastern Woodlands, Desert Pueblo, Navajo, Apache, Plains, California and Northwest Indians and Eskimos. Library. Established 1914.

MORRIS MUSEUM OF ARTS & SCIENCES
Box 125, Normandy Hts. & Columbia Rds.
MORRISTOWN 07961
Description: Woodland Indians Gallery: Shows the

development of Woodland culture from the Paleo-Indian through Archaic to Woodland and historic periods. North American Indian Gallery: Exhibits on the Northwest Coast, the Southwest, and the Plains Indians. Library. Museum shop.

THE NEWARK MUSEUM
49 Washington St., P.O. Box 540
NEWARK 07101
(201) 596-6550
Mary Sue Sweeney Price, Director
Anne M. Spencer, Curator of Ethnology
Description: Maintains a permanent Native American Gallery with Indian art and artifacts representative of major culture areas of the U.S., and some from Canada. Includes pottery and textiles of the Southwest, extensive basket collection, bead and quillwork. Publications. Library. Established in 1909.

PRINCETON UNIVERSITY-MUSEUM OF NATURAL HISTORY
Guyot Hall
PRINCETON 08540
Description: Exhibits Northwest Coast Indian art; also, artifacts, mainly Tlingit, of Yukatat and Sitka areas, Alaska, period 1876-1886. Publications. Library.

POWHATAN RENAPE NATION INDIAN HERITAGE MUSEUM
P.O. Box 225
RANCOCAS 08073
(609) 261-4747
Description: Shows the Life of the Creation; and exhibits crafts and artifacts of of the Powhatan Renape Nation.

SETON HALL UNIVERSITY MUSEUM
South Orange Ave. - Fahy Hall
SOUTH ORANGE 07079
(201) 761-9543
Dr. Herbert C. Kraft, Director
Description: An archaeology and Indian museum featuring Eastern Woodlands Indian artifacts, with emphasis on New Jersey prehistory - Paleo-Indian to European contact. Includes petroglyphs, effigies, ceramics. *Publications*: Occasional publications concerning the Lenape/Delaware Indians, prehistoric archaeology; report of excavations, etc. Library. Established 1960.

THE LENAPE INDIAN MUSEUM & VILLAGE
Waterloo Village
STANHOPE 07874
(201) 347-0900
John T. Kraft, Curator

NEW JERSEY STATE MUSEUM
205 West State St.
TRENTON 08625
Description: Maintains a collection of ethnographic artifacts of the Lenni Lenape; also, Plains Indian beadwork, and material from Southwest, Eskimo and Northeast Indians. Library.

NEW MEXICO

ACOMA MUSEUM
P.O. Box 309, Pueblo of Acoma
ACOMITA 87034
(505) 552-6606
Juan S. Juanico, Director
Description: Indian history and culture museum

with photo archives and documents relating to the history of Acoma; also artifacts. *Publication*: One Thousand Years of Clay, catalog. Library.

M. TULAROSA BASIN HISTORICAL SOCIETY
P.O. Box 518
1301 White Sands Blvd.
ALAMOGORDO 88310
(505) 437-4760
Terry Benson, Director
Description: Maintains a collection of Indian artifacts from the area.

INDIAN PUEBLO CULTURAL CENTER
2401 12th St., NW
ALBUQUERQUE 87104
(800) 766-4405 (outside NM)
(505) 843-7270 Fax 842-6959
Rafael Gutierrez, Executive Director
Pat Reck, Curator
Description: The Main Museum consists of prehistoric to contemporary arts and crafts. A vast collection that traces the development of the Pueblo culture. Pueblo House Children's Museum offers a unique "hands on" experience for children. *Special programs*: Arts and craft demonstration program each weekend. Library/Archives. Gift Shop. Established 1991.

MAXWELL MUSEUM OF ANTHROPOLOGY
University and Ash, NE
ALBUQUERQUE 87131
(505) 277-4404
J.J. Brody, Director
Description: Exhibits Navajo weaving, Mimbres and Pueblo pottery, Hopi kachinas, North American Indian basketry. *Publications*: Seven Families in Pueblo Pottery; Anasazi Pottery, et al. Library. Navajo and Pueblo silver jewelry for sale.

AZTEC MUSEUM
125 N. Main St.
AZTEC 87410
(505) 334-9829

AZTEC RUINS NATIONAL MONUMENT
P.O. Box 640, Ruins Rd.
AZTEC 87410
(505) 334-6174 Fax 334-6372
Charles B. Cooper, Supt.
Dana Howlett, Curator
Description: Prehistoric Pueblo Indian ruin. Two-(cultural) phase inhabitation, Chaco Canyon and Mesa Verde. *Archaeology Museum*: Anasazi artifacts gathered from excavations of area sites, and from sites in the Lower San Juan Basin. Library. Open June-August. A National Historic Landmark. Established 1923.

CORONADO STATE MONUMENT
P.O. Box 95
BERNALILLO 87004
(505) 867-5351
Nathan Stone, Manager
Description: Site of a partially reconstructed Pueblo Indian village ruin occupied circa 1300-1600. Includes a completely reconstructed underground ceremonial kiva, which was the first to be discovered bearing ceremonial murals. Exhibits material from the excavations & Pueblo Indian culture.

CHACO CULTURE NATIONAL HISTORIC PARK
Star Rte. 4, Box 6500
BLOOMFIELD 87413
(505) 786-7014
C.T. Wilson, Supt.; Philip LoPiccolo, Curator

Description: A National Historic Landmark - 13 major prehistoric Anasazi sites, and over 400 smaller village sites. *Museum*: Features 26 exhibits on Anasazi and Navajo cultures. *Special collections*: Large archaeological collection of two million artifacts and samples; Associated Documentation mostly Chaco Project including: 2,000 maps, Field Notes and Archives, 35,000 photographs and negatives, and over 5,000 color slides. Library. *Publications*: 1,500 published and unpublished manuscripts housed in Albuquerque, NM.

RED ROCK MUSEUM
Box 328, Red Rock State Park
CHURCH ROCK 87311
  (505) 863-1337 Fax 863-9352
  Joan Barnette, Curator
Description: Indian arts and crafts museum exhibiting crafts and artifacts of prehistoric Anasazi and Navajo, Hopi, Zuni, Rio Grande Pueblos, Apache and Plains Indians. *Special collection*: Zuni kachina dolls. Library. Established 1951.

DEMING LUNA MIMBRES MUSEUM
301 S. Silver St.
DEMING 88030
  (505) 546-2382
  Treva L. Mester, Coordinator
Description: Exhibits Mimbrano Indian artifacts, and pottery.

JICARILLA ARTS & CRAFTS MUSEUM
P.O. Box 147
DULCE 87528

SAN JUAN COUNTY ARCHAEOLOGICAL RESEARCH CENTER & LIBRARY
6131 U.S. Highway 64
FARMINGTON 87401
  (505) 632-2013
  Larry L. Baker, Executive Director
Description: Contains exhibits of artifacts taken from the Anasazi-Salmon Ruin: 1.5 million prehistoric Pueblo artifacts, replicated domiciles and exhibits representing Navajo, Ute, Jicarilla and Hispanic cultures; slides of rock art; oral history tapes; maps. *Special programs*: Educational programs and guided tours to student groups. *Publications*: 3,000+ archaeological reports; and historical publications. Research library. Established 1973.

BANDELIER NATIONAL MONUMENT
HCR 1 Box 1, Rte. 4, Suite 15
LOS ALAMOS 87544
  (505) 672-3861
  John D. Hunter, Supt.
Description: Approximately 29,000 acres of ruins of the Pueblo (Anasazi) culture, dating from about 1200-1600 A.D. Publications. Library. A National Historic Landmark.

MESCALERO APACHE CULTURAL CENTER MUSEUM
P.O. Box 176
MESCALERO 88340
  (505) 671-4495

GADSEN MUSEUM
Barker Rd. and Hwy. 28
P.O. Box 147
MESILLA 88046
  (505) 526-6293
  Mary Veitch Alexander, Curator/Owner
Description: Collections include Indian artifacts from the Southwest.

SALINAS NATIONAL MONUMENT
Route 1, Box 496
MOUNTAINAIR 87036
  (505) 847-2585
  Thomas B. Carroll, Supt.
Description: Located on the site of prehistoric pithouses, 800 A.D.; prehistoric Indian ruins 1 100-1670 A.D.; four Spanish Mission ruins, 1627-1672. An archaeology museum maintains a collection of artifacts from the ruins. Library.

PECOS NATIONAL HISTORICAL PARK
P.O. Drawer 418
PECOS 87552
  (505) 757-6414/6032
  Linda L. Stoll, Superintendent
  Ann Rasor, Interpreter
Description: Pecos preserves the ruins of the great Pecos Pueblo (1400-1838) and two associated Spanish colonial missions, 17th & 18th centuries; visitor center displays over 100 artifacts, historical timeline and ten minute introductory film. Special collection: Kidder Collection - 15,000 artifacts excavated from Pecos Pueblo from 1915-1929. *Publication*: Pecos: Gateway to Pueblo and Plains: The Anthology. Library. Established 1965.

PICURIS PUEBLO MUSEUM
P.O. Box 228
PENASCO 87553

EASTERN NEW MEXICO UNIVERSITY BLACKWATER DRAW MUSEUM
Station 9
PORTALES 88130
  (505) 562-2202 F AX 562-2578
  Dr. John Montgomery, Director
Description: Maintains collection of Paleo-Indian archaeology & anthropology.

PALEO-INDIAN INSTITUTE
Eastern New Mexico University
P.O. Box 2154
PORTALES 88130
  Dr. George Agogino, Director
Description: Maintains exhibits illustrating the life of the paleo-archaic and modern Indian. Library.

EL MORRO NATIONAL MONUMENT
RAMAH 87321
  (505) 783-5132
  Douglas Eury, Supt.
Description: Archaeological site of Inscription Rock, prehistoric Pueblo ruins. Library.

STRADLING MUSEUM OF THE HORSE
RUIDOSO 88345
  Anne C. Stradling, Director
Description: Equine and Indian Museum. Library.

INSTITUTE OF AMERICAN INDIAN ARTS MUSEUM
P.O. Box 20007
SANTA FE 87504
  (505) 988-6463 Fax 988-6446
  Charles A. Dailey, Director
  Manuelita Lovato, Curator
Special collection: Student Honors Collection--Contains approximately 6,000 items--paintings, graphics, sculpture, ceramics, textiles, costumes, jewelry, and ethnological material of Native-American students' work. Also, more than 1,000 items of non-student work done by Indian artists throughout the U.S. *Special programs*: Art festival, lectures, workshops; arts and crafts for sale. *Publication*: Spawning the Medicine River, quarterly. Native-American Videotape Archives and Library.

MUSEUM OF INDIAN ARTS & CULTURE--LABORATORY OF ANTHROPOLOGY
P.O. Box 2087, 708 Camino Lejo
SANTA FE 87504
  (505) 827-6344 Fax 827-6349
  Dr. Stephen Becker, Director
  Bruce Bernstein, Chief Curator
  Louise Stiver, Collections
  Ed Ladd, Ethnology
  Dr. Stephen Lekson, Archaeology
  Pearl Sunrise, Resource Center
Description: Consists of over 15,000 ethnographic objects and more than 26,000 archaeological objects, with emphasis on artifacts from the prehistoric, ethnographic, and present-day Indian Southwest. Features permanent exhibitions of Southwestern Indian culture. Papers in Anthropology; Research Records; Lab Notes; and Archaeological Surveys. Library. Established 1987.

MUSEUM OF NEW MEXICO FINE ARTS MUSEUM
P.O. Box 1727, 127 E. Palace Ave.
SANTA FE 87501
Special collection: Indian Arts Fund Collection--Contains pottery, jewelry, and costumes; art of the Southwest.

SAN ILDEFONSO PUEBLO MUSEUM
Route 5, Box 315-A
SANTA FE 87501
  (505) 455-2424

SCHOOL OF AMERICAN RESEARCH
660 Garcia St., Box 2188
SANTA FE 87504
  (505) 982-3583 Fax 989-9809
  Dr. Douglas W. Schwartz, President
Description: Maintains collections of Pueblo Indian pottery, Navajo and Pueblo textiles and jewelry, Native American paintings; Southwestern Indian basketry, and kachinas; and other ethnographic objects. Operates the Indian Arts Center.

WHEELWRIGHT MUSEUM OF THE AMERICAN INDIAN
P.O. Box 5153, 704 Camino Lejo
SANTA FE 87502
  (505) 982-4636
  Richard W. Lang, Director
  LaRayne Parrish, Curator
Description: Collections of Southwest ethnology--Navajo textiles and silver; Navajo, Apache, and Hopi basketry; Pueblo pottery; Navajo, Apache, and Pueblo cradleboards; Navajo sandpainting reproductions. *Special programs*: Lecture series; textile and basket-weaving workshops; craft demonstrations; Indian arts and crafts and books for sale. *Publication*: Quarterly newsletter. Library.

WESTERN NEW MEXICO UNIVERSITY MUSEUM
P.O. Box 680
SILVER CITY 88062
  (505) 538-6386
  Dr. Cynthia Ann Bettison, Director
  Sidney Basilius, Curator
Special collection: Eisele Collection of Ancient Mimbres, Casa Grandes & Upper Gila River Pottery and Artifacts. Also dozens of picture bowls depicting life and culture of the ancient Mimbres culture of circa 600 A.D.; collection of Mogollon Culture artifacts, including lithics, pottery, and fiber. *Publication*: Newsletter. Established 1974.

KIT CARSON MEMORIAL FOUNDATION
P.O. Drawer B, Old Kit Carson Rd.
TAOS 87571
　(505) 758-4741
　Jack Boyer, Director
Description: Displays artifacts of prehistoric Indian culture of Taos and the Southwest. Library.

MILLICENT ROGERS MUSEUM
P.O. Box A
TAOS 87571
　(505) 758-2462
　Arthur H. Wolf, Director
　Michael Stephens, Curator
Description: Exhibits prehistoric and historic Southwest and Plains Native-American art and material culture.

ZUNI ARCHAEOLOGY PROGRAM
P.O. Box 339
ZUNI 87327
　(505) 782-4814
　Roger Anyon, Director
Description: Archaeological site record files are maintained as are a comprehensive map file and air photo file of the Reservation and surrounding areas. Unpublished manuscripts on Zuni history and archaeology are maintained. Historic photographs. Publications: Report Series; Research Series. Library. Founded 1975.

NEW YORK

NEW YORK STATE MUSEUM
Cultural Education Center
Empire State Plaza
ALBANY 12224
Special collections: Morgan Collection–Mid 19th century Seneca ethnographic material; The Beauchamp Collection--Onondaga ethnographic material; The Parker Collection--Late 19th and 20th century Iroquois ethnological and general New York archaeological materials. Publications. Library.

SIX NATIONS INDIAN MUSEUM
ANCHIOTA 12968

OWASCO TEYETASTA
RT. 38A Emerson Park
Mail: 203 Genessee St.
AUBURN 13021
　(315) 253-8051
　Peter L. Jones, Director
Description: Indian History Museum - maintains a collection of Point Peninsula, Owasco, Cayuga Indian artifacts from Cayuga County; Ely Parker, Redjacket items, and John S. Clark maps. Crafts for sale. Library.

KATERI GALLERIES
The National Shrine of North American Martyrs
AURIESVILLE 12016
　(518) 853-3033
　Rec. Robert J. Boyle, S.J., Director
　Rev. John M. Dovlan, S.J., Curator
Description: Located on the site of the martyrdom of Father Isaac Jogues, French Jesuit priest, and his companions who were killed by the Mohawk Indians in 1642. Also, the 1656 Birthplace of Kateri Tekakwitha. *Special collection*: Mohawk Indian Culture Collection–Indian artifacts and handicrafts; Indian longhouse dioramas. *Publication*: Pilgrim, quarterly magazine. Library.

TONAWANDA-SENECA MUSEUM
Tonawanda-Seneca Reservation
BASOM 14013

THE BROOKLYN CHILDREN'S MUSEUM
145 Brooklyn Ave.
BROOKLYN 11213
Description: Exhibits Plains Indian material; also, Southwestern, Eastern Woodlands and Northwest Indian artifacts. Library.

BUFFALO AND ERIE COUNTY HISTORICAL SOCIETY MUSEUM
Humboldt Park
BUFFALO 14211
Description: Maintains a collection of Niagara frontier Indian artifacts, including clothing, masks, and tools, mostly of Iroquois village life. Publications. Library.

THE ROCKWELL MUSEUM
111 Cedar St.
CORNING 14830
　(607) 937-5386
　Kent Ahrens, Director
　Robyn G. Peterson, Curator of Collections
Description: Houses a fine arts collection that emphasizes the subject matter of the American West and a complementary collection of several hundred Native American artifacts focusing on the period from about 1870-1940 and upon the cultures of the Plains and the Southwest. *Special programs*: Teacher training and outreach programs on the Iroquois. Library. *Publications*: Newsletter for members; exhibition catalogs. Established 1976.

MUSEUM OF THE HUDSON HIGHLANDS
The Boulevard, P.O. Box 181
CORNWALL-ON-HUDSON 12520
　(914) 534-7781
　Charles I. Keene, Director
Special collection: Eastern Woodlands Indians–Exhibits more than 80 stone artifacts; 40 modern reproductions made by a group of Iroquois. *Special program*: Native American educational aides for programs and presentations to school groups, kindergarten to fourth grades. An Indian Loan Kit comprised of an Iroquois pack basket filled with artifacts and reproductions is designed for teachers to use to complement the NYS fourth grade history curriculum. Library. Established 1962.

BLACK BEAR MUSEUM
P.O. Box 47
ESOPUS 12429
　Roy Black Bear, Owner

THE MOHAWK-CAUGHNAWAGA MUSEUM
Route 5, Box 554
FONDA 12068
　(518) 853-3678
　Rev. Nicholas Weiss, Chairman
　Volkert Veeder, Curator
Description: Located on the site of the 1666-1693 excavated Caughnawaga Indian Village. Displays North, South and Central American Indian artifacts, with emphasis on the Iroquois of central New York State. *Publication*: Mohawk Indian-Mo and Their Valley. Library.

TEKAKWITHA SHRINE
Route 5, Box 627, RD 1
FONDA 12068
　(518) 853-3646
　Rev. Nicholas Weiss, Director

Description: Religious Shrine and Historic Archaeological Site, 1666-1693; Mohawk Indian Castle: residence of Kateri Tekakwitha.

LONGYEAR MUSEUM OF ANTHROPOLOGY
Colgate University
HAMILTON 13346
　(315) 824-7543
Description: Features large collections of local Oneida Iroquois and Mesoamerican archaeological materials.

AKWESASNE MUSEUM
Akwesasne Cultural Center
St. Regis Mohawk Nation
RR 1, Box 14C
HOGANSBURG 13655
　Carol White, Director
　(518) 358-2240 Fax 358-2649
Description: Showcases Mohawk culture by exhibiting contemporary Iroquoian art and historic artifacts. *Special programs*: Changing art exhibit; contemporary baskets by master basketmakers of Akwesasne; slide-tape shows on Iroquoian art; Native arts and basketmaking classes; produces movies, slide shows, and video; sells original handicrafts through Sweetgrass Gift Shop. *Publication*: Kariwenhawi, newsletter. Library.

IROQUOIS INDIAN MUSEUM
P.O. Box 7, Caverns Rd.
HOWES CAVE 12092
　(518) 296-8949
　Dr. Christina B. Johannsen Hanks, Director
　Stephanie E. Shultes, Curator
　Mike Butler, Nature Park Manager
Description: A 45-acre nature park with educational trails explaining the ethnobotany of Iroquois culture. Maintains an extensive collection of contemporary Iroquois fine art and craftwork; archaeological materials of the Northeast and Schoharie Valley occupations from the Archaic Period to the Contact Period (1700's); photographic collections of contemporary Iroquois arts, ethnographic objects, events and people. *Special programs*: Children's museum - a restatement of the adult museum designed to break down stereotypes and to introduce to children the Iroquois people of today; educational programs; 3 Annual Iroquois Indian Festivals (Memorial Day weekend, mid-July weekend, and Labor Day weekend). *Publications*: Museum Notes, quarterly newsletter; Directory of Iroquois Artists & Crafts People; "Joe Jacobs, Iroquois Art," "Pete Jones: Iroquois Art," and Visual Voices of the Iroquois," all three exhibition catalogs. Library. Established in 1980.

SENECA INDIAN HISTORICAL SOCIETY
12199 Brant Reservation Rd.
IRVING 14081
　Twylah Nitsch, Director

STE. MARIE AMONG THE IROQUOIS
P.O. Box 146, Onondaga Lake Park
LIVERPOOL 13088
　(315) 457-2990
　Robert Geaci, Director; Valerie Bell, Curator
Description: A reconstruction of a 1656 French settlement among the Onondaga Iroquois. Maintains archaeological material from area sites-- Onondaga cultural material. *Special programs*: Living History Program--interpretation of Onondaga Indian culture; lectures. *Publication*: Onondaga Portrait of a Native People. Library.

AMERICAN INDIAN COMMUNITY HOUSE GALLERY/MUSEUM
708 Broadway at Waverly Place
NEW YORK 10003
 (212) 226-7433
 Lloyd E. Oxendine, Curator
Description: Displays native-American art work.

AMERICAN MUSEUM OF NATURAL HISTORY
79th St. & Central Park West
NEW YORK 10024
 (212) 769-5375
 Ian Tattersall, Ph.D., Chairman
 Stanley A. Freed, Ph.D., Curator
Special collections: Eskimo Exhibit, and Indians of the Northwest Coast--Artifacts of the Coast Salish, Nootka, Haida, Tsimpshean, Thompson, Bella Coola, Tlingit, and Kwakiutl; also, shamanistic regalia and ceremonial objects. *Publications*: Natural History; Curator; Bulletin; Anthropological Papers. Library and Reading Room.

GEORGE GUSTAV HEYE CENTER -NATIONAL MUSEUM OF THE AMERICAN INDIAN
Smithsonian Institution
1 Bowling Green
NEW YORK 10004
 (212) 283-2420 Fax 491-9302
 Dr. Duane King, Assistant Director
 Richard West, Director (Washington, DC office)
 Vine Deloria, Jr., Vice-Chair, Board of Trustees
 Peter Scott Brill, Curator of Exhibits
 Sharon Dean, Head, Photo Archives
 Lee A. Callander, Registrar
 Carolyn Rapkievian, Public Prog. Coord,
 Judith A. Brundin, Head Education Dept.
 Martha Kreipe de Montano, Mgr. Resource Ctr.
 Elizabeth Weatherford, Film & Video Center
 Barbara J. Christ, Manager, Museum Store
 Ellen Jamieson, Publications Manager
Description: Acknowledged to be one of the largest and finest assemblage of artifacts representing the native cultures of North, Central & South America, the Museum (founded 1916) is a national treasury unsurpassed for its potential for education and research. Its areal and temporal scope is vast, ranging from Alaska to Chile and from the Paleo-Indian period to the present, encompassing societies as diverse as the 20th century hunting band societies of the Arctic and subarctic and the ancient agricultural civilizations of the Aztec and Inca. The artifacts in the collections range from precious ornaments to commonplace tools, from projectile points to abstract paintings by contemporary Indian artists. The Central & South American and the Caribbean collections include ancient ornaments of Mexican jade and turquoise, ancient gold, silver, basketry, fabrics, and pottery, stone, and shell sculptures from the Antilles. The North American collections include silver and turquoise jewelry, weavings, and pottery from the Southwest; painted wooden sculptures from the Northwest Coast; ancient carved shell artifacts from the Southeast; and carved ivory and stone from the Arctic. Spec*ial programs*: Education Department offers guided tours, visiting Native American artists and artisans, and a lecture series; The Film and Video Center researches and exhibits film and video productions concerned with Inuit & Indian peoples of the Americas; The Indian Information Center makes available to the public a wide variety of information concerning the native peoples of the Americas; The Museum Store offers a wide variety of contemporary Indian crafts from many tribes, and books, slides, etc. *Publications*: Indian Notes; quarterly newsletter; Museum schedule of exhibits & public programs; exhibition catalogs,

archaeological reports, ethnological studies, bibliographies & biographies published by the Museum for sale; Native American Film & Video Catalog. Photogra*phic Archives*: Contains approximately 70,000 photographs documenting Native American life in the Western Hemisphere. Slides & prints are available for purchase. Library.

NATIVE AMERICAN CENTRE FOR THE LIVING ARTS, INC.
25 Rainbow Mall
NIAGARA FALLS 14303
 (716) 284-2427
 Duffy Wilson, Executive Director
 Elwood Green, Curator
Description: Maintains a collection of Native-American archaeological and ethnological artifacts; Native-American archives and iconography. *Publications*: Turtle, quarterly tabloid; Art Catalogues, book. Library.

SIX NATIONS INDIAN MUSEUM
Roakdale Rd., HCR 1 Box 10
ONCHIOTA 12968
 (518) 891-0769
 Ray Fadden, Owner
Description: Dedicated to preserving the culture of the Iroquois Confederacy (Mohawks, Senecas, Onondagas, Oneidas, Cayugas and Tuscaroras), the Museum exhibits pre-Columbian, historic, as well as contemporary items of Iroquois culture--clothing, tools, crafts, baskets, and objects of art; a collection of charts, posters, and written material; miniature Abenaki, Lakota, Delaware and Mohegan villages. *Special program*: Lectures on Native-American history and culture.

MUSEUMS AT HARTWICK
Hartwick College
ONEONTA 13820-9989
 (607) 431-4480
 Jane des Grange, Director
 Dr. David Anthony, Curator of Collection
Yager Museum: A collection of upper Susquehanna Indian artifacts, and Southwest basketry and pottery. Library. Founded 1928

ROCHESTER MUSEUM & SCIENCE CENTER
657 East Ave., Box 1480
ROCHESTER 14603
 (716) 271-4320
 Richard Shultz, President; Betty Prisch, Curator
 Charles F. Hayes, III, Director of Research
Description: Exhibits Native American material related to archaeology, ethnology, and physical anthropology, with emphasis on Seneca, Iroquoian ethnology. Collection includes Iroquois Indian arts and artifacts; paintings by Seneca artist Ernest Smith. *Special collections*: Lewis Henry Morgan mid 19th Century collection of Woodlands, Plains, and Southwestern material; Indian Arts Project collection produced by Iroquois arts and crafts workers in the 1930's and 40's. "At the Western Door", permanent exhibit detailing story of contact between Seneca Iroquois and Europeans in western New York, A.D. 1550 to present. *Publications*: Monthly newsletter; Research Records. Research library. Established in 1912.

SENECA-IROQUOIS NATIONAL MUSEUM
Allegany Indian Reservation
P.O. Box 442, Broad St. Extension
SALAMANCA 14779
 (716) 945-1738
 Judith Greene, Director
Description: Devoted to the presentation of the prehistory, history, and contemporary heritage of

the Seneca Nation of Indians, and, in a wider sense, the Iroquois culture. Collection holdings include archaeological, ethnographic, archival materials, as well as a large photo collection. *Special program*: Living Artists Series--lectures. *Publication*: 1981 Collections of the Seneca-Iroquois National Museum. Library. Museum shop.

SHINNECOCK NATIONAL MUSEUM
Shinnecocok Tribe Cultural Complex
P.O. Box 59
SOUTHAMPTON 11968
 (516) 283-1643
 David Martine, Director
Monthly cable show "Voices of Native America," Channel 25 cable vision.

SOUTHOLD INDIAN MUSEUM
Bayview Rd., Box 268
SOUTHOLD 11971
 (516) 765-5577
 Walter L. Smith, President
Description: Collections include Native American articles and artifacts; and handiworks of Eskimos.

GANONDAGAN STATE HISTORIC SITE
P.O. Box 239, 1488 Victor Holcomb Rd.
VICTOR 14564
 (716) 924-5848
 G. Peter Jemison, Director
Description: Located at the late 17th century Seneca Indian settlement. Maintains collections of site related artifacts. Also contemporary Iroquois arts and crafts. Small reference library. *Publications*: Si Wong Geh, newsletter; Art from Ganondagan; War Against the Seneca by John Mohawk. *Hours*: 9-5 Wed.-Sun., mid-May to end of October.

NORTH CAROLINA

CHEROKEE INDIAN CYCLORAMA WAX MUSEUM
P.O. Box 398, Highway 19E
CHEROKEE 28719
 (704) 497-4521 (April-October)
 (704) 497-2111 (November-March)
Description: Explains over 300 years of Cherokee history by the use of life-size wax figures depicting actual events. A large scale electronically lighted map of the Southeast shows the vast empire of the Cherokee Nation, covering over eight southern states, fade away to the present Qualla Indian Reservation. Displays portray the techniques in making Cherokee crafts and tools. Includes "Trail of Tears". Open April-October.

MUSEUM OF THE CHEROKEE INDIAN
U.S. Highway 441 North, Box 770-A
CHEROKEE 28719
 (704-497-3481
 Juanita Hughes, Curator
 Maxine Hill, General Manager
Description: Exhibits Cherokee Indian artifacts, relics and documents. *Publication*: Journal of Cherokee Studies, semiannual. Library.

SCHIELE MUSEUM REFERENCE LIBRARY & CENTER FOR SOUTHEASTERN NATIVE AMERICAN STUDIES
P.O. Box 953, 1500 E. Garrison Blvd.
GASTONIA 28053-0953
 (704) 865-6131
 Steve Watts & Melissa Turney,
  Native American Education
 Alan May, Archaeologist

Ms. M. Turner, Registrar & Librarian
Description: Maintains extensive holdings of Native-American artifacts, clothing, utensils, rugs, pottery, jewelry, costumes, arts and crafts, etc. spanning known history; collections of 12 major cultural areas throughout the U.S. and Canada; specialized collections on Southeast Indians, especially pottery; also, lithic material from the Southeast with special sections relating to local areas of North Carolina. The Catawba Village: A replicated Southeastern Indian village, circa 1550, representing Catawba and Southeastern Indian architecture and lifestyles from the 16th through 19th centuries. *Special programs*: Catawba Village Study-Tour Program designed for grades 4 and up, where students explore the ways and means of aboriginal life; contract courses; workshops; The Southeastern Indian Culture Study Group; annual Native-American Fall Festival in September. Library.

INDIAN MUSEUM OF THE CAROLINAS
607 Turnpike Rd.
LAURINBURG 28352
(919) 276-5880
Dr. Margaret Houston, Director
Description: Exhibits Indian ethnographic material and modern Native American art and artifacts of North and South Carolina, and the Southeast U.S. Comparative displays show artifacts from other geographic areas. *Special programs*: Evening speakers program; guided tours. Library.

TOWN CREEK INDIAN MOUND
STATE HISTORIC SITE
Rt. 3, Box 50
MT. GILEAD 27306
(910) 439-6802
Archie C. Smith, Site Manager
Description: A reconstructed 15th century Indian ceremonial center, based on archaeological data and early documents, includes major temple on top of an earthen mound, minor temple, mortuary, game pole, and palisade surrounding the ceremonial area. *Museum*: Exhibits area interpreting way of life of the Indians at Town Creek, includes artifacts discovered during excavation of the site. *Special program*: 18-minute slide presentation on way of life of the Indians at Town Creek. Established in 1937.

NATIVE AMERICAN RESOURCE CENTER
Pembroke State University
PEMBROKE 28372
(919) 521-4214
Dr. Stanley Knick, Director & Curator
Description: Museum housing various collections of archaeological and ethnographic artifacts from Native Americans in North and South America, with emphasis on Eastern Woodlands. *Publications*: Spirit, quarterly newsletter; Robeson Trails Archaeological Survey. Library. Established 1979.

NORTH CAROLINA DIVISION OF
ARCHIVES & HISTORY MUSEUM
109 E. Jones St.
RALEIGH 27611

CATAWBA MUSEUM OF ANTHROPOLOGY
2113 Brenner Ave., Heath Hill Forest
SALISBURY 28144
(704) 637-4111/4447
Dee Dee Joyce, Director/Curator
Description: Exhibits on the prehistoric and historic culture of American Indians, primarily from the Mid-Atlantic and Southeast Plains.

MUSEUM OF ANTHROPOLOGY
Wake Forest University
Box 7267, Wingate Dr.,
WINSTON-SALEM 27109
(919) 759-5282
Dr. Mary Jane Berman, Director/Curator
Description: An anthropology museum exhibiting North and South American Indian artifacts. *Special programs*: School tours and lectures, kindergarten to 8th grade; traveling exhibitions. Library. *Publication*: Newsletter. Established 1963.

NORTH DAKOTA

TURTLE MOUNTAIN CHIPPEWA
HERITAGE CENTER
Hwy. 5, Box 257
BELCOURT 58316
(701) 477-6140
Denise Lajimodierre, CEO and Chair
Description: Maintains collections of Chippewa Indian artifacts and contemporary art.

STATE HISTORICAL SOCIETY OF ND
North Dakota Heritage Center
Capitol Grounds
BISMARCK 58505
(701) 224-2666
James E. Sperry, Superintendent
Description: Collections include ethnological, ethnographical, and prehistory materials of all types dating throughout the eras of known occupation of the northern Great Plains by human beings (circa 10,000 B.C. to present.) *Publications*: North Dakota History: Journal of the Northern Great Plains; Plains Talk, Newsletter. Archives & Library.

BUFFALO TRAILS MUSEUM
Box 22
EPPING 58843
(701) 859-3512/4361
Duane Syverson, Director
Elmer Halvorson, Curator
Description: Depicts Indian culture native to the region (Upper Missouri area.) Exhibits Plains Indian artifacts; Diorama of Assiniboin Indian Village; Diorama of Fortified Hidatsa Village. *Publication*: Museum brochure. Library. Founded 1966.

STANDING ROCK RESERVATION MUSEUM
FORT YATES 58538

NORTH DAKOTA MUSEUM OF ART
P.O. Box 7305, University Station
GRAND FORKS 58202
(701) 777-4195
Laurel J. Reuter, Director
Displays American Indian art.

MUSEUM OF THE BADLANDS
P.O. Box 198
MEDORA 58645
(701) 623-4444
Description: Exhibits attire and crafts of North American Indian tribes.

FORT ABRAHAM LINCOLN STATE
HISTORICAL PARK MUSEUM
Route 2, Box 139
MANDAN 58554
(701) 663-9571
Charles Erickson, Director
Dale Carlson, Curator
Description: Houses artifacts from the Mandan tribe. Also, a reconstructed Mandan Indian Village.

Special program: Cultural Indian Celebration held each August. Library. Established 1934.

THREE AFFILIATED TRIBES MUSEUM
Fort Berthold Reservation
NEW TOWN 58763

KNIFE RIVER INDIAN VILLAGES
NATIONAL HISTORIC SITE
RR 1 Box 168
STANTON 58571
(701) 745-3300 Fax 745-3708
Michael Holm, Area Manager
Description: Collections of Hidatsa/Mandan cultural artifacts.

OHIO

AKRON ART INSTITUTE
69 E. Market St.
AKRON 44308
Special collection: Dr. Edgar B. Foltz Collection–American Indian art and artifacts–kachinas, jewelry, musical instruments, blankets, beadwork, basketry, pottery. Library.

MOUND CITY GROUP NATIONAL MONUMENT
16062 State Route 104
CHILLICOTHE 45601
(614) 774-1125
William Gibson, Supt.
Robert Petersen, Park Ranger
Description: A 240 acre park preserving 23 burial mounds and two Hopewell earthen enclosures. Collections illustrate the wide spread Hopewell trade network between B.C. 200 and 500 A.D. *Museum*: Exhibits of Hopewell artifacts. Library. Established 1923.

CINCINNATI ART MUSEUM
Eden Park
CINCINNATI 45202
(513) 721-5204
Millard Rogers, Jr., Director; Bill Mercer, Curator
Description: Displays archaeological and ethnological specimens. Archaeological--principally Mound Builder, also Adena, Hopewell, Fort Ancient cultures from Ohio; stone, bone, metal, shell, and pottery from Tennessee and Arkansas; Casas Grandes pottery. Ethnological material principally Northwest Coast, Plains and Pueblo pottery. Some prehistoric Woodlands material in collection. *Special collection*: A permanent exhibit gallery for Native American art; periodic speial temporaryt exhibitions and programming (speakers and art demonstrations) rlated to Native American art. *Publication*: "Art of the First Americans" exhibition catalog. Library. Established 1881.

JOHNSON-HUMRICKHOUSE MUSEUM
300 N. Whitewoman St., Roscoe Village
COSHOCTON 43812
(614) 622-8710
Midge Derby, Director
Description: Native American Gallery exhibits paleo to modern North American Indian and Eskimo arts, crafts, basketry, beadwork, blankets and jewelry. Chronologically arranged prehistoric artifacts date back thousands of years and include projectile points, primitive tools and pottery made by Ohio's aboriginal people. Special collection: Indian-made baskets are displayed georgaphically, depicting various designs and styles from tribes coast to coast. *Publication*: Quarterly newsletter. Reference library. Established 1931.

**RUTHERFORD B. HAYES
PRESIDENTIAL CENTER**
Spiegel Grove
FREMONT 43420
  (419) 332-2081
  Roger Bridges, Supt.; James Snider, Curator
Description: A collection of artifacts, largely of the
Plains Indians, the Sioux, and some Pueblo; pre-
historic Ohio Indian artifacts. *Publications*: The
Statesman (newsletter); The Hayes Historical
Journal. Library.

MOUNDBUILDERS STATE MEMORIAL
7091 Brownsville Rd. SE
GLENFORD 43739
  (614) 787-2476
  James Kingery, Site Manager
  Dr. Brad Lepper, Curator
Description: The site museum is centered around
an original flint pit; two Hopewell quarries are
placed there. Collections include art objects and
other media representing achievements of the
Adeba and Hopewell cultures 1000 B.C. to 700
A.D. *Special collection*: Display objects made of
flint; depict Native Americans quarrying and chip-
ping the mineral.

FORT ANCIENT MUSEUM
LEBANON 45036
  (513) 932-4421
Description: Located 7 miles southeast of Lebanon, 240 feet above the Little Miami River, the
prehistoric Hopewell Indians (ca. 100 B.C. - A.D.
500) constructed earth and stone walls 4-23 feet
high. Around A.D. 1200, groups of Fort Ancient
Indians established themselves in villages. Exhibits models and life study groups of the Hopewell
and Fort Ancient people who occupied the site.
A National Historic Landmark.

SCHOENBRUNN VILLAGE STATE MEMORIAL
P.O. Box 129, East High Ave.
NEW PHILADELPHIA 44663
  (216) 339-3636
  Susan Goehring, Site Manager
Description: Founded by David Zeisberger in 1772
as a Moravian mission to the Delaware Indians.
Restored to appear as it did over 200 years ago.
Museum: Tells the story of the Christian Delawares
and the Moravian missionaries at Schoenbrunn.
Special program: Volunteer interpreters conduct
daily life demonstrations in period costume. *Pub-
lication*: Schoenbrunn and the Moravian Missions
in Ohio. Established 1923.

**MOUNDBUILDERS STATE MEMORIAL
THE OHIO INDIAN ART MUSEUM**
99 Cooper Ave.
NEWARK 43055
  (614) 344-1920
  James Kingery, Site Manager
  Dr. Brad Lepper, Curator
Description: Prehistoric Indian Art Museum and
Historic Site depicting The Great Circle Earth-
works--ceremonial grounds of prehistoric Hopewell Indians, circa 1000 B.C. - 700 A.D. Exhibits
art objects and other relics representing Adena
and Hopewell cultures. The art museum is the
nation's first museum devoted to prehistoric Native American art. Programs are scheduled for the
general public.

INDIAN MUSEUM OF LAKE COUNTY, OHIO
c/o Lake Erie College
391 W. Washington
PAINESVILLE 44077
  (216) 352-3361

  Gwen G. King, Director
Description: Houses pre-contact artifacts, and
crafts and art of Native North American cultures
from 1800 to present.

SERPENT MOUND MUSEUM
State Route 73, Box 234
PEEBLES 45660
  (513) 587-2796
  William E. Gustin, Manager
Description: Indian Museum exhibiting material of
Adena Indian culture.

HISTORIC INDIAN MUSEUM
Piqua Historical Area/Ohio Historical Society
9845 N. Hardin Rd.
PIQUA 45356-9707
  (513) 773-2522
  John C. Neilson, Site Manager
Description: Restored 1829 home and outbuild-
ings of federal Indian agent John Johnston, well
respected by the Indians of Ohio and handled
many of the important treaties. A museum contains artifacts of Native American tools, art, canoes, costumes, etc. Describes the lifestyle of the
Native American after the white man came to the
U.S. and the changes before and after. A collection of McKenney-Hall prints as well as Catlin prints
are displayed. A life-size diorama of Native Americans and French trader in museum. Established
1972.

OKLAHOMA

APACHE TRIBAL MUSEUM
P.O. Box 1220
ANADARKO 73005
  (405) 247-9493

DELAWARE TRIBAL MUSEUM
c/o Delaware Executive Board
P.O. Box 825
ANADARKO 73005

INDIAN CITY, U.S.A.
Highway 8, Box 695
ANADARKO 73005
  (405) 247-5661
  George F. Moran, Director
Description: Features reconstructed Plains Indian
dwellings; also, Indian history museum located on
site of 1887, Tonkawa Massacre. Exhibits Indian
artifacts, pottery, dance costumes, and dolls.

**THE NATIONAL HALL OF FAME
FOR FAMOUS AMERICAN INDIANS**
Highway 62, Box 808
ANADARKO 73005
  (405) 247-5795
  Allie Reynolds, President
  Paul T. Stonum, Executive V.P.
Description: An outdoor museum containing sculp-
tured bronze portraits of famous American Indi-
ans in a landscaped area. Includes portraits of Will
Rogers, Jim Thorpe, Pocahontas, Chief Joseph,
Sacajawea, Chief Quanah Parker, Charles Curtis,
Osceola, Sequoyah, Pontiac, Hiawatha, et al.
Special programs: Annual dedication ceremonies
in August, when an honoree is inducted; educa-
tional seminars regarding inductee's history and
contribution to the American way of life.

SOUTHERN PLAINS INDIAN MUSEUM
Highway 62 East, Box 749
ANADARKO 73005
  (405) 247-6221

  Rosemary Ellison, Curator
Description: Presents the richness and diversity
of historic arts created by the tribal peoples of
western Oklahoma, including the Kiowa, Comanche, Kiowa-Apache, Southern Cheyenne, Southern Arapaho, Wichita, Caddo, Delaware, and Fort
Sill Apache. Exhibits the creative achievements
of Native American artists and craftspeople of the
U.S. Highlighting the exhibit is a display of the
varied traditional costumes of Southern Plains
men, women and children, presented in complete
detail on life-size figures; four dioramas and a
mural illustrating historic Indian cultural subjects,
created by artist and sculptor, Allan Houser, a Fort
Sill Apache and native Oklahoman. *Special programs*: Annual series of one-person exhibitions;
demonstrations of Native American arts and crafts
techniques; hosts events honoring Native-Americans; The American Indian Exposition, in August,
features a week-long event of dance contests, arts
and crafts; tours and Gallery discussions. *Publications*: Illustrated catalogs and brochures. Craft
shop. Administered by the Indian Arts and Crafts
Board. Established in 1947.

WICHITA TRIBAL MUSEUM
P.O. Box 729
ANADARKO 73005
  (405) 247-2425
Description: General collection consists of very
small displays depicting traditional homes, clothing, food, and/or household items; cultural artifacts
of religious significance; pictures of tribal members and places of importance with explanations
of mythology, religious occasions or ceremonials.
Also traditional construction of dwellings with a
display of a grass lodge diorama; and displays of
various items found by archaeologists at several
digging sites. *Publications*: Wichita Tribal Newsletter, quarterly; book - "The Wichita People," by
W.W. Newcomb, Jr.; two pamphlets: "Wichita
Memories" and "Southern Plains Lifeways,"
Apache and Wichita.

FORT SILL APACHE MUSEUM
Route 2, Box 121
APACHE 73006

WOOLAROC MUSEUM
Route 3, State Highway 123
BARTLESVILLE 74003
  (918) 336-0307
  Robert R. Lansdown, Director
Description: Exhibits arts and crafts of the South-
west Indian tribes, as well as archaeological ma-
terial from Oklahoma excavations. Publications.
Library.

MEMORIAL INDIAN MUSEUM
P.O. Box 483
Second & Allen Sts.
BROKEN BOW 74728
  (405) 584-6531
  LaMarr Smith, Director
Description: A collection of prehistoric Indian
artifacts, Indian skeletal remains, early beadwork;
displays modern textiles and basketry. *Research*:
Prehistoric Caddo Indians and their pottery.
Library.

COMANCHE CULTURAL CENTER MUSEUM
P.O. Box 344
CACHE 73527

KIOWA TRIBAL MUSEUM
P.O. Box 369
CARNEGIE 73015

(405) 654-2300

Exhibit: "The View From Rainy Mountain." The New Kiowa Murals by Parker Boyiddle, Mirac Creepingbear, and Sherman Chaddleson. Each artist produced three 6'x8' paintings depicting periods of Kiowa existence. Listening to their elders, they selected highlights from the creation stories, pre-history, and historic periods. A tenth mural, a collaborative painting, represents Kiowa reality today and its journey into tomorrow.

WILL ROGERS MEMORIAL
P.O. Box 157
CLAREMORE 74018
(918) 341-0719
Dr. Reba N. Collins, Director

Description: Consists of four main galleries displaying the personal effects and memorabilia belonging to Will Rogers, his wife Betty, and infant son, Fred are buried in the tomb adjoining the Memorial building. *Special collection*: The original manuscripts and papers belonging to Will Rogers. An annual Will Rogers Day celebration is held on November 4, to commemorate his birthday. *Publication*: Will Rogers Times, irregular newsletter. Library.

NO MAN'S LAND HISTORICAL MUSEUM
P.O. Box 278, Sewell St.
GOODWELL 73939
(405) 349-2670
Joan Kachel, Director
Dr. Harold S. Kachel, Curator

Special collections: William E. Baker Archaeology Collection, W. Guy Clark Collection, and Duckett alabaster carvings. Contains artifacts of the Plains Indians (buffalo hunters) and the Basketmaker Indian, all collected by local residents of the Oklahoma Panhandle on their land to preserve the Indian cultures that preceded them on the land. Library. Established 1932.

CHEROKEE COURTHOUSE
Rte. 2 Box 37-1
GORE 74435
(918) 489-5663
John Pruitt, Curator
Description: Displays and exhibits on the history of the Cherokee Indians

MUSEUM OF THE RED RIVER
812 E. Lincoln Rd.
IDABEL 74745
(405) 286-3616
Mary Herron, Director/Curator

Description: Collections include art and artifacts of Native peoples of the Western Hemisphere, historic, prehistoric and contemporary. Emphasis on prehistory and early American Indian history of southeast Oklahoma. Exhibits prehistoric Caddoan ceramics, stone tools; also, historical Choctaw items. Library. Publications: Archaeological site reports. Established 1975.

COMANCHE CULTURAL CENTER
P.O. Box 908
LAWTON 73502
(405) 429-1990

MUSEUM OF THE GREAT PLAINS
P.O. Box 68, 601 Ferris Ave.
LAWTON 73502
Steve Wilson, Director; Dan Provo, Curator
Description: Maintains exhibits and artifacts representing the Plains Indian material culture from prehistoric times to present. *Publications*: Great Plains Journal; Newsletter; books for sale. Library.

ATALOA LODGE MUSEUM
Bacone College
2299 Old Bacone Rd.
MUSKOGEE 74403
(918) 683-4581 ext. 283
Dr. Dennis Tanner, President
Thomas R. McKinney, Director

Description: Historic site. Displays Native American artifacts: rugs, beadwork, blankets, basketry, pottery & quillwork. *Special collections*: Large collection of San Ildenfonso pottery; items that were personal property of Native American chiefs; signed documents-President Abraham Lincoln & Chief John Ross of the Cherokee Nation. Library. *Publications*: Baconian and Smoke Signals, booklets; brochures on the museum. Established 1932.

FIVE CIVILIZED TRIBES MUSEUM
Agency Hill on Honor Heights
MUSKOGEE 74401
(918) 683-1701
Lynn Hart Thornley, Director

Description: Exhibits art, artifacts, books, documents, and letters pertaining to the history and culture of the Cherokees, Choctaws, Creeks, Chickasaws, and Seminoles. Housed in the Indian Agency Building built in 1875. Depicts "Trail of Tears" travel and artifacts. Art Gallery of Traditional Indian Art, only by artists of Five Tribes heritage. Maintains an extensive art and sculpture collection, Jerome Tiger Originals; original carvings and sculptures of Willard Stone. *Special program*: Sponsors four competitive art shows annually - crafts, sculpture, paintings. *Publications*: Quarterly newsletter; Pow Wow Chow Cookbook; The Cherokees; The Muskogee Book; Limited edition artist signed art prints. Library.

FRED JONES, JR. MUSEUM OF ART
University of Oklahoma
410 W. Boyd St.
NORMAN 73019
(405) 325-3272
Thomas R. Topevzer, Curator

Special collection: American Indian Painting Collection--Contains more than 200 original paintings by American Indian artists. Library.

OKLAHOMA MUSEUM OF NATURAL HISTORY
University of Oklahoma
1335 Asp Ave.
NORMAN 73019
(405) 325-4711
Dr. Michael A. Mares, Director

Description: Maintains a permanent exhibit on Oklahoma prehistory and historic Indian tribes; North American archaeological and ethnological specimens, depicting the development of Southern Plains, Southwest and Northwest Coast Indian cultures; also, material from the Spiro Mounds. *Special programs*: Educational; slide/tape programs: Wichita Memories, The Plains Apache, Native American Games, and Spiro Mounds. *Publications*: Newsletter; "Heritage at Risk"; Oklahoma Indian Artifacts. Founded 1899.

STATE MUSEUM OF OKLAHOMA
Oklahoma Historical Society
2100 N. Lincoln Blvd.
Wiley Post Historical Blvd.
OKLAHOMA CITY 73105
(405) 521-2491
Bill Pitts, Dir.; Stan Byers & Jeff Briley, Curators
Description: Maintains Indian and Regional History Museum exhibiting Native-American art and artifacts. *Research*: U.S. Indian Policy. *Special collections*: Newspapers of Indian Territory; Indian

Archive Department--contains more than three million documents pertaining to Indian history. Established 1893.

RED EARTH INDIAN CENTER MUSEUM
2100 NE 52 St.
OKLAHOMA CITY 73111
(405) 427-4228
Scott Tigert, Curator
Exhibits ethnographic items, late 1700s to present; paintings.

CREEK COUNCIL HOUSE MUSEUM
Creek Council House
OKMULGEE 74447
(918) 756-2324
Bruce M. Shackleford, Director
Description: Displays arts and artifacts of the Muscogee Creek Nation. *Publications*: History and Legends of the Creek; Indians of Oklahoma; Creek Nation Capitol. Arts and crafts for sale.

FORT ANCIENT MUSEUM
6123 St. Rte. 350
OREGONIA 45054
(513) 932-4421
Jack K. Blosser, Area Manager
Description: Maintains a collection of artifacts relating to prehistoric Indian life and culture.

OSAGE TRIBAL MUSEUM
Osage Agency Reserve
PAWHUSKA 74056
Description: Exhibits Osage artifacts, paintings, and pictures. Workshops. Library.

PONCA CITY CULTURAL CENTER & MUSEUM
1000 E. Grand
PONCA CITY 74601
(405) 767-0427
La Wanda French, Director
Description: Collections feature clothing, utensils, photographs, weapons, art, musical instruments, and ceremonial materials of the tribes of the Ponca City area: the Osage, Kaw, Ponca, and Otoe; also, Hopi pottery and kachinas; relics from the early French-Indian trading post in Oklahoma; Northwest Coast material, and Quileute and other northern tribes' material. Library.

SEQUOYAH'S HOME HISTORIC SITE
Rt. 1, Box 141
SALLISAW 74955
(918) 775-2413
Dillard Jordan, Manager
Description: An Historic Building, 1829, log cabin of Sequoyah, inventor of Cherokee Syllibary. Located 11 miles northeast of Sallisaw on State Hwy. 101. Includes personal furnishings and artifacts of the life of Sequoyah and western Cherokees. Special program: Computer program designed to help teach Cherokee language on site. Library. Established 1936.

POTAWATOMI INDIAN NATION ARCHIVES & MUSEUM
1901 S. Gordon Cooper
SHAWNEE 74801

SHAWNEE INDIAN MISSION
SHAWNEE 74801

SAC & FOX TRIBAL RV PARK & MUSEUM/CULTURAL CENTER
Route 2, Box 246
STROUD 74079
(918) 968-3526/(405) 275-4270

Jessica Patterson, Director/Curator
Special collections: The Frank Hanison Collection, and Jim Thorpe Collection--Contains displays of pictures, treaties and documents, old tribal rolls; exhibits paintings and artifacts by tribal members. *Special programs*: All-Indian Rodeo, and Arts and Crafts Show; annual Pow-W ow.

CHOCTAW CHIEF'S HOUSE
P.O. Box 165
SWINK 74761
(405) 873-2492
  Gale Carter, Site Attendant
Description: An Historic 1832 Old Chief's House with furniture and furnishings of the 1800's.

CHEROKEE NATIONAL MUSEUM (TSA-LA-GI)
Cherokee Heritage Center
P.O. Box 515
TAHLEQUAH 74464
(918) 456-6007
  Duane H. King, Director
Description: Located on the site of the original 1851 Cherokee Female Seminary and Ancient Village. Collections on Cherokee history, heritage and culture. *Publication*: Columns Newsletter. Library.

CHICKASAW COUNCIL HOUSE MUSEUM
P.O. Box 717
TISHOMINGO 73460
(405) 371-3351
  Faye Orr, Director; Vickie Luster, Genealogist
Description: Indian museum exhibiting items pertaining to the history and culture--government, education, religious and social life--of the Chickasaw Indians. Emphasis is placed on the Chickasaw Governors, their families and administrations, from 1855 to the present day . Library.

TONKAWA TRIBAL MUSEUM
P.O. Box 70
TONKAWA 74653
(405) 628-5301
  Virginia Combrink, Director
  Anna Beard & Cynthia Gould, Curators
Description: Tonkawa artifacts located in Tribal Housing Building. Established 1970..

PHILBROOK ART CENTER
P.O. Box 52510, 2727 S. Rockford Rd.
TULSA 74152
(918) 749-7941
  Jesse G. Wright, Jr., President/Director
Special collections: Clark Field Collection--American Indian basketry and pottery; Roberta Campbell Lawson Collection--American Indian costumes and artifacts; Philbrook Collection--American Indian paintings; The Butler Museum of American Indian Art Collection; The Elizabeth Cole Butler Collection of Native American Art. Library.

GILCREASE MUSEUM
1400 Gilcrease Museum Rd.
TULSA 74127
(918) 596-2700
  Fred A. Myers, Director
Description: The world's largest collection of art of the American West. The story of many cultures of North America is told through art, documents and artifacts from the pre-Columbian era through the 20th century. Exhibits artifacts relating to the culture of the Five Civilized Tribes. *Publications*: Gilcrease Magazine, quarterly; Catlin Catalogue. Library.

YELLOW BULL MUSEUM
Northern Oklahoma College
1220 E. Grand
TONKAWA 74653

CHOCTAW NATION MUSEUM
HC 64, Box 3270
TUSKAHOMA 74574
(918) 569-4465
  Donna Jo Heflin, Curator
Description: The Choctaw Capitol building, a three-story red brick and sandstone structure was completed in 1884 and houses the courtroom which seats three tribal judges appointed by the present Choctaw Chief. Exhibits artifacts such as bone spoons, clay pots, and arrowheads; also items moved over the Trail of Tears are dispolayed; a spinning wheel and iron pots; vintage clothing, old documents and Choctaw pottery . Guided tours available.

SEMINOLE NATION MUSEUM
524 S. W ewoka Ave., Box 1532
WEWOKA 74884
(405) 257-5580
  Jan Wyrick, Director
  Margaret Jane Norman, Curator
Description: Maintains exhibits and artifacts relating to the history of the Oklahoma Seminoles, the Freedmen, early pioneers and oil boom history of the area. *Special exhibits*: Dioramas depicting the Indian Stick Ball Game, The Seminole Whipping Tree, a life-size replica of the Florida Seminole home (Chickee), and exhibits depicting the Florida Seminoles, The Seminole Hunter W arrior, Law-Man (Lighthorseman), and Medicine Man. *Publication*: Este Cate, a history of the Seminoles written by Museum Director, Tuskahoma B. Miller. Library. Established 1974.

PLAINS INDIANS AND PIONEERS MUSEUM
P.O. Box 1167, 2009 W illiams Ave.
WOODWARD 73802
(405) 256-6136
  Sarah Taylor, Director
Description: Collection consists of archival materials, agricultural equipment, items from early settlers, and local Plains Indian items, including beadwork, tools and clothing. *Special programs*: Monthly lectures; slide program, Plains Indian Heritage of Northwestern Oklahoma, for local and statewide use. Publications.

OREGON

UNIVERSITY OF OREGON
MUSEUM OF NATURAL HISTORY
1680 E. 15th Ave.
EUGENE 97403
(503) 346-3024
  Theodore Stern & C. Melvin Aikens, Curators
Description: Holdings include archaeological collections, primarily from Oregon and Alaska, and ethnographic collections from around the world. *Programs*: Occasional workshops on Native American issues. Co-sponsors annual event "Celebrating Traditions: Native American Arts and Cultures" with local Indian education programs offices. Small reference library. *Publications*: Fieldnotes, quarterly newsletter; museum bulletin series.

COLLIER STATE PARK LOGGING MUSEUM
P.O. Box 428
KLAMATH FALLS 97601

Description: Located on the Klamath Indian Reservation, the museum exhibits Indian stone utensils and unexcavated pit houses. Library .

FAVELL MUSEUM OF WESTERN
ART & INDIAN ARTIFACTS
125 West Main, Box 165
KLAMATH FALLS 97601
(503) 882-9996
  Gene Favell, Owner
Description: Exhibits of contemporary original Western and wildlife art; 60,000 arrowheads; pictographs, baskets, pottery, and mortors. *Publication*: A Treasury of Our Western Heritage, a book. Established 1972.

LINFIELD ANTHROPOLOGY MUSEUM
Linfield College
McMINNVILLE 97128
(503) 472-4121
Special collection: John Dulin Native American Art Collection.

HOCKING COUNTY HISTORICAL
SOCIETY MUSEUM
LOGAN 43138
  Tim Dunkle, President
Description: Collects, preserves, studies, and displays all items and papers pertaining to the history of Hocking County, Ohio from Indian days to present. Scheduled tours of museum. *Publications*: History of Hocking County, Logan Celebrating A Century and a Half of Progress (1988) contains two Leland Connor articles, Hocking Canal. Established 1960.

PORTLAND ART MUSEUM
1219 S.W. Park
PORTLAND 97205
(503) 226-2811 Ext. 231
  Dan Monroe, President
  Paul Faulstick, Curator-Native American Art
Special collections: Axel Rasmussen Collection of Northwest Indian Art--Contains approximately 500 objects--items of dress, tools and equipment used in hunting and fishing; also, Eskimo pieces; Pueblo Indian ceramic pieces and prehistoric stone sculpture from the Columbia River basin. also, the Butler Collection-includes about 1,800 pieces dating from the 18th century to the 20th century from virtually every tribe and geographic region in the U.S. *Publication*: Art in the Life of the Northwest Coast Indian. Library .

PENNSYLVANIA

LENNI LENAPE HISTORICAL SOCIETY
Museum of Indian Culture
R.D. #2, Fish Hatchery Rd.
ALLENTOWN 18103
(215) 797-2121
  Carla J.S. Messinger, Director
  Nome Alexander, Curator
Description: The heritage of the Lenni Lenape (Delaware Indians), the earliest known inhabitants of the Lehigh Valley. The museum exhibits artifacts and a traditional village and gardens. *Special interest programs*: preschool, school age, special education classes, adults; Corn Planting Ceremony, in May; Roasting Ears of Corn Ceremony, in August; and A Time of Thanksgiving, in October; slide/lectures, and arts and crafts workshops; speaker's bureau. *Publications*: The Time of the Autumn Moon; Quarterly newsletter; Library . Gift Shop. Established 1979.

CUMBERLAND COUNTY HISTORICAL SOCIETY MUSEUM
21 North Pitt St.
CARLISLE 17013
Special collection: Carlisle Indian School Collection-- Contains photographs, publications, and memorabilia. *Publications*: An Account of Illustrated Talks to Indian Chiefs, by Charles F. Himes; and The Indian Industrial School at Carlisle: Its Origin, Purpose, Progress and Difficulties, by Richard H. Pratt. Library.

BUSHY RUN BATTLEFIELD PARK
P.O. Box 468
HARRISON CITY 15636
Description: Located on the site of Chief Pontiac's rebellion of 1763. Museum: Contains copies of maps and letters relating to the Campaign of 1763, Pontiac's War; exhibits Indian artifacts.

HERSHEY MUSEUM
170 W. Hersheypark Dr.
HERSHEY 17033
(717) 534-3439
David L. Park, Jr., Director
James D. McMahon, Jr., Curator
Description: The Hershey Museum began as the Hershey Indian Museum in 1933 and showcased the collection of Col. John Worth. He put together his extensive collection at the end of the 19th century. The museum has artifacts from the Eastern Woodland tribes, including archaeological objects from the Susquehannocks, as well as items representing Southwest, Plains, and Northwest Coast tribes. Also maintains an Eskimo collection.

READING PUBLIC MUSEUM & ART GALLERY
500 Museum Rd.
READING 19611
(215) 371-5850
Bruce L. Dietrich, Director
Description: Exhibit includes examples of cultural materials, pottery, clothing, tools, toys, ceremonial objects of the following cultural areas: Woodland, Plains, Southwest Desert, California, Northwest Coast, and Inuit. *Special collections*: Study collection of southeastern Pennsylvania lithic objects, approximately 10,000 pieces; study collection of mound pottery; Speck Collection–Delaware material collected during Speck's research of Oklahoma and Canadian dwellings of Delaware peoples. *Special program*: A Museum-School Native-American Studies Project--Elementary education programs for local schools using exhibit areas and Museum classroom lessons. Publications. Library.

EVERHART MUSEUM OF NATURAL HISTORY, SCIENCE & ART
Nay Aug Park
SCRANTON 18510
Description: Maintains American Indian Gallery with exhibits of American Indian art covering five major regions of the U.S. Library.

RHODE ISLAND

HAFFENREFFER MUSEUM OF ANTHROPOLOGY
Brown University, Mt. Hope Grant
BRISTOL 02809
(401) 253-8388
Shepard Krech, III, Director
Barbara Hail, Curator
Thierry Gentis, Asst. Curator
Description: Located on the traditional lands of the Wampanoag peoples, the museum houses artifacts from the native peoples of the Americas. Exhibits tribal arts from around the world. Collections of over 10,000 ethnographic objects and over 100,000 archaeological specimens. Extensive prehistoric Arctic collections including Ipiutak and northern Athapaskan. Special programs: Education programs for school children; lectures and seminars. Publications: 17th Century Wampanoag Burial Ground in Warren, Rhode Island; Hau, Kola! The Plains Indian Collection of the Haffenreffer Museum of Anthropology. Library.

TOMAQUAG INDIAN MEMORIAL MUSEUM
Dovecrest Indian Cultural Center
368 Summit Rd.
EXETER 02822
(401) 539-7795
Description: Archaeology, ethnology, and natural history exhibits related to southern New England Indian cultures. *Publications*: Indians of Southern New England, by Princess Red Wing; Musical Expressions of Early Indians of Rhode Island; Indian Communications. Library.

MUSEUM OF PRIMITIVE ART & CULTURE
1058 Kingston Rd., P.O. Drawer A
PEACE DALE 02883
(401) 783-5711
Sarah Peabody Turnbaugh, Director
Description: An archaeological and ethnology museum exhibiting artifacts from around the world, with an emphasis on North America and especially the Northeast. Special programs: Community-oriented multicultural programming; evening lecture series; public education program. *Publication*: The Nineteenth-Century American Collector: A Rhode Island Perspective (centennial catalog), 1992. Established 1892.

RHODE ISLAND HISTORICAL SOCIETY MUSEUM
52 Power St.
PROVIDENCE 02906
(401) 331-8575
Nina Zannieri, Curator
Description: Maintains a collection of 11,000 objects and artifacts pertaining to Rhode Island history; displays Narragansett and Wampanoag Tribes' artifacts--stone bowls, baskets, metal combs, jewelry, hair ornaments. *Publication*: Rhode Island History, journal. Library.

MUSEUM OF NATURAL HISTORY
Roger Williams Park
PROVIDENCE 02906
(401) 785-9450 Ext. 225
Elizabeth R.T. Fradin, Director
Marilyn Massaro, Curator
Description: Archaeological and ethnological collections from North America. *Special program*: An educational kit - Native Americans in the Northeast: An Archaeological Perspective. Exhibits feature Woodland Indian culture--model village; canoe; model Pueblo; Plains and Northwest Coast Indian artifacts; Eskimo material; American Indian plants; and maps. *Publication*: The Explorer Newsletter. Library. Established 1896.

SOUTH CAROLINA

CHESTER COUNTY HISTORICAL SOCIETY MUSEUM
124 Saluda St.
CHESTER 29706
Louis Warmoth, President
Special collection: The Gatlin Catawba Indian Collection– Displays more than 30,000 artifacts.

McKISSICK MUSEUM
University of South Carolina
COLUMBIA 29208
(803) 777-7251
George D. Terry, Director
Catherine W. Horne, Curator
Description: Exhibits more than 200 Catawba Indian pottery and baskets from the 19th & 20th centuries; Folk Art Resource Center with primary and secondary sources on SC Indians.

SOUTH DAKOTA

DACOTAH PRAIRIE MUSEUM
21 South Main St., Box 395
ABERDEEN 57401
Description: Exhibits Sioux Indian artifacts--beadwork, quillwork, decorated ceremonial and functional leather items, pictographs, ghost dress, and pictures. Library. Sales Shop features contemporary Sioux handicrafts.

AGRICULTURAL HERITAGE MUSEUM
South Dakota State University
BROOKINGS 57007
Special collection: Indian Agricultural Heritage Collection of South Dakota. Reference Library.

AKTA LAKOTA MUSEUM
St. Joseph Indian School
P.O. Box 89
CHAMBERLAIN 57325
(605) 734-3455
Jim O'Donnell, Director
Description: The Akta Lakota Museum is a tribute to the Sioux Nation striving to preserve and promote Sioux heritage and culture. Displays Native American art and artifacts; a collection of first class beadwork and quillwork. *Programs*: Visiting artists present lectures and shows; school tours; Native American history research. Library. Established 1991.

INDIAN MUSEUM OF NORTH AMERICA & CRAZY HORSE MEMORIAL
Avenue of the Chiefs-The Black Hills
CRAZY HORSE 57730
(605) 673-4681 Fax 673-2185
Anne Ziolkowski, Director
Description: Exhibits Plains Indian artifacts, works of art, displays from other tribes of North America. *Special collection*: Sculpture, furniture and art work of Korczak Ziolkowski, sculptor of Crazy Horse Memorial. *Publications*: Books - Crazy Horse and Korczak; The Saga of Sitting Bull's Bones; 40th Anniversary of Crazy Horse Memorial; Indian Museum of North America; and Crazy Horse Coloring books; and serial publication, Crazy Horse Progress, 3/yr. Library. Established 1974.

HARVEY V. JOHNSON AMERICAN INDIAN CULTURAL CENTER MUSEUM
Cheyenne River Reservation
P.O. Box 857
EAGLE BUTTE 57625

AMERICAN INDIAN CULTURE RESEARCH CENTER
Blue Cloud Abbey
MARVIN 57251
  (605) 432-5528 Fax 432-4754
  Rev. Stanislaus Maudlin, Director
Description: Maintains a collection of Maria Pottery; artifacts; 30,000 photos of Dakota Indians. Special programs: Workshops and seminars; Indin studies courses; assistance grants to Indian college students. Research Library.

OSCAR HOWE CULTURAL CENTER
119 West Third
MITCHELL 57301
Description: A collection of twelve paintings by Oscar Howe, Sioux artist.

ROBINSON MUSEUM
500 E. Capitol, Memorial Bldg.
PIERRE 57501
  (605) 773-3797
  David B. Hartley, Director
Special collection: Plains Indian Collection—Contains primarily Sioux Indian artifacts. *Publication*: South Dakota History, quarterly. Library.

SOUTH DAKOTA STATE HISTORICAL SOCIETY
Cultural Heritage Center
PIERRE 57501-2217
  (605) 773-3458
  David B. Hartley, Museum Director
  Sarah Ackermann, Curator of Exhibits
  Claudia J. Nicholson, Curator of Collections
Description: Exhibits Sioux items collected by Delorme W. Robinson prior to 1910 and the Mary C. Collins collection of Lakota items. Lakota game pieces collected by J. Walker, paintings by Oscar Howe. Established 1901.

THE HERITAGE CENTER
Red Cloud Indian School
Highway 18 W.
PINE RIDGE 57770
  (605) 867-5491 Fax 867-1104
  Brother C.M. Simon, S.J., Director/Curator
Description: Maintains Indian Art Museum which is housed in 1888 Holy Rosary Mission, scene of Battle day after the Wounded Knee Massacre; maintains a collection of paintings by Native American artists from many different tribes; also, starquilt collection; Oglala Sioux beadwork and quillwork collection; and small pottery collection; graphics, Inuit prints, and Northwest Coast prints. *Special program*: Traveling shows; Red Cloud Indian Art Show held every summer. *Publications*: Standing Soldier: A Retrospective; Five Families: An Art Exhibition. Library. Established 1982.

WHITE RIVER VISITOR CENTER
Rocky Fort RR
PORCUPINE 57772
  (605) 455-2878
  (608) 698-7058
  Fr. Norman Volk, Director
Description: Maintains Indian cultural exhibits and an audiovisual program.

SIOUX INDIAN MUSEUM
P.O. Box 1504, 515 West Blvd.
RAPID CITY 57709
  (605) 348-0557
Description: Administered by the Indian Arts and Crafts Board. Exhibits historic Sioux arts and other Native-American arts and crafts of the U.S.; a permanent exhibit presents the rich diversity of historic Sioux arts and two special exhibition galleries are devoted to changing presentations promoting the creative works of outstandingly talented contemporary Native artists and craftsmen. *Special program*: One-person exhibition series with demonstrations of Native American arts and crafts techniques in a variety of media; tours. Publications. Museum Sales Shop. Established 1939.

BUECHEL MEMORIAL LAKOTA MUSEUM
350 South Oak St., Box 499
ST. FRANCIS 57572
  (605) 747-2745 Fax 747-2361
  Ben Black Bear, Chairman
  Donna DuBray, Director
Description: Sioux Indian Museum exhibits ethnographic material (over 3,000 artifacts, and 2,100 photos) of the reservation period of the Rosebud and Pine Ridge Sioux. Special collections: "Crying for a Vision" - photo exhibit; Rosebud Sioux quilts. *Publications*: A Grammar of Lakota; Everyday Lakota; Dictionary; Bible History in Lakota; Lakota Prayer Book; Lakota Names and Traditional Uses of Native Plants by Sigangu People; Crying for a Vision; A Rosebud Sioux Trilogy; Betteloyun Manuscripts; Walker Papers; Buechel's Diary; and documents relating to Sioux culture. Indian arts and crafts for sale. Resource Library. Established 1947.

CENTER FOR WESTERN STUDIES
Augustana College
P.O. Box 727
SIOUX FALLS 57197
  (605) 336-4007
  Harry F. Thompson, Curator of Collections
Description: An Historical Research and Archival Agency which maintains a collection of Native American (mostly Sioux) art work and artifacts. *Research*: Native Americans. *Publications*: Sundancing at Rosebud and Pine Ridge; Yanktmai Sioux Water Colors; The Last Contrary; Tomahawk and Cross. Library, Archives.

SIOUXLAND HERITAGE MUSEUM
THE PETTIGREW MUSEUM
131 North Duluth
SIOUX FALLS 57104
Special collections: The Pettigrew-Drady Indian Collection: Chief emphasis is on Dakota (Sioux) Indian artifacts, circa 1870-1920, including: clothing, tools, pipes, weapons, tepee, Ghost Dance shirt; and a Photograph Collection covering 1870-1900. Library.

TEKAKWITHA FINE ARTS CENTER
P.O. Box 208
SISSETON 57262
  (608) 698-7058
  Fr. Norman Volk, Director
Description: Maintains a collection of two dimensional art of the lake Traverse Dakotah Sioux Reservation. *Activities*: Sponsors art festivals, concerts, workshops, and the annual Coteau Heritage Festival.

BEAR BUTTE STATE PARK
2209 Thompson St.
STURGIS 57785

  (605) 347-3176
  William A. Gullet, Park Manager
Description: Located on a Native-American traditional religious site. *Museum*: Exhibits archaeological site materials; Native-American clothing and religious artifacts. *Research*: Native-American Indian religion, anthropology, archaeology and geography.

W.H. OVER STATE MUSEUM
414 East Clark
VERMILLION 57069-2390
  (605) 677-5228
  Allen Schroeder, Director
  Cleo Kosters, Curator of Collections
Description: Displays Sioux artifacts from the late 19th century to the present. Special collections: Clark Memorial Collection of Lakota Artifacts; and Stanley J. Morrow Historical Photographs, 1869-1883. Library. Established 1883.

DAKOTA TERRITORIAL MUSEUM
P.O. Box 1033
YANKTON 57078
Description: Exhibits Indian artifacts from the Dakota Territory, and the history of Yankton.

TENNESSEE

RED CLAY STATE HISTORICAL PARK
1140 Red Clay Park Rd., S.W.
CLEVELAND 37311
  (615) 478-0339
  Lois I. Osborne, Park Manager
Description: The 1832-1838 seat of the Cherokee Government, and site of 11 General Councils on national affairs. *Collection*: Paleo, Archaic, Mississippian, Woodland, and historical period artifacts. *Research*: Cherokee Removal Story, 1832-1838. Small research library of Cherokee history.

OLD STONE FORT ARCHAEOLOGICAL AREA
Route 7, Box 7400
MANCHESTER 37355
  (615) 723-5073
  Ward Weems, Site manager
Description: The Old Stone Fort is a 2,000-year-old American Indian ceremonial site. It consists of mounds and walls which combine with cliffs and rivers to form an enclosure measuring 1-1/4 mile around. *Special programs*: educational and entertaining programs. An exhibit hall complex includes exhibits relating to the history, archaeology, and legends surrounding the Old Stone Fort and its builders.

CHUCALISSA ARCHAEOLOGICAL MUSEUM
C.H. Nash Museum
1987 Indian Village Dr.
MEMPHIS 38109
  (901) 785-3160
  Dan S. Beasley, Interim Director
  Mary L. Kwas & Camille Wharey, Curators
Description: Preserves the site of a 15th-century Mississippian-period village (in western Tennessee) partially reconstructed with life-size dioramas. The exhibit hall displays Southeast Indian culture, a collection of Indian artifacts from the site and adjacent areas. *Special programs*: group tours; demonstrations of hunting technologies; lecture series; Choctaw Indian Heritage Festival; outreach material to schools. *Publication*: Chucalissa Revisited. Library. Established 1955.

CUMBERLAND MUSEUM & SCIENCE CENTER
800 Ridley Blvd.
NASHVILLE 37203
 (615) 259-6099
 Bill Bradshaw, Director
Description: Maintains approximately 4,000 objects on Native-Americans; small exhibit on Native-Americans in their environment. Special program: School programs on Native-Americans and archaeology. *Publication*: Museum Notes, monthly newsletter.

TENNESSEE STATE MUSEUM
James K. Polk Cultural Center
505 Deaderick St.
NASHVILLE 37243
 (615) 741-2692
 Lois Riggins Ezzell, Executive Director
 Dan Pomeroy, Director of Colections
Description: A collection of over 10,000 artifacts of prehistoric and historic Indian cultures in Tennessee, including stone implements, ceremonial objects and ornaments, and pottery. *Publication*: Art and Artisans of Prehistoric Middle Tennessee, by Stephen D. Cox. Library. Established in 1937.

PINSON MOUNDS STATE ARCHAEOLOGICAL AREA
Ozier Rd., Route 1, Box 316
PINSON 38366
 (901) 988-5614
 Mary L. Kwas, Area Supervisor
Description: A Middle Woodland Period ceremonial site with mounds and earthworks. *Collection*: Historic and prehistoric material from throughout Tennessee and on-site fieldwork. *Special program*: Indian Culture Festival. Library.

SEQUOYAH MUSEUM
VONORE 37885

TEXAS

CADDOAN MOUNDS STATE HISTORIC PARK
Route 2, Box 85-C
ALTO 75925
 (409) 858-3218
 David D. Turner, Supt.
Description: An archaeological site of prehistoric Caddoan village and ceremonial center, with three earthen mounds occupied 750-1300 A.D. *Collection*: Dioramas and prehistoric artifacts of early Caddoan culture excavated at the site—ceramic vessels, stone tools, etc.; replicated Caddo house on site. Activities: School tours, techer packet; outreach-off site presentations. *Publication*: Caddoan Mounds, Temples and Tombs of an Ancient People. Reference library. Established 1979.

TEXAS MEMORIAL MUSEUM
University of Texas, 2400 Trinity St.
AUSTIN 78705
 (512) 471-1604
 Dr. William Reeder, Director
 P. Lynn Denton, Curator
Description: Collections include artifacts from Native Americans throughout the U.S.; and a series of exhibits highlighting the major native North American cultural groups which includes: costumes and artifacts of Indians of the Plains, Woodlands, Southwest, Northwest Coast, and Eskimo populations. *Publications*: Newsletter; monographs; bulletin series. Library. Established 1936.

PANHANDLE-PLAINS HISTORICAL MUSEUM
WTAMU Box 967
CANYON 79016
 (806) 656-2244
 Walter R. Davis, II, Director
Description: Hall of the Southern Plains: Exhibit of over 5,000 items from 70 groups, the majority from Southern Plains tribes--Comanche, Kiowa, Cheyenne, Arapaho, Apache and includes important collections of basketry, pottery, and beadwork; Nanvjo weavings; material on the Indian wars; trade goods. *Special programs*: Educational programs include Interpretive overviews and special-focus tours for students (grades K-12) and adults; Outreach programs - Native American Dance and Traditional Clothing; Life of the Southern Plains Indian. *Publication*: Panhandle Plains Historical Review, newsletter. Research Center houses archival material - more than 17,000 books (a 1,200 volume art library) and over 250,000 historical photographs. Museum Store. Established 1933.

NATIVE AMERICAN CULTURAL HERITAGE CENTER
Dallas Independent School District
DALLAS 75204

TIGUA PUEBLO MUSEUM
Tigua Arts and Crafts Center
Texas Indian Reservation
EL PASO 79907
 (915) 859-7913

YSLETA DEL SUR PUEBLO MUSEUM
P.O. Box 17579, 119 S. Old Pueblo Rd.
Tigua Indian Reservation
EL PASO 79917
 (915) 859-7913/3916
 Raymond Ramiriz, Superintendent
Description: Historic House, 1700-1850 Alderite/ Candelaria House; on grounds of 1680 Ysleta and Sur Pueblos and Mission Church. Maintains a collection of art of the Pueblos.

ALABAMA-COUSHATTA INDIAN MUSEUM
Rte. 3, Box 640, US Hwy. 190
LIVINGSTON 77351
 (713) 563-4391; (800) 444-3507
 Tony Byars, Superintendent
 Jo Ann Battise, Tribal Administrator
Description: Located on the Alabama-Coushatta Indian Reservation, the museum contains a dioramic historical display of tribes, and a Living Indian Village. Indian arts and crafts for sale.

AMERICAN INDIAN HORSE MUSEUM
American Indian Horse Registry
Rt. 3, Box 64
LOCKHART 78644
 (512) 398-6642
 Nanci Falley, President
 Scottie Stevenson, Curator
Description: Museum: A collection of horse tack, art and books representing 19th century Southwest U.S. Library. Publication: American Indian Horse News. Appointment only. Established 1979.

CADDO INDIAN MUSEUM
701 Hardy St.
LONGVIEW 75604
 (214) 759-5739
 Mrs. James L. Jones, Director
Description: Collection includes approximately 30,000 artifacts pertaining to the prehistoric and historic Indian cultures who inhabited east Texas, primarily tribes of the Kad had acho, Hasinai, and Natchitoches confederacies of the Caddo Indians;

extensive ceramic and stone pre-Columbian burial artifacts belonging to the prehistoric Indians of east Texas.

THE MUSEUM OF TEXAS TECH UNIVERSITY
P.O. Box 4499
LUBBOCK 79409
Description: Exhibits Yaqui, Comanche and other Indian artifacts. Publications. Library.

SFASU ANTHROPOLOGY LAB
NACOGDOCHES 75962
Special collection: Caddo Indian Artifacts Collection—beads, pottery, arrow points, pipes, etc. from the site of new Lake Nacogdoches, as well as from various Indian sites across the County.

CROCKETT COUNTY MUSEUM
404 11th St., Box 667
OZONA 76943
Special collection: Frank Mills Indian Collection—ornaments, jewelry, pottery, weapons, utensils, implements and ceremonial costumes. Cave exhibits. Library.

WITT MEMORIAL MUSEUM
3801 Broadway
SAN ANTONIO 78209
Description: Displays artifacts of the Plains Indian, Apache, Navajo, California Indians, Comanche-Kiowa, Eastern Woodlands, Northwest Coast, and Eskimo and Arctic Indians, including basketry, pottery, blankets and costumes. Library.

SUNSET TRADING POST OLD WEST MUSEUM
Rt. 1, Box 365C
SUNSET 76270
 (817) 872-2027
 Jack N. Glover, Owner/Curator
Description: Exhibits Indian artifacts. *Publication*: Sex Life of American Indians. Library.

UTAH

EDGE OF THE CEDARS STATE HISTORICAL MONUMENT & MUSEUM
P.O. Box 788, 660 West 400 North
BLANDING 84511
 (801) 678-2238
 Stephen J. Olsen, Museum/Park Manager
 Timothy "Todd" Prince, Curator
Description: Located on the Anasazi Ruin dating from 700-1200 A.D., ancient dwellings of the Anasazi Indian culture. Maintains artifacts of prehistoric Anasazi Indian Tribe; Anasazi pottery; also, Navajo, Ute and Paiute Indian artifacts. *Special collection*: Rock Art Exhibit. Indian arts and crafts for sale. Reference Library. Publication: Spirit Windows--Native American Rock Art of Southeastern Utah. Established 1978.

ANASAZI STATE PARK
P.O. Box 1329
BOULDER 84716
 (801) 335-7308
 Larry Davis, Park Manager
 William R. Latady, Curator
Description: Located on a 1050-1200 A.D. excavated Anasazi village site. *Museum*: Maintains and exhibits a collection of artifacts representative of the Kayenta Anasazi culture; diorama of Anasazi village (Coombs site). *Special programs*: Priitive techology demonstrations; guided tours of ruins; 14 video presentations. Small library. Established 1970.

UTE TRIBAL MUSEUM
P.O. Box 190, Highway 40
FORT DUCHESNE 84026
 (801) 722- 4992
 Clifford Duncan, Director
Description: Located on the site of U.S. Cavalry and Old Fort Duchesne. Maintains Indian produced artwork in various media artifacts. *Research*: Ute history archives; personal interviews with elderly to document verbal Indian history . *Publication*: A History of Northern Ute People. Library.

COLLEGE OF EASTERN UTAH PREHISTORIC MUSEUM
451 E. 400 North (mailing)
155 E. Main (physical)
PRICE 84501
 (801) 637-5060
 Don Burge, Director; Pam Miller , Curator
Description: Utah archaeological exhibits, including 9th century Indian material of the Fremont culture. Emphasis on Nine Mile Canyon cultural and rock art area, Anasazi artifacts, lifesize Ute Indian diorama, Ute lifeways. *Special collections*: Pillings Figurines - set of 10 Fremont Indian clay figurines; two protohistoric painted hides and one Shoshone painted robe by Charlie W ashakie. *Special programs*: lectures, children's programs; tours to archaeological sites. *Publication*: Quarterly newsletter . Library. Established in 1960.

MUSEUM OF PEOPLES AND CULTURES
Brigham Young University
105 Allen Bldg.
PROVO 84602
 (801) 378-6112
 Dr. Joel C. Janetski, Director
 Dr. Marti Lu Allen, Curator/Asst. Director
Description: An archaeology and ethnology museum exhibiting artifacts of prehistoric and historic native cultures. Permanent exhibitions highlight Hohokam, Anasazi, Mogollon, Casas Grandes, Fremont, and Polynesian collections. *Special collection*: Anasazi material generated during two decades of research in Montezuma canyon and the Abajo mountain area. *Activities*: Free tours; training in museum practices and archaeological field techniques. Publications. Library .

UTAH FIELD HOUSE OF NATURAL HISTORY STATE PARK
235 E. Main St.
VERNAL 84078
 (801) 789-3799
 Alden H. Hamblin, Supt.
 Sue Ann Bilbey, Curator
Description: Ute Indian Hall: Exhibits Ute Indian artifacts. Library. Established 1948.

VIRGINIA

SOUTHWEST VIRGINIA MUSEUM
Box 742, 10 W. First St.
BIG STONE GAP 24219
 (703) 523-1322
 Janet H. Blevins, Park Manager
Description: Maintains artifacts representing the culture of the southern Appalachians, including artifacts of the Cherokee and Shawnee Nations. Developing a children's program on Native Americans. Library. Established 1948.

AMERICAN INDIAN HERITAGE FOUNDATION MUSEUM
6051 Arlington Blvd.
FALLS CHURCH 22044
 (703) 237-7500

LANCASTER LIBRARY
Longwood College
FARMVILLE 23909
 (804) 395-2241
Special collection: O'Brien Collection of over 5,000 prehistoric Virginia Indian artifacts.

SYMS-EATON MUSEUM
418 W. Mercury Blvd.
HAMPTON 23666
 (804) 727-6248
 Charles E. Smith, Manager
Description: Historic Kecoughtan Indian V illage; exhibits artifacts from V illage area. *Publication*: Indian Recipe.

PAMUNKEY CULTURAL CENTER MUSEUM
Pamunkey Indian Reservation
Rt. 1, Box 2220
KING WILLIAM 23086
 (804) 843-4792
Description: A collection of Pamunkey Indian artifacts from the area. V ideos available.

HISTORIC CRAB ORCHARD MUSEUM
P.O. Box 12, Route 19 and 460
TAZEWELL 24651
 (703) 988-6755
 Nellie White Bundy , Director
Description: Located on Big Crab Orchard Archaeological and Historic Site, exhibiting prehistoric Woodlands Indian artifacts. *Publication*: Quarterly newsletter . Library.

MATTAPONI INDIAN MUSEUM & TRADING POST
Mattaponi Indian Reservation
WEST POINT 23181
 (804) 769-2194
JAMESTOWN SETTLEMENT
P.O. Box JF
WILLIAMSBURG 23187
 (804) 253-7302
 Sara Patton, Supt.
 Dr. Thomas Davidson & Daniel Hawks, Curators
Description: Museum of V irgiia history focusing on 17th century English colonization and the Powhatan Indians. Exhibits prehistoric artifacts of the Virginia coastal plain. Also, other Indian artifacts and pioneer items; reconstruction of Powhatan's Indian Lodge. Publications. Library . Established 1957.

WASHINGTON

LELOOSKA FAMILY MUSEUM
5618 Lewis River Rd.
ARIEL 98603

WHATCOM MUSEUM OF HISTORY & ART
121 Prospect St.
BELLINGHAM 98225
 (206) 676-6981

CHELAN COUNTY HISTORICAL MUSEUM & PIONEER VILLAGE
600 Cottage Ave., Box 22
CASHMERE 98815
 (509) 782-3230

Description: Recreates the history of the Columbia River Indians before the arrival of the first pioneers and maintains an extensive collection of artifacts.

LEWIS COUNTY HISTORICAL MUSEUM
599 N.W. Front St.
CHEHALIS 98532
 (206) 748-0831
 James Buckman, President
Description: Maintains a collection of Chehalis Indian artifacts. Indian archive collection in library .

ALPOWAI INTERPRETIVE CENTER
Highway 12
CLARKSTON 99403
 (509) 758-9580
Description: An ethnology and Indian museum exhibiting Nez Perce Indian artifacts from 1880-1920; Nez Perce canoe. *Research*: Nez Perce Indians.

COLVILLE CONFEDERATED TRIBES MUSEUM
P.O. Box 233
COULEE DAM 99116
 (509) 633-0751 Fax 633-2320
 Andrew C. Joseph, Director/Curator
Description: Museum exhibits include an 1801 Thomas Jefferson Peace Medal, given to Nez Perce on the Snake River in 1805. There is an authentic Indian V illage Sweatlodge and Tulle Mat Tipi, a fishing scene (12,000 - 100 years ago), and a cledar and bear grass basketmaking display and video. The collection includes arrowheads and spearpoints, pestals and other tools. *Special collection*: Tribal membership photos from 1855 to 1950. *Publication*: "Salish" Okanagan/Colville Indian language cassette tapes with dictionary ($24.95), by staf f. Gift Shop.

MAKAH CULTURAL & RESEARCH CENTER
P.O. Box 95
NEAH 98357
 (206) 645-2711
Description: Contains exhibits pertaining to the Makah Indian history and culture.

COLVILLE CONFEDERATED TRIBES MUSEUM
Box 150
NESPELEM 99155
 (509) 634-4711
 Arnold N. Marchand, Director
Description: Contributes culturally as well as educationally to the communities of the five counties touched by the Colville Tribes. Maintains a gallery and gift shop.

SACAJAWEA INTERPRETIVE CENTER ·
Sacajawea State Park
R.R. 9, Box 2503
2503 Sacajawea Park Rd.
PASCO 99301
 (509) 545-2361
Description: Interpretive Center focus is Indians of the Columbia Basin Plateau (stone, bone tools, tool making, physical culture) and the Lewis and Clark Expedition, including the park's namesake, Sacajawea; photo-essay of culture and lifestyle. *Special programs*: Photo-essay and slide show of Lewis and Clark Expedition; summer interpretive programs related to area Indians and the Lewis and Clark Expedition. *Publications*: Pacific Northwest Resources (resource book for area teachers). Library. Open from mid April-mid September. Established 1940.

FORT OKANOGAN INTERPRETIVE CENTER
c/o Alta Lake State Park
HCR 88, Box 40
PATEROS 98846
(509) 923-2400
Mike Nickerson, Supt.
Steve Wang, Chief-Interpretive Services
Description: Exhibits fur trade items, and Indian and pioneer artifacts--basketry, weapons, etc. *Special program*: Verbal presentation of the history of Fort Okanogan area.

**SACRED CIRCLE GALLERY
OF AMERICAN INDIAN ART**
Daybreak Star Arts Center
Discovery Park, P.O. Box 99100
SEATTLE 98199
(206) 285-4425
Description: Maintains collections of original art by contemporary Native American artists. *Activities*: Native artist exhibitions.

WASHINGTON STATE MUSEUM
Thomas Burke Memorial
University of Washington
SEATTLE 98195
(206) 543-5590
Patrick V. Kirch, Director
Dr. James D. Nason, Chair-Anthropology Div.
Bill Holm, Curator-Northwest Coast Indian Art
Description: Exhibits Northwest Coast Indian art and artifacts; maintains ethnological and archaeological collections of the Pacific Rim and Islands. Publications.

**CHENEY COWLES MUSEUM
OF NATIVE AMERICAN CULTURES**
Eastern Washington State Historical Society
2316 West 1st Ave.
SPOKANE 99204
(509) 456-3931
Glenn Mason, Director
Lynn Harrison, Larry Schoonover
& Beth Sellars, Curators
Description: American Indian collections consist of over 35,000 items representing all cultural groups of the Americas, with special emphasis on the Plateau tribes. In 1992, the Museum of Native American Cultures turned over its holdings to make the combined collections one of the largest and most extensive in the Northwest. Major collections of Plateau baskets, beadwork, cornhusk bags, regalia and other examples of material culture. *Publications*: Exhibit catalogs, "Beadwork of the Native American" and "The Chap C. Dunning Collection." Book - Cornhusk Bags of the Plateau Indian; Text/fiche of 170 cornhusk bags (both sides illustrated.) Exhibition poster on sale, Native American Collection. Library. Established 1916.

**STEILACOOM TRIBAL CULTURAL
CENTER & MUSEUM**
1515 Lafayette St., P.O. Box 88419
STEILACOOM 98388
(206) 584-6308
Joan K. Ortez, Director
Description: Promotes cultural and educational exhibits to insure the preservation of the history and culture of the Steilacoom tribe. *Special exhibits*: Gallery I - changing gallery with a new exhibit on a Native American theme about every six months; Gallery II - a permanent exhibit on the history and contemporary lifestyles of the Steilacoom Tribe, beginning with first European contact in 1792; Gallery III - "Visions of the Past...Legacy to the Steilacoom Tribe" - prehistory of traditional homeland of Steilacoom Tribe.

Special programs: Education programs - tours in education about Coast Salish culture; lectures, conferences, and cultural demonstrations. Gift Shop. Library. Established 1988.

SUQUAMISH MUSEUM
15838 Sandy Hook NE
P.O. Box 498
SUQUAMISH 98392
(206) 598-3311
Leonard Forsman, Superintendent
Charles Sigo, Curator
Description: The Museum is dedicated to preservation of Suquamish and other Puget Sound Indian culture and history. *Exhibit*: The Eyes of Chief Seattle - The history and culture of the Puget Sound Indians; Old Man House - The people and their way of life at D'Suq'W ub' and it tells the history of a 600 foot traditional longhouse located on what is now known as the Port Madison Indian Reservation, home to the Suquamish Indian Tribe of 750 members. *Publications*: Suquamish Museum Newsletter; "Eyes of Chief Seattle" Exhibit Catalogue. Library - Suquamish Tribal Archives. Established 1983.

PUYALLUP TRIBE MUSEUM
2215 E. 22nd St.
TACOMA 98404
(206) 597-6479

**WASHINGTON STATE HISTORICAL
SOCIETY MUSEUM**
315 N. Stadium Way
TACOMA 98403
(206) 593-2830
David Nicandri, Director
Lynn D. Anderson, Head of Museum Collections
Description: Exhibits and collections focusing on the history of the people and forces that shaped the development of Washington and about 5,500 objects focusing on tribes of the Pacific Northwest, including basketry, tools, carvings, clothing, and personal artifacts; 200,000 rare pictures and maps. *Special collection*: Washington: Home, Frontier, Crossroads includes a section on the indigenous peoples of Washington. *Publications*: Columbia, quarterly journal of popular history; The Indian Woodcarvings of Harvey Kyllonen; Northwest Indian Basketry; They Walked Before: The Indians of Washington State. Library. Established 1891.

TOPPENISH MUSEUM
1 South Elm
TOPPENISH 98945
(509) 865-4510
Tish Cooper, Director
Description: Historic Museum housed in 1923 first Agency Building for the Yakima Indian Nation. Exhibits artifacts and Indian baskets. Library.

YAKIMA NATION MUSEUM
Yakima Nation Cultural Center
P.O. Box 151
TOPPENISH 98948
(509) 865-2800 Ext. 720
Brycene Neaman, Curator
Description: Collection reflects traditional crafts of the Yakima people, including utility & ceremonial items; also, items from Southwest & Plains tribes, but mainly items important to Yakima (or Columbia Basin Plateau area) tribes & bands culture & history. Includes baskets, clothing, stones, pipes; Navajo blankets, kachinas and jewelry; several large oil paintings of Columbia Plateau family elders. *Publications*: Time Ball; Mother Nature Is Our Teacher. Library. Established 1980.

**WEST VIRGINIA STATE GOVERNMENT
ARCHIVES AND HISTORY MUSEUM**
Dept. of Archives and History
Capitol Complex-Science and Cultural Center
CHARLESTON 25305

MOUND MUSEUM
Tenth St. and Tomlinson Ave.
MOUNDSVILLE 26041

RED CLIFF TRIBAL MUSEUM
Arts and Crafts Cultural Center
P.O. Box 529
BAYFIELD 54814
(715) 779-5609/5805
Francis Montano, Director

LOGAN MUSEUM OF ANTHROPOLOGY
Beloit College
700 College St.
BELOIT 53511-5595
(608) 363-2677
Henry Moy, Director; Irina Khazanov, Curator
Description: Exhibits material (over 200,000 artifacts) of North American Indian ethnology (Great Lakes, Plains, and Southwest), Arikara-Mandan archaeology, Archaic and Woodland archaeology, and northern Wisconsin. *Special collection*: The Albert Green Heath Collection of Native American artifacts. Library. *Publications*: Bulletin; exhibit catalogs; occasional papers. Established 1893.

**STOCKBRIDGE-MUNSEE HISTORICAL
LIBRARY & MUSEUM**
Route 1, Box 300
BOWLER 54416
(715) 793-4270
Bernice Miller Pigeon, Director

HISTORYLAND-OJIBWA NATION MUSEUM
Route 2, Box 715
CABLE 54821
Description: The museum is geared toward the Indian people with the hope that they will continue to identify themselves as Indians and preserve their cultural arts. Exhibits Ojibwa crafts & artifacts.

CHIPPEWA VALLEY MUSEUM
P.O. Box 1204, Carson Park
EAU CLAIRE 54701
Description: Maintains a collection of artifacts and photographs of the Chippewa, Menominee and Winnebago Indians. Library.

CHIEF OSHKOSH MUSEUM
7631 Egg Harbor Rd.
EGG HARBOR 54209
(414) 868-3240
Jeanette L. Hutchins, Director/Curator
Description: Indian Museum exhibiting Indian artifacts, craftwork and possessions belonging to the late Chief Oshkosh, last Chief of the Menominees. Open May-October. Established 1975.

**LAC DU FLAMBEAU MUSEUM
& CULTURAL CENTER**
P.O. Box 804
LAC DU FLAMBEAU 54538
(715) 588-3303

Description: Displays artifacts from the Lac du Flambeau Chippewa Indian Reservation.

MUSEUM OF THE STATE HISTORICAL SOCIETY OF WISCONSIN
30 N. Carroll St. (exhibit facility)
816 State St. (collections)
MADISON 53703/6
 (608) 264-6555
 William C. Crowley, Director of Museum
 Joan E. Freeman, Curator of Anthropology
Description: Historic Wisconsin and Plains Indian artifacts and prehistoric archaeological artifacts from Wisconsin. *Special collections*: H.P. Hamilton Collection--Contains old copper implements from Wisconsin. Ethnological collections are from all Wisconsin tribes, Plains Indians, Northwest Coast, and Eskimo. *Special programs*: Classroom lessons on Wisconsin Indian life; photograph, manuscript and tape collections. *Publications*: Magazine of History; six volumes on History of Wisconsin. Library. Established 1846.

RAHR-WEST ART MUSEUM
610 North 8th St.
MANITOWOC 54220
 (414) 683-4501
 Richard Quick, Director
Special collection: Exhibits stone, copper, and bead artifacts from a personal collection obtained in the Manitowoc County area. Library. Established 1941.

MILWAUKEE PUBLIC MUSEUM
800 W. Wells St.
MILWAUKEE 53233
 (414) 278-2786
 Barry Rosen, PhD, President/CEO
 Ann McMullen, Curator of N.A. Ethnology
 Carter Lupton, Head Curator-Anthropology
Description: Maintains a collection of approximately 22,000 North American ethnographic American Indian items representing over 180 Native Ameriacn groups and tribes, including Inuit; archaeological collections from Midwest sites. *Special collection*: Dioramas, including "A Tribute to Survival" and the Crow Indian Bison Hunt. *Special programs*: Study collections; tours of American Indian areas for school and other groups. *Publications*: Lore, quarterly; North American Indian Lives; Building a Chippewa Indian Birchbark Canoe; Prehistoric Indians of Wisconsin; et al. Reference Library. Founded 1882.

ONEIDA NATION MUSEUM
P.O. Box 365
ONEIDA 54155
 (414) 869-2768
 Jan Malcolm, Director
Description: Exhibits approximately 1,000 artifacts and photographs - primarily ethnographic pieces - relating to the history, beliefs and crafts of the Oneida and related Iroquois people. The collection is composed of a variety of cultural material mostly from the 20th century, including wood, basketry, dress, beadwork, silverwork and other objects of the Oneida Indians. Small reference library. Established 1979.

OSHKOSH PUBLIC MUSEUM
1331 Algoma Blvd.
OSHKOSH 54901
 (414) 424-0452
 Robert Hruska, Director/Curator
Description: Maintains a collection of Wisconsin Indian archaeological and ethnographical artifacts. Library.

JOHN MICHAEL KOHLER ARTS CENTER
P.O. Box 489, 608 New York Ave.
SHEBOYGAN 53082
 (414) 458-6144
 Ruth DeYoung Kohler, Director
Special collection: Kuehne Collection of Prehistoric Wisconsin Indian Artifacts--6,000 pieces, including pottery, projectiles, copper, celts, grooved axes, etc. Library. Facilities available for research.

FAIRLAWN HISTORICAL MUSEUM
906 East 2nd St.
SUPERIOR 54880
 (715) 394-5712
 Thomas C. Hendrickson, Jr., Director
Special collections: David F. Barry Collection of Sioux Indian Portraits; and, Catlin Lithographs of Indians of the Plains. Exhibits artifacts. Library.

WAUKESHA COUNTY MUSEUM
101 W. Main St.
WAUKESHA 53186
 (414) 548-7186
 Anita Baerg-Vatndal, Director
 Cathy Baumbach, Curator
Description: Located on Mound of the Turtle, prehistoric Indian burial mound. Focuses on Waukesha County from Native American settlement to the present, Exhibiting Native American artifacts from the area. Research Center Library. Established in 1914. *Publication*: Landmark, 6x/year times.

WINNEBAGO INDIAN MUSEUM
3889 N. River
WISCONSIN DELLS 53965
 (608) 254-2268
 Roxanne Tallmadge Johnson, Acting Manager
 Bernadine Tallmadge, Curator
Description: An extensive collection of stone artifacts, clothing, methods of ornamentation (i.e., beadwork, quillwork, metal) as well as oil paintings. *Special programs*: On-site lectures describing current and traditional issues; festival. Established 1953.

WYOMING

BRADFORD BRINTON MEMORIAL MUSEUM
P.O. Box 460, 239 Brinton St.
BIG HORN 82833
 (307) 672-3173
 Kenneth L. Schuster, Director
 Dorothy Savage, Curator
Description: Exhibits Native Americanobjects of art - costumes, bead & quill work, tools, baskets, blankets, weapons, and interpretive materials; mostly Plains tribes, but also some from the Southwest and Northwest Coast. Library. Established 1961.

WYOMING STATE MUSEUM
Barrett Bldg., 22nd & Central Ave.
CHEYENNE 82002
 (307) 777-7022/4
 Dr. Dona Bachman, Director
Description: Displays Sioux, Arapaho, Cheyenne, Blackfeet, Shoshone, & Flathead Indian artifacts.

PLAINS INDIAN MUSEUM
Buffalo Bill Historical Center
P.O. Box 1000, 720 Sheridan Ave.
CODY 82414
 (307) 587-4771
 Peter Hassrick, Director
 Emma Hansen, Curator
Description: Contains over 5,000 ethnographic items representing the Northern, Central, and Southern Plains people- Sioux, Cheyenne, Shoshone, Crow, Arapaho, Blackfeet, Gros Ventre. Exhibits provide an introduction to economic, religious and social lives of Plains Indians, and include a re-creation of an 1890 Sioux camp as well as a gallery of contemporary art. *Programs*: Annual Northern Plains Pow wow in June at the Robbie Pow Wow Grounds; the Plains Indian Art Seminar, a symposium relating to Plains Material culture each Fall; and a variety of temporary exhibitions which explore elements of the Plains Indian culture. The McCracken Research Library. Publications: Catalogues of exhibitions. Established 1917.

ARAPAHOE CULTURAL MUSEUM
Wind River Reservation
P.O. Box 127
ETHETE 82520

UNIVERSITY OF WYOMING ANTHROPOLOGY MUSEUM
Anthropology Building
LARAMIE 82071
 (307) 766-5136
 George W. Gill, Curator
Description: Maintains a collection of American Indian artifacts.

GRAND TETON NATIONAL PARK
MOOSE 83013
Colter Bay Indian Art Museum: Displays approximately 1,500 items of American Indian art (collected by David Vernon) from most culture areas, with emphasis on Northern Plains and Eastern Woodlands, 1875-1925. Special programs: Native-American culture films, guided tours, and Native-American crafts demonstrations. Programs conducted during summer months.

RIVERTON MUSEUM
700 E. Park Ave.
RIVERTON 82501
 (307) 856-2665
Description: Collections include Shoshone and Arapaho costumes and artifacts.

These alpha-geographically arranged listings, like those in the Museums section, include libraries with both large and small holdings, pertaining, in whole or part, to the subject of the North American Indian.

ALABAMA

POARCH CREEK INDIAN HERITAGE CENTER LIBRARY
HCR 69A, Box 85B
ATMORE 36502
(205) 368-9136
Sandra Ridley, Director
Description: Maintains a collection on Southeastern Creek Indians, specialifically , and 5 Civilized Tribes, generally.

ALASKA

ANCHORAGE MUSEUM OF HISTORY & ART LIBRARY
121 West Seventh Ave.
ANCHORAGE 99501
(907) 343-4326
M. Diane Brenner , Museum Archivist
Description: Collection includes over 1,000 volumes on the Tlingit, Haida, Northwest Coast, Athapaskan, Aleut & Eskimo cultures with an emphasis on material culture; 1890-1960 photograph collection. Interlibrary loans. Open to public.

ARCTIC ENVIRONMENTAL INFORMATION & DATA CENTER
University of Alaska, Anchorage
707 A St.
ANCHORAGE 99501
(907) 257-2733
Research activities: Conducts field studies and provides assistance on resource management issues in Alaska, including Native land selection under the Alaska Native Claims Settlement Act.

INSTITUTE OF SOCIAL & ECONOMIC RESEARCH
University of Alaska, Anchorage
3211 Providence Dr.
ANCHORAGE 99508
(907) 786-7710
Edward L. Gorsuch, Director
Research activities: Conducts Alaska Native studies, federal-state relations, eceonimic development, natural resources management, social and economic impact studies, etc. *Publication*: Alaska Review of Social and Economic Conditions.

SIMON PANEAK MEMORIAL MUSEUM LIBRARY
P.O. Box 21085
ANAKTUVUK PASS 99721
(907) 661-3413 Fax 661-3414
Grant Spearman, Curator
Description: 2,000 volumes concerning the natural and cultural history of the Arctic with special emphasis on the Brooks Range of Alaska.

ALASKA'S MOTION PICTURE FILM ARCHIVE CENTER
P.O. Box 95203, University of Alaska
FAIRBANKS 99701
(907) 479-7296
Reg Emmert, Director

Description: A repository of Alaskan archival film. Catalog of available films is available.

ALASKA NATIVE LANGUAGE CENTER RESEARCH LIBRARY
University of Alaska, Fairbanks
Eielson Bldg., 2nd Floor , P.O. Box 757680
FAIRBANKS 99775-7680
(907) 474-7874 Fax 474-6586
Dr. Michael E. Krauss, Director
Description: Collection contains more than 8,000 items: books, journals, papers, and archival material in or on 20 Alaska Native languages and languages connected to Alaskan languages. Special activities: Publish books in and on Alaska Native languages. Open to scholars.

CENTER FOR CROSS-CULTURAL STUDIES
University of Alaska, Fairbanks
FAIRBANKS 99775
(907) 474-7143
Dr. Gerald V. Mohatt, Director
Research activities : Current projects include improving science education of Alaska Native teachers.

INSTITUTE OF ALASKA NATIVE ARTS INFORMATION CENTER
P.O. Box 70769, 455 Third Ave. #117
FAIRBANKS, AK 99707
(907) 456-7491
Patricia Petrivelli, Executive Director
Resource library with over 66 titles; audio and video tapes. Also consists of an artists registry of hard copy files and slides, and photographic files.

ELMER E. RASMUSON LIBRARY
University of Alaska
FAIRBANKS 99701
Special collections : Skinner Collection—Contains material regarding Alaska and the Polar regions (Arctic and Antarctic); over 4,000 volumes on the Athapaskan, Haida, Tlingit, Tsimshean, and Eskimo. University Archives & Manuscript Collections (Alaskana only)--Consists of journals, records, historic photos, tape recordings (Alaska Native Stories); 4,000 historic photos of Alaska natives.

AHTNA, INC. LIBRARY
P.O. Box 649
GLENNALLEN 99588
(907) 822-3476
Description: Contains mostly publications dealing with land and resources in interior Alaska, with some on native culture (Athabascan.)

CHILKAT VALLEY HISTORICAL SOCIETY SHELDON MUSEUM & CULTURAL CENTER LIBRARY
Box 269
HAINES 99827
(907) 766-2366
Rebecca Nelson, Curator
Description: Material on Tlingit and other Indian art and culture; local history; Alaska history. Also, archives with unpublished local documents (diaries, city records, school records, etc.)

ALASKA STATE DIVISION OF STATE LIBRARIES HISTORICAL LIBRARY
Pouch G
JUNEAU 99801

ROBBIE BATHOLOMEW MEMORIAL LIBRARY
Tongass Historical Museum
629 Dock St.
KETCHIKAN 99901

(907) 225-5600 Fax 225-5075
Roxana Adams, Director
Description: Collection of about 650 books; regional archives and photographs on Alaskan native culture.

TOTEM HERITAGE CENTER LIBRARY
629 Dock St.
KETCHIKAN 99901
(907) 225-5900 Fax 225-5075
Roxanna Adams, Museum Director
Description: City of Ketchikan's museum department and archives holdings include photographs on all Alaska villages with totem poles; index to all Alaska totem poles; vertical file on Northwest Coast Indian art and culture. Covers Tlingit, Haida and Tsimshian tribes - art, anthropology , totem poles. *Programs*: Art and crafts slides available for use; lecture series on traditional Alaska Native arts and culture.

KODIAK AREA NATIVE ASSN. LIBRARY
402 Center Ave.
KODIAK 99615
(907) 486-5725
General book collection. Museum/Cultural Center & Research Library in planning stages.

NOME LIBRARY/KEGOAYAH KOZGA PUBLIC LIBRARY
Front St., Box 1 168
NOME 99762
(907) 443-5133
Dee J. McKenna, Librarian
Description: Collection contains about 15,000 books, 3,000 cassette tapes, 1,200 AV programs, photographs, and bilingual and oral history materials on Alaska, Eskimos, and Gold Rush artifacts.

SITKA NATIONAL HISTORICAL PARK LIBRARY
106 Metlakatla, P.O. Box 738
SITKA 99835
(907) 747-6281 Fax 747-5938
Michele M. Hellickson, Director
Description: Contains about 2,000 books; tapes and films; and special papers on Tlingit Indians, Northwest Coast Indian arts and culture, as well as titles on Russian American history and natural history.

ARIZONA

CANYON DE CHELLY NATIONAL MONUMENT LIBRARY
P.O. Box 588
CHINLE 86503
(602) 674-5436

TUZIGOOT NATIONAL MONUMENT LIBRARY
P.O. Box 68
CLARKDALE 86324
(602) 634-5564

CASA GRANDE RUINS NATIONAL MONUMENT LIBRARY
1100 N. Ruins Dr.
COOLIDGE 85228
(602) 723-3172
Description: Contains a collection of 1,500 volumes on Hohokam archaeology and culture; Indians of area.

THE AMERIND FOUNDATION
RESEARCH LIBRARY
P.O. Box 248
DRAGOON 85609
(602) 586-3666
Anne I. Woosley, Director
Description: Maintains a collection of 20,000
volumes focusing on American archaeology, ethnology, Greater American Southwest; ethnology,
history and art; many on the American Indian. Not
available to the public.

CLINE LIBRARY
Northern Arizona University
P.O. Box 6022
FLAGSTAFF 86011
(602) 523-5551 Fax 523-3770
Randall R. Butler, Archivist
Special Collections & Archives Department: Sub-
jects include Navajo and Hopi Indians, and South-
western U.S. *Special collections*: Alexander and
Dorothea Lieghton Collection; Apachean Lan-
guage Collection, including Chiricahua dialects-
320 cassettes.

HAROLD S. COLTON MEMORIAL LIBRARY
Museum of Northern Arizona
Route 4, Box 720
FLAGSTAFF 86001
(602) 774-5211 Fax 779-1527
Dorothy A. House, Librarian
Description: Special collections on Hopi and Na-
vajo Indians, and archaeology of the Southwest-
ern U.S. A major repository of documentation on
Native American art.

WUPATKI NATIONAL MONUMENT LIBRARY
HC 33, Box 444A
FLAGSTAFF 86001
(602) 527-7152

NAVAHO INITIATIVE PROJECT
P.O. Box 920
FORT DEFIANCE 86504
(602) 724-3351
James Muneta, Contact
Research activities: Research on and develop-
ment of services for handicapped Native Ameri-
cans. *Publication*: Satellite (quarterly newsletter).

HUBBELL TRADING POST LIBRARY
P.O. Box 150
GANADO 86505
(602) 755-3475
Description: Contains materials relevant to Native
American and Southwest history; Navajo culture,
Indian arts and crafts, oral interviews, and trading
posts and Indian traders; and NPS planning docu-
ments, standards and policies.

AK-CHIN HIM-DAK LIBRARY
P.O. Box 897
MARICOPA 85239
(602) 568-9480
Elaine F. Peters, Director
Description: Collection of Native American publi-
cations, videos and audios, oral histories; Archives
of tribal records.

COLORADO RIVER INDIAN TRIBES
PUBLIC LIBRARY/ARCHIVES
Tribal Administration Center
Route 1, Box 23-B
PARKER 85344
(602) 669-9211 x 285 Fax 669-5675
Amelia Flores, Library Director
Description: Holdings include 12,000 volumes in

the general sections. Extensive collection on the
Native American. Archives includes over 1,000
documents, videotape and oral history tapes, personal correspondence, and works of historians,
ethnologists and anthropologists; also microfilm
relating to the history and culture of the four tribes
of the Colorado River Indian Reservation - the
Mohave, Chemehuevi, Navajo and Hopi. Also includes a Photograph Collection. Interlibrary loans.
Established in 1958

BROWN & BAIN, P.A. LIBRARY
2901 N. Central
PHOENIX 85012
(602) 351-8039 Fax 351-8516
Ellen Hepner, Librarian
Description: A special collection on
American Indian law.

DOROTHY CUMMINGS MEMORIAL LIBRARY
American Indian Bible College
10020 N. 15th Ave.
PHOENIX 85021
(602) 944-3335
John S. Rose, Director
Description: Maintains a special Native American
collection of books, audiocassettes, & microfiche.

HEARD MUSEUM LIBRARY & ARCHIVES
22 East Monte Vista Rd.
PHOENIX 85004-1480
(602) 252-8840 Fax 252-9757
Mario Nick Klimiades, Librarian/Archivist
Description: Maintains a collection of approximately 30,000 volumes in the areas of Native
American art and culture with an emphasis on the
Southwest, ethno-arts, and anthropology; journals
and newsletters; pamphlet file; archives of manuscripts, posters and library prints, photographs and
negatives, and museum papers; sound recordings
include audiocassettes and record albums of primarily native Southwestern music, taped lectures,
and interviews; 300 films & videos; and thousands
of slides. *Special program*: Native American Artists Resource Collection - includes files on about
10,000 traditional to contemporary artists working in all media. Collectors, students, and art en-
thusiasts can contribute information to the collection. Open to the public for reference only - ap-
pointments are necessary for archives & videos
and sound recordings.

MARICOPA COUNTY LAW LIBRARY
East Court Bldg., 2nd Floor
101 W. Jefferson St.
PHOENIX 85003
(602) 262-3461 Fax 262-3677
Elizabeth Kelley Schneider, Director
Description: Collection on Native American law.

PHOENIX INDIAN MEDICAL CENTER
HEALTH SCIENCES LIBRARY
4212 North 16th St.
PHOENIX 85016
(602) 263-1200 Fax 263-1669
Jean Crosier, Administrative Librarian
Description: Basic professional & medical collection with small Native American collection includes
medical, cultural, fiction and non-fiction titles about
& written by Native Americans; also focus is on
Southwestern tribes (approx. 200 books and documents). Open to the public.

PHOENIX PUBLIC LIBRARY
Arizona Room
12 E. McDowell Rd.
PHOENIX 85004

(602) 262-4636
Description: Subjects cover Southwestern Indians.
Special collection: James Harvey McClintock pa-
pers, 1864-1934.

PUEBLO GRANDE MUSEUM LIBRARY
4619 East Washington St.
PHOENIX 85034
(602) 275-3452
Description: Collection primarily on Southwest
archaeology with volumes pertaining to the American Indian. Open to scholars by appointment.

STATE OF ARIZONA --
DEPT. OF LIBRARY & ARCHIVES
State Capitol, 1700 W. Washington
PHOENIX 85007
(602) 542-3701 Fax 542-4400
Sharon G. Womack, Director
Description: Contains over 105,000 volumes on
Arizona and the Southwest, including material on
Southwestern Indians. Numerous exhibits supple-
ment library research.

SHARLOT HALL/PRESCOTT HISTORICAL
SOCIETIES LIBRARY/ARCHIVES
415 W. Gurley St.
PRESCOTT 86301
(602) 445-3122
Sue Abbey, Archivist
Description: Subjects cover Anglo and Indian
history of the Southwest, especially Arizona.

SMOKI PEOPLE LIBRARY
P.O. Box 123
PRESCOTT 86302
(602) 778-5228
Description: A collection of 600 volumes on North
& South American Indian dance and ceremonials.

YAVAPAI-PRESCOTT TRIBAL LIBRARY
530 E. Merritt
PRESCOTT 86301
(602) 445-8790 Fax 778-9445
Joy E. Dromey, Director
Description: Maintains a special Indian collection
(non-circulating) of approximately 3,500 volumes;
& an archaeology collection of about 200 volumes,
both mostly Southwest. Open to the public.

SAFFORD-THATCHER STAKES
FAMILY HISTORY CENTER
Church of Jesus Christ of Latter-Day Saints
1803 S. 8th Ave.
SAFFORD 85546
(602) 428-3194
Lorin W. Moffett, Director
Description: A special collection on Indian tribes.
Genealoical Society Series; microfiche; films.

THE ARIZONA COLLECTION
Dept. of Archives & Manuscripts
University Libraries, A.S.U.
P.O. Box 871006
TEMPE 85287
(602) 965-4932 Fax 965-0776
Edward C. Oetting, Dept. Head
Description: A research repository containing over
30,000 volumes in addition to primary source
materials covering prehistoric Arizona to the
present. There are ephemeral materials and photographs. Contains information on prehistoric, historic, and current tribes in Arizona. *Special collections*: Manuscript material includes papers of
Carlos Montezuma, the Odd Halseth Papers and
the Thomas H. Dodge Collection. Open to the
public.

CENTER FOR INDIAN EDUCATION
Arizona State University
College of Education
Farmer Education Bldg., Rm. 415
TEMPE 85287
 (602) 965-6292
 Karen Swisher, Director
Description: Covers all phases of American Indian education and related interdisciplinary issues.
Publication: Journal of American Indian Education.

THE LABRIOLA NATIONAL
AMERICAN INDIAN DATA CENTER
Dept. of Archives & Manuscripts
University Libraries, Arizona State University
Box 871006
TEMPE 85287
 (602) 965-6490 Fax 965-0776
 Patricia A. Etter, Curator
Description: Serves as a national repository of documents and materials on Native Americans. Center collects bilingual educational and curriculum materials focusing on all American Indian/Alaska Native tribes. Includes literature, manuscripts, encyclopedias, and general reference works dealing with American Indian history and culture. 3,000 books, films, slides, cassette tapes, and video in addition to CD-ROM indexes. Specialized database gives access to hundreds of pamphlets, brochures, newsletters, articles, and other material dealing with Native Americans. Open to the public.

MARY MILDRED McCARTHY LIBRARY
Charles Cook Theological School
708 S. Lindon Lane
TEMPE 85281
 (602) 968-9354
 Mark Thomas, Librarian
Description: A special collection of about 1,500 books on Native American history and culture.

NATIONAL INDIAN TRAINING &
RESEARCH CENTER LIBRARY
2121 South Mill Ave., Suite 216
TEMPE 85282
 (602) 967-9484
Description: Contains 1,000 volumes relating to Indian education.

NAVAJO NATIONAL MONUMENT LIBRARY
TONALEA 86044
 (602) 672-2366
Description: A collection of approximately 600 volumes on Navajo history and archaeology.

NAVAJO COMMUNITY COLLEGE LIBRARY
TSAILE 86556
 (602) 724-3311
Special collection: Collection of over 45,000 volumes and an extensive pamphlet file on more than 100 Indain-related topics. Central to the collection is the Moses Donner Indian Collection--An extensive collection of publications on Indians.

ARIZONA HISTORICAL SOCIETY LIBRARY
949 E. 2nd St.
TUCSON 85719
 (602) 628-5774
 Margaret S. Bret-Harte, Librarian
Description: Holdings include 35,000 volumes related to Arizona and the Southwest. Manuscript Division contains 500 collections of historical documents.

ARIZONA STATE MUSEUM LIBRARY
Bldg. 26, University of Arizona
TUCSON 85716
 (602) 621-6281
 Mary Graham, Associate Librarian
Description: A major U.S. repository of documentation on Native American art. Contains approximately 43,000 volumes of published materials as well as archives of unpublished documents, field notes, diaries, with emphasis on prehistory and ethnology of Greater Southwest and Northern Mexico, and cultures of Arizona and New Mexico; many of which are on the subject of Native Americans; extensive microfilm collection.

COLLEGE OF LAW LIBRARY
University of Arizona
TUCSON 85721
 (602) 621-5455
 Ronald L. Cherry, Librarian
Description: Maintains a special collection on law relating to the American Indian. Subjects includes Federal laws, Indian constitutions, laws and codes, tribal court reports, U.S. Congressional hearings and reports, periodicals, treatises, and treaties. Interlibrary loans. Open to the public.

NATIVE AMERICAN RESEARCH
& TRAINING CENTER
University of Arizona
1642 E. Helen
TUCSON 85719
 (602) 621-5075
 Jennie R. Joe, Ph.D., Director
Research activities: Health and rehabilitation of disabled and chronically ill Native Americans. Studies the impact of government policy on the delivery of health care. Serves as a national resource for all North American tribes and Alaska natives.

MISSION SAN XAVIER DEL BAC LIBRARY
Route 11, Box 645
TUCSON 85706
 (602) 294-2624
Description: A collection of about 5,000 volumes pertaining to Aztec and Native-American ethnography and anthropology.

SOUTHWEST FOLKLORE CENTER
University of Arizona
TUCSON 85706
 (602) 626-3392
Description: Contains four videotaped conversations: Navajo singer Andrew Natonabah, writers Leslie Marmon Silko and N. Scott Momaday, and Papago storyteller Ted Rios. Two videotapes.

WESTERN ARCHAEOLOGICAL &
CONSERVATION CENTER LIBRARY
P.O. Box 41058, 1415 N. Sixth Ave.
TUCSON 85717
 (602) 792-6501
Description: Collection includes 15,000 volumes on archaeology, anthropology, history of the Southwest, California and Hawaii; 1,000 volumes pertain to the American Indian.

NAVAJO NATION LIBRARY SYSTEM
Window Rock Public Library
P.O. Drawer K
WINDOW ROCK 86515
 Irving Nelson, Manager
 (602) 871-6376/7303 Fax 871-7304
Purpose: To plan, develop, and implement a library and information system which will serve the residents of the Navajo Nation. To be the primary source of information for all who are interested in the Navajo people, their land and culture. *Special collections*: General Reference Collection: 2,500 books and documents; Environmental Assessment Collection: 200 folders; Navajo Nation Government Documents Collection: 1,000 documents and publications; Navajo Times Today Collection: 120 boxes of hard copy and micro-film copies; Vertical File Collection: 930 folders of articles; Correll Collection: 30 filing cabinets of historical documents; Native American Music Collection: 350 cassettes; Oral History Collection: 200 cassettes; Native American Research Library Collection: 2,000 books. Subjects covered are Navajo Indians; Southwest archaeology, Indians of America, and Arizona history. Bookmobile services: 2 bookmobiles provide services to 90 communities across the reservation within Arizona, New Mexico and Utah. Audio Visual Services. Computer Software Service: Uses hypercard application on a MacIntosh Computer to create interactive computer software, "Information on the Navajo Nation."

HOMOLOVI RUINS STATE PARK LIBRARY
523 W. 2nd St.
WINSLOW 86047
 (602) 289-4106
 Karen Berggren, Park Manager
Description: Covers the Anasazi culture; prehistory of Southwestern U.S.; Hopi, Navajo, and other Northern Arizona Indian cultures.

ARKANSAS

ARKANSAS STATE UNIVERSITY
MUSEUM LIBRARY & ARCHIVES
P.O. Box 490, State University
JONESBORO 72467
 (501) 972-2074 Fax 972-5706
 Connie Coldwell, Museum Secretary
Description: Contains over 1,200 books and reference material on Indian history and culture with focus on Southeast, Southwest and Plains groups related to Arkansas native tribal groups; ethnology and archaeology exhibits. Interlibrary loans via Dean B. Ellis Library. Open to the public.

AMERICAN INDIAN & ALASKA NATIVE
PERIODICALS RESEARCH CLEARINGHOUSE
Stabler Hall 502
University of Arkansas
33rd and University Ave.
LITTLE ROCK 72204

SOUTHWEST ARKANSAS
REGIONAL ARCHIVES
P.O. Box 134
WASHINGTON 71862
 (501) 983-2633
 Mary Medearis, Director
Description: Subjects cover the history of Southwest Arkansas, Caddo Indians

CALIFORNIA

AMERICAN INDIAN LORE
ASSOCIATION LIBRARY
P.O. Box 9698
ANAHEIM 92802
Description: A collection of 1,000 volumes on North American Indian lore, ethnology, anthropology, and folklore

CENTER FOR INDIAN
COMMUNITY DEVELOPMENT
Humboldt State University
ARCATA 95521
 (707) 826-3711
 Lois J. Risling, Director
Description: Covers community economic and organizational development, assessment of local needs for archaeological research, regeneration of American Indian languages and literatures and the application of computer systems to publication of Indian languages. Publishes textbooks and instructional material in and about Hupa, Karuk, Tolowa, Yurok, and other Indian languages. *Publication*: The Messenger, quarterly newsletter.

MALKI MUSEUM LIBRARY
11-795 Fields Rd.
Morongo Indian Reservation
BANNING 92220
 (714) 849-7289
Description: Collection consists of 500 volumes on southern California Indians.

BANCROFT LIBRARY & THE HEARST
MUSEUM OF ANTHROPOLOGY LIBRARY
University of California - 103 Kroeber Hall
BERKELEY 94720
 (510) 642-3681 (Bancroft)
 (510) 642-3781 (Heart Museum Library)
Description: Major U.S. repositories of documentation on Native American art.

NATIVE AMERICAN STUDIES LIBRARY
University of California
343 Dwinelle Hall
BERKELEY 94720
Description: A collection of 2,000 books on Native-Americans, anthropology, and sociology; microfilm, records, tapes, videotapes; journals and newspapers.

CABOT'S OLD INDIAN PUEBLO
MUSEUM LIBRARY
67-616 East Desert View Ave.
DESERT HOT SPRINGS 92240
 (619) 329-7610 Fax 329-1956
 Colbert H. Eyraud, Director
Description: Contains ten 4-drawer file cabinets of Desert Hot Springs newspapers; a collection of historical papers of city on microfilm, dated 1940-1980 at public library; City Government meetings, dated 1976-1990.

FRESNO COUNTY FREE LIBRARY
2420 Mariposa St.
FRESNO 93721
 (209) 488-3209 Fax 488-1971
 John K. Kallenberg, Librarian
Description: Covers American Indians of Fresno County, including Mono, Miwok, and Yokut tribes. *Special collection*: Ta-Kwa-Teu-Nee-Ya-Y Collection of about 200 books.

AMERICAN INDIAN RESOURCE CENTER
Los Angeles County Public Library
6518 Miles Ave.
HUNTINGTON PARK 90255
 (213) 583-1462 Fax 587-2061
 Tom Lippert, Librarian
Description: Maintains a collection of 6,000 volumes (Southwest, Plains, Woodlands); 50 periodical titles; 70 16mm films; 50 videocassettes; 400 audiocassettes; 300 phonorecords; current events clipping file (8 drawers, 350 subject head-

ings); 700 reels Indian census. *Special programs*: Information and referral services; outreach program; meeting room (free for Indian groups). Interlibrary loans. Open to public. Affiliated with Los Angeles County Public Library.

CABAZON TRIBAL REFERENCE LIBRARY
Cabazon Band of Mission Indians
84-245 Indio Springs Dr.
INDIO 92203

LAKE COUNTY HISTORICAL
SOCIETY LIBRARY
P.O. Box 1011
LAKEPORT 95453
 (707) 279-4466
 Norma Wright, President
Description: Covers Pomo Indian history and culture. Includes photographs, manuscripts, oral history tapes, and genealogical data.

LOMPOC MUSEUM LIBRARY
200 South H St.
LOMPOC 93436
 (805) 736-3888
 Roger Colten, Director
Description: Contains over 1,000 volumes on Chumash Indians, Indians of southern California, and Lompoc history and archaeology. Open to public.

AMERICAN INDIAN STUDIES
CENTER & LIBRARY
University of California
3220 Campbell Hall
LOS ANGELES 90024
 (310) 825-7315
 Dr. Duane Champaigne, Director
 Velma Salabiye, Librarian
Description: Coordinates educational, research, and action-oriented programs designed to meet the needs of American Indian students at UCLA and the American Indian communities in general. *Activities*: Encourages the development of new courses; promotes hiring of Native American faculty; sponsors research on American Indians; publishes journals, books, monographs, and other media reflecting contemporary Indian research and issues. *Library*: Approximately 6,000 volumes comprise the Library's core collection, covering the subject of the Indians of North America, with a strong emphasis on California and the Southwest. The primary focus is on American Indian life, culture, and state-of-affairs in historical and contemporary perspectives. Augmenting the circulating and reference collections are serials/periodicals, and a vertical file. *Publication*: American Indian Culture and Research Journal.

BRAUN RESEARCH LIBRARY
OF THE SOUTHWEST MUSEUM
234 Museum Dr., P.O. Box 41558
LOS ANGELES 90065
 (213) 221-2164 Fax 224-8223
 Kim Walters, Librarian
Description: Collection consists of 50,000 volumes of books and serials; includes 700 manuscript collections, 1,300 sound recordings, and 120,000 photographs. The Photo Archive is strongest on Indians of the Southwest, with many pictures of Native Americans of Alaska, the Northwest Coast, California, and the Plains. *Special collections*: The Papers of Frederick Webb Hodge, Frank Hamilton Cushing, George Bird Grinnell, Charle F. Lummis, and George Wharton James.

LOS ANGELES PUBLIC LIBRARY
History/Genealogy Department
433 S. Spring St. - 90013 (location)
630 West Fifth St. (mailing)
LOS ANGELES 90071
 (213) 612-3314 Fax 612-0519
 Jane Nowak, Dept. Manager
Description: Maintains a special collection on the American Indian; 8,000 volumes on the Indians of the Americas with an emphasis on the Southwestern U.S. Monographs, periodicals, pamphlet material, and specialized newsletters and newspapers are accessed through the general catalog and through the Indian file, a detailed computer based index. Interlibrary loans.

UNIVERSITY OF CALIFORNIA
AT LOS ANGELES LIBRARY
Special Collections
405 Hilgard Ave.
LOS ANGELES 90024
 (213) 825-1201
Description: A major U.S. repository of documentation on Native American art.

MARIN MUSEUM OF THE
AMERICAN INDIAN LIBRARY
P.O. Box 864, 2200 Novato Blvd.
NOVATO 94948
 (415) 897-4064
 Katharine J. Volz, Executive Director
Description: A reference library of approximately 1,000 volumes/periodicals oriented heavily to California Indians, especially Coast Miwok.

OAKLAND PUBLIC LIBRARY
American Indian Library Project
Dimond Branch Library
3565 Fruitvale Ave.
OAKLAND 94602
 (510) 530-3881 Fax 530-1623
Description: 1,500+ volumes on Native American literature, culture, history.

NATIONAL ARCHIVES & RECORDS
ADMINISTRTION-PACIFIC SIERRA REGION
1000 Commodore Dr.
SAN BRUNO 94066
 (415) 876-9009 Fax 876-0920
 Waverly B. Lowell, Director
Description: Archival records of the Federal Government in Nevada, Northern California, Hawaii, the Pacific Ocean areas. Includes original records of the Bureau of Indian Affairs, California and Nevada; microfilm.

DEPT. OF AMERICAN INDIAN
STUDIES LIBRARY
San Diego State University
SAN DIEGO 92182
 (619) 594-6991
Description: The Golsh Collection: Consists of rare documents & books.

INDIAN CENTER OF SAN JOSE LIBRARY
SAN JOSE 95127
 (408) 259-9722
Description: Contains 4,000 books on Indian history, culture, tribal groups, and literature. *Special collection*: The Indian Tribal Series: Consists of tribal newsletters, periodicals, films, filmstrips, and records. *Publication*: Newsletter.

PALOMAR COMMUNITY COLLEGE LIBRARY
1140 W. Mission Rd.
SAN MARCOS 92069

(619) 744-1150
Judy J. Carter, Director
Description: A collection of 3,500 volumes pertaining to American Indian culture, history, arts and crafts, and social problems; Bureau of Ethnology Reports.

HUNTINGTON LIBRARY
1151 Oxford Rd.
SAN MARINO 91108
(310) 792-6141
Description: A major U.S. repository of documentation on Native American art.

MESA GRANDE RESERVATION LIBRARY
P.O. Box 270
SANTA YSABEL, CA 92070
(619) 782-3835
Small tribal library.

HELD-POAGE RESEARCH LIBRARY
603 West Perkins St.
UKIAH 95482-4726
(707) 462-6969
Lila J. Lee, Director
Description: Local history and ethnography collection of over 6,000 volumes; many on American Indians. *Special collections*: Estle Beard Collection-research material for Genocide & Vendetta: The Round Valley Wars of Northern California; the Edith Van Allen Collection for Indian Uses of native plants; California and western states anthropology and archaeology; and Photographic Negative Collection; artifacts, maps.

UNIVERSAL CITY STUDIOS RESEARCH DEPARTMENT LIBRARY
UNIVERSAL CITY 91608
Special collection: 7,500 books dealing with Western Americana and the American Indian.

YOSEMITE MUSEUM LIBRARY
P.O. Box 577
YOSEMITE NATIONAL PARK 95389
(209) 372-0282
Linda Eade, Librarian
Description: Contains approximately 20,000 volumes and a large archival and photographic collection relating to Yosemite and Central California Indian people.

COLORADO

CENTER FOR STUDIES OF ETHNICITY AND RACE IN AMERICA
University of Colorado
Ketchum 30, CB 339
BOULDER 80309
(303) 492-8852
Dr. Evelyn Hu-DeHart, Director
Research activities: Comparative race and ethnicity and specific ethnic groups, including Native Americans.

CENTER FOR THE STUDY OF NATIVE LANGUAGES OF THE PLAINS & SOUTHWEST
University of Colorado
Dept. of Linguistics
Campus Box 295
BOULDER 80309
(303) 492-2748
Dr. Allen R. Taylor, Director
Research activities: Collects data and conducts research on Native American languages of the Great Plains and Southwest, including the Siouan

languages, Gros Ventre, Kiowa, and Wichita. Also includes the Lahkota Project, which offers instructional materials to aid in learning Dakota Sioux language.

NATIONAL INDIAN LAW LIBRARY
Native American Rights Fund
1522 Broadway
BOULDER 80302
(303) 447-8760
Deana J. Harragarra Waters, Director
Description: Serves as a clearinghouse for all legal materials pertinent to Indian law, including Federal and tribal law. Includes cases, briefs, pleadings, orders, legal opinions, government documents, memoranda, treatises, studies, books, articles, reports, and legislative histories pertinent to Federal Indian Law. *Publications*: National Indian Law Catalogue, An Index to Indian Legal Materials and Resources; Bibliography on Indian Economic Development, Second Edition; Indian Claims Commission Decisions and Index. Interlibrary loans. Open to the public.

COLORADO SPRINGS FINE ARTS CENTER LIBRARY
30 West Dale St.
COLORADO SPRINGS 80903
(719) 634-5581
Roderick Dew, Director
Description: A collection of about 9,000 volumes on Indians of the Southwest, Mexico and Guatemala, with emphasis on art, textiles and pottery. Contains a large collection of periodicals, some from the late 19th century. Open to the public.

CROW CANYON CENTER FOR SOUTHWESTERN ARCHAEOLOGY
23390 County Rd. K
CORTEZ 81321
(303) 565-8975
Ian Thompson, Director
Research activities: Archaeological investigation, including excavation and cataloging of artifacts. Specializes in Anasazi Indian culture, excavates sites in the Four Corners area of the southwest U.S. Research expeditions open to the public.

COLORADO HISTORICAL SOCIETY STEPHEN H. HART LIBRARY
1300 Broadway
DENVER 80203
(303) 866-2305 Fax 866-5739
Katherine Kane, Director
Description: Walker Colection (Sioux); W.H. Jackson photos (Southwestern tribes); many other photos - emphasis on the Ute, Cheyenne, Arapaho, Navajo, Hopi, Zuni; extensive ethnological collections on Plains and Southwest Indians; Mesa Verde Plains and Mountain Indian materials; source materials on the history of the Indian wars; materials from the Rosebud Indian Agency, 1885-1890; and photograph collection. Open to the public.

FOURTH WORLD CENTER FOR THE STUDY OF INDIGENOUS LAW AND POLITICS
University of Colorado at Denver
Campus Box 190, P.O. Box 173364
DENVER 80217
(303) 556-2850
Glenn T. Morris, Prof.

FREDERIC H. DOUGLAS MEMORIAL LIBRARY
Denver Art Museum
100 West 14th Ave. Pkwy.
DENVER 80204

(303) 640-1613 Fax 640-5513
Margaret Goodrich, Librarian
Description: Holdings include more than 50,000 volumes; 80 journals; and a special collection on the American Indians.

RESOURCE CENTER LIBRARY
National Urban Indian Council
National Indian Employment Resource Center
100068 University Park Sta., Box 10068
DENVER 80210
Description: Maintains American Indian/Alaskan Native off-reservation documents. Contains publications on employment-related subjects; extensive listings of employment opportunities and other books concerning Indian people, law, foundations and population. Not available to the public.

CENTER OF SOUTHWEST STUDIES
Fort Lewis College Library
DURANGO 81301
(303) 247-7456 FAX 247-7588
Richard N. Ellis, Director
Description: Covers subjects of Southwestern U.S. history and American Indians. Special collection: Indians of the Southwest. Includes microfilm, maps and photos, manuscripts, personal papers; archives; artifacts.

GRAND CANYON NATIONAL PARK LIBRARY
P.O. Box 129
GRAND CANYON 86023
(602) 638-7701
Robert S. Chandler, Director
Description: Maintains a collection of approximately 10,000 volumes; 16,000 bxw photos. Material on the Grand Canyon, natural history, archaeology, etc.

MUSEUM OF WESTERN COLORADO ARCHIVES
248 S. 4th St.
GRAND JUNCTION 81501
(303) 242-0971
Judy Prosser-Armstrong, Archivist
Description: Covers the history of western Colorado; anthropology of southwestern Indians.

KOSHARE INDIAN LIBRARY
Koshare Indian Museum
P.O. Box 580
LA JUNTA 81050
Description: Collection contains 2,000 volumes on Indian history, religion, legends, art, handicrafts, etc. Reference use only.

MESA VERDE RESEARCH LIBRARY
P.O. Box 38
MESA VERDE NATIONAL PARK 81330
(303) 529-4475 Fax 529-4498
Beverly J. Cunningham, Librarian
Description: Maintains more than 6,500 volumes on archaeology and ethnography, with many on the Indians of the Mesa Verde area, and North America. Interlibrary loans.

CONNECTICUT

CONNECTICUT HISTORICAL SOCIETY LIBRARY
1 Elizabeth St.
HARTFORD 06105
(203) 236-5621
Christopher P. Bickford, Executive Director

Description: Collection contains 70,000 volumes and two million manuscripts relating to Connecticut and New England history and genealogy.

CONNECTICUT STATE LIBRARY
231 Capitol Ave.
HARTFORD 06115
Description: Maintains an American Indian collection emphasizing languages and history; its core deriving from the library of J. Hammond Trumball.

MASHANTUCKET PEQUOT RESEARCH LIBRARY
P.O. Box 3060, Indiantown Rd.
LEDYARD 06339
(203) 536-7200
Charlene Jones, Tribal Librarian
Description: A non-circulating research facility devoted to preserving and reclaiming the cultural heritage of the tribe. In addition, special emphasis is placed on supporting scholars and students at all academic levels studying issues related to Native North American peoples. *Programs*: Exhibits a dramatic multi-media presentation, "The Mashantucket Pequots: A Proud Tradition", focuses on the story of the 1637 massacre that killed hundreds of Pequot, and deprived survivors of their ancestral land; the Archaeological Researh Project - special trips to some of the more than 200 archaeological sites on the Reservation can be arranged; Teacher In-Service Training; and Research Assistance.

YALE UNIVERSITY LIBRARY
120 High St.
NEW HAVEN 06520
(203) 436-8335
Description: A major U.S. repository of documentation on Native American art.

INDIAN & COLONIAL RESEARCH CENTER EVA BUTLER LIBRARY
P.O. Box 525
OLD MYSTIC 06372
(203) 536-9771
Kathleen Greenhalg, Librarian
Description: Subjects cover Native Americans, genealogy, and colonial history.

THE INSTITUTE FOR AMERICAN INDIAN STUDIES & RESEARCH LIBRARY
38 Curtis Rd., Box 1260
WASHINGTON GREEN 06793
(203) 868-0518 Fax 868-1649
Alberto C. Meloni, Director
Purpose: The discovery, preservation, and interpretation of Native American cultures of the Northeastern Woodlands rgion of the U.S. *Activities*: Conducts surveys for prehistoric and historic evidence of human occupation; excavations of historic sites. *Research Library*: Collection of 2,000 volumes, periodicals, archival documents, and maps. For use by members, scholars and students with letters from professors. By appointment only.

DELAWARE

NANTICOKE INDIAN MUSEUM LIBRARY
Rt. 4, Box 107A
MILLSBORO 19966
(302) 945-7022
Odette Wright, Curator
Description: A collection of about 500 books on the Nanticoke and other tribes.

DISTRICT OF COLUMBIA

AMERICAN HISTORICAL ASSN. LIBRARY
400 A St., S.E.
WASHINGTON 20003
(202) 544-2422

INDIAN EDUCATION INFORMATION SERVICE
ComTec, Inc.
519 Capitol Ct., NE #100
WASHINGTON 20002

DAUGHTERS OF THE AMERICAN REVOLUTION - NATIONAL SOCIETY LIBRARY
1776 D St., NW
WASHINGTON 20006
(202) 879-3229 Fax 879-3252
Eric G. Grundset, Library Director
Description: Subjects cover American Indian history, genealogy and culture.

INDIAN ARTS & CRAFTS BOARD LIBRARY
U.S. Dept. of the Interior
18th & C Sts., NW, Room 4004-MIB
WASHINGTON 20240
(202) 208-3773
Geoffrey Stamm, Acting General Manager
Description: Covers contemporary Native American arts and crafts. Acts as a clearinghouse for all matters pertaining to the development of authentic Native American arts and crafts.

LIBRARY OF CONGRESS
1st and Independence, S.E.
WASHINGTON 20540
(202) 707-5522
James H. Billington, Librarian
GENERAL REFERENCE & BIBLIOGRAPHY DIVISION: A collection of approximately 16,000 volumes covering virtually all subjects relating to North American tribes. Includes various bibliographies, catalogs, and guides to other collections containing material on Indians, such as Dictionary Catalog of the Edward E. Ayer Collection of Americana and American Indians, the Dictionary Catalog of the American Indian Collection, Huntington Free Library and Reading Room, New York, and the Biographical and Historical Index of American Indians and Persons Involved in Indian Affairs. *MICROFORM READING ROOM*: Contains much Indian-related material from a variety of print and nonprint sources. For example: North American Indians: Photographs from the National Anthropological Archives, Smithsonian Institution, compiled by Herman Viola--contains approximately 4,700 photographs on microfiche of Indians and Indian artifacts; individual and group portraits; Doctoral Dissertation Series. University Microfilms has published North American Indians: Dissertation Index, written between 1904-1976 at North American universities; Early State Records--The study of colonial relations with Indians; also includes public and private collections noted for Indian-related material, such as: The Connecticut Archives Indian Volumes, 1647-1820; The Henry O'Reilly Papers, 1744-1825--Relating to the Six Nations and Indians of the Old Northwest; Records of the Five Civilized Tribes, 1840-1905; The Penn Manuscripts, 1687-1801; and, The Timothy Horsfield Papers, 1733-1771--The last two collections involving Indians in Pennsylvania and surrounding areas; Pamphlets in American History--Microfiche collection of rare pamphlets includes many dealings with American Indians; British Manuscripts Project--contains abundant source

material on Indians especially for the period of the French and Indian War. *MANUSCRIPT DIVISION*: The Papers of the President, military officers, agents in Indian affairs, and other public and private individuals who dealt with Indians at various periods, such as those of Thomas A. Jesup, Henry L. Dawes, Edward S. Godfrey, Henry Rowe Schoolcraft, Philip Sheridan, Samuel P. Heintzelman, and John M. Schofield. Important collections available on microfilm include the papers of the American Missionary Society, the American Indian Correspondence Collection, and the Moravian Archives, as well as the papers of Timothy Pickering, Henry Knox, and Lyman C. Draper. Transcripts and photocopies of collections in foreign archives and libraries, such as the Indian records in the Public Archives of Canada. *SERIAL AND GOVERNMENT PUBLICATIONS DIVISION*: The Senate Confidential Executive Documents and Reports: Dating from the 17th Congress (1821)--comprised of formerly confidential documents which relate primarily to treaties. Patrons who wish to use this material should write to the Chief of this Division of the Library of Congress, or phone (202) 707-5647. *PRINTS AND PHOTOGRAPHS DIVISION*: Maintains holdings of nearly 4,000 prints, photographs, and engravings. The Edward S. Curtis Collection--Contains more than 1,600 photographs of Indians of the Plains, the Central Plateau, the Northwest Coast, the Southwest, and California; The Heyn-Matzen Collection--Contains approximately 550 photographs, mostly of Sioux, Crow and other Plains tribes; The John Grabill Collection--Consists mainly of photographs of Western frontier life, but includes many of Indians; also more than 200 stereo views of Indians, and a miscellaneous collection of uncataloged and unsorted prints and photographs. Copies of the division's material not covered by copyright may be purchased from the Library's Photoduplication Service. *ARCHIVE OF FOLK CULTURE*: Joseph C. Hickerson, Head. The Smithsonian-Densmore Collection--Contains more than 3,500 cylinder recordings of songs of 35 tribal groups, compiled from 1907-1932; Peabody Museum Collection--Compiled in the 1890's by anthropologist Jesse Walter Fewkes, this collection contains more than 50 recordings reproducing the music and language of tribes like the Passamaquoddy, Hopi and Zuni; The Willard Rhodes Collection--Contains the music of 50 Indian tribes, recorded on disc and tape from 1940-1952, when Rhodes worked for the B.I.A. 20 longplaying records of selections from these and other collections are available for purchase. The Federal Cylinder Project- Judith A. Gray, Ethno-musicologist - began in 1979 to organize, catalog, duplicate for preservation, and disseminate wax cylinder recordings, most of which document the music and lore of American Indian cultures. Includes recordings of 15 Native American groups initially resident in the Northeastern and Southeastern woodlands-Passamaquoddy, Chippewa, Menominee, Seminole, and Winnebago recordings. Also recordings from the Great Basin/Plateau regions and 20 collections from the Pacific Northwest and Arctic areas. Maintains a file of bibliographies and related lists. For information and descriptive literature write the Archive, or phone (202) 707-5510. *MOTION PICTURE, BROADCASTING AND RECORDED SOUND DIVISION*: Contains films of ceremonial dances and of everyday Indian life; maintains several filmographies and guides to titles of films about Indians. For information regarding viewing films and video tapes write Division.

NATIONAL ANTHROPOLOGICAL ARCHIVES
Smithsonian Institution
WASHINGTON 20560
(202) 357-1976
Description: A major U.S. repository of
documentation on Native American art.

**NATIONAL ARCHIVES &
RECORDS ADMINISTRATION**
8th and Pennsylvania Ave., N.W.
WASHINGTON 20408
(202) 501-5425
James Rush, Jr., Ass't Chief
Description: Civil Reference Branch: Contains
records of the Bureau of Indian Affairs, and tribal
enrollment records for the period prior to 1958;
Motion Picture Branch: Consists of films showing
Indian life-ways in the 1930's, and Plains Indian
sign language.

NATIONAL GEOGRAPHIC SOCIETY LIBRARY
17th and M Sts., N.W.
WASHINGTON 20036
(202) 857-7000

**NATIONAL INDIAN EDUCATION
ASSOCIATION LIBRARY**
1819 H St., N.W., Suite 800
WASHINGTON 20006
Description: Library of material written be, about,
and for American Indians and Alaskan natives.
Holdings include about 5,000 books, 1,000 films
and filmstrips, microfiche, tapes, cassettes, journals and newspapers on native Americans.

NATURAL RESOURCES LIBRARY
U.S. Department of the Interior
1849 C St., NW
WASHINGTON 20240
(202) 208-5815
Victoria Nozero, Project Director
Description: Holdings include all publications issued by the Bureau of Indian Affairs: Native American treaties, history, policy; and Native American
education. Open to the public.

**SMITHSONIAN INSTITUTION - NATIONAL
ANTHROPOLOGICAL ARCHIVES**
Natural History Bldg.
10th & Constitution Ave., NW
WASHINGTON 20560
(202) 357-1976
Description: Contains over 5,000 cubic feet on all
branches of anthropology. Maintains the Bureau
of Ethnology Collection and others: Extensive collection of manuscripts, photographs, administrative records, maps and other material relating to
North American Indians, anthropological institutions, and the history of anthropology.

U.S. DEPT. OF THE INTERIOR LIBRARY
18th & C Sts., NW
WASHINGTON 20240
(202) 343-5810
Robert Uskavitch, Chief-Information Services
Description: Maintains a large collection of Indian
reference material.

**U.S. DEPT. OF JUSTICE
ENVIRONMENT LIBRARY**
10th & Pennsylvania Ave., NW, Rm. 2333
WASHINGTON 20530
(202) 514-2768 Fax 371-0570
Lee Decker, Branch Librarian
Description: Serves the Environment & Natural
Resources Division at the Dept. of Justice, includ-

ing the Indian Resources section; holdings of
18,000 volumes, many of which are on Indian
claims and natural resources as related to Indian
lands.

WILKINSON, CRAGUN & BARKER LIBRARY
1735 New York Ave., N.W.
WASHINGTON 20006
Description: Maintains a special collection of
American Indian-Federal Government legal ma-
terial.

FLORIDA

TEMPLE MOUND MUSEUM LIBRARY
P.O. Box 4009, 139 Miraclestrip Pkwy SE
FORT WALTON BEACH 32548
(904) 243-6521
Steve Tuthill, Museum Director
Description: Collection consists of 1,500 volumes
on the archaeology of the site, and Indians of the
region; slides and photographs.

SEMINOLE TRIBE LIBRARY
6073 Stirling Rd.
HOLLYWOOD 33024
(305) 964-4860
Norman H. Tribbett, Librarian/Director
Description: Contains books, manuscripts, periodicals, photographs and microfilm on the history
and culture of the Seminole Indian Tribe of Florida.

JOHN C. PACE LIBRARY
Special Collections Department
The University of West Florida
11000 University Parkway
PENSACOLA 32514-5750
(904) 474-2213
Dean DeBolt, Librarian
Description: Collection of manuscripts, archival
records, microfilms, and research materials include the history of the Creek Indians of the Southeast from earliest contact with white man, up to
the present-day attempts to gain recognition as
tribal groups.

FLORIDA HISTORICAL SOCIETY LIBRARY
University of South Florida
TAMPA 33620
Description: Holdings are mainly of Seminole
Indian material.

GEORGIA

NEW ECHOTA HISTORIC SITE LIBRARY
1211 Chatsworth Highway
CALHOUN 30701
(404) 629-8151
Jeff Stancil, Curator
Description: General works on the Cherokee Indians and microfilm of the 1828-1834 Cherokee
Phoenix newspaper, and the 1836-37 property
evaluations of the Cherokee Nation.

OCMULGEE NATIONAL MONUMENT LIBRARY
1207 Emery Highway
MACON 31201
(912) 742-0447
Description: A collection of over 1,000 volumes
on anthropology, archaeology, and prehistoric and
historic Indians of the area; history of the SE U.S.

CHIEFTAINS MUSEUM LIBRARY
501 Riverside Parkway
ROME 30162
(404) 291-9494
Josephine Ransom, Director
Description: Holdings include books and magazines dealing with Cherokee history, local history;
videocasettes. Hours: Tue-Fri 11-4PM; Sunday 2-
5PM; $1/adults.

**UNIVERSITY OF HAWAII AT MANOA
CENTER FOR ORAL HISTORY**
Social Science Research Institute
Porteus Hall 724, 2424 Maile Way
HONOLULU 96822
(808) 956-6259
Warren S. Nishimoto, Director
Description: A resource center for researchers,
students, and the general community. Collection
includes books, photo displays, catalogs, bro-
chures, and videotapes based on oral histories.
Research activities: Records and preserves
through oral interviews the recollections of Hawaii's
people. Transcript topics include life histories of
Native Hawaiians. *Publications*: Oral History Recorder, quarterly newsletter.

HAWAII

BISHOP MUSEUM LIBRARY & ARCHIVES
1525 Bernice St.
HONOLULU 96817
(808) 847-3511
Description: A major U.S. repository of
documentation on Native American art.

IDAHO

**IDAHO STATE HISTORICAL
SOCIETY LIBRARY**
610 North Julia Davis Dr.
BOISE 83702
(208) 334-3356
Arthur A. Hart, Director
Description: Collections include more than 200
volumes of Lapwai Agency records of 1871-1883;
diaries and private papers. The Alice Fletcher-Jane
Gay Nez Perce Allotment Photograph Collection,
1882-1892; Idaho Superintendency and other Indian records (National Archives microfilm); Indian
files in the territorial section of State Archives; Nez
Perce and Shoshone literature.

**PACIFIC NORTHWEST
ANTHROPOLOGICAL ARCHIVES**
Laboratory of Anthropology
University of Idaho
MOSCOW 83844-1111
(208) 885-6123 Fax 885-5878
Roderick Sprague, Director
Description: Originals or copies of virtually all
sources of material pertaining to Pacific Northwest
ethnography, archaeology, physical anthropology,
and anthopological linguistics. Also personal papers of Don Crabtree, Alfred W. Bowers, and Frank
C. Leonhardy. Also includes the Don Crabtree
Lithic Technology collection of publications, reprints, correspondence, and specimens. Holdings
number ca. 5,000. Area most strongly covered is
the Plateau, secondly the Northwest. Open to the
public.

**NEZ PERCE NATIONAL
HISTORICAL PARK LIBRARY**
P.O. Box 93
SPALDING 83551
 (208) 843-2261 x 41/42 Fax 843-2001
 Susan Buchel, Curator
Description: Collection consists of about 1,700 volumes on Nez Perce Indian history and culture, and culture and history of other Columbia Plateau and Pacific Northwest tribes. Special collection: 5,000 historical photographs. Open to the public by special arrangements (2-3 weeks advance notice needed.)

ILLINOIS

**FIELD MUSEUM OF NATURAL
HISTORY LIBRARY**
Roosevelt Rd. at Lake Shore Dr.
CHICAGO 60605
 (312) 922-9410
Description: A major U.S. repository of documentation on Native American art.

**MacARTHUR FOUNDATION
LIBRARY VIDEO PROJECT**
P.O. Box 409113
CHICAGO 60640
 (800) 847-3671
 Mary M. Kirby, Director
Description: A non-profit organization providing public librarians, native American organizations, and tribal libraries with a listing of Native American videos suggested by a panel of Native Americans. Many of these works are independent films normally not seen on TV or in collections by major distributors. *Publications*: Videoforum, first issue is on Native American videos.

THE NEWBERRY LIBRARY
D'Arcy McNickel Center for the
History of the American Indian
60 West Walton
CHICAGO 60610
 (312) 943-9090
 Frederick E. Hoxie, Academic V.P.
Description: E.E. Ayer Collection consists of thousands of volumes, manuscripts, prints and photographs on the American Indian; Indian-White contact and response; Native-American linguistics; Government-Indian relations prior to the New Deal; and maps. Other library holdings supplement this collection.

**CAHOKIA MOUNDS STATE
HISTORIC SITE LIBRARY**
7850 Collinsville Rd.
EAST ST. LOUIS 62201
 (618) 344-5268
Description: Contains research data on the excavations at Cahokia Mounds Site; and generally related Mississippian Site; volumes on Illinois and Midwestern archaeology.

THE MITCHELL INDIAN MUSEUM LIBRARY
Kendall College
2408 Orrington Ave.
EVANSTON 60201
 (708) 866-1395 Fax 866-1320
 Dr. Thomas Kerr, CEO
Description: Collection focuses on the history, anthropology, archaeology, education, literature, religion, art, crafts, and social problems of the American Indian.

INDIANA

THE ARCHIVES OF TRADITIONAL MUSIC
Indiana University, Morrison Hall 117
BLOOMINGTON 47405
 (812) 855-4679 Fax 855-6673
 Ruth M. Stone, Director
Description: A library of sound recordings of world music, including a significat number of recordings of Native American music and language, and other oral data made from the late 1890s to the present. *Special collection*: Edward S. Curtis Collection of American Indian Music. *Special program*: Outreach program that helps Native American communities obtain copies of recordings of their own music and enhances the existing documentation of these materials. *Publication*: Resound, quarterly. Established 1954.

INDIANA UNIVERSITY MUSEUM LIBRARY
Student Bldg. 107
BLOOMINGTON 47401
Description: A collection of 2,000 volumes on the American Indian.

**AMERICAN INDIAN STUDIES
RESEARCH INSTITUTE**
Indiana University
422 N. Indiana Ave.
Bloomington 47408
 (812) 855-4086
 Douglas R. Parks

THE POTAWATOMI MUSEUM LIBRARY
P.O. Box 631
FREMONT 46737
Description: Holdings include 1,000 reference books on the American Indian. By appointment.

**MUSEUM OF INDIAN HERITAGE
REFERENCE LIBRARY**
500 W. Washington St.
INDIANAPOLIS 46204
 (317) 293-4488
 Vicki Cummings, Director
Description: Collections consist of approximately 2,000 volumes on Native American ethnology, archaeology, art, and language; also, periodicals; Bureau of American Ethnology annual reports; historical accounts of early contact; treaties; and literature. Tribal works emphasize Northwest Coast, Eskimo, Southwest, California, Great Plains, Eastern Woodlands, and works on Central and South American tribes.

IOWA

**IOWA STATE HISTORICAL
MUSEUM LIBRARY**
East 12th & Grand Ave.
DES MOINES 50319
 (515) 281-5111

**STATE HISTORICAL SOCIETY
OF IOWA LIBRARY**
402 Iowa Ave.
IOWA CITY 52240-1806
 (319) 335-3916 Fax 335-3924
 David Crosson, Administrator
Description: A collection of 130,000 books and bound periodicals, microforms, newspapers, maps, etc. of which there is a small collection of

books relating to tribes that lived in Iowa, census data, public records, documents from Indian Claims Commission court cases, theses, manuscripts, maps, paintings and drawings, and several hundred Mesquakie Indian photographs.

**EFFIGY MOUNDS NATIONAL
MONUMENT LIBRARY**
151 Hwy. 76
HARPERS FERRY 52146
 (319) 873-3491
Description: Books and periodicals relating to prehistoric Indians, archaeology, history of Iowa, Wisconsin, Mississippi River, natural resources, and specifically on the archaeology and ethnography of Effigy Mounds region.

MORNINGSIDE COLLEGE LIBRARY
SIOUX CITY 51106
Description: Contains a special collection on the American Indian.

KANSAS

**CULTURAL HERITAGE &
ARTS CENTER LIBRARY**
P.O. Box 1275
DODGE CITY 67801
Description: Consists of more than 2,000 books, films, and records on North American Indians, with emphasis on Indians of the Southwest.

MENNONITE LIBRARY & ARCHIVES
Bethel College
300 E. 27th
NORTH NEWTON 67117
 (316) 283-2500 Fax 284-5286
 Dale R. Schrag, Director
Special collection: Includes the H.R. Voth Manuscript and Photograph Collection on Hopi Indians; and Rodolphe Petter Manuscript Collection on Cheyenne Indians. Also includes microfilm, audiotapes, and maps.

**PAWNEE INDIAN VILLAGE
MUSEUM LIBRARY**
Rt. 1, Box 475
REPUBLIC 66964
 (913) 361-2255
 Richard Gould, Director
Description: Collection includes hand research material on the Pawnee as well as more general history on Kansas.

**KANSAS STATE HISTORICAL
SOCIETY LIBRARY**
120 West 10th St.
TOPEKA 66612-1291
 (913) 296-4776 Fax 296-1005
 David A. Haury, Director
Description: Holdings include a special collection of approximately 4,750 books on the American Indians and the West; also Kansas State public records and documents; microfilm, maps, paintings and drawings, photographs, etc.

**MID-AMERICA ALL INDIAN
CENTER LIBRARY**
650 North Seneca
WICHITA 67203
 (316) 262-5221
Description: Contains a collection of over 400 volumes on the American Indian.

KENTUCKY

J.B. SPEED ART MUSEUM LIBRARY
2035 S. Third St., P.O. Box 2600
LOUISVILLE 40201
 (502) 636-2893 Fax 636-2899
 Ruth Cloudman, Curator
Description: Collection includes over 14,300 books, 72 periodical subscriptions; artists pamphlet files: 54 drawers. *Special collection*: Frederick Weygold's books on American Indians.

LOUISIANA

GRINDSTONE BLUFF MUSEUM LIBRARY
P.O. Box 7965, 501 Jenkins Rd.
SHREVEPORT 71107
Description: Collection consists of approximately 3,600 volumes, with emphasis on Caddo and other area Indians.

MAINE

ABBE MUSEUM LIBRARY
P.O. Box 286
BAR HARBOR 04609
 (207) 288-3519
 Rebecca Cole-Will, Curator
Description: Includes over 5,000 volumes on Native Americans, archaeology, Maine prehistory and Maine Native peoples. Open to members and scholars by appointment only.

MAINE TRIBAL UNITY MUSEUM LIBRARY
Quaker Hill Rd.
UNITY 04988
 (207) 948-3131
Description: A collection of more than 500 volumes on the Indians of Maine and American Indians in general.

MASSACHUSETTS

**ROBERT S. PEABODY MUSEUM
OF ARCHAEOLOGY LIBRARY**
Phillips Academy
ANDOVER 01810
 (617) 749-4490
 James W. Bradley, Director
Description: 5,000 archaeological, anthropological and ethnological sources; rare book, journals; and historical photographs.

**CHILDREN'S MUSEUM
RESOURCE CENTER**
300 Congress St.
BOSTON 02210
 (617) 426-6500
Description: Holdings include 10,000 cultural materials relating to the American Indian.

TOZZER LIBRARY
Harvard University
21 Divinity Ave.
CAMBRIDGE 02138
 (617) 495-2248
 Lynne M. Schmelz-Keil, Librarian
Description: A major U.S. repository of documen-

tation on Native American art. Collection consists of over 175,000 volumes relating to the major subfields of anthropology, including archaeology, biological anthropology; cultural anthropology, and linguistics; strong collection on Mayan archaeology and ethnology. *Publications*: Author and Title Catalogues of the Tozzer Library (microfiche); Bibliographic Guide to Anthropology and Archaeology, annual; Anthropological Literature: An Index to Periodical Articles and Essays, quarterly. Interlibrary loans. Open to the public.

BOSTON INDIAN COUNCIL LIBRARY
105 S. Huntington
JAMAICA PLAIN 02130
 (617) 232-0343
Description: A collection of various materials related to Indian programs, history and culture.

PLIMOTH PLANTATION LIBRARY
P.O. Box 1620
PLYMOUTH 02362
 (508) 746-1622
 Nanepashemet, Manager
Description: In addition to Pilgrim related topics, there is a growing body of southern New England Native literature.

STEPHEN PHILLIPS LIBRARY
Peabody Essex Museum
East Indian Square
SALEM 01970
 (508) 745-1876
Description: Collection contains 1,000 books, plus periodicals and pamphlets on the history and culture of North American Indians, with emphasis on the Northeastern section of the U.S. Special collections: Papers of Native American researchers Frank Speck and E. Tappan Adney. Interlibrary loans. Open to the public.

CHAPIN LIBRARY OF RARE BOOKS
Williams College
WILLIAMSTOWN 01267
 (413) 597-2241
Description: Collection of 16th, 17th & 18th-century documents relating to Indians of North and South America.

AMERICAN ANTIQUARIAN SOCIETY LIBRARY
185 Salisbury St.
WORCESTER 01609
 (617) 755-5221
Description: A collection of five million books, prints, maps, and periodicals on American history, archaeology, and life through 1876.

MICHIGAN

**UNIVERSITY OF MICHIGAN -
WILLIAM L. CLEMENTS LIBRARY**
South University St.
ANN ARBOR 48104
Description: Collection consists of over 40,000 books and bound periodicals on Americana to 1830, including Indian relations.

CRANBROOK INSTITUTE OF SCIENCE
500 Lone Pine Rd., Box 801
BLOOMFIELD HILLS 48303
 (313) 645-3260
Description: Collection includes over 18,000 volumes on anthropology and ethnology; also, about 200 journal subscriptions.

GENESEE INDIAN CENTER LIBRARY
124 West First St.
FLINT 48502-1311
 (313) 239-6621
Description: Contains a collection of reference books and records on American Indian history and culture.

BISHOP BARAGA ASSOCIATION ARCHIVES
444 S. 4th St., Box 550
MARQUETTE 49855
 (906) 225-1141 Fax 225-0437
 Regis Walling, Archivist
Description: Maintains a special collection on Native Americans, with microfilm of the Office of Indian Affairs of early 1800s.

**LAKE SUPERIOR STATE COLLEGE -
MICHIGAN COLLECTION**
SAULT STE. MARIE 49783
Description: Collection of 1,000 volumes on the history of Michigan's Upper Peninsula, including Indians and local history.

MINNESOTA

**BECKER COUNTY HISTORICAL
SOCIETY LIBRARY**
915 Lake Ave.
DETROIT LAKES 56501
Description: Holdings include 1,500 volumes pertaining to the White Earth Indian Reservation, covering twelve townships of Becker County, MN.

**MINNEAPOLIS COLLEGE OF ART &
DESIGN–LEARNING RESOURCE CENTER**
200 East 25th St.
MINNEAPOLIS 55404
Special collection: The American Indian Book Collection.

MINNEAPOLIS ATHENAEUM
300 Nicollet Mall
MINNEAPOLIS 55404-1992
 (612) 372-6525 Fax 372-6546
 Edward R. Kukla, Director
Description: Holdings include approximately 500 volumes dealing with Indian affairs and activities on 18th and 19th century travel books. Specializing in the following tribes: Dakota (Sioux); Mandan; Ojibwa (Chippewa).

**UPPER MIDWEST INDIAN
CULTURE CENTER LIBRARY**
P.O. Box 727, Pipestone National Monument
PIPESTONE 56164
Description: Collection of 500 volumes on Indian history of the northern Plains.

**MINNESOTA HISTORICAL
SOCIETY RESEARCH CENTER**
345 Kellogg Blvd. W.
ST. PAUL 55102-1906
 (612) 296-2143 Fax 297-7436
 Denise E. Carlson, Head of Reference
Description: A major U.S. repository of documentation on Native American art. Maintains a collection of material on the Ojibwe and Dakota tribes, plus a small amount on Winnebago; includes information on Indian education, state census schedules with listings of Indian people, and correspondence on Indian matters in the Governor's papers. Collections include books, photos, newspapers, periodicals, oral histories, sound and vi-

sual recordings, and artworks. Also, Dakota and Ojibwe dictionaries, histories of Native peoples in Minnesota, and material on the U.S.-Dakota conflicts of 1862. *Activities*: Mini-classes on genealogy resources, house history research, etc. Interlibrary loans. Open to the public.

MISSISSIPPI

JP MUSEUM OF INDIAN ARTIFACTS LIBRARY
Route 1, Box 715, Hwy. 49 (LYMAN)
SAUCIER 39574
Description: Contains a collection on Indian history and culture; artifact reference.

THE GRAND VILLAGE OF THE NATCHEZ INDIANS--LIBRARY
400 Jefferson Davis Blvd.
NATCHEZ 39120
(601) 446-6502
 James F. Barnett, Jr., Director
Description: A collection of 300 volumes on archaeology and Southeastern Indians. Special programs: Seminars, workshops, and educational programs. Open to public for reference only .

NATCHEZ TRACE PARKWAY LIBRARY
R.R. 1, NT 143
TUPELO 38801
Description: Maintains a special collection of 200 items of papers and letters relating to Choctaw and Chickasaw Indians.

MISSOURI

SOUTHEAST MISSOURI STATE UNIVERSITY LIBRARY
CAPE GIRARDEAU 63701
Description: Extensive collection on North American archaeology and Indians.

KANSAS CITY MUSEUM LIBRARY
3218 Gladstone Blvd.
KANSAS CITY 64123
 (816) 483-8300
 David Ucko, President
Description: Maintains a general reference library with about 4,000 volumes covering primarily local and regional history , Native American art and history, natural sciences, material culture, and museum-related publications.

NATIONAL ARCHIVES-K.C. BRANCH
2312 East Bannister Rd.
KANSAS CITY 64131
 (816) 926-7271
 R. Reed Whitaker , Director
Description: Collection consists of Federal Indian records created on Indian reservations and schools in North and South Dakota, Minnesota, Kansas and Nebraska. The tribes included on these reservations include the Chippewa and the various tribes of the Sioux Confederation, as well as the Iowa, Kickapoo, Omaha, Potawatomi, Ponca, Sac and Fox, Winnebago and Munsee; also, records of the Bismarck, Flandreau, Haskell, Pierre, Pipestone, Rapid City , and Wahpeton Indian schools; some records relate to tribes and reservations in Wisconsin, primarily the Menominee. Information contained are: censuses, tribal enrollment rosters, annuity payrolls, indi-

vidual Indian bank account ledgers, land allotment rolls, employee payrolls and student case files; also extensive series of superintendent's (agent's) correspondence files.

UNIVERSITY OF MISSOURI, K.C.
GENERAL LIBRARY
5100 Rockhill Rd.
KANSAS CITY 64110
Special collection : Snyder Collection of Americana--25,000 volumes--historical and Indian-related works.

MISSOURI HISTORICAL SOCIETY LIBRARY
Jefferson Memorial Bldg.
ST. LOUIS 63112
Description: Holdings include more than 2,000 volumes on the American Indian.

MONTANA

CENTER FOR NATIVE AMERICAN STUDIES
Univerity of Montana
BOZEMAN 59717
(406) 994-3881
 Dr. Wayne J. Stein, Director
Research activities : American Indian studies, including research on Montana tribal histories and culture and Indian-white relations.

MUSEUM OF THE PLAINS INDIAN LIBRARY & ARCHIVES
P.O. Box 400, Highway 89
BROWNING 59417
 (406) 338-2230
Description: Collection consists of volumes on Plains ethnology and archaeology; Montana ethnology and history; and Blackfeet life and history .

WHITE SWAN MEMORIAL LIBRARY
Custer Battlefield National Monument
P.O. Box 39
CROW AGENCY 59022
 (406) 638-2621
 Mardell Plainfeather , Librarian
Elizabeth & George Custer Collection - correspondence with statesmen and military personnel of the period; 2,000 photographs, including military personnel, the Custer family; Native Americans (Crow, Sioux, Cheyenne); 5,000 cartridges; 3,000 letters. Not open to the public.

CROW INDIAN HOSPITAL MEDICAL LIBRARY
U.S. Public Health Service
CROW AGENCY 59022

MILES ROMNEY MEMORIAL LIBRARY
Bitter Root Valley Historical Society
Old Court House, 205 Bedford Ave.
HAMILTON 59840
 (406) 363-3338
 Helen Ann Bibler , Director
Description: Subjects include pioneer and Indian history .

HISTORICAL SOCIETY OF MONTANA LIBRARY & ARCHIVES
225 North Roberts
HELENA 59601
Description: Holdings include 50,000 volumes on Montana history, frontier life, Indians and Indian affairs, Lewis and Clark Expedition, and other related subjects.

UNIVERSITY OF MONTANA- SCHOOL OF LAW LIBRARY
MISSOULA 59801
Description: Maintains a special collection on Indian law; 120 treaties.

BIG HOLE NATIONAL BATTLEFIELD LIBRARY
P.O. Box 237
WISDOM 59761
(406) 689-3155
 Crystal Coffey-Avey, Librarian
Description: Collection contains over 400 volumes on Nez Perce history , culture; military history of the 1870s, and opening of the W estern frontier. *Special program* : Interpretive program in summer on Nez Perce and military culture. Open to the public.

NEBRASKA

CENTER FOR GREAT PLAINS STUDIES
University of Nebraska
1213 Oldfather Hall
LINCOLN 68588-0314
Description: A collection of Western art and fiction with emphasis on Plains Indian nations. A collection of videotapes on several Nebraska tribes for use as elementary and secondary school curriculum material. Ten one-hour tapes concentrate on oral tradition and include storytelling, history , and elders' reminiscences by members of the Lakota, Brule Sioux, Santee Sioux, Omaha, Pawnee and Winnebago tribes. V ideotapes in inch cassette and inch reel-to-reel formats are available at the cost of duplication and cassette.

UNIVERSITY OF NEBRASKA STATE MUSEUM
Nebraska Hall
LINCOLN 68588
 (402) 472-6365
 Hugh H. Genoways, Director
Research activities : Studies include the culture and history of the Plains Apache. *Publication* : Bulletin of the University of Nebraska State Museum

NATIVE AMERICAN PUBLIC BROADCASTING CONSORTIUM LIBRARY
P.O. Box 83111
LINCOLN 68501
 (402) 472-3522
Description: A collection of videotapes and films include Native-American programs which have been screened and evaluated by the Consortium for technical quality and accuracy of portrayal and content. Topics include: history, culture, education, economic development, current events and the arts.

NEBRASKA STATE HISTORICAL SOCIETY LIBRARY/ARCHIVES
P.O. Box 82554, 1500 R St.
LINCOLN 68501
 (402) 471-3270
 Andrea Paul, Archivist; James Potter, Historian
Description: Holdings include more than 70,000 volumes on Nebraska history , Indians of the Great Plains, genealogy; 465 photographs in the John A. Anderson Photograph Collection of Brule Sioux.

NEVADA

**COLLEGE CAREER & VOCATIONAL
RESOURCE LIBRARY**
Nevada Urban Indians
2100 Capurro Way
Sparks, NV 89431
 (702) 356-8111
 Missy Shemick, Director
Description: Provides information on all major colleges with Native American Studies Programs from across the nation. Includes brochures and applications, scholarships, grants and vocational schools.

NEW HAMPSHIRE

**NEW ENGLAND ANTIQUITIES
RESEARCH ASSOCIATION**
305 Academy Rd.
Pembroke, NH 03275
 (603) 485-5655
 Daniel Leary, President
Research activities: Anthropology, archaeology; Native American studies of stoneworks and related structures in the northeastern U.S. Archaeology in Maine and New Hampshire. *Publication*: NEARA Journal.

NEW JERSEY

BRIDGETON FREE PUBLIC LIBRARY
Special Collections
150 E. Commerce St.
BRIDGETON 08302
 (609) 451-2620
 Patricia W. McCulley, Director
Description: 2,000 volumes on Cumberland County history, local genealogy, and Woodland Indians. Holdings include 20,000 Indian artifacts collected within a 30-mile radius of library.

NEWARK MUSEUM LIBRARY
43-49 Washington St.
NEWARK 07101
 (201) 596-6625 Fax 642-0459
 Margaret DiSalvi, Librarian
Description: Collection covers American Indian art, crafts, life, ethnology, etc. Open to the public.

PRINCETON UNIVERSITY LIBRARIES
PRINCETON 08540
 (609) 452-3180
Description: A major U.S. repository of documentation on Native American art.

SETON HALL UNIVERSITY MUSEUM LIBRARY
South Orange Ave.
SOUTH ORANGE 07079
 (201) 761-9543
Description: Contains a collection of 1,000 volumes on prehistoric Indians of New Jersey.

NEW MEXICO

ACOMA MUSEUM LIBRARY & ARCHIVES
P.O. Box 309, Pueblo of Acoma
ACOMITA 87034

 (505) 552-6606
Description: Contains photographs & documents relating to the history of Acoma Pueblo.

AMERICAN INDIAN LAW CENTER LIBRARY
University of New Mexico-School of Law
P.O. Box 4456, Station A, 1117 Stanford N.E.
ALBUQUERQUE 87196
 (505) 277-5462
Description: Maintains a special collection on American Indian law.

**MAXWELL MUSEUM OF ANTHROPOLOGY
CLARK FIELD ARCHIVES**
University of New Mexico
University and Ash N.E.
ALBUQUERQUE 87131
 (505) 277-4404
 Garth L. Bawden, Director
Description: Collection of 2,500 volumes on archaeology, anthropology and ethnology, with emphasis on the Southwestern U.S.

**NATIVE AMERICAN STUDIES - INFORMATION
& MATERIALS RESOURCE COLLECTION**
University of New Mexico
1812 Las Lomas Dr. NE
ALBUQUERQUE, NM 87131
 (505) 277-3917 Fax 277-1818
 Alison Freese, PhD, Information Specialist
Description: A resource/research center with books, journals, Native newspapers, videos, and newsclippings on Native issues, specializing in stereotyping, Native American economic development, Southwestern history, Native American literature, Native perspectives of American history, and a Quincentennial archive. *Special programs*: Speakers series; computer networking with tribal offices, schools, and libraries. *Publication*: Monthly newsletter. Open to the public.

**INDIAN PUEBLO CULTURAL CENTER
RESEARCH LIBRARY/ARCHIVES**
2401 12th St., NW
ALBUQUERQUE 87104
 (505) 843-7270 Fax 842-6959
 Rafael Gutierrez, Executive Director
Description: Collection consists of microfilm, old photos, books, materials, and statistical information on Pueblo Indians.

**AZTEC RUINS NATIONAL
MONUMENT LIBRARY**
P.O. Box 640
AZTEC 87410
 (505) 334-6174
Description: A collection of 300 volumes on the ethnography and archaeology of Southwestern Indians and prehistoric Pueblo Indians.

**CHACO CULTURE NATIONAL
HISTORICAL PARK LIBRARY**
Star Route 4, Box 6500
BLOOMFIELD 87413
 (505) 786-5384
Description: Study library housing hundreds of volumes on prehistory and history of Chaco area, Southwestern archaeology, ethnology, including journals, photographs, and records of historic period.

SALMON RUIN MUSEUM LIBRARY
San Juan County Archaeological Research Ctr.
6131 U.S. Hwy. 64
FARMINGTON 87401
 (505) 632-2013 Fax 632-1707
 Vivian Price, Librarian

Description: Research library focusing upon archaeology and history of the Four Corners area, including archaeological reports, historical documents, slides of Navajo rock art; 1,000 books, 1,200 pamphlets, 35 oral history tapes, photographs and color slides, transcriptions, and maps; and an on-loan collection of Navajo material. Open to the public. Established 1973.

**GALLUP INDIAN MEDICAL
CENTER LIBRARY**
PHS – Indian Health Service
P.O. Box 1337, East Nizhoni Blvd.
GALLUP 87301
Description: Maintains a special collection on the Navajo Indians.

GALLUP PUBLIC LIBRARY
115 West Hill
GALLUP 87301
Description: A collection of rare, out-of-print and contemporary titles on Southwestern tribes: Navajo, Hopi and Zuni.

NAVAJO NATION LIBRARY SYSTEM
Book Distribution Services
P.O. Box 1484
GALLUP 87301
 (505) 863-6058 Fax 863-2145
 LeManuel Bitsoi, Contact
Purpose: To distribute free book materials, non-book materials, and equipment to elegible organizations and individuals. See listing under Window Rock, AZ for more information.

**BANDELIER NATIONAL
MONUMENT LIBRARY**
LOS ALAMOS 87544
 (505) 672-3861
Description: Contains a collection of 2,000 volumes on the archaeology of the area, and Pueblo Indians.

SALINAS NATIONAL MONUMENT LIBRARY
Route 1, Box 496
MOUNTAINAIRE 87036
 (505) 847-2585

NAVAJO NATION LIBRARY SYSTEM
Navajo Community Library
P.O. Box 1296
NAVAJO 87328
 Fax (505) 777-2598
See listing under Window Rock, AZ.

PALEO-INDIAN INSTITUTE LIBRARY
Eastern New Mexico University
Campus Box 2154
PORTALES 88130

**EL MORRO NATIONAL
MONUMENT LIBRARY**
RAMAH 87321
 (505) 783-5132
Description: A collection of 400 volumes on the archaeology of the prehistoric site and historic Pueblos.

FORT BURGWIN RESEARCH CENTER
Southern Methodist University
P.O. Box 300
RANCHOS DE TAOS 87557
 (505) 758-8322
 Dr, William B., Stallcup, Jr. Research Director
Research activities: Includes field studies in prehistoric pithouses and Pueblo settlements. Performs archaeological site preservation technology.

**STRADLING MUSEUM
OF THE HORSE LIBRARY**
RUIDOSO 88345
Description: Maintains a collection of 1,000 volumes on Indian history; Indian rugs.

**ANTHROPOLOGY FILM CENTER
FOUNDATION LIBRARY**
P.O. Box 493
SANTA FE 87594-0493
 (505) 983-4127
Description: A study collection of films, especially those produced by graduates of the Film Center training program.

INDIAN ARTS RESEARCH CENTER
School of American Research
P.O. Box 2188
SANTA FE 87501
 (505) 982-3584
  Michael Hering, Director
Description: Collection of Southwest cultural materials, focusing on Native American arts of the Southwest, such as ceramics, basketry, textiles, jewelry, paintings and kachinas. *Publications*: Exploration Magzine (annual); annual report.

**INSTITUTE OF AMERICAN INDIAN ARTS
LIBRARY - NATIVE AMERICAN VIDEOTAPES
ARCHIVES**
P.O. Box 20007, Alexis Hall - St. Michael's Dr.
SANTA FE 87504
 (505) 988-6423 Fax 988-6446
  Mary L. Young, Librarian
Description: Collection consists of about 20,000 volumes on North American Indian art, history and culture; 800 videotapes, recording tribal and reservation history, tribal projects and activities, such as the reservation medical center or tribal government--30,000 Smithsonian photographs of Native American culture; more than 900 recordings of Native-American music; 9,000 slides of art of all types and Native American art objects; 15 linear feet of school archives. Open to the public for research only.

MUSEUM OF NEW MEXICO LIBRARY
Museum of Indian Arts & Culture &
Laboratory of Anthropology
708 Camino Lejo
SANTA FE 87504
 (505) 827-6344 Fax 827-6349
  Laura Holt, Librarian
Description: A major U.S. repository of documentation on Native American art. Southwest anthropology research library of approximately 5,000 volumes with holdings in 1,000 journal titles; as well as the personal library of Sylvanus G. Morley with many rare Mesoamerican titles.

NEW MEXICO STATE LIBRARY
325 Don Gaspar
SANTA FE 87503
 (505) 827-3800 Fax 827-3820
  Karen Watkins, Acting Director
Description: Contains 11,000 books on Southwest history; New Mexico newspapers. Interlibrary loans. Open to the public.

**WHEELWRIGHT MUSEUM OF THE AMERICAN
INDIAN - MARY CABOT WHEELWRIGHT
RESEARCH LIBRARY**
P.O. Box 5153, 704 Camino Lejo
SANTA FE 87501
 (505) 982-4636
  Steve Rogers, Curator

Description: Maintains over 10,000 volumes on the art, history, and religions of the Navajo and other tribes; archives contain 1,000 examples of Navajo ceremonial art, 3,000 Navajo ceremonial music recordings, 100 Navajo myth texts, 1,000 Navajo sandpaintings on slides, and 100 music and prayer tapes. Open to public by appointment.

NAVAJO COMMUNITY COLLEGE LIBRARY
SHIPROCK 87420
 (505) 368-5291
Description: Collection of books, periodicals, video tapes, pamphlets, and maps. *Special collections*: Native American Speial collection, and the Caswell and Betty Silver Southwest Geoscience Collection.

**GILA CLIFF DWELLINGS NATIONAL
MONUMENT–VISITOR CENTER LIBRARY**
Route 11, Box 100
SILVER CITY 88061
Description: A collection of books on prehistoric Mogollon Indians, archaeology and natural history.

**KIT CARSON MEMORIAL
FOUNDATION LIBRARY**
P.O. Box CCC
TAOS 87571
 (505) 758-4741
Description: Contains a collection of 5,500 volumes on the prehistoric Indian culture of Taos and the Southwest.

ZUNI ARCHAEOLOGY PROGRAM LIBRARY
P.O. Box 339
ZUNI 87327
 (505) 782-4814
Description: Comprehensive holdings concerning Zuni prehistory, archaeology, history, and land use. Unpublished field notes, ethnographic interviews, papers, and published works are on file.

NEW YORK

TONAWANDA INDIAN COMMUNITY LIBRARY
P.O. Box 326, 372 Bloomingdale Rd.
AKRON 14001-0326
 (716) 542-5618
  Ramona Charles, Director

INSTITUTE FOR ARCHAEOLOGICAL STUDIES
SUNY at Albany-Social Science, Rm. 263
1400 Washington Ave.
ALBANY 12222
 (518) 442-4700
  Prof. Dean R. Snow, Director
Description: Northeastern archaeology, ethnology and linguistics. Supports research activities on Native Northeasten peoples, primarily Algonquian and Iroquois tribes. *Publication*: Man in the Northeast.

**CAYUGA MUSEUM OF HISTORY & ART--
LIBRARY & ARCHIVES**
203 Genessee St.
AUBURN 13021

NATIONAL KATERI CENTER LIBRARY
The National Shrine of N.A. Martyrs
AURIESVILLE 12016
 (518) 853-3033
  Rec. Robert J. Boyle, S.J., Director

HUNTINGTON FREE LIBRARY
9 Westchester Square
BRONX 10461
 (718) 829-7770
  Mary B. Davis, Librarian
Description: A major U.S. repository of documentation on Native American art. One of the leading research sources on Indians of the Western Hemisphere, this non-circulating collection contains more than 40,000 volumes on the archaeology, ethnology, and history of the native peoples of the Americas, as well as exceptional selections in Indian languages, codices, current Native American affairs, and Indian biography and related ephemera; maintains a large collection of Indian newspapers, manuscripts and field notes, and microform and audio-visual material. Open to the public by appointment.

**THE BROOKLYN MUSEUM
LIBRARY & ARCHIVES**
200 Eastern Parkway
BROOKLYN 11238
 (718) 638-5000 ext. 307
Description: A major U.S. repository of documentation on Native American art.

**BUFFALO & ERIE COUNTY
HISTORICAL SOCIETY LIBRARY**
5 Nottingham Court
BUFFALO 14216
Description: Holdings include books and manuscripts related to the Seneca Indians and other Indians of the Niagara frontier.

**THE MOHAWK-CAUGHNAWAGA
MUSEUM LIBRARY**
Route 5, Box 554
FONDA 12068
 (518) 853-3678
Description: A collection of 4,500 volumes on American Indians and American history.

**AKWESASNE LIBRARY
& CULTURAL CENTER**
St. Regis Mohawk Reservation
RR 1, Box 14C
HOGANSBURG 13655
 (518) 358-2240 Fax 358-2649
  Carol White, Director
Description: Public library with holdings of 27,000 volumes; with special collection on the North American Indian. *Publication*: Ka-ri-wen-hawi, monthly newspaper. Interlibrary loans. Open to the public.

IROQUOIS INDIAN MUSEUM LIBRARY
P.O. Box 7, Caverns Rd.
HOWES CAVE 12092
 (518) 296-8949
  Dr. Christina B. Johannsen-Hanks, Director
Description: A collection of books, periodicals, pamphlets and files relating to the Iroquois.

THE SENECA NATION LIBRARY
The Cattaraugus Reservation Branch
1490 Rte. 438
IRVING 14081
 (716) 532-9449
  Ethel E. Bray, Library Director
  Ann John, Branch Supervisor
Description: A collection of books and periodicals, with a special collectionon the history of the Iroquois Indians on microfilm; videotapes, and college and career catalogs. *Special programs*: Native American Art Show; speakers and displays;

exhibits and cultural presentations; Native American film programs. *Publication*: Seneca Nation Arts and Crafts Director. Allegany Reservation Branch in Salamanca, NY. Interlibrary loans.

AMERICAN MUSEUM OF NATURAL HISTORY DEPARTMENT OF LIBRARY SERVICES
Central Park West at 79th St.
NEW YORK 10024
(212) 769-5406
Nina J. Root, Dept. Chairperson
Description: A major U.S. repository of documentation on Native American art. Out of a collection of 410,000 volumes, approximately 50,000 volumes on the anthropology of North American Indian tribes (ethnology and archaeology - especially strong holdings on Northwest Coast cultures) along with accounts and descriptions of explorers; 125,000 photographs, primarily black-and-white of the early 20th century and some recent color photographs of artifacts. Maintains a special film collection with a limited number of films on Indians. Interlibrary loans. Open to the public.

THE NEW YORK PUBLIC LIBRARY
42nd St. & Fifth Ave.
NEW YORK 10018
(212) 930-0826
Timothy Troy, Bibliographer
of American Indian Material
Description: A major U.S. repository of documentation on Native American art. Maintains one of the largest collections of Indian bibliographical material in the world. Includes material from all cultural areas and time periods, from pre-Columbian eras to the present. The collections range through the disciplines of anthropology, archaeology, history, linguistics, and literature. Contains writings by Indians, runs of related periodicals and serials, pictures (photographs and engravings), works on Indian place names, and a collection of Indian captivity journals. Collects contemporary Native-American literature (in English or Indian languages.) The Library has materials in all written Indian languages from throughout the Western Hemisphere. Many items concerning the Indians of the Americas, particularly 16th & 17th century material in Spanish and English, are located in various special collections.

NATIVE AMERICAN CENTRE FOR THE LIVING ARTS LIBRARY
25 Rainbow Mall
NIAGARA FALLS 14303
(716) 284-2427
Elwood Green, Director
Description: A collection of 3,000 volumes on Native-American history, art, culture and crafts. Special collection: Smithsonian Institution Bureau of American Ethnology Reports (30 volumes); native periodicals; native music and oral history tapes. Inter-library loan.

SIX NATIONS INDIAN MUSEUM
ONCHIOTA 12968
(518) 891-0769
Description: Collection includes charts, posters, and other written material concerning many aspects of Iroquois history and culture.

YAGER LIBRARY
Hartwick College
ONEONTA 13820
(607) 432-4200
Description: A collection of over 1,000 volumes on North American Indian history and culture.

ROCHESTER MUSEUM & SCIENCE CENTER - RESEARCH DIV. - NEW YORK STATE ARCHAEOLOGICAL ASSOCIATION LIBRARY
Rochester Museum and Science Center
P.O. Box 1480, 657 East Ave.
ROCHESTER 14603
(716) 271-4320
Leatrice Kemp, Librarian
Description: Field and laboratory work in anthropology (especially American Indian and Genesee Valley region during 16th-20th centuries. *Library*: Contains more than 26,000 volumes: ethnographic and archaeological material - books, manuscripts and photographs on the history and technology of the Genesee Valley region, with emphasis on Iroquois.

THE SENECA NATION LIBRARY
The Allegany Reservation Branch
P.O. Box 231
SALAMANCA 14779
(716) 945-3157
Ethel E. Bray, Library Director
Dorsie Familo, Branch Supervisor
Description: A collection of books and periodicals, with a special collection on the history of the Iroquois Indians on microfilm; videotapes, and college and career catalogs. *Special programs*: Native American Art Show; speakers and displays; exhibits and cultural presentations; Native American film programs. Publication: Seneca Nation Arts and Crafts Director. Cattaraugus Reservation Branch in Irving, NY. Interlibrary loans.

NORTH CAROLINA

MUSEUM OF THE CHEROKEE INDIAN LIBRARY
P.O. Box 770-A, U.S. Hwy. 441 North
CHEROKEE 28719
(704) 497-3481
Description: Collection contains more than 3,000 volumes on Cherokee Indian history and culture. Reference use only.

SCHIELE MUSEUM REFERENCE LIBRARY
Center for SE Native American Studies
P.O. Box 953, 1500 East Garrison Blvd.
GASTONIA 28053-0953
(704) 866-6900 Fax 866-6041
Melissa Turney, Registrar/Librarian
Description: Contains a collection of more than 6,000 volumes serving the Reference Centers for the Library of Congress. 20 of holdings, including subject index files, graduate papers, monographs, as well as bound volumes, are on broad areas of Native-American topics representing all major Indian groups in U.S. and Canada with special emphasis on Indians of the Southeast. *Special collections*: Lilly Hobbs Schiele Collection; W.M. Modisette Collection; The Red Dawn Collection; and, The McCuen Collection. Open to the public by appointment only.

INDIAN MUSEUM OF THE CAROLINAS LIBRARY
607 Turnpike Rd.
LAURINBURG 28352
(919) 276-5880
Description: Maintains a collection of 500 volumes on Indian literature, archaeology, and history. Reference.

NATIVE AMERICAN LIBRARY
Lumbee Indian Education
Lumbee Regional Development Association
P.O. Box 637, East Main St.
PEMBROKE 28372

NATIVE AMERICAN RESOURCE CENTER & LIBRARY
Pembroke State University
College Rd.
PEMBROKE 28372
(919) 521-4214
Dr. Robert C. Hersch, Librarian
Description: Research into Lumbee Indians, American Indian tribal histories and culture. Conducted in conjunction with tribal organizations. *Library*: A collection of 500 volumes with emphasis on Lumbee Indians of North Carolina; audio-visual material; archival documents. *Publications*: SPIRIT! (quarterly newsletter); Robeson Trails Archaeological Survey.

NORTH DAKOTA

STATE HISTORICAL SOCIETY OF NORTH DAKOTA LIBRARY
North Dakota Heritage Center
Capitol Grounds
BISMARCK 58505
(701) 224-2666
Description: Holdings include 20,000 volumes on North Dakota history and the history of the American Indian; extensive photographs archive; government documents; genealogical collections; sound and visual recordings, including Native-American music.

CENTER FOR RURAL HEALTH
University of North Dakota
501 Columbia Rd.
GRAND FORKS 58203
(701) 777-3848
Jack M. Geller, Ph.D., Director
Description: Research into rural health care delivery, including Native American health care. Publication: Focus on Rural Health (semiannual).

CHESTER FRITZ LIBRARY
University of North Dakota
GRAND FORKS 58202

MEMORIAL LIBRARY
Minot State University
500 University Ave. W.
MINOT 58701
(701) 857-3200 Fax 857-3581
Description: Maintains a 1,500 volume collection focusing on Indians of the North Central U.S. and South Central Canada.

FORT BERTHOLD RESERVATION PUBLIC LIBRARY
Box 788
NEW TOWN 58763
(701) 627-4738
Quincee Baker, Director
Description: A collection of 10,000 books, videos, and microfiche serving the Three Affiliated Tribes: Arikara, Hidatsa, and Mandan, and the Fort Berthold Community College. An Indian studies collection reflect the cultural interests of tribal residents. Emphasis recently has been placed on children's programming and services. Established in 1985.

OHIO

AKRON ART INSTITUTE LIBRARY
69 East Market St.
AKRON 44308

MOUND CITY GROUP NATIONAL MONUMENT LIBRARY
16062 State Route 104
CHILLICOTHE 45601
(614) 774-1125
Description: A collection of 1,500 volumes on Hopewell and Adena Indian culture, and other Indian culture of Ohio; archaeological research on Hopewell and Adena cultures is conducted at Monument.

CINCINNATI ART MUSEUM LIBRARY
Eden Park
CINCINNATI 45202

RUTHERFORD B. HAYES PRESIDENTIAL CENTER LIBRARY
Spiegel Grove
FREMONT 43420
(419) 332-2081
Rebecca Hill & Barbara Paf f, Librarians
Description: Contains a collection of 1,000 books and pamphlets on Plains Indians, Sioux, and Wyandot. Also microfilm sets of the record of the Michigan Supt. of Indian Affairs, 1814-1851; correspondence of Reverend J.B. Finley, minister to the Wyandot Indians; diary of J.G. Bourke, ethnologist, 1872-1895. Interlibrary loans. Open to public.

OKLAHOMA

WOOLAROC MUSEUM LIBRARY
State Highway 123, Route 3
BARTLESVILLE 74003
(918) 336-0307
Description: A collection of 1,000 volumes on American Indians and Oklahoma history .

MEMORIAL INDIAN MUSEUM LIBRARY
P.O. Box 483, Second & Allen Sts.
BROKEN BOW 74728
(405) 584-6531
Description: Maintains a collection of over 3,000 volumes on American Indian history and culture.

KIOWA TRIBAL LIBRARY
P.O. Box 369
CARNEGIE 73015
(405) 654-2300
Grace Bointy, Librarian
Description: Maintains a collection of books and documents on Kiowa Indian tribal history and culture.

WILL ROGERS MEMORIAL LIBRARY
P.O. Box 157
CLAREMORE 74018
(918) 341-0719
Patricia Lowe, Librarian
Description: Contains the original papers of Will Rogers; also, 2,500 volumes concerning Will Rogers and his times; 6,000 photos of Roger's family and others; and Will Rogers memoirs.

MUSEUM OF THE RED RIVER LIBRARY
812 E. Lincoln Rd.
IDABEL 74745
(405) 286-3616
Maintains a collection of approximately 2,500 books relating to American Indians, with emphasis on Choctaw Indians.

INSTITUTE OF THE GREAT PLAINS LIBRARY & ARCHIVES
P.O. Box 68, 601 Ferris Ave.
Elmer Thomas Park
LAWTON 73502
(405) 353-5675
Description: Collection consists of a special collection of approximately 10,000 volumes on Plains Indian history and prehistory; documents and photos.

MIAMI TRIBE OF OKLAHOMA LIBRARY
202 S. Eight Tribes Trail
MIAMI 74355
(918) 542-4505 Fax 542-7260
Karen Alexander, Librarian
Description: A collection of 8,000 volumes serving all Native Americans of all tribes, emphasizing the Northeast Eight Tribes of Oklahoma. Special programs: Computer classes, author talks, homebound delivery. Affiliated with the Miami and Ottawa Tribes of Oklahoma. Open to the public.

BACONE COLLEGE LIBRARY
2299 Old Bacone Rd.
MUSKOGEE 74403
(918) 683-4581 ext. 263
Frances A. Donelson, Librarian
Description: Maintains a rare book collection of over 10,000 books on Native American culture, including some of the original Dawes Commission papers. Open to the public.

OKLAHOMA ANTHROPOLOGICAL SOCIETY LIBRARY
1000 Horn St.
MUSKOGEE 74403
(405) 364-2279
Description: Holdings of more than 35,000 volumes; archives contain over three million documents of the Five Civilized Tribes; newspaper library of thirty million pages.

UNIVERSITY OF OKLAHOMA LAW LIBRARY
300 Timberdell Rd.
NORMAN 73019
(405) 325-4311 Fax 325-6282
Nina Miley, Interim Director
Description: Maintains a collection on American Indian law and law relating to Native Americans, including mineral rights, water issues, land titles, jurisdiction, and the like, with emphasis on Oklahoma tribes. Special collection: Native Peoples Collection - 2,300 titles on indigenous peoples, mostly Native American. Interlibrary loans. Open to the public.

WESTERN HISTORY COLLECTION-DIVISION OF MANUSCRIPTS & LIBRARY
University of Oklahoma
401 West Brooks St.
NORMAN 73019
(405) 325-3641
Description: A major U.S. repository of documentation on Native American art. Contains a collection of 40,000 books and pamphlets; 200,000 historic photos; four million manuscripts; principally regional; Indian, Oklahoma, & Southwest history .

COOKSON INSTITUTE LIBRARY
623 Culbertson Dr.
OKLAHOMA CITY 73105
Description: A collection of 1,000 volumes on American Indian thought with emphasis on Cherokee, Arawak, Maya, and Caddo Indians. Available to research scholars associated with the Institute.

INSTITUTE FOR THE DEVELOPMENT OF INDIAN LAW LIBRARY
Oklahoma City University-School of Law
2501 N. Blackwelder
Oklahoma City 73106
(405) 521-5188
K. Kirke Kickingbird, Executive Director
Description: A collection of books on federal Indian law, with special emphasis on Indian sovereignty, self-confidence and self-government, and clarification of historical and legal foundations of modern Indian rights. Distributes films, videotapes and filmstrips. Founded 1971.

OKLAHOMA HISTORICAL SOCIETY INDIAN ARCHIVES DIVISION
2100 N. Lincoln Blvd.
OKLAHOMA CITY 73105
(405) 521-2481
Jack Wettengel, Public Information Director
Description: Collection of 40,000 volumes; holdings include approximately 6,000 books covering the subject areas of the Creek Nation, and Indian and pioneer history; three million documents on American Indian history; and newspapers of Indian territories.

RED EARTH INDIAN CENTER MUSEUM
2100 NE 52 St.
OKLAHOMA CITY 73111
(405) 427-4228
Barbara Jobe, Executive Director
Collection of approximately 300 books and periodicals.

CREEK COUNCIL HOUSE MUSEUM RESEARCH LIBRARY
Town Square
OKMULGEE 74447
(918) 756-2324
Tommy A. Steinsiek, Librarian
Description: Contains a collection of 250 volumes on Muscogee Creek culture and history; records of early day Creek Government; diaries and journals of past principal chiefs; also, Indian readers, dictionaries, documents and newspapers on Oklahoma and Indian history .

OKLAHOMA STATE UNIVERSITY LIBRARY
Curriculum Materials Laboratory
STILLWATER 74074
Description: Maintains a children's collection of books on the Indians of North America.

SAC & FOX NATIONAL PUBLIC LIBRARY
Route 2, Box 246
STROUD 74079
(918) 968-3526 Fax 968-3887
Jan Vassar, Library Director
Description: Maintains a 4,000 volume collection of both general and a special collection of books on the North American Indian, particularly Oklahoma tribes. The archive division includes Sac and Fox history, photographs and annuity records. Programs: Photo and art exhibits; seminars on tribal archives; arts and crafts shop; book sales; Sac & Fox language classes.

CHEROKEE HERITAGE CENTER LIBRARY
P.O. Box 515, TSA-LA-GI
TAHLEQUAH 74464
Description: A collection of 2,500 volumes on Cherokee heritage, including manuscripts and photographs.

JOHN VAUGHN LIBRARY
Northeastern State University
TAHLEQUAH 74464
(918) 456-5511 ext. 3252 Fax 458-2197
Delores Sumner, Special Collections Librarian
Special collections: Approximately 9,000 books on Cherokee history; tribes of Oklahoma; Native-American mythology and religion; Oklahoma history; Indian Territory history; Native-American history, culture, social structures, and conditions; local towns, counties, city histories; Oklahoma tribal rolls; houses microfilm copies of important regional historical newspapers of the late 1800's and early 1900's such as the Cherokee Advocate, Indian Chieftain, and Tahlequah Arrow; U.S. Office of Indian Affairs, and the Historical Information Relating to Military Posts and Other Installations. Also with the Indian Affairs microfilms are records from the U.S. Army and the U.S. Department of War (1800-1823). Contains microfilm of Native American and Oklahoma-related subjects; John Ross Letters; Indian Affairs Miscellaneous Letters; Ballenger Miscellaneous Letters; Ballenger Manuscripts Relating to Cherokee History; Andrew Nave Collections (Business Accounts and Letters); Letters To and From Stand Watie. All bound volumes typed from the originals. Originals are housed in Archives. *Special program*: Symposium on the American Indian held annually at NSU. Interpretive exhibition of historical photographs for the 100th Anniversary of NSU Seminary Hall symbolizing the legacy of Cherokee education. Open to the public.

CHICKASAW COUNCIL HOUSE LIBRARY
P.O. Box 717
TISHOMINGO 73460
(405) 371-3351
Faye Orr, Director
Description: Contains about 150 volumes on Chickasaw Indian history, geography and genealogy.

INDIAN HEALTH CARE RESOURCE CENTER
P.O. Box 184, 915 S. Cincinnati
TULSA 74119
(918) 582-7225

ROBERTA CAMPBELL LAWSON INDIAN LIBRARY
Philbrook Museum of Art
P.O. Box 52510, 2727 S. Rockford Rd.
TULSA 74152-0510
(918) 748-5306 Fax 743-4230
Thomas Young, Librarian
Description: A major U.S. repository of documentation on Native American art. A collection of approximately 2,000 volumes on Indian art and history. Reference only. Open to the public by appointment.

THOMAS GILCREASE INSTITUTE OF AMERICAN HISTORY & ART LIBRARY
1400 Gilcrease Museum Rd.
TULSA 74127
(918) 596-2700 Fax 596-2770

Sarah Erwin, Curator of Archival Collections
Description: A major U.S. repository of documentation on Native American art. Contains a collection of about 7,500 volumes relating to most American Indian tribes with emphasis on the Five Civilized Tribes. Includes 40,000 manuscript items, 10,000 imprints, and 10,000 photographs. *Special collections*: John Ross Papers (Cherokee); Peter Pitchlynn Papers (Choctaw); John Drew Papers (Cherokee); Cherokee Papers; Chickasaw Papers; Choctaw Papers; Creek Papers; and Seminole Papers. Open to the public by appointment only.

THE McFARLAND LIBRARY
University of Tulsa
TULSA 74104
(918) 592-6000
Description: The repository for many unique primary documents and published works pertinent to Native-Americans and governmental relations of the historic period in eastern Oklahoma and adjacent areas.

UNIVERSITY OF TULSA COLLEGE OF LAW LIBRARY
3120 E. Fourth Place
TULSA 74104
(918) 592-6000
Description: A collection of over 750 volumes on Indian law.

SEMINOLE NATION LIBRARY
P.O. Box 1532, 524 South Wewoka
WEWOKA 74884
(405) 257-5580
Description: Contains books, and documents on the history of the Seminoles, the history of Wewoka, and the history of oil in Oklahoma; Special exhibit: Cultural Continuities in Seminole County, Oklahoma--provides detailed information on the clans, bands, churches, and homes of the Seminoles; and the Dawes rolls for reference into Seminole genealogy.

OREGON

NATIONAL INDIAN CHILD WELFARE ASSOCIATION LIBRARY
3611 SW Hood St., Suite 201
Portland, OR 97201
(503) 222-4044
Terry L. Cross, Executive Director
A clearinghouse of over 3,000 articles, books, periodicals on Indian child welfare, mental health, and social work issues.

THE REX ARRAGON LIBRARY
Portland Art Museum
1219 SW Park Ave.
PORTLAND 97205
(503) 226-2811 Ext. 231

PENNSYLVANIA

CUMBERLAND COUNTY HISTORICAL SOCIETY – HAMILTON LIBRARY
21 North Pitt St.
CARLISLE 17013
Description: Maintains a special collection of magazines and journals published by the Carlisle Indian School.

HARCOURT LIBRARY-GETTYSBURG COLLEGE
American Indian Research & Resource Institute
GETTYSBURG 17325
(717) 337-6265
Dr. Frank W. Porter, III, Director
Description: Harcourt Library maintains a special collection on Native Americans; also the Herman Finkelstein Primitive Mask Collection. Founded 1983.

INDIAN RIGHTS ASSOCIATION LIBRARY
c/o Davis
108 Delancey St.
PHILADELPHIA 19106-4303
Description: Contains a collection of 500 texts on assorted subjects ranging from Indian history and political analysis to tribally specific accounts; extensive periodical and federal Indian law files.

AMERICAN PHILOSOPHICAL SOCIETY LIBRARY
104 South 5th St.
PHILADELPHIA 19106
(215) 627-0706
Description: A major U.S. repository of documentation on Native American art. *Special collection*: American Indian linguistics; Franz Boas collection of 18th and 19th century Indian vocabularies.

FREE LIBRARY OF PHILADELPHIA
Social Science & History Department
Logan Square
PHILADELPHIA 19103
Special collection: The Wilberforce Eames Collection on American Indians.

UNIVERSITY OF PENNSYLVANIA-MUSEUM LIBRARY
33rd & Spruce Sts.
PHILADELPHIA 19104
(215) 898-7840
Description: A major U.S. repository of documentation on Native American art. Collection of 50,000 volumes on world archaeology, anthropology and ethnology. *Special collection*: Brinton Collection--Aboriginal American linguistics and ethnology.

COUNCIL OF THREE RIVERS AMERICAN INDIAN CENTER LIBRARY
200 Charles St.
PITTSBURGH 15238
(412) 782-4457
Description: Cultural library on Indian tribes, cultures, customs and traditions. Maintains the Indian Child Welfare Resource Library.

AMERICAN INDIAN EDUCATION POLICY CENTER LIBRARY
Penn State University, 320 Rackley Bldg.
UNIVERSITY PARK 16803
(814) 865-1489
Dr. L.A. Napier, Director
Description: Maintains a collection of 1,000 volumes on American Indian education.

RHODE ISLAND

HAFFENREFFER MUSEUM OF ANTHROPOLOGY LIBRARY
Brown University, Mt. Hope Grant
BRISTOL 02809
(401) 253-8388
Barbara A. Hall, Associate Director

Description: A major U.S. repository of documentation on Native American art. Contains a collection of 2,500 vols. in the field of anthropology , with material on American Indian culture & history .

TOMAQUAG INDIAN MEMORIAL MUSEUM LIBRARY
Summit Rd.
EXETER 02822
 (401) 539-7795

CENTER FOR THE STUDY OF RACE & ETHNICITY IN AMERICA
Brown University, Box 1886
PROVIDENCE 02912
 (401) 863-3080
 Rhett S. Jones, Director

JOHN CARTER BROWN LIBRARY
Brown University, Box 1894
PROVIDENCE 02912
 (401) 863-2725 Fax 863-3477
 Norman Fiering, Librarian
Description: A collection of historical sources pertaining to the discovery , exploration, colonization, settlement, and development of the New W orld (especially those relating to Native American populations and development.) Includes native language materials published in colonial era. *Activities*: Exhibitions, lectures, conferences, publications for sale. Research fellowships awarded.

RHODE ISLAND HISTORICAL SOCIETY LIBRARY
52 Power St.
PROVIDENCE 02906

SOUTH CAROLINA

SOUTH CAROLINA DEPARTMENT OF ARCHIVES AND HISTORY
P.O. Box 11669, 1430 Senate St.
COLUMBIA 29211
 (803) 734-8577
 George L. V ogt, Director
Special collections : Cherokee Indian Treaties, 1759-77; Journals of the Commissioners of Indian Trade, 1710-18; Documents Relating to Indian Affairs, 1750-65; Evidence of Leasehold and Taxes Paid, Catawba Indian Lands, 1791-1856; Supt. of the Catawba Nation Record Book of Plots and Leases, 1810-25, and Accounts of Rents, 1810-1831; Records of the Commissioner to Carry into Effect the Treaty of Nation Ford 1840: and Journal of a Journey to the Catawba Nation, 1727-28.

SOUTH DAKOTA

CRAZY HORSE MEMORIAL FOUNDATION LIBRARY
Ave. of the Chiefs
CRAZY HORSE 57730
 (605) 673-4681
Description: A collection of over 12,000 volumes on American Indian art, culture and history .

BADLANDS NATIONAL MONUMENT LIBRARY
P.O. Box 72
INTERIOR 57750
Description : Maintains a collection of 1,000 books and 500 bound periodicals on the Badlands and Indians of South Dakota.

THE OGLALA LAKOTA HISTORICAL CENTER LIBRARY
Oglala Lakota College, P .O. Box 490
KYLE 57752
 (605) 455-2321
Description: Holdings include tribal college and government records; personal papers of Dr . Valentine T. McGillycuddy; photographs and oral histories, and other historical material.

AMERICAN INDIAN CULTURE RESEARCH CENTER
Blue Cloud Abbey, P.O. Box 98
MARVIN 57251
 (605) 432-5528 Fax 432-4754
 Rev. Stanislaus Maudlin, Director
Description: Collection of more than 3,000 books on Native American culture. *Purpose*: To support Indian leaders, and educators in their ambitions for rebuilding the Indian community; aids in teaching the non-Indian public of the culture and philosophy of the Indian. *Programs*: Compiled oral history and photographic collection; distributes films, records and tapes; provides assistance grants to Indian college students; conducts workshops and seminars; maintains speakers bureau. *Publication* : Blue Cloud Quarterly . Distributes films, books, records and tapes. Founded 1967.

SOUTH DAKOTA HISTORICAL SOCIETY - STATE ARCHIVES
900 Governors Dr .
PIERRE 57501-2217
 (605) 773-3804 Fax 773-6041
 Colleen Kirby, Librarian
 Linda Sommer , State Archivist
Description: Contains a collection of 1,400 volumes on Indian history and culture, with emphasis on Sioux Indians. Open to the public.

THE HERITAGE CENTER LIBRARY
Red Cloud Indian School, Hwy . 18 W.
PINE RIDGE 57770
 (605) 867-5491
 Brother C.M. Simon, S.J., Director
Description: Collection of 1,000 volumes on Lakota history and culture; Native American art.

LAKOTA ARCHIVES & HISTORICAL RESEARCH CENTER
Sinte Gleska University
P.O. Box 490
ROSEBUD 57570
 (605) 747-2263 Fax 747-2098
 Marcella Cash, Director
Description: Archival repository for the records of the Rosebud Sioux Tribe and Sinte Gleska College; Native American Periodicals and Oral History collections; and manuscript material related to the Rosebud Sioux Reservation, including records of the Episcopal Mission which date back to the 1870's. Open to the public.

THE CENTER FOR WESTERN STUDIES LIBRARY
Augustana College, Box 727
SIOUX FALLS 57197
 (605) 336-4007 Fax 336-5447
 Harry F. Thompson, Curator of Collections
Description: The collections focus is Northern Plains history and cultures, including native (mostly Sioux) and immigrant peoples. A reference library of 30,000 volumes on the American W est with emphasis on South Dakota and the Northern Plains plus 3,000 linear feet of archives and manuscripts. Includes the Papers of the Riggs family of missionaries to the Sioux. *Activities*: Annual Da-

kota History Conference in the spring; annual art show; book publications on the Northern Plains with special emphasis on Sioux life and art. Interlibrary loans. Open to the public.

E.Y. BERRY LIBRARY-LEARNING CENTER
Black Hills State University , 1200 University
SPEARFISH 57799
 (605) 642-6833 Fax 642-6298
 Dora Ann Jones, Special Collections Librarian
Description: Subjects deal with Dakota Indians and North American Indians.

BUECHEL MEMORIAL LAKOTA MUSEUM LIBRARY
350 South Oak St., Box 499
ST. FRANCIS 57572
 (605) 747-2745 Fax 747-2361
 Donna DuBray, Director
Description: Native American literature, slides, and documents.

INSTITUTE OF AMERICAN INDIAN STUDIES LIBRARY
University of South Dakota
Dakota Hall, 414 E. Clark St.
VERMILLION 57069
 (605) 677-5209
 Dr. Herbert Hoover , Director
Description: American Indian Research Project: Maintains a collection of 1,500 oral interview tapes with emphasis on tribes of the northern plains; subject matter is widely varied; also a collection of about 1,000 books on ethnology and contemporary affairs of the northwest Plains Indians. Open to public by appointment.

SOCIAL SCIENCE RESEARCH INSTITUTE
University of South Dakota
VERMILLION 57069
 (605) 677-5401
 Prof. Harlowe Hatle, Jr ., Director
Description: Research includes studies in medical and educational problems on American Indian reservations. Conducts anthropological studies.

W.H. OVER STATE MUSEUM LIBRARY
414 E. Clark St.
VERMILLION 57069
 (605) 677-5228
 Allen Schroeder , Director
Description : Collection on local histroy , Indian history, and northern Plains ethnography and history .

TENNESSEE

RED CLAY STATE HISTORICAL PARK LIBRARY
Route 6, Box 733
CLEVELAND 37311
 (615) 472-2626
Description: A collection on Cherokee history and Removal.

CHUCALISSA ARCHAEOLOGICAL MUSEUM–LIBRARY
1987 Indian V illage Dr.
MEMPHIS 38109
 (901) 785-3160
 Gerald P. Smith, Director
 Mary L. Kwas, Curator of Education
Description: Contains a collection of 2,000 volumes on Indian history , culture and archaeology . Material available to public upon request.

INDIAN HERITAGE COUNCIL LIBRARY
Box 2302, Henry St.
MORRISTOWN 37816
  (615) 581-4448
  Louis Hooban, Librarian
Description: A collection of originals: Great American Indian Bible, the Scorced Earth, Indian Nation, and other books. *Special activities*: Publishes Indian books approved by the Board and that are deemed worthy and cost effective. Open to the public by appointment.

TENNESSEE STATE LIBRARY & ARCHIVES
403 7th Ave. North
NASHVILLE 37219
  (615) 741-2764 Fax (615) 741-6471
  Dr. Edwin Gleaves, State Librarian & Archivist
Description: Reference works deal mainly with Tennessee history and items of material culture; Indian-related works deal with tribes of the Southeastern U.S., and are concerned mostly with genealogical research; photographic archives. *Special programs*: Conducts occasional workshops and seminars dealing with Indian genealogical research; exhibit of Indian materials constructed during the Year of the American Indian. *Publication*: Bibliography of Indian genealogical research. Interlibrary loans. Open to public.

**PINSON MOUNDS STATE
ARCHAEOLOGICAL AREA LIBRARY**
Rt. 1, Box 316, Ozier Rd.
PINSON 38366
  (901) 988-5614
Description: Consists of 400 volumes on the archaeology of Pinson Mounds area.

TEXAS

**AMARILLO PUBLIC LIBRARY-
LOCAL HISTORY COLLECTION**
413 E. 4th, Box 2171
AMARILLO 79189
  (806) 378-3054 Fax 378-4245
  Mary Kay Snell, Director of Services

**PANHANDLE-PLAINS HISTORICAL
MUSEUM--LIBRARY & ARCHIVES**
P.O. Box 967, W.T. Sta.
CANYON 79016
  (806) 656-2261 Fax 656-2250
  Lisa Lambert, Librarian
Description: A collection of about 400 titles on the Indians of the Southern Plains, such as Comanche, Apache, Kiowa, Navaho, Cheyenne, & Indians of Oklahoma; & archaeology of the Texas Panhandle. Photographs of individual tribe members, maps, brochures, periodicals, etc. Open to the public.

**AMON CARTER MUSEUM
PHOTOGRAPHIC ARCHIVES**
3501 Camp Bowie Blvd.
FORT WORTH 76107-2631
  (817) 738-1933
  Barbara McCandless, Asst. Curator of Photog.
Description: E.A. Brininstool Collection: 3,500 items (2,680 prints, 550 negatives) - B/W images of natives 1868-1937, sometimes staged environments as well as natural landscapes; photographs of geographic locations, monuments, battlefields of the Plains & Indian wars. Helen M. Post Collection: 11,000 pieces (6,000 prints, 4,000 negatives) - B/W documentation from 1936-41 of Indian reservation life, primarily Sioux, Navajo and Crow on a personal and intimate level.

**SUNSET TRADING POST
OLD WEST MUSEUM--LIBRARY**
Route 1
SUNSET 76270
  (817) 872-2027
Description: A collection of over 500 volumes on American Indians, and the frontier.

UTAH

**EDGE OF THE CEDARS STATE HISTORICAL
MONUMENT & MUSEUM LIBRARY**
P.O. Box 788, 660 West 400 North
BLANDING 84511
  (801) 678-2238
  Stephen J. Olsen, Museum/Park Manager
Description: Materials related directly to archaeology, and Native American cultures of the American Southwest, particularly the Four Corners area.

UTE TRIBAL MUSEUM LIBRARY
Ute Tribe, P.O. Box 190, Highway 40
FORT DUCHESNE 84026
  (801) 722-4992
Description: Maintains a collection of books on the Ute Indians; American Indian history and culture; and early Western American history.

AMERICAN WEST CENTER
University of Utah
1023 Annex
SALT LAKE CITY 84112
  (801) 581-7611
  Dr. Floyd A. O'Neill, Director
Description: Research includes American Indian history and traditions.

UNIVERSITY OF UTAH--MARRIOTT LIBRARY
Ethnic Reading Room
SALT LAKE CITY 84112

UTAH STATE HISTORICAL SOCIETY LIBRARY
300 Rio Grande
SALT LAKE CITY 84101
  (801) 533-5755
  Melvin T. Smith, Director
Description: A collection of books and periodicals on the history of Utah, Mormons, Indians, and the West.

WASHINGTON

CENTER FOR PACIFIC NORTHWEST STUDIES
Western Washington University
High St.
BELLINGHAM 98225
  (206) 676-3284/3125
  Dr. James W. Scott
Purpose: To collect materials of every sort--manuscripts, business records, maps, photographs, tapes, etc.--of the people and activities of the Pacific Northwest, past and present. *Publications*: Publishes two series: Occasional Papers (21 to-date) and Informational Papers (5 to-date.) Archive-Library. Founded 1971.

LEWIS COUNTY HISTORICAL LIBRARY
599 N.W. Front St.
CHEHALIS 98532
  (206) 748-0831
Description: Holdings of about 1,600 volumes in the Indian archive collection.

MAKAH CULTURAL & RESEARCH CENTER
P.O. Box 160
NEAH BAY 98357
  (206) 645-2711
Description: Studies Makah language, culture, and ethnohistory; comparative Wakashan linguistics and Nootkin studies. *Publication*: Portraits In Time.

NISQUALLY TRIBAL LIBRARY
4814 She-Nah-Num Dr. SE
OLYMPIA 98513
  (206) 456-5221
  Ann Dickerson, Librarian
Description: Maintains a 3,500-item collection of books, Native American periodicals, and videos. Emphasis is on Native American and children's materials. Serves the community's members, both tribal and nontribal. *Programs*: Literacy and vocational education.

**NORTH AMERICAN INDIAN MISSION
(NAIM) MINISTRIES LIBRARY**
P.O. Box 151
POINT ROBERTS 98281
  (604) 946-1227
  William Lottis, General Director
Description: Collection contains 600 volumes with audio and video tapes.

**AMERICAN INDIAN HERITAGE
SCHOOL LIBRARY**
1330 N. 90th St.
SEATTLE 98103
  (206) 298-7895
Description: Large Native American collection - both print and audio-video.

UNIVERSITY OF WASHINGTON LIBRARIES
Special Collections and Preservation Division
Allen Library, FM-25
SEATTLE 98195
  (206) 543-1929 Fax 685-8049
  Gary L. Menges, Librarian
Description: A major U.S. repository of documentation on Native American art. Extensive holdings of published and photographic material on native Americans of the northwest coast of North America, Alaska, and Pacific Northwest plateau area. *Special collection*: Native Americans of the Pacific Northwest: A Photographic Record: Over 4,000 photographs plus a 17,000 entry index - microfiche (112 sheets), $115 per set; Viola E. Garfield Albums on Totem Art: 1,749 photographs - microfiche (60 sheets), $60 per set. Open to public.

**EASTERN WASHINGTON STATE
HISTORICAL SOCIETY LIBRARY**
West 2316 First Ave.
SPOKANE 99204
  Glenn Mason, Director
Description: Collection contains approximately 5,000 volumes on the American Indian, 10,000+ Indian-related photos, ephemera, manuscripts and original artwork.

**OREGON PROVINCE ARCHIVES--
CROSBY LIBRARY**
Gonzaga University
SPOKANE 99258
  (509) 328-4220 Fax 484-2804
  Fr. Neill R. Meany, S.J., Archivist
Special collections: Jesuit Missions Collection-- 150 volumes of Jesuit missionaries among Indians of Northwest--Blackfeet, Coeur d' Alenes, Yakimas, Cheyennes. Northwest Mission Papers--500 boxes, 45,000 items--correspondence, dia-

ries, photos, microfilm, relating to Jesuit Mission-
ary activity in Alaska, and the Northwest States,
including the Athapaskans and Eskimos to the
previous tribes mentioned. The Indian Language
Collection--50,600 pages--manuscript dictionaries,
grammars, catechisms, gospels, prayer books,
sermons in the Indian languages of the Rocky
Mountains, and the Eskimo languages of Alaska.
Among the languages are: Assiniboine, Blackfoot,
Crow, Chinook, Columbia, Colville, Gros V entre,
Inuit, Kalispel, Nez Perce, Okanagan, Sioux,
Tlingit, and Yakima. Most are contained on micro-
film.

**STEILACOOM TRIBAL
CULTURAL CENTER LIBRARY**
1515 Lafayette St., P.O. Box 88419
STEILACOOM 98388
  (206) 584-6308
  Joan K. Ortez, Director
Description: Research material - books, articles,
videotapes and other materials, all on Native
Americans.

SUQUAMISH MUSEUM LIBRARY
15838 Sandy Hook NE, Box 498
SUQUAMISH 98392
  (206) 598-3311
Description: The Suquamish Tribal Archives has
a large collection of written documents, oral history tapes and transcripts, historical photographs,
maps, and historical and cultural texts, relating to
the Suquamish and other Puget Sound tribes.

**WASHINGTON STATE HISTORICAL
SOCIETY SPECIAL COLLECTIONS**
315 North Stadium W ay
TACOMA 98403
  (206) 593-2830 Fax 597-4186
  Edward W. Nolan, Curator of Special Collections
Description: A collection of books, pamphlets,
manuscripts and photographs dealing with the
Pacific Northwest Indians in general and W ashington tribes in particular . Complete set of Edward
Curtis with folios; papers of Louis Mann (Indian
activist), 1914-36; Judge George Boldt (Indian fishing rights decision); R.B. Milroy papers (Indian
agent in Washington Territory, 1880-90), fragmentary; Yakima India Agency Records, 1880-1900,
fragmentary; photo collections include 600 negatives of Makah tribe taken by Morse; and a file of
newspaper clippings. Open to the public.

TOPPENISH MUSEUM LIBRARY
1 South Elm
TOPPENISH 98945
  (509) 865-4510
Description: Maintains a collection of 18,500 volumes including many on the Indians of the Northwest, and Native-American history and culture.

YAKAMA CULTURAL HERITAGE LIBRARY
P.O. Box 151, Yakama Nation Cultural Center
TOPPENISH 98948
  (509) 865-2800
  Sherry Hokansen, Librarian
Description: Collection contains 500 volumes on
Native Americans and Yakama history; also, older
books from Yakima Agency--reports, periodicals,
magazines and photo collection. *Special collection*: Nippo Strongheart Collection of rare books,
articles, etc.

WEST VIRGINIA

**ERIC CLEARINGHOUSE ON RURAL
EDUCATION & SMALL SCHOOLS**
Appalachia Educational Laboratory
P.O. Box 1348
CHARLESTON 25325
  (800) 624-9120; (304) 347-0400 Fax 347-0487
  Craig Howley, Co-director
Description: Holdings include 300,000 (education-
related professional literature in English) documents on microfiche, including many on American Indians (North & South America) and Alaskan Natives. *Special programs*: Workshops on
how to use ERIC database; free searches of ERIC
database; free Digests on topics of current interest. Publications: Newsletter; book for sale. Open
to the public.

WISCONSIN

**STOCKBRIDGE MUNSEE
HISTORICAL LIBRARY**
Route 1, Box 300
BOWLER 54416
  (715) 793-4270
  Bernice Miller Pigeon, Director

HOARD HISTORICAL MUSEUM LIBRARY
407 Merchant Ave.
FORT ATKINSON 53538
Description: Maintains a special collection of rare
books on the Black Hawk W ar, 1800-1840.

**STATE HISTORICAL SOCIETY
OF WISCONSIN LIBRARY**
816 State St.
MADISON 53706
  (608) 264-6535 Fax 264-6404
  R. David Myers, Director
Description: A major U.S. repository of documen-
tation on Native American art. *Special collection*:
"Largest library in the nation devoted to North
American history." Extensive holdings on North
American Indians; Native American newspapers
and periodicals; manuscripts and photographs.

MILWAUKEE PUBLIC MUSEUM LIBRARY
800 W. Wells St.
MILWAUKEE 53233
  (414) 278-2786 Fax 278-6100
  Judith Turner, Librarian
Description: Maintains a collection of 125,000 volumes of monographs and periodicals in the subject areas of natural and human history; literature
on the archaeology , ethnology, ethnohistory and
material culture of American Indians is well-repre-
sented; 300,000 item Photographic Collection is
especially strong in photographs depicting Native
American culture and objects. Interlibrary loans.
Open to the public.

OSHKOSH PUBLIC MUSEUM LIBRARY
1331 Algoma Blvd.
OSHKOSH 54901
  (414) 424-0452

WYOMING

**BRADFORD BRINTON
MEMORIAL MUSEUM LIBRARY**
P.O. Box 23
BIG HORN 82833
  (307) 672-3173

**WYOMING STATE MUSEUM HISTORICAL
RESEARCH COLLECTION**
2301 Central Ave., Barrett Bldg.
CHEYENNE 82002
  (307) 777-7016 Fax 777-6005
  Barbara Allen, Supervisor
Description: Collection of books, periodicals,
maps, oral history, military and census records;
primary sources for Native American history, especially W yoming tribes. Affliated with the State
of Wyoming Dept. of Commerce.

THE McCRACKEN RESEARCH LIBRARY
Buffalo Bill Historical Center
P.O. Box 1000, 720 Sheridan Ave.
CODY 82414
  (307) 587-4771
  Albert C. Minnick, Librarian
Description: A collection of 15,000 volumes of
which 25% relate to the Plains Indian Museum
and its collections; some material on the
Sheepeaters; vertical files on specific tribes, e.g.
Blackfeet; photographs--The Cheyenne Sun
Dance, Crow Indians, 19th to 20th century . *Spe-
cial collections*: Yellowstone National Park-Indians;
Photographs by Anne Black, D.H. Barry, J.H.
Sharp, L.A. Huffman; Bureau of American Ethnol-
ogy Annual Reports, 1880's to 1940's.

This section lists radio and television stations, programs, and projects throughout the U.S. Listings are arranged alpha-geographically.

ALABAMA

WASG - 550 AM & WYDH - FM
Alabama Native American Broadcasting Co.
1210 S. Main St.
ATMORE 36502
　(205) 368-2511 Fax 368-4227
　Jerry Gehman, News Director
　David Gehman, Operations Manager
Commercial station. "Our company is comprised of partners who are members of the Poarch Band of Creek Indians, a federally recognized tribe, located adjacent to Atmore, Alabama. WASG airs and produces many programs aimed at and for members of the tribe and airs other American Indian programs produced by other Indian media." Begun 1981.

ALASKA

NATIVE BROADCAST CENTER
Alaska Public Radio Network
810 E. Ninth Ave.
ANCHORAGE 99501
　(907) 277-2776 Fax 263-7450
　Diane Kaplan, President & CEO
　D'Anne Hamilton, Host & Producer
　(National Native News)
The Native Broadcast Center, a project of the Alaska Public Radio Network, is designed to provide public broadcast training at all skill levels for Native Americans. The Center will provide culturally-sensitive training that is currently non-existent in the areas of management, development, engineering, operations, production and news. The Center is also designed to introduce more Native Americans to public broadcasting. National Native News is the country's only daily Native news service which is carried by over 170 stations in live five-minute headline weekday newscasts across the country.

ONE SKY PRODUCTIONS, LTD.
2611 Fairbanks St. #D
ANCHORAGE 99503
　(907) 272-8111 Fax 272 7007
　Jeanie Greene, Host/Director/Producer
　John Tepton & Gary Fife, Moderators (One Sky)
Programs: "Heartbeat Alaska" and "One Sky." "Heartbeat Alaska," a 30-minute news program hosted by Ms. Greene, is seen on Channel 13, Channel 7, and RATNET, and focuses on the life and times of rural Alaska residents. It airs over networks in Anchorage, Fairbanks and Juneau and is beamed 20 247 Alaska communities via the Rural Alaska Television Network (RATNET); "One Sky," which airs immediately after "Heartbeat Alaska," is a discussion style forum for rural issues.

ASRC COMMUNICATIONS, INC.
P.O. Box 129
BARROW 99723
　(907) 852-8633
Barrow Cable TV.

KBRW - 680 AM
Silakkuagvik Communications, Inc.
P.O. Box 109, 1695 Okpik St.
BARROW 99723
　(907) 852-6811/6300 Fax 852-4791
　Don Rinker, Manager
Inuit station. Non-commercial station.

KYUK - 640 AM
Bethel Broadcasting, Inc.
P.O. Box 468, 640 Radio St.
BETHEL 99559
　(907) 543-3131 Fax 543-3130
　John McDonald, Manager
　Mike Martz, Executive Producer (TV)
Yupik Eskimo station. Begun 1975.

KCUK - FM
Kashunaniut School District
CHEVAK 99563
　(907) 858-7014 Fax 858-7114
　Peter Tuluk, Manager
Noncommercial station.

KDLG - 670 AM
P.O. Box 670
DILLINGHAM 99576
　(907) 842-5281 Fax 842-5645
　Casey Jackson, Manager
Noncommercial station. Begun 1975.

KUAC-TV
FAIRBANKS 99701
　Mark Badger, Executive Producer
　Greg Ruff, Program Director

KZPA-AM
P.O. Box 126
FORT YUKON 99740
　(907) 662-2587 Fax 662-2222
　Marilyn Savage, Manager
Athabascan. Noncommercial station.

KTOO - FM
224 4th St., Box 224
JUNEAU 99801
　(907) 586-1670

KOTZ - 720 AM
P.O. Box 78
KOTZEBUE 99752
　(907) 442-3435 Fax 442-2292
　Rob Rawls, Manager
Inupiaq Eskimo. Noncommercial station.

KSKO 870AM
P.O. Box 195
McGRATH 99627
　(907) 524-3001 Fax 524-3436
　Betsy McGuire, manager
Athabascan. Noncommercial station.

METLAKATLA INDIAN COMMUNITY CABLE TV
P.O. Box 8
METLAKATLA 99926
　Bonnie Scudero, Contact

KUHB - FM
Pribiloff School District
ST. PAUL 99660
　(907) 546-2254 Fax 546-2327
　Alicia Misikin, Manager
Aleut. Noncommercial station.

KNSA - AM
P.O. Box 178
UNALAKLEET 99684
　(907) 624-3101 Fax 624-3130
　Henry Ivanoff, Manager
Inupiaq Eskimo. Noncommercial station.

ARIZONA

CHANNEL 3
P.O. Box 5968
PHOENIX 85010
　Mary Kim Titla, Contact

KTVK - CHANNEL 3 (ABC)
3435 N. 16th St.
PHOENIX 85016
　(602) 263-3333
　Roy Track, Host & Executive Producer
Program: 21st Century Native-American.
Public affairs program. Sunday, 12:00 PM.

KNCC - FM
Navajo Community College
TSAILE 85445
　(602) 724-3311

KGHR - 91.5 FM
Navajo/Greyhills High School
P.O. Box 160
TUBA CITY 86045
　(602) 283-6271 Fax 283-6604 Ext. 50
　Stu Schader, Acting Manager
Noncommercial station.

KUAT - AM
University of Arizona
TUCSON 85721
Program: Desert Visions.
Native American Radio Program.

KNNB - 88.1 FM
White Mountain Apache Tribe
P.O. Box 310
WHITERIVER 85941
　(602) 338-5229 Fax 338-1744
　Phoebe Nez, Manager
Native American Radio Program.
Noncommercial station.

KTNN - 660 AM
Navajo Nation
P.O. Box 2569
WINDOW ROCK 86515
　(602) 871-2582 Fax 871-3479
　Roy Hubbell, Manager
Commercial station.

NAVAJO NATION OFFICE OF BROADCAST SERVICES
P.O. Box 308
WINDOW ROCK 86515

CALIFORNIA

KZFR - 90.1 FM
CHICO 95929
　Mark Franco, Host & Producer
　Rick Wilson, Co-producer
Pow Wow Highway.

ROUND VALLEY RADIO PROJECT
P.O. Box 8
COVELO 95428
Native American Radio Project.

KIDE - 91.3 FM
Hoopa Valley Tribe
P.O. Box 1220
HOOPA 95546
  (916) 625-4245 Fax 625-4594
  Frank Starkey, Acting Manager
The first and only Native owned and operated radio station in California. Owned by Hoopa Valley Tribe. Noncommercial station.

THE AMERICAN INDIAN HOUR
American Indian Liberation Crusade
4009 S. Halldale Ave.
LOS ANGELES 90062
  (213) 299-1810
  Dr. Henry E. Hedrick, President
The radio voice of the American Indian Liberation Crusade (see National Associations section.) Broadcasts on 17 radio stations across the country.

NATIVE AMERICAN MEDIA
1015 Gayle Ave., Suite 1024
LOS ANGELES 90024
  (310) 475-6845
  Mike Roberts

KMTP - TV Channel 32
Indian News Network
1918 McAllister St.
SAN FRANCISCO 94115
  (415) 396-5687
  Alvin Mariweather
60 minute news program aired last Monday of each month.

KPFA - 94.1 FM
International Indian Treaty Council
710 Clayton St.
SAN FRANCISCO 94117
  (415) 566-0251 Fax 566-0442
Living on Indian Time. Weekly news show.

KPOO - 89.5 FM
P.O. Box 11008
SAN FRANCISCO 94101
  (415) 346-5373
Red Voices of Native Nations. Tuesday, 7:00 PM.

COLORADO

KGNU 88.5FM - Public Radio
P.O. Box 885
BOULDER 80306
  (800) 737-3030; (303) 449-4885 Fax 447-9955
  Theresa Halsey & Mary Bowannie, Hosts & producers
  Sam Fuqua, News & Public Affairs Director
Program: Indian Voices airs weekly from 3-3:30pm on Sundays, reaching Denver, Boulder, Fort Collins, and Colorado Springs.

KSUT - 91.3 FM
Southern Ute Tribe
P.O. Box 737
IGNACIO 81137
  (303) 563-0255 Fax 563-0396
  Carlos Sena, Manager
Noncommercial station.

HAWAII

KUAI - 720 AM
P.O. Box 720
ELEELE 96705
  (808) 335-3171
Ethnic oriented.

KAHU - 1060 AM
400 Hualani
HILO 96720
  (808) 959-2056
Ethnic format.

KPUA - 670 AM
1145 Kilauea Ave.
HILO 96720
  (808) 935-5461
Ethnic oriented.

KCCN, KINE & HAWAIIAN BROADCASTING COS.
900 Fort St., Suite 400
HONOLULU 96813
  (808) 536-2728 FAX 536-2528
  Michael W. Kelly & Rhoda-Ann Kihikihi, V.P.s
KCCN 1420AM - traditional Hawaiian music
KCCN 100FM - contemporary Hawaiian music
KINE 105.1FM - classic Hawaiian music from the 70's to the 90's

KRON - 790 AM
KONA 96740
  (808) 323-2200
Ethnic format.

KLUA - 93.9 FM
74-5605 Luhia St.
KONA 96740
  (808) 329-8688
Ethnic format.

KPOA - 93.5 FM
658 Front St.
LAHAINA 96761
  (808) 667-9110
Ethnic format.

KMVI - 550 AM
250 Waiehu Beach Rd.
WAILUKU 96793
  (808) 242-6611 Fax 244-8017
Ethnic format.

MAINE

WQDY - AM/FM
281 Main St.
CALAIS 04619

WRKD - AM
415 Main St.
ROCKLAND 04841

MINNESOTA

FIRST AMERICANS NETWORK
Native American Television, Inc.
P.O. Box 8120
Minneapolis, MN 55408

  (612) 825-9525
  Lynne C. Gray, President
Produces weekly television programs: "First Americans Journal," "Indian News Network," "Sovereignty On Our Own Terms," "Native American Forum."

FIRST PERSON RADIO
Migizi Communications
3123 E. Lake St., Suite 200
MINNEAPOLIS 55406
  (612) 721-6631

WUSA - TV
1113 W. Broadway
MINNEAPOLIS 55411
  Mark Houle, Contact

RED LAKE CHIPPEWA TRIBAL COUNCIL RADIO PROJECT
RED LAKE 56671
  (218) 679-3331
  Francis Downwind, Contact
Native American Radio Project.

KTCA-TV Channel 2
172 E. 4th St.
ST. PAUL 55101
  (612) 646-4611
  Susan Robeson, Director
  Tom Beaver, Host.
Native American TV Program.

MONTANA

BLACKFEET MEDIA
Blackfeet Tribe
P.O. Box 850
BROWNING 59417
Native-American Radio Project.

KBFT - FM
P.O. Box 819
BROWNING 59417

KFBB - TV Channel 5
P.O. Box 1139
GREAT FALLS 59401
  (406) 453-4377
  Darnell Doore, Contact
Program: Native-American TV Program. On the Air 4th Sunday of each month at 11:30 AM.

1230-AM RADIO
HARDIN 59034
  Sterling Watan, Owner
Recently bought former KKUL-AM radio station. Broadcasting at 1230 on the AM dial, under new call letters, will serve Big Horn & Rosebud counties.

KOBL - TV
Dull Knife Memorial College
P.O. Box 98
LAME DEER 59043
  Ron Holt, Director

KZIN - FM; KSEN 1150 AM
830 Oilfield Ave.
SHELBY 59474
On the Air Monday, Wednesday, and Friday at 9:10 AM.

NEBRASKA

KCSR - AM
CHADRON 69337
(308) 432-5545

KHNE - 89.1 FM
P.o. Box 190
LINCOLN 68503
(402) 472-3611

OMAHA CABLE TV SERVICE
Omaha Indian Reservation
P.O. Box 368
MACY 68039

NEW MEXICO

KABR - 1500 AM
P.O. Box 907
ALAMO 87825
(505) 854-2543
Trowen Hulett, Owner
Navajo language.

KNME - TV
1130 University Blvd., NE
ALBUQUERQUE 87102
Jeffrey Harjo, Contact

KOAT - TV
P.O. Box 25982
ALBUQUERQUE 87125
Duane Boyd, Contact

KCIE - 90.5 FM
Jicarilla Apache Tribe
P.O. Box 603
DULCE 87528
(505) 759-3681 Fax 759-3005
Lee Martinez, Jr., Manager
Noncommercial station.

KABR - 1500 AM
Alamo Navajo School Board
P.O. Box 907
MAGDALENA 87825
(505) 854-2632 Fax 854-2641
Patsy Apachito, Manager
Noncommercial station.

KTDB - 89.7 FM
Ramah Navajo School Board
P.O. Box 40
PINEHILL 87357
(505) 775-3215 Fax 775-3551
Bernie Bustos, Manager
Public radio; talk; ethnic (Indian cultural affairs) news. Begun 1972.

KSHI - 90.0 FM
Zuni Pueblo
P.O. Box 339
ZUNI 87327
(505) 782-4811 Fax 782-2700
Arden Kucate, Manager
Noncommercial station.

NEW YORK

WBAI - FM
505 Eighth Ave.
NEW YORK 10018
(212) 279-0707
Jim Buck, Host & Producer
Program: Sequoyah. Weekly half-hour Native American news program. Airs Mondays 8:30 PM.

CKON - 97.3 FM
Akwesasne Communication Society
P.O. Box 140
ROOSEVELTOWN 13683
(518) 358-3426 Fax 575-2935
Kallen M. Martin, General Manager
Program: National Native News,
12 noon, 4pm, 8pm daily .

CHANNEL 25 CABLE VISION
Shinnecock Indian Tribe
Box 59, Rte. 27A, Montauk Hwy.
SOUTHAMPTON 11968
(516) 283-1643
David Martine, Director
Program: Voices of Native America. Monthly .

NORTH CAROLINA

EASTERN BAND OF CHEROKEE
Indian Cable TV Service
P.O. Box 455
CHEROKEE 28719

WPSU - TV
Pembroke State University
PEMBROKE 28372

WYRU - 1160 AM
Lumbee Tribe
P.O. Box 0711
RED SPRINGS 28377
(919) 843-5946 Fax 521-8694
Gene Hanrahan, Manager
Commercial station. Religious format.
Begun 1970.

NORTH DAKOTA

KEYA - 88.5 FM
Turtle Mountain Chippewa Tribe
P.O. Box 190
BELCOURT 58316
(701) 477-5686 Fax 477-3252
Michael V. Vann, President
Betty Hanley, Manager
Noncommercial station.

KAEN - 89.5 FM
Standing Rock Sioux Radio Project
P.O. Box D
FORT YATES 58538
(701) 854-7226
Alex Looking Elk, Contact

FORT BERTHOLD COMMUNICATIONS ENTERPRISE
KMHA - 91.3 FM
HCR 3, Box 1
NEW TOWN 58763
(701) 627-3333 Fax 627-3907

Pete Coffey, Jr., Producer
Mandan-Hidatsa-Arikara Native-American
Radio Project.

STANDING ROCK CABLE TV SERVICE
Standing Rock Tribal Council
FORT YATES, ND 58538

OKLAHOMA

KIOWA TRIBAL RADIO STATION
P.O. Box 361
CARNEGIE 73015
(405) 654-2300

KOTV - TV
302 S. Frankfort
TULSA 74107
George Tiger, Contact

OREGON

KTWI-KTWS - 96.5 FM
Warm Springs Confederated Tribes
20450 Empire Ave.
BEND 97701
(503) 389-9500 Fax 388-5448
John Stoltz, Manager
Commercial station.

KBOO - FM
20 SE 8th Ave.
PORTLAND 97214
(503) 231-8032
Indian World - A radio program which airs Native American music, social events, interviews, poetry, legends, and news which relates to all Indians in North and South America. Airs on Mondays from 8-9 p.m.

CONFEDERATED TRIBES TELECOMMUNICATION PROJECT
P.O. Box 584
WARM SPRINGS 97761
Native-American Radio Project.

KWSO - 91.9 FM
Warm Springs Confederated Tribes
P.O. Box 489
WARM SPRINGS 97761
(503) 553-1968 Fax 553-3348
Mike Villalobos, Manager
Warm Springs Confederated Tribes

SOUTH DAKOTA

YANKTON SIOUX TRIBE RADIO PROJECT
KONA, Inc. - Marty School
P.O. Box 222
MARTY 57361
(605) 384-5431
Vince Two Eagles, Coordinator

KILI - 90.1 FM
Oglala Lakota Sioux
P.O. Box 150
PORCUPINE 57772
(605) 867-5002 Fax 867-5634
Tom Casey, Manager
Larry Swalley, Program Director

Wilson Two Lance, Production Coordinator
Native-American Radio Project, noncommercial
station, with programming dedicated to providing
education, traditions, culture, and entertainment
for the people of the Lakota (Sioux) Nation. Focuses on contemporary issues which affect the
people such as treaty rights, healthcare, education, attitutdes of sovereignty, environmental issues, among others.

KINI - 96.1 FM
Rosebud Lakota Sioux
P.O. Box 146
ST. FRANCIS 57572
  (605) 747-2291 Fax 747-5057
  Bernard Whiting, Manager
Noncommercial station.

KSWS - 89.3 FM
Sisseton Wahpeton Sioux Tribe
P.O. Box 268
SISSETON 57262
  (605) 698-7972 Fax 698-7897
  Mike Simon, Manager

KUSD - TV
414 E. Clark St.
VERMILLION 57069

SOUTH DAKOTA PUBLIC BROADCASTING
South Dakota Public Radio Network
P.O. Box 5000, Cherry & Dakota St.
VERMILLION 57069
  (605) 677-5861 Fax 677-5010
  Tom Sorensen, News Director & Host
  Leonard Bruguier, Voices of the Plains' Host
  Ross King, Program Director
Programs: South Dakota Forum & Voices of the
Plains - A ten-station network producing a variety
of news programs, features and call-in talk shows
dealing with Native issues. Suggestions for topics
are welcome.

UTAH

AMERICAN INDIAN TV SERVICES
Room 234 - HRCB
Brigham Young University
PROVO, UT 84602
  Howard Rainer, Contact

WASHINGTON

OLYMPIC TV CABLE
P.O. Box 88
PORT ORCHARD 98366

QUINAULT TRIBE RADIO PROJECT
P.O. Box 332
TAHOLAH 98587
  (206) 276-4353
  Gilbert Thunder Corwin, Coordinator
Commercial station.

WISCONSIN

WOJB - 88.9 FM
Lac Court Oreilles Ojibwe Broadcasting Corp.
Route 2, Box 2788
HAYWARD 54843
  (715) 634-2100 Fax 634-4797
  Camille Lacapa-Morrison, Manager
  David Kellar, Program Director
  Joan Kozak, Asst. Program Director
  Dave Collins, Sherrole Benton, Eric Schubring,
  Jeff St. Germaine, Producers
Provides public radio service with 100,000 watt
audio production and radio services. Publicat *ion*:
Monthly program guide ($10 per year).

WIRC - FM
University of Wisconsin
216 College of Professional Studies
STEVENS POINT 54481
  (715) 346-2746

WYOMING

KIEA - FM
Wind River Indian Education Association
Wyoming Indian High School
ETHETE 82520
  (307) 332-2793
Native American Radio Project.

NATIONAL INDIAN GAMING ASSOCIATION
904 Pennsylvania Ave., SE
Washington, DC 20003
  (202) 546-7711
  Rick Hill, Chairperson
  S. Timothy Wapato, Executive Director
Activities: Holds Indian Gaming Enterprise and Management Law Seminars; and Annual Convention and Trade Show. Professional training for tribal casino management, staff, and for tribal start up operations.

NATIONAL INDIAN GAMING & HOSPITALITY INSTITUTE
Menominee Indian Tribe of Wisconsin
P.O. Box 1210
Keshena, WI 54135
  (715) 799-5600 Fax 799-1308
  Dr. Verna Fowler, Contact
Purpose: To explore & address economic, social and cultural issues related to the development of gaming enterprises on American Indian reservations; to provide certificate & associate degree education programs designed to expand the trained workforce with expertise in Indian gaming nationally; to establish a central clearinghouse and library; and a new gaming product development center.

ALABAMA

CREEK BINGO PALACE
P.O. Box 09
Atmore, AL 36504

ARIZONA

At least 8 Arizona tribes have signed gaming compacts wit the State of Arizona. The only legal casino gaming in Arizona is conducted by the Indian tribes.

AK-CHIN INDIAN CASINO
Route 2, Box 27
Maricopa, AZ 85239
  (602) 568-2227
  Martin J. Antone, Sr., Contact
Owned by the Ak-Chin Indian Tribe. *Location*: 25 miles south of Phoenix. *Facility*: 72,000 sq. feet, with a gaming area of 29,500 sq. feet. 475 slots, 40 table games.

MOJAVE CASINO
500 Merriman Ave.
Needles, CA 92363
  (619) 326-4591
  Don Laughlin, Operator
Owned by Fort Mojave Indian Tribe. *Location*: South of Bullhead City, Arizona, on Hwy. 95, 1 mile northeast of the Needles bridge. *Facilities*: 20,000 square feet. 250 slots, table games.

FORT McDOWELL CASINO
Route 1 Box 798
Scottsdale, AZ 85264
  (800) THE-FORT
  (602) 837-1424 Fax 837-0844
  Betty Humphries, Contact
Owned by the Mohave-Apache Tribe of Fort McDowell. *Location*: 2 miles past Shea Blvd. of Hwy. 87. 35 miles northeast of Phoenix. *Facility*: 60,000 sq. ft. 475 slots. 75 table games.

TOHONO O'ODHAM INDIAN CASINO
P.O. Box 837
Sells, AZ 85634
  (602) 383-2221
  Bruce Phillips, Contact
Owned by the Tohono-O'Odham Tribe. *Location*: 56 miles west of Tucson on Hwy. 86. *Facilities*: 2,600 electronic gaming machines.

PASCUA YAQUI INDIAN CASINO
7474 S. Camino de Oeste
Tucson, AZ 85746
  (602) 883-2838
Owned by Pascua Yaqui Indian Tribe. *Location*: South of downtown Tucson. *Facility*: 1,800 electronic gaming machines.

THE WHITE MOUNTAIN APACHE CASINO
P.O. Box 700
Whiteriver, AZ 85941
  (602) 338-4346
Owned by the White Mountain Apache Tribe. *Location*: South of Show Low, Arizona. *Facility*: 1,800 electronic gaming machines.

CALIFORNIA

CACHE CREEK INDIAN BINGO
P.O. Box 65
Brooks, CA 95606

CASINO MORONGO
Box 366
Cabazon, CA 92230
  (800) 252-4499; (714) 849-4455
Owned by the Morongo Band of Mission Indians. *Location*: I-10, between Banning and Palm Springs. *Facility*: 35 tables.

SYCUAN GAMING CENTER
5440 Dehasa Rd.
El Cajon, CA 92019
  (619) 445-6002
Owned by the Sycuan Band of Mission Indians. *Location*: 18 miles east of San Diego on Interstate Hwy. I-8. *Facility*: 62 tables

TABLE MOUNTAIN RANCHERIA BINGO
P.O. Box 445
Friant, CA 93626

SAN MANUEL INDIAN BINGO
5797 N. Victoria Ave.
Highland, CA 92346

INDIO BINGO PALACE & CASINO
84-245 Indio Springs Dr.
Indio, CA 92201
  (619) 342-5000
Owned by the Cabazon Band of Mission Indians. *Location*: 24 miles east of Palm Springs on Interstate Hwy. I-10. *Facility*: 25 tables.

JACKSON CASINO/INDIAN BINGO
16000 Bingo Way
Jackson, CA 95642
  (800) 822-WINN
Facility: 6 tables.

BARONA CASINO
1000 Wild Cat Canyon Rd.
Lakeside, CA 92040
  (619) 433-2300

Owned by the Barona Mission Indians. *Location*: 21 miles east of San Diego on Hwy. 67. *Facility*: 18 tables.

CAHUILLA INDIAN CASINO
The Agua Caliente Band of Mission Indians and Caesars World will be building a 40,000 sq. ft. casino near Palm Springs, California.

COLORADO

SKY UTE LODGE & CASINO
Hwy. 172, Box 340
Ignacio, CO 81137
  (303) 563-4531
Owned by the Ute Mountain Ute Indians. *Location*: 26 miles southeast of Durango, Colorado. *Facility*: 100 slots; table games.

UTE MOUNTAIN CASINO
3 Weeminuche Dr.
Towaoc, CO 81334
  (800) 442-1818; (303) 565-8800
Owned by the Ute Mountain Ute Indians. *Location*: 11 miles south of Cortez on Hwy. 160 & 666. *Facility*: 317 slots; table games.

CONNECTICUT

FOXWOODS HIGH STAKES BINGO & CASINO
State Rd. 2, Box 410
Ledyard, CT 06339
  (800) PLAY-BIG
  (203) 885-3000 Fax 885-3101
  G. Michael Brown, President
Owned by the Mashantucket-Pequot Indians. *Location*: Southeastern Connecticut, northeast of New London, Connecticut, 8 miles west of I-95 off exit 92. *Facility*: 150,000 sq. ft. 3,200 slots; 120 table games.

FLORIDA

SEMINOLE INDIAN BINGO
4150 N. State Rd. 7
Hollywood, FL 33021

MICCOSUKEE INDIAN BINGO
P.O. Box 44021, Tamiami Station
Miami, FL 33144

SEMINOLE BINGO OF TAMPA
5223 N. Orient Rd.
Tampa, FL 33610

IDAHO

SHOSHONE-BANNOCK GAMING ENTERPRISE
P.O. Box 868
Fort Hall, ID 83203
  Dave Archuleta, Contact

IOWA

CASINO OMAHA
P.O. Box 89
Onawa, IA 51040
  (800) 858-UBET; (712) 423-3700
Owned by the Omaha Tribe of Nebraska. *Location*: 32 miles south of Sioux City, Iowa; or 60 miles north of Omaha Nebraska. Facility: 325 slots; 25 table games. Opened April 1992.

MESQUAKI BINGO & CASINO
1504 305th St.
Tama IA 52339
  (800) 728-4263 (515) 484-2108
Owned by the Sac & Fox Indian Tribe of Mississippi in Iowa. *Location*: 40 miles west of Cedar Rapids, Iowa. *Facility*: Slots & table games.

LOUISIANA

GRAND CASINO COUSHATA
Coushatta Nation Reservation
Kinder, LA 70648
Owned by the Coushatta Indian Nation. *Location*: 35 northeast of Lake Charles. *Facility*: 100,000 sq. ft. with 900 slots & 45 table games. Opened Spring 1994.

TUNICA-BILOXI CASINO
Tunica-Biloxi Nation Reservation
P.O. Box 311
Marksville, LA 71351
  Earl Barbry, Contact
Owned by the Tunica-Biloxi Indian Nation. *Location*: 30 miles south of Alexandria, Louisiana. Facility: 100,000 sq. ft. 900 slots & 45 table games. Opened Spring 1994.

MICHIGAN

Michigan has seven full-scale Nevada style Indian tribe casinos. They were in operation before the National Gaming Act of 1988. All have completed compact agreements with the state of Michigan.

OJIBWA CASINO
Rte. M38, Box 284A
Baraga, MI 49944
  (800) 323-8045
  (906) 353-6333 Fax 353-7618
Owned by the Keweenaw Bay Indian Tribe. *Location*: 5 miles north of Baraga in Upper Michigan. *Facility*: 18 table games.

CHIP-INN CASINO & MOTEL
P.O. Box 351, Hwy. U.S. 2 & 41
Harris, MI 49845
  (906) 466-2686
Owned by the Hannahville Indian Community-Potawatomi Tribe. *Location*: 13 miles west of Escanaba. *Facility*: 3,000 sq. ft. Slots & 34 table games. A new $1.6 million complex opened May, 1991.

SAGINAW CHIPS CASINO
707 E. Broadway
Mount Pleasant, MI 48858
  (800) 338-9092; (517) 772-0827
Owned by the Chippewa Tribe. *Location*: 75 miles north of Lansing on Hwy. 20. *Facility*: 36 table games.

LEELANAU SANDS CASINO & BINGO
Grand Traverse Band Indian Reservation
Route 1 Box 157A
Suttons Bay, MI 49682
  (616) 271-4104
Owned by the Chippewa & Ottawa Tribes. *Location*: Lower peninsula on the coastline of Lake Michigan, 5 minutes north of Suttons Bay. *Facility*: Slots & table games.

KEWADIN SHORES CASINO
3039 Mackinaw Trail
St. Ignace, MI 49781
  (906) 643-7071
Owned by Sault Ste. Marie Chippewa Tribe. Location: Upper peninsula at the north end of the Mackinac Bridge, across the Straits of Mackinaw from Mackinaw City. Facility: Slots & 20 table games.

VEGAS KEWADIN CASINO
2186 Skunk Rd.,
Saulte Ste. Marie, MI 49783
  (800) 626-9878
  (906) 632-0530 Fax 635-9155
Owned by the Sault Ste. Marie Tribe. *Location*: Upper peninsula on the Canadian border and the International bridge to Ontario. *Facility*: Slots & 30 table games.

LAC VIEUX DESERT CASINO
Watersmeet, MI 49969
  (906) 358-4227
Owned by the Lac Vieux Chippewa Tribe. *Location*: East of U.S. Hwy. 45, just east of Land O' Lakes, Wisconsin. *Facility*: Slots & table games.

MINNESOTA

There are 13 Indian gaming facilities operating in Minnesota. The compact agreements are all based on the National Indian Gaming Act of 1988. The tribes offer slots, blackjack, and bingo.

THE PALACE BINGO & CASINO
Bingo Palace Dr., Leech Lake Reservation
Cass Lake, MN 56633
  (800) 228-6676; (218) 335-6787
Owned by the Leech Lake Chippewa Tribe. *Location*: 12 miles east of Bemidji on U.S. Hwy. 2. *Facility*: 15,000 sq. ft. Slots & 20 table games; 800 seat bingo hall.

BIG BUCKS CASINO & BINGO
105 University Ave.
Cloquet, MN 55720
  (800) 365-1613; (218) 879-4691
Owned by the Fond du Lac Chippewa Tribe. *Location*: Intersection of I-35 and U.S. Hwy. 210, on the Fond du Lac Reservation. *Facility*: 67,000 sq. ft. Slots & 25 table games; bingo hall.

FOND DE LUTH CASINO
129 E. Superior St.
Duluth, MN 55802
  (800) 873-0280
  (218) 722-0280 Fax 722-7505
Owned by the Fond du Lac Chippewa Tribe. *Location*: On the shore of Lake Superior in northeast Minnesota. *Facility*: 45,00 sq. ft. Slots & 16 table games; bingo hall.

GRAND PORTAGE HOTEL & CASINO
P.O. Box 307, US Hwy. 61
Grand Portage, MN 55605
  (800) 232-1384
Owned by the Grand Portage Chippewa. *Location*: On Lake Superior, 5 miles south of he Canadian border. *Facility*: Slots & 6 table games; bingo hall.

GRAND CASINO HINCKLEY
777 Lady Luck Dr.
Hinckley, MN 55037
  (800) GRAND-21
  Fax (612) 384-7777 Fax 449-7757
Owned by Mille Lacs Chippewa. *Location*: 76 miles east of Duluth, on Hwy. 48, 1 mile east of I-35. *Facility*: 120,000 sq. ft.; slots & 52 table games; bingo hall.

SHOOTING STAR CASINO
777 Casino Blvd.
Mahnomen, MN 56557
  (800) 453-STAR; (218) 935-2711
Owned by the White Earth Chippewa Tribe. *Location*: 35 miles north of Detroit Lakes, on U.S. Hwy. 59. *Facility*: 70,000 sq. ft. slots & 12 table games; bingo hall.

JACKPOT JUNCTION CASINO
P.O. Box 420
Morton, MN 65270
  (800) LETTER-X; (507) 644-3000
Owned by Fond du Lac Chippewa tribe. *Location*: 6 miles east of Redwood Falls, on US Hwy. 71 in southwest Minnesota. *Facility*: slots & 40 table games; bingo hall.

GRAND CASINO MILLE LACS
777 Grand Ave.
Onamia, MN 56359
  (800) 626-LUCK
  (612) 532-7777 Fax 449-5992
Owned by Mille Lacs Chippewa Tribe. *Location*: 90 miles north of Minneapolis, on US Hwy. 169, 8 miles south of Garrison. *Facility*: 120,000 sq. ft. Slots & 48 table games; 500 seat bingo hall.

MYSTIC LAKE CASINO & BINGO HALL
2400 Mystic lake Blvd.
Prior Lake, MN 55372
  (800) 262-7799
  Leonard Prescott, CEO
Owned by Shakopee Mdewakanton Sioux Tribe. *Location*: 25 miles southwest of Minneapolis on Shakopee Sioux Reservation. *Facility*: 130,000 sq. ft. Slots & 76 table games; 1,100 seat bingo hall.

FORTUNE BAY CASINO & BINGO HALL
1430 Boisforte Rd.
Tower, MN 55790
  (800) 992-PLAY; (218) 753-6400
Owned by Bois Forte Chippewa Tribe. *Location*: 5 miles west of Tower, on US Hwy. 169, on the Bois Forte Reservation. *Facility*: 40,000 sq. ft. Slots & 15 game tables; bingo hall.

NORTHERN LIGHTS CASINO
Bingo Palace Dr., Box 1003
Walker, MN 56484
  (800) 252-PLAY; (218) 547-2744
Owned by Leech Lake Chippewa Tribe. *Location*: On the Leech Lake Reservation, 4 miles south of Walker at junction of Hwys. 200 & 371. *Facility*: 30,000 sq. ft. Slots & 36 table games; bingo hall.

TREASURE ISLAND CASINO
5734 Sturgeon Lake Rd.
Prairie Island Reservation
Welch, MN 55089
Owned by Prairie Island Sioux Tribe. *Location*: 45 miles southeast of St. Paul, on US Hwy . 61. *Facility*: 100,000 sq. ft. Slots & 70 tables; bingo hall.

MISSOURI

EASTERN SHAWNEE TRIBAL BINGO
P.O. Box 350
Seneca, MO 64865

MONTANA

FORT BELKNAP BINGO ENTERPRISES
P.O. Box 338
Harlem, MT 59526

NEW MEXICO

ISLETA BINGO PALACE
11000 Broadway S.E.
Albuquerque, NM 87105

BINGO OF MESCALERO
P.O. Box 190
Mescalero, NM 88340

NEW YORK

ONEIDA INDIAN BINGO
4 Territory Rd.
Oneida, NY 13421

MOHAWK BINGO PALACE
P.O. Box 480
Hogansburg, NY 13655

ST. REGIS CASINO
Owned and operated by the St. Regis Mohawk Indian Tribe. *Location*: in Massena, NY about 50 miles southwest of Montreal. *Facility*: 40,000 sq. ft. Table games: dice, roulette and card games. Opened Summer 1994.

SENECA BINGO
P.O. Box 231
Salamanca, NY 14779

TURNING STONE CASINO
P.O. Box 126
Verona, NY 13478
(315) 361-7711
Owned by the Oneida Indian Nation. *Location*: Upstate New York 35 miles east of f Hwy. I-90. *Facility*: 68,000 sq. ft. Slots & table games; 1,600 seat bingo hall.

NORTH CAROLINA

CHEROKEE BINGO
P.O. Box 1629
Cherokee, NC 28719

NORTH DAKOTA

TURTLE MOUNTAIN CASINO
P.O. Box 900
Belcourt, ND 58316
(701) 477-3171
Owned by the Turtle Mountain Band of Chippewa Indians. *Location*: In north central North Dakota near the Canadian border . *Facility*: 25,000 sq. ft. Slots & table games.

DEVILS LAKE SIOUX CASINO
P.O. Box 359
Fort Totten, ND 58335
(701) 766-4221
Ownd by the Devils.Lake Sioux Tribe. *Location*: in northeast central North Dakota near Devils Lake on US Hwy. 2. *Facility*: Slots & table games.

STANDING ROCK SIOUX CASINO
P.O. Box D
Fort Yates, ND 58538
(701) 854-7231
Owned by the Standing Rock Sioux Tribe. *Location*: In south central ND south of Bismarck on the Missouri River. *Facility*: Slots & table games.

OKLAHOMA

ADA GAMING CENTER
P.O. Box 1340
Ada, OK 74820

BRISTOW INDIAN BINGO
121 West Lincoln
Bristow, OK 74010

CHEYENNE & ARAPAHO BINGO
P.O. Box 95
Concho, OK 73022

CHOCTAW INDIAN BINGO PALACE
P.O. Box 1919
Durant, OK 74702

COMANCHE NATION GAMES
P.O. Box 347
Lawton, OK 73502

KAW NATION BINGO
P.O. Box 171
Newkirk, OK 74647

THUNDERBIRD ENTERTAINMENT CENTER
15700 East State Hwy . 9
Norman, OK 73071

GOLDSBY GAMING CENTER
Rte. 1 Box 104P
Norman, OK 73072

CREEK NATION OKMULGEE BINGO
P.O. Box 790
Okmulgee, OK 74447
CIMARRON BINGO CASINO
P.O. Box 190
Perkins, OK 74059

CHEROKEE NATION'S OUTPOST BINGO
P.O. Box 1000
Roland, OK 74954

POTAWATOMI BINGO
9101 S. Gordon Cooper Dr .
Shawnee, OK 74801

SULPHUR GAMING CENTER
West First & Muskogee
Sulphur, OK 73086

UNITED KEETOOWAH BINGO
2450 S. Muskogee Ave.
Tahlequah, OK 74465

TOUSO ISHTO GAMING CENTER
P.O. Box 149
Thackerville, OK 73459

CREEK NATION TULSA BINGO
P.O. Box 700833
Tulsa, OK 74170

OREGON

COW CREEK INDIAN BINGO
146 Chief Miwaleta Lane
Canyonville, OR 97417
Peter Ingenito, General Manager

UMATILLA CASINO & BINGO
P.O. Box 638
Pendleton, OR 97801
(503) 276-3165
John Barkley, General Manager
Owned by the Confederated Tribes of the Umatilla Indians. *Location*: In northeast Oregon just south of I-84 east of Pendleton. *Facility*: 40,000 sq. ft. Slots & table games.

SOUTH DAKOTA

There are four Indian casinos operating in the State. Six other Indian tribes are negotiating with the state seeking approval for casino gaming based on the National Indian Gaming Act of 1988

FORT RANDALL CASINO
RR 1, Box 100
Lake Andes, SD 57356
(800) 553-3003
(605) 487-7871 Fax 487-7354
Sam Weddel & Raymond Stone, Contacts
Owned by the Yankton Sioux Tribe. *Location*: on Hwy. 46, in East Pickstown, 50 miles west of Yankton on the Missouri River near the Nebraska border. *Facility*: 24,000 sq. ft. Slots & 20 table games. Opened in June, 1990.

ROYAL RIVER CASINO
P.O. Box 326, Veterans St.
Flandreau, SD 57028
(800) 234-2WIN
(605) 997-3746 Fax 997-2388
Joe Massa, Contact
Owned by the Flandreau Santee Sioux Tribe. *Location*: On Hwy. 34 - the Santee Sioux Reservation, 45 miles north of Sioux Falls. *Facility*: 15,000 sq. ft. Slots & 25 table games.

GOLDEN BUFFALO CASINO
Sitting Bull St.
Lower Brule, SD 57548
(605) 473-5770

Owned by the Lower Brule Sioux Tribe. *Location*: 45 miles southeast of Pierre, on the Lower Brule Sioux Reservation. *Facility*: Slots & table games.

BEAR SOLDIER JACKPOT BINGO
P.O. Box 876
McLaughlin, SD 57642

DAKOTA SIOUX ENTERTAINMENT CENTER & CASINO
Rt. 1 Box 107, 107 Sioux Valley Rd.
Watertown, SD 57201
 (605) 882-2051
 Wiley Shepher, Contact
Owned by the Sisseton-Wahpeton Sioux Tribe. *Location*: 8 miles north of Watertown off I-29. *Facility*: Slots & 25 table games

WASHINGTON

SWINOMISH INDIAN BINGO
P.O. Box 1075
Anacortes, WA 98221
 Claudine Bruner, Contact

MUCKLESHOOT CASINO
39015 172 St. SE
Auburn, WA 98002
 (206) 939-3311 Fax 939-5311
New Indian casino.

LUMMI CASINO
2559 Lummi View Dr.
Bellingham, WA 98226
 (800) 776-1337
 (206) 758-7559 Fax 758-7545
Owned by the Lummi Indian Tribe. *Location*: 10 miles off I-5 near Bellingham. *Facility*: 53 tables.

NOOKSACK CASINO
5048 Mount Baker Hwy., Box 157
Deming, WA 98244
 (800) 233-2573
 (206) 592-5176 Fax 592-5753
Owned by the Nooksack Indian Tribe. *Location*: 14 miles off I-5, east on Hwy. 542 near Deming. *Facility*: 43 Table games.

TULALIP BINGO & CASINO
6330 33rd Ave. NE
Marysville, WA 98271
 (206) 653-7395
 Steve Griffis, General Manager
Owned by the Tulalip Tribe. *Location*: 30 miles of Seattle off I-5 in Snohomish County. *Facility*: 70 table games. Employs about 500 people of which about 70% are tribal members. An expansion is planned where 1,000 people will be employed. Opened 1992.

JAMESTOWN BAND OF KLALLAM INDIANS CASINO
305 Old Blyn Hwy.
Sequim, WA 98382
 (206) 683-1109 Fax 683-4366
New Indian casino.

B.J.'S BINGO
4411 Pacific Hwy. E.
Tacoma, WA 98424
 Mackenzie Tunnetsege, G.M.

WISCONSIN

HO-CHUNK GOLDEN NICKEL CASINO
912 Sauk Rd.
Baraboo, WI 53940
 (608) 356-0279
Owned by the Wisconsin Winnebago Indian Tribe. *Location*: On Hwy. 12, south of Lake Delto, 40 miles north of Madison. *Facility*: Slots, video poker & blackjack.

MAGIC PINES BINGO & CASINO
Rte. 5, Box 433-G
Black River Falls, WI 54615
 (715) 284-9098
 Gordon Thunder, Contact
Owned by the Wisconsin Winnebago Indian Tribe. Location: 44 miles southeast of Eau Claire on Hwy. 54. *Facility*: Slots & video poker.

RAINBOW BINGO & CASINO
P.O. Box 460
Black River Falls, WI 54615
 (715) 886-4560
Owned by the Wisconsin Winnebago Indian tribe. *Location*: In Nekoosa, Wisconsin, on the Wisconsin River, south of Stevens Point. *Facility*: Slots, video poker & blackjack.

MOHICAN NORTH STAR CASINO/BINGO
Rte. 2, Box 59
Bowler, WI 54416
 (800) 952-0195; (715) 793-4090
 Louis Raywinkle, Contact
Owned by the Stockbridge-Munsee Mohican Indians of WI. *Location*: 50 miles northwest of Green Bay. *Facility*: Slots, video poker & blackjack.

GRAND ROYALE CASINO
Rte. 1, Box 625
Crandon, WI 54520
 (800) 236-WINN; (715) 478-5565
Owned by the Sokoagan Chippewa Indian Tribe. *Location*: On Hwy. 55 in Mole Lake, 8 miles south of Crandon. *Facility*: Slots, video poker & blackjack.

REGENCY RESORT CASINO
Rte. 1, Box 625
Crandon, WI 54520
 (715) 478-5290
Owned by the Sokoagan Chippewa Indian Tribe. *Location*: On Hwy. 55 in Mole Lake, 8 miles south of Crandon. *Facility*: Slots, video poker & blackjack.

HOLE IN THE WALL CASINO
P.O. Box 98
Danbury, WI 54830
 (715) 656-3444
Owned by the St. Croix Chippewa Indians of Wisconsin. *Location*: On Hwys. 77 & 35, 45 miles south of Duluth, Minnesota. *Facility*: Slots, video poker & blackjack.

ONEIDA BINGO & CASINO
2100 Airport Dr.
Green Bay, WI 54155
 (800) 238-4263; (414) 497-8118
 Louise King, Contact
Owned by the Oneida Tribe of Wisconsin. *Location*: Near Green Bay airport. *Facility*: 1,350 slots; video poker & keno; and 40 blackjack tables.

GRAND CASINO
Rte. 5, Box 505
Hayward, WI 54843
 (715) 634-4422/5643
Owned by the Lac Courte Orielle Band of Lake Superior Indians. *Location*: Northwest Wisconsin, 55 miles east of Duluth, Minnesota; on County Rd. E, 9 miles south of Hayward. *Facility*: Slots; video poker & keno; blackjack.

SAND LAKE BINGO & CASINO
c/o St. Croix Tribal Center
P.O. Box 287
Hertel, WI 54845
 (715) 349-2195
Owned by the St. Croix Chippewa Indians of Wisconsin. *Location*: In northwest Wisconsin on Hwy. 70. *Facility*: Slots, video poker, blackjack.

MENOMINEE NATION CASINO
Hwy. 47, P.O. Box 7060
Keshena, WI 54135
 (800) 421-3077; (715) 799-4592
Owned by Menominee Indian Tribe of Wisconsin. *Location*: 40 miles northwest of Green Bay on Hwy. 47. *Facility*: Slots & table games.

LAND OF THE TORCHES CASINO
567 Peace Pipe Rd., Box 67
Lac du Flambeau, WI 54538
 (715) 588-7070
Owned by the Lac du Flambeau Band of Lake Superior Chippewa. *Location*: Hwy. 47, 160 miles northwest of Green Bay. *Facility*: Slots, video poker & keno, blackjack.

POTAWATOMI BINGO
1721 West Canal St.
Milwaukee, WI 53233

BAD RIVER CASINO
P.O. Box 9
Odanah, WI 54861
 (715) 682-7131
Owned by the Bad River Band of Lake Superior Tribe of Chippewa Indians. *Location*: 45 miles east of Duluth, and 12 miles east of Ashland, on US Hwy. 2 near Lake Superior. *Facility*: Slots, video poker & keno, blackjack.

ST. CROIX CASINO
777 US Hwy. 8 West
Turtle Lake, WI 54889
 (800) 846-8946
 (715) 987-4777 Fax 986-2800
Owned by the St. Croix Chippewa Indians of Wisconsin. *Location*: In northwest Wisconsin on US Hwy. 8, 23 miles from the border of Minnesota. *Facility*: Slots, video poker, blackjack.

NORTHERN LIGHTS CASINO & BINGO
Hwy. 32, P.O. Box 140
Wabeno, WI 54566
 (800) 487-9522; (715) 473-2021
Owned by the Forest County Potawatomi Indian Tribe. *Location*: In northeast Wisconsin, 65 miles north of Green Bay on Hwy. 32. *Facility*: Slots, video poker, blackjack.

ISLE VISTA CASINO
Route 3, Box 3365
Washburn, WI 54891
 (715) 779-3712
Owned by the Red Cliff Band of Lake Superior Chippewa. *Location*: 3 miles north of Bayfield, WI,, on the shores of Lake Superior. *Facility*: Slots, video poker & keno, blackjack.

This section lists Indian-related films, videos, recordings, filmstrips, picture-sets, and maps. Films and videos are color/sound unless otherwise stated in the listing. Entries are arranged alphabetically by title. At the end of each entry there are code letters which correspond to the distributor and address listed at the end of the section.

FILMS & VIDEOS

ABNAKI: THE NATIVE PEOPLE OF MAINE
Jay Kent, Producer/Director/W riter;
Michel Chalufour , Editor
Chronicles the history of the Penobscot, Maliseet, Passamaquoddy & Micmac. The land claims suit of the Passamaquoddy & Penobscot tribes of Maine. Members of the tribe discuss issues, from educational systems hostile to Indian culture to tourism. Produced for the Maine Tribal Governors, Inc. 1982. Grades 7 and up. 29 minutes, color . Purchase: 16mm, $525; video, $149.95. CC.

ABORIGINAL RIGHTS: I CAN GET IT FOR YOU WHOLESALE
TV Ontario, Producer
Historical photos and on-sight footage trace the history of aboriginal rights in North America from Mexico to Canada. 1976. 60 minutes, color . Video. Rental: $80/week. NAPBC.

ACORNS: STAPLE FOOD OF CALIFORNIA INDIANS
Clyde B. Smith, Producer
A film on the gathering, storing and processing of acorns, a staple food of the Pomo Indians. Includes scenes showing original primitive methods. 1962. Grades 7 and up. 28 minutes, color . Purchase: 16mm, $560; video, $195. Rental, $50. UC & PSU.

ACTS OF DEFIANCE
Documents the long dispute over sovereign rights between the Mohawk of Kanesatake & the Province of Quebec. 1992. 104 minutes, color . VHS. Rental, $29. IU.

ADAM: MINORITY YOUTH
Adam, an American Indian youth, speaks candidly about his cultural heritage and his place in today's society. 1971. Grades 4 and up. 10 minutes, color . Purchase: 16mm, $225; video, $135. 16mm rental, $31. PHOENIX.

AGAIN, A WHOLE PERSON I'VE BECOME
Will Sampson, Narrator
Three American Indian tribal leaders describe the wisdom of their shared culture. Grades 7 and up. 19 minutes, color . 16mm. Purchase: 16mm, $390; video, $360. Rental: 16mm, $45. SH. Rental, $21. PSU.

AGE OF THE BUFFALO
An indictment of the mass slaughtering of buf falos & systematic subduing of the Indians. Uses live footage & rare paintings to tell its story . 1964. Grades 4-8. 14 minutes, color . Rental: $14. UCT.

AIDS AND THE NATIVE AMERICAN F AMILY
Addresses people's needs for cultural and family support. Includes preventive AIDS information for all ages. 1989. 1 1 minutes, color. Video. Purchase: $50. UP.

SUZANNE AKIMNACHI MAKES A BURCH-BARK BERRY BASKET
David E. Young, Trudy Nicks
& David Strom, Producers
A Beaver Indian from northern Alberta, Suzanne documents in detail the entire production process. 1989. 23 minutes, color . Video. Purchase: $70; rental, $20. UADA.

AKWESASNE: ANOTHER POINT OF VIEW
A portrait of the Mohawk people as they confront two choices: survival or assimilation. Explores some of the social, political, and legal obstacles faced by traditional Mohawks in recent years in their struggle to retain traditional rights. 1981. 28 minutes, color. Purchase: 16mm, 3/4" U-matic; $495, video, $290; rental, 16mm, $50. ICARUS.

THE ALASKA NATIVE CLAIMS SETTLEMENT ACT SERIES
Bob Walker, Director
In five educational programs, explores the terms and implications of this major legislation. Examines its history; how it has settled native land claims and established native corporations; and what its impact may be in the future. 1979. 16-30 minutes, color. Video. In Inupiaq or English. NA TC.

ALASKA: SETTLING A NEW FRONTIER
National Geographic Society
Recounts the history of Alaska and views life in Eskimo villages. 1966. Grades 3 and up. 22 minutes, color. For grades 3 and up. 16mm. Rental, $17.50. PSU.

ALASKA: THE YUP'IK ESKIMOS
Susan Duncan, Executive Producer;
Larry Lansburgh & Gail Evanari, Co-producers;
Gail Evanari, W riter
Focuses on charges in Yup'ik culture and way of life, with commentary provided by people from four communities: Bethel, Eek, Chevak, and Tooksook Bay. Also depicts changes in village life. For grades 7-12; suitable for adult audiences. A study guide in English or Yup'ik is available. 1985. 27 minutes, color. Video. CHE (free loan).

THE ALASKAN ESKIMO
Sarah Elder & Len Kamerling, Producers
A series of four films produced jointly with village councils to ensure authentic Alaskan Eskimo material and point of view . Now available on video. DER.

DENNIS ALLEY WISDOM DANCERS VIDEO
Dennis Alley presents eight dances, including hoop, Northern traditional, shield and spear , eagle, and war dance. Introduction by Willie Nelson. 30 minutes, color. Video. Purchase: $19.95. CAN.

AMERICA'S INDIAN HERITAGE: REDISCOVERING COLUMBUS (OHIO)
Roger Kennedy, director of the Smithsonian's National Museum of American History focuses on Columbus, Ohio and the earthworks, mound-builders of ancient North America. This documentary ties together the connections across thousands of miles and thousands of years of ideas. 56 minutes, color. Video. 1992. Purchase: $159; rental, $75. FH.

THE AMERICAN AS ARTIST: A PORTRAIT OF BOB PENN
SD ETV, Producer
Penn offers his insights into the essence of being an artist and a Native-American in the U.S. 1976. 29 minutes, color. Video. Rental, $40. NAPBC.

THE AMERICAN EXPERIENCE: GERONIMO & THE APACHE RESISTANCE
Neil Goodwin
Portrays the profound transformation of a once-proud Indian society faced with the loss of its land and traditions. 1988. Grades 9 and up. 58 minutes, color. Video. Rental, $12. PSU.

THE AMERICAN EXPERIENCE: INDIANS, OUTLAWS, & ANGIE DEBO
Barbara Abrash & Martha Sandlin
Recounts the life of Angie Debo (1890-1988), a courageous maverick scholar whose work in behalf of Native American tribal sovereignty and land rights is considered the cornerstone of Indian history. Grades 9 and up. 58 minutes, color . 1988. Video. Rental, $12. PSU.

THE AMERICAN INDIAN
Center for Educational Telecommunications
Examines the history of the American Indian from the turn of the century to the present day . 28 minutes. 1980. 3/4" VHS. DT.

THE AMERICAN INDIAN - AFTER THE WHITE MAN CAME
Examines the profound impact white expansion had upon the many tribes of Native-Americans. The formation of U.S. governmental policies as well as contemporary social issues are discussed. Narrated by Iron Eyes Cody . 1972. 27 minutes, color. 16mm & video. Purchase: 16mm, $410; video, $150. HF . Rental: $16. UCT.

AMERICAN INDIAN ARTISTS: Parts I & II
Tony Schmitz and Don Cirillo, Directors
Part I: Six programs, profiling seven contemporary Native American artists: Grace Medicine Flower & Joseph Lonewolf, potters; Fritz Scholder , R.C. Gorman, and Helen Hardin, painters; Allen Houser, sculptor; and Charles Loloma, jeweler . 1976. Part II: Three programs—Larry Golsh's artistry in gold and precious stones; James Quick-To-See Smith, painter; and Dan Namingha, artist, 1984. 30 minutes each, color . Video. Part 1 - Rental: $40 each artist, $200/series; Part 2 - Purchase: $150/series; Rental: $80/series. NAPBC.

THE AMERICAN INDIAN - BEFORE THE WHITE MAN
Norman Foster, Producer
Presents a study of the American Indian from early migration routes to the development of the main tribes of North America. Narrated by Iron Eyes Cody. Grades 4-12. 19 minutes, color .16mm & video. Purchase: 16mm, $335; video, $150. HF .

THE AMERICAN INDIAN DANCE THEATRE - FINDING THE CIRCLE
Includes dances from many Indian tribes as performed on stage and at outdoor pow wows on their U.S. and international tours. Includes hoop dance, eagle dance, Apache Crown dance, Zuni rainbow dance, pow wow dances, plains snake and buffalo dance and others. 1990. 60 minutes, color . Video. Purchase: $35.00. CAN.

AMERICAN INDIAN IN TRANSITION
A North American Indian mother , living on a reservation, describes her family & tribal problems-relating her past & her dreams for the future. 1976. 22 minutes, color. 16mm. Rental: $1 1. UCT.

THE AMERICAN INDIAN INFLUENCE ON THE U.S.
Albert Saparof f, Producer
Narrated by Barry Sullivan, this film depicts how

life in the U.S. today has been influenced by the American Indian. Discusses the Pueblo Indians and the Spanish, Chief Massasoit and the Pilgrims, Hiawatha, Sitting Bull, General Custer , Buffalo Bill, President Jackson, Sequoyah, Will Rogers, Jim Thorpe and Buf fy St. Marie. 1972. Grades 5 and up. 20 minutes, color . 16mm & video. Purchase: $495; rental: $40. DP . Rental: $20. UK & UMN.

AMERICAN INDIAN OF T ODAY
(LOS INDIOS NORT AMERICANOS DE HOY)
Examines current trends that are shaping the future of American Indians in their adjustment to new ways of making their living. 1957. 16 minutes. Spanish edition. 16mm. UA.

AMERICAN INDIAN RHYTHMS
Documentary of Indian dancers from various tribes show authentic Indian dances. 1930. 10 minutes, bxw. EG.

THE AMERICAN INDIAN SPEAKS
Documentary lets the Indian speak about his people & heritage, about the white man & the future. Visits with the Muskogee, Cree, Sioux & Nisqually. 1973. Grades 7 and up. 23 minutes, color. 16mm. Purchase: BF . Rental: IU, PSU, UCLA & UMN.

AMERICAN INDIAN
SWEAT LODGE CEREMONY
Shows the entire ceremony . A little hut of the woods used as a sauna/steambath. Also shows the sacred pipe ceremony. With Bill Elwell. 1987. 90 minutes, color. Video. Purchase: $39.95. AV.

THE AMERICAN INDIAN T ODAY
This is a lesson which contains material on American Indians circa 1969. 30 minutes. 1969. 1/2" reel. NETV.

AMERICAN INDIANS AS
SEEN BY D.H. LAWRENCE
His wife Frieda speaks intimately about his beliefs & thoughts. Aldous Huxley presents selections from Lawrence, which reveal his deep insights into the religious & ceremonial impulses of Indian culture as shown by various ritual dances. 1966. Grades 7 and up. 14 minutes, color . Rental: $8. UCT.

AMERICAN INDIANS BEFORE
EUROPEAN SETTLEMENT
David Baerreis, Ph.D.
Where they came from, how they lived, and unique aspects of their cultures as related to their environment are examined. 1959. 1 1 minutes. Grades 4 to 12. Purchase: 16mm, $270; video, $190. COR. Rental: UA & UCT.

AMERICAN INDIANS OF T ODAY
Describes the achievements and problems of Indians. 1957. Grades 3 and up. 16 minutes, bxw . 16mm. Rental: PSU & UCT.

THE AMERICAN INDIAN'S SACRED GROUND
The mythical and geological aspects of the Native American sacred grounds are examined, with discussions on architecture, communication, and the natural and spiritual world; filmed at sited across the U.S. 60 minutes. 1991. VHS. KP

AMERICAN INDIANS: YESTERDAY & TODAY
Don Klugman
Shows that various Indian tribes have dif ferent histories and ways of life. A young Shoshone-Paiute man from the Owens V alley in California,

an elderly Northern Cheyenne man from Lame Deer, Montana, and a young Seneca woman from New York State tell about their history and modern lifestyles of their tribes. 1982. 19 minutes, color . Grades K-8. 16mm. Purchase: $375; Rental: $40. FF.

AMERINDIAN LEGACY
Explores the many important contributions first made by the Amerindians. 1992. Grades 4 and up. 29 minutes, color . Purchase: 16mm, $525; video, $285. Rental: 16mm, $55. PHOENIX.

AMIOTTE
Bruce Baird, KUSD-TV, Producer
Explores Sioux painter Arthur Amiotte's art and the reasons for returning to his native culture and religion. 1976. 29 minutes, color . Video. Rental: $40. NAPBC.

AMISK
Alanis Obomsawin, Director/Producer
The traditional lands of the Cree of Misstassini in northern Quebec are being threatened by a Hydro-Electric Power project. Shows a festival, with Cree music and dance, to raise money to fight against this project. 1977. 38 minutes, color . 16mm. NFBC.

THE ANASAZI & CHACO CANYON
This program looks at the fascinating finds at Chaco Canyon, the home of the Anasazi, ancestors of the Navajo. Also, the possible explanation for the disappearance of the highly advanced Anasazi culture. 1993. 43 minutes, color . Purchase: $149; rental: $75. FH.

ANCESTRAL VOICES
Joy Harjo & Mary Tall Mountain
Native American Poetry . 60 minutes. V ideo. $59.95. PBS

ANCIENT INDIAN CUL TURES
OF NORTHERN ARIZONA
Explores the ruins and ancient cultures of the Sinagua and Anasazi of Montezuma Castle, Wupatki, Tuzigoot, W alnut Canyon and Sunset Crater. 27 minutes, color . Video, $29.95. VVP. CH.

ANCIENT FORESTS: THE RAGE OVER TREES
Narrated by Paul Newman
Looks at the head-to-head struggle over the Pacific Northwest's National Forests. 60 minutes, color. Video. Rental: $10. HO.

ANCIENT PLACES
Focuses on the Native American cultures of the Southwest. 1981. 30 minutes, color . 16mm. KS.

ANCIENT SPIRIT. LIVING WORD -
THE ORAL TRADITION
The presentations and opinions of the Native Americans featured in this program culminate in a portrait of oral tradition, how it works and where it leads. 1983. 58 minutes, color . Video. Purchase: $150; Rental: $80. NAPBC.

THE ANCIENTS OF NORTH AMERICA
A dry cave/rock shelter with human remains was discovered in southeastern Utah. The site, dated 5500 BC,offers a unique opportunity to examine the culture & remains of a people more than 7000 years old. 28 minutes, color . Video. Purchase: $149; rental: $75. FH.

...AND THE MEEK SHALL INHERIT THE EARTH
Examines the American Indians of Menominee

County, Wisconsin. 1972. 59 minutes, color . 16mm. Rental: $25.25. IU & UMN.

...AND WOMAN WOVE IT IN A BASKET
Bushra Azzouz & Marlene Farnum, Producer/directors
The spiritual & cultural importance of basket-weaving to Oregon's Klickitat Indians is explored in this portrait of master craftswoman Nettie Kuneki. 1989. 70 minutes, color . Video & 16mm. Purchase: $350. WMM.

ANGOON - 100 YEARS LATER
Laurence Goldin, Producer/director/writer
Provides the history and culture of the Tlingit Indians while telling of the 1882 destruction of the Tlingit Indian village of Angoon, Alaska, by U.S. Naval forces. 1982. 30 minutes, color . Video. Rental: $40. NAPBC.

ANGOTEE: ST ORY OF AN ESKIMO BOY
Douglas Wilkinson, Director
A documentary account of an Indian boy's life from infancy to maturity . 1953. 31 minutes, color . Grades 6 and up. In English or French. Purchase: 16mm, $525; video, $385. Rental, $35. IFB. Rental only, PSU.

ANNIE & THE OLD ONE
Miska Miles, W riter
A dramatized film for young people with non-professional Navajo actors, about the relationship between a ten-year-old girl and her grandmother (the Old One.) 1976. Grades 1-8. 15 minutes, color. Purchase: 16mm, $320; V ideo, $190; rental, $44. PHOENIX. Rental: UA, UCT & IU.

ANNIE MAE--BRAVE HEARTED WOMAN
Lan Brookes Ritz, W riter/producer/director
A documentary portrait of Annie Mae Pictou Aquash, a young Native American woman and activist for human rights, found dead on the prairie in South Dakota in 1974, a year after the Wounded Knee uprising. Explores the events leading up to her death and investigates her unsolved murder. 1982. 80 minutes, color . 16mm; Purchase: $1,090. Rental: $150. BBP and NAPBC.

ANOTHER WIND IS MOVING: THE OFF-
RESERVATION INDIAN BOARDING SCHOOL
A documentary film about how dif ficult it is for Native Americans to learn about their culture. 59 minutes, color. 1986. V ideo. Purchase: $195; rental: $60. UC & STULL.

THE APACHE INDIAN
Shows the life of Apache Indians on their reservation in the White Mountains of W yoming; their ancient ceremonies, and contemporary education, work, and the role of the tribal council in determining the direction of tribal af fairs. 1975 revised edition. 10 minutes, color . Grades K-6. Purchase: 16mm, $265; video, $185. COR. Rental: 16mm, $9. UA & IU.

APACHE MOUNTAIN SPIRITS
John H. Crouch, Producer
Bob Graham, Director
An explanation of the role of the "Gaan", the Mountain Spirits who are the source of sacred power for the Apache. 1985. 58 minutes, color . Video. In English and Apache with English subtitles. NAPBC. & SVP.

ARCHAEOLOGY: PURSUIT OF MAN'S PAST
15 minutes. 16mm. Rental. UA.

ARCHAEOLOGY: QUESTIONING THE PAST
Betty Goerke, Producer
Includes two sequences of digging, one at an ancient Indian site in northern California and the other at Sand Canyon, an Anasazi pueblo site near Mesa Verde National Park in Colorado. Designed for students in introductory archaeology classes. 1988. 25 minutes, color. Video. Purchase, $195; Rental, $50. UC.

ARCHAEOLOGY SERIES
Three, 20-minute tapes explores various aspects of the archaeology of Yup'ik Eskimo sites throughout Southwest Alaska, including an examination of the Smithsonian Museum's huge collection of artifacts collected by Edward Nelson. 1983. 60 minutes, color. Video. Purchase: $24.95. KYUK.

ARCTIC SPIRITS
Katherine Marielle & Peter Raymont, Producers
Peter Raymont, Director
An investigation of the rise of evangelical Christianity in Inuit villages in the Canadian Arctic. Follows three Canadian evangelists on their crusades in Arctic Quebec and the Northwest Territories. Interview Inuit. 1983. 27 minutes, color. 16mm & video. IP.

ARROW TO THE SUN
Gerald McDermott
From the Acoma Pueblo in New Mexico comes this classic tale of a boy's search for his father: the universal search for identity, purpose, and continuity. 1973. Grades K-8. 12 minutes, color. 16mm & video. Purchase: Video, $79. FI. Rental: 16mm, UCT.

THE ART OF BEING INDIAN: FILMED ASPECTS OF THE CULTURE OF THE SIOUX
SD-ETV, Producer
Presents an overview of the cultural heritage of the Sioux from their early days in the Northeast to the Dakotas. Illustrates with paintings and sketches by George Catlin, Seth Eastman, and Karl Bochner; photography by Edward S. Curtis, Stanley Morrow, and the St. Francis Mission; and contemporary paintings by Sioux artist Bob Penn. 1976. 30 minutes, color. Video. Rental: $40. NAPBC.

THE ART OF NAVAJO WEAVING
Explores the traditional art of Navajo weaving and its origins. Shows the Durango Collection. 56 minutes. Video, $29.95. AA & CH.

AS LONG AS THE GRASS IS GREEN
A summer experience with the children of the Woodland Indians of North America. Nonnarrative. 11 minutes, color. 1973. VHS. AP.

AS LONG AS THE GRASS SHALL GROW
Lynn Brown, Writer/Producer
A series of eight programs designed for classroom use with pre-school age children. Combines elements of Seneca life to teach children to count to ten in Seneca, and at the same time helps build positive self-images. 1978. 15 minutes each, color. Video. The SN.

AT THE TIME OF WHALING
Leonard Kamerling & Sarah Elder
Depicts an Eskimo whale hunt at Gambell, Alaska, a Yup'ik-speaking community on St. Lawrence Island in the Bering Sea. 1974. 38 minutes, color. Purchase: 16mm, $650, video, $400; rental, $60; video, $40. DER.

AUGUSTA
Anne Wheeler, Director
Portrait of Augusta Evans, an 88 year-old granddaughter of a Shuswap chief, who lives alone in a cabin in the caribou country of British Columbia, Canada. She discusses her past and present. 1978. 17 minutes, color. Purchase: 16mm, $300; Video, $195; rental, $25. PHOENIX & NFBC.

THE BALLAD OF CROWFOOT
Willie Dunn, Director
Graphic history of the Canadian West created by a film crew of Canadian Indians who reflect on the traditions, attitudes, and problems of their people. 1970. 11 minutes, bxw. Grades 4 and up. 16mm. Rental: PSU, UCT & IU.

BASKETRY OF THE POMO
Clyde B. Smith, Producer
A series of three 1962, color films. An Introductory Film shows Indians gathering raw materials for baskets, and demonstrates, in slow motion and animation, the ten Pomo basketmaking techniques. 30 minutes. Purchase: 16mm, $600; video, $195. Rental: 16mm, $50. Techniques: A more detailed film on Pomo basketry techniques, showing precisely how the various weaves are executed. 33 minutes. Purchase: 16mm, $660; video, $195. Rental: 16mm, $50. Forms and Ornamentation: Illustrates the great variety of shapes, sizes, and design elements of Pomo baskets. 21 minutes. Purchase: 16mm, $420; video, $195. Rental, 16mm, $50. UC Rental only, IU.

BATTLE AT BAD AXE
Documentary re-tells the story of a dramatic event (The Black Hawk War) which forged the destiny of American settlement of western Wisconsin & the Upper Midwest. 29 minutes, color. Video. Rental: $10. HO.

BEAR DANCE
James Ciletti; narrated by James & Matthew Box, et al
Describes the traditional Bear Dance, a Ute courtship ritual that welcomes the advent of spring. 1988. Grades 3-8. 13 minutes, color. Purchase: $250. EB.

BEAUTIFUL TREE--CHISHKALE
Clyde B. Smith, Producer
The Southwestern Pomo called the tan oak chishkale (the beautiful tree.) Cooking methods and processing techniques used in making acorn bread are demonstrated. 1965. 20 minutes, color. Purchase: 16mm, $410; video, $195. Rental, $50. UC & PSU. Rental only, IU.

BEFORE THE WHITE MAN CAME
John E. Maple
A feature film made in the Big Horn Mountains of Montana and Wyoming in the early 1920's with the cooperation of the Crow. An all-Indian cast presents authentic rites and ceremonies. 50 minutes, bxw. 16mm. UUT & BL.

BE-TA-TA-KIN
A cliff-dwelling of the Indians who lived in Arizona at the time of the Crusades. Shows the canyons and mesas of these early Indians; their lives, agriculture, and industry. 11 minutes, color. Grades 9 and up. Rental, $13.50. NYU and PSU.

THE BELL THAT RANG TO AN EMPTY SKY
William Farley
A film essay using animation techniques and suggestive cutting to make a comment on the relationship between the expansion of white society onto Indian territories and the increase of wealth in the Federal Treasury. Commentary by Russell Means. 1977. Five minutes. 16mm. CANYON.

BETWEEN TWO RIVERS
Tells the story of the Indians' continuing battle for identity. The tragedy of Thomas Whitehawk caught between the world of the white man and the Indian. 1970. 26 minutes, color. 16mm. Rental: UCT & UMN.

BETWEEN TWO WORLDS
Peter Raymont; Producer
Barry Greenwald, Director
Reviews the tragedies and contradictions of Canada's colonization of the Inuit people; in particular, the effects upon the life of Joseph Idlout, one of the world's most famous Inuit. 1991. 58 minutes, color. Purchase: 16mm, $895, video, $390; rental, 16mm, $125. ICARUS.

BEYOND TRADITION - CONTEMPORARY INDIAN ART & ITS EVOLUTION
Presents more than 300 examples of prehistoric, historic and contemporary American Indian art. Carvings, paintings, sculptures, baskets, rugs, jewelry and pottery.The evolution of Indian art is traced through the centuries. 1989. 45 minutes, color. Video. Purchase: $29.95. CAN & HVC. Rental: $10. HO; $16. UMN.

BIG CITY TRAIL: THE URBAN INDIANS OF TEXAS
Focuses on the 20,000 American Indian living in the Dallas/Ft. Worth area. Discusses the challenges these people face as they adjust to urban life, while resisting its homogenization. 28 minutes. Teacher's guide. $35. UT-ITC.

BILL REID
Jack Long, Director
Haida carver and jewelry-maker, Bill Reid, speaks of his work and what his Haida heritage has meant for him as an artist. 1979. 28 minutes. 16mm, NFBC.

THE BIRTH OF CALIFORNIA
A documentary of the prehistory & history of California in the early days of exploration. 1927. 22 minutes, bxw. EG.

THE BISON HUNTERS
The painter George Catlin describes his enchantment with the life of the Plains Indians. 13 minutes, color. Video. Purchase: $69.95. FH.

BLACK COAL, RED POWER
Shelly Grossman, Producer
Examines the effects coal strip-mining has had on the Navajo and Hopi reservations in Arizona. 1972. 41 minutes, color. 16mm. Rental. IU & UA.

THE BLACK HILLS ARE NOT FOR SALE
Sandra Osawa, Producer
Taped at the 1980, International Survival Gathering in South Dakota, Sioux people tell why the Black Hills are not for sale. Provides historical background on the Laramie Treaty of 1868 which guaranteed the Sioux ownership of their lands. 1980. 28 minutes, color. Video. UP.

THE BLACK HILLS: WHO OWNS THE LAND?
NETV, Producer
A two-part program examines the roots of this problem, presenting the facts and beliefs that have fueled over a century of debate. Part 1. The Treaty

of 1868 - Focuses on the original treaties; Part 2. Black Hills Claim - Highlights the physical and legal battles waged to gain and regain the Black Hills of SD. 30 minutes each. Color . Video. Purchase: $50 per program; $70/series. NETV .

BLUNDEN HARBOR
Shows a group of Pacific Northwest Kwakiutl Indians living in Blunden Harbor and sustaining themselves by the sea. Includes the Legend of Killer Whale, and a dance ceremony . 1951. Grades 7 and up. 20 minutes, bxw . Rental, $14. PSU.

BOLDT DECISION: IMPACTS AND IMPLEMENTATION
A discussion of the court ruling by U.S. Judge George Boldt who ruled that treaty Indians in Washington are entitled to half the harvestable catch of salmon and steelhead. 1976. 60 minutes. 3/4" U-matic. UW.

BOLDT DECISION: UPDATE
A look at the impact of the Boldt decision. 60 minutes, color. 1977. 3/4" U-matic. UW .

BORN TO BE A NATION
Documents the proceedings of the 1976, International American Indian Treaty Conference on the Yankton Sioux Reservation. Native American leaders speak of the history of treaties recognizing Indian sovereignty and of the attempts by non-Indian interests to ignore those treaties because of resources found on Indian lands. 1976. 15 minutes, bxw. Reel & video. UCV.

BOWS & ARROWS
Jim Hamm
Describes the art of making bows & arrows. 59 minutes. VHS, $26.95. CMM.

BOX OF TREASURES
Chuck Olin, Producer/director
In 1921 the Kwakiutl people of Alert Bay, British Columbia, Canada, held their last secret potlatch. Fifty years later, the masks, blankets, and copper heirlooms that had been confiscated by the Canadian government were returned. The Kwakiutl built a cultural center to house these treasures and named it U'Mista something of great value that has come back. 1980. 28 minutes, color . Purchase: 16mm, $480; video, $350. Rental. 16mm, $45; video, $35. DER (U.S.); CFDW (Canada).

BOY OF THE NAVAJOS
Depicts life among the Navajos as seen through the eyes of Tony, a present day Navajo Indian boy . Revised 1975 edition. Grades K-6. 1 1 minutes, color. Purchase: 16mm, $270; video, $190. COR. Rental. UA, IU.

BOY OF THE SEMINOLES (INDIANS OF THE EVERGLADES)
Wendell W. Wright, PhD
A visit to the Seminole tribe in the Everglades of Florida. 1956. Grades K-6. 1 1 minutes. Purchase: 16mm, $270; video, $190. COR.

BRAVEHEART
Indian tries to make it in white man's world, falls in love with white woman, alienates his tribe. Finally returns to Indian ways. 1925. 68 mins., bxw . EG.

THE BROKEN CORD WITH LOUISE ERDRICH AND MICHAEL DORRIS
Two Native American authors share their insights into the traditions & conditions of Native America today. 30 minutes. Video. $39.95. PBS.

BROKEN JOURNEY
Gary Robinson, Producer
A documentary which looks at the disease of alcohol through the personal stories of Native American inmates, men and women who have been incarcerated because of alcohol-related problems. 1986. 30 minutes, color . Purchase: $150; Rental: $40. NAPBC.

BROKEN RAINBOW
Victoria Mudd & Maria Florio, Producers/writers editors; Victoria Mudd, Director
A feature length documentary narrated by Martin Sheen, this film is concerned with the relocation of traditional Navajo from their homes in Big Mountain, Arizona. It provides a sympathetic view of the Navajo perspective on the history of the lands in dispute. Won the Academy Award for best documentary in 1985. 70 minutes, color . 16mm & video. DC.

BROKEN TREATY AT BATTLE MOUNTAIN
Joel Freedman, Director; narrated by Robert Redford
Shows the dramatic story of the traditional W estern Shoshone Indians of Nevada and their struggle to regain 24 million acres of land stolen from them by the U.S. Government. Also, a portrait of the traditional Indian way of life. 1974. 60 minutes, color. 16mm & video. Purchase: $250. CIN. Rental. UN & UW.

BRYAN BEAVERS: A MOVING POTRAIT
A Maidu Indian of California talks about his past, Indian spirits, his ancestral history , and his life. 1969. 30 minutes, color . Grades 9 and up. 16mm rental, $15.90. IU

BUCKEYES: FOOD OF CALIFORNIA INDIANS
Clyde B. Smith, Producer
Shows harvesting, stone boiling, and leaching of buckeyes (horse chestnuts) by Niseanan Indians, a centuries-old method of changing poisonous nuts into edible mush or soup. 1961. 13 minutes. Color. Purchase: 16mm, $280; video, $195. Rental, 16mm, $40. UC & PSU.

BUFFALO, BLOOD, SALMON & ROOTS
George Burdeau, W riter/Director
Filmed at the Flathead, Kalispel and Coeur d' Alene Reservations in western Montana, the Idaho panhandle and eastern W ashington, this film shows the old tribal ways of gathering and preserving food. 1976. 28 minutes, color . 16mm & video. NAPBC and PBS.

4-BUTTE-1: A LESSON IN ARCHAEOLOGY
Clyde B. Smith and Tony Gorsline
Shows the excavations and analyzes the artifacts of a Maidu Indian village in California Sacramento Valley. 1968. 33 minutes, color . Purchase: 16mm, $660; VHS, $195, Rental: $50. UC. Rental only: 16mm, $24.50; VHS, $24. PSU.

BY NO MEANS CONQUERED PEOPLE
Verity Lund and John Moore;
Richard Erdoes, photography
Presents issues that the Longest W alk, 1978, was organized around. The Walk was made across the U.S. to demonstrate their concern about proposed legislation: eleven bills, one of which would abrogate all treaties between the U.S. & Indian tribes. Dick Gregory & Clyde Bellacourt were speakers at the gathering. 1979. 26 minutes, bxw . VHS. VL.

BY SPIRITS MOVED
Explores spiritual beliefs & rituals of the Inuit (Es-

kimo) & other tribal people, and compares the role of the shaman with leadership in W estern culture. 20 minutes. VHS. $50. TOP.

BY THE WORK OF OUR HANDS
Designed to be used with the text of the same name. However , it can be used independently . Focuses on drum making, and both oak and cane basket making. Teacher's guide. 30 minutes. Grades 3-8. Purchase: video, $85. Rental, $10/two weeks. CHP.

BY THIS SONG I WALK: NAVAJO SONG
Larry Evers with Andrew Natonabah
Natonabah sings as he travels through Canyon de Chelly where the Navajo believe the songs were originally created and he discusses the songs and their origin. In Navajo with English subtitles. 1978. 25 minutes, color . Video. Purchase: $175. NR. Rental, $52.50. ATL.

CAHOKIA LEGACY
Cahokia Mounds and Cahokia Archaeology. 20 minutes, color. Video, $10. CMM.

CAHOKIA MOUNDS VIDEO LIBRARY
Cahokia: A Prehistoric Legacy, 17 minutes, color; The Cahokia Arrow Point, 13 minutes, color; Woodhenge Dedication Lectures, 1985; In Search Of...Ancient Indian Astronomies, series, 84 minutes, color; 1987 Cahokia Culture Lecture Series, 155 minutes, color . 2 week rentals, $2 per tape. CMM.

THE CALIFORNIA MISSIONS
Philomen Long, Director/writer
Martin Sheen, Narrator
Documentary exploring the heritage of the California missions, emphasizing the clash pf cultures between the Spanish Franciscan missionaries & the native CA Indians. 1990. 22 minutes. Purchase: 16mm, $450; video, $195; rental, $50. UC.

CALIFORNIA RIVIERA
Looks at the history , culture, archaeology , and oceanographyof southern California. Includes an interview with the present members of the Juaneno Indian tribe. 50 minutes. 1989. VHS and Beta. NU.

CALUMET, PIPE OF PEACE
Discusses rituals surrounding the calumet or peace pipes. Describes Indian use of pipes and tobacco, and shows traditional Indian methods of fashioning, decorating and consecrating pipe bowl and stem. 1964. 23 minutes, color . Purchase: 16mm, $460; video, $195. Rental: $50. UC. Rental only: PSU.

CANADA: PORTRAIT OF A NATION
Covers the environmental problems, and the social & political gains being made by the country's native Indians & Inuits. Grades 4-8. 5 VHS cassettes. 16 minutes each. $49. each. SVE.

CANADA'S ORIGINAL PEOPLES: THEN AND NOW
TV Ontario, Producer
Contrasts the life of native Canadians before the arrival of Europeans with contemporary native life in Canada. 1977. 20 minutes, color . Video. Rental, $40. NAPBC.

CANYON de CHELLY & HUBBELL TRADING POST
Visits both national parks containing Anasazi cliff dwellings and Navajo craftsmen. 30 minutes. 1979. VHS & Beta. VVP.

CELEBRATION & THE PIPE IS THE ALTAR
Chris Spotted Eagle, Producer/director
Two companion pieces presents aspects of contemporary Native American culture for Indians living in the Minneapolis-St. Paul area. CELEBRATION (1979), filmed at the Honor the Earth Pow Wow held annually on the Lac Courte Oreilles Reservation in Wisconsin, depicts the strengths of Native American life: pow wow dancing, feasting, Indian sports, give-aways, etc. In THE PIPE IS THE ALTAR (1980) spiritual leader Amos Owen, a Sioux Indian living on the Prairie Island Reservation near Red Wing, Minnesota, shares his daily prayer ritual using the ceremonial pipe. 26 minutes, color. Video (VHS, Beta). IN, MAI.

CELEBRATION OF THE RAVEN
Ken Kuramoto
Bill Reid is the acknowledged master of contemporary art in the ancient native tradition of the Haida. Since 1959, he has created a series of large works of sculpture, culminating in his 1980 masterwork, The Raven and the First Men. Traces the evolution of this celebrated work of art. 1981. 12 minutes, color. Video. CFDW.

CELEBRATION OF SURVIVAL
American Indians join with others at the National Cathedral in Washington, DC, on October 12, 1992 to mark 500 years of colonialism. Bishop Steve Charleston presiding delivers a powerful message. 53 minutes, color. Video. Rental: $10. HO.

A CENTURY OF SILENCE...
PROBLEMS OF THE AMERICAN INDIAN
Correlates the current problems of the American Indian to the past 100 years of contact with the white culture. Also addresses issues of cultural conflict, assimilation, and activism within the Indian community. 28 minutes, color. 1978. VHS and Beta. AP.

CESAR'S BARK CANOE
Bernard Gosselin, Director
Cesar Newashish, a Cree Indian, peels the bark from a birch tree and with his pocket knife and axe, constructs a canoe. Subtitles in Cree, French and English. 1971. 58 minutes, color. Grades 7-adult. EDC.

THE CHACO LEGACY
Graham Chedd, Director
Explores the excavations of the first monumental stone ruins discovered in North America, the Pueblo Bonito community in Chaco Canyon, New Mexico. Teachers guide. 1980. Grades 9 and up. 59 minutes, color. Purchase: 16mm, $600. Rental, $60. DER. Purchase: Video, $59.95. PBS. Rental: 16mm, $24; video, $12. PSU and IU.

CHARLES KILLS ENEMY, MEDICINE MAN
This film shows Kills Enemy in a Sweat Lodge Ceremony and a Lowanpi Ceremony. 30 minutes, color. 16mm. Purchase: $300; rental: $30. AICRC.

CHARLEY SQUASH GOES TO TOWN
An animated, imaginative simplification of the acculturation-identity crisis of an Indian. 1969. Grades 6 and up. 5 minutes, color. 16mm. Rental: UA & UCT.

CHEROKEE
Philip Hobel, Executive Producer
Examines the modern Cherokee's efforts to preserve native traditions. Cherokees are shown performing ceremonies and activities of the past, and discusses their heritage and hopes for the future.

1975. 26 minutes. Purchase: 16mm, $400; video, $340. Rental, $55 each. CG.

CHEYENNE AUTUMN
Based on an actual incident, this film tells of the valiant efforts of the Cheyenne Indians to escape to their Wyoming homeland from their wretched Oklahoma lands. 1965. 156 minutes. Rental. UM.

*CHIEF SEATTLE TELLS HIS OWN STORY
An actor depicts the hisoric personality, explaining the time he lived in; the political, social, & ethical battles they fought, and the contributions he made. Grades 4-8. 20 minutes. VHS, $89. SVE.

CHILDREN OF THE LONG-BEAKED BIRD
Peter Davis and Swedish TV
Portrait of Dominic Old Elk, a 12 year old Crow Indian, exploring his life and interests; a view of Native American life and history. Seeks to erase many stereotypes. 1976. 29 minutes, color. Grades 3 and up. Purchase: 16mm, 485; Video, $100; Rental: $50. BULL. Rental: $40. NAPBC.

CHILDREN OF THE PLAINS INDIANS
A view of Indian life on the Great Plains before the arrival of white settlers, featuring scenes of tribal activities. 20 minutes, bxw. 1962. Video. CRM. Rental: UCT.

CHOCTAW HERITAGE VIDEO
William Brescia, Producer
"By the Work of Our Hands" - Documents tribal members expert in making crafts: split-oak baskets, cane baskets, and drums. 1983. 30 minutes; "More Than Just a Week of Fun" - Shows events of the Choctaw Fair, held on the reservation every summer. 1984. 12 minutes; and "Choctaw Tribal Government" - Explains the structure and functions of Mississippi Choctaw tribal government, and a view of life on the Choctaw reservation today. 1985. Grades 5 and up. 17 minutes, color. Video. CVP.

CHOCTAW STORY
Bob Ferguson
Highlights the achievements of the tribal administration of Chief Phillip Martin, since 1979. 1985. 28 minutes, color. Video. CVP.

CIRCLE OF LIFE, Parts 1 & 2
American Indian youth on teenage pregnancy. Stresses the importance of education, prenatal care, and family planning. Part 1, 43 minutes; Part 2, 32 minutes, color. Video. Rental: $16. UMN.

CIRCLE OF LIFE: THE ALABAMA-COUSHATTAS
Documentary exploring the cultural identity of the Alabama-Coushattas. 24 minutes. Teacher's guide. $35. UT-ITC.

CIRCLE OF SONG
Cliff Sijohn and George Burdeau
Presents the Indian concept of the Circle of Life on which important life events and the songs and dances associated with them are point. In two parts. 1976. 28 minutes each, color. 16mm & video. NAPBC & PBS.

CIRCLE OF THE SPIRIT
A saga of Native Americans in the Catholic Church. 60 minutes, color. Video. Rental: $10. HO.

CIRCLE OF THE SUN
Colin Low, Director
Documents the life and ceremonial customs of the

Blood Indians of Alberta, Canada, and contrasts their present existence on the reservation. 1960. Grades 7 and up. 30 minutes, color. 16mm & video. $27. NFBC. Rental: UA, IU & UMN.

CIRCLE OF WARRIORS
Featurs nine Native Americans living with HIV infections and AIDS, discussing various aspects of their lives. A discussion guide is provided with the video. 27 minutes, color. VHS. Purchase: $75. NNA.

A CIRCLE OF WOMEN
Modern women meet women elders of Native American tribes in an effort to link their cultures. 60 minutes, color. 1991. IVA.

CIVILIZED TRIBES
Philip Hobel, Executive Producer
Life is reconstructed at the Seminole Reservation in Florida to simulate that of their Seminole ancestors. Also focuses on their present conditions. 26 minutes, color. 1972. Purchase: 16mm, $400; video, $340. Rental $55 each. CG. 16mm rental only, IU.

CLASH OF CULTURES
Scott Nielsen and Dick Blofson
Four elders from the Lakota tribe, drawing on the oral tradition of Indian life in the late 19th-century, explain the cultural attitudes of the Indians and the clash of attitudes with white settlers. 28 minutes. 1978. 16mm & VHS. UMA & KS.

CLASH OF CULTURES ON THE GREAT PLAINS (1865-1890)
Describes the traditional relationship of the Lakota people to their environment & explore conflicts with outsiders who moved into the area during the 1860s & 1870s. Grades 9-12. Teacher's guide. 20 minutes. VHS, $125. AIT.

CLOUDED LAND
Randy Croce, Producer
A sensitive examination of Native American land claims of the White Earth Reservation in Minnesota. 1987/1989. 58 minutes, color. Purchase: 3/4" $160; 1/2" VHS - $110. Rental: IN & UMN.

CLUES TO ANCIENT INDIAN LIFE
Discusses the kind of clues ancient indians left behind, and the importance of preserving these artifacts for study. 1962. 10 minutes. Video. AIMS.

COLLIDING WORLDS
The lives of the Mono women, representing three generations, are intertwined to form the body of this film. Shows how traditional Mono ways have clashed & collided with modern technology. 1978. 30 minutes, color. 16mm. Rental: $37. UCLA.

COLOURS OF PRIDE
Henning Jacobson
Four Indian artists of Canada are interviewed in their home studios by Tom Hill, a Seneca from the Six Nations Reserve in Ontario. 1974. 24 minutes, color. 16mm. NFBC.

COLUMBUS CONTROVERSY:
CHALLENGING HOW HISTORY IS WRITTEN
Nick Kaufman, Director
Examines the Columbus controversy using footage from the classroom of Bill Bigelow, along with historians John Mohawk and William McNeil. 1991. 24 minutes, color. Video. Purchase: $89. SRA Rental only: $10. HO.

COLUMBUS DIDN'T DISCOVER US
Robbie Leppzer, Director
Wil Echevarria, Producer
Features interviews with indigenous activists, filmed at the Quincentennial gathering in 1990 in Ecuador of 300 native peoples of North, South and Central America. A moving testimony of the impact of the Columbus legacy on the lives of indigenous peoples resulting from the European invasion. 1992. 24 minutes, color . Video. Purchase: institutions, $89.95; community groups, $39.95; and indigenous organizations, $29.95. Rental: institutions, $45; community groups, $20. TTP & OY. Rental only: $10. HO.

COME FORTH LAUGHING: VOICES OF THE SUQUAMISH PEOPLE
Suquamish Tribal Cultural Center , Producer
Provides an account of the life of the Suquamish Indian Tribe living in the Puget Sound region of Washington State over the past one hundred years. 1983. 15 minutes. Color and b&w . 16mm and video. SUQ.

A COMMON DESTINY
Gayil Nalls, Producer/Director
John Steele, Producer
Comprised of two shorter films: "W alk in Both Worlds" - Jewell Praying W olf James, a Lummi tribesman speaks of his ancestors and presents the 1853 message of Chief Seattle. "W e do not own the freshness of the air or the sparkle of the water. How Can you buy them from us? ..."; also talks of the white man's reltaionship to the earth; and that Native American knowledge and needs are being ignored. And, "The Hopi Prophecy" - Thomas Banyacya, now in his 80s, is a spokesman for Hopi high religious leaders, interprets the prophetic symbols of a sacred petroglyph in Arizona for visitors from other tribes, and speaks about the damage that industry has caused on the reservation. 1990. 52 minutes, color . Video. Purchase: $24.95. MFV .

COMPLETING OUR CIRCLE
Looks at the tradityions of the Plains and W est Coast Indians, the Inuit, and the first Europeans and settlers in W estern Canada. Presents their arts and crafts. 1978. 27 minutes, color . Video. Purchase: CRM. Rental: 16mm, $23. UMN.

CONCERNS OF AMERICAN INDIAN WOMEN
Will George, Director
Interviews with Marie Sanchez, North Cheyenne judge, and Dr . Connie Uri, Choctaw-Cherokee physician and law student. 1977. 30 minutes, color . Video. MAI.

THE CONQUERED DREAM
Features sequences on Eskimo art and folklore, traditional hunting methods, health problems and education of today's Eskimo. 51 minutes. CEN.

CONQUISTA
Narrated by Richard Boone
A look at how the history of Old W est was af fected by the fateful meeting of the Plains Indian and the horse. 1974. 20 minutes, color . Video. CFH. Rental: 16mm, $14. UCT .

CONSONANTS WITH COYOTE
Animated Navajo language film. Consonants with common sounds to both Navajo & English. 9 minutes. All grades. 16mm & video. SAN.

CONTRARY WARRIORS: A STORY OF THE CROW TRIBE
Connie Poten & Pamela Roberts, Producers
narrated by Peter Coyote
An award-winning documentary on the Crow people of southeastern Montana, as told by the members of the tribe, documents the life of 97-year-old Robert Yellowtail as a focus for the telling of Crow history . 1985. 60 minutes, color . 16mm & video. Purchase: $250. DC. Rental: 16mm, $47.50. UMN.

CONTRASTS
Portrays the Plains Indians warriors and the U.S. Cavalrymen that faced of f against each other in the 1870's. Filmed at the actual site of the Reno retreat crossing at the Battle of the Little Big Horn. 45 minutes, color. Video. Purchase: $25. OAP .

A CONVERSATION WITH VINE DELORIA, JR.
Larry Evers, University of Arizona
The writer discusses the gulf between Indian and non-Indian culture and the schizophrenia of white expectations for the Indian. 1978. 29 minutes, color. Purchase: Video, $175. NR. Rental, video. $37.50. ATL.

1987 COOK INLET FRIENDSHIP POTLATCH
Highlights of Alaska Native traditional dances, music, Native Olympic games & other activities. 1988. 12 minutes, color . Video. $7. NDM.

COPPERMINE
Ray Harper, Director
Story about the clash of cultures. The Copper Inuit lived in Canada's central arctic until early 1900's when southern Canadians, Americans & British moved into the area. 1993. 56 minutes, color . Purchase: 16mm, $775; video, $250. Rental: $80.

CORN & THE ORIGINS OF SETTLED LIFE IN MESO-AMERICA
Jack Churchill, Director
Presents the work of three scholars, Michael Coe, Paul Mangelsdorf, and Richard MacNeish. 1964. 40 minutes. 16mm. EDC.

COYOTE TALES
Don Mose, Director; Kent Tibbitts, Producer
A series of five animated Navajo language and culture-based curriculum films in the Navajo language. 5 legendary coyote stories: Coyote and Beaver, 4 minutes; Coyote and Lizard, 7 minutes; Coyote and Rabbit, 10 minutes; Coyote and Skunk, 9 minutes; and Coyote and Toad, 8 minutes, color. 16mm & video. SAN.

A CREE HEALER
Consists of interviews with the healer and shows segments where he prepares for the sweatlodge ceremony. The interview concerns the issues and controversies encountered by this native healer in openly discussing the subject. 22 minutes, color . Video. UADA.

CREE HUNTERS OF MISTASSINI
Tony Ianzelo and Boyce Richardson, Directors
The setting up of a winter camp by 16 Cree Indians. Indian life observed in the bush. 1974. Grades 7 and up. 58 minutes, color . 16mm & video. Purchase: NFBC. Rental: DEC, PSU, UCT & UMN.

CREE WAY
Tony Ianzelo and Boyce Richardson, Director
Provides a view of a successful bilingual education project which connects Cree children to their past and future. 1977. 28 minutes. 16mm. NFBC.

CREEK NATION VIDEO
Gary Robinson, Producer/director
For the past decade The Muscogee Creek Nation Communications Center , located in Okmulgee, Oklahoma, has been producing videotapes to present accurate and contemporary views of the Creek Nation. 17 programs on culture, history , and current affairs have been produced. A copy of any program is available at no charge, if a cassette is supplied. For a complete list of titles and information about production services of fered contact MCN.

CROOKED BEAK OF HEAVEN
David Attenborough, W riter/Narrator
A Haida chief bestows lavish gifts on his tribesmen and then smashes his most valuable possessions, a potlatch ceremony . Contrasted with footage made of the Kwakiutl by Edward S. Curtis in 1912. 1976. 52 minutes, color . 16mm. Rental: TW, UCLA, UCT, UI & UMN.

CROW DOG
Mike Cuesta and David Baxter , Directors
Documentary portrait of Sioux medicine man, Leonard Crow Dog, the spiritual leader of 89 American Indian tribes and the spokesman for the traditionalists. 1979. 57 minutes, color . Purchase: 16mm, $795; video, $595. Rental, $95. CG. Rental only, $30. UT.

CROW DOG'S PARADISE
A look at a Sioux Indian enclave where the Crow Dog family preserves the spiritual and intellectual heritage of their traditional American Indian culture. 1979. Grades 9 and up. 28 minutes. 16mm & video. Purchase: VHS, $89; 3/4", $1 19. CC. Rental: VHS, $16; 16mm, $21.75. UMN.

CROW/SHOSHONE SUNDANCE... A TRADITIONAL CEREMONY
Documents the traditional Crow Lifeways & philosophies through authentic & legendary Crow/Shoshone Sundance Ceremony . 1991. 56 minutes, color. Video. Rental: $16. UMN.

CRY OF THE YUROK
Details the Yuroks, California's largest Native American tribe,with the many problems that beset them as they try to survive. 58 minutes, color . Purchase: $149; rental, $75. FH.

CULTURAL CHANGES
The pre-reservation life of the buf falo hunting Indians of the southern Plains is told through the use of pictographic drawings made by Kiowa & Cheyenne young men imprisoned in Fort Marion, Florida, in 1875. 1970. 17 minutes, color . 16mm. Rental: $13. UMN.

THE CUP'IK OF ALASKA--ESKIMOS: A CHANGING CULTURE
Despite many technological & material changes, their resources are the same as their ancestros, and they still depend on ancient knowledge that helps them adjust to their environment. 1992. Grades 4 and up. 32 minutes, color . Purchase: 16mm, $615; video, $375. Rental: $16mm, $95. PHOENIX.

CUSTER'S LAST FIGHT
Thomas Ince, Producer
The 1925 release of the 1912 Ince film, with two reels added to fill out the story . 45 minutes, color.Video. Purchase: $25. OAP .

THE DAKOTA CONFLICT
Floyd Red Crow Westerman
& Garrison Keillor, Narrators
Recounts the war (sometimes called "the Great Sioux Uprising") that began the 30 year struggle for the Great Plains, a struggle that continued at the Little Big Horn and ended at Wounded Knee. Uses diaries, old photographs, sketchbooks, newspaper archives, trail transcripts, and oral histories passed down through the generations. 60 minutes, color. Video. Rental: $10. HO; $16. UMN.

DANCE TO GIVE THANKS
Looks at the 184th annual He-De-Wa-Chi (Festival of Joy) of the Omaha Indian Tribe. Learn aboiut the history of the festival and see traditional dance by tribal members. 30 minutes. VHS & 3/4" U-matic. NAPBC.

DANCING FEATHERS
Paul Stephens; Producer/Writer
Eric Jordan, Director
In this "Spirit Bay" program, Tafia, a young Ojibway girl, is apprehensive about performng a jingle dance at an upcoming powwow in Toronto. 1983. Grades 3-8. 28 minutes, color. 16mm & video. Purchase: $149. ALT.

DANCING IN MOCCASINS: KEEPING NATIVE AMERICAN TRADITIONS ALIVE
Examines the needs & problems of today's Native Americans, both those who live on the reservation & those who have chosen the mainstream. The conclusion focuses on celebration & survival as reflected in the continuing tradition of the Pow Wow. 49 minutes, color. Video, Purchase: $149; rental: $75. FH.

A DANCING PEOPLE
Dancers & musicians from nine Yup'ik Eskimo villages gathered in the Yukon town of St. Mary's for 'Yupiit Yuraryariat.' Three days of dancing, gift-giving, and contests. 1983. 30 minutes, color. Video. $24.95. KYUK.

DANCING TO GIVE THANKS
NETV, Producer; JR Mathews, Host
Celebrates the traditions and family customs of the Omaha Indian Tribe. Filmed at the Omaha Tribal headquarters near Macy, Nebraska. Interprets dance themes & traditions. 1988. 30 minutes, color. Video. Rental: $20. GPN. Purchase: $150; Rental: $40. NAPBC.

DAUGHTERS OF THE ANASAZI
John Anthony
The legendary Acoma potter, Lucy Lewis, and her daughters Emma & Delores demonstrate the traditional way of making fine pottery from grinding the clay to forming the coils & bowls, polishing, painting & firing. 1990. 28 minutes, color. Video. Purchase: $24.95. FILM & FI. Rental: $16. UMN.

DAUGHTERS OF THE COUNTRY
Norma Bailey, Producer
Focuses on four women of Native American heritage who find themselves drawn into the world of the white man and then rejected by it. Their stories move from 18th century to present day. Includes: Part 1 - "Ikwe," an Indian girl who lives in a remote area of North America in 1770; Part 2 - "Mistress Madeleine," she is half Native American in 1850; Part 3 - "Places Not Our Own," about a family in pre-Depression era in North America; and Part 4 - "The Wake," about Joan in 1985, a single American Indian parent with two small children whose father deserted them. 1987. 57 min-

utes each, color. Purchase: 16mm, $775 each; VHS, $150 each. Rental: $80 each. NFBC.

ROBERT DAVIDSON
Michael Brodie & Bill Roxborough, Producers/directors
Features one of the best known of contemporary artists, Robert Davidson. He is shown making a deer skin drum, with the entire process well portrayed. Discusses his technique, the philosophy behind the art of the Haida, and his personal connection to it. 1981. 29 minutes, color. In English or French. Video. MVS & VOI.

THE DAWN RIDERS: NATIVE AMERICAN ARTISTS
Robert and Dona DeWeese
Three prominent Indian painters, Woody Crumbo (Potawatomi), Blackbear Bosin (Kiowa-Comanche) and Dick West (Cheyenne) talk about their work and influences on their art. 1969. 27 minutes. 16mm. LF.

DE GRAZIA
Ted De Grazia, well-known Arizona artist, discusses how his life among the Indians and Mexicans of the Southwest is reflected in his work. 1967. 29 minutes. 16mm. Rental. UA.

THE DEATH MARCH OF DE SOTO
Archaeologists chart the conquistador's trail across Florida's Gulf Coast to the Gulf of the Mississippi and uncover now-extinct Native American cultures, their people victims of brutality, disease, and neglect. 1993. 28 minutes, color. Video. Purchase: $149; rental: $75. FH.

THE DEATH OF THE BISON
The stories of the Indian chiefs, of Crazy Horse and Sitting Bull and their great battles to the events at Wounded Knee in 1973 demonstrates that the conflicts of the past have yet to be resolved. 13 minutes, color. Video. Purchase: $69.95. FH.

DESERT DANCE
Includes single voice chanting with Native American flute by Carlos Nakai, drums, rattles, wind & rain. Cassette, $12. CH.

DESERT PEOPLE (PAPAGO)
1949. 25 minutes. Rental. UA.

DESERT REGIONS: NOMADS & TRADERS
A look at the Navajo Indians of Monument Valley and Bedouins of Jordan. 1980. 15 minutes, color. Video. PHOENIX.

DIARY: NATIVE AMERICAN MINNESOTANS
Documents the personal stories of several Native Americans living in Minnesota. Describes the process of getting in touch with their roots & fitting into the white American culture. 1992. 35 minutes, color. Video. Rental: $16. UMN.

A DIFFERENT DRUM
The story of a young Comanche boy who is torn between his family's desire for him to attend college and his own natural aptitude for auto mechanics. 1974. 21 minutes. Rental. UK.

DINEH: THE PEOPLE
Jonathan Reinis & Stephen Hornick
Documentary focusing on the impending relocation of several thousand Navajo from a joint-use land area surrounding the Hopi Reservation which is located in the midst of the Navajo Reservation. Portrays the cultural and economic conditions

under which the Navajo attempt to survive while striving to preserve their traditional values. 1976. 77 minutes, color. Video. Purchase: $150; Rental: $80/week. NAPBC.

DISCOVERING AMERICAN INDIAN MUSIC
Bernard Wilets
Songs and dances of tribes from various parts of the country performed in authentic costumes. All ages. 1971. Grades 4 and up. 24 minutes, color. Purchase: $480. BARR. Rental: IU, UMN, UCLA, UCT, UT & UK.

THE DISPOSSESSED
Sympaheic view of the Pit River Indians' struggle to regain lands in northern California taken from them in 1853 and now controlled by Pacific Gas & Electric Co.Shows the Indians' impoverished living conditions, and describes how PG&E dams have destroyed salmon runs on which they depend. Traces the legal history of the land dispute. 1970. 33 minutes, color. 16mm. Rental: UCLA.

DISTANT VOICE...THUNDER WORDS
Discusses the role of the oral tradition in modern Native American literature. Includes interviews with storytellers and other experts. 1990. 60 minutes, color. Video. NAPBC.

THE DIVIDED TRAIL: A NATIVE AMERICAN ODYSSEY
Jerry Aronson & Michael Goldman
Follows the lives of three Chippewa as they moved from various stages of activism and discontent into vocational alternatives. 1977. 30 minutes, color. Purchase: 16mm, $495; Video, $345; Rental, $42.50. PHOENIX. Rental: Video, $19.65. IU; 16mm, $24.25. UMN

DO WE WANT US TO?
The story about the heritage of the Tlinget Indians. 1979. Grades 7 and up. 20 minutes, color. Video. NAC. Rental: $10. UCT.

DOCTOR, LAWYER, INDIAN CHIEF
Carol Geddes, Director
Gail Valaskakis, Narrator
Focuses on five Native Indian women from across Canada; each talks about her personal dif ficulties in getting to where she is today, and about her life experiences. Includes: Sophie Pierre, the chief of St. Mary's Band in B.C.; Lucille McLeod, job-counselor for native women; Margaret Joe, the first native women to have become a minister in the Yukon government; Corrine Hunt, of the Kwakiutl Nation, operates the hydraulic equipment on a commercial fishing boat of f the coast of B.C.; and Roberta Jamieson, Canada's first native Indian woman lawyer. 1987. 29 minutes, color. Purchase: 16mm, $550; VHS, $250. Rental: $60. NFBC.

DREAM DANCES OF THE KASHIA POMO
Clyde B. Smith, Producer
Pomo women dance the Bole Maru nearly a century after it first evolved, blending the native Kaksu cult with the Maru or dream religion. Five dances are shown. The shaman expresses her religious beliefs in her own words. 1964. 30 minutes, color. Purchase: 16mm, $600; video, $195. Rental: $50. UC. Rental: IU & PSU.

DREAMSPEAKER
An emotionally disturbed boy runs away from an institution and is adopted by an old Indian shaman. The Indian vision of life and death are reviewed. 1977. 75 minutes, color. Grades 9 and up. Rental, $42. PSU

THE DRUM
Alaska Native Human Resource Dev . Project
Shows a Native American ritual. Grades 4-12.
1987. 15 minutes, color . VHS. $260. NDM

THE DRUM IS THE HEART
Randy Croce, Producer
Narrated entirely by Indian participants, ranging
from children to elders, this film focuses on the
Blackfeet, Blackfoot, Blood and Peigan tribes that
make up the Blackfoot Nation at their celebrations,
speaking about their contemporary lives and traditional values. 1982. 29 minutes, color . Video.
Purchase: 3/4" - $120; 1/2" - $80. Rental: 3/4" -
$45; 1/2" - $30. IN.

THE DRUMMAKER
Presents an Ojibwa Indian, W illiam Bineshi Baker ,
Sr., on the Lac Court Oreilles Reservation in northern Wisconsin, one of the last of his people to
continue the art of drummaking. Step-by-step he
constructs a dance drum, and expresses his beliefs about tradition, as well as frustrations. 1978.
37 minutes, bxw. Purchase: 16mm, $390; VHS,
$175. Rental, 16mm, $22; VHS, $12.50. PSU.

THE DRUMMER
Thomas Vennum, Jr.
William Bineshi Baker , Jr., an Ojibwa, living on the
Lac Courte Oreilles Reservation in northern Wis-
consin constructs a drum step-by-step. 1978. 37
minutes, bxw. Purchase: 16mm. PSU.

DRUMS OF THE AMERICAN INDIAN
Suitable for practicing traditional dance steps.
Cassette, $12. CH.

THE DRUMS OF WINTER (UKSUUM CAUY AI)
Sarah Elder & leonard Kamerling
A dcoumentary exploring the traditional dance,
music and spiritual world of the Yup'ik Eskimo
people of Emmonak, a remote village at the mouth
of the Yukon River on the Bering Sea coast. 1988.
90 minutes, color . Purchase: 16mm, $1300; video,
$600. Rental: 16mm, $130; video, $80. DER.

THE EAGLE & THE CONDOR
KBYU-TV, Provo Utah, Producer
Examines the interaction between the Native
American cultures of North and South America.
Native American entertainers of BYU's Laminite
Generation tour South America performing and
discussing dif ferences and similarities in cultures.
1975. 29 minutes, color . Video. Purchase: $150;
Rental: $40. NAPBC.

THE EAGLE & THE MOON
Wango Weng, Director
An animated Haida story presenting elements of
Haida culture such as the class and their totem
poles. 1971. 10 minutes. 16mm. W ALL.

THE EARLY AMERICANS
Traces the rise of man from his arrival in North
America as an ice age wanderer , to builder of complex societies more than 2,000 years before Columbus. 1976. 42 minutes, color . Grades 9 and
up. Video. Rental, $18. UA & PSU.

THE EARLY AMERICANS, 1776
Daniel Wilson Productions
Describes the lifestyles of Americans west of the
Appalachians in 1776 in New Mexico, Hawaii,
Alaska & the Spanish Mission of California. Grades
7 and up. 28 minutes, color . Rental: $10. UCT .

EARLY MAN IN NORTH AMERICA
A film about early man in North America. 1972. 12
minutes. VHS. FILMS.

EARTH CIRCLES
Emphasizes the traditional closeness with nature
that is a fundamental aspect of Native American
life.Images are from W oodlands Indian prints &
photos of wildlife in natural habitat. Study guide
included. 10 minutes. VHS. $50. TOP.

THE EARTH IS OUR HOME
Elizabeth Patapof f, Producer/writer
Produced in cooperation with members of the
Burns Paiute tribe in Oregon to preserve a record
of their traditional way of life and skills. 1979. 29
minutes, color. 16mm & video. MP

EARTHSHAPERS
A look at the sacred mounds created by the W ood-
land Native people. Grades 7 and up. 14 minutes,
color. Video. NAPBC. Rental: $10. UCT .

EASTER IN IGLOOLIK: PETER'S ST ORY
Paulle Clark, Producer
A photographed look at Inuit life in a modern Arc-
tic community, Igloolik, in Canada's Northwest
Territories. 1987. Grades 7 and up. 24 minutes,
color. Purchase: 16mm, $495; V ideo, $350;
Rental: $50. BULL.

EDUCATIONAL VIDEO
Two videos in one. Time Journey - explores the
prehistoric time period of North America; and, Indian Diversity - examines the life of modern Indian cultures, Choctaw , Ponca, Pueblo, and Peo-
ria/Miami. Plus two Indian stories. Includes handbook. $14. CMM.

THE EIGHTH FIRE
National Council of Churches; PBS
Examines racism & treaty issues aimed at Wisconsin Chippewa, Pacific Northwest, & Lakota
tribal communities. The Eighth Fire is the final
prophecy of the Chippewa people that represent
the healing & bringing together of all races. Traditional Chippewa. 60 minutes, color . Video. Purchase: $20; rental: $10. HO.

THE ELDERS SPEAK OUT.."NOW I LISTEN
Elders from around the country speak out on the
needs of Native American, Native Alaskam & Native Hawaiian elders. 20 minutes. V ideo. Purchase:
$360; rental: $45. SH.

**ELLA MAE BLACKBEAR:
CHEROKEE BASKETMAKER**
Scott & Sheila Swearingen, Producer/directors
Fran Ringold, Narrator
Ella Mae Blackbear practices the ancient art of
Cherokee basketmaking as it has survived in Okla-
homa after the Cherokees' removal to the Indian
Territory in the late 1830's. 1982. 25 minutes, color .
Video. FC.

EMERGENCE
Barbara Wilk, Producer/writer/animator
Tells the story of the events leading to the entrance
of the Dineh, the Navajo people, onto the surface
of this earth through a number of underworlds.
The traditional chants heard in the film are versions of the origin myths sung as part of certain
Navajo healing rituals. 1981. 14 minutes. Color
animation. 16mm, video. Purchase: VHS, $89; 3/
4", $119. CC & PR.

**EMERGENCE: A GRASS ROOTS ACCOUNT
OF INDIAN ACTIVISM**
Walter Verbanie
Documents how the Potawatomi in Kansas lost
lands through disadvantageous treaties and divi-
sions in the tribe between members of the Mis-
sion and Prairie bands. 1977. 35 minutes. 16mm.
MAI.

THE EMERGING ESKIMO
Deals with the impact of the white man upon the
native Eskimos. 15 minutes. Grades 1-8. Rental.
UK.

THE ENCHANTED ARTS: PABLITA VELARDE
Irene-Aimee Depke, Producer/director
Presents a portrait of Santa Clara Pueblo, Pablita
Velarde, one of the first Indian women to pursue
painting professionally . 1977. 28 minutes, color .
Video. DEPKE.

**END OF THE TRAIL: THE
AMERICAN PLAINS INDIANS**
Surveys the westward movement in America during the last century and the tragic impact of that
movement on the American Indians. 1967. Grades
6 and up. 53 minutes, b&w . 16mm. CRM. Rental:
IU, UA, UCT & UMN.

ESKIMO ARTIST - KENOJUAK
John Geeney , Director
Inuit artist Kenojuak shows the sources of her inspiration and methods used to transfer her carvings to stone. 1964. 20 minutes, color . Grades 7
and up. Purchase: 16mm, $410; and video, $300.
Rental, $50. NFBC. Rental, $17. UK and PSU.

ESKIMO CHILDREN
Portrays the activities of a typical Eskimo family
living on Nunivak Island of f the Alaskan coast.
1941. 11 minutes, bxw. Grades 4 and up. In English & Spanish. 16mm. Rental only . IU, UA & UK.

ESKIMO: FIGHT FOR LIFE
Asen Balikci, Advisor and Narrator
Shows the careful division of tasks among the different members of a group of Netsilek Eskimos
camped together during the winter seal hunting
season. 1970. Grades 7 and up. 51 minutes.
16mm. EDC & UW .

ESKIMO HUNTERS
Presents the life of the Eskimos who live in the
cold areas of Northwestern Alaska. 1949. 21 minutes, bxw. 16mm. Rental only . IU & UK.

THE ESKIMO IN LIFE & LEGEND
Shows how the Inuit's way of life, his legends, and
his art of stone carving are interrelated. 1960. 22
minutes. Grades 7 and up. Rental. EB, UA.

THE ESKIMO SEA HUNTERS
How Eskimo people live in regions where the
weather is always cold. 1949. 20 minutes/bxw.
Rental. UK.

ESKIMOS: A CHANGING CUL TURE
Wayne Mitchell
Examines the lives of two generations of Inuit
Eskimos who live on Nunivak Island in the Bering
Sea off the coast of Alaska. 1971. 17 minutes,
color. Grades 4 and up. Purchase: 16mm, $355;
video, $225. Rental, $53. PHOENIX. Rental only ,
IU & BYU.

THE ESKIMOS OF POND INLET
Hugh Brody
Studies the Inuits (Eskimos) of Pond Inlet, Baffin Island. 1977. 52 minutes, color . Video. Purchase: FI. Rental: $19. PSU.

ESTE MVSKOKE/THE MUSCOGEE PEOPLE
Marty Fulk & Gene Hamilton, Assoc. producers
Gary Robinson, Script
Tim Bigpond, Narrator
Beginning with the "origin of clans," this program provides an overview of the history , culture, and modern achievements of the Creek Nation. 1985. 24 minutes, color. Video. MCN & ODE.

THE ETERNAL DRUM
Don Priest, Producer
Looks at the social & spiritual significance of the contemporary American Indian Pow W ow & explains the traditions & the altruistic foundations of the American Indian societies. Grades 6 and up. 25 minutes. VHS. $195. NDM

EVERY DAY CHOICES:
ALCOHOL & AN ALASKA TOWN
Sarah Elder, Producer/director/editor
Shows how insidious, destructive, and pervasive the problem of alcohol is in native communities in the north, Yup'ik Eskimo villages in the Bethel, Alaska area. The film addresses stereotyped ideas of Native American alcoholism. 1985. 93 minutes, color. 16mm & video. NH.

EXCAVATION OF MOUND 7
Archaeology work in the field and in the lab to piece together the mysteries of the Pueblo Indians of New Mexico. 1973. 44 minutes. VHS, U-matic. NAC.

THE EXILES
Kent Mackenzie, Producer
Classic depiction of one anguished but typical night in the lives of three young American Indians who have left the reservation and come to live in downtown Los Angeles. 1961. 72 minutes, bxw . 16mm & video. Purchase: $250; rental: $75. UC. Rental: UA, UCLA, UMN, UK, IU & PSU.

EXPEDITION ARIZONA:
MISSIONS OF OLD ARIZONA
Reviews the buildings of San Xavier del Bac which is still used by the Papago people after 260 years, and the contributions of Father Kino to Indian culture. 1960. 27 minutes, bxw . Rental. UA.

EXPEDITION ARIZONA:
SHARDS OF THE AGES
Shows three ancient cultures: the Hohokam of the desert, the Mogollon of the mountains, and the Anasazi of the plateau regions of Arizona. 1960. 27 minutes, bxw . Rental. UA.

EYANOPAPI: THE HEART OF SIOUX
Details the historical and religious significance of the South Dakota Black Hills to the Sioux Nation. Grades 9 and up. 30 minutes. Purchase: VHS, $250; 3/4", $280. CC.

EYES OF THE SPIRIT
Corey Flintoff, Producer/writer
Alexie Isaac, Director/camera
Ina Carpenter, Narrator
Documents the work of a group of dancers, the Bethel Native Dancers, and three master carvers, in preserving and teaching Yup'ik Eskimo traditions and reviving the use of masks in Native dancing. 1983. 30 minutes. Color . VHS. $24.95. KYUK.

THE FACE OF WISDOM:
STORIES OF ELDER WOMEN
Catherine Busch-Johnston, Producer/Director
hosted by Julie Harris
Series of 8 videotapes, including one entitles: "Nellie Red Owl," a Native American elder of the Sioux tribe of South Dakota. Born only 16 years after her tribe's massacre at W ounded Knee, she lives with the conviction that her land & native traditions must never again be compromised. 1993. 30 minutes, color. Video. Purchase: $125. PHOENIX.

FACE TO FACE
Contains 5 extended interviews with Native Americans living with AIDS. Each discusses various aspects of their lives. A discussion guide is priovidd with the video. 47 minutes. VHS, $100. NNA.

FACES OF CULTURE: 22 - NEW ORLEANS' BLACK INDIANS: A CASE STUDY IN THE ARTS
Follows the Black Indian tribes of New Orleans, a blend of American Indians and blacks. 1983. 30 minutes, color. Video. Rental, $14. PSU.

THE FAITHKEEPER
Betsy McCarthy, Producer/director
Relates the guding philosophy of Native Americans to our own today. Bill Moyers is the guest of Oren Lyons, who taks about the past and future of Native American peoples. L yons is chief of the Turtle Clan of the Onondaga Nation and a prominenet member of the environmental movement. He describes how the U.S. democracy was modelled on the Iroquois Federation; discusses respect for nature; Native American prophecies about the environmental disasters we now face; and recounts the legends of his clan. 1992. 58 minutes, color. Video. Purchase: $29.95. MFV .

FAMILY LIFE OF THE NAVAJO INDIANS
Fries, Kluckhohn & W oolf, Producers
Highlights some of the ways in which the Navajo child develops into adulthood. 1943. 31 minutes, bxw. 16mm. Rental, $15. NYU & UT .

A FAMILY OF LABRADOR
Kent Martin, Director
A story of corporate development and changing ways of life for Indian, Inuit and people of mixed ancestry. 1978. 59 minutes, color . Video. $27. NFBC.

FEATHERS
Larry Littlebird, W riter;
Frank Marrero (WGBH), Producer
Dramatizes personal and social problems encountered by teenagers over how far they , as Indians, should go in joining the mainstream of American life. Emphasizes the closeness of family and community life. 1980. 30 minutes, color . Video. WGBH.

FEDERAL INDIAN LAW
Joel Freedman; Joan Kaehl, W riter
Traces the development of federal Indian law through treaties, statutes, and court decisions. By using real life examples, it illustrates the impact that federal Indian law can have on tribal economics and community lifestyles, and how law can be made to work for your tribe. Narrated by Kirke Kickingbird, Kiowa attorney and founder of the Institute for the Development of Indian Law . 1980. 19 minutes. 16mm. IDII

THE FEMININE: ANCIENT VISION, MODERN WISDOM
Wabun Wind
Discusses matriarchy, patriarchy, women's power, moon cycles and menstrual cycles, stereotyping of women, sexuality , relationships, and raising children. 65 minutes. V ideo. Purchase: $29.95. BTP & CH.

THE FIGHTING CHEYENNE
Depicts the Cheyenne Indians' battles with white travelers on the trail. Relates the historic tale of Dull Knife and his Cheyenne band. 30 minutes. 16mm. Rental. UT .

FINDING THE CIRCLE: AMERICAN INDIANB DANCE THEATRE
Native American dancing - its colors & sacred ritual. 56 mins.color . VHS. Purchase: $36. CH.

FIRES OF SPRING
Henry T. Lewis, Ph.D., W riter/Producer
Shows how, among the Slavey and Beaver tribes of northern Alberta, Canada, fire was used to carefully maintain and improve selected habitats of plants, game and furbearing animals. 1980. 33 minutes. Purchase: 16mm, $250 (Canadian); video, $125. BINS. Rental: 16mm, $17.50. PSU; $20.50, UMN.

THE FIRST AMERICAN MELTING POT
The gradual arrival of new Indian groups on the Plains and their clash with bison-hunting horse culture. 1981. 30 minutes, color . Video. KS.

THE FIRST AMERICANS
Story of Raymond Tracey, a young Indian man trying to get back to his roots & determine who the American Indians are. Grades 3-8. Produced in 1989 by Children's Television International & American Indian Heritage Foundation. In six 15-minute programs. $29.95 each, $131.70/set. Teacher's Guide, $2. GPN.

THE FIRST AMERICANS
Studies the major Indian tribes of the U.S.- their customs, culture and the land that belonged to them. Students will explore the special characteristics of individual tribes. Grades 4-6. 1988. 60 minutes. Video. Purchase: $132. Also available as filmstrips and cassettes. TA.

THE FIRST AMERICANS
In two parts. Part I: And Their Gods-- (20 minutes, color) The migration of people into the Americas and the eventual setting and dif ferentiating of these people into tribes. 1 1 minutes. Part II: Some Indians of the Southlands-- (32 minutes, color) Depicts customs & beliefs of certain Indians in the southern half of U.S.: Natchez, the Moundbuilders, the Hopi, Zuni and Navajo. Grades 4-9. 1969. Purchase: 16mm, Part 1-$220; Part 2-$300; V ideo, 2 parts, $250. IFF; UT - 16mm rental, $20. Rental only, 16mm. IU & UCT.

THE FIRST AMERICANS
Discusses the 30,000 years of cultural development of the American Indian. 1979. 30 minutes. 3/4" U-matic. CET.

THE FIRST AMERICANS-SOME INDIANS OF THE SOUTHLAND
The customs, beliefs and history that shaped the daily patterns of life in the early cultures of the Natchez, the "Moundbuilders," the Hopi, the Zuni, and the Navajo. 1976. 18 minutes, color . Grades 7 and up. 16 mm. Rental, $14. IU.

FIRST FRONTIER
Chronicles the long process of defeat and destruction of the Native American community beginning with the 1540 penetration into North America by DeSoto and his forces, then the French and British. Made with the cooperation of the Mississippi Band of Choctaw and the Poarch Band of Creek Indians. 58 minutes, color . Video. Purchase: $250. BE.

THE FIRST NORTHWESTERNERS:
THE ARCHAEOLOGY OF EARLY MAN
  Louis and Ruth Kirk, Producers
Examines the first northwest environment of more than 10,000 years ago and the first humans known to have lived there. 1979. 29 minutes, color . Purchase: 16mm, $425; beta, $225; VHS, $215. UW .

FIRST PEOPLES
Explain how ancient people came to North America and compare their lifestyles before Europeans arrived. Myths & legends are included. Grades 4-8. 15 minutes. VHS, $125. AIT.

A FISHING PEOPLE: THE TULALIP TRIBE
  Heather Oakson
Tells the story of their history as a fishing people and provides an overview of the tribe's current involvement with fishing as an industry . 1980. 17 minutes, color. The TT.

FOLKLORE OF THE MUSCOGEE
(CREEK) PEOPLE
  Rex Daugherty, Exec. producer
  Gary Robinson, W riter
Host Dr. Ruth Arrington (Creek Nation) describes the nature of folklore within Creek culture, and explains the breakdown of folklore into three categories: legends, myths and fables. Grades 3-12. 1983. 29 minutes, color . Video. Purchase: $150; Rental: $40. MCN & NAPBC.

FOLLOWING THE STAR
Story of Russian Orthodox Christmas as practiced by the Yup'ik Eskimos of the Kuskokwim River Delta. 1987. 30 minutes, color . VHS. $24.95. KYUK.

FONSECA: IN SEARCH OF COYOTE
  Mary Louise King & Fred Aronow, Producers
Noted Native American artist Harry Fonseca relates the development of his "Coyote" series of paintings and drawings; shows how Fonseca's anthropomorphic coyote grew out of traditional North American India art forms and legends surrounding the famous "trickster ." 1983. 30 minutes, color. Video. Purchase: $95; rental, $50. UC. Rental: $16. UMN.

FOREST SPIRITS
  NEWIST, Producer
A series of seven 30-minute programs on the Oneida & Menominee tribes of W isconsin. 1: To Keep a Heritage Alive—Oneida children learn their native tongue, religious code and moral ethic. 2: The Learning Path--The educational system and the Native American. 3: Land Is Life—Documents Oneida's troubles over land. 4: Ancestors Of Those Yet Unborn—Menominee lifestyle. 5: Living W ith Tradition—Menominee traditions and reaf firmation of heritage. 6 & 7: Dreamers With Power--Part 1: Explores stereotypes and truths about Menominee Reservation life; and Part 2: Menominee's history . Grades 4 and up. 1975-76. Color . Video. Purchase: $350/series; $65/program. Rental: $17.50/program. Teacher's Guide, $1. NAPBC & GPN.

FOREVER IN TIME: THE
ART OF EDWARD S. CURTIS
  Robert W. Mull, Producer
Curtis (1868-1952), one of the world's foremost photographers, captured in photos and on film the culture and lifestyle of the American Indian. He recorded tribal chants, narratives of Indian life and vocabulary translations. This documentary chronicles Curtis's career , featuring interviews with surviving family members, and blending his motion picture footage, sound recordings and photographic portraits, and an original music score. 1990. 50 minutes, color & bxw . Video. Purchase: $295; rental, $75. CG. Rental: $20. UMN.

FORGET THE FISH...CULTURAL ASPECTS
OF NURSING CARE FOR NAVAJOS
Reality-based story about a new nurse, Ann Davis, and her experiences with a Navajo patient & his wife. Her encounter with a medicineman helps her learn how to work with Navajo medicine people within the hospital setting. 1984. 25 minutes, color . Video. Rental: $18.50. UMN.

THE FORGOTTEN AMERICAN
A documentary filmed in the Southwest and in the urban Indian communities of Los Angeles and Chicago. Shows the impoverishment of the American Indian, his loss of identity and self-respect. 1968. 25 minutes, color . 16mm. Purchase/rental. MAI-CFV. Rental: PSU, UA, UCT & UCLA.

FORGOTTEN FRONTIER
  KAET-TV Phoenix, Producer
Documents Spanish mission settlements of southern Arizona, and the conversion and teaching of skills to Indians. 1976. 30 minutes, color . Video. Rental, $40/week. NAPBC.

FORT PHIL KEARNEY: THE HATED
POST ON THE LITTLE PINEY
A tour of Fort Phil Kerney , Fetterman Hill and the Wagon Box Fight, where the Sioux under Red Cloud clashed with the U.S. Army for control of northern W yoming's Powder River Country and the Bozeman Trail. 30 minutes. V ideo, $30. OAP.

FORTY-SEVEN CENTS
  Lee Callister & W endy Carrel, Producers
Focuses on the land claims of the Pit River Indians in northern California and the processes by which Indians are unfairly treated. 1973. 25 minutes, bxw. 16mm & video. Purchase: $95; rental: $50. UC & CG. Rental: 16mm, $14.75. UMN.

FOSTER CHILD
  Gil Cardinal, Director
At age 35, Gil Cardinal searches for his natural family and an understanding of the circumstances that led to his coming into foster care as an infant. This is a documentary about the process of that discovery and a renewed sense of his Metis culture. 1988. 43 minutes, color . Purchase: 16mm, $650; video, $300. Rental: $70. NFBC.

THE FOUR CORNERS: A
NATIONAL SACRIFICE AREA?
  Christopher McLeod, Glenn Switkes
  & Randy Hayes, Producers/directors
The Four Corners area of Utah, Colorado, New Mexico, and Arizona is rich in the history for Native Americans and also rich in coal, oil shale, and uranium. This film raises questions about the "hidden costs" of energy development in the Southwest. Features interviews with region's inhabitants and leaders - Navajo uranium miners, tribal of fic-ers, governors, ranchers, energy company spokesmen, and federal government of ficials. 1983. Grades 9 and up. 58 minutes, color . Purchase: 16mm, $850; V ideo, $450; Rental: $85. BULL.

FOUR CORNERS OF EARTH
  Bureau of Florida Folklife & WFSU-TV
Explores the roles and culture of Seminole women whose traditional values keep pace with the forces of today's technology . 1985. 30 minutes, color . Rental: $40/week. NAPBC.

FRANZ BOAS, 1852-1942
  T.W. Timreck
A profile of Franz Boas, his work with Northwest American Indian tribes and his teaching of anthropology. 1980. 59 minutes, color . Purchase: Beta or VHS, $250; rental, $90/week. PBS. Purchase: 16mm, $600; rental, $60. Educator's guide. DER. Rental: 16mm, $24. PSU. V ideo renta!, $14.65. IU.

FROM THE ELDERS
  Katrina W aters, Producer & Director
A series of films from the Alaska Native Heritage Film Project presenting the stories and thoughts of one of three highly regarded Alaska Native elders. Provides a window of understanding into the Eskimo experience. Joe Sun - Immaluuraq (Joe Sun in English) tells of the legendary Inupiaq prophet, Maniilaq, who was his great uncle. 19 minutes, color. Purchase: 16mm, $390, video, $200. Rental: 16mm, $35, video, $30. In lirgu's Time - an elder from the Siberian Yup'ik Eskimo village of Hambell on St. Lawrence Island. Purchase: 16mm, $390, video, $200. Rental: 16mm, $35, video, $30. The Reindeer Thief - Pelaasi, an elder from Gambell speaks Siberian Yup'ik and tells about Chukchi, the Reindeer People. 13 minutes, color. Purchase: 16mm, $260, video, $150. Rental: 16mm, $25, video, $20. 1988. DER.

FROM THE FIRST PEOPLE
  Leonard Kamerling and Sarah Elder
Shows change and contemporary life in Shungnak, a village on the Kobuk River in northwestern Alaska. An old man shares his feelings about the changes he has seen. 1976. 45 minutes. Purchase: 16mm, $650; video, $400; Rental, $60; video, $40. DER. Rental: 16mm & video, $22.50. PSU.

FROM HAND TO HAND: BETHEL
NATIVE ARTIST PROFILES
  Gretchen McManus, Producer/camera/editor;
  Martha Larson, Narrator
Collection of short profiles of Yup'ik Eskimo artists and their work. Features practitioners who discuss the place of their art in traditional Yup'ik culture. Storyknifing, Lucy Beaver , Skin Sewer, Nick Charles, Carver, and Uncle John, Carver . 1985. 45 minutes. In Yup'ik or English. VHS. $24.95. KYUK.

FULL CIRCLE
  Maria Gargiulo & John de Graaf
Documentary which relates the success story of Native American tribes of W ashington state by depicting the diverse lives of tribal elders, business leaders, traditional artists, environmental activists, salmon fisherman, and innovative teachers. 1990. 50 minutes, color . Video. Purchase: $295; rental, $60. UC.

GAME OF STAVES
Clyde B. Smith, Producer

Pomo boys demonstrate the game of staves, a variation of the dice game using six staves and 12 counters, played by most of the Indian tribes of North America. Explains the individualized pyrographic ornamentation of the staves and counters. 1962. 10 minutes, color . Purchase: 16mm, $220; video, $195. Rental: $45. UC. Rental only: PSU.

GANNAGARO
Alexandra J. Lewis-Lorentz, Producer

The Seneca, one of the five Iroquois nations of New York State, lived at Gannagaro, an ancient Seneca village located just outside of V ictor, New York. It was destroyed by the French in July , 1687. This film pieces together life at this 17th century Seneca village. 1986. 30 minutes, color . Video. Purchase: $150; Rental: $40. NAPBC.

GATHERING UP AGAIN: FIESTA IN SANTA FE
Jeanette DeBouzek, Director

Examines the Santa Fe Fiesta; documents preparation for the fiesta; shows the formation of ethnic identities, the ongoing impact of the cultures of conquest on Native Americans in the region. 1992. Grades 7-12. Purchase: $275; rental: $75. CG.

GATECLIFF: AMERICAN INDIAN ROCK-SHELTER
Led by Dr. David Hurst Thomas, amateur archaeologists attempt to discover the identity of ancient inhabitants of this shallow rock-shelter in Monitor Valley, Nevada. Teacher's guide. 1974. 24 minutes. Purchase: 16mm, $345; video, $315. NGS.

GERONIMO & THE APACHE RESISTANCE
Dscendants of those Apaches who fought so long ago tell their story , explaining the mysteries of Apache power. The story of Geronimo and his people is told, and his battles and broken promises that provoked them are discussed. 1989. 60 minutes, color. Video. Purchase: $19.95. CAN. $59.95. PBS.

GERONIMO: THE FINAL CAMPAIGN
Host Will Rogers, Jr . draws viewers into Geronimo's fascinating history . Grades 9 and up. 30 minutes, color . Purchase: VHS, $250; 3/4", $280. CC. Rental: V ideo, $17.75. IU.

GERONIMO JONES
A young American Indian of Apache & Papago descent, living on a reservation with his mother and grandfather , explores the conflicts he faces, torn between pride in his heritage and his future in modern American society. 1970. 21 minutes, color. 16mm & video. Purchase: $250; rental, $75. COR. Rental: HO, UCT & UMN.

THE GIFT OF THE SACRED DOG
Cecily Truett, Producer; Larry Lancit, Director
LeVar Burton, Series host
Michael Ansara, Narrator

The narrator reads the book Gift of the Sacred Dog, written & illustrated by Paul Goble, as its illustrations are shown, presenting a tale of ancient times told with minor variations by several tribes of the Great Plains, in which a boy brings to his people the first horse, known to some tribes as the "sacred dog." A documentary sequence presents Dan Old Elk and his family who live at Crow Agency, Montana, & shows them perparing for and participating in the festivities of the annual Crow Indian Fair, including tipi raising and powwow dancing. 1983. 30 minutes, color . Video. GPN.

GIFT OF THE WHALES
A Native American boy discovers a naturalist studying whales of f the coast of his small Alaskan village.Grade 1-5. 30 minutes. V ideo. $19.95. VC.

GIFTS OF SANTA FE
Marguerite J. Moritz, Producer

Tells the story of the Santa Fe Indian Market, the largest and most prestigious competition of Native Amerian artists in the world. 1988. 22 minutes, color. Video. Purchase: $150; Rental: $40. NAPBC

GIRL OF THE NAVAJOS
Norman Nelson

A story about two Navajo girls who become friends. 1977. Grades K-6. 15 minutes, color . 16mm & video. Purchase: video, $250. COR. Rental: 16mm, $16.50. UMN.

GIVEAWAY AT RING THUNDER
Jan Wahl, Producer/writer
Christine Lesiak, W riter/narrator/editor

Documents a giveaway held during the annual Ring Thunder powwow on the Rosebud Sioux Reservation in South Dakota. The Menard family is celebrating the giving of Indian names to three children. Opens with archival photographs of Lakota Sioux life and a reflection on traditional customs in earlier times. 1982. 15 minutes, color . Video. NETV.

GLOOSCAP
India legend of how humans and animals were created to live in peace and plenty , and how evil intervened. 26 minutes, color . Video, Purchase: $89.95. FH.

GLOOSKAP
Recounts the Canadian Indian legend of the creation, as told by Glooskap, Father of all Indian children. He shows them how to survive and how to live in peace with man and nature. 1971. 12 minutes, color. Grades 4-9. Purchase: 16mm, 260; Video, $160; rental, $37. PHOENIX.

GONE WEST
In Two Parts: Part I - The Lewis and Clark Expedition; Part II - The gold rush begins a mass migration west. Both parts show the af fect of white migrations on Indian nations. 1972. 26 minutes each. Rental. UK.

A GOOD DAY TO DIE
Old Army Press, Producer

Computer graphics combine with aerial photographs to show Custer Battlefield; scenes from the Indian village; re-created by re-enactors including Sioux & Cheyenne Indians. 60 minutes, color. Video. Purchase: $25. OAP .

GOOD MEDICINE
Chris Gaul, W riter/Producer

Documentary on Native American medicine, narrated by John Bolindo, Kiowa-Navajo who was at the time of the film the executive director of the National Indian Health Board. Emphasizes the holistic nature of Indian medicine. Settings include the Rosebud and Navajo Reservations. 1979. 59 minutes, color . Video. Purchase: WQED; 16mm, LU.

THE GOOD MIND
Robert Stiles, Producer
Steve Charleston, Narrator

Explores the similarities between Christian and Native American beliefs and practices of traditional Native American tribes in the words and life styles of contemporary Indians. 1983. 30 minutes. VHS, U-matic. NAPBC.

GRAND CANYON
Dr. Joseph Wood Krutch journeys on mule down the canyon to the Colorado River . The Havasupai Indian settlement at Bright Angel Creek is compared with the outside world. 1966. 26 minutes. Rental. UA.

GREAT AMERICAN INDIAN HEROES
The personal stories of leaders and chiefs who won the trust of their people and inspired their tribes in war and peace. Includes Tecumseh, Osceaola, Black Hawk, Pontiac, Chief Joseph, Sitting Bull, Geronimo, and Joseph Brant. Grades 4-6. 1988. V ideo. Purchase: $176. Also available as filmstrips and cassettes. TA.

THE GREAT MOVIE MASSACRE
Narrated by Wil Sampson

Explores the motion picture image of the Indian warrior. 1982. VHS, Beta, U-matic. VT .

THE GREAT SPIRIT WITHIN THE HOLE
Chris Spotted Eagle, KTCA, Producer/director

A narrative around the words of Indian people in our nation's prisons. The movie demonstrates how freedom of Indian religious practice aids in rehabilitation. Narrated by Will Sampson, with original soundtrack by Buf fy Sainte-Marie. 1983. 60 minutes, color. Purchase: video, 3/4" - $160; 1/2" - $110. Rental, 3/4" - $60; 1/2" - $40. IN. Rental: 16mm, $16. UMN.

THE GREEN CORN FESTIVAL
Gary Robinson, Producer/director
Mike Bigler, Narrator

Describes and explains the Green Corn Festival ceremonial activities practiced today by the Creek Indians of Oklahoma. Opens with archival footage shot in the 1940's, underscoring the longevity of the ceremonial. 1982. 20 minutes, color . Video. MCN.

HAA SHAGOON
Joe Kawaky, Producer

Documents a day of Tlingit Indian ceremony held along the Chilkoot River , ancestral home of the Chilkoot Tlingit of Alaska. Ceremony consists of time-honored prayers, songs and dances. 1983. 29 minutes, color. English & Tlingit with English subtitles. Purchase: 16mm, $580; video, $195. Rental, $50. UC.

HAD YOU LIVED THEN: LIFE IN THE WOODLANDS BEFORE THE WHITE MAN CAME
Indians show how there ancestors lived before the white man came and how deer were important in the survival of the Indians.1976. 12 minutes. VHS, U-matic. AIMS.

HAIDA CARVER
Richard Gilbert, Director

Shows a young Haida Indian artist on the Pacific coast of Canada shaping miniature totems from argillite, a soft dark slate. 1964. Grades 9 and up. 12 minutes, color . Purchase: 16mm, 225; video, $195. Rental: IFB, UA & UCLA.

HANDS OF MARIA
A pictorial study of Maria Martinez, an Indian potter, and of her work which has brought fame to her and to her pueblo. 1968. 17 minutes. Rental. UA.

HAROLD OF ORANGE
Dianne Brennan, Producer
Richard Weise, Director
Gerald Vizenor, Writer
Confronts with ironic humor the issue of the inter-connection between reservation communities and the powerful bureaucracies on which they often must rely, presenting both a group of young Indian "tricksters" & a well-intentioned, though woefully paternalistic, white institution. 1983. 32 minutes, color. 16mm & Video. FIC. Rental: $10. HO.

HASKIE
Jack L. Crowder
The story of a young Navajo Indian boy, who wants to become a medicine man but instead attends a boarding school to meet the requirements of compulsory education. 1970. 25 minutes, color. 16mm. Rental, $15.90. IU.

HAT CREEK
Amarcord Productions
Hat Creek, a small community near Lillooet, British Columbia, Canada faces major environmental changes because of strip-mining and a coal-fired generating plant. Shows the affect it has had on the largely Indian population. 1981. 28 minutes, color. Video. CFDW.

HAUDENOSAUNEE: WAY OF THE LONGHOUSE
Robert Stiles & John Akin, Producers/directors
Oren Lyons, Narrators
Documents the traditional culture of the six nations of the Iroquois Confederacy, the League of Haudenosaunee. Also documents the resiliency of Iroquois culture in the face of pressures to assimilate. 1982. Grades 6-9. 13 minutes, color. Purchase: 16mm, $245, video, $160; rental, 16mm, $35. ICARUS.

HEALING THE HURTS
Phil Lucas, Producer
The people of Alkali Lake, Albert, Canada participate in a ceremonial healing process focused on healing the hurt and shame of residential schools across North America. 60 minutes. Video. Purchase: $150. FOUR.

HEALTH CARE CRISIS AT ROSEBUD
South Dakota ETV, Producer
Explores and offers some possible solutions to a serious shortage of physicians on the Rosebud Sioux Reservation in South Dakota. 1973. 20 minutes. Color. Video. Rental: $40/week. NAPBC.

HEART OF THE EARTH SURVIVAL SCHOOL and CIRCLE OF THE WINDS
Chris Spotted Eagle, Producer/director
Presents aspects of contemporary Native American culture for Indians living in the Minneapolis-St. Paul area. Heart of the Earth Survival School (1980) documents an alternative Native American school in Minneapolis; and Circle of the Winds (1979) documents a Native American student art exhibition. 32 minutes, color. Video. IN.

HEART OF THE NORTH
Presents the ideas & traditions of five contemporary artists from the Woodlands & Plains in their own words & images. Issues impoertant to Indian artists are discussed while the five are shown quarrying, carving, painting, and designing. Includes study guide. 24 minutes. VHS. $50. TOP.

THE HEART OF WETONA
Chief's daughter is wronged by white man. 1918. 69 minutes, bxw. EG.

HER GIVEAWAY: A SPIRITUAL JOURNEY WITH AIDS
Mona Smith, Producer/director
A candid portrait of Carole Lafavor, member of the Ojibwe tribe, activist, mother, registered nurse & person with AIDS. 1988. 21 minutes, color. Video. Purchase: $195. WMM. Rental: $16. UMN.

HERITAGE
An overview of early Native American life, before Columbus. Introduces us to oral traditions of Indian people & through slides tells of the differences & similarities in Native art, music, and religion, before the time of Columbus. 28 minutes, color. Grades 9 and up. Video, Purchase: $55. UP.

HERITAGE IN CEDAR: NORTHWEST COAST: INDIAN WOODWORKING, PAST & PRESENT
Louis and Ruth Kirk
From Oregon to Alaska, tribesmen lived in houses built of cedar planks and traveled in canoes hollowed from cedar logs. This film explores the Northwest Coast Indian legacy by going to abandoned villages and to living villages, to archaeological digs and to museums. 1979. 29 minutes, color. Purchase: 16mm, $425; or VHS, $215. UW.

HERITAGE OF THE SEA: MAKAH INDIAN TREATY RIGHTS
Louis and Ruth Kirk
Examines fishing as the Makahs presently practice it, regard it, and view it historically. In two parts: Part I - Makah reminiscenses about the past and comments on the future of their tribal salmon management programs. Part II - Represents comments by Makah fisherman and elders. 29 minutes each, color. Purchase: 16mm, $425 each; beta, $225, or VHS, $215 each. UW.

HERMAN RED ELK: A SIOUX INDIAN ARTIST
South Dakota ETV, Producer; Bill Hopkins, Project Director
Red Elk speaks of his lifelong interest in art and of the influences of his grandfather's teachings. Points out the role of skin painting in Plains Indian history. 1975. 29 minutes, color. Video. Rental: $40/week. NAPBC.

HISATSINOM - THE ANCIENT ONES
The history of an Anasazi outpost, Kayenta. People & culture are discussed. A portrait of the Anasazi historical sites at the Navajo National Monument. Grades 7 and up. 24 minutes, color. Rental: $10. UCT.

HISTORY OF SOUTHERN CALIFORNIA
In two parts: Part I, From Prehistoric Times to the Founding of Los Angeles - major sequences include, prehistoric life, Indian economy, European explorations, and establishment of pueblos, missions and presidios; Part II, Rise and Fall of the Spanish and Mexican Influences. 1967. Grades 4-9. 17 minutes each. Rental. UA.

HOHOKAM: AT PEACE WITH THE LAND
Bill Land
The archaeologist Emil Haury discusses his excavations at the earliest Hohokam site, Snaketown, which dates from approximately 2,000 years ago, and their descendants, the Pima and Papago, who still live in the region near Phoenix, Arizona. 1976. 20 minutes, color. 16mm. UA.

HOME OF THE BRAVE
Helena Solberg-Ladd, Producer/director
David Meyer, Writer
This documentary examines the contemporary plight of Indian peoples of North and South America, focusing on the impact of development on native people, the crisis of identity, and the prospects for political organization to protect Indian lives and land. Includes interviews with numerous Indian leaders.1985. 53 minutes, color. Purchase: 16mm, $850; video, $595. Rental, $90. CG.

HONORABLE NATIONS
Chana Gazit & David Steward, Directors/writers
For 99 years the residents of Slamanca, a town in upstate New York, rented the land beneath their homes from the Seneca Nation for $1 a year under the terms of a lease agreement imposed by Congress. This documentary charts the conflicts that arose when the lease's impendent expiration pitted the town's citizenry against the Seneca Nation. 1991. 54 minutes, color. Video. Purchase: $395. FIL. Rental: $20. UMN.

HONORED BY THE MOON
Provides examples of traditional roles & beliefs of Indian women & men. Covers homosexuality & homophobia in the Indian community. 1989. 15 minutes, color. Video. Rental: $16. UMN.

THE HONOUR OF ALL
Phil Lucas, Producer/director
Two part series that recreates the story of the Alkali Lake Indian Band's heroic struggle to overcome & conquer its widespread alcoholism. Narrated by Andy Chelsea, Chief of the Alkali Lake Indian Band of British Columbia, Canada. 2 parts: Part 1: (56 minutes) examines the problem; Part 2: (43 minutes) outlines the community development process. 1987. Video. Purchase: $150/series; $75/prog. NAPBC & GPN. Rental: $10. HO.

THE HOPI
Museum of Northern Arizona, Producer
Scenes of family life, work and rituals as seen through the role of corn in Hopi daily life. Shows how communal values and survival skills that have kept their culture alive for centuries are passed on. 15 minutes, color. Purchase: $19.95. CAN.

THE HOPI INDIAN
Observes Hopi men and women in daily routines and in special celebrations, such as the secret Hopi wedding ceremony. Revised 1975. 11 minutes, color. Grades K-6. Purchase: 16mm, $270; video, $190. COR. Rental: 16mm, $16.50. UA, PSU & IU.

HOPI INDIAN ARTS & CRAFTS
1945 & 1975 Editions. Shows traditional skills as the Hopi work at weaving, basket-making, silversmithing and ceramics. Grades K-6. 11 minutes, color. Purchase: 16mm, $250; video, $175. Rental, $40. COR, IU & UA.

THE HOPI INDIAN & THE NAVAJO INDIANS
Documentary. 1925. 10 minutes, bxw. EG.

HOPI KACHINAS
Shows an artisan in the complete process of carving, assembling and painting a doll; also, Hopi life and dance. 1960. 10 minutes. 16mm. UA.

HOPI SNAKE DANCE
Preparation of dancers, handling of snakes, costumes and part of a dance. 1951. 10 minutes, bxw. 16mm. UW.

HOPI: SONGS OF THE FOURTH WORLD
Pat Ferrero, Producer/director
narrated by Ronnie Gilbert
The study of the Hopi that captures their deep spirituality and reveals their integration of art and daily life. In two parts: Part I - Story of emergence into 4th world; explanation of com (color and directions) and planting; Hopi courtship and marriage ceremonies; Hopi kachinas. Part II - Hopi religion; interviews with Hopi painter and potter; women's roles; child-raising and traditional education; games, clowns and Hopi humor . A study guide/resource book. 1983. Grades 4 and up. 16mm, 58 minutes, color . 30 minute version for high school audiences-video only . Purchase: $350. NDF. Rental. UN, UMN & UW .

THE HOPI WAY
Shelly Grossman; Mary Louise Grossman, W riter
The history of the Hopi is briefly discusses by David Mongnongyi who shows pictographs made by Hopi ancestors. Presents a concise picture of Hopi traditionalism and current threats to that way of life. 1972. Grades 4 and up. 23 minutes. 16mm. Purchase. FILMS. Rental, $16.20. UA.

HOPIIT
Victor Masayesva, Jr., Producer/director/camera; Ross Macaya & Victor Masayesva, Sr., Narrators
Provides an impressionistic view of a year in the Hopi community, including ordinary scenes of Hopi life. 1982. 15 minutes, color . Purchase: Video, 3/ 4" - $120, and 1/2" - $80; Rental: 3/4" - $45, 1/2" - $30. IN & IS. Rental: ATL.

HOPIS—GUARDIANS OF THE LAND
Dennis Burns, Producer
Explores the traditional Hopi way of life and the threat of men's desecration of the land and life they have known. 1971. 10 minutes, color . Purchase: 16mm, $150; VHS, $89. FF . Rental: $13. FF & UMN.

HOW BEAVER STOLE FIRE
Caroline Leaf
A retelling, through animation, of a Northwest American Indian legend of how the Animal People all worked together to capture fire from the Sky People. 1972. Grades K-4. 12 minutes, color . 16mm. Purchase: AIMS. Rental: UCT, BYU & UI.

HOW MAN ADAPTS TO HIS PHYSICAL ENVIRONMENT
The film uses as examples the Pueblo Indians, Navahos, and the early Caucasians. 1970. 20 minutes. Rental: UA & IU.

HOW PANTHER GOT TEAR MARKS
Presentation of a traditional Karuk story is told in both English & the Karuk language. Grades 4-6. 11 minutes. VHS. $59.95. K-T .

HOW TO BUILD AN IGLOO
Douglas Wilkinson, Director
Two Inuit Eskimos give a step-by-step demonstration of Igloo construction. 1950. Grades K-8. 1 1 minutes, bxw. Purchase: 16mm, $275; VHS, $200. Rental: $40. NFBC & SEF .

HOW THE WEST WAS WON... AND HONOR LOST
Ross Devenish, Producer
A re-enactment, using photographs, paintings and newspaper accounts, telling the story of the white man's treatment of American Indians in the westward push for land. Broken treaties, railroad building, decimation of the buffalo, and the massacre at Wounded Knee. 1970. 25 minutes, color . 16mm. PSU & IU.

HOW THE WEST WAS LOST
Document Associates and BBC, Co-Producers
Highlights the prime of Plains Indian civilization and focuses upon the temporary Indian ef fort to maintain a sense of their own identity . 1972. 26 minutes, color . Purchase: 16mm, $400; video, $340. Rental, $55 each. CG.

HOW THE WEST WAS LOST
Documentary of the epic struggle for the American West; witnesses the tragic plight of five Native American Nations: the Navajo, Nez Perce, Apache, Cheyenne & Lakota. In three volumes: Vol. 1 - Navajo & Nez Perce; V ol. 2 - Apache & Cheyenne; & Vol. 3 - Lakota & Northern Cheyenne. 100 minutes each, color . Video. Rental: $10 each; $25/set. HO.

HUNGER IN AMERICA
CBS, Producer
A researched study of hunger and malnutrition in the U.S., showing views of Navajo Indians in Arizona, as well as other impoverished groups. 1968. Grades 7 and up. 58 minutes, color . 16mm. Rental, $31. UT.

RICHARD HUNT CARVES A BEAR MASK
A Kwakiutl artist from British Columbia, carves a bear mask. Documents in detail the entire production process. 1988. 25 minutes, bxw . Video. Purchase: $70; rental, $20. UADA.

HUICHOL SACRED PILGRIMAGE TO WIRIKUTA
Larain, Boyll
Documentary following the anual pilgrimage and peyote hunt of the Huichol Indians of western Mexico. Focuses on the sacred sites, the traditional Huichol shamans and elders. Includes songs and music. 1991. 29 minutes, color . Video. Purchase: $195; rental, $50. UC.

HUNTERS & BOMBERS: THE INNU FIGHT BACK
The Innu, indigenous inhabitants of Labrador-Quebec in northeast Canada, are fighting back against the Dutch, German, and British air forces which use the region for supersonic low-level bomber training. 52 minutes, color . Video. Purchase: $149; rental: $75. FH.

HUPA INDIAN WHITE DEERSKIN DANCE
Portrays the 10-day deerskin ceremony still held by the Hupa Indians of northwestern California. 1958. Grades 4 and up. 1 1 minutes, color . 16mm. Rental: BARR & UCLA.

HUTEETL: KOYUKON MEMORIAL POTLATCH
Curt Madison, Producer/director/editor
Catherine Attla & Eliza Jones, Narrators
A documentary of an Athapascan Indian potlatch in interior Alaska. 1983. 60 minutes. Color . In English and Koyukon Athabascan with English subtitles. Video. Purchase: $150; Rental: $80. KYUK and NAPBC.

I AM DIFFERENT FROM MY BROTHER: DAKOTA NAME-GIVING
Tony Charles, Director
A real-life docu-drama depicting the Name-Giving Ceremony of three young Flandreau Dakota Sioux Indian children. 1981. Grades 3-9. 20 minutes, color. Video. Purchase: $150; Rental: $40/ week. NAPBC.

I HEARD THE OWL CALL MY NAME
Roger Gimbel, Producer
A story about how an Anglican priest, who with a short time to live learns acceptance of death from the Indians. 1974. Grades 7 and up. 78 minutes, color. 16mm. Rental: V ideo, $20; 16mm, $50.50. UA & UMN.

I KNOW WHO I AM
Sandra Sunrising Osawa, Producer
Focuses on cultural values important to Indian tribes of the Pacific coast and was shot on the Makah, Puyallup and Nisqually reservations. 1979. 28 minutes, color. Video. UP.

I WILL FIGHT NO MORE FOREVER
Richard T. Efron, Director
Stan Margulies, Producer
A dramatization of the struggle of the Nez Perce Indians and their leader Chief Joseph, who attempted to take his people to Canada to avoid being placed on a reservation. 1975. 106 minutes, color. 16mm. FILMS & UA. V ideo, $29.95. CH. Rental: HO & UCT.

I'D RATHER BE POWWOWING
George P. Horse Capture, Producer
Larry Littlebird, Director
Presents an unstereotyped portrait of a contemporary Indian, Al Chandler (a Gros V entre from the Fort Berthold Indian Reservation in North Dakota) a senior technical representative for a large corporation and explores the values that are central to his identity .Chandler and his son travel to a powwow celebration at the Rocky Boys Reservation near Havre, Montana. 1983. 27 minutes, color . 16mm & video. Purchase: $50. BB.

ICE PEOPLE
An anthropological study showing that the modern Eskimo must adapt again. 1970. Grades 6 and up. 23 minutes, color . 16mm. Rental: IU & UA.

IHANBLA WAKTOGLAG WACIPI
Henry Smith
A dance showcasing Solaris, a modern dance theatre company, and Sioux Indian dancers drawn from the nine reservations of the Lakota Nation in South Dakota. 1981. 60 minutes, color . Video. SO.

I'ISAW: HOPI COYOTE STORIES
Larry Evers, University of Arizona
With Helen Sekaquaptewa. In Hopi with English subtitles. 1978. 18 minutes. VHS. Purchase: $150. NR. Rental (with Nawatniwa: A Hopi Philosophical Statement) - two programs on one tape, $52.50. ATL.

THE IMAGE MAKER & THE INDIANS
George I. Quimby, Bill Holm and David Gerth
Shows how the famous pioneer cinematographer , Edward S. Curtis, made the first full-length documentary film of Native Americans among the Northwest Coast Indians of 1914. Edited and restored in 1973. 17 minutes; color/bxw . Purchase: 16mm, $275; and VHS, $165. UW .

IMAGES OF INDIANS
Robert Hagopian & Phil Lucas, Producers/Directors/W riters
A five-part series, narrated by Will Sampson, examines the stereotypes drawn by the movies and questions what the ef fect of the Hollywood image has been on the Indian's own self-image. (1) "The Great Movie Massacre" - Indian's warrior image. (2) "Heathen Injuns and the Hollywood Gospel" - The distortion and misrepresentation of Indian

religion and values in Hollywood movies. (3) "How Hollywood Wins the West" - Deals with the one-sided presentation of Indian history despite the frequent use of Indian culture in Hollywood films. (4) "The Movie Reel Indians" - The image of Indians as savage murderers is commented on by Dennis Banks & Vine Deloria. (5) "Warpaint and Wigs" - Examines how the movie, Nobel Savage and the Savage-Savage, has affected the Native American self-image. 1980. Curriculum package contains a curriculum guide, student resource pages, video, and other learning resources (map, books, posters). Video, 30 minutes each. $250. PLP. Video. Purchase: $56.95 each, $237.50 for series. FOUR, GPN & NAPBC.

IMAGINING INDIANS
Victor Masayesva, Jr.
Visits tribal communities in Arizona, Montana, New Mexico, South Dakota, Washington, and the Amazon. 1992. 60 minutes, color. 16mm & video. Purchase: $750; rental: $110. Video. Purchase: $245; rental: $60. DER.

IN THE BEST INTEREST OF THE CHILD
Will Sampson, Narrator
Documents the legal issues involved in Indian child welfare cases. Trys to educate the public to the Indian Child Welfare Act. 1981. Grades 9 and up. 15 minutes, color. 16mm. Purchase: 16mm, $390; Video, $360. Rental: $45. SH. Rental: $21. PSU.

IN THE HEART OF BIG MOUNTAIN
Captures an intimate portrait of the traumatic consequences of relocation on one Navajo family. Through Katherine Smith's eyes and words, as a Navajo matriarch, the viewer experiences life on one of the most remote and traditional places in Indian country - Big Mountain, Arizona. 1988. 28 minutes, color. Video. Purchase: $75. UP.

IN THE LAND OF THE WAR CANOES: KWAKIUTL INDIAN LIFE ON THE NORTHWEST COAST
Edward S. Curtis; Edited & Restored by George Quimby and Bill Holm
A saga of Kwakiutl Indian life filmed in 1914 in Vancouver Island, British Columbia, Canada. 43 minutes, bxw. Purchase: 16mm, $650; Beta, $425, VHS, $400. UW. Rental: 16mm, $26. UA & PSU.

IN OUR OWN BACKYARDS: URANIUM MINING IN THE U.S.
Pamela Jones & Susanna Styron
Explores the impact of uranium mining on the environment in the Southwest, and on the health of workers and nearby residents. 1981. Grades 7 and up. 29 minutes, color. Purchase: 16mm, $515; Video, $100; Rental: $50. BULL.

IN SEARCH OF THE LOST WORLD
Traces the origins of the lost civilizations of the Americas; tells the story of Indian cultures: complex, urbane & ancient. 1972. 52 minutes, color. 16mm. Rental. UA & UCLA.

IN THE WHITE MAN'S IMAGE
Covers the policies, methods, and tragic long-term consepquences of attempts to "civilize" Native Americans in the 1870s. 1992. 60 minutes, color. Video. Purchase: $59.95. NAPBC. Rental: $10. HO; $16. UMN.

INCIDENT AT OGLALA: THE LEONARD PELTIER STORY
Michael Apted, Director
Robert Redford, Narrator
Documents the 71-day siege of Wounded Knee in May 1973, covering actions taken by members of the American Indian Movements, and the federal authorities. 1991. 90 minutes, color. Video. SFMPC.

INDIAN AMERICA
The story of the American Indian and his desperate struggle against extinction. Indian activists, tribal leaders, and poor sheep herders tell about themselves & their heritage. 1970. Grades 4-adult. 80 mins, color. 16mm & video. Purchase: 16mm, $600; video, $350. SEF. Rental. UA & UMN.

INDIAN ART OF THE PUEBLOS
Bert Van Bork
An introductory survey of traditional art forms being produced by contemporary Pueblo artists of Arizona and New Mexico, including artists Blue Corn and Lucy Lewis. The film stresses that Pueblo artists and craftsmen are preserving their culture. 1976. 13 minutes. 16mm. EB.

INDIAN ARTIFACTS OF THE SOUTHWEST
Examines the arts and crafts of several Southwestern tribes, including: Zuni, Hopi and Navajo. Stresses the history and tradition which are apparent in the objects. 1972. 15 minutes. 16mm. Rental. IU.

INDIAN ARTISTS OF THE SOUTHWEST
Deals with the history of American Indian paintings and its rich heritage from petroglyphs to the modern artists. Shows techniques, symbolism and style. 1972. 15 minutes, color. Grades 4 and up. 16mm. Rental; $23. IU, PSU & UA.

INDIAN ARTS AT THE PHOENIX HEARD MUSEUM
KAET-TV Phoenix, Producer
Dick Peterson, Director
Explores six major areas of Native American Art: 1: Basketry - Naomi White, guest; 2: Painting - Larry Golsh and Pop Chalee, guests; 3: Pottery - Mabel Sunn, guest; 4: Textiles - Martha Began and Lillian Dineyazhe; 5: Jewelry - John E. Salaby; and 6: Katchinas. 1975. 30 minutes each, color. Video. Purchase: $150 each. Rental, $40 each/ week. NAPBC.

INDIAN BOY IN TODAY'S WORLD
Presents a picture of life on the Makah Reservation and shows how the way of life on the Reservation is changing as a result of interaction with the outside world--the conflict of Indian and non-Indian cultures. 1971. Grades 4 and up. 14 minutes, color. Rental. UA & IU.

INDIAN BOY OF THE SOUTHWEST
Toboya, a Hopi Indian boy, tells of his life and his home on a high mesa in the Southwestern desert of the U.S. 1983 revised edition. Grades 4-9. 19 minutes, color. Purchase: 16mm, $400; Video, $260; Rental; $58. PHOENIX. Rental only: UA.

THE INDIAN BROTHERS
A sympathetic portrait of the American Indian. 1911. Directed by D.W. Griffith. 12 minutes, bxw. EG.

INDIAN CANOES ALONG THE WASHINGTON COAST
Louis and Ruth Kirk
This film demonstrates how and with what tools a canoe is carved; also, river and salt water races are shown. 1971. 18 minutes. Purchase: 16mm, $250; beta, $175; and VHS, $165. UW.

INDIAN CONVERSATION
Portrays two Indians, one raised in an urban environment, the other on a reservation. Both are college graduates and explore their identities as Indians. 1974. 13 minutes. 16mm. Rental. UK.

INDIAN COUNTRY?
Document Associates and BBC
Indian journalist, Richard LaCourse, discusses the revolution of attitudes within the younger American Indians creating a new mood of militancy. Also, interviews with Indian educators discussing the efforts to preserve the integrity of the Native American culture. 1972. 26 minutes, color. Purchase: 16mm, $400; Video, $340; Rental; $55 each. CG.

INDIAN CRAFTS: HOPI, NAVAJO, AND IROQUOIS
Nancy Creedman, Producer
Illustrates the wide range of arts practiced by the Indians: basketweaving, pottery-making, kachina carving, weaving, jewelry-making, and mask carving by the Hopi, Navajo and Iroquois. 1980. 11 minutes, color. Grades 4-9. Purchase: 16mm, $255; video, $150. Rental. $35. PHOENIX.

INDIAN DIALOGUE
David Hughes, Director
Indians of Canada discuss many problems that cause them concern. 1967. 28 minutes, bxw. Video. $27. NFBC.

INDIAN FAMILY OF LONG AGO: BUFFALO HUNTERS OF THE PLAINS
Tells the story of the Sioux Indian buffalo hunters who roamed the great western plains of the U.S. more than 200 years ago. 1957. Grades 4-9. 15 minutes, color. 16mm. Rental: UA, UCT & UMN.

INDIAN FAMILY OF THE CALIFORNIA DESERT
A woman from the Cahuilla Indian Tribe from the desert of Palm Springs recalls her primitive life and illustrates her tribe's culture. 1967. 16 minutes. Grades 4-9. 16mm. UA.

INDIAN FOR A CHANGE
Uses portraits of five Indian men and women to show the life of the American Indian as it really is, as opposed to the romanticized stereotype commonly accepted. 1970. 28 minutes, color. 16mm & video. Purchase: 16mm, $295; video, $110. NAC. Rental: Video, $10. UCT.

INDIAN HOUSE: THE FIRST AMERICAN HOME
Remnants of the dwellings of Indians in the Southwest represent the oldest homes in America. 1950. 11 minutes/bxw. 16mm. Rental. UA.

INDIAN HUNTER-GATHERERS OF THE DESERT: KILIWA
R.C. Michelsen, J. Albrecht & V.W. Kjonegaard
Focuses on subsistence activities of Baja California Indians. 1975. 14 minutes, color. 16mm. Rental, $15. PSU.

INDIAN INFLUENCES IN THE U.S.
David A. Baerreis, Ph.D.
Presents many aspects of Indian heritage in the mainstream of American society today, in music, art and the foods we eat. 1964. Grades 4-9. 11 minutes, color. 16mm. Rental. IU, UA & UK.

INDIAN LAND: THE NATIVE AMERICAN ECOLOGIST
Herbert McCoy, Jr., Director/Producer
American Indians discuss their traditional veneration for the Earth. 21 minutes; color/bxw. FILMS.

Audiovisual Aids

INDIAN LEGENDS: GLOOSCAP
Records a segment of the creation myth of the North American Micmac Indians. 1985. 26 minutes, color. Video. Rental, $29. PSU.

INDIAN LEGENDS OF CANADA
Daniel Bertolino, Director
This series of 15 films (13 parts) provides an authentic backdrop against which to study the first native peoples of Canada. The Winter Wife (Ojibwa); The Windigo (Montagnais); The Invisible Man, Megmuwesug and Magic Box (MicMac); The Path of Souls (3 films, Ojibwa); Moowis, Where Area You Moowis (Algonguian), and The Return of the Child (Carrier); Mandamin, Or the Legend of Corn (Ojibwa); Pitchie the Robin and The Path Without End (Ojibwa); The Spirit of the Dead Chief (Chippewa); Glooscap (Abnaki).1981-1983. 26 minutes each. Color. Available in Native languages with English or French narration. Purchase: 16mm, $675 each; and VHS, $450 each. Rental: $65 each; series, $8,450. ITFE, FH & THA.

INDIAN MAINSTREAM
Thomas Parsons
Emphasizes rediscovery of language and rituals which have been suppressed over the last three generations, and the need to pass on the Indian heritage to the young before it is forgotten. Sponsored by the Dept. of Labor to regenerate the Indian culture of the tribes in northern California, specifically the Hupa, Karok, Tocowa, and Yurok tribes. 1971. 25 minutes, color. Grades 9 and up. Purchase: 16mm, $425; video, $375. Rental: 16mm, $48. SH. Rental, $18. PSU.

INDIAN PAINT
Norman Foster, Director
The heroic efforts of a 15-year-old Indian boy, son of a tribal chief, to raise a "painted" colt. The portrayal of Indian life in the far West before the coming of the white man. 1965. 91 minutes, color. 16mm. Rental: UCT.

INDIAN POTTERY OF SAN ILDEFONSO
Rick Krepela
Documentary of renowned Pueblo artist Maria Martinez making hand fired black pottery using techniques redeveloped after they had fallen from use. Maria, in her mid-eighties at the time, works closely with her son Popovi Da at San Ildefonso Pueblo, New Mexico. 1972. 27 minutes, color. 16mm & video. Purchase: 16mm, $285; video, $110. NAC. Rental: UCT.

INDIAN RELOCATION: ELLIOT LAKE: A REPORT
Probes the Canadian government's experiment to move 20 Indian families from their rugged northern Ontario reserves to a new town. Questions the wisdom of the program. 1967. 30 minutes, bxw. 16mm. Rental: $28. UCLA.

INDIAN RIGHTS, INDIAN LAW
Joseph and Sandra Consentino, Directors
Film documentary focusing on the Native American Rights Fund, its staff and certain casework. 1978. 60 minutes. Grades 10-adult. 16mm. Rental, $24. IRA, FILMS, PSU.

INDIAN SELF-RULE: A PROBLEM OF HISTORY
Selma Thomas, Producer
Michael Cotsones, Director
Traces the history of white-Indian relations from 19th century treaties through the present, as tribal leaders, historians, teachers, and other Indians gather at a 1983 conference organized to reevaluate the significance of the Indian Reorganization Act of 1934. The experience of the Flathead Nation of Montana, the Navajo Nation of the Southwest, and the Quinault people of the Olympic Peninsula, Washington, illustrates some of the ways Indians have dealt with shifting demands upon them. 1985. 58 minutes, color. Video. Purchase: $400; rental, $60. DER.

INDIAN SPEAKS
Reveals some of the general cultural deprivation of Indians in Canada & depicts aspects of life on a reserve. Describes the gradual disappearance of the Indian culture & the plight of individual Indians who wish to preserve it. 1967. Grades 7 and up. 41 minutes, color. 16mm. Rental: $15.55. UMN.

INDIAN STEREOTYPES IN PICTURE BOOKS
This video & accompanying script is about stereotypic images as a process over time; and learning to recognize these images. 25 minutes, color. Video. Rental: $10. HO.

INDIAN SUMMER
A summer experience of Chippewa Indian children on a woodland reservation, their relationship to animals & to the environment. 1975. Grades K-4. 11 minutes, color. Rental: $8. UCT.

INDIAN TIME
Native Multi-media Productions, Inc.
Presents Shingoose, Buffy Sainte-Marie, Charlie Hill, Laura Vinson, Tom Jackson, Bill Brittain and special guest, Max Gail in a variety special of America's finest Native American entertainers. 1988. 48 minutes, color. Purchase: $150; Rental: $80. NAPBC.

INDIAN TO INDIAN
Shows Indians who are part of the work force explaining their lives and work. Describes how, though part of the work force, they retain their tribal heritages. 1970. 26 minutes, color. 16mm & Video. Purchase: 16mm, $275; video, $110. NAC.

INDIAN TREATY RIGHTS BY THE RIGHT REV. WILLIAM WANTLAND
Rev. Wantland (Seminole), an attorney & Episcopol Bishop, gives a 30 minute summary on "What is Soverignty." Video. Purchase: $20; rental: $10. HO.

INDIAN TRIBAL GOVERNMENT
Filmed at the Gila River Indian Reservation, this film shows how effective tribal governments operate and what tribal members should expect from their governments. 1980. 16 minutes, color. 16mm. IDIL.

THE INDIANS
The story of the conflict between the Indian and the white man in the Colorado Territory during the time when white traders, trappers and settlers moved into the Great Plains. 1969. 31 minutes. Grades 4-12. Purchase: VHS, $99. GA. Rental. UA.

INDIANS IN THE AMERICAS
Surveys (using panoramas, still photos, and paintings) the development of the American Indian civilizations from the first nomadic hunter to the European explorers. Revised 1985 edition. 22 minutes, color. Grades 4-12. Purchase: 16mm, $475; video, $285. Rental: 16mm, $55. PHOENIX. Rental: 16mm, $25; video, $23.50. IU & PSU.

INDIANS, THE NAVAJOS
A contemporary motion picture report that examines the winds of change that have been sweeping across the lives of 140,000 Navajos on the largest Indian reservation in the world. 1975. 14 minutes, color. 16mm. Rental: $9. UCT.

INDIANS OF CALIFORNIA
Tells the story of a primitive people as they lived before the white man came to the Pacific Coast. In two parts: Part 1, Village Life - includes trading, house building, basket-making, use of a tule boat, the sweat house, songs and dances. 15 minutes. Part 2, Food - includes bow and arrow making, a deer hunt, gathering and preparing acorns, a family meal, and the story teller. 14 minutes. 1955. Also, a LP record, California Indian Songs, $5.00. BARR & UA.

INDIANS OF EARLY AMERICA
Classifies all of the Indians of early America according to four general geographic regions, and represents each region by one dominant and characteristic tribe. 1957. Grades 4 and up. 22 minutes, bxw. In English & Spanish. 16mm. Rental: $13. IU, UA, PSU & UMN.

INDIANS OF THE EASTERN WOODLANDS: THE LEGACY OF THE AMERICAN INDIANS
Camera One, Producer; hosted by Wes Studi
Examines the Effigy Mounds, ancient structures & the Woodland Indians; examines the legends & cultures of the various tribes. Ancient America Series. 1994. 60 minutes, color. $19.98. WKV.

INDIAN OF NORTH AMERICA
John K. White, Consultant; produced by SVE
A series of three, 20 minute VHS cassettes exploring the diverse cultures of Native Americans. Grades 4-6. Volume 1: Indians of the Northeast/ Southest; Volume 2: Indians of the Plains/Northwest Coast; Volume 3: Indians of the Southwest/ Far North. $SVE, $89 each.

INDIANS OF NORTH AMERICA
Schlessinger Video Productions
Twenty, 30-minute programs portray the history & culture of particular Indian communities, with insights and commentary from historians & contemporary tribal members attacking myths & stereotypes that remain even today. Includes photographic images, sketchings, portraits, and maps. *Programs*: The Apache; The Aztec; The Cherokee (Southeast); The Cheyenne; The Comanche; The Iroquois; The Maya; The Navajo; The Seminole; The Yankton Sioux; The Chinook; The Creek; The Crow, The Huron; The Lenape; The Menominee; The Narragansett; The Potawatomi; The Pueblo; and A History of Native Americans. 1993-94. Grades 4-10. Closed captioned for the hearing impaired. Purchase: $39.95 each; $799/ set. LV & GPN.

INDIANS OF THE NORTHWEST: THE LEGACY OF THE AMERICAN INDIANS
Camera One, Producer; hosted by Wes Studi
The origin of the totem pole; examines the legends & cultures of the various tribes. Ancient America Series. 1994. 60 minutes, color. $19.98. WKV.

INDIANS OF THE PLAINS: LIFE IN THE PAST
This film describes how the Plains Indians depended on the buffalo for almost all the necessities of life. Also, quillwork, beadwork and painting are presented. 11 minutes. 16mm. Rental. UT & PSU.

INDIANS OF THE PLAINS:
SUN DANCE CEREMONY
Pictures erection of the tepee or tent for lodging. Features the Sweat Lodge, Sun Dance Ceremony and Grass Dance. 1954. Grades 4 and up. 11 minutes, color. 16mm. Rental: $15. UMN, UT & PSU.

INDIANS OF THE SOUTHWEST: THE
LEGACY OF THE AMERICAN INDIANS
Camera One, Producer; hosted by Wes Studi From Anasazi to Hohokam to Navajo & Pueblo; examines the legends & cultures of the various tribes. Ancient America Series. 1994. 60 minutes, color. $19.98. WKV.

INDIANS OF THE SOUTHWEST
Focuses on the history and culture of the Indians of the Southwest; their descendants, the Pueblos, and other tribes that settled in the Southwest, including the Navajos, Hopi and Zuni. 16 minutes. Grades 4-9. 16mm. FILMS.

INDIANS OF THE UPPER MISSISSIPPI SERIES
This three part program documents the success of two tribes of Native Americans, the Winnebago & Menominee. Interviews reveal how these tribes won their struggle to stay on their ancestral lands & retain their culture & heritage. 86 minutes. VHS, $275. Parts: History, 28 minutes, $99.95; Culture, 29 minutes, $99.9; Politics, 29 minutes, $99.95. CC.

INDIANS, OUTLAWS & ANGIE DEBO
95-year-old Angie Debo, an early 20th century scholar and pioneer, recalls her life as the daughter of 19th century Oklahoma homesteaders. Deb unearthed troubling documents regarding a criminal conspiracy by major political figures to rob the Five Civilized Indian Tribes of Oklahoma of their mineral-rich lands. 1988. 60 minutes, color. Video. Purchase: $59.95. PBS. Rental: $10. HO; $16. UMN.

THE INDIANS WERE THERE FIRST
Shows the path of the ancestors of the first North American Indians across the landbridge from Asia; the various tribes and some of their characteristics; and in particular, the distribution of Iroquois at the end of the 16th-century and the nature of their social and political organization. 13 minutes, color. Video. Purchase, $69.95. FH.

INSTITUTE FOR THE DEVELOPMENT
OF INDIAN LAW
A series of five seven minute films providing a review of vital areas of federal Indian law and their effect on tribal government. They include: A Question of Indian Sovereignty, Indian Treaties, Indians and the U.S. Government, Indian Jurisdiction, and The Federal-Indian Trust Relationship. Purchase: 16mm, $550/set. IDIL.

INUGHUIT: THE PEOPLE AT
THE NAVAL OF THE EARTH
Arctic Eskimos of Thule, the world's northernmost community, tell their own story. 1985. 85 minutes, color. 16mm & video. Purchase: $1,250; rental: $175. ACF.

INUIT
Bo Boudart, Director
Documents the first Inuit Circumpolar Conference of 1977. Provides an overview of the issues that concern Native peoples in the Arctic. 1978. 28 minutes, color. 16mm. BO.

INUIT KIDS
Paulle Clark, Producer/Director
Helps children get the feel of Arctic life by sharing moments in the lives of two 13-year-old Inuit boys who are friends. 1986. 15 minutes, color. Grades 2-8. Purchase: 16mm, $315; Video, $245; Rental: $30. BULL.

INUPIAT ESKIMO HEALING
Nellie Moore, Producer
Daniel Housberg, Director
Looks at the practice of medicine in northern Alaska today by following several traditional doctors and their patients in three Inupiat villages. 1985. 30 minutes, color. In English and Inupiaq with English subtitles. Video. NATC.

IROQUOIS SOCIAL DANCE I & II
Nick Manning
Presents, in two parts, social dances of the Mohawk Indians, filmed on the Reserve at St. Regis, Canada. Part I, 15 minutes; Part II, 11 minutes. Teacher's guide. Video. Purchase: $49 (both). RM.

IS THERE AN AMERICAN STONEHENGE?
Mayer, Producer
Relates Dr. John Eddy's efforts to prove his theory of a Wyoming solar observatory built and used by ancient American Indians. Grades 4-adult. 1982. 30 minutes, color. Rental. IU & UT.

ISHI IN TWO WORLDS
Richard Tomkins, Producer
The story of the Yahi Indians of California. Ishi, the last of the Yahi, was the last person in North America known to have lived a totally aboriginal existence. 1967. Grades 9 and up. 19 minutes, color. Rental: UCLA, UT, PSU & UA.

ISHI, THE LAST YAHI
The story of Ishi, the last wild Indian in North America. For more than 40 years, Ishi had lived in hiding with a tiny band of survivors in northern California. He suddenly appeared in 1911, and was the last Yahi Indian alive. He related Yahi stories & demonstrated the traditional of life he once knew. Using Alfred Kroeber's notes & recordings taken at the time, the film provides a unique look at indigenous life in America before the arrival of Europeans. 1994. 57 minutes. Purchase: 16mm, $1,195; video, $325. Rental, Video, $75. UC.

ITAM HAKIM, HOPIIT
Victor Masayesva, Jr., Producer/director/camera
Ross Macaya, one of the last members of the Hopi tribal storytelling clan, recounts his life story and various epochs in Hopi history. 1984. 60 minutes. Color. In Hopi or English. Purchase: Video 3/4" - $200, and 1/2" -$140. Rental: 3/4" - $75, 1/2" - $50. ISP (sales); IN (sales & rentals).

IT'S NOT JUST A TIME FOR FUN
Looks at the annual Choctaw Fair held every June on the Choctaw Reservation. Introduces all the activities of the Fair. All grades. 15 minutes. Purchase: VHS, $85; rental, $10 (two weeks). CHP.

IYAHKIMIX, BLACKFEET
BEAVER BUNDLE CEREMONY
Sacred bundles are collections of artifacts and sacred natural objects belonging to clan ancestors and passed on to their descendants. The ritual consists of dancing with the chanting to the bundle's individual parts. Presents the religion's ritual in its entirety. 58 minutes. 16mm. UAB.

JAUNE QUICK-TO-SEE SMITH
Jack Peterson, Producer
Anthony Schmitz, Director
Joy Harjo, Writer; N. Scott Momaday, Narrator
An imaginative introduction to the work and thought of an outstanding contemporary Native American painter. It conveys Jaune's personal vision and its relation to her painting. 1983. 29 minutes, color. 16mm & video. NAPBC.

JOE KILLS RIGHT--OGLALA SIOUX
Jon Alpert (DTC-TV)
Portrait of a young Sioux man living in New York City. Scenes of Joe living in one of New York City's worst neighborhoods. He loses his job, begins drinking and using drugs, then enters a treatment center. After, he returns to the reservation. Includes dialogue of educational and health services on the reservation. 1980. 25 minutes. beta & VHS. DTC.

JOHN CAT
Based on the story by W.P. Kinsella. An encounter with an older Indian leads two younger ones to a painful awareness of racial prejudice. 26 minutes, color. Video. Purchase: $149. BE.

JOHN KIM BELL
Anthony Azzopardi, Producer
Tells the story of a talented and passionate young man who has broken through social barriers and stepped into the limelight. Bell is the first Native American pursuing a career as a symphonic conductor. Film tracks Bell's early interest and development in music. 1983. 36 1/2 minutes. Color. Video. Purchase: $150; Rental: $40. NAPBC.

JOHNNY FROM FORT APACHE
Records the readjustments in lifestyle the Russells, an Indian family, experience when they move from the reservation to San Francisco. 1971. 15 minutes. Grades 4-adult. 16mm. Rental. UA and IU.

JOSHUA'S SOAPSTONE CARVING
Joshua Qumaluk, an Eskimo, helps his Uncle Levi hunt, fish & trap. He learns to carve soapstone sculptures to sell. 23 mins. Grades 4-9. Purchase: 16mm, $495; video, $290. Rental: $60. COR.

JOURNEY TO THE SKY: A HISTORY OF
THE ALABAMA COUSHATTA INDIANS
Robert Cozens, & KUHT-TV, Executive Producers; Paul Yeager, Director/writer/camera; Marcellus Bearheart
Williams, and Robert Symonds, Narrators
Alabama Chief, Fulton Battise relates in his native dialect the fantasy tale of three youths traveling to the ends of the earth and beyond. Describes the struggle of a people to preserve their way of life. 1982. 53 minutes. Color. Video. Rental: $80/ week. NAPBC.

JUST DANCING
Eskimo dancing. 1987. 60 minutes. VHS. $24.95. KYUK.

KAINAI
Raoul Fox, Director
On the Blood Indian Reserve, near Cardston, Alberta, Canada, a pre-fab factory has been built to employ the residents. 27 mins. 16mm. NFBC.

KAMIK
Elise Swerthone
Inuit, Ulayok Kavlok, a hunte/seamstress, makes seal skin boots called Kamik. 15 mins. Purchase: 16mm, $350; VHS, $200. Rental: $40. NFBC.

KAMINURIAK: CARIBOU IN CRISIS
Inuit Broadcasting Corp.
& Don Snowden, Producers
Focuses on the ecological and cultural practices in the North which has affected the Caribou herds in the Inuit regions of Northern Canada. 33 interviews, 4-20 minutes each, presenting both sides of the issue and contrasting approaches to wildlife management. 1982-3. Color. Video. In Inuktitut & English. IBC.

KANEHSATAKE: 270 YEARS OF RESISTANCE
Alanis Obomsawin, Producer
Documents the confrontation between Mohawks & Canadian government forces in Quebec in 1990, outside the town of Oka. Raises vital questions about basic social injustices, the role of politicians, police, the military, and the press. 120 minutes, color. Video. Purchase: $275; rental: $90. BULL.

KARUK BASKET MAKERS, A WAY OF LIFE
Shows women & girls engaged in learning the art of basketmaking from Karuk elders who still practice it. Types & uses of baskets are discussed. Grades 4-6. 22 minutes. VHS. $69.95. K-T.

KASHIA MEN'S DANCES: SOUTHWESTERN POMO INDIANS
Clyde B. Smith, Producer
Preserves four authentic Pomo dances as performed in full costume on the Kashia Reservation on the northern California coast. 1963. 40 minutes, color. Purchase: 16mm, $800, video, $195. Rental: $60. UC. Rental: IU, PSU & UCLA.

KECIA: WORDS TO LIVE BY
Gryphon Productions
15 year-old Kecia speaks of her expereicnes--how she contracted the HIV virus, and her pride in her Native American traditions. Grades 7 and up. 22 minutes. 1992. NDM. $240.

KEEP YOUR HEART STRONG: LIFE ALONG THE POW WOW TRAIL
Deb Wallwork, Producer
Provides an inside view of contemporary Native American culture in its most accessible and popular form - the Pow Wow. 1986. 58 minutes, color. Video. Purchase: $150; Rental: $80. NAPBC. Rental: $16. UMN.

KEEPER OF THE WESTERN DOOR
Eight short films made on the Cattaraugus and Allegany Reservations in western New York. Each program investigates Seneca life. The Music and Dance of the Senecas, 11 minutes; A Seneca Language Class, 11 minutes; Preparing Seneca Food, 18 minutes; The Seneca People--Past and Present, 13 minutes; A Visit to the Basketmaker, 12 minutes; A Visit to the Beader, 15 minutes; A Visit to the Seneca Museum, 15 minutes; A Visit With a Seneca Artist, 17 minutes. 1980. Video. SN.

KEVIN ALEC
Beverly Shaffer, Director
Kevin, an 11 year-old Indian boy from the Fountain Indian Reserve in British Columbia, Canada, whose parents are dead, lives with his grandmother. He leaves, participates and builds pride in the value of tribal life. 1976. 16 minutes. Grades 1-8. Purchase: 16mm, $290; video, $145; rental: $28. MG.

KLEENA
H. Leslie Smith, Director
Dann Firehouse, Writer
A small group of Kwakiutl Indians, organized by Peter Knox, the grandson of a famed carver Mungo Martin, sets out from their community at Alert Bay to participate in a traditional fishing activity. Narration gives economic and social facts related to kleena, the oil extracted from the oil-rich eulachon fish, a feast food for potlatches. 1981. 20 minutes, color. 16mm & video. CFDW.

KWA' NU' TE': MICMAC & MALISEET ARTISTS
Catherine Martin & Kimberlee McTaggart, Dirs.
Interviews with eight Native American artists at work talking about the power of creation. 1993. 42 minutes, color. Purchase: 16mm, $650; VHS, $250. Rental: $70. NFBC.

THE KWAKIUTL OF BRITISH COLUMBIA
Franz Boas; Bill Holm, Editor
A documentary film made by noted anthropologist Dr. Franz Boas, in 1930 at Fort Rupert on Vancouver Island. Includes scenes depicting traditional Kwakiutl dances, crafts, games, oratory and actions of a shaman. 1950. 55 minutes. Silent/bxw. Purchase: 16mm, $500; beta, $350; VHS, $340. UW. Rental, $19. IU.

KYUK VIDEO
John A. McDonald, Executive producer
Located in Bethel, Alaska, KYUK-TV, begun in 1972, has produced works on the lifestyles and native culture of the Yukon-Kuskokwim Delta, both in English and Yup'ik. Documentaries focusing on the Yup'ik Eskimo way of life and the people's viewpoints on contemporary events and the continuation of their cultural traditions. Several productions include: Eyes of the Spirit; From Hand to Hand: Bethel Native Artist Profiles; A Matter of Trust; They Never Asked Our Fathers; Yupiit Yuraryarait/A Dancing People; Just a Small Fishery; Old Dances, New Dancers; Parlez-Vois Yup'ik; People of Kashunuk. For a complete list of video programs contact KYUK.

LA CROSSE STICK MAKER
Jack Ofield, Director/Producer
Helen-Maria Erawan, Writer/Narrator
Onondaga craftsmen of the sovereign Onondaga Nation, located in New York State, demonstrate the ancient craft of steaming and binding wood to make lacrosse sticks. They discusses tools and techniques, play a game and reflect on their cultural heritage and lifestyle. 1974. Grades 5 and up. 9 minutes, color. Purchase: 16mm, $125; video, $50. Rental, $30 each. NPP & BGF.

THE LAKOTA: ONE NATION ON THE PLAINS
Fran Cantor
Narrated by N. Scott Momaday, this film opens by evoking traditional Lakota philosophy, and conveys history as it is understood in the Lakota tradition. 1976. 29 minutes, color. 16mm & video. UMA & KS.

LAKOTA QUILLWORK: ART & LEGEND
H. Jane Nauman, Producer/director/editor
A documentary on Lakota quillworking, demonstrated and explained, with a re-enactment scene as it might have appeared 150 years ago. Two well-known quillworkers demonstrate sewn and wrapped quilling. 1985. 27 minutes, color . In English & Lakota. 16mm & video. OW.

LAMENT OF THE RESERVATION
Thames TV, Producer
Discusses the living conditions of the 600,000 Indians on barren reservations, pointing out high infant mortality and suicide rates. Grades 7 and up. 23 minutes, color. 16mm. Rental. UT & IU.

LAND OF THE CREE
Life among the Cree Indians of Canada, with the women doing all the work. 1935. 10 minutes, bxw . EG.

LAND OF THE EAGLE
BBC & WNET's Nature Series
George Page, host & narrator
An 8-part series presenting an account of European colonization of North America. Narratives from American Indians communicate the spiritual naturalism - harmony between man and nature that existed until the "White Man" arrived. 1991. 8/60 minute programs. Video. Individual programs, $39.95. $249.95 complete. A 32-page teacher guide is provided free with series purchase. PBS.

THE LAST DAYS OF OKAK
Anne Budgell & Nigel Markham, Directors
Shows what happens to a community (the Inuit of Labrador) when a disaster (1918-19 flu epidemic) that overwhelms its people also largely destroys the values by which they lived. 1985. 24 minutes, color. Purchase: 16mm, $500; video, $225. Rental: $50. NFBC.

THE LAST MENOMINEE
Describes what is happening to the Menominee Indians of Menominee County, Wisconsin. 1966. Grades 10 and up. 30 minutes, bxw. 16mm. Purchase: $250; rental, $12.15. IU.

THE LAST MOOSESKIN BOAT
Raymond Yakeleya, Director
The Shoteah Dene of the Northwest Territories built mooseskin boats to carry their families and cargo downriver to trading posts. A member of the Dene constructs the last boat of this type to be housed in a museum in Yellowknife. 1982. 28 minutes. Video. Purchase: $27. NFBC.

THE LAST OF THE CADDOES
Ken Harrison, Producer/director/writer/editor
Set in rural Texas in the 1930s, this film follows James Edward Hawkins through a summer of self-discovery. Jimmy, age 12, learns that he is part Indian and seeks to learn about his heritage. 1982. 29 minutes, color. Purchase: 16mm, $525; video, $315. Rental, $52.50. PHOENIX.

LAST SALMON FEAST OF THE CELILO INDIANS
Produced prior to the Dalles Dam inundation of the last major salmon fishery of the Wy-am Pum, a branch of lower Deschute Indians, the Yakimas and the Warm Springs, and other central Oregon tribes. 1955. 18 minutes, bxw. Purchase: 16mm, $150; rental, $10. OHS.

LAST STAND AT LITTLE BIGHORN
N. Scott Momaday, Narrator
Re-examines the Battle of the Little Bighorn from both the white & Native American perspectives. 1992. 54 minutes, color. Video. Purchase: NAPBC. Rental: $10. HO.

THE LEARNING PATH
Loretta Todd, Director
Native control of Native education in Canada, to preserve their languages and identities. Schools i

Edmonton and nearby Saddle Lake Reserve. 1991. 57 minutes, color. Video. Purchase: $27. NFBC.

LEGEND OF THE BOY & THE EAGLE
The Hopi legend of Tutevina, the young Indian boy who is banished from his tribe for freeing the sacrificial bird. 21 minutes. 16mm. WD.

THE LEGEND OF THE BUFFALO CLAN
A lesson for teaching traditions, proper behavior, cultural history, and spiritual beliefs. The Buffalo chief does an authentic healing ceremony, reviving the child. 1993. 29 minutes, color. Purchase: 16mm, $525; video, $285. Rental: 16mm, $55. PHOENIX.

LEGEND OF THE MAGIC KNIVES
A totem village in the Pacific Northwest provides the setting for this portrayal of an ancient Indian legend, recounted by means of figures on a totem pole and authentic Indian masks. 1970. 11 minutes, color. Grades 4 and up. 16mm. Rental. $14. PSU & IU.

LEGENDS & LIFE OF THE INUIT
Richard Robesco, Director
Animated film looks at life today in an Inuit community and presents five legends. 1978. 58 minutes, color. Video. Purchase: $27. NFBC.

LEGENDS OF THE INDIANS
These stories of various Native American tribes are re-enacted by Native Americans to remember who they are and what they believe. The Return of the Child (Algonquin); The Legend of the Corn (Ojibway); The Winter Wife (Chippewa); Moowis, Where Are You, Moowis? (Algonquin); The Path of the Souls (Ojibway); Glooscap, Creation Legend; The World Between & The Path of Life. 26 minutes each, color. Video. Purchase: Complete series, $675; $89.95 each. FH.

LEGENDS OF THE SIOUX
Filmed in South Dakota, this film relates many of the legends of the Sioux Indians. 27 minutes. 16mm. Rental. UK.

LENAPE: THE ORIGINAL PEOPLE
Thomas Agnello, Producer/director/editor
David Oestreicher, Research coordinator
Briefly sketches Delaware, or Lenape history; focuses on two elders living in Dewey, Oklahoma, who retain the language and knowledge of old customs and beliefs. Edward Thompson describes his participation in a Big House Ceremony in 1924; and Nora Thompson Dean, also know as Touching Leaves Woman. Scenes of the first reunion of Lenape held in 1983 are included. 1986. 22 minutes, color. Purchase: 16mm, $325; video, $95. Rental: $45. AG.

LETTER FROM AN APACHE
Barbara Wilk, Producer/writer/animator
Fred Hellerman, Narrator
An animated film presenting experiences of a Yavapai Indian of the early 20th century. The narration is adapted from a letter written by Carlos Montezuma, M.D., known as Wassajah, to Frederick W. Hodge to provide autobiographical information for the 1907 Handbook of American Indians. 1983. Grades 4-9. 11 minutes. Purchase: 16mm, $240; VHS, $89; 3/4", $119. BARR & CC.

LEWIS & CLARK AT THE GREAT DIVIDE
CBS News; hosted by Walter Cronkite
The expedition nearly ends prematurely in 1805 when a young Indian girl turns out to be a Shoshoni chief's sister. Grades 3-8. 22 minutes, color. 16mm & video. Purchase: 16mm, $490; video, $285; rental, $72. PHOENIX.

LIKE THE TREES
Rose, a Metis Indian from northern Alberta, leaves the city to find her roots among the Woodland Cree. 15 minutes. 16mm. NFBC.

A LITTLE WHILE MORE YET
Jan Marie Martell
Stephen Charleson, from the Hesquiat Band of the West Coast of Vancouver Island, talks about the difficulties in making the transition from his native community to a city environment. 1976. 15 minutes. 16mm or video. Purchase or rental. CFDW.

LITTLE WHITE SALMON INDIAN SETTLEMENT
Harry Dawson, Director
Leo Alexander, Advisor/narrator
Cooks Landing, the site of one of the oldest Indian fishing villages in North America, is the subject of this documentary produced in cooperation with members of the Yakima Indian Tribe. 1972. Grades 9 and up. 30 minutes, color. 16mm. Rental: PSU & UCLA.

LIVE & REMEMBER
Henry Smith, Producer
Using some footage of Vision Dance, as well as new interviews and footage shot on Rosebud Reservation in South Dakota, this film examines the role and sacred nature of dance, music and oral tradition in Lakota culture and what it means to be Indian living in America today. 1986. Grades 9 and up. 29 minutes, color. Purchase: VHS, $89; 3/4", $119. CC. Purchase: VHS, $56.95. NAPBC. Rental: $21. UMN.

THE LIVING STONE
John Freeney, Director
Contemporary Inuit Eskimos of Cape Dorset on Baffin Island continue an ageless tradition of creative craftsmanship carving stone into evocative portrayals of Inuit life. 1958. Grades 7 and up. 33 minutes, color. Purchase: 16mm, $550; video, $350. Rental: $60. NFBC. Rental. IU.

LIVING TRADITIONS: FIVE INDIAN WOMEN ARTISTS
Denise Mayotte, Kathee Prokop & Fran Belvin,Producers/directors/editors
Sherry Wilson, Narrator
The relationship between traditional Indian values and the handiwork of five Indian women artists from Minnesota is examined. Shows the role of culture handed down from generation to generation. 1984. 27 minutes, color. Video. IN.

THE LONG WALK
KQED-TV San Francisco
Explores the contemporary life of the Navajo and describes their history. 1970. 60 minutes, color. 16mm. FW.

THE LONG WALK OF FRED YOUNG
Michael Barnes
The story of a child, Fred Young, who only spoke the Ute and Navajo languages, went to a medicine man when he was sick. Today, he is Dr. Frederick Young a nuclear physicist. 1979. 58 minutes. 16mm & video, WGBH. Rental: 16mm, $27.50. UMN.

THE LONGEST TRAIL
Alan Lomax, Producer/Editor
Forrestine Paulay, Editor
Exploration of the dance traditions of the American Indian showing more than 50 Native American dances. Focuses on Native America, showing patterns of movement linking dances of Indians and Inuit from the Arctic Circle to Tierra del Fuego into one tradition. Also seeks to demonstrate a connection between these cultures and indigenous cultures in Siberia. 1986. 58 minutes, color. Purchase: 16mm, $995; video, $295. Rental, $60. UC. Rental: $23. UMN.

THE LONGEST WALK: S.F. TO D.C. 1978
A documentary of the spiritual and political walk across the nation from Alcatraz Island to Washington, D.C. to protest anti-Indian legislation and inform local communities about eleven bills then currently before Congress. 60 minutes. Also available are three 20 minute videotapes which are supplemental reference information: John Trudell-Pueblo Rally Speech; A Look Behind Indian Legislation; and, Dennis Banks–AIM Leader in Exile. Video. Purchase: $170 (Documentary), $75 (each supplement.) Rental: $50 (Documentary), $35 (each supplement.) CLP.

THE LONGEST WAR
Diane Orr, Director
An interview with Dennis Banks, founder of the American Indian Movement (AIM). Shows scenes of the occupation of Wounded Knee and the burning of the Courthouse at Custer, South Dakota in 1973. Interviews with participants at Wounded Knee. 1974. 30 minutes, color. 16mm & video. BF.

THE LONGHOUSE PEOPLE
Tom Daly, Producer
The life and religion of the Iroquois today. Shows a rain dance, a healing ceremony, and a celebration of a new chief. 1951. Grades 9 and up. 24 minutes, color. Purchase: 16mm, $500; video, $300. Rental, $50. NFBC. Rental: IU & UCLA.

THE LOON'S NECKLACE
Crawley Films, Producer
A Spanish language film recreating a Salish legend which tells how the loon came to receive his distinguished neckband. Authentic ceremonial masks establish the characters of the story. 1949, restored, 1990. 11 minutes, color. Grades 4 and up. 16mm & video. Purchase: $225. EB. Rental, $14. PSU, UMN, UT & IU.

LORD OF THE SKY
Ludmila Zeman & Eugen Spaleny, Director
Based on the legends of the Native poeples of the Pacific Northwest, this animated film is an artistic unity of form & content. An environmental parable. 13 minutes. Purchase: 16mm, $350; VHS, $200. Rental: $40. NFBC.

LOS INDIOS NAVAJOS
A Spanish language film which shows the Navajo people in their own environment. 1939. 11 minutes; bxw. Grades 4-8. UA.

LOST IN TIME
Bruce Kuerten & Maryanne Culpepper, Producers; Dennis King, Narrator
Observes the work of archaeologists in the Tennessee Valley. Traces the history of the early native peoples, describing American prehistory beginning with the migration of Paleolithic hunters into the New World over the Bering land bridge.

Briefly discusses the changes of Indian culture leading to the complex settled lifestyles of the Indians who built the great mounds of the Black Warrior River Valley in Alabama. 1985. 60 minutes, color. Purchase: video, $250. AT & BE. Edited version, 30 minutes, $195. BE.

LOUISE ERDRICH & MICHAEL DORRIS
Bill Moyers, Host

Native American husband & wife team who write novels together. Their writings & beliefs in family, community & lifestyle reflect their heritage. 1988. 27 minutes, color. Video. Rental: $16. UMN.

LOVING REBEL

A documentary profile of Helen Hunt Jackson, one of the 19th-century's foremost advocates of Native American rights and one of its most celebrated writers. This video features readings from her writings as well as rare photographs & drawings of her world. 1987. Grades 9 and up. 26 minutes, color. Purchase: VHS, $89; 3/4", $119. CC. Rental: $19. UMN.

LUCY COVINGTON:
NATIVE AMERICAN INDIAN
Steve Heiser, Director

Filmed on the Colville Reservation in eastern Washington, Lucy Covington, chairperson of the Colville tribe and granddaughter of Chief Moses, gives an account of her part in the effort to prevent federal termination of the tribe. She talks about the Indian heritage and Indian identity, and how the land is central to these. 1978. Grades 7 and up. 15 minutes, color. 16mm. EB. Rental: Video, $12. PSU & UCT.

LUCY SWAN

An Indian woman born on the Rosebud Reservation at the turn of the century remembers the old ways but does not entirely discount the new. 16mm. Purchase: $300; rental: $30. AICRC.

LUMAAQ - AN ESKIMO LEGEND
Co Hoedeman, Director

Lumaaq tells the story of a legend widely believed by the Povungnituk Inuit. 1975. Grades 7 and up. 8 minutes, color. Video. Purchase: $22. NFBC.

MAGIC IN THE SKY
Peter Raymont, Director/Writer

An examination of the impact of Canadian (CBC) TV on Inuit Eskimos on the Arctic coast of Quebec, and their efforts to establish their own network. Mirrors the struggle of any culture to preserve its unique identity. 1981. Grades 7 and up. 57 minutes, color. Purchase: 16mm, $775; video, $350. Rental: $80. NFBC.

MAKE MY PEOPLE LIVE: THE
CRISIS IN INDIAN HEALTH CARE
Linda Harrar, Producer/director/writer
Lee Grant, Narrator

Investigates the state of health care for Indians. Details Native American life in four vastly different regions and discusses legislative and other issues, providing an introduction not only to health concerns but also to contemporary life of Native Americans across the country. Sites visited range from the impoverished Rosebud Sioux Reservation to the Tlingit villages of Alaska; and from the Navajo Nation to the Creek Nation of Oklahoma. 1984. 60 minutes, color. 16mm (sales only), 3/4" video (sales & rentals). AVP; rental, 1/2' video, $11. UT; 16mm rental, $37.50. PSU

MAKE PRAYERS TO THE RAVEN
Mark Badger, Producer/camera/editor
Barry Lopez, Narrator

Public television series introducing the lifeways and traditions of interior Alaska's Koyukon Indians. Focuses on their relationship to the land, and explores their spiritual beliefs. Includes the Koyukon communities of Alatna, Allakaket, Hughes, and Huslia - located just below the Arctic Circle. Color. All video formats. KUAC.

MAKOCE WAKAN: SACRED EARTH
Robby Romero, Director/writer

Focuses on Native American sacred sites & their importance to Native American culture. Personal & poitical insights on the importance of protecting Native American sacred sites: Ben Nighthorse Campbell (Cheyenne); Richard Moves Camp (Oglala Lakota); Audrey Shenandoah (Onondaga); Franklin Stanley (San Carlos Apache); Suzan Shown Harjo (CVheyenne/Hodulgee Muscogee); Ola Cassadore (San Carlos Apache); and Leon Shenandoah (Iroquois). 1993. 30 minutes. VH-1.

THE MAN & THE GIANT: AN ESKIMO LEGEND
Co Hoedeman, Director

An Inuit legend acted out by the Inuit people themselves. They use their traditional form of singing, katadjak, or throat singing. 1978. 8 minutes, color. Video. Purchase: 16mm, $225; Video, $125. Rental. $17. PHOENIX & NFBC.

MAN OF LIGHTNING
Gary Moss, Producer

Based on two Cherokee Indian legends, this film is a drama of the long-vanished world of the Cherokee years before European contact. 1982. 29 minutes, color. Video. Rental: $40/week. NAPBC.

MAN ON THE RIM: THE PEOPLING OF
THE PACIFIC, 4 - FLAMING ARROWS

Over 20,000 years ago Siberian hunters crossed the Bering Strait land bridge into Alaska and poured ito the American prairie. The Indian emerged in North America. 1988. 58 minutes, color. Video. Rental, $24. PSU.

MARIAI INDIAN POTTERY
OF SAN ILDEFONSO
National Park Service

Indian pottery maker Maria Martinez demonstrates the traditional India ways of pottery making. 27 minutes. Video, $29.95. CH.

MARIA & JULIAN'S BLACK POTTERY
Arthur E. Baggs, Jr.

Shows famous potters Maria and Julian Martinez in the step-by-step process of creating the famed black-on-black pottery that revived at San Ildefonso Pueblo, New Mexico. 1938/1977. 11 minutes, color. 16mm/silent. Purchase, 16mm, $190; VHS, $105. Rental: 16mm, $14; VHS, $13. PSU.

MARIA OF THE PUEBLOS

The life of the famous Pueblo potter, Maria Martinez. Provides an understanding of the culture, philosophy, art and economic condition of the Pueblo Indians of San Ildefonso, New Mexico. 1971. Grades 4 and up. 15 minutes, color. Purchase: 16mm, $345; video, $240. Rental: $50. COR. Rental: 16mm, $14. UCT.

MARKS OF THE ANCESTORS: ANCIENT
INDIAN ROCK ART OF ARIZONA
Echo Productions

Produced in cooperation with the Museum of Northern Arizona, this video explores six different rock art sites. 40 minutes, color. VHS. $24.95. TC.

THE MARMES ARCHAEOLOGICAL DIG
Louis & Ruth Kirk, Producers

Presents the oldest fully documented discovery of early man in the Western Hemisphere. 1971. 18 minutes, color. Purchase: 16mm, $250; beta, $175; VHS, $165. UW.

MASHPEE
Maureen McNamara & Mark Gunning, Producers/directors/writers/editors

Illustrates the land claims of the Mashpee Wampanoags of Massachusetts since 1976. Provides the complex background of the controversy, with interviews of Mashpee leaders, real estate developers, historians, legal experts, and trial lawyers presenting their sides of the story. 1985. 50 minutes, color. Video. McN.

THE MASKS OF CULTURE
Gryphon Productions

Explains the importance the wooden mask in tribal ceremonies. Grades 8 and up. 25 minutes. VHS. $250. NDM.

A MATTER OF CHOICE

The Hopi Nation and their efforts to find a place In the modern world. 60 minutes, color. Video. Purchase: $60. PBS.

A MATTER OF PROMISES

Introduces students to members of Native American tribes who describe their struggles to maintain their cultural identity and political sovereignty. 60 minutes, color. Video. Purchase: $60. PBS.

A MATTER OF TRUST
Bill Sharpsteen, Producer/writer/editor/host
Bryan Murray, Narrator

Focuses on the Alaska Native Claims Settlement Act passed by Congress in 1971 and the problems it has posed for Alaska's Indians and Inuit. 1983. 28 minutes, color. Video. KYUK.

MATTHEW ALIUK: ESKIMO IN TWO WORLDS
Bert Sulzman, Writer/Director

The relationship of an Eskimo boy assimilated into the city life of Anchorage. Tells the story of a proud people's struggle for cultural survival in a changing world. 1973. 18 minutes, color. Purchase: 16mm, $270. Rental: $25. LCA.

MEDICINE FIDDLE

Documentary celebrates the fiddling & dancing traditions of Native & Metis families on both sides of the U.S. & Canadian border. Features Ojibwe, Menominee, Metis & Ottawa fiddlers & dancers. 1990. 81 minutes, color. Video. Purchase: $295; rental: $75. UC.

MEDICINE LINE
Ken Mitchell, Director

A brief acount of Chief Sitting Bull of the Lakota Sioux during his years in exile in Canada. 1987. 10 minutes. Video. Purchase: $22. NFBC.

MEDOONAK, THE STORMMAKER
Les Krizsan, Director

A MicMac Indian legend. 1975. Grades 7-12. 13 minutes, color. Purchase: 16mm, $250; video, $210. Rental: $17.50. IFB & UA.

MEET THE SIOUX INDIAN
Shows the transient life of the Sioux Indians. 1949. Grades K-6. 11 minutes, color. Purchase: 16mm, $195. IFB. Rental: UCT.

MENOMINEE
This documentary examines the historical development of the many social and political problems faced by the Menominee Indians of northwestern Wisconsin. 1974. 59 minutes, color. Video. Rental: $80/week. NAPBC.

MESA VERDE
  National Park Service
Mesa Verde's cliff dwellings is interpreted. 23 minutes, color. Video. Purchase: $29.95. CH.

**MESA VERDE: MYSTERY
OF THE SILENT CITIES**
Views (using extensive aerial photography) the ruined cities and multiply family cliff dwellings of the 13th-century Indians of the Mesa Verde. 1975. 14 minutes, color. 16mm. Rental, $11.20. IU.

MESQUAKIE
  Alan Weber and Michael Bartell
Looks at the Mesquakie Indian settlement at Tama, Iowa, where carious activities of the traditional days are shown through old photographs and present-day film footage. 1976. 10 minutes. ISU.

MIGHTY WARRIORS
During the mass migration west, the white man encountered the Plains Indians. Familiar battles are depicted in the light of the true facts. 1964. Grades 4 and up. 30 minutes, bxw. 16mm. Purchase: $250; rental, $12.15. IU. Rental only, $16. PSU.

MI'KMAQ
A series of five programs recreating, in dramatized form, the seasonal round of Micmac life in Nova Scotia, Canada, before European contact as it might have been experienced by a single, extended Micmac family. Performed by Native people in the Micmac language. Available in French and English. Teacher's guide. Grades 6-adult. Video. NS.

**MILLENIUM: TRIBAL WISDOM
& THE MODERN WORLD**
  Biniman Productions &
  Adrian Malone Productions
Filmed in 15 countries, this ten-hour series tells the stories of people in 11 tribal cultures across the globe in an attempt to discover different ways of thinking about life as the turn of the century approaches. Two of the cultures covered include the Mohawk, and the Navajo. #6 - Touching the Timeless (Navajo); and #9 - The Tightrope of Power ((Mohawk & Ojibwe-Cree). 1992. 60 minutes each. VHS. Purchase: PBS. Rental, $14 each. PSU.

**MINORITIES IN AGRICULTURE:
THE WINNEBAGO**
  Ralph A. Swain, Briar Cliff College
Highlights the economic development programs of the Winnebago Tribe of Nebraska. 1984. 29 minutes, color. Video. Rental: $40/week. NAPBC.

MINORITY YOUTH: ADAM
The narration of a teenage American Indian's view of himself, his race, and his cultural heritage that is in danger of being lost. 1971. 10 minutes, color. 16mm. Rental, $9. IU.

MISS INDIAN AMERICA
  KBYU-TV, Provo, Utah
Covers the 20th annual Miss Indian America Pageant in 1973 at Sheridan, Wyoming. Contest represents 30 American Indian tribes from all over the U.S. 59 minutes, color. Video. Purchase: $150; Rental: $80/week. NAPBC.

MISSION LIFE: ALTA CALIFORNIA 1776
22 minutes. 16mm. Rental. UA.

MISSION OF FEAR
  Fernand Dansereau, Director
The story of the 20th century Jesuit martyrs who lived with their Huron converts, Indians of Midland, Ontario. 79 minutes, bxw. NFBC.

MISSION SAN XAVIER DEL BAC
33 minutes. 16mm. Rental. UA.

**MISSIONS OF CALIFORNIA:
NEW WAYS IN NEW WORLD**
21 minutes. 16mm. Rental. UA.

MISSIONS OF THE SOUTHWEST
15 minutes. 16mm. Rental. UA.

MOCCASIN FLATS
A young boy learns to come to terms with his Native American heritage, and learns to be proud of his background and finally claims his Native American name, Moccasin Flats. 26 minutes. Purchase, VHS, $149. CC.

MODOC
  Peter Winograd
By the use of archival photos by Edward S. Curtis and news clippings, this film tells the story of the Modoc Indians of California and their struggle to remain on their own lands. 1979. 15 minutes. bxw. 16mm and beta. EM.

**MOHAWK BASKETMAKING:
A CULTURAL PROFILE**
  Frank Semmens, Producer
Features a sensitive and personal look at the life and work of master basketmaker Mary Adams. 1980. 28 minutes. Color. Purchase: 16mm, $385; rental, $22; video, $70; rental, $12.50. PSU.

**MONUMENT VALLEY:
LAND OF THE NAVAJOS**
Shows the life of the Navajo Indians in the four-corner area where Arizona, New Mexico, Colorado and Utah meet. 1959. 17 minutes. Grades 6-adult. 16mm. UA.

THE MOON'S PRAYER
Stories of the Northwest tribes struggles to reverse the unsound environmental practices that have been inflicted upon their land. 60 minutes, color. Video. Rental: $10. HO.

MORE LEGENDS OF THE INDIANS
These are authentic stories from various Indian tribes, told by Native Americans to remember who they are and what they believe. 8-part series: Windigo; The Pleiades; The Magic Box; Pitchie the Robin; The Spirit of the Dead Chief; The Path Without End; The Invisible Man; & Megmoowesoo. 26 minutes each, color. Purchase: $89.95 each; $685 for all 8 parts. FH.

**MORE THAN BOWS & ARROWS:
THE LEGACY OF THE AMERICAN INDIANS**
  Roy Williams, Director; narrated by N.
  Scott Momaday; produced by Camera One

Documents the contributions of Native Americans to the development of the U.S. & Canada. N. Scott Momaday is a prominent Kiowa Indian writer and educator. 1994. 58 minutes, color. Purchase: $20. WKV; $35. HO; $39.95. COP. Rental: Video, $10. UMN, PSU & HO.

MOTHER CORN
  KBYU-TV, Provo, Utah
Examines the historical significance of various types of corn among Native American cultures. 1977. 29 minutes, color. Video. Purchase: $150; Rental: $40/week. NAPBC.

MOTHER OF MANY CHILDREN
  Alanis Obomsawin, Director
Agatha Marie Goodine, 108 year-old member of the Hobbema tribe, contrasts her memories with the conflicts that most Indian and Inuit woman face today. 1977. 58 minutes, color. Grades 9 and up. Purchase: 16mm, $775; VHS, $350. Rental, $80. NFBC.

MOUNTAIN WOLF WOMAN: 1884-1960
  Naomi Russell, Narrator
Tells the life story of an American Indian in her own words & narrated by her granddaughter. Based on the book by Nancy Oestreich Lurie. Includes an authentic Winnebago wedding song, baskets, beads, wigwams, & scenes from a pow-wow. 1990. 17 minutes, color. Video. Rental: $16. UMN.

MOVABLE FEAST
Presents Indian & Eskimo ways of hunting, gathering, preparing, and celebrating food, through images by Native artists from all over North America. Includes study guide. 30 minutes, color. Video. $50. TOP.

**MUNGO MARTIN: A SLENDER
THREAD/THE LEGACY**
  Barb Cramer/The U'Mista Cultural Society
From the time of his birth, Mungo Martin was exposed to cultural rituals and traditions of his people. At a young age he learned the basic skills of designing, carving and painting in the Northwest Coast traditional style of the Kwakwakawakw. 1991. 17 minutes, color. Purchase: Video, $195. CFDW.

MUSIC & DANCE OF THE MOHAWK
  Frank Semmens, Producer/director
Traces the origin, development and meaning behind Iroquois social songs; and the making of Iroquois musical instruments. 1983. 25 minutes, color. 16mm & video. AM & IM.

MUSIC & DANCE OF THE SENECAS
Covrs various aspects of the Seneca Indian culture. Introduces a variety of musical instruments with explanations. of how each one was taken from nature. 1981. 20 minutes, color. 3/4" U-matic. Rental: $25. UCLA.

**MY FATHER CALLS ME SON:
RACISM & NATIVE AMERICANS**
  David Fanning, Exec. Producer for KOCE-TV
Examines the problem of discrimination and some of the parallel pressures against Indian people to give up their uniqueness and become more like whites. 1975. 29 minutes, color. Video. PBS.

**MY HANDS ARE THE TOOLS OF MY SOUL:
ART & POETRY OF THE AMERICAN INDIAN**
  Arthur Barron & Zina Voynoz
A survey of American Indian achievements in po-

etry, music, sculpture, philosophy and history. Dialogue in tribal language as well as English. 1975. 52 minutes, color. 16mm & video. FI & TF. Rental: 16mm, PSU & UCT.

THE MYSTERY OF THE ANASAZI
Russ Morash, Director; WGBH, Producer
A study of the ruins of the Anasazi, the builders, ancestors of the Navajo. 1973. 50 minutes, color. 16mm & video. TW & ISU. 16mm rental, $31. PSU.

THE MYSTERY OF THE LOST RED PAINT PEOPLE: THE DISCOVERY OF A PREHISTORIC NORTH AMERICAN SEA CULTURE
T.W. Timreck & William Goetzmann, Producers
Follows U.S., Canadian, and European scientists from the barrens of Labrador - where archaeologists uncover an ancient stone burial mound - to sites in the U.S., France, England, Denmark and Norway where monumental standing stones testify to links among seafaring cultures across immense distances. 1987. Grades 9 and up. 57 minutes, color. Purchase: 16mm, $895; Video, $495; Rental: $90. BULL. Rental: 16mm, $39. PSU.

THE MYTHICAL TRIBE
History of the Sioux tribe from their victory at Little Big Horn to their defeat at Wounded Knee. 1981. 30 minutes, video. KS.

MYTHS & MOUNDBUILDERS
Graham Chedd, WGBH, Producer
Archaeologists probe mysterious mounds in the Eastern U.S. uncovering clues about a lost Indian civilization. Educator's guide. 1981. Grades 9 and up. 58 minutes, color. Video. Purchase: $30. NDM, PBS, DER, CAN & CH. Rental: $14. PSU & IU; $10. HO.

NANOOK OF THE NORTH
Robert Flaherty
A documentary studying the life of an Eskimo hunter and his constant struggle for survival against the menaces of nature. 1948. 65 minutes, 16mm/bxw/silent. Grades 4 and up. Original silent version, MMA. Purchase: 16mm, $26; video, $12.50. PSU. 1975 (51 minutes) restored version with musical score-rental, $22. PSU. 16mm rental, $20.25. IU.

NANOOK REVISITED
This program revisits the site of Flaherty's filming, and learns that he staged much of what he filmed, sired children to whose future he paid no heed, and is himself part of Inuit myth. 60 minutes, color. Purchase: $149; rental: $75. FH.

NATIONS WITHIN A NATION
Dept of Sociology, OK State U.
Examines the historical, legal and social backgrounds of the issue of the right of sovereignty-self-government. Examples of tribal government in operation are drawn from Taos Pueblo, the Mescalero Apache Tribe, the Muscogee (Creek) Nation and the Sac and Fox Tribe. 1986. 59 minutes, color. Video. Purchase: $150; Rental: $80. NAPBC.

NATIVE AMERICAN ARTS
Indian Arts and Crafts Board
The development of Native American arts in the U.S. Shows that contemporary artists and craftsmen (Indian Eskimo and Aleut) are making unique and significant contributions to the cultural life of our nation. 1974. 20 minutes, color. 16mm & video. Purchase: 16mm, $210. Rental: UCT & NAC.

NATIVE AMERICAN IMAGES
Carol Patton, Producer
Profiles the lives, philosophies and works of Paladine H. Royce (Ponca), Donald Van (Cherokee) and Steve Forbes, three artists living in Austin, Texas. Forbes is a non-Indian who has devoted himself to the portrayal of contemporary Native Americans. 1984. 29 minutes. Color. Video. Rental: $40. NAPBC.

NATIVE AMERICAN INDIAN SACRED PURIFICATION SWEAT LODGE CEREMONY
42 minute version of "American Indian Sweat Lodge Ceremony." Video. Purchase: $24.95. AV.

NATIVE AMERICAN MYTHS
An animated film introduced by Native American narrator Ned Romero, who briefly explains the relevant background information for each of five authentic myths: Sky Woman, a Seneca myth; How Raven Gave Daylight to the World, Haida myth; The First Strawberry, Cherokee myth; The People Came Out of the Underworld, Hopi myth. 1976. 23 minutes. Color. Grades 4-12. 16mm rental, $21. PSU, EB and UT.

THE NATIVE AMERICAN POWWOW
An introduction to the powwow and information guide on how to enjoy a powwow. Illustrates the variety of dances; history of the powwow, interviews with tribal elders. 1994. 58 minutes. VHS, $29.95. AUDIO.

THE NATIVE AMERICAN SERIES
Consists of three films, helps young people understand the origin of the American Indians, and the effect the coming Europeans had on the Indians. Indian Origins - The First 50,000 Years; Indian Cultures - From 2000 B.C. to 1500 A.D.; and The Indian Experience - After 1500 A.D. 19 minutes each, color. Video. Purchase: $305 each. BE.

NATIVE AMERICAN TALES
Video 1: The Dancing Stars (Iroquois) & The Friendly Wolf (Plains Indians); Video 2: The Fire Bringer (Paiute) & How Saynday Brought the Buffalo to the Indians (Kiowa); Video 3: The Angry Moon (Tlingit); Video 4: Coyote & Cottontail & Coyote and the Beaver People (Navajo). Grades K-5. Teacher's guide. 15 minutes each. $125 each. AIT.

A NATIVE AMERICAN'S VIEW: COLUMBUS & EUROPEAN SETTLEMENT
Native American storyteller, Helen Herrara Anderson, answers 9 questions about Columbus & European explorers commonly asked her by her students. Grades 4-7. 8 minutes. VHS. 1992. $145. NDM.

NATIVE AMERICANS
TBS Productions
The history of Native American peoples as told by Native American people. 8 hrs. VHS. Native Americans, P.O. Box 2203, S. Burlington, VT 05407.

THE NATIVE AMERICANS
A six-hour documentary told by Native Americans of today. 1994. TBS.

NATIVE GRACE
A selection of prints of Native American peoples, landscapes, creatures and plants done by famous artists who recorded the earliest days of exploration in North America. 30 minutes. $29.95. CH.

NATIVE INDIAN FOLKLORE
a 5-video compilation: Christmas at Moose Factory (James Bay); The Man, the Snake and the Fox (Ojibway legend); Medoonak the Stormmaker (Micmac legend); Salmon People (West Coast Indians); Summer Legend (Micmac legend). 1986. 71 minutes. Video. Purchase: $35. NFBC.

NATIVE LAND; NOMADS OF THE DAWN
Alvin H. Perlmutter, Producer
John Peaslee, Director
Jamake Highwater, Writer/host
Examines the history and culture of the Native Americans who discovered and civilized the North and South American continents. Focuses on the function of myths as the basis of cosmology of ancient (and contemporary) society. 1986. 58 minutes, color. Video. Purchase: $495; rental, $95. CG. Rental: $27.50. UMN.

NATWANIWA: A HOPI PHILOSOPHICAL STATEMENT
Larry Evers, University of Arizona
With George Nasoftie, a ceremonial leader, talks of cultivation of the land--how every crop and action has significance for his future life. In Hopi with English subtitles. 27 minutes. Video. $175. NR.

NAVAJO
KBYU, Provo, Utah
Teaching children the way and heritage of the Navajo people. 1979. 29 minutes, color. Video. Purchase: $150; Rental: $40/week. NAPBC.

NAVAJO
The Navajos of the Grand Canyon. 16 minutes. Grades 7-12. 16mm. FILMS.

THE NAVAJO
Museum of Northern Arizona, Producer
Navajos tell their story of survival in northern Arizona. A child learns to tend sheep, a mother teaches how to card, spin, dye and weave wool for rugs. A family sacrifices a sheep. Story is cast against their history and the vital role of women in religious, social and cultural life. 1990. 15 minutes, color. Video. Purchase: $19.95. CAN.

THE NAVAJO
A visit to the Navajo Reservation in northeastern Arizona to discover the values held by this indigenous community. Navajo medical practices, religious rituals and beliefs are compared to modern practices, with a discussion of the problems of reconciling traditional Navajo ways with modern technology. 1959. 58 minutes, bxw. Grades 9 and up. Rental: UA & IU.

THE NAVAJO
Fred J. Pain, Jr.
The history, customs, and life of the Navajo Indian Nation (15 million acres within the Southwestern part of the U.S.) are described in this film. 1972. 21 minutes, color. 16mm. Purchase: $300; video, $180. Rental: 16mm, $13.40. IU.

NAVAJO CANYON COUNTRY
Depicts the way of life of the Navajos and provides some of the historical background of Indian life in Arizona and New Mexico. 1954. 13 minutes. 16mm. Rental. IU & PSU.

NAVAJO CHILDREN
Deals with the semiannual migration of a Navajo family to its summer home. 1938. 11 minutes, bxw. 16mm. Rental. UK.

NAVAJO CODE TALKERS
Tom McCarthy
Documentary using interviews and archival footage to show the vital role a small group of Navajo Marines played in the South Pacific during World War II. Interviews with Peter McDonald, Navajo Chairman; Carl Gorman, artist & scholar; and R.C. Gorman, Taos artist. 1986. 28 minutes, color. Video. Purchase: $56.95; rental: $40. NAPBC, NMFV & OW. Rental: $17.50. UMN.

NAVAJO COUNTRY
Shows the nomadic life of the Navajo Indian in northwestern Arizona. 1951. Grades 1-6. 10 minutes, color. 16mm & video. Purchase: 16mm & video, $175. Rental: $17.50. IFB. Rental. UA & IU.

NAVAJO COYOTE TALES: LEGEND TO FILM
Animate in English and Navajo. Shows how coyote films were animated on computer. 1972. Grades 6 and up. 18 minutes, color. 16mm. Purchase: 16mm, $260. SAN. Rental: SAN & UCLA.

NAVAJO FILMS THEMSELVES SERIES
Sol Worth & John Adair
Concerned with seeing how Navajo Indians, taught the technology of filmmaking might show a definite Navajo perspective in their films. Five films are descriptive of processes; two are concerned with man's relationship to nature. "A Navajo Weaver," by Susie Benally; "A Navajo Silversmith," by Johnny Nelson; "Old Antelope Lake," by Mike Anderson; "The Shallow Well Project," by Johnny Nelson; "Second Weaver," by Alta Kahn; and, "The Spirit of the Navajo," by Maxine & Mary Jane Tsosie. 1966. Grades 9 and up. 9-27 minutes, bxw. Video. Purchase: $420 (3 cassettes); $85/title. MMA.

NAVAJO GIRL
Life on an Indian reservation in northeast Arizona. Focuses on the life of a ten year old girl and her family. 1973. 20 minutes. Grades 3-12. Purchase: VHS, $99. GA.

THE NAVAJO INDIAN
Provides a picture of the changing life styles of the Navajos who live on an Arizona reservation. 1975 revised edition. 10 minutes, color. Grades K-6. Purchase: 16mm, $265; video, $185. COR. Rental only, $16.50. PSU; $9. IU.

NAVAJO INDIANS
Portrays the Navajos in their native environment. 1939. 11 minutes. Grades 4-9. 16mm/bxw. Rental. UA, PSU, UK & IU.

NAVAJO LIFE
Shows the National Monument of Canyon de Chelly, describing the life of the Navajo Indians living in the canyon. 1961. 9 minutes, color. 16mm. Rental, $9.35. IU.

NAVAJO MOON
This documentary-type story, photographed on the Navajo reservation in New Mexico, provides an inside look at the lives of three Navajo children. 28 minutes, color. Purchase: $89.95. FH.

THE NAVAJO MOVES INTO THE ELECTRONIC AGE
Briefly describes the background of the Navajo before World War II. Then points out how the tribal council invested income from oil discoveries into projects to benefit the entire tribe. 19 minutes. 16mm. Rental. UK and UA.

NAVAJO NIGHT DANCES
Walter P. Lewisohn, Producer
Deals with a Navajo family at the Nine Day Healing Chant, a feast, and the Arrow, Feather and Fire Dance rituals. 1957. 12 minutes. 16mm. Rental: UK & UA.

NAVAJO - A PEOPLE BETWEEN TWO WORLDS
Francis R. Line
Effects of modern culture upon the largest remaining Indian tribe on a reservation in Arizona. 1958. 18 minutes. 16mm. Rental, $14. PSU.

NAVAJO, RACE FOR PROSPERITY
Document Associates & BBC
Offers a contemporary view of life on the Navajo reservation and focuses upon the development of industries on the reservation. 1972. 26 minutes, color. Purchase: 16mm, $400; video, $340. Rental, $55. CG.

NAVAJO ROUND DANCE
A group of Navajo high school students perform the traditional Navajo Round Dance. Navajo music soundtrack, no narration. 1971. 3 minutes, color. 16mm. Rental: $18. UCLA.

NAVAJO RUG WEAVING
Shows how the Navajo Indians weave their famous rugs. Explains the different operations; Provides a clase view of the weaving technique. 10 minutes, color, silent. 16mm. Rental: $21. UCLA.

NAVAJO: SHEPHERDS OF THE DESERT
Describes a day in the life of a typical Navajo family. 1970. Nine minutes. Grades 4 and up. 16mm. Rental. UA.

NAVAJO SILVERSMITH
Traces a Navajo artisan's creation of some small Yeibachai figures from the mining of the silver to the finished works. 21 minutes, bxw. Grades 9 and up. Rental: 16mm, $15. PSU.

NAVAJO SILVERSMITHING
Focuses on a Navajo craftsman, Tom Burnside, on an Arizona reservation, who has come to grips with modern technology while still maintaining the values of his own culture. 1961. Grades 7 and up. 11 minutes, color. Rental: PSU, UCT & UA.

NAVAJO: A STUDY IN CULTURAL CONTRAST
Portrays the culture, social organization, and physical environment of the Navajo Indian. 1969. Grades 6 and up. 15 minutes, color. 16mm. Rental: PSU, UCT & IU.

NAVAJO: THE LAST RED INDIANS
Michael Baines
Contains scenes of Navajo ceremonies including diagnosing illnesses by trance-like hand trembling and a sing or healing ceremony. The integration of traditional healing practices with those of white doctors is shown. 1972. 35 minutes, color. 16mm & video. TW & UA.

THE NAVAJO WAY
Robert Northshield, Director
Survival as a tribe within American society is said to come from the involvement with tradition, the Navajo way. Reflects the spiritual life of the traditional community. 1975. 52 minutes. color. 16mm. FILMS.

THE NAVAJOS & ANNIE WAUNEKA
Annie Wauneka, awarded the Freedom Medal by President Kennedy for her achievements in public health education among her fellow Navajo Indians, visits the homes of her people instructing them in simple health measures. 1965. 26 minutes. Grades 9-adult. 16mm. Rental. UA.

NAVAJOS OF THE 70's
Deals with the customs, history, economics, current problems and future prospects of the Navajo Indians. Grades 1-8. 15 minutes. 16mm. Rental: UK.

NAWATNIWA: A HOPI PHILOSOPHICAL STATEMENT
George Nasoftie
Ceremonial leader from Shongopavi relates the Hopi ceremonial cycle to agriculture and the sacred teachings. 1978. 20 minutes. Video. With I'isaw: Hopi Coyote Stories - two programs on one tape. Rental, $52.50. ATL.

NEHI CHEII TOAD COUNTS HIS CORN
Math concept of place value taught using coyote and toad. Available in English and Navajo version. Animated. Ten minutes. Grades 2-8. 16mm & video. Rental, $10/week. SAN.

NESHNABEK: THE PEOPLE
Gene Bernofsky; Donald Stull, Project Director
Based on footage of the Prairie Band Potawatomi of Kansas by amateur anthropologist Floyd Schultz between 1927-1941, this film was edited & supplied with a soundtrack based on recent interviews with elderly Potawatomi. Covers reservation life, culture and the people. 1979. 30 minutes, 16mm, bxw. STULL, UK & KS.

NETSILIK ESKIMO 1
Gilles Blais, Director
A 2-part video: 1) The Eskimo: Fight for Life, 51 minutes - This ethnographic documentary studies the traditional forms of play, work and education of the Netsilik Inuit during their last migratory camp in the 1960s; and 2) The Netsilik Eskimo Today, 18 minutes - shows the actual life of an Eskimo family in the settlement of Pelly Bay inside the Arctic Circle. Purchase: $35. NFBC.

NETSILIK ESKIMO SERIES
Quenten Brown, Ph.D., Director
Nine films in 21 half-hour parts. Titles include: At The Autumn River Camp: Two Parts: Part 1, In late autumn, the Inuit travel through soft snow and build karmaks in the river valley. Fishing through ice. 26 minutes. Part 2, The men build an igloo, make a sleigh; women work on parka; children play. 33 minutes. At The Caribou Crossing Place: Two Parts: Part 1, Early autumn; caribou hunting and skins. 30 minutes. Part 2, Caribou hunting. 29 minutes. At The Spring Sea Ice Camp: Three Parts: Part 1, Two Inuit families travel across the wide sea ice; build small igloos. 27 minutes. Part 2, The men hunt seal through ice, then skin it. 27 minutes. Part 3, Hunting and fishing; women sewing; breaking camp moving ashore to tents for summer. 27 minutes. At The Winter Sea Ice Camp: Four Parts: Part 1, Seal hunting; making camp for winter. 36 minutes. Part 2, Women with furs; men hunting; children play; games. 36 minutes. Part 3, Community igloos; games; hunting and fishing. 30 minutes. Part 4, Family activities; games and music. 35 minutes. Building A Kayak: Two Parts: Part 1, Summer, ice melts, time to build a kayak. 33 minutes. Part 2, Building a kayak. 33 minutes. Stalking Seal On The Spring Ice: Two Parts: Part

1, Seal hunt and skinning; use of fur and meat. 25 minutes. Part 2, Seal hunt. 34 minutes. The Eskimo: Fight For Life; People of the Seal: Eskimo Summer/Winter; Yesterday, Today: The Netsilik Eskimo. 1969. Grades 7-adult. 16mm & video. Purchase: $145 each; rental: $30. DER, CDA & UEVA. Rental: UCT, IU & PSU.

THE NEW CAPITALISTS: ECONOMICS IN INDIAN COUNTRY

Portrays developments on some 30 reservations from Alaska to Florida. Examines the quantum leap into the 20th century being made by Native Americans. Provides insight into Native American culture. Narrated by Eric Sevareid. Adult. 1984. 60 minutes. Color. 3/4" and 1/2" Video. Free loan to Indian organizations and the business and investment community. Purchase: 3/4" - $75, 1/2" $55. OP.

THE NEW INDIANS

Shows a young Creek woman as she attends an intertribal conference; a Kwakiutl chief; a Navajo woman attorney; etc. 1977. 59 minutes. Purchase: 16mm, $595; video, $545. NGS.

THE NEW PEQUOT - A TRIBAL PORTRAIT

Connecticut Public Television, Producer
A documentary exploring the history and future of Connecticut's Mashantucket Pequot Indians. 1989. 60 minutes. Color. Video. Purchase: $150; Rental: $80. NAPBC.

NEZ PERCE - PORTRAIT OF A PEOPLE

Deals with the cultural heritage of the Nez Perce and shows how the Nez Perce National Historical Park has influenced and preserved that culture. 23 minutes, color. Purchase: 16mm & video, $110. NAC. Rental: Video, $10. UCT.

NI'BTHASKA OF THE UMONHON - A SERIES

Chet Kincaid, Producer
A three-program series about a 13 year-old boy from the Omaha tribe as he goes through the first summer of his manhood. Program 1: Turning of the Child; Program 2: Becoming a Warrior; Program 3: The Buffalo Hunt. 1987. 30 minutes each. Color. Purchase: $150 each; Rental: $40 each, $80/series. NAPBC.

NINOS NAVAJOS

Spanish language film. 11 minutes. 16mm/bxw. Rental. UA.

NINSTINTS: SHADOW KEEPERS OF THE PAST

Spreitz-Husband Productions
'Ninstints' located on Anthony Island, is the site of the last stand of totem poles anywhere on the Northwest Coast still remaining in their original location. The Haida abandoned the village in the late 1800's after falling prey to the white man's diseases and the intrusion of his lifestyle into the wider Haida culture. A study guide is available with the film. 1983. 27 1/2 miutes. 16mm & video. Purchase or rental. CFDW.

NISHNAWBI-ASKI: THE PEOPLE & THE LAND

Phyllis Wilson, Director
Illustrates the different ways the Cree and Ojibway of the Nishnawbi-Aski region are reacting to change. 1977. 28 minutes. Video. Purchase: $27. NFBC.

NO ADDRESS

Alanis Obomsawin, Director/writer
Focuses on the young native people who are homeless in Montreal. Describes three organizations that are helping the homeless of Montreal: the Montreal Native Friendship Centre, Dernier Recours, and La Mission Colombe. 1988. 56 minutes, color. Purchase: 16mm, $775; VHS, $350. Rental: $80. NFBC.

NOMADIC INDIANS OF THE WEST: THE LEGACY OF THE AMERICAN INDIANS

Camera One, Producer; hosted by Wes Studi
The world of the Plains Indians; examines the legends & cultures of the various tribes. Ancient America Series. 1994. 60 minutes. $19.98. WKV.

THE NORTH AMERICAN INDIAN

Narrated by Marlon Brando
In three parts: Part 1: Treaties Made, Treaties Broken--presents the conflict between the Nisqually and Washington State over fishing rights. 18 minutes. Part 2: How the West Was Won, And Honor Lost--presents a chronology of Indian-white relations from the landing of Columbus to the defeat of Geronimo in 1866. 25 minutes. Part 3: Lament of the Reservation--presents the living conditions of the Sioux Indians on Pine Ridge Reservation in the Badlands of South Dakota. Also looks at another reservation in Washington State where suicide is above the national average. 1970. 24 minutes. Music by Buffy St. Marie. Grades 6 and up. 16mm. Rental: $18 each. UMN, IU & PSU.

NORTH AMERICAN INDIAN ARTS & CRAFTS SERIES

Geoff Voyce
Commissioned by the Canadian National Indian Arts & Crafts Corporation, these film shows individual artists in their local setting and their artistic processes examined. The following films are available in English, French and Indian languages. A collection of ethnographic documentaries on outstanding Native American artists & artisans. Each artist recounts the history of their people and their craft while they work. A Teacher's Guide contains 200+ pp. of craft activities, history, maps, glossaries, print & non-print bibliographies (free with purchase of two or more videos. The titles include: A Pair of Moccasins for Mary Thomas, 15 minutes, (Shuswap); A Corn Husk Doll by Deanna Skye, 11 minutes (Cayuga); A Malecite Fancy Basket, 12 minutes (Malecite-Canada); A Moon Mask by Freda Deising, 10 minutes (Haida); Beads & Leather of Manitoba, 18 minutes (Cree-Canada); A Willow Basket by Florine Hotomani, 11 minutes (Assiniboine-Canada); Tony Hunt, a Kwakiutl Artist, 10 minutes; Joe Jacobs - Stone Carver, 11 minutes (Cayuga); Porcupine Quill Work, 11 minutes (Odawa-Canada); A Micmac Scale Basket, 12 minutes (Micmac-Canada); A Ceremonial Pipe by Guy Siwi, 10 minutes (Abenaki); Robert Bellegard, a Prairie Artist, 12 minutes (Cree-Canada); Sara Smith, Mohawk Potter, 18 minutes (Mohawk); Birch Bark Biting by Angelique Mirasty, 6 minutes (Cree-Canada); Wooden Flowers of Nova Scotia by Matilda Paul, 14 minutes (Micmac-Canada); Iroquoian Pottery by Bill Parker, 18 minutes; A Silver Chalice by Jeff Gabriel, 10 minutes (Mohawk); Fort Albany Carver, Lawrence Mark, 14 minutes (Cree-Canada). 1977-1979. Purchase: VHS, $49 each; 16mm, $129 each. Rental: $40 each. AMP & ITFE.

NORTH AMERICAN INDIAN LEGENDS

Dramatizes several Indian legends with special effects photography to emphasize their mythical quality. 1973. 21 minutes, color. Grades 1-8. Purchase: 16mm, $435; Video, $275; Rental, $65. PHOENIX. Rental. IU and UA.

NORTH AMERICAN INDIAN TODAY

Covers contemporary attitudes of Indians as well as their cultural past. 1977. 25 minutes. Purchase: 16mm, $395; video, $360. NGS.

NORTH AMERICAN INDIANS & EDWARD S. CURTIS

Teri C. McLuhan, Producer/director
Focuses on Edward S. Curtis (1868-1952), photographer, whose life work was concerned with preserving a record of North American Indians and Alaskan Eskimos. 1985. 30 minutes. Color. 16mm, 3/4" video. PHOENIX.

NORTH OF 60: DESTINY UNCERTAIN

TV Ontario, Producer
Five 30 minute programs exploring areas of Canada's Northwest Territories, the Yukon and Alaska. Depicts the reality of life in the far north, and the future of this land and the culture of its original inhabitants. 1983. 28 1/2 minutes each. Color. See NAPBC for titles and prices.

NORTHERN GAMES

Traditional games of the Inuit. 1981. 25 minutes. Video. Purchase: $27. NFBC.

THE NORTHERN LIGHTS

Alan Booth, Director
Explores the phenomenon of the aura borealis and illustrates how the legends & tales of the indigenous people of the north have helped us to understand the lights. 1993. 48 minutes. Purchase: 16mm, $710; VHS, $300. Rental: $70. NFBC.

NORTHWEST ARCTIC VIDEO

Bob Walker, Director
The Northwest Arctic Television Center at Kotzebue, Alaska, produces programs about cultural, social, and political issues pertinent to the region, including documentaries of traditional skills, public affairs programs, and
and looks at specific aspects of cultural transition in Inupiat Eskimo culture; programs on Inuit studies are also available. Series include: The Alaska Native Claims Settlement Act Series; Inupiat Legends of the Northwest Arctic Series; Traditional Inupiat Eskimo Health Series; Traditional Inupiat Eskimo Technology Series. For a complete list of programs contact NATC.

NORTHWEST COAST INDIANS: A SEARCH FOR THE PAST

Louis and Ruth Kirk
Archaeologists and students reconstruct the Ozette Indian Village at Cape Alava, Washington, an abandoned seafaring hunter's village site. 1973. 26 minutes. Purchase: 16mm, $340; VHS, $200; VHS, $200. UW.

NORTHWEST INDIAN ART

Walter P. Lewisohn, Producer
Shows material collected from six different museums, including double-faced mechanical masks. 1966. Ten minutes. 16mm. Rental. UK.

NORTHWESTERN AMERICAN INDIAN WAR DANCE CONTEST

Covers an annual contest portraying The War Dance, The Feather Dance, The Fancy Dance, and The Hoop Dance. 1971. 12 minutes. Purchase: 16mm, $200; VHS, $150; VHS, $140. UW.

NOW & FOREVER

Shows scenes of Oregon Indians from 1915 to 1945. 80 minutes/bxw. Rental. OHS.

NOW THAT THE BUFFALO'S GONE
Shows how Europeans, who came to America looking for freedom of speech and religion, forgot those freedoms when it came to the Indians. 1991. 20 minutes, color. Video. Purchase: $149; rental, $75. FH. Rental: 16mm, $13.40.

NOW THAT THE BUFFALO'S GONE
Ross Deveish, Director
Analyzes the history of massacres, broken promises, worthless treaties, and land-grabbing that the Indian nations as a whole have suffered. Narrated by Marlon Brando. 1969. 65 minutes, color. Grades 9 and up. Purchase: 16mm, $995; video, 225. Rental, $80/3 days. MG. Rental only: 16mm, $35.50; VHS, $23. PSU.Rental: 16mm, $20. UCLA.

NUHONIYEH: OUR STORY
Mary & Allen Code
Explores the history & current circumstances of the Sayisi Dene, "a people of the ecological & cultural borderlands between Tundra & forest in Canada. 1993. 55 minutes. VHS. Purchase: $245; rental: $60. DER.

OBSIDIAN POINT-MAKING
Clyde B. Smith, Producer
A Tolowa Indian demonstrates an ancient method of fashioning an arrow point from obsidian. Describes various tribes' folklore customs connected with obsidian-chipping and explains the significance, history, and uses of obsidian points. 1964. 13 minutes, color. Purchase: 16mm, $280; video, $195. Rental: 16mm, $45. UC. Video rental, $19.50. PSU.

OJIBWAY & CREE CULTURAL CENTRE VIDEO
Dennis Austin, Executive Producer
Since 1979, the Ojibway and Cree Cultural Centre in Timmins, Ontario, has produced over 25 videotapes which portray traditional craft techniques, tales, and profiles of elders. The programs reflect the heritage of Indians in eastern Canada. For a complete list of programs contact O&C.

OLD DANCES, NEW DANCERS
Documents the first annual Young People's Eskimo Dance Awareness Festival organized at Chevak, Alaska. 1984. 30 minutes. VHS. $24.95. KYUK.

OMAHA TRIBE - FILM SERIES
David Conger, Director
Documentary of Native American life on a reservation presented through portraits of several Omaha people of different ages. The Land, The People, and The Family. 1979. 30 minutes each. Color. 16mm and video. Purchase: $50 each; $105/series. GPN, NETV.

ON THE PATH TO SELF-RELIANCE
Peter J. Barton Productions
Narrated by James Billie, Chairman of the Seminole Tribe of Florida, this film provides an overview of tribal history and current tribal economic development. 1982. 45 minutes. Color. Video. Rental: $80/week. NAPBC.

ON THE SPRING ICE
Walrus as well as whales are hunted by the Eskimos of Gambell on St. Lawrence Island. 45 minutes, color. Purchase: 16mm, $700; video, $400. Rental: 16mm, $60; video, $40. DER.

1,000 YEARS OF MUSCOGEE (CREEK) ART
Gary Robinson, Producer
Traces the development of Creek Indian art forms from the prehistoric period of the mound-builders to the present. Examines over 175 examples of Creek art. 1982. 28 minutes. Color. Video. Rental: $40/week. NAPBC.

ONENHAKENRA: WHITE SEED
Frank Semmons, Producer/director/camera
Explores the development of Iroquois culture; focuses on corn and people's reflections on its use as a way of presenting the audience with a view of Mohawk traditions. Features local people of Akwesasne. 1984. 20 minutes. Color. 16mm, 3/4" and 1/2" video. AM.

THE ORIGIN OF THE CROWN DANCE: AN APACHE NARRATIVE & BA'TS'OOSEE: AN APACHE TRICKSTER CYCLE
Larry Evers, University of Arizona
With Rudoplh Kane. In Apache with English subtitles. 40 minutes. VHS. Purchase: $220. NR. Rental, $52.50. ATL.

ORIGINS
Takes the viewer across the continent looking at the history, geography, language and circumstance, and the roles each had in naming the places we all know. Includes the legacy of Indian languages (26 of the United States have Indian names.) 1989. 30 minutes, color. Video. Purchase: $30. COP.

OSCAR HOWE: THE SIOUX PAINTER
KUSD-TV, Producer
Vincent Price adds his narrative to the personal commentary of Oscar Howe, focusing on his art, philosophy and cultural heritage, as he designs and paints the brilliant Sioux Eagle Dancer. 1973. 27 minutes. Color. Grades 9-adult. 16mm and video. COR. Purchase: $150; Rental: $40. NAPBC.

THE OTHER SIDE OF THE LEDGER: AN INDIAN VIEW OF THE HUDSON'S BAY COMPANY
Martin Defalco and Willie Dunn, Directors
Presents the view of spokesmen for Canadian Indian and Metis groups. With archival materials and contemporary examples, this film includes scenes from a conference in which Hudson's Bay Co. officials respond to Native people's objections. 1972. 42 minutes. Video. Purchase: $27. NFBC.

OUR LAND, OUR TRUTH
Maurice Bulbulian, Director
Ethnographic description of the Inuit of James Bay. 1983. 54 minutes. Video. Purchase: $27. NFBC.

OUR LIVES IN OUR HANDS
Karen Carter & Harold Prins, Producers
Karen Carter, Director
Presents the story of the Micmac basketmakers of Aroostook County, Maine, focusing on Donald Sanipass, and members of his extended family.Touches on survival of their language and tribal lands. 1986. 49 minutes, color. Purchase: 16mm, $600; video, $300. Rental: 16mm, $60; video-3/4" and 1/2", $40. DER.

OUR PROUD LAND
Written and narrated from the Navajo point of view, this film presents a number of sequences of modern day life of the Navajo Indians. 30 minutes. 16mm. Rental. UK.

OUR SACRED LAND
Chris Spotted Eagle, Producer/director
Focuses on the story of the continuing struggle of the Sioux to regain the Black Hills of South Dakota. Examines the reasons why many Sioux have refused to accept the $105 million recently awarded by the Federal Government for the lands confiscated. 1984. 28 minutes, color. 16mm & Video. Purchase: $290. NAPBC & SE. Rental: $10. HO & IN.

OUR SONGS WILL NEVER DIE
Yurok, Karuk & Tolowa cultural summer camps are established for the purpose of reconstructing early village dnce sites. 35 mins. Purchase: 16mm, $425; rental: $48. Purchase: Video, $375. SH.

OUR TOTEM IS THE RAVEN
Features Chief Dan George in a contemporary tale of a young Indian boy's initiation into manhood and his acceptance of his Indian heritage. 1972. 21 minutes, color. Purchase: 16mm, 435; Video, $250; Rental, $58. PHOENIX. Rental: $14. IU & UMN.

THE OWL & THE LEMMING: AN ESKIMO LEGEND
Co. Hoedeman, Director
An example of the Inuit art and folklore. 1971. Six minutes. All ages. Purchase: 16mm, $150; video, $150. Rental, $35. NFBC. 16mm rental only, $8.70. IU.

THE OWL & THE RAVEN: AN ESKIMO LEGEND
Co Hoedeman, Director
An Inuit legend is retold using puppets of sealskin in traditional Inuit design and accompanied by a music track of Inuit songs. 1974. Seven minutes. Grades 1-6. All ages. Purchase: 16mm, $200; video, $150. Rental, $35. NFBC.

THE OWL WHO MARRIED A GOOSE: AN ESKIMO LEGEND
Caroline Leaf, Director
An example of commitment and love. 1974. 8 minutes, b&w. All ages. 16mm & video. CF. Rental, $14. PSU.

PABLITA VELARDE
Irene-Aimee Depke, Producer
Santa Clara Indian artist Pablita Velarde reminisces about her childhood at the Pueblo, her struggling years in a medium traditionally closed to Indian women, her philosophy and her existence in the white man's world, away from the pueblo. She demonstrates her "earth painting" technique, which begins with her gathering the stones and minerals from New Mexico soil. She closes with a visit to a classroom of first-graders, where she tells them a Santa Clara legend, "Why the Coyote Bays at the Moon." 29 minutes, color. Video. DEPKE.

PADDLE TO SEATTLE
Mark Mascarin, Producer/Director
Documents a cooperative project undertaken by the Quileute & Hoh peoples of La Push, Washington, namely to embark on a journey made many times by their ancestors - a six day, 170 mile "paddle to Seattle." 1990. Grades 9-12. 45 minutes, color. Video. Purchase: $78. QTS.

PAGES ON THE PAST
A series of four films which tell the story of the peoples of the Pacific Northwest from the time of

the Ice Age to the coming of Lewis and Clark. An Age of Ice: How the peoples of the Northwest adapted and endured; After the Flood: Floods 13,000 years ago signalling the end of the Ice Age; Landmarks In Time: The time of the eruption of Mt. Mazama about 7,000 years ago; and, History In the Making: Portrays the expansion of Native American civilization throughout the region up to the coming of Lewis and Clark. Study guide and maps. 30 minutes each. Grades 9 and up. Purchase: 16mm, (An Age of Ice only) $450; video, $250 each ($900/series). Rental: 16mm & video, $50/week. TBM.

PARALEGAL FILM SERIES
In four parts; one part demonstrates how Native Americans can protect themselves against consumer fraud, employment discrimination, etc. 16mm & video. ICVT.

CYNTHIA ANN PARKER: BLUE EYED COMANCHE
Jillian Preet, Writer/ Editor/Narrator
Story about a settler child who was abducted by the Comanche Indians. Archival photos & paintings evoke the triumph & tragedy of the American frontier. 1987. Grades 4 and up. 12 minutes, color. Video. Purchase: $49. FI.

THE PATH OF OUR ELDERS
Several Pomo elders portray a way of life that has been handed down throughout the generations 1986. Grades 4 and up. 20 minutes, color. Video. Purchase: $360; rental: $45. SH. Rental: $20.50. UMN.

PAUL KANE GOES WEST
Gerald Budner, Director
Artist Paul Kane traveled Canada in the mid-19th century depicting the Indians through his sketches and paintings. 1972. 14 minutes. Grades 4-12. Video. NFBC, EB.

PEACEFUL ONES
Shows life and customs of the Hopi in the painted desert, including cultivating the land, harvesting crops, weaving, kachinas, and snake dance. 1953. 12 minutes. Grades 4-adult. 16mm. Rental. UT, PSU and UA.

THE PEOPLE (INDIAN)
An analysis of Indian literature. 1981. 30 minutes, video. KS.

THE PEOPLE AT DIPPER
Richard Gilbert, Jack Olfield
Shows life among the Chippewayan Indians of a reserve in northern Saskatchewan. 1966. 18 minutes. Video. Purchase: $27. NFBC.

PEOPLE OF THE BUFFALO
Austin Campbell
Dramatic contemporary paintings of life on the Western Plains, portray the unique relationship between the Indians and buffalo. 1968 revised edition. 14 minutes, color. Grades 5 and up. Rental. PSU, IU, EB and UA.

PEOPLE OF THE FIRST LIGHT
WGBY-TV Springfield, Mass.
7-29 minute films about Native Americans living in Rhode Island, Massachusetts and Connecticut: The Narragansetts, Pequots, Wampanoags, Mohegans, Nipnucs and Paugausetts, descendents of the original Eastern Woodland Algonquin Indians. *Indians In Southern New England (The Survivors); The Wampanoags of Gay Head*

(Community Spirit and Island Life); The Boston Indian Community (Change and Identity); The Narragansett (Tradition); Indians of Connecticut (The Importance of Land); The Indian Experience: Urban and Rural (Survival); The Mashpee Wampanoags (Tribal Identity.) 1979. Color. Video. GPN and NAPBC.

PEOPLE OF KASHUNUK
A family portrait through sight & sound of the Yup'ik Eskimo village of Chevak. 1983. 30 minutes. VHS. $24.95. KYUK.

PEOPLE OF THE MACON PLATEAU
Introduction to the Indian cultures of the Macon Plateau with emphasis on the Mississippian Indian culture. Grades 7 and up. 12 minutes, color. Video. Rental. $10. UCT.

PEOPLE OF THE SEAL
Michael McKennirey & George Pearson, Producers
Part I: Eskimo Summer - Documents the summer activities of th Netsilik Inuit, which take place on the land. Part II: Eskimo Winter - Search for seal holes; building igloos; seal hunting. 1971. 52 minutes each. Grades 7-adult. Video. Purchase: $27 each. NFBC. 16mm & video, EDC.

PEOPLE OF THE SUN: THE TIGUAS OF YSLETA
Documentary surveying the history of the Tigua Indians as they struggle to gain recognition as a tribe & walk the fine line between being Texans in El Paso & Pueblo Indians. Teacher's guide. 56 minutes. $45. UT-ITC.

THE PEYOTE ROAD
Gary Rhine, Producer/Director
A feature length documentary exploring the history of the use of the cactus Peyote as a religious sacrament by North American Indigenous people. Interviews with experts Dr. Huston Smith, Dr. Milner Ball and NAC Roadman Reuben Snake. 60 minutes, color. Purchase: VHS, $29.95; 16mm, $750. KF. Rental: Video, $10. HO.

PETROGLYPHS: IMAGES IN STONE
Marianne Kaplan
A documentary focusing on the petroglyphs of the Coastal Salish, Kwakiutl and West Coast People and uses the carvings to depict their rituals and myth. 1985. 10 minutes. 16mm or video. Purchase or rental. CFDW.

PINE NUTS
Clyde B. Smith, Producer
Members of the Paviotso and Paiute tribes demonstrate how the pine nut, from the pinon tree, were harvested and prepared as food, using ancient techniques. 1961. 13 minutes, color. Purchase: 16mm, $280; video, $195. Rental: 16mm, $45, UC. Rental only: Video, $15.50. PSU.

PLAY & CULTURAL CONTINUITY: Part 4, MONTANA INDIAN CHILDREN
On the Flathead Indian Reservation and surrounding countryside, the play of Indian children ranges from the universal domestic activities and monster play themes of those mirroring individualistic cultural elements, such as wrapping of babies, drumming, singing, and hunting. 1975. 29 minutes, color. 16mm rental, $17.50. PSU.

POMO BASKETWEAVERS: A TRIBUTE TO THREE ELDERS
This three-part series provides an in-depth intro-

duction to the culture, history, and basketweaving traditions of the Pomo. Part 1: The People, the Baskets - presents an overview of Pomo culture & features a portrait of basketweaver, Laura Somersal. An introduction to Pomo basket-weaving, showing the varies types of styles & different techniques. Part 2: A History of Change, a Continuing Tradition - recounts the history of the Pomo & explores the changes in the art & traditions of Pomo basketweaving. Features a biographical tribute to Elsie Allen, one of the most revered of all Pomo basketweavers. Part 3: The People, the Plants, and the Rules - examines the close relationship of the Pomo to their environment & explores the spiritual rules & responsibilities of the Pomo to the natural world. Features a portrait of Mabel McKay, a famed dream weaver & Indian doctor. 1994. 29 minutes each. Video. Purchase: $175 each; rental: $50 each. UC.

POMO SHAMAN
William Heick, Producer
A shortened version of the complete research documentary, "Sucking Doctor." The second and final night of a shamanistic curing ceremony among the Kashia group of Southwestern Pomo Indians. 1964. 20 minutes, bxw. Purchase: 16mm, $410; Video, $195. Rental, $50. UC. 16mm rental: $14.50. PSU & IU.

PORTAGE
Reviews the history of Canadian fur trapping and shows the building of a birch bark canoe by Indian craftsmen. 1941. 22 minutes, color. Grades 6 and up. 16mm. Rental, $12.75. IU.

PORTRAIT OF LUCY SWAN
Elderly Lucy Swan, Cheyenne River Sioux, reminisces about family and tribal history. Illustrates past/present living conditions on the reservation. Adult. 30 minutes. 16mm. Rental, $15. NILB.

POTLATCH PEOPLE
Document Associates & BBC
Presents the Indians of the Pacific Northwest and the ceremonial potlatch feast. 1972. 26 minutes, color. Purchase: 16mm, $400; video, $340. Rental, $55. CG.

POTLATCH: A STRICT LAW BIDS US DANCE
Dennis Wheeler, Director
Features the outlawed Kwakiutl Potlatch ceremony. The confiscation of an enormous and valuable collection of dancing masks and costumes. Shows a Potlatch given by the Cranmer family. Narrated by Gloria Cranmer Webster. 1975. 53 minutes. 16mm & video. Purchase/rental. CFDW.

POUNDMAKER'S LODGE: A HEALING PLACE
Alanis Obomsawin, Director
Drug and alcohol abuse and treatment in St. Albert, Alberta. 1987. 29 minutes. Video. Purchase: $27. NFBC.

POW-WOW!
Displays North American Indian dances at a gathering of more than 20 tribes. Chiricahua Apaches perform their ancient sacred Fire Dance; Comanches execute the Gourd Dance; the Intertribal Dance; and, the War Dance. Indians speak of their traditions, ceremonies and heritage. All ages. 1980. 16 minutes. Purchase: 16mm, $375; video, $250. COR. Rental: $16mm, $20. UMN.

POWWOW AT DUCK LAKE
Bonnie Sherr Klein, Director
A discussion at Duck Lake, Saskatchewan, where

Indian-Metis problems are openly and strongly presented before a gathering of Metis Indians and Whites. 1967. 14 minutes. Video. Purchase: $22. NFBC.

THE POWER OF THE WORD WITH BILL MOYERS: 3 - ANCESTRAL VOICES
Features three poets with distinctive heritages that ionfluence their work: Joy Harjo (Creek-Cherokee), Garrett Hongo (Japanese-American), and Mary TallMountain (Native American born in Alaska.) 1989. 58 minutes, color. Video rental, $12. PSU.

POWERLESS POLITICS
Sandy Johnson Osawa–KNBC-TV, Producer
Provides an overview of the legal relationship between the U.S. and Indian tribes showing how shifts and emphasis in the government Indian policy have had far reaching effects on Indian life. 1975. 28 minutes. Video. Purchase: $55. UP and BYU-N.

PREHISTORIC MAN
Traces the development of the Indians in the American West. 1967. Grades 7 and up. 17 minutes, color. Rental. UA & UCT.

PRIDE, PURPOSE & PROMISE: PAIUTES OF THE SOUTHWEST
Mitchell Fox, Producer/writer
Interviews with tribal leaders and members of the Kaibab Reservation in Arizona, the Shivwits Reservation in Utah, and the Moapa Reservation in Nevada. Discusses Southern Paiute tribal self-determination, tribal lands, history, education and economic development, and the present day Indian reservation life. 1984. 28 minutes, color. Video. Rental: $40. NAPBC.

THE PRIMAL MIND
Alvin H. Perlmutter, Producer
Jamake Highwater, Writer/host
Documentary which explores the basic dif ferences between Native American and Western cultures, while examining two cultures' contrasting views of nature, time, space, art, archaeology, dance and language. 1984. 58 minutes, color. Purchase: 16mm, $895; video, $595. Rental: 16mm, $100. CG. Rental: VHS, $39. PSU.

PRINCESS OF THE POW-WOW
A documentary focusing on Ella Aquino, a Lummi Indian woman, who has devoted her life toward the advancement of Indian culture and concerns. Examines issues of battles over land and fishing rights on behalf of the Puget Sound Indians. 22 minutes. Color. Video. Purchase: $50. GPN.

THE PROBABLE PASSING OF ELK CREEK
Rob Wilson, Director
Documentary focusing on the controversy between a little town, Elk Creek, and the Grindstone Indian Reservation over a government planned reservoir. 1983. 60 minutes, color. Purchase: 16mm, $895; 3/4" and 1/2" video, $595. Rental, $95. CG. NAPBC (members only).

THE PSORIASIS RESEARCH PROJECT - A CREE HEALER
Documents the healer's treatment practices under controlled conditions in a western health clinic. It also shows treatment of the same patients in a more traditional sweatlodge ceremony. 1985. 35 minutes. Color. Video-3/4" U-Matic, $125; VHS, Beta, $100. In A CREE HEALER, which serves as an introduction to the psoriasis video, Russell Willier talks about traditional native medicine and

the controversies he has encountered in openly discussing this subject. 1985. 22 minutes. Color. Video. 3/4" U-Matic, $100; VHS, Beta, $75. Combines on One Tape, 3/4" U-Matic, $200, and VHS, Beta, $150. UADA.

PUEBLO ARTS
The soil used by the Pueblos to build homes is also used to create objects of art. 11 minutes. Color. Purchase: 16mm, $175; video, $140. Rebtal, $17.50. IFB.

PUEBLO BOY
Tells the story of a young Indian boy being instructed in the ancient and modern ways and traditions of his people, the Pueblos of the Southwest. 24 minutes. 16mm. Rental. UK.

PUEBLO INDIANS OF TAOS, NM
1927 documentary of of the lives, customs and characters of the Pueblos of the area and some of the whites who lived among them. 10 minutes, bxw. EG.

THE PUEBLO PEOPLES: FIRST CONTACT
George Burdeau, Director; co-produced with Larry Walsh; hosted by Conroy Chino
Describes the early encounter between this peaceful Indian tribe and the distructive Spanish explorer Coronado. Told through the images and legends of the Pueblo people. 1990. 30 minutes, color. Video. Purchase: $50. PBS. Rental: Video, $14. PSU.

THE PUEBLO PRESENCE
Hugh and Suzanne Johnston, WNET-13
Examines the continuity of ancient Pueblo civilization into the present. Zuni historian Andrew Napetcha discusses the ancestry of Pueblo peoples. Art, religion, ceremonials, language, architecture, and daily activities and relationship to the natural world. 1981. 58 minutes. 16mm and VHS. JOHNSTON.

PUEBLO RENAISSANCE
Philip Hobel, Executive Producer
Provides an authentic view of the sacred traditions, ancient religious and agricultural ceremonies of the Pueblo people. 1972. 26 minutes, color. Purchase: 16mm, $400; video, $340. Rental, $55. CG and IU.

THE PUEBLO EXPERIENCE: MAKING A NEW WORLD
Richard Marquand, Director/Producer
The story of a 17 year-old girl, Charity, in Puritan Massachusetts in 1640. Captured by the Indians then returned, Charity rebels against the Puritan doctrine and treatment of the Indians. 1975. 31 minutes. All ages. Purchase: 16mm, $425; rental, $40. LCA.

QAGGIQ
Zacharias Kunuk, Producer/director
A drmatization of past Arctic life, directed by an Inuit videomaker & improvised by Igloolik community members, far-flung families arrive via dogsled for a joyful reunion. 1989. 58 minutes, color. Video. Purchase: $1,250. IIP.

QUEEN VICTORIA & THE INDIANS
Animated film adaptation is based on a true story by noted American artist George Catlin. In the late 1840's a small group of Ojibwes journeyed to London to dance at the opening of the Indian Gallery. Grades 4-9. 11 minutes. Purchase: 16mm, $240; VHS, $89; 3/4", $119. CC.

THE RAINBOW OF STONE
When drought threatens the grazing lands of the Navajos, an old chief tells his grandson the tribal legend of a wonderful country beyond The Rainbow of Stone. 1949. 23 minutes, color. 16mm. Rental: UCT & UT.

RAMONA: A STORY OF PASSION & PROTEST
Helen Hunt Jackson's novel of 1884 crystalized opinion about whites' maltreatment of Indians. This film uses feature film clips to recap the plot & historical sources & sites. 28 minutes, color. Video. Purchase: $89.95. FH.

REAFFIRMATION & DISCOVERY THE FIRST POW-WOW ON HAWAII
Story of two women whose lives & vision come together in the creation of the first pow wow on the big island, Hawaii - of the connection made between Native Americans & Native Hawaiians, 29 mins. Video. Purchase: $250; rental: $45. SH.

THE REAL PEOPLE SERIES
KSPS-TV Spokane, Washington
Nine, 30-minute programs on Indian tribes of Northwest. The Colville, the Flathead, the Couer d'Alene, the Kalispel, the Kootenai, the Nez Perce and the Spokane. Examines the lifestyles, culture and lore of these seven tribes. Teacher's guide. 1976. Color. Grades 5-adult. 16mm & video. Purchase: $450/series, $65/program. Rental: $17.50/program. GPN & NAPBC.

THE RED DRESS
Michael Scott, Director
Tells the story of conflicting loyalties to the past, the demands of the present day, traditional values and family affections. 1978. 28 minutes. Grades 7-adult. Purchase: 16mm, $500; video, $300. Rental, $50. NFBC.

RED ROAD - TOWARD THE TECHNO-TRIBAL
KBDI-TV, Producer
Documentary presenting and exploring contemporary views of Native American philosophy, spirituality and prophecy. 1984. 27 minutes. Color. Video. Purchase: $150; Rental: $40. NAPBC.

RED SUNDAY
John McIntyre, Narrator
The story of the Custer battle, told in art work, photographs, modern re-enactment and aerial photography. 1975. 28 minutes, color. Purchase: Video, $25. OAP. Rental: 16mm, $15. IU.

REDISCOVERY: THE EAGLE'S GIFT
Peeter Prince
On a remote island off the Northwest coast of British Columbia, native and non-native youth learn about the unique Haida culture. They explore ancient villages, caves, totem and burial grounds, as they learn the drum song, dances and drama of the "Haida Potlatch". 1984. 29 minutes. 16mm and video. Purchase or rental. CFDW.

RELOCATION & THE NAVAJO-HOPI LAND DISPUTE
Victoria Mudd, Director/producer
In 1974, Congress passed the Navajo-Hopi Land Settlement Act, partitioning 1.8 million acres of disputed land i Arizona equally between the Navajo and Hopi Indian tribes. This film examines the historical and political forces behind the land dispute, and documents the struggle of 9,000 displaced Navajos to retain their homes, their culture, and their dignity. 1981. 23 minutes, color. 16mm rental, $20. PSU.

RETURN OF THE RAVEN - THE EDISON CHILOQUIN STORY
Barry Hood Films, Producer
In 1954, in a policy which became known as "Klamath Termination," the Klamath Tribe of Oregon joined over 100 tribes throughout the country in loss of federal recognition. This is the true story of Klamath Termination and Edison Chilquin's ten-year struggle to preserve traditional values. 1985. 47 minutes. Color. Video. Rental: $80. NAPBC.

RETURN OF THE SACRED POLE
Michael Farrell, Producer/director/writer
narrated by Roger Welsch
Documentary charting the return of a treasured religious object to the Omaha people, the sacred pole (Washabagel) that forms the center of Omaha spiritual life. 1990. 28 minutes, color. Video. Purchase: $39.95. GPN.

RETURN TO SOVEREIGNTY: SELF-DETERMINATION & THE KANSAS KICKAPOO
Donald D. Stull, Producer/writer
David M. Kendall, Director/writer/editor
Bernard Hirsch, Writer/narrator
A documentary film about the Kickapoo Indians of Kansas and their struggle to regain control of their future. Explores Indian self-determination & the Education Assustance Acts. 1987. 46 minutes, color. Video. Purchase, $95; and rental, $50. UC. KS (loan).

1492 REVISITED
Provides an alternative, "indigenous" perspective on the quincentennary of Columbus' arrival. Features artwork from the touring national exhibition Counter Colon-Ialismo as well as challenging commentary by artists & scholars. Also raises important questions about the nature of history and its construction. 1993. 28 minutes, color. Video. Purchase: $225; rental: $50. UC.

REVIVAL
Michael Brodie & Bill Roxborough, Producers/directors; Doreen Jensen, Narrator
Presents four contemporary artists of the Northwest Coast: Reg Davidson and Dorothy Grant, both Haida; Nishga artist Norman Tait overseas the printing of a silkscreen design of the beaver; and Noreen Jensen, Gitskan carver. These artists look to the artists of old to interpret the design vocabulary of the Northwest Coast tradition. 1983. 29 minutes. Color. 3/4" and 1/2" video. MBP and VOI.

RICHARD CARDINAL: CRY FROM A DIARY OF A METIS CHILD
Alanis Obomsawin, Director/writer
Based on the diary of a young man who committed suicide at 17 years of age. Richard had lived in 28 foster homes, group homes, shelters and lockups throughout Alberta. The new Alberta Welfare Act is, in part, Richard's legacy, whereby numerous tribes are now administering their own social services. 1986. 29 minutes, color. Purchase: $550; VHS, $250. Rental: $60. NFBC.

RICHARD'S TOTEM POLE
Richard Harris, 16, is a Gitskan Indians living in British Columbia, Canada, while helping his father a master totem pole carver, he begins to take an interest in his heritage. Through his carving he discovers his roots, culture and family traditions. 25 minutes. Grades 4-adult. Purchase: 16mm, $495; video, $290. Rental, $60. COR.

THE RIGHT TO BE MOHAWK
George Hornbein, Lorna Rasmussen & Anne Stanaway, Producers/Directors
Members of the Mohawk Nation at Akwesasne describe their efforts to maintain identity & sovereignty in an ever-changing society. 1989. Grades 9-12. 17 minutes, color. 16mm & video. Purchase: $250. NDF.

RIO GRANDE: WHERE FOUR CULTURES MEET
Explores the cultural and economic interdependence and interaction of Mexican, Spanish, Indian, and Anglo-American peoples of the Rio Grande Valley. Grades 7 and up. 15 minutes. 16mm. Rental, $15. UT.

RITA JOE: THE SONG SAYS IT ALL
About the life & work of the contemporary Micmac poet, Rita Joe. 1988. 27 minutes. Video. NS.

RITUAL CLOWNS
Victor Masayesva, Producer/director
Hopi videomaker, Victor Masayesva meshes ancient oral tradition, live-action video & computer-generated animation to analyze the evolving, yet universal role of the clown in Southwest tribal cultures. 1988. 18 minutes, color. Video. Purchase: $200. EAI.

RIVER PEOPLE
The Pima Indians reconstruct their old ways of life for this film. 1949. 25 minutes. Grades 4-adult. Rental. UA.

RIVER PEOPLE: BEHIND THE CASE OF DAVID SOHAPPY
Michael Conford, Michele Zacchero
narrated by Ruby Dee
Focuses on the case of David Sohappy, a Yakima spiritual leader, who was sentenced to a five-year prison term for selling 317 salmon out of season. Claiming an ancestral right to fish along the Che Wana, the indigenous name for the Columbia River, Sohappy openly defied state & federal fishing laws and has become a symbol of resistance for Native peoples of the Northwest. 1990. 50 minutes, color. Video. Purchase: $395. FIL.

ROAD TO INDEPENDENCE
Transportation & independence for elders. A story of how the need is being met by the Chickasaw Nation & Delaware Tribe of Oklahoma. 14 minutes. Video. Purchase: $200; rental: $45. SH.

THE ROADS LESS TAKEN
OPBS/Dorothy Velasco, Producer
The travels & travails of the pioneers who journeyed west in the mid-1840's are documented, with the focus on the exploration of less traveled routes and the impact on the Native Americans along the way. 1993. Grades 7 and up. 26 minutes. Purchase: VHS, $260. NDM

ROCK ART TREASURES OF ANCIENT AMERICA: THE CALIFORNIA COLLECTION
Dave Caldwell, Producer/director; Scott Beach, Narrator
Focuses on three major types of rock art - carvings, paintings, and ground figures - at three sites in southern California. Also contemporary Indian storytellers from tribes near these sites. 1983. 25 minutes. Color. 16mm, 3/4" and 1/2" video. DCP.

ROOTS TO CHERISH
Evaluates young Indian pupils. A concept film designed to identify & illustrates consequences of cultural differences upon school performance; ways to conduct a more appropriate evaluation; and suggestions for program modifications. 30 minutes. 16 mm. purchase, $425; rental, $48. Video, purchase, $375. SH.

ROPE TO OUR ROOTS
Bo Boudart, Producer/director/writer
Presents the Inuit Circumpolar Conference, an international organization of Eskimos and Inuit from Alaska, Canada, and Greenland founded in 1977. Discusses the commonalities and differences in life styles and concerns of the delegates. 1981. 30 minutes. Color. 16mm, 3/4" and 1/2" VHS. BO.

ROSEBUD TO DALLAS
Jed Riffe & Robert Rouse
Tells the story of five families who come to Dallas from the Rosebud Sioux Reservation in South Dakota to make a better life through vocational education and on the job training. 1977. 60 minutes. VHS. THRC.

ROUND DANCE
A group of dancers perform a round dance. Three minutes. All grades. Purchase: 16mm, $110. Rental, $10/week. Also available in video. SAN.

THE RUNAWAY
NETV, Producer
14 year-old Darlene Horse runs away from a difficult home situation. Social workers and a Native American alcoholism counselor help the family through appreciation of their culture and use of counseling groups. 1989. 29 minutes. Color. Video. Purchase: $150; Rental: $40. NAPBC.

RUNNING ON THE EDGE OF THE RAINBOW: LAGUNA STORIES & POEMS
Larry Evers, University of Arizona
With Leslie Marmon Silko--reflects on the nature of Laguna storytelling, its functions and the problems she has faced as an Indian poet. 28 minutes. Purchase: VHS & Beta, $175. NR. Rental: VHS, $37.50. ATL.

SACAJAWEA
Neil Affleck
A 16 year-old Shoshone girl joins the Lewis & Clark Expedition. Still photos and drawings offer scope to the land they travelled while animation brings to life Sacajawea and the adventures she shared. She is followed into her later years as a traveller, mediator between Indian and white man and speaker in the councils of her tribe. 1990. 18 minutes, color. Grades 4-9. Purchase: 16mm, $425; VHS, $385; Rental, $45. FF.

SACAJAWEA
A young Indian guide of Lewis & Clark Expedition to the Pacific Northwest. Sacajawea recounts the events prior to the sighting of the Pacific Ocean in 1805. 24 minutes, color. Video. Purchase: $79. FH.

THE SACRED CIRCLE
Donald K. Spence, Producer/director
Adrian Hope, Narrator
In two parts: Part I: Invites the viewer through a bold series of symbolic imagery to participate in the mystical harmony of the Native world. Culminates in the ritual expression of the Sun Dance. The film combines animation, documentary photographs, paintings and on location realism, augmented by lyrical narrative. Part II: Recovery--moves from the frontal assault on Native culture

by missionaries and others in the last century to a series of vignettes reflecting its contemporary face, while conveying the tragedy of cultural loss. 1980. 29 minutes each. Color. VHS. UAL.

SACRED GROUND
The story of the North American Indian's relationship to the land. Their intimate involvement and reverence for places throughout the land that hold a special religious and traditional significance for their race. Provides a detailed look at the specific geographic places all over America that are and always were sacred to the American Indian. Original music by Dr. Louis Ballard, and narrated & hosted by Cliff Robertson. 50 minutes. Video, $19.95. NV.

THE SACRED TREE
Curriculum package including text, four videos, six resource books, posters and other visual aids. Presents many of the universal concepts and teachings handeed down through the ages in Native societies throughout North America concerning the nature, purposes and possibilities of human existence. $450. FOUR.

SALMON ON THE RUN
Steve Christiansen, Producer/director
A documentary on salmon, focusing on conditions threatening the survival of the salmon species of the Northwest Coast. It shows how the special salmon fishing rights of the Yurok Indians of California have brought them into conflict with sports fisherman and small-scale commercial fisherman. 1980-81. 58 minutes, color. Video. AVP.

SANANGUAGAT: INUIT MASTER WORKS OF 1,000 YEARS
Derek May, Director
An exhibition of Inuit carvings from public and private collections. Views of daily life in the Iglootik settlement of the Northwest Territories. 1974. 25 minutes, color. Grades 7 and up. Purchase: 16mm, $500; video, $300. Rental, $50. NFBC. Rental, $19.50. PSU.

SCHOOL IN THE BUSH
Dennis Sawyer, Producer
Tony Ianzelo, Photographer
Cree values & culture. Touches on the jarring dichotomies experienced by (Canadian) Native children in city schools. Uses excerpts from two documentaries, "Cree Hunters of the Mistassini," & "Our Land is Our Life." 1986. Grades 7-12. 15 minutes, color. 16mm & video. Purchase: $200. NFBC.

THE SEA IS OUR LIFE
Bo Boudart
Inuit speak out about the effects of offshore drilling. Shows the growing political awareness and their efforts to organize. 1979. 16 minutes. 16mm. BO.

THE SEARCH FOR THE FIRST AMERICANS
This program follows the trail of America's first inhabitants. 1993. 60 minutes, color. Video. Purchase: $89.95. FH.

SEASONS OF A NAVAJO
John Borden, Producer/camera
Will Lyman, Narrator
Documentary on the lifestyles & traditions of modern Navajo families in Canyon de Chelly, Arizona - sacred songs, ceremonies and oral traditions. Aspects of Navajo life rarely seen on film are shown. Also filmed is the kinaalda, the ritual for young women. 1984. 60 minutes, color. In English

& Navajo with English subtitles. Video. Purchase: $29.50, AUDIO; $59.95. PBS. Rental, $14. PSU.

SECRETS OF THE LITTLE BIGHORN
By retracing the pattern of bullets & cartridge cases across the battlefield, archaeologists have been able to generate a computer simulation of the final, fatal moments of the Battle of the Little Bighorn. The reconstyruction shows a Native American triumph rather than Custer's defeat. 1993. 28 minutes, color. Video. Purchase: $149; rental: $75. FH..

SEDNA; THE MAKING OF A LEGEND
John Paskievich, Director
Follows a team of Inuit carvers and a white man from Vancouver as they craft the first monumental sized Inuit sculpture for a private corporation. 1992. 58 minutes. Video. Purchase: $27. NFBC.

SEEKING THE FIRST AMERICANS
Graham Chedd
Archaeologists from Texas and Arkansas search for clues to the identity of the first North Americans. 58 minutes, color. Adult. Purchase: 16mm, $600; rental, $60. Educator's guide. DER. Purchase: beta/VHS, $60. PBS. Rental only, IU.

SEMINOLE INDIANS
A study of Seminole life on the hummocks of the Everglades in Florida. 1951. 11 minutes, color. Purchase: 16mm & video, $175. Rental, $17.50. IFB.

THE SENECAS
Ron Hagell
Through interviews and narration, this film views the contemporary Seneca Indian of New York State and their history. 1980. 29 minutes. VHS. WXXI.

SEPARATE VISIONS
Peter Blystone & Nancy Tongue, Producers
Profiles four pioneering American Indian artists: Baje Whitethorne, a Navajo painter: Brenda Spencer, a Navajo weaver; John Fredericks, a Hopi kachina carver; and Nora Naranjo-Morse, a Santa Clara sculptor. 1989. 40 minutes, color. Video. Purchase: $195; rental, $50. UC. Rental: $16. UMN.

THE SETTLERS
Allied Film Artists, Inc., Producer
Explores the reasons for and history and impact of America's westward expansion. Including the destruction of Native American cultures. 1978. 22 minutes, color. Purchase: 16mm, $450; Video, $275; Rental, $62. PHOENIX.

SEQUOYAH
The story of the Cherokee Indian who developed the first written American Indian language. 15 minutes. 16mm. WD.

SEYEWAILO: THE FLOWER WORLD
Larry Evers, University of Arizona
Yaqui Deer Songs as they are sung and danced to at a fiesta, the pahko. Yaqui with English subtitles. 51 minutes. Purchase: VHS & Beta, $290. NR. Rental: VHS, $52.50. ATL.

THE SHADOW CATCHER: EDWARD S. CURTIS & THE NORTH AMERICAN INDIAN
T.C. McLuhan, Director/Producer
A film about Edward S. Curtis, photographer, anthropologist and filmmaker.Features marked Kwakiutl dancers, a Navajo Yebechai Ceremony,

and Curtis' own initiation into the Hopi Snake Fraternity. Soundtrack features original Indian music and contemporary Comanche variations. 1975. 88 minutes, color. Grades 9 and up. Purchase: 16mm, 975; video, $585; Rental, $100. PHOENIX. Rental: IRA, PSU, IU, UCT, UK, UMN, UCLA & UA.

SHAMANISM
Serge King & Terry Eaton, Producers
Terry Eaton discusses Native American spiritual values and traditions. 57 minutes. VHS video. TPH.

SHEM PETE MEMORIAL POTLATCH
Highlights of potlatch held in Tyonek, Alaska on October 7, 1989. Remarks by Bonnie McCord, Emil McCord, Sr., Jim Kari, Jim Fall, et al. Features the Tyuonek Dancers, the Northern Lights Intertribal Pow-wow Club, Paul Theodore of Knik & the Dena'ina Indian cloth ceremony. 1990. 45 minutes. VHS. $15. NDM.

SHENANDOAH FILMS
Vern & Carole Korb, Producers
Carole Korb, Director
A Yurok-owned production company, which has made numerous films, filmstrips, and slide tapes about Indian culture, particularly in northern California. Focuses on improving the education, employment skills, and cultural pride of Indian children and youth. Among the productions are: *Again, A Whole Person I Have Become* - Narrated by Will Sampson, this film features a Wintu medicine woman, a Karok spiritual leader, and a Tolowa headman who speak of wisdom of the old ways. 1985, 20 minutes; *In the Best Interest of the Child: Indian Child Welfare Act* - Narrated by Will Sampson, this film depicts an Indian child's removal from his home, to be placed in a non-Indian foster home. Tells of the problems of foster care and the provisions of the Act. 1984, 20 minutes; *Our Songs Will Never Die* - Narrated by Juni Donahue. Yurok, Karok, and Tolowa summer camps have been established in California, where young people work together with tribal elders. 1983, 35 minutes; *The Path of Our Elders* - Narrated by Pat Tswelmaldin. Pomo elders show how traditions are passed on, demonstrating traditional song and dance and the preparation and weaving of basketry. 1986, 20 minutes, video only; and *Roots to Cherish* - Directed by Marilyn Miles & Don Mahler, narrated by Carl Degado. A concerned mother, a Maidu educator, a traditional Hupa teacher, and a guidance counselor speak of the consequences their cultural differences have for Indian students. 1983, 30 minutes, color. 16mm & video. For a complete list of titles contact SH.

SHINNECOCK: THE STORY OF A PEOPLE
Dana Rogers, Producer
Joseph E. Miller, Director/writer
The Indians of the East Coast region who were the first to come into contact with the white man, when the original settlers arrived from Europe. Consequently, these Indians were the first to lose much of their own culture. 1976. 20 minute, color. Purchase: 16mm, $375; video, $215; Rental, $35. PHOENIX.

SHUNGNAK: A VILLAGE PROFILE
Daniel Housberg, Director
Focuses on a tiny Inupiat Eskimo community in northwest Alaska, 75 miles north of the Arctic Circle. Villagers discuss their subsistence practices, and the contrast between past and present. 1985. 30 minutes. Color. 3/4" and 1/2" video. NATC.

THE SILENT ENEMY
H.P. Carver
Chief Yellow Robe, a noted Sioux, who acts in the film, points out the usefulness of the film in preserving an authentic image of the old days. Documents a band of Ojibwa in winter. 1930. 88 minutes. 16mm/bxw. FCE and BL.

SINEW-BACKED BOW & ITS ARROWS
Clyde B. Smith, Producer
Follows the construction of a sinew-backed bow, by a Yurok craftsman. Also demonstrates the making of arrows. 1961. 24 minutes, color. Purchase: 16mm, $480; video, $195. Rental, $50. UC. Rental: 16mm, $20. PSU.

SINGERS OF TWO SONGS
A story of Indian artists as they live in two worlds: traditional & contemporary. 25 minutes. Video Purchase: $375; rental: $48. SH.

SINUMWAK
Jim & Justine Bizzocchi
Follows the (Bella Coola) process from catching oolichan (fish) to feasting on the result, while the many uses of oolichan grease are discussed. 1979. 20 minutes. Purchase: 16mm, $325; and video, $225. CFDW.

SIOUX LEGENDS
Charles & Jane Nauman
Recreates some of the legends closest to the philosophy and religion of the Sioux culture. Demonstrates the Indian feeling of identification with the forces of nature. 1973. Grades 4 and up. 20 minutes, color. Purchase: 16mm, $415; video, $70; rental, $30. AIMS. Rental: IU & UCT.

SISKYAVI - THE PLACE OF CHASMS
Victor Masayesva, Producer/Director
Combines documentary footage with video effects to present a subtle study of the conflicts between Hopi tradition & technology as applied to the Hopi culture. 1991. Grades 9-12. 28 minutes, color. Video. Purchase: $200. EAI.

SITTING BULL: A PROFILE IN POWER
The tragic but heroic saga of Indian/U.S. relations in this interview with Sitting Bull, portrayed by August Schellenberg. 1977. 26 minutes, color. Purchase: 16mm, $325; rental, $30. LCA. Rental: 16mm, $20. UMN.

THE SIX NATIONS
Nick Gosling, Director
The President of the Seneca Nation and the Mayor of the town of Salamanca discuss the various aspects of Indian and white coexistence. The Iroquois League consists of the Mohawk, Oneida, Onondaga, Seneca, Cayuga and Tuscarora India tribes. Grades 7 and up. 1976. 26 minutes, color. Purchase: 16mm, $400; video, $340. Rental, $55. CG. Rental, $30. UT.

SKOKOMISH INDIAN BASKETS: THEIR MATERIALS AND TECHNIQUES
Documents the varied techniques of basket-making by the Skokomish Indians from the Puget Sound region in western Washington State. 1977. 28 minutes/bxw/silent. Super 8mm and video. Rental. UW.

SNAKETOWN
This study of the Snaketown archaeological excavation in southern Arizona, explores the Hohokam Indian culture. 1969. 40 minutes, color. Video. Purchase: $95; rental, $50. UC.

SOMEDAY, I'LL BE AN ELDER
Narrated by Will Sampson
This film is about a pilot substance prevention program, "Project Renewal." A story featuring Karuk tribal members as they conduct a 3 week summer camp program which emphasizes the renewal of traditional ways & values. 25 minutes. Purchase: 16mm, $425; Video, $375. Rental: 16mm, $48. SH.

SOMEPLACE YOU DON'T WANT TO GO
Vivid scenes show hardcore drug & alcohol abuse. Designed to educate elementary & high school Indian youth to drug & alcohol abuse. 22 minutes. Video. Purchase: $360; rental: $45. SH.

SOMETIMES WE FEEL
William Maheras, Director
Brad Stanley, Writer/Producer
A young Indian tells of a life of sorrow, poverty, neglect, and isolation on an Arizona reservation. Ten minutes. 16mm. Rental. UA.

SOMEWHERE BETWEEN
Hy Perspectives Media Group
Looks at the history of Canadian government legislation affecting Indian women and their traditional role in Indian society. 1982. 50 minutes. 16mm & video. Purchase or rental. CFDW.

A SONG FOR DEAD WARRIORS
Examines the reasons for the Wounded Knee occupation in the Spring of 1973 by Oglala Sioux Indians. Features many of the personalities involved, including Russell Means, tribal chairman Dick Wilson, Chief Charley Red Cloud, and Medicine Man Frank Fools Crow. 1973. 25 minutes, color. 16mm. Rental: UCLA & UNI.

SONGS IN MINTO LIFE
Curt Madison, Producer/director
A documentary which explores the creativity and tradition in the songs of Tanana Indians living near Minto Flats, Alaska. Shows activities during the four seasons, with elders singing both contemporary songs and traditional khukal'ch'leek songs. 1985. 30 minutes, color. In English & Tanana Athapascan. Video. Purchase: $56.95. KYUK, NAPBC & RTP.

SONGS OF MY HUNTER HEART: LAGUNA STORIES & POEMS
Harold Littlebird
Author sings traditional and popular Pueblo songs. Includes his song-poem Talking 49 which describes the singing which takes place around a drum after a powwow. 1978. 34 minutes in Engliush and Keres. VHS. Rental, $52.50. ATL.

SONGS OF MY HUNTER HEART: LAGUNA SONGS & POEMS
Larry Evers, University of Arizona
Harold Littlebird continues the oral tradition of his people by incorporating contemporary themes into his work which retains the Pueblo reverence for the Spoken word. 1978. 34 minutes. Purchase: Video, $220. NR.

SOUTHWEST CULTURAL VIDEO SERIES
Designed & developed to help the classroom teacher. Four videos: *Storytelling in Clay & Language* - Native American sculptor Dorothy Trujillo demonstrating how to make a clay storyteller doll. 26 minutes. *Creating Portraits in Art & Language* - Sam English, a Native American painter, is shown demonstrating the art of self-portraiture to 3rd & 4th graders. 17 minutes. *Space in Dance & Po-*

etry - Jerome Marcus, a Taos Pueblo Indian, demonstrates the grass dance for 5th & 6th graders, and Jennifer Predock-Linnell, a modern dancer, is shown demonstrating a variety of creative dance movements to these students. 26 minutes. *Mask, Dance & Character* - Rosalie Jones, artistic director of Daystar Dancers, demonstrates Native American dance steps & use of costumes, masks, and button blankets for theatrical production. 17 minutes, color. VHS. Purchase: $49.95 each; $100 each with curriculum package. ALA.

SOUTHWEST INDIAN ARTS AND CRAFTS
Shows techniques in Navajo rug-making; San Ildefonso and Acoma pottery; Hopi and Zuni jewelry and kachina dolls; and Pima and Papago basket-making. 1973. 14 minutes. Grades K-12. Purchase: 16mm, $320; video, $225; Rental, $40. COR. Rental. IU and UK.

SOUTHWEST INDIAN OF EARLY AMERICA
Uses Indian actors, dioramas, and narration to help recreate what life might have been like about 600 years ago for the Hohokam and Anasazi Indians of northern Arizona and New Mexico. 1973. 14 minutes. Grades 4-8. Purchase: 16mm, $350; video, $245. COR. Rental. IU and UK.

SOVEREIGNTY & THE U.S. CONSTITUTION
By Senator Daniel S. Inouye, Chairman of the Senate Select Committee on Indian Affairs. 20 minutes, color. Video. Purchase: $20; rental: $10. HO.

SPIRIT BAY SERIES
Eric Jordan & Paul Stephens, Producers
Keith Leckie, Director
An entertainment series of 13 films which reflect some of the reality of reserve life and debunks stereotypes about Indians. Filmed on the Rocky Bay Reserve in Ontario, it depicts a remote northern Indian community through the experiences of its children, and shows how its residents have adapted to white society while retaining ties to the land. 1982-86. Grades 4 and up. 28 minutes each, color. In English, French, or Ojibwa. Video. $149 each. ALT & BE (U.S.); ML (Canada).

SPIRIT IN THE EARTH
The legend of a Western Indian tribe, describing the phenomenon of Old Faithful in terms of the Plains' Indians concept of original sin. 22 minutes. Rental. UK.

THE SPIRIT OF CRAZY HORSE
Milo Yellow Hair, Narrator
Reveals the modern Sioux struggle to regain their heritage, and how places like Wounded Knee became sites for a fight that continues still. Presents the militant confrontations of the 1960's & 1970's, the explosive results of 100 years of confinement on Indian reservations. 1989. 58 minutes, color. Purchase: Video, $19.95. CAN. Purchase: Video, $25. AUDIO; $40. PBS. Rental: Video, $10. HO, UMN & PSU.

SPIRIT OF THE HUNT
Narrated by Will Sampson, this film features a spiritual search for the essential elements of what the Buffalo meant historically and in the present to people of the Chippewa, Cree and Dogrib tribes. Historical footage combined with a modern hunt, illustrates the central concept. 1982. Grades 9 and up. 29 minutes, color. Purchase: 16mm, $675. TC. Purchase: VHS, $160; 3/4", $190. CC. Rental: 16mm, $20.50. UMN.

THE SPIRIT OF THE MASK
Peter von Puttkamer, Director
Gryphon Productions
Documentary explores the spiritual & psychological powers of the masks of the Northwest Coast Native people. Features ceremonies as well as commentary by important Indian spiritual leaders, Relates the colonial history of the Northwest Coast Indians.1992. 50 minutes, color. Video. Purchase: $295; rental: $70. UC.

SPIRIT OF THE WHITE MOUNTAINS
Documents the activities of the White Mountain Apaches, and how they support themselves by developing the natural resources of their reservation. 1959. 13 minutes. Grades 4-9. 16mm. Rental. IU & UA.

SPIRIT RIDER
Raised in foster homes, 16-year-old Native American Jesse Threebears is reluctantly repatriated to the reservation of his birth. 1993. Grades 4 and up. 98 mins, color. Video. Purchase: $29.95. FI.

THE SPIRIT WITHIN
Gil Cardinal & Wil Campbell, Directors
Story of how Native prisoners in four western Canadian correctional facilities have won the right to practice their traditional spirituality. 1990. 51 minutes, color. Purchase: 16mm, $775; VHS, $350. Rental: $80. NFBC.

SPIRITS OF THE CANYON: ANCIENT ART OF THE PECOS INDIANS
Artist Amado Pena & archaeologists analyze the paintings & pictographs on the walls of the majestic southwest Texas canyons that date from about 3000 BC until the arrival of the conquistadors in the 16th century. 1992. 30 minutes, color. Video. Purchase: $149; rental: $75. FH.

ST. MARY'S POTLATCH
Three vilages participated in this huge potlatch, celebrating the traditional Yup'ik Eskimo Messenger feast, at which young people are honored as they come of age. 1981. 30 minutes. VHS. $24.95. KYUK.

STANDING ALONE
Colin Low, Director
25 years ago, Pete Standing Alone was the subject of a film by Colin Low which stressed the conflicts facing a young man of the Blood tribe caught between Indian and the white ways. Now middle-aged, Standing Alone lives on the Blood Indian Reserve in Alberta and is active in family and tribal affairs. Through his eyes are seen many aspects of contemporary Blood life. Also considers the economic and political pressures which affect Indian tribes. 1983. 58 minutes. Color. 16mm, 3/4" and 1/2" video. Purchase: 16mm, $775; VHS, $150. Rental: $80. NFBC

STANDING BUFFALO
Joan Henson, Director
An account of rug-making cooperative organized by Sioux Indian women of the Standing Buffalo Reserve in the Qu'Appelle Valley of southern Saskatchewan. 1968. 23 miutes. Video. Purchase: $27. NFBC.

STAR LORE
Faith Hubley, Producer/director
An animated, original and visually dynamic rendering of six Native American sky myths. Stories chosen include: an Inuit tale, and a Pawnee tale. 1984. 8 1/2 minutes. Color. 16mm, 3/4" video. PFV.

STARBLANKET
Donald Brittain, Director
Video about Noel Starblanket and his methods of learning the political process. Looks at his Canadian reserve and what life was like for his people. 1973. 27 minutes. Purchase: $27. NFBC.

STARTING FIRE WITH GUNPOWDER
David Poisey & William Hansen, Directors
Chronicles the origins and achievement of the Inuit Broadcasting Corp. Explores how Inuit TV is a critical element in the creation of a modern Inuit nation in Canada's Arctic. 1991. 57 minutes. Video. Purchase: $27. NFBC.

STEVE CHARGING EAGLE
A film about an American Indian man from Red Scaffold, South Dakota. Quiet, proud, a man of responsibility, he performs in a War Dance competition. 30 minutes, color. 16mm. Purchase: $300; rental: $30. AICRC.

STICKS & STONES WILL BUILD A HOUSE
Traces the development of Indian architecture in the Southwestern U.S. 1970. 30 minutes. Rental, $19. IU.

STONE AGE AMERICANS
Jules Powers & Daniel Wilson, Producers
Discovery Series, NBC
Introduces the vanished Indians of the Mesa Verde in Colorado. The film presents the history of these farmer Indians by examining the cliff dwellings and artifacts discovered in 1888. 21 minutes. 16mm. Rental. UA.

STOP RUINING AMERICA'S PAST
Covers the problem of the destruction of archaeological sites by urban and industrial expansion, as illustrated by the case histories of two prehistoric Indian communities in Illinois - Cahokia Mounds and Hopewell Mounds. 1968. 22 minutes, bxw. 16mm. Rental: UA.

STORIES OF NORTH AMERICA. Part II
Includes Stories of Native American Peoples - Joe Bruchac tells "The Earth on Turtle's Back" & "The Race With the Buffalo." 30 minutes, color. Video. Purchase: $70. NGS.

THE STORY OF TUKTU SERIES
Lawrence Hyde, Director
A children's adventure series, starring Tuktu, an Inuit boy, in 13 film adventures. 1966-1968. Approximately 14 minutes each. Grades 1-8. FILMS.

STORYTELLER
A docuimentary, focusing on an important Pueblo tradition, this video tells the story of the increasingly popular clay sculpture of Helen Cordero of Cochiti Pueblo, New Mexico. Grades 7 and up. 23 minutes, color. Purchase: VHS, $79; 3/4", $109. CC.

THE STRENGTH OF LIFE
Scott & Sheila Swearingen, and Gary Robinson, Producers/directors/writers/editors
Portrays Creek-Cherokee artist Knokovtee Scott reviving an ancient art form of producing jewelry made with engraved shells, its motifs based on the incised shell tradition of the moundbuilder cultures of the ancient Southeast. 1984. 26 minutes. Color. 3/4" and 1/2" video. FC, NAPBC.

SUCKING DOCTOR
William Heick, Producer
A documentary presenting the final night of a cur-ing ceremony held by the Kashia group of Southwestern Pomo Indians. The Indian Sucking Doctor is a prophet of the Bole Maru religion, spiritual head of the Kashia community. 1964. 45 minutes, bxw. Video. Purchase: $295; rental $60. UC. Rental: 16mm, PSU & UCLA.

THE SUMMER OF JOHNSON HOLIDAY - NAVAJO BOY
Johnson Holiday lives in Monument Valley. During the summer he herds the family sheep and goats; during the winter he attends the white man's school. 12 minutes. Grades 1-8. Rental. UK.

SUMMER OF THE LOUCHEUX: PORTRAIT OF A NORTHERN INDIAN FAMILY
Graydon McCrae, Producer/director
Profiles the Andre family, a Loucheux or Kutchin, one of the northernmost Indian peoples, living in both Canada and Alaska. 1983. Grades 7 and up. 28 minutes, color. 16mm & video. In English or Loucheux. TAM (Canada, sales only.) 16mm rental, $27.50. UMN & PSU.

SUN BEAR: ON POWER & EARTH CHANGES
"On Power" - Sun Bear, medicine teacher and founder of the Bear Tribe, teaches people the first steps toward finding their own path of power. "Earth Changes" - Sun Bear draws on his own visions and Native prophecies to help people understand and come into harmony with these times of change. 65 minutes each. VHS & Beta. $29.95 each.

THE SUN DAGGER
Anna Sofaer, Producer/Writer
Albert Ihde, Director/Editor
Tells the story of Anna Sofaer, A Washington, DC artist who having climbed to the top of a high butte in Chaco Canyon, New Mexico, saw a dagger of light pierce an ancient spiral rock carving. After careful study, she found that the dagger marks solstices, equinoxes, and the 19-year lunar cycle. Narrated by Robert Redford, this film explores the Anasazi culture that produced this calendar and thrived over 1,000 years ago in the Chaco Canyon environment. 1982. Grades 7 and up. 60 & 30 minute versions. Color. Purchase: 16mm, $550; video, $250; Rental: $50. BULL. Rental: 30 minute-16mm version, UCT, UT & PSU. Video rental (30 minute version): $40. NAPBC.

SUN, MOON & FEATHER
Bob Rosen & Jane Zipp, Producers/directors
Documentary about three Native American sisters growing up in Brooklyn during the 1930s & 1940s. Blends musical theater (song & dance reenactments of family & tribal stories) and personal memoir (scenes filmed in Brooklyn home). 1989. 30 minutes, color. Purchase: 16mm, $425; video, $250. Rental: $55. CG.

SUNFLOWER JOURNEYS
Explores the heritage of Kansas. Each 30-minute video contains three separate stories. Includes: Native Americans (#209-200 Series, 1989); Glaciated Region - Iowa Tribe Powwow (#303-300 Series, 1990); Natives & Newcomers - Medicine Lodge Peace Treaty & Indian Self Determination (#502-500 Series, 1992); Indian Art Market (#513-500 Series, 1992); Artifacts of Culture - Sacred Spaces (#607-600 Series, 1993); Native Americans (#704-700 Series, 1994); Three Dimensional Art (#705-700 Series, 1994). KS.

SURVIVING COLUMBUS
Chronicles the Pueblo Indians' 450 years of con-

tact with Europeans nd their long struggle to preserve their culture, land & religion. Includes stories of Pueblo elders, interviews with Pueblo scholars & leaders, historical accounts as told by the Pueblo Indians of New Mexico & Arizona. VHS. 1992. Grades 7 and up. 120 minutes, color. Purchase: NAPBC. Rental, $14. UMN & PSU.

TAHTONKA: PLAINS INDIANS
BUFFALO CULTURE
Charles and Jane Nauman, Producers
A re-enactment of the Plains Indian's culture from the pre-horse era to the time of the Wounded Knee massacre. 1966. 30 minutes, color. Grades 4-adult. Purchase: 16mm, $495 and video, $70. Rental, $50. AIMS & NILB. Rental: $20. UMN.

TAKING TRADITION TO TOMORROW
N. Scott Momaday, Ph.D., Narrator
A video presentation and study guide, featuring significant cultural and scientific contributions that American Indians have made to society. Grades 7-college level. 32-page study guide. 30 minutes. Video. $69.95. AISES.

TALES OF THE TUNDRA
Traditional Yup'ik Eskimo storytellers explore the legends of Southwest Alaska. 1992. 30 minutes. VHS. $24.95. KYUK.

TALES OF WESAKECHAK
Marla Dufour, Storytellers Production
A series of 13 fifteen-minute programs based on well known Canadian Cree legends. Wesakechak, the teacher of the first Indian people. 1984. Color. Rental: $300/series; $40 each. NAPBC.

TALKING HANDS
Demonstrates the sign language of the Plains Indians. Tells the story of the Battle of the Washita in sign language with background narration. 20 minutes. 16mm. Rental: $15. UT.

THE TAOS PUEBLO
Paulle Clark, Producer/Director
Spend a day at the 1000-year-old pueblo in Toas, New Mexico to discover more about the traditions that the resident Indians are trying to preserve. See young children doing ceremonial dances; learn about building homes with adobe clay; breadbaking; and making pottery. Includes study guide. 1986. 9 mins, color. Grades 2-8. Purchase: 16mm, 225; video, $165. Rental: $20. BULL.

TEACHING INDIANS TO BE WHITE
Reviews the issues surrounding schooling of Native American children, where native children find it nearly impossible to balance the white view they are taught with the language & values they learn at home. The Seminole in Florida resist being integrated, the Miccosukee decided not to fight, and the Cree took back their own schools. 1993. 28 minutes, color. Video. Rental: $16. UMN.

TEN THOUSAND BEADS FOR NAVAJO SAM
Focuses on Sam Begay, a full-blooded Navajo, who has left the reservation to make a new alien, but secure, life for himself and his family in Chicago. 1971. 25 minutes, color. 16mm. Rental. IU & UCLA..

THAT ONE GOOD SPIRIT -
AN INDIAN CHRISTMAS STORY
Larry Cesspooch, Writer/Director
A clay animated tale of a young Ute Indian boy. 1981. 16 minutes. Color. Grades K-3. Video. Rontal: $40/week. NAPDC.

THE THEFT OF FIRE
Title V Indian Education Program staff
Based on a traditional Yurok story retold by elder Jimmie James, this video version features a running translation in Yurok & English. *Curriculum Unit*: discusses the traditional use of fire as a land management tool by Native Americans. Illus. by Frank Tuttle (Pomo/Maidu). Grades 6-8. 14 minutes. VHS. $69.95 (includes Curriculum Unit.

THESE ARE MY PEOPLE
Michael Mitchell, Director
Two Mohawk spokesmen explain historical and other aspects of Longhouse religion, culture and government which are interwoven. 1969. 13 minutes. Video. Purchase: $22. NFBC.

THEY NEVER ASKED OUR FATHERS
Corey Flintoff, Producer/writer; John A. McDonald, Director/editor; John Active, Narrator
Through interviews and scenes of various aspects of Yup'ik life on Nunivak Island, 20 miles from the mainland of southwest Alaska, this video presents the situation of a native people whose daily affairs are dominated by the federal government located thousands of miles away. 1980. 60 minutes. In English and Yup'ik with English subtitles. VHS. $24.95. KYUK.

THEY PROMISED TO TAKE OUR LAND
Document Associates & BBC
Discusses the misunderstanding by the white man of the value of land to the Indian. 1976. 26 minutes, color. Purchase:16mm, $400; video, $340. Rental, $55. CG. Rental: $30. UT.

THIEVES OF TIME
Gerald Richman
Describes the problems of pot hunters looting valuable archaeological sites in Arizona. 1978. 28 minutes. video. MAI.

THIS SIDE OF THE RIVER
Monona Wali
Focuses on concerns of Onondaga Indians of New York State. Discusses social problems and political awareness. 1978. 30 minutes. and VHS; bxw. WALI.

THIS WAS THE TIME
Eugene Boyko and William Brind, Directors
A recreation of Haida Indian life in a village in the Queen Charlotte Islands. Portrays the potlatch and totems which existed. 16 minutes. 16mm. NFBC.

THIS WORLD IS NOT OUR HOME
Introduction to the history, culture, and traditions of the Pomo people of northern California, as seen through the eyes of Elvina Brown, a tribal elder. 1993. 13 minutes, color. Video. Purchase: $125; rental: $40. UC.

THOSE BORN AT MASSET:
A HAIDA STONEMOVING & FEAST
Covers the Haida ritual, the modern equivalent of the traditional memorial potlatch. 1976. 70 minutes/bxw. 16mm and video. UW.

THREE STONE BLADES
Valerie L. Smith, Director
A dramatization of an Inuit legend from the Bering Strait reconstructing aboriginal Eskimo customs and values. 1971. 15 1/2 minutes. Color. Purchase: 16mm, $275; video, $225. Rental, $20. IFB. Rental only. UA.

THREE WARRIORS
Keith Merrill, Director
Portrays the problems encountered by a 13 year-old on the Warm Springs Indian Reservation in Oregon, and his coming to terms with his heritage. 1977. 105 minutes, color. 35mm & 16mm. ZAENTZ.

THROUGH THIS DARKEST NIGHT
Susan Malins, Producer; Daniel Salazar, Dir.
Vivian Locust & Richard Peters, Narrators
Presents Indian people's experiences during the early reservation period, including some drawn from period accounts. Three speakers: a man speaks of the upheaval experienced when the buffalo were finally gone; a woman describes how she used her strength and traditional skills to ensure that her family would survive; and a third speaker tells of being sent to boarding school and the isolation and humiliation of that experience. 1986. 12 minutes, color. Video. ADL & DAM.

THUNDER IN THE DELLS
Lance Tallmadge, a Wisconsin Winnebago, presents the history of his tribe and their legal struggle to remain in the Wisconsin Dells area in the mid-19th Century. Shows the effects of over 120 years of tourism on the Winnebagos, and discusses the importance of their traditional songs and dances to their well-being and survival. Also the preparation and weaving of black ash wood baskets. 1989. Grades 7 and up. 28 minutes, color. Purchase: VHS, $295; 3/4", $325. CC.

TIKINAGAN
Gil Cardinal
Account of the difficulties along the path to Native self-determination. Foster care and a child welfare agency in Northwestern Ontario, Canada. 1991. 57 minutes, color. Video. Purchase: $27. NFBC.

TIME IMMEMORIAL
Hugh Brody, Director
Native land claims in Canada today; Aboriginal rights in Canada. Takes place in Nass Valley where the Nishga'a people bear witness to their struggle and that of their ancestors. 1991. 57 minutes, color. Video. Purchase: $27. NFBC.

TIME OF THE CREE
Bob Rodgers and Gail Singer
Records a salvage archaeological dig near Southern Indian Lake on the Churchill River in northern Manitoba, Canada. Shows a Cree family in the area living a traditional way of life. 1974. 26 minutes. 16mm. RODGERS.

A TIME TO BE BRAVE
Eric Jordan, Producer/editor
Paul Stephens, Director/writer
Filmed in Ontario, Canada, this film focuses on the Shibagabo family - living on their trapline in winter. Scenes of the family at home and of tracking and trapping establish a good sense of daily life. 1982. 28 minutes, color. 16mm & video. BE.

TIWA TALES: LITTLE FILTH & THE TLACHEES
Chuck Banner, Maggie Banner &
Joseph Leonard Concha, Producers/Directors
A grandfather relates an ancient story. Interwoven with claymation live-action & video effects, bring to life the tale. 1990. Grades 2-8. 17 minutes, color. Video. Purchase: $31.95. MP.

TO EVERY NATION...FROM EVERY TRIBE
An Episcopol film about the history of mission work among Indians to the present day. 28 minutes, color. Video. Rental: $10. HO.

TOM SAVAGE: BOY OF EARLY VIRGINIA
Dramatizes the story of a boy given to the Indians. Depicts his new life, and his learning of their language, skills and tribal customs. 1958. Grades 4-9. 22 minutes. Rental: UA.

TOMORROW'S YESTERDAY
  KBYU-TV Provo, Utah, Producer
Shows how the Pueblo people adapt to the challenges of modern civilization while maintaining their identity and culture. 1971. 29 minutes, color. Video. Rental: $40/week. NAPBC.

TOTEM POLE
  Clyde B. Smith, Producer
Illustrates the seven types of totem poles and relates each to a social system and mythology that laid great stress on kinship, rank, and ostentatious displays of wealth. The carving of a pole by Mungo Martin, a famous carver and chief of the Kwakiutl is shown. 1963. 27 minutes, color. Purchase: 16mm, $540; video, $195. Rental, $50. UC. Rental: 16mm, $27; video, $26. PSU.

TOTEMS
Shows the enormous cedar totems, with their ritualistic & religious carvings, made by the Wes Coast Indians of British Columbia. 1944. 11 minutes, color. 16mm. Rental: $19. UCLA.

TRADITIONAL USE OF PEYOTE
  Gary Rhine, Producer/Director
A summary of the Native American Church Crisis. The U.S. Supreme Court "Smith Decision." 17 minutes, color. Video. Purchase: $19. KF. Rental: $10. HO.

**TRAGEDY & TRIUMPH -
THE CHEROKEE STORY**
The history of the Eastern Band of Cherokee told through tradition and a glimpse of their lives today in Western North Carolina. 30 minutes. V ideo. $29.95. CH.

TRAIL OF BROKEN TREATIES
  Document Associates & BBC, Producer
Examines the past and present injustices and focuses on the attempt of Indian leaders to improve the situation. 1972. 26 minutes, color. Purchase: 16mm, $400; video, $340. Rental: $55. CG.

TRAIL OF THE BUFFALO
Eight minutes. 16mm. Rental: UA.

THE TRAIL OF TEARS
Traces westward expansion and the damage created to Indian culture. 13 minutes, color. Purchase: $69.95. FH.

TRAIL OF TEARS
  WETA-TV Washington, D.C.
Focuses on the forced removal of the Cherokees from their homelands and their exodus to the W est, and the Cherokee's struggle to maintain their identity and their heritage. 20 minutes. Grades 7-12. 16-page teacher's guide, $1.95. Purchase: 16mm, $300; video, $150. AIT.

**TRANSITIONS: DESTRUCTION
OF MOTHER TONGUE**
  Darrell Kipp & Joe Fisher
This program explores the relationship between language, thought & culture, and the impact of language disappearance in Native American communities. 1991. 25 minutes, color. Video. Rental: $10. HO.

THE TREASURE: INDIAN HERITAGE
Two teenage Indian brothers, after their father is arrested for defending tribal fishing rights, begin to weigh the worth of their heritage against today's commercial considerations. 1970. 13 minutes, color. Purchase: 4280; video, $175; Rental, $38. PHOENIX.

TREATIES
  Sandra Osawa, Writer/Producer
  Julian Finkelstein, Director
Retraces Indian treaty history from Colonial times to the present. Discusses the treaty as a legal concept and historical reality. A speech made by Chief Seattle during a treaty session in 1855 is dramatized by host, Nez Perce actor, John Kauffman. 1975. 28 minutes. Video. Purchase: $55. UP and BYU-N.

TREATIES MADE–TREATIES BROKEN
Discusses the land grabbing, broken promises and treaties made by the white man with the Nisqually Indian tribe of Washington State. 1970. 18 minutes, color. 16mm. Rental. UT and IU.

TREATIES, TRUTH & TRUST
Presents 10 of the most commonly asked questions on treaty rights. The answers are given by Wisconsin tribal leaders & religious leaders from various communities. 14 minutes, color. Video. Purchase: $20; rental: $10. HO.

TREATY 8 COUNTRY
  Anne Cubitt & Hugh Brody, Producers/directors
Documents subsistence hunting of the Beaver Indians of the Halfway River Band in northeast British Columbia, and records their views on the current situation over the abrogation of their treaty rights. 1982. 44 minutes. Color. 16mm (sales and rentals); 3/4" and 1/2" (sales only). CFDW.

THE TREATY OF 1868
  NETV, Producer
Examines the roots of the dispute over the Lakota Sioux claim to the Black Hills of South Dakota. A series, two 30-minute videos. Program 1: The Treaty of 1868; Program 2: The Black Hills Claim. 1987. Color. Rental: $65/series; $40 each. NAPBC.

THE TREE IS DEAD
Describes one of the last Indian reservations in the State of Minnesota, Red Lake, and the disintegration of their own culture. 1955. Grades 4 and up. 11 minutes, bxw. 16mm. Rental: $13. UMN.

THE TRIAL OF LEONARD PELTIER
  Paul Burtness, et al
The U.S. Government's murder case against American Indian Movement leader Leonar Peltier. Voices criticism of Native American's experiences with the Federal government, both on their reservations and with the proceedings of Peltier's case. 1977. 16 minutes/b&w. Video. Purchase: $75; rental, $35. UCV.

THE TRIAL OF STANDING BEAR
  NETV, Producer
Tells the story of one man's struggle of self-determination in th 1879 court case "Standing Bear vs. Crook. The dramatic portrayal of the courageous Ponca Chief Standing Bear explores the personal side of the story as the Poncas were forced from their home on the Niobrara River (now northern Nebraska) to inhospitable Territory that is now modern-day Oklahoma. 1988. 120 minutes. Color. Video. Purchase: $40. GPN & NAPBC.

**THE TRIBE & THE PROFESSOR:
OZETTE ARCHAEOLOGY**
  Louis and Ruth Kirk, Producers
Professor Richard Daugherty and his students from Washington State University returned to Ozette Indian Village to resume archaeological investigation begun in 1966. Results in the reconstruction of the Makah's past. Revised 1978 edition. 44 minutes. Purchase: 16mm, $550; beta, $425; VHS, $400. UW.

TRIBE OF THE TURQUOISE WATERS
Records the life of the Havasupai Indians in Arizona, and how their lives are shaped by their environment. Shows food preparation & the use of sweat lodges. 1952. Grades 6 and up. 13 minutes, color. 16mm. Rental: UA & UCLA.

**TRUST FOR NATIVE AMERICAN
CULTURES & CRAFTS VIDEO**
  Todd Crocker, Producer/narrator/editor
  Henri Vaillancourt, Director/writer
Documents aspects of the material culture of northern Native Americans i Eastern Canada. Programs include: Beavertail Snowshoes - the construction of traditional Cree Indian beavertail snowshoes, 1981, 40 minutes; Building an Algonquin Birchbark Canoe, 1984, 57 minutes; and Indian Hide Tanning -the Cree of northern Quebec show s moose and caribou hide tanning process, 1981, 35 minutes. Color. 3/4" & 1/2" video. In English and native languages. TR.

TUBUGHNA, THE BEACH PEOPLE
  Emil McCord, Sr., Film Coordinator
Documentary about life in the Athabascan village of Tyonek, Alaska from 1964 to 1984. 1988. 57 minutes. VHS. $29.95. CIRI.

TUKTU STORIES
  Lawrence Hyde, Writer/Editor
A series of 13 stories on Inuit culture. 1969. 14 minutes each. 16mm. Grades 3-9. See FILMS for titles and prices.

**TULE TECHNOLOGY: NORTHERN PAIUTE
USES OF MARSH RESOURCES IN WESTERN
NEVADA**
  Thomas Vennum, Jr., Producer
  Louella George, Narrator
A film about Northern Paiute Indian people who have lived near the Stillwater marshes of western Nevada for generation. Focuses on Wuzzie George and members of her family constructing a duck egg bag, cattail house, duck decoy, and tule boat. 1983. 42 minutes, color. Purchase: 16mm, $420; video, $70. Rental: 16mm, $23; video, $12.50. PSU.

TUNUNEREMIUT: THE PEOPLE OF TUNUNAK
Portrays aspects of the lives of the people (Eskimos) of Tununak, a village on the southwestern coast of Alaska. 1973. 35 minutes, color. Purchase: 16mm, $550; video, $400. Rental: 16mm, $50; video, $40. DER.

TURNAROUND
  Moira Simpson, Producer/director/camera
  Janet Wright, Narrator
Aurora House provides a 6-12 week program for overcoming both chemical and personal depen-

dencies. This film is about women who are learning to face painful truths with courage. One of the women is Marlene, who grew up in an environment of poverty and neglect. A Native Indian, she is committed to her work within the Native community. Four short films (Recovery Series) reflects the ongoing life of an Aurora House client after she has left treatment. 1984. 47 minutes. Color. 16mm, video. NFBC.

TURTLE SHELLS
Gary Robinson, Producer
Christine Hanneha, a Muscogee Creek Indian of Oklahoma demonstrates an ancient method of fashioning turtle shell leg rattles. 1987. 26 minutes. Color. Video. Purchase: $150; Rental: $40. NAPBC.

THE 21ST ANNUAL WORLD ESKIMO-INDIAN OLYMPICS
Skip Blumberg, Producer/Director
Portraits of two Inupiat Eskimo athletes preparing for the Olympics and speaking of their Eskimo heritage. 1983. 27 minutes, color. Video. Purchase: $200. EIA.

TWO INDIANS - RED REFLECTIONS OF LIFE
Documentary study of two North American Indian high school students and their classmates. 1973. 26 minutes. 16mm. Rental. UK.

UMEALIT: THE WHALE HUNTERS
John Angier (WGBH)
The Inuit and the controversy of whale hunting for subsistence versus the international effort to save the whales. 1980. 58 minutes. video. WGBH.

UNDERSTANDING A.I.R.F.A.
Gary Rhine, Producer/Director
A summary of the 1993 Congressional Amendment to the American Indian Religious Freedom Act which concerns protection of the use of sacred sites, eagle feathers and Peyote, and guarantees prisoner's rights. Features testimony by Indian law professor Vine Deloria, Native American rights attorney Walter Echo-Hawk, and Senator Daniel Inouye, Chair of the Senate Select Committee on Indian Affairs. 15 minutes, color. Video Purchase: $19. KF. Rental: $10. HO.

UNIVERSITY OF CALIFORNIA: AMERICAN INDIAN FILM SERIES
Samuel A. Barrett and Clyde Smith
Each of 12 films uses the memories and oral traditions of contemporary Indians as well as anthropological records to document their cultural skills. Tribes filmed include: Southwestern Pomo, Kwakiutl, Yurok, Paviotso, Washo, Tolowa, Nisenan, and Brule Sioux. See UC for titles & prices.

UNLEARNING INDIAN STEREOTYPES
VHS tape & discussion guide. A teaching unit for elementary teachers & children's librarians contains: a study of stereotyping in picture books; 10 classroom don'ts for teachers; guidelines for publishers, illustrators, & writers; role playing strategies; Native American perspectives on Columbus Day, Thanksgiving, & Washington's Birthday. Rental: $10. HO.

URBAN FRONTIER
Seattle Indian Center, Producer
Narrated by Dr. John Fuller and Will Sampson, this film provides an insight into the historical problems that have confronted Indian culture, and that have set the stage for the difficulties of adaptation

in today's fast-paced society. A story which is told by Indians themselves, and illustrates how Indians have banded together in cities to form urban Indian centers; how they are putting their traditional values to work to help solve their problems. Two versions, 26 minutes & 17 minutes. Purchase: 16mm--27 minute version, $290; video, $65; 16mm--17 minute version, $215; video, $45. Rental (16mm only): 26 minute version, $30; 17 minute version, $20. COP. Rental: 16mm (26 min.), $16. UMN.

URBAN INDIANS
The story of Joe Killsright, an Oglala Sioux Indian from Pine Ridge Reservation who comes to New York City for a job and the problems he encounters as a result.20 minutes. Color. Video. Purchase: $175; Rental, $40. DTC.

UTE INDIAN TRIBE VIDEO
Larry Cesspooch, Producer/director
Since 1979, the Ute Indian Tribe, from the Uintah and Ouray Ute Reservation in Colorado, has been documenting Ute traditions and tribal concerns on video. Includes interviews, historical photographs, and other materials to illustrate this decisive period in Ute history. Programs include: Ute Bear Dance Story - 1983, 15 minutes; NOOdtVweep/ Ute India Land - 1986, 18 minutes. Color. 3/4" and 1/2" video. UTE.

THE VANISHING AMERICAN
Richard Dix
Indian pre-history is the prelude to the story of Reservation Indians who are cheated by the Indian Agent, even after the Indians go fight in WW I. 1926. Grades 7 and up. 110 minutes, bxw. EG. Rental: $16. UMN.

VILLAGE OF NO RIVER
Barbara Lipton, Writer/Director/Producer
Yup'ik Eskimo film, 1935-1940 and 1979-1980, illustrating change and continuity in the culture. Discusses present problems and concerns. 1981. 58 minutes. 16mm/bxw. In English and Yup'ik with English subtitles. NM.

VILLAGES IN THE SKY
Shows life in the high mesa villages of the Hopi. Women are shown making baskets and pottery, and baking; also, dances. 1952. Grades 6 and up. 12 minutes, color. 16mm. Rental: UT, UA & UCLA.

A VIOLATION OF TRUST
Bill Jersey, Producer/director
Jim Belson, Producer/writer
Presents a conference, the American Indian International Tribunal, which indicts the U.S. government for its violation of trust relationship guaranteed by treaties. American Indian activists (Bob Gregory-Inupiat Eskimo; the late Philip Deere-Muscogee Creek; Oren Lyons-Onondaga; Janet McCloud-Tulalip-Duwamish; Dennis Banks-Ojibwa; and Matthew King-Oglala Sioux) forcefully articulate their aims and goals. 1982. 26 minutes, color. Video. CAT.

VISION DANCE
Henry Smith and Skip Sweeney, Directors
Showcases the talents of SOLARIS Dance Theatre and Lakota Sioux Indian Dancers drawn from nine reservations of the Lakota Nation in South Dakota. Lakota legends, myths and spirit qualities are juxtaposed with modern dance interpretations. 1982. 58 minutes. Purchase: or Video, $300; rental, $76. SOLARIS.

VISION QUEST
Dramatization of the spiritual experience required of 14 year old Western Indian boy before his acceptance as a man and a warrior. Shows phases of Indian life. 1961. 30 minutes, color. Grades 7 and up. 16mm rental, $19. PSU.

A VISIT TO WILD RICE COUNTRY
A visit with the Chippewa Indians shows that harvesting techniques have changed very little in a thousand years. 1975. Grades 1-6. 10 minutes, color. 16mm. Rebtal: $14.35. UMN.

VOICES OF NATIVE AMERICANS
Audrey Barnes, Producer
Diane Wildman, Writer/host
A look at the different approaches to current problems being taken by Native American leaders in the U.S.. A documentation of two conferences: the first conference, on tradition and modernization-participants include moderator Jamake Highwater, lawyer David Harrison (Osage), psychiatric nurse Phyllis Old Dog Cross (Mandan/Hidatsa), Roy Sampsel (Choctaw), David Powless (Oneida), and LaDonna Harris (Comanche); the second gathering presents a more politically radical native leadership; this segment is available as a separate production "A Violation of Trust" (see listing). 1983. 58 minutes, color. All video formats. ABP.

WALKING IN A SACRED MANNER
Stephen Cross, Director
Joseph Epes Brown, Consultant
Opens with photography by Edward S. Curtis and the words of many Native American orators, this film conveys the respect felt by Native Americans for the natural world. 1982. 23 minutes, color. Purchase: 16mm, $425; video, $340. Rental: IFB, UCT, UA & IU.

WALKING WITH GRANDFATHER
Phil Lucas, Producer/director
A series of six, 15-minute programs - stories, drawing upon the rich oral traditions of North American Indian people of several tribes. Presents basic human values. Teacher's guide. 1988. Color. VHS. Teacher's Guide, $12. Purchase: $325/series; $70/program. FOUR (Canada); PLP & GPN (U.S.)

WANAGI IS GONE
Bruce Baird
The uncovering of a massive ancient grave site raises questions about the excavations of such sites and examines Indian traditional views as well as scientific significance. 1978. 30 mins. 2 quad, 1 videotape, VHS. KUSD.

WANDERING SPIRIT SURVIVAL SCHOOL
Marvin Midwicki, Les Holdway,
Christopher Wilson
Canadian children learn Indian legends, traditions, languages and crafts. 1978. 28 minutes, color. Video. Purchase: $27. NFBC.

THE WARPATH
Western expansion and the breaking of treaties which led to war between the setlers and Indians. 13 minutes, color. Video. Purchase: $69.95. FH.

WARRIOR CHIEFS IN A NEW AGE
Dean Curtis Bear Claw
As a young man in the late 1800's, Chiefs Plenty Coups & Medicine Crow had prophetic visions concerning the future of the Crow people. Protrait of the transitional leaders tells the story of how these visions helped lead the Crow Indian Nation into the 20th century. 28 mins, color. Rental: $10. HO.

WARRIORS
Deb Wallwork, Producer
Honoring Native American veterans of the Vietnam War. 1986. 57 minutes, color. Video. Purchase: $56.95. NAPBC. Purchase: 3/4" - $160, 1/2" - $110; Rental: 3/4" - $60, 1/2" - $40. IN.

WARRIORS AT PEACE
Depicts the life of the Apache Indians in eastern Arizona with emphasis on their customs and traditions. 1953. 12 minutes, color. Grades 4 and up. Rental: UA, UCLA & UK.

WASHOE
Veronika Pataky
Depicts the transition of the Washoe Tribe in Nevada from traditional customs to the 20th century. 1968. Grades 7 and up. 57 minutes, bxw. 16mm. In Washoe with English narration. Rental: UW, UK, IU, UCLA & UMN.

THE WATER IS SO CLEAR THAT A BLIND MAN COULD SEE
New Mexico's Taos Indians believe that all life (plant and animal) is sacred and live without disturbing their environment. Lumber companies are trying to get permission from the Federal Government to lumber the Taos Indian area. 1970. 30 minutes, color. 16mm. Rental: PSU, UCT & IU.

THE WAY
Sandra Osawa (KNBC-TV)
A sketch of Native American religion and its place in contemporary Indian life. Focuses on the Cherokee, Cheyenne and Ojibwa religious practices, and Indian spirituality. 1975. 28 mins. VHS. BYU-N.

A WAY OF LIFE
CBC Northern Services, Producer
The lifestyle of Henry Evaluarjuk, Inuit carver, who, with his family and two other families, chose to live on an uninhabited and secluded inlet on Baffin Island. 1983. 28 minutes. 2 quad, 1 videotape, and VHS. Rental, $40/week. NAPBC.

THE WAY WE LIVE
Four, 10-15 minute video tapes showing several aspects of traditional Yup'ik Eskimo culture. 1981. 60 minutes. VHS. $24.95. KYUK.

WAY OF OUR FATHERS
Bradley Wright
Members of several northern California Indian tribes depict unique elements of a way of life as it flourished before the imposition of European culture. 33 minutes, color. Grades 9 and up. Video. Purchase: $95; rental: $50. UC. Rental: 16mm, $24.50. PSU.

WE ARE ONE
Chet Kincaid, Producer
Eight, 20-minute programs about the life and culture of a Native American family in early 19th century Nebraska\ Focuses on 13-year-old Ni'bthaska and his younger sister Mi'onbathin and on the daily rituals and rites of passage that make up their lives. 1986. Color. Video. Rental: $250/series; $40 each. NAPBC.

WE ARE A RIVER FLOWING
Nick Clark, Producer
An exploration of Northern Irish and Native American cultures. A Ten-year-old girl from Belfast travels to the Pine Ridge Indian reservation as a part of a program for children of political turmoil. 1985. 28 minutes. Color. Video. Purchase: 3/4" - 120, 1/2" - 80; Rental: 3/4" - 45, 1/2" - 30. IN.

WE ARE THESE PEOPLE
Featuring Will Sampson, this film is designed to foster an appreciation for the richness of Native American cultures & promote social support by reinforcing traditional values. 15 minutes, color. Video. Purchase: $350; rental: $45. SH. Rental: 16mm, $21. UMN.

WE BELONG TO THE LAND
Reaffirms the relationship between Indain & the land; and explores lifestyles in natural resource careers of forestry, game management, range management, & related fields. 30 minutes. 16mm purchase, $425; rental, $48. Video purchase, $375. SH.

WE OF THE RIVER
Documentary chronicles the arrival and the emergence into the 20th century of the Yup'ik Eskimo people who have lived in this area for more than 12,000 years. 1985. 60 minutes. VHS. $24.95. KYUK.

WE OWE IT TO OURSELVES AND TO OUR CHILDREN
Video uses cartoon images and live action Native health educators to discuss the causes, symptoms, treatments, and prevention of HIV & STDs. 8 minutes. VHS, $5. NNA.

WE REMEMBER
Raymond Yakeleya
The history of the Dene people as told by Yakeleya, a Slavey Indian, and some of the elders of the Slavey and Loucheau tribes of Canada - their past, present and thoughts for the future. 1979. In two parts. 1979. 30 minutes each. 16mm and video. Purchase or rental. CFMDC.

A WEAVE OF TIME
Susan Fanshel, with John Adair & Deborah Gordon, Producers; Susan Fanshel, Director
Follows the lives of four generations of the Burnsides, a Navajo family from the Pine Springs community in Arizona on the Navajo reservation. In 1938 anthropologist John Adair filmed daily activities and artistic techniques; explores many aspects of Navajo life. 1986. 60 minutes. b&w & color. 16mm, 3/4" (sales only) and 1/2" (sales & rentals). DC.

WEAVERS OF THE WEST
A film which shows the Navajo's process of rugmaking. 1954. 13 minutes, color. Rental: IU.

WEDDING OF PALO
F. Dalsheim and Knud Rasmussen
Rasmussen, the Danish Inuit anthropologist and explorer directed this film based on a traditional Inuit tale about the courtship and marriage of a young man and woman. 1937. 72 minutes. 35mm/16mm/bxw. In Inuit with English subtitles. MMA.

WELCOME TO NAVAHO LAND
Paul Auguston
Navajo children's drawings are animated with the children telling the stories their work illustrates. Navajo songs. In two parts: Part I, 12 minutes; Part 2, 20 minutes. video. UMC.

WESTWARD EXPANSION
Follows the chain of events leading to the Indian Removal Act, manifest destiny, the Civil War, and the Indian wars. 1969. 25 minutes, color. Grades 6 and up. 16mm. Rental, $15.25. IU.

WHAT MORE CAN I DO?...A NURSE'S EXPERIENCE WITH A NAVAJO CANCER PATIENT
Story of a community health nurse, who through persistence & sensitivity, learns to integrate her own values & perceptions with those of a Navajo cancer patient & his family. 1986. 27 minutes, color. 3/4" U-mat. Rental: $16. UMN.

WHEN THE WHITE MAN CAME
Describes life among the major tribes across the U.S. when the Europeans arrived in the late 15th Century. 13 minutes, color. Video. Purchase: $69.95. FH.

WHERE HAS THE WARRIOR GONE?
Explores the life of Ted Cly, a typical Navajo father living on a reservation in Utah. 13 minutes. Grades 1-8. Rental. UK.

WHERE THE SPIRIT LIVES
Bruce Pittman, Director; music by Buffy St. Marie
The story of Amelia, a young Blackfoot Indian girl, and her plight to escape the horrors that white society has forced upon her. Set in 1937 amid the Canadian Rockies. Amelia was kidnapped from her reserve by the government and placed in an Indian Residential School. 1989. 97 minutes, color. Video. Purchase: $295. BE. Rental: $16. UMN.

WHITE MAN'S WAY
Christine Lesiak & NETV, Producer
Beginning in the late 1800s, an experiment that endeavored to transform the American Indian took place; the federal government built the U.S. Indian School in Genoa, Nebraska, a military-style school for Indian children from more than 20 tribes. Here they taught the white man's language, traditions, lifestyles and were forbidden to practice their own. 1986. 30 minutes, color. Video. Purchase: $40. NAPBC & GPN. Rental: $16. UMN.

WHY COYOTE HAS THE BEST EYES
Discusses the importance of stories & storytelling within Indian culture. An elder of the Hupa tribe shares his knowledge of nature & heritage with Indian children on the Hoopa Reservation. Grades K-3. 10 minutes. $59.95. K-T.

WHY DID GLORIA DIE?
NET, Producer
Depicts the tragic life of Gloria Curtis, a Chippewa woman who died of hepatitis at age 17. Deals with the adjustments one must make from reservation to urban life. 1973. 27 minutes, color. 16mm & video. Rental: $20. IU & UMN.

WILD RICE: THE TAMING OF A GRAIN
Waterstone Films, Producer
Traces the history of wild rice, a Native North American food, and the first wild grain to be brought into cultivation in modern history. 1988. Grades 7 and up. 18 minutes. Purchase: VHS, $250. NDM.

WINTER ON AN INDIAN RESERVATION
A film about children on a forest reservation. 1973. Grades K-4. 11 minutes, color. 16mm. Rental: $9. UCT.

RUSSELL & YVONNE WILLIER TAN A MOOSE HIDE
David E. Young, Trudy Nicks, Ruth McConnell, & David Strom, Producers
Russell and Yvonee are Woods Cree Indians from northern Alberta. Documents the entire production process. 1989. 30 minutes, color. Video. Purchase: $70; rental, $20. UADA.

WINDS OF CHANGE: A MATTER OF CHOICE
Carol Cotter, Writer/producer
Examines the struggle of Native Americans to maintain individual identities & sovereign Indian nations within the U.S. Hopi tribal membersprovide insights into the personal side of acculturation & assimilation, focusing on the exodus of their youth to the cities. Original score by R. Carlos Nakai. Hosted by Hattie Kauffman & N. Scott Momaday. 1990. 58 minutes, color. Video. Purchase: PBS. Rental: $12. PSU; $16. UMN.

WINDS OF CHANGE: A MATTER OF PROMISES
PBS, Producer
Kiowa author, N. Scott Momaday explores the plight of the American Indian in today's society. A visit to the Onondaga of New York, the Navajo in Arizona, and the Lummi in Washington. 58 minutes, color. Video. Purchase: $19.95. PBS & CAN. Rental: $10. HO & PSU; $16. UMN.

WINTER WOLF: LEARNING ABOUT NATIVE AMERICAN CULTURE
Follows a young Native American girl as she seeks to understand age-old conflicts between mankind & wolves. 30 minutes. Purchase: VHS, $49. GA.

WIPING THE TEARS OF SEVEN GENERATIONS
Gary Rhine, Producer/Director
A documentary that examines U.S. history through the Lakota Sioux perspective, with emphasis on The Wounded Knee Massacre and The Bigfoot Memorial Ride. In English & Lakota with English subtitles. 1992. Grades 4 and up. 57 minutes, color. Purchase: Video, $30; 16mm, $750. Rental: Video, $85; 16mm, $200. KF & OY. Rental: $10. HO & UMN.

WITH HAND & HEART
Oak Creek Films, Producer
Documentary on the history of Southwestern Native American art as seen through a selected group of contemporary practitioners & storytellers. 1986. Grades 7 and up. 28 minutes. Purchase: VHS, $240. NDM.

WOMEN IN AMERICAN LIFE
Five videos depicting women's roles in American history. How westward expansion, immigration, the two world wars, and government legislation have affected the lives of Native Americans. 1990. KS.

WOODEN BOX: MADE BY STEAMING AND BENDING
Clyde B. Smith, Producer
The Indians of the Northwest Pacific Coast developed woodworking; a specialty was steaming and bending of a single wooden slab to form a box. This film follows, carefully, every stage of making the Kwakiutl box. 1962. 33 minutes, color. Purchase: 16mm, $660; video, $195. Rental: $50. UC. Rental only:16mm, $24.50. PSU.

WOODLAND INDIANS OF EARLY AMERICA
Roy A. Price, Ed.D.
Authentic reconstructions and scenes in the eastern and Great Lakes regions provide settings for this study of Woodland Indian life (Chippewa) prior to European influence. Revised 1980 edition. 10 minutes, color. Grades K-6. Purchase: 16mm, $265; video, $185. COR. Rental: 16mm, $16.50. IU, UMN & PSU.

WOODLAND TRADITIONS: THE ART OF THREE NATIVE AMERICANS
Features three Woodland Indian artists who tell in their own words how & why they create. Follows the artists step-by-step from the point of inspiration through the actual creation to the final work of art. 1984. 27 minutes, color. Video. Rental: $16. UMN.

WOONSPE (EDUCATION & THE SIOUX)
SD ETV
Explores the problems of Native American education. 1974. 28 minutes, color. Video. Rental: $40. NAPBC.

WORDS & PLACE: NATIVE LITERATURE FROM THE AMERICAN SOUTHWEST
Denny Carr, Director; Larry Evers, Producer
Series of eight videotapes (produced by the University of Arizona, in cooperation with KUAT (Tucson, 1976-77) focus on traditional & modern Native American literature as told or written by individuals of various Southwestern tribes: Apache, Yaqui and Hopi people speak of their traditional philosophy, rituals & songs. Titles: "By This Song I Walk" (A Navajo Song); "Seyewailo: The Flower World" (Yaqui Deer Songs); "The Origin of the Crown Dance" (An Apache Narrative) & "Ba'ts'oosee" (An Apache Trickster Cycle); "Iisaw" (Hopi Coyote Stories); "Natwaniwa" (A Hopi Philosophical Statement); "Running on the Edge of the Rainbow" (Laguna Stories & Poems); "Songs of My Hunter Heart" (Laguna Songs & Poems); "A Conversation With Vine Deloria, Jr." 18-51 minutes. Video. Purchase: $150 to $290 each, $1425/series. NR. Rentals: see ATL.

A WORLD OF IDEAS WITH BILL MOYERS 1 & 2: LOUISE ERDRICH & MICHAEL DORRIS
Louise Erdrich and Michael Dorris, a Native American wife-husband team who write novels based on their heritage. 1. Discuss the values and difficulties of modern Native Americans, the concept of "ironic survival humor," and the Native American's ability to live on the land in harmony with nature. 29 minutes, color. 2. Observe how alcoholism & despair have shattered the lives of many Native Americans. Grades 9 and up. Rental: video, $11 & $14. PSU & IU.

YAQUI
Arizona artist Ted De Grazia narrates this filmic story of his paintings that depict the Yaqui Indian Ceremony. 1973. Grades 4 and up. 19 minutes, color. 16mm. Rental: UA.

THE YAQUI CUR
D.W. Griffith, Director
A young Yaqui brave is converted to Christianity, and refuses to fight when his tribe is attacked by Zuni neighbors. He later redeems himself. 1913. 12 minutes, bxw. EG.

YESTERDAY'S CHILDREN
Skokomish youth interview two elders on the Skokomish Reservation on Hood Canal in western Washington State. The elders talk about their lives and changes they have experienced. Teacher's guide and lesson plans. 30 minutes, color. Grades 9 and up. Purchase: Video, $110. Rental: $25. DSP.

YESTERDAY, TODAY: THE NETSILIK ESKIMO
Gilles Blais
Traces the adaptation of the Netsilik from a migratory people to settlers in a government village.

Filmed ten years after the documentary film, The Eskimo: Fight for Life. 1974. 58 minutes, color. Grades 7 and up. 16mm. EDC & UA. Video, $27. NFBC.

YOU ARE ON INDIAN LAND
Mort Ransen, Director
Report of a protest demonstration by Mohawk Indians of the St. Regis Reservation on the international Bridge between Canada and U.S. 1969. 36 minutes, bxw. Purchase: Video, $27. NFBC. Rental: 16mm, $17.50. PSU.

YOU CHOOSE
Features Nathan Chasing His Horse. Designed to discourage youth from chewing or smoking tobacco. 20 minutes, color. Video. Purchase: $360; rental: $45. SH.

1987 YUP'IK DANCE FESTIVAL
Villages from the Yukon & Kuskokwim Delta sent dancers to Bethel to participate in one of the largest festivals in recent memory. 1988. 120 minutes, color. Video. $24.95. KYUK.

FILMSTRIPS & SLIDES

AKWESASNE RESERVATION SLIDE SHOW
A complete package of slide carousel, tape and script. Includes Iroquois legends, corn husk doll-making, Mohawk basketmaking, Iroquois Wampum & Cradleboards. 1984. 10 minutes. Rental, $15. AM.

AMERICA'S 19th CENTURY WARS
Covers the Indian Wars. Includes teacher's guide. Grades 7-12. Six filmstrips/cassettes. $141. LL.

AMERICAN INDIAN FOLK LEGENDS
Myths and legends of the American Indian. The White Buffalo; The First Tom-Tom; First Winter, First Summer; The Four Thunders, two parts; How Fire Came to Earth. Six filmstrips; records or cassettes. $130. RH.

AMERICAN INDIAN LEGENDS
Four filmstrips: The Magic Food (Iroquois); The Basket Lady (Ute); When the People Lived in the Dark (Cherokee); Mountain Spirit Dance (Mescalero Apache). 4 cassettes, guide. $129. SVE.

AMERICAN INDIAN LEGENDS
Adventure stories showing many customs and rituals of American Indians. Aids vocabulary growth. Grades 3-5. Six filmstrips / cassettes, $119.00; six filmstrips (captioned), $55. RH.

AMERICAN INDIAN LIFE
Nine color filmstrips comparing and contrasting the ways of life of Indians in different sections of the U.S. Grades 1-6. CMC.

AMERICAN INDIAN NATURE LEGENDS
The wonders of nature and reverence for life are interwoven into these American Indian legends. Grades 3-6. 6 filmstrips, 6 cassettes. $132. TA.

THE AMERICAN INDIAN: A STUDY IN DEPTH
Dr. Ethel J. Alpenfels traces the history and development of the American Indians over the past 400 centuries. Six color filmstrips/cassettes. PHM.

AMERICAN INDIANS & HOW THEY REALLY LIVED

The heritage and history of American Indians are revealed. Indian crafts and customs are depicted. Includes Hopi and Navajo, Seminoles, Crow , Chinook, and the Iroquois tribes. Grades 3-7. 5 filmstrips. $50; $10, individual. TA.

AMERICAN INDIANS OF THE NORTH PACIFIC COAST

Their history, arts and crafts, myths and ceremonies. Grades 4-6. Six filmstrips/cassettes. $119. COR.

AMERICAN INDIANS OF THE NORTHEAST

A study of the rise and fall of the Algonquin and Iroquois Indian empires, migrants from Asia to the Northeastern U.S. and southern Canada. Who they are, their history, religion, handicrafts. Grades 4-6. Six filmstrips/cassettes. $119. COR.

AMERICAN INDIANS OF THE PLAINS

Presents the history, tribes, culture, arts and crafts, and religion of the Plains Indians. Grades 4-9. Six filmstrips/cassettes. $119. COR.

AMERICAN INDIANS OF THE SOUTHEAST

A full-blooded Cherokee explains their life today . Reveals the life of the Southeastern Indian tribes from prehistoric times to the present. Grades 4-9. Six filmstrips/cassettes. $119. COR.

AMERICAN INDIANS OF THE SOUTHWEST

A history-oriented presentation of the Pueblo tribes, examining their customs and languages. Grades 4-9. Six filmstrips/cassettes. $1 19. COR.

AMERICAN MUSEUM OF NATURAL HISTORY- -PHOTOGRAPHIC & FILM COLLECTION

Contains thousands of bxw photographs, color slides, and color transparencies of Native Americans; may be rented for reproduction, or purchased. For films, short footage segments may be available for reproduction upon payment of film/ video duplication costs and use fees. AM.

THE BATTLE OF THE LITTLE BIGHORN

A detailed study of the impact of Custer's defeat by the Sioux and Cheyenne. Grades 7-12. Filmstrip/cassette. $26. LL.

BATTLE OF THE LITTLE BIG HORN

A series of 78 slides or filmstripdepicting the Battle which took place in 1876. Includes a booklet, teacher's guide, cassette tape, map and poster . $36.60. SI.

CAHOKIA SLIDE PACKAGE

Seven sets of 5 slides each with a cassette tape and written text, illustrating the history of Indian culture at Cahokia, as well as the archaeological techniques used to explore and study the site. $2 per strip. CMM.

CLIMBING THE HILL

A specialized filmstrip developed for men and women who are interested in following the kind of leadership demonstrated by the old Dakota Holy Men. $15. AICRC.

CONTEMPORARY INDIAN & ESKIMO CRAFTS OF THE U.S.

74 full-color, 35mm slides with lecture text booklet illustrating the great variety of distinctive craft forms created by numerous contemporary Native American craftsmen. $50. TIPI.

CONTEMPORARY NATIVE AMERICAN MASKS

20 color slides. $30. ATL.

CONTEMPORARY SIOUX PAINTING

77 full-color and bxw, 35mm slides with lecture text booklet. Illustrates the historic development of expressive forms of painting created by Sioux artists during the past 200 years. $50. TIPI.

THE CORPS OF DISCOVERY: THE LEWIS & CLARK EXPEDITION

An exploration that had a significant impact on opening up Western America. Grades 7-12. Two filmstrips; cassette. $31. LL.

COSTUMES & MASKS OF THE SOUTHWEST TRIBES

Shows Navajo, Apache, Hopi & Pueblo ceremonial attire, including masks & costumes. 27 slides, no narration. 1977. $10. UCLA.

DAKOTA WAY & THE SACRAMENTS

Filmstrip, with cassette & guide. $10. AICRC.

THE DRUM IS THE HEART

Randy Croce, Producer
Focuses on the Blackfeet, Blackfoot, Blood and Peigan tribes that make up the Blackfoot Nation at their celebrations, speaking about their contemporary lives and traditional values. Filmstrip and slide set. Purchase and rental. UCV and BM.

THE EARTH KNOWERS: THE NATIVE AMERICANS SPEAK

Statements of Indian wise men who relied on religious and cultural experience to deal with technological and social reorganization. Guide. Grades 7-12. Filmstrip/cassette. $26. LL.

ESKIMOS OF ALASKA (ARCTIC LIFE)

Four color filmstrips providing a picture of the life of Eskimos in Alaska. Emphasis is placed on activities of children. Grades 4-8. CMC.

EVERYTHING NEW

Audio tape with slides tells the story of creation; traditional chants and songs include Eskimo, and North American Indian people. 1973. 19 minutes. $7.00. UT.

EXPLORING & COLONIZING

In 4 parts. One filmstrip on the First Americans. 4 filmstrips, 4 cassettes, 28 skill sheets, guide. $89. SVE.

FAMOUS INDIAN CHIEFS

Examines eight famous Indian chiefs: Pontiac (Ottawa), Joseph Brant (Mohawk), Tecumseh (Shawnee), Black Hawk (Sauk), Osceola (Seminole), Chief Joseph (Nez Perce), Sitting Bull (Sioux), and Geronimo (Apache). Grades 4-6. Eight filmstrips; cassettes. $149. COR.

THE FAR NORTH

Deals with the art and culture of the Alaskan Eskimo Aleuts and the Athapascan and Tlingit Indians, focusing on the art and ways of life. 1975. 48 color slides. Free rental. NGA.

THE FIRST AMERICANS

Six sound filmstrips which studies the major Indian tribes of the U.S. - their customs, culture and the land that belonged to them. Indians of the Northeast, Southwest, Great Lakes, Plains, Southeast, and Northwest. Grades 4-6. $132.00; $22 each. Available os a video. TA.

THE FIRST PEOPLE OF NORTH AMERICA: INDIANS AND INUIT

Presents an historical overview of the various native cultures existing in North America. The distinctive lifestyles of native peoples of dif fering geographic regions are examined with an emphasis on environmental factors. One filmstrip is devoted to the study of the Inuit of the Arctic. Six filmstrips; cassettes; one sound filmstrip guide with discussion questions; one script booklet. $160. UL.

FOLKTALES OF ETHNIC AMERICA

Includes The Brahman, The Tiger, and The Six Judges (Indian); and The Blind Boy and the Loon (Alaskan.) Grades 3-6. Six filmstrips/cassettes. $119. RH.

THE FRENCH & INDIAN WARS: ROAD TO THE AMERICAN REVOLUTION?

Reviews the outstanding developments which lead to independence, including the French and Indian War 1689-1762. Grades 7-12. Two filmstrips/cassettes. $31. LL.

GHOST DANCE TRAGEDY AT WOUNDED KNEE

66-slide program which brings the Wounded Knee incident of December of 1890 alive -- its historical and religious background, and the events of that infamous day when members of the Seventh Cavalry (Custer's old regiment) confronted the Sioux who had gathered at the Pine Ridge agency. Includes booklet, teacher's guide, cassette tape, and 2 maps. $36.60. SI.

GREAT AMERICAN INDIAN HEROES

Personal stories of leaders and chiefs who won the trust of their people and inspired their tribes in war and peace. 8 sound filmstrips: Tecumseh, Osceola, Black Hawk, Pontiac, Chief Joseph, Sitting Bull, Geronimo, and Joseph Brant. Grades 4-6. $176; $22. each. Available as a video. TA.

HOMES OF ANCIENT PEOPLE

A color filmstrip showing the ruins of ancient Indian homes at Mesa Verde, Canyon de Chelly, and Walnut Canyon. Grades 4-8. CMC.

HOW THE INDIANS DISCOVERED A NEW WORLD

Paleo-Indian transition from hunting to farming, trade and communications. Grades 6-12. Two filmstrips; cassettes. $33. RH.

HUNGER WALKS AMONG INDIANS

Indian Ministries Task Force on the work they have done to alleviate hunger problems of Native Americans. 85 slides; cassette. Rental, $5. NILB.

INDIAN AMERICANS: STORIES OF ACHIEVEMENT

A four filmstrip set which portrays, in illustrations and soundtracks, the contributions of four great Indian Americans: Hiawatha, Ely S. Parker , Washakie, and Pocahontas. Four records or cassettes; teacher's guide. WD.

INDIAN ART IN AMERICA: THE ARTS & CRAFTS OF THE NORTH AMERICAN INDIANS

51 slides. MAI.

INDIAN HERITAGE

Six color filmstrips that explore the life and culture of the American Indian. Includes: Americans Before Columbus, Indian Children, Indian Homes, Indian Celebrations, Indian Legends, Indians Who Showed the Way. Grades 2-6. $60; $10 each. TA.

AN INDIAN JESUS
Richard West, a Cheyenne Indian, is a Christian and an artist. Through his paintings, he helps us see Jesus through Native American eyes. 42 frames; color. Reading script and guide. Grades 3-12. $10. FP.

INDIAN LEADERS OF TOMORROW
American Indian Science &
Engineering Society, Producer
For encouraging Native American youth to further their education & pursue professional careers. Slide/tape. Purchase: $200; rental: $40. SH.

INDIAN PAINTING
63 subjects (slide sets.) See MAI
for ordering information.

INDIAN ROCK ART
Portrays one of the most ancient art forms in New Mexico, illustrating the timeless images of a mysterious art. 12 minute slide-tape program. Available for loan or purchase. MNM.

INDIAN SOVEREIGNTY--INDIAN TREATIES--INDIANS AND THE U.S. GOVERNMENT--INDIAN JURISDICTION FEDERAL INDIAN TRUST RELATIONSHIP
A series of five instructional programs of four filmstrips each, explaining the legal concepts and the history behind many of the present areas of controversy involving Indian tribes. Researched by the Institute for the Development of Indian Law, Inc. Includes response sheet master for practice quizes; trainer's guide for each. Pre/Post tests available, $6 per topic. $120 each; $480 per set. COOK.

INDIAN VALUES IN A NEW WORLD
Council Energy Resource Tribes, Producer
A teenage brother & sister are troubled by their uncertain future as high school graduation nears. Through their grandfather they meet various role models who apply traditional values in pursuing their post-secondary education. Slide/tape. Purchase: $200; rental: $40. SH.

INDIAN VILLAGE ARCHAEOLOGY
Documents the rediscovery of ancient Ozette by archaeologists. 1972. 88 color frames; teacher's guide and cassette. UW.

INDIANS OF HISTORIC TIMES
Slide sets on the following areas: Eskimo and Arctic (33 subjects); Northwest Coast (221 subjects); Woodlands and Northeast (118 subjects); Southeast (38 subjects); Plains and Plateau (446 subjects); Southwest (184 subjects); and, Far West (73 subjects). See MAI for ordering information.

INDIANS OF NORTH AMERICA
North America's native peoples from ancient to modern times. A series of five sound filmstrips: The First Americans; The Eastern Woodlands; The Plains; West of the Shining Mountains; and, Indians Today. 13-14 minutes each. Grades 5-12. $99.50. NGS.

INDIANS OF NORTH AMERICA
Six filmstrips: Indians of the Northeast, Southeast, Plains, Northwest Coast, Southwest, Far North. Grades 4-6. Includes 6 cassettes, guide. $179. SVE.

INDIANS: THE SOUTHWEST & THE PLAINS INDIANS
The history of the American Indian people and how they live today. The Southwest Indians and The Sundance People. Two filmstrips, cassettes each, $48 each. Grades 6-8. RH.

INSIDE THE CIGAR STORE: IMAGES OF THE AMERICAN INDIAN
Focuses on the contradictory stereotypes of the American Indian which have been perpetuated by mass media and textbooks, and pleads for the replacement of the inaccurate images with the knowledge about contemporary American Indian people. Filmstrip/cassette. MRC.

LEGENDS OF THE MICMAC
The use of puppetry and mask-making in providing an instructive introduction to one of the earliest tribes to settle in North America. Grades 2-5. Four filmstrips, cassettes; teacher's guide. $95. RH.

THE LIFE OF THE AMERICAN INDIAN
Two sound filmstrips: The Eastern Woodlands and the Plains - explains how eastern tribes utilize their environment; and The Northwest Coast and the Southwest - Southwestern Indians farm arid lands and dance for rain, while Northwest Coast Indians fish and hold potlatches. 1977. 13-14 minutes each. Grades K-4. $50. NGS.

THE MAKE-BELIEVE INDIAN: NATIVE AMERICANS IN THE MOVIES
Gretchen Bataille and Charles L.P. Silet
Demonstrates the influence of early travel narratives, literature, the visual arts, and the wild west shows on the Native American image in the movies. Examples are drawn from silent films, serials, and contemporary feature films. 140 slides and carousel tray; audio-cassette; bibliography; script; suggestions. Purchase: $99; rental, $15/3 days. MRC.

THE MAN FROM DEER CREEK, THE STORY OF ISHI
A Yahi Indian in 1911, the last of his tribe, and the last to grow up without contact with American civilization. Grades 7-12. Two filmstrips, cassette. $41. LL.

THE MARMES MAN DIG
Louis and Ruth Kirk, Producer
An account of an archaeological discovery in eastern Washington State. The remains of early man in the Western Hemisphere. A graphic exposition of the techniques of archaeology. 1968. 61 color frames. $10. UW.

MICMAC: THE PEOPLE AND THEIR CULTURE
A kit of nine filmstrips provide an overview of Micmac culture—structures, transportation, hunting and fishing, recreation and domestic crafts. Grade 6. NOVA.

NAKED CLAY: 3,000 YEARS OF UNADORNED POTTERY OF THE AMERICAN INDIAN
Features American Indian artistry in modelled ceramics. Includes a 72-page catalog. 90 slides. MAI.

NATIVE AMERICAN LITERATURE
Literature by and about the Native American: The writings of John Smith, Cotton Mather, William Byrd; the Noble Savage; Cooper's novels, Longfellow's "Hiawatha;" the characteristics of Indian literature; song, dance, myth & rituals; the Cherokee alphabet; Chief Joseph's oratory; the work of Momaday. Two 15-minute filmstrips. $49.95. FH.

NATIVE PEOPLES OF THE SOUTHWEST
The Heard Museum
A multi-media instructional materials program designed to develop concepts and skills by focusing on traditional and contemporary Native American cultures. Five levels of instructional units are: Level 2: Inde: The Western Apache, Apache family life; Level 3: Hopi: The Desert Farmers, Hopi communities; Level 4: Anasazi: The Ancient Villagers, archaeology and culture history of livin Pueblo Indians; Level 5: O'odham: Indians of the Sonoran Desert, cultural geography & human adaptations to the desert environment; Level 6: Dine: The Navajo, culturees change & evolve. Each program consists of color slides, audio cassettes, overhead transparencies, 30 student booklets and teacher's guide, and artifacts. $295 each. Complete set, $1472. CA.

NAVAJO CULTURAL FILMSTRIPS & SLIDES
Contains 23 filmstrips with cassettes ranging in time from five minutes to 20 minutes. All grades. See SAN for titles and prices.

NORTH AMERICAN ARCHAEOLOGICAL SLIDE SET SERIES
Paleoindians of Northeastern U.S.: 64 slides, $120; Sloan Dalton Site: 68 slides, $122; Ohio Hopewell: 100 slides, $161; Mississippian Cultures: 85 slides, $151; The Southeastern Ceremonial Complex: 86 slides, $151; Early Caddoan Cultures: 78 slides, $140; Late Caddoan Cultures: 70 slides, $122; Spiro Mounds: 80 slides, $140; The Tunica Treasure: 79 slides, $140; Poverty Point: 63 slides, $120; The Art of the Taino: 59 slides, $110; Weeden Island Culture: 65 slides, $120; Fort Center: 54 slides, $102;The Gulf of Georgia: 80 slides, $140; Stone Sculpture of the Fraser River: 50 slides, $94; Ozette: 58 slides, $110; Hoko River Complex: 80 slides, $140; Mesa Verde: 86 slides, $152; Canyon de Chelly: 78 slides, $140; Chaco Canyon: 65 slides, $120; Native American Rock Art of the Colorado Plateau: 52 slides, $102. PR.

NORTHWEST COAST INDIAN TRADITIONS TODAY: A CONTEMPORARY LOOK AT REMNANTS OF A HERITAGE
Louis and Ruth Kirk, Producers
Features dugout canoes hollowed from cedar logs, the netting and preparation of fish, baskets made from swamp and saltwater marsh grasses, etc. 1972. 90 color/sound frames. 15 minutes. Cassette/booklet. $25. UW.

OUR HEARTS BEAT AS ONE
Provides an historical view of tribes in Oregon. Two carousel slide trays; 160 slides. Grades 6-adult. Rental, $15. NILB.

OZETTE ARCHAEOLOGY
Louis and Ruth Kirk, Producers
Tells the story of the past and the present as it is being continually uncovered at the Ozette Archaeological Dig, Cape Alava, Washington State. Summarizes the resources available to the Makah Indians living on the Northwest Coast of the Olympic Peninsula. 1979. 153 color; sound frames. 21 minutes. Cassette - booklet. $25. UW.

THE PAINTINGS OF CHARLES BIRD KING
King painted many prominent Amerian Indians. 34 slides. $31. SI.

A POINT OF PARTNERSHIP
Depicts the work of the National Indian Lutheran Board. All ages. 12 mins. Filmstrip/cassette. NILB.

PRE-COLUMBIAN CULTURES
A series of slide sets. United States (231 subjects); Canada (three subjects). All archaeological specimens are of pottery. MAI.

PUEBLO INDIANS OF NEW MEXICO
Examines the history and culture of the Pueblo Indians. Includes images of the people, ancient and modern villages, crafts and ways of life many of which are drawn from the Museum of New Mexico's collection of historic photographs and rare old hand-tinted glass slides. 17 minute slide-tape program. Available for loan or purchase. MNM.

THE PURITAN EXPERIENCE:
MAKING A NEW WORLD
Life in Massachusetts--the Higgin's family daughter, a captive of the Indians for a while, resents the Puritans' treatment of the Indians, and challenges strict Puritan authority. Grades 7-12. Two filmstrips, cassettes. $60. LL.

READ ALONG AMERICAN INDIAN LEGENDS
Stimulates reading interest with tales of Indian lore. Vocabulary-building captions. Program guide. Grades 2-5. Six filmstrips, cassettes. $119. RH.

THE SACRED PIPE
A filmstrip of the Sacred Pipe, the central instrument of the Dakota religion. Gives the proper understanding of the origin and use of the Pipe. $15. AICRC.

SANDSTONE COUNTRY: THE CANYONS AND INDIANS OF THE SOUTHWEST
Louis and Ruth Kirk, Producers
Arizona and Utah apartment-dwelling Indians before Columbus, reveals the ancient cities and the geological history. Teacher's guide. 1970. 70 color frames. $10. UW.

SICA HOLLOW
An historical and religious filmstrip. One of the old story of the flood--localized on the Sisseton-Wahpeton Reservation. $15. AICRC.

THE SIOUX
Black Elk's words from a broken treaty. Study of the Sioux, past and present, are analyzed to show the Indian in confrontation with cultural crisis and identity loss. Includes a script. Grades 7-12. Filmstrip/cassette. $30. LL.

SIX NATIVE AMERICAN FAMILIES
The Life of a Mohawk Family; The Life of a Sioux Family; The Life of a Seminole Family; The Life of a Navajo Family; The Life of a Pueblo Family; The Life of a Kwakiutl Family. Grades K-6. 6 filmstrips, 6 cassettes, guide. $149. SVE.

THE SOUTHWEST: EARLY INDIAN CULTURES: THE SPANISH HERITAGE: THE EARLY ANGLO PERIOD: THE MODERN SOUTHWEST
The influence of the desert environment on the culture and lifestyle of the Indians. Four sound filmstrips, two cassettes. Script/guide. $90. UL.

SOUTHWEST INDIAN FAMILIES
A day in the lives of four real families from four different tribes: Navajo, Zuni, Apache and Hopi. Grades 1-3. Four filmstrips, four cassettes; four filmstrips/captioned. $40. COR.

SUBMULOC SHOW/COLUMBUS WOHS
Represents the theme of turning back the history of the Columbian legacy. 36 color slides. $60. ATL.

SURVIVAL: A HISTORY OF NORTHWEST INDIAN TREATY FISHING RIGHTS
A slide presentation produced by the Point No Point Treaty Council. Recounts the history of Indian fishing before the arrival of white people in the Northwest, and of treaties and legal decisions culminating in the 1974 Boldt Decision. Teacher's guide and student handouts and worksheets. 20 minutes. Grades 4-adult. Purchase: $195; rental, $30. DSP.

TALES OF THE PLAINS INDIANS
Gives insight into the religion, culture, and relationship to nature of the Blackfeet, Sioux, Pawnee and Cheyeen tribes. Grades 3-5. Six filmstrips, cassettes. $119. RH.

TEXAS INDIANS: ALABAMA-COUSHATTA INDIANS - Presents the early history and present customs of the Alabamas and the Coushattas who have lived together in the Piney Woods of east Texas. 1971. 8 minutes. Filmstrip, $20; Slide set, $40; **THE INDIAN TEXANS** - Tribes of the 20th century who live together in Texas. The Dallas Intertribal Council's annual ceremonials are highlighted in this program. 1971. 7 minutes. Filmstrip, $25; slide set, $45; **THE TIGUA INDIANS: OUR OLDEST TEXANS** - Discusses the early (1680) settlement of the Tigua Pueblo Indians of Ysleta, near present El Paso, Texas, and the progress they are making through the Texas Commission on Indian Affairs to become completely self-sufficient and financially independent. 1971. 8 minutes. Filmstrip, $20; slide set, $25. UT-ITC.

TRIBAL ARCHIVES
In two parts: Part 1: An Introduction - Discusses what an archives is, what you need to establish one, and how you will benefit from an archives program. Slide/tape program; 110 slides; 1983, 13 minutes. Part 2: Getting Started - A slide/tape program. Includes a booklet containing script, a bibliography, a glossary, and a list of resources. 1986. Purchase: $80 each; rental, $17 each. SI-OMP.

TWO EAGLES LEGEND
This filmstrip is a morality story; a young man, betrayed by his friend, is saved by two young eagles. (In Dakota tradition, the Eagle is always a symbol of God's presence.) $15. AICRC.

UNLEARNING INDIAN STEREOTYPES
Works with myths and images from books and television. 15 minutes. Grades 3-6. Filmstrip, cassette. Rental, $5. NILB.

A VISIT TO THE FATHER
Authentic Navajo origin legend in four filmstrip episodes. Translated and illustrated by Navajo artist Auska Kee. All ages. $67.50 with cassettes. CEN.

VOICES FROM THE CRADLEBOARD
Slide presentation of traditional child rearing practices, such as the use of legends and the cradleboard, which emphasizes the importance of children in past and present Indian societies. 30 minutes. Grades 9-adult. Purchase: $185; rental, $30. DSP.

WHITE MAN AND INDIAN:
THE FIRST CONTACTS
Depicts the first explorers and their halting, initial contacts with the Indians of Eastern America. Grades 7-12. Two filmstrips, cassettes. $31. LL.

WOLF GIRL

This filmstrip is a morality story. In non-Indian myth, the Wolf is always an evil animal. Indian people, however, have discovered the wolf to be a friend and a helpful animal. $15. AICRC.

WOMEN OF SWEETGRASS, CEDAR & SAGE: CONTEMPORARY ART BY NATIVE AMERICAN WOMEN
20 color slides. ATL.

RECORDINGS

AH-K' PAH-ZAH
Douglas Spotted Eagle & Dan James
Dan James on synthesizer and Douglas Spotted Eagle on Native American flute. 60 minutes. Cassette, $9.98. CAN.

AKA GRAFITTI MAN
A unique blend of poetry & music by songwriter/poet John Trudell. Cassette, $10.60; CD, $16.

ALASKAN ESKIMO SONGS AND STORIES
Lorraine D. Koranda; illustrated by Robert Mayokok
42 stories and songs on one LP. Sung in Eskimo and told in English. 1971. 50 page booklet. UW.

ALL ONE EARTH: SONGS FOR THE GENERATIONS
Performed by Michael J. Caduto
A new dimension to the lessons of the Keepers books12 songs; 10 original compositions. 47 minutes. 1993. Cassette, $9.95; CD, $14.95. FUL.

AMERICAN INDIAN DANCES
Recordings of the following Indian dances: Rabbit Dance, Sun Dance and Omaha Dance (Sioux); Devil Dance (Apache); Eagle Dance (San Ildefonso); Harvest Dance and Rain Dance (Zuni); Squaw Dance (Navajo); War Dance and Dog Dance (Plains); Snake Dance and Pow-Wow Dance (Flathead). LP. $9.98. CAN.

AMERICAN INDIAN GOSPEL/CHRISTIAN MUSIC
American Indian Hymn Singers - Christian Hymns in Creek - Arbor Shade Singers -Vol. 1: What a Beautiful Day, Vol. 2: Nizhonie Christmas, Vol. 3: Let It Shine; The Chinle Galileans; Country Gospel Singers; Johnny Curtis - Vol. 1: Apache Country Gospel Songs, Vol. 2: Leavin' This Reservation, Vol. 3: Johnny Curtis - With Apache Gospel Sounds, Vol. 4: In Loving Memories, Vol. 5: Spirit of God, Vol. 6: In Loving Memories; Larry Emerson - Vol. 1: Larry Emerson and Skyward -10 gospel songs, Vol. 2: Now is the Tim; The Gospel Light Singers -Volume One - 12 songs, Vol. 2: Jesus Died for Me Long Ago, Vol. 3: To My Mansion in the Sky, Vol. 4: Life's Railway to Heaven, Vol. 5: I'm Bound for that City, Vol. 6: If That Isn't Love; Harvey Family: Vol. 1: The Curtis Harvey Family, Vol. 2: Let's Tell the World; Murphy Platero: Murphy Platero and the Morning Star Band-When Shall It Be; Smith Family: Smith Family Gospel Singers with The Thunders. Cassettes. $7.98 each. CAN.

AMERICAN INDIAN LANGUAGES
Cherokee Phrase Cards (with syllabary pronunciation tape), $12.95; Introduction to Cherokee (2 tapes plus 50-page workbook & glossary), $35.95; Cherokee Dictionary - Durbin Feeling, $18.95; Choctaw Language Sampler (audiotape with booklet), $14.95; Introduction to Choctaw (2 tapes plus 60-page workbook), $35.95; Choctaw Dic-

tionary - Cyrus Byington, hard cover, $59, soft cover, $39; The Lord's Prayer & 23rd Psalm - read in Choctaw by Charlie Jones (audiocassette with both printed in Choctaw), $9.95; Ontroduction to Chickasaw (2 tapes plus workbook), $35.95; Introduction to Kitoah Cherokee-Eastern dialect (2 tapes, with workbook), $35.95; Chickasaw Language Sampler (audio tape with phrase booket), $14.95; Chickasaw Glossary - Albert S. Gatchet, 1889, $15.95; Kiowa Language Sampler (audio tape with pronunciation guide), $12.95; Cherokee Syllabary (8 1/2 x 11 aged parchment), $1.95. VIP.

AMERICAN INDIAN LEGENDS
Recorded in both Indian & English. Cherokee: "The Rabbit & the Bear," & "Why the Hog's Tail is Flat" (Sam Hider, storyteller), $12.95; Choctaw: "Choctaw Creation Story," "The Little People," & "Why the Rabbit's Tail is Short," (Charlie Jones - storyteller), $12.95; Kiowa: "The Little Eagle" (EvaLu Ware Russell, storyteller), $12.95. VIP

AMERICAN INDIAN MEDICINE
Rolling Thunder, a Medicine Man, describes the difficulties Indians have had in preserving their philosophy and culture, while being captives in the white man's society. 60 minutes. cassette. BSR.

AMERICAN INDIAN MUSIC FOR THE CLASSROOM
Dr. Louis Ballard sings 27 songs of 22 Indian tribes in the authentic style of the tribal musician. He analyzes the song content so that the listener acquires an understanding of both the musical and cultural meaning of Indian vocal music. 4 LPs or cassettes. Includes a study guide, 20 study photographs, a complete set of spirit masters, and a bibliography of books for students who wish to pursue a further study of Indian cultures. Grades 1-12. $75. CAN.

THE AMERICAN INDIAN ORAL HISTORY COLLECTION
Dr. Joseph H. Cash & Dr. Herbert Hoover, Eds. In two volumes, the series contains 30 interviews on audiocassettes conducted by historians and anthropologists for students and scholars. The tapes offer a broad account of the experience of being an Indian, from recollections of 19th- century Indian-white relations and indigenous Indian culture to the experience of today's young Indians struggling to survive in White America without sacrificing their ethnic identity. Includes the following: Volume I - The Sundance (Crow); Medicine Men and Women I & II (Cheyenne River Sioux, Crow and Rosebud Sioux); The Buffalo Hunt I & II (Crow); Kinship, I, II & III (Crow); Legends (Chippewa); The Drum Society (Mille Lacs Chippewa); Little Bighorn; The BIA (Oglala Sioux); The BIA (Rosebud Sioux); Indian Students (Oglala Sioux); Life in 1900 (Cheyenne River Sioux). Volume II - A. Traditional Ways of Life: Religion (Rosebud Sioux , Winnebago & Northern Cheyenne, 5 tapes); Traditional Foods (Cheyenne River Sioux); Traditional Social Customs (Sisseton & Yankton Sioux); Legends (Spokane). B. Indian Leaders and Uprisings: Crazy Horse and Struck-by-the-Ree (Sioux); The Minnesota Uprising of 1862, I&II (Sioux). C. Contemporary Indian Problems: The City Vs. The Reservation (Spokane, Winnebago, Sioux); Problems of the Reservation (Crow Creek Sioux); Problems of the Urban Indian (Yankton Sioux & Winnebago); India Schools (Oglala Sioux). 30 minutes each. $15 each; Either Volume (15 tapes), $190; $350 per set (30 tapes). NR.

AMERICAN INDIAN STAR TALES: THE FEATHER MOON
Stories told by Lynn Moroney about the sky, the stars, & the planets. Music composed & performed on a Plains Indian flute. Cassette, $10. CH.

AMERICAN INDIANS IN FACT AND SYMBOL
In two parts by Dr. Joseph Henderson: Part 1: The American Indian and the Jungian Orientation -- Dr. Henderson offers an historical sketch of the white man's attitudes and actions toward American Indians. Part 2: The American Indian–A Sioux Shaman -- Dr. Henderson speaks of Black Elk, who at the age of nine had a vision which later evolved into the seven secret rites of the soul. Three hours, two tapes. BSR.

ANAPAO
Indian tales. Spoken and written by Jamake Highwater. Cassette. $10.98. FR.

ANCESTRAL VOICES
Carlos Nakai
Flute & guitar combo with songs. $11.50. CMM.

THE ANGRY INDIANS
Documentary on American Indian Conference at the University of Chicago in 1961, whose objectives were to get Indians from all parts of the U.S. together so that they could discuss their common problems and determine what they want from the U.S. Government and people. 26 minutes. Cassette. AUDIO.

ANIMAL STORIES (in English)
Stories colected from the Navajo, Cheyenne, Hopi, Kwakiutl, Tlingit, and Iroquois. Narrated by Gerald Hausman. 1 cassette (60 minutes), $10.95. AUDIO.

ANTHOLOGY OF NORTH AMERICAN INDIAN & ESKIMO MUSIC
A two-record set, compiled by Michael I. Asch, of the music of many of the tribes of North America, including: music of the Plains Indians; Indians of the Southwest; Northwest Coast Indians; Sub-Arctic; Arctic; Northeast Indians; and Southeast Indians. LPs. $19.96. FR.

APACHE INDIAN RECORDS & TAPES
Apache-Cassadore; Remembering Murphy Cassa, 2 Vols.; Songs of the Arizona Apache-San Carlos & White Mountain; Songs of the White Mountain Apache. Cassettes. $7.98 each. CAN.

THE ARCHIVE OF FOLK CULTURE-NATIVE AMERICAN RECORDINGS
Contains the following material: 1) The Jesse Walter Fewkes' 1890 cylinders of Passamaquoddy Indians--earliest field recordings made anywhere in the world; 2) More than 3,500 cylinders assembled between 1895 and 1940 by Francis Densmore and others for the Smithsonian Institution, Bureau of American Ethnology; 3) Several hundred discs and tapes 1940 to 1952 by Willard Rhodes for the Bureau of Indian Affairs; and 4) numerous other collections. The following recordings were edited by William N. Fenton ($8.95 each): Songs From the Iroquois Longhouse; Seneca Songs From Coldspring Longhouse. The following were recorded and edited by Frances Densmore ($8.95 each): Songs of the Chippewa; Songs of the Sioux; Songs of the Yuma, Cocopa, and Yaqui; Songs of the Pawnee and Northern Ute; Songs of the Papago; Songs of the Nootka and Quileute; Songs of the Menominee, Mandan and Hidatsa. The following songs were recorded

and edited by Willard Rhodes ($8.95 each): Northwest (Puget Sound); Kiowa; Indian Songs of Today; Delaware, Cherokee, Choctaw and Creek; Great Basin: Paiute, Washo, Ute, Bannock, Shoshone; Plains: Comanche, Cheyenne, Kiowa, Caddo, Wichita, Pawnee; Sioux; Navajo; Apache; Pueblo: Taos, San Ildefonso, Zuni, Hopi; Omaha Indian Music: Historic Recordings from the Fletcher/LaFlesche Collection, $10.95. Copies of most of the Archive's recorded collections can be ordered from: The Archive of Folk Culture, Library of Congress, Washington, D.C. 20540. (202) 707-5510. Photocopies of folklore & ethnomusicology material which are not protected by copyright or other restrictions may also be ordered.

ARCHIVES OF TRADITIONAL MUSIC
Indiana University, Morrison Hall
Bloomington, IN 47405
(812) 335-8632
Dorothy Sara Lee
Maintains extensive recorded material on the North American Indian.

AS LONG AS THE GRASS SHALL GROW
Peter LaFarge sings 13 of his own songs. A 12-page brochure includes words and transcriptions of songs. LP. $9.98. CAN.

AUTHENTIC INDIAN LEGENDS
Each program has an Indian-language version on one side and an English version on the other. The Little Eagle (Kiowa), Creation, Little People, and Rabbit's Short Tail (Choctaw); The Rabbit and the Bear, and Why the Hog's Tail Is Flat (Cherokee); Raccoon (Passamaquoddy). One cassette each (30 minutes). $11.95 each. AUDIO.

AUTHENTIC INDIAN MUSIC #1
Field recorded in North America. Casettee. $12.95. VIP.

BASIC MEDICAL NAVAJO
An elementary course for physicians & nurses who treat Navajo speakers. Each section consists of dialogues, vocabulary, questions & instructions, grammatical explanations & notes. 1 cassette (60 minutes) and 141 pp. text, $39. AUDIO.

BEGINNING CHEROKEE
Ruth Bradley Holmes & Betty Sharp Smith
A set of two cassettes for learning the Cherokee language. 3 hours, 332-page text. $39. CAN, CH & AUDIO.

BEGINNING PASSAMAQUODDY
Provides basic phrases, structures and vocabulary needed to speak Passamaquoddy in everday situations. Includes one cassette for basic phrasework, encyclopedia-type reference text with 3 cassettes for a spoken presentation of the material of the program, and one cassette for mastering the vowel sounds. 3.5 hours, 50 pp. phrasebook & 112 pp. reference text, and vowel sounds booklet. $59.50. AUDIO.

BEGINNING TLINGIT
A sytematic & structural introduction to Tlingit grammar with phrases & conversations for everyday use. 2 cassettes (2 hours) and 208 pp. spiral-bound text in album. $55. AUDIO.

BLACKFEET GRASS DANCE SONGS
11 grass dance songs sung by Allen White Grass, Pat Kennedy & Stanley Whiteman. Recorded at Browning, Montana, July 2, 1960. Cassette/LP, $10. AIS

BLACKFEET RECORDS & TAPES
Blackfeet Pow-Wow Songs; Carlson Singers; From the Land of the Blackfeet (LP); Hand Game Songs - Thomas Big Spring and Floyd Heavy Runner; Heart Butte Singers, 2 Vols.; Kicking Woman Singers, 5 Vols.; Little Corner Singers - Pow Wow Songs; Spotted Eagle Singers - Inter-tribal Pow Wow Songs; Two Medicine Lake Singers, 2 Vols.; Young Grey Horse Society, 2 Vols.; Black Lodge Singers - Pow Wow Songs, 6 Vols. Cassettes, $7.98 each. CAN.

THE BLESSING WAYS
Sharon Burch (Navajo) & A. Paul Ortega (Mescalero Apache) sing of Navajo culture, especially about women and their ways. Cassette, $10. FTW .

BOOTS & SADDLES
Book-on-cassette depicting Elizabeth (Libbie) Custer's experiences during her stay in the Dakotas with her husband General George Armstrong Custer. Edited from the original 1886 edition. 2 cassettes, $14.95. MCP.

BREAKTHROUGH NAVAJO
Self-study audiocassette/book programs developed by Alan Wilson to give instruction in the Navajo language and to provide a deeper understanding of the culture & lifestyle of the Navajo. An Introductory Course: 2 cassettes (3 hours) & 234 pp. text, $49; Speak Navajo: Intermediate: 2 cassettes (2 hours) & 180 pp. text, $49. AUDIO.

BUDDY RED BOW
Two cassettes: Black Hills Dreamer - country western songs; and Journey to the Spirit World. Cassettes, $9.98 each. CAN and FWT.

BUFFALO BIRD WOMAN - MY LIFE ON THE NOTHERN PLAINS (1840-1890)
Narrative by Buffalo Bird Woman tells how th Hidatsa lived on the Missouri River in western North Dakota during the late 1800's. 2 cassettes, $14.95. MCP.

BUFFALO SPIRIT
Original compositions by Fernando Cellicion. Cassette. $4.50. GDA.

CADDO TRIBAL DANCES
4 turkey dance songs, 4 duck dance songs, 4 green corn dance songs, 4 bell dance songs, 2 fish dance songs, and 2 stirrup dance songs sung by Mr. & Mrs. Houston Edmonds, Mr. & Mrs. Lewis Edmonds, and Lowell Edmonds. Recorded at Anadarko, Oklahoma, March 1955.

CANADIAN INDIAN RECORDS & TAPES
Assiniboine Jr. - 10 pow wow songs recorded in Manitoba, $9.98; Elk's Whistle - 13 pow wow songs recorded in Saskatoon, Saskatchewan, $9.98; Dakota Hotain Singers, Vol. 1 - 14 songs from Sioux Valley, Manitoba, and Vol. 2 - songs of the Dakota, $9.98 each; Whitefish Bay Singers - pow wow songs by a popular Ojibway drum from Whitefish Bay, Ontario, $9.98; Chiniki Lake Singers (from Morley, Alberta) 4 Vols., $7.98 each; Vic Thunderbird and the Thunderchild Singers; Old Agency Drummers-13 grass dance and chicken dance songs from the Blood Reserve, Standoff, Alberta, $7.98. Cassettes. CAN.

CANYON TRILOGY
Carlos Nakai with his Native American flute, journeys to the past, records in a canyon to simulate the ambience of the now abandoned cliff-dwelling villages. Cassette, $12. CH.

CEREMONIAL SONGS & DANCES OF THE CHEROKEE
Kevin Lewis sings 50 songs accompanied by a gourd or drum. Cassette, $10. CAN, CMM & CH.

CHEROKEE LANGUAGE WORKBOOK & INSTRUCTIONAL CASSETTE TAPE
Prentice Robinson
Booklet, 30 pp. and one cassette, $25. CH.

CHEROKEE LEGENDS I
Kathi Smith
30 minute cassette. $9. CH

CHICKASAW
Gregg Howard
Language course containing words, phrases, and sentences around the themes of everyday living. Also includes recipes of authentic dishes; legends & bibliography of information on the Chickasaw Nation. 1994. 2 cassettes & 95-page book. $39.95. AUDIO.

CHICKEN SCRATCH - POPULAR DANCE MUSIC OF THE INDIANS OF SOUTHERN ARIZONA
Chicken Scratch is a couples social dance passed down from generation to generation among the desert tribes of Southern Arizona. The music is primarily polkas and chotes played on guitars, accordions, saxophones, and drums, and is performed at church, fiestas, tribal celebrations, family affairs, and weekend social dances. A series of 42 LPs and cassettes based on the Scratch Dance. See CAN for titles.

CHIPPEWA-CREE CIRCLE DANCE
13 cirlce dance songs sung by Rocky Boy Singers, Paul Eagleman, Charles Gopher, Bill Baker, John Gilbert Meyers, and Windy Boy. Recorded at Crow Agency, Montana, August 1966. Cassette/LP, $10, AIS.

CHIPPEWA-CREE GRASS DANCE
14 grass dance songs sung by Rocky Boy Singers, Paul Eagleman, Charles Gopher, Bill Baker, John Gilbert Meyers, and Windy Boy. Recorded at Crow Agency, Montana, August 1966. Cassette/LP, $10, AIS.

CHOCTAW SINGING
Charlie Jones, Singer
With lyric booklet in Choctaw. Cassette. $14.95. VIP.

COMANCHE CHURCH HYMNS
Traditional hymns in the Comanche language. Cassette. CAN & GDA.

COMANCHE FLUTE MUSIC
Flute songs and narration by Doc Tate Nevaquaya as he discusses the flute & songs. LP. $9.98. CAN.

COMING LIGHT: CHANTS TO HONOR THE MOTHER EARTH
19 original chants on a 45-minute cassette. $10. CH.

THE CONTEST IS ON
Trick dance songs. Vol. 1 - Chiefly Ponca and Pawnee; Vol. 2 - Part of the annual Osage War Dance, Ponca Pow Wow and Ponca Heluska. Cassettes, $7.98 each. CAN & GDA.

CONVERSATION WITH TONY HILLERMAN
Rebekkah Presson
1992. Cassette, $9.95. LP.

COVERSATIONAL LAKOTA
Set of 6 tapes, $60. Set of 6 books (16 pp. each), $30. CAN.

COYOTE LOVE MEDICINE
Jessica Reyes uses the Native American courting flute with ritual percussion instruments & synthesizers. Cassette, $12. CH.

COYOTE LOVE MEDICINE
Jessica Reyes uses the Native American courting flute with ritual percussion instruments & synthesizers. Cassette, $12. CH.

CROW GRASS & OWL DANCE SONGS
12 grass dance songs & 1 owl dance song sung by Lloyd Old Coyote, Frank Bakcbone, Sr., Robert Other Medicine, & Lindsey Bad Bear; 3 owl dance songs sung by Warren Bear Cloud & John Strong Enemy. Cassette/LP, $10. AIS.

CRY FROM THE EARTH
Music of the North American Indians. 33 songs from 24 different tribes. LP. $9.98. CAN.

CULTURAL PLURALISM & THE RECOVERY OF THE CLASSIC
Uses poetry of the American Indian and reservation treaties of the 19th century to reveal the wisdom and philosophy of Indian leaders. 1972. 59 minute cassette. NCTE.

DAKOTA LANGUAGE (SANTEE) BY AGNES ROSS
Beginning language and simple sentence material. CAN.

DAKOTA THEOLOGY
30 minutes, bxw. VHS. $5.00. AICRC.

DANCING DAKOTA
Songs & stories of North Dakota singer/songwriter , Chuck Suchy. Cassette, $10; CD, $15. MCP.

THE DAWNING: CHANTS OF THE MEDICINE WHEEL
17 original chants on a 60-minute cassette. $10. CH.

DESERT DANCE
Carlos Nakai with his Native American flute, drums, voice, rattles, wind and rain in his ritual expression of nature's beauty. Cassette, $12. CH.

DREAM CATCHER
Flute music by Tokeya Inajin (Kevin Locke). Cassette, $10.60; CD, $16. MCP.

DRUMS OF THE AMERICAN INDIAN
One side of drum beat; and other side includes a collection of different drums and beats accompanied by shaker, rattle, deer toes or bells. 40 minutes. Cassette. $4.50. GDA.

EARTH SPIRIT
Carlos Nakai presents sounds of the Native American flute and introduces the mysterious & sacred sounds of the eagle bone whistle. 59 minutes. Cassette, $11.50. CMM.

EASTERN INDIANS TAPES
Iroquois Social Dance Songs, 3 Vols.; Beginning Cherokee-book & 2 tapes ($33.93); Songs & Dances of Eastern Indians From Medicine Spring (Cherokee) & Allegany (Seneca); Ceremonial Songs and Dances of the Cherokee. Cassettes, $8.98-9.98 each. CAN.

ECHOES OF THE UPPER MISSOURI
Flute music by Keith Bear (debut release). Cassette, $10; CD, $15. MCP.

EMERGENCE
Songs of the rainbow by Carlos Nakai (flute music). Cassette, $11.50. CMM.

ENGLISH & AMERICAN INDIAN STUDIES
Robert Lewis sets forth dos and donts for English teachers who plan to use Native American materials. 1972. 35 minutes. NCTE.

ESKIMO MUSIC OF ALASKA & THE HUDSON BAY
Record & notes by Laura Boulton. LP. $9.98. CAN.

ESKIMO SONGS FROM ALASKA
Twenty contemporary and ancient songs recorded by Miriam C. Stryker on St. Lawrence Island. Edited by Charles Hoffman. Includes an illustrated brochure. LP. $9.98. CAN.

EVERYDAY KIOWA PHRASES
Provides a brief introduction to some of the most common words & phrases used in Kiowa. 1 cassette, $12.95. AUDIO.

EYE OF THE CAT
Roger Zelazny
A shape-shifting extraterrestrial stalks a legendary Navajo tracker in a futuristic confrontation. 5 hours. Cassettes, $24.95. LP.

FEATHERSTONE CASSETTES
Gordon Bird Sings Traditional/Contemporary American Indian Songs-12 songs from the Mandan, Hidatsa and Arikara Nations; Dakota Songs by Wahpe Kute-12 traditional/contemporary songs of the Dakota Nation; New Town Singers-Live at Dakota Dance Clan Celebration; Mandaree Singers-Live at New Town, N.D.; Old Scout Singers-Live at White Shield, N.D.; Wahpe Kute-Live at Dakota Dance Clan Celebration, Sisseton, S.D.; Eagle Whistles-Live at Mandaree, N.D.; Leroy Strong and Johnny Smith "The Buckaroos"; Little Earth Singers-Live in the Twin Cities (Minneapolis/St. Paul, MN); Ft. Yates Singers-Live at Ft. Yates, N.D.; Rock Creek Singers-Live at Ft. Yates, N.D.; Mandaree Singers-Live at Bismarck, N.D.-Vol. 2; Eagle Whistles-Live at Bismarck, N.D.-Vol. 2; Assiniboine Singers-Live at Dakota Tipi; Dakota Tipi Live-Minneapolis Buckaroos, Red Nation Singers and the Assiniboine Singers; Red Nation Singers-Live at Ft. Totten Days; Dakota Language (Santee) by Agnes Ross; The White Buffalo Calf Woman as Told by Martin High Bear; Lakota Wiikijo Olowan by Kevin Locke, 2 Vols.; All Nation Singers-Flandreau Indian School; Songs of the People by Georgia Wettlin-Larsen. Cassettes. $8.25 each. CAN.

THE FLASH OF THE MIRROR
Flute music by Tokeya Inajin (Kevin Locke). Cassette, $10; CD, $15. MCP.

THE FLOOD & OTHER LAKOTA STORIES
Kevin Locke
Locke performs traitional Native American flute music between stories he tells. All stories reveal the values and beliefs of the Lakota. 60 minutes. 1993. Cassette. $11. CHA.

FLUTE/NEW AGE TAPES
Each flute artist has his own style influenced by his tribal heritage, personal experiences and feelings. N. Carlos Nakai, Gordon Bird, Fernando

Cellicion, Robert Tree Cody, Herman Edwards, Daniel C. Hill, Kevin Locke, Frank Montano, Cornel Pewewardy, John Rainer, Jr., Rainmaker, Stan Snake, Douglas Spotted Eagle, Robert Two Hawks, & Tom Mauchahty-Ware. See CAN for tape titles.

THE FLUTE PLAYER
Flute music by Bryan Akipa. Cassette, $10; CD, $15. MCP.

FLUTE PUEBLO
Traditional Zuni Pueblo flute music of Fernando Cellicion. 10 songs from Zuni, Laguna, Sioux & Acoma tribes. Cassette, $10. CMM.

FOOLS CROW, HOLY MAN
A retrospective of noted Ceremonial Chief & spiritual leader of the Oglala Sioux. Cassette, $10.60. MCP.

FORT OAKLAND RAMBLERS: OKLAHOMA INTERTRIBAL & CONTEST SONGS
Ponca Flag Song, 6 intertribal songs, 2 patriotic giveaway songs, 4 contest songs, & 1 Ponca veterans' song sung by a variety of singers. Recorded at White Eagle, Oklahoma, 1992. Cassette/LP, $10. IH.

GHOST WALK: NATIVE AMERICAN TALES OF THE SPIRIT
Gerald Hausman, Narrator; Ray Griffin, Music 1992. Cassette, $9.95. LP.

THE GIFT OF THE GREAT SPIRIT
Tehanetorens
These lesson stories, including The Story of the Monster Bear, are told by Mohawk Elder Tehanetorens in his inimitable style. 1988. All grades. Cassette, $9.95. OY.

GREAT AMERICAN INDIAN SPEECHES
Narrated by Vine Deloria, Jr. and Arthur S. Junalaska. Includes speeches of Geronimo, Standing Bear, Cochise, Black Elk and others. Grades 7-12. Two cassettes. $19.95. LL.

HAWAIIAN
D.M. Kahananui & A.P. Anthony
A beginning-level course that uses the aural-oral Method & emphasizes the development of conversational skills through dialogs & drills. 8 cassettes (8.5 hours); 431 pp., $95. AUDIO.

HAWAIIAN DRUM DANCE CHANTS: SOUNDS OF POWER IN TIME
Elizabeth Tatar
Compilation of historic & contemporary recordings from 1923. Cassette or CD. $12.95. BMP.

HEALING SONGS OF THE AMERICAN INDIANS
Healing songs of the Chippewa, Sioux, Yuman, Northern Ute, Papago, Makah and Menominee Indians. Text included. LP. $9.98. CAN.

HEART SONGS OF BLACK HILLS WOMAN
Paula Horne (Dakota Sioux) speaks her prose of each song in English before she sings it in her Native tongue. Cassette, $11; CD, $16. MCP.

AN HISTORICAL ALBUM OF BLACKFOOT INDIAN MUSIC
Includes Medicine Pipe songs, Sun Dance songs, Owl Dance songs, Gambling songs. Historical recordings dating back to the turn of the century. LP. $9.98. CAN.

HO HWO SJU LAKOTA SINGERS TRADITIONAL SONGS BY THE SIOUX
Includes the Sioux National Anthem, among other traditional songs of the Sioux. Cassette, $10. IH.

HOPI
Frank Waters
Myths of Native American lore. 28 minutes. Cassette, $9.95. LP.

HOPI KATCINA SONGS
Includes six other songs by Hopi Chanters. 17 songs and dances recorded by Dr. Jesse Walter Fewkes in Arizona in 1924. Text included. LP. $9.98. CAN.

HUNTER'S HEART
Larry Littlebird
A Pueblo Indian's introduction to the ritual of hunting. 40 minutes. Cassette, $9.95. LP.

IN THE LONG TIME AGO
11 legendary Cherokee stories told by Rogers Clinch, Sr., a Cherokee elder. He explains modern relevance to ancient stories. Cassette, $10. FTW.

INDIAN CHIPMUNKS
Alvin Ahoy-boy and his Indian Chipmunk Singers from Yuk-a-Day, Canada, sing pow wow songs. 2 Vols. Cassettes. $7.98 each. CAN & GDA.

INDIAN COUNTRY-WESTERN
Apache Spirit, 10 Vols. ($8.50 each)Three guys and a girl from Whiteriver, Arizona singing a combination of their own original compositions and popular country-western standards; Cody Bearpaw, 2 Vols. ($7.98 each); Louis Becenti - Eddie's Club in Gallup, NM presents Louis Becenti singing 12 country-western standards ($7.98); El Coochise, 3 Vols. ($7.98 each) - Hopi, Apache, and Navajo musicians provide back up for the vocals of Hopi musician and singer El Coochise; The Fenders, 2 Vols. ($7.98 each) - Navajo country-western band; Bill Johnson & the Jamborees, 3 Vols. (7.98 each) - A Navajo country-western band; Harold Mariano & the Variations, 3 Vols. ($7.98 each); Joe Montana and the Roadrunners, 3 Vols. ($8.98 each) - Hualapai Indian group from Peach Springs, Arizona; Navajo Clan, 3 Vols. ($7.98 each); Navajo Sundowners, 13 Vols. ($8.50 each) - A popular country-western group from Farmington, NM; Night Ryders - Composed of members of the Hopi and White Mountain Apache tribes. ($7.98); Jimi Poyer - Juke Box Music ($7.98); The Rockin' Rebels - Navajo group ($8.50); Sioux Savages - A Sioux-Navajo band from Tuba City, AZ ($7.98); The Thunders, 3 Vols. ($7.98 each); Undecided Takers - Navajo country-western and rock group from Kayenta, AZ ($7.98 each); Wingate Valley Boys - Navajo band from Fort Wingate, NM ($7.98); Zuni Midnighters, 4 Vols. - country-western dance band from Zuni Pueblo, NM ($7.98 each); Isleta Poorboys - Just Play 'N Good, songs by Clarence Jojola of Isleta Pueblo, NM. ($8.50) Cassettes. CAN.

INDIAN HOUSE RECORDS & TAPES
Includes the following records & cassettes: Round Dance Songs of Taos Pueblo, 2 vols.; Taos Round Dance, 2 parts; Taos Pueblo Round Dance; Ditch-Cleaning & Picnic Songs of Picuris Pueblo; Turtle Dance Songs of San Juan Pueblo; Cloud Dance Songs of San Juan Pueblo; Zuni Fair-Live; Navajo Sway Songs; Night & Daylight Yeibichei; Navajo Skip Dance & Two Step Songs; Navajo Round Dance; Navajo Gift Songs & Round Dance; Na-

vajo Corn Grindings & Shoe Game Songs; Klagetoh Maiden Singers; Navajo Songs About Love - The Klagetoh Swingers, Six volumes; The San Juan Singers - Navajo Skip Dance Songs; Turtle Mountain Singers - Navajo Social Dance Songs, 2 vols.; Navajo Skip Dance & Two-Step Songs - The Rock Point Singers, 2 vols.; Southern Maiden Singers - Navajo Skip Dance & Two-Step Songs; Navajo Peyote Ceremonial Songs, 4 vols.; War Dance Songs of the Ponca, 2 vols.; Ponca Peyote Songs, Three volumes; Cheyenne Peyote Songs, 2 vols.; Comanche Peyote Songs, 2 vols.; Handgame of the Kiowa, Kiowa Apache, & Comanche, 2 vols.; Kiowa Gourd Dance, 2 vols.; Kiowa 49 - War Expedition Songs; Kiowa Church Songs, 2 Vols.; War Dance Songs of the Kiowa–O-ho-mah Lodge Singers, 2 vols.; Flute Songs of the Kiowa & Comanche - Tom Mauchahty-Ware; Kiowa & Kiowa-Apache Peyote Songs; Songs of the Muskogee Creek, 2 parts; Stomp Dance - Muskogee, Seminole, Yuchi, 4 vols.; Blackfoot A-1 Club Singers, 2 vols; Old Agency Singers of the Blood Reserve, 2 parts; The Badland Singers - Assiniboine-Sioux Grass Dance; Sounds of the Badland Singers; The Badland Singers - Live at Bismarck; The Badland Singers at Home; Kahomini Songs - The Badland Singers; The Badland Singers, Live at United Tribes, 2 vols.; Ashland Singers - North Cheyenne War Dance; Ho Hwo Sju Lakota Singers - Traditional Songs of the Sioux; Love Songs of the Lakota, performed on Flute by Kevin Locke; Ironwood Singers - Songs of the Sioux, Live at the 106th Rosebud Sioux Fair; Yankton Sioux Peyote Songs, 8 vols.; Songs of the Native American Church - Sung by Rev. Joseph M. Shields; Rocky Boy Singers: Grass Dance & Jingle Dress Songs, 2 Vols.; Rocky Boy Chippewa-Cree Grass Dance Songs; Red Earth Singers, Live at Bismarck, 2 vols.; Sounds of Indian America - Plains & Southwest; Pueblo Songs of the Southwest; Turtle Mountain Singers-Welcome to Navajo Land & Early This Morning I Heard My Horse Calling; Eagle Society-Blackfoot Grass Dance Songs, Siksika Nation; Red Earth Singers of Tama, Iowa - "Live". American Indian Soundchiefs: Blackfeet Grass Dance Songs; Crow Grass Dance & Owl Dance Songs; Ponca & Pawnee Warriors Dance Songs; Ponca Tribal Songs; Caddo Tribal Dances; Kiowa-Comanche Peyote Songs; Cassette or LP recordings available for most selections. $10 for each cassette or LP. See HI for further information.

INDIAN MUSIC OF THE CANADIAN PLAINS
Recordings of the Blood, Cree, Blackfoot and Assiniboine Indians made on the reservation. Includes war songs, greeting songs, stick games, Dance songs, etc. LP. $9.98. CAN.

INDIAN MUSIC OF THE PACIFIC NORTHWEST COAST
A two-record set containing 27 songs and dances recorded by Dr. Ida Halpern, mostly from the Kwakiutl Tribe with Nootka and Tlingit songs and dances included. LP. $19.96. CAN.

INDIAN MUSIC OF THE SOUTHWEST
Includes Hopi, Zuni, Navajo, Taos, San Ildefonso, Santa Ana, Mohave, Papago, Pima and Apache music. Record and notes by Dr. Laura Boulton. LP. $9.98. CAN.

INDIAN ROCK MUSIC
Hamana (2 LPs-$7.98 each): Hamana, and Butchamana and the Big Bang Brothers Band; Many Hogans: American Clan; Mr. Indian and

Time: Medicine Dream; Redbone (2 LPs-$7.98 each): Message from a Drum, and Beaded Dreams Through Turquoise Eyes; Sand Creek: Endless Flight ($7.98); Winterhawk (3 cassettes-$8.50 each): Electric Warriors, Dog Soldier, and Winterhawk; XIT (7 cassettes-$8.98 each): Plight of the Redman, Silent Warrior, Entrance, Backtrackin', Relocation, Drums Across the Atlantic, and Tom Bee-Color Me Red. CAN.

INDIAN THEME CONTEMPORARY
B.Y.U. Musical Production - Lamanite Generation, 1985, Go My Son, and From the Eagle's Bed; Vincent Craig, Vol. 1 - (Navajo performer), and The Navajo Code Talker Song (45 rpm record); A. Paul Ortega - Mescalero Apache: Two Worlds, Three Worlds, and Blessing Ways; Buddy Red Bow - Journey to the Spirit World; Floyd Westerman: Custer Died for Your Sins, and The Land is Your Mother; Francis Country: The Peyote Dream; Homeland - 10 songs by Bugs Moran; Burt Lambert and the Northern Express: Just Arriving (LP-$7.98); Billy Thunderkloud and the Chieftones: Off the Reservation (LP-$5.98), and What Time of Day. Cassettes. $8.98 each. CAN.

INDIAN WISDOM STORIES
Dramatized legends recorded and produced by American Indians with authentic Salish Indian language chants, drum songs, and sound effects. Told by Jay Silverheels, Mohawk Indian actor. Includes 2 cassettes; four color filmstrips; a script for each story; a teacher's guide by Dr. Jerry Blanche (Choctaw Indian educator). Grades 4-6. CAN.

INTERTRIBAL GROUPS & COLLECTIONS
Bala Sinem Choir, 2 Vols. (American Indian Songs for Choir & Walk in Beauty My Children); Crow Celebration-10 Great Drums at Crow Fair; Denver Indian Singers-Arikara & Sioux (LP); Great Plains Singers & Songs; Hopi Sunshield Singers-Northern Style Pow Wow Songs; Kyi-Yo Pow Wow-9 Northern Plains Drums; Omak Pow Wow 1980 (Washington)-6 Drums from the Northwest; Pow Wow Songs - Music of the Plains Indians ($9.98-LP); The Song of the Indian-8 Tribal Groups & Soloists; White Eagle Singers-Intertribal Pow Wow Songs and Love Songs, 5 Vols.; Santa Fe Pow Wow, 2 Vols; Songs of the Earth, Water, Fire and Sky; Pow Wow Songs-Music of the Plains Indians. Cassettes, $7.98-$9.98 each; also available on compact disc, $16.98 each. CAN.

INTRODUCTION TO CHOCTAW
Provides a brief introduction to some of the most common words and phrases used in Choctaw. The seections revolve around the themese of everyday living, The native speaker is Charles G. Jones, past president of the Choctaw Indian Council. 2 cassettes (2 hours, 20 minutes); 60 pp. looseleaf binder album, $32.95. AUDIO.

INTRODUCTORY LAKOTA
All recordings are by native speakers; text contains 15 lessons, the last lesson being a comprehensive review. Exercises for written practice are included, using the English alphabet. 15 cassettes (12 hours), 102 pp. text, 9 pp final exam. Purchase: $175. AUDIO.

IROQUOIS SOCIAL DANCE SONGS
Traditional Iroquois social dance songs from the Six Nations Reserve in Ontario, Canada. Singers are: George Buck, Raymond Spragge, Jacob Thomas and Wm. Guy Spittal. 3 Vols. Cassettes. $7.98 each. CAN.

IROQUOIS STORIES
Joseph Bruchac
1988. All Grades. Cassette, $9.95. OY.

JOHNNY DAMAS & ME
The music of John Trudell, with the Graffiti Band. Cassette, $14.50; CD, $16.50. ICC.

JOURNEYS
Native American flute music. Carlos Nakai performs on several wooden flutes. Cassette, $11.50. CMM.

KEEPERS OF THE ANIMALS & KEEPERS OF THE EARTH
Told by Joseph Bruchac, featuring the complete, unabridged stories from "Keepers of the Animals" and Keepers of the Earth" Represents the art of traditional Native American storytelling, performing stories drawn from the native cultures of North America. 110 & 133 minutes, respectively (two tapes each). Cassette, $16.95 each. FUL.

KEEPERS OF THE DREAM
Flute music by Tokeya Inajin (Kevin Locke). Cassette, $10.60; CD, $16. MCP.

KIOWA CIRCLE & TWO-STEP SONGS
12 round dance songs sung by Leonard Cozad, Jasper Sankadota, Oscar Tahlo & Laura Tahlo. Recorded in 1964. Cassette/LP, $10. AIS.

KIOWA & COMANCHE PEYOTE SONGS
13 songs sung by Nelson Big Bow. Recorded at Crow Agency, Montana, August 1966. Cassette/LP, $10. AIS.

KIOWA-COMANCHE PEYOTE SONGS
6 songs sung by Nelson Big Bow, 6 songs sung by Edgar Gouladdie, 4 songs sung by Harding Big Bow & 7 songs sung by Walter Ahhaity. Cassette/LP, $10. AIS.

KIOWA FLAG SONG
Oklahoma Round Dance, Kiowa War Mothers & Comanche "49". Cassette. $45. GDA.

KIOWA HYMNS
Traditional church hymns for solo voice in the Kiowa language sung by Ralph Kotay. 2 cassettes. $15.95. CAN. $9. GDA.

KIOWA & KIOWA-APACHE PEYOTE RITUAL SONGS
4 songs sung by Emmett Williams, 4 songs sung by Nathan Doyebi, 4 songs sung by Edgar Gouladdie, & 8 songs sung by Nelson Big Bow. Cassette/LP, $10, AIS.

KIOWA MYTHS & LEGENDS
Kiowa Jill Momaday brings these traditional Native American tales to life. Each is accompanied by authentic tribal music. 2 cassettes (180 minutes), $21. AUDIO.

KIOWA PEYOTE MEETING
Documents the vision-producing peyote ritual. Recorded with the Anadarko, Oklahoma tribes and consists of both words & syllables with emotional connotations. 3 LP record set. Edited by Harry E. Smith. $29.94. CAN.

KIOWA PEYOTE RITUAL SONGS
18 ritual songs sung by the following: James Aunguoe, Ernest Redbird, Allen Tsontokoy, Francis Tsontokoy, & Oscar Tahlo. Cassette/LP, $10. AIS.

KIOWA PEYOTE RITUAL SONGS
15 Kiowa songs sung by Edward Hunmmingbird. Recorded at Crow Agency, ontana, in August 1966. Casette/LP, $10. AIS.

KIOWA ROUND DANCE SONGS
16 round dance songs, 2 Comanche 49 songs, 2 Kiowa War Mother's songs and a Kiowa Flag Song. Cassette. $7.98. CAN.

KIOWA SONGS & DANCES
Dance and war songs of the Kiowa Indians. LP. $9.98. CAN.

KIOWA STORYTELLER
Stories in the age-old oral tradition told by master storyteller & Pulitzer-Prize winner, N. Scott Momaday (Kiowa). 1 cassette (60 minutes), $10.95. AUDIO.

KOKOPELI DREAMS
Flute music by Fernando Cellicion. Cassette/CD, $4.50. GDA.

KWAKIUTL INDIAN MUSIC OF THE PACIFIC NORTHWEST
25 songs including Raven, Hagok, Hamatsa, Thunderbird, Potlatch, Whale and others. Two LP records. $19.96. CAN.

LAKOTA LOVE SONGS & STORIES
Flute music by Tokeya Inajin (Kevin Locke). Cassette, $10. MCP.

LAUGHTER: THE NAVAJO WAY
Humorous stories of the Navajo. Each story is presented in Navajo with a word-for-word translation, colloquial English equivalents, and an explanation of the story with cultural notes. 1 cassette (80 minutes) and 143 pp. text, $39. AUDIO.

LEARN TO PLAY NATIVE AMERICAN FLUTE
Dave Powell
Instruction for playing the Native American wood flute. Includes instructions and demonstrations, and lessons for playing four tunes are also included. 32 minutes. Cassette. $9.95. CAN.

LEGENDS OF NORTH AMEICAN INDIANS
Music by Jackie Crow Hiendlmayr. Cassette, $10.50. CMM.

LENAPE LANGUAGE LESSONS
Introductory-level course of the language of the Lennape (Delaware Indians) consists of 4 lessons on 2 audio cassettes (71 minutes) and two 30 pp. texts. $29.50. AUDIO.

LET'S 49!
25 singers record 49 songs from Oklahoma. Cassette. CAN & GDA.

LET'S SPEAK MOHAWK
Beginning-level course in conversational Mohawk provides the pronunciation, grammar, structures, and vocabulary needed to communicate in everday situations. 3 cassettes, and 102 pp. text. $39.95. AUDIO.

LIBRARY OF CONGRESS
LPs: Seneca Songs from the Coldspring Longhouse; Songs of the Yuma, Cocopa, Yaqui; Songs of the Pawnee & Northern Ute; Songs of the Papgo; Songs of the Nootka & Quiliute; Songs of the Menominee, Mandan & Hidatsa. Cassettes: Songs of the Kiowa; Indian Songs of Today; Songs of the Paiute, Washo, Ute, Bannock, Shoshone,

Songs of the Comanche, Cheyenne, Kiowa, Caddo, Wichita, Pawnee; Songs of the Sioux; Songs of the Navajo; Songs of the Apache; Pueblo: Taos, San Ildefonso, Zuni, Hopi; Omaha Indian Music. Cassettes & LPs, $9.98 each. CAN.

LONG AGO TIME
Cassette, $10. CMM.

LOVE FLUTE
Audio companion to Paul Goble's book put to the music of Bryan Akipa's flute. Cassette, $11; CD, $16. MCP.

THE LOVING WAYS
Joanne Shenedoah (Oneida) and A. Paul Ortega (Mescalero Apache) sing songs which reflect Native American philosophy and culture. Cassette, $8.98. CAN & FWT.

MAKE ME A HOLLOW REED
Flute music by Tokeya Inajin (Kevin Locke). Cassette, $10. MCP.

MIDWEST INDIANS RECORDS & TAPES
Chippewa War Dance Songs; Chippewa Grass Dance Songs; The Kingbird Singers; Mesquakie Bear Singers with War Dance Songs; Songs of the Chippewa; White Earth Pow-Wow; Winnebago Songs; Ojibway Music from Minnesota ($9.98); Honor the Earth Pow Wow - Songs of the Great Lakes Indians (Cassette, $9.98; compact disc, $16.98). Cassettes, $7.98 each. CAN.

MIGRATIONS
Ia Tulip
First album by flutist Ia Tulip of Sedona, Arizona. Cassette, $9.98. CAN.

MITAKUYE OYASIN: LAKOTA SUNDANCE SONGS
I6 songs with booklet of words in Lakota and English. 2 cassettes. $16. BOND.

MORNING STAR
Flute music by Tom Marchanty-Ware, featuring, "Crazy Horse Song." Cassette, $4.50. GDA.

MUSIC OF THE ALASKAN KUTCHIN INDIANS
Traditional Athabascan language songs including love, medicine, crow and other plus jigs, reels and square dances played on a violin. Recorded in 1972 in the Fort Yukon area of Alaska. LP. $9.98. CAN.

MUSIC OF THE ALGONKIANS
19 songs, most of them about hunting. Includes those of the Woodland Indians: Cree, Montagnais, Naskapi. LP. $9.98. CAN.

MUSIC OF THE AMERICAN INDIANS OF THE SOUTHWEST
Includes the Navajo, Zuni, Hopi, San Ildefonso, Taos, Apache, Yuma, Papago, Walapai and Havasupai tribal music. Recorded by Willard Rhodes in cooperation with the Bureau of Indian Affairs. Notes by Harry Tschopik, Jr. and Willard Rhodes. LP. $9.98. CAN.

MUSIC OF THE PAWNEE
Contains 45 Pawnee Indian songs sung by Mark Evarts and recorded in 1935 by Dr. Gene Weltfish. Reflects all aspects of Pawnee life. LP. $9.98. CAN.

MUSIC OF THE PLAINS APACHE
15 songs recorded and edited by Dr. John Beatty. Includes children's songs, lullabies, church songs, dance songs, hand game songs, and peyote songs. Notes and background of songs included. LP. $9.98. CAN.

MUSIC OF THE PUEBLOS, APACHE, AND NAVAJOS
Recorded by David P. MacAllester and Donald N. Brown. 12 LP. TM.

MUSIC OF THE SIOUX AND THE NAVAJO
Sioux recordings include, among others, Rabbit Dance, Sun Dance, love songs; Navajo recordings include: Squaw Dance, Night Chant, riding song, etc. Notes included. Recorded by Willard Rhodes in cooperation with the Bureau of Indian Affairs. LP. $9.98. CAN.

CARLOS R. NAKAI - NATIVE AMERICAN FLUTE MUSIC
Includes the following cassettes: Winter Dreams, Changes, Trilogy, Natives, Cycles, Journeys, Earth Spirit, Carry the Gift, Sundance, Desert Dance. $15 each tape. RC.

NATIVE AMERICAN ANIMAL STORIES
Gerald Hausman
Stories collected from the Navajo, Cheyenne, Hopi, Kwakiutl, Tlingit, and Iroquois. 53 minutes. Cassette, $9.95. LP.

NATIVE AMERICAN FLUTE MUSIC
Kevin Locke: Lakota Wiikijo Olowan, 2 Vols. ($8.25 each); Tom Mauchahty-Ware: The Traditional & Contemporary Indian Flute of Tom Mauchahty-Ware ($7.98); Carlos Nakai: Changes - Native American Flute Music, Vol. 1, Cycles - Native American Flute Music, Vol. 2, and Journeys: Native American Flute Music, Vol. 3 ($8.98 each); Stan Snake: Dan of Love ($8.98). Cassettes. CAN.

NATIVE AMERICAN LANGUAGES
Self-study audiocassette/book programs celebrating the languages, lives, legends and music of the Navajo, Lakota, Kiowa, Cherokee, Choctaw, Lenape, and Passaquoddy Indians; and Hawaiian Natives. Separate programs include: *Navajo* - Breakthrough Navajo-2 cassettes (3 hours) and 234 pp. text, $49; Laughter: The Navajo Way (humorous stories of the Navajo-1 cassette (80 minutes), and 143 pp. text, $39; Basic Medical Navajo-1 cassette (1 hour), and 141 pp. text, $39. *Lakota* - Introductory Lakota-15 cassettes (12 hours), and 102 pp. text, $175. *Kiowa*-1 cassette, $12.95. *Cherokee* - Beginning Cherokee-2 cassettes (3 hours), and 332 pp. text, $39.00. *Lenape* - Lenape Language Lessons-2 cassettes (71 minutes), and 2-30 pp. text., $29.50. *Passamaquoddy* - Beginning Passamaquoddy-5 cassettes (3.5 hours), 50 pp. phrasebook, 112 pp. text and vowel sounds booklet, $59.50. *Hawaiian* - Let's Speak Hawaiian-8 cassettes (8.5 hours), and 430 pp. text, $95. AUDIO.

NATIVE AMERICAN LISTEN & COLOR LIBRARY
Library of educational coloring books with accompanying cassettes portrays the symbols, settings, dress, & tribal decorations of 95 Indian tribes grouped into six major division: Northeast, Northwest, Southwest, Plains, Southeast, California. Each tribe is described and illustrated. 1994. Six, 32-page booklets, six, 60-minute cassettes. $39.95. AUDIO.

NATIVE AMERICAN MUSIC
Authentic music of four Native American tribes. Songs of the Cherokee, Songs of the Lenape, Songs of the Navajo, Songs of the Sioux. $11.95 each. AUDIO.

NATIVE AMERICAN WISDOM
Kent Nerburn & Louise Mengelkoch, Editors Features flute music by R. Carlos Nakai. Read by Kent Nerburn, Paula Bruce & Marc Allen. The unabridged reading of the book, and the Native American oral tradition. Speeches and writings of peoples from many tribes. 1993. Cassette, 83 minutes. $10.95. NWL.

NATIVES
Peter Kater and Carlos Nakai with an improvisational exploration and expression of the seven directions. Cassette, $12. CH.

NAVAJO
  Alan Wilson
Self-study audio-cassette/book programs on the Navajo language. Also provides a deeper understanding of the Navajo culture and life style. Includes the following programs: Breakthrough Navajo: An Introductory Course, 2 cassettes (3 hrs.) and 234-page text, $49; Speak Navajo: Intermediate, 2 cassettes (2 hrs.) and 180-page text, $49; Laughter: The Navajo Way (Humorous Stories of the Navajo), 1 cassette (80 mins.) and 143-page text, $39; and Basic Medical Navajo, 1 cassette (60 mins.) and 141-page text, $39. AUDIO.

NAVAJO CREATION STORIES
Sacred Twins & Spider Woman (stories); accompanied by drums & song, Geri Keams, Streak-of-Black-Forest Navajo Clan, brings listener into the circle & beauty way. 1994. 1 cassette, 60 minutes. $11.95. AUDIO.

NAVAJO & ENGLISH CASSETTES
20 cassettes. Grades K-6. See SAN for titles and prices.

NAVAJO EXPERIENCE STORIES
24 cassettes and booklets. Grades 1-6. See SAN for titles and prices

NAVAJO INDIAN RECORDS & TAPES
Beclabito Valley Singers, Vol. 3&4; Bita Hochee Travelers, Vols. 1,3&4; Chinle Valley Boys, 4 Vols.; Chinle Valley Singers, 2 Vols.; Chinle Valley Traditional Song and Dance Festival, 2 Vols.; Cove Nava-Tune Singers; Dennehotso Swinging Wranglers, 3 Vols.; Dine' Ba'Aliil of Navajoland (Navajo Songs and Dances)(LP); Four Corners Singers (Teec Nos Pos, Navajo Two Step & Love Songs), 7 Vols.; Four Corners Yei-Be-Chai; Lupton Valley Singers ($8.98); Memories of Navajoland; Davis Mitchell, 3 Vols.; Nanaba Midge Sings Traditional Navajo Songs; Natay, Navajo Singer; Navajo - Songs of the Dine; Navajo Squaw Dance Songs; Rock Point Singers, Vols. 3&4; San Juan Singers; Toh-Den-Nas-Shai Singers; Traditional Navajo Songs; Tsi Yi-Tohi Singers (Woodspring), 2 Vols.; Yei-Be-Chai Songs; Sweethearts of Navajoland, 2 Vols.; D.J. Nez, 2 Vols.Chinle Swingin' Echoes, 2 Vols.; Lupton Valley Singers, Vol. 1; Navajo Nation Swingers; Whippoorwill Singers, Vol. 1; Navajo Songs from Canyon de Chelly; Southwestern Singers. Cassettes & CDs. $7.98-$9.98; compact discs available, $16.98 each. CAN.

NAVAJO NIGHTS
  Gerald Hausman
Navajo healing stories. 50 minutes. Cassette, $11.95. AUDIO & LP.

NAVAJO PLACE NAMES
Arranged in alphabetical order, non-Navajo name first, then the Navajo name followed by literal translation of the complete Navajo term. 1 cassette & 100-page text which includes pronunciation guide and entire text of place names. $16.95. AUDIO.

THE NEW KICKING WOMAN SINGERS, Vol. 5
Intertribal Pow Wow Songs recorded live at Many Farms, AZ Pow Wow. 1988. Cassette, $7.98. CAN.

NEW WORLD RECORDS
A series of recordings compiled by Charlotte Heth, an ethnomusicologist and member of the Cherokee tribe. Includes: Songs of Love, Luck, Animals and Music - music of the Yurok and Tolowa Indians of Northern California; Songs and Dances of the Eastern Indians from Medicine Spring and Allegany - ritual, ceremonial and social music from the Cherokee (Oklahoma) and Seneca (Iroquois-Salamanca, NY); Oku Shareh - turtle dance songs recorded at San Juan Pueblo, NM; Songs of Earth, Water, Fire and Sky - an anthology of nine tribes: San Juan Pueblo, Seneca; Northern Arapaho; North Plains; Creek; Yurok, Navajo, Cherokee, and Southern Plains; Pow Wow Songs - Music of the Plains Indians. Cassettes. CAN.

NIGHT RIDERS & SKY BEINGS
Tsonakwa's second tape contains magical tales of the unseen world of the spirit told with warmth & power. 42 minutes. Cassette. $9.95. TOP & CH.

NOOTKA - INDIAN MUSIC OF THE PACIFIC NORTHWEST COAST
Includes canoe paddling songs, medicine songs, various animal songs, potlatch songs. Two LP record set. $19.96. CAN.

NORTHERN PLAINS RECORDS & TAPES
Arapaho War Dance Songs and Round Dances; Arikara Grass Songs - White Shield Singers (LP); Cree Pow-Wow Songs, 2 Vols. - By the Parker Singers from Rocky Boy's Reservation; Flathead Stick Game Songs; Hays Singers - Gros Ventre Songs; Hidatsa Songs - By the Little Shell Singers (LP); The Mandaree Singers - Contemporary Pow-Wow Songs, 2 Vols.; Pow-Wow Songs from Rocky Boy, 2 Vols.; Social Songs of the Arapaho Sun Dance - By Wind River Singers; Stick Game Songs; War Dances of the Crow; Sage Point Singers; Music of the Nez Perce; Nez Perce Stories. Cassettes, $7.98-$9.98 each. CAN.

NORTHWEST INDIAN RECORDS & TAPES
Canyon Wellpinit Singers - Spokane WA; The Chemiwai Singers; Songs & Stories from Neah Bay Makah (LP); Songs of the Warm Springs Indian Reservation; Songs of a Yakima Encampment; Stick Game Songs by Joe Washington - Lummi; Treaty of 1855 - Intertribal Pow-Wow Songs; Umatilla Tribal Songs; Yakima Nation Singers of Satus Longhouse. Cassettes, $7.98. CAN.

OJIBWAY MUSIC FROM MINNESOTA: A CENTURY OF SONG FPR VPICE & DRUM
  booklet by Thomas Vennum, Jr.
15 songs; 15-page booklet on Ojibway music and pow wows. Cassette & booklet, $9.95. CAN.

OJIBWE INTERMEDIATE VOCABULARY
Ojibwe Mekana
One, 60-minute tape & translation book. $21. ICC.

OJIBWE VOCABULARY FOR ADVANCED LEARNERS
Ojibwe Mekana
Two, 60-minute language tapes; Ojibwe/English booklet. $33. ICC.

OJIBWE VOCABULARY FOR BEGINNERS
Ojibwe Mekana
One, 60-minute language tape; Ojibwe/English work manual. $22. ICC.

OKLAHOMA POWWOW
18 specialty dance songs, including, "Eagle Dance." Casette, $4.50. GDA.

OUT OF THE FIRE
Tom Minton flute music. Cassette. $9.95. VIP.

PAPAGO-PIMA INDIAN RECORDS & TAPES
Papago Dance Songs (Chelkona & Keihina Dance Songs) (LP); Songs from the Pima; Traditional Papago Music; Traditional Pima Dance Songs. Cassettes. $7.98 each. CAN.

PASSAMAQUODDY BRIEF HISTORIES
One cassette (30 minutes) in Passamaquoddy & bilingual, with 20 pp. booklet. $11.95. AUDIO.

PETER LA FARGE--ON THE WARPATH
Includes 14 contemporary protest songs by Peter La Farge, accompanied by Nick Navarro, Indian drums. LP. $9.98. CAN.

PEYOTE CANYON
Paul Guy, Jr. and Teddy Allen (Navajos) sing peyote songs. Cassette, $10. FTW.

PEYOTE MUSIC
Peyote - A Collection; Chants of Native American Church, Vol. 2 (LP); Intertribal Peyote Chants-Bill Denny, 5 Vols.; Kiowa Peyote Songs; Lord's Prayer Songs-Alfred Armstrong; Navajo Wildcat Peak-Peyote Songs, 5 Vols.; Navajo Wildcat Peak-Youth; Peyote Healing Chants of Native American Church (LP); Peyote Prayer Songs, 2 Vols.; Peyote Songs, Vol. 2.; Billy Nez-Peyote Songs from Navajoland; Nez & Yazzie-Peyote Voices; Guy and Allen. Cassettes. $7.98-$9.98 each. CAN.

PONCA TRIBAL SONGS
Songs sung by Lamont Brown, Sylvester Warrior, Alberta Waters, & henry Snake. Recorded in 1967. Cassette/LP, $10. AIS.

PONCA WARRIORS DANCE SONGS & PAWNEE WARRIORS DANCE SONGS
10 Ponca warrior dance songs vy Sylvester Warrior, Albert Waters & Francis Eagle; Pawnee Flag Song & 12 warrior dance songs sung by Frank Murrie, Lamont Pratt, Phillip Jim & Mrs. Jacob Leader. Cassette/LP, $10. AIS.

POW WOW SONGS FROM OKLAHOMA
32 War Dance Songs from the O-Ho-Mah Lodge, Cheyenne, Pawnee and Ponca tribes sung by Tom Ware, Millard Clark, et al. 2 Vols. Cassettes. $15.96. CAN & GDA.

POW WOW SONGS OF THE MENOMINEE
Summer Cloud Singers in honor of the life of "Nepenanakwat" Johnson Awonohopay. Cassette, $12. ICC.

POW WOW & SPECIALTY DANCE SONGS FROM OKLAHOMA
18 songs including Comanche Flag Song, round, gourd, war eagle, hoop, etc. dance songs. Kiowa and Comanche singers. Cassette, $10. CMM & CAN.

POWWOW SONGS
1 audiocassette (48 minutes), $10.95. AUDIO.

PUEBLO INDIAN TAPES
Hopi Butterfly; Hopi Social Dance Songs, 2 Vols.; Songs from Laguna; Pueblo Indian Songs from San Juan; Zuni - Ceremonial Songs; Grand Canyon Hopi Dancers, recorded 1958-15 minutes ($6.95). Cassettes, $7.98 each. CAN.

REFLECTIONS
Tsonakwa tells stories & reminisces about his early life. 11 short tales told in "intimate leisurely style. 53 minutes. Cassette, $9.95.

THE RENAISSANCE OF THE AMERICAN INDIAN
Describes the social barriers the American Indian has had to face; his experiences in various careers, and the anachronistic traditions of Indian culture that confuses his progress. 1968. Cassette. AUDIO.

ROBERT TREE CODY: LULLABIES & TRADITIONAL SONGS
Native American flute music. Cassette, $12. CH.

ROCK POINT SINGERS, Vol. 4
Traditional love tunes. 14 skip and two-step dance songs. Cassette, $7.98. CAN

ROUND DANCE SONGS WITH ENGLISH LYRICS
48 songs. By Tom Mauchahty-Ware & Millard Clark. 4 LPs. $7.98 each. CAN & GDA.

SACRED FEELINGS
Douglas Spotted Eagle combines the nature sounds of the earth-mother with Native American flute. Cassette, $12. CH.

SALISH
Language course for beginners in the Salish language, spoken today principally in British Columbia. 30 lessons providing vocabulary, phrases, and sentences on subjects of everyday interest, such as work, weather, directions, food & money. 1994. 2 cassettes & 88-page text which includes 22 pp. index. $29.95. AUDIO.

SAN XAVIER FIDDLE BAND
O'odham old time fiddle music. 12 polkas, chotes and mazurkas. Cassette, $7.98. CAN

SELF-DETERMINATION FOR AMERICAN INDIANS: 1) DEVELOPMENT OF THEIR LANDS; 2) CULTURES IN CONFLICT
Recorded and edited by Henry W. Hough: 1) Traces the history of reservations and discusses the present development of resources on Indian reservations. 2) Why Indians cling to their way of life although proud of their American citizenship. 1968. Cassettes, 25 minutes each. AUDIO.

SEMINOLE INDIANS OF FLORIDA
Dr Frances Densmore on cylinders. Includes corn dance, Cypress Swamp hunting and buffalo dance songs; plus songs for treatment of the sick and songs concerning removal of Seminole to Oklahoma. LP. $9.98. CAN.

SENECA SOCIAL DANCE MUSIC
30 songs from Allegany Reservation, Cattaraugus Co., New York. Recorded by M.F. Reimer. LP. $9.98. CAN.

SENECA SONGS FROM COLDSPRING LONGHOUSE
Songs include the Drum Dance, Bear Society, Fish Dance, and others. Recorded and edited in 1941-1945 by Willard N. Fenton. 16-page brochure. LP. $8.98, LC and $9.98, CAN.

THE SEVENTH DIRECTION
Flute music by Tokeya Inajin (Kevin Locke). Cassette, $10. MCP.

SIGNALS FROM THE HEART
Collection of "49's" songs using traditional drumming and style. Performed by Common Man Singers of the Standing Rock Sioux Reservation in North Dakota. Cassette, $10.60; CD, $16. MCP.

SIOUX RECORDS & TAPES
Celebration on an Indian Theme; Denver Dakota Singers -Pow Wow Songs; Fort Kipp Celebration; Fort Kipp '77 Live; Fort Kipp Sioux Singers; Grass Dance Songs from Devil's Lake - By the Lake Region Singers; Ironwood Singers; Montana Grass Songs - By the Fort Kipp Singers; Porcupine Singers, 6 Vols. - At Ring Thunder, Traditional Sioux Songs, Concert in Vermillion, At the University of South Dakota, Rabbit Songs; Rock Creek Singers - Hunkpapa Sioux; Sioux Favorites; Sioux Grass Songs and Round Dances; Sioux Songs From Devils Lake - By the Lone Buffalo Singers; Sioux Songs of War and Love; Sisseton-Wahpeton Songs (LP); and Songs of the Sioux. Rock Creek Singers; Sioux-Assiniboine Singers, 2 Vols.; Red Nation Singers; Taku Wakan: Lakota Sundance Songs; Taku Skanskan: Lakota Yuwipi Songs. Cassettes, $7.98-9.98 each. CAN.

A SKY OF DREAMS
Neoprimitive solos for flutes of the world. By Barry Stramp of the Coyote Oldman duo. Cassette, $10; compact disc, $15. FTW & CH.

SMOKESIGNS
Rick Eby
Flute & synthesizer music. Cassette. $12.95. VIP.

SONGS & DANCES OF THE FLATHEAD INDIANS
A complete musical culture of the Salish people. Illustrated notes included. LP. $9.98. CAN.

SONGS & DANCES OF THE GREAT LAKES INDIANS
Music of the Algonquins and Iroquois. Recorded in Iowa, Wisconsin, Michigan and New York State by Gertrude P. Kurath. Text included. LP. $9.98. CAN.

SONGS FROM THE IROQUOIS LONGHOUSE
Selections include: Creator's Songs; Midwinter Festival Chants; Medicine Men's Celebration (Onondaga.) Recorded and edited by William N. Fenton in cooperation with the Smithsonian Institution. 34-page brochure. LP. $8.95, LC and $9.98, CAN.

SONGS OF THE CHEROKEE
Ceremonial songs & dances (caasette); songs & dances of the Cherokee of North Carolina & the Seneca (cassette). $11.95 each. AUDIO.

SONGS OF EARTH, WATER, FIRE & SKY
Traditional dance songs recorded on location by Pueblo, Seneca, Arapaho, Plains, Creek, Yurok, Navajo & Cherokee tribes. Cassette, $12. CH.

SONGS OF THE NATIVE AMERICAN CHURCH
Peyote songs by Billy McClellan. 2 Vols. $9. GDA.

SONGS OF THE NAVAJO
Traditional Navajo songs (cassette); traditional Sioux songs (cassette); Taku Wakan: Lakota Sundance Songs (cassette). $11.95 each. AUDIO.

SONGS, POEMS AND LIES
Lorenzo Baca (Isleta Pueblo/Mescalero Apache) sings songs with traditional chants and original poetry. Cassette, $10. FTW.

SONGS & STORIES FROM NEAH BAY - MAKAH
Legends and little songs by a favorite Makah storyteller, Helen Peterson. LP. $7.98. CAN.

SOUNDS OF INDIAN AMERICA – PLAINS & SOUTHWEST RECORDED LIVE AT THE GALLUP CEREMONIALS
Includes the Buffalo Dance, Jemez Eagle Dance, Ute Bear Dance, San Juan Butterfly Dance, Zuni Rain Song Dance by the Olla Maidens, Navajo Feather Dance, Taos Belt Dance, Pawnee Ghost Dance, Zuni Doll Dance, Crow Sun Dance, Kiowa Attack Dance. Cassette, $10. IH.

SOUTHERN PLAINS-OKLAHOMA INDIANS RECORDS & TAPES
Brave Scout Singers-Northern Style Otoe, Missourian & Pawnee; Gourd Dance Songs of the Kiowa-Koomsa Tribal Singers; Kiowa Back Leggings Society Songs-Bill Kaulaity; Kiowa Gourd Dance Songs; Kiowa "49" & Round Dance Songs; Kiowa Scalp & Victory Dance Songs-Koomsa Tribal Singers; Ponca War Dances-Ponca India Singers; Pow Wow - Southern Style War Dances; Songs of the Caddo, 2 Vols. (LP). Cassettes. $7.98 each. CAN.

SOUTHERN THUNDER: INTERTRIBAL SONGS OF OKLAHOMA
Osage Flag Song, 14 intertribal songs, 2 Pawnee veterans' songs, & 1 Pawnee war dance song sung by a few different singers. Recorded at Hominy, Oklahoma, 1992. Cassette/LP, $10. IH.

SOUTHERN THUNDER: REACHIN' OUT
14 intertribal songs by a number of singers. Recorded at Hominy, Oklahoma, 1993. Cassette/LP, $10. IH.

SPIRIT HORSES
Carlos Nakai with contemporary concerto for Native American flute and chamber orchestra. Cassette, $12. CH.

SPIRIT JOURNEY - CORNEL PEWEWARDY
Dr. Pewewardy (Comanche/Kiowa) demonstrates his talents of singer, flute player & keeper of the drum. Cassette, $10.60; CD, $16. MCP.

SPIRIT OF SONG
Original digital recording of the "Spirit of Song" singers from spring of 1990. Features the voices of Sissy & Credric Goodhouse, Earl & Tom Bullhead, Dave Archambault. Cassette, $11. MCP.

SPIRITS OF THE PRESENT: THE LEGACY FROM NATIVE AMERICA
Focuses on Native American histories, cultures, and modern realities. Explores American Indian

religious fredom, the sovereignty of Native nations, stereotyping of Native people by sports teams and other commercial entities, and Native American art. 1991. 5 audiocassettes. $29.95. PUSA (800) 253-6476.

STAR LORE
Lynn Moroney (Cherokee/Chickasaw), tells the star lore to be found in the myths of Native Americans. Authentic music by Native American flute player. The Feather Moon, 1 casette; The Star Husband, 1 casette. 1994. 45 minutes each. $10.95 each. AUDIO.

STARGAZER
  Gerald Hausman
Navajo supernatural myths & divination stories. 60 minutes. Cassette, $11.95. AUDIO & LP.

STORYTELLER
  N. Scott Momaday
Stories in the Native American oral tradition shared by a storytelling master of the Kiowa origin. 60 minutes. Cassette, $9.95. LP.

SUNRISE
Flute music by Tom Mauchanty-Ware, featuring, "Zuni Sunrise Song." Cassette. $4.50. GDA.

SYMBOLIC SHAMANISM: A STUDY OF NAVAJO MEDICINE MEN
Dr. Donald Sandner describes the healing process of medicine men and attempts to explain the sandpaintings, how they are made, how images are evoked for each patient, and how cures are performed. Two hours/two cassettes. BSR.

SYMBOLS OF HOPI
Jill McManus, a jazz musician, has created a jazz album by arranging two songs each by a pair of Hopi composers who work within their own dance music tradition, and added three originals in the spirit of Hopi and Pueblo music. Includes two Hopi ceremonial songs, "Corn Dance" and "Cloud Blessing." Louis Mofsie, director of the famed Thunderbird Dance Troup, opens Mark Lomayestewa's Corn Dance on the cottonwood drum. CJ.

TEAR OF THE MOON
Coyote Old Man. Compositions on Native American flute & Incan Pan Pipes. Cassette, $12. CH.

THE THIRD CIRCLE - SONGS OF LAKOTA WOMEN
Traditional & contemporary Lakota women's songs sung by Sissy Goodhouse. Cassette, $10; CD, $15. MCP.

THUNDER CHORD
Coyote Oldman. Native American flutes and panpipes. Cassette, $12. CH.

THUNDERDRUMS
Scott Fitzgerald uses drums from both Native America and Africa for sounds of nature. Cassette, $10; compact disc, $16. FTW.

TOUCH THE FIRE
Native American poetry by Bob Annesley. Cassette, $4.50. GDA.

TRACKS WE LEAVE
16 impressionistic compositions featuring William Eaton, with R. Carlos Nakai, Rich Rodgers, Claudia Tulip, Arvel Bird & Udi Arouh. Notes on the instruments and performers included. 55 min-

utes. Cassette, $8.98; compact disc, $14.98. CAN & CH.

THE TRADITIONAL & CONTEMPORARY INDIAN FLUTE
Flute music by Tom Mauchanty-Ware. Cassette. $4.50. GDA.

THE TRADITIONAL & CONTEMPORARY INDIAN FLUTE
Flute songs by Fernando Cellicion. Cassette, $4.50. GDA.

TRADITIONAL INDIAN FLUTE OF FERNANDO CELLICION
10 flute songs. Cassette, $4.50. GDA.

TRIBAL MUSIC INTERNATIONAL
Music from the Hopi; Music from San Juan Pueblo; Red Eagle Wing Pow Wow Songs; Flute and Prayer Songs; Music from the Alliance West Singers; and 65th Inter-Tribal Ceremonial-Gallup Ceremonial; Music from Zuni Pueblo. Cassettes. $8.98 each. CAN.

TRIBAL SONGS
Ceremonial and social songs and dances of eight Native American Indian tribes: Tohono O'odham (Papago), Apache, Sioux, Navajo, Crow, Ute, Shawnee, & New Taos. Cassette. $12.95. AUDIO.

TURTLE ISLAND ALPHABET
Gerald Hausman's anthology of myths & stories which study the symbols & images central to the Native American culture. 1 cassette (90 minutes), $10.95. AUDIO.

TURTLE MOUNTAIN SINGERS: EARLY THIS MORNING I HEARD MY HORSE CALLING
10 Navajo social dance songs sung by John Comanche, Jimmie Castillo, Samuel Harrison, & Kee Trujillo, . Recorded at Taos, New Mexico, 1990. Cassette/LP, $10. IH.

TURTLE MOUNTAIN SINGERS: WELCOME TO NAVAJO LAND
10 Navajo social dance songs sung by John Comanche, Jimmie Castillo, Samuel Harrison, Ernest Chavez, Kee Trujillo, Johnny B. Dennison & Benson Trujillo. Recorded at Lybrook, New Mexico, 1990. Cassette/LP, $10. IH.

UTES
Includes six northern war dance songs, three bear dances, and three sun dance songs. Singers from Ignacio, Colorado, and from the White Mesa, Utah. Cassette. $7.98. CAN.

A VOICE FOR THE AMERICAN INDIAN
A program on Indian culture and history, and the current struggles for political rights and power. Produced by Pacifica, KPFA. 1971. 54 minutes. AUDIO.

WALKING THE RED ROAD
Earl Bullhead, a Lakota of the Standing Rock Reservation in North Dakota, sings traditional Lakota songs recorded in a contemporary style. Cassette, $10.60; CD, $16. MCP.

WAR WHOOPS AND MEDICINE SONGS
33 songs collected at the Upper Dells of the Wisconsin River where more than 200 American Indians from five different tribes assembled for the annual Star Rock Indian Ceremonial. Includes an illustrated brochure. Edited by Charles Hofman. LP. $9.98. CAN.

WASHO PEYOTE SONGS: SONGS OF THE AMERICAN INDIAN NATIVE CHURCH
Recorded by Dr. Warren d'Azevedo. LP. $9.98. CAN.

WESTERN CANADIAN INDIAN RECORDS & TAPES
A-1 Club Singers - Vol. 2; Blackfoot A-1 Singers; Blackfoot Oldtimers - Songs from the Past; Calgary Drummer; Chiniki Lake Drummers; Crowfoot Drummers - Blackfoot, Alberta; The Drums of Poundmaker - With the Tootoosis Family, 2 Vols. (LP); Fraser Valley Spotted Lake Inter-Tribal Singers; Little Pine Singers - Cree Pow-Wow Songs; Pigeon Lake Singers - Cree Tribal Songs, 2 Vols.; Pow Wow Songs - Treaty 6 Ermine Skin Band; Sarcee Broken Knife Singers, 2 Vols.; Sarcee Oldtimers; Pezhin Wachipi (Grass Dance) (LP); Scalp Lock Singers; Sioux Pow-Wow Songs; Songs from the Blood Reserve - Kaispai Singers; Songs from the Battleford Pow-Wow; Songs of the Sarcee (LP); Stony Pow-Wow Songs - Eden Valley Pow-Wow Club; Two Nation Singers - Round Dance Songs; Little Boy Singers - Pow Wow Songs, 2 Vols.; Northern Cree Singers, Vols. 3 - Live at Fort Duchesne; Blackstone Singers, Vol. 1 - Contest Songs - Live at Fort Duchesne; Sioux Assiniboine - Dakota Kahomini Songs; The Red Bull Singers, 2 Vols.; Dakota Hotain Singers, 2 Vols.; Cathedral Lakes Singers, 2 Vols.; White-fish Bay Singers, 2 Vols.; Plains Ojibway Singers, Vol. 1; Stoney Eagle. Cassettes & LPs, $7.98-$9.98 each. CAN.

THE WHITE BUFFALO CALF WOMAN AS TOLD BY MARTIN HIGH BEAR
Cassette, $8.25. CAN.

WHITE EAGLE SINGERS, Vol. 5
11 intertribal pow wow songs recorded live at the Numaga Indian Days in Reno-Sparks, Nevada. Cassette, $7.98. CAN.

WINTER DREAMS
Native American Christmas music. Carlos Nakai and William Eaton arranged these old traditional European Christmas songs. Cassette, $12. CH.

WOODLAND WINDS - THE WOODLAND CONSORT
Fusion of Native & Western instruments, with Ojibway flute. Cassette, $11; CD, $16. MCP.

WOPILA - A GIVEAWAY: LAKOTA STORIES
  Dovie Thompson
Features the traditional flute music of Kevin Locke within the prose of tha artist. Grades PS-4. Cassette, $10.60. MCP.

THE WORLD IN OUR EYES
Storyteller Reuben Silverbird's view of the essence of our country's most ancient heritage. Tells of the Great Spirit, Mother Earth, Father Sky, the circle, the rain, the eagle and other elements of the creation stories. Two cassettes, $20. CH.

A YAQUI WAY OF KNOWLEDGE
The group Wild Strawberries in a series of tone poems inspired by Carlos Castaneda's best-selling book of the same title. Cassette, $10; compact disc, $16. FTW.

ZANGO MUSIC DISTRIBUTION
Specializing in Native American music, including R. Carlos Nakai, Coyote Oldman, Black Lodge Singers, John Trudell, Kevin Locke, Jackalope, and others. 300 titles. Catalog. ZANGO.

PRINTS &PHOTOGRAPHS, PICTURE SETS, POST CARDS, CALENDARS, POSTERS & KITS

ALASKAMEUT '86
Exhibition poster features masks by John Kailukiak, Kathleen Carlo and James Schoppert. 24x18", full color. $8.50, postpaid. IANA.

ARTS FROM THE ARCTIC
Exhibition poster featuring the artwork of Alvin Amason. 18x22", full color. $12.50, postpaid. IANA.

ATHABASCAN OLD-TIME FIDDLING POSTER
Features musicians and dancers. 18x24", black and silver duotone. $7.50, postpaid. IANA.

THE BEAUTY OF NATIVE AMERICAN CHURCH-POSTER
By Haroldton Begaye. 21 x 17. $3.95. CAN.

BENDING TRADITION
Exhibition poster featuring bentwood art by traditional and contemporary artists. 24" x 18" full color. Institute of Alaska Native Arts, $8.50, postpaid. IANA.

BOSTON CHILDREN'S MUSEUM BORROW A KIT
The Indians Who Met the Pilgrims: Presents the Wampanoag people of Massachusetts past and present; Hopi Culture: Describes a public kachina dance and its connection to contemporary Hopi culture. These two kits may be used as curriculum units, include cultural objects, oral history, texts and guides, A-V materials, and classroom activities; prepared with the participation of Native American people. Two other kits, The Navajo and Northwest Coast Indians, contain cultural objects and related labels for classroom exhibit. CMB.

CAHOKIA ARTIFACTS POSTER
Full color poster showing artifacts found at Cahokia Mounds site. 38" x 25". $10. CMM.

CAHOKIA MOUNDS MURAL
Entrance scene in new Interpretive Center - artists conception of ancient city. 20" x 37". $10. CMM.

CATLIN'S NORTH AMERICAN INDIAN PORTFOLIO
The 1845 American edition is supplemented with six additional prints from the original British edition. Each set contains 31 plates measuring 16x22". Strictly limited to 950 sets. 1989. $1,250. A.

CHEROKEE POEM
8.5" x 11 poster. $2.50. VIP.

CHEROKEE POSTER
Kevin Smith, artist
17" x 21". $7.95. VIP.

CHOCTAW T-SHIRT
Kevin Smith, artist
$13.95. VIP.

CLOVIS CULTURE
Poster. $15. CMM.

EARLY PALEO INDIAN PERIOD
Poster. $15. CMM.

EARLY TEXAS INDIAN MURAL POSTERS
George Nelson
Series of posters, full-color photographs of the actual 24" x 10" murals on the Institute of Texan Cultures' Floor. "A Caddo Farming Community in East Texas"; "Desert Farmers of Southwest Texas: The Mogollon Culture"; An Apache Encampment in the Texas Hill Country." Each poster, 36" x 21". $10 each; $25 for all three. UT-ITC.

EDUCATIONAL AID KITS
Children's touchable exhibits contained in a large footlocker-type trunk. Artifacts are compiled from the Museum of New Mexico's collections and various other sources in Santa Fe. Includes: Anglo Pioneer Family; Apache Family; Navajo Family; Pueblo Indian Family; and Spanish Frontier Family. Grades 1-6. Available for loan in the State of New Mexico only. Free one month rental. MNM.

GEORGE CATLIN'S NORTH AMERICAN INDIANS
Box of 20 5x7" notecards & envelopes. 4 different designs. $11.95. A.

HOOP DANCER PRINT
Milton Denny, artist
$2.50. VIP.

HOWARD ROCK & HIS LEGACY
Exhibition poster featuring *The Dance of Kakimok*, a painting by the late Howard Rock. 16x20", full color. $7.50, postpaid. IANA.

INDIAN DWELLING & HOMES OF THE U.S. POSTER
Revised 1984. 29" x 23". $5.25. CMM.

INDIAN PHOTOGRAPHS FROM THE SMITHSONIAN
There are four sets of five prints each. Set 1) Selected portraits: Kicking Bear, Geronimo, Chief Joseph, Quanah Parker, and Wolf Robe; Set 2-4) Lifestyles, Northwestern Indians - Southwestern Indians - Plains Indians. 11 x 14. SI.

THE INDIANS OF THE PLAINS
Contains 46, 11 x 14 photographs explaining the Plains Indians culture, government, society and habits; and how they were discovered in 1805. $73.50. DPA.

INTERWOVEN EXPRESSIONS
Exhibition poster featuring 20 Alaska Native baskets representative of all of the Alaska Native cultures. 24x18", full color. $8.50, postpaid. IANA.

KIOWA EAGLE PRINT
Ruth Blaylock Jones, artist
$3. VIP.

LIBRARY OF CONGRESS PRINTS & PHOTOGRAPHS DIVISION
Recently completed the processing and cataloging of 3,500 images of American Indians photographed over an 85-year period ending in the 1940s. Also an extensive collection of Edward S. Curtis photographs, more than 1,600 photos. The images are now accessible to researchers in the division's reading room in the Library's Madison building in Washington, DC. LC.

MUSEUM OF THE AMERICAN INDIAN-PHOTO-GRAPHIC ARCHIVES
Covers all areas and aspects of Native American life in the Western Hemisphere. Includes photographs by Curtis, Matteson and Jackson; Pepper,

Wildschut and Verrill. 42,000 negatives, 28,000 bxw prints, and 5,000 color transparencies and slides; bxw prints, 5x7 or 8x10 format; 35mm color slides; and 4x5 color transparencies. A slide list is available for a modest fee. MAI.

MUSEUM OF NEW MEXICO PHOTOGRAPHIC PORTFOLIOS
Includes three Native American photographic portfolios: Pueblo Indians of New Mexico; Apache Indians of New Mexico; and, Navajo Indians of New Mexico. Each set contains 16 photographs illustrating important aspects of the subject group's life and history during the late 19th and early 20th centuries. Large bxw photographs printed on heavy glossy paper. Each portfolio also contains a brief history of the group plus a vocabulary list, bibliography, and descriptive captions for the photographs. $6.95 each. MNM.

NATIONAL NATIVE AMERICAN MONTH - NOVEMBER 1994
Designed by Gerald Dawavendewa, a Hopi/Cherokee artist. Entitled "Spiritual Winds." $7. ROD.

NATIVE AMERICAN INDIAN TRIBES - MAP
Shows four geographical areas. 20" x 16". $3. CMM.

NATIVE AMERICAN VISIONS CALENDAR
12 exquisite Sam English (Ojibwa artist) full-color prints; calendar with 10x14 print and appointment calendar below; and selected quotes from historic and present-day tribal leaders. Available in August for upcoming year. $10.95. AB & FUL.

NAVAJO CURRICULUM MATERIALS - DRUGS & ALCOHOL
Drug & Alcohol Myths - poster set, 11x17-3 colors - 12 posters drawn with Indian people depicting common myth about drug and alcohol use and abuse. $5.10 per set; $8.95 laminated; *Fetal Alcohol Syndrome* - poster set, 11x17-2 color - 8 posters stating facts about fetal alcohol syndrome and its effect on new born babies. $3.40 per set; $6.80 laminated. SAN.

NAVAJO GUIDES, CULTURAL MANUALS, & TEXTBOOKS
See SAN for titles and prices.

NAVAJO INDIAN CULTURAL CARD SETS & POSTERS
Contains 16 in all. All grades. See SAN for titles and prices.

NAVAJO INSTRUCTIONAL PROGRAMS, KITS & PACKETS
See SAN for titles and prices.

NEW TRADITIONS
Exhibition poster features The Hunter, by the late Sam Fox of Dillingham, AK. 18x30", blue & black duotone. $7.50, postpaid. IANA.

OLD WOMAN PRINT
Milton Denny, artist
$3. VIP.

PEYOTE PRAYER-POSTER
By Doug Standing Rock. 28 x 21". $3.95. CAN.

THE PLAINS INDIANS
Two sets of 18 different photographs, featuring the fully captioned art of Howard Terpning, renowned painter of Plains Indian history. $73. DPA.

POSTCARDS OF HISTORIC TAHLEQUAH
BxW postcards of the capital of the Cherokee
Nation. 4 sets available. $6 for each set of 6 views,
all 4 sets, 24 cards, $10. VIP.

SACRED PEYOTE WATER BIRD-POSTER
By Doug Standing Rock. 21 x 14". $3.95. CAN.

**SELECTED PORTRAITS OF PROMINENT
NORTH AMERICAN INDIANS**
8x10 glossy or matte prints. SI.

SIX INDIAN CRAFTS POSTCARDS
  Eiteljorg Museum
Full-color postcards of items on display at the
Eiteljorg Museum of American Indian and West-
ern Art in Indianapolis, Indiana. 6 cards, $1. TC.

SOUTHWEST INDIAN STICKERS
  Madeleine Orban-Szontagh
24 full-color, pressure-sensitive, designs adapted
from the Hopi, Navajo and Pueblo tribes. 8 pp.
$1. TC.

STORY IN STONE
Artifacts poster. 24" x 36". $10. CMM.

**TEACHING RESPECT
FOR NATIVE PEOPLES**
A brief list of how, and how not to, teach about
Native peoples in the classroom. 18" x 24". $10.
OY.

A TREASURED HERITAGE
Exhibition poster featuring 11 works by Alaska
Native artists representative of Yup'ik and Inupiaq
Eskimo, Tlingit, Haida, Tsimshian and Athabascan
Indian cultures. 24x18", full color. $8.50, postpaid.
IANA.

WHEN EARTH BECOMES AN "IT"
This poem, about what will happen if Mother Earth
continues not to be respected, was a gift to us
from Cherokee/Appalachian poet Awiatka. 11" x
14". $10. OY.

WOVOKA POSTER
I6 1/2 x 23" poster of the Northern Paiute Ghost
Dance Prophet. $5.00. YPT.

XIT RELOCATION POSTER
23 x 35". $1.95. CAN.

MAPS

AMERICAN INDIAN HISTORY MAP
Documents the last 500 years of American Indian
history. 24 x 36" full color shaded relief map with
matte finish, printed on two sides. Informational
booklet. $3.50. ATL

AMERICAN INDIAN NATIONS
A composite graphic of contemporary Indian
America. 24x36" full-color shaded relief map. Illustrates the diminished land base as Indians were
forced westward be encroahing settlers. Locations of over 300 federally recognized reservations.
Reservations with gaming facilities are indicated.
$13 postpaid. TE.

ATLAS OF THE NORTH AMERICAN INDIANS
  Carl Waldman; Map & illus. by Molly Braun
1989. $16.95. FOF.

COLOR MAP
Shows the distribution of Indian tribes in New York
City and vicinity during the 17th century. $1.50.
MAI.

**CONOZCA SUS RAICES / KNOW YOUR
ROOTS: A MAP OF THE INDIGENOUS
PEOPLES OF MEXICO & CENTROAMERICA**
  Dolan H. Eargle, Jr., Editor
A full color, 18"x24" poster, bilingual - Spanish &
English with color-coded legend of contemporary
ethnic homelands grouped by linguistic families.
Mexico to Panama. Biblio. Trees Co. Press, $5.

**DISTRIBUTION OF INDIAN
TRIBES OF NORTH AMERICA**
Map by Dr. A.L. Kroeber. 21x28" map of the time
of first contact with white men. SM.

**EARLY INDIAN TRIBES, CULTURE
AREAS, & LINGUISTIC STOCK**
  William Sturtevant-U.S. Geological Survey
Multi-colored map, shows geographic extent of
major an minor Indian tribes, their culture areas,
and 18 linguistic stocks for Alaska and the 48
states. Biblio. $3.10. WE.

**THE GABRIELINO INDIANS AT THE
TIME OF THE PORTOLA EXPEDITION**
Map by Allen M. Welts. 22x15 map showing locations of ancient Indian villages in southern California. SM.

**HISTORICAL MAP, WARM SPRINGS
INDIAN RESERVATION**
Map by Ralph M. Shane and Ruby D. Leno, show-
ing historical trails, sites and modern Kah-Nee-
Ta. 15x18 color. OHS.

INDIAN LAND AREAS--GENERAL
A multicolor map that indicates the location and
size of Federal Indian reservations, Indian groups,
etc. SD.

INDIAN RESERVATIONS MAP
Black and white map of the U.S. showing where
the Indian tribes, reservations, and settlements are
located. IRA.

**INDIAN TRIBES & LANGUAGES
OF OLD OREGON TERRITORY**
22x33 color map. OHS.

INDIANS OF NORTH AMERICA
An archaeological and ethnological map. 32x37"
with ethnological descriptive notes and illustrations. 1979. NGS.

**MAP`N`FACTS: NATIVE PEOPLES
OF NORTH AMERICA**
Two full-color maps show--before Columbus--and
today. 23x35. Two bxw maps on reverse set forth
population and language groups. $4.50. FP.

MAP OF NORTH AMERICAN INDIANS
16 x 20 color map on durable enamel finished
paper, $2.95; laminated, $4.95. CH.

NAVAJOLAND
A full-color illustrated map of the Southwestern
U.S. where the Navajos live. Covers four states
and 16 million acres. KC.

**QUINCENTENNIAL MAP OF
AMERICAN INDIAN HISTORY**
  George Russell
Represents a geographic history of 500 years of

the American Indian. Identifies military forts & dates
of activity, major battles & dates, and Indian lands
& reservations. The margins contain texts that discuss various topics & time periods. Accompanied
with a pamphlet, The American Indian Digest providing additional information. 2nd Ed. 1992. $15.
TE.

THREE MAPS OF INDIAN COUNTRY
Haskell Indian Junior College, Lawrence Kansas
66044. No charge.

MICROFICHE

AKWESASNE NOTES
Vols. 1-9, 1969-1981. 168 fiches. $588. KM.

**AMERICAN CULTURE
SERIES I (ACSI), 1493-1806**
Series I: A Compact Overview of American Books
& Pamphlets - 1493-1806 - this collection includes
accounts of Indians and Indian captives. Micro-
film. UM.

AMERICAN INDIAN PERIODICALS
From the State Historical Society of Wisconsin.
Tribal news, political issues, humor, community
services, scholarly research. Silver halide film; 12
reels (approximate) 35mm silver halide microfilm.
$585. From the Princeton University Library on
Microfiche. Part 1, 96 titles: 2,068 fiche and two
reels 35mm film, $5,000; Part 2, 34 titles: 401 fiche
and two reels 35mm film, $1,000. See NR for in-
dividual titles and prices.

AMERINDIAN: AMERICAN INDIAN REVIEW
Vols. 1-23, 1952-1974. 23 fiches, $80.50. KM.

**ARCTIC EXPEDITION DIARIES OF
VILHJALMUR STEFANSSON, 1878-1925**
An Account of Eskimo Life and Culture Preserved
on Microfilm. A record of native Arctic culture and
geography with detailed documentation of Eskimo
life before it was altered by white cultural values.
Chronicles three expeditions made by V.
Stefansson between 1906 and 1918. Provides
factual and insightful accounts of Eskimo hunting
trips, religious beliefs, legends and family traditions. Includes translations of Eskimo words and
phrases, extensive charts and maps; and sketches
illustrating Eskimo clothes. 5 reels of 35mm microfilm. UM.

CHEROKEE ALMANAC
1838-1860. Text in English and Cherokee. 1 reel,
35mm. $50. KM.

THE JOHN COLLIER PAPERS, 1922-1968
The Author of a Sweeping Federal Indian Reform
Strategy - Assimilation was the U.S. Indian policy
from the late 1880's through the 1920's, and provoked widespread animosity as it eroded tribal
culture, religion, history, and freedom. Collier's accomplishments in effecting major Indian rights re-
forms as executive secretary of the American Indian Defense Association and later as Commissioner of Indian Affairs during FDR's administration marked a turning point in federal Indian policy.
His Indian New Deal proposed tribal self-government, culture preservation, and religious freedom
for native Americans. Includes correspondence,
speeches, government documents, court records
and news clippings which record Collier's private
thoughts and public impact during those years.
59 reels of 35mm microfilm. UM.

CONSTITUTION & LAWS OF THE AMERICAN INDIAN
Includes a hardbound copy of A Bibliography of the Constitution and Laws of the American Indian, and a listing of titles filmed. 157 separate constitutions. 7 reels, 35mm. $360. Contact KM for a complete list of tribes and nations included.

DUKE INDIAN ORAL HISTORY COLLECTION
Consists of the tape-recorded verbal testimonies of knowledgeable Indian people, members of most of the Indian tribes of Oklahoma, concerning their history, culture and philosophy of life. 310 fiches with Index on 8 reels. 35mm. $1,450. KM.

ENCYCLOPEDIA ARCTICA
16 volumes of articles on the Arctic Region written by leading specialists from around the world. Compiled by by noted explorer and scholar Vilhjalmur Stefansson. Features articles and information on: The Sciences, Trade, Biographies, and Maps, diagrams and charts. 27 reels of 35mm microfilm. UM.

VIOLA E. GARFIELD ALBUMS ON TOTEM ART
Anthropologist Viola E. Garfield (1899-1983) amassed a collection of 26 volumes of photographs and information on the totem art of the Native Americans of the Pacific Northwest Coast from Seattle to southeastern Alaska. Microfiche-60 sheets, $60 per set. UWL.

HISTORY OF THE PACIFIC NORTHWEST AND CANADIAN NORTHWEST
Microfilm collection which makes available a number of rare primary source materials on the early history of the two regions. 511 texts, from reports of expeditions to political pamphlets. 50 reels, $2,325. 20-page microfilm reel index and Table of Contents, $30. RP.

INDIAN CULTURE & HISTORY
A new microform index to Wisconsin Native American periodicals, 1879-1981. Edited by James P. Danky. Six computer-output microfiche; 42:1 reduction ratio. 1984. $30. GP.

INDIAN HISTORIAN
American Indian Historical Society. New series: Vols. 1-12, 1967-1979. 48 fiches. $168. KM.

INDIAN PIONEER PAPERS: 1860-1935
Consists of interviews of elderly early day settlers in Oklahoma collected in the late 1930's. Consists of typescripts of 7105 interviews. A subject index is included. 1019 fiches. $3.057. KM.

INDIAN RIGHTS ASSOCIATION PAPERS, 1864-1973
Documents the struggle for American Indian civil liberties, and includes information on Indian affairs, and supported federal and state court cases in its efforts to secure basic rights for Native Americans. Includes correspondence, printed materials, Herbert Welsh Papers, 1877-1934, photographs, and Council on Indian Affairs Papers, 1943-1968. 136 reels of 35mm microfilm. UM.

INDIAN TRUTH
Indian Rights Association. Nos. 1-260, 1924-1984. 59 fiches. $177. KM.

INDIAN'S FRIEND
National Indian Association. Vols. 1-63, 1888-1951. 3 reels, 35mm. $150. KM.

INDIANS - U.S. GOVERNMENT PRINTING OFFICE PUBLICATIONS
1927-1970. 168 fiches. $588. Contact KM for complete list of titles.

INDIANS OF NORTH AMERICA
1760-1952. Includes works by James B. Finley, Hampton Institute, and Peter Williamson. 2 reels, 35mm. $100. KM.

IROQUOIS INDIANS: A DOCUMENTARY HISTORY
Provides 8,000 reproductions of records from the early 1600s to the 1840s compiled by the D'Arcy McNickle Center for the History of the American Indian at the Newberry Library. Focuses on the Mohawk, Oneida, Onondaga, Cayuga, Seneca and Tuscarora nations comprising the Iroquois Confederacy. Includes a guide with chronological calendar and index of names, places, and tribes cited. 35mm microfilm. 1984. RP.

THE LAKE MOHONK CONFERENCE OF FRIENDS OF THE INDIAN
From 1883 to 1916 the center of the movement to reform federal Indian policy was the annual Lake Mohonk Conference, and its significance on Indian-white relations in the U.S. Details the opinions and programs of a distinguished group of American reformers. Microfiche (80 fiche), $200. Index volume, $25. NR.

THE BEYNON MANUSCRIPT
The Literature, Myths and Traditions of the Tsimshian People - Represents the most extensive body of Tsimshian literature available for linguistic, anthropological and theological scholarship. Provides documentation on North American Indian myths and traditions. The Tsimshian people, native to the territory along the international border between Alaska and British Columbia, originated the totem pole and other art forms characteristic of the Pacific Northwest coastal region. William Beynon was a native speaker of the Tsimshian language. He recorded the history, ethnography and literature of his people. Includes narratives of clan histories and myths, and descriptions of traditional ceremonies, practices and beliefs. 4 reels of 35mm microfilm. UM.

NATIVE AMERICANS OF THE PACIFIC NORTHWEST: A PHOTOGRAPHIC RECORD
A comprehensive graphic documentation of Pacific Northwest and Alaska Native Americans. Over 4,000 images were selected resulting in a 17,000 entry catalog. Microfiche-112 sheets, $115 per set. UWL.

THE PAGAENT OF AMERICA
A vital, authentic pictorial history of the U.S. Volume 1: Adventures in the Wilderness - covers the early navigators, settlers, and explorers as they fought Native Americans and each other for mastery of the New World; Volume 6: The Winning of Freedom - from the early struggles with the Indians through the War of 1812. Microfiche. Each volume begins with an essay or outline. UM.

THE PAPERS OF PANTON, LESLIE & CO.
Ethnographic collection for the study of the American Indians of the Southwest. Documents trading activities with the Cherokee, Chickasaw, Choctaw, and Creek Nations, and is a key collection for the study of the origins and early development of the Seminole Indians. Includes a guide to listed documents. 35mm microfilm; approximately 10,000 documents on 26 reels. $2,400. RP.

THE PAPERS OF JOHN PEABODY HARRINGTON IN THE SMITHSONIAN INSTITUTION, 1907-1957
Consists of over 750,000 pages of his documents. Includes a detailed guidebook giving the contents of each reel. Individual reels, $75. See KM for titles and prices.

PARRAL PAPERS
Spanish-American History of the Southwest and Mexico - spanning the years 1631-1821, this Spanish-written collection includes official records, directives, treaties, court transcripts, wills, letters, and other documents relating to the Spanish Colonial Era. Includes information on Indian uprisings, plus an account of the 1720 peace treaties with the Apaches and the Texans. 324 reels of 35mm microfilm. Includes index in English or Spanish. UM.

PRE-1900 CANADIANA
Primary resource materials which preserve and document printed materials from Canada's past. Covers Canadian culture, politics, ethnology, sociology, history, geography, art, economics, literature, religion and natural sciences. 35mm microfilm. UM.

RECORDS OF THE MORAVIAN MISSION AMONG THE INDIANS OF NORTH AMERICA
Microfilm collection of the Indian missionary records at the archives of the Moravian Church in Bethlehem, PA, provides important information on the history and activities of the Moravian Church in North America. Includes a 111-page Guide and two-volume, 135,000 entry index. 35mm microfilm. 40 reel;s, $19.10; 2-volume Index, $400. RP.

RECORDS OF THE U.S. INDIAN CLAIMS COMMISSION
Includes 550,000 pages--6,140 silver halide microfiche, $12,000. Historical, anthropological and economic reports of the American Indian. The Decisions, Volumes 1-47 & Appeals, 355 fiche, $750; Expert Testimony, 400 volumes, 100,000 pages, 1,270 fiche, $2,500/Supplement 1: 48 titles on 125 fiche, $250;2: 97 titles on 209 fiche, $400. Transcripts of Oral Expert Testimony, 400 volumes, 100,000 pages, 1,398 fiche, $2,800/Supplement; 77 titles, 420 fiche, $850. The Briefs, 3,000 volumes, 125,000 pages, 1,536 fiche, $3,000. GAO Reports, 80 volumes, 25,000 pages, 300 fiche, $600/Supplement; 11 titles, 34 fiche, $75. Index to Decisions, $25. Index to Expert Testimony, $25. Legislative History of the Indian Claims Commission Act, 12 fiche, $35. Docket Books, 41 fiche, $80. Journal, 32 fiche, $60. NR.

SELECTED WORKS BY AMERICAN INDIAN AUTHORS
12 titles, 1860-1939. 2 reels, 35mm. $100. Contact KM for complete listing of authors.

SMITHSONIAN INSTITUTION BUREAU OF AMERICAN ETHNOLOGY BULLETINS & ANNUAL REPORTS
Includes primary sources of information on the culture and history of North and South American Indian Tribes. Includes material on the prehistory, language, society and culture of many extinct tribal groups. Focuses on the history f Indian tribes within the U.S., with substantive information on the Indian tribes of Alaska, Hawaii, Mexico, Central America, and Canada. 42 reels of 35mm microfilm. Comes with a guide to Microfilm Edition of Smithsonian Publications Relating to the North American Indian. UM.

U.S. BOARD OF INDIAN COMMISSIONERS. ANNUAL REPORT OF THE BOARD OF INDIAN COMMISSIONERS TO THE SECRETARY OF THE INTERIOR
Reports 1-63, 1869-1932. 3 reels, 35mm. $150. KM.

U.S. BUREAU OF INDIAN AFFAIRS
17 titles, 1966-1970. 17 fiches, $59.50. Contact KM for complete listing of titles.

WASAJA/THE INDIAN HISTORIAN. A NATIONAL NEWSMAGAZINE OF INDIAN AMERICA
Vols. 1-19, 1973-1982. 82 fiches. $287. KM.

WESTERN AMERICANA
Includes federal and state documents, directories, guidebooks, state and regional histories, memoirs, reminiscences and travel accounts, and conventional and secondary histories of the West. Two sub-collections may be purchased separately: Indians, and Other Ethnic Influences. Microfiche. UM.

WESTERN AMERICANA: FRONTIER HISTORY OF THE TRANS-MISSISSIPPI WEST, 1550-1900
Includes a broad selection of printed sources relating to the discovery, exploration, settlement, and development of North America. Provides information on Indian/White relations including missions, trade, government relations, and Indian wars. A 2-volume guide and index accompanies each order. 35mm microfilm. 617 reels; divided into 11 units of 56-57 reels each, $2,880 each. RP.

COMPUTER NETWORK

INDIAN NATION NETWORK (INN) ELECTRONIC BULLETIN BOARD (EBB)
Devoted entirely to issues affecting and relating to Indian country. Access INN with a phone line, modem, computer, and communications software. Features such issues as religious freedom, environmental degradation on Indigenous lands, stereotypes, and treaty rights. INN equips users with tools necessary for meaningful advocacy and action by offering Congressional bills significant to Native Americans, hearing write-ups, Federal Register Notices relating to Indian country, listing of federally recognized tribes, telephone/addresses of Congressional Committees, events in Indian Country, and more. $25/year. HO.

CD-ROMs

THE AMERICAN INDIAN: A MULTIMEDIA ENCYCLOPEDIA
Covers more than 150 tribes of native peoples of the U.S., Canada, and northern Mexico - focusing on the history, culture, words, images, legends, and leaders. Includes the complete texts of four titles: Atlas of the North American Indian; Who Was Who in Native American History; Encyclopedia of Native American Tribes; and Voices of the Winds. There are sound bites of authentic Indian songs, over 900 VGA photographs, over 1,000 biographies, 250 color illustrations, the full text of over 250 documents from the 18th and 19th centuries, mor than 100 legends from over 60 tribes, maps, time lines, and lsitings of tribal locations, historical societies, and museums. $295. FOF.

BIBLIOGRAPHY OF NATIVE NORTH AMERICANS ON DISC - CD-ROM
Timothy O'Leary & M. Marlene Martin, Editors
Based on th Human Relations Area File's Ethnographic Bibliography of North Ameica, 4th Ed. 1975, and Supplement, 1973-87, 1990. IBM compataible. ABC-CIIO.

ETHNIC NEWSWATCH
A full text multicultural general reference database on CD-ROM. Contains more than 70 newspapers published by the ethnic and minority press in America. Contains about 90,000 fully ndexed articles from more than 100 newspapers and magazines. Includes Native American newspapers, i.e., News From Indian Country, Navajo TimesSho-Ban News, Seminole Tribune, Tundra Times, Cherokee Advocate, Lakota Times, et al. SII.

THE INDIAN QUESTION: THE HISTORY OF THE AMERICAN INDIANS FROM 19TH CENTURY ORIGINAL SOURCE DOCUMENTS
CD-ROM consisting of a library of Indian resources: Full text of all treaties; artistic view of the images and scenes-over 700 engravings; Books by Black Hawk and Right Hand Thunder; accounts from original observers. Includes *Henry R. Schoolcraft's* Archives of Aboriginal Knowledge; extensive data on Chippewa, Cherokees, Sioux, and many other tribes; linguistic coverage-large vocabulary lists, including a highly detailed analysis of Algonquin by Schoolcraft. The artwork of George Catlin's Letters and Notes on the Manners, Customs and Conditions of the North American Indians. For IBM compatible multimedia PCs. $99.95. OC.

NORTH AMERICAN INDIANS - CD-ROM
A database of text and image on the history of Native Americans. Includes information on leadership, tribal heritage, religion, family life, and customs. IBM compatible. QP, 1991. $69.95.

COMPUTER GRAPHICS

NATIVE AMERICAN CLIP ART COLLECTIONS
Art Bernstein
For IBM PC & Macintosh: **The Santa Fe Collection** - Pueblo Indians and Spanishinfluence, $179; **Plains Collections** - Indians of the Great Plains, $149; **Northwest Collections** - tribes of the Northwest to Alaska. 500 EPS images, 125 EPS borders. RT.

GAMES

POW WOW! THE GAME
Sarah Seeney Sullivan
A Native American board game featuring Native American concepts and designs that will challenge and entertain family members ages 8 and up. Includes Native American trivia cards. $19.95. LE.

TRAVELING EXHIBITS

AKWESASNE TRAVELLING EXHIBITS
Teionkwahontasen Basketmakers of Akwesasne: Ten panel, color and bxw photo display detailing the history of basketry. *Tsinikaiatotenne Ne*

Akwesasne - A Portrait of Akwesasne: Ten panel bxw historical photo display of Akwesasne family, religion, sports and lifestyles of the Mohawk of Akwesasne. *Our Strength Our Spirit*: Art exhibit by contemporary artists of Akwesasne. Catalog available. Cost negotiable. AM.

THE BUFFALO TOUR
The Institute for the Study of Natural Systems
P.O. Box 637
Mill Valley, CA 94942
(415) 383-5064
James A. Swan, Project Director
Pete Sears, Musical Director
To support bison restoration on Indian reservations, a musical concert tour program is being produced by a coalition of Indian leaders, entertainers and ecologists. The tour will begin in 1992 and hold a series of concerts around the U.S. which will culminate in the first annual Buffalo Festival, which will be held in late July of 1993, in the LaCrosse, Wisconsin, area in cooperation with the first International Bison Conference. Each concert will include Indian and non-Indian artists, as well as educational materials and programs, Indian arts and crafts sales, and a chance for local community involvement.

CAHOKIA TRAVELING DISPLAYS
A large free-standing exhibit on Cahokia with texts, photos and artifacts. Depicts the phases of Illinois prehistory. A booklet, Illinois Archaeology, is included. Two weeks, no charge. Must be picked up by the borrower. CMM.

MUSEUM OF NEW MEXICO TRAVELING EXHIBITS
Maintains the following traveling exhibits: Art of the Rainmakers: Prehistoric Indian Art and Architecture; Crystal to Burnt Water: Navajo Regional Style Textiles; People of the Sun: Photographs by Buddy Mays; The Portrait: Historic Photographs of New Mexicans; Sacred Paths: Aspects of the Native American and Hispanic Religious Experience in the Southwest; Traditions in Transition: Contemporary Basket Weaving of the Southwestern Indians; and, Turquoise and Tobacco: Trade Systems in the Southwest. The exhibits include historical and contemporary artifacts, drawings, prints, photographs, and paintings which have been assembled for exhibition in museums, libraries, community and art centers, and any other public space with controlled access. Pieces in the exhibitions are framed and matted with descriptive or interpretive labels printed directly on the mats and faced with plexiglass. In addition, each exhibition contains a title and statement panel. The exhibitions are offered free of charge and are transported in sturdy, custom-built crates. MNM.

TEXAS INDIANS WHO LIVED IN HOUSES
Students can learn to cook Indian bread, make an adobe brick, or plant a garden. The trunk contains artifact reproductions, filmstrips, activity cards, audio cassettes, and books. Grades 3-8. Rental fee: $100 (30 days) UT-ITC.

FESTIVALS OF NATIVE AMERICAN FILM & VIDEO

AMERICAN INDIAN FILM FESTIVAL & VIDEO EXHIBITION
333 Valencia St., Suite 322
San Francisco, CA 94103

(415) 554-0525
Michael Smith, Contact
Held in November, this festival is the oldest inter-national film exhibition dedicated to the presenta-tion of Native Americans in cinema. It is competi-tive and features seven categories: documentary feature; documentary short, feature, docudrama, live short subject, animated short subject & indus-trial. Founded 1975.

AMERICAN INDIAN FILM & VIDEO COMPETITION
2101 N. Lincoln
Jim Thorpe Bldg., Rm. 640
Oklahoma City, OK 73105
(405) 521-2931
Patrick Whelan, Contact
All entries are publicly presented at the Red Earth Festival in Oklahoma City. Finalists in each cat-egory are screened & awards presented at the University of Tulsa during the conference. Founded 1992.

DREAMSPEAKERS: THE FIRST PEOPLES WORLD FILM CELEBRATION
9914 76th Ave.
Edmonton, Alberta
Canada T6E 1K7
(403) 439-3456 Fax 439-2066
Russell Mulvey, Contact
Held in September, this noncompetitive event in-cludes around 60 hours of public screenings. Also a Professional Development Symposium compo-nent each year.

NATIVE AMERICAN FILM & VIDEO FESTIVAL
Film & Video Center
George Gustav Heye Center
National Museum of the American Indian
Smithsonian Institution
1 Bowling Green
New York, NY 10004
(212) 283-2420
Millie Seubert & Elizabeth Weatherford, Contacts
A noncompetitive showcase of film, video & audio productions with a focus on works by indepen-dent & tribal community leaders. Each festival screens about 40 documentaries, short features & animations, introduced by their producers & members of the native communities represented. Established in 1979.

TWO RIVERS NATIVE FILM & VIDEO FESTIVAL
Native Arts Circle
1433 E. Franklin
Minneapolis, MN 55404
(612) 870-7173
Juanita Espinoza, Contact
Presents a prize known as the "New Visionary" award. Established in 1991.

TRIBAL FILM/VIDEO PRODUCERS

CHICKASAW NATION
c/o Cultural Center
P.O. Box 1548
Ada, OK 74820
(405) 436-2603 Fax 436-4287
Glenda Galvan, Contact
More than 200 oral histories have been recorded (a portion of these exist on audio only). Estab-lished 1986.

CHOCTAW VIDEO PRODUCTION (CVP)
P.O. Box 6010
Philadelphia, MS 39350
(601) 656-5251 Fax 656-6696
Bob Ferguson, Contact
In addition to 3/4" documentary & instructional vid-eos on Choctaw history & culture, this production unit also does contract work for other tribes, in-cluding the Creek of Alabama, the Seneca of New York, and the Tunica-Biloxi of Louisiana. CVP also maintains a 24-hour TV station. Established 1983.

CREEK NATION VIDEO
c/o Muskogee Creek Nation
Communication Center
P.O. Box 580
Okmulgee, OK 74447
(918) 758-8700 Fax 758-0824
Produces documentaries containing various ar-chival material & video shot in the last 20 years on the history of the Creek people. The collection is divided into a four-volume video history; each volume contains 5-7 titles.

OJIBWAY & CREE CULTURAL CENTER
152 3rd Ave.
Timmins, Ontario
Canada P4N 1C6
(705) 267-7911 Fax 267-4988
Esther Wesley, Contact
Produces documentaries on tribal practices, crafts & oral histories of elders, which are ideal for gen-eral audiences & classroom use. Maintains a cata-log of about 20 titles with an average running time of 20 minutes. Established 1978.

SUQUAMISH MUSEUM
c/o Suquamish Tribal Cultural Center
P.O. Box 498
Suquamish, WA 98392
(206) 598-3311 Fax 598-4666
Marilyn Jones or Alan Preston, Contacts
The Suquamish do not currently mantain an ac-tive video production unit, but the museum does hold several self-produced educational titles in-cluding "Come Forth Laughing," which features oral histories of Suquamish elders, and "Waterborne," which illustrates the processes in-volved in making canoes. Titles run under 30 min-utes each.

TULALIP TRIBE
6700 Totem Beach Rd.
Marysville, WA 98271
(206) 653-0255
Lita Sheldon, Contact
Video production within the tribe is divided nto two categories: industrial (public relations) video & domentation of oral histories. The public relations tapes are brief introductions to Tulalip culture: "My Indian People" (1991, 7 minutes); and "Tulalip Tribe: Administration for Native Americans" (1990, 10 minutes). Also oral history shorts. Established 1989.

UTE INDIAN TRIBE
c/o Audio-Visual Dept.
P.O. Box 190
Fort Duchesne, UT 84026
(801) 722-3736 Fax 722-4023
Larry Cesspooch, Contact
Approximately half of the 250 videotapes produced functions as legal documentation of meetings & agreements with local, staff and federal officials. The remainder serves as educational preserva-tion of Ute history & culture practices. Much of this work is intended for audiences ages 5-13. In-cludes many oral histories as well as a variety of tribal ceremonies. Working on a low-power televi-sion station. Established 1979.

(A) Abbeville Press, 488 Madison Ave., New York, NY 10022 (800) 278-2665

(AA) Arts America, 12 Havermeyer Place, Greenwich, CT 06830 (203) 637-1454

(AB) AISA Books, 1630 30th St., Suite 301, Boulder, CO 80301 (303) 492-8658

(ABC) ABC-Clio, P.O. Box 1911, Santa Barbara, CA (800) 422-2546

(ABP) Audrey Barnes Productions, New York, NY (212) 921-1816

(ACF) Arthur Cantor Films, 2112 Brodway, Suite 400, New York, NY 10023 (212) 496-5710

(ADL) Anti-Defamation League of B'nai Brith, 823 UN Plaza, New York, NY 10017 (212) 490-2525

(AF) Aurora Films, P.O. Box 020164, Juneau, AK 99802-0164 (907) 586-6696

(AG) Agnello Films, 31 Maple St., Ridgefield, NJ 07660 (201) 933-6698

(AICRC) American Indian Culture Research Center, Blue Cloud Abbey, P.O. Box 98, Marvin, SD 57251 (605) 432-5528

(AIMS) AIMS Media, 9710 DeSoto Ave., Chatsworth, CA 91311 (800) 367-2467; in CA, AK & HI (818) 785-4111 Fax (818) 376-6405

(AIS) American Indian Soundchiefs, Box 472, Taos, NM 87571 (505) 776-2953

(AISES) American Indian Science & Engineering Society, Video Department, 1630 30th St., # 301 Boulder, CO 80303 (303) 492-8658 Fax 492-7090

(AIT) Agency for Instructional Technology, Box A, Bloomington, IN 47402 (800) 457-4509

(ALA) A.L. Atkins, Special Projects, 223 Onate Hall, Universityof New Mexico, Albuquerque, NM 87131 (505) 277-5204

(ALT) The Altschul Group, 1560 Sherman Ave., #100, Evanston, IL 60201 (800) 323-5448

(AM) Akwesasne Museum, RR 1 Box 14C, Hogansburg, NY 13655 (518) 358-2240

(AMNH) American Museum of Natural History, Dept. of Library Services, C.P.W.. & 79 St., New York, NY 10024 (212) 873-1300 x 346

(AMP) Arthur Mokin Productions, P.O. Box 1866, Santa Rosa, CA 95402 (800) 238-4868

(AP) Atlantis Productions, 1252 La Granada Dr., Thousand Oaks, CA 91360 (805) 495-2790

(AT) Auburn Television, Auburn University, Auburn, AL 36849 (205) 826-4110

(ATL) ATLATL, 2303 N. Central, Ste. 104, Phoenix, AZ 85004 (602) 253-2731

(AUDIO) Audio-Forum, Jeffrey Norton Publishers, 96 Broad St., Guilford, CT 06437 (800) 243-1234

(AV) Artistic Video, 87 Tyler Ave., Sound Beach, NY 11789 (516) 744-0449

(AVP) Ambrose Video Publishing, 1290 Ave. of the Americas, New York, NY 10104 (800) 526-4663; in NY (212) 696-4545

(BARR) Barr Films, P.O. Box 7878, Irwindale, CA 91706 (800) 234-7878

(BB) Buffalo Bill Historical Center, Education Dept., Box 1000, Cody, WY 82414 (307) 587-4771

(BBP) Brown Bird Productions, 1971 N. Curson Ave., Hollywood, CA 90068 (213) 851-8928

(BE) Beacon Films, 930 Pitner Ave., Evanston, IL 60202 (800) 323-5448

(BF) Britannica Films, 310 S. Michigan Ave., Chicago, IL 60604 (312) 347-7958

(BGF) Bowling Green Films Dist. by Jack Ofield Productions, P.O. Box 12792, San Diego, CA 92112 (619) 462-8266

(BINS) Boreal Institute for Northern Studies, U. of Alberta, CW-401 Biological Sciences Bldg., Edmonton, AB, Canada T6G 2E9 (403) 432-4409

(BL) Blackhawk, P.O. Box 66930, Los Angeles, CA 90066-0330

(BM) Blackfeet Media, P.O. Box 850, Browning, MT 59417 (406) 338-7179 ext. 268

(BMP) Bishop Museum Press, P.O. Box 19000A, Honolulu, HI 96817 (808) 848-4134

(BO) Bo Boudart Films, 1032 Marker Ave., Palo Alto, CA 94301 (415) 856-2004

(BOND) Jim Bond, I.T., 35113 Brewster Rd., Lebanon, OR 97355 (503) 258-3645

(BTP) Bear Tribe Publishing, P.O. Box 9167, Spokane, WA 99209 (509) 326-6561

(BYU) Brigham Young University, Educational Media Ctr., 101 Fletcher Bldg., Provo, UT 84602 (801) 378-2713

(BYU-N) Brigham Young University Native American Series, Multi-Cultural Ed. Dept., 115 BRMB, Provo, UT 84602

(BULL) Bullfrog Films, P.O. Box 149, Oley, PA 19547 (800) 543-3764

(CA) Cloud Associates, P.O. Box 39016, Phoenix, AZ 85069 (800) 888-7820; (602) 866-7820

(CAN) Canyon Records & Indian Arts, 4143 N. 16th St., Phoenix, AZ 85016 (602) 266-4823

(CANYON) Canyon Cinema, 2325 3rd St., # 338, San Francisco, CA 94107 (415) 626-2255

(CAT) Catticus Corporation, 2600 10th St., Berkeley, CA 94710 (510) 548-0854

(CC) Centre Communications, 1800 30th St., # 207, Boulder, CO 80301 (800) 886-1166; (303) 444-1166

(CDA) Curriculum Development Associates, 1211 Connecticut Ave., NW, Suite 414, Washington, DC 20036 (202) 293-1760

(CEN) Centron Films, 708 West Ninth St. Lawrence, KS 66044

(CET) Center forEducational Telecommunications, 9596 Walnut St., Dallas, TX 75243 (214) 952-0303

(CF) Churchill Films, 12210 Nebraska Ave., Los Angeles, CA 90025-3600 (800) 334-7830 (213) 657-5110 (for those in CA)

(CFDW) Canadian Filmmakers Distribution West, 1131 Howe St., Suite 100, Vancouver, BC, Canada V6Z 2L7 (604) 684-3014

(CFH) Center for Humanities, P.O. Box 1000, Mt. Kisco, NY 10549 (800) 431-1242; (914) 666-4100

(CG) The Cinema Guild, 1697 Broadway, Suite 506, New York, NY 10019 (800) 723-5522; Fax (212) 246-5525

(CH) Cherokee Publications, P.O. Box 256, Cherokee, NC 28719 (704) 488-2988

(CHA) Caedmon: Harper-Audio, 10 E. 53 St., New York, NY 10022 (212) 207-7000

(CHE) Chevron USA, Community Affairs, 575 Market St., San Francisco, CA 94105 (415) 894-5193; Study Guide: Chevron USA, 742 Bancroft Way, Berkeley, CA 94710

(CIMA) CIMA, 52 E. 1st St., New York, NY 10003 (212) 673-1666

(CIN) Cinnamin Productions, 19 Wild Rose Rd., Westport, CT 06880 (203) 221-0613 (phone & fax)

(CIRI) The CIRI Foundation, P.O. Box 93330, Anchorage, AK 99509 (907) 274-8638

(CJ) Concord Jazz, Box 845, Willow Pass Rd., Concord, CA 94522 (415) 682-6770

(CVP) Choctaw Video Productions, Rt. 7, Box 21, Philadelphia, MS 39350 (601) 656-5251

(CMB) The Children's Museum, Boston, Museum Wharf, 300 Congress St., Boston, MA 02210 (617) 426-6500

(CMM) Cahokia Mounds Museum Society, Video Rental, P.O. Box 382, Collinsville, IL 62234 (618) 344-9221

(COOK) Cook School, 708 S. Lindon Ln. Tempe, AZ 85281

(COP) Camera One Productions, 8523 15th Ave., NE, Seattle, WA 98115 (800) 726-3456; Fax (206) 523-3668

(COR) Coronet-MTI Films & Video, 108 Wilmot Rd., Deerfield, IL 60015 (800) 621-2131; in IL, HI & AK (312) 940-1260

(CP) Centre Productions, 1800 30th St., Suite 207, Boulder, CO 80301 (800) 824-1166; (303) 444-1168

(CRM) CRM/McGraw Hill Films, 2233 Faraday Ave., Carlsbad, CA 92008 (619) 431-9800

(CT) Coast Telecourses, 11460 Warner Ave., Fountain Valley, CA 92708 (714) 241-6109

(DAR) Denver Art Museum, Education Dept., 100 W. 14th Ave. Pkwy., Denver, CO 80204 (303) 575-2312

(DC) Direct Cinema Limited, P.O. Box 10003 ,Santa Monica, CA 90410 (800) 525-0000; Fax (310) 396-3233

(DCP) Dave Caldwell Productions, 26934 Halifax Pl., Hayward, CA 94542 (415) 538-4286

(DEPKE) Irene-Aimee Depke, 5627 N. Neva Ave., Chicago, IL 60631 (312) 774-2589

(DER) Documentary Educational Resources, 101 Morse St., Watertown, MA 02172 (800) 569-6621; Fax 926-9519

(DP) Dana Productions, 6249 Babcock Ave., N. Hollywood, CA 91606 (213) 877-9246

(DPA) Documentary Photo Aids, P.O. Box 956, Mt Dora, FL 32757 (800) 255-0763; Fax (904) 383-5679

(DSP) Daybreak Star Press Film & Video, United Indians of All Tribes Foundation, Daybreak Star Cultural/Educational Center , Discovery Park, P.O. Box 99253, Seattle, WA 98199 (206) 285-4425

(DT) Dallas Telecourses, 9596 Walnut St., Mesquite, TX 75243 (214) 952-0303

(DTC) DTC-TV Downtown Community TV 87 Lafayette St., New York, NY 10013 (212) 966-4510

(EAI) Electronic Arts Intermix, 536 Broadway , 9th Fl., New York, NY 10012 (212) 966-4605

(EB) Encyclopedia Britannica, Ed. Corporation, 425 N. Michigan Ave., Chicago, IL 60611 (800) 558-6968; in IL (312) 347-7400

(EDC) Education Development Center , 55 Chapel St., Newton, MA 02158 (800) 225-4276; in MA (617) 969-7100

(EG) Em Gee Film Library , 6924 Canby, #103, Reseda, CA 91335 (818) 881-8110

(FC) Full Circle Communications, 1131 South College, Tulsa, OK 74104

(FF) FilmFair Comunications, Gregg Ohara Films, P.O. Box 2187, Beverly Hills, CA 90213

(FH) Films for the Humanities, P.O. Box 2053, Princeton, NJ 08543 (800) 257-5126; (609) 275-1400 Fax 275-3767

(FI) Films Incorporated Video, 5547 N. Ravenswood Ave., Chicago, IL 60640 (800) 343-4312; Fax (312) 878-0416

(FIC) Film in the Cities, 2388 University Ave., St. Paul, MN 55114 (612) 646-6104 Fax 646-3879

(FIL) Filmakers Library, 124 E. 40th St., New York, NY 10016 (212) 808-4980 Fax 808-4983

(FILM) Film Project, John Anthony, 4305 N. Meridian, Indianapolis, IN 46208 (317) 283-2703

(FILMS) Films, Inc., 5547 N. Ravenswood Ave., Chicago, IL 60640 (800) 323-4222

(FL) Flower Films, 10341 San Pablo Ave., El Cerrito, CA 94530 (415) 525-0942

(FM) Facets Multimedia, 1517 W. Fullerton Ave., Chicago, IL 60614 (312) 281-9075

(FOF) Facts on File, 460 Park Ave. S., New York, NY 10016 (800) 322-8755; in NY (212) 683-2244

(FOUR) Four Worlds Development Project, Faculty of Education, The University of Lethbridge, 4401 University Dr., Lethbridge, AB, Canada T1K 3M4 (403) 329-2065 Fax 329-3081

(FP) Friendship Press Distribution Office, P.O. Box 37844, Cincinnati, OH 45237 (513) 761-2100

(FU) Fulton Films, 64 Orchard Hill Rd., Newton, CT 06070 (203) 426-2580

(FUL) Fulcrum Publishing, 350 Indiana St., Suite 350, Golden, CO 80401 (800) 992-2908

(FW) Film Wright, 4530 18th St., San Francisco, CA 94114 (415) 863-6100

(FWT) Four Winds Trading Co., 685 S. Broadway , Suite A, Boulder, CO 80303 (800) 456-5444; (303) 499-4484

(GA) Guidance Associates, P.O. Box 1000, Mt. Kisco, NY 10549 (800) 431-1242; Fax (914) 666-5319

(GAUL) Chris Gaul, 1919 Old Turkey Point Rd., Baltimore, MD 21211 (301) 686-7273

(GDA) Gray Deer Arts, P.O. Box 2341, Edmond, OK 73083 (405) 340-6323

(GP) Greenwood Publishing, 88 Post Rd. W. Box 5007, Westport, CT 06881

(GPN) Great Plains National, P.O. Box 80669, Lincoln, NE 68501 (800) 228-4630; or (402) 472-2007 Fax (402) 472-1785

(HF) Handel Film Corporation, 8730 Sunset Blvd., West Hollywood, CA 90069 (800) 395-8990;

(HO) HONOR, Inc., 2647 N. Stowell Ave., Milwaukee, WI 53211 (414) 963-1324

(HVC) Home Vision Cinema, 5547 N. Ravenswood Ave., Chicago, IL 60640 (312) 878-2600 (800) 826-3456

(IANA) Institute of Alaska Native Arts, P.O. Box 70769, Fairbanks, AK 99707 (907) 456-7491
(IBC) Inuit Broadcasting Corp., 251 Laurier Ave., West, Suite 703, Ottawa, ON, Canada K1P 5J6 (613) 235-1892

(ICARUS) Icarus-First Run Films, 153 Waverly Place, 6th Fl., New York, NY 10014 (800) 876-1710; Fax (212) 989-7649

(ICVT) Institute for Career & Vocational Training, 5819 Uplander Way, Culver City, CA 90230 (213) 204-2080

(IDIL) Institute for the Development of Indian Law , 1104 Glyndon St., SE, Vienna, VA 22180 (703) 938-7822

(IF) Image Film, 37 Burkhard Place, Rochester, New York, NY 14620 (716) 473-8070

(IFB) International Film Bureau, 332 S. Michigan Ave., Chicago, IL 60604 (800) 432-2241; for rentals: College Film Center (same address) (312) 922-6621

(IFF) International Film Foundation, 155 W. 72nd St., Rm. 306, New York, NY 10023 (212) 580-1111

(IH) Indian House, P.O. Box 472, Taos, NM 87571 (800) 545-8152; in NM (505) 776-2953

(IIP) Igloolik Isuma Productions, P.O. Box 223, Igloolik, NWT, Canada X0A 0L0 (819) 934-8809 Fax 934-8782

(IM) Image Film, 132 Hampshire Dr ., Rochester, NY 14618 (716) 473-8070

(IN) Intermedia Arts Minnesota, 425 Ontario St., SE, Minneapolis, MN 55414 (416) 627-4444

(IP) Investigative Productions, 48 Major St., Toronto, ON, Canada M5S 2L1 (416) 968-7818

(IRA) Indian Rights Association, Film Rental Program, c/o Janney Montgomery , 1601 Market St., Philadelphia, PA 19103 (215) 665-4523

(IS) IS Productions, P.O. Box 747, Hotevilla, AZ 86030

(ISU) Iowa State University, Media Resources Center, 121 Pearson Hall, Ames IA 50010 (515) 294-1540

(ITFE) International Tele-Film Enterprises, 47 Densley Ave., Toronto, ON, Canada M6M 5A8 (416) 241-4483

(IU) Indiana University, Instructional Support Svcs., Bloomington, IN 47405 (800) 552-8620

(IVA) Island Visual Arts, 8920 Sunset Blvd., 2nd Floor, Los Angeles, CA 90069 (213) 288-5382

(JOHNSTON) Hugh & Suzanne Johnston, 16 Valley Rd., Princeton, NJ 08540 (609) 924-7505

(KC) KC Publications, Box 14883, Las Vegas, NV 89114 (703) 731-3123

(KF) Kifaru Productions, 1550 California St., # 275, San Francisco, CA 94109 (415) 381-6560

(KM) Kraus Microform, Route 100, Millwood, NY 10546 (800) 223-8323

(KP) Knapp Press, 5900 Wilshire Blvd., Los Angeles, CA 90036 (800) 521-2666; (213) 937-5486

(KS) Kansas State Historical Society , 6425 S.W. Sixth St., Topeka, KS 66615 (800) 766-3777

(K-T) K-T Curriculum Project,
P.O. Box 1401, Hoopa, CA 95546

(KUAC) KUAC-TV, University of Alaska,
Fairbanks, AK 99775 (907) 474-7492

(KUHT) KUHT-TV, 4513 Cullen Blvd.,
Houston, TX 77004 (713) 749-7371

(KUSD) KUSD-TV, 414 E. Clark St.,
Vermillion, SD 57069 (605) 677-5861

(KUTV) KUTV, Promotion Dept., P.O. Box 30901,
Salt Lake City, UT 84301 (801) 973-3375

(KYUK) KYUK Video Productions,
Pouch 468, Bethel, AK 99559 (907) 543-3131

(LC) Library of Congress, Motion Picture,
Broadcasting & Recorded Sound Division;
and Prints & Photographs Division,
Washington, DC 20540 (202) 707-2905

(LCA) Learning Corporation of America;
Distributed by COR

(LE) Lenapehoking Enterprises, P.O. Box 310,
Cheswold, DE 19936 (800) 897-4263

(LL) Listening Library, P.O. Box L,
Old Greenwich, CT 06870 (800) 243-4504

(LP) Lotus Press, Ltd., 2801 Rodeo Rd.,
Suite B-570, Santa Fe, NM 87505 (800) 648-4125

(LU) Lumiere, 826 Savanah Ave.,
Pittsburgh, PA 15221 (412) 241-1127

(LV) Library Video Co., P.O. Box 1110,
Bala Cynwyd, PA 19004 (800) 843-3620

(MAI) National Museum of the American Indian,
Film & Video Archives & Photographic Archives,
The George Gustav Heye Center-Smithsonian
Institution, One Bowling Green, New York, NY
10004 (212) 283-2420

(MAN) Robert N. Manning, 53 Hamilton Ave.,
Staten Island, NY 10301

(MB) Margaret Brandon, 140 Ridgeway Rd.,
Woodside, CA 94062 (415) 369-0139

(MBP) Michael Brodie Productions,
590 Transit Rd., Victoria, BC, Canada
V8S 4Z5 (604) 598-2308

(McN) Maureen McNamara, 12 Vincent St.,
Cambridge, MA 02140 (617) 661-0402

(MCN) Muscogee Creek Nation Community
Center, P.O. Box 580, Okmulgee, OK 74447
(918) 756-8700

(MCP) Meyer Creative Productions, P.O. Box
1738, Bismarck, ND 58502 (800) ND-SOUND

(MFV) Mystic Fire Video, 225 Lafayette St.,
Suite 1206, New York, NY 10012 (212) 941-0999

(MG) The Media Guild, 11562 Sorrento Valley Rd.,
Suite J, San Diego, CA 92121 (619) 755-9191

(ML) Magic Lantern Communications, Ltd.,
775 Pacific Rd., Unit #38, Oakville, ON,
Canada L6L 6M4 (416) 827-1155 in Canada
(800) 263-1717

(MMA) Museum of Modern Art, 11 West 53rd St.,
New York, NY 10019 (212) 956-4204

(MNM) Museum of New Mexico,
Programs & Ed. A-V Specialist,
Santa Fe, NM 87503 (505) 827-2070

(MP) Mixtech Productions, P.O. Box 1100-304,
Taos, NM 87571 (505) 758-9052

(MRC) Media Resources Center,
121 Pearson Hall, Iowa State University,
Ames, IA 50011 (515) 294-1540

(NAC) National Audiovisual Center,
GSA, Order Section NA/REF SECT EC,
Washington, DC 20409 (202) 763-1896

(NAPBC) Native American Public Broadcasting
Consortium, P.O. Box 83111, Lincoln, NE 68501
(402) 472-3522

(NATC) Northwest Arctic Television Center,
P.O. Box 51, Kotzebue, AK 99752 (907) 442-3472

(NCTE) National Council of Teachers of English,
1111 Kenyon Rd., Urbana, IL 61801

(NDF) New Day Films, 121 W. 27th St., Suite 902,
New York, NY 10001 (212) 645-8210

(NDM) New Dimension Media, 85803 Lorane
Hwy., Eugene, OR 97405 (800) 288-4456

(NETCHE) NETCHE is now NETV

(NETV) Nebraska Educational Television, P.O. Box
83111, Lincoln, NE 68501 (800) 228-4630; in HI
& NE (402) 472-2007

(NFBC) National Film Board of Canada, 1251 Ave.
of the Americas, 16th Floor, New York, NY 10020
(800) 542-2164; Fax (717) 822-8226

(NGA) National Gallery of Art, Extension Services,
Washington, DC 20565

(NGS) National Geographic Society, Educational
Services, P.O. Box 98018, Washington, DC 20090
(800) 368-2728; Fax (301) 921-1575

(NH) Northern Heritage Films (For information on
distribution and new productions contact MAI)

(NM) The Newark Museum, 49 Washington St.,
Newark, NJ 07101 (201) 733-6600

(NMFV) New Mexico Film & Video, Box 272,
Tesuque, NM 87574 (505) 983-3094

(NNA) National Native American AIDS Prevention
Center, 3515 Grand Ave., Suite 100, Oakland, CA
94610 (510) 444-2051 Fax 444-1593.

(NOVA) Nova Scotia Dept. of Education,
Education Media Services, 6955 Bayers Rd.,
Halifax, NS, Canada B3L 4S4 (902) 453-2810

(NPP) New Pacific Productions, P.O. Box 12792
,San Diego, CA 92112 (619) 462-8266

(NR) Norman Ross Publishing, 330 W. 58th St.,
New York, NY 10019 (800) 648-8850

(NU) New & Unique Videos, 2336 Summac Dr.,
San Diego, CA 92105 (619) 282-6126

(NV) New Visions, P.O. Box 599, Aspen, CO 81612
(303) 925-2640 Fax 925-9369

(NWL) New World Library, 58 Paul Dr., San Rafael,
CA 94903 (800) 972-6657; Fax (415) 472-2100

(NYU) New York University Film Library,
26 Washington Pl., New York, NY 10003

(O&C) Ojibway & Cree Cultural Center,
84 Elm South, Timmons, ON, Canada
P4N 1W6 (705) 267-7911

(OAP) Old Army Press, P.O. Box 2243,
Fort Collins, CO 80522 (800) 627-0079

(OC) Objective Computing, P.O. Box 51246,
Indianapolis, IN 46251 (800) 745-9904

(ODE) Oklahoma Dept. of Education,
Media Resources, Oliver Hodge Bldg.,
Oklahoma City, OK 73105

(OHS) Oregon Historical Society, Education Dept.,
1230 S.W. Park Ave., Portland, OR 97205
(503) 222-1741 ext. 36

(OP) Odyssey Productions, 2800 NW Thurman
St., Portland, OR 97210 (503) 223-3480

(OW) One West Media, 535 Cordova Rd.,
Suite 410, Santa Fe, NM 87501 (505) 983-8685

(OY) Oyate, 2702 Mathews St., Berkeley,
CA 94720 (510) 848-6700 Fax 848-4815

(PBS) PBS Video, 1320 Braddock Place,
Alexandria, VA 22314 (800) 344-3337;
Fax (703) 739-5269

(PFV) Pyramid Film & Video, Box 1048,
Santa Monica, CA 90406 (800) 421-2304

(PHOENIX) Phoenix/BFA Films, 2349 Chaffee Dr.,
St. Louis, MO 63146 (800) 221-1274;
Fax (314) 569-2834

(PIE) Pacific International Enterprises,
1133 S. Riverside, #1, Medford, OR 97501
(503) 779-0990

(PLP) Phil Lucas Productions, P.O. Box 1218,
Issaquah, WA 98027 (206) 392-9482

(PMI) Public Media, Inc., 5547 N. Ravenswood
Ave., Chicago, IL 60640 (800) 323-4222, Ext. 343;
in IL (312) 878-7300, Ext. 343

(PR) Pictures of Record, 119 Kettle Creek Rd.,
Weston, CT 06883 (203) 227-3387 Fax 222-9673

(PSU) The Pennsylvania State University,
Audio-Visual Services, Special Services Bldg.,
1127 Fox Hill Rd., University Park, PA 16803
(800) 826-0132; In PA, HI & AK (814) 865-6314

(PUSA) Penguin USA, Academic Marketing Dept.,
375 Hudson St., New York, NY 10014 (800) 253-6476

(QP) Quanta Press, 1313 Fifth St. SE,
Minneapolis, MN 55414

(QTS) Quileute Tribal School, Old Coast Guard
Rd., P.O. Box 39, La Push, WA 98350 (206) 374-6163 Fax 374-6311

(RC) Reservation Creations, P.O. Box 27626, Tucson, AZ 85726 (602) 622-4900

(RH) Random House--School Division, Dept. 9020, 400 Hahn Rd., W estminster, MD 21157 (800) 638-6460; in MD (800) 492-0782; in AK & HI (301) 876-2286

(RITZ) Lan Brook Ritz, Brown Bird Productions, 1971 N. Curson Ave., Hollywood, CA 90046 (213) 851-8928

(RM) Robert N. Manning, 53 Hamilton Ave., Staten Island, NY 10301 (718) 981-0120

(RP) Research Publications, 12 Lunar Dr./Drawer AB, Woodbridge, CT 06525 (800) 732-2477; in CT call collect; in AK & HI (203) 397-2600;

(ROD) ROD Enterprises, 1001 S. Park Ave., Tucson, AZ 85719 (602) 622-3522

(RODGERS) Distributed by Gail Singer Films, 82 Willcocks St., Toronto, ON, Canada M5S 1C8 (416) 923-4245

(RT) RT Computer Graphics, 602 San Juan de Rio, Rio Rancho, NM 87124 (800) 891-1600; (505) 891-1600 Fax 891-1350

(RTP) River Tracks Productions, Box 9, Manley Hot Springs, AK 99756

(SAN) San Juan School District Media Center, Curriculum Division, 28 W est 200 North (15-7), Blanding, UT 84511 (801) 678-2281

(SE) Spotted Eagle Productions, 2524 Hennepin Ave. So., Minneapolis, MN 55405 (612) 377-4212

(SEF) Sterling Educational Films, 241 E. 34th St., New York, NY 10016 (212) 759-5727

(SFMPC) Spanish Fork Motion Picture Co. (address unknown)

(SH) Shenandoah Film Productions, 538 G St., Arcata, CA 95521 (707) 822-1030 Fax 822-5334

(SHSW) State Historical Society of Wisconsin, 816 State St., Madison, WI 53706

(SI) Smithsonian Institution, Services Branch, National Anthropological Archives, Washington, DC 20560 (202) 357-4560

(SI-OMB) Smithsonian Institution, Of fice of Museum Programs, A-V Loan Program, W ashington, DC 20560 (202) 357-3101

(SII) Softline Information, Inc., 65 Broad St., Stamford, CT 06901 (800) 524-7922; Fax (203) 975-8347

(SM) Southwest Museum, Highland Park, Los Angeles, CA 90042

(SN) Seneca Nation of Indians, P .O. Box 442, Salamanca, NY 14779 (716) 945-1738

(SO) Solaris, 264 West 19th St., New York, NY 10011 (212) 741-0778

(SRA) Science Research Associates, P.O. Box 543, Blacklick, OH 43004 (800) 843-8855

(STULL) Donald D. Stull, 2900 W estdale Rd., Lawrence, KS 66044 (913) 842-8055

(SUPT) Superintendent of Documents, G.P.O., Washington, DC 20402

(SUQ) Suquamish Museum, P.O. Box 498, Suquamish, W A 98392 (206) 598-331 1

(SVE) Society for Visual Education, 55 E. Monroe St., 34th Floor, Chicago, IL 60603 (800) 829-1900 Fax (800) 624-1678

(SVP) Silvercloud Video Productions, 1321 E. King Rd., Tucson, AZ 85719 (602) 326-7647

(TA) Troll Associates, Instructional Materials, 100 Corporate Dr., Mahwah, NJ 07430 (800) 526-5289; Fax (201) 529-9347

(TAM) Tamarack Films, 1 1032-76 St., Edmonton, AB, Canada T5B 2C6 (403) 477-7958

(TC) Treasure Chest, P.O. Box 5250, Tucson, AZ 85703 (800) 969-9558

(TE) Thunderbird Enterprises, c/o George Russell, 8821 N. First St., Phoenix, AZ 85020 (800) 835-7220

(TM) Taylor Museum, Colorado Springs Fine Arts Center, 30 West Dale, Colorado Springs, CO 80903

(TBM) Thomas Burke Memorial, W ashington State Museum, DB-10, University of W ashington, Seattle, W A 98195 (206) 543-5884

(TBS) Turner Broadcasting System, Atlanta, GA

(THA) Thomas Howe Associates Ltd., 1100 Homer St., V ancouver, BC, Canada V6B 2X8 (604) 687-4215

(THRC) Texas Human Resources Center, U. of Texas, Arlington, Library, P.O. Box 19497, Arlington, TX 76019 (817) 273-2767

(TIPI) Tipi Shop, P.O. Box 1542, Rapid City, SD 57709

(TOP) The Origins Program, 4632 V incent Ave. S., Minneapolis, MN 55410

(TPH) Theosophical Publishing House, 306 W. Geneva Rd., Wheaton, IL 60189 (800) 654-9430; in IL (312) 665-0123

(TR) The Trust for Native American Cultures & Crafts, Box 142, Greenville, NH 03048 (603) 878-2944

(TT) Tulalip Tribe, 3901 Totem Beach Rd., Marysville, W A 98270 (206) 653-0220

(TTP) Turning Tide Productions, P.O. Box 864, Wendell, MA 01379 (508) 544-8313

(TW) Time-Warner Video, P.O. Box 4367, Huntington Station, NY 11750 (800) 854-7200

(TWN) Third World Newsreel, 335 W . 38th St., 5th Floor, New York, NY 10018 (212) 947-9277

(UA) University of Arizona, Media Services-Film Library, Tucson, AZ 85706 (602) 626-3282

(UAB) University of Alberta, Motion Picture Division, Edmonton, AB, Canada (403) 432-3302

(UADA) University of Alberta, Dept. of Anthro., 13-15 HM Tory Bldg., Edmonton, ON T6G 2H4 Canada (403) 432-3879

(UAL) University of Alberta, Audio Visual Services, L2-6A Humanities Bldg., Edmonton, AB, Canada T6G 2E1 (403) 432-4962

(UC) University of California, Extension Media Center, 2000 Center St., Berkeley , CA 94704 (510) 642-0460; Fax 643-9271

(UCLA) University of California, Los Angeles, Instructional Media Library , Powell Library-46, Los Angeles, CA 90024 (310) 825-0755

(UCT) University of Connecticut, Film Library , U-1, Storrs, CT 06268 (203) 486-2530

(UCV) University Community V ideo, 425 Ontario, S.E., Minneapolis, MN 55414 (612) 376-3333

(UI) University of Illinois Film Center , 506 S. W right St. #378, Urbana, IL 61801 (800) 367-3456; in IL (800) 252-1357

(UK) University of Kansas, Audio Visual Center, 645 New Hampshire St., Lawrence, KS 66044 (913) 864-3352

(UL) United Learning, 6633 W . Howard St., P.O. Box 718, Niles, IL 60648 (800) 323-9468

(UM) University Microfilms International, 300 North Zeeb Rd., An Arbor, MI 48106 (800) 521-0600; (313) 761-4700 ext. 789

(UMA) University of Mid-America (See GPN)

(UMC) Utah Media Center , 20 South W est Temple, Salt Lake City, UT 84101

(UMN) University of Minnesota, Film & V ideo, 1313 Fifth St. SE, #108, Minneapolis, MN 55414 (800) 847-8251; in MN (612) 373-3810

(UN) University of Nevada Film Library , Getchell Library, Reno, NV 89557 (702) 784-6037

(UP) Upstream Productions, 420 1st Ave. W., Seattle, W A 98119 (206) 281-9177 Fax 284-6963

(UT) University of Texas, Film Library, Education Annex G-5, 20th at San Jacinto, Austin, TX 78713 (512) 471-3572

(UTE) Ute Indian Tribe Audio-Visual, P.O. Box 129, Fort Duchesne, UT 84026 (801) 722-5141

(UTFL) The University of Texas Film Library , Drawer W, Austin, TX 78711 (512) 471-3573

(UT-ITC) The University of Texas, Institute of Texan Cultures at San Antonio, P.O. Box 1226, San Antonio, TX 78294-1226 (800) 776-7651; (210) 558-2235 Fax 558-2205

(UUT) University of Utah, Instructional Media Center, 207 Milton Bennion Hall, Salt Lake City , UT 84112 (801) 581-3170

(UW) University of W ashington, Instructional Media Services, 23 Kane Hall, DG-10, Seattle, W A 98195 (206) 543-9909

(UWL) University of Washington Libraries, Special Collection Division--Microforms, Suzzallo Library, FM-25, Seattle, WA 98195

(VC) The Video Catalog, P.O. Box 64428, St. Paul, MN 55164-0428 (800) 733-2232

(VH) VH-1, 1515 Broadway, New York, NY 10036 (212) 258-7800

(VL) Verity Lund, Henry Street Settlement, 265 Henry St., New York, NY 10002 (212) 766-9200

(VOI) Video Out International, 1160 Hamilton St., Vancouver, British Columbia, Canada V6B 2S2 (604) 688-4336

(VT) Video Tech, 19346 3rd Ave. NW, Seattle, WA 98177 (206) 546-5401

(VVP) Victorian Video Productions, P.O. Box 1540, Colfax, CA 95713 (800) 848-0284; (916) 346-6184

(WALI) Monona Wali, 886 S. Bronson Ave., Los Angeles, CA 90005 (213) 650-7341

(WALL) Alfred Wallace, 420 Riverside Dr., New York, NY 10025 (212) 865-8817

(WD) Walt Disney Educational Media Co., 500 South Buena Vista, Burbank, CA 91521

(WE) World Eagle, 64 Washburn Ave., Wellesley, MA 02181

(WGBH) WGBH Distribution Office, 125 Western Ave., Boston, MA 02134 (617) 492-2777

(WKV) Wood Knapp Video, 5900 Wilshire Blvd., Los Angeles, CA 90036 (800) 521-2666; Fax (213) 930-2742

(WMM) Women Make Movies, 462 Broadway, 5th Floor, New York, NY 10013 (212) 925-0606 Fax 925-2052

(WNET) WNET-13 Video Distribution, 356 W. 58th St., New York, NY 10019 (212) 560-3045

(WQED) WQED-TV, Distribution Dept. 4802 Fifth Ave., Pittsburgh, PA 15213 (412) 622-1356

(WXXI) WXXI-TV, 280 State St., P.O. Box 21 Rochester, NY 14601 (716) 325-7500

(YPT) Yerington Paiute Tribe Publications, 171 Campbell Lane, Yerington, NV 89447

(ZAENTZ) The Saul Zaentz Productions Co., 2600 Tenth St., Berkeley, CA 94710 (800) 227-0602

(ZANGO) Zango Music Distribution, 3700 Bennett Creek Rd., Cottage Grove, OR 97424 (800) 688-0187 Fax (503) 942-1564.

(ZC) Zia Cine, P.O. Box 493, Santa Fe, NM 87504 (505) 983-4127

Arranged alphabetically by publication title, this section lists those periodicals which deal directly or indirectly with the history, culture, and contemporary issues of the North American Indian and Eskimo.

ABORIGINE
P.O. Box 892
Gallup, NM 87301

ABSARAKA
Crow Indian Tribe
Crow Agency, MT 59022

ABSENTEE SHAWNEE NEWS
P.O. Box 1714
Shawnee, OK 74801

ACCESS
Office of Minority Business Enterprise
Department of Commerce
Washington, D.C. 20230

ACTION NEWS
P.O. Box 607
New Town, ND 58763

AGUA COUNCIL LETTER
960 E. Tahquitz Wat, Suite 106
Palm Springs, CA 92262

AHTNA KANAS
Ahtna, Inc.
P.O. Box 649
Glennallen, AK 99588
(907) 822-3476
Bimonthly shareholder newsletter of Ahtna, Inc., the Copper River Native Association.

AI REGISTRY FOR THE PERFORMING ARTS
1717 N. Highland Ave. #614
Hollywood, CA 90028
Geraldine Keams, Editor

AICH NEWSLETTER
American Indian Community House
404 Lafayette St., 2nd Floor
New York, NY 10003
(212) 598-0100
Reports on activities of the organization, which serves the needs of Native Americans residing in the New York metropolitan area. News and reviews of interest to American Indians. 5x/yr. Donations requested. Begun 1969.

AIRS NEWSLETTER
2734 E. Pierson St.
Phoenix, AZ 85016

AK-CHIN O'ODHAM RUNNER
Ak Chin Indian Reservation
42507 Peters & Nall Rd.
Maricopa, AZ 85239
(602) 568-2095
Cyndee Justus, Editor
Monthly newspaper includes articles, photos, puzzles and recipes provided by Ak-Chin members. Articles deal with events that pertain to the people of Ak-Chin Indian community. Advertising accepted. No charge. Begun 1986.

AKWE:KON JOURNAL
Akwe: kon Press
300 Caldwell Hall, Cornell University
Ithaca, NY 14853
(607) 255-4308 Fax 255-0185
Jose Barreiro, Editor-in-Chief

Susan Dixon, Managing Editor
Jennifer Bedell, Editorial Assistant
Written primarily for academics or members of Native American communities. A national Native American scholarly quarterly magazine that features articles on Native American history, arts, politics, environmental issues, economics, and current events; includes new fiction, poetry, book reviews, interviews and features on Native American artists. Quarterly. $15/year; $18/year, Canada; $20/year, foreign; $35/year, institutions.

AKWESASNE NOTES
Mohawk Nation, P.O. Box 196
Rooseveltown, NY 13683
(518) 358-9531 Fax 575-2064
Teresa David, Publisher
Douglas M. George - Kanentiio, Editor
Covers news by and about indigenous people in the Americas: poetry, cultural essays, book reviews, current event lists, pow-wows, conferences, and letters. Bimonthly tabloid. 12,000 cir. $15/year. Complimentary copies, exchanges. Microfilm/fiche available. Begun 1968.

ALAMO NEWSLETTER
Alamo Navajo High School
P.O. Box 907
Magdalena, NM 87825

ALASKA FEDERATION OF NATIVES (AFN) NEWS
1577 C St. #100
Anchorage, AK 99501
(905) 274-3611
Julia E. Kitka, Editor
Monthly newsletter.

ALASKA GEOGRAPHIC
The Alaska Geographic Society
P.O. Box 93370
Anchorage, AK 99509-3370
(907) 258-2515 Fax 278-6582
Penny Rennick, Editor
Deals with the culture, history or region of Alaska or northwestern Canada including extensive coverage of Alaska's native peoples. Quarterly magazine. 8,000 cir. $39/year; prices of individual issues vary. Begun 1975.

ALASKA NATIVE MAGAZINE
Alaska Native News, Inc.
Anchorage, AK 99522
(907) 243-8730
Celeste Worl, Publisher; Ricardo W orl, Editor
Focuses on social, political, and economic issues involving the Native community. 48 pp. Bimonthly. Annual subs., $21; $2.50/copy. Begun 1982.

ALASKA NATIVE BROTHERHOOD NEWSLETTER
P.O. Box 112
Juneau, AK 99801

ALASKA NATIVE EDUCATION
P.O. Box 1250
Fairbanks, AK 99707

ALASKA STATE MUSEUM NEWSLETTER
Pouch FM
Juneau, AK 99811
(907) 465-2901

ALLIGATOR TIMES
Seminole Tribe, 6073 Stirling Rd.
Hollywood, FL 33024
Monthly Seminole news.

ALMANACK
Plimoth Plantation
Wampanoag Indian Program
P.O. Box 1620
Plymouth, MA 02362
(508) 746-1622
Nanepashemet, Editor
Membership newsletter.

AMERICAN ANTHROPOLOGICAL ASSOCIATION NEWSLETTER
1703 New Hampshire Ave., N.W.
Washington, D.C. 20009
(202) 232-8800
Published ten times per year.

AMERICAN ANTHROPOLOGIST
American Anthropological Association
1703 New Hampshire Ave., N.W.
Washington, D.C. 20009
(202) 232-8800 Fax 667-5345
Janet Dixon Keller, Editor
Devoted to cross-field and theoretical articles; book reviews. Quarterly journal. 9,000 cir. $85/year. Advertising. Begun 1889.

AMERICAN ANTIQUARIAN SOCIETY NEWSLETTER
185 Salisbury
Worcester, MA 01609
(617) 755-5221

AMERICAN ETHNOLOGIST
American Anthropological Association
1703 New Hampshire Ave., N.W.
Washington, DC 20009
(202) 232-8800 Fax 667-5345
Don Brenneis, Editor
Concerned with 'ethnology' in the broadest sense; book reviews. Quarterly journal. 3,000 cir. $50/year. Advertising. Begun 1974.

THE AMERICAN HISTORICAL REVIEW
American Historical Association
400 A St., SE
Washington, DC 20003
(202) 544-2422
Published five times per year.

AMERICAN INDIAN
Telecommunications Corporation
P.O. Box 333
Lapwai, ID 83540

AMERICAN INDIAN ALASKA NATIVE MENTAL HEALTH RESEARCH JOURNAL
University Press of Colorado
P.O. Box 849
Niwot, CO 80544
(303) 530-5337 Fax 530-5306
Provides better understanding of current mental health issues and concerns of Native Americans and Alaska Natives.

AMERICAN INDIAN/ALASKA NATIVE TRADERS DIRECTORY
Arrowstar Publishing
100134 University Park Station
Denver, CO 80210-0134
(303) 231-6599
Natl. Indian Trader Assn., Editor
Published annually. Begun 1985.

AMERICAN INDIAN ART MAGAZINE
7314 East Osborn Dr., Suite B
Scottsdale, AZ 85251

(602) 994-5445
Mary G. Hamilton, Publisher
Roanne P. Goldfein, Editor
Mary B. O'Halloran. Editorial
Art journal devoted exclusively to the art forms of
the American Indian. Art forms are presented by
full-color photographs and articles written by leading scholars in the field. Also includes book and
exhibition reviews and listings of major museum
and gallery exhibitions. Quarterly .15,000 cir. $5/
copy. $20/year; $24/year, foreign. Advertising.
Begun 1975.

AMERICAN INDIAN BASKETRY MAGAZINE
P.O. Box 66124
Portland, OR 97266
(503) 233-8131
  John M. Gogol, Editor & Publisher
Quarterly. Contains articles, book reviews, and lists
of new exhibits; sponsors research & communications in the study of American Indian basketry.
5,000 cir. $7/copy; $30/year. Advertising. Began
1979.

AMERICAN INDIAN BUSINESS MAGAZINE
Communications Group
206 S. Galena Ave.
Freeport, IL 61032
(815) 232-5176
  Floyd Roberts, Editor
Bimonthly.

AMERICAN INDIAN COURTLINE
NAICCA/Arrow, Inc.
1000 Connecticut Ave., NW #1206
Washington, DC 20036

**AMERICAN INDIAN CULTURAL RESOURCES:
A PRESERVATION HANDBOOK**
Oregon Commission on Indian Affairs
454 State Capitol
Salem, OR 97310
(503) 378-5481

**AMERICAN INDIAN CULTURE
& RESEARCH JOURNAL**
University of California, Los Angeles
American Indian Studies Center
3220 Campbell Hall, 405 Hilgard Ave.
Los Angeles, CA 90024-1548
(310) 206-7508 Fax 206-7060
  Duane Champagne, Editor
An interdisciplinary research forum for scholars
and innovators in the areas of historical and con-
temporary American Indian life and culture. Book
reviews; essays, poems, and monographs. Quar-
terly. $20/individuals; $30/institutions. Advertising.
Begun 1971.

AMERICAN INDIAN DEFENSE NEWS
American Indian Defense of Americas
P.O. Box 3121
Hutchison, KS 67504
(316) 665-3614
  Chief Thunderbird Webber, Editor
Quarterly newsletter dealing with Indian problems
in North and South America. 1,000+ cir. $5.95/
year; $10 for lifetime membership. Begun 1974.

AMERICAN INDIAN DIRECTIONS
The Seventh Generation Fund
P.O. Box 10
Forestville, CA 95436
(707) 887-1559
Newsletter on Indian issues for the
philanthropic community.

AMERICAN INDIAN GRADUATE RECORD
4520 Montgomery Blvd., NE, Suite 1-B
Albuquerque, NM 87109
(505) 881-4584
  Oran LaPointe, Editor
This newsletter describes graduate opportunities
for American Indians and Alaska Natives. No subscription price since it is usually circulated to students, Indian higher education programs and those
who are interested in contributing to the organization. Published 1-1/year. Begun 1972.

AMERICAN INDIAN HORSE NEWS
American Indian Horse Registry
Route 3, Box 64
Lockhart, TX 78644
(512) 398-6642
  Nanci Falley, Editor
Quarterly breed publication of the AIHR.

AMERICAN INDIAN JOURNAL
Institute for the Development of Indian Law
2600 Summit Dr.
Edmond, OK 73034-5984
  Lynn Kickingbird, Editor
Contains scholarly articles on American Indian
history and law, as well as articles of current interest in Indian affairs. Book reviews. Quarterly. 350
cir. $13/copy; $50/year. Advertising. Begun 1971.

AMERICAN INDIAN LAW NEWSLETTER
American Indian Law Center
P.O. Box 4456, Station A
Albuquerque, NM 87196
(505) 277-5462
  Marc Mannes, Editor
Includes articles on American Indian law, Indian-
related policy issues, service programs, legislation at the national, regional, state, local and tribal
government levels; also provides information on
projects impacting the political, administrative, and
leadership capabilities of tribal government. Book
reviews. Bimonthly. 500 cir. $15/year. Complimen-
tary copies available upon request for subscription information. Open to exchanges with other
publications. Begun 1968

AMERICAN INDIAN LAW REVIEW
University of Oklahoma Law Center
300 Timberdell Rd., Rm. 378
Norman, OK 73019
(405) 325-2840 Fax 325-6282
  Michael Waters, Editorial Advisor
This journal documents and analyzes legal, cultural, and historical issues of interest to Native
American communities. Includes articles by legal
professionals and scholars, notes written by students, and recent developments in the federal
courts on American Indian issues. Book reviews.
Advertising. Contest: The American Indian Law
Writing Competition. Semiannual. $20/year. Back
copies available from William S. Hein & Co. by
calling toll-free (800) 828-7571.

**AMERICAN INDIAN LAW STUDENTS
ASSOCIATION NEWSLETTER**
American Indian Law Center
University of New Mexico-School of Law
1117 Stanford Dr., NE
Albuquerque, NM 87196
(505) 277-5462
Published irregularly.

**AMERICAN INDIAN LAWYER
TRAINING PROGRAM NEWSLETTER**
319 MacArthur Blvd.
Oakland, CA 94610

AMERICAN INDIAN LIBRARIES NEWSLETTER
American Indian Library Association
School of Library and Information Studies
University of Oklahoma, 401 W. Brooks
Norman, OK 73019
(405) 325-3921 Fax 325-7648
  Lotsee Patterson, Editor
  Lana Grant, Production Manager
Contains information of interest to those interested
in library services to Native Americans in the U.S.
and Canada. Includes news, items of interest, re-
views, advertisements, and Association informa-
tion. Quarterly newsletter. 1,500 Cir. $10 mem-
bership in Association for individuals, $5, students,
$25, institutions. Send subscriptions to: Joan
Howland, Law Library, University of MN, 229 19th
Ave., Minneapolis, MN 55455. Begun 1976.

AMERICAN INDIAN NEWS
Office of Native American Programs
P.O. Box 217
Fort Washakie, WY 82514

AMERICAN INDIAN QUARTERLY
University of Nebraska Press
P.O. Box 880484
Lincoln, NE 68588
(402) 472-3581 Fax 472-6214
  Morris W. Foster, Editor
  Devon Mihesuah & Blake Thurman,
    Associate Editors
  Robert Black, Book Review Editor
An interdisciplinary journal of Native American
Studies including the history, anthropology, litera-
ture, and the arts of Native North America. Book
reviews. Published quarterly. AIQ is a peer-re-
viewed academic journal with a circulation of 850.
$25/year, individuals; $45/year, institutions. Adver-
tising. Begun 1979.

AMERICAN INDIAN REPORT
The Falmouth Institute, Inc.
3918 Prosperity Ave., Suite 302
Fairfax, VA 22031
(703) 641-9100 Fax 641-1558
  Marguerite Carroll, Editor
A monthly subscription newsletter focusing on legal decision, federal regulations, available grants,
education, health, news and issues affecting American Indians and Alaska natives. $79, annual sub-
scription. A complimentary issue is available upon
request. Begun 1985.

AMERICAN INDIAN REVIEW
National Urban Indian Council
100068 University Park Station
Denver, CO 80210
(303) 750-2695

**AMERICAN INDIAN RESOURCE
CENTER NEWSLETTER**
6518 Miles Ave.
Huntington Park, CA 90255

**AMERICAN INDIAN SCIENCE &
ENGINEERING SOCIETY --NEWSLETTER**
1630 30th St., Suite 301
Boulder, CO 80301
(303) 492-8658
Quarterly.

AMERICAN INDIAN SERVICES DIRECTORY
NAES College Press, 2838 W. Peterson
Chicago, IL 60659-3813
(312) 761-5000
  Ronald Bowan, Editor
  Florence Dunham, Publisher

**AMERICAN INDIAN SOCIETY
OF WASHINGTON NEWSLETTER**
22258 Cool Water Dr.
Ruther Glen, VA 22546
(804) 448-3707
Mitchell Bush, Editor
Reports on Indian life in Washington, D.C. It features a calendar of coming events, and a section on events of interest to local Indians. Monthly. 500 cir. $8/year. Advertising. Begun 1966.

AMERICAN INDIAN STUDIES NEWSLETTER
University of Minnesota
1314 Social Sciences Bldg.
Minneapolis, MN 55455

**AMERICAN INDIAN STUDY CENTER--
NEWSLETTER**
211 South Broadway
Baltimore, MD 21231

**AMERICAN INDIANS FOR DEVELOPMENT --
NEWSLETTER**
P.O. Box 117, 236 West Main St.
Meriden, CT 06450
(203) 238-4009
Jose E. Rodriguez-Sellas,
and Patricia Benedict, Editors
Contains articles and Indian related themes (poems, recipes, etc.) Also contains job information for Americn Indians, general news about Native issues and cultural activities. Bimonthly. No subscription charge. Donations accepted. Complimentary copies available upon request. Begun 1983.

**AMERICAN INDIANS UNLIMITED--
NEWSLETTER**
240 Michigan Union, 530 South St.
Ann Arbor, MI 48104

**AMERICAN INSTITUTE OF
INDIAN STUDIES NEWSLETTER**
University of Pennsylvania
Philadelphia, PA 19102

AMERICAN JOURNAL OF ARCHAEOLOGY
Archaeological Institute of America
675 Commonwealth Ave.
Boston, MA 02215
(617) 353-9361
Quarterly. Professional archaeological journal with book reviews on New World archaeology.

AMERICAN NATIVE PRESS
American Indian & Alaska Native Newspapers
& Periodicals Resources
2801 S. University
Little Rock, AR 72204
(501) 569-3160
Dan Littlefield, Editor
Native American book reviews. Quarterly newsletter. 1,100 cir. Begun 1983.

AMERICAN QUARTERLY
American Studies Association
307 College Hall, University of Pennsylvania
Philadelphia, PA 19104-6303
(215) 898-6252
Janice Radway, Editor
Contains scholarly articles on various aspects of American culture. Advertising. Published six times per year; last issue of year contains book reviews. Subscription: $30/year (libraries).

AMERICAN WEST
Buffalo Bill Memorial Association
Buffalo Bill Historical Center
P.O. Box 1000
Cody, WY 82414
(307) 587-4771
Published six times per year.

AMERICANS BEFORE COLUMBUS
National Indian Youth Council
318 Elm St., SE
Albuquerque, NM 87102
(505) 247-2251
Sherry Robinson
Covers tribal rights and values through education and litigation. Bimonthly newsletter. Free to members; $20/year to non-members.

AN-CHI-MO-WIN
Rocky Boys Reservation
Chippewa Cree Tribe
Box Elder, MT 59521

ANICA NEWS HIGHLIGHTS
Alaska Native Industries
4634 E. Marginal Way South
Seattle, WA 98101

ANISHINAABE NEWS
648 Holton Hall
University of Wisconsin
Milwaukee, WI 53201

ANISHINABE DEE-BAH-GEE-MO-WIN
White Earth Reservation Tribal Council
P.O. Box 418
White Earth, MN 56591
(218) 983-3285
Norma L. Felty, Editor

ANISHANAABE NEWS
G48 Holton Hall
Milwaukee, WI 53201

ANISHNABE NEWS
P.O. Box 55
Stillwater, MN 55082

ANISHNAWBE JOURNAL
Pine Point School
Ponsford, MN 56575

ANTHROPOLOGICAL LINGUISTICS JOURNAL
Indiana University-Dept. of Anthropology
Student Bldg. 130
Bloomington, IN 47405
(812) 855-1203
Douglas R. Parks, Editor
Published jointly with the American Indian Studies Research Institute.

**ANTHROPOLOGICAL LITERATURE: AN
INDEX TO PERIODICAL ARTICLES & ESSAYS**
Tozzer Library-Harvard University
Cambridge, MA 02138
Quarterly index that provides access to scholarly articles on Native Americans.

**ANTHROPOLOGICAL PAPERS
OF THE UNIVERSITY OF ALASKA**
Dept. of Anthropology
University of Alaska, 310 Eielson
Fairbanks, AK 99775
(907) 474-7288 Fax 474-7720
Linda J. Ellana, Ph.D., Editor

Articles dealing with northern socio-cultural anthropology and archaeology. Semiannually. $8/issue. Begun 1956.

**ANTHROPOLOGICAL PAPERS OF THE
AMERICAN MUSEUM OF NATURAL HISTORY**
Central Park West at 79th St.
New York, NY 10024
Contains the current reports of the Museum's Department of Anthropology.

THE APACHE SCOUT
Mescalero Apache Tribe
Mescalero, NM 88340

ARAPAHOE AGENCY COURIER
Arapahoe Agency, Wyoming 82510

**ARCHAEOLOGICAL
CONSERVANCY NEWSLETTER**
415 Orchard Dr.
Santa Fe, NM 87501
(505) 982-3278
Published quarterly.

ARCHAEOLOGY MAGAZINE
135 William St.
New York, NY 10038
(212) 732-5154
Peter A. Young, Editor
Provides consistent treatment of the archaeology of North and South American Indians; book reviews on the art and archaeology of the Americas. Bimonthly by the Archaeological Institute of America. Subscription, $20 per year; $26, foreign; $3.95 each issue. All subscriptions to Box 50260, Boulder, CO 80321. Advertising.

**ARCHAEOLOGY OF
EASTERN NORTH AMERICA**
Archeological Society of Connecicut
P.O. Box 260, Curtis Rd.
Washington, CT 06793

ARCTIC REPORTER
P.O. Box 253
Barrow, AK 99723

ARCTIC VILLAGE ECHOES
Arctic Village School
Arctic Village, AK 99722

ARIZONA TRIBAL DIRECTORY
Arizona Commission on Indian Affairs
1645 West Jefferson
Phoenix, AZ 85007-3004
(602) 255-3123
Diane C. Dankerl, Editor
Indian tribes and associations, government agencies and other organizations concerned with Indian affairs in Arizona. Annual.

ARROW GAZETTE
Bureau of Indian Affairs
2800 Cottage Way
Sacramento, CA 95825
(916) 978-4691
News from the California B.I.A.

ARTIFACTS
The Institute for American Indian Studies
38 Curtis Rd., P.O.Box 1260
Washington Green, CT 06793
(203) 868-0518
Alberto C. Meloni, Director
Quarterly membership magazine.

ARTS & CULTURE OF THE NORTH
Box 1333, Gracie Square Station
New York, NY 10028
 (212) 879-9019
Newsletter devoted to Eskimo art and culture.
Back issues available. Publication ceased 1984.

THE ASSOCIATION
American Indian & Alaska Social Work
410 N.W. 18th St., Suite 101
Portland, OR 97209

**ASSOCIATION OF AMERICAN INDIAN
PHYSICIANS--NEWSLETTER**
1235 Sovereign Row #C-7
Oklahoma City, OK 73108
 (405) 631-0447
Quarterly.

**ASSOCIATION OF CONTRACT TRIBAL
SCHOOLS (ACTS) NEWSLETTER**
c/o St. Francis Indian School
P.O. Box 155
St. Francis, SD 57572
 (605) 747-2296
Monthly.

ATNI NEWSLETTER
824 NE 20th Ave., Suite 310
Portland, OR 97232
 (503) 230-0293

ATOKA INDIAN CITIZEN
P.O. Box 160
Atoka, OK 74525

ATTAN-AKAMIK
Rankikus Rd., Box 225
Rankokous, NJ 08073

AU-AUTHM ACTION NEWS
Salt River Tribal Office
Route 1, Box 216
Scottsdale, AZ 85251

AWARENESS INFORMATION
Nez Perce Nuclear Waste Program
P.O. Box 305
Lapwai, ID 83540

AWATTIM AWAHAN
c/o Salt River Tribal Office
Route 1, Box 700
Scottsdale, AZ 85251

B

BACONE COLLEGE--SMOKE SIGNALS
Muskogee, OK 74401

BAYFIELD SCHOOL COMMUNICATOR
Urban-Rural School Development Program
Joint District No. 1
Bayfield, WI 54814

BEAR FACTS NEWSLETTER
Room 18, Eshelman Hall, 3rd Floor
University of California
Berkeley, CA 94720

BEAR TRACK
Phoenix College
1202 W. Thomas Rd.
Phoenix, AZ 85013

BEAVER TRAILS
Coos, Lower Umpqua & Siuslaw Tribe
533 Buchanan
Coos Bay, OR 97420

BEEFLINE
917 Larson Bldg.
6 South 2nd St.
Yakima, WA 98901

BELLS OF ST. ANN
St. Ann's Indian Mission
Belcourt, ND 58316

BERING STRAITS AGLUKTUK
Bering Straits Native Corporation
P.O. Box 1008
Nome, AK 99762

BILLINGS INDIAN NEWSLETTER
Billings American Indian Council
P.O. Box 853
Billings, MT 59103

BISHINIK
Choctaw Nation of Oklahoma
P.O. Drawer 1210
Durant, OK 74702
 (405) 924-8280 Fax 924-1150
 Judy Allen, Editor
Monthly tribal newspaper.

BIZHII
Cibecue Community School
Cibecue, AZ 85911
 (602) 332-4480
Student magazine. Published 4x/year.

BLACKFEET TRIBAL NEWS
Blackfeet Media
P.O. Box 850
Browning, MT 59417

BOIS FORTE NEWS
Nett Lake, MN 55772

**BOSTON INDIAN MULTISERVICE
CENTER NEWSLETTER**
105 South Huntington Ave.
Jamaica Plain, MA 02130

BTIR TRIBAL NEWSLETTER
Burns Paiute Reservation
HC 71, 100 Pa Si Go St.
Burns, OR 97720

THE BUCKSKIN
Route 3
Eaufaula, OK 74432

BUFFALO GALLERY NEWSLETTER
127 S. Fairfax St.
Alexandria, VA 22314

BUFFALO GRASS NEWSLETTER
Native American Services Agency
2228 South Ave. West
Missoula, MT 59801
 (406) 329-3373
 Bill Walls, Director
Contains the news and events of the
Missoula Indian community. Bimonthly.

BUFFALO TRACKS
Intertribal Bison Cooperative
520 Kansas City St., Suite 209
Rapid City, SD 57701

 (605) 394-9730 Fax 394-7742
 Carla Brings Plenty, Editor
An 8-page quarterly newsletter for members.

THE BULLETIN
Institute of American Indian Studies
University of South Dakota
414 East Clark St.
Vermillion, SD 57069
 (605) 677-5209
 Leonard R. Bruguier & Margaret S. Quintal, Edis.
A semi-annual bulletin published in October & May
featuring information, essays, feature columns on
American Indians. No advertising. No subscrip-
tion price - contributions appreciated. Complimen-
tary copies available upon request. Begun 1956.

BULLHEAD
2205 Moore St.
Ashland, KY 41101
 Joe Napora, Editor
Poetry, prose and graphics, focusing on
the Serpent Mounds of Ohio. 52 pp.

**BUREAU OF CATHOLIC INDIAN
MISSIONS NEWSLETTER**
2021 H St., N.W.
Washington, D.C. 20006
 (202) 331-8542 Fax 331-8544
Covers news and concerns of the Bureau, espe-
cially those issues pertaining to the Catholic
Church and the Indian community. Updates on
legislation affecting the Indian community. 10x/yr.
No charge. Begun 1977.

**BUREAU OF INDIAN AFFAIRS
RESEARCH BULLETIN**
Indian Education Center
615 1st St., Box 26567
Albuquerque, NM 87125-6567

**BUREAU OF INDIAN AFFAIRS
TRIBAL NEWSLETTER**
Phoenix Area Office
Box 10, 1 N. 1st St.
Phoenix, AZ 85001-0010

BUSINESS ALERT
First Nations Financial Report
69 Kelly Rd.
Falmouth, VA 22405
 (703) 371-5615
 Jo Lynn Gentry, Editor
Contains the articles on finance, legislative policy
and law; with articles on how tribes or individuals
can use this legislation, law or policy to their-his/
her benefit. Quarterly newsletter. Free to tribes;
$10 to others. Advertising accepted. Begun 1986.

**BUYERS GUIDE TO PRODUCTS
MANUFACTURED ON AMERICAN
INDIAN RESERVATIONS**
U.S. Government Printing Office
Washington, D.C. 20402
 (202) 275-3314

C

CABAZON CIRCLE NEWSLETTER
Cabazon Band of Mission Indians
84-245 Indio Springs Dr.
Indio, CA 92203
 (619) 342-2593 Fax 347-7880

**CAOS; NEW MEXICO
ARCHAEOLOGY & HISTORY**
CAOS Publishing and Research
P.O. Box 3 CP
Las Cruces, NM 88003

CAHOKIAN
Cahokia Mounds Museum Society, Publisher
P.O. Box 382
Collinsville, IL 62234
  (618) 344-9221
  Richard Y. Norrish, Editor
Newsletter.

CALIFORNIA NEWSDRUM
225 Valencia St.
San Francisco, CA 94103

CALISTEM ERINI
Calista Corporation
601 West 5th St. #200
Anchorage, AK 99501

THE CALUMET
United Southern and Eastern Tribes
1101 Kermit Dr., Suite 800
Nashville, TN 37217
  (615) 361-8700
Bimonthly newsletter.

CAMP CRIER
Fort Belknap Agency
RR 1, Box 66
Halem, MT 59526

CANYON SHADOWS
General Delivery
Supai, AZ 86435

CAP NEWSLETTER
Rosebud Sioux Tribe
Rosebud, SD 57570

CAPITAL NEWS
Santo Domingo, NM 87052

**CAREER DEVELOPMENT OPPORTUNITIES
FOR NATIVE AMERICANS**
B.I.A-Bureau of Higher Education
P.O. Box 26567
Albuquerque, NM 87125-6567
  (505) 766-3131
  Mary F. Asbill, Editor

THE CAROLINA INDIAN VOICE
P.O. Box 1075, College Plaza
Pembroke, NC 28372
  (919) 521-2826
  Connie Brayboy, Editor
Community newspaper to give Indians in North
Carolina (and other minorities) a united voice to
be heard from coast to coast. Weekly. $12/year in
NC; $15/year, elsewhere. Advertising accepted.
Begun 1973.

CAVO TRANSPORTER
Chey-Arap Veterans Organization
P.O. Box 34
Concho, OK 73022

**CENTER FOR INDIAN
EDUCATION NEWSLETTER**
Arizona State University
302 Farmer Education Bldg., Rm. 302
Tempe, AZ 85287

**CENTER FOR THE STUDY OF
EARLY MAN -- CURRENT RESEARCH**
University of Maine
495 College Ave.
Orono, ME 04473

**THE CENTER FOR WESTERN
STUDIES NEWSLETTER**
Box 727, Augustana College
Sioux Falls, SD 57197
  (605) 336-4007 Fax 336-5447
  Harry F. Thompson, Managing Editor
Contains articles describing the programs of the
Center, which often focus on Native Americans,
specifically Sioux culture. Announces research
projects, exhibits, and publications by or about
Sioux Indians. 3x/year. Membership, $15.00.

CHAR-KOOSTA
Confederated Salish and Kootenai Tribes
P.O. Box 278
Pablo, MT 59855-0278
  (406) 675-3000 Fax 675-2806
  Ron Bick, Editor
Weekly newspaper featuring news of interest to
Native Americans focusing on memerbs of the
Confederated Salish and Kootenai Tribes, Mon-
tana and reservation reisdents. Book reviews.
3,900 circ. $18/year, local; $20/year, in state; $25/
year, out-of-state; $45/year, foreign. Advertising.
Begun 1957.

CHEHALIS NEWSLETTER
P.O. Box 536
Oakvilke, WA 98568

CHEMAWA AMERICAN
Chemawa Indian School
5495 Chugach St., N.E.
Chemawa, OR 97303

CHEMAWA CHATTER
Indian Health Service
Chemawa Indian Health Center
3750 Chemawa Rd. NE
Salem, OR 97305
  (503) 399-5931

CHEROKEE ADVOCATE
Cherokee Nation Communications Dept.
P.O. Box 948
Tahlequah, OK 74465-0948
  (918) 456-0671 Fax 456-6485
  Lynn Howard, Editor
  Norma Harvey, Publication Coordinator
Contains news and information about programs
and services, and tribal government of the Chero-
kee Nation. Book reviews. Monthly newspaper.
5,000 circ. $12.50/year. Advertising. Begun 1977.

CHEROKEE BOYS CLUB NEWSLETTER
P.O. Box 507
Cherokee, NC 28719
  (704) 497-9101
  Stan Bienick, Editor
Quarterly newsletter. 2,500 circ. Begun 1965.

CHEROKEE ONE FEATHER
Eastern Band of Cherokee Indians
P.O. Box 501
Cherokee, NC 28719-0501
  (704) 497-5513
  Richard Welch, Editor
  Pat Taylor, Circulation Manager
Provides information on tribal policies and news.
Book reviews. Weekly tabloid. 2,000 circ. $20/yr.
Advertising. Begun 1966.

CHEROKEE TIMES
76 River Rd.
Cherokee, NC 28719

THE CHESOPIEAN JOURNAL
The Chesopiean
7507 Pennington Rd.
Norfolk, VA 23505
Published three to six times per year.
Subscription: $10/year.

CHEYENNE-ARAPAHO BULLETIN
Cheyenne-Arapaho Business Committee
P.O. Box 38
Concho, OK 73022
  (405) 262-0345

**CHEYENNE RIVER AGENCY
NEWS BULLETIN**
Eagle Butte, SD 57625

CHICKASAW TIMES
Chickasaw Nation Tribal Government
P.O. Box 1548
Ada, OK 74821-1548
  (405) 436-2603
  Emil Farve, Publisher & Editor
Contains information on tribal goals, operations,
procedures, services, accomplishments, or opin-
ions of Chickasaw citizens. Book reviews. Monthly
newspaper. 8,500 cir. Begun 1970.

CHOCTAW COMMUNITY NEWS
Mississippi Band of Choctaw Indians
Route 7, Box 21
Philadelphia, MS 39350-9807
  (601) 656-5251
  Julie Kelsey, Editor
Monthly tribal newspaper containing articles; pri-
marily concerned with local events which involve
Mississippi Choctaws. Book reviews. 5,000 cir.
Limited advertising. Free subscription by request,
donations accepted. Begun 1970.

**CHOCTAW PRODUCTIONS
& CABLE PROGRAMMING**
Mississippi Band of Choctaw Indians
Route 7, Box 21
Philadelphia, MS 39350-9807
  (601) 656-5251

THE CIRCLE
Boston Indian Council
105 S. Huntington Ave.
Jamaica Plain, MA 02130-4799
  (617) 232-0343
  Helen Blue, Editor
Monthly newspaper containing information on urban Indians, particularly in the Boston area, as
well as significant events involving Native peoples
in New England and throughout the U.S. and
Canada. Book reviews. 5,000 circ. $10/yr. Adver-
tising. Begun 1976.

THE CIRCLE
Minneapolis American Indian Center
1530 East Franklin Ave.
Minneapolis, MN 55404
  (612) 871-4749 Fax 871-6878
  Ruth Denny, Editor
  Michael Bassett, Assistant Editor
Monthly tabloid size newspaper covering the news
and events of the Native Americans in Minnesota.
Includes reviews of books, movies, arts, etc.
15,000 circ. Advertising accepted. Begun 1979.

CLAN DESTINY
Seneca Indian Historical Society
Irving, NY 14081

**COALITION FOR INDIAN
EDUCATION NEWSLETTER**
8200 Mountain Rd. NE Suite 203
Albuquerque, NM 87110
(505) 262-2351
Dr. Dean Chavers, Editor
Triannual newsletter includes updates on federal
legislation & association activities. Price- included
in membership dues. Advertising accepted. Begun 1991.

COCHITI LAKE SUN
P.O. Box 70
Cochiti, NM 87041

COCOPAH NEWSLETTER
P.O. Box G
Somerton, AZ 85350

COEUR D'ALENE COUNCIL FIRES
Coeur D'Alene Tribal Council
Plummer, ID 83851

COKTV TVLEME
Seminole Nation of Oklahoma
P.O. Box 1498
Wewoka, OK 74884

**COLLEGE GUIDE FOR
AMERICAN INDIAN STUDENTS**
AISES Books
1630 30th St., Suite 301
Boulder, CO 80301
(303) 492-8658
Data on colleges, universities, and financial aid,
all geared to American Indian students; resources
and references specifying to American Indian students; articles on preparation for college, etc. Published annually as a full-color, special issue of
Winds of Change. $5.00.

COLORADO HISTORY NEWS
Ute Indian Museum, Ouray Memorial Park
P.O. Box 1736
Montrose, CO 81402
Glen Gross, Editor

THE COLUMNS
Cherokee National Historical Association
P.O. Box 515
Tahlequah, OK 74464
(918) 456-6007
Myrna Moss, Editor
Quarterly newsletter.

COMANCHE
Comanche Tribe of Oklahoma
P.O. Box 908
Lawton, OK 73502

COMMUNICATOR
Migizi Communications, Inc.
3123 E. Lake St., Suite 200
Minneapolis, MN 55406
(612) 721-6631

COMMUNIQUE
Order of the Indian Wars
P.O. Box 7401
Little Rock, AR 72217
(501) 225-3996
Jerry L. Russell, Editor
Monthly newsletter.

CONFEDERATED INDIAN TRIBES
Washington State Penitentiary
P.O. Box 520
Walla Walla, WA 99362

**CONFEDERATED TRIBES OF COOS,
LOWER UMPQUA & SIUSLAW INDIANS -
TRIBAL NEWSLETTER**
455 South 4th St.
Coos Bay, OR 97420
(503) 267-5454
Monthly.

**CONFEDERATED TRIBES OF SILETZ-
SPRINGFIELD AREA OFFICE NEWS**
188 West B St., Bldg. P
Springfield, OR 97477
(503) 746-9658

CONFEDERATED UMATILLA JOURNAL
P.O. Box 638
Pendleton, OR 97801

CONTEMPORARY INDIAN AFFAIRS
Navajo Community College
Tsaile, AZ 86556

CORNELL WEB
Cornell University
400 Caldwell Hall
Ithaca, NY 14853
(607) 255-4308 Fax 255-0185
Jose Barreiro, Editor
Published twice a year - 8 pages of news on Native American students and faculty at Cornell. No
charge.

THE CORNPLANTER
Rhode Island Indian Council
444 Friendship St.
Providence, RI 02907

THE COUNCIL
Tanana Chiefs Conference
122 1st Ave.
Fairbanks, AK 99701

COUNCIL DRUM NEWS
Inter-Tribal Council
45 Lexington N.W.
Grand Rapids, MI 49504
Monthly newsletter.

COUNCIL FIRES
Coeur D'Alene Tribal Council
Plummer, ID 83851

COUNCIL FOR AMERICAN INDIAN MINISTRY
122 W. Franklin
Minneapolis, MN 55404

**COUNCIL OF ENERGY RESOURCE
TRIBES (CERT) REPORT**
1580 Logan St., Suite 400
Denver, CO 80203
(303) 832-6600

COUNCIL SIGNALS
Montana Dept. of Indian Affairs
State Capitol
Helena, MT 59620

COYOTE ON THE TURTLE'S BACK
Institute of American Indian Arts
College of Santa Fe Campus
Alexis Hall, St. Michael's Dr.
Santa Fe, NM 87501

(505) 988-6463
Published annually.

**CRAFTS: AMERICAN INDIAN
PAST & PRESENT**
Written Heritage
8009 Wales St.
New Orleans, LA 70126-1952
(504) 246-3742
Jack Heriard, Editor
Annual journal covering American Indian crafts and
material culture. 7,000 cir. $7/copy. Begun 1988.

CRAZY HORSE PROGRESS
Crazy Horse Memorial Foundation
Avenue of the Chiefs--The Black Hills
Crazy Horse, SD 57730-9988
(605) 673-4681
Robb DeWall, Editor
Published 3x/year. No charge.

CREEK NATION NEWS
Creek Nation of Oklahoma
P.O. Box 580
Okmulgee, OK 74447

CRIT NEWSLETTER
Colorado River Indian Tribes
Rte. 1, Box 23-B
Parker, AZ 85344
(602) 669-9211 Fax 669-5675
Quarterly tribal newsletter.

CRITFC NEWS
729 NE Oregon St.
Portland, OR 97232

CROSS & FEATHER NEWS
Tekakwitha Conference National Center
P.O. Box 6768
Great Falls, MT 59406
(406) 727-0147 (phone & fax)
Richard L. King, Executive Director
Staff: Wilson Boni, Billie Jo Moore, Terri Jarvey,
and Christine Collins. *Description*: A quarterly
newsletter containing articles addressing religious,
social, and legislative issues concerning Native
American Catholics or people involved with the
blessed Kateri Tekakwitha (a Mohawk who lived
from 1656 to 1680, and who is now a candidate
for Sainthood in the Roman Catholic Church.) Also
includes reports on workshops, conferences, and
meetings. $10, membership. Begun 1979.

CROW NEWS
Crow Tribal Government
Crow Agency, MT 59022

CROWNDANCER
San Carlos Apache Tribe
P.O. Box 0
San Carlos, AZ 85550

CULTURAL BROTHERHOOD
Council of Native Nations
SCI Huntington Prison
Huntington, PA 16652

CULTURAL DEMOCRACY
Alliance for Cultural Democracy
P.O. Box 7591
Minneapolis, MN 55407
(612) 729-4090 Fax 721-2160
A magazine devoted to cultural rights, neighbor-
hood, ecology, and arts activism. Membership,
$25/year.

CULTURAL NOTES
Indian Arts Board, Rm. 4004
U.S. Dept. of the Interior
18th & C Sts.
Washington, DC 20240

CULTURAL SURVIVAL QUARTERLY
Cultural Survival
215 First St.
Cambridge, MA 02142
 (617) 621-3818 Fax 621-3814
 Melanie Tang, Publications Asst.
International advocate for the human rights of indigenous peoples. Includes news, resources, and
general-interest articles. $5/issue.

CURRENT ANTHROPOLOGY
Wenner-Gren Foundation for
Anthropological Research
1865 Broadway
New York, NY 10023
 (212) 957-8750
Bimonthly journal.

CURTIS (CARL T.) HEALTH CENTER NEWS
Omaha Indian Reservation
Macy, NE 68039

**CUSTER BATTLEFIELD NATIONAL
MONUMENT NEWSLETTER**
P.O. Box 39
Crow Agency, MT 59022
 (406) 638-2622
Published quarterly.

D

DAKOTA STUDENT
University of North Dakota
Box 8177, University Station
Grand Forks, ND 58201

DAKOTA WOWAPIPHI
P.O. Box 157
Marty, SD 57361

DANCING PRAYERS
Orre Drumrite Walking Heritage
P.O. Box 221689
Anchorage, AK 99522-1689
 Elizabeth A. Wells, Editor
Quarterly publication devoted to tradition,
culture, and heritage. Begun 1990.

DARTMOUTH NATIVE ALUMNI NEWS
P.O. Box A-162
Hanover, NH 03755

DAYBREAK
P.O. Box 315
Williamsville, NY 14231-0315
 (607) 272-1749
 Oren Lyons, Publisher
 John Mohawk, Editor
Covers Amerian Indian world views. Quarterly
newspaper. $3/copy; $12/year. Begun 1987.

DAYBREAK STAR INDIAN READER
Bernie Whitebear
P.O. Box 99100
Seattle, WA 98199
 (206) 285-4425
 Kathryn Onetta, Director
A 24-page, monthly (October through May)

children's learning resource featuring culturally
focused articles of interest to students in grades
4-6. Includes creative writing exercises, games
and puzzles, legends, math and science activities, book and movie reviews. See publisher for
multiple copy rates.

DE-BAH-JI-MON
P.O. Box 308
Cass Lake, MN 56633

DELAWARE NEWSLETTER
P.O. Box 825
Anadarko, OK 73005

**DENVER INDIAN HEALTH
BOARD NEWSLETTER**
2035 East 18th Ave. 5
Denver, CO 80206

**DENVER NATIVE AMERICANS
UNITED NEWSLETTER**
4407 Morrison Rd.
Denver, CO 80219
 (303) 937-0401

**DEPT. OF AMERICAN INDIAN
STUDIES NEWSLETTER**
University of Minnesota-West Bank Campus
1314 Social Science Bldg.
Minneapolis, MN 55455

DESERT CONNECTIONS
American Indian Professional Training Program
in Speech-Language Pathology & Audiology
Dept. of Speech & Hearing Sciences
University of Arizona
Tucson, AZ 85721
 (602) 621-1969/1644
 Betty Nunnery, Program Coordinator
A network publication for Native American speech-
language pathologists and audiologists.

DEVILS LAKE SIOUX TRIBE NEWSLETTER
Public Information Office
Fort Totten, ND 58335

DINESH D'SOUVA
Dartmouth Review
P.O. Box 343
Hanover, NH 03755

**DIRECTORY OF AMERICAN INDIAN
BUSINESSES**
National Center for American
Indian Enterprise Development
953 Juanita Ave.
Mesa, CA 85204
 (800) 423-0452; (602) 831-7524
 Steven L.A. Stallings, Editor
Annual.

DIRECTORY OF INDIAN MUSEUMS
North American Indian Museums Association
c/o Seneca Iroquois National Museum
Allegany Indian Reservation, P.O. Box 442
Salamanca, NY 14779
 (716) 945-1738
Annual.

**DIRECTORY OF NATIVE AMERICAN
PERFORMING ARTISTS**
ATLATL
2303 N. Central Ave., Suite 104
Phoenix, Arizona 85004
 (602) 253-2731 Fax 256-6385
 Wendy Weston-Ben, Editor

A directory of Native American authentic traditional
dance, singers, musicians, storytellers, dancers,
contemporary adaptations, popular culture and
other Native American performers available for
booking. $5.50 per copy.

**DIRECTORY OF NATIVE AMERICANS
IN SPEECH-LANGUAGE PATHOLOGY
& AUDIOLOGY**
American Indian Professional Training Program
in Speech-Language Pathology & Audiology
Dept. of Speech & Hearing Sciences
University of Arizona
Tucson, AZ 85721
 (602) 621-1969/1644
 Betty Nunnery, Program Coordinator

DISTANT VISIONS
Institute of American Indian Art
College of Santa Fe
Santa Fe, NM 87503

**DISTRICT OF COLUMBIA (D.C.) DIRECTORY
OF NATIVE AMERICAN FEDERAL & PRIVATE
PROGRAMS**
American Indian Education Program
The Phelps-Stokes Fund
1228 M St., N.W.
Washington, D.C. 20005
 (202) 638-7066
250 entries. Published annually. $5.00;
$25/year for updates.

DNA IN ACTION
DNA Legal Services
P.O. Box 36
Window Rock, AZ 86515

**DOMESTIC ABUSE IS NOT
AN INDIAN TRADITION**
Ne-Naiah-Kaha-Kok
Box 82
Keshena, WI 54135
 (715) 799-4398

THE DRAGONFLY
Two Rivers Gallery
Minneapolis American Indian Center
1530 Franklin Ave. E.
Minneapolis, MN 55404
 Sammy Watso & Mason Riddle, Directors
A cultural arts department newsletter.

DRUMBEAT
U.S. Penitentiary
Leavenworth, KS 66048

DRUMBEAT
Crow Creek Reservation High School
Stephan, SD 57346

DRUMBEAT
Charlotte-Mecklenburg School
428 W. Blvd.
Charlotte, NC 28203

DRUMBEAT
2400 Southeast Circle Dr.
Bartlesville, OK 74006

THE DRUMBEAT
Confederated Tribes of Siletz-Salem Area Office
3789 River Rd. N. Suite D
Keizer, OR 97303
 (503) 390-9494
Monthly newsletter.

DSUQ' WUB' SIATSUB
Suquamish Tribe
P.O. Box 498
Suquamish, WA 98392

DUCK VALLEY ROUNDUP
P.O. Box 219
Owynee, NV 89832

DWOQ'WUB'STATSUB
Suquamish Tribe
P.O. Box 498
Suquamish, WA 98392-0498

DXWHIIDA
National Coalition to Support Indian Treaties
814 N.E. 40th St.
Seattle, WA 98105

E

E'YANAPAHA
Devil's Lake Sioux Tribe
Public Information Office
Fort Totten, ND 58335

EAGLE BUTTE NEWS
P.O. Box 210
Eagle Butte, SD 57625

EAGLE FEATHER TALK
P.O. Box 1268
Castle Dale, UT 84313

EAGLE FREE PRESS
Phoenix Indian Center, Inc.
333 W. Indian School Rd.
Phoenix, AZ 85013-3215
  (602) 256-2000

THE EAGLE
Eagle Wing Press, Inc.
P.O. Box 579MO
Naugatuck, CT 06770
  (203) 729-0035
  Ed Sarabia, Chairperson
  Ida Rees, Vice Chairperson
  Richard Carlson, Editor
Bimonthly newspaper presenting positive American Indian press to non-Indian public. Funds generated beyond publication costs are committed to a scholarship fund which provides monies to American Indian/Alaskan Native post high school students studying education or journalism. Bimonthly. Annual subscription, $10; $2.50 per copy. Advertising. Begun 1981.

EAGLE'S EYE
Brigham Young University
Office of Student Programs
4th Floor, ELWC
Provo, UT 84602
  (801) 378-6263 Fax 378-6864
  Ken Sekaquaptewa, Publisher
Quaterly magazine for Native American students at BYU. Book reviews. 3,500 cir. $10/year; $3/copy. Begun 1967.

EAGLE'S VOICE
Sinte Gleska College
Box 8
Mission, SD 57555
  (605) 856-2321
Contains literature on Native American experiences on high plains. Text also in lakota. 1975.

EARLY SITES RESEARCH SOCIETY NEWSLETTER
c/o James Whittall, Archaeology Director
Long Hill
Rowley, MA 01969
  (617) 948-2410
Published bimonthly.

EARTH WALK
Council for Native American Indian Progress
280 Broadway, Suite 316
New York, NY 10007
  (212) 732-0485
Newsletter.

EARTHSONG
The Heard Museum
22 E. Monte Vista Rd.
Phoenix, AZ 85004-1480
  (602) 252-8840 Fax 252-9757
  Mary H. Brennan, Editor
Newsletter targeted at Museum members. Content includes articles on upcoming exhibitions and events, as well as behind-the-scenes features on Museum happenings. Published four times a year.

ECH-KA-NAV-CHA
500 Merrian
Needles, CA 92363

ECHO--TOWAOC COMMUNITY NEWSPAPER
Ute Mountain Tribe
Towaoc, CO 81334

EL PALACIO
Museum of New Mexico
Box 2087
Santa Fe, NM 87504-2087
  (505) 827-6794
  Karen Meadows, Editor
Articles on anthropology, archaeology, fine arts, folk arts, Southwest history and geography. Book reivews. Triannual magazine. 3,000 cir. $6/copy; $18/year. Begun 1913.

ELDER VOICES
National Indian Council on Aging
6400 Uptown Blvd., NE #510-W
Albuquerque, NM 87110-4203
  (505) 888-3302 Fax 888-3276
  Larry Curley, Editor
Covers issues affecting Native American elders, including serviecs and related legislative issues. Published periodically. Begun 1977.

ELKO COMMUNITY NEWS
Nevada Intertribal Council
806 Holman Way
Sparks, NV 89431
  (702) 355-0600

EOP NEWSLETTER
350 Waldo Hall, Oregon State University
Corvallis, OR 97331

ETHNIC DIRECTORY OF CALIFORNIA NORTHWEST COAST OF U.S.
Western Publishers
P.O. Box 30193, Station B
Calgary, Alberta, Canada

ETHNIC REPORTER
National Association for Ethnic Studies
Department of English
Arizona State University
Tempe, AZ 85287-0001
  (602) 965-3391 Fax 965-1093

  Gretchen Bataille, Editor
Covers NAES activities. Semiannual newsletter. $35/year, individuals; $45/year, institutions; $5/copy. Advertising. Begun 1975.

ETHNOHISTORY
Duke University Press for the
American Society for Ethnohistory
6697 College Station
Durham, NC 27708
  (919) 684-2173 Fax 684-8644
  Shepard Krech, III, Editor
Studies of native peoples in the Americas and throughout the world. Quarterly journal. 1,200 cir. $34/year, institutions; $21, individuals. Begun 1953.

ETHNOMUSICOLOGY
Society for Ethnomusicology
P.O. Box 2984
Ann Arbor, MI 48106
  (313) 665-9400
Published three times per year.

EXPLORE INDIAN COUNTRY
Indian Country Communications, Inc.
Route 2, Box 2900-A
Hayward, WI 54843
  (715) 634-5226 Fax 634-3243
  Paul DeMain, CEO
  Terri Bisonette, Editor
Published monthly for tourist and casino patrons, including articles and letters related to gaming, entertainment, music, historical information, museums, hotels. Also, casino and bingo information located in Indian country. $25/year. Advertising accepted.

EYAPAHA
American Indian Center Newsletter
4115 Connecticut
St. Louis, MO 63116

EYAPIOAYE
Assiniboine and Sioux Tribes
Poplar, MT 59255

F

FAIRBANKS NATIVE ASSN. NEWSLETTER
201 First Ave.
Fairbanks, AK 99701
  (907) 452-1648
Monthly newsletter.

FAMILY SERVICES NEWSLETTER
Family Services Program
Toiyabe Indian Health Project
P.O. Box 1296
Bishop, CA 93515
  (619) 873-6394 Fax 873-3935
Focuses on concerns of Indian families, such as drugs and alcohol, child abuse and neglect, and women's concerns. Quarterly. No charge. Begun 1980.

FEATHER REVIEW
P.O. Box 149
Mountain View, OK 73062
  (405) 347-2875
  Deborah Ahtone, Editor/Publisher
Monthly state wide Indian and government agencies newspaper. $15/year.

FIRST NATIONS BUSINESS ALERT
First Nations Development Institute
The Stores Bldg., 11917 Main St.
Fredericksburg, VA 22408
  (703) 371-5615 Fax 371-3505
Quarterly newsletter providing business news
about and of interest to tribes. No charge to tribes;
$10/year, others. Advertising.

**FIRST NATIONS NATIONAL
MARKETING DIRECTORY**
First Nations Development Institute
The Stores Bldg., 11917 Main St.
Fredericksburg, VA 22408
  (703) 371-5615 Fax 371-3505
Includes in-depth profiles of businesses, with indexes by product type and business name; calendar of events (trade shows, craft fairs, pow-
wows, expos, etc.). Also lists national trade associations. The Directory os made available to over
2,000 Indian arts & crafts producers throughout
the nation.

**FIVE CIVILIZED TRIBES
MUSEUM NEWSLETTER**
Agency Hill on Honor Heights
Muskogee, OK 74401
  (918) 683-1701

FIVE FEATHERS NEWS
Tribe of Five Feathers
P.O. Box W
Lompoc, CA 93436

FIVE TRIBES JOURNAL
Five Civilized Tribes Foundation
c/o Chickasaw Nation, P.O. Box 1548
Ada, OK 74820

FLAGSTAFF INDIAN CENTER NEWSLETTER
2717 N. Steves Blvd. #11
Flagstaff, AZ 86004

FLANDREAU SPIRIT
Flandreau Indian High School
Flandreau, SD 57028

FOCUS: INDIAN EDUCATION
Minnesota Department of Education
Capitol Square Bldg.
St. Paul, MN 55101

FOLKLIFE CENTER NEWS
American Folklife Center
The Library of Congress
Washington, D.C. 20540
  (202) 707-6590
Provides information about current projects; and
lists current publications. Quarterly newsletter.

FOND DU LAC NEWS
105 University Dr.
Cloquet, MN 55720

FORT APACHE SCOUT
White Mountain Apache Tribe
P.O. Box 898
Whiteriver, AZ 85941-0898
  (602) 338-4813
  Stewart Nicholas, Production Manager
Biweekly newspaper covering news of the tribe
and its people. 2,600 cir. $10/year. Advertising.
Begun 1962.

FORT HALL NEWSLETTER
Bureau of Indian Affairs
Fort Hall, ID 83203

FORT McDOWELL BAJA NEWS
P.O. Box 17779
Fountain Hills, AZ 85268

**FOUNDATION FOR INDIAN
LEADERSHIP NEWSLETTER**
P.O. Box 5335
Santa Fe, NM 87502
  (505) 988-6291

FOUR DIRECTIONS
Kiva Club
1812 Las Lomas, NE
Albuquerque, NM 87131

**THE FOUR DIRECTIONS: AMERICAN
INDIAN LITERARY QUARTERLY**
Snowbird Publishing Co.
P.O. Box 729
Tellico Plains, TN 37385
  (615) 982-7261 Fax 681-3418
  Joanna & William Meyer, Editors
Quarterly journal of poetry, short stories, and es-
says; book & media reviews; all by Native writers.
$21/yr. $6/issue.

**FOUR DIRECTIONS FOR
PEACE & MEDICINE LODGE**
Council for Native American Indian Progress
280 Broadway, Suite 316
New York, NY 10007
  (212) 732-0485
Newsletter.

FOUR WINDS
Hundred Arrows Press
P.O. Box 156
Austin, TX 78767-0156
  (512) 472-8877/956-7048
Quarterly magazine focusing on Native American
art, literature and history. $22/year.

FOUR WINDS NEWSLETTER
Confederated Indian Tribes
Washington State Penitentiary
P.O. Box 520
Walla Walla, WA 99362

FUTURES
Futures for Children
805 Tijeras, NW
Albuquerque, NM 87102
  (800) 545-6843; (505) 247-4700 Fax 247-2831
Seeks to find sponsors for American Indian children to contribute toward the child's education and
clothing. Provides sponsors and donors for the
program. Includes news and events. Published
semiannually. No chare. Begun 1961.

G

GALLERY NOTES
The Indian Museum
Mid-America All Indian Center
650 North Seneca
Wichita, KS 67203

GILA RIVER INDIAN NEWS
P.O. Box 459
Sacaton, AZ 85247

GILCREASE JOURNAL
Thomas Gilcrease Museum Association
1400 Glcrease Museum Rd.
Tulsa, OK 74127-2100

  (918) 596-2700 FAX 596-2770
  Carol Haralson Editor
Features stories concerning the art, artifacts, and
archival materials of the Gilcrease Museum. Includes photographic and artistic reproductions
from the collections. The collections emphasize
the Old West and the American Indian. Semiannual. 4,500 cir. $40/year membership; $6/copy;
$25/year for libraries. Begun 1958.

**GRAND RAPIDS
INTERTRIBAL NEWSLETTER**
45 Lexington, NW
Grand Rapids, MI 49504

**GRAND RONDE HUNTING
& FISHING NEWSLETTER**
P.O. Box 38
Grand Ronde, OR 97347

GREAT LAKES AGENCY NEWS
Great Lakes Indian Agency
Ashland, WI 54806

GREAT LAKES INDIAN NEWS BUREAU
Route 5, Box 5355
Hayward, WI 54843

GREAT LAKES PATHFINDER
460 W. Spruce St.
Sault Ste. Marie, MI 49783

GREAT PLAINS JOURNAL
Institute of the Great Plains
Museum of the Great Plains
P.O. Box 68, 601 Ferris
Elmer Thomas Park
Lawton, OK 73502
  (405) 353-5675
Contains articles concerning the history, archae-
ology, ecology or natural history of the ten-state
Great Plains region. Published annually.

GREAT PLAINS QUARTERLY
Center for Great Plains Studies
University of Nebraska, 1214 Oldfather Hall
Lincoln, NE 68588-0313
  (402) 472-6058
  Frances W. Kaye, Editor
A scholarly, interdisciplinary journal which publishes refereed articles in the geography, history,
literature, anthropology, ethnology, folklore, fine
arts, sociology, political science, economics, and
agriculture of the Great Plains region. Book reviews. Advertising accepted. Subscription: Individuals: U.S. - $15/year, $28/2 years; Canada -
$18/year; $34/2 years; Overseas - $21/year, $40/
2 years. Institutions: U.S. $20/year, $33/2 years;
Canada - $23/year, $39/2 years; Overseas - $26/
year, $45/2 years. $5 (single issue). Complimentary copies available.

GREAT PLAINS RESEARCH
Center for Great Plains Studies
University of Nebraska, 1215 Oldfather Hall
Lincoln, NE 68588-0317
  (402) 472-3082 Fax 472-1123
  Clare V. McKanna, Jr., Editor
A biannual multidisiciplinary journal, publishes original scholarly papers in the natural and social sciences dealing with issues of regional concern. It
includes reports on symposia and conferences
and reviews of books. U.S. - $25/year, individu-
als; $50, institutional; Canada - $28/year, individuals, $53, institutional; other foreign - $35/year, individuals, $60, institutional. Complimentary cop-
ies available.

GREAT PROMISE MAGAZINE
1103 Hatteras
Austin, TX 78753
 (512) 480-9922
 David Prego, Editor
Staff: Vince Bland, Annette Arkeketa, Tricia Tingle & Barbara Woelk. A quarterly magazine for and about American Indian children, grades 5-8. Includes articles, drawings and photographs; material carefully designed to help American Indian children protect and preserve their heritage while at the same time helping them prepare for the future. Readers will learn how American Indian children live across the nation, whether they live on reservations or in cities. Also features profiles of successful young Indian men and women. Each issue contains a study guide for teachers and parents. $25/year donation.

H

HARVARD INDIAN NEWSLETTER
Native American Program
Graduate School of Education
Harvard University
Cambridge, MA 02138

HASKELL INDIAN JUNIOR COLLEGE LEARNING RESOURCE CENTER NEWSLETTER
P.O. Box H1305
Lawrence, KS 66044

HAWAIIAN COUNCIL OF AMERICAN INDIAN NATIONS NEWSLETTER
P.O. Box 17627
Honolulu, HI 96817

HEALING OUR HEARTS
National Association for Native American Children of Alcoholics
1402 Third Ave. #1110
Seattle, WA 98101
 (206) 467-7686 Fax 467-7689
 Anna M. Latimer, Editor
Quarterly newsletter. 5,000 cir.
No charge for members.

HEALTH NOTES
St. Croix Chippewas of Wisconsin
St. Croix Tribal Center
P.O. Box 287
Hertel, WI 54845

HEALTH REPORTER
National Indian Health Board
50 S. Steele St., Suite 500
Denver, CO 80209
 (303) 394-3500
Published six times per year.

HEART OF AMERICA INDIAN CENTER NEWSLETTER
1340 East Admiral
Kansas City, MO 64106

HELLO CHOCTAW
P.O. Box 59
Durant, OK 74701

HISTORICAL ARCHAEOLOGY
Society for Historical Archaeology
P.O. Box 30446
Tucson, AZ 85751
 (602) 886-8006 Fax 886-0182

 Ronald L. Michael, Editor
Quarterly journal containing articles on theoretical perspectives, comparative studies, artifact and site analysis, and book reviews. Focuses on A.D. 1400 to present. $30/students; $50, individuals; $65/institutions, annual membership dues. Begun 1967.

HO CHUNK WO-LDUK
Wisconsin Winnebago Business Committee
P.O. Box 311
Tomah, WI 54660

HONGA
American Indian Center of Omaha
3610 Dodge St. #2078
Omaha, NE 68131-3207

HONORING THE CHILDREN
National Indian Child Welfare Association
3611 SW Hood St., Suite 201
Portland, OR 97201
 (503) 222-4044 Fax 222-4007
 Larry Douglas, Editor
Annual magazine aimed at promoting positive parenting techniques by giving information on parenting, child abuse and neglect prevention; FAS/E information, child safety tips, etc. Issues are free and sent to Indian child welfare programs, tribes, medical and dental offices located near reservations across the U.S. and Canada.

HOPI ACTION NEWS
Winslow Mail
Winslow, AZ 86047

HOPI CRIER
Hopi Day School
Oraibi, AZ 86039

HOPI TUTU-VE-NI
Office of Public Relations
P.O. Box 123
Kykotsmovi, AZ 86039

HOW NI KAN
Citizen Band Potawatomi Tribe
1901 S. Gordon Cooper
Shawnee, OK 74801
 (405) 275-3121
 Patricia Sulcer, Editor
Monthly tribal newsletter. Subscription: $6/year.

HUMAN DEVELOPMENT NEWS
(NATIVE AMERICAN NEWS INSERT)
HHH Bldg., Room 350G
200 Indepedence Ave., S.W.
Washington, D.C. 20201

HUNTER
North American Indian League
P.O. Box 7
Deer Lodge, MT 59731-0007
 Cloyce Little Light, Editor
Monthly magazine. 200 cir. $5/year.

I

ICE
American Indian Film Institute
333 Valencia St., Suite 212
San Francisco, CA 94103

ICHANA
National Committee on Indian Work of the Episcopal Church
815 Second Ave.
New York, NY 10017
 (212) 867-8400
Focuses on American Indian affairs. Informs readers of programs and projects of the Committee and other groups affiliated with the Episcopal Church. Quarterly. No charge. Begun 1979.

IMPACT
Public Information Division of Save the Children
54 Wilton Rd.
Westport, CT 06881
 (203) 221-4000
 Lee Mullane, Editor
Published quarterly.

IN HARMONY
Institute for the Study of Natural Systems
P.O. Box 637
Mill Valley, CA 94942
 (415) 383-5064
Semiannual newsletter including articles on the preservation of Native American sacred sites. 8,000 cir. $15/year. Begun 1987.

INDEX TO REPRODUCTIONS IN ART PERIODICALS
Data Arts, P.O. Box 30789
Seattle, WA 98103-0789
 Quarterly index to reproductions in in art periodicals for American Indian arts, African arts, arts of Asia, and art in America. $44/year. Begun 1987.

INDIAN AFFAIRS
Association on American Indian Affairs
245 Fifth Ave., Suite 1801
New York, New York 10016
 (212) 689-8720 Fax 685-4692
Covers current news about and of interest to American Indians and to those interested in Indian affairs. Published three times a year with occasional special issues. 45,000 cir. $10/year. Begun 1949.

INDIAN AFFAIRS NEWSLETTER
Bureau of Indian Affairs
1951 Constitution Ave., N.W.
Washington, D.C. 20245

INDIAN AMERICAN QUARTERLY
P.O. Box 443
Hurst, TX 76053

INDIAN ARCHIVES
Antelope Indian Circle
P.O. Box 790
Susanville, CA 96130

INDIAN ARIZONA TODAY
IDDA
4560 N. 19th Ave. #200
Phoenix, AZ 85015-4113

INDIAN ARTIFACT MAGAZINE
Indian Artifact Magazine, Inc.
RD #1, Box 240
Turbotville, PA 17772-9599
 (717) 437-3698
 Gary L. Fogelman, Editor
Concentrates on American Indain pre-history: artifacts, tools, lifestyles, customs, archaeology, tribes, etc. Book reviews included. Published quarterly. Advertising accepted. $17/year. Sample, $5. Begun 1982.

INDIAN ARTS & CRAFTS ASSN. (IACA) NEWSLETTER
122 La Veta Dr., NE, Suite B
Albuquerque, NM 87108
 (505) 265-9149
 Helen Skredergard, Editor
Contains information on markets, meetings, new members, applications, and other news of interest to those in the industry; helps in the education of consumers. Advertising accepted from members only. Published monthly for IACA members and a limited press list. Begun 1974.

INDIAN AWARENESS CENTER NEWSLETTER
Fulton County Historical Society
37 E 375 N
Rochester, IN 46975
 (219) 223-4436
 Shirley Willard, Editor
Covers projects and activities of the Center which encourages the awareness, appreciation, and preservation of Native American culture and traditions, especially that of the Potawatomi and Miami Indians of northern Indiana. Quarterly. $5/yr, individuals, $7.50, institutions. Begun 1984.

INDIAN BOOKS FROM THE FOUR WINDS
P.O. Box 3300
Rapid City, SD 57709
 (605) 343-6064 (phone & fax)
 Ray Gowan, Editor & Publisher
A newspaper format catalog featuring over 800 Indian books. Semiannual. $2.00. Begun 1989.

INDIAN BUSINESS & MANAGEMENT MAGAZINE
National Center for American Indian
Enterprise Development
953 E. Juanita
Mesa, AZ 85204
 (602) 491-1332

INDIAN BUSINESS REVIEW
Native American Business Alliance
8435 SE 17th Ave.
Portland, OR 97202
 (503) 233-4841
Covers programs and projects of the Alliance and its efforts to promote economic development for all Indians. Quarterly. $10/year; free to members.

INDIAN CENTER TASK FORCE NEWS
4040 30th St., Suite A
San Diego, CA 92104

INDIAN COMMUNICATIONS
Dovecrest Indian Cultural Center
390 Summit Rd.
Exeter, RI 02822
Monthly newsletter.

INDIAN COUNTRY
Sac & Fox Settlement
Tama, IA 52339

INDIAN COUNTRY TODAY
1920 Lombardy Dr.
Rapid City, SD 57701

INDIAN COURTS
National American Indian Court Judges
1000 Connecticut Ave., NW, Suite 401
Washington, DC 20036
 (202) 296-0685
Quarterly newsletter.

INDIAN CRUSADER
American Indian Liberation Crusade, Inc.
4009 S. Halldale Ave.
Los Angeles, CA 90062
 (213) 299-1810
 Basil M. Gaynor and Henry E. Hedrick, Editors
Reports on programs to aid Indian reservations. Quarterly. No charge (tax deductible donations accepted.) Begun 1954.

INDIAN EDUCATION
National Indian Education Association
1819 H St., N.W. Suite 800
Washington, D.C. 20006

INDIAN EDUCATION NEWS
Coos County Indian Education
Coordination Program
9140 Cape Arago Hwy.
Coos Bay, OR 97420
 (503) 888-4584

INDIAN EDUCATION NEWSLETTER
United Sioux Tribes of South Dakota
P.O. Box 1193
Pierre, SD 57501

INDIAN EDUCATION UPDATE
National Indian Training and Research Center
2121 S. Mill Ave., Suite 216
Tempe, AZ 85282
 (602) 967-9484
Quarterly newsletter.

INDIAN EDUCATOR
United Indians of All Tribes Foundation
Day Break Star Arts Center
Discovery Park, Box C-99305
Seattle, WA 98199
 (206) 285-4425
Monthly newsletter.

INDIAN, ESKIMO, ALEUT OWNED & OPERATED ARTS BUSINESS SOURCE DIRECTORY
Indian Arts & Crafts Board
Room 4004, U.S. Dept. of the Interior
Washington, DC 20240
 (202) 343-2773
Published annually.

INDIAN EXTENSION NEWS
New Mexico State University
Box 3AP
Las Cruces, NM 88003

INDIAN FORERUNNER
Eight Northern Pueblos
P.O. Box 927
San Juan Pueblo, NM 87566

INDIAN HEALTH NEWSLETTER
Indian Unit-FHSS, 714-744 P St.
Sacramento, CA 95814

INDIAN HEALTH UNIT NEWSLETTER
BMCH, 2141 Berkeley Way
Berkeley, CA 94704

INDIAN HERITAGE PARENTS' NEWS
Seattle School District
5950 Delridge Way, SW
Seattle, WA 98106

INDIAN HIGHWAYS
Cook Christian Training School
708 South Lindon Lane
Tempe, AZ 85281

THE INDIAN HISTORIAN
American Indian Historical Society
1451 Masonic Ave.
San Francisco, CA 94117
 (415) 626-5235
 Jeanette Henry, Editor
Magazines covering American Indian culture and history. 1964. Quarterly. $10. Back issues available.

INDIAN LAW PROJECT NEWSLETTER
Connecticut Legal Services
114 East Main St.
Meriden, CT 06450

INDIAN LAW REPORTER
American Indian Lawyer Training Program
319 MacArthur Blvd.
Oakland, CA 94610
 (510) 834-9333 Fax 834-3836
 Patricia Zell, Editor
 Christine Miklas, Managing Editor
Legal reporting service reporting current developments in Indian law. Monthly journal. 650 cir. $396/year. Begun 1973.

INDIAN LAW SUPPORT CENTER REPORTER
Native American Rights Fund
1506 Broadway
Boulder, Colorado 80302
 (303) 447-8760 Fax 443-7776
Monthly newsletter providing local legal services attorneys with information on developments in the area of Indian law. Includes summaries of recent court decisions in Indian country; Federal Register highlights, and new publications & materials. $36/year.

THE INDIAN LEADER
Haskell Indian Junior College
155 Indian Ave.
Lawrence, KS 66046
 (913) 749-8477

INDIAN LIFE: CHRISTIAN MEDIA FOR NATIVE NORTH AMERICANS
Intertribal Christian Communications
P.O. Box 32
Pembina, ND 58271
 (204) 661-9333 Fax 661-3982
 Tim Nielsen, Editor

INDIAN NEWS
United Indiamn Women, Inc.
5352 SE 89th St.
Portland, OR 97266

INDIAN NEWS: WEEK-IN-REVIEW
Bureau of Indian Affairs
1951 Constitution Ave., N.W.
Mail Stop 4160 MIB
Washington, D.C. 20240

INDIAN NOTES
P.O. Box 66
Wellpinit, Washington 99040

INDIAN PROGRAMS
University of Arizona
Tucson, AZ 85721

INDIAN PROGRESS
Associated Committee of Friends
on Indian Affairs
P.O. Box 2326
Richmond, IN 47375
 (317) 962-9169

Harold Smuck, Editor
News about Native Americans at Friends Centers in Oklahoma, Alabama, and Iowa. Published three times per year and sent to those persons interested in India affairs and those persons contributing to the Committee. Complimentary copies sent upon written request. Begun 1869.

INDIAN QUEST
708 S. Lindon Place
Tempe, AZ 85281

INDIAN READER
806 E. Brooks Rd.
Memphis, TN 38116

THE INDIAN RELIC TRADER
P.O. Box 88
Sunbury, OH 43074
Janie Jinks-Weidner, Editor
Features articles on prehistoric relics, current archaeological findings and research; calendar of events and meetings; sources for books and supplies. Advertising. Subscription: $8/year; sample copies available, $1.00 each.

INDIAN RECORD
Bureau of Indian Affairs
1951 Constitution Ave., N.W.
Washington, D.C. 20245

INDIAN REPORT
Friends Committee on National Legislation
245 Second St., NE
Washington, DC 20010
(202) 547-6000 Fax 547-6019
Melissa Shirk, Editor
Quarterly newsletter containing articles focusing on issues and national legislation of interest to American Indians and Alaskan natives. Complimentary copies available upon request. Begun 1977.

INDIAN STUDIES QUARTERLY
400 Caldwell Hall, Cornell University
Ithaca, NY 14853
(607) 256-8402
Ray Fougnier, Director
Jose Barreiro, Editor
Contains articles, national tribal news, media notes, poetry, and book reviews. Published quarterly. Subscription: $12/year, U.S.; $18/year, Canada; $28/year, Europe.

INDIAN TIME
Akwesasne Notes
P.O. Box 196, Mohawk Nation
Rooseveltown, NY 13683-0196
(518) 358-9535/9531
Promotes unity for all Mohawk groups through communicating information on the environment, health, women, youth and Iroquois history; also Native American and Canadian news. An eight page weekly newspaper of the St. Regis Mohawk Reservation (New York-Quebec-Ontario.) Advertising. Subscription: $33/year, U.S.; $40/year, Canada. Sample copies, $1.00 each. Begun 1983.

INDIAN TOWNSHIP NEWSLETTER
Princeton, ME 04668

INDIAN TRADER
Indian Trader, Inc.
P.O. Box 1421
Gallup, NM 87305
(505) 722-6694

Martin Link, Publisher; William Donovan, Editor
Covers American Indian arts and crafts, cultures and history, contemporary Indian news items, and western Americana. Book reviews. Monthly newspaper. 4,000 cir. $2/copy; $18/year; $30/year, foreign. Advertising. Begun 1969.

INDIAN TRUTH
Indian Rights Association
c/o Janney Montgomery
1601 Market St.
Philadelphia, PA 19103
(215) 665-4523
Janney Montgomery, Executive Officer
Highlights news events from throughout Indian country with feature articles on current, and critical topics; coverage of major Indian news from Congress, the Courts, and Indian country. Book reviews. Bimonthly news journal. Subscription: $20/year. Complimentary copies on exchange basis only.

INDIAN VOICE
American Indian Folklore Group
P.O. Box 55
Stillwater, MN 55082

INDIAN VOICE
Southwest Indian Polytechnic Institute
P.O. Box 10146
Albuquerque, NM 87184

INDIAN VOICE, STOWW
P.O. Box 578
Sumner, WA 98390

INDIAN YOUTH OF AMERICA NEWSLETTER
Indian Youth of America, Inc.
P.O. Box 2786
609 Badgerow Bldg.
Sioux City, IA 51106
(800) 828-4492; (712) 252-3230
Patricia Trudell Gordon & Sharon Gullette, Edis.
Contains articles; and short fiction by Native American writers. Also a calendar of events and career opportunities. Quarterly. Complimentary copies available upon request. No charge. Advertising. Begun 1987.

INDIAN WORLD
3110 State Office Annex
117 University Ave.
St. Paul, MN 55101

INDIAN YOUTH OF AMERICA NEWSLETTER
P.O. Box 2786
Sioux City, IA 51106
(800) 828-4492; (712) 276-0794
Patricia Trudell Gordon, Executive Director
A quarterly of fiction and poetry from Native American authors. $2.50 each issue.

INDIANS OF ALL TRIBES CLUB
P.O. Box 777
Monroe, WA 98272

INDIGENOUS WOMAN
Indigenous Women's Network
P.O. Box 174
Lake Elmo, MN 55042
Articles touch on the rights of political prisoners, environmental struggles, and Native spirituality. Profiles of indigenous women who have impacted their community, such as Norma Kassi, a Native Gwichin of the Athapaskan nation. Art of indigenous women is featured. Semiannual, $25.00.

INDIGENOUS WORLD
275 Grand View Ave., Apt. 103
San Francisco, CA 94114

THE INFOMANT
University of South Dakota
414 E. Clark St.
Vermillion, SD 57069

INI-MI-KWA-ZOO-MIN
Minnesota Chippewa Tribe
P.O. Box 217
Cass Lake, MN 56633
Betty Blue, Editor

INTER-COM NEWSLETTER
Native American Educational Service
2838 W. Peterson Ave.
Chicago, IL 60659
(312) 761-5000
Faith Smith, Editor
Monthly newsletter.

INTER-TRIBAL AMERICA MAGAZINE
Inter-Tribal Indian Ceremonial Association
P.O. Box 1
Church Rock, NM 87311
(505) 863-3896
Laurence D. Linford, Editor
Reports on the activities of the Association. Quarterly newsletter.

INTER-TRIBAL ASSOCIATION–NEWSLETTER
Inter-Tribal Association
Vietnam Era Veterans Center
1223 Sherry Lane
Cherokee, OK 74801
(405) 273-6790
Provides news of interest on American Indians who served in the Vietnam War. Quarterly.

**INTER-TRIBAL TIMBER
COUNCIL NEWSLETTER**
Intertribal Timber Council
4370 NE Halsey St.
Portland, OR 97213

INTER-TRIBAL TIMES NEWSPAPER
Inter-Tribal Council, Inc.
P.O. Box 1308
Miami, OK 74355
(918) 542-4486 Fax 540-2500
Liz Gaines, Editor
Newakis Burkybile, Advertising Sales Rep.
Involves at least seven Northeastern Oklahoma area tribal newsletters, each using a full page to announce their monthly news. Also included is a national, state, and local news that holds intyerest for local tribal members. Monthly. 10,000 circulation in northeastern Oklahoma, Arkansas, Missouri and Kansas. $18/year. Advertising. Begun 1994.

INTER-TRIBAL VOICE
1740 W. 41st St.
Tulsa, OK 74107

INTERTRIBAL NEWS
Native American Center
Fort Lewis College, College Hts.
Durango, CO 81137
(303) 247-7221 Fax 247-7108
Rick Wheelock, Faculty Sponsor
Indian student tabloid-size newspaper. Published biweekly - Fall & Winter trimesters only. 1,000 cir (approx. 450 Indian students). No charge. Advertising accepted. Begun 1981.

ISLETA EAGLE PRIDE
Isleta Elementary School
P.O. Box 312
Isleta, NM 87022
 (505) 869-2321
School newspaper.

ITZA VOICE
Kaweah Indian Nation
P.O. Box 3121
Hutchinson, KS 67504-3121
 (316) 665-3614
 Chief Thunderbird Webber, Editor
Quarterly journal of the Kaweah Indian Nation.
Book reviews. 5,000 cir. $5.95/year. Advertising.

J

JICARILLA CHIEFTAIN
Jicarilla Apache Tribe
P.O. Box 507
Dulce, NM 87528-
 (505) 759-3242 Ext. 224 Fax 759-3005
 Mary Polanco, Editor; Lori Vicenti, Co-Editor
 Shane S. Valdez, Computer Specialist
Biweekly newsletter containing information of general importance to tribal members, as well as national and state news pertaining to other tribes and Indian affairs. Book reviews. 1,200 cir. $12/year, local; $24/year, foreign. Advertising. Begun 1960.

JOURNAL OF ALASKA NATIVE ARTS
Institute of Alaska Native Arts
P.O. Box 70769
Fairbanks, AK 99707
 (907) 456-7491 Fax 451-7268
 Jan Steinbright, Editor
A 16-page quarterly journal containing interviews with Alaska Native artists; news of opportunities of interest to artists; and photographs, poetry and issues affecting Alaska Native artists. 2,700 cir. $25/year.

JOURNAL OF AMERICAN FOLKLORE
American Folklore Society
Maryland State Arts Council
15 W. Mulberry St.
Baltimore, MD 21201
 (301) 685-6740
Published 6x/year.

JOURNAL OF AMERICAN INDIAN EDUCATION
Center for Indian Education
Arizona State University, Box 871311
Tempe, AZ 85287-1311
 (602) 965-6292 Fax 965-8115
 Dr. Karen Swisher, Editor
 Laura Williams & Rick Noguchi, Staff
Publishes papers directly related to the education of North American Indians and Alaskan Natives. Emphasis is on research - basic and applied. Published three times per year (October, January, and May.) Submits five complimentary copies of the Journal to authors of accepted manuscripts. 700 cir. $16/year, U.S.; $18.50/year, Canada & foreign. Available on microfilm from Xerox University Microfilms, 300 North Zeeb Rd., Ann Arbor, Michigan 48106. Begun 1961.

JOURNAL OF AMERICAN INDIAN FAMILY RESEARCH
Histree
23011 Moulton Parkway , D-12
Laguna Hills, CA 92653-1223
 (714) 859-1659
 Larry Watson, Editor
Records and research aids for American Indian family research. Book reviews. Quarterly. 600 cir. $25/year; $7/copy. Advertising. Begun 1980.

JOURNAL OF AMERICAN INDIAN RESEARCH MONTHLY NEWSLETTER
Histree
23011 Moulton Parkway , D-12
Laguna Hills, CA 92653-1223
 (714) 859-1659
 Larry Watson, Editor
Covers current events and activities in the Native American community; calendar of events. 100 cir. $59/year. Begun 1988.

JOURNAL OF ARIZONA HISTORY
Arizona Historical Society
949 East Second St.
Tucson, AZ 85719
Contains articles, critical essays, and book reviews on the history of Arizona and the Southwest, and northern Mexico when appropriate. Articles often include appraisals of American Indian life and lore, the Indian wars and Anglo-Indian relations. Published quarterly.

JOURNAL OF CALIFORNIA AND GREAT BASIN ANTHROPOLOGY
Department of Anthropology
University of California
Riverside, CA 92521-0001
 (714) 787-7317
 Philip J. Wilke, Editor
Publishes original manuscripts on the ethnography, languages, arts, archaeology, and prehistory of the Native peoples of California, the Great Basin, and Baja California. Book reviews. Semiannual. $18/year. Advertising. Begun 1974. Back issues may be obtained from Coyote Press, P.O. Box 3377, Salinas, California 93912.

JOURNAL OF CHEROKEE STUDIES
Museum of the Cherokee Indian
P.O. Box 770-A
Cherokee, NC 28719
 (704) 497-3481
 Duane King, Editor
Published semiannually.

JOURNAL OF NEW WORLD ARCHAEOLOGY
Institute of Archaeology
405 Hilgard Ave.
Los Angeles, CA 90024
 (213) 825-4711
 Dr. Ernestine S. Elster
Contains contributions on original research throughout America. Published infrequently. $20 per issue.

JOURNAL OF THE WEST
Box 1009, 1531 Yuma
Manhattan, KS 66502-4228
 (913) 539-1888
 Robin Higham, Editor
Covers western history and culture containing articles, book reviews, pieces about the West. A Quarterly. Advertising accepted. $30/year, individuals; $40/year, institutions. Begun 1962.

K

KA NUHOU
Hawaii Home Lands Dept.
Community Relations/Information Office
335 Merchant St., Room 342
Honolulu, HI 96813
 (808) 586-3822
Monthly newsleter providing information to and about the beneficiaries of the Hawaiian Homes Commission Act of 1920.

KA WAI OLA O
Office of Hawaiian Affairs
711 Kapi'olani Blvd., Suite 500
Honolulu, HI 96813
 (808) 586-3777
Monthly newspaper with articles and information for the Native Hawaiian community. 55.000 circ. Begun 1982. No charge.

KALI-WISAKS
Nobert Hill Center
P.O. Box 365
Oneida, WI 54415

KALIHUI SAKS
P.O. Box 365
Oneida, WI 54155

KANA KAWITAQ
Kodiak Area Native Association
Kodiak, AK 99615

KARIWENHAWI NEWSLETTER
St. Regis Mohawk Reservation
RR 1, Box 14C
Hogansburg, NY 13655
 (518) 358-2272
 Carol White, Editor
Covers news of the Reservation community and the Akwesasne Library/Cultural Center. Monthly. 1,100 cir. No charge. Advertising. Begun 1970.

KE KIA'I, THE GUARDIAN
Native Hawaiian Advisory Council
1088 Bishop St., Suite 1204
Honolulu, HI 96813
 (808) 523-1445 Fax 599-4380
Monthly newsletter with information to the native Hawaiian community assisting them in asserting and exercising control over their resources.

KEE-YOKS
Swinomish Tribal Community
P.O. Box 388
La Connor, WA 98257

KEYAPI NEWS
P.O. Box 200
Fort Thompson, SD 57339

KINZUA PLANNING NEWSLETTER
Seneca Nation, P.O. Box 231
Salamanca, NY 14779

KIOWA INDIAN NEWS
Kiowa Tribe
P.O. Box 397
Carnegie, OK 73015
 (405) 347-2875
 Deborah Ahtone, Editor
Monthly tribal newspaper. No charge to tribal members.

KIOWA VIDEO
Kiowa Nation of Oklahoma
P.O. Box 369
Carnegie, OK 73015

KIVA: THE JOURNAL OF SOUTHWESTERN ANTHROPOLOGY & HISTORY
Arizona Archaeological & Historical Society
Arizona State Museum, University of Arizona
Tucson, AZ 85721
  (602) 621-4011
  Gayle Harrison Hartmann, Editor
Covers original research relating to the prehistoric and historic archaeology and ethnology of the southwestern U.S. and northwestern Mexico. Quarterly. 1,100 cir. $25/year.

KLAH'CHE'MIN
Squaxin Tribal Center
SE 70 Squaxin Lane
Shelton, WA 98584

KLALLAM NEWSLETTER
Port Gamble-Klallam Nation Tribal Council
P.O. Box 280
Kingston, WA 98346

KLAMATH NEWSLETTER
Klamath Tribe
P.O. Box 436
Chiloquin, OR 97624
  (503) 783-2219
Monthly tribal newsletter

KROEBER ANTHROPOLOGY SOCIETY PAPERS
Dept. of Anthropology, University of California
Berkeley, CA 94720-0001
  (415) 642-6932
Contains original research in all aspects of anthropology and related disciplines; also bibliographies and texts. Biannual journal. 450 cir. $15/copy. Begun 1949.

KUMTUX
Native American Task Force
Church Councl of Greater Seattle
4759 15th Ave. NE
Seattle, WA 98105
  Jeanette Mills, Editor
Monthly calendar of Indian-related events in Washington State. $18/yr.

L

LAC COURTE OREILLES JOURNAL
LCO Graphic Arts, Route 2
Hayward, WI 54843
  (715) 634-8934

LAC DU FLAMBEAU UPDATE
LDF Tribal Office
P.O. Box 67
Lac du Flambeau, WI 54538

LAGH'-WEGH A-MOO-E'SHA
Confederated Tribes of the Umatilla
P.O. Box 638
Pendleton, OR 97801

THE LAKOTA FUND NEWSLETTER
P.O. Box 340
Kyle, SD 57750
  (605) 455-2500

Elsie Meeks, Executive Director
A fund formed to help build a private sector economy on the Reservation by providing loans and technical assistance & business training; and arts & crafts marketing assistance tribal members.

LAKOTA OYATE-KI
Oregon State Penitentiary
2605 State St.
Salem, OR 97310

THE LAKOTA TIMES
1920 Lombardy Dr., Box 2180
Rapid City, SD 57709
  (605) 341-0011 Fax 341-6940
  Tim Giago, Publisher
  Amanda War Bonnett, Editor
  Avis Little Eagle, Associate Editor
  Konnie LeMay, Managing Editor
  Karen Little Thunder, General Manager
A weekly newspaper serving 21 Indian reservations in North and South Dakota, Nebraska and Montana. With the addition in 1991 of a Washington, D.C. bureau, the Lakota Times also covers the U.S. Capitol from an Indian perspective. 10,000 cir. (the largest independent Indian-owned wekly). $30/year, local; $38/year, others; $53/year, foreign. Advertising. Begun 1980.

LEONARD PELTIER FREEDOM WEEKEND NEWS
53 W. Jackson Blvd. #557
Chicago, IL 60604
  (312) 427-4457

LETAN WANKATAKIYA
Dakota Hall, Room 18
University of South Dakota
Vermillion, SD 57069

LINCOLN INDIAN JOURNAL
Lincoln Indian Center
1100 Military Rd.
Lincoln, NE 68508

LINKAGES
TCI, Inc.
3410 Garfield St., N.W.
Washington, DC 20007
  (202) 333-6350 Fax 965-0246
  Thomas Clary, Publisher; Nancy Gale, Editor
Covers American Indian child welfare; BIA social service progams; Indian family law; Indians against alcohol & drug abuse. News of conferences and workshops. Book reviews. Bimonthly newsletter. 4,500 cir. Begun 1984.

LORE
Friends of the Museum, Inc.
Milwaukee Public Museum
800 West Wells St.
Milwaukee, WI 53233
  (414) 278-2752
Published quarterly.

LUMBEE OUTREACH
Lumbee Regional Development Association
P.O. Box 68
Pembroke, NC 28372

LUMMI INDIAN NEWS
2616 Kwina Rd.
Bellingham, WA 98226
  (206) 734-8180
A bi-weekly community newsletter.

LUMMI SQUOL QUOL
2616 Kwina Rd.
Bellingham, Washington 98226
  (206) 734-8180

M

MAINE INDIAN NEWSLETTER
Maine Indian Affairs Commission
State Health Station No. 38
Augusta, ME 04333

MAKAH DAKAH
P.O. Box 547
Neah Bay, WA 98357

MAKAH VIEWERS
P.O. Box 115
Neah Bay, WA 98357

MANASSEH-JOURNAL OF THE TRIBES
Eagle Communications
29 Brimmer St.
Brewer, ME 04412
  Reginald Roberts, Jr., Publisher
Quarterly. $24/year.

MANATABA MESSENGER
P.O. Box 810
Parker, AZ 85344

MANDAN, HIDATSA & ARIKARA TIMES
Three Affiliated Tribal Council
P.O. Box 220, Tribal Administration Bldg.
New Town, ND 58763
  (701) 627-4781 Fax 627-3805

MANIILAQ DIRECTORY
Maniilaq Association
P.o. Box 256
Kotzebue AK 99752
  (907) 442-3311
  Marie N. Greene, President
Annual directory of members.

MANY SMOKES METIS/EARTH
Awareness Magazine
Bear Tribe Medicine Society
P.O. Box 9167
Spokane, WA 99206

MARIN MUSEUM OF THE AMERICAN INDIAN–MUSEUM QUARTERLY
P.O. Box 864, 2200 Novato Blvd.
Novato, CA 94948
  (415) 897-4064

MARYLAND AMERICAN INDIAN DIRECTORY
Maryland Commission on Indian Affairs
100 Community Place
Crownsville, MD 21032
  (410) 514-7651

MARKUP
National Council of Churches
110 Maryland Ave., NE
Washington, DC 20002

MASINAIGAN
Great Lakes Indian Fish & Wildlife Commission
P.O. Box 9
Odanah, WI 54861
  (715) 682-6619
Monthly newspaper.

THE MASTERKEY
Southwest Museum
234 Museum Dr., BOX 41558
Los Angeles, CA 90065
(213) 221-2164 Fax 224-8223
Steven Le Blanc, Editor
Devoted to the anthropology and archaeology of the Americas; contains articles, book reviews, and a conservation column. Book reviews. Quarterly journal. 5,500 cir. $15/year. Begun 1927.

MAWIW-KILUN
Tribal Governors, Inc.
Indian Township
Princeton, ME 04668
Contains community news, tribal activities, health and social service articles. Published bimonthly.

MAY WUTCHE AQUE'NE
American Indians for Development
P.O. Box 117, 236 W. Main St.
Meridien, CT 06450
(203) 238-4009
Patricia Benedict, Editor
Contains historical articles on social issues, culture, medicine, archaeology; literature on or about American Indians. Primary focus is on Connecticut, but encompass the U.S. and areas of interest of aboriginal issues throughout the world. Published bi-yearly. $5 per issue plus $1 for shipping. Donations accepted. Advertising accepted. Begun 1989.

McKINLEY MISSION NEWSLETTER
American Indian Evangelical Society
P.O. Box 231
Toppenish, WA 98848

A MEASURE OF EXCELLENCE
Inter-Tribal Indian Ceremonial Association
P.O. Box 1
Church Rock, NM 87311
(505) 863-3896
Laurence D. Linford, Editor
A full-color annual publication focusing on each year's top art award-winners at the Ceremonial.

MCRC NEWSLETTER
P.O. Box 95
Neah Bay, WA 98357

MEDICINE BAG
Salt LakeCity Indian Health Center
508 East South Temple, No. 219
Salt Lake City, UT 84102
(801) 532-2034

MEDIUM RARE
Native American Journalists Association
1433 E. Franklin Ave., Suite 11
Minneapolis, MN 55404-2135
(612) 874-8833 Fax 874-9007
Gordon Regguinti, Editor
Theresa Lumbar & Robyn Dudley, Staff
Bi-monthly newsletter distributed to members of the association. The only publication by, for and about Native American communicators. 1,800 cir.

MEETING GROUND
D'Arcy McNickle Center for the
History of the American Indian
Newberry Library
60 W. Walton St.
Chicago, IL 60610
(312) 943-9090
Jay Miller, Editor
Contains information on Center activities,
research, teaching materials. Book reviews. Semi-annual newsletter. 4,000 cir. No charge. Begun 1974.

MENOMINEE TRIBAL NEWS
Menominee Indian Tribe
P.O. Box 397
Keshena, WI 54135
(715) 799-5168 Fax 799-4525
Yvonne M. Kaquatosh-Aragon, Editor
Michelle Mahkimetas &
Michael Sturdevant, Reporters
Biweekly tribal newspaper. 1,100 cir. 50¢/copy. Advertising. Begun 1976.

MICCOSUKEE EVERGLADES NEWS
Miccosukee Tribe of Florida
Box 440021, Tamiami Station
Miami, FL 33144

THE MICHIGAN INDIAN
Baker Olen Bldg. West, Room 313
3423 N. Logan St.
Lansing, MI 48926

MID-AMERICA ALL INDIAN CENTER NEWSLETTER
650 North Seneca
Wichita, KS 67203

MILLE LAC NEWS
Star Route
Onamia, MN 56395

MINNESOTA HISTORY
Minnesota Historical Society
690 Cedar St.
St. Paul, MN 55101
Deals with events, places, and personalities in Minnesota history, often touching upon events related to Minnesota's Indian tribes. Quarterly.

MINNESOTA WINNEBAGO NEWSLETTER
St. Paul Urban League
401 Selby Ave.
St. Paul, MN 55103

MISKWEEWA PINAYWIN
Lakes Publishing Co.
Detroit Lakes, Minnesota 56501

MITTARK, WAMPANOAG INDIANS
P.O. Box 1048
Mashpee, Massachusetts 02649

THE MOCCASIN
P.O. Box 1711
Globe, AZ 85502-1711

MOCCASIN TELEGRAPH
Community Action Program
Grand Portage, MN 55605

MOCCASIN TELEGRAPH
2951 Ellenwood Dr.
Fairfax, VA 22031
(703) 280-1028 (phone & fax)
Lee Francis, III, PhD, Editor
Joseph Bruchac, III, Co-Editor
D.L. "Don" Birchfield, Contributing Editor
A monthly news journal for Native writers and storytellers particularly members of Wordcraft Circle of Native Writers and Storytellers. Includes original poetry, fiction, and essays by Native writers. Also reports on writer's conferences and workshops, and profiles of Native authors. $24/yr. $2 for sample copy.

MOCCASIN TRAIL
Oklahoma Tribes Assistance Program
1840 East 15th St.
Tulsa, OK 74114

MONTANA INTER-TRIBAL POLICY BOARD NEWSLETTER
Department of Indian Affairs
6301 Grand Ave.
Billings, MT 59103

MONTANA, THE MAGAZINE OF WESTERN HISTORY
Montana Historical Society
Roberts and Sixth Ave.
Helena, MT 59601
Deals with Western history, often touching upon the Indian's involvement. Quarterly.

THE MORNING STAR PEOPLE
St. Labre Indian School
Ashland, MT 59003

MOUNTAIN LIGHT NEWS AND VIEWS FROM THE SOUTHWEST
Southwest learning Centers of Santa Fe
P.O. Box 8627
Santa Fe, NM 87504
Semiannual.

MUKLUKS HEMCUNGA
Organization of the Forgotten American
P.O. Box 1257
Klamath Falls, OR 97601

MULTICULTURAL EDUCATION
Caddo Gap Press
3145 Geary Blvd., Suite 275
San Francisco, CA 94118
(415) 750-9978
Quarterly journal of the National Association for Multicultural Education (NAME). Features articles, interviews, practical advice, reviews, and resources for multicultural educators. 40 pp. $40/year.

THE MULTICULTURAL LINK
Paramount Publishing
Secondary Education Group
113 Sylvan Ave.
Englewood Cliffs, NJ 07632
(201) 461-7992
Irving Hamer, Publisher
Educator-based newsletter features brief essays, book reviews, practical activities, and resources. Subscriptions are complimentary.

MULTICULTURAL REVIEW
Greenwood Publishing Group
88 Post Rd. W., Box 5007
Westport, CT 0686-3571 Fax 222-1502
Brenda Mitchell-Powell, Editor
Quarterly journal that reviews of multicultural materials and information on the subject of multiculturalism. $59/year. Advertising.

THE MUSCOGEE NATION NEWS
The Muscogee (Creek) Nation
P.O. Box 580
Okmulgee, OK 74447
(918) 756-8700 Fax 758-0824
Jim Wolfe, Editor
Stephanie Berryhill, Associate Editor
Monthly tribal news tabloid of the Muscogee (Creek) Nation. No charge to tribal members. 8,100 cir. $12/year to non-tribal members. Begun 1971.

MUSEUM OF THE AMERICAN INDIAN NEWSLETTER
The George Gustav Heye Center
Smithsonian Institution
One Bowling Green
New York, NY 10004
 (212) 283-2420
 Elizabeth A. Beim, Editor
Quarterly. Begun 1977.

MUSEUM OF THE FUR TRADE QUARTERLY
HC 74, Box 18
Chadron, NE 69337

MUSEUM OF THE GREAT PLAINS NEWSLETTER
P.O. Box 68
Lawton, OK 73502
 (405) 353-5675

MUSEUM OF INDIAN HERITAGE NEWSLETTER
500 W. Washington St.
Indianapolis, IN 46204
 (317) 293-4488
Quarterly.

MUSTANG NEWS
Little Wound School Board
P.O. Box 500
Kyle, SD 57752-0500

N

NA TINI XWE
Hoopa Valley Business Council
P.O. Box 1438
Hoopa, CA 95546

NACIE NEWSLETTER
National Advisory Council on Indian Education
Switzer Bldg., 330 C St., SW #4072
Washington, DC 20202
 (202) 205-8353 Fax 205-8897

NARF LEGAL REVIEW
Native American Rights Fund
1506 Broadway
Boulder, CO 80302
 (303) 447-8786
 Susan Arkekete, Editor
Covers NARF's involvement in Indian legal issues.
Discusses current Indian law issues. Staff news,
activities, and announcements of NARF services
and publications. Quarterly newsletter. No charge.
Begun 1973.

NARRAGANSETT INDIAN TRIBE NEWSLETTER
P.O. Box 268
Charleston, RI 02813

NASP NEWS
Native American Student Program
University of California-233 Library South
Riverside, CA 92521
 (714) 787-3821

NATION NOTES
Penobscot Nation Newsletter
Community Bldg.
6 River Rd., Indian Island
Old Town, ME 04468

NATIONAL AMERICAN INDIAN CATTLEMAN'S ASSOCIATION NEWSLETTER & YEARBOOK
c/o Tim Foster, President
1541 Foster Rd.
Toppenish, WA 98948
 (509) 854-1329
Monthly newsletter.

NATIONAL AMERICAN INDIAN COURT JUDGES ASSOCIATION NEWSLETTER
1000 Connecticut Ave., N.W., 501
Washington, D.C. 20036

NATIONAL ASSOCIATION OF BLACKFEET INDIANS BULLETIN
P.O. Box 340
Browning, MT 59417

NATIONAL CENTER FOR AMERICAN INDIAN ALTERNATIVE EDUCATION JOURNAL
Box 18329, Capitol Hill Station
Denver, CO 80218
 (303) 861-1052
Published biennially.

NATIONAL CENTER FOR AMERIAN INDIAN ENTERPRISE DEVELOPMENT REPORTER & REVIEW
953 E. Juanita Ave.
Mesa. AZ 85204
 (602) 831-7524
 Steven L.A. Stallings, Editor
The voice of American Indian business.
Quarterly journals.

NATIONAL CONGRESS OF AMERICAN INDIANS NEWS
900 Pennsylvania Ave., SE
Washington, DC 20003
 (202) 546-9404

NATIONAL COALITION TO SUPPORT INDIAN TREATIES NEWSLETTER
814 N.E. 40th St.
Seattle, WA 98105

NATIONAL INDIAN ARTS & CRAFTS DIRECTORY
National Indian Traders Association
3575 South Fox
Englewood, CO 80110
 (303) 762-6579
Published biennially.

NATIONAL INDIAN EDUCATION NEWSLETTER
1819 H St., NW, Suite 800
Washington, DC 20006
Published bimonthly.

NATIONAL INDIAN HEALTH BOARD (NIHB) HEALTH REPORTER
P.O. Box 6940
Denver, CO 80206
 (303) 270-5598
Bimonthly newsletter, No charge.

NATIONAL INDIAN SOCIAL WORKERS ASSOCIATION - THE ASSOCIATION
P.O. Box 27463
Albuquerque, NM 87125
 Mary Kihega, Sec.-Treas.
Contains a calendar of events and news of members, research, and awards. Quarterly newsletter. Price included in membership dues.

THE NATIONS NEWS
Nations Ministries
P.O. Box 70
Honobia, OK 74549
 (918) 755-4570
 Riley Donica, Editor
Quarterly newsletter.

NATIVE AMERICAN ANNUAL
Native American Publishing Co., Inc.
P.O. Box 6338, 760 Mays Blvd., Suite 6
Incline Village, NV 89450
 (702) 831-7726
 Margaret Clark-Price, Editor
A non-political media created as a communicative tool to assist in cultural awareness profiling tribal history, location and present day activities throughout the U.S. $8.95. Quarterly supplements.

NATIVE AMERICAN AUTHORS DISTRIBUTION PROJECT
The Greenfield Press
2 Middle Grove Rd., P.O. Box 308
Greenfield Center, NY 12833
Distributes work only by Native American authors, more than 360 titles from 80 different publishers, mostly books, but including current and back issues of Native periodicals. Catalog.

NATIVE AMERICAN COMMUNITY & CAREER
P.O. Box 1281
Scottsdale, AZ 85252

THE NATIVE AMERICAN CONNECTION
Spotted Horse Tribal Gifts
P.O. Box 414
Coos Bay, OR 97420
 Diane McAlister, Editor
Monthly newsletter covering Native Amrerican craftmaking.

NATIVE AMERICAN CONNECTIONS
Gloria J. Davis, Publisher
P.O. Box 579
Winchester, CA 92596
 (909) 926-1728
 Dayne E. Lopez, Editor
A yearbook/directory, published in July for Native Americans and businesses. Begun 1993.

NATIVE AMERICAN COUNCIL
204 Hagestad Student Center
University of Wisconsin
River Falls, WI 54022

NATIVE AMERICAN COUNCIL NEWS
204 Hagested Student Center
University of Wisconsin
River Falls, WI 54022

NATIVE AMERICAN CULTURAL CENTER NEWSLETTER
2115 E. Main St.
Rochester, NY 14609

NATIVE AMERICAN DIRECTORY
National Native American Co-op
P.O. Box 1000
San Carlos, AZ 85550
 (602) 622-4900
 Fred Synder, Editor
Provides information about American Indian events, organizations, and crafts. Includes pow-wows & celebrations, Indian rodeos, conventions, arts & crafts shows; also, Indian crafts guilds & cooperatives and Indian performing artists, dancers and exhibitors. Published periodically.

NATIVE AMERICAN EDUCATION PROGRAM NEWSLETTER
234 W. 109th St., Room 507
New York, NY 10025

NATIVE AMERICAN EDUCATIONAL SERVICE RULE
2838 W. Peterson Ave.
Chicago, IL 60659
(312) 761-5000
Faith Smith, Editor
Quarterly journal.

NATIVE AMERICAN JOURNALIST ASSOCIATION NEWS
School of Journalism & Mass Communication
University of Colorado
Campus Box 287
Boulder, CO 80309
(303) 492-7397

NATIVE AMERICAN LAW DIGEST
The Falmouth Institute, Inc.
3918 Prosperity Ave., Suite 302
Fairfax, VA 22031
(703) 641-9100 Fax 641-1558
Gregory Smith, Esq., Editor
A monthly summary of all court and administrative decisions significant to the Indian community. This comprehensive law digest covers all issues affecting tribes and tribal organizations. In addition to summarized cases, the digest publishes numerous law review articles covering topics such as Indian gaming, Indian taxation, sovereign immunity and tribal self-governance. $299 per year. Includes in the subscription price is a 3-ring binder and tabs for easy storage and retrieval of the cases and articles.

NATIVE AMERICAN POLICY NETWORK NEWSLETTER
Barry University, 11300 NE 2nd Ave.
Miami Shores, FL 33161
(305) 899-3000 Fax 899-3279
Prof. Michael E. Melody, Editor
An offset newsletter for 425 policy makers, political scientists and Native American leaders, issued three times per year. Articles and news relevant to Native American policy issues. Book reviews. 1,500 cir. $5/year. Begun 1980.

NATIVE AMERICAN PUBLIC BROADCASTING CONSORTIUM NEWSLETTER
P.O. Box 83111
Lincoln, NE 68501
(402) 472-3522
Matthew Jones, Editor
Quarterly newsletter. 1,100 cir. Begun 1981.

NATIVE AMERICAN SCHOLAR
Bureau of Indian Affairs
Higher Education Program
P.O. Box 26567
Albuquerque, NM 87125-6567
(505) 766-3170

NATIVE AMERICAN STUDENTS OF THE NORTHWEST NEWSLETTER
University of Idaho
Moscow, ID 83843

NATIVE AMERICAN STUDIES
Edwin Mellon Press
240 Portage Rd., Box 450
Lewiston, NY 14092
(716) 754-8566 Fax 754-4335

NATIVE ARTS UPDATE
ATLATL
2303 N. Central, Suite 104
Phoenix, AZ 85004
(602) 253-2731 Fax 256-6385
Wendy Weston Ben, Editor
Quarterly newsletter promoting contemporary Native American artists and cultural organizations. Includes issues, regional highlights, interviews, exhibition listings, opportunities, and book reviews. 2,000 cir. $25/year.

NATIVE CALIFORNIAN INDIAN NEWSLETTER
Office Planning/Research
1400 10th St., 109
Sacramento, CA 95814

THE NATIVE MAGAZINE
Tod Bedrosian, Publisher
7427 Braeridge Way
Sacramento, CA 95831
(916) 421-5121 (phone & fax)
Deborah Hirsch, Editor
Becky Lemon & Virginia Willis, Staff
Monthly magazine with readership primarily in california and Nevada. $15 per year; $2/copy.

THE NATIVE MONTHLY READER
RedSun Institute
P.O. Box 122
Crestone, CO 81131
(719) 256-4848 Fax 256-4849
A scholastic newspaper for grades 5 through 12, reaches over 5,000 students monthly throughout the U.S. and Canada. Focuses on Native American topics presented in a positive format, highlighting the numerous contributions Native people are making in the arts, their culture and tradition.

NATIVE NATIONS
310 W. 52nd St.
New York, NY 10019
(212) 765-9731
Alex Ewen, Editor
Monthly magazine. Begun 1991.

THE NATIVE NEVADAN
Reno-Sparks Indian Colony
98 Colony Rd.
SPARKS, NV 89502-1288
(702) 359-9449
Becky Lemon, Editor
Covers all facets of Native American life, primarily in Nevada and California. Book reviews. Monthly newspaper. 2,200 cir. $15/year; $2/copy. Advertising. Begun 1964.

NATIVE NEWS
School District 4J Indian Education Program
3411-A Willamette St.
Eugene, OR 97405
(503) 687-3489
Twila Souers & Ann Dunn, Editors
For families and Native American children enrolled in Eugene, Bethel and Fern Ridge School District public schools, and for Native American community members. Monthly newsletter. Complimentary copies available upon request.

NATIVE NEWS & B.I.A. BULLETIN
Bureau of Indian Affairs
P.O. Box 3-8000
Juneau, AK 99801

NATIVE PEOPLES
5333 N. 7th St. #224C
Phoenix, AZ 85014

(602) 252-2236 Fax 252-6180
Gary Avey, Editor & Publisher
A quarterly magazine portraying the arts and lifeways of Native peoples of the Americas. Includes book and audio/video reviews, Native American foods, childrens corner, and in the news section on Native American role models.. Quarterly journal. $5/copy; $18/year; $25/year, foreign. Advertising. Begun 1987.

NATIVE PLAYWRIGHTS NEWSLETTER
P.O. Box 1364
Madison, WI 53701
Quarterly of news and reviews of Native playwrights' works (i.e. Bruce King, LeAnne Howe, Carlotta Kauffman, etc.) History of Native theater. $10/yr.

NATIVE PRESS RESEARCH JOURNAL
University of Arkansas, Little Rock
Stabler Hall 502, 2801 S. University
Little Rock, AR 72204
Daniel F. Littlefield, Jr.
Suspended publication. Back issues available.

NATIVE SELF-SUFFICIENCY
Seventh Generation Fund
Tribal Sovereignty Program
P.O. Box 10
Forestville, CA 95436-0010
(707) 887-1559
Paula Hammett, Editor
Focuses on practical information for increasing community self-reliance. Emphasis is on appropriate technologies and how they can and are being used as alternative tools for economic development on Indian land. Book reviews. Quarterly newspaper. 2,000 cir. $6/year. Begun 1978.

NATIVE SUN
Detroit American Indian Center
22720 Plymouth Rd.
Detroit, MI 48239
(313) 535-2966
Andrew Butterfly, Editor
Reports on news and activities of the center; and issues of importance to American Indians of Wayne County, Michigan. Monthly newsletter. 200 cir. $1/copy; $8/year. Begun 1975.

NATIVE VISION
American Indian Contemporary Arts
Monadnock Bldg.
685 Market St., Suite 250
San Francisco, CA 94105
(415) 495-7600

NATIVE WRITERS INK
Institute of Alaska Native Arts
P.O. Box 80583, 524 Third Ave.
Fairbanks, AK 99708
(907) 456-7491/7406

NATIVES NEWS
Natives Program
200 N. Monroe
Eugene, OR 97402

NAVAHO-A MAGAZINE FOR THE DINEH
Maazo Publishing
Box 1245
Window Rock, AZ 86515
(602) 729-2233
Covers Navajo Indian culture. Quarterly. $12/year; $28/year, foreign.

NAVAJO AREA NEWSLETTER
Bureau of Indian Affairs
Box M
Window Rock, AZ 86515
  (602) 871-5156
  Frank Hardwick, Editor
Contains information of interest to Navajo Area,
B.I.A.'s employees on education, personnel actions, Bureau policy, etc. Monthly. 4,000 cir. No charge.

NAVAJO COMMUNITY COLLEGE NEWSLETTER
Publications Department
Tsaile, AZ 86556

NAVAJO EDUCATION NEWSLETTER
Navajo Area Office
Bureau of Indian Affairs
Window Rock, AZ 86515

NAVAJO NATION ENQUIRY
P.O. Box 490
Window Rock, AZ 86515

THE NAVAJO TIMES
The Navajo Nation
P.O. Box 310
Window Rock, AZ 86515
  (602) 871-5400
  Mark Trahant, Editor & Publisher
  Angie Damon, Circulation Manager
  Michael Kellogg, Advertising Director
  Paul Natonabah, Art Director
Only American Indian daily newspaper reporting Navajo, national and regional news. Book reviews. 4,500 cir. $90/year. Advertising. Begun 1959. Formerly "Navajo Nation Times".

NAVAJOLAND PUBLICATIONS
Navajo Tribal Museum
Window Rock, AZ 86515

NEBRASKA INDIAN TERRITORY NEWS
P.O. Box 94914
Lincoln, NE 68509

NEW MEXICO HISTORICAL REVIEW
1013 Mesa Vista Hall
University of New Mexico
Albuquerque, NM 87131
  (505) 277-5839
  Dr. Paul A. Hutton, Editor
Covers New Mexico and Southwest history. Includes articles, book reviews, essays and notes, and history news notes dealing with American Indian topics. Quarterly journal. $20/year, institutions; $18/year, individuals; single copies, $5. Advertising accepted. Begun 1926.

NEW MEXICO INDIAN AFFAIRS SOURCE
LaVilla Revera Bldg.
224 E. Palace Ave.
Santa Fe, NM 87501

THE NEW PHOENIX
The Free Cherokees
800 Oak Dr.
Mechanicsburg, MD 20659
Official newsletter of the Free Cherokees, an independent tribe dedicated to the preservation of authentic Native American teachings. $16/year.

NEWS FROM INDIAN COUNTRY
Indian Country Communications, Inc.
Route 2, Box 2900-A
Hayward, WI 54843
  (715) 634-5226 Fax 634-3243
  Paul DeMain, Editor
  Pat Calliotte, Associate Editor
Staff: Terri Bisonette, Assistant Editor; Kim Kutz, Advertising; Tammy Tribble, Subscriptions; D.L. Birchfield, Book Review Editor. *Description*: National bi-monthly newspaper (24 issues annually) with circulation in Canada and 14 other countries. Covers news and community events of the American Indian, business activities, and cultural events. Special features on treaty rights, legislation; year-round pow-wow locations, etc. Monthly newspaper. $26/yr. - 3rd Class, $40 - 1st Class. Advertising, EEO/AA Job Search. Begun 1977.

NEWS FROM NATIVE CALIFORNIA
Heyday Books
P.O. Box 9145
Berkeley, CA 94709
  (510) 549-3564
  Malcolm Margolin, Publisher
  Jeannine Gendar, Editor
Written for major figures and organizations in the California Indian community, from individuals on reservations to government officials. Quarterly magazine. 3,300 circ.$17.50/year; $4.50, single issue. Begun 1987.

NEZ PERCE TRIBAL NEWSPAPER
P.O. Box 305
Lapwai, ID 85341

NI-MI-KWA-ZOO-MIN
Minnesota Chippewa Tribe
P.O. Box 217
Cass Lake, MN 56633

NISHNAWBE NEWS
Organization of North American Indian Students
Northern Michigan University
140 University Center
Marquette, MI 49855
  Mike Wright, Editor
Monthly magazine. 8,500 cir. $5/year. Begun 1971.

NMIEA NEWSLETTER
New Mexico Indian Education Assn.(NMIEA)
P.O. Box 16356
SANTA FE, NM 87506
  (505) 989-5569

NO NA LIMA HANA NO'EAU
Alu Like, Inc.
1024 Mapunapuna St.
Honolulu, HI 96819
  (808) 836-8940
Monthly newsletter of Alu Like,, a private, nonprofit community based advocate for Native Hawaiian social & economic self sufficiency. Begun 1989.

NORTH AMERICAN INDIAN MUSEUMS ASSOCIATION NEWSLETTER
c/o Iroquois Indian Museum
P.O. Box 7, Caverns Rd.
Howes Cave, NY 12092
  (518) 296-8949

NORTH CAROLINA HISTORICAL REVIEW
North Carolina Div. of Archaeology & History
109 East Jones St.
Raleigh, NC 27601

NORTH DAKOTA HISTORY: JOURNAL OF THE NORTHERN PLAINS
State Historical Society of North Dakota
612 E. Boulevard Ave.
Bismarck, ND 58505
  (701) 224-2799 Fax 224-3710
  Janet Daley Lysengen, Editor
  Ann Rathke, Historian
A quarterly scholarly journal dedicated to the history and culture of the state of North Dakota and the northern plains. 1,900 cir. $4/issue; $25/year, institutions; single memberships, $30; family memberships, $40, in ND Heritage Foundation.

NORTH DAKOTA QUARTERLY
University of North Dakota Press
P.O. Box 7209
Grand Forks, ND 58202
  (701) 777-3322 Fax 777-3650
  Robert W. Lewis, Editor
Quarterly university journal in the humanities, arts, and social sciences, with a special interest in Native American writing and writing about it. $20/year; $5 per copy.

NORTHERN CHEYENNE NEWS
P.O. Box 401
Lame Deer, MT 59043

NORTHWEST ARCTIC NUNA
Maniilaq Association
P.O. Box 256
Kotzebue, AK 99752
  (907) 442-3311
Monthly newsletter includes local news and program information. No charge. Advertising.

NORTHWEST ETHNIC NEWS
Ethnic Heritage Council
305 Harrison St. #326
Seattle, WA 98109
  (206) 443-1410 Fax 443-1408
  Sarah Sarai, Editor
Monthly newspaper covering arts and issues relevant to ethnic communities of the Pacific Northwest. 13,000 cir. $12/year. Begun 1984.

NORTHWEST INDIAN FISHERIES COMMISSION NEWS
6730 Marti Way E.
Olympia, WA 98506
Monthly

NPAIHB HEALTH NEWS & NOTES
Northwest Portland Area Indian Health Board
520 SW Harrison, Suite 440
Portland, OR 97201
  (503) 228-4185
Quarterly.

NUGGUAM
Quinault Tribal Affairs
P.O. Box 1118
Taholah, WA 98587

O

O-HE-YOY NOH
Seneca Nation of Indians
Plummer Bldg., Box 231
Salamanca, NY14779
  Eldena Halftown, Editor
Monthly newsletter devoted to the Seneca Nation of Indians. 500 cir. Begun 1970.

OGLALA WICAHPI
Journalism Department
Oglala Lakota College
P.O. Box 490
Kyle, SD 57752

**OKLAHOMA ANTHROPOLOGICAL
SOCIETY NEWSLETTER**
Oklahoma Anthropological Society
Route 1, Box 62B
Cheyenne, OK 73628
(918) 682-5091
Frieda Odell, Editor & Publisher
Information on statewide archaeological investigations.; articles of Oklahoma history and prehistory. Book reviews. Monthly newsletter (Septem-
ber-May). 600 cir. Subscription: $12/year. individu-
als; $17/year, institutions; $20/year, foreign. Begun 1952.

**OKLAHOMANS FOR INDIAN
OPPORTUNITY NEWSLETTER**
555 Constitution
Norman, OK 73069

OLD NORTHWEST CORP. NEWSLETTER
Sonotabac Prehistoric Indian Mounds & Museum
2401 Wabash Ave.
Vincennes, IN 47591
(812) 885-4330/7679
Published monthly.

ON THE WAY UP
American Indian Science & Engineering Society
1310 College Ave., Suite 1220
Boulder, CO 80302
(303) 492-8658
Published three times per year.

ONEIDA NATION NEWSLETTER
Oneida Indian Nation
223 Genesee St.
Oneida, NY 13421
(315) 697-8251 Fax 697-7581
Ray Halbritter, Representative
Provides tribal and reservation news.

ORDER OF THE INDIAN WARS JOURNAL
P.O. Box 7401
Little Rock, AR 72217
(501) 225-3996
Jerry L. Russell, Editor/Publisher
Contains reprinted articles on the history of the
Indian wars. Quarterly.

**OREGON COMMISSION ON
INDIAN SERVICES NEWSLETTER**
454 State Capitol
Salem, OR 97310
(503) 986-1067 Fax 986-1071
Quarterly.

**OREGON DIRECTORY OF
AMERICAN INDIAN RESOURCES**
Commission on Indian Services
454 State Capitol
Salem, OR 97310
(503) 986-1067 Fax 986-1071
Gladine G. Ritter, Editor
1993-95. Published biennially.

OREGON INDIAN EDUCATION NEWSLETTER
Oregon Indian Educaion Association
2125 N. Flint
Portland, OR 97227
(503) 275-9600

**OREGON INDIANS: CULTURE,
HISTORY & CURRENT AFFAIRS**
The Oregon Historical Society Press
1230 SW Park Ave.
Portland, OR 97205

ORIC NEWS
Orange County Indian Center
P.O. Box 250
Garden Grove, CA 92642

OSAGE NATION NEWS
Osage Tribal Council
Tribal Administration Bldg.
Pawhuska, OK 74056

OSHKABEWIS
Indian Studies Program
Bemidji State University
Bemidji, MN 56601

OURSELVES
Minnesota Chippewa Tribe
P.O. Box 217
Cass Lake, MN 56633

OUTLOOK
P.O. Box 1249
Utah State University
Logan, UT 84322

**OWENS VALLEY INDIAN EDUCATION
CENTER NEWSLETTER**
P.O. Box 1648
Bishop, CA 93514

OYATE-ANISHNANABE NEWS
American Indian Student Cultural Center
104 Jone Hall, 27 Pleasant SE
Minneapolis, MN 55404

OYATE NAT E NATA YAZADI PHEZUTA
University of Colorado
Campus Box 135
Boulder, CO 80309

OYATE-VISION
P.O. Box 393
Pine Ridge, SD 57770

OYATE WO'WAPI
Tahana Whitecrow Foundation
P.O. Box 18181
Salem, OR 97305
Quarterly.

P

PACEMAKER
1663 Bristol Pike
Cornwall Heights, PA 19020

THE PADRE'S TRAIL
P.O. Box 645
St. Michael's, AZ 86511

PAHA SAPA WAHOSE
c/o Student Special Services
Black Hills State College
Spearhead, SD 57783

PAN-AMERICAN INDIAN ASSOCIATION NEWS
P.O. Box 244
Nocatee, FL 33864

(813) 494-6930
Chief Piercing Eyes, Editor
Heritage revival for native Americans and other
tribal peoples. Help in genealogy; networking of
groups and resources. Book reviews. Irregular. 16-
page tabloid. 5,000 cir. $5/year; $10/year, foreign.
Advertising. Begun 1984.

PANA PANA NEWSLETTER
National Indian Youth Council
318 Elm, SE
Albuquerque, NM 87102

PANHANDLE-PLAINS HISTORICAL REVIEW
Panhandle-Plains Historical Museum
P.O. Box 967, W.T. Station
2401 Fourth Ave.
Canyon, TX 79016
(806) 655-7194

PAPAGO BULLETIN
P.O. Box 364
Sells, AZ 85634

PASCUA PUEBLO NEWS
4821 West Calle Vicam
Tucson, AZ 85706

PATHFINDER NEWSLETTER
American Indian Heritage Foundation
6051 Arlington Blvd.
Falls Church, VA 22044
(703) 237-7500 fax 532-1921
Informs Indians and non-Indians about the culture and heritage of Native Americans. Addresses
the spiritual and physical needs of American Indians and aims to encourage Indian youth. Quarterly. Membership, $20/yr. Begun 1982.

THE PEOPLE BEFORE COLUMBUS
Southwest Indian Student Coalition
1812 Los Lomas
Albuquerque, NM 87131
(503) 277-6065
Annual journal.

THE PEOPLE'S VOICE
Kanienkehaka Teritory
P.O. Box 216
Hogansburg, NY 13655
(518) 358-3022
Cindy Terrance, Editor
Weekly newspaper for the St. Regis Mohawk
Reservation (both U.S. and Canadian portions);
also serves Mohawk people in Kahnawake Que-
bec (near Montreal) and California. Begun 1987.

THE PEQUOT TIMES
Mashantucket Pequot Tribal Nation
P.O. Box 3060, Indiantown Rd.
Ledyard, CT 06339-3060
(203) 536-7200 Fax 572-7955
Bruce MacDonald, Editor
Monthly newspaper for tribal members, tribal em-
ployees, public officials and the general public.
Covers stories of interest about the reservation,
tribal cultural events and issues affecting Native
Americans nationally. Also reports on news about
tribal enterprises such as Foxwoods Resort Ca-
sino. Free circulation of 10,000.

PHOENIX INDIAN CENTER NEWSLETTER
333 W. Indian School Rd.
Phoenix, AZ 85013-3215
(602) 256-2000

PIERRE CHIEFTAIN
Pierre Indian School
Pierre, SD 57501

PIERRE INDIAN LEARNING CENTER NEWS
Star Route 3
Pierre, SD 57501

PILGRIM
Shrine of Our Lady of Martyrs
Noeltner Rd.
Auriesville, NY 12016
 (518) 853-3033 Fax 853-3051
 John J. Paret, S.J., Editor
Newsletter for persons interested in the three
martyrs venerated here: Sts. Isaac Joques, Rene
Goupil, and John Lalande - and in the Shrine it-
self, and in Blessed Kateri Tekakwitha, the young
Mohawk-Algonquin woman who was born here.

PIMA-MARICOPA ECHO
Gila River Indian Community
P.O. Box 97
Sacaton, AZ 85247

PLAINS ANTHROPOLOGIST
Plains Anthropological Society
University of Arkansas, Dept. of Anthropology
Fayetteville, AR 72701
 (501) 575-5446 Fax 575-2642
 Marvin Kay, Editor
A quarterly journal containing articles on the Plains
area of the U.S. Book reviews. 1,500 cir. $20/year,
individuals; $35/year, institutions. Begu 1954.

PLAINS TALK
State Historical Society of North Dakota
612 E. Boulevard Ave.
Bismarck, ND 58505
 (701) 224-2799 Fax 224-3710
Quarterly newsletter about the activities of the ND
State Historical Society and ND Heritage Foun-
dation. No charge to members of the ND Heritage
Foundation.

POARCH CREEK NEWS
Poarch Band of Creek Indians
Route 3, Box 243-A
Atmore, AL 36502

POCAHONTAS TRAILS - QUARTERLY
Pocahontas Trails Genealogical Society
6015 Robin Hill Dr.
Lakeport, CA 95453
Focuses on the pursuit and study of the genealogy of Pocahontas and Powhatan. Membership
dues. Begun 1983.

**POINT NO POINT TREATY
COUNCIL NEWSLETTER**
7999 NE Salish Lane
Kingston, WA 98346

**PORTLAND PUBLIC SCHOOLS
INDIAN EDUCATION ACT PROJECT
NEWSLETTER**
Portland Public Schools
8020 N.E. Tillamook
Portland, OR 97213
 (503) 280-6474

POTTERY SOUTHWEST
Albuquerque Archaeological Society
6207 Mossman Place NE
Albuquerque, NM 87110

 (505) 881-1675
Carries news and queries on prehistoric pottery
of the Indians of New Mexico, Arizona, Utah, Colorado, and parts of Texas and Mexico. Quarterly.
$3/yr. Begun 1974.

PREVENTION QUARTERLY
Falmouth Institute
3918 Prosperity Ave., Suite 205
Fairfax, VA 22031
 (703) 641-0251
 Bonnie Paquin, Contact
Covers news, programs, and issues in the area of
Indian alcohol and substance abuse prevention
and treatment.

PUEBLO HORIZON
Indian Pueblo Cultural Center, Inc.
2401 12th St., N.W.
Albuquerque, NM 87102

PUEBLO COUNCIL NEWS
P.O. Box 3256
Albuquerque, NM 87190

PUEBLO TIMES
Pueblo Times Publishing Co.
1860 Don Pasqual Rd.
Los Lunas, NM 87031
 (505) 865-4508
 George E. Gorospe, Owner/Publisher
Weekly (Wednesday) newspaper for the 19 Indian Pueblos of northern New Mexico. Distribution includes part of the Navajo Nation. Circulation about 10,000. Begun 1985.

**PYRAMID LAKE INDIAN
RESERVATION NEWSLETTER**
P.O. Box 256
Nixon, NV 89424

Q

QUALLA RESERVATION NEWS
Cherokee Agency
Cherokee, NC 28719

QUECHAN NEWS
Fort Yuma Indian Reservation
P.O. Box 1352
Yuma, Arizona 85364
 (619) 572-0213 Fax 572-2102

QUILEUTE INDIAN NEWS
Quileute Tribal Council
P.O. Box 279
La Push, WA 98350
 (206) 374-6163 Fax 374-6311
 Anne Cooper, Editor
Monthly.

QUIN-A-MONTH-A'
Stockbridge Historical Museum
Route 1, Box 300
Bowler, WI 54416

QUINAULT NATURAL RESOURCES
Quinault Department of Natural Resources
 and Economic Development
P.O. Box 189
Tahola, WA 98587
 Jacqueline Storm

R

THE RAVEN CHRONICLES
P.O. Box 95918
Seattle, WA 98145
Multi-cultural journal of the arts and literature, in-
cluding native American literature. $12/yr. $3
sample issue.

THE RAWHIDE PRESS
Spokane Tribal Business Council
P.O. Box 359
Wellpinit, WA 99040-0359
 (509) 258-7320
 Bertha Seyler, Editor
Monthly newspaper covering news regarding In-
dian affairs including historical features, biogra-
phies, etc. on Indian culture. Book reviews. 800
cir. $12/year. Advertising. Begun 1972.

RED ALERT
Americans for Indian Opportunity
1010 Massachusetts Ave., N.W., Suite 200
Washington, D.C. 20001
 (202) 371-1280

RED CLIFF TRIBAL NEWS
P.O. Box 529
Bayfield, WI 54814

RED CLOUD COUNTRY
Red Cloud Indian School
Holy Rosary Mission
Pine Ridge, SD 57770
 (605) 867-5491
 Fr. Roger, S.V., Editor
Contains information about Red Cloud School.
Sent to donors, friends and benefactors of the
school. Quarterly newsletter. $10/year.

RED HILLS NEWSLETTER
Kaibab Tribal Council
Tribal Affairs Bldg.
Fredonia, AZ 86022

RED LAKE NEWSLETTER
Red Lake Reservation
Red Lake, MN 56671

RED MEN MAGAZINE
Great Council of U.S.
Improved Order of Red Men
P.O. Box 683
Waco, TX 76703
 (817) 756-1221
Published three times per year.

REDSKIN
Phoenix Indian High School
37 E. Indian School Rd.
Phoenix, AZ 85012

RED VOICES
American Indian Training Institute, Inc.
4153 Northgate Blvd.
Sacramento, CA 95834
 (916) 920-0731

**THE RENEGADE: A STRATEGY
JOURNAL OF INDIAN OPINION**
Survival of American Indian Associations
7803-A Samurai Dr., SE
Olympia, WA 98503
 (206) 459-2679
Published annually.

THE RENO TALKING LEAF
Nevada Urban Indians, Inc.
917 E. 6th St.
Reno, NV 89512
  (702) 329-2573/4
Contains community events, atcivities, services
and resources, and educational articles. Monthly
newsletter.

REPORT TO INDIAN COUNTRY
Senate Committee on Indian Affairs
838 Hart Senate Office Bldg.
Washington, D.C. 20510

RESERVATION TIMES
Seneca Nation Education Department
1500 Route 438
Irving, NY 14081

RIDGE NOTES
Chieftains Museum
501 Riverside Pkwy., Box 373
Rome, GA 30162
  (706) 291-9494
  Janine E. Joslin, Editor
Quarterly membership newsletter focusing on
museum activities and historical articles on the
region's history.

RISING SUN
United American Indians
225 Chestnut
Philadelphia, PA 19106

ROCKY BOY'S NATIVE VOICE
Rocky Boy's Health Board
Box Elder, MT 59521

ROCKY BOY'S NEWS
Rocky Boy's Route
Box Elder, MT 59521

WILL ROGERS TIMES
Will Rogers Memorial
P.O. Box 157
Claremore, OK 74018
  (918) 341-0719

ROSEBUD SIOUX HERALD
P.O. Box 430
Rosebud, SD 57570

ROUGH ROCK NEWS
Dine'Biolta'Daahani
Rough Rock Demonstration School
P.O. Box 217
Chinle, AZ 86503
Provides a view of the life-style and attitudes of a
desert community that is determined to control its
own destiny. Published monthly Sept.-June.

S

SAC AND FOX NEWS
Route 2, Box 246
Stroud, OK 74079

SAIIC NEWSLETTER
South and Meso American Indian
Information Center
P.O. Box 28703
Oakland, CA 94604
  (510) 834-4263 Fax 834-4264
Contains articles about issues of importance to
indigenous people in Central and South America.

**SAN JUAN COUNTY ARCHAEOLOGICAL
RESEARCH CENTER NEWSLETTER**
6131 U.S. Highway 64
Farmington, NM 87401
  (505) 632-2013
  Jo Lynn Davenport-Smith, Editor
Quarterly newsletter focusing on the
activities and programs of the Center.

SANDPAINTER
P.O. Box 791
Chinle, AZ 86503

**SCHOHARIE MUSEUM OF THE
IROQUOIS INDIAN--MUSEUM NOTES**
P.O. Box 7
Howes Cave, NY 12092
  (518) 296-8949
  Dr. John P. Ferguson, Editor
A newsletter reporting on the Museum's activities;
scholarly articles on the Iroquois. Subscription:
$10/year. Complimentary copies available.

SCREAMING EAGLE
2400 Southeast Circle Dr.
Bartlesville, OK 74006

SEALASKA SHAREHOLDER
Sealaska Corporation
One Sealaska Plaza, 400
Juneau, AK 99801
  Ross Soboleff, Editor

SEASONS
The National Native American
AIDS Preven tion Center
3515 Grand Ave., Suite 100
Oakland, CA 94610
  (510) 444-2051 Fax 444-1593
  Andrea Green Rush, Editor
A quarterly newsletter featuring articles by Native
Americans with HIV and Native American health
educators, and health care providers. 3,000 cir.
No charge.

SECCI NEWSLETTER
Southeastern Cherokee Confederacy
318 Crestview Dr.
Valdosta, GA 31602
  White Wolf Crider & Elk Dreamer Crider, Editors
Monthly newsletter of the Southeastern Cherokee
Confederacy.

THE SEMINOLE TRIBUNE
Seminole Tribe of Florida
6333 N.W. 30th St.
Hollywood, FL 33024
  (305) 964-4853
  Betty Mae Jumper, Editor-in-Chief
  Twila Perkins, Editor
Biweekly newspaper providing news about the
Seminole Tribe from five reservations in Florida;
also, news about other tribes across the country.
Book reviews. $15/year. 5,000 cir. Advertising.
Begun 1973.

SENECA TRIBAL NEWSLETTER
Cattauragus Indian Reservation
1490 Route 438
Irving, NY 14081
  Debbie Hoag, Editor

SENTINEL
White Shield School
HC 1-Box 45
Roseglen, ND 58775
  (701) 743-4350

THE SENTINEL
National Congress of American Indians
900 Pennsylvania Ave., S.E.
Washington, DC 20003-2140
  (202) 546-9404
  Emily Segar, Editor
Focuses on national issues af fecting Native Americans. Examines federal legislation and governmental policy developments that affect Indians.
Book reviews. Monthly magazine. 3,000 cir. $25/
year, individuals; $50/year, institutions. Advertis-
ing. Begun 1944

SHAMAN'S DRUM
Cross-Cultural Shaman's Network
Box 430
Willets, CA 95490
  (707) 459-0486
  Timothy White, Editor
Covers experiential international shamanism, na-
tive medicine ways and spirituality. Book reviews.
Quarterly magazine. 19,000 cir.$5/copy; $15/year,
individuals; $35/year, institutions; $20/year, for-
eign. Advertising. Begun 1985.

SHENANDOAH NEWSLETTER
736 W. Oklahoma St.
Appleton, WI 54914
  (414) 832-9525
  Paul A. Skenandore (Scan doa), Publisher/Ed.
Discusses the history and legal rights of the native poeples of Great Turtle Island. Reports news
of treaty and discrimination disputes. Monthly.
1,000 cir. $14.50/year, individuals; $19.50/year, institutions. Begun 1973.

SHO-BAN NEWS
Shoshone-Bannock Tribal Council
P.O. Box 900
Fort Hall, Idaho 83203
  (208) 238-3887/8
  Terry A. Tetreault, Editor
Weekly tribal newspaper covering local, state and
national news of interest to Native Americans. Ad-
vertising accepted. Subscription: $15/year,
Shoshone-Bannock tribal members; $20/year,
non-members; $30/year, foreign; 35¢ each.
Complimentary copies available upon request
(send first class stamp). Begun 1976.

SILETZ NEWSLETTER
Confederated Tribes of Siletz
P.O. Box 549
Siletz, OR 97380
  (503) 444-2532 ext. 134
Monthly.

THE SINGING WINDS NEWSLETTER
Council of Three Rivers American Indian Center
200 Charles St.
Pittsburgh, PA 15238
  (412) 782-4457
  Russell Simms, Editor
Monthly newsletter focusing on the
activities of the Center.

SINTE GLESKA COLLEGE NEWS
Library-Media Center
Box 107, Rosebud Reservation
Mission, SD 57555

SIOUX JOURNAL
Cheyenne River Sioux Tribal Council
P.O. Box 590
Eagle Butte, SD 57625

SIOUX MESSENGER
Yankton Sioux Tribe
Route 248
Marty, SD 57361

SIOUX SAN SUN
PHS Indian Hospital
Rapid City, SD 57701

SISSETON AGENCY NEWS
Bureau of Indian Affairs
Sisseton, SD 57262

SMALL TRAILS
American Indian Community House
404 Lafayette
New York, NY 10003

SMITHSONIAN RUNNER
Smithsonian Institution
Office of Public Affairs
Rm. 2410, Arts & Industries Bldg.
Washington, DC 20560
A newsletter for Native Americans
from the Smithsonian.

SMOKE SIGNALS
Baltimore American Indian Center
113 South Broadway
Baltimore, MD 21231
 (410) 675-3535
 Archie Lynch, Editor
Contains news and events concerning the Native American community of the Baltimore metropolitan area. No charge; donations accepted.

SMOKE SIGNALS
Bacone College
Muskogee, OK 74401

SMOKE SIGNALS
Colorado River Indian Tribes
Route 1, Box 23-B
Parker, AZ 85344

SMOKE SIGNALS
St. Paul American Indian Center
341 University Ave. West
St. Paul, MN 55101

SMOKE SIGNALS
Northeastern Native American Association, Inc.
P.O. Box 230266
Hollis, NY 11423
 (718) 978-7057
 Paul "Wassaja" Gibson, President
Quarterly newsletter.

SMOKE SIGNALS
Confederated Tribes of the Grand
Ronde Community of Oregon
9615 Grand Ronde Rd.
Grand Ronde, OR 97347
 (800) 422-0232; (503) 879-5211
 Fax (503) 879-5964
 Tracy Olson, Newsletter Director
Deals mainly with issues, controversies, events and politics involving the Confederated Tribes of the Grand Ronde. Monthly newsletter, 2,300 cir. (tribal members, government officials, community members). No charge.

SMOKE SIGNALS
Dallas Inter-Tribal Center
209 E. Jefferson Blvd.
Dallas, TX 75203

 (214) 941-1050 Fax 941-6537
 Cindy McKnight, Editor
Covers the news and events of the Native American community in the Dallas area. Quarterly newsletter. 1,200 cir. (nationwide distribution). No charge.

SMOKE SIGNALS
Route 2, Box 400
Odanah, WI 54806

SMOKE SIGNALS: BUSINESS DIRECTORY
Arrowstar Publishing
100134 University Park Sta.
Denver, CO 80210-0134
 (303) 231-6599
 J. Bell, Editor
Lists over 3,500 American Indian/Alaska Native owned and operated businesses. $24.95, plus $2.50 shipping and handling.

SMOKE TALK
Brotherhood of American Indians
P.O. Box 500
Steilacoom, WA 98388

SMOKI CEREMONIALS & SNAKE DANCE
Smoki People, P.O. Box 123
Prescott, AZ 86302
 (602) 778-5228
Published annually.

SOCIETY FOR HISTORICAL ARCHAEOLOGY NEWSLETTER
P.O. Box 30446
Tucson, AZ 85751
 (602) 886-8006 Fax 886-0182
 Norman F. Barka, Editor
Presents information on current research and recent publications, forums on archaeological conservation and urban archaeology, and information on Society activities. Quarterly newsletter. Annual membership dues - $30/students; $50, individuals; $65/institutions. Begun 1967.

SOTA-EYE-YE-YAPI
P.O. Box 509
Agency Village, SD 57262

THE SOURCE
New Mexico Office of Indian Affairs
O1A, Villa Rivera Bldg.
224 E. Palace Ave.
Santa Fe, NM 87501
 (505) 827-6440 Fax 827-7308
Provides information on intergovernmental relations, commissioner activities, culture, arts, and educational issues of the American Indians. Triannually. Begun 1985.

SOUTH DAKOTA HISTORY
South Dakota State Historical Society
900 Governors Dr.
Pierre, SD 57501-2217
 (605) 773-3458
 Nancy Tystad Koupal, Editor
A quarterly scholarly, refereed journal designed for professional historians and lay readers interested in western and Great Plains history. Includes scholarly articles, edited documents, and other annotated, unpublished primary materials that contribute to the knowledge of the history of South Dakota and the surrounding region. Book reviews. 2,300 circ. $20/yr.; $30, foreign.

SOUTH FLORIDA HISTORY MAGAZINE
Historical Association of Southern Florida
101 West Flagler St.
Miami, FL 33130
 (305) 375-1492 Fax 375-1609
 Stuart McIver & Mary Ann Wilson, Editors
Focuses on southern Florida and the Caribbean including stories on folklife as well as history. Quarterly. $35/yr.

SOUTHEASTERN CHEROKEE CONFEDERACY NEWS
Route 4, 120 Will Hatcher Rd.
Albany, GA 31705-9430
 (912) 787-5722
 Chief William "Rattlesnake" Jackson, Editor
Covers tribal events. 4-page bimonthly newsletter. Advertising accepted. Begun 1976.

SOUTHERN CALIFORNIA INDIAN CENTER, INC. - NEWS
P.O. Box 2550, 12755 Brokkhurst St.
Garden Grove, CA 92746
 (213) 977-1366
 Cathi Garfield, Editor
Community articles, news on local pow wow; promotes in-house programs. Monthly newsletter. Complimentary copies are available upon request. Begun 1985.

SOUTHERN CHEYENNE & ARAPAHO NATION NEWS
P.O. Box 91
Concho, OK 73002

SOUTHERN PUEBLOS AGENCY BULLETIN
Bureau of Indian Affairs
1000 Indian School Rd., NW
Albuquerque, NM 87103

SOUTHERN UTE DRUM
P.O. Box 737, Tribal Affairs Bldg.
Ignacio, CO 81137

SOUTHWEST ASSOCIATION ON INDIAN AFFAIRS NEWSLETTER
P.O. Box 1964
Santa Fe, NM 87501

SOUTHWEST MUSEUM NEWS
P.O. Box 41558
Los Angeles, CA 90041
 (213) 261-2164 ext. 233

SOUTHWEST RESOURCE & EVALUATION NEWSLETTER
National Indian Training Research Center
2121 South Mill Ave., Suite 218
Tempe, AZ 85282

SOUTHWESTERN ASSOCIATION OF INDIAN AFFAIRS, INC. QUARTERLY
Roswell Printing Company
110 North Pennsylvania
Roswell, NM 88201-4620
 (505) 983-5220
 John Bott, Editor
Quarterly journal covering Indian arts, crafts and writing. 1,000 cir. $15/Year. Begun 1964.

SOVEREIGN NATIONS
Tribal Self-Governance Demonstration Project
Alumni Indian Business Council
2616 Kwina Rd.
Bellingham, WA 98226

SPAWING THE MEDICINE RIVER
Institute of American Indian Arts Museum
P.O. Box 20007
SANTA FE 87504
(505) 988-6463 Fax 988-6446
Charles A. Dailey, Director
Philip Foss, Jr., Editor
Published quarterly.

SPEAKING LEAVES
American Indian Cultural Group
P.O. Box 2000
Vacaville, CA 95688

**SPEAKING OF OURSELVES
NI-MI-KWA-ZOO-MIN**
Minnesota Chippewa Tribe
P.O. Box 217
Cass Lake, MN 56633

SPILYAY TYMOO
Confederated Tribes of Warm Springs
P.O. Box 870
Warm Springs, OR 97761
(503) 553-1644
Bi-weekly newsletter.

SPIRIT!
Native American Resource Center
Pembroke State University
Pembroke, NC 28372
(919) 521-4214
Contains news of projects and events of the
Center. Quarterly. No charge. Begun 1987.

SPIRIT OF CRAZY HORSE
Leonard Peltier Defense Committee
P.O. Box 583
Lawrence, KS 66044
(913) 842-5796
Bimonthly newspaper.

SPIRIT TALK
P.O. Box 430
The Blackfoot Nation
Browning, MT 59417
(800) 350-2882; (406) 338-2882
Fax (406) 338-5120
Long Standing Bear Chief, Editor
A quarterly magazine in celebration of Indian culture. Topics include: respect for the earth, the sacredness of the family, stories and legends, profiles of significant people, Indian music and dance,
Indian art and artisans, history, Indian foods, uses
of plants; books, movie and video reviews; cultural seminars; places to visit in Indian Country;
and events in Indian Country: celebrations, rodeos
and fairs. 50,000 cir. $4.75, single copies; $18/
year. Advertyising. Begun 1994.

SPRINGFIELD AREA OFFICE NEWS
Confederated Tribes of Siletz
1293 N. 18th St., Suite B
Springfield, OR 97477

SQUOL - QUOL
Lummi Tribal Office
2616 Kwina Rd.
Bellingham, WA 98255

**STANDING ROCK SIOUX
TRIBAL NEWSLETTER**
P.O. Box D
Fort Yates, ND 58538

STEALING OF CALIFORNIA
Native American Training Association Institute
P.O. Box 1505
Sacramento, CA 95807

**STOCKBRIDGE MUNSEE
TRIBAL NEWSLETTER**
RR 1
Bowler, WI 54416

STOWW INDIAN VOICE
P.O. Box 578
Sumner, WA 98390

**STUDIES IN AMERICAN
INDIAN LITERATURES**
Association for the Study of
American Indian Literatures
Box 112, University of Richmond
Richmond, VA 23173
(804) 289-8311 Fax 289-8313
Robert M. Nelson, Editor
Quarterly scholarly journal focusing exclusively on
American Indian literature, primarily academic, and
those involved one way or another with the study
of or creation of Native American literatures (oral
as well as print, old time as well as contemporary;
also includes reviews, interviews, bibliographies,
scholarly and theoretical articles. 300 cir. $25/yr.,
individuals; $35/yr., institutions.

SUISA NEWS
Survival International USA
2121 Decatur Place, N.W.
Washington, DC 20008

SUNDEVIL ROUNDUP
Rough Rock Community High School
Star Route 1
Rough Rock, AZ 85021

SUNLODGE BUFFALO TALES
c/o Gene Barbee
P.O. Box 02
Fort Spring, WV 24936
(304) 445-2836
Gene Barbee, Editor
Quarterly magazine. $12/year.

SUQUAMISH MUSEUM NEWSLETTER
P.O. Box 498
Suquamish, WA 98392
(206) 598-3311
Leonard Forsman, Editor

**SUSQUEHANNA VALLEY
NATIVE AMERICAN EAGLE**
Box 99, Walnut Valley Farm
LOGANVILLE, PA 17342
(717) 428-1440
Rick Edmund & Jerry Dietz, Co-Editors
Bi-monthly newsletter for Native and non-Native
people interested in current events, powwows,
festivals, and historic articles on native people of
the mid-Atlantic region. Also includes recipes, poetry, etc. $6/year.

SURFACE SCATTER
Marin Museum of the American Indian
P.O. Box 864, 2200 Novato Blvd.
Novato, CA 94947
(415) 897-4064
Quarterly newsletter.

T

TA NEWSLETTER OF UIATF
Daybreak Star Press
P.O. Box 99253
Seattle, WA 98199

TALKING LEAF NEWSPAPER
Los Angeles Indian Center
Los Angeles, CA 90017
(213) 413-3156
Mike Burgess, Managing Editor
George Howell, Operations Editor
Robert Melson, Circulation Manager
Monthly American Indian newspaper providing
news of North American Indian people written for,
by and about Native Americans; also, news of Los
Angeles County area. Microfilm. $10/year, $15/
two years; foreign, $13/year, $20/two years.

TALKING PEACEPIPE
Southeast Michigan Indians, Inc.
P.O. Box 861
Warren, MI 48090
(313) 756-1350
Monthly newsletter. Advertising. $3/year.

TEKAKWITHA CONFERENCE NEWSLETTER
Tekakwitha Conference National Center
1800 9th Ave. S., Box 6759
Great Falls, MT 59406-6759
(406) 727-0147
Gilbert Hemauer
Quarterly. 15,000 cir. Begun 1979.

TEQUESTA
Historical Association of Southern Florida
101 West Flagler St.
Miami, FL 33130
(305) 375-1492 Fax 375-1609
Arva Moore Parks, Editor
Annual scholarly journal focusing on southern
Florida and the Caribbean. 3,500 cir. $35/annual
dues. Begun 1941.

THEATA
Cross Cultural Communications Department
University of Alaska, Alaskan Native Program
Fairbanks, AK 99708
(907) 474-7181
Pat Kwachka, Editor
Alaskan Native college students writing on tradi-
tional and contemporary topics. Annual journal.
4,000 cir. $5/year. Begun 1973.

THE THUNDERER
American Indian Bible Institute
100020 North 15th Ave.
Phoenix, AZ 85021

TI SWANNI ITST
Skokomish Indian Tribal Center
Route 5, Box 432
Shelton, WA 98584

TLIN TSIM HAI
Ketchikan Indian Corporation
429 Deermount
Ketchikan, AK 99901

TLINGIT/HAIDA TRIBAL NEWS
Tlingit/Haida Central Council
One Sealaska Plaza, Suite 300
Juneau, AK 99801
(312) 784-1050

**TODAY'S MINORITIES: THE
VOICE OF AMERICA'S FUTURE**
3220 N St., NW
Washington, DC 20007
 (800) 398-2201; (800) 735-5397
 Charles Bivonia, Jr., Editor
Quarterly newspaper. $15/yr.; $18/2 yrs.

TOMAHAWK
Oregon State University
P.O. Box 428
Warm Springs, OR 97761

TONAWANDA INDIAN NEWS
P.O. Box 64, Bloomingdale Rd.
Akron, NY 14001

TOSAN
P.O. Box 162
Dayton, OH 45401

TRAIL OF VISIONS
Black River Falls School District
North Third
Black River Falls, WI 54660

TRAILBLAZER
Cook Inlet Native Association
Anchorage, Alaska 99503
 (907) 278-4641

TRC NEWS
Tribal Research Center-NAES College
2838 W. Peterson Ave.
Chicago, IL 60659
 (312) 761-5000
Reports on the activities of the center.
Monthly newsletter. Begun 1987.

TREATY COUNCIL NEWS
International Indian Treaty
Council Information Office
123 Townsend St. #575
San Francisco, CA 94107
$10/year, individuals; $15/year, institutions.

TRENDS IN INDIAN HEALTH
Indian Health Service
5600 Fisher's Lane
Rockville, MD 20857
 (301) 443-1083
Annual publication.

TRIBAL COLLEGE
American Indian Higher Education Consortium
P.O. Box 898
Chestertown, MD 21620
 (301) 778-0171 Fax 778-0151
The official journal of the Consortium, focusing on
post-secondary education for Native Americans.
4x/yr. $14/yr.

TRIBAL DIRECTORY
Arizona Commission on Indian Affairs
1645 West Jefferson
Phoenix, AZ 85007

TRIBAL TRIBUNE
Colville Confederated Tribes
P.O. Box 150
Nespelem, WA 99155
 (509) 634-8835 Fax 634-4617
 Sheila Whitelaw, Editor
Monthly newspaper of the Confederated Tribes
of the Colville Reservation. 4,500 cir. $15/year in
Washington; $20/year outside Washington.

TU'KWA HONE' NEWSLETTER
Burns Paiute Tribe
HC-71, 100 Pa'Si'Go' St.
Burns, OR 97720
 (503) 573-2088
Weekly tribal newsletter.

TUNDRA DRUMS
P.O. Box 468
Bethel, AK 99559

THE TUNDRA TIMES
Eskimo, Indian, Aleut Publishing Co.
P.O. Box 92247
Anchorage, AK 99509
 (907) 274-2512 Fax 274-2512
 Anna Pickett, Business Managerr
Weekly newspaper consisting of articles about and
of interest to the indigenous peoples of Alaska.
Advertising accepted. $30/year. Begun 1962.

TURTLE MOUNTAIN TIMES
Turtle Mountain Tribe
Belcourt, ND 58316
 (701) 477-6451 Fax 477-6836
 Brenda Greenwood & Orie Richard, Co-editors
 Bryant LaVallie, Manager
Weekly tribal newspaper.

TURTLE QUARTERLY
Native American Center for the Living Arts
25 Rainbow Blvd. S.
Niagara Falls, NY 14303
 (716) 284-2427
 Millicent Knapp, Editor
 Millicent Green & Tim Johnson, Staff
Quarterly magazine which conveys the present
realities of Native American life. Includes articles
with emphasis on clture, art, history, philosophy
and cosmology; also covers environmental and
legal issues; fiction, reviews, photos, and special
children's section. $4/issue; $15/year, U.S.; $21,
Canadian, $38, foreign. 3,000 cir. Begun 1989.

TURTLETALK
Massachusetts Center for
Native American Awareness
P.O. Box 5885
Boston, MA 02114
 (617) 884-4227
 Burne Stanley, Editor
Quarterly newsletter.

TWIN LIGHT TRAIL
Intertribal Native American Indian News
P.O. Box 52
London, England N1O 3TQ

U

UMATILLA AGENCY NEWSLETTER
Bureau of Indian Affairs
P.O. Box 520
Pendleton, OR 97801

**UNITED INDIANS OF ALL TRIBES
FOUNDATION--TA NEWSLETTER**
United Indians of All Tribes
P.O. Box 99100
Seattle, WA 98199

UNITED LENAPE NATION NEWSLETTER
P.O. Box 1198
Fredonia, AZ 86022

UNITED LUMBEE NATION TIMES
United Lumbee Nation of N.C. and America
P.O. Box 512
Fall River Mills, CA 96028-0512
 (916) 336-6701
 Silver Star Reed, Editor
 Morning Hawk Lawson & Little Fox Gordon, Staff
Tribal newspaper containing articles and informa-
tion concerning members of the Lumbee Nation
of Indians. Published 3-4 times per year. 1,200
cir. $1.25/copy. Complimentary copies available
upon request. Advertising. Begun 1979.

UNITED SIOUX TRIBES NEWS
P.O. Box 1193
Pierre, SD 57501

UNITED TRIBES NEWS
Office of Public Information
3315 S. Airport Rd.
Bismarck, ND 58501
 (701) 255-3285
Monthly newspaper.

**UNITED TRIBES OF SOUTH DAKOTA
NEWSLETTER**
P.O. Box 1193
Pierre, SD 57501

UNITY MAGAZINE
Getting Together Publications
P.O. Box 29293
Oakland, CA 94604
 (510) 482-1432 Fax 482-1433
 (800) 39-UNITY to advertise
 Nic Paget-Clarke, Publisher
A multicultural, English/Spanish, nationally-distrib-
uted magazine which brings together views on
theme issues: education, environmental justice,
health care. Quarterly. Advertising. Begun 1993.

UNITY NEWS
United National Indian Tribal Youth (UNITY)
P.O. Box 25042
Oklahoma City, OK 73125
 (405) 424-3010 Fax 424-3018
 Sherry Kast, Communications Specialist
 J.R. Cook, Executive Director
Quarterly newspaper for Native American youth,
youth advisors and coordinators, and others interested in American Indian and Alaskan Native
youth. Contents promotes the activities, training
sessions and conferences of UNITY, and promotes
the positive actions and readership ability of outstanding Native youth ages 15-24. No charge.

**UNIVERSITY OF MINNESOTA, DEPT. OF
AMERICAN INDIAN STUDIES NEWSLETTER**
West Bank Campus, 1314 Social Sciences Bldg.
Minneapolis, MN 55455

UNIVERSITY OF SOUTH DAKOTA BULLETIN
Institute of Indian Studies
Dakota Hall, Room 12
414 E. Clark St.
Vermillion, SD 57069
 (605) 677-5209 Fax 677-5073
 Leonard Bruguier, Editor
Newsletter concerning the activities of the insti-
tute and information of general interest to Native
American people of South Dakota and across the
nation. Quarterly. 2,300 circ. Begun 1955.

THE USET CALUMET
1101 Kermit Dr., Suite 800
Nashville, TN 37212

UTAH INDIAN JOURNAL
Division of Indian Affairs
University of Utah
Salt Lake City, UT 84112

UTAH NAVAJO BAA HANE
Utah Navajo Department Council
Blanding, UT 84511

UTE BULLETIN
Ute Indian Tribe
P.O. Box 220
Fort Duchesne, UT 84026
  (801) 722-5141
  Carleen Kurip, Editor
Monthly newspaper covering American Indian interests. Book reviews. 1,500 cir. $1/copy; $6/year. Advertising. Begun 1974.

UTS'ITISCTAAN'I
American Indian Rehabilitation
Research and Training Center
Institute for Human Development
Northern Arizona University
CU Box 5630
Flagstaff, AZ 86011
  (602) 523-4791
Covers activities of the Center, which aims to improve the lives of American Indians with disabilities. Contains articles on rehabilitation. Semiannual. No charge. Begun 1983.

V

VALLEY ROUND UP
Shoshone-Paiute Business Council
P.O. Box 219
Owyhee, Nevada 89832

VIDEOFORUM
MacArthur Foundation Library Video Project
P.O. Box 409113
Chicago, IL 60640
  (800) 847-3671
  Mary M. Kirby, Director
First issue is on Native American videos.

VISIONS
Communications Publishing Group, Inc.
3100 Broadway, Suite 225
Kansas City, MO 64111
  (816) 756-3039
  Georgia Lee Clark, President & Editor
A resource guide for Native-American students containing individual profiles, scholarships and financial aid information, calendar of events, etc. Semiannually in March & September. $1.50 each.

THE VOICE
Denver Indian Center
4407 Morrison Rd.
Denver, CO 80219
Monthly newsletter reporting on local programs, activities, issues. $10/yr.

W

WAHPETON HIGHLIGHTS
Wahpeton Indian School
Wahpeton, ND 58075

WAHPETON INDIAN SCHOOL WEEKLY BULLETIN
Wahpeton, ND 58075

WALKER RIVER PAIUTE TRIBAL NEWS NOTES
Schurz, NV 89427

WAMIDIOTA NEWSLETTER
Fort Lewis College
Division of Intercultural Studies
120 Miller Student Center
Durango, CO 81301

WANA CHINOOK TYMOO
Columbia River Inter-Tribal Fish Commission
729 N.E. Oregon, Suite 200
Portland, OR 97232
  (503) 238-0667 Fax 235-4228
  Laura Berg, Editor; Carol Craig & Dan Kane, Staff
Columbia River salmon stories. Quarterly magazine. 6,000 cir.

WANBLI HO: A LITERARY ARTS JOURNAL
Lakota Studies/Creative Writing Program
Sinte Gleska College, P.O. Box 8
Mission, SD 57555
  Victor Douville, Editor
Features short fiction, poetry, literary articles, oral tradition texts, and artwork. Focuses on contemporary and traditional Native-American literature and art. Published twice a year. Subscription: $7.50/year; $4.50 each issue.

WARM SPRINGS TRIBAL NEWSLETTER
Warm Springs Confederated Tribes
Warm Springs, OR 97761

WARPATH
United Native Americans
2434 Faria Ave.
Pinole, CA 94564
  (415) 758-8160
  Lehman L. Brightman, Editor
Monthly newsletter.

THE WARRIOR
American Indian Center
1630 West Wilson
Chicago, IL 60640

WASHOE NEWSLETTER
Washoe Tribal Council
919 Hwy 395 South
Gardnerville, NV 89410
  (702) 265-4191 Fax 265-6240
Tribal newsletter.

THE WEB
American Indian Program
300 Caldwell Hall - Cornell University
Ithaca, NY 14853
  (602) 255-4308
  Jennifer Bedell, Coordinator
Focuses on Native American students at Cornell University. Reports on activities, awards, projects, scholarships, , and alumni. Semiannul. No charge. Begun 1986. Semiannual newsletter of the American Indian program of Cornell University.

WHISPERING WIND
Written Heritage
8009 Wales St.
New Orleans, LA 70126
  (504) 246-3742
  Jack B. Heriard, Editor

Bimonthly magazine of American Indian crafts and material culture. Includes old photos, powwow dates and reports, color photos, and book reviews. 16,000 cir. $18/year. Advertising. Begun 1967.

WHISPERING WINDS
Tule River Tribal Council
Porterville, CA 93258

WHITE EARTH RESERVATION NEWS
P.O. Box 274
White Earth, MN 56591

WHITE MOUNTAIN APACHE NEWSPAPER
P.O. Box 700
White River, AZ 85941

WHITE MOUNTAIN EAGLE
P.O. Box 1570
Show Low, AZ 85901

THE WICAZO SA REVIEW
(The Red Pencil Review)
Rte. 8, Box 510, 3755 Blake Ct. N.
Rapid City, SD 57701-4618
  (605) 341-3228
  Elizabeth Cook-Lynn, Editor
  Robert Warrior, Contributing Editor
Journal of American Studies devoted to the development of Native American Studies as an academic discipline. *Contributing editors*: William Willard, Roger Buffalohead, Beatrice Medicino, Larry Evers, Ted Jojola, Cecil Joie, A. Blair Stonechild, Jack Forbes, Steven Crum. Associated with Eastern Washington University and U.C.-Davis, Native American Studies Depts and A.A.I.R. Bi-annual. 600 cir. $20/year. Begun 1985.

WICOZANNI WOWAPI
Native American Community Board
P.O. Box 572
Lake Andres, SD 57356
  (605) 487-7072 Fax 487-7964
  Charon Asetoyer, Editor
Newsletter of the Native American Community Board concerned with Native American issues. No charges; donations accepted. Quarterly.

WI GUABA
Havasupai Tribal Council
P.O. Box 10
Supai, AZ 86435

WILDFIRE MAGAZINE
Beart Tribe Medicine Society
P.O. Box 9167
Spokane, WA 99209
  (509) 326-6561
  Sun Bear, Publisher
  Matthew Ryan, Editor
Concerned with healthy living, including in-depth interviews, environmental issues, book reviews, etc. Semiannual. 10,000 cir. $4/copy; $15/year; $23/year, Canada; $27/year, foreign. Library rates: $7.50/year-U.S., $15/year, Canada. $2.50 per copy. Advertising. Began 1961.

WILLIAM & MARY QUARTERLY
Institute of Early American History and Culture
P.O. Box 8781
Williamsburg, VA 23187-8781
  (804) 221-1120 Fax 221-1047
  Michael McGiffert, Editor
  Ann Gross, Managing Editor
Scholarly journal containing articles on American Indians, including Caribbean and Southwestern,

in the period up to about 1820--including their relations with other groups in early America. 3,600 cir. $25/year, individuals; $30, institutions; $12.50, students.

WIN-AWAENEN-NISITOTUNG
Saulte Ste. Marie Tribe of Chippewa Indians
2218 Shunk Rd.
Sault Ste. Marie, Michigan 49783-9326
(906) 635-6050
Susan Matrious and Leslie Eger, Editors
Contains local and some national news; photographs and written features. Monthly newspaper. $7/year. Complimentary copies available upon request. Advertising.

WIND RIVER JOURNAL
Shoshone Tribe, P.O. Box 157
Fort Washakie, Wyoming 82514

WIND RIVER NEWS
P.O. Box J
Lander, WY 82520

WIND RIVER RENDEZVOUS
St. Stephan's Mission Foundation
P.O. Box 278
St. Stephan, WY 82524-0278
(307) 856-6797
Ron Mamot, Editor
Covers the history of Western USA, cultural contribution of the Native American, and pastoral programs for the Arapaho and Shoshoni people at St. Stephens Mission. Quarterly magazine. 41,000 cir. $10/year. Begun 1971.

WINDS OF CHANGE
A.I.S.E.S. Publishing, Inc.
1630 30th St., Suite 301
Boulder, CO 80301
(303) 444-9099 Fax 444-6607
James Weidlein, Editor
Designed to provide positive program information and succesful role models for Indian students and professionals of all disciplines (not just science and engineering.) Inforamtion about education and career opportunities, as well as tribal culture and events. A new section highlights articles and information about environmental concerns and issues of interest to Native Americans. Quarterly magazine. 50,000 cir. $24/year.

WINNEBAGO INDIAN NEWS
Winnebago Tribal Council
Winnebago, NE 68071

WOLF CRY NEWSLETTER
Northwest Cherokee Wolf Band
Southeastern Cherokee Confederacy, Inc.
P.O. Box 592
Talent, OR 97540
(503) 535-5003
Chief-Robert Silver Badger Ponder, Editor
Deals with Tribal business, Native American affairs and issues (non-radical), Tribal heritage, culture and customs of the Nortwest Cherokee Wolf Band. Bi-monthly. $15/year to non-tribal members. Complimentary copies available upon request to Native American oriented businesses. Begun 1980.

WOLF SONGS
Ti Ospaye
P.O. Box 200
Wanblee, SD 57577
(605) 462-6544
Gilbert C. Walking Bull, Editor
Quarterly newsletter. $10/year.

WOPEEDAM
Immaculate Conception Mission
Stephan, SD 57346

WOTANIN WOWAPI
Fort Peck Assiniboine & Sioux Tribes
P.O. Box 1027
Poplar, MT 59255
(406) 768-5155 Ext. 2370
Bonnie Red Elk, Editor
Weekly newspaper of articles and photos of news pertinent to the Assiniboine and Sioux people residing on the Fort Peck Reservation. Also contains complete tribal government meetings; also a historical review of the tribes. Complimentary copies available upon request. Advertising. Begun 1976.

WUSKUSU YERTUM
Mashantucket Pequot Tribe
Box 160, Indian Town Rd.
Ledyard, CT 06339

Y

YA-KA-AMA INDIAN EDUCATIONNEWSLETTER
6215 East Side Rd.
Forestville, CA 95436

YAKIMA NATION REVIEW
Yakima Indian Nation
P.O. Box 310
Toppenish, WA 98948
(509) 865-5121
Richard V. LaCourse, Editor
Contains articles pertaining to and affecting Indian people, human interest articles involving Indian population, governmental action on national, state and local levels relevant to the Yakima Tribal Government structure. Biweekly magazine. 10,000 cir. $15/year. Complimentary copies available upon request. Advertising. Begun 1970.

YAQUI BULLETIN
4730 West Calle Tetakusin
Tucson, AZ 85910

YUGTARVIK REGIONAL MUSEUM NEWSLETTER
P.O. Box 338
Bethel, AK 99559
Monthly.

YUPIIT GANLAUCIAT
Association of Village Council President
Pouch 219
Bethel, AK 99559

Z

ZUNI CARRIER
Zuni Pueblo
Zuni, New Mexico 87327

ZUNI LEGAL AID NEWSLETTER
Zuni, New Mexico 87327

ZUNI TRIBAL NEWSLETTER
Box 339, Zuni Tribal Office
Zuni, New Mexico 87327

Product codes A-Z are located on page 338.
IACA stands for Indian Arts & Crafts Assn.

ALASKA

ALASKAN TREASURES
1013 E. Dimond #514
Anchorage, AK 99515
(907) 333-5839
Fred, Eva & Angie Larson
Wholesale, retail. *Products*: C,G,H,I,L,X,Y.
Membership: IACA.

**"OOM-INGMAK" - MUSK OX
PRODUCERS' COOPERATIVE**
604 H St.
Anchorage, AK 99501
(907) 272-9225
Sigrun C. Robertson, Owner
Retail, mail order. Tundra/coastal villager's co-op.
250 Eskimo ladies who handknit hats and scarves
and accessories from the Qiviut (the underwool
of the domestic musk ox. Brochure.

SOUTHWEST REFLECTIONS
P.O. Box 202815, 3101 Penland Pkwy . #112
Anchorage, AK 99520
(907) 258-9988
Nancy & Weyman Perez
Retail. *Products*: A,B,E,G,H,J,M,P,Q,R,S,V,W.
Membership: IACA.

TAHETA ARTS & CULTURAL GROUP
605 "A" St.
Anchorage, AK 99501
(907) 272-5829
Jim L. Richards, Manager
Wholesale, retail, mail order . Eskimo, Indian and
Aleut non-profit cooperative. *Products*: A,B,P,X.

YUGTARVIK REGIONAL MUSEUM SHOP
P.O. Box 388, Third Ave.
Bethel, AK 99559
(907) 543-2098
Penni K. Abraham, Manager
Wholesale, mail order . *Products*: B,H,I,P,X.

**ST. LAWRENCE ISLAND ORIGINAL
IVORY COOPERATIVE LTD.**
P.O. Box 189
Gambell, AK 99742
(907) 985-5112/5649
Clement Ungott
Mail order. Eskimo Cooperative. *Products*: X.

CHILKAT VALLEY ARTS
P.O. Box 145
Haines, AK 99827
(907) 766-2990/2216
Sue Folletti
Retail. *Products*: L,P. Totemic designs
of the Northwest Coast Tlingit Indians.

INUA
P.O. Box 4243
Homer, AK 99603
(907) 235-6644
William E. Lovett, Owner
Retail, wholesale. *Products*: Native crafts from
Alaska - B,C,H,I,L,N,P,S,X,Z. *Appraisals*: B,L,X.
Membership: IACA. *Branch*: Boulder, CO.

AMOS WALLACE
P.O. Box 478
Juneau, AK 99802
(907) 586-9000
Amos Wallace, Owner
Wholesale/mail order . Tlingit crafts. *Products*: P.
Special orders on totem poles, masks & paddles.

**NANA MUSEUM OF THE
ARCTIC CRAFT SHOP**
P.O. Box 49
Kotzebue, AK 99752
(907) 442-3304/3747
Pete Schaef for
Retail/mail order by special request.
Products: B,H,I,L,P,X.

SAVOONGA NATIVE STORE
P.O. Box 100
Savoonga, AK 99769
Paul Rookok, Sr., Manager
Mail order. *Products*: L, P,X. Eskimo ivory
carvings, jewelry. Price list available.

MARDINA DOLLS
P.O. Box 611
Wrangell, AK 99929
(907) 874-3854
Marleita Wallace
Wholesale, mail order . *Products*: A,H,I.
Tlingit-Tsimsian art, clothing, dolls.

ARIZONA

THE BOULDERS
P.O. Box 2090
Carefree, AZ 85377
(602) 9009 Fax 488-4118
Melissa Brasch, William Nassikas,
Kenneth Humes
Retail. *Products*: B,G,J,N,P,Q,U,V.
Membership: IACA.

D.Y. BEGAY; NAVAJO TEXTILE STUDIO
P.O. Box 1770
Chinle, AZ 86503
(201) 391-2236
Retail, by appointment only . *Products*: V. Traditional and contemporary Navajo weavings–rugs,
blankets and tapestries. Special orders accepted.

THUNDERBIRD LODGE
Canyon de Chelly , Box 548
Chinle, AZ 86503
(602) 674-5841
Mary Jones
Retail. *Products*: All. *Membership*: IACA.

M & M SALES
Box 567, 1111 Spanish Trail
Eager, AZ 85925
(602) 333-2333
Blackie & Mary Mitscher
Wholesale. *Product*: P. Zuni handmade jewelry .
Catalog.

BLACK MESA TRADERS
2930 E. Matterhorn Dr .
Flagstaff, AZ 86004-2213
(602) 526-8354 Fax 774-9079
Rita Alexander & Rodger Berg
Wholesaler. *Products*: A,B,C,F,G,H,I,M,P,
Q,S,X,Z. *Appraisals*: Q. Specializes in Kachinas.
Membership: IACA. Catalog.

MILT'S INDIAN ARTS
P.O. Box 22007
Flagstaff, AZ 86002
(602) 526-0442
Milton Forsman
Wholesale. *Products*: B,V,W,X.

TURQUOISE HOGAN
4 N. Leroux St.
Flagstaff, AZ 86001
(602) 774-0174
Mary Jane & Franklin Kahn, Owners
Wholesale, retail. *Products*: A,B,C,P,Q,U,V.

DEE'S EXQUISITE JEWELRY
P.O. Box 235
Fredonia, AZ 86022
(602) 643-7093
Melvin Martin and Dolores Savala
Retail.

MELJOY INDIAN TRADERS
165 Amarilla Dr.
Globe, AZ 85501
(602) 425-0216
Melvin & Joyce Montgomery
Wholesale, retail. *Products*: B,C,H,I,S.
Membership: IACA.

GRAND CANYON SQUIRE INN
Box 130, Hwy. 64/180
Grand Canyon, AZ 86023
(602) 638-2681
Raymond Curley, Manager
Retail. *Products*: A,B,C,J,P,U,V,W,X.

PRINGLE'S SOUTHWEST, LTD.
P.O. Box 503
Green Valley, AZ 85614
(602) 648-1388
Don & Phyllis Pringle
Retail. *Products*: B,N,P,S,U,V.

SHONTO TRADING CO.
336 N. Calle de las Profetas
Green Valley, AZ 85614
Gary Vaughn
Retail. *Products*: All.

CHEE'S INDIAN STORE, INC.
P.O. Box 66, I-40 Allentown Rd., Exit 351
Houck, AZ 86506
(602) 688-2603
Clara Chee & Harrison Lauber
Karen Chee & Paul Schell
Retail. *Products*: All. *Membership*: IACA.

THE GIFT SHOP OF JEROME
P.O. Box 396, 114 Jerome Ave.
Jerome, AZ 86331
(602) 634-5105
Anna Rae Adams
Wholesale, retail. *Products*: A,B,C,E,F,H,I,J,
N,O, P,Q,R,S,T,U,W,X,Y. *Membership*: IACA..

McGEE'S INDIAN ART
P.O. Box 607, Hwy. 264
Keams Canyon, AZ 86034
(602) 738-2295 Fax 738-5250
William B. & C.F. McGee
Wholesale, retail. *Products*: B,E,F,G,H,I,J,K,N,
O,P,Q,S,U,V,W,X,Z. *Membership*: IACA.

MORNING STAR INDIAN JEWELRY
Box 987, 531 Oak St.
Kingman, AZ 86402
(602) 753-6434
 Sarah J. Ellis
Retail. *Products*: All.

ALBERT LONG: TRADER/CRAFTSMAN
P.O. Box 40
Lake Havasu City, AZ 86405
(602) 453-5925
 Albert Long, Owner
Mail order. *Products*: I,P. Brochure available.

INDIAN JOE
329 S. Lake Havasu
Lake Havasu City, AZ 86403
 Joe & Teri Zwierzycki
Retail. *Products*: A,B,C,H,J,K,N,O,P,Q,R,S,
T,U,V,W,X,Z. *Membership*: IACA.

PERCHARO JEWELRY
RR 2, Box 790
Laveen, AZ 85339
(602) 237-4249
 Nathaniel & Lisa Percharo
Retail/mail order. *Product*: P.

GALA DISTRIBUTING
1125 W. Baseline Rd. #2-138
Mesa, AZ 85210
(602) 820-6326
 James Grover
Wholesale, retail. *Products*: J,N,O,P,Q,U.
Repair & restoration.

HEARTLINE TRADING
911 N. Somerset Cir.
Mesa, AZ 85205
(602) 969-6232
 Barbara Stechnij
Retail. *Products*: C,N,O,P,Q,R,U,V,Y.
Membership: IACA.

INDIAN JEWELRY USA
Box 2424, 6101 E. Main
Mesa, AZ 85204-0090
(602) 985-5146
 Jack & Ranelle Adam
Wholesale, retail. *Products*: A,C,D,I,J,K,N,O,P,
Q,R,S,T,U,W,X,Z. *Appraisals*: C,J,N,O,P,Q,
R,S,T,U,W,X,Z. *Membership*: IACA.

THE KIVA INDIAN SHOP
5809 E. Lawndale St.
Mesa, NM 85205
(505) 982-4906
 Catherine Katona, Owner
Retail. *Products*: B,C,N,P,Q,U.

WHITE EAGLE TRADING CO.
911 N. Somerset Cr.
Mesa, AZ 85205
(602) 969-6232
 Mark & Barbara Stechnij
Wholesale, retail. *Products*: B,N,P,Q,U,V,W.

HUDSON TRADING CO.
P.O Box 1254
Oracle, AZ 85623
(602) 896-2901
 Raymond & Velveeta Volante
Wholesale. *Products*: B,C,N,P,Q,S,U,V.
Membership: IACA.

HOPI KIVA
P.O. Box 96
Oraibi, AZ 86039
(602) 734-2423/6667
 Michael C. Sockyma, Sr., Owner
Mail order. *Products*: P. Specializes in Hopi
overlay jewelry in silver and gold. Brochure.

BLAIR'S DINNEBITO TRADING POST
Box 2903, 626 N. Navajo
Page, AZ 86040
(602) 645-3008
 Elijah & James Blair
Wholesale, retail. *Products*: A,B,C,D,E,G,H,I,J,
K,M,N,P,Q,R,T,U,V,W,X. *Membership*: IACA.

WAHWEAP GIFT SHOP
P.O. Box 1597
Page, AZ 86040
(602) 645-2433
 Kathy M. Parsons, Manager
Retail. *Products*: All.

**COLORADO RIVER INDIAN TRIBES
MUSEUM**
Rt. 1, Box 23-B, Mohave Rd. & 2nd Ave.
Parker, AZ 85344
 Charles A. Lamb, Manager
Retail. *Products*: B,E,J,Q,U,V.

SAR JO INDIAN ARTS
13909 N. 69th Dr.
Peoria, AZ 85381
(602) 979-4665
 Joseph Levine
Wholesale. *Products*: B,I,J,O,P,Q,S,Y,Z.
Membership: IACA.

CANYON RECORDS & INDIAN ARTS
4143 N. 16th St.
Phoenix, AZ 85016
(602) 266-4823
 Bob Nuss, Owner
Retail, wholesale, mail order.
Products: C,D,H,V,Y. Brochure.

HEARD MUSEUM STORE
22 E. Monte Vista
Phoenix, AZ 85004
(602) 252-8344
Retail. *Products*: A,B,C,E,I,K,N,O,P,Q,S,U,
V,W,X. *Membership*: IACA.

MUSIAL'S NAVAJO ARTS
19209 No. 40th Place
Phoenix, AZ 85024
(602) 569-2283
 Kalley Musial
Wholesale, retail. *Products*: B,F,G,I,K,M,P,U,V,Z.
Membership: IACA.

NAVAJO SILVERCRAFT
P.O. Box 2725
Phoenix, AZ 85002
(602) 253-1594
 Jane Yikazbaa Popovich
Retail. *Product*: P.

ROCKING HORSE DESIGNS
2415 W. Glenrosa
Phoenix, AZ 85015
(602) 265-1061
 Lani Randall
Wholesale, retail. *Product*: P. *Appraisals*: P.
Membership: IACA.

ARROWHEAD TRADING POST
P.O. Box 1253, 6 N. Hwy.
Pine, AZ 85544
(602) 476-3140
 Dorothea L. Poland
Retail. *Products*: A,C,E,H,I,J,N,O,P,Q,T,V,W.
Membership: IACA.

GILA RIVER ARTS & CRAFTS CENTER
P.O. Box 457
Sacaton, AZ 85247
(602) 562-3411
 Jon A. Long, Manager
Retail, mail order. *Products*: B,C,Q,P,U,V.

BROWN'S TURQUOISE SHOP
2248 First Ave.
Safford, AZ 85546
(602) 428-6433
 Bernice Brown
Retail, wholesale. *Products*: B,C,E,F,I,J,K,N,
O,P,Q,S,T,U,V,W,X,Z. *Membership*: IACA.

PHILLIP TITLA STUDIO
P.O. Box 497
San Carlos, AZ 85550
(602) 475-2361
 Phillip Titla, Owner
Retail, mail order. *Products*: A,I,X. Brochure.

THE EASTERN COWBOYS
4235 N. 86th Place
Scottsdale, AZ 85251
(602) 945-9804
 Jay & Edith Sadow, Owners
Wholesale. *Products*: All. Catalog.

GODBERS JEWELRY, INC.
Box 831, 7542 E. Main
Scottsdale, AZ 85252
(602) 949-1133
 Allie Mae & Ken Godber
Wholesale. *Products*: A,B,K,N,O,P,Q,U,V,W,X.
Membership: IACA.

GREY WOLF
7101 Stetson Dr.
Scottsdale, AZ 85251
(602) 423-0004
 Anne & Sid Billings
Wholesale, retail. *Products*: A,B,C,F,H,I,J,M,
N,O,P,Q,R,U,V,W,X,Z. *Membership*: IACA.

LEONA KING GALLERY
7171 E. Main
Scottsdale, AZ 85251
(602) 945-1209
 Sam & Sue King
Wholesale, retail. *Products*: A,B,C,H,J,N,O,P,
Q,R,S,U,V,X. *Appraisals*: A,U,X. *Membership*:
IACA.

RUTH KIERNAN ENTERPRISES
9490 E. Cactus Rd.
Scottsdale, AZ 85260
(602) 860-2551
 Ruth & Philip Kiernan
Wholesale. *Products*: C,I,J,N,O,P,Q.
Membership: IACA.

SEWELL'S INDIAN ARTS
7087 5th Ave.
Scottsdale, AZ 85251
(602) 945-0962
 Sandy, Sam & Nadiya Daiza
Retail. *Products*: A,B,F,G,H,I,J,K,N,O,P,Q,R,S,
T,U,V,W,Z. *Appraisals*: P,Q. *Membership*: IACA.

Arts & Crafts Shops & Cooperatives

SOUTHWEST EVENTS ETC.
8233 Paseo del Norte #A600
Scottsdale, AZ 85258
 (602) 991-5131 Fax 991-0715
 Nancy & Chris Pavlik
Retail. *Products*: A,B,E,G,N,O,P,Q,R,S,U,V,W,X.
Membership : IACA>

TRADER GENE
Box 1725, 14437 N. 73rd St.
Scottsdale, AZ 85252
 (800) 258-3746; (602) 945-5826 Fax 443-0355
 Gene Benner
Wholesale. *Products*: I,N,P,Q,V,W,X,Y.

TURQUOISE HOGAN, INC.
P.o. Box 657
Scottsdale, AZ 85252-0657
 (602) 949-5122 (Phone & Fax)
 Judith & Donald Barajas, Owners
Wholesale, retail. *Products*: N,P,Z.
Membership : IACA.

DAWA'S HOPI ARTS & CRAFTS
P.O. Box 127 (Hopi Reservation)
Second Mesa, AZ 86043
 (602) 734-2430
 Bernard Dawahoya, Owner
Retail/mail order . *Product*: P.
Specializes in Hopi overlay silver jewelry .

HOPI GALLERY
Hopi Cultural Center
P.O. Box 316
Second Mesa, AZ 86043
 (602) 734-2238
 Phil Sekaquaptewa, Owners
Retail, wholesale, mail order .
Products: A,B,P,Q,U,V. Brochure, catalog.

**HOPI ARTS & CRAFTS -
SILVERCRAFT COOPERATIVE GUILD**
P.O. Box 37, Hwy. 264
Second Mesa, AZ 86043
 (602) 734-2463 Fax 734-6647
 Milland S. Lomakema, Executive Director
Retail, wholesale, mail order . *Products*:
A,B,E,F,I,J,P,Q,S,U,X. Brochure, catalog.

SECAKUKU ENTERPRISES & SHOP
P.O. Box 67
Second Mesa, AZ 86043
 (602) 734-2401; 737-2632
 Dorothy & Ferrell Secakuku, Owners
Retail, wholesale. *Products*: A,B,Q,U.

"...AND INDIANS
Artesania Plaza
251 Hwy. 179 #B-7,8
Sedona, AZ 86336
 (602) 282-2026
 Michael & Dianne Hoedel
Retail, wholesale. *Products*: A,B,C,H,I,J,
N,P,Q,R,U,X.

BLUE-EYED BEAR
299 N. Hwy. 89-A
Sedona, AZ 86336
 Bud & Linda Johnson
Retail. *Products*: N,P,U,V,W,X.
Membership : IACA.

DINETKAH SILVER GALLERY
Hozho Bldg. #B-4, 431 Hwy . 179
Sedona, AZ 86336
 (602) 282-3525, Sue O'Dell
Retail. *Products*: A,B,C,J,N,O,P,Q,U,V,W.

GARLAND'S INDIAN JEWELRY
Box 1848, Indian Gardens Hwy . 89-A
Sedona, AZ 86336
 (602) 282-6632
 William T. Garland, Owner
 Britt Burns, Manager
Wholesale, retail. *Products*: B,K,N,O,P,Q,
R,S,T,U,W. *Appraisals*: P. *Membership* : IACA.

GARLAND'S NAVAJO RUGS
Box 851, 41 1 Hwy. 179
Sedona, AZ 86336
 (602) 282-4070
 Daniel J. Garland
Retail. *Products*: B,K,Q,S,U,V,W.
Appraisals: V. *Membership* : IACA.

THE HUMIOVI
P.O. Box 1463
Sedona, AZ 86339
 (602) 282-3002
 John & Kathy Runnion
Wholesale/retail. *Products*:
B,C,F,H,I,N,O,P,Q,U,V,W,X.

TURQUOISE TORTOISE GALLERY
Hozho Center, 431 Hwy. 179
Sedona, AZ 86336
 (602) 282-2262
 Peggy J. Lanning-Eisler
Wholesale, retail. *Products*: A,B,C,E,H,N,O,
P,Q,S,T,W. *Membership* : IACA.

INDIAN PONY TRADING POST
Box 767
Sonoita, AZ 85637
 (602) 394-2264
Retail. *Products*: A,B,C,U,W,X.

THE TRADING POST
8817 Montana
Sun Lakes, AZ 85248
 (602) 895-6072
 Tom & Marilyn DeYoung
Wholesale, retail. *Products*: C,N,P,Q,R.
Membership : IACA.

TEEC NOS POS ARTS/CRAFTS
P.O. Box Z
Teec Nos Pos, AZ 86514-0113
 (602) 656-3228
 Bill & Kay Foutz
Wholesale, retail. *Products*: B,C,E,G,I,K,P,Q,U,
V,W,X. *Membership* : IACA. Catalog.

**ARLENE'S SOUTHWEST TRADING CO.
& ARLENE'S GALLERY**
P.O. Box 340, 400/404/415 Allen St.
Tombstone, AZ 85638
 (602) 457-3344
 Arlene L. Klein
Wholesale, retail. *Products*: A,B,C,D,E,F,G,H,
I,J,K,M,N,Q,R,S,T,U,V,W,X. *Membership* : IACA.

HATATHLI GALLERY
Navajo Community College Dev . Foundation
Tsaile, AZ 86556
 (602) 724-331 1 ext. 156
 Janice C. Hillis, Manager
Wholesale, retail. *Products*: A,C,P,V,W.

**SAN JUAN SOUTHERN PAIUTE
YINGUP WEAVERS ASSOCIATION**
P.O. Box 1336
Tuba City, AZ 86045
 (602) 526-7143
 Evelyn James, Manager
Wholesale, retail, mail order . *Product*: B.
Paiute basketry.

TUBA TRADING POST
Box 247, Main & Moenave Sts.
Tuba City, AZ 86045
 (602) 283-5441 Fax 283-4144
 Mark & Janet Shipley
Wholesale, retail. *Products*: A,B,E,H,I,J,N,
P,Q,U,V,W,X. *Membership* : IACA.

OLD PRESIDIO TRADERS
Box 4023, #14 Tubac Rd.
Tubac, AZ 85646
 (602) 398-9333
 Lisa & Garry Hembree
Retail.

TURQUOISE TORTOISE GALLERY
Box 2321, La Pradera Mall, Hwy . 82
Tubac, AZ 85646
 (602) 398-2041
 Esther & Larry Fitzpatrick
Retail. *Products*: A,B,C,E,H,J,N,O,P,Q,T,V,W.
Membership : IACA.

BAHTI INDIAN ARTS
4300 N. Campbell Ave.
Tucson, AZ 85701
 (602) 577-0290
 Mark Tomas Bahti, Owner
Retail. *Products*: All. *Membership* : IACA.

BLACK ARROW TRADERS
2400 N. Calle de Maurer
Tucson, AZ 85749-9582
 (602) 749-4119
 Sophie & Jack Guth
Wholesale, retail. *Products*: B,C,I,N,O,P,Q,V,W.
Membership : IACA.

DESERT SON, INC.
4759 E. Sunrise Dr.
Tucson, AZ 85718
 (602) 299-0818
 Stephen Osborne
Retail. *Products*: H,M,P,Q,U,V.
Membership : IACA. Catalog.

GUARDIAN RAINBOW
P.O. Box 32078
Tucson, AZ 85751
 (602) 885-8369 Fax 722-5872
 Keith & Doris Palmer
Wholesale, retail. *Products*: B,N,P,Q,U,V.
Appraisals: P,Q,U,V. *Membership* : IACA.

K & G CO., INC.
63647 E. Edgeview Lane
Tucson, AZ 85737
 Gloria Snook
Retail. *Products*: A,C,F,H,I,J,N,O,P,Q,
T,U,V,W,X,Y. *Membership* : IACA.

MORNING STAR TRADERS, INC.
2020 E. Speedway Blvd.
Tucson, AZ 85719
 (602) 881-2112
 Richard Rosenthal
Retail. *Products*: B,D,C,K,M,N,O,P,Q,T,U,V.
Membership : IACA.

NATIVE AMERICAN COLLECTIBLES
2241 S. Double O Place
Tucson, AZ 85713
  John & Ruth Gruber
Wholesale, retail. *Products*: B,J,N,O,P,Q,U,V,X.
Appraisals: V. *Membership*: IACA.

NORTHERN HERITAGE ART CO., LTD.
3256 E. Grant Rd.
Tucson, AZ 85716
  (602) 795-9890 Fax 795-31 11
  David & Adele Waine
Wholesale, retail. *Products*: A,B,D,J,L,X.
Catalog.

SO WEST GALLERY
6310 E. Calle Pegaso
Tucson, AZ 85710
  (602) 623-1871
  Linda & Harry Sheraw
Wholesale, retail. *Products*: A,B,G,H,J,P,Q,U,X.
Membership: IACA. *Branch*: 201 N. Court Ave.,
Tucson, AZ.

**TAYLOR'S INDIAN
STUDIO/OWL EAR STUDIO**
2901 W. Sahuaro Divide
Tucson, AZ 85741
  (800) 487-0180; (602) 297-4456 Fax 544-4382
  Urshel Taylor, Owner
Wholesale, retail, mail order. *Products*: A,N,X.
Membership: IACA. Brochure.

THUNDERBIRD SHOP, INC.
40 W. Broadway
Tucson, AZ 85701
  (602) 623-1371
  Sam & Frank Patania
Retail. *Products*: B,C,N,O,P,U,V,X.
Membership: IACA.

TOWAYALANE TRADING CO.
6590 E. Tanque Verde, Suite A
Tucson, AZ 85715
  (602) 886-3542
  Joe & Jan Douthitt
Wholesale. *Products*: A,B,C,D,G,I,J,K,N,
P,Q,S,U,V,W. *Membership*: IACA.

TREASURE CHEST PUBLISHING
1802 W. Grant Rd. #101
Tucson, AZ 85745
  (602) 623-9558 Fax 624-5888
  Sterling Mahan & Oscar Branson
Wholesale. *Products*: D. *Membership*: IACA.
Catalog.

TREASURES & TRIFLES
3030 N. Willow Creek Dr.
Tucson, AZ 85712
  (602) 881-2124
  James & Elsie Deer
Retail. *Products*: A,B,N,O,P,S,Y,Z.
Appraisals: B,N,O,P,S. *Membership*: IACA.

VINCENT MEIER
P.O. Box 5862
Tucson, AZ 85703
  (602) 325-3209
  Vincent Meier
Wholesale. *Products*: B,C,I,N,P,Q,R,U,V,W.

MANY NATION
Box 460, 13251 E. Benson Hwy.
Vail, AZ 85641
  (602) 762-5266
  Rosalie & Bob Baker

Wholesale, retail. *Products*: All.
Membership: IACA. Catalog.

BENALLY'S INDIAN ARTS
P.O. Box 780
Window Rock, AZ 86515
  (602) 871-5727
  Ronald F. Benally
Wholesale.

NAVAJO ARTS & CRAFTS ENTERPRISE
P.O. Drawer A
Window Rock, AZ 86515
  (602) 871-4090 Fax 871-3340
  Raymond Smith & Russ Morgan
Wholesale/retail. Tribal Enterprise.
Products: A,B,C,E,H,I,K,N,P,Q,U,V,W,X,Y,Z.
Branch shops: P.O. Box 464, Cameron, AZ
86020 (602) 679-2244; 812 North Hwy . 666,
Gallup, NM 87301 (505) 722-6709.

NAVAJO TRIBAL ENTERPRISE
Hwy. 264 & Rte. 12
Window Rock, AZ 86515
  (602) 871-4095 Fax 871-3340
Wholesale/retail. Tribal Enterprise.
Products: A,B,C,E,H,I,K,N,P,Q,U,V,W,X,Y,Z.

MARQUIS INDIAN ARTS
340 Main St.
Yuma, AZ 85364
  (602) 783-2726
  Jim Harlin, Owner

CALIFORNIA

HHS ENTERPRISES E.T.C.
2305 Roark Dr.
Alhambra, CA 91803-4535
  (818) 449-0933 Fax 449-5340
  Hermann & Maria Schmidt
Wholesale, retail. *Products*: All. *Appraisal*:
A,M,N,O,P,Q,R,T,U,X. *Membership*: IACA.

SANTA FE CRAFTS
P.O. Box 298
Altadena, CA 91003-0298
  (800) 421-7661; (818) 398-1789 Fax 398-1575
  Barbara Goldeen
Wholesale. *Products*: B,G,I,M,N,O,P,Q,S,T,U.
Membership: IACA.

TREASURES OF SANTA FE
376 1st St.
Benicia, CA 94510
  (707) 747-9251
  Jack & Jean Hastings
Retail. *Products*: All. *Membership*: IACA.

**TATEWIN-PETAKI AMERICAN INDIAN
ARTS & CRAFTS**
P.O. Box 549
Big Bear City, CA 92314
  (714) 585-1435
  Wendy Holt, Owner
Special orders and commissions. *Products*:
C,H,I,beadwork, dolls, leatherwork, tapestries.

BEAR MOUNTAIN TRADING CO.
P.O. Box 6503, 42626 Moonridge Rd.
Big Bear Lake, CA 92315
  (714) 585-9676 Fax 585-0310
  Gerry & Patty Taylor
Retail. *Products*: A,B,C,F,G,H,I,J,N,O,
P,Q,R,S,T,U,V,W,X. *Membership*: IACA.

EASTERN SIERRA TRADING CO.
P.O. Box 731
Bridgeport, CA 93517
  (619) 932-7231
  Joe & Mary Lent, Owners
Retail. *Products*: B,C,P,U. b

KNOTT'S BERRY FARM
8039 Beach Blvd.
Buena park, CA 90620
  (714) 220-5270
  Fred Wagner, Mechandise Div.
Retail. *Products*: All. *Membership*: IACA.

THE WRIGHT STUFF
1811 W. Burbank Blvd.
Burbank, CA 91506
  (818) 954-8943 Fax 954-9370
  Peter & Marcie Wright
Retail. *Products*: N,P,Q,U. *Membership*: IACA.

THE WOODEN INDIAN
3019 State St.
Carlsbad, CA 92008
  (619) 729-1596 (Phone & Fax)
  LaVon & Pete Ritter
Retail. *Products*: A,B,C,D,E,I,J,N,O,P,Q,R,S,T,
U,V,W,X,Z. *Appraisals*: A,B,C,N,O,P,Q,U,V,W.
Membership: IACA.

BUNTE & SHAW TRADING CO.
651 Citadel Ave.
Claremont, CA 91711
  (714) 626-0121
  Howard Bunte & Theresa Shaw
Retail. *Products*: A,N,O,P,V. *Membership*: IACA.

THREE FLAGS TRADING POST
Walker Rt. 1, Box 115, Hwy. 395
Coleville, CA 96107
  (916) 495-2955
  Tom & Marlene Stewart
Retail. *Products*: A,B,C,F,H,I,J.

BEARCLOUD TRADING POST
Gallery & Miwok Heritage Museum
P.O. Box 308
Columbia, CAS 95310

WHITE PELICAN
34475 Golden Lantern
Dana Point, CA 92629
  (714) 240-1991
  Chuck & Cathy Mullen
Retail. *Products*: A,B,C,E,F,G,H,I,J,N,O,
P,Q,R,S,T,U,V,W,X. *Membership*: IACA.

DELUNA JEWELERS
521 Second St.
Davis, CA 95616
  (916) 753-3351
  Richard Luna, Owner
Wholesale, retail, mail order.
Products: B,C,P,U,V,X.

AMERICAN INDIAN STORE
1095 Magnolia
El Cajon, CA 92020
  (619) 583-5389
  G. Roy Cook, Owner
Mail order. *Products*: A,C,H,P,Q,U,V,Z.
Catalog.

ONE SQUAW ENTERPRISES
220 Glen Arbor Dr.
Encinitas, CA 92024
  (619) 942-5534

Sandie & Dick Powers
Retail. *Products*: B,C,F,J,N,O,P,Q,U,W,Z.

AMERICAN INDIAN ART & GIFT SHOP, NCIDC, INC.
241 F St.
Eureka, CA 95501
(707) 445-8451 Fax 445-8479
Terry Coltra, manager
Retail, wholesale. *Products*: A,B,C,D,E,M,P,Q,U, V,W,X,Y. *Membership*: IACA. Special orders accepted. Small outlet in Yreka, CA. Brochure/Price list.

KAROK ORIGINALS BY VIT
P.O. Box 3317
Eureka, CA 95502
(707) 442-8800
Linda C. Vit, Owner
Wholesale, retail, mail order .
Products: P,V. Special orders accepted.
Catalog and wholesale price list.

THE WESTERNER
110 N. Main St.
Fallbrook, CA 92028
(619) 728-1462
Juanita Walden
Retail. *Products*: A,B,C,F,H,J,N,P,Q,U,V,W,X.
Membership: IACA.

ANCIENT ECHOES
12776 Brookhurst St.
Garden Grove, CA 92640
(714) 638-0908
Mary Ray, Owner
Retail. *Products*: A,D,J,P,Q,X

THE TURQUOISE NUT
321 N. Verdugo Rd.
Glendale, CA 91206
(818) 243-1001
Tom & Helen Snyder
Wholesale, retail. *Products*: All.
Membership: IACA.

MAR-BILL INDIAN STORE
1620 San Vicente Dr.
Hemet, CA 92543
(509) 996-2470
Mary Luther
Retail. *Products*: B,C,D,E,H,I,J,K,N,
O,P,Q,R,S,U,V,W,X. *Membership*: IACA.
Branch: Winthrop, WA.

GEORGE N. BLAKE
P.O. Box 1304
Hoopa, CA 95546
(916) 625-4619
Wholesale, retail. *Products*: J,U,X.

GENE AUTRY WESTERN HERITAGE MUSEUM STORE
4700 Western Heritage Way
Los Angeles, CA 90027
(213) 667-2000
Joanne Hale, Executive Director
Susan DeLand, Director of Merchandising
Blue Gehrens, Manager
Retail. *Products*: All. *Membership*: IACA.
Catalog.

ROCKY MOUNTAIN HOUSE
2574 S. Bundy Dr.
Los Angeles, CA 90064
(310) 393-8912
Ron Daleo

Wholesale. *Products*: B,C,H,J,N,P,S,U,V,W.
Membership: IACA.

TRIBAL ARTS
P.O. Box 19965
Los Angeles, CA 90019
(213) 292-6808 Fax 295-1045
Judy Cross
Wholesale, retail. *Products*: O,P,T.
Membership: IACA.

YO'ZHO
10392 Almayo Ave.
Los Angeles, CA 90064
(213) 858-7700
Paula Palmer
Retail. *Product*: P.

THE INDIAN STORE
Box 308, 50 University Ave.
Los Gatos, CA 95031
(408) 354-9988
Janice L. Benjamin
Retail. *Products*: A,B,C,D,E,G,I,J,L,N,O,P,
Q,S,U,V,W,X. *Membership*: IACA.

FIEGE'S COLLECTIBLES
15236 Lassan St.
Mission Hills, CA 91345
(818) 892-6826
Kathleen & Gary Fiege
Wholesale, retail.

JERRY ROELEN ENTERPRISES
P.O. Box 3086
Mission Viejo, CA 92690
(714) 728-0186
Jerry & Jay Roelen
Retail. *Membership*: IACA.

OPHELIA JOHNSON'S INDIAN VARIETY SHOP
10256 Central Ave.
Montclair, CA 91763
(714) 625-2611
Retail/mail order . *Products*: B,C,I,P,U.

WINDSPIRIT GALLERY INDIAN ARTS
P.O. Box 651
Newbury Park, CA 91319
(805) 493-4990
Michael & Lori Dee Jekelis
Wholesale, retail. *Products*: A,B,C,E,F,G,H,J,K,
L,N,O,P,Q,S,T,U,V,W,X. *Membership*: IACA.
Catalog.

WESTERN PACIFIC TRADING CO.
40879 Hwy. 41, Suite 1A
Oakhurst, CA 93644
(209) 683-2900
Bill & Barbara Giles
Retail. *Products*: All. *Membership*: IACA.

INTERTRIBAL TRADING POST
523 E. 14th St.
Oakland, CA 94606
(410) 452-1235
Rose M. Anderson, Manager
Wholesale/retail. *Products*: C,H,P,V.

J.J. TAYLOR'S PUEBLO
3864 Piedmont Ave.
Oakland, CA 94611
(510) 652-4040 Fax 428-9132
Fred Banuelos, Owner
Retail. *Products*: A,B,E,F,G,I,J,M,N,O,P,
Q,S,T,U,V,W. *Membership*: IACA.

OJAI INDIAN SHOP
318 E. Ojai Ave.
Ojai, CA 93023-2739
(805) 646-2631
George & Wendy LaBraque
Retail. *Products*: All. *Appraisals*: B,V.

THE SOUTHWEST
P.O. Box 32
Ontario, CA 91762
(714) 981-5711
Debbie Zugzda
Retail. *Products*: B,C,E,I,J,L,N,O,P,Q,S,U,V.

REDROCK ARTS
1295 Adobe Lane
Pacific Grove, CA 93950
(408) 624-5149
Steve & Carol Bishop
Retail. *Products*: A,B,N,O,P,U,V.

LA QUINTA TRADING CO., LTD.
Box 3512, 73-625 Hwy . 111
Palm Desert, CA 92261
(619) 568-4188 Fax 568-6955
Randy Gillet
Retail. *Products*: A,B,C,F,H,I,J,K,M,N,O,
P,Q,S,U,V,W,X,Z. *Membership*: IACA.

SOUTHWEST COLLECTIBLES
73-170 El Paseo
Palm Desert, CA 92210
(619) 346-2209 Fax 568-2473
Joe & DeeDee Polzin
Wholesale, retail. *Products*: A,H,J,P,Q,R,S,
U,V,W,X.

INDIAN VILLAGE, INC.
#43 Town & Country Village
Palo Alto, CA 94301-2326
(415) 328-7090
Beth & Ron Hale
Retail. *Products*: A,B,C,E,G,H,J,M,N,O,P,Q,
R,S,T,U,V,W,X. *Membership*: IACA.

PALOMAR MOUNTAIN GENERAL STORE & TRADING CO.
P.O. Box 100, Jct. S6 & S7
Palomar Mountain, CA 92060
(619) 742-3496 Fax 742-4233
Brian Beck
Retail. *Products*: B,C,E,J,L,M,N,O,P,Q,U,V,X.
Membership: IACA.

THE INDIAN SHOP
P.O. Box 614
Pauma Valley, CA 92061
(619) 749-0130
Leo & Monte Calec
Wholesale, retail. *Products*: A,B,H,I,J,P,V.

MOON DANCER
1706 S. Catalina Ave.
Redondo Beach, CA 90277
(310) 316-7200
Paula Hausvick, Owner
Retail. *Products*: All. *Membership*: IACA.

GALLERY OF THE AMERICAN WEST
121 "K" St.
Sacramento, CA 95814
(916) 446-6662
Leon W. Hodge
Retail. *Products*: A,B,C,N,O,P,Q,S,T,U,V,
W,X,Z. *Appraisals*: B,N,O,P,Q,T,U,V,W.
Membership. IACA..

PAINTED DESERT
36 W. Alisal
Salinas, CA 93901
(408) 757-2536
Emmy & Bob Ames
Retail. *Products*: All. *Membership*: IACA.

BAZAAR DEL MUNDO GALLERY
2754 Calhoun St.
San Diego, CA 92110
(619) 296-3161 Fax 297-2706
Diane Powers
Retail. *Products*: A,C,N,O,P,Q,T,U,V,W,X.
Membership: IACA.

ENBEE COLLECTIBLES
6435 Crystalaire Dr.
San Diego, CA 92120
(619) 582-3185
Norman & Bernice Harris
Wholesale/retail. *Products*: B,U,X.

TRAILS WEST SILVER & LEATHER CO.
821 W. Harbor Dr.
San Diegio, CA 92101
(619) 232-0553
Betty Lou McAdams
Retail. *Products*: All. *Appraisals*: P.
Membership: IACA.

SKY LOOM
502 S. Darwood
San Dimas, CA 91773
(714) 599-3071
Bob & Deborah Anderson
Wholesale, retail.

**AMERICAN INDIAN CONTEMPORARY
ARTS GALLERY**
685 Market St., Suite 250,
Monadniock Bldg.
San Francisco, CA 94105
(415) 495-7600
Janeen Antoine & Kathryn Stewart
Wholesale/retail. *Products*: A,P,U,V,X.

THE INDIAN TRADING POST
527 Grant Ave.
San Francisco, CA 94108
(415) 788-1018
Satoshi S. Fujikake
Retail. *Products*: C,F,I,N,P,Q,U,V,W,X.

KACHINA
2801 Leavenworth #J-22
San Francisco, CA 94133
(415) 441-2636
Farideh Petri
Wholesale, retail. *Membership*: IACA.
Branch: Tiburon, CA.

MAYFLOWER GIFT SHOP
2770 40th Ave.
San Francisco, CA 94116
(415) 982-1890
Doug & Julie Shinn
Retail. *Products*: All.

WHITE BUFFALO GALLERY
900 North Point
San Francisco, CA 94109
(415) 931-0665
Ata Petri
Retail. *Products*: A,B,C,E,H,J,N,O,P,Q,
R,U,V,W,X. *Membership*: IACA.

THE TRADING POST
919 The Alameda
San Jose, CA 95126
(408) 298-7748 Fax 732-1363
Lee & Marilyn Gardner
Retail. *Products*: A,B,C,E,F,G,H,I,J,K,N,O,
P,Q,S,U,V,W,X. *Membership*: IACA..

REYNA'S GALLERIES
Box 1022, 106 Third St.
San Juan Bautista, CA 95045
(408) 623-2379
Sonne & Elaine Reyna
Wholesale, retail. *Products*: All. *Appraisals*: All.
Catalog.

DONNA GOLD
P.O. Box 55277
Sherman Oaks, CA 91413-0277
(818) 789-2559 Fax 789-1510
Donna Gold
Wholesale, retail. *Products*: A,B,C,E,J,L,M,Q,S,
U,V,W,X. Northwest Coast Indian masks, rattles,
bowls, graphics. Mail order only .

TWO BEARS GALLERY
14755 Ventura Blvd. #1-619
Sherman Oaks, CA 91403
(310) 393-4776
Lou A. Finley.
Retail. *Products*: A,B,E,F,G,H,I,J,L,N,O,P,U,V,X.
Membership: IACA. *Branch*: 1205 Montana
Ave., Santa Monica, CA.

KACHINA
41 Reed Ranch Rd.
Tiburon, CA 94920
(415) 389-8524
Farideh Petri
Wholesale, retail. *Membership*: IACA.
Branch: San Francisco, CA.

CHIEF GEORGE PIERRE TRADING POST
620 The Village (Redondo Beach)
P.O. Box 3202
Torrance, CA 90510
(213) 372-1048
Chief George Piere, Owner
Wholesale, retail, mail order . *Products*: C,P,Q,V.

AB-ORIGINALS
P.O. Drawer 850
Trinidad, CA 95570
(707) 677-3738
Joy & Lisa Sundberg & Elaine Clary , Owners
Wholesale, retail. *Products*: H,P. Fashionable
accessories such as chokers, hair pieces,
necklaces, earrings, beaded neck ties, belts.

ADOBE ROAD, INC.
1000 Universal Center Dr ., Shop 157
University City, CA 91608
(818) 622-3623
Prudence J. Gallop
Wholesale, retail. *Products*: A,B,C,E,F,H,I,J,K,M,
N,O,P,Q,R,S,T,U,V,W,X. *Membership*: IACA.

SOUTHWEST ACCENTS
P.O. Box 55458
Valencia, CA 91385
(818) 792-3235
Betty F. Broadbent
Retail. *Products*: All.

RED FLUTE TRADERS
9620 Las Cruces
Ventura, CA 93004
(805) 647-6437
Floyd & Sue Beller
Wholesale, retail. *Products*: B,C,O,P,Q,V.
Membership: IACA.

LAILAN
1937 Main St. #148
Watsonville, CA 95076
(408) 761-1852
Derek & Sima Cockshut
Retail. *Products*: A,P,U,W,X.

KACHINA ART GALLERY
Box 4800, 12301 Whittier Blvd.
Whittier, CA 90607
(213) 941-5635
Lynn & Mercedes Stermolle
Retail. *Products*: A,B,C,H,I,J,N,P,Q,
R,S,U,V,W,X. *Membership*: IACA.

MATOSKA TRADING CO.
P.O. Box 2004
Yorba Linda, CA 92686
(909) 393-0647
Brent Schellhase, Owner
Retail, wholesale, mail order .
Products: A,C,D,H,J,Y. Catalog, $3.

THE ANSEL ADAMS GALLERY
P.O. Box 455, The Village Mall
Yosemite, CA 95389
(209) 372-4413 Fax 372-4714
Michael & Jeanne Adams
Retail. *Products*: A,B,C,E,F,J,N,O,P,Q,
S,T,U,V,V,X. Catalog.

YOSEMITE PARK & CURRY CO.
P.O. Box 578
Yosemite Lodge (209) 372-1438
Ahwahnee Hotel (209) 372-1409
Yosemite, CA 95389
Cassandra Martin, Manager (Y osemite Lodge)
Georgine Gray , Manager (Ahwahnee Hotel)
Retail. *Products*: All. *Membership*: IACA.

BARKER'S INDIAN TRADING POST
P.O. Box 2732, 6495 W ashington St.
Yountville, CA 94599-2732
(707) 944-8012
Frank & Wilda Barker
Wholesale/retail. *Products*: A,B,C,P,U,V,W,X.
Membership: IACA.

GEODES & GEMS
56925 Yucca Trail, Suite A
Yucca Valley, CA 92284
(619) 365-9614
Robert & Marjorie Clayton
Wholesale, retail. *Products*: A,B,C,D,J,K,L,N,O,
P,Q,R,S,U,V,W,X,Y,Z. *Membership*: IACA.

COLORADO

EAGLE PLUME'S
9853 Highway 7
Allenspark, CO 80510
(303) 747-2861 (phone & fax)
Ann Strange Owl-Raben, Nico Strange
Owl-Hunt, Dayton Raben, Owners
Retail. *Products*: B,C,D,P,Q,U,X.
American Indian arts & crafts.

BYRNE-GETZ GALLERY
P.O. Box 4737, 413 E. Hyman Ave.
Aspen, CO 81611
(303) 925-2155
Marion Byrne-Getz
Retail. *Products*: A,B,C,P,U,V,X,Z. *Appraisals*: P.

SQUASH BLOSSOM, INC.
450 S. Galena
Aspen, CO 81611
(303) 925-3214
Lisa A. Smith
Retail. *Products*: A,B,C,D,I,J,N,P,Q,T,U,V,X.
Appraisals: A,C,D,P,Q,S,T,U,V,W,X.
Membership: IACA. Catalog.

FOUR WINDS TRADING CO.
685 A S. Broadway
Boulder, CO 80306
(800) 456-5444; (303) 499-4484
Richard & Cat Carey
Retail. *Product*: D. *Membership*: IACA.

INUA-'THE SPIRIT OF ALASKA'
3111 Washington St.
Boulder, CO 80304
(303) 442-0371
William & Catrin Lovett
Wholesale, retail. *Products*:
B,C,G,H,I,L,N,P,S,X,Z. *Appraisals*: B,L,X.
Membership: IACA. *Branch*: Homer, AK.

SANTA FE AMBIANCE
1116 Pearle St.
Boulder, CO 80302
(303) 444-7200
Deborah Smith-Klein & Melinda Theis
Retail. *Products*: A,B,C,G,I,J,L,N,O,P,
Q,R,S,T,U,V,W,X. *Membership*: IACA.

A.M. INDIAN ARTS, INC.
12 E. Bijou St.
Colorado Springs, CO 80903
(719) 471-3235
Samuel M. Eppley
Retail. *Products*: A,B,C,U,V,W,X.

ARIZONA ROOM
8085 Edgerton
Colorado Springs, CO 80919
(719) 592-9106
Linda & Carl Radunsky
Retail. *Products*: A,B,N,P,Q,U,V,X.
Membership: IACA.

BROADMOOR DRUG CO.
P.O. Box 1439, 4 Hazel Ave.
Colorado Springs, CO 80901
(719) 577-5740
Ben B. Finch
Retail. *Products*: B,N,O,P,T,U.

THE FLUTE PLAYER GALLERY
2511 W. Colorado Ave.
Colorado Springs, CO 80904
(719) 632-7702
John & Linda Edwards
Wholesale, retail. *Products*: G,K,N,O,P,Q,R,S,U,
V,W,X. *Appraisals*: P,T,U,V. *Membership*: IACA.

HIDDEN INN
529 S. 31st St.
Colorado Springs, CO 80904
(719) 632-2303
Al Dickey
(719) 632-2303
Retail. *Membership*: IACA.

**THE SQUASH BLOSSOM
& COGSWELL GALLERY**
2531 W. Colorado
Colorado Springs, CO 80904
(303) 632-1899
John Cogswell & Chris Jones
Retail. *Products*: A,B,C,D,J,N,O,P,Q,S,T, U,V,W,X.
Appraisals: A,B,C,J,N,O,P,Q,S,T, U,V,W,X. Gallery
specializes in Pueblo pottery; Navajo weavings;
Hopi kachinas; Kiowa sculptures; Navajo, Hopi
and Pima/Papago baskets; Navajo, Hopi and Zuni
jewelry; Zuni fetishes; Navajo sandpaintings.
Membership: IACA. Catalog.

CLIFF DWELLER
Box 9, 1004 E. Main St.
Cortez, CO 81321
(303) 565-3424
J.D. Tipton, Jr.
Retail. *Products*: A,B,C,E,F,I,J,K,N,O,P,Q,
R,S,U,V,W,X. *Membership*: IACA.

DON WOODARD'S INDIAN TRADING POST
27688 E. Hwy. 160
Cortez, CO 81321-9366
(303) 565-3986
Don Woodard, Owner
Retail. *Products*: All. Appraisals.
Membership: IACA.

MESA VERDE POTTERY
P.O. Box 9
Cortez, CO 81321
(800) (303) 565-4492
Jay Tipton, Jr.
Wholesale, retail. *Products*: All.
Membership: IACA. Catalog.

THE BLACK BEAR
8753 E. Monmouth Place
Denver, CO 80237-2935
(303) 779-1316
John & Mary Claire W alter
Retail. *Products*: A,N,O,P,Q,S,U,V,W.
Membership: IACA.

BOUCHER TRADING CO.
8505 E. Temple Dr. #473
Denver, CO 80237-2542
(303) 770-7718
Robert G. Boucher
Wholesale, retail. *Product*: P. *Membership*: IACA.

D & H GIFTS
1281 Phillips Dr.
Denver, CO 80233-1259
(303) 457-3606 Fax 457-9944
H. & Diane Yamamoto
Wholesale, retail. *Products*: P.W. *Membership*:
IACA. *Branch*: 11480 N. Cherokee St., Unit I,
Denver.

DENVER ART MUSEUM SHOP
100 W. 14th Ave. Pkwy.
Denver, CO 80204
(303) 640-2672
Mary Jane Butler
Retail. *Products*: C,I,N,P,U. *Membership*: IACA.

**DENVER MUSEUM OF
NATURAL HISTORY SHOP**
2001 Colorado Blvd., City Park
Denver, CO 80205-5716
(303) 370-6366 Fax 331-6492
Thielma Gamewell & Ron V eenstra
Retail. *Products*: A,B,C,E,F,G,I,J,K,L,N,O,
P,Q,S,T,U,W,X. *Membership*: IACA.

KOHLBERG'S LTD.
1720 Champa St.
Denver, CO 80202
(303) 292-4578/3864
Mrs. Eric Kohlberg
Retail. *Products*: All. *Appraisals*: B,C,D,M,N,O,
P,Q,T,U,V,W. *Membership*: IACA..

O.B. ENTERPRISES
Box 234, 451 E. 58th Ave. #2590
Denver, CO 80216-1404
(800) 525-6376; (303) 295-2718 Fax 295-2714
Mike & Gail O'Neil
Wholesale. *Products*: A,B,C,I,J,M,N,O,P,
Q,U,V,W,X. *Membership*: IACA.

**PATH-OF-THE-SUN IMAGES,
GALLERY AND DESIGN SERVICES**
3020 Lowell Blvd.
Denver, CO 80211
(303) 477-8442
Susanne Aikman & John Chingman, Owners
Wholesale, retail, mail order . *Products*: A,X,Z.
Traditional and contemporary crafts.
Repairs beadwork.

SAND CREEK ARTS
5344 Altura St.
Denver, CO 80239
(303) 371-7636
William W. Phillips
Wholesale, retail. *Product*: A.
Membership: IACA.

SHALAKO
3023 East 2nd Ave.
Denver, CO 80206
(303) 295-2713
Angie Yava & Mike O'Neil
Retail. *Products*: A,B,C,I, J,N,O,P,Q,U,V,W, X.
Membership: IACA.

THE SQUASH BLOSSOM
1415 Larimer Square
Denver, CO 80202
(303) 572-7979
John Cogswell
Retail. *Products*: A,B,C,D,E,F,G,I,J,N,O,
P,Q,T,U,V,X,Z. *Membership*: IACA. Catalog.

TRADER GENE
451 E. 58th St. #1090
Denver, CO 80216
(303) 296-6435
Harold Benner & Robert Staab
Wholesale. *Products*: All. Appraisals.

WESTERN TRADING POST
P.O. Box 9070
Denver, CO 80209-0070
(303) 777-7750
Ronald Eberhart
Retail. *Products*: A,B,C,D,E,F,G,H,I,J,N,P,
Q,R,U,V,W,X,Y,Z. *Appraisals*: B,V,
Membership: IACA. Catalog.

GLEN COMFORT STORE
2380 Big Thompson Canyon
Drake, CO 80515
(303) 586-3878
Harold M. Tregent
Retail. *Products*: B,I,K,L,N,O,P,Q,S,U,V,W,X.
Membership: IACA.

DIAMOND CIRCLE INDIAN GIFT SHOP
651 Main Ave.
Durango, CO 81301-5423
  Skip & Marsha Wells
Retail. *Products*: All.

DURANGO TRADING CO.
602 Eagle Pass
Durango, CO 81301
  Sharleen & L.D. Daugherty
Wholesale/retail. *Products*: U,V.
Membership: IACA.

HELL BENT LEATHER & SILVER
741 Main Ave.
Durango, CO 81301
  (303) 247-9088
  Lovvis Downs & Charles Glass
Retail. *Products*: C,N,O,P,Q,R,U,V,Y.
Membership: IACA.

TOH-ATIN GALLERY
Box 2329, 145 W. 9th St.
Durango, CO 81301
  (800) 525-0384
  (303) 247-8277 Fax 259-5390
  Jackson & Antonia Clark
Wholesale, retail. *Products*: A,B,D,E,G,J,K,N,O,
P,Q,R,S,T,U,V,W,X. Appraisals: V. Catalog.

RED MAN HALL
P.O. Box 608, 125 W. Park Ave.
Empire, CO 80438
  (303) 569-3243
  Francine & Richard Frajola
Retail. *Products*: A,B,C,N,P,Q,S,U,W,X.
Membership: IACA.

FALL RIVER TRADING POST
1875 Fall River Rd.
Estes Park, CO 80517
  (505) 586-6573
  Wendell & Ann Keller
Retail. *Products*: A,B,C,H,I,J,N,O,P,Q,
R,S,T,U,V,W,X. *Membership*: IACA.

GRANDPA'S
Box 861, 230 W. Elkhorn Ave.
Estes Park, CO 80517
  (800) 242-4218; (303) 586-3539
  Bob & Betty Hockaday
Retail. *Products*: A,B,C,H,I,J,K,M,N,O,P,Q,
R,S,U,V,W,X. *Membership*: IACA.

SERENDIPITY TRADING CO.
117 E. Elkhorn Ave., Box 3945
Estes Park, CO 80517
  (303) 586-8410 Fax 586-0463
  Sam, Sue Charles King, Owners
Retail, wholesale, mail order. *Products*: A,B,C,
G,J,L,M,N,O,P,Q,U,V,W,X. *Membership*: IACA.
Brochure & catlog. *Branch shop*: Leona King
Gallery, Scottsdale, AZ.

SILVER FEATHER TRADING CO.
1209 Washington Ave.
Golden, CO 80401
  (303) 279-0595
  David & Kay Dawn Todd
Wholesale, retail. Products: C,F,I,J,N,P,Q,U,W.
Membership: IACA.

HARVEY INDIAN GALLERY
P.O. Box 3524, 130 N. 6th St.
Grand Junction, CO 81502
  (303) 243-4093

Jim & Nancy Harvey
Retail. *Products*: All. *Membership*: IACA.

NATIONAL PARK VILLAGE NORTH
3450 Fall River Rd.
Estes Park, CO 80517
  (303) 586-3183
  H.W. Stewart, Owner
Retail. *Products*: B,F,G,I,K,M,P,U,V,Z.
Membership: IACA.

**ROCKY MOUNTAIN NATIONAL
PARK-TRAIL RIDGE STORE**
P.O. Box 2680
Estes Park, CO 80517-2680
  (303) 586-9319 Fax 586-8590
  Don Wallace, VP
Retail. *Products*: All. *Winter address*: Forever
Resorts, P.O. Box 29041, Phoenix, AZ 85038
Membership: IACA.

SERENDIPITY TRADING
Box 3945, 117 E. Elkhorn Ave.
Estes Park, CO 80517
  (303) 586-8410
  Sam, Sue & Charles King
Retail. *Products*: All.

BENZAV TRADING CO.
P.O. Box 911, 1716 E. Lincoln Ave.
Fort Collins, CO 80522
  (303) 482-6397
  Steven Pickelner
Wholesale. *Products*: B,C,H,M,O,P,T,U,V.

SIOUX VILLA CURIO
114 6th St.
Glenwood Springs, CO 81601
  (303) 945-6134
  John Gilcrest
Retail. *Products*: C,O,P. *Membership*: IACA.

BANWARTH ENTERPRISES
8 Zodiac St.
Golden, CO 80401
  Kay Dawn Todd
  (303) 279-4870
Wholesale, retail. *Product*: P.

HARVEY SALES CO.
Box 3524, 130 N. 6th St.
Grand Junction, CO 81502
  (303) 243-4093
  Jim & Nancy Harvey
Retail. *Products*: All.

THUNDEROCK
128 N. 5th St.
Grand Junction, CO 81501
  (303) 242-4890
  Max & Judith Barnstead
Retail. *Products*: A,B,C,E,I,J,K,N,O,P,Q,S,
U,V,W,X,Z. *Membership*: IACA..

EAGLE DANCER TRADING CO.
P.O. Box 547
Grand Lake, CO 80447-0547
  (303) 726-9209; 627-3394
  Dick & Nina Stasser
Retail. *Products*: All. *Membership*: IACA.
Branch: Winter Park, CO.

BEN NIGHTHORSE
P.O. Box 639
Ignacio, CO 81137
  (303) 563-4623
Mail order. *Product*: jewelry.

SKY UTE INDIAN GALLERY
P.O. Box 550
Ignacio, CO 81137
  (303) 563-4531
  Elise Redd & John Cole
Retail. Tribal Enterprise.
Products: A,C,P,U,W,X,Z.

SOUTHERN UTE MUSEUM & GIFT SHOP
P.O. Box 737
Ignacio, CO 81137
  (303) 563-4649
  Janis Peabody, Manager
Wholesale, retail. *Products*: All. *Appraisals*: All.
Membership: IACA.

THE SOUTHWESTERN COLLECTION
12600 W. Colfax Ave., Suite A120
Lakewood, CO 80215
  (303) 237-2719
  Jacqueline B. Aucoin
Retail. *Products*: A,B,E,F,G,J,N,P,Q,R,U,V,W.
Membership: IACA. *Branch*: 6921 Hwy. 73,
Evergreen, CO.

WALTON'S
12550 W. Second Dr.
Lakewood, CO 80228
  (303) 988-5580
  Roger Alan Walton
Wholesale, retail. *Products*: G,Q,U,X.

BONANZA TRADING
316 Harrison Ave.
Leadville, CO 80461
  (719) 486-3020
  Clyde & Mary McVicar
Retail. *Products*: A,B,C,E,F,H,I,J,N,O,P,
Q,U,V,W,X. *Membership*: IACA.

SOUTHWESTERN GALLERY
1212 W. Littleton Blvd.
Littleton, CO 80120
  (303) 795-7338
  Beverly J. Nelson, Owner
Retail, mail order. *Products*: A,N,P,Q,U,V,W,X.
Membership: IACA.

TOUCH OF SANTA FE
Box 620549, 6574 S. Broadway
Littleton, CO 80162
  (303) 730-2408
  Ruth Venable
Retail. *Products*: All.

DEER TRACK TRADERS LTD.
P.O. Box 448
Loveland, CO 80539-0448
  (303) 669-6750 Fax 667-8464
  Alpine & Sue Rodman
Wholesale. *Products*: A,B,C,D,E,F,G,I,N,P,Q,
S,U,V,W,X. *Membership*: IACA. Catalog.

ANASAZI TRADING POST
P.O. Box 320, 344 Main St.
Lyons, CO 80540
  (303) 823-5681
  Susan & Daniel Martin
Retail. *Products*: All. *Membership*: IACA.

ARA MESA VERDE CO.
P.O. Box 277, 109 S. Main
Mancos, CO 81328
  (303) 533-7731
  Bob Marshall
Retail. *Products*: A,B,C,E,F,I,J,K,N,O,P,Q,R,
S,U,V,W,X. *Membership*: IACA.

MANITOU JACK'S
742 Manitou Ave.
Manitou Springs, CO 80829
(719) 685-5004
Kendra Homer & Dawn Carnel
Wholesale, retail. *Products*: A,P,U,W,X,Y,Z.
Membership: IACA.

NAVA SOUTHWEST
61336 Hwy. 90
Montrose, CO 81401
(303) 325-4850
Douglas & Rebecca Dodson
Wholesale, retail. *Products*: All. Summer
address: Box 37, Ouray 81427

RED ROCKS TRADING POST
16351 County Rd. 93
Morrison, CO 80465
(303) 697-8935
William S. Carle
Retail. *Products*: A,H,P,Q,U. *Membership*: IACA.

WINTERCOUNT
Box 889, 303 W. Main St.
New Castle, CO 81647
(303) 984-3685
Tom & Diane Voight
Wholesale, retail. *Products*: A,D. T-shirts &
Calendars. *Membership*: IACA. Catalog.

BUCKSKIN TRADING CO.
P.O. Box 1876, 636 Main St.
Ouray, CO 81427
(303) 325-4044
P. David & Jan Smith
Retail. *Products*: A,B,C,D,F,H,I,J,K,L,M,N,O,
P,Q,R,S,T,U,V,W,X,Z. *Membership*: IACA.

NORTH MOON
P.O. Box 51
Ouray, CO 81427
(303) 325-4885
Sandra K. Boles
Retail. *Products*: C,L,N,P. *Membership*: IACA.
Branch shop: Telluride, CO.

FILTER PRESS
Box 5, 785 Hwy. 105
Palmer Lake, CO 80133-0005
(719) 481-2523
Gilbert Campbell
Retail. *Product*: D.

EAGLES NEST
P.O. Box 5952, 100 Elbert Lane
Snowmass Village, CO 81615
(303) 923-2007
Annalisa & Edward Frederickson
Retail, wholesale. *Products*: A,E,H,I,J,K,N,P,Q,R,S,U,V,W.
Membership: IACA.

TAWA INDIAN GALLERY
P.O. Box 322
South Fork, CO 81154
Beverly S. O'Rourke
Retail. *Products*: A,B,H,N,O,P,.Q,U,V,W,Z.
Summer address: Box 322, South Fork, CO
81154 (719) 873-5838.

THE COLLECTOR'S ROOM
P.O. Box 3226, Vail National Bank #302
108 s. Frontage Rd. West
Vail, CO 81657
(303) 476-9019
Paul & Betty Numerof
Retail. *Products*: P. *Membership*: IACA.

SQUASH BLOSSOM, INC.
198 Gore Creek Dr.
Vail, CO 81657
(303) 476-3129 F AX 476-8984
John Cogswell
Retail. *Products*: A,B,C,E,H,I,J,K,M,N,O,P,Q,
R,S,T,U,V,W,X,Z. *Appraisals*: A,J,M,N,O,P,Q,
R,S,T,U,V,W. Catalog.

EAGLE DANCER TRADING CO., INC.
Box 3462, 223 Cooper Creek Sq.
Winter Park, CO 80482
(303) 726-9209; 627-3394
Dick & Nina Stasser
Retail. *Products*: All. *Membership*: IACA.
Branch: Grand Lake, CO.

ELK HORN ART GALLERY
P.O. Box 197
Winter Park, CO 80482
(800) 285-4676; (303) 726-9292 Fax 726-8292
Tom Coblentz, Owner
Retail, wholesale. *Products*: Works of art by Na-
tive American artists, Jo Anne Bird, Robert Red
Bird, and Michael C. McCullough. Also published
limited edition prints with dealerships available.
Menbership: IACA. Brochure.

CONNECTICUT

BLACK DIAMOND TRADING CO.
P.O. Box 1151
Danbury, CT 06813-1151
(203) 792-9656
Thomas J. Valeri
Wholesale. *Product*: P. *Membership*: IACA.

SOUTHWEST INDIAN ARTS
98 The Laurels
Enfield, CT 06082
(203) 749-7332 (phone & fax)
Bud August, Owner
Retail. *Products*: B,C,F,M,N,P,Q,U,V,W.
Membership: IACA.

RALPH W. STURGIS
97 Raymond St.
New London, CT 06320
(203) 442-8005
Retail. *Products*: X.

YAH-TA-HEY GALLERY
279 Captains Walk
New London, CT 06320
(203) 443-3204
Dorothy Noga
Retail. *Products*: A,B,E,I,J,N,P,Q,V,W,X.
Membership: IACA.

TEARS OF THE MOON
885 Rockrimmon Rd.
Stamford, CT 06903
(203) 329-3818
Wendy Cannold
Retail. *Products*: A,C,F,H,L,M,N,P,Q,U,X.

DISTRICT OF COLUMBIA

FAMCO & NAICA GALLERIES
1227 Savannah St., SE
Washington, DC 20032
(202) 561-1354

Walter H. De Vore, Jr.
Wholesale, retail.

THE INDIAN CRAFT SHOP
1849 C St., NW, Suite 1023
Washington, DC 20240
(202) 208-4056
Susan M. Pourian, Manager
Retail. *Products*: All. *Membership*: IACA.
Branch: See below.

THE INDIAN CRAFT SHOP
3222 M St., NW
Washington, DC 20007
(202) 342-3918
Abby Kent, Manager
Retail. *Products*: All. *Membership*: IACA.

NAICA COLLECTIBLES
5223 Wisconsin Ave., NW, Suite 138
Washington, DC 20015
(202) 561-1354
W. Howard DeVore, Owner
Wholesale, retail, mail order.
Products: C,P,U,X. Catalog.

FLORIDA

SHARED VISIONS GALLERY
10355 Prestwick Rd.
Boynton Beach, FL 33436
(407) 272-4495
Kathleen & Chad Ragland
Wholesale, retail. *Products*:
A,B,I,L,N,P,Q,U,V,W,X. *Membership*: IACA.
Branch shop: 504 E. Atlantic Ave., Delray
Beach, FL 33483.

TURTLE ISLAND TRADERS
P.O. Box 9563
Bradenton, FL 34206
(813) 747-5653
C.G. "Bud" Horton, Owner
Retail. *Products*: D,M,S,X.

SUNDANCER GALLERY
6 Florida Ave.
Cocoa Village, FL 32922
(407) 631-0092
Joan & Jim McCarthy, Owners
Retail, wholesale. *Products*: Southwest & Native
American art & craftwork, and turquoise jewelry.
Branch shop: This N' That, Cocoa Village.

THUNDERBIRD SHOP
16754 Willow Creek Dr.
Delray Beach, FL 33484
Louis & Sheila Brilliant
Retail. *Products*: All.

THE PLAINSMEN GALLERY
542 Douglas Ave.
Dunedin, FL 34698
(813) 446-4396
Betty Brown & Maria Alcoz
Retail. *Products*: A,B,N,P,Q,V.

GREEN'S RINGS & THINGS
P.O. Box 129
Everglades City, FL 33929
(813) 695-3559
Jeri & Larry Green
Wholesale, retail. *Products*: A,C,H,P,U,V,W.

AMERICAN INDIAN IMAGEMAKERS
6321 N.W. 34th St.
Hollywood, FL 33024
  (305) 983-7708
  Jo Motlow North, Owner
Wholesale, retail by appointment only .
Products: A,H,P.

MICCOSUKEE GIFT SHOP
& CULTURAL CENTER
Box 440021, Tamiami Station
Miami, FL 33144
  (305) 223-8380
  Jim Kay, Manager
Retail, wholesale. Miccosukee Tribal Enterprise.
Products: B,C,H,I,X.

NIZHONI DREAM CATCHERS
2190 D Anchorage Lane
Naples, FL 33942
  (813) 643-2026
  Patricia Sauselein & Ralph Stevens
Retail. Products: A,B,C,E,G,H,J,K,N,O,
P,Q,U,V,W,X. Membership: IACA.

PRODIGY GALLERY
4320 Gulf Shore Blvd. N., Suite 206
Naples, FL 33940
  (813) 263-5881 Fax 263-5882
  Karen Weinert-Kim & Sam Miller
Retail. Products: All. Membership: IACA.

ME'SHIWI
433 Harrell Dr.
Orlando, FL 32828
  (407) 568-5162
  Terrence & Olivia Halote, Owners
Retail. Products: A,P,Q,U.

SUNDANCE INDIAN CRAFTS
1440 N.W. 122nd Ave.
Pembroke Pines, FL 33026
  (305) 437-5419
  Karen Ashford
Retail. Products: N,O,P,U,V. Membership: IACA.

JOLIMA INDIAN CRAFTS
1403 N. 57th Ave.
Pensacola, FL 32506
  (904) 455-0874
  John & Marie Varnes, Owners
Wholesale; retail by appointment only .
Products: B,C,J,P. Special orders accepted.

RED CLOUD
208 Beach Dr. NE
St. Petersburg, FL 33701-3414
  (813) 821-5824
  Pamela R. Glawe
Retail. Products: All. Membership: IACA.

ABORIGINALS: ART OF THE FIRST PERSON
2340 Periwinkle Way
Sanibel, FL 33957
  (813) 395-2200 Fax 482-7025
  Susanne Waites
Wholesale, retail. Products: A,B,C,D,H,I,J,M,
N,O,P,U,V,W,X. Appraisals.

SAGEBRUSH GALLERY
812 Angel Wing Dr.
Sanibel, FL 33957
  (813) 472-6971/395-1 155
  Myles & Barbara Murray
Retail. Products: A,C,G,I,J,N,P,Q,R,U,V,W.
Membership: IACA.

SEMINOLE CULTURAL CENTER
5221 Orient Rd.
Tampa, FL 33610
  (813) 623-3549
  Leslie Stevens, Manager
Retail/mail order . Products: B,C,H,X.

PAIRS OF WELLINGTON, INC.
13873 Wellington Trace, Suite B-3
Wellington, FL 33414
  (407) 798-5590
  Merlin & Pierluigi Nuti
Retail. Products: N,O,P. Membership: IACA.

GEORGIA

NATIVE AMERICA
P.O. Box 7711
Athens, GA 30604
  (706) 543-8425
  Jane Scott & Mike Duemmel, Owners
Retail. Products: D,N,P,Q,W,X.
Membership: IACA.

COYOTE TRADING CO.
419 Moreland Ave. NE
Atlanta, GA 30307
  (404) 221-1512
  David Simpson
Retail. Products: A,N,O,P,Q,U.
Membership: IACA.

OGLE WANAGI ARTS & CRAFTS GALLERY
842 b. N. Highland Ave.
ATLANTA 30306
  (404) 872-4213
  Tom Perkins & Vickie Dunken, Owners
Retail. Products: P,Q,U,V.

OUT OF THE WOODS GALLERY
22-B Bennett St., NW
Atlanta, GA 30309
  (404) 351-0446
  Deb Douglas
Retail. Products: All.

SOUTHWEST INDIAN ARTISANS
P.O. Box 941759
Atlanta, GA 30341
  (404) 729-1624
  Martha J. Hueglin
Wholesale/retail. Products: A,B,J,N,O,
P,Q,U,V,X. Membership: IACA.

TRACEY SOUTHWEST
3500 Peachtree Rd., Phipps Plaza
Atlanta, GA 30326
  (404) 237-5929
  Patti Hathcoat
Retail. Products: A,C,D,E,F,G,H,I,J,N,
P,R,S,U,V,X. Membership: IACA.

RAY'S INDIAN ORIGINALS
90 Avondale Rd.
Avondale Estates, GA 30002
  (404) 299-2397/4999
  Ray Belcher, Owner
Wholesale/retail. Products: A,B,P,Q,,U,V

ANASAZI ARTS & CRAFTS
P.O. Box 2174
Calhoun, GA 30703-2174
  (706) 629-8163
  Faye Gregory & A.H. Hart

Retail. Products: A,B,E,F,H,I,J,M,N,P,Q,
R,T,U,V,W,X. Membership: IACA.

CHESTATEE CROSSING
P.O. Box 2064, Hall's Block Bldg.,
Dahlonega, GA 30533
  (404) 864-9099
  Mary Brogdon & Kitty Jarrard
Retail. Products: A,C,D,F,G,H,J,N,P,R,U,V,X,Y.
Membership: IACA.

TEKAKWITHA
P.O. Box 338
Helen, GA 30545
  (404) 878-2938
  Ruth Lammers
Retail. Products: All. Membership: IACA.

NATIVE AMERICA OF JEFFERSON
Village Fair Mall
Jefferson, GA 30549
  (706) 543-8425
  Jane Scott & M.J. Duemmel
Retail. Products: A,C,D,E,F,G,H,J,N,O,
P,Q,R,T,U,W. Membership: IACA.
Branch shop: Athens, GA.

ANASAZI ARTS & CRAFTS
6624 Dawson Blvd.
Norcross, GA 30093
  (404) 446-0856 Fax 629-8163
  A.H. Hart & Faye Gregory, Owners
Retail. Products: Native American arts & crafts;
Southwestern furnishings & accessories.

STONE BEAR GALLERY
120 Strand Hill Rd.
Tyrone, GA 30290
  (404) 631-3424
  M. Barry Bartlett
Retail. Products: A,E,P,U,X. Membership: IACA.

HAWAII

THE SANTA FE COLLECTION
469 Ena Rd. #3004
Honolulu, HI 96815
  (808) 947-9169 (Phone & Fax)
  Raymond & Louann Suppa
Retail. Products: A,B,N,O,P,Q,R,S,U,V,W,X.
Membership: IACA.

IDAHO

ANGLETON
107 N. 9th St.
Boise, ID 83702
  (208) 343-1861
  Hugh R. Angleton
Retail. Products: A,B,C,P,U,V,W,X.
Membership: IACA.

KAMIAKIN KRAFTS
P.O. Box 358
Fort Hall, ID 83203
  (208) 785-2546
  Atwice Goudy Osborne, Owner
Retail/mail order . By appointment only .
Products: C,H. Price list available.

TRADING POST CLOTHES HORSE
P.O. Box 368
Fort Hall, ID 83203
(208) 237-8433
Gayle Shappert, Manager
Wholesale, retail, mail order . Shoshone-Bannock
Tribal Enterprise. *Products*: C,H,J. Special order
accepted. Brochure and price list available.

ARTIFACTS
P.O. Box 991, 351 Leadville
Ketchum, ID 83340
(208) 726-2406
Mark McIntire
Retail. *Products*: B,C,D,E,G,H,I,J,K,L,M,N,
O,P,Q,R,S,U,V,W,X,Y. *Membership*: IACA.

HEARTLINE GALLERY
Box X, 317 East Lake
McCall, ID 83638
(800) 736-0231; (208) 634-2544
Elizabeth Cook
Retail. *Products*: A,B,C,E,G,H,J,L,M,N,P,Q,
R,S,T,U,V,X. *Membership*: IACA.

ILLINOIS

TRIBAL EXPRESSIONS
7 Dunton Ave.
Arlington Heights, IL 60005
(708) 590-5390
Retail. *Products*: B,E,J,L,P,V.
Membership: IACA.

GALL SOUTHWEST SILVER JEWELRY CO.
9014 W. 31st St.
Brookfield, IL 60513
(708) 387-0460
Geraldine M. Gall
Retail. *Products*: All.

SOUTHWEST EXPRESSIONS
1459 W. Webster St.
Chicago, IL 60614
(312) 525-2626 Fax 525-7130
T.J. Harris
Retail. *Products*: A,E,G,J,M,N,P,Q,S,U,W,X.
Membership: IACA.

SILVER LINING GALLERY
128 N. Main St.
Edwardsville, IL 62025
(618) 692-1000
Lorraine Levy & Alison Sale
Retail. *Products*: A,B,C,D,H,J,L,N,P,Q,
S,U,V,W,X. *Membership*: IACA.

NATIVE AMERICAN ART
810 Dempster
Evanston, IL 60202
(708) 864-0400
Mary L. Dwyer
Retail. *Products*: All. *Membership*: IACA.

TA-TONKA GALLERY & TRADING POST
19 S. Ash St.
Frankfort, IL 60423
(815) 469-0775
Tina Rzepka, Owner
Retail. *Products*: All. Native American creations.
Membership: IACA.

SKYSTONE TREASURES
715 Valley Rd.
Glencoe, IL 60022
(708) 835-3355
Patricia Schwartz
Retail. *Products*: A,C,G,M,N,O,P,S,T,U.
Appraisals: P. *Membership*: IACA.

OBELISK, LTD.
5130 Center Ave.
Lisle, IL 60532
(708) 955-0010
Nancy C. Kelly
Retail. *Products*: A,C,E,L,N,P,Q,U,V,X.

BEAR PAW, INC.
217 Ferry St.
Rockton, IL 61072
(815) 624-7427
Patricia Davies & Joe Skeen
Wholesale, retail. *Products*: B,C,H,J,L,M,Q,U,V.

SOUTHWEST TRADING CO.
203 W. Main St.
St. Charles, IL 60174
(708) 584-5707
Steven & Janet Fabiani
Retail. *Products*: A,B,C,E,I,J,K,M,N,O,P,Q,
R,S,U,V,W,X. *Membership*: IACA..

FOUR FEATHERS
120 Mill St.
Utica, IL 61373
(815) 667-4499
Judith Rigby
Retail. *Products*: A,B,C,E,H,J,P,Q,R,S,U,V,W.
Membership: IACA.

INDIANA

INDIAN CREEK TRADING POST
121 E. Chestnut St.
Corydon, IN 47112
(812) 738-1212
Retail, mail order . *Products*: D.

SKYSTONE N' SILVER
1350 S. Lake Park Ave.
Hobart, IN 46342
(219) 942-9022
Pam Phillips, Owner
Retail *Products*: All. *Appraisals*: A,M,P,Q,V.
Membership: IACA. Brochure.

ONE EARTH GALLERY & GIFTS
1022 Main St.
Lafayette, IN 47901
(317) 742-7564
David R. Kurtz
Retail. *Products*: All. Price list.

RAINBOW ART & FRAME
1708 S. 25th St.
Terre Haute, IN 47802
(812) 232-1337
Connie Hickman
Retail. *Products*: A,B,C,D,F,G,J,K,N,
Q,R,U,V,W,X. *Membership*: IACA.

DAYS PAST
1215 W. Grant St.
Countryside Antique Mall
Thorntown, IN 46071
(317) 436-7200

Dan Bunderle, Owner
Retail. *Products*: M,P,Q,U,V,W,X.
Membership: IACA.

AMERICAN TREASURES
115 N. Chauncey Ave.
West Lafayette, IN 47906
(317) 743-6153
David R. Kurtz, Owner
Retail. *Products*: All. Price list available.

KANSAS

**EDDIE MORRISON - WOOD
CARVINGS, SCULPTURES**
223 N. Young
Caldwell, KS 67022
(316) 845-2355
Retail, mail order . Commissions accepted.

TRADITIONS OF THE SOUTHWEST
P.O. Box 1647
Garden City, KS 67846
(316) 276-2101
Lonnie & Abbie Winterrowd
Wholesale, retail. *Products*: A,B,C,E,H,I,J,N,O,
P,Q,R,S,T,U,V,W,X. *Membership*: IACA.

**LAURIE HOUSEMAN-
WHITE HAWK ENTERPRISES**
RR #3, Box 155-B
Lawrence, KS 66044
(913) 842-1948
Laurie White Hawk, Owner
Retail (by appointment only), wholesale, mail or-
der. *Products*: Original Gouache paintings; limited
edition prints; cards & posters. Brochure.

CHINOOK WINDS
RR 2, Box 180
Oskaloosa, KS 66066
(913) 863-2312
Betty & Elden White
Retail. *Products*: C,H,P,V.; various other
products by other Indian craftsmen.

THE SANTA FE CONNECTION
Box 7466, 4563 Indian Creek Pkwy .
Overland Park, KS 66207
(913) 897-4107
William & Sue Park
Retail. *Products*: A,B,C,G,L,N,P,Q,U,V,W,X.
Membership: IACA.

WESTERN HERITAGE
9647-A Metcalf Ave.
Overland Park, KS 66212
(913) 341-8767
Tom & Joan Vogt
Retail.

INDIAN CENTER MUSEUM GIFT SHOP
Mid-America All-Indian Center
650 N. Seneca
Wichita, KS 67203
(316) 262-5221 ext. 41 Fax 262-4216
Carrie Morehouse, Manager
Retail. *Products*: A,B,C,I,P,Q,U.

KENTUCKY

BUFFALO ARROW HEADS
6365 Bethel Ch. Rd.
Kevil, KY 42053
(502) 462-3210
Al Puckett, Owner
Mail order. *Products*: Traditional arrow heads
& crafts.

MARTIN YONAH CONE
506 Center Point East
Munfordville, KY 42765
Retail. *Products*: H,J,P,X. Jewelry repair &
design. Special orders accepted.

LOUISIANA

NATIVE AMERICAN ARTS OF THE SOUTH
P.O. Box 217
Elton, LA 70532
(318) 584-5130
Rosalene L. Medford, Owner
Wholesale, retail, mail order . *Products*: B,U.
Special orders accepted. Price list.

MAINE

NOWETAH'S INDIAN STORE & MUSEUM
Rt. 27, Box 40
New Portland, ME 04954
(207) 628-4981
Nowetah Timmerman, Owner/curator
Retail, mail order . *Products*: A,B,C,E,H,J,
P,Q,S,U,V,W. Catalogs available.

PENOBSCOT QUILLWORKS
P.O. Box 195
Old Town, ME 04468
(207) 827-6117
Martin Neptune & Jennifer Sapiel
Wholesale, retail. *Products*: Jewelry.

WABANAKI ARTS
P.O. Box 453
Old Town, ME 04468
(207) 827-3447
Stan Neptune, Owner
Wholesale, retail, mail order . *Products*: B,C,J,L,
M,X; traditional Penobscot bows and fish spers.

LONGACRE ENTERPRISES, INC.
Box 196, Old Eastport Rd.
Perry, ME 04667
(800) 642-5024; (207) 853-2762
Cliv Dore, Owner
Wholesale, mail order . *Products*: Passamaquoddy
baskets, beadwork, boxes, children's items, dolls,
drums/pipes, miniatures. Repairs & restoration.
Price list available.

BASKET BANK
Aroostook Micmac Council
P.O. Box 772
Presque Isle, ME 04769
(207) 764-1972
Alice B. Worcester, Manager
Mail order; some wholesale, retail. *Product*:
baskets. Special orders accepted. Brochure
available.

RUNNING WATER CRAFT & GIFT SHOP
R.R. 1, Box 866
Wells, ME 04090
(207) 646-1206
Barbara A. Beckwith
Retail. *Products*: All.

THE CENTER OF NATIVE ART
(Rt. 1, Woolwich 04579)
RFD 3, Box 247 (mail)
Woolwich, ME 04579
(207) 442-8399
Chuck & Marli Hagen, Owners
Retail. *Products*: A,B,C,D,E,F,H,J,P,Q,
U,V,W,X,Y. *Membership*: IACA. Catalog.

MARYLAND

SPIRIT CATCHER
996 Headwater Rd.
Annapolis, MD 21403
(410) 263-1776
Russell & Ellen Jones, Owners
Retail. *Products*: A,B,C,I,J,N,O,P,Q,R,U,V,W,X.
Membership: IACA.

DIFFERENT
505 Vogts Lane
Baltimore, MD 21221
(410) 391-0163
Carol Sullivan & Littletree Hughes, Owners
Retail, wholesale, mail order . *Products*: Jewelry
- custom design, original, and unique creations;
contemporary and traditional styles.

THE WHITE BUFFALO
7101 Democracy Blvd.
Bethesda, MD 20817
(301) 469-0859
Lori & Bob Curtis
Retail. *Products*: A,B,D,F,G,H,I,J,K,N,O,P,Q,
R,S,U,V,W,X,Z. *Membership*: IACA.

NATIVE AMERICAN COLLECTIBLES, INC.
7908 Colonial Lane
Clinton, MD 20735
(301) 868-5849
John & Ruth Gruber
Wholesale, retail. *Products*: B,J,N,O,P,Q,U,V,X.
Appraisals: B,N,V.

PRAIRIE BUFFALO
1397 Generals Hwy.
Crownsville, MD 21032
(301) 923-0760
Myra Raven-Sky
Wholesale, retail. Products: A,C,D,E,G,H,I,J,K,
N,P,Q,R,U,V,W,X. *Membership*: IACA.

THE INDIAN CONNECTION
141 Olen Dr.
Glenburnie, MD 21061
(301) 768-8201
Littletree "Buffy" Hughes, Owner
Retail, wholesale. *Products*: A,H,P,V,W.

THE EARTH ART GALLERY
P.O. Box 236
Woodstock, MD 21163
(301) 465-6106
Jane Goss & Al Finley, Owners
Retail, mail order . *Products*: A,B,D, N,P, S,U,X.
Presently working craft shows & pow wows.
Catalog.

MASSACHUSETTS

DANCING SPIRITS
2456 Mass Ave., Suite 103
Cambridge, MA 02140
(617) 868-7368
Sharon Basch
Retail. *Products*: A,B,C,D,E,F,G,H,J,K,M,
N,P,Q,S,U,V,X. *Membership*: IACA.

THE SANTA FE TRAIL
24 North St.
Hingham, MA 02043
(617) 740-0019
Margaret Cadieux
Retail. *Products*: A,B,E,G,J,K,N,O,P,Q,
R,U,V,W,X. *Membership*: IACA.

SILVER STAR, WAMPANOAG CRAFTS
c/o Anita G. Nielsen
190 Wood St., P.O. Box 402
Middleboro, MA 02346
(617) 947-4159
Mail order. *Products*: B,C,H.

THE KHALSA COLLECTION
P.O. Box 604
Millis, MA 02054-0604
(508) 376-2804 Fax 376-0845
Arjankaur Khalsa
Wholesale, retail. *Products*: D,F,N,O,P,Q,R,T.
Membership: IACA.

PEACEWORK GALLERY & CRAFTS
263 Main St.
Northampton, MA 01060
(413) 586-7033
Robert Nelson & Daisy Mathias, Owners
Retail. *Products*: All. *Membership*: IACA.

NEW ENGLAND TRADERS
Wilbraham St., Rt. 20
Palmer, MA 01069
(413) 596-3129
Bob & Linda Schultz
Retail. *Products*: A,B,C,D,F,H,I,J,M,N,O,
P,Q,R,S,U,V. *Membership*: IACA.

THE AMERICAN INDIAN STORE
139 Water St.
Quincy, MA 02169-6535
(617) 328-1951
Arlene F. Roberts
Retail. *Products*: A,B,C, P,U,X. Appraisals.

SUN BASKET
8-1/2 Bearskin Neck
Rockport, MA 01966
(508) 546-7546
Mary Curran, Owner
Retail. *Products*: All. *Membership*: IACA.

MOHAWK TRADING POST
874 Mohawk Trail, Rt. 2
Shelburne, MA 01370
(413) 625-2412 Fax 625-8134
Laurene L. York, Owner
Retail, mail order (Minnetonka moccasins).
Products: A,B,C,D,E,H,I,J,M,N,P,Q,U,V,W,X,Y.
Membership: IACA. Brochure, catalog.

THE CORNER CAPE
P.O. Box 853, 1 Bank St.
Wellfleet, MA 02667

(508) 349-9694/9539
Althea Robida
Retail. *Products*: C,N,O,P,Q,S,T,U,X.
Membership: IACA.

JOSEPH JOHNS
7 Russell St.
W. Peabody, MA 02535
(617) 535-2426
Joseph Johns, Owner
Special orders only. *Products*: carvings wood, slate
or bone, based on forms and motifs of the
Mushkogean culture. Illustrative material available
upon request.

G/M GALLERIES
12 Main St.
W. Stockbridge, MA 01266
(413) 232-8519
George & Marie Woodcock
Retail. *Products*: A,B,C,J,L,M,N,O,P,Q,T,U,V,Z.
Appraisals. Repair & restoration.

MICHIGAN

BEAR TRACKS DBA BUNDY'S BUNGALOW
125 Irwin St.
Brooklyn, MI 49230
(517) 592-3439 Fax 592-8022
Caryn Howard, Owner
Retail. *Products*: H,P,V. Pendleton blankets,
coats, crafts, Tshirts.

FLYING FEATHERS
P.O. Box 868
East Lansing, MI 48226
(517) 484-7093
Rick Hewitt, Owner
Retail. *Products*: books, tapes, crafts supplies.

NOC BAY TRADING CO.
P.O. Box 295
1133 Washington Ave.
Escanaba, MI 49829
(906) 789-0505
Mail order. *Products*: craft supplies and
materials. Catalog, $3.00.

INDIAN EARTH ARTS & CRAFTS STORE
Genesee Valley Indian Association
609 W. Court St.
Flint, MI 48503
(313) 239-6621
Cora Starlin, Manager
Wholesale, retail, mail order. *Products*: art,
baskets, beadwork, moccasins, pottery,
quillwork.

GLEN ARBOR CITY LIMITS
Box 444, 6610 Western Ave.
Glen Arbor, MI 49636
(616) 334-4424
Beverly Gilmore & Barbara Weber
Retail. *Products*: All.

INDIAN ARTS & CRAFTS STORE
Native American Arts & Crafts Council
P.O. Box 1049, Goose Creek Rd.
Grayling, MI 49738
(517) 348-3190
Robin L. Menefee, Executive Director
Retail, mail order by request only. *Products*: art,
baskets, beadwork, boxes, leatherwork.

COYOTE WOMAN GALLERY
339 State St.
Harbor Springs, MI 49740
(419) 636-3300
Terri & John Freudenberger
Retail. *Products*: A,B,C,D,E,G,H,I,J,L,M,
N,O,P,Q,R,S,U,V,X. *Membership*: IACA.
Branch: Bryan, OH.

ANNA M. CRAMPTON
14360 Woodbury Rd.
Haslett, MI 48840
(517) 339-8856
Retail (by appointment only). *Products*: B,C.

MONADNOCK TRADING CO., INC.
309 E. Central Ave., P.O. Box 400
Mackinac City, MI 49701
(616) 436-5131
Lawrence Goldman
Retail. *Products*: All. *Membership*: IACA.

SOUTHWEST MIRAGE
36643 Suffolk
Mt. Clemens, MI 48043
(313) 791-3384
Frank & Joann Spatafore
Retail. *Products*: dolls, drums/pipes, fetishes,
heishi, jewelry, kachinas, pottery, sandpaintings.

ELI THOMAS
2795 S. Leaton Rd.
Mt. Prospect, MI 48858
(517) 773-4299
Wholesale, retail. Product: baskets.

**INDIAN HILLS TRADING CO.
& INDIAN ART GALLERY**
1681 Harbor Rd.
Petoskey, MI 49770
(616) 347-3789
Victor S. Kishigo, Owner
Retail, mail order (by special request).
Products: baskets, beadwork, drums,
quillwork, jewelry, pottery, Navajo rugs.

NATIVE WEST
863 W. Ann Arbor Trail
Plymouth, MI 48170
(313) 455-8838
Annette & Ken Horn
Retail. *Products*: A,E,G,J,K,N,P,Q,R,U,V,W,X.
Membership: IACA.

SWEETGRASS ARTS & CRAFTS
206 Greenough St.
Sault Ste. Marie, MI 49783
(906) 635-6050
Susan Moore, Manager
Wholesale, retail. *Products*: A,B,C,E,X.

MINNESOTA

LADY SLIPPER DESIGNS
RR #3, Box 556
Bemidji, MN 56601
(218) 751-0835
Lisa Bruns, Manager
Wholesale. *Products*: birch bark baskets &
canoes. Special orders accepted. Catalog.

PAINTED TIPI, LTD.
387 W. Market
Bloomington, MN 55425

(612) 854-9193 Fax 645-5745
Retail. *Products*: All. *Appraisals*: A,C,D,
H,M,P,Q,T,U,V. *Membership*: IACA.

KENOO
Box 97, Ojibwe Tribal Enterprises
Callaway, MN 56521
(800) 726-1863; Fax (218) 375-4765
Dave Reinke, Marketing Manager
Wholesale. *Products*: B,C,D,E,J,P,S.
Membership: IACA. Catalog.

MA-EN-GUN STUDIO/GALLERY
5901 Rhode Island Ave. N.
Crystal, MN 55428
(612) 535-0091
Robert DesJarlait, Owner
Retail. *Products*: murals, original paintings,
drawings and graphics. Special orders and
commissions accepted.

**CHIPPEWA INDIAN
CRAFTS AND GIFT SHOP**
Red Lake Indian Reservation
Goodridge, MN 56725
(218) 378-4210/4322
Dan & Ed Needham, Owners
Wholesale, retail, mail order. *Products*: special-
izes in carved catlinite peacepipe bowls with deco-
rated stems; drums, cradleboards; birch bark tipis.
Special orders accepted. Color brochure, $2.00.

IKWE MARKETING
Route 1
Isage, MN 56570
(218) 573-341 1/3049
Margaret Smith & Winona LaDuke, Managers
Retail/mail order. *Products*: baskets, beadwork,
quillwork, rugs/quilts.

EARTH CIRCLES
4251 Nicolet Ave. So.
Minneapolis, MN 55409
(612) 823-8244
Retail. *Products*: C,D,V.

WOODLAND INDIAN CRAFTS
1530 E. Franklin Ave.
Minneapolis, MN 55404
(612) 874-7766
Elaine & Charles Stately, Owners
Retail/, mail order. *Products*: B,C,H,P,V.

PIPESTONE INDIAN SHRINE ASSOCIATION
Pipestone National Monument
P.O. Box 727
Pipestone, MN 56164
(507) 825-5463 Fax 825-2903
Maddie Redwing, Business Manager
Retail, wholesale, mail order. *Products*: C,J,P,U.
Carvings in pipestone (catlinite) including pipes
and jewelry; beaded pipe bags. Brochure.

AMBER WOODS STUDIO
810 Summit Ave.
St. Paul, MN 55071
(612) 856-2328
David D. DuBois, Co-owner
Retail. *Products*: A,X.

CBR, INC. TOUCH THE EARTH
2040 St. Clair Ave.
St. Paul, MN 55105
(612) 690-1050 Fax 690-0440
Carol Howe
Retail, wholesale.

STORMCLOUD TRADING CO.
725 Snelling Ave. N.
St. Paul, MN 55104
 (612) 645-0343 Fax 645-5745
 Sandra Graves, Owner; Jim Priest, Manager
Retail, wholesale, mail order . *Products*: A,C,D,
E,M,P,Q,U,V. Appraisals. *Membership*: IACA.

JOHN T. SHOPTEESE
14471 Kipling Ave. S.
Savage, MN 55378
Wholesale, retail. *Products*: P.X.
Custom orders accepted.

MISSISSIPPI

**CHOCTAW MUSEUM OF THE SOUTHERN
INDIAN GIFT SHOP**
Route 7, Box 21
Philadelphia, MS 39350
 (601) 656-5251
 Martha Ferguson, Manager
Retail, mail order . *Products*: B,C,H,I,U.
Special orders accepted. Price list available.

SOARING EAGLE INDIAN JEWELRY
906 Spring St.
Waynesboro, MS 39367
 (601) 735-1195
 Carolyn Stagg-White
Retail. *Products*: B,P,U. *Membership*: IACA.

MISSOURI

TURNER ARTWORKS
14323 Spring Dr.
De Soto, MO 63020
 (314) 337-4105
 Kevin Skypainter Turner, Owner
Retail, wholesale, mail order . *Products*: A,P.
Brochure, catalog.

AMERICAN INDIAN STORE
500 Nichols Rd. #206
Kansas City, MO 64112-2011
 (816) 561-0343
 Michael & Karen Shoemaker
Retail. *Products*: A,B,C,E,F,I,J,L,N,
P,Q,R,U,V,W,X,Z.

SOUTHWEST STAR FINE ARTS
11123 E. 85 Terrace
Raytown, MO 64138
 (800) 992-8939
 Roy A. Beers
Wholesale/retail. *Products*: U. Appraisals: U.
Membership: IACA. Catalog.

SILVER FOX TRADING POST
5104 King Hill Ave.
St. Joseph, MO 64504
 (816) 238-7560
Retail, wholesale. *Products*: Indian crafted
items & artifacts.

MONTANA

BUFFALO CHIPS INDIAN GALLERY
327 S. 24th St. West
Billings, MT 59102-5669
 (406) 656-8954
 Thom Myers
Retail, wholesale. *Products*: All.
Appraisals: C,H,I,P,V,Z. Catalog.

WOLF CREEK TRADING CO.
2 W. Main St.
Bozeman, MT 59715
 (800) 255-9653; (406) 585-1700 Fax 585-8885
 Walter Eisenstein & Ivy Sinn
Retail. *Products*: A,C,E,F,H,I,J,L,M,N,P,
R,U,V,X,Y. *Membership*: IACA.

BLACKFEET CRAFTS ASSOCIATION
P.O. Box 51
Browning, MT 59417
 Mary F. Hipp, Manager
Retail, mail order . *Products*: C,H,P.

BLACKFEET TRADING POST
P.O. Box 626
Browning, MT 59417
 (406) 338-2050
 Nora Lukin, Owner
Retail, mail order . *Products*: A,B,C,H,U.
Special order accepted.

NORTHERN PLAINS INDIAN CRAFTS ASSN.
P.O. Box E
Browning, MT 59417
 (406) 338-5661
 Jackie Parsons, Manager
Mail order. *Products*: B,C,H,I,P.

YELLOWSTONE TRADING POST
Box 1129, Hwy. 212
Cooke City, MT 59020
 (406) 838-2265
 Bernie & Phyllis Kiley
Retail. *Products*: A,C,F,H,I,J,N,P,Q,W.
Membership: IACA.

JAY CONTWAY ART
434 McIver Rd.
Great Falls, MT 59404
 (406) 452-7647
 Jay Contway
Wholesale, retail. *Products*: A,P,V,X.
Membership: IACA. Catalog.

WOLF CHIEF GRAPHICS
907 Ave. "C", NW
Great Falls, MT 59404
 (406) 452-4449
 King Kula, Owner
Retail, wholesale, mail order . *Products*: A,X.
Brochure.

**H. EARL & MARGARET TURNER
CLACK MEMORIAL MUSEUM**
P.O. Box 1484
Havre, MT 59501
 (406) 265-9913
 Elinor Clack
Retail. *Products*: A,C,F,I,M. *Appraisals*: C.

NEENEY
Box 84
Joplin, MT 59531
 (406) 292-3890
 Robert Harvey Allen, Owner
Retail. *Products*: C,N,P.

**NORTHERN CHEYENNE
ARTS & CRAFTS ASSOCIATION**
Northern Cheyenne Indian Reservation
Lame Deer, MT 59043
 Carol A. White Wolf, Manager
Retail, wholesale. *Products*: C,H,P.

PLAINS GALLERY
P.O. Box 126
Lame Deer, MT 59043
 Donald Hollowbreast, Owner
Retail, wholesale. *Products*: A. Oil paintings,
watercolors, pen & ink drawings.

THE TIPI GIFT SHOP
Rt. 2, Box 3110E
Livingston, MT 59047
 (406) 222-8575
 Evelyn Denham & Rex Moore
Retail, mail order . *Products*: A,B,C,H,J,P,V.

COUP MARKS
Box 532
Ronan, MT 59864
 (406) 246-3216
 Lorrain Big Crane & Dwight Billedeaux, Mgrs.
Retail. *Products*: A,C,I,J,H,X. Special orders
accepted

**DOUG ALLARD'S TRADING POST &
MUSEUM**
Box 460, #1 Museum Lane
St. Ignatius, MT 59865
 (406) 745-2951
 Doug Allard
Retail, wholesale. *Products*: A,C,E,F,H,I,J,N,P,
R,S,U,V,W,Y,Z. *Appraisals*: All. *Membership*:
IACA. Catalog.

**FLATHEAD INDIAN MUSEUM, TRADING
POST & ART GALLERY**
P.O. Box 464
St. Ignatius, MT 59865
 (406) 745-2951
 L. Doug Allard, Owner
Retail, wholesale, mail order . *Products*: A,C,H,P.
Special orders accepted on beadwork and
buckskin items.

HAMILTON STORES, INC.
P.O. Box 250, Yellowstone National Park
West Yellowstone, MT 59758
 (406) 646-7325 Fax 646-7323
 David Reynolds & Eleanor Hamilton Povah
Retail. *Products*: B,C,D,E,G,H,I,J,K,M,N,O,
P,Q,S,T,U,V,W,X. *Membership*: IACA.

NEBRASKA

THE TURQUOISE SHOP
905 N. Jeffers St.
North Platte, NE 69101
 (308) 532-7023
 Betty J. Kind
Retail. *Products*: N,O,P,U,W,Y.

THE PLAINS GALLERY
7830 Dodge St.
Omaha, NE 68114
(402) 397-7338
 Dorothy & John Head
Retail. *Products*: All. *Membership*: IACA. *Branch shop*: Eppley Air Field, N.Terminal, Omaha, NE (402) 346-1260.

NEVADA

LEHMAN CAVES GIFTS
Great Basin National Park
Baker, NV 89311
(702) 234-7221
 Tonia T. Harvey
Retail. *Products*: A,B,C,D,E,F,G,H,I,K, N,O,P,S,U,V. *Membership*: IACA.

STEWART INDIAN MUSEUM TRADING POST
5366 Snyder Ave.
Carson City, NV 89701
(702) 882-1808
 Edward C. Johnson, Manager
Retail. *Products*: B,C,I,P,V.

FORUNATE EAGLE'S ROUND HOUSE GALLERY
7133 Stillwater Rd.
Fallon, NY 89406
(702) 423-2220
 Adam Fortunate Eagle Nordwall, Owner
Retail. *Products*: A,C,H,J,P,U,X.

JEWELERS AT DEL RIO
P.O. Box 70, Verdi (89439)
2900 S. Casino Dr., Laughlin (89029)
(702) 298-6863 Fax 298-6893
 Mike & John Hoeck
Retail. *Products*: A,H,N,O,P,Q,R,S,V,W,X.

MALOTTE STUDIO
South Fork Reservation, Star Route
Lee, NV 89829
(702) 744-4305
 Jack Malotte, Owner
By appointment only. *Products*: original drawings, graphic design and illustrations.

MOAPA TRIBAL ENTERPRISES
P.O. Box 340, Paiute Tribal Enterprise
Moapa, NV 89025-0340
(702) 865-2787 Fax 379-4012
 Vince Pillig, manager
Wholesale, retail. *Products*: A,B,C,D,F,G,I,J, N,P,Q,R,S,U,V,W,X. *Membership*: IACA.

MAGGI HOUTEN
P.O. Box 265
Nixon, NV 89424
(702) 476-0205
 Margaret Houten, Owner
Mail order. *Products*: B,C.

EARTH WINDOW
401 W. 2nd St.
Reno, NV 89503
(702) 329-2573
 Mary Jo Weise, Manager
Retail. *Products*: A,C,H,P.

MICHAEL & SON'S BLACK HILLS TRADING CO.
2001 E. 2nd St.
Reno, NV 89502
(702) 829-9933
 David & Shannon Lorenz
Wholesale, retail. *Products*: B,G,H,I,J,N,O, P,Q,S,U,W,Z. *Membership*: IACA.

ARNOLD ARAGON - SCULPTURE & ILLUSTRATION
Box 64
Schurz, NV 89427
(702) 773-2542
Wholesale, retail. *Products*: A,X.

WINTER MOON TRADING CO.
P.O. Box 189
Schurz, NV 89427
(702) 773-2510
 Georgina & Elvin Willie, Owners
Retail, mail order. *Products*: A,B,C,P,U.

WESTERN INTERNATIONAL
395 Freeport Blvd. #2
Sparks, NV 89431
(800) 634-6737; (702) 359-4400 Fax 359-4439
 John & Shirley Fritz
Wholesale. *Products*: D. *Membership*: IACA. Catalog.

INDIAN OUTPOST
Box 829, 20 South C St.
Virginia City, NV 89440
(702) 847-9025
 Paul & Marilyn Slick
Wholesale, retail. *Products*: A,B,C,N,P,Q,S,U,X.

THE INDIAN TRADING POST
Box 671, Virginia City Mall #7
Virginia City, NV 89440
(702) 847-0242
 Winson Hong, Owner
Wholesale, retail. *Products*: All. *Membership*: IACA.

NEW HAMPSHIRE

AMERICAN INDIAN ARTS
P.O. Box 476
Epsom, NH 03234
(603) 736-9946
 Lynn & Gardner Gray
Retail.

FOUR WINDS TRADING CO.
222 Elm St. Plaza
Milford, NH 03055
(603) 672-2729
 Colleen & Leo Trudeau, Owners
Retail. *Products*: All. *Membership*: IACA.

KACHINA JUGGLER
278 State St.
Portsmouth, NH 03801
(603) 436-0253
 Kevin & Elisa Marconi-Davis
Retail. *Products*: A,B,C,E,F,G,H,I,J,L, N,P,Q,R,U,V,W,X. *Membership*: IACA.

NEW JERSEY

LITTLE WHIRLWIND IROQUOIS CRAFTS
721 E. Chanese Lane
Absecon, NJ 08201
(609) 652-1540
 Richard W. Frohman, Jr., Owner
Wholesale, retail. *Products*: traditional Iroquois pipes and carvings of soapstone and catlinite; bone chokers, leatherwork; featherwork by Gerrie Kirscher.

TRADER SUE
329 Front St.
Belvidere, NJ 07823
(201) 475-5566
 James Edwards & Jamie Shearer
Wholesale, retail. *Products*: A,B,C,E,F,G,I,K, N,O,P,Q,S,U,V,W,X,Z. *Membership*: IACA.

BLUE ZAT GEMS INDIAN ROOM
130 Atlantic St.
Bridgeton, NJ 08302
(609) 451-8059
 Russell & Doris Harris
Wholesale/retail. *Products*: art, jewelry, rugs/ weavings/wall hangings, sandpaintings, sculpture/carvings.

ARCHEOCRAFT
22 Rose Terrace
Chatham, NJ 07928
(201) 635-1447
 Kenneth O'Brien
Retailer. *Product*: Pottery.

CROSSROADS
9 Main St.
Madison, NJ 07940
(908) 879-6062
 Jan Keyes, Owner
Retail. *Products*: A,B,C,D,H,L,P,U,V,X. All Native-made crafts. *Membership*: IACA. Catalog.

JEAN MUIZNIEKS
13 Channing Way
Cranbury, NJ 08512
(609) 799-0448/1793
 Jean Muiznieks
Wholesale/retail. *Products*: C,N,O,P.

THE MORNING DANCER COLLECTION
130F The Orchard
Cranbury, NJ 08512-2421
(908) 548-8423
 Holly Sandiford & Chip Greenberg
Wholesale, retail. *Products*: B,P,U. *Membership*: IACA.

TURQUOISE LADY
10 Horace Court
Cranbury, NJ 08512
(609) 936-1044
 Jayne Davis
Retail. *Products*: P. *Membership*: IACA.

TURQUOIS INDIAN
23-27 Broadway
Fair Lawn, NJ 07410
(201) 797-1060
 Dennis & Ingred Taormina
Retail. *Products*: A,B,C,H,I,J,N,O,P,Q,R,S,T,U, V,W,X,Z. *Appraisals*: P. *Membership*: IACA.

SOUTHWEST AMERICAN INDIAN JEWELRY
76 Still Well Rd.
Kendall Park, NJ 08824
 (609) 799-0448
 Jean M. Muiznieks
Wholesale, retail. *Products*: C,N,O,P.
Membership: IACA.

SEIDEN AMERICAN INDIAN DESIGNS
P.O. Box 99, 14 Ridgewood Dr.
Livingston, NJ 07039
 (201) 992-4788 Fax 994-2795
 Matthew & Gella Seiden
Wholesale, retail. *Products*: N,P,Q,S,Y.
Membership: IACA.

CROSSROADS
65 Main St.
Madison, NJ 07940
 (201) 514-1616
 Jan Keyes, Owner
Retail. *Products*: A,B,C,D,H,L,P,U,V,X.
All Native-made crafts. *Membership*: IACA.
Catalog.

SPIDER WOMAN
141 Idolstone Lane
Matawan, NJ 07747
 (908) 583-0829
 John & Shaharazad Kleindienst
Retail. *Products*: C,I,N,O,P,Q,R,U.
Membership: IACA. *Branch*: Secaucus, NJ.

WAY OF THE ARROW
72 South St.
New Providence, NJ 07971
 (908) 464-2270
 Dot Hovi
Retail. *Products*: J,N,O,P,Q,S,T,U,V,W,Z.
Membership: IACA.

LONE BEAR INDIAN CRAFT CO.
300 Main St. #3F
Orange, NJ 07050
 James Lone Bear Revey, Owner
Mail order. *Products*: Woodland Indian
craftwork. Price list.

MOON LAKE INDIAN JEWELRY
175 Hayes Dr.
Saddle Brook, NJ 07662
 (201) 797-8367
 Bernard Ahrens
Retail. *Products* P,Q. Repairs & restoration.

SPIDER WOMAN
700 Plaza Dr.
Secaucus, NJ 07794
 (201) 223-1313
 John & Shaharazad Kleindienst
Retail. *Products*: C,I,N,O,P,Q,R,U.
Membership: IACA. *Branch*: Matawan, NJ.

ADOBE EAST GALLERY
445 Springfield Ave.
Summit, NJ 07901
 (908) 273-8282 Fax 277-1483
 Tedd & Phyllis Schwartz
Retail. *Products*: A,P,Q,U,V,X.
Membership: IACA.

COYOTE JUNCTION
7 Glenview Rd.
Towaco, NJ 07082
 (201) 299-0506
 Joseph & Susan Ascione

Wholesale/retail. *Products*: G,N,O,P,Q,U,W.
Membership: IACA.

NEW MEXICO

BLUE JAY'S POTTERY & GIFTS
P.O. Box 717
Acoma, NM 87034
 (505) 782-2124
 Angelina Medina & Calsue Murray
Wholesale/retail. *Products*: A,H,P,S,U,X.

LILLY'S GALLERY
P.O. Box 342
Acoma, NM 87034
 (505) 552-9501
 Lillian Salvador, Owner
Wholesale/retail/mail order.
Products: traditional Acoma pottery & figurines.

SQUASH BLOSSOM
306 10th St.
Alamagordo, NM 88310
 (505) 437-8126
 Cliff & Sue Hall, Owners
Retail, mail order. *Products*: American Indian
arts & crafts, primarily Navaho, Zuni, Hopi, and
New Mexico Pueblos. *Appraisals*: P,V. *Membership*: IACA.

AMERICAN HERITAGE INDIAN ARTS
9709 Trumbull SE
Albuquerque, NM 87123
 (800) 395-3962; (505) 271-1981
 Cynthia Judd & D.L. Uher, Sr.
Wholesale/retail. *Products*: H.J.V.
Membership: IACA. Catalog.

AMERICAN WEST TRADING CO.
1208 San Pedro NE, Suite 1 17
Albuquerque, NM 871 10
 Ken Kaemmerle
 (505) 265-8549
Wholesale. *Products*: L,Q,U,V,X. *Membership*:
IACA.

AMERINJECO TRADING CO.
P.O. Box 13345
Albuquerque, NM 87192
 (800) 874-1976; (505) 293-4727 (phone & fax)
 Layne E. Fuller, Director
Wholesale. *Products*: N,O,P,Q,R,U,V,W,X.
Membership: IACA. catalog available.

ANITRAS, INC.
1701 Central NW
Albuquerque, NM 87104
 (800) 824-4149; (505) 242-1060
 Anita Becker & William Blythe
Wholesale. *Product*: P. Catalog available.

ARMADILLO TRADING CO.
201 Wellesley Dr., SE
Albuquerque, NM 87106-1419
 (505) 266-7698
 Chuck Hall
Wholesaler. *Product*: U. *Membership*:IACA.

BEAR PAW INDIAN ARTS
326 San Felipe, NW, Old Town
Albuquerque, NM 87104
 (505) 843-9337
 Jim, Mary & Marian Trujillo, Owners
Retail, wholesale. *Products*: A,B,I,J,P,U,W.

BIEN MUR INDIAN MARKETING CENTER
Sandia Pueblo Tribal Enterprise
P.O. Box 91148, I-25 & Tramway
Albuquerque, NM 87199
 (505) 821-5400 Fax 821-7674
Retail, wholesale. *Products*: Authentic Native
American arts & crafts. *Membership*: IACA.
Brochure.

BING CROSBY'S INDIAN ARTS
2510 Washington NE
Albuquerque, NM 871 10
 (800) 545-6556; (505) 888-4800 Fax 883-6206
 Bing Crosby, Sharon Tomlinson, Jonathan Cox
Wholesale. *Products*: A,E,F,H,I,J,N,O,P,Q,R,
S,U,V,X. *Membership*: IACA. Catalog available.

CACTUS BOB'S TRADING CO.
401-B San Felipe NW
Albuquerque, NM 87140
 (505) 764-9696
 Robert Tingler
Wholesale. *Products*: B,C,H,J,P,R,S,U,V,X.
Membership: IACA. Catalog available.

CARLISLE SILVER CO., INC.
P.O. Box 26627, 750 Rankin Rd., NE
Albuquerque, NM 87125
 (505) 345-5304 Fax 345-5445
 H. William Pollack, III
Retail, wholesale. *Products*: A,N,O,P,Q,U,V,W, .
Catalog available.

CHRISTIN WOLF, INC.
2425 Monroe NE #B (871 10)
206 1/2 San Felipe NW (87104)
Albuquerque, NM
 (505) 242-4222
 Jerry McKenzie
Wholesale/retail. *Products*: N,O,P,R.

CHRISTOPHER'S ENTERPRISES
P.O. Box 25621
Albuquerque, NM 87125-0621
 (505) 294-4581 Fax 294-4585
 Christopher & Deborah Cates
Wholesale. *Products*: P. *Membership*: IACA.
Catalog available.

CIBOLA TRAIL TRADERS EAST
P.O. Box 3362
Albuquerque, NM 87190-3362
 (505) 869-2044
 Garry & Sue Zens
Wholesale. *Products*: N,P,U. *Membership*:
IACA. *Branch*: P.O. Box 1500, Peralta, NM
87042.

D'ANZE
P.O. Box 27206, 4908 4th St. NW
Albuquerque, NM 87125-7206
 (505) 345-2587
 Dee Ann Price
Wholesale. *Product*: P. *Membership*: IACA.

DISTINCTIVE INDIAN JEWELRY
1028 Stuart Rd., NW
Albuquerque, NM 871 14
 (505) 897-4152
 Ted & Randy Brackett
Wholesale. *Products*: N,O,P,Q,T,V.
Membership: IACA.

GERTRUDE ZACHARY, INC.
1613 Second NW
Albuquerque, NM 87102
 (505) 243-3711

Gertrude Schmidt
Wholesale. *Products*: P,Q,U.

THE GOLDEN FLEECE
10025 Acoma SE
Albuquerque, NM 87123
(505) 294-1604
Raphael Seidel
Wholesale. *Product*: P. Appraisals.

GRANDFATHER EAGLE
202-A San Felipe NW
Albuquerque, NM 87104
(505) 242-5376
Mark & Sally Ann Blythe
Wholesale, retail. *Products*: A,H,J,N,O,P,Q,R,S,
U,V,X,Y. *Membership*: IACA. Catalog.

GUS'S TRADING CO.
2026 Central S.W.
Albuquerque, NM 87104
(505) 843-6381
Wholesale.

HILL'S INDIAN JEWELRY
3004 2nd St., NW
Albuquerque, NM 87107-1418
(800) 545-6500
(505) 345-4110 Fax 345-5208
Martha & Hershel Hill
Wholesale. Product: P.

HOUSE OF THE SHALAKO
First Plaza Galeria #65
Albuquerque, NM 87102
(505) 242-4579
Gary & Sue Zens
Retail. *Products*: B,C,D,K,N,O,P,Q,S,U,V,W.
Membership: IACA.

INDIAN PUEBLO CULTURAL CENTER, INC.
2401 12th St., NW
Albuquerque, NM 87102
(800) 288-0721; (505) 843-7270
John Hihelcic, Manager
Wholesale, retail, mail order .
Products: B,J,P,U,V,WX.

JAMES ROGERS SILVERSMITHS
3137 San Mateo Blvd., NE
Albuquerque, NM 87110
(505) 889-9327 Fax 889-9329
James Rogers
Wholesale. *Product*: P. Catalog available.

JUDY CROSBY'S AMERICANA ARTS
2119 San Mateo Blvd. NE
Albuquerque, NM 87110
(505) 266-2324
Judy Crosby, Owner
Wholesale. *Products*: N,O,P,Q,R,S,U,W,X.
Membership: IACA.

KENNEDY INDIAN ARTS
P.O. Box 6526, 602 Montano NW
Albuquerque, NM 87197
(505) 344-7538
John & Georgiana Kennedy, Owner
Wholesale. *Products*: A,B,C,E,F,G,H,I,J,K,N,
O,P,Q,S,T,U,V,X. *Membership*: IACA.

KHALSA TRADING CO.
1423 Carlisle NE
Albuquerque, NM 87110
(505) 255-8278 Fax 255-3877
S.S. Gurubachan Khalsa & Kulbir Puri
Wholesale *Product*: Jewelry.

L.G. KINGS TRADING CO.
900 Coors SW
Albuquerque, NM 87105
(505) 836-2824
Leonard G. King
Wholesale. *Membership*: IACA.

MILAINES SANTA FE SILVER
2013 Ridgecrest Dr. SE
Albuquerque, NM 87108
(505) 268-8073 Fax 255-0659
Wayne Desantis
Wholesale. *Products*: A,N,P,U,X.
Membership: IACA. Catalog.

NAVAJO GALLERY
323 Romero NW, Suite #1
Albuquerque, NM 87104
(505) 843-7666
Barbara Griffith, Manager
Wholesale/retail/and some mail order . *Products*:
paintings, sculpture, lithographs, and drawings
by R.C. Gorman.

OLD TOWN TRADING POST
Box 7036, 208 San Felipe NW
Albuquerque, NM 87194-7036
(505) 243-0859
Bruce Mollenkopf
Wholesale/retail. *Products*: B,C,E,F,G,H,I,J,K,
N,O,P,Q,R,S,U,W,X. *Membership*: IACA.

R.L. COX FUR & HIDE CO., INC.
Box 25321, 708 1st St., NW
Albuquerque, NM 87125
(505) 242-4980
R.L. Cox
Wholesale. *Product*: U. *Membership*: IACA.

RED MOON
P.O. Box 81942, 10700 Acoma SE
Albuquerque, NM 87198
(800) 880-4353; (505) 293-4353 Fax 293-4738
Richard Donfro, Jr.
Wholesale, retail. *Products*: H,J,N,O,U,V,X.
Membership: IACA. Catalog.

RIO GRANDE ALBUQUERQUE
6901 Washington NE
Albuquerque, NM 87109
(505) 345-8511
Hugh Bell
Wholesale. *Product*: Y. *Membership*: IACA.

RUNNING DEER STUDIO
617 Figueroa St. NE
Albuquerque, NM 87123
(505) 579-4263
Rose Kerstetter, Owner
Retail. *Product*: tradional & contemporary
Iroquois-style pottery, clay sculptures.

SAM ENGLISH STUDIO/GALLERY, LTD.
400 San Felipe, NW, Old Town
Albuquerque, NM 87104
(505) 843-9332
Samuel F. English, Owner
Wholesale/retail. *Products*: original paintings by
Sam English; B,C,P,U.X. Special orders taken..

SANTA FE SILVER FOX
7000 Louisiana NE #1005
Albuquerque, NM 87109
Joan & Robert Fox
Wholesale, retail. *Products*: I,N,O,P,Q,U.
Membership: IACA.

SECRET SOURCE, INC.
133 Virginia NE
Albuquerque, NM 87108
(505) 255-0385 Fax 265-1973
Alfonso & Delores Jaramillo
Wholesale. *Product*: P. *Membership*: IACA.

SHAFFER'S INDIAN ART
P.O. Box 21700
Albuquerque, NM 87154
(505) 293-2217/264-0549
Richard L. Shaffer
Wholesale. *Products*: B,E,N,P,Q,S,U.
Membership: IACA.

SILVER HILLS
3821 Hawkins NE
Albuquerque, NM 87109
(505) 345-7088 Fax 345-7170
Rita Yokoi, Owner
Wholesale. *Products*: American Indian
handcrafted jewelry, specializing in jewelry from
Santo Domingo Pueblo. *Membership*: IACA.

SILVER NUGGET
416 Juan Tabo NE
Albuquerque, NM 87123
(505) 293-6861 Fax 292-0367
Gary DePriest
Wholesale/retail. *Products*: I,N,P,Q,Z.
Membership: IACA. Catalog.

SILVER SUN
2042 S. Plaza NW
Historic Old Town
Albuquerque, NM 87104
(800) 662-3220
(505) 242-8265/246-9692 Fax 246-9719
Deanna Olson & Kathy Sanchez
Wholesale, retail. *Products*: F,H,J,N,O,P,,S,Z.
Branch: 2011 Central NW, Albuquerque, NM;
and Santa Fe, NM. *Membership*: IACA. Catalog.

SOUND OF AMERICAN RECORDS (SOAR)
5200 Constitution Ave. NE
Albuquerque, NM 87110
(505) 268-6110 Fax 268-0237
Tom Bee, Owner
Retail, wholesale, mail order . *Products*: D.
Brochure.

SPIRIT OF SANTA FE
7000 Louisiana Blvd. NE #703
Albuquerque, NM 87109
Martha Vilanueva Russell
Retail.

STARBOY ENTERPRISES
8007 Indian School Rd. NE
Albuquerque, NM 87110
(505) 298-9454
Wayne M. Starboy, Owner
Retail, wholesale, mail order . *Product*: Star
qults. Special orders only. Brochure.

SUNBEAR TRADING CO.
3900 Elfego Rd. NW
Albuquerque, NM 87107
(505) 722-5555
John & Sheila Kennedy
Wholesale.

TECOLOTTE TILES & GALLERY
400 San Felipe, NW
Albuquerque, NM 87104-1462
(505) 243-3403 Fax 296-6865
Richard & Priscilla Jupp

Retail. *Products*: A,E,G,I,P,U.
Membership: IACA. Catalog.

TRACEY LTD.
2403 San Mateo NE, Suite S3
Albuquerque, NM 871 10
  (800) 458-2500; (505) 883-8868 Fax 883-8806
  Ray Tracey & Kristen Middleton
Wholesale. *Products*: P. *Branch*: 2407 E. Boyd
#8A, Gallup, NM. *Membership*: IACA. Catalog.

THE TREASURE TRADERS
6000 Lomas NE
Albuquerque, NM 871 10
  (505) 268-4343
  Arnie & Norma Jean Sidman
Retail. *Products*: A,B,H,I,J,O,P,Q,R,S,U,X.

TWO GREY HILLS
7712 Republic Dr. NE
Albuquerque, NM 87109
  (505) 821-4282
  Rick Richardson
Wholesale. *Products*: A,G,K,M,N,O,P,Q,S,
T,U,V,W,Z. *Membership*: IACA.

UTILITY SHACK, INC.
11035 Central NE
Albuquerque, NM 87123
  (505) 292-0174
  Linda & David Stout
Wholesale/retail. *Products*: All.
Appraisals: B,P,U,V.

WADE'S AMERICAN INDIAN TRADERS
627 Fairway NW
Albuquerque, NM 87107
  (505) 343-9100 Fax 343-9101
  Clare Wade
Wholesale, retail. *Products*: A,B,C,F,I,J,K,N,O,
P,Q,R,S,T,V,W,X,Y,Z. *Membership*: IACA.

WRIGHT'S COLLECTION
6600 Indian School NE, Park Sq.
Albuquerque, NM 871 10
  (505) 883-6122
  Sam Chernoff, Owner
  Wayne Bobrick, Director
Retail. *Products*: A,B,D,F,G,I,J,K,N,O,
P,Q,S,T,U,V,W,X,Z. *Membership*: IACA.

YELLOWHORSE
4314 Silver SE
Albuquerque, NM 87108-2723
  (505) 266-0600
  Artie Yellowhorse
Wholesale. *Product*: P. *Membership*: IACA.

ZACH-LOW, INC.
Box 10314, 7500 2nd St. NW
Albuquerque, NM 87184
  (800) 821-7443; (505) 848-1623
  Joe & Katy Lowry
Wholesale. *Products*: B,C,I,N,P,Q,S,U,W.
Catalog available.

ZACHARY TURQUOISE, INC.
7500-B 2nd NW
Albuquerque, NM 87107
  (505) 898-9278 Fax 344-7581
  Robert Zachary
Wholesale. *Products*: P. Brochure.

THE ED YOUNGS, INC.
P.O. Box 866
Belen, NM 87002
  (505) 864-1242

  Ed Young, President
Wholesale. *Products*:
C,F,G,J,N,O,P,Q,S,T,U,X,Z.
Membership: IACA. Catalog.

TA-MA-YA CO-OP ASSOCIATION
Santa Ana Pueblo
Star Route Box 37
Bernalillo, NM 87004
  (505) 867-3301
  Clara Paquin, President
Wholesale, retail. *Products*:Pueblo pottery,
embroidery, weaving and clothing.

SOUTHWEST SUNSET INTERIORS
702 W. Broadway
Bloomfield, NM 87413
  (505) 632-3805
  Brad & Marcia Magee
Wholesale/retail.

INDIAN PONY ART GALLERY
P.O. Box 1852, 56 Comanche Dr.
Carlsbad, NM 88221-1852
  (505) 887-0065 Fax 887-9610
  Robert & Wanda Spencer
Retail. *Products*: A,B,C,D,H,I,J,K,N,P,Q,T,U,V,X.
Membership: IACA.

THE PLAINS COMPANY
P.O. Box 186, 1014 E. Ave.
Carrizozo, NM 88301
  (505) 648-2472 Fax 648-2983
  Woody Schlegel
Retail. *Products*: A,P,U,V,X. *Membership*: IACA.

RHONDA HOLY BEAR
P.O. Box 70
Chamisal, NM 87521
  (505) 587-2018
Wholesale to galleries only/mail order. *Products*:
Plains and other tribal doll-figurines, handcrafted
costume. Price list available.

CLINES CORNERS OPERATING CO.
#1 Yacht Club Dr.
Clines Corners, NM 87070
  (505) 472-5488 Fax 472-5487
  Doug Murphy
Retail. *Products*: A,B,C,E,F,H,I,J,N,O,P,
Q,R,S,U,W. *Membership*: IACA.

THE BEAR TRACK
P.O. Box 15, 502 Burro Ave.
Cloudcroft, NM 88317
  (505) 682-3046
  Nita & Donald Lane
Retail. *Products*: A,B,C,E,F,G,I,J,K,N,O,P,Q,
R,S,T,U,V,W,X. *Membership*: IACA.

NOEL BENNETT
P.O. Box 1175
Corrales, NM 87048
  (505) 898-7211
Author, "Navajo Rugs, How to Tell...etc."

BIG SKY TRADERS
P.O. Box 461
Corrales, NM 87048
  (800) 827-1992; (505) 899-1990
  Phil & Margene Gibbs
Wholesale. *Products*: B,J,K,N,P,W,X.
Membership: IACA.

CROWNPOINT RUG WEAVERS' ASSN.
P.O. Box 1630
Crownpoint, NM 87313

  (505) 786-5302
  Ena B. Chavez, Manager
Navajo rugs sold at auction.

THE SILVER EAGLE
P.O. Box 158
Crownpoint, NM 87313
  (505) 786-5591 Fax 786-5593
  Jim Clinton
Wholesale/retail. *Products*: B,C,K,P,Q,U,V,W.
Membership: IACA.

APACHE MESA GALLERY & GIFTS
Box 233, Jicarilla Inn, Hwy. 64
Dulce, NM 87528
  (505) 759-3663
  Eileen Vigil, Manager
Wholesle/retail. *Products*: A,B,C,P,U,V.
Special orders accepted.

**JICARILLA ARTS & CRAFTS SHOP/
MUSEUM**
P.O. Box 507
Dulce, NM 87528
  (505) 759-3515
  Brenda Julian, Director
Retail/mail order. *Products*: A,B,C,E,H.

PASSAGES EXPRESST
P.O. Box 1184
Espanola, NM 87532
  Char Pully, Owner
Wholesale, retail, mail order. *Products*: dolls,
pocupine quill and leatherwork.

SINGING WATER GALLERY
Rt. 1, Box 472-C
Espanola, NM 87532
  (505) 753-9663
  Joe Baca, Owner
Retail, wholesale. *Products*: A,H,U.
Appraisals: U.

TERESITA NARANJO
Rt. 1, Box 455, Santa Clara Pueblo
Espanola, NM 87532
  (505) 753-9655
Wholesale/retail. *Product*: Santa Clara pottery.
Special orders accepted.

ARROYO TRADING CO., INC.
2111 W. Apache St.
Farmington, NM 87401-3204
  (505) 326-7427
  Vince & Helen Ferrari
Wholesale/retail. *Products*: A,C,E,G,W,X.
Author brochure, "Introduction to Sandpainting."
Catalog available.

THE FIFTH GENERATION TRADING CO.
232 W. Broadway
Farmington, NM 87401
  (505) 326-3211 Fax 326-0097
  Joe Tanner, Jr.
Wholesale. *Products*: B,G,J,K,P,Q,S,T,U,V,W,X.
Membership: IACA.

NAVAJO BEADWORKS
2111 W. Apache
Farmington, NM 87401
  (505) 326-7427
  Loree Ferari
Wholesale/retail. *Product*: C (Navajo beadwork).

RUSSELL FOUTZ INDIAN ROOM
301 W. Main St.
Farmington, NM 87401

(505) 325-9413
Russell Foutz
Wholesale. *Products*: B,G,K,P,Q,V,W,X.
Membership: IACA.

ASHCROFT TRADERS
695 County Rd. 6100
Fruitland, NM 87416
(505) 598-9159
W.L. & Lori Ashcroft
Wholesale, retail. *Products*: B,K,P,T,V,W.
Membership: IACA. *Appraisals*: V. Catalog
available.

ANASAZI TRADERS OF GALLUP
400 E. Hwy. 66
Gallup, NM 87301
(800) 777-6952; (505) 863-9294 Fax 863-2088
Tom Mortensen
Wholesale. *Products*: A,I,J,K,N,P,Q,R,U,W,X,
Y,Z. *Memebership*: IACA. Catalog available.

ANDY'S TRADING CO.
612 W. Wilson
Gallup, NM 87301
(505) 863-3762
Greg & Cambria Masci
Wholesale, retail. *Products*: B,C,P,Q,T,V.

ATKINSON TRADING CO.
P.O. Box 566, 1300 S. 2nd
Gallup, NM 87305
(800) 338-7380
(505) 722-4435 Fax 863-5624
Joe Atkinson, Owner; Roger Morris, Manager
Wholesale, retail. *Products*: J,K,N,P,Q,R,U,V.
Membership: IACA.

FELIX INDIAN JEWELRY
P.O. Box 195
Gallup, NM 87301
(505) 722-5369
Felix Gomez
Wholesale. *Product*: P. *Membership*: IACA.

FIRST AMERICAN TRADERS
2201 W. 66th Ave.
Gallup, NM 87301-6809
(505) 722-6601 Fax 722-6300
Dominic Biava
Wholesale, retail. *Products*: A,I,J,K,N,O,P,Q,U,
V, W,X. *Membership*: IACA. Catalog available.

THE INDIAN DEN TRADING CO.
1111 Caesar Dr.
Gallup, NM 87301
(505) 722-4141
Edward Gomez
Wholesale, retail. *Membership*: IACA.

INDIAN VILLAGE, INC.
2209 W. Hwy. 66
Gallup, NM 87301
(505) 722-5524 Fax 863-9093
Nathan Ramadoss, Owner
Retail, wholesale, mail order. *Products*: I,N,P,Q,
U,W,X. *Membership*: IACA.

JOHNNY MURPHY'S TRADING CO.
1206 E. 66th Ave.
Gallup, NM 87301
(505) 722-5088
John E. Murphy
Retail, wholesale. *Products*: B,C,N,P,T.
Membership: IACA.

THE NUGGET GALLERY
1512 E. 66th St.
Gallup, NM 87301
(505) 863-3615
Chet Jones
Retail, wholesale. *Products*: B,D,K,N,
P,Q,S,V,X,Y,Z.

O.B.'s INDIAN AMERICA
3330 E. Hwy. 66
Gallup, NM 87301
(505) 722-4431 Fax 722-6394
Bill & Harlene O'Neil
Wholesale. *Products*: All. *Membership*: IACA.

OUTLAW TRADERS
600 Belle Dr.
Gallup, NM 87301
(505) 722-6703
Diane & Larry Jinks
Retail, wholesale. *Products*: A,B,C,N,
P,Q,R,U,V,X.

PAT YELLOWHORSE ORIGINALS
1302 S. 2nd St.
Gallup, NM 87301
(505) 863-6809
Pat & Mary Yellowhorse
Wholesale/retail. *Products*: B,D,F,I,K,N,P,Q,
U,V,W,X,Z. Catalog.

RED SHELL JEWELRY
P.O. Box 764, 601 S. Second
Gallup, NM 87305
(505) 722-6963
John Hornbek
Wholesale, retail. *Products*: B,C,E,G,O,P,Q,V.
Appraisals: B,C,P,V. *Membership*: IACA.

SHAFFER'S INDIAN ART
P.O. Box 5300
Gallup, NM 87301
(505) 722-2526
Richard L. Shaffer
Wholesale. *Products*: A,B,E,F,I,N,P,Q,S,U.

SUNBURST HANDCRAFTS, INC.
306 County Rd. #1
Gallup, NM 87301
(505) 863-4541
Lionel McKinney
Wholesale. *Products*: jewelry.

TOBE TURPEN'S INDIAN TRADING CO.
1710 S. 2nd St.
Gallup, NM 87301-5895
(505) 722-3806
Tobe J. Turpen & Art Quintana
Wholesale, retail. *Products*: A,B,C,G,I,J,
K,N,P,Q,U,V,W. *Membership*: IACA.

TRACEY-KNIFEWING, INC.
Box 443, 2407 E. Boyd #8A
Gallup, NM 87305
(505) 863-3635 Fax 722-4218
Ray Tracey & Warren Lyons
Wholesale. *Product*: P. *Membership*: IACA.
Catalog.

ANCIENT MESAS GIFTS SOUTHWESTERN
P.O. Box 220, I-40 Exit 89
Grants, NM 87020
(505) 285-4335
Patricia McClure & Kraig Williams
Retail. *Products*: A,B,C,E,G,I,J,N,O,P,Q,T,U,V.
Membership: IACA.

LEGACY GALLERY & STUDIO
P.O. Box 418
Isleta, NM 87022
(505) 869-3317
Spencer Moss & Michael Kirk
Wholesale. *Product*: Jewelry.

TELLER POTTERY
P.O. Box 135
Isleta, NM 87022
(505) 869-3118
Stella Teller
Wholesale. *Product*: U. *Membership*: IACA.

CAROL G. LUCERO
P.O. Box 319
Jemez Pueblo, NM 87024
Wholesale, retail. *Products*: art, figurines,
pottery, storytellers, Christmas ornaments.

CAROL VIGIL
P.O. Box 443, Hwy. 4
Jemez Pueblo, NM 87024
Retail, mail order. *Product*: Jemez pottery.

ASHCROFT TRADERS
P.O. Box 1005
Kirtland, NM 87417
(505) 598-9159
W.L. & Lori Ashcroft
Wholesale, retail. *Products*: B,K,P,T,V,W.
Membership: IACA. *Appraisals*: V. Catalog.

55 SILVER & SUPPLY
P.O. Box 688, 4187 U.S. Hwy. 64
Kirtland, NM 87417
(505) 598-5322
John & Jacqueline Foutz
Wholesale, retail. *Products*: B,P,Y.
Membership: IACA.

LAGUNA PUEBLO MART, INC.
Box 63, Exit 114 off I-40 West
Laguna, NM 87026
(505) 552-9585 Fax 552-7446
Arne & Ron Fernandez
Wholesale, retail. *Products*: B,C,Q,S,U.

THE SILVERSMITH, INC.
Box 531, Mesilla Plaza
Mesilla, NM 88046
(505) 523-5561
Charles & Diane Rogers
Retail. *Products*: H,N,P,Q,S,U,W.
Membership: IACA.

THE WILLIAM BONNEY GALLERY
P.O. Box 27, 3 Calle de Parian
Mesilla, NM 88046
(505) 526-8275
Dan & Della McKinney
Retail. *Products*: A,B,I,J,N,Q,R,S,U,V,W,X.
Membership: IACA.

WINDMILL TRADING CO.
Box 1297, 788 Hwy. 22
Pena Blanca, NM 87041-1297
(505) 465-2416
Susan M. Rodin
Wholesale, retail. *Products*: O,P,Y.
Membership: IACA.

ZUNI RIVER TRADING CO.
P.O. Box 85
Ramah, NM 87321
(505) 473-9230

Susan Heller , Leo Brereton
Wholesale. *Products*: N,P.

SANDS TURQUOIS
Box 37, 300 Clayton Rd.
Raton, NM 87740
(505) 445-2737
Worth Wilkins
Retail. *Products*: H,J,N,O,P,U,W.

MASSACHUSETTS BAY CO.
3703 Oakmount SE
Rio Rancho, NM 87124
(505) 891-1821
Dean & Jacie Davis
Wholesale, retail. *Products*: E,N,O,P,Q,S,U.
Membership: IACA.

NATIVE VISIONS
4110 La Merced
Rio Rancho, NM 87124
(505) 891-0624
Soia Burdette & Doug Gomez
Wholesale, retail. *Products*:P,U.

TWO SQUAWS
1109 W. Second
Roswell, NM 88201
(505) 623-1921
Pat Mitchell & Garry Zens
Retail. *Products*: B,C,E,I,K,N,O,P,Q,S,T,
U,V,W,X,Z. *Membership*: IACA.

PUEBLO POTTERY
P.O. Box 366
San Fidel, NM 87049
(800) 933-5771; (505) 552-6748 (phone & fax)
Arthur & Carol Cruz
Wholesale, retail. *Products*: A,B,C,E,G,H,J,N,
P,Q,S,U,V,W. *Appraisals*: U. Shop located in
Acomita, NM. Catalog.

OKE OWEENGE ARTS & CRAFTS
P.O. Box 1095
San Juan Pueblo, NM 87566
(505) 852-2372
Joyce Ortiz, Manager
Retail, mail order . *Products*: A,B,C,H,I,P,X.
Special orders accepted. Price list available.

ANASAZI INDIAN ARTS
P.O. Box 319
Santa Cruz, NM 87567-0319
(505) 753-4730
Joe & Belle Becker
Wholesale. *Products*: U.V. *Membership*: IACA.

AGUILAR INDIAN ARTS
Rt. 5, Box 318C
Santa Fe, NM 87501
Alfred Aguilar, Owner
Retail, some wholesale, mail order .
Products: A,U.

CASE TRADING POST
P.O. Box 5153, Wheelwright Museum
Santa Fe, NM 87502
(505) 982-4636
Robb, Lucas, Owner
Retail. *Products*: All.

CRISTOF'S
106 W. San Francisco St.
Santa Fe, NM 87501
(505) 988-9881
Louis "Buzz" Trevathan, Jr.
& Pam Nicosin, Owners

Retail. *Products*: P,V,W,X. *Membership*: IACA.
Brochure.

HOGAN IN THE HILTON
100 Sandoval St.
Santa Fe, NM 87504-2131
(505) 984-0932
Paula Hausvick
Retail. *Products*: B,C,E,F,I,J,M,N,O,P,Q,
R,S,U,V,W,X. *Membership*: IACA.

INSTITUTE OF AMERICAN INDIAN ARTS
MUSEUM SALES
P.O. Box 20007
Santa Fe, NM 87504
(505) 988-6281
Richard Hill, Manager
Retail. *Products*: graphics, jewelry ,
metalwork, paintings, sculpture, textiles.

OTTOWI TRADING CO., INC.
P.O. Box 9152
Santa Fe, NM 87504
(505) 982-6881
Anthony Whitman
Wholesale, retail. *Products*: N,O,P,S,U,V.
Appraisals: U. *Membership*: IACA. Catalog.

PACKARD'S INDIAN TRADING CO., INC.
61 Old Santa Fe Trail
Santa Fe, NM 87501
(505) 983-9241
Richard H. Canon
Retail. *Products*: B,P,U,V,W,X.
Membership: IACA.

PEYOTE BIRD TRADING
P.O. Box 99
Santa Fe, NM 87504-0099
(505) 983-2480 Fax 982-8094
Mark Alexander
Wholesale. *Products*: N,O,P,U. Catalog.

POPOVI DA STUDIO OF INDIAN ART
San Ildefonso Pueblo
Santa Fe, NM 87501
(505) 455-2456
Anita M. Da, Owner
Wholesale/retail. *Prodcuts*: A,B,P,U,V..

RODICH, INC.
903 W. Alameda #1 14
Santa Fe, NM 87501
(505) 984-1801
Bob & Jane Matthews
Retail. *Products*: A,N,P,U,V,W,X.
Membership: IACA.

SCRIPSIT
3089 Plaza Blanca
Santa Fe, NM 87505
(505) 471-1516
Glen Billy, Owner
Wholesale, retail/mail order . *Product*: calligraphy
on paper and leather . Special orders accepted.

SILVER SUN
656 Canyon Rd.
Santa Fe, NM 87501
(800) 562-2036
(505) 983-8743
Deanna Olson, Cheryl Ingram, Kathy Sanchez
Wholesale, retail. *Products*: A,F,N,O,P,U,W.
Membership: IACA. Catalog.

TED MILLER CUSTOM KNIVES
P.O. Box 6328
Santa Fe, NM 87502
(505) 984-0338
Wholesale, retail, some mail order . Price list.

TRADE ROOTS
28 Burro Alley
Santa Fe, NM 87501
(800) 477-6687; (505) 982-8168 Fax 982-8688
Jeffrey Lewis
Wholesale, retail. *Products*: N,P.
Membership: IACA. Catalog.

FOUR CORNERS TRADING CO., INC.
P.O. Box 1814
Shiprock, NM 87420
(505) 368-5003
Larry A. Wray
Wholesale/retail. *Products*: V,W,X.

FOUTZ TRADING CO.
P.O. Box 1894
Shiprock, NM 87420-1894
(800) 383-0615; (505) 368-5790 Fax 368-4441
Bill & Kay Foutz
Wholesale, retail. *Products*: C,E,G,K,P,Q,
U,V,W,X. *Membership*: IACA. Catalog.

SHIPROCK TRADING CO.
P.O. Box 906, Hwy. 64
Shiprock, NM 87420
(505) 368-4585 Fax 368-5583
Ed Foutz & Jed Foutz, Owners
Retail, wholesale. *Products*: A,B,C,I,P,Q,U,
V,W,X. Appraisals. *Membership*: IACA.

ALL ONE TRIBE DRUMS
P.O. Drawer N, 803 N. Pueblo Rd.
Taos, NM 87571
(505) 751-0019 Fax 751-0509
Feeny Lipscomb, Charles Conley , Bruce Ross
Wholesale, retail. *Products*: A,B,C,D,F,H,I,J,N,,
P,Q,U,V,X. *Membership*: IACA. Catalog.

BROKEN ARROW INDIAN ARTS & CRAFTS
P.O. Box 1601, 222 N. Plaza
Taos, NM 87571
(505) 758-4304
Joel & Jess Payne
Retail. *Products*: A,B,C,G,I,J,K,N,O,P,Q,S,T,
U,V,W,X,Z. *Membership*: IACA.

CARL'S INDIAN TRADING POST & WHITE
BUCKSKIN GALLERY
Box 813, E. Kit Carson Rd. & Dragoon Ln.
Taos, NM 87571
(505) 758-2378
Mary Schlosser, Owner
Wholesale, retail. *Products*: A,B,J,N,P,Q,U,V,W.

CHUCK LEWIS EDITIONS, INC.
216 M N. Santa Fe Rd. #403
Taos, NM 87571
(505) 758-5692
Chuck Lewis, President
Wholesale. *Products*: A,E,U,X.
Membership: IACA. Catalog.

MILLICENT ROGERS MUSEUM STORE
P.O. Box A
Taos, NM 87571
(505) 758-4316 Fax 758-5751
Melody Gladin-Kehoe, Manager
Retail. *Products*: B,D,U,V. *Branch shop*:
Millicent Rogers Plaza Store, Taos Plaza, NM.

NAVAJO GALLERY
P.O. Box 1756
Taos, NM 87571
(505) 758-3250
R.C. Gorman, Owner
Wholesale, retail, and some mail order .
Products: paintings, sculpture, lithographs,
and drawings by R.C. Gorman.

SILVER & SAND TRADING CO.
129 A N. Plaza
Taos, NM 87571
(505) 758-9698
Harold & Wanda Allcorn
Wholesale, retail. *Products*: A,B,C,F,G,I,J,
N,O,P,Q,S,T,U,V,W,X. *Membership*: IACA.

SIX DIRECTIONS
Box 1042, 104 S. Plaza
Taos, NM 87571
(505) 758-5844
Neva & Otis Wilson
Wholesale, retail. *Products*: All.
Membership: IACA.

TAOS DRUMS
P.O. Box 1916, Hwy. 68
Taos, NM 87571
(800) 424-3786; (505) 758-3796 Fax 758-9844
Bruce & Pat Allen
Wholesale, retail. *Products*: J.
Membership: IACA.

TEHN-TSA INDIAN ARTS & CRAFTS
P.O. Box 471, Taos Pueblo
Taos, NM 87571
(505) 758-0173
Victor Trujillo, Owner
Wholesale, retail. *Products*: A,C,Q,P,U ;
paintings by Victor Trujillo.

TONY REYNA INDIAN SHOP
P.O. Box 1892, Taos Pueblo
Taos, NM 87571
(505) 758-3835
Tony Reyna, Owner
Retail. *Products*:A,P,J,Q.

WESTERN HERITAGE GALLERY
P.O. Box 1042
Taos, NM 87571
(505) 758-4489
Neva & Otis Wilson
Retail. *Products*: A,J,L,M,N,O,P,Q,R,U,V,W,X.
Membership: IACA.

MILLICENT ROGERS MUSEUM STORE
115 E. McCarthy Plaza
Taos Plaza, NM 87571
(505) 758-4316 Fax 758-5751
Melody Gladin-Kehoe, Manager
Retail. *Products*: B,D,U,V. *Branch shop*:
Millicent Rogers Plaza Store, Taos Plaza, NM.

**CONTINENTAL DIVIDE INDIAN
HANDCRAFTS**
Box 1059
Thoreau, NM 87323
(505) 862-7350
Willie Janish
Wholesale. *Product*: P. *Membership*: IACA..

SOUTHWEST INDIAN SILVERSMITHS
30 Steeplechase Dr.
Tijeras, NM 87059
(505) 281-5276

Channah Pruter-Edwards
Wholesale. *Products*: N,O,P,U.
Membership: IACA.

THE TEE PEE
P.O. Box 734
Tucumcari, NM 88401
(505) 461-3773
Mike & Betty Callens
Retail. *Products*: A,E,H,P,Q,U.
Membership: IACA.

JOE MILO'S TRADING CO.
P.O. Box 296
Vanderwagen, NM 87326
(505) 778-5531 Fax 778-5314
Joe Milosevich
Wholesale, retail. *Products*: A,B,C,H,I,J,K,N,O,
P,Q,R,,S,T,U,V,W,X,Y,Z. *Membership*: IACA.

CIRCLE W PAWN & TRADING CO.
Box 256, 3316 Hwy. 64
Waterflow, NM 87421
(505) 598-9179
Charles Webb
Wholesale/retail. *Products*: B,C,P,T,V,X.
Membership: IACA.

HOGBACK TRADING CO.
3221 Hwy. 64
Waterflow, NM 87421
(505) 598-5154/9243
Tom & Ann Wheeler
Wholesale, retail. *Products*: A,B,D,I,J,K,
N,O,P,Q,R,,T,U,V,W. *Membership*: IACA.

CAROLYN BOBELU
P.O. Box 443
Zuni, NM 87327
(505) 782-2773
Wholesale, retail, mail order . *Product*: P.
Special orders accepted.

PUEBLO OF ZUNI ARTS & CRAFTS
Box 425, Hwy. 53
Zuni, NM 87327-0339
(505) 782-5531 Fax 782-2136
Jim Ostler, Manager
Wholesale/retail. Tribal Enterprise.
Products: A,C,I,M,N,P,S,U,V,X. Catalog.

QUANDELACY FAMILY
P.O. Box 266
Zuni, NM 87327
(505) 782-2797
Faye Quandelacy
Wholesale, retail. *Products*: N,P,X.

ZUNI CRAFTSMEN COOPERATIVE ASSN.
P.O. Box 426, Zuni Pueblo
Zuni, NM 87327
(505) 782-4425
Loencita W. Mahkee, Manager
Wholesale, retail, mail order .
Products: A,C,N,P,U. Brochure.

ZUNI INDIAN JEWELRY
Drawer F
Zuni, NM 87327
(505) 782-2869
Carlton & Julie Jamon
Wholesale, retail. *Products*: C,N,P,V,X.
Membership: IACA.

NEW YORK

AMERICAN WEST BOUTIQUE
P.O. Box 58, 475 Main St.
Armonk, NY 10504
(914) 273-4056 Fax 273-5325
Mark & Laura Faller
Retail. *Products*: A,C,D,F,H,J,N,O,
P,Q,R,T,U,W,X. *Membership*: IACA.

TURQUOISE INDIAN
South Shore Mall, Captree Corners
Bay Shore, NY 11706
(516) 968-5353 Fax 277-1532
John & Jane Fuchs
Wholesale, retail. *Products*: All.
Membership: IACA.

KIVA TRADING CO.
117 Main St.
Cold Spring Harbor, NY 11724
(516) 367-2875 Fax 351-4984
Richard & Vivian Sutton
Wholesale, retail. *Products*: A,B,C,H,J,M,
N,O,P,Q,R,T,U,V,X. *Membership*: IACA.

THE ROCKWELL MUSEUM SHOP
111 Cedar St.
Corning, NY 14830
(607) 937-5386 Fax 974-4536
Juanita M. Malavet, Manager
Retail. *Products*: Native American arts & crafts
from the Southwest. Art reproduction of the
permanent collections; books and educational
tapes. *Membership*: IACA. Catalog.

PRODIGY
126 W. Main St.
Endicott, NY 13760
(607) 748-0190
Kim Weinert-Kim, Owner
Retail. *Products*: All.

BLACK BEAR TRADING POST
Rt. 9, Box 47
Esopus, NY 12429
(914) 384-6786
Roy Blackbear, Owner
Wholesale, retail. *Products*: B,C,H,P,Q,X.

SHELL & STONE TURQUOISE GALLERY
511 E. Genesee St.
Fayetteville, NY 13066-1548
(315) 637-4550
Frank & Rosemary Rodriguez, Owners
Retail. *Products*: All. *Appraisals*: A, N, P,
Q,S,U,V. *Membership*: IACA.

IROQUOIS BONE CARVINGS
3560 Stony Point Rd.
Grand Island, NY 14072
(716) 773-4974
Stanley R. Hill, Owner
Wholesale/retail/mail order on craftwork only .
Products: beadwork, carvings, bone jewelry;
dolls, drums, moccasins. Brochure available.

AMERICAN INDIAN TREASURES, INC.
P.O. Box 579
Guilderland, NY 12084-0579
Lillian Samuelson
Retail. *Product*: A. *Membership*: IACA

MOHAWK IMPRESSIONS
Box 20, Mohawk Nation
Hwy. 37, St. Regis Reservation
Hogansburg, NY 13655
 (518) 358-2467
 Gail General, Pam Brown,
 Charles Clench, Owners
Wholesale, retail, mail order . *Products*: A,B,C,
I,N,P. Special orders accepted. Brochure &
price list available.

SWEETGRASS GIFT SHOP
Akwesasne Museum, Rt. 37
Hogansburg, NY 13655
 (518) 358-2240
 Donna Cole, Manager
Wholesale, retail, mail order . *Products*: baskets,
beadwork, quillwork. Special order accepted.
Brochure and price list available.

CAYUGA TRADING POST
P.O. Box 523
Ithaca, NY 14850
 (607) 257-3138
 Roy Schreck
Wholesale, retail. *Products*: B,C,D,F,J,P,X.
Membership: IACA.

GREY OWL INDIAN CRAFTS
P.O. Box 340
Jamaica, NY 11434
 (718) 527-6000
 Jim Feldman, Owner
Mail order. *Products*: Native American craft
supplies. 4,000+ items. Catalog, $3; free to
Native Americans.

LITTLE FEATHER TRADING POST
P.O. Box 3165
Jamaica, NY 11431
 (718) 658-0576
 Marion Nieves, Owner
Retail, wholesale, mail order . *Products*: C,H,P.

SACRED EARTH STUDIOS
197 Longfellow Dr.
Mastic Beach, NY 11951
 (516) 399-4539
 Jamie Reason, Owner
Wholesale, retail, mail order from dealers only .
Products: carvings, featherwork.

ADIRONDACK ARTWORKS
Rte. 3 Main St.
Natural Bridge, NY 13665
 (315) 644-4645
 Donn & Nicole Alfredson
Retail. *Products*: A,B,C,D,E,F,J,N,P,Q,R,U,V,X.
Appraisals: J,P,X. *Membership*: IACA. Catalog.

ONONDAGA INDIAN TRADING POST
Onondaga Indian Reservation
Nedrow, NY 13120
 (315) 469-4359
 Dewasenta, Owner
Wholesale, retail. *Products*: Iroquois baskets,
beadwork, cornhusk dolls.

**AMERICAN INDIAN COMMUNITY HOUSE
GALERY/MUSEUM**
404 Lafayette St., 2nd Floor
New York, NY 10003
 (212) 598-0100
 Lloyd E. Oxendine, Manager
Wholesale/retail. *Products*: A,B,P,X.

FIRST PEOPLES GALLERY
114 Spring St.
New York, NY 10012
 (212) 343-0167
 Victoria Torrez
Wholesale, retail. *Products*: A,B,C,E,G,
H,J,L,N,P,Q,U,V,X. *Membership*: IACA.

SAKIA
100 LaSalle St., Suite 17D
New York, NY 10027
 (212) 866-2193
 Eugene A. Cam
Wholesale, retail.

UNIQUE NATIVE CRAFTS
505 LaGuadia Pl., #19-D
New York, NY 10012
 (212) 777-8394
 Audrey Bernstein, Owner
Retail. *Products*: Native American jewelry/crafts
from Alaska to Chile. *Membership*: IACA.

VENTURA INDIAN COLLECTION
175 E. 74th St.
New York, NY 10021
 (212) 988-8050
 Bebe Ventura & Stan Rosenfeld
Wholesale, retail. *Products*: P.
Membership: IACA.

**NATIVE AMERICAN CENTER
FOR THELIVING ARTS, INC.**
25 Rainbow Mall
Niagara Falls, NY 14303
 (716) 284-2427
 Wanda Chew , Manager
Retail, wholesale. *Products*: A,B,C,H,I,P,U,V.

TAOS TRADERS
80 Main St.
Nyack, NY 10960
 (914) 353-2949
Retail. *Products*: A,D,I,J,N,P.

MINERAL & NEEDLE CRAFT CREATIONS
P.O. Box 614
Oceanside, NY 11572
 (516) 536-2220
 Thelma Kirsch
Retail, wholesale. *Products*: A,B,C,D,H,I,J,L,M,
N,O,P,Q,R,S,U,V,W,X,Y. Appraisals: A,B,C,D,J,
L,M,N,O,P,Q,R,U,V,W,X. *Membership*: IACA.

FULL WOLF MOON
49 Wolden Rd.
Ossining, NY 10562
 (914) 762-7083
 Jude Westerfield
Retail. *Products*: P,X. *Membership*: IACA.

PAINTED PONY TRADING CO. LTD.
14 E. Broadway
Port Jefferson, NY 11777
 (516) 473-5155
 Evelyn Magers & Kathryn Magers-Larsen
Retail. *Products*: All. *Membership*: IACA.

TEARS OF THE MOON
209 Eastwoods Rd.
Pound Ridge, NY 10576
 (914) 764-1944
 Wendy Alexander
Retail. Products: A,B,C,H,I,J,L,M,N,O,
P,Q,T,U,V,X,Y. *Membership*: IACA.

CHRISJOHN FAMILY ARTS & CRAFTS
RD #2, Box 315
Red Hook, NY 12571
 (914) 758-8238
 Richard Chrisjohn, Owner
Wholesale, retail, mail order . *Products*: masks and
other wood carvings, bone jewelry , traditional
silverwork, dolls, pipes. Brochure available.

M & J ENTERPRISES
42 Eagle Ridge Cir.
Rochester, NY 14617
 (716) 342-5225
 Mary Catherine Hickey
Retail. *Products*: P,V,X. *Membership*: IACA.

PURPLE COYOTE, LTD.
274 Merrick Rd.
Rockville Centre, NY 11570
 (516) 536-6410
 James & Eileen Mirman
Retail. *Products*: A,B,D,EF,G,H,I,J,M,N,
P,Q,U,V,W,X. *Membership*: IACA.

AMERICAN INDIAN CRAFTS
719 Broad St.
Salamanca, NY 14779
 (716) 945-1225
 Lane & Lance Hoag, Owners
Wholesale, retail, mail order . *Products*: Mohawk
baskets, Seneca beadwork, Navajo and Zuni
jewelry, Ute pottery. Brochure available.

**SENECA-IROQUOIS NATIONAL
MUSEUM GIFT SHOP**
Box 442, Broad St. Extension
Salamanca, NY 14779
 (716) 945-1760
Retail, mail order . *Products*: B,C,H,U,X.
Brochure.

TUSKEWE KRAFTS
2089 Upper Mountain Rd.
Sanborn, NY 14132
 (716) 297-1821 Fax 297-0318
 John Wesley Patterson, Jr., Owner
Retail, wholesale, mail order . *Products*: field lacrosse and box lacrosse sticks. Brochure/price list.

STEVE'S TRADING POST
75 Garth Rd.
Scarsdale, NY 10583
 (914) 472-8094
 Steve Katz, Owner
Retail. *Products*: A,B,H,J,M,N,Q,R,U,V,X. Demon-
strations and exhibits by featured artists: Stella
Teller, Jim Jackson, Joe Cajero, Jr., Richard Begay,
Jerome Begay, Phil Poseyesva, Henry Shelton,
Mark Silversmith, et al. *Membership*: IACA.

THE MEXICAN SHACK
Route 100
Somers, NY 10589
 (914) 232-8739 Fax 232-7830
 Steven & Mary Delzio
Retail. *Products*:
A,B,C,D,F,J,K,N,O,P,Q,R,S,U,V,W,X,Z.
Appraisals: Jewelry. Repairs & restoration.
Membership: IACA.

SOUTHWEST STUDIO CONNECTION
65 Main St.
Southamtpon, NY 11968
 (516) 283-9649
 Kerry Sharkey-Miller
Retail. *Products*: A,G,N,O,P,U,X.
Membership: IACA. .

NATIVE PEOPLES ARTS & CRFATSHOP
P.O. Box 851, 210 Fabius St.
Syracuse, NY 13201
(315) 476-7425
Carol Moses, Manager
Retail, mail order by special request.
Products: B,H,U,X.

PETER B. JONES
Box 174, Cattaraugus Reservation
Versailles, NY 14168
(716) 532-5993
Roberta & Peter Jones, Owners
Wholesale, retail. *Products*: original works in
clay, ceramic sculptures, wall hangings, pottery ,
pipes.

THE VILLAGE POTTER
P.O. Box 220
Walker Valley, NY 12588
(914) 361-4401
Lois & Charles Garrison
Wholesale, retail. *Membership*: IACA.
ranch: 172 Sullivan St., W urtsboro, NY I2790.

M. ZACHARY GALLERIES, INC.
347 Maple St.
W. Hempstead, NY 11552
(516) 538-4659
Lorraine & Martin Schmidt
Retail. *Products*: B,P,Q,U,V,X.

FORTUNOFF
1300 Old Country Rd.
Westbury, NY 11590
(516) 542-4105 Fax 542-4188
Helene & Alan Fortunof f
Retail. *Product*: P. Catalog.

WHITE BUFFALO
13 Mill Hill Rd.
Woodstock, NY 12498
(914) 679-8723
Gloria Turk
Retail. *Products*: A,D,E,G,H,I,J,N,P,R,V,X.
Membership: IACA.

NORTH CAROLINA

CROWN DRUGS
400 Commerce Place
Bermuda Quay
Advance, NC 27006
(919) 998-6800 Fax 998-6846
Conrad Stonestreet, Ray Gentry ,
Douglas Sprinkle
Wholesale/retail. *Membership*: IACA.

SACRED HOOP TRADING POST
207 Purefoy Rd. #A
Chapel Hill, NC 27514
(919) 933-7595
Terrance Brayboy, Owner
Wholesale/retail/mail order . *Products*: baskets,
pottery, Lumbee original paintings, wood &
stone carvings.

EL CAMINO INDIAN GALLERY
P.O. Box 482
Cherokee, NC 28719
(704) 497-3600
Nathan Robinson, Owner
Retail. *Products*: B,C,H,I,P,X. Seminole crafts.

QUALLA ARTS & CRAFTS
Box 310, Hwy. 441 North
Cherokee, NC 28719
(704) 497-3103
Betty DuPree, Manager
Retail. Eastern Cherokee Tribal Enterprise.
Products: B,C,I,J,U,X. Catalog, $2.00.

WHITE BUFFALO
2617 Shady Grove Rd.
Durham, NC 27703
(919) 846-2771 (Phone & Fax)
Donald, Marty & Steve Koehler
Retail. *Products*: All. *Membership*: IACA.
Branch: Raleigh, NC.

HALIWA-SAPONI TRIBAL POTTERY & ARTS
P.O. Box 99, Hwy. 561
Hollister, NC 27844
(919) 586-4017
Linda Cooper-Mills, Executive Director
Wholesale/retail/mail order . *Products*: C,U,V,X.
Special orders accepted. Price list available.

WAYAH'STI INDIAN TRADITIONS
P.O. Box 130, Rt. 561
Hollister, NC 27844
(919) 586-4519
Patricia & Arnold Richardson, Owners
Mail order. *Products*: beadwork, leatherwork,
pipes, pottery , sculpture/carvings. Special orders
accepted. Price list available.

TUSCARORA INDIAN HANDCRAFT SHOP
Rt. #4, Box 172
Maxton, NC 28364
(919) 844-3352
Leon Locklear, Owner
Retail/mail order . *Products*: costumes,
leatherwork, jewelry . Special orders accepted.
Price list available.

NEW BERN NET & CRAFT CO.
2703 Hwy. 70 East
New Bern, NC 28560
(919) 633-2226 Fax 633-5760
Louise & Johnnie Thompson
Retail. Products: B,C,E,G,I,K,N,O,P ,R,S,U,Y.
Membership: IACA.

DESERT RAINBOW
3121-103 Edwards Mill Rd.
Raleigh, NC 27612
(919) 783-5345
Paulette Drury & Larry Hinshaw
Retail. *Products*: All.

WHITE BUFFALO
7909 Falls of Neuse
Raleigh, NC 27615
(919) 846-2771 (Phone & Fax)
Donald, Marty & Steve Koehler
Retail. *Products*: All. *Membership*: IACA.
Branch: Durham, NC.

LUMBEE INDIAN ARTS & CRAFTS
Rt. 1, Box 310AA
Rowland, NC 28383
(919) 521-9494
Hope Sheppard & Jane Oxendine, Owners
Mail order . *Products*: B,C.

EARTHWORKS ENVIRONMENT AL GALLERY
110 N. Main St.
Waynesville, NC 28786
(704) 452-9500

Susan & Jerold Johnson
Wholesale, retail. *Products*: A,C,D,E,F,G,H,I,J,
K,N,O,P,Q,R,S,U,V,W,X. *Membership*: IACA.

NORTH DAKOTA

**GREAT PLAINS NATIVE
AMERICAN ARTS CO-OP**
c/o NDIAA, 401 N. Main St.
Mandan, ND 58554-3164
(701) 221-5328
Carol Good Bear
Wholesale, retail. *Products*: A,B,C,E,F,H,I,J,P,
R,V,X,Y,Z. *Membership*: IACA. Catalog.

**THREE AFFILIATED TRIBES MUSEUM,
ARTS & CRAFTS**
New Town, ND 58763
(701) 627-4477
Gertrude Silletti, Manager
Retail. *Products*: beadwork, jewelry , quilts.

OHIO

DREAM CATCHERS
262 N. Roanoke
Austintown, OH 44515
(216) 793-7468
Kathleen & Shawne Bowman
Wholesale, retail. *Products*: A,C,F,G,J,N,O,
P,Q,R, S,U,V,W,Y. *Membership*: IACA.

TESOTA TRADING CO.
P.O. Box 24
Birmingham, OH 44816
Michael Savulak
Retail. *Products*: B,C,N,O,P,Q,S,U,Y.

COYOTE WOMAN GALLERY
P.O. Box 868,
Bryan, OH 43506
(419) 636-3300
Terri & John Freudenberger
Retail. *Products*: A,B,C,D,E,G,H,I,J,L,M,N,O,
P,Q,R,S,U,V,X. *Membership*: IACA. *Branch*:
Harbor Springs, MI.

QUEMAHONING COLLECTION
8060 Oxford Lane
Chesterland, OH 44026
(216) 247-0430
Retail. *Products*: A,B,C,E,J,N,O,P,Q,R,T,
U,V,W,X. *Membership*: IACA.

AMERICAN INDIAN ARTS & CRAFTS
3547 Raymar Dr .
Cincinnati, OH 45208
(513) 871-1858
Dan & Pat Stricker
Retail. *Products*: A,B,C,D,E,F,G,H,I,J,K,L,
N,O,P,Q,R,S,T,U,V,W,X,Z. *Branch*: 3512 1/2
Erie Ave. *Membership*: IACA.

BUFFALO GALLERY
130 E. Main St.
Lebanon, OH 45036
(513) 932-0792
William V. Jordan
Wholesale, retail. *Products*: A,B,C,D,E,H,I,J,K,
N, P,Q,R,S,U,V,X. *Appraisals*: A. *Membership*:
IACA.

SANTA FE TRADERS
5682 Mayfield Rd.
Lyndhurst, OH 44124
  (216) 461-8073
  Mary Lee & John Petranic
Retail. *Products*: A,D,E,G,H,J,N,P,Q,R,U,V,W,X.
Membership: IACA.

DESERT SUN
101 E. Wayne St.
Maumee, OH 43537
  (419) 893-9630
  Thomas & Denise Lawson
Retail. *Products*: A,B,C,E,G,H,J,K,N,P,Q,S,
U,V,W,X,Z. *Membership*: IACA.

SOUTHWEST EXPRESSIONS OF OHIO, INC.
25576 Mill St.
Olmsted Falls, OH 44138
  (216) 235-1177 (Phone & Fax)
  Randi & John MacWilliams
Retail, wholesale. *Products*: Native American
arts & crafts and Southwest home decor .
Membership: IACA. Brochure.

**EARTH SPIRIT-NATIVE
AMERICAN ART GALLERY**
5758 N. Main #1
Sylvania, OH 43560
  (419) 885-7012
  Chris & Pam Clayworth, Owners
Retail. *Products*: A,D,J,M,P,Q,U,V,W.
Membership: IACA.

OKLAHOMA

NATIVE AMERICAN ARTS
Box 2103, 3727 Gov. Harris Dr.
Ada, OK 74820
  (405) 436-5506
  Jack Pettigrew, Owner
Wholesale/retail/mail order . By appointment
only. *Products*:A,P,X. Price list available.

BRUCE C. CAESAR
Box 1183, 112 Prairie Village
Anadarko, OK 73005
  (405) 247-2303
Wholesale/retail. *Product*: jewelry. Specilizes in
Native Amerian church type ornaments. Special
orders accepted.

CIRCLE TURTLE GALLERY
Box 986, 1st & Broadway
Anadarko, OK 73005
  (405) 247-5224
  Linda S. Poolaw , Owner
Wholesale/retail. *Products*: A,B,U,X.
Special orders accepted.

DIXON PALMER HEADDRESSES & TIPIS
Rt. 3, Box 189
Anadarko, OK 73005
  (405) 247-3983
  Dixon Palmer, Owner
Retail. By appointment only . Special orders only .

**OKLAHOMA INDIAN ARTS & CRAFTS
COOPERATIVE**
Box 966, Southern Plains Indian Museum
Anadarko, OK 73005
  (405) 247-3486
  LaVerna Capes, Manager
Retail, wholesale, mail order . *Products*: A,H,I,P.
Price list.

TOEHAY-POTTERY
Route 3
Anadarko, OK 73005
  (405) 247-5268
  Thelma Toehay Chapman, Owner
Retail. *Products*: A,C,H,U.

ARROWHEAD TRADING POST
2700 N. Old Hwy. 66
Catoosa, OK 74015
  (918) 266-3663
  Douglas A. Jennings
Retail. *Products*: All.

TOUCHING LEAVES INDIAN CRAFTS
927 Portland Ave.
Dewey, OK 74029
  (918) 534-2859
  Louise Dean, Owner; Jim Clear-Sky , Manager
Mail order. *Products*: beadwork, jewelry,
leatherwork. Catalog available, $1.00.

TIM RAMSEY
P.O. Box 472
El Reno, OK 73036
  (405) 262-1677
Retail/some mail order . *Products*: C,H; tipi
accessories. Special orders accepted.

BILL GLASS, JR., STUDIO
HC64, Box 1410
Locust Grove, OK 74352
  (918) 479-8884
Retail/mail order . *Products*: U,X.
Special orders accepted.

AMERICAN INDIAN HANDICRAFTS
Box 533, 325 N. Dawson, Hwy . 18
Meeker, OK 74855
  (405) 279-3343
  Shalah Rowlen, Owner
Wholesale/retail. *Products*: C,H.
Brochure & price list available.

BUFFALO SUN
P.O. Box 1556
Miami, OK 74355
  (918) 542-8870
  Revard Moore, Owner
Retail, wholesale, mail order . *Products*:
Traditional and contemporary Indian fashions
and accessories, jewelry , leatherwork

DOUG MAYTUBBIE
200 E. Lockheed Dr .
Midwest City, OK 73110
  (405) 733-8534
Retail, wholesale. *Products*: A,X. Price list.

SONJA K. AYRES STUDIO
P.O. Box 249
Muldrow, OK 74948
  (918) 427-4593
  Sonya K. Ayres, Owner
Retail, wholesale. *Products*: A,J,U,P.

SAM KIDD ORIGIALS
Rt. 2, Box 129
Muldrow, OK 74948
  (918) 427-3793
Retail. *Product*: A.

**FIVE CIVILIZED TRIBES
MUSEUM TRADING POST**
Agency Hill, Honor Hts. Dr .
Muskogee, OK 74401
  (918) 683-1701

  Peggy Denton, Manager
Retail, mail order . *Products*: A,B,P,X.
Brochure available.

TIGER ART GALLERY
2110 E. Shawnee St.
Muskogee, OK 74403
  (918) 687-7006
  Johnny Tiger, Jr. & Peggy Tiger, Owners
Retail, wholesale, mail order . *Products*: A,H.
Brochure & price list available.

THE DANCING RABBIT
814 N. Jones
Norman, OK 73069
  (405) 360-0512
  Patta LT Joest, Owner
Wholesale, retail. By appointment only .
Products: C,P. Special orders accepted.

THE GALLERIA
1630 W. Lindsey
Norman, OK 73069
  (405) 329-1225
  Reba Reece & Clarence Olson, Owners
Retail. *Products*: A,B,C,P,U,X.

CHOCTAW INDIAN TRADING POST, INC.
1500 N. Portland Ave.
Oklahoma City, OK 73107
  (405) 947-2490 Fax 512-0005
  Angela A. Askew, Manager
Retail. *Products*: All. *Membership*: IACA

CONNIE SEABOURN STUDIO
P.O. Box 23795
Oklahoma City, OK 73132
  (405) 728-3903
Mail order. *Products*: A.

MAVIS V. DOERING
5918 NW 58th St.
Oklahoma City, OK 73122
  (405) 787-6082
Retail. Product: baskets.

STUDIO-GALLERY
2148 Huntleigh Dr .
Oklahoma City, OK 73120
  (405) 751-5751
  Adele Collins, Owner
Retail. By appointment only . *Product*: original
paintings. Commissions accepted.

MONKAPEME
P.O. Box 457
Perkins, OK 74059
  (405) 547-2948
  Remonia O. Jacobsen, Owner
Special order only . *Product*: clothing,
leatherwork.

ADAMS STUDIOS
Rt. 3, Box 615A
Ponca City, OK 74604
  (405) 765-5086
  Jack & Anna Adams, Owners
Retail. *Products*: A,C,P,R,U.
Special orders accepted. Brochure.

SNAKE CREEK WORKSHOP
Box 147, Hwy. 33
Rose, OK 74364
  (918) 479-8867
  Knokovtee Scott, Owner
Retail/mail order . *Product*: mussel shell gorget
necklaces. Brochure & price list available.

MISTER INDIAN'S COWBOY STORE
1000 S. Main
Sapulpa, OK 74066
 (918) 224-6511
 Jo Arrington, Manager
Retail/some mail order . *Products*: A,C,H,J,U,V.

KELLY HANEY ART GALLERY
P.O. Box 103, 214 E. Oak
Seminole, OK 74868
 (405) 382-3915
 Enoch Kelly Haney , Owner
Retail/mail order . *Products*: A,B,P,U,X.
Brochure available.

SUPERNAW'S OKLAHOMA INDIAN SUPPLY
Box 216, 303 East W .C. Rogers Blvd.
Skiatook, OK 74070
 (918) 396-1713
 Kugee Supernaw , Owner
Wolesale, retail, mail order . *Products*: C,H,P,Y.
Catalog, $1.00.

THE STILWELL COLLECTION
P.O. Box 1287, 1203 W . Locust, Hw. 100-W
Stilwell, OK 74960
 (918) 696-3607 Fax 696-3723
 Debi Kilgore
Wholesale, retail. Products: B,C,P ,V,Y.
Membership: IACA.

CHEROKEE ARTS & CRAFTS CENTER
Box 948, Hwy. 62 at Tsa-La-Gl Motor Inn
Tahlequah, OK 74464
 (918) 456-0511 ext. 307
 Nita Mccarter, Manager
Retail, mail order . Tribal Enterprise. *Products*:
C,H,I,P,U,V,X. Special orders accepted.

CHEROKEE CREATIONS
P.O. Box 948
Tahlequah, OK 74465
 (918) 456-0671
 Linda Lewis, Director
Wholesale/retail.

**CHEROKEE NATIONAL
MUSEUM GIFT SHOP**
P.O. Box 515, TSA-LA-GI
Tahlequah, OK 74464
 (918) 456-6007
 Betty Jo Smith, Manager
Retail, mail order . *Products*: A,B,X Price list.

TAH-MELS
Box 1123, Hwy. 62
Tahlequah, OK 74465
 (918) 456-5461
 E.G. & Betty Thompson, Owners
Wholesale/retail/mail order . *Products*: A,B,C,H,
P,U,V,X. Jewelry repair. Special orders.

JOYCE JOHNSON
4735 E. Latimer Place
Tulsa, OK 74115
 (918) 835-3069
Mail order. *Products*: Cherokee baskets.
Brochure & price list available.

J. BALES STUDIO
One Plaza Soufe
Tahlequah, OK 74464
 (405) 247-3993
 Jean E. Bales, Owner
By appointment only . *Products*: paintings/prints,
pottery, sculpture. Special orders accepted.

GILCREASE MUSEUM SHOP
1400 Gilcrease Museum Rd.
Tulsa, OK 74127
 (918) 582-2423
 Susan Logsdon
Wholesale, retail. *Products*: All.
Membership: IACA. Catalog.

LYON'S INDIAN STORE
700 S. Main
Tulsa, OK 74119
 (918) 582-6372
 Larry & Janie L yon
Retail, mail order . *Products*: C,H,P,V,Y.
Membership: IACA. Brochure; catalog for craft
supplies only. *Branch shop*: Woodland Hills
Mall, Tulsa, OK.

ZADOKA POTTERY
12515 E. 37th St.
Tulsa, OK 74146
 (918) 663-9455
 David Thompson, Owner
Wholesale/retail/mail order . *Product*: Earthen-
ware storage vessels, vases and bowls.

JANET L. SMITH STUDIO
1106 SE 7th St.
Broken Arrow, OK 74467
 (918) 251-8952
By appointment only . *Product*: traditional and
contemporary Cherokee watercolors, original
paintings.

JACK GREGORY
Rt. 1, Box 79, Hwy. 59
Watts, OK 74964
 (918) 723-5408
By appointment only . *Product*: wood carvings.
Special orders accepted.

WEWOKA TRADING POST
Box 1532, 524 S. W ewoka Ave.
Seminole Nation Historical Society
Wewoka, OK 74884
 (405) 257-5580
Retail, mail order . *Products*: A,C,H,I,P,V.
Special orders accepted. Brochure & catalog.

OREGON

RED BEAR CREATIONS
358 N. Lexington Ave.
Bandon, OR 97411
 (503) 347-9725
 Red She Bear, Owner
Retail, Wholesale. *Products*: Traditional star
quilts & drum covers made to order . Brochure.

OARD'S
SR2 1604 Buchanan Rd.
Burns, OR 97720
 (503) 493-2535
 Mavis Oard
Retail. *Products*: All. *Membership*: IACA.

SPOTTED HORSE TRIBAL GIFTS
P.O. Box 414
Coos Bay, OR 97420
 Diane McAlister Owner
Retail, wholesale, mail order . Native American
owned and operated mail order business.
Products: Native American craftmaking kits,
patterns, supplies, tapes, books, crafts.

Cherokee research. Publishes "The Native
American Connection Newsletter , monthly.

ART OF THE VINEYARD, INC.
1430 Willamette, Suite 24
Eugene, OR 97401
 William & Jacqueline Kaufman
Retail. *Products*: A,B,D,L,P,V.
Membership: IACA.

AMERICAN SHADOWS
1800 SE Hwy. 101, Suite G
Lincoln City, OR 97367
 (503) 996-6887
 Patricia L. Erickson
Retail. *Products*: A,B,C,I,J,N,P,Q,R,S,U,W,X.
Membership: IACA.

WESTERN IMAGES
4744 S. Immonen Rd.
Lincoln City, OR 97367
 (503) 996-3774
 Hudy Troutner & Sally Binninger
Retail. *Products*: A,B,C,D,H,I,J,N,P,Q,U,V,W,X.
Membership: IACA.

NADINE VAN MECHELEN
Rt. 1, Box 270
Pendleton, OR 97801
 (503) 276-2566
Wholesale/retail. By appointment only . *Product*:
Dolls dressed in authentic Indian costume for
collectors. Special orders accepted.

THE BEAD GOES ON
8721 S.E. Foster Rd.
Portland, OR 97266
 (503) 788-9533
 Kellie LaBonty
Retail/wholesale. *Products*: Native American
artwork and craft supplies. Special orders.

RAINEY DAY NATIVE AMERICAN ART
4504 N.E. Sandy Blvd.
Portland, OR 97213
 (503) 287-1380
Retail, wholesale, mail order . *Products*: A,B,
D,H,I,P,U,V,W,X,U. Catalog available.

**QUINTANA'S GALLERY
OF NATIVE AMERICAN ART**
139 N.W. 2nd Ave.
Portland, OR 97209
 (503) 223-0339
 Cecil Quintana, Owner
Retail. *Products*: A,B,C,P,U,V,X. Paintings and
sculpture featuring Northwest Coast Indian art.
Accepts art work on consignment.

PENNSYLVANIA

INDIAN POST
1645 Hausman Rd.
Allentown, PA 18104
 (215) 395-5530
 Carolyn Foreback, Owner
 Connie Foreback, Manager
Retail. *Products*: A,B,D,H,J,P,V,W,X.
Membership: IACA.

**LENNI LENAPE HISTORICAL SOCIETY
MUSEUM OF INDIAN CULTURE STORE**
R.D. #2, Fish Hatchery Rd.
Allentown, PA 18103

(610) 797-2121
Carla J.S. Messinger , Manager
Retail. *Products*: A,C,D,H,I,P.

TURQUOISE 'N TREASURES
21 E. High St.
Elizabethtown, P A 17022
(717) 367-1848
Nancy Barnitz
Retail. *Products*: A,C,E,I,J,M,N,O,P,Q,U,V,W.
Membership: IACA.

EICHER INDIAN MUSEUM SHOP
Ephrata Community Park
P.O. Box 601
Ephrata, PA 17522
(717) 738-3084
Beverly Flaherty, Manager
Retail. *Products*: A,B,C,I,L,N,O,P,Q,U,V,W,X.

SOUTHWEST SELECTIONS
The Art Works at Doneckers
100 N. State St., Gallery 1 12
Ephrata, PA 17522-2230
(717) 738-9593
Jeanne Loomis
Retail. *Products*: N,O,P,Q,T,U,V,W.
Membership: IACA.

SILVER ARROWS GALLERY
P.O. Box 3175, 2 York St.
Gettysburg, PA 17325
(717) 334-8422
Dona M. Fuss
Retail. *Products*: A,B,C,H,J,K,L,M,N,
P,Q,R,U,V,WX. *Membership*: IACA.

FITCH'S TRADING POST
230 N. 3rd St.
Harrisburg, P A 17101-1502
(717) 233-6832
Delores Fitch-Basehore;
Richard & Deirdre Basehore
Retail, mail order . *Products*: Native American
fine art representing 32 tribes in North America
and tribe in Central America. *Appraisals*: All.
Membership: IACA.

WESTERN LEGENDS GALLERY
1311 Old Ford Rd.
Huntingdon V alley, PA 19006
(215) 659-7530
Robert & Annette Grif fith
Retail. *Products*: A,C,G,J,L,M,N,O,P,Q,
R,U,V,W,X. *Membership*: IACA.

THE TURQUOISE SHOPPE
26 E. Main St.
Lititz, PA 17543
(717) 626-1616
Carol Stocker
Retail. *Products*: B,C,F,G,H,I,J,K,N,P,Q,
R,U,V,W,X. *Membership*: IACA.

SOUTHWEST VISIONS
36 W. Mechanic St.
New Hope, PA 18938
(215) 862-0323 Fax 797-1934
Sandie & Nikki Anthony
Retail. *Products*: A,B,C,F,G,I,J,N,P,Q,R,U,V,W,X.
Membership: IACA. Catalog.

DANDELION
1618 Latimer St.
Philadelphia, P A 19103
(215) 972-0999
Beth Fluke

Retail. *Products*: A,C,D,E,F,G,H,I,J,N,P,U,V,X,Y.
Membership : IACA. Branch: 1718 Sansom St.,
Philadelphia, P A.

NATIVE DREAMS GALLERY LTD.
184 E. Evergreen Ave.
Philadelphia, P A 19118
(215) 242-4443
Ethel & Richard Saunders
Retail. *Products*: A,B,C,J,L,M,N,P,Q,U,V.
Membership: IACA.

SOUTHWEST IMAGES
1041 Hilltown Plaza, Rt. 1 13
Souderton, PA 18964
(215) 721-9606
Marla & Bill Hammerschmidt, Owners
Retail. *Products*: A,E,G,J,M,N,P,Q,S,U,W,X.
Membership : IACA.

SHADY LAMP WORKSHOP
1800 Mearns Rd., Bldg. JJ
Warminster, PA 18974
(215) 672-2350 Fax 672-6401
Eileen & Jack Wilson
Wholesale, retail. Products: A,B,F,G,P,V.
Membership : IACA. *Branch shop*: Peddler's
Village, Lahaska, P A 18931.

SIMPLY SOUTHWEST
10 S. 5th Ave.
West Reading, P A 19611
(610) 373-3160
Randy & Paulette Nein
Retail. *Products*: A,D,I,J,N,P,Q,R,U,W,X.
Specializing in silver and turquoise jewelry .
Membership : IACA. Brochure.

TOMAR SER VICES, INC.
P.O. Box 233
Wexford, PA 15090
(412) 367-2310
Todd & Mary Grant
Wholesale/retail. *Products*: AB,C,E, P,U,V,
W,X,Z.

RHODE ISLAND

THE TURQUOISE
Rockland Rd.
N. Scituate, RI 02857
(401) 647-2579
Arietta Tapner, Owner
Retail/mail order . *Products*: A,B,H,P,U.

DOVE INDIAN TRADING POST
Main St.
Rockville, RI 02873
(401) 539-2094/2786
Eleanor F. Dove, Owner
Retail. *Products*: C,H,P,U.

SOUTH CAROLINA

SOUTHWESTERN CREA TIONS
c/o Laser Images
270 Harbison Ct. #A
Columbia, SC 29212-2232
(803) 750-4854
Robert L. Gibson
Retail.

SARA AYERS
1182 Brookwood Cr.
West Columbia, SC 29169
(803) 794-5436
Mail order. *Product*: U. Special orders
accepted. Price list.

WESTERN VISIONS, INC.
4728 C Hwy. 17 South
North Myrtle Beach, SC 29582
(800) 745-5691; (803) 272-2698
Grace C. Krueger
Retail. *Products*: All. *Membership*: IACA.

SOUTH DAKOTA

FEATHERSTONE PRODUCTIONS
P.O. Box 487
Brookings, SD 57006
(605) 693-3183
JoAnne & Gordon Bird, Owners
Retail, wholesale, mail order . *Products*: A,M,X.

**ST. JOSEPH LAKOTA
DEVELOPMENT COUNCIL**
St. Joseph's Indian School
Chamberlain, SD 57326
(605) 734-6021 ext. 307
Cy Maus, Manager
Retail, wholesale, mail order . *Products*:
A,C,H,I,P,V. Special order accepted for quilts.
Brochure/price list.

GALLERY OF INDIAN ARTS
Mt. Rushmore
Keystone, SD 57751
(605) 574-2515
Charles & Kay Steuerwald
Retail. *Products*: A,I,J,N,O,PU,V,W,X.

THE INDIANS
P.O. Box 162
Keystone, SD 57751
(605) 666-4864
Eugene & Lucille Jellif fe
Retail. *Products*: A,B,C,D,E,H,J,P,U,V,W,Z.

CHEYENNE CROSSING ST ORE
HC-37, Box 1220
Lead, SD 57754
(605) 584-3510
Jim & Bonnie LeMar
Retail. *Products*: A,C,E,H,J,P,R,U,V.
Membership: IACA.

OYATE KIN CULTURAL COOPERATIVE
c/o Wesley Hare, Jr.
Marty, SD 57361
Mail order. *Products*: C,E,H,V.
Special orders accepted.

RINGS 'N' THINGS
P.O. Box 906
Mission, SD 57555
(605) 856-4548
Paul Szabo, Owner
Retail wholesale, mail order . *Products*: C,E.
Special orders accepted.

JACKSON ORIGINALS
Box 1049
Mission, SD 57555
(605) 856-2541
Jackie Colomb, Owner

Retail, wholesale, mail order . By appointment only. *Product:* contemporary apparel. Price list.

MAKOCE WANBLI
333 E. 5th St.
Pierre, SD 57501
(605) 473-5622
Dennis Eagle Horse, Owner
Retail, wholesale, mail order . *Products:* A,H,I,J. Traditional Plains Indian items. Special orders accepted. Price list.

CRAZY HORSE
P.O. Box 153
Pringle, SD 57773
(603) 436-3629
Lynn & Gardner Gray
Retail. *Products:* All.

LAKOTA JEWELRY VISIONS
909 E. St. Patrick, Suite 16
Rapid City, SD 57701
(605) 343-0603
Mitchell Zephier , Owner
Retail, wholesale, mail order . *Products:* Traditional & contemporary jewelry . Special orders accepted. Brochure/price list.

SIOUX TRADING POST
913 Mt. Rushmore Rd.
Rapid City, SD 57701
(800) 456-3394 (mail order)
(605) 348-4822 fax 348-9624
Ray Hillenbrand, Manager
Retail, wholesale, mail order . Plains Indian arts & crafts. *Products:* C,E,H,I,J,M,P,Q,V,X,Y. *Membership:* IACA. Brochure; catalog, $2.
Branch shops: Mission, SD, and Santa Fe, NM.

TIPI SHOP, INC.
Box 1542, 515 West Blvd.
Rapid City, SD 57709
(605) 343-8128
Melvin Miner , Manager
Retail, wholesale, mail order .
Products: B,C,D,E,H,J,P,Q,U,Y. Catalog.

BRULE SIOUX ARTS & CRAFTS COOP.
P.O. Box 230
St. Francis, SD 57572
(605) 747-2019
Retail, wholesale. *Products:* A,C,E,V.

WALL DRUG STORE, INC.
Box 401, 510 Main St.
Wall, SD 57790
(605) 279-2175
Ted H. Hustead
Retail. *Products:* A,B,C,D,F,H,I,J,P,R,U. *Membership:* IACA.

TENNESSEE

RUNNING BEAR TRADING POST
P.O. Box 0549
Cookeville, TN 38503-0549
(615) 372-8023
William Alan Miller
Wholesale, retail. *Products:* N,O.P.Q. *Membership:* IACA.

TEXAS

NATIVE AMERICAN IMAGES, INC.
P.O. Box 156, 2104 Nueces
Austin, TX 78767
(512) 472-3049
Ted Pearsall
Wholesale. *Product:* A. *Membership:* IACA.

BONHAM GALLERY
P.O. Box 938
Burleson, TX 76097
(800) 333-5287; (817) 335-3491
H.E. Eugene Bonham, M.D.
Retail, wholesale. *Product:* Art.

L. DAVID EVENINGTHUNDER
Contemporary Native American Art
Box 1197, 201 River Creek V illage
Coldspring, TX 77331
(409) 653-2565
L. David Eveningthunder , Owner
Retail, wholesale, mail order . *Products:* A,H,J,M. Commissioned art work by Eveningthunder . Brochure.

AMERICAN WEST TRADING CO.
1701 Laura Lane
College Station, TX 77840
Ken Kaemmerle
(505) 265-8549
Wholesale. *Products:* L,Q,U,V,X. *Membership:* IACA.

CRAZY CROW TRADING POST
Box 314, 107 N. Fannin
Denison, TX 75020
(214) 463-1366
Ginger & Rex Reddick, Owners
Wholesale/retail/mail order . *Products:* C,H,P. Catalog available, $2.00.

TIGUA INDIAN RESERVATION CULTURAL CENTER
Box 17579, 122 S. Old Pueblo Rd.
El Paso, TX 79917
(915) 859-3916
Pat Gomez, Manager
Retail. Tribal Enterprise. *Products:* P,U.

YSLETA DEL SUR PUEBLO CULTURAL CENTER
122 S. Old Pueblo
El Paso, TX 79907
(915) 859-3916 Fax 859-2889
Vince Munoz, General Manager
Wholesale, retail. Tribal Enterprise.
Products: A,P,Q,U,V.

GUILDHALL, INC.
2535 Weisenberger
Fort Worth, TX 76107
(800) 356-6733
(817) 332-6733 Fax 332-8100
John M. Thompson, III
Wholesale, retail. *Products:* A,B,C,E,H,L,X. *Membership:* IACA.

PUEBLO ART
P.O. Box 330386
Fort Worth, TX 76163
(817) 292-0668
Bob & Pat Gordon
Wholesale, retail. *Products:* All. *Membership:* IACA.

NAVAJO TURQUOISE
2311 Strand
Galveston, TX 77550
(409) 763-2821
Lynn Dye
Retail. *Products:* B,C,E,G,H,J,M,N,O,P,Q, R,S,T,U,V,W,X,Z. *Membership:* IACA.

PUEBLO CONNECTION
334 S. Main St.
Grapevine, TX 76051
(817) 481-7724
Patrick & Beverly Fairchild
Retail. *Products:* All. Appraisals: V. *Membership:* IACA.

CACTUS BOB'S TRADING CO.
P.O. Box 431732
Houston, TX 77243-1732
(713) 461-9686
Robert Tingler
Wholesale. *Products:* B,C,H,J,P,R,S,U,V,X. *Membership:* IACA. Catalog available.

NARRANJO'S WORLD OF AMERICAN INDIAN ART
Box 7973, 4617 Montrose, Suite 150
Houston, TX 77270-7973
(713) 660-9690
Stella Naranjo Thompson, Manager
Wholesale/retail/mail order . *Products:* baskets, beadwork, dolls, jewelry , leatherwork, pottery , rugs. Price list available.

ZAPOTEC ART/SOUTHWEST SPIRIT
1728 Sunset Blvd.
Houston, TX 77005-1714
(713) 529-0890 Fax 526-4655
Michael C. McBride
Wholesale, retail. *Products:* All. *Membership:* IACA.

INDIAN CREEK JEWELRY
5920 Lalagray Lane
Hurst, TX 76148
(817) 268-4921
Betty Beaver
Retail. *Products:* C,N,O,P,U.

TW RECREATIONAL SERVICES
Mt. Rushmore, Box 178
Keystone, SD 57751
(605) 574-2515
Bruce Van Vort
Retail. *Membership:* IACA.

CROW'S NEST ART GALLERY
230 Jefferson
La Porte, TX 77571
(713) 471-4371 Fax 471-2468
Fern Yung, Owner
Retail. *Products:* All. *Membership:* IACA. Brochure.

WOODEN PENNY TRADING POST
105 Bois D'Arc
Lake Jackson, TX 77566
(409) 297-8953 Fax 265-6813
Richard Wood, Owner
Retail/mail order . *Products:* All. Catalog.

EAGLE DANCER
159 Gulf Fwy. South
League City, TX 77573
(713) 332-6028
Joseph Skywolf, Owner
Retail. *Products:* B,C,I I,I,P,U,V,X.

TRIBAL ENTERPRISE
Alabama-Coushatta Indian Reservation
Route 3, Box 640
Livingston, TX 77351
  (713) 563-4391; (800) 392-4794 (TX)
  Nelson Celestine, Manager
Retail/mail order . *Products*: B,C,H,U.

BLUE GEM SHOP & GALLERY
321 Dodson St.
Midland, TX 79701
  (800) 747-1391; (915) 683-1391 Fax 682-5809
  Dorothy L. Davis
Retail. *Products*: A,B,C,D,F,G,I,K,L,N,O,P,Q,
R,S,U,V,W,X. *Membership*: IACA. Appraisals.

ANNESLEY STUDIO
P.O. Box 3
Missouri City, TX 77459
  (713) 729-8960
  Robert H. Annsley, Owner
Mail order, some wholesale, retail.
Products: A,X.

TIGER'S TURQUOISE SHOP
3807 Meeks Dr.
Orange, TX 77630
  (409) 886-7906
  Abe Tiger, Owner
Retail. *Products*: B,C,P,U,V.

THE VICTORIAN DREAMER & THE COWBOY
1511 Browning Rd.
Orange, TX 77630
  (409) 882-9339
  Josephine & Robert Walter
Retail. Products: A,B,E,K,N,O,P,Q,S,U,V,W.
Membership: IACA.

WHITEWOLF PHOTOGRAPHY
P.O. Box 297
Redwater, TX 75573
  Ron Whitewolf Morgan, Owner
Mail order. *Products*: original photographs of
Indian and western themes. Brochure.

GALLERY OF THE SOUTHWEST
13485 Blanco Rd.
San Antonio, TX 78216
  (210) 493-3344
  R.D. & Ann K. Carlyon
Wholesale, retail. *Products*: A,B,C,D,F,G,H,I,J,
N,O,P,Q,R,T,U,V,W,X. *Membership*: IACA.

RATTLESNAKE AND STAR
209 N. Presa
San Antonio, TX 78205
  (512) 225-5977
  Gustin Aldrete
Retail. *Products*: B,C,I,P,U,V,X.

THE RESERVATION
8802 Broadway
San Antonio, TX 78217
  (210) 820-3916 Fax 820-0633
  Matt & Helen Walence
Wholesale/retail. *Products*: All. *Appraisals*: P,U.
Membership: IACA. Catalog.

TEXAS HILLCOUNTRY ENTERPRISES
2810 Thousand Oaks, Suite 287
San Antonio, TX 78232
  (210) 590-8911
  Ben T. Treadway, Owner
Retail, wholesale. *Products*: American Indian
jewelry & handicrafts. *Membership*: IACA.

**BOB & DOT NATION'S
TWO NATIONS TRADING CO.**
Box 2441, 109 Shadowyck Ave.
Universal City, TX 78148
  (512) 658-1185
  Bob & Dot Nation
Wholesale/retail. *Products*: A,B,C,E,F,G,I,J,
N,O,P,Q,S,T,U,V,X. *Membership*: IACA.

BRAZOS ART
P.O. Box 796, 1407 Woodland Hills
Whitehouse, TX 75791
  (903) 839-7573
  Linda Busby
Wholesale/reatil. *Products*: A,B,C,E,H,
J,N,O,P,U,V,X. *Membership*: IACA.

THE TURQUOISE LADY
2310 Brook St.
Wichita Falls, TX 76301-6124
  (817) 766-2626
  Edna Redding
Retail. *Products*: All. *Appraisals*: P.

UTAH

COW CANYON TRADING POST
P.O. Box 88
Bluff, UT 84512
  (801) 672-2208
  Liza Doran
Wholesale, retail. *Products*: B,C,F,H,
M,P,S,U,V,X.

RUBY'S INN GENERAL STORE
Bryce, UT 84764
  (801) 834-5341
  Fred Syrett, Manager
Retail. *Products*: All. *Membership*: IACA.

LEMA INDIAN TRADING CO.
Box 474, 60 N. Main & 860 S. Main
Moab, UT 84532
  (801) 259-5055/5942/5217
  Anthony & Carolyn Lema
Wholesale, retail. *Products*: A,B,C,I,J,K,N,O,
P,Q,S,U,V,W,X. *Membership*: IACA.

EAGLECRAFTS, INC.
168 W. 12th St.
Ogden, UT 84404
  (801) 393-3991 Fax 745-0903
Mail Order. Arts & Crafts supplies. Catalog.

BRYCE CANYON TRADING POST
Box 371, 2938 E. Hwy. 12
Panguitch, UT 84759
  (801) 676-2688
  Barbara Sheen & Gayle Collins
Retail. *Products*: A,B,C,D,F,H,I,J,K,N,O,
P,Q,R,S,T,U,V,W. *Membership*: IACA.

RED CANYON INDIAN STORE
Box 717, 3279 Hwy. 12
Panguitch, UT 84759
  (801) 676-2690
  Arthur Tebbs
Retail. *Products*: B,C,E,F,H,I,J,K,N,O,P,Q,
R,S,T,U,V,W. *Membership*: IACA.

SOUTHWESTERN EXPRESSIONS
Box 1162, 333 Main St. Mall
Park City, UT 84060
  (801) 649-1612

  Monty J. Coates
Retail. *Products*: A,B,I,J,K,M,N,O,P,Q,
R,S,U,V,W,X. *Membership*: IACA. .

KEN HOYT, INC.
P.O. Box 201, 408 N. 400 W
St. George, UT 84771-0201
  (801) 628-2269
  Ken & Lisa Hoyt
Wholesale, retail. *Products*: All.
Appraisals: Q,U,V. *Membership*: IACA.

AIR TERMINAL GIFTS, INC.
AMF Box 22031, 750 N. Airport Rd.
Salt Lake City, UT 84122
  (801) 575-2540
Retail. *Products*: A,B,C,F,H,I,J,K,N,O,P,Q,S,T,
U,V,W,X. *Appraisals*: N,O,P. *Membership*: IACA.

ZION NATURAL HISTORY ASSOCIATION
Council Hall/Capitol Hill
Salt Lake City, UT 84116
  (801) 538-1398
  Mary-Delle Gunn
Retail. *Products*: I,N,P,U,V,W.
Membership: IACA.

ZION NATURAL HISTORY ASSOCIATION
Zion National Park
Springdale, UT 84767
  (801) 538-1398
  Jamie Gentry
Retail. *Products*: I,N,P,U,V,W.
Membership: IACA.

PIONEER CENTER
391 N. Main St.
Springville, TX 84663
  (801) 489-6853
  Norma L. Suth, Owner
Wholesale, retail. *Products*: B,P,U,V.
Pueblo pottery.

VERMONT

LONG AGO & FAR AWAY
Box 809, Rt. 7A North
Manchester Center, VT 05255
  (802) 362-3435
  Grant & Betsy Turner
Retail. *Products*: A,B,C,D,E,H,I,J,K,L,N,O,
P,Q,R,S,U,V,W,X. *Appraisals*: B,C,D,L,P,V.
Membership: IACA

VIRGINIA

RED ROCK TRADING CO.
315 Cameron St.
Alexandria, VA 22314
  (703) 548-5990
  Ted & Joan Dunham
Wholesale/retail. *Products*: All. *Appraisals*:
A,B,P,T,U,V,X. *Membership*: IACA.

VERART JEWELRY
328 So. Pickett St.
Alexandria, VA 22304
  (703) 370-5573
  Vera & William Brennan
Retail. *Products*: beadwork, children's items,
fetishes, heishi, jewelry, miniatures, pottery,
sandpaintings.

THE SILVER PHOENIX
1624 Crystal Square Arcade
Crystal City Underground
Arlington, VA 22202
(703) 979-8027
James Grayhawk Armagost, Owner
Retail, mail order . *Products*: A,C,D,H,J,
N,O,P,Q,R,S,U,V,W. *Appraisals*: P.

TURQUOISE EAGLE GALLERY
4350 N. Fairfax Dr.
Arlington, VA 22203
(703) 525-9777 Fax 525-9782
Judy Cross, Owner
Wesley Mathews, Manager
Retail, wholesale, mail order . *Products*: All.
Appraisals: B,L,P,Q,T,U,V. *Membership*: IACA.

AMERIND GALLERY
P.O. Box 588, 885 Roanoke Rd.
Daleville, VA 24083
(703) 992-1066
Lnda Anderson
Retail. *Products*: A,B,D,E,I,J,L,N,O,
P,Q,S,U,V,W,X. *Membership*: IACA.

FIRST NATIONS ARTS
11917 Main St.
Fredericksburg, VA 22408
(703) 371-5615 Fax 371-3505
Dennis Fox, Jr., Rebecca Adamson
Wholesale, retail. *Products*: A,B,C,D,E,F,G,H,I,J,
L,N,P,Q,U,V,W,X. *Membership*: IACA. Catalog.

THE SILVER PHOENIX, INC.
Rte. 3, Box 990
Gainesville, VA 22065
James Grayhawk Armagost, Owner
Retail, mail order . *Products*: A,C,D,H,J,N,O,
P,Q,R,S,U,V,W. *Appraisals*: P.

**PAMUNKEY POTTERY
& CRAFTS TRADING POST**
Rt. 1, Pamunkey Indian Reservation
King William, VA 23086
(804) 843-2851
Mrs. James Bradby, Manager
Retail. Tribal Enterprise. *Products*: C,S,U,Y.

EAGLE SPIRIT
1038 E. Ocean View Ave.
Norfolk, VA 23503
(804) 491-2964
Carol Quanty
Retail. *Products*: A,C,D,E,H,N,P,Q,S,U,V,W,X.
Membership: IACA.

THE SILVER PHOENIX, INC.
2946-D Chain Bridge Rd.
Oakton, VA 22124
(703) 255-3393
James Grayhawk Armagost, Owner
Retail, mail order . *Products*: A,C,D,H,J,N,O,
P,Q,R,S,U,V,W. *Appraisals*: P. *Branch*: Crystal
City, Arlington, VA; The Cabin, Gainesville, VA.

VIA GAMBARO STUDIO, INC.
P.O. Box 1117
Stafford, VA 22554
(703) 659-0130
Retha Walden Gambaro, Owner
Retail. *Products*: J,V,X. Special orders accepted.

GEORGTOWN COTTON & CO.
2070 Chain Bridge Rd., Suite G-99
Vienna, VA 22182
(703) 790-0711 Fax 442-7543

Maureen Donovan & Moses Robbins
Retail. *Products*: C,N,O,P,S,T.
Membership: IACA.

EAGLE DANCER
1505 Brookfield Cove
Virginia Beach, VA 23464
(804) 490-0477
Jacqueline LaCrone
Retail. *Products*: A,B,C,E,G,H,I,J,N,O,P,Q,
R,S,U,V,W. *Membership*: IACA.

THE TRADING POST
Box 403, Rt. 211W
Washington, VA 22747
(703) 675-3990
Jeanie Redfield
Retail. *Products*: All. *Membership*: IACA.

EASTERN WIND CRAFTS
Mattaponi Indian Reservation
Rt. 2, Box 233
West Point, VA 23181
(804) 769-0289
Lionel Custalow , Owner
Retail, wholesale, mail order . *Products*: C,J.

RIVER OF HIGH BANKS CRAFT SHOP
Mattaponi Indian Reservation
Rt. 2, Box 270
West Point, VA 23181
(804) 769-4711
Christine Rippling Water Custalow, Owner
Retail, wholesale, mail order . *Products*:
C,H,U,X. Brochure.

SNYDER ART STUDIOS
P.O. Box 1565
Woodbridge, VA 22193
(703) 670-0074
Kim L. Snyder, Owner
Retail, mail order . *Products*: A,H,V,X.
Special orders and commissions accepted.

WASHINGTON

MARCH POINT INDIAN ARTS
815 S. March Point Rd.
Anacortes, WA 98221
(206) 293-5632
Marvi & Joan Wilbur, Owners
Retail, mail order . *Products*: B,H,I,P,U,V,X.

POTLATCH GIFTS
Northwind Trading Co.
P.O. Box 217
Anacortes, WA 98221
(206) 293-6404
Tim King, Manager
Wholesale, retail, mail order . *Products*:
A,B,H,P,U,X. Special orders accepted on wood
carvings and clothing. Brochure & price list.

LELOOSKA FAMILY GALLERY
5618 Lewis River Rd.
Ariel, WA 98603
(206) 225-9522/8828
Patty Fawn, Manager
Retail, some mail order . *Products*: A,I,L,P,X.
All items primarily Northwest Coast.

M.J.R. ENTERPRISE
126 SW 301
Federal Way, WA 98023

(206) 941-7333
Ron E. English
Wholesale, retail. *Products*: B,P,Q,W.

**FRAN & BILL JAMES, LUMMI INDIAN
CRAFTSMEN**
4339 Lummi Rd.
Ferndale, WA 98248
(206) 384-5292/758-2522
Retail, some mail order . *Products*: C,L,V.
Special orders accepted.

INDIAN ISABELLE'S LUMMI WORKSHOP
4435 Haxton Way
Ferndale, WA 98248
(206) 734-5216
Isabelle Warbus, Owner
Retail. *Products*: B,H,P. Special orders.

MAKAH CULTURAL RESEARCH CENTER
P.O. Box 160, Rt. 112
Neah Bay, WA 98357
(206) 645-2711/2
Greg W. Arnold, Manager
Retail. *Products*: B,C,H,J,J,L. Price list.

**TIN-NA-TIT KIN-NE-KI
INDIAN ARTS & GIFTS**
P.O. Box 1057, 993 Hwy . 20 East
Republic, WA 99166
(509) 775-3077
Ot-Ne-We & Jim Swayne, Owners
Retail. *Products*: A,B,C,E,H,I,J,P, U,W,X.
Brochure.

DAYBREAK STAR ARTS GALLERY
Discovery Park, P.O. Box 99253
Seattle, WA 98199
(206) 285-4425
Diane Svarney, Manager
Retail. *Products*: A,B,P, V,X.
Commissions accepted.

**SACRED CIRCLE GALLERY
OF AMERICAN INDIAN ART**
c/o Daybreak Star Arts Center
P.O. Box 99100
Seattle, WA 98199
(206) 285-4425
Steve Charles, Manager
Retail. *Products*: A,B,H,R,U, X.
Commissions accepted.

SUQUAMISH MUSEUM
P.O. Box 498
Hwy. 305, Port Madison Reservation
Suquamish, WA 98392
(206) 598-3311
Leonard Forsman, Manager
Retail, mail order . *Products*: B,I,M,X.
Special orders accepted.

TREASURES INDIAN JEWELRY
P.O. Box 64237
Tacoma, WA 98464
(800) 327-0852; (206) 564-2366
Dave & Judy MacMillan
Wholesale, retail. *Products*: A,C,I,P,Q,
U,V,W,Y,Z.

BEAD LADY/CHEROKEE RAINBOWS
315-B Roosevelt
Wenatchee, WA 98801
Dorothea C. Orndorf f, Owner
Mail order (special orders only). *Products*: C,H.
Beadwork repairs. By appointment only .

MAR-BILL INDIAN STORE
281 Riverside
Winthrop, WA 98862
(509) 996-2470
  Mary Luther
Retail. *Products*: B,C,D,E,H,I,J,K,N,O,
P,Q,R,S,U,V,W,X. *Membership*: IACA.
Branch: Winthrop, WA.

WISCONSIN

BEAR TRAP TRADING POST
Rt. 2, Box 419C
Ashland, WI 54806
(715) 682-2209
Retail. *Products*: crafts & supplies.

BUFFALO ART CENTER
Box 51, Hwy. 13
Bayfield, WI 54814
(715) 779-5858
  Mardella Soulier, Manager
Retail. *Products*: A,C,E,H,P,X.

LIL TP
1114 Woodward Ave.
Beloit, WI 53511
(608) 365-1009
  Jim & Katy King, Owners
Retail. *Products*: C,P.

MAPLE PLAIN CRAFT SHOPPE
Rt. 3, Box 142A, Hwys. 63 & 48
Cumberland, WI 54829
(715) 822-8706
  Margaret & Pauline Hart, Owners
Wholesale, retail. *Products*: C,H,I,
Special orders accepted for dance outfits.

AMERICAN INDIAN GIFT STORE
132 Main St., Box 73
Hayward, WI 54843
(715) 634-2655
  Gerald B. Diamond, Owner
Retail. *Products*: Authentic American Indian
made crafts. *Membership*: IACA

C & S LTD.
4303 75th St.
Kenosha, WI 53142-4265
(414) 694-3960
  Gayle Chiodo
Retail. *Products*: A,B,C,H,I,J,K,N,O,P,Q,
R,S,U,V,W,X. *Membership*: IACA.

WA-SWA-GON ARTS & CRAFTS
Box 477, Hwy. 47
Lac du Flambeau, WI 54538
(715) 588-7636
  Elizabeth Vetterneck, Manager
Mail order. *Products*: C,E,H,V,X.

TOUCH THE EARTH
220 Main St.
LaCrosse, WI 54601
(608) 785-2980
  Dinah & Ron Klemmedson
Retail. *Products*: hand-crafted silver jewelry
and pottery; art, beads and supplies.

KATY'S AMERICAN INDIAN ARTS
1803 Monroe St.
Madison, WI 53711
(608) 251-5451/0014
  Katy Schalles
Retail. *Products*: All. *Appraisals*: B,N,O,P,
Q,S,T,U,V,W. *Membership*: IACA.

WHITE THUNDER WOLF TRADING CO.
320 E. Clybourn St.
Milwaukee, WI 53202
(414) 278-7424 Fax 278-8244
  White Thunder Wolf, Owner
Products: Art, jewelry, drums, music, books,
beads & supplies, crafts, gifts.

JO'S LOG CABIN TRADING POST
Box 294, Hwy. 54
Oneida, WI 54155
(414) 869-2505
Retail. *Products*: Crafts, Leatherwork,
silver turquoise jewelry.

ONEIDA NATION MUSEUM
P.O. Box 365
Oneida, WI 54155
(414) 869-2768
  Shirley Tourtillott, Manager
Retail, wholesale, mail order. Tribal Enterprise.
Products: B,C,D,E,H,I,U. Special orders
accepted on beadwork and quillwork. Brochure.

TURTLE CLAN TRADERS
1090 Sunlite Dr.
Oneida, WI 54155
(414) 434-6777
  Sue Skenandore
Wholesale, retail. *Products*: C,H,P,Y,Z.

SHEILA S. SMITH
1795 Poplar Lane
Seymour, WI 54165
(414) 833-7366
Retail. *Products*: Iroquois costumes and
accessories. Special orders accepted.

WINNEBAGO PUBLIC INDIAN MUSEUM
Box 441, Hwy. 13 & River Rd.
Wisconsin Dells, WI 53965
(608) 254-2268
  Bernadine Tallmadge, Owner
Retail/mail order. *Products*: B,C,H,P,V.
Brochure and price list available.

WYOMING

**BUFFALO BILL HISTORICAL CENTER
MUSEUM SHOP**
P.O. Box 2630, 720 Sheridan Ave.
Cody, WY 82414-2630
(307) 587-3243 Fax 587-5714
Wholesale/retail. *Products*: All.
Catalog available.

LA RAY TURQUOISE CO.
P.O. Box 83
Cody, WY 82414
(307) 587-9564
  Ray & Laura Vallie, Owners

Wholesale/retail/mail order. *Products*: Ojibwa
beadwork, Navajo rugs, silverwork. Special and
custom orders accepted.

STEWART'S TRAPLINE GALLERY
Box 823, 120 E. Ramshorn
Dubois, WY 82513
(307) 455-2800
  Mark & Catherine Stewart
Wholesale, retail.

FORT WASHAKIE TRADING CO.
53 N. Fork Rd., Box 428
Fort Washakie, WY 82514
(307) 332-3557
  Jeri Greeves, Owner
Retail, wholesale, mail order. *Products*:
B,C,H,F,H,I,P,U,V. Special orders accepted.
Brochure.

BOYER'S INDIAN ARTS & CRAFTS
P.O. Box 647, 30 W. Broadway
Jackson, WY 83001
(307) 733-3773
  Dick & John Boyer
Retail. *Products*: B,C,D,H,I,J,K,N,O,P,Q,
R,S,U,V,X. *Membership*: IACA.

RAINDANCE TRADERS
Box 3262, 103 E. Broadway
Jackson, WY 83001-3262
(307) 733-1081
  Barbara & Terry Kennedy
Retail. *Products*: All.

TWO GREY HILLS
Box 1252, 110 E. Broadway
Jackson, WY 83001-1252
(307) 733-2677
  Gary Mattheis
Retail. *Products*: B,K,N,O,P,Q,U,V,W.
Membership: IACA.

WARBONNET
Box 3494, 60 E. Broadway
Jackson, WY 83001
(800) 950-0154; (307) 733-6158
  Greg & Sue Koschtial, Owners.
Retail, wholesale, mail order. *Products*: A,L,M,
P,Q,U,V,W,X. *Appraisals*: P,T,V. Brochure &
Catalog.

GRAND TETON NATIONAL PARK
Signal Mountain Lodge
P.O. Box 50
Moran, WY 83013
(307) 543-2831 Fax 543-2569
  Don Wallace, VP Retail
Retail. *Products*: A,N,P,S,W. *Membership*: IACA.
Winter address: Forever Resorts, P.O. Box
29041, Phoenix, AZ.

TW RECREATIONAL SERVICES, INC.
Yellowstone Park, WY 82190
(307) 344-5354 Fax (406) 848-7048
  Peter White
Retail. *Products*: All. *Membership*: IACA.

TRIBAL ENTERPRISES

Bien Mur Indian Marketing Center
Albuquerque, NM
(Sandia Pueblo Tribal Enterprise)

KENOO, Callaway, MN
(Ojibwe Tribal Enterprise)

MOAPA TRIBAL ENTERPRISES
Moapa, NV
(Paiute Tribal Enterprises)

NAVAJO ARTS/CRAFTS ENTERPRISES
Window Rock, AZ (Navajo Tribal Enterprise)

PUEBLO OF ZUNI ARTS & CRAFTS
Zuni, NM (Zuni Pueblo Tribal Enterprise)

QUALLA ARTS & CRAFTS, Cherokee, NC
(Eastern Cherokee Tribal Enterprise)

SOUTHERN UTE MUSEUM & GIFT SHOP
Ignacio, CO (Southern Ute Tribal Enterprise)

FOREIGN AMERICAN INDIAN ARTS & CRAFTS SHOPS

AUSTRALIA

AMERICAN INDIAN TRADING CO.
P.O. Box 367
Manly, N.S.W. 2095
011-02-938-5278
Ann O'Bryan, Kerry O'Bryan, Suzy Rochester
Wholesale, retail. *Products*: A,C,J,N,O,
P,Q,R,V,W. *Membership* : IACA.

THE CORN MAIDEN
P.O. Box 45
Ormeau, 4208 Queensland
011-61-07-210-0518
Kym Quinn
Wholesale, retail. *Products*: A,C,D,H,I,J,N,P,
Q,R,U,W. *Membership* : IACA. *Branch*: 66
Charlotte St., Brisbane 4000.

THE COWBOY FROM DOWN UNDER
Dolphin Arcade-Surfer's Paradise
Queensland 4217
011-61-07-592-0525
Wholesale, retail. *Products*: A,D,I,J,M,N,O,
P,Q,R,V. *Membership* : IACA.

THUNDER DOWN UNDER
P.O. Box 903, 85 Grafton St.
Mareeba, Queensland 4880
011-61-07-051-1040
Greg & Jana Whittaker
Wholesale, retail. *Products*: A,C,D,H,I,J,N,P,
R,T,V,W. *Membership* : IACA.

TWO FEATHERS TURQUOISE GALLERY
1 The Crescent
Sassafras 3787, Victoria
011-61-03-755-1072 (Phone & Fax)
Jacqueline & Paul Johnson
Wholesale, retail. *Products*: A,B,C,D,E,F,G,H,
I,J,N,O,P,Q,S,U,V,W,X. *Membership* : IACA.

VELVET IMPORTS
P.O. Box 349 Donacster
Melbourne, Victoria

011-61-03-848-2207
Bob & Zandra Heywood
Retail. *Products*: A,C,E,H,J,N,O,P,Q,V,W.
Membership : IACA.

BELGIUM

SPRL. CURIOS
36 Rue de Dampremy
6000 - Charleroi
011-32-07-132-1339 Fax 136-0324
Leon Gobillon
Wholesale, retail. *Products*: P,S,X.
Membership : IACA.

CANADA

ARCTIC CO-OPERATIVES LTD.
1741 Wellington Ave.
Winnipeg, Manitoba R3H 0G1
(204) 786-4481
Terry Thompson
Wholesale. *Membership* : IACA.

WOLFWALKER ENT.
30 Hatt St.
Dundas, Ontario L9H 2E8
(416) 627-1400
Wolf & Myrna Prudek
Wholesale, retail. *Products*: A,L,N,P,Q,U,X.
Membership : IACA.

GERMANY

VONHAND DESIGN
Frankfurter Str. 8
61118 Bad Vilbel
011-49-61-018-7938
Oliver Will & Isolde Eberle
Wholesale, retail. *Products*: A,C,D,H,J,M,
N,O,P,Q,T,U,V,W. *Membership* : IACA.

ARIZONA-GALERIE
GAST & MORTELL GMBH
Grosse Bockenheimer
Strasse 37
6000 Frankfurt/Main 1
011-49-06-928-7379 Fax 928-3362
Anja & Hildegard Gast
Retail. *Products*: A,C,E,H,I,J,N,O,P,Q,
R,T,U,V,W,Y,Z. *Membership* : IACA.

NAVAJO SILVER
Schmiedstrasse 2
3342 Gields
011-49-05-339-541 Fax 339-740
Hans-Jurgen & Le-Thu Grimm
Wholesale, retail. *Products*: A,C,E,I,J,N,O,P,
Q,S,X,Y,Z. *Membership* : IACA. *Branch Shop*:
Weenderstrasse 75, 3400 Gottingen.

TRADING POST
Wilstorfer Str. 72
21073 Hamburg
011-49-40-765-9699 Fax 765-6879
Wholesale, retail. *Products*: C,H,J,N,O,
P,Q,R,W,X. *Membership* : IACA.

CHEROKEE WIGWAM
Ringseestr 9
85053 Ingolstadt-Sud
0-11-49-03-416-9541
A. Weger, Liselotte Nichols
Wholesale/retail. *Products*: P,W.
Membership : IACA.

RIO GRANDE
Yantener Str. 42
Meerbusch-Strl"mp 40670
02159-6466
Carl Shroeter, Owner
Retail, wholesale. *Products*: All Indian arts &
crafts. Brochure & catalog. Branch shops.

FORM IM-UND EXPORT GMBH
Havensteinstr. 31
42 Oberhausen 1
011-49-20-880-1593 Fax 880-6199
Carl Shroeter
Wholesale, retail. *Products*: A,C,E,H,
J,O,P,Q,R,T,U,V,W,X. *Appraisal*: P.
Membership : IACA.

RED CLOUD INDIAN STORE
Rossbachstr. 16
88212 Ravensburg
011-47-7-511-3755 (phone & fax)
Michael Gribulis & Katharina Meyer
Wholesale, retail. *Products*: A,C,E,H,J,P,Q,T,X.
Membership : IACA.

AMERICAN ART GALLERY
Bahnhofstrasse 29
D-6632 Saarwellingen
011-49-6-838-6791
Hubert & Marlene Masloh
Wholesale, retail. *Product*: A.
Membership : IACA.

JAPAN

GALLERY SEDONA
16-61 Kita 5-Chome, Higashikaigan
Chigasaki, Kanagawa-Pref. 253
011-81-0467-87-081 1 Fax 0467-88-0058
Shigeo Niida, Owner
Retail, some mail order . *Products*: A,C,D,I,N,
P,Q,S,U,V,W. *Membership* : IACA. Brochure.
Kamakura branch shop: Goshoudou Bld. 2-8-16,
Komachi, Kamakura, Kanagawa. 248

INDIAN CRAFT CO., LTD.
5-5-10 Akasada
Minato, Tokyo 107
011-81-03-586-3737
Ms. Ayako Umemoto & Sumie Matsuda
Wholesale. *Products*: O,P,U,V,W.
Membership : IACA.

NETHERLANDS

CLASSIC WESTERN HOUSE
Kalverstraat 154
1012 XE Amsterdam
011-31-020-622-3329
Henk & Ilona Stots
Retail. *Products*: A,C,D,E,H,J,M,N,P,Q,R,V.
Membership : IACA.

PRODUCT CODES

A ART - PRINTS, POSTERS, CARDS

B BASKETS

C BEADWORK

D BOOKS, MUSIC, ED. MATERIALS

E BOXES, BARK, QUILL,
FEATHERWORK, METALS

F CHILDREN'S ITEMS

G CHRISTMAS ORNAMENTS

H CLOTHING, LEATHERWORK,
MASKS, MOCCASINS,
HEADDRESSES

I DOLLS

J DRUMS, FLUTES,
PIPES, TOMAHWKS

K DYE CHARTS

L ESKIMO, INUIT, NORTHWEST
COAST ARTS

M ETHNOGRAPHIC ARTIFACTS
& REPRODUCTIONS

N FETISHES

O HEISHI

P JEWELRY & SILVERWORK

Q KACHINAS

R KNIVES

S MINIATURES, TOYS

T PAWN

U POTTERY, STORYTELLERS,
NATIVITY SETS

V RUGS, WEAVINGS,
WALL HANGINGS

W SANDPAINTINGS

X SCULPTURE, CARVINGS

Y SUPPLIES, FINDINGS,
STONES, SHELLS

Z REPAIR, RESTORATION

Please call to confirm dates and locations

JANUARY

Annual Florida Everglades Powwow
West Palm Beach, Florida
(305) 927-2382 Attn: James Jumper
Dates: Dec. 31-Jan. 3

New Year's Indoor Contest Powwow
Amigos Indoor Sports Arena
South Tucson, Arizona
(602) 622-4900
Dates: Jan. 1-3

Santa Monica Indian Show-Sale - Powwow
Civic Auditorium, 1855 Main St.
Santa Monica, California
(310) 430-5112 Attn: Allicia & Don Bullock
Dates: Jan. 8-10

Colorado Indian Market
Boulder, Colorado
(303) 447-9967
Dates: Jan. 8-10

Providence Intertribal Society Social
Trinity United Methodist Church
375 Broad St.
Providence, Rhode Island
(401) 421-0888
Dates: Jan., March

American Indianist Society Powwow
Quinsigamond Village Community Center
16 Greenwood St.
Worcester, Massachusetts
(508) 852-6271
Dates: Jan. 10

Native American Student Council
Annual Winter Powwow
University of Washington
Seattle, Washington
(206) 543-4635
Dates: Jan. 15-16

Native American Awareness Day Powwow
Massachusetts Center for
Native American Awareness
Cambridge, Massachusetts
(617) 884-4227
Dates: Jan. 16

TIHA Powwow
San Antonio, Texas
(817) 498-2873
Dates: 3rd Saturday in January

Greater Lowell Indian Cultural Association
Midwinter Powwow
VA Hospital
Bedford, Massachusetts
(508) 453-7182
Dates: Jan. 23

Mashpee Wampanoag
Winter Social & Potluck
Mashpee United Church
Village Community Center
Mashpee, Massachusetts
(508) 477-0208
Dates: Monthly

FEBRUARY

Sinte Gleska College Founders Day Powwow
Sinte Gleska College
Rosebud, South Dakota
(605) 747-2263
Dates: Jan. 31-Feb. 2

Lincoln's Birthday & Self-Government
Sovereignty Celebration
Warm Springs, Oregon
(503) 553-3393 Attn: Anna Clements
Dates: Feb. 5-7

Hosaga Annual Powwow
Springfield College-Dana Gym
Springfield, Massachusetts
(413) 783-3428
Dates: Feb. 6

Honor Our Ancestors Traditional Powwow
Negaunee Community Center
Negaunee, Michigan
(906) 249-3153
Dates: Feb. 11-14

Annual Council of Indian Students Traditional Winter Powwow
Bemidji State University
Bemidji, Minnesota
(218) 755-2094 Attn: Tony Troyer

Seminole Tribal Fair & Rodeo
Hollywood Reservation
Hollywood, Florida
(305) 321-1051
Dates: 2nd weekend in Feb.

United Native American Tribes Powwow
Porterville Fairgrounds
Porterville, California
(209) 781-1706
Dates: Feb. 13-14

Annual O'Odham Tash
Casa Grande, Arizona
(602) 836-4723
Dates: Feb. 18-21

Arizona Indian Market
Casa Grande, Arizona
(602) 762-5266
Dates: Feb. 19-21

Three Fires Society Winter Ceremonies
Eagle Lodge
Lac Courte Oreilles Reservation, Wisconsin
(715) 634-1442/4078
Dates: Feb. 19-22

Annual Native American Heritage Assn.
of Radford University Powwow
Radford, Virginia
(703) 633-1871
Dates: Feb. 19-22

Annual Ira H. Hayes Recognition Day
Veteran's Park
Sacaton, Arizona
(602) 562-3310
Dates: Feb. 20

Annual Stanley Purser Powwow
Port Gamble Tribal Center
Port Gamble, Washington
(206) 297-2253
Dates: Feb. 20

Washington's Birthday Celebration
Toppenish Community Center
Toppenish, Washington
(509) 865-5121
Dates: Washington's birthday weekend

Annual Michigan State University Powwow
West Lansing, Michigan
(517) 353-7745
Dates: Feb. 20-21

Annual Tony White Cloud Memorial World
Champion Hoop Dance Competition
The Heard Museum
Phoenix, Arizona
(602) 252-8840 ext. 512 or 545
Dates: Feb. 20-21

Lima Council for Native American Indians
Traditional Powwow
UAW Hall, 1440 Bellefontaine Ave.
Lima, Ohio
(419) 228-1097
Dates: Feb. 20-21

Nindinawe Maaganag Nimiwin
Competetive Powwow
North Pines High School
Eagle River, Wisconsin
(715) 588-3346
Dates: Feb. 20-21

All Indian Day
Graham County Fairgrounds
Safford, Arizona
(602) 428-6260
Dates: Feb. 27

MARCH

Annual Indian Festival Bazaar
St. John Indian School
Laveen, Arizona
(602) 550-2400
Dates: March 1

Carmel American Indian Festival
Carmel, California
(408) 623-2379 Attn: Sonny/Elaine Reyna
Dates: 1st weekend in March

Rimrock Rendezvous & Powwow
"A Celebration of Contemporary
& Traditinal Native American Art"
Chico Mall
Chico, California
(916) 343-0696
Dates: March 5-6

Annual Gathering of the Clans
Metlakatla, Alaska
(907) 886-6332 ext. 310
Dates: March 5-6

Massachusetts Center for Native American
Awareness Day Celebration
South Shore, Massachusetts
(617) 884-4227
Dates: March 6

Annual College Park Powwow
University of Maryland
College Park, Maryland
(301) 270-2991
Dates: March 6-7

Miami Valley Council for Native Americans -
Annual Benefit Powwow
Dayton, Ohio
(513) 275-8599 Attn: James Cain

Crafton Hill Powwow
Yucaipa, California
(714) 785-4377
Dates: March 6-7

Annual Heard Museum Guild •
Indian Fair & Market
The Heard Museum
Phoenix, Arizona
(602) 252-8840 Attn: Mary Brennan

Annual Central Wisconsin Indian Center
Powwow
Rothchild Pavilion
Rothchild, Wisconsin
(715) 845-2613
Dates: March 6-7

WA AK Powwow
St. Xavier Mission
Tucson, Arizona
(602) 294-5727
Dates: March 6-7

Speelyi Mi Arts & Crafts Fair
Yakima, Washington
(509) 865-5121
Dates: 2nd weekend in March

E-Peh-Tes Powwow
Lapwai, Idaho
(208) 843-2253
Dates: 2md weekend in March

Annual North American Indian Student
Alliance Powwow
Montezuma Hall Aztec Center
San Diego State University
San Diego, California
(619) 594-6991/4251
Dates: March 12-13

Bear River Benefit
Lac du Flambeau, Wisconsin
(715) 588-3286
Dates: March 13

Cal State U.-Long Beach, Annual Powwow
1250 Bellflower
Long Beach, California
(310) 985-5293
Dates: March 13-14

Annual Native Arts & Crafts Show & Sale
Scottsdale, Arizona
(602) 569-0728
Dates: 3rd weekend in March

Florida Indian Hobbyist Association
Powwow
Indian River Community College
Ft. Pierce, Florida
(407) 464-4973
Dates: 3rd weekend in March

Annual Great Falls Native American Art
Association Exhibit & Sale
Ponderosa Inn
Great Falls, Montana
(406) 791-2212 Attn: Gladys Cantrell
Dates: March 18-21

St. Joseph's Feast Day
Laguna Pueblo Plaza
Laguna Pueblo, New Mexico
(505) 552-6654
Date: March 19

Native American Awareness Day
Northland College
Ashland, Wisconsin
(715) 682-4531
Date: March 19

Annual Indian Awareness Powwow
Crow Creek High School
Stephan, South Dakota
(605) 852-2258
Date: March 19

Annual American Indian Festival & Market
Museum of Natural History of Los Angeles Co.
900 Exposition Blvd.
Los Angeles, California
(213) 744-3488 Attn: Shelley Stephens
Dates: March 19-20

Texas Indian Market
Arlington Convention Center
Arlington, Texas
(806) 355-1610 Attn: Randy Wilkerson
Dates: March 19-21

Annual Denver March Powwow
Denver Coliseum
Denver, Colorado
(303) 936-4826 Attn: Grace Gillette

Annual Celebration of Sobriety & Powwow
College of Great Falls
MacLaughlin Center
Great Falls, Montana
Dates: March 19-21

Annual Birthday Celebration for Slow Turtle
National Guard Armory
Middle Burrow, Massachusetts
(617) 884-4227
Date: March 20

Carolina Indian Circle Powwow
University of North Carolina
Chapel Hill, North Carolina
(919) 929-0883
Date: March 20

NASA Spring Contest Powwow
Oklahoma State University
Stillwater, Oklahoma
(405) 744-5481

Annual Homestead Intertribal Powwow
Homestead High School
Cupertino, California
(408) 241-7999 Attn: Gwen Steirer

Annual Ann Arbor Contest Powwow
Chrysler Arena
Ann Arbor, Michigan
(313) 763-9044
Dates: March 20-21

Annual United Indians of Milwaukee
Traditional Powwow
State Fair Park
Milwaukee, Wisconsin
(414) 384-8070
Dates: March 20-21

Spring Powwow
Leech Lake Reservation
Cass Lake, Minnesota
(218) 335-6211
Dates: March 20-21

Scottsdale All Indian Powwow
Salt River Reservation
Scottsdale, Arizona
(602) 569-0728
Dates: 4th weekend in March

Annual Traditional Intertribal Powwow
Armed Forces Armory
Rochester, Minnesota
(507) 281-4772
Dates: March 26-27

Edisto Indian Cultural Festival
Summerville, South Carolina
(803) 871-2126
Dates: March 26-27

Annual Heart of the Earth Contest Powwow
Minneapolis Convention Center
Minneapolis, Minnesota
(612) 331-8862

Annual Waila Festival
Arizona Historical Society Museum
Tucson, Arizona
(602) 622-808 Attn: Angelo Joaquin
Date: March 27

Sugar Row Powwow
Laconia Indian Historical Association
Laconia, New Hampshire
(603) 783-9922
Date: March 27

Annual American Indian Powwow
Cal State U.-Stanislaus
Turlock, California
(800) 828-7733
Date: March 27

Salem Area Spring Powwow
Polk County Fairgrounds
Richreal, Oregon
(503) 623-8971 Attn: Cookie Spencer

Sucker Ceremony
Chiloquin High School
Chiloquin, Oregon
(503) 783-2219 ext. 162 Attn: Gordon Bettles

American Indian Students Association
Powwow
University of Massachusetts
Amherst, Massachusetts
(617) 413-5103
Dates: March 27-28

Annual Natchez Powwow
Grand Village of the Natchez Indians
Natchez, Mississippi
(601) 442-0200 Attn: Chuck Borum
Dates: March 27-28

Traditional Powwow
Dominic Jacobetti Center
Michigan University Campus
Marquette, Michigan
(906) 227-2138
Date: March 28

APRIL

**UC Davis Native American Cultural Days
& D-Q University Powwow**
Davis, California
(916) 758-0470 Attn: Karen Bohay
Date: Late March, Early April

Annual Chief Seattle Powwow
Connolly Center-Seattle Unversity
Seattle, Washington
(206) 296-6000 ect. 6076
Date: Early April

Annual Raleigh Powwow
Raleigh, North Carolina
(919) 821-7400
Date: Early April

**Annual Native American
Cultural Awareness Weekend**
North Carolina State University
Raleigh, North Carolina
(919) 839-2214 Attn: Reggie Oxendine

**North Florida Indian Cultural
Association Powwow**
Orange Springs, Florida
(904) 799-7981
Date: 1st weekend in April

Annual Spring Powwow
University of Wyoming
Laramie, Wyoming
(307) 766-6189
Date: 1st weekend in April

American Indian Club Powwow
Montana State University
Bozeman, Montana
(406) 994-4880
Dates: April 2-3

Annual Tulsa Indian Art Festival
Expo Square Pavilion
Tulsa, Oklahoma
(918) 838-3875 Attn: Monetta Trepp

Annual Powwow
Humboldt State University
Arcata, California
(707) 826-4994
Dates: April 2-4

Kansas City Indian Market
Overland, Kansas
(806) 355-1610 Attn: Randy Wilkerson
Dates: April 2-4

Annual Native American Spring Festival
Virginia Wesleyan College
1518 Wesleyan Dr.
Norfolk, Virginia
(804) 481-7342
Date: April 3

Annual Native American Festival
Ocean Stables
Virginia Beach, Virginia
(804) 481-7342
Date: April 3

Nighthawk Dancers Annual Powwow
Little Falls High School
Little Falls, New York
(315) 823-2570
Date: April 3

Northern Virginia Powwow
White Oak, Maryland
(703) 451-8617
Date: April 3

Annual Indian Creek Traders Expo
Midlands Mall
Council Bluffs, Iowa
(712) 325-1770
Dates: April3-4

American Indian Day
Boston Children's Museum
Boston, Massachusetts
(617) 426-6500 ext. 261
Date: April 4

Annual Central Michigan University Powwow
Mt. Pleasant, Michigan
(517) 772-5700
Dates: April 4-5

Annual Spring Powwow
Native American Student Council
University of Washington
Seattle, Washington
(206) 543-4635
Dates: 2nd weekend in April

Cocopah Indian Patent Day
Sommerton, Arizona
(602) 627-2102
Dates: 2md weekend in April

Navajo Community College Powwow
Tsaile, Arizona
(605) 724-3311 ext. 219
Dates: April 9-10

Annual Davis Lake Powwow
Suffolk, Virginia
(804) 539-1191
Dates: April 9-10

**Annual Honoring of the Elders
& 1st Annual SANAI Powwow**
University of Santa Cruz
Santa Cruz, California
(408) 459-2296
Dates: April 9-11

**Annual Northwest Indian
Youth Conference Powwow**
Seattle, Washington
(206) 343-3111
Dates: April 9-11

University of Iowa Powwow
Iowa City, Iowa
(319) 335-8298
Dates: April 9-11

Celilo-Wyam Salmon Feast
Celilo, Oregon

(503) 298-1559
Dates: April 9-11

Annual Indian Awareness Day Powwow
Morningside College Campus
Sioux City Iowa
(712) 274-5147
Date: April 10

**University of Wisconsin-Superior
Annual Indian Awareness Powwow**
Superior, Wisconsin
(715) 394-8358
Date: April 10

Native American Awareness Day Celebration
Wellesley Middle School
Wellesley, Massachusetts
(617) 884-4227
Date: April 10

Annual Traditional Powwow
Itasca Community College
Grand Rapids, Minnesota
(218) 327-4491
Date: April 10

Native American Ponatom
Natick, Massachusetts
(617) 884-4227
Date: April 10

Cultural Awareness Powwow
Napa Valley College
Napa, California
(707) 226-5075 Attn: Charlie Toledo
Date: April 10

Oyate/AISES Spring Powwow
University of Colorado
Boulder, Colorado
(303) 492-8874
Date: April 10

**Annual 1st Peoples International
Trade Expo & Powwow**
Macomb Community College
Warren, Michigan
(313) 756-1350
Dates: April 10-11

**Annual Tewaquchi American
Indian Club Powwow**
Cal State University-Fresno
Fresno, California
(209) 278-3277
Dates: April 10-11

Annual Southwest Nations Powwow
New Mexico State University
Las Cruces, New Mexico
(505) 646-4207
Dates: April 10-12

"Art Under the Oaks" Indian Market
Five Civilized Tribes Museum
Muskogee, Oklahoma
(918) 683-1701
Dates: 3rd weekend in April

American Indian Powwow
West Valley College
Saratoga, Califonia
(408) 867-2200 ext. 5601
Dates: 3rd weekend in April

American Indian Days Powwow
Chico State University
Chico, California
(916) 895-5396
Dates: 3rd weekend in April

**Annual Octagon American Indian
Preservation Society Powwow**
Lee Civic Center
Fort Myers, Florida
(813) 543-1130
Dates: April 16-18

Annual Haliwa-Saponi
Haliwa School
Hollister, North Carolina
(919) 586-3787
Dates: April 16-18

Rock Creek Annual Salmon Feast
Rock Creek, Washington
(509) 773-3787
Date: April 16-18

Annual ASU Spring Competition Powwow
Arizona State University
Tempe, Arizona
(602) 965-2230 Attn: Lee Williams

Annual NASA Powwow
Eastern Washington University
Cheney, Washington
(509) 359-2441
Dates: April 16-17

**Annual Sherman High School
Intertribal Powwow**
Riverside, California
(714) 276-6309 Attn: Mary Basquez
Date: April 17

ITSC Powwow
University of California-Berkeley
Berkeley, California
(510) 642-6613 Attn: Ruth Hopper

Annual South Beach Sobriety Powwow
Westport, Washington
(206) 267-6212 Attn: Rose Shipman
Dates: April 17-18

Annual Powwow
Western Washington State University
Bellingham, Washington
(206) 676-3000
Dates: April 17-18

All Indian Days Powwow
Scottsdale Community College
Scottsdale, Arizona
(602) 946-4228
Dates: April 17-18

Annual Native Arts & Crafts Show
Suquamish Tribal Center
Suquamish, Washington
(206) 598-3311
Dates: April 17-18

Annual American Indian Week
Indian Pueblo Cultural Center
Albuquerque, New Mexico
(800) 288-0721
Dates: April 19-25

A.I.R.O. Powwow
University of Wisconsin-Stevens Point
Stevens Point, Wisconsin
(715) 346-3576
Dates: 4th weekend in April

Annual KYI-Yo Youth Conference & Powwow
Missoula, Montana
(406) 243-5831
Dates: 4th weekend in April

Texas Gulf TIA-PIAH Powwow
Sallas County Park
New Carey, Texas
(713) 523-0583 Attn: Janelle Walker

"Gathering of Nations" Powwow
University of New Mexico
Albuquerque, New Mexico
(505) 836-2810
Dates: April 23-24

**Annual University of
Minnesota-Duluth Powwow**
Sports Arena
Duluth, Minnesota
(218) 726-8141
Dates: April 23-25

Keeper of the Earth Spring Powwow
Fullerton Union High School Stadium
Fullerton, California
(800) 428-3872
Date: April 24

Annual Powwow- Mills College
Oakland, California
(510) 430-2080
Date: April 24

Annual NASA Powwow
Colorado State University
Fort Collins, Colorado
(303) 491-8946 Attn: Debra Wadena
Dates: April 24-25

South Umpqua Powwow
Myrtle Creek, Oregon
(503) 863-4942
Date: April 24

Annual New England NAI Powwow
Foxboro, Massachusetts
(508) 791-5007
Dates: April 24-25

Annual Spring Traditional Powwow
UAW 933 Hall
Indianapolis, Indiana
(317) 545-5057
Dates: April 24-25

Celebrating Life Not Genocide Powwow
Ohio State University
Columbus, Ohio
(614) 443-6120
Dates: April 24-25

Annual Eau Claire Traditional Powwow
Eau Claire, Wisconsin
(715) 836-3367
Date: April 24

Agua Caliente Heritage Festival
Palm Springs, California
(619) 325-5673
Dates: April 24-25

MAY

American Indian Festival & Powwow
Jackson, Mississippi
(601) 371-8242 Attn: Linda Swindoll
Dates: April 30-May 2

Annual Spring Challenge Powwow
Minneapolis, Minnesota
(612) 721-9800
Dates: April 30-May 2

Annual Wildflower Festival
Tule Indian Reservation
near Fresno, California
(209) 781-1519 Attn: Leona Dabney
Date: May 1

**Annual San Francisco
State University Powwow**
San Francisco, California
(415) 338-1929
Date: May 1

Annual Strawberry Festival
Kule Koklo Village, Pt. Reyes
Marin County, California
(415) 663-1092

**Madison Area Technical College
Traditional Powwow**
Madison, Wisconsin
(608) 246-6584 Attn: Karen Martin
Date: May 1

**Native American Indian Association
Annual Powwow**
Metrolina Indian Center
Charlotte, North Carolina
(704) 331-4818
Date: May 1

Cupa Days
Pala Cultural Center
Pala Reservation, California
(619) 742-1590
Dates: 1st weekend in May

Southern Ute Bear Dance
Ignacio, Colorado
(303) 563-4525
Dates: 1st weekend in May

**Louisiana Indian Heritage
Association Powwow**
Folsom, Louisiana
(504) 244-5866
Dates: 1st weekend in May

Annual American Indian Spring Market
Mission San Juan Bautista
San Juan Bautista, California
(408) 623-2379 Attn: Elaine Reyna
Dates: 1st weekend in May

Annual Powwow
Turtle Center for the Living Arts
Niagara Falls, New York
(716) 284-2427
Dates: May 1-2

Annual UCLA Contest Powwow
Los Angeles, California
(310) 825-7315
Dates: May 1-2

Mohawk Trail Powwow
Claremont, Massachusetts
(413) 339-4096
Dates: May 1-2

**Wampanoag New Year
Ceremony & Indian Gathering**
Wampanoag Indian Reservation
Freetown, Massachusetts
(508) 947-7466
Dates: May 1-2

Corn Planting Ceremony
Lenni Lenape Historical Society
Allentown, Pennsylvania
(215) 797-2121
Date: 1st Sunday in May

Portland State University Spring Powwow
Portland, Oregon
(503) 725-4452
Dates: 2nd weekend in May

Mother's Day Powwow
Lassen Community College
Susanville, California
(916) 257-5222
Dates: 2nd weekend in May

Root Festival
Lapwai, Idaho
(208) 843-2253
Dates: 2nd weekend in May

Montana State University Annual Powwow
Bozeman, Montana
(406) 994-3881
Dates: 2nd weekend in May

Tse-Ho-Tso Intertribal Powwow
Window Rock High School
Fort Defiance, Arizona
(602) 729-5704
Dates: 2nd weekend in May

CSRIHA Mother's Day Powwow
Augusta, Georgia
(404) 863-6931 Attn: Grady Burnett
Dates: 2nd weekend in May

**Annual Contemporary Indian
Art Exhibition & Sale**
(benefits Crow Canyon Archaeological Center)
Chicago, Illinois
(708) 234-3310
Dates: May 6-8

Northern Montana College Powwow
Havre, Montana
(406) 265-3700 ext. 3040
Dates: May 7-8

East Tennessee League Powwow
Knoxville, Tennessee
(615) 693-0079
Dates: May 7-9

Annual United Tribes All Nations Powwow
Bismarck, North Dakota
(701) 255-3285 ext. 217/219
Dates: May 7-9

Annual Cherokee County Powwow
Canton, Georgia
(404) 735-6275
Dates: May 7-9

Annual Intertribal Gathering & Powwow
Fontana, California
(714) 984-6215
Dates: May 7-9

Feather River Festival
Native American Village
Oroville, California
(916) 538-7986
Date: May 8

Dartmouth College Annual Powwow
Hanover, New Hampshire
(603) 646-2110
Date: May 8

Palomar College Powwow
San Marcos, California
(619) 744-1150 ext. 2425
Date: May 8

LIHA Annual Auction & Powwow
Laconia, New Hampshire
(603) 783-9922
Date: May 8

**Nipmuck Council Planting
Moon Ceremony & Potluck**
Nipmuck Reservation
Webster, Massachusetts
(508) 943-4569
Date: May 8

**Friends of Native Americans &
Mystic River Association Powwow**
Lake Winchester, Massachusetts
(617) 646-0743
Date: May 8

Annual Mt. Scenario Powwow
American Indian Program
Mt. Scenario College
Ladysmith, Wisconsin
(715) 532-5511 ext. 272
Date: May 8

**Moon When the Ponies
Shed Traditional Powwow**
Ohio State University
Canton, Ohio
(614) 443-6120
Dates: May 8-9

**Annual Traditional Wacipi
Honoring All Mothers**
Simmons Jr High School
Aberdeen, South Dakota
(605) 226-2533 Attn: Stella Flute
Dates: May 8-9

Annual Heal Mother Earth Powwow
Fairgrounds
York, Pennsylvania
(804) 929-6911 Attn: George Whitewolf
Dates: May 8-9

Haskell Indian Jr. College Powwow
Lawrence, Kansas
(913) 749-8404
Dates: May 8-9

Mother's Day All Indian Rodeo
Browning, Montana
(406) 338-7406
Date: 2nd Sunday in May

San Diego American Indian Cultural Days
Balboa Park
San Diego, California
(619) 281-5964
Dates: 3rd weekend in May

Red Mountain Powwow & Indian Rodeo
Fort McDermitt, Nevada
(702) 532-8259
Dates: 3rd weekend in May

Mat'Alyma Root Festival
Kamiah, Idaho
(208) 935-2144
Dates: 3rd weekend in May

**De Anza College Powwow
& Arts & Crafts Fair**
Cupertino, California
(408) 864-8963
Dates: 3rd weekend in May

Tygh Valley All Indian Rodeo
Tygh Valley, Oregon
(503) 553-1161 ext. 214 Attn: Ginger Smith
Dates: 3rd weekend in May

Annual Tuscarora Nation Powwow
Tribal Grounds
Maxton, North Carolina
(919) 844-3352
Dates: May 14-15

Indian Nations Rendezvous & Trade Fair
Denver, Colorado
(303) 238-7540
Dates: May 14-16

Takini Skyhawk & Stampede & Wacipi
Takini School
Howes, South Dakota
(605) 538-4399
Dates: May 14-16

**Annual H.V. Johnston
Cultural Center Powwow**
Eagle Butte, South Dakota
(605) 964-2542 Attn: Matt Uses Knife
Dates: May 14-16

GLICA Spring Planting Festival
Tyngsborough State Forest
Tyngsboro, Massachusetts
(508) 453-7182
Dates: May 14-16

Annual New Jersey Indian Center Powwow
Old Bridge, New Jersey
(908) 525-0066
Dates: May 14-16

**Longview Kelso Indian
Education Intertribal Powwow**
Kelso, Washington
(206) 577-2451 Attn: Dena Taylor
Dates: May 14-16

Prairie Band Potawatomi Powwow
Horton, Kansas
Date: May 15

Native American Club Powwow
Hamlet, North Carolina
(919) 582-7071
Date: May 15

Annual Spring Powwow
University of Oregon
Eugene, Oregon
(503) 346-3723
Dates: May 15-16

Annual Eagle Point Powwow
Ojai, California
(805) 494-1558
Dates: May 15-16

Mankato State University Powwow
Mankato, Minnesota
(507) 389-5230
Dates: May 15-16

AISA University of Minnesota Annual Powwow
Minneapolis, Minnesota
(612) 624-2555
Dates: May 15-16

Annual Aurora University-Schingoethe Center for Native American Cultures Traditional Powwow
Aurora, Illinois
Dates: May 15-16

Massachusetts Center for Native American Awareness Annual Powwow
Middleboro, Massachusetts
(617) 884-4227
Dates: May 15-17

DE-UN-DA-GA Powwow
Yellow Creek State Park
Penn Run, Pennsyvania
(412) 547-8442
Dates: 4th weekend in May

YA-KA-AMA Spring Fair
6215 Eastside Rd.
Forrestville, California
(707) 887-1541
Dates: 4th weekend in May

Annual Zuni Artists Exhibition
Museum of Northern Arizona
Flagstaff, Arizona
(602) 774-521 1
Dates: 4th weekend in May

Annual University of Utah Powwow
Jon Huntsman Center
Salt Lake City, Utah
(801) 581-8151
Dates: May 21-22

Spavinaw Days
Spavinaw, Oklahoma
(918) 589-2758
Dates: May 21-22

Pyramid Lake Powwow
Nixon, Nevada
(702) 574-031 1
Dates: May 21-22

Annual Gissiwas Creek Powwow
Marion, Michigan
(616) 281-3640
Dates: May 21-23

Heart of the Circle Powwow
St. Croix Tribal Center
Hertel, Wisconsin
Dates: May 21-23

Call to Cream Ridge Powwow
Cream Ridge, New Jersey
(908) 475-3872
Dates: May 21-23

Klamath Memorial Powwow
Klamath Falls, Oregon
(503) 883-7466 Attn: Gina Moses
Dates: May 21-23

Annual Celebration of Sobriety
Red Lake, Minnesota
(218) 679-3392
Dates: May 21-23

Upper Mattaponi Spring Festival
King William, Virginia
(804) 769-2408
Date: May 22

Nisenan-Maidu Bigtime
Roseville, California
(916) 785-5144 Attn: Mary Orr
Date: May 22

Annual Veterans Memorial Powwow
Keshena, Wisconsin
(715) 799-5168
Dates: May 22-23

Annual Texas Gulf Coast Championship Powwow
Traders Village, NW Hwy. 290
Houston, Texas
(713) 890-5500
Dates: May 22-23

Massachusetts Center for Native American Awareness Powwow
Topsfield, Massachusetts
(617) 884-4227
Dates: May 22-23

Mohawk Trail Powwow
Indian Plaza Mohawk Trail
Charlemont, Massachusetts
(413) 339-4096
Dates: May 22-23

Annual Spring Juried Arts Festival
Rancocas Indian Reservation
Rancocas, New Jersey
(609) 261-4747
Dates: May 22-24

Indian Powwow
Rockome Gardens
5 miles west of Arcola, Illinois
(217) 268-4106 Attn: Jeane Lambeth

Oneida Vietnam Veterans Powwow
Norbert Hill Center
Oneida, Wisconsin
(414) 869-1261
Date: May 24

Annual Memorial Weekend Celebration
Cecil B. DeMille Middle School
7025 Parkcrest Ave.
Long Beach, California
(714) 785-4377

Annual Red Road Celebration
Casa de Fruta, near
Hollister, California
(408) 426-821 1
Dates: Memorial Day weekend

Omaha Memorial Day Celebration
Macy, Nebraska
(402) 837-5391
Dates: Memorial Day weekend

Weaseltail Powwow
White Swan, Washington
(509) 865-5121
Dates: Memorial Day weekend

Choctaw Annual Rodeo
Jones Academy
Hartshorne, Oklahoma
(405) 924-8280
Dates: Memorial Day weekend

Kenel Powwow
Kenel, South Dakota
(701) 854-7231
Dates: Memorial Day weekend

Native American Awareness Day
Grays Harbor Community College
Aberdeen, Washington
(800) 562-4839 ext. 21 1 Attn: Patty Smith
Date: May 28

Upper Skagit Cultural Day
2284 Community Plaza
Sedro Wooley, Washington
(206) 856-5501 Attn: Sherry Burnham
Date: May 28

Fredericksburg Powwow
Fredericksburg, Virginia
(410) 675-3535
Dates: May 28-30

American Indian Arts & Crafts Festival
Palm Springs, California
(619) 329-3407 Attn: Ray Kingfisher
Dates: May 28-30

Annual Grand Casino Powwow
Hinckley, Minnesota
(612) 384-7771
Dates: May 28-31

Santa Fe Powwow & Indian Art Market
Pojoaque Pueblo (13 miles north of
Santa Fe, New Mexico)
(505) 983-5220
Dates: May 28-31

Otsinigo Indian Powwow
Apalachin, New York
(607) 625-2221
Dates: May 28-30

Annual Championship Dance Contest
Pierre Indian Learning Center
Pierre, South Dakota
(605) 224-8661
Dates: May 28-30

Annual Tribal Elder Day Celebration
Ghost Hawk Park
Rosebud, South Dakota
(605) 747-2381
Date: May 29

Honoring Powwow for American Indian Children
Rancho Santiago Community College
Santa Ana, California
(714) 360-1025
Date: May 29

**Annual Delaware Contest
Powwow & Stomp Dancing**
Copan, Oklahoma
(918) 336-4925
Dates: May 29-30

Annual Inter-Agency Committee Powwow
Bishop, California
(619) 873-6394 Attn: Leslie Davis
Dates: May 29-30

Annual Spring Powwow
Green River Community College
Muckleshoot Tribal Center
Auburn, Washington
(206) 226-2589

Annual NAC Powwow
Lake County Fairgrounds
Grays Lake, Illinois
(708) 740-9270
Dates: May 29-30

Abenaki Nation & State Parks Dept. Powwow
Salisbury, Massachusetts
(508) 682-4511
Dates: May 29-30 & August 21-22

Annual Fort Garland Powwow
The Old Fort
Fort Garland, Colorado
(719) 384-4850 Attn: Sherry Manyik
Date: May 30

JUNE

Wisconsin Indian Arts Festival
Chippewa Valley Museum
Eau Claire, Wisconsin
(715) 834-7871
Dates: May 30-June 15

Ute Mountain Bear Dance
Towaoc, Colorado
(303) 565-3751 ext. 200
Dates: June 3-7

Medicine Ways Conference & Powwow
University of California
Riverside, California
(714) 787-4143
Dates: 1st weekend in June

**Annual Winds of the
Northwest Contest Powwow**
Olympia, Washington
(206) 456-1311
Dates: 1st weekend in June

**Indian Intertribal Agency
Committee Powwow**
Bishop, California
(619) 873-6394 Attn: Leslie Davis
Dates: 1st weekend in June

Annual Festival & Powwow
Maryland Indian Heritage Society
Brandywine, Maryland
(301) 372-1932
Dates: 1st weekend in June

Morton Powwow
Morton, Minnesota
(507) 697-3250
Dates: 1st weekend in June

Four Moons Powwow
California Steel & Arts Foundation
Fontana, California
(714) 624-1072 Attn: Ray Wade
Dates: 1st weekend in June

Alabama Coushatta Powwow
(17 miles East of Livingston, Texas)
(409) 563-4391 Attn: Roland Poncho
Dates: June 4-5

Honoring of Elders Gathering & Powwow
Santa Clara County Park
Santa Clara, California
(408) 728-8471
Dates: June 4-6

**Santa Monica Indian Ceremonial
Show, Sale, Powwow**
Santa Monica Civic Auditorium
Santa Monica, California
(310) 430-5112 Attn: Don Bullock

LCO Ojibwe School Contest Powwow
Hayward, Wisconsin
(715) 634-8924
Dates: June 4-6

Tiinowit Annual International Powwow
Yakima, Washington
(509) 877-4093 Attn: Hazel Olney
Dates: June 4-6

NIYC Annual Powwow
Southwestern Indian Polytechnic Institute
Albuquerque, New Mexico
(505) 247-2251
Dates: June 4-6

Richmond Title V Indian Program Powwow
Richmond, California
(510) 237-1643
Date: June 5

Worcester Intertribal Center Powwow
Rutland, Massachusetts
(508) 754-3300
Dates: June 5-6

Annual Day of the Eagle Powwow
East Jordan, Michigan
(616) 536-7583
Dates: June 5-6

Annual Powwow
Siskiyou County Fairgrounds
Yreka, Califronia
(916) 842-9200 Attn: Florine Super
Dates: June 5-6

AISSI Annual Festival & Powwow
American Indian Cultural Center
Brandywine, Maryland
(301) 372-1932
Dates: June 5-6

Dove Crest Strawberry Moon Festival
Rhode Island
(401) 539-7795
Date: June 6

Big Wind Crowheart Powwow
Crowheart, Wyoming
(307) 856-1117
Dates: 2nd weekend in June

Annual Trade Feast
Miwok Park
Novato, California
(415) 897-4064
Dates: 2nd weekend in June

Sac & Fox All Indian Pro Rodeo
Stroud, Oklahoma
(405) 273-0579
Dates: 2nd weekend in June

First Peoples Powwow
Camp Rotary, Michigan
(313) 756-1350
Dates: 2nd weekend in June

**Annual American Indian
Film & Video Competition**
Oklahoma City, Oklahoma
(918) 747-8276 Attn: Gloria Pasternak
Dates: June 10-12

Red Earth Native American Cultural Festival
Oklahoma City, Oklahoma
(405) 427-5228
Dates: June 11-13

Cannon Ball Annual Flag Day Celebration
Cannon Ball, North Dakota
(701) 544-3430
Dates: June 11-13

Annual Cheyenne Homecoming Powwow
Lame Deer, Montana
(406) 477-6284 Attn: LeRoy Pine
Dates: June 11-13

Return to Pimitoui Powwow
Peoria, Illinois
(309) 685-7843
Dates: June 11-13

Annual White Earth Powwow
White Earth, Minnesota
(218) 983-3285
Dates: June 11-13

DQ University Graduation Powwow
Davis, California
(916) 758-0470 Attn: Karen Bohay
Date: June 12

Annual Chipeta Park Powwow
Nederland, Colorado
(303) 258-0224 Attn: David Clyne
Date: June 12

Strawberry Moon Festival
Heffenreffer Museum
Bristol, Rhode Island
(401) 253-8388
Date: June 12

**Gathering of Native Americans
Arts & Crafts Show**
Albuquerque, New Mexico
(505) 768-3466
Date: June 12

Museum of Man - Annual Indian Fair
San Diego, California
(619) 239-2001 Attn: Carla Edwards

Lenni Lenape Nanicoke Powwow
Salem, New Jersey
(609) 935-8392
Dates: June 12-13

Annual Southern Cascades Powwow
Intermountain Fairgrounds
McArthur, California
(916) 243-1741 Attn: Bev LeBeau

Klamath Salmon Festival
Klamath, California
(707) 482-5585
Dates: June 12-13

Traditional Powwow
Comstock Riverside Park
Grand Rapids, Michigan
(517) 487-5409
Dates: June 12-13

**Wollomononuppoag Indian
Council Powwow**
Attleboro, Massachusetts
(508) 822-5061
Dates: June 12-13

Red Cloud Indian Art Show
Heritage Center
Pine Ridge, South Dakota
(605) 867-5491 Attn: Brother Simon
Dates: June 15 - August 15

Annual Silver Star Powwow & Indian Market
Kaiser Convention Arena
Oakland, California
(510) 763-1495
Dates: 3rd weekend in June

Annual Sam Yazzi, Jr. Memorial Powwow
Lukachukai, Arizona
(602) 787-2301
Dates: 3rd weekend in June

Annual All My Relations Powwow & Feast
Swinomish Gym
La Conner, Washington
(206) 466-2355 Attn: Alex Paul
Dates: 3rd weekend in June

City of Roses Powwow
Delta Park
Portland, Oregon
Dates: 3rd weekend in June

Homecoming of the Three Fires
Comstock Riverside Park
Grand Rapids, Michigan
(616) 774-8331
Dates: 3rd weekend in June

TIHA Powwow
Llano City Park
Llano, Texas
(817) 498-2873
Dates: 3rd weekend in June

Red Bottom Celebration
Fraser, Montana
(406) 477-6284
Dates: 3rd weekend in June

Community Powwow
Arapahoe, Wyoming
(307) 856-6117
Dates: Father's Day weekend

All Indian Rodeo
Birch Creek, Montana
(406) 338-7522
Dates: Father's Day weekend

Red Mountain Powwow
Ft. McDermitt, Nevada
(702) 532-8259 Attn: Helen Snapp
Dates: June 18-20

NAIA Powwow
Halle Stadium
Memphis, Tennessee
(901) 276-4741
Dates: June 18-20

AICA Annual Powwow
Van Hoy Campground
Union Grove, North Carolina
(704) 464-5579
Dates: June 18-20

Annual Traditional Gathering
Powwow Grounds
Mole Lake, Wisconsin
(715) 478-3957
Dates: June 18-20

Porcupine Powwow
Porcupine, North Dakota
(701) 554-3430 Attn: Clay Dogskin
Dates: June 18-20

Chief Joseph & Warriors Memorial Powwow
Lapwai, Idaho
(208) 843-2253
Dates: June 18-20

Ring Thunder Traditional Powwow
St. Francis Indian School
Rosebud, South Dakota
(605) 747-2381 ext. 120
Dates: June 18-20

Annual Wakeby Lake Powwow
Glen Farms
Portsmouth, Rhode Island
(401) 683-5167
Dates: June 18-20

Eastern Delaware Nations Powwow
Forksville, Pennsylvania
(717) 924-9082
Dates: June 18-20

Creek Nation Festival
Okmulgee, Oklahoma
(405) 756-8700
Dates: June 18-20

Carthage Powwow
Carthage, Missouri
(417) 358-4974
Dates: June 18-20

Annual Yavapai Prescott All Indian Powwow
Prescott, Arizona
(602) 445-8790
Dates: June 18-20

Virginia Indian Heritage Festival
Jamestown Settlement
Williamsburg, Virginia
(804) 229-1607
Date: June 19

Trail of Tears Art Show
Cherokee Historical Society
Tahlequah, Oklahoma
(918) 456-6007 Attn: Myrna Moss
Date: June 19

Big Foot Memorial Riders Honoring Wacipi
Soldier Creek, South Dakota
(605) 747-2336 Attn: Dorothy Jones
Dates: June 19-20

**Annual Stewart Indian School
Powwow & Reunion**
Stewart Indian School Museum
Carson City, Nevada
(702) 882-1802
Dates: June 19-20

Annual Yosemite Indian Days Big Time
Yosemite Valley, California
(209) 372-0294 Attn: Jay Johnson
Dates: June 19-20

Summer Powwow
Harford City, Indiana
(317) 348-1223
Dates: June 19-20

Annual Eagle Mountain Powwow
Ferndale, Washington
(206) 647-6238 Attn: Ted Solomon
Dates: June 19-20

**Worcester Indian Cultural Art Lodge
Powwow**
Sterling, Massachusetts
(508) 754-3300
Dates: June 19-20

Pequot & Narragansett Joint Powwow
Westerly, Rhode Island
(401) 346-1100
Dates: June 19-20

Indian Hills Powwow
Tehachapi, California
(805) 822-4623
Dates: June 19-20

Connecticut River Powwow Society
Strawberry Moon Powwow
Rocky Hill, Connecticut
(203) 684-5407
Dates: June 19-20

Annual Lansing Indian Center Powwow
Lansing, Michigan
(517) 487-5409
Dates: June 19-20

Annual Sokaogon Traditional Powwow
Crandon, Wisconsin
(715) 478-5190
Dates: June 20-22

Indian Days Celebration
Rosebud, South Dakota
(605) 474-2381 Attn: Rose Cordier
Dates: June 23-25

Badlands Celebration
Brockton, Montana
(406) 768-5151
Dates: 4th weekend in June

**Shoshone Indian Days & Treaty Days
Celebration**
Fort Washakie, Wyoming
(307) 332-4173
Dates: last weekend in June

San Joaquin Indian Council Powwow
Manteca, California
(209) 858-2421
Dates: last weekend in June

Annual Anishinaabe Way Powwow
Hayward, Wisconsin
(715) 634-3041/5841
Dates: June 25

Plains Indian Powwow
Buffalo Bill Historical Center
Cody, Wyoming
(307) 587-4771 Attn: Faith Bad Bear
Dates: June 25-26

Annual Heber City Powwow
Heber City, Utah
(801) 359-6906
Dates: June 25-27

Big Sky Indian Art Market
Native American Cultural Institute of Montana
Eastern Montana College
Billings, Montana
(406) 657-2200
Dates: June 25-27

Stommish Water Festival
Lummi Stommish Grounds
Ferndale, Washington
(206) 734-8289 Attn: Levi Jefferson
Dates: June 25-27

Graduation Powwow
Oglala Lakota College
Kyle, South Dakota
(605) 455-2321
Dates: June 25-27

Flagstaff All Indian Days Powwow
Flagstaff, Arizona
(602) 774-1330
Dates: June 25-27

Annual Great Lakes Powwow
Wilson, Michigan
(906) 466-2342 Attn: Audrey Gamez
Dates: June 25-27

Annual Festival of Native American Arts
Cococino Center for the Arts
Flagstaff, Arizona
(602) 779-6921
Dates: June 25 - Aug. 1

American Indian Music Festival
Oakland, California
(510) 452-1235
Date: June 26

Annual "Keeping the Traditions" Powwow
Miami Valley Council for Native Americans
Xenia, Ohio
(513) 275-8599 Attn: James Cain
Dates: June 26-27

PI-UME-SHA Treaty Days & Powwow
Warm Springs, Oregon
(503) 553-1161
Dates: June 26-27

St. Francis Indian Day Celebration
St. Francis Indian School
Rosebud, South Dakota
(605) 747-2298
Dates: June 26-27

Coquille Indian Tribe Powwow
Brandon, Oregon
(503) 888-4274 Attn: Sharon Parrish
Dates: June 26-27

Annual Potowatomi Powwow
Shawnee, Oklahoma
(405) 964-3855
Dates: June 27-29

Santee Annual Wacipi
Santee, Nebraska
(402) 857-3509
Dates: June 28-30

JULY

Annual Pawnee Homecoming
Pawnee, Oklahoma
(918) 762-2552
Dates: July 1-4

Annual Northern Cheyenne Powwow
Lame Deer, Montana
(406) 477-6284
Dates: July 1-4

Arlee Powwow & Celebration
Arlee, Montana
(406) 745-3525 Attn: Pat Pierre
Dates: July 1-5

Early Summer Greasy Grass
No Water Districts Powwow
Amateur Rodeo & Celebration
Lodge Grass, Montana
(406) 638-2601

Calico Dancers Annual Good Time Powwow
S. Glen Falls, New York
(518) 793-3471
Dates: July 2-3

Bear Soldier Powwow
MacLaughlin, South Dakota
(701) 854-7231 ext. 200
Dates: July 2-4

Annual Sisseton-Wahpeton Wacipi
Agency Village
Sisseton, South Dakota
(605) 698-3911
Dates: July 2-4

Annual Red Cliff Traditional Powwow
Red Cliff, Wisconsin
(715) 779-3701
Dates: July 2-4

Annual Traditional Powwow
Sault Ste. Marie, Michigan
(906) 635-6050
Dates: July 2-4

Kiowa Gourd Clan Celebration
Carnegie, Oklahoma
(405) 726-2996 Attn: Glenn Hamilton
Dates: July 2-4

Quapaw Tribal Powwow
Quapaw, Oklahoma
(918) 542-1853
Dates: July 2-4

Mashpee Wampanoag Powwow
Mashpee, Massachusetts
(508) 477-0208
Dates: July 2-4

AICO Powwow
McHenry, Maryland
(301) 963-7284
Dates: July 2-4

Annual 4th of July Celebration
Mescalero Apache Reservation
Mescalero, New Mexico
(505) 671-4495
Dates: July 2-5

4th of July Powwow & Open Rodeo
Nespelem, Washington
(509) 634-4711
Dates: July 2-11

Heat Moon Festival & Potluck
Nipmuck Reservation
Webster, Massachusetts
(508) 943-4569
Dates: July 3

Mountain Springs Powwow & Festival
Shartlesville, Pennsylvania
(215) 488-6859
Dates: July 4th weekend

Annual Northern Ute Powwow & Rodeo
Fort Duchesne, Utah
(801) 722-5141 ext. 156
Dates: July 4th weekend

July 4th Celebration
Tonto Apache Reservation
Payson, Arizona
(602) 474-5000
Dates: July 4th weekend

Leech Lake Powwow
Cass Lake, Minnesota
(218) 335-6211
Dates: July 4th weekend

Shoshone Paiute Annual Powwow
Owyhee, Nevada
(702) 757-3161
Dates: July 4th weekend

Iron Lightning Powwow
Eagle Butte, South Dakota
(605) 964-2542
Dates: July 4th weekend

Chief Taholah Days
Taholah, Washington
(206) 276-8211
Dates: July 4th weekend

Annual Chumash Intertribal Powwow
Santa Ynez, California
(805) 686-1416
Dates: July 4th weekend

Annual 4th of July Powwow
Three Rivers Indian Lodge
Manteca, California
(209) 858-2421
Dates: July 4th weekend

Annual Oneida Powwow
Oneida, Wisconsin
(414) 833-6760
Dates: July 4th weekend

Wakpamni Lake Powwow
Batesland, South Dakota
(605) 867-5821
Dates: July 4th weekend

July 4th Celebration Powwow & Rodeo
Window Rock, Arizona
(602) 871-6645/6702/6478
Dates: July 4th weekend

4th of July Celebration in Hoopa Valley
Hoopa, California
(916) 625-4211/4239
Dates: July 4th weekend

Fort Kipp Celebration
Fort Kipp, Montana
(406) 786-3369
Dates: July 4th weekend

July 4th Celebration
Hopi Reservation
Oraibi, Arizona
(602) 734-2441
Dates: July 4th weekend

Indian Days Encampment & Powwow
White Swan, Washington
(509) 865-5121
Dates: July 4th weekend

Native American Indian Powwow
Charlemont, Massachusetts
(413) 339-4096
Dates: July 4th weekend & August 21-22

Arts & Crafts Fair
Indian Pueblo Cultural Center
Albuquerque, New Mexico
(505) 843-7270
Dates: July 4th weekend

Nambe Waterfall Ceremonial
Nambe Pueblo, New Mexico
(505) 455-2036
Dates: July 4

National Powwow
Iroquois County Fairgrounds
Crescent City, Illinois
(708) 969-7131 Attn: Byron Loehman
Dates: July 7-10

Sac & Fox Nation Annual Powwow
Stroud, Oklahoma
(918) 968-3526 Attn: Ron Harrie
Dates: July 8-11

North American Indian Days
Browning, Montana
(406) 338-7276 Attn: Elma Lawrence
Dates: July 8-11

American Indian Art Festival
San Luis Obispo, California
(408) 623-2379 Attn: Elaine Reyna
Dates: 2nd weekend in July

Little Hoop Traditional Powwow
Mission, South Dakota
(605) 747-2342
Dates: 2nd weekend in July

Hays Powwow
Hays, Montana
(406) 358-2205
Dates: 2nd weekend in July

Afraid of His Horse Ceremonial
Pine Ridge, South Dakota
(605) 867-5670
Dates: 2nd weekend in July

Arikara Celebration & Powwow
White Shield, North Dakota
(701) 627-4781
Dates: 2nd weekend in July

Bear River Powwow
Lac du Flambeau, Wisconsin
(715) 588-3286
Dates: 2nd weekend in July

Passamaquoddy Tribe Annual Indian Days
Peter Dana Point
Princeton, Maine
(207) 796-2301 ext. 15
Dates: July 9-10

Taos Powwow
Taos Pueblo Buffalo Field
Taos, New Mexico
(800) 732-TAOS; (505) 758-9593
Dates: July 9-11

Annual Black Hills & Northern Plains Powwow & Art Expo
Rushmore Plaza Civic Center
Rapid City, South Dakota
(605) 341-0925
Dates: July 9-11

Apache Tears Spirit Powwow
Crescent, Oregon
(503) 433-2461 Attn: Linda Wilcox
Dates: July 10-11

Annual Cedar Grove Powwow
Chico, California
(916) 894-5068
Dates: July 10-11

Algonquin Indian School Powwow
Roger Williams Park
Providence, Rhode Island
(401) 781-2626
Dates: July 10-11

Indian League of America Powwow
Barryville, New York
(718) 836-6255 Attn: Jim Kavanaugh
(914) 858-8309 Attn: Patricia Rice
Dates: July 10-11

Annual Celebration of the Feast Day of the Blessed Katerai Tekakwitha
Miami, Oklahoma
(918) 674-2587
Date: July 11

Colorado Indian Market
Currigan Hall
Denver, Colorado
(303) 447-9967
Dates: July 11-13

International Brotherhood Days
Porcupine, South Dakota
(703) 578-5685
Dates: July 11-18

Honor the Earth Powwow
Hayward, Wisconsin
(715) 634-2100
Dates: July 13-18

Annual Feast
Cochiti Pueblo, New Mexico
(505) 465-2244
Dates: July 15-18

Comanche Homecoming
Walters, Oklahoma
(405) 492-4988
Dates: July 15-18

Quileute Days
La Push, Washington
(206) 374-6163
Dates: 3rd weekend in July

Antelope Powwow
Mission, South Dakota
(605) 856-2703
Dates: 3rd weekend in July

Standing Arrow Powwow
Elmo, Montana
(406) 849-5541
Dates: 3rd weekend in July

All Indian Stampede & Pioneer Days
Fallon, Nevada
(702) 423-2544
Dates: 3rd weekend in July

Flandreau Santee Sioux Wacipi
Flandreau, South Dakota
(605) 997-3891
Dates: 3rd weekend in July

Ethete Powwow
Ethete, Wyoming
(307) 332-2056
Dates: 3rd weekend in July

Charlotte Native American Festival
Charlotte, North Carolina
(704) 527-7187
Dates: July 16-18

Council Oak Powwow
Dighton, Massachusetts
(508) 669-5008
Dates: July 16-18

Little Beaver Powwow
Jicarilla Apache Tribe
Dulce, New Mexico
(505) 759-3242
Dates: July 16-18

Annual Corn Creek Traditional Powwow
Rosebud, South Dakota
(605) 462-6281
Dates: July 16-18

Mandaree Celebration & Powwow
Mandaree, North Dakota
(701) 759-3311
Dates: July 16-18

Kansas City Indian Club Powwow
Wyandotte County Fairgrounds
Kansas City, Kansas
(816) 331-2823 Attn: Shirley Harris
Dates: July 16-18

Native American Events

Kickapoo Tribe of Kansas Powwow
Horton, Kansas
(913) 486-2131
Dates: July 16-18

Cheyenne Frontier Days
Cheyenne, Wyoming
(800) 227-6336
Dates: July 16-25

Annual Big Time Festival
Kule Loklo Village
Pt. Reyes, California
(415) 663-1092
Dates: July 17

Annual Aspen/Snowmass Celebration
Snowmass Village, Colorado
(303) 920-2873
Dates: July 17-18

Allegany Indian Powwow
Salamanca, New York
(716) 945-2034
Dates: July 17-18

**Annual Eight Northern Indian
Pueblos Artist & Craftsman Show**
San Juan Pueblo, New Mexico
(505) 852-4265 ext. 112 Attn: Leon Tafoya
Dates: July 17-18

Bay City Powwow
Bay City, Michigan
(517) 772-5700
Dates: July 17-18

Keeper of the Western Door Powwow
St. Bonaventure University
Olean, New York
(716) 945-4971
Dates: July 17-18

Annual Homecoming Celebration
Veterans Park
Winneabgo, Nebraska
(402) 878-2272/2772
Dates: July 22-24

Chief Joseph Days
Joseph, Oregon
(503) 432-1015
Dates: 4th weekend in July

**Annual White Mountain Native
American Art Festival & Indian Market**
Blue Ridge School
Pinetop, Arizona
(602) 367-4290
Dates: 4th weekend in July

Milk River Powwow
Fort Belknap, Montana
(406) 535-2621
Dates: 4th weekend in July

Annual Eastern Navajo Fair
Crownpoint, New Mexico
(505) 786-5244
Dates: July 22-25

Annual Seafair Indian Days
Daybreak Star, Discovery Park
Seattle, Washington
(206) 285-4425
Dates: July 23-25

Fort Totten Annual Wacipi
Fort Totten, North Dakota
(701) 766-4221 Attn: Elmer White
Dates: July 23-25

Little Eagle Monument Celebration
Little Eagle, South Dakota
(701) 854-7564
Dates: July 23-25

Annual Keewanaw Bay Traditional Powwow
Ojibway Campground
Baraga, Michigan
(906) 353-6623
Dates: July 23-25

Cherokee of Hoke County Powwow
Davis Bridge, North Carolina
(919) 875-6668
Date: July 24

Honoring Our Heritage Powwow
Mt. Morris, Michigan
(313) 239-6621
Dates: July 24-25

**Annual Rising-Falling Water
Festival & Powwow**
Tribal Grounds
Fredericksburg, Virginia
(804) 769-1018
Dates: July 24-25

Thunderbird Dancers Powwow
Queens County Farm Museum
Floral Park, New York
(201) 587-9633
Dates: July 24-25

Village Indian Trade Days
Knife River Indian Villages
Stanton, North Dakota
(701) 745-3309 Attn: Fred Armstrong
Dates: July 24-25

Navajo Artists Exhibition
Museum of Northern Arizona
Flagstaff, Arizona
(602) 774-5211
Dates: Last weekend in July

Annual Native American Fair & Powwow
Hassanamisco Reservation
Grafton, Massachusetts
(508) 393-2080
Date: July 25

Annual Native American Exhibition
Red Lodge, Montana
(406) 446-1370
Dates: July 26 - Aug. 7

Fort Randall Powwow
Lake Andes, South Dakota
(605) 384-3641
Dates: July 29 - Aug. 2

**Takozakpaku Intertribal
Return of the Eagles Powwow**
Vancouver, Washington
(206) 696-4061 ext. 3413
Dates: July 30 - Aug. 1

Kalispel Powwow
Usk, Washington
(509) 445-1147 Attn: Susan Finley
Dates: July 30 - Aug. 1

Wososo Wakpala District Celebration
He Dog & Upper Cutmeat, South Dakota
(605) 747-2263 Attn: Lorraine Walking Bull
Dates: July 30 - Aug. 1

Indian Hill Powwow
Oklahoma City, Oklahoma
(405) 391-9580
Dates: July 30 - Aug. 1

Kaw Nation Powwow
Kaw City, Oklahoma
(405) 269-2552
Dates: July 30 - Aug. 1

Annual Little Elk's Retreat
Mt. Pleasant, Michigan
(517) 772-5700
Dates: July 31 - Aug. 1

MCNAA Native American Powwow
Walpole, Massachusetts
(617) 884-4227
Dates: July 31 - Aug. 1

American Indian Federation Annual Powwow
Richmond, Massachusetts
(508) 372-6754
Dates: July 31 - Aug. 1

Annual Indian Art Show
Owens, Kentucky
(812) 547-4881
Dates: July 31 - Aug. 1

AUGUST

Rocky Boy Powwow
Rocky Boy Agency
Havre, Montana
(406) 395-4291/4707
Dates: 1st weekend in August

Indian Days Fair & Powwow
Sierra Mono, California
(209) 877-2115
Dates: 1st weekend in August

Annual Festival
Pojoaque Pueblo, New Mexico
(505) 455-2278
Dates: 1st weekend in August

American Indian Federation Powwow
University of Rhode Island
Kingston, Rhode Island
(401) 231-6716
Dates: 1st weekend in August

YA-KA-AMA Acorn Festival
Forrestville, California
(707) 887-1541
Dates: 1st weekend in August

**United Lumbee Nations High
Eagle Warrior Society Powwow**
Round Mountain, California
(916) 234-2038 Attn: Jim Johnson
Dates: 1st weekend in August

Menominee Contest Powwow
Keshena, Wisconsin
(715) 799-5166/5144
Dates: 1st weekend in August

Omaha Tribal Powwow
Macy, Nebraska
(402) 837-5391
Dates: Full moon Aug. weekend

Mesquakie Powwow
Tama, Iowa
(515) 484-4578
Dates: Aug. 5-8

Annual Passamaquoddy Powwow
Pleasant Point Reservation
Perry, Maine
(207) 853-2551
Dates: Aug. 6-7

Annual IICOT Powwow of Champions
Tulsa, Oklahoma
(918) 836-1523
Dates: Aug. 6-8

Lower Brule Fair & Powwow
Lower Brule, South Dakota
(605) 473-5561/5565
Dates: Aug. 6-8

Parmelee Traditional Powwow
Parmelee, South Dakota
(605) 747-2136/2381
Dates: Aug. 6-8

Massacre Canyon Powwow
Trenton, Nebraska
(308) 285-3322
Dates: Aug. 6-8

Houston Indian Market
Houston, Texas
(806) 355-1610 Attn: Randy Wilkerson
Dates: Aug. 6-8

Oglala Nation Powwow & Rodeo
Pine Ridge, South Dakota
(605) 867-5821
Dates: Aug. 6-8

Standing Rock Wacipi
Fort Yates, South Dakota
(701) 854-7451/3431
Dates: Aug. 6-8

Annual Virginia Native American Cultural Center Powwow
Ashland, Virginia
(804) 994-2897 Attn: Reg Tupponce
Date: Aug. 7

Saquache Powwow
Sagauche, Colorado
(719) 655-2699 Attn: Ruth Horn
Dates: Aug. 7-8

Annual LacVieux Desert Powwow
Waters Meet, Michigan
(906) 358-4106
Dates: Aug. 7-8

Annual Native American Festival
Prescott, Arizona
(602) 445-1270 Attn: Ann Hale
Dates: Aug. 7-8

Mohican Contest Powwow
Stockbridge-Munsee Reservation
Bowler, Wisconsin
(715) 793-4111/4270
Dates: Aug. 7-8

Annual Leonard J. Pamp Memorial Traditional Powwow
Burlington, Michigan
(616) 729-9434
Dates: Aug. 7-8

Narragansett Indian Powwow
Charleston, Rhode Island
(401) 364-1100/9832
Dates: 2nd Sunday in August

Annual Elders & Youth Powwow
Pipestone National Monument
Pipestone, Minnesota
(612) 724-3129

Annual Inter-Tribal Indian Ceremonial
Church Rock, New Mexico
(800) 233-4528
Dates: Aug. 10-15

Paumanauke Powwow
Copiaque, New York
(212) 757-0207
Dates: 2nd weekend in August

Bullhead Powwow
Bullhead, South Dakota
(701) 854-7231
Dates: 2nd weekend in August

United Peoples Powwow
Ft. Missoula Historical Museum
Missoula, Montana
(406) 728-2180
Dates: 2nd weekend in August

Omak Stampede
Omak, Washington
(800) 933-6625
Dates: 2nd weekend in August

Nesika Illahee Powwow
Siletz, Oregon
(503) 444-2532 Attn: Karen Bell
Dates: 2nd weekend in August

Little Shell Powwow
Newtown, North Dakota
(701) 627-4781
Dates: 2nd weekend in August

Shoshone-Bannock Festival & Rodeo
Ft. Hall, Idaho
(208) 238-3700
Dates: 2nd weekend in August

Native American Craft Days
Bridgeport, California
(619) 934-3342
Dates: 2nd weekend in August

Heart Butte Indian Days
Heart Butte, Montana
(406) 338-7276
Dates: 2nd weekend in August

Annual Crow Fair Celebration, Powwow & All Indian Rodeo
Crow Agency, Montana
(406) 638-2601
Dates: Aug. 12-15

Sac & Fox Annual Powwow
Tama, Iowa
(515) 484-4678/5358
Dates: Aug. 12-15

Grand Ronde Powwow
Grand Ronde, Oregon
(503) 879-5211
Dates: Aug. 13-15

Annual Southern California Indian Center Powwow
Orange County Fairground
Costa Mesa, California
(714) 530-0225
Dates: Aug. 13-15

Annual Crow Creek Powwow
Stephan, South Dakota
(605) 245-2305/2434
Dates: Aug. 13-15

Clear Creek All Indian Powwow
Nevada, Missouri
(417) 944-2745
Dates: Aug. 13-15

Annual West Texas Homecoing Powwow
Amarillo, Texas
(806) 273-6504
Dates: Aug. 13-15

Hoopa Sovereignty Day Celebration
Hoopa, California
(916) 625-4211
Date: 2nd Saturday in Agust

Annual Fiesta
Zia Pueblo, New Mexico
(505) 867-3304
Date: Aug. 14

Festival of the River
Arlington, Washington
(206) 435-2755
Dates: Aug. 14-15

Roaming Buffalo Singers Annual Powwow
Plainfield, Massachusetts
(508) 226-5712
Dates: Aug. 14-15

Annual Cataldo Mission Pilgrimage
Mass Feast & Powwow
Cataldo, Idaho
(208) 274-5871
Date: Aug. 15

Honoring All Veterans Powwow
Lebanon, Indiana
(317) 482-3315
Dates: Aug. 16-18

Annual Indian Exposition
Anadarko, Oklahoma
(405) 247-2733
Dates: Aug. 16-21

Twin Buttes Celebration & Powwow
Twin Buttes, North Dakota
(701) 627-4781
Dates: 3rd weekend of August

Wazi Paha Oyate Festival
Kyle, South Dakota
(605) 455-2321
Dates: 3rd weekend of August

Quinnetuqut
Haddam, Connecticut
(203) 282-1404
Dates: 3rd weekend of August

White River Powwow
White River, South Dakota
(605) 259-3670
Dates: 3rd weekend of August

Wakpala Powwow
Wakpala, South Dakota
(701) 854-7231
Dates: 3rd weekend of August

Eagle Spirit Celebration
Satus, Washington
(509) 865-5121
Dates: 3rd weekend of August

AICI Annual Traditional Powwow
Lebanon, Indiana
(317) 482-3315
Dates: 3rd weekend of August

Chief Looking Glass Powwow
Kamiah, Idaho
(208) 935-2144
Dates: 3rd weekend of August

Annual Chief Seattle Days
Suquamish, Washington
(206) 598-3311
Dates: Aug. 20-22

Klamath Treaty Days Celebration
Chiloquin, Oregon
(503) 783-2005/2219
Dates: Aug. 20-22

Annual American Indian Powwow
Baltimore, Maryalnd
(301) 675-3535
Dates: Aug. 20-22

Annual Makah Days
Neah Bay, Washington
(206) 645-2201
Dates: Aug. 20-22

Annual O-Sa-Wan Powwow
Marengo, Illinois
(815) 568-7997
Dates: Aug. 20-22

Annual NiMiW Intertribal Powwow
Spirit Mountain
Duluth, Minnesota
(218) 722-2781

Connecticut River Powwow
Farmington Polo Grounds
Farmington, Connecticut
(203) 388-3391
Dates: Aug. 20-22

Celebrating Our Traditions Powwow
Peshawbestown, Michigan
(616) 271-3538 ext. 228
Dates: Aug. 21-22

Santa Fe Indian Market
Santa Fe, New Mexico
(505) 983-5220
Dates: Aug. 21-22

Annual Rosebud Fair & All Indian Rodeo
Rosebud, South Dakota
(605) 747-2381
Dates: Aug. 21-24

Annual St. Croix Wild Rice Powwow
Webster, Wisconsin
(715) 349-2195
Dates: Aug. 26-28

Annual Ponca Powwow
White Eagle
Ponca City, Oklahoma
(405) 762-8104
Dates: Aug. 26-29

Council of Three Rivers Powwow
Indian Center-200 Charles St.
Pittsburgh, Pennsylvania
(412) 782-4457
Dates: 4th weekend in August

Mohegan Tribe Powwow
Uncasville, Connecticut
(203) 848-8983
Dates: 4th weekend in August

**Spokane Falls Northwest
Indian Encampment & Powwow**
Spokane, Washington
(509) 634-4711 Attn: Eddie Palmenteer
Dates: Aug. 27-29

**Native American Veterans
Memorial Association Powwow**
Salt Palace
Salt Lake City, Utah
(801) 825-3639
Dates: Aug. 27-29

Annual MowWeh Traditional Powwow
Rapid River, Michigan
Dates: Aug. 27-29

Red Scaffold Powwow
Red Scaffold, South Dakota
(605) 964-4594
Dates: Aug. 27-29

Cherry Creek Powwow
Cherry Creek, South Dakota
(605) 964-2542
Dates: Aug. 27-29

Native American Heritage Days
Fort Laramie Treaty Days
Fort Laramie National Historic Site, Wyoming
(307) 837-2221
Dates: Aug. 27-29

**Appalachian State University
Annual Powwow**
Boone, North Carolina
(704) 256-2724
Dates: Aug. 27-29

Annual Bad River Powwow
New Odanah Powwow Grounds
Odanah, Wisconsin
(715) 682-7111
Dates: Aug. 27-29

Seminole Intertribal Powwow
Seminole Municipal Park
Seminole, Oklahoma
(405) 257-6573
Dates: Aug. 27-29

Delaware Indian Heritage Festival & Powwow
Dover, Ohio
(216) 343-1047
Dates: Aug. 27-29

Annual Muskegon Traditional Powwow
Muskegon, Michigan
(616) 759-7016
Dates: Aug. 28

Nansemond Indian Tribal Festival
Chuckaluck, Virginia
(804) 483-4236
Dates: Aug. 28-29

Lake Quinsigamond Powwow
Worcester, Massachusetts
(508) 832-8173
Dates: Aug. 28-29

MCNAA Apsqe Powwow
Walpole, Massachusetts
(617) 884-4227
Dates: Aug. 28-29

Annual South Charleston Powwow
South Charleston, West Virginia
(501) 253-7364
Dates: Aug. 28-30

SEPTEMBER

Numaga Indian Days Celebration
Reno-Sparks Indian Colony
Reno, Nevada
(712) 324-4600 Attn: Dan Thayer
Dates: Labor Day Weekend

White Mountain Apache Tribal Fair & Rodeo
White River, Arizona
(602) 383-4621
Dates: Labor Day Weekend

Annual Cheyenne River Sioux Fair & Rodeo
Eagle Butte, South Dakota
(605) 964-6685
Dates: Labor Day Weekend

Cherokee National Holiday & Powwow
Tahlequah, Oklahoma
(918) 456-0671
Dates: Labor Day Weekend

Cheyenne & Arapaho Powwow
Colony, Oklahoma
(405) 323-3542/4877
Dates: Labor Day Weekend

Wee-Gitchie-Ne-Me-E-Dim Powwow
Leech Lake Reservation
Cass Lake, Minnesota
(218) 335-6211
Dates: Labor Day Weekend

**Puyallup Tribe's Annual
Powwow & Salmon Bake**
2002 E. 28th
Tacoma, Washington
Dates: Labor Day Weekend

Indian Nations of Kansas Powwow
Lake Shawnee
Topeka, Kansas
(913) 272-5489 Attn: Mike Ballard
Dates: Labor Day Weekend

Eufaula Powwow
Eufaula, Oklahoma
(405) 689-5066/5407
Dates: Labor Day Weekend

Spokane Tribal Fair & Powwow
Wellpinit, Washington
(509) 258-4581
Dates: Labor Day Weekend

Awokpamani Omaha Traditional Powwow
Poplar, Montana
(406) 768-5155
Dates: Labor Day Weekend

Tulalip Powwow
Marysville, Washington
(206) 653-4585
Dates: Labor Day Weekend

Pyramid Lake Rodeo & Elders Day
Nixon, Nevada
(702) 574-0140
Dates: Labor Day Weekend

Stockton, California Indian Days
Edison High School
Stockton, California
(209) 952-6931
Dates: Labor Day Weekend

Camp Pollock Powwow
Sacramento, California
(916) 485-9838
Dates: Labor Day Weekend

Labor Day Powwow
Ethete, Wyoming
(307) 856-6117
Dates: Labor Day Weekend

Turtle Mountain Ni-Mi-W in Celebration
Dunseith, North Dakota
(701) 477-6451 ext. 126
Dates: Labor Day Weekend

Shoshone Indian Fair
Fort Washakie, Wyoming
(307) 323-9423
Dates: Labor Day Weekend

Annual White Buffalo Council Powwow
Denver, Colorado
(303) 936-2688 Attn: John Emhula
Dates: Labor Day Weekend

Shinnecock Powwow
Shinnecock Reservation
Southampton, New York
(516) 283-3776
Dates: Labor Day Weekend

Choctaw Nation Labor Day Festival
Tushkahoma Capitol Grounds
Clayton, Oklahoma
(405) 924-8280 Attn: Nancy Belvin
Dates: Labor Day Weekend

Kee-Boon-Mein-Kaa Powwow
South Bend, Indiana
(616) 782-6323
Dates: Labor Day Weekend

Labor Day Weekend Powwow
Caddo Tribal Grounds
Binger, Oklahoma
(405) 656-2344

Bull Creek Traditional Powwow
Dixon, South Dakota
(506) 747-2381
Dates: Labor Day Weekend

Annual Navajo Nation Fair
Window Rock, Arizona
(602) 871-6478/6659
Dates: Labor Day Weekend

Tecumseh Lodge Annual Powwow
Tipton, Indiana
(317) 773-4233
Dates: Labor Day Weekend

Omaha Urban Indian Powwow
Omaha, Nebraska
(402) 451-8026
Dates: Labor Day Weekend

Annual Pacific Coast Indian Club Powwow
Barona Indian Reservation
Lakeside, California
(619) 484-4784
Dates: Labor Day Weekend

Mountain Eagle Festival
Hunter Mountain
Catskill, New York
(315) 363-1315
Dates: Labor Day Weekend

Annual Arkansas Festival
Eureka, Arkansas
(501) 253-7364
Dates: Labor Day Weekend

Annual Seneca Intertribal Powwow
Kenneth Young Gallery
Lawtons, New york
(716) 337-3946
Dates: Labor Day Weekend

Indian Arts & Crafts Market
Santo Domingo Pueblo, New Mexico
(505) 465-2812
Dates: Labor Day Weekend

Annual AIM Powwow
Fort Snelling, Minnesota
(612) 724-3129
Dates: Labor Day Weekend

Annual Powwow
Camp Calumet
Lake Ossipee, New Hampshire
(603) 647-5374
Dates: Labor Day Weekend

Labor Day Powwow
C.B. Smith Park
Fort Lauderdale, Florida
(305) 476-7672

Annual California All Indian Market Mission
San Juan Bautista, California
(408) 623-2379
Dates: 1st weekend in September

Michinemackinong Powwow
Marquette Museum
St. Ignace, Michigan
(906) 643-8173 Attn: Shirley Brown
Dates: Sept. 3-5

Annual Nansemond Indian Tribal Festival
Chuckatuck, Virginia
(804) 485-9809
Date: Sept. 4

Annual All Nations Powwow
Rock Island, Illinois

(309) 788-9063
Dates: Sept. 4-5

Iroquois Indian Festival
Cobleskill, New York
(518) 296-8949
Dates: Sept. 4-5

Annual Labor Day Traditional Powwow
Columbus, Ohio
(614) 433-6120
Date: Labor Day

Protect the Earth Powwow
Lac Court, Wisconsin
(715) 766-2725
Date: Labor Day

Cultural Center Celebration
Yakima Nation Cultural Heritage Center
Toppenish, Washington
(509) 865-2800
Dates: 2nd weekend in Sept.

Trail of Tears Intertribal Powwow
Hopkinsville, Kentucky
(502) 886-8033 Attn: Beverly Baker
Dates: 2nd weekend in Sept.

Indian Heritage Festival & Powwow
Martinsville, Virginia
(703) 666-8600 Attn: Mabel Peters
Dates: Sept. 10-11

Annual Raccoon Mountain Indian Festival
Chattanooga, Tennessee
(706) 735-6275 Attn: Chipa Wolf
Dates: Sept. 10-11

Coharie Powwow
Clinton, North Carolina
(919) 564-6909
Dates: Sept. 10-11

Annual Championship Powwow
Grand Priarie, Texas
(214) 647-2331 Attn: Doug Beich
Dates: Sept. 10-12

**United Tribes International
Championship Powwow**
United Technical College
Bismarck, North Dakota
(701) 255-3285 ext. 217, 219
Dates: Sept. 10-12

United Tribes Indian Art Exposition
Bismarck Civic Center
Bismarck, North Dakota
(701) 255-3285
Dates: Sept. 10-12

Annual Frontier Day & Powwow
Council Bluffs, Iowa
(712) 325-1770
Dates: Sept. 10-12

Annual Southern Ute Tribal Fair & Powwow
Ignacio, Colorado
(800) 772-1236 Attn: Alden Naranip
Dates: Sept. 10-12

Annual Indian Summer Festival
San Jose, California
(408) 971-9622
Dates: Sept. 10-12

Seminole Nation Day Powwow
Miccosukee Mission
Wewoka, Oklahoma
(405) 257-6287
Dates: Sept. 10-12

Annual Moberly Powwow
Rothwell Park
Moberly, Missouri
(816) 263-3009
Dates: Sept. 10-12

Annual Daow-Aga Powwow
Lake Tahoe, Nevada
(800) 225-6382 Attn: Jim Jeffers
Dates: Sept. 10-12

Annual Sycuan Powwow
El Cajon, California
(619) 445-2613
Dates: Sept. 10-12

Shakopee Mdewakanton Powwow
Mystic Lake Casino
Prior Lake, Minnesota
(612) 445-8900
Dates: Sept. 10-12

Indian Summer Powwow
Milwaukee, Wisconsin
(414) 383-7425
Dates: Sept. 10-12

Annual Lawrence Indian Arts Show
Haskell Indian Junior College
Lawrence, Kansas
(913) 864-4245 Attn: Maria Martin
Dates: Sept. 10-24

Annual WVNAC/NASC Intertribal Powwow
West Virginia University
Morgantown, WV
(304) 363-8151
Date: Sept. 11

Annual California Indian Council Foundation Powwow
Newberry, California
(310) 457-5496
Dates: Sept. 11-12

Lenni Lenape Festival
Lebanon, New Jersey
(215) 797-2121
Dates: Sept. 11-12

Annual Nipmuck Powwow
Oxford, Massachusetts
(508) 943-4569
Dates: Sept. 11-12

Annual Nanticoke Indian Powwow
Millsboro, Delaware
(302) 945-3400
Dates: Sept. 11-12

Indian Ceremonial Harvest Dancers & Feast
Starved Rock, Illinois
(815) 667-4976
Dates: Sept. 11-12

Grand Valley American Indian Lodge Powwow
Riverside Park
Grand Rapids, Michigan
(616) 791-4014 Attn: Ike Peters
Dates: Sept. 11-12

Annual Iroquois Arts Festival
Dutchess County Fairgrounds
Rhinebeck, New York
(914) 758-6526
Dates: Sept. 11-12

Annual Kit-Han-Ne Powwow
West Kittanning, Pennsylvania
(412) 548-8823
Dates: Sept. 11-12

Native American Appreciation Day
Cumberland, Maine
(207) 339-9520
Dates: Sept. 11-12

Chief Red Blanket Memorial Powwow
Haverhill, Massachusetts
(617) 884-4227
Dates: Sept. 11-12

Pine Nut Festival
Walker River Paiute Reservation
Schurz, Nevada
(702) 773-2306
Dates: Sept. 11-18

Gojiiya Feast Day
Jicarilla Apache Reservation
Dulce, New Mexico
(505) 759-3242

Pendleton Roundup
Pendleton, Oregon
(800) 524-2984
Dates: Sept. 15-18

Guilford Native Ameican Association Cultural Festival & Powwow
Jamestown, North Carolina
(919) 273-8686
Dates: Sept. 16-18

Annual Children's Powwow
Hannahville Reservation
Wilson, Michigan
(800) 682-6040
Dates: Sept. 16-18

Choctaw Powwow
Canadian, Oklahoma
(405) 924-8280
Dates: 3rd weekend in Sept.

Eagle Plume Society Powwow
Nespelem, Washington
(509) 634-4711
Dates: 3rd weekend in Sept.

American Indian Cultural Festival
Pismo Beach, California
(408) 623-2379
Dates: 3rd weekend in Sept.

Indian Summer Festival
Bartlesville, Oklahoma
(918) 336-5272/8708
Dates: Sept. 17-18

GLICA Maple Syrup Festival
Tyngsborough, Massachusetts
(508) 453-7182
Dates: Sept. 17-19

Ogden Powwow
Fort Buenaventura State Park
Ogden, Utah

(801) 621-4414
Dates: Sept. 17-19

Annual Honoring of the Youth Powwow
Monterey, California
(408) 375-0095 Attn: White Bear
Dates: Sept. 17-19

Annual American Indian Days
O'Fallon, Missouri
(314) 272-1964
Dates: Sept. 17-19

Annual Choctaw Intertribal Association
Pittsburg County Powwow
McAlester, Oklahoma
(918) 423-2667 Attn: Dena Cantrell
Dates: Sept. 17-19

Annual Santa Rosa Junior College Powwow
Santa Rosa, California
(707) 528-6170
Dates: Sept. 18

Festival of San Jose De Los Lagunas & Arts & Crafts Fair
Old Laguna Pueblo, New Mexico
(505) 552-6654
Dates: Sept. 18

Kituwah-American Indian National Arts Exposition & Powwow
Asheville, North Carolina
(704) 252-3880 Attn: Gail Gomez
Dates: Sept. 23-26

Fall Festival & Intertribal Contest Powwow
Sioux City American Indian Center
Sioux City, Iowa
(712) 255-8957
Dates: 4th weekend in September

Chickahominy Festival
Charles City, Virginia
(804) 829-2186/2261
Dates: Sept. 24-25

Annual Middle Tennessee Powwow
Lebanon, Tennessee
(615) 444-4899 Attn: Don Yahola
Dates: Sept. 24-25

California Indian Days
Roseville, California
(916) 920-0285 Attn: Loranda Sanchez
Dates: Sept. 24-26

Annual Northern Plains Tribal Arts Show
Sioux Falls, South Dakota
(800) 658-4797
Dates: Sept. 24-26

Annual Black Eagle Powwow
Spanaway, Washington
(206) 535-3888
Dates: Sept. 24-26

Annual Michigan Celebration
University of Michigan
Dearborn, Michigan
(313) 593-5390
Dates: Sept. 24-26

Traditional Gathering
Cliffwood Beach, New jersey
(908) 390-1642
Dates: Sept. 24-26

California Indian Day Celebration
Auberry, California
(209) 855-8523
Dates: Sept. 25

Sapulpa Indian Day Powwow
Sapulpa, Oklahoma
(918) 224-9322
Dates: Sept. 25

Indian Trail Powwow
Indian Trail, North Carolina
(704) 821-6361
Dates: Sept. 25-26

Native Heritage Celebration
Porterville, California
(209) 784-4509
Dates: Sept. 25-26

Annual California Indian Days Celebration
Balboa Park
San Diego, California
(619) 281-5964
Dates: Sept. 25-26

The Mounds Traditional Powwow
Whitewater, Wisconsin
(414) 563-4860
Dates: Sept. 25-26

Annual St. Louis Indian Western Art Show & Sale
Gateay Indian Art Club
St. Louis, Missouri
(314) 938-6130 Attn: Virgil Laux
Dates: Sept. 25-26

Turning Leaves Festival
Old Indian Festival Area
Thornton, Indiana
(317) 436-2202
Dates: Sept. 25-26

Annual Council of Three Rivers Powwow
Tribal Bldg., Dorceyville
Pittsburgh, Pennsylvania
(412) 782-4457
Dates: Sept. 25-26

Annual Western Michigan State University Powwow
Kalamazoo, Michgian
(616) 375-5376
Dates: Sept. 25-26

Annual Traditional Intertribal Powwow
Black Rock State Park
Watertown, Connecticut
(203) 729-0035
Dates: Sept. 25-26

Eagle Wing Press American Indian Powwow
Watertown, Connecticut
(203) 238-4009
Dates: Sept. 25-26

Baxoje Fall Powwow
White Cloud, Kansas
(913) 595-3367
Dates: Sept. 25-26

Indian Summer
Bartlesville, Oklahoma
(918) 336-8708
Dates: Sept. 27-29

OCTOBER

Shiprock Navajo Fair
Shiprock, New Mexico
(505) 368-4679/4892
Dates: Sept. 30 - Oct. 3

Two Rivers Native Film & Video Festival
Holiday Inn Metrodome
Minneapolis, Minnesota
(612) 292-3221 Attn: Juanita Espinosa
Dates: Sept. 30- Oct. 3

Native American Powwow
Hagerstown, Maryland
(410) 675-3535 Attn: Barry Richardson
Dates: October

Homecoming Powwow
American Indianist Society
Spencer, Massachusetts
(508) 852-6271
Dates: 1st weekend in October

Cumberland Native American Powwow
Fayetteville, North Carolina
(919) 483-8442
Dates: October 1-2

Okiciyapo Festival
Lawrenceville, Georgia
(404) 921-4840 Attn: Paul Eddy
Dates: October 1-2

Annual Mesa College Powwow
San Diego, California
(619) 627-2706
Dates: October 1-2

Cherokees of Georgia Gathering & Powwow-Tribal Grounds
St. George, Georgia
(904) 275-2953
Dates: October 1-3

Annual Sacred Beginnings Powwow
South Puget Sound Community College
Olympia, Washington
(206) 866-7642 Attn: Dave Wells
Dates: October 1-3

Day of the Wolf Annual Intertribal Powwow
Louisville, Kentucky
(502) 955-7965
Dates: October 1-3

Wolf Moon Powwow
Lucerne Valley, California
(619) 248-7048
Dates: October 1-3

Dighton Intertribal Council Powwow
Somerset, Massachusetts
(508) 669-5008
Dates: October 1-3

Monacan Indian Tribal Bazaar
Amherst, Virginia
(804) 946-2531
Date: October 2

Annual West Valley College Powwow
Saratoga, California
(408) 867-2200 ext. 3642
Dates: October 2

Annual Powwow
Nowata, Oklahoma
(918) 273-3821
Dates: October 2-3

Indian Summer Powwow
Camden, Arkansas
(501) 231-4205
Dates: October 2-3

Running Water Powwow
Rome, Georgia
(404) 295-4382
Dates: October 2-3

Annual Fall Festival
Philadelphia, Pennsylvania
(215) 574-9020
Dates: October 2-3

Annual Western Michigan University Powwow
Kalamazoo, Michigan
(616) 349-5387
Dates: October 2-3

Annual Cherokee Heritage Art Show
Museum of the Cherokee Indian
Cherokee, North Carolina
(704) 497-3481
Dates: October 2-30

Narragansett Nation Annual Fall Festival
Indian Long House Rt. 2
Charlestown, Rhode Island
(401) 364-1100
Dates: October 3

Annual Native American Powwow
Pee Dee Trade School
McColl, South Carolina
(803) 523-5269/6790
Dates: October 8-9

Spirit of the People Powwow
Oklahoma City, Oklahoma
(800) 375-3737
Dates: October 8-9

Annual Intertribal Arts Experience
Dayton, Ohio
(513) 376-4358
Dates: October 8-10

Bay Area Indian Alliance Powwow
Oakland, California
(510) 452-1235
Dates: October 8-11

Harvest Festival
Greater Lowell Indian Cultural Association
Tyngsborough, Massachusetts
(508) 453-7182
Dates: October 8-11

Annual Intertribal Powwow
United Indians of Virginia
Chicahominy Reservation
Providence Forge, Virginia
(804) 865-6814 Attn: Ray Adams
Dates: October 9

Salem Area Fall Powwow
Rickreal, Oregon
(503) 623-8971 Attn: Cookie Spencer
Dates: October 9

Providence Intertribal Social
Providence, Rhode Island
(401) 423-0888
Dates: October 9

Harvest Moon Festival & Potluck
Nipmuck Reservation
Webster, Massachusetts
Dates: October 9

American Indian Gathering
Community College of Beaver County
Monaca, Pennsylvania
(412) 775-8561 Attn: Alex Gladis
Dates: October 9-10

**Paucatuck Eastern Pequot
Harvest Moon Powwow**
Connecticut Rivber Powwow Association
North Stonington, Connecticut
(203) 684-6984
Dates: October 9-10

Annual Juried Arts Festival
Rankocas Reservation
Rancocas, New Jersey
(609) 261-4747
Dates: October 9-10

Native American Indian Powwow
Charlemont, Massachusetts
(413) 339-4096
Dates: October 9-11

Annual Chumash Intertribal Powwow
Santa Ynez, California
(805) 686-1416
Dates: October 9-11

A Time of Thanksgiving
Lenni Lenape Historical Society
Allentown, Pennsylvania
(215) 797-2121
Dates: 2nd Sunday in October

Native American Student Art Show
The Heard Museum
Phoenix, Arizona
(602) 252-8840
Dates: October 10-18

Fall Festival & Powwow
Native American Indian Assn. of Tennessee
Nashville, Tennessee
(615) 726-00806
Dates: 3rd weekend in October

Apache Days
Globe, Arizona
(602) 425-4495
Dates: 3rd weekend in October

Timutla Art Exposition & Fashion Show
Umatilla Tribal Complex
Pendleton, Oregon
(503) 278-0552
Dates: 3rd weekend in October

**Annual Native American Heritage
Festival & Powwow**
Heritage Festival & Powwow
Roanoke, Virginia
(703) 342-5714
Dates: October 15-16

Waccamaw Siouan Powwow
Buckhead Bolton, North Carolina

(919) 655-8778
Dates: October 15-16

Reservationwide Championship W ardancing
St. Ignatius, Montana
(406) 745-3523 Attn: Pat Pierre
Dates: October 15-16

Four Nations Powwow
Lewiston, Idaho
(208) 843-2003
Dates: October 15-17

Five Civilized Tribes Masters Show
Five Civilized Tribes Museum
Muskogee, Oklahoma
(918) 683-1701
Dates: October 16

Fort Mojave Days
Needles, California
(602) 326-4591
Dates: October 16-17

Fire Hawk & Blue Sky Annual Powwow
Pomfret, Connecticut
(203) 429-2668
Dates: October 16-17

Annual Apigsigtag Ta Powwow
University of New Hampshire
Durham, New Hampshire
(603) 862-2050
Dates: October 16-17

Comanche War Dance & Powwow
Cache, Oklahoma
Dates: 4th weekend in October

Meherrin Indian Tribe Powwow
Winton, North Carolina
(919) 348-2166
Dates: Oct. 22-23

Las Vegas Indian Days
Community College, Pecos & Cheyenne
North Las Vegas, Nevada
(702) 642-6674
Dates: Oct. 22-24

NASA Powwow
University of Arkansas
Fayetteville, Arkansas
Date: Oct. 23

**Best of the Best Powwow &
Native American Arts Festival**
Rockland Community College
Suffern, New York
(914) 357-8424
Dates: Oct. 23-24

Annual AITA Powwow
Tribal Center
Toledo, Ohio
(419) 249-2601
Dates: Oct. 24-15

Amigos Social Powwow
Tucson, Arizona
(602) 622-4900
Dates: Oct. 28-30

Annual South Texas Powwow
Mission, Texas
(512) 686-6696 Attn: Robert Soto
Dates: last weekend in October

Mid Columbia River Powwow
Celilo, Oregon
(503) 298-1559
Dates: Oct. 29-31

La Ka Le'l Be Powwow
Carson Indian Colony
Carson City, Nevada
(702) 885-9759 Attn: Jack Malone
Dates: Oct. 29-31

National Indian Days Powwow
Parker, Arizona
(602) 669-921 1/2357
Dates: Oct. 29-31

**Oklahoma Federation of Indian
Women Youth Powwow**
Oklahoma City, Oklahoma
Dates: Oct. 30

NOVEMBER

Indian Arts & Crafts Exhibition & Sale
Stewart Museum
Carson City, Nevada
(702) 882-1808
Dates: Nov. 1 - Dec. 31

Pima Maricopa Art Festival
Sacaton, Arizona
(602) 963-4323
Dates: 1st weekend in November

Carmel American Indian Festival
Carmel, California
(408) 623-2379
Dates: 1st weekend in November

Annual AIA Orlando Powwow
Orlando, Florida
(407) 862-9676
Dates: Nov. 5-7

Annual Veterans Powwow
University of Maryland
College Park, Maryland
(301) 540-0966
Dates: Nov. 6-7

Annual Eastern Michigan Powwow
Ypsilanti, Michigan
(313) 487-2377
Dates: Nov. 6-7

Oglewanagi Powwow
Akron, Ohio
(216) 225-3416 Attn: Donna Seward
Dates: 2nd weekend in Novemeber

Annual American Indian Film Festival
San Francisco, California
(415) 554-0525 Attn: Michael Smith
Dates: Nov. 10-14

Veterans Powwow
LCO Ojibwe Reservation
Hayward, Wisconsin
(715) 799-5100/5166
Date: Nov. 11

Pawnee Veterans Day Gathering & Dance
Pawnee, Oklahoma
(918) 762-3962/3624
Date: Nov. 11

Veterans Day Powwow
Owyhee, Nevada
(702) 757-3161
Date: Nov. 11

Veterans Day Powwow
Chemawa Indian School
Salem, Oregon
(503) 399-5721
Date: Nov. 11

Veterans Day Powwow
Blue Earth Indian Nation
Council Bluffs, Iowa
(712) 325-1770
Date: Nov. 11

Veterans Day Celebration
Toppenish, Washington
(509) 865-5121
Dates: Veterans Day weekend

Veterans Day Powwow
Nespelem, Washington
(509) 634-4711
Dates: Veterans Day weekend

Veterans Day Memorial Powwow
Hopi Civic Center
Oraibi, Arizona
(602) 734-2441 ext. 215
Dates: Veterans Day weekend

Veterans Day Rodeo & Fair
San Carlos Apache Reservation
San Carlos, Arizona
(602) 475-2361
Dates: Veterans Day weekend

Annual American Indian
Art Festival & Market
Dallas, Texas
(214) 891-9648/8221
Dates: Nov. 12-14

Pomona Valley Indian Ceremonial
Show/Sale/Powwow
Pomona, California
(310) 430-5112 Attn: Alicia Bullock
Dates: Nov. 12-14

Red Nations Powwow
Dallas, Texas
(214) 263-4039
Dates: Nov. 12-14

National Museum of the American Indian
Powwow
New York, New York
(212) 598-0100 ext. 29
Date: Nov. 13

Restoration Celebration
Siletz, Oregon
(503) 444-2532 Attn: Karen Bell
Date: Nov. 13

Veterans Powwow
DQ University
Davis, California
(916) 758-0470 Attn: karen Bohay
Date: Nov. 13

Annual Indoor Native Arts & Crafts Show
Bloomsburg, Pennsylvania
(717) 389-4574 Attn: Madeline Foshay
Dates: Nov. 13-14

Great Plains Indian Art Show & Sale
Sioux Falls, South Dakota
(605) 336-4007
Dates: Mid-November

Mashpee Wampanoag
Winter Social & potluck
Mashpee, Massachusetts
(508) 477-0208
Date: Nov. 20

National Native American
Heritage Day Powwow
Concord, Massachusetts
(617) 884-4227
Date: Nov. 20

All Nations Indian Youth Powwow
Tulsa, Oklahoma
(918) 762-3962
Date: Nov. 20

Annual Powwow
Fort Duchesne, Utah
(801) 722-5141
Dates: Thanksgiving weekend

American Indian Market
Phoenix, Arizona
(602) 252-1594
Dates: 4th weekend in November

Thanksgiving Powwow
Indland Native American Association
San Bernardino, California
(714) 889-2444
Dates: Thanksgiving weekend

Thanksgiving Season Indoor Powwow
South Tucson, Arizona
(602) 622-4900
Dates: Thanksgiving weekend

DECEMBER

Quinapiac Dancers Winter Dance
Milford, Connecticut
(203) 263-3610
Dates: 1st weekend in December

All Indian Rodeo
Colorado River Reservation
Parker, Arizona
(602) 669-2357
Dates: 1st weekend in December

Annual Powwow
University of St. Thomas
St. Paul, Minnesota
(612) 872-6523
Dates: Dec. 4-5

Annual "Eyes That Shine From the Heart"
Powwow & Arts & Crafts Fair
Reno, Nevada
(702) 853-7444 Attn: Sonny Silverheels
Dates: Dec. 8-12

Christmas Powwow
DQ University
Davis, California
(916) 758-0470 Attn: Karen Bohay
Date: Dec. 11

Annual Chicago American
Indian Center Powwow
Chicago, Illinois
(312) 275-5871 Attn: Diane Maney
Dates: Dec. 12-14

Miccosuke Art Festival
Miccosukee Reservation
Miami, Florida
(305) 223-8380 ext. 346 Attn: Debbie Tiger
Dates: Dec. 26 - Jan 1

This section contains a listing of Canadian Indian Reserves and Bands, with land areas of at least 1,000 acres. Many bands have more than one reserve in each province. In these cases, the land areas (indicated by an asterisk before the Reserve) are added together to provide a total for that Province. The Reserves are in bold type followed by the Bands and Acreage. Arranged alphabetically by Reserve and Province.

ALBERTA

ALEXANDER INDIAN BAND
Box 510
Morinville, AB T0G 1P0
(403) 939-5887
Joseph Stanley Arcand, Chief

ALEXIS INDIAN BAND
Box 7
Glenevis, AB T0E 0X0
(403) 967-2225
Howard Mustus, Chief

ATHABASCA CHIPEWYAN
Box 366
Fort Chipewyan, AB T0P 1B0
(403) 697-3730
Patrick Marcel, Chief

BEARSPAW (STONEY)
Box 40
Morley, AB T0L 1N0
(403) 881-3770
Johnny Ear, Chief

BEAVER LAKE INDIAN BAND
Box 960
Lac La Biche, AB T0A 2C0
(403) 623-4549
Alphonse Lameman, Chief
Cultural/Educational Centre
Alex Redcrow, Diretor

BIGSTONE CREE BAND
General Delivery
Desmarais, AB T0G 0T0
(403) 891-3836
Eric Alook, Chief

BLOOD INDIAN BAND
Box 60
Standoff, AB T0L 1Y0
(403) 737-3753
Roy Fox, Chief

BOYER RIVER INDIAN BAND
P.O. Box 270
High Level, AB T0H 1Z0
(403) 927-3500
Harvey Bulldog, Chief

CHINIKI (STONEY)
Box 40
Morley, AB T0L 1N0
(403) 881-3770
Kenneth Soldier, Chief

COLD LAKE FIRST NATIONS BAND
Box 1769
Grand Centre, AB T0A 1T0
(403) 594-7183
Baptiste Blackman, Chief

CREE INDIAN BAND
Box 90
Fort Chipewyan, AB T0P 1B0
(403) 697-3740
Archie Waquan, Chief
Cultural/Educational Centre
Terry Marten, Director

DENE THA' TRIBE BAND
Box 120
Chateh, AB T0H 0S0
(403) 321-3842
Harry Chonkolay, Chief

DRIFTPILE INDIAN BAND
General Delivery
Driftpile, AB T0G 0V0
(403) 355-3868
Eugene Germain Laboucan, Chief

DUNCAN'S INDIAN BAND
Box 148
Brownvale, AB T0H 0L0
(403) 597-3777
Donald Testawich, Chief

ENOCH INDIAN BAND
Box 2, Site 2, RR #1
Winterburn, AB T0E 2N0
(403) 470-4505
Howard Peacock, Chief

ERMINESKIN INDIAN BAND
Box 219
Hobbema, AB T0C 1N0
(403) 420-0008
John Baptiste Ermineskin, Chief

FORT McKAY INDIAN BAND
Box 5360
Fort McMurray, AB T9H 3G4
(403) 828-4220
Mary Dorothy McDonald, Chief

FORT McMURRAY INDIAN BAND
Box 8217, Clearwater Station
Fort McMurray, AB T9H 4J1
(403) 334-2293
Robert Cree, Chief

FROG LAKE INDIAN BAND
General Delivery
Frog Lake, AB T0A 1M0
(403) 943-3737
Elmer Thomas Abraham, Chief

GOODSTONEY (STONEY)
Box 40
Morley, AB T0L 1N0
(403) 881-3770
John Snow, Chief

GROUARD INDIAN BAND
General Delivery
Grouard, AB T0G 1C0
(403) 523-4471
Frank Thomas Halcrow, Chief

HEART LAKE INDIAN BAND
Box 447
Lac La Biche, AB T0A 2C0
(403) 623-2130
Eugene Monias, Chief

HORSE LAKE INDIAN BAND
Box 303
Hythe, AB T0H 2C0

(403) 356-2248
Dale Robert Horseman, Chief

JANVIER INDIAN BAND
9206 McCormack Dr.
Fort McMurray, AB T9H 1C7
(403) 559-2259
Walter Janvier, Chief

KEHEWIN INDIAN BAND
Box 6218
Bonnyville, AB T9N 2G8
(403) 826-3333
Gordon Gadwa, Chief
Community Education Centre
Jim Hawkins, Director

LITTLE RED RIVER CREE NATION INDIAN BAND
Box 1165
High Level, AB T0H 1Z0
(403) 759-3912
A.J. Sewepagaham, Chief

LOUIS BULL INDIAN BAND
Box 130
Hobbema, AB T0C 1N0
(403) 585-3978
Simon Threefingers, Chief

LUBICON INDIAN BAND
Box 6731
Peace River, AB T8S 1S5
(403) 629-3945
Bernard Ominayak, Chief

MONTANA INDIAN BAND
Box 70
Hobbema, AB T0C 1N0
(403) 585-3744
Leo Cattleman, Chief

O'CHIESE INDIAN BAND
Box 1570
Rocky Mountain House, AB T0M 1T0
(403) 989-3943
Caroline Beaver Bones, Chief

PAUL INDIAN BAND
Box 89
Duffield, AB T0E 0N0
(403) 892-2691
Walter Rain, Chief

PEIGAN NATION
Box 70
Brocket, AB T0K 0H0
(403) 965-3940
Leonard Walter Bastien, Chief

SADDLE LAKE BAND
Goodfish Lake Group
Goodfish Lake, AB T0A 1R0
(403) 428-9501
Ernest Houle, Chief

SADDLE LAKE INDIAN BAND
Box 100
Saddle Lake, AB T0A 3T0
(403) 726-3829
Carl Quinn, Chief
Cultural Education Program
Keith Lapatak, Director

SAMSON INDIAN BAND
Box 159
Hobbema, AB T0C 1N0

(403) 421-4926
Victor Buffalo, Chief

SAWRIDGE INDIAN BAND
Box 326
Slave Lake, AB T0G 2A0
(403) 849-4311
Walter Patrick Twinn, Chief

SIKSIKA NATION BAND
Box 249
Gleichen, AB T0J 1N0
(403) 264-7250
Strater Crow Foot, Chief
Cultural/Education Centre
(403) 734-3862 Fax 734-2709
Floria Duck, Coordinator

STURGEON LAKE INDIAN BAND
Box 757
Valleyview, AB T0H 3N0
(403) 524-3307
Ronald Sunshine, Chief

SUCKER CREEK BAND
Box 65
Enilda, AB T0G 0W0
(403) 523-4426
Jim Badger, Chief

SUNCHILD CREE INDIAN BAND
Box 747
Rocky Mountain House, AB T0M 1T0
(403) 989-3740
Harry Goodrunning, Chief

SWAN RIVER INDIAN BAND
Box 270
Kinuso, AB T0G 1K0
(403) 775-3536
Charles Henry Chalifoux, Chief

TALLCREE INDIAN BAND
Box 367
Fort Vermillion, AB T0H 1N0
(403) 927-3727
Bernard John Meneen, Chief

TSUT'INA K'OSA NATION (SARCEE)
3700 Anderson Rd., S.W., Box 135
Calgary, AB T2W 3C4
(403) 281-4455
Roy Albert Whitney, Chief
Sarcee Cultural Program
(403) 238-2677 Fax 251-5871
Jeanette Starlight, Director

WHITEFISH LAKE INDIAN BAND
General Delivery
Atikameg, AB T0G 0C0
(403) 767-3914
Eddie Tallman, Chief

WOODLAND CREE INDIAN BAND
General Delivery
Cadotte Lake, AB T0H 0N0
(403) 629-3803
John Cardinal, Chief

BRITISH COLUMBIA

ADAMS LAKE INDIAN BAND
Box 588
Chase, B.C. V0E 1M0

(604) 679-8841
Harvey Jules, Chief

AHOUSAHT INDIAN BAND
General Delivery
Ahousaht, B.C. V0R 1A0
(604) 670-9563
Louie M. Frank, Sr., Chief

AITCHELITZ INDIAN BAND
8150 Aitken Rd., R.R. #1
Sardis, B.C. V2R 1A9
(604) 792-2404
Johnny George, Chief

ALEXANDRIA INDIAN BAND
Box 4, R.R. #2
Quesnel, B.C. V2J 3H6
(604) 993-4324
Thomas Billboy, Chief

ALEXIS CREEK INDIAN BAND
Box 69
Chilanko Forks, B.C. V0L 1H0
(604) 481-3335
Irvine Charleyboy, Chief

ALKALI INDIAN BAND
Box 4479
Williams Lake, B.C. V2G 2V5
(604) 440-5611
William Chelsea, Chief

ANAHAM INDIAN BAND
General Delivery
Alexis Creek, B.C. V0L 1A0
(604) 394-1212/3
Andrew Harry, Chief

ANDERSON LAKE INDIAN BAND
Box 88
D'Arcy, B.C. V0N 1L0
(604) 452-3221
Lawrence Patrick, Chief

ASHCROFT INDIAN BAND
Box 440
Ashcroft, B.C. V0K 1A0
(604) 453-9154
Mae Boomer, Chief

BEECHER BAY INDIAN BAND
3843 East Sooke Rd.
RR 1, Box 2
Sooke, B.C. V0S 1N0
(604) 478-3585
Patricia Ann Chipps, Chief

BELLA COOLA INDIAN BAND
Box 65
Bella Coola, B.C. V0T 1C0
(604) 799-5613
Edward Moody, Chief

BLUEBERRY RIVER INDIAN BAND
Box 3009
Buick, B.C. V0C 2R0
(604) 630-2584
Joe Apsassin, Chief

BONAPARTE INDIAN BAND
Box 669
Cache Creek, B.C. V0K 1H0
(604) 457-9624
Nels Terry Porter, Chief

BOOTHROYD INDIAN BAND
Box 295
Boston Bar, B.C. V0K 1C0
(604) 867-9211
Wilfred Campbell, Chief

BOSTON BAR INDIAN BAND
S.S. #1
Boston Bar, B.C. V0K 1C0
(604) 867-9349
Herman Phillips, Chief

BRIDGE RIVER INDIAN BAND
Box 190
Lillooet, B.C. V0K 1V0
(604) 256-7423
Susan James, Chief

BROMAN LAKE INDIAN BAND
P.O. Box 760
Burns Lake, B.C. V0J 1E0
(604) 698-7330
Maureen Ogen, Chief

BURNS LAKE INDIAN BAND
P.O. Box 9000
Burns Lake, B.C. V0J 1E0
(604) 692-7097
Robert Charlie, Chief

BURRARD INDIAN BAND
3082 Chumlye Dr.
North Vancouver, B.C. V7H 1B3
(604) 929-3455
Leonard George, Chief

CAMPBELL RIVER INDIAN BAND
1400 Weiwaikum Rd.
Campbell River, B.C. V9W 5W8
(604) 286-6949
Roy Roberts, Chief

CANIM LAKE INDIAN BAND
P.O. Box 1030
100 Mile House, B.C. V0K 2E0
(604) 397-2227
Gabriel Roy Christopher, Chief

CANOE CREEK INDIANBAND
General Delivery
Dog Creek, B.C. V0L 1J0
(604) 440-5645 Fax 440-5679
William Harry, Chief

CAPE MUDGE INDIAN BAND
Box 220
Quathiaski Cove, B.C. V0P 1N0
(604) 285-3316
Ralph Dick, Sr., Chief

CAYOOSE CREEK INDIAN BAND
Box 484
Lillooet, B.C. V0K 1V0
(604) 256-4136
Perry Redan, Chief

CHAWATHIL INDIAN BAND
Box 1659
Hope, B.C. V0X 1L0
(604) 869-9994
Herman W. Dennis Peters, Chief

CHEAM INDIAN BAND
10704 No. 9 Highway
Rosedale, B.C. V0X 1X0
(604) 794-7924
Theodore (Sam) Douglas, Chief

CHEHALIS INDIAN BAND
RR 1, Chehalis Rd.
Agassiz, B.C. V0M 1A0
(604) 796-2116
Virginia Peters, Chief

CHEMAINUS INDIAN BAND
RR 1
Ladysmith, B.C. V0R 2E0
(604) 245-7155
Robert Daniels, Chief

**CHESLATTA CARRIER
NATION INDIAN BAND**
Box 909
Burns Lake, B.C. V0J 1E0
(604) 694-3334
Marvin Charlie, Chief

CLAYOQUOT INDIAN BAND
Box 18
Tofino, B.C. V0R 2Z0
(604) 725-3233/4
Francis F. Frank, Chief

COLDWATER INDIAN BAND
Bag 4600
Merritt, B.C. V0K 2B0
(604) 378-6174
Gordon Antoine, Chief

COLUMBIA LAKE INDIAN BAND
Box 130
Windermere, B.C. V0B 2L0
(604) 342-6301
Joseph Nicholas, Chief

COMOX INDIAN BAND
3320 Comox Rd.
Courtenay, B.C. V9N 3P8
(604) 339-7122
Norman Frank, Chief

COOK'S FERRY INDIAN BAND
Box 1000
Spences Bridge, B.C. V0K 2L0
(604) 458-2224
Percy Minnabarriet, Chief

COQUITLAM INDIAN BAND
65 Colony Farm Rd.
Port Coquitlam, B.C. V3C 3V4
(604) 941-4995
Winnifred Joe, Chief

COWICHAN INDIAN BAND
Box 880
Duncan, B.C. V9L 3Y2
(604) 748-3196
Dennis Alphonse, Chief

COWICHAN LAKE INDIAN BAND
Box 1376
Lake Cowichan, B.C. V0R 2G0
(604) 745-3548
E. Cyril Livingstone, Chief

DEASE RIVER INDIAN BAND
Good Hope Lake, Box 3500
Cassier, B.C. V0C 1E0
(604) 239-3000
Roy Carlick, Chief

DITIDAHT INDIAN BAND
Box 340
Port Alberni, B.C. V9Y 7M8
G. Jackie Thompson, Chief

DOIG RIVER INDIAN BAND
Box 55
Rose Prairie, B.C. V0C 2H0
(604) 787-4466
Gerry Attachie, Chief

DOUGLAS INDIAN BAND
Box 339
Harrison Hot Springs, B.C. V0M 1K0
(604) 820-3082
Neil Phillips, Chief

EHATTESAHT INDIAN BAND
Box 716
Campbell River, B.C. V9W 6J3
(604) 287-4353
Earl J. Smith, Chief

ESQUIMALT INDIAN BAND
1113A Admirals Rd.
Victoria, B.C. V9A 6V2
(604) 381-7861
Andrew Benedict Thomas, Chief

FORT GEORGE INDIAN BAND
RR 1, Site 27, Comp. 60
Prince George, B.C. V2N 2H8
(604) 963-8451
Peter Quaw, Chief

FORT NELSON INDIAN BAND
RR 1, 293 Alaska Highway
Fort Nelson, B.C. V0C 1R0
(604) 774-7688/7257
Sally Behn, Chief

FORT WARE INDIAN BAND
1257 4th Ave. #3
Prince George, B.C. V2I 3J5
(604) 563-4161
Emil McCook, Chief

FOUNTAIN INDIAN BAND
Box 1330
Lillooet, B.C. V0K 1V0
(604) 256-4227
Roger Adolf, Chief

GITANMAAX INDIAN BAND
Box 440
Hazelton, B.C. V0J 1Y0
(604) 842-5297
Garry Patsey, Sr., Chief

GITANYOW INDIAN BAND (KITWANCOOL)
P.O. Box 340
Kitwanga, B.C. V0J 2A0
(604) 849-5222
Elmer Derrick, Chief

GITLAKDAMIX INDIAN BAND
New Aiyansh, B.C. V0J 1A0
(604) 633-2215
Herbert Morven, Chief

GITSEGUKLA INDIAN BAND
36 Cascade Ave., R.R. #1
South Hazelton, B.C. V0J 2R0
(604) 849-5595
Donald Ryan, Chief

GITWANGAK INDIAN BAND
Box 400
Kitwanga, B.C. V0J 2A0
(604) 849-5591
Glenford Williams, Chief

GITWINKSIHLKW INDIAN BAND
Box 1
Gitwinksihlkw, B.C. V0J 3T0
(604) 633-2294
Harry Nyce, Chief

GLEN VOWELL INDIAN BAND
Box 157
Hazelton, B.C. V0J 1Y0
(604) 842-5241
Marvin N. Sampson, Chief

**GWA'SALA-'NAK
WAXDA'ZW INDIAN BAND**
Box 998
Port Hardy, B.C. V0N 2P0
(604) 949-8343
Paddy Walkus, Chief

HAGWILGET INDIAN BAND
Box 460
New Hazelton, B.C. V0J 2J0
(604) 842-6258
Jack Sebastian, Chief

HALALT INDIAN BAND
RR 1
Chemainus, B.C. V0R 1K0
(604) 246-4736/7
George Norris, Chief

HALFWAY RIVER INDIAN BAND
Box 59
Wonowon, B.C. V0C 2N0
(604) 787-4452
Gerry Hunter, Chief

HARTLEY BAY INDIAN BAND
Hartley Bay, B.C. V0V 1A0
(604) 851-2500/25
William Clifton, Chief

HEILTSUK INDIAN BAND
Box 880
Waglisa, B.C. V0T 1Z0
(604) 957-2381
Cecil Reid, Chief

HESQUIAHT INDIAN BAND
Box 880
Tofino, B.C. V0R 2Z0
Richard Lucas, Sr., Chief

HIGH BAR INDIAN BAND
c/o Fraser Canyon Indian Admin.
P.O. Box 400
Lytton, B.C. V0K 1Z0
(604) 455-2279
Rosemarie Haller, Chief

HOMALCO INDIAN BAND
Box 789
Campbell River, B.C. V9W 6Y4
(604) 287-4922
Richard Harry, Chief

INGENIKA INDIAN BAND
101-1551 Oglivie
Prince George, B.C. V2N 1W7
(604) 562-8882
Gordon Pierre, Chief

ISKUT INDIAN BAND
Iskut, B.C. V0J 1K0
(604) 234-3331
Louis Louie, Chief

KAMLOOPS INDIAN BAND
315 Yellowhead Highway
Kamloops, B.C. V2H 1H1
(604) 828-9700
Clarence Thomas Jules, Chief

KANAKA BAR INDIAN BAND
Box 210
Lytton, B.C. V0K 1Z0
(604) 455-2279
James Frank, Chief

KATZIE INDIAN BAND
10946 Katzie Rd.
Pitt Meadows, B.C. V3Y 1Z3
(604) 465-8961
Ed Pierre, Chief

KINCOLITH INDIAN BAND
Kincolith, B.C. V0J 1B0
(604) 326-4212
Stuart Doolan, Chief

KISPIOX INDIAN BAND
R.R. #1, Box 25
Kispiox, B.C. V0J 1Y0
(604) 842-5248/9
Brian Williams, Chief

KITAMAAT INDIAN BAND
Haisla, P.O. Box 1101
Kitamaat Village, B.C. V0T 2B0
(604) 639-9361
Gerald Victor Amos, Chief

KITASOO INDIAN BAND
Klemtu, B.C. V0T 1L0
(604) 839-1255
Percy Star, Chief

KITKATLA INDIAN BAND
Kitkatla, B.C. V0V 1C0
(604) 628-9305
Francis Lewis, Chief

KITSELAS INDIAN BAND
4562 Queensway
Terrace, B.C. V8G 3X6
(604) 635-5084
Melville Stanley Bevan, Chief

KITSUMKALUM INDIAN BAND
House of Sim-Oi-Ghets
Box 544
Terrace, B.C. V8G 4B5
(604) 635-6177/8/9
Steve Roberts, Chief

KITWANCOOL INDIAN BAND
Box 340
Kitwanga, B.C. V0J 2A0
(604) 849-5222
Elmer Derrick, Chief

KLAHOOSE INDIAN BAND
Box 9
Squirrel Cove, B.C. V0P 1T0
(604) 935-6650
Arlene Hope, Chief

KLUSKUS INDIAN BAND
395A Kinchant St.
Quesnel, B.C. V2J 2R5
(604) 992-8186
Roger Jimmie, Chief

KWA-WA-AINEUK
Box 344
Port McNeill, B.C. V0N 2R0
(604) 949-8732
Charlie Williams

KWAKIUTL INDIAN BAND
Box 1440
Port Hardy, B.C. V0N 2P0
(604) 949-6012
Alfred Hunt, Chief

KWAW-KWAW-A-PILT INDIAN BAND
Box 412
Chilliwack, B.C. V2P 6H7
(604) 858-0662
Harold Henry, Chief

KWIAKAH INDIAN BAND
1440 Island Highway
Campbell River, B.C. V9W 2E3
(604) 286-1295
Stephen G. Dick, Chief

**KWICKSUTAINEUK-AH-K
WAW-AH-MISH INDIAN BAND**
General Delivery
Simoon Sound, B.C. V0P 1S0
Alice Smith, Chief

KYUQUOT INDIAN BAND
Kyuquot, B.C. V0P 1J0
(604) 332-5259
Richard H. Leo, Chief

LAKAHAHMEN INDIAN BAND
41290 Lougheed Highway
Deroche, B.C. V0M 1G0
(604) 826-7976
George Campo, Chief

LAKALZAP INDIAN BAND
Greenville, B.C. V0J 1X0
(604) 621-3212/3
Henry Moore, Chief

LAKE BABINE INDIAN BAND
P.O. Box 879
Burns Lake, B.C. V0J 1E0
(604) 692-7555
Wilf Adams, Chief

LANGLEY INDIAN BAND
P.O. Box 117
Fort Langley, B.C. V0X 1J0
(604) 888-4546
Alfred J. Gabriel, Chief

LAX-KW-ALAAMS INDIAN BAND
206 Shashaak St.
Port Simpson, B.C. V0V 1H0
(604) 625-3474
Lawrence Helin, Chief

LILLOOET INDIAN BAND
P.O. Box 615
Lillooet, B.C. V0K 1V0
(604) 256-4118
William Machell, Chief

LITTLE SHUSWAP INDIAN BAND
P.O. Box 1100
Chase, B.C. V0E 1M0
(604) 679-3203
Felix Arnouse, Chief

LOWER KOOTENAY INDIAN BAND
Box 1107
Creston, B.C. V0B 1G0
(604) 428-4428
Wayne Louie, Chief

LOWER NICOLA INDIAN BAND
R.R., Site 17, Comp. 18
Merritt, B.C. V0K 2B0
(604) 378-5157
Darryl C. Moses, Chief

LOWER SIMILKAMEEN INDIAN BAND
P.O. Box 100
Keremeos, B.C. V0X 1N0
(604) 499-5528
Barnett Allison, Chief

LYACKSON INDIAN BAND
P.O. Box 1798
Ladysmith, B.C. V0R 2E0
(604) 245-3829
Gordon Thomas, Chief

LYTTON INDIAN BAND
P.O. Box 20
Lytton, B.C. V0K 1Z0
(604) 455-2304/2353
Byron James Spinks, Chief

MALAHAT INDIAN BAND
P.O. Box 111
Mill Bay, B.C. V0R 2P0
(604) 743-3231
Randolph Daniels, Chief

**MAMALELEQALA QWE'QWA'SOT'ENOX
INDIAN BAND**
1400 Weiwakum Rd.
Campbell River, B.C. V9W 5W8
(604) 287-2955
Robert Sewid, Chief

MASSET INDIAN BAND
P.O. Box 189
Masset, B.C. V0T 1M0
(604) 626-3337
Michael Nicoll, Chief

MATSQUI INDIAN BAND
Box 229, RR 1, 31753 Harris Rd.
Matsqui, B.C. V0X 1S0
(604) 826-6145
David McKay, Chief

McLEOD LAKE INDIAN BAND
McLeod Lake, B.C. V0J 2G0
(604) 750-4415
Harry Chingy, Chief

METLAKATLA INDIAN BAND
Box 459
Prince Rupert, B.C. V8J 3R1
(604) 628-9294
Danny V. Leighton, Chief

MORICETOWN INDIAN BAND
RR 1, Site 15, Box 1
Smithers, B.C. V0J 2N0
(604) 847-2133
Stanislaus G. Nikal, Chief

MOUNT CURRIE INDIAN BAND
P.O. Box 165
Mount Currie, B.C. V0N 2K0
(604) 894-6115
Fraser Andrew, Chief

MOWACHAHT INDIAN BAND
Box 459
Gold River, B.C. V0P 1G0
(604) 283-2532
Lawrence Andrews, Chief

MUSQUEAM INDIAN BAND
6370 Salish Dr.
Vancouver, B.C. V6N 2C6
(604) 263-3261
Wendy Grant, Chief

NADLEH WHUTEN BAND
Box 36
Fort Fraser, B.C. V0J 1N0
(604) 690-7211
Ernie Nooski, Chief

NAK'AZDLI
Box 1329
Fort St. James, B.C. V0J 1P0
(604) 996-7171
Leonard Thomas, Chief

NANAIMO INDIAN BAND
1145 Totem Rd.
Nanaimo, B.C. V9R 1H1
(604) 753-3481
Robert E. Thomas, Chief

NANOOSE INDIAN BAND
RR 1, Box 124
Lantzville, B.C. V0R 2H0
(604) 390-3661
Leonard W. Edwards, Chief

NAZK0 INDIAN BAND
Box 4534
Quesnel, B.C. V2J 3H8
(604) 992-9810
Stanley Boyd, Chief

NEE-TAHI-BUHN INDIAN BAND
RR 2, Box 28
Burns Lake, B.C. V0J 1E0
(604) 694-3301
Pius Jack, Chief

NEMAIAH VALLEY INDIAN BAND
Nemaiah Valley P.O.
Nemaiah Valley, B.C. V0L 1X0
Roger William, Chief

NESKONLITH INDIAN BAND
Box 608
Chase, B.C. V0E 1M0
(604) 679-3295
Madene Joyce Manuel, Chief

NICOMEN INDIAN BAND
Box 328
Lytton, B.C. V0K 1Z0
(604) 455-2279
Cyril H. Spence, Chief

NIMPKISH INDIAN BAND
Box 210
Alert Bay, B.C. V0N 1A0
(604) 974-5556
Patrick Alfred, Chief
Cultural/Educational Centre, Jim Coke, Director

NOOAITCH INDIAN BAND
Box 6000
Merritt, B.C. V0K 2B0
(604) 378-6141
Linday May Shackelly, Chief

NORTH THOMPSON INDIAN BAND
Box 220
Barriere, B.C. V0E 1E0
(604) 672-9995
Nathan L. Matthew, Chief

NUCHATLAHT INDIAN BAND
Box 40
Zeballos, B.C. V0P 2A0
(604) 761-4520
Walter Michael, Chief

OHAMIL INDIAN BAND
C4, Site 22, RR 2
Hope, B.C. V0X 1L0
(604) 869-2627
Audrey Diana Kelly, Chief

OHIAHT INDIAN BAND
Box 82, Station A
Nanaimo, B.C. V9R 5K4
(604) 752-3994
K. Dennis Telford, Chief

OKANAGAN INDIAN BAND
Site 8, Comp. #20, RR #7
Vernon, B.C. V1T 7Z3
(604) 542-4328
Albert Saddleman, Chief

OPETCHESAHT INDIAN BAND
Box 211
Port Alberni, B.C. V9Y 7M7
(604) 724-4041
Daniel Watts, Chief

OREGON JACK CREEK BAND
Box 940
Ashcroft, B.C. V0K 1A0
(604) 453-9098
Robert S. Pasco, Chief

OSOYOOS INDIAN BAND
Site 25, Box 1, RR 3
Oliver, B.C. V0H 1T0
(604) 498-4906
Clarence Louie, Chief

OWEEKENO INDIAN BAND
P.O. Box 3500
Port Hardy, B.C. V0N 2P0
Frank Johnson, Chief

PACHEENAHT INDIAN BAND
General Delivery
Port Renfrew, B.C. V0S 1K0
(604) 647-5521
Kenneth Jones, Chief

PAUQUACHIN INDIAN BAND
Box 517
Brentwood Bay, B.C. V0S 1A0
(604) 656-0191
Edwin Mitchell, Chief

PAVILION INDIAN BAND
Box 609
Cache Creek, B.C. V0K 1H0
(604) 256-4204
Marvin Bob, Chief

PENELAKUT INDIAN BAND
Box 360
Chemainus, B.C. V0R 1K0
(604) 246-2321
Earl Wilbur Jack, Chief

PENTICTON INDIAN BAND
RR 2, Site 80, Comp. 19
Penticton, B.C. V2A 6J7
(604) 493-0048
Archie Jack, Chief

PETERS INDIAN BAND
Peters Rd., RR 2
Hope, B.C. V0X 1L0
(604) 794-7059
Frank Peters, Chief

POPKUM INDIAN BAND
Box 68, RR 1
Rosedale, B.C. V0X 1X0
(604) 794-7924/5630
James Murphy, Chief

PROPHET RIVER INDIAN BAND
Box 3250
Fort Nelson, B.C. V0C 1R0
(604) 774-1025
Liza Wolf, Chief

QUALICUM INDIAN BAND
Site 347, C-1, RR 3
Qualicum Beach, B.C. V0R 2T0
(604) 757-9337
Robert M. Recalma, Chief

QUATSINO INDIAN BAND
Box 100
Coal Harbour, B.C. V0N 1K0
(604) 949-6245
Stephen Clair, Chief

RED BLUFF INDIAN BAND
1515 Arbutus Rd., Box 4693
Quesnel, B.C. V2J 3J9
(604) 747-2900
Frank Boucher, Chief

SAMAHQUAM INDIAN BAND
Box 3068
Mission, B.C. V2V 4J3
(604) 894-5262
Allan Smith, Chief

SAULTEAU INDIAN BAND
Box 414
Chetwynd, B.C. V0C 1J0
(604) 788-3955
Stewart Cameron, Chief

SCOWLITZ INDIAN BAND
Box 76
Lake Errock, B.C. V0M 1N0
(604) 826-5813
Clarence Martin Pennier, Chief

SEABIRD ISLAND INDIAN BAND
Box 650
Agassiz, B.C. V0M 1A0
(604) 796-2177
Archie Charles, Chief

SECHELT INDIAN BAND
Box 740
Sechelt, B.C. V0N 3A0
(604) 688-3017
Thomas Paul, Chief

SEMIAHMOO INDIAN BAND
RR 7, 16010 Beach Rd.
White Rock, B.C. V4B 5A8
(604) 536-1794/6191
Bernard Charles, Chief

SETON LAKE INDIAN BAND
General Delivery
Shalalth, B.C. V0N 3C0
(604) 259-8227/8
  Rooney J. Louie, Chief

SHACKAN INDIAN BAND
Box 6000
Merritt, B.C. V0K 2B0
(604) 378-6141
  Percy Anthony Joe, Chief

SHESHAHT INDIAN BAND
Box 1218
Port Alberni, B.C. V9Y 7M1
(604) 724-1225
  Adam Shewish, Chief

SHUSWAP INDIAN BAND
Box 790
Invermere, B.C. V0A 1K0
(604) 342-6361
  Paul Ignatius Sam, Chief

SISKA INDIAN BAND
Box 358
Lytton, B.C. V0K 1Z0
(604) 455-2219
  Guy Dunstan, Chief

SKAWAHLOOK INDIAN BAND
Box 1668
Hope, B.C. V0X 1L0
(604) 796-9877
  Ana Delores Chapman, Chief

SKEETCHESTN INDIAN BAND
P.O. Box 178
Savona, B.C. V0K 2J0
(604) 373-2493
  Ronald Eric Ignace, Chief

SKIDEGATE INDIAN BAND
Box 699, R.R. #1
Queen Charlotte City, B.C. V0T 1S0
(604) 559-4496
  Paul E. Pearson, Chief

SKOOKUMCHUCK INDIAN BAND
P.O. Box 190
Pemberton, B.C. V0M 2L0
(604) 894-6037
  Paul Williams, Chief

SKOWKALE INDIAN BAND
P.O. Box 365
Sardis, B.C. V2R 1A7
(604) 792-0730
  Sam Archie, Chief

SKUPPAH INDIAN BAND
P.O. Box 116
Lytton, B.C. V0K 1Z0
(604) 455-2279
  John McIntyre, Chief

SKWAH INDIAN BAND
P.O. Box 178
Chilliwack, B.C. V2P 6H7
(604) 792-9204/5
  Leslie Williams, Chief

SKWAY INDIAN BAND
P.O. Box 174
Chilliwack, B.C. V2R 6H7
(604) 792-2852
  Cecelia James, Chief

SLIAMMON INDIAN BAND
RR 2, Sliamon Rd.
Powell River, B.C. V8A 4Z3
(604) 483-9646
  Gene Louie, Chief
  Cultural/Educational Centre
  Clair Noble, Coordinator

SODA CREEK INDIAN BAND
Site 15, Comp. 2, RR 4
Williams Lake, B.C. V2G 4M8
(604) 297-6323
  Beverly Ann Sellers, Chief

SONGHEES INDIAN BAND
1500 A-Admirals Rd.
Victoria, B.C. V9A 2R1
(604) 386-1043
  John P. Albany, Chief

SOOKE INDIAN BAND
RR 3, 2184 Lazzar Rd.
Sooke, B.C. V0S 1N0
(604) 642-3957
  Lawrence D. Underwood, Chief

SOOWAHLIE INDIAN BAND
Box 696
Vedder Crossing, B.C. V0X 1Z0
(604) 858-4603
  William Commodore, Chief

SPALLUMCHEEN INDIAN BAND
Box 430
Enderby, B.C. V0E 1V0
(604) 838-6496
  Cindy Williams, Chief

SPUZZUM INDIAN BAND
RR 1
Yale, B.C. V0K 2S0
(604) 863-2205
  James Johnson, Chief

SQUAMISH INDIAN BAND
Box 86131
N. Vancouver, B.C. V7L 4J5
(604) 985-7711
  Joseph Mathias, Chief

SQUIALA INDIAN BAND
Box 392
Chilliwack, B.C. V2P 6J7
(604) 792-8300
  Robert B. Jimmie, Chief

STELLAQUO INDIAN BAND
Box 760
Fraser Lake, B.C. V0J 1S0
(604) 699-8747
  Robert Mitchell, Chief

ST. MARY'S INDIAN BAND
Site 15, Mission Rd., R.R. #1
Cranbrook, B.C. V1C 4H4
(604) 426-5717
  Agnes McCoy, Chief

STONE INDIAN BAND
General Delivery
Hanceville, B.C. V0L 1K0
(604) 394-4295/6
  Tony Myers, Chief

STONY CREEK INDIAN BAND
RR 1, Site 12, Comp. 26
Vanderhoof, B.C. V0J 3A0

(604) 567-9293
  Geoffrey Thomas, Chief
  Cultural/Educational Centre
  Judy Labatch, Director

SUMAS INDIAN BAND
3092 Sumas Mountain Rd.
Abbotsford, B.C. V2S 4N4
(604) 852-4040
  Lester Vernon Ned, Chief

TAHLTAN INDIAN BAND
Telegraph Creek, B.C. V0J 2W0
(604) 235-3241
  Ronnie Carlick, Chief

TAKLA LAKE INDIAN BAND
General Delivery
Takla Landing, B.C. V0J 2T0
  Roy French, Chief

TAKU RIVER TLINGIT INDIAN BAND
Box 132
Atlin, B.C. V0W 1A0
(403) 651-7615
  Sylvester Jack, Sr., Chief

TANAKTEUK INDIAN BAND
Box 327
Alert Bay, B.C. V0N 1A0
(604) 974-5489
  William McKenzie, Chief

TLA-O-QUI-AHT FIRST NATIONS BAND
Box 18
Tofino, B.C. V0R 2Z0
(604) 725-3223/34
  Francis F. Frank, Chief

TLATLASIKWALA INDIAN BAND
c/o Whe-La-La-U Area Council
Box 150
Alert Bay, B.C. V0N 1A0
(604) 974-5501
  Thomas Wallace, Chief

TL'AZT'EN NATION
Box 670
Fort St. James, B.C. V0J 1P0
(604) 648-3212
  Edward John, Chief

TLOWITSIS-MUMTAGILA INDIAN BAND
Box 150
Coquitlam, B.C. V3J 1P5
(604) 974-5501
  John Smith, Chief

TOBACCO PLAINS INDIAN BAND
Box 21
Grasmere, B.C. V0B 1R0
(604) 887-3461
  Josephine Shottanana, Chief

TOOSEY INDIAN BAND
General Delivery
Riske Creek, B.C. V0L 1T0
(604) 659-5655
  Francis Laceese, Chief

TOQUAHT INDIAN BAND
Box 759
Ucluelet, B.C. V0R 3A0
(604) 726-4230
  Burt Mack, Chief

TSARTLIP INDIAN BAND
P.O. Box 70
Brentwood Bay, B.C. V0S 1A0
(604) 652-3988
Daniel Sam, Sr., Chief

TSAWATAINEUK INDIAN BAND
General Delivery
Kingcome Inlet, B.C. V0N 2B0
Patricia Dawson, Chief

TSAWOUT INDIAN BAND
Box 121
Saanichton, B.C. V0S 1M0
(604) 652-9101
Louie Claxton, Chief

TSAWWASSEN INDIAN BAND
Box 102
Delta, B.C. V4K 3N5
(604) 943-2112
Frederick A. Jacobs, Chief

TSEYCUM INDIAN BAND
Box 2501
Sidney, B.C. V8L 4C1
(604) 656-0858
David Bill, Chief

TSEYCUM
Box 2596
Sidney, B.C. V8L 4C1
(604) 656-0858
David Bill, Chief

TZEACHTEN INDIAN BAND
Box 278
Sardis, B.C. V2R 1A6
(604) 858-3888
Kenneth Malloway, Chief

UCHUCKLESAHT INDIAN BAND
Box 157
Port Alberni, B.C. V9Y 7M7
(604) 724-1832
Charlie Cootes, Chief

UCLUELET INDIAN BAND
Box 699
Ucluelet, B.C. V0R 3A0
(604) 726-7342
Robert Mundy, Chief

ULKATCHO INDIAN BAND
Box 3430
Anahim Lake, B.C. V0L 1C0
(604) 742-3260
Jimmy Stillas, Chief

UNION BAR INDIAN BAND
Box 788
Hope, B.C. V0X 1L0
(604) 869-9466
Andrew Alex, Chief

UPPER NICOLA INDIAN BAND
Box 3700
Merritt, B.C. V0K 2B0
(604) 350-3342/3
George Saddleman, Chief

UPPER SIMILKAMEEN INDIAN BAND
Box 100
Keremeos, B.C. V0X 1N0
(604) 499-5528
Edward Allison, Chief

WEST MOBERLY INDIAN BAND
General Delivery
Moberly Lake, B.C. V0X 1X0
(604) 788-3663
George Desjarlais, Chief

WESTBANK INDIAN BAND
515 Highway 97 South
Kelowna, B.C. V1Z 3J2
(604) 769-5666
Robert Louie, Chief

WHISPERING PINES BAND
RR 1, Site 8, Comp. 4
Kamloops, B.C. V2C 1Z3
(604) 579-5772
Richard LeBourdais, Chief

WILLIAMS LAKE INDIAN BAND
RR 3, Box 4
Williams Lake, B.C. V2G 1M3
(604) 296-3507
Eric M. Gilbert, Chief

YAKWEAKWIOOSE INDIAN BAND
7176 Chilliwack River Rd., RR 2
Sardis, B.C. V2R 1B1
(604) 858-6726
Frank Malloway, Chief

YALE INDIAN BAND
Box 1869
Hope, B.C. V0X 1L0
(604) 863-2423
Robert Hope, Chief

MANITOBA

BARREN LANDS INDIAN BAND
General Delivery
Brochet, MB R0B 0B0
(204) 323-2300
Fred Bighetty, Chief

BERENS RIVER INDIAN BAND
Berens River P.O.
Berens River, MB R0B 0A0
(204) 382-2161
Lester O. Everett, Chief

BIRDTAIL SIOUX INDIAN BAND
Box 22
Beulah, MB R0M 0B0
(204) 568-4540
Henry Skywater, Chief

BLOODVEIN INDIAN BAND
General Delivery
Bloodvein, MB R0C 0J0
(204) 395-2148
Helen Cook, Chief

BROKENHEAD INDIAN BAND
Scanterbury, MB R0E 1W0
(204) 766-2494
Wendell Sinclair, Chief
Cultural Program-Harvey Olson, Director

BUFFALO POINT FIRST NATION BAND
Box 37
Middlebro, MB R0A 1B0
(204) 437-2133
James Thunder, Chief

CHEMAWAWIN FIRST NATION BAND
Easterville, MB R0C 0V0
(204) 329-2161
Alpheus Brass, Chief

CHURCHILL
Tadoule Lake, MB R0B 2C0
(204) 684-2022
Peter Thorassie, Chief

CRANE RIVER INDIAN BAND
Crane River, MB R0B 0J0
(204) 732-2490
John H. MacDonald, Chief

CROSS LAKE INDIAN BAND
Cross Lake, MB R0B 0J0
(204) 676-2218 Fax 676-21 17
Sydney Garrioch, Chief
Cultural/Education Centre
John Paupanekis, Coordinator

DAKOTA OJIBWAY TRIBAL COUNCIL
702 Douglas St.
Brandon, MB R7A 5V2
(204) 725-3560 Fax 726-5966
Hubert Pierre, Director
Cultural/Education Center

DAKOTA PLAINS INDIAN BAND
Box 110
Portage La Prairie, MB R1N 3P1
(204) 252-2288
Ernie Smoke, Chief

DAKOTA TIPI INDIAN BAND
Box 1569
Portage La Prairie, MB R1N 3P1
(204) 857-4381
Dennis Pashe, Chief

DAUPHIN RIVER INDIAN BAND
Gypsumville, MB R0C 1J0
(204) 659-6370
Emery Stagg, Chief

EBB AND FLOW INDIAN BAND
Ebb and Flow, MB R0L 0R0
(204) 448-2113
Alfred Beaulieu, Chief

FAIRFORD INDIAN BAND
Fairford, MB R0C 0X0
(204) 659-5705
Edward Anderson, Chief

FISHER RIVER INDIAN BAND
Koostatak, MB R0C 1S0
(204) 645-2171
Lorne Cochrane, Chief

FORT ALEXANDER INDIAN BAND
Fort Alexander, MB R0E 0P0
(204) 367-2287
Jerry Fontaine, Chief

FOX LAKE INDIAN BAND
Box 369
Gilliam, MB R0B 0L0
(204) 652-2219
Robert Wavey, Chief

GAMBLERS INDIAN BAND
Box 293
Binscarth, MB R0J 0G0
(204) 532-2464
Louis Tanner, Chief

GARDEN HILL FIRST NATION INDIAN BAND
Island Lake, MB R0B 0T0
(204) 456-2085
Geordie Little, Chief

GOD'S LAKE INDIAN BAND
God's Lake Narrows, MB R0B 0M0
(204) 335-2552
Peter Watt, Chief

GOD'S RIVER INDIAN BAND
God's River, MB R0B 0N0
(204) 335-2011
Marcel Okimaw, Chief

**GRAND RAPIDS FIRST
NATION INDIAN BAND**
Box 500
Grand Rapids, MB R0C 1E0
(204) 639-2219
Harold Turner, Chief

HOLLOW WATER INDIAN BAND
Wanipigow, MB R0E 2E0
(204) 363-7278
Roderick Bushie, Chief

INDIAN BIRCH BAND
Birch River, MB R0L 0E0
(204) 236-4201
Charles Audy, Chief

INTERLAKE RESERVES TRIBAL COUNCIL
P.O. Box 580
Ashern, MB R0C 0E0
(204) 659-4465 Fax 659-2147
Rene E. Toupan, Tribal Administrator
Cultural/Educational Program

JACKHEAD INDIAN BAND
Dallas, MB R0C 0S0
(204) 276-2366
Bert Traverse, Chief

KEESEEKOOWENIN INDIAN BAND
Box 100
Elphinstone, MB R0J 0N0
(204) 625-2004
Randy Bone, Chief

LAKE MANITOBA INDIAN BAND
Vogar, MB R0C 3C0
(204) 768-3492
Raymond Swan, Chief

LAKE ST. MARTIN INDIAN BAND
Box 69
Gypsumville, MB R0C 1J0
(204) 659-4539
David E. Traverse, Chief

LITTLE BLACK RIVER INDIAN BAND
O'Hanley, MB R0E 1K0
(204) 367-4411
Franklin Abraham, Chief

LITTLE GRAND RAPIDS INDIAN BAND
Little Grand Rapids, MB R0B 0V0
(204) 397-2264/42
Oliver Owens, Chief

LITTLE SASK. INDIAN BAND
Gypsumville, MB R0C 1J0
(204) 659-4584
Hector Shorting, Chief

LONG PLAIN INDIAN BAND
General Delivery
Edwin, MB R0H 0G0
(204) 252-2731
Peter Yellowquill, Chief

MATHIAS COLOMB INDIAN BAND
Pukatawagan, MB R0B 1G0
(204) 553-2090/89
Pascal Bighetty, Chief

MOOSE LAKE INDIAN BAND
Moose Lake, MB R0B 0Y0
(204) 678-2113
Jim Tobacco, Chief

NELSON HOUSE INDIAN BAND
General Delivery
Nelson House, MB R0B 1A0
(204) 484-2332
Norman Linklater, Chief

NORTHLANDS INDIAN BAND
Lac Brochet, MB R0B 2E0
(204) 337-2001
Simon Samuel, Chief

NORWAY HOUSE INDIAN BAND
P.O. Box 218
Norway House, MB R0B 1B0
(204) 359-6721
Alan James Ross, Chief
Cultural Education Centre
Joyce Osborne, Director
(204) 359-6313

OAK LAKE SIOUX INDIAN BAND
Box 146
Pipestone, MB R0M 1T0
(204) 854-2959
Marcel Yuhada, Chief

OXFORD HOUSE INDIAN BAND
Oxford House, MB R0B 1C0
(204) 538-2156
Gabriel Hart, Chief

PAUINGASSI INDIAN BAND
Pauingassi, MB R0E 1M0
(204) 397-2371
David Owen, Chief

PEGUIS INDIAN BAND
Box 219
Hodgson, MB R0C 1N0
(204) 645-2359/60
Louis J. Stevenson, Chief
Peguis Cultural Centre
Daphne Stevenson, Band Manager

PINE CREEK INDIAN BAND
Camperville, MB R0L 0J0
(204) 524-2478
Clifford McKay, Chief

POPLAR RIVER FIRST NATION BAND
Negginan, MB R0B 0Z0
(204) 244-2267
Vera Mitchell, Chief

RED SUCKER LAKE INDIAN BAND
Red Sucker Lake, MB R0B 1H0
(204) 469-9300
Fred Harper, Chief

ROLLING RIVER INDIAN BAND
P.O. Box 145
Erickson, MB R0J 0P0
(204) 636-2211
Dennis Whitebird, Chief
Cultural/Educational Centre.

ROSEAU RIVER INDIAN BAND
P.O. Box 30
Ginew, MB R0A 2R0
(204) 427-2312
Lawrence Henry, Chief

SAGKEENG
Fort Alexander, MB R0E 0P6
(204) 367-2287
Jerry Fontaine, Chief

SANDY BAY INDIAN BAND
Marius, MB R0H 0T0
(204) 843-2462
Angus Starr, Chief

SHAMATTAWA FIRST NATION BAND
Shamattawa, MB R0B 1K0
(204) 565-2340/2455
Tommy McKay, Chief

SHOAL RIVER INDIAN BAND
Pelican Rapids, MB R0L 1L0
(204) 587-2012
Ronald Cook, Chief

SIOUX VALLEY INDIAN BAND
P.O. Box 38
Griswold, MB R0M 0S0
(204) 855-2671
Robert J. Bone, Chief

SPLIT LAKE INDIAN BAND
Split Lake, MB R0B 1P0
(204) 342-2045
Norman Flett, Chief

ST. THERESA POINT INDIAN BAND
St. Theresa Point, MB R0B 1J0
(204) 462-2106
Jack Flett, Chief

SWAN LAKE INDIAN BAND
Box 368
Swan Lake, MB R0G 2S0
(204) 836-2101
Roy McKinney, Chief

THE PAS INDIAN BAND
Box 297
The Pas, MB R9A 1K4
(204) 623-5483/4
Francis Flett, Chief

VALLEY RIVER INDIAN BAND
Shortdale, MB R0L 1W0
(204) 546-3334
Mervin Lynxleg, Sr., Chief

WAR LAKE INDIAN BAND
General Delivery
Ilford, MB R0B 0S0
(204) 288-4315/6
Alex Ouskan, Chief

WASAGAMACK INDIAN BAND
Wasagamack, MB R0B 1Z0
(204) 457-2337
Elijah Knott, Chief

WATERHEN INDIAN BAND
Skownan, MB R0L 1Y0
(204) 628-3373
    Harvey Nepinak, Chief

**WAYWAYSEECAPPO
FIRST NATION INDIAN BAND**
P.O. Box 340
Rossburn, MB R0J 1V0
(204) 859-2883/79
    Murray Clearsky, Chief

YORK FACTORY INDIAN BAND
York Landing, MB R0B 2B0
(204) 342-2210
    Eric Saunders, Chief

NEW BRUNSWICK

BIG COVE INDIAN BAND
Box 1, RR 1, Site 11
Rexton, NB E0A 2L0
(506) 523-9183
    Albert Levi, Vice-Chief
Cultural/Educational Centre
    Eva Sock, Director

BOUCTOUCHE MICMAC BAND
RR 2 Kent Co.
Buctouche, NB E0A 1G0
(506) 743-6493
    William Sanipass, Chief
Cultural/Educational Centre

BURNT CHURCH INDIAN BAND
RR 2
Lagaceville, NB E0C 1K0
(506) 776-8331/8612
    Wilbur Dedam, Chief
Cultural/Educational Centre
    Alex Dedam, Director

EDMUNDSTON INDIAN BAND
Box 382
Edmundston, NB E3V 3L1
(506) 735-3370/3379
    Richard Wallace, Chief

EEL GROUND INDIAN BAND
Site 3, Box 9, RR 1
Newcastle, N.B. E1V 3L8
(506) 622-2181/8
    Roger J. Augustine, Chief
Cultural/Educational Centre
(506) 622-2181 Fax 622-8667
    Howard McKay, Director

EEL RIVER INDIAN BAND
Box 1444
Dalhousie, NB E0K 1B0
(506) 684-2360/9
    Thomas Everett Martin, Chief
Education Committee:
    Mae Labillois, Chairperson
(506) 684-5268/3360 Fax 684-5840

FORT FOLLY INDIAN BAND
Box 21, RR 1
Dorchester, NB E0A 1M0
(506) 379-6224
    Dave Thomas, Chief

INDIAN ISLAND INDIAN BAND
Box 288, RR 1
Rexton, NB E0A 2L0
(506) 523-9187
    Wendall Paul Barlow, Chief

KINGSCLEAR INDIAN BAND
RR 6, Box 6, Comp. 19
Fredericton, NB E3B 4X7
(506) 363-3028/9 Fax 363-4324
    Stephen Sacobie, Chief
Cultural Education Program
    Ian Graham, Contact

OROMOCTO INDIAN BAND
Box 417
Oromocto, NB E2V 2J2
(506) 357-2083 Fax 357-2089
    Rupert J. Sacobie, Chief
Cultural Education Program
    Bob Atwin, Director

PABINEAU INDIAN BAND
Box 1, RR 5, Site 26
Bathurst, NB E2A 3Y8
(506) 548-9211
    Benjamin Peter Paul, Chief
Cultural Education Program.

RED BANK INDIAN BAND
Box 120
Red Bank, NB E0C 1W0
(506) 836-2366 Fax 836-7660
    Michael Ward, Chief
Arts and Crafts Committee
    Marlene Ward, Contact

ST. MARY'S INDIAN BAND
247 Paul St.
Fredericton, NB E3A 2V7
(506) 472-9511 Fax 458-2850
    Richard "Sonny" Polchies, Chief
Cultural Education Program
    Daniel Paul, Director

TOBIQUE INDIAN BAND
RR 3, Box 840
Perth, NB E0J 1V0
(506) 273-2282/3 Fax 273-3035
    Stewart Paul, Chief
Cultural Education Program
    Gertrude Nicholas & Delbert Moulton, Directors

WOODSTOCK INDIAN BAND
Box 8, Siye 1, RR 1
Woodstock, NB E0J 2B0
(506) 328-3304
    Len Tomah, Chief
Cultural Education Program
    Gary Paul, Coordinator

NEWFOUNDLAND

FIRST NATION COUNCIL OF DAVIS INLET
Davis Inlet, Labrador, NF A0P 1A0
(709) 478-8827
    Prote Poker, Chief

**FIRST NATION COUNCIL
OF NORTH WEST RIVER**
Box 160
North West River, Labrador NF A0P 1M0
(709) 497-8522
    Daniel Ashini, Chief

MIAWPUKEK INDIAN BAND
Baie d'Espoir
Conne River, NF A0H 1J0
(709) 882-2146
    Shayne McDonald, Chief

NORTHWEST TERRITORY

AKLAVIK INDIAN BAND
Box 118
Klavik, NT X0E 0A0
(403) 978-2340
    Eugene Pascal, Chief

ARCTIC RED RIVER INDIAN BAND
General Delivery
Arctic Red River, NT X0E 0B0
(403) 953-3201
    Peter Ross, Chief

COLVILLE LAKE
Fort Good Hope, NT X0E 0H0
    Richard Kochon, Chief

**DECHI LAO'TI COUNCIL
(SNARE LAKE) DENE**
Snare Lake, NT X1A 1C0
(403) 920-9812
    Joseph Judas, Chief

DENE NATION
Denedeh National Office
P.O. Box 2338
Yellowknife, NT Y1A 2P7
(403) 873-4081 Fax 920-2254
    Billy Erasmus, President

DOG RIB RAE INDIAN BAND
P.O. Box 8
Fort Rae, NT X0E 0Y0
(403) 392-6471
    Edward Erasmus, Chief

FITZ/SMITH (ALTA-N.W.T.) NATIVE BAND
P.O. Box 960
Fort Smith, NT X0E 0P0
(403) 872-2986
    Henry Beaver, Chief

FORT FRANKLIN INDIAN BAND
General Delivery
Fort Franklin, NT X0E 0G0
(403) 589-3151
    Raymond Taniton, Chief

FORT GOOD HOPE INDIAN BAND
General Delivery
Fort Good Hope, NT X0E 0H0
(403) 598-2231
    Everett Kakfwi, Chief

FORT LIARD INDIAN BAND
General Delivery
Fort Liard, NT X0G 0A0
(403) 770-4141
    Harry Deneron, Chief

FORT McPHERSON
Box 86
Fort McPherson, NT X0E 0J0
(403) 952-2330
    James Ross, Chief

FORT NORMAN INDIAN BAND
General Delivery
Fort Norman, NT X0E 0K0
(403) 588-3341
David Etchinelle, Chief

FORT PROVIDENCE INDIAN BAND
General Delivery
Fort Providence, NT X0E 0J0
(403) 699-341 1/41
Joachim Bonnetrouge, Chief

FORT RESOLUTION INDIAN BAND
General Delivery
Fort Resolution, NWT X0E 0M0
(403) 394-5281
Bernadette Unka, Chief

FORT SIMPSON INDIAN BAND
Box 469
Fort Simpson, NT X0E 0N0
(403) 695-3328/51
Jim Antoine, Chief

FORT WRIGLEY INDIAN BAND
General Delivery
Fort Wrigley, NT X0E 1E0
(403) 581-3321
Alma Ekenale, Chief

HAY RIVER INDIAN BAND
Box 1638
Hay River, NT X0E 0R0
(403) 874-6701/17
Pat Martel, Chief

INUVIK NATIVE BAND
P.O. Box 2570
Inuvik, NT X0E 0T0
(403) 979-3344
Cece McCauley, Chief

KAKISA LAKE BAND
General Delivery
Kakisa Lake, NT X0E 0L0
(403) 699-9949
Lloyd Chicot, Chief

LAC LA MARTRE BAND
General Delivery
Lac La Martre, NT X0E 1P0
(403) 573-3012
Isidore Zoe, Chief

LUTSEL K'E DENE INDIAN BAND
General Delivery
Snowdrift, NWT X0E 1A0
(403) 370-3551
Antoine Michel, Chief

NAHANNI BUTTE INDIAN BAND
General Delivery
Nahanni Butte, NWT X0E 0N0
Peter Marcellais, Chief
(403) 695-7223

PEHDZEH K'I (WRIGLEY) DENE
Wrigley, NT X0E 1R0
(403) 581-3321
Alma Ekenale, Chief

RAE LAKES DENE
Rae Lakes, NT X0E 1R0
(403) 997-3441
Henry Gon, Chief

RAINBOW VALLEY
Box 2514
Yellowknife, NT X1A 2P8
(403) 873-8951
Darrel Beaulieu, Chief

**SAMBAA K'E (TROUT LAKE)
DENE INDIAN BAND**
General Delivery
Trout Lake, N.W.T. X0E 0N0
(403) 695-9800
Edward Jumbo, Chief

SNOWDRIFT INDIAN BAND
Lutsel K'e Dene Council
Snowdrift, NT X0E 1A0
(403) 370-3051
Antoine Michel, Chief

YELLOWKNIVES DENE INDIAN BAND
Box 2514
Yellowknife, NT X1A 2P8
(403) 873-4307
Jonas Sangris, Chief

NOVA SCOTIA

ACADIA INDIAN BAND
RR 4, Box 5914C
Yarmouth, NS B5A 4A8
(902) 682-2150
Diana D. Robinson, Chief

AFTON INDIAN BAND
Afton (Antigonish Co.), NS B0H 1A0
(902) 386-2881
Noel Francis, Chief

ANNAPOLIS VALLEY INDIAN BAND
Cambridge Reserve, Box 89
Cambridge Station, NS B0P 1G0
(902) 538-7149
Lawrence Leo Toney, Chief

BEAR RIVER INDIAN BAND
Box 210 (Digby County)
Bear River, NS B0S 1B0
(902) 467-3802
Frank S. Meuse, Jr., Chief

CHAPEL ISLAND INDIAN BAND
RR 1
St. Peters, NS B0E 3B0
(902) 535-3317
George W. Johnson, Chief
Cultural/Educational Centre
(902) 535-2307
Dr. Marie Bastiste, Director

ESKASONI INDIAN BAND
Eskasoni, NS B0A 1J0
(902) 379-2800/1
Leonard Paul, Chief

HORTON INDIAN BAND
Box 449
Hantsport, NS B0P 1P0
(902) 825-4369
Joseph B. Peters, Chief

MEMBERTOU INDIAN BAND
111 Membertou St.
Sydney, NS B1S 2M9
(902) 539-6688/9850
Terrance Paul, Chief

MILLBROOK INDIAN BAND
Box 634
Truro, NS B2N 5E5
(902) 895-4365
Lawrence Alexander Paul, Chief

PICTOU LANDING INDIAN BAND
Box 249
Trenton, NS B0K 1X0
(902) 752-4912
Roderick P. Francis, Chief

SHUBENACADIE INDIAN BAND
Box 350
Shubenacadie, NS B0N 2H0
(902) 758-2049
Stephen J. Knockwood, Chief

WAGMATCOOK INDIAN BAND
Box 237
Baddeck, NS B0E 1B0
(902) 295-2598
Francis Pierro, Chief
Cultural/Educational Centre

WHYCOCOMAGH INDIAN BAND
Box 149
Whycocomagh, N.S. B0E 3M0
(902) 756-2337/2440
Roderick A. Googoo, Chief

ONTARIO

ALDERVILLE INDIAN BAND
RR 46
Roseneath, ON K0K 2X0
(416) 352-2011
Nora Bothwell, Chief

ALBANY INDIAN BAND
(Sinclair Island)
General Delivery
Fort Albany, ON P0L 1H0
(705) 278-1044
Edmund Metatawabin, Chief

ALBANY INDIAN BAND
(Village of Kashechewan)
General Delivery
Kashechewan, ON P0L 1S0
(705) 275-4440/13
Dan Koosees, Chief

ALGONQUIN OF GOLDEN LAKE BAND
Golden Lake, ON K0J 1X0
(613) 625-2800
Clifford Milnese, Chief

AROLAND INDIAN BAND
Box 390
Nakina, ON P0T 2H0
(807) 329-5970
William Magiskan, Chief

ATTAWAPISKAT INDIAN BAND
General Delivery
Attawapiskat, ON P0L 1A0
(705) 997-2166
Reg Louttit, Chief

BATCHEWANA INDIAN BAND
236 Frontenac St.
Sault Ste. Marie, ON P6A 5K9
(705) 759-0914 Fax 759-9171
Harvey Bell, Chief

Darlene Syrette, Band Administrator
Cultural/Educational Centre
Kathy Jones-Pine, Coordinator

BEARSKIN LAKE INDIAN BAND
Bearskin Lake P.O., ON P0V 1E0
(807) 363-2518
Steven Fiddler, Chief

BEAUSOLEIL INDIAN BAND
Cedar Point P.O.
Christian Island, ON L0K 1C0
(705) 247-2051
Jeffrey Monaque, Chief

BEAVERHOUSE
Box 1022
Kirkland Lake, ON P2N 3L4
(705) 567-4713
Isaac Mathias, Chief

BIG GRASSY INDIAN BAND
General Delivery
Morson, ON P0W 1J0
(807) 488-5552
Fred Copenace, Chief

BIG ISLAND INDIAN BAND
General Delivery
Morson, ON P0W 1J0
(807) 488-5602
Pauline Big George, Chief

BIG TROUT LAKE INDIAN BAND
Big Trout Lake, ON P0V 1G0
(807) 537-2263
Stanley Sainnawap, Chief

BRUNSWICK HOUSE INDIAN BAND
Box 1319
Chapleau, ON P0M 1K0
(705) 864-0174
Joseph Saunders, Sr., Chief

CALDWELL INDIAN BAND
Box 163, 215 Main St.
Bothwell, ON N0P 1C0
(519) 695-3642
Larry Johnson, Chief

CAT LAKE INDIAN BAND
2 Back Rd. West
Cat Lake, ON P0V 1J0
(807) 347-2100
Albert Wesley, Chief

CHAPLEAU CREE BAND
Box 400
Chapleau, ON P0M 1K0
(705) 864-0784
Doreen Cachagee, Chief

CHAPLEAU OJIBWAY INDIAN BAND
Box 279
Chapleau, ON P0M 1K0
(705) 864-1090
Joanne Nakogee, Chief

**CHIPPEWAS OF GEORGINA
ISLAND INDIAN BAND**
Box A-3, RR 2
Sutton West, ON L0E 1R0
(705) 437-1337
Eric Charles, Chief

**CHIPPEWAS OF KETTLE &
STONY POINT INDIAN BAND**
RR 2
Forest, ON N0N 1J0
(519) 786-2125
Thomas S. Bressette, Chief

CHIPPEWAS OF NAWASH INDIAN BAND
RR 5
Wiarton, ON N0H 2T0
(519) 534-1689
Ralph Akiwenzie, Chief

**CHIPPEWAS OF RAMA
FIRST NATION INDIAN BAND**
Rama Rd. P.O. 35
Rama, ON L0K 1T0
(705) 325-3611
George C. St. Germain, Chief

CHIPPEWAS OF SARNIA
978 Tashmoo Ave.
Sarnia, ON N7T 7H5
(519) 336-8410
Phillip Maness, Chief

CHIPPEWAS OF SAUGEEN
RR 1
Southampton, ON N0H 2L0
(519) 797-2218
Vernon Roote, Chief

CHIPPEWAS OF THE THAMES
RR 1
Muncey, ON N0L 1Y0
(519) 264-1528
Delbert Riley, Chief

COCKBURN ISLAND BAND
303-50 Larch St.
Sudbury, ON P3E 1B9
(705) 674-2372
Norma Fox-Wagosh, Chief

CONSTANCE LAKE INDIAN BAND
Constance Lake Indian Reserve
Calstock, ON P0L 1B0
(705) 463-4511
Mark Spence, Chief

COUCHICHING INDIAN BAND
Box 723
Fort Frances, ON P9A 3M9
(807) 274-3228
Joan Mainville, Chief

CURVE LAKE INDIAN BAND
Curve Lake, P.O. ON K0l 1R0
(705) 657-8045
Mel Jacob, Chief

DALLES INDIAN BAND
Box 1770
Kenora, ON P9N 3X7
(807) 548-1929
Jerry Perrault, Chief

DEER LAKE INDIAN BAND
Box 335
Red Lake, ON P0V 1V0
(807) 775-0053
Fred Meekis, Chief

DOKIS INDIAN BAND
Dokis Bay
Monetville, ON P0M 2K0

(807) 763-2200
Tim Restoule, Chief

EABAMETOONG FIRST NATION BAND
P.O. Box 70, Eabamet Lake
via Pickle Lake, ON P0T 1L0
(807) 242-7361
Harvey Yesno, Chief

EAGLE LAKE INDIAN BAND
Eagle River, ON P0V 1S0
(807) 755-5526
Arnold Gardner, Chief

FLYING POST INDIAN BAND
Box 937
Nipigon, ON P0T 2J0
(807) 886-2443
Frances Ray, Chief

FORT ALBANY
General Delivery
Fort Albany, ON P0L 1H0
(705) 278-1044
Edmund Metatawabin, Chief

FORT SEVERN INDIAN BAND
Fort Severn, ON P0V 1W0
(807) 478-2572
Elias (Ennis) Crow, Chief

FORT WILLIAM INDIAN BAND
Box 786, Station "F"
Thunder Bay, ON P7C 4Z2
(807) 623-9543
Christi Pervais, Chief

GARDEN RIVER FIRST NATION BAND
Box 7, Site 5, RR 4
Sault Ste, Marie, ON P6A 5K9
(705) 942-4011
Darrell E. Boissoneau, Chief

GINOOGAMING FIRST NATION
Box 89
Longlac, ON P0T 2A0
(807) 876-2241/2
Leslie O'Nabigon, Chief

GRASSY NARROWS INDIAN BAND
Grassy Narrows, ON P0X 1B0
(807) 925-2201
Raphael Fobister, Chief

GULL BAY INDIAN BAND
Gull Bay P.O.
via Armstrong, ON P0T 1P0
(807) 982-2188
John Roger King, Chief

HENVEY INLET INDIAN BAND
Pickerel, ON P0G 1J0
(705) 857-2331
Charlotte Contin, Chief

HORNEPAYNE
Box 465, Spruce St.
Homepayne, ON P0M 1Z7
(807) 868-2039
Dave Taylor, Chief

ISLINGTON INDIAN BAND
General Delivery
Whitedog, ON P0X 1P0
(807) 927-2068
Roy McDonald, Chief

KASABONIKA INDIAN BAND
Box 106
Kasabonika Lake, ON P0V 1Y0
(807) 535-2547
Jeremiah McKay, Chief

KEE-WAY-WIN INDIAN BAND
Sandy Lake, ON p)v 1V0
(807) 774-1215
Halum (Alijum) Kakepetum, Chief

KINGFISHER LAKE INDIAN BAND
Kingfisher Lake, ON P0V 1Z0
(807) 532-0067
James Mamawka, Chief

LAC LA CROIX INDIAN BAND
P.O. Box 640
Fort Frances, ON P9A 3M9
(705) 485-2431
Leon Jourdain, Chief

LAC DES MILLES LACS INDIAN BAND
136 Mai St. South
Kenora, ON P2N 1S9
Kevin Chicago, Chief

LAC LA CROIX
Box 640
Fort Frances, ON P9A 3N9
(807) 485-2431
Steve Jourdain, Chief

LAC SEUL INDIAN BAND
General Delivery
Lac Seul, ON P0V 2A0
(807) 582-3211
Roger Southwind, Chief

LANSDOWNE HOUSE INDIAN BAND
via Pickle Lake, ON P0T 1Z0
(807) 479-2570
Alex Moonias, Jr., Chief

LONG LAKE No. 58 INDIAN BAND
Box 609
Long Lac, ON P0T 2A0
(807) 876-2292
Sydney Abraham, Chief

MAGNETAWAN INDIAN BAND
P.O. Box 15, R.R. #1
Britt, ON P0G 1A0
(705) 383-2477
Joan Noganosh, Chief

MARTIN FALLS INDIAN BAND
Ogoki Post
via Nakina, ON P0T 2L0
(807) 349-2509
Eli Moonias, Chief

MATACHEWAN INDIAN BAND
General Delivery
Matachewan, ON P0K 1M0
(705) 565-2288
Barnie Batisse, Chief

MATTAGAMI INDIAN BAND
Box 99
Gogama, ON P0M 1W0
(705) 894-2072
GeraldLuke, Chief

McDOWELL LAKE INDIAN BAND
P.O. Box 315
Red Lake, ON P0V 2M0

(807) 727-2803
Albert James, Chief

MICHIPICOTEN INDIAN BAND
Box 26, Site 7, RR 1
Wawa, ON P0S 1K0
(705) 856-4456
Evelyn Stone, Chief

MISSANABIE CREE
217 John St.
Sault Ste. Marie, ON P6A 1P4
(705) 942-0123
Arthur Nolan, Spokesperson

MISSISSAUGA INDIAN BAND
P.O. Box 1299
Blind River, ON P0R 1B0
(705) 356-1621
Douglas Daybutch, Chief

MISSISSAUGAS OF NEW CREDIT
RR #6
Hagersville, ON N0A 1H0
(416) 768-1133/4/5
Maurice LaForme, Chief

MISSISSAUGAS OF SCUGOG
RR #5
Port Perry, ON L9L 1B6
(416) 985-3337
Yvonne Edgar, Chief

MOCREBEC INDIAN GOVERNMENT
Box 4
Moose Factory, ON P0L 1W0
(705) 658-4769
Randy

MOHAWKS OF AKWESASNE INDIAN BAND
P.O. Box 579
Cornwall, ON K6H 5T3
(613) 575-2250
Michael Mitchell, Chief

**MOHAWKS OF THE BAY
OF QUINTE INDIAN** BAND
R.R. #1
Deseronto, ON K0K 1X0
(613) 396-3424
Earl Hill, Chief

MOHAWKS OF GIBSON
Box 327
Bala, ON P0C 1A0
(613) 762-3343
Stephen Stock, Chief

MOOSE DEER POINT INDIAN BAND
P.O. Box 119
Mactier, ON P0C 1H0
(705) 375-5209
Edward Williams, Chief

MOOSE FACTORY INDIAN BAND
P.O. Box 190
Moose Factory, ON P0L 1W0
(705) 658-4619
Norman F. Wesley, Chief

**MORAVIAN OF THE
THAMES INDIAN BAND**
RR #3
Thamesville, ON N0P 2K0
(519) 692-3936
Richard Snake, Chief

MUNSEE-DELAWARE NATION INDIAN BAND
R.R. #1
Muncey, ON N0L 1Y0
(519) 289-5396
Leroy Dolson, Chief

MUSKRAT DAM INDIAN BAND
Muskrat Dam, ON P0V 3A0
(807) 471-2573
Frank Beardy, Chief

NAICATCHEWENIN INDIAN BAND
Box 12, RR #1
Devlin, ON P0W 1C0
(807) 486-3407
Roseanna Councillor, Chief

NEW POST INDIAN BAND
RR #2, Box 2, Comp. 0
Cochrane, ON P0L 1C0
(705) 272-5685
Peter Archibald, Sr., Chief

NEW SLATE FALLS INDIAN BAND
Slate Falls via Sioux Lookout, ON P0V 2T0
Gordon Carpenter, Chief

NIBINAMIK INDIAN BAND
Summer Beaver via Pickle Lake, ON P0T 3B0
(807) 593-2131
Sandy Yellowhead, Chief

NICIKOUSEMENECANING BAND
Box 68
Fort Francis, ON P9A 3M5
(807) 481-2536
Kelvin Morrison, Chief

NIPIGON INDIAN BAND
Nipigon Ojibway First Nation
Box 241, Rocky Bay Reserve
Beardmore, ON P0T 2B0
(807) 885-5441
Joseph Thompson, Chief

NIPISSING FIRST NATION
Box 70, Site 12D, RR #1
Sturgeon Falls, ON P0H 2G0
(705) 753-2050 Fax 753-0207
Phil Goulais, Chief
Maggie Penasse-Mayer, Deputy Chief
Tribe in residence: Ojibway. *In residence*: 1,971.
Area: 52,000 acres. *Councillors*: June Commanda,
Lorraine Commanda, Gerald Beaucage, Paul
Goulais, Roy McLeod, Ken Dokis. *Activities*: Annual Pow-wow, feast, elders gathering. Library.

NORTH CARIBOU LAKE INDIAN BAND
Weagamow Lake, ON P0V 2Y0
(807) 469-5191
Caleb Sakchekapo, Chief

NORTH SPIRIT LAKE INDIAN BAND
Box 70
North Spirit Lake, ON P0V 2G0
Peter Campbell, Chief

NORTHWEST ANGLE No. 33 BAND
Angle Inlet, MN 5671 1
(807) 733-2200
Kenneth Sandy, Chief

NORTHWEST ANGLE No. 37 BAND
General Delivery
Sioux Narrows, ON P0X 1N0
(807) 226-5353
Joseph Powassin, Chief

OJIBWAYS OF HIAWATHA
RR #2
Keene, ON K0L 2G0
(705) 295-4421
Frank Frank Cowie, Chief

OJIBWAYS OF ONEGAMING BAND
Box 160
Nestor Falls, ON P0X 1K0
(807) 484-2162
Anthony Copenace, Chief

OJIBWAYS OF THE PIC RIVER FIRST NATION
Heron Bay, ON P0T 1R0
(807) 229-1749
Roy Michano, Chief

OJIBWAYS OF WALPOLE ISLAND
RR #3
Wallaceburg, ON N8A 1R0
(519) 627-1481
Robert L. Williams, Chief

ONEIDAS OF THE THAMES INDIAN BAND
RR #2
Southwold, ON N0L 2G0
(519) 652-3244
Alfred L. Day, Chief

OSNABURG INDIAN BAND
Osnaburg, ON P0V 2H0
(807) 928-2414
Aloysius L. Kaminaiwash, Chief

PAYS PLAT INDIAN BAND
P.O. Box 819
Schreiber, ON P0T 2S0
(807) 824-2541
Aime Bouchard, Chief

PIC MOBERT INDIAN BAND
Mobert, ON P0M 2J0
(807) 822-2131/4
James Kwissiwa, Chief

PIKANGIKUM INDIAN BAND
Pikangikum, ON P0V 2L0
(807) 773-5578
John James Suggashie, Chief

POPLAR HILL INDIAN BAND
Box 5004
Poplar Hill, ON P0V 2M0
(807) 772-8838
Gary Owen, Chief

RAINY RIVER INDIAN BAND
Box 450
Emo, ON P0W 1E0
(807) 482-2479
Willie Wilson, Chief

RAT PORTAGE INDIAN BAND
P.O. Box 1850
Kenora, ON P9N 3X8
(807) 548-5663
George Kakeway, Chief

RED ROCK INDIAN BAND
P.o. Box 1030
Nipigon, ON P0T 2J0
(807) 887-2510/1
Betty Paakunainen, Chief

ROCKY BAY INDIAN BAND
MacDiarmid, ON P0T 2B0

(807) 885-3401
James Hardy, Chief

SACHIGO LAKE INDIAN BAND
Sachigo Lake, ON P0V 2P0
(807) 595-2577
Titus Tait, Chief

SAGAMOK ANISHNAWBEK
Box 160
Massey, ON P0P 1P0
(705) 865-5421
Nelson Toulouse, Chief

SAND POINT INDIAN BAND
921 Athapasca St.
Thunder Bay, ON P7C 3E5
(807) 774-3421
Dan R. McGuire, Chief

SANDY LAKE INDIAN BAND
Sandy Lake, ON P0V 1V0
(807) 774-3421
Jonas Fiddler, Chief

SAUGEEN INDIAN BAND
RR #1
Southampton, ON N0H 2L0
(519) 797-2218
Richard Kahgee, Chief

SAUGEEN NATION INDIAN BAND
Savant Lake, ON P0V 2S0
(807) 584-2908
Edward Machimity, Chief

SEINE RIVER INDIAN BAND
Box 124
Mine Centre, ON P0W 1H0
(807) 599-2224
Andrew Johnson, Chief

SERPENT RIVER INDIAN BAND
48 Indian Rd., Box 14
Cutler, ON P0P 1B0
(705) 844-2418
Earl Commanda, Chief

SHAWANAGA INDIAN BAND
RR #1
Nobel, ON P0G 1G0
(705) 366-2526
Howard Pamajewon, Chief

SHEGUIANDAH INDIAN BAND
Box 101
Sheguiandah, ON P0P 1X0
(705) 368-2781
Maxie Assinewai, Chief

SHESHEGWANING INDIAN BAND
Box C-1
Sheshegwaning, ON P0P 1X0
(705) 283-3292
Joseph Endanawas, Chief

SHOAL LAKE No. 39 INDIAN BAND
Kejick P.O.
Shoal Lake, ON P0X 1E0
(807) 733-2560
Eli Mandamin, Chief

SHOAL LAKE No. 40 INDIAN BAND
Kejick P.O.
Shoal Lake, ON P0X 1E0
(807) 733-2315
Lloyd Redsky, Chief

SIX NATIONS OF THE GRAND RIVER INDIAN BAND
Box 1
Ohsweken, ON N0A 1M0
(519) 445-2201
William Montour, Chief

STANGECOMING INDIAN BAND
Box 609
Fort Frances, ON P9A 3M6
(807) 274-2188
Janice Henderson, Chief

SUCKER CREEK INDIAN BAND
RR #1, Box 21
Little Current, ON P0P 1K0
(705) 368-2228
Patrick Madahbee, Chief

TEMAGAMI INDIAN BAND
Bear Island
via Temagami, ON P0H 2H0
(705) 237-8943
Gary Potts, Chief

THESSALON INDIAN BAND
Box 9, R.R. #3
Thessalon, ON P0R 1L0
(705) 842-2323
Alfred Bisaillon, Chief

WEBAUSKANG INDIAN BAND
Box 1730
Kenora, ON P9N 3X7
(807) 543-2555
Barney Petiquan, Chief

WABIGOON LAKE OJIBWAY NATION
Box 41
Dinorwic P.O., ON P0V 1P0
(807) 938-6684
John Kooshet, Chief

WAHGOSHIG INDIAN BAND
Box 722
Matheson, ON P0K 1N0
(705) 567-4891
Clifford Diamond, Chief

WAHNAPITAE INDIAN BAND
Box 128
Wahnapitae, ON P0M 3C0
(705) 694-5632
Norman Recollect, Chief

WALPOLE ISLAND INDIAN BAND
RR #3
Wallaceburg, ON N8A 4K9
(519) 627-1481
Robert L. Williams, Chief

WAPEKEKA INDIAN BAND
Angling Lake, ON P0V 1B0
(807) 537-2315
Norman Brown, Chief

WASAUKSING (PARRY ISLAND)
Box 253
Parry Sound, ON P2A 2X4
(705) 746-2531
John I. Rice, Chief

WASHAGAMIS BAY INDIAN BAND
Box 625
Keewatin, ON P0X 1C0
(807) 543-2532
Alfred Sinclair, Chief

WAUZHUSHIK ONIGUM
Box 1850
Kenora, ON P9N 3X7
(807) 548-5663
George Kakeway, Chief

WAWAKAPEWIN INDIAN BAND
Long Dog Lake, ON P0V 1G0
(807) 442-2567
Jermiah Nanokeesic, Chief

WEBEQUI INDIAN BAND
Box 176
Webequi, ON P0T 3A0
(807) 353-6531
Roy Spence, Chief

WEENUSK INDIAN BAND
Box 1
Pewaukuk, ON P0L 2H0
(705) 473-2554
Joseph Bird, Chief

WEST BAY INDIAN BAND
Box 2
West Bay, ON P0P 1G0
(705) 377-5362
Stewart Roy, Chief

WHITEFISH BAY INDIAN BAND
Pawitik, ON P0X 1L0
(807) 226-5411
George Crow, Chief

WHITEFISH LAKE INDIAN BAND
Box 39
Naughton, ON P0M 2M0
(705) 692-3651
Larry Naponse, Chief

WHITEFISH RIVER INDIAN BAND
Birch Island, ON P0P 1A0
(705) 285-4335
Leona Nahwegahbow, Chief

WHITESAND INDIAN BAND
Box 68
Armstrong, ON P0T 1A0
(807) 583-2177
Doug Sinoway, Chief

WIKWEMIKONG INDIAN BAND
Box 112
Wikwemikong, ON P0P 2J0
(705) 859-3122
Henry Peltier, Chief

WUNNUMIN INDIAN BAND
Wunnumin Lake, ON P0V 2Z0
(807) 442-0051/59/63
Simon Winnepetonga, Chief

PRINCE EDWARD ISLAND

ABEGWEIT INDIAN BAND
Box 220
Cornwall, PEI C0A 1H0
(902) 675-3842
George James Sark, Chief

LENNOX ISLAND INDIAN BAND
Lennox Island, PEI C0B 1P0
(902) 831-2779
Jack J.T. Sark, Chief

Cultural/Educational Centre
Charlie Sark, Director

QUEBEC

ABENAKIS DE WOLINAK
Reserve indienne de W olinak
4680 Boul. Danube
Becancour, P.Q. G0X 1B0
(819) 294-6696
Raymond Bernard, Chief

ABITIBIWINNI (ALGONQUIN)
Box36, Pikogan
Amos, P.Q. J9T 3A3
(819) 732-6591
Harry McDougall, Chief

ATTIKAMEKS DE WEYMONTACHIE
331, rue Simon Ottawa
Via St-Michel des Saints
Manouane, PQ J0K 1M0
(819) 971-8813
Henri Ottawa, Chief

**BARRIERE LAKE
(ALGONQUIN) INDIAN BAND**
Rapid Lake, V ia Val D'or
Parc de la Verendrye, PQ J0W 2C0
(819) 824-1734
Jean-Maurice Matchewan, Chief

BANDE INDIENNE DE BETSIAMITES
20, rue Messek, C.P. 40
Betsiamites, P.Q. G0H 1B0
(418) 567-2265
Jean-Louis Bacon, Chief

CHISASIBI INDIAN BAND
P.O. Box 150
Chisasibi, P.Q. J0M 1E0
(819) 855-2878
Violet Pachano, Chief

CONSEIL DES ATTIKAMEKS D'OBEDJIWAN
Reserve Indienne d'Obedjiwan
Via Roberval, PQ G0W 3B0
(819) 974-8837
Paul Mequish, Chief

EASTMAN (CREE) INDIAN BAND
Eastman, P.Q. J0M 1W0
(819) 977-0211
Ted Moses, Chief

GASPE (MICMAC)
Box 69, Fontenelle
Gaspe, P.Q. G0E 1H0
(418) 368-6005
Placide Jeannotte, Chief

GRAND LAC VICTORIA (ALGONQUIN)
Louvicourt, P.Q. J0Y 1Y0
(819) 736-2351 (LacSimon)
Henri Papatisse, Chief

KENESATAKE INDIAN BAND
Box 607
Oka, P.Q. J0N 1E0
(514) 479-8373
Jerry Peltier, Grand Chief

KIPAWA (ALGONQUIN) INDIAN BAND
Kebaoweck Indian Reserve
Box 787
Temiscamingue, P .Q. J0Z 3R0
(819) 627-3455
Jimmy Constant, Chief

KITIGAN ZIBI ANISHINABEG INDIAN BAND
P.O. Box 309
Maniwaki, PQ J9E 3C9
(819) 449-5170
Jean-Guy Whiteduck, Chief
Cultural Education Centre
Bertha Tenasco, Director
(819) 449-5039

LAC SIMON (ALGONQUIN)
Lac Simon, PQ J0Y 3M0
(819) 736-2351
Louis Jerome, Chief
Centre Amikwan-Jeanette Papatie, Coord.

LONG POINT (ALGONQUIN) INDIAN BAND
Box 1
Winneway River, P.Q. J0Z 2J0
(819) 722-2441
Jerry Polson, Chief

LES ATIKAMEKW DE MANOUANE
135, rue KICIK
Manouane, P.Q. J0K 1M0
(819) 971-8813
Henri Ottawa, Chief

MICMACS OF GESGAPEGIAG
Maria Indian Reserve
Box 1280
Maria, P.Q. G0C 1Y0
(418) 759-3441/2 Fax 759-5856
Douglas Martin, Chief
John Martin, Education Director

BANDE INDIENNE DE MINGAN
Box 319
Mingan, P.Q. G0G 1V0
(418) 949-2234
Jean-Charles Pietacho, Chief

MISTASSINI INDIAN BAND
Mistassini Lake, Baie-Du-Poste
via Chibougamau, P .Q. G0W 1C0
(418) 923-3253/9
Henry Mianscum, Chief

MOHAWKS OF KAHNAWAKE
Box 720
Kahnawake, PQ J0L 1B0
(514) 632-7500 Fax 638-5958
Joseph Norton, Grand Chief
Grand Chief and 1 1 council chiefs. *Tribe served*: Mohawk of the Six Nations Iroquois Confederacy. *In residence*: 5,500. *Total acreage*: 12,500. *Boundaries*: Triangular in shape, bounded on north by St. Lawrence River with survey boundaries east & west. *Special programs*: Social services; alcohol and drug abuse prevention; heath services program; social assistance; economic and financial services; community development; human resource development. Mohawk Council.

MONTAGNAIS DES ESCOUMINS
27, rue de la Reserve, Box 820
Les Escoumins, P.Q. G0T 1K0
(418) 233-2509
Denis Ross, Chief

MONTAGNAIS DE LA ROMAINE
La Romaine, P.Q. G0G 1M0
(418) 229-2917
Georges Bacon, Chief

MONTAGNAIS DE PUKUA SHIPI INDIAN BAND
St-Augustin, P.Q. G0G 2R0
(418) 947-2726
Charles Mark, Chief

MONTAGNAIS DE SCHEFFERVILLE
Case Postale 1390
Schefferville, P.Q. G0G 2T0
(418) 585-2601
Alexandre McKenzie, Chief

MONTAGNAIS DE UASHAT ET MALIOTENAM
Box 8000
Sept-Iles, PQ G4R 4L9
(418) 962-0327
Elie Jacques Jourdain, Chief

MONTAGNAIS DE NATASHQUAN
Natashquan, PQ G0G 2E0
(418) 726-3529
Joseph Tettaut, Chief

MONTAGNAIS DU LAC ST-JEAN
151, rue Quiatchouan
Pointe-Bleue, PQ G0W 2H0
(418) 275-2473
Remi Kurtness, Chief

NASKAPIS OF SCHEFFERVILLE INDIAN BAND
Box 1390
Schefferville, PQ G0G 2T0
(418) 585-2601
Alexandre McKenzie, Chief

CONSEIL DE LA NATION HURONNE-WENDAT
255, Place Chef Michel Laveau
Wendake, PQ G0A 4V0
(418) 843-3767
Max (Magella) Gros-Louis, Grand Chief
Elected chiefs: Roger Picard, Reine Laine, Rene Duchesneau, Arold Bastien, Michel Picard, Raymond Gros Louis. *Tribe served*: Huron - Wendat. *In residence*: 837. *Total acreage*: 300. School and museum.

NEMASKA (CREE) INDIAN BAND
Lac Champion
Nemiscau, PQ J0Y 3B0
(819) 673-2512
Lawrence Jimiken, Chief

BANDE INDIENNE D'OBEDJIWAN
Reserve indienne d'Obedjiwan
via Roberval, PQ G0W 3B0
(819) 974-8837
Hubert Clary, Chief

ODANAK (ABENAQUIS)
58, rue Wabanaki
Odanak, PQ J0G 1H0
(514) 568-2810 Fax 568-3553
Albert O'Bomsawin, Chief

WEMINDJI (CREE) INDIAN BAND
16 Beaver Rd., Box 60
James Bay, PQ J0M 1L0
(819) 978-0264
Walter Hughboy, Chief

RESTIGOUCHE (MICMAC) INDIAN BAND
17 Riverside West
Restigouche, PQ G0C 2Ro
(418) 788-2136
Ronald Jacques, Chief

TEMISKAMING (ALGONQUIN) INDIAN BAND
Box 336
Notre-Dame-Du-Nord, PQ J0Z 3B0
(819) 723-2335
Carol McBride, Chief

VIGER INDIAN BAND
39-3400 Losch Blvd.
St. Hubert, PQ J3Y 5T6
(514) 656-9731
Gaetane Aubin, Grand Chief

WASKAGANISH BAND
Box 60
Waskaganish, PQ J0M 1R0
(819) 895-8843
Billy Diamond, Chief

WASWANIPI (CREE) INDIAN BAND
Waswanipi River, PQ J0Y 3C0
(819) 753-2587/2388
Allan Happyjack, Chief

BANDE INDIENNE DE WEYMONTACHIE
Reserve indienne de Weymontachie
via Sanmaur, PQ G0A 4M0
(819) 666-2237/2259
Marcel Boivin, Chief

WHAPMAGOOSTUI INDIAN BAND
Box 390
Poste de la Baleine, PQ J0M 1G0
(819) 929-3503
Robbie Dick, Chief

WOLF LAKE INDIAN BAND
Box 1060
Temiscamingue, PQ J0Z 3R0
(819) 627-3628
Harold St. Denis, Chief

SASKATCHEWAN

AHTAHKAKOOP INDIAN BAND
Box 220
Shell Lake, SK S0J 2G0
(306) 468-2326
Barry Ahenakew, Chief

BEARDY'S INDIAN BAND
Box 340
Duck Lake, SK S0K 1J0
(306) 467-4523
Richard J.H. Gamble, Chief

BIG C INDIAN BAND
P.O. Box 145
La Loche, SK S0M 1G0
(306) 822-2021
Frank Piche, Chief

BIG RIVER INDIAN BAND
P.O. Box 519
Debden, SK S0J 0S0
(306) 724-4700
John Keenatch, Chief

BLACK LAKE INDIAN BAND
Black Lake, SK S0J 0H0
(306) 284-2044
Daniel Robillard, Chief

BUFFALO RIVER INDIAN BAND
Dillon, SK S0M 0S0
(306) 282-2033
Gordon Billette, Chief

CANOE LAKE INDIAN BAND
Canoe Narrows, SK S0M 0K0
(306) 829-2150
Frank Iron, Chief

CARRY THE KETTLE INDIAN BAND
Box 57
Sintaluta, SK S0G 4N0
(306) 727-2135
James L. O'Watch, Chief

COTE INDIAN BAND
Box 1659
Kamsack, SK S0A 1S0
(306) 542-2694
Hector Badger, Chief

COWESSESS INDIAN BAND
Box 607
Broadview, SK S0G 0K0
(306) 696-2520
Lionel Sparvier, Chief

CUMBERLAND INDIAN BAND
Box 278
Cumberland House, SK S0E 0S0
Harvey Young, Chief

CUMBERLAND HOUSE INDIAN BAND
Box 220
Cumberland House, SK S0E 0S0
(306) 888-2152
Pierre Settee, Chief

DAY STAR INDIAN BAND
Box 277
Punnichy, SK S0A 3C0
(306) 835-2834
Cameron Kinequon, Chief

ENGLISH RIVER INDIAN BAND
Patuanak, SK S0M 2H0
(306) 396-2055
Louis George, Jr., Chief

FISHING LAKE INDIAN BAND
Box 508
Wadena, SK S0A 4J0
(306) 338-3838
Allan Paquachan, Chief

FLYING DUST INDIAN BAND
Box 2410
Meadow Lake, SK S0M 1V0
(306) 236-4437
Richard Gladue, Chief

FOND DU LAC INDIAN BAND
Fond du Lac, SK S0J 0W0
(306) 686-2102
Napolean Mercredi, Chief

GORDON INDIAN BAND
Bpx 248
Punnichy, SK S0A 3C0
(306) 835-2232
Wayne Morris, Chief

HATCHET LAKE INDIAN BAND
Wollaston Lake, SK S0J 3C0
(306) 633-2003
Joe Tsannie, Chief

ISLAND LAKE INDIAN BAND
Box 460
Loon Lake, SK S0M 1L0
(306) 837-4845
Ernest Crookedneck, Chief

JAMES SMITH INDIAN BAND
Box 680
Kinistino, SK S0J 1H0
(306) 864-3636
Walter Constant, Chief

JOHN SMITH INDIAN BAND
Box 9
Birch Hills, SK S0J 0G0
(306) 764-1282
Austin Bear, Chief

JOSEPH BIGHEAD INDIAN BAND
Box 309
Pierceland, SK S0M 2K0
(306) 839-2277
Ernest Sundown, Chief

KAHKEWISTAHAW INDIAN BAND
Box 609
Broadview, SK S0G 0K0
(306) 696-3291
Louis Taypotat, Chief

KAWACATOOSE INDIAN BAND
Box 10
Quinton, SK S0A 3G0
(306) 835-2125
Richard Poorman, Chief

KEESEEKOOSE INDIAN BAND
Box 1120
Kamsack, SK S0A 1S0
(306) 542-2516
Albert James Musqua, Chief

KEY INDIAN BAND
Box 70
Norquay, SK S0A 2V0
(306) 594-2020
Dennis O'Soup, Chief

KINISTIN INDIAN BAND
Box 2590
Tisdale, SK S0E 1T0
(306) 873-5590
Albert Scott, Chief

LAC LA RONGE INDIAN BAND
Box 480
La Ronge, SK S0J 1L0
(306) 425-2183
Harry Cook, Chief

LITTLE BLACK BEAR INDIAN BAND
Box 102
Goodeve, SK S0A 1C0
(306) 334-2269
Clarence A. Bellegarde, Chief

LITTLE PINE INDIAN BAND
Box 70
Paynton, SK S0M 2J0
(306) 398-4942
Johnson Kakum, Chief

LUCKY MAN INDIAN BAND
401 Packham Place
Saskatoon, SK S3A 3K2
(306) 374-2828
Andrew King, Chief

MAKWA SAHGAIEHCAN INDIAN BAND
Box 340
Loon Lake, SK S0M 1L0
(306) 837-2150
Gerald Kisyeinwakup

MISTAWASIS INDIAN BAND
Box 250
Leask, SK S0J 1M0
(306) 466-4800
Noel Daniels, Chief

MOOSE WOODS INDIAN BAND
Box 149, RR #5
Saskatoon, SK S7K 3J8
(306) 477-0908
Charles R. Eagle, Chief

MOOSOMIN INDIAN BAND
Box 45
Cochin, SK S0M 0L0
Gerald SwiftW olfe, Chief
(306) 386-2014

MOSQUITO GRIZZLY BEAR'S HEAD BAND
Cando, SK S0K 0V0
Jenny Spyglas, Chief
(306) 937-7707

MUSCOWPETUNG INDIAN BAND
Box 1310
Fort Qu'Appelle, SK S0G 1S0
(306) 723-4710
Paul Poitras, Chief

MUSKEG LAKE INDIAN BAND
Box 248
Leask, SK S0J 1M0
(306) 466-4959
Harry Lafond, Chief

MUSKOWEKWAN INDIAN BAND
Box 298
Lestock, SK S0A 2G0
(306) 274-2061
Albert Pinacie, Chief

NEKANEET INDIAN BAND
Box 548
Maple Creek, SK S0N 1N0
(306) 662-3660
Gordon Oakes, Chief

OCEAN MAN
Box 157
Stoughton, SK S0G 4T0
(306) 457-2697
Laura Big Eagle, Chief

OCHAPOWACE INDIAN BAND
Box 550
Whitewood, SK S0J 5C0
(306) 696-2637
Denton George, Chief

OKANESE INDIAN BAND
Box 759
Balcarres, SK S0G 0C0
(306) 334-2532
Marie Ann Daywalker, Chief

OKEMASIS INDIAN BAND
Box 312
Duck Lake, SK S0J 1J0
(306) 466-4959
Don Eyahpaise, Chief

ONE ARROW INDIAN BAND
Box 1, RR 1
Wakaw, SK S0K 4P0
(306) 423-5900
Richard John, Chief

ONION LAKE BAND
Box 900
Lloydminster, SK S9V 1C3
(306) 344-2107
Donald Cardinal, Chief

PASQUA INDIAN BAND
Box 968
Fort Qu'Appelle, SK S0G 0C0
(306) 332-5697
Lindsay Cyr, Chief

PEEPEEKISIS INDIAN BAND
Box 518
Balcarres, SK S0G 0C0
(306) 334-2573
Enoch Poitras, Chief

PELICAN LAKE INDIAN BAND
Box 9
Leoville, SK S0J 1N0
(306) 984-2313
Leo Thomas, Chief

PETER BALLANTYNE INDIAN BAND
Box 100
Pelican Narrows, SK S0P 0E0
(306) 632-2125
Ronald Michel, Chief

PHEASANT RUMP NAKOTA
Box 418
Carlyle, SK S0G 0R0
(306) 462-2002
Kelvin J. McArthur, Chief

PIAPOT INDIAN BAND
Box 4
Craven, SK S0G 0W0
(306) 781-4848
Art Kaiswatum, Chief

POUNDMAKER INDIAN BAND
Box 220
Paynton, SK S0M 2J0
(306) 398-4971
Teddy Antoine, Chief

RED EARTH INDIAN BAND
Box 109
Red Earth, SK S0E 1K0
(306) 768-3640
Philip Head, Chief

RED PHEASANT INDIAN BAND
Box 70
Cando, SK S0K 0V0
(306) 937-7717
Mike Baptiste, Chief

SAKIMAY INDIAN BAND
Box 339
Grenfell, SK S0G 2B0
(306) 697-2831
Samuel Bunnie, Chief

SANDY LAKE INDIAN BAND
Box 220
Shell Lake, SK S0J 2G0
(306) 468-2326
  Barry L. Ahenakew, Chief

SAULTEAUX INDIAN BAND
Box 1
Cochin, SK S0M 0L0
(306) 386-2324
  Gabriel Gopher, Chief

SHOAL LAKE OF THE CREE NATION
Pakwaw Lake, SK S0E 1G0
(306) 768-3551
  Dennis Whitecap, Chief

STANDING BUFFALO INDIAN BAND
Box 128
Fort Qu'Appelle, SK S0G 1S0
(306) 332-4685
  Mel Isnana, Chief

STARBLANKET INDIAN BAND
Box 456
Belcarres, SK S0G 0C0
(306) 334-2206
  Irvin Starr, Chief

STURGEON LAKE INDIAN BAND
Box 5, Site 12, RR #1
Shellbrook, SK S0J 2E0
(306) 764-1872
  Wesley Daniels, Chief

SWEETGRASS INDIAN BAND
Box 147
Gallivan, SK S0M 0X0
(306) 937-3555
  Edward Standinghorn, Chief

THUNDERCHILD INDIAN BAND
Box 340
Turtleford, SK S0M 2Y0
(306) 845-3224
  Charles Paddy, Sr., Chief

TURNOR LAKE INDIAN BAND
Turnor Lake, SK S0M 3E0
(306) 894-2030
  Jean Campbell, Chief

WAHPETON LAKE INDIAN BAND
Box 128
Prince Albert, SK S6V 3B0
(306) 764-6649
  Lorne Waditaka, Chief

WATERHEN LAKE INDIAN BAND
Waterhen Lake, SK S0M 0B0
(306) 236-6717
  Robert Fiddler, Chief

WHITE BEAR INDIAN BAND
Box 700
Carlyle, SK S0C 0R0
(306) 577-2461
  Bernard Shepherd, Chief

WILLIAM CHARLES
Box 106
Montreal Lake, SK S0J 1Y0
(306) 663-5349
  Edward Henderson, Chief

WITCHEKAN LAKE INDIAN BAND
Box 27
Spiritwood, SK S0J 2M0
  Mike Fineday, Chief

WOOD MOUNTAIN INDIAN BAND
Box 104
Wood Mountain, SK S0H 4L0
(306) 266-4422
  William Goodtrack, Chief

**YELLOWQUILL (NUTT LAKE)
INDIAN BAND**
Box 97
Rose Valley, SK S0E 1M0
(306) 322-2281
  Henry Neapetung, Chief

YOUNG CHIPPEWAYAN
409-19th St. E.
Prince Albert, SK S6V 4A1
(306) 486-2326
  Alfred Snake, Chief

YUKON TERRITORY

CARCROSS/TAGISH INDIAN BAND
Box 130
Carcross, YT Y0B 1B0
(403) 821-4251
  Doris McLean, Chief

CHAMPAGNE/AISHIHIK INDIAN BAND
Box 5309
Haines Junction, YT Y0B 1L0
(403) 634-2288
  Paul Birckel, Chief
Cultural/Educational Centre
  Kathy Kushniruk, Director

DAWSON INDIAN BAND
Box 599
Dawson City, Y.T. Y0B 1G0
(403) 993-5387
  Steve Tailor, Chief

DEASE RIVER INDIAN BAND
Good Hope Lake
Bag 3500
Cassier, BC V0C 1E0
(403) 993-3000
  Roy Carlick, Chief

KLUANE INDIAN BAND
Mile 1093, Alaska Highway
Burwash Landing, YT Y1A 1H0
(403) 841-4274 Fax 841-5900
  Agnes Johnson, Chief

KWANLIN DUN INDIAN BAND
154 Tlingit St.
Whitehorse, YT Y1A 2Z1
(403) 667-6465
  Ann Smith, Chief
Cultural/Educational Centre
  Dorothy Sam, Director

LIARD RIVER INDIAN BAND
Box 328
Watson Lake, YT T0A 1C0
(403) 536-2131
  Dixon Lutz, Chief

LIARD RIVER INDIAN RESERVE #3
Box 489
Watson Lake, YT T0A 1C0
(604) 779-3161
  George Miller, Deputy Chief

**LITTLE SALMON -
CARMACKS INDIAN BAND**
General Delivery
Carmacks, YT Y0B 1C0
(403) 863-5576
  Roddy Blackjack, Chief

NA-CHO NY'A'K-DUN INDIAN BAND
Box 220
Mayo, YT Y0B 1M0
(403) 996-2265
  Robert Hager, Chief

OLD CROW INDIAN BAND
General Delivery
OLD CROW, YT Y0B 1N0
(403) 966-3261
  Howard Linklater, Director
Cultural/Educational Centre

ROSS RIVER INDIAN BAND
General Delivery
Ross River, YT Y0B 1S0
(403) 969-2278/9
  Clifford McLeod, Chief

SELKIRK INDIAN BAND
General Delivery
Pelly Crossing, Y.T. Y0B 1P0
(403) 537-3331
  Patrick Van Bibber, Chief

TA'AN KWACH'AN COUNCIL
22 Nisutlin Dr.
Whitehorse, YT Y1A 3S5
(403) 668-3613
  Glenn Grady, Chief

TAKU RIVER TLINGITS
Box 132
Atlin, YT V0W 1A0
(403) 651-7615
  Sylvester Jack, Sr., Chief

TESLIN INDIAN BAND
General Delivery
Teslin, Y.T. Y0A 1B0
(403) 390-2532
  David Keenan, Chief
Cultural/Educational Centre
  Eric Morris, Director

**VUNTUT GWITCHIN
(OLD CROW) INDIAN BAND**
General Delivery
Old Crow, Y.T. Y0B 1N0
(403) 966-3261
  Roger Kaye, Chief

**WHITE RIVER FIRST
NATION INDIAN BAND**
General Delivery
Beaver Creek, Y.T. Y0B 1A0
(403) 862-7802
  Billy Blair, Chief

ABORIGINAL INSTITUTE OF CANADA
4 Newgale St.
Ottawa, ON K2H 5R2

**ABORIGINAL TRAPPERS
FEDERATION OF CANADA**
Box 1869, 225 Pitt St.
Cornwall, ON K68 6N6
    (613) 933-6279 Fax 936-0505

ABORIGINAL YOUTH COUNCIL OF CANADA
120-1 Laval St.
Ottawa, ON K1L 1Z4
    (613) 741-7488 Fax 230-6273

**ANTHROPOLOGICAL
ASSOCIATION OF CANADA**
1575 Forlan Dr .
Ottawa, ON K2C 0R8
    (613) 225-3405

ARCTIC CO-OPERATIVES LIMITED
1741 Wellington St.
Winnipeg, MB R3H 0G1
    (204) 786-4481
    Bill Lyall, President

**ASSEMBLY OF FIRST NATIONS (AFN)
NATIONAL INDIAN BROTHERHOOD**
55 Murray St., Suite 500
Ottawa, ON K1N 5M3
    (613) 236-0673 Fax 238-5780
    Ovide Mercredi, National Chief
Head Office: Territory of Akwesasne, Hamilton's
Island, Summerstown, ON K0C 2E0 (613) 931-
1012 Fax 931-2438. Ottawa Office: 47 Clarence
St., Suite 300, Ottawa, ON K1N 9K1 (613) 236-
0673 Fax 238-5780. Harry Alen, Northern Region
(403) 667-7631; Gordon Peters, Ontario Region
(416) 972-0212; Konrad Sioui, Quebec and Labrador Region (418) 842-5020; Leonard Tomah,
Atlantic Region (506) 328-3304; Ken Young,
Manitoba Region (204) 956-0610; Bill Wilson, British Columbia Region (604) 339-6605; Roland
Crowe, Saskatchewan Region (306) 721-2822.
There are approximately 633 First Nations groups
across Canada. *Purpose*: To represent the views
and interests of Canada's First Nations in discussions with other levels of government on the issues: education, housing, economic development,
health, and forestry; to inform other Canadians
about the opportunities and issues relating to First
Nation's self-government. *Activities*: The AFN
Resource Centre; Educational scholarships;
Awards in honour of "Heroes of Our Time". *Publications*: AFN Bulletin, $18/year . Library. Founded
1969.

**ASSOCIATION OF IROQUOIS
AND ALLIED INDIANS**
920 Commissioners Rd. East
London, ON N5Z 3J1
    (519) 681-3551

**ASSOCIATION FOR NATIVE DEVELOPMENT
IN THE PERFORMING & VISUAL ARTS**
204-9 St. Joseph St.
TORONTO, ON M4Y 1J6
    (416) 972-0871

AVATAQ CULTURAL INSTITUTE
Inukjuak, PQ J0M 1M0
    (819) 254-8919
    Johnny Epoo, President

**CANADA – DEPARTMENT OF INDIAN
AFFAIRS & NOTHERN DEVELOPMENT**
Ottawa, ON K1A 0H4
    (819) 997-8205 or 997-0380
    Tom Siddon, Minister

**CANADIAN ALLIANCE IN SOLIDARITY
WITH THE NATIVE PEOPLES**
16 Spadina Rd., Suite 302
Toronto, ON M5R 2S7
    (416) 964-0169
    Catherine Jerrall, Coordinator
Membership: 1,250. Native and non-native people
working together to bring a better understanding
to non-native people. *Purpose*: To bring awareness issues to the public as identified by native
people. *Committees*: Aboriginal Rights, Child
Welfare Native, Focus on the Canadian Constitution, Justice, Native Rights, and Prisons. *Publications*: Phoenix, quarterly journal; Resource/Read-
ing List; Indian Giver: A Legacy of North American Native Peoples.Native Rights in Canada, Third
Edition. Maintains small resource center . Annual
meeting. Founded 1960.

**THE CANADIAN ARCTIC
CO-OPERATIVE FEDERATION**
Box 2039
Yellowknife, NT X1A 2P5
    (403) 873-3481

CANADIAN HISTORICAL SOCIETY
395 Wellington St.
Ottawa, ON K1A 0N3

CANADIAN NATIVE ARTS FOUNDATION
99 Atlantic Ave., Suite 315
Toronto, ON M6K 3J8
    (416) 588-3328 Fax 588-9198
    John Kim Bell, President

**CANADIAN SOCIETY FOR
CIRCUMPOLAR HEALTH**
Box 519
Ft. Qu'Appelle, SK
    (306) 332-6261 Fax 332-5985
    Dr. Jean Goodwill, President

**CENTRE FOR NUTRITION & THE
ENVIRONMENT OF INDIGENOUS PEOPLE**
Assembly of First Nations
300-47 Clarence St.
Ottawa, ON K1N 9K1
    (613) 236-0637 Fax 238-5780
    Laurie Montour , Director

**COMMITTEE FOR ORIGINAL
PEOPLE'S ENTITLEMENT**
P.O. Box 2000
Inuvik, NT X0E 0T0
    (403) 979-3510

CONSEIL ATTIKAMEK-MONTAGNAIS
80 Boulevard Bastien
Village des Hurons
Lorette, PQ G0A 4V0
    (418) 842-0277

COUNCIL OF ELDERS
RR #9
Fredericton, NB E3B 4X9
    (506) 472-7934
    Wallace Labillois, Chairperson

FIRST NATIONS CONFEDERACY
286 Smith St., Suite 203
Winnipeg, MB R3C 1K4

    (204) 994-8245 Fax 943-1482
    Chief Raymond Swan, Chairperson

FOUR ARROWS
P.O. Box 1332, Station B
Ottawa, ON K1P 5L4
    (613) 234-5887
    Rarihokwats, Coordinator
Membership: 100. Persons seeking to protect the
human and political rights of indigenous peoples
of the Americas. *Purpose*: To promote intercultural
exchange, spiritual strength, and communication
among Indian people; encourages self-suf ficiency
projects. *Activities*: Sponsors programs in educational & agricultural development. Founded 1968.

GRAND COUNCIL TREATY No. 3
P.O. Box 1720
Kenora, ON P9N 3X7
    (807) 548-4215

GRAND COUNCIL OF THE CREES
1, Place Ville Marie, Suite 3434
Montreal, PQ H3B 3N6
    (514) 861-5837 Fax 861-0760
    Matthew Coon-Come, Chairperson

INDIAN CLAIMS COMMISSION
255 Albert St., Suite 200
P.O. Box 1750, Station B
Ottawa, ON K1P 1A2
    (613) 943-2737 Fax 943-0157
    Harry S. LaForme, Chief Commissioner

INDIAN & INUIT NURSES OF CANADA
47 Clarence St., 3rd Floor
Ottawa, Ontario K1N 9K1
    (613) 230-1864 F AX 238-5780
    Madeleine Dion Stout, President

INDIAN RIGHTS FOR INDIAN WOMEN
19 Slackville St.
Toronto, ON M5A 3E1
    (416) 368-3524

**INDIGENOUS BAR
ASSOCIATION OF CANADA**
1338 Wellington St.
Ottawa, ON K1Y 3B7
    (613) 729-9491

INDIGENOUS SURVIVAL INTERNATIONAL
47 Clarence St., Suite 300
Ottawa, ON K1N 9K1
    (613) 236-0673 Fax 238-5780
    David Monture, Executive Director

**INSTITUTE FOR ENCYCLOPEDIA OF HUMAN
IDEAS ON ULTIMATE REALITY & MEANING**
Regis College, 15 St. Mary St.
Toronto, ON M4Y 2R5
    (416) 922-2476
    Tibor Horvath, Director
Purpose: Interdisciplinary research on human effort to find meaning in our world; specifically how
63 North American and 72 South American Indian
linguistic families with their 474 and 505 members
respectively expressed the meaning of their lives
and their concepts of ultimate reality and meaning. *Activities*: Biennial meetings and publications
of essays in journal; scholars-experts in any of
979 American Indian groups listed in the Outline
of the Research are welcome to submit essays
following the guidelines of the Institute. *Publication*: Ultimate Reality and Meaning; newsletter .
Library. Founded 1970.

INTERTRIBAL CHRISTIAN COMMUNICATIONS
P.O. Box 3765, Station B
Winnipeg, MB R2W 3R6
(204) 661-9333
George McPeek, Director
Purpose: To assist the Indian church in its broadest sense to speak to the social, cultural and spiritual concerns of its own native people. *Activities/programs*: Seminars dealing with grief resolution. *Publications*: Indian Life Magazine; The Grieving Indian; Christian education curricula for Native youth.

INUIT ART FOUNDATION
2081 Marivale Rd.
OTTAWA, ON K2G 1G9
(613) 224-8189 Fax 224-2907

INUIT BROADCASTING CORP.
251 Laurier West, Suite 703
Ottawa, ON K1P 5J6
(613) 235-1892 Fax 230-8824
Rosemarie Kuptana, President

INUIT CIRCUMPOLAR CONFERENCE
170 Laurier Ave., Suite 510
Ottawa, ON K1P 5V5
(613) 563-2642 Fax 234-1991
Mary Simon, President

INUIT COMMITTEE ON NATIONAL ISSUES
176 Gloucester St., 3rd Floor
Ottawa, ON K2P 0A6
(613) 234-8532

INUIT CULTURAL INSTITUTE
Eskimo Point, NT X0C 0E0
(819) 857-2803
Tom Owlijoot, Executive Director

INNUIT NON-PROFIT HOUSING CORPORATION
176 Gloucester St., 3rd Floor
Ottawa, ON K2P 0A6
(613) 238-1549
Joelee Arreak, Housing Corp. President

INUIT TAPIRISAT OF CANADA
170 Laurier Ave. West, Suite 510
Ottawa, ON K1P 5V5
(613) 238-8181 Fax 234-1991
Rosemarie Kuptana, President
Purpose: National voice of Inuit in Canada. *Activities*: Lobby for Inuit rights, self-government, economic development, environment, and cultural preservation & development. *Publication*: Inuktitut Magazine. Library. Founded 1971.

INUIT TUNGAVINGAT NUNAMINI
Povungnituk, PQ J0M 1C0
(819) 988-2963

INUIT WOMEN'S ASSOCIATION (PAUKTUUTIT)
200 Elgin St., Suite 804
Ottawa, ON K2P 1L5
(613) 238-3977 Fax 238-1787
Eva Voisey, President

INUIT WOMEN'S ASSN. OF CANADA
251 Laurier Ave. W., Suite 600
Ottawa, ON K1P 5J6
(613) 236-6057 Fax 235-4957

INUIT YOUTH COUNCIL
176 Gloucester St., 3rd Floor
Ottawa, ON K2P 0A6
(613) 238-8181
John Bennett, Coordinator

INUVIALUIT DEVELOPMENT CORP.
P.O. Box 704
Inuvik, NT X0E 0T0
(403) 979-2320
Roy Goose, President

INUVIALUIT DEVELOPMENT CORP.
P.O. Box 2000
Inuvik, NT X0E 0H0
(403) 979-3510
Frank Hansen, Chairman

MAKIVIK CORPORATION
4898 Maisonneuve West
Montreal, PQ H3Z 1M8
(514) 483-2780
Mark R. Gordon, President

METIS NATIONAL COUNCIL
558 Whitewood Crescent
Saskatoon, SK S7J 4L1
(306) 373-8855

NATIONAL ABORIGINAL COMMUNICATIONS SOCIETY
298 Elgin St., Suite 105
Ottawa, ON K2P 1M3
(613) 230-6244 Fax 230-6227

NATIONAL ABORIGINAL FORESTRY ASSN.
Algonquin Golden Lake First Nation
Box 100
Golden Lake, ON K0J 1X0
(613) 625-8000

NATIONAL ABORIGINAL NETWORK ON DISABILITY
RR 3
Cornwall, ON K6H 5R7
(613) 563-1066

NATIONAL ASSOCIATION OF FRIENDSHIP CENTRES
251 Laurier Ave. West, Suite 600
Ottawa, ON K1P 5J6
(613) 563-4844 Fax 235-4957
Jerome Berthelette, Executive Director
Purpose: To act in the capacity of social advocate for Canadian Native Peoples in an urban setting by qualifying or lobbying for special projects funding in the areas of Native self-sufficiency, alcohol, drug and solvent abuse counseling, courtwork representation, etc. *Activities*: Handles core support to new and satellite centres, as well as training support, capital constructions, and renovations of existing centres. *Publication*: Monthly newsletter. Library.

NATIONAL COMMITTEE OF INDIAN CULTURAL EDUCATIONAL CENTRES
R.R. 3
Cornwall Island, ON K6H 5R7
(613) 932-9452
Barbara Barnes, President
Harold Tarbell, Coordinator

NATIONAL INDIAN ARTS & CRAFTS CORP.
1 Nicholas St., Suite 1106
Ottawa, ON K1N 7B6
(613) 232-2436 Fax 233-7708

Wellington Staats, President
Claudette Fortin, Executive Director
A national native owned non-profit development organization. *Purpose*: To develop Indian arts and crafts industry; the promotion and development of viable native arts and crafts enterprises and industries. *Activities/programs*: Maintains a business referral and information service (BRS) answering inquiries from producers, distributors and other interested parties; sponsors exhibitions. *Publication*: Canadian Indian Artscraft, a national quarterly trade magazine. Library - maintains a collection of resource material including artists profiles, reference books and trade magazines; a series of video tapes entitled "NIACC Indian Arts and Crafts Film Series' available for viewing through a separate distribution company, titles available upon request. Founded 1975.

NATIONAL INDIAN EDUCATION FORUM
Box 1440
Morinville, AB T0G 2E4
(403) 939-3551

NATIONAL NATIVE ADVISORY COUNCIL ON ALCOHOL AND DRUG ABUSE
177 Nepean St., Suite 202
Ottawa, ON K2P 0B4
(613) 230-0402

NATIONAL NATIVE ASSOCIATION OF TREATMENT DIRECTORS
8989 MacLeod Trail S.W., Suite 410
Calgary, AB T2H 0M2
(403) 253-6232 Fax 252-9210
Betty Bastien, Executive Director

NATIONAL OFFICE FOR THE DEVELOPMENT OF INDIAN CULTURAL EDUCATION
222 Queen St., 5th Floor
Ottawa, Ontario K1P 5V9
(613) 232-5315

NATIVE COUNCIL OF CANADA
384 Bank St., 2nd Floor
Ottawa, ON K2P 1Y4
(613) 238-3511 Fax 230-6273
Dan Smith, President

NATIVE EMPLOYMENT SERVICES ASSOCIATION (NESA)
200 Markum Place
10235-124th St.
Edmonton, AB T5H 1P9
(800) 667-NESA; (403) 428-9350
Fax (403) 426-6650

NATIVE FISHING ASSOCIATION
202-1755 E. Hasting St.
Vancouver, BC V5L 1T1
(604) 255-5457 Fax 255-0955
David Barrett, Executive Director

NATIVE INDIAN/INUIT PHOTOGRAPHER'S ASSOCIATION
134 James St. S.
Hamilton, ON L8P 2Z4
(416) 529-7477 Fax 522-6713
Yvonne Maracle, Executive Director

NATIVE INVESTMENT & TRADE ASSOCIATION
6200 Comstock Rd.
Richmond, BC V7C 2X4
(604) 275-0307 (phone & fax)

NATIVE LAW CENTRE
University of Saskatchewan
150 Diefenbaker Centre
Saskatoon, SK S7K 3S9
 (306) 966-6189
 Don Purich, Director
Purpose: To provide a head start program for
people of native ancestry who wish to enter law
school; to research problems related to native legal rights, e.g. land claims; to provide a resource
to lawyers and researchers working in the area of
native law; and, to back up the courses in native
law taught in the College of Law , University of
Saskatchewan. *Activities*: Summer program of
legal study for native people; research. *Prizes*:
Harvey Bell Memorial Prize, $1,000 for a student
graduating from law school; Native Law Students
Association Writing Competition, $200 book prize;
book prize to student in summer program, $150.
Publication : Canadian Native Law Reporter , quarterly journal; books for sale. Library .

**NATIVE MENTAL HEALTH
ASSOCIATION OF CANADA**
Box 89
Shannonville, ON K0K 3A0
 (613) 966-0888
 Clare Clifton Brant, Chairperson
Purpose: To provide mental health care services
to Native peoples of Canada. *Activities*: Work-
shops; training programs; and information and
referral services.

NATIVE WOMEN'S ASSN. OF CANADA
251 Laurier Ave. West, Suite 600
Ottawa, ON K1P 5J6
 (613) 236-6057 Fax 235-4957

 Gail Stacey-Moore, Speaker
Goals: To enhance, promote and foster the social, econimic, cultural and political well-being of
First Nations and Metis women with First Nations
and Canadian societies. Awards granted. Founded
1974.

**NATIVE THEATRE SCHOOL
INDIGENOUS THEATRE CELEBRATION**
Association for Native Development in the
Performing and Visual Arts
27 Carlton St., Suite 208
Toronto, ON M5B 1L2
 (416) 977-2512

NUNASI CORPORATION
280 Albert St., Suite 902
Ottawa, ON K1A 5G8
 (613) 238-4981
 Pat Lyall, President

NUNAVUT CONSTITUTIONAL FORUM
63 Sparks St., Room 300
Ottawa, ON K1P 5A6
 (613) 594-0158
 John Amgoalik, President

OJIBWAY CULTURAL FOUNDATION
Box 278, West Bay Indian Reserve
Manitoulin, ON P0P 1G0
 (705) 377-4902 Fax 377-5460

OKALAKATIGET SOCIETY
P.O. Box 160
Nain, LB A0P 1L0
 (709) 922-2955
 Fran Williams, President

TAGRAMIUT NIPINGAT, INC.
185 Dorval Ave.
Dorval, PQ H9S 5J9
 (514) 631-1394
 George Kakayak, President

TRADITIONAL NATIVE HEALING SOCIETY
P.O. Box 1882
High Prairie, AB T0G 1E0
 (403) 523-4355
 Russell & Yvonne Miller, Contacts
Goals: To increase the awareness of the benefits
of Indian healing practices and to provide greater
access to Native healers for both Natives and non-
Natives. Founded 1986 by a Cree Medicine Man.

TUNGAVIK FEDERATION OF NUNAVUT
176 Gloucester St., 2nd Floor
Ottawa, ON K2P 0A6
 (613) 238-8181

TUNGGASUK CULTURAL INSTITUTE
P.O. Box 40
Nain, LB A0P 1L0
 (709) 922-2942
 Lucy Brennan, Director

UNITED NATIVE NATIONS
1682 West 7th Ave., Suite 300
Vancouver, BC V6J 4S6
 (604) 732-1201

**WORLD COUNCIL OF
INDIGENOUS PEOPLE**
555 King Edward Ave.
Ottawa, ON K1N 6N5
 (613) 230-9030 Fax 230-9340

ALBERTA

ATHABASCA NATIVE FRIENDSHIP CENTRE
Box 3207
ATHABASCA, AB T0G 0B0
(403) 675-4128

**BONNYVILLE CANADIAN
NATIVE FRIENDSHIP CENTRE**
Box 5399
BONNYVILLE, AB T9N 2G5
(403) 826-3374 Fax 826-2540
Karen "K.C." Collins, Executive Director

KEHEWIN CULTURAL EDUCATION CENTRE
Box 6218
BONNEYVILLE, AB T9N 2G8
(403) 826-3333 Fax 826-2355
Eva Fagnon, Director

OLDMAN RIVER CULTURAL CENTRE
Box 70
BROCKET, AB T0K 0H0
(403) 965-3939 Fax 965-3713
Brian Yellowhorn, Coordinator

ALBERTA FAMILY & SOCIAL SERVICES
Hillburst Professional Bldg.
203-301 14th St., N.W.
CALGARY, AB T2N 2A1 (403) 297-8435

CALGARY NATIVE FRIENDSHIP SOCIETY
140 - 2nd Ave. S.W.
CALGARY, AB T3E 6N7
(403) 264-1155 Fax 265-9675
Laverna McMaster, Executive Director

NATIVE AWARENESS CENTRE
One Pallister Sq., 125-9th St. S.E.
CALGARY, AB T2G 0T8
(403) 292-3900 Fax 292-2134

**PLAINS INDIAN CULTURAL
SURVIVAL SCHOOL**
1723 33 St. S.W.
CALGARY, AB T3C 1P4
(403) 246-5378

SARCEE CULTURAL PROGRAM
Box 135
CALGARY, AB T2W 3C4
(403) 238-2677 Fax 251-5871

NINASTAKO CULTURAL CENTRE
Box 1299
CARDSTON, AB T0K 0K0
(403) 737-3774 Fax 737-2336

INDIGENOUS PEOPLES RESOURCE ASSN.
221-1011 17th Ave., S.W.
EDMONTON, AB T0J 0A8
(403) 228-9683

TSUT'INA K'OSA
Sarcee Cultural Program
Box 135, 3700 Anderson Rd., S.W.
CALGARY, AB T2W 3C4
(403) 238-2677; FAX 251-5871
Jeanette Starlight, Director

NINASTAKO CULTURAL CENTRE
P.O. Box 1299
CARDSTON, AB T0K 0K0
(403) 737-3774 Fax 737-2336
C. Gloria Wells, Executive Director

**ABORIGINAL MULTI-MEDIA
SOCIETY OF ALBERTA (AMMSA)**
15001, 112 Ave.
EDMONTON, AB T5M 2V6
(403) 455-2700
Fred Didzena, President
Bert Crowfoot, General Manager
Newspaper: Windspeaker - Gary Gee, Editor

**ALBERTA INDIAN
ARTS & CRAFTS SOCIETY**
501, 10105-109th St.
EDMONTON, AB T5J 1M8
(403) 426-2048
Leonie Willier, President

**ALBERTA NATIVE COMMUNICATIONS
SOCIETY**
11427 Jasper Ave.
EDMONTON, AB

**ALBERTA NATIVE FRIENDSHIP CENTRE
ASSOCIATION**
201-11445 124th St., N.W.
EDMONTON T5M 0K4
(403) 455-7185 Fax 452-7076
Fred Campiou, President
Tony Callihoo, Coordinator

**ALBERTA NATIVE RIGHTS FOR NATIVE
WOMEN**
14211 - 130th Ave.
EDMONTON T5L 4K8
(403) 453-2808/454-8462

**ANDERSON NATIVE HERITAGE & CUL-
TURAL CENTRE**
10826-124th St. N.W.
EDMONTON, AB T5M 0H3
(403) 455-9317

CANADIAN NATIVE FRIENDSHIP CENTRE
11016 - 127th St.
EDMONTON, AB T5M 0T2
(403) 452-7811 Fax 452-8754
Gerald Cuthbert, Executive Director

INDIAN ASSOCIATION OF ALBERTA
11630 Kingsway Ave.
EDMONTON T5G 0X5
(403) 452-4330; Fax 451-0010
Roy Louis, President

NATIVE COUNCIL OF CANADA
9012-112th Ave.
P.O. Box 6084, Station "C"
EDMONTON, AB T5B 4K5
(403) 429-6003 Fax 428-6964
Doris Ronnenberg, President

NATIVE HERITAGE & CULTURAL CENTRE
10826-124th St.
EDMONTON, AB T5M 0H3
(403) 452-6296

**PRAIRIE TREATY NATIONS ALLIANCE
(PRAIRIE REGIONAL COUNCIL)**
11630 Kingsway Ave.
EDMONTON T5G 0X5
(403) 452-4330

EDSON FRIENDSHIP CENTRE
Box 6508
EDSON, AB T7E 1T9
(403) 723-5494
Sharron Johnstone, Executive Director

**NISTAWOYOU ASSOCIATION
FRIENDSHIP CENTRE**
8310 Manning Ave.
FORT McMURAY, AB T9H 1W1
(403) 743-8555 Fax 791-4041
Eleanor Grandjamb, Executive Director

GRAND CENTRE FRIENDSHIP CENTRE
Box 1978
GRAND CENTRE, AB T0A 1T0
(403) 594-7526 Fax 794-7360
Elaine Janvier, Executive Director

GRANDE PRAIRIE FRIENDSHIP CENTRE
10507 98th Ave.
GRANDE PRAIRIE, AB T8V 4L1
(403) 532-5722 Fax 539-5121
Irene Loutitt, Executive Director

HIGH LEVEL NATIVE FRIENDSHIP CENTRE
Box 1735
HIGH LEVEL, AB T0H 1Z0
(403) 926-3355 Fax 926-2850
Howard Walker, Executive Director

**HIGH PRAIRIE NATIVE FRIENDSHIP
CENTRE**
Box 1448
HIGH PRAIRIE, AB T0G 1E0
(403) 523-4511 Fax 523-5686
Loraine Duguay, Executive Director

**LAC LA BICHE CANADIAN
NATIVE FRIENDSHIP CENTRE**
Box 2338, 10210 - 101 St.
LAC LA BICHE, AB T0A 2C0
(403) 623-3249
Ray Mason, Executive Director

ALBERTA NATIVE WOMEN'S ASSN.
471 Columbia Blvd.
LETHBRIDGE, AB T1K 4T7
(403) 381-8845
Carrie Cotton, President

SIK-OOK-KOTOK CENTRE
10-535 - 13th St. N.
LETHBRIDGE, AB T1H 2S6
(403) 328-2414 Fax 327-0087
Mike Bruised Head, Executive Director

**LLOYDMINSTER NATIVE
FRIENDSHIP CENTRE**
5010 41st St.
LLOYDMINSTER, AB T9V 1B7
(403) 875-6558 Fax 825-6875
George Hougham, Executive Director

NAKODA INSTITUTE
Stoney Tribal Administration
P.O. Box 120
MORLEY, AB T0L 1N0
(403) 881-3770/3868/3949
Ian Getty, Director

ALBERTA NATIVE WOMEN'S ASSOCIATION
9423-84TH Ave.
PEACE RIVER, AB T8S 1G0
(403 624-6190
Carrie Cotton, President

SAGITAWA FRIENDSHIP CENTRE
Box 5083, 10108 - 100 Ave.
PEACE RIVER, AB T8S 1R7
(403) 624-2443 Fax 624-2728
Diane Pudolchuck, Executive Director

NAPI FRIENDSHIP ASSOCIATION
Box 657
PINCHER CREEK, AB T0K 1W0
(403) 627-4224 Fax 627-2916
Carol Specht, Executive Director

RED DEER NATIVE FRIENDSHIP SOCIETY
5217 Gaetz Ave.
RED DEER, AB T4N 4B4
(403) 340-0020 Fax 342-1610
Caroline Yellowhorn, Executive Director

ROCKY MOUNTAIN FRIENDSHIP SOCIETY
4917 - 52nd St., Box 1927
ROCKY MOUNTAIN HOUSE, AB T0M 1T0
(403) 845-2788 Fax 845-3093
Carrie Mason, Executive Director

SADDLE LAKE CULTURAL EDUCATION PROGRAM
Box 102
SADDLE LAKE, AB T0A 3T0
(403) 726-3829; F AX 726-3788
Fred Cardinal, Director

SLAVE LAKE NATIVE FRIENDSHIP CENTRE
416 - 6th Ave.
SLAVE LAKE, AB T0G 2A2
(403) 849-3039 Fax 849-7297
Peggy Roberts, Executive Director

MANNIWANIS NATIVE FRIENDSHIP CENTRE
Box 2519
ST. PAUL, AB T0A 3A0
(403) 645-4630
Bob Harison, Executive Director

INDIAN NEWS MEDIA
Box 120
STANDOFF, AB T0L 1Y0
(403) 653-3301
Gerri Manyfingers, Executive Director
Marie Smallface Marule, President
Blackfoot Radio Network; Bull Horn V ideo
Newspaper: Kainai News-Mary W easel Fat, Editor

VOICE OF ALBERTA NATIVE WOMEN'S SOCIETY
P.O. Box 87
STANDOFF, AB T0L 1Y0
(403) 737-3753/3939

INDIAN ASSOCIATION OF ALBERTA
P.O. Box 516
WINTERBURN, AB T0E 2N0
(403) 470-5751
Roy Louis, President
Purpose: To advance the social and economic welfare of the Treaty Indians of Alberta; to promote programs designed to serve the educational and cultural interests of the Native people's it represents; to work in conjunction with other Indian bands and/or chiefs and councils to work with with Federal, Provincial and Local Governments for the benefit of the Treaty Indians of Alberta. Founded 1944.

TREATY VOICE OF ALBERTA
WINTERBURN, AB T0E 2N0
(403) 487-4141
Women's Indian Association.

BRITISH COLUMBIA

NIMPKISH CULTURAL EDUCATION CENTRE
Box 210, Nimpkish First Nation
ALERT BAY, BC V0N 1A0
(604) 974-5591 Fax 974-5700

U'MISTA CULTURAL CENTRE
Box 253
ALERT BAY, BC V0N 1A0
(604) 974-5403 Fax 974-5466
Wendy Jakobsen, Administrator

BELLA COOLA-NUXALK EDUCATION AUTHORITY
P.O. Box 778
BELLA COOLA, BC V0T 1C0
(604) 799-5453/591 1
Stewart Clellamin, Coordinator

SAANICH CULTURAL EDUCATION CENTRE
Box 368, 7449 W . Saanich Rd.
BRENTWOOD, BC V0S 1A0
(604) 652-1811 Fax 652-6929
Philip Paul, Director

LAKE BABINE CULTURAL EDUCATION CENTRE
Box 879, Lake Babine First nation
BURNS LAKE, BC V0J 1E0
(604) 692-7555 Fax 692-7559

TANSI FRIENDSHIP CENTRE
P.O. Box 418
CHETWYND, BC V0C 1J0
(604) 788-2996 Fax 788-9545
Bev Davies, Executive Director

NAWICAN FRIENDSHIP CENTRE
1320 - 102 Ave., P.O. Box 593
DAWSON CREEK, BC V1G 4H4
(604) 782-5202
Keith Hall, Executive Director

COWICHAN CULTURAL EDUCATION CENTRE
Box 880, Cowichan First Nation
DUNCAN, BC V9L 3Y2
(604) 748-3196

VALLEY NATIVE FRIENDSHIP CENTRE SOCIETY
P.O. Box 1015
DUNCAN, BC V9L 3Y2
(604) 748-2242 Fax 748-2238
Debbie Williams, Executive Director

FORT NELSON-LIARD NATIVE FRIENDSHIP SOCIETY
P.O. Box 1266
FORT NELSON, BC V0C 1R0
(604) 774-2993 Fax 774-3730
Don Potkins, Executive Director

FORT ST. JOHN FRIENDSHIP SOCIETY
10208 - 95th Ave.
FORT ST. JOHN, BC V1J 1J2
(604) 785-8566 Fax 785-1507
Shirley Churchill, Executive Director

B.C. NATIVE WOMEN'S SOCIETY
345 Yellowhead Highway
KAMLOOPS, BC V2H 1H1
(604) 374-9412
Janet Gottfriedson, President

INTERIOR INDIAN FRIENDSHIP CENTRE
125 Palm St.
KAMLOOPS, BC V1J 8J7
(604) 376-1296 Fax 376-2275
Ruth Williams, Executive Director

SECWEPEMC CULTURAL EDUCATION SOCIETY
345 Yellowhead Highway
KAMLOOPS, BC V2H 1H1
(604) 828-9779
Muriel Sasakamoose, Executive Director

CENTRAL OKANAGAN INDIAN FRIENDSHIP CENTRE
442 Leon Ave.
KELOWNA, BC V1Y 6J3
(604) 763-4905 Fax 861-5514
Tillie Gof fic, Executive Director

LILLOOET FRIENDSHIP CENTRE
P.O. Box 1270, 357 Main St.
LILLOOET, BC V0K 1V0
(604) 256-4146 Fax 256-7928
Susan James, Executive Director

ED JONES CULTURAL/EDUCATION CENTRE
Box 189
MASSET, BC V0T 1Z0
(604) 626-5128
John Enrico, Director

CONAYT FRIENDSHIP CENTRE
2067 Quilchena Ave., Box 1989
MERRITT, BC V0K 2B0
(604) 378-5107 Fax 378-6676
Ross Albert, Executive Director

NATIVE WOMEN'S ASSOCIATION OF CANADA - WEST REGION
Box 213
MERRITT, BC V0K 2V0
(604) 378-5969
Sharon McIvor, Director

MISSION INDIAN FRIENDSHIP CENTRE
33150 A First Ave.
MISSION, BC V2V 1G4
(604) 826-1281 Fax 826-4056
Christina Cook, Executive Director

TS'ZIL BOARD OF EDUCATION
P.O. Box 174
MOUNT CURRIE, BC V0N 2K0
(604) 894-6335/6517
Bernita Saul, Administrator

TILLICUM HAUS SOCIETY
602 Haliburton St.
NANAIMO, BC V9R 4W5
(604) 753-8291 Fax 753-6560
Grace Nielson, Executive Director

OKANAGAN INDIAN EDUCATIONAL RESOURCES SOCIETY
257 Brunswick St.
PENICTON, BC V2A 5P9
(604) 493-7181
Jeanette Armstrong, Director

PORT ALBERNI FRIENDSHIP CENTRE
3555 Fourth Ave., Box 23
PORT ALBERNI, BC V9Y 4C3
(604) 723-8281 Fax 723-1877
Wally Samuel, Executive Director

SILIAMMON CULTURAL CENTRE
R.R. 2, Sliammon Rd.
POWELL RIVER, BC V8A 4Z4
   (604) 483-9317 Fax 483-9769
   Elizabeth Harry, Education Coordinator

**PRINCE GEORGE NATIVE
FRIENDSHIP CENTRE**
144 George St.
PRINCE GEORGE, BC V2L 1P9
   (604) 564-3568 Fax 563-0924
   Dan George, Executive Director

**FRIENDSHIP HOUSE ASSOCIATION
OF PRINCE RUPERT**
P.O. Box 512
PRINCE RUPERT, BC V8J 3R5
   (604) 627-1717
   Fred Anderson, Executive Director

**QUESNEL TILLICUM SOCIETY
FRIENDSHIP CENTRE**
319 N. Fraser Dr.
QUESNEL, BC V2J 1Y8
   (604) 992-8347 Fax 992-5708
   Doug Sanderson, Executive Director

**COQUALEETZA EDUCATION
TRAINING CENTRE**
7201 Vedder Rd., Box 370
SARDIS, BC V2R 1A7
   (604) 858-9431 Fax 858-7692
   Shirley D. Leon, Manager

DZEL K'ANT FRIENDSHIP CENTRE
P.O. Box 2920
SMITHERS, BC V0J 2N0
   (604) 847-3525 Fax 847-3600
   Von Sarac, Acting Executive Director

KERMODE FRIENDSHIP SOCIETY
3313 Kalum St.
TERRACE, BC V8G 2N7
   (604) 635-4906 Fax 635-3013
   Sadie Parnell, Executive Director

ALLIED INDIAN & METIS SOCIETY
2716 Clark Dr.
VANCOUVER, BC V5N 3H6
   (604) 874-9610 Fax 876-1858
   Marge White, Executive Director

**B.C. ABORIGIAL PEOPLES'
FISHERIES COMMISSION**
990 Homer St., Suite 204
VANCOUVER, BC V6B 2W7
   (604) 682-4897 Fax 682-3550
   Ken Malloway, Chairperson

CANADIAN INDIAN VOICE SOCIETY
429 E. 6th St., North
VANCOUVER, BC V7L 1P8

FIRST NATIONS CONGRESS OF B.C.
990 Homer St., Suite 403
VANCOUVER, BC V6B 2W7
   (604) 682-8516 Fax 682-8057
   Bill Wilson, Vice-Chief

INDIAN ARTS & CRAFTS SOCIETY OF B.C.
540 Burrard St., Suite 505
VANCOUVER, BC V6C 2K1
   (604) 682-8988
   Noel C. Derriksan, President

**INDIAN HOMEMAKERS ASSN.
OF BRITISH COLUMBIA**
102 - 423 W. Broadway
VANCOUVER, BC V5Y 1R4
   (604) 876-4929

NATIVE BROTHERHOOD OF B.C.
#200 - 1755 E. Hastings
VANCOUVER, BC V5L 1T1
   (604) 255-3137 Fax 251-7107
   Robert Clifton, President

**NATIVE COMMUNICATIONS
SOCIETY OF B.C.**
1161 W. Georgia St.
VANCOUVER, BC V6E 3H4
   (604) 684-7375 Fax 684-5375
   Emma Williams, President
   Tim Isaac, Managing Editor
Newspaper: Kahtou.

**UNION OF BRITISH COLUMBIA
INDIAN CHIEFS**
73 Water St., Suite 200
VANCOUVER, BC V6B 1A1
   (403) 684-0231 Fax 684-5726
   Saul Terry, President

UNITED NATIVE NATIONS
33 East Broadway
VANCOUVER, BC V5T 1V4
   (604) 879-2420 Fax 879-3778
   Ron George, President
   Ernie Crey, Vice President

VANCOUVER INDIAN CENTRE SOCIETY
1607 E. Hastings St.
VANCOUVER, BC V5L 1S7
   (604) 251-4844 Fax 251-1986
   Art Paul, Executive Director

**STONEY CREEK ELDERS CULTURAL
SOCIETY**
Siye 12, Comp. 15, R.R. 1
VANDERHOOF, BC V0J 3A0
   (604) 567-4314 Fax 567-4215
   Winnie Bernier, Sec.-Treasurer

ALLIED INDIAN & METIS SOCIETY
R.R. #7, Comp. 24, Siye 11
VERNON, BC V1T 7Z3
   (604) 549-7413
   Dave Parker, Executive Director

UNITED NATIVE FRIENDSHIP CENTRE
2902 - 29th Ave.
VERNON, BC V1T 5E6
   (604) 542-1247 Fax 542-3707
   Bertha Phelan, Executive Director

**B.C. ASSN. OF INDIAN
FRIENDSHIP CENTRES**
307 - 733 Johnson St,
VICTORIA, BC V8W 1M3
   (604) 380-1447 Fax 380-7381
   Marie Anderson, President
   Florence Wylie, Coordinator

VICTORIA NATIVE FRIENDSHIP CENTRE
533 Yates St., Penthouse
VICTORIA, BC V8W 1K7
   (604) 384-3211 Fax 384-1586
   Edmond Constantineau, Executive Director

HEILTSUK CULTURAL EDUCATION CENTRE
Box 880
WAGLISLA, BC V0T 1Z0

   (604) 957-2381/2626 Fax 957-2544
   Jennifer Carpenter, Program Manager

CARIBOO FRIENDSHIP SOCIETY
99 3rd Ave. S.
WILLIAMS LAKE, BC V2G 1J1
   (604) 398-6831 Fax 398-6115
   Gail Madrigga, Executive Director

LABRADOR

LABRADOR FRIENDSHIP CENTRE
P.O. Box 767, Station "B"
GOOSE BAY, LB A0P 1E0
   (709) 896-8302
   Renne Simms, Executive Director

LABRADOR METIS ASSOCIATION
P.O. Box 254, Station "C"
GOOSE BAY, LB A0P 1E0
   (709) 896-2682
   Reg Michelin, President
   Ruby Durno, Vice-President

LABRADOR NATIVE FRIENDSHIP CENTRE
P.O. Box 767, Station "B"
HAPPY VALLEY, LB A0P 1E0
   (709) 896-8302 Fax 896-2812
   Rennie Simms, Executive Director

LABRADOR NATIVE WOMEN'S ASSN.
Box 1101, Station "B"
HAPPY VALLEY, LB A0P 1M0
   (709) 896-8420
   Annette Blake, President

LABRADOR CULTURAL INSTITUTE
NAIN, LB A0P 1L0
   (709) 922-2941

LABRADOR INUIT ASSOCIATION
P.O. Box 70
NAIN, LB A0P 1L0
   (709) 922-2942; FAX 922-2931
   Joe Dicker, President

OKALAKATIGET SOCIETY
P.O. Box 160
NAIN, LB A0P 1L0
   (709) 922-2955
   Fran Williams, President

TORNGUSOK CULTURAL INSTITUTE
P.O. Box 40
NAIN, LB A0P 1L0
   (709) 922-2139 Fax 922-2931
   Gary Baikie, Director

LABRADOR NATIVE WOMEN'S ASSN.
P.O. Box 10
NORTH WEST RIVER, LB A0P 1M0
   (709) 497-8375/8298
   Beatrice Watts, President

NASKAPI-MONTAGNAIS INNU ASSN.
NORTHWEST RIVER, LB A0P 1M0
   (709) 497-8392
   Greg Penashue, President

NASKAPI-MONTAGNAIS INNU ASSN.
P.O. Box 119
SHESHATSIU, LB A0P 1M0
   (709) 497-8353
   Greg Penashue, President

MANITOBA

BRANDON FRIENDSHIP CENTRE
303 - 9th St.
BRANDON, MB R7A 4A8
(204) 727-1407
Louise Phaneuf-Miron, Executive Director

DAUPHIN FRIENDSHIP CENTRE
210 First Ave. NE
DAUPHIN, MB R7A 1A7
(204) 638-5707
Stan Guiboche, Executive Director

WEST REGION TRIBAL COUNCIL
Indian Cultural Education Program
21-4th Ave., N.W.
DAUPHIN, MB R7N 1H9
(204) 638-8225 F AX 638-8062
Wally Swain, Program Head

**FLIN FLON INDIAN & METIS
FRIENDSHIP CENTRE**
57 Church St., Box 188
FLIN FLON, MB R8A 1M7
(204) 687-3900
Marcie Johnson, Executive Director

LYNN LAKE FRIENDSHIP CENTRE
625 Gordon Ave., Box 460
LYNN LAKE, MB R0B 0W0
(204) 356-2445 Fax 356-8223
Vicki Stoneman, Executive Director

SAGKEENG CULTURAL CENTRE, INC.
Box 749
PINE FALLS, MB R0E 1M0
(204) 367-8740 Fax 943-1482
Art Boubard, Director

PORTAGE FRIENDSHIP CENTRE
21 Royal Rd. S., Box 1 118
PORTAGE LA PRAIRIE, MB R1N 3C5
(204) 239-6333
Richard Chaske, Executive Director

KA-WAWIYAK FRIENDSHIP CENTRE
Box 74
POWERVIEW, MB R0E 1P0
(204) 367-2892
Rhonda Houston, Executive Director

NATIVE WOMEN'S ASSN. OF MANITOBA
P.O. Box 177
RIVERTON, MB R0C 2R0
(204) 373-2396/378-2460

**RIVERTON & DISTRICT
FRIENDSHIP CENTRE**
P.O. Box 359
RIVERTON, MB R0C 2R0
(204) 378-2927
Marlane Monkman, Executive Director

**INDIAN COUNCIL OF FIRST
NATIONS OF MANITOBA, INC.**
Box 13, Group 10, R.R. #2
SAINT ANNE, MB R0A 1R0
(204) 422-5193 Fax 422-8860
Andrew Kirkness, Grand Chief

BROKENHEAD CULTURAL CENTRE
SCANTERBURY, MB R0E 1W0
(204) 766-2494 F AX 766-2270
Harvey Olson, Director

INDIAN & METIS FRIENDSHIP CENTRE
347 Phyllis St.
SELKIRK, MB R1A 2J5
(204) 482-5896
Elsie Bear, Executive Directort

SELKIRK FRIENDSHIP CENTRE
425 Eveline St.
SELKIRK, MB R1A 2J5
(204) 482-7525
Jim Sinclair, Executive Director

**SWAN RIVER INDIAN &
METIS FRIENDSHIP CENTRE**
1413 Main St., Box 1448
SWAN RIVER, MB R0L 1Z0
(204) 734-9301 Fax 734-3090
Elbert Chartrand, Executive Director

**INDIAN COUNCIL OF FIRST
NATIONS OF MANITOBA, INC.**
P.O. Box 2857
THE PAS, MB R9A 1M6
(204) 623-7227 Fax 623-4041

MANITOBA METIS WOMEN'S ALLIANCE
Box 1503
THE PAS, MB R9A 1L4
(204) 623-7881

THE PAS FRIENDSHIP CENTRE
Box 2638, 81 Edwards Ave.
THE PAS, MB R9A 1M3
(204) 623-6459
Judy Elaschuk, Executive Director

MA-MOW-WE-TAK FRIENDSHIP CENTRE
122 Hemlock Crescent
THOMPSON, MB R8N 0R6
(204) 778-7337 Fax 677-3195
Larry Soldier, Executive Director
Cathy V. Menard, Program Coordinator
A social service organization existing to administer and implement programs to meet the nedsof native people either migrating to or living in urban areas. *Special programs* : Counseling and referral service; social and recreational programs; cultural awareness and community development. Native Resource Library: consisting of audio/visual and reading material. *Publication* : Interagency Quarterly Newsletter. Founded 1976.

MANITOBA KEEWATINOWI OKIMAKANAK
3 Station Rd.
THOMPSON, MB R8N 0N3
(204) 778-4431 Fax 778-7655
Chief Robert W avey, Chairperson

THE ABORIGINAL WOMEN OF MANITOBA
78 Grey Friars
WINNIPEG, MB R3T 3J5
(204) 269-0033
Pauline Busch, President

ASSEMBLY OF MANITOBA CHIEFS
400-286 Smith St.
WINNPEG, MB R3C 1K4
(204) 956-0610 Fax 956-2109
Ovide Mercredi, V ice-Chief

FIRST NATIONS CONFEDERACY
333 Garry St., 2nd Floor
WINNIPEG, MB R3B 2G7
(204) 944-8245
075-5238 Telex
Chief Ken Courchene, Chairperson

FOUR NATIONS CONFEDERACY
500 - 275 Portage Ave.
WINNIPEG, MB R3B 2B3
(204) 944-8245

INDIAN & METIS FRIENDSHIP CENTRE
239 Magnus Ave.
WINNIPEG, MB R2W 2B6
(204) 586-8441
Stirling Ranville, Executive Director

INDIAN CRAFTS & ARTS MANITOBA, INC.
348 Hargrave St.
WINNIPEG, MB R3B 2J9
(204) 944-1469
Pat Bruderer, President

**INDIGENOUS WOMEN'S
COLLECTIVE OF MANITOBA, INC.**
120-388 Donald St.
WINNIPEG, MB R2B 2J4
(204) 944-8709/10 F AX 949-1336
Winnie Greisbretch, President

**MANITOBA ABORIGINAL
RESOURCE ASSOCIATION**
286 Smith St., 5th Floor
WINNIPEG, MB R3C 1K4
(204) 947-1647 Fax 942-3687

**MANITOBA ASSOCIATION
OF FRIENDSHIP CENTRES**
604 - 213 Notre Dame Ave.
WINNIPEG, MB R3B 1N3
(204) 943-8082 Fax 983-8674
David Chartrand, President
Grace Buhr, Coordinator

**MANITOBA INDIAN CULTURAL
EDUCATION CENTRE**
119 Sutherland Ave.
WINNIPEG, MB R2W 3C9
(204) 942-0228 Fax 947-6564
Dennis Daniels, Executive Director

MANITOBA METIS FEDERATION
211 Portage Ave., Room 100
WINNIPEG, MB R3B 2A2
(204) 956-2070

NATIVE WOMEN'S TRANSITION CENTRE
730 Alexander Ave.
WINNIPEG, MB R3E 1H9
(204) 783-5237

**SOUTHEAST RESOURCE
DEVELOPMENT COUNCIL**
201-511 Ellice Ave.
WINNIPEG, MB R3B 1Y8
(204) 477-6050
Phil Fontaine, V ice-Chief

WINNIPEG INDIAN COUNCIL
650 Burrows Ave.
WINNIPEG, MB R2W 2A8
(204) 586-8561

WINNIPEGOSIS FRIENDSHIP CENTRE
P.O. Box 278
WINNIPEGOSIS, MB R0L 2G0
(204) 367-8820

NEW BRUNSWICK

CULTURAL/EDUCATIONAL CENTRE
Pabineau Indian Band
R.R. #5, Box 1, Site 26
BATHURST, NB E2A 3Y8
(506) 548-9211
Chief Benoit Paul, Director

KITIKMEOT INUIT ASSOCIATION
P.O. Box 88
CAMBRIDGE BAY, N.W.T. X0E 0C0
(403) 983-2458
(403) 983-2158 FAX
John Maksagak, President

COUNCIL OF ELDERS
R.R. #9
FREDERICTON, NB E3B 4X9
(506) 450-6664
Wallace Labillois, Chairperson

EDUCATION ASSISTANCE PROGRAM
New Brunswick Aboriginal Peoples Council
320 St. Mary's St.
FREERICTON, NB E3A 2S4
(506) 458-8422 Fax 450-3749

**FOUR WINDS NATIVE
FRIENDSHIP CENTRE**
173 King St.
FREDERICTON, NB E3B 1C8
(506) 459-5283

**NEW BRUNSWICK ABORIGINAL
PEOPLES COUNCIL**
320 St. Mary's St.
FREDERICTON, NB E3A 2S4
(506) 458-8422/3 Fax 450-3749
Phil Fraser, President
Raymond Gould, Vice President

**NEW BRUNSWICK INDIAN
ARTS & CRAFTS ASSOCIATION**
212 Queen St., Suite 402
FREDERICTON, NB E3V 1A7
(506) 459-7312
David Paul, President

**NEW BRUNSWICK NATIVE
INDIAN WOMEN'S COUNCIL**
65 Brunswick St., Room 258
FREDERICTON, NB E3B 1G5
(506) 458-1114 Fax 453-1723
Carol Wortman, President

UNION OF NEW BRUNSWICK INDIANS
35 Dedam St.
FREDERICTON, NB E3A 2V2
(506) 458-9444 Fax 458-2850
Ronald Perley, President

**ASSEMBLY OF FIRST NATIONS-
ATLANTIC REGION**
P.O. Box 1587
WOODSTOCK, NB E0J 2B0
(506) 328-3303 FAX 328-2420
Leonard Tomah, Vice-Chief

NEWFOUNDLAND

FEDERATION - NEWFOUNDLAND INDIANS
BENOIT'S COVE, NF A0L 1A0
(709) 789-2797
Gerard Webb, President
Calvin Francis, Vice-President

**MI'KMAW ARTS & CRAFTS
NEWFOUNDLAND CORPORATION**
CONNE RIVER, NF A0H 1J0
(709) 882-2293
Marilyn John, President

COUNCIL OF THE CONNE RIVER MICMACS
Conne River Reserve, Micmac Territory
CONNE RIVER, NF A0H 1J0
(709) 882-2470 Fax 882-2292
Chief Marilyn John, Contact

LABRADOR METIS ASSOCIATION
Box 599, Station "B"
GOOSEBAY, NF A0P 1E0
(709) 896-5112

LABRADOR FRIENDSHIP CENTRE
Box 767, Station "B"
HAPPY VALLEY-GOOSE BAY, NF A0P 1E0
(709) 896-8302 Fax 896-2812

LABRADOR NATIVE WOMEN'S ASSN.
Box 1101, Station "B"
HAPPY VALLEY, NF A0P 1E0

LABRADOR CULTURAL INSTITUTE
NAIN, NF A0P 1L0
(709) 922-2139

NEWFOUNDLAND INDIAN GOVERNMENT
Box 375
ST. GEORGE'S A0N 1Z0
(709) 647-3733
Canadian Native Association.

LABRADOR INUIT ASSOCIATION
302-95 Lemarchant
ST. JOHN'S, NF A1C 2H1
(709) 754-2587 Fax 754-2364

**NATIVE PEOPLE'S SUPPORT GROUP
OF NEWFOUNDLAND & LABRADOR**
Box 582, Station "C"
ST. JOHN'S, NF A1C 5K8

ST. JOHN'S NATIVE FRIENDSHIP CENTRE
Box 2414, Station "C"
ST. JOHN'S, NF A1C 6E7
(709) 726-5902 Fax 754-2364
Myrtle Blandford, Executive Director

NORTHWEST TERRITORY

INUIT CULTURAL INSTITUTE
Bag 2000
ARVIAT, NWT X0E 0E0
(403) 857-2803 Fax 857-2740
Roy Goose, Executive Director

KITIKMEOT INUIT ASSOCIATION
P.O. Box 88
CAMBRIDGE BAY, NWT X0E 0C0
(403) 983-2458 Fax 983-2158
John Maksagak, President

ZHAHTI KOE FRIENDSHIP CENTRE
FORT PROVIDENCE, NWT X0E 0Y0
(403) 699-3801
Esther Lazore, Executive Director

RAE EDZO FRIENDSHIP CENTRE
Box 95
FORT RAE, NWT X0C 0G0
(403) 392-6000 Fax 392-6093
Bertha Rabesca, Director

DEH CHO SOCIETY
Box 470
FORT SIMPSON, NWT X0E 0N0
(403) 695-2577 Fax 695-2141
Bertha Norwegian, Executive Director

UNCLE GABE'S FRIENDSHIP CENTRE
Box 957
FORT SMITH, NWT X0E 0P0
(403) 872-3013 Fax 872-5313
Roger Rawlyk, Executive Director

BAFFIN REGION INUIT ASSOCIATION
P.O. Box 219
FROBISHER BAY, NWT X0A 0H0
(819) 979-5391

SOARING EAGLE FRIENDSHIP CENTRE
Box 396
HAY RIVER, NWT X0E 0R0
(403) 874-6581 Fax 874-3362
Abby Crook, Executive Director

**COMMITTEE FOR ABORIGINAL
PEOPLE'S ENTITLEMENT (COPE)**
Box 2000
INUVIK, NWT X0E 0T0
(403) 979-3510
Inuit Association.

INGAMO HALL FRIENDSHIP CENTRE
Box 1293
INUVIK, NWT X0E 0P0
(403) 979-2166 Fax 979-2873
Shirley Kisoun, Executive Director

BAFFIN REGIONAL INUIT ASSOCIATION
Box 219
IQALUIT, NWT X0A 0H0
(819) 979-5301

BAFFIN REGIONAL INUIT ASSOCIATION
Box 219
PROBISHER BAY, NWT X0L 0G0
(819) 979-5391
(819) 979-4325 FAX
Louis Tapardjuk, President

RAE EDZO FRIENDSHIP CENTRE
Box 35
RAE, NWT X0E 0Y0
(403) 392-6000 Fax 392-6093
Bertha Rabesca, Executive Director

KEEWATIN INUIT ASSOCIATION
RANKLIN INLET, NWT X0C 0G0
(819) 645-2805 Fax 645-2885
Jack Anawak, President

KEEWATIN WILDLIFE FEDERATION
RANKLIN INLET, NWT X0C 0G0
(819) 979-5301

SAPPUJJIJIT FRIENDSHIP CENTRE
Box 58
RANKLIN INLET, NWT X0C 0G0

(403) 645-2600 Fax 645-2538
Cecilia Papak, Executive Director

DENE CULTURAL INSTITUTE
Box 207
YELLOWKNIFE, NWT X1A 2N2
(403) 873-6617 Fax 873-3867
Joanne Barnaby, Executive Director

METIS ASSOCIATION OF THE N.W.T.
P.O. Box 1375
YELLOWKNIFE, NWT X1A 2P1
(403) 873-3505
Gary Bohnet, President
David Krutko, Vice-President
Gordon Lennie, Vice-President

NATIVE WOMEN'S ASSOCIATION OF N.W.T.
P.O. Box 2321
YELLOWKNIFE, NWT X1A 2P7
(403) 873-5509
Helen Hudson-MacDonald, President

N.W.T. COUNCIL OF FRIENDSHIP CENTRES
Box 2667
YELLOWKNIFE, NWT X1A 2P9
(403) 873-2864 Fax 873-5185
Tom Eagle, President

N.W.T. NATIVE ARTS & CRAFTS SOCIETY
Box 2765
YELLOWKNIFE, NWT X1A 2R1
(403) 920-2854
Sonny McDonald, President

TREE OF PEACE FRIENDSHIP CENTRE
Box 2667
YELLOWKNIFE, NWT X1A 2P9
(403) 873-2864 Fax 873-5185
Tom Eagle, Executive Director

NOVA SCOTIA

MICMAC NATIVE FRIENDSHIP CENTRE
2158 Gottingen St.
HALIFAX, NS B3K 3B4
(902) 420-1576 Fax 423-6130
Gordon V. King, Executive Director
Purpose: To provide Native Indians with an education and occupational training in computer technology and office automation. A licensed trade school granting a Certificate to all students who graduate. Small library.

UNION OF NOVA SCOTIA INDIANS
Box 100
SHUBENACADIE, NS B0N 2H0
(902) 758-2048/3856

MICMAC ASSOCIATION OF CULTURAL STUDIES
Box 961
SYDNEY, NS B1P 6J4
(902) 539-8037 Fax 539-6645
Peter Christmas, Executive Director

NATIVE COMMUNICATIONS SOCIETY PF NOVA SCOTIA
Box 344
SYDNEY, NS B1P 6H2
(902) 539-0045 Fax 564-0430

UNION OF NOVA SCOTIA INDIANS
P.O. Box 961
SYDNEY, N.S. B1P 6J4
(902) 539-4107
Alex Christmas, President

NATIVE COUNCIL OF NOVA SCOTIA
P.O. Box 1320, Abenaki Rd.
TRURO, NS B2N 5N2
(902) 895-1523 Fax 895-0024
Dwight Dorey, President
Florence Walsh, Sec/Treas.

NOVA SCOTIA MICMAC ARTS & CRAFTS SOCIETY
Box 978
TRURO, NS B2N 5G7
(902) 892-7128

NOVA SCOTIA NATIVE WOMEN'S ASSN.
P.O. Box 805
TRURO, NS B2N 5E8
(902) 893-7402
Clara Gloade, President

SOCIETY OF CANADIAN ARTISTS OF NATIVE ANCESTRY
Box 848
WOLFVILLE, NS B0P 1X0
Leonard Paul, President

ONTARIO

ATIKOKAN NATIVE FRIENDSHIP CENTRE
307 - 309 Main St., Box 961
ATIKOKAN, ON P0T 1C0
(807) 597-1213 Fax 597-1520
Roberta McMahon, Executive Director
Personnel: Roberta McMahon, Community Development Worker; Ange Sponchia, Youth Programmer. Purpose: To help create a better quality of life for urban Natives. Special programs: Youth programs; craft teachings, Powwow's; traditional teachings; fundraising activities. Founded 1983.

BARRIE NATIVE FRIENDSHIP CENTRE
202-105 Dunlop St. E.
BARRIE, ON L4M 1A6
(705) 721-7689
Ken Geroux, Director

PINE TREE NATIVE CENTRE OF BRANT
344 Colborne St.
BRANTFORD, ON N3S 3N3
(519) 752-5132
Nancy Hill, President

WOODLAND INDIAN CULTURAL CENTRE
Box 1506, 184 Mohawk St.
BRANTFORD, ON N3T 5V6
(519) 759-2650 Fax 759-8912
Joanna Bedard, Executive Director

ININEW FRIENDSHIP CENTRE
Box 1499, 190 Third Ave.
COCHRANE, ON P0L 1C0
(705) 272-4497 Fax 272-6097
Howard Restoule, Executive Director

AKWESASNE COMMUNICATIONS SOCIETY
Box 372
CORNWALL, ON K6H 5T1
(613) 938-1113

DRYDEN NATIVE FRIENDSHIP CENTRE
53 Arthur St.
DRYDEN, ON P8N 1J7
(807) 223-4180
Irene St. Goddard, Executive Director

FORT ERIE NATIVE FRIENDSHIP CENTRE
796 Buffalo Rd.
FORT ERIE, ON L2A 5H2
(416) 871-8931 Fax 871-9655
Wayne Hill, Executive Director

UNITED NATIVE FRIENDSHIP CENTRE
Box 752
FORT FRANCIS, ON P9A 3N1
(807) 274-8541 Fax 274-4110
Frank Bruyere, Executive Director

THUNDERBIRD FRIENDSHIP CENTRE
Box 430, 301 Beamish Ave. W.
GERALDTON, ON P0T 1M0
(807) 854-1060 Fax 854-0861
Terry Dowhank, Executive Director

GUELPH NATIVE FREINDSHIP CENTRE
Unit 52, 180 Marksam Rd.
GUELPH, ON N1H 8GB
(519) 763-5935 Fax 767-0322
Sherman Maness, Vice-President

HAMILTON REGIONAL INDIAN CENTRE
183 James St. South
HAMILTON, ON L8P 3A8
(416) 546-1446 Fax 546-1449
Cathy Staats, Executive Director

NORTHERN ONTARIO INDIAN HOMEMAKERS ASSOCIATION
General Delivery
HERON BAY, ON P0T 1R0
(807) 229-1486
Indian Women's Association.

KAPUSKASING INDIAN FRIENDSHIP CENTRE
Box 26
KAPUSKASING, ON P5N 1A8
(705) 337-1935
Dorothy Wynne, Executive Director

GRAND COUNCIL TREATY No. 3
Box 1720
KENORA, ON P7N 3X7
(807) 548-4215 Fax 548-5041
Robin Greene, Grand Chief

LAKE OF THE WODS OJIBWAY CULTURAL CENTRE
Box 1720
KENORA, ON P9N 3X7
(807) 548-5744 Fax 548-5041
Joseph Tom, Director

NE-CHEE FRIENDSHIP CENTRE
Box 241
KENORA, ON P9N 3X3
(807) 468-5440 Fax 468-5340
Joe Seymour, Executive Director

GEEWAEDIN FRIENDSHIP CENTRE, INC.
Box 1359
KIRKLAND, ON P2N 3P2
(705) 567-6737
Eva Smith, Contact

**ASSOCIATION OF IROQUOIS
& ALLIED INDIANS**
466 Ha ilton Rd. East
LONDON, ON N5Z 1R9
(519) 434-2761 F AX 679-1653
Harry Dixtator, President

N'AMERIND FRIENDSHIP CENTRE
260 Colborne St.
LONDON, ON N6B 2S6
(519) 672-0131 Fax 672-0717
Rossalyn McCoy-Mestes, Executive Director

OJIBWE CULTURAL FOUNDATION
P.O. Box 278
West Bay Indian Reserve
MANITOULIN, ON P0P 1G0
(705) 377-4902 Fax 377-5460
Mary Lou Fox, Director

**GEORGIAN BAY NATIVE
FRIENDSHIP CENTRE**
366 Midland Ave.
MIDLAND, ON L4R 3K7
(705) 523-5589
Fred Jackson, Executive Director

MOOSONEE NATIVE FRIENDSHIP CENTRE
Box 478
MOOSONEE, ON P0L 1Y0
(705) 336-2808
Bill Morrison, Executive Director

NIAGARA REGIONAL NATIVE CENTRE
RR #4, Queenston & Taylor Rd.
NIAGARA-ON-THE-LAKE, ON L0S 1H0
(416) 688-6484
Vince Hill, Executive Director

NORTH BAY INDIAN FRIENDSHIP CENTRE
980 Cassells St.
NORTH BAY, ON P1B 4A6
(705) 472-2811
Bill Butler, Executive Director

ASSEMBLY OF FIRST NATIONS-ALBERTA
47 Clarence St., Suite 300
OTTAWA, ON K1N 9K1
(613) 236-0673 F AX 238-5780
Lawrence Courtrielle, V ice-Chief

INUIT DEVELOPMENT CORPORA TION
280 Albert St., Suite 902
OTTAWA, ON K1P 5G8
(613) 238-4981

NATIONAL ABORIGINAL YOUTH COUNCIL
120-1 Laval St.
OTTAWA, ON K1L 7Z4
(613) 741-7488
Janet August, Vice-President

ODAWA NATIVE FRIENDSHIP CENTRE
396 Maclaren St.
OTTAWA, ON K2P 0M8
(613) 238-8591 Fax 238-6106
Jim Eagle, Executive Director

TUNGAVIK FEDERATION OF NUNAVUT
130 Slater St., Suite 1200
OTTAWA, ON K1P 6E2
(613) 238-1096
Donat Milortuk, President

PARRY SOUND FRIENDSHIP CENTRE
13 Bowes St.
PARRY SOUND, ON 92A 2K7

(705) 746-5970
Vera Pawis-Tabobondung, Executive Director

**ONTARIO METIS &
NON-STATUS INDIAN ASSN.**
5385 Yonge St., Suite 30
PELLETIER-WILLOWDALE, ON M2N 5R7
(416) 226-2890

RED LAKE INDIAN FRIENDSHIP CENTRE
Box 244
RED LAKE, ON P0V 2M0
(807) 727-2847
Donna Prest, Executive Director

ONTARIO METIS & ABORIGINAL ASSN.
158 Sackville Rd.
SAULT STE. MARIE, ON P6B 4T6
(800) 461-5112
(705) 949-5161 Fax 949-3561
Olaff Bjornaa, President
Henry Wetelainen, V ice-President

**SAULT STE. MARIE INDIAN
FRIENDSHIP CENTRE**
29 Wellington St.
SAULT STE. MARIE, ON P6A 2K9
(705) 256-5634
Mary Desmoulin, Executive Director

NISHNAWBE-GAMIK FRIENDSHIP CENTRE
Box 1299, 52 King St.
SIOUX LOOKOUT, ON P0V 2T0
(807) 737-1903 Fax 737-1805
Laura Wynn, Executive Director

**WAWATAY NATIVE
COMMUNICATIONS SOCIETY**
Box 1180, 16 Fifth Ave.
SIOUX LOOKOUT, ON P0V 2T0
(807) 737-2951 Fax 737-3224

**N'SWAKAMOK NATIVE
FRIENDSHIP CENTRE**
110 Elm St.
SUDBURY, ON P3C 1T5
(705) 674-2128
Marie Meawasige, Executive Director
Established to help Native people to help
themselves. Founded 1972.

ONTARIO NATIVE WOMEN'S ASSOCIATION
115 N. May St.
THUNDER BAY, ON P7C 3N8
(807) 623-3442 F AX 623-1104
Carol Nobigan, President

**THUNDER BAY INDIAN
FRIENDSHIP CENTRE**
401 N. Cumberland St.
THUNDER BAY, ON P7A 4P7
(807) 345-5840 Fax 344-8945
Ann Cox, Executive Director

OJIBWAY & CREE CULTURAL CENTRE
152 Third Ave.
TIMMINS, ON P4N 1C6
(705) 267-7911 Fax 267-4988
Esther Wesley, Director
Purpose: To encourage and support Native
People's involvement in the development of self-
determination of the Nishnawbe-Aski Nation; to
involve and provide opportunities for people; to
support and maintain the use of Native languages;
to produce and circulate educational printed and
audio-visual material; to promote and encourage
the establishment of a library and information ser-

vices in the community . *Activities/programs* : Native Language program; Ojibway Cree Resource
Center; Ojibway Cree media productions; Indian
education programs. Grand Council Treaty #9 -
Signed between the crown, the Provincial Government and the Cree-Ojibway of what is now
known as Northern Ontario in 1905-06. This was
one of a number of treaties made across Canada,
following the Royal Proclamation of 1763. The area
under Treat #9 covers about 210,000 square miles.
There are over 40 Indian commuities scattered
throughout the area. 30 of these are accessible
by air only. The Indian People of the Treat #9 area
are known as the Nishnawbe-Aski. *Publications* :
Catalogue of Materials Available for Sale. Library .
Founded 1976.

TIMMINS NA TIVE FRIENDSHIP CENTRE
170 Second Ave.
TIMMINS, ON P4N 1G1
(705) 268-6262
Christine Cummings, Executive Director

CHIEFS OF ONTARIO
22 College St., 2nd Floor
TORONTO, ON M5G 1K2
(416) 972-0212 Fax 972-0217
Andrea Chrisjohn, Executive Director
Gordon Peters, ON Regional Chief

**INDIAN ARTS & CRAFTS
OF ONTARIO CORP.**
2 Carlton St., Suite 1518
TORONTO, ON M5B 1J3
(416) 997-4442
Wellington Staats, President

NATIVE CANADIAN CENTRE OF T ORONTO
16 Spadina Rd.
TORONTO, ON M5R 2S7
(416) 964-9087 Fax 964-21 11
Gayle Mason, Executive Director

NISHNAWBE-ASKI NATION
14 College St., 6th Floor
TORONTO, ON M5C 1K2
(416) 920-2376 Fax 920-1765
Bentley Cheechoo, Grand Chief

OBONSAWIN-IRWIN CONSULTING, INC.
20 Carleton St., Suite 126
TORONTO, ON M5B 2H5
(416) 591-6995
Roger Obonsawin, President

**ONTARIO FEDERATION OF
INDIAN FRIENDSHIP CENTRES**
234 Eglinton Ave. East, Suite 207
TORONTO, ON M4P 1K5
(416) 484-1411 Fax 484-6893
Vera Pawis Tabobondung, President
Sylvia Maracle, Executive Director
Assists and supports the 18 Indian Centres under
its membership in Ontario. Promotes development
of new centres, and provides programs and services to its member centres. Publications. Library .

**ONTARIO INDIAN RIGHTS
FOR INDIAN WOMEN**
100 Bain Ave., No. 2 Maples
TORONTO, ON M4K 1E8

UNION OF ONTARIO INDIANS
27 Queen St. East, 2nd Floor
TORONTO, ON M5C 1R2
(416) 693-1305 Fax 693-1620
Joe Miskokomon, President

K. Gayle Mason, Executive Director
Represents 40 Indian bands and their 35,000 members. A political organization of fering technical and support services to member bands. Library.

OJIBWE CULTURAL FOUNDATION
Excelsior Post Office
WEST BAY, ON P0P 1G0
(705) 377-4902
Mary Lou Fox Radulovich, Director

THE ONTARIO ARCHAEOLOGICAL SOCIETY
126 Willowdale Ave.
WILLOWDALE, ON M2N 4Y2
(416) 730-0797
Christine L. Caroppo, Director
Purpose: To preserve, promote, investigate record and publish an archaeological record of the Province of Ontario. Activities/progams: Excavations; workshops; annual Symposium; tours and trips; public lectures; volunteer program "Passport to the Past."Publications: Ontario Archaeology - refereed journal; Monographs in Ontario Archaeology - periodic; special publications - directories, etc. Founded 1950.

CAN AM INDIAN FRIENDSHIP CENTRE
Box 441, Station "A"
WINDSOR, ON N9A 6L7
(519) 252-8331 Fax 252-4943
Terry Doxtator, Executive Director

PRINCE EDWARD ISLAND

ABORIGINAL WOMEN'S ASSN. OF P.E.I.
P.O. Box 213
CHARLOTTETOWN, PEI C1A 7K4
(902) 892-1015
Mary Moore, President

NATIVE COUNCIL OF P.E.I.
33 Allen St.
CHARLOTTETOWN, PEI C1A 2V6
(902) 892-5314
Graham Tuplin, President

LENNOX ISLAND CULTURAL EDUCATIONAL CENTRE
Box 134
LENNOX ISLAND, PEI C0B 1P0
(902) 831-2779 Fax 831-2493
Charles Sark, Director

QUEBEC

CREE INDIAN CENTRE
95 rue Jaculet
CHIBOUGAMAU, PQ G8P 2G1
(418) 748-7667 Fax 748-6954
Judy Parceaud, Executive Director

JAMES BAY CREE CULTURAL ED. CENTRE
Box 390
CHISASIBI, PQ J0M 1E0
(819) 855-2473
Jane Pachano, Director

KATIVIK SCHOOL BOARD
185 Dorval Ave.
DORVAL, PQ H9S 3G6
(819) 636-8720

NATIVE ALLIANCE OF QUEBEC & LAURENTIAN ALLIANCE OF METIS & NON-STATUS INDIANS
21 Brodeur Ave.
HULL, PQ J8Y 2P6
(819) 770-7763 Fax 770-6070
Rheal Boudrias, President

AVATAQ CULTURAL INSTITUTE, INC.
INUKJUAK, PQ J0M 1M0
(819) 254-8919
Barrie Gunn, Director

CONFEDERTION OF INDIANS OF QUEBEC
P.O. Box 729
KAHNAWAKE, PQ J0L 1B0
(514) 632-7321

KANIEN'KEHAKA: RAOTITIONHKWA
Kahnawake Indian Band
Box 1988
KAHNAWAKE, PQ J0L 1B0
(514) 638-0880 Fax 638-4009
Jessica Hill, Coordinator

QUEBEC INDIAN RIGHTS FOR INDIAN WOMEN
P.O. Box 614
KAHNAWAKE, PQ J0L 1B0
(514) 632-6304

KANESATAKE CULTURAL CENTRE
P.O. Box 607
KANESATAKE, PQ J0N 1E0
(514) 479-8524
Chief George Martin, Contact

KATIVIK REGIONAL GOVERNMENT
P.O. Box 9
KUUJJUAQ, PQ J0M 1C0
(819) 964-2960

CENTRE D'AMITIE AUTOCCHTONE DE LA TUQUE
315, rue St. Paul
LA TUQUE, PQ G9X 3P3
(819) 523-6121 Fax 523-8637
Rosanne Petiquay, Executive Director

CENTRE D'AMITIE AUTOCCHTONE DE QUEBEC
234, St. Louis St.
LORETTEVILLE, PQ G2A 1L4
(418) 843-5818 Fax 843-8960
Jocelyn Gros-Louis, Executive Director

CENTRE AMIKWAN
Conseil de Band du Lac Simon
via LOUVICOURT, PQ J0Y 1M0
(819) 736-3161
Francois Larose, Director

CENTRE D'AMITIE AUTOCCHTONE D' INNU
Boite Group 81
MALIOTENAM, PQ G4R 4K2
(418) 968-2026
Serge Jourdain, Executive Director

RIVER DESERT CULTURAL EDUCATION CENTRE
P.O. Box 309
MANIWAKI, PQ J9E 3B3
(819) 449-5039 Fax 449-5673
Bertha Tenasco, Director

ASSOCIATION DES FEMMES AUTOCHTONES DU QUEBEC
1410 Rue Stanley, 7 ieme etage
MONTREAL, PQ H3A 1P8
(514) 873-7029

AVATAQ CULTURAL INSTITUTE, INC.
INUKJUAK J0M 1M0
(819) 254-8919 Fax 254-8148
Johnny Epoo, President
Office: 294 Carre St. Louis
MONTREAL, PQ H2X 1A4
(514) 844-0109 Fax 848-9648
Arantxa Comas, Contact
Purpose: To preserve and promote Nunavik (Northern Quebec) Inuit language and culture. Activities/programs: Building a community museum; language program; traditional medicine project; place name project; genealogy project; photo exhibits; retrieval of anthropological material; transcribe and translate recorded information. Documentation Center comprises historical photographs colection, interview with elders, and library and archives.

LE REGROUPEMENT DES CENTRES D'AMITIE AUTOCHTONES DU QUEBEC
5333 Sherbrooke est. Apt. 1009-B
MONTREAL, PQ H1T 3W2
(514) 254-2257

NATIVE FRIENDSHIP CENTRE
3730 Cote Des Neiges Rd.
MONTREAL, PQ H3H 1V6
(514) 937-5338 Fax 937-4437
Ida Williams, Executive Director

QUEBEC NATIVE WOMEN'S ASSOCIATION
1450 City Councillors, Suite 440
MONTREAL, PQ H3A 2E5
(514) 844-0314 Fax 844-2108
Michele Rouleau, President

OKA CULTURAL CENTRE
P.O. Box 640
OKA, PQ J0N 1E0
(514) 479-8524
Mary Cree, Director

CONFEDERACY OF INDIANS OF QUEBEC
P.O. Box 443
RESTIGOUCHE, PQ G0C 2R0
(418) 788-5336

RESTIGOUCHE INST. OF CULTURAL ED.
Restigouche Indian Band
17 Riverside West
RESTIGOUCHE, PQ G0C 2R0
(418) 788-2136 Ext. 56 Fax 788-2058
Romey Labillois, Director

ASSOCIATIONS DES METIS ET DES INDIENS HORS RESERVES, INC.
2023 Boulevard De'l'anse
ROBERVAL, PQ G8H 2N1
(418) 275-0198

CENTRE D'ENTRAIDE ET D'AMITIE
910, 10e Ave., Box 1769
SENNETERRE, PQ J0Y 2M0
(819) 737-2324 Fax 737-831 1
Louis Bordeleau, Executive Director

INNU FRIENDSHIP CENTRE
100 Laure Blvd., Suite 100
SEPT-LES, PQ G4R 1Y1
(418) 968-2026

**ALGONQUIN COUNCIL
OF WESTERN QUEBEC**
351 Central Ave.
VAL D'OR, PQ J2P 1P6
(819) 770-7763 Fax 770-6070
Roger Brindamour, Director

CENTRE D'ENTRAIDE AUTOCHTONE
1101 - 6 eme rue
VAL D'OR, PQ J9P 3W4
(819) 825-6857 Fax 825-9120
Diane Decoste, Executive Director

GRAND COUNCIL OF THE CREES
1462 rue de la Quebecoise
VAL D'OR, PQ J9P 5H4
(819) 825-3402 Fax 825-6892
Matthew Coon-Come, Grand Chief

**INSTITUT EDUCATIF ET CULTUREL
ATTIKAMEK-MONTAGNAIS**
40, rue Francois Grox-Louis, #7
VILLAGE DES HURONS, P.Q. G0A 4V0
(418) 843-0258
Johanne Robertson, Director

LES ARTISANS INDIENS DU QUEBEC
540 Max Gros-Louis St.
VILLAGE DES HURONS, P.Q. G0A 4V0
(418) 845-2150
Alex Vicaire, President

NATION HURONNE-WENDAT
Cultural/Educational Centre
VILLAGE DES HURONS, P.Q. G0A 4V0
(418) 843-3767
M. Regent Sioui, Director

R.C.A.A.Q.
30 rue de l'ours
VILLAGE DES HURONS, PQ G0A 1L4
(418) 842-6354 Fax 842-9795
Ida Williams, President
Diane Decoste, Coordinator
Linda Sioui, Translator

**LA FEDERATION DES COOPERATIVES
NOUVEAU-QUEBEC**
8102 route Trans-Canadienne
VILLE ST. LAURENT, PQ H4S 1R4
(514) 332-0880 Fax 332-2788
Paulosie Rasuoluak, President

**INSTITUT EDUCATIF ET CULTUREL
ATTIKAMEK-MONTAGNAIS**
7-40, rue Francois Gros-Louis
WENDAKE, PQ G0A 4V0
(418) 843-0258 F AX 843-7313
Johanne Robertson, Director

LES ARTISANS INDIENS DU QUEBEC
540 Max Gros-Louis St.
Village des Hurons
WENDAKE, PQ G0A 4V0
(418) 845-2150
Therese Sioui, President

NATION HURONNE-WENDAT
Village des Hurons
WENDAKE, PQ G0A 4V0
(418) 843-3663 Fax 842-1 108
Danielle Laine, Director

**SECRETARIAT OF FIRST
NATIONS OF QUEBEC**
430 Koska, Village des Hurons-W endat
WENDAKE, PQ G0A 4V0
(418) 842-5020 Fax 842-2660
Konrad Sioui, V ice-Chief

SASKATCHEWAN

BUFFALO NARROWS FRIENDSHIP CENTRE
P.O. Box 189
BUFFALO NARROWS, SK S0M 0J0
(306) 235-4633
Norman Hansen, Executive Director

NINASTAKO CENTRE
Box 1299
CARDSTON, AB T0K 0K0
(403) 737-3774
Gloria Wells, Director

MOOSE MOUNTAIN FRIENDSHIP CENTRE
P.O. Box 207, Main St.
CARYLE, SK S0C 0R0
(306) 453-2425
Diette Standing Ready, Executive Director

NATIVE COUNCIL OF SASKATCHEWAN
P.O. Box 2045
CUMBERLAND HOUSE, SK S0E 0S0
(306) 888-2149
Harvey Young, President

QU'APPELLE VALLEY FRIENDSHIP CENTRE
P.O. Box 240
FORT QU'APPELLE, SK S0G 1S0
(306) 332-5616 Fax 332-5091
J. Peter Dubois, Executive Director
Personnel: W. Arliss Dellow, Program Director; Robyn Donsion, Coordinator (Y outh Alternative Measures Program). *Purpose*: To identify and cater to the social, cultural, and recreational needs of the Indian and Metis people of Fort Qu'Appelle and District; to enhance community participation by the people of Indian descent; and to promote better understanding and relations between Native and non-Native citizens. *Programs*: Youth Alternative Measures; Identification Program (fingerprinting children); Drug & Alcohol Counseling; Literacy, et al. *Publication*: Qu'Appelle V alley Quill, quarterly newsletter.

LA LOUCHE FRIENDSHIP CENTRE
P.O. Box 59
LA LOUCHE, SK S0M 1G0
(306) 822-2332
Mabel Park, Executive Director

KIKINAHK FRIENDSHIP CENTRE, INC.
320 Boardman St., Box 254
LA RONGE, SK S0J 1S0
(306) 425-2051
Norm Bouvier, Executive Director

NORTHWEST FRIENDSHIP CENTRE
P.O. Box 1780
MEADOW LAKE, SK S0M 1V0
(306) 236-3766
Gladys Joseph, Executive Director

MOOSE JAW NATIVE FRIENDSHIP CENTRE
42 High St. E.
MOOSE JAW, SK S6H 0B8
(306) 693-6966 Fax 692-3509
Ed Pelletier, Executive Director

**BATTLEFORDS INDIAN
& METIS FRIENDSHIP CENTRE**
11501 - 8th Ave., Box 667
NORTH BATTLEFORD, SK S9A 2Y9
(306) 445-8216 Fax 445-2335
Daryl Larose, Executive Director

**ABORIGINAL WOMEN'S
COUNCIL OF SASKATCHEWAN**
62-17th St. W est
PRINCE ALBER T, SK S6V 3X3
(306) 763-6005 Fax 373-9123
Lil Sanderson, Contact

INDIAN & METIS FRIENDSHIP CENTRE
1409 - 1st Ave. East
PRINCE ALBERT S6V 6Z1
(306) 764-3431 Fax 763-3205
Eugene Arcand, Executive Director

**ABORIGINAL FRIENDSHIP
CENTRES OF SASKATCHEWAN
REGINA FRIENDSHIP CENTRE**
1440 Scarth St.
REGINA, SK S4R 2E9
(306) 525-5459 Fax 525-3005
Sharon Ironstar, President
Dona Racette, Executive Director

**FEDERATION OF SASKATCHEWAN
INDIAN NATIONS**
Indian Governments of Saskatchewan
109 Hadsman Rd.
REGINA, SK S4N 5W5
(306) 721-2822 Fax 721-2707
Roland Crowe, President

INDIAN & METIS FRIENDSHIP CENTRE
303 McGee Crescent
REGINA, SK S4R 6K8
(306) 543-2745
Walter Schoenthal, Executive Director

**SASKATCHEWAN INDIAN
ARTS & CRAFTS CORPORATION**
2431-8th Ave.
REGINA, SK S4R 5J7
(306) 352-1501
Dorothy Thomas, President

**SASKATCHEWAN
ARCHAEOLOGICAL SOCIETY**
#5 - 816 1st Ave. North
SASKATOON S7K 1Y3
(306) 664-4124 Fax 665-1928
Tim Jones, Executive Director
Purpose: To actively promote and encourage the study, preservation and proper use of the archaeological resources of Saskatchewan. *Activities*: Educational programs; field school; seminars; field trips; Certification program; operates the Regional Archaeology V olunteers Program. Member Funding Grants - 4 grants for members to complete special projects. *Publication*: Tracking Ancient Hunters: Prehistoric Archaeology in Saskatchewan; Avonlea, Yesterday and Today, Annotated Bibliography of Saskatewan Archaeology and Prehistory; Bimonthly newsletter; annual Journal. Founded 1963.

**SASKATCHEWAN INDIAN CULTURAL
CENTRE**
120-33rd St. East, Box 3085
SASKATOON, SK S7K 3S9
(306) 244-1 146 Fax 665-6520
Linda Pelly-Landrie, President

**SASKATCHEWAN NATIVE
WOMEN'S ASSOCIATION**
1401 Egbert Ave.
SASKATOON S7N 2L8
 (306) 652-6564/373-1957

**SASKATOON INDIAN &
METIS FRIENDSHIP CENTRE**
168 Wall St.
SASKATOON, SK S7K 1N4
 (306) 244-0174 Fax 664-2536
 Maurice J. Blondeau, Director

YORKTON FRIENDSHIP CENTRE
283 Myrtle Ave.
YORKTON, SK S3N 1R5
 (306) 782-2822
 Ivan Cote, Executive Director

YUKON

COUNCIL FOR YUKON INDIANS
22 Nisutlin Dr.
WHITEHORSE, YUKON Y1A 3S5
 (403) 667-7631 Fax 668-6577
 Judy Gingell, Chairperson
 Harry Allen, Vice-Chief (403) 668-7358
Cultural Education Society Resource Center
 Rose Marie Blair-Smith,
  Vice-Chairperson (Social Programs)
 Dayle MacDonald, Vice-Chairperson
  (Economic Development)

SKOOKUM JIM FRIENDSHIP CENTRE
3159 - 3rd Ave.
WHITEHORSE, YU Y1A 1G1
 (403) 668-4465 Fax 668-4725
 Ruby Van Bibban, Executive Director

YE SA TO COMMUNICATIONS SOCIETY
22 Nisutlin Dr.
WHITEHORSE, YU Y1A 3S5
 (403) 667-2775 Fax 667-6923

**YUKON INDIAN ARTS & CRAFTS
CO-OPERATIVE LIMITED**
4230 Fourth Ave.
WHITEHORSE, YU Y1A 1K1
 (403) 667-2779
 Stan Peters, President

**YUKON INDIAN CULTURAL
EDUCATION SOCIETY**
22 Nisutlin Dr.
WHITEHORSE, YU Y1A 2B0
 (403) 667-7631 Fax 668-6577
 Pat Martin, Coordinator

YUKON INDIAN WOMEN'S ASSOCIATION
22 Nisutlin Dr.
WHITEHORSE Y1A 3S5
 (403) 667-6161 Fax 668-6577
 Nina Bolton, President

ALBERTA

LUXTON MUSEUM
BANFF
Western Canadian Indian museum.

OLDMAN RIVER CULTURAL CENTRE
P.O. Box 70
BROCKET T0K 0H0
(403) 965-3939

GLENBOW-ALBERTA INSTITUTE MUSEUM
Glenbow Centre
9th Ave. and First St., S.E.
CALGARY

TSUT'INA K'OSA (SARCEE)
3700 Anderson Rd., S.W.
P.O. Box 67
CALGARY T2W 3C4
(403) 238-2676/7
Helen McGinnis, Director

PROVINCIAL MUSEUM OF ALBERTA
12845 - 102 Ave.
EDMONTON T5N 0M6
(403) 427-1730
John Fortier, Director
Dr. Patricia A. McCormack, Curator-Ethnology
Description: Collections focus on the material culture and lifeways of indigenous peoples of Alberta (Beaver, Slavey, Chipewyan, Northern and Plains Cree, Blackfoot, Blood, Peigan, Sarsi, Assiniboine, Kutenai, Sauteaux, Metis) and other groups relevant to the histories of indigenous peoples in Alberta (e.g. Iroquois.) Contains about 12,000 items, strong in both functional and religious Plains materials; tipis and moccasins are extensive; Inuit clothing and other items from the Canadian Arctic. *Special programs*: Research and collecting projects--Native lifeways and material cultures in Alberta, focusing on 20th century items. *Publications*: Storyteller, monthly; books for sale. Library.

BLACKFOOT CULTURAL STUDIES
Box 339
GLEICHEN T0J 1N0
(403) 264-9658

MUSKWACHEES CULTURAL COLLEGE
HOBBEMA
Fred Carneau, Director

SADDLE LAKE CULTURAL ED. PROGRAM
SADDLE LAKE T0A 3T0
(403) 726-3829

BRITISH COLUMBIA

ALERT BAY MUSEUM
Fir St., Box 208
ALERT BAY
Indian museum displaying Salish Indian relics.

U'MISTA CULTURAL CENTRE
P.O. Box 253
ALERT BAY V0N 1A0
Gloria Cranmer Webster, Director

ATLIN MUSEUM
Fourth & Trainor Sts.
ATLIN
Exhibits Tlingit Indian artifacts.

CAMPBELL RIVER MUSEUM
P.O. Box 101, 1235 Island Highway
CAMPBELL RIVER
Indian museum displaying Northwest Coast material.

**ST. MARY'S BAND
ADMINISTRATIVE OFFICE**
Site #15, Mission Rd., SS #1
CRANBROOK V1C 4H4
Sophie Pierre, Director

'KSAN MUSEUM
P.O. Box 333, High Level Rd.
HAZELTON V0J 1Y0
(604) 842-5723/5544
Eve Hope, Director & Curator
Description: Museum is part of a reconstructed Indian village. Maintains a collection of Northwest Coast Indian artifacts, specifically Gitksan. *Special program*: Kitanmax School of Northwest Coast Indian Art - a 2-year program in wood carving, design, tool making, serigraph. *Publications*: Weget Wanders On - prints and legends; Gathering What the Great Nature Provided; Robes of Dover. Founded 1959.

KAMLOOPS MUSEUM & ARCHIVES
207 Seymour St.
KAMLOOPS V2C 2E7
(604) 828-3576
Ken Favrholdt, Director & Curator
Description: General history collection related to the natural and human history of the Kamloops district including artifacts and exhibits related to Native Indians of area. *Special collection*: Extensive archives including files on interior Salish Indians and local Shuswap Indians. Exhibits Indian artifacts, mostly Shuswap Indians, with some material relevant to other tribes of the Interior Salish. *Publication*: The Dispossessed (Salish Indians); local history publications. Archives and library. Founded 1937.

**SECWEPEMC CULTURAL
EDUCATION SOCIETY**
345 Yellowhead Highway
KAMLOOPS V2H 1H1
(604) 374-1096
Muriel Sasakamoose, Director
Linda Jules, Curator
Description: Contains canoes, a tule mat lodge, archaeological material, baskets, church and religious artifacts, photos, beadwork, trade items, leatherwork. *Programs*: Educational; Language; Trades training; Communications; Band management training; Native Life Skills Coaches training; Indian Lands management; workshops and conferences. *Publication*: Secwepemc News - monthly newspaper. Library.

**MUSEUM OF NORTHERN
BRITISH COLUMBIA**
P.O. Box 669
PRINCE RUPERT V8J 3S1
(604) 624-3207
Elaine Moore, Curator/Director
Description: Exhibits a collection of ethnographic artifacts representing Tsimshian native people (coast, Gitksan and Nisgha) and Haida and Tlingit to a lesser extent; Northwest Coast Indian artifacts, and other cultural remains relating to regional history. *Publication*: The Curator's Log, quarterly newsletter; book, Arts of the Salmon People; Totem Poles of Prince Rupert", illustrated guide; Guide to the Collection. Library.

KWAGIULTH MUSEUM
P.O. Box 8
QUATHIASKI COVE V0P 1N0
Estelle Inman, Executive Director

ED JONES HAIDA MUSEUM
Second Beach Skidgate
QUEEN CHARLOTTE CITY V0T 1S0
(604) 559-4643

**UNIVERSITY OF BRITISH COLUMBIA
MUSEUM OF ANTHROPOLOGY**
6393 N.W. Marine Dr.
VANCOUVER V6T 1W5
(604) 228-5087
Description: Major research and study collections include Northwest Coast archaeology and ethnology, and ethnological specimens from other North American Indian cultures. *Publications*: Anthropology at the Academy, newsletter; The Elkus Collection of Southwestern Indian Art; Hopi Kachina: Spirit of Life. Library.

THE VANCOUVER MUSEUM
1100 Chestnut
VANCOUVER V6J 3J9
(604) 736-4431
Dr. David Hemphill, Director
Lynn Maranda, Curator of Anthropology
Special collections: Lipsett Native Indian collection; Ryan Collection of Haida argillite carvings. *Publication*: Muse News. Library. Founded 1894.

BRITISH COLUMBIA PROVINCIAL MUSEUM
Heritage Court, 601 Belleville St.
VICTORIA

PROVINCIAL ARCHIVES OF B.C.
Parliament Bldg.
VICTORIA

MANITOBA

ESKIMO MUSEUM
James St.
CHURCHILL R0B 0E0

**CROSS LAKE CULTURAL
EDUCATION CENTRE**
Cross Lake Indian Reserve
CROSS LAKE R0B 0J0
(204) 676-2268/2218

CULTURAL CENTER
Fort Alexander Band
P.O. Box 1610
PINE FALLS R0E 1M0
(204) 367-8740

**SAGKEENG CULTURAL
EDUCATION CENTRE**
Box 749
PINE FALLS R0E 1M0
Art Boubard, Director

**MANITOBA INDIAN CULTURAL
EDUCATION CENTRE**
119 Sutherland Ave.
WINNIPEG R2W 3C9
(204) 942-0228
Dennis Daniels, Director
Description: Maintains a collection of artifacts of native peoples of Manitoba. Library of books, films, tape/slides, and audio-visual presentations, arti-

facts, educational kits. *Publications*: Manitoba Elders, $6; Lifestyles of Manitoba Indians, $2 coloring book. Founded 1975.

MANITOBA MUSEUM OF MAN & NATURE
190 Rupert Ave.
WINNIPEG

NEW BRUNSWICK

PAPINEAU INDIAN CULTURAL CENTRE
P.O. Box 8, Site 22
BATHURST E2A 3Y8
(506) 548-9211

BIG COVE CULTURAL CENTRE
Big Cove Reserve, RR 1
REXTON E0A 2L0
(506) 523-6384

THE NEW BRUNSWICK MUSEUM
277 Douglas Ave.
SAINT JOHN

NORTHWEST TERRITORIES

INUMMARIT COMMITTEE-
SOD HOUSE MUSEUM
c/o Hamlet of Arctic Bay, General Delivery
ARCTIC BAY X0A 0A0
Dorothee Komangapik, Director

INUIT SILATTUQSARVINGAT
Inuit Cultural Institute
ESKIMO POINT X0C 0E0
(819) 857-2803
Luke Suluk, Director

DENE MUSEUM/ARCHIVES
c/o General Delivery
FORT GOOD HOPE X0E 0U0

SIPALASEEQUTT MUSEUM SOCIETY
PANGNIRTUNG X0A 0R0
Koaguk Akulujuk, Director

DENE CULTURAL INSTITUTE
P.O. Box 207
YELLOWKNIFE X1A 2N2
(403) 873-6617
Joanne Burnaby, Executive Director

NOVA SCOTIA

NOVA SCOTIA MUSEUM
1747 Summer St.
HALIFAX B3H 3A6
(902) 429-4610
Candace Stevenson, Director
Description: Contains an extensive collection and exhibit of Micmac material culture--stone tools, basketry, birchbark objects, quill boxes, and bone implements. *Publications*: Micmac Quillwork; Elitekey; Red Earth; Withe Baskets, Traps and Brooms. Library.

ONTARIO

WOODLAND INDIAN CULTURAL
EDUCATIONAL CENTRE
P.O. Box 1506, 184 Mohawk St.
BRANTFORD N3T 5V6
(519) 759-2653
Tom Hill, Director

JOSEPH BRANT MUSEUM
1240 North Shore Blvd.
BURLINGTON
Description: A collection of Joseph Brant (Iroquois) memorabilia; general material on the Iroquois culture. Library.

NORTH AMERICAN INDIAN
TRAVELLING COLLEGE
RR 3
CORNWALL ISLAND K6H 5R7
(613) 932-9452
Barbara Barnes, Director

GOLDEN LAKE ALGONQUIN MUSEUM
P.O. Box 28
GOLDEN LAKE K0J 1X0

LAKE OF THE WOODS
OJIBWAY CULTURAL CENTRE
P.O. Box 1720
KENORA P9N 3X7
(807) 548-5744

THE McMICHAEL CANADIAN
ART COLLECTION
10365 Islington Ave.
KLEINBERG L0J 1C0
(416) 893-1121
Jean Blodgett, Curator of Native
Indian and Inuit Art
Description: Collection includes contemporary Canadian Woodland and Plains paintings, drawings and sculpture; some Northwest Coast Indian material culture. *Special program*: School program and resource package entitled: "Contemporary Expressions: Indian Art." *Publications*: Quarterly newsletter; exhibition catalogs. Library. Founded 1965.

MUSEUM OF INDIAN ARCHAEOLOGY
U. of Western Ontario, Lawson-Jury Bldg.
LONDON N6G 3M6
(519) 473-1360
William D. Finlayson, Ph.D., Exec. Director
Debra Bodner, Curator
Description: Large (over one-half million specimens) archaeological collections from throughout southern Ontario; small ethnographic collection from Ontario, Canadian Plains, and the Arctic. *Lawson Prehistoric Indian Village*: An open-air facility featuring excavation, reconstruction and interpretation of a prehistoric Neutral village. *Programs*: Exhibition Gallery; study and layout space; tours and lectures; Research Associate Program; Archaeological Contracting and Consulting Services; archaeological field schools and courses. *Publications*: Newsletter; Bulletin; Research Reports. Library.

SAINTE-MARIE AMONG THE HURONS
MUSEUM
R.R. 1
MIDLAND

OJIBWA CULTURAL FOUNDATION
Excelsior Post Office, West Bay
MANITOULIN ISLAND T0P 1G0
(705) 377-4902/4899

NATIONAL MUSEUM OF MAN
NATIONAL MUSEUMS OF CANADA
OTTAWA K1A 0M8
(819) 994-6113 (Archaeological Survey of Can)
(613) 996-4540 (Canadian Ethnological Svc.)
Ian G. Dyck, Ph.D., Chief-Archaeology
A. McFadyen Clark, Chief Ethnologist
Archaeological Collection: Contains approximately 2,500,000 specimens from Canada and Alaska; collections from the Eastern Woodlands (Ontario eastward to the Atlantic Provinces) and the Eskimo (Arctic) areas; the Arctic Coast, Northwest Coast, Plateau, western Boreal forest, and Plains. *Ethnological Collection*: Approximately 50,000 artifacts, 90 of which are Canadian Indian and Inuit material (including modern works of Indian and Inuit art) with emphasis on Inuit and Pacific Coast Indian traditional material culture. *Programs*: Responsible for the survey and rescue of Canada's prehistoric sites; to record the languages and cultures of Canadian Indians, Inuit and Metis. Publications. Library.

LAURENTIAN UNIVERSITY
MUSEUM & ARTS CENTRE
John St.
SUDBURY P3E 2C6
(705) 674-3271
Pamela Krueger, Director/Curator
Description: Collection areas relate to contemporary native and Inuit artists of Canada, and native and Indian artists of Northern Ontario; over 800 works by over 600 Canadian artists, historical and contemporary; over 25 different exhibitions are presented each year. *Special programs*: Talks and tours; lectures; art courses; film series. *Publications*: Communique, published every six weeks; exhibition catalogues. Library. Founded 1967.

OJIBWAY & CREE CULTURAL CENTRE
59 - 71 Third Ave.
TIMMINS P4N 1C2
(705) 267-7911

ROYAL ONTARIO MUSEUM
100 Queens Park
TORONTO M5S 2C6
(416) 978-3654 (Ethnology)
(416) 978-3668 (Archaeology)
Edward S. Rogers, Ph.D., Curator-Ethnology
Peter L. Storck, Ph.D., Curator-Archaeology
Ethnology: Collections of material for the following geographical areas & tribes: Arctic--Eastern Canadian Eskimo, Netsilik Eskimo, Copper Eskimo, Western Canadian Eskimo; Northwest Coast--Kwakiutl, Tsimshian, Haida, Gitskan, Bella Bella; Northeast Coast--Iroquois, Cree Ojibwa, Montagnais-Naskapi; Plains--Blackfoot, Cree and Saulteaux, Canadian Plains. Archaeology: Provincial collections of Ontario archaeological material; and material from the rest of Canada; material from the U.S., including the Southwest and Mississippi Valley cultures. *Publications*: Archaeological Newsletter; Rotunda, quarterly magazine; Monographs and Papers; Round Lake Ojibwa (monograph); contemporary native arts catalogs; Native People of Canada (7 booklets); books for sale. Library.

PRINCE EDWARD ISLAND

**PRINCE EDWARD ISLAND HERITAGE
FOUNDATION MUSEUM**
P.O. Box 922
CHARLOTTETOWN

QUEBEC

CANADIAN MUSEUM OF CIVILIZATION
100 Laurier St., Box 3100 Station "B"
HULL J8X 4H2
(819) 992-3497
Dr. George MacDonald, Director
Description: Concerned with the national representation of artwork, artifacts and documentation
relative to archaeology, ethnology, physical anthropology, folk culture and history. Maintains reference library.

KANIEN'KEHA...RAOTITOHKWA
P.O. Box 750
KAHNAWAKE J01 1B0
(514) 638-0880

**RIVER DESERT CULTURAL
EDUCATION CENTRE**
River Desert Band, P.O. Box 309
MANIWAKI J9E 3B3
(819) 449-4575

MUSEE DES ABENAKIS
108 rue Waban-Aki
ODANAK J0G 1H0
Nicole O'Bomsawin, Director

OKA CULTURAL CENTRE
P.O. Box 640
OKA J0N 1L0
(514) 479-8373

AMERINDIAN MUSEUM
406 Amisk
POINTE-BLEUE G0W 2H0
Carmen Gill Casavante, Director

**HISTORICAL MUSEUM
OF INUIT POVUNGNITUK**
POVUNGNITUK G0M 1P6

**INSTITUT CULTUREL ET EDUCATIF
ATTIKAMEK-MONTAGNAIS**
Boulevard Bastien
VILLAGE HURON G0A 4V0
(418) 842-0277

SASKATCHEWAN

**BATTLEFORD NATIONAL
HISTORIC PARK MUSEUM**
P.O. Box 70
BATTLEFORD

PRAIRIE PIONEER MUSEUM
P.O. Box 273
CARIK

MOOSE JAW ART MUSEUM
Crescent Park
MOOSE JAW

**THE SASKATOON GALLERY &
CONSERVATORY CORP. MUSEUM**
Mendel Art Gallery
950 Spadina Crescent East
SASKATOON

VIGFUSSON MUSEUM
University of Saskatchewan
Room 69, Arts Bldg.
SASKATOON

ALBERTA

HISTORICAL RESOURCES LIBRARY
Provincial Archives of Alberta
12845 102 Ave.
EDMONTON T5N 0M6
(403) 427-1750
FAX (403) 454-6629
Margaret E. Bhatnagar, Librarian
Description: A collection of 20,000 volumes on local history (Alberta), western Canadian history, archaeology and ethnology. *Publications*: Bibliography and Literature Guide. Interlibrary loans. Open to public.

UNIVERSITY OF ALBERTA
BOREAL INSTITUTE FOR NORTHERN STUDIES LIBRARY
EDMONTON T6G 2E9

UNIVERSITY OF ALBERTA
COLLEGE OF ST. JEAN LIBRARY
8406 91st St.
EDMONTON T6C 4G9
Description: Maintains a collection of 50,000 volumes, many of which are on the anthropology and ethnology of North American Indians.

BRITISH COLUMBIA

UNIVERSITY OF BRITISH COLUMBIA LIBRARY
Humanities & Social Sciences Division
1956 East Mall
VANCOUVER V6T 1W3
(604) 228-2725 Fax 228-6465
Description: Maintains a strong academic collection, specializing in the Indians of the Northwest Pacific Coast (especially British Columbia) but also Canadian aboriginal peoples in general. Interlibrary loans. Open to the public.

UNIVERSITY OF BRITISH COLUMBIA MUSEUM OF ANTHROPOLOGY LIBRARY
6393 N.W. Marine Dr.
VANCOUVER V6T 1W5
(604) 228-5087

MANITOBA

ESKIMO MUSEUM LIBRARY
242 La Verendrye St.
CHURCHILL R0B 0E0
(204) 675-2541
A collection of ethnographic material on the Eskimos.

DEPARTMENT OF CULTURAL AFFAIRS & HISTORICAL RESOURCES PROVINCIAL ARCHIVES
200 Vaughan St.
WINNIPEG R3C 0V8
Focus Program: A collection of master tapes and duplicates made with Indian people in Manitoba.

HUDSON'S BAY COMPANY LIBRARY
77 Main St.
WINNIPEG R3C 2R1

NEWFOUNDLAND

MEMORIAL UNIVERSITY OF NEWFOUNDLAND
Centre for Newfoundland Studies
Elizabeth Ave.
ST. JOHNS A1B 3Y1
(709) 737-7476 Fax 737-3188
Anne Hart, Librarian
Description: Holdings include materials on Beothuk, Naskapi-Montagnais, Micmac, Dorset, Innu, Maritime Archaic, and Inuit peoples. Also an archives, holding a small collection of manuscript material on some of these peoples.

NOVA SCOTIA

DALHOUSIE UNIVERSITY MARITIME SCHOOL OF SOCIAL WORK LIBRARY
6420 Coburg Rd.
HALIFAX B3H 3J5
Special collection: Native Peoples Collection-- books and journals on Indians, Eskimos and Metis.

NOVA SCOTIA MUSEUM LIBRARY
1747 Summer St.
HALIFAX B3H 3A6
Description: Contains a collection of books on Micmac material culture and ethnography.

ONTARIO

ASSEMBLY OF FIRST NATIONS - RESOURCE CENTRE
47 Clarence St., 3rd Floor
OTTAWA K1N 9K1
(613) 236-0673 Fax 238-5780
Kelly Whiteduck, Coordinator
Description: Maintains a collection of 10,000 volumes on treaty and aboriginal rights, with special collections on education, alcohol and drug abuse, lands revenue & Trust Review, etc.; books and monographs (unpublished reports); 100 Native-American periodicals; and law cases. Open to public as a reference library - Monday-Friday, 9 AM - 5 PM.

CANADA—DEPT. OF INDIAN AFFAIRS NORTHERN DEVELOPMENTAL LIBRARY
OTTAWA K1A 0H4
(819) 997-0811 Fax 997-051 1/4/8
Mrs. Ramma Kamra, Librarian
Holdings include over 51,000 titles (200,000 volumes); 20,000 bound periodical volumes; 1,200 current subscriptions; 3,500 government documents; 3,000 reels of microfilm; 6 drawers of microfiche. Subject coverage: Canadian native peoples; the Canadian North, the environment, natural resources, Canadian history, and economic development. books on North American Indians and Eskimos.

THE NATIONAL MUSEUMS OF CANADA LIBRARY
360 Lisgar St.
OTTAWA K1A 0M8
Description: Maintains a collection of 35,000 volumes on anthropology, including many on the Indians & native peoples of Canada. Museo-cinematography: Ethnographic Film Programs.

LAURENTIAN UNIVERSITY MUSEUM & ARTS CENTRE LIBRARY
Laurentian University, Dept. of Cultural Affairs
SUDBURY P3E 2C6
(705) 675-1151 Fax 674-3065
Pamela Krueger, Librarian
Description: A collection of books covering all areas of art with special sections on native and Inuit peoples. Open to the public.

ROYAL ONTARIO MUSEUM LIBRARY
100 Queen's Park
TORONTO M5S 2C6
Description: A collection of 50,000 volumes, and 20 journals of anthropological interest; many books on the Indians and native peoples of Canada.

QUEBEC

CANADIAN MUSEUM OF CIVILIZATION MEDIATHEQUE
P.O. Box 3100, Station "B" - 100 Laurier St.
HULL J8X 4H2
(819) 953-6456
FAX 953-4378
M. Boudreau, Reference Librarian

SASKATCHEWAN

NATIVE LAW LIBRARY
Native Law Centre
University of Saskatchewan
150 Diefenbaker Centre
SASKATOON S7N 0W0
(306) 966-6189
Linda Fritz, Native Law Librarian
Description: A collection of 6,000 books, journals and legal decisions in all areas of native law including self-government, constitutional developments, membership rights, child welfare and international law. A major retrospective cataloguing project has recently been completed, making historical documents from various native organizations and older published works accessible. Archival collection of materials from the Mackenzie Valley Pipeline Inquiry; and a complete collection of native law cases.

ABORIGINAL CIRCUIT
Box 2868
Winnipeg, MB R3C 4B4
(204) 663-4543 Fax 255-5057

AFN BULLETIN
Assembly of First Nations
47 Clarence St., Suite 300
Ottawa, ON K1N 9K1
(613) 236-0673
Bi-monthly newsletter . $18.00/year .

ALBERTA NATIVE NEWS
530-10036 Jasper Ave.
Edmonton, AB T5J 2W2
(403) 421-7966

ANISHINABE NEWS
Nipissing First Nation
Box 711
North Bay, ON P1B 8J8
(705) 497-9127 Fax 497-9135

**ANTHROPOLOGICAL
JOURNAL OF CANADA**
Anthropological Association of Canada
1575 Forlan Dr .
Ottawa, ON K2C 0R8

ARROWS OF FREEDOM
c/o Drumheller Native Brotherhood
of Indian & Metis
Box 3000
Drumheller, AB T0J 0Y0
(403) 823-2542

ARTSCRAFT
The National Indian Arts & Crafts Corporation
1 Nicholas St., Suite 1 106
Ottawa, ON K1N 7B6 - Canada
(613) 232-2436
Claudette Fortin, Editor
A quarterly publication which includes feature articles on Indian arts and crafts; regional profiles and artist's profiles; and book reviews. No advertising. Subscription, $16 per year . Begun 1989.

**ASSOCIATION FOR NATIVE DEVELOPMENT
IN THE PERFORMING & VISUAL ARTS
NEWSLETTER**
27 Carlton St., Suite 208
Toronto, ON M5B 1L2

**BATCHEWANA FIRST
NATION NEWSLETTER**
236 Frontenac St.
Sault Ste. Marie, ON P6A 5K9
(705) 759-0914 Fax 759-9171
Darlene Syrette, Editor

BROTHER OF TIME
Native Brotherhood of Millhaven
P.O. Box 280
Bath, ON K0H 1G0

CANADIAN ETHNIC STUDIES
Research Centre for Canadian Ethnic Studies
University of Calgary
2500 University Dr ., N.W
Calgary, AB T2N 1N4
(403) 220-7257 Fax 282-8606
J.S. Frideres, Editor
Book reviews. Triannual journal. 1,250 cir . $30/year; institutions, $36/year . Begun 1969.

**CANADIAN HISTORICAL ASSOCIATION
NEWSLETTER/BULLETIN**
395 Wellington St.
Ottawa, ON K1A 0N3

CANADIAN INDIAN ARTCRAFTS
National Indian Arts and Crafts Corporation
One Nicholas St., Suite 1 106
Ottawa, ON K1N 7B6
Published quarterly .

CANADIAN JOURNAL OF ANTHROPOLOGY
Department of Anthropology
University of Alberta
Edmonton, AB T6G 2H4

CANADIAN JOURNAL OF ARCHAEOLOGY
Department of Anthropology
University of Victoria
Victoria, B.C. V8W 2Y2

**CANADIAN JOURNAL
OF NATIVE EDUCATION**
University of Alberta
5-109 Education N. Bldg.
Edmonton, AB T6G 2G5
(403) 492- 2769 Fax 492-0762
Carl Urion, Editor
Semiannual. Covers the education of native peoples in North America with special focus on Canada. Includes Inuit, Metis and Indian people. Book reviews. 750 cir . $8/copy; $15/year . Advertising. Begun 1973.

CANADIAN JOURNAL OF NATIVE STUDIES
Department of Native Studies
Brandon University
Brandon, MB R7A 6A9
Samuel W . Corrigan, Editor
An international refereed periodical published twice annually . It is the official publication of the Canadian Indian/Native Studies Association.

CANADIAN NATIVE LAW REPORTER
Native Law Centre
University of Saskatchewan
Room 141, Diefenbaker Centre
Saskatoon, SK S7N 0W0
(306) 966-6189
Zandra MacEachem, Editor
Contributing editors : Donald Purich, Phil Lancaster, Norman K. Zlotkin, and Nancy Ayers. A specialized law report series, providing full, comprehensive coverage of native law judgements in Canada. *Research features* : subject index, statutes judicially considered; year end cumulative indexes; articles and case comments. Advertising. Published quarterly . *Subscription* : $50/year (Canadian). Back issues: 1984-1985, $45/year; 1979-1983, $30/year . Begun 1978.

THE CARIBOU
Box 375
St. George's, NF A0N 1Z0
(709) 647-3723

**CENTRAL OKANAGON FRIENDSHIP
SOCIETY NEWSLETTER**
442 Leon Ave.
Kelowna, BC V1Y 6J3
(604) 861-4905 Fax 861-5514

CREE AJEMON
James Bay Cree Communications Society
MISTASSINI, PQ G0W 1C0
(418) 923-3191

Diane Reid, Editor
Bulletin.

DAKOTA TIME
Box 149
Griswold, MB R0M 0S0
(204) 855-2250

DAN SHA NEWS
Ye Sa to Communications Society
22 Nisutlin Dr.
Whitehorse YT Y1A 3S5
(403) 667-2775 Fax 668-6577
Joanne MacDonald, Publisher
Eric Huggard, Editor
Monthly newspaper covering Yukon Indian issues and community events. 2,700 cir . $12/year, individuals; $25/year, institutions. Advertising. Begun 1973.

DANNZHA
Ye Sa To Communications Society
22 Nisutlin Dr .
Whitehorse, Yukon Y1A 3S5
(403) 667-7636/2775

ELBOW DRUMS
Calgary Indian Friendship Society
140 - 2nd Ave., S.W.
Calgary 1, AB

ENOCH ECHO
Enoch Tribal Administration
Box 2, Site 2, RR 1
Winterbum, AB T0E 2N0
(403) 470-4505

ESKIMO
P.O. Box 10
Churchill, MB R0B E0E
(204) 675-2252
Guy Mary-Rousselier, Editor
Semiannual magazine on missionary history in the central and eastern Canadian Arctic and Inuit traditions. Published in French. Begun 1944.

ESQUIMALT NEWS
542C Fraser St.
Victoria, BC V9A 6H7
(604) 381-5664 Fax 361-9283

ETHNIC DIRECTORY OF CANADA
Western Publishers
P.O. Box 30193, Station B
Calgary, AB
(403) 289-3301
Vladimir Markotic, Editor
Published once every few years.
Complimentary copies available.

ETUDES/INUIT/STUDIES
Inuksiutit Katimajiit Association
Department of Anthropology, Laval University
Quebec, P.Q. G1K 7P4
(418) 656-2353 Fax 656-3023
Francois Therien, Editor
Semiannual journal devoted to the study of Inuit societies of Siberia, Greenland, and Canada, either traditional or contemporary , in the perspective of social sciences and humanities: archaeology, linguistics, symbolism, demography , ethnohistory and law . Contains articles in French and English on the Inuit culture, language and history . Book reviews. 750 cir . $12/copy; $27/year , individuals; $43/year , institutions. Back issues available. Advertising. Begun 1976.

THE FIRST CITIZEN
P.O. Box 760, Station A
Vancouver, BC

FIRST NATIONS MAGAZINE
CKND-TV
603 St. Mary;s Rd.
Winnipeg, MB R2M 4A5
 (204) 233-3304 Fax 233-5615

FOUR WORLDS EXCHANGE
Box 143
Pincher Creek, AB T0K 1W0
 (403) 627-4411
 Michael Bopp, Editor

FRIENDSHIP CENTRE NEWS
16 Spadina Rd.
Toronto, ON M5R 2S7
 (416) 964-9087

**GATHERINGS: THE EN'OWKIN JOURNAL
OF FIRST NORTH AMERICAN PEOPLES**
Theytus Books Ltd.
P.O. Box 20040
Penticton, B.C. Canada V2A 8K3
Published annually by the En'owkin Centre of the
International School of Writing, a Native writer's
school in Canada, affiliated with the University of
Victoria. Contents are poetry & fiction. 300 pages.

HA-SHILTH-SA
Box 1383
Port Alberni, B.C. V9Y 7M2
 (604) 724-5757 Fax 723-0463

HOLMAN ESKIMO PRINTS
Canadian Arctic Producers Limited
P.O. Box 4132. Postal Station E
Ottawa, ON K1S 5S2

INDIAN & INUIT GRADUATE REGISTER
Canada Dept. of Indian Affairs & Northern Affairs
10 Wellington
Ottawa, ON K1A 0H4

INDIAN ECHO
Canadian Department of Justice
Penitentiary Branch
Ottawa, ON

INDIAN FREE PRESS N'AMERIND
London's Indian Friendship Centre
613 Wellington St.
London, ON

INDIAN LIFE MAGAZINE
Intertribal Christian Communications
Box 3765 Station B
Winnipeg, MB R2W 3R6
 (204) 661-9333
 George McPeek, Director
 Jim Uttley, Editor & Publisher
Bimonthly. Contains feature news, first-person
articles, photo features, family-life material and
legends. Focus is primarily on dealing with problems and issues within contemporary North American Indian society. 150,000 cir. $1.50/copy; $7/
year. Advertising. Begun 1967.

INDIAN MAGAZINE NEWSLETTER
Canadian Broadcasting Company, Publishers
P.O. Box 500, Station A
Toronto 116, ON

INDIAN NEWS
Canada Department of Indian Affairs
and Northern Development
10 Wellington
Ottawa, ON K1A 0H4

INDIAN RECORD
480 Aulneau St.
Winnipeg, MB R2H 2V2
 (204) 233-6430
 Rev. G. Laviolette, OMI, Editor
Contains articles on the Canadian Indians from
coast to coast. Published four times per year. Advertising. Subscription: $4/year, $7/two years, $10/
three years.

THE INDIAN VOICE
Canadian Indian Voice Society
429 East 6th St. North
Vancouver, B.C. V7L 1P8
 (604) 876-0944
 Donna Doss, Editor
Quarterly newsletter covering areas affecting the
native Indian. 2,800 cir. $1/copy; $7/year. Advertising. Begun 1969.

INDIAN WORLD MAGAZINE
Union of British Columbia Indian Chiefs
440 West Hastings, 3rd Floor
Vancouver, B.C. V6B 1L1
 (604) 684-0231

INDIANS OF QUEBEC
c/o Coalition of Nations
P.O. Box 810
Caughnawaga, Q.P. J0L 1B0
 (514) 632-7321

INUKTITUT
Inuit Tapirisat of Canada
170 Laurier W.
Ottawa, ON K1P 5V5
 (613) 238-8181 Fax 234-1991
 John Bennett & Alootook Ipellie, Editors
Quarterly magazine promoting the exchange of
cultural information among Inuit groups in Canada
and to inform non-Inuit about Iuit life. 10,000 cir.
$7/copy. Advertising. Begun 1959.

INUVIALUIT
Committee for Original People's Entitlement
P.O. Box 200
Inuvik, N.W.T. X0E 0T0

JOURNAL OF INDIGENOUS STUDIES
Gabriel Dumont Institute of Native
Studies & Applied Research
121 Broadway Ave. East
Regina, SK S4N 0Z6
 (306) 522-5691 Fax 565-0809
 Catherine I. Littlejohn, Editor
Semiannual. 200 cir. Individuals, $10/copy;
$20/year; Institutions, $15/copy, $30/year.
Begun 1989.

KAHTOU COMMUNICATIONS, INC.
Native Communications Society of B.C.
203-540 Burrard St.
Vancouver, B.C. V6C 2K1
 (604) 684-7375 Fax 684-5375
 Tim Isaac, Managing Editor
Biweekly newspaper. $15/year.

KAINAI NEWS
Indian News Media
P.O. Box 120
Standoff, AB T0L 1Y0

 (403) 653-3301 Fax 653-3437
 Mary Weasel Fat, Editor
A weekly newspaper that covers issues of interest to status, non-status and Metis people of southern Alberta. Extensive coverage of the Treaty 7
tribes located in southern Alberta. The tribes are
Blackfoot, Blood, Peigan, Carcee and Stoney.
Coverage is extended to the urban cities of Calgary
and Lethbridge. Advertising accepted. Complimentary copies are available upon request. Maintains a Calgary Bureau locate at Calgary Friendship Centre. $20/year; 50¢ per copy. Begun 1968.

KATERI
P.O. Box 70
Kahnawake, P.Q. J0L 1B0
 (514) 525-3611
 Rev. Henri Bechard, S.J., Editor
"Its aim is to promote the canonization of Blessed
Kateri Tekakwitha; articles on life of the Beata, nes
concerning the native peoples of North America,
with special emphasis on her own people, the
account of favors due to her intercession." Published quarterly. Subscription: $3/year. No adver-
tising. Complimentary copies available upon request. Begun 1949.

KINATUINAMOT ILENGAJUK
Okalakatiget Society
Box 160
Nain, Labrador A0P 1E0
 (709) 922-2955 Fax 922-2293
 Ken Todd, Editor
Newsletter.

THE LABRADORIAN
Box 39, Station "B"
Goose Bay, NF A0P 1E0
 (709) 896-3341

LE METIS
410 McGregor St.
Winnipeg, MB R2W 4X5
 (204) 589-4327 Fax 586-6462

MACKENZIE TIMES
Box 499
Fort Simpson, NT X0E 0N0
 (403) 695-3330 Fax 695-2922

MAL-I-MIC NEWS
320 St. Mary's St.
Fredericton, NB E3A 2S4
 (506) 458-8422 Fax 450-3749

**MANITOBA INDIAN EDUCATION
ASSOCIATION NEWSLETTER**
816-294 Portage Ave.
Winnipeg, MB R3C 3C9
 (204) 943-3707 Fax 947-6564

MASENAYEGUN
239 Magnus Ave.
Winnipeg, MB R2W 2B6
 (204) 586-8441

MESSENGER
William Head InstituteIndian Education Club
Box 10
Metochosin, BC
 M. Walkus, Editor
Quarterly newsletter. $1/year. Begun 1970.

MICMAC NEWS
Nova Scotia Native Communications Society
Box 344
Sydney, N.S. B1P 6H2

(902) 539-0045 Fax 564-0430
Roy Gould, Publisher
Brian Douglas, Editor
Bimonthly newspaper containing local provincial and national issues on Canadian Indians. $7/yr .

MICMAC-MALISEET NEWS
Confederacy of Mainland Micmacs
Box 1590
Truro, NS B2N 5V3
(902) 895-6385 Fax 893-1520

THE MIDDEN
Archaeological Society of British Columbia
P.O. Box 520, Station A
Vancouver, B.C. V6C 2N3
Kathryn Bernick, Editor
Contains articles, book reviews, news items related to British Columbia archaeology--prehistoric and historic periods. Published five times per year . Subscription: $10/year; $12/year , overseas.

MIDNIGHT SUN
c/o Settlement Council
Igloolik, NT X0E 0L0

MIRAMICHI NEWS
Miramichi Indian Agency
P.O. Box 509
Chatham, NB

MOOSE TALK
Box 125
Moosonee, ON P0L 1Y0
(705) 336-2510

MOSAIK
696 Buckingham Rd.
Winnipeg, MB R3R 1C2
(204) 888-8245
Ted Alcuitas, Editor & Publisher
Monthly tabloid of news and views on multicultural events and issues that impact on the multicultural community, Book reviews. 3,500 cir. $35/year; $45/year, foreign. Advertising. Begun 1983.

MUSEUM OF INDIAN ARCHAEOLOGY NEWSLETTER
University of Western Ontario
Lawson-Jury Bldg.
London, ON N6G 3M6
(519) 473-1360
Debra Bodner, Editor

NATIVE ALLIANCE FOR RED POWER
P.O. Box 6152
Vancouver, B.C.

NATIVE BROTHERHOOD NEWS
P.O. Box 60
Mission, B.C. V2Y 4L1

NATIVE BROTHERHOOD NEWSCALL
Saskatchewan Pentitentiary
P.O. Box 160
Prince Albert, SK S6V 5R6

NATIVE ISSUES
Native Peoples Support Group
of Newfoundland and Labrador
P.O. Box 582, Station C
St. John's, NFLD A1C 5K8

NATIVE NETWORK NEWS
120-12520 St. Albert Trail
Edmonton, AB T5L 4H4
(403) 454-7076

NATIVE PERSPECTIVE
Box 2550
LacLa Biche, AB T0A 2C0
(403) 623-3333

NATIVE PRESS
Native Communications Society-W estern N.W.T.
P.O. Box 1919, Aquarius Bldg.
Yellowknife, N.W.T. X1A 2P4
(403) 873-2661 Fax 920-4205
Lee Selleck, Editor
Weekly newspaper serving 26 communities in the Western Northwest Territories. Book reviews. 5,600 cir. $1/copy; $25/year . Advertising. Begun 1971.

NATIVE SCENE MAGAZINE
202-115 Bannatyne Ave.
Winnipeg, MB R3B 0R3
(204) 943-6475 Fax 942-1380

THE NATIVE SISTERHOOD
P.O. Box 515
Kingston, ON K7L 4W7

NATIVE SPORTS NEWS
205-15517 Stony Plain Rd.
Edmonton, AB T3P 3Z1
(403) 486-7766

NATIVE STUDIES REVIEW
University of Saskatchewan
Native Studies Department
15 McLean Hall
Saskatoon, SK S7N 0W0
Semiannual journal.

NATIVEBEAT
Box 1260
Fo.est, ON N0N 1J0
(519) 786-2142 (phone & fax)

NDOODEMAK (MY FRIENDS/RELATIVES)
Manitoba Association for Native Languages
119 Sutherland Ave.
Winnipeg, MB R2W 3C9
(204) 943-3707 Fax 943-9312

NEIGHBOURHOOD PROFILE
Box 2868
Winnipeg, MB R3C 4B4
(204) 256-2699 Fax 254-5302

NEW BREED
Saskatchewan Native Communications Corp.
202 - 173 Second Ave. South
Saskatoon, SK S7K 1K6
(306) 653-2253
Ona Fiddler-Bertelg, Editor
Newspaper.

NEWS & VIEWS
Canada Department of Indian Affairs
and Northern Development
10 Wellington
Ottawa, ON K1A 0H4

NEWS OF THE NORTH
Box 2820
Yellowknife, NT X1A 2R1
(403) 873-4031 Fax 873-8507

NICOLA INDIAN
Nicola Valley Indian Administration
P.O. Box 188
Merritt, B.C. V0K 2B0
(604) 378-6411/1235

NORTHERN REPORTER
Box 310, Station "B"
Goose Bay, NF A0P 1E0
(709) 896-2595

NORTHERN SENTINEL
626 Enterprise Ave.
Kitimat, BC V8C 2E4
(604) 632-6144

THE NORTHIAN
University of Saskatchewan
Saskatoon, SK S7N 0W0

NUNATSIAQ NEWS
Box 8
Iqaluit, NT X0A 0H0
(819) 979-5357 Fax 979-4763

ONTARIO ARCHAEOLOGY
The Ontario Archaeological Society
126 Willowdale Ave.
Willowdale, ON M2N 4Y2
(416) 730-0797
Charles Garrad, Administrator
A learned refereed journal dedicated to the archaeoogy and prehistory of Ontario and the Northeast. Back issues are available for sale. Included in membership. Begun 1956.

ONTARIO INDIAN
Union of Ontario Indians
27 Queen St. East, 2nd Floor
Toronto, ON M5C 2M6
(416) 366-3527
Dennis Martel, Editor
Published monthly . $10 per year. Begun 1978.

ONTARIO NATIVE EXPERIENCE
Ontario Federation of Friendship Centres
234 Eglington Ave., East, Suite 203
Toronto, ON M4P 1K5

ONTARIO NATIVE WOMEN'S ASSOCIATION NEWSLETTER
278 Bay St.
Thunder Bay, ON

OWNEWS
Original Women's Network, Inc.
A-356 Stella Ave.
Winnipeg, MB R2W 2T9
(204) 582-2383 Fax 582-6468

PAPERS OF THE ALGONQUIAN CONFERENCE - Carleton University
Dept. of Linguistics
Ottawa, ON K1S 5B6
(613) 788-2809
William Cowan, Editor
Publishes papers given at annual Algonquian Conference. 300 cir. $25/copy. Begun 1974.

PEACE HILLS COUNTRY NEWSPAPER
Box 509
Hobbema, AB T0C 1N0
(403) 474-6283

PENTICTON INDIAN BAND NEWSLETTER
RR 2, Site 50, Comp. 8
Penticton, BC V2A 6J7
(604) 493-0048 Fax 493-2882

PEREGRINE PRESS
16120 8th Ave.
Surrey, BC V4A 1A2
(604) 536-1790 Fax 538-0666

PHOENIX
Canadian Alliance in
Solidarity With Native Peoples
39 Spadina Rd.
Toronto, ON M5R 2S9
  (416) 972-6232
Quarterly magazine. Curent issues seen from a
Native perspective; also poetry and book reviews.
$20/year.

PRAIRIE FORUM
Canadian Plains Research Center
University of Regina
Regina, SK S4S 0A2
  (306) 585-4795 Fax 586-9862
  Alvin Finkel, Editor
Semiannual journal of research relating to the
Canadian Plains. Book reviews. 400 cir . $13/copy;
$20/year, individuals; $25/year , institutions. Adver-
tising. Begun 1976.

**RECHERCHES AMERINDIENNES AU
QUEBEC**
Societe de Recherches Amerindiennes au
Quebec
6742 rue St. Denis
Montreal, PQ H2S 2S2
  (514) 277-6178
  Carole Levesque, Editor
Quarterly journal on the Native peoples of Quebec with an anthropological perspective. Text
mainly in French. Book reviews. 1,500 cir . $8/copy.
$24/year, individuals; $30/year , institutions. Advertising. Begun 1971.

RENCONTRE
Secretariat aux Affaires Autochtones
875 Grande Allee est.
Quebec, PQ G1R 4Y8
  (418) 643-3166
  Ann Picard, Publisher
Quarterly government publication for Quebec's
Amerindian & Inuit peoples. Begun 1979.

REX MAGAZINE
443 W. 3rd St.
N. Vancouver, BC V7M 1G9
  (604) 985-0799 Fax 980-3861

**THE RUNNER: NATIVE MAGAZINE
FOR COMMUNICATIVE ARTS**
c/o ANDPVA
39 Spadina Rd., 2nd Floor
Toronto, ON M5R 2S9
  (416) 972-0871 Fax 972-0892
  Gary Farmer, Editor/Publisher
Promotes the talents, products and services of
established and upcoming Native individuals and
groups in the arts and communication fields. Includes news for Native writers, actors, film makers and radio and television people. Quarterly . $20/
yr., individuals; $24/yr ., institutions.

**SASKATCHEWAN ARCHAEOLOGICAL
SOCIETY NEWSLETTER**
Saskatchewan Archaeological Society
816 1st Ave. North #5
Saskatoon, SK S7K 1Y3
  (306) 664-4124
  Jim Finnigan, Editor
A bi-monthly publiction. No advertising.
Included in membership. Begun 1963.

SASKATCHEWAN ARCHAEOLOGY
Saskatchewan Archaeological Society
816 1st Ave. North #5
Saskatoon, SK S7K 1Y3

  (306) 664-4124
  Terry Gibson, Editor
An annual publication. Included with membership.
Begun 1980.

SASKATCHEWAN INDIAN
Saskatchewan Indian Media Corp.
2103 Airport Dr., #107
Saskatoon, SK S7L 6W2
  (306) 665-2175
  Alex Greyeyes, Publisher
  Doug Cuthand, Editor
Monthly magazine providing communication
among Saskatchewan's almost 50,000 Treaty Indians through information news, stories and editorial opinion. Book reviews. 8,500 cir . $15/year;
$3/copy. Advertising. Begun 1987.

**SASKATCHEWAN INDIAN FEERATED
COLLEGE JOURNAL**
College W. Bldg., 127
Regina, SK S4S 0A2
  (306) 584-8333
  Joel Demay, Editor
Semiannual. $15/year , individuals; $25/year ,
institutions. Begun 1984.

THE SCOUT
Indian-Metis Friendship Centre
Brandon Friendship Centre
836 Lorne Ave.
Brandon, MB R7A 0TB

SECWEPEMC NEWS
Secwepemc Cultural Education Society
345 Yellowhead Highway
Kamloops, B.C. V2H 1H1
  (604) 828-9784
To inform the Shuswap Nation of current political,
social and economic issues and events af fecting
their lives and promoting the preservation of
Shuswap history, language and culture. Published
six times per year.

STO:LO NATION NEWS
Box 370
Sardis, BC V2R 1A7
  (604) 858-3366 Fax 858-4790

TAQRALIK
Northern Quebec Inuit Association
P.O. Box 179
Fort Chimo, P.Q. J0M 1C0

THE TALKING LEAVES
Native Brotherhood Association
P.O. Box 880
Kingston, ON

TAWOW
Canada Department of Indian Affairs
and Northern Development
10 Wellington
Ottawa, ON K1A 0H4

TEKAWENNAKE NEWSPAPER
Tekawennake Publications
Box 130
Ohsweken, ON N0A 1M0
  Roberta Green, Editor
Weekly tabloid. Advertising.

**TEKAWENNAKE SIX NATIONS
NEW CREDIT REPORTER**
Woodland Indian Cultural Education Center
184 Mohawk St., Box 1506
Brantford, ON N3T 5V6

  (519) 753-5531
  Roberta Green, Editor & Publisher
Weekly native newspaper for and about native
peoples. Book reviews. 1,550 cir . $30/year; $1/
copy. Advertising. Begun 1967.

THREE SISTER'S MUL TI-MEDIA
Box 1260
Forest, ON N0N 1J0
  (519) 786-2142 (phone & fax)

TORONTO NATIVE TIMES
16 Spadina Rd.
Toronto, ON M5R 2S8
  (416) 964-9087

TREATY No. 3 COUNCIL FIRE
37 Main St. South
Kenora, ON P9N 1S8

TRENT NATIVE NEWS
Department of Native Studies
Trent University
Petersborough, ON K9J 7B7

TRIBAL INDIAN NEWS N'AMERIND
London's Indian Friendship Centre
613 Wellington St.
London, ON

TUSAAYAKSAT (Newspaper)
Inuvialuit Communications Society
Box 1704, McKenzie Rd., Semmler Bldg.
Inuvik, NWT X0E 0T0
  (403) 979-2067; 977-2202
  Vincent Teddy, Editor & President

TYENDINAGA TERRITORY NEWSLETTER
c/o Mohawk Band Of fice, RR 1
Deseronto, ON K0K 1X0
  (613) 396-3424

UNITY
Association of Iroquois and Allie Indians
R.R. 2
Southwold, ON N0L 2G0
  Shelly Bressette, Editor
Quarterly newsletter covering news and issues of
importance to the Indian peoples.

**WA-WA-TAY CREE COMMUNICATIONS
NETWORK**
Fort Albany, ON P0L 1H0
  (705) 278-1 147

WAWATAY NEWS
Wawatay Communications Society
Box 1180, 16-5th Ave.
Sioux Lookout, ON P0V 2T0
  (807) 737-2951 Fax 737-3224
  Megan Williams, Editor
Bilingual, semi-monthly newspaper which carries
all types of news for and about Nishnawbe-Aski
Nation. Advertising accepted. Circulation 10,000/
\Subscription: $1 1/year (individuals) in Canada;
$12, U.S., and $16, foreignBegun 1973.

WEETAMAH
595 Notre Dame Ave.
Winnipeg, MB R3B 1S6
  (204) 774-0431

**THE WESTERN CANADIAN
ANTHROPOLOGIST**
University of Saskatchewan
Dept. of Anthropology/Archaeology
Saskatoon, SK S7N 0W0

(306) 966-4175
Satya Sharma, Editor
Annual journal cotaining material of interest to
anthropologists. Book reviews. 400 cir . $10/
copy. Begun 1968.

WESTERN NATIVE NEWS
530-10036 Jasper Ave.
Edmonton, AB T5J 2W2
(403) 425-3508
201-1593 W. 3rd St.
Vancouver, BC V6J 1J8
(604) 736-3015

WHISPERING PINES
Northern Association of Community Councils
504-63 Albert St.
Winnipeg, MB R3B 1G4
(204) 947-2227

WINDSPEAKER
Aboriginal Multi-Media Society of Alberta
15001 112th Ave.
Edmonton, AB T5M 2V6
(403) 455-2700 Fax 452-1428
Gary Gee, Editor
Biweekly newspaper. 10,000 cir. $26/year; $40,
foreign. Advertising. Begun 1983.

WINNIPEG INDIAN TIMES
Indian and Metis Friendship Centre
73 Princess St.
Winnipeg 3, MB

ALBERTA

UNIVERSITY OF CALGARY
Native Studies Department
CALGARY T2N 1N4
Faculty: Jean-Guy Goulet, PhD

UNIVERSITY OF ALBERTA
School of Native Studies
11023 90th Ave.
EDMONTON T6G 2Z6
(403) 492-2991

UNIVERSITY OF ALBERTA
Native Health Care Career Program
Faculty of Medicine
2J2.11 W.C. MacKenzie Sciences Centre
EDMONTON T6G 2R7
(403) 492-6350 Fax 492-7303
Anne-Marie Hodes, Coordinator

UNIVERSITY OF ALBERTA
Indigenous Law Programs
Faculty of Law
4th Floor, Law Centre
EDMONTON T6G 2H5
(403) 492-7749 FAX 492-4924

GRANT MacEWAN COMMUNITY COLLEGE
Native Communications Department
EDMONTON

OLD SUN COMMUNITY COLLEGE
P.O. Box 339
GLEICHEN T0J 1N0
(403) 734-3862; 264-9658
Blackfoot Cultural Centre
Gerald Sitting Eagle, Coordinator

MASKWACHEES CULTURAL COLLEGE
P.O. Box 360
HOBBEMA, AB T0C 1N0
(403) 585-3925 Fax 585-2080
Dr. Fred Carnew, Director

UNIVERSITY OF LETHBRIDGE
Department of Native American Studies
4401 University Dr.
LETHBRIDGE T1K 3M4
(403) 329-2635
Don Frantz, Chairperson
Martin Heavy Head, Native Student Services
Instructors: Don Frantz, Tony Hall, Christine
Miller, Alfred Young Man, Leroy Little Bear.

BRITISH COLUMBIA

SIMON FRASER UNIVERSITY
The Secwepeme Cultural Education Society
345 Yellowhead Highway
KAMLOOPS V2H 1H1
Chief Ron Ignace, Co-chair
Muriel Sasakamoose, Executive Director
(604) 374-0616 (Sheila Dick-education
coordinat)
(604) 372-5396 (Marianne Boelscher-
instructor)
Currently in its first year of offering a university
program for Native Indian students with focus on
social science research and Native studies.

UNIVERSITY OF BRITISH COLUMBIA
Department of Anthropology.
6303 N.W. Marine Dr.
VANCOUVER V6T 2B2
(604) 228-2878
Instructors: David F. Aberle, PhD, Harry B. Haw-
thorn, PhD (Indians of Canada); J.E. Michael Kew,
PhD (Indians of Canada), Louise M. Jackson, PhD,
Bruce G. Miller, PhD, William Robin Ridington,
PhD (Native American cosmology); and Wolfgang
George Jilek, M.D. *Special program*: Summer
Field School in Archaeology. *Special facilities*:
Research laboratories in archaeology, ethno-meth-
odology and socio-linguistics, and ethnography;
Museum of Anthropology.

UNIVERSITY OF BRITISH COLUMBIA
Museum of Anthropology
6393 N.W. Marine Dr.
VANCOUVER V6T 1W5
(604) 228-5087
Michael M. Ames, Ph.D., Director/Professor
Moya Waters, Administrative Officer
Special programs: Anthropology and archaeology
of Northwest Coast of British Columbia, indigenous
arts, material culture, ceramics, and development
of innovative teaching pograms in museology and
the arts. *Financial aid*: The Lois McConkey Memorial Fellowship for Native Indian Work-Study
Program - a fellowship for secondary school and
university students of North American Indian descent. Research results published occasionally in
professional journals and books; also publishes
notes, catalogues, and museum visitory profiles.

UNIVERSITY OF BRITISH COLUMBIA
First Nations Health Care Professions Program
Woodward Instructional Resources Centre
407-2194 Health Sciences Mall
VANCOUVER, BC V6T 1Z6
(604) 822-5613 Fax 822-2495

UNIVERSITY OF BRITISH COLUMBIA
Native Indian Teachers Education Program
6375 Biological Science Rd.
VANCOUVER, BC V6T 1Z5
(604) 822-5240 FAX 822-6501

UNIVERSITY OF BRITISH COLUMBIA
Native Law Progfam
1822 East Mall
VANCOUVER, BC V6T 1Z1
(604) 822-5559 Fax 822-8108

UNIVERSITY OF BRITISH COLUMBIA
TS'KEL Program (MEd, MA, EdP, PhD)
Faculty of Education
VANCOUVER, BC V6T 1Z4
(604) 822-5857 FAX 822-6501

UNIVERSITY OF VICTORIA
Department of Anthropology
VICTORIA V8W 2Y2
(604) 721-7046
Instructors: Kathleen A. Berthiaume, PhD, Leland
H. Donald, PhD, N. Ross Crumrine, PhD, Eric A.
Roth, PhD. *Special facilities*: Provincial Archives
and Museum; archaeological, ethnological and lin-
guistic (especially in Coast Salish languages
through the Lingistics Department) field training;
Pacific Studies; and Interdisciplinary Studies Pro-
gram.

MANITOBA

UNIVERSITY OF BRANDON
Department of Native Studies
BRANDON

UNIVERSITY OF MANITOBA
Department of Native Studies
532B Fletcher Ave
WINNIPEG R3T 2N2
(204) 474-9266
Freda Ahenakew, PhD, Chairperson
Instructors: Freda Ahenakew, PhD, Emma
LaRocque, PhD, Paul L.A.H. Chartrand, PhD, Fred
Shore, PhD, John D. Nichols, PhD, H. Christoph
Wolfart, PhD (Linguistics), Richard T. Carter, Jr.,
PhD (Linguistics). *Publications*: Algonquian and
Iroquoian Linguistics, quarterly; Algonquian and
Iroquoian Memoirs (monograph series.)

UNIVERSITY OF MANITOBA
Department of Anthropology
WINNIPEG R3T 2N2
(204) 474-9361
Instructors: Louis Allaire, PhD, Richard T. Carter,
Jr., PhD (Linguistics), Joan B. Townsend, PhD, H.
Christoph Wolfart, PhD (Linguistics), John D.
Nichols, PhD (Native Studies), William Koolage,
PhD, Gregory Monks, PhD, Dwight A. Rokala,
PhD, & David H. Stymeist, PhD. *Special programs*:
Population biology and medical anthropology of
North American Indians; indigenous languages of
Canada, especially Siouan and Algonquian (Cree
Language Project.) Special facilities: Anthropol-
ogy Laboratories; The Provincial Archives.

UNIVERSITY OF WINNIPEG
Department of Anthropology
515 Portage Ave.
WINNIPEG R3B 2E9
(204) 786-9875
Instructors: Gary R. Granzberg, PhD (Chair), Wing
Sam Chow, PhD, William H. Morgan, PhD. *Special program*: Archaeological Field School. *Special facilities*: Algonkian ethnological collections;
Hudson's Bay Company Archives Research Centre; ethnology, archaeology, and physical anthropology laboratories.

NEW BRUNSWICK

UNIVERSITY OF NEW BRUNSWICK
Department of Anthropology
FREDERICTON E3B 5A3
(506) 453-4975
Instructors: William G. Dalton, PhD, Vincent O.
Erickson, PhD, Peter R. Lovell, PhD, and Gail R.
Pool, PhD. *Special resources*: Local fieldwork
opportunities (Maliseet-Micmac Indian communi-
ties); archaeology-anthropology laboratory. Ar-
chives. Library.

NEWFOUNDLAND

**MEMORIAL UNIVERSITY
OF NEWFOUNDLAND**
Department of Anthropology
ST. JOHN'S A1C 5S7
(709) 737-8870

(709) 737-8870

Instructors: Gordon Inglis, PhD, John C. Kennedy, PhD, Thomas F. Nemec, PhD, Adrian Tanner, PhD, and James A. Tuck, PhD. Special foci: Field research programs--Arctic, Subarctic, and circumpolar (especially Lapps, Algonquin, Inuit and white settlers); northern North Atlantic (Newfoundland, Labrador, Baffin, Iceland.) *Special facility*: Killam Arctic Library.

ONTARIO

NORTH AMERICAN INDIAN TRAVELLING COLLEGE
R.R. 3
CORNWALL ISLAND, ON K6H 5R7
(613) 932-9452 Fax 932-0092
Barbara Barnes, President

UNIVERSITY OF WESTERN ONTARIO
Department of Anthropology
LONDON, ON N6A 5C2
(519) 679-3430
Instructors: Chet Creider, PhD, Chair; Margaret Seguin, PhD (Director-Center for Research and Teaching of Native Languages), Michael W. Spence, PhD, William R. Thurston, PhD, and Lisa Valentine, PhD. *Special facilities*: Center for Research and Teaching of Native Languages, administered within the Department, offers research funds and facilities for faculty and students working on Canadian native languages; Museum of Indian Archaeology.

UNIVERSITY OF WESTERN ONTARIO
Journalism Program for Native People
Middlesex College
LONDON, ON N6A 5B7
(519) 661-3380 Fax 661-3292

YORK UNIVERSITY
Faculty of Environmental Studies
Native/Canadian Relations Dept.
4700 Keele St.
NORTH YORK, ON M3J 1P3
(416) 736-5252 Fax 736-5679
Peter Homenuck, Director
"Native/Canadian Relations (masters level program) focuses on the multi-faceted, unique, bicultural relationships, between, on the one hand, the Native community and its organizations and, on the other, the broader Canadian society and its institutions, together with the issues that result from the relationships. An important component of Native/Canadian Relations is research conducted on the expressed need of Bands, Native communities, Native organizations, and government departments."

TRENT UNIVERSITY
Department of Anthropology
PETERBOROUGH K9J 7B8
(705) 748-1310 Fax 748-1246
Special Program: Native Studies. *Instructors*: Susan M. Jamieson, PhD, Kenneth E. Kidd, PhD (Prof. Emeritus), Evelyn M. Todd, PhD, and Joan M. Vastokas, PhD. *Special facility*: Archaeological Centre.

ALGOMA UNIVERSITY COLLEGE
Ojibway Language
1520 Queen St. E.
SAULT STE. MARIE, ON P6A 2G4
(705) 949-2301

LAURENTIAN UNIVERSITY
Native Institute of Research & Learning
Native Studies Department
Ramsey Lake Rd.
SUDBURY, ON P3E 2C6
(705) 673-5661
Instructors: Roger Spielmann, PhD, Patrick J. Julig, PhD, Kathryn T. Molohon, PhD.

LAKEHEAD UNIVERSITY
Department of Anthropology
THUNDER BAY, ON P7B 5E1
(807) 343-8632
Special programs: Native Studies; Boreal Studies. Instructors: Paul Driben, PhD, and Joe D. Stewart, PhD (Chair).

LAKEHEAD UNIVERSITY
Native Language Teaching
Faculty of Education
955 Oliver Rd.
THUNDER BAY, ON P7B 5E1
(807) 343-8110

LAKEHEAD UNIVERSITY
School of Nursing
THUNDER BAY, ON P7B 5E1
(807) 343-8446 Fax 343-8023
Native Nurses Entry Program

UNIVERSITY OF TORONTO
Department of Anthropology
Sidney Smith Hall
TORONTO, ON M5S 1A1
(416) 978-5416
Instructors: Gary Coupland, PhD, Ivan Kalmer, PhD, Martha A. Latta, PhD, Richard B. Lee, PhD, Krystyna Siesiechowicz, PhD, and Rosamund Vanderburgh. Special program: Northern Yukon Research Project; excavations at historic and prehistoric Huron villages & older sites in Ontario; research among Canadian Indians, rural and urban.

UNIVERSITY OF WATERLOO
Department of Anthropology
WATERLOO N2L 3G1
(519) 885-1211 ext. 2520
Courses: Prehistoric man in America/Great Lakes area - A survey; Inuit and Eskimo cultures; the contemporary Canadian Indian scene; comparative policies on native minorities; early man in the new world. *Instructors*: Thomas S. Abler, PhD, and Sally M. Weaver, PhD. *Award*: Graham Goddard Anthropology Medal--silver medal awarded annually to a 3rd and 4th year anthropology major or honours student who has demonstrated an interest in native peoples of North America.

QUEBEC

McGILL UNIVERSITY
Department of Anthropology
855 Sherbrooke St. West
MONTREAL H3A 2T7
(514) 398-4300 Fax 398-7476
Jerome Rousseau, Dept. Chair
Special programs: Canadian Studies Program; Northern Studies Minor; a group of Iroquoian archaeologists forms a core of an intimate group in archaeology. *Instructors*: Carmen Lambert, PhD, Toby Morantz, PhD, and Colin Scott, PhD.

UNIVERSITY OF MONTREAL
Department of Anthropology
CP 6128, Succursale 'A'
MONTREAL H3C 3J7
(514) 343-6560
Instructors: Franklin Auger (Doct. en Anth), Asen Balikci, PhD, Pierre Beaucage, PhD, Claude Chapdelaine, PhD, Norman Clermont, PhD, Louise I. Paradis, PhD, Remi Savard (Doct. en Ethnol.), Gilles Lefebvre, Ph.D. (Linguistics), and Marcel Rioux, M.A. (Sociology). *Special programs*: Northeast archaeology; Summer Field Programs (Inuit and Canadian Indian areas--ethnology .)

UNIVERSITE LAVAL
Department of Anthropologie
Cite Universitaire
STE-FOY G1K 7P4
(418)656-5867
Courses: ethnologie des Amerindiens; ethnologie des Inuit; dossiers autochtones contemporains. Instructors: Paul Charest, Gerry McNulty, Bernard Saladin d'Anglure, Francois Trudel, PhD, Louis-Jacques Dorais, Pierre Miranda, and Yvan Simonis. *Special programs*: North American Indian; Canadian Inuit. *Special facility*: Centre d'etudes nordiques. *Publications*: Etudes Inuit Studies; Anthropologie et Societes.

SASKATCHEWAN

SASKATCHEWAN INDIAN FEDERATED COLLEGE
University of Regina
118 College West
REGINA, SK S4S 0A2
(306) 584-8333 Fax 584-8334
Dr. Oliver Brass, President
Prof. Paul J. Dudgeon, V.P. Academic
Programs: Undergraduate and graduate degree programs within an environment of Indian cultural affirmation. Elders are available to provide counseling and advice based on traditional Indian values. *Personnel*: Gloria Mehlmann, Director, Research and Development; Richard Laye, Director, Public Relations; Rolando Ramirez, Director, Centre for International Indigenous Studies and Development; Blair Stonechild, Dean; Brian Opikokew, Dean of Students; Robert Anderson, Registrar; Phyllis Lerat, Librarian. *Department Heads*: Bob Boyer, Indian Fine Arts; Edgar Epp, School of Social Work; Dr. Brent Galloway, Indian Languages, Literature & Linguistics; Dr. Pam Janz, Indian Education; David Reed Miller, PhD, Indian Studies. *Publication*: Saskatchewan Indian Federated College Journal, Bi-annual.

UNIVERSITY OF REGINA
Department of Anthropology
REGINA, SK S4S 0A2
(306) 584-4189
Richard K. Pope, Head
Instructors: George W. Arthur, PhD, Head; J.J. McHugh, PhD, Richard K. Pope, and C.R. Watrall, PhD, David Reed Miller, PhD, Patrick Douard, PhD. *Special facilities*: Canadian Plains Research Centre; Saskatchewan Archives; Saskatchewan Indian Federated College. Publications.

SASKATCHEWAN INDIAN CULTURAL COLLEGE
University of Saskatchewan Campus
SASKATOON, SK S7K 3S9
(306) 244-1146

UNIVERSITY OF SASKATCHEWAN
College of Education
SASKATOON, SK S7N 0W0
 (306) 966-7686
Indian Teachers Education Program

UNIVERSITY OF SASKATCHEWAN
National Native Access to Nursing Program
College of Nursing
SASKATOON, SK S7N 0W0
 (306) 966-6224
Indian Health Careers Program

UNIVERSITY OF SASKATCHEWAN
Dept. of Anthropology & Archaeology
SASKATOON, SK S7K 3S9
 (306) 966-4176
 Ernest G. Walker, PhD, Head
Special Program: Native Studies and Ethnicity.
Instructors: Alexander M. Ervin, PhD, Mary C.
Marino, PhD, Zenon S. Pohorecky, Ph.D., Ernest
G. Walker, PhD, Robert G. Williamson, PhD, Urve
Linnamae, PhD (part-time), and James B.
Waldram, PhD (Native Studies Dept.). *Special
programs*: Emphasis is given to research in the
Prairie Provinces of western Canada, Arctic, Sub-
arctic and Northwest Territories of Canada; sum-
mer fieldwork in archaeology and ethnology in
Saskatchewan and/or NWT. *Special facilities*: In-
dian and Northern Curriculum Resources Centre,
College of Education, with a specialized collec-
tion in North American Indian and crosscultural
education; Saskatchewan Provincial Archives;
Reference Library.

UNIVERSITY OF SASKATCHEWAN
A103, Health Sciences Bldg.
SASKATOON, SK S7N 0W0
 (306) 966-6224 Fax 966-8718
National Native Access to Nursing Program

UNIVERSITY OF SASKATCHEWAN
Native Law Centre
141 Diefenbaker Centre
SASKATOON, SK S7N 0W0
 (306) 966-6189 Fax 966-8517
 Donald J. Purich, JD, Director
Established in 1973 to promote the development
of the law and the legal system in ways which
would better accommodate the advancement of
native communities in Canadian society. One of
the Centre's best known activities is its annual pre-
law orientation and screening program for native
students, the Program of Legal Studies for Native
People. *Instructors*: Linda Fritz, JD, Norman
Zlotkin, JD, Donald Purich, JD, Fergus O'Connor,
JD, and Zandra MacEachern, JD. *Special programs*: Research - aboriginal land rights; rights of
indigenous peoples in international law; Indians
and taxation and other areas. Summer program.
Publications: The Canadian Native Law Reporter,
quarerly journal, which provides full text reporting
of current native law cases; Canadian Native Law
Cases, 9 volumes. Library.

UNIVERSITY OF SASKATCHEWAN
Native Studies Department
104 McLean Hall
SASKATOON, SK S7N 0W0
 (306) 966-6208

YUKON

YUKON COLLEGE PROGRAM
Box 2799
WHITEHORSE, YU Y1A 5K4

ALBERTA

CKUA - AM/FM
Native Voice of Alberta. On the Air 4:30 PM, Sunday, in the following cities: Edmonton, Grand Prairie, Medicine Hat, Lethbridge, Red Deer, and Peace River.

'YR' RADIO
Native Voice of Alberta. On the Air 9:30 AM, Sunday, in the following cities: Hinton, Whitecourt, Edson, Jasper, Grand Cache.

CFAC - FM
Treaty No. 7 Radio Program
CALGARY, AB
News Information Program. On the Air 10:30 to 10:45 AM, Sunday.

CFWE RADIO (NATIVE PERSPECTIVE)
Aboriginal Multi Media Society of Alberta
15001 112 Ave.
EDMONTON, AB T5M 2V6
(403) 455-2700 Fax 455-6739
Fred Didzena, President
Bert Crowfoot, General Manager
Thomas Droege, Host/Producer
Gary Gee, Editor (Windspeaker-newspaper)

GREAT NORTH PRODUCTIONS
300-10359 82nd Ave.
EDMONTON, AB T6E 1Z9
(403) 439-1260 Fax 431-0197

GREAT PLAINS PRODUCTIONS
202-10138 81st Ave.
EDMONTON, AB T2E 1X1
(403) 448-9360 Fax 431-0197

CJOK - FM
FORT McMURRAY, AB
Native Voice of Alberta. On the Air 7:30 PM, Sunday.

HOBBEMA BROADCASTING CABLE TV
Box 660
HOBBEMA, AB T2E 1X1
(403) 585-2111

CFWE - 89.9 FM (CATCH THE SPIRIT)
Aboriginal Multi Media Society of Alberta
P.O. Box 2250
LAC LA BICHE, AB T0A 2C0
(403) 423-2800 Fax 623-2811
Ray Fox, Host, Station Manager
Program: Native Perspective. Aboriginal programming - news magazine format - Cree/English 50/50 split. Broadcast 6-9 AM, Monday-Friday, via satellite. Alberta's only aboriginal radio station, rebroadcasts in 29 Native communities in Northern Alberta as well as across Canada and the U.S.

CILA - FM (RED ROCK RADIO)
LETHBRIDGE, AB
Native Rock Program. On the Air 1:00 to 2:00 PM, Sunday.

CJOC - FM
LETHBRIDGE, AB
Native-American Radio Program catering to tribes of southern Alberta. On the Air 11:30 AM to 12:00 PM, Sunday.

CIOK - FM
ST. PAUL, AB
Native Voice of Alberta. Airs 8:00 PM, Sunday.

INDIAN NEWS MEDIA
Box 120
STANDOFF, AB T0L 1Y0
(403) 653-3301
Marrie Smallface Marule, President
Gerri Manyfingers, Executive Director
Mary Weasel Fat, Editor (Kainai News)
Blackfoot Radio Network; Bull Horn Audio Video; Newspaper.

CKTA - FM
TABOR, AB
Native-American Elders Program.
On the Air 10:30 to 11:00 AM, Sunday.

BRITISH COLUMBIA

NNB-BC RADIO
Northern Native Broadcasting
Box 1090
TERRACE, BC V8G 4V1
(604) 638-8137
Ray Jones, General Manager

THE NATIVE CANADIAN MEDIA CORPS.
600-444 Robson St.
VANCOUVER, BC V6B 2B5
(604) 688-3877

NATIVE RADIO STATION CITR
206-6138 Sub Blvd.
VANCOUVER, BC V6T 2A5
(604) 228-3017 Fax 228-6093

THE NATIVE VOICE
200-1755 E. Hastings St.
VANCOUVER, BC V5L 1T1
(604) 255-3137

NATIVE VOICE BROADCAST SYSTEM
533 Yates St.
VICTORIA, BC V8W 1K7
(604) 383-3211 Fax (384-1586
Radio & TV broadasting.

LABRADOR

OKALAKATIGET SOCIETY
P.O. Box 160
NAIN, LB A0P 1E0
(709) 922-2896/2955
Robert Lyall, President
Ken Todd, Executive Director
Radio, TV. *Publication*: Kinatuinamot Ilengajuk (newsletter).

MANITOBA

CROSS LAKE TV - SATELLITE STATION
CROSS LAKE, MB R0B 0J0
(204) 676-2146

NATIVE MEDIA NETWORK
Box 848
PORTAGE LA PRAIRIE, MB R1N 3C3
(204) 239-1920

NATIVE COMMUNICATIONS, INC.
76 Severn Crescent
THOMPSON, MB R8N 1M6
(204) 778-8343 Fax 778-6559
Ron Nadeau, Chairperson & CEO
Henry Wilson, Dirctor of Broadcasting

BLIND TREK
9-819 Grant Ave.
WINNIPEG, MB R3M 1Y1
(204) 287-2311
30 minute live phone in show, Ch. 11

FIRST CITIZEN TV TALK SHOW
517 Craig St.
WINNIPEG, MB R3G 3C2
(204) 774-8432

NATIVE MEDIA NETWORK
204-424 Logan Ave.
WINNIPEG, MB R3A 0R4
(204) 943-6475 Fax 942-1380

OUR NATIVE LAND TV
CBC Radio, P.O. Box 160
WINNIPEG, MB

THETA PRODUCTIONS, INC.
205-698 Corydon Ave.
WINNIPEG, MB R3M 0X9
(204) 284-0398

WOODSMOKE & SWEETGRASS
CKY TV, Polo Park
WINNIPEG, MB R3G 0L7
(204) 775-0371 Fax 783-4841

NEWFOUNDLAND

ATJIQANGITUT &LABRADORIMUIT
Box 160
NAIN, NF A0P 1L0
(709) 922-2955 Fax 922-2293
Radio & TV, respectively.

NORTHWEST TERRITORIES

INUVIALUIT COMMUNICATIONS SOCIETY
P.O. Box 1704
Semmler Bldg., McKenzie Rd.
INUVIK, NWT X0E 1C0
(403) 979-2067
Vincent Teddy, President

IBC-TV
Inuit Broadcasting Corp.
P.O. Box 700
IQALIUT, NWT X0A 0H0
(819) 979-5853
Jobi Weetaluktuk, Executive Producer
Lynda Gunn, Regional Manager

INUVIALUIT DEVELOPMENT CORP.
Box 173
TUKTOYAKTUK, NWT X0E 1C0
(403) 977-2202
Vincent Teddy, President

CKNM-FM
Native Communications Society-Western NWT
Box 1919, Aquarius Bldg.
YELLOWKNIFE, NWT X1A 2P4

(403) 873-2661
Percy Kinney, Radio Manager
Pat Burke, Chairperson
Catherine MacQuarrie, Executive Director
Lee Selleck, Editor
Publication: Native Press (newspaper)

NOVA SCOTIA

**NATIVE COMMUNICATIONS
SOCIETY OF NOVA SCOTIA**
P.O. Box 344
SYDNEY, NS B1P 6H2
(902) 539-0045
Roy A. Gould, Executive Director

**NATIVE COMMUNICATIONS
SOCIETY OF NOVA SCOTIA**
P.O. Box 1005
TRURO, NS B2N 5G7
(902) 895-6217
Brian Douglas, Editor
Publication: Micmac News.

ONTARIO

BEARSKIN LAKE RADIO STATION
BEARSKIN LAKE, ON P0V 1E0
(807) 363-2578

**AUDIO-VISUAL STUDIO - WOODLANDS
CULTURAL EDUCATION CENTRE**
184 Mohawk St.
BRANTFORD, ON N3S 2X2
(519) 759-2650

CKON - FM 97.3
Indian Time
Box 1496, RR #3
CORNWALL ISLAND, ON K6A 5B7
(613) 938-1113

THREE SISTER'S MULTI-MEDIA
Box 1260
FOREST, ON N0N 1J0
(519) 786-2142 Fax 786-2142

KENOMADIWIN RADIO
P.O. Box 609, Longlac No. 58 Reserve
LONG LAKE , ON P0T 2A0
(807) 876-2865

CHMD - AM
James Bay Broadcasting Corp.
P.O. Box 400
MOOSONEE, ON P0L 1Y0
(705) 336-2301

INUIT BROADCASTING CORP. (IBC)
251 Laurier Ave., Suite 703
OTTAWA, ON K1P 5J5
(613) 235-1892 Fax 230-8824
Doug Saunders, President
Debbie Brisebois, Executive Director

**NORTHEN SERVICES
PROGRAM, CBC NORTH**
Box 3220, Station "C"
OTTAWA, ON K1Y 1E4
(613) 724-1200 Fax 598-3558

WAWATAY COMMUNICATIONS SOCIETY
Box 1180, 16-5th Ave.
SIOUX LOOKOUT, ON P0L 1W0
(807) 737-2951 Fax 737-3224
Lawrence Martin, Executive Director
Megan Williams, Ed. - WaWaTay (newspaper)
MOOSE FACTORY, ON P0L 1Wo
(705) 658-4556
Vern Cheechoo, Sr. Producer (Radio & TV)

QUEBEC

TAQRAMIUT NIPINGAT, INC.
185 Dorval Ave., Suite 501
DORVAL, PQ H9S 5J9
(514) 631-1394 Fax 631-6258
George Kakayuk, President

SENECA SATELLITE SERVICES, INC.
430 Old Chateauguay Rd.
KAHNAWAKE, PQ J0L 1B0
(514) 632-8133 Fax 632-8448

**JAMES BAY CREE
COMMUNICATIONS SOCIETY**
1, Place Ville Marie, Suite 3434
MONTREAL, PQ H3B 3N9
(514) 861-5837 Fax 861-0760
Soloman Awashish, Radio Director
Diane Reid, Director General
Publication: Cree Ajemon.

**SANS RESERVE COMMUNICATIONS
AUTOCHTONES**
3575, boul. Saint-Laurent
MONTREAL, PQ H2X 2T7
(514) 843-6098

TEWEGAN COMMUNICATIONS SOCIETY
351 Central Ave.
VAL D'OR, PQ J9P 1P6
(819) 825-5192 Fax 631-6528
Noe Mitchell, Executice Director

**CHISASIBI TELECOMMUNICATIONS
ASSOCIATION**
Reserve Indienne Wemidji
WEMIDJI, PQ J0M 1L0
(819) 855-2527

SOCAM - AM
Societe de Communications
Atikamekw Montagnais
80 Boulevard Bastien
Village des Hurons
WENDAKE, PQ G0A 4V0
(418) 843-3873
Bernard Hervieau, Producer
Diane Savard, General Manager

SASKATCHEWAN

MISSINIPI BROADCASTING CORP.
Box 1529, LaRonge Ave.
LA RONGE, SK S0J 1L0
(306) 425-4003
Robert Merasty, Executive Director
Rick Laliberte & William Dumais, Directors
Radio: Missinipi Atchimowin

RAM REBROADCASTING, INC.
Box 3075
PRINCE ALBERT, SK S6V 3M4
(306) 763-0396

CJUS - FM
SASKATOON, SK
Native Voice of Alberta. Airs 4:30 PM, Sunday.

GEMINI PRODUCTIONS, INC.
Box 7773
SASKATOON, SK S7K 4R5
(306) 665-8575 Fax 665-0008

MOCCASIN TELEGRAPH
c/o Saskatchewan Indian
1630 Idylwyld Dr.
SASKATOON, SK S7K 3S9

QUEST
c/o Saskatchewan Indian Institute of Tech.
Moose Woods Reserve
RR 5, GB 139
SASKATOON, SK S7K 3J8
(306) 244-4444 Fax 244-1391

**SASKATCHEWAN NATIVE
COMMUNICATIONS CORP.**
173 Second Ave. S., Suite 202
SASKATOON, SK S7K 1K6
(306) 653-2253
Gary Laplante, Chairperson
Ona Fiddler-Bertelg, Editor/Manager
Publication: New Breed

O & O BROADCASTING, INC.
Thunderchild Reserve
TURTLEFORD, SK S0M 2Y0
(306) 845-3170

YUKON

CHON-FM
Northern Native Broadcasting of Yukon
4228-A 4th Ave.
WHITEHORSE, YUKON Y1A 1K1
(403) 688-6629 Fax 668-6612
Ken Kane, Chairperson
Marion Telep, Radio Director
Radio broadcasting.

KAI PRODUCTIONS
4228-A 4th Ave.
WHITEHORSE, YUKON Y1A 1K1
(403) 668-2420
TV productions.`

YE SA TO COMMUNICATIONS SOCIETY
Nisutlin Dr.
WHITEHORSE, YUKON Y1A 3S5
(403) 667-7636/2775
Elizabeth Jackson, President
Publication: Dan Sha (newspaper).

An alphabetical listing of approximately 4,500 in-print books about or relating to Indians of North America. In each listing, the reader will find--where sufficient material has been provided--the title, author or editor, information on pagination, whether illustrated, indexed, etc., name of publisher, the year of publications, and price. The address of the publishers are contained in the Publishers Index. An asterisk (*) preceding a title indicates it is of primarily juvenile or young adult interest; the specific age group for which such titles are intended has been noted, if available. If you require material on a particular subject or interest area, refer to the subject listings in the Subject Classifications section, located at the end of this section.

A

*A,B,C'S THE AMERICAN INDIAN WAY
Children learn the alphabet while learning about American Indians. Grades K-2. Illus. Paper. Sierra Oaks, $6.95.

*ABC'S OF OUR SPIRITUAL CONNECTION
Kim Soo Goodtrack
First Nations people's common ethics and cultural values that identify them in their everday lives. Grades 3-8. Illus. 56 pp. Paper. Theytus, 1994. $9.95.

A.D. 1250: ANCIENT PEOPLES OF THE SOUTHWEST
Lawrence W. Cheek
Focuses on the cultures of the Anasazi, Sinagua, Mogollon, Hohokam, and Salado. 176 pp. University of Arizona Press, 1994. $49.95.

THE ABENAKI
Colin G. Calloway
Grades 5 and up. Illus. 104 pp. Chelsea House, 1988. $17.95.

*ABENAKI CAPTIVE
M.L. Dubois
Grades 4-7. 144 pp. Lerner, 1994. $19.95.

THE ABNAKIS & THEIR HISTORY
E. Vetromile
Reprint of 1866 edition. AMS, $22.50.

ABORIGINAL AMERICAN INDIAN BASKETRY; STUDIES IN TEXTILE ART WITHOUT MACHINERY
Otis Tufton Mason
Reprint of 1904 edition. Illus. 688 pp. The Rio Grande Press, $40.

ABORIGINAL CHIPPED STONE IMPLEMENTS OF NEW YORK
William M. Beauchamp
Reprint of 1897 edition. AMS, $14.50.

ABORIGINAL INDIAN BASKETRY
Otis T. Mason
Reprint of 1904 edition. Illus. 688 pp. Rio Grande, $35.

ABORIGINAL MONUMENTS OF THE STATE OF NEW YORK
E.B. Squier
Reprint of 1849 edition. Illus. 200 pp. Sourcebook, $18.95.

ABORIGINAL OCCUPATION OF NEW YORK
William M. Beauchamp
Reprint of 1900 edition. AMS, $22.

ABORIGINAL REMAINS OF TENNESSEE
J. Jones
Reprint of 1880 edition. Illus. 186 pp. Sourcebook, $16.95.

ABORIGINAL SOCIETY IN SOUTHERN CALIFORNIA
William D. Strong
Reprint of 1929 edition. Paper. Malki Museum Press, $37.50.

ABORIGINAL SUBSISTENCE TECHNOLOGY ON THE SOUTHEASTERN COASTAL LAIN DURING THE LATE PREHISTORIC PERIOD
Lewis H. Larson
Illus. Maps. Biblio. 260 pp. University Press of Florida, 1980. $29.95.

ABORIGINAL USE OF WOOD IN NEW YORK
William M. Beauchamp
Reprint of 1905 edition. AMS, $27.50.

THE ABORIGINES OF SOUTH DAKOTA
Charles E. Deland
Reprint of 1906 edition. AMS, $30.

AN ABRIDGEMENT OF THE INDIAN AFFAIRS CONTAINED IN FOUR FOLIO VOLUMES
Peter Wraxall
Transacted in the Colony of New York from the Year 1687 to 1751. Reprint of 1915 edition. Ayer Co., $24.50.

*ABSALOKA
Council for Indian Education, 1971. 75¢.

ABSARAKA: HOME OF THE CROWS
Margaret I. Carrington
Illus. 285 pp. University of Nebraska Press, 1983. $22.50; paper, $6.95.

AN ACCOUNT OF THE ORIGIN & EARLY PROSECUTION OF THE INDIAN WAR IN OREGON
Charles S. Drew
Reprint of 1860 edition. 48 pp. Ye Galleon, $7.50.

ACCULTURATION & PERSONALITY AMONG THE WISCONSIN CHIPPEWA
Victor Barnouw
Reprint of 1950 edition. Paper. AMS, $19.50.

ACCULTURATION IN SEVEN INDIAN TRIBES
Ralph Linton
Reprint. Peter Smith, $13.25.

ACOMA
H.L. James
Revised edition. Presents Acoma, the "sky city" of New Mexico. Illus. 96 pp. Paper. Schiffer, $14.95.

ACOMA
Tryntje Van Ness Seymour
Text & original photographs tell the story of Acoma. Limited edition of 75. Illus. 64 pp. Lime Rock Press, 1980. $295.00. Delux edition of 25 signed copies available, $750.

ACOMA & LAGUNA POTTERY
Rick Dillingham; with Melinda Elliott
Traces the development of pottery making at the two pueblos. Illus. Maps. Biblio. 256 pp. Paper. University of Washington Press & School of American Research, 1994. $24.95.

ACROSS ARCTIC AMERICA, NARRATIVE OF THE FIFTH THULE EXPEDITION
Knud Rasmussen
Reprint of 1927 edition. Greenwood, $35.

*ACROSS THE TUNDRA
Marjorie Vandervelde
Tale of two Eskimo boys hunting alone. Grades 4-9. 40 pp. Council for Indian Education, 1972. $9.95; paper. $3.95.

ACTS & RESOLUTIONS OF INDIAN NATIONS-TRIBAL COUNCILS
A series of books on laws, treaties and unions among Indians of certain nations. See Scholarly Resources for titles and prices.

A.D. 1250: ANCIENT PEOPLES OF THE SOUTHWEST
text by Lawrence W. Cheek
Details ancient cultures such as the Anasazi, Mogollon, etc. 200 full-color photos and drawings. 176 pp. Treasure Chest, 1994. $49.95.

ADAMS: MANUFACTURING OF FLAKED STOINE TOOLS AT A PALEOINDIAN SITE IN WESTERN KENTUCKY
Thomas N. Sanders
Illus. 165 pp. Paper. Persimmon Press, $15.95.

THE ADKINS SITE: A PALAEO-INDIAN HABITATION & ASSOCIATED STONE STRUCTURE
Richard M. Gramly
Illus. 130 pp. Paper. Persimmon Press, $13.95.

ADOBE WALLS: THE HISTORY & ARCHAEOLOGY OF THE 1874 TRADING POST
Lindsay Baker & Billy Harrison
Illus. 430 pp. Texas A&M University Press, 1986. $39.50.

*ADVENTURES IN STORYTELLING
Set of three titles with accompanying audiocassette. *The Animals' Ballgame, Loon and Deer Were Traveling,* and *Naughty Little Rabbit and Old Man Coyote.* Grades K-4. Illus. 24-48 pp. Childrens Press, $37.

ADVENTURES ON THE WESTERN FRONTIER
Maj. Gen. John Gibbon
A record of the lives of the Indians, soldiers and white settlers; Indian warfare; Sioux Campaign of 1876. Illus. 288 pp. Indiana University Press, 1994. $24.95.

AFRICANS & CREEKS: FROM THE COLONIAL PERIOD TO THE CIVIL WAR
Daniel F. Littlefield, Jr.
Illus. Greenwood Press, 1979. $35.

AFRICANS & SEMINOLES: FROM REMOVAL TO EMANCIPATION
Daniel F. Littlefield, Jr.
Illus. Greenwood Press, 1977. $35.

AFTER & BEFORE THE LIGHTNING
Simon J. Ortiz
Prose & verse poems of winter in South Dakota on the Rosebud Sioux Reservation. 160 pp. University of Arizona Press, 1994. $32.50; paper, $15.95.

AFTER THE BUFFALO WERE GONE: THE LOUIS WARREN HILL, SR., COLLECTION OF INDIAN ART
Ann T. Walton
Illus. 256 pp. Paper. University of Washington Press, 1985. $24.95.

AFTER COLUMBUS: THE SMITHSONIAN CHRONICLE OF THE NORTH AMERICAN INDIANS
Herman J. Viola
The facts & implications of Indian & white interaction in America. Illus. 288 pp. Smithsonian Books, 1991. $34.95.

AFTER THE LITTLE BIG HORN
Robert J. Ege
Illus. Paper. Werner Publications, $3.95.

AFTER REMOVAL: THE CHOCTAW IN MISSISSIPPI
Samuel Wells & Roseanna Tubby, Editors
154 pp. Illus. University Press of Mississippi, 1986. $30.

AFTER THE TRAIL OF TEARS: THE CHEROKEES' STRUGGLE FOR SOVEREIGNTY, 1839-1880
William G. McLoughlin
450 pp. University of North Carolina Press, 1994. $39.95; paper, $17.95.

AGAINST BORDERS: PROMOTING BOOKS FOR A MULTICULTURAL WORLD
Hazel Rochman
Illus. 288 pp. Paper. ALA Books, 1993. $16.95.

*AGALIHA': INDIAN SELF-ESTEEM CURRICULUM ACTIVITY BOOK
Indian Developed Curriculum & Pubg. Corp.
Encourages Indian students to feel pride in their heritage. Grades 1-8. 62 pp. Daybreak Star Press, $12.95.

THE AGATE BASIN SITE: A RECORD OF THE PALEOINDIAN OCCUPATION OF THE NORTHWESTERN HIGH PLAINS
George Frisom and Dennis Stanford
440 pp. Academic Press, 1982. $44.50.

AGENTS OF REPRESSION: THE FBI's SECRET WARS AGAINST THE BLACK PANTHER PARTY & THE AMERICAN INDIAN MOVEMENT
Ward Churchill & James V. Wall
325 pp. South End Press, 1988. $30.00; paper, $15.

THE AGRICULTURAL & HUNTING METHODS OF THE NAVAHO INDIANS
Willard W. Hill
Reprint of 1938 edition. AMS, $19.50.

AGRICULTURAL TERRACING IN THE ABORIGINAL NEW WORLD
Robin Donkin
Illus. 196 pp. Paper. University of Arizona Press, 1979. $8.50.

AGRICULTURE OF THE HIDATSA INDIANS: AN INDIAN INTERPRETATION
Gilbert L. Wilson
Reprint of 1917 edition. AMS, $24.50.

AH MO: INDIAN LEGENDS FROM THE NORTHWEST
Arthur Griffin, Editor
Illus. 64 pp. Paper. Hancock House, 1990. $7.95.

*AH MO: INDIAN LEGENDS FROM WASHINGTON STATE
Arthur E. Griffin, Editor
Grades 2-5. Illus. 75 pp. Paper. Bainbridge, 1989.

AHTNA ATHABASKAN DICTIONARY
James Kari, Editor
Contains 6,000 Ahtna language entries. 700 pp. Alaska Native Language Center, 1990. $50; paper, $25.

*AHYOKA & THE TALKING LEAVES
Peter & Connie Roop
Fictionalized story of Sequoyah & daughter. Grades 3-6. Illus. 60 pp. AISES, $12.

AIDS REGIONAL DIRECTORY: RESOURCES IN INDIAN COUNTRY
Laurie McLemore, MD, Director
Second edition. Association of Native American Medical Students, 1994. $23, postpaid.

AIRLIFT TO WOUNDED KNEE
Bill Zimmerman
Illus. 348 pp. Ohio U. Press, 1976. $14.95.

AISES CALENDAR
12 Sam English full-color prints. 10x14" and appointment calendar; selected quotes from historic & present-day tribal leaders. Annual in August. AISES. $11.

AKWE:KON LITERARY ISSUE
An anthology of new fiction and poetry from 14 Native American authors. Akwe:kon Press, $8.

AKWESASNE HISTORICAL POSTCARDS; PEACEMAKER & HIAWATHA POSTERS
Akwesasne Museum, 50/postcard; 75/poster.

ALAAWICH
Lucy Arvidson
Paper. Malki Museum Press, 1978. $3.

ALASKA DAYS WITH JOHN MUIR
Samuel Hall Young
Illus. 240 pp. Paper. Gibbs Smith, 1991. $9.95

THE ALASKA ESKIMOS AS DESCRIBED IN THE POSTHUMOUS NOTES OF KNUD RASMUSSEN
Knud Rasmussen
Reprint of 1952 edition. AMS, $52.

THE ALASKA ESKIMOS: A SELECTED ANNOTATED BIBLIOGRAPHY
Arthur Hippler & John Wood
Paper. University of Alaska, 1977. $15.

ALASKA 1899: ESSAYS FROM THE HARRIMAN EXPEDITION
George Bird Grinnell
Records Grinnell's observations of native Alaskans. Illus. 136 pp. Paper. Universityof Washington Press, 1994. $14.95.

ALASKA: A HISTORY OF THE 49TH STATE
Claus M. Naska & Herman Slotnick
Second edition. Photos. Maps. 368 pp. Paper. University of Oklahoma Press, $16.95.

ALASKA HISTORY SERIES
Richard Pierce, Editor/Publisher
See Limestone Press for titles and prices.

*ALASKA IN THE DAYS THAT WERE BEFORE
Tanya Hardgrove
A Native elder tells stories from his life. Grades 3-10. 31 pp. Council for Indian Education, 1985. $8.95; paper, $2.95.

ALASKA IN TRANSITION: THE SOUTHEAST REGION
George W. Rogers
Reprint of 1959 edition. Paper. Books on Demand, $99.50.

ALASKA NATIVE ARTS & CRAFTS
Alaska Geographic
In-depth review of the art and artifacts of Alaska's Native people. 210 pp. Alaska Natural History Association & The Alaska Geographic Society, $19.95.

THE ALASKA NATIVE CLAIMS SETTLEMENT ACT, 1991, & TRIBAL GOVERNMENT
Thomas A. Morehouse
Illus. 29 pp. University of Alaska, Institute of Social and Economic Research, 1988. $2.

ALASKA NATIVE LANGUAGE CENTER PUBLICATIONS
Contains numerous titles covering the Inupiaq Eskimo, Central Yup'ik Eskimo, Alutiiq (Sugpiaq) Eskimo, Aleut, Siberian Yup'ik EskimoAhtna Athabaskan, Tanaina Athabaskan, Ingalik (Deg Hit'an) Athabaskan, Holikachuk Athabaskan, Upper Kuskokwim, Koyukon Athabaskan, Han Athabaskan, Lower Tanana Athabaskan, Tanacross Athabaskan, Upper Tanana Athabaskan, Kutchin (Gwich'in) Athabaskan, Eyak, Tlingit, and Haida. Also research papers, maps, and other sources of materials. Alaska Native Language Center.

ALASKA NATIVE LANGUAGES: PAST, PRESENT & FUTURE
Michael E. Krauss
Illus. 110 pp. Paper. Alaska Native Language Center, 1980. $6.

ALASKA NATIVES & AMERICAN LAWS
David S. Case
A review & analysis of legal principles applicable to Alaska Natives in several substanbtive areas. 608 pp. University of Alaska Press, 1985. $25.

ALASKA NATIVES: A GUIDE TO CURRENT REFERENCE SOURCES IN THE RASMUSON LIBRARY
Mark C. Goniwiecha
78 pp. Paper. University of Alaska, Rasmuson Library. $10.

ALASKA'S NATIVE PEOPLE
Lael Morgan, Editor
Illus. 304 pp. Paper. Alaska Northwest & The Alaska Geographic Society, 1979. Album style, $24.95.

ALASKAMEUT '86
Exhibition catalog featuring interviews with and the artwork of 14 maskmakers representative of Aleut, Yup'ik, Inupiaq, Tlingit and Athabascan cultures. Illus. 48 pp. Paper. Institute of Alaska Native Arts, 1986. $10.50, postpaid.

ALASKAN ESKIMO CEREMONIALISM
Margaret Lantis
Reprint of 1947 edition. AMS, $22.50.

ALASKAN ESKIMO WORDS
Knud Rasmussen
Reprint of 1941 edition. AMS, $30.

***ALASKAN IGLOO TALES**
Keithahn; illus. by Ahgupuk
Grades 3 and up. Paper. Graphic Arts Center, $12.95.

ALBERNI PREHISTORY
Alan D. McMillan & Denis St. Claire
Archaeological & ethnographic Investigations on Western Vancouver Island. Illus. 221 pp. Paper. Theytus, 1982. $9.95.

ALCATRAZ! ALCATRAZ: THE INDIAN OCCUPATION OF 1969-71
Adam Fortunate Eagle
A personal account written by one of the organizers. 160 pp. Paper. Heyday Books, $9.95.

ALEUT DICTIONARY
Knut Bergsland, Compiler
Documents all the recorded vocabulary of the Aleut language; 1,600 Aleut place names are plotted on 33 maps; over 600 Aleut men's names; English index qith 14,000 Aleut words & suffixes. 739 pp. Paper. Alaska Native Language Center, 1994. $37.50.

ALEUT TALES & NARRATIVES
Waldemar Jochelson; edited by
Knut Bergsland & Moses Dirks
Aleut folklore in Aleut with English translations. 87 stories. Illus. 715 pp. Alaska Native Language Center, 1990. $25.

ALEUTS: SURVIVORS OF THE BEPING LAND BRIDGE
William S. Laughlin
Paper. Holt, Rinehart & Winston, 1981. $9.95.

***ALGONQUIAN**
Rita & Mary D'Apice
Grades 5-8. Illus. 32 pp. Rourke Corp., 1990. $9.95.

ALGONQUIN LEGENDS
Charles G. Leland
Study of myths & folklore of the Micmac, Passamaquoddy & Penobscot tribes. Illus. 416 pp. Paper. Dover, $8.95.

***ALL ABOUT ARROWHEADS & SPEAR POINTS**
Howard E. Smith, Jr.
Grades 4-7. Illus. 80 pp. Henry Holt & Co., 1989. $14.95.

ALL MY RELATIONS: AN ANTHOLOGY OF CONTEMPORARY CANADIAN NATIVE FICTION
Thomas King, Editor
236 pp. Paper. University of Oklahoma Press, $14.95.

ALL ROADS ARE GOOD: NATIVE VOICES ON LIFE & CULTURE
Foreword by W. Richard West, Jr.
& Preface by Clara Sue Kidwell
23 accomplished figures from diverse indigenous cultures throughout the Americas selects objects of cultural, spiritual, artistic, or personal significance from the National Museum of the American Indian's collection & reflects on their cultuial heritage. Illus. 224 pp. Smithsonian Institution Press, 1994. $55; paper, $29.95.

ALL THAT REMAINS: A WEST VIRGINIA ARCHAEOLOGISTS DISCOVERIES
Robert Pyle; Betty L. Wiley, Editor
Illus. Paper. Cannon Graphics, 1991.

ALLAN HOUSER
Barbara H. Perlman
The art of Allan Houser. 133 color & 183 bxw illus. 266 pp. Smithsonian Books, 1991. $50.

ALMANAC OF THE DEAD
Leslie Marmon Silko
Fiction. 792 pp. Paper. Penguin USA, $13.

ALOHA SAMPLER
24 pp. Paper. Hawaiian songs. World Around Songs, $2.45.

ALWAYS GETTING READY, UPTERRLAINARLUTA: YUP'IK ESKIMO SUBSISTENCE IN SOUTHWEST ALASKA
James H. Barker, photos & text
Illus. Photos. 144 pp. Paper. University of Washington Press, $29.95.

AMERICA, LAND OF THE RISING SUN
Don Smithana
Illus. 256 pp. Paper. Anasazi Publishing, 1992. $9.95.

AMERICA ON PAPER: THE FIRST HUNDRED YEARS
Lynn Glaser
Revised and enlarged edition. Illus. 288 pp. Associated Antiquaries, 1989. $32.50.

AMERICA STREET: A MULTICULTURAL ANTHOLOGY OF STORIES
Anne Mazer, Editor
Persea Books, 1993.

AMERICA'S FASCINATING INDIAN HERITAGE
Readers Digest Editors
Synthesis of North American Indian heritage. Illus. Photos. 416 pp. Reader's Digest & Cherokee Publications, 1978. $29.50.

AMERICA'S FIRST FIRST WORLD WAR: THE FRENCH & INDIAN WAR, 1754-1763
Timothy Todish; Monte Smith, Editor
Illus. 120 pp. Paper. Eagles View Publishing, 1987. $8.95.

AMERICA'S INDIAN STATUES
Marion Gridley
Paper. Brown Book Co., 1966. $3.95.

THE AMERICAN BUFFALO IN TRANSITION
John Rorabacher
North Star Press, $6.50.

THE AMERICAN EAGLE
Tom & Pat Leeson, photographers
Photos of the eagle with text exploring the historic symbolism, the Native American traditions & myths, and the legends which comprise the portrait of the bald eagle. Illus. 88 color photos. 128 pp. Beyond Words Publishing, $39.95; paper, $24.95.

AMERICAN FOLK MASTERS: THE NATIONAL HERITAGE FELLOWS
Steve Siprin, Editor
Documents in text and photographs the winners and their skills, including numerous Native American artists. Pottery, baskets, weavings, and musical instruments are shown. 256 pp. Harry N. Abrams, 1992. $49.50.

THE AMERICAN INDIAN
Raymond F. Locke, Editor
Paper. Mankind, 1976. $1.75.

AMERICAN INDIAN
Lee F. Harkins, Editor
Reprint. Liveright, 1970. Slipcased, $99.99.

THE AMERICAN INDIAN & ALASKA NATIVE HIGHER EDUCATION FUNDING GUIDE
Gregory W. Frazier
100 pp. Arrowstar, 1990. $21.90.

AMERICAN INDIAN & ALASKA NATIVE NEWSPAPERS & PERIODICALS, 1826-
1924/1925-1970
Daniel Littlefield, Jr. and James Parins
Two volumes. 482 pp. 577 pp. Greenwood, 1984/86. $85 each.

AMERICAN INDIAN & ALASKA NATIVE TRADERS DIRECTORY
Gregory Frazier
140 pp. Arrowstar, 1990. $21.45.

American Indian/Alaska Native Tribal & Village HIV-1 Policy Guidelines
48 pp. National Native American AIDS Prevention Center, 1991.

THE AMERICAN INDIAN: THE AMERICAN FLAG
Richard A. Pohrt
Illus. 152 pp. Flint Institute of Arts, $12.50; paper, $9.

AMERICAN INDIAN ARCHERY
Reginald & Gladys Laubin
Illus. 192 pp. University of Oklahoma Press, 1980. $27.95; paper, $14.95.

AMERICAN INDIAN ARCHIVAL MATERIAL: A GUIDE TO HOLDINGS IN THE SOUTHEAST
R. Chepesiuk and A. Shankman, Editors
323 pp. Greenwood, 1982. $46.95.

AMERICAN INDIAN AREAS & ALASKA NATIVE VILLAGES, 1980
38 pp. Supt. of Documents, 1984. $2.75.

AMERICAN INDIAN ART, 1920-1972
Paper. Peabody Museum, 1973. $2.

AMERICAN INDIAN ARTS & CRAFTS SOURCE BOOK
Anthony J. Cusmano, Editor
Paper. Media Publications, 1987. $6.95.

THE AMERICAN INDIAN AS SLAVEHOLDER & SUCCESSIONIST
Annie Heloise Abel
Reprint of 1919 edition. Illus. Map. 400 pp. Paper. University of Nebraska Press, $12.95.

AMERICAN INDIAN AUTOBIOGRAPHY
H. David Brumble, III
336 pp. University of California Press, 1988. $35.

AMERICAN INDIAN BASKETRY
Otis Tufton Mason
800 pp. Paper. Hothem House & Dover, 1988.
$16.95.

THE AMERICAN INDIAN, 1492-1976:
A CHRONOLOGY & FACT BOOK
Henry C. Dennis
Second edition. 177 pp. Oceana , 1977. $8.50.

AMERICAN INDIAN BOOKS
Joe Thompson
A mail order catalog listing of over 100 books on
Indians and archaeology. American Indian Books,
No charge.

AMERICAN INDIAN CHILDREN AT SCHOOL,
1850-1930
Michael C. Coleman
Study revealing white society's program of civiliz-
ing Indian schoolchildren. 230 pp.University Press
of Mississippi, 1993. $38.50.

*THE AMERICAN INDIAN COLORING BOOK
Tom Underwood
Reprint of 1969 edition. Grades 1-4. 24 pp.
Paper. Cherokee Publications, $3.

AMERICAN INDIAN COOKING & HERB LORE
J. Ed Sharpe and Thomas Underwood
Contains dozens of recipes. Illus. 32 pp. Paper .
Cherokee Publications, $3.50.

THE AMERICAN INDIAN CRAFT BOOK
Marz Minor and Nono Minor
Illus. 416 pp. Paper. University of Nebraska
Press, 1978. $9.95.

AMERICAN INDIAN DESIGN & DECORATION
Leroy H. Appleton
Reprint of 1971 edition. Illus. 280 pp. Peter
Smith, $17.50. Paper. Dover, $9.95.

AMERICAN INDIAN DIGEST: FACTS
ABOUT TODAY'S AMERICAN INDIANS
George Russell
Contemporary American Indian demographics
with regard to population, tribes and reservation.
Includes maps, reservation roster, graphics, tables,
and reference sources. 64 pp. Paper. Thunderbird
Enterprises, $12.

AMERICAN INDIAN ECOLOGY
Donald J. Hughes
Revised Second Edition. Illus. Biblio. 190 pp.
Texas Western Press, 1995. $20.

AMERICAN INDIAN EDUCATION: DIREC-
TORY OF ORGANIZATIONS & ACTIVITIES
IN AMERICAN INDIAN EDUCATION
ERIC/CRESS, $4.50.

AMERICAN INDIAN EDUCATION: GOVERN-
MENT SCHOOLS & ECONOMIC PROGRESS
Evelyn C. Adams
Reprint of 1946 edition. Ayer Co. $16.

THE AMERICAN INDIAN & THE END
OF THE CONFEDERACY, 1863-1866
Annie Heloise Abel
Reprint of 1919 edition. Illus. Map. 420 pp.
Paper. University of Nebraska Press, $12.95.

AMERICAN INDIAN ENCYCLOPEDIA -
CD-ROM
3 reference books on CD-ROM; text, pictures,
sound. Facts-on-File, $295.

AMERICAN INDIAN ENERGY
RESOURCES & DEVELOPMENT
Roxanne D. Ortiz, Editor
Includes Transnational Energy Corporations and
American Indian Development, by Richard
Nafziger, and The Role of Policy in American In-
dian Mineral Development, by Lorraine Turner
Ruffing. 80 pp. Paper. University of New Mexico,
Native American Studies, 1980. $5.

AMERICAN INDIAN ENGLISH
William L. Leap
Documents and examines the diversity of English
in American Indian speech communities. 352 pp.
University of Utah Press, 1993. $37.50.

AMERICAN INDIAN ENVIRONMENTS:
ECOLOGICAL ISSUES IN NATIVE
AMERICAN HISTORY
C. Vecsy & R.W. Venables, Editors
Reprint of 1980 edition. Illus. 236 pp. Paper.
Syracuse University Press, $15.95.

AMERICAN INDIAN EXPERIENCE: A
PROFILE, 1524 TO PRESENT
Philip Weeks, Editor
Illus. 336 pp. Paper. Harlan Davidson, $16.95.

AMERICAN INDIAN FOOD & LORE
Carolyn Neithammer
Illus. 195 pp. Paper. Macmillan, 1974. $12.95.

AMERICAN INDIAN FOODS & VEGETABLES
Harriet L. Smith
Illus. Paper. SSS Publishing, 1982. $4.50.

AMERICAN INDIAN GHOST DANCE, 1870
& 1890: AN ANNOTATED BIBLIOGRAPHY
Shelley Osterreich
110 entries. 96 pp. Greenwood Press, 1991.
$37.95.

AMERICAN INDIAN HOLOCAUST & SUR-
VIVAL: A POPULATION HISTORY SINCE
1492
Russell Thornton
Illus. 352 pp. Paper. University of Oklahoma
Press, 1987. $12.95.

AMERICAN INDIAN IDENTITY:
TODAY'S CHANGING PERSPECTIVES
Clifford E. Trafzer
Seven American Indians provide essays. 51 pp.
Paper. Sierra Oaks Publishing, 1986. $10.95.

THE AMERICAN INDIAN IN
THE CIVIL WAR, 1862-1865
Annie Heloise Abel
Reprint of 1919 edition. Illus. Map. 400 pp.
Paper. University of Nebraska Press, $12.95.

THE AMERICAN INDIAN IN
ALABAMA & THE SOUTHEAST
John F. Phillips
Illus. 213 pp. American Indian Books, 1986.
$10.95; paper, $8.95.

*THE AMERICAN INDIAN IN AMERICA, Vol. II
Jayne Clark Jones
Grades 5 and up. Illus. 96 pp. Paper. Lerner,
$5.95.

AMERICAN INDIAN IN ENGLISH LITERA-
TURE OF THE 18th CENTURY
Benjamin H. Bissell
Reprint of 1925 edition. Illus. 225 pp. Shoe
String Press, $26. Gordon Press, $59.95.

THE AMERICAN INDIAN IN FILM
Michael Hilger
Illus. 206 pp. Scarecrow Press, 1986. $21.

THE AMERICAN INDIAN IN GRADUATE
STUDIES: A BIBLIOGRAPHY OF THESES
AND DISSERTATIONS
Frederick J. Dockstader
Two volumes. Paper. National Museum of the
American Indian, 1973. $10 each; $18 per set.

THE AMERICAN INDIAN
IN NORTH CAROLINA
Douglas L. Rights
Illus. 298 pp. Paper. John F. Blair & Cherokee
Publications, $14.95.

THE AMERICAN INDIAN IN SHORT FICTION:
AN ANNOTATED BIBLIOGRAPHY
Peter G. Beidler and Marion F. Egge
215 pp. Scarecrow Press, 1979. $18.50.

AMERICAN INDIAN IN THE U.S.,
PERIOD 1850-1914
Warren K. Moorehead
Facsimile of 1914 edition. Bibliographies Reprint
Series. Ayer Co., $35.

AMERICAN INDIAN INDEX:
A DIRECTORY OF INDIAN COUNTRY
Gregory W. Frazier
Lists American Indian and Alaska Native groups.
325 pp. Arrowstar Publishing, 1985. $21.45.

AMERICAN INDIAN & INDO-EUROPEAN
STUDIES: PAPERS IN HONOR OF
MADISON S. BELLER
Kathryn Klar, et al, Editors
495 pp. Mouton, 1980. $82.

AMERICAN INDIAN ISSUES
IN HIGHER EDUCATION
206 pp. American Indian Studies Center, 1981.
$14.

AMERICAN INDIAN LACROSSE,
LITTLE BROTHER OF WAR
Thomas Vennum, Jr.
An account of the Native American game, and its
functions in Indian life. Illus. 376 pp. Smithsonian
Institution Press, 1994. $44.95; paper, $15.95.

AMERICAN INDIAN LANGUAGE SERIES
Includes: Mayan Linguistics, 267 pp., $5.00;
Hualapai Reference Grammar, 575 pp., $17.50;
and Chem'ivillu' (Let's Speak Cahuilla), 316 pp.,
$17.50. The American Indian Studies Center.

AMERICAN INDIAN LANGUAGES, Vol. 5
William Bright, Editor
585 pp. Mouton de Gruyter, 1989. $99.

AMERICAN INDIAN LAW
500 pp. The Michie Co., $46. Supplement, $6.

AMERICAN INDIAN LAW IN A NUTSHELL
William C. Canby, Jr.
Second edition. 336 pp. Paper. West Publishing,
1988. $12.95.

THE AMERICAN INDIAN LAW SERIES
A series of seven pamphlets: Indian Sovereignty;
Indian Treaties; Indians and the U.S. Government;
Indian Jurisdiction; The Federal Indian Trust Re-
lationship; Indian Water Rights; and Introduction
to Oil and Gas. Institute for the Development of
Indian Law..

AMERICAN INDIAN LEADERS: STUDIES IN DIVERSITY
R. David Edmunds, Editor
Illus. 270 pp. Paper. University of Nebraska Press, 1980. $8.95.

AMERICAN INDIAN LEGAL MATERIALS: A UNION LIST
Laura N. Gasaway, et al
Lists important works of Indian law, history, and policy. 200 pp. E.M. Coleman, 1979. $49.50.

AMERICAN INDIAN LEGAL STUDIES TEACHER'S MANUAL & TEXT
Institute for the Development of Indian Law . $20 each.

AMERICAN INDIAN LIFE
Elsie C. Parsons, Editor
Reprint of 1967 edition. Illus. 425 pp. Paper. University of Nebraska Press, $32.

AMERICAN INDIAN LINGUISTICS & LITERATURE
William Bright
159 pp. Mouton de Gruyter, 1984. $41.25.

AMERICAN INDIAN LITERATURE: AN ANTHOLOGY
Alan R. Velie
Illus. 384 pp. University of Oklahoma Press, 1979. $32.95; paper, $15.95.

AMERICAN INDIAN LITERATURES: AN INTRODUCTION, BIBLIOGRAPHIC REVIEW, & SELECTED BIBLIOGRAPHY
LaVonne Brown Ruoff
Includes journals, films & videos, and Indian authors and their works. Also provides and index and chronology of notable American Indian events. 200 pp. Paper. Modern Language Assn., 1990. $19.50.

AMERICAN INDIAN MAGIC: SCARED POW WOWS & HOPI PROPHECIES
Brad Steiger
Illus. 210 pp. Paper. Global Communications, 1986. $17.95.

AMERICAN INDIAN MEDICINE
Rolling Thunder
Sweetlight Books, 1972. $10.

AMERICAN INDIAN MEDICINE
Virgil J. Vogel
The contribution of the American Indian to pharmacology & medicine. Illus. 622 pp. Paper. University of Oklahoma Press, 1977. $21.95.

THE AMERICAN INDIAN: A MULTIMEDIA ENCYCLOPEDIA - CD-ROM
Incorporates four Facts on File publications: Atlas of the North American Indian; Native American Legends; Indians & Non-Indians from Early Contacts through 1900; and Encyclopedia of Native American Tribes. Also over 1,000 reproductions of images and maps from NARA publications and documents. Facts on File, 1993. $295.

*AMERICAN INDIAN MUSIC & MUSICAL INSTRUMENTS
George S. Fichter
Grades 5-10. David McKay, 1978. $8.95.

AMERICAN INDIAN MYTHOLOGY
Alice Marriott and Carol K. Rachlin
Illus. 210 pp. Paper. New American Library, 1972. $3.95.

AMERICAN INDIAN MYTHS & LEGENDS
Richard Erdoes & Alfonso Ortiz
160 tales from 80 tribal groups from across North America. Illus. 528 pp. Paper. AISES & Cherokee Publications, $17.

AMERICAN INDIAN PAINTERS: A BIOGRAPHICAL DIRECTORY
Jeanne Snodgrass
National Museum of the American Indian, 1968.

AMERICAN INDIAN PAINTING & SCULPTURE
Patricia Janis Broder
Survey of work by this century's leading Native American artists. 74 full-color illustrations, including 4 gatefolds. 168 pp. Abbeville Press, $45.

THE AMERICAN INDIAN PARFLECHE: A TRADITION OF ABSTRACT PAINTING
Gaylord Torrence
Explains the origin and chronology of parfleches - rawhide with painted designs. Illus. Map. 272 pp. University of Washington Press, 1992. $60; paper, $35.

THE AMERICAN INDIAN: PAST & PRESENT
Roger L. Nichols
Third edition. 280 pp. Paper. McGraw-Hill, $14.50.

THE AMERICAN INDIAN: PERSPECTIVES FOR THE STUDY OF SOCIAL CHANGE
Fred Eggan
185 pp. Cambridge University Press, 1981. $37.50.

AMERICAN INDIAN POLICY
Theodore W. Taylor
Illus. 230 pp. Lomond, 1983. $23.50. Microfilm, $12.95.

AMERICAN INDIAN POLICY & AMERICAN REFORM: CASE STUDIES OF THE CAMPAIGN TO ASSIMILATE THE AMERICAN INDIANS
Christine Bolt
228 pp. Unwin Hyman, Inc., 1987. $44.95.

AMERICAN INDIAN POLICY & CULTURAL VALUES: CONFLICT & ACCOMMODATION
Jennie R. Joe, Editor
169 pp. Paper. American Indian Studies Center, 1987. $10.

AMERICAN INDIAN POLICY IN THE FORMATIVE YEARS: THE INDIAN TRADE & INTERCOURSE ACTS, 1790-1834
Francis P. Prucha
310 pp. Paper. University of Nebraska Press, 1970. $5.95.

AMERICAN INDIAN POLICY IN THE TWENTIETH CENTURY
Vine Deloria, Jr., Editor
272 pp. University of Oklahoma Press, 1985. $21.95; paper. $12.95.

AMERICAN INDIAN POTTERY
Sharon Wirt
Studies pottery styles of the early natives and their significance. Illus. 32 pp. Paper. Hancock House, 1984. $3.95.

AMERICAN INDIAN POTTERY: AN IDENTIFICATION & VALUE GUIDE
John W. Barry
Second Edition. Illus. 214 pp. Apollo Books, 1984. $29.95.

AMERICAN INDIAN PRAYERS & POETRY
J. Edward Sharpe, Editor
Illus. 32 pp. Paper. Cherokee Publications, 1985. $3.

THE AMERICAN INDIAN: PREHISTORY TO THE PRESENT
Arrell Gibson
618 pp. Paper. D.C. Heath & Co., 1980. $15.50.

AMERICAN INDIAN PROPHETS: RELIGIOUS LEADERS & REVITALIZATION MOVEMENTS
Clifford E. Trafzer
138 pp. Paper. Sierra Oaks, 1986. $11.95.

THE AMERICAN INDIAN READER SERIES
Jeannette Henry, Editor
Five volumes covering separate subject areas: Anthropology, 174 pp.; Education, 300 pp.; Literature, 248 pp.; History, 149 pp.; and Current Affairs, 248 pp. Paper. The Indian Historian, 1972-75. $4.50 each.

AMERICAN INDIAN REFERENCE BOOKS FOR CHILDREN & YOUNG ADULTS
Barbara Kuipers
An annotated bibliography of 200 entries for grades 3-12. 190 pp. Libraries Unlimited & AISES, 1991. $25. Available on diskette.

AMERICAN INDIAN RESOURCE MATERIALS IN THE WESTERN HISTORY COLLECTION
Donald DeWitt
Illus. 290 pp. University of Oklahoma Press, 1990. $32.95.

AMERICAN INDIAN SCULPTURE: A STUDY OF THE NORTHWEST COAST
Paul S. Wingert
Reprint of 1949 edition. AMS, $27.50.

AMERICAN INDIAN SOCIETIES: STRATEGIES & CONDITIONS OF POLITICAL & CULTURAL SURVIVAL
Duane Champagne, Editor
2nd revised edition. 160 pp. Cultural Survival, 1989. $19.95; paper, $10.

AMERICAN INDIAN SPORTS HERITAGE
Joseph B. Oxendine
Illus. 352 pp. Human Kinetics Pubs., 1988. $32.

*AMERICAN INDIAN STEREOTYPES IN THE WORLD OF CHILDREN: A READER & BIBLIOGRAPHY
Arlene B. Hirschfelder
312 pp. Scarecrow Press, 1982. $22.50.

*AMERICAN INDIAN STORIES
12 book series on the lives/achievements of great Native Americans: Carlos Montezuma, Geronimo, Hole-in-the-Day, Ishi, Jim Thorpe, John Ross, Maria Tallchief, Osceola, Plenty Coups, Sarah Winnemucca, Sitting Bull, & Wilma Mankiller. Grades 4-5. Illus. Raintree, 1993. $19.95 each.

AMERICAN INDIAN STORIES
Zitkala-Sa
Presents the pain and difficulty of growing up Indian in a white man's world. 200 pp. Paper. University of Nebraska Press, 1985. $7.95.

AMERICAN INDIAN TREATIES: THE HISTORY OF A POLITICAL ANOMALY
Francis P. Prucha
University of California Press, 1994.

THE AMERICAN INDIAN TREATY SERIES
Compiles treaties and agreements made between the U.S. Government and Indian Tribes. Nine volumes. Separate books for treaties and agreements of the Sioux Nation, the Pacific Northwest, the Northern Plains, eastern Oklahoma, the Southwest (western Oklahoma), the Five Civilized Tribes, the Chippewa, and the Great Lakes region. 102-278 pp each. Institute for the Development of Indian Law, 1973-1975.

AMERICAN INDIAN TRIBAL AUTONOMY & AMERICAN SOCIETY IN THE 1980's: A BIBLIOGRAPHY
Tim J. Watts
48 pp. Vance Bibliographies, 1988. $12.50.

AMERICAN INDIAN TRIBAL COURTS: THE COSTS OF SEPARATE JUSTICE
American Bar Foundation Staff
153 pp. Paper. American Bar Assn., 1978. $5.

AMERICAN INDIAN TRIBAL GOVERNMENTS
Sharon O'Brien
Examines the impact of federal policies on Indian tribes. Illus. 380 pp. Paper. University of Oklahoma Press, 1989. $17.95.

*AMERICAN INDIAN TRIBES
The first book "Indians," is an overview of the Indian Tribes; tribes covered: Choctaw, Apache, Cherokee, Chippewa, Eskimo, Hopi, Navajo, Seminole, Sioux, Cheyenne, Shoshone, Nez Perce, Anasazi, Cayuga, Crow, Mandans, Mohawk, Oneida, Onandaga, Pawnee, Seneca, Tlingit, Tuscarora. Grades 2-3. Illus. Photos. 48 pp. each. Paper. Childrens Press, $.95 each; $125/ set of 27 books.

THE AMERICAN INDIAN UNDER RECONSTRUCTION
Annie H. Abel
Reprint of 1925 edition. Reprint Services, $49.

THE AMERICAN INDIAN & THE U.S.: A DOCUMENTARY HISTORY
Wilcomb E. Washburn, Editor
Four volumes. Greenwood Press, 1973. $195 per set; $50 each.

AMERICAN INDIAN UTENSILS: HOW TO MAKE BASKETS, POTTERY & WOODENWARE WITH NATURAL MATERIALS
Evelyn Wolfson
Illus. David McKay Co., 1979. $8.95.

AMERICAN INDIAN WARRIOR CHIEFS: TECUMSEH, CRAZY HORSE, CHIEF JOSEPH, GERONIMO
Jason Hook
Illus. 210 pp. Sterling Publishing, $24.95; paper, $14.95.

AMERICAN INDIAN WARS
Philip Katcher
Paper. tackpole Books, 1989. $10.95.

AMERICAN INDIAN WATER RIGHTS & THE LIMITS OF LAW
Lloyd Burton
Illus. 174 pp. University Press of Kansas, 1991. $29.95; paper, $12.95.

AMERICAN INDIAN & WHITE CHILDREN: A SOCIOPSYCHOLOGICAL INVESTIGATION
R.J. Havighurst and B.L. Neugarten
Reprint of 1969 edition. University of Chicago Press, $17.

AMERICAN INDIAN WOMEN: A GUIDE TO RESEARCH
Gretchen M. Bataille & Kathleen M. Sands
Contains 1,500 annotated citations to resources and materials pertaining to American Indian women. 423 pp. Garland, 1991. $57.00.

AMERICAN INDIAN WOMEN: TELLING THEIR LIVES
Gretchen M. Bataille and Kathleen M. Sands
210 pp. Paper. University of Nebraska Press, 1984. $7.95.

AMERICAN INDIAN WOMEN'S CALENDAR
12 beautiful women representing 18 different tribes. 10x13" Annual. Elan Marketing, $12 postpaid.

*AMERICAN INDIANS
Grades Preschool-12. Aerial Photography Services, $2.85.

AMERICAN INDIANS
Describes the Federal Government's economic policy affecting Indian tribes and Alaska natives. 45 pp. Paper. Supt. of Documents, 1984. $2.50.

*AMERICAN INDIANS
Bearl Brooks
Grades 4-6. 24 pp. ESP, 1977. Workbook, $5.

*THE AMERICAN INDIANS
Roland W. Force
Grades 7-12. Illus. 112 pp. Chelsea House, 1990. $17.95.

*AMERICAN INDIANS
Patricia Kindle & Susan Finney
Grades 4-8. Illus. 64 pp. Workbook. Good Apple, 1985. $6.95.

*AMERICAN INDIANS
Florence Randall
Grades K-6. Revised edition. Illus. Paper. Highlights for Children, 1972. $2.95.

AMERICAN INDIANS
F. Starr
Reprint of 1899 edition. AMS Press, $21.50.

AMERICAN INDIANS
William T. Hagan
Revised 1979 edition. A history of the relationship between the white man and the Indian. Illus. 190 pp. Paper. University of Chicago Press, $8.95.

*THE AMERICAN INDIANS
Time-Life Book Editors
A series of books which reveals the customs & cultures, myth, magic & folklore of the American Indian. The titles in the series are: *The First Americans*, *The Spirit World*, *European Challenge*, *People of the Desert*, *The Way of the Warrior*, *The Buffalo Hunter*, *Realm of the Iroquois*, *The Mighty Chieftains*, *Keeper of the Totem*, *Cycles of Life*, *The War of the Plains*, *Tribes of the Southern Woodlands*, *The Indians of California*, *People of the Ice & Snow*, *People of the Lakes*, *Tribes of the Atlantic Coast*, *The War of the West II*, *Plains Indians II*, *The Way of Beauty*, *Indians of the Western Range*, & *Villagers and Cliff Dwellers*. Grades 4 and up. Illus. 176 pp. each. Paper. Time-Life Books, $14.95 each.

THE AMERICAN INDIANS
Edward H. Spicer
176 pp. Paper. Harvard University Press, 1982. $6.95.

AMERICAN INDIANS, AMERICAN JUSTICE
Vine Deloria, Jr. & Clifford M. Lytle
Reprint of classic indictment of mistreatment of Indian peoples. 278 pp. Paper. University of Texas Press, 1983. $12.95.

AMERICAN INDIANS: ANSWERS TO TODAY'S QUESTIONS
Jack Utter
Illus. Photos. Maps. 330 pp. National Woodlands Publishing Co., 1993. $21.95; paper, $14.95.

AMERICAN INDIANS & CHRISTIAN MISSIONS: STUDIES IN CULTURAL CONFLICT
Henry W. Bowden
256 pp. University of Chicago Press, 1981. $18.00; paper, $12.95.

AMERICAN INDIANS DISPOSSESSED: FRAUD IN LAND CESSIONS FORCED UPON THE TRIBES
Walter H. Blumenthal
Facsimile of 1955 edition. Ayer Co., $18.

AMERICAN INDIANS: FACTS & FUTURE TOWARD ECONOMIC DEVELOPMENT FOR NATIVE AMERICAN COMMUNITIES
Subcommittee on Economy in Government
Reprint of 1969 edition. Ayer Co., $13.

AMERICAN INDIANS: THE FIRST OF THIS LAND
C. Matthew Snipp
450 pp. Paper. Russell Sage, 1989. $16.95.

*THE AMERICAN INDIANS IN AMERICA: VOLUME II: THE LATE 18TH CENTURY TO THE PRESENT
Jayne Clark Jones
Grades 5 and up. 72 pp. Lerner Publications, 1991. $11.95; paper, $5.95.

AMERICAN INDIANS IN COLORADO
Donald J. Hughes
Illus. Paper. Pruett, 1987. $8.95.

AMERICAN INDIANS & THE LAW
Lawrence Rosen
Reprint of 1976 edition. 230 pp. Transaction Publishers, $24.95.

AMERICAN INDIANS OF THE SOUTHWEST
Bertha P. Dutton
Revised edition. Illus. 320 pp. Paper. University of New Mexico Press, 1983. $15.95.

AMERICAN INDIANS: A SELECT CATALOG OF NATIONAL ARCHIVES MICROFILM PUBLICATIONS
91 pp. National Archives, 1984. $2.

THE AMERICAN INDIANS & THEIR MUSIC
Frances Densmore
Examines different types of Indian music and instruments. Includes a general discussion of Native American history and customsReprint of 1926 edition. Johnson Reprint.

AMERICAN INDIANS, TIME & THE LAW: NATIVE SOCIETIES IN A MODERN CONSTITUTIONAL DEMOCRACY
Charles F. Wilkinson
Examines Indian law from pre-Columbian times to the present. 227 pp. Yale University Press, 1987. $25.00; paper, $9.95.

AMERICAN INDIANS TODAY: ANSWERS TO YOUR QUESTIONS
Bureau of Indian Affairs
Pamphlet providing an overview of the role of federal government and its relationship to Native Americans. Includes general statistics, map, and bibliography. 36 pp. Paper. U.S. Government Printing Office, 1991.

*AMERICAN INDIANS TODAY: ISSUES & CONFLICTS
Judith Harlan
Grades 7 and up. Illus. 128 pp. Franklin Watts, 1987. $12.90.

AMERICAN INDIANS & WORLD WAR II: TOWARD A NEW ERA IN INDIAN AFFAIRS
Alison Bernstein
Illus. 288 pp. University of Oklahoma Press, 1991. $21.95.

AMERICAN PROTESTANTISM & U.S. INDIAN POLICY, 1869-1882
Robert H. Keller, Jr.
Illus. 400 pp. University of Nebraska Press, 1983. $32.50.

THE AMERICAN PUEBLO INDIAN ACTIVITY BOOK
Walter Yoder
40 pages of activities. 48 pp. Paper. Sunstone Press, $7.95.

AMERICAN PURITANISM & THE DEFENSE OF MOURNING: RELIGION, GRIEF, & ETHNOLOGY IN MARY WHITE ROWLANDSON'S CAPTIVITY NARRATIVE
Mitchell Breitwieser
224 pp. University of Wisconsin Press, 1990. $40.00; paper, $15.50.

THE AMERICAN RACE: A LINGUISTIC CLASSIFICATION & ETHNOGRAPHIC DESCRIPTION OF THE NATIVE TRIBES OF NORTH & SOUTH AMERICA
Daniel G. Brinton
Reprint of 1901 edition. Johnson Reprint. $25.

THE AMERICAN REVOLUTION IN INDIAN COUNTRY
Colin G. Calloway
Cambridge University Press, 1995.

*THE AMERICAN REVOLUTIONARIES: A HISTORY IN THEIR OWN WORDS
Milton Meltzer
Grades 7 and up. Illus. 256 pp. Harper & Row, Junior Books, 1987. $13.89.

AMERICAN SOCIETY FOR PROMOTING THE CIVILIZATION & GENERAL IMPROVEMENT OF THE INDIAN TRIBES WITHIN THE U.S.
Reprint of 1824 edition. Kraus, $20.

AMERICAN SOURCES OF MODERN ART
Holger Cahill
Reprint of 1933 edition. Illus. Ayer Co., $15.

AN AMERICAN URPHILOSOPHIE: AN AMERICAN PHILOSOPHY - BP (BEFORE PRAGMATISM)
Robert Bunge
218 pp. University Presses of America, 1984. $27.25.

THE AMERICAN WEST
Paper. Mankind, 1991. $1.75.

THE AMERICAN WEST
Dee Brown
An account of the demise of the Native Americans of the Plains. Illus. 304 pp. Scribners, 1994. $25.

THE AMERICAN WEST IN THE TWENTIETH CENTURY: A BIBLIOGRAPHY
Richad W. Etulain & co-editors
Compiled over 8,000 entries focusing on the West after 1900. 464 pp. University of Oklahoma Press, 1994. $60.

AMERICAN WOODLAND INDIANS
Michael Johnson
Paper. Stackpole Books, 1990. $10.95.

AMERICANIZING OF THE AMERICAN INDIANS: WRITINGS BY THE FRIENDS OF THE INDIAN, 1880-1900
Francis P. Prucha, Editor
368 pp. Harvard University Press, 1973. $25.50. Paper. University of Nebraska Press, $6.95.

AMERINDIANS & THEIR PALEO-ENVIRONMENTS IN NORTHEASTERN NORTH AMERICA, Volume 288
Walter Newman and Bert Salwen
New York Academy of Science, 1977. $37.

AMONG THE APACHES
Frederick Schwatka
Reprint of the 1887 articles. Collected observations of several visits to the Apache Indian agencies. Tells of life as it was. Illus. 30 pp. Paper. Filter Press, 1974. $2.50.

AMONG THE CHIGLIT ESKIMOS
E. Petitot
202 pp. Paper. CCI, 1981. $10.

AMONG THE ESKIMOS OF WALES, ALASKA: 1890-93
Harrison R. Thornton
Reprint of 1931 edition. AMS< $27.50.

*AMONG THE PLAINS INDIANS
Lorenz Engel
Based upon the journals of the German explorer Maximilian, as well as upon the records of George Catlin during the early 1830's. Grades 5-12. Illus. 112 pp. Lerner, 1970. $9.95.

AMONG THE SIOUX OF DAKOTA: EIGHTEEN MONTHS EXPERIENCE AS AN INDIAN AGENT, 1869-70
D.C. Poole
Reprint of 1881 edition. Illus. Photos. Map. 241 pp. Paper. Minnesota Historical Society, 1988. $8.95.

AN ANALYSIS OF COASTAL ALGONQUIAN CULTURE
Regina Flannery
Reprint of 1939 edition. AMS, $22.50.

AN ANALYSIS OF COEUR D'ALENE INDIAN MYTHS
Gladys A. Reichard
Reprint of 1947 edition. Kraus, $23.

AN-NIK-A-DEL: THE HISTORY OF THE UNIVERSE AS TOLD BY THE MODES-SE INDIANS OF CALIFORNIA
C.H. Meriam, Editor
Reprint of 1928 edition. AMS.

ANASAZI
Pike
Paper. Random House, $17.

*THE ANASAZI
Grades K-4. Illus. 48 pp. Childrens Press, $11.45.

*ANASAZI, THE ANCIENT VILLAGERS
Susan Shaffer
Grade 4. Illus. with 30 student booklets and teacher's manual; transparencies, slides & audio-cassette. Heard Museum, 1987. $295.

ANASAZI PLACES: THE PHOTOGRAPHIC VISION OF WILLIAM CURRENT
Jeffrey Cook
Illus. 101 bxw photos. 144 pp. University of Texas Press, 1992. $45.

ANASAZI RUINS OF THE SOUTHWEST IN COLOR
William M. Ferguson & Arthur H. Rohn
Illus. 320 pp. Paper. University of New Mexico Press, 1987. $24.95.

*AN ANASAZI WELCOME
Kay Matthews; illus. by Barbara Belknap
Grades Preschool-3. Illus. 40 pp. Paper. Red Crane Books, $6.95.

*ANCESTOR'S FOOTSTEPS
T. Moore
Two stories of young men who prove themselves. Grades 6 to 9. Illus. 40 pp. Council for Indian Education, 1978. $9.95; paper, $3.95.

THE ANCESTORS: NATIVE AMERICAN ARTISANS OF THE AMERICAS
Anna C. Roosevelt & James G.E. Smith, Eds.
Illus. 197 pp. Paper. University of Washington Press & National Museum of the American Indian, 1979. $17.50.

ANCESTRAL VOICE: CONVERSATIONS WITH N. SCOTT MOMADAY
Charles L. Woodard, Editor
He explores his individual and Kiowa tribal identity, his philosophies on language and literature, and his painting theories and practices. Illus. 230 pp. Center for Western Studies, $21.50; paper, $9.95. Paper. University of Nebraska Press, $9.95.

ANCIENT AMERICA
Marian Wood
Facts on File, 1990. $17.95.

ANCIENT ARCHITECTURE OF THE SOUTHWEST
William N. Morgan
Explores concurrent Mogollon, Hohokam, and Anasazi architecture. Illus. 320 pp. University of Texas Press, 1994. $55.

ANCIENT ART OF THE AMERICAN WOODLAND INDIAN
David S. Brose
Illus. 240 pp. Detroit Institute of Arts, $29.95.
Harry N. Abrams, 1985. $35.

THE ANCIENT AMERICAS: THE MAKING OF THE PAST
Earl H. Swanson, et al
Illus. 160 pp. Peter Bedrick Books, 1989. $24.95; paper, 16.95.

ANCIENT ART OF OHIO
Lar Hothem
Reviews most of the artifact types in all of Ohio's prehistoric periods. Illus. 272 pp. Hothem House, 1994. $43, postpaid.

ANCIENT CHIEFDOMS OF THE TOMBIGBEE
John H. Blitz
256 pp. Paper. University of Alabama Press, 1993. $24.95.

ANCIENT CULTURE OF THE FREMONT RIVER IN UTAH
Noel Morss
Reprint of 1931 edition. Paper. Kraus, $24.

ANCIENT DRUMS, OTHER MOCCASINS: NATIVE NORTH AMERICAN CULTURAL ADAPTATION
Harriet J. Kupferer
Illus. 352 pp. Prentice-Hall, 1988. $34.67.

ANCIENT INDIAN POTTERY OF THE MISSISSIPPI RIVER VALLEY
Hathcock
2nd Edition. Illus. 236 pp. Hothem House, 1988. $48, postpaid.

*ANCIENT INDIANS: THE FIRST AMERICANS
Roy Gallant
Grades 5-11. 128 pp. Enslow Publishers, 1989. $15.95.

ANCIENT LIFE IN THE AMERICAN SOUTHWEST
Edgar Hewett
Reprint of 1930 edition. Illus. Biblo-Moser, $25.

ANCIENT MODOCS OF CALIFORNIA & OREGON
Carrol Howe
Reprint of 1979 edition. Illus. 264 pp. Paper. Binford & Mort, $12.95.

ANCIENT NORTH AMERICA: THE ARCHAEOLOGY OF A CONTINENT
Brian M. Fagan
Revised edition. Paper. Thames & Hudson, 1995. $31.95.

ANCIENT NORTH AMERICANS
Jesse Jennings, Editor
Illus. 642 pp. W.H. Freeman, 1983. $29.95.

ANCIENT ROAD NETWORKS & SETTLEMENT HIERARCHIES IN THE NEW WORLD
Charles Trombold
300 pp. Cambridge University Press, 1991.

ANCIENT SOCIETY
Lewis H. Morgan
The primitive institutions of the Indians. Reprint of 1877 edition. 608 pp. Paper. University of Arizona Press, $19.95.

ANCIENT TEXANS
Harry J. Shafer
Illus. 256 pp. Texas Monthly Press, 1986. $35.

ANCIENT TREASURES: A GUIDE TO ARCHAEOLOGICAL SITES & MUSEUMS IN THE U.S. & CANADA
Franklin Folsom & Mary Elting
3rd Edition. University of New Mexico Press, 1983.

ANCIENT TRIBES OF THE KLAMATH COUNTRY
Carol B. Howe
Illus. Paper. Binford-Metropolitan, 1968. $9.95.

ANCIENT VOICES, CURRENT AFFAIRS: THE LEGEND OF THE RAINBOW WARRIORS
Steven McFadden
Explores the myth of the rainbow warriors through the teachings of indigenous peoples of the Americas, Australia, and Tibet. Illus. 176 pp. Paper. Bear & Co., $9.95.

ANCIENT WALLS: INDIAN RUINS OF THE SOUTHWEST
Chuck Place
Illus. 112 pp. Fulcrum Publishing, 1991. $34.95; paper, $19.95.

ANCIENT WASHINGTON: INDIAN CULTURES OF THE POTOMAC VALLEY, Vol. 6
Robert Humphrey & Mary Chambers
George Washington University, $5.

AND EAGLES SWEEP ACROSS THE SKY: INDIAN TEXTILES OF THE NORTH AMERICAN WEST
Dena S. Katzenberg
Illus. Baltimore Museum, 1977. $6.98.

AND STILL THE WATERS RUN: THE BETRAYAL OF THE FIVE CIVILIZED TRIBES
Angie Debo
Reprint of 1940 edition. Illus. 448 pp. Paper. University of Oklahoma Press, $13.95.

ANGEL SITE: AN ARCHAEOLOGICAL, HISTORICAL, AND ETHNOLOGICAL STUDY
Glenn A. Black
Excavations of Angel Mounds community in southwestern Indiana. 2 Vols. Illus. 620 pp. Indiana Historical Society, 1967. $35.

ANGELS TO WISH BY
Joseph Juknialis
Paper. Resource Publications, 1984. $7.95.

ANISHINABE: SIX STUDIES OF MODERN CHIPPEWA
J. Anthony Paredes, Editor
Illus. 447 pp. University Press of Florida, 1980. $41.95.

ANNALS OF SHAWNEE METHODIST MISSION & INDIAN MANUAL LABOR SCHOOL
Martha B. Caldwell
Reprint of 1939 edition. Illus. 120 pp. Paper. Kansas State Historical Society, $3.

AN ANNOTATED BIBLIOGRAPHY OF AMERICAN INDIAN & ESKIMO AUTOBIOGRAPHIES
H. David Brumble, III
182 pp. University of Nebraska Press, 1981. $16.50.

AN ANNOTATED BIBLIOGRAPHY OF AMERICAN INDIAN PAINTING
Doris O. Dawdy
50 pp. Paper. National Museum of the American Indian, 1968. $2.50.

ANNOTATED STATUTES OF THE INDIAN TERRITORY
Reprint of 1899 edition. AMS, $98.50.

*ANPAO: AN AMERICAN INDIAN ODYSSEY
Jamake Highwater
Grades 5-9. Harper & Row Junior Books, 1977. $13.50; paper, $3.95.

ANTHOLOGY: OBSERVATIONS ON MISSISSIPPI VALLEY & TRANS-MISSISSIPPI INDIANS
Jean A. Delanglez; Mildred M. Wedel, Editor
399 pp. Garland Publishing, 1985. $50.

ANTHROPOLOGIA ANTHROPOLOGICA: THE NATIVE RACES OF AMERICA
James G. Frazier and Robert A. Downie, Editors
Reprint of 1939 edition. Illus. AMS, $47.50.

ANTHROPOLOGICAL OBSERVATIONS ON THE CENTRAL ESKIMOS
Kaj Birket-Smith; W.E. Calvert, Translator
Reprint of 1928 edition. Illus. AMS, $42.50.

ANTHROPOLOGICAL PAPERS OF UNIVERSITY OF ALASKA
Linda Ellanna, Editor of Series
See Dept. of Anthropology, University of Alaska, Fairbanks, AK 99775 (907) 474-7288 for a complete listing with prices.

ANTHROPOLOGICAL STUDIES ON THE QUICHUA & MACHIGANGA INDIANS
Harry B. Ferris
Reprint of 1921 edition. Paper. Elliots Books.

ANTHROPOLOGY & THE AMERICAN INDIAN
Report of a symposium held in 1970 by the American Anthropological Association on the issues raised by Vine Deloria's book, Custer Died for Your Sins. 125 pp. Paper. Indian Historian Press, 1973. $2.50.

THE ANTHROPOLOGY OF KODIAK ISLAND
Alex Hrdlicka
Reprint of 1944 edition. Illus. AMS, $60.50.

ANTHROPOLOGY ON THE GREAT PLAINS
W. Raymond Wood and Margot Liberty, Editors
Illus. 310 pp. University of Nebraska Press, 1980. $27.95.

ANTIQUITIES OF THE NEW ENGLAND INDIANS
Charles C. Willoughby
Reprint of 1935 edition. Illus. AMS, $34.

ANTHROPOLOGY OF THE NORTH PACIFIC RIM
William Fitzhugh & Valerie Chaussonnet, Eds.
Investigates the anthropology, history, and art of the North pacific rim. Illus. 368 pp. Smithsonian Institution Press, 1993. $49.

ANTIQUITIES OF THE SOUTHERN INDIANS PARTICULARLY OF THE GEORGIA TRIBES
C.C. Jones, Jr.
Reprint of 1887 edition. Illus. 548 pp. AMS Press, $57.50; Reprint Co., $30.

THE ANTIQUITY & ORIGIN OF NATIVE AMERICANS
Clark S. Larseon
171 pp. Garland Publishing, 1985. $80.

ANY OTHER COUNTRY EXCEPT MY OWN
Hadley A. Thomas
The evolution of the Dine from prehistory to the present. The story of the Navajo. Illus. 270 pp. paper. Cross Cultural Publications, 1994. $19.95.

APACHE
Will L. Comfort
274 pp. Paper. University of Nebraska Press, 1985. $7.95.

*APACHE
Barbara McCall
Grades 5-8. Illus. 32 pp. Rourke Corp., 1990. $9.95.

*THE APACHE
Patricia McKissack
Grades K-4. Illus. 48 pp. Childrens Press, $11.45.

*THE APACHE
Michael Melody
Grades 5 and up. Illus. 104 pp. Paper. Chelsea House, 1988. $9.95.

APACHE AGENT: THE STORY OF JOHN P. CLUM
W. Clum
Illus. 300 pp. Gordon Press, 1977. $59.95 (library binding.)

APACHE AUTUMN
Robert Skimin
Novel deals with the struggle of the Apaches tomaintain their way of life against insurmountable odds. 427 pp. St. Martins Press, 1993. $22.95.

AN APACHE CAMPAIGN IN THE SIERRA MADRE
John G. Bourke
Illus. 150 pp. Paper. University of Nebraska Press, 1987. $4.95.

APACHE DAYS & AFTER
Thomas Cruse; E. Cunningham, Editor
Illus. 364 pp. University of Nebraska Press, $27.95; paper, $9.95.

APACHE GOLD & YAQUI SILVER
J. Frank Dobie
Legend & lore. Explores the mysterious and alluring sagas of lost mines and adventure. Illus. 380 pp. Paper. University of Texas Press, $12.95.

APACHE INDIAN BASKETS
Clara Lee Tanner
Illus. 204 pp. University of Arizona Press, 1982. $39.95.

THE APACHE INDIANS
Frank C. Lockwood
Illus. 348 pp. University of Nebraska Press, 1987. $26.50; paper, $9.95.

APACHE LEGENDS: SONGS OF THE WILD DANCER
Lou Cuevas
Illus. 128 pp. Naturegraph, $8.95.

AN APACHE LIFE-WAY: THE ECONOMIC, SOCIAL, AND RELIGIOUS INSTITUTIONS OF THE CHIRICAHUA INDIANS
Morris E. Opler
Reprint of 1941 edition. Based on the author's two years of field work. Illus. Maps. 500 pp. Cooper Square Publishers, $33.50.

APACHE MEDICINE-MEN
John G. Bourke
Intensive studies of 19th century American Indian life. Reprint. Photos. Illus. 176 pp. Paper. Dover, $7.95.

APACHE MOTHERS & DAUGHTERS: FOUR GENERATIONS OF A FAMILY
Ruth McDonald Boyer
& Narcissus Duffy Gayton
Family history of four generations of Chiricahua Apache women from 1848 to the present. Illus. Maps. 416 pp. University of Oklahoma Press, 1993. $24.95.

APACHE, NAVAHO, & SPANIARD, 2nd Ed.
Jack D. Forbes
Apache & Navaho response to Spanish advance in the 17th century into northern mexico and the Southwest U.S. Illus. Maps. Biblio. 328 pp. Paper. University of Oklahoma Press, 1994. $14.95.

APACHE ODYSSEY: A JOURNEY BETWEEN TWO WORLDS
Morris E. Opler; G. and L. Spindler, Editors
A biographical narrative of a Mescalero Apache. A study of an incipient shaman, and of shamanism. Reprint of 1969 edition. Illus. 320 pp. Paper. Irvington, $16.95.

APACHE RESERVATION: INDIGENOUS PEOPLES & THE AMERICAN STATE
Richard J. Perry
Discusses reservation issues and the historical development of the reservation system. Illus. Maps. 276 pp. Paper. University of Texas Press, 1993. $15.95.

APACHE WARS: AN ILLUSTRATED BATTLE HISTORY
E. Lisle Reedstrom
Illus. 256 pp. Sterling, 1990. $24.95.

APACHE WOMEN WARRIORS
Kimberly M. Buchanan
54 pp. Paper. Texas Western, 1986. $5.

APACHEAN CULTURE HISTORY AND ETHNOLOGY
Keith H. Basso; Morris E. Opler, Editor
Reprint of 1971 edition. Illus. 172 pp. Paper. Books on Demand, $45.80.

APACHES AT WAR AND PEACE: THE JANOS PRESIDIO, 1750-1858
William B. Griffen
Illus. 313 pp. University of New Mexico Press, 1988. $35.

THE APACHES: A CRITICAL BIBLIOGRAPHY
Michael Melody
96 pp. Paper. Indiana University, 1977. $6.95.

THE APACHES: EAGLES OF THE SOUTHWEST
Donald Worcester
Illus. Maps. 408 pp. Paper. University of Oklahoma, 1979. $14.95.

*THE APACHES & NAVAJOS
Craig & Katherine Doherty
Grades 3 and up. Illus. 64 pp. Paper. Franklin Watts, 1991. $4.95.

APALACHEE: THE LAND BETWEEN THE RIVERS
John H. Hann
Illus. Biblio. 464 pp. University Press of Florida, 1988. $39.95.

APOLOGIES TO THE IROQUOIS
Edmund Wilson
Illus. Paper. Syracuse University Press, $15.95.

APPALACHIAN INDIAN FRONTIER: THE EDMOND ATKIN REPORT & PLAN OF 1755
Edmond Atkin; Wilbur R. Jacobs, Editor
Illus. 125 pp. Peter Smith, 1967. $11.25. Paper. University of Nebraska Press, $3.95.

APPALACHIAN MOUNTAIN CHEROKEE
David Michael Wolfe
Booklet specifically to Cherokee people of the present day Appalachian Mountain region encompassing the mountainous regions of WV, KY, Ohio and PA.. 24 pp. David. M. Wolfe.

APPLICATION OF A THEORY OF GAMES TO THE TRANSITIONAL ESKIMO CULTURE
Robert G. Glassford
Reprint of the 1976 edition. Ayer Co., $23.50.

APPROACHES TO TEACHING MOMADAY'S THE WAY TO RAINEY MOUNTAIN
Kenneth M. Roemer, Editor
175 pp. Modern Language Association, 1988. $32.00; paper, 17.50.

*THE ARAPAHO
Loretta Fowler
Grades 5 and up. Illus. Chelsea House, 1989. $17.95.

THE ARAPAHO
Alfred L. Kroeber
Discusses Arapaho culture; dance and design, Indian symbolism. Illus. 480 pp. University of Nebraska Press, 1983. $10.95.

THE ARAPAHO INDIANS: A RESEARCH GUIDE & BIBLIOGRAPHY
Zdenek Salzmann, Compiler
Greenwood Press, 1988. $35.

THE ARAPAHO SUN DANCE, THE CEREMONY OF THE OFFERINGS LODGE
G.A. Dorsey
Reprint of 1903 edition. Kraus, $88.

ARAPAHOE POLITICS, 1851-1978: SYMBOLS IN CRISES OF AUTHORITY
Loretta Fowler
Illus. 375 pp. University of Nebraska Press, 1982. $32.95; paper, $9.95.

THE ARAPAHOES, OUR PEOPLE
Virginia C. Trenholm
Illus. Paper. University of Oklahoma Press, 1986. $12.95.

ARARAPIKVA: TRADITIONAL KARUK INDIAN LITERATURE FROM NORTHWESTERN CALIFORNIA
translated & introduced by Julian Lang
Bilingual text. 112 pp. Heyday Books, 1994. $11.

ARCHAEOASTRONOMY IN THE NEW WORLD: AMERICAN PRIMITIVE ASTRONOMY
A.F. Aveni, Editor
230 pp. Cambridge University Press, 1982. $39.50.

ARCHAEOLOGICAL EXPLORATIONS ON THE MIDDLE CHINLE
Noel Morss
Reprint of 1927 edition. Paper. Kraus, $16.

ARCHAEOLOGICAL COLLECTIONS FROM THE WESTERN ESKIMOS
Therkel Mathiassen
Reprint of 1930 edition. Illus. AMS, $37.50.

ARCHAEOLOGICAL EXCAVATIONS AT KUKULIK, ST LAWRENCE ISLAND, AK
Otto W. Geist and Froelich G. Rainey
Reprint of 1936 edition. AMS, $32.50.

ARCHAEOLOGICAL EXPLORATIONS ON THE MIDDLE CHINLE, 1925
Noel Morss
Reprint of 1927 edition. Kraus, $16.00.

ARCHAEOLOGICAL GEOLOGY OF NORTH AMERICA
N.P. Lasca & J. Donahue, Editors
Illus. Geological Society of America, 1990. $62.50.

ARCHAEOLOGICAL INVESTIGATIONS IN THE ALEUTIAN ISLANDS
Vladimir I. Iokhelson
Reprint of 1925 edition. AMS, $37.50.

ARCHAEOLOGICAL INVESTIGATIONS IN THE UPPER SUSQUEHANNA VALLEY, NEW YORK STATE (VOLUME 1)
Robert E. Funk
Illus. 400 pp. Persimmon Press, 1994. $66.95.

THE ARCHAEOLOGICAL INVESTIGATIONS OF FORT KNOX II, FORT KNOX CO., INDIANA, 1803-1813
Marlesa Gray
Illus. 312 pp. Paper. Indiana Historical Society, 1988. $32.00.

ARCHAEOLOGICAL INVESTIGATIONS OF THE KIOWA & COMANCHE INDIAN AGENCY COMMISSARIES
Daniel J. Crouch
Illus. Paper. Museum of the Great Plains, 1978. $11.30.

ARCHAEOLOGICAL PERSPECTIVES ON THE BATTLE OF LITTLE BIGHORN: THE FINAL REPORT
Douglas D. Scott
Illus. 328 pp. University of Oklahoma Press, 1989. $24.95.

ARCHAEOLOGICAL RECONNAISSANCE OF FORT SILL, OKLAHOMA
C.R. Ferring
Illus. Paper. Museum of the Great Plains, 1978. $20.30.

THE ARCHAEOLOGICAL REPORTS OF FREDERIC WARD PUTNAM
Frederic W. Putnam
Reprint of 1973 edition. Illus. AMS Press, $46.50.

AN ARCHAEOLOGICAL STUDY OF THE MISSISSIPPI CHOCTAW INDIANS
John H. Blitz
Illus. 120 pp. Paper. Mississippi Department of Archives and History, 1985. $7.50.

ARCHAEOLOGY AS ANTHROPOLOGY: A CASE STUDY
William Longacre
Focuses on organizational and behavioral aspects of societies which emerged approximately 1500 B.C. through 1350 AD. 57 pp. Paper. University of Arizona Press, 1970. $5.95.

ARCHAEOLOGY & CERAMICS AT THE MARKSVILLE SITE
Alan Toth
Illus. Paper. University of Michigan, Museum of Anthropology, 1975. $4.00.

ARCHAEOLOGY & ETHNOHISTORY OF THE OMAHA INDIANS; THE BIG VILLAGE SITE
John M. O'Shea & John Ludwickson
Illus. 380 pp. University of Nebraska Press, 1992. $40.

ARCHAEOLOGY, HISTORY, & CUSTER'S LAST BATTLE; THE LITTLE BIGHORN REEXAMINED
Richard Allan Fox, Jr.
Illus. 416 pp. U. of Oklahoma Press, $29.95.

ARCHAEOLOGY IN THE CITY: A HOHOKAM VILLAGE IN PHOENIX, ARIZONA
Michael H. Bartlett, et al
Describes the process of salvage archaeology as it interprets artifacts. 80 pp. Paper. University of Arizona Press, 1986. $8.95.

ARCHAEOLOGY IN VERMONT
John C. Huden, Editor
Illus. Paper. Charles E. Tuttle, 1970. $6.50.

ARCHAEOLOGY OF ABORIGINAL CULTURE CHANGE IN THE INTERIOR SOUTHEAST: DEPOPULATION DURING THE EARLY HISTORIC PERIOD
Marvin T. Smith
Illus. Biblio. 198 pp. University Press of Florida, 1987. $29.95; paper, $16.95.

ARCHAEOLOGY OF ALKALI RIDGE, SOUTHEASTERN UTAH
J.O. Brew
Reprint of 1946 edition. Paper. Kraus, $79.00.

THE ARCHAEOLOGY OF CAPE NOME, AK
John Bockstoce
Illus. 133 pp. Paper. University of Pennsylvania Museum, $25.00.

ARCHAEOLOGY OF THE CENTRAL ESKIMO
Therkel Mathiassen
Reprint of 1927 edition. Two parts in one volume. AMS, $137.50.

ARCHAEOLOGY OF COOK INLET, ALASKA
Frederick De Laguna
Reprint of 1934 edition, AMS, $57.50.

ARCHAEOLOGY OF THE FROBISHER VOYAGES
William Fitzhugh & Jacqueline S. Olin, Editors
An account of the Frobisher voyage into the Canadian Arctic, 1576-1578. Illus. Maps. 368 pp. Smithsonian Institution Press, 1993. $45.

ARCHAEOLOGY OF THE LOWER OHIO RIVER VALLEY
Jon Muller
Academic Press, 1986. $76.50; paper, $37.50.

ARCHAEOLOGY OF MISSISSIPPI
Calvin S. Brown
Reprint of 1926 edition. Illus. 230 pp. University Press of Mississippi, 1993. $42; paper, $19.95.

THE ARCHAEOLOGY OF MISSOURI
Carl H. Chapman
Examines the cultural adaptation of Missouri's first inhabitants. 320 pp. University of Missouri Press, 1975. $26.00.

ARCHAEOLOGY OF NEW YORK STATE
William A. Ritchie
Reprint of 1969 revised edition. Illus. Harbor Hill Books, 1980. $22.50.

*THE ARCHAEOLOGY OF NORTH AMERICA
Dean R. Snow
Grades 7-12. Illus. 128 pp. Chelsea House, 1989. $17.95.

ARCHAEOLOGY OF THE CENTRAL ESKIMO
Therkel Mathiassen
Reprint of 1927 edition. Two parts in one Illus. AMS, $137.50.

ARCHAEOLOGY OF THE FLORIDA GULF COAST
G.R. Willey
Reprint of 1949 edition. Illus. AMS Press, $72.50.

ARCHAEOLOGY OF THE LOWER OHIO RIVER VALLEY
Jon Muller
Academic Press, 1986. $76.50; paper, $ 37.50.

ARCHAEOLOGY OF THE ONEIDA IROQUOIS, Volume 1
Peter Pratt
Franklin Pierce College, Fund for Anthropology, 1976. $5.50.

ARCHAEOLOGY OF PRECOLUMBIAN FLORIDA
Jerald T. Milanich
Illus. Maps. Biblio. 456 pp. University Press of Florida, 1994. $24.95.

THE ARCHAEOLOGY OF SUMMER ISLAND: CHANGING SETTLEMENT SYSTEMS IN NORTHERN LAKE MICHIGAN
David S. Brose
Illus. Paper. University of Michigan, Museum of Anthropology, 1970. $3.00.

THE ARCHAEOLOGY OF THREE SPRINGS VALLEY: A STUDY IN FUNCTIONAL CULTURAL HISTORY
Brian D. Dillon & Matthew A. Boxt, Editors
Illus. 200 pp. Paper. University of California, Los Angeles, 1989. $19.00.

ARCHAEOLOGY OF THE U.S.
Samuel F. Haven
Reprint of 1856 edition. AMS Press, $37.50.

ARCHAIC HUNTERS AND GATHERERS IN THE AMERICAN MIDWEST
James A. Brown; James L. Phillips, Editor
Academic Press, 1983. $32.50.

**ARCHITECTURE OF ACOMA PUEBLO:
THE 1934 HISTORIC AMERICAN BUILDINGS
SURVEY PROJECT**
Peter Nabokov
Illus. 144 pp. Paper . Ancient City Press, $15.95.

**ARCHITECTURE OF THE PUEBLO INDIANS:
AN ANNOTATED BIBLIOGRAPHY**
Glenna Dunning
22 pp. Vance Bibliographies, 1988. $6.25.

**THE ARCHITECTURE OF SOCIAL
INTEGRATION IN PREHISTORIC PUEBLOS**
William Lipe & Michelle Hegmon, Editors
Illus. 175 pp. Paper . Crow Canyon Archaeological Center, 1990. $21.95.

ARCHIVES OF CALIFORNIA PREHISTORY
A series of 41 volumes on the archaeology of California. See Coyote Press for titles and prices.

ARCTIC ART: ESKIMO IVORY
James G. Smith
Examples of Eskimo art from the Museum's collection. The text discusses the people of the Arctic. 127 pp. Paper . National Museum of the American Indian, $19.95.

ARCTIC ARTIST
C. Stuart Houston, Editor
The journal and paintings of George Back, midshipman with Sir John Franklin, 1819-1822, Arctic explorer. Covers various native peoples. Illus. 392 pp. McGill-Queen's University Press, $45.

ARCTIC DREAMS
Alootook Ipellie
Inuit mythology. Illus. 200 pp. Paper . Theytus, 1993. $16.95.

ARCTIC ESKIMO
C. Whittaker
Reprint of 1937 edition. A record of fifty years experience and observations among the Eskimo. Illus. Map. AMS Press, $21.50.

**ARCTIC HANDBOOK OF NORTH
AMERICAN INDIANS, Vol. 5**
David Damas & William C. Sturtevant, Editors
Illus. 862 pp. Smithsonian, 1985. $29.00.

*ARCTIC HUNTER
Diane Hoyt-Goldsmith
An Inupiat experiences ancient & modern cultures. Grades 4-6. Illus. 32 pp. Holiday House, 1992. $15.95; paper , $6.95.

ARCITIC LANGUAGES: AN AWAKENING
450 pp. Paper . UNIPUB, 1990. $45.00.

ARCTIC LIFE: CHALLENGE TO SURVIVE
M. Jacobs and J. Richardson, III, Editors
Illus. 208 pp. Paper . Carnegie Museum, 1982. $17.50.

*ARCTIC MEMORIES
Normee Ekoomiak
Bilingual - English/Inuit. Grades 3 and up. Illus. 32 pp. Henry Holt & Co., 1988. $15.95.

**ARCTIC SCHOOLTEACHER:
KULUKAK, ALASKA, 1931-1933**
Abbie Morgan Madenwald
Story of Abbie Morgan's experiences teaching Eskimo children in the Alaskan village of Kulukak in 1931. Reprint. Illus. Maps. Paper . University of Oklahoma Press, $11.95.

**ARCTIC VILLAGE" A 1930s
PORTRAIT OF WISEMAN, ALASKA**
Robert Marshall
Illus. Maps. 400 pp. University of Alaska Press, 1991. $28; paper , $20.

**AN AREAL-TYPOLOGICAL STUDY OF
AMERICAN INDIAN LANGUAGES NORTH
OF MEXICO**
J. Sherzer
Paper. Elsevier-Nelson, 1976. $31.75.

**ARIKARA NARRATIVE OF THE CAMPAIGN
AGAINST THE HOSTILE DAKOTAS: JUNE
1876**
O.G. Libby, Editor
Illus. Amereon Ltd., 1920. $17.00.

ARIZONA TRAVELER: INDIANS OF ARIZONA
Illus. 48 pp. Paper . Renaissance House Publishers, 1990. $4.95.

ARK OF EMPIRE: THE AMERICAN FRONTIER
Dale Van Every
Reprint of 1963 edition. Ayer Co. Pubs., $17.00.

**ARMS, INDIANS & THE MISMANAGEMENT
OF NEW MEXICO**
D. Vigil; David Weber, Ed. & Translator
Texas Western, $10.00; paper , $5.00.

**THE ARMY & THE NAVAJO: THE BOSQUE
REDONDO RESERVATION EXPERIMENT,
1863-1868**
Gerald Thompson
Chronicles the federal government's attempt to find solutions to problem of raids by Navajo and Apache Indians. 196 pp. Paper . University of Arizona Press, 1976. $7.50.

**AN ARMY WIFE ON THE FRONTIER:
THE MEMOIRS OF ALICE BLACKWOOD
BALDWIN, 1867-77**
Robert & Eleanor Cariiker
118 pp. Signature Books, 1975. $7.95.

**AROUND THE WORLD IN FOLKTALE
& MYTH: AMERICAN INDIAN**
Lu Keatley; H.E. & L.K. Fraumann, Editors
96 pp. Paper . Specialty Books International, 1989. $99.87.

ARROW-MAKER
Mary H. Austin
Revised 1915 edition. AMS Press, $12.50.

**ARROWHEADS & SPEAR POINTS OF THE
PREHISTORIC SOUTHEAST: A GUIDE TO UN-
DERSTANDING CULTURAL ARTIFACTS**
Linda Crawford Culberson
Illus. 118 pp. 230 pp.University Press of Mississippi, 1993. $29.95; paper , $12.95.

**ARROWHEADS & STONE ARTIFACTS:
A PRACTICAL GUIDE FOR THE SURFACE
COLLECTOR & AMATEUR ARCHAEOLOGIST**
C.G. Yeager
A handbook for identifying various stone artifacts. Illus. 158 pp. 1992. Paper . $11.95. The Arrowheads Video shows where to look & what to look for. VHS or Beta, 30 minutes. $22.95. Pruett Pubg.

**THE ARROYO HONDO
ARCHAEOLOGICAL SERIES**
Douglas W. Schwartz, General Editor
5 volumes. Illus. Biblio. Paper . School of American Research, 1990. $10-15.

ART & ENVIRONMENT IN NATIVE AMERICA
M.E. King and I.R. Traylor, Jr. Editors
Illus. 169 pp. Paper . Texas Tech Press, 1974. $8.

**ART & ESKIMO POWER: THE LIFE &
TIMES OF ALASKAN HOWARD ROCK**
Lael Morgan
Illus. 260 pp. Paper . Epicenter Press, 1988. $24.95; paper , $16.95.

**ART IN THE LIFE OF THE NORTHWEST
COAST INDIANS**
Describes the Rasmussen Collection of Northwest Coast Indian art. Published by the Portland Art Museum, 1219 SW Park Ave., Portland, OR 97205 (503) 226-2811.

ART OF THE AMERICAN INDIAN
Levin, et al: Vandervelde, Editor
Paper. Council for Indian Education, 1973. $1.95.

**ART OF THE AMERICAN INDIAN FRONTIER:
THE CHANDLER-POHRT COLLECTION**
David Penney, Editor
Illustrates the many objects in the collection. Includes memoirs, essay, and text. Illus. Photos. 368 pp. paper . University of Washington Press, 1992. $35.

**ART OF CLAY: TIMELESS
POTTERY OF THE SOUTHWEST**
Lee M. Cohen
Al Qoyawayma featured. Illus. Color photos. 140 pp. Clear Light Publishers, $34.95.

**THE ART OF THE INDIAN
BASKET IN NORTH AMERICA**
Carol Fallon
Illus. 56 pp. Paper . Spencer Museum of Art, 1975. $2.50.

**THE ART OF NATIVE AMERICAN
BASKETRY: A LIVING LEGACY**
Frank W. Porter, III, Editor
Illus. Greenwood Publishing, 1990. $49.95.

ART OF THE NORTHERN TLINGIT
Aldona Jonaitis
Illus. 232 pp. University of Washington Press, 1985. $30.

ART OF THE NORTHWEST COAST INDIANS
Robert B. Inverarity
Second edition. Illus. 244 pp. Paper . University of California Press, 1967. $14.95.

**ART OF THE RED EARTH PEOPLE:
THE MESQUAKIE OF IOWA**
Gaylord Torrence & Robert Hobbs
Illus. 144 pp. University of Washington Press, 1989. $50; paper , $24.95.

ART OF THE TOTEM
Marius Barbeau
Explains the historic origins & the significance of totem art among northwest tribes. Illus. 64 pp. Paper . Hancock House, 1984. $6.95.

**ART OF A VANISHED RACE: THE
MIMBRES CLASSIC BLACK-ON-WHITE**
Victor Giamattei & Nanci Reichert
Illus. 2nd Ed. 100 pp. Paper . High-Lonsome Books, 1990. $11.95.

**ARTIFACTS OF THE
NORTHWEST COAST INDIANS**
Hilary Stewart
Illus. 172 pp. Paper. Hancock House, $12.95.

THE ARTISTS BEHIND THE WORK
Suzi Jones, Editor
Features the life history & craft of four Alaska
Native artists: Nicholas Charles, a Yup'ik
Eskimo; Frances Demientieff, an Athabaskan
bead worker & skin sewer; Lena Sours, an
Inupiat skin sewer; and Jennie Thlunaut, a
Chilkat Tlingit basket & blanket maker. Illus.
Maps. Paper. University of Alaska Museum,
1986. $17.50.

ARTISTS OF THE TUNDRA & THE SEA
Dorothy J. Ray
Illus. 192 pp. Paper. University of Washington
Press, 1980. $10.95.

ARTS & CRAFTS OF THE CHEROKEE
Rodney Leftwich
Illus. 146 photos. 160 pp. Paper. Cherokee
Publications, $8.95.

ARTS & CRAFTS OF HAWAII
Sir Peter H. Buck
Hawaiian material culture in 14 separate sections.
Reprint of 1957 edition. Illus. Paper. Bishop Mu-
seum, $7.95 each; $99.95 per set.

ARTS FROM THE ARCTIC
An exhibition catalog documenting the Arts from
the Arctic exhibition. Illus. 80 pp. Institute of Alaska
Native Arts, 1993. $22.50, postpaid.

**THE ARTS IN SOUTH DAKOTA:
A SELECTIVE, ANNOTATED BIBLIOGRAPHY**
Ron MacIntyre, Rebecca Bell, Arthur Amiotte
A companion volume to An Illustrated History of
the Arts in South Dakota. A section on Dakota/
Lakota arts. Illus. 282 pp. Center for Western
Studies, $12.50.

**ARTS OF THE INDIAN AMERICAS:
NORTH, CENTRAL & SOUTH: LEAVES
FROM THE SACRED TREE**
Jamake Highwater
Illus. 320 pp. Paper. HarperCollins, 1985.
$22.50.

**ARTS OF THE NORTH AMERICAN INDIAN:
NATIVE TRADITIONS IN EVOLUTION**
Edwin L. Wade, Editor
Illus. 320 pp. Hudson Hills Press, 1986. $50;
paper, $27.50.

**AS LONG AS THE RIVER SHALL RUN:
AN ETHNOHISTORY OF PYRAMID
LAKE INDIAN RESERVATION**
Marta Knack and Omer C. Stewart
416 pp. U. of California Press, 1984. $42.50.

**AS MY GRANDFATHER TOLD IT: TRADI-
TIONAL STORIES FROM THE KOYUKUK
SITSY YUGH NOHOLNIK TS'IN**
Catherine Attla
University of Alaska Press, $12.

**THE ASCENT OF CHIEFS: CAHOKIA &
MISSISSIPPIAN POLITICS IN NATIVE
NORTH AMERICA**
Timothy R. Pauketat
Analysis of the origins of Cahokia. 256 pp.
Paper. U. of Alabama Press, 1994. $28.95.

ASHES & SPARKS
R. Dell Davis
Illus. 185 pp. J. Franklin Publishers, 1989.
Includes audiotape. $24.95.

**AN ASIAN ANTHROPOLOGIST IN THE
SOUTH: FIELD EXPERIENCES WITH
BLACKS, INDIANS & WHITES**
Choong S. Kim
University of Tennessee Press, 1977. $17.95;
paper, $8.95.

**ASPECTS OF UPPER GREAT LAKES
ANTHROPOLOGY: PAPERS IN HONOR
OF LLOYD A. WILFORD**
Elden Johnson, Editor
Illus. 190 pp. Paper. Minnesota Historical
Society, 1974. $9.50.

**THE ASSAULT ON INDIAN TRIBALISM: THE
GENERAL ALLOTMENT LAW (DAWES ACT)
OF 1887**
Wilcomb E. Washburn
88 pp. Paper. Krieger Publishing, 1975. $7.50.

THE ASSINIBOINE
R.H. Lowie
Reprint of 1909 edition. Illus. AMS Press, $22.45.

*ATARIBA AND NIGUAYONA
adapted by Harriet Rohmer & Jesus Guerrero;
illus. by Consuelo Mendez
Taino tales. Grades 1-6. Illus. Children's Book
Press, $13.95.

ATHAPASKAN LINGUISTICS
Eung-Do Cook, Editor
Current perspectives on a language family.
645 pp. Mouton de Gruyter, 1989. $125.

**ATHABASCAN OLD-TIME FIDDLING
COMMEMORATIVE BOOKLET**
Festival booklet featuring musicians, dancers
and history. Illus. 20 pp. Institute of Alaska
Native Arts, 1992. $8.50, postpaid.

**ATHABASKAN STORIES FROM ANVIK
COLLECTED BY JOHN W. CHAPMAN**
James Kari, retranscribed by
16 stories. 186 pp. Alaska Native Language
Center, 1981. $12.

**ATHAPASKAN VERB THEME
CATEGORIES: AHTNA**
James Kari
230 pp. Paper. Alaska Native Language Center,
1979. $10.

**THE ATHABASKANS: PEOPLE
OF THE BOREAL FOREST**
Richard K. Nelson
Focuses on the Athabaskans' implements, trans-
lated tales & poems, and describes their signifi-
cance. Illus. Maps. 68 pp. paper. University of
Alaska Museum, 1983. $9.95.

**ATKA, AN ETHNOHISTORY OF THE
WESTERN ALEUTIANS**
Lydia T. Black
Illus. 219 pp. Limestone, 1984. $26.

ATLAS OF AMERICAN INDIAN AFFAIRS
Francis P. Prucha
Graphically presents the history of Native
Americans in 109, full-page, black & white
maps. Includes references. Illus. Biblio. 190 pp.
University of Nebraska Press, 1990. $47.50.

ATLAS OF GREAT LAKES INDIAN HISTORY
Helen H. Tanner, Editor
Illus. 240 pp. University of Oklahoma Press,
1987. $75; paper, $29.95.

ATLAS OF THE NORTH AMERICAN INDIAN
Carl Waldman; map & illus. by Molly Braun
Extensive text, numerous illustrations, and more
than 100 two-color maps on the history, culture,
and locations of Native Americans in North &
Central America. Illus. Biblio. 288 pp. Paper.
Facts on File, $29.95; paper, $17.95.

**ATTITUDES OF COLONIAL POWERS
TOWARD THE AMERICAN INDIAN**
Howard Peckham and Charles Gibson, Eds.
Paper. University of Utah Press, 1969. $9.95.

*AUNT MARY, TELL ME A STORY
as told by Mary Chiltoskey
28 Cherokee legends & tales. Grades 3 and up.
Illus. 82 pp. Paper. Cherokee Publications, $3.50.

**AUTHENTIC AMERICAN INDIAN
BEADWORK & HOW TO DO IT**
Pamela Stanley-Millner
Illus. 48 pp. Paper. Dover & Cherokee
Publications, 1985. $3.50.

AUTHENTIC INDIAN DESIGNS
Maria Naylor, Editor
2,500 illustrations from reports of the Bureau of
American Ethnology. Reprint of 1975 edition. Illus.
220 pp. Paper. Hothem House & Dover, $9.95.

**AUTHENTIC MEMOIRS OF WILLIAM
AUGUSTUS BOWLES, ESQ.**
W.A. Bowles
He was the ambassador from the United Nations
of Creeks and Cherokees to the Court of London.
A classic adventure story casting light on condi-
tions along the troubled southern frontier during
the 1780s and 1790s. Reprint of 1791 edition. Ayer
Co., $19.95.

***AUTHENTIC NORTH AMERICAN INDIAN
CLOTHING FOR SPECIAL TIMES SERIES**
Little Bears Go Visiting Series. Preschool -3. Arc-
tic Circle; California; Columbia River Plateau;
Columbia River Plateau Yakima; Great Basin;
Oregon; Pacific Northwest Coast; Plains; South-
east; Southwest; and Woodlands. See Celia Totus
Enterprises for prices.

***AUTHENTIC NORTH AMERICAN
INDIAN INDIAN CRADLEBOARDS**
Baby Bears Go Visiting Series. Columbia River
Plateau and California; Great Basin, Southeast
and Southwest; Pacific Northwest Coast, Wood-
lands & Arctic Circle; and Plains. See Celia Totus
Enterprises for prices.

**THE AUTOBIOGRAPHY
OF A KIOWA APACHE INDIAN**
Charles S. Brant, Editor
Autobiography of Jim Whitewolf. Reprint. 144
pp. Map. Paper. Dover, $4.95.

AUTOBIOGRAPHY OF A PAPAGO WOMAN
Ruth Underhill
Reprint of 1936 edition. Paper. Kraus, $12.

**THE AUTOBIOGRAPHY
OF A WINNEBAGO INDIAN**
Paul Radin
Reprint of 1920 edition. 91 pp. Paper.
Dover, $3.95.

AUTOBIOGRAPHY OF A YAQUI POET
Refugio Savala; Kathleen Sands, Editor
Yaqui culture. 228 pp. Paper . University of
Arizona Press, 1980. $1 1.95.

B

*BABY RATTLESNAKE
told by L ynn Moroney
Folktale. Grades K-6. Illus. Childrens Press,
$13.95.

BACAVI: A HOPI VILLAGE
Peter Whitely
144 pp. Paper . Northlan, 1988. $14.95.

*BACK IN THE BEFORETIME:
TALES OF THE CALIFORNIA INDIANS
Jane L. Curry, Editor
Grades 3-7. Illus. 144 pp. Macmillan, 1987.
$12.95.

BACKGROUND HISTORY OF THE
COEUR D'ALENE INDIAN RESER VATION
Jerome Peltier
100 pp. Ye Galleon Press.

BACKGROUND OF TREATY-MAKING
IN WESTERN WASHINGTON
Barbara Lane
32 pp. Institute for the Development of Indian
Law, $15.

BACONE INDIAN UNIVERSITY
Howard Meredith & John Williams
A history of the nation's oldest continuing Indian
institution of higher learning from 1880 to 1980.
Illus. 163 pp. Indian University Press, 1980. $14,
postpaid.

BACKWARD: AN ESSAY ON
INDIANS, TIME & PHOT OGRAPHY
Will Baker
Illus. 420 pp. North Atlantic, 1983. $24.95;
paper, $12.95.

Bad Men & Bad Towns
Wayne C. Lee
Chronicles the violent events in Nebraska from
1823-1925, including Indian conflicts. Illus. paper .
The Caxton Printers, 1994. $14.95.

*A BAG OF BONES: LEGENDS OF
THE WINTU INDIANS OF NORTHERN
CALIFORNIA
Marcelle Masson
Grades 4 and up. Illus. Photos. Map.
Naturegraph, 1966. $16.95; paper , $8.95.

THE BARK CANOES & SKIN
BOATS OF NORTH AMERICA
Edwin Adney and Howard Chapelle
Reprint of 1964 second edition. Illus. 242 pp.
Smithsonian Books, $24.95.

BASHFUL NO LONGER: AN ALASKAN
ESKIMO ETHNOHISTORY, 1778-1988
W.H. Oswalt
University of Oklahoma Press.

BASIC CALL TO CONSCIOUSNESS
Oren L yons, et al, Editors
A collection of position papers delivered to the
United Nations by the traditional Six Nations

Council in 1977. Illus. Photos. 128 pp. Paper .
The Book Publishing Co.. $7.95.

BASKETMAKER CAVES IN THE PRAYER
ROCK DISTRICT, NORTHEASTERN AZ
Elizabeth A. Morris
158 pp. Paper . University of Arizona Press,
1980. $13.95.

BASKETMAKER CAVES OF
NORTHEASTERN ARIZONA
S.J. Guernsey and A.V. Kidder
Reprint of 1921 edition. Illus. Paper . Kraus, $20.

BASKETRY
F.J. Christopher
Covers selection of material, patterns and weaving procedures are explained and illustrated. 130
pp. Paper. Cherokee Publications, $2.95.

BASKETRY DESIGNS
OF THE SALISH INDIANS
Livingston Farrand
Reprint of 1900 edition. AMS, $22.50.

BASKETRY OF THE PAPAGO
& PIMA INDIANS
Mary Lois Kissell
Reprint of 1916 edition. Illus. 158 pp.
Rio Grande Press, $15.

BASKETRY OF THE SAN CARLOS
APACHE INDIANS
Helen H. Roberts
Reprint of 1929 edition. Illus. 105 pp. Paper .
Rio Grande Press, $10.

BATTLE CANYON
Robert Hilgardner
Illus. 110 pp. Paper. Mid-America Publishing
House, 1986. $8.95.

BATTLE OF HORSESHOE BEND
W.H. Brantley, Jr.
Illus. Paper . Southern University Press, 1955,
$3.75.

THE BATTLE OF THE LITTLE BIGHORN
Mari Sandoz
Illus. 191 pp. Paper . University of Nebraska
Press, 1978. $4.95.

BATTLE OF THE ROSEBUD:
PRELUDE TO THE LITTLE BIGHORN
Neil C. Mangum
Illus. 200 pp. Upton & Sons, 1987. $35.

THE BATTLE OF WISCONSIN HEIGHTS
Crawford B. Thayer, Editor
Illus. 416 pp. Paper . Thayer Associates, 1983.
$9.95.

BATTLE ROCK, THE HERO'S ST ORY
Bert & Margie W ebber, Editors
A true account-Oregon Coast Indian attack.
Illus. Maps. Biblio. 75 pp. Paper . Webb
Research Group, $8.95.

BATTLEFIELD & CLASSROOM: FOUR
DECADES WITH THE AMERICAN INDIAN,
1867-1904
Richard H. Pratt; Robert Utley , Editor
Reprint of 1964 edition. 390 pp. University of
Nebraska Press, $29.95.

BATTLEFIELDS & BURIAL GROUNDS:
THE INDIAN STRUGGLE T O PROTECT
ANCESTRAL GRAVES IN THE U.S.
Roger C. Echohawk & W alter R. Echohawk
Examines the historical & cultural roots behind the
double standard perpetuated by American soci-
ety. Illus. 80 pp. Lerner , 1994. $19.95.

BATTLES & SKIRMISHES OF THE GREA T
SIOUX WAR, 1876-77: THE MILIT ARY VIEW
Jerome A. Greene, Editor
Illus. Maps. 256 pp. University of Oklahoma
Press, 1993. $24.95.

BAYOU SALADO
Virginia M. Simmons
Illus. 280 pp. Paper . Century One, 1982. $8.95.

BEADS & BEADWORK
OF THE AMERICAN INDIAN
William C. Orchard
Revised 1929 second edition. Illus. 170 pp.
Hothem House, $15.95, postpaid; Eagle's V iew
Publishing, $15.95; paper , $9.95.

BEADS TO BUCKSKINS
Peggy Sue Henry
Nine volumes. Illus. 96 pp. each. Paper .
Cherokee Publications & Treasure Chest,
$10.95 each.

A BEADWORK COMPANION
Jean Heinbuch
Step-by-step, illustrated projects designed to
teach Native American beadwork. Illus. 1 12 pp.
Paper. Eagle's V iew Publishing, 1992. $10.95.

BEAR CHIEF'S WAR SHIRT
James W. Schultz and W ilbur Betts
Illus. 240 pp. Paper . Mountain Press, 1984.
$8.95.

BEAR HEART: THE HEIRSHIP CHRONICLES
Gerald Vizenor
Sebtiments of Manifest Destiny . 260 pp. U. of
Minnesota Press, 1990. $24.95; paper , $12.95.

THE BEAR RIVER MASSACRE
Newell Hart
Illus. 300 pp. Cache V alley, 1982. $35.

*THE BEAR THAT TURNED
WHITE; & OTHER NATIVE TALES
Maurine Grammer , retold by
Stories with messages intended to teach young
people about various aspects of Native
American culture or tradition. Grades 4-10. Illus.
108 pp. Northland Publishing, $1 1.95.

THE BEAR TRIBE'S SELF-RELIANCE BOOK
Sun Bear, Wabun & Nimimosha
Contains Native American philosophy , legends
and prophecy. Illus. 202 pp. Paper . Prentice Hall
Press, 1989. $8.95.

THE BEAR WHO ST OLE THE CHINOOK:
TALES FROM THE BLACKFOOT
Frances Fraser
144 pp. Paper. University of W ashington Press,
1991. $12.95.

THE BEAUTIFUL & THE DANGEROUS:
DIALOGUES WITH THE ZUNI INDIANS
Barbara Tedlock
Illus. 336 pp. Penguin USA, $23; paper , $12.

**BECOMING BRAVE: THE PATH
TO NATIVE AMERICAN MANHOOD**
  Laine Thom, Editor
Illus. 120 pp. Chronicle Books, 1992. $29.95;
paper, $18.95

*BEFORE COLUMBUS
  Muriel Batherman
Daily life of earliest inhabitants, based on archaeo-
logical findings. Focus on Pueblos. Illus. Paper.
Houghton Mifflin Co., 1990. $4.95.

BEFORE THE LITTLE BIGHORN
  Fred H. Werner
Revised and enlarged 1983 edition.
Paper. Werner Publications, $4.95.

BEFORE THE LONG KNIVES CAME
  Millie House
Illus. 94 pp. Kennebec River Press, 1987.

BEFORE MAN IN MICHIGAN
  R. Ray Baker
Reprint. Paper. George Wahr Publishing, $12.50.

**BEFORE THE WILDERNESS: ENVIRON-
MENTAL MANAGEMENT BY NATIVE
CALIFORNIANS**
  Tom Blackburn & Kat Anderson
Includes the full text of *Patterns of Indian Burning*.
Illus. 476 pp. Ballena Press, 1994. $41.50; paper,
$31.50.

BEGINNING CHEROKEE
  Ruth B. Holmes & Betty S. Smith
A Cherokee language grammar. Revised edition.
Illus. 346 pp. Paper. University of Oklahoma Press,
1978. $21.95. Set of two cassettes, $20.

BEHIND THE TRAIL OF BROKEN TREATIES
  Vine Deloria, Jr.
Historical review of Indian political recognition and
land title with respect to other nations. 310
pp.Paper. University of Texas Press, 1974. $12.95.

**BEING & BECOMING INDIAN:
BIOGRAPHICAL STUDIES OF
NORTH AMERICAN FRONTIERS**
  James A. Clifton, Editor
337 pp. Wadsworth, 1988. $32.95. Paper.
Waveland Press, $14.95.

**BEING COMANCHE: A SOCIAL HISTORY
OF AN AMERICAN INDIAN COMMUNITY**
  Morris W. Foster
Won the 1992 Erminie Wheeler-Voegelin Prize of
the American Society of Ethnohistory. Illus. Uni-
versity of Arizona Press & University of Oklahoma
Press, 1992. $29.95; paper, $14.95.

**BEHIND THE TREE OF PEACE:
A SOCIOLOGICAL ANALYSIS
OF IROQUOIS WARFARE**
  George Snyderman
Reprint of 1948 edition. AMS, $17.

**BELIEF & WORSHIP IN
NATIVE NORTH AMERICA**
  Ake Hultkrantz; Christopher Vecsey, Editor
358 pp. Syracuse University Press, 1981. $30.

**BELIEFS & HOLY PLACES: A SPIRITUAL
GEORGAPHY OF THE PIMERIA ALTA**
  James S. Griffith
The Tohono O'odham, their places and
traditions are covered. 218 pp. University of
Arizona Press, 1992. $32.50; paper, $15.95.

***BELLE HIGHWALKING: THE NARRATIVE
OF A NORTHERN CHEYENNE WOMAN**
  Katheryne Weist, Editor
Grades 5-12. 66 pp. Council for Indian
Education, 1979. $9.95; paper, $3.95.

BENDING TRADITION
Exhibiton catalog featuring traditional and contemporary bentwood containers, Aleut headgear and
sculptures. Illus. 48 pp. Institute of Alaska Native
Arts, 1990. $12.50, postpaid.

**THE BENTEEN-GOLDIN LETTERS
ON CUSTER & HIS LAST BATTLE**
  John M. Carroll
Illus. Paper. Amereon Ltd., 1985. $18.95.

*THE BENTWOOD BOX
  Nan McNutt
Grades 3-8. Illus. 35 pp. Paper. N. McNutt
Associates, 1989. $9.95.

BEOTHUK & MICMAC
  Frank G. Speck
Reprint of 1922 edition. AMS Press, $41.

**THE BEOTHUCKS, OR RED INDIANS,
THE ABORIGINAL INHABITANTS OF
NEWFOUNDLAND**
  James P. Howley
Reprint of 1915 edition. AMS Press, $49.50.

**O.E. BERNINGHAUS - TAOS, N.M., MASTER
PAINTER OF AMERICAN INDIANS AND
FRONTIER WEST**
  Gordon E. Sanders
Illus. 152 pp. Taos Heritage Press, 1985. $40.

**A BETTER KIND OF HATCHET: LAW, TRADE,
DIPLOMACY IN THE CHEROKEE NATION**
  John P. Reid
262 pp. Penn State U. Press, 1975. $27.50.

**BETWEEN INDIAN & WHITE WORLDS:
THE CULTURAL BROKER**
  Margaret Connell Szasz
14 portraits of cultural brokers between the
Indian & White. Illus. Maps. Biblio. 448 pp.
University of Oklahoma Press, 1994. $45.

***BETWEEN SACRED MOUNTAINS: NAVAJO
STORIES & LESSONS FROM THE LAND**
  Sam & Janet Bingham, Editors
Grades 4-12. Illus. 290 pp. University of Arizona
Press, $35; paper, $25.95.

**BETWEEN TWO CULTURES:
KIOWA ART FROM FORT MARION**
  Moira F. Harris; with Rodney C. Loehr
Reproduction of the drawings by Wo-Haw com-
pleted during his imprisonment. Illus. 148 pp. Pogo
Press, 1989. $39.95.

**BETWEEN WORLDS: INTERPRETERS,
GUIDES, & SURVIVORS**
  Frances Karttunen
Tells the story of 16 men & women who served as
interpreters & guides to explorers, soldiers, an-
thropologists, missionaries, and conquerors. In-
cludes the stories of Sacajawea, Sarah
Winnemucca, Charles Eastman, and Ishi. Rutgers
University Press, 1994. $24.95.

**BEYOND THE COVENANT CHAIN:
THE IROQUOIS & THEIR NEIGHBORS
IN INDIAN NORTH AMERICA, 1600-1800**
  Daniel Richter & James Merrell, Editors

Illus. 288 pp. Syracuse University Press, 1987.
$27.50.

**BEYOND THE HUNDREDTH MERIDIAN:
JOHN WESLEY POWELL & THE SECOND
OPENING OF THE WEST**
  Wallace Stegner
Exploration of the Colorado River, the Grand Can-
yon, and homeland of Indian tribes of the Ameri-
can Southwest. Illus. 464 pp. Paper. Penguin USA,
$12.

**BEYOND THE RIVER & THE BAY:
THE CANADIAN NORTHWEST IN 1811**
  Eric Ross
Illus. Paper. U. of Toronto Press, 1970. $9.95.

**BEYOND TRADITION: CONTEMPORARY
INDIAN ART & ITS EVOLUTION**
  Lois Jacka
Illus. 224 pp. Northland, 1988. $55.

**BEYOND THE VISION: ESSAYS
ON AMERICAN INDIAN CULTURE**
  William K. Powers
Illus. 220 pp. University of Oklahoma Press,
1987. $35.

**A BIBLIOGRAPHICAL GUIDE TO THE
HISTORY OF INDIAN-WHITE RELATIONS
IN THE U.S.**
  Francis P. Prucha
Lists and discusses more than 9,000 items includ-
ing materials in the National Archives. Paper. Uni-
versity of Chicago Press, 1977. $12.

**BIBLIOGRAPHIES OF THE LANGUAGES
OF THE NORTH AMERICAN INDIANS**
  James C. Pilling
Reprint of 1894 edition. Consists of nine parts
in three volumes. AMS Press, $125 per set.

**BIBLIOGRAPHY OF AMERICAN INDIAN
LAND CLAIMS**
  Richard H. Weil
46 pp. Vance Bibliographies, 1987. $12.50.

**BIBLIOGRAPHY: NATIVE AMERICAN
ARTS & CRAFTS OF THE U.S.**
A selection of books and pamphlets chosen and
annotated for their pertinence to the field of con-
temporary Native American arts and crafts of the
U.S. 8 pp. Indian Arts and Crafts Board. No charge.

**BIBLIOGRAPHY OF THE
ALGONQUIAN LANGUAGES**
  James C. Pilling
Reprint of 1891 edition. Reprint Services, $75.

**BIBLIOGRAPHY OF ARTICLES & PAPERS
ON NORTH AMERICAN INDIAN ART**
  Anne D. Harding and Patricia Bolling
Reprint of 1938 edition. Gordon Press, 1980.
Library binding, $75.

**A BIBLIOGRAPHY OF THE
ATHAPASKAN LANGUAGES**
  Richard T. Parr
Paper. National Museum of Canada, $3.95.

BIBLIOGRAPHY OF THE BLACKFOOT
  Hugh Dempsey & Lindsey Moir
255 pp. Scarecrow, 1989. $27.50.

BIBLIOGRAPHY OF THE CATAWBA
  Thomas J. Blumer
575 pp. Scarecrow, 1987. $59.50.

BIBLIOGRAPHY OF THE CHICKASAW
Anne Kelley Hoyt
230 pp. Scarecrow, 1987. $25.

A BIBLIOGRAPHY OF CONTEMPORARY NORTH AMERICAN INDIANS: SELECTED & PARTIALLY ANNOTATED WITH STUDY GUIDES
William H. Hodge; intro. by Paul Prucha
320 pp. Interland Publishing, 1976. $27.50.

BIBLIOGRAPHY OF THE CONSTITUTIONS & LAWS OF THE AMERICAN INDIANS
Lester Hargrett
Reprint of 1947 edition. Illus. Paper. Kraus, $31. Also available on microfilm.

BIBLIOGRAPHY OF THE ENGLISH COLONIAL TREATIES WITH THE AMERICAN INDIAN
H. De Puy
Reprint of 1917 edition. Reprint Services, $49. Paper. Scholarly Press, $10; AMS, $11.50.

BIBLIOGRAPHY OF LANGUAGE ARTS MATERIALS FOR NATIVE NORTH AMERICANS, 1975-1976
G. Edward Evans, Karin Abbey & Dennis Reed
Paper. American Indian Studies Center, 1977. 153 pp., $5.

BIBLIOGRAPHY OF LANGUAGES OF NATIVE CALIFORNIA: INCLUDING CLOSELY RELATED LANGUAGES OF ADJACENT AREAS
William Bright
234 pp. Scarecrow Press, 1982. $20.

BIBLIOGRAPHY OF NATIVE NORTH AMERICANS ON DISC - CD-ROM
Timothy O'Leary & M. Marlene Martin, Editors
Based on th Human Relations Area File's Ethnographic Bibliography of North Ameica, 4th Ed. 1975, and Supplement, 1973-87, 1990. IBM compataible. ABC-Clio.

BIBLIOGRAPHY OF THE NAVAHO INDIANS
Clyde Kluckhohn and K. Spencer
Reprint of 1940 edition. AMS, $16.

BIBLIOGRAPHY OF NORTH AMERICAN INDIAN MENTAL HEALTH
Dianne Kelso and Carolyn Attneave, Editors
Illus. 404 pp. Greenwood Press, 1981. $46.95.

BIBLIOGRAPHY OF THE OSAGE
Terry P. Wilson
172 pp. Scarecrow Press, 1985. $20.

BIBLIOGRAPHY OF THE SIOUX
Jack W. Marken & Herbert T. Hoover
388 pp. Scarecrow Press, 1980. $27.50.

BIG BEAD MESA: AN ARCHAEOLOGICAL STUDY OF NAVAHO ACCULTURATIONS
D.L. Keur
Reprint of 1941 edition. Paper. AMS Press & Kraus Reprint, $12.50.

BIG BEAR: THE END OF FREEDOM
Hugh A. Dempsey
Illus. 227 pp. Paper. University of Nebraska Press, 1985. $8.95.

BIG CYPRESS: A CHANGING SEMINOLE COMMUNITY
M. Garbarino; Spindler, Editors
131 pp. Paper. Waveland, 1972. $8.50.

THE BIG HORN MEDICINE WHEEL, THE BIRTH & DEATH OF HUMANITY
Jay Ellis Ransom
Illus. Paper. Western America Institute, 1992. $9.95.

THE BIG MISSOURI WINTER COUNT
Roberta C. Cheney
Illus. 48 pp. Naturegraph, 1979. $11.95; paper, $4.95.

BIGHORSE THE WARRIOR
Tiana Bighorse; Noel Bennett, Editor
Stories of the sufferings of the Navajo people. 115 pp. University of Arizona Press, 1990. $15.95; paper, $10.95.

BILINGUAL EDUCATION FOR AMERICAN INDIANS
U.S. Bureau of Indian Affairs
Francesco Cordasco, Editor
Reprint of 1971 edition. Ayer Co. Pubs., $22.

*BILL RED COYOTE IS A NUT
Hap Gilliland
Grades 1-8. 32 pp. Paper. Council for Indian Education, 1981. $8.95; paper, $2.95.

THE BINGO PALACE
Louise Erdrich
A novel of gaming & competetion dancing and traditional Anishinabe culture. HarperCollins, 1994.

A BIOBIBLIOGRAPHY OF NATIVE AMERICAN WRITERS, 1772-1924: SUPPLEMENT
Daniel F. Littlefield, Jr. & James W. Parsons
350 pp. Scarecrow Press, 1985. $29.50.

BIOGRAPHICAL DICTIONARY OF INDIANS OF THE AMERICAS
Contains nearly 2,000 detailed biographies of significant Indians past and present, and over 900 portraits. Second edition. 3 vols. American Indian Publishers, 1992. $375 per set.

BIOGRAPHICAL & HISTORICAL INDEX OF AMERICAN INDIANS & PERSONS INVOLVED IN INDIAN AFFAIRS
U.S. Dept. of the Interior
Biographical material on Native Americans who were involved in any way with the U.S. government up to 1965. G.K. Hall, 1966.

BIOGRAPHY OF FRANCIS SLOCUM, THE LOST SISTER OF WYOMING: A COMPLETE NARRATIVE OF HER CAPTIVITY & WANDERINGS AMONG THE INDIANS
John F. Meginness
Reprint of 1891 edition. 260 pp. Ayer Co., $21.

BIRCHBARK CANOE: THE STORY OF AN APPRENTICESHIP WITH THE INDIANS
David Gidmark
Illus. 160 pp. Paper. Prairie House, $9.95.

BIRDS, BEADS & BELLS: REMOTE SENSING OF A PAWNEE SACRED BUNDLE
Diane Good
Illus. 25 pp. Kansas State Historical Society, 1989. $7.95.

THE BIRTH OF AMERICA
R.F. Locke
Mankind, $1.75.

BISHOP MUSEUM & THE CHANGING WORLD OF HAWAI'I
Nelson Foster
Presents artifacts, cultural objects, art, photos and archival materials from the museum's collections. Illus. 96 pp. Bishop Museum Press, 1994. $24.95.

BISON CULTURAL TRADITIONS OF THE NORTHERN PLAINS
Lauren M. McKeever
A report on the bison cultural presentationnn June 17, 1993 at Ethete, Wyoming on the Wind River Indian Reservation. Booklet. The InterTribal Bison Cooperative, 1993.

BLACK AFRICANS & NATIVE AMERICANS
Jack D. Forbes
352 pp. Basil Blackwell, Inc., 1988. $60.

BLACK, BROWN & RED: THE MOVEMENT FOR FREEDOM AMONG BLACK, CHICANO, LATINO & INDIAN
John Alan, Editor
Illus. 78 pp. Paper. News & Letters, $9.95.

THE BLACK CANOE: BILL REID & "THE SPIRIT OF HAIDA GWAII"
Robert Bringhurst; photos by Ulli Steltzer
Photos of sculpture by Bill Reid, The Spirit of Haida Gwaii; with translations from oral narratives. Illus. 176 pp. University of Washington Press, $45.

BLACK EAGLE CHILD
Ray A. Young Bear
The Facepaint Narratives. 261 pp. University of Iowa Press, $24.95.

BLACK ELK: HOLY MAN OF THE OGLALA
Michael F. Steltenkamp
Portrays the Sioux spiritual leader as a victim of Western subjugation. 211 pp. Illus. Maps. University of Oklahoma Press, 1993. $19.95.

*BLACK ELK: A MAN WITH VISION
Carol Greene
Grades K-3. Illus. 50 pp. Childrens Press, 1990. $11.95.

BLACK ELK: THE SACRED WAYS OF A LAKOTA
Wallace B. Elk & William Lyon
225 pp. Paper. HarperCollins, 1992. $8.95.

BLACK ELK SPEAKS
John Neihardt
Illus. 300 pp. Paper. Cherokee Pubns., $8.95.

BLACK HAWK: AN AUTOBIOGRAPHY
Donald Jackson, Editor
Reprint of 1955 edition. Maps. 177 pp. Paper. University of Illinois Press, $5.95.

*BLACK HAWK, FRONTIER WARRIOR
Joanne Oppenheim
Grades 4-6. Illus. 48 pp. Troll Associates, 1979. $9.59; paper, $2.50.

*BLACK HAWK & JIM THORP
Greison Bloom & Hap Gilliland
Biographies of two Salk heros. Grades 5-12. 71 pp. Council for Indian Education. $10.95; paper, $4.95.

THE BLACK HAWK WAR, 1831-1832
Ellen M. Whitney, Editor
Two volumes. Illinois State Historical Library.

THE BLACK HAWK WAR, INCLUDING A REVIEW OF BLACK HAWK'S LIFE
Frank E. Stevens
A detailed history of the war, with data on many participants. Illus. 323 pp. Paper. Heritage Books, $22.

THE BLACK HAWK WAR, WHY?
Lloyd H. Efflandt
Illus. 40 pp. Paper. Rock Island Arsenal Historical Society, 1987. $1.95.

THE BLACK HILLS; OR, THE LAST HUNTING GROUND OF THE DACOTAHS
Annie D. Tallent
Reprint of 1899 edition. Illus. 594 pp. Brevit Press, limited leather edition, $50. Facsimile edition. Illus. Ayer Co., $62.

BLACK HILLS: SACRED HILLS
Tom Eagle & Ron Zeilinger
Illus. 60 pp. Paper. Tipi Press, 1987. $2.50.

BLACK HILLS, WHITE JUSTICE: THE SIOUX NATION VERSUS THE U.S., 1775 TO THE PRESENT
Edward Lazarus
Case study in the history of Indian/white relations in North America. HarperCollins, 1993. $27.95.

BLACK INDIANS: A HIDDEN HERITAGE
William Katz
Describes historic links between African & Native Peoples in the Americas. Grades 5 and up. Illus. 208 pp. Macmillan, 1986. $15.95.

BLACK, RED & DEADLY: BLACK & INDIAN GUNFIGHTERS OF THE INDIAN TERRITORIES
Art Burton
Illus. 288 pp. Eakin Press, 1992. $19.95.

BLACK ROBE FOR THE YANKTON SIOUX: FR. SYLVESTER EISENMAN, O.S.B. (1891-1948)
Mary E. Carson
Illus. 295 pp. Paper. Tipi Press, 1989. $11.95.

BLACK SAND: PREHISTORY IN NORTHERN ARIZONA
Harold S. Colton
Reprint of 1960 edition. Illus. 132 pp. Greenwood, $35.

THE BLACKFEET: AN ANNOTATED BIBLIOGRAPHY
Bryan R. Johnson
232 pp. Garland, 1988. $35.00.

THE BLACKFEET: ARTISTS OF THE NORTHERN PLAINS: THE SCRIVER COLLECTION OF BLACKFEET INDIAN ARTIFACTS & RELATED OBJECTS, 1894-1990
Bob Scriver
Illus. 320 pp. Lowell Press, 1992. $50.

BLACKFEET CRAFTS
John C. Ewers
Reprint of 1945 edition. Illus. 68 pp. Paper. R. Schneider, Publishers, $5.95.

BLACKFEET INDIAN STORIES
George Bird Grinnell
Reprinted from 1913 ed. With original N.C. Wyeth painting, Spring, on front cover. Illus. 224 pp. Paper. Globe Pequot Press, $10.95.

BLACKFEET INDIANS
W. Reiss and F.B. Linderman
Reprint. Gordon Press, 1977. $75.95.

THE BLACKFEET: RAIDERS ON THE NORTHWESTERN PLAINS
John C. Ewers
Reprint of 1958 edition. Illus. 377 pp. Paper. University of Oklahoma Press, $15.95.

BLACKFEET: THEIR ART & CULTURE
John C. Ewers; Herb Bryce, Editor
Illus. 96 pp. Paper, Hancock House, 1985. $6.95.

THE BLACKFOOT CONFEDERACY, 1880-1920: A COMPARATIVE STUDY OF CANADA & U.S. INDIAN POLICY
Hana Samek
Illus. 248 pp. University of New Mexico Press, 1987. $27.50.

BLACKFOOT CRAFTWORKER'S BOOK
Adolf & Beverly Hungry Wolf
A collection of photos of traditional clothing, accessories, utensils, cradleboards, etc. Illus. 80 pp. Paper. The Book Publishing Co., $11.95.

A BLACKFOOT-ENGLISH VOCABULARY
C.C. Uhlenbeck and R.H. Van Gulik
Reprint of 1934 edition. AMS, $45.

BLACKFOOT LODGE TALES: THE STORY OF A PRAIRIE PEOPLE
George B. Grinnell
Reprint of 1892 edition. 310 pp. Corner House, $20. Paper. University of Nebraska Press, $9.95.

BLACKFOOT MUSICAL THOUGHT: COMPARATIVE PERSPECTIVES
Bruno Nettl
214 pp. Kent State University, 1989. $21.

A BLACKFOOT SOURCEBOOK
Clark Wisler
Reprint. 510 pp. Garland, $65.

BLANKETS & MOCCASINS: PLENTY COUPS & HIS PEOPLE, THE CROWS
G. Wagner & W. Allen
Illus. 304 pp. University of Nebraska Press, 1987. $24.95; paper, $8.95.

BLESSED ASSURANCE: AT HOME WITH THE BOMB IN AMARILLO TEXAS
A.G. Mojtabai
Illus. 272 pp. Paper. University of New Mexico Press, 1988. $10.95.

BLESSINGWAY
Leland C. Wyman
The central rite of Navajo religion. Presents Navajo origin myths and ritual poetry. Illus. 660 pp. University of Arizona Press, 1970. $35.

BLOOD AT SAND CREEK: THE MASSACRE REVISITED
Bob Scott
Illus. Biblio. 256 pp. Paper. The Caxton Printers, 1994. $8.95.

BLOODLINES: ODYSSEY OF A NATIVE DAUGHTER
Janet Campbell Hale
Autobiographically-based book of essays traces the life experiences of the author and her family. Random House, 1993. $18. Paper. Elliott Bay Books. $12.95.

*BLUE JACKET: WAR CHIEF OF SHAWNEES
Allen W. Eckert
Grades 7-adult. 177 pp. Paper. Landfall Press, 1983. $5.95.

BLUE STAR: THE STORY OF CORABELLE FELLOWS, TEACHER AT DAKOTA MISSIONS, 1884-1888
Kunigunde Duncan
A church-sponsored teacher among the Sioux and Cheyenne in the Dakota Territory in the 1880s. Illus. Photos. Map. Paper. Minnesota Historical Society Press, 1989. $8.95.

*BLUE STONE: AN ANASAZI INDIAN BOY
Charles Fellers; Maxine Hughes, Editor
Grades Preschool-K. Illus. 60 pp. Paper. Laughing Fox Legends, $6.95.

*BLUE THUNDER
Richard Throssel
Grades 5-12. 32 pp. Paper. Council for Indian Education, 1976. $8.95; paper, $2.95.

BO'JOU, NEEJEE!: PROFILES OF CANADIAN INDIAN ART
Ted J. Brasser
Source of ethnographic information on central Indian artifacts. Illus. 204 pp. Paper. National Museums of Canada and University of Chicago Press, 1976. $19.95.

*BOAT RIDE WITH LILLIAN TWO BLOSSOM
Patricia Polacco
A story which xplores the magic of myth. Illus. 32 pp. Philomel, 1989. $14.95.

BONE DANCE: NEW & SELECTED POEMS, 1965-1993
Wendy Rose
Poetry anthology of a Native American author's work. 108 pp. Paper. University of Arizona Press, 1994. $10.95.

BONE GAME
Louis Owens
A novel (murder mystery) by Louis Owens, of Choctaw-Cherokee-Irish descent. 256 pp. University of Oklahoma Press, 1994. $19.95.

THE BOOK OF THE AMERICAN INDIAN
Hamlin Garland
Reprint of 1923 edition. Reprint Services, $59.

BOOK OF AUTHENTIC INDIAN LIFE CRAFTS
Oscar E. Norbeck
Revised edition. Illus. 260 pp. Galloway, 1974. $10.95.

BOOK OF THE ESKIMOS
Peter Freuchen
Paper. Fawcett, 1981. $2.95.

BOOK OF THE GODS & RITES & THE ANCIENT CALENDAR
Fr. Diego Duran; Fernando Horcasitas and Doris Heyden, Translators
Illus. Paper. University of Oklahoma Press, 1970. $14.95.

BOOK OF THE HOPI
Frank Waters
Reveals the Hopi view of life, kept secret for generations. Illus. 360 pp. Paper. Penguin USA, 1977. $9.95.

**THE BOOK OF INDIAN
CRAFTS & COSTUMES**
Bernard S. Mason
Describes the crafts and customs of the Indians
of the Woodlands and Plains. Reprint of 1946
edition. Illus. 118 pp. Paper. Books on Demand,
$32.

**THE BOOK OF INDIAN
CRAFTS & INDIAN LORE**
Julian H. Salomon
A general discussion of the Indians of the U.S.
Reprint. Illus. Biblio. Index. 418 pp. Gordon Press,
$69.95.

THE BOOK OF THE INDIANS
S.G. Drake
Reprint of 1841 edition. AMS Press, $49.

THE BOOK OF THE NAVAJO
Raymond Friday Locke
Navajo history and legends. The Navajo's own
history taken from the authentic Navajo "Singer"
folktales & extensive historical and anthropological research. 5th Ed. Illus. 512 pp. Paper. Mankind Publishing, $6.95.

THE BOOK OF ONE TREE
Annette R. Schober
Fiction. Story of of the struggle many Native Americans have today as they cope with urban life. 64
pp. Northland Publishing, $9.95.

**A BOOK OF TALES, BEING MYTHS OF THE
NORTH AMERICAN INDIANS**
Charles E. Woods
Reprint. Gordon Press, $59.95.

BOOKS ON AMERICAN INDIANS & ESKIMOS
Mary J. Lass-Woodfin
American Library Association, 1977. Text
edition, $25.

**BOOKS WITHOUT BIAS:
THROUGH INDIAN YES**
Beverly Slapin & Doris Seale, Editors
Illus. 2nd Edition. 470 pp. Oyate, $25.

BORDER TOWNS OF THE NAVAJO NATION
Aaron Yava
Second edition. Illus. 80 pp. Paper.
Holmgangers, 1975. $4.

**BORN A CHIEF: THE NINETEENTH CEN-
TURY HOPI BOYHOOD OF EDMUND
NEQUATEWA, AS TOLD TO ALFRED F.
WHITING**
P. David Seaman, Editor
193 pp. Paper. U. of Arizona Press, 1993. $13.95.

**BOSQUE REDONDO: A STUDY OF CUL-
TURAL STRESS AT THE NAVAJO RESERVA-
TION**
Lynn R. Bailey
Illus. 275 pp. Westernlore, $8.50.

**BOUNDARIES & PASSAGES: RULE & RITUAL
IN YUP'IK ESKIMO ORAL TRADITION**
Ann Fienup-Riordan
Traditional Yup'ik rules and rituals. Illus. Maps.
Biblio. U. of Oklahoma Press, 1994. $47.50.

**BOWS & ARROWS OF
THE NATIVE AMERICANS**
J. Hamm
Lyons & Burford, 1991. $19.95.

**THE BOX OF DAYLIGHT:
NORTHWEST COAST INDIAN ART**
Bill Holm
Illus. 160 pp. University of Washington Press,
1983. $40.

*THE BOY WHO DREAMED OF AN ACORN
Leigh Casler; illus. by Shonto Begay
Based on a Native American rite known as the
Spirit Quest. Grades PS-3. Illus. 32 pp. Putnam,
1994. $15.95.

*BOY WHO FOUND THE LIGHT
Dale Dearmond
Grades 4-7. Little, Brown & Co., 1990. $16.95.

*THE BOY WHO LIVED WITH THE SEALS
Rafe Nartin; illus by David Shannon
A Chinook Indian tale about loss & redemption.
Grades PS-3. Illus. 32 pp. Putnam, 1993. $14.95.

**THE BOZEMAN TRAIL: HISTORICAL AC-
COUNTS OF THE BLAZING OF THE OVER-
LAND ROUTES INTO THE NORTHWEST & THE
FIGHTS WITH RED CLOUD'S WARRIORS**
Grace Hebard
Reprint of 1922 edition. Two volumes. AMS,
$63.50 per set.

**BRAIDED LIVES: AM ANTHOLOGY OF
MULTICULTURAL WRITING**
Minnesota Humanities Commission, copiler
Illus. Paper. Minnesota Humanities Commis-
sion, 1992.

**JOSEPH BRANT: IROQUOIS ALLY OF THE
BRITISH**
Robert A. Hecht; D. Steve Rahmas, Editor
32 pp. SamHar Press, 1975. $3.95; paper,
$2.50.

**BRAVE ARE MY PEOPLE:
INDIAN HEROES NOT FORGOTTEN**
Frank Waters
Biographies and history. Illus. 180 pp. Clear Light
Publishers & AISES, 1994. $24.95; paper, $14.95.

**BRAVE EAGLE'S ACCOUNT
OF THE FETTERMAN FIGHT**
Paul Goble, Writer & Illus.
Illus. 64 pp. Paper. University of Nebraksa
Press, 1992. $9.95

BREAD & FREEDOM
Ted Zuern
160 pp. Paper. Tipi Press, 1991. $11.95.

BREATH OF THE INVISIBLE
John Redtail Freesoul
Illus. 226 pp. Paper. Theosophical Publishing
House, 1986. $8.95.

BREATHTRACKS
Jeannette C. Armstrong
Poetry by an Okanagan author/artist. Illus.
112 pp. Theytus, 1991. $9.95.

**A BRIEF HISTORY OF THE COEUR
D'ALENE INDIANS, 1806-1909**
Jerome Peltier
94 pp. Paper. Ye Galleon, $6.95.

A BRIEF HISTORY OF THE INDIAN PEOPLES
William W. Hunter
Ayer Co., $16.75.

A BRIEF HISTORY OF THE PEQUOT WAR
John Mason
Facsimile of 1736 edition. Ayer Co., $9.

**A BRIEF & TRUE REPORT OF THE
NEW FOUND LAND IN VIRGINIA**
Thomas Harriot
Reprint of 1588 edition. Illus. 106 pp. Paper.
Dover, $8.95.

**THE BRIGHT EDGE: A GUIDE TO THE
NATIONAL PARKS OF THE COLORADO
PLATEAU**
Stephen Trimble
Illus. 76 pp. Paper. Museum of Northern
Arizona, 1979. $5.95.

**BRINGING HOME ANIMALS: RELIGIOUS
IDEOLOGY & MODE OF PRODUCTION OF
THE MISTASSINI CREE HUNTERS**
Adrian Tanner
St. Martin's Press, 1979. $27.50.

**BRITISH ADMINISTRATION OF THE
SOUTHERN INDIANS, 1756-1783**
Helen Shaw
Reprint of 1931 edition. AMS Press, $24.50.

THE BROKEN CORD
Michael Dorris
Story about an Indian family's ordeal with "Fetal
Alcohol Syndrome." 300 pp. Paper. Paper.
Harper Perennial, Greenfield Review Press, or
Cherokee Publications, $11.

*BROKEN ICE
Hap Gilliland
Grades 1-8. 35 pp. Paper. Council for Indian
Education, 1972. $8.95; paper, $2.95.

**BROKEN PATTERN - SUNLIGHT
& SHADOWS OF HOPI HISTORY**
Vada Carlson
The intrusion of the Spanish; life of the Hopi. Illus.
208 pp. Naturegraph, $16.95; paper, $8.95.

**THE BROKEN RING: THE DESTRUCTION
OF THE CALIFORNIA INDIANS**
Van H. Sarner
Illus. Westernlore, 1982. $13.95.

*BROTHER EAGLE, SISTER SKY
Susan Jeffers
Grades 4 and up. Text based on the famous
Chief Seattle speech of the mid-1950's. Illus. 26
pp. Four Winds Trading Co., $15.

*BROTHERS OF THE HEART
Joan Blos
Grades 4 and up. Illus. Macmillan, 1987.
$13.95; paper, $3.95.

**BROTHERS OF LIGHT, BROTHERS OF
BLOOD: PENITENTS OF THE SOUTHWEST**
Marta Weigle
Illus. 320 pp. Paper. Ancient City Press, 1988.
$12.95.

BRUCHKO
Olson
Paper. Strang Communications Co., 1977. $5.95.

**BRULE: THE SIOUX PEOPLE
OF THE ROSEBUD**
Paul Dyck
Reprint. Illus. Center for Western Studies, $50.

BUCKSKIN HOLLOW REFLECTIONS
Maggie Culver Fry
Book of peotry by the author who was a former Oklahoma poet laureate. 95 pp. The Five Civilized Tribes Museum. $4.50.

THE BUCKSKINNER'S COOKBOOK
Over 200 authentice recipes of Indian, Canadian, Alaskan, etc. cooking; food at trading posts. Illus. The Fur Press, $5.

BUFFALO BIRD WOMAN'S GARDEN: AGRICULTURE OF THE HIDATSA INDIANS
Buffalo Bird Woman as told to Gilbert Wilson
Reprint of 1917 edition. Illus. 129 pp. Paper. Minnesota Historical Society Press, 1987. $7.95.

BUFFALO HEARTS
Sun Bear
An account of Native American history, culture, and religion from a Native viewpoint. Illus. 128 pp.Paper. Bear Tribe Publishing, 1976. $5.95.

BUFFALO HUMP & THE PENATEKA COMANCHES
Jodyce & Thomas Schilz
Illus. 78 pp. Texas Western Press, 1989. $12; paper, $7.50.

*BUFFALO HUNT
Russell Freedman
The Plains Indians and the buffalo. Grades 4-6. Illus. 52 pp. Holiday House, 1988. $18.95.

*BUFFALO & INDIANS ON THE GREAT PLAINS
Noel Grisham & Betsy Warren
Grades K-4. Illus. Eakin, 1985. $8.95.

BUFFALO PEOPLE: PREHISTORIC ARCHAEOLOGY ON THE CANADIAN PLAINS
Liz Bryan
The University of Alberta Press, $24.95, paperback, $14.95.

*BUFFALO WOMAN
Paul Goble
Grades K-6. Illus. Macmillan, 1987. $13.95; paper, $4.95.

BUFFALO WOMAN COMES SINGING
Brooke Medicine Eagle
The Spirit Song of the Rainbow Medicine Woman. Illus. 495 pp. Paper. Ballantine Books, $12.50.

BUILDING A CHIPPEWA INDIAN BIRCHBARK CANOE
Robert E. Ritzenhaler
Second revised edition. 42 pp. Milwaukee Public Museum, 1984. $4.

BUILT LIKE A BEAR
James P. Dowd
190 pp. Ye Galleon, 1979. $16.

BULL CREEK
Jesse D. Jennings & Dorothy Sammons-Lohse
Paper. University of Utah Press, 1982. $15.

BULLYING THE MOQUI
Charles F. Lummis; edited by Robert Easton & Mackenzie Brown
Reprints articles that Lummis published in "Out West" in 1903. Text is story of the attempts to forcibly "civilize" the Hopi Indians of Arizona. Illus. 132 pp. Center for Anthropological Studies, $30.

BURIAL MOUNDS OF THE RED RIVER HEADWATERS
Lloyd A. Wilford
Illus. 36 pp. Paper. Minnesota Historical Society, 1970. $2.

BURIALS OF THE ALGONQUIAN, \SIOUAN & CADDOAN TRIBES WEST OF THE MISSISSIPPI
David Bushnell, Jr.
Reprint of 1927 edition. Scholarly Press, $59.

BURR'S HILL: A 17th CENTURY AMPANOAG BURIAL GROUND IN WARREN, R.I.
Susan G. Gibson, Editor
Illus. 182 pp. Paper. University of Washington Press, 1980. $19.95.

BURY MY HEART AT WOUNDED KNEE: AN INDIAN HISTORY OF THE AMERICAN WEST
Dee Brown
Illus. 480 pp. Henry Holt & Co., 1971. $24.95. Paper. Washington Square Press, $4.95.

THE BUSINESS OF FANCYDANCING
Sherman Alexie
Stories and poems. 84 pp. Hanging Loose Press, $18.00; paper, $10.

*THE BUTTON BLANKET
Nan McNutt
Grades K-3. Illus. 2nd Ed.. 45 pp. Paper. N. McNutt Associates & Workshop Publications, $7.95.

BY CANOE & MOCCASIN. SOME NATIVE PLACE NAMES OF THE GREAT LAKES
Basil Johnston
Illus. Greenfield Review Press, $10.95.

BY CHEYENNE CAMPFIRES
George B. Grinnell
A collection of war stories, mystery stories, tales of creation. Illus. 319 pp. Paper. University of Nebraska Press, 1971. $10.95.

BY THE PROPHET OF THE EARTH: ETHNOBOTANY OF THE PIMA
L.S.M. Curtin
Reprint of 1949 edition. Illus. 156 pp. Paper. University of Arizona Press. $8.95.

C

THE CADDO NATION: ARCHAEOLOGICAL & ETHNOHISTORIC PERSPECTIVES
Timothy K. Perttula
Illus. 344 pp. University of Texas Press, 1992. $37.50.

THE CADDOAN, IROQUOIAN & SIOUIAN LANGUAGES
Wallace L. Chafe
98 pp. Paper. Mouton de Gruyter, 1976. $20.

CADDOAN TEXTS, PAWNEE, SOUTH BAND DIALECT
Gene Weltfish
Reprint of 1937 edition. AMS, $32.

CAHOKIA MOUNDS MUSEUM SOCIETY BOOKS/VIDEOS
See Cahokia Mounds Museum Society for catalog.

*THE CAHUILLA
Lowell Bean & Lisa Bourgeault
Grades 5 and up. Illus. 112 pp. Chelsea House, 1989. $17.95.

CAHUILLA DICTIONARY
Hansjakob Seiler & Kojiro Hioki
Paper. Malki Museum Press, 1979. $14.95.

CAHUILLA GRAMMAR
Hansjakob Seiler & Kojiro Hioki
Paper. Malki Museum Press, 1979. $12.

THE CAHUILLA INDIANS OF SOUTHERN CALIFORNIA
John L. Bean & Harry W. Lawton
Paper. Malki Museum Press, 1965. $2.

THE CAHUILLA LANDSCAPE: THE SANTA ROSA & SAN JACINTO MOUNTAINS
Lowell J. Bean, Sylvia Brakke Vane, et al
Illus. 116 pp. Ballena Press, 1991. $19.95; paper, $14.95.

CALENDAR HISTORY OF THE KIOWA INDIANS
James Mooney
Reprint of 1895 17th Annual Report of the BIA. Illus. 460 pp. Paper. Smithsonian, $24.95.

CALIFORNIA
Robert F. Heizer, Editor
Illus. 800 pp. Smithsonian, $25.

CALIFORNIA ARCHAEOLOGY
Michael J. Moratto
Paper. Academic Press, 1984. $74.50; paper, $35.

CALIFORNIA INDIAN COUNTRY: THE LAND & THE PEOPLE
Dolan H. Eargle, Jr., Editor
A pictorial guide to contemporary Native American peoples and places of California. 1st edition. 180 pp. Paper. Trees Co. Press, 1992. $12.70.

CALIFORNIA INDIAN NIGHTS ENTERTAINMENT
E. Gifford and G. Block, Compilers
Reprint of 1930 edition. Illus. 325 pp.AMS Press, $32.50. Paper. U. of Nebraska Press, $9.95.

CALIFORNIA INDIAN SHAMANISM
Lowell J. Bean, Editor
Illus. 274 pp. Ballena Press, 1992. $33; paper, $27.50.

CALIFORNIA INDIAN WATERCRAFT
Richard W. Cunningham
Illus. Paper. E Z Nature Books, 1989. $12.95.

*CALIFORNIA INDIANS
C.L. Keyworth
Grades 5-8. Illus. 95 pp. Facts on File, 1990. $18.95.

*CALIFORNIA INDIANS: AN EDUCATIONAL COLORING BOOK
Linda Spizzirri & staff, Editors
Grades 1-8. Illus. 32 pp. Paper. Spizzirri, 1986. $1.95.

CALIFORNIA INDIANS & THE ENVIRONMENT
News from Native California
Special Report #1. Greenfield Review Press, $5.

***CALIFORNIA INDIANS,
AN ILLUSTRATED GUIDE**
George Emmanuels
Grades 7 and up. Illus. 175 pp. Diablo Books,
$19.95; apper, $14.95.

*CALIFORNIA'S INDIANS & THE GOLD RUSH
Clifford E. Trafzer
Grades 4-7. Illus. 60 pp. Paper. Sierra Oaks,
1990. $10.95.

**CALIFORNIA INDIANS:
PRIMARY RESOURCES**
Sylvia Vane & Lowell J. Bean
A guide to manuscripts, artifacts, documents, se-
rials, music, and illustrations. Illus. 300 pp. Paper.
Ballena Press, 1990. $33.

CALIFORNIA INDIANS: A SOURCE BOOK
Robert F. Heizer and M.A. Whipple. Editors
A collection of writings. Second revised edition.
Illus. University of California Press, 1971. $38.00;
paper, $15.95.

CALIFORNIA NATIVE AMERICAN TRIBES
Mary Null Boule
A series of 26 individual books on each tribe of
California. Pre-European tribal life of each tribe.
Grades 3-5. Illus. Merryant Publishers.

**CALIFORNIA SPECIAL INDIAN CENSUS
1910**
Larry S. Watson, indexed & edited by
268 pp. paper. Histree, 1993. $24.95.

CALIFORNIA'S GABRIELINO INDIANS
Bernice Johnston
Illus. 198 pp. Southwest Museum, 1962. $12.50.

**CALIFORNIA JOE: NOTED
SCOUT & INDIAN FIGHTER**
Joe E. Milner & Earle R. Forrest
Illus. 400 pp. University of Nebraska Press,
1987. $28.95; paper, $9.95.

CALIFORNIA NATIVE AMERICAN TRIBES
Mary N. Boule
Grades 1-8. Illus. Paper. Merryant Publishers,
1991. $68.95, boxed edition.

CALIFORNIA POWWOWs
Karen Doris Wright
Powwow dates and locations in the state of Cali-
fornia. Annual. 90 pp. California Powwow. $10.

**CALUMET & FLEUR-DE-LYS; ARCHAEOL-
OGY OF INDIAN & FRENCH CONTACT IN
THE MIDCONTINENT**
John Walthal & Thomas Emerson, Editors
Illus. 320 pp. Smithsonian Institution Press,
1992. $45.

**CAMERON CREEK VILLAGE, A SITE IN
THE MIMBRES AREA IN GRANT COUNTY,
NEW** MEXICO (Santa Fe, NM)
Wesley Bradfield
Reprint of 1929 edition. Illus. 244 pp. Kraus, $30.

**CAMP BEALE'S SPRINGS
AND THE HUALAPAI INDIANS**
Dennis G. Casebier
Illus. 240 pp. Tales Mojave Rd., 1980. $18.50.

**CAMP, CLAN & KIN AMONG THE COW
CREEK SEMINOLES OF FLORIDA**
Alexander Spoehr
Reprint of 1941-47 eds. Illus. Paper. Kraus, $20.

**CAMPAIGNING WITH CUSTER AND THE NINE-
TEENTH KANSAS VOLUNTEER CAVALRY ON
THE WASHITA CAMPAIGN, 1868-69**
David L. Spotts
Illus. 215 pp. University of Nebraska Press,
1988. $19.95; paper, $6.95.

**CAMPAIGNING WITH KING: CHARLES KING,
CHRONICLER OF THE OLD ARMY**
Don Russell; Paul Hedrin, Editor
Illus. 215 pp. U. of Nebraska Press, 1991. $25.

BEN NIGHTHORSE CAMPBELL
Herman J. Viola
Biography of the Native American, U.S. Congress-
man from Colorado. Illus. Random House, $23.

CAN THE RED MAN HELP THE WHITE MAN?
Sylvester M. Morey, Editor
130 pp. Illus. Paper. Myrin Institute, 1970. $3.50.

***CANADA: THE LANDS,
PEOPLE, & CULTURES SERIES**
Bobbie Kalman, Editor
4 vols. Canada: The Land; Canada: The People;
Canada: The Culture; and Canada Celebrates
Multiculturalism. Grades 3-9. Ilus. 32 pp. each.
Crabtree, 1993. $15.95; paper, $7.95 each.

**CANADA'S FIRST NATIONS: A HISTORY OF
FOUNDING PEOPLES FROM EARLIEST TIMES**
O.P. Dickason
University of Oklahoma Press.

**CANADA'S INDIANS:
CONTEMPORARY CONFLICTS**
J. Frideres
Paper. Prentice-Hall, 1974. $12.95.

THE CANADIAN DAKOTA
Wilson D. Wallis
Reprint of 1947 edition. AMS Press, $32.50.

A CANADIAN INDIAN BIBLIOGRAPHY
Tom Abler, et al Editors
Reprint of 1974 ed. Paper. Books on Demand,
$16.

**CANADIAN INDIAN POLICY:
A CRITICAL BIBLIOGRAPHY**
Robert J. Surtees
Illus. 120 pp. Paper. Indiana U. Press, 1982. $4.95.

CANADIAN NATIVE LAW CASES
Brian Slattery and Linda Charlton
Three volumes. Volume 1, 1763-1869, 478 pp,
1980, $50; Volume 2, 1870-1890, 634 pp.,
1981, $65; Volume 3, 1891-1910, 663 pp.,
1985, $65. Native Law Centre Publications.

CANADIAN PREHISTORY SERIES
Each book includes time charts, graphs, maps,
photos and drawings which picture the life of native peoples of Canada before the arrival of
Jacques Cartier. The titles are: Canadian Arctic
Prehistory, by Robert McGhee, the prehistoric
ancestors of the Inuit. 136 pp., $8.50; The Dig, by
George MacDonald and Richard Inglis, the story
of the Coast Tsimshian people. 102 pp., $7.50;
Maritime Provinces Prehistory, by James A. Tuck,
the story of the Micmacs nd Malecites. 112 pp.,
$12.95; Newfoundland and Labrador Prehistory,
by James A. Tuck. 135 pp. $5.50; Six Chapters of
Canada's Prehistory, by J.V. Wright. 118 pp. $5.50;
Quebec Prehistory, by J.V. Wright. 128 pp. $5.50;
Ontario Prehistory, by J.V. Wright. 132 pp. Paper.
$5.50. Paper. National Museums of Canada.

THE CANADIAN SIOUX
James H. Howard
210 pp. U. of Nebraska Press, 1984. $18.95.

**A CANNNONEER IN NAVAJO COUNTRY:
JOURNAL OF PRIVATE JOSIAH M. RICE,
1851**
Richard H. Dillon, Editor
Illus. Old West, 1970. $17.50.

CANOEING WITH THE CREE
Eric Sevareid
Reprint of 1935 edition. Illus. 206 pp. Paper.
Minnesota Historical Society, $6.95.

**CANTE OHITIKA WIN (BRAVE-HEARTED
WOMEN): IMAGES OF LAKOTA WOMEN
FROM THE PINE RIDGE RESERVATION,
SOUTH DAKOTA**
Caroline Reyer
With the writings of Beatrice Medicine and Debra
Lynn White Plume; photos by Thomas Gleason
and Tom Casey. Illus. 90 pp. University of South
Dakota Press, $19.95; paper, $13.95.

**CANYON DE CHELLY:
ITS PEOPLE & ROCK ART**
Campbell Grant
290 pp. Paper. University of Arizona Press,
1978. $16.95.

**CANYON DE CHELLY: THE
STORY BEHIND THE SCENERY**
Charles Supplee, et al
Photos. Maps. 48 pp. Paper. KC Pubns., $6.95.

CAPTAIN JACK, MODOC RENEGADE
Doris P. Payne
Illus. Paper. Binford & Mort, 1979. $9.95.

THE CAPTIVE
Mary Rowlandson
The true story of the captivity of Mrs. Mary
Rowlandson. Reprint of 1682 edition. Revised.
Illus. 96 pp. Paper. American Eagle Publications,
$4.95.

CAPTIVITY OF MARY SCWANDT
Mary Schwandt
Paper. Ye Galleon Press, $3.50.

**CAPTIVITY OF THE OATMAN GIRLS:
AMONG THE APACHES & MOJAVE INDIANS**
Royal B. Stratton
Reprint of 1857 edition. Illus. 300 pp. Paper.
University of Nebraska Press, $7.95.

**CAPTIVITY TALES:
AN ORGINIAL ANTHOLOGY**
Reprint of 1974 ed. Illus. Ayer Co. Pubs., $20.

**CAPTURED BY THE INDIANS:
15 FIRSTHAND ACCOUNTS, 1750-1870**
Frederick Drimmer, Editor
180 pp. Paper. Hothem House & Dover, 1985.
$7.95.

THE CARIBOU ESKIMOS
Kaj Birket-Smith
Reprint of 1929 edition. AMS, $137.50.

**CARLOS CASTANEDA, ACADEMIC OPPOR-
TUNISM, & THE PSYCHEDELIC SIXTIES**
Jay Courtney Fikes
Illustrates the chronic ignorance about Native
American religions. 275 pp. Madison Books, 1992.
$24.95; paper, $14.95.

STOKES CARSON: TWENTIETH-CENTURY TRADING ON THE NAVAJO RESERVATION
Willow Roberts
246 pp. University of New Mexico Press, 1987. $24.95; paper, $13.95.

CARTIER'S HOCHELAGA & THE DAWSON SITE
James Pendergast & Bruce Trigger
Illus. 470 pp. University of Toronto Press, 1972. $34.95.

CARVED HISTORY: A GUIDE TO THE TOTEM POLES OF SITKA NATIONAL HISTORICAL PARK
Alaska Natural History Association.

CASE & AGREEMENT IN INUIT
Reineke Bok-Bennema
308 pp. Mouton de Gruyter, 1991. $75.

THE CASE OF THE SENECA INDIANS IN THE STATE OF NEW YORK
Reprint of 1980 Edition. 366 pp. E.M. Coleman. $32.50.

A CASE STUDY OF A NORTHERN CALIFORNIA INDIAN TRIBE: CULTURAL CHANGE TO 1860
Robert M. Peterson
R & E Research Associates, 1977. $11.95.

CASPER COLLINS: THE LIFE & EXPLOITS OF AN INDIAN FIGHTER OF THE SIXTIES
Agnes Spring
Reprint of 1927 edition. AMS Press, 16.

CATAWBA NATION
Charles Hudson, Jr.
152 pp. Paper. University of Georgia Press, 1970. $8.50.

CATAWBA TEXTS
Frank G. Speck
Reprint of 1934 edition. AMS Press, $18.

*THE CATAWBAS
James H. Merrell
Grades 7-12. Illus. 112 pp. Chelsea House, 1989. $17.95.

CATCH THE WHISPER OF THE WIND
Cheewa James
Compilation of 70 quotations from U.S. and Canadian tribes, with an accompanying cassette of songs in original tribal languages. Illus. Revised edition. 128 pp. Cassette and book. BookWorld, 1994. $21.95; book only, $11.95.

CATHECHISM & GUIDE: NAVAHO-ENGLISH
Berard Haile
Reprint of 1937 edition. Paper. St. Michaels Historical Museum, $3.

CATHLAMET ON THE COLUMBIA
Thomas N. Strong
New edition. Illus. 178 pp. Binford & Mort, 1981. $12.95.

THE CATHOLIC INDIAN MISSIONS IN MAINE (1611-1820)
Sr. Mary Leger
Reprint of 1929 edition. AMS Press, $26.

GEORGE CATLIN
Joseph R. Millichap
Illus. Paper. Boise State University, 1977. $2.95.

THE GEORGE CATLIN BOOK OF AMERICAN INDIANS
Hassrick
Reproductions of Catlin's famous paintings. 48 color & 121 bxw illustrations. 203 pp. Hothem House, 1988. $24.95.

CATLIN'S NORTH AMERICAN INDIAN PORTFOLIO
George Catlin
Reprint. Illus. Abbeville Press, 1989. $1,250.

CATLIN'S NORTH AMERICAN INDIAN PORTFOLIO: A REPRODUCTION
George Catlin
Reprint of 1845 edition. Ohio U. Press, $250.

CAUSES OF THE MARYLAND REVOLUTION OF 1689
F.E. Sparks
Reprint of 1896 edition. Johnson Reprint, $12.

CAUTANTOWWIT'S HOUSE: AN INDIAN BURIAL GROUND ON THE ISLAND OF CONANICUT IN NARRAGANSETT BAY
William Simmons
Reprint of 1970 edition. Illus. 198 pp. Paper. Books on Demand, $49.50.

CAVALIER IN BUCKSKIN: GEORGE ARMSTRONG CUSTER & THE WESTERN MILITARY FRONTIER
Robert M. Utley
Illus. 250 pp. Paper. University of Oklahoma Press, 1991. $10.95.

*THE CAYUGA
Grades K-4. Illus. 48 pp. Childrens Press, $11.45.

THE CAYUSE INDIANS: IMPERIAL TRIBESMEN OF THE OLD OREGON
Robert Ruby & John Brown
Illus. 350 pp. Paper. Pacific Northwest National Parks, 1989. $11.95.

*CEDAR PLANK MASK
Nan McNutt
Grades 3-6. Illus. 35 pp. Paper. N. McNutt Associates, $9.95.

CELEBRATE NATVE AMERICA! AN AZTEC BOOK OF DAYS
Richard Balthazar
Explains the complex Aztec count of days. Illus. 80 pp. Paper. Five Flower Press, $18.95.

A CELEBRATION OF BEING
Susanne Page
Illus. 175 pp. Paper. Northland Press, $24.95.

CENSUS ROLL OF THE OLD SETTLER PARTY CREEKS 1857
Larry S. Watson, indexed by
83 pp. Paper. Histree, 1981. $12.50.

CENTENNIAL CAMPAIGN: THE SIOUX WAR OF 1876
John S. Gray
Illus. 408 pp. Paper. U. of Oklahoma Press, $14.95.

THE CENTRAL ESKIMO
Franz Boas
A record of Eskimo life in the 1880s. Reprint of 1884 edition. Illus. 280 pp. Paper. University of Nebraska Press, $9.95.

A CENTURY OF DISHONOR: A SKETCH OF THE U.S. GOVERNMENT'S DEALING WITH SOME OF THE INDIAN TRIBES
Helen Jackson
Reprint of 1888 edition. 515 pp. Scholarly Press, $75.

CERAMIC DECORATION SEQUENCE AT AN OLD INDIAN VILLAGE SITE NEAR SICILY ISLAND, LOUISIANA
James A. Ford
Reprint of 1935 edition. Kraus, $16.

CEREMONIAL PATTERNS IN THE GREATER SOUTHWEST: BOUND WITH FACTIONALISM IN ISLETA PUEBLO
Ruth Underhill & David French
Reprint of 1948 edition. AMS, $20.

CEREMONIAL SONGS OF THE CREEK & YUCHI INDIANS
Frank G. Speck
Reprint of 1911 edition. AMS Press, $20.

CEREMONIES OF THE PAWNEE
James R. Murie; Douglas R. Parks, Editor
Reprint of 1981 edition. Illus. 500 pp. Paper. University of Nebraska Press, $19.95.

CEREMONY
Leslie Marmon Silko
A novel which captures the search for the identity of the American Indian. 262 pp. Paper. Penguin USA, $8.

*CEREMONY IN THE CIRCLE OF LIFE
White Deer Autumn (Gabriel Horn)
A tale of how Little Turtle is visited by the Star Spirit and taught the mysteries of life through love & understanding pf Mopther Earth & her four seasons. Grades 1-5. Illus. 32 pp. Levite of Apache, $14.95. Paper. Beyond Words Publishing, $6.95.

CEV'ARMIUT QANEMCIIT QULIRAIT-LLU: ESKIMO NARRATIVES & TALES FROM CHEVAK, ALASKA
Anthony C. Woodbury, Editor
5 Chevak Yup'ik elders tell of traditional life, shamans, and history of the people of Chevak. Illus. 88 pp. Paper. University of Alaska Press, 1989. $9.

CHACO & HOHOKAM: PREHISTORIC REGIONAL SYSTEMS IN THE AMERICAN SOUTHWEST
Patricia Crown & W. James Judge
Illus. 380 pp. School of American Research, 1991. $35; paper, $15.95.

THE CHACOAN PREHISTORY OF THE SAN JUAN BASIN
R. Gwinn Vivian
525 pp. Academic Press, 1990. $85.

CHAINBREAKER: THE REVOLUTIONARY WAR MEMOIRS OF GOVERNOR BLACK-SNAKE
Chainbreaker; Benjamin Williams & Thomas Abler, Editors
Illus. Maps. 310 pp. University of Nebraska Press, 1989. $35.

CHALLENGE: THE SOUTH DAKOTA STORY
Robert Karolevitz
Illus. 325 pp. Brevet Press, $19.95; paper, $12.95.

**CHAMPIONS OF THE CHEROKEES:
EVAN & JOHN B. JONES**
William G. McLoughlin
492 pp. Princeton University Press, 1989. $35.

**CHANGING CONFIGURATIONS IN THE
SOCIAL ORGANIZATION OF A BLACKFOOT
TRIBE DURING THE RESERVE PERIOD**
E.S. Goldfrank; L.M. Hanks and J. Richardson
Bound with Observations on Northern Blackfoot
Kinship. Illus. 81 pp. University of Washington
Press, 1945. $15.

CHANGING CULTURE OF AN INDIAN TRIBE
Margaret Mead
Reprint of 1932 edition. AMS Press, $32.50.

**CHANGING MILITARY PATTERNS OF THE
GREAT PLAINS INDIANS**
Frank R. Secoy
Historical study of tribal change, conflicts and
movements. Maps. 120 pp. Paper. University
of Nebraska Press, $7.95.

**CHANGING PHYSICAL ENVIRONMENT
OF THE HOPI INDIANS OF ARIZONA**
John Hack
Reprint of 1942 edition. Paper. Kraus, $26.

*****CHANT OF THE RED MAN**
Hap Gilliland
A fable for Americans. Grades 7-adult. Illus. 84
pp. Paper. Council for Indian Education, 1976.
$10.95; paper, $4.95.

**CHAPTERS ON THE ETHNOLOGY OF
THE POWHATAN TRIBES OF VIRGINIA**
Frank G. Speck
Reprint of 1928 edition. AMS Press, $27.50.

**CHARACTER & INFLUENCE OF INDIAN
TRADE IN WISCONSIN: A STUDY OF THE
TRADING POST AS AN INSTITUTION**
F.J. Turner; David and Harry Miller, Editors
Reprint of 1891 edition. Johnson Reprint, $10.
University of Oklahoma Press, $11.95.

*****CHARLES EASTMAN: PHYSICIAN,
REFORMER, & NATIVE AMERICAN LEADER**
Grades 4 and up. Illus. 128 pp. Childrens Press,
$13.95.

*****CHARLIE YOUNG BEAR**
Katherine Van Ahnen &
Joan Azure Young Bear
Grades K-3. 48 pp. Paper. Roberts Rinehart,
1994. $4.95.

*****THE CHARM OF THE
BEAR CLAW NECKLACE**
Margaret Zehmer Searcy
2 Stone Age Indian siblings living in what is now
the Southeastern U.S. Grades 3-8. Illus. 80 pp.
Pelican Publishing, $13.95; paper, $6.95.

**CHEHALIS RIVER TREATY COUNCIL
& THE TREATY OF OLYMPIA**
Robert & Barbara Lane
75 pp. Institute for the Development of Indian
Law, $15.

**CHEMEHUEVI INDIANS
OF SOUTHERN CALIFORNIA**
Ronald Miller & Peggy Miller
Paper. Malki Museum Press, 1070. $2.

CHEM'IVULLU: LET'S SPEAK CAHUILLA
316 pp. Paper. American Indian Studies Center,
1982. $17.50.

*****THE CHEROKEE**
Emilie U. Lepthien
Grades K-4. Illus. 48 pp. Childrens Press, $11.45.

*****THE CHEROKEE**
Barbara McCall
Grades 5-8. Illus. 35 pp. Rourke., 1989. $9.95.

*****THE CHEROKEE**
Theda Perdue
Grades 7-12. Illus. 112 pp. Chelsea House,
1989. $17.95; paper, $9.95.

*****CHEROKEE ABC COLORING BOOK**
Daniel Pennington
Words in English & Cherokee characters with
phoentic pronunciations. Grades K-3. Paper.
Cherokee Publications, $3.50.

**CHEROKEE AMERICANS, EASTERN BAND
OF CHEROKEES IN THE 20TH CENTURY**
John R. Finger
Illus. Maps. 250 pp. Paper. University of
Nebraska Press, 1991. $9.95

**CHEROKEE ARCHAEOLOGY: A STUDY
OF THE APPALACHIAN SUMMIT**
Bennie C. Keel
Illus. 290 pp. Paper. Cherokee Publications &
University of Tennessee Press, 1975. $14.95.

**CHEROKEE BY BLOOD: RECORDS OF
EASTERN CHEROKEE ANCESTRY IN THE
CHEROKEE CROWN OF TANNASSY**
William O. Steel
Sir Alexander Cuming's effort to charm the Chero-
kees into loyalty to England before the Revolu-
tionary War. 162 pp. Cherokee Publications, $7.95.

**CHEROKEE BY BLOOD: RECORDS OF
EASTERN CHEROKEE ANCESTRY IN THE
U.S. COURT OF CLAIMS, 1906-1910**
Jerry Wright Jordan
Series presents detailed abstracts of those appli-
cations including numerous verbatim transcriptions
of affidavits by the applicants. 8 vols. Heritage
Books, 1988-1992. $25 each.

CHEROKEE COOKLORE
Contains many Cherokee recipes; chart of herbs;
Cherokee food preparation and a menu from a
Cherokee Indian Feast. Reprint of 1949 edition.
Illus. 72 pp. Paper. Cherokee Publications, $3.50.

CHEROKEE DANCE & DRAMA
Frank G. Speck & Leonard Broom
Reprint of 1951 edition. Illus. 160 pp. Paper.
University of Oklahoma Press, $9.95.

CHEROKEE DICTIONARY
Durbin Feeling
Paper. VIP Publishing, $18.95.

**CHEROKEE & EARLIER REMIANS
ON UPPER TENNESSEE RIVER**
Mark Harrington
Reprint of 1922 edition. AMS.

**CHEROKEE-ENGLISH INTERLINER, FIRST
EPISTLE OF JOHN OF THE NEW TESTAMENT**
Ralph E. Dawson, III and Shirley Dawson
25 pp. Indian University Press of Oklhoma,
1982. Spiral binding, $5.

**THE CHEROKEE EXCAVATIONS: HOLOCENE
ECOLOGY AND HUMAN ADAPTATIONS IN
NORTHEASTERN IOWA**
Duane C. Anderson and Holmes Semken, Eds
Academic Press, 1980. $54.50.

**THE CHEROKEE FREEDMEN: FROM
EMANCIPATION TO AMERICAN CITIZENSHIP**
Daniel F. Littlefield, Jr.
Greenwood Press, 1978. $35.

*****CHEROKEE FUN & LEARN BOOK**
J. Ed Sharpe
Grades 4-6. 20 pp. Cherokee Publications,
1970. $3.

THE CHEROKEE GHOST DANCE
William G. McLoughlin
525 pp. Mercer University Press, 1984. $34.95.

CHEROKEE HERITAGE
Duane King, Editor
The official guidebook to the Museum of the Chero-
kee Indian. Photos. 130 pp. Paper. Cherokee
Publications, $4.

**THE CHEROKEE INDIAN NATION:
A TROUBLED HISTORY**
Duane H. King
Illus. 276 pp. University of Tennessee Press
& Cherokee Publications, 1979. $16.95.

**CHEROKEE LANGUAGE WORKBOOK
& INSTRUCTIONAL CASSETTE TAPE**
Prentice Robinson
30 pp. & cassette. Cherokee Publications, $25.

*****CHEROKEE LEGENDS
\& THE TRAIL OF TEARS**
Tom Underwood
Grades 4-12. Illus. 32 pp. Cherokee Publications,
1956. $3.

CHEROKEE NATION CODE ANNOTATED
Reviewed by Joan S. Howland
New edition. Recodification of the Cherokee Nation statutes. Contains tribal legislation passed
through 1992. 2 vols. West Publishing, 1993. $55.

CHEROKEE NEW TESTAMENT
American Bible Society
In the Cherokee language. 408 pp. Paper.
Cherokee Publications, $3.95.

**THE CHEROKEE PEOPLE: THE STORY
OF THE CHEROKEES FROM EARLIEST
ORIGINS TO CONTEMPORARY TIMES**
Thomas E. Mails
Illus. 368 pp. Cherokee Publications, 1992. $50.

THE CHEROKEE PERSPECTIVE
L. French & J. Hornbuckle, Editors
The Cherokee today. Photos. 244 pp. Paper.
Cherokee Publications, $7.95.

CHEROKEE PLANTS
Hamel & Chiltoskey
Resource dictionary for plants and their uses by
the Cherokee in food, medicine & religion. Illus.
72 pp. Paper. Cherokee Publications, $3.50.

**CHEROKEE PREHISTORY: THE PASGAH
PHASE IN THE APPALACHIAN SUMMIT
REGION**
Roy S. Dickens, Jr.
Illus. 260 pp. U. of Tennessee Press, 1976.
$26.95.

THE CHEROKEE PERSPECTIVE
Laurence French & Jim Hornbuckle, Editors
Illus. 245 pp. Appalachian Consortium &
Cherokee Publications, 1981. $7.95.

A CHEROKEE PRAYERBOOK
Howard Meredith and Adeline Smith
44 pp. Paper. Indian University Press, 1981. $2.

**CHEROKEE PSALMS,
A COLLECTION OF HYMNS**
J. Ed Sharpe; Daniel Scott, translated by
Illus. 33 pp. Cherokee Publications, 1991. $3.

**CHEROKEE REMOVAL:
BEFORE AND AFTER**
William L. Anderson, Editor
Maps. 176 pp. Paper. University of Georgia
Press, 1991. $12.95.

CHEROKEE REMOVAL
Larry S. Watson, indexed & edited
Reprint of Senate Document 120 & 121.
400 pp. Paper. Histree, 1994. $49.95.

**CHEROKEE REMOVAL: THE WILLIAM
PENN ESSAYS AND OTHER WRITINGS
BY JEREMIAH EVARTS**
Francis P. Prucha, Editor
320 pp. U. of Tennessee Press, 1981. $28.95.

CHEROKEE RENASCENCE, 1794-1833
William G. McLaughlin
472 pp. Princeton U. Press, 1987. $29.50.

CHEROKEE ROOTS
Bob Blankenship
Trace your Cherokee ancestry. Includes over
15,000 name entries from 1835 to 1924. Two vols.
Vol. 1, Eastern Cherokee Rolls (164 pp), $10; and
Vol. 2, Western Cherokee Rolls (306 pp.), $18.
Paper. 1992. Both vols. $25. Also the 1898 Dawes
Roll "Plus", 275 pp. 1994. Paper, $25; and 1909
Gujon Miller Roll "Plus", 62,769 names and re-
lated informtion. 225 pp. 1994. Paper, $30. Heri-
tage Books.

CHEROKEE SONG BOOK
Agnes Cowen
A collection of favorite songs and hymns written
in the Cherokee language. 112 pp. Paper. Cherokee Publications, $5.95.

**THE CHEROKEE STRIP LIVE STOCK
ASSOCIATION: FEDERAL REGULATION
& THE CATTLEMAN'S LAST FRONTIER**
William W. Savage, Jr.
Documents the role of federal governmental agen-
cies in dealing with both white ranhcers & Indian
entrepreneurs. Illus. Map. 160 pp. Paper. Univer-
sity of Oklahoma Press, $12.95.

*CHEROKEE SUMMER
Diane Hoyt-Goldsmith
A proud Cherokee girl lives in two worlds.
Grades 4-6. Illus. 32 pp. Holiday House, 1993.
$15.95.

THE CHEROKEE TRAIL
O.K. Armstrong
260 pp. Paper. Indian University Press, 1994.
$18.50, postpaid.

**CHEROKEE TRAGEDY: THE RIDGE FAMILY
& THE DECIMATION OF A PEOPLE**
Thurman Wilkins
Reprint of 1970 revised second edition. Illus.

432 pp. University of Oklahoma Press, $24.95.
Paper. Cherokee Publicatios, $12.95.

CHEROKEE VISION OF ELOH'
Howard Meredith & Virginia E. Milan;
Wesley Proctor, Translator
A legendary histor of the Cherokee people.
Bilingual in Cherokee and English. 49 pp. Paper.
Indian University Press, 1981. $10.50, postpaid.

CHEROKEE WORDS
Mary Ulmer Chitoskey
A simplified, illustrated Cherokee/English dictio-
nary. 72 pp. Paper. Cherokee Pubns, $3.50.

THE CHEROKEES
Grace Steele Woodward
Reprint of 1963 edition. Illus. 376 pp. Paper.
University of Oklahoma Press, $17.95.

**THE CHEROKEES & CHRISTIANITY, 1794-
1870: ESSAYS ON ACCULTURATION &
CULTURAL PERSISTENCE**
William G. McLoughlin; Walter Comser, Jr., Ed.
Examines how the process of religious accultura-
tion worked wityhin the Cherokee Nation during
the 19th century. 368 pp. University of Georgia
Press, 1994. $45.

CHEROKEES AT THE CROSSROADS
John Gulik
With a new chapter by Sharlotte N. Williams. The
cultural patterns of the Eastern Cherokees during
1956-1958. 222 pp. Institute for Research in Social Science, 1973. $7.

CHEROKEES, AN ILLUSTRATED HISTORY
Billy M. Jones & Odie B. Faulk
Overview of the Cherokee people, 1735 to
1984. Illus. 166 pp. The Five Civilized Tribes
Museum, 1984. $25.

**THE CHEROKEES IN
PRE-COLUMBIAN TIMES**
Cyrus Thomas
Reprint of 1890 edition. AMS Press, $16.50.

**CHEROKEES IN TRANSITION: A STUDY OF
CHANGING CULTURE & ENVIRONMENT
PRIOR TO 1775**
Gary C. Goodwin
Illus. Paper. University of Chicago, Dept. of
Geography, 1977. $10.

CHEROKEES & MISSIONARIES, 1789-1839
William G. McLoughlin
375 pp. Yale University Press, 1984. $37.50.

THE CHEROKEES PAST & PRESENT
J. Edward Sharpe
Illus. 32 pp. Cherokee Pubns., 1970. $3.50.

**THE CHEROKEES OF
THE SMOKEY MOUNTAINS**
Horace Kephart
Photos. Map. 48 pp. Paper.
Cherokee Publications, $3.50.

**THE CHEROKEES:
A POPULATION HISTORY**
Russell Thornton
Illus. Maps. 250 pp. Paper. University of
Nebraska Press, 1990. $11.95.

*CHEYENNE
Sally Lodge
Grades 5-8. Illus. 35 pp. Rourke Corp., $9.95.

CHEYENNE
George A. Dorsey
How the Cheyenne lived and worked before the
white man arrived. In two parts: The Ceremonial
Organization, and The Sun Dance. Reprint of 1905
edition. Illus. 72 pp. Kraus, $34.00. Paper. Ye
Galleon Press, $12.

*THE CHEYENNE
Dennis B. Fradin
Grades K-4. Illus. 48 pp. Childrens Press, 1988.
$11.45.

*THE CHEYENNE
Stanley Hoig
Grades 7-12. Illus. 112 pp. Chelsea House,
1989. $17.95; paper, $9.95.

CHEYENNE & ARAPAHO MUSIC
Frances Densmore
Reprint of 1936 edition. 111 pp. Southwest
Museum, $5.

**THE CHEYENNE & ARAPAHO ORDEAL:
RESERVATION & AGENCY LIFE IN THE
INDIAN TERRITORY, 1875-1907**
Donald J. Berthrong
Illus. Maps. Biblio. 418 pp. Paper. University
of Oklahoma Press, 1976. $15.95.

CHEYENNE AUTUMN
Mari Sandoz
The story of the Northern Cheyennes, who fled
the reservation in 1878 to return to their ancestral
hunting grounds. Illus. Photos. 275 pp. Paper.
AISES, $9.95.

***CHEYENNE FIRE FIGHTERS: MODERN
INDIANS FIGHTING FOREST FIRES**
Henry Tall Bull and Tom Weist
Grades 4-12. Paper. Council for Indian
Education, 1973. $1.95.

**THE CHEYENNE IN PLAINS INDIAN
TRADE RELATIONS, 1795-1840**
Joseph Jablow
A study of the effects of the fur trade and
diffusion of the horse upon the Cheyenne.
Reprint of 1951 edition. Illus. Maps. Biblio.
110 pp. AMS, $20.

**THE CHEYENNE INDIANS: SKETCH
OF THE CHEYENNE GRAMMAR**
J. Mooney and R.C. Petter
Reprint of 1907 edition. Paper. Kraus, $15.

**CHEYENNE INDIANS, THEIR
HISTORY & WAYS OF LIFE**
George B. Grinell
Reprint of 1923 edition. Two vols: Vol. 1, 358
pp.; Vol. 2, 478 pp. Illus. MAP. Paper. University
of Nebraska Press, $12.95 each.

*CHEYENNE LEGENDS OF CREATION
Henry Tall Bull and Tom Weist
Grades 4-9. Paper. Council for Indian Education,
1972. $1.95.

CHEYENNE MEMORIES
John & MargotLiberty Stands in Timber
Illus. 350 pp. Paper. University of Nebraska
Press,1972. $10.95.

**THE CHEYENNE NATION: A SOCIAL
& DEMOGRAPHIC HISTORY**
John H. Moore
Illus. 390 pp. U. of Nebraska Press, 1987. $32.50.

*CHEYENNE SHORT STORIES
Grades 3-8. 32 pp. Council for Indian Education,
1977. $8.95; apper, $2.95.

*CHEYENNE WARRIORS
Henry Tall Bull and Tom Weist
Grades 2-12. 32 pp. Paper. Council for Indian
Education, 1976. $8.95; paper, $2.95..

**THE CHEYENNE WAY: CONFLICT AND
CASE LAW IN PRIMITIVE JURISPRUDENCE**
Karl Llewellen and E. Adamson Hoebel
Reprint of 1941 edition. Illus. 375 pp. University
of Oklahoma Press, $27.95; paper, $14.95.

**CHEYENNES & HORSE SOLDIERS: THE
1857 EXPEDITION & THE BATTLE OF
SOLOMON'S FORK**
William Chalfant
Illus. 430 pp. University of Oklahoma Press,
1989. $27.95.

**THE CHEYENNES: INDIANS
OF THE GREAT PLAINS**
E. Adamson Hoebel
A portrait of the Cheyenne Indians. Second edi-
tion. 125 pp. Paper. Holt, Rinehart, 1978. $9.95.

**THE CHEYENNES, MA HEO O'S PEOPLE:
A CRITICAL BIOGRAPHY**
Peter J. Powell
Illus. 160 pp. Paper. Indiana University Press,
1980. $4.95.

THE CHEYENNES OF MONTANA
Thomas Marquis; Tom Weist, Editor
Reference Publications, 1978. $19.95.

**THE CHICAGO AMERICAN INDIAN COMMU-
NITY, 1893-1988: AN ANNOTATED BIBLIOG-
RAPHY & GUIDE TO SOURCES IN CHICAGO**
David Beck
Illus. 296 pp. Paper. Academy Chicago
Publishers, 1989. $39.95.

*THE CHICHI HOOHOO BOGEYMAN
Virginia Driving Hawk Sneve
Three Indian girls encounter a weird creature while
secretly exploring an old fort on the South Dakota
priaire. Grades 3-5. Illus. Paper. University of Nebraska Press & AISES, 1993. $6.95.

*THE CHICKASAW
Duane Hale
Grades 5 and up. Illus. Chelsea House, 1989.
$17.95.

CHICAKSAW: AN ANALYTICAL DICTIONARY
Pamela Munro & Catherine Willmond
The first scholarly dictionary of the Chickasaw
language. Biblio. 608 pp. University of Oklahoma Press, 1994. $39.95.

CHICKASAW GLOSSARY
Albert S. Gatchet
Reprint of 1889 edition. VIP Publishing, $15.95.

THE CHICKASAWS
Arrell M. Gibson
Illus. 352 pp. Paper. University of Oklahoma
Press, 1971. $17.95.

CHIEF JOSEPH
Matthew Grant & Dan Zadra
Creative Education, 1987. $16.45

**CHIEF JOSEPH COUNTRY:
LAND OF THE NEZ PERCE**
Bill Gulick
Reprint of 1981 edition. Illus. 27 maps. Biblio.
316 pp. The Caxton Printers, $39.95.

**CHIEF JOSEPH: GUARDIAN
OF THE NEZ PERCE**
Jason Hook
Illus. 52 pp. Sterling, 1989. $12.95.

***CHIEF JOSEPH OF THE NEZ PERCE
INDIANS: CHAMPION OF LIBERTY**
Grades 4 and up. Illus. 130 pp. Childrens Press,
$13.95.

**CHIEF JOSEPH'S ALLIES: THE PALOUSE
INDIANS & THE NEZ PERCE WAR OF 1877**
Richard D. Scheuerman
Illus. Paper. Sierra Oaks, 1987. $10.95.

CHIEF JOSEPH'S OWN STORY
Joseph Young
Autobiography. 38 pp. Paper. Ye Galleon, $4.95.

***CHIEF JOSEPH'S OWN STORY
AS TOLD BY CHIEF JOSEPH IN 1879**
Autobiography. Grades 4 and up. 32 pp. Council
for Indian Education, 1972. $8.95; paper, $2.95.

**CHIEF JUNALUSKA OF THE
CHEROKEE INDIAN NATION**
John F. Phillips
Biography. Illus. 90 pp. American Indian Books,
1988. $9.00; paper, $6.

CHIEF LEFT HAND: SOUTHERN ARAPAHO
Margaret Coel
Biography. Illus. Maps. 352 pp. University of
Oklahoma Press, 1981. $19.95.

***CHIEF PLENTY COUPS: LIFE OF THE
CROW INDIAN CHIEF**
Flora Hatheway
Grades 4-12. 36 pp. Council for Indian Eduction,
1971. $8.95; paper, $2.95.

CHIEF POCATELLO, THE "WHITE PLUME"
Brugham D. Madsen
Illus. 142 pp. Paper. University of Utah Press,
1986. $6.95.

*CHIEF RED HORSE TELLS ABOUT CUSTER
Jessie B. McGaw
Grades 4-12. Illus. 40 pp. Lodestar Books,
1981. $9.95.

***CHIEF SARAH: SARAH WINNEMUCCA'S
FIGHT FOR INDIAN RIGHTS**
Dorothy N. Morrison
Grades 4 and up. Illus. 195 pp. Paper. Oregon
Historical Society Press, 1990. $5.95.

**CHIEF SEATTLE'S
UNANSWERED CHALLENGE**
John M. Rich
Reprint of 1970 edition. 61 pp. Paper.
Ye Galleon Press, $4.95.

*CHIEF STEPHEN'S PARKY
Ann Chandonnet; Hap Gilliland, Editor
Historical fiction looks at 1898 Alaska and a year
in th life of Athapascan Chief Stephen's wife, Olga.
Grades 4-12. Illus. 72 pp. Paper. Roberts Rinehart,
1972. $7.95.

CHIEF WASHAKIE
Mae Urbanek
Illus. 150 pp. Urbanek, $5.

**CHIEFLY FEASTS: THE ENDURING
KWAKIUTL POTLATCH**
Aldona Jonaitis
Portait of Kwakiutl culture. Illus. 300 pp.
University of Washington Press, 1991. $60.

**CHIEFS & CHALLENGERS: INDIAN
RESISTANCE & COOPERATION IN
SOUTHERN CALIFORNIA**
George H. Phillips
An historical and ethnographic study of the Cali-
fornia Indians. University of California Press, 1975.
$27.50.

**THE CHIEFS HOLE-IN-THE-DAY
OF THE MISSISSIPPI CHIPPEWA**
Mark Diedrich
Legends recounting the lives of four generations
of Chippewa leaders. Illus. 58 pp. Paper. Coyote
Books (MN), $8.95.

*CHII-LA-PE & THE WHITE BUFFALO
John Nicholson
Adventures of a young Crow Indian boy. Grades
2-10. 44 pp. Council for Indian Education. $9.95;
paper, $3.95.

A CHILD'S ALASKA
Claire Rudolf Murphy
Photos by Charles W. Mason. Children's photo-
essay. Grades K-4. Illus. Photos. 48 pp. Graphic
Arts Center, $14.95.

**CHILDHOOD & FOLKLORE: A PSYCHOANA-
LYTIC STUDY OF APACHE PERSONALITY**
L. Bryce Boyer
Psychohistory Press, 1979. $16.95; paper,
$8.95.

**CHILDHOOD & YOUTH IN JICARILLA
APACHE SOCIETY**
Morris E. Opler
Reprint of 1946 edition. Illus. 180 pp. AMS
Press, $21. Paper. Southwest Museum, $5.

**THE CHILDREN OF AATAENTSIC: A
HISTORY OF THE HURON PEOPLE TO 1660**
Bruce G. Trigger
An analysis of the internal dynamism of Huron
culture. Reprint of 1976 edition. Illus. University
of Toronto Press, $80; paper, $29.95.

**CHILDREN AT RISK: MAKING A DIFFER-
ENCE THROUGH THE COURT APPOINTED
SPECIAL ADVOCATE PROJECT**
Michael Blady
ILLUS. 318 pp. NCJW, 1982. Workbook, $7.50.

*CHILDREN INDIAN CAPTIVES
Roy D. Holt
Grades 4-7. Eakin Publications, 1980. $6.95.

CHILDREN OF THE CIRCLE
Adolf & Star Hungry Wolf
A photographic history of Native American children from 1870s to 1920s. Includes over 20 tribes
from American West. Illus. 160 pp. Paper. Center
for Western Studies & The Book Publishing Co.,
$9.95.

THE CHILDREN OF THE COLD
Frederick Schwatka
Reprint of 1899 edition. AMS, $14.50.

CHILDREN OF COTTONWOOD: PIETY & CER-EMONIALISM IN HOPI INDIAN PUPPETRY
Armin Geertz & Michael Lomatuway'ma
Illus. 412 pp. University of Nebraska Press, 1987. $24.95; paper, $14.95.

CHILDREN OF THE FIRST PEOPLE: A PHOTOGRAPHIC ESSAY
Dorothy Haegart
Illus. 127 pp. Paper. Left Bank, 1984. $18.95.

CHILDREN OF SACRED GROUND: AMERICA'S LAST INDIAN WAR
Catherine Feher-Elston
Illus. 256 pp. Northland, 1988. $19.95.

CHILDREN OF THE SALT RIVER
Mary R. Miller
Paper. Resource Center for Language Semiotic, 1977. $11.

CHILDREN OF THE SUN
William E. Curtis
Reprint of 1883 edition. AMS Press, $15.

CHILDREN OF THE TWILIGHT: FOLK TALES OF INDIAN TRIBES
Emma-Lindsay Squier
Gordon Press, 1977. $34.95.

CHILDREN'S ATLAS OF NATIVE AMERICANS
Provides an in-depth view of Native American cultures; origins, cliff dwellers and mound builders, and the great civilizations of Central & South America, e.g. Mayans, Aztecs, and Incas. Grades 3-7. Illus. Maps. 80 pp. Rand McNally, $14.95.

CHILIES TO CHOCOLATE: FOOD THE AMERICAS GAVE THE WORLD
Nelson Foster & Linda Cordell, Editors
The foods Native Americans enjoyed before the arrival of the Europeans. 191 pp. Paper. University of Arizona Press, 1992. $13.95.

CHILLS & FEVER: HEALTH & DISEASE IN THE EARLY HISTORY OF ALASKA
Robert Fortuine
Illus. 395 pp. University of Alaska Press, 1989. $29.95.

CHINIGCHINICH
Geronimo Boscana
Malki Museum Press, 1978. $27.50.

CHINIGCHINIX, AN INDIGENOUS CALIFORNIA INDIAN RELIGION
James R. Moriarty
Illus. Maps. 70 pp. Southwest Museum, 1969. $12.50.

CHINLE TO TAOS
R.C. Gorman
Exhibition catalog-retrospective of R.C. Gorman at the Millicent Rogers Museum in June 1988. Illus. 64 pp. Navajo Gallery, $20.

***CHINOOK**
Jessie Marsh
Grades K-6. 32 pp. Paper. Council for Indian Education, 1976. $8.95; paper, $2.95.

CHINOOK: A HISTORY & DICTIONARY
Edward Thomas
Second edition. 184 pp. Binford & Mort, $12.95.

THE CHINOOK INDIANS: TRADERS OF THE LOWER COLUMBIA RIVER
Robert H. Ruby & John A. Brown
Illus. 400 pp. Paper. University of Oklahoma Press, 1988. $13.95.

***THE CHINOOK - NORTHWEST**
Clifford L. Trafzer
Grades 7-12. Illus. 112 pp. Chelsea House, 1990. $17.95.

***THE CHIPPEWA**
Alice Osinski
Grades K-4. Illus. 48 pp. Childrens Press, 1987. $13.27; paper, $3.95.

CHIPPEWA & DAKOTA INDIANS
Subject catalog of books, pamphlets, periodical articles and manuscripts in the Minnesota Historical Society. 131 pp. Paper. Minnesota Historical Society, 1970. $7.50.

CHIPPEWA & THEIR NEIGHBORS: A STUDY IN ETHNOHISTORY
Harold Hickerson; G. and L. Spindler, Editors
Reprint of the 1970 edition. 151 pp. Paper. Waveland Press, $9.50.

CHIPPEWA CHILD LIFE & ITS CULTURAL BACKGROUND
M. Inez Hilger
Reprint of 1951 edition. Illus. Photos. Biblio. 204 pp. Paper. Minnesota Historical Society, $10.95.

***CHIPPEWA CUSTOMS**
Frances Densmore
Authoritative source for tribal history, customs, legends, traditions, art, music, economy & leisure activity of the Chippewa (Ojibway) Indians of the U.S. & Canada. Reprint of 1929 edition. Illus. Biblio. 204 pp. Paper. Minnesota Historical Society, $9.95.

CHIPPEWA INDIANS
David A. Horr, Editor
Seven volumes. Illus. Maps. Garland Publishing, $51 each. See publisher for titles and descriptions.

CHIPPEWA INDIANS AS RECORDED BY REV. FREDERICK BARAGA IN 1847
Rev. Frederick Baraga, Editor
82 pp. Studia Slovenica, 1976. $5.

CHIPPEWA MUSIC
Francis Densmore
Reprint of 1911 & 1913 editions. 2 vols in 1. 110 pp. Da Capo Press, $20.

CHIPPEWA TREATY RIGHTS: THE RESERVED RIGHTS OF WISCONSIN'S CHIPPEWA INDIANS IN HISTORICAL PERSPECTIVE
Ronald N. Satz
History of the Chippewa's treaty rights in Wisconsin. GLIFWC, 1991.

1826 CHIPPEWA TREATY WITH THE U.S. GOVERNMENT
Robert Keller
45 pp. Institute for the Development of Indian Law, $10.

THE CHIPPEWAS OF LAKE SUPERIOR
Edmund J. Danziger, Jr.
Illus. University of Oklahoma Press, 1979. $21.95.

***THE CHIPEWYAN**
James G. Smith
Grades 5 and up. Illus. Chelsea House, 1989. $17.95.

THE CHIRICAHUA APACHE, 1846-1876: FROM WAR TO RESERVATION
D.C. Cole
Illus. 225 pp. University of New Mexico Press, 1988. $32.50.

CHIRICAHUA & MESCALERO APACHE TEXTS
Harry Hoijer and Morris E. Opler
Reprint of 1838 edition. AMS Press, $36.50.

JESSE CHISHOLM: TEXAS TRAIL BLAZER & PEACEMAKER
Ralph B. Cushman
Illus. 288 pp. Eakin Press, 1992. $22.95.

***CHOCOLATE CHIPMUNKS & CANOES: AMERICAN INDIAN WORDS COLORING BOOK**
written & illus. by Juan Alvarez
Grades Preschool-3. Illus. 32 pp. Paper. Red Crane Books, 1991. $3.95.

***THE CHOCTAW**
E. Lepthien
Grades K-4. Illus. 48 pp. Childrens Press, 1987. $11.45.

***THE CHOCTAW**
Jesse O. McKee
Grades 5 and up. Illus. Chelsea House, 1989. $17.95.

***A CHOCTAW ANTHOLOGY, I & II**
Papers written by Choctaw high school and college prep students on Choctaw history, culture and current events. Grades 7-12. Choctaw Heritage Press, I--$2.75; II--$7.00. $8.50/set.

THE CHOCTAW BEFORE REMOVAL
Carolyn K. Reeves, Editor
University Press of Mississippi, 1985. $27.50.

CHOCTAW DICTIONARY
Cyrus Byington
VIP Publishing, $59; paper, $39.

CHOCTAW MUSIC
Frances Densmore
Reprint of 1943 edition. Illus. 110 pp. Da Capo Press, $22.50.

A CHOCTAW SOURCEBOOK
John H. Peterson, Editor
Reprint. 257 pp. Garland Publishing, $30.

CHOCTAW VERB AGREEMENT & UNIVERSAL GRAMMAR
William D. Davies
Kluwer Academic, 1986. $48.00; paper, $19.50.

CHOCTAWS & MISSIONARIES IN MISSISSIPPI, 1818-1918
Clara Sue Kidwell
University of Oklahoma Press, 1994.

CHOTEAU CREEK: A SIOUX REMINISCENCE
Joseph Iron Eye Dudley
Growing up on the Yankton Sioux Reservation in South Dakota. 1993 Christopher Award Winner. Illus. 180 pp. U. of Nebraska Press, 1992. $19.95.

CHRISTIAN HARVEST
Bill B. DeGeer
104 pp. Carlton Press, 1988. $8.95.

CHRISTIAN INDIANS & INDIAN NATIONALISM, 1855-1950: AN INTERPRETATION IN HISTORICAL & THEOLOGICAL PERSPECTIVES
George Thomas
271 pp. Peter Lang, 1979. $41.

CHRISTIANITY & NATIVE TRADITIONS: INDIGENIZATION & SYNCRETISM CHRONICLES OF AMERICAN INDIAN PROTEST
Antonio R. Gualtieri
The actual views of Arctic missionaries of various denominations. 200 pp. Cross Cultural Publications, $19.95.

CHRONICLES OF BORDER WARFARE: HISTORY OF THE SETTLEMENTS BY WHITES OF NORTHWESTERN VIRGINIA
Alexander S. Withers
Reprint of 1895 edition. Ayer Co., $36.

CHRONOLOGICAL LIST OF ENGAGEMENTS BETWEEN THE REGULAR ARMY OF THE U.S. & VARIOUS TRIBES OF HOSTILE INDIANS...1790-1898
George W. Webb
Reprint of 1939 edition. AMS, $16.50.

CHRONOLOGY OF THE AMERICAN INDIAN
Examination of Indian history. Revised edition. 300 pp. American Indian Publishers, 1984. $85.

TO THE CHUKCHI PENINSULA & TO THE TLINGIT INDIANS 1881/1882: JOURNALS & LETTERS BY AUREL & ARTHUR KRAUSE
translated by Margot Krause McCaffrey
The expedition that brought knowledge of southern Alaska and its people the Tlingit. Illus. Maps. 230 pp. Paper. University of Alaska Press, 1993. $17.50.

*THE CHUMASH
Robert O. Gibson
Grades 5 and up. Illus. 105 pp. Paper. Chelsea House, 1989. $9.95.

CHUMASH HEALING
Phillip L. Walker & Travis Hudson
Medical & healing practices of a California Indian tribe--the Chumash of the Santa Barbara area. Illus. 161 pp. Malki Museum Press, 1993. $16.95; paper, $12.95.

THE CHUMASH INDIANS OF SOUTHERN CALIFORNIA
Eugene Anderson
Paper. Malki Museum Press, 1973. $2.

CHUMASH: A PICTURE OF THEIR WORLD
Bruce W. Miller, III
Illus. 144 pp. Paper. Sand River Press, 1988. $8.95.

CHURCH PHILANTHROPY FOR NATIVE AMERICANS & OTHER MINORITIES
Phyllis A. Meiners, Editor
Profiles over 50 grant programs & more than 25 loan programs from church & religious institutions for Native American, Hispanic, and other minority groups. 11 denominations are included; each listing includes contact persons, special interests, sample grants, application deadlines & procedures, etc. CRC Publishing, 1994. $118.95.

CHURCHMEN & THE WESTERN INDIANS, 1820-1920
Clyde Milner, II, and Floyd O'Neil
Illus. 272 pp. University of Oklahoma Press, 1985. $19.95.

THE CIBECUE APACHE
Keith H. Basso
106 pp. Paper. Waveland Press, 1970. $8.50.

A CIRCLE OF NATIONS: VOICES & VISIONS OF AMERICA INDIANS
John Gattuso
Reflection of the lives of contemporary American Indians through the eyes of well known Indian writers & photographers including Paula Gunn Allen, Leslie Marmon Silko, Joy Harjo, Simon ortiz, White Deer of Autumn, David Neel, Monty Roessel & Ken Blackbird. Illus. 128 pp. Beyond Words Publishing, $39.95. Available in two-tape audiocassette, $15.95.

A CIRCLE OF POWER
William Higbie
Story of a Plains Indian boy seeking manhood. Illus. 90 pp. Eagle's View, 1991. $13.95; paper, $7.95.

*CIRCLE OF WONDER: A NATIVE AMERICAN CHRISTMAS STORY
N. Scott Momaday
Illus. 42 pp. Clear Light Publishers, 1993. $14.95.

THE CIRCLE WITHOUT END: A SOURCEBOOK OF AMERICAN INDIAN ETHICS
Gerald & Francis Lombardi
Illus. 212 pp. Naturegraph, 1980. $16.95; paper, $8.95.

CIRCLES, CONSCIOUSNESS & CULTURE
James A. Mischke
Native American religious activities. Paper. Navajo Community College Press, 1984. $2.50.

CIRCLES OF POWER
Ronald McCoy
Devoted to shields. Illus. 32 pp. Paper. Four Winds Trading Co., $6.

CIRCLES OF THE WORLD: TRADITIONAL ART OF THE PLAINS INDIANS
Richard Conn
Illus. 152 pp. Paper. Denver Art Museum, 1982. $14.95.

CIVILIZATIONS OF ANCIENT AMERICA
Sol Tax, Editor
29th Congress of Americanists. Reprint of 1952 ed. Illus. 328 pp. Cooper Square Pubs., $35.

CLAIMING BREATH
Diane Glancy
Focuses on contemporary American Indian, women, and writer. 115 pp. University of Nebraska Press, 1992. $15.95. 1993 American Book Award Winner.

CLAIMS FOR DEPREDATIONS BY SIOUX INDIANS
38th U.S. Congress
Material on the Sioux Indian War of 1962. 25 pp. Paper. Ye Galleon Press, 1975. $2.50.

*CLAMBAKE, A WAMPANOAG TRADITION
Russell M. Peters
Grades 3-6. Illus. 48 pp. Lerner, 1992. $14.95.

*CLAMSHELL BOY
Terri Cohlene
Grades 4-8. Illus. 50 pp. Rourke Corp., 1990. $14.95.

WILLIAM CLARK: JEFFERSONIAN MAN ON THE FRONTIER
Jerome O. Steffen
Reprint of 1977 edition. Illus. University of Oklahoma Press, $16.95; paper, $7.95.

CLASSIFICATION AND DEVELOPMENT OF NORTH AMERICAN INDIAN CULTURES: A STATISTICAL ANALYSIS OF THE DRIVER-MASSEY SAMPLE
Harold E. Driver and James L. Coffin
Illus. Paper. American Philosophical Society, 1975. $15.

THE CLASSIFICATION & DISTRIBUTION OF THE PIT RIVER INDIAN TRIBES OF CALIFORNIA
Clinton H. Merriam
Reprint of 1926 edition. AMS Press, $15.

CLIFF DWELLERS OF THE MESA VERDE
Gustaf Nordenskiold
Reprint of 1893 edition. Illus. Map. 382 pp. AMS, $97.50.

CLOTHED-IN-FUR & OTHER TALES: AN INTRODUCTION TO AN OJIBWA WORLD VIEW
Thomas W. Overholt and J. Biard Callicott
198 pp. University Presses of America, 1982. $32.25; paper, $14.25.

CLOWNS OF THE HOPI: TRADITION KEEPERS & DELIGHT MAKERS
Barton Wright; photos by Jerry Jacka
Looks at Hopi clowns, their purposes and historical backgrounds. Illus. 148 pp. Northland Publishing, $12.95.

*CLUES FROM THE PAST: A RESOURCE BOOK ON ARCHAEOLOGY
Pam Wheat & Brenda Whorton, Editors
Grades 3 and up. Illus. 200 pp. Paper. Hendrick-Long, 1990. $17.95.

COAST SALISH
Reg Ashwell
Illus. 88 pp. Paper. Hancock House, $4.95.

COAST SALISH ESSAYS
Wayne Suttles
Illus. 286 pp. University of Washington Press, 1988. $30; paper, $14.95.

THE COAST SALISH OF BRITISH COLUMBIA
Homer Barnett
Reprint of 1955 edition. Illus. 320 pp. Greenwood, $25.00.

*THE COAST SALISH PEOPLE
Frank W. Porter
Grades 5 and up. Illus. Chelsea House, 1989. $17.95.

*COCA-COLA CULTURE: ICONS OF POP
The Icarus World Issues
Addresses such global ironies as the image of Native Americans in American advertising. Grades 7-12. 176 pp. The Rosen Publishing Group, 1992. Hard cover, $18.95, paperback, $8.95.

COCHISE: CHIRICAHUA APACHE CHIEF
Edwin R. Sweeney
Biography of Cochise, the most resourceful & most feared Apache chief. Illus. 512 pp. University of Oklahoma Press, 1992. $27.95.

THE COCHISE CULTURAL SEQUENCE IN SOUTHEASTERN ARIZONA
E.B. Sayles, et al
192 pp. Paper. University of Arizona Press, 1983. $15.95.

COCHITI: A NEW MEXICO PUEBLO, PAST & PRESENT
Charles H. Lange
Illus. 650 pp. Paper. University of New Mexico Press, 1990. $22.50.

COCOPA ETHNOGRAPHY
William H. Kelly
A study of the Cocopa Tribe of the Colorado River Delta during the late 1880s. Paper. University of Arizona Press, 1977. $13.50.

COGEWEA, THE HALF-BLOOD
Mourning Dove
302 pp. University of Nebraska Press, 1981. $30; paper, $9.95.

FELIX S. COHEN'S HANDBOOK OF FEDERAL INDIAN LAW
Felix S. Cohen
Facsimile of 1942 edition. University of New Mexico Press, $25.00. 950 pp. Michie Co., 1982. $80.00.

COLDWATER INDIAN ARTIFACTS PRICE GUIDE
Puckett
Covers most of the point and blade types of the Southeastern U.S. and adjoining states. Illus. 294 pp. Hothem House, 1993. $20.

MICHAEL COLEMAN
Illus. Paper. University of Nebraska Press, 1979. $12.95.

COLLECTED WORKS OF EDWARD SAPIR
William Bright & Philip Sapir, Editors
Vol. V: American Indian Languages, 584 pp., 1990; Vol. VI: American Indian Languages, 559 pp. 1991; Vol. VII: Wishram Texts & Ethnography, 518 pp. 1990; Vol. X: Southern Paiute & Ute Linguistics & Ethnography, 932 pp. 1993. Mouton de Gruyter.

COLLECTING NORTH AMERICAN INDIAN KNIVES
Lar Hothem
Illus. 300 pp. Paper. Books Americana, 1986. $14.95.

COLLECTING THE NAVAJO CHILD'S BLANKET
Joshua Baer
Illus. 60 pp. Paper. Morning Star Gallery, 1986. $21.

COLLECTING SHAWNEE POTTERY: A PICTORIAL REFERENCE & PRICE GUIDE
Mark Supnick
Illus. 64 pp. Paper. M. Supnick, 1983. $12.95.

COLLECTING THE WEST: THE C.R. SMITH COLLECTION OF WESTERN AMERICAN ART
Richard H. Saunders
Illus. 224 pp. U. of Texas Press, 1988. $35.

COLLEGE GUIDE FOR AMERICAN INDIAN STUDENTS
Winds of Change Special issue
Data on colleges, universities, and financial aid; resources and references; and articles on preparation for college, cultural support on campus; interviews with students. All geared to American Indian students. AISES, $5.

JOHN COLLIER'S CRUSADE FOR INDIAN REFORM, 1920-1954
Kenneth R. Philp
Commissioner of Indian Affairs under FDR, Collier rejected the idea of Americanizing Indians in favor of preserving their traditions. 304 pp. Paper. University of Arizona Press, 1977. $8.95.

COLLOQUIAL NAVAJO: A DICTIONARY
Robert W. Young & William Morgan
A practical guide to colloquial terms and idiomatic expressions of the Navajo language. 461 pp. Paper. Hippocrene Books, 1994. $16.95.

*A COLORING BOOK OF AMERICAN INDIANS
Grades K-3. Paper. Bellerophon, $3.95.

*A COLORING BOOK OF HIDATSA INDIAN STORIES
Roberta Krim & Thomas Thompson
Grades K-3. 32 pp. Paper. Minnesota Historical Society Press, $2.50.

THE COLOUR OF RESISTANCE: A CONTEMPORARY COLLECTION OF WRITING BY ABORIGINAL WOMEN
Connie Fife
A collection of writing by 45 Native women from throughout North America, some of the strongest voices in Native literature. Paper. Sister Vision Press, 1993.

COLUMBIA RIVER BASKETRY: GIFT OF THE ANCESTORS, GIFT OF THE EARTH
Mary Dodds Schlick
Illus. Map. 240 pp. University of Washington Press, 1992. $60; paper, $35.

COLUMBUS & BEYOND: VIEWS FROM NATIVE AMERICANS
A look at Columbus by prominent Native writers including Paula Gunn Allen, Lee Francis III, Linda Hogan, Simon Ortiz, Carter Revard & Ray Young Bear. Southwest Parks & Monuments, $7.95.

*COLUMBUS DAY
Vicki Liestman; illus. by Rick Hanson
Grades K-3. Deals with the mistreatment of the Indians by Columbus & the Spaniards. Illus. 50 pp. Lerner, 1991. $15.95; paper, $5.95

COLUMBUS: HIS ENTERPRISE: EXPLODING THE MYTH
Hans Koning
Depicts Columbus for who he was and describes the consequences of his actions on the Native people & the environment. Monthly Review Press, 1991. $8.95.

COLUMBUS ON TRIAL
Anthology. Coluiimbus and his crimes against Native society. Greenfield Review Press, $10.

COLUMBUS & OTHER CANNIBALS
Jack Forbes
Collection of essays dealing with some past & contemporary problems that have come about &

continued in America since Columbus. Published by Autonomedia. Available from Greenfield Review Press, $10.

*THE COMANCHE
Willard Rollings
Grades 7-12. Illus. 112 pp. Chelsea House, 1989. $17.95; paper, $9.95.

COMANCHE DICTIONARY & GRAMMAR
Lile Robinson & James Armagost
Paper. Summer Institute of Linguistics, 1990.

COMANCHE MOON: A PICTURE NARRATIVE ABOUT CYNTHIA ANN PARKER, HER TWENTY-FIVE YEAR CAPTIVITY AMONG THE COMANCHE INDIANS-AND HER SON QUANAH PARKER, THE LAST CHIEF OF THE COMANCHES
Jack Jackson
129 pp. Paper. Texas State Historical Association, 1979. $5.95.

COMANCHE TREATIES DURING THE CIVIL WAR
R.J. DeMallie
30 pp. Institute for the Development of Indian Law, $10.

COMANCHE TREATIES: HISTORICAL BACKGROUND
R.J. DeMallie
20 pp. Institute for the Development of Indian Law, $7.50.

COMANCHE TREATIES OF 1835 WITH THE U.S.
R.J. DeMallie
20 pp. Institute for the Development of Indian Law, $7.

COMANCHE TREATIES OF 1846 WITH THE U.S.
R.J. DeMallie
16 pp. Institute for the Development of Indian Law, $6.50.

COMANCHE TREATIES OF 1850, 1851, 1853 WITH THE U.S.
R.J. DeMallie
60 pp. Institute for the Development of Indian Law, $12.50.

COMANCHE TREATIES WITH THE REPUBLIC OF TEXAS
R.J. DeMallie
20 pp. Institute for the Development of Indian Law, $7.50.

*COMANCHE WARBONNET
Troxey Kemper
Fiction. About famous Comanche chief Quanah Parker. Paper. Navajo Community College Press, $12.50.

COMANCHERO FRONTIER: A HISTORY OF NEW MEXICO-PLAINS INDIAN RELATIONS
Charles L. Kenner
History of the Comancheros, or Mexicans who traded with the Comanche Indians in the early Southwest. Illus. Maps. Biblio. 250 pp. Paper. University of Oklahoma Press, 1994. $14.95.

COMANCHES
T.R. Fehrenbach
Alfred A. Knopf, 1974. $29.95.

**THE COMANCHES: LORDS
OF THE SOUTH PLAINS**
Ernest Wallace and E. Adamson Hoebel
Illus. Map. 400 pp. University of Oklahoma
Press, $22.95; paper , $10.95.

**"COME BLACKROBE":
DE SMET & THE INDIAN TRAGEDY**
John J. Killoren, S.J.
Evaluation of DeSmet, known as "Blackrobe," an
evangelist among the Coeur d'Alenes, the
Flatheads, the Kalispels, the Blackfeet, and the
Kutenais. Illus. Maps. Biblio. University of Okla-
homa Press, 1994. $29.95.

*COME TO OUR SALMON FEAST
Martha F. McKeown
Grades 4-9. Illus. 80 pp. Binford & Mort, 1959.
$7.95.

**COMMAND OF THE WATERS:
IRON TRIANGLES, FEDERAL WATER
DEVELOPMENT, & INDIAN WATER**
Daniel McCool
Illus. 324 pp. University of California Press, 1987.
$38. Paper. University of Arizona Press, $16.95.

**THE COMMISSIONERS OF
INDIAN AFFAIRS, 1824-1977**
Robert Kvasnicka & Herman Viola
Discusses the leaders of the Bureau of Indian
Affairs. Illus. University of Nebraska Press,
1977.

**COMMONERS, TRIBUTE, & CHIEFS: THE
DEVELOPMENT OF ALGONQUIAN CUL-
TURE IN THE POTOMAC VALLEY**
Stephen R. Potter
Archaeological and documentary information on
the Indianpeoples who lived in the Potomac
Valley from A.D. 200 to 1650. 280 pp. University
Press of Virginia, 1993. $29.95.

**COMMUNICATING EFFECTIVELY WITH
NON-INDIAN SERVICE PROVIDERS**
A handbook for Indian parents that summarizes
five effective communication skills to use when
talking with non-Indian professionals. Southwest
Communication Resources, $10.00.

**COMMUNICATION & DEVELOPMENT:
A STUDY OF TWO INDIAN VILLAGES**
Y.V. Rao
Reprint of 1966 edition. Paper. Books on
Deamnd, $38.

**COMMUNITY-BASED RESEARCH: A
HANDBOOK FOR NATIVE AMERICANS**
Susan Guyette
358 pp. Paper. American Indian Studies Center ,
$15.

**A COMPANY OF HEROES:
THE AMERICAN FRONTIER, 1775-1783**
D. Van Every
Reprint of 1962 edition. Ayer Co. Publishers,
$17.

**COMPARATIVE HOKAN-
COAHUILTECAN STUDIES**
Margaret Langdon
Illus. 114 pp. Paper. Mouton, 1974. $20.

**COMPARATIVE STUDIES
IN AMERINDIAN LANGUAGES**
Esther Matteson, et al
251 pp. Paper. Mouton, 1972. $55.75

**A COMPARATIVE STUDY OF
LAKE IROQUOIAN ACCENT**
Karin Michelson
Kluwer Academic, 1988. $89.

**COMPARATIVE VOCABULARIES &
PARALLEL TEXTS IN TWO YUMAN
LANGUAGES OF ARIZONA**
Leslie Spier
Reprint of 1946 edition. Paper. AMS, $15.

**THE COMPLETE AMERICAN ESKIMO:
A SPECIAL KIND OF COMPANION DOG**
Barbara Beynon; Seymour Weiss, Editor
256 pp. Howell Book House, 1990. $21.95.

**THE COMPLETE BOOK
OF NATURAL SHAMANISM**
Robert J. Titus
Snowbird Publishing Co., $11.45 postpaid.

**THE COMPLETE GUIDE TO TRADITIONAL
NATIVE AMERICAN BEADWORK**
Joel Monture
A definitive study of authentic tools, materials,
techniques & styles. Illus. Greenfield Review
Press, $14.

***THE COMPLETE HOW-TO
BOOK OF INDIAN CRAFT**
W. Ben Hunt
Grades 7-adult. 188 pp. Paper, Macmillan,
1973. $8.95.

**THE COMPLETE VISITOR'S GUIDE
TO MESOAMERICAN RUINS**
Joyce Kelly
Illus. 550 pp. University of Oklahoma Press,
1982. $39.95.

**CONCEPT OF THE GUARDIAN
SPIRIT IN NORTH AMERICA**
Ruth Benedict
Reprint of 1923 edition. Paper. Kraus, $12.

**CONCERNING THE LEAGUE: THE
IROQUOIS LEAGUE TRADITION AS
DICTATED IN ONONDAGA BY JOHN
ARTHUR GIBSON**
Hanni Woodbury, Editor
Paper. Syracuse University Press, 1993. $80.

A CONCISE BLACKFOOT GRAMMAR
Christianus C. Uhlenbeck
Reprint of 1938 edition, AMS Press, $27.50.

**A CONCISE DICTIONARY OF INDIAN
TRIBES OF NORTH AMERICA**
Barbara Leitch et al.
Revised edition. Reference Pubns., 1995. $75.

**CONCISE ENCYCLOPEDIA
OF THE AMERICAN INDIAN**
Bruce Grant
Over 800 entries covering legends, lore, weap-
ons and wars, beliefs, tools, information on each
tribe. Illus. 352 pp. Cherokee Pubns, 1989. $9.95.

**THE CONDITION OF AFFAIRS IN INDIAN
TERRITORY & CALIFORNIA**
Charles C. Painter
Reprint of 1888 edition. AMS Press, $14.

**THE CONFLICT BETWEEN THE CALI-
FORNIA INDIAN & WHITE CIVILIZATION**
Sherburne F. Cook
Reprint of 1888 edition. Four volumes in one.

AMS, 27.50. Paper. University of California
Press, $10.95.

**CONFLICT & SCHISM IN
NEZ PERCE ACCULTURATION**
Deward Walker
Illus. 171 pp. Paper. University of Idaho Press,
1968. $10.95.

**THE CONFLICT OF EUROPEAN AND
EASTERN ALGONKIAN CULTURES, 1504-
1700: A STUDY IN CANADIAN CIVILIZATION**
Alfred Bailey
Second edition. Paper. University of Toronto
Press, 1969. $9.95.

**CONOZCA SUS RAICES / KNOW YOUR
ROOTS: A MAP OF THE INDIGENOUS
PEOPLES OF MEXICO & CENTROAMERICA**
Dolan H. Eargle, Jr., Editor
A full color, 18"x24" poster, bilingual - Spanish &
English with color-coded legend of contemporary
ethnic homelands grouped by linguistic families.
Mexico to Panama. Biblio. Trees Company Press,
$5.

**THE CONQUEST OF PARADISE:
CHRISTOPHER COLUMBUS
& THE COLUMBIAN LEGACY**
Kirkpatrick Sale
Reexamination of colonialism and its wake of
ecological destruction. 464 pp. Paper. Penguin
USA, 1993. $12.95.

**CONRAD WEISER & THE INDIAN
POLICY OF COLONIAL PENNSYLVANIA**
Joseph S. Walton
Reprint of 1900 edition. Ayer Co., $34.95.

**CONSERVATISM AMONG THE IROQUOIS
AT THE SIX NATIONS RESERVE**
Annemarie Shimony
Paper. Syracuse University Press, 1994.

CONTEST FOR EMPIRE, 1500-1775
Essays by George Waller, James Brown, John
Tepaske, George Rawlyk, Jack Sosin, and Thomas Clark. 95 pp. paper. Indiana Historical Society, 1975. $2.75.

CONQUERING HORSE
Frederick Manfred
370 pp. Paper. University of Nebraska Press,
1983. $8.95.

CONQUEST OF APACHERIA
Dan Thrapp
Illus. University of Oklahoma Press, 1967.
$24.95; paper, $13.95.

**THE CONQUEST OF THE COEUR
D'ALENES, SPOKANES & PALOUSES**
Benjamin F. Manring
Illus. 312 pp. Ye Galleon Press, 1975. $19.95.

**CONSIDERATIONS ON THE PRESENT
STATE OF THE INDIANS & THEIR REMOVAL
TO THE WEST OF THE MISSISSIPPI**
Lewis Cass
Reprint of 1828 edition. Ayer Co. Publishers,
$13.50.

**THE CONSTITUTION OF THE FIVE NATIONS/
THE IROQUOIS BOOK OF THE GREAT LAW**
Arthur C. Parker
Paper. The Greenfield Review Press, $5.95.

**CONSTITUTION OF THE
STATE OF SEQUOYAH**
Reprint of 1906 edition. Three volumes in one.
AMS Press, $18.

**THE CONSTITUTIONS & LAWS OF
THE AMERICAN INDIAN TRIBES**
This program presents the complete collection of
the written constitutions and laws of the American
Indian tribes to 1906 when tribal governments in
Indian territory were abolished. The constitutions
for the following tribes are included: The
Chickasaw, Osage, Cherokee, Choctaw,
Muskogee, Creek, and Sac and Fox. Two series.
53 volumes. See Scholarly Resources for titles,
descriptions and prices.

**CONSUMER'S GUIDE TO SOUTHWESTERN
INDIAN ARTS & CRAFTS**
  Mark T. Bahti
Guide to determining the quality and authenticity
of rugs, blankets, jewelry, and pottery. Includes
buying tips, and a list of hallmarks of well known
silversmiths. Illus. 32 pp. Paper. Treasure Chest,
$3.

**THE CONSUMER'S RIGHTS
UNDER WARRANTIES**
Institute for Development of Indian Law, $3.50.

**CONTEMPORARY ARCHAEOLOGY: A
GUIDE TO THEORY & CONTRIBUTIONS**
  Mark P. Leone, Editor
Illus. 476 pp. Paper. Southern Illinois University
Press, 1972. $17.95.

**CONTEMPORARY ARTISTS & CRAFTSMEN
OF THE CHEROKEE INDIANS**
Illus. 145 pp. Qualla Arts & Crafts & Cherokee
Publications, 1990. $9.95.

**CONTEMPORARY FEDERAL POLICY
TOWARD AMERICAN INDIANS**
  Emma R. Gross
165 pp. Greenwood, 1989. $39.95.

**CONTEMPORARY INDIAN ART FROM
THE CHESTER & DAVID HERWITZ FAMILY
COLLECTION**
  Thomas W. Sokolowski
Illus. 88 pp. Paper. Grey Art Gallery Study
Center, 1985. $15.

**CONTEMPORARY INDIAN ARTISTS:
MONTANA, WYOMING & IDAHO**
Catalog of an exhibition presented at the Museum
of the Plains Indian in Browning, Montana. Re-
views the diversity of paintings by contemporary
Indian artists of the Northern Plains region. Illus.
Map. 80 pp. Northern Plains Indian Crafts Asso-
ciation, 1972. $7, postpaid.

CONTEMPORARY NAVAJO AFFAIRS
  Norman Eck
243 pp. Navajo Curriculum, 1982. $15.

**CONTEMPORARY NAVAJO WEAVING;
THOUGHTS THAT COUNT**
  Ann Lane Hedlund
Discusses what it means to be a Navajo weaver,
including history of the rugs, their designing and
making, buying & collecting, and the future of
weaving. Illus. 32 pp. Paper. Museum of Northern
Arizona, $6.95.

**CONTEMPORARY SOUTHERN PLAINS
INDIAN METALWORK**
Explores an important tradition of distinctive jewelry and ornamentation created of nickel-silver by
modern tribal craftsmen of the Southern Plains
region. Illus. Map. 80 pp. Catalog. Oklahoma Indian Arts & Crafts Cooperative, $8, postpaid.

**CONTEMPORARY SOUTHERN
PLAINS INDIAN PAINTING**
An historic survey of contemporary painting by
Indian artists of the tribally diverse Southern Plains
region. Illus. Map. 80 pp. Catalog. Oklahoma In-
dian Arts & Crafts Coop., 1972. $7, postpaid.

**CONTENT & STYLE OF AN ORAL LITERA-
TURE: CLACKAMAS CHINOOK MYTHS &
TALES**
  Melville Jacobs
285 pp. U. of Chicago Press, 1959. $17.50.

**CONTINENT LOST - A CIVILIZATION WON:
INDIAN LAND TENURE IN AMERICA**
  J.P. Kinney; Dan C. McCurry & Richard E.
Rubinstein, Editors
Reprint of 1937 edition. Illus. 336 pp. Ayer Co.,
$36.50.

**CONTINENTS IN COLLISION: THE IMPACT
OF EUROPE ON THE NORTH CONTINUITIES
OF HOPI CULTURE CHANGE**
  Richard O. Clemmer
Paper. Acoma Books, 1978. $9.50.

CONTRACTS & YOU
Institute for Development of Indian Law, $3.50.

**CONTRIBUTIONS TO ANTHROPOLOGY:
SELECTED PAPERS OF A. IRVING
HALLOWELL**
  A. Irving Hallowell
University of Chicago Press, 1976. $40.

**CONTRIBUTIONS TO THE ARCHAEOLOGY
& ETHNOHISTORY OF GREATER MESO-
AMERICA**
  William J. Folan, Editor
368 pp. Southern Illinois U. Press, 1985. $28.95.

**CONTRIBUTIONS TO
CHIPEWYAN ETHNOLOGY**
  Kaj Birket-Smith
Reprint of 1930 edition. AMS Press, $38.50.

**CONTRIBUTIONS TO THE
ETHNOGRAPHY OF THE KUTCHIN**
  Cornelius Osgood
Reprint of 1936 edition. 190 pp. Paper.
HRAF Press, $15.

**A CONVERSATIONAL DICTIONARY
OF KODIAK ALUTIIQ**
  Jeff Leer, Editor
119 pp. Paper. AK Native Language Center, $4.

**CONVERSATIONS WITH LOUISE
ERDRICH & MICHAEL DORRIS**
  Allan Chavkin & Nancy Feyl Chavkin, Editors
224 pp. University Press of Mississippi, 1994.
$37.50; paper, $15.95.

**CONVERTING THE WEST:
A BIOGRAPHY OF NARCISSA WHITMAN**
  Julie Roy Jeffrey
Pioneer missionary to the Cayuse Indians of
Oregon Territory. Illus. Maps. 256 pp. University
of Oklahoma Press, $24.95.

**COOKING WITH SPIRIT; NORTH
AMERICAN INDIAN FOOD & FACT**
  Lisa Railsback & Darcy Williamson
Cookbook, healing guide & folklore anthology. Illus.
111 pp. Paper. Cherokee Publications & Four
Winds Trading Co., $12.95.

**COPING WITH THE FINAL TRAGEDY:
DYING & GRIEVING IN CROSS CULTURAL
PERSPECTIVE**
  David & Dorothy Counts, Editors
285 pp. Baywood, 1992. $34.95; paper, $24.95.

COPPER PALADIN: THE MODOC TRAGEDY
  Walter H. Palmberg
Looks at some of the leading figures in one of
the most costly Indian wars. 194 pp. Dorrance
Publishing, 1982. $12.

**THE COPPERS OF THE NORTHWEST
COAST INDIANS: THEIR ORIGIN, DEVELOP-
MENT, & POSSIBLE ANTECEDENTS**
  Carol F. Jopling
Illus. Paper. American Philosophical Society,
1987. $25.

**THE COQUILLE INDIANS:
YESTERDAY, TODAY & TOMORROW**
  Roberta L. Hall
Illus. 250 pp. Paper. SSS Pubg., 1984. $9.95.

**CORN AMONG THE INDIANS OF THE
UPPER MISSOURI**
  George F. Will and George E. Hyde
323 pp. U. of Nebraska Press, 1964. $25.95.

***CORN IS MAIZE -
THE GIFT OF THE INDIANS**
  Aliki
Grades K-3. Illus. 34 pp. paper. AISES, $4.50.

CORN RECIPES FROM THE INDIANS
32 pp. Paper. Cherokee Publications, $3.50.

**CORNHUSK BAGS OF THE PLATEAU
INDIANS**
  Cheney Cowles Memorial Museum
Microfiche. Illus. University of Chicago Press,
1976. $30.

**THE CORPORATION & THE INDIAN: TRIBAL
SOVEREIGNTY & INDUSTRIAL CIVILIZATION
IN INDIAN TERRITORY, 1865-1907**
  H. Craig Minor
Illus. Map. 252 pp. Paper. University of
Oklahoma Press, 1976. $14.95.

**THE CORPORATE & FOUNDATION
FUNDRAISING MANUAL FOR NATIVE
AMERICANS**
A step-by-step guide to securing private sector
grants, outlining basic fundraising and research
procedures. Helps Native American planners diversify their funding base with private sector dollars. CRC Publishing, 1993. $129.95.

THE COSMOLOGY OF THE GITA
  Institute for Indian Studies Staff, Editors
187 pp. Foundation for Classical Reprints, 1986.
$127.45.

**COSTUMES OF THE PLAINS INDIANS &
STRUCTURAL BASIS TO THE DECORATION
OF COSTUMES AMONG THE PLAINS INDIANS**
  Clark Wissler
Reprint of 1915 edition. Illus. 88 pp. AMS Press,
$17.

C.N. COTTON & HIS NAVAJO BLANKETS
Lester L. Williams
Avanyu Publishing, 1989.

*COULD IT BE OLD HIARI
Marjorie Vandervelde
Grades 5-9. 30 pp. Council for Indian Education, 1975. $8.95; paper, $2.95.

COUNCIL FIRES ON THE UPPER OHIO
Randolph C. Downs
Illus. Paper. University of Pittsburgh Press, 1969. $8.75.

COUNCIL OF THE RAINMAKERS ADDRESS BOOK
David Dawangyumptewa, artist
24 paintings of Hopi artist David Dawanyumptewa's paintings. 110 pp. Northland Publishing, 1993. $12.95.

COUNTING COUP & CUTTING HORSES: INTERTRIBAL WARFARE ON THE NORTH-ERN PLAINS, 1738-1889
Anthony McGinnis
Illus. 258 pp. Paper. Cordillera Press, 1989. $14.95.

A COUNTRY BETWEEN: THE UPPER OHIO VALLEY & ITS PEOPLES, 1724-1774
Michael N. McConnell
History of Indians in Upper Ohio Valley. Illus. Maps. 350 pp. University of Nebraska Press, 1992. $40.

*COURAGEOUS SPIRITS: ABORIGINAL HEROES OF OUR CHILDREN
Joann Archibald; editorial by Richard Wagamese
Grades 4 and up. Illus. 76 pp. Paper. Theytus, 1993. $9.95; teachers guide, $5.95.

THE COVENANT CHAIN: INDIAN CEREMO-NIAL & TRADE SILVER
Jaye Frederickson and Sandra Gibb
Reprint of 1980 edition. Illus. 168 pp. University of Chicago Press, $24.95; paper, $19.95.

*COYOTE & THE FISH
Lorna Garrod
An Mimbre Indian trickster story on the first Rainbow trout. Grades 3-7. Illus. 36 pp. Filter Prss, 1993. $2.50.

*COYOTE & KOOTENAI
Louie Gingras and Jo Rainboldt
Grades 2-6. Paper. Council for Indian Education, 1977. $1.95.

*COYOTE & LITTLE TURTLE
as told by Hershel Talashoema; edited & translated by Emory Sekaquaptewa & Barbara Pepper
A traditional Hopi tale. Grade 1-4. Illus. 95 pp. Clear Light Publishers, $14.95; paper, $9.95.

*COYOTE STEALS THE BLANKET: A UTE TALE
Janet Stevens
Grades K-3. Illus. 32 pp. Holiday House, 1993. $15.95; paper, $5.95.

*COYOTE STORIES
Mourning Dove
Reprint of 1933 edition. Grades 4 and up. Illus. 246 pp. University of Nebraska Press & AISES, $8.95.

*COYOTE STORIES FOR CHILDREN: TALES FROM NATIVE AMERICA
Susan Strauss; illus by Gary Lund
Coyote tales with true-life anecdotes about coy-otes & Native wisdom. Grades 1-6. Illus. 50 pp. Beyond Words Publishing, $10.95; paper, $6.95.

*COYOTE TALES
Evelyn Dahl Reed
Stories from the Indian Pueblos. Grades 4 and up. 64 pp. Paper. Sunstone Press, $6.95.

*COYOTE TALES OF THE MONTANA SALISH
as told by Pierre Pichette; transcribed by Harriet Miller & Elizabeth Harrison
13 folk tales about the mischievous & amazing folk hero. Grades 4 and up. Illus. Maps. 80 pp. Paper. Northern Plains Indian Crafts Association, 1972. $7, postpaid.

COYOTE: A TRICKSTER TALE FROM THE AMERICAN SOUTHWEST
Gerald McDermott
Grades Pre-school to 3. Illus. 32 pp. Harcourt Brace, 1994. $14.95.

COYOTE WAS GOING THERE: INDIAN LITERATURE OF THE OREGON COUNTRY
Jarold Ramsey, Editor/Compiler
Illus. 336 pp. Paper. University of Washington Press, 1977. $16.95.

*COYOTE & THE WINNOWING BIRDS
as told by Eugene Sekaquaptewa; edited & translated by Emory Sekaquaptewa & Barbara Pepper
A traditional Hopi tale. Grades 1-4. Illus. 100 pp. Clear Light Publishers, $14.95; paper, $9.95.

*COYOTE'S POW-WOW
Hap Gilliland
Grades K-4. 31 pp. Paper. Council for Indian Education, 1972. $8.95; paper, $2.95.

COYOTEWAY: A NAVAJO HOLYWAY HEALING CEREMONIAL
Karl W. Luckert
Includes more than 100 photos, plus song and prayer texts. Illus. 243 pp. Paper. University of Arizona Press, 1979. $13.95.

*CRAFTS OF THE NORTH AMERICAN INDIANS: A CRAFTSMAN'S MANUAL
Richard C. Schneider
Grades 9-12. Reprint of 1972 edition. Illus. 325 pp. Paper. R. Schneider, Publishers, $19.95.

CRANIOMETRY OF SOUTHERN NEW ENGLAND INDIANS
Marian V. Knight
Reprint of 1915 edition. Paper. Elliots Books, $150.

CRANIONETRIC RELATIONSHIPS AMONG PLAINS INDIANS: CULTURAL, HISTORICAL & EVOLUTIONARY IMPLICATIONS
Patrick J. Key
204 pp. Paper. University of Tennessee Press, 1983. $19.95.

CRASHING THUNDER: THE AUTO-BIOGRAPHY OF AN AMERICAN INDIAN
Paul Radin, Editor
250 pp. Paper. University of Nebraska Press, 1983. $8.95.

*CRAZY HORSE
Judith St. George
An account of the Sioux Wars and the character of the Plains people; and the life story of Crazy Horse. Grades 6 and up. Illus. 192 pp. Putnam, 1994. $16.95.

CRAZY HORSE CALLED THEM WALK-A-HEAPS
Neil Baird Thompson
The story of the foot soldier in the Prairie Indian Wars. Illus. North Star Press, $9.95.

CRAZY HORSE & CUSTER: THE PARALLEL LIVES OF TWO AMERICAN WARRIORS
Stephen E. Ambrose
Illus. 544 pp. Paper. New American Library, 1986. $15.

CRAZY HORSE, HOKA HEY: IT IS A GOOD TIME TO DIE!
Vinson Brown
Personal study of Crazy Horse. 192 pp. Naturegraph, $16.95; paper, $8.95.

CRAZY HORSE & KORCZAK: THE STORY OF AN EPIC MOUNTAIN CARVING
Robb DeWall
Illus. 154 pp. Crazy Horse Memorial Foundation, $9.50.

CRAZY HORSE MEMORIAL, 40TH ANNIVERSARY
Illus. Crazy Horse Memorial Foundation.

CRAZY HORSE: SACRED WARRIOR OF THE SIOUX
Illus. 52 pp. Sterling, 1989. $12.95.

CRAZY HORSE: THE STRANGE MAN OF THE OGLALAS
Mari Sandoz
Illus. 428 pp. Paper. University of Nebraska Press & AISES. $11.95.

THE CRAZY HORSE SURRENDER LEDGER
Thomas R. Buecker, Editor
Illus. Paper. Nebraska State Historical Society, 1994.

CREATION MYTHS OF PRIMITIVE AMERICA
Jeremiah Curtin
Ayer Co., 1980. $31.00.

*CREATION OF A CALIFORNIA TRIBE: GRANDFATHER'S MAIDU INDIAN TALE
Paper. Sierra Oaks Publishing, $6.95.

*CREATION TALES FROM THE SALISH
W.H. McDonald
Grades 3-9. Paper. Council for Indian Education, 1973. $1.95.

CREATION'S JOURNEY: NATIVE AMERICAN IDENTITY & BELIEF
Tom Hill & Richard W. Hill, Sr.
Draws on the vast collections of the National Museum of the American Indian to retell the story of native life from the Arctic to the Tierra del Fuego. Illus. 256 pp. Smithsonian Institution Press, 1994. $60.

*THE CREEK
Michael D. Green
Grades 5 and up. Illus. 104 pp. Chelsea House, 1989. $17.05.

CREEK CENSUS 1832
Larry S. Watson, indexed by
155 pp. Paper. Histree, 1988. $48.95.

CREEK-CHOCTAW-CHICKASAW LAND FRAUD IN PUBLIC LAND SALES
Larry S. Watson, indexed & edited by
150 pp. Paper. Histree, 1990. $19.95.

CREEK INDIAN HISTORY: A HISTORICAL NARRATIVE OF THE GENEALOGIES, TRADITIONS & DOWNFALL OF THE ISPOCOGA OR CREEK INDIAN TRIBE OF INDIANS BY ONE OF THE TRIBE
George Stiggins; Virginia P. Brown, Editor
Illus. 160 pp. Birmingham Public Library, 1989. $24.95.

CREEK INDIAN STIDHAM ROLL 1886 WITH INDEX
Larry S. Watson, indexed by
74 pp. Paper. Histree, 1980. $9.95.

CREEK INDIANS OF TASKIGI TOWN
Frank G. Speck
Reprint of 1907 edition. Paper. Kraus, $15.00.

CREEK (MUSKOGEE) NEW TESTAMENT CONCORDANCE
Lee Chupco, Rev. Ward Coachman, et al
The first New Testamint Concordance printed for an American Indian language. 167 pp. Indian University Press, 1982. $11, postpaid.

CREEK SOLDIER CASULATY LISTS - SEMINOLE WAR 1836
49 pp. Paper. Histree, 1987. $9.95.

A CREEK SOURCEBOOK
William C. Sturtevant, Editor
Reprint od 1983 edition. 780 pp. Garland Publishing, $100.00.

THE CREEK VERB
Henry O. Harwell & Deloris T. Harwell
A linguistic study of the Creek (Muskogee) verb and grammar. 57 pp. Indian University Press, 1981. $8.50, postpaid.

A CREEK WARRIOR FOR THE CONFEDERACY: THE AUTOBIOGRAPHY OF CHIEF G.W. GRAYSON
G.W. Grayson; W. David Baird, Editor
Illus. Maps. 200 pp. Paper. University of Oklahoma Press, 1988. $14.95.

CREEKS & SEMINOLES: THE DESTRUCTION & REGENERATION OF THE MUSCOGULGE PEOPLE
J. Leitch Wright, Jr.
Illus. Maps. 383 pp. Paper. University of Nebraska Press, 1987. $12.95.

THE CRESCENT HILLS PRHISTORIC QUARRYING AREA
David J. Ives
35 pp. Paper. Museum of Anthropology, University of Missouri, 1975. $1.80.

*CRICKETS & CORN: FIVE STORIES ABOUT NATIVE NORTH AMERICAN CHILDREN
Peg Black
Five Native American children make important discoveries about it means to be Native people. paper. Friendship Press, $3.50.

CRIMINAL JURISDICTION ALLOCATION IN INDIAN COUNTRY
Ronald B. Flowers
126 pp. Associate Faculty Press, 1983. $17.50.

CRIMSONED PRAIRIE: THE INDIAN WARS
S.L. Marshall
Reprint of 1972 edition. Illus. 285 pp. Paper. Da Capo Press, $10.95.

CRITICAL FICTIONS: THE POLITICS OF IMAGINATIVE WIRITING
Philomena Mariani, Editor
292 p. Paper. Bay Press, $15.95.

CROSSBLOODS: BONE COURTS, BINGO, & OTHER REPORTS
Gerald Vizenor
From reservation treaties to cultural schizophrenia and the rise of the American Indian Movement. Illus. 335 pp. University of Minnesota, 1990. $34.95; paper, $14.95.

CROSSCURRENTS ALONG THE COLORADO: THE IMPACT OF GOVERNMENT POLICY ON THE QUECHEN INDIANS
Robert Bee
184 pp. Paper. University of Arizona Press, 1981. $7.50.

*THE CROW
Frederick E. Hoxie
Grades 5 and up. Illus. Chelsea House, 1989. $17.95.

*THE CROW
Ruth Hagman
Grades K-4. Illus. 50 pp. Childrens Press, 1990. $14.60; paper, $4.95.

*CROW CHIEF
Paul Goble
Grades PS-3. Illus. 32 pp. Orchard Books, $15.

THE CROW & THE EAGLE: A TRIBAL HISTORY FROM LEWIS & CLARK TO CUSTER
Keith Algier
Relates the saga of the Crow Nation in the 1800s. Illus. Maps. Biblio. 399 pp. Paper. The Caxton Printers, 1994. $14.95.

CROW INDIAN ART: PAPERS PRESENTED AT THE CROW INDIAN ART SYMPOSIUM SPONSORED BY THE CHANDLER INSTITUTE
R. Pohrt, Jr. and B. Lanford;
F. Dennis Lessurd, Editor
Illus. 68 pp. Paper. Chandler Institute, 1984. $12.

CROW INDIAN BEADWORK
William Wildschut and John C. Ewers
A descriptive and historical study. Second ed.. Illus. 108 pp. Eagles View, $14.95; paper, $8.95.

CROW INDIAN MEDICINE BUNDLES
William Wildschut; John C. Ewers, Editor
Reprint of 1960 edition. Illus. 187 pp. Paper. National Museum of the American Indian, $9.95.

THE CROW INDIANS
Robert H. Lowie
Reprint of 1935 edition. 350 pp. Paper. University of Nebraska Press, $10.95.

CROW MAN'S PEOPLE: THREE SEASONS WITH THE NAVAJO
Nigel Pride
Illus. 222 pp. Universe Books, 1985. $15.00.

CROWN & CALUMET: BRITISH-INDIAN RELATIONS, 1783-1815
Colin G. Calloway
Illus. 360 pp. University of Oklahoma Press, 1987. $22.95.

A CRY FROM THE EARTH: MUSIC OF THE NORTH AMERICAN INDIANS
John Bierhorst
Illus. 113 pp. Paper. Ancient City Press, 1992. $14.95. Cassette, $10.95.

CRY OF THE EAGLE: ENCOUNTERS WITH A CREE HEALER
David Young & Grant Ingram
University of Toronto Press, $22.50; paper, $14.95.

CRY OF THE THUNDERBIRD: THE AMERICAN INDIAN'S OWN STORY
Charles Hamilton, Editor
Illus. 283 pp. University of Oklahoma Press, 1972. $21.95; paper, $9.95.

CRYING FOR A DREAM
Richard Erdoes
Focus is on the natural & sacred world of North America's indigenous peoples, includes elements of the Sioux ceremonial cycle & portraits of native peoples from the plains, mesas, and deserts. Describe the sun dance, sacred pipe, yuwipi, the vision quest. Illus. 128 pp. Paper. Bear & Co., 1989. $24.95.

*THE CRYING FOR A VISION
Walter Wangerin, Jr.
Saga of Wask Mani - a Lakota orphan with a mysterious past and powers. Grades 7 and up. 288 pp. Simon & Schuster, 1994. $15.

CRYING FOR A VISION: A ROSEBUD SIOUX TRILOGY 1886-1976
John Anderson, Eugene Buechel, et al
Photos cover nearly a century of life i the Rosebud country of South Dakota. Illus. Morgan & Morgan, $19.95.

CRYSTALS IN THE SKY: AN INTELLECTUAL ODYSSEY INVOLVING CHUMASH ASTRONOMY, COSMOLOGY AND ROCK ART
Travis Hudson & Ernest Underhay
Illus. 165 pp. Paper. Ballena Press, 1978. $18.95.

DELFINA CUERO: HER AUTOBIOGRAPHY & HER ETHNOBOTANIC CONTRIBUTIONS
Florence Shipek
Includes "The Autobiography of Delfina Cuero." Illus. 120 pp. Ballena Press, 1991. $16.00; paper, $12.00.

CULTURAL CHANGE & CONTINUITY ON CHAPIN MESA
Arthur H. Rohn
Illus. 330 pp. U. Press of Kansas, 1977. $29.95.

CULTURAL & ENVIRONMENTAL HISTORY OF CIENEGA VALLEY, SOUTHEASTERN ARIZONA
Frank W. Eddy and Maurice E. Cooley
62 pp. University of Arizona Press, 1983. $7.95.

CULTURAL PERSISTENCE: CONTINUITY IN MEANING & MORAL RESPONSIBILITY AMONG THE BEARLIKE ATHAPASKANS
Scott Rushforth with James Chisholm
Ethnographic description of Athapaskan-speaking Indians of Canada's Northwest Territories. 187 pp. University of Arizona Press, 1991. $37.50.

CULTURE, CHANGE & LEADERSHIP IN A MODERN INDIAN COMMUNITY: THE COLORADO RIVER INDIAN RESERVATION
Katherine E. Blossom
101 pp. Paper. Cherokee Publications, 1979. $6.00.

CULTURES IN CONTACT: THE EUROPEAN IMPACT ON NATIVE CULTURAL INSTITU-TIONS IN EASTERN NORTH AMERICA A.D. 1000-1800
William W. Fitzhugh, Editor
Illus. 326 pp. Smithsonian Books, 1985. $29.95; paper, $15.95.

CURRENT RESEARCH IN INDIANA ARCHAEOLOGY & PREHISTORY: 1987 & 1988
Christopher S. Peebles
Illus. 51 pp. Paper. Indiana Historical Society, 1989. $2.75.

CUSHING AT ZUNI: THE CORRESPON-DENCE & JOURNALS OF FRANK HAMILTON CUSHING, 1879-1884
Jesse Green, Editor
Illus. 450 pp. University of New Mexico Press, 1990. $45.00.

CUSTER BATTLEFIELD, A HISTORY AND GUIDE TO THE BATTLE OF THE LITTLE BIGHORN
Robert M. Utley
Illus. 112 pp. Paper. U.S. Government Printing Office, 1988. $4.75.

*CUSTER & CRAZY HORSE
Jim Razzi
Grades 3-7. Paper. Scholastic, Inc., 1989. $2.75.

CUSTER DIED FOR YOUR SINS: AN INDIAN MANIFESTO
Vine Deloria, Jr.
Federal Indian policy from a Native American perspective. Reprint of 1969 edition. 276 pp. Paper. University of Oklahoma Press, $8.95.

THE CUSTER FIGHT & OTHER TALES OF THE OLD WEST
Larry Underwood & Dee A. Brown
Illus. 180 pp. Paper. Media Periodicals, 1989. $9.95.

CUSTER & THE LITTLE BIG HORN: A PSYCHOBIOGRAPHICAL INQUIRY
Charles K. Hofling
130 pp. Paper. Wayne State University Press, 1986. $10.95.

THE CUSTER STORY: THE LIFE & INTIMATE LETTERS OF GENERAL GEORGE A. CUSTER & HIS WIFE ELIZABETH
Marguerite Merington, Editor
Reprint of 1950 edition. 340 pp. Chatham Pres, $9.95.

THE CUSTER TRAGEDY: EVENTS LEADING UP TO & FOLLOWING THE LITTLE BIG HORN CAMPAIGN OF 1876
Fred Dustin
Reprint of 1939 edition. Illus. 310 pp. Upton & Sons, $45.00.

CUSTER'S CHIEF OF SCOUTS: THE REMINISCENCES OF CHARLES A. VARNUM
Charles A. Varnum; John M. Carroll, Editor
Illus. 192 pp. University of Nebraska Press, 1987. $18.95; paper, $6.95.

CUSTER'S DEFEAT & OTHER CONFLICTS IN THE WEST
Illus. 110 pp. Paper. Sunflower University Press, 1979. $15.00.

CUSTER'S FALL: THE NATIVE AMERICAN SIDE OF THE STORY
Presents an interpretation of the Battle of the Little Big Horn, and of the death of General Custer. Illus. 288 pp. Paper. Penguin USA, $10.

CUSTER'S LAST BATTLE
Richard A. Roberts
60 pp. Paper. Monroe County Library, 1978. $8.00.

*CUSTER'S LAST STAND
Quentin Reynolds
Grades 5-9. Illus. 160 pp. Random House, 1964. $8.99; paper, $2.95.

CUSTER'S PRELUDE TO GLORY
Herbert Krause & Gary Olson
Illus. 280 pp. Brevet Press, $19.95.

CUSTER'S SEVENTH CAVALRY AND THE CAMPAIGN OF 1873
Lawrence A. Frost
Illus. 255 pp. Upton & Sons, 1986. $45.00.

*CUT FROM THE SAME CLOTH: AMERICAN WOMEN OF MYTH, LEGEND, & TALL TALE
Robert D. San Souci, Editor
15 tales. Grades 8 and up. Illus. 140 pp. Philomel Books, 1993. $16.95.

CYCLES OF CONQUEST: THE IMPACT OF SPAIN, MEXICO & THE U.S. ON INDIANS OF THE SOUTHWEST, 1533-1960
Edward H. Spicer
More than 400 years of cultural history of some 25 Southwestern tribes. Illus. 609 pp. Paper. University of Arizona Press, 1962. $19.95.

CYCLORAMA OF GEN. CUSTER'S LAST FIGHT: A REPRODUCTION OF THE ORIGINAL DOCUMENT COMPLETE IN ALL RESPECTS
John M. Carroll, intro by
Reprint of 1889 edition. Illus. 104 pp. Upton & Sons, $30.00.

D

DAHCOTAH: OR, LIFE & LEGENDS OF THE SIOUX AROUND FORT SNELLING
Mary Eastman
Facsimile of 1849 edition. Illus. Ayer Co., $24.50.

DAILY AFFIRMATIONS FROM THE DIVINE CREATOR
Willie C. Hooks
75 pp. Paper. JTE Associates, 1990. $7.95.

A DAKOTA-ENGLISH DICTIONARY
Stephen R. Riggs
Reprint of 1852 edition. 680 pp. Paper. Minnesota Historical Society Press, $24.95.

*DAKOTA INDIANS COLORING BOOK
Chet Kozlak
Grades 1-3. Map. 32 pp. Paper. Minnesota Historical Society Press, $2.50.

*DAKOTA & OJIBWE PEOPLE IN MINNESOTA
Frances Densmore
Grades 5-8. Illus. 55 pp. Paper. Minnesota Historical Society, 1977. $3.50.

THE DAKOTA OR SIOUX IN MINNESOTA: AS THEY WERE IN 1834
Samuel W. Pond
192 pp. Paper. Minnesota Historical Society Press, 1986. $8.95.

DAKOTA ORATORY: GREAT MOMENTS IN THE RECORDED SPEECH OF THE EAST-ERN SIOUX, 1695-1874
compiled & illus. by Mark Diedrich
Illus. 102 pp. Paper. Coyote Books (MN), 1989. $16.95.

DAKOTA PANORAMA
J. Leonard Jennewein & Jane Boorman
Illus. 468 pp. Paper. Brevet Press, $14.95.

DAKOTA SIOUX INDIAN DICTIONARY
Paul Warcloud
English to Sioux translations of over 4,000 words. Developed for beginners interested in the Sioux language by artist and author Paul Warcloud. 192 pp. Paper. Center for Western Studies, $5.95.

DAKOTA: A SPIRITUAL GEOGRAPHY
Kathleen Norris
An evokation of the Great Plains, weaves together the lives of farmers, townsfolk, Native Americans, and a community of Benedictine monks. 224 pp. Paper. Houghton Mifflin, 1994. $9.95.

DAKOTA TEXTS
Ella C. Deloria
Reprint of 1932 edition. AMS Press, $34.50. Paper. Dakota Press, $10.95.

DAKOTA WAR WHOOP
H.E. McConkey
Reprint of 1864 edition. Ross & Haines, $15.

DAKOTA WAY OF LIFE SERIES
Incorporates Indian legends & culture with Christian teaching. using Indian designs, Indian art & photographs of Indian people. Pre-school, Teacher's Guide, $7.50; Grades 1-12, Student text, $2.50; Teacher Guide, $4.75. American Indian Culture Research Center.

DAMMED INDIANS: THE PICK-SLOAN PLAN & THE MISSOURI RIVER SIOUX, 1944-1980
Michael L. Lawson
Reprint of 1982 edition, with a new preface by the author, and a new foreword by Vine Deloria, Jr. Illus. 288 pp. Paper. University of Oklahoma Press, $14.95.

DANCES OF THE TEWA PUEBLO INDIANS: EXPRESSIONS OF LIFE
Jill D. Sweet
Illus. 100 pp. Paper. School of American Research, 1985. $9.95.

DANCES & STORIES OF THE AMERICAN INDIAN
Bernard S. Mason
Reprint of 1944 edition. Illus. Paper. Books on Demand, $53.20.

DANCES WITH WOLVES
Blake
Plains Indian struggle for survival during the late 1800s. Illus. Center for Western Studies, 1989. $16.95.

DANCING COLORS: PATHS OF NATIVE AMERICAN WOMEN
C.J. Brafford & Laine Thom
Illus. 120 pp. Chronicle Books, 1992. $29.95; paper, $18.95.

*DANCING DRUM
Terri Cohlene
Grades 4-8. Illus. 50 pp. Rourke Corp., 1990. $19.95; paper, $14.95.

DANCING GODS: INDIAN CEREMONIALS OF NEW MEXICO & ARIZONA
Erna Fergusson
Illus. 328 pp. Paper. University of New Mexico Press, $12.95.

THE DANCING HEALERS: A DOCTOR'S JOURNEY OF HEALING WITH NATIVE AMERICANS
Carl Hammerschlag
128 pp. Harper & Row, 1988. $14.45.

DANCING ON THE RIM OF THE WORLD: AN ANTHOLOGY OF CONTEMPORARY NORTHWEST NATIV AMERICAN WRITING
Andrea Lerner, Ed
266 pp. University of Arizona Press, 1990. $37.50; paper, $16.95.

*DANCING TEPEES: POEMS OF AMERICAN INDIAN YOUTH
Virginia Sneve
Grades K-3. Illus. 32 pp. Holiday House, 1989. $15.95; paper, $5.95.

DANCING WITH CREATION
Martha Kirk
Paper. Resource Publications, 1983. $7.95.

DANCING WITH INDIANS
Angela Shelf Medearis
An African-American family attends a Seminole celebration & participants. Illus. 32 pp. Holiday House, 1991. $14.95; paper, $5.95.

DANGEROUS PASSAGE: THE SANTA FE TRAIL & THE MEXICAN WAR
William Y. Chalfant
Tells the story of the Santa Fe Trail and the Indians who onces lived on it. Ilus. Photos. Biblio. University of Oklahoma Press, 1994. $29.95.

DARING DONALD McKAY: OR, THE LAST WAR TRIAL OF THE MODOCS
Keith and Donna Clark, Editors
Illus. Paper. Oregon Historical Society, 1971. $2.95.

DARK LADY DREAMING
Amy Cordova
A contemporary Native American/Hispanic artist discusses the methods and spiritual commitments inher work. Illus. 15 pp. The origins Program, $5.95.

*THE DARK SIDE OF THE MOON
Tom Kovach
Grades 1-4. Illus. 32 pp. Council for Indian Education, $8.45; paper, $2.45.

DAUGHTERS OF THE EARTH
Carolyn Niethammer
Paper. Macmillan, 1977. $11.95.

DAWN IN ARCTIC ALASKA
Diamond Jenness
Illus. 225 pp. Paper. University of Chicago Press, 1985. $8.95.

DAWN LAND
Joseph Bruchac
First novel by a Native American storyteller. 332 pp. Fulcrum Publishing & AISES, 1992. $19.95. Also on audiocassettes, $16.95.

THE DAWN OF THE WORLD: MYTHS & TALES OF THE MIWOK INDIANS OF CALIFORNIA
C. Hart Merriam, Editor
Illus. Maps. 273 pp. University of Nebraska Press, 1993. $30; paper, $9.95.

*DAWN RIDER
Jan Hudson
Details of tribal life. Fiction. Grades 4-8. 192 pp. Philomel, 1990. $14.95.

DAWNLAND ENCOUNTERS: INDIANS & EUROPEANS IN NORTHERN NEW ENGLAND
Colin G. Calloway
Illus. 300 pp. Paper. University Press of New England, 1991. $15.95.

*THE DAY OF THE OGRE KACHINAS: A HOPI INDIAN FABLE
Peggy Spence
Grades K-3. Illus. 48 pp. Paper. Roberts Rinehart, 1994. $4.95.

DEAD TOWNS OF ALABAMA
W. Stuart Harris
176 pp. Ilus. University of Arizona Press, 1977. $10.95.

DEAD VOICES: NATURAL AGONIES IN THE NEW WORLD
Gerald Vizenor
Using tales drawn from traditional tribal stories, this book illuminates the centuries of conflict between American Indians & Europeans. 152 pp. Paper. University of Oklahoma Press, 1994. $9.95.

DEATH IN THE DESERT: THE FIFTY YEARS' WAR FOR THE GREAT SOUTHWEST
Paul Wellman
Illus. 318 pp. University of Nebraska Press, 1987. $27.95; paper, $8.95.

THE DEATH OF BERNADETTE LEFTHAND
Ron Querry
Alcohol & witchcraft and a mysterious murder in Navajo territory. 232 pp. Red Crane Books, 1993, $23.95; paper, $12.95.

*DEATH OF THE IRON HORSE
Paul Goble
Grades K-3. Illus. Macmillan, 1987. $13.95.

THE DEATH OF JIM LONELY
James Welch
Novel about a modern American Indian, with no tribe and no real home. 192 pp. Paper. Penguin USA, $8.

*THE DEATH OF JIMMY LITTLEWOLF: AN INDIAN BOY AT BOYS RANCH
R.L. Templeton
Grades 4-7. Eakin Publications, 1980. $6.95.

DEATH ON THE PRAIRIE: THE THIRTY YEARS' STRUGGLE FOR THE WESTERN PLAINS
Paul Wellman
Illus. 322 pp. University of Nebraska Press, 1987. $27.95; paper, $8.95.

THE DEATH & REBIRTH OF THE SENECA
Anthony F. Wallace
416 pp. Paper. Random House, 1972. $6.36.

DEATH, TOO, FOR THE HEAVY-RUNNER
Ben Bennett
Illus. 192 pp. Paper. Mountain Press, 1982. $7.95.

DEATH VALLEY: GEOLOGY, ECOLOGY, ARCHAEOLOGY
Charles B. Hunt
256 pp. University of California Press, 1975. $19.95; paper, $11.95.

DEBERT: A PALEO-INDIAN SITE IN CENTRAL NOVA SCOTIA
George MacDonald
Third revised edition. Illus. 205 pp. Paper. Persimmon, 1985. $13.95.

DECEMBER'S CHILD: A BOOK OF CHUMASH ORAL NARRATIVES
Thomas Blackburb, Editor
360 pp. Univerity of California Press, 1976. $25.00; paper, $10.95.

THE DECORATIVE ART OF THE INDIANS OF THE NORTH PACIFIC COAST
Franz Boas
Reprint of 1897 ed. Illus. AMS Press, $14.00.

DECORATIVE ART OF THE SOUTHWESTERN INDIANS
Dorothy S. Sides
Reprint of 1962 edition. Illus. 100 pp. Paper. Dover, $4.95.

DEER TRACK: A LATE WOODLAND VILLAGE IN THE MISSISSIPPI VALLEY
Charles McGimsey & Michael Conner, Editors
Illus. 134 pp. Paper. Center for American Archaeology, 1985. $7.95.

DEERSKINS & DUFFELS: THE CREEK INDIAN TRADE WITH ANGLO-AMERICA, 1685-1815
Kathryn E. Holland Braund
Illus. Maps. 310 pp. University of Nebraska Press, 1993. $37.50.

*THE DEFENDERS
Ann McGovern
Grades 3-7. Illus. 128 pp. Paper. Scholastic, Inc., 1987. $2.50.

DELFINA CUERO: HER AUTOBIOGRAPHY
Florence C. Shipek
Illus. 101 pp. Ballena Press, 1991. $16; paper , $12.

THE DELAWARE INDIANS: A HISTORY
C.A. Weslager
570 pp. Paper. Rutgers University Press, 1990. $19.95.

THE DELAWARE & SHAWNEE ADMITTED TO CHEROKEE CITIZENSHIP & THE RELATED WYANDOTTE & MORAVIAN DELAWARE
Toni Jollay Prevost
Contains information on migration patterns; missionary school data; 1860 & 1870 federal census of Wyandotte County , Kansas. 129 pp. Paper. Heritage Books, 1992. $21.50.

THE DELAWARES: CRITICAL BIBLIOGRAPHY
C.A. Weslager
Paper. Indiana University Press, 1978. $4.95.

DELIBERATE ACTS: CHANGING HOPI CULTURE THROUGH THE ORAIBI SPLIT
Peter M. Whiteley
373 pp. University of Arizona Press, 1988. $45.

DELIGHT MAKERS
Adolph F. Bandelier
A fictional reconstruction of prehistoric Indian culture in the American Southwest by a 19th century archaeologist. Illus. 490 pp. Paper . Harcourt Brace, 1971. $12.95.

THE DEMOGRAPHICS OF AMERICAN INDIANS
Statistics based on 1980 census. Illus. 25 pp. Paper. AISES, $6.

DENA'INA LEGACY K'TL'EGH'I SUKDU: THE COLLECTED WRITINGS OF PETER KALIFORNSKY
Peter Kalfornsky; James Kari & Alan Boraas, Eds.
Illus. Photos. Maps. 485 pp. Paper . CIRI & Alaska Native Language Center , 1991. $16.

DENA'INA NOUN DICTIONARY
James Kari, Compiled by
Illus. 355 pp. Paper . Alaska Native Language Center, 1977. $8.

DENE NATION: THE COLONY WITHIN
Mel Watkins
Paper. University of Toronto Press, 1977. $12.95.

DENETSOSIE
B. Johnson and S.M. Callaway , Editors
Revised edition. Illus. 51 pp. Navajo Curriculum, 1974. $5.

DENIZENS OF THE DESERT: A TALE IN WORD & PICTURE OF LIFE AMONG THE NAVAJO INDIANS
Elizabeth Forster & Laura Gilpin
Martha Sandweiss, Editor
Illus. 160 pp. University of New Mexico Press, 1988. $24.95.

FRANCES DENSMORE & AMERICAN INDIAN MUSIC
Charles Hofmann
127 pp. Paper. National Museum of the American Indian, 1968. $5.

DESCRIPTION – NATURAL HISTORY OF THE COASTS OF NORTH AMERICA
N. Denys; W.F. Ganong, Editor
Reprint of 1908 edition. Greenwood Press, $42.

DESCRIPTION OF A JOURNEY & VISIT TO THE PAWNEE INDIANS
Dottlieb Oehler and David Smith
32 pp. Ye Galleon, $7.50; paper , $4.95.

DESERT FORAGERS & HUNTERS: INDIANS OF THE DEATH VALLEY REGION
William J. and Edith W allace
Illus. Paper. Acoma Books, 1979. $3.25.

DESERT IMMIGRANTS: THE MEXICAN OF EL PASO, 1880-1920
Mario T. Garcia
Illus. 328 pp. Yale University Press, 1981. $32.50; paper, $11.95.

*THE DESERT IS THEIRS
Byrd Baylor
Grades P-3. Illus. Macmillan, 1987. $13.95; paper, $4.95.

THE DESERT LAKE: THE ST ORY OF NEVADA'S PYRAMID LAKE
Sessions S. Wheeler
Prehistory and history of the basin, including its famous Indian battles. Illus. Biblio. 139 pp. Paper . The Caxton Printers, $7.95.

DESERT LIGHT: MYTHS & VISIONS OF THE GEAT SOUTHWEST
John Miller , Editor
Illus. 120 pp. Paper . Chronicle Books, 1990. $18.95.

THE DESERT SMELLS LIKE RAIN: A NATURALIST IN PAPAGO INDIAN COUNTRY
Gary P. Nabhan
176 pp. Paper. North Point Press, 1987. $8.95.

DESIGNING WITH THE WOOL
Noel Bennett
Illus. 128 pp. Paper . Northland, 1979. $8.95.

DESIGNS & FACTIONS: POLITICS, RELIGION, & CERAMICS ON THE HOPI THIRD MESA
Lydia Wyckoff
Illus. 210 pp. Paper . University of New Mexico Press, 1990. $24.95.

DESIGNS ON PREHIST ORIC HOPI POTTERY
Jesse W. Fewkes
Reprint. Illus. 290 pp. Paper . Dover, 1973. $7.95.

THE DESTRUCTION OF AMERICAN INDIAN F AMILIES
Steven Unger , Editor
Paper. Association on American Indian Affairs, 1977. $4.25.

THE DESTRUCTION OF CALIFORNIA INDIANS
Robert F. Heizer
Reveals how thousands of California natives died from 1847 to 1865. Illus. Paper . University of Nebraska Press, 1993. $12.95.

THE DEVELOPMENT OF CAPIT ALISM IN THE NAVAJO NATION: A POLITICAL-ECONOMIC HIST ORY
Lawrence D. W eiss
180 pp. MEP Pubns, 1984. $29.95; paper ,$10.95.

THE DEVELOPMENT OF SOUTHEASTERN ARCHAEOLOGY
Jay K. Johnson, Editor
352 pp. Paper. University of Alabama Press, 1993. $29.95.

THE DEVIL IN THE NEW WORLD: THE IMPACT OF DIABOLISM IN NEW SP AIN
Fernando Cervantes
Reveals how Native American reinterpreted the view of Christianity presented to them. He deals with the social history of the interaction between the two cultures. Illus. 192 pp. Yale University Press, 1994. $22.50.

DEZBA, NAVAJO WOMAN OF THE DESERT
Gladys A. Reichard
Illus. 220 pp. Paper . Rio Grande Press, $12.

THE DIARIO OF CHRIST OPHER COLUMBUS'S FIRST VOY AGE TO AMERICA 1492-1493
trans. by Oliver Dunn & James Kelley , Jr.
Illus. 504 pp. University of Oklahoma Press, 1993. $65; paper , $24.95.

THE DIARY OF ELI SHELDON GLOVER
Eli S. Glover
75 pp. Ye Galleon Press, 1987. $12.95.

DICTIONARY OF THE ALABAMA LANGUAGE
Cora Sylestine, Heather Hardy , et al
The language of the Alabama-Coushatta Indian Reservation in Polk County , Texas. Over 8,000 entries. 765 pp. University of Texas Press, $35.

DICTIONARY OF THE AMERICAN INDIAN
John Stoutenburgh, Jr .
Sourcebook of American Indian history and lore. 480 pp. Cherokee Publications, $9.95.

DICTIONARY CATALOG OF THE EDWARD E. AYER COLLECTION OF AMERICANA & AMERICAN INDIANS
Newberry Library Staff
16 Volumes and First Supplement. G.K. Hall, 1970. $1,280.00; First Supplement, $365.

DICTIONARY OF DAILY LIFE OF INDIANS OF THE AMERICAS
2 vols. 2,000 pp. American Indian Publishers, 1982. $165. per set.

DICTIONARY OF INDIAN TRIBES OF THE AMERICAS
2nd edition. 3 vols. Illus. 2,000 pp. American Indian Publishers, 1981. $375 per set.

DICTIONARY OF INDIANS OF NORTH AMERICA
Harry Waldman, Editor
Reprint of 1978 edition. 3 vols. Scholarly Press, $145.

DICTIONARY OF MESA GRANDE DIEGUENO
Ted Couro & Christina Hutcheson
First dictionary published of a Yuman Indian language. Paper. Malki Museum Press, 1979. $7.50.

DICTIONARY OF NATIVE AMERICAN MYTHOLOGY
Sam D. Gill & Irene F. Sullivan
Describes past & present rituals, traditions, and myths of over 100 Native American cultures. Biblio. 425 pp. ABC-Clio, 1992. $65.

DICTIONARY OF THE OJIBWAY LANGUAGE
Frederica Baraga
Compiled nearly 150 years ago. Reprint of 1878 edition. 736 pp. Paper . Minnesota Historical Society, $24.95.

A DICTIONARY OF THE OSAGE LANGUAGE
Francis La Fleche
Reprint of 1932 edition. Scholarly Press, $69.

A DICTIONARY OF PAPAGO USAGE
M. Mathiot
504 pp. Mouton de Gruyter , $50.

DICTIONARY OF PREHISTORIC INDIAN ARIFACTS OF THE AMERICAN SOUTHWEST
Franklin Barnett
Reprint of 1973 edition. Illus. 128 pp. Paper . Hothem House, $12.95.

DIGEST OF AMERICAN INDIAN LAW: CASES & CHRONOLOGY
H. Barry Holt & Gary Forrester
140 pp. Fred B. Rothman & Co., 1990. $35.

DIGEST OF DECISIONS RELATING TO INDIAN AFFAIRS
U.S. Bureau of Indian Affairs
Reprint of 1901 edition. Kraus, $29.

*DINE, THE NAVAJO
Suan L. Shaffer, Editor
Grade 6. Illus. Includes 30 student booklets, one teacher's resource binder which includes transparencies, color slides and audiocassette. Heard Museum, 1987. $295.

THE DINE: ORIGIN MYTHS OF THE NAVAHO INDIANS
Aileen O'Brien
Reprint of 1956 edition. Reprint Services, $75.

DINE BAHANE: NAVAJO CREATION STORY
Paul G. Zolbrod
368 pp. Paper. University of New Mexico Press & AISES, 1984. $15.95.

DINETAH: NAVAJO HISTORY
Robert A. Roessel; T.L. McCarty, Editor
Volume III. Illus. 180 pp. Navajo Curriculum, 1983. $15.

DIPLOMATS IN BUCKSKINS: HISTORYOF INDIAN DELEGATIONS IN WASHINGTON CITY
Herman J. Viola
Illus. 234 pp. Smithsonian, 1981. $21.95.

DIRECTORY OF AMERICAN INDIAN LAW ATTORNEYS
150 pp. Native Word Research & Publishing, 1990-91. $35.00.

DIRECTORY OF FINANCIAL AID TO MINORITIES
Gail Schlachter, Editor
Includes a section on financial aid to Native Americans. 450 pp. Biennial.

DIRECTORY OF NATIVE AMERICAN PERFORMING ARTISTS
Lists artists and groups available for booking and performances. Includes storytellers, musicians, dancers, poets, singers, and craft demonstrators. Atlatl, 1991. $3.

DIRECTORY OF NATIVE EDUCATION RESOURCES IN THE NORTHWEST REGION
Lists about 600 organizations in the 5-state region that provide educational services to Native Americans and Alaska Natives. 73 pp. paper . NWREL, 1994. $7.

DIRTY BOY: A JICARILLA TALE OF RAID & WAR
Morris E. Opler
Reprint of 1938 edition. Kraus, $15.

DISCOVER INDIAN RESERVATIONS: A VISITOR'S WELCOME GUIDE
Veronica Tiller
Lists reservations by state,providing a tribal profile, location, sites, events, etc. for each. Paper. Council Publications, 1992. AISES, $19.95.

DISCOVERED LANDS, INVENTED PASTS: TRANSFORMING VISIONS OF THE AMERICAN WEST
Jules David Prown, et al
Presents a major reinterpretation of western American art of the past three centuries. Includes depictions of Indians by early explorers. Illus. 232 pp. Yale University Press, 1992. $40; paper , $25.

DISCOVERY OF THE YOSEMITE & THE INDIAN WAR OF 1851 WHICH LED TO THE EVENT
Lafayette H. Bunnell
Original source history of Yosemite Valley. Reprint of 1911 edition. 340 pp. Paper . Yosemite Association, $9.95.

DISEASE CHANGE & THE ROLE OF MEDICINE: THE NAVAJO EXPERIENCE
Stephen Kunitz
Paper. U. of California Press, 1989. $10.95.

DISEASE, DEPOPULATION & CULTURE CHANGE IN NORTHWESTERN NEW SPAIN, 1518-1764
Daniel T. Reff
Illus. 415 pp. U. of Utah Press, 1990. $30.

DISPOSSESSING THE AMERICAN INDIAN: INDIAN & WHITESON THE COLONIAL FRONTIER
Wilbur R. Jacobs
Illus. 256 pp. Paper . University of Oklahoma Press, 1972. $9.95.

THE DISPOSSESSION OF THE AMERICAN INDIAN, 1887-1934
Janet A. McDonnell
Illus. 176 pp. Indiana U. Press, 1991. $20.

DISPUTED WATERS: NATIVE AMERICA & THE GREAT LAKE FISHERY
Robert Doherty
210 pp. U. Press of Kentucky , 1990. $24.

DIVING FOR NORTHWEST RELICS
James S. White
Illus. Binfort-Metropolitan, 1979. $8.95; paper , $6.50.

DIVISIVENESS & SOCIAL CONFLICT: AN ANTHROPOLOGICAL APPROACH
Alan R. Beals and Bernard J. Siegel
185 pp. Stanford University Press, 1966. $19.50.

DIX-HUIT ANS CHEZ LES SAUVAGES: VOYAGES ET MISSIONS DE MONSEIGNEUR HENRY FARAUD
Henry Faraud
Reprint of 1866 edition. Johnson Reprint, $28.

DO THEM NO HARM
Zoa L. Swayne
Lewis and Clark Expedition among the Nez Perce Indians in the Clearwater Valley in Idaho. Illus. 350 pp. Legacy House, 1990. $25.95.

*DOCTOR COYOTE
John Bierhorst; illus. by Wendy Watson
Grades 2-6. Illus. Macmillan, 1988. $15.95.

DOCTORS OF MEDICINE IN NEW MEXICO: A HISTORY OF HEALTH & MEDICAL PRACTICE, 1886-1986
Jake W. Spidle, Jr.
Illus. 400 pp. University of New Mexico Press, 1986. $29.95.

DOCUMENTS OF U.S. INDIAN POLICY
Francis P. Prucha, Editor
Selection of primary documents important in Indian-white relations. Illus. 2nd Edition. 340 pp. University of Nebraska Press, 1990. $35.00; paper , $12.95.

*DOGSONG
Gary Paulsen
Grades 7 and up. Illus. Macmillan, 1989. $13.95.

DOING FIELDWORK: WARNINGS & ADVICE
Rosalie H. Wax
Reprint of 1971 edition. 396 pp. Paper . University of Chicago Press, $20.

DON'T BLAME THE INDIANS: NATIVE AMERICANS & THE MECHANIZED DOORS OF PERCEPTION
Aldous Huxley
Paper. Harper & Row, 1970. $3.95.

*THE DOUBLE LIFE OF POCAHONTAS
Jean Fritz
Dispels myths & describes the life of the girl whose active conscience made her a pawn, exploited by her own people and the white world. Grades 4-8. Illus. 96 pp. Putnam, 1983. $13.95.

THE DOVE ALWAYS CRIED: NARRATIVES OF INDIAN SCHOOL LIFE
Marguerite Bigler Stoltz
Author's experiences as a teacher in schools for Indian children in the 1920s-30s, plus tales by some of her pupils. Paper . Pocahontas Press, 1994. $8.95.

DR. JOHN McLOUGHLIN, MASTER OF FORT VANCOUVER, FATHER OF OREGON
Nancy Wilson; Bert Webber, Editor
Treatment of Indians is included. Illus. Maps. Biblio. Paper. Webb Research Group, $12.95.

DRAGONFLY'S TALE
Kristina Rodanas
Native American folklore. Paper . Clarion Books, 1993. $14.95.

DRAMATIC ELEMENTS IN AMERICAN INDIAN CEREMONIALS
Virginia S. Heath
Paper. Haskell House, 1970. $22.95.

DRAWINGS OF THE SONG ANIMALS; NEW & SELECTED POEMS
Duane Niatum
Poetry. Drawing on his native heritage, Niatum interweaves the themes of aging and human community. 136 pp. Holy Cow! Press, 1994. $18.95; paper, $10.95.

THE DREAM DANCE OF THE CHIPPEWA & MENOMINEE INDIANS OF NORTHERN WISCONSIN
Samuel A. Barrett
Reprint of 1911 edition. AMS Press & Garland Publishing, $24.50.

*DREAM FEATHER
Stan Padilla
Story of a young boy's spiritual awakening. Grades 5 and up. Illus. 60 pp. Paper. The Book Publishing Co., 1991. $11.95.

THE DREAM SEEKERS: NATIVE AMERICAN VISIONARY TRADITIONS OF THE GREAT PLAINS
Lee Irwin
Demonstrates the central importance of visionary dreams as sources of empowerment and innovation in Plains Indian religion. Biblio. 320 pp. University of Oklahoma Press, 1994. $26.95.

*DREAM WOLF
Paul Goble
Grades 4 and up. Illus. Macmillan, 1988. $13.95.

*DREAMCATCHER
Audrey Osofsky; illus. by Ed Young
Free verse text with glimpses of Ojibwe life. Grades PS-3. Illus. 32 pp. Orchard Books, $15.

*DREAMPLACE
George Ella Lyon
When a young girl visits the Pueblo where the Anasazi lives, she sees images of its past inhabitants' history. Grades PS-3. Illus. 32 pp. Orchard Books, $16.

DREAMER-PROPHETS OF THE COLUMBIA PLATEAU: SMOHALLA & SKOLASKIN
Robert Ruby & John Brown
Illus. 275 pp. U. of Oklahoma Press, 1989. $23.95.

DREAMERS WITH POWER: THE MENOMINEE
George & Louise Spindler
Reprint of 1971 edition. Illus. 208 pp. Paper. Waveland Press, 1984. $9.95.

DRESS CLOTHING OF THE PLAINS INDIANS
Ronald P. Koch
Illus. 238 pp. Paper. Center for Western Studies & University of Oklahoma Press, 1977. $13.95.

DRINKING BEHAVIOR AMONG THE SOUTH-WESTERN INDIANS: AN ANTHROPOLOGI-CAL PERSPECTIVE
Jack Waddell & Michael Everett, Editors
248 pp. Paper. University of Arizona Press, 1980. $16.95.

DRIFTING THROUGH ANCESTOR DREAMS
Ramson Lomatewama
Poetry. Illus. 72 pp. Northland Publishing, $9.95.

DRINKING CAREERS: A 25-YEAR STUDY OF THREE NAVAJO POPULATIONS
Stephen J. Kunitz & Jerrold E. Levy
First long-term follow-up study of alcohol use among Native Americans. 300 pp. Yale University Press, 1994. $28.50.

DRUM SONGS: GLIMPSES OF DENE HISTORY
Kerry Abel
Examines the history of the Dene, one of the aboriginal peoples of Canada's western subarctic. Illus. Maps. McGill-Queen's University Press, 1993. $44.95; paper, $19.95.

DRY BONES, DAKOTA TERRITORY REFLECTED
John & Pauline Gregg
Ancient diseases in the northern Plains; problems concerning the prehistory of the Great Plains native populations. Paper. University of South Dakota Press, 1987. $25.

THE DULL KNIFE BATTLE
Fred H. Werner
Paper. Werner Publications, 1981. $6.95.

THE DUNBAR-ALLIS LETTERS ON THE PAWNEE
John Dunbar and Samuel Allis
Reprint. 192 pp. Garland Publishing, $35.

DURING MY TIME: FLORENCE EDENSHAW DAVIDSON, A HAIDA WOMAN
Margaret B. Blackman
Illus. 228 pp. Paper. University of Washington Press, 1982. $12.95.

THE DUST ROSE LIKE SMOKE: THE SUBJUGATION OF THE ZULU & THE SIOUX
James O. Gump
Illus. Maps. 260 pp. University of Nebraska Press, 1994. $30..

DWELLERS AT THE SOURCE: SOUTH-WESTERN INDIAN PHOTOGRAPHS OF A.C. VROMAN
William Webb & Robert Weinstein
Illus. 223 pp. University of New Mexico Press, 1987. $42.50; paper, $27.50.

THE DYNAMICS OF GOVERNMENT PROGRAMS FOR URBAN INDIANS IN THE PRAIRIE PROVINCES
Raymond Breton and Gail Grant
628 pp. Paper. Gower, 1984. $19.95.

DYNAMICS OF SOUTHWEST PREHISTORY
Linda Cordell & George Gumerman, Editors
Illus. 390 pp. Smithsonian Press, 1989. $39.95.

E

*EAGLE FEATHER FOR A CROW
Alice Durland Ryniker
Grades Grades 2-6. A Crow Indian boy growing up. Illus. 80 pp. The Lowell Press, $9.95.

AN EAGLE NATION
Carter Revard
Poetry. 125 pp. University of Arizona Press, $35; paper, $14.95.

EAGLE TRANSFORMING: THE ART OF ROBERT DAVIDSON
Robert Davidson; photos by Ulli Steltzer
Discusses the place of art in Haida culture. Illus. 174 pp. University of Washington Press, $39.95.

EARLY ACCOUNT OF THE CHOCTAW INDIANS
John Swanton
Reprint of 1918 edition. Paper. Kraus Reprint, $15.

EARLY AMERICAN INDIAN DOCUMENTS: TREATIES & LAWS, 1607-1789
Alden T. Vaughan
20 volumes. 7,000 pp. University Publications, 1983. $1,500 per set.

EARLY AMERICAN WRITINGS
Giles Gunn, Editor
Includes writings from Cherokee, Hopi, and other Amerindian genesis legends. 720 pp. Penguin USA, 1994. $12.95.

EARLY ENCOUNTERS - NATIVE AMERI-CANS & EUROPEANS IN NEW ENGLAND FROM THE PAPERS OF W. SEARS NICKERSON
Delores Bird Carpenter, Editor
19 essays from the papers of Warren Sears Nickerson (1880-1966), New England historian, antiquarian, and genealogist. Illus. 200 pp. Michigan State University Press, $28.85.

EARLY EXPLORERS OF NORTH AMERICA
C. Keith Wilbur, MD, Editor
Recreates the clash of two dissimilar cultures. 144 pp. Paper. Gobe Pequot Press, $11.95.

EARLY HISTORY OF THE CREEK INDIANS & THEIR NEIGHBORS
John Swanton
Reprint of 1922 edition. Johnson Reprint & Scholarly Press, $46.

EARLY INDIAN TRADE GUNS: 1625-1775
T.M. Hamilton
Illus. Paper. Museum of the Great Plains, 1968. $6.95.

EARLY INTERVENTION WITH AMERICAN INDIAN FAMILIES: AN ANNOTATED BIBLI-OGRAPHY
Readings containing information about the influence of Indian culture and its affect on Indian families whose young children have health impairments or disabilities. Southwest Communication Resources, $10.

EARLY LATE WOODLAND OCCUPATIONS IN THE FALL CREEK LOCALITY OF THE MISSISSIPPI VALLEY
David T. Morgan & C. Russell Stafford, Editors
Illus. 145 pp. Paper. Center for American Archaeology, 1987. $7.95.

EARLY MAN IN THE NEW WORLD
Richard J. Shutler, Jr., Editor
Illus. 200 pp. Sage, 1983. $32.00; paper, $16.95.

EARLY POTTERY IN THE SOUTHEAST: TRADITION & INNOVATION IN COOKING TECHNOLOGY
Kenneth E. Sassaman
312 pp. Paper. University of Alabama Press, 1993. $27.95.

EARLY PREHISTORIC AGRICULTURE IN THE AMERICAN SOUTHWEST
W.H. Wills
Illus. 196 pp. University of Washington Press & School of American Research, $27.50.

THE EARLY PREHISTORIC SOUTHEAST: A SOURCEBOOK
Jerald T. Milanich, Editor
400 pp. Garland Publishing, 1985. $55.

EARLY PUEBLOAN OCCUPATIONS: TESUQUE BY-PASS AND UPPER RIO GRANDE VALLEY
Charles McNutt
Illus. Paper. University of Michigan, Museum of Anthropology, 1969. $3.

EARLY TREATIES WITH THE SOUTHERN CHEYENNE & ARAPAHO
Raymond J. DeMallie
35 pp. Institute for the Development of Indian Law, $10.

EARLY WHITE INFLUENCE UPON PLAINS INDIAN PAINTING: GEORGE CATLIN & CARL BODMER AMONG THE MANDAN, 1832-34
John C. Ewers
Illus. Paper. Territorial Press, 1989. $4.50.

THE EARLY YEARS OF NATIVE AMERICAN ART HISTORY: THE POLITICS & SCHOLARSHIP OF COLLECTING
Janet Catherine Berlo, Editor
Anthology of academic essays on the development of Native American artifact collections and the historiography of Native American material culture. Illus. 244 pp. University of Washington Press, 1993. $30.

EARTH ELDER STORIES
Alexander Wolfe
Stories by a Salteaux leader who lived in Canada's Northwest Territories and the U.S. Great Plains in the 1800s. Greenfield Review Press, $9.95.

EARTH FIRE: A HOPI LEGEND OF THE SUNSET CRATER ERUPTION
E. Malotki & M. Lomatuway'ma
Illus. 150 pp. Paper. Northland, 1987. $19.95.

EARTH IS MY MOTHER, SKY IS MY FATHER
Trudy Griffin-Pierce
Space, time, astronomy in Navajo Sand Painting. Illus. 230 pp. AISES, $29.95.

THE EARTH IS OUR MOTHER: A GUIDE TO THE INDIANS OF CALIFORNIA, THEIR LOCALES & HISTORY SITES
Dolan Eargle, Jr.
4th edition. 200 pp. Paper. Trees Co. Press, 1993-94. $12.95.

EARTH MAGIC: SKY MAGIC: NORTH AMERICAN INDIAN TALES
Rosalind Kerven
Illus. 95 pp. Cambridge University Press, 1991. $12.95; paper, $7.95.

EARTH MEDICINE: ANCESTOR'S WAYS OF HARMONY FOR MANY MOONS
Jamie Sams
364 daily offerings organized according to the cycles of the moon. Insights into the spirituality of the earth. 400 pp. Paper. Treasure Chest, 1994. $12.

EARTH POWER COMING: SHORT FICTION IN NATIVE AMERICAN LITERATURE
Simon J. Ortiz
Contemporary fiction by 30 contemporary Native American writers. Paper. Navajo Community College Press, $14.

EARTHDIVERS: TRIBAL NARRATIVES ON MIXED DESCENT
Gerald Vizenor
A series of stories that convey the oral tradition of modern American Indian life. Illus. 195 pp. University of Minnesota Press, 1981. $14.95.

*EARTHMAKER'S TALES: NORTH AMERICAN INDIAN STORIES ABOUT EARTH HAPPENINGS
Gretchen W. Mayo
Grades 5 and up. Illus. 96 pp. Walker & Co., 1989. $11.95.

THE EARTHSHAPERS
Karen Speerstra
Details of daily life, great tribal gfestivals, and reasons behind the gigantic mounds. Illus. 80 pp. Naturegraph, 1977, $15.95; paper, $5.95.

THE EASTERN BAND OF CHEROKEES, 1819-1900
John R. Finger
Illus. 304 pp. Paper. University of Tennessee Press & Cherokee Publications, 1984. $14.50.

THE EASTERN CHEROKEES
William H. Gilbert
Reprint of 1943 edition. AMS Press, $27.50.

EASTERN OJIBWA-CHIPPEWA-OTTAWA DICTIONARY
Richard Rhodes
623 pp. Mouton de Gruyter, $125.

EASTMAN JOHNSON'S LAKE SUPEROR INDIANS
Patricia Condon Johnson
Paintings and drawings of the native Ojibwe at Lake Superior in 1856 & 1857. Illus. 72 pp. Johnston Publishing, $12.95.

ECOCIDE OF NATIVE AMERICA: ENVIRONMENTAL DESTRUCTION OF INDIAN SLANDS & PEOPLES
Donald A. Grinde, Jr. & Bruce E. Johansen
Illus. 224 pp. Clear Light Publishers, 1994, $24.95.

THE ECONOMIC BOTANY OF THE KIOWA INDIANS
Paul A. Vestal and Richard E. Schultes
Reprint of 1939 edition. AMS Press, $21.50.

ECONOMIC DEVELOPMENT ON AMERICAN INDIAN RESERVATIONS
Roxanne D. Ortiz, Editor
157 pp. Paper. University of New Mexico, Native American Studies, 1979. $8.95.

ECONOMICS OF THE IROQUOIS
Sara Stites
Reprint of 1905 edition. AMS Press, $18.

THE ECONOMICS OF SAINTHOOD: RELIGIOUS CHANGE AMONG THE RIMROCK NAVAJOS
Kendall Blanchard
Illus. 244 pp. Fairleigh Dickinson, 1976. $22.50.

EDUCATION ASSISTANCE FOR AMERICAN INDIANS & ALASKA NATIVES
Master of Public Health Program for American Indians
School of Public Health, 1994. No charge.

EDUCATION & CAREER OPPORTUNITIES HANDBOOK
The CIRI Foundation
Lists over 200 scholarships, grant & loan programs for which Alaska Natives may be eligible. Annual. CIRI, $5.

THE EDUCATION OF LITTLE TREE
Forrest Carter
A moving account of a Cherokee as he grows up with his grandparents. 220 pp. Paper. University of New Mexico Press , $10.95.

EDWARD SHERIFF CURTIS: VISIONS OF A VANISHING RACE
Florence Curtis Graybill & Victory Boesen
Paper. Houghton Mifflin, $19.95.

EFFECTIVE PRACTICES IN INDIAN EDUCATION
Floy Pepper
Techniques and ideas to help teachers of Indian children. 211 pp. Teacher's Monograph, 211 pp. $14.80; Curriculum Monograph, 186 pp. $24.45; and Administration Monograph, 86 pp. $11.30. NWREL.

THE EFFECTS OF WHITE CONTACT UPON BLACKFOOT CULTURE
Oscar Lewis
Reprint of 1942 edition. AMS, $20.00.

EL GRINGO: OR, NEW MEXICO AND HER PEOPLE
William W. Davis
Reprint of 1857 edition. Illus. 436 pp. Ayer Co. Publishers, $24.00.

THE ELDER AMERICAN INDIAN
Frank Dukepoo
South Dakota State University Press, 1978. $3.50.

THE ELDERS: PASSING IT ON
Essays, art, photos, and poetry by Native American artists about their elders. Illus. 31 pp. Paper. The Origins Program, $5.95.

ELDERBERRY FLUTE SONG, CONTEMPORARY COYOTE TALES
Peter Blue Cloud
Illus. Greenfield Review Press, $10.

THE ELDERS ARE WATCHING
Dave Bouchard; illus. by Roy H. Vickers
Environmental message. Illus. 66 pp. Paper. Fulcrum Publishing, 1993. $12.95.

ELEMENTARY FORMS OF THE RELIGIOUS LIFE
E. Durkheim; J.W. Swain, Translator
Totems. Paper. Free Press, 1965. $16.95.

ELEVEN YEARS A CAPTIVE AMONG THE SNAKE INDIANS
James Kimball
13 pp. Ye Galleon, 1986. $4.95.

JOHN ELIOT'S INDIAN DIALOGUES: A STUDY IN CULTURAL INTERACTION
J. Eliot; H.W. Bowden and J. Rhonda, Editors
Illus. 173 pp. Greenwood Press, 1980. $35.

THE ELKUS COLLECTION: SOUTHWEST INDIAN ART
Dorothy K. Washburn, Editior
Illus. 222 pp. Paper. University of Washington Press, 1986. $19.95.

ELNGUQ
Anna W. Jacobson
The first novel written in Yup'ik. Reflects a traditional Native Alaskan way of life. 114 pp. Alaska Native Language Center, $13.50, postpaid.

THE EMBATTLED NORTHEAST:
THE ELUSIVE IDEAL OF ALLIANCE IN ABENAKI-EUROAMERICAN RELATIONS
Kenneth Morison
University of California Press, 1984. $37.50.

THE EMIGRANT INDIANS OF KANSAS:
A CRITICAL BIBLIOGRAPHY
William E. Unrau
Illus. 96 pp. Paper. Indiana U. Press, 1980. $4.95.

EMIL W. HAURY'S PREHISTORY
OF THE AMERICAN SOUTHWEST
Emil W. Haury; J. Jefferson Reid & David Doyel, Editors
A collection of Haury's published works. 506 pp. Paper. University of Arizona Press, 1986. $17.50.

EMPIRE OF FORTUNE: CROWNS, COLONIES,
& TRIBES IN THE SEVEN YEARS WAR IN AMERICA
Francis Jennings
W.W. Norton & Co., 1988. $27.

EMPOWERING NORTHERN & NATIVE COMMUNITIES FOR SOCIAL, POLITICAL & ECONOIC CONTROL: AN ANNOTATED BIBLIOGRAPHY OF RELEVANT LITERATURE
M.G. Stevenson, C.G. Hickey
Inuit literature on models for community empowerment. 64 pp. Paper., CCI, 1994. $15.

ENCHANTED MOCCASINS AND OTHER LEGENDS OF THE AMERICAN INDIANS
Cornelius Mathews, Editor
Reprint of 1877 edition. AMS Press, $24.75.

ENCYCLOPEDIA OF FRONTIER BIOGRAPHY
Dan L. Thrapp, Editor
Contains over 5,500 biographies of the men and women who have played major roles in frontier history. GFrom the earliest European explorers to contemporary historians. Includes Indians and Indian agents. 4 vols. The Arthur H. Clark Co. The original three-volume work was published in 1988 and costs $195; paper. $60. Volume 4, Suplemental, 1993. $65.

ENCYCLOPEDIA OF MULTICULTURALISM
Examines American history and society through the experiences of ethnic groups, including Native Americans. 6 Vols. Illus. 2,000 pp. Bibliographies. Marshall Cavendish Corp., 1992.

ENCYCLOPEDIA OF NATIVE AMERICAN RELIGIONS
Arlene Hirschfelder & Paulette Molin
Ceremonies, individuals, places, and concepts from Native American groups across America. 1,200 entries. Includes biographies of religious leaders and Christian missionaries. Illus. 367 pp. Facts on File, 1992. $45.

ENCYCLOPEDIA OF NATIVE AMERICAN TRIBES
Carl Waldman
Contains concise descriptions on history and culture for more than 150 Indian tribes in the U.S., Canada, and Mexico; also a glossary of terms and classified bibliography. Illus. 308 pp. Facts on File, 1987. $35

ENCYCLOPEDIA OF WORLD CULTURES,
Vol. 1 - North America
An overview of American Indian cultures. Articles of traditional cultural practices and beliefs. G.K. Hall, 1991.

THE END OF INDIAN KANSAS: A STUDY OF CULTURAL REVOLUTION, 1854-1871
H. Craig Miner & William E. Unrau
Illus. 196 pp. Paper. University Press of Kansas, 1977. $9.95.

ENDURING CULTURE: A CENTURY OF PHOTOGRAPHY OF THE SOUTHWEST INDIANS
Marcia Keegan
Illus. 120 pp. Clear Light, 1991. $29.95.

THE ENDURING INDIANS OF KANSAS: A CENTURY & A HALF OF ACCULTURATION
Joseph B. Herring
Illus. 248 pp. University Press of Kansas, 1990. $25; paper, $12.95.

THE ENDURING NAVAHO
Laura Gilpin
Illus. 243 photos. 321 pp. University of Texas Press, 1968. $60.

ENDURING SEEDS: NATIVE AMERICAN AGRICULTURE & WILD PLANT CONSERVATION
Gary P. Nabhan
Native ecology, seeds, and roots. 220 pp. Paper. North Point Press, 1991. $11.95.

THE ENDURING STRUGGLE
George H. Phillips, Jr.; N. Hundley and John Schutz, Editors
Illus. 110 pp. Paper. Boyd & Fraser, 1981. $6.95.

ENDURING TRADITIONS:
ART OF THE NAVAJO
Lois Essary Jacka; illus. by Jerry Jacka
Presents modern-day crafts from 192 Navajo artists. 205 full-color photos. 208 pp. Northland Publishing, 1994. $55.

ENDURING VISIONS: ONE THOUSAND YEARS OF SOUTHWESTERN INDIAN ART
D. Erdman and P.M. Hortstein, Editors
Illus. Paper. Aspen Center for Visual Arts, 1979. $12.95.

ENEMY ANCESTORS: THE ANAZASI WORLD, WITH A GUIDE TO SITES
Gary Matlock
128 pp. Paper. Northland Publishing, 1988. $19.95.

AN ENGLISH--BLACKFOOT VOCABULARY
C.C. Uhlenbeck and R.H. Van Gulik
Reprint of 1930 edition. AMS Press, $26.50.

ENGLISH--CHEYENNE DICTIONARY
Paper. Council for Indian Education, 1976. $4.95.

AN ENGLISH-DAKOTA DICTIONARY
John P. Williamson
Reprint of 1902 edition. 288 pp. Paper. Minnesota Historical Society Press, $12.95.

ENGLISH--ESKIMO, ESKIMO–ENGLISH DICTIONARY
P. Shalom Publications, $24.50; thumb-index edition, $29.50.

ENGLISH-ESKIMO, ESKIMO-ENGLISH DICTIONARY
A. Thibert
Revised edition. Paper. IBD Ltd., $18.75.

ENGLISH INSTITUTIONS & THE AMERICAN INDIAN
James A. James
Reprint of 1894 edition. Paper. Johnson Reprint, $9.00. AMS, $11.50.

ENGLISH TO CHOCTAW & CHOCTAW TO ENGLISH DICTIONARIES
Cyrus Byingtons
Choctaw Museum.

ENGLISH-ESKIMO & ESKIMO-ENGLISH VOCABULARIES
R. Wells, Compiler; John Kelly, Translator
72 pp. AMS, $11.50. Paper. Charles E. Tuttle, 1982. $6.95.

THE ENSLAVEMENT OF THE AMERICAN INDIAN
Barbara Olexer
Illus. 280 pp. Library Research Associates, 1982. $18.95.

ENWHISTEETKWA: WALK IN WATER
Jeanette Armstrong
An Okanagan child of 11 in 1860 encounters non-Indian people. Grades K-4. Illus. 44 pp. Paper. Theytus, 1982. $5.95.

ESCAPE FROM INDIAN CAPTIVITY
John Ingles; Roberta Steele, Editor
39 pp. Paper. Roberta Ingles Steele, 1982. $3.50.

*THE ESKIMO
Jean Aigner
Grades 5 and up. Illus. Chelsea House, 1989. $17.95.

*THE ESKIMO
Alice Osinski
Grades 2-3. Illus. 45 pp. Childrens Press, $13.27; paper, $4.95.

THE ESKIMO ABOUT BERING STRAIT
Edward W. Nelson
The Alaskan Eskimos of the 19th century. Reprint of 1899 edition. Illus. 520 pp. Paper. Smithsonian Institution Press, $29.95.

*THE ESKIMO: ARCTIC
Jean S. Aigner
Grades 5 and up. Illus. Chelsea House, 1989. $17.95.

ESKIMO ART: TRADITION & INNOVATION IN NORTH ALASKA
Dorothy J. Ray
Illus. 356 pp. University of Washington Press, 1977. $35.00.

ESKIMO ARTISTS
Hans Himmelheber
The cultural and artistic heritage of the Yup'ik Eskimo in southwestern Alaska during the late 1930s. Illus. Photos. Map. 96 pp. Paper. University of Alaska Press, 1993. $15.00.

ESKIMO CAPITALISTS:
OIL, POLITICS & ALCOHOL
Samuel Z. Klausner and Edward A. Foulks
Illus. 360 pp. Rowman & Littlefield, 1982. $43.50.

ESKIMO CHILDHOOD & INTERPERSONAL RELATIONSHIPS: NUNIVAK BIOGRAPHIES & GENEALOGIES
Margaret Lantis
A collection of life stories of 18 Eskimos. Reprint of 1960 edition. Illus. Map. 326 pp. AMS, $32..

ESKIMO ESSAYS: YUP'IK LIVES & HOW WE SEE THEM
Ann Fienup-Riordan
Illus. 232 pp. Rutgers University Press, 1990. $30; paper, $15.

*AN ESKIMO FAMILY
Bryan and Cherry Alexander
Grades 2-5. Illus. 39 pp. Lerner Pubns., 1985. $8.95.

*THE ESKIMO: INUIT & YUPIK
Grades K-4. Illus. 48 pp. Childrens Press, $1 1.45.

ESKIMO LIFE OF YESTERDAY
Revellion Freres
48 pp. Paper. Hancock House, $3.95.

ESKIMO MASKS: ART & CEREMONY
Dorothy J. Ray
Discusses masks in the context of 19th century aboriginal Eskimo culture. Illus. 252 pp. Paper . U. of Washington Press, 1975. $19.95.

ESKIMO MEDICINE MAN
Otto George
Illus. 324 pp. Paper. Oregon Historical Society, 1979. $7.95.

THE ESKIMO OF BAFFIN LAND & HUDSON BAY
Franz Boas
Reprint of 1907 edition. AMS, $64.50.

ESKIMO OF NORTH ALASKA
Norman A. Chance
Paper. Holt, Rinehart & Winston, 1966. $9.95.

ESKIMO POEMS FROM CANADA & GREENLAND
Tom Lowenstein, Translator
University of Pittsburgh Press, 1973. $17.95.

ESKIMO SCHOOL ON THE ANDREAFSKY: A STUDY OF EFFECTIVE BICULTURAL EDUCATION
Judith S. Kleinfeld
209 pp. Praeger Publishers, 1979. $36.95.

THE ESKIMO STORYTELLER: FOLKTALES FROM NOATAK, ALASKA
Edwin S. Hall, Jr.
Illus. 510 pp. University of Tennessee Press, 1975. $34.95; paper, $16.95.

THE ESKIMO TRIBES
Hinrich J. Rink
Reprint of 1891 edition. Covers their distribution and characteristics, especially in regard to language. Map. Two volumes in one. AMS, $37.50.

*ESKIMOS
Kate Petty
Grades 1-3. Illus. 32 pp. Franklin Watts, 1987. $10.40.

*ESKIMOS
Nancy M. Davis
Grades Preschool-5. Illus. 32 pp. Paper . DaNa Pubns, 1986. $4.95.

*ESKIMOS
Derek Fordham
Grades 5 and up. Silver Burdette, $13.96.

THE ESKIMOS
Ernest S. Birch, Jr.
Illus. 128 pp. University of Oklahoma Press, 1988. $22.50.

ESKIMOS & ALEUTS
Don E. Dumond
Illus. 180 pp. Paper. Thames & Hudson, 1977. $11.95.

*ESKIMOS - THE INUIT OF THE ARCTIC
J.H. Smith
Grades 4-8. Illus. 48 pp. Rourke Corp., 1987. $12.66.

THE ESKIMOS OF BERING STRAIT, 1650-1898
Dorothy Jean Ray
Oral tradition of this region. Quotes & details of cross-cultural contact for the past 250 years. Illus. Maps. 360 pp. Paper. U. of Washington Press & Alaska Natural History Association, $16.95.

ESKIMOS, REVISED
Jill Hughes
Illus. 32 pp. Franklin Watts, 1984. $11.90.

AN ESSAY TOWARDS AN INDIAN BIBLIOGRA-PHY: BEING A CATALOGUE OF BOOKS, RE-LATING TO THE HISTORY, ANTIQUITIES, LAN-GUAGES, CUSTOMS, RELIGION, WARS, LIT-ERATURE, & ORIGIN OF THE AMERICAN IN-DIANS IN THE LIBRARY OF THOMAS W. FIELD
Thomas W. Field
Reprint of 1873 edition. 440 pp. William Reese Co., $35.

ESSAYS IN ANTHROPOLOGY PRESENTED TO A.L. KROEBER IN CELEBRATION OF HIS SIXTIETH BIRTHDAY, JUNE 11, 1936
Alfred L. Kroeber
Facsimile of the 1936 edition. Ayer Co., $27.50.

ESSAYS IN NORTH AMERICAN INDIAN HISTORY
Gillis
255 pp. Paper. Kendall-Hunt, 1990. $24.95.

ESTHETIC RECOGNITION OF ANCIENT AMERINDIAN ART
George Kubler
Illus. 300 pp. Yale University Press, 1991. $32.50.

ESTIYUT OMAYAT: CREEK WRITING
Lewis Oliver
Illus. 17 pp. Paper. Indian University Press, 1985. $3.60, postpaid.

ETERNAL ONES OF THE DREAM: MYTH & RITUAL, DREAMS & FANTASIES - THEIR ROLE IN THE LIVES OF PRIMITIVE MAN
Geza Roheim
Paper. International Universities Press, $19.95.

ETHICS: ATTORNEY VS. TRIBE, WHO'S IN CONTROL
Panel discussion materials discuss ethical con-siderations of representing Indian tribes from the tribal perspective. 75 pp. Feeral Bar Association, 1988. $15.

ETHNIC HERITAGE IN MISSISSIPPI
Barbara Carpenter, Editor
Essays. Illus. 192 pp.University Press of Mississippi, 1993. $35; paper, $15.95.

ETHNIC IDENTITY AND THE BOARDING SCHOOL EXPERIENCE OF WEST-ETHNIC STUDIES, Vol. II; CHICANO & NATIVE AMERI-CAN STUDIES
Gary Y. Okihiro
146 pp. Paper. Markus Wiener Publishing, 1989. $16.95.

ETHNOBIOLOGY OF THE PAPAGO INDIANS
Edward F. Castetter and Ruth Underhill
Reprint of 1935 edition. AMS, $14.

THE ETHNOBOTANY OF THE COAHUILLA INDIANS OF SOUTHERN CALIFORNIA
David P. Barrows
Reprint of 1900 edtition. Paper. Malki Museum Press, $12.

ETHNOBOTANY OF THE FOREST POTAWATOMI INDIANS
Huron H. Smith
Reprint of 1933 edition. AMS, $29.

ETHNOBOTANY OF THE GOSIUTE INDIANS OF UTAH
Ralph V. Chamberlin
Reprint of 1911 edition. Paper. Kraus, $12.

ETHNOBOTANY OF THE HOPI
Alfred F. Whiting
Reprint of 1939 edition. AMS Press, $16.

ETHNOBOTANY OF THE MENOMINEE INDIANS
Huron H. Smith
Reprint of 1923 edition. Greenwood, $35.

ETHNOBOTANY OF THE MESKWAKI INDIANS
Huron H. Smith
Reprint of 1928 edition. Bound with Ethnobotany of the Menomini Indians. AMS, $40.50.

ETHNOBOTANY OF THE NAVAJO
Francis H. Elmore
Reprint of 1944 edition. AMS Press, $22.50.

ETHNOBOTANY OF THE RAMAH NAVAHO
Paul A. Vestal
Reprint of 1952 edition. Paper. Redwood Seed, $9.50.

ETHNOGRAPHIC BIBLIOGRAPHY OF NORTH AMERICA
J. O'Leary; supplement by Martin & O'Leary
5 vols. of original publication by geographic ar-eas, subdivided by tribe. 1975. Supplement is ar-ranged by author, with extensive subject and tribal indexes. 1990. HRAF Press.

ETHNOGRAPHICAL COLLECTIONS FROM THE NORTHWEST PASSAGE
Kaj Birket-Smith; W.E. Calvert, Translated by
Reprint of 1945 edition. Illus. AMS, $82.00.

AN ETHNOGRAPHY OF DRINKING & SOBRIETY AMONG THE LAKOTA
Beatrice Medicine, Editor
University of Nebraska Press, 1994.

**ETHNOGRAPHY & FOLKLORE OF THE INDI-
ANS OF NORTHWESTERN CALIFORNIA: A
LITERATURE REVIEW & ANNOTATED BIBLI-
OGRAPHY**
Joan Berman; G. Breschini & T. Haversat, Eds.
120 pp. Paper. Coyote Press, 1986. $7.45.

**ETHNOGRAPHY & PHILOLOGY
OF THE HIDATSA INDIANS**
Washington Matthews
U.S. Geoological Survey of the Territories.
Pubn. 7. Reprint of 1897 edition. Johnson
Reprint, $25.00.

**ETHNOGRAPHY OF FRANZ BOAS:
LETTERS & DIARIES OF FRANZ BOAS
WRITTEN ON THE NORTHWEST COAST
FROM 1886-1931**
Franz Boas; Ronald P. Rohner, Editor
Reprint. Illus. University of Chicago Press, $16.

**AN ETHNOGRAPHY OF THE
HURON INDIANS, 1615-1649**
Elisabeth Tooker
Reprint of 1964 edition. 195 pp. Syracuse
University Press, $29.95; paper, $14.95.
Scholarly Press, $49.

ETHNOGRAPHY OF THE KUTENAI
H.H. Turney-High
Reprint of 1941 edition. Paper. Kraus, $23.

ETHNOGRAPHY OF THE NORTHERN UTES
Anne M. Smith
Illus. Paper. Museum of New Mexico Press,
1974. $14.95.

ETHNOGRAPHY OF THE TANAINA
Cornelius Osgood
A study of the Tanaina of Cook Inlet, Alaska.
Reprint of 1937 edition. Illus. 229 pp. Paper.
HRAF Press, $15.

**ETHNOHISTORY IN THE ARCTIC:
THE BERING STRAITS ESKIMO**
Dorothy J. Ray; Richard A. Pierce, Editor
Illus. 280 pp. Limestone Press, 1983. $27.

**ETHNOLOGICAL RESULTS OF
THE POINT BARROW EXPEDITION**
John Murdock
The only major early ethnography of northern Alaskan Eskimos. Reprint of 1892 9th Annual Report
of the BIA. Illus. 480 pp. Paper. Smithsonian Institution Press, $29.95.

**ETHNOLOGY OF THE INDIANS
OF SPANISH FLORIDA**
David H. Thomas
Reprint. 415 pp. Garland, $60.00.

ETHNOLOGY OF THE IOWAY INDIANS
Alanson Skinner
Reprint of 1926 edition. AMS Press.

ETHNOLOGY OF THE TEXAS INDIANS
Thomas R. Hester
Reprint. 440 pp. Garland, $57.00.

ETHNOLOGY OF THE YUCHI INDIANS
Frank G. Speck
Reprint of 1909 edition. Illus. AMS, $28.

**THE EUROPEAN & THE INDIAN: ESSAYS IN
THE ETHNOHISTORY OF COLONIAL NORTH
AMERICA**
James Axtell

Illus. 256 pp. Oxford University Press, 1982.
$27.50; paper, $9.95.

EVA: AN ARCHAIC SITE
Thomas Lewis and Madeline Lewis
Illus. Paper. University of Tennessee Press,
1961. $5.95.

**EVENTS LEADING TO
INDIAN CONSOLIDATION**
Annie Able; edited by Larry S. Watson
100 pp. Paper. Histree, 1994. $24.95.

**EVERYDAY LAKOTA: AN ENGLISH-
SIOUX DICTIONARY FOR BEGINNERS**
Joseph S. Karol & Stephen L. Rozman
Includes 3,800 entries, 300 phrass, idiom drills,
expressions of time, coinage, native birds,
etc.Intended to enable speakers of English to
begin to learn Lakota. 122 pp. Paper. Center for
Western Studies, $5.95.

**EVERYDAY LIFE OF THE
NORTH AMERICAN INDIAN**
Jon M. White
Illus. 256 pp. Holmes & Meier, 1979. $24.50.

**THE EVOLUTION OF THE CALUSA: A NON
AGRICULTURAL CHIEFDOM ON THE SOUTH-
WEST FLORIDA COAST**
Randolf J. Widmer
Illus. 393 pp. Paper. University of Alabama
Press, 1988. $18.95.

**THE EVOLUTION OF NORTH AMERICAN
INDIANS**
David Hurst Thomas, Editor
A 31-volume series of outstanding dissertations.
Garland Publishing, $2,230/set; also sold sepa-
rately.

**EVOLUTION OF THE ONONDAGA
IROQUOIS: ACCOMODATING CHANGE,
1500-1655**
James Bradley
Illus. 288 pp. Syracuse University Press, 1987.
$24.95.

EXCAVATIONS AT MAGIC MOUNTAIN
Cynthia Irwin-Williams
Paper. Denver Museum of Natural History,
1966. $4.95.

**EXCAVATION OF MAIN
PUEBLO AT FITZMAURICE RUIN**
Franklin Barnett
Illus. 178 pp. Paper. Museum of Northern
Arizona, 1974. $7.50.

**EXCAVATIONS OF LOS MUERTOS &
NEIGHBORING RUINS IN THE SALT RIVER
VALLEY, SOUTHERN ARIZONA**
Emil W. Haury
Reprint of 1945 edition. Paper. Kraus, $40.00.

**EXCAVATIONS AT SNAKETOWN:
MATERIAL CULTURE**
Harold S. Gladwin, et al
Reconstructs the building of the Hohokam
civilization. Reprint of 1965 edition. 305 pp.
University of Arizona Press, $19.95.

**EXCAVATIONS, 1940, AT UNIVERSITY
INDIAN RUIN**
Julian Hayden
Illus. Maps. 234 pp. Paper. Southwest Parks
and Monuments, 1957. $2.00.

**EXECUTIVE ORDERS ESTABLISHING THE
PAPAGO RESERVATIONS -- WITH A BRIEF
CHRONOLOGICAL HISTORY**
Lynn Kickingbird & Curtis Berkey
57 pp. Institute for the Development of Indian
Law, $12.00.

**EXECUTIVE ORDERS RELATING TO
INDIAN RESERVATIONS FROM 1855-
1912; AND FROM 1912-1922**
Reprint of 1922 edition. Two volumes in one.
Scholarly Resources, $45.00.

**EXEMPLAR OF LIBERTY: NATIVE AMERI-
CAN & THE EVOLUTION OF AMERICAN
DEMOCRACY**
Donald A. Grinde, Jr. & Bruce E. Johansen
American Indian Studies Center, 1991.

**EXILED IN THE LAND OF THE FREE:
DEMOCRACY, THE INDIAN NATIONS
& THE U.S. CONSTITUTION**
Preface by Sen. Daniel K. Inouye;
Foreword by Peter Matthiessen
8 essays - Oren Lyons, John Mohawk, Vine
Deloria, Jr., Laurence Hauptman, Howard
Berman, Donald Grinde, Jr., Curtis Berkey, and
Robert Venables. Illus. 335 pp. Clear Light
Publishers, 1991. $24.95; paper, $14.95.

EXILES OF FLORIDA
Joshua R. Giddings
Facsimile of 1858 edition. Illus. Ayer Co., $15.

**EXPANSION & AMERICAN INDIAN
POLICY, 1783-1812**
Reginals Horsman
Reprint. 224 pp. Paper. University of Oklahoma
Press, $12.95.

**EXPEDITION AGAINST THE
SAUK & FOX INDIANS, 1832**
Henry Smith
Reprint of 1833 edition. 19 pp. Paper. Ye
Galleon Press, $2.50.

**EXPEDITION TO THE PAWNEE
PICT VILLAGE IN 1834**
Thompson Wheelock
Reprint. Paper. Ye Galleon Press, $3.95.

EXPLORATIONS IN THE FAR NORTH
F. Russell
Reprint of 1898 edition. AMS, $25.00.

**EXPLORATIONS IN THE INTERIOR OF THE
LABRADOR PENINSULA, THE COUNTRY OF
THE MONTAGNAIS & NASQUAPEE INDIANS**
H.Y. Hind
Reprint of 1863 edition. Kraus, $55.00.

**EXPLORATIONS IN
NORTHEASTERN ARIZONA**
Samuel J. Guernsey
Reprint of 1931 edition. Paper. Kraus, $24.00.

**EXPLORATIONS OF KEY DWELLERS'
REMAINS ON THE GULF COAST OF
FLORIDA**
F.H. Cushing
Reprint of 1896 edition. AMS, $22.00.

**EXPLORING IOWA'S PAST: A GUIDE
TO PREHISTORIC ARCHAEOLOGY**
Lynn M. Alex
Illus. 180 pp. Paper. University of Iowa Press,
1980. $8.95.

**EXPLORING THE OUTDOORS
WITH INDIAN SECRETS**
Allan A. Macfarlan
Illus. 224 pp. Paper. Stackpole, 1982. $10.95.

EXPLORING THE WEST
Herman J. Viola
Story of those who risked everything to open
upo the West. Includes the Lewis & Clark
Expedition. Illus. 256 pp. Smithsonian Books,
$24.96.

**EXPLORING YOUR CHEROKEE ANCESTRY:
A BASIC GENEALOGICAL RESEARCH
GUIDE**
T.G. Mooney
58 pp. Paper. Cherokee Publications, $12.00.

*EXTRAORDINARY AMERICAN INDIANS
Grades 4 and up. Illus. Biblio. 150 pp. Childrens
Press, $22.95.

**THE EYAK INDIANS OF THE
COPPER RIVER DELTA, ALASKA**
Kaj Birket-Smith and F. De Laguna
Reprint of 1938 edition. Illus. AMS Press, $42.50.

***THE EYE OF THE NEEDLE: BASED ON A
YUP'IK TALE TOLD BY BETTY HUFFMAN**
Teri Sloat, retold by & Illus.
Grades Preschool-4. E.P. Dutton, 1990. $13.95.

**THE EYES OF CHIEF SEATTLE:
THE SUQUAMISH MUSEUM**
Illus. 56 pp. Paper. University of Washington
Press, 1985. $8.95.

EYEWITNESS AT WOUNDED KNEE
Richard E. Jensen, R. Eli Paul, and John E.
Carter
Illus. Maps. 272 pp. University of Nebraska
Press, 1991. $40.

F

FACES IN THE MOON
Betty Louise Bell
Story of three generations of Cherokee women.
192 pp. University of Oklahoma Press, 1994.
$19.95.

**FACES OF A RESERVATION: A PORTRAIT OF
THE WARM SPRINGS INDIAN RESERVATION**
Cynthia D. Stowell
Illus. 220 pp. Oregon Historical Society, 1987.
$29.95.

**FACIAL PAINTINGS OF THE INDIANS
OF NORTHERN BRITISH COLUMBIA**
Franz Boas
Reprint of 1898 edition. AMS, $24.50.

**FACING WEST: THE METAPHYSICS OF
INDIAN HATING & EMPIRE-BUILDING**
Richard Drinnan
Makes connection between suppression of
native nations and suppression of liberation
movements throughout the world. Schocken
Books, 1990. $16.95.

FAINTLY SOUNDS THE WAR CRY
Fred H. Werner
Paper. Werner Publications, 1983. $5.95.

**THE FAITHFUL HUNTER
& OTHER ABENAKI STORIES**
Joseph Bruchac
Abenaki traditional legends. Illus.
Bowman Books, $7.95.

*THE FALCON BOW
James Houston
Grades 3-6. Illus. Macmillan, 1989. $12.95.

**THE FALCON: A NARRATIVE OF THE CAPTIV-
ITY & ADVENTURES OF JOHN TANNER**
Louise Erdrich, Editor
John Tanner was captured by the Shawnee Indi-
ans in 1789 and ultimately sold to and adopted by
the Ojibwas. 304 pp. Penguin USA, 1993. $12.50.

**THE FALL OF NATURAL MAN: THE AMERICAN
INDIAN & THE ORIGINS OF COMPARATIVE
ETHNOLOGY**
Anthony Pagden
272 pp. Cambridge U. Press, 1982. $49.50.

*FALSE FACE
Welwyn Wilton Katz
Grades 5-9. Illus. Macmillan, 1989. $13.95.

THE FALSE FACES OF THE IROQUOIS
William N. Fenton
Illus. 560 pp. University of Oklahoma Press,
1987. $95; paper, $42.95.

*FAMILY, CLAN, NATION
Grades 4-5. 50 pp. Capstone Press, 1989.
$10.95.

**FAMILY HISTORY OF THE
BROTHERTOWN INDIANS**
Larry S. Watson
Reprint of Love's study of Brothertown families.
Tribal origins, connections with Brothertown,
New York. 53 pp. Histree, 1986. $12.95.

*FAMINE WINTER
John W. Schultz
Grades 4-10. Paper. Council for Indian
Education, 1984. $1.00.

*FAMOUS AMERICAN INDIAN LEADERS
Bearl Brooks
Grades 4-6. 24 pp. ESP. Workbook, $5.

FAMOUS CHIEFS OF THE EASTERN SIOUX
Mark Diedrich
Illus. 81 pp. Paper. Coyote Books (MN), 1987.
$10.95.

FAMOUS INDIAN CHIEFS
Charles Johnston
Reprint of 1909 edition. Ayer Co., $30.

**FAMOUS INDIANS OF
NORTHWEST NEBRASKA**
Dr. James A. Hanson
Biographies of 12 famous chiefs including Red
Cloud and Crazy Horse. Illus. 40 pp. The Fur
Press, $2.

**FANTASIES OF THE MASTER RACE:
LITERATURE, CINEMA & THE COLONIZA-
TION OF AMERICAN INDIANS**
Ward Churchill
Examines the connection between culture &
genocide in the 500 years since Columbus.
Essays on Tony Hillerman's novels, Sun Bear,
Dances With Wolves 312 pp. Common Courage
Press, $29.95; paper, $14.95.

**FAREWELL, MY NATION: THE AMERICAN
INDIAN & THE U.S., 1820-1890**
Philip Weeks; John Franklin
& A.S. Eisenstadt, Editors
Illus. 265 pp. Paper. Harlan Davidson, 1990.
$16.95.

**FARMERS, HUNTERS, & COLONISTS:
INTERACTION BETWEEN THE SOUTH-
WEST & THE SOUTHERN PLAINS**
Katherine A. Spielmann, Editor
217 pp. University of Arizona Press, 1991. $35.

**FATHERS & CROWS: VOL. 2 OF SEVEN
DREAMS: A BOOK OF NORTH AMERICAN
LANDSCAPES**
William T. Vollmann
Fictional history of the clash of Indians &
Europeans in the New World. 1,008 pp. Paper.
Penguin USA, $14.

**THE FAUNEL REMAINS FROM
ORROYO HONDO, NEW MEXICO**
Richard W. Lang and Arthur Harris
Illus. 150 pp. Paper. Scholarly American
Research, 1984. $15.

A FEAST FOR EVERYONE
Grades 4-5. 50 pp. Capstone Press, 1989.
$10.95.

**FEASTING WITH CANNIBLAS: AN
ESSAY ON KWAKIUTL COSMOLOGY**
Stanley Walens
Illus. 236 pp. Princeton University Press, 1981.
$20.00.

**FEASTING WITH MINE ENEMY: RANK &
EXCHANGE AMONG NORTHWEST COAST
SOCIETIES**
Abraham Rosman & Paula Rubel
Illus. 221 pp. Paper. Waveland Press, 1986.
$9.95.

**THE FEATHERED SUN: PLAINS
INDIANS IN ART & PHILOSOPHY**
Frithjof Schuon
165 pp. World Wisdom Books, 1990. $37.50;
paper, $25.00.

***FEATHERS IN THE WIND:
THE STORY OF OLIVE OATMAN**
Lillian M. Fisher
Account of capture of two young pioneer girls
by Apaches. Grades 5-10. Illus. Biblio. Paper.
Pocahontas Press, $12.95.

**THE FEDERAL BUY INDIAN PROGRAM:
PROMISE VERSUS PERFORMANCE**
Moses Lukaczer
126 pp. Mojave Books, 1976. $9.00; paper ,
$7.00.

**FEDERAL CONCERN ABOUT CONDITIONS
OF CALIFORNIA INDIANS 1853-1913: EIGHT
DOCUMENTS**
Robert F. Heizer
Paper. 152 pp. Ballena Press, 1979. $7.95.

FEDERAL INDIAN LAW CASES & MATERIALS
David H. Getches, et al
Second ed. 868 pp. Richard West, 1986. $35.95.

*FEDERAL INDIAN POLICY
Lawrence C. Kelly
Grades 5 and up. Illus. Chelsea House, 1989.
$17.95.

FEDERAL INDIAN RELATIONS, 1774-1788
Walter H. Mohr
Reprint of 1933 edition. AMS, $19.45.

**FEDERAL INDIAN TAX RULES: A COMPILA-
TION OF IRS RULES RELATING TO INDIANS**
Hans Walker, Jr.
240 pp. Paper. Institute for the Development of
Indian Law, 1989. $50.00.

FEDERAL-INDIAN TRUST RELATIONSHIP
Institute for Development of Indian Law, 1981.
$12.00.

**FEDERAL PROGRAMS OF ASSISTANCE TO
AMERICAN INDIANS: A REPORT PREPARED
FOR THE SENATE SELECT COMMITTEE ON
INDIAN AFFAIRS OF THE U.S. SENATE**
Roger Walke, Editor
335 pp. U.S. Government Printing Office, Dec.
1991. No charge.

FEMININE FUR TRADE FASHIONS
Patterns for Indian dresses and moccasins from
the Crees to the Pueblos. Illus. 48 pp. Paper. The
Fur Press, $2.00.

FETISHES & CARVINGS OF THE SOUTHWEST
Oscar T. Branson
Illus. Paper. Treasure Chest, 1976. $9.95.

**A FEW SUMMER CEREMONIALS AT THE
TUSAYON PUEBLOS: NATAL CEREMONIES
OF THE HOPI INDIANS & A REPORT ON THE
PRESENT CONDITION OF A RUIN IN ARZIONA
CALLED CASA GRANDE**
J. Fewkes and J. Owens
Reprint of 1892 edition. AMS Press, $30.00.

**A FEW SUMMER CEREMONIALS
AT ZUNI PUEBLO: ZUNI MELODIES,
RECONNAISANCE OF RUINS IN OR
NEAR THE ZUNI RESERVATION**
J. Fewkes and B. Gilman
Reprint of 1891 edition. AMS Press, $25.00.

**A FIELD GUIDE TO MYSTERIOUS PLACES
OF THE WEST**
Salvatore Michael Trento
Includes many Native American sites. Illus. 256
pp. Paper. Pruett Publishing, 1994. $18.95.

**FIFTEEN FLOWER WORLD VARIATIONS: A
SEQUENCE OF SONGS FROM THE YAQUI
DEER DANCE**
Jerome Rothenberg
Illus. 60 pp. Paper. Membrane Press, 1985.
$12.00.

FIFTH ANNUAL INDIAN LAW SEMINAR
Federal Bar Association Conference of 1980.
100 pp. Federal Bar Association, $15.00.

FIFTY YEARS BELOW ZERO
Charles D. Brower
Reprint of 1942 edition. Illus. Dodd-Mead, $12.95.

**FIG TREE JOHN: AN INDIAN
IN FACT & FICTION**
Peter G. Beidler
152 pp. Paper. U. of Arizona Press, 1977. $4.95.

*THE FIGHT FOR FREEDOM, 1750-1783
N. Farr and D. Postert; L. Block, Editor
Grades 4-12. Illus. Pendulum, 1976. $2.95;
paper, $1.25.

FIGHT WITH FRANCE FOR NORTH AMERICA
A.G. Bradley
Reprint of 1900 edition. Illus. Ayer Co.
Publishers, $25.50.

FIGHTIN': NEW & COLLECTED STORIES
Simon Ortiz
Collection of contemporary short stories.
Thunder's Mouth Press, 1983. $6.95.

THE FIGHTING CHEYENNES
George F. Grinnell
Reprint of 1956 edition. Illus. 450 pp. University
of Oklahoma Press, $29.95; paper, $14.95.

**FIGHTING TUSCARORA: THE AUTOBIOG-
RAPHY OF CHIEF CLINTON RICKARD**
Barbara Graymont, Editor
Reprint of 1973 edition. Illus. Maps. 212 pp.
Paper. Syracuse University Press, $15.95.

**FIGHTING WITH PROPERTY: A STUDY OF
KWAKIUTL POTLATCHING & WARFARE**
Helen Codere
Reprint of 1950 edition. AMS, $30.00.

**A FINAL PROMISE: THE CAMPAIGN TO
ASSIMILATE THE INDIANS, 1880-1920**
Frederick E. Hoxie
365 pp. University of Nebraska Press, 1984.
$27.50. Paper. Cambridge University Press,
$13.95.

**FINAL REPORT OF INVESTIGATIONS
AMONG THE INDIANS OF THE SOUTH-
WESTERN U.S.**
A.F. Bandelier
Reprint of 1890-1892 edition. Two volumes
in one. AMS, $84.00; index, $17.00.

**FINAL REPORT OF THE U.S.
DE SOTO EXPEDITION COMMISSION**
John R. Swanton
Report of the Indians' and Spaniards' actions, their
societies, and the ecology; early southeastern
American life. Reprint of 1939 congressional com-
mittee report. 12 maps. 400 pp. Smithsonian In-
stitution Press, $29.95.

**FINDING THE CENTER: NARRATIVE
POETRY OF THE ZUI INDIANS**
Dennis Tedlock, tr.
Illus. 300 pp. University of Nebraska Press,
1978. $26.95; paper, $7.95.

**FINDING A WAY HOME: INDIAN & CATHOLIC
SPIRITUAL PATHS OF THE PLATEAU TRIBES**
Patrick J. Twohy
Illus. 296 pp. Paper. Patrick J. Twohy, 1990.
$12.

FINGER WEAVING: INDIAN BRAIDING
Alta R. Turner
Illus. 48 pp. Paper. Cherokee Pubns., 1989. $4.

FIRE ALONG THE SKY
Robert Moss
350 pp. St. Martin's Press, $19.95.

**FIRE & THE SPIRITS: CHEROKEE
LAW FROM CLAN TO COURT**
Rennard Strickland
Illus. Maps. 280 pp. Paper. University of
Oklahoma Press, $14.95.

FIRESTICKS: A COLLECTION OF STORIES
Diane Glancy
Drama, poetry & Cherokee history. 152 pp.
University of Oklahoma Press, $19.95.

THE FIRST AMERICANS
William H. Goetzmann; Owen Andrews, Ed.
Illus. Photos from The Library of Congress. 144
pp. Starwood Publishing, $34.95.

THE FIRST AMERICANS
Illus. 64 pp. Includes text, teacher's guide, tests
and answer key. 5 workbooks. Science Research
Associates, $21.25.

*THE FIRST AMERICANS COLORING BOOK
William Sauts &Netamuxwe Bock
Grades 3-5. Illus. Paper. 64 pp. Middle Atlantic
Press, $4.95.

*FIRST AMERICANS SERIES, 8 Vols.
Provides an overview of Native American history
and culture. Each volume covers a region of the
U.S. Grades 5-8. Illus. 768 pp. Facts on File, 1990-
91. $18.95/volume.

***THE FIRST AMERICANS:
TRIBES OF NORTH AMERICA**
Jane W. Watson
Grades 1-4. Illus. Pantheon, 1980. $6.95.

FIRST AMONG THE HURONS
Max Gros-Louis & Marcel Bellier
Reprint of 1973 edition. Paper. Books on
Demand, $41.80.

**FIRST ARTIST OF THE WEST: GEORGE
CATLIN PAINTINGS & WATERCOLORS FROM
THE COLLECTION OF GILCREASE MUSEUM**
Joan Carpenter Troccoli
74 color prints; 24 bxw prints; biblio. 176 pp.
Paper. University of Oklahoma Press, $29.95.

*FIRST BOOKS
A series of books for Grades 3-5 covering history
& culture of various tribes. Titles are: The
Chippewa, by Jacqueline D. Greene; The Inuits,
by Shirlee P. Newman; The Pawnee, by Arthur
Myers; The Pueblos, by Suzanne Powell; and The
Zunis, by Craig & Katherine Doherty. Illus. Franklin
Watts, 1993.

*FIRST CAME THE INDIANS
M.J. Wheeler; illus by James Houston
Grades 1-5. Illus. 32 pp. Macmillan, 1983. $1 1.95.

**FIRST ENCOUNTERS: SPANISH
EXPLORATIONS IN THE CARIBBEAN
& THE U.S., 1492-1570**
Jerald T. Milanich & Susan Milbrath, Editors
Illus. Maps. Biblio. 222 pp. University Press of
Florida, 1989. $49.95; paper, $22.95.

**FIRST HORSES: STORIES
OF THE NEW WEST**
Robert Franklin Gish
Collection of original short stories on multi-ethnic
complexities of the 1950s and 1960s in Albuquerque, NM. Illus. 134 pp. University of Nevada Press,
1993. $19.95; paper, $10.95.

THE FIRST KOSHARE
Alicia Otis
Story of Koshare clown figure in Native
American humor. 128 pp. Paper. Sunstone
Press, $8.95.

FIRST MAN WEST
  A. Mackenzie; W. Sheppe, Editor
Reprint of 1962 edition. Illus. 366 pp.
Greenwood, $35.

FIRST PEOPLE OF MICHIGAN
  Wilbert B. Hinsdale
Reprint of 1930 edition. Paper. George Wahr
Publishing, $12.95.

**FIRST SCALP FOR CUSTER: THE SKIRMISH
AT WARBONNET CREEK, NEBRASKA, JULY
17,** 1876
  Paul L. Hedrin
Illus. 106 pp. University of Nebraska Press,
1981. $12.95; paper, $5.95.

**THE FIRST SOCIAL EXPERIMENTS
IN AMERICA**
  Lewis Hanke
Peter Smith, 1964. $11.25.

***THE FIRST THANKSGIVING**
  Jean Craighead George
Its hero is Squanto, a Pawtuxet man, once kidnapped by European traders. Grades PS-3. Illus.
32 pp. Philomel, 1993. $15.95.

**FISH DECOYS OF THE
LAC DU FLAMBEAU OJIBWAY**
  Art & Brad Kimball
Illus. 96 pp. Aardvark Publications, 1988. $46;
paper, $19.50.

FIVE CIVILIZED TRIBES
  Grant Foreman
A brief history. Booklet. University of Oklahoma
Press, 1971. $4.

**THE FIVE CIVILIZED TRIBES:
A BIBLIOGRAPHY**
  Library Resources Div.
Paper. Oklahoma Historical Society, 1991. $5.

FIVE HUNDRED ESKIMO WORDS
  Kaj Birket-Smith
Reprint of 1928 edition. AMS, $25.

**FIVE INDIAN TRIBES OF THE UPPER MIS-
SOURI: SIOUX, ARICKARAS, ASSINIBOINES,
CREES & CROWS**
  Edwin Denig
Illus. Paper. University of Oklahoma Press,
1961. $8.95.

THE FLAG IN AMERICAN INDIAN ART
  Toby Herbst & Joel Kopp
Illus. 120 pp. University of Washington Press,
1993. $40; paper, $24.95.

***14 FLAGS OVER OKLAHOMA**
  Lucilia Wise
Illus. Five Civilized Tribes Museum, 1984. $1.

THE FLATHEAD INDIANS OF MONTANA
  H.H. Turney-High
Reprint of 1937 edition. Paper. Kraus, $13.

***FLECHA AL SOL: UN CUENTO DO LOS
INDIOS PUEBLO**
  Gerald McDermott
Grades Preschool-3. Illus. 50 pp. Paper.
Puffin Books, 1991. $3.95.

THE FLIGHT OF THE NEZ PERCE
  Mark H. Brown
Illus. 408 pp. Paper. U. of Nebraska
Press, 1982. $10.95.

FLIGHT OF THE NEZ PERCE
  Bill Schneider
Illus. 32 pp. Paper. Falcon Press, 1988. $4.95.

**FLIGHT OF THE SEVENTH MOON:
THE TEACHING OF THE SHIELDS**
  Lynn F. Andrews
Illus. 208 pp. Harper & Row, 1984. $13.50.

***FLINT'S ROCK**
  Hap Gilliland
A young Cheyenne boy must leave his home on
the Montana reservation to live with his sister in
the city. Grades 3-7. Paper. Roberts Rinehart,
1995. $8.95.

***THE FLOOD**
Grades 3-12. Paper. Council for Indian
Education, 1976. $2.95.

**FLORIDA PLACE-NAMES OF INDIAN
ORIGIN & SEMINOLE PERSONAL NAMES**
  William A. Reed
Paper. Books on Demand. $24.30.

**THE FLORIDA SEMINOLE
& THE NEW DEAL, 1933-1942**
  Harry Kersey, Jr.
Illus. Biblio. 230 pp. University Press of Florida,
1989. $25.95.

THE FLORIDA WARS
  Virginia Peters
Illus. Maps. Biblio. Index. 331 pp. The Shoe
String Press, 1979. $28.

**FLORIDA'S PREHISTORIC STONE TECHNOL-
OGY: A STUDY OF THE FLINTWORKING
TECHNIQUES OF EARLY FLORIDA STONE
IMPLEMENT-MAKERS**
  Barbara Purdy
Illus. 165 pp. U. Press of Florida, 1981. $31.95.

FLORIDA'S SEMINOLE INDIANS
  Wilfred Neill and E. Ross Allen
Illus. Paper. Great Outdoors, 1965. $4.95.

***THE FLUTE PLAYER:
AN APACHE FOLKTALE**
  Michael Lacapa
Grades 1-3. Illus. 65 pp. Northland Press, 1990.
$14.95.

**FLUTES OF FIRE: ESSAYS OF THE
LANGUAGES OF NATIVE CALIFORNIA**
  Leanne Hinton
Collection of essays on native California
languages. 288 pp. Heyday Books, 1994. $18.

**FOLK-LORE OF THE MESQUAKIE
INDIANS OF NORTH AMERICA**
  May A. Owen
Includes a catalogue of beadwork and other
objects in the collection of the folklore society.
Paper. Kraus, $12.

**FOLK MEDICINE OF THE DELAWARE
AND RELATED ALGONKIAN INDIANS**
  Gladys Tantaquidgeon
Illus. 145 pp. Pennsylvania Historical & Museum
Commission, 1972. $7.50; paper, $5.50.

FOLK-TALES OF THE COAST SALISH
  E.T. Adamson, Editor
Reprint of 1934 edition. Kraus, $40.

**FOLK-TALES OF THE SALISHAN
AND SAHAPTIN TRIBES**
  Franz Boas, Editor
Reprint of 1917 edition. Kraus, $21.

FOLKLORE OF THE MENOMINI INDIANS
  Alanson B. Skinner and John V. Satterlee
Reprint of 1915 edition. AMS Press, $22.

**FOLLOWING THE GUIDON: INTO THE INDIAN
WARS WITH GENERAL CUSTER AND THE
SEVENTH CAVALRY**
  Elizabeth B. Custer
Covers the period between 1867 to 1869 when
Custer engaged in extensive military activity
against the Plains Indians. Reprint. Illus. 342 pp.
Paper. University of Oklahoma Press, $12.95.

***FOLLOWING INDIAN TRAILS**
  Nicolas Grenier
Grades K-5. Illus. 38 pp. Young Discovery
Library, 1988. $4.95.

**FOLLOWING THE INDIAN WARS: THE STORY
OF THE NEWSPAPER CORRESPONDENTS
AMONG THE INDIAN CAMPAIGNERS**
  Oliver Knight
Illus. Maps. 384 pp. Paper. University of
Oklahoma Press, $17.95.

FOOD FROM DRYLAND GARDENS
  David A. Cleveland
How-to guide to sustainable Native farming.
Illus. 380 pp. Paper. AISES, $21.95.

FOOLS CROW: WISDOM & POWER
  Thomas Mails
Teton Sioux holy man Frank Fools Crow describes
his life. Illus. Maps. 250 pp. Center for Western
Study, $16.95. Paper. University of Nebraska
Press & AISES, $10.95.

FOOLS CROW
  James Welch
Novel. Illus. Paper. Penguin USA, $10.

FOR AN AMERINDIAN AUTOHISTORY
  Georges E. Sioul
The author, a Huron, presents guidelines for the
study of Native history from an Amerindian point
of view. McGill-Queen's U. Press, 1992. $29.95.

**THE FORGOTTEN ARTIST: INDIANS OF
ANZA-BORREGO & THEIR ROCK ART**
  Manfred Knaak; Rose Houk
& Harry Daniel, Editors
Illus. 128 pp. Anza-Borrego, 1988. $36.95;
paper, $24.95.

**THE FORGOTTEN CENTURIES: INDIANS &
EUROPEANS IN THE AMERICAN SOUTH,
1521-1704**
  Charles Hudson & Carmen Chaves Tesser
17 Essays of the history of the early South. Illus.
Maps. 496 pp. University of Georgia Press, 1994.
$50; paper, $25.

**FORGOTTEN FOUNDERS: BENJAMIN
FRANKLIN, THE IROQUOIS AND THE
RATIONALE FOR AMERICAN REVOLUTION**
  Bruce E. Johansen
167 pp. Harvard Common Press, 1982. $12.95.

FORGOTTEN FOUNDERS: HOW THE AMERICAN INDIAN HELPED SHAPE DEMOCRACY
Bruce E. Johansen
185 pp. Paper. Harvard Commons Press, 1982. $12.95.

THE FORGOTTEN SIOUX: AN ETHNO-HISTORY OF THE LOWER BRULE RESERVATION
Ernest L. Schusky
Illus. 272 pp. Nelson-Hall, 1975. $23.95.

FORKED TONGUES: SPEECH, WRITING & REPRESENTATION IN NORTH AMERICAN INDIAN TEXTS
David Murray, Editor
188 pp. Indiana University Press, 1991. $39.95; paper, $14.50.

FORLORN HOPE: THE BATTLE OF WHITE-BIRD CANYON AND THE BEGINNING OF THE NEZ PERCE WAR
John D. McDermott
Illus. 230 pp. Idaho State Historical Society, 1978. $9.95; paper, $4.95.

FORMAL EDUCATION IN AN AMERICAN INDIAN COMMUNITY: PEER SOCIETY & THE FAILURE OF MINORITY EDUCATION
Murray Wax, Rosalie Wax & Robert Dumont
Revised edition. 145 pp. Paper. Waveland Press, 1989. $8.95.

THE FORMATIVE CULTURES OF THE CAROLINA PIEDMONT
J.L. Coe
Reprint of 1964 edition. American Philosophical Society, $12.

FORMULATING AMERICAN INDIAN POLICY IN NEW YORK STATE, 1970-1986
Laurence Hauptman
Illus. 288 pp. State University of New York Press, 1988. $57.50; paper, $19.95.

THE FORT BELKNAP ASSINIBOINE OF MONTANA: A STUDY IN CULTURE CHANGE
David Rodnick
Reprint of 1938 edition. AMS Press, $24.50.

FORT GIBSON HISTORY
Grant Foreman
A brief history of Fort Gibson in Indian Territory. The Five Civilized Tribes Museum. Booklet, $2.50.

FORT LARAMIE & THE SIOUX
Remi Nadeau
Illus. 375 pp. Paper. University of Nebraska Press, 1982. $9.95.

FORT MEADE & THE BLACK HILLS
Robert Lee
An authoritative history of the fort that served the northern plains from the Indian Wars until World War II. 321 pp. Center for Western Study. $40.

FORT SUPPLY, INDIAN TERRITORY: FRONTIER OUTPOST ON THE PLAINS
Robert Carriker
Illus. 275 pp. Paper. University of Oklahoma Press, 1990. $12.95.

FORTH TO THE WILDERNESS: THE FIRST AMERICAN FRONTIER, 1754-1774
D. Van Every
Reprint of 1961 edition. Ayer Co. Pubs, $17.

FORTY MILES A DAY ON BEANS AND HAY: THE ENLISTED SOLDIER FIGHTING THE INDIAN WARS
Don Rickey, Jr.
Illus. Paper. University of Oklahoma Press, 1977. $10.95.

FOUR MASTERWORKS OF AMERICAN INDIAN LITERATURE
John Bierhorst, Editor
Reprint of 1974 edition. 371 pp. Paper. University of Arizona Press, $15.95.

FOUR WINDS, POEMS FROM INDIAN RITUALS
Gene M. Hodge
36 PP. Paper. Sunstone Press, 1979. $4.95.

FOUR WINDS CATALOG
Richard & Cat Carey
Catalog of Native American titles, periodicals and audio tapes. Four Winds Trading Co.

FOURTEEN FAMILIES IN PUEBLO POTTERY
Rick Dillingham
Introduced seven new families and explores the development of the craft. Illus. 304 pp. University of New Mexico Press, $75; paper, $37.50.

THE FOURTH BIENNIAL NATIVE AMERICAN FINE ARTS INVITATIONAL, OCTOBER 21, 1989-SPRING 1990
Margaret Archuleta
Illus. 32 pp. Paper. The Heard Museum, 1989. $5.

THE FOURTH WORLD OF THE HOPIS: THE EPIC STORY OF THE HOPI INDIANS AS PRESERVED IN THEIR LEGENDS & TRADITIONS
Harold Courlander
Illus. 239 pp. Paper. University of New Mexico Press, 1987. $11.95.

THE FOURTH WORLD, AN INDIAN REALITY
George Manuel and Michael Posluns
Illus. Free Press, 1974. $7.95.

*FOX SONG
Joseph Bruchac; illus. by Paul Morin
Story of a modern Abenaki child learning to accept death. Grades PS-3. Illus. 32 pp. Philomel, 1993. $14.95.

FOX TEXTS
William Jones
Reprint of 1907 edition. AMS Press, $42.

THE FOX WARS: THE MESQUAKIE CHALLENGE TO NEW FRANCE
R. David Edmunds & Joseph L. Peyser
The Foxes occupied central Wisconsin, where for a long time they had warred with the Sioux. Struggling to maintain their identity in the face of colonial New France, the Foxes were eventually defeated and took sanctuary among the Sac Indians. Illus. Maps. 304 pp. University of Oklahoma Press, 1994. $14.95.

FRAGMENTS OF HAWAIIAN HISTORY
John Papal'i; trans. by Mary Kawena Pukui
Describes life under the Kamehamehas, presenting personal experiences. Illus. 212 pp. Paper. Bishop Museum, $19.95.

FRAUD AGAINST INDIAN SOLDIERS
Larry S. Watson, indexed & edited by
250 pp. Paper. Histree, 1994. $24.95.

THE FREEING OF THE DEER AND OTHER NEW MEXICO INDIAN MYTHS
Carmen Espinosa
Illus. 93 pp. University of New Mexico Press, 1985. $10.95.

THE FREMONT CULTURE: A STUDY IN CULTURE DYNAMICS ON THE NORTHERN ANASAZI FRONTIER
James H. Gunnerson
Paper. Peabody Museum, 1969. $15.

FRIEND AND FOE: ASPECTS OF FRENCH-AMERICAN CULTURAL CONTACT IN THE 16th & 17th CENTURIES
Cornelius J. Jaenen
Illus. Columbia University Press, 1976. $25.

*FROM ABENAKI TO ZUNI: A DICTIONARY OF NATIVE AMERICAN TRIBES
Evelyn Wolfson
Grades 5 and up. Walker & Co., 1988. $17.95.

FROM THE DEEP WOODS TO CIVILIZATION: CHAPTERS IN THE AUTOBIOGRAPHY OF AN INDIAN
Charles A. Eastman
Illus. 255 pp. Paper. University of Nebraska Press, 1977. $7.95.

FROM DROUGHT TO DROUGHT
Florence H. Ellis
Illus. 220 pp. Paper. Sunstone, 1988. 1988. $14.95.

FROM THE HEART OF CROW COUNTRY
Joseph Medicine Crow
The Crow Indians' own stories. Illus. Photos. 130 pp. Random House & AISES, $17.

FROM INDIAN LEGENDS TO THE MODERN BOOKSHELF
Edith Mosher & Nella Williams
Reprint of 1931 edition. Paper. George Wahr Publishing, $12.95.

FROM INDIANS TO CHICANOS: THE DYNAMICS OF MEXICAN-AMERICAN CULTURE
James D. Virgil
Illus. 245 pp. Paper. Waveland Press, $9.95.

FROM MASSACRE TO MATRIARCH: SIX WEEKS IN THE LIFE OF FANNY SCOTT
Clara Talton Fugate
Illus. 50 pp. Paper. Pocahontas Press, 1989. $8.95.

FROM THE LAND OF THE TOTEM POLES: THE NORTHWEST COAST INDIAN ART COLLECTION AT THE AMERICAN MUSEUM OF NATURAL HISTORY
Aldona Jonaitis
Illus. 272 pp. Paper. University of Washington Press, 1988. $40.

FROM A NATIVE DAUGHTER: COLONILAISM & SOVEREIGNTY IN HAWAII
Haunani Kay Trask
Common Courage Press, 1993. $11.

FROM THE SANDS TO THE MOUNTAIN: A STUDY OF CHANGE & PERSISTENCE IN A SOUTHERN PAIUTE COMMUNITY
Pamela Bunte & Robert Franklin
350 pp. University of Nebraska Press, 1987 $22.95.

FROM THIS EARTH: THE ANCIENT ART OF PUEBLO POTTERY
Stewart Peckham
Illus. 180 pp. Museum of New Mexico Press, 1990. $45.

FROM VILLAGE, CLAN AND CITY
Alyce Sadongei, Editor
A chapbook of eleven Native American writers. Includes poetry and short stories. Atlatl, 1989. $3.

FROM YORKTOWN TO SANTIAGO WITH THE SIXTH U.S. CAVALRY
W.H. Carter
Reprint of 1900 edition. Illus. 335 pp. State House Press, $24.95.

FRONTIER PATROL: THE ARMY & THE INDIANS IN NORTHEASTERN CALIFORNIA, 1861
Loring White
28 pp. Association of Northern California Records, 1974. $4.

FRONTIER REGULARS: THE U.S. ARMY & THE INDIAN, 1866-1891
Robert M. Utley
Reprint of 1977 edition. Illus. 500 pp. Paper. University of Nebraska Press, $12.95.

*FRONTIERSMEN
Gail Stewart
Grades 3-8. Illus. 32 pp. Rourke Corp., 1990. $12.95.

THE FRONTIERSMEN
Allan Eckert
Little, Brown & Co., 1967. $25.

*FROZEN FIRE
James Houston
Grades 7 and up. Illus. Macmillan, 1989. $13.95; paper, $4.95.

FRY BREADS, FEAST DAYS & SHEEPS
Kris Hotvedt
48 pp. Paper. Sunstone, 1987. $6.95.

FULL COLOR AMERICAN INDIAN DESIGNS FOR NEEDLEPOINT RUGS
Dorothy Sides
32 pp. Paper. Dover, 1975. $3.50.

FUNCTIONS OF WAMPUM AMONG THE EASTERN ALGONKIAN
Frank G. Speck
Reprint of 1919 edition. Paper. Kraus, $12.

FUNDAMENTALS OF AGE-GROUP SYSTEMS
Frank H. Stewart
Academic Press, 1977. $39.50.

*THE FUR TRADER AND THE INDIAN
Lewis O. Saum
Illus. 336 pp. Grades 9 and up. University of Washington Press, 1965. $18; paper, $9.95.

*FUR TRAPPERS AND TRADERS: THE INDIANS, THE PILGRIMS & THE BEAVER
Beatrice Siegel
Grades 3-7. Illus. 64 pp. Walker & Co., 1981. $11.85.

FURTHER STUDY OF PREHISTORIC SMALL HOUSE-RUINS IN THE SAN JUAN WATERSHED
P.M. Prudden
Reprint of 1918 edition. Paper. Kraus, $15.

THE FUS FIXICO LETTERS
Alexander Posey; Edited by Daniel F. Littlefield & Carol A. Pretty Hunter
Humorous articles by Posey, the Creek political humorist. Reprint. University of Nebraska Press, $37.50.

G

THE GABRIELINO
Bruce W. Miller
A historical look at the Indians of the Los Angeles Basin. Illus. 120 pp. Paper. Sand River Press, $7.95.

GAGI WDULST: BROUGHT FORTH TO RECONFIRM THE LEGACY OF A TAKU RIVER TLINGIT CLAN
Elizabeth Nyman & Jeff Leer
Ancient legends and traditional stories of the Tlingit of the Taku region. Illus. Photos. 261 pp. Alaska Native Language Center, $26.95.

GALENA & ABORIGINAL TRADE IN EASTERN NORTH AMERICA
John A. Walthall
Illus. 66 pp. Paper. Illinois State Museum, 1981. $2.50.

THE GAMES OF AMERICAS: A BOOK OF READINGS
Brian Sutton-Smith
Reprint of 1975 edition. Illus. Ayer Co., $42.

GAMES OF THE NORTH AMERICAN INDIANS
Stewart Culin
Reprint of 1907 edition. Two vols. 867 pp. Vol. 1: Games of Chance; Vol. 2: Games of Skill. Illus. 865 pp. Paper. University of Nebraska Press, $13.95 each. Dover, $16.95.

GATHERING THE DESERT
Gary Paul Nabhan; illus. by Paul Mirocha
Reveals how Southwestern desert peoples have used indigenous plants over the centuries. 209 pp. University of Arizona Press, 1985. $24.95; paper, $17.95.

A GATHERING OF SPIRIT: WRITING & ART BY NORTH AMERICAN INDIAN WOMEN
Beth Brant, Editor
Illus. 240 pp. Paper. Sinister Wisdom Books, 1984. $9.50. Firebrand Books, $9.95.

GATHERINGS II
Greg Young-Ing, Editor
Features the works of several high profile First Nations authors and artists. Illus. 240 pp. Paper. Theytus, 1991. $12.95.

GATHERINGS III
Greg Young-Ing, Editor
Features a wide array of work by First Nation authors from across North America. Illus. 240 pp. Paper. Theytus, 1992. $12.95.

GATHERINGS IV: RE-GENERATION: EXPANDING THE WEB TO CLAIM OUR FUTURE
Don Fiddler, Editor
Poetry, short fiction, essays, songs, oratory, pictograph writing, drama, criticism, biography, artworks and cartoons. 250 pp. paper. Theytus, 1993. $12.95.

GENERAL & AMERINDIAN ETHNO-LIN-GUISTICS: IN REMEMBRANCE OF STANLEY NEWMAN
Mary Key & Henry Hoenigwald, Editors
500 pp. Mouton de Gruyter, 1989. $125.

GENERAL CROOK IN THE INDIAN COUNTRY
John G. Bourke
Reprint of 1974 edition. Illus. 44 pp. Paper. Filter Press, $2.50.

GENERAL ORDERS OF 1757 ISSUED BY THE EARL OF LOUDON AND PHINEAS LYMAN IN THE CAMPAIGN AGAINST THE FRENCH
Loudon and Lyman
Facsimile of 1899 edition. Ayer Co. Pubs., $14.

GENERATION TO GENERATION
Edward Benton-Benai
Ojibway traditional teaching story. Illus. 24 pp. Indian Country Communication, 1991. $6.

GENERATIONS IN CLAY: PUEBLO POTTERY OF THE AMERICAN SOUTHWEST
Alfred E. Dittert, Jr. & Fred Plog
Illus. 156 pp. Paper. Northland Publishing, 1980. $17.95.

THE GENIUS OF SITTING BULL: 13 HEROIC STRATEGIES FOR TODAY'S BUSINESS LEADERS
Emmett C. Murphy with Michael Snell
Illus. 340 pp. Prentice Hall, 1993. $18.95.

GENOCIDE AGAINST THE INDIANS: ITS ROLE IN THE RISE OF U.S. CAPITALISM
George Novak
Reprint of 1970 edition. 31 pp. Booklet. Pathfinder Press, $3.

GENUINE NAVAJO RUGS: HOW TO TELL
Noel Bennett
Illus. 24 pp. Paper. Filter Press, 1979. $2.50.

GEOGRAPHIA AMERICAE WITH AN ACCOUNT OF THE DELAWARE INDIANS
Peter Linderstrom
Based on Surveys & Notes Made in 1654-1656. Reprint of 1925 edition. Ayer Co., $37.

GEOGRAPHICAL NAMES OF THE KWAKIUTL INDIANS
Franz Boas
Reprint of 1934 edition. AMS Press, $25.

*GEORGE CATLIN
Mark Sufrin
Grades 4-8. Illus. Macmillan, 1987. $14.95.

GEORGIA VOICES, Vol. Two: Nonfiction
Hugh Ruppersburg, Editor
Includes selections from Native American writers. 592 pp. University of Georgia Press, 1994. $40; paper, $19.95.

GERANIUMS FOR THE IROQUOIS: A FIELD GUIDE TO AMERICAN INDIAN MEDICINAL PLANTS
Daniel E. Moerman; Keith Irvine, Editor
Illus. Reference Publications, 1982. $24.95.

GERMAN ARTIST ON THE TEXAS FRONTIER: FRIEDRICH RICHARD PETRI
William K. Newcomb, Jr.
Illus. 250 pp. University of Texas Press, 1978. $35.

GERONIMO
Alexander B. Adams
Illus. 380 pp. Da Capo Press, $14.95.

***GERONIMO**
Russell Shorto
Grades 5-7. Illus. 144 pp. Silver Burdette, 1989.
$11.98; paper, $7.95.

GERONIMO CAMPAIGN
Odie B. Faulk
Illus. Oxford University Press, 1969. $27.95.

**GERONIMO & THE END
OF THE APACHE WARS**
C.L. Sonnichson, Editor
Illus. 140 pp. Paper . University of Nebraska
Press, 1990. $6.95.

**GERONIMO: LAST RENEGADE
OF THE APACHE**
Jason Hook
Illus. 52 pp. Sterling, 1989. $12.95.

GERONIMO: THE MAN, HIS TIME, HIS PLACE
Angie Debo
Illus. 500 pp. Paper . University of Oklahoma
Press & AISES, 1982. $18.95.

GHOST DANCE
David H. Miller
Illus. 325 pp. University of Nebraska Press,
1985. $27.95; paper , $8.95.

**GHOST DANCE MESSIAH:
THE JACK WILSON STORY**
Paul Bailey
Westernlore, $12.95.

**GHOST-DANCE RELIGION &
THE SIOUX OUTBREAK OF 1890**
James Mooney; Anthony Wallace, Editor
Reprint. Illus. Maps. 520 pp. University of
Nebraska Press, $65; paper , $25.

**THE GHOST-DANCE RELIGION
& WOUNDED KNEE**
James Mooney
Explores messianic cult behind Indian resistance.
Reprint. Illus. 544 pp. Paper . Dover, $12.95.

GHOST VOICES
Donald M. Hines
Yakima Indian myths, legends, humor and hunting stories. Illus. 435 pp. Biblio. Great Eagle Publishing, 1993. $23.95.

FORT GIBSON HISTORY
Grant Foreman
A brief history of Fort Gibson in Indian territory .
Booklet. Five Civilized Tribes Museum, $2.50.

**THE GIFT OF AMERICAN NATIVE PAINT-
INGS FROM THE COLLECTION OF EDGAR
WILLIAM & BERNICE CHRYSLER
GARBISCH**
Illus. 68 pp. Paper . Chrysler Museum,1975. $5.

THE GIFT OF CHANGING WOMAN
Tryntje Van Ness Seymour
Henry Holt & Co., 1993.

**THE GIFT OF THE GILA MONSTER:
NAVAJO CEREMONIAL TALES**
Introduced & retold by Gerald Hausman
Mythology/ceremonial songs of the Navajo. Illus.
224 pp. Paper. Simon & Schuster , 1993. $11.

**GIFT OF POWER: THE LIFE & TEACHINGS
OF A LAKOTA MEDICINE MAN**
Archie Fire Lame Deer & Richard Erdoes
Illus. 304 pp. Bear & Co., 1992. $21.95; paper ,
$14.95.

***THE GIFT OF THE SACRED DOG**
Paul Goble
Grades K-3. Illus. Macmillan, 1989. $13.95;
paper, $4.95.

THE GIFT OF THE SACRED PIPE
Vera L. Drysdale and Joseph E. Brown
Illus. 128 pp. University of Oklahoma Press,
1982. $34.50.

**THE GIFT OF SPIDER WOMAN: SOUTH-
WESTERN TEXTILES, THE NAVAJO
TRADITION**
Joe B. Wheat
Illus. 48 pp. Paper . University of Pennsylvania,
1984. $14.95.

***GIFTS OF THE SEASON: LIFE
AMONG THE NORTHWEST INDIANS**
Carol Batdorf
Grades 1-6. Illus. 25 pp. Hancock House, 1990.
$5.95.

**GIGYAYK VO JKAI (WALK STRONG!)
YUMAN POETRY WITH MORPHOLOGICAL
ANALYSIS**
Lucille Watahomigie & Akira Yamamoto, Eds.
Poetry. 141 pp. Paper . Malki Museum Press,
1983. $12.

***THE GIRL WHO LOVED WILD HORSES**
Paul Globe
Story of a Plains Indian girl devoted to the care of
her tribe's horses. Grades K-3. Illus. Macmillan,
1986. $13.95; paper , $3.95.

***THE GIRL WHO MARRIED A GHOST**
John Bierhorst; photos by Edward Curtis
Grades 7 and up. Illus. Macmillan, 1989. $12.95.

**GIVE OR TAKE A CENTURY:
AN ESKIMO CHRONICLE**
Joseph E. Senungetuk
The first professional, full-length work to be pub-
lished by an Eskimo author . Illus. Map. 206 pp.
Paper. The Indian Historian Press, 1971. $6.

**GIVING: OJIBWAY STORIES & LEGENDS
FROM THE CHILDREN OF CURVE LAKE**
Curve Lake Reserve, Canada
Paper. Greenfield Review Press, $7.95.

**GIVING VOICE TO BEAR: NORTH AMERI-
CAN INDIAN MYTHS, RITUALS, & IMAGES
OF THE BEAR**
David Rockwell
Stories, both oral and written, in which rituals describe the bear as central to initiation, shamantic
rites, healing & hunting ceremonies, and new year
celebrations. Illus. 224 pp. Roberts Rinehart Publishers, 1994. $25; paper , $14.95..

GLIMPSES OF THE ANCIENT SOUTHWEST
David E. Stuart
Describes the prehistoric life in Chaco Canyon,
Folsom, esa Verde, Bandelier, Mibres, and other
sites. Illus. Maps. 128 pp. Paper . Ancient City
Press, $9.95.

**GLORY REMEMBERED: WOODEN
HEADGEAR OF ALASKA SEA HUNTERS**
Lydia T. Black
Illus. 176 pp. Paper . University of Washington
Press, $24.95.

***THE GOAT IN THE RUG**
Charles L. Blood & Martin Link;
illus. by Nancy W. Parker
Grades P-3. Illus. Macmillan, 1989. $14.95;
paper, $3.95.

**GOD GAVE US THIS COUNTRY: TECUMSEH
& THE FIRST AMERICAN CIVIL WAR**
Bil Gilbert
Macmillan, 1989. $21.95.

GOD IS RED: A NATIVE VIEW OF RELIGION
Vine Deloria, Jr.
Revised edition. 320 pp. Fulcrum, $24.95;
paper, $16.95.

**GODS OF THE POPOL VUH: XMUKANE,
K'UCUMATZ, TOJIL, & JURAKAN**
Mary H. Preuss
Illus. 106 pp. Paper . Labyrinthos, 1988. $20.

**THE GOLDEN WOMAN: THE COLVILLE
NARRATIVE OF PETER J. SEYMOUR**
Anthony Mattina, Editor
Northwest Indian version of a European folktale.
357 pp. University of Arizona Press, 1985. $29.95.

**A GOOD MEDICINE COLLECTION;
LIFE IN HARMONY WITH NATURE**
Adolph Hungry Wolf
Legends, lore, and spiritual seeking of North
America's native people. Illus. 200 pp. Paper .
The Book Publishing Co., 1990. $9.95.

***GOODBIRD THE INDIAN: HIS STORY**
Edward Goodbird as told to Gilbert L. Wilson
Grades 7 and up. Illus. 1 10 pp. Paper . Minne-
sota Historical Society Press, 1985. $5.95.

R.C. GORMAN'S ENGAGEMENT CALENDAR
10.5 x 12.5". Clear Light Publishers, $12.

***THE GOSPEL OF THE GREAT SPIRIT**
Joshua M. Bennett
Grades 8 and up. Illus. Morning Star Publishing,
1990. $21.

THE GOSPEL OF THE REDMAN
Ernest T. Seton
Reprint of 1930 edition. Compilation of Indian
thought & culture. Illus. 126 pp. Paper .
Naturegraph, $4.95.

**GOVERNMENT & RELIGION
OF THE VIRGINIA INDIANS**
S.R. Hendren
Reprint of 1895 edition. Paper . Johnson Reprint,
$9.00. AMS Press, $11.50.

**GRAMMAR & DICTIONARY OF
THE LANGUAGE OF THE HIDATSA**
Washington Matthews
Reprint of 1873 edition. AMS Press, $27.50.

**A GRAMMAR & DICTIONARY
OF THE TIMUCUA LANGUAGE**
Julian Granberry
Describes the grammar and lexicon of the extinct
17th-century Timucua language of Central and
North Florida. 352 pp. Paper . U. of Alabama Press,
1993. $29.95.

A GRAMMAR OF COMANCHE
Jean Ormsbee Charney
288 pp. University of Nebraska Press, 1994. $35.

A GRAMMAR OF DIEGUENO NOMINALS
Larry P. Gorbet
Garland, 1976. $51.

GRAMMAR OF THE LANGUAGE OF THE LENNI LENAPE OR DELAWARE INDIANS
D. Zeisberger; trans. by Peter S. Du Ponceau
Reprint of 1827 edition. AMS Press, $29.50.

GRAMMAR OF THE MIKMAQUE LANGUAGE OF NOVA SCOTIA
A. S. Maillard; Joseph M. Bellenger, Editor
Reprint of 1864 edition. AMS Press, $28.50.

A GRAMMAR OF SOUTHEASTERN POMO
Julius A. Moshinsky
Paper. University of California Press, 1974. $18.50.

A GRAMMAR OF THE WAPPO LANGUAGE
P.A. Radin
Reprint of 1929 edition. Kraus, $51.00.

THE GRAND CANYON: INTIMATE VIEWS
Robert C. Euler; Frank Tikalsky, Editor
University of Arizona Press, 1993.

GRAND ENDEAVORS OF AMERICAN INDIAN PHOTOGRAPHY
Paula Richardson Fleming
& Judith Lynch Luskey
Illus. Smithsonian Institution Press, $39.95.

THE GRAND PORTAGE STORY
Carolyn Gilman
History of legendary fur-trade crossroads in northern Minnesota. Illus. Photos. Maps. Biblio. 168 pp. Paper. Minnestoa Historical Society Press, $8.50.

THE GRAND VILLAGE OF THE NATCHEZ INDIANS REVISITED
Robert Neitzel; Patricia Galloway, Editor
215 pp. Paper. Mississippi Dept. of Archaeology, 1983. $15.00.

*GRANDFATHER GREY OWL TOLD ME
Althea Bass
Grades 4 and up. Paper. Council on Indian Education, 1973. $1.95.

*GRANDFATHER & THE POPPING MACHINE
Henry Tall Bull & Tom Weist
Grades 2-12. 32 pp. Council for Indian Education, 1970. $8.95; paper, $2.95.

*GRANDFATHER ORIGIN STORY: THE NAVAJO INDIAN BEGINNING
Richard Redhawk
Grades 3-6. Paper. Sierra Oaks, 1988. $5.95.

*GRANDMOTHER FIVE BASKETS
Lisa Larrabee & Lori Sawyer
12-year old Anna finds it fun to help Grandmother Five Baskets basket weave (Poarch Creek). Grades 3-7. 64 pp. Harbinger House, $14.95; paper, $9.95.

*GRANDMOTHER STORIES: NORTHWESTERN INDIAN TALES
Nashone
Grades 5-12. Illus. Paper. Sierra Oaks, 1987. $5.95.

*GRANDMOTHER'S CHRISTMAS STORY: A TRUE QUECHAN INDIAN STORY
Grades 3-7. Illus. Paper. Sierra Oaks Publishing, $6.95.

GRANDMOTHERS OF THE LIGHT: A MEDICINE'S WOMAN'S SOURCEBOOK
Paula Gunn Allen
250 pp. Paper. Beacon Press, 1991. $19.95.

GREAT AMERICAN INDIAN BIBLE
Homer "Louis" Hooban, Editor
Indian Heritage Publishing, 1990.

GREAT BASIN ATLATL STUDIES
T.R. Hester; R.F. Heizer, Editor
Illus. 60 pp. Paper. Ballena Press, 1974. $6.95.

GREAT BASIN INDIAN POPULATION FIGURES (1873 TO 1970) & THE PITFALLS THEREIN BOUND WITH BIG SMOKEY VALLEY SHOSHONI
Joy Leland
Illus. 276 pp. 2 Vols. University of Nevada Systems, 1976. $11.00 per set.

A GREAT BASIN SHOSHONEAN SOURCEBOOK
David Thomas
779 pp. Garland, 1986. $100.

GREAT BLACK ROBE
Jean Pitrone
Illus. Daughters of St. Paul, 1965. $4; paper, $3.

*THE GREAT CHANGE
White Deer of Autumn (Gabriel Horn)
A tale of a wise grandmother explaining a meaning of death to her questioninf granddaughter. Grades 3 and up. Illus. 36 pp. Levite of Apache & Beyond Words Publishing, 1992. $14.95.

*THE GREAT CHIEFS
B. Capps
Grades 7-12. Illus. Silver Burdette, 1975. $19.94.

THE GREAT CHIEFS
William W. Johnson
Illus. 240 pp. Time-Life Books, 1975. $14.95.

GREAT EXCAVATIONS: TALES OF EARLY SOUTHWESTERN ARCHAEOLOGY, 1888-1939
Melinda Elliott
Stories of the early Southwestern archaeologists. Illus. 230 pp. School of American Research, 1995.

THE GREAT FATHER: THE U.S. GOVERNMENT & AMERICAN INDIANS
Francis Prucha
Two volumes. Illus. 1.250 pp. University of Nebraska Press, 1984. $80.00. Abridged edition, $27.50; paper, $9.95.

*GREAT INDIAN CHIEFS
50 stories of the great chiefs. Grades 3-5. Illus. Paper. Bellerophon, $3.95.

*GREAT INDIANS OF CALIFORNIA
Coloring book. Grades K-3. Paper. Bellerophon, $3.95.

THE GREAT JOURNEY: THE PEOPLING OF ANCIENT AMERICA
Brian Fagan
Illus. 288 pp. Paper. Thames & Hudson, 1987. $12.95.

*THE GREAT RACE: OF THE BIRDS & ANIMALS
Paul Goble
Grades K-3. Illus. 32 pp. Paper. Macmillan, 1991. $4.95.

THE GREAT SIOUX WAR: THE BEST FROM MONTANA, THE MAGAZINE OF WESTERN HISTORY
Paul L. Heden
Illus. 330 pp. Montana Historical Society Press, 1991. $27.50; paper, $11.95.

THE GREAT FATHER: THE U.S. GOVERNMENT & THE AMERICAN INDIAN
Francis Paul Prucha
Detailed chronological overview of the interaction between the federal government and Indian tribes. 2 vols. University of Nebraska Press, 1984.

GREAT INDIAN CHIEFS
Albert Britt
Facsimile of 1938 edition. 280 pp. Ayer Co. Publishers, $21.50.

*GREAT INDIANS OF CALIFORNIA
Maurice Vallejo, et al
Grade 6. Illus. 48 pp. Paper. Bellerophon Books, 1981. $3.95.

THE GREAT KIVA
Phillips Kloss
Poetry. Illus. 112 pp. Sunstone Press, $37.50; paper, $14.95.

GREAT NORTH AMERICAN INDIANS
Frederick Dockstader
Van Nostrand Reinhold, 1977.

GREAT SALT LAKE TRAIL
H. Inman and W.F. Cody
Reprint of 1897 edition. Illus. Ross & Haines, $15.

THE GREAT SIOUX TRAIL
Joseph Altsheler
Amereon Ltd., $20.95.

GREAT WESTERN INDIAN FIGHTS
Potomac Coral of the Westerners
Illus. 352 pp. Paper. University of Nebraska Press, 1966. $7.95.

*GREEN MARCH MOONS
Mary TallMountain; illus. by J.E. Senungetuk
Details Native Alaskan life. Grades 5 and up. Illus. Paper. New Seed Press, $7.95.

GROS VENTRE OF MONTANA
Regina Flannery
Reprint of 1956 edition. Two volumes: Volume 1: Social Life; Volume 2: Religion and Ritual. Illus. Gros Ventre Treaty, $21.00 per set.

THE GROWING PATH
Describes traditional Indian infant stimulation practices. Illus. 16 pp. Southwest Communication Resources, $10.00.

*GROWING UP IN SIOUXLAND
Arthur R. Huseboe & Sandra Looney
Grades 4 and up. Illus. 74 pp. Paper. Center for Western Studies, $5.

GROWING UP INDIAN
Evelyn Wolfson
Illus. 96 pp. Walker & Co., 1986. $10.95.

*GUARDIAN SPIRIT QUEST
Ella Clark
Grades 5-10. Paper. Council for Indian
Education, 1974. $2.45.

**GUESTS NEVER LEAVE HUNGRY: THE
AUTOBIOGRAPHY OF JAMES SEWID, A
KWAKIUTL INDIAN**
James Sewid; James P. Spradley, Editor
Reprint of 1969 edition. Illus. 310 pp. University
of Toronto Press, 1969. $16.95.

**GUIDE TO AMERICAN INDIAN DOCUMENTS
IN THE CONGRESSIONAL SERIAL SET:
1817-1899**
Steven L. Johnson
503 pp. N. Ross, 1977. $35.

**GUIDE TO AMERICA'S INDIANS: CERE-
MONIALS, RESERVATIONS & MUSEUMS**
Arnold Marquis
Illus. 400 pp. Paper. University of Oklahoma
Press, 1974. $14.95.

**A GUIDE TO THE ANASAZI & OTHER
ANCIENT SOUTHWEST INDIANS**
Eleanor Ayer
Illus. Map. 48 pp. Paper. Renaissance House,
1991. $4.95.

**A GUIDE TO CHEROKEE DOCUMENTS
IN FOREIGN ARCHIVES**
William L. Anderson and James A. Lewis
768 pp. Scarecrow Press, 1983. $40.

**A GUIDE TO CHEROKEE DOCUMENTS
IN THE NORTHEASTERN U.S.**
Paul Kutsche
541 pp. Scarecrow Press, 1986. $79.50.

A GUIDE TO COMMUNITY EDUCATION
Institute of the Development of Indian Law,
$7.50.

**GUIDE TO FEDERAL FUNDING FOR
GOVERNMENTS & NONPROFITS:
NATIVE AMERICAN EDITION**
Describes general assistance funds for which
Native Americans are eligible. Covers federal pro-
grams that are relevant to Indian Tribal govern-
ments, Indian villages, nonprofits serving Native
American needs, and state and local governments
encompassing Native American populations. 3
Volumes. 2,456 pages. Government Information
Services. $329.95, includes 12 monthly grant
updates

**GUIDE TO INDIAN ARTIFACTS OF THE
NORTHEAST**
Roger W. Moeller
Illus. 32 pp. Paper. Hancock House, 1984.
$3.95.

GUIDE TO INDIAN HERBS
Ray Stark; Margaret Campbell
Illus. 48 pp. Paper. Hancock House, 1984.
$6.95.

**GUIDE TO THE INDIAN TREATIES
& OTHER DOCUMENTS 1778-1902**
Histree. $15.95.

**A GUIDE TO THE INDIAN
TRIBES OF OKLAHOMA**
Muriel H. Wright
Reprint of 1951 edition. Illus. 320 pp. University
of Oklahoma Press, $10.05; paper, $10.95.

**A GUIDE TO THE INDIAN TRIBES
OF THE PACIFIC NORTHWEST**
Robert Ruby & John Brown
Illus. Maps. 304 pp. Paper. University of
Oklahoma Press, 1986. $19.95.

**GUIDE TO MULTICULTURAL
RESOURCES, 1995-96**
Alex Boyd, Editor
Current information on multicultural organizations,
services and trends. Lists over 3,000 organizations including many Native American associations, institutions, and government agencies. 512
pp. Paper. Highsmith Press, $49.

**GUIDE TO THE PALAEO-INDIAN
ARTIFACTS OF NORTH AMERICA**
Richard M. Gramly
2nd revised edition. An authoritative treatment of
the variety of stone, bone, ivory and antler arti-
facts at North American Palaeo-Indian sites from
Alaska to Florida. Illus. 90 pp. Paper. Persimmon
Press, 1992. $15.95.

**GUIDE TO PREHISTORIC
RUINS OF THE SOUTHWEST**
Oppelt
Surveys many prehistoric sites, and provides
background facts. Illus. 208 pp. Paper. Hothem
House, $12.95.

A GUIDE TO PROPOSAL WRITING
Institute of the Development of Indian Law, $7.50.

**GUIDE TO THE RECORDS AT THE NATIONAL
ARCHIVES-LOS ANGELES BRANCH RELAT-
ING TO AMERICAN INDIANS OF CALIFORNIA**
Larry S. Watson
30 pp. Paper. Histree. $12.95.

**GUIDE TO RECORDS IN THE NATIONAL
ARCHIVES RELATING TO AMERICAN
INDIANS**
Edward E. Hill, Compiler
Illus. 468 pp. Illus. 368 pp. Smithsonian
Institution Press, 1981. $25.00.

**GUIDE TO RESEARCH ON
NORTH AMERICAN INDIANS**
Arlene B. Hirschfelder
A basic guide to the literature for general readers,
students, and scholars interested in the study of
American Indians. 340 pp. American Library As-
sociation, 1983. $75.00.

**A GUIDE TO UNDERSTANDING
CHIPPEWA TREATY RIGHTS**
Booklet. GLIFWC, 1991. No charge

**GUNS ON THE EARLY FRONTIERS: A HIS-
TORY OF FIREARMS FROM COLONIAL TIMES
THROUGH THE YEARS OF THE WESTERN
FUR TRADE**
Carl P. Russell
395 pp. University of Nebraska Press, 1980.
$28.95.

**GYAEHLINGAAY: TRADITIONS, TALES, &
IMAGES OF THE KAIGANI HAIDA**
Carol M. Eastman & Elizabeth A. Edwards
Provides the historical, cultural, and linguistic back-
ground of each story. Illus. 138 pp. Paper. Univer-
sity of Washington Press, $22.50.

H

**HAA SHUKA, OUR ANCESTORS;
TLINGIT ORAL NARRATIVES**
Nora Marks & Richard Dauenhauer, Editor
A Tlingit author tells stories that deal with "coming
of age, alienation, identity and self concept," etc.
Illus. 532 pp. Paper. University of Washington
Press, $22.50.

**HAA KUSTEEYI, OUR CULTURE:
TLINGIT LIFE STORIES**
Nora Marks & Richard Dauenhauer, Editor
Introduction to Tlingit social & political history
featuring biographies and life histories of over
50 men & women. Illus. 600 pp. University of
Washington Press, 1994. $40; paper, $24.95.

**HAA TUWUNAAGU YIS, FOR HEALING
OUR SPIRIT: TLINGIT ORATORY**
Nora Marks & Richard Dauenhauer, Editor
Tlingit texts with English translations and detailed
annotations; biographies of the elders. Illus. Biblio.
606 pp. Paper. University of Washington Press,
$22.50.

**HABOO: NATIVE AMERICAN STORIES
FROM PUGET SOUND**
Vi Hilbert, Editor & Translator
Illus. 228 pp. Paper. University of Washington
Press, 1985. $19.95.

**HAIDA MONUMENTAL ART: VILLAGES
OF THE QUEEN CHARLOTTE ISLANDS**
George F. MacDonald
Includes about 300 photos of houses & totem
poles constructed by the Haida Indians of the
Queen Charlotte Islands, British Columbia during
the late 19th century. Illus. 240 pp. Paper. Univer-
sity of Washington Press, $39.95.

HAIDA POTLATCH
Ulli Steltzer
Illus. 96 pp. University of Washington Press,
1984. $14.95.

**HAIDA: THE QUEEN CHARLOTTE ISLAND
INDIANS: THEIR ART & CULTURE**
Leslie Drew
Illus. 112 pp. Paper. Hancock House, $9.95.

HAIDA SONGS & TSIMSHIAN TEXTS
John Swanton and Franz Boas
Reprint of 1912 edition. AMS Press, $34.00.

**HAIDA TEXTS & MYTHS:
SKIDGATE DIALECT**
John Swanton
Reprint of 1905 edition. Scholarly Press, $79.00.

HAIDA: THEIR ART & CULTURE
Leslie Drew
Illus. 111 pp. Paper. Hancock House, $7.95.

HALFBREED
Maria Campbell
Tells you what it is like to be a half breed woman.
157 pp. Paper. University of Nebraksa Press,
1982. $6.95

**THE HALL OF THE NORTH AMERICAN
INDIAN**
Hillel Burger & Ian Brown; Barbara Isaac, Ed.
Illus. 135 pp. Paper. Peabody Museum, 1990.
$25.00.

HALLMARKS OF THE SOUTHWEST: WHO MADE IT?
Indian Arts & Crafts Association Staff
Illus. 244 pp. Schiffer, 1989. $45.00.

HAMPTON INSTITUTE SCHOOL RECORDS 1878-1891
Larry Watson, Editor
Record of Indian students who attended to 1890. 175 pp. Histree. $24.95.

THE HAN INDIANS: A COMPILATION OF ETHNOGRAPHIC & HISTORICAL DATA ON THE ALASKA--YUKON BOUNDARY AREA
Cornelius Osgood
Paper. Yale University, Anthropology, 1971. $7.50.

HAND TREMBLING, FRENZY WITCHCRAFT, & MOTH MADNESS: A STUDY OF NAVAJO SEIZURE DISORDERS
Jerrold E. Levy, et al
176 pp. University of Arizona Press, 1987. $27.95.

HANDBOOK OF THE AMERICAN FRONTIER - FOUR CENTURIES OF INDIAN-WHITE RELATIONSHIPS: THE SOUTHEASTERN WOODLANDS, Vol. 1
J. Norman Heard
Vol. I: The Southeastern Woodlands, 421 pp. 1987. $39.50; Vol. II: The Northeastern Woodlands, 417 pp. 1990; Vol. III: The Great Plains 280 pp. 1993 Scarecrow Press, $39.50.

HANDBOOK OF AMERICAN INDIAN GAMES
Allan & Paulette Macfarlan
150 authentic Indian games. Illus. 288 pp. Paper. Dover & Cherokee Publications, 1985. $6.95.

HANDBOOK OF THE AMERICAN INDIAN LANGUAGES
Franz Boas
Reprint. 4 vols. Reprint Services, $225 per set.

HANDBOOK OF AMERICAN INDIAN RELIGIOUS FREEDOM
Christopher Vecsey
175 pp. Paper. Crossroad Pubg., 1991. $14.95.

HANDBOOK OF AMERICAN INDIANS NORTH OF MEXICO, 1907-1910
Frederick Hodge
Reprint of 1912 ed. 2 vols. Illus. Greenwood, $49.60.

A HANDBOOK OF CREEK (MUSCOGEE) GRAMMAR
Anna Bosch
Vocabulary, spelling, and pronunciation. 35 pp. Paper. Indian University Press, 1994 second printing. $7, postpaid.

HANDBOOK OF FEDERAL INDIAN LAW
Felix S. Cohen, Editor
Standard reference work on federal Indian law. Reprint of 1942 edition. The Michie Co., $80. Paper. AMS Press, $25.

HANDBOOK OF FEDERAL INDIAN LAW WITH REFERENCE TABLES & INDEX
Felix S. Cohen
Reprint of 1941 ed. 686 pp. William S. Heinman, $75.

HANDBOOK OF THE INDIANS OF CALIF.
A. L. Kroeber
Reprint of 1925 edition. Illus. 995 pp. Reprint Services, $95.00. Paper. Hothem House, $16.95.

HANDBOOK OF NATIVE AMERICAN HERBS
Alma R. Hutchens
Covers many Indian plants and their uses. Illus. 250 pp. Paper. AISES, $10.

HANDBOOK OF NORTH AMERICAN INDIANS
Seven handbooks discuss the culture, history, and language of North American Indians. Vol. 2: Great Basin, 863 pp., 1986, $27; Vol. 5: Arctic, 861 pp., 1984, $29; Vol. 6: Subarctic, 853 pp., 1981, $25; Vol. 7: Northwest Coast, 795 pp., 1990, $38; Vol. 8: California, 800 pp., 1978, $25; Vol. 9: Southwest - Puebloan Peoples, 701 pp., 1979, $23; Vol. 10: Southwest - Non-Puebloan People, 884 pp., 1983, $25; Vol. 15: Northeast, 924 pp., 1978, $27. Illus. Smithsonian.

A HANDBOOK OF NORTHEASTERN INDIAN MEDICINAL PLANTS
James A. Duke
Illus. 212 pp. Quarterman, 1986. $30.00.

HANDBOOK OF NORTHERN ARIZONA POTTERY WARES
Harold S. Colton and Lyndon L. Hargrave
Reprint of 1937 edition. AMS Press, $32.50.

HANDBOOK OF TRIBAL NAMES OF PENNSYLVANIA 1908
Thomas K. Donnalley, Editor
160 pp. Paper. Histree, 1986. $19.95.

THE HANDSOME PEOPLE: A HISTORY OF THE CROW INDIANS AND THE WHITES
Charles Crane Bradley
Grades 8-adult. 310 pp. Council for Indian Education, $20.95; paper, $14.95.

HANO: A TEWA INDIAN COMMUNITY IN ARIZONA
Edward P. Dozier
Paper. Holt, Rinehart & Winston, 1966. $9.95.

*HAPPILY MAY I WALK: AMERICAN INDIANS & ALASKA NATIVES TODAY
Arlene Hirschfelder
Grades 5 and up. 160 pp. Macmillan, 1986. $13.95.

HARMONY BY HAND: ART OF THE SOUTHWEST INDIANS
Patrick Houlihan
Illus. 108 pp. Chronicle Books, 1987. $30.00; paper, $18.95.

HARPER'S ANTHOLOGY OF TWENTIETH CENTURY NATIVE AMERICAN POETRY
Duane Niatum, Editor
Anthology of poetry by 36 Native Americans. Harper & Row, 1988. $16.95.

HART'S PREHISTORIC PIPE RACK
Hart
Covers prehistoric Indian pipes for the Mississippi River into the Eastern U.S. Illus. 272 pp. Hothem House, 1978. $47.50, postpaid.

HASINAI: A TRADITIONAL HISTORY OF THE CADDO CONFEDERACY
Vynola Newkumet & Howard Meredith
Illus. 168 pp. Texas A&M U. Press, 1988. $16.95.

THE HASINAIS: THE SOUTHERN CADDOANS AS SEEN BY THE EARLIEST EUROPEANS
Herbert Bolton
Illus. 200 pp. U. of Oklahoma Press, 1987. $19.95.

HAU, KOLA! THE PLAINS INDIAN COLLECTION OF THE HAFFENREFFER MUSEUM OF ANTHROPOLOGY
Barbara A. Hail
Illus. 256 pp.Paper. University of Washington Press, 1980. $25.

EMIL W. HAURY'S PREHISTORY OF THE AMERICAN SOUTHWEST
Emil W. Haury; J. Reid & D. Doyel, Editors
506 pp. University of Arizona Press, 1986. $ 45.

HAVASUPAI ETHNOGRAPHY
Leslie Spier
Reprint of 1928 edition. AMS Press, $57.50.

HAVASUPAI HABITAT: A.F. WHITING'S ETHNOGRAPHY OF A TRADITIONAL NDIAN CULTURE
Steven A. Weber & David P. Seaman, Editors
288 pp. University of Arizona Press, 1985. $35.

HAVASUPAI LEGENDS: RELIGION & MYTHOLOGY OF THE INDIANS OF GRAND CANYON
Carma Lee Smithson & Robert C. Euler
Illus. Paper. U. of Utah Press, 1994. $12.95.

HAVASUPAI RELIGION & MYTHOLOGY
Carma Smithson and Robert Euler
Reprint of 1964 ed. 120 pp. AMS Press, $14.

THE HAVASUPAI WOMAN
Carma Smithson
Reprint of 1959 ed. Illus. 178 pp. AMS Press, $16.75.

HAVASUPAI YEARS
Madge Knobloch
Journal of teacher teching on the Havasupai reservation in the bottom of the Grand Canyon in 1931-33. 124 pp. Council for Indian Education, $11.95; paper, $5.95.

HAVSUW BAAJA: PEOPLE OF BLUE GREEN WATER
Lois Hurst
Revised 1985 edition. Havasupai Council, $18.

HAWAII: THE ALOHA STATE
Helen Bauer; revised & updated by Dr Ann Rayson
Hawaiian history from ancient times through statehood to the present. 192 pp. The Bess Press, $27.95; paper, $17.95. Teacher's workbook, $6.95.

HAWAII: OUR ISLAND STATE
Potter, Kasdon, Hazama
Hawaiian history. Illus. 421 pp. The Bess Press, $25.95.

HAWAII PONO: AN ETHNIC & POLITICAL HISTORY
Lawrence H. Fuchs
History of Hawaii; native Hawaiian cultural contributions and the impact of American settlers from the time they assumed control of the islands in 1893 until statehood in 1959. Illus. 528 pp. Paper. The Bess Press, $14.95.

HAWAIIAN ANTIQUITIES
David Malo; translated by Nathaniel Emerson
Authentic sources of information on the ancient beliefs & practices of Hawaiians. Illus. 302 pp. Paper. Bishop Museum, $19.95.

HAWAIIAN CORDAGE
Catherine C. Summers
Traditional Hawaiian material culture is examined. Illus. 144 pp. Paper. Bishop Museum, $24.95.

HAWAIIAN MEDICINE BOOK: HE BUKE LAAU LAPAAU
Malcolm Naea Chun, translator
A translation (both Hawaiian and English) of a mo'elelo (legend), chants, and description of Hawaiian medicine. 96 pp. The Bess Press, $14.95.

HAWAIIAN NAME BOOK
Patrick Ka'ano'i & Robert Snakenberg
Gives origins, derivations, and melodic Hawaiian translations of hundreds of English first names. 64 pp. The Bess Press, $6.95.

HAWAIIAN PETROGLYPHS
J. Halley Cox; with Edward Stasack
Explores all the known petroglyph sites in the Hawaiian Islands. Illus. Photos. 108 pp. Paper. Bishop Museum, $13.95.

HAWAIIAN SENTENCE BOOK
Robert Snakenberg; illus. by Robin Burningham
Illus. lessons expand on the basic Hawaiian Word Book. Cassette. 112 pp. The Bess Press, $16.95.

HAWAIIAN WORD BOOK
Illus. by Robin Burningham
200 illustrated words present various aspects of Hawaiian culture. Cassette. 104 pp. The Bess Press, $16.95.

THE HAWAIIANS OF OLD
Betty Dunford
Shows the detail and complexity of the ancient Hawaiian culture. Revised edition. 230 pp. The Bess Press, $27.95. Teacher's manual, 88 pp. $6.95. Also, an eight-part filmstrip & cassettes, $289.

HAWAII'S ROYAL HISTORY
Helen Wong & Dr. Ann Rayson
Focuses on the monarchy period and the history of Hawai'i and the arrival and settlement of the early Hawaiians. 240 pp. The Bess Press, $27.95; paper, $17.95; workbook, $6.95.

THE HAWK IS HUNGRY; AND OTHER STORIES
D'Arcy McNickle; Birgit Hans, Editor
16 stories by McNickle, one of the most influential Native Americans of this century. 180 pp. University of Arizona Press, 1992. $29.95; paper, $14.95.

HE WALKED THE AMERICAS
L. Taylor Hansen
Illus. Amherst Press, 1963. $13.95.

HE WHO HUNTED BIRDS IN HIS FATHER'S VILLAGE: THE DIMENSIONS OF A HAIDA MYTH
Gary Snyder
154 pp. Paper. Grey Fox, 1979. $5.95.

HEAD & FACE MASKS IN NAVAHO CEREMONIALISM
Bernard Haile
Reprint of 1947 edition. AMS Press, $17.50.

HEADED UPSTREAM: INTERVIEWS WITH ICONOCLASTS
Jack Loofflor

Illus. 168 pp. Paper. Harbinger House, Inc., 1989. $10.95.

HEAR THE CREATOR'S SONG: A GUIDE TO THE STUDY THEME "NATIVE PEOPLES OF NORTH AMERICA"
Remmelt & Kathleen Hummelen
Includes five study sessions for groups using the book, Stories of Survival," and offers a selection of poetry, myths, songs and artwork of Native cultures across North America. Paper. Friendship Press, $4.50.

HEAR ME MY CHIEFS: NEZ PERCE LEGEND & HISTORY
Lucullus V. McWhorter
Reprint of 1952 edition. Illus. Maps. Biblio. 640 pp. The Caxton Printers, $27.95; paper. $19.95.

THE HEARD MUSEUM: HISTORY & COLLECTIONS
Ann Marshall & Mary Brennan
Illus. 50 pp. Paper. The Heard Museum, 1989. $8.95.

HEART BAGS & HAND SHAKES: THE STORY OF THE COOK COLLECTION
Dorothy Cook Meade
By the granddaughter of Capt." James H. Cook describes the unique friendships which Cook forged with Sioux & Cheyenne families in western Nebraska from the late 1800s to the 1940. Illus. 60 pp. Paper. National Woodlands Publishing, 1994. $10.95.

*HEART BUTTE: A BLACKFEET INDIAN COMMUNITY
John Reyhner
Grades K-4. 18 pp. Paper. Council for Indian Education, 1984. $1.95.

A HEART FULL OF TURQUOISE: PUEBLO INDIAN TALES
Joe Hayes, retold by
Illus. 80 pp. Paper. Mariposa Print Publishing, 1988. $9.50.

HEART OF THE DRAGONFLY
Allison Bird
Discusses the development and history of the cross necklaces worn by Pueblo & Navajo Indians. Illus. Photos. 208 pp. Paper. Avanyu Publishing, $39.95.

*HEETUNKA'S HARVEST: A TALE OF THE PLAINS INDIANS
retold by Jennifer Berry Jones
Grades 1-6. Illus. 32 pp. Roberts Rinehart, 1994. $15.95.

HEIAU OF THE ISLAND OF HAWAI'I: A HISTORIC SURVEY OF NATIVE HAWAIIAN TEMPLE SITES
John F.G. Stokes
Archaeological study of Hawaiian heiau during 1906-7. Illus. 196 pp. Paper. Bishop Museum, $29.95.

THE HEIRS OF COLUMBUS
Gerald Vizenor
190 pp. University Press of New England, 1991. $22.95; paper, $12.95.

HELEN HUNT JACKSON & HER INDIAN REFORM LEGACY
Valerie Sherer Mathes
Conflict in Indian policy and reform of the period.

Illus. Map. 253 pp. University of Texas Press, 1990. $27.95.

*HER SEVEN BROTHERS
Paul Goble
Grades 3 and up. Illus. Macmillan, 1989. $13.95.

*THE HERITAGE
Nancy Armstrong et al
Grades 3-6. Council for Indian Education, 1977. $2.95.

THE HERITAGE OF KLICKITAT BASKETRY: A HISTORY & ART PRESERVED
Nettie Kuneki and Marie Teo
Illus. 48 pp. Paper. Oregon Historical Society, 1982. $4.95.

HERNANDO DE SOTO & THE INDIANS OF FLORIDA
Jerald T. Milanich & Charles Hudson
Illus. 42 maps Biblio. 307 pp. University Press of Florida, 1993. $34.95.

THE HERO OF BATTLE ROCK:A TRUE ACCOUNT - OREGON COAST INDIAN ATTACK
Bert Webber
Illus. 56 pp. Paper. Ye Galleon, 1978. $6.95.

*HEROES & HEROINES IN TLINGIT-HAIDA LEGENDS: & THEIR COUNTERPARTS IN CLASSICAL MYTHOLOGY
Mary L. Beck
Grades 8 and up. Illus. 120 pp. Paper. Alaska Northwest, 1989. $12.95.

*HIAWATHA
Megan McCiard & George Ypsilantis
Grades 5-7. Illus. 144 pp. Silver Burdette, 1989. $11.98; paper, $7.95.

*HIAWATHA - MESSENGER OF PEACE
Dennis B. Fradin
The real Hiawatha of Iroquois history. Grades 3-6. Illus. Photos. 40 pp. AISES, $14.95.

*THE HIDATSA
Mary J. Schneider
Grades 7-12. Illus. 112 pp. Chelsea House, 1989. $17.95.

HIDATSA EAGLE TRAPPING
Gilbert L. Wilson
Reprint of 1928 edition. AMS Press, $14.

THE HIDATSA EARTHLODGE
Gilbert L. Wilson; Bella Weitzner, Editor
Reprint of 1934 edition. AMS Press, $29.

HIDATSA SHRINE & THE BELIEFS RESPECTING IT
G.H. Pepper and G.L. Wilson
Reprint of 1908 edition. Kraus, $15.

HIDATSA SOCIAL & CEREMONIAL ORGANIZATION
Alfred W. Bowers
Extensive personal and ritual narratives. Illus. 530 pp. Paper. University of Nebraska Press, 1992. $15.95.

THE HIDDEN HALF: STUDIES OF PLAINS INDIAN WOMEN
Patricia Albers and Beatrice Medicine
286 pp. University Presses of Ameica, 1983. $31.50; paper, $15.

THE HIDDEN LANGUAGE OF THE SENECA: LANGUAGE OF THE STONES; LANGUAGE OF THE TREES; ENTERING THE SILENCE THE SENECA WAY; CHANTS AND DANCES
Twylah Nitsch
Scriptorium Press, 1987.

THE HILL CREEK HOMESTEAD AND THE LATE MISSISSIPPIAN SETTLEMENT IN THE LOWER ILLINOIS VALLEY
Michael D. Connor, Editor
Illus. 239 pp. Paper. Center for American Archaeology, 1985. $9.95.

HISTOIRE DES ABENAKIS: A BIBLIOGRA-PHY OF CANADIANA
J. Maurault
Reprint of 1866 edition. Johnson Reprint, $45.

HISTORIC HOPI CERAMICS: THE THOMAS V. KEARN COLLECTION OF THE PEABODY MUSEUM OF ARCHAEOLOGY & ETHNOLOGY, HARVARD UNIVERSITY
Edwin L. Wade and Lea S. McChesney
Illus. 550 pp. Paper. Peabody-Harvard, 1981. $30.

THE HISTORIC INDIAN TRIBES OF LOUISI-ANA: FROM 1542 TO THE PRESENT
Fred B. Kniffen, et al
Illus. 344 pp. Louisiana State University Press, 1987. $24.95.

HISTORIC NAVAJO WEAVING, 1800-1900: THREE CULTURES-ONE LOOM
Tyrone Campbell
Revised edition. Illus. 40 pp. Paper. Avanyu, 1987. $14.75.

HISTORIC POTTERY OF THE PUEBLO INDIANS, 1600-1800
Larry Frank & Francis Harlow
Illus. 175 pp. Schiffer, 1989. $35.

HISTORICAL ACCOUNT OF THE DOINGS & SUFFERINGS OF THE CHRISTIAN INDIANS IN NEW ENGLAND IN THE YEARS 1675, 1676, 1677
Daniel Gookin
Reprint of 1836 ed. Ayer Co. Publishers, $21.

HISTORICAL ATLAS OF THE AMERICAN WEST
Warren A. Beck & Ynez D. Haase
Includes a section on aboriginal settings and Native American tribes, European contacts and settlements, etc. 78 maps. 200 pp. Paper. University of Oklahoma Press, $19.95.

HISTORICAL ATLAS OF ARKANSAS
Gerald T. Hanson & Carl H. Moneyhon
Includes a section on Arkansas' aboriginal setting and Native American tribes, European contacts and settlements, etc. 71 maps. 176 pp. Paper. University of Oklahoma Press, $19.95.

HISTORICAL ATLAS OF COLORADO
Thomas J. Noel, et al
Includes a section on Colorado's aboriginal setting and Native American tribes, European contacts and settlements, etc. 60 maps. Biblio. 192 pp. Paper. University of Oklahoma Press, 1994. $19.95.

HISTORICAL ATLAS OF LOUISIANA
Charles R. Goins & John M. Caldwell
Includes a section on Louisiana's aboriginal set-ting and Native American tribes, European con-tacts & settlements, etc. 99 maps. 240 pp. University of Oklahoma Press, $65; paper, $29.95.

HISTORICAL ATLAS OF MISSOURI
Milton D. Rafferty
Includes a section on Missouri's aboriginal set-ting and Native American tribes, European con-tacts and settlements, etc. 113 pp. of maps. 256 pp. University of Oklahoma Press, $34.95; paper, $18.95.

HISTORICAL ATLAS OF OKLAHOMA
John W. Morris, Charles R. Goins & Edwin C. McReynolds
Includes a section on Oklahoma's aboriginal set-ting and Native American tribes, European con-tacts & settlements, etc. 83 maps. 206 pp. Uni-versity of Oklahoma Press, $32.95; paper, $18.95.

HISTORICAL ATLAS OF TEXAS
A. Ray Stephens & William M. Holmes
Includes a section on Texa's aboriginal setting and Native American tribes, European contacts and settlements, etc. 64 maps. 160 pp. University of Oklahoma Press, $34.95; paper, $18.95.

HISTORICAL BACKGROUND OF THE SANTA ANA PUEBLO
Tom Luebben
25 pp. Institute for the Development of Indian Law, $8.50.

HISTORICAL BACKGROUND TO CHIPPEWA TREATIES
Robert Keller
25 pp. Institute for the Development of Indian Law, $12.50.

AN HISTORICAL CHRONOLOGY OF THE KIOWA TRIBE
John Belindo
12 pp. Institute for the Development of Indian Law, $5.50.

HISTORICAL COLLECTIONS OF GEORGIA
George White
Reprint of 1920 edition. 787 pp. Genealogical Publishing, $35.

HISTORICAL COLLECTIONS OF THE INDIANS OF NEW ENGLAND
Daniel Gookin
Reprint of 1836 edition. Ayer Co., $23.50.

HISTORICAL DEMOGRAPHY OF THE PIMA & MARICOPA INDIANS, 1846-1974
Cary W. Meister
Reprint. Two volumes. 770 pp. Garland, $154.

THE HISTORICAL DEVELOPMENT OF THE CONCEPT OF NUNAVUT: AN ANNOTATED BIBLIOGRAPHY OF THE LITERATURE SINCE THE 1930'S
R.L. Minion
Paper. CCI, 1994. $15.

HISTORICAL DICTIONARY OF NORTH AMERICAN ARCHAEOLOGY
Edward Jelks & Juliet Jelks
An alphabetical listing of over 1,800 entries pro-viding descriptions for cultures, mounds, ruins, and archaeological sites. Sources of information, and list of references. Biblio. 760 pp. Greenwood Pub-lishing, 1988. $95.

HISTORICAL INTRODUCTIONS TO STUDIES AMONG THE SEDENTARY INDIANS OF NEW MEXICO & A REPORT ON THE RUINS OF THE PUEBLO AT PECOS
Adolf F. Bandelier
Reprint of 1881 edition. Paper. AMS Press, $19.

AN HISTORICAL JOURNAL OF THE CAMPAIGNS IN NORTH AMERICA IN THE YEARS 1757-1760
A.G. Doughty
Facsimile of 1916 edition. Two volumes. Greenwood Press, $125.00/set.

HISTORICAL MEMOIRS, RELATING TO THE HOUSATONIC INDIANS
Samuel Hopkins
Reprint of 1911 edition. Johnson Reprint, $17.

HISTORICAL SKETCH OF THE FLATHEAD INDIAN NATION
Peter Ronan
Reprint of 1890 ed. 108 PP. Ross & Haines, $15.

HISTORICAL & STATISTICAL INFORMATION RESPECTING THE HISTORY, CONDITION & PROSPECTS OF THE INDIAN TRIBES OF THE U.S.
H.R. Schoolcraft; Francis Nichols, Editor
Reprint of 1857 edition. Seven volumes. Illus. AMS Press, $1.500 per set.

THE HISTORY & CULTURE OF IROQUOIS DI-PLOMACY: AN INTERDISCIPLINARY GUIDE TO THE TREATIES OF THE SIX NATIONS & THEIR LEAGUE
Francis Jennings & William Fenton, Editors
Illus. 296 pp. Syracuse University Press, 1985. $35.

HISTORY, EVOLUTION & THE CONCEPT OF CULTURE: SELECTED PAPERS BY ALEXANDER LESSER
Sidney W. Mintz
192 pp. Cambridge University Press, 1989. $34.50.

HISTORY, MANNERS & CUSTOMS OF THE INDIAN NATIONS WHO ONCE INHABITED PENNSYLVANIA & NEIGHBORING STATES
John Heckewelder
Reprint of 1819 edition. Illus. 450 pp. Heritage Books & Ayer Co., $29.95.

HISTORY, MYTHS & SACRED FORMULAS OF THE CHEROKEES
James Mooney
Primary source book on Cherokee contains 126 legends obtained on the Cherokee Reservation in N.C. in 1887-88. Illus. 700 pp. Paper. Cherokee Publications, $15.95.

HISTORY OF ALABAMA, & INCIDENTALLY OF GEORGIA & MISSISSIPPI, FROM THE EARLIEST PERIOD
Albert J. Pickett
Reprint of 1851 edition. Illus. Ayer Co., $52.95.

HISTORY OF BAPTIST INDIAN MISSIONS
Isaac McCoy
Reprint of 1840 edition. Johnson Reprint, $36.

A HISTORY OF THE BUREAU OF INDIAN AFFAIRS & ITS ACTIVITIES AMONG INDIANS
Curtis E. Jackson and Marcia J. Galli
Paper. R & E Research Associates, 1977. $15.

HISTORY OF CANADA, OR NEW FRANCE
F. Du Creaux; J.B. Conacher, Editor
Reprint of 1951 edition. Two volumes.
Greenwood Press, $26.75 each.

**HISTORY OF THE CATHOLIC MISSIONS
AMONG THE INDIAN TRIBES OF THE U.S.,
1529-1854**
John D. Shea
Reprint of 1855 edition. Ayer Co., $26.50;
AMS Press, $28.50.

**HISTORY OF THE CHEROKEE INDIANS
& THEIR LEGENDS & FOLKLORE**
Emmet Starr
Reprint of 1921 edition. Kraus, $52.

*A HISTORY OF THE CHEYENNE PEOPLE
Tom Weist
Grades 6-12. ilius. 227 pp. Paper . Council for
Indian Education, 1977. $15.95; paper , $9.95.

**HISTORY OF EVENTS RESULTING IN INDIAN
CONSOLIDATION WEST OF THE MISSISSIPPI**
Annie H. Abel
Reprint of 1908 edition. AMS Press, $14.50.

**HISTORY OF THE FIVE INDIAN NATIONS:
DEPENDING ON THE PROVINCE OF NEW
YORK IN AMERICA**
Cadwallader Colden
Reprint. Paper. Cornell University Press, $8.95.

**HISTORY OF THE FIVE INDIAN
NATIONS OF CANADA**
Cadwallader Colden
Reprint of 1922 edition. 2 vols. 205 pp. AMS
Press, $55.00. Reprint Services, $79.00

**HISTORY OF INDIAN ARTS
EDUCATION IN SANTA FE**
Winona Garmhausen
Illus. 144 pp. Paper . Sunstone Press, 1988.
$15.95.

A HISTORY OF INDIAN EDUCATION
Jon Reyhner & Jeanne Eder
Overview from first missionaries to present.. 150
pp. Council for Indian Education, $1 1.95; paper,
$5.95.

A HISTORY OF INDIAN POLICY: SYLLABUS
Judith Bachman
Paper. National Book, $6.75; cassette recording,
$146.10.

HISTORY OF THE INDIAN WARS
Samuel Penhallow
Reprint of 1726 edition. 208 pp. Corner House,
$18.50.

**HISTORY OF THE INDIAN WARS IN NEW EN-
GLAND, FROM THE FIRST SETTLEMENT T O
THE TERMINATION OF THE WAR WITH KING
PHILIP IN 1677**
William Hubbard
Reprint of 1865 edition. 2 vols. in one. 595 pp.
Map. Paper. Heritage Books, $35.

**HISTORY OF INDIAN-WHITE RELA TIONS,
Vol. 4**
William Sturtevant; W ilcomb E. W ashburn, Ed.
Illus. 852 pp. Smithsonian, 1989. $47.00.

HISTORY OF THE INDIANS OF CONNECTICUT
John DeForest
Reprint of 1861 odition. Reprint Services, $59.

HISTORY OF THE INDIANS OF THE U.S.
Angie Debo
Illus. 464 pp. Paper . University of Oklahoma
Press, 1974. $17.95.

HISTORY OF THE NATIVE AMERICANS
Alvin Josephy, Editor
Six biographies of Native American leaders and
the tribes theyu represent. Includes separate
books for Hiawatha, King Philip, Geronimo, Sitting Bull, Sequoyah & Tecumseh. Illus. Mapos. 128
-144pp each. Silver Burdett Press, 1993. $10.95
each; paper, $7.95. $65.70/set; paper , $47.70/set.

**A HISTORY OF THE NEW YORK IROQUOIS,
NOW COMMONLY CALLED THE SIX NATIONS**
William M. Beauchamp
Reprint of 1905 ed. Illus. AMS Press, $37.50.

**HISTORY OF THE NAVAJOS:
THE RESERVATION YEARS**
Garrick & Roberta Bailey
Illus. 376 pp. School of American Research &
University of Washington Press, 1986. $32.50;
paper, $17.50.

HISTORY OF NEW FRANCE
Marc Lescarbot
Reprint of 1907 edition. Three volumes.
Greenwood Press, $27.50, $37.75, & $35.25.

**HISTORY OF THE NEW YORK INDIANS
AND INDIANS OF THE PRINTUP FAMILY**
A.D. Printup
Illus. 89 pp. DeWitt & Sheppard, 1985. $66.66.

HISTORY OF THE OJIBWAY INDIANS
Peter Jones
Reprint of 1861 edition. Ayer Co., $24.50.

HISTORY OF THE OJIBWAY PEOPLE
William W. Warren
First hand descriptions & stories from relatives,
tribal leaders & acquaintamces. Reprint of 1885
edition. Illus. 41 1 pp. Paper. Minnesota Historical
Society Press, 1984. $12.95.

**HISTORY OF THE ORIGINAL
PEOPLES OF NORTHERN CANADA**
Keith J. Crowe
Revised edition. Paper . McGill-Queen's
University Press, 1991. $19.95.

**HISTORY OF PHILIP'S WAR, COMMONLY
CALLED THE GREAT INDIAN WAR OF 1675 &
1676. ALSO THE FRENCH & INDIAN WARS AT
EASTWARD IN 1689, 1690, 1692, 1696, & 1704**
Thomas Church, Esq.; notes by Samuel Drake
Reprint. 360 pp. Paper . Heritage Books, $23.50.

**HISTORY OF THE SANTEE SIOUX:
U.S. INDIAN POLICY ON TRIAL**
Roy W. Meyer
Reprint of 1967 edition. Illus. 452 pp. Paper. .
University of Nebraska Press, $17.95.

**HISTORY OF THE SECOND
SEMINOLE W AR, 1835-1842**
John K. Mahon
Revised 1967 edition. Illus. Biblio. 391 pp.
Paper. University Press of Florida, $15.95

**HISTORY OF THE SPIRIT LAKE MASSACRE
& OF MISS ABIGAIL GARDINER'S THREE
MONTH CAPTIVITY AMONG THE INDIANS**
L.P. Lee
Reprint of 1857 ed. Ye Galleon Press, $7.50.

**HISTORY & PRESENT DEVELOPMENT
OF INDIAN SCHOOLS IN THE U.S.**
Solomon R. Ammon
Reprint of 1935 edition. Paper . R & E
Associates, $10.95.

**THE HISTORY & PRESENT
STATE OF VIRGINIA**
R. Beverley; Louis B. W right, Editor
Reprint of 1947 edition. Illus. 366 pp. Paper .
Books on Demand, $76.40.

**HIV PREVENTION IN NA TIVE AMERICAN
COMMUNITIES: A MANUAL FOR NATIVE
AMERICAN HEALTH & HUMAN SER VICE
PROVIDERS**
Updates AIDS: The Basics. It highlights Native
American HIV prevention educators and pro-
grams. Includes overviews of HIV and AIDS. Na-
tional Native American AIDS Prevention Center ,
$20.

**HIWASSEE ISLAND: AN ARCHAEOLOGICAL
ACCOUNT OF FOUR TENNESSEE INDIAN
PEOPLES**
Thomas N. Lewis and Madeline Kneberg
Illus. 328 pp. University of Tennessee Press,
1984. $28.50; paper , $14.95.

**THE HOE & THE HORSE ON THE PLAINS:
A STUDY OF CULTUREAL DEVELOPMENT
AMONG NORTH AMERICAN INDIANS**
Preston Holder
An ethnological study; fieldwork with the Arikara;
Plains ethnography . Illus. Maps. 200 pp. Paper .
University of Nebraska Press, 1970. $8.95.

**HOGANS: NAVAJO HOUSES
& HOUSE SONGS**
David & Susan McAllester
Illus. 115 pp. Paper. University Press
of New England, 1987. $14.95.

**THE HOHOKAM: ANCIENT
PEOPLE OF THE DESERT**
David Grant Noble
Illus. Maps. 88 pp. Paper . School of
American Research, 1989. $10.95.

**THE HOHOKAM INDIANS
OF THE TUCSON BASIN**
Linda Gregonis & Karl J. Reinhard
A layman's guide to Hohokam lifeways. 48 pp.
Paper. University of Arizona Press, 1979. $4.95.

**HOHOKAM & PATAYAN: PREHISTORY
OF SOUTHWESTERN ARIZONA**
R. McGuire and M. Schif fer, Editors
Academic Press, 1982. $49.50.

**HOKAHEY! A GOOD DAY TO DIE! THE
INDIAN CASUALTIES OF THE CUSTER
FIGHT**
Richard G. Hardorf f
Identifies the fallen Indians, by name and the
location where they were killed. Illus. 176 pp.
The Arthur H. Clark Co., $27.50.

*HOKSILA & THE RED BUFF ALO
Moses N. Crow
Grades 3 and up. Illus. 40 pp. Paper . Tipi Press,
1991. $5.95.

**THE HOLLYWOOD INDIAN: STEREOTYPES
OF NATIVE AMERICANS IN FILMS**
Illus. 80 pp. New Jersey State Museum, 1981.
$5.95.

HOLOCENE HUMAN ECOLOGY IN NORTHEASTERN NORTH AMERICA
G.P. Nicholas, Editor
Illus. 340 pp. Plenum Publishing, 1988. $34.50.

HOLY WIND IN NAVAJO PHILOSOPHY
James K. McNeley
115 pp. Paper. U. of Arizona Press, 1981. $12.95.

A HOMELAND FOR THE CREE: REGIONAL DEVELOPMENT IN JAMES BAY, 1971-1981
Richard F. Salisbury
Shows how the first James Bay project was negotiated between the Cree and the Quebec government. McGill-Queen's University Press, 1986. $19.95.

HOMOL'OVI II: ARCHAEOLOGY OF AN ANCESTRAL HOPI VILLAGE, ARIZONA
E. Charles Adams & Kelley Ann Hays, Editors
Excavations. 139 pp. Paper. University of Arizona Press, 1992. $15.95.

HONOR DANCE: NATIVE AMERICAN PHOTOGRAPHS
John Running and William A. Allard
Illus. 168 pp. U. of Nevada Press, 1985. $40.

THE HOOP OF PEACE
Jan Havnen-Finley
Kevin Locke, a Lakota, is one of a few hoop dancers. He depicts the sacred Great Hoop of Peace. Illus. Photos. 48 pp. Paper. Naturegraph, $7.95.

THE HOPEWELL MOUND GROUP OF OHIO
Warren and Moorhead
Reprint of 1922 edition. Illus. AMS Press, $42.50.

HOPEWELL VILLAGE: A SOCIAL & ECONOMIC HISTORY OF AN IRON-MAKING COMMUNITY
J.E. Walker
University of Pennsylvania Press, 1966. $26.50; paper, $14.95.

HOPEWELLIAN STUDIES
Joseph Caldwell and Robert Hall, Editors
Facsimile edition. Illus. 156 pp. Illinois State Museum, 1977. $4.

HOPI
Susanne and Jake Page
Illus. 240 pp. Harry N. Abrams, 1982. $55.

*THE HOPI
Ann Tomchek
Grades K-4. Illus. 48 pp. Childrens Press, 1987. $11.45.

*THE HOPI
Nancy Bonvillain
Part of the *Indians of North America* series. Grades 4 and up. Illus. 112 pp. Paper. Chelsea House, 1991. $7.95.

*THE HOPI
Elaine Landau
Tells the story of the Hopi way of life. Part of the *Indian of Americas* seriesFull-color illustrations. Grades3 and up. 64 pp. Paper. Franklin Watts, 1994. $5.95.

THE HOPI APPROACH TO THE ART OF KACHINA DOLL CARVING
Erik Bromberg
Presents the diversity of Hopi kachina dolls. Illus. 94 pp. Paper. Schiffer, $9.95.

HOPI BIBLIOGRAPHY: COMPREHENSIVE & ANNOTATED
W. David Laird
3,000 sources. 735 pp. Paper. University of Arizona Press, 1977. $35.

THE HOPI CHILD
Wayne Dennis
Reprint of 1940 edition. Illus. 232 pp. Ayer Co. Publishers, $16.

HOPI COOKERY
Juanita Tiger Kavena
Includes over 100 authentic Hopi recipes. 1 15 pp. Paper. University of Arizona Press, 1980. $11.95.

HOPI COYOTE TALES: ISTUTUWUTSI
Ekkehart Malotki & Michael Lomatuway'ma
Illus. 350 pp. Paper. University of Nebraska Press, 1984. $13.95.

*HOPI, THE DESERT FARMERS
Susan L. Shaffer, Editor
Grade 3. Illus. Includes 30 student booklets and teacher's manual with transparencies, slides & audiocassette. The Heard Museum. $295.

HOPI DICTIONARY: HOPI-ENGLISH, ENGLISH-HOPI, GRAMMATICAL APPENDIX
P. David Seaman
600 pp. Paper. Northern Arizona University. $35.

HOPI & HOPI-TEWA POTTERY
32 pp. Paper. Museum of Northern Arizona, 1982. $4.

HOPI INDIAN ALTER ICONOGRAPHY
Armin W. Geertz
Illus. 39 pp. Paper. E.J. Brill, 1987. $39.

HOPI JOURNALS
A.M. Stephen; Elsie C. Parsons, Editor
Reprint of 1936 edition. Two vols. AMS Press, $115 per set; $57.50 each.

HOPI KACHINA DOLLS & THEIR CARVERS
Theda Bassman
Illustrates contemporary kachina dolls and the lives of the 25 carvers who make them. Illus. 192 pp. Schiffer, $59.95.

HOPI KACHINA DOLLS WITH A KEY TO THEIR IDENTIFICATION
Harold S. Colton
Revised 1971 edition. Illus. 159 pp. Paper. University of New Mexico Press, $10.95.

HOPI KACHINAS
Edwin Earle and Edward A. Kennard
Second edition. Illus. 50 pp. National Museum of the American Indian, 1971. $12.50. Portfolio of 28 color plates from the book, $3.50.

HOPI KACHINAS: THE COMPLETE GUIDE TO COLLECTION KACHINA DOLLS
Barton Wright
Includes buying tips and the history of the cultural roles played by the various figures. Illus. 152 pp. Northland Publishing, $12.95.

HOPI KACHINAS: A POSTCARD COLLECTION
Cliff Bahnimptewa, illustrator
20 full-color postcards. Illus. Northland Publishing, $7.95.

HOPI KATCINAS
Jesse W. Fewkes
Reprint of 1903 edition. Illus. 150 pp. Rio Grande Press, $25. Paper. Hothem House & Dover, $7.95.

HOPI MUSIC & DANCE
Robert Rhodes
Illus. 36 pp. Paper. Navajo Community College Press, $3.25.

*HOPI MYSTERIES
Jack Woolgar and Barbara J. Rudnicki
Grades 5-9. 32 pp. Council for Indian Education, 1974. $8.95; paper, $2.95.

HOPI OF THE SECOND MESA
Ernest and Pearl Beaglehole
Reprint of 1935 edition. Paper. Kraus, $15.

HOPI PHOTOGRAPHERS–HOPI IMAGES
Victor Masayesva & Erin Younger, Editors
Illus. 111 pp. Paper. University of Arizona Press, 1983. $19.95.

THE HOPI PHOTOGRAPHS: KATE CORY
Marnie Gaede, et al
Illus. 157 pp. University of New Mexico Press, 1988. $35.00; paper, $19.95.

HOPI POTTERY SYMBOLS
Alex Patterson
Based on work by Alexander M. Stephen. Includes tentative meanings and a glossary of Hopi words. Illus. 308 pp. Paper. Johnson Books, $17.95.

HOPI RUIN LEGENDS
Kiqotutuwutsi
Seven narratives, each about the destruction of a different village. All told in Hopi with English translations. 510 pp. U. of Nebraska Press, 1993. $50.

*HOPI SHIELDS & THE BEST DEFENSE
Eugene L. Hartley
Hopi boy learns about their traditional shields and their tradition of peace. Grades 2-6. 32 pp. Paper. Council for Indian Education, $3.95.

HOPI SILVER: THE HISTORY & THE HALLMARKS OF HOPI SILVERSMITHING
Margaret Wright
Illus. 4th revised edition. 135 pp. Paper. Northland Publishing, 1989. $12.95.

HOPI SNAKE CEREMONIES, AN EYEWITNESS ACCOUNT
Jesse W. Fewkes
Illus. 160 pp. Paper. Avanyu Pubg, 1986. $16.95.

HOPI SNAKE DANCE
D.H. Lawrence; W. David Laird, Editor
Illus. 60 pp. Paper. Membrane Press, 1985. $12.

A HOPI SOCIAL HISTORY: ANTHROPOLOGICAL PERSPECTIVES ON SOCIOCULTURAL PERSISTENCE & CHANGE
Scott Rushforth & Steadman Upham
Illus. 320 pp. Paper. U. of TX Press, 1992. $16.95.

HOPI SONGS
B. Gilman
Reprint of 1908 edition. AMS Press, $35.

HOPI TIME
E. Malotki
A linguistic analysis of the temporal concepts in the Hopi Language. 677 pp. Mouton de Gruyter, $125.

THE HOPI VILLAGES: ANCIENT PROVINCE OF TUSAYAN
John W. Powell
Illus. Maps. 48 pp. Paper. Filter Press, 1972. $2.50.

HOPI VOICES & VISIONS
Michael Kabotie, et al, Editors
80 pp. Paper. Street Press, 1984. $7.50.

THE HOPI WAY
Robert Boissiere
Illus. 90 pp. Paper. Sunstone Press, $8.95.

THE HOPI WAY: TALES FROM A CHANGING CULTURE
Mando Sevillano; drawings by Mike Castro
Illus. 102 pp. Paper. Northland Publishing, 1986. $12.95.

HOPI & ZUNI CEREMONIALISM
Elsie C. Parsons
Reprint of 1933 edition. Paper. Kraus, $15.

HOPIS, TEWAS, & THE AMERICAN ROAD
Willard Walker & Lydia Wyckoff, Editors
Illus. 189 pp. University of New Mexico Press, 1986. $25.00; paper, $15.95.

HORN & BONE IMPLEMENTS OF THE NEW YORK INDIANS
W.M. Beauchamp
Reprint of 1902 edition. AMS Press, $19.50.

TOM HORN, GOVERNMENT SCOUT & INDIAN INTERPRETER
Tom Horn
Reprint of 1904 edition. A first-hand account of the Apache Indian wars of the American Southwest. 318 pp. Paper. The Rio Grande Press, $12.

THE HORSE & THE DOG IN HIDATSA CULTURE
Gilbert L. Wilson
Reprint of 1924 edition. AMS Press, $23.

THE HORSE IN BLACKFOOT INDIAN CULTURE
John C. Ewers
Bound with comparative material from other western tribes. Reprint of 1955 edition. Illus. 374 pp. Paper. Smithsonian Books, $19.95.

*THE HORSE & THE PLAINS INDIAN
Raymond Schuessler & Tom Weist
Grades 4-10. 32 pp. Council for Indian Education, $8.95; paper, $2.95.

THE HORSEMEN OF THE AMERICAS: AN EXHIBITION FROM THE HALL OF THE HORSEMEN OF THE AMERICAS
Sheila Ohlendorf and William D. Wittliff
Illus. Paper. University of Texas, Humanities, 1968. $5.00.

*HOSKILA & THE RED BUFFALO
Moses Big Crow
A story from Lakota Sioux traditions. Grades 3 and up. Illus. Paper. Tipi Press, $5.95.

HOSTEEN KLAH: NAVAHO MEDICINE MAN & SAND PAINTER
Franc J. Newcomb
Illus. 227 pp. Paper. University of Oklahoma Press, 1971. $9.95.

*THE HOUR OF THE WOLF
Patricia Calvert
Grades 6 and up. Illus. Macmillan, 1989. $12.95.

HOUSE MADE OF DAWN
N. Scot Momaday
Pulitzer Prize winning first novel. 210 pp. Paper. AISES, $11.

HOUSE OF THREE TURKEYS: ANASAZI REDOUBT
Dave Bohn & Stephen Jett
Illus. Paper. Capra Press, 1977. $3.95.

HOUSES BENEATH THE ROCK: THE ANASAZI OF CANYON DE CHELLY & NAVAJO NATIONAL MONUMENT
David Noble, Editor
Illus. Maps. 56 pp. Paper. Ancient City Press, 1992. $8.95.

*HOUSES OF BARK: TIPI, WIGWAM, & LONGHOUSE
Grades 3-7. Illus. 25 pp. Tundra Books, 1990. $12.95.

*HOW THE BIRCH TREE GOT ITS STRIPES
Freda Ahenakew, Editor
Easy to read story written by Cree students. Grades 4-8. Illus. 1988. Distributed by Inland Books.

HOW CAN ONE SELL THE AIR? CHIEF SEATTLE'S VISION
Eli Gifford & R. Michael Cook
New edition. Illus. 80 pp. Paper. The Book Publishing Co. & AISES, 1993. $6.95.

*HOW FOOD WAS GIVEN: AN OKANAGAN LEGEND
illus. by Barb Marchand
Grades K-6. Illus. Paper. Theytus, 1991. $12.95.

HOW GEORGE ROGERS CLARK WON THE NORTHWEST & OTHER ESSAYS IN WESTERN HISTORY
R.G. Thwaites
Facsimile of 1903 edition. Ayer Co. Publishers, $21.50.

*HOW GLOOSKAP OUTWITS THE ICE GIANTS; & OTHER TALES OF THE MARITIME INDIANS, VOL. 1, 1989
Howard Norman
Grades 5 and up. Little, Brown & Co., 1989. $14.95.

HOW INDIANS USE WILD PLANTS FOR FOOD, MEDICINE & CRAFTS
Frances Densmore
Reprint of 1927 edition. Illus. 120 pp. Paper. Cherokee Publications, Hothem House & Dover, $4.95.

*HOW NAMES WERE GIVEN: AN OKANAGAN LEGEND
Illus. by Barb Marchand
Grades K-6. Illus. Paper. Theytus, 1991. $12.95.

*HOW THE PLAINS INDIANS LIVED
George Fichter
Grades 6 and up. David McKay, 1980. $10.95.

*HOW RABBIT STOLE THE FIRE: A NORTH AMERICAN INDIAN FOLK TALE
Joanna Troughton, retold by and illus by
Preschool-2. Illus. 28 pp. Peter Bedrick Books, 1986. $13.95.

HOW TO COLLECT NORTH AMERICAN INDIAN ARTIFACTS
Robert F. Brand
Illus. 151 pp. Robert F. Brand and American Indian Books, $11.95.

HOW TO ENROLL IN AN INDIAN/ALASKA NATIVE TRIBE
A step-by-step plan for an individual who is interested in enrolling in a tribe. Includes forms and instructions. Arrowstar Publishing, 1994. $19.95.

HOW TO RESEARCH AMERICAN INDIAN BLOOD LINES
Cecilia S. Carpenter
Illus. 110 pp. Paper. Heritage Quest, 1987. $9.

HOW TO TAKE PART IN LAKOTA CEREMONIES
William Stolzman
A step-by-step guide to the Pipe, Sweatbath, Vision Quest, Yuwipi, Lowanpi, and Sundance Ceremonies of the Lakota (Sioux). Illus. 72 pp. Paper. Center for Western Studies, $3.95.

HOW TO TAN SKINS THE INDIAN WAY
Evard H. Gibby
Explains brain tanning as it was done by Native Americans. Illus. 32 pp. Paper. Eagle's View Publishing, 1991. $4.50.

*HOW TURTLE SET THE ANIMALS FREE: AN OKANAGAN LEGEND
illus. by Barb Marchand
Grades K-4. Illus. Paper. Theytus, 1991. $12.95.

HOWARD'S CAMPAIGN AGAINST THE NEZ PERCE INDIANS, 1878
Thomas A. Sutherland
Ye Galleon Press, 1982. $14.95.

HULA PAHU: HAWAIIAN DRUM DANCES: Vol. I: HA'A & HULA PAHU SACRED MOVEMENTS
Adrienne L. Kaeppler
Analyzes dance movements & explains their evolution from early ha'a (ritual) traditions. Illus. 289 pp. Paper. Bishop Museum Press, 1994. $35.

HUMAN & CULTURAL DEVELOPMENT
J.T. Robinson, et al
66 pp. paper. Indiana Historical Society, 1974. $2.75.

HUMAN ECOLOGY: ISSUES IN THE NORTH Vols. I & II
R. Riewe & J. Oakes
Volume I - papers from the 1991 lecture series addressing traditional native nutrition and spirituality; health, housing & social problems; Inuit bird skin clothing. 135 pp., 1992; Volume II - collection of papers featuring presentations in the 1992 & 1993 lecture series focusing on relationships between aboriginal people & the Alberta government's education system; health & environmental legislation. 1994. CCI, $15 each.

THE HUMAN SIDE OF HISTORY
R.F. Locke, Editor
Paper. Mankind, $1.75.

*THE HUNT
Samuel Stanley and Pearl Oberg
Grades 5-9. 32 pp. Paper. Council for Indian Education, 1976. $1.95.

THE HUNT FOR WILLIE BOY: INDIAN-HATING & POPULAR CULTURE
James A. Sandos & Larry E. Burgess
The story of the Paiute-Chemehuevi Indian, Willie Boy, and his flight from justice. Illus. Map. Biblio. University of Oklahoma Press, 1994. $21.95.

*THE HUNTER & THE RAVENS
Mary Holthaus
Eskimo legends. Grades K-3. 32 pp. Council for Indian Education,1976. $8.95; paper, $2.95.

*THE HUNTER & THE WOODPECKER
Christine Crowl
Grades Preschool-6. Illus. 12 pp. Paper . Tipi Press, 1990. $2.50.

HUNTERS OF THE BUFFALO
R. Stephen Irwin
Illus. 52 pp. Paper . Hancock House, 1984. $3.95.

HUNTERS OF THE EASTERN FOREST
R. Stephen Irwin
52 pp. Paper . Hancock House, 1984. $3.95.

HUNTERS OF THE ICE
R. Stephen Irwin
Illus. 84 pp. Paper . Hancock House, 1984. $5.95.

HUNTERS OF THE NORTHERN FOREST
R. Stephen Irwin
Illus. 52 pp. Paper . Hancock House, 1984. $3.95.

HUNTERS OF THE NORTHERN FOREST: DESIGNS FOR SURVIVAL AMONG THE ALASKAN KUTCHIN
Richard K. Nelson
Illus. 320 pp. Second edition. Paper . University of Chicago Press, 1986. $12.95.

HUNTERS OF THE NORTHERN ICE
Richard K. Nelson
Illus. Paper. University of Chicago Press, 1972. $12.95.

HUNTERS OF THE RECENT PAST
Peter Ucko, et al, Editors
450 pp. Unwin Hyman, 1989. $85.00.

HUNTERS OF THE SEA
R. Stephen Irwin
Illus. 52 pp. Hancock House, 1984. $3.95.

HUNTING A SHADOW: THE SEARCH FOR BLACK HAWK
Crawford Thayer
Illus. 496 pp. Paper . Thayer Associates, 1984. $9.95.

HURON: FARMERS OF THE NORTH
B.G. Trigger
Paper. Holt, Rinehart & Winston, 1969. $9.95.

*THE HURON: GREAT LAKES
Nancy Bonvillain
Grades 5 and up. Illus. Chelsea House, 1989. $17.95.

HYEMEYOHSTS STORM'S "SEVEN ARROWS" FICTION & ANTHROPOLOGY IN THE NATIVE AMERICAN NOVEL
Bernd Peyer
220 pp. Paper. Coronet Books, 1979. $43.50.

I

*I AM THE EAGLE FREE (SKY SONG): A SIX NATIONS LEGEND AS INTERPRETED BY SIMON PAUL-DENE
Grade K-4. Illus. 36 pp. Paper . Theytus, 1992. $10.95.

I AM ESKIMO: AKNIK MY NAME
Paul Green & Abbe Abbott
Reprint of 1959 edition. Illus. 86 pp. Paper . Alaska Northwest, $12.95.

I AM HERE; TWO THOUSAND YEARS OF SOUTHWEST INDIAN CULTURE
Stewart Peckham
Museum of New Mexico Press, 1988. $34.95; paper, $24.95.

I AM LOOKING TO THE NORTH FOR MY LIFE; SITTING BULL, 1876-1881
Joseph Manzione
What happened to the Sioux after the Little Bighorn. Illustrates how two countries, the U.S. and Canada, struggled to control their potentially explosive common border . Illus. 300 pp. Paper . University of Utah Press, 1994. $14.95.

*I AM REGINA
Sally Keehn; illus. by Jan Schoenherr
Fictionalized account of a girl held captive by the Delaware Indians from 1755 to 1764. Grades 4-8. Illus. 240 pp. Philomel, 1991. $15.95.

I BECOME PART OF IT: SACRED DIMENSIONS IN NATIVE AMERICAN LIFE
D.M. Dooling & Paul Jordan-Smith, Editors
Illus. 304 pp. Paper . Parabola Magazine, 1989. $14.95.

*I CAN READ ABOUT ESKIMOS
Grades 2-4. Paper . Troll Associates, 1979. $1.95.

*I CAN READ ABOUT THE INDIANS
Elizabeth I. Warren
Grades 2-4. Illus. Paper . Troll Associates, 1974. $1.95.

I FOUGHT WITH GERONIMO
Jason Betzinez & Wilbur Nye
Illus. 214 pp. University of Nebraska Press, 1987. $19.95; paper , $7.95.

I HAVE COME TO STEP OVER YOUR SOUL: A TRUE NARRATIVE OF MURDER & INDIAN JUSTICE
Charles W. Sasser
298 pp. Scarborough House, 1987. $17.95.

I HAVE SPOKEN: AMERICAN HISTORY THROUGH THE VOICES OF THE INDIANS
Virginia I. Armstrong, Editor
Paper. Swallow Press, 1971. $7.95.

I'ISHIYATAM (DESIGNS)
K.S. Saubel & A. Galloway
Paper. Malki Museum Press, 1978. $3.

I SEND A VOICE
Evelyn Eaton
A first person account of what actually transpires inside of an Amerindian Sweat Lodge. Illus. 180 pp. Theosophical Publishing House, 1978. $12.95; paper , $4.95.

*I SING FOR THE ANIMALS
Grades 4 and up. Illus. Macmillan, 1989. $9.95.

I TELL YOU NOW: AUTOBIOGRAPHICAL ESSAYS BY NATIVE AMERICAN WRITERS
Brian Swann & Arnold Krupat
283 PP. Paper. U. of NE Press, 1989. $10.95.

I WILL DIE AN INDIAN
E. Richard Hart, Editor
116 pp. Paper . Howe Brothers, $5.95.

I WILL FIGHT NO MORE FOREVER: CHIEF JOSEPH & NEZ PERCE WAR
Merrill D. Beal
Reprint of the 1963 edition. Illus. 384 pp. Paper . University of Washington Press, $14.95.

THE IDEA OF FERTILIZATION IN THE CULTURE OF THE PUEBLO INDIANS
Herman K. Haeberlin
Reprint of 1916 edition. Paper . Kraus, $15.00.

*IF YOU LIVED WITH THE SIOUX INDIANS
Ann McGovern
Grades K-3. Illus. 96 pp. Paper . Scholastic, Inc., 1974. $2.95.

IF YOU POISON US: URANIUM & NATIVE AMERICANS
Peter H. Eichstaedt
Story of how America's frantic entry into the nuclear age impacted Native American communities. Illus. 272 pp. Red Crane Books, 1994. $19.95.

IF YOU TAKE MY SHEEP...THE EVOLUTION & CONFLICTS OF NAVAJO PASTORALISM, 1630-1868
Lynn R. Bailey
Illus. 304 pp. Westernlore, $14.95.

IGLOO LIFE
62 pp. Paper . Albert Saifer, Publisher, $15.00.

IGNOBLE SAVAGE: AMERICAN LITERARY RACISM, 1790-1890
Louise Barnett
220 pp. Greenwood, 1976. $29.95.

*IKTOMI & THE BERRRIES: A PLAINS INDIAN STORY
Paul Goble
Grades PS-3. Illus. 32 pp. Orchard Books, 1989. $15.

*IKTOMI & THE BOULDER
Paul Goble
Grades PS-3. Illus. 32 pp. Orchard Books, 1990. $15.

*IKTOMI & THE BUFFALO SKULL: A PLAINS INDIAN STORY
Paul Goble, as told by & Illus.
Grades PS-3. Illus. 32 pp. Orchard Books, 1991. $15.

*IKTOMI & THE DUCKS
Paul Goble
Grades PS-3. Illus. 32 pp. Orchard Books, 1992. $15.

*IKWA OF THE MOUND-BUILDER INDIANS
Margaret Zehmer Searcy
Story of a young Indian Girl living in the Southeastern U.S. before colonization. Grades 3-8. Illus. Map. Photos. 800 pp. Pelican Publishing, $13.95: paper, $6.95.

THE ILLINOIS & INDIANA INDIANS
H.W. Beckwith
Facs. of 1884 ed. Ayer Co., $13.

AN ILLUSTRATED HISTORY OF THE ARTS IN SOUTH DAKOTA
Arthur R. Huseboe
With a major section on Sioux arts by leading Lakota artist Arthur Amiotte. Illus. 396 pp. Center for WEestern Studies, $24.95.

IMAGES FROM THE INSIDE PASSAGE: AN ALASKAN POORTRAIT BY WINTER & POND
Vicoria Wyatt
A catalog for an exhibition documenting the work of Lloyd Winter and E. Percy Pond. Includes photos of Alaskan natives, landscapes and village scenes. 144 pp. University of Alaska Press, 1989. $40; paperback, $19.95.

IMAGES IN OSAGE: AN ILLUSTRATED GUIDE TO THE SYLVESTER J. TINKER COLLECTION
Diane L. Good
Paper. KS State Historical Society, 1990. $5.95.

IMAGES OF A PEOPLE: TLINGIT MYTHS & LEGENDS
Mary Helen Pelton & Jacqueline DiGennaro
22 Tlingit legends. Illus. 150 pp. Libraries Unlimited & AISES, 1992. $22.

IMAGES OF A VANISHED LIFE: PLAINS INDIAN DRAWINGS FROM THE COLLECTION OF THE PENNSYLVANIA ACADEMY OF FINE ARTS
John C. Ewers, et al
Illus. 50 pp. Pennsylvania Academy of Art, 1985.

IMAGINE OURSELVES RICHLY: MYTHIC NARRATIVES O." NORTH AMERICAN INDIANS
Christopher Vecsey
Illus. 272 pp. Crossroad Pubg. Co., 1988. $22.95.

*THE IMMIGRANT EXPERIENCE
David Reimers
Grades 5 and up. Illus. 112 pp. Chelsea House, 1989. $17.95.

THE IMPERIAL OSAGES: SPANISH--INDIAN DIPLOMACY IN THE MISSISSIPPI VALLEY
Gilbert Din and Abraham P. Nasatir
Illus. 432 pp. U. of OK Press, 1983. $39.95.

IN THE ABSENCE OF THE SACRED: THE FAILURE OF TECHNOLOGY & THE SURVIVAL OF THE INDIAN NATIONS
Jerry Mander
446 pp. Four Winds Trading Co., 1992. $25.

*IN THE BEGINNING
Ella Clark, Editor
Grades 5-12. Paper. Council for Indian Education, 1977. $2.95.

IN THE BEGINNING: THE NAVAHO CREATION MYTH
Stanley Fishler
Reprint of 1953 edition. AMS Press, $26.50.

IN THE DAYS OF VICTORIO: RECOLLECTIONS OF A WARM SPRINGS APACHE
Eve Ball
Records an Apache's own account of their history from 1878-1886. 222 pp. Paper. U. of Arizona Press, 1970. $10.95.

IN HONOR OF EYAK: THE ART OF ANNA NELSON HARRY
Michael E. Krauss
Illus. 157 pp. Paper. Alaska Native Language Center, 1982. $10.00; two cassettes, $9.00.

IN HONOR OF MARY HAAS: FROM THE HAAS FESTIVAL CONFERENCE ON NATIVE AMERICAN LINGUISTICS
William Shipley, Editor
826 pp. Mouton, 1988. $175.00.

IN THE LAND OF THE GRASSHOPPER SONG: TWO WOMEN IN THE KLAMATH RIVER INDIAN COUNTRY 1908-1909
Mary Arnold and Mabel Reed
Illus. 329 pp. University of Nebraska Press, 1980. $27.50; paper, $7.95.

IN MAD LOVE AND WAR
Joy Harjo
Poetry. Illus. 70 pp. Paper. University Press of New England, 1990. $10.95.

IN PURSUIT OF THE PAST: AN ANTHROPOLOGICAL & BIBLIOGRAPHIC GUIDE TO MARYLAND & DELAWARE
Frank W. Porter, III
268 pp. Scarecrow, 1986. $27.50.

IN A SACRED MANNER WE LIVE: PHOTOGRAPHS OF THE AMERICAN INDIAN AT THE BEGINNING OF THE TWENTIETH CENTURY
Don D. Fowler
Illus. 196 pp. Paper. Barre, 1972. $5.95.

IN THE SHADOW OF THE SUN: CONTEMPORARY CANADIAN INDIAN & INUIT ART
Gerhard Hoffmann
Illus. 600 pp. U. of Chicago Press, 1989. $60.

IN THE SPIRIT OF CRAZY HORSE
Peter Matthiessen
American Indian Movement and the Leonard Peltier case. 688 pp. Paper. Penguin USA, 1992. $14.

IN THE SPIRIT OF MOTHER EARTH: NATURE IN NATIVE AMERICAN ART
Jeremy Schmidt & Laine Thom
Illustrates the relationship between art and nature. 100 full-color & 15 bxw photos. 120 pp. Chronicle Books, 1994. $35; paper, $19.95.

*IN THE TRAIL OF THE WIND: AMERICAN INDIAN POEMS & RITUAL ORATIONS
John Bierhorst, Editor
Grades 8 and up. Paper. Farrar, Strauss & Giroux, 1987. $3.50.

IN VAIN I TRIED TO TELL YOU: ESSAYS IN NATIVE AMERICAN ETHNOPOETICS
Dell Hymes
416 pp. University of Pennsylvania Press, 1981. $48.75; paper, $17.95.

INCOME & HEALTH IN A NORTH INDIAN VILLAGE
Mike Shepperdson
200 pp. Gower, 1987. $49.95.

INCONSTANT SAVAGE: ENGLAND & THE NORTH AMERICAN INDIANS, 1500-1660
H.C. Porter
500 pp. Biblio Distribution Centre, 1979. $34.95.

*THE INCREDIBLE ESKIMO
Raymond Coccola & Paul King;
J. Cameron, Editor
Life among the Barren Land Eskimo. Grade 9. Illus. 435 pp. Paper. Hancock House, 1986. $16.95.

*INDE, THE WESTERN APACHE
Susan Shaffer
Grade 2. Illus. Includes 30 student booklets and teacher's resource binder with overhead transparencies, slides, audiocassette. The Heard Museum, 1987. $295.

INDEH: AN APACHE ODYSSEY
Eve Ball, et al
Illus. 356 pp. Paper. University of Oklahoma Press, 1988. $12.95.

INDEX TO THE DECISIONS OF THE INDIAN CLAIMS COMMISSION
Norman A. Ross
168 pp. N. Ross, 1973. $25.

INDEX TO THE EXPERT TESTIMONY PRESENTED BEFORE THE INDIAN CLAIMS COMMISSION
Norman A. Ross
112 pp. N. Ross, 1973. $25.

INDEX TO LITERATURE ON THE AMERICAN INDIAN
Jeanette Henry, Editor
Four volumes. Paper. The Indian Historian Press, 1975. $12 each.

INDEX TO THE RECORDS OF THE MORAVIAN MISSION AMONG THE INDIANS OF NORTH AMERICA
Carl J. Fliegel, Compiler
4 vols. 1,400 pp. Research Publications, 1970. $400 per set.

INDIAN AFFAIRS
Larry Woiwode
320 pp. Farrar, Straus & Giroux, 1991. $18.95.

INDIAN AFFAIRS IN GEORGIA,
1732-1756
John P. Corry
Reprint of 1936 edition. AMS Press, $21.50.

INDIAN AFFAIRS IN OREGON & WASHINGTON TERRITORIES
James Buchanan
23 pp. Paper. Ye Galleon Press, 1988. $3.95.

INDIAN AFFAIRS IN TERRITORIES OF OREGON AND WASHINGTON: FIRST SESSION, 35th CONGRESS, I858
J. Ross Brown
Ye Galleon Press, 1973. $4.95.

INDIAN AFFAIRS: LAWS & TREATIES
Charles J. Kappler, Editor
Reprint of 1941 edition. 5 vols. 4,667 pp. Supt. of Documents, $90.00; AMS Press, $475.

INDIAN AFFAIRS AND THEIR ADMINISTRATION, WITH SPECIAL REFERENCE TO THE FAR WEST, 1849-1860
A.W. Hoopes
Reprint of 1932 edition. Kraus, $26.

INDIAN AGENTS OF THE OLD FRONTIER
Flora W. Seymour
Reprint of 1941 edition. Octagon Books, 1973. $27.50. Kraus, $30.

**INDIAN AGRICULTURE IN AMERICA:
PREHISTORY TO THE PRESENT**
R. Douglas Hurt
Illus. 304 pp. University Press of Kansas, 1988.
$29.95.

**INDIAN AMERICA: A GEOGRAPHY
OF NORTH AMERICAN INDIANS**
M. Wallace Ney
Illus. Maps. 56 pp. Paper. Cherokee Publications,
1977. $4.95.

**INDIAN AMERICA: A
TRAVELER'S COMPANION**
Eagle & Walking Turtle
Illus. 3rd Edition. 460 pp. Paper. John Muir,
1993. $18.95.

INDIAN AMERICANS: UNITY & DIVERSITY
Murray L. Wax
Prentice-Hall, 1971. $21.

**INDIAN ANTIQUITIES OF
THE KENNEBEC VALLEY**
Charles Willoughby; Arthur E. Spiess, Editor
Illus. 160 pp. Maine State Museum, 1980. $22.

**INDIAN ARROWHEADS -
IDENTIFICATION & PRICE GUIDE**
Overstreet & Peake
3rd edition. Illus. 800 pp. Hothem House, 1993.
$22, postpaid.

INDIAN ART & CULTURE
Della Kew and P.E. Goddard
Reprint of 1978 second edition. Illus. 96 pp.
Paper. Hancock House, $9.95.

**INDIAN ART FROM THE GEORGE
P. BICKFORD COLLECTION**
Cleveland Museum of Art Staff
Reprint of 1974 edition. Illus. Paper. Books on
Demand, $33.

INDIAN ART IN THE ASHMOLEAN MUSEUM
J.C. Harle & Andrew Topsfield
Illus. 128 pp. University of Chicago Press, 1988.
$50; paper, $22.50.

INDIAN ART OF THE U.S.
F.H. Douglas and R. D'Harmoncourt
Reprint of 19451 edition. Illus. Ayer Co., $20.00.

**INDIAN ART TRADITIONS
ON THE NORTHWEST COAST**
Roy L. Carlson, Editor
Illus. 214 pp. Paper. University of Washington
Press, 1984. $14.95.

INDIAN ARTIFACTS
Russell
Flint & stone artifacts, with identification &
classification. Illus. 170 pp. Hothem House,
1981. $11.50, postpaid.

INDIAN ARTIFACTS OF THE MIDWEST
Lar Hothem
Covers six states: KY, OH, IN, IL, MO, IA. 2nd
edition. Illus. 206 pp. Paper. Hothem House,
$16.95, postpaid.

INDIAN ARTISTS AT WORK
Ulli Steltzer
Illus. 144 pp. University of Washington Press,
1977. $30; paper, $14.95.

**INDIAN ARTS & CRAFTS BOARD - SOURCE
DIRECTORY**
A directory of Native American owned & operated
businesses located throughout the U.S. that market a wide range of authentic contemporary Native American arts & crafts. Illus. 48 pp. Indian Arts
& Crafts Board. No charge.

***THE INDIAN AS A SOLDIER AT FORT
CUSTER, MONTANA, 1890-1895: LT. SAMUEL
C. ROBERTSON'S FIRST CAVALRY CROW
INDIAN CONTINGENT**
Richard Upton
Grades 7-12. Illus. 147 pp. Upton Sons, 1985.
$27.50.

**THE INDIAN AWAKENING
IN LATIN AMERICA**
Yves Materne, Editor
Friendship Press, $5.95.

**INDIAN AXES & RELATED
STONE ARTIFACTS**
Lar Hothem
2nd edition. Illus. 214 pp. Paper. Hothem House,
1993. $16.95, postpaid.

INDIAN BASKET WEAVING
Navajo School of Indian Basketry
Illus. Paper. Dover, 1971. $3.95.

**INDIAN BASKET WEAVING: HOW TO WEAVE
POMO, YUROK, PIMA & NAVAJO BASKETS**
Sandra Corrie Newman
Describes the weaving techniques & the
importance of the craft to these Native peoples.
Illus. 110 pp. Northland Publising, $12.95.

INDIAN BASKETRY
George W. James
Reprint. Illus. 271 pp. Paper. Hothem House &
Dover, $6.95.

**INDIAN BASKETRY, & HOW TO MAKE
BASKETS**
George W. James
Enlarged 1903 edition. 2 vols. in 1. Illus. Biblio.
424 pp. The Rio Grande Press, $30.

INDIAN BASKETS
Sarah & William Turnbaugh
Illus. 256 pp. Paper. Schiffer, $24.95.

INDIAN BASKETS & CURIOS
Reproduction of 1902 Frohman Trading Co.
Illus. 28 pp. catalog. Paper. Binford & Mort,
$6.50.

**INDIAN BASKETS OF THE
PACIFIC NORTHWEST & ALASKA**
Lobb; photos by Al Wolfe
Illus. 130 pp. Graphic Arts Center Publishing,
1990. $29.50.

INDIAN BASKETS OF THE SOUTHWEST
Clara Lee Tanner
Illus. 242 pp. University of Arizona Press, 1983.
$55.

**INDIAN BASKETWEAVING: HOW TO WEAVE
POMO, YUROK, PIMA, & NAVAJO BASKETS**
Sandra C. Newman
Illus. 108 pp. Paper. Northland Publishing, 1984.
$12.95.

**INDIAN BATTLES ALONG THE ROGUE
RIVER: ONE OF AMERICA'S WILD AND
SCENIC RIVERS**
Frank K. Walsh
Second edition. Illus. 32 pp. Paper. Te-Cum-
Tom, 1972. $4.95.

**INDIAN BATTLES, MURDERS, SEIGES, AND
FORAYS IN THE SOUTHWEST: THE NARRA-
TIVE OF COLONEL JOSEPH BROWN**
Joseph Brown
Illus. Paper. Territorial Press of Tennessee,
1989. $4.50.

**INDIAN BATTLES & SKIRMISHES
ON THE AMERICAN FRONTIER,
1790-1898**
Joseph P. Peters, Compiler
Reprint of 1966 edition. 256 pp. Ayer Co., $30.50.

***INDIAN BEAD--WEAVING PATTERNS: CHAIN
WEAVING DESIGNS & BEAD LOOM WEAVING-
-AN ILLUSTRATED HOW--TO GUIDE**
Horace R. Goodhue
Grades 3-12. Illus. 80 pp. Paper. Bead Craft,
1984. $9.95.

INDIAN BLANKETS & THEIR MAKERS
George W. James
Enlarged 1892 edition. Illus. Biblio. 352 pp. The
Rio Grande Press, $40. Paper. Hothem House
& Dover, $9.95.

*INDIAN BOYHOOD
Charles Eastman (Ohiyesa)
A Santee Sioux recalls his boyhood among
the Sioux Indians of the Plains. Grades 3-7.
Illus. 290 pp. Paper. AISES, $9.95.

*INDIAN CANOEING
Pierre Pulling
Grades 6-12. Illus. Paper. Council for Indian
Education, 1976. $2.95.

**THE INDIAN CAPTIVE: A NARRATIVE OF THE
ADVENTURES & SUFFERINGS OF MATTHEW
BRAYTON, IN HIS 34 YEARS OF CAPTIVITY
AMONG INDIANS OF NORTHWEST U.S.**
John H. Bone
Reprint. 65 pp. Paper. Ye Galleon Press,
$12.95.

**THE INDIAN CAPTIVE: OR, A NARRATIVE OF
THE CAPTIVITY & SUFFERINGS OF ZADOCK
STEELE**
Zadeck Steele
Reprint of 1908 edition. Ayer Co., $14.

INDIAN CAPTIVITIES
A series of Indian capitivity narratives.
See Garland for titles and prices.

**INDIAN CAPTIVITIES:
OR, LIFE IN THE WIGWAM**
S.G. Drake
Reprint of 1851 edition. AMS Press, $27.50.

**INDIAN CAPTIVITY NARRATIVE:
A WOMAN'S VIEW**
Frances R. Kestler
670 pp. Garland, 1990. $97.00.

*INDIAN CHIEFS
H. Upton
Grades 3-8. Illus. 32 pp. Rourke Corp., 1990.
$17.26.

*INDIAN CHIEFS
Russell Freedman
Six western chiefs. Grades 4-6. Illus. Photos. Map. 160 pp. Holiday House, 1987. $18.95; paper, $9.95.

INDIAN CHIEFS OF PENNSYLVANIA
C. Sipe
Reprint of 1927 edition. Ayer Co., $37.50.

INDIAN CHIEFS OF SOUTHERN MINNESOTA
Thomas Hughes
Reprint. Ross & Haines, $10.00.

THE INDIAN CHRONICLES
Jose Barreiro
Historical novel that recounts the invasion of the Americas by the Spaniards as seen by Christopher Columbus's adopted Indian son. 303 pp. Arte Publico Press, $19.95.

INDIAN CLAIMS COMMISSION ACT
U.S. Senate Committee on Indian Affairs
Reprint of 1935 edition. AMS, $21.50.

INDIAN CLOTHING BEFORE CORTES: MESOAMERICAN COSTUMES FROM THE CODICES
Patricia R. Anawalt
Illus. 250 pp. University of Oklahoma Press, 1981. $49.50.

INDIAN CLOTHING OF THE GREAT LAKES: 1740-1840
Sheryl Hartman; Monte Smith, Editor
Illus. 134 pp. Eagles View Publishing, 1988. $15.95; paper, $9.95.

INDIAN CLUB EXERCISE: PUMPING IRON
S. Kehoe
Illus. 125 pp. Paper. Albert Saifer, 1984. $25.

INDIAN COOKING
Traditional recipes. Illus. 64 pp. Paper. Cherokee Publications, $3.50.

INDIAN CORN OF THE AMERICAS: GIFT TO THE WORLD
Jose Barreiro, Editor
Explores the meaning of corn to Indian people through tradition, myth, agriculture, economics, histry, and language. Akwe:kon Press & AISES. $10.

*INDIAN COSTUMES
Robert Hofsinde (Gray-Wolf)
Grades 3-7. Illus. 96 pp. William Morrow, 1968. $11.80.

INDIAN COUNTRY
Peter Matthiessen
350 pp. Peter Smith, 1984. $24.95. Paper. Penguin USA, $11.

INDIAN COUNTRY: A GUIDE TO NORTHEASTERN ARIZONA
Tom Dollar
Provides an overview of Indian arts & crafts. Illus. Maps. 64 pp. Paper. University of Arizona Press, 1993. $9.95.

*INDIAN COUNTRY: A HISTORY OF NATIVE PEOPLE IN AMERICA
Karen D. Harvey & Lisa D. Harjo
Excerpts from Ada Deer and M. Scott Momaday. Complete lesson plans utilizing a whole-language approach. Grades 4-9. Illus. 360 pp. North Ameri-

can Press, 1994. $27.95; Teacher's Guide - additional lesson plans and support materials including maps, graphs, documents. $12.95.

INDIAN CRAFT
Chief McIntosh & Harvey Shell
Concise instruction in the art of Indiancraft. Illus. 144 pp. Paper. Naturegraph, $17.95; paper, $9.95.

*INDIAN CRAFTS
K. Brandt
Grades 2-6. Illus. 32 pp. Troll Associates, 1985. $8.95; paper, $2.50.

*INDIAN CRAFTS
Janet and Alex D'Amato
Grades 1-4. Illus. Lion Press, $11.95.

INDIAN CRISIS: THE BACKGROUND
J.S. Hoyland
Reprint of 1943 edition. Ayer Co., $17.00.

INDIAN CULTURE & EUROPEAN TRADE GOODS: THE ARCHAEOLOGY OF THE HISTORIC PERIOD IN THE WESTERN GREAT LAKES REGION
George I. Quimby
Reprint of 1966 edition. Greenwood Press, 1978. $22.50.

INDIAN DANCES OF NORTH AMERICA: THEIR IMPORTANCE TO INDIAN LIFE
Reginald & Gladys Laubin
Illus. 540 pp. Paper. University of Oklahoma Press, $22.95.

INDIAN DAYS OF LONG AGO
Edward S. Curtis
Reprint of 1978 edition. Illus. 221 pp. Ten Speed Press, $8.95; paper, $5.95.

INDIAN DEPREDATIONS IN TEXAS
J.W. Wilbarger
Reprint. Illus. 690 pp. Eakin Press, $32.95.

INDIAN DESIGNS
David & Jean Villasenor
Shows quilt patterns, applique, needlepoint, stitchery, fabric painting, etc. Illus. 48 pp. Paper. Naturegraph, 1983. $7.95.

*INDIAN DESIGNS: STAINED GLASS COLORING BOOK
John Green
Eight images from North American Indian life, emphasizing artistic and ceremonial themes. Paper. Dover, $1.

INDIAN DOCTOR
Poisons, Ailments & Herbs. Plants to use for treatment and how to prepare; dictionary of herbs and what to use them for. Reprint. 54 pp. Paper. Cherokee Publications, $3.50.

INDIAN DRINKING: NAVAJO PRACTICES & ANGLO-AMERICAN THEORIES
Jerold E. Levy and Stephen J. Kunitz
Reprint of 1974 edition. Books on Demand, $67.30.

INDIAN EDUCATION
Jack Rudman
Three volumes. Elementary, Secondary and Guidance. 1989. Paper. National Learning Corp., $16.00 each.

INDIAN EDUCATION & CIVILIZATION
A. Fletcher, U.S. Bureau of Education
Reprint of 1888 edition. Kraus, $36.00.

INDIAN EDUCATION IN AMERICA
Vine Deloria, Jr.
8 essays on education & culture. 70 pp. Paper. AISES, $9.

INDIAN EDUCATION IN AMERICAN COLONIES, 1607-1783
Margaret C. Szasz
Illus. 343 pp. University of New Mexico Press, $37.50; paper, $16.95.

INDIAN EDUCATION: SELECTED STATUTES & REGULATIONS
423 pp. Center for Law & Education, 1980. $15.00.

INDIAN, ESKIMO & ALEUT BASKETRY OF ALASKA
Gogol
Basketry items of the Attu, Yakutat, Tlingit, Haida and Tsimshian. Vol. 6 of American Indian Basketry, 1982. Illus. 34 pp. Hothem House, $7.95, postpaid.

INDIAN, ESKIMO, ALEUT OWNED & OPERATED ARTS BUSINESSES SOURCE DIRECTORY
Indian Arts & Crafts Board.

INDIAN & ESKIMO ARTIFACTS OF NORTH AMERICA
Reginald P. Bolton
Outlet Book Co., 1981. $9.98.

*Indian Fairy Tales
Jacobs
Grades 3 and up. Peter Smith.

INDIAN FAMILIES OF THE NORTHWEST COAST: THE IMPACT OF CHANGE
Claudia Lewis
Reprint of 1970 edition. Paper. Books on Demand, $59.00.

*INDIAN FESTIVALS
Keith Brandt
Grades 3-6. Illus. 32 pp. Troll Associates, 1985. $8.95; paper, $2.50.

INDIAN FIGHTING IN THE FIFTIES IN OREGON & WASHINGTON TERRITORIES
Philip Sheridan
95 pp. Ye Galleon Press, 1988. $14.95; paper, $9.95.

INDIAN FIGHTS & FIGHTERS
Cyrus Brady
Illus. 495 pp. University of Nebraska Press, 1971. $33.95; paper, $8.95.

INDIAN FISHING: EARLY METHODS ON THE NORTHWEST COAST
Hilary Stewart
Illus. 450 drawings, 75 photos. 182 pp. Paper. University of Washington Press, 1977. $19.95.

INDIAN FLINTS OF OHIO
Lar Hothem
Covers prehistoric tools and weapons of the eastern Midwest. 165 artifact types with names and descriptions. Illus. 188 pp. Paper. Hothem House, $11.95.

***INDIAN FOLK TALES
FROM COAST TO COAST**
Jessie Marsh
Grades 3-6. Illus. Paper. Council for Indian Education, 1978. $1.95.

**INDIAN FOODS & FIBERS
OF ARID AMERICA**
Walter Ebeling
University of California Press, 1986. $77.50.

**THE INDIAN FRONTIER OF THE
AMERICAN WEST, 1846-1890**
Robert M. Utley
Illus. 350 pp. Paper. University of New Mexico Press, 1984. $14.95.

**INDIAN GAMES & DANCES
WITH NATIVE SONGS**
Alice C. Fletcher
Reprint of 1915 edition. AMS Press, $14.50.

**INDIAN GIVERS: HOW THE INDIANS OF THE
AMERICAS TRANSFORMED THE WORLD**
Jack M. Weatherford
Native Americans "gave" Europeans food, the idea of a federal government system, and many other innovations that are thought of as European. 275 pp. Crown, 1989. $17.95; paper, $8.95.

INDIAN HANDCRAFTS
C. Keith Wilbur, MD
How to craft dozens of practical objects using traditional Indian techniques. Illus. 144 pp. Paper. Globe Pequot, 1989. $14.95.

**INDIAN HEALING; SHAMANIC CEREMONI-
ALISM IN THE PACIFIC NORTHWEST TODAY**
W.G. Jilek
Illus. 184 pp. Paper. Hancock House, $16.95.

INDIAN HERBALOGY OF NORTH AMERICA
Hutchens
An illustrated encyclopedic guide to over 200 medicinal plants found in North America. 382 pp. Paper. Cherokee Publications, $17.

**INDIAN HERITAGE, INDIAN PRIDE:
STORIES THAT TOUCHED MY LIFE**
Jimalee Burton
Illus. 160 pp. Paper. University of Oklahoma Press, 1974. $18.95.

INDIAN HERITAGE OF AMERICA
Alvin M. Josephy, Jr.
Enlarged 1968 ed. 450 pp. Paper. Houghton Mifflin.

THE INDIAN HERITAGE OF AMERICANS
John Frank Phillips
The tools of the American Indians are examined; some achievements of the American Indians. 54 pp. Paper. American Indian Books, 1981. $2.95.

INDIAN HEROES & GREAT CHIEFTAINS
Charles A. Eastman
Illus. 255 pp. Paper. University of Nebraska Press, 1991. $9.95.

INDIAN & HIS PROBLEM
Francis E. Leupp
Reprint of 1910 edition. Johnson Reprint, $24.00; Ayer Co., $24.50.

**INDIAN HISTORY, BIOGRAPHY & GENEAL-
OGY: PERTAINING TO THE GOOD SACHEM
MASSASOIT OF THE WAMPANOAG TRIBE,**

& HIS DESCENDANTS
E.W. Pierce
Reprint of 1878 edition. Ayer Co., $21.

THE INDIAN HISTORY OF THE MODOC WAR
Jeff C. Riddle
Illus. 292 pp. Urion Press, 1975. $14.95; paper, $7.95.

*INDIAN HOMES
Keith Brandt
Grades 3-6. Illus. 32 pp. Troll Associates, 1985. $8.94; paper, $2.50.

THE INDIAN HOW BOOK
Arthur C. Parker
Authentic history & information on American Indian crafts, customs, food, clothing, religion & recreation. Reprint. Illus. 335 pp. Paper. Dover & Cherokee Publications, $5.95.

THE INDIAN HUNTERS
R. Stephen Irwin, MD; illus. by J.B. Clemens
The lives of the first North American hunters. 296 pp. Paper. Hancock House, 1994. $16.95.

**INDIAN HUNTING, TRAPPING & FISHING
RIGHTS IN THE PRAIRIE PROVINCES OF
CANADA**
Kent McNeil
64 pp. University of Saskatchewan, 1983. $20.

**INDIAN HUNTS & INDIAN
HUNTERS OF THE OLD WEST**
F. Hibben; as told to him by Juan de Dios
An account of the old West as told to him by Juan de Dios, a Navajo captured by the Spanish in a slaving raid. Reprint. Illus. Photos. 228 pp. Safari Press, 1989. $24.95.

THE INDIAN IN AMERICA
Wilcomb Washburn
Illus. 330 pp. Harper & Row, 1975. $19.45; paper, $8.95.

THE INDIAN IN AMERICAN HISTORY
William T. Hagan
32 pp. Paper. American Historical Association, 1971. $3.50.

INDIAN IN AMERICAN HISTORY
Virgil Vogel
Paper. Equity & Excellence, 1968. $1.25.

THE INDIAN IN AMERICAN LIFE
Gustavus E. Lindquist
Reprint of 1944 edition. AMS Press, $17.50.

THE INDIAN IN AMERICAN LITERATURE
Albert Keiser
Gordon Press, $59.95.

**THE INDIAN IN HIS WIGWAM: OR, CHARAC-
TERISTICS OF THE RED RACE IN AMERICA**
Henry R. Schoolcraft
Reprint of 1848 edition. AMS Press, $29.

AN INDIAN IN WHITE AMERICA
Mark Monroe; edited by Carolyn Reyer
Autobiography of Mark Monroe, A Lakota Sioux Indian who overcame his personal struggles to help his community. Illus. 256 pp. Temple University Press, 1994. $49.95; paper, $19.95.

INDIAN ISSUES
E.B. Eiselein
Presents a brief introduction to current issues

facing both urban and reservation Indians. Spiral bound. Spirit Talk Press, 1993. $12.

**INDIAN JEWELRY OF THE AMERICAN
SOUTHWEST**
William & Sarah Turnbaugh
ILLUS. 96 PP. Paper. Schiffer, $12.95.

THE INDIAN JOURNALS, 1859-1862
Lewis Henry Morgan;
L. White & C. Walton, Editors
Morgan's researches among the tribes of Kansas & Nebraska. Reprint of 1958 edition. Paper. Dover, $10.95.

INDIAN JUSTICE
John Howard Payne
First newspaper account of an Indian trial in Indian Territory. First published in "The New York Journal of Commerce" on April 17 & April 29, 1841. 105 pp. The Five Civilized Tribes Museum, 1984. $6.95.

**INDIAN JUSTICE: A
RESEARCH BIBLIOGRAPHY**
Vincent J. Webb
CPL Biblios, 1976. $6.50.

INDIAN KNOLL
William S. Webb
Reprint of 1974 edition. Books on Demand, $70.50.

INDIAN LAND CESSIONS IN THE U.S.
Charles C. Royce
Reprint of 1900 edition. Illus. Ayer Co., $75.

INDIAN LAND LAWS
S.T. Bledsoe; Stuart Bruchey, Editor
Reprint of 1909 edition. Ayer Co., $47.50.

**INDIAN LAND TENURE: BIBLIOGRAPHICAL
ESSAYS & A GUIDE TO THE LITERATURE**
Irme Sutton
300 pp. Illus. N. Ross, 1975. $25.00.

INDIAN LANDS
Malcom Rosholt
Illus. 352 pp. Paper. Krause Publications, $17.50.

INDIAN LAW CONFERENCE SERIES
Federal Bar Assn. Editors
Material includes annual updates of legislation and litigation; jurisdictional issues, bibliographies, etc. 1977-92. See Federal Bar Association for editions and prices.

THE INDIAN LAWYER
James Welch
A young American Indian lawyer is torn between the trappings of his profession & his Indian heritage. Illus. 352 pp. Paper. Penguin USA, $8.95.

INDIAN LEADERSHIP IN THE WEST
Walter Williams, Editor
92 pp. Paper. Sunflower U. Press, 1984. $15.

INDIAN LEGACY OF CHARLES BIRD KING
Herman J. Viola
Illus. 152 pp. Smithsonian, 1976. $27.50.

**INDIAN LEGENDS FROM
THE NORTHERN ROCKIES**
Ella E. Clark
Reprint of 1966 edition. Illus. Map. 356 pp. Paper. University of Oklahoma Press, $13.95.

INDIAN LEGENDS FROM THE PACIFIC NORTHWEST
Ella E. Clark
Reprint of the 1953 edition. Illus. Paper. University of California Press, $10.95.

INDIAN LIFE AT THE OLD MISSIONS
Edith B. Webb
Reprint of 1952 edition. Illus. 385 pp. University of Nebraska Press, $35.00.

INDIAN LIFE & INDIAN HISTORY
George Copway
Reprint of 1860 edition. AMS, $21.00.

INDIAN LIFE OF THE YOSEMITE REGION: MIWOK MATERIAL CULTURE
S.A. Barrett & E.W. Gifford
Study of the Miwok Indian culture based upon data obtained from Miwok informants shortle after 1900. Reprint of 1933 edition. Illus. Maps. Biblio. 261 pp. Paper. Yosemite Association, $7.50.

INDIAN LIFE ON THE UPPER MISSOURI
John C. Ewers
Illus. 228 pp. University of Oklahoma Press, 1968. $15.95; paper, $9.95.

INDIAN LIFE: TRANSFORMING AN AMERICAN MYTH
William Savage, Editor
Illus. 300 pp. Paper. University of Oklahoma Press, 1978. $12.95.

INDIAN LIVES: ESSAYS ON 19th & 20th CENTURY NATIVE AMERICAN LEADERS
L.G. Moses & Raymond Wilson
Illus. 232 pp. University of New Mexico Press, 1985. $19.95; paper, $10.95.

INDIAN MEDICINE POWER
Brad Steiger; Marah Ren, Editor
224 pp. Schiffer Publishing & Cherokee Publications, 1984. $12.95.

INDIAN MINIATURE PAINTINGS & DRAWINGS: THE CLEVELAND MUSEUM OF ART CATALOGUE OF ORIENTAL ART
L. York Leach
Part One. Illus. 350 pp. Indian University Press, 1986. $65.00.

INDIAN MISSIONS
Pierre-Jean DeSmet
67 pp. Ye Galleon, 1985. $12.00.

INDIAN MONEY AS A FACTOR IN NEW ENGLAND CIVILIZATION
W.B. Weeden
Reprint of 1884 edition. AMS Press, $11.50. Paper. Johnson Reprint, $9.00.

INDIAN MOUNDS OF THE ATLANTIC COAST
McDonald & Woodward
A guide to the prehistoric mounds and mound-like features of the AStlantic Coast region. Illus. Paper. Hothem House, 1987. $12.95.

INDIAN MOUNDS OF THE MIDDLE OHIO VALLEY
McDonald & Woodward
Adena and Hopewell Mounds and earthworks of the region. Illus. Maps. 130 pp. Paper. Hothem House, 1986. $9.95.

INDIAN MYTH & LEGEND
D. Mackenzie
Reprint of 1913 edition. Longwood, $50.00.

INDIAN MYTHS
Ellen Emerson
Gordon Press, $59.95.

*INDIAN MYTHS FROM THE SOUTHEST
Beatrice Levin
Grades 4-12. Council for Indian Education, 1974. $1.95.

INDIAN NATION
Homer "Louis" Hoban
Indian Heritage Publishing, 1991.

INDIAN NEW ENGLAND BEFORE THE MAYFLOWER
Howard S. Russell
Illus 384 pp. Paper. University Press of New England, 1980. $16.95.

INDIAN NULLIFICATION OF THE UNCONSTITUTIONAL LAWS OF MASSACHUSETTS, RELATIVE TO THE MARSHPEE TRIBE: OR, THE PRETENDED RIOT EXPLAINED
William Apes
Reprint of 1835 edition. 175 pp. E.M. Coleman, $17.50.

INDIAN ORATORY: FAMOUS SPEECHES BY NOTED INDIAN CHIEFTAINS
W.C. Vanderwerth
Reprint of 1971 edition. Illus. 291 pp. Paper. University of Oklahoma Press, $12.95.

INDIAN ORIGINS & THE BOOK OF MORMON
Dan Vogel
154 pp. Paper. Signature Books, 1986. $8.95.

INDIAN OUTBREAKS
Daniel Buck
Reprint of 1965 edition. Ross & Haines, $12.50.

THE INDIAN PEOPLES OF EASTERN AMERICA: A DOCUMENTARY HISTORY OF THE SEXES
James Axtell, Editor
Illus. 256 pp. Paper. Oxford University Press, 1981. $12.95.

INDIAN PLACE NAMES IN ALABAMA
William A. Read
Illus. 128 pp. University of Alabama Press, 1984. $20.00; paper, $8.95.

INDIAN PLACE NAMES IN ILLINOIS
Virgil J. Vogel
Paper. Illinois State Historical Society, 1963. $2.

INDIAN PLACE NAMES IN MICHIGAN
Virgil J. Vogel
Illus. 224 pp. University of Michigan Press, 1986. $29.50; paper, $14.95.

INDIAN PLACE-NAMES IN NORTH AMERICA
N. Holmer, et al
Reprint. Two volumes. Paper. Kraus, $15.00/set.

INDIAN PLACE NAMES OF NEW ENGLAND
John C. Huden
408 pp. Paper. National Museum of the American Indian, 1962. $7.50.

INDIAN PLACE-NAMES: THEIR ORIGINS, EVOLUTION, & MEANINGS, COLLECTED IN KANSAS FROM THE SIOUAN, ALGONQUIAN, SHOSHONEAN, CADDOAN, IROQUOIAN, AND OTHER TONGUES
John Rydjord
Illus. Maps. 392 pp. University of Oklahoma Press, $32.95; paper, $17.95.

INDIAN POLICE & JUDGES: EXPERIMENTS IN ACCULTURATION & CONTROL
William T. Hagan
220 pp. University of Nebraska Press, 1980. $18.50; paper, $4.95.

INDIAN POLICY IN U.S. HISTORICAL ESSAYS
Francis P. Prucha
Illus. 272 pp. University of Nebraska Press, 1981. $22.50.

INDIAN POPULATION IN THE U.S. & ALASKA, 1910, 1937
U.S. Bureau of the Census
Reprint of 1915 and 1937 editions. Kraus, $51.00 and $21.00 respectively.

INDIAN PORTRAITS OF THE PACIFIC NORTHWEST
George M. Cochran
Third edition. Illus. 64 pp. Paper. Binford & Mort, 1987. $5.95.

INDIAN POTTERY OF THE SOUTHWEST: A SELECTED BIBLIOGRAPHY
Marcia Muth
Illus. 35 pp. Paper. Sunstone Press, 1991. $6.95.

INDIAN PUEBLO COLOR BOOK
O.T. Branson
32 pp. Paper. Treasure Chest, 1984. $1.95.

THE INDIAN QUESTION - CD-ROM
Objective Computing
Includes original 1850s encyclopedia on American Indians, edited by Henry Schoocraft, over 4200 pages of first hand accounts, history, essays, and more; collection of authentic myths; Notebooks of George Catlin; guides to National Archives; lives of famous Indian chiefs. Illus. 10,000 pp. of text. Directory Marketplace, $75.

INDIAN QUILLWORKING
Christy A. Hensler
Illus. 64 pp. Paper. Hancock House, $6.95.

INDIAN RAWHIDE: AN AMERICAN FOLK ART
Mable Morrow
Illus. 200 pp. University of Oklahoma Press, 1975. $28.95; paper, $15.95.

*INDIAN READING SERIES
A supplementary reading program for elementary classrooms representing the oral tradition of 16 Northwest tribes in Idaho, Montana, Oregon, and Washington. Contains 99 booklets written at six reading levels, teacher's manuals, and a parent/teacher guide. Stories and legends. Sundance Educational Publishers. $403 (postpaid) for completye series.

INDIAN RECIPE BOOK
United Tribes Technical College
Authentic recipes. Illus. Arrow Graphics, $6., postpaid.

INDIAN REFERENCE SOURCES: AN ANNO-TATED GUIDE TO INDIAN REFERENCE MATE-RIAL, SOCIAL SCIENCES & PURE & APPLIED SCIENCES, VOL. 2
H.D. Sharma, Intro. by
2nd Edition. University Books Ltd., 1989. $35.

INDIAN RELICS OF NORTHEAST ARKANSAS & SOUTHEAST MISSOURI
Dethrow
Summary of prehistoric artifacts in stone, bone, etc. Also pottery. Illus. 152 pp. Hothem House, 1985. $20.

INDIAN REMOVAL: THE EMIGRATION OF FIVE CIVILIZED TRIBES OF INDIANS
Grant Foreman
Illus. 424 pp. University of Oklahoma Press, 1976. $21.95; paper, $12.95.

INDIAN RESERVATIONS: A STATE & FEDERAL HANDBOOK
Confederation of American Indians Staff
Alpha-geographical listing of reservations with information on land status, culture, government, facilities, recreation, and vital statistics for each. 330 pp. McFarland & Co., 1986. $45.

THE INDIAN RIGHTS ASSOCIATION: THE HERBERT WELSH YEARS, 1882-1904
William T. Hagan
301 pp. University of Arizona Press, 1985. $35.

INDIAN RIGHTS MANUALS
A Manual for Protecting Indian Natural Resources, 151 pp., $25.00; A Self-Help Manual for IndianEconomic Development, 300 pp., $35.00; A Manual on Tribal Regulatory Systems, 110 pp., $25.00; Handbook of Federal Indian Laws, 130 pp., $15.00. Native American Rights Fund.

INDIAN ROCK ART IN WYOMING
Mary H. Hendry
Illus. 240 pp. Hendry Publications, 1983. $25.

INDIAN ROCK ART OF THE COLUMBIA PLATEAU
James D. Keyser
Illus. Maps. 140 pp. University of Washington Press, 1992. $35; paper, $17.50.

INDIAN ROCK ART OF THE SOUTHWEST
Polly Schaafsma
Reprint of 1980 edition. Illus. 390 pp. University of New Mexico Press, 1980. $29.95.

INDIAN ROCK CARVINGS
Beth Hill
Illus. 50 pp. Paper. Hancock House, 1990. $4.95.

INDIAN ROOTS OF AMERICAN DEMOCRACY
Jose Barreiro, Editor
Book version of best selling special issue of *Akwe:kon Journal*. Explores the influence of the Iroquois Great Law of Peace on the formation of U.S. democracy. New and previously published works by Donald Grinde, Richard Hill, Sally Roesch Wagner and others. Akwe:kon Press, $12.

INDIAN RUNNING: NATIVE AMERICAN HISTORY & TRADITION
Peter Nabokov
Second edition. Illus. Map. 208 pp. Paper. Ancient City Press & AISES, 1987. $14.95.

INDIAN SCHOOL DAYS
Basil H. Johnston
Map. 256 pp. University of Oklahoma Press, 1989. $19.95.

INDIAN SCOUT CRAFT & LORE
Charles Eastman
Reprint. Illus. 190 pp. Paper. Dover, $4.95.

INDIAN SELF-RULE: FIRST-HAND ACCOUNTS OF INDIAN-WHITE RELATIONS - ROOSEVELT TO REAGAN
Kenneth R. Philp
350 pp. Howe Brothers, 1985. $21.50; paper, $12.50.

THE INDIAN'S SIDE OF THE INDIAN QUESTION
William Barrows
Reprint of 1887 edition. Ayer Co. Publishers, $13.

INDIAN SIDE OF THE WHITMAN MASSACRE
T.E. Jessett
Reprint. 45 pp. Paper. Ye Galleon Press, $4.95.

INDIAN SIGN LANGUAGE
William Tomkins
Illus. 110 pp. Paper. Cherokee Publications, $2.95.

THE INDIAN SIGN LANGUAGE
W.P. Clark
450 pp. Paper. University of Nebraska Press, 1982. $11.95.

***INDIAN SIGN LANGUAGE**
Robert Hofsinde (Gray-Wolf)
Shows how to form more than 500 words in Indian sign language; 200 drawings. Grades 5 and up. 96 pp. William Morrow, 1956. $11.88.

INDIAN SIGN LANGUAGES
William Tomkins
Original title: Universal Sign Language of the Plains Indians of North America. Reprint of 1969 edition. Illus. 108 pp. Paper. Cherokee Publications & Dover, $3.50.

INDIAN SILVER JEWELRY OF THE SOUTH-WEST, 1868-1930
Larry Frank, with Millard Holbroo, II
Illus. 224 pp. Paper. Schiffer, 1989. $19.95.

INDIAN SLAVE TRADE IN THE SOUTHWEST: A STUDY OF SLAVE-TAKING & THE TRAFFIC IN INDIAN CAPTIVES FROM 1700-1935
L.R. Bailey
Reprint of 1966 edition. Illus. Westernlore, $12.95.

INDIAN SLAVERY IN COLONIAL TIMES WITHIN THE PRESENT LIMITS OF THE U.S.
A.W. Lauber
Reprint of 1913. AMS Press, $11.50.

INDIAN SLAVERY IN THE PACIFIC NORTH-WEST
Robert H. Ruby & John A. Brown
Illus. Maps. Biblio. 336 pp. The Arthur H. Clark Co., $37.50.

INDIAN, SOLDIER & SETTLER: EXPERI-ENCES IN THE STRUGGLE FOR THE AMERICAN WEST
Robert M. Utley
Illus. 86 pp. Paper. University of Washington Press, 1977. $3.95.

INDIAN STORIES & LEGENDS OF THE STILLAGUAMISH, SAUKS, AND ALLIED TRIBES
Nels Bruseth
Upper Puget Sound Indian material. 35 pp. Paper. Ye Galleon Press, 1977. $4.95.

INDIAN STORIES FROM T! . 'UEBLOS: TALES OF NEW MEXICO AND ARIZONA
F.G. Applegate
Reprint of 1929 edition. Illus. 198 pp. Paper. The Rio Grande Press, 1977. $10.00.

INDIAN STORY & SONG FROM NORTH AMERICA
A. Fletcher
Reprint of 1900 edition. AMS Press, $9.50.

INDIAN SUMMER: TRADITIONAL LIFE AMONG THE CHOINUMNE INDIANS OF CALIFORNIA'S SAN JOAQUIN VALLEY
Thomas Jefferson Mayfield
144 pp. Heyday Books, $16.

INDIAN SURVIVAL ON THE CALIFORNIA BORDERLINE FRONTIER, 1819-60
Albert Hurtado
Yale University Press, 1988. $25.00.

***INDIAN TALES**
J. De Angulo
Reprint of 1962 edition. Grades 5-12. Illus. 256 pp. Paper. Farrar, Straus & Giroux, $7.95.

INDIAN TALES FROM PICURIS PUEBLO
John P. Harrington, Collected by
Illus. 112 pp. Ancient City Press, 1989. $22.95; paper, $10.95.

INDIAN TALES & LEGENDS
J.E.B. Gray
Over 35 stories. Peter Smith, $20.50.

***INDIAN TALES OF THE NORTHERN PLAINS**
Sally Old Coyote and Joy Yellow Tail Toineeta
Grades 2-5. Council for Indian Education, 1972. $1.95.

***INDIAN TALK: HAND SIGNALS OF THE NORTH AMERICAN INDIANS**
Iron Eyes Cody
Grades 1-12. Illus. Photos. 112 pp. Naturgraph, 1970. $15.95; paper, $7.95.

INDIAN TERMS OF THE AMERICAS
Lotsee Patterson & Mary Ellen Snodgrass
Defines a variety of terms from Native American history; a compendium of vocabulary, people, places and events. Illus. 275 pp. Libraries Unlimited, 1994. $35.

THE INDIAN TESTIONY
Amiya Chakravarty
Paper. Pendle Hill, 1983. $2.50.

INDIAN THOUGHT & ITS DEVELOPMENT
Schweitzer
Peter Smith.

THE INDIAN TIPI: ITS HISTORY, CONSTRUCTION & USE
Reginald & Gladys Laubin
Second edition. Illus. 350 pp. Paper. U. of Oklahoma Press, 1977. $17.95.

THE INDIAN TODAY
C. Eastman
Reprint of 1915 edition. AMS Press, $17.50.

INDIAN TRADE GOODS
Arthur Woodward
Trade goods used in exchange with Indians of the Pacific Northwest, and the way natives adapted these to their own use. Second edition. Illus. 40 pp. Paper. Binford & Mort, $5.95.

THE INDIAN TRADERS
Frank McNitt
Illus. 430 pp. Paper. University of Oklahoma Press, 1989. $15.95.

INDIAN TRADERS ON THE MIDDLE BORDER: THE HOUSE OF EWING, 1827-1854
Robert A. Trennert, Jr.
Illus. 280 pp. University of Nebraska Press, 1981. $23.95.

INDIAN TRADERS OF THE SOUTH-WESTERN SPANISH BORDER LANDS: PANTON & FORBES CO. 1783-1847
W.S. Coker and T.D. Watson
Illus. Maps. Biblio. 448 pp. University Press of Florida, 1985. $44.95.

INDIAN TREATIES
Institute for the Development of Indian Law, 1980. $12.00.

INDIAN TREATIES, 1778-1883
C.J. Kappler, Editor
Contains a listing of every treaty and agreement made between the U.S. and Native Americans. Reprint of 1904 edition. Illus. Map. 1,100 pp. Interland, $75.

INDIAN TREATIES BY TRIBE
28 volumes. Indexed. Histree. Set, $515.00. See publisher for separate editions and prices.

INDIAN TRIBAL CLAIMS DECIDED IN THE COURT OF CLAIMS OF THE U.S.: BRIEFED & COMPILED JUNE 30, 1947
E.B. Smith, Editor
2 Volumes. Greenwood, 1976. $65.00 each.

INDIAN TRIBE OF THE NORTHWEST
Reg Ashwell
Illus. 64 pp. Paper. Hancock House, 1990. $6.95.

INDIAN TRIBES OF THE LOWER MISSISSIPPI VALLEY & ADJACENT COAST OF THE GULF OF MEXICO
John R. Swanton
Reprint of 1911 edition. Scholarly Press, $150.

INDIAN TRIBES OF NORTH AMERICA
John R. Swanton
Outlines tribal histories. Reprint of 1952 edition. Illus. Biblio. 726 pp. Paper. Smithsonian Press, $35. 1991 reprint. Native American Book Publishers, $125; paper, $69.

INDIAN TRIBES OF NORTH AMERICA WITH BIOGRAPHICAL SKETCHES & ANECDOTES OF THE PRINCIPAL CHIEFS
McKenney & Hall
Reprint. 3 Volumes. Scholarly Press, $275.00.

INDIAN TRIBES OF NORTH AMERICA
John R. Swanton
Reprint. Paper. Smithsonian Institution Press, $35.

INDIAN TRIBES OF THE NORTHERN ROCKIES
Adolf Hungry Wolf
Illus. Maps. Biblio. 135 pp. Paper. The Book Publishing Co., $9.95.

THE INDIAN TRIBES OF OHIO: HISTORICALLY CONSIDERED, A PRELIMINARY PAPER
W.K. Moorehead
Reprint of 1899 edition. AMS Press, $18.50.

INDIAN TRIBES OF WASHINGTON, OREGON & IDAHO
John R. Swanton
Reprint. Yel Galleon Press, $9.95; paper, $4.95.

INDIAN TRIBES OF WASHINGTON TERRITORY
George Gibbs
56 pp. Paper. Ye Galleon, 1978. $4.95.

INDIAN USE OF THE SANTA FE NATIONAL FOREST: A DETERMINATION FROM ETHNOGRAPHIC SOURCES
Eva Friedlander & Pamela Pinyan
Illus. Maps. 51 pp. Center for Anthropological Studies, 1980. $8 (postpaid).

INDIAN USES OF NATIVE PLANTS
Describes the uses and documents the plants, giving detailed descriptions and methods of preparation. Includes traditional recipes, dictionary of plants. Illus. 81 pp. Paper. Cherokee Pubns, $6.95.

INDIAN VILLAGE SITE & CEMETARY NEAR MADISONVILLE, OH
E.A. Hooten
Reprint of 1920 edition. Paper. Kraus, $20.00.

INDIAN VILLAGES OF THE ILLINOIS COUNTRY: HISTORIC TRIBES & SUPPLEMENT
Wayne C. Temple
Facsimile edition. Illus. 218 pp. Paper. Illinois State Museum, 1977. $5.00. Supplement, 4 pp. 39 maps. $5.00.

INDIAN VOICES: THE NATIVE AMERICAN TODAY
Jeanette Henry, Editor
The Second Convocation of Indian Scholars, 1971, discussing education, health and medicine, communications, etc. of American Indians. 250 pp. Paper. The Indian Historian Press, 1974. $9.95.

THE INDIAN WAR OF 1864
Capt. Eugene F. Ware
Illus. Center for Western Studies, $25.

*INDIAN WARRIORS & THEIR WEAPONS
Robert Hofsinde (Gray-Wolf)
Grades 4-7. Illus. 96 pp. William Morrow, 1965. $11.88.

*THE INDIAN WARS
Richard B. Morris; illus. by Leonard E. Fisher
Grades 5 and up. Illus. 74 pp. Lerner, 1985. $13.50.

INDIAN WARS
Robert Utley & W. Washburn
Illus. 317 pp. Paper. Houghton Mifflin & Cherokee Publications, 1985. $10.95.

INDIAN WARS OF NEW ENGLAND
H.M. Sylvester; R.H. Kohn, Editor
Reprint of 1910 edition. 3 vols. AMS & Ayer Co, $121.50/set.

INDIAN WARS OF PENNSYLVANIA
C. Hale Sipe
Reprint of 1929 edition. Illus. Ayer Co., $54.

INDIAN WARS OF THE RED RIVER VALLEY
William Leckie
Illus. 135 pp. Paper. Sierra Oaks, 1987. $11.95.

INDIAN WARS OF THE WEST
Timothy Flint
Reprint of 1833 edition. Ayer Co., $26.95

INDIAN WARS & PIONEERS OF TEXAS
John H. Brown
Reprint of 1896 edition. Illus. 775 pp. State House Press, $100.

INDIAN WATER IN THE NEW WEST
Thomas R. McGuire, et al, Editors
Collection of essays on Indian water rights. 260 pp. University of Arizona Press, 1993. $35.

*INDIAN WAY: LEARNING TO COMMUNICATE WITH MOTHER EARTH
Gary McLain
Grades 3 and up. Illus. 110 pp. Peter Smith, $24.95. Paper. John Muir, 1990. $9.95.

INDIAN WEAVING, KNITTING, AND BASKETRY OF THE NORTHWEST COAST
Elizabeth Hawkins
Illus. 32 pp. Paper. Hancock House, 1978. $3.50.

INDIAN–WHITE RELATIONS IN THE U.S.: A BIBLIOGRAPHY OF WORKS PUBLISHED, 1975-1980
Francis P. Prucha
180 pp. University of Nebraska Press, 1982. $16.95; paper, $7.95.

INDIAN-WHITE RELATIONS: A PERSISTENT PARADOX
Jane Smith & Robert Kvasnicka, Editors
278 pp. Howard University Press, 1976. $15; paper, $6.95.

INDIAN–WHITE RELATIONSHIPS IN NORTHERN CALIFORNIA, 1849-1920
Norris Bleyhl
109 pp. Association of Northern California Records, 1978. $12.00.

INDIAN & WHITE: SELF–IMAGE & INTERACTION IN A CANADIAN PLAINS COMMUNITY
Niels W. Braroe
Illus. 206 pp. Stanford University Press, 1975. $22.50; paper, $7.95.

INDIAN & THE WHITEMAN IN CONNECTICUT
Chandler Whipple
Illus. 95 pp. Paper. The Berkshire Traveller, 1972. $3.50.

*AN INDIAN WINTER
Russell Freedman
The culture of the Mandan & Hidatsa. Grades 4-6. Illus. 96 pp. Holiday House, 1992. $21.95.

INDIAN WOMEN CHIEFS
Carolyn T. Foreman
Reprint of 1954 edition. Zenger, $15.95.

*INDIANS
Teri Martini
Grades K-4. Illus. 48 pp. Childrens Press, 1982. $11.45.

*THE INDIANS
Ben Capps
Grades 7 and up. Illus. Silver Burdette, 1973.
$19.94; Time-Life Books, $14.95.

*INDIANS
Nancy Davis & Teresa Moon
Grades K-5. Illus. 33 pp. Paper. DaNa
Publications, 1986. $4.95.

*INDIANS
Edwin Tunis
Revised 1959 edition. Grades 5-12. Illus.
Harper & Row, Junior Books, $24.89.

INDIANS
Rich Steber
Illus. 60 pp. Paper. Bonanza, 1987. $4.95.

*INDIANS: AN ACTIVITY BOOK
John Artman
Grades 4-8. Good Apple, 1981. $6.95.

INDIANS & ALCOHOL IN EARLY AMERICA
Peter C. Mancall
Explores the liquor trade's devastating impact
on the Indian communities of colonial America.
Cornell University Press, 1995. $29.95.

**INDIANS ALONG THE OREGON TRAIL: THE
TRIBES OF NEBRASKA, WYOMING, IDAHO,
OREGON, WASHINGTON IDENTIFIED**
Bert Webber
Includes village locations, language groups, popu-
lations to 1989. Illus. Biblio. 208 pp. Paper. Webb
Research, 1989 expanded edition. $17.95.

**INDIANS, THE AMERICAN
HERITAGE LIBRARY**
William Brandon
Chronicles 20,000 years of Indian history. 420
pp. Paper. Cherokee Publications, $10.95.

**INDIANS & THE AMERICAN WEST
IN THE TWENTIETH CENTURY**
Donald L. Parman
Follows the Indians' continuing struggle to hold
on to their land, their resources, and their identity.
Illus. 256 pp. Indiana University Press, 1994.
$29.95; paper, $12.95.

**INDIANS, ANIMALS, & THE FUR TRADE:
A CRITIQUE OF KEEPERS OF THE GAME**
Shepard Krech, Editor
210 pp. Paper. University of Georgia Press,
1981. $10.00.

**INDIANS ARE US? CULTURE & GENOCIDE
IN NATIVE NORTH AMERICA**
Ward Churchill
Discusses the commercialization of Native Ameri-
can cultures which is threatening the indigenous
struggles for sovereignty and freedom. 400 pp.
Common Courage Press, 1993. $29.95; paper,
$14.95.

INDIANS & ARTIFACTS IN THE SOUTHEAST
Bierer
Over 1,000 illustrations, many artifact types.
Includes trails, maps, and tribal data. 506 pp.
Paper. Hothem House, 1980. $25.95.

THE INDIANS' BOOK
Natalie Curtis
Lore, music, narratives, drawings by Indians.
149 songs in full notation. Reprint. Illus. 584 pp.
Paper. Dover & Cherokee Publications, $14.95.

**INDIANS & BUREAUCRATS: ADMINISTERING
THE RESERVATION POLICY DURING THE
CIVIL WAR**
Edmund J. Danziger, Jr.
250 pp. University of Illinois Press, 1974. $22.95.

**INDIANS, BUREAUCRATS & LAND: THE
DAWES ACT & THE DECLINE OF INDIAN
FARMING**
Leonard A. Carlson
231 pp. Greenwood Press, 1981. $35.00.

***THE INDIANS & THE
CALIFORNIA MISSIONS**
Linda Lyngheim
Grades 4-6. Illus. Revised edition. 160 pp. Langtry
Publications, 1990. $14.95; paper, $10.95.

**INDIANS & A CHANGING FRONTIER:
THE ART OF GEORGE WINTER**
Sarah E. Cooke & Rachel Ramadhyani, Eds.
Watercolors & drawings of the Potawatomi Indians in northern Indiana just before their removal
west of the Mississippi in the mid 1800's. Illus.
270 pp. Indiana University Press, 1993. $49.95.

INDIANS & CRIMINAL JUSTICE
Laurence French, Editor
224 pp. Rowman & Littlefield, 1982. $23.95.

**INDIANS & EUROPEANS: SELECTED
ARTICLES ON INDIAN-WHITE RELATIONS
IN COLONIAL NORTH AMERICA**
Peter C. Hoffer
393 pp. Garland, 1988. $60.00.

INDIANS IN AMERICAN HISTORY
Frederick E. Hoxie
Illus. 336 pp. Paper. Harlan Davidson, 1988.
$16.95.

THE INDIANS IN AMERICAN SOCIETY
Francis P. Prucha
U. of California Press, 1985. $20; paper, $8.95.

INDIANS IN MINNESOTA
Elizabeth Ebbott; Judith Rosenblatt, Editor
Survey of contemporary experience of Ojibway &
Dakota Indians on and off the reservations in Min-
nesota. Illus. 330 pp. Paper. University of Minne-
sota Press, 1985. $13.95.

*INDIANS IN NEW YORK STATE
Kenneth Job; Bernard Whitman, Editor
Grades 4-7. Illus. 50 pp. Paper. IN Education,
Inc., 1989. $5.00.

THE INDIANS IN OKLAHOMA
Rennard Strickland
Illus. Paper. U. of Oklahoma Press, 1980. $7.95.

INDIANS IN OVERALLS
Jaime De Angulo
Revised edition. 120 pp. Paper. City Lights,
1990. $6.95.

INDIANS IN PENNSYLVANIA
Paul A. Wallace
Illus. 200 pp. Pennsylvania Historical and Museum
Commission, 1981. $8.95; paper, $5.95.

**INDIANS IN PRISON; INCARCERATED
NATIVE AMERICANS IN NEBRASKA**
Elizabeth S. Grobsmith
Illus. 265 pp. University of Nebraska Press,
1994. $37.50.

INDIANS IN 17th CENTURY VIRGINIA
Ben C. McCary
Reprint of 1957 edition. 93 pp. Paper.
University Presses of Virginia, $3.95.

**THE INDIANS & INTRUDERS IN CENTRAL
CALIFORNIA, 1769-1849**
G.H. Phillips
University of Oklahoma Press.

**THE INDIANS' LAND TITLE IN CALIFORNIA:
A CASE IN FEDERAL EQUITY, 1851-1942**
Ruth C. Dyer
Paper. R & E Research Associates, 1975. $10.95.

**INDIANS LAST FIGHT
OR THE DULL KNIFE RAID**
Dennis Collins
Reprint of 1915 edition. AMS Press, $25.00.

**THE INDIAN'S NEW WORLD: CATAWBAS &
THEIR NEIGHBORS FROM EUROPEAN CON-
TACT THROUGH THE ERA OF REMOVAL**
James H. Merrell
Illus. 382 pp. University of North Carolina Press,
1989. $32.50.

*INDIANS OF AMERICA
Preschool-12. Aerial Photography. $2.85.

***INDIANS OF AMERICA: GERONIMO, CRAZY
HORSE, OSCEOLA, PONTIAC, SQUANTO,
CHIEF JOSEPH**
Dan Zadra
Grades 2-4. 6 volumes. Creative Education.
1987. $19.95 each; paper, $13.95 each.

INDIANS OF THE AMERICAN SOUTHWEST
Steven Walker
Discusses different prehistoric & presentday cul-
tures. Photos & Illus. 64 pp. Paper. Treasure Chest,
$8.95.

***INDIANS OF THE AMERICAS
COLORING BOOK**
Connie Asch
Grades K-6. Illus. 32 pp. Paper.
Treasure Chest, 1987. $1.95.

**INDIANS OF THE AMERICAS: SELF-
DETERMINATION & INTERNATIONAL
HUMAN RIGHTS**
Roxanne D. Ortiz
360 pp. Praeger, 1984. $38.95; paper, $13.95.

**INDIANS OF ARIZONA: A GUIDE
TO ARIZONA'S HERITAGE**
Eleanor H. Ayer
Illus. Map. 48 pp. Paper. Renaissance House,
1990. $4.95.

**INDIANS OF CALIFORNIA:
THE CHANGING IMAGE**
James J. Rawls
Illus. 312 pp. University of Oklahoma Press,
1984. $21.95; paper, $9.95.

**THE INDIANS OF CALIFORNIA:
A CRITICAL BIBLIOGRAPHY**
Robert F. Heizer
Paper. 80 pp. Indiana University Press, 1976.
$4.95.

THE INDIANS OF CANADA
Diamond Jenness
Sixth Edition. Paper. University of Toronto Press,
1963. $17.95.

INDIANS OF CANADA: CULTURAL DYNAMICS
J. Price
Illus. 262 pp. Paper. Sheffield, Wisc., 1979. $8.95.

INDIANS OF THE CHICAGO AREA
Terry Straus
2nd Edition. 185 pp. Paper. American Indian Press, 1990. $16.95.

*INDIANS OF THE EASTERN WOODLANDS
Rae Bains
Grades 2-6. Illus. 32 pp. Troll Associates, 1985. $8.94; paper, $2.50.

INDIANS OF THE FEATHER RIVER: TALES & LEGENDS OF THE CONCOW MAIDU OF CALIFORNIA
Donald Jewell; Sylvia Vane
& Lowell Bean, Eds.
Illus. 184 pp. Paper. Ballena Press, 1987. $12.95.

INDIANS OF THE GREAT BASIN: A CRITICAL BIBLIOGRAPHY
Omer C. Stewart
152 pp. Paper. Indiana University Press, 1982. $5.95.

THE INDIANS OF THE GREAT PLAINS
Norman Bancroft-Hunt;
photos by Werner Foreman
Presents a vivid image of the lives of the the Great Plains Indians. Reprint of 1982 edition. Ilus. 128 pp. Paper. University of Oklahoma Press, $21.95.

*INDIANS OF THE GREAT PLAINS STENCILS
Mira Bartok & Christine Ronan
Five easy-to-do art projects that explore the myths, legends and festivals of the Plains Indians. Grades 3 and up. 32 pp. Paper. Harper & Row, $9.95.

INDIANS OF THE HIGH PLAINS: FROM THE PREHISTORIC PERIOD TO THE COMING OF EUROPEANS
George E. Hyde
Illus. Paper. University of Oklahoma Press, 1976. $9.95.

THE INDIANS OF THE HOUSATONIC & NAUGATUCK VALLEYS
Samuel Orcutt
Reprint of 1882 edition. AMS Press.

INDIANS OF KANSAS: THE EURO-AMERICAN INVASION & CONQUEST OF INDIAN KANSAS
William E. Unrau
Paper. Kansas State Historical Society, 1991. $10.95.

*THE INDIANS OF LOUISIANA
Fred B. Kniffen
Legends and tales. A list of tribes in Louisiana, and a glossary of state Indian names are included with the history. Grades 3-8. Illus. 112 pp. Pelican Publishing, $13.95.

INDIANS OF THE LOWER HUDSON REGION: THE MUNSEE
Julian Harris-Salomon
Illus. 95 pp. Rockland County Historical Society, 1983. $15.95; paper, $8.95.

THE INDIANS OF MAINE & THE ATLANTIC PROVINCES: A BIBLIOGRAPHIC GUIDE
Roger B. Ray
Reprint of 1972 edition. Paper. Maine Historical Society, $5.

INDIANS OF MANHATTAN ISLAND & VICINITY
Alanson B. Skinner
Reprint of 1915 edition. AMS Press, $21.

THE INDIANS OF NEW ENGLAND: A CRITICAL BIBLIOGRAPHY
Neal Salisbury
128 pp. Paper. Indiana University Press, 1982. $4.95.

*THE INDIANS OF NEW JERSEY: DICKON AMONG THE LENAPE
M.R. Harrington
Grades 4-6. Illus. 352 pp. Paper. Rutgers University Press, 1963. $12.95.

*THE INDIANS OF NORTH AMERICA SERIES
Dr. Frank W. Porter, III, Editor
Grades 4 and up. 16 titles. Illus. 96-128 pp. each. Chelsea House, 1987. $12.95 each; paper, $7.95 each; $120/set.

INDIANS OF NORTH AMERICA
Series of books on the history & culture of North American Indian peoples. Includes: The Cherokee: Southeast; The Choctaw: Southeast; The Comanche: Great Plains; The Kiowa: Great Plains; The Lenape: Middle Atlantic; The Navajos: Southwest; The Yankton Sioux: Great Plains. Illus. Audio-Forum. Hardcover, $18.95 each.

*INDIANS OF NORTH AMERICA
Daniel Jacobson
Grades 4-12. Illus. 96 pp. Franklin Watts, $10.40.

INDIANS OF NORTH AMERICA
Harold E. Driver
Second revised edition. Illus. Paper. University of Chicago Press, 1969. $16.95.

INDIANS OF NORTH AMERICA: METHODS & SOURCES FOR LIBRARY RESEARCH
Marilyn Haas
175 pp. Shoe String Press, 1984. $25.

INDIANS OF NORTH AMERICA: SURVEY OF TRIBES THAT INHABIT THE CONTINENT
Paula Franklin
Illus. David McKay, 1979. $12.95.

*INDIANS OF THE NORTH AMERICAN PLAINS
Virginia Luling
Grades 6 and up. 64 pp. Silver Burdette, $13.96.

INDIANS OF THE NORTH PACIFIC COAST
Tom McFeat, Editor
Examines the culture of the Tlingit, the Haida, the Tsimshian, the Bella Coola, the Kwakiutl, the Nootka, and the Salish peoples of the Northwest Coast. 286 pp. Paper. University of Washington Press, $9.95.

INDIANS OF NORTH & SOUTH AMERICA: BIBLIOGRAPHY BASED ON THE COLLECTION AT THE WILLARD E. YAGER LIBRARY - MUSEUM, HARTWICK COLLEGE, ONEONTA, N.Y.
Carolyn E. Wolf and Karen R. Folk
565 pp. Scarecrow Press, 1977. $42.50.
Supplement, 660 pp. 1988. $59.50.

INDIANS OF NORTHEAST NORTH AMERICA
Christian F. Feest
Illus. 50 pp. Paper. E.J. Brill, 1986. $48.

*INDIANS OF NORTHWEST CALIFORNIA
Title V program staff & tribal resource people
A curriculum book dealing with Native American culture; information on tribal groups in Northwest California which can be integrated into language, literature, social studies, science & math curriculum. Videos available. Grades K-5. Illus. 325 pp. binder. K-T Curriculum Project. $49.95.

INDIANS OF THE NORTHWEST COAST
D. Allen
Photographic study of the northwest people, their land, houses, dances, totem poles, and artifacts. 32 pp. Paper. Hancock House, $3.50.

INDIANS OF THE NORTHWEST COAST
Peter R. Gerber
Facts on File, 1989. $40.

*INDIANS OF OKLAHOMA
LUCILIA WISE
Illus. The Five Civilized Tribes Museum. $1.

*INDIANS OF THE PACIFIC NORTHWEST
Karen Liptak
Grades 5-8. Illus. 96 pp. Facts on File, 1990. $18.95.

INDIANS OF THE PACIFIC NORTHWEST
Ruth Underhill
Reprint of 1945 edition. AMS Press, $27.50.

INDIANS OF THE PACIFIC NORTHWEST: A HISTORY
Robert H. Rubie and John A. Brown
Illus. 300 pp. University of Oklahoma Press, 1981. $29.95; paper, $17.95.

INDIANS OF PECOS PUEBLO
Ernest A. Hooton
Elliots Books, 1930. $200.

INDIANS OF THE PIKE'S PEAK REGION
Irvin Howbert
An account of the Sand Creek massacre of 1864, with material on the Ute Indians of the area east of the Rockies. Reprint of 1914 edition. Illus. Maps. 262 pp. Rio Grande Press, $15.

*INDIANS OF THE PLAINS
Elaine Andrews
Grades 5-8. Illus. 96 pp. Facts on File, 1991. $18.95.

*INDIANS OF THE PLAINS
Rae Bains
Grades 2-6. Illus. 32 pp. Troll Associates, 1985. $8.94; paper, $2.50.

*INDIANS OF THE PLAINS
Ruth Thompson
Grades K-4. Illus. 32 pp. Franklin Watts, 1991. $11.40.

INDIANS OF THE PLAINS
Robert H. Lowie
Reprint. 250 pp. University of Nebraska Press, $21.00; paper, $7.95.

THE INDIANS OF POINT OF PINES, ARIZONA: A COMPARATIVE STUDY OF THEIR PHYSICAL CHARACTERISTICS
Kenneth A. Bennett
Reprint of 1973 edition. Pape...
Books on Demand, $20.80

**THE INDIANS OF PUGET SOUND:
THE NOTEBOOKS OF MYRON EELS**
Myron Eels; George Castile, Editor
Illus. 496 pp. University of Washington Press,
1985. $40.

**INDIANS OF THE RIO GRANDE DELTA: THEIR
ROLE IN THE HISTORY OF SOUTHERN TEXAS
& NORTHEASTERN MEXICO**
Martin Salinas
Maps. 207 pp. Paper. University of Texas Press,
1990. $11.95.

INDIANS OF THE RIO GRANDE VALLEY
A.F. Bandelier and E. Hewett
Reprint of 1937 edition. AMS Press, $33.

INDIANS OF THE SOUTH
Maxine Alexander, Editor
Illus. 120 pp. Paper. Institute of Southern
Studies, 1985. $4.

INDIANS OF THE SOUTHEASTERN U.S.
John Swanton
Reprint of 1946 edition. Illus. 13 maps. 1,068
pp. Greenwood Publishing, $59.50. Paper.
Smithsonian Institution Press, $29.95.

**INDIANS OF THE SOUTHEASTERN
U.S. IN THE LATE 20TH CENTURY**
J. Anthony Paredes, Editor
Surveys American Indian communities still surviv-
ing in the southeastern U.S. from Virginia to
Florida. 256 pp. Paper. University of Alabama
Press, 1992. $21.95.

INDIANS OF SOUTHERN CALIFORNIA
Ruth Underhill
Reprint of 1941 edition. AMS Press, $14.00.

INDIANS OF SOUTHERN ILLINOIS
Irvin Peithman
Photocopy spiral edition. Illus. 172 pp.
Charles C. Thomas, 1964. $14.50.

*INDIANS OF THE SOUTHWEST
Karen Liptak
Grades 5-8. Illus. 96 pp. Facts on File, 1990.
$18.95.

INDIANS OF THE SOUTHWEST
George A. Dorsey
Reprint of 1903 edition. Illus. AMS Press,
$19.50.

INDIANS OF THE SOUTHWEST
Pliny E. Goddard
Reprint of 1913 edition. 248 pp.
The Rio Grande Press, $20.00.

**INDIANS OF THE SOUTHWEST: A CENTURY
OF DEVELOPMENT UNDER THE U.S.**
Edward E. Dale
Illus. Paper. University of Oklahoma Press,
1976. $9.95.

**THE INDIANS OF THE SUBARCTIC:
A CRITICAL BIBLIOGRAPHY**
June Helm
104 pp. Paper. Indiana Unviersity Press, 1976.
$6.95.

**THE INDIANS OF TEXAS: AN ANNOTATED
RESEARCH BIBLIOGRAPHY**
Michael L. Tate
514 pp. Scarecrow, 1986. $52.50.

**THE INDIANS OF TEXAS: FROM
PREHISTORIC TO MODERN TIMES**
W.W. Newcomb, Jr.
Reprint of 1961 edition. Illus. 422 pp. University
of Texas Press, $29.95; paper, $12.95.

***INDIANS OF THE TIDEWATER COUNTRY:
OF MARYLAND, VIRGINIA, DELAWARE &
NORTH CAROLINA**
Thelma Ruskin; Carol Buchanan
& Robert Ruskin, Editors
Grades 4-5. Illus. 132 pp. Maryland Historical
Press, 1986. $15.00.

THE INDIANS OF TODAY
G.B. Grinnell
Reprint of 1911 edition. Illus. AMS Press, $34.50.

**INDIANS OF THE U.S.: FOUR CENTURIES
OF THEIR HISTORY & CULTURE**
Clark Wissler
Paper. Doubleday, 1966. $6.95.

INDIANS OF UPPER CALIFORNIA
F.P. Wrangell
25 pp. Paper. Ye Galleon, $3.00.

INDIANS OF THE UPPER TEXAS COAST
Laurence Aten
338 pp. Academic Press, 1983. $44.50.

INDIANS OF THE URBAN NORTHWEST
Marian W. Smith
Reprint of 1949 edition. AMS Press, $37.50.

**THE INDIANS OF WASHTENAW COUNTY,
MICHIGAN**
Wilbert B. Hinsdale
Reprint of 1927 edition. Paper. George Wahr,
$12.95.

*INDIANS OF THE WEST
Rae Bains
Grades 3-6. Illus. 32 pp. Troll Associates, 1985.
$8.94; paper, $2.50.

**INDIANS OF THE WESTERN
GREAT LAKES, 1615-1760**
W. Vernon Kinietz
Reprint of 1965 edition. 440 pp. Paper.
University of Michigan Press, $14.95.

THE INDIANS OF YELLOWSTONE PARK
Joel Janetski
Illus. 116 pp. Paper. University of Utah Press,
1987. $8.95.

INDIANS OF THE YOSEMITE
Galen Clark
Illus. 132 pp. Paper. Diablo Books, 1988. $8.95.

**INDIANS: OR, NARRATIVES OF MASSACRES
& DEPREDATIONS ON THE FRONTIER IN
WAWASINK AND ITS VICINITY DURING THE
AMERICAN REVOLUTION**
Abraham G. Bevier
Reprint of 1846 edition. 90 pp. Paper. Library
Research Associates, $4.50.

**INDIANS, SETTLERS, & SLAVES IN A FRON-
TIER EXCHANGE ECONOMY: THE LOWER
MISSISSIPPI VALLEY BEFORE 1783**
Daniel H. Usner, Jr.
Examines the economic and cultural interactions
among the Indians, Europeans & slaves of colo-
nial Louisiana. 320 pp. University of North Caro-
lina Press, 1991. $32.50; paper, $12.95.

**THE INDIAN'S SIDE
OF THE INDIAN QUESTION**
W. Barrows
Reprint of 1887 edition. Ayer Co., $13.00.

THE INDIANS & THEIR CAPTIVES
James Levermier and Henry Cohen, Editors
Greenwood Press, 1977. $35.00.

THE INDIANS & THE U.S. CONSTITUTION
Institute for the Development of Indian Law, $7.95.

INDIANS & THE U.S. GOVERNMENT
Institute for the Development of Indian Law, $12.

*INDIANS WHO LIVED IN TEXAS
Betsy Warren
Reprint of 1970 edition. Grades 2-12. Illus. 48 pp.
Hendrick-Long, $9.95.

**INDIGENOUS ECONOMICS: TOWARD
A NATURAL WORLD ORDER**
Jose Barreiro, Editor
Iroquois, Anishnabe, Algonquin, Dene Indian,
among other, viewpoints are represented in this
book that features Fourth World analysis of envi-
ronment and developmnent issues. Akwe:kon
Press, $10.

**INDIGENOUS PEOPLES & TROPICAL FOR-
EST: MODELS OF LAND USE & MANAGE-
MENT FROM LATIN AMERICA**
Jason Clay
116 pp. Cultural Survival, 1988. $20; paper, $8.

INGALIK MATERIAL CULTURE
C. Osgood
Reprint of 1940 edition. Illus. Biblio. 500 pp.
Paper. HRAF Press, $25.

***THE INLAND WHALE: NINE STORIES
RETOLD FROM CALIFORNIA INDIAN
LEGENDS**
Theodora Kroeber
Grades 8 and up. Reprint of 1959 edition. Illus.
Paper. University of California Press, $9.95.

**INSECTS AS FOOD: ABORIGINAL
ENTOMOPHAGY IN THE GREAT BASIN**
Mark Q. Sutton; Thomas C. Blackburn, Editor
Illus. 115 pp. Paper. Ballena Press, 1988. $17.95.

**INSIDE PASSAGE: LIVING WITH KILLER
WHALES, BALD EAGLES & KWAKIUTL
INDIANS**
Michael Modzelewski
Illus. 215 pp. HarperCollins, 1991. $19.95.

INSIGHT GUIDE: NATIVE AMERICA
A travel guide to Indian reservations, historic sites,
festivals & ceremonies. Houghton Mifflin, $19.95.

**THE INSTITUTE OF AMERICAN
INDIAN ARTS, ALUMNI EXHIBITION**
Intro. by Lloyd K. New
Illus. 72 pp. Paper. Amon Carter Museum, 1974.
$3.25.

**INTELLECTUAL CULTURE
OF THE COPPER ESKIMOS**
Knud Rasmussen
Reprint of 1932 edition. AMS, $74.50.

**INTELLECTUAL CULTURE
OF THE HUDSON BAY ESKIMOS**
Knud Rasmussen
Reprint of 1930 ed. 3 vols. AMS, $160 per set.

INTELLECTUAL CULTURE OF THE IGLULIK ESKIMOS
Knud Rasmussen
Reprint of 1929 edition. AMS, $105.

INTERIOR LANDSCAPES: AUTOBIOGRAPHICAL MYTHS & METAPHORS
Gerald Vizenor
Illus. 280 pp. University of Minnesota Press, 1990. $17.95.

THE INTERIOR SALISH TRIBES OF BRITISH COLUMBIA: A PHOTOGRAPHIC COLLECTION
Leslie H. Tepper
Illus. 277 pp. Paper. University of Chicago Press, 1988. $17.95.

INTERPRETING THE INDIAN: TWENTIETH-CENTURY POETS & THE NATIVE AMERICAN
Michael Castro
242 pp. Paper. University of Oklahoma Press, 1993. $12.95.

INTRODUCTION TO AMERICAN INDIAN ART
O. LaFarge, et al
Reprint of 1932 edition. Two volumes in one. Illus. 200 pp. Paper. The Rio Grande Press, $17.50.

INTRODUCTION TO CHEROKEE: A CHEROKEE LANGUAGE STUDY COURSE
Sam Hider
Teaches the fundamental of the language using tapes and work book. Also a history of the language. 44 pp. 2 cassette tapes. Cherokee Publications, $35.

INTRODUCTION TO HANDBOOK OF AMERICAN INDIAN LANGUAGES by Franz Boas; **INDIAN LINGUISTIC FAMILIES OF AMERICA NORTH OF MEXICO,** by J.W. Powell
Reprint. Two vols. in one. 225 pp. Paper. University of Nebraska Press, $9.95.

INTRODUCTION TO HOPI POTTERY
Francis H. Harlow
32 pp. Illus. Paper. Museum of Northern Arizona, 1978. $2.50.

AN INTRODUCTION TO THE LUISENO LANGUAGE
Villiana Hyde
Paper. Malki Museum Press, 1979. $8.

INTRODUCTION TO NAVAHO CHANT PRACTICE
C. Kluckhohn and L.C. Wyman
Reprint of 1940 edition. Paper. Kraus, $23.

AN INTRODUCTION TO THE PREHISTORY OF INDIANA
James H. Kellar
Revised 1983 edition. Illus. Biblio. 78 pp. Paper. Indiana Historical Society, $4.95.

INTRODUCTION TO THE STUDY OF INDIAN LANGUAGES WITH WORDS, PHRASES, AND SENTENCES TO BE COLLECTED
J.W. Powell
Gordon Press, 1977. $69.95.

INTRODUCTION TO THE STUDY OF MORTUARY CUSTOMS OF THE NORTH AMERICAN INDIANS; WITH A FURTHER CONTRIBUTION TO THE STUDY OF THE MORTUARY CUSTOMS OF NORTH AMERICAN INDIANS
H.C. Yarrow
Reprint of 1881 edition. AMS Press, $33.

INTRODUCTION TO THE STUDY OF NORTH AMERICAN ARCHAEOLOGY
Cyrus Thomas
Reprint of 1898 edition. AMS, $45.

INTRODUCTION TO THE STUDY OF SOUTHWESTERN ARCHAEOLOGY
Alfred V. Kidder
Illus. Paper. Yale University Press, 1962. $16.95.

*INTRODUCTION TO TRIBAL GOVERNMENT
Yerington Paiute Tribe
Grades 9-12. 94 pp. Paper. Yerington Paiute Tribe Publications, $13.

INTRODUCTION TO WISCONSIN INDIANS: PREHISTORY TO STATEHOOD
Carol I. Mason
Illus. 321 pp. Paper. Sheffield Publishing, 1988. $15.50.

AN INTRODUCTORY GUIDE TO ENTREPRENEURSHIP FOR AMERICAN INDIANS
Enid, et al, Editors
50 pp. American Association for Community & Junior Colleges, 1990. $11.

INUA: SPIRIT WORLD OF THE BERING SEA ESKIMOS
William Fitzhugh & Susan Kaplan
Illus. 296 pp. Smithsonian, 1982. $35.00; paper, $19.95.

*INUIT
Elizabeth Hahn
Grades 5-8. Illus. 32 pp. Rourke Corp., 1990. $13.26.

INUIT ARTISTS PRINT WORKBOOK
Sandra B. Barz, Editor
Illus. 324 pp. Paper. Arts and Culture of the North, 1981. $58.

INUIT: THE NORTH IN TRANSITION
Ulli Steltzer
Illus. 224 pp. Paper. University of Chicago Press, 1983. $22.50.

THE INUIT PRINT, L'ESTAMPE INUIT
Helga Goetz
The art of the Canadian Inuit. Illus. 267 pp. University of Chicago Press, 1977. $24.95; paper, $17.95.

INUIT WOMEN ARTISTS
Odette Leroux, et al
Reminiscences of 12 Inuit women artists. Illus. 256 pp. University of Washington Press, 1994. $45.

INUIT YOUTH: GROWTH & CHANGE IN THE CANADIAN ARCTIC
Richard Condon
275 pp. Paper. Rutgers U. Press, 1987. $15.

INUPIALLU TANNILLU UQALUNISA ILANICH: ABRIDGED INUPIAQ & ENGLISH DICTIONARY
Edna A. MacLean
Illus. 168 pp. Paper. Alaska Native Language Center, 1981. $10.

THE INUPIAT & ARCTIC ALASKA: AN ETHNPOGRAPHY OF DEVELOPMENT
Norman Chance
250 pp. Paper. Holt, Rinehart & Winston, 1990. $10

THE INVASION OF AMERICA: INDIANS, COLONIALISM, & THE CHANT OF CONQUEST
Francis Jennings
Illus. 384 pp. Paper. W.W. Norton, 1976. $9.95.

THE INVENTED INDIAN: CULTURAL FICTIONS & GOVERNMENT POLICIES
James A. Clifton, Editor
388 pp. Paper. Transaction Publishers, 1990. $24.95.

AN INVENTORY OF THE MISSION INDIAN AGENCY RECORDS
James Young, Dennis Moristo & G. David Tanenbaum
66 pp. Paper. American Indian Studies Center, 1976. $5.

AN INVENTORY OF THE PALA INDIAN AGENCY RECORDS
James Young, Dennis Moristo and G. David Tanenbaum
87 pp. Paper. American Indian Studies Center, 1976. $5.

THE INVISIBLE CULTURE: COMMUNICATION IN CLASSROOM & COMMUNITY ON THE WARM SPRINGS INDIAN RESERVATION
Susan Urmston Philips
A classic in the field of educational anthropology & sociolinguistics. 147 pp. Paper. Waveland Press, 1993. $9.95.

THE INVISIBLE MUSICIAN
Ray A. Young Bear
Poetry. Draws upon ancient traditions while creating dramatic versions of the harshness of modern tribal life. 120 pp. Holy Cow! Press, $15; paper, $8.95.

INVOLVEMENT OF CANADIAN NATIVE COMMUNITIES IN THEIR HEALTH CARE PROGRAMS: A REVIEW OF THE LITERATURE SINCE THE 1970'S
D.E. Young & L.L. Smith
Identifies ovber 60 models of Native community involvement in health care in Canada. 90 pp. paper. CCI, 1993. $15.

IOWA INDIANS
O.J. Fargo
2 vols. 51 pp & 71 pp. Paper. Green Valley Area Education Agency, 1988. $1.50 each.

THE IOWAY INDIANS
Martha R. Blaine
Illus. University of Oklahoma Press, 1979. $29.95.

AN IRON HAND UPON THE PEOPLE: THE LAW AGAINST THE POTLATCH ON THE NORTHWEST COAST
Douglas Cole & Ira Chaikin
Illus. 248 pp. U. of WA Press, 1990. $26.95.

IROQUOIAN COSMOLOGY
John H. Hewitt
Reprint of 1928 edition. AMS Press, $60.

THE IROQUOIS
Frank G. Speck
Second edition. Illus. 95 pp. Paper. Cranbrook Institute, 1955. $4.50.

*THE IROQUOIS
Barbara Graymont
Grades 7-12. Illus. 104 pp. Chelsea House, 1989. $17.95; paper, $9.95.

*THE IROQUOIS
Barbara McCall
Grades 5-8. Illus. 32 pp. Rourke Corp., 1989.
$13.26.

IROQUOIS: ART & CULTURE
Carrie Lyford
Illus. 100 pp. Paper. Hancock House, $6.95.

IROQUOIS BOOK OF RITES
Horatio Hale, Editor
Reprint of 1883 edition. AMS Press, $30.

IROQUOIS CRAFTS
Carrie A. Lyford
Reprint of 1945 edition. Illus. 100 pp.
Paper. R. Schneider, Publishers, $5.95.

**THE IROQUOIS EAGLE DANCE: AN
OFFSHOOT OF THE CALUMET DANCE**
William Fenton
Illus. 325 pp. Paper. Syracuse University Press,
1991. $17.95.

IROQUOIS FOLK LORE
William M. Beauchamp
Reprint of 1922 edition. AMS Press, $21.

IROQUOIS IN THE AMERICAN REVOLUTION
Barbara Graymont
Illus. Maps. 359 pp. Syracuse University Press,
1972. $24.95; paper, $12.95.

**THE IROQUOIS IN THE CIVIL WAR:
FROM BATTLEFIELD TO RESERVATION**
Laurence M. Hauptman
The ware and effects of the war on the Iroquois
families at home. 240 pp. Syracuse University
Press, 1993. $29.95.

**IROQUOIS INDIANS: A DOCUMENTARY
HISTORY - GUIDE TO THE MICROFILM
COLLECTION**
Mary Druke, Editor
718 pp. Research Publications, 1985. $180.

IROQUOIS LAND CLAIMS
Christopher Vecsey & William Starna, Editors
Illus. 240 pp. Syracuse University Press, 1988.
$24.95; paper, $14.95.

IROQUOIS MEDICAL BOTANY
James W. Herrick & Dean R. Snow
A guide to understanding the use of herbal medi-
cines in traditional Iroquois culture. Illus. 240 pp.
Syracuse University Press, 1994. $29.95.

**IROQUOIS MUSIC & DANCE: CEREMONIAL
ARTS OF TWO SENECA LONGHOUSES**
Gertrude P. Kurath
Reprint of 1964 edition. Reprint Services, $49.

THE IROQUOIS & THE NEW DEAL
Laurence Hauptman
Illus. 276 pp. Syracuse University Press, 1988.
$24.95; paper, $10.95.

AN IROQUOIS SOURCEBOOK
Elisabeth Tooker, Editor
Reprint. Three volumes. Vol. 1, Political & Social
Organization, 400 pp., $55; Calendric Rituals, 292
pp., $40; and Medicine Society Rituals, 360 pp.,
$50. Garland Publishing.

***IROQUOIS STORIES: HEROES &
HEROINES, MONSTERS & MAGIC**
Retold by Joseph Bruchac;
illus. by Daniel Burgevin
A collection of 30 tales told in the Longhouses of
the Iroquois Indians. Grades 3-7. Illus. 200 pp.
Paper. The Crossing Press, 1991, $9.

**IROQUOIS STUDIES: A GUIDE TO DOCUMEN-
TARY & ETHNOGRAPHIC RESOURCES FROM
WESTERN NEW YORK & THE GENESEE VAL-
LEY**
Russell A. Judkins, Editor
Illus. 98 pp. Paper. State University of New York
at Geneseo.

**THE IROQUOIS STRUGGLE FOR SURVIVAL:
WORLD WAR II TO RED POWER**
Laurence Hauptman
Illus. 384 pp. Paper. Syracuse University Press,
1986. $15.95.

THE IROQUOIS TRAIL
W. Beauchamp
Reprint of 1892 edition. AMS Press, $21.50.

**THE IROQUOIS TRAIL: DICKON AMONG
THE ONONDAGAS & SENECAS**
Mark Harrington
215 pp. Paper. Rutgers U. Press, 1991. $9.95.

**IRREDEEMABLE AMERICA: THE
INDIANS' ESTATE & LAND CLAIMS**
Imre Sutton
Illus. University of New Mexico Press, 1985.

**ISHI IN TWO WORLDS: A BIOGRAPHY OF
THE LAST WILD INDIAN IN NORTH AMERICA**
T. Kroeber
Reprint of 1961 edition. Illus. University of
California Press, $25.00; paper, $11.95.

*ISHI: THE LAST OF HIS PEOPLE
Grades 2-4. Illus. 32 pp. Childrens Press, $10.95.

ISHI MEANS MAN
Thomas Merton
Five essays about Native American Indians. Illus.
75 pp. Unicorn, 1976. $17.50; paper, $6.95.

**ISHI'S JOURNEY FROM THE CENTER
TO THE EDGE OF THE WORLD**
James A. Freeman
Ishi tale, the last Yahi Indian. Illus. Photos.
224 pp. Paper. Naturegraph, $8.95.

ISLAND BETWEEN
Margaret E. Murie
Fiction. Saga of Toozak the Eskimo, his people,
his early years, marriage and manhood. Illus. 228
pp. University of Alaska Press, 1977. $9.95

ISLAND IMMIGRANTS
J.D. Cleaver
40 pp. Paper. Oregon Historical Society, 1986.
$2.95.

**ISSUES FOR THE FUTURE OF
AMERICAN INDIAN STUDIES**
Susan Guyette
267 pp. Paper. American Indian Studies Center,
1985. $10.

**IT WILL LIVE FOREVER: TRADITIONAL
YOSEMITE ACORN PREPARATION**
Bev Ortiz
Illus. 160 pp. Paper. Heyday Books, $11.95.

**IT'S YOUR MISFORTUNE & NONE OF MY
OWN: A NEW HISTORY OF THE AMERICAN
WEST**
Richard White
U. of Oklahoma Press, $42.95; paper , $21.95.

IVALU, THE ESKIMO WIFE
Peter Freuchen
Reprint of 1935 edition. AMS, $27.50.

J

WILLIAM JACKSON, INDIAN SCOUT
James W. Schultz
Reprint of 1976 ed. 200 pp. Borgo Press, $19.95.

*JAMES AT WORK
Looks at reservation life through the eyes of a
Choctaw Indian boy. Grades Preschool-3. 14 pp.
Choctaw Heritage Press, $2.75.

JEFFERSON'S AMERICA: 1760-1815
Norman Risjord
350 pp. Madison House, 1991. $32.95; paper,
$17.95.

**THE JEROME AGREEMENT BETWEEN THE
KIOWA, COMANCHE & APACHE TRIBES &
THE U.S.**
R.J. DeMalle
38 pp. Institute for the Development of Indian
Law, $11.

**JEWELRY BY SOUTHWEST AMERICAN
INDIANS: EVOLVING DESIGNS**
Nancy Schiffer
Illus. 256 pp. Schiffer, 1990. $59.95.

JICARILLA APACHE TEXTS
Pliny Goddard
Reprint of 1911 edition. AMS Press.

JICARILLA APACHE TRIBAL CODE
Equity Publishing, 1987.

**THE JICARILLA APACHE TRIBE:
A HISTORY, 1846-1970**
Veronica E. Tiller
Revised edition. Illus. Photos. Maps. 300 pp.
University of Nebraska Press, 1991. $12.95.

**THE JICARILLA APACHES:
A STUDY IN SURVIVAL**
Dolores Gunnerson
Illus. 327 pp. Northern IL U.. Press, 1973. $22.

JOHN ROSS: CHEROKEE CHIEF
Gary E. Moulton
Biography. 292 pp. Paper. University of
Georgia Press, $11.95.

*JIM THORPE
Guernsey Van Riper, Jr.
Grades 3-7. Illus. Paper. Macmillan, 1989. $3.95.

***JIM THORPE: WORLD'S
GREATEST ATHLETE**
Grades 4 and up. Illus. 130 pp.
Childrens Press, $13.95.

*JOHN HAWK: A SEMINOLE SAGA
Beatrice Levin
A novel recounting the horror and the hostilities
of the Seminole wars. Grades 7 and up. Illus.
182 pp. Paper. Roberts Rinehart, 1994. $9.95.

JOHNSON OF THE MOHAWKS
Arthur Pound & Richard E. Day
Reprint of 1930 edition. Ayer Co., $44.
Gordon Press, $59.95.

**EASTMAN JOHNSON'S
LAKE SUPERIOR INDIANS**
Patricia C. Johnston
Illus. 72 pp. Johnston Publishing & University
of Washington Press, 1983. $12.95.

***PHILIP JOHNSTON & THE
NAVAJO CODE TALKERS**
Syble Lagerquist
Grades 4-12. 31 pp. Paper. Council for Indian
Education, 1975. $2.45.

*JOSEPH: CHIEF OF THE NEZ PERCE
Dean Pollock
Grades 5 and up. Illus. 64 pp. Paper.
Binford & Mort, 1990. $7.95.

***ALVIN JOSPEHY'S HISTORY OF
THE NATIVE AMERICANS SERIES**
Alvin M. Josephy, Jr.
Grades 5-7. Six books. Illus. 864 pp. Silver
Burdette Press, 1989. $71.88 per set; paper,
$47.70 per set.

**JOURNAL OF THE ADVENTURES
OF MATTHEW BUNN**
Matthew Bunn
Facsimile of the 1962 edition. Paper.
Newberry Library Center, $2.

**JOURNAL OF CAPTAIN WILLIAM TRENT
FROM LOGSTOWN TO PICKAWILLANY,
A.D. 1752**
William Trent
Reprint of 1871 edition. Ayer Co., $11.

JOURNAL OF CHEROKEE STUDIES
Issues of the Journal (official publication of the
Museum of the Cherokee) 1976-1986. Illus. 4 Vols.
1,200 pp. Cherokee Publications, $125/set.

**THE JOURNAL OF...NARRATING AN
ADVENTURE FROM ARKANSAS THROUGH
INDIAN TERRITORY, ETC.**
Jacob Fowler
A trip from Arkansas to New mexico and encoun-
ters with the Cherokee, Kiowa, Pawnee &
Arapaho. Reprint of 1898 edition. 183 pp. Ross
Haines, $15.

**A JOURNAL OF SIBLEY'S INDIAN EXPOSI-
TION DURING THE SUMMER OF 1863 AND
RECORD OF THE TROOPS EMPLOYED**
Arthur M. Daniels
Reprint. Illus. 154 pp. Thueson, $30.

**JOURNAL OF SOUTHERN
TREATY COMMISSION 1865**
Larry S. Wayson, Editor
80 pp. Paper. Histree, 1994. $16.95.

**JOURNAL OF TWO VISITS MADE TO SOME
NATIONS OF INDIANS ON THE WEST SIDE OF
THE RIVER OHIO IN THE YEARS 1772 & 1773
BY THE REV. DAVID JONES, MINISTER OF
GOSPEL AT FREEHOLD, N.J.**
David Jones
Reprint of 1774 edition. Ayer Co., $21.95.

**THE JOURNALS OF THE
LEWIS & CLARK EXPEDITION**
Meriweather Lewis & William Clark;

Gary Moulton, Editor
Three volumes. Illus. University of Nebraska
Press, 1987. $40.00 each.

**JOURNALS OF JOSEPH N. NICOLLET:
1836-1837**
Martha Bray; Andre Fertey, Translator
Illus. 288 pp. Minnesota Historical Society
Press, 1970. $16.50.

**JOURNALS OF THE MILITARY EXPEDITION
OF MAJOR GENERAL JOHN SULLIVAN:
AGAINST THE SIX NATIONS OF INDIANS IN
1779**
Maj. Gen. John Sullivan
Reprint of 1887 edition. Ayer Co., $39.

**JOURNEY FROM PRINCE OF WALES' FORT
IN HUDSON'S BAY TO THE NORTHERN
OCEAN, 1769-1772**
Samuel Hearne
Reprint of 1795 edition. Illus. Maps. 437 pp.
Charles E. Tuttle, $20.00; Greenwood Press,
$32.75.

**A JOURNEY INTO MOHAWK & ONEIDA COUN-
TRY, 1634-1635: THE JOURNAL OF HARMEN
MEYNDERTSZ VAN DEN BOGAERT**
Charles Gehring
Illus. 120 pp. Syracuse University Press, 1988.
$17.50.

JOURNEY TO ALASKA IN 1868
E. Teichmann
Reprint of 1925 edition. Argosy, $20. Delux
edition, $50.

**JOURNEY TO THE ANCESTRAL SELF:
TAMARACK SONGS**
Teaches that the lifeways of all native peoples are
essentially one. Illus. 224 pp. Paperback. Teaching Drum Outdoor School, $14.95. With voice cas-
sette, $26.

**JOURNEY TO THE FOUR DIRECTIONS:
TEACHINGS OF THE FEATHERED SERPENT**
Jim Berenholtz
Ceremoial musician & visionary traveler Jim
Berenholtz shares the story of his mystical awak-
ening & remarkable training. Illus. Map. 288 pp.
Paper. Bear & Co., $14.95.

**JOY BEFORE NIGHT:
EVELYN EATON'S LAST YEARS**
Terry Eaton
Illus. 173 pp. Paper. Theosophical Publishing
House, 1988. $6.95.

**THE JUAN PARDO EXPEDITION; EXPLORA-
TION OF THE CAROLINAS & TENNESSEE,
1566-1568**
Charles Hudson, Editor
Illus. 354 pp. Smithsonian Institution Press,
1990. $42.

JUH, AN INCREDIBLE INDIAN
Dan L. Thrapp
Juh was a chief and Geronimo only a war
leader. The full account of his Apache shadowy
life and career. Illus. Map. 42 pp. Paper. Texas
Western Press, 1993. $12.50.

**THE JUMANOS: HUNTERS & TRADERS OF
THE SOUTH PLAINS**
Nancy Parrott Hickerson
Describes encounters with Native North
Americans by Spanish explorers. Illus. Maps.

340 pp. Paper. University of Texas Press, 1994.
$17.95.

***THE JUNIOR LIBRARY
OF AMERICAN INDIANS**
25 titles. Illus. 72-80 pp. each. Chelsea
House Publishers, 1992. $12.95 each.

*JUST A WALK
Jordan Wheeler; illus. by Bill Cohen
Children's stories by a Cree author. Grades K-4.
Illus. 50 pp. Paper. Theytus, 1994. $8.95.

K

*KA-HA-SI & THE LOON
Terri Cohlene
Grades 4-8. Illus. 48 pp. Rourke Corp., 1990.
$14.95.

FRED KABOTIE: HOPI INDIAN ARTIST
Fred Kabotie and Bill Belknap
Illus. 150 pp. Museum of Northern Arizona,
$24.95; Northland Press, 1977. $35.00.

KACHINA CEREMONIES & KACHINA DOLLS
Martina M. Jacobs
Illus. 72 pp. Paper. Carnegie, 1980. $1.50.

**KACHINA DOLLS: THE
ART OF HOPI CARVERS**
Helga Teiwes
Provides an understanding of the secular contexts
of contemporary Hopi kachina wood sculpture.
Illus. 201 pp. University of Arizona Press, 1986.
$50; paper, $24.95.

**THE KACHINA DOLLS OF CECIL
CALNIMPTEWA: THEIR POWER,
THEIR SPLENDOR**
Theda Bassman; photos by Gene Balzer
Features 127 dolls in full-color. Includes a biogra-
phy of the author. Illus. 112 pp. Treasure Chest,
1993. $70.

**KACHINA TALES FROM
THE INDIAN PUEBLOS**
Gene M. Hodge, Ed.
Illus. 96 pp. Paper. Sunstone Press, $8.95

KACHINA: A SELECTED BIBLIOGRAPHY
Marcia Muth
Over 100 references to kachinas and an essay.
Illus. 32 pp. Paper. Sunstone Press, $4.95.

**KACHINAS: A HOPI
ARTIST'S DOCUMENTARY**
Barton Wright; illus. by Cliff Bahnimptewa
237 color plates. Illus. 272 pp. Northland
Publishing, 1973. $45.00.

KACHINAS IN THE PUEBLO WORLD
Poly Schaafsma
14 noted scholars examine the role of the
kachina in the Pueblo culture. 41 full-color
photos and bxw drawings. 232 pp. University of
New Mexico Press, $40.

KACHINAS, SPIRIT BEINGS OF THE HOPI
J. Brent Ricks & Alexander E. Anthony, Jr.
Based on 79 paintings by Neil David, Sr., Hopi
Indian artist and Kachina carver. Illus. Photos.
200 pp. Avanyu Publishing, $50.

**KAHBE NAGWIWENS - THE MAN
WHO LIVED IN THREE CENTURIES**
  Carl A. Zapffe
  Illus. 100 pp. Paper. Historical Heart Associates,
  1975. $10.

**KAHTNUHT'ANA QENAGA: THE KENAI
PEOPLE'S LANGUAGE**
  Peter Kalifornsky; James Kari, Editor
  Second edition. Illus. 140 pp. Paper. Alaska
  Native Language Center, 1982. $6.

KALAUPAPA: A PORTRAIT
  photos by Wayne Levin
  Portrait of Kalaupapa Settlement. Illus.
  104 pp. Bishop Museum, $28.

THE KALISPEL INDIANS
  John Fahey
  Illus. 256 pp. University of Oklahoma Press,
  1986. $18.95.

**PAUL KANE, THE COLUMBIA WANDERER:
SKETCHES, PAINTINGS & COMMENT, 1846-
1847**
  Thomas Vaughan, Editor
  Illus. 80 pp. Paper. Oregon Historical Society,
  1971. $3.95.

**KANIENKEHAKA (MOHAWK NATION): STATE
POLICIES & COMMUNITY RESISTANCE**
  Donna Goodleaf
  Account of the "Oka Crisis" with Mohawkl perspec-
  tive of the issues & events. 250 pp. Paper. Theytus,
  1993. $12.95.

**KANSAS INDIANS: A HISTORY
OF THE WIND PEOPLE, 1673-1873**
  William E. Unrau
  Illus. Paper. University of Oklahoma Press,
  1971. $10.95.

**THE KARANKARA INDIANS,
THE COAST PEOPLE OF TEXAS**
  A.S. Gatschet
  Reprint of 1891 edition. Paper. Kraus, $15.

KARUK: THE UPRIVER PEOPLE
  Maureen Bell
  The history of the Karuk; also present-day Karuk
  life & culture are presented. Photos. 144 pp.
  Naturegraph, $16.95; paper, $8.95.

**KASKA INDIANS: AN ETHNOGRAPHIC
RECONSTRUCTION**
  John J. Honigmann
  163 pp. Paper. HRAFP, 1964. $15.

**KAWAIISU: A GRAMMAR & DICTIONARY,
WITH TEXTS**
  Maurice L. Zigmond, et al
  416 pp. Paper. U. of California Press, 1991.
  $42.

**K'ETAALKKAANEE: THE ONE WHO
PADDLED AMONG THE ANIMALS**
  Catherine Attla
  University of Alaska Press, $12.

*KEEPER OF FIRE
  James Magorian
  Grades 4-12. Illus. 78 pp. Council for Indian
  Education, 1984. $10.95; paper, $4.95.

***KEEPERS OF THE ANIMALS: NATIVE AMERI-
CAN STORIES & WILDLIFE ACTIVITIES FOR
CHILDREN**

  Michael Caduto & Joseph Bruchac;
  illus. by John Kahionhes Fadden
  Grades K-12. Illus. 286 pp. Fulcrum Publishing &
  AISES, 1991. $19.95. Teacher's Guide, 66 pp.
  paper, $9.95. Two audiocassettes, $16.95.

**KEEPERS OF THE CULTURE:
WOMEN IN A CHANGING WORLD**
  Janet Mancini Billson
  Explores women's lives in seven distinct and intact North American cultures: Iroquois, Inuit, Blood,
  mennonite, West Indian, Chinese & Ukranian. 350
  pp. Lexington Books, 1995. $23.

***KEEPERS OF THE EARTH: NATIVE AMERI-
CAN STORIES & ENVIRONMENTAL ACTIVI-
TIES FOR CHILDREN**
  Michael Caduto & Joseph Bruchac; illus. by
  John Kahionhes Fadden
  Grades K-12. Illus. 234 pp. Fulcrum Publishing
  & AISES, 1988. $19.95. Teacher's Guide, 48 pp.
  paper, $9.95. Two audiocassette, $16.95.

**KEEPERS OF THE GAME: INDIAN-ANIMAL
RELATIONSHIP OF THE FUR TRADE**
  Calvin Martin
  Illus. University of California Press, 1978.
  $27.95; paper, $11.95.

***KEEPERS OF LIFE: DISCOVERING PLANTS
THROUGH NATIVE AMERICAN STORIES AND
EARTH ACTIVITIES FOR CHILDREN**
  Michael Caduto & Joseph Bruchac; illus. by
  John Kahionhes Fadden
  Grades K-12. Illus. 288 pp. Fulcrum Publishing,
  1994. $22.95. Teacher's Guide, 48 pp. paper,
  $9.95. Two audiocassette, $16.95.

***KEEPERS OF THE NIGHT: NATIVE AMERI-
CAN STORIES & NOCTURNAL ACTIVITIES
FOR CHILDREN**
  Michael Caduto & Joseph Bruchac; illus. by
  John Kahionhes Fadden
  Grades K-12. Illus. 160 pp. Paper. Fulcrum
  Publishing, $14.95.

KENEKUK, THE KICKAPOO PROPHET
  Joseph B. Herring
  Illus. Maps. 170 pp. University Press of Kansas,
  1988. $19.95.

KERESAN TEXTS
  Franz Boas
  Reprint of 1928 ed. 2 vols. AMS Press, $60/set.

**A KEY INTO THE LANGUAGE
OF WOODSPLINT BASKETS**
  Ann McMullen & Russell Handsman, Editors
  Illus. 196 pp. Paper. American Indian Archaeo-
  logical Institute, 1987. $20.

KICKAPOO TALES
  William Jones; trans. by T. Michelson
  Reprint of 1915 edition. AMS Press, $24.

KIIKAAPOU: THE KANSAS KICKAPOO
  Donald D. Stull
  Illus. 214 pp. Paper. Kickapoo Tribal Press,
  1984. $12.

KILIWA DICTIONARY
  Mauricio J. Mixco
  207 pp. Paper. U. of Utah Press, 1985. $25.

THE KILIWA INDIANS OF LOWER CALIF.
  P. Meigs
  Reprint of 1939 edition. AMS Press.

**KILIWA TEXTS: WHEN I HAVE
DONNED MY CREST OF STARS**
  Mauricio J. Mixco
  Illus. 250 pp. Paper. University of Utah Press,
  1983. $25.

THE KILLING OF CHIEF CRAZY HORSE
  Robert A. Clark, Editor
  Three eyewitness accounts of the killing of Crazy
  Horse. Illus. 152 pp. Paper. University of Nebraska
  Press, 1988. $6.95.

**THE KILLING OF NED CHRISTIE:
CHEROKEE OUTLAW**
  Bonnie Speer
  180 pp. Reliance Press, 1990. $19.95; paper,
  $13.95.

**KINAALADA: A NAVAJO
PUBERTY CEREMONY**
  Shirley M. Begay and Verna Clinton-Tullie
  Illus. 171 pp. Navajo Curriculum, 1983. $15;
  paper, $11.

**KINAALDA: A STUDY OF THE NAVAHO
GIRL'S PUBERTY CEREMONY**
  Charlotte Johnson Frisbie
  Illus. Paper. University of Utah Press, $24.95.

**KING ISLAND TALES - UGIUVANGMIUT
QULIAPYUIT**
  Eskimo history & legends from the Bering
  Strait. University of Alaska Press, $19.95.

**KING OF THE DELAWARES:
TEEDYUSCUNG, 1700-1763**
  Anthony Wallace
  Reprint of 1949 edition. 330 pp. Ayer Co.,
  $23.50. Paper. Syracuse University Press,
  $15.95.

**KINO'S HISTORICAL
MEMOIR OF PRIMERIA ALTA**
  Eusebio F. Kino
  Reprint of 1919 edition. Two vols. in one.
  AMS Press, $52.50.

**KINSHIP & THE DRUM DANCE IN
A NORTHERN DENE COMMUNITY**
  M.L. Asch
  Illus. 113 pp. CCI, $25; paper, $15.

**KINSMEN OF ANOTHER KIND: DAKOTA--
WHITE RELATIONS IN THE UPPER MISSIS-
SIPPI VALLEY, 1650-1862**
  Gary C. Anderson
  400 pp. University of Nebraska Press, 1984. $30.

**KINSMEN THROUGH TIME: AN ANNOTATED
BIBLIOGRAPHY OF POTAWATOMI HISTORY**
  David R. Edmunds
  237 pp. Scarecrow Press, 1987. $27.50.

*THE KIOWA: GREAT PLAINS
  John Wunder
  Grades 5 and up. Illus. Chelsea House, 1989.
  $17.95.

**KIOWA MEMORIES; IMAGES
FROM INDIAN TERRITORY, 1880**
  Ron McCoy
  Illus. 67 pp. Morning Star Gallery, 1987. $21.

KIOWA TALES
  Elsie Parsons
  Reprint of 1929 edition. Kraus, $16.

THE KIOWA TREATY OF 1853
R.J. DeMallie
60 pp. Institute for the Development of
Indian Law, $12.50.

***KIOWA VOICES: CEREMONIAL
DANCE, RITUAL & SONG**
Maurice Boyd
Grades 3-12. Illus. 165 pp. Paper. Texas
Christian University Press, 1981. $29.95.

**KIOWA VOICES: MYTHS,
LEGENDS & FOLKTALES**
Maurice Boyd
Volume II. Illus. 323 pp. Texas Christian
University Press, 1983. $39.95.

THE KIOWAS
Mildred P. Mayhall
Revised 1972 edition. Illus. 2nd edition. Paper.
University of Oklahoma Press, $12.95.

**KITCHI-GAMI: LIFE AMONG THE LAKE
SUPERIOR OJIBWAY**
Johann G. Kohl; trans. by L. Wraxall
Illus. 477 pp. Paper. Minnesota Historical
Society Press, 1985. $12.95.

**KIVA ART OF THE ANASAZI AT
POTTERY MOUND, N.M.**
Frak Hibben
Illus. 145 pp. KC Publications, 1975. $35; paper,
$14.95.

KLAMATH ETHNOGRAPHY
L. Spier
Reprint of 1930 edition. Kraus, $56.

**THE KLAMATH TRIBE: A PEOPLE
& THEIR RESERVATION**
Theodore Stern
Reprint of 1965 edition. AMS, $45.

**KNOWLEDGE OF THE ELDERS: THE
IROQUOIS CONDOLENCE CANE TRADITION**
A study guide designed for high school students.
Looks at a living tradition of the Eastern Wood-
lands as told by Jacob Thomas, and elder of the
Cayuga Nation. Akwe:kon Press, $8.

KOASATI GRAMMAR
Geoffrey D. Kimball
Illus. Map. 650 pp. University of Nebraska
Press, 1991. $75.

**KOKOPELLI: FLUTEPLAYER
IMAGES IN ROCK ART**
Dennis Slifer & Jim Duffield
Extensive survey of rock art depictions of the
humpbacked fluteplayer. Photos, Illus. maps. Pa-
per. 150 pp. Ancient City Press, 1994. $14.95.

KOMANTCIA
Harold Keith
A tale of captivity by the Comanche Indians.
300 pp. Levite of Apache, $17.

KORCZAK: STORYTELLER IN STONE
The biography of Korczak Ziolkowski, the sculpture of Crazy Horse from Thunderhead Mountain.
Illus. 80 pp. Paper. Crazy Horse Memorial Foundation, 2.95.

THE KORYAK
V.I. Iokhel'Son
Reprint of 1908 edition. AMS Press, $94.50.

KOSSATI GRAMMAR
Geoffrey Kimball
Illus. 640 pp. University of Nebraska Press,
1991. $70.

*KOU-SKELOWH "WE ARE THE PEOPLE"
Barb Marchand, Editor & Illus.
Entirely done by Okanagan First Nation people.
Grades K-4. Illus. 28 pp. Paper. Theytus, 1990.
$12.95.

KOVIASHUVIK: A TIME & PLACE OF JOY
Sam Wright
228 pp. Sierra Club Books, 1989. $17.95.

KUMTUX
Jeanette Mills, Editor
A monthly calendar of events in and related to
Indian Country in Washington State. Native Ameri-
can Task Force, Church Council of Greater Se-
attle. $18/yr.

*KUNU: WINNEBAGO BOY ESCAPES
Kenneth Thomasma; Jack Brouwer. Illus.
Historical novel of the forced migration of
Winnebago Indians in 1863. Grades 4 and up. Illus.
Baker Book House, $10.99; paper, $6.99.

**KUSIQ: AN ESKIMO LIFE HISTORY FROM
THE ARCTIC COAST OF ALASKA**
Waldo Bodfish, Sr.
Illus. Maps. 330 pp. Paper. University of Alaska
Press, 1991. $21.

*THE KWAKIUTL
Stanley Walens
Grades 5 and up. Illus. Chelsea House, 1989.
$17.95.

KWAKIUTL ART
Audrey Hawthorne
Illus. 292 pp. Paper. University of
Washington Press, 1988. $35.

**KWAKIUTL CULTURE AS
REFLECTED IN MYTHOLOGY**
Franz Boas
Reprint of 1935 edition. Kraus, $21.

KWAKIUTL ETHNOGRAPHY
Franz Boas; Helen Codere, Editor
Illus. University of Chicago Press, 1967. $30.

**KWAKIUTL: INDIANS
OF BRITISH COLUMBIA**
R.P. Rohner and E. Rohner
111 pp. Paper. Waveland Press, 1970. $8.50.

THE KWAKIUTL OF VANCOUVER ISLAND
Franz Boas
Reprint of 1909 edition. AMS Press, $58.

KWAKIUTL STRING FIGURES
Julia Averkieva & Mark Sherman
Study of 112 string figures and tricks collected
among the Kawkiutl Indians by Averkieva. Illus.
164 drawings. 232 pp. University of Washington
Press, $35.

KWAKIUTL TALES
Franz Boas
Reprint of 1910 edition. AMS Press, $42.50.

KWAKIUTL TALES: NEW SERIES
Franz Boas
Reprint of 1943 ed. 2 vols. AMS Press, $20 each.

KWAKIUTL TEXTS
Franz Boas & George Hunt
Reprint of 1905 edition. AMS Press, $49.50.
Second series reprint of 1906 edition. AMS Press,
$49.50.

A KWAKIUTL VILLAGE AND SCHOOL
Harry F. Wolcott
Reprint of 1967 edition. Illus. 132 pp. Paper.
Waveland Press, 1984. $7.95.

**KWAKWAKA'WAKW SETTLEMENT SITES,
1775-1920**
Robert Galois
Demographics & settlement patterns of the
Kawakiutl in British Columbia betweem 1775 and
1920. 60 maps. 350 pp. University of Washington
Press, $60.

***KWULASULWUT: STORIES
FROM THE COAST SALISH**
Ellen White; illus. by David Neel
Grades K-6. Illus. 76 pp. Paper. Theytus, 1992.
$12.95.

***KWULASULWUT: SALISH CREATION
STORIES**
Ellen White; illus. by David Neel
Grades K-6. Illus. 25 pp. Paper. Theytus, 1995.
$9.95.

L

LABRADOR ESKIMO
Ernest Hawkes
Reprint of 1916 edition. Johnson Reprint, $16.

**LACHLAN McGILLIVRAY, INDIAN TRADER:
THE SHAPING OF THE SOUTHERN COLO-
NIAL FRONTIER**
Edward J. Cashin
The career of the Indian trader from 1736 to 1776.
Illus. 352 pp. University of Georgia Press, $45.

**LAKE PERTHA & THE
LOST MURALS OF CHIAPAS**
J. David Wonham
Illus. 19 pp. Paper. Pre-Columbian Art, 1985. $10.

LAKOTA BELIEF & RITUAL
James R. Walker
Illus. 370 pp. Paper. University of Nebraska
Press & AISES, 1980. $15.95.

LAKOTA LIFE
Ron Zeilinger
Illus. 75 pp. Paper. Tipi Press, 1986. $3.95.

LAKOTA MYTH
James R. Walker; Elaine A. Jahner, Editor
428 pp. Paper. University of Nebraska Press,
1983. $14.95.

**LAKOTA RECOLLECTIONS OF THE CUSTER
FIGHT: NEW SOURCES OF INDIAN-MILITARY
HISTORY**
Richard G. Hardorff, Editor
A collection of sixteen interviews with partici-
pants in the Battle of the Little Big Horn. Illus.
Maps. 211 pp. The Arthur H. Clark Co., $32.50.

LAKOTA SOCIETY
James R. Walker; Raymond J. DeMallie, Editor
Illus. 250 pp. University of Nebraska Press,
1982. $27.50; paper, $10.95.

LAKOTA STAR KNOWLEDGE:
STUDIES IN STELLAR THEOLOGY
  R. Goodman, S. Redbird, Jr., et al
Illus. 60 pp. Paper. AISES, $15.

LAKOTA WOMAN
  Mary Crow Dog
Illus. 275 pp. Paper. HarperCollins, 1991. $9.95.

LAMAR ARCHAEOLOGY: MISSISSIPPIAN
CHIEFDOMS IN THE DEEP SOUTH
  Mark Williams & Gary Shapiro, Editors
256 pp. Paper. University of Alabama Press,
1990. $20.95.

LAME DEER: SEEKER OF VISIONS: THE
LIFE OF A SIOUX MEDICINE MAN
  John Fire/Lame Deer and Richard Erdoes
Chief Lame Deer, the chief medicine man for the
western Sioux tribes, tells of the modern Indian
experience. Paper. Simon & Schuster, 1972.
$11.

THE LANCE & THE SHIELD: THE LIFE &
TIMES OF SITTING BULL
  Robert M. Utley
Biography of a great Sioux leader. Henry Holt,
1993. $19.95.

THE LAND OF THE CLIFF-DWELLERS
  Frederick H. Chapin
Reprint of 1892 edition. AMS Press, $23.50.
Paper. University of Arizona Press, $9.95.

LAND OF THE FOUR DIRECTIONS
  Frederick J. Pratson
A photographic portrayal of American Indians of
Maine. Illus. 140 pp. Paper. Chatham Press,
$3.95.

THE LAND OF THE OJIBWE
  MHS Education Dept.
Describes the movement of the Ojibwe through-
out the Western Great Lakes region and beyond.
Maps. 48 pp. Paper. Minnesota Historical Society
Press, 1973. $1.50.

THE LAND OF RED CLOUD:
AMONG NORTH AMERICA'S INDIANS
  Peter Korniss
136 pp. International Specialized Book Service,
1982. $19.95.

LAND OF THE SPOTTED EAGLE
  Luther Standing Bear
Illus. 275 pp. Paper. University of Nebraska
Press, 1978. $8.95.

LANDFILL MEDITATION:
CROSSBLOOD STORIES
  Gerald Vizenor
200 pp. University Press of New England. 1991.
$30; paper, $14.95.

LAND RIGHTS OF INDIGENOUS CANADIAN
PEOPLES
  Brian Slattery
478 pp. University of Saskatchewan, 1979. $70.

LANDLORD TENENT RELATIONS
Institute for the Development of Indian Law, $3.50.

LANGUAGE & ART IN
THE NAVAJO UNIVERSE
  Gary Witherspoon
Illus. 234 pp. University of Michigan Press,
1977. $24.95; paper, $15.95.

LANGUAGE, CULTURE & HISTORY:
ESSAYS BY MARY R. HAAS
  Mary R. Haas; Anwar S. Dil, Editor
398 pp. Stanford University Press, 1978. $32.50.

LANGUAGE, HISTORY, & IDENTITY:
ETHNOLINGUISTIC STUDIES OF THE
ARIZONA TEWA
  Paul V. Kroskrity
250 pp. University of Arizona Press, 1993. $50.

LANGUAGE OF THE PAPAGO OF ARIZONA
  John A. Hason
Paper. Books on Demand, $22.

LANGUAGE RENEWAL AMONG
AMERICAN INDIAN TRIBES
  Robert N. St. Clair and William L. Leap
176 pp. Paper. National Clearinghouse Bilingual
Education, 1982. $8.95.

LANGUAGES OF THE ABORIGINAL SOUTH-
EAST: AN ANNOTATED BIBLIOGRAPHY
  Karen M. Booker
265 pp. Scarecrow Pres, 1991. $32.50.

LANGUAGES OF NATIVE AMERICA: HISTORI-
CAL & COMPARATIVE ASSESSMENT
  Lyle Campbell and Marianne Mithun, Editors
1,040 pp. University of Texas Press, 1979. $35.

LANGUAGES OF THE TRIBES OF THE
EXTREME NORTHWEST: ALASKA, THE
***THE LAST CHEROKEE WARRIORS**
  Phillip Steele
Grades 6-12. Second edition. Illus. 1 11 pp.
Pelican Publishing, 1978. $7.95; paper, $5.95.

THE LAST CONTRARY: THE STORY OF
WESLEY WHITEMAN (BLACK BEAR)
  Warren Schwartz
Illus. 146 pp. Center for Western Studies, 1990.
$12.95.

LAST DAYS OF THE SIOUX NATION
  Robert M. Utley
Historical study of the reaction of the Sioux to the
reservation system in the mid 1800s. Illus. Maps.
Biblio. 314 pp. Paper. Center for Western Studies
& Yale University Press, 1963. $15.

THE LAST LIGHT BREAKING: LIVING
AMONG ALASKA'S INUPIAT ESKIMOS
  Nick Jans
Map. 224 pp. Graphic Arts Center, 1994.
$21.95.

LAST OF THE CURLEWS
  Fred Bodsworth
Illus. 176 pp. Dodd, Mead, 1987. $16.95; paper,
$8.95.

***THE LAST OF THE MOHICANS**
  James Fenimore Cooper; illus. by N.C. Wyeth
Grades 5 and up. Illus. 400 pp. Macmillan, $24.95.
Paper. Center for Western Studies, $5.95.

LAST RAMBLES AMONGST THE INDIANS
OF THE ROCKY MOUNTAINS & THE ANDES
  George Catlin
Reprint of 1867 edition. Reprint Services, $79.

THE LATE PREHISTORIC SOUTHEAST: A
SOURCEBOOK
  Chester DePratter
548 pp. Garland, 1987. $70.

LAST WARRIOR
  MacDonald
Orion Books, $25.

LATE WOODLAND SITES IN THE
AMERICAN BOTTOM UPLANDS
  Charles Bentz, et al
Illus. Paper. University of Illinois Press, 1988.
$17.50.

LAUGHING BOY
  Oliver La Farge
A novel about a young Navajo lover & his mate.
Winner of the 1929 Pulitzer Prize. 192 pp.
Paper. Penguin USA, $4.95.

AUGUSTINE LAURE, S.J.
MISSIONARY TO THE YAKIMAS
  Victor Garrard
36 pp. Paper.Ye Galleon Press, 1977. $7.50;
paper, $5.95.

THE LAUREL CULTURE IN MINNESOTA
  James B. Stoltman
Illus. 146 pp. Paper. Minnesota Historical
Society, 1973. $5.50.

LAW & THE AMERICAN INDIAN:
READINGS, NOTES AND CASES
  Monroe E. Price and Robert Clinton
Second edition. 800 pp. Michie Co., 1983.
$28.50.

LAW ENFORCEMENT ON INDIAN
RESERVATIONS AFTER OLIPHANT
V. SUQUAMISH INDIAN TRIBES
Institute for the Development of Indian Law, $2.

LAW & GOVERNMENT OF
THE GRAND RIVER IROQUOIS
  John A. Noon
Reprint of 1949 ed. Paper. Johnson Reprint, $19.

LAW & IDENTITY: LAWYERS, NATIVE
AMERICANS & LEGAL PRACTICE
  Linda Medcalf
Paper. Books on Demand, 1978. $37.

LAW & STATUS AMONG THE KIOWA
INDIANS
  Jane Richardson
Reprint of 1940 edition. AMS, $23.50.

LAWS OF THE COLONIAL & STATE GOV-
ERNMENTS RLATING TO INDIANS & INDIAN
AFFAIRS, 1633-1831
Reprint of 1832 edition. 322 pp. E.M. Coleman,
$27.50.

LEAGUE OF THE IROQUOIS
  L.H. Morgan
Reprint of 1904 edition. 477 pp. Peter Smith.
$15.50. Paper. Carol Publishing Group, $7.95.

LEARN HAWAIIAN AT HOME
  Kahikahealani Wight
Self-study program, with vocabulary and useful
phrases; glossaries, and cassette tape. Illus. 176
pp. The Bess Press, $29.95.

LEASING INDIAN WATER: UPCOMING
CHOICES IN THE COLORADO RIVER BASIN
  Gary Weatherford & Mary Wallace
66 pp. Paper. Conservation Forum, 1988.
$10.50.

LEFT BY THE INDIANS
E. Fuller & C. Schlicke
61 pp. Ye Galleon Press, 1988.

LEFT-HANDED: A NAVAJO AUTOBIOGRAPHY
Walter & Ruth Dyk
Illus. 624 pp. Columbia University Press, 1980. $37.50.

THE LEGACY OF ANDREW JACKSON: ESSAYS ON DEMOCRACY, INDIAN RE-MOVAL & SLAVERY
Robert Remini
120 pp. Paper. Louisiana State University Press, 1990. $6.95.

THE LEGACY: TRADITION & INNOVATION IN NORTHWEST COAST INDIAN ART
Peter Macnair, Alan Hoover & Kevin Neary
Illus. 194 pp. Paper. University of Washington Press, $26.95.

LEGAL CONSCIENCE, SELECTED PAPERS
Felix S. Cohen; Lucy K. Cohen, Editor
Reprint of 1960 edition. 505 pp. Shoe String Press, $45.

LEGAL INFORMATION SERVICE
32 vols. on Canadian Indian legal affairs. See University of Saskatchewan for titles and prices.

LEGAL ISSUES IN INDIAN JURISDICTION
63 pp. National Attorney's General, 1976. $3.50.

LEGAL PROCESS & THE RESOLUTION OF INDIAN CLAIMS
Eric Golvin
Studies in Canadian aboriginal rights. 29 pp. University of Saskatchewan, 1981. $6.50.

THE LEGAL STATUS OF THE INDIAN
Robert Weil
Reprint of 1888 edition. 76 pp. AMS Press, $12.50.

*A LEGEND FROM CRAZY HORSE CLAN
Big Crow & Moses Nelson;
Renee S. Flood, Editor
Grades 3 and up. Illus. 36 pp. Paper. Center for Western Studies, 1987. $3.95.

*THE LEGEND OF THE BLUEBONNET, retold
Tomie dePaola
An old tale of Texas..a courageous little Comanche girl sacrifices her most beloved possession, Grades PS-3. Illus. 32 pp. Putnam, 1983. $14.95; paper, $5.95.

*THE LEGEND OF THE INDIAN PAINT-BRUSH, retold
Tomie dePaola
An Indian brave dreams of creating a painting that will capture the beauty of a sunset. Grades PS-3. Illus. 40 pp. Putnam, 1988. $14.95.

THE LEGEND OF NATURAL TUNNEL
Clara Talton Fugate; illus. by Caren Ertmann
Illus. 40 pp. Paper. Pocahontas Press, 1989. $5.95.

*THE LEGEND OF TOM PEPPER & OTHER STORIES
Arthur Griffin
Grades 2-5. Illus. 100 pp. Bainbridge Press, 1990.

LEGENDS IN STONE, BONE & WOOD
Tsonakwa
Abenaki legends, history, and photographed works of art. The Greenfield Review Press, $10.95.

*LEGENDS OF CHIEF BALD EAGLE
Harry B. Shows and Hap Gilliland
Grades 2-10. Paper. Council for Indian Education, 1977. $2.95.

*LEGENDS OF THE GREAT CHIEFS
Emerson N. Matson
Authentic legends and little-known incidents re-called during first-hand interviews with actual de-scendants of some of the most famous chiefs. Grades 8-12. Illus. 144 pp. Paper. Storypole, 1972. $5.95.

LEGENDS OF THE LAKOTA
James LaPointe; illus. by Louis Amiotte
Illus. 184 pp. The Indian Historian Press, 1975. $11.00; paper, $6.

LEGENDS OF THE LONGHOUSE
Jesse Complanter
Iroquois tales told by Jesse Corplanter. Illus. Greenfield Review Press, $10.

LEGENDS OF THE MICMACS
Silas Rand
Reprint of 1894 edition. Johnson Reprint, $42.

LEGENDS OF THE MIGHTY SIOUX
Montana Lisle Reese, Editor
45 traditional legends of the Sioux written by el-ders on the Rosebud & Yankton reservations. Reprint of 1941 edition. Center for Western Stud-ies, $14.95; paper, $5.95.

LEGENDS OF OUR NATIONS
Collection of traditional Native tales from across Canada & U.S. Paper. Greenfield Review Press, $6.

LEGENDS OF THE YOSEMITE MIWOK
Frank LaPena, Craig D. Bates & Steven P. Medley, Editors
Revised edition. Illus. 64 pp. Paper. Yosemite Association, 1993. $10.95.

LEGENDS TOLD BY THE OLD PEOPLE
Adolph Hungry Wolf
Illus. 80 pp. Paper. Cherokee Publications & The Book Publishing Co., 1990. $5.95.

LEGENDS, TRADITIONS AND LAWS OF THE IROQUOIS: OR, SIX NATIONS, HISTORY OF THE TUSCARORA INDIANS
Elias Johnson
Reprint of 1881 edition. AMS Press, $24.50.

THE LEMHI: SACAJAWEA'S PEOPLE
Brigham Madsen
Illus. Maps. Biblio. 214 pp. Paper. The Caxton Printers, 1980. $7.95.

THE LENAPE
Herbert Kraft
Illus. 300 pp. New Jersey Historical Society, 1987. $24.95.

*THE LENAPE: MIDDLE ATLANTIC
Robert Grumet
Grades 5 and up. Illus. Chelsea House, 1989. $17.95.

LENAPE HISTORY & NUMBERS POSTERS
The Middle Atlantic Press, $5 each.

THE LENAPE & THEIR LEGENDS
W. Olum; Daniel G. Brinton, Editor
Reprint of 1884 edition. Scholarly Press, $30.

LESCHI, LAST OF THE NISQUALLIES
Cecilia Carpenter
Illus. 56 pp. Paper. Heritage Quest, 1986. $5.

LESSONS FROM CHOUTEAU CREEK: YANKTON MEMORIES OF DAKOTA IN-TRIGUE
Renee Sansom-Flood
Reprint. Illus. Paper. Center for Western Studies, $10.95.

LESSONS IN HOPI
Milo Kalectaca; Ronald W. Langacker, Editor
30 grammar lessons, ten exemplary dialogs, and Hopi--English, English--Hopi lexicons. 234 pp. Paper. University of Arizona Press, 1978. $11.95.

**LET ME BE FREE:
THE NEZ PERCE TRAGEDY**
David Lavender
Illus. 400 pp. HarperCollins, $30.

*LET ME TELL YOU A STORY
Yerington Paiute Tribe
Grades 2-8. Illus. 95 pp. Paper. Yerington Paiute Tribe Publications, $8. Companion Activity Work-book, 105 pp., $10.

LET MY PEOPLE KNOW: AMERICAN INDIAN JOURNALISM, 1828-1978
James E. and Sharon M. Murphy
300 pp. The Indian Historian Press and University of Oklahoma Press, 1979. $19.95.

*LET'S LOOK INSIDE A TEPEE
Betsy Warren
Grades 3 and up. Illus. 30 pp. Paper. Ranch Gate Books, 1989. $3.50.

*LET'S REMEMBER...INDIANS OF TEXAS
Betsy Warren
Grades 3-8. Illus. 32 pp. Paper. Hendrick-Long, $4.50.

LETTER FROM THE SECRETARY OF THE IN-TERIOR - INFORMATION IN RELATION TO THE EARLY LABORS OF THE MISSIONARIES
90 pp. Paper. Ye Galleon Press, 1988. $7.50.

LETTERS OF THE LEWIS & CLARK EXPEDI-TION, WITH RELATED DOCUMENTS, 1783-1854
Donald Jackson, Editor
Second edition. Two volumes. 832 pp. University of Illinois Press, 1978. $49.95.

LETTERS & NOTES ON THE MANNERS, CUSTOMS & CONDITIONS OF THE NORTH AMERICAN INDIANS
George Catlin
Reprint of 1841 edition. Two vols. Illus. 572 pp. Reprint Services, $79.00. Paper. Hothem House & Dover, $17.90.

LETTERS TO HOWARD: AN INTERPRETATION OF THE ALASKA NATIVE LANDS CLAIM
Fred Bigjim
Collection of 24 letters on critical issues of the Alaska Native Land Claims. Greenfield Review Press, $12.

*LEWIS & CLARK
Francene Sabin
Grades 3-6. Illus. 32 pp. Troll Associates,
1985. $8.94; paper, $2.50.

LEWIS & CLARK AMONG THE INDIANS
James P. Ronda
Illus. Maps. 320 pp. Paper. University of
Nebraska Press, 1984. $10.95.

THE LEWIS & CLARK EXPEDITION
Patrick McGrath
Grades 5 and up. Illus. 64 pp. Silver Burdette,
1985. $14.96; paper, $7.95.

**LEWIS & CLARK & THE SHAHAPTIAN
SPEAKING AMERICANS**
Cheryl Halsey & Robert Beale
Illus. 24 pp. Paper. Ye Galleon, $2.95

***MERIWEATHER LEWIS & WILLIAM CLARK:
SOLDIERS, EXPLORERS, & PARTNERS IN
HISTORY**
David Petersen & Mark Coburn
Grades 4 and up. Illus. 152 pp. Childrens Press,
1988. $15.95.

LEWIS & CLARK: VOYAGE OF DISCOVERY
Dan Murphy
Illus. 64 pp. Paper. KC Publications , 1977. $4.50.

**LIBRARY OF ABORIGINAL
AMERICAN LITERATURE**
Daniel G. Brinton, Editor
Reprint of 1890 edition. Eight volumes.
AMS Press, $240.00 per set; $30.00 each..

LIBRARY OF AMERICAN LINGUISTICS
John Shea, Editor
Reprint of 1860-1864 editions. 13 volumes.
AMS Press, $370.00 per set; $28.50 each.

**LICENSE FOR EMPIRE: COLONIALISM BY
TREATY IN EARLY AMERICA**
Dorothy V. Jones
University of Chicago Press, 1982. $25.

**LIFE & ADVENTURES OF JAMES P.
BECKWOURTH, MOUNTAINEER, SCOUT &
PIONEER, AND CHIEF OF THE CROW NATION
OF INDIANS**
J. Beckwourth; T.D. Bonner, Editor
Reprint of 1856 edition. 650 pp. Ayer Co., $36.95.
Paper. University of Nebraska Press, $10.95.

LIFE & ADVENTURES OF FRANK GROUARD
Joe De Barthe; Edgar Stewart, Editor
Reprint of 1958 edition. Illus. Books on Demand,
$74.50.

LIFE AMONG THE APACHES
John C. Cremony
322 pp. Paper. University of Nebraska Press,
1983. $8.50.

**LIFE AMONG THE CHOCTAW INDIANS
AND SKETCHES OF THE SOUTHWEST**
Henry C. Benson
Reprint of 1860 edition. Johnson Reprint, $79.

**LIFE AMONG THE INDIANS: OR, PERSONAL
REMINISCENCES & HISTORICAL INCIDENTS
ILLUSTRATIVE OF INDIAN LIFE & CHARAC-
TER**
James Finley; D.W. Clark, Editor
Facsimile of the 1857 edition. Ayer Co., $31.

**LIFE AMONG THE MODOCS:
UNWRITTEN HISTORY**
Joaquin Miller
Reprint of 1873 edition. 440 pp. Urion Press,
1982. $19.95; paper, $8.95.

**LIFE AMONG THE PAIUTES:
THEIR WRONGS & CLAIMS**
Sarah Hopkins
Reprint of 1883 edition. Paper.
Chalfant Press, 1971. $13.50.

**LIFE & ART OF THE NORTH
AMERICAN INDIAN**
John Warner
Book Sales, 1990. $15.98.

LIFE & DEATH IN MOHAWK COUNTRY
Bruce E. Johansen; illus. by
John Kahionhes Fadden
Disputed land claims along the U.S. & Canadian
border. Illus. 202 pp. North American Press,
1992. $23.95.

THE LIFE I'VE BEEN LIVING
Moses Cruikshank
Biography of Moses Cruikshank, an Athabaskan
elder and skilled storyteller from Interior Alaska.
Reprint of 1986 edition. Illus. 132 pp. Paper.
University of Alaska Press, $9.95.

**LIFE IN CUSTER'S CAVALRY: DIARIES &
LETTERS OF ALBERT & JENNIE BARNITZ,
1867-1868**
Albert & Jennie Barnitz; Robert Utley, Editor
Illus. 302 pp. Paper. University of Nebraska
Press, 1987. $7.95.

LIFE IN THE PUEBLOS
Ruth Underhill; Willard Beatty, Editor
Interprets Pueblo lifestyles for the general public.
Illus. Maps. 168 pp. Paper. Ancient City Press,
$12.95.

LIFE & JOURNALS OF KAH-KE-WA-QUO-NA
Peter Jones
Reprint of 1860 edition. AMS Press, $26.

**LIFE, LETTERS & TRAVELS OF FATHER
PIERRE JEAN DE SMET, S.J., 1801-1873**
Pierre Jean de Smet
Missionary Labors & Adventures Among the Wild
Tribes of the North American Indians. Reprint of
the 1905 edition. 4 vols. Ayer Co., $88.

**THE LIFE & TIMES OF DAVID ZEISBERGER:
THE WESTERN PIONEER & APOSTLE OF
THE INDIANS**
Edmund De Schweinitz
Reprint of 1870 edition. Ayer Co., $39.

**LIFE & TIMES OF RED JACKET
OR SA-GO-YE-WAT-HA**
William Stone
Reprint of 1841 edition. Scgholarly Press, $49.

**LIFE LIVED LIKE A STORY: LIFE STORIES
OF THREE YUKON NATIVE ELDERS**
Julie Cruikshank
Illus. Maps. 415 pp. University of Nebraska
Press, 1991. $50; paper, $14.95.

**LIFE OF GEORGE BENT:
WRITTEN FROM HIS LETTERS**
George E. Hyde; Savoie Lottinville, Editor
Illus. 389 pp. Paper. University of Oklahoma
Press, 1983. $14.95.

**THE LIFE OF BLACKHAWK,
DICTATED BY HIMSELF**
J.B. Patterson
Enlarged edition. Ye Galleon Press, 1975. $12.

**THE LIFE OF HAROLD SELLERS COLTON:
A PHILADELPHIA BRAHMIN IN FLAGSTAFF**
Jimmy Herbert Miller
Paper. Navajo Community College Press, 1991.
$15.95.

**LIFE OF JOSEPH BRANT
(THAYENDANEGEA)**
W.L. Stone
Includes the border wars of the American Revolu-
tion and sketches of Indian campaigns,1783-
1795. Reprint of 1838 edition. 2 vols. Kraus,
$56.00 per set.

THE LIFE OF OKAH TUBBEE
Okah Tubbee; Daniel Littlefield, Jr., Editor
159 pp. University of Nebraska Press, 1988.
$19.95.

**LIFE OF TECUMSEH & HIS BROTHER THE
PROPHET: WITH AN HISTORICAL SKETCH
OF THE SHAWANOE INDIANS**
B. Drake
Reprint of 1841 edition. Ayer Co., $21.95.

**LIFE OF TOM HORN, GOVERNMENT SCOUT
& INTERPRETER, WRITTEN BY HIMSELF, TO-
GETHER WITH HIS LETTERS AND STATE-
MENTS BY HIS FRIENDS: A VINDICATION**
Tom Horn
Paper. U. of Oklahoma Press, 1964. $7.95.

**THE LIFE & TIMES OF LITTLE TURTLE:
FIRST SAGAMORE OF THE WABASH**
Harvey L. Carter
Illus. 296 pp. U. of Illinois Press, 1987. $24.95.

**LIFE & TIMES OF DAVID ZEISBERGER:
THE WESTERN PIONEER & APOSTLE
OF THE INDIANS**
Edmund De Schweinitz
Reprint of 1870 edition. Ayer Co., $39.

LIFE UNDER THE SUN
Charles Lovato
Lithograph art. Illus. Sunstone Press, $35;
signed & numbered hard cover edition, $125.

LIFE WITH THE ESKIMO
Illus. 16 pp. Paper. Hancock House, $2.95.

LIGHT ON THE LAND
Art Davidson; photos by Art Wolfe
Landscape photography with essays and Native
writings from around the world. Illus. 100 color
photos. 196 pp. Beyond Words Publishing, 1994.
$75.

THE LIGHT PEOPLE: A NOVEL
Gordon Henry, Jr.
A young Chippewa boy is trying to learn the where-
abouts of his parents. 272 pp. University of Oklahoma Press, 1994. $22.95.

**LIGHTNING INSIDE OF YOU & OTHER
NATIVE AMERICAN RIDDLES**
John Bierhorst, Editor
140 riddles translated from 20 Indian languages.
Grades 3 and up. Illus. 100 pp. Paper. AISES,
$14.

THE LIGHTNING WITHIN
Alan R. Velie, Editor
Anthology of American Indian fiction: N. Scott Momaday, James Welch, Louise Erdich, and Michael Doris. 170 pp. University of Nebraksa Press, 1991. $22; paper , $9.95.

LIKE BEADS ON A STRING: A CULTURE HISTORY OF THE SEMINOLE INDIANS IN NORTH PENINSULA FLORIDA
Brent Weisman
Illus. 216 pp. Paper . University of Alabama Press, 1989. $15.95.

THE LILLOOET INDIANS
James A. Teit
Reprint of 1906 edition. AMS Press, $30.

LINCOLN & THE INDIANS: CIVIL WAR POLICY & POLITICS
David A. Nichols
256 pp. University of Missouri Press, 1978. $26.

*LINDA'S INDIAN HOME
Grades 3-7. Illus. Binford & Mort, 1969. $6.95.

THE LIPAN APACHES IN TEXAS
Thomas F. Schilz
Illus. 58 pp. Texas Western, 1987. $10; paper , $5.

LIST OF DOCUMENTS CONCERNING THE NEGOTIATION OF RATIFIED INDIAN TREATIES: 1801-1869
U.S. National Archives
Reprint of 1949 edition. Kraus, $40.

LITERATURE BY & ABOUT THE AMERICAN INDIAN: AN ANNOTATED BIBLIOGRAPHY
Anna L. Stensland, Compiler
Describes more than 775 books on Native American experiences, new and old. Second edition. 382 pp. Paper . National Council of Teachers of English, 1979. $10.95.

LITTLE BIG HORN DIARY: CHRONICLE OF THE 1876 INDIAN WAR
James Willert
Second Edition. Illus. 520 pp. J. Willert, 1982. $60.

LITTLE BIT KNOW SOMETHING: STORIES IN A LANGUAGE OF ANTHROPOLOGY
Robin Ridington
Illus. 300 pp. University of Iowa Press, 1990. $28.50; paper, $10.95.

*LITTLE BOY WITH THREE NAMES: STORIES OF TAOS PUEBLO
Ann Nolan Clark
Reprint. Grades 3 and up. Illus. 80 pp. Paper . Ancient City Press, $8.95.

LITTLE CROW, SPOKESMAN FOR THE SIOUX
Gary Anderson
Illus. Photos. Maps. 259 pp. Paper . Minnesota Historical Society Press, 1986. $10.95.

*LITTLE FIREFLY
Terri Cohlene
Grades 4-8. Illus. 50 pp. Rourke Corp., 1990. $19.95; paper, $14.95.

*LITTLE HERDER IN AUTUMN
Ann Nolan Clark
Reprint. Grades 3 and up. Illus. 96 pp. Paper. Ancient City Press, $8.95.

A LITTLE HISTORY OF THE NAVAJOS
Oscar Lipps
Reprint of 1909 edition. Illus. 176 pp. Avanyu, $19.95.

LITTLE-KNOWN SMALL HOUSE RUINS IN THE COCONIMO FOREST
M.R. & N.S. Colton
Reprint of 1918 edition. Paper . Kraus, $15.

*LITTLE SOUTHWEST INDIAN GIRL PAPERDOLLS
Kathy Allert
Outfits represent Navajo, Pueblos, and Apache tribes. Grades 3 and up. 16 pp. Paper . Dover, $1.

LIVING ARCTIC: HUNTERS OF THE CANADIAN NORTH
Hugh Brody
Illus. Maps. 270 pp. Paper . University of Washington Press, 1990. $16.95.

LIVING THE SKY: THE COSMOS OF THE AMERICAN INDIAN
Ray A. Williamson
Illus. 404 pp. Paper . University of Oklahoma Press, 1987. $14.95.

LIVING THE SPIRIT: A GAY AMERICAN INDIAN ANTHOLOGY
Will Roscoe, Editor
Illus. 240 pp. St. Martin Press, 1988. $16.95.

THE LIVING TRADITION OF MARIA MARTINEZ
Susan Peterson
Revised edition. Illus. 300 pp. Kodansha, 1989. $70; paper, $34.95.

*LIVING WITH THE ESKIMOS
Grades K-5. Illus. 40 pp. Childrens Press, $11.45.

THE LIVINGSTON INDIAN RECORDS, 1666-1723
Lawrence H. Leder, Editor
Reprint of 1956 edition. 240 pp. E.M. Coleman, $25.

LOGS OF THE CONQUEST OF CANADA
W. Wood, Editor
Reprint of 1909 edition. Greenwood Press, $29.

LONG BEFORE COLUMBUS: HOW THE ANCIENTS DISCOVERED AMERICA
Hans Holzer
Illus. 160 pp. Paper . Bear & Co., $12.95.

LONG DEATH
Ralph Andrist
Ilus. Paper. Macmillan, 1969. $8.95.

THE LONG HOUSE OF THE IROQUOIS
Spencer Adams
Reprint of 1944 edition. Illus. AMS Press, $27.50.

LONG JOURNEY TO THE COUNTRY OF THE HURONS
G. Sagard-Theodat; George M. Wrong, Editor
Reprint of 1939 edition. Greenwood Press, $29.25.

LONG LANCE: THE TRUE STORY OF AN IMPOSTER
Donald B. Smith
Illus. 325 pp. Paper . University of Nebraska Press, 1983. $8.95.

*THE LONG SEARCH
Richard A. Boning
Grades 5-11. Illus. 48 pp. B. Loft, 1972. $7.95.

*LONG SHADOWS: INDIAN LEADERS STANDING IN THE PATH OF MANIFEST DESTINY 1600-1900
Jack Jackson
Grades 3-8. Illus. 128 pp. Paramount, 1985. $17.95.

A LONG & TERRIBLE SHADOW: WHITE VALUES, NATIVE RIGHTS IN THE AMERICAS, 1492-1992
Thomas R. Berger
Surveys and examines the history of the Americas since their discovery by Europeans. Illus. 196 pp. Paper . University of Washington Press, 1993. $14.95.

THE LONG WALK: HISTORY OF THE NAVAJO WARS, 1846-1868
Lynn R. Bailey
Illus. 300 pp. Westernlore, $10.95.

LOOK TO THE MOUNTAIN: AN ECOLOGY OF INDIGENOUS EDUCATION
Gregory Cajete, PhD
Studies indigenous educational philosophy by a Native American scholar. Looks to Indian education for tomorrow and into the 21st century . Illus. Biblio. 248 pp. Paper . Kivaki Press, 1994. $16.95.

LOOKING AT INDIAN ART OF THE NORTHWEST COAST
Hilary Stewart
Illus. 112 pp. Paper. University of Washington Press, 1979. $14.95.

LOOKING AT THE LAND OF PROMISE: PIONEER IMAGES OF THE PACIFIC NORTHWEST
William H. Goetzmann
Contains the work of many important early artists who painted and drew scenes in the Pacific Northwest. Some of the artists recorded th customs of the American Indians. Illus. Biblio. 122 pp. Washington State U. Press, 1988. $35; paper , $20.

LOOKING AT TOTEM POLES
Hilary Stewart
Guide to totem poles in outdoor locations accessible to tourists and interested viewers; with legends most often associated with the poles. Illus. 100 drawings, 30 photos. 192 pp. Paper. University of Washington Press, $14.95.

LOOKING AT THE WORDS OF OUR PEOPLE
Jeanette Armstrong, Editor
An anthology of First Nation literary criticism. 150 pp. paper. Theytus, 1993. $12.95.

LOON LEGENDS
Corrine A. Dwyer
Illus. North Star Press, $9.95.

LORE OF THE GREAT TURTLE: INDIAN LEGENDS OF MACKINAC RETOLD
Dirk Gringhuis
Illus. 96 pp. Paper . Mackinac Island State Park, 1970. $3.75.

LOST COPPER
Wendy Rose
Poetry. 127 pp. Paper. Malki Museum Press, 1980. $12.

**LOST & FOUND TRADITIONS:
NATIVE AMERICAN ART, 1965-1985**
Ralph T. Coe
Illus. 288 pp. University of Washington Press,
1986. $35.00; paper, $24.95.

**LOST HARVESTS: PRAIRIE INDIAN RE-
SERVE FARMERS & GOVERNMENT POLICY**
Sarah Carter
350 pp. University of Toronto Press, 1990. $34.95.

**LOST TRIBES & SUNKEN CONTINENTS:
MYTH & METHOD IN THE STUDY OF
AMERICAN INDIANS**
Robert Wauchope
Reprint of 1961 ed. Paper. Books on Demand,
$44.30.

**THE LOST UNIVERSE:
PAWNEE LIFE & CULTURE**
Gene Weltfish
Illus. 525 pp. University of Nebraska Press,
1977. $35; paper, $10.95.

**LOUD HAWK: THE U.S. VERSUS THE
AMERICAN INDIAN MOVEMENT**
Kenneth S. Stern
Explains what happened to the American Indian
Movement (AIM). Documents official government
misconduct on the Pine Ridge Reservation in
1975. Illus. 384 pp. University of Oklahoma Press,
1994. $24.95.

*LOUISIANA INDIAN TALES
Elizabeth Butler Moore & ASlice Wilbert
Couvillon
Tales for children to learn of Louisiana Indian heri-
tage. Grades 3-8. Illus. 112 pp. Pelican Publish-
ing, $11.95.

*LOUISIANA INDIANS
Carrel & Brenda Muller
Grades 3 and up. Illus. 64 pp. Bonjour Books,
1985. $7.50.

*LOVE FLUTE
Paul Goble
Story of a shy young man, incorporating the traditional Native American flute, Plains Indian culture,
and the beauty of a legend. Grades K-
3. Illus 32 pp. Meyer Creative Productions &
AISES, $15.95.

LOWER CHINOOK ETHNOGRAPHIC NOTES
Verne F. Ray
Reprint of 1938 edition. AMS Press.

**LOWER UMPQUA TEXTS & NOTES
ON THE KUSAN DIALECTS**
Leo J. Frachtenberg
Reprint of 1914 edition. AMS Press, $24.

***LUCY LEARNS TO WEAVE:
GATHERING PLANTS**
Virginia Hoffman
Grades 1-4. Illus. 46 pp. Paper. Navajo
Curriculum Center Press, 1974. $2.75.

**LULU LINEAR PUNCTATED: ESSAYS IN
HONOR OF GEORGE IRVING QUIMBY**
Robert Dunnell & Donald Grayson
Illus. 354 pp. Paper. University of Michigan,
Museum of Anthropology, 1983. $12.

*THE LUMBEE
Karen Blu
Grades 5 and up. Illus. Chelsea House, 1989.
$17.95.

**THE LUMBI PROBLEM: THE MAKING
OF AN AMERICAN INDIAN PEOPLE**
Karen I. Blu
Illus. 280 pp. Cambridge University Press, $39.50.

*LUMBERMAN
Gail Stewart
Grades 3-8. Illus. 32 pp. Rourke Corp., 1990.
$17.26.

LUMINARIES OF THE HUMBLE
Elizabeth Woody
Collection of poems focusing on the land & people
of the Pacific Northwest. 130 pp. University of Arizona Press, 1994. $35; paper, $15.95.

**LUMMI INDIANS OF NORTHWEST WASH-
INGTON**
Bernhard J. Stern
Reprint of 1934 edition. AMS Press, $22.

**CHARLES F. LUMMIS: THE CENTENNIAL
EXHIBITION**
Daniela P. Moneta, Editor
Illus. 82 pp. Paper. Southwest Museum, 1985.
$14.95.

LURE OF THE ARCTIC
Bernice Chappel; Marjorie Klein, tr
Illus. 256 pp. Paper. Wilderness Adventure.

LUSHOOTSEED DICTIONARY
Dawn Bates, Thom Hess & Vi Hilbert
Update of *Thom Hess's Dictionary of Puget Salish*
(1976). 406 pp. Paper. University of Washington
Press, $30.

M

MAASAW: PROFILE OF A HOPI GOD
E. Malotki & M. Lomatuway'ma
Illus. 275 pp. University of Nebraska Press,
1987. $24.95; paper, $ 14.95.

THE MACKENZIE ESKIMOS
Knud Rasmussen
Reprint of 1942 edition. AMS, $42.50.

**MAD BEAR: SPIRIT, HEALING, &THE SACRED
IN THE LIFE OF A NATIVE AMERICAN MEDI-
CINE MAN**
Doug Boyd
Profiles Mad Bear, a Tuscarora Indian, renowned
medicine man, and dynamic Indian-rights activist
during the 1960s and 1970s. He died in 1985. 352
pp. Paper. Simon & Schuster, 1994. $12.

MADAM DORIAN
Jerome Peltier
44 pp. Ye Galleon Press, $7.50; paper, $4.95.

**MADONNA SWAN: A LAKOTA WOMAN'S
STORY**
as told through Mark St. Pierre
Biography of a Lakota Sioux woman from the
Cheyenne River Sioux Reservation. Illus. Maps.
224 pp. Center for Western Studies, 1989.95. Paper. University of Oklahoma Press, $10.95.

**A MAGIC DWELLS: A POETIC &
PSYCHOLOGICAL STUDY OF THE
NAVAHO EMERGENCE MYTH**
Sheila Moon
206 pp. Paper. Wesleyan University Press,
1970. $7.95.

**MAGIC IMAGES: CONTEMPORARY
NATIVE AMERICAN ART**
Edwin Wade and Rennard Strickland
Illus. 125 pp. Paper. Southwestern Art Associa-
tion and U. of Oklahoma Press, 1982. $16.95.

***THE MAGIC LAKE: A MYSTICAL
HEALING LAKE OF THE CHEROKEE**
Tom Underwood
Grades 1-3. Illus. 20 pp. Cherokee Publications,
1982. $3.

THE MAGIC OF BANDELIER
David E. Stuart
Illus. Maps. 132 pp. Paper. Ancient City Press,
$10.95.

**THE MAIDU INDIAN MYTHS
& STORIES OF HANC'IBYJIM**
William Shipley, editor & translator
192 pp. Paper. Heyday Books, $12.95.

MAIDU MYTHS & TALES
Hanc'ibyjim
Illus. Heyday Books, $12.

**THE MAIN STALK: A SYNTHESIS
OF NAVAJO PHILOSOPHY**
John R. Farella
221 pp. Paper. University of Arizona Press,
1984. $13.95.

***MAISONS D'ENCORE: TIPI,
WIGWAM ET LONGUE MAISON**
Bonnie Shemie
Grades 3-7. Illus. 25 pp. Tundra Books, 1990.
$12.95.

MAJOR RICHARDSON'S SHORT STORIES
David Beasley, Editor
Ottawa Indian novelist of the mid-1800s.
134 pp. Paper. Theytus, 1985. $6.95.

THE MAKAH INDIANS
Elizabeth Colson
Reprint of 1953 edition. Illus. 308 pp.
Greenwood, $25.

MAKE PRAYERS TO THE RAVEN
Richard Nelson
Ethnographic study of the Koyukon Athabascan
people. 281 pp. Paper. Alaska Natural History
Association, $13.95

MAKING ARROWS THE OLD WAY
Doug Wallentine
How to make Native American arrows. Illus.
28 pp. Paper. Eagle's View Publishing, $4.

**MAKING INDIAN BOWS & ARROWS...
THE OLD WAY**
Doug Wallentine
Explores in detail acquiring tools and wood, designing, and making Native American bows and
arrows. Illus. 98 pp. Paper. Eagle's View Publishing, $9.95.

MAKING NATIVE AMERICAN POTTERY
Michael Simpson
How indigenous people gathered & processed clay; designs, finishes, firing pottery, etc. Photos. 80 pp. Naturegraph, $15.95; paper, $7.95.

MAKING TWO WORLDS ONE & THE STORY OF ALL-AMERICAN INDIAN DAYS
Hila Gilbert
Illus. 60 pp. Paper. Connections Press, 1986. $8.

MALAESKA; THE INDIAN WIFE OF THE WHITE HUNTER
Anna S. Stephens
Fiction. A portrait of the early Dutch settlers of New York and the Indians they encountered. Reprint of 1929 edition. Ayer Co., $17.

MAN IN NORTHEASTERN NORTH AMERICA
Frederick Johnson, Editor
Reprint of 1946 edition. AMS Press, $42.50.

MAN OF THE PLAINS: RECOLLECTIONS OF LUTHER NORTH, 1856-1882
Luther North; Donald Danker, Editor
Illus. 350 pp. University of Nebraska Press, 1961. $25.

THE MAN TO SEND RAIN CLOUDS
Kenneth Rosen, Editor
18 stories, including the work of Leslie Marmon Silko, Simon J. Ortiz, Anna Lee Walters, and Larry Littlebird & members of the Circle Films. 192 pp. Paper. Penguin USA, $9.

MAN WHO KILLED THE DEER
Frank Waters
Reprint of 1974 edition. 266 pp. Ohio University Press, $9.95; paper, $6.95.

THE MAN WHO MARRIED THE MOON & OTHER PUEBLO INDIAN FOLK-STORIES
Charles Lummis
Reprint of 1894 edition. Illus. AMS Press, $19.45.

MAN'S KNIFE AMONG THE NORTH AMERICAN INDIANS: A STUDY IN THE MAN'S RISE TO CIVILIZATION: THE CULTURAL ASCENT OF THE INDIANS OF NORTH AMERICA
Peter Farb
Illus. Maps. Biblio. 336 pp. Paper. Penguin USA, $12.95.

MAN'S RISE TO CIVLIZATION: THE CULTURAL ASCENT OF INDIANS OF NORTH AMERICA
Peter Farb
Illus. Photos. Maps. Biblio. 336 pp. Paper. Penguin USA, $12.95.

MANDAN & HIDATSA MUSIC
F. Densmore
Reprint of 1923 edition. Illus. 236 pp. Da Capo Press, $27.50.

MANDAN--HIDATSA MYTHS & CEREMONIES
M.W. Beckwith, Editor
Reprint of 1938 edition. Kraus, $32.

*THE MANDANS
Emilie Lepthien
Grades K-4. 50 pp. Childrens Press, 1989. $11.45.

MANDANS, A STUDY OF THEIR CULTURE, ARCHAEOLOGY & LANGUAGE
George Will and H.J. Spinden
Reprint of 1906 edition. Illus. Paper. Kraus, $15.

MANIFEST MANNERS: POSTINDIAN WARRIORS OF SURVIVANCE
Gerald Vizenor
190 pp. University Press of New England, 1994. $30; paper, $13.95.

MANKILLER: A CHIEF & HER PEOPLE
Wilma Mankiller & Michael Wallis
An autobiography by the Principal Chief of the Cherokee Nation. 293 pp. St. Martin's Press & AISES, 1993. $22.95.

*WILMA P. MANKILLER: CHIEF OF THE CHEROKEE
Biography of her childhood to the present, 1992. Includes list of important dates and an index. Grades 3-7. Illus. 20 pp. Cherokee Publications, $3.

RAY MANLEY'S COLLECTING SOUTH-WESTERN INDIAN ARTS & CRAFTS
Clara L. Tanner, et al
Third revised edition. Illus. Paper. Ray Manley, 1979. $6.

RAY MANLEY'S "THE FINE ART OF NAVAJO WEAVING"
Steve Getzwiller
Illus. Paper. Ray Manley, 1984. $9.95.

RAY MANLEY'S HOPI KACHINA
Clara L. Tanner
Illus. Paper. Ray Manley, 1980. $6.

RAY MANLEY'S INDIAN LANDS
Clara L. Tanner
Illus. Ray Manley, 1979. $10.00; paper, $7.95.

A MANUAL OF NAVAHO GRAMMAR
Berard Haile
Reprint of 1926 edition. AMS Press, $26.

MANY SMOKES, MANY MOONS: A CHRONOLOGY OF AMERICAN INDIAN HISTORY THROUGH INDIAN ART
Jamake Highwater
130 pp. HarperCollins, 1978. $15.95.

MANY TRAILS: INDIANS OF THE LOWER HUDSON VALLEY
Catherine C. Brawer, Editor
Illus. 112 pp. Paper. Publishing Center for Cultural Research, 1983. $14.50.

*MANY WINTERS
Nancy Winters
Grades 6-12. Illus. 80 pp. Doubleday, 1974. $13.95.

A MAP OF VIRGINIA: THE PROCEEDINGS OF THE ENGLISH COLONIE IN VIRGINIA
John Smith
Reprint of 1612 edition. 164 pp. Walter J. Johnson, $18.50.

MAP'N'FACTS: NATIVE PEOPLES OF NORTH AMERICA
Two maps show "then" and "now" in the life of Native North Americans. Friendship Press, $4.50.

THE MARCH OF THE MONTANA COLUMN: A PRELUDE TO THE CUSTER DISASTER
James Bradley
Illus. 216 pp. Paper. University of Oklahoma Press, 1991. $9.95.

MARIA
Richard L. Spivey
The famous San Ildefonso potter Maria Martinez developed her legendary black-on-black ware around 1919. Illus. Biblio. 176 pp. Northland Publishing, 1989 revised & expanded edition. $19.95.

MARIA MAKING POTTERY
Hazel Hyde
Illus. 32 pp. Paper. Sunstone Press, $4.95.

*MARIA MARTINEZ: PUEBLO POTTER
Grades 2-4. Illus. 32 pp. Childrens Press, $10.95.

MARIA: THE POTTER OF SAN ILDEFONSO
Alice Marriott
Reprint of 1948 edition. Illus. 320 pp. Revised edition. University of Oklahoma Press, $19.95; paper, $11.95.

MARICOPA MORPHOLOGY & SYNTAX
Lynn Gordon
Paper. University of California Press, 1986. $25.

*MARK OF OUR MOCCASINS
Colleen Reece
Grades 5-12. Paper. Council for Indian Education, 1982. $2.95.

MARQUIS DE MORES AT WAR IN THE BAD LANDS
Usher Burdick
27 pp. Paper. Ye Galleon Press, 1986. $3.50.

MARTYRS OF THE OBLONG & LITTLE NINE
Defost Smith
Reprint of 1948 edition. Brown Book Co., $6.

THE MARU CULT OF POMO INDIANS: A CALIFORNIA GHOST DANCE SURVIVAL
Clement W. Meighan and Francis A. Riddele
134 pp. Southwest Museum, 1972. $12.50.

THE MARVELOUS COUNTRY
Samuel Cozzens
Cochise & the Apaches; Indian life, struggles & customs. Reprint of 1874 edition. 532 pp. Ross & Haines, $20.

MARY & I: FORTY YEARS WITH THE SIOUX
Stephen Riggs
Reprint of 1971 edition. 412 pp. Ross & Haines, $15. Corner House, $21.

MARYLAND'S ATTITUDE IN THE STRUGGLE FOR CANADA
J. Black
Reprint. Paper. Johnson Reprint, $9.

MARXISM & NATIVE AMERICANS
Ward Churchill, Editor
250 pp. South End Press, 1984. $20; paper, $12.50.

MASCOUTENS OR PRAIRIE POTAWATOMI INDIANS: SOCIAL LIFE & CEREMONIES
Alanson Skinner
Reprint of 1924 edition. Greenwood Press, $35.

MASHKIKI: OLD MEDICINE NOURISHING THE NEW
Edwin Haller & Larry Aitken
Examines learning by American Indian & Alaskan Native students. 214 pp. University Press of America, 1992. $39.50; paper, $24.50.

THE MASHPEE INDIANS: TRIBE ON TRIAL
Jack Campisi
Illus. 177 pp. Paper. Syracuse University Press, 1991. $13.95.

MASKED GODS: NAVAHO & PUEBLO CEREMONIALISM
Frank Waters
Reprint of 1950 edition. 438 pp. Paper. Ohio University Press, $10.95.

MASKS OF THE SPIRIT: IMAGE & METAPHOR IN MESOAMERICA
Roberta & Peter Markman
Illus. 375 pp. U. of California Press, 1989. $65.

MASSACRE!
Frank Laumer
Illus. Maps. Biblio. 188 pp. Paper. University Press of Florida, 1968. $14.95.

MASSACRE AT BAD AXE
Crawford Thayer
Illus. 544 pp. Paper. Thayer Associates, 1981. $9.95.

MASSACRE AT FORT BULL: THE DELERY EXPEDITION AGAINST ONEIDA CARRY, 1756
Gilbert Hagerty
Illus. Mowbray, 1971. $8.

MASSACRE ON THE GILA: AN ACCOUNT OF THE LAST MAJOR BATTLE AMONG AMERICAN INDIANS
Clifton Kroeber & Bernard Fontana
232 pp. Paper. University of Arizona Press, 1986. $15.95.

MASSACRE: A SURVEY OF TODAY'S AMERICAN INDIAN
Robert Gessner
Reprint of 1931 edition. 418 pp. Da Capo Press, $45.

MASSACRE: THE TRAGEDY AT WHITE RIVER
Marshall Sprague
Illus. 365 pp. University of Nebraska Press, 1980. $28.95; paper, $8.95.

MATERIAL ASPECTS OF POMO CULTURE
Samuel Barrett
Reprint of 1952 edition. AMS Press, $57.50.

MATERIAL CULTURE OF THE BLACKFOOT INDIANS
Clark Wissler
Reprint of 1910 edition. AMS Press, $17.50.

THE MATERIAL CULTURE OF THE CROW INDIANS
Robert H. Lowie
Reprint of 1922 edition. AMS Press, $11.50.

MATERIAL CULTURE OF THE IGLULIK ESKIMOS
Therkel Mathiassen
Reprint of 1928 edition. AMS, $67.50.

MATERIAL CULTURE OF THE MENOMINI
Alanson Skinner
Reprint of 1921 edition. AMS Press.

MATERIAL CULTURE & THE STUDY OF AMERICAN LIFE
Ian M. Quimby
Illus. Paper. W.W. Norton & Co., 1978. $7.95.

MAUI: THE MISCHIEF MAKER
as told by Dietrich Varez
The myth of the demi-god Maui. Illus. Bishop Museum, $12.95.

THOMAS MAYHEW, PATRIARCH TO THE INDIANS, 1593-1682
L.C. Hare
Reprint of 1932 edition. Illus. AMS Press, $20.

McINTOSH & WEATHERFORD, CREEK INDIAN LEADERS
Benjamin Griffith
Illus. 300 pp. U. of Alabama Press, 1988. $26.95.

THE McKENNEY-HALL PORTRAIT GALLERY OF AMERICAN INDIANS
Portraits of famous American Indians. First published in 1836, this new volume includes historical materials and biographical profiles on each. Illus. 370 pp. Cherokee Publications, $14.95.

JOHN McMURTRY & THE AMERICAN INDIAN: A FRONTIERSMAN IN THE STRUGGLE FOR THE OHIO VALLEY
Richard K. McMurtry
Illus. Paper. Current Issues, 1980. $14.95.

ME & MINE: THE LIFE STORY OF HELEN SEKAQUAPTEWA
as told to Louise Udall
262 pp. Paper. U. of Arizona Press, 1969. $11.95.

*ME RUN FAST GOOD: BIOGRAPHIES OF TEWANIMA (HOPI), CARLOS MONTEZUMA (APACHE) AND JOHN HORSE (SEMINOLE)
Beatrice Levin and Marjorie Vanderveld
Grades 5-9. 32 pp. Paper. Council for Indian Education, 1983. $1.95.

MECHANISMS & TRENDS IN THE DECLINE OF THE COSTANOAN INDIAN POPULATION OF CENTRAL CALIFORNIA: NUTRITION & HEALTH IN PRE-CONTACT CALIFORNIA & MISSION PERIOD ENVIRONMENTS
Ann Stodder: Gary Breschini & Trudy Harverset, Editors
Illus. 78 pp. Paper. Coyote Press, 1986. $6.20.

MEDICINAL & OTHER USES OF NORTH AMERICAN PLANTS
Charlotte Erichsen-Brown
Historical citations document uses of plants with special reference to the Eastern Indian tribes. Illus. 122 pp. Paper. Dover, $4.95.

MEDICINAL USES OF PLANTS BY INDIAN TRIBES OF NEVADA
Percy Train, et al
Reprint of 1957 edition. Quarterman, $30.

MEDICINE AMONG THE AMERICAN INDIANS
Eric Stone
Reprint of 1932 edition. Illus. AMS Press, $20.

THE MEDICINE BOWS: WYOMING'S MOUNTAIN COUNTRY
Scott Thybony, et al
The region was an important fur trading center and one of the last refuges of the Cheyenne, Arapaho, and Sioux Indians. Illus. Biblio. 180 pp. Paper. The Caxton Printers, $7.95.

MEDICINE CARDS: THE DISCOVERY OF POWER THROUGH THE WAYS OF ANIMALS
Jamie Sams & David Carson
224 pp. Bear & Co., 1988. $26.95.

THE MEDICINE CREEK TREATY OF 1854
Lynn Kickingbird & Curtis Berkey
31 pp. Institute for the Development of Indian Law, $10.

*MEDICINE MAN
Grades 4-5. Illus. 48 pp. Capstone Press, 1989. $10.95.

THE MEDICINE-MAN OF THE AMERICAN INDIAN & HIS CULTURAL BACKGROUND
W. Corlett
Reprint of 1935 edition. AMS Press, $47.50.

THE MEDICINE MEN: OGLALA SIOUX CEREMONY & HEALING
Thomas H. Lewis
Describes traditional healing practices of the Oglala Sioux of Pine Ridge Reservation. Illus. 220 pp. University of Nebraska Press, 1990. $22; paper, $9.95.

MEDICINE MEN OF THE APACHE, A PAPER FROM THE NINTH ANNUAL REPORT OF THE BUREAU OF AMERICAN ETHNOLOGY (1887-1888)
John Bourke
Reprint of 1970 edition. Illus. 187 pp. The Rio Grande Press, $22.50.

MEDICINE RIVER
Thomas King
Breaks down stereotypes about Indians. A young Blackfoot Indian returns to his birthplace in Alberta. 480 pp. Paper. Penguin USA, $11.

*MEDICINE WALK
Ardath Mayhar
Grades 4-8. Illus. Macmillan, 1989. $11.95.

MEDICINE WHEEL: EARTH ASTROLOGY
Sun Bear & Wabun
Learn about the different moons, totems, powers of the directions and elemental clans. Illus. 228 pp. Paper. Simon & Schuster, $10.

MEDICINE WOMEN, CURANDERAS & WOMEN DOCTORS
Bobette Perrone, et al
Illus. 272 pp. Paper. University of Oklahoma Press, 1989. $12.95.

THE MEDICINE WHEEL: EARTH ASTROLOGY
Sun Bear & Wabun
Illus. 203 pp. Paper. Cherokee Publications, $8.95.

MEDITATION WITH NATIVE AMERICANS: LAKOTA SPIRITUALITY
Paul Steinmetz
The songs & thoughts of the Lakota, along with a section on the Native American Church & Christian influences. Illus. 144 pp. Paper. Bear & Co., 1984. $7.95.

MEDITATIONS WITH ANIMALS: A NATIVE AMERICAN BESTIARY
Gerald Hausman
Shows the healing roles animals have played since the beginning. Illus. 144 pp. Paper. Bear & Co., 1986. $7.95.

MEDITATIONS WITH THE HOPI
Robert Boissiere
The author's interpretation of the essence of Hopi experience. Illus. 144 pp. Paper. Bear & Co., 1984. $7.95.

MEDITATIONS WITH THE NAVAJO
Gerald Hausman
Prayer, songs & stories of healing & harmony. Illus. 144 pp. Paper. Bear & Co., 1987. $7.95.

MEET CREE: A GUIDE TO THE CREE LANGUAGE
C.H. Wolfart and J.F. Carroll
120 pp. University of Nebraska Press, 1981. $12.50.

MEET THE LAKOTA, VOL. ONE: THE PEOPLE
Rose LaVera
An introduction to the Lakota, written in English & in Lakota by Alvin Horse Looking. Illus. Paper. The Greenfield Review Press, $5.95.

*MEET THE NORTH AMERICAN INDIANS
Elizabeth Paine
Grades 2-6. Illus. Random House, 1965. $8.99; paper, $5.95.

MEMOIR OF INDIAN WARS & OTHER OCCURENCES BY THE LATE COLONEL STUART OF GREENBRIER
John Stuart; Charles Stuart, Editor
Reprint of 1833 edition. Ayer Co., $11.50.

MEMOIRS OF A CAPTIVITY AMONG THE INDIANS OF NORTH AMERICA, FROM CHILDHOOD TO THE AGE OF NINETEEN
John Hunter
Reprint of 1823 edition. Johnson Reprint, $28.

MEMOIRS OF A CHICKASAW SQUAW: A JOURNAL OF THE CHICKASAW REMOVAL
Velma Taliaferro; Molly Griffis, Editor
Illus. 65 pp. Paper. Levite of Apache Publishing, 1987. $5.

MEMOIRS OF LT. HENRY TIMBERLAKE
H. Timberlake
Reprint of 1927 edition. Ayer Co., $25.95.

MEMOIRS OF A WHITE CROW INDIAN
Thomas Leforge; Thomas Marquis, Narrator
380 pp. University of Nebraska Press, 1974. $31.50; paper, $10.95.

MEMOIRS, OFFICIAL & PERSONAL
Thomas L. McKenney; Herman J. Viola, Editor
Insight into Indian affairs by Thomas McKenney, Director of Indian Affairs, 1816-1830. 340 pp. Paper. University of Nebraska Press, 1973. $6.95.

*THE MENOMINEE
Patricia Ourada
Grades 5 and up. Illus. Chelsea House, 1989. $17.95.

MENOMINEE DRUMS: A HISTORY
Patricia K. Ouranda
Illus. 300 pp. University of Oklahoma Press, 1979. $22.95.

MENOMINEE DRUMS: TRIBAL TERMINATION & RESTORATION, 1954-1974
Nicholas C. Peroff
Illus. 304 pp. University of Oklahoma Press, 1982. $21.95.

THE MENOMINI INDIANS OF WISCONSIN
Felix Keesing
304 pp. University of Wisconsin Press, 1987. $30; paper, $11.95.

MENOMINEE MUSIC
Francis Densmore
Reprint of 1932 edition. Illus. 286 pp. Da Capo Press, $29.50. Reprint Services, $75.

MENOMINI TEXTS
L. Bloonfield
Reprint of 1928 edition. AMS Press, $58.

MEREJILDO GRIJALVA, APACHE CAPTIVE, ARMY SCOUT
Edwin R. Sweeney
Presents a detailed acount of his life. Illus. Map. Biblio. Paper. Texas Western Press, 1993. $12.50.

MESA VERDE NATIONAL PARK
Ruth Radlauer
Updated edition. Grades 3 and up. Illus. 50 pp. Childrens Press, 1984. $14.60; paper, $4.50.

MESA VERDE: THE STORY BEHIND THE SCENERY
Linda Martin
Archaeological sites of Anasazi culture. Photos. Maps. 48 pp. Paper. KC Publications, $6.95.

THE MESCALERO APACHES
C.L. Sonnichsen
Illus. 300 pp. Paper. University of Oklahoma Press, 1980. $11.95.

MESSAGES FROM MOTHER EARTH: DAILY AFFIRMATIONS
Willie Hooks
60 pp. Paper. JTE Associates, 1989. $6.95.

METAL WEAPONS, TOOLS & ORNAMENTS OF THE TETON DAKOTA INDIANS
James A. Hanson
Illus. 118 pp. University of Nebraska Press, 1975. $16.50.

METALLIC ORNAMENTS OF THE NEW YORK INDIANS
W.M. Beauchamp
Reprint of 1930 edition. 160 pp. AMS Press, $16.

METHOD & THEORY IN HISTORICAL ARCHAEOLOGY
Stanley South
Academic Press, 1977. $42.95.

THE MEXICAN KICKAPOO INDIANS
Felipe & Dolores Latorre
Illus. Map. 416 pp. Paper. Dover, $11.95.

THE MICROFILM EDITION OF THE WASHINGTON MATTHEWS PAPERS & GUIDE
Wheelwright Museum Staff
Illus. 126 pp. University of New Mexico Press, 1985. $15. Microfilm (ten rolls), $400.

THE MIDDLE FIVE: INDIAN SCHOOLBOYS OF THE OMAHA TRIBES
Francis La Flesche
Illus. 152 pp. University of Nebraska Press, 1978. $17.50; paper, $4.50.

THE MIDDLE GROUND: INDIANS, EMPIRES, & REPUBLICS IN THE GREAT LAKES REGION, 1650-1815
Richard White
Illus. 560 pp. Cambridge University Press, 1991. $69.50; paper, $19.95.

MIGRATION LEGEND OF THE CREEK INDIANS
A.S. Gatschet
Reprint of 1884 edition. AMS Press, $30.

BARTLEY MILAM: PRINCIPAL CHIEF OF THE CHEROKEE NATION
Howard Meredith
157 pp. Paper. Indian University Press, 1985. $5.

THE MILITARY CONQUEST OF THE SOUTHERN PLAINS
William H. Leckie
Reprint of 1963 edition. Illus. Books on Demand, $56.10.

THE MILITARY & THE U.S. INDIAN POLICY, 1865-1903
Robert Wooster
256 pp. Yale University Press, 1988. $22.50.

MILLENIUM: TRIBAL WISDOM & THE MODERN WORLD
David Maybury-Lewis
Illus. Penguin USA, $45.

THE MIMBRES, ART & ARCHAEOLOGY
Jesse Walter Fewkes; into. by J.J. Brody
Reprint of 1914 edition. Illus. 182 pp. Paper. Avanyu Publishing, $16.95.

MIMBRES DESIGNS
Fred Kabotie
Prepared interpretations of 12 Mimbres designs. Draws upon the traditional beliefs of his tribe. bxw art is printed on heavy faun-colored all-rag folded sheets. Limited edtiion of 100. Illus. 64 pp. Lime Rock Press, 1982. $295.

MIMBRES INDIAN TREASURE: IN THE LAND OF BACA
Roy Evans, R. Evelyn & Lyle Ross
Illus. 352 pp. The Lowell Press, 1985. $29.95.

MIMBRES MYTHOLOGY
Pat Carr
Illus. 78 pp. Texas Western Press, 1989. $12; paper, $7.50.

MINIATURE ARTS OF THE SOUTHWEST
Nancy Schiffer
Arts of American Indian tribes in the Southwest are occasionally made in miniature. This book presents a wide array of these miniatures of all the major craft styles of the region. Illus. 64 pp. Paper. Schiffer, $9.95.

MINNESOTA'S BROWNS VALLEY MAN & ASSOCIATED BURIAL ARTIFACTS
Albert E. Jenks
Reprint fo 1937 edition. Paper. Kraus, $15.

MIRROR & PATTERN: GEORGE LAIRD'S WORLD OF CHEMEHUEVI MYTHOLOGY
Carobeth Laird
Myths of the Chemehuevi. 373 pp. Malki Museum Press, $25.

*THE MISHOMIS BOOK, THE VOICE OF THE OJIBWAY
Edward Benton-Banai
Ojibway traditions, culture and ceremonies. Grades 4 and up. Illus. Indian Country Communication, $14. Also, The Mishomis Coloring Book Series - 5 history coloring books. $4.25 each.

MISSION INDIANS IN CALIFORNIA
Larry S. Watson, Compiler
A report on the condition of the Indians of Southern California written in part by Helen Hunt Jackson, 48th Congress 1st Session. 80 pp. Paper . Histree, 1988. $14.95.

MISSION OF SORROWS: JESUIT GUEVAVE & THE PIMAS, 1691-1767
John L. Kessell
Paper. Books on Demand, $60.

MISSION SAN XAVIER DEL BAC: A PHOTOGRAPHIC ESSAY ON THE DESERT PEOPLE & THEIR CHURCH
Bernard Fontana; Helga Teiwes, Photographer
Illus. 32 pp. Paper . University of Arizona Press, 1973. $3.50.

*THE MISSIONS: CALIFORNIA'S HERITAGE
Mary Null Boule
21 individual booklets of detailed facts of each Mission's history. Grades 4-6. Illus. Meerant Publishers.

THE MISSIONS OF CALIF0RNIA, A HISTORY OF GENOCIDE
Rupert Costo & Jeanette Henry
Paper. Indian Historian Press, $12.50.

MISSIONS & PUEBLOS OF THE OLD SOUTHWEST
Earle R. Forrest
Reprint of 1929 edition. 398 pp. Paper . The Rio Grande Press, $12.

MISSISSIPPI CHOCTAWS AT PLAY: THE SERIOUS SIDE OF LEISURE
Kendall Blanchard
248 pp. University of Illinois Press, 1981. $22.95.

THE MISSISSIPPIAN EMERGENCE
Bruce D. Smith, Editor
Collection of 11 essays examines the evolution of ranked chiefdoms in the midwestern and southeastern U.S. from 700-1220 A.D. Illus. 272 pp. Smithsonian Institution Press, 1990. $45.

MISSISSIPPIAN MORTUARY PRACTICES
Goldstein
Covers burial details and Indian social organization. Illus. 196 pp. Paper. Hothem House, 1980. $12.50, postpaid.

MISSISSIPPIAN ST0NE IMAGES IN ILLINOIS
Thomas E. Emerson
Illus. 50 pp. Paper . Univerity of Illinois Archaeology, 1982. $3.75.

MITAKUYE OYASIN: WE ARE ALL RLATED
Allen C. Ross
Comparative culture studies. Illus. 215 pp. Paper. Bear & Center for Western Studies, $12.

MIWOK MATERIAL CULTURE
S.A. Barrett and E.W . Gifford
Illus. 257 pp. Paper . Yosemite, $6.95.

MIXED-BLOODS & TRIBAL DISSOULTION: CHARLES CURTIS & THE QUEST FOR INDIAN IDENTITY
William Unrau
Illus. 224 pp. University Press of Kansas, 1989. $27.50.

MOBILITY & ADAPTATION: THE ANASAZI OF BLACK MESA, ARIZONA
Shirley Powell
304 pp. Southern Illinois University Press, 1983. $29.95.

THE MOCASSIN MAKER
E. Pauline Johnson
Reprint of 1913 edition. 267 pp. Paper . University of Arizona Press, 1987. $12.95.

MOCCASINS ON PAVEMENT: THE URBAN INDIAN EXPERIENCE, A DENVER PORTRAIT
Michael Taylor, et al
Illus. Paper. Denver Museum of Natural History , 1978. $2.50.

MODEL COURT DEVELOPMENT PROJECT: FULL FAITH & CREDIT FOR INDIAN COURT JUDGEMENTS
National Center for State Courts Staf f
750 pp. National Center for State Courts, manuscript - $3.12.

MODERN BLACKFEET: MONTANANS ON A RESERVATION
Malcolm McFee
Illus. 134 pp. Paper . Waveland Press, 1984. $8.95.

MODERN HAWAIIAN HIST ORY
Dr. Ann Rayson
Chronicles Hawaii's last century; text includes graphics and photos from the state archives. Illus. 288 pp. The Bess Press, $27.95. W orkbook, $6.95.

MODERN INDIAN PSYCHOLOGY
John F. Bryde
Paper. Dakota Press, 1971. $9.00.

MODERN INDIANS OF ALABAMA: REMNANTS OF THE REMOVAL
Marie Cromer
Illus. 390 pp. Paper . Southern University Press, 1987. $16.50.

MODERN PRIMITIVE ARTS OF MEXICO, GUATEMALA & THE SOUTHWEST
C. Oglesby
Facsimile of 1939 edition. Ayer Co., $16.

THE MODERN SIOUX: SOCIAL SYSTEMS & RESERVATION CULTURE
Ethel Nurge, Editor
Reprint of 1970 edition Illus. 350 pp. Paper . Books on Demand, $92.

MODERN TRANSFORMATIONS OF MOENKOPI PUEBLO
Shuichi Nagata
Illus. 350 pp. Paper . University of Illinois Press, 1970. $10.95.

*THE MODOC
Odie & Laura Faulk
Illus. 104 pp. Chelsea House, 1988. $17.95.

MODOCS & THEIR WAR
Keith A. Murray
Reprint of 1959 edition. Illus. 358 pp. Paper . University of Oklahoma Press, $9.95.

MOGOLLON CULTURE IN THE FORESTDALE VALLEY, EAST-CENTRAL ARIZONA
Emil W . Haury
Reprint. 454 pp. University of Arizona Press, 1985. $45.

MOHAVE ETHNOPSYCHIATRY & SUICIDE: THE PSYCHIATRIC KNOWLEDGE & THE PSYCHIC DISTURBANCES OF AN INDIAN TRIBE
George Devereux
Reprint of 1961 edition. Scholarly Press, $95.

*THE MOHAWK
Grades K-4. Illus. 48 pp. Childrens Press, $1 1.45.

MOHAWK FRONTIER: THE DUTCH COMMUNITY OF SCHENECTADY, NEW YORK, 1661-1710
Thomas E. Burke, Jr.
Explores Schenectady's origins and its destruction in 1690. Tells the story of the Indians, French and African slaves, et al. 264 pp. Cornell University Press, $36.95.

THE MOHAWK THAT REFUSED TO ABDICATE
David P. Morgan
Kalmbach Publishing, 1975. $25.

THE MOHICANS OF STOCKBRIDGE
Patrick Frazier
The ethnohistory of the colonial Northeast. Illus. Map. 310 pp. University of Nebraska Press, 1992. $35.

MOKI SNAKE DANCE
Walter Hough
Travel guide published in 1899 describes the drama of Snake Dance ceremonial of the Moki (Hopi) Indians of Arizona. Snake Legend. Illus. Photos. 80 pp. Paper . Avanyu Publishing, $5.95.

MOLLY MOLASSES & ME: A COLLECTION OF LIVING ADVENTURES
Ssipsis & Georgia Mitchell
Illus. 2nd edition. 75 pp. Paper . Robin Hood Books, $8.

*THE MONEY GOD
Dolly Hildreth, et al
Grade 6. Paper. Council for Indian Education, 1972. $1.95.

THE MONGREL: A STORY OF LOGAN FONTANELLE OF THE OMAHA INDIANS
Anthony J. Barak; Jim Reisdorf f, Editor
Illus. 145 pp. Paper . South Platte Press, 1988. $9.95.

MONTANA'S INDIANS: YESTERDAY & TODAY
William Bryan
Illus. 142 pp. Paper . American Geographic Publishing, 1986. $13.95.

MONTEREY IN 1786: THE JOURNAL OF JEAN FRANCOIS DE LA PEROUSE
Intro by Malcolm Margolin
Account of Carmel Mission and the relations between the missionaries and the Indian neophytes, shortly after the death of Junipero Sera. Illus. 104 pp. Paper. Heyday Books, $8.95.

MONTEZUMA'S DINNER
Lewis Morgan
2nd edition. Paper . New York Labor News, 75¢.

MONUMENT VALLEY: THE STORY BEHIND THE SCENERY
K.C. DenDooven
The story of the Navajo who lived there, the Gouldings who established the trading post, and a young photographer in 1937. Illus. Photos. 48 pp. Paper. KC Publications, $6.95.

MOON OF POPPING TREES
Rex Alan Smith
The tragedy of Wounded Knee and the end of the Indian wars, 1851-1891. Maps. 225 pp. Paper. University of Nebraska Press, 1981. $8.95.

*MOON SONG
Byrd Baylor; illus. by Ronald Himler
Grades 3-7. Illus. Macmillan, 1989. $11.95.

MORAL EDUCATION AMONG THE NORTH AMERICAN INDIANS
Claude A. Nichols
Reprint of 1930 edition, AMS Press, $22.50.

MORE AH MO: INDIAN LEGENDS FROM THE NORTHWEST
Tren J. Griffin
New Edition of Ah Mo. Illus. 64 pp. Paper. Hancock House, 1994. $7.95.

LEWIS H. MORGAN ON IROQUOIS MATERIAL CULTURE
Elisabeth Tooker
A collection of 500 Iroquois objects, researched in 1849-50, provides information on Irqouois culture. Illus. 400 pp. University of Arizona Press, 1994. $65; paper, $40.

*MORNING GIRL
Michael Dorris
Grades 3 and up. Illus. Paper. Hyperion. $3.50.

MORPHOLOGY OF THE HUPA LANGUAGE
P.E. Goddard
Reprint of 1905 edition. Kraus Reprint, $56.

MORTUARY CUSTOMS OF THE SHAWNEE & OTHER EASTERN TRIBES
Ermine W. Voegelin
Reprint of 1944 edition. AMS Press, $26.

MOTHER EARTH: AN AMERICAN STORY
Sam D. Gill
196 pp. University of Chicago Press, 1987. $24.95.

MOTHER EARTH, FATHER SKY: ANCIENT CHANTS BY PUEBLO & NAVAJO INDIANS OF THE SOUTHWEST
Marcia Keegan
Reprint of 1974 edition. Illus. 112 pp. Clear Light, 1974. $24.95.

MOTHER EARTH SPIRITUALITY: NATIVE AMERICAN PATHS TO HEALING OUR- SELVES & OUR WORLD
Ed McGaa & Eagle Man
Illus. 304 pp. Paper. HarperCollins, 1990. $14.95.

THE MOUNDBUILDERS
Robert Silverberg
276 pp. Paper. Ohio University Press, 1986. $6.95.

MOUNDS FOR THE DEAD
Dragoo
Study of the Adena (Early Woodland) Indians; their lifeway, mounds, burial pratice, artifacts. Reprint of 1963 edition. Illus. Paper. Hothem House, $14.95.

MOUNTAIN IN THE CLOUDS: A SEARCH FOR THE WILD SALMON
Bruce Brown
Illus. 2nd Edition. 256 pp. Paper. Macmillan, 1990. $12.95.

THE MOUNTAIN MEADOWS MASSACRE
Juanita Brooks
Story of a wagon train in southern Ultah was attacked by Indians & Mormans. Illus. Maps. 352 pp. Paper. University of Oklahoma Press, $17.95.

MOUNTAIN WINDSONG: A NOVEL OF THE TRAIL OF TEARS
Robert J. Conley
A love story and the Cherokee Removal of 1835-1838 from their traditional lands in North Carolina. 240 pp. University of Oklahoma Press, $19.95.

MOUNTAIN WOLF WOMAN, SISTER OF CRASHING THUNDER: THE AUTOBIOGRA- PHY OF A WINNEBAGO INDIAN
Nancy O. Lurie, Editor
Illus. 164 pp. Paper. University of Michigan Press, 1961. $7.95.

THE MOUNTAINWAY OF THE NAVAJO
Leland Wyman
The examination of a Navajo song ceremonial and its various branches, phases and ritual. Illus. 271 pp. University of Arizona Press, 1975. $14.50.

MOURNING DOVE: A SALISHAN AUTOBIOGRAPHY
Mourning Dove; Jay Miller, Editor
Illus. 265 pp. University of Nebraska Press, 1990. $30; paper, $12.95.

MOVEMENT FOR INDIAN ASSIMILATION, 1860-1890
Henry E. Fritz
Reprint of 1963 edition. Illus. 244 pp. Greenwood Press, $35.

MOVING WITHIN THE CIRCLE: CONTEMPO- RARY NATIVE AMERICAN MUSIC & DANCE
Bryan Burton
Book/audio tape set. Features songs, dances, and flute tunes of the Haliwa-Saponi Dancers, R. Carlos Nakai, the Porcupine Singers, and more. World Music Press, $29.95.

*MUCKWA: THE ADVENTURES OF A CHIPPEWA INDIAN BOY
Wilson G. Dietrich
Illus. Winston-Derek, $6.95.

*THE MUD FAMILY
Betsy James; illus. by Paul Morin
Story depicting the lives of the Anasazi, ancestor of the Pueblo peoples of the Southwest. Grades PS-3. Illus. 32 pp. Putnam, 1994. $15.95.

MUD WOMAN: POEMS FROM THE CLAY
Nora Naranjo-Morse
Poetry by a noted Pueblo potter. Illus. 127 pp. University of Arizona Press, 1992. $45; paper, $19.95.

MUKAT'S PEOPLE: THE CAHUILLA INDIANS OF SOUTHERN CALIFORNIA
Lowell J. Bean
Illus. 300 pp. Paper. University of California Press, 1972. $7.95.

MULEWETAM: THE FIRST PEOPLE
Jane H. Hill & Rosinda Nolasquez
Paper. Malki Museum Press, 1991. $18.

MULTICULTURAL RESOURCE BOOK & APPOINTMENT CALENDAR
Detailed entries marking birthdays, historical/cultural events, and days of religious observance associated ith over 30 different cultural and religious tradition, including 30 entries dealing with Native Americans. Book, 6"X9"; Resource Calendar, 11"x17". Biblio. Index. Annual. Amherst Educational Publishing, $21.95 each.

MULTIDISCIPLINARY RESEARCH AT GRASSHOPPER PUEBLO, ARIZONA
W.A. Longacre and S.J. Holbrook, Editors
138 pp. Paper. University of Arizona Press, 1982. $12.95.

MUMIGCISTET KALIKAIT: A YUP'IK LANGUAGE TERM BOOK
Oscar Alexie, et al, Editors
175 pp. Paper. University of Alaska, Fairbanks Center, 1990.

*MARY MUSGRAVE: GEORGIA INDIAN PRINCESS
Helen Todd
Grades 6-12. 152 pp. Paper. Cherokee, 1981. $6.95.

MUSHROOM STONES OF MESO-AMERICA
Karl H. Meyer
Illus. Paper. Acoma Books, 1977. $4.95.

MUSIC AND DANCE RESEARCH ON THE SOUTHWESTERN INDIANS
Charlotte Frisbie
109 pp. Harmonie Park Press, 1977. $18.

MUSIC OF ACOMA, ISLETA, COCHITI & ZUNI PUEBLOS
Francis Densmore
Reprint of 1957 edition. Illus. 142 pp. Da Capo Press, $25.

MUSIC OF THE INDIANS OF BRITISH COLUMBIA
Francis Densmore
Reprint of 1943 edition. Illus. 118 pp. Da Capo Press, $21.50.

MUSIC OF THE NATIVE NORTH AMERICAN FOR FLUTE & RECORDER
Daniel Chazanoff
Music notation book with spiral binding; includes melodies from the Great Lakes and Eastern Woodlands Indians, Southeast, Plains, Southwestern, Pueblo, Great Basin-Plateau, Northwest and California Indians. 32 pp. $9.95. Canyon Records & Indian Arts. See Audio-Visual Distributors under CAN.

THE MUSIC OF THE NORTH AMERICAN INDIAN
Francis Densmore
13 volumes. Da Capo Press, 1972. $325 per set.

MUSKOGEE CITY & COUNTY
Odie B. Faulk
History through the 1970s of the Muskogee area of Oklahoma. Illus. 197 pp. The Five Civilized Tribes Museum, 1984. $19.95.

MY ADVENTURES IN ZUNI
Frank H. Cushing
Illus. Filter Press, 1967. $8, paper, $3.

MY FRIEND THE INDIAN
  James McLaughlin
  Illus. 475 pp. Paper . University of Nebraska
  Press, 1989. $11.50.

**MY GRANDFATHER'S HOUSE: TLINGIT
SONGS OF DEATH & SORROW**
  David Cloutier
  Illus. 40 pp. Paper . Holmgangers, 1980. $3.

MY HEART SOARS
  Chief Dan George
  Illus. 96 pp. Paper . Hancock House, $7.95.

MY INDIAN BOYHOOD
  Chief Luther Standing Bear
  Illus. 200 pp. University of Nebraska Press,
  1988. $19.95; paper , $6.95.

*MY LIFE AS AN INDIAN
  James W. Schultz
  Reprint of 1981 edition. Grades 6 and up. 328
  pp. Paper. Green Hill, $12.95.

MY LIFE ON THE PLAINS
  George A. Custer; Milo M. Quaife, Editor
  Illus. 632 pp. Paper . University of Nebraska
  Press, 1966. $11.95.

MY LUISENO NEIGHBORS
  Eleanor Beemer
  Illus. 91 pp. Acoma Books, 1980. $9.95.

MY PEOPLE THE SIOUX
  L. Standing Bear; E.A. Brininstool, Editor
  Reprint of 1928 edition. Illus. 288 pp. Paper .
  University of Nebraska Press, $6.95.

MY SPIRIT SOARS
  Chief Dan George
  Illus. 96 pp. Paper . Hancock House, $7.95.

**MY WORK AMONG THE
FLORIDA SEMINOLES**
  James Glenn; Harry Kersey , Jr., Editor
  Illus. Maps. 121 pp. University Press of Florida,
  1982. $16.95.

*MYSTERY AT ECHO CLIFFS
  Kate Abbott
  Story for children contains information about Navajo customs and history . Grades 4-9. Illus. 184
  pp. Paper . Red Crane Books, $11.95.

*MYSTERY OF COYOTE CANYON
  Timothy Green
  Col. Kit Carson's military campaign against the
  Navajos, artifacts of the Anasazi, and the ruins
  of Cliff dwellings in Canyon de Chelly are some
  of the historical themes in this story . Grades 6
  and up. Illus. Map. 150 pp. Paper . Ancient City
  Press, 1994. $11.95.

**MYSTERY OF SACAJAWEA:
INDIAN GIRL WITH LEWIS & CLARK**
  Harold P. Howard
  Story of Shoshone guide Sacajawea of the Lewis
  & Clark Expedition. Illus. 200 pp. Paper . Center
  for Western Studies, $4.95.

*MYSTERY TRACKS IN THE SNOW
  Hap Gilliland
  Identifies over 100 North American animal
  tracks. Grades 4-adult. Council for Indian
  Education, $14.95; paper . $7.95.

**THE MYSTIC LAKE SIOUX: SOCIOLOGY
OF THE MDEWAKANTONWAN SANTEE**
  Ruth Landes
  Illus. Map. 234 pp. University of Wisconsin
  Press, 1969. $25.

MYSTIC WARRIORS OF THE PLAINS
  Thomas E. Mails
  Illus. 608 pp. Center for W estern Studies.
  Leather edition, $400.

**MYSTICS, MAGICIANS,
& MEDICINE PEOPLE**
  Doug Boyd
  Simon & Schuster. $12.

***MYTH, MUSIC & DANCE
OF THE AMERICAN INDIAN**
  Ruth DeCesare; Sandy Feldstein, et al, Editors
  Grades 4-12. Illus. 80 pp. Teacher's edition, $12.95
  with cassette, $19.95; student edition, 16 pp.
  $3.95; student songbook, 24 pp., $4.95.   Alfred
  Publishing, 1988.

**MYTH OF HIAWATHA, AND OTHER ORAL
LEGENDS, MYTHOLOGIC & ALLERGORIC,
OF THE NORTH AMERICAN INDIAN**
  H.R. Schoolcraft
  Reprint of 1856 edition. Kraus Reprint, $28.

**THE MYTH OF THE SAVAGE: & THE
BEGINNINGS OF THE FRENCH COLONIAL-
ISM IN THE AMERICAS**
  Olive Dickason
  272 pp. University of Nebraska Press, 1984. $30.

**THE MYTH & PRAYERS OF THE
GREAT STAR CHANT & THE MYTH
OF THE COYOTE CHANT**
  Recorded by Mary C. Wheelwright;
  ed. by David McAllester
  Illus. 190 pp. Paper . Navajo Community
  College Press, 1989. $27.

**THE MYTHIC WORLD OF THE ZUNI: AS
WRITTEN BY FRANK HAMILTON CUSHING**
  Barton W right, Editor
  Reprint of 1896 edition. Illus. 190 pp.
  University of New Mexico Press, $19.95.

**THE MYTHICAL PUEBLO RIGHTS DOCTRINE:
WATER ADMINISTRATION IN HISPANIC NEW
MEXICO**
  Daniel Tyler
  Illus. 65 pp. Texas Western, 1989. $12; paper ,
  $7.50.

**THE MYTHOLOGY OF THE
BELLA COOLA INDIANS**
  Franz Boas
  Reprint of 1898 edition. AMS Press, $32.50.

MYTHOLOGY OF THE BLACKFOOT INDIANS
  C. Wissler and D. Duvall
  Reprin tof 1909 edition. Illus. 88 pp. AMS Press,
  $17.

**THE MYTHOLOGY OF NORTH AMERICA:
INTRO TO CLASSIC AMERICAN GODS,
HEROES & TRICKSTERS**
  John Bierhorst
  Illus. 256 pp. Paper . William Morrow , 1986.
  $6.95.

MYTHOLOGY OF THE THOMPSON INDIANS
  J. Teit
  Reprint of 1912 edition. AMS Press, $41.50.

**MYTHOLOGY & VALUES: AN ANALYSIS
OF NAVAHO CHANTWAY MYTHS**
  Katherine Spencer
  Reprint of 1957 edition. 248 pp. Paper .
  University of Texas Press, 1957. $6.95.

**MYTHS & FOLKTALES OF THE
ALABAMA-COUSHATTA INDIANS**
  Howard N. Martin
  45 stories. The Encino Press, 1982. $10.95.

**MYTHS & HUNTING STORIES OF
THE MANDAN AND HIDATSA SIOUX**
  M.W. Beckwith
  Reprint of 1930 edition. AMS Press, $16.

***MYTHS & LEGENDS OF THE HAIDA
INDIANS OF THE NORTHWEST**
  Dr. Reid
  Grade 5. Illus. Paper . Bellerophon Books, 1978.
  $3.95.

***MYTHS & LEGENDS OF THE INDIANS OF THE
SOUTHWEST: HOPI, ACOMA, TEWA, ZUNI**
  Bertha Dutton and Caroline Olin
  Grade 5. Illus. Paper . Bellerophon Books, 1978.
  $3.95.

***MYTHS & LEGENDS OF THE INDIANS
OF THE SOUTHWEST: NAVAJO, PIMA
& APACHE**
  Bertha Dutton and Caroline Olin
  Grade 5. Illus. Paper . Bellerophon Books, 1978.
  $3.95.

**MYTHS & LEGENDS OF
THE LIPAN APACHE INDIANS**
  M. Opler
  Reprint of 1940 edition. Kraus Reprint, $48.

MYTHS & LEGENDS OF THE SIOUX
  Marie L. McLaughlin
  38 Sioux legends. Illus. 200 pp. Paper .
  University of Nebraska Press, 1990. $8.

**MYTHS & SACRED FORMULAS
OF THE CHEROKEES**
  James Mooney
  Obtained on the Cherokee Reservation in NC in
  1887-1888 covering daily life and thought of the
  Cherokee. 400 pp. Paper . Cherokee Publica-
  tions, $15.95.

**MYTHS & SYMBOLS, OR ABORIGINAL
RELIGIONS IN AMERICA**
  Stephen Peet
  Reprint of 1905 edition. Illus. Longwood, $45.

**MYTHS & TALES FROM
THE SAN CARLOS APACHE**
  P.E. Goddard
  Reprint of 1918 edition. AMS Press, $16.50.

**MYTHS & TALES OF THE
CHIRICAHUA APACHE INDIANS**
  M. Opler
  Reprint of 1942 edition. Kraus Reprint, $30.

**MYTHS & TALES OF THE
JICARILLA APACHE INDIANS**
  M. Opler
  Reprint of 1938 edition. Kraus Reprint, $37.

**MYTHS & TALES OF THE
SOUTHEASTERN INDIANS**
  John Swanton
  Reprint of 1929 edition. AMS Press, $20.

**MYTHS & TALES OF THE
WHITE MOUNTAINS APACHE**
  G. Goodwin, Editor
Reprint of 1938 edition. Kraus, $32. Paper.
University of Arizona Press, $16.95.

MYTHS OF THE CHEROKEE
  James Mooney
Reprint of 1900 edition. Scholarly Press, $89.

**MYTHS OF THE CHEROKEE & SACRED
FORMULAS OF THE CHEROKEES**
  James Mooney
Historical sketch & 126 Cherokee myths.
Reprint. Illus. 350 pp. Charles & Randy Elder,
Publishers, $24.95; paper, $16.95.

**MYTHS OF THE MODOCS: INDIAN
LEGENDS FROM THE NORTHWEST**
  Jeremiah Curtin
Reprint of 1912 edition. Ayer Co.

**MYTHS OF THE NEW WORLD INDIANS: A
TREATISE ON THE SYMBOLISM & MYTHOL-
OGY OF THE RED RACE OF AMERICA**
  D.G. Brinton
Reprint of 1876 edition. Illus. 360 pp. Longwood,
$30; Greenwood, $35.

**THE MYTHS OF THE
NORTH AMERICAN INDIANS**
  Lewis Spence
Anthology of the myths & legends of the
Algonquins, Iroquois, Pawnees & Sioux. Illus. 480
pp. Paper. Dover, 1989. $8.95.

N

**NACIMIENTOS: NATIVITY SCENES BY
SOUTHWEST INDIAN ARTISANS**
  Guy & Doris Monthan
2nd revised edition. Illus. 110 pp. Paper. Avanyu
Publishing, 1990. $29.95.

*NA YO PISA
A noun recognition book for young readers. Includes three scenes from reservation life are
shown, home-school-town. Grades K-3. 7 pp.
Choctaw Heritage Press, $3.

**NAIRNE'S MUSKHOGEAN JOURNALS: THE
1708 EXPEDITION TO THE MISSISSIPPI RIVER**
  Capt. Thomas Nairne; Alexander Moore, Editor
Muskhogean society in Colonial white-Indian
relations. 92 pp.University Press of Mississippi,
1988. $18.50.

**THE NAKED MAN, VOL. 4:
MYTHOLOGIQUES**
  Claude Levi-Strauss;
  John & Doreen Weightman, translators
Reprint. 760 pp. Paper. University
of Chicago Press, 1990. $21.95.

THE NAMES
  N. Scott Momaday
170 pp. Paper. University of Arizona Press,
1987. $9.95.

**NAMING CANADA: ESSAYS ON PLACE
ANMES FROM CANADIAN GEOGRAPHIC**
  Alan Rayburn
Native place names are stamped across the en-
tire country, reflecting the First Nations' contribu-

tions to Canadian history. Illus. 300 pp. University
of Toronto Press, 1994. $55; paper, $18.95.

**NANA'S RAID: APACHE WARFARE
IN SOUTHERN NEW MEXICO**
  Stephen H. Lekson
Illus. 78 pp. Texas Western Press, 1989. $12;
paper, $7.50.

NANISE: A NAVAJO HERBAL
  Vernon O. Mayes & Barbara Bayless Lacy
Identifies and illustrates 100 plants found today
on the Navajo Reservation. Illus. Paper. Navajo
Community College Press, $27.

*THE NANTICOKE
  Frank Porter
Grades 5 and up. Illus. 104 pp. Chelsea House,
1987. $17.95.

NANTICOKE COMMUNITY OF DELAWARE
  F.G. Speck
Reprint of 1915 edition. Illus. 88 pp. AMS Press,
$18.

THE NANTICOKE & CONOY INDIANS
  F.G. Speck
Reprint of 1927 edition. AMS Press, $10.

THE NANTICOKE INDIANS
  C.A. Weslager
Reprint of 1948 edition. 350 pp. AMS Press,
$20. University of Delaware Press, $28.50.

*THE NARRAGANSETT
  William Simmons
Grades 7-12. Illus. 112 pp. Chelsea House,
1989. $17.95.

**NARRATIVE CHANCE: POSTMODERN DIS-
COURSE ON NATIVE AMERICAN INDIAN LIT-
ERATURES**
  Gerald Vizenor, Editor
238 pp. University of New Mexico Press, 1989.
$29.95. Paper. University of Oklahoma Press,
$14.95.

**NARRATIVE OF THE CAPTIVITY OF
EBENEZER FLETCHER**
  Ebenezer Fletcher
Reprint. 28 pp. Paper. Ye Galleon, $3.

**NARRATIVE OF THE CAPTIVITY
OF ISAAC WEBSTER**
  Isaac Webster
25 pp. Paper. Ye Galleon Press, 1988. $3.95.

**A NARRATIVE OF THE
CAPTIVITY OF MRS. JOHNSON**
  Johnson
Rerint of 1814 edition. Illus. 230 pp. Paper.
Heritage Book, $18.50.

**A NARRATIVE OF THE EARLY DAYS & RE-
MEMBRANCES OF OCEOLA NIKKANOCHEE,
PRINCE OF ECONCHATTI, A YOUNG SEMI-
NOLE INDIAN, et al**
  Andre G. Welch
Reprint of 1841 edition. Illus. 305 pp. University
Press of Florida, $19.95.

**NARRATIVE OF THE EXPEDITION TO
THE SOURCE OF ST. PETER'S RIVER**
  W.H. Keating
Facsimile of 1825 edition. Illus. Ross & Haines,
$20.

**A NARRATIVE OF THE
LIFE OF MRS. MARY JEMISON**
  James Seaver
196 pp. Paper. Syracuse University Press,
1990. $12.95.

**A NARRATIVE OF THJE MANNER IN WHICH
THE CAMPAIGN AGAINST THE INDIANS, IN
THE YEAR 1791, WAS CONDUCTED**
  Arthur St. Clair
Reprint of 1812 edition. Ayer Co., $29.95.

**NARRATIVE OF THE MISSION OF THE
  BRETHREN AMONG THE DELAWARE
AND MOHEGAN INDIANS**
  J. Heckewelder
Reprint of 1820 edition. Ayer Co., $29.

**NARRATIVE OF OCCURENCES IN THE
INDIAN COUNTRIES OF NORTH AMERICA**
  S.H. Wilcocke
Reprint of 1817 edition. Beekman Publishers,
$19.95.

NARRATIVE OF WILLIAM BIGGS
  William Biggs
Reprint. 35 pp. Paper. Ye Galleon Press, $6.95.

**NARRATIVES OF CAPTIVITY AMONG THE
INDIANS OF NORTH AMERICA: A LIST OF
BOOKS & MANUSCRIPTS ON THE SUBJECT
IN THE EDWARD A. AYER COLLECTION OF
THE NEWBERRY LIBRARY**
Lists 339 narratives. Reprint of 1912 edition.
185 pp. Omnigraphics, $35.

**NARRATIVES OF THE
INDIAN WARS, 1675-1699**
  Charles Lincoln, Editor
Reprint of 1913 edition. 312 pp. Barnes and
Noble Imports, $21.50.

**NATION-STATES &
INDIANS IN LATIN AMERICA**
  Greg Urban & Joel Sherzer
370 pp. University of Texas Press, 1991.
$37.50.

NATIONAL ABORIGINAL DIRECTORY
Canadian aboriginal directory of tribal groups and
organizations. 328 pp. Paper. Arrowfax Canada,
$25.

**NATIONAL DIRECTORY OF PHILAN-
THROPY FOR NATIVE AMERICANS**
  Phyllis A. Meiners, Editor
Profiles 39 private sector (24 foundations, 12
corporations, and 3 religious institutions) grant
makers; prominent funders of Native American
programs. 140 pp. CRC Publishing, 1993.
$69.95.

**NATIONS REMEMBERED: AN ORAL HISTORY
OF THE CHEROKEES, CHICKASAWS,
CHOCTAWS, CREEKS, & SEMINOLES, 1865-
1907**
  Theda Perdue
Illus. Maps. 246 pp. Paper. University of
Oklahoma Press, $11.95.

**NATIONS WITHIN A NATION: HISTORICAL
STATISTICS OF AMERICAN INDIANS**
  Paul Stuart
Historical statistics on Native American tribes.
Biblio. 251 pp. Greenwood, 1987. $45.

THE NATIONS WITHIN: THE PAST & FUTURE OF AMERICAN INDIAN SOVEREIGNTY
Vine Deloria, Jr. and Clifford Lytle
336 pp. Paper. Pantheon, 1984. $11.95.

NATIVE ACCOUNTS OF NOOTKA ETHNOGRAPHY
E. Sapir and M. Swadesh
Reprint of 1955 edition. AMS Press, $34.50.

NATIVE AMERICA
John Gattuso
A narrative approach to identify and describe the sites and activities of the Native American. Includes discussion of Amerian Indian art, Indians and alcohol, and ancestral grounds. Illus. Biblio. 389 pp. Paper. Prentice-Hall, 1992. $19.95.

NATIVE AMERICA: ARTS, TRADITIONS & CELEBRATIONS
Christine Mather
Illus. Crown Publishers, 1990. $40.

NATIVE AMERICA IN THE TWENTIETH CENTURY
Contains 282 signed articles (written by historians, anthropologists, and other specialists - 40% of whom are Native American) on present-day tribal groups providing information on 20th-century American Indians & Alaska Natives. 75 photos. 20 maps. 818 pp. Garland Publishing, 1994. $95.

NATIVE AMERICA: PORTRAIT OF THE PEOPLES
Duane Champagne, Editor
A selection of articles covering Native American history, religion, arts, language and present-day lifeways and issues. Also hundreds of biographies. Illus. 200 photos and drawings. Maps. 814 pp. Paper. Visible Ink Press, $18.95.

Native American AIDS Statistics
Statistics from the U.S. CDC on reported cases of AIDS among Native Americans. Graphs. National Native American AIDS Prevention Center. No charge.

*NATIVE AMERICAN ANIMAL STORIES
told by Joseph Bruchac
Illus. 160 pp. Paper. Fulcrum Publishing & AISES, 1991. $11.95. Audiocassette, $16.95.

NATIVE AMERICAN ANNUAL, Vol. I
Margaret Clark-Price
Illus. 100 pp. Native American Publishing, 1985. $8.95.

NATIVE AMERICAN ARCHITECTURE
Peter Nabaokov & Robert Easton
Illus. 432 pp. Oxford University Press, 1988. $50.

NATIVE AMERICAN ARCHIVES: AN INTRODUCTION
John A. Fleckner
72 pp. Paper. Society of American Archivists, 1985. $7.

NATIVE AMERICAN ART
David W. Penney & George C. Longfish
Traces the development of American Indian art from the handmade tools of the Archaic Period to contemporary creations. 290 full-color black & white photos, 320 pp. Levin Associates, 1994. $85.

THE NATIVE AMERICAN ART LOOK BOOK
Dawn Weiss and Barbara Zaffran, Editors
An activity book from The Brooklyn Museum. Presents objects from the museum's collection of Native American art–pottery, basketry, and wood carvings. Illus. 48 pp. Paper. W.W. Norton & Co., 1993. $14.95.

NATIVE AMERICAN ART AT PHILBROOK
Philbrook Art Center
Paper. Philbrook Art Center,1980. $9.95; University of Oklahoma Press, $11.95.

NATIVE AMERICAN ART & THE NEW YORK AVANTE-GARDE
W. Jackson Rushing
The influence Native American art had on American modernist art of 1910-1950. Illus. 288 pp. University of Texas Press, 1995. $39.95.

NATIVE AMERICAN ARTISANS SURVEY
A survey of American Indian artists in Arizona. Atlatl, 1992. $5.

NATIVE AMERICAN BASKETRY: AN ANNOTATED BIBLIOGRAPHY
Frank W. Porter, III, compiled by
1,000+ entries on all aspetcs of Native American basket making. 249 pp. Greenwood, 1988. $39.95.

NATIVE AMERICAN BEADWORK
Georg J. Barth
Covers all aspects of traditional Indian beadwork. Illus. 220 pp. R. Schneider, Publishers, 1993. $27.95; paper, $19.95.

NATIVE AMERICAN BIBLIOGRAPHY SERIES
Jack W. Marken, General Editor
Begun in 1980, titles in this series have focused on individual tribes, geographic areas, literature, languages, and collections of documents. See publisher for titles & prices. Scarecrow Press.

*NATIVE AMERICAN BIOGRAPHIES
11 biographies: Squanto, Sacajawea, Pocahontas, Sitting Bull, Jim Thorpe, Pontiac, Sequoyah, Black Hawk, Tecumseh, Chief Joseph, and Osceola. Illus. 48 pp. each. Troll Associates, $2.95 each; $30/set.

NATIVE AMERICAN BIOGRAPHIES
Virginia Seeley, Editor
Illus. Photos. 240 pp. Paper. AISES, $11.

THE NATIVE AMERICAN BOOK OF CHANGE
Gabriel Horn
Chronicles the struggles of the American Indians since Europeans came into their world. Focuses on the clash between tribes and those seeking to exploit these people and their resource. Papr. Beyond Words or Greenfield Review Press, $4.95.

NATIVE AMEICAN CHECKLIST
Barbara Beaver, Compiler
Contains over 900 titles relating to Native Americans. Covers art, history, literature, religion, travel, and women's studies. Also audiovisual materials and children's books. 20 pp. Paper. Bookpeople. No charge to schools and lbraries.

NATIVE AMERICAN DANCE: CEREMONIES & SOCIAL TRADITIONS
Charlotte Heth, General Editor
Essays on Native American dance traditions & their meaning, origin, abnd evolution. Illus. 208 pp. Starwood Pubg, 1992. $45; paper, $24.95

NATIVE AMERICAN DESIGNS
Caren Caraway
Combines five regional books: *Eastern Woodland Indian Designs*, *Northwest Indian Designs*, *Plains Indian Designs*, *Southeastem Woodland Indian Designs*, and *Southwest American Indian Designs*. Illus. 240 pp. Paper. Stemmer House, 1993. $27.95. Regional books, $5.95 each.

NATIVE AMERICAN DIRECTORY: ALASKA, U.S. & CANADA
Fred Snyder, Editor
Third edition. 375 pp. Paper. Native American Co-Op, 1994. $47.95.

NATIVE AMERICAN DISCOURSE: POETICS & RHETORIC
Joel Sherzer & Anthony Woodbury
Illus. 256 pp. Cambridge University Press, 1987. $44.50.

NATIVE AMERICAN ESTATE: THE STRUGGLE OVER INDIAN & HAWAIIAN LANDS
Linda S. Parker
256 pp. University of Hawaii Press, 1989. $24.

NATIVE AMERICAN FOLKLORE, 1879-1979
Frances Malpezzi
Covers all aspects of oral literature, including dance and ritual. Swallow Press, 1984.

NATIVE AMERICAN HERITAGE, Third Ed.
Merwyn Garbarino & Robert F. Sasso
A text providing a broad overview of the diversity of American Indian cultures. In 4 parts: prehistory, the construct of culture areas; various culture traits, and exploring the interactions between Native Americans and non-natives. Illus. Maps.Paper. Waveland Press, 1994$17.95.

NATIVE AMERICAN HISTORICAL DEMOGRAPHY: A CRITICAL BIBLIOGRAPHY
Henry Dobyns
104 pp. Paper. Indian University Press, 1982. $4.95.

NATIVE AMERICAN IN AMERICAN LITERATURE: A SELECTIVELY ANNOTATED BIBLIOGRAPHY
Roger O. Rock
225 pp. Greenwood Press, 1985. $36.95.

*NATIVE AMERICAN LEADERS OF THE WILD WEST
William R. Sanford
7 biographies: Chief Joseph, Crazy Horse, Geronimo, Quanah Parker, Red Cloud, Sitting Bull, and Osceola. Grades 4-10. Illus. Maps. Biblio. 48 pp. each. Enslow Publishing, 1994. $14.95 each; $104.65/set.

*NATIVE AMERICAN LEGENDS
Terri Cohlene
Grades 4-8. Illus. 6 books. 288 pp. Rourke Corp., 1990. $89.70.

NATIVE AMERICAN LEGENDS
131 legends from many North American Indian tribes and information and background of each legend. 265 pp. Paper. Cherokee Pubns,$11.95.

NATIVE AMERICAN LEGENDS: THE SOUTHEAST
George Lankford
Illus. 268 pp. August House, 1987. $19.95; paper, $9.95.

NATIVE AMERICAN PAINTED BUFFALO HIDES
George P. Horse Capture,
Anne Vitart, and Richard West, Editors
Collection of 100 photos of painted buffalo hides. Includes introductory and historical essays by two Native American art experts. Illus. 168 pp. W.W. Norton & Co., 1993. $35.

*NATIVE AMERICAN PEOPLE
Rita D'Apice, et al
Grades 5-8. Illus. 6 book set. 192 pp. Rourke Corp., $59.70 per set.

NATIVE AMERICAN PERIODICALS & NEWS-PAPERS, 1828-1982: BIBLIOGRAPHY, PUBLISHING RECORD AND HOLDINGS
James P. Danky, Editor
Maureen E. Hady, Compiler
Lists 1,200 Native American periodicals in 146 libraries in North America. Illus. 565 pp. Greenwood, 1983. $50.95.

NATIVE AMERICAN PORTRAITS
Nancy Hathaway
Illus. 120 pp. Chronicle Books, 1990. $29.95; paper, $16.95.

NATIVE AMERICAN PRESS IN WISCONSIN & THE NATION: PROCEEDINGS OF THE CONFERENCE ON THE NATIVE AMERICAN PRESS IN WISCONSIN & THE NATION, APRIL, 1982
James P. Danky and Maureen B. Hady
197 pp. Paper. University of Wisconsin Library School, 1982. $6.50.

NATIVE AMERIAN PROPHECIES: EXAMINING THE HISTORY, WISDOM & STARTLING PREDICTIONS OF VISIONARY NATIVE AMERICANS
Scott Peterson
256 pp. Paragon House, 1991. $22.95; paper, $12.95.

NATIVE AMERICAN READER: STORIES, SPEECHES & POEMS
Anthology of stories. The Denali Press, $25.

NATIVE AMERICAN RELIGIONS
Sam Gill
192 pp. Paper. Wadsworth, 1982.

NATIVE AMERICAN RELIGIONS: AN INTRODUCTION
Denise Lardner Carmody
& John Tully Carmody
Surveys major aspects of the traditional religious lives of native peoples in all parts of the Americas. Illus. 288 pp. paper. Paulist Press, 1993. $14.95.

NATIVE AMERICAN RELIGIONS: A GEOGRAPHICAL SURVEY
John J. Collins
420 pp. Edwin Mellen Press, 1991. $79.95.

NATIVE AMERICAN RELIGIONS: NORTH AMERICA
Lawrence E. Sullivan, into by
Paper. Macmillan, 1989. $12.95.

NATIVE AMERICAN RELIGIOUS ACTION: A PERFORMANCE APPROACH TO RELIGION
Sam D. Gill; Frederick Denny, Editor
125 pp. University of South Carolina Press, 1987. $21.95.

NATIVE AMERICAN RENAISSANCE
Kenneth Lincoln
320 pp. University of California Press, 1983. $30; paper, $11.95.

NATIVE AMERICAN REPATRIATION OF CULTURAL PATRIMONY ACT (S.1980) & THE NATIVE AMERICAN GRAVE & BURIAL PROTECTION ACT (S.1021)
Norvert S. Hill, Editor
Testimony before the Senate Select Committee on Indian Affairs made on behalf of the American Indian Science & Engineering Society. AISES, 1990.

NATIVE AMERICAN RESEARCH INFORMATION SERVICE
William Carmack, et al
275 pp. Paper. American Indian Studies Center, 1983. $15.

NATIVE AMERICAN RESURGENCE & RENEWAL: A READER & BIBLIOGRAPHY
Robert N. Wells, Jr.
Native American self determination. Treaty rights and tribal soverignty. 671 pp. Scarecrow Press, 1994. $65.

NATIVE AMERICAN SPIRIT
Calendar. Pictures taken from book, *The Spirit of Native America*. 12x12". Chronicle Books, $9.95.

*NATIVE AMERICAN STORIES
Joseph Bruchac;
illus. by John Kahiuonhes Fadden
Grades 4 and up. 156 pp. Paper. Fulcrum Publishing & AISES, $11.95; audio tape, $16.95..

THE NATIVE AMERICAN STRUGGLE: CONQUERING THE RULE OF LAW: A COLLOQUIUM
Margaret A. Gilbert-Temple, Managing Editor
Speeches, articles and review essays. 226 pp. Paper. New York University, Review of Law & Social Change. Volume XX, 1993. $7.

NATIVE AMERICAN SWEAT LODGE: HISTORY & LEGENDS
Joseph Bruchac
Explains the history, the meaning and the use of the sweat lodge. Paper. Crossing Press, $12.95.

*NATIVE AMERICAN TESTIMONY: AN ANTHOLOGY OF INDIAN & WHITE RELATIONS, FIRST ENCOUNTER TO DISPOSSESSION
Peter Nabokov, Editor
Grades 7-and up. Illus. 220 pp. Harper & Row, 1992. $25.

NATIVE AMERICAN TESTIMONY: A CHRONICLE OF INDIAN-WHITE RELATIONS FROM PROPHECY TO THE PRESENT, 1492-1992
Peter Nabokov, Editor
Collection of essays by Native Americans. 512 pp. Paper. Penguin USA, $10.

THE NATIVE AMERICAN TODAY
Joan Isom & Claude Noble, Editors
118 pp. Paper. Northeastern State University, 1986. $6.95.

NATIVE AMERICAN TRIBALISM: INDIAN SURVIVALS AND RENEWALS
D'Arcy McNickle
Illus. 120 pp. Paper. Oxford University Press, 1973. $9.95.

NATIVE AMERICAN TRADITIONS
Sam Gill
200 pp. Paper. Wadsworth Publishing, 1983. $12.95.

NATIVE AMERICAN VISIONS CALENDAR
12 exquisite Sam English (Ojibwa artist) full-color prints; calendar with 10x14 print and appointment calendar below; and selected quotes from historic and present-day tribal leaders. Available in August for upcoming year. Fulcrum Publishing, $10.95.

NATIVE AMERICAN VOICES
David A. Rausch & Blair Schlepp
Native American history and culture from an evangelical perspective. Describes native cultures before the coming of the Europeans. 192 pp. Paper. Baker Book House, 1993. $10.99.

NATIVE AMERICAN WISDOM
Kent Nerburn & Louise Mengelkoch, Editors
Collection of philosophical and religious thoughts, quotations from Chief Joseph, Sitting Bull, Red Cloud, Black Elk, Ohiyesa, and others. 128 pp. New World Library, 1991. $9.95. Audiocassette, $10.95.

NATIVE AMERICAN WISDOM, 3 Vols.
Terry P. Wilson, Text by
Hopi: Following the Path of Peace; *Lakota: Seeking the Great Spirit*; and *Navajo: Walking in Beauty*. Illus. 64 pp. each. Chronicle Books, 1990. $9.95 each; $29.95/set.

NATIVE AMERICAN WOMEN
Calendar. Features photos from the book, *Native American Portraits*. 12x12". Chronicle Books, $9.95.

NATIVE AMERICAN WOMEN: A BIOGRAPHICAL DICTIONARY
Gretchen M. Bataille, Editor
Profiles more than 200 Native American women born in the U.S. and Canada. Covers both historical and contemporary figures; bibliograpies of primary & secondary works. Illus. 352 pp. Garland Publishing, 1993. $40.

NATIVE AMERICAN WOMEN: A CONTEXTUAL BIBLIOGRAPHY
Rayna Green
700 entries about or by Native North American women. 128 pp. Indiana U. Press, 1983. $25.

*THE NATIVE AMERICANS
Polly and John Zane
Grades 1-12. Teacher's edition. Proof Press, 1976. $32.

*NATIVE AMERICANS
Preschool-8. Illus. 32 pp. Paper. Smithsonian, $29.50.

THE NATIVE AMERICANS
Carter Smith, Editor
Illus. 288 pp. Facts on File, 1990. $14.50.

NATIVE AMERICANS AS SHOWN ON STAGE, 1753-1916
Eugene Jones
219 pp. Scarecrow, 1988. $22.50.

NATIVE AMERICANS: ETHNOLOGY & BACKGROUNDS OF THE NORTH AMERICAN INDIANS
Robert Spencer
Second edition. Illus. Harper & Row, $38.50.

NATIVE AMERICANS: FIVE CENTURIES OF CHANGING IMAGES
Patricia Trenton & Patrick Houlihan
Illus. 305 pp. Harry N. Abrams, 1989. $49.50.

NATIVE AMERICANS: 23 INDIAN BIOGRAPHIES
Dr. Roger W. Axford
Offers insight into Native American life—the stories of 23 individuals and their careers. 120 pp. A.G. Halldin Publishing, 1980.

NATIVE AMERICANS INFORMATION DIRECTORY
Julia C. Furtaw, Editor
Information sources on Native Americans, including organizations, agencies, institutons, programs, and publications. Covers American Indians, Alaskan Natives, Native Hawaiians, and Aboriginal Canadians. 371 pp. Biennial. Gale Research, 1993. $75.

NATIVE AMERICANS: THE NEW INDIAN RESISTANCE
William Meyer
Paper. Books on Demand, 1971. $24.

NATIVE AMERICANS & NIXON: PRESIDENTIAL POLITICS & MINORITY SELF–DETERMINATION, 1969-1972
Jack D. Forbes
148 pp. Paper. American Indian Studies Center, 1982. $12.

NATIVE AMERICANS: NORTH AMERICA
Frederick E. Hoxie & Harvey Markowitz
Illus. 324 pp. Scarecrow, 1991. $40.

NATIVE AMERICANS OF CALIFORNIA & NEVADA
Jack D. Forbes
Revised editin. 240 pp. Illus. Photos. Naturegraph, $17.95; paper, $9.95.

NATIVE AMERICANS OF THE NORTHWEST COAST: A CRITICAL BIBLIOGRAPHY
Robert S. Grumet
Illus. 128 pp. Paper. Indiana University Press, 1979. $5.95.

NATIVE AMERICANS OF THE PACIFIC COAST
Vinson Brown
Life as it was 300 years ago along the Pacific Coast. Illus. Photos. 272 pp. Naturegraph, 1979. $17.95; paper, $9.95.

*NATIVE AMERICANS: THE PEOPLE & HOW THEY LIVED
Eloise Potter & John Funderburg
Grades 4-12. Illus. 80 pp. North Carolina State Museum of Natural Sciences, 1986. $18.95; paper, $14.95.

*NATIVE AMERICANS: A PERSONAL HISTORY BOOK
This interctive workbook includes a chronological overview of the history of an American culture; open-ended exercises for research projects. Index & answer key. SVE, $7.95; package of ten, $69.

NATIVE AMERICANS OF TEXAS
Sandra L. Myers
Surveys the history of the Native American people of Texas from prehistoric times to the present. Illus. Map. Biblio. 46 pp. American Press, 1981. $3.95.

*NATIVE AMERICANS OF WASHINGTON STATE: A CURRICULUM GUIDE FOR THE ELEMENTARY GRADES
A guide to aid the elementary classroom teacher in implementing Native American curriculum in the classroom. Grades 1-6. 40 pp. Daybreak Star Press, $5.50.

NATIVE AMERICANS ON FILM & VIDEO
Elizabeth Weatherford, with Emilia Seubert, Editors
Detailed descriptions of films and videotapes about Indians and Inuit of the Americas. Two volumes Volume I, 151 pp., 1981; Volume II, 112 pp., 112 pp. Paper. National Museum of the American Indian, $5 & $7.

NATIVE AMERICANS & PUBLIC POLICY
Fremont J. Lyden & Lyman H. Legters, Editors
17 essays covering such topics as problems of national policy, questions of legal sovereignty, and Native resources and economy. 330 pp. University of Pittsburgh, 1992. $39.95.

*NATIVE ARTISTS OF NORTH AMERICA
Reavis Moore
Five Native American artists. Grades 8 and up. Illus. 48 pp. Paper. John Muir, 1991. $14.95.

NATIVE ARTS NETWORK
Atlatl convenes native artists and administrators to discuss issues in the field. Special reports document these biennial conferences. 1986, 1990, 1992, 1994. Atlatl, $5.

NATIVE ARTS OF NORTH AMERICA
Christian F. Feest
Revised edition. Illus. 220 pp. Paper. Thames & Hudson, 1992. $19.95.

THE NATIVE ARTS OF NORTH AMERICA, AFRICA & THE SOUTH PACIFIC: AN INTRODUCTION
George Corbin
Illus. 352 pp. Paper. Harper & Row, 1988. $24.95.

NATIVE BASKETRY OF WESTERN NORTH AMERICA
Joan M. Jones
Illus. 72 pp. Paper. Illinois State Museum, 1979. $2.

THE NATIVE BROTHERHOODS: MODERN INTER-TRIBAL ORGANIZATIONS ON THE NORTHWEST COAST
P. Drucker
Reprint of 1958 edition. Reprint Services, $79.

NATIVE CALIFORNIAN: A THEORETICAL RETROSPECTIVE
Lowell J. Bean & Thomas Blackburn
Anthology of 16 papers on Native Californians. 453 pp. Paper. Ballena Press, 1976. $21.95.

NATIVE CANADIAN ANTHROPOLOGY & HISTORY: A SELECTED BIBLIOGRAPHY
Shepard Krech III
Revised edition. 3,000 sources emphasizes recent publications on Canada's Native peoples. 224 pp. University of Oklahoma Press, 1994. $28.95.

NATIVE CAROLINIANS: THE INDIANS OF NORTH CAROLINA
Theda Perdue
Illus. 75 pp. Paper. North Carolina Division of Archives & Cherokee Publications, 1985. $4.50.

NATIVE CEMETARIES & FORMS OF BURIAL EAST OF THE MISSISSIPPI
David Bushnell
Reprint of 1920 edition. Scholarly Press, $59.

THE NATIVE CREATIVE PROCESS: A COLLABORATIVE DISCOURSE
Douglas J. Cardinal & Jeanette Armstrong; illus. by Greg Young-Ing
Authors share their visions and insights into the creative process from the perspective of their Native ancestry. Illus. 127 pp. Paper. Theytus, 1991. $24.95.

NATIVE FACES; INDIAN CULTURES IN AMERICAN ART
P. Trenton and P.T. Houlihan
Illus. 120 pp. Paper. Southwest Museum, 1984. $15.95.

NATIVE HARVESTS: RECIPES & BOTANICALS OF THE AMERICAN INDIAN
Barrie Kavasch
Illus. Paper. Random House, 1979. $7.95.

NATIVE HEALER: INITIATION INTO AN ANCIENT ART
Lake Medicine Grizzlybear
Paper. Theosophical Publishing House, 1991. $10.95.

NATIVE HEART: AN AMERICAN INDIAN ODYSSEY
Gabriel Horn (White Deer of Autumn)
An autobography. One man's sacred journey as he strugles to live the way of his ancestors in modern America. 304 pp. Paper. New World Library, $13.95.

A NATIVE HERIATGE: IMAGES OF THE INDIAN IN ENGLISH-CANADIAN LITERATURE
Leslie Monkman
208 pp. University of Toronto Press, 1981. $35.

NATIVE LAND
Mary Ann Wells
Documented chronicle about the lands that became the state of Mississippi. Illus. Maps. 256 pp. University Press of Mississippi, 1995. $45; paper, $15.95.

NATIVE LAND & FOREIGN DESIRES
Lilikala Kame'eleihiwa
Explores the 1848 Mahele written from a Hawaiian standpoint. Illus. 424 pp. Bishop Museum, $54.95; paper, $39.95.

NATIVE LAW BIBLIOGRAPHY
Linda Fritz
100 pp. University of Saskatchewan, 1984. $20.

NATIVE LIGHT FOR A DARK WORLD
Donald Matheson
272 pp. Carlton Press, 1988. $14.95.

NATIVE NORTH AMERICAN ALMANAC
Duane Champagne, Editor
Covers the range of Native history and culture in the U.S. and Canada. Includes a chronology, demographic and distribution descriptions and histories, and discussions. Illus. 1,300 pp. Gale Research, 1993. $95.

NATIVE NORTH AMERICAN ART HISTORY-- SELECTED READINGS
Zena Mathews and Adona Jonaitis
Illus. 500 pp. Paper. Peek Publns, 1982. $19.95.

NATIVE NORTH AMERICAN MUSIC & ORAL DATA: A CATALOGUE OF SOUND RECORDINGS, 1893-1976
Dorothy S. Lee
480 pp. Indian University Press, 1979. $25.

NATIVE NORTH AMERICAN SPIRITUALITY OF THE EASTERN WOODLANDS: SACRED MYTHS, DREAMS, VISION SPEECHES, HEALING FORMULAS, RITUALS & CEREMONIES
Elisabteh Tooker, Editor
302 pp. Paulist Press, 1979. $14.95.

NATIVE NORTH AMERICANS: AN ETHNOHISTORICAL APPROACH
Daniel Boxberger
450 pp. Kendall-Hunt, 1991. $25.95.

NATIVE NORTH AMERICANS IN DOCTORAL DISSERTATIONS, 1971-1975: A CLASSIFIED & INDEXED RESEARCH BIBLIOGRAPHY
S. Gifford Nickerson
CPL Biblios, 1977. $7.50.

NATIVE PEOPLE IN CANADA: CONTEMPORARY CONFLICTS
James Frideres
Second Edition. 350 pp. Prentice-Hall, 1983.

NATIVE PEOPLE, NATIVE LANDS: CANADIAN INDIANS, INUIT & METIS
Bruce Cox
300 pp. Paper. Oxford U. Press, 1988. $16.95.

*NATIVE PEOPLE, NATIVE WAYS SERIES
White Deer of Autumn (Gabriel Horn)
Stories about the Native American experience. In 4 vols. *Native American Book of Knowledge* (Vol. I): stories - "We Have Always Been Here", & "Prophets, Poets & Peacemakers: Before Columbus"; *Native American Book of Life* (Vol. II): stories - "The Children, Always the Children," & "By the Magic of the Strawberry Moon"; *Native American Book of Change* (Vol. III): stories: "Prophets, Poets, & Peacemakers: After the Conquest," & "Dad's Signs, Now Mine"; *Native American Book of Wisdom* (Vol. IV): stories - "From the Great Mystery: Wakan-Tanka," & "Medicine Man." 96 pp. Paper. Beyond Words Publishing, $4.95 each.

THE NATIVE PEOPLE OF ALASKA
Steve J. Langdon
Introductory guide to the Eskimos, Indians, and Aleuts. Focus is on their life-styles, traditions, and culture. Photos. Maps. Biblio. 90 pp. Revised edition. Paper. Alaska Natural History Association & Greatland Graphics, 1993. $7.95.

NATIVE PEOPLES OF THE NORTHEAST WOODLANDS: AN EDUCATIONAL RESOURCE PUBLICATION
Judith Brundin
Illus. 255 pp. National Museum of the American Indian, 1990. $29.95.

NATIVE PEOPLES OF THE SOUTHWEST
Susan L. Shaffer, Editor
Grades 2-6. Illus. Includes 150 student booklets with 5 teacher resource binders with overhead transparencies, slides & audiocassette; artifacts, posters, etc. The Heard Museum, 1987. $1,475.

NATIVE PLANTERS IN OLD HAWAII: THEIR LIFE, LORE & ENVIRONMENT
E.S. Craighill Handy & Elizabeth Green Handy
Hawaiian culture through the cultivation of the soil. Illus. 641 pp. Paper. Bishop Museum, $49.95.

THE NATIVE RACES
H.H. Bancroft
Reprint of 1888 edition. Five volumes. Bancroft Press, $200 per set.

NATIVE RELIGIONS OF NORTH AMERICA
Ake Hultkrantz
144 pp. Paper. Harper & Row, 1988. $7.95.

NATIVE ROOTS: HOW THE INDIAN ENRICHED AMERICA
Jack Weatherford
Illus. Crown Publishers, 1992. $21.

NATIVE SHELL MOUNDS OF NORTH AMERICA: EARLY STUDIES
Bruce Trigger
544 pp. Garland, 1986. $70.

NATIVE TRIBES MAP
Alfred L. Kroeber
Paper. University of California Press, $5.95.

THE NATIVE TRIBES OF OHIO
Helen Cox Tregillis
Tells the story from the very beginning of the Eries to the later tribes before their removal west of the Mississippi; brief biographies and list of resources. Illus. 130 pp. Maps. Paper. Heritage Books, $15.50.

NATIVE WILD GAME: FISH & WILD FOODS COOKBOOK
340+ recipes from many tribes. 283 pp. Cherokee Publications, $19.95.

NATIVE WRITINGS IN MASSACHUSETTS
Ives Goddard & Kathleen Bragdon
Illus. 838 pp. American Philosophical Society, 1988. $60.

NATIVES & NEWCOMERS: CANADA'S "HEROIC AGE" RECONSIDERED
Bruce G. Trigger
A tale of Canada's early development that finally gives Native people their rightful place. paper. University of Toronto Press, 1986. $22.95.

*NATOSI: STRONG MEDICINE
Peter Roop
Blackfeet raiding party captures their first horses from the Crows. Grades 3-8. 32 pp. Council for Indian Education, $8.95; paper, $2.95.

A NATURAL EDUCATION: NATIVE AMERICAN IDEAS & THOUGHTS
Stan Padilla, Editor & Illus.
Collection of quotations from traditional Native Americans on the importance of educating young people to the natural way. Revised edition. Illus. 80 pp. Paper. The Book Pubg. Co., 1994. $8.95.

THE NATURAL HISTORY OF NORTH CAROLINA
John Brickell
Reprint of 1737 ed. Illus. Johnson Reprint, $36.

THE NATURAL MAN OBSERVED: A STUDY OF CATLIN'S INDIAN GALLERY
William Truettner
Illus. 323 pp. Smithsonian Institution Press, 1979. $47.50.

THE NATURAL WORLD OF THE CALIFORNIA INDIANS
Robert Heizer and Albert Elsasser
Illus. Paper. U. of California Press, 1980.$10.95.

A NATURALIST IN INDIAN TERRITORY: THE JOURNALS OF S.W. WOODHOUSE, 1849-50
John S. Tomer & Michael J. Brodhead
A young Philadelphia physician was appointed surgeon-naturalist of two expeditions to survey Creek-Cherokee boundary in Indian Territory. Illus. Maps. 288 pp. University of Oklahoma Press, 1994. $29.95.

NATURE POWER: IN THE SPIRIT OF OKANAGAN STORYTELLER
Harry Robinson: Wendy Wickwire, Editor
Stories by Robinson who died in 1990. 256 pp. Paper. University of Washington Press, $17.95

THE NAVAHO
Clyde Kluckhohn and Dorothea Leighton
Revised 1973 edition. Illus. 365 pp. Harvard University Press, $18.50; paper, $8.95.

THE NAVAJO
James F. Downs
Illus. 136 pp. Paper. Waveland Press, 1984. $8.95.

*THE NAVAJO
S. Stan
Grades 5-8. Illus. 32 pp. Rourke Corp., 1989. $13.26.

*THE NAVAJO
Grades K-4. Illus. 48 pp. Childrens Press, $11.45.

NAVAJO AGING: THE TRANSITION FROM FAMILY TO INSTITUTIONAL SUPPORT
Stephen J. Kunitz & Jerrold E. Levy
191 pp. University of Arizona Press, 1991. $35.

THE NAVAJO & HIS BLANKET
Uriah S. Hollister
Reprint of 1903 edition. Illus. 176 pp. The Rio Grande Press, $17.50.

NAVAHO ART & CULTURE
George T. Mills
Reprint of 1959 edition. Illus. 273 pp. Greenwood Press, $41.50.

NAVAJO ART, HISTORY & CULTURE
Stephen Wallace, et al
79 pp. Paper. Navajo Curriculum Center Press, 1984. $5.

THE NAVAJO ART OF SANDPAINTING
Douglas Congdon-Martin
Contains over 400 full color photos of sandpaintings. Illus. 64 pp. Paper. Schiffer, 1990. $9.95.

NAVAJO ARTS & CRAFTS
Robert Roessel
Illus. 176 pp. Navajo Curriculum Center Press, 1989. $15.

NAVAJO ARTS & CRAFTS
Nancy Schiffer
Photos and explanations of each craft. Illus. 64 pp. Paper. Schiffer, $12.95.

THE NAVAJO ATLAS: ENVIRONMENTS, RESOURCES, PEOPLES & HISTORY OF THE DINE BIKEYAH
James Goodman
Illus. 120 pp. Paper. University of Oklahoma Press, 1987. $12.95.

NAVAJO BLESSINGWAY SINGER: THE AUTOBIOGRAPHY OF FRANK MITCHELL, 1881-1967
Charlotte Frisbie & David McAllester, Editors
446 pp. Paper. University of Arizona Press, 1978. $14.95.

A NAVAJO BRINGING-HOME CEREMONY: THE CLAUS CHEE SONNY VERSION OF DEERWAY AJILEE
Karl W. Luckert
Illus. 224 pp. paper. University of Nebraska Press and Museum of Northern Arizona, 1980. $14.95.

*THE NAVAJO BROTHERS & THE STOLEN HERD
Maurine Grammer; illus by Fred Cleveland
Story of two Navajo teenagers who regain their family's sheep from thieves. Grades 4-9. Illus. 120 pp. paper. Red Crane Books, $9.95.

NAVAJO: A CENTURY OF PROGRESS, 1868-1968
Martin Link, Editor
Illus. 110 pp. Navajo Tribal Museum, 1968. $6.

NAVAJO CHANGES: A HISTORY OF THE NAVAJO PEOPLE
Teresa McCarty and staff, Editors
107 pp. Navajo Curriculum Center Press, 1983. $10.

*NAVAJO CHILDREN
Nancy Armstrong
Grades 2-6. Paper. Council for Indian Education, 1975. $1.95.

NAVAHO CLASSIFICATION OF THEIR SONG CEREMONIALS
L.C. Wyman and C. Kluckhohn
Reprint of 1938 edition. Paper. Kraus, $15.00.

NAVAJO CODE TALKERS
Doris Paul
Story of Navajo platoon during World War II and of the intricate and unbreakable code language they created. Illus. 171 pp. Dorrance Publishing, 1973. $14.50.

A NAVAJO CONFRONTATION & CRISIS
Floyd A. Pollock
Traces the development of Navajo-federal relations during the 1930s and 1940s. Navajo Community College Press, $10.

*NAVAJO COYOTE TALES
William Morgan
Grades 4 and up. Illus. 50 pp. Paper. Ancient City Press, 1989. $8.95.

NAVAJO COYOTE TALES: THE CURLY TO AHEEDLIINII VERSION
Father Berard Haile
Reprint. Illus. 150 pp. Paper. University of Nebraska Press, 1984. $8.95.

NAVAJO CREATION MYTH: THE STORY OF EMERGENCE
H. Klah
Reprint of 1942 edition. AMS Press, $24.50.

A NAVAJO CRISIS & CONFRONTATION
Floyd A. Pollock
Navajo Community College Press, 1984. $15.

*NAVAJO CULTURAL GUIDES, EXPERIENCE STORIES, & CULTURAL READERS
See San Juan District Media Center for titles, prices and grade levels.

*THE NAVAJO DESIGN BOOK
Grades 1-6. Paper. Fun Publications, 1975. $3.95.

NAVAJO DICTIONARY ON DIAGNOSTIC TERMINOLOGY
Dine Center for Human Development
Paper. Navajo Community College Press, 1991. $10.

NAVAJO EDUCATION IN ACTION: THE ROUGH ROCK DEMONSTRATION SCHOOL
Robert A. Roessel, Jr.
149 pp. Navajo Curriculum Press, 1977. $10.

NAVAJO EDUCATION, 1948-1978: ITS PROGRESS & PROBLEMS
Robert A. Roessel, Jr.
Illus. 339 pp. Navajo Curriculum Press, 1979. $14.95.

*NAVAJO-ENGLISH CHILDREN'S PICTURE DICTIONARY
Roman Delos-Santos; Raymond Johnson, illustrator
Grades 4-8. Navajo Community College Press, 1995.

NAVAJO-ENGLISH DICTIONARY
Leon Wall & William Morgan
Includes over 9,000 entries, a section on Navajo pronunciation, everyday expressions, etc. 165 pp. Paper. Hippocrene Books, $8.95.

THE NAVAHO (OR CORRAL) FIRE DANCE
B. Haile
Reprint of 1946-7 editions. 3 vols. in 1. Paper. St. Michaels, $7.50.

NAVAJO FOREIGN AFFAIRS: 1795-1846
Frank D. Reeve; ed. by Eleanor Adams & John Kessell
Paper. 54 pp. Navajo Community College Press, 1983. $4.

NAVAHO GRAMMAR
G.A. Reichard
Reprint of 1951 edition. AMS Press, $47.

NAVAJO GRAVES: AN ARCHAEOLOGICAL REFLECTION OF ETHNOGRAPHIC REALITY
Albert E. Ward
Discusses select Navajo burials from northeastern Arizona and northwestern New Mexico. Illus. 54 pp. Center for Anthropological Studies, 1980. $8.

NAVAJO HISTORY
Ethelou Yazi, Editor
Revised edition. Volume I. Illus. 100 pp. Paper. Navajo Curriculum Center Press, 1982. $11.

THE NAVAJO HUNTER TRADITION
Karl W. Luckert
Hunter myths and rituals are examined in conjunction with other deities and the rise of shamanism. 239 pp. Paper. U. of Arizona Press, 1975. $9.50.

*THE NAVAJO INDIAN BOOK
Grades 1-6. Paper. Fun Publications, 1975. $3.95.

NAVAJO INDIAN MEDICAL ETHNOBOTANY
L. Wyman and S. Harris
Reprint of 1941 edition. Paper. Kraus and AMS Press, $16.50.

NAVAHO INDIAN MYTHS
Aileen O'Bryan, Editor
Tribal fables & legends recorded in the 1920s from an elderly chief. Reprint. 187 pp. Paper. Dover, $5.95.

THE NAVAJO INDIANS
D. and M. Coolidge
Reprint of 1930 edition. AMS Press, $28.50.

THE NAVAJO INDIANS
Henry F. Dobyns & Robert C. Euler
An account of the Navajo Indians, past and present. Illus. Maps. 121 pp. Center for Anthropological Studies, $8.

NAVAJO INDIANS & FEDERAL INDIAN POLICY, 1900-1935
Laurence C. Kelly
Paper. Books on Demand, $57.80.

NAVAJO INFANCY: AN ETHNOLOGICAL STUDY OF CHILDREN DEVELOPMENT
James S. Chisholm
267 pp. Aldine de Gruyter, 1983. $36.95.

NAVAJO KINSHIP & MARRIAGE
Gary Witherspoon
Illus. 150 pp. Paper. University of Chicago Press, 1975. $10.95.

NAVAJO LAND USE: AN ETHNOARCHAEOLOGICAL STUDY
Klara B. Kelley
Academic Press, 1985. $39.50; paper, $19.50.

NAVAJO LEADERSHIP & GOVERNMENT
Title IV Materials Development Staff
149 pp. Navajo Curriculum Center Press, 1977. $7.50.

NAVAHO LEGENDS
Washington Matthews
Reprint of 1897 edition. Illus. Paper. University of Utah Press, $19.95.

NAVAJO LIVESTOCK REDUCTION: A NATIONAL DISGRACE
Ruth Roessel, Editors
Illus. 224 pp. Navajo Community College Press, 1974. $15.

*NAVAJO LONG WALK
Nancy Armstrong
Grades 3-7. 88 pp. Paper. Roberts Rinehart, 1994. $7.95.

*NAVAHO MAGIC OF HUNTING
Elsie Kreischer
Narrative poem telling of a boy's first deer hunt. Grades 4-9. 32 pp. Council for Indian Education, $8.95; paper, $2.95.

NAVAJO MEDICINE BUNDLES OR JISH: ACQUISITION, TRANSMISSION & DISPOSITION IN THE PAST & PRESENT
Charlotte Frisbie
Illus. 627 pp. U. of New Mexico Press, 1987. $42.

NAVAJO MEDICINE MAN SAND PAINTINGS
Gladys Reichard
Reprint. Illus. 132 pp. Paper. Dover, $12.95.

**NAVAJO MOUNTAIN &
RAINBOW BRIDGE RELIGION**
Karl W. Luckert
Translated by I.W. Goosen and H. Bilagody, Jr.
Illus. 164 pp. University of Nebraska Press,
1977. $9.95.

THE NAVAJO NATION
Peter Iverson
Illus. 275 pp. Greenwood Press, 1981. $35.00.
Paper. University of New Mexico Press, $9.95.

**NAVAJO NATIVE DYES: THEIR PREPARA-
TION & USE**
Nonobah Bryan & Stella Young
Reprint of 1940 edition. Illus. 75 pp. Paper. Filter
Press, $3.50.

NAVAJO ORAL HISTORY
Alfred W. Yazzie
Gene and Isaac Johnson, Editors
Illus. 56 pp. Paper. Rough Rock Demonstration
School, 1984.

NAVAJO ORAL TRADITIONS
Alfred W. Yazzie; Jeri Eck, Editor
Illus. 72 pp. Paper. Navajo Curriculum Center
Press, 1984.

**NAVAJO PICTORIAL WEAVING 1880--1950:
FOLK ART IMAGES OF NATIVE AMERICANS**
Tyrone Campbell & Joel Kopp
160 full color photos of Navajo rugs. Illus. 112
pp. New American Library, 1991. $32.50; paper,
$22.50.

NAVAJO: PORTRAIT OF A NATION
Joel Grimes
Calendar. 12 full-color photos of the people,
places, and landscapes from the Navajo nation.
14x12". Treasure Chest. $10.95.

NAVAHO POTTERY MAKING
H. Tschopik
Reprint of 1941 edition. Illus. Paper. Kraus, $13.

**NAVAJO POTTERY: TRADITIONS & INNOVA-
TIONS**
Russell Hartman & Jan Musial
Illus. Biblio. Paper. Northland Publishing, 1987.
$12.95.

**THE NAVAJO PROJECT: ARCHAEOLOGICAL
INVESTIGATIONS PAGE TO PHOENIX 500
KV SOUTHERN TRANSMISSION LINE**
Donald Fiero, et al
282 pp. Museum of Northern Arizona, 1978.
$9.95.

NAVAJO & PUEBLO SILVERSMITHS
John Adair
Reprint of 1944 edition. Illus. University of
Oklahoma Pres, $17.95.

**NAVAHO RELIGION:
A STUDY OF SYMBOLISM**
Gladys A. Reichard
Reprint of 1963 edition. 856 pp. Paper.
Princeton University Press, $19.95.

**NAVAJO REPORTER: OFFICIAL REPORTS
OF CASES ARGUED & DECIDED IN THE
SUPREME COURT & THE DISTRICT COURTS
IN THE NAVAJO NATION**
Volume 5. Navajo Community College Press.
$50.

**NAVAJO RESOURCES &
ECONOMIC DEVELOPMENT**
Philip Reno
Formerly, Mother Earth, Father Sky and. Illus. 200
pp. Paper. University of New Mexico Press, and
Native American Studies Center, 1981. $8.95.

**NAVAJO ROUNDUP: SELECTED CORRE-
SPONDENCE OF KIT CARSON'S EXPEDI-
TION AGAINST THE NAVAJO, 1863-1865**
Lawrence C. Kelly
Paper. Books on Demand, $57.20.

**NAVAJO RUGS: HOW TO FIND, EVALUATE,
BUY & CARE FOR THEM**
Don Dedera
Illus. 2nd edition. 128 pp. Paper. Northland
Press, 1990. $12.95.

NAVAJO RUGS, PAST & PRESENT
Gilbert Maxwell
100 pp. Paper. Treasure Chest, 1987. $7.

NAVAJO SACRED PLACES
Klara Bonsack Kelley & Harris Francis
Illus. Maps. 264 pp. Indiana University Press,
1994. $29.95; paper, $12.95.

NAVAJO SANDPAINTING ART
Eugene B. Joe, et al
Illus. 32 pp. Paper. Treasure Chest, 1978.
$5.95.

**NAVAJO SANDPAINTING: FROM
RELIGIOUS ACT TO COMMERCIAL ART**
Nancy J. Parejo
275 pp. Paper. University of New Mexico Press,
1991. $19.95.

**NAVAJO SANDPAINTING: THE HUCKEL
COLLECTION**
Leland C. Wyman
Illus. Paper. Taylor Museum, 1971. $5.

NAVAJO SHEPARD & WEAVER
Gladys Reichard
Reprint of 1936 edition. Illus. 280 pp. Paper.
Rio Grande Press. $12.

*THE NAVAJO: SOUTHWEST
Peter Iverson
Grades 5 and up. Illus. Chelsea House, 1989.
$17.95.

**NAVAHO SYMBOLS OF HEALING: A
JUNGIAN EXPLORATION OF RITUAL,
IMAGE & MEDICINE**
Donald Sandner
Illus. 304 pp. Paper. Inner Traditions Interna-
tional, 1991. $12.95.

**NAVAJO TEXTILES: THE WILLIAM
RANDOLPH HEARST COLLECTION**
Nancy Blomberg
Illus. 257 pp. University of Arizona Press, 1988.
$45; paper, $35.

NAVAJO TEXTS
P. Goddard
Reprint of 1933 edition. AMS Press, $16.

**NAVAJO & TIBETAN SACRED WISDOM:
THE CIRCLE OF THE SPIRIT**
Peter Gold
Shows the parallels between cultures. Illus.
Paper. Inner Traditions, 1994. $29.95.

**NAVAJO TRADER: ESSAYS ON A REGION &
ITS LITERATURE**
Gladwell Richardson; Philip Reed Rulon, Editor
217 pp. Paper. University of Arizona Press,
1986. $13.95.

NAVAHO TRADING DAYS
Elizabeth Hegemann
Illus. 399 pp. University of New Mexico Press,
1987. $24.95; paper, $14.95.

NAVAJO: TRADITION &
CHANGE IN THE SOUTHWEST
Wolfgang Lindig; photos by Helga Teiwes
Illus. Photos. Biblio. 240 pp. Facts on File, 1991.
$45.

THE NAVAJO TREATY, 1868
K C Publications, 1968. $3.50; paper, $1.

NAVAJO TRIBAL CODE
Equity Publishing, 1987. $130.

NAVAJO WAR DANCE
B. Haile
Reprint of 1946 edition. Paper. St. Michaels, $6.

NAVAJO WEAVERS & SILVERSMITHS
W. Matthews
Facsimile of 1968 edition. Illus. 43 pp. Paper.
Filter Press. $2.50.

**A NAVAHO WEAVING,
ITS TECHNIC & HISTORY**
Charles A. Amsden
A comprehensive study of primitive textile weav-
ing. Reprint of 1934 edition. Illus. 460 pp. The Rio
Grande Press, $17.50. Paper, Dover, $8.95.

NAVAJO WEAVING, NAVAJO WAYS
Harriet & Seymour Koenig; Betty Himmel,
Editor
56 pp. Paper. Katonah Galleries, 1986. $12.

**NAVAJO WEAVING: THREE
CENTURIES OF CHANGE**
Kate Peck Kent
Illus. 150 pp. Paper. School of American
Research & University of Washington Press,
1985. $16.95.

NAVAJO WEAVING TODAY
Nancy Schiffer
Full-color photos of contemporary Navajo
blankets and rugs, with text. Illus. 64 pp. Paper.
Schiffer, $12.95.

**THE NAVAJO WEAVING TRADITION, 1650
TO THE PRESENT**
Alice Kaufman & Christopher Selser
Detailed history and appreciation of the Navajo
weavings. Discusses traders, the weaving process, and contemporary weaving. 200 full-color
photos. Illus. 160 pp. Paper. E.P. Dutton, $25.95.

NAVAHO WITCHCRAFT
C. Kluckhohn
Reprint of 1944 edition. Paper. Beacon Press,
$10.95.

**NAVAJOLAND: FAMILY
SETTLEMENT & LAND USE**
Clara Kelley & Peter Whitely
Paper. Navajo Community College Press,
$14.50.

NAVAJOLAND PLANG CATALOG
  Vernon Mayes & James Rominger
List of more than 1,100 plants known to grow on
the Navajo Reservation. 72 pp. Paper . National
Woodlands Publishing, 1994. $7.

**NAVAJOLAND: A PORTFOLIO OF NAVAJO
LIFE DURING THE 1940's & 1950's**
  Ray Manley
A pictorial study, in bxw, of the Navajo people.
Illus. 52 pp. Paper . Ray Manley, $9.95.

*THE NAVAJOS
  Peter Iverson
Grades 5 and up. Illus. Chelsea House, 1990.
$17.95; paper, $9.95.

*THE NAVAJOS
  Virginia Driving Hawk Sneve
The creation myth of the Navajos; history , cus-
toms, and facts about the tribe today . Grades 2-6.
Illus. 32 pp. Holiday House, 1993. $15.95.

THE NAVAJOS
  R. Underhill
Reprint of 1956 edition. Illus. 288 pp. Paper .
University of Oklahoma Press, $9.95.

THE NAVAJOS: A CRITICAL BIBLIOGRAPHY
  Peter Iverson
Paper. Indian University Press, 1976. $4.95.

THE NAVAJOS' LONG WALK FOR EDUCATION
  H. Thompson; Broderick Johnson, Editor
Illus. 248 pp. Navajo Community College Press,
1975. $15.

THE NAVAJOS & THE NEW DEAL
  Donald L. Parman
Illus. 320 pp. Yale University Press, 1976.
$37.50.

*NAYA NUKI: SHOSHONE GIRL WHO RAN
  Kenneth Thomasma; Eunice Hundley , Illus.
Indian lore, survival skills, and the W es before the
white man. Grades 4-9. Illus. Baker Book House,
$10.99; paper, $6.99.

**NCH'I-WANA "THE BIG RIVER" MID-
COLUMBIA INDIANS & THEIR LAND**
  Eugene S. Hunn
Illus. 384 pp. Paper . University of W ashington
Press, 1990. $19.95.

*NEEKNA & CHEMAI
  Jeanette Armstrong
Two little Okanagan girls teach about the seasonal
life patterns of the Okanagan Indian people.
Grades 2-8. Illus. paper. Theytus, 1991. $12.95.

**NEETS'AII GWIINDAII: LIVING
IN THE CHANDALAR COUNTRY**
  Katherine Peter
Illus. 108 pp. Paper . Alaska Native Language
Center, 1992. $12.

**NEGOTIATORS OF CHANGE: HISTORICAL
PERSPECTIVES ON NATIVE WOMEN**
  Nancy Shoemaker, Editor
Collection of articles on th history of women &
gender in American Indian societies. Illus. 320 pp.
Routledge, 1994. $59.95; paper , $17.95.

**NEGRO--INDIAN RELATIONSHIPS
IN THE SOUTHEAST**
  L. Foster
Reprint of 1935 edition. AMS Press, $14.50.

NEHALEM TILLAMOOK T ALES
  Melville Jacobs, et al, Editors
275 pp. Oregon State University Press, 1990.
$19.95; paper , $9.95.

**NEITHER WOLF NOR DOG: ON FORGOTTEN
ROADS WITH AN INDIAN ELDER**
  Kent Nerburn
A journey into the Native American experience.
224 pp. New W orld Library, 1994. $11.95.

**THE NELSON ISLAND ESKIMO: SOCIAL
STRUCTURE & RITUAL DISTRIBUTION**
  Norman Chance
Paper. Holt, Rinehart & W inston, 1966. $9.95.

**NEON POWWOW: NEW NATIVE
AMERICAN VOICES OF THE SOUTHWEST**
  Anna Lee W alters, Editor
Anthology of 34 selections of contemporary Southwest Native American poetry , short fiction and
playwriting. 130 pp. Paper . Northland Publishing,
1993. $12.95.

THE NETSILIK ESMIKO
  Asen Balikci
Revised edition. Illus. 264 pp. Paper .
Waveland, 1989. $9.50.

THE NETSILIK ESKIMOS
  Knud Rasmussen
Reprint of 1931 edition. AMS, $105.

NEVADA: A HISTORY OF CHANGES
  David Thompson
Includes a chapter on Indians. Illus. 232 pp.
Paper. The Grace Dangberg Foundation,
$17.50.

*NEVADA TRIBAL HISTORY & GOVERNMENT
  Yerington Paiute Tribe
Grades 7-12. An introductory social studies unit
about Nevada Tribes. Illus. 32 pp. Yerington
Paiute Tribe Publications, $5.

**NEVER IN ANGER: PORTRAIT
OF AN ESKIMO FAMILY**
  Jean L. Briggs
Illus. Paper. Harvard University Press, 1970.
$10.95.

**THE NEW AMERICAN STATE PAPERS:
INDIAN AFFAIRS, 1789-1860, SUBJECT SET ,
13 Volumes**
  Loring B. Priest, Editor
  Thomas C. Cochran, General Editor
Contains reports of the commissioners of Indian
Affairs, personal accounts of Indian life and
culture, etc. Facsimile reprint. Illus. Scholarly
Resources, $750 per set.

**NEW DEAL ADOBE: THE CIVILIAN CONSER-
VATION CORPS & THE RECONSTRUCTION
OF MISSION LA PURISIMA, 1934-1942**
  Christine Savage
Illus. 160 pp. Paper . Fithian Press, 1991. $9.95.

**THE NEW DEAL & AMERICAN INDIAN
TRIBALISM: THE ADMINISTRATION OF THE
INDIAN REORGANIZATION ACT, 1934-1945**
  Graham D. Taylor
210 pp. University of Nebraska Press, 1980.
$18.95.

**NEW DIRECTIONS IN
AMERICAN INDIAN HIST ORY**
  Colin Calloway, Editor
288 pp. Paper . University of Oklahoma Press,
1988. $14.95.

**NEW DIRECTIONS IN FEDERAL INDIAN
POLICY: A REVIEW OF AMERICAN INDIAN
POLICY REVIEW COMMISSION**
Collection of articles presented as papers at a
1978 conference sponsored by the American
Indian Studies Center , UCLA. 150 pp. Paper .
American Indian Studies Center , 1979. $10.

**NEW ECHOTA LETTERS: CONTRIBUTIONS
OF SAMUEL L. WORCESTER T O THE
CHEROKEE PHOENIX**
  Jack & Anna Kilpatrick, Editors
The Phoenix was the first newspaper printed in
part in an American Indian language. A white mis-
sionary, Worcester, writes of a crucial period in
Cherokee history . 136 pp. SMU Press, 1968.
$14.95.

THE NEW ENGLAND INDIANS
  C. Keith W ilbur, MD
Describes how New England's 18 major Indian
tribes actually lived. 400 Illus. Biblio. 1 10 pp.
Paper. Globe Piquot Press, 1978. $14.95.

NEW ENGLAND'S PROSPECT
  W. Wood; Alden T. Vaughan, Editor
Reprint of 1634 edition. Illus. 144 pp. Paper .
University of Massachusetts Press, $11.95.

**NEW HOPE FOR THE INDIANS: THE GRANT
PEACE POLICY & THE NAVAJOS IN THE
1870s**
  Norman Bender
Illus. 288 pp. University of New Mexico Press,
1990.

NEW HORIZONS IN AMERICAN INDIAN ART
Illus. 16 pp. Paper . Southwest Museum, 1976.
$2.00.

NEW INDIAN SKETCHES
  P.J. DeSmet
Reprint of 1904 edition. 146 pp.
Ye Galleon, $14.95.

NEW LIGHT ON CHACO CANYON
  David Grant Noble, Editor
Illus. 108 pp. Paper . School of American
Research, $11.95.

**NEW NATIVE AMERICAN DRAMA:
THREE PLAYS**
  Hanay Geiogamah, Editor
Illus. University of Oklahoma Press, 1980.
$14.95; paper , $7.95.

NEW & OLD VOICES OF W AH'KON-TAH
  Robert Dodge & Jos. McCullough
144 pp. Paper. International Publishers, 1985.
$4.95.

**A NEW ORIGINAL VERSION OF BOSCANA'S
HISTORICAL ACCOUNT OF THE SAN JUAN
CAPISTRANO INDIANS OF SOUTHERN
CALIFORNIA**
  G. Boscana & J. Harrington
Reprint of 1934 edition. Illus. AMS Press.

NEW PERSPECTIVES ON THE PUEBLOS
  A. Ortiz, Editor
Illus. 360 pp. Paper . U. of NM Press, 1970. $12.

NEW RELATION TO GASPESIA: WITH THE CUSTOMS & RELIGION OF THE GASPESIAN INDIAN
C. Le Clercq
Reprint of 1910 edition. Greenwood Press, $33.75.

THE NEW RESOURCE WARS: NATIVE & ENVIRONMENTAL STRUGGLE AGAINST MULTINATIONAL CORPORATIONS
Al Gedicks
Illus. 250 pp. South End Press, 1994. $15.

A NEW SERIES OF BLACKFOOT TEXTS
C.C. Uhlenbeck
Reprint of 1912 edition. AMS Press, $38.50.

NEW TRAILS IN MEXICO: AN ACCOUNT OF ONE YEAR'S EXPLORATION IN NORTH-WESTERN SONORA, MEXICO, & SOUTH-WESTERN ARIZONA, 1909-1910
Carl Lumholtz
An early look at the Papagos. Reprint of 1912 edition. 411 pp. Paper. University of Arizona Press, $18.95.

NEW VOICES FROM THE LONGHOUSE: AN ANTHOLOGY OF MODERN IROQUOIS LITERATURE
Joseph Bruchac
Greenfield Revue Press, 1988. $12.95.

NEW VOICES IN NATIVE AMERICAN LITERARY CRITICISM
Arnold Krupat, Editor
Smithsonian Institution Press, $79; paper, $34.95.

NEW WORLD ARCHAEOLOGY & CULTURE HISTORY: COLLECTED ESSAYS & ARTICLES
Gordon Willey
Illus. 450 pp. University of New Mexico Press, 1990. $39.95.

NEW WRITERS OF THE PURPLE SAGE
Russell Martin, Editor
Includes some Native American writers. 368 pp. Penguin USA, $11.

NEW YORK CITY IN INDIAN POSSESSION
Reginald P. Bolton
Second Edition. Illus. 170 pp. Paper. AMS & National Museum of the American Indian, 1975. $6.

NEWBERRY LIBRARY/CENTER FOR THE HISTORY OF AMERICAN INDIAN BIBLIO-GRAPHICAL SERIES
Francis Jennings
A series of bibliographies of Native American groups, geographic areas, and subjects. Indiana University Press, 1976-84.

NEWE NATEKWINAPPEH: SHOSHONI STORIES & DICTIONARY
W. Miller
Reprint of 1972 edition. AMS Press, $24.00.

***NEZ PERCE**
Kathi Howes
Grades 5-8. Illus. 32 pp. Rourke Corp., 1990. $9.95.

***THE NEZ PERCE**
Clifford E. Trafzer
Historical look at the Nez Perce. Grades 7 and up. Illus. Chelsea House Publishers, 1993. $7.95.

***THE NEZ PERCE**
Virginia Driving Hawk Sneve
The creation myth of the Nez Perce; their history, customs, and facts about the tribe today. Grades 4-6. Illus. 32 pp. Holiday House, 1994. $15.95; paper, $6.95.

***THE NEZ PERCE**
Alice Osinski
Grade K-4. Illus. 48 pp. Childrens Press, 1984. $11.45.

NEZ PERCE COUNTRY
223 pp. Paper. Nez Perce National Historical Park.

NEZ PERCE INDIANS
H.J. Spinden
Reprint of 1908 edition. Paper. Kraus, $13.00.

THE NEZ PERCE INDIANS & THE OPENING OF THE NORTHWEST
Alvin M. Josephy, Jr.
Abridged edition. Illus. 683 pp. Paper. University of Nebraska Press, 1979. $14.95.

NEZ PERCE JOSEPH
O. Howard
Reprint of 1881 edition. Illus. 274 pp. Da Capo Press, 1972. $32.50.

NEZ PERCE NARRATIVES
Aski Haruo & Deward Walker
Paper. University of California Press, 1989. $64.

***THE NEZ PERCE: NORTHWEST**
Peter Nabokov
Grades 5 and up. Illus. Chelsea House, 1989. $17.95.

NEZ PERCE TEXTS
Haruo Aoki
Paper. University of California Press, 1979. $25.

NEZ PERCE TEXTS
A. Phinney
Reprint of 1934 edition. AMS Press, $49.50.

NEZ PERCES: TRIBESMEN OF THE COLUMBIA PLATEAU
Francis Haines
Reprint of 1955 edition. Illus. Paper. University of Oklahoma Press, $13.95.

NI-KSO-KO-WA: BLACKFOOT SPIRITUAL-ITY, TRADITIONS, VALUES, & BELIEFS
Long Standing Bear Chief
Presents an overview of Blackfoot beliefs from a modern day viewpoint. Paper. Spirit Talk Press, 1992. $9.95.

NICOLAS POINT, S.J.: HIS LIFE & NORTH-WEST INDAIN CHRONICLES
Cornelius Buckley
356 pp. Loyola University Press, 1989. $15.95.

***NIGHT WALKER & THE BUFFALO**
Althea Bass
An old Southern Cheyenne warrior tells stories that relate the old ways to the new. Grades 5-9. 32 pp. Council for Indian Education, $8.95; paper, $2.95.

NIHANCAN'S FEAST OF BEAVER: ANIMAL TALES OF THE NORTH AMERICAN INDIANS
Edward Lavitt & Robert McDowell
Illus. 112 pp. Museum of New Mexico Press, 1990. $18.95; paper, $12.95.

THE NIGHT CHANT: A NAVAHO CEREMONIAL
W. Matthews
Reprint of 1902 edition. AMS Press, $70.

NIGHT FLYING WOMAN: AN OJIBWAY NARRATIVE
Ignatia Broker; illus. by Steven Premo
Life experiences of author's great-great grand-mother from the 1860s through the 1940s. Illus. 135 pp. Minnesota Historical Society, 1983. $12.95; paper, $7.50.

***NIGHTWALKER & THE BUFFALO**
Althea Bass
Grades 4-9. Paper. Council for Indian Education, 1972. $1.95.

NISQUALLY INDIAN ALLOTMENT ROLL 1887
Larry S. Watson, indexed & edited by
175 pp. Paper. Histree, 1994. $24.95.

NO MORE INDIANS
Ralph Taylor & Bearl Brooks
Grades 4-6. 24 pp. Workbook. ESP, Inc., $5.

NO MORE BUFFALO
Bob Scriver
Illus. 150 pp. Lowell Press, 1982. $35.

***NO ONE LIKE A BROTHER**
Hap Gilliland
Grades 4-12. 32 pp. Council for Indian Education, 1970. $8.95; paper, $2.95.

NO PLACE TO GO: EFFECTS OF COMPUL-SORY RELOCATION ON NAVAJOS
Thayer Scudder, et al
Illus. 208 pp. Institute for the Study of Human Issues, 1982. $19.95.

NO TURNING BACK: A HOPI INDIAN WOMAN'S STRUGGLE TO LIVE IN TWO WORLDS
Polingaysi Qoyawayma
187 pp. Paper. University of New Mexico Press, 1977. $10.95.

NOBLE RED MAN: LAKOTA WISDOMKEEPER MATHEW KING
Harvey Arden
Illus. 128 pp. Beyond Words Publishing, $16.95.

NOCCALULU: LEGEND, FACT & FUNCTION
Jeffrey R. Jones; Jerry Pogue & David Underhill, Editors
Illus. 72 pp. Jeffrey & Jones, 1989. $17.00; paper, $7.

THE NOME LACKEE INDIAN RESERVATION, 1854-1870
Donald L. Hislop
99 pp. Association for Northern California Records, 1978. $7.

NOOTKA AND QUILEUTE MUSIC
F. Densmore
Reprint of 1939 edition. Illus. 416 pp. Da Capo Press, $42.50.

***NORTH AMERICAN INDIAN**
Grades 4-6. Paper. Price Stern, $1.95

THE NORTH AMERICAN INDIAN
David Hurst Thomas, Editor
21-volume set reproducing over 375 articles in facsmilie. Garland Publishing.

THE NORTH AMERICAN INDIAN
Edward S. Curtis
20 vols. in 4 vols. describes Indians of the U.S. and Alaska. Reprint of 1907-1930 editions. Illus. 1,800 pp. Johnson Reprint, $85 each. Supplement/four volumes, $95 each.

NORTH AMERICAN INDIAN ALMANAC
Duane Cjampagne, Editor
Information on the civilization and culture of the indigenous peoples of the U.S. and Canada. Documentary excerpts, biographies, and 400 maps and illustrations. 800 pp. Gale Research, 1993. $95.

North American Indian Anthropology: Essays on Society & Culture
Raymond J. De Mallie & Alfonso Ortiz
Essay exploring the blending of structural & historical approaches to American Indian anthropology. Illus. Maps. 448 pp. University of Oklahoma Press, 1994. $32.95.

NORTH AMERICAN INDIAN ART
Peter T. and Jill L. Furst
Illus. 265 pp. Paper. Rizzoli International, 1982. $25.

NORTH AMERICAN INDIAN ARTIFACTS: A COLLECTOR'S ID & VALUE GUIDE
Lar Hothem
Revised 5th edition with 2,000 new photos and pricing. Illus. 512 pp. Paper. Hothem House, 1993. $22.95.

NORTH AMERICAN INDIAN ARTS: PRICES & AUCTIONS
Laurence & Maurine Smith
Annual. Arlist.

THE NORTH AMERICAN INDIAN, BEING A SERIES OF VOLUMES PICTURING & DESCRIBING THE INDIANS OF THE U.S. & ALASKA
Edward S. Curtis
20 Volumes. Reprint of 1907-1930 editions. Johnson Reprint, $1,800 per set; $85 each. Supplement in 4 vols., $95 each.

NORTH AMERICAN INDIAN BURIAL CUSTOMS
H.C. Yarrow; Monte Smith, Editor
Illus. 150 pp. Paper. Cherokee Publications, Eagle's View Publishing. $9.95.

THE NORTH AMERICAN INDIAN COLLECTION OF THE LOWE ART MUSEUM
intro. by Richard Conn
Illus. 158 pp. Paper. University of Washington Press, 1992. $24.95.

NORTH AMERICAN INDIAN DESIGNS
Caren Caraway
5 titles: *Eastern Woodland Indian Designs*, *Northwest Indian Designs*, *Plains Indian Designs*, *Southeastern Woodland Indian Designs*, and *Southwest American Indian Designs*. 50 pp. each. Paper. Stemmer House Publishers, $5.95 each.

261 NORTH AMERICAN INDIAN DESIGNS
Madeline Orban-Szontagh
Illus. 48 pp. Paper. Dover, $3.95.

NORTH AMERICAN INDIAN DESIGNS FOR ARTISTS & CRAFTSPEOPLE
Eva Wilson
128 pp. Paper. Dover, 1987. $6.95.

NORTH AMERICAN INDIAN LANDMARKS: A TRAVELER'S GUIDE
George Cantor
Explores more than 300 sites relevant to American Indian history and culture. Illus. 409 pp. Visible Ink Press, 1993. $34.95; paper, $17.95.

NORTH AMERICAN INDIAN LANGUAGE MATERIALS, 1890-1965
G. Edward Evans and Jeffrey Clark
An update of James C. Pilling's nine American Indian linguistic bibliographies published for the U.S. Bureau of Ethnology. 187 entries. 153 pp. Paper. American Indian Studies Center, 1979. $5.

NORTH AMERICAN INDIAN LIFE: CUSTOMS & TRADITIONS OF 23 TRIBES
Elsie Clews Parsons, Editor
27 fictionalized essays by noted anthropologists. Studies by Paul Rodin, Robert Lowie, Stewart Culin, Franz Boas, and Elsie Clews Parson. 480 pp. Paper. Dover, $10.95.

NORTH AMERICAN INDIAN LIVES
Nancy O. Lurie
Illus. 72 pp. Paper. Waveland Press, 1985. $6.95.

*NORTH AMERICAN INDIAN MASKS
Frieda Gates
Grades 5 and up. Illus. 64 pp. Walker & Co., 1982. $8.95.

*NORTH AMERICAN INDIAN MEDICINE PEOPLE
Karen Liptak
Grades 5-8. Illus. 65 pp. Franklin Watts, 1990. $11.90.

NORTH AMERICAN INDIAN MYTHOLOGY
Cottie Burland
Illus. 144 pp. Peter Bedrick Books, 1985. $19.95.

NORTH AMERICAN INDIAN POINTS
Books Americana
Illus. Second edition. 208 pp. Paper. Books Americana, 1984. $7.95.

THE NORTH AMERICAN INDIAN PORTFOLIOS FROM THE LIBRARY OF CONGRESS
Bodmer, Catlin, McKenney & Hall
Illus. 272 pp. Paper. Abbeville Press, $10.95.

*NORTH AMERICAN INDIAN STORIES
Gretchen Mayo
Grades 5 and up. 4 titles: Earthmaker's Tales, More Earthmaker's Tales, Star Tales & More Star Tales. Illus. 48 pp. each. Walker & Co., 1991. $5.95 each.

*NORTH AMERICAN INDIAN SURVIVAL SKILLS
Karen Liptak
Grades 5-8. Illus. 65 pp. Fraklin Watts, 1990. $11.90.

NORTH AMERICAN INDIAN TRADE SILVER
Carter
Study of the historic silver objects made for, and treasured by, the Indians. Illus. 256 pp. Paper. Hothem House, 1988. $18.95.

NORTH AMERICAN INDIAN TRAVEL GUIDE
Ralph & Lisa Shanks
U.S. & Canada's Indian & Eskimo events & places of interest. Over 100 tribal offices; over 900 places and events to visit. 5th Ed. Illus. 295 pp. Paper. Costano Books, 1993. $19.95.

NORTH AMERICAN INDIAN WARS - CD-ROM
In the process of being completed. Quanta Press.

NORTH AMERICAN INDIANS
Illus. 32 pp. Paper. Hancock House, $3.

NORTH AMERICAN INDIANS
George Catlin; Peter Mathiessen, Editor & intro by.
Collection of George Catlin's letters, and illustrated with 50 of his drawings. Reprint. 560 pp. Paper. Penguin USA, $11.

NORTH AMERICAN INDIANS
Paula Fleming & Judith Luskey
256 pp. Harper & Row, 1986. $34.50.

*NORTH AMERICAN INDIANS
Marie Gorsline and Douglas Gorsline
Preschool-2. Paper. Random House, 1978. $1.95.

NORTH AMERICAN INDIANS
Bill Yenne & Susan Garratt
Describes the culture and heritage of the indigenous people of America in nine different regions before and up to the arrival of the white man. Includes several short biographies. Maps. Illus. 192 pp. Hardcover. Cahill & Co., $16.

THE NORTH AMERICAN INDIANS: AN ACCOUNT OF THE AMERICAN INDIANS NORTH OF MEXICO
Rose Amelia Palmer, Editor
Compiled from original sources. Reprint of 1938 edition. 458 pp. Books on Demand, $123.70.

NORTH AMERICAN INDIANS BURIAL CUSTOMS
H.C. Yarrow; Monte Smith, Editor
Illus. 150 pp. Paper. Eagles View, 1988. $9.95.

NORTH AMERICAN INDIANS - CD-ROM
A database of text and image on the history of Native Americans. Includes information on leadership, tribal heritage, religion, family life, and customs. IBM compatible. Quanta Press, 1991. $69.95.

NORTH AMERICAN INDIANS COLORING ALBUM
Rite Warner, Illustrator
Illus. 32 pp. Paper. Troubador Press, 1978. $3.95.

NORTH AMERICAN INDIANS: A COMPREHENSIVE ACCOUNT
Alice B. Kehoe
Illus. 564 pp. Paper. Prentice-Hall, 1981. $20.95.

NORTH AMERICAN INDIANS: A DISSERTATION INDEX
University Microfilms International, 1976. $28.

NORTH AMERICAN INDIANS IN HISTORICAL PERSPECTIVE
Eleanor Burke Leacock & Nancy O. Lurie, Eds.
Illus. 498 pp. Paper. Waveland Press, 1988. $18.95.

*NORTH AMERICAN INDIANS OF ACHIEVEMENT
Dr. Frank W. Porter, III
Grades 4 and up. 22 titles. Includes Sitting Bull, Will Rogers, Jim Thorpe, Sarah Winnemucca, Joseph Brant, Quanah Parker, et al. Illus. 104-128 pp. each. Chelsea House, $12.95; paper, $7.95.

THE NORTH AMERICAN INDIANS: PHOTOGRAPHS BY EDWARD S. CURTIS
Edward S. Curtis
Illus. 96 pp. Aperture, 1972. $25.

THE NORTH AMERICANS OF YESTERDAY
F.S. Dellenbaugh
A comparative study of North American Indian life, customs and products, on the theory of the ethnic unity of the race. Reprint of 1901 edition. Gordon Press, $69.95.

NORTH COUNTRY CAPTIVES: SELECTED NARRATIVES OF INDIAN CAPTIVITY FROM VERMONT & NEW HAMPSHIRE
Colin G. Calloway
Eight narratives. 160 pp. Paper. University Press of New England, 1992. $15.95.

NORTH DAKOTA INDIANS: AN INTRODUCTION
Mary Schneider
275 pp. Paper. Kendall-Hunt, 1986. $19.95.

FRANK J. NORTH: PAWNEE SCOUT, COMMANDER AND PIONEER
Ruby E. Wilson
Illus. 335 pp. Ohio University Press, 1982. $19.95.

NORTH POLE LEGACY: BLACK, WHITE & ESKIMO
S. Allen Counter
Illus. 236 pp. University of Massachusetts Press, 1991. $24.95.

NORTH SLOPE INUPIAQ DIALOGUES
Edna MacLean
13 pp. Paper. Alaska Native Language Center, $2.50.

NORTHEAST
Bruce G. Trigger
Illus. 942 pp. Smithsonian, 1979. $27.

A NORTHEASTERN ALGONQUIAN SOURCEBOOK
Edward S. Rogers, Editor
364 pp. Garland Publishing, 1985. $50.

THE NORTHERN ALGONQUIAN SUPREME BEING
J.M. Cooper
Reprint of 1934 edition. AMS Press, $14.

NORTHERN ATHAPASKAN ART: A BEADWORK TRADITION
Kate Duncan
Illus. 272 pp. University of Washington Press, 1988. $45.

THE NORTHERN & CENTRAL NOOTKAN TRIBES
Philip Drucker
Reprint. Reprint Services, $75.

*NORTHERN CHEYENNE FIRE FIGHTERS
Henry Tall Bull & Tom Weist
Grades 4-adult. 39 pp. Council for Indian Education$9.95; paper, $3.95.

THE NORTHERN MAIDU
Marie Potts
Illus. Map. 48 pp. Naturegraph, 1977. $13.95; paper, $5.95.

THE NORTHERN MAIDU
R. Dixon
Reprint of 1905 edition. AMS Press, $31.50.

THE NORTHERN NAVAJO FRONTIER, 1860-1900: EXPANSION THROUGH ADVERSITY
Robert McPherson
Illus. 142 pp. University of New Mexico Press, 1988. $22.50.

THE NORTHERN PAIUTE INDIANS OF CALIFORNIA & NEVADA
R. Underhill
Reprint of 1941 edition. AMS Press, $14.

THE NORTHERN SHOSHONE
R. Lowie
Reprint of 1909 edition. AMS Press, $16.

NORTHERN TALES: TRADITIONAL STORIES OF ESKIMO & INDIAN PEOPLES
Howard Norman, Editor
370 pp. Pantheon Press, 1990. $24.95.

THE NORTHERN TRADITIONAL DANCER
C. Scott Evans & J. Rex Reddick
Illus. 50 pp. Paper. Reddick Enterprises, 1990. $9.95.

NORTHERN UTE MUSIC
F. Densmore
Reprint of 1922 edition. Illus. 236 pp. Da Capo Press, $27.50.

NORTHERN VOICES: INUIT WRITING IN ENGLISH
Penny Petrone
Illus. 330 pp. University of Toronto Press, 1988. $27.50.

WALTER NORTHWAY
Yvonne Yarber & Curt Madison, Editors
Della Northway, et al, trs
Illus. 55 pp. Paper. Alaska Native Language Center, 1987. $7.

NORTHWEST CHIEFS: GUSTAV SOHON'S VIEWS OF THE 1855 STEVENS TREATY COUNCILS
Paper. Washington State Historical Society, 1986. $9.50.

NORTHWEST COAST INDIAN ART: AN ANALYSIS OF FORM
Bill Holm
Illus. 133 pp. Paper. University of Washington Press, 1965. $14.95.

*THE NORTHWEST COAST INDIAN ART SERIES
Nan McNutt
Grades 3-6. Illus. 120 pp. Nan McNutt & Associates, 1991. $29.85.

NORTHWEST COAST INDIAN GRAPHICS: AN INTRODUCTION TO SILK SCREEN PRINTS
Edwin S. Hall, Jr., et al
Illus. 144 pp. University of Washington Press, 1981. $35.

NORTHWEST NATIVE HARVEST
Carol Batdorf
96 pp. Paper. Hancock House, 1990. $7.95.

NORTHWEST NEBRASKAS INDIAN PEOPLE
Dr. James A. Hanson
Scholarly story of 6 successive tribes in the region including the Kiowa and Apache. Illus. 48 pp. The Fur Press. $2.

NORTHWEST PASSAGE: THE GREAT COLUMBIA RIVER
Wiliam Dietrich
The settlers & Native American struggle over these lands. Maps. 432 pp. Simon & Schuster, 1995. $25.

NORTHWESTERN INDIAN IMAGES: A PHOTOGRAPHIC LOOK AT PLATEAU INDIANS
Richard Scheuerman
Illus. Paper. Sierra Oaks, 1989. $9.95.

THE NORTHWESTERN INDIAN TRIBES IN EXILE: MODOC, NEZ PERCE, & PALOUSE REMOVAL TO THE INDIAN TERRITORY
Clifford Trafzer
Illus. 137 pp. Paper. Sierra Oaks, 1987. $11.95.

NOT FOR INNOCENT EARS: SPIRITUAL TRADITIONS OF A DESERT CAHUILLA MEDICINE WOMAN
Ruby Modesto & Guy Mount
Ethnographic portrait of the spiritual beliefs, healing strategies, personal history & cultural heitage of a Desert Cahuila medicine woman & her people. Illus. 128 pp. Paper. Sweetlight, 1980. $9.95.

NOTABLE NATIVE AMERICANS
Sharon Malinowski, Editor
Biographies of about 275 notable Native Americans from all areas of endeavor, both past and present. 400 pp. Gale Research, 1995.

NOTEBOOK ON ART, HISTORY & CULTURE
Stephen Wallace, et al
80 pp. Navajo Curriculum Center Press.

NOTES FROM INDIAN COUNTRY
Tim Giago
Includes columns on communications, culture, education and athletics, government, health, humor, litigation, politics, religion, and people as observed by Giago. Greenfield Review Press, $10.

NOTES & OBSERVATIONS ON THE KWAKIOOL PEOPLE OF THE NORTHERN PART OF THE VANCOUVER ISLAND & ADJACENT COASTS, MADE DURING THE SUMMER OF 1885: WITH A VOCABULARY OF ABOUT 700 WORDS
George M. Dawson
37 pp. Paper. Ye Galleon Press, $4.95.

NOTES OF A TWENTY-FIVE YEARS' SERVICE IN THE HUDSON'S BAY TERRITORY
John McLean; W.S. Wallace, Editor
Reprint of 1932 edition. Greenwood Press, $29.50.

NOTES ON THE BUFFALO-HEAD DANCE OF THE BEAR GENS OF THE FOX INDIANS
Truman Michelson
Reprint of 1928 edition. Scholarly Press, $29.

NOTES ON THE CADDO
E. Parsons
Reprint of 1941 edition. Paper. Kraus, $20.

NOTES ON COCHITI, NEW MEXICO
Noel Dumarest
Reprint of 1919 edition. Paper . Kraus, $12.

NOTES ON THE EASTERN CREE & NORTHERN SALTEAUX
A.B. Skinner
Reprint of 191 1 edition. AMS Press, $15.50.

NOTES ON THE GYNECOLOGY AND OBSTETRICS OF THE ARIKARA TRIBE OF INDIANS
Melvin Gilmore
Paper. Acoma Books, 1980. $2.50.

NOTES ON HOPI ECONOMIC LIFE
E. Beaglehle
Reprin tof 1937 edition. AMS Press, $18.50.

NOTES ON IROQUOIS ARCHAEOLOGY
A.B. Skinner
Reprint of 1921 edition. AMS Press, $26.

NOTES ON SHOSHONEAN ETHNOGRAPHY
Frank Lockwood
Reprint of 1924 edition. AMS Press.

NOTES ON THE SOCIAL ORGANIZATION & CUSTOMS OF THE MANDAN, HIDATSA AND CROW INDIANS
R.H. Lowie
Reprint of 1917 edition. AMS Press, $13.45.

NOTES ON ZUNI
E.C. Parsons
Reprint of 1917 edition. 2 vols. Paper . Kraus, $12 each.

NOTICES OF EAST FLORIDA: WITH AN ACCOUNT OF THE SEMINOLE NATION OF INDIANS
W. Simmons; George Buker , Editor
Reprint of 1822 edition. 123 pp. University Press of Florida, $14.95.

NOTICIAS DE NUTKA: AN ACCOUNT OF NOOTKA SOUND IN 1792
Jose Mozino; Iris Engstrand, Editor
200 pp. Paper. University of Washington Press, 1991. $14.95.

NOW THAT THE BUFFALO'S GONE: A STUDY OF TODAYS AMERICAN INDIANS
Alvin M. Josephy
Illus. 334 pp. Paper . University of Oklahoma & AISES, 1984. $16.95.

NUDES & FOODS, VOLUME II
R.C. Gorman
A new collection of nudes, recipes, and anecdotes by Navajo artist, R.C. Gorman. Illus. 112 pp. Navajo Gallery , 1989. $20.

*A NUMU HISTORY-THE YERINGTON PAIUTE TRIBE
Michael Hittman
Grades 7-12. Illus. 68 pp. Paper . Yerington Paiute Tribe Publications, $12.50.

*THE NUMU WAY
Yerington Paiute Tribe
Grades 4 and up. Traditional arts, crafts, food, music, medicine, customs, clothing and games of the Yerington Paiute Tribe. 94 pp. Paper. Yerington Paiute Tribe Publications, $8. W orkbook, 71 pp., $10.

NUNAVUT ATLAS
Rick Riewe, Editor
The atlas assisted the Inuit in selecting the lands they retained after the settlement of the Nunavut claim. The relationship between Inuit & the natural environment. Illus. Maps. 259 pp. CCI, $15.

O

O BRAVE NEW WORDS: NATIVE AMERICAN LOANWORDS IN CURRENT ENGLISH
Charles L. Cutler
Covers more than one thousand North American Indian, Eskimo, and Aleut words in the English vocabulary. Surveys the thousands of Native American place-names in North America. Map. Biblio. 304 pp. University of Oklahoma Press, 1994. $24.95.

OBJECTS OF BRIGHT PRIDE: NORTHWEST COAST INDIAN ART FROM THE MUSEUM OF NATURAL HISTORY
Allen Wardwell
Second revised edition. Illus. 130 pp. Paper . University of Washington Press & American Federation of Arts, 1988. $30.

OBJECTS OF CHANGE: THE ARCHAEOLOGY & HISTORY OF ARIKARA CONTACT WITH EUROPEANS
J. Daniel Rogers
Illus. 336 pp. Smithsonian Press, 1990. $35.

OBJECTS OF MYTH & MEMORY: AMERICAN INDIAN ART AT THE BROOKLYN MUSEUM
Diana Fane, Ira Jacknis & Lise Breen
Illus. 320 pp. University of Washington Press, 1992. $60; paper, $29.95.

OBSERVATIONS OF THE ETHNOLOGY OF THE SAUK INDIANS
A.B. Skinner
Reprint of 1923-1925 edition. Illus. 180 pp. Greenwood Publishing, $35.

OBSERVATIONS ON THE INTELLECTUAL CULTURE OF THE CARIBOU ESKIMOS
Knud Rasmussen
Bound with Iglulik & Caribou Eskimo Texts. Reprint of 1930 edition. AMS Press.

OCCUPATION OF WOUNDED KNEE
Robert Hecht; Siguid C. Rahmas, Editor
32 pp. SamHar Press, 1982. $3.95; paper, $2.50.

OCEANIC, AMERICAN INDIAN, & AFRICAN MYTHS OF SNARING THE SUN
K. Luomala
Reprint of 1940 edition. Kraus, $12.

OCMULGEE ARCHAEOLOGY, 1936-1986
David J. Hally
Illus. Maps. 264 pp. University of Georgia Press, 1994. $40.

ODE SETL'OGHWNH DA': LONG AFTER I AM GONE
Teddy Charlie
Stories of traditional knowledge and skills by Tanana Athabaskan. Illus. Map. 30 pp. Alaska Native Language Center, 1992. $6.50

THE ODYSSEY OF CHIEF STANDING BUFFALO & THE NORTHERN SISSETON SIOUX
Mark Diedrich
Illus. 120 pp. Paper. Coyote Books (MN), 1988. $16.95.

OF THE CROW NATION
E. Denig; John Ewers, Editor
Reprint of 1953 edition. AMS Press, $14.50.

OF EARTH & LITTLE RAIN: PAPAGO INDIANS
Bernard L. Fontana
Illus. 170 pp. Paper. University of Arizona Press, 1981. $13.95

OF MOTHER EARTH & FATHER SKY
Fred Bia and T.L. McCarthy
Illus. 69 pp. Navajo Curriculum Center Press, 1983. $17; paper, $12.

OF VISION & VALOR: GENERAL OLIVER O. HOWARD - A BIOGRAPHY
Gerald Weland
Illus. 200 pp. Daring Books, 1991. $17.95.

OFFERING
Diane Glancy
Poetry. Commemorating Indian chief Sequoyah's achievement in absorbing and transforming a foreign language into his own native Cherokee. 88 pp. Paper. Holy Cow! Press, $6.95.

OFFERING SMOKE: THE SACRED PIPE & NATIVE AMERICAN RELIGION
Jordan Paper
Illus. 192 pp. Paper. University of Idaho Press, 1989. $22.95.

OFFICE OF INDIAN AFFAIRS, 1824-1880: HISTORICAL SKETCHES
Edward E. Hill
255 pp. N. Ross, 1974. $25.

OFFICE OF INDIAN AFFAIRS: ITS HISTORY, ACTIVITIES & ORGANIZATIONS
L.F. Schmeckebier
Reprint of 1927 edition. AMS Press, $37.50.

OGLALA LAKOTA CRAZY HORSE: A PRELIMINARY GENEALOGICAL STUDY & AN ANNOTATED LISTING OF PRIMARY SOURCES
Richard G. Hardorff
Illus. Amereon Ltd. $17.95; paper, $11.95.

OGLALA RELIGION
William Powers
Illus. 250 pp. Paper. University of Nebraska Press, 1977. $6.95.

OGLALA WOMEN: MYTH, RITUAL & REALITY
Marla N. Powers
Illus. 242 pp. University of Chicago Press, 1986. $24.95; paper, $12.95. Paper. Center for Western Studies, $12.95.

OHIYESA: CHARLES EASTMAN, SANTEE SIOUX
Raymond Wilson
Illus. 242 pp. U. of Illinois Press, 1983. $10.95.

THE OHLONE WAY: INDIAN LIFE IN THE SAN FRANCISCO & MONTEREY BAY AREAS
Malcolm Margolin
Illus. 182 pp. Paper. Heyday Books, 1978. $12.95.

OIL AGE ESKIMOS
Joseph Jorgensen
University of California Press, 1990. $42.50.

OIL & GAS
Institute for the Development of Indian Law, 1980. $12.

OJIBWA CRAFTS
Carrie A. Lyford
Reprint of 1943 edition. Illus. 216 pp.
Paper. R. Schneider, Publishers, $8.95.

*THE OJIBWA: GREAT LAKES
Helen H. Turner
Grades 5 and up. Illus. Chelsea House, 1989. $17.95.

OJIBWA SOCIOLOGY
R. Landes
Reprint of 1937 edition. AMS Press, $22.

OJIBWA TEXTS
W. Jones and T. Michelson, Editors
Reprint of 1917 edition. Two volumes.
AMS Press, $96.50.

OJIBWA WOMAN
R. Landes
Reprint of 1938 edition. AMS Press, $27.50.

THE OJIBWAS: A CRITICAL BIBLIOGRAPHY
Helen H. Tanner
88 pp. Paper. Indiana Univerity Press, 1976. $4.95.

OJIBWAY CEREMONIES
Basil Johnston; Illus. by David Beyer
Illus. 190 pp. Paper. University of Nebraska Press, 1990. $7.95.

THE OJIBWAY DREAM
Arthur Shilling
Illus. 48 pp. Tundra Books, 1986. $29.95.

OJIBWAY HERITAGE
Basil Johnston; Illus. by David Beyer
Illus. Map. 175 pp. Paper. University of Nebraska Press, 1990. $8.95.

*OJIBWAY INDIANS COLORING BOOK
Chet Kozlak
Grades 1-6. Map. 32 pp. Paper. Minnesota Historical Society Press, $2.50.

OJIBWAY MUSIC FROM MINNESOTA: A CENTURY OF SONG FOR VOICE & DRUM
Thomas Vennum, Jr.
LP record/cassette & booklet. Minnesota Historical Society, 1990. $9.95.

THE OJIBWAY OF WALPOLE ISLAND, ONTARIO: A LINGUISTIC STUDY
Nils M. Holmer
Reprint of 1953 edition. AMS Press, $18.

OJIBWAY ORATORY
compiled & illus. by Mark Diedrich
Illus. 110 pp. Paper. Coyote Books (MN), 1990. $16.95.

OJIBWAY TALES
Basil Johnston
Illus. 188 pp. Paper. University of Nebraska Press, 1993. $9.

OJIBWE LANGUAGE BOOK
Coy Eklund
Ojibwe/English translations and phrases. 272 pp. Indian Country Communications, $24.

OJIBWE VOCABULARY FOR BEGINNERS; INTERMEDIATE VOCABULARY; & VOCABU-LARY FOR ADVANCED LEARNERS
Ojibwe Mekana
Tape and booklet. Indian Country Communications, Beginners, $22; Intermediate Vocabulary, $21; Advanced Learners, $33.

OKANAGAN SOURCES
Jean Webber, Editor
Essays by First Nation authors providing historical accounts of Okanagan Valley. 206 pp. Paper. Theytus, 1990. $16.95.

OKANOGAN HIGHLAND ALBUM
Mary L. Loe, et al
Illus. 510 pp. Statesman-Examimer, 1990. $19.95.

*OKEMOS: STORY OF A FOX INDIAN OF HIS YOUTH
George Fox and Lela Puffer
Grades 3-9. Paper. Council for Indian Education, 1976. $1.95.

*OKLA APILACI: COMMUNITY HELPERS
Text in Choctaw with English translation.
All participants are Choctaw. Different professions on reservation are featured. Grades Preschool-3. 14 pp. Choctaw Heritage Press, $3.50.

OKLA HANNALI
R.A. Lafferty
The history of the Choctaw Indians. 240 pp. Paper. University of Oklahoma Press, $9.95.

OKLAHOMA DELAWARE CEREMONIES: FEASTS & DANCES
F.G. Speck
Reprint of 1937 edition. AMS Press, $21.50.

OKLAHOMA SEMINOLES: MEDICINES, MAGIC AND RELIGION
James H. Howard and Willie Lena
Illus. 300 pp. University of Olahoma Press, 1984. $19.95.

*O'KOHOME: THE COYOTE DOG
Hap Gilliland
Grades 4-9. Illus. 47 pp. Paper. Council for Indian Education, 1989. $10.45.

OKTOKAHEKAGAPI: (FIRST BEGINNINGS) SIOUX CREATION STORY
Thomas Simms
Presents the creation mystery legend in English & Lakota. Illus. 36 pp. paper. Center for Western Studies, $3.50.

OLD FATHER STORY TELLER
Pablita Velarde
6 legends from Santa Clara Pueblo. Illus. 56 pp. Clear Light Publishers, 1992. $24.95; paper, $14.95.

OLD FATHER'S LONG JOURNEY
Beulah Karney
Illus. 192 pp. Paper. CLC Press, 1985. $15.95; paper, $7.95.

OLD FORT KLAMATH: AN OREGON FRONTIER POST, 1863-1890
Buena Cobb Stone; Bert Webber, Editor
History of the the many military posts in the west over 100 years ago. Fort Klamath and its part in Modoc Indian War. Biblio. 112 pp. Paper. Webb Research Group, $10.95.

OLD FRONTIERS: THE STORY OF THE CHEROKEE INDIANS FROM THE EARLIEST TIMES TO THE DATE OF THEIR REMOVAL TO THE WEST, 1838
J.P. Brown
Reprint of 1838 edition. Illus. Ayer Co., $38.50.

OLD INDIAN DAYS
Charles A. Eastman
Stories of Sioux bands of the Upper Midwest in pre-reservation times. 300 pp. Paper. University of Nebraska, $8.95.

OLD INDIAN LEGENDS
Zitkala-Sa
Illus. 180 pp. Paper. University of Nebraska Press, 1985. $6.95.

OLD INDIAN TRAILS
Walter McClintock
Records the native customs, legends, religious rites, and daily life of the Blackfoot. Illus. 400 pp. Paper. Houghton & Mifflin, 1992. $10.95.

OLD LIGHT ON SEPARATE WAYS: THE NARRAGANSETT DIARY OF JOSEPH FISH, 1765-1776
Wiliam & Cheryl Simmons, Editors
Illus. 150 pp. University Press of New England, 1982. $22.50.

OLD MEXICAN, NAVAHO INDIANS: A NAVAHO AUTOBIOGRAPHY
Walter Dyk, Editor
Reprint of 1947 edition. Paper. Johnson Reprint, $19.

OLD NAVAJO RUGS: THEIR DEVELOPMENT FROM 1900-1940
Marian E. Rodee
Illus. 96 pp. Paper. University of New Mexico Press, 1981. $15.95.

THE OLD NORTH TRAIL: LIFE, LEGENDS & RELIGION OF THE BLACKFEET INDIANS
Walter McClintock
Illus. 540 pp. Paper. University of Nebraska Press, 1968. $14.95.

*THE OLD ONES: A CHILDREN'S BOOK ABOUT THE ANASAZI INDIANS
J. Brian & Jodi Freeman
Grades K-4. Illus. 65 pp. Paper. Think Shop, Inc., 1986. $2.95.

*THE OLD ONES TOLD ME: AMERICAN INDIAN STORIES FOR CHILDREN
Berry Keeper
Grades 4-6. Illus. 36 pp. Paper. Binfort & Mort, 1989. $4.95.

OLD ORAIBI
M. Titiev
A study of the Hopi Indians of Third Mesa. Reprint of 1944 edition. Illus. Paper. Kraus, $48.

OLIVER LA FARGE & THE AMERICAN INDIAN: A BIOGRAPHY
Robert A. Hecht
Illus. Photos. 400 pp. Scarecrow Press, 1991. $Cloth, $42.50; Paper, $25.

OMAHA & PONKA LETTERS
James Dorsey
Reprint of 1891 edition. Scholarly Press, $49.

OMAHA SECRET SOCIETIES
R. Fortune
Reprint of 1932 edition. AMS Press, $27.50.

OMAHA SOCIOLOGY
J. Dorsey
Reprint of 1884 edition. Johnson Reprint, $18.

THE OMAHA TRIBE
A. Fletcher and F. LaFlesche
Reprint of 1911 edition. Two vols. Illus. Musical examples. Vol. 1, 312 pp.; Vol. 2, 355 pp. Johnson Reprint, $50 per set. Paper. University of Nebraska Press, $12.95 each, $25.90 per set.

*OM-KAS-TOE: BLACKFEET TWIN CAPTURES & ELKDOG
Kenneth Thomasma; Jack Brouwer, Illus.
The Blackfeet tribe in the early 1700s. Grades 4 and up. Illus. Baker Book House, $10.99; paper, $6.99.

ON THE APACHE INDIAN RESERVATIONS & ARTIST WANDERINGS AMONG THE CHEYENNES
Frederic Remington
Reprint of 1974 edition. Illus. 36 pp. Paper. Filter Press, $2.50.

ON THE BORDER WITH CROOK
John G. Bourke
490 pp. Paper. University of Nebraska Press, 1971. $11.95.

*ON THE CLIFFS OF ACOME
John Dressman
Children's story for all ages outlining the history of the celebrated New Mexico cliffs. Illus. 48 pp. Paper. Sunstone Press, $5.95.

ON THE EDGE OF SPLENDOR: EXPLORING GRAND CANYON'S HUMAN PAST
Douglas W. Schwartz
Illus. 80 pp. Paper. School of American Research, $12.95.

ON THE GLEAMING WAY: NAVAJOS, EASTERN PUEBLOS, ZUNIS, HOPIS, APACHES & THEIR LAND, & THEIR MEANING TO THE WORLD
John Collier
Illus. 163 pp. Paper. Ohio University Press, 1962. $5.95.

ON THE LANDING
Michael W. Simpson
A book of poems by a young Indian poet. 49 pp. Paper. Indian University Press, 1986. $3.60, postpaid.

ON THE MUSIC OF THE NORTH AMERICAN INDIANS
Theodore Baker; Ann Buckley, Translator
Da Capo Press, 1977. $25.

ON OUR OWN GROUND: THE COMPLETE WRITINGS OF WILLIAM APESS, A PEQUOT
Barry O'Connell, Editor & intro.
An autobiography by a Native American in the early 1800s. 432 pp. University of Massachusetts Press, $50.00; paper, $16.95.

ON TIME FOR DISASTER: THE RESCUE OF CUSTER'S COMMAND
Edward J. McClernand
Illus. 176 pp. Paper. University of Nebraska Press, 1989. $6.95.

ON THE TRANSLATION OF NATIVE AMERICAN LITERATURES
Brian Swann, Editor
23 scholars in linguistics, folklore, English, and anthropology, provide a working introduction to the history, methods, and problems of translating Native American l;iteratures. Illus. 498 pp. Smithsonian Institution Press, 1993. $45; paper, $19.95.

ONCE THEY MOVED LIKE THE WIND: COCHISE, GERONIMO, & THE APACHE WARS
David Roberts
History of final battlkes of the Indian wars. Illus. 368 pp. Paper. Simon & Schuster. $14.

ONE HOUSE, ONE VOICE, ONE HEART: NATIVE AMERICAN EDUCATION AT THE SANTA FE INDIAN SCHOOL
Sally Hyer
Illus. 170 pp. Museum of New Mexico Press, 1990. $29.95; paper, $22.50.

ONE HUNDRED YEARS OF NATIVE AMERICAN ARTS: SIX WASHINGTON CULTURES
Delbert McBride; Penelope Loucas, Editor
Illus. 16 pp. Paper. Tacoma Art Museum, 1989. $1.

*ONE INDIAN & TWO CHIEFS
Ralph Salisbury
Grades 4 and up. Short stories. Navajo Community College Press, 1993. $14.95.

ONE MORE STORY: CONTEMPORARY SENECA TALES
Duwayne Bowen
Tales of the supernatural drawn from modern day Seneca life. Illus. Bowman Books, $9.95.

ONE OF THE KEYS: 1676-1776-1976: WAMPANOAG INDIAN CONTRIBUTION
Milton A. Travers
A list of words and definitions from the language of the historical Indians of southeastern Massachusetts. Illus. 64 pp. Christopher Publishing, 1975. $8.95.

ONE SMART INDIAN
Robert J. Seidman
Paper. Penguin USA, $13.95.

ONE THOUSAND USEFUL MOHAWK WORDS
Mohawk-English, English-Mohawk dictionary includes words, idioms, and expressions common in everyday speech. 158 pp. Audio-Forum, $9.95.

ONE THOUSAND YEARS ON MOUND KEY
R. Schell
Revised 1968 edition. Illus. Island Press, $3.95; paper, $1.95.

*THE ONEIDA
Grades K-4. Illus. 48 pp. Childrens Press, $11.45.

THE ONEIDA INDIAN EXPERIENCE
Jack Campisi & Laurence Hauptman
245 pp. Syracuse University Press, 1988. $29.95; paper, $14.95.

THE ONEIDA LAND CLAIMS: A LEGAL HISTORY
George Shattuck
290 pp. Syracuse University Press, 1991. $29.95; paper, $15.95.

ONEIDA VERB MORPHOLOGY
Floyd G. Lounsbury
111 pp. Paper. HRAF Press, 1976. $15.

ONEONTA STUDIES
Guy E. Gibbon and
Robert F. Spencer, Editors
122 pp. Paper. University of Minnesota, Department of Anthropology, 1983. $7.50.

THE ONLY LAND I KNOW: A HISTORY OF THE LUMBEE INDIANS OF NORTH CAROLINA
Adolph Dial and David Eliades
Illus. 240 pp. The Indian Historian Press, 1974. $9.75; paper, $6.00.

ONLY LAND THEY KNEW: THE TRAGIC STORY OF THE AMERICAN INDIANS IN THE OLD SOUTH
J. Leitch Wright, Jr.
Illus. 372 pp. Macmillan, 1981. $19.95. Paper. Free Press, $9.95.

*ONLY THE NAMES REMAIN: THE CHEROKEES & THE TRAIL OF TEARS
Alex Bealer
Grades 4-6. Little, Brown & Co., 1972. $14.95.

THE ONLY TRUE PEOPLE: A HISTORY OF THE NATIVE AMERICANS OF THE COLORADO PLATEAU
Kathleene Parker
Features brief histories of the Ute, Navajo, Jicarilla Apache, Paiute, Havasupai & Pueblo people. Illus. 96 pp. Paper. Thunder Mesa Publishing.

*THE ONONDAGA
Grades K-4. Illus. 48 pp. Childrens Press, $11.45.

ONONDAGA: PORTRAIT OF A NATIVE PEOPLE
Dennis Connors, Editor;
photos by Fred R. Wolcott
Collection of photographs & history of the Onondaga people. Illus. 120 pp. Paper. Syracuse University Press, 1985. $15.95.

*O'ODAM, INDIANS OF THE SONORAN DESERT
Susan Shaffer
Grade 5. Illus. Includes 30 student booklets and teacher's resource binder with overhead transparanecies, slides, and audiocasstte. The Heard Museum, 1992. $295.

OPENING IN THE SKY
Armand Garnet Ruffo
Poetry by an Ojibway person. Explores issues of identity, alienation, liberation, love and loss. Illus. 64 pp. Paper. Theytus, 1994. $9.95.

**ORAIBI MARAU CEREMONY - BRIEF
MISCELLANEOUS HOPI PAPERS**
H.R. Voth
Reprint of 1912 edition. Paper. Kraus, $48.

**ORAIBI SOYAL CEREMONY AND ORAIBI
POWAMU CEREMONY, AND MISHONGNOVI
CEREMONIES OF THE SNAKE AND ANTE-
LOPE FRATERNITIES AND ORAIBI SUMMER
SNAKE CEREMONY**
G.A. Dorsey and H.R. Voth
Reprint of 1901-1903 editions. 4r vols. in one.
Paper. Kraus Reprint, $77.

**ORAYVI REVISITED: SOCIAL STRATIFICA-
TION IN AN "EGALITARIAN" SOCIETY**
Jerrold E. Levy
Re-examination of the Orayvi village split of
1906. Illus. Maps. 216 pp. University of
Washington Press, $35.

**THE ORDEAL OF THE LONGHOUSE: THE
PEOPLES OF THE IROQUOIAN LEAGUE IN
THE ERA OF EUROPEAN COLONIZATION**
Daniel K. Richter
Illus. Maps. 580 pp. University of North Carolina
Press, 1993. $45; paper, $17.95.

The Ordeal of Running Standard
Thomas Fall
Dramatizes the dilemma of two young Indians,
Running Standing (Kiowa) and his Cheyenne
wife. 320 pp. Paper. University of Oklahoma
Press, $14.95.

**THE ORDERS OF THE DREAMED: GEORGE
NELSON ON CREE & NORTHERN OJIBWA
RELIGION & MYTH, 1823**
Jennifer Brown & Robert Brightman
Illus. Maps. 226 pp. Minnesota Historical
Society, 1988. $24.95.

**THE OREGON & CALIFORNIA TRAIL:
DIARY OF JANE GOULD IN 1862**
Bert Webber, Editor
Indian massacres. 92 pp. paper. Webb
Research Group, $7.50.

**OREGON INDIANS: CULTURE, HISTORY
& CURRENT AFFAIRS; AN ATLAS &
INTRODUCTION**
Jeff Zucker & Bob Hogfoss
Second edition. Illus. 192 pp. Paper. Oregon
Historical Society, 1988. $15.95.

OREGON TRAIL
F. Parkman; E.N. Feltskog, Editor
Reprint of 1964 edition. Illus. 854 pp. Paper.
Books on Demand, $160.

*OREGON TRAIL
F. Parkman
Grades 6-12. Paper. Airmont, 1964. $1.50;
New American Library, $3.50.

OREGON'S SALTY COAST
James A. Gibbs; with Bert Webber
Details of the Oregon coast from early explore,
from what they found to Indian encounters. In-
cludes all state parks and other places. Illus. Maps.
Biblio. Paper. Webb Research Group, $14.95.

**ORGANIZING THE LAKOTA: THE POLITICAL
ECONOMY OF THE NEW DEAL ON THE
PINE RIDGE & ROSEBUD RESERVATIONS**
Thomas Biolsi
245 pp. University of Arizona Press, 1992. $35.

**THE ORIGIN & DEVELOPMENT
OF THE PUEBLO KATSINA CULT**
E. Charles Adams
Examines the concept of the katsina and the reli-
gion that developed around it. 253 pp. University
of Arizona Press, 1991. $40; paper, $13.95.

**ORIGIN LEGEND OF THE
NAVAJO ENEMY WAY**
B. Haile
Reprint of 1938 edition. 328 pp. AMS Press,
$37.50.

ORIGIN LEGEND OF THE NAVAJO FLINTWAY
G.B. Grinnell
Reprint of 1943 edition. AMS Press, $49.50.

ORIGIN OF ANCIENT AMERICAN CULTURES
Paul Shao
Illus. 375 pp. Iowa State U. Press, 1983. $42.75.

**ORIGINAL JOURNALS OF THE
LEWIS & CLARK EXPEDITION**
Reuben Thwaites, Editor
Reprint of 1904 edition. 8 volumes. Ayer Co.,
$224. per set.

**THE ORIGINAL VERMONTERS: NATIVE
INHABITANTS, PAST & PRESENT**
Wm. A. Haviland & Marjory W. Power
Revised 1994 ed. Illus. 340 pp. Paper.
University Press of New England. $22.50.

ORIGINS OF PRE-COLUMBIAN ART
Terence Grieder
Illus. 250 pp. University of Texas Press, 1982.
$19.95.

**THE ORIGINS OF SOUTHWESTERN
AGRICULTURE**
R.G. Matson
356 pp. University of Arizona Press, 1991. $60.

**ORNAMENTAL ARTIFACTS OF THE NORTH
AMERICAN INDIAN: IDENTIFICATION &
VALUE GUIDE**
Hothan
Illus. 256 pp. Paper. Hothem House, 1991.
$19.95.

ORNAMENTAL & CEREMONIAL ARTIFACTS
Lar Hothem
Covers many classes of higher-grade and top-
quality artifacts. Illus. 133 pp. Paper. Hothem
House, 1990. $19.95.

*THE OSAGE
Terry P. Wilson
Grades 5 and up. Illus. 104 pp. Chelsea House,
1988. $17.95.

**THE OSAGE CEREMONIAL
DANCE I'N-LON-SCHKA**
Alice A. Callahan
Illus. Maps. 12 music examples. 192 pp. Paper.
University of Oklahoma Press, 1990. $10.95.

**THE OSAGE: CHILDREN
OF THE MIDDLE WATERS**
John Joseph Matthews
An account of the Sioux Osage tribe from the
oral history of his people in the period before the
coming of the Europeans to the recorded history
since, and his own life among them. Reprint of
1961 edition. Illus. 854 pp. Paper. University of
Oklahoma Press, $19.95.

OSAGE INDIAN CUSTOMS & MYTHS
Louis F. Burns
Illus. 240 pp. Ciga Press & The Osage Mission,
1984. $20.

OSAGE INDIANS: BANDS & CLANS
Louis F. Burns
196 pp. Ciga Press & The Osage Mission, 1984.
$20.

**OSAGE LIFE & LEGENDS:
EARTH PEOPLE - SKY PEOPLE**
Robert Liebert
History of the Osage Tribe. Illus. 144 pp.
Naturegraph, 1987. $16.95; paper, $8.95.

**OSAGE MISSION BAPTISMS, MARRIAGES,
& INTERMENTS, 1820-1886**
Louis Burns, Editor
870 pp. Ciga Press & The Osage Mission, 1986.
$35.

**THE OSAGES, DOMINANT POWER
OF LOUISIANA TERRITORY**
Wallace T. Talbott
96 pp. Carlton Press, 1989. $8.95.

**OTHER DESTINIES: UNDERSTANDING
THE AMERICAN INDIAN NOVEL**
Louis Owens
Critical analysis of novels written between 1854
and today by American Indian authors. Traces how
ten Native American authors have come to terms
with discovering their identity in contemporary
America. Biblio. 304 pp. Paper. University of Oklahoma Press, 1992. $12.95.

OTHER MEN'S SKIES
Robert M. Bunker
Reprint of 1956 edition. Kraus, $26.

THE OTHER SIDE OF NOWHERE
Peter Blue Cloud
Collection of mythic and rythmic coyote stories.
Illus. Greenfield Review Press, $10.

OTO
W. Whitman
Reprint of 1937 edition. AMS Press, $22.

**OTTAWA & CHIPPEWA INDIANS
OF MICHIGAN, 1870-1909**
Raymond C. Lantz
Three censuses taken by the BIA. 288 pp.
Heritage Books, 1991. $21.

**OUR CHIEFS & ELDERS: WORDS &
PHOTOGRAPHS OF NATIVE LEADERS**
David Neel
Series of portraits of Native American chiefs & el-
ders. Illus. 64 duotone photos. 192 pp. University
of Washington Press, $29.95.

OUR FRIENDS: THE NAVAJO
Ruth Roessel, Editor
Formerly *Papers on Navajo Life & Culture*. Illus.
Paper. Navajo Community College Press, 1976.
$8.

**OUR HOME FOREVER: THE HUPA
INDIANS OF NORTHERN CALIFORNIA**
Bryon Nelson
Illus. 225 pp. Paper. Howe Brothers, 1988. $9.95.

OUR INDIAN WARDS
  G.W. Manypenny
Reprint of 1880 edition. Da Capo Press, $35.

OUR LIVES IN OUR HANDS: MICMAC INDIAN BASKETMAKERS
  Bunny McBridge
Illus. 96 pp. Paper. Tilbury House, 1991. $10.95.

OUR RED BROTHERS & THE PEACE POLICY OF PRESIDENT ULYSSES S. GRANT
  Lawrie Tatum
Illus. 375 pp. University of Nebraska Press, 1970. $28.95.

OUR STORIES, OUR LIVES
  CIRI Foundation
Collection of personal experiences & traditional stories told by 23 Alaska Native elders--Eskimos, Indians & Aleuts of the Cook Inley region. Illus. 245 pp. Paper. CIRI, $15.95.

OUR VOICES, OUR LAND
  Stephen Trimble, Editor
Illus. 176 pp. Northland, 1988. $35.

OUR VOICES, OUR VISION
  AISES teachers
American Indians speak out for educational excellence. 10 pp. Paper. AISES, $3.

OUR WESTERN BORDER, ITS LIFE, COMBATS, ADVENTURES, FORAYS, MASSCRES, CAPTIVITIES, SCOUTS, RED CHIEFS, PIONEERS, WOMEN: 100 YEARS AGO, CAREFULLY WRITTEN & COMPILED
  C. Knight
Reprint of 1876 edition. Illus. Johnson Reprint, $50.

OUR WILD INDIANS: 33 YEARS PERSONAL EXPERIENCE AMONG THE RED MEN OF THE GREAT WEST
  R.I. Dodge
Reprint of 1883 edition. 657 pp. Ayer Co., $55.

OUR VOICES, OUR LAND
  Stephen Tribmle, Editor
Photographic collection shows Native Americans in various settings. Illus. 176 pp. Northland Publishing, $19.95.

OURAY - CHIEF OF THE UTES
  P. David Smith
Illus. 220 pp. Paper. Wayfinder Press, 1986. $9.95.

OUT OF THE NORTH: THE SUBARCTIC COLLECTION OF THE HAFFENREFFER MUSEUM OF ANTHROPOLOGY, BROWN UNIVERSITY
  Barbara Hail & Kate Duncan
Shows about 185 pieces made by Cree, Ojibwa, and Athapascan peoples, with historical & interpretive essays. Illus. 291 bxw photos. 301 pp. Paper. University of Washington Press, $25.

OUTCROPPINGS FROM NAVAJOLAND
  David Levering
Poems. Navajo Commuity College Press, $5.

AN OUTLINE OF BASIC VERB INFLECTIONS OF OKLAHOMA CHEROKEE
  Charles D. Van Tuyl
79 pp. Paper. Indian University Press, 1994. $15.50, postpaid.

AN OUTLINE OF SENECA CEREMONIES AT COLDSPRING LONGHOUSE
  William N. Fenton
Bound with: The Shawnee Female Deity, by C.F. Voegelin; Human Wolves Among the Navaho, by William Morgan; Musical Areas in Aboriginal North America, by Helen H. Roberts; and Rank & Potlatch Among the Haida, by George P. Murdock. Reprint of 1936 edition. HRAF Press, $15.

AN OUTLINE OF THE DOCUMENTARY HISTORY OF THE ZUNI TRIBE: SOMATOLOGICAL OBSERVATIONS OF INDIANS OF THE SOUTHWEST
  A.F. Bandelier and H.F. Ten Kate
Reprint of 1892 edition. AMS Press, $25.

OVERCOMIG OBSTACLES & IMPROVING OUTCOMES: EARLY INTERVENTION SERVICES FOR INDIAN CHILDREN WITH SPECIAL NEEDS
Southwest Communication Resources, $10.

OVERLAND TO STARVATION COVE: WITH THE INUIT IN SEARCH OF FRANKLIN, 1878-1880
  Heinrich Klutschak; William Barr, Editor & tr.
Illus. University of Toronto Press, 1987. $30.

*OWL IN THE CEDAR TREE
  N. Scott Momaday; illus. by Don Perceval
Details of Navaho culture and religious beliefs, and the conflict between traditional and contemporary ways. Grades 4-8. Illus. 125 pp. Paper. University of Nebraksa Press, 1992. $9.95.

OYATE CATALOG
Bibliography of books for grades K-12. Includes evaluation of texts, resource materials and fiction; as well as distribution of children's books, with an emphasis on writing and illustration by Native people. 20 pp. Oyate.

OZARK BLUFF-DWELLERS
  Mark R. Harrington
Reprint of 1960 edition.Illus. 185 pp. Paper. National Museum of the American Indian, $5.

P

*PACHEE GOYO: HISTORY & LEGENDS FROM THE SHOSHONE
  Rupert Weeks
Paper. Jelm Mountain Publications, 1981. $6.

*PACIFIC COAST INDIANS OF NORTH AMERICA
  Grant Lyons
Grades 3 and up. Illus. 96 pp. Julian Messner, 1983. $9.29.

PACIFIC NORTHWEST AMERICANA
  Charles W. Smith, Editor
Bibliography of 11,000+ books, pamphlets, newspapers, speeches & historical documents relating to the history of the Pacific Northwest. Also a listing of libraries. Reprint of 1950 edition. 392 pp. Paper. Supplement, 1949-74 by R.E. Moore & N.H. Purcell, Eds. Binford & Mort, $20 each.

THE PACIFIC NORTHWEST: ITS DISCOVERY & EARLY EXPLORATION BY SEA, LAND, & RIVER
  Edward W. Nuffield
288 pp. Paper. Hancock House, $16.95.

PACIFYING THE PLAINS: GENERAL ALFRED TERRY & THE DECLINE OF THE SIOUX, 1866-1890
  John Bailey
Greenwood Press, 1979. $35.

PAGES FROM HOPI HISTORY
  Harry C. James
An authentic account of the Hopi way of life. 258 pp. Paper. U. of Arizona Press, 1974. $14.95.

PAI KA LEO
A collection of Hawaiian songs for children performed by six Hawaiian professional musicians. Cassette. 40 pp. The Bess Press, $11.95.

PAINTBRUSHES & PISTOLS: HOW THE TAOS ARTISTS SOLD THE WEST
  Sherry Clayton-Taggett & Ted Schwartz
Illus. 288 pp. Paper. John Muir, 1990. $17.95

PAINTED TIPIS BY CONTEMPORARY PLAINS INDIAN ARTISTS
Explores the esthetic qualities and significance of 12 painted tipi covers specially created in 1972-73 by contemporary Plains Indian artists. Illus. Map. 80 pp. Oklahoma Indian Arts & Crafts Cooperative, $8, postpaid.

PAINTING IN THE NORTH: ALASKAN ART IN THE ANCHORAGE MUSEUM OF HISTORY & ART
University of Washington Press, 1993.

THE PAIUTE, INDIANS OF NORTH AMERICA
  Pamela Bunte & Robert Franklin
350 pp. U. of Nebraska Press, 1989. $22.95.

PAIUTE SORCERY
  B. Whiting
Reprint of 1950 edition. Paper. Johnson Reprint, $19.

*THE PAIUTE: SOUTHWEST
Pamela Bunte & Robert Franklin
Grades 5 and up. Illus. Chelsea House, 1989. $17.95.

A PALEO-INDIAN SITE IN EASTERN PENNSYLVANIA: AN EARLY HUNTING CULTURE
  John Witthoft
Facsimile of the 1952 edition. Illus. 32 pp. Paper. Persimmon Press, $4.95.

THE PAMUNKEY INDIANS OF VIRGINIA
  Garland Pollard
Reprint of 1894 edition. Reprint Services, $49.

A PAPAGO CALENDAR RECORD
  Ruth Underhill
Reprint of 1938 edition. Paper. Kraus & AMS Press, $15.

A PAPAGO GRAMMAR
  Ofelia Zepeda
190 pp. Paper. University of Arizona Press, 1983. $15.95.

PAPAGO INDIAN POTTERY
Bernard Fontana, et al.
Reprint of 1962 edition. AMS, $32.50.

PAPAGO INDIAN RELIGION
Ruth Underhill
Reprint of 1946 edition. AMS Press, $37.50.

PAPAGO INDIANS AT WORK
Jack Waddell
Illus. 160 pp. Paper. University of Arizona
Press, 1969. $14.25.

**THE PAPAGO INDIANS OF ARIZONA &
THEIR RELATIVES THE PIMA**
Ruth Underhill
Reprint of 1940 edition. AMS Press, $16.50.

PAPAGO MUSIC
F. Densmore
Reprint of 1929 edition. Illus. 276 pp. Da Capo
Press, $27.50.

THE PAPAGO & PIMA INDIANS OF ARIZONA
Ruth Underhill
Illus. 64 pp. Paper. Filter Press, 1979. $2.50.

**PAPAGO/PIMA TO ENGLISH, ENGLISH
TO PAPAGO/PIMA DICTIONARY**
Dean & Lucille Saxton, et al
5,000+ entries, plus appendixes on culture. 2nd
edition. 145 pp. University of Arizona Press, 1983.
$17.95.

**A PAPAGO TRAVELER: THE
MEMORIES OF JAMES McCARTHY**
James McCarthy; John Westover, Editor
200 pp. Paper. University of Arizona Press,
1985. $12.95.

**PAPER MEDICINE MAN: JOHN GREGORY
BOURKE & HIS AMERICAN WEST**
Joseph C. Porter
Illus. 352 pp. University of Oklahoma Press,
1986. $29.95.

**THE PAPERS OF JOHN PEABODY
HARRINGTON IN THE SMITHSONIAN INSTITU-
TION, 1907-1957: PART 3, SOUTHERN CALI-
FORNIA-BASIN; & PART 4: SOUTHWEST**
Elaine L. Mills
Microfilm and guidebook for each part. Kraus,
1986. Part 3, $8,800; Part 4, $2,610.

**THE PAPERS OF PANTON, LESLIE & CO.:
GUIDE TO THE MICROFILM COLLECTION**
Documents trading activities with the Cherokee,
Chickasaw, Choctaw and Creek Nations. Over
8,000 documents on 26 reels. 764 pp. Research
Publications International, $2,700.00.

**A PARENT'S GUIDE TO THE BIA
SPECIAL EDUCATION PROCESS**
Handbook for parent's rights. Southwest
Commuication Resources, $5.00.

CYNTHIA ANN PARKER: INDIAN CAPTIVE
Catherine T. Gonzales
Eakin Publications, 1980. $6.95.

**CYNTHIA ANN PARKER:
THE LIFE & LEGEND**
Margaret S. Hacker
Recounts her experiences a s a captive of the
Comanches (1836-60). Illus. Biblio. Paper. Texas
Western Press, 1990. $12.50.

PARKER ON THE IROQUOIS
Arthur Parker; William Fenton, Editor
Bound with The Code of Handsome Lake, the
Seneca prophet; The Constitution of the Five Na-
tions; and, Iroquois Uses of Maize and Other Food
Plants. Illus. 530 pp. Paper. Syracuse University
Press, 1968. $15.95.

**PARTIAL RECALL: PHOTOGRAPHS
OF NATIVE NORTH AMERICANS**
Lucy R. Lippard, Editor
Explorations by 12 Native American artists and
writers into the images that have shaped our ideas
of "Indianness," and the complex relationship of
photopgraphy to identity. Illus. 100 photos. 200
pp. Paper. W.W. Norton & Co., 1992. $35.00.

**A PARTICUAR HISTORY OF THE FIVE YEARS
FRENCH & INDIANS WARS IN NEW ENGLAND
& PARTS ADJACENT**
Samuel G. Drake
Reprint of 1870 edition. Ayer Co., $19.

**PARTNERS IN FURS: A HISTORY OF THE FUR
TRADE IN EASTERN JAMES BAY, 1600-1870**
Daniel Francis & Toby Morantz
Illus. 205 pp. Paper. University of Toronto Press,
1982. $17.95.

PASCUA: A YAQUI VILLAGE IN ARIZONA
Edward H. Spicer
Reprint of 1940 edition. Illus. 325 pp. Paper.
University of Arizona Press, 1984. $15.95.

**PASQUALA: THE STORY OF A CALIFORNIA
INDIAN GIRL**
Gail Faber & Michele Lasagna
Grades 4-8. Illus. 95 pp. Magpie Publications,
1990. $12.95; paper, $9.95.

PASSAMAQUODDY DICTIONARY
Passamaquoddy-English, English-
Passamaquoddy. 184 pp. $14.95. A.

PASSAMAQUODDY TEXTS
J.D. Price
Reprint of 1921 edition. AMS Press, $19.00.

THE PASTOR'S\HANDBOOK
Jack Dunigan
Paper. Life Lines, 1985. $6.95.

THE PATH OF POWER
Sun Bear, Wabun & Barry Weinstock
The life story of Sun Bear, medicine teacher of
the Ojibwa and founder of the Bear Tribe
Medicine Society. Illus. 270 pp. Paper.
Cherokee Publications, $9.95.

PATHFINDERS OF THE WEST
Agnes C. Laut
Reprint of 1904 edition. Ayer Co., $27.50.

***PATHKI NANA: KOOTENAI G
IRL SOLVES A MYSTERY**
Kenneth Thomasma; Jack Brouwer, Illus.
Grades 4-8. Illus. Baker Book House, $10.99;
paper, $6.99.

**PATHS OF THE PEOPLE: THE
OJIBWE IN THE CHIPPEWA VALLEY**
Tim Pfaff
Illus. Maps. 100 pp. Paper. University of
Washington Press, 1992. $12.95.

**PATHWAYS TO SELF-DETERMINATION:
CANADIAN INDIANS & THE CANADIAN STATE**
Leroy Little Bear, et al, Editors
192 pp. Paper. University of Toronto Press,
1984. $12.95.

***PATRICK DES JARLAIT: CONVERSATIONS
WITH A NATIVE AMERICAN ARTIST**
Neva Williams, Editor
Includes photos of his paintings. Grades 5 and
up. Illus. 56 pp. Lerner, 1995. $21.50.

**THE PATRIOT CHIEFS: A CHRONICLE
OF AMERICAN INDIAN RESISTANCE**
Alvin M. Josephy, Jr.
Indian resistance to the white man through the
stories of nine outstanding leaders. 384 pp. Pa-
per. Penguin USA, $9.95.

PATTERNS OF CULTURE
Ruth Benedict
Reprint of 1961 edition. Paper. Houghton-Mifflin,
$8.70.

**PATTERNS OF LIFE, PATTERNS OF ART: THE
RAHR COLLECTIONS OF NATIVE AMERICAN
ART - HOOD MUSEUM OF ART, DARTMOUTH
COLLEGE**
Gregory Schwarz & Barbara Hail
Illus. 80 pp. Paper. University Press of New
England, 1987. $19.95.

**PATTERNS & SOURCES
OF NAVAJO WEAVING**
W.D. Harmsen
Revised edition. Illus. Harmsen Publishing, 1978.

*THE PAWNEE
Dennis B. Fradin
Grades K-4. Illus. 50 pp. Childrens Press,
$13.27; paper, $3.95.

**THE PAWNEE GHOST DANCE HAND GAME:
GHOST DANCE REVIVAL & ETHNIC IDENTITY**
A. Lesser
Reprint of 1933 edition. Illus. 468 pp. AMS
Press, $37.00. University of Wisconsin, $22.00;
paper, $8.95.

**PAWNEE HERO STORIES & FOLKTALES
WITH NOTES ON THE ORIGIN, CUSTOMS &
CHARACTER OF THE PAWNEE PEOPLE**
George Grinnell
Reprint of 1961 edition. Illus. 425 pp. University
of Nebraska Press, $35.00.

THE PAWNEE INDIANS
George E. Hyde
Illus. 384 pp. University of Oklahoma Press,
1974. $12.95.

PAWNEE & LOWER LOUP POTTERY
Rogert Grange, Jr.
Volume 3. Paper. Nebraska State Historical
Society, 1968. $6.00.

PAWNEE MUSIC
F. Densmore
Reprint of 1929 edition. 160 pp.
Da Capo Press, $21.50.

PAWNEE PASSAGE: 1870-1875
Martha Blaine
Illus. 352 pp. University of Oklahoma Press,
1990. $27.95.

PAWNEES: A CRITICAL BIBLIOGRAPHY
Martha P. Blaine
Illus. 128 pp. Paper. Indiana University Press, 1981. $4.95.

THE PEACE CHIEFS OF THE CHEYENNES
Stan Hoig
Illus. University of Oklahoma Press, 1980. $17.95.

PEACE WITH THE APACHES OF NEW MEXICO & ARIZONA
V. Colyer
Facsimile of 1872 edition. Ayer Co., $12.

PECOS RUINS: GEOLOGY, ARCHAEOLOGY, HISTORY, AND PREHISTORY
David Grant Noble
Describes the development of Pecos Pueblo from prehistoric times to the Anglo period of 19th century. Illus. Maps. 32 pp. Paper. Ancient City Press, 1990. $6.95.

PELE: THE FIRE GODDESS
as told by Dietrich Varez
The ancient myth of Pele. Illus. Bishop Museum, $12.95.

PELTS, PLUMES & HIDES: WHITE TRADERS AMONG THE SEMINOLE INDIANS, 1870-1930
Harry Kersey, Jr.
Reprint of 1975 edition. Illus. Map. Biblio. 158 pp. Paper. University Press of Florida, $14.95.

PENHALLOW'S INDIAN WARS
E. Wheelock, Editor
Reprint of 1924 edition. Ayer Co., $20.

PENITENTE SELF-GOVERNMENT: BROTHERHOODS & COUNCILS, 1797-1947
Thomas Steele & Rowena Rivera
Illus. 210 pp. Ancient City Press, 1985. $29.95; paper, $12.95.

*WILLIAM PENN'S OWN ACCOUNT OF LENNI LENAPE OR DELAWARE INDIANS
Albert C. Myers, Editor
Grades 7 and up. Illus. 96 pp. Paper. Mid Atlantic Press, 1986. $7.95.

PENNSYLVANIA'S INDIAN RELATIONS TO 1754
S.P. Uhler
Reprint of 1951 edition. AMS Press, $22.50.

*THE PENOBSCOT
Jill Duvall
Grades K-3. Illus. Childrens Press, 1993.

PENOBSCOT SHAMANISM
F.G. Speck
Reprint of 1919 edition. Paper. Kraus, $28.00.

THE PEOPLE CALLED APACHE
Thomas Mails
Reprint. Illus. Center for Western Studies, $150.

PEOPLE FROM OUR SIDE: A LIFE STORY WITH PHOTOGRAPHS & ORAL BIOGRAPHY
Peter Pitseolak & Dorothy Harley Eber
During his lifetime, Inuit photographer Peter Pitseolak witnessed the arrival of missionaries, fur traders, law, government, and alcohol in the eastern Canadian Arctic. Reprint of 1975 edition. Illus. University of Toronto Press, $39.95; paper, $19.95.

THE PEOPLE: INDIANS OF THE AMERICAN SOUTHWEST
Stephen Trimble, words & illus.
Introduction to the native peoples of the American Southwest. Illus. Maps. 536 pp. Paper. University of Washington Press & School of American Research, 1994. $29.95.

THE PEOPLE NAMED THE CHIPPEWA: NARRATIVE HISTORIES
Gerald Vizenor
History of the Chippewa experience based on memoirs, court records, and the oral tradition of the Anishinaabe. Illus. Map. 175 pp. Paper. University of Minnesota Press, 1984. $12.95.

THE PEOPLE: NATIVE AMERICAN THOUGHTS & FEELINGS
Illus. 64 pp. Paper. The Book Pubg. Co., $5.95.

PEOPLE OF THE BLUE WATER: A RECORD OF LIFE AMONG THE WALAPAI & HAVASUPAI INDIANS
Flora G. Iliff
Reprint of 1954 edition. Paper. University of Arizona Press. $13.95.

*THE PEOPLE OF THE BREAKING DAY
Marcia Sewall
Grades 1-8. Illus. Macmillan, 1989. $14.95.

*PEOPLE OF THE BUFFALO
Maria Campbell
Grades 5 and up. Paper. Salem House, $6.95.

PEOPLE OF THE CRIMSON EVENING
Ruth Underhill
Papago life of long ago. Illus. 64 pp. Paper. Filter Press, $3.

PEOPLE OF THE DESERT & SEA: ETHNO-BOTANY OF THE SERI INDIANS
Richard Felger & Mary Moser
Illus. 435 pp. Paper. University of Arizona Press, 1984. $35.

PEOPLE OF THE HIGH COUNTRY: JACKSON HOLE BEFORE THE SETTLERS
Gary Wright
Illus. 191 pp. Paper. Peter Lang Publishing, 1984. $20.

*PEOPLE OF THE ICE: HOW THE INUIT LIVED
Heather Siska
Grades 5 and up. Illus. Paper. Salem House, $6.95.

*PEOPLE OF THE LONGHOUSE: HOW THE IROQUOIAN TRIBES LIVED
Jillian & Robin Riddington
Grades 5 and up. Illus. Paper. Salem House, $9.95

PEOPLE OF THE MAGIC WATERS: THE CAHUILLA INDIAN OF PALM SPRINGS
John Brumgardt and Larry Bowles
Illus. ETC Publications, 1981. $9.95.

PEOPLE OF THE MESA: THE ARCHAEOLOGY OF BLACK MESA, ARIZONA
Shirley Powell & George Gummerman
Illus. 200 pp. Southern Illinois University Press, 1987. $19.95.

PEOPLE OF THE MIDDLE PLACE: A STUDY OF THE ZUNI INDIANS
Dorothea Leighton and John Adair
189 pp. Paper. HRAF Press, 1966. $15.

PEOPLE OF PASCUA
Edward H. Spicer; Kathleen Sands & Rosamond Spicer, Editors
The history & culture of the Tucson area Yaqui. 331 pp. University of Arizona Press, 1988. $40.

THE PEOPLE OF THE POLAR NORTH: A RECORD...
Knud Rasmussen; G. Herring, Editor
Reprint of 1908 edition. AMS, $56.50.

PEOPLE OF THE SACRED MOUNTAIN: A HISTORY OF THE NORTHERN CHEYENNE CHIEFS & WARRIOR SOCIETIES, 1830-1879
Peter Powell
Two volumes. Illus. 1,376 pp. Harper & Row, 1981. $125 per set.

THE PEOPLE OF THE SAINTS
George Mills
Illus. Paper. Taylor Museum, 1967. $5.

PEOPLE OF THE SHINING MOUNTAINS: THE UTES OF COLORADO
Charles S. Marsh
Illus. 190 pp. Paper. Pruett Publishing, 1984. $11.95.

PEOPLE OF TERRA NULLIUS: BETRAYAL & REBIRTH IN ABORIGINAL CANADA
Boyce Richardson
The right of Aboriginals to self-government. Illus. Map. 408 pp. Paper. University of Washington Press, $19.95.

*PEOPLE OF THREE FIRES
George Cornell
History, culture & dynamics of Michigan's Indigenous peoples: Ottawa, Potawatomi & Ojibway. Greenfield Review Press, $14.95.

PEOPLE OF THE TONTO RIM; ARCHAEOLOGICAL DISCOVERY IN PREHISTORIC ARIZONA
Charles L. Redman, Editor
Illus. 224 pp. Paper. Smithsonian Books, 1993. $14.95

PEOPLE OF THE TOTEM: THE INDIANS OF THE PACIFIC NORTHWEST
Norman Bancroft-Hunt & Werner Forman
Reprint of 1979 edition. Illus. Map. 128 pp. Paper. University of Oklahoma Press, $22.95.

*PEOPLE OF THE TRAIL: HOSW THE NORTHERN FOREST INDIANS LIVED
Jillian & Robin Ridington
Grades 5 and up. Illus. Paper. Salem House, $6.95.

PEOPLE OF THE TWILIGHT
Diamond Jenness
Reprint of 1959 edition. Paper. University of Chicago Press, $9.95.

*THE PEOPLE SHALL CONTINUE
Simon Ortiz; illus. by Sharol Graves
Epic story of Native American peoples, a "teaching story." Grades 4-8. Illus. Children's Book Press, 1987. $14.95.

THE PEOPLE SPEAK: NAVAJO FOLK ART
Chuck & Jan Rosenak; photos by Lynn Lown
Guide for collectors of Native American art. Illus. 160 pp. Northland Publishing, $40.

A PEOPLE'S ARMY: MASSACHUSETTS SOLDIERS & SOCIETY IN THE SEVEN YEAR'S WAR
Fred Anderson
Illus. 292 pp. University of North Carolina Press, 1984. $27.50.

THE PEOPLE'S HEALTH: ANTHROPOLOGY & MEDICINE IN A NAVAJO COMMUNITY
John Adair, et al
Illus. 313 pp. University of New Mexico Press, 1988. $27.50; paper, $14.95.

THE PEQUOTS IN SOUTHERN NEW ENGLAND: THE FALL & RISE OF AN AMERICAN INDIAN NATION
Laurence Hauptman & James Wherry
Illus. Maps. 288 pp. University of Oklahoma Press, 1990. $24.95; paper. $12.95.

PERCH LAKE MOUNDS, WITH NOTES ON OTHER NEW YORK MOUNDS & SOME ACCOUNTS OF INDIAN TRAILS
William Beauchamp
Reprint of 1905 edition. AMS, $14.50.

*PERIL AT THUNDER RIDGE
Anthony Dorame
Myron, a Native American teenager, conveys his people's philosophy that a balanced environment is crucial to man. Grades 6-10. Illus. 128 pp. Paper. Red Crane Books, $9.95.

PERSISTENCE IN PATTERN IN MISSISSIPPI CHOCTAW CULTURE
Patti C. Black, Editor
Illus. 44 pp. Paper. Mississippi Department of Archives & U. Press of Mississippi, 1987. $9.95.

A PERSISTENT VISION: ART OF THE RESERVATION DAYS
Richard Conn
Illus. 192 pp. Denver Art Museum, 1986. $35.00; paper, $19.95.

PERSONAL MEMOIRS OF A RESIDENCE OF 30 YEARS WITH THE INDIAN TRIBES ON THE AMERICAN FRONTIERS, 1812-1842
H.R. Schoolcraft
Reprint of 1851 edition. AMS Press, $37.50; Ayer Co., $54.

PERSONAL NARRATIVE OF JAMES O. PATTIE
James O. Pattie; Richard Batman, Editor
Frontier attitudes toward Indians and Mexicans. Illus. 216 pp. Mountain Press, $24.95; paper, $12.95.

PERSONAL RECOLLECTIONS & OBSERVATIONS OF GENERAL NELSON A. MILES
N.A. Miles
Revised 1896 edition. Illus. Da Capo Press, $69.50.

PERSPECTIVES ON HEALTH CARE DELIVERY SYSTEMS FOR AMERICAN INDIAN FAMILIES
Article. Southwest Communication Resources, $5.00.

PERSPECTIVES ON THE SOUTHEAST: LINGUISTICS, ARCHAEOLOGY, & ETHNOHISTORY
Patricia B. Kwachka
11 essays focusing on questions relating to the distribution, organization, and relationships of southeastern Native American groups. Illus. Maps. U. of Georgia Press, 1994. $30; paper, $20.

PETROGLYPHS OF OHIO
James Swauger
Illus. 350 pp. Ohio University Press, 1984. $49.95.

PETROGLYPHS & PUEBLO MYTHS OF THE RIO GRANDE
Carol Patterson-Rudolph
Describes individual rock art symbols focusing on their meaning within the context of a language system. Illus. Photos. 162 pp. Paper. Avanyu Publishing, 1991. $29.95.

THE PEYOTE BOOK: A STUDY OF NATIVE MEDICINE
Guy Mount, Compiler/editor
A collection of ancient legends, healing testimonials, spiritual & philosophical perceptions, songs, stories & illustrations inspired by the Good Medicine. 3rd edition. Illus. Biblio. 144 pp. Sweetlight, 1992. $9.95.

THE PEYOTE CULT
Weston La Barre
Illus. Paper. 4th Ed. The Shoe String Press, 1975. $15; 5th Ed. University of Oklahoma Press, 1989. $14.95.

PEYOTE: THE DEVINE CACTUS
Edward F. Anderson
Questions the use of peyote in Native American religious ceremonies, with a firsthand account of a peyote ceremony. Illus. 248 pp. Paper. University of Arizona Press, 1980. $10.95.

PEYOTE HUNT: THE SACRED JOURNEY OF HUICHOL INDIANS
Barbara Myerhoff
Illus. 285 pp. Paper. Cornell University Press, 1974. $11.95.

PEYOTE MUSIC
D. McAllester
Reprint of 1949 ed. Paper. Johnson Reprint, $19.

PEYOTE RELIGION
Omer C. Stewart
Encyclopedic history. Illus. Maps. 472 pp. University of Oklahoma Press, 1987. $34.95; paper, $15.95.

THE PEYOTE RELIGION AMONG THE NAVAHO
David F. Aberle
2nd Ed. Illus. Maps. 528 pp. Paper. University of Oklahoma Press, 1982. $19.95.

PEYOTISM IN THE WEST: A HISTORICAL & CULTURAL PERSPECTIVE
Omer Stewart, Editor
Illus. 168 pp. Paper. University of Utah Press, 1984. $17.50.

*PHANTOM HORSE OF COLLISTER'S FIELDS
Gail Johnson
Grades 4-12. Paper. Council for Indian Education, 1974. $1.95.

THE PHOENIX INDIAN SCHOOL: FORCED ASSIMILATION IN ARIZONA, 1891-1935
Robert A. Trennert, Jr.
Illus. 272 pp. University of Oklahoma Press, 1988. $24.95.

THE PHOENIX OF THE WESTERN WORLD: QUETZALCOATL & THE SKY RELIGION
Burr C. Brundage
Illus. 320 pp. University of Oklahoma Press, 1982. $24.50.

PHONETICAL STUDY OF THE ESKIMO LANGUAGE, BASED ON OBSERVATIONS MADE ON A JOURNEY IN NORTH GREENLAND, 1900-1901
William Thalbitzer
Reprint of 1904 edition. AMS, $30.

PHONOLOGICAL ISSUES IN NORTH ALASKAN INUPIAQ
Lawrence D. Kaplan
280 pp. Paper. Alaska Native Language Center, 1981. $15.

PHONOLOGICAL VARIATION IN WESTERN CHEROKEE
Lawrence Foley
250 pp. Garland, 1980. $35.

THE PHOTOGRAPH & THE AMERICAN INDIAN
Alfred L. Bush & Lee Clark Mitchell
Illus. 352 pp. Princeton University Press, 1994. $75.

PICTOGRAPHIC HISTORY OF THE OGLALA SIOUX
Amos Brad Heart Bull and Helen Blish
Illus. 530 pp. University of Nebraska Press, 1968. $35.

PICTORIAL WEAVINGS OF THE NAVAJOS
Nancy Schiffer
Over 200 photos of pictorial weavings. Paper. Schiffer, $12.95.

*A PICTURE BOOK OF SITTING BULL
David A. Adler; illus. by Samuel Byrd
Grades K-3. Illus. 32 pp. Holiday House, 1993. $15.95.

PICTURE-WRITING OF THE AMERICAN INDIANS
Garrick Mallery
Reprint. Two vols. 1,300 Illus. 822 pp. Paper. Dover, $25.90/set.

PICTURE-WRITING OF TEXAS INDIANS
A.T. Jackson
Reprint of 1938 edition. AMS Press.

*PIECES OF WHITE SHELL: A JOURNEY TO NAVAJOLAND
Terry T. William
Grades 7-12. Illus. 176 pp. Charles Scribners Sons, 1984. $14.95. Paper. University of New Mexico Press, $9.95.

A PILLAR OF FIRE TO FOLLOW: AMERICAN INDIAN DRAMAS, 1808-1859
Priscilla F. Sears
149 pp. Bowling Green University Press, 1982. $11.95; paper, $5.95.

PIMA INDIAN BASKETRY: ILLUSTRATED WITH PHOTOGRAPHS FROM THE COLLECTION OF THE HEARD MUSEUM
  H. Thomas Cain
Illus. 40 pp. Paper. The Heard Museum, 1962. $5.

PIMA INDIAN LEGENDS
  Anna Moore Shaw
111 pp. Paper. University of Arizona Press, 1968. $9.95.

*THE PIMA-MARICOPA: SOUTHWEST
  Henry Dobyns
Grades 5 and up. Illus. Chelsea House, 1989. $17.95.

PIMA & PAPAGO INDIAN AGRICULTURE
  E.F. Castetter and W. Bell
Reprint of 1942 edition. AMS Press, $21.

A PIMA PAST
  Anna Moore Shaw
262 pp. Paper. University of Arizona Press, 1994. $15.95.

A PIMA REMEMBERS
  George Webb
Recollections of childhood and Pima Indian lifeways. 126 pp. Paper. University of Arizona Press, 1959. $10.95.

PIMAN & PAPAGO RITUAL ORATORY
  Donald M. Bahr
The author's personal relationship with the Pima and Papago. Illus. Paper. The Indian Historian Press, 1975. $7.

PIMAN SHAMANISM & STAYING SICKNESS: KA: CIM MUMKIDAG
  Donald Bahr, Juan Gregorio, David Lopez
Describes and analyzes a non-Western system of medicine. 332 pp. Paper. University of Arizona Press, 1974. $9.95.

PIONEER HISTORY: BEING AN ACCOUNT OF THE FIRST EXAMINATIONS OF THE OHIO VALLEY & THE EARLY SETTLEMENT OF THE NORTHWEST TERRITORY
  S.P. Hildreth
Reprint of 1848 edition. Ayer Co., $29.

PIONEER MISSIONARY TO THE BERING STRAIT ESKIMOS
  Louis Renner, et al
Illus. Binford-Metropolitan, 1979. $12.50.

PIONEERING IN MONTANA: THE MAKING OF A STATE, 1864-1887
  Stuart Granville; Paul Phillips, Editor
Reprint of 1977 edition. Illus. 265 pp. University of Nebraska Press, $21.50; paper, $7.95.

THE PIONEERS OF NEW FRANCE IN NEW ENGLAND
  J.P. Baxter
Reprint of 1894 ed. 450 pp. Heritage Books, $25.

PIPE, BIBLE & PEYOTE AMONG THE OGLALA LAKOTA: A STUDY IN RELIGIOUS IDENTITY
  Paul Steinmetz
270 pp. U. of Tennessee Press, 1990. $29.95.

THE PIPE & CHRIST: A CHRISTIAN-SIOUX DIALOGUE
  William Stolzman
Illus. 3rd Edition. 222 pp. Paper. Center for Western Studies, 1991. $7.95.

PETER PITCHLYNN: CHIEF, LIFE & TIMES, 1800-1891
  Rowena Alcorn
Paper. Ye Galleon, 1986. $5.95.

PETER PITCHLYNN: CHIEF OF THE CHOCTAWS
  W. David Baird
Illus. Maps. 288 pp. Paper. University of Oklahoma Press, $14.95.

PLACE FOR WINTER: PAUL TIULANA'S STORY
  Vivian Senungetuk & paul Tiulane
Second edition. Illus. 150 pp. CIRI Foundation, 1989. $17.95.

THE PLACE IN FLOWERS WHERE POLLEN RESTS
  Paul West
500 pp. Macmillan, 1990. $9.95.

PLACE & VISION: THE FUNCTION OF LANDSCAPE IN NATIVE AMERICAN FICTION
  Robert M. Nelson
Explores the role of physical landscape in three contemporary Native American novels. 189 pp. Peter Lang, 1994. $39.95.

A PLAINS ARCHAEOLOGY SOURCEBOOK: SELECTED PAPERS OF THE NEBRASKA STATE HISTORICAL SOCIETY
  Wald R. Wedie, Editor
314 pp. Garland, 1985. $40.

THE PLAINS CREE
  D.G. Mandelbaum
Reprint of 1940 edition. AMS Press, $21.

PLAINS CREE TEXTS
  L. Bloomfield
Reprint of 1934 edition. AMS Press, $36.

*THE PLAINS INDIAN BOOK
Grades 1-6. Paper. Fun Publishing, 1974. $3.95.

PLAINS INDIAN CULTURE
  O.J. Fargo
Illus. 50 pp. Paper. Green Valley Area, 1990. $1.50.

PLAINS INDIAN DESIGNS
  Caren Caraway
Illus. 48 pp. Stemmer House, 1984. $5.95.

PLAINS INDIAN MYTHOLOGY
  Alice Marriott & Carol Rachlin
A collection of traditional stories gleaned from oral sources, with poetyry. Illus. 224 pp. Paper. Penguin USA, 1975. $4.95.

PLAINS INDIAN PAINTING: A DESCRIPTION OF ABORIGINAL AMERICAN ART
  John Ewers
Reprint of 1939 edition. AMS Press, $24.50.

PLAINS INDIAN RAIDERS: THE FINAL PHASES OF WARFARE FROM THE ARKANSAS TO THE RED RIVER
  Wilbur S. Nye
Illus. 438 pp. Paper. U. of Oklahoma Press, 1974. $14.95.

PLAINS INDIAN SCULPTURE: A TRADITIONAL ART FROM AMERICA'S HEARTLAND
  John C. Ewers
Illus. 240 pp. Paper. Smithsonian Books, 1986. $27.50.

*PLAINS INDIAN WARRIOR
  R.A. May
Grades 3-8. Illus. 32 pp. Rourke Corp., 1990. $14.

*PLAINS INDIANS
  Kate Petty
Grades 3 and up. Illus. 32 pp. Franklin Watts, 1988. $10.40.

THE PLAINS INDIANS
  Colin F. Taylor
Covers the cultural diversity of many different tribes. Includes Blackfoot, Cheyenne, Sioux, Comanche, Crow, and others. 250 full-color and b&w illus. 240 pp. Random House, 1994. $25.

PLAINS INDIANS, A.D. 500-1500: THE ARCHAEOLOGICAL PAST OF HISTORIC GROUPS
  Karl H. Schlesler, Editor
Traces Indian ethnic continuity & cultural diversity in the Great Plains during the millennium preceding European arrival. Illus. Maps. Biblio. University of Oklahoma Press, 1994. $39.95.

PLAINS INDIANS: AN EDUCATIONAL COLORING BOOK
Grades 1-8. Illus. 32 pp. Paper. Spizzirri Publishing, 1981. $1.95.

THE PLAINS INDIANS & NEW MEXICO, 1751-1778
  Alfred B. Thomas
Reprint of 1940 edition. AMS Press.

PLAINS INDIANS OF NORTH AMERICA
  Robin May
Grades 4-8. Illus. 48 pp. 6 book set. Rourke Corp., $75.96 per set; $12.66 each.

THE PLAINS INDIANS OF THE 20th CENTURY
  Peter Iverson, Editor
11 essays dealing with the complex cultural problems of the 20th century Plains Indian reservations. Illus. 288 pp. University of Oklahoma Press, 1985. $24.95; paper, $14.95.

*PLAINS INDIANS PUNCH-OUT PANORAMA
  A.G. Smith
Construction of tribal settlement; pieces illustrate their way of life. 27 full-color pieces, and 4 b&x diagrams. Grades 3 and up. 12 pp. paper. Dover, $3.95.

PLANNING PROCESS ON THE PINE RIDGE & ROSEBUD INDIAN RESERVATION
  Richard E. Brown
University of South Dakota, Government Research Bureau, 1969. $1.

PLANTS USED AS CURATIVES BY CERTAIN SOUTHEASTERN TRIBES
  Lyda Taylor
Reprint of 1940 edition. AMS Press, $14.50.

PLANTS USED IN BASKETRY BY THE CALIFORNIA INDIANS
  Ruth Merrill
Reprint. Illus. Acoma Books, 1980. $2.95.

A PLEA FOR THE INDIANS
John Beeson
184 pp. Ye Galleon Press, 1981. $14.95.

PLEASING THE SPIRITS: A CATLOGUE OF A COLLECTION OF AMERICAN INDIAN ART
Douglas C. Ewing
More than 500 objects of Native American art from across North America, Illus. 402 pp. University of Washington Press, 1992. $90.

PLENTY-COUPS, CHIEF OF THE CROWS
F. Linderman
Reprint of 1962 edition. Illus. 325 pp. Paper. University of Nebraska Press, $7.95.

PO PAI MO: THE SEARCH FOR WHITE BUFFALO WOMAN
Robert Boissiere
Illus. 96 pp. Paper. Sunstone Press, 1983. $8.95.

POCAHONTAS
Ingri D'Aulaire
Paper. Doubleday, 1989. $7.95.

POCAHONTAS & CO: THE FICTORIAL AMERI-CAN INDIAN WOMAN IN 19th CENTURY LIT-ERATURE: A STUDY OF METHOD
Asebrit Sundquist
350 pp. Humanities Press, 1986. $39.95.

*POCAHONTAS: DAUGHTER OF A CHIEF
Grades K-3. Illus. 48 pp. Childrens Press, $11.95.

POCAHONTAS'S PEOPLE: THE POWHATAN INDIANS OF VIRGINIA
Helen Rountree
Illus. 416 pp. University of Oklahoma Press, 1990. $29.95.

THE POINT ELLIOTT TREATY, 1855
Lynn Kickingbird & Curtis Berkey
28 pp. Institute for the Development of Indian Law, $9.

POINT HOPE, AN ESKIMO VILLAGE IN TRANSITION
James W. Vanstone
Reprint of 1962 edition. AMS, $31.50.

THE POINT-NO-POINT TREATY, 1855
Lynn Kickingbird & Curtis Berkey
29 pp. Institute for the Development of Indian Law, $9.

POINT OF PINES, ARIZONA: A HISTORY OF THE UNIVERSITY OF ARIZONA ARCHAEO-LOGICAL FIELD SCHOOL
Emil W. Haury
140 pp. University of Arizona Press, 1989. $19.95.

POLISHED STONE ARTICLES USED BY THE NEW YORK ABORIGINES BEFORE AND DUR-ING EUROPEAN OCCUPATION
W.M. Beauchamp
Reprint of 1905 edition. AMS Press, $17.50.

THE POLITICAL ECONOMY OF NORTH AMERICAN INDIANS
John H. Moore, Editor
Collection of articles on macroeconimics and intercultural conflict. Illus. 320 pp. University of Oklahoma Press, 1993. $32.95.

POLITICAL ORGANIZATIONS & LAW-WAYS OF THE COMANCHE INDIANS
E.A. Hoebel
Reprint of 1940 edition. Kraus Reprint, $13.

POLITICAL ORGANIZATION OF THE PLAINS INDIANS: WITH SPECIAL REFERENCE TO THE COUNCIL
M.G. Smith
Reprin tof 1924 edition. AMS Press, $15.

THE POLITICAL OUTSIDERS: BLACKS & INDIANS IN A RURAL OKLAHOMA COUNTY
Brian F. Rader
Paper. R & E Research Associates, 1978. $13.95.

POLITICS & ETHNICITY ON THE RIO YAQUI: POTAM REVISITED
Thomas R. McGuire
Yaqui culture. 186 pp. University of Arizona Press, 1986. $24.95.

THE POLITICS OF INDIAN REMOVAL: CREEK GOVERNMENT & SOCIETY IN CRISES
Michael D. Green
Illus. 250 pp. University of Nebraska Press, 1982. $22.50.

POLITICS & POWER: AN ECONOMIC & POLITICAL HISTORY OF THE WESTERN PUEBLO
Steadman Upham
Academic Press, 1982. $24.50.

THE POLLEN PATH: A COLLECTION OF NAVAJO MYTHS
Retold by M.S. Link
Reprint of 1956 edition. Illus. 210 pp. Stanford University Press, $19.50.

POMO BASKETMAKING - A SUPREME ART FOR THE WEAVER
Elsie Allen
Step-by-step instructions for recreating beautiful & useful baskets. Illus. Photos. 67 pp. Naturegraph, $14.95; paper, $6.95.

POMO INDIAN BASKETRY
S.A. Barrett
Second Edition. Reprint of 1908 edition. Illus. 288 pp. Paper. Rio Grande Press, $10.

*POMO INDIANS OF CALIFORNIA & THEIR NEIGHBORS
Vinson Brown; Albert Alsasser, Editor
Grades 4-12. Illus. Naturegraph, 1969. $16.95; paper, $8.95.

PONY TRACKS
F. Remington
Reprint of 1961 edition. Illus. Paper. University of Oklahoma Press, 1977. $7.95.

THE POOL & IRVING VILLAGES: A STUDY OF HOPEWELL OCCUPATION
John McGregor
Reprint of 1958 edition. Illus. Books on Demand, $61.

POPULATION CHANGES AMONG THE NORTHERN PLAINS INDIANS
Clark Wissler
Bound with: "Cultural Relations of the Gila River & Lower Colorado Tribes," by Leslie Spier; "Hopi Huntingn & Hunting Ritual," by Ernest Beaglehole;

"Navaho Warfare," by W.W. Hill; "The Economy of a Modern Teton Dakota Community," by Mekeel H. Scudder; and "The Distribution of the Northern Athapaskan Indians." Reprinted from the 1936 edition. HRAF Press, $15.

THE POPULATION OF CALIFORNIA INDIANS, 1769-1970
Sherburne F. Cook
Includes six essays on the native California popu-lation at the time of initial settlement in 1769. 239 pp. University of California Press, 1976. $40.

THE PORTABLE NORTH AMERICAN INDIAN READER
Frederick W. Turner, III
Third Edition. A collection of myths, tales, poetry, speeches, and passages from Indian autobiogra-phies, and recent writings. 640 pp. Penguin USA, 1977. $9.95.

PORTAGE LAKE: MEMORIES OF AN OJIBWE CHILDHOOD
Maude Kegg; edited by John Nichols
A child's view of traditional Anishinaabe lifeways coming into contact with Euro-American settlers. 272 pp. Paper. University of Minnesota Press, 1993. $16.95.

PORTFOLIO II
Kathryn Stewart
Illus. 50 pp. American Indian Contemporary Arts, 1988.

PORTRAIT INDEX OF NORTH AMERICAN INDIANS IN PUBLISHED COLLECTIONS
Patrick Frazier, Library of Congress
Identifies and indexes hundreds of pictures, prints, drawings, and lithographs of Native American por-traits contained in 75 sources.Illus. Biblio. 142 pp. Paper. U.S. Government Printing Office, $16.

PORTRAITS OF THE WHITEMAN
Keith Basso
130 pp. Paper. Cambridge University Press, 1979. $12.95.

ALEX POSEY: CREEK POET, JOURNALIST, & HUMORIST
Daniel F. Littlefield, Jr.
Illus. Map. 350 pp. University of Nebraska Press, 1992. $39.95.

*POTAWATOMI
James A. Clifton
Grades 5 and up. Illus. 105 pp. Chelsea House, 1988. $17.95.

*THE POTAWATOMI: GREAT LAKES
Grades 7-12. Illus. 112 pp. Knowledge Unlimited, $16.95.

POTAWAOMI INDIANS OF MICHIGAN, 1843-1904, INCLUDING SOME OTTAWA & CHIPPEWA, 1843-1866, & POTAWATOMI OF INDIANA, 1869 & 1885
Raymond C. Lantz
Covers annuity rolls on the Ottawa, Chippewa and Potawatomi of Michigan abd Indiana. Roll num-bers are given. 92 pp. Paper. Heritage Books, 1992. $14.

POTAWATOMIS: KEEPERS OF THE FIRE
R. David Edmunds
Illus. 374 pp. University of Oklahoma Press, 1978. $22.95; paper, $12.95.

POTLATCH: NATIVE CEREMONY & MYTH ON THE NORTHWEST COAST
Mary Beck; illus. by Oliver
Paper. Alaska Northwest Books, $12.95.

THE POTTERY FROM ARROYO HONDO PUEBLO: Tribalization & Trade in the Northern Rio Grande
Judith A. Habicht-Mauche
Includes *The Stone Artifacts from Arroyo Hondo Pueblo*, by Carl J. Phagan. Illus. Maps. Biblio. Paper. School of Americn Research, 1990. $30.

POTTERY OF THE GREAT BASIN & ADJACENT AREAS
Suzanne Griset
Illus. 170 pp. Paper. University of Utah Press, 1986. $17.50.

POTTERY OF THE PAJARITO PLATEAU AND OF SOME ADJACENT REGIONS IN NEW MEXICO
A.V. Kidder
Reprint of 1915 edition. Paper. Kraus, $12.

POTTERY TECHNIQUES OF NATIVE NORTH AMERICA: AN INTRODUCTION TO TRADITIONAL TECHNOLOGY
John K. White
University of Chicago Press, 1976. $38.00. Includes four-color fiches.

POW WOW
A young Indian boy, Red Elk, explains what is happening at the Pow Wow celebration. Illus. 32 pp. Paper. Cherokee Publications, $3.95.

*POW-WOW
Mimi Chenfeld and Marjorie Vandervelds
Grades 5-12. Paper. Council for Indian Education, 1972. $2.95.

POW WOW CALENDAR
Liz Campbell, Editor
Lists, month-by-month, Native American powwows, dances, crafts fairs and other cultural events. Annual. Illus. 70 pp. The Book Publishing Co., $5.95.

POW WOW CHOW
A cookbook with collection of recipes from women of Five Tribes heritage. 354 pp. Spiral bound. The Five Civilized Tribes Museum. $12.95.

THE POW WOW HIGHWAY
David Seals
An up-to-date account of being Indian in America. 304 pp. Paper. Penguin USA, $9.95.

POW WOW: & OTHER YAKIMA INDIAN TRADITIONS
Helen Willard
23 stories. Illus. 128 pp. Roza Run, 1990. $29.95; paper, $19.95.

POW WOW: ON THE RED ROAD
Fred Synder
Lists over 700 American Indian events in the U.S. and Canada for 1993 thru 1997. Native American Co-Op, $25.

THE POWER OF SILENCE
Carlos Castaneda; Jane Rosenman, Editor
290 pp. Pocket Books, 1991. $8.95.

POWER QUEST: THE JOURNEY INTO MANHOOD
Carol Betdorf
Illus. 224 pp. Paper. Hancock House, $12.95.

THE POWHATAN INDIANS OF VIRGINIA: THEIR TRADITIONAL CULTURE
Helen Rountree
Illus. Maps. 225 pp. Paper. University of Oklahoma Press, $11.95.

POWHATAN FOREIGN RELATIONS 1500-1722
Helen C. Rountree, Editor
Examines the Powhatans and their relationships with both European & Indian "foreigners". 321 pp. University Press of Virginia, 1993. $29.95.

POWHATAN'S MANTLE: INDIANS IN THE COLONIAL SOUTHEAST
Peter Wood, Gregory Waselkov & M. Thomas Hatley
Illus. Maps. 360 pp. Paper. University of Nebraska Press, 1989. $19.95.

*THE POWHATAN TRIBES: MIDDLE ATLANTIC
Christina Feest
Grades 5 and up. Illus. Chelsea House, 1989. $17.95.

A PRACTICAL GRAMMAR OF THE ST. LAWRENCE ISLAND: SIBERIAN YUP'IK ESKIMO LANGUAGE
Steven A. Jacobson
105 pp. Paper. Alaska Native Language Center, 1990. $10.

*PRAIRIE LEGENDS
M. Earring, et al
Grades 6-9. Paper. Council for Indian Education, 1978. $2.95.

*PRAIRIE SMOKE
Melvin R. Gilmore
The life of the Indians of the Missouri Valley, as reflected in their mythology. Grades 7 and up. Reprint of 1929 edition. Illus. 225 pp. Paper. Minnesota Historical Society Press, $7.95.

*THE PRAYING FLUTE
Tony Shearer
Grades 4 and up. 112 pp. Paper. Naturegraph, 1988. $7.95.

PRE-COLUMBIAN ARCHITECTURE, ART & ARTIFACTS SLIDE CATALOG
H.L. Murvin
40 pp. Paper. H.L. Murvin, 1983. $3.95.

PRE-COLUMBIAN ART
Elizabeth P. Benson, Editor
University of Chicago Press, 1976. $25.

PRE-COLUMBIAN ART FROM THE LAND COLLECTION
Alana Cordy-Collins & H.B. Nicholson; L. K. Land, Editor
Illus. 275 pp. Paper. California Academy of Sciences, 1979. $25.

PREHISTORIC ARCHITECTURE IN THE EASTERN U.S.
Morgan
A source for information on the major prehistoric earthworks east of the Mississippi. Illus. 197 pp. Hothem House, 1980. $19.95.

PREHISTORIC BIOLOGICAL RELATIONSHIP IN THE GREAT LAKES REGION
Richard Wilkinson
Illus. Paper. University of Michigan, Museum of Anthropology, 1971. $3.50.

PREHISTORIC HOPI POTTERY DESIGNS
Jesse Fewkes
Pre-Columbian design from Sikyatki site. Reprint. 564 Illus. 288 pp. Paper. Dover, $8.95.

PREHISTORIC HOUSEHOLDS AT TURKEY CREEK PUEBLO, ARIZONA
Julie Lowell
Illus. 110 pp. Paper. University of Arizona Press, 1991. $21.95.

PREHISTORIC HUNTERS OF THE HIGH PLAINS
George Frison
Reprint of 1978 edition. Illus. 2nd Edition. 460 pp. Hothem House, $64.95.

PREHISTORIC INDIAN ROCK ART: ISSUES & CONCERNS
Jo Anne Van Tilburg & Clement Meighan, Eds.
Illus. 66 pp. Paper. UCLA Institute of Archaeology, 1981. $6.

PREHISTORIC INDIANS
Barnes & Pendleton
A guide to understanding the early Indian cultures of the Four Corners (AZ, NM, UT, CO) area. Includes artifacts, cultures, rpck art and ruins. Illus. 256 pp. Paper. Hothem House, 1988. $7.50.

PREHISTORIC INDIANS OF THE SOUTHEAST: ARCHAEOLOGY OF ALABAMA AND THE MIDDLE SOUTH
John Walthall
Illus. 288 pp. University of Alabama Press, 1980. $25.

PREHISTORIC INDIANS OF WISCONSIN
Robert Ritzenthaler
Third revised edition. Illus. 62 pp. Paper. American Indian Books, and Milwaukee Public Museum, 1985. $7.95.

PREHISTORIC LITHIC INDUSTRY AT DOVER, TENNESSEE
Richard M. Gramly
An investigation of quarries and workshops used by lithic craftsmen of the Mississippian archaeological culture, the Flintkappers of Dover. Illus. 150 pp. Paper. Persimmon Press, $21.95.

PREHISTORIC MAN ON THE GREAT PLAINS
Waldo Wedel
Illus. University of Oklahoma, 1961. $28.95.

PREHISTORIC MAN OF THE SANTA BARBARA COAST
David Rogers
Reprint of 1929 edition. AMS Press, $57.50.

THE PREHISTORIC PEOPLES OF MINNESOTA
Elden Johnson
Revised edition. Illus. 35 pp. Paper. Minnesota Historical Society Press, 1988. $3.95.

PREHISTORIC PEOPLES OF SOUTH FLORIDA
William E. McGoun
176 pp. Paper. University of Alabama Press, 1993. $19.95.

PREHISTORIC ROCK ART
Barnes
Guide to the prehistoric and historic petroglyphs and pictographs of the Four Corners and Great Basin. Illus. 304 pp. Paper. Hothem House, 1986. $8.50.

PREHISTORIC SOUTHWESTERN CRAFT ARTS
Clara L. Tanner
Discusses baskets, pottery, textiles, ornaments, and other crafts of the Southwest's prehistoric peoples. Illus. 226 pp. University of Arizona Press, 1976. $27.50.

PREHISTORIC SOUTHWESTERNERS FROM BASKETMAKER TO PUEBLO
C.A. Amsden
Reprint of 1949 edition. Illus. Maps. 165 pp. Paper. Southwest Museum, $5.

PREHISTORIC STONE IMPLEMENTS OF NORTHEASTERN ARIZONA
R.B. Woodbury
Reprint of 1954 edition. Illus. Kraus, $32.

PREHISTORIC WEAPONS IN THE SOUTHWEST
Stewart Peckham
Illus. Paper. Museum of New Mexico Press, 1965. $1.50.

PREHISTORY IN THE NAVAJO RESERVOIR DISTRICT
Frank W. Eddy
Illus. Paper. Museum of New Mexico Press, 1966. Two parts, $8.95 each.

THE PRE-HISTORY OF THE BURNT BLUFF AREA
James E. Fitting, Editor
Paper. University of Michigan, Museum of Anthropology, 1968. $3.

THE PREHISTORY OF FISHTRAP, KY
R.C. Dunnell
Paper. Yale University, Anthropology, 1972. $7.

A PRELIMINARY STUDY OF THE PUEBLO OF TAOS, NEW MEXICO
M.L. Miller
Reprint of 1898 edition. AMS Press, $10.

PRESBYTERIAN MISSIONARY ATTITUDES TOWARD AMERICAN INDIANS, 1837-1893
Michael C. Coleman
Based upon correspondence of missionaries in the field. Illus. 222 pp. University Press of Mississippi, 1985. $32.

PRESENT STATE OF NEW ENGLAND
Co Mather
Reprint of 1690 edition. Haskell House, $59.95.

PRESERVING TRADITIONAL ARTS: A TOOL-KIT FOR NATIVE AMERICAN COMMUNITIES
Susan Dyal
205 pp. American Indian Studies Center, 1985. $20.

PRESIDENT WASHINGTON'S INDIAN WAR: THE STRUGGLE FOR THE OLD NORTHWEST, 1790-1795
Wiley Sword
Illus. 432 pp. University of Oklahoma Press, 1985. $24.95.

THE PRETEND INDIANS - IMAGES OF NATIVE AMERICANS IN THE MOVIES: AN ANALYTICAL SURVEY OF TWENTIETH CENTURY INDIAN ENTERTAINERS
Gretchen Bataille & Charles Silent
Iowa State University Press, 1978.

PRETTY-SHIELD, MEDICINE WOMAN OF THE CROWS
F. Linderman
An Indian woman's side of life. Reprint of 1932 edition. Illus. 256 pp. Paper. University of Nebraska Press, 1974. $6.95.

THE PRIMAL MIND: VISION & REALITY IN INDIAN AMERICA
Jamake Highwater
Examines Indian ritual, art, oral traditions, architecture, and ceremonial dance and how it comes into contact and conflict with the "civilized" Western world. 240 pp. Paper. New American Library, $9.95.

PRIMITIVE ARTS & CRAFTS
Roderick U. Sayce
Reprint of 1993 ed. Illus. Biblo-Moser . $24.

PRIMITIVE MAN IN OHIO
W.K. Moorehead
Reprint of 1892 edition. AMS Press, $27.50.

PRIMITIVE PRAGMATISTS: THE MODOC INDIANS OF NORTHERN CALIFORNIA
Verne V. Ray
Illus. University of Washington Press, 1963. $11.50.

PRISON OF GRASS: CANADA FROM A NATIVE VIEWPOINT
Howard Adams
Adams, PhD & leader in the Canadian Native rights movement. Updated edition. Greenfield Review Press, $18.95.

PROCEEDINGS OF THE COMMISSIONERS OF INDIAN AFFAIRS
Franklin Hough
Reprint. Scholarly Press, $59.

PROCEEDINGS OF THE FORT CHIPEWYAN/FORT VERMILLION BICENTENNIAL CONFERENCE, SEPT. 23-24, 1988, EDMONTON, ALBERTA
Patricia McCormack &
R. Geoffrey Ironside, Editors
Focusses on the Aboriginal beginnings, histories, present conditions, and future prospects of the regions. Illus. 319 pp. CCI, $25.

PROCEEDINGS OF THE GREAT PEACE CONFERENCE
Institute for the Development of Indian Law , $10.

PROCEEDINGS OF THE 1973 HOHOKAM CONFERENCE
Donald Weaver, Jr., Susan Burton &
Minnabell Laughlin, Compilers & Editors
Monograph documenting two days of intensive discussions on Hohokam archaeology . Maps. 105 pp. Center for Anthropological Studies, $12 (postpaid).

PROFILES IN WISDOM: NATIVE ELDERS SPEAK ABOUT THE EARTH
Steven McFadden, Editor
Illus. 256 pp. Paper. Bear & Co., 1991. $12.95.

PROMISES OF THE PAST: A HISTORY OF INDIAN EDUCATION
David H. DeJong
304 pp. North American Press, 1993. $24.95.

PROPERTY CONCEPTS OF THE NAVAHO INDIANS
B. Haile
Reprint of 1954 edition. AMS Press, $12.50. Paper. St. Michaels, $6.

THE PROPHET DANCE OF THE NORTHWEST AND ITS DERIVATIVES: THE SOURCE OF THE GHOST DANCE
L. Spier
Reprint of 1935 edition. AMS Press, $18.

PROPHETIC WORLDS: INDIANS & WHITES ON THE COLUMBIA PLATEAU
Christopher C. Miller
174 pp. Rutgers University Press, 1985. $35.

THE PROTECTOR DE INDIOS IN COLONIAL NEW MEXICO, 1659-1821
Charles R. Cuttler
Illus. 140 pp. University of New Mexico Press, 1986. $17.50; paper, $8.95.

PROTO-ATHAPSKAN VERB STEM VARIATION: PART ONE: PHONOLOGY
Jeff Leer
100 pp. Paper. Alaska Native Language Center, 1979. $5.

THE PROVIDERS
Stephen Irwin
Illus. 296 pp. Paper. Hancock House, 1984. $12.95.

PSYCHOCULTURAL CHANGE AND THE AMERICAN INDIAN: AN ETHNOHISTORICAL ANALYSIS
Laurence French
Garland, 1987. $34.

PSYCHOLOGICAL RESEARCH ON AMERICAN INDIAN AND ALASKA NATIVE YOUTH: AN INDEXED GUIDE TO DISSERTATIONS
Spero M. Manson, et al, Editors
Illus. 230 pp. Greenwood Press, 1984. $36.95.

*PTEBLOKA; TALES FROM THE BUFFALO
M. Grant Two Bulls
Grades 3 and up. Illus. 20 cartoons. 24 pp. Paper. Dakota Press, 1991. $3.

*PUEBLO
Mary D'Apice
Grades 5-8. Illus. 32 pp. Rourke Corp., 1990. $9.95.

*THE PUEBLO
Alfonso Ortiz
A history of the people. Grades 7 and up. Illus. Chelsea House Publishers, $7.95.

*THE PUEBLO
Charlotte Yue
Grades 4-7. Paper. Houghton Mifflin, 1990. $4.95.

PUEBLO BIRDS & MYTHS
Hamilton A. Tyler
Discusses birds place in Pueblo ritual, ceremony , myth, and folklore. Illus. Biblio. 280 pp. Paper. Northland Press,1979. $19.95.

PUEBLO CRAFTS
Ruth Underhill; Willard Beatty, Editor
Reprint of 1944 edition. Illus. 148 pp. Paper .
R. Schneider, Publishers, $7.95.

PUEBLO CULTURES
B. Wright
Illus. 30 pp. Paper . E.J. Brill, 1986. $36.75.

**PUEBLO DESIGNS: 176 ILLUSTRATIONS
OF THE RAIN BIRD**
H.R. Mera; drawings by Tom Lea
Reprint of 1970 edition. Illus. 1 15 pp. Peter
Smith, $14.25. Paper . Dover, $7.95.

A PUEBLO GOD & MYTHS
Hamilton Tyler
Illus. 336 pp. Paper . University of Oklahoma
Press, 1984. $9.95.

PUEBLO INDIAN EMBROIDERY
N.R. Mera
Illus. 80 pp. William Gannon, 1975. $15.

PUEBLO INDIAN FOLK-STORIES
Charles F. Lummis
Seven elders tell folk-stories. Illus. 257 pp. Paper .
University of Nebraska Press, 1992. $8.95.

PUEBLO INDIAN JOURNAL
E.C. Parsons
Reprint of 1925 edition. Paper . Kraus, $20.

**PUEBLO INDIAN LAND GRANTS
OF THE RIO ABAJO NEW MEXICO**
H.O. Brayer
Reprint of 1938 edition. Ayer Co., $12.

**THE PUEBLO INDIAN REVOLT OF 1696 & THE
FRANCISCAN MISSIONS IN NEW MEXICO:
LETTERS OF THE MISSIONARIES & RELATED
DOCUMENTS**
translated & edited by J. Manuel Espinosa
Portrait of the conflict between Franciscan mis-
sionary zeal and the Pueblo holy men. Illus. Map.
336 pp. Paper . University of Oklahoma Press,
$15.95.

**PUEBLO INDIAN TEXTILES:
A LIVING TRADITION**
Kate P. Kent
Illus. 136 pp. Paper . School of American Research
& University of Washington Press, 1983. $16.95.

**PUEBLO INDIAN WATER RIGHTS:
STRUGGLE FOR A PRECIOUS RESOURCE**
Charles T. DuMars, et al, Editors
183 pp. University of Arizona Press, 1984.
$24.95.

THE PUEBLO INDIAN WORLD
E. Hewett and B. Dutton; John Harrington,
Editor
Reprint of 1945 edition. AMS Press, $37.50.

THE PUEBLO INDIANS
Joe Sando
The history of the Pueblos; includes the
constitution of the All Indian Pueblo Council.
Illus. 246 pp. Paper . The Indian Historian Press,
1976. $12.25.

**THE PUEBLO INDIANS OF NEW MEXICO:
THEIR LAND ECONOMY & CIVIL ORGANIZA-
TION**
S.B. de Aberle
Reprint of 1948 edition. Paper . Kraus, $12.

THE PUEBLO INDIANS OF NORTH AMERICA
Edward P. Dozier
Reprint. Illus. 224 pp. Paper . Waveland Press,
$9.95.

PUEBLO INDIANS OF SAN ILDEFONSO
W. Whitman
Reprint of 1947 edition. AMS Press, $22.

**PUEBLO MOTHERS & CHILDREN: ESSAYS
BY ELSIE CLEWS PARSONS, 1915-1924**
Barbara Babcock, Editor
Illus. Maps. 140 pp. Ancient City Press, $29.95;
paper, $16.95.

PUEBLO: MOUNTAIN, VILLAGE, DANCE
Vincent Scully
Second edition. Illus. 440 pp. University of
Chicago Press, 1989. $60; paper, $19.95.

**PUEBLO NATIONS: EIGHT CENTURIES
OF PUEBLO INDIAN HISTORY**
Joe S. Sando
Illus. 280 pp. Clear Light Publishing, 1991.
$22.95; paper, $14.95.

PUEBLO & NAVAJO INDIAN LIFE TODAY
Kris Hotvedt
Revised ed. of *Fry Breads, Feast Days and Sheep*.
Illus. 64 pp. Paper. Sunstone Press, $8.95.

THE PUEBLO OF JEMEZ
E.C. Parsons
Reprint of 1925 edition. AMS Press, $47.50.

PUEBLO OF SAN FELIPE
L. White
Reprint of 1932 edition. Paper. Kraus, $34.

PUEBLO OF SANTA ANA, NEW MEXICO
L. White
Reprint of 1942 edition. Paper. Kraus, $31.

PUEBLO OF SANTO DOMINGO, NM.
L. White
Reprint of 1935 edition. Paper. Kraus, $23.

**PUEBLO PEOPLE CALENDAR: A PHOTO-
GRAPHIC PORTFOLIO OF PUEBLO INDIANS**
Marcia Keegan
Clear Light, $12.

**THE PUEBLO POTTER: A STUDY OF
CREATIVE IMAGINATION IN PRIMITIVE ART**
Ruth L. Bunzel
Reprint of 1926 edition. Illus. 134 pp. Peter
Smith, $55. Paper. Hothem House, $7.95.

**PUEBLO POTTERY MAKING: A STUDY
OF THE VILLAGE OF SAN ILDEFONSO**
C.E. Guthe
Reprint of 1925 edition. AMS Press, $30.

**PUEBLO POTTERY OF
THE NEW MEXICO INDIANS**
Betty Toulouse
Illus. Paper. Museum of NM Press, 1977. $8.95.

**PUEBLO PROFILES: CULTURAL IDENTITY
THROUGH CENTURIES OF CHANGE**
Joe S. Sando
Tells the stories of political leaders, educators, and
artists who took part in the events and movements
that have shaped Pueblo Indian life from the time
of the Pueblo Revolt to the present day. Illus. 224
pp. Clear Light Publishers, 1994. $22.95; paper,
$12.95.

**PUEBLO SHIELDS FROM THE FRED
HARVEY FINE ARTS COLLECTION**
Barton Wright
Illus. 96 pp. The Heard Museum, 1976. $9.50.

***THE PUEBLO: SOUTHWEST**
Alfonso Ortiz
Grades 5 and up. Illus. Chelsea House, 1989.
$17.95.

PUEBLO STORIES & STORYTELLERS
Mark Bahti
48 pp. Paper. Treasure Chest, 1988. $9.95.

***PUEBLO STORYTELLER**
Diane Hoyt-Goldsmith
Grades 3-7. Illus. 32 pp. Holiday House, 1991.
$15.95; paper, $6.95..

**THE PUEBLO STORYTELLER:
DEVELOPMENT OF A FIGURATIVE
CERAMIC TRADITION**
Barbara Babcock, et al.
Illus. 201 pp. University of Arizona Press, 1986.
$50; paper, $24.95.

***A PUEBLO VILLAGE**
Hilda Aragon, Illustrator
Preschool-7. Illus. 8 pp. Paper.
Pueblo of Acoma Press, $1982. $4.

***THE PUEBLOS**
Suzanne Powell
Includes maps, a glossary and bibliography . Part
of *Indians of the Americas* series. Full-color illus-
trations. Grades 3 and up. 64 pp. Paper. Franklin
Watts, $5.95.

**PUEBLOS: PREHISTORIC INDIAN
CULTURES OF THE SOUTHWEST**
Max Bruggman, photos by
Illus. 240 pp. Facts on File, 1990. $45.

**PUMPKIN SEED POINT:
BEING WITHIN THE HOPI**
Frank Waters
175 pp. Ohio University Press, 1973. $9.95;
paper, $6.95.

**THE PUNISHMENT OF THE STINGY
& OTHER INDIAN STORIES**
George Bird Grinnell
Reprint of 1901 ed. Illus. 275 pp. Paper.
University of Nebraska Press. $7.95.

**PURITAN JUSTICE & THE INDIAN: WHITE
MAN'S LAW IN MASSACHUSETTS, 1630-
1763**
Yasuhide Kawashima
Illus. Map. Biblio. 336 pp. University Press of
New England, 1986. $40.

**PURITANS AMONG THE INDIANS: ACCOUNTS
OF CAPITIVITY & REDEMPTIONS 1676-1724**
Alden Vaughan and Edward Clark
Illus. 352 pp. Harvard University Press, 1981.
$23.50.

**PUSHED INTO THE ROCKS: SOUTHERN CALI-
FORNIA INDIAN LAND TENURE, 1769-1986**
Florence Shipek
Illus. 230 pp. U. of Nebraska Press, 1988.
$25.95.

PUYALLUP-NISQUALLY
M.W. Smith
Reprint of 1940 edition. AMS Press, $34.50.

Q

QAWIARAQ INUPIAQ LITERACY MANUAL
Lawrence Kaplan
50 pp. Paper. Alaska Native Language Center, 1987. $5.

QUAIL SONG: A PUEBLO INDIAN FOLKTALE
Valerie Carey, retold by
Illus. Putnam, 1990. $14.95.

QUANAH PARKER, COMANCHE CHIEF
William T. Hagan
Present Parker as a man torn between two worlds. Illus. Maps. 160 pp. University of Oklahoma Press & AISES, $17.95.

*QUANAH PARKER: GREAT CHIEF OF THE COMANCHES
Catherine Gonzales; Melissa Roberts, Editor
Grades 1-5. Illus. 48 pp. Eakin Press, 1987. $9.95.

QUANAH: A PICTORIAL HISTORY OF THE LAST COMANCHE CHIEF
Pauline D. Robertson and R.D. Robertson
Illus. 192 pp. Paramount, 1985. $19.95.

*THE QUAPAW INDIANS: A HISTORY OF THE DOWNSTREAM PEOPLE
W. David Baird
Grades 5 and up. Reprint of 1980 edition. Illus. 104 pp. University of Oklahoma Press, $24.95; Chelsea House, $17.95.

THE QUAPAW & THEIR POTTERY
Hathcock
The ceramic output of the Quapaw Indians, 1650-1750. Illus. 176 pp. Hothem House, 1983. $35.

*THE QUAPAWS
W.D. Baird
Grades 5 and up. Illus. 105 pp. Chelsea House, 1989. $17.95.

QUARTER-ACRE OF HEARTACHE
Claude C. Smith
In the words of Big Eagle of the Golden Hill Tribe, Paugussett Nation, his legal struggle to save the token parcel of land that remain of the original Paugussett reservation. Illus. Maps. 160 pp. Pocahontas Press, 1985. $12.95; paper, $8.95.

QUEESTO: PACHEENAHT CHIEF BY BIRTHRIGHT
Chief Charles Jones with Stephen Bosustow
Memoirs of hereditary Chief of the Pacheenaht people of Vancouver Island's West Coast. 125 pp. Theytus, 1982. $14.95.

*QUEST FOR COURAGE
Stormy Randolph
A lame Blackfeet boy overcomes his handicap by going on a vision quest. Grades 3-17. Illus. 102 pp. Paper. Roberts Rinehart, 1993. $8.95.

QUIET PRIDE: AGELESS WISDOM OF THE AMERICAN WEST
J. Bourge Hathaway;
photos by Robert A. Clayton
Collectio of photograhs and narration that preserves the stories, wisdom & insight of Native and non-Native American elders. Illus. 80 color photos. 128 pp. Beyond Words Pubg, 1993. $39.95.

QUIET TRIUMPH: FORTY YEARS WITH THE INDIAN ARTS FUND, SANTA FE
Mitchell Wilder
Illus. 18 pp. Paper. Amon Carter Museum, 1965. $2.

QUILL & BEADWORK OF THE WESTERN SIOUX
Carrie A. Lyford
Reprint of 1940 edition. Illus. 116 pp. Paper. R. Schneider, Publishers, $6.95.

A QUILLWORK COMPANION: AN ILLUSTRATED GUIDE TO TECHNIQUES OF PORCUPINE QUILL EMBROIDERY
Jean Heinbuch
Describes and illustrates all of the basic and advanced designs used by the American Indian. Also explains birchbark and loom quillwork. Illus. 92 pp. Eagle's View Publishing, $15.95; paper, $9.95.

QULIAQTUAT MUMIAKRAT ILISAQTUANUN SAVAAKSRIAT
Edna MacLean
Illus. 35 pp. Paper. Alaska Native Language Center, 1986. $4.

R

RACE, DISCOURSE, & THE ORIGIN OF THE AMERICAS, A NEW WORLD VIEW
Vera Lawrence Hyatt & Rex Nettleford
Collection of essays. Illus. 448 pp. Smithsonian Institution Press, 1994. $42.

RACE RELATIONS IN BRITISH NORTH AMERICA 1607-1783
Bruce Glasrud and Alan Smith
368 pp. Nelson-Hall, Inc., 1982. $27.95.

RACIAL PREHISTORY IN THE SOUTHWEST & THE HAWIKUH ZUNIS
C.C. Seltzer
Reprint of 1944 edition. Paper. Kraus, $16.

*THE RAINBOW BRIDGE: A CHUMASH LEGEND
Tom & Kerry Nechodom
Grades 4 and up. Illus. 32 pp. Paper. Sand River Press, $6.95.

*RAINBOW CROW
Nancy Van Laan
Preschool-3. Illus. 40 pp. Alfred K. Knopf, 1989. $12.95.

RAINBOW MEDICINE: A VISIONARY GUIDE TO NATIVE AMERICAN SHAMANISM
Wolf Moondance
Teaches self-worth through ancient ceremonies, using ordinary objects, herbs, and foods. Illus. 192 pp. Paper. Sterling, $12.95.

RAINHOUSE & OCEAN: SPEECHES FOR THE PAPAGO YEAR
Ruth Underhill, et al
Illus. 160 pp. Paper. Museum of Northern Arizona,1980. $12.95.

THE RAIN--MAKERS: INDIANS OF ARIZONA & NEW MEXICO
M. Coolidge
Reprint of 1929 edition. 376 pp. AMS Press, $35.

THE RAINMAKERS
E.J. Bird
Illus. 150 pp. Lerner, 1993. $19.95.

*THE RAMILUK STORIES: ADVENTURES OF AN ESKIMO FAMILY IN THE PREHISTORIC ARCTIC
Eugene Vickery
Grades 5 and up. Illus. 125 pp. Stonehaven Publishers, 1989. $16.00; paper, $10.95.

RAMONA
Helen Hunt Jackson : into. by Michael Dorris
Ethical novel of the Native American struggle, and the horror of the American political past. 384 pp. Paper. Penguin USA, $3.50.

THE RANGE SITE: ARCHAIC THROUGH LATE WOODLAND OCCUPATIONS
John Kelly, et al
Illus. 480 pp. Paper. University of Illinois Press, 1987. $23.95.

RANK & WARFARE AMONG THE PLAINS INDIANS
Bernard Mishkin
Reprint of 1940 edition. AMS, $20. Paper. University of Nebraska Press, $6.95.

THE RAPE OF THE INDIAN LANDS: AN ORIGINAL ANTHOLOGY
Paul Gates and Stuart Bruchey, Editors
Ayer Co., 1978. $23.

RARE & UNUSUAL ARTIFACTS OF THE FIRST AMERICANS
Ray Parman, Jr.
Illus. 300 pp. Paper. Fred Pruett, 1989. $24.95.

KNUD RASMUSSEN'S POSTHUMOUS NOTES ON EAST GREENLAND LEGENDS & MYTHS
Knud Rasmussen; H. Osterman, Editor
Reprint of 1939 edition. AMS, $27.

RAVEN: A TRICKSTER TALE FROM THE PACIFIC NORTHWEST
Gerald McDermott
Grades K-3. Illus. Harcourt Brace, 1994. $14.95.

RAVEN'S CRY
Christie Harris; illus. by Bill Reid
Fictionalized retelling of the near destruction of the Haida Nation. Illus. 196 pp. Paper. University of Washington Press, $12.95.

RAVEN'S GUIDE TO AIDS PREVENTION RESOURCES
Alaska Native Health Board
Designed to provide infomation & resources available for American Indians and Alaska Natives on AIDS and AIDS prevention. Includes agencies, programs & servics, books & periodicals, brochures, videos, posters, and other materials. 42 pp. National Native American AIDS Prevention Center, 1991.

RAVEN'S JOURNEY: THE WORLD OF ALASKA'S NATIVE PEOPLE
Susan A. Kaplan
Illus. 210 pp. University of Pennsylvania Museum, 1986. $39.95; paper, $24.95.

*RAVEN'S LIGHT
Susan Hand Shetterly;
illus. by Robert Shetterly
Grades 1-5. Illus. Macmillan, 1989. $13.95.

THE RAVEN STEALS THE LIGHT
 Bill Reid & Robert Bringhurst
Illus. 94 pp. Paper . University of Washington
Press, $17.95.

THE RAVEN TALES
 Peter Goodchild
Illus. 144 pp. Indepdent Publishers Group & Chi-
cago Review Press, 1991. $16.95; paper , $9.95.

**RAVENSONG: A NATURAL & FABULOUS
HISTORY OF RAVENS & CROWS**
 Catherine Feher-Elston
Extensive personal interviews with Native Ameri-
cans . Illus. 224 pp. Paper . Northland Publishing,
$16.95.

REACHING BOTH WAYS
 Helen P. Wolf: Barbara Ketcham, Editor
Illus. 135 pp. Paper . Jelm Mountain, 1989. $9.95.

**READERS DIGEST - AMERICA'S
FASCINATING INDIAN HERITAGE**
Random House, $30.

**READING COMPREHENSION & LANGUAGE
PROFICIENCY AMONG ESKIMO CHILDREN**
 Virginia Streif f; Francesco Cordasco, Editor
Ayer Co., 1978. $30.

**READING THE FIRE: ESSAYS IN THE
TRADITIONAL INDIAN LITERATURES
OF THE FAR WEST**
 Jarold Ramsey
250 pp. U. of Nebraska Press, 1983. $21.95.

READINGS ON JAMES BAY
Articles on the hydroelectric projects planned for
the James Bay region of northern Canada where
Cree people live. Akwe;kon Press, $8.

**READJUSTMENT OF INDIAN AFFAIRS:
HEARINGS**
 U.S. Congress, Committee on Indian Affairs
Reprint of 1934 edition. AMS Press, $36.

**THE REAL PEOPLE & THE CHILDREN OF
THUNDER: THE YUP'IK ESKIMO ENCOUNTER
WITH MORAVIAN MISSIONARIES JOHN &
EDITH KILBUCK**
 Ann Fienup-Riordan
Illus. Maps. 432 pp. University of Oklahoma
Press, 1992. $35.

**REBELLION FROM THE ROOTS:
INDIAN UPRISING IN CHIAPAS**
 John Ross
250 pp. Common Courage Press, 1994.
$29.95; paper , $14.95.

**THE RE-ESTABLISHMENT OF THE INDIANS
IN THEIR PUEBLO LIFE THROUGH THE
REVIVAL OF THEIR TRADITIONAL CRAFTS**
 H. Burton
A study in home extension education. Reprint of
1936 edition. Kraus, $18; AMS Press, $22.50.

**RECENTLY DISCOVERED TALES
OF LIFE AMONG THE INDIANS**
 James Willard Schultz; Warren L. Hanna, Ed.
Collection of stories from Schultz's earliest writ-
ings from 1880 to 1894. Illus. 152 pp. Paper . Moun-
tain Press, $10.

**RECKONING WITH THE DEAD, THE LARSEN
BAY REPATRIATION & THE SMITHSONIAN
INSTITUTION**
 Tamara L. Bray & Thomas W. Killion, Editor
Presents the Larsen Baym Alaska, repatriation
request of the Smithsonian. Illus. 352 pp. Paper .
Smithsonian Institution Press, 1994. $29.95.

**RECONCILING THE PAST: TWO
BASKETRY KA'AI & THE LEGENDARY
LILOA & LONOIKAMAKAHIKI**
 Roger G. Rose
Anthropological literature. Illus. Paper . Bishop
Museum, $12.95.

RECONSTRUCTION IN INDIAN TERRITORY
 M. Thomas Bailey
A story of avarice, discrimination, and opportun-
ism. Associated Faculty Press, 1972. $23.95.

**RECOVERING THE WORD: ESSAYS
ON NATIVE AMERICAN LITERATURE**
 Brian Swann & Arnold Krupat, Editors
600 pp. University of California Press, 1987.
$60.00; paper , $17.95.

RED BROTHER
 R. Ray Baker
Reprint of 1927 edition. Paper .
George Wahr Publishing, $12.50.

**RED CAPITALISM: AN ANALYSIS OF THE
NAVAJO ECONOMY**
 Larry Galbreath
150 pp. Paper . Books on Deamnd, 1973.
$41.80.

RED CHILDREN IN WHITE AMERICA
 Ann H. Beuf
168 pp. U. of Pennsylvania Press, 1977. $19.95.

RED CLOUD & THE SIOUX PROBLEM
 James Olson
Illus. 388 pp. University of Nebraska Press,
1965. $28.95; paper , $9.95.

**RED CLOUD'S FOLK: A HISTORY
OF THE OGLALA SIOUX INDIANS**
 George E. Hyde
Reprint of 1937 edition. Illus. 350 pp. Paper .
University of Oklahoma Press, $9.95.

RED CROW: WARRIOR CHIEF
 Hugh A. Dempsey
Illus. 256 pp. University of Nebraska Press,
1980. $21.95.

**RED EAGLE & THE WARS WITH
THE CREEK INDIANS OF ALABAMA**
 G.C. Eggleston
Reprint of 1878 edition. AMS Press, $22.50.

**RED EAGLES OF THE NORTHWEST: THE
STORY OF CHIEF JOSEPH & HIS PEOPLE**
 F. Haines
Reprint of 1939 edition. Illus. 376 pp. AMS
Press, $32.50.

**RED FOX: BRIG.-GENERAL STAND WATIE'S
CIVIL WAR YEARS IN INDIAN TERRITORY**
 Wilfred Knight
Watie was the last Confederate General in the Civil
War to surrender. He and his Indian troops fought
unsung battles in Indian Territory throughout the
war. Illus. Map. Biblio. 320 pp. The Arthur H. Clark
Co., $27.50.

*RED FROG MAN: A HOHOKAM LEADER
 Charles Fellers; Maxine Hughes, Editor
Grades 1-6. Illus. 64 pp. Paper . Laughing Fox,
1990. $6.95.

**RED HAWK'S ACCOUNT OF
CUSTER'S LAST BATTLE**
 Paul Goble
Illus. 64 pp. Paper . University of Nebraksa
Press, 1992. $9.95

**RED-HEADED RENEGADE -- CHIEF
BENGE OF THE CHEROKEE NATION**
 Clara Talton Fugate
Illus. Paper . Pocahontas Press, 1994.

RED HUNTERS & THE ANIMAL PEOPLE
 C. Eastman
Reprint of 1904 edition. Illus. AMS Press, $21.

**THE RED KING'S REBELLION: RACIAL
POLITICS IN NEW ENGLAND, 1675-1677**
 Russell Bourne
Illus. 288 pp. Macmillan, 1990. $22.95. Paper .
. Oxford University Press, $9.95.

**RED LAKE COURT OF INDIAN OFFENES:
MANAGEMENT AUDIT**
52 pp. National Center for State Courts, 1982.
Manuscript, $3.12

**RED LAKE COURT OF TRIBAL
OFFENSES COURT MANUAL**
450 pp. National Center for State Courts, 1982.

**RED LAKE NATION:
PORTRAITS OF OJIBWAY LIFE**
 Charles Brill
Illus. 192 pp. University of Minnesota Press,
1992. $24.95.

RED MAN IN THE U.S.
 G. Lindquist
Reprint of 1923 edition. Illus. 487 pp.
Augustus M. Kelley, $45.

**RED MAN'S AMERICA: A HISTORY
OF INDIANS IN THE U.S.**
 Ruth Underhill
Revised edition. Illus. 398 pp. Paper . University
of Chicago Press, 1971. $13.95.

**RED MAN'S LAND/WHITE MAN'S LAW: A
STUDY OF THE PAST & PRESENT STATUS
OF THE AMERICAN INDIAN**
 Wilcomb Washburn
Provides a clear discussion of the legal history of
Indian-white relations. Illus. Harper & Row , 1975.

**RED MAN'S RELIGION: BELIEFS & PRAC-
TICES OF THE INDIANS NORTH OF MEXICO**
 Ruth Underhill
Illus. 350 pp. Paper . University of Chicago
Press, 1965. $10.95.

RED MEN IN RED SQUARE
 Bud Smith & Chief Big Eagle
Story of Chief Big Eagle of the Golden Hill Tribe of
Connecticut (*Quarter-Acre of Heartache* , 1985)
and his travel to Russia and discovery of the
Indianists-Soviet citizens who study the ways,
crafts, and religion of Native American tribes. Illus.
Pocahontas Press, 1994. $15.95; paper , $12.95.

RED OVER BLACK: BLACK SLAVERY AMONG THE CHEROKEE INDIANS
R. Halliburton, Jr.
Illus. Greenwood Press, 1977. $35.

RED POWER: THE AMERICAN INDIANS' FIGHT FOR FREEDOM
Alvin M. Josephy, Jr.
Documents which have led the Federal Government toward a long overdue policy of self-determination for Native Americans. Reprint of 1970 edition. 252 pp. Paper . University of Nebraska Press, $8.95.

*RED POWER ON THE RIO GRANDE
Franklin Folsom
Pueblo Indian uprising of 1680 against Spanish control in the Southwest. Grades 9-adult. 144 pp. Council on Indian Education, 1989. $12.95; paper, $8.95.

THE RED RECORD OF THE SIOUX
W. Johnson
Reprint of 1891 edition. AMS Press, $64.50.

THE RED RECORD; THE WALLA OLUM
David McCutchen
Epic journey - 6,000 miles, 2,000 years. Illus. 200 pp. Paper. AISES, $14.95.

*RED RIBBONS FOR EMMA
Grades 3-12. Illus. 48 pp. New Seed Press, 1981. $12.

THE RED SWAN: MYTHS & TALES OF THE AMERICAN INDIANS
John Bierhorst, Translator
Reprint of 1976 edition. 386 pp. Paper . Farrar, Straus & Giroux, $10.95.

RED, WHITE & BLACK: SYMPOSIUM ON INDIANS IN THE OLD SOUTH
Charles Hudson
Paper. University of Georgia Press, 1971. $8.

RED & WHITE: INDIAN VIEWS OF THE WHITE MAN, 1492-1982
Annette Rosensteil
Illus. 192 pp. Universe Books, 1983. $14.95.

THE REDEEMED CAPTIVE RETURNING TO ZION
John Williams
The captivity and deliverance of Rev . John Williams of Deerfield, Mass. Reprint of 1908 ed. Kraus, $23.00; facsimile of 1853 edition. Ayer Co., $19.

THE GEORGE REEVES SITE: LATE ARCHAIC, LATE WOODLAND, EMERGENT MISSISSIP-PIAN, & MISSISSIPPIAN COMPONENTS
Dale McElrath & Fred Finney
Illus. 464 pp. Paper . University of Illinois Press, 1987. $22.95.

REFLECTIONS OF SOCIAL LIFE IN THE NAVAHO ORIGIN MYTH
K. Spencer
Reprint of 1947 edition. AMS Press, $20.

REFLECTIONS OF THE WEAVER'S WORLD: THE GLORIA F. ROSS COLLECTION OF CON-TEMPORARY NAVAJO WEAVING
Ann Lund Hedlund
Illustrates the Denver Art Museum's permanent collection of contemporary Navajo weaving. Illus. 112 pp. Paper . University of Washington Press, $29.95.

REFLECTIONS ON THE ALASKA NATIVE EXPERIENCE: SELECTED ARTICLES & SPEECHES BY ROY M. HUHNDORF
Roy M. Huhndorf
21 selections from a series of articles written by Huhndorf, President of Cook Inlet Region, Inc., for the editorial section of the *Anchorage Times* during the period of 1981 through 1984. 61 pp. CIRI, 1991. No charge.

REGULARS IN THE REDWOODS: THE U.S. ARMY IN NORTHERN CALIFORNIA, 1852-61
William F. Strobridge
The clash between settlers and Indians during California's early statehood. Detailed account of the Regular Army's attempts to maintain peace.Illus. Map. Biblio. 283 pp. The Arthur H. Clark Co., $29.95.

RELATIONS OF NATURE TO MAN IN ABORIGINAL AMERICA
C. Wissler
Reprint of 1926 edition. AMS Press, $22.

THE RELATION OF SENECA FALSE FACE MASKS TO SENECA & ONTARIO ARCHAE-OLOGY
Zena P. Mathews
Garland Publishing, 1978. $44.

THE RELATIONSHIP SYSTEMS OF THE TLINGIT, HAIDA & TSIMSHIAN
T. Durlach
Reprint of 1928 edition. AMS Press, $27.50.

RELIGION & CEREMONIES OF THE LENAPE
M.R. Harrington
Reprint of 1921 edition. AMS Press, $39.50.

RELIGION & HOPI LIFE IN THE 20TH CENTURY
John D. Loftin
195 pp. Indiana University Press, 1991. $22.95; paper, $8.95.

RELIGION IN NATIVE NORTH AMERICAN
Christopher Vecsey
Illus. 210 pp. Paper. University of Idaho Press, 1990. $22.95.

THE RELIGION OF THE CROW INDIANS
R.H. Lowie
Reprint of 1922 edition. AMS Press, $15.

RELIGION OF THE KWAKIUTL INDIANS
Franz Boas
Two volumes. Reprint of 1930 edition. AMS Press, $60/set; $30. each.

THE RELIGIONS OF THE AMERICAN INDIANS
Ake Hultkrantz
U. of California Press, 1979. $25; paper, $11.95.

*REMEMBER MY NAME
Sara H. Banks
Deals with the Cherokee Indian Removal of 1838. An 11-year-old Cherokee, Annie Rising Fawn, shows courage and an adventurous spirit. Grades 3 to 8. Illus. 120 pp. Paper. Roberts Rinehart. $8.95.

REMEMBER NATIVE AMERICA! THE EARTHWORKS OF ANCIENT AMERICA
Richard Balthazar
Documents and illustrates Indian mounds and other earthworks from 23 states. Paper. Five Flower Press, 1993. $14.95.

REMEMBER YOUR RELATIVES, YANKTON SIOUX IMAGES, Vol. 1, 1851-1904; Vol. 2, 1865-1915
Renee Sansom-Flood, et al
Illus. Vol. 1, 55 pp.; Vol. 2, 150 pp. Paper. Yankton Sioux Tribe, 1985 & 1989. $8.50 each.

REMINGTON & RUSSELL: THE SID RICHARDSON COLLECTION
Brian W. Dippie, Editor
Revised edition. Illus. 240 pp. University of Texas Press, 1994. $70; paper, $34.95.

REMINISCENCE OF THE INDIANS
C. Washburn
Reprint of 1869 edition. Johnson Reprint, $27.

REMINISCENCES OF SEATTLE, WASHING-TON TERRITORY & THE U.S. SLOOP-OF-WAR DECATUR DURING THE INDIAN WAR OF 1855-1856
Thomas Phelps
Reprint. Ye Galleon Press, $7.50.

REMOVAL OF THE CHEROKEE INDIANS FROM GEORGIA
W. Lumpkin
Reprint of 1907 edition. Ayer Co., $45.50.

THE REMOVAL OF THE CHEROKEE NATION: MANIFEST DESTINY OF NATIOAL DISHONOR
Louis Filler and Allen Guttman, Editors
Reprint of 1962 edition. 128 pp. Paper. Krieger Publishing, $9.50; paper, $7.50.

THE REMOVAL OF THE CHOCTAW INDIANS
Arthur H. DeRosier, Jr.
An accurate account of a major Indian removal with the policies, treaties and agonies that were a part of it. Illus. 210 pp. Paper. Cherokee Publications, $9.95.

RENEGADE TRIBE: THE PALOUSE INDIANS & THEIR INVASION OF THE INLAND PACIFIC NORTHWEST
Clifford Trafzer & Richard Scheuerman, Editor
Illus. Maps. Biblio. 224 pp. Paper. Washington State University Press, 1986. $15.95.

RENEWING THE WORLD: PLAINS INDIAN RELIGION & MORALITY
Howard L. Harrod
213 pp. University of Arizona Press, 1987. $24.95; paper, $13.95.

REPORT OF CHARLES A. WETMORE, SPECIAL U.S. COMMISSIONER OF MISSION INDIANS OF SOUTHERN CALIFORNIA
Norman Tanis, Editor
Paper. California State University, Northridge, 1977. $10.

REPORT OF THE COMMISSIONER OF INDIAN AFFAIRS FOR THE TERRITORIES OF WASHINGTON, IDAHO & OREGON, 1870
75 pp. Ye Galleon, 1981. $12.50.

REPORT OF THE COMMISSIONER OF INDIAN AFFAIRS: REPORTS FOR THE YEARS 1824-1899
U.S. Office of Indian Affairs
65 volumes. Reprint of 1899 edition. AMS Press, $2,330.50 per set.

REPORT OF A VISIT TO SOME OF THE TRIBES OF INDIANS, LOCATED WEST OF THE MISSISSIPPI RIVER

John Long and Samuel Taylor
34 pp. Ye Galleon Press, 1973. $7.50.

REPORT OF THE MOUND EXPLORATIONS OF THE BUREAU OF ETHNOLOGY
Cyrus Thomas
Reprint of 1894 edition. Illus. 786 pp. Paper. Smithsonian Books, $29.95.

REPORT TO THE SECRETARY OF WAR OF THE U.S., ON INDIAN AFFAIRS
J. Morse
Reprint of 1822 edition. Illus. 400 pp. Augustus M. Kelley, $45.

REPOSSESSION AND YOU
Institute for the Development of Indian Law , $3.50.

REQUIEM FOR A PEOPLE: THE ROGUE INDIANS & THE FRONTIERSMEN
Stephen D. Beckham
Illus. University of Oklahoma Press, 1975. $16.95; paper, $9.95.

THE RESERVATION
Ted C. Williams
Tales of life on the Tuscarora Indian Reservation in New York State, from the late 1930's to the 1950's. Illus. 260 pp. Paper. Syracuse University Press, 1976. $10.95.

THE RESERVATION BLACKFEET, 1885-1945: A PHOTOGRAPHIC HISTORY OF CULTURAL SURVIVAL
William E. Farr
Illus. 240 pp. Paper. University of Washington Press, 1984. $19.95.

RESERVATION TO CITY: INDIAN URBANIZA-TION & FEDERAL RELOCATION
Elaine M. Neils
200 pp. Paper. University of Chicago, Department of Geography, 1971. $12.

RESOURCE READING LIST
Canadian Alliance in Solidarity
with Native People
Bibliography of books by and about Native peoples. paper. Greenfield Review Press, $15.

RESPECT FOR LIFE: THE TRADITIONAL UP-BRINGING OF AMERICAN INDIAN CHILDREN
S.M. Morey and O.L. Gilliam, Editors
Illus. 202 pp. Paper. Myrin Institute, 1974. $4.95.

RESTITUTION: THE LAND CLAIM CASES OF THE MASHPEE, PASSAMAQUODDY & PENOBSCOT INDIANS OF NEW ENGLAND
Paul Brodeur
Illus. 160 pp. New England University Press, 1985. $21.95; paper, $9.95.

THE RETURN OF CHIEF BLACK FOOT
Victoria Mauricio
Illus. 140 pp. Paper. Donning Co., 1981. $5.95.

*RETURN OF THE INDIAN SPIRIT
Vinson Brown
Grades 4 and up. A young Indian boy's coming of age through the beliefs and ways of his people. Illus. 60 pp. Paper. Cherokee Publications, $5.95.

THE RETURN OF THE NATIVE: AMERICAN INDIAN POLITICAL RESURGENCE
Stephen E. Cornell
Illus. 288 pp. Paper. Oxford U. Press, 1988. $12.95.

RETURN OF THE SUN, TALES FROM THE NORTHEASTERN WOODLANDS
Joseph Bruchac
Varies tales illustrating both the wealth of humor and depth of respect for life and earth of the Indigenous Northeast American people. Illus. Paper. Crossing Press, $9.95.

RETURN OF THE THUNDERBEINGS
Donn Le Vie, Jr. & Iron Thunderhorse
Illus. 288 pp. Paper. Bear & Co., 1990. $14.95.

RETURN TO CREATION: A SURVIVAL MANUAL FOR NATIVE & NATURAL PEOPLE
Medicine Story, pseud.
Illus. 210 pp. Paper. Bear Tribe, 1991. $9.95.

RETURNING THE GIFT: POETRY & PROSE FROM THE FIRST NORTH AMERICAN NATIVE WRITERS' FESTIVAL
Joseph Bruchac, Editor
A collection of submissions by 92 writers at the "Returning the Gift Festival" held in 1992. Bruchac comments on the current state of Native literature. 400 pp. University of Arizona Press, 1994. $45; paper, $19.95.

THE RICHEY CLOVIS CACHE: EARLIEST AMERICANS ALONG THE COLUMBIA RIVER
Richard M. Gramly
Illus. 70 pp. Paper. Persimmon Press, $12.95.

JOHN ROLLIN RIDGE: HIS LIFE & WORKS
James W. Parins
Illus. 270 pp. University of Nebraska Press, 1991. $30.

*RIEL'S PEOPLE: HOW THE METIS LIVED
Maria Campbell
Grades 5 and up. Paper. Salem House, $6.95.

RIG VEDA AMERICANS
Daniel G. Brinton, Editor
Reprint of 1890 edition. AMS, $30.

*RIGHT AFTER SUNDOWN: TEACHING STORIES OF THE NAVAJO
Marilyne Virginia Mabery; Raymond Johnson, Illustrator
12 short stories. Grades 4 and up. Paper. Navajo Community College Press, 1991. $14.95.

*THE RINGS ON WOOT-KEW'S TAIL: INDIAN LEGENDS OF THE ORIGIN OF THE SUN, MOON & STARS
Will Gerber, et al
Grades 3-9. Paper. Council for Indian Education, 1973. $1.95.

RISE & FALL OF THE CHOCTAW REPUBLIC
Angie Debo
Reprint of 1934 edition. Second Edition. Illus. Maps. Biblio. 317 pp. Paper. University of Oklahoma Press, $11.95.

*RISING FAWN & THE FIRE MYSTERY
Marilou Awiakta
Story about the Trail of Tears. Grades 4 and up. Illus. Paper. St. Luke's Press, 1984. $6.95.

THE RISING OF A NEW MOON: A CENTURY OF TABWA ART
Allen Roberts & Evan Maurer
Illus. 304 pp. Paper. University of Washington Press, 1985. $39.95.

RITUAL IN PUEBLO ART: HOPI LIFE IN HOPI PAINTING
Byron Harvey, III
Illus. 265 pp. Paper. National Museum of the American Indian, 1970. $10.

RIVER OF SORROWS - LIFE HISTORY OF THE MAIDU-NISENAN INDIANS
Richard Burrill
Historical fiction reveals their lifeways. Illus. Photos. Maps. 192 pp. Naturegraph, 1978. $16.95; paper, $8.95.

RIVER OF TEARS
Maud Emery
The events of the massacre at Bute Inlet. Illus. 96 pp. Paper. Hancock House, 1994. $9.95.

*RIVERMAN
Gail Stewart
Grades 3-8. Illus. 32 pp. Rourke Corp., 1990. $17.26.

THE ROAD: INDIAN TRIBES & POLITICAL LIBERTY
Russell Barsh and J. Youngblood Henderson
Paper. University of California Press, 1979. $9.95.

THE ROAD OF LIFE & DEATH: A RITUAL DRAMA OF THE AMERICAN INDIANS
Paul Radin
370 pp. Paper. Princeton University Press, 1991. $14.95.

THE ROAD TO DISAPPEARANCE: A HISTORY OF THE CREEK INDIANS
Angie Debo
Reprint of 1941 edition. Illus. Paper. University of Oklahoma Press, $15.95.

THE ROAD TO NUNAVUT: THE PROGRESS OF THE EASTERN ARCTIC INUIT SINCE THE SECOND WORLD WAR
R. Quinn Duffy
376 pp. University of Toronto Press, 1987. $35.

ROADS TO CENTER PLACE: AN ANASAZI ATLAS
Kathryn Gabriel
Illus. 250 pp. Paper. Johnson Books, 1991. $12.95.

ROADSIDE HISTORY OF ARIZONA
Marshall Trimble
Illus. 480 pp. Mountain Press, 1990. $24.95; paper, $15.95.

ROADSIDE HISTORY OF OKLAHOMA
Francis L. & Robert B. Fugate
Tales of early explorers. Illus. 472 pp. Mountain Press, 1990. $24.95; paper, $15.95.

ROADSIDE HISTORY OF OREGON
Bill Gulick
Illus. 448 pp. Mountain Press, 1991. $24.95; paper, $15.95.

THE ROARING OF THE SACRED RIVER
Steven Foster with Meredith Little
The wilderness quest for vision and self-healing. Illus. 240 pp. Paper. Prentice Hall Press, $9.95.

THE ROAD OF LIFE & DEATH: A RITUAL DRAMA OF THE AMERICAN INDIANS
Paul Radin
Reprint. 368 pp. Paper. Princeton University Press, $14.95.

THE ROAD ON WHICH WE CAME: A HISTORY OF THE WESTERN SHOSHONE
Steven J. Crum
Illus. University of Utah Press, 1993. $29.95.

ROADSIDE HISTORY OF NEW MEXICO
Francis L. & Roberta Fugate
Illus. 484 pp. Mountain Press, 1990. $24.95;
paper, $15.95.

ROBERT DAVIDSON: EAGLE OF THE DAWN
Ian Thom, Editor
On the works of Davidson, master carver of masks and totems, print maker, painter, and jeweler. Illus. 192 pp. University of Washington Press, $50.

ROCK ART OF THE AMERICAN INDIAN
Campbell Grant
Illus. 192 pp. Paper. Outbooks, 1972. $16.95.

ROCK ART OF THE AMERICAN SOUTHWEST
Scott Thybony; photos by Fred Hirschmann
100 color photos of rock art throughout the Southwest. 128 pp. Graphic Arts Center, 1994. $29.50.

THE ROCK ART OF UTAH
Polly Schaafsma
Illus. Paper. U. of Utah Press, 1976. $19.95.

ROCK ART OF WESTERN SOUTH DAKOTA
James D. Keyser & linea Sundstrom
An illustrated compendium of prehistoric petroglyphs and pictographs found in caves and on canyon walls throughout western South Dakota. 220 pp. Paper. Center for Western Studies, $9.95.

ROCK ISLAND: HISTORICAL INDIAN AR-CHAEOLOGY IN THE NORTHERN LAKE MICHIGAN BASIN
Ronald Mason
Illus. 275 pp. Paper. Kent State University Press, 1986. $19.95.

THE ROCKS BEGIN TO SPEAK
LaVan Martineau
Illus. 210 pp. K C Publications, 1973. $17.50.

ROCKY MOUNTAIN WEST IN 1867
Louis Simonin; translated by Wilson Clough
Illus. University of Nebraska Press, 1966. $16.95.

THE ROLES OF MEN AND WOMEN IN ESKIMO CULTURE
N.M. Giffen
Reprint of 1930 edition. AMS Press, $14.

THE ROLL CALL OF THE IROQUOIS CHIEFS: A STUDY OF A MNEMONIC CANE FROM THE SIX NATIONS RESERVE
W.N. Fenton
Reprint of 1950 edition. AMS Press, $20.

*THE ROLLING HEAD: CHEYENNE TALES
Henry Tall Bull and Tom Weist
Grades 3-9. Paper. Council for Indian Education, 1971. $1.95.

ROLLING THUNDER: A PERSONAL EXPLO-RATION INTO THE SECRET HEALING POWER OF AN AMERICAN INDIAN MEDICINE MAN
Doug Boyd
273 pp. Paper. Dell, 1974. $9.95.

THE ROMANCE OF INDIAN LIFE
Mary Eastman
300 pp. Paper. Irvington, 1986. $8.95.

ROOTED LIKE THE ASH TREES
Richard Carlson, Editor
Collection of writings by members of New England tribes: the Micmac & Penobscot from Maine, the Paugusset of Connecticut, and the Abenakis of Vermont. Paper. Eagle Wing Press, $5.

THE ROOTS OF DEPENDENCY: SUBSIS-TENCE, ENVIRONMENT, & SOCIAL CHANGE AMONG THE CHOCTAWS, PAWNEES, & NA-VAJOS
Richard White
Illus. Maps. 435 pp. University of Nebraska Press, 1988. $35; paper, $12.

ROOTS OF OPPRESSION: THE AMERICAN INDIAN QUESTION
Steve Talbot
240 pp. International Publishing Co., 1981. $14; paper, $5.25.

THE ROOTS OF TICASUK: AN ESKIMO WOMAN'S FAMILY STORY
Emily I. Brown
Illus. Photos. Map. 120 pp. Paper. Alaska Northwest Publishing, 1981. $9.95.

JOHN ROSS & THE CHEROKEE INDIANS
R.C. Eaton
Reprint of 1921 edition. AMS Press, $24.50.

THE ROUND VALLEY INDIANS OF CALIFOR-NIA: AN UNPUBLISHED CHAPTER IN ACCUL-TURATION IN SEVEN AMERICAN INDIAN TRIBES
Paper. Books on Demand, $35.30.

*THE ROUGH-FACE GIRL
Rafe Martin; illus. by David Shannon
An Algonquin tale. Grades PS-3. Illus. 32 pp. Putnam, 1992. $15.95.

RUGS & POSTS: THE STORY OF NAVAJO WEAVING & THE ROLE OF THE INDIAN TRADER
H.L James
Illus. Maps. 160 pp. Paper. Schiffer, 1988. $19.95.

THE RUNNING INDIANS: THE TARAHUMARA OF MEXICO
Dick & Mary Lutz
An account of the Tarahumara Indians of northern Mexico. Illus. 112 pp. Paper. Dimi Press, $11.95.

RUXTON OF THE ROCKIES
George F. Ruxton; R. LeRoy, Editor
Illus. 344 pp. Paper. University of Olahoma Press, 1979. $9.95.

S

SAANII DAHATAAL - THE WOMEN ARE SINGING: POEMS & STORIES
Luci Tapahonso
95 pp. Paper. U. of Arizona Press, 1993. $9.95.

THE SABIN COLLECTION
Selected Americana from Sabin's dictionary of books relating to America from its discovery to the present time. Includes Bibliotheca Americana-over 100,000 entries dating from 1493 to 1890s. See Research Publications for titles and prices.

THE SAC & FOX INDIANS
W.T. Hagan
Reprint of 1958 edition. Illus. 320 pp. University of Oklahoma Press, $21.95; paper, $12.95.

*SACAGAWEA
Grades 3-8. Illus. Paper. Macmillan, 1988. $3.95.

*SACAGEWEA: INDIAN INTERPRETER TO LEWIS & CLARK
Grades 4 and up. Illus. 130 pp. Childrens Press, $13.95.

SACRED BUNDLES OF THE SAC & FOX INDIANS
M.R. Harrington
Reprint of 1914 edition. Illus. 192 pp. AMS Press, $30.00.

SACRED CIRCLES: TWO THOUSAND YEARS OF NORTH AMERICAN INDIAN ART
Ralph Coe
Illus. 260 pp. Paper. Nelson Atkins, $12.95. University of Washington Press, 1977. $15.

SACRED ENCOUNTERS: FATHER DE SMET & THE INDIANS OF THE ROCKY MOUNTAIN WEST
Jacqueline Peterson; with Laura Peers
Displays the similarities and differences between European Christianity and Native American beliefs. 200 color illustrations and 20 bxw photos. University of Oklahoma Press, 1993. $49.95; paper, $24.95.

SACRED FEATHERS: THE REVEREND PETER JONES (KAHKEWAQUONABY) & THE MISSISSAUGA INDIANS
Illus. 390 pp. University of Nebraska Press, 1987. $22.95.

THE SACRED GEOGRAPHY OF THE AMERICAN MOUND-BUILDERS
Maureen Korp
170 pp. Edwin Mellen Press, 1990. $49.95.

SACRED GROUND
Ron Zeilinger
Illus. 152 pp. Paper. Tipi Press, 1986. $5.95.

*THE SACRED HARVEST: OJIBWAY WILD RICE GATHERING
Gordon Regguinti
Grades 3-6. Illus. 48 pp. Lerner, 1992. $14.95.

THE SACRED HOOP: RECOVERING THE FEMININE IN AMERICAN INDIAN TRADITIONS
Paula G. Allen
Essays, poetry, keen insights. 328 pp. Paper. Beacon Press, 1987. $12.95.

SACRED LANGUAGE: THE NATURE OF SUPERNATURAL DISCOURSE IN LAKOTA
William K. Powers
Illus. 264 pp. Paper. University of Oklahoma Press, 1986. $14.95.

SACRED PATH CARDS: THE DISCOVERY OF SELF THROUGH NATIVE TEACHINGS
Jamie Sams
Illus. 295 pp. HarperCollins, 1990. $29.95; paper, $14.95.

THE SACRED PIPE: BLACK ELK'S ACCOUNT OF THE SEVEN RITES OF OGLALA SIOUX
Joseph Epes Brown, Editor
Reprint of 1953 edition. Illus. 176 pp. University of Oklahoma Press, $26.95; paper , $9.95.

SACRED PLACES: HOW THE LIVING EARTH SEEKS OUR FRIENDSHIP
James Swan
Discusses varieties of Native American sacred places and the dilemma of sacred places in a modern world, and includes a guide to sacred places on public lands throughout the U.S. Illus. 240 pp. Paper . Bear & Co., 1990. $14.95.

SACRED SCROLLS OF THE SOUTHERN OJIBWAY
Selwyn Dewdney
University of Toronto Press, 1974. $30.

SACRED SITES OF THE INDIANS OF THE AMERICAN SOUTHWEST
Raymond Locke
Illus. 130 pp. Roundtable Publishing, 1992. $29.95.

*SACRED SONG OF THE HERMIT THRUSH: AN IROQUOIS TALE
by Tehanetorens
Mohawk legend. Grades 3 and up. Illus. 64 pp. Paper. The Book Publishing Co.. $5.96.

SACRED STORIES OF THE SWEET GRASS CREE
L. Bloomfield
Reprint of 1930 edition. AMS Press, $34.50.

THE SACRED TREE
Four Worlds Development Project
Reflections on Native American spirituality . Paper. Four Winds Trading Co., $9.95.

THE SACRED: WAYS OF KNOWLEDGE, SOURCES OF LIFE
Peggy Beck, Anna Walters & Nia Francisco
Illus. 384 pp. Navajo Community College Press, 1977. $16.

SACRED WORDS: A STUDY OF NAVAJO RELIGION AND PRAYER
Sam Gill
Illus. 283 pp. Greenwood Press, 1981. $35.

SADIE BROWER NEAKOK, AN INUPIAQ WOMAN
Margaret Blakman
Illus. 326 pp. Paper . University of Washington Press, 1989. $14.95.

SAGA OF THE COEUR D'ALENE INDIAN NATION
Joseph Seltice; Edward J. Kowrach, Intro.
Ye Galleon Press, 1990.

THE SAGA OF SITTING BULL'S BONES: THE UNUSUAL STORY BEHIND SCULPTOR KORCZAK ZIOLKOWSKI'S MEMORIAL TO CHIEF SITTING BULL
Robb DeWall
Illus. 320 pp. Crazy Horse Foundation, 1984. $15.95.

SAGEBRUSH SOLDIER: PRIVATE WILLIAM EARL SMITH'S VIEW OF THE SIOUX WAR OF 1876
Sherry Smith
Illus. 176 pp. University of Oklahoma Press, 1989. $19.95.

SAGEBRUSH TO SHAKESPEARE
Carrol B. Howe
Provides informtion on prehistoric Indian cultures; and the peope who discovered and developed the region of Southern Oregon and Northern California. Illus. 216 pp. Paper . Binford & Mort, 1984. $10.

SAINT CLAIR PAPERS: THE LIFE & PUBLIC SERVICES OF ARTHUR ST. CLAIR, WITH HIS CORRESPONDENCE AND OTHER PAPERS
W.H. Smith
Facsimile of 1881 edition.   Two volumes. Illus. Da Capo Press, $115 per set; Ayer Co., $62 each.

RAMONA SAKIESTEWA - PATTERNED DREAMS: TEXTILES OF THE SOUTHWEST
Suzanne Baizerman
52 pp. Paper . Wheelright Museum, 1989. $9.95.

SALINAN INDIANS OF CALIFORNIA & THEIR NEIGHBORS
Betty Brusa
History, vocabulary. Illus. 96 pp. Naturegraph, 1975. $15.95; paper , $7.95.

SALINAS: ARCHAEOLOGY, HISTORY, PREHISTORY
David Grant Noble, Editor
Illus. Maps. 40 pp. Paper . Ancient City Press, 1990. $7.95.

SALINAS PUEBLO MISSIONS (ABO, QUARIA, GRAN QUIVIRA) NATIONAL MONUMENT, NEW MEXICO
Dan Murphy
Tells the story of Estancia Basin from Ice Age geology to Indian villages, to European invasion to designation as a national monument. Illus. 64 pp. Paper. Southwest Parks & Monumnets Association, 1993. $9.95.

*SALISH FOLK TALES
Katheryn Law
Grades 2-8. Paper . Council for Indian Education, 1972. $2.95.

SALISH INDIAN SWEATERS
Priscilla Gibson-Roberts
Dos Tejedoras, 1989. $17.50.

SALISH WEAVING
Paul Gustafson
Illus. 132 pp. University of W ashington Press, 1980. $27.50.

THE SALT RIVER PIMA-MARICOP A INDIANS
John L. Myers & Robert Gryder
Illus. 176 pp. Heritage Publishers, 1988.

SALVATION AND THE SAVAGE: AN ANALYSIS OF PROTESTANT MISSIONS AND AMERICAN INDIAN RESPONSE, 1787-1862
R.F. Berkhofer
Reprint of 1965 edition. Greenwood Press, $35.00. Paper. Macmillan, $4.95.

*SAM & THE GOLDEN PEOPLE
Marjorie V andervelde
Grades 5-9. 40 pp. Council for Indian Education, 1972. $8.95; paper , $2.95.

SAN CARLOS APACHE TEXTS
Pliny Goddard
Reprint of 1919 edition. AMS Press.

SAN DIEGO COUNTY INDIANS AS FARMERS & WAGE EARNERS
Teo Couro
Paper. Acoma Books, $1.

SAN GABRIEL DEL YUNGUE AS SEEN BY AN ARCHAEOLOGIST
Florence H. Ellis
Illus. Paper. Sunstone, 1988. $10.95.

SANAPIA: COMANCHE MEDICINE WOMAN
David E. Jones
Reprint of 1972 edition. 107 pp. Paper . Waveland Press, $7.95.

SAND IN A WHIRLWIND: THE PAIUTE INDIAN WAR, 1860
Ferol Egan
Illus. 316 pp. Paper . University of Nevada Press, 1985. $9.95.

THE SANDAL & THE CAVE: THE INDIANS OF OREGON
Luther S. Cressman
Illus. 96 pp. Paper . Oregon State University Press, 1981. $6.95.

SANDPAINTINGS OF THE NAVAJO SHOOTING CHANT
Franc Newcomb & Gladys Reichard
Reprint. Illus. 132 pp. Paper . Dover, $11.95.

SANPOIL & NESPELEM: SALISHAN PEOPLES OF NORTHEASTERN WASHINGTON
Verne F. Ray
Reprint of 1933 edition. AMS Press, $24.50.

SANTA FE: HIST ORY OF AN ANCIENT CITY
David Grant Noble
Illus. 168 pp. School of American Research, 1990. $29.95; paper , $16.95.

SAPAT'QQAYN: TWENTIETH CENTURY NEZ PERCE ARTISTS
72 pp. Paper . Nez Perce National Historical Park.

SASQUATCH: THE APES AMONG US
John Green
Illus. 492 pp. Paper . Hancock House, $12.95.

SASQUATCH: BIGFOOT: THE CONTINUING MYSTER Y
Thomas N. Steenburg
An Indian legend told to early explorers. Illus Maps. 128 pp. Paper . Hancock House, $11.95.

SATANTA, THE GREAT CHIEF OF THE KIOWAS & HIS PEOPLE
C. Wharton
Reprint of 1935 edition. AMS Press, $29.50.

THE SAUKS & THE BLACK HA WK WAR
P.A. Armstrong
Reprint of 1887 edition. Illus. AMS Press, $47.50.

THE SAVAGE & HIS TOTEM
P. Hadfield
Reprint of 1938 edition. AMS Press, $20.

SAVAGE SCENE: THE LIFE & TIMES OF JAMES KIRKER, FRONTIER KING
William McGaw
Illus. 288 pp. Hastings House, 1972. $10.95.

THE SVANAH RIVER CHIEFDOMS: POLITI-CAL CHANGE IN THE LATE PREHISTORIC SOUTHEAST
David G. Anderson
Illus. 488 pp. Paper. University of Alabama Press, 1994. $39.95.

SAYULA POPOLUCA VERB DERIVATION
Lawrence Clark
80 pp. Paper. Summer Institute of Linguistics, 1983. $8.50. Microfiche, $2.

SCALP CEREMONIAL OF ZUNI
E.C. Parsons
Reprint of 1924 edition. Paper. Kraus, $15.

SCARLET PLUME
Frederick Manfred
365 pp. Paper. University of Nebraska Press, 1983. $8.95.

SCARLET RIBBONS: AMERICAN INDIAN TECHNIQUE FOR TODAYS QUILTERS
Helen Kelley
Illus. 120 pp. Paper. Collector Books, 1987. $15.95.

SCHAT-CHEN: HISTORY, TRADITIONS & NARRATIVES OF THE QUERES INDIANS OF LAGUNA & ACOMA
John Gunn
Reprint of 1917 edition. AMS Press, $22.

SCHOLARS & THE INDIAN EXPERIENCE: CRITICAL REVIEWS OF RECENT WRITINGS IN THE SOCIAL SCIENCES
W.R. Swagerty
280 pp. Indiana University Press, 1984. $22.50; paper, $9.95.

SCHOOLCRAFT: LITERARY VOYAGER
Philip Mason, Editor
208 pp. Michigan State U. Press, 1962. $5.

SCHOOLCRAFT SERIES
Philip P. Mason, Editor
Schoolcraft was explorer, historian, and Indian agent. Includes three volumes: Schoolcraft's Expedition to Lake Itasca; Schoolcraft's Indian Legends; and Schoolcraft's Narrartive Journal of Travels. Reprints. Michigan State University, $35 each; paper, $16. each.

SCHOOLCRAFT'S INDIAN LEGENDS FROM ALGIC RESEARCHES
H.R. Schoolcraft; M. Williams, Editor
Reprint of 1956 edition. 322 pp. Greenwood Press, $22.50.

SCIENCE ACTIVITIES FOR TEACHERS
AISES teachers
Created by & for teachers at American Indian schools. Illus. 220 pp. Paper. AISES, $11.

SCIENCE OF ALCOHOL CURRICULUM - TEACHER UNIT
AISES, Editors
Teacher training manual - Grades 5-8. Illus. Paper. AISES, $60.

SCIENTIST ON THE TRAIL
A.F. Bandelier; George P. Hammond, Editor
Reprint of 1949 edition. Ayer Co., $17.

SCOORWA: JAMES SMITH'S INDIAN CAPTIVITY NARRATIVE
James Smith

Reprint. Illus. 176 pp. Paper. Ohio Historical Society, $5.95.

SCOUT & RANGER
James Pike
Reprint of 1932 edition. Illus. 164 pp. Da Capo Press, $25.

*SCOUTS
Gail Stewart
Grades 3-8. Illus. 32 pp. Rourke Corp., 1990. $17.26.

SCRAPBOOK OF THE AMERICAN WEST
E. Lisle Reedstrom
Illus. 260 pp. Paper. The Caxton Printers, 1989. $17.95.

SCULPTURING TOTEM POLES
Walt Way; Jack Ekstrom, Editor
Illus. 26 pp. Paper. Vestal, 1985. $5.

SEAHB SIWASH
Leon L. Stock
Illus. 352 pp. Todd & Honeywell, 1981. $15.

*SEAL FOR A PAL
Paul E. Layman
Grades 4-9. 31 pp. Council for Indian Education, 1972. $8.95; paper, $2.95.

THE SEARCH FOR AN AMERICAN INDIAN IDENTITY: MODERN PAN-AMERICAN MOVEMENTS
Hazel W. Hertzberg
Illus. 362 pp. Syracuse University Press, 1971. $18.95; paper, $10.95.

*SEARCH FOR IDENTITY
Hap Gilliland, et al
5 stories of Indian youth attempting to find their place in life. Grades 6-10. Council for Indian Education, 1991. $10.95; paper, $4.95.

SEARCH FOR THE PUREBLOODS
Charles B. Wilson
Second edition. Illus. 56 pp. Paper. University of Oklahoma Press, 1989. $10.95.

SEARCHING FOR FOOTSTEPS TO THE PAST: SURFACE FINDS ALONG THE KASKASKIA RIVER
James Smith
Illus. 160 pp. Paper. Mayhaven Publishing, 1991. $29.95.

SEARCHING, TEACHING, HEALING: AMERICAN INDIANS & ALASKAN NATIVES IN BIOMEDICAL RESEARCH CAREERS
Edwin H. Haller & Ruth A. Myers
Illus. 176 pp. Paper. Futura, 1986. $9.50.

SEASONS OF THE KACHINA: PROCEED-INGS OF THE CALIFORNIA STATE UNIVER-SITY HAYWOOD CONFERENCES ON THE WESTERN PUEBLOS, 1987-1988
Lowell J. Bean
Illus. 175 pp. Ballena Pres, 1989. $32.95; paper, $21.95.

THE SECOND LONG WALK: THE NAVAJO-HOPI LAND DISPUTE
Jerry Kammer
258 pp. Paper. University of New Mexico Press, 1980. $12.95.

SECRET OF THE TOTEM
Andrew Lang
Reprint of 1905 edition. AMS Pres, $16.75.

THE SECRET SAGA OF FIVE-SACK
Henry L. Reimers
25 pp. Paper. Ye Galleon Press, 1975. $4.95.

SECRETS FROM THE CENTER OF THE WORLD
Joy Harjo & Stephen Strom
Prose. 76 pp. Paper. University of Arizona Press, 1989. $12.95.

SEEDS OF CHANGE: A QUINCENTENNIAL COMMEMORATION
Herman J. Viola & Carolyn Margolis, Editors
Illus. 352 pp. Smithsonian Books, 1991. $39.95.

SEEDS OF EXTINCTION: JEFFERSONIAN PHILANTHROPY AND THE AMERICAN INDIAN
Bernard Sheehan
320 pp. University of North Carolina Press, 1973. $30. Paper. W.W. Norton, $8.95.

SEEING WITH THE NATIVE EYE: CONTRIBUTIONS TO THE STUDY OF NATIVE AMERICAN RELIGION
Walter H. Capps
Paper. Harper & Row, 1976. $6.95.

SELECTED WRITINGS OF EDWARD SAPIR IN LANGUAGE, CULTURE & PERSONALITY
E. Sapir; David G. Mandelbaum, Editor
Reprint of 1949 edition. University of California Press, $45; paper, $15.95.

SELECTION OF SOME OF THE MOST INTERESTING NARRATIVES OF OUTRAGES COMMITTED BY THE INDIANS IN THEIR WARS WITH THE WHITE PEOPLE
Archibald Loudon
Reprint of 1808 ed. 2 vols. in 1. Ayer Co., $45.

SELF-DETERMINATION & THE SOCIAL EDUCATION OF NATIVE AMERICANS
Guy B. Senese
Greenwood, 1991. $39.95.

SELF-RELIANCE VS. POWER POLITICS: AMERICAN & INDIAN EXPERIENCES IN BUILDING NATION-STATES
J. Ann Tickner
352 pp. Columbia University Press, 1986. $35.

SELF & SAVAGERY ON THE CALIFORNIA FRONTIER: A STUDY OF THE DIGGER STEREOTYPE
Allan Lonnberg
Illus. 98 pp. Paper. Coyote Press, 1980. $10.

SELU: SEEKING THE CORN-MOTHER'S WISDOM
Marilou Awiakta; illus. by Mary Adair
Presents the Corn-Mother's wisdoms as traditionally taught by representative Native peoples. Illus. 352 pp. Fulcrum Publishing & AISES, 1993. $19.95; paper, $14.95.

THE SEMANTICS OF TIME; ASPECTUAL CAT-EGORIZATION IN KOYUKON ATHABASKAN
Melissa Axelrod
Athabaskan studies. 200 pp. University of Nebraska Press, 1993. $40.

*THE SEMINOLE
B. Brooks
Grades 5-8. Illus. 32 pp. Rourke Corp., 1989.
$13.26.

*THE SEMINOLE
Merwin Garbarino
Grades 7-12. Illus. 112 pp. Paper.
Chelsea House, 1989. $9.95.

*THE SEMINOLE
Emilie U. Lepthien
Grades 2-4. Illus. 48 pp. Childrens Press, 1985.
$11.45.

SEMINOLE INDIANS OF FLORIDA, 1850-1874
Raymond C. Lantz
Annuity & per capita rolls of the BIA and National
Archives. 415 pp. Paper. Heritage Books, 1994.
$30.

**THE SEMINOLE & MICCOSUKEE TRIBES:
A CRITICAL BIBLIOGRAPHY**
Harry A. Kersey, Jr.
Examines over 200 major works relating to the
ethnohistorical development of the Seminole and
Miccosukee tribes of Florida. 116 pp. Paper. Indi-
ana University Press, 1987. $7.95.

SEMINOLE MUSIC
F. Densmore
Reprint of 1956 edition. Illus. 276 pp.
Da Capo Press, $27.50.

SEMINOLE PATCHWORK
Margaret Brandenbourg
Illus. 96 pp. Paper. Sterling, 1987. $10.95.

SEMINOLE PATCHWORK BOOK
Cheryl G. Bradkin
Illus. 48 pp. Paper. Burdett Design, 1980. $7.50.

THE SEMINOLE SEED
Robert N. Peck
420 pp. Pineapple Press, 1983. $14.95.

A SEMINOLE SOURCEBOOK
W.C. Sturtevant, Editor
856 pp. Garland Publishing, 1985. $90.

*THE SEMINOLE: SOUTHEAST
Grades 7-12. Illus. 112 pp. Knowledge
Unlimited, $16.95.

*THE SEMINOLES
Martin Lee
Grades 3 and up. Illus. 64 pp. Paper.
Franklin Watts, 1991. $4.95.

*THE SEMINOLES
Virginia Driving Hawk Sneve
The creation myth of the Seminoles; history, cus-
toms, and facts about the tribe today. Grades 2-6.
Illus. 32 pp. Holiday House, 1994. $15.95.

SEMINOLES
Edwin McReynolds
Reprint of 1957 edition. Illus. Paper.
University of Oklahoma Press, $11.95.

THE SEMINOLES OF FLORIDA
James W. Covington
History of the Florida Seminoles. Illus. Maps.
Biblio. 416 pp. University Press of Florida, 1994.
$49.95; paper, $18.95.

*THE SENECA
Grades K-4. Illus. 48 pp. Childrens Press,
$11.45.

SENECA MYTHS & FOLK TALES
A. Parker
Reprint of 1923 edition. 485 pp. AMS Press, $35.
Paper. University of Nebraska Press, $11.95

SENECA THANKSGIVING RITUALS
Wallace L. Chafe
Reprint. Reprint Services, $75.

**The Seneca & Tuscarora Indians: An
Annotated Bibliography**
Marilyn L. Haas, Editor
Citations to journal articles, books, theses, and
government documents published up to 1992.
465 pp. Scarecrow Press, 1994. $55.

THE SENECA WORLD OF GA-NO-SAY-YEH
Joseph A. Francello
225 pp. Peter Lang, 1989. $37.10.

SENATE DOCUMENT #512
Contains thousands of pages of material in the form
of census documents, payrolls, records and correspondence and other material documenting the
removal of the Indians from the 30th November
1831, through 27th December 1833. In five volumes. See publisher for prices and titles. Histree.

SEPARATE REALITY
Carlos Castaneda; Jane Rosenman
275 pp. Pocket Books, 1991. $8.95; paper, $4.95

SEQUOYAH
Grant Foreman
The life of the creator of the Cherokee alphabet.
Illus. 85 pp. Paper. Cherokee Publications, $6.95.

*SEQUOYAH
Robert Cwiklik; Nancy Furstinger, Editor
Grades 5-7. Silver Burdett Press, 1989. $11.98;
paper, $7.95.

*SEQUOYAH (CHEROKEE HERO)
Joanne Oppenheim
Biograpgy for children. Grades 4 and up. Illus.
48 pp. Paper. Cherokee Publications, $2.95.

SEQUOYAH & THE CHEROKEE ALPHABET
Robert Cwiklik
Illus. 130 pp. Paper. Cherokee Publications,
$7.95.

***SEQUOYAH: FATHER OF THE CHEROKEE
ALPHABET**
David Petersen
Grades 2-4. Illus. 32 pp. Childrens Press,
$10.95. Paper. Cherokee Publications, $3.95.

*SEQUOYAH & HIS MIRACLE
William Roper
Biography of the Cherokee who invented writing
for his people. Grades 5-12. 32 pp. Council for
Indian Education, $8.95; paper, $2.95.

THE SERI
Alfred Kroeber
Reprint of 1931 edition. AMS, $11.50.

THE SERI INDIANS OF SONORA
Bernice Johnston
Illus. 16 pp. Paper. University of Arizona Press,
1980. $3.95.

**THE SERRANO INDIANS
OF SOUTHERN CALIFORNIA**
Frank Johnston
Malki Museum Press, 1967. $1.75.

SERRANO SONGS & STORIES
Guy Mount
Recorded at Morongo Indian Reservation in south-
ern California by Sarah Martin, Louis Marcus and
Magdalina Nombre. Introduction to Serrano cul-
ture is provided by author, Guy Mount. Sweetlight
Books, 1993. $5.

**SETTING IT FREE: AN EXHIBITION OF MOD-
ERN ALASKAN ESKIMO IVORY CARVING**
Dinah Larsen & Terry Dickey, Editors
Illus. Map. Paper. University of Alaska Museum,
1982. $10.

**SETTLEMENT, SUBSISTENCE, &
SOCIETY IN LATE ZUNI PREHISTORY**
Keith W. Kintigh
132 pp. Paper. University of Arizona Press,
1985. $19.95.

SEVEN ARROWS
Hyemeyohsts Storm
The story of the Shield and the Medicine Wheel.
A teaching story. Illus. 375 pp. Paper. Cherokee
Publications, $14.95.

SEVEN FAMILIES IN PUEBLO POTTERY
Maxwell Museum of Anthropology
Illus. 116 pp. University of New Mexico Press,
1974. $7.95.

**SEVEN ROCK ART SITES
IN BAJA CALIFORNIA**
Clement W. Meighan & V.L. Pontoni, Editors
Illus. 236 pp. Paper. Ballena Press, 1979. $10.95.

THE SEVEN VISIONS OF BULL LODGE
told by his daughter Garter Snake
George Horse Capture, Editor
A record of the spiritual life of Bull Lodge (1802-
86). Illus. 125 pp. Paper. University of Nebraska
Press, 1992. $8.95.

SHADOW COUNTRY
Paula G. Allen
149 pp. Paper. American Indian Studies Center,
1982. $7.50.

**SHADOW DISTANCE:
A GERALD VIZENOR READER**
Gerald Vizenor
340 pp. University Press of New England, 1994.
$40; paper, $17.95.

**SHADOW OF THE HUNTER:
STORIES OF ESKIMO LIFE**
Richard K. Nelson
Illus. 282 pp. Paper. University of Chicago
Press, 1980. $10.95.

**THE SHADOW OF SEQUOYAH: SOCIAL
DOCUMENTS OF THE CHEROKEES, 1862-
1964**
Jack and Anna Kilpatrick, Editors
143 pp. Paper. Books on Demand, $36.00.

SHADOWCATCHERS
Steve Wall
Teachings of Native American elders from 13
different tribes. Illus. 288 pp. Harper & Row,
1994. $27.50.

SHADOWS IN GLASS: THE INDIAN PHOTOGRAPHS OF BEN WITTICK
Patricia Broder
Rowman & Littlefield, 1990. $39.95.

SHADOWS OF THE BUFFALO: A FAMILY ODYSSEY AMONG THE INDIANS
Adolf and Beverly Hungry W olf
Pat Golbitz, Editor
Illus. 288 pp. Paper . William Morrow , 1985. $6.95.

SHADOWS OF THE INDIAN: STEREOTYPES IN AMERICAN CULTURE
Raymond Stedman
Illus. 300 pp. University of Oklahoma Press, 1982. $24.95; paper , $14.95.

SHADOWS ON THE KOYUKUK: AN ALAS-KAN NATIVE'S LIFE ALONG THE RIVER
Huntington & Rearden
Illus. Map. Paper . Alaska Northwest Books, $12.95.

THE SHAMAN & THE MEDICINE WHEEL
Evelyn Eaton
Illus. 206 pp. Theosophical Publishing, 1982. $13.95.

THE SHAMAN'S TOUCH: OTOMI INDIAN SYMBOLIC HEALING
James Dow
illus. 180 pp. University of Utah Press, 1986. $13.95.

SHAMANIC ODYSSEY: THE LUSHOOTSEED SALISH JOURNEY TO THE LAND OF THE DEAD
Jay Miller; Sylvia V ane, Editor
Illus. 217 pp. Ballena Press, 1988. $39.95; paper, $28.95.

SHAMANISM IN WESTERN NORTH AMERICA
W.Z. Park
Reprint of 1938 edition. 166 pp. Cooper Square Publishers, $32.50.

SHAMANS & KUSHTAKAS: NORTH COAST TALES OF THE SUPERNATURAL
Mary Beck; illus. by Oliver
Illus. 128 pp. Paper . Alaska Northwest Books, 1991. $12.95.

SHANDAA: IN MY LIFETIME
told by Belle Herbert; edited by
Bill Pfisterer & Jane McGary
19th century life on the upper Yukon River. Stories are in Gwich'in Athabaskan with English translations. Illus. 207 pp. Paper . University of Alaska Press, 1988. $14.95.

SHAPES OF THEIR THOUGHTS: REFLECTIONS OF CULTURAL CONTACT IN NORTHWEST COAST INDIAN ART
Victoria Wyatt
Illus. 80 pp. Paper . University of Oklahoma Press, 1984. $9.95.

SHARED VISIONS: NATIVE AMERICAN PAINTERS AND SCULPTORS IN THE TWENTIETH CENTURY
Margaret Archuleta & Rennard Strickland, Eds
Presents works by Native American artists influenced by Euro-American conceptions of art. Prepared by The Heard Museum. Illus. 1 10 pp. Paper. W.W. Norton & Co., 1992. $20.

SHARING THE DESERT: THE TOHONO O'ODHAM IN HISTORY
Winston Erickson
Traces the development of relations between the tribe and other peoples. 200 pp. University of Arizona Press, 1994. $35.

SHARING A HERITAGE: AMERICAN INDIAN ARTS
Charlotte Heth
214 pp. Paper . American Indian Studies Center, 1984. $15.

*SHARING OUR WORLDS
A photographic documentary of children from three families sharing their multicultural experiences. Grades 2-6. Illus. 32 pp. Daybreak Star Press, $4.75.

THE SHARPEST SIGHT: A NOVEL
Louis Owens
Mystery. 272 pp. University of Oklahoma Press, 1991. $19.95.

THE SHASTA
R. Dixon
Reprint of 1907 ed. 256 pp. AMS Press, $26.50.

*SHASTA INDIAN TALES
Rosemary Holsinger
Myths. Illus. 48 pp. Naturegraph, 1978. $13.95; paper, $5.95.

THE SHASTA INDIANS OF CALIFORNIA & THEIR NEIGHBORS
Elizabeth Renfro
Shasta origins, shamanism, mythology , philosophy, ceremonies, etc. Illus. Photos. 128 pp. Naturegraph, $16.95; paper , $8.95.

SHAWNEE: THE CEREMONIALISM OF A NATIVE AMERICAN TRIBE & ITS CULTURAL BACKGROUND
James Howard
Illus. 460 pp. Ohio University Press, 1981. $28.95; paper , $14.95.

SHAWNEE HOME LIFE: THE PAINTING OF ERNEST SPYBUCK
Lee Callander and Ruth Slivka
Illus. 32 pp. Paper . National Museum of the American Indian, 1984. $8.95.

THE SHAWNEE PROPHET
R. David Edmunds
Illus. 275 pp. University of Nebraska Press, 1983. $23.50; paper , $7.95.

SHAWNEES TRADITIONS
C.C. Trowbridge; V. Kinietz & E. Voegelin, Editors
Reprint of 1939 edition. AMS Press, $17.

THE SHEFFIELD SITE: AN ONEONTA SITE ON THE ST. CROIX RIVER
Guy E. Gibbon
Illus. 62 pp. Paper . Minnesota Historical Society, 1973. $4.

SHEM PETE'S ALASKA
James Kari & James Fall, Editors
Geography of the Cook Inlet region of Alaska. Contains over 700 Dena'ina place names of the western Cook Inlet region. Illus. Maps. 330 pp. Paper. CIRI & Alaska Native Language Center , 1987. $15.

SHONTO: STUDY OF THE ROLE OF THE TRADER IN A MODERN NAVAJO COMMUNITY
W.Y. Adams
Reprint of 1963 edition. Reprint Services, $75.

A SHORT ACCOUNT OF THE DESTRUCTION OF THE INDIES
Bartlome de las Casas
translated by Nigel Grif fin
Eyewitness record & protest of Spanish atrocities in the territory of Columbus. Reprint. Illus Maps. 192 pp. Paper . Penguin USA, $9.95.

A SHORT BIOGRAPHY OF JOHN LEETH; WITH AN ACCOUNT OF HIS LIFE AMONG THE INDIANS
E. Jeffries; R.G. Thwaites, Editor
The experiences of a trade-hunter in the Indian country of Pennsylvania & Ohio. Ayer Co., $18.

A SHORT HISTORY OF THE INDIANS OF THE U.S.
Edward H. Spicer
Reprint of 1969 edition. 320 pp. Paper . Krieger Publishing, $1 1.95.

SHORT-TERM SEDENTISM IN THE AMERI-CAN SOUTHWEST: THE MIMBRES VALLEY SALADO
Ben Nelson & Steven LeBlanc
Illus. 315 pp. Paper . University of New Mexico Press, 1986. $35.

SHOSHONE TALES
Anne M. Smith, Editor
Collected in 1939, from the Shoshone oral tradition. Illus. 188 pp. U. of Utah Press, 1993. $24.95.

*THE SHOSHONI
Alden Carter
Grades 3-5. Illus. 65 pp. Franklin W atts, 1989. $11.90.

*THE SHOSHONI
Dennis Fradin
Grades K-4. Illus. 48 pp. Childrens Press, 1988. $11.45.

THE SHOSHONI-CROW SUN DANCE
Fred W. Voget
Illus. 368 pp. U. of Oklahoma, 1984. $19.95.

THE SHOSHONI FRONTIER & THE BEAR RIVER MASSACRE
Brigham D. Madsen
Illus. 336 pp. U. of Utah Press, 1985. $19.95.

THE SHOSHONIS: SENTINELS OF THE ROCKIES
V. Trenholm and M. Carley
Illus. Paper. U. of Oklahoma Press, 1964. $14.95.

SHOTO CLAY: FIGURINES & FORMS FROM THE LOWER COLUMBIA
Robert Slocum & Kenneth Matsen
Descriptions and classifications of the clay work done by the little-known Shoto Indians, who once lived in the lower Columbia near V ancouver, Wash. Illus. 32 pp. Paper . Binford & Mort, $5.95.

A SHOVEL OF STARS: THE MAKING OF THE AMERICAN WEST, 1800 TO THE PRESENT
Ted Morgan
The forced removal of the Indians to reservations in Oklahoma. Illus. Maps. 544 pp. Simon & Schuster, 1995. $30.

THE SHUSWAP
J. Teit
Reprint of 1909 edition. AMS Press, $57.50.

THE SHUSWAP LANGUAGE
A.H. Kuipers
297 pp. Paper. Mouton de Gruyter, 1974.
$64.25.

**SIBERIAN YUP'IK ESKIMO: THE LANGUAGE
& ITS CONTACTS WITH CHUKCHI**
Willem J. de Reuse
Examines a number of interrelated grammatical
subsystems of Central Siberian Yup'ik, an Eskimo
language, spoken on St., Lawrence Island, Alaska.
424 pp. University of Utah Press, 1994. $50.

**SIGN LANMGUAGE AMONG NORTH AMERI-
CAN INDIANS COMPOARED WITH THAT OF
OTHER PEOPLES AND DEAF-MUTES**
Garrick Mallery, with Kroeber & Voegelin
318 pp. Mouton de Gruyter, 1972.

**SIGN LANGUAGE: CONTEMPORARY
SOUTHWEST NATIVE AMERICA**
Skeet McAuley
Illus. 80 pp. Aperture, 1989. $24.95.

**SIGNS FROM THE ANCESTORS: ZUNI
CULTURAL SYMBOLISM & PERCEPTIONS
OF ROCK ART**
Jane M. Young
Illus. 333 pp. Paper. University of New Mexico
Press, 1988. $24.95.

*SILAS & THE MAD-SAD PEOPLE
Grades 1-5. New Seed, 1981. $5.

**SILENT ARROWS: INDIAN
LORE & ARTIFACT HUNTING**
Earl F. Moore
Third Edition. Illus. Tremaine, 1973. $12.95.

**THE SILVER ARROW & OTHER INDIAN
ROMANCES OF THE DUNE COUNTRY**
E.H. Reed
Gordon Press, 1977. $59.95.

*SING FOR A GENTLE RAIN
J. Alison James
Grades 7 and up. Illus. Paper. Macmillan, $3.95.

**SINGING AN INDIAN SONG:
A BIOGRAPHY OF D'ARCY McNICKLE**
Dorothy R. Parker
Traces the coursr of D'Arcy McNickle's life. Illus.
330 pp. University of Nebraska Press, 1992.
$35.

**SINGING FOR POWER: THE SONG MAGIC
OF THE PAPAGO INDIANS OF SOUTHERN
ARIZONA**
Ruth Underhill
Reprint of 1938 edition. 158 pp. Paper.
University of Arizona Press, $10.95.

**THE SINGING SPIRIT: EARLY STORIES
BY NORTH AMERICAN INDIANS**
Bernd Peyer, Editor
Native American fiction. 175 pp. Paper.
University of Arizona Press, 1990. $9.95.

**THE SINKAIETK OR SOUTHERN
OKANAGON OF WASHINGTON**
Leslie Spier, et al, Editors
Reprint of 1938 edition. AMS Press.

*SINOPAH, THE INDIAN BOY
James W. Schultz
Grades 4-7. Illus. 104 pp. Paper. Confluence
Press, 1983. $15.95; paper, $7.95.

THE SIOUAN TRIBES OF THE EAST
James Mooney
Reprint of 1894 edition. Illus. Johnson Reprint,
$12.

*THE SIOUX
Virginia Driving Hawk Sneve
Their creation myth, history, beliefs & ways of life.
Grades 4-6. Illus. 32 pp. Holiday House, $15.95;
paper, $6.95.

*THE SIOUX
B. Brooks
Grades 5-8. Illus. 32 pp. Rourke Corp., 1989.
$12.67.

THE SIOUX
Royal B. Hassrick; with Dorothy
Maxwell & Cile Bach
Illus. Paper. University of Oklahoma Press, $17.95.

*THE SIOUX
Elaine Landau
Grades 3 and up. Illus. 64 pp. Paper.
Franklin Watts, 1991. $4.95.

*THE SIOUX
Alice Osinski
Grades K-4. Illus. 48 pp. Children's Press, 1984.
$11.45.

*THE SIOUX
Virginia Driving Hawk Sneve
The creation myth of the Sioux; history,
customs, and facts about the tribe today.
Grades 2-6. Illus. 32 pp. Holiday House, 1993.
$15.95.

SIOUX COLLECTIONS
T. Emogene Paulson, Editor
University of South Dakota Press, 1982. $14.95.

SIOUX CREATION STORY
Thomas Simms
Illus. 36 pp. Paper. Tipi Press, 1987. $3.50.

**SIOUX INDIAN RELIGION:
TRADITION & INNOVATION**
Raymond DeMallie & Douglas Parks, Editors
Illus. 252 pp. Paper. University of Oklahoma
Press & Center for Western Studies, 1987.
$12.95.

***THE SIOUX INDIANS: HUNTERS
AND WARRIORS OF THE PLAINS**
Sonia Bleeker
Grades 3-6. Illus. Wiliam Morrow, 1962. $11.88.

**SIOUX: LIFE & CUSTOMS
OF A WARRIOR SOCIETY**
R.B. Hassrick, et al
Reprint of 1964 edition. Illus. 400 pp. University
of Oklahoma Press, $22.95; paper, $11.95.

SIOUX MUSIC
William Fenton
Reprint. Scholarly Press, $59.

**THE SIOUX OF THE ROSEBUD:
A HISTORY IN PICTURES**
Henry and Jean Hamilton

Illus. 320 pp. Paper. U. of Oklahoma Press,
and American Indian Books, 1971. $19.95.

THE SIOUX UPRISING OF 1862
Kenneth Carley
Revised edition. Illus. Photos. Map. 102 pp.
Paper. Minnesota Historical Society Press,
1976. $7.50.

**SITANKA: THE FULL STORY
OF WOUNDED KNEE**
Forrest W. Seymour
An account of the major events preceding, during
and immediately after the battle of 1890 at
Wounded Knee. Christopher Publishing, 1981.
$10.75.

SITES OF O'AHU
Elspeth Sterling & Catherine Summers
Study of archaeological & historical sites of O'ahu.
Illus. Maps. 372 pp. Paper. Bishop Museum,
$29.95.

*SITTING BULL
Sheila Black; Nancy Furstinger, Editor
Grades 5-7. Illus. 144 pp. Silver Burdett, $1 1.98;
paper, $7.95.

SITTING BULL
Kathie B. Smith
Grades K-5. Illus. 25 pp. Julian Messner, 1987.
$7.79. Paper. Wanderer Books, $2.25.

**SITTING BULL, CHAMPION
OF THE SIOUX: A BIOGRAPHY**
Stanley Vestal
Reprint of 1957 edition. Illus. University of
Oklahoma Press, $24.95.

*SITTING BULL & THE PLAINS INDIANS
John Hook
Grades 4-8. Illus. 65 pp. Frankin Watts, 1987.
$12.40.

*SITTING BULL: WARRIOR OF THE SIOUX
Jane Fleischer
New edition. Grades 4-6. Illus. 48 pp. Troll
Associates, 1979. $9.59; paper, $2.50.

SITTING ON THE BLUE-EYED BEAR
Gerald Hausman
Navajo mythology & history. Sunstone Press, $10.

SIX MONTHS AMONG THE INDIANS
Darius B. Cook
Reprint of 1889 edition. Illus. 101 pp. Avery
Color, $7.49. Paper. Hardscrabble Books, $4.50.

SIX NATIONS GUIDES
Carol Cornelius
By teachers for teachers. Illus. 50 pp. Paper.
AISES, $15, teacher's guide; $4, student's guide.

SIX NATIONS SERIES
The only curriculum overview currently available
for 7th through 12th grade units on New York State
Indians. Separate guides available for teachers
and students. Akwe;kon Press, Teacher's guide,
$15. Student's guide, $4.

**SIX WEEKS IN THE SIOUX TEPEES:
A NARRATIVE OF INDIAN CAPTIVITY**
Sarah Wakefield
Bound with other captivity narratives. Reprint of
1863 edition, et al. Ye Galleon Press, $13.

SIXTH ANNUAL INDIAN LAW CONFERENCE: PROCEEDINGS OF THE FEDERAL BAR ASSOCIATION, APRIL 1981
Federal Bar Associatio Staff
113 pp. Federal Bar Association, 1981. $15.

THE SIXTH GRANDFATHER: BLACK ELK'S TEACHINGS GIVEN TO JOHN G. NEIHARDT
Raymond J. De Mallie, Editor
Illus. Maps. 475 pp. Paper. University of Nebraska Press, 1984. $11.95.

SIXTY YEARS OF INDIAN AFFAIRS: POLITICAL, ECONOMIC & DIPLOMATIC, 1789-1850, CHAPEL HILL, NORTH CAROLINA
G.D. Harmon
Reprint of 1941 edition. Kraus, 29.

SKELETAL BIOLOGY IN THE GREAT PLAINS, MIGRATION, WARFARE, HEALTH, & SUBSISTENCE
Douglas W. Owsley & Richard L. Jantz
Illus. 408 pp. Smithsonian Institution Press, 1994. $45.

SKELETAL REMAINS OF THE CENTRAL ESKIMOS
Knud Fischer-Moller; W.E. Calvert, tr.
Reprint of 1937 edition. AMS, $32.50.

A SKETCH OF THE CREEK COUNTRY IN THE YEARS 1798 & 1799
Benjamin Hawkins
Bound with Letters of Benjamin Hawkins. Reprint of 1848 edition. Illus. 592 pp. Reprint Co., 27.50.

SKETCHES OF INDIAN LIFE IN THE PACIFIC NORTHWEST
Alexander Diomedi
96 pp. Ye Galleon Press, 1978. $14.95.

SKETCHES OF MISSION LIFE AMONG THE INDIANS OF OREGON
Zachariah Mudge
Ye Galleon Press, 1983. $12.50.

SKETCHES OF A TOUR TO THE LAKES
Thomas L. McKenney
A sourcebook of early Indian life among the Ojibwe & the Sioux. Reprint of 1827 edition. Illus. 494 pp. Ross & Haines, $25.

SKETCHES OF WESTERN ADVENTURE
John McClung
Reprint of 1832 edition. Ayer Co., $13.

THE SKIN BOATS OF SAINT LAWRENCE ISLAND, ALASKA
Steohen R. Braund
Illus. 145 pp. University of Washington Press, 1988. $19.95.

SKULKING WAY OF WAR
Patrick Malone
Madison Books, 1991. $29.95.

***SKUNNY WUNDY: SENECA INDIAN TALES**
Arthur C. Parker, Editor;
Illus by George Armstrong
Children's tales handed down by Native American storytellers. Grades 4 and up. Illus. 224 pp. Paper. Syracuse University Press, 1994. $12.95.

THE SKY CLEARS: POETRY OF THE AMERICAN INDIANS
Arthur G. Day, Editor
Reprint of 1951 edition. 204 pp. Paper. University of Nebraska Press, $7.95.

THE SKY IS MY TIPI
Mody Boatright, Editor
Reprint of 1949 edition. Illus. 254 pp. Southern Methodist University Press, $13.95.

***SKY WATCHERS OF AGES PAST**
Malcolm E. Weiss
Grades 5-9. Houghton Mifflin, 1982. $7.95.

SKYSCRAPERS HIDE THE HEAVENS: THE HISTORY OF INDIAN-WHITE RELATIONS IN CANADA
J.R. Miller
Illus. 408 pp. U. of Toronto Press, 1989. $35.

SLASH
Jeannette C. Armstrong
A novel which traces the pain, and the alienation felt by the modern First Nation peoples of Canada. 254 pp. Paper. Theytus, 1990. $12.95.

SLAVEHOLDING INDIANS
Annie H. Abel
Reprint. 3 Volumes. Scholarly Press, $200.

SLAVERY & THE EVOLUTION OF CHEROKEE SOCIETY, 1540-1866
Maps. 222 pp. University of Tennessee Press, 1979. $19.95; paper, $9.95.

***SLEEPY RIVER**
Hannah Bandes; illus. by Jeanette Winter
Grades PS-3. Illus. 32 pp. Philomel, 1993. $14.95.

JOHN SIMPSON SMITH, 1810-1871
Stan Hoig
Reprint of 1974 edition. Illus. 30 pp. Arthur H. Clark, $22.50. Paper. Pueblo County Historical Society, $3.50.

SMALL BONES, LITTLE EYES
Nila Northsun & Jim Sagel; Kirk Robertson, Editor
72 pp. Paper. Duck Down Press, 1982. $5.

SMALL POX & THE IROQUOIS WARS: AN ETHNOHISTORICAL STUDY OF THE INFLUENCE OF DISEASE & DEMOGRAPHIC CHANGE IN IROQUOIAN CULTURE HISTORY, 1630-1700
Stephen Clark
Illus. 125 pp. Paper. Coyote Press, 1981. $11.25.

***SMALL WORLD OF ESKIMOS**
Bernard Planche; Sarah Matthews, tr.
Grades K-3. Franklin Watts, 1980. $10.40.

SMITH & OTHER EVENTS: TALES OF THE CHILCOTIN
Paul St. Pierre
Collection of short stories of the Chilcotin Indians of British Columbia, Canada. 332 pp. Paper. University of Oklahoma Press, 1994. $11.95.

THE SMITHSONIAN & THE AMERICAN INDIAN, MAKING A MORAL ANTHROPOLOGY IN VICTORIAN AMERICA
Curtis M. Hinsley
A guide to changing attitudes and values about Indians. Illus. Paper. Smithsonian Institution Press, 1981. $17.95.

THE SMITHSONIAN BOOK OF NORTH AMERICAN INDIANS: BEFORE THE COMING OF THE EUROPEANS
Philip Kopper; Alexis Doster, III, Editor
Illus. 288 pp. Smithsonian, 1986. $29.97.

SMOKING TECHNOLOGY OF THE ABORIGINES OF THE IROQUOIS AREA OF NEW YORK STATE
Edward S. Rutsch
252 pp. Fairleigh Dickinson University Press, 1972. $25.

SMOKY-TOP: THE ART & TIMES OF WILLIE SEAWEED
Bill Holm
Illus. 160 pp. University of Washington Press, 1983. $24.95.

SMOOTHING THE GROUND; ESSAYS ON THE NATIVE AMERICAN ORAL LITERATURE
Brian Swann, intro. by
364 pp. University of California Press, 1983. $40; paper, $14.95.

THE SNAKE CEREMONIALS AT WALPI
J.W. Fewkes, et al
Reprint of 1894 edition. AMS Press, $25.

THE SNAKE COUNTRY EXPEDITION OF 1830-1831: JOHN WORK'S FIELD JOURNAL
John Work; Francis D. Haines, Editor
Reprint of 1971 edition. Ilus. 224 pp. Paper. Books on Demand, $52.

THE SNAKE DANCE OF THE HOPI INDIANS
Earle Forrest
Reprint of 1961 edition. Illus. 175 pp. Westernlore, $10.95.

THE SNAKE DANCE OF THE MOQUIS OF ARIZONA
John G. Bourke
Reprint of 1884 edition. Illus. 371 pp. Paper. University of Arizona Press, $16.95.

SNARES, DEADFALLS & OTHER TRAPS OF THE NORTHERN ALGONQUIAN & NORTHERN ATHAPASKANS
J.M. Cooper
Reprint of 1934 edition. AMS Press, $17.50.

SNOWBIRD CHEROKEES: PEOPLE OF PERSISTENCE
Sharlotte Neely
Examines the Cherokees of Snowbird, North Carolina. Illus. Maps. 192 pp. Paper. University of Georgia Press, $14.95.

A SNUG LITTLE PURCHASE: HOW RICHARD HENDERSON BOUGHT KAINTUCKEE FROM THE CHEROKEES IN 1775
Charles Brashers
Illus. Associated Creative Writers, 1979. $7.95; paper, $4.95.

SOCIAL & CEREMONIAL ORGANIZATION OF COCHITI
E. Goldfrank
Reprint of 1927 edition. Paper. Kraus, $15.

SOCIAL & ECONOMIC CHANGE AMONG THE NORTHERN OJIBWA
R.W. Dunning
Paper. University of Toronto Press, 1959. $8.95.

SOCIAL LIFE OF THE CROW INDIANS
R. Lowie
Reprint of 1912 edition. AMS Press, $11.50.

SOCIAL LIFE OF THE NAVAJO INDIANS
G. Reichard
Reprint of 1928 edition. AMS Press, $31.

**SOCIAL ORGANIZATION
OF THE PAPAGO INDIANS**
R. Underhill
Reprint of 1939 edition. AMS Press, $32.50.

**SOCIAL ORGANIZATION
OF THE TEWA OF NEW MEXICO**
E.C. Parsons
Reprint of 1929 edition. Paper. Kraus, $34.

**SOCIAL ORGANIZATION
OF THE WESTERN PUEBLOS**
Fred Eggan
Reprint of 1950 edition. Illus. Paper. University
of Chicago Press, 1973. $12.50; paper, $2.95.

**SOCIAL ORGANIZATION AND RITUALISTIC
CEREMONIES OF THE BLACKFOOT
INDIANS**
C. Wissler
Reprint of 1912 edition. Illus. 312 pp. AMS
Press, $24.

**SOCIAL ORGANIZATION AND SOCIAL
USAGES OF THE INDIANS OF THE CREEK
CONFEDERACY**
John Swanton
Reprint of 1928 edition. Johnson Reprint, $37.

SOCIAL STUDIES
Teacher Resource Handbook. 408 pp. Kraus,
1994. $19.95.

**A SOCIAL STUDY OF 150 CHIPPEWA
INDIAN FAMILIES OF THE WHITE EARTH
RESERVATION OF MINNESOTA**
Inez Hilger
Reprint of 1939 edition. AMS Press, $26.

SOCIETIES OF THE PLAINS INDIANS
C. Wissler
Reprint of 1916 edition. 13 parts in one. Illus.
1,034 pp. AMS Press, $70.

***SOFT CHILD: HOW RATTLESNAKE
GOT ITS FANGS**
Joe Hayes & Kay Sather
Tohono O'odham tale. Grades Pre-K-3. Illus.
32 pp. Paper. Harbinger House, $8.95.

**THE SOKOKIS: NATIVE AMERICANS
OF NEW HAMPSHIRE**
Dorothea M. Thompson
Grade 4. Illus. 150 pp. Paper. Thompson
Press, 1986. $9.95.

**SOLDIERING IN DAKOTA:
AMONG THE INDIANS IN 1863-1865**
F. Myers
Reprint of 1888 edition. Ayer Co., $12.
Facsimile. 50 pp. Ye Galleon Press, $4.95.

SOLDIERS OF THE CROSS
J.B. Salpointe
Reprint of 1898 edition. Documentary
Publications, $24.95.

**SOME KIND OF POWER: NAVAJO
CHILDREN'S SKIN-WALKER NARRATIVES**
Margaret K. Brady
224 pp. University of Utah Press, 1984. $20.

**SOME NEWSPAPER REFERENCES CON-
CERNING INDIAN--WHITE RELATIONSHIPS IN
NORTHEASTERN CALIFORNIA, 1850-1920**
Norris Bleyhl
209 pp. Association of Northern California
Records, 1979. $9.

**SOME SEX BELIEFS & PRACTICES
IN A NAVAHO COMMUNITY**
F.L. Bailey
Reprint of 1950 edition. Paper.
Peabody Museum, $10; Kraus, $12.

**SOME WARMER TONE: ALASKA
ATHABASKAN BEAD EMBROIDERY**
Kate C. Duncan, Editor
Illus. Maps. 64 pp. Paper. University of Alaska
Museum, 1984. $12.

*SON OF THE DINE'
J. Walter Wood
Grades 5-9. Paper. Council for Indian
Education, 1972. $1.95.

**SON OF OLD MAN HAT:
A NAVAHO AUTOBIOGRAPHY**
Walter Dyk & Left Handed, recorded by
380 pp. Paper. University of Nebraska Press,
1967. $10.95.

*SON OF THUNDER
Stig Holmas
The sole survivor of a Mexican Army massacre is
adopted by Cochise. Grades 7 and up. 128 pp.
Harbinger House, 1993. $16.95; paper, $10.95.

**THE SONG OF THE LOOM: NEW
TRADITIONS IN NAVAJO WEAVING**
Frederick Dockstader
Illus. 132 pp. Hudson Hills Press, 1987. $35;
paper, $25.

*SONG OF THE SEVEN HERBS
Walking Night Bear & Stan Padilla
Grades 3 and up. Illus. 60 pp. Paper. Cherokee
Publications & The Book Publishing Co., $10.95.

**SONG OF THE SKY: VERSIONS OF
NATIVE AMERICAN SONG-POEMS**
Brian Swann; rev. ed. by Barry O'Connell
Paper. University of Massachusetts Press,
1994. $14.95.

*SONG OF THE WILD VIOLETS
Peggy Thompson, Writer & Illus.
Grades 3 and up. Illus. 36 pp. Paper.
The Book Publishing Co., $5.95.

SONGS
Charley J. Greasybear
Tom Trusky & Judson Crews, Editors
Paper. Ahsahta Press, 1979. $4.95.

**SONGS FROM THIS EARTH ON TURTLE'S
BACK: AN ANTHOLOGY OF POETRY BY
AMERICAN INDIAN WRITERS**
Joseph Bruchac
300 pp. Paper. Greenfield Revue Press, 1983.
$9.95.

SONGS OF INDIAN TERRITORY
Illus. 2nd Edition. Includes recorded tape.
Paper. Center of the American Indian, 1991.

**SONGS OF THE SPIRIT:
SCULPTURE BY DOUG HYDE**
Patrick T. Houlihan & Charles Dailey
Essays. 24 pp. Paper. Southwest Museum. $4.95.

SONGS OF THE TETON SIOUX
Harry Paige
Illus. Westernlore, 1969. $9.50.

SONGS OF THE TEWA
Herbert J. Spinden, Editor/Translator
Tewa poetry. Reprint of 1933 edition. Illus.
125 pp. Paper. Sunstone Press, $12.95.

SONGS OF THE WIGWAM
Contains more than a dozen songs portraying
native life and thought in the forest around the
Great Lakes. 24 pages. 95 each; 65 each, 15 or
more. World Around Songs, $2.45

**SONORA: A DESCRIPTION
OF THE PROVINCE**
Ignaz Pfefferkorn
Ethnographic account of the Pima, Opata, and
Eudeve Indians of the Sonora region. Reprint of
1949 edition. 329 pp. Paper. University of Arizona
Press, $12.95.

THE SONS OF THE WIND
D.M. Dooling
Mythology of the Oglala Lakota Sioux, 126 pp.
Paper. Meyer Creative Productions, $10.

**A SORROW IN OUR HEART:
THE LIFE OF TECUMSEH**
Allan W. Eckert
862 pp. Bantam Books, $27.50.

SOUL CONCEPTS OF THE NAVAHO
Berard Haile
Reprint of 1964 edition. Paper. St. Michaels
Historical Museum, $6.50.

**THE SOUL OF THE INDIAN; & OTHER
WRITINGS FROM OHIYESA**
Charles Eastman; edited by Kent Nerbum
Ohiyesa, a Dakota Indian, has been described
as "the Native American Thoreau." Also known
as Charles Alexander Eastman. 128 pp. New
World Library, $12.95.

**THE SOUL OF THE INDIAN:
AN INTERPRETATION**
Charles A. Eastman
Reprint of 1911 edition. 175 pp. Paper.
University of Nebraska Press, 1980. $6.95.

***SOUN TETOKEN: NEZ PERCE
BOY TAMES A STALLION**
Kennth Thomasma; Eunice Hundley, Illus.
Recounts the days of the Nez Perce tribe during
the War of 1877. Grades 4 and up. Illus. Baker
Book House, $10.99; paper, $6.99.

**THE SOUND OF RATTLES & CLAPPERS: A
COLLECTION OF NEW CALIFORNIA INDIAN
WRITING**
Greg Sarris, Editor
Poetry & fiction by 10 Native Americans of
California Indian ancestry documents history.
161 pp. University of Arizona Press, 1994. $30;
paper, $14.95.

THE SOUND OF STRINGS
Harold Keith
The Comanches during the mid-1800s. 182 pp.
Levite of Apache, $17.

**SOURCES OF FINANCIAL AID AVAILABLE
TO AMERICAN INDIAN STUDENTS**
Leslie A. Kedelty, Editor
Major sources of financial aid, and admissions and financial aid process information. Includes program reps, BIA area offices, and job opportunities. 78 pp. Annual. Paper. Indian Resource Development (IRD), $5.

**SOURCING PREHISTORIC CERAMICS
AT CHODISTAAS PUEBLO, ARIZONA**
Maria Nieves Zedeno
Prehistoric pottery identification. Illus. 110 p. Paper. University of Arizona Press, 1994. $12.95.

**SOUTH DAKOTA LEADERS: FROM PIERRE
CHOUTEAU, JR. TO OSCAR HOWE**
Herbert T. Hoover & Larry Zimmerman
Includes biographies of Sitting Bull and Crazy Horse. Paper. University of South Dakota Press, 1989. $27.50.

**SOUTH FLORIDA'S VANISHED PEOPLE:
TRAVELS IN THE HOMELAND OF ANCIENT
CALUSA**
Byron Voegelin
Island Press, 1977. $6.95.

***SOUTHEAST INDIANS: AN
EDUCATIONAL COLORING BOOK**
Linda Spizzirri & Staff
Grades K-5. Illus. 32 pp. Paper. Spizzirri, 1985.
$1.95.

**THE SOUTHEASTERN CEREMONIAL
COMPLEX, ARTIFACTS & ANALYSIS**
Patricia Galloway, Editor
Illus. 400 pp. U. of Nebraska Press, 1989. $60.

**THE SOUTHEASTERN CEREMONIAL
COMPLEX & ITS INTERPRETATION**
J.H. Howard and C.H. Chapman
Illus. 169 pp. Paper. Missouri Archaeological
Society, 1968. $4.

**SOUTHEASTERN FRONTIERS: EUROPEAN,
AFRICANS, & THE AMERICAN INDIANS,
1513-1840: A CRITICAL BIBLIOGRAPHY**
James H. O'Donnell, III
136 pp. Paper. Indiana U. Press, 1982. $4.95.

THE SOUTHEASTERN INDIANS
Charles Hudson
Illus. 573 pp. Paper. Hothem House &
University of Tennessee Press, 1976. $17.95.

**SOUTHEASTERN INDIANS
SINCE THE REMOVAL ERA**
Walter Williams, Editor
Illus. 270 pp. Paper. University of Georgia
Press, 1979. $12.

**SOUTHEASTERN POMO CEREMONIALS:
THE KUKSU CULT & ITS SUCCESSORS**
Abraham M. Halpern
Paper. University of California Press, 1988. $20.

**SOUTHEASTERN WOODLAND
INDIAN DESIGNS**
Caren Caraway
Illus. 48 pp. Paper. Stemmer House, 1985. $5.95.

SOUTHERN ARIZONA FOLK ARTS
James Griffith
235 pp. University of Arizona Press, 1988.
$29.95; paper, $14.95.

**SOUTHERN ATHAPASKAN MIGRATION:
A.D. 200-1750**
128 pp. Navajo Community College Press,
1987. $18.80.

THE SOUTHERN CADDO: AN ANTHOLOGY
H.F. Gregory & David H. Thomas, Editors
550 pp. Garland, 1986. $75.

SOUTHERN CALIFORNIA INDIAN TRAILS
Larry S. Watson
Illus. 30 pp. Bibliography. Paper. Histree, $9.95.

SOUTHERN CHEYENNE WOMEN'S SONGS
Virginia Giglio
Book & tape set. Illus. Maps. 34 song transcriptions. 272 pp. University of Oklahoma Press, $29.95 (book); tape, $9.95; book & tape set, $35.

THE SOUTHERN CHEYENNES
Donald Berthrong
Illus. Maps. Biblio. 456 pp. Paper. University
of Oklahoma Press, 1963. $15.95.

THE SOUTHERN FRONTIER, 1670-1732
Verner Crane
Reprint of 1956 ed. Greenwood Press, $22.50.

SOUTHERN INDIAN MYTHS & LEGEDS
Virginia Borwn & Laurella Owens, Editors
Illus. 160 pp. Beechwood Books, 1985. $15.95.

**THE SOUTHERN INDIANS &
BENJAMIN HAWKINS, 1796-1816**
Florette Henri
Illus. 392 pp. U. of Oklahoma Press, 1986. $26.95.

**SOUTHERN INDIANS IN THE
AMERICAN REVOLUTION**
James O'Donnell, III
Reprint of 1973 edition. 188 pp. Paper.
Books on Demand. $46.30.

**THE SOUTHERN INDIANS: THE STORY OF
THE CIVILIZED TRIBES BEFORE REMOVAL**
R.S. Cotterill
Reprint of 1954 edition. 259 pp. Paper.
University of Oklahoma Press, 1954. $9.95.

SOUTHERN PAIUTE
E. Sapir
Bound with Texts of the Kaibab Paiutes and Uintah Utes; Southern Paiute Dictionary. Reprint of 1931 edition. AMS Press, $72.

SOUTHERN PAIUTE ETHNOHISTORY
Robert Euler
Reprint of 1966 ed. Illus. 176 pp. AMS Press, $24.

SOUTHERN PAIUTE ETHNOLOGY
I.T. Kelly
Reprint of 1964 edition. AMS Press, $24.

SOUTHERN PLAINS ALLIANCES
Howard Meredith
University Press of Kansas, 1994.

**SOUTHERN PLAINS LIFEWAYS:
APACHE & WICHITA**
Pamphlet on the Apache & Wichita Tribes.
Wichita Tribal Office.

**SOUTHERN UTE INDIANS
OF EARLY COLORADO**
Verner Z. Reed; William Jones, Editor
Illus. Paper. Outbooks, 1980. $3.95.

SOUTHWEST
Alfonso Ortiz, Editor
Illus. 701 pp. Smithsonian, 1980. $23.

**SOUTHWEST COOKS! THE TRADITION
OF NATIVE AMERICAN CUISINES**
Lynn Kirst & Jeanette O'Malley, Editors
Illus. 108 pp. Paper. Southwest Museum, 1991.
$14.95.

**SOUTHWEST: HANDBOOK
OF NORTH AMERICAN INDIANS**
Illus. 868 pp. Smithsonian, 1983. $25.00.

SOUTHWEST INDIAN ARTS & CRAFTS
Mark Bahti
Illus. 48 pp. KC Publications, 1983. $8.95;
paper, $4.50.

SOUTHWEST INDIAN CRAFT ARTS
Clara L. Tanner
Covers baskets, jewelry, textiles, silver, pottery, carving and minor crafts of recent and contemporary tribes. Illus. 206 pp. University of Arizona Press, 1968. $27.50.

**SOUTHWEST INDIAN DESIGNS;
WITH SOME EXPLANATIONS**
Mark T. Bahti
Recreates about 200 symbols and their variations. Includes are symbols and explanations of Zuni, Navajo, Hopi, Tewa, Acoma, Pueblo, Mimbres, and Hohokam designs. Illus. 32 pp. Paper. Treasure Chest, 1994. $4.95.

SOUTHWEST INDIAN IRON-ON TRANSFERS
Madeline Orban-Szontagh
24 designs based on authentic Native American art and artifact motifs. 32 pp. Paper. Dover, $1.

**SOUTHWEST INDIAN PAINTING:
A CHANGING ART**
Clara L. Tanner
Represents Indian easel art from 200 artists from Arizona and New Mexico; 300 illustrations. Revised edition. 477 pp. University of Arizona Press, 1980. $50.

**SOUTHWEST INDIAN SILVER
FROM THE DONEGHY COLLECTION**
Louise Lincoln, Editor
Illus. 189 pp. University of Texas Press, 1982.
$29.95.

*SOUTHWEST INDIANS COLORING BOOK
Peter Copeland
Ready-to-color depictions and descriptions of Southwest Indians of the past and present, 1840s-1980s. Grades 1 -4. Illus. Paper. Dover, $2.95.

***SOUTHWEST INDIANS: AN
EDUCATIONAL COLORING BOOK**
Linda Spizzirri, Editor
Grades 1-8. Illus. 32 pp. Paper. Spizzirri, 1981.
$1.95.

**SOUTHWEST INDIANS:
A PHOTOGRAPHIC PORTRAIT**
Bill Harris
A photographic tour of Native American culture in the Southwest. 100 full-color photos. 128 pp.
Random House, $15.

SOUTHWEST MUSEUM PUBLICATIONS
Southwest Museum.

SOUTHWESTERN INDIAN ARTS & CRAFTS
Tom Bahti; updated by Mark Bahti
Come to know silverwork, turquoise, beadwork, pottery, baskets, ironwood carvings, Navajo sandpainting, Zuni fetishes, Hopi kachinas, and Navajo rugs. Illus. Photos. Maps. 48 pp. KC Publications, $8.95; paper, $6.95.

SOUTHWESTERN INDIAN BASKETS: THEIR HISTORY & THEIR MAKERS
Andrew H. Whiteford
Illus. 236 pp. Paper. School of American Research & University of Washington Press, 1988. $18.95.

SOUTHWESTERN INDIAN CEREMONIALS
Tom Bahti; updated by Mark Bahti
Illus. Photos. Map. 64 pp. KC Publications, 1982. $8.95; paper, $6.95.

SOUTHWESTERN INDIAN DESIGNS
Madeleine Orban-Szontagh
250 authentic motifs drawn from Navajo jewelry & rugs, Pueblo pottery, Hopi ceremonial dress, & other sources. Illus. 48 pp. Paper. Dover, $3.95.

SOUTHWESTERN INDIAN RECIPE BOOK
Zora G. Hesse
Favorite foods of many tribes. Illus. 60 pp. Paper. Filter Press, $3.

SOUTHWESTERN INDIAN RITUAL DRAMA
Charlotte Frisbie
Illus. 372 pp. Paper. Waveland, 1989. $14.95.

SOUTHWESTERN INDIAN TRIBES
Tom Bahti; updated by Mark Bahti
Covers 32 Southwestern Indian cultures. Illus. Photos. Maps. 72 pp. KC Publications, 1968. $8.95; paper, $6.95.

SOUTHWESTERN POTTERY: AN ANNOTATED BIBLIOGRAPHY & LIST OF TYPES & WARES
Norman T. Oppelt
Illus. 333 pp. Scarecrow, 1988. $35.

SOVEREIGNTY & SYMBOL: INDIAN-WHITE CONFLICT AT GANIENKEH
Gail Landsman
Illus. 250 pp. U. of New Mexico Press, 1988. $19.95.

SPANISH EXPLORERS IN THE SOUTHERN U.S., 1528-1543
Frederick Hodge & Theodore Lewis, Editors
Reprint fo 1907 edition. Illus. 410 pp. Barnes & Noble, $21.50.

SPANISH-AMERICAN BLANKETRY: ITS RELATIONSHIP TO ABORIGINAL WEAVING IN THE SOUTHWEST
H.P. Mera
Reprint of 1948 edition. Illus. 96 pp. Paper. School of American Research, $14.95.

SPANISH & INDIAN PLACE NAMES OF CALIFORNIA: THEIR MEANING & THEIR ROMANCE
Nellie Sanchez; Carlos Cortes, Editor
Reprint of 1930 edition. Illus. Ayer Co., $23.

THE SPANISH BORDERLANDS SOURCEBOOKS
David Hurst Thomas, Editor
27 volumes set with more than 450 articles in fac-simile. The ethnology of precontact and contact period Native American groups who inhabited the various subregions of Northwest Mexico, Texas, Spanish Florida, Alta and Baja California. Garland Publishing, 1991. $2,165, or by volume.

THE SPANISH FRONTIER IN NORTH AMERICA
David J. Weber
Definitive history of the Spanish colonial period in North America. Describes the influences by the Spaniards and the effect of Native North Americans on the Spanish settlers from Florida to California. Illus. 600 pp. Yale University Press, 1992. $40; paper, $16.

THE SPANISH MISSIONS OF NEW MEXICO, AFTER 1680
John Kessell & Rick Hendricks, Editors
Reprint. 536 pp. Garland Publishing, $75.

*THE SPARK IN THE STONE: SKILLS & PROJECTS FROM THE NATIVE AMERICAN TRADITION
Peter Goodchild
Grades 5 and up. Illus. 130 pp. Paper. Cherokee Pubns. & Chicago Review Press, 1991. $11.95.

*SPARROW HAWK
Meridel le Sueur; illus. by Robert DesJarlait
Fictional look at youth and race relations. Grades 4 and up. 192 pp. Holy Cow! Press, $13.95

SPEAKING OF INDIANS
Ella Deloria
Describes traditional values, costumes, kinship patterns and religious attitudes of the Sioux. Reprint of 1944 edition. Paper. Friendship Press or Greenfield Review Press, $6.95.

SPEAKING OF INDIANS; WITH AN ACCENT ON THE SOUTHWEST
Bernice Johnston
Answers hundreds of questions about Indians. Reprint of 1970 edition. Illus. 112 pp. Paper. Books on Demand, $28.

SPEECHES ON THE PASSAGE OF THE BILL FOR THE REMOVAL OF THE INDIANS
U.S. 21st Congress
Reprint of 1830 edition. Kraus, $29.

*SPELYI & OTHER INDIAN LEGENDS
Arthur Griffin, Editor
Grades 2-5. Illus. Bainbridge Press, 1989.

SPIDER WOMAN STORIES
G.M. Mullett
Hopi mythology. 142 pp. Paper. University of Arizona Press, 1979. $9.95.

SPIDERWOMAN: A STORY OF NAVAJO WEAVERS & CHANTERS
Gladys Reichard
Reprint of 1934 edition. 344 pp. Paper. The Rio Grande Press, $12.

SPIDERWOMAN'S DREAM
Alicia Otis
Southwestern Indian mythology. Illus. 64 pp. Paper. Sunstone Press, $7.95.

SPIDERWOMAN'S GRANDDAUGHTERS: TRADITIONAL TALES & CONTEMPORARY WRITING BY NATIVE AMERICAN WOMEN
Paula G. Allen, Editor
256 pp. Paper. Fawcett, 1990. $11.95.

SPIRIT & ANCESTOR: A CENTURY OF NORTHWEST COAST INDIAN ART AT THE BURKE MUSEUM
Bill Holm
Illus. 256 pp. University of Washington Press, 1987. $50; paper, $29.95.

THE SPIRIT & THE FLESH: SEXUAL DIVERSITY IN AMERICAN INDAIN TRADITION
Walter L. Williams
Illus. 365 pp. Paper. Beacon Press, 1988. $9.95.

SPIRIT OF THE HARVEST: NORTH AMERICAN INDIAN COOKING
Beverly Cox & Martin Jacobs
255 pp. Four Winds Trading Co., $35.

SPIRIT HEALING: NATIVE AMERICAN MAGIC & MEDICINE
Mary Dean Atwood; illus. by Bert Seabourn
A self-help guide to the Native American spiritual growth process. 160 pp. Paper. Sterling, 1992. $12.95.

SPIRIT MOUNTAIN: AN ANTHOLOGY OF YUMAN STORY & SONG
Leanne Hinton and Lucille Watahomigie, Eds.
344 pp. University of Arizona Press, 1984. $45; paper, $24.95.

THE SPIRIT OF THE ALBERTA INDIAN TREATIES
Richard Price
202 pp. Paper. Gower, 1979. $8.95.

SPIRIT OF NATIVE AMERICA: BEAUTY & MYSTICISM IN AMERICAN INDIAN ART
Anna Lee Walters
Illus. 120 pp. Chronicle Books, 1990. $30; paper, $18.95.

SPIRIT OF THE NEW ENGLAND TRIBES: INDIAN HISTORY & FOLKLORE, 1620-1984
Wm. S. Simmons
Map. 330 pp. Paper. University Press of New England, 1986. $17.95.

SPIRIT OF THE HARVEST: NORTH AMERICAN INDIAN COOKING
Beverly Cox & Marvin Jacobs
Recipes. Illus. 255 pp. Center for Western Studies, 1991. $29.95.

*SPIRIT OF THE WHITE BISON
Beatrice Culleton
Plains Nations sory of the deliberate destruction of the bison. Grades 4 and up. Illus. 64 pp. Book Publishing Co., 1989. $5.95.

*SPIRIT QUEST
Susan Sharpe
Grades 4-6. Illus. Macmillan, 1987. $12.95.

*SPIRIT QUEST: THE INITIATIONS OF AN INDIAN BOY
Carol Batdorf
Grades 4 and up. Illus. 160 pp. Paper. Hancock House, $9.95.

THE SPIRIT SINGS: ARTISTIC TRADITIONS OF CANADA'S FIRST PEOPLES
Glenbow Museum Staff
Illus. 265 pp. Firefly Books Ltd., 1990. $50.

A SPIRITED RESISTANCE: THE NORTH AMERICAN INDIAN STRUGGLE FOR UNITY, 1745-1815

Gregory Evans Dowd
260 pp. The Johns Hopkins University Press,
$24.95.

SPIRITUAL LEGACY OF
THE AMERICAN INDIAN
Joseph Epes Brown
Reprint of 1964 edition. Illus. 135 pp. Paper.
Meyer Creative Productions, $9.95.

SPIRITUAL WISDOM OF
THE NATIVE AMERICANS
John Heinerman
Illus. 170 pp. Paper. Cassandra Press, 1989.
$9.95.

SPOKEN CREE: WEST COAST
OF JAMES BAY
C. Douglas Ellis
715 pp. Paper. University of Nebraska Press,
1983. $21.

*SPORTS & GAMES THE INDIANS GAVE US
Alex Whitney
Grades 7 and up. David McKay, 1977. $7.95.

*SPOTTED EAGLE & BLACK CROW:
A LAKOTA LEGEND
Emery Bernhard
Betrayed by his brother, a warrior is rescued by
eagles. Grades K-3. Illus. 32 pp. Holiday House,
1993. $15.95.

*THE SPOTTED HORSE
Henry Tall Bull
Grades 2-10. 32 pp. Council for Indian
Education, 1970. $8.95; paper, $2.95.

SPOTTED TAIL'S FOLK: A HISTORY
OF THE BRULE SIOUX
George E. Hyde
Revised 1974 edition. Illus. 361 pp. Paper.
University of Oklahoma Press, $12.95.

*SQUANTO & THE FIRST THANKSGIVING
Joyce K. Kessel; illus. by Lisa Donze
Grades K-3. Illus. 50 pp. Lerner, 1983. $15.95;
paper, $5.95.

*SQUANTO, FRIEND OF THE PILGRIMS
Clyde Bulla
Grades 4-6. 110 pp. Paper. Scholastic, Inc.,
1990. $2.75.

STALLING'S ISLAND MOUND,
COLUMBIA COUNTY, GEORGIA
W.H. Claflin, Jr.
Reprint of 1931 edition. Paper. Kraus, $15.

*STAR BOY
Paul Goble
Grades K-6. Illus. Macmillan, 1989. $14.95;
paper, $4.95.

THE STAR LAKE ARCHAEOLOGICAL
PROJECT: ANTHROPOLOGY OF A HEADWA-
TERS AREA OF CHACO WASH, NEW MEXICO
Walter Wait and Ben Nelson, Editors
Illus. 480 pp. Southern Illinois University Press,
1983. $24.95.

STAR QUILT
Roberta Hill Whiteman
Poetry. Illus. 92 pp. Paper. Holy Cow! Press,
$6.95.

*STAR TALES: NORTH AMERICAN
INDIAN STORIES ABOUT THE STARS
Gretchen Mayo
Grades 5 and up. 96 pp. Walker & Co., 1987.
$11.95.

STAR WOMAN: WE ARE MADE FROM
STARS & TO THE STARS WE MUST RETURN
Lynn V. Andrews
256 pp. Warner Books, 1986. $16.95.

STAR WARRIOR:
THE STORY OF SWIFTDEER
Bill Wahlberg
The story of Harley SiftDeer Reagan, a medicine
teacher, the leder of the Deer Tribe Metis Medicine Society. Illus. 196 pp. paper. Bear & Co., 1993.
$12.95.

THE STATE OF NATIVE AMERICA: GENO-
CIDE, COLONIZATION & RESISTANCE
M. Annette Jaimes, Editor
Essays by Native American authors and activists
on contemporary Native issues including the
quincentenary. 480 pp. Paper. South End Press,
1991. $16.

THE STATE OF SEQUOYAH: AN IMPRES-
SIONISTIC LOOK AT EASTERN OKLAHOMA
Jerald C. Walker; Daisy Decazes, photos by
Traces the background of what is now eastern
Oklahoma. The story of Indian removal, "Trail of
Tears", and the development of the state. Illus.
120 pp. The Lowell Press, $25.

STATE & RESERVATION: NEW PERSPEC-
TIVES ON FEDERAL INDIAN POLICY
George Pierre Castile & Robert L. Bee, Editors
Essays focus on the rise, change, and persistence
of the Native American reservation system. 259
pp. University of Arizona Press, 1992. $35; paper,
$19.95.

STATE-TRIBAL RELATIONS:
INTO THE 21st CENTURY
Judy Zelio & James Reed
Analysis of government-to-government relations;
describes the issues and discusses agreements.
Case studies. 120 pp. National Conference of
State Legislatures, 1993. $25.

STATE-TRIBAL RELATIONSHIPS - REPORTS
*1991 State Legislation Relating to Native Ameri-
cans*, Report, Vol. 16, No. 9 - 19 pp. $5; *State-
Tribal Transportation Agreements*, Report No. 14,
No. 4 - 1989. $5; *States and the Indian Gaming
Regulatory Act*, Report Vol. 17, No. 16 - 1992, 18
pp. $5; *Promoting Effective State-Tribal Relations:
A Dialogue* - examines how states and tribes can
work together. 1990. 19 pp. $10; *Jurisdiction Over
Nuclear Waste Transportation on Indian Tribal
Lands: State-Tribal Relationships*, Report Vol. 16,
No. 4. 1991. 11 pp. $5. National Conference of
State Legislatures.

STATISTICAL RECORD OF
NATIVE NORTH AMERICANS
Marlita A. Reddy, Editor
Statistics on all aspects of Native American family
life, education, business and industry. Compiled
from government records, and private associations. Includes 1,000 charts, graphs, and tables;
200 current and extinct tribes are detailed. Illus.
1,650 pp. Gale Research, 1993. $89.50.

STATUS & HEALTH IN PREHISTORY; A
CASE STUDY OF THE MOUNDVILLE
CHIEFDOM
Mary Lucas Powell
Illus. 352 pp. Smithsonian Institution Prfess,
1988. $35.

STATUS TERMINOLOGY & THE SOCIAL
STRUCTURE OF NORTH AMERICAN
INDIANS
Munro S. Edmonson
Reprint of 1958 edition. AMS, $20.

STATISTICS OF INDIAN TRIBES,
AGENCIES AND SCHOOLS
U.S. Bureau of Indian Affairs
Reprint of 1903 edition. Kraus, $24.

*STOLEN PRINCESS:
A NORTHWEST INDIAN LEGEND
Willard N. Morss and Janet M. Herren
Grades 4-8. Illus. 79 pp. Paper. J.M. Herren,
1983. $8.95.

STONE AGE IN THE GREAT BASIN
Emory Strong
Illus. 280 pp. Paper. Binford & Mort, 1967.
$12.95.

STONE AGE OF THE COLUMBIA RIVER
Emory Strong
Illus. Photos and maps. 256 pp. Paper.
Binford & Mort, 1967. $9.95.

STONE AGE SPEAR & ARROW POINTS
OF THE MIDCONTINENTAL & EASTEN U.S.
Noel D. Justice
A modern survey & reference. Illus. 302 pp.
Indiana University Press, 1988. $37.95.

STONE ARTIFACTS OF TEXAS INDIANS -
A FIELD GUIDE
Turner & Hester
Illus. 308 pp. Paper. Hothem House, 1985.
$14.95.

THE STONE CANOE
Peyton
12 stories told by the People of the Rapids, the
northernmost Ojibway. Illus. 151 pp. Paper.
Hothem House, 1989. $14.95.

STONE ORNAMENTS USED BY
INDIANS IN THE U.S. & CANADA
Warren Moorhead
Reprint of 1917 edition. AMS Press, $55.

STORIES FROM INDIAN WIGWAMS
AND NORTHERN CAMPFIRES
E.R. Young
Reprint. Gordon Press, 1977. $59.95.

STORIES FROM THE LAND
32 pp. Paper. Museum of Northern Arizona,
1981. $3.

STORIES & LEGENDS OF THE BERING
STRAIT ESKIMOS
Clark M. Garber
Reprint of 1940 edition. 260 pp. AMS, $24.50.

STORIES OF MAASAW, A HOPI GOD
Ekkehart Malotki & Michael Lomatuway'ma
Illus. 275 pp. University of Nebraska Press,
1987. $24.95; paper, $14.95.

**STORIES OF THE ROAD
ALLOWANCE PEOPLE**
 Maria Campbell
Collection of short stories about Metis political movement. 127 pp. Paper. Theytus, 1994. $12.95.

***STORIES OF OUR BLACKFEET
GRANDMOTHERS**
 Mary C. Boss-Ribs & Jenny Running-Crane
Grades 1-6. Paper. Council for Indian Education, 1984. $1.45.

STORIES OF THE SIOUX
 Luther Standing Bear
Illus. 95 pp. Paper. University of Nebraska Press, 1988. $5.95.

**STORIES OF SURVIVAL: CONVERSATIONS
WITH NATIVE NORTH AMERICANS**
 Remmelt & Kathleen Hummelen
Stories that depicty concerns of Native peoples in Northeastern cities, Arctic communities, prairie towns, and reservations. Paper. Friendship Press, $5.95.

**STORIES OF TRADITIONAL
NAVAJO LIFE & CULTURE**
 Broderick H. Johnson, Editor
22 stories written by Navajo men & women. Illus. 335 pp. Paper. Navajo Community College Press, 1977. $15.

**STORIES WE LIVE BY /
BAAK'AATUGH TS'UHUNITY**
 Catherine Attla
University of Alaska Press, $18.

STORM IN THE MOUNTAIN
 Vernon Crow
Story of William H. Thomas' Legion of Cherokee Indians formed during the Civil War. Illus. Photos. Maps. 300 pp. Paper. Cherokee Publications, $7.95.

**STORM PATTERNS: POEMS
FROM TWO NAVAJO WOMEN**
 Della Frank & Roberts D. Joe
20 poems. Illus. Navajo Community College Press, 1993. $12.

**STORMS BREWED IN OTHER MEN'S
WORLDS; THE CONFRONTATIONS OF INDI-
ANS, SPANISH, AND FRENCH IN THE SOUTH-
WEST, 1540-1795**
 Elizabeth A.H. John
Maps. 805 pp. Paper. University of Nebraska Press, 1981. $13.50

THE STORY OF THE CHEROKEE
 Tom B. Underwood
Reprint of 1961 edition. Illus. 48 pp. Paper. Cherokee Publications, $3.95.

THE STORY OF CYNTHIA ANN PARKER
 Jack C. Ramsay, Jr.
Took into captivity, she had a son, the "white Indian," Quanah, the last and most famous of the Comanche war chiefs. Illus. 225 pp. Eakin Press, $16.95.

STORY OF DEEP DELIGHT
 Thomas McNamee
Relates the life stories of three young men - the last Chickasaw Indian chief, a mid-19th century slave, and a present-day artist. 480 pp. Paper. Penguin USA, $11.

*THE STORY OF GERONIMO
Grades 3-6. Illus. 32 pp. Childrens Press, $9.95.

**THE STORY OF INDIAN MUSIC:
ITS GROWTH & SYNTHESIS**
 O. Gosvami
Reprint. 332 pp. Scholarly Press, $75.

*THE STORY OF LITTLE BIG HORN
 R.C. Stern
Grades 3-6. Illus. 32 pp. Childrens Press, 1983. $9.95.

THE STORY OF OKLAHOMA
 W. David Baird & Danney Goble
The up-t-date history of the Sooner State, includ-ing a collection of primary sources on life in Indian Territory. Illus. Maps. Biblio. 528 pp. University of Oklahoma Press, 1994. $28.95.

THE STORY OF THE MEADOWLARK
 Scott B. Smith
Illus. 47 pp. Stump Publishing, 1986. $15.

STORY OF THE RED MAN
 Flora W. Seymour
Facsimile of 1929 edition. Ayer Co., $27.50.

*THE STORY OF THE TRAIL OF TEARS
 R. Conrad Stein
Grades 3-6. Illus. 32 pp. Childrens Press, 1985. $9.95.

*THE STORY OF WOUNDED KNEE
 R.C. Stein
Grades 3-6. Illus. 32 pp. Childrens Press, 1983. $9.95.

**STORYTELLERS & OTHER
FIGURATIVE POTTERY**
 Douglas Congdon-Martin
In 1964, Helen Cordero of Cochiti Pueblo created the first storyteller, a clay image of her grandfa-ther with five children clinging to him. This book presents over 400 pieces, by nearly 150 artists, in full color and organized by pueblo. Illus. 144 pp. Paper. Schiffer, $19.95.

**STRAIGHT TONGUE: MINNESOTA
INDIAN ART FROM THE BISHOP
WHIPPLE COLLECTIONS**
 Louise Casagrande and Melissa Ringheim
Illus. 94 pp. Paper. University of Washington Press, 1980. $9.95.

**STRAIGHT WITH THE MEDICINE: NARRA-
TIVES OF WASHOE FOLLOWERS OF THE TIPI
WAY**
 Warren L. D'Azevedo
Narratives compiled in the 1950s from seven fol-lowers of the Native American Church. Illus. 64 pp. Paper. Heyday Books, 1985. $5.95.

**STRAINS OF CHANGE: THE IMPACT
OF TOURISM ON HAWAIIAN MUSIC**
 Elizabeth Tatar
Illus. 29 pp. Paper. Bishop Museum, $9.95.

STRANGE BUSINESS
 Rilla Askew
Short story collection of Choctaw Indians' place in the fictitious town of Cedar, Okla. 192 pp. Paper. Penguin USA, $10.

**STRANGE JOURNEY: THE VISION
LIFE OF A PSYCHIC INDIAN WOMAN**
 Louise Lone Dog
105 pp. Paper. Naturegraph, $8.95.

**A STRANGER IN HER NATIVE LAND:
ALICE FLETCHER & THE AMERICAN
INDIANS**
 Joan Mark
Illus. 430 pp. University of Nebraska Press, 1988. $35; paper, $16.95.

**STRANGERS IN A STOLEN LAND:
AMERICAN INDIANS IN SAN DIEGO**
 Richard L. Carrico
Illus. Paper. Sierra Coaks, 1987. $10.95.

**STRANGERS IN THEIR OWN LAND:
A CHOCTAW PORTFOLIO**
 Photos by Carole Thompson
A booklet of 30 b&w photos with text showing daily life rituals of the Mississippi Choctaw. 40 pp. Pa-per. University Press of Mississippi, 1983. $4.95.

**STRANGERS IN THEIR OWN LAND: AN
AMERICAN INDIAN HISTORY GUIDE**
 Sandra Sheffield & Jude Urich
55 pp. Paper. Open Book Publishers, 1988. $6.95.

**STRATEGIES FOR SURVIVAL: AMERICA
INDIANS IN THE EASTERN U.S.**
 Frank W. Porter, III, Editor
248 pp. Greenwood, 1986. $36.95.

**STRUCTURAL CONSIDERATIONS OF METIS
ETHNICITY: AN ARCHAEOLOGICAL, ARCHI-
TECTURAL AND HISTORICAL STUDY**
 David Burley, Gayle Horsfall & John Brandon
Illus. University of South Dakota Press, 1992. $44.95; paper, $25.95.

**A STRUCTURAL & LEXICAL COMPARISON
OF THE TUNICA, CHITIMACHA & ATAKAPA
LANGUAGES**
 John Swanton
Reprint of 1919 edition. Scholarly Press, $19.

**THE STRUCTURE OF TWANA CULTURE:
WITH COMPARATIVE NOTES ON THE
STRUCTURE OF YUROK CULTURE**
 William Elmendorf & A.L. Kroeber
An account of Washington's Twana Indians of the southern coast Salish region. Illus. Maps. Illus. 576 pp. Paper. Washington State University Press, 1992. $25.

**A STRUCTURED APPROACH TO LEARNING
THE BASIC INFLECTIONS OF THE CHERO-
KEE VERB**
 Durbin D. Feeling
190 pp. Paper. Indian University Press, 1994. $29, postpaid.

**STRUGGLE FOR EMPIRE: A BIBLIOGRAPHY
OF THE FRENCH & INDIAN WARS**
 James G. Lydon
275 pp. Garland Publishing, 1985. $40.

**STRUGGLE FOR THE LAND: INDIGENOUS
RESISTANCE TO GENOCIDE, ECOCIDE &
EXPROPRIATION IN CONTEMPORARY
NORTH AMERICA**
 Ward Churchill; preface by Winona LaDuke
Essays. 480 pp. Common Courage Press, $29.95; paper, $17.95.

JOHN STUART AND THE SOUTHERN COLONIAL FRONTIER: A STUDY OF INDIAN RELATIONS, WAR, TRADE, LAND PROBLEMS IN THE SOUTHERN WILDERNESS, 1754-1775
J. Alden
Reprint of 1944 edition. Illus. 384 pp. Gordian Press, $40.

STUDIES IN AMERICAN INDIAN LANGUAGES
Jesse Sawyer
University of California Press, 1974. $40.

STUDIES IN AMERICAN INDIAN LITERATURE: CRITICAL ESSAYS & COURSE DESIGNS
Paula G. Allen
385 pp. Modern Language Association of America, 1983. $35; paper, $18.

STUDIES IN SOUTHEASTERN INDIAN LANGUAGES
James Crawford, Editor
463 pp. Brown Book & Cherokee Publications, 1975. $25.

A STUDY IN CULTURE CONTACT & CULTURE CHANGE: THE WHITEROCK UTES IN TRANSITION
G.O. Lang
Reprint of 1953 edition. AMS Press, $10.50.

A STUDY IN THE ETYMOLOGY OF THE INDIAN PLACE NAME
G.A. McAleer
Reprint. Gordon Press, 1977. $59.50.

STUDY OF AMERICAN INDIAN RELIGIONS
Ake Hultkrantz
Illus. 142 pp. Scholars Press, 1983. $26.95.

A STUDY OF THE DELAWARE INDIAN BIG HOUSE CEREMONY: IN NATIVE TEXT DICTATED BY WITAPANOXWE
F.G. Speck
Reprint of 1931 edition. AMS Press, $24.

A STUDY OF DELAWARE INDIAN MEDICINE PRACTICE & FOLK BELIEFS
Gladys Tantiquidgeon
Reprint of 1942 edition. AMS Press, $18.

STUDY OF NAVAJO SYMBOLISM
Reprint of 1956 edition. Three parts in one. Part I: Navago Symbols in Sandpaintings and Ritual Objects, F.J. Newcomb; Part II: Navajo Picture Writing, S.A. Fishler; Part III: Notes on Corresponding Symbols in Various Parts of the World, M.C. Wheelwright. Paper. Kraus, $23.

STUDY OF OMAHA INDIAN MUSIC
A.C. Fletcher
Includes transcriptions of 92 songs, words and music. Reprint of 1893 edition. Paper. Kraus, $20.

A STUDY OF PUEBLO ARCHITECTURE: TUSAYAN & CIBOLA BUREAU OF AMERICAN ETHNOLOGY, 8th ANNUAL REPORT
Victor Mindeleff
Illus. 425 pp. Paper. Smithsonian, 1989. $19.95.

STYLE TRENDS IN PUEBLO POTTERY IN THE RIO GRANDE & LITTLE COLORADO CULTURAL AREAS FROM THE 16th to 19th CENTURY
Harry P. Mera
Reprint of 1939 edition. AMS Press.

SU SITE: EXCAVATIONS AT A MOGOLLON VILLAGE, WESTERN NEW MEXICO, 1st to 3rd SEASONS
Paul Martin
Reprint of 1940-1947 editions. Paper. Kraus, $34.

THE SUBARCTIC ATHAPASCANS: A SELECTED, ANNOTATED BIBLIOGRAPHY
Arthur E. Hippler and John R. Wood
380 pp. Paper. University of Alaska Institute of Social Sciences, 1974. $15.

SUBJUGATION & DISHONOR: A BRIEF HISTORY OF THE TRAVAIL OF THE NATIVE AMERICANS
Philip Weeks and James B. Gidney
160 pp. Paper. Krieger Publishing, 1981. $8.50.

SUBSTANCE OF A JOURNAL DURING A RESIDENCE AT THE RED RIVER COLONY
John West
Reprint of 1824 edition. Johnson Reprint, $19.

SUMMER IN THE SPRING: ANISHINAABE LYRIC POEMS & STORIES
Gerald Vizenor
Ne edition. Anthology. Includes translations and a glossary of the Anishinaabe (Chippewa) words in which the poems and stories originally were spoken. Illus. with tribal pictomyths. 176 pp. Paper. University of Oklahoma Press, $8.95.

SUMMER PEOPLE, WINTER PEOPLE
Sandra A. Edelman
Guide to Indian Pueblos in New Mexico. Illus. 32 pp. Sunstone Press, $4.95.

SUMMONING THE GODS: SANDPAINTING OF THE NATIVE AMERICAN SOUTHWEST
Ronald McCoy
Illus 32 pp. Paper. Museum of Northern Arizona, 1988. $4.95.

SUN BEAR: THE PATH OF POWER
Sun Bear, et al
Illus. 272 pp. Paper. Bear Tribe, 1984. $9.95.

THE SUN CAME DOWN: TRADITIONAL BLACKFEET STORIES
Percy Bullchild
Illus. 384 pp. Paper. Harper & Row, 1985. $12.95.

SUN CHIEF: THE AUTOBIOGRAPHY OF A HOPI INDIAN
Leo W. Simmons, Editor
Revised 1963 edition. Illus. Paper. Yale University Press, $12.95.

SUN CIRCLES & HUMAN HANDS: THE SOUTHEASTERN INDIANS, ART & INDUSTRIES
E.L. Fundaburk and M.D. Forman, Editors
Reprint of 1957 edition. Illus. 232 pp. Hothem House & Southern Publications, $24.

*SUN DANCE FOR ANDY HORN
Shelly Frome
Grades 9-12. 124 pp. Council for Indian Education, 1990. $12.95; paper, $7.95.

THE SUN DANCE OF THE CROW INDIANS
R. Lowie
Reprint of 1915 edition. AMS Press, $12.50.

THE SUN DANCE & OTHER CEREMONIES OF THE OGLALA DIVISION OF THE TETON DAKOTA
J.R. Walker
Reprint of 1917 edition. AMS Press, $21.50.

*THE SUN DANCE PEOLE: THE PLAINS INDIANS, THEIR PAST & PRESENT
Richard Erdoes
Grades 5-8. Illus. 224 pp. Alfred A. Knopf, 1972. $5.95.

THE SUN DANCE RELIGION: POWER FOR THE POWERLESS
Joseph G. Jorgensen
Illus. 372 pp. Paper. University of Chicago Press, 1972. $14.95.

SUNDOGS
Lee Maracle
Novel about a young First Nation's family during 1992 and the Meech Lake Accord and the "Oka Crisis." 214 pp. Paper. Theytus, 1992. $12.95.

THE SUN GIRL
E. White, pseud.
Reprint of 1941 edition. Illus. 52 pp. Museum of Northern Arizona. $4.75.

*SUN JOURNEY: A STORY OF ZUNI PUEBLO
Ann Nolan Clark
Grades 8 and up. Illus. 96 pp. Ancient City Press, 1988. $19.95; paper, $9.95.

SUN MEN OF THE AMERICAS
Grace Cooke
De Vorss & Co., $6.95.

SUN TRACKS
Ofelia Zepeda, Editor
American Indian literary series sponsored by the American Indian Studies Program, Dept. of English, University of Arizona.

SANDANCING AT ROSEBUD & PINE RIDGE
Thomas E Mails
Reprint. Illus. Center for Western Studies, Delux edition, $125.

*SUNPAINTERS: ECLIPSE OF THE NAVAJO SUN
Baje Whitehorne, Writer/Illustrator
Insight into how Native Americans have traditionallu honored natural phenomena. Grades 1 and up. Illus. 32 pp. Northland Publishing, 1994. $14.95.

SUNSHINE ON THE PRAIRIE: THE STORY OF CYNTHIA ANN PARKER
Jack C. Tamsay; Edwin Eakin, Editor
Illus. 225 pp. Eakin Press, 1989. $16.95.

A SUPPLEMENT GUIDE TO MANUSCRIPTS: RELATING TO THE AMERICAN INDIANS IN THE LIBRARY OF THE AMERICAN PHILOSOPHICAL SOCIETY
Daythal Kendall
American Philosophical Society, 1983. $15.

SUPPLEMENT TO THE HANDBOOK OF MIDDLE AMERICAN INDIANS, Vol. 1: ARCHAEOLOGY
Victoria R. Bricker & Jeremy A. Sabloff, Editors
Illus. 475 pp. University of Texas Press, 1981. $55.

SUPPLEMENT TO THE HANDBOOK OF MIDDLE AMERICAN INDIANS, Vol. 2: LINGUISTICS
Victoria Bricker & Munro Edmonson, Editors
224 pp. University of Texas Press, 1984. $35.

SUPPLEMENT TO THE HANDBOOK OF MIDDLE AMERICAN INDIANS, Vol. 3: LITERATURE
Victoria Bricker & Munro Edmonson, Editors
207 pp. University of Texas Press, 1985. $35.

*SUQUAMISH TODAY
A documentary on the Suquamish of Port Madison Reservation, WA. Teacher's guide. Grades 4-8. Illus. 21 pp. Daybreak Star Press, $4.50.

A SURPRISING ACCOUNT OF THE CAPTIVITY & ESCAPE OF PHILIP McDONALD & ALEXANDER McLEOD, FROM THE CHIKKAMAUGGA INDIANS
McDonald and McLeod
Reprint. 23 pp. Ye Galleon Press, $7.50.

SURVIVAL ARTS OF THE PRIMITIVE PAIUTES
Margaret Wheat
Illus. 120 pp. Paper. University of Nevada Press, 1977. $14.95.

SURVIVAL: LIFE & ART OF THE ALASKAN ESKIMO
The Newark Museum; Text by Barbara Lipton
Text and photographs of Alaska and objects: tools, utensils, dress, art created by the Eskimo. Illus. 96 pp. Paper. Newark Museum Publications, 1977. $7.95.

THE SURVIVAL OF THE BARK CANOE
John McPhee
Illus. 146 pp. Paper. Farrar, Straus & Grioux, 1975. $7.95.

SURVIVAL OF THE SPIRIT: CHIRICAHUA APACHES IN CAPTIVITY
H. Henrietta Stockel
Relates the struggle for survival of the Chiricahua Apaches after being moved from the Southwest to Florida and Alabama then Oklahoma. Illus. 350 pp. University of Nevada Press, 1993. $24.95.

SURVIVAL SKILLS OF THE NORTH AMERICAN INDIANS
Peter Goodchild
Illus. 224 pp. Independent Publishers Group, 1985. $16.95; paper, $9.95.

SURVIVAL THIS WAY: INTERVIEWS WITH AMERICAN INDIAN POETS
Joseph Bruchac
365 pp. Paper. University of Arizona Press, 1987. $16.95.

*SUSETTE LA FLESCHE: ADVOCATE FOR NATIVE AMERICAN RIGHTS
Grades 4 and up. Illus. 120 pp. Childrens Press, $13.95.

SUSQUEHANNA'S INDIANS
Barry C. Kent
Illus. 438 pp. Pennsylvania Historical and Museum Commission, 1984. $15.95.

SWAMP SAILORS: RIVERLINE WARFARE IN THE EVERGLADES, 1835-1842
George Buker
Illus. Maps. Biblio. 152 pp. University Presses of Florida, 1975. $15.

MADONNA SWAN: A LAKOTA WOMAN'S STORY
Mark St. Pierre, Editor
Illus. 210 pp. University of Oklahoma Press, 1991, $19.95.

SWAN AMONG THE INDIANS: LIFE OF JAMES G. SWAN, 1818-1900
Lucile McDonald
A record of the Makah Indian culture and artifacts. Illus. 280 pp. Binford & Mort, $14.95.

SWARTS RUIN: A TYPICAL MIMBRES SITE IN SOUTHWESTERN NEW MEXICO
H.S. and C.B. Cosgrove
Reprint of 1932 edition. Paper. Kraus, $60.

THE SWEET GRASS LIVES ON: FIFTY CONTEMPORARY NORTH AMERICAN INDIAN ARTISTS
Jamake Highwater
Illus. 192 pp. Harper & Row, 1980. $35.

SWEET MEDICINE: THE CONTINUING ROLE OF THE SACRED ARROWS, THE SUN DANCE, & THE SACRED BUFFALO HAT IN NORTHERN CHEYENNE HISTORY
Peter J. Powell
Illus. 986 pp. University of Oklahoma Press, 1969. $62.50.

*SWEETGRASS
Jan Hudson
A novel set in the 19th century western Canadian prairie. 160 pp. Philomel, 1989. $13.95.

SYMBOL & SUBSTANCE IN AMERICAN INDIAN ART
Zena Mathews; Amy Hobar, Editor
24 pp. Paper. Metropolitan Museum of Art, 1984. $2.95.

SYMBOLIC & DECORATIVE ART OF THE OSAGE PEOPLE
Illus. The Osage Mission.

SYMBOLIC IMMORTALITY: THE TLINGIT POTLATCH OF THE 19TH CENTURY
Sergei Kan
The first comprehensive analysis of the mortuary practices of the Tlingit Indians of southeastern Alaska. 2 maps, 2 charts. 384 pp. Smithsonian Institution Press, 1989. $35; paper, $15.95.

SYMPOSIUM ON LOCAL DIVERSITY IN IROQUOIS CULTURE
William Fenton
Reprint of 1951 edition. Scholarly Press, $49.

SYNTAX & SEMANTICS: THE SYNTAX OF NATIVE AMERICAN LANGUAGES
Eung-Do Cook and Donna B. Gerdts
Volume 16 of Syntax and Semantics. Academic Press, 1984. $75.

T

TACACHALE: ESSAYS ON THE INDIANS OF FLORIDA & SOUTHEASTERN GEORGIA DURING THE HISTORIC PERIOD
J.T. Milanich & Samuel Proctor, Editors
Illus. Maps. 217 pp. U. Press of Florida, 1978. $23.95.

MARGARET TAFOYA: A TEWA POTTER'S HERITAGE & LEGACY
Mary Ellen & Laurence Blair
Susan McDonald, Editor
Illus. 200 pp. Schiffer, 1986. $45.

TAH-KOO WAH-KAN: OR, THE GOSPEL AMONG THE DAKOTAS
S. Riggs
Reprint of 1869 edition. 534 pp. Ayer Co., $33.

*THE TAINOS: THE PEOPLE WHO WELCOMED COLUMBUS
Francine Jacobs; illus. by Patrick Collins
Describes the early beginnings of the Tainos' culture. Grades 6 and up. Illus. 112 pp. Putnam, 1992. $15.95.

TALES THE ELDERS TOLD: OJIBWAY LEGENDS
Basil H. Johnston; illus. by Shirley Cheechoo
Illus. 64 pp. University of Toronto Press, $15.95.

*TALES FROM THE CHEROKEE HILLS
Jean Starr
33 Cherokee folktales. 94 pp. Paper. John F. Blair & Cherokee Publications, $8.95.

TALES FROM THE MOHAVES
Herman Grey
96 pp. Paper. University of Oklahoma Press, 1980. $4.95.

TALES OF THE ANISHINAUBACK: OJIBWAY LEGENDS
Basil H. Johnston; illus. by Maxine Noel
Native myths. Illus. 80 pp. University of Toronto Press, $24.95.

TALES OF THE BLACK HILLS
Helen Rezatto
Collection of legends, including legends by the Sioux. Illus. 288 pp. Paper. Center for Western Studies, $9.95.

TALES OF THE COCHITI INDIANS
Ruth Benedict
Reprint of 1931 edition. Scholarly Press, $49.

TALES OF KANKAKEE LAND
C.H. Bartlett
Reprint of 1907 edition. Hardscrabble Books, $7.50.

TALES OF THE NEZ PERCE
Donald M. Hines
232 pp. Ye Galleon, 1984. $14.95.

TALES OF THE NORTH AMERICAN INDIAN
Stith Thompson, Editor
Illus. 416 pp. Paper. Indiana University Press, 1966. $9.95.

TALES OF THE NORTHWEST: ON SKETCHES OF INDIAN LIFE & CHARACTER
W.J. Snelling
Collection of short stories on Plains Indians. Reprint of 1830 edition. 288 pp. Ross & Haines, $15.

*TALES OF A PUEBLO BOY
Lawrence J. Vallo
Stories of growing up in an Indian Pueblo. Grades 3-9. Illus. 48 pp. Paper. Sunstone Press, $5.95.

TALES OF A SHAMAN'S APPRENTICE
Mark Plotkin, PhD
Penguin USA, $22.

TALES OF TICASUK:
ESKIMO LEGENDS & STORIES
Emily Ivanoff Brown
Reprint. Illus. 135 pp. University of Alaska Press, 1990. $15; paper , $8.95.

TALES & TRADITIONS OF THE ESKIMO
H.J. Rink
Reprint of 1875 edition. AMS, $34.50.

TALKING LEAVES: CONTEMPORARY NATIVE AMERICAN SHORT STORIES, ANTHOLOGY
Craig Lesley, Editor
Anthology of 38 contemporary Native American short stories. 385 pp. Dell Publishing & Cherokee Publications, 1991. $10.

TALKING TO THE MOON: WILDLIFE ADVENTURES ON THE PLAINS & PRAIRIES OF OSAGE COUNTRY
John Joseph Matthews
Keen & intimate observations of nature; Native American comparisons, cowboy reflections & humor. University of Oklahoma Pres, $16.

TALKING WITH THE CLAY:
THE ART OF PUEBLO POTTERY
Stephen Trimble
Illus. 124 pp. Paper . University of Washington Press & School of American Research, 1987. $15.95.

TANAINA TALES FROM ALASKA
Bill Vaudrin
133 pp. Paper . University of Oklahoma Press, 1981. $5.95.

THE TAOS INDIANS
Blanche C. Grant
Reissue of 1925 edition. Illus. 198 pp. Paper . Rio Grande Press, $10.

THE TAOS INDIANS & THE BATTLE FOR BLUE LAKE
R.C. Gordon-McCutchan
Story of the Taos Indians' 60 year struggle to regain their sacred tribal lands. Illus. 256 pp. Red Crane Books, 1991. $25.95.

TAOS: 1847: THE REVOLT IN CONTEMPORARY ACCOUNTS
Michael McNierney, Editor
102 pp. Paper . Johnson Books, 1980. $4.95.

TAOS TALES
E. Parsons
Reprint of 1940 edition. Kraus, $26.

THE TAOS TRAPPERS: THE FUR TRADE IN THE FAR SOUTHWEST
David J. Webber
Illus. 280 pp. Paper . University of Oklahoma Press, 1980. $8.95.

TAPESTRIES IN THE SAND: THE SPIRIT OF NATIVE AMERICAN SANDPAINTING
David Villasenor
Illus. 112 pp. Naturegraph, $16.95; paper , $8.95.

*THE TARHUMARA: MIDDLE AMERICA
John G. Kennedy
Grades 5 and up. Illus.Chelsea House, 1989. $17.95.

TATL'AHWT'AENN NENN' THE HEAD WATERS PEOPLE'S COUNTRY
James Kari, et al, Editors
Illus. 220 pp. Paper . Alaska Native Language Center, 1986. $10.

A TEACHER'S GUIDE TO THE LENAPE
Karen Waldauer, Editor
Three separate kits: 1. Introduction to the Lenape, $22.50; 2. Lenape Lore/Folk Medicines, $15.50; 3. Lenape Lore/Clothing, Shelter , Crafts, Weapons, Tools & Specialties, $15.50. Illus. Charts, quizzes, posters. The Middle Atlantic Press.

TEACHING ABOUT AMERICAN INDIANS IN CONNECTICUT
17 pp. U. of Connecticut Education, 1982. $2.

TEACHING ABOUT NATIVE AMERICANS
Karen D. Harvey, Lisa D. Harjo, Jane K. Jackson
NCSS Publications, $8.95 (members); $10.95 (non-members).

TEACHING AMERICAN INDIAN HISTORY: AN INTERDISCIPLINARY APPROACH
Larry L. Vantine
Paper. R & E Research Associates, 1978. $11.95.

TEACHING AMERICAN INDIAN STUDENTS
Jon Reyhner
Summarizes the latest research on Indian education, and provides practical suggestions for teachers, and resources. Map. Biblio. 344 pp. Paper . University of Oklahoma Press, 1992. $14.95.

TEACHING GUIDE FOR INDIAN LITERATURE
Diana Campbell
Volume I, 110 pp. Grades 4-6; Volume II, 55 pp. Grades 6 and up. Navajo Curriculum Center , 1983. $4.50 each.

TEACHING THE NATIVE AMERICAN
Hap Gilliland
A guide to adapting instruction to the needs of American Indian students. 196 pp. Council for Indian Education, 1987. $22.95; paper , $15.95.

TEACHINGS FROM THE AMERICAN EARTH: INDIAN RELIGION & PHILOSOPHY
Dennis and Barbara Tedlock, Editors
Illus. 280 pp. Paper . Liveright, 1975. $10.95.

TEACHINGS OF NATURE
Adolf Hungry Wolf
Illus. 94 pp. Paper . The Book Publishing Co., $8.95.

TECHNIQUE OF NORTH AMERICAN INDIAN BEADWORK
Monte Smith
Features examples and photos of beadwork from 1835 to the present time. Illus. 106 pp. Eagle's View Publishing, $15.95; paper , $10.95.

THE TECHNIQUE OF PORCUPINE QUILL DECORTION AMONG THE INDIANS OF NORTH AMERICA
William C. Orchard; Monte Smith, Editor
Revised 1917 edition. Illus. 88 pp. Paper . Eagles View Publishing, $8.95.

TECHNIQUES OF BEADING EARRINGS
Deon DeLange
Illus. 72 pp. Paper . Eagle's View Publishing, $7.95.

*TECUMSEH
Grades 3-6. Illus. 32 pp. Childrens Press, $11.45.

*TECUMSEH
Russell Shorto; Nancy Furstinger , Editor
Grades 5-7. Illus. 145 pp. Silver Burdett Press, 1989. $11.98; paper, $7.95.

TECUMSEH & THE QUEST FOR INDIAN LEADERSHIP
R. David Edmunds
Paper. Scott Foresman & Co., 1984. $7.95.

TECUMSEH: VISIONARY CHIEF OF THE SHAWNEE
Jason Hook
Illus. 52 pp. Sterling, 1989. $12.95.

TEEPEE NEIGHBORS
Grace Coolidge
200 pp. Paper. University of Oklahoma Press, 1984. $7.95.

TEEPEES ARE FOLDED: AMERICAN INDIAN POETRY
Sally Old Coyote
Council for Indian Education, 1991. $5.95.

TEJANO ORIGINS IN 18TH CENTURY SAN ANTONIO
Gerald Poyo & Gilberto Hinojoso
Illus. 200 pp. U. of Texas Press, 1991. $19.95.

TELLICO ARCHAEOLOGY
Jefferson Chapman
12,000 years of Native American occupation in the Little Tennessee and Tellico Rivers region of Tennessee. Illus. 142 pp. Paper . Hothem House & University of Tennessee Press, 1985. $14.95.

TEMALPAKH: CAHUILLA INDIAN KNOWLEDGE & USAGE OF PLANTS
Lowell J. Bean & Katherine Siva Saubel
Paper. Malki Museum Press, 1972. $20; paper , $16.

THE TEN GRANDMOTHERS
A. Marriott
Reprint of 1945 edition. Illus. 305 pp. Paper . University of Oklahoma Press, $10.95.

TEN MONTHS AMONG THE TENTS OF THE TUSKI
William Hooper
Reprint of 1853 edition. AMS, $31.

THE TEN YEAR'S WAR: INDIAN-WHITE RELATIONS IN PENNSYLVANIA, 1755-1765
Stephen F. Auth
Reprint. 256 pp. Garland, $51.

TENA'S TEXTS & TALES FROM ANVIK, ALASKA
John Chapman
Reprint of 1914 edition. AMS, $30.

*TENDOY, CHIEF OF THE LEMHIS
David Crowder
Grades 5-9. Illus. Paper. Caxton, 1969. $2.75.

TENNESSEE'S INDIAN PEOPLES: FROM WHITE CONTACT TO REMOVAL, 1540-1840
Ronald N. Satz
Illus. 110 pp. U. of Tennessee Press, 1979. $9.95; paper , $3.50.

TENTING ON THE PLAINS
Elizabeth B. Custer
Reprint of 1887 edition. 403 pp.
Comer House, $21.

TENSION & HARMONY: THE NAVAJO RUG
32 pp. Paper. Museum of Northern Arizona, 1982. $4.

TENTING ON THE PLAINS; OR, GENERAL CUSTER IN KANSAS & TEXAS
Elizabeth B. Custer
Portrays the aftermath of the Civil War in Texas, and life in Kansas. Detailed dscriptions of an army officer's home life on the frontier during theis major period of Indian unrest. Reprint. Illus. Maps. 424 pp. Paper. University of Oklahoma Press, $12.95.

TERMINATION & RELOCATION: FEDERAL INDIAN POLICY, 1945-1960
Donald L. Fixico
Illus. 286 pp. Paper. University of New Mexico Press, $13.95.

TERRITORIAL SUBDIVISIONS & BOUND- ARIES OF THE WAMPANOAG, MASSACHU- SETT & NAUSET INDIANS
F.G. Speck
Reprint of 1928 edition. AMS Press, $15.

TETON SIOUX MUSIC & CULTURE
Frances Densmore
Explores the role of music in all aspects of Sioux life. Reprint of 1918 edition. Illus. 644 pp. Paper. University of Nebraska Press, $19.95.

TEWA TALES
Esie Clews Parsons
Collection of more than 100 tales. Reprint of 1926 edition. Kraus, $26. Paper. University of Arizona Press, $16.95.

TEWA WORLD: SPACE, TIME, BEING, AND BECOMING IN A PUEBLO SOCIETY
Alfonso Ortiz
Paper. University of Chicago Press, 1969. $9.95.

THE TEXAS CANNIBALS: OR, WHY FATHER SERRA CAME TO CALIFORNIA
S. Morrill
28 pp. Holmes Book Co., 1964. $5.

THE TEXAS CHEROKEES: A PEOPLE BETWEEN FIRES, 1819-1840
Dianna Everett
Illus. Maps. 192 pp. University of Oklahoma Press, 1990. $22.95.

TEXTBOOKS & THE AMERICAN INDIAN
Jeanette Henry and Rupert Costo, Editors
269 pp. Paper. The Indian Historian Press, 1969. $5.

THAT'S WHAT SHE SAID: CONTEMPORARY POETRY & FICTION BY NATIVE AMERICAN WOMEN
Rayna Green, Editor
Illus. 352 pp. Indiana University Press, 1984. $29.95; paper, $12.95.

THEIR DAY IN COURT: A HISTORY OF THE INDIAN CLAIMS COMMISSION
H.D. Rosenthal
Facsimile reprint. 330 pp. Garland, $70.

THEIR NUMBER BECOME THINNED: NATIVE AMERICAN POPULATION DYNAMICS IN EASTERN NORTH AMERICA
Henry F. Dobyns
Illus. 382 pp. University of Tennessee Press, 1983. $34.95; paper, $16.95.

THEIR STORIES OF LONG AGO
Belle Deacon
A bilingual colection of traditional Athabascan tales from Alaska. Illus. Alaskan Native Language Center, $10.

THEMES IN SOUTHWEST PREHISTORY
George J. Gumerman, Editor
Illus. 370 pp. Paper. University of Washington Press & School of American Research, 1994. $22.50.

THEORETICAL PERSPECTIVES ON NATIVE AMERICAN LANGUAGES
Donna Gerdts & Karin Michelson, Editors
Illus. 290 pp. State University of New York Press, 1989. $24.50; paper, $12.95.

*THERE STILL ARE BUFFALO
Ann Nolan Clark; Willard Beatty, Editor
illus. by Steve Tongier
Grades 1-6. Illus. 50 pp. Paper. Ancient City Press, 1992. $8.95.

THESE ARE MY CHILDREN
A. Murray
116 pp. Ye Galleon Press, 1977. $14.95.

*THESE WERE THE SIOUX
Marie Sandoz
The philosophy and practical wisdom of the Sioux Indians, including their beliefs and customs. Reprint of 1961 edition. Grades 6-12. Illus. 118 pp. Paper. University of Nebraska Press, $74.50; paper, $24.50.

THEY CALLED IT PRAIRIE LIGHT: THE STORY OF CHILOCCO INDIAN SCHOOL
K. Tsianina Lomawaima
Illus. Maps. 395 pp. University of Nebraska Press, 1994. $29.95.

THEY HAVE NO RIGHTS
Walter Ehlich
266 pp. Paper. Jefferson National, 1979. $7.95.

THEY LED A NATION
Virginia Driving Hawk Sneve; N. Jane Hunt, Ed
A pictorial and biographical documentation of 20 historic Sioux leaders. Ilus. 46 pp. Paper. Brevet Press, $4.95.

THEY SANG FOR THE HORSES: THE IMPACT OF THE HORSE ON NAVAJO & APACHE FOLKLORE
LaVerne Clark; illus. by Ted DFeGrazier
The weaving of the horse into existent mythology of the Navajo and Apache tribes. Illus. 225 pp. Paper. University of Arizona Press, 1966. $14.95.

THEY WALKED BEFORE: THE INDIANS OF WASHINGTON STATE
Cecilia Carpenter
Illus. Revised edition. 75 pp. Paper. Tahoma Publications, 1989. $10.

THIRTEEN MOONS ON TURTLE'S BACK
Joseph Bruchac & Jonathan London; illus. by Thomas Locker

Retelling of Native American legends. Storytelling poems. Illus. Philomel Press, 1992. $15.95.

THIS FOOL HISTORY, AN ORAL HISTORY OF DAKOTA TERRITORY
Sylvia G. Wheeler
A play representing the meeting of Indian and white cultures in Dakota Territory. University of South Dakota Press, 1991. $19.95.

THIS IS OUR LAND
Val J. McClellan
Illus. Two vols. Western Publishers, 1978. $13.95 each.

*THIS LAND IS MY LAND
George Littlechild
Grades 1-6. Story by a Canadian Plains Cree. Illus. Children's Book Press, $15.95.

THIS LAND WAS THEIRS: A STUDY OF THE NORTH AMERICAN INDIAN
Wendell H. Oswait
Fourth edition. 500 pp. Paper. Mayfield Publishing, 1987. $24.95.

THIS PATH WE TRAVEL: CELEBRATIONS OF CONTEMPORARY NATIVE AMERICAN CREATIVITY
National Museum of the American Indian, Smithsonian Institution
Combining photography with collected observations, this book documents a group of Native American artists examining the relationships between native and contemporary and traditional and innovative artistic endeavors. Illus. 128 pp. Fulcrum Publishing, 1994. $24.95; paper, $18.95.

THE THOMPSON INDIANS OF BRITISH COLUMBIA
J. Teit; Franz Boas, Editor
Reprint of 1900 edition. AMS Press, $47.50.

THOREAU AND THE AMERICAN INDIANS
Robert F. Sayre
Princeton U. Press, 1977. $29.50; paper, $13.50.

THOSE TREMENDOUS MOUNTAINS: THE STORY OF THE LEWSI & CLARK EXPEDITION
David Hawke
Illus. 290 pp. Paper. W.W. Norton & Co., 1985. $7.70.

A THOUSAND YEARS OF AMERICAN INDIAN STORYTELLING
Rupert Costo & Jeanette Henry Costo
Collection of Native American tales. Indian Historian Press, $12.

THE THREE SISTERS; EXPLORING AN IROQUOIS GARDEN
Marcia Eames-Sheavly
Illus. Photos. 20 pp. Paper. AISES, $4.25.

THREE STRANDS IN THE BRAND: A GUIDE FOR ENABLERS OF LEARNING
Paula Underwood
Paper. Greenfield Review Press, $8.95.

THREE YEARS AMONG THE COMANCHES: THE NARRATIVE OF NELSON LEE, THE TEXAS RANGER
Nelson Lee
200 pp. Paper. U. of Oklahoma Press, 1991. $8.95.

A THRILLING NARRATIVE OF THE SUFFER-INGS OF JANE ADELINE WILSON DURING HER CAPTIVITY AMONG THE COMANCHE INDIANS
Jane A. Wilson
Reprint. 28 pp. Ye Galleon Press, $7.50; paper, $4.95.

THROUGH DAKOTA EYES: NARRATIVE ACCOUNTS OF THE MINNESOTA INDIAN WAR OF 1862
Gary Anderson; Alan Woolworth, Editor
Illus. Photos. Maps. 316 pp. Minnesota Historical Society Press, 1988. $24.95; paper, $11.95.

THROUGH INDIAN EYES, THE NATIVE EXPERIENCE IN BOOKS FOR CHILDREN
Beverly Slapin & Doris Seale, Editors
Articles, stories, poetry, and reviews of books dealing with Native Americans. Bibliography. 312 pp. Paper. Oyate, 1991. $24.95.

THROUGH INDIAN EYES, VOL. 1: THE WHEEL OF LIFE
Donald & Jean Johnson
Revised edition. Illus. Paper. Center for International Training & Education, 1985. $8.95.

THROUGH NAVAJO EYES: AN EXPLORATION IN FILM COMMUNICATION & ANTHROPOLOGY
Sol Worth and John Adair
Illus. 320 pp. Indiana University Press, 1973. $20; paper, $7.95.

THROUGH WHITE MEN'S EYES: A CONTRIBUTION TO NAVAJO HISTORY
J. Lee Correll
Illus. 6 vols., 2,832 pp. University of Arizona Press, 1979. $255 per set.

THUNDER OVER THE OCHOO, 4 Vols.
Andrew Gale Ontko
The Shoshoni Indian history in four volumes: Volume I - covers hundreds of years from pre-Columbian times to the collapse of the world fur trade in 1840, Vol. I meets the Shoshoni Indians before arrival of the Europeans; Volume II - Covers the 20 year period between 1840 and 1860; Volume III - Covers between 1860 and 1869; and Volume IV - Covers the 45 year interval between 1867 and 1912. Illus. 450 pp each. Maverick Distributors, $16.95 each.

THUNDER RIDES A BLACK HORSE: MESCALERO APACHES & THE MYTHIC PRESENT
Claire F. Farrer
A 4-day, 4-night Mescalero Apache girls' puberty ceremonial. Waveland Press, 1994.

*THUNDER WATERS: EXPERIENCES OF GROWING UP IN DIFFERENT INDIAN TRIBES
Frances Snow, et al
Grades 3-8. Council for Indian Education, 1975. $7.95; paper, $1.95.

THE TIGUAS: PUEBLO INDIANS OF TEXAS
Bill Wright
Illus. Biblio. 180 pp. Texas Western Press, 1994. $40.

TILLAMOOK INDIANS OF OREGON COAST
John Sauter and Bruce Johnson
Illus. Binford-Metropolitan, 1974. $9.95; paper, $6.95.

TIME AMONG THE NAVAJO: TRADITIONAL LIFEWAYS ON THE RESERVATION
Kathy Hooker
Illus. 100 pp. Paper. Museum of New Mexico Press, 1991. $19.95.

THE TIME OF THE AUTUMN MOON
Harold E. Sommons, Editor
Booklet devoted to the history, present life, and possible future of the Lenni Lenape (Delaware) Indians of Eastern Pennsylvania. 34 pp. Lenni Lenape Historical Society. $5, postpaid.

A TIME OF GATHERING: NATIVE HERITAGE IN WASHINGTON STATE
Robin K. Wright, Editor
Illus. 256 pp. Paper. University of Washington Press, 1989. $29.95.

TIME: SPACE & TRANSITION IN ANASAZI PREHISTORY
Michael S. Berry
112 pp. University of Utah Press, 1982. $20.

TIME'S FLOTSAM: OVERSEAS COLLECTIONS OF CALIFORNIA
Thomas Blackburn & Travis Hudson
Illus. 226 pp. Santa Barbara Museum of Natural History, 1990. $34.95.

TIMOTHY: NEZ PERCE CHIEF, LIFE AND TIMES, 1800-1891
Rowena Alcorn
Paper. Ye Galleon Press, 1986. $5.95.

*THE TIPI: A CENTER OF NATIVE AMERICAN LIFE
Charlotte Yue
Grades 4-7. Illus. 96 pp. Paper. Alfred A. Knopf, 1983. $10.95.

TLAPACOYA POTTERY IN THE MUSEUM COLLECTION
Muriel Weaver
Illus. 48 pp. Paper. National Museum of the American Indian, 1967. $3.50.

*THE TLINGIT
Grades K-4. Illus. 48 pp. Childrens Press, $11.45.

TLINGIT ART & CULTURE
Don Kaiper
Illus. 95 pp. Hancock House, 1990. $4.95.

TLINGIT INDIANS OF ALASKA
Anatoli Kamenski; translated by Sergei Kan
Marvin Falk, Editor
Illus. Biblio. 166 pp. Paper. University of Alaska Press, 1985. $15.

THE TLINGIT INDIANS
George Thornton Emmons
Frederica de Laguna, Editor
Illus. 65 drawings, 127 photos. 530 pp. University of Washington Press, $60.

TLINGIT MYTHS & TEXTS
John Swanton
Reprint of 1909 edition. Scholarly Press, $79.

TLINGIT TALES: POTLATCH & TOTEM POLES
Lorle Hayes
Illus. 48 pp. Naturegraph, $14.95; paper, $6.95.

TO THE AMERICAN INDIAN: REMINIS-CENCES OF A YOUROK WOMAN
Lucy Thompson
Illus. Revised edition. 325 pp. Paper. Heyday Books, 1991. $13.95.

TO THE ARCTIC BY CANOE
C. Stuart Houston
The journal & paintings of Robert Hood, midshipman with Sir John Franklin, Arctic explorer. Reveals the adverse effects on Native peoples and their environment of the coming of the Europeans. Illus. 280 pp. Paper. University of Toronto Press, 1994. $22.95.

TO THE CHUKCHI PENINSULA & TO THE TLINGIT INDIANS 1881/1882: JOURNALS & LETTERS BY AUREL & ARTHUR KRAUSE
translated by Margot Krause McCaffrey
Studies & observations of the region's natural history, art and ethnography. Illus. Maps. 230 pp. Paper. University of Alaska Press, 1993. $17.50.

TO HAVE THIS LAND: THE NATURE OF INDIAN/WHITE RELATIONS, SOUTH DAKOTA, 1888-1891
Philip S. Hall
Illus. Paper. Center for Western Studies & University of South Dakota Press, 1991. $10.95.

TO LIVE IN TWO WORLDS: AMERICAN INDIAN YOUTH TODAY
Brent Ashabranner
Grades 7-11. Illus. Putnam Publishing Group, $13.95.

TO LIVE ON THIS EARTH: AMERICAN INDIAN EDUCATION
Estelle Fuchs and Robert Havighurst
Revised 1983 edition. 408 pp. Paper. University of New Mexico Press, $11.95.

TO PLEASE THE CARIBOU: PAINTED CARI-BOU-SKIN COATS WORN BY THE NASPAKI, MONTAGNAIS, & CREE HUNTERS OF THE QUEBEC-LABRADOR PENINSULA
Dorothy K. Burnham
Description and illustrations of 60 painted Caribou-skin coats. Illus. 763 drawings, photos. 328 pp. U. of Washington Press, $60; paper, $35.

TO PRESERVE A CULTURE: THE TWENTIETH-CENTURY FIGHT OVER INDIAN REORGANI-ZATION
Jon F. Rice, Jr.
Illus. 60 pp. The Committee, 1981. $2.

TO RUN AFTER THEM: CULTURAL & SOCIAL BASES OF COOPERATION IN A NAVAJO COMMUNITY
Louise Lamphere
230 pp. Paper. University of Arizona Press, 1977. $13.95.

TO SING OUR OWN SONGS: COGNITION & CULTURE IN INDIAN EDUCATION
Paper. Association on American Indian Affairs, 1985. $2.50.

TO TOUCH THE WIND: AN INTRODUCTION TO NATIVE AMERICAN PHILOSOPHY & BELIEFS
Edward Morton
128 pp. Paper. Kendall-Hunt, 1988. $13.95.

TOBA TUCKER: A SHINNECOCK PORTRAIT
John Strong & Madeleine Burnside
Illus. 25 pp. Paper. Guild Hall, 1987. $7.

TOBACCO, PEACE PIPES & INDIANS
Louis Seig
Illus. 51 pp. Paper. Filter Press, 1971. $2.50.

TOBACCO, PIPES & SMOKING CUSTOMS OF THE AMERICAN INDIANS
G.A. West
Reprint of 1934 edition. Greenwood Press, $57.50.

THE TOBACCO SOCIETY OF THE CROW INDIANS
R.H Lowie
Reprint of 1919 edition. AMS Press, $13.45.

TOMAHAWK & CROSS: LUTHERAN MISSIONARIES AMONG NORTHERN PRAIRIE INDIANS, 1858-1866
Gerhard Schmutterer
Illus. 220 pp. Paper. Center for Western Studies, 1989. $12.95.

TOMAHAWKS ILLUSTRATED
Kuck
Illus. 112 pp. Paper. Hothem House, 1977. $9.

TOMOCHICHI: INDIAN FRIEND OF THE GEORGIA COLONY
Helen Todd
Illus. 208 pp. Cherokee Publishing, 1977. $12.95.

TONKAWA, AN INDIAN LANGUAGE OF TEXAS
Harry Hoijer
Paper. J.J. Augustin, Inc., Publisher, $5.

THE TONKAWA PEOPLE: A TRIBAL HISTORY FROM EARLIEST TIMES TO 1893
Deborah Newlin; Gale Richardson, Editor
Illus. 120 pp. Paper. West Texas Museum, $5.

TOP OF THE HILL
Morris Taylor
Tale that crosses generations and cultures. 64 pp. Paper. Naturegraph, $4.95.

TOPICS IN MOJAVE SYNTAX
Pamela E. Munro
Garland Publishing, 1976. $51.

TOPOGRAPHICAL DESCRIPTION OF THE STATE OF OHIO, INDIANA TERRITORY & LOUISIANA
Jervis Cutler
Reprint of 1812 edition. Illus. Ayer Co., $17.

TOPOGRAPHICAL MEMOIR
Thomas Cram
126 pp. Ye Galleon, 1978. $12.95.

THE TOTEM CARVERS: CHARLIE JAMES, ELLEN NEEL, AND MUNGO MARTIN
Phil Nuytten
Illus. 132 pp. University of Washington Press, 1983. $32.

*TOTEM POLE
Diane Hoyt-Goldsmith
The background of totem poles & the creation of one. Grades 4-6. Illus. 32 pp. Holiday House, $15.95; paper, $6.95.

*THE TOTEM POLE INDIANS OF THE NORTHWEST
Don E. Beyer

Grades 3 and up. Illus. 64 pp. Paper. Franklin Watts, 1991. $4.95.

*TOTEM POLES
Put the parts together and you will have a pole from floor to ceiling. Grades 3-5. Paper. Bellerophon, $4.95.

TOTEM POLES OF THE NORTHWEST
D. Allen
Illus. 32 pp. Paper. Hancock House, $3.95.

TOTEM POLES OF THE PACIFIC NORTHWEST COAST
Edward Malin
Presents totem poles from the Tlingit settlements of Alaska to the Kwakiutl villages of Vancouver Island. 54 historic photos, and 14 color photos of contemporary poles; 199 line drawings. <aps. 195 pp. Paper. Timber Press, 1994 first paper edition. $19.95.

*TOTEM POLES TO COLOR & CUT OUT, Vol. 2: Tlingit
Grades 3-5. Paper. Bellerophon, $4.95.

*TOTEM POLES TO COLOR & CUT OUT, Vol. 3: Kwakiutl
Grades 3-5. Paper. Bellerophon, $4.95.

TOTEMISM
C. Levi-Strauss
Paper. Beacon Press, 1963. $9.95.

TOUCH THE EARTH: A SELF PORTRAIT OF INDIAN EXISTENCE
T.C. McLuhan
Selection of statements and writings by North American Indians on Indian history and life. Illus. 185 pp. Hardcover. Cahill & Co., $10.

TOUR THROUGH THE SOUTHERN & WESTERN TERRITORIES OF THE U.S. OF NORTH AMERICA, THE SPANISH DOMINIONS ON THE RIVER MISSISSIPPI & THE FLORIDAS, THE COUNTRIES OF THE CREEK NATIONS, & MANY UNINHABITED PARTS
John Pope
Reprint of 1792 edition. Ayer Co., $11.

TOVANGER
Anne Galloway
Paper. Malki Museum Press, 1978. $3.

TOWN & TEMPLES ALONG THE MISSISSIPPI
David Dye & Cheryl Cox, Editors
Illus. 280 pp. Paper. University of Alabama Press, 1990. $22.95.

THE TRADE GUN SKETCHBOOK
Full-size plans to build seven different Indian trade guns from the Revolution to the Indian Wars. Illus. 48 pp. Paper. Thr Fur Press, $2.00.

TRADERS OF THE WESTERN MORNING: ABORIGINAL COMMERCE IN PRECOLUMBIAN NORTH AMERICA
John U. Terrell
Illus. Maps. 145 pp. Southwest Museum, 1967. $12.50.

TRADITION & CHANGE ON THE NORTHWEST COAST: THE MAKAH, NUU CHAH-NULTH, SOUTHERN KWAKIUTL & NUXALK
Ruth Kirk

Illus. 200 photos. 256 pp. Paper. University of Washington Press, 1988. $29.95.

TRADITION & INNOVATION: A BASKET HISTORY OF THE INDIANS OF THE YOSEMITE-MONO LAKE REGION
Craig D. Bates & Martha J. Lee
Study of the history and basketry of the Miwok and Paiute people. Illus. 252 pp. Yosemite Association, 1991. $49.95.

TRADITIONAL DRESS
Adolph Hungry Wolf
Illus. 80 pp. Paper. The Book Publishing Co., 1990. $5.95.

TRADITIONAL INDIAN BEAD & LEATHER CRAFTS
Monte Smith & Michele Van Sickle
Illus. 100 pp. Paper. Eagle's View Publishing, 1987. $8.95.

TRADITIONAL INDIAN CRAFTS
Monte Smith
Illus. 96 pp. Paper. Eagle's View Publishing, 1987. $7.95.

TRADITIONAL LITERATURES OF THE AMERICAN INDIAN: TEXTS & INTERPRETATIONS
Karl Kroeber, Editor
Illus. Paper. University of Nebraska Press, 1981. $8.95.

TRADITIONAL NARRATIVES OF THE ARIKARA INDIANS, 4 Vols.
Douglas Parks
Vol. 1, *Stories of Alfred Morsette*, 684 pp; Vol. 2, *Stories of Other Narrators*, 660 pp. University of Nebraska Press, 1991. $125 per set. Audiocassette, $20. Vols. 3 & 4, *Free Translations*. Illus. Maps. 400 pp. & 320 pp. $75.

TRADITIONAL OJIBWA RELIGION & ITS HISTORICAL CHANGES
Christopher Vecsey
American Philosophical Society, 1983. $12.

TRADITIONS IN TRANSITION: CONTEMPORARY BASKET WEAVING OF THE SOUTHWESTERN INDIANS
Barbara Maudlin
Illus. 64 pp. Paper. Museum of New Mexico Press, 1984. $8.95.

TRADITIONS & LAWS OF THE IROQUOIS: OR, SIX NATIONS, & HISTORY OF THE TUSCARORA INDIANS
Elias Johnson
Reprint of 1881 edition. AMS Press, $24.

TRADITIONS OF THE ARAPAHO
G.A. Dorsey and A.L. Kroeber
Reprint of 1903 edition. Paper. Kraus, $48.

TRADITIONS OF THE CADDO
G.A. Dorsey
Reprint of 1905 edition. AMS Press, $16.50.

TRADITIONS OF THE CHILCOTIN INDIANS
L. Farand
Reprint of 1900 edition. AMS Press, $24.50.

THE TRADITIONS OF THE HOPI: THE STANLEY McCORMIC HOPI EXPEDITION
H.R. Voth, Translator
Reprint of 1905 edition. Paper. AMS Press, $39; and Kraus, $36.

**TRADITIONS OF THE
NORTH AMERICAN INDIANS**
J.A. Jones
Three volumes. Gordon Press, $300 per set.

TRADITIONS OF THE OSAGE
G. Dorsey
Reprint of 1904 edition. AMS Press, $12.50.

TRADITIONS OF THE QUINAULT INDIANS
L. Farrand and W.S. Kahnweiler
Reprint of 1902 edition. 54 pp. AMS Press,
$24.50.

TRADITIONS OF THE SKIDI PAWNEE
G.A. Dorsey
Reprint of 1904 edition. Illus. Kraus, $34.

**TRADITIONS OF THE THOMPSON
RIVER INDIANS OF BRITISH COLUMBIA**
J.A. Teit
Reprint of 1898 edition. Kraus, $16.

***THE TRAIL ON WHICH THEY WEPT:
THE STORY OF A CHEROKEE GIRL**
Dorothy & Thomas Hoobler
The Trail of Tears through the eyes of a young
Cherokee girl. Grades 3-5. Illus. 64 pp. Silver
Burdett Press, 1992. $7.95; paper. $3.95

**THE TRANSFORMATION OF BIGFOOT:
MALENESS, POWER & BELIEF AMONG
THE CHIPEWYAN**
Henry Sharp
Illus. 190 pp. Smithsonian, 1988, $22.50.

THE TRAGEDY OF THE BLACKFOOT
W. McCluntock
Reprint of 1930 edition. Illus. 53 pp.
Southwest Museum, $5.

*TRAGEDY OF TENAYA
Allan Shields
Grades 6-and up. 60 pp. Paper. Council for
Indian Education, 1974. $9.95; paper, $3.95.

TRAGIC SAGA OF THE INDIANA INDIANS
Harold Allison
350 pp. Turner Publishing Co., 1987. $15.

THE TRAIL OF THE HARE
Joel Savishinsky
Illus. 285 pp. Gordon & Breach, 1974. $40.

TRAIL OF TEARS
John Ehle
Portrayal of the Cherokee Nation, filled with
legend, lore & religion. 424 pp. Paper. Cherokee
Publications, $11.95.

TREKWAYS OF THE WIND
Nils-Aslak Valkeapaa; trans.
by Ralph Salisbury, et al
Studies Native American poetry. 300 pp.
University of Arizona Press, 1994. $20.

THE TRIAL OF LEONARD PELTIER
Jim Messersmith
Paper. South End Press, 1991. $12.

THE TRAIL OF LEWIS & CLARK: 1804-1904
O. Wheeler
Reprint of 1904 edition. 2 vols. AMS Press,
$57.50 per set.

THE TRAIL OF TEARS
Gloria Jahoda
355 pp. Brown Book Co., 1975. $12.95.

**TRAIL OF TEARS: THE RISE & FALL
OF THE CHEROKEE NATION**
John Ehle
430 pp. Doubleday, 1988. $19.95. Paper.
Cherokee Publications, $10.95.

***THE TRAIL ON WHICH THEY WEPT:
THE STORY OF A CHEROKEE GIRL**
Dorothy and Thomas Hoobler
pictures by S.S. Burrus
A young girls story of their Trail of Tears.
Ages 9-11. Illus. 64 pp. Silver Burdett Press.

**TRAITS OF AMERICAN
INDIAN LIFE & CHARACTER**
P. Ogden
Reprint of 1933 second edition. AMS Press,
$17.50; Ye Galleon, $19.95.

**THE TRANSFORMATION OF BIGFOOT:
MALENESS, POWER, & BELIEF AMONG
THE CHIPEWYAN**
Henry S. Sharp
192 pp. Smithsonian Institution Press, 1988. $30.

*TRAPPERS & TRADERS
Gail Stewart
Grades 3-8. Illus. 32 pp. Rourke Corp., 1990.
$17.26.

**A TRAVELERS GUIDE TO SOUTHWEST
INDIAN ARTS & CRAFTS**
Charlotte Smith Neyland
Illus. Map. 48 pp. Paper. Renaissance House,
1992. $4.95.

**TRAVELS IN THE GREAT WESTERN
PRAIRIES**
T.J. Farnham
Reprint of 1843 edition. 2 vols. in 1. 612 pp. Da
Capo Press, $75.

**TRAVELS IN NORTH AMERICA, INCLUDING
A SUMMER WITH THE PAWNEES**
C. Murray
Reprint of 1839 Second Edition. 878 pp. Da
Capo Press, $85.

**A TREASURED HERITAGE: WORKS
OF MASTERS & APPRENTICES**
Exhibition catalog featuring biographies and the
works of 54 Alaska Native master artists and their
apprentices. Illus. 64 pp. Paper. Institute of Alaska
Native Arts, 1988. $12.50, postpaid.

TREASURES OF THE MOUND BUILDERS
Lar Hothem
Covers 135 Adena and Hopewell mounds in
Ohio, with name, location, when and by whom
excavated, artifacts found. Photos. Illus. 146 pp.
Paper. Hothem House, 1989. $11.95.

**A TREASURY OF OUR WESTERN HERI-
TAGE: THE FAVELL MUSEUM OF WESTERN
ART & INDIAN ARTIFACTS**
Illus. Favell Museum, 1986. $19.75.

**TREATIES & AGREEMENTS OF THE INDIAN
TRIBES OF THE PACIFIC NORTHWEST**
Institute for the Development of Indian Law , $12.

**THE TREATIES OF CANADA, WITH THE
INDIANS OF MANITOBA & NORTHWEST
TERRITORIES**
Alexander Morris
Reprint of 1880 edition. AMS Press.

**TREATIES ON TRIAL: THE CONTINUING CON-
TROVERSY OVER NORTHWEST INDIAN FISH-
ING RIGHTS**
Fay G. Cohen, et al
Illus. 280 pp. Paper. University of Washington
Press, 1986. $11.95.

**TREATISE ON THE HEATHEN SUPERSTI-
TIONS: THAT TODAY LIVE AMONG THE INDI-
ANS NATIVE TO THIS NEW SPAIN, 1629**
Ruiz de Alarcon; J. Richard Andrews & Ross
Hassig, Editors
Illus. 430 pp. Paper. University of Oklahoma
Press, 1987. $16.95.

TREATY MANUSCRIPTS SERIES
A series of treaties. See Institute for the
Development of Indian Law for titles and prices.

TRENDS IN INDIAN HEALTH
Indian Health Service
Annual compendium of tables and charts that
describe the IHS program, and health ststaus of
American Indian and Alaska Natives. Paper. U.S.
Government Printing Office. No charge.

**TRIBAL ASSETS: THE REBIRTH
OF NATIVE AMERICA**
Robert White
Henry Holt & cO., 1990. $24.95.

**TRIBAL DISPOSSESSION & OTHER
OTTAWA INDIAN UNIVERSITY FRAUD**
William E. Unrau and H. Craig Miner
Illus. 224 pp. U. of OK Press, 1985. $19.95.

TRIBAL DISTRIBUTION IN OREGON
J.V.Berreman
Reprint of 1937 edition. Paper. Kraus, $15.

TRIBAL GOVERNMENT: A NEW ERA
Includes Choctaw Tribal constitution and all
Choctaw treaties with U.S. Government.
Choctaw Heritage Press, $6.

**TRIBAL GOVERNMENT OF THE
OGLALA SIOUX OF PINE RIDGE, S.D.**
Ira Grinnell
University of South Dakota, Government
Research Bureau, 1967. $5.

TRIBAL GOVERNMENT TEXTBOOK
National Congress of American Indians.

**TRIBAL SECRETS: RECOVERING AMERI-
CAN INDIAN INTELLECTUAL TRADITIONS**
Robert Allen Warrior
Presents a narrative account of the litrary produc-
tions and political and cultural interactions of Ameri-
can Indian writers of this century. 192 pp. U. of
Minnesota Press, 1994. $39.95; paper, $16.95.

***TRIBAL SOVEREIGNTY:
INDIAN TRIBES IN U.S. HISTORY**
Four scholarly papers which consider the issue of
tribal sovereignty. Papers by: Dr. Fay Cohen, Dr.
D'Arcy McNickle, Dr. Roger Buffalohead, and Dr.
Mary Young. Studies the impact of non-Indian
settlement and U.S. Government policy. Teacher's
guide. Grades7-12. Illus. 60 pp. Daybreak Star
Press, $5.50.

TRIBAL WARS OF THE SOUTHERN PLAINS
Stan Hoig
Indian conflicts from the Spaniards in the 16th century through the U.S.-Cheyenne Battle of the Sand Hills in 1875. Illus. Maps. 272 pp. University of Oklahoma Press, 1992. $22.95.

TRIBALLY CONTROLLED COLLEGES: MAKING GOOD MEDICINE
Wayne J. Stein
History of the early years of the American Indian tribally controlled college movement. 180 pp. Peter Lang Publishing, 1992. $35.95.

TRIBALLY CONTROLLED COMMUNITY COLLEGES
Norman T. Oppelt
History of American Indian higher education. Paper. Navajo Community College Press, 1991. $20.

TRIBES OF CALIFORNIA
S. Powers
Covers American Indian ethnography of California. Reprint of 1877 edition. Illus. 482 pp. University of California Press, $45.50; paper, $11.95.

TRIBES OF THE COLUMBIA VALLEY AND THE COAST OF WASHINGTON & OREGON
A.B. Lewis
Reprint of 1906 edition. Paper. Kraus, $15.

TRIBES THAT SLUMBER: INDIANS OF THE TENNESSEE REGION
T. Lewis and M. Kneberg
Reprint of 1958 edition. Illus. 208 pp. Paper. Hothem House & University of Tennessee Press, $14.95.

THE TRICKSTER OF LIBERTY: TRIBAL HEIRS TO A WILD BARONAGE
Gerald Vizenor
Novel of a traditional tribal trickster figure; moves from oral stories into contemporary narrative. Illus. 160 pp. University of Minnesota Press, 1988. $19.95; paper, $9.95.

TRICKSTER: STUDY IN AMERICAN INDIAN MYTHOLOGY
Paul Radin
Reprint of 1956 edition. 223 pp. Greenwood, $35.00. New edition. 223 pp. Paper. Shocken Books, 1972. $6.95.

A TRIP TO A POW WOW
Paper. Sierra Oaks Publishing, $6.95.

TRUE COPY OF THE RECORD OF THE OFFICIAL PROCEEDINGS AT THE COUNCIL IN THE WALLA WALLA VALLEY, 1855
Darrell Scott & Isaac Stevens
125 pp. Ye Galleon, 1985. $12.95.

A TRUE DISCOURSE OF THE PRESENT ESTATE OF VIRGINIA
R.A. Hamor
Reprint of 1615 edition. 70 pp. Walter J. Johnson, $30.

TRUE STORIES OF NEW ENGLAND CAPTIVES CARRIED TO CANADA DURING THE OLD FRENCH & INDIAN WARS
Alice C. Baker
Illus. 420 pp. Paper. Heritage Books, 1991. $27.50.

THE TRUTH ABOUT GERONIMO
Britton Davis; M.M. Quaife, Editor
Illus. 293 pp. Paper. University of Nebraska Press, 1976. $7.95.

TRUTH OF A HOPI
Edmund Nequatewa
Stories of Hopi origins, legends, clans. 110 pp. Paper. AISES, $12.95.

TSONAKWA & YOLAIKIA: LEGENDS IN STONE, BONE & WOOD
Gerard Rancourt Tsonakwa
Indian stories discussing Native American beliefs about the earth and shared life. Illus. 64 pp. The Origins Program, $10.95.

TSEE-MA'HEONE-NEMEOTOTSE: CHEYENNE SPIRITUAL SONGS
David Graber, Editor
227 pp. Faith & Life, 1982. $29.95.

THE TSIMSHIAN: IMAGES OF THE PAST; VIEWS FOR THE PRESENT
Margaret Seguin, Editor
Illus. 364 pp. Paper. University of Washington Press, $20.

TSIMISHIAN TEXTS
Franz Boas
Reprint of 1902 edition. Scholarly Press, $49.

THE TSIMSHIAN: THEIR ARTS & MUSIC
Viola Garfield, et al.
Reprint of 1951 edition. AMS, $45.

THE TSIMSHIAN & THEIR NEIGHBORS OF THE NORTH PACIFIC COAST
Jay Miller & Carol Eastman, Editors
Illus. 366 pp. University of Washington Press, 1985. $35.

TUBERCULOSIS AMONG CERTAIN INDIAN TRIBES OF THE U.S.
Ales Hrdlicka
Reprint of 1909 edition. 96 pp. Scholarly Press, $49.

*TUL-TOK-A-NA: THE SMALL ONE
Kathleen Allan Myer
A Yosemite Indian legend. Grades 1-5. 32 pp. Council for Indian Education, 1991. $4.95.

TULAPAI TO TOKAY: A BIBLIOGRAPHY OF ALCOHOL USE & ABUSE AMONG NATIVE AMERICANS OF NORTH AMERICA
David R. McDonald & Pat Mail
372 pp. HRAFP, 1981, $25.

TULIP: THE UNIVERSAL - UNION LIST OF INDIAN PERIODICALS
Murai & Sarla Nagar
215 pp. Paper. International Library Center, 1989. $45.

*THE TUNICA-BILOXI: SOUTHEAST
Jeffrey Brain
Grades 5 and up. Illus. Chelsea House, 1989. $17.95.

TURQUOISE & THE INDIAN
Bennett
Study of raw gem materials, turquoise mines and locations, and the beginning of gem-working and Indian jewelry style progression. Reprint of 1970 edition. Illus. 152 pp. Hothem House, $9.95.

TURQUOISE JEWELRY
Nancy Schiffer
Full color photos of a variety of Southwest Indian-made jewelry with many types of turquoise. Illus. 64 pp. Paper. Schiffer, $9.95.

TURQUOISE & THE NAVAJO
Lee Hammons
Illus. 32 pp. Paper. Primer Publishers, $1.95.

TURTLE DREAM
Gerald Hausman
Illus. Mariposa Print, 1989. $9.95.

TURTLE MEAT & OTHER STORIES
Joseph Bruchac
18 stories, myths and legends reveal the transforming power Native American writing in a contemporary world. Illus. 128 pp. Holy Cow! Press, 1993. $18.95; paper, $10.95.

TUSAYAN KATCINAS & HOPI KATCINA ALTARS
Jesse Walter Fewkes
Discusses the ceremonies of the Tusayan (Hopi) Indians and the Cibola (Zuni) Indians. Illus. 120 pp. Paper. Avanyu Publishing, 1991. $17.95.

*THE TUSCARORA
Grades K-4. Illus. 48 pp. Childrens Press, $11.45.

THE TUSCARORA LEGACY OF J.N.B. HEWITT: MATERIALS FOR THE STUDY OF THE TUSCARORA LANGUAGE & CULTURE
Blair Rudes & Dorothy Crouse
670 pp. Paper. University of Chicago Press, 1988. $39.95.

TWANA GAMES
A handbook of games played by Twana people of the Skokomish Reservation in western Washington State. Illus. 20 pp. Daybreak Star Press, $3.50.

TWANA NARRATIVES: NATIVE HISTORICAL ACCOUNTS OF A COAST SALISH CULTURE
William W. Elmendorf
Illus. Maps. 416 pp. University of Washington Press, $40.

THE TWENTIETH CENTURY FICTIONAL AMERICAN INDIAN WOMAN & FELLOW CHARACTERS: A STUDY OF GENDER & RACE
Asebrit Sundquist
304 pp. Humanities Press, 1991, $39.95.

THE TWILIGHT OF THE SIOUX
John Neihardt
295 pp. Paper. University of Nebraska Press, 1971. $9.95.

TWO CROWS DENIES IT: A HISTORY OF CONTROVERSY IN OMAHA SOCIOLOGY
R.H. Barnes
Illus. 288 pp. University of Nebraska Press, 1984. $24.95.

TWO CULTURES MEET: PATHWAYS FOR AMERICAN INDIANS INTO MEDICINE
Larry Aitken & Edwin Haller
110 pp. Paper. Garrett Park Press, 1990. $10.95.

TWO GREAT SCOUTS & THEIR PAWNEE BATTALION: THE EXPERIENCES OF FRANK J. NORTH & LUTHER H. NORTH, PIONEERS IN THE GREAT WEST, 1856-1882, & THEIR DEFENCE OF THE BUILDING OF THE UNION PACIFIC RAILROAD
George Grinnell
Reprint of 1929 edition. Paper. Books on Demand, $76.50.

TWO LEGGINGS: THE MAKING OF A CROW WARRIOR
Peter Nabakov
Illus. 250 pp. Paper. University of Nebraska Press, 1970. $7.95.

*TWO OLD WOMEN: AN ALASKA LEGEND OF BETRAYAL, COURAGE & SURVIVAL
Velma Wallis
Portrait of Native subsistence life in the boreal forest. Told with an ecological perspective. Grades 6 and up. Illus. 160 pp. Graphic Arts Center & Greenfield Review Press, $16.95. Paper. Alaska Natural History Association, $9.

TWO WORLDS: THE INDIAN ENCOUNTER WITH THE EUROPEAN, 1492-1509
S. Lyman Tyler
275 pp. University of Utah Press, 1988. $25.

U

UGIUVANGMIUT QULIAPYUIT KING ISLAND TALES
Lawrence D. Kaplan
Eskimo history and legends from Bering Strait. Illus. Maps. 258 pp. Paper. University of Alaska Press, 1988. $19.95.

UKOMNO'M: THE YUKI INDIANS OF NORTHERN CALIFORNIA
Virginia P. Miller
Illus. 108 pp. Paper. Ballena Press, 1979. $8.95.

UNBROKEN CIRCLES: TRADITIONAL ARTS OF CONTEMPORARY WOODLAND PEOPLES
Looks at the preservation of culture through the artistic media that have been used by Native people since before Columbus. Akwe:kon Press, $10.

UNCLE SAM'S STEPCHILDREN: THE REFORMATION OF U.S. INDIAN POLICY, 1865-1887
L.B. Priest
Reprint of 1942 edition. 310 pp. Paper. University of Nebraska Press, $6.95.

THE UNCOVERED PAST: ROOTS OF NORTHERN ALBERTA SOCIETIES
Patricia A. McCormack & R. Geoffrey Ironside, Editors
Illus. Maps. 290 pp. CCI, $30; paper, $20.

UNDER THE INDIAN TURQUOISE SKY
Rosemary Davey
Illus. 93 pp. Ye Galleon Press, 1985. $9.

UNDER YOUR FEET: THE STORY OF THE AMERICAN MOUND BUILDERS OF THE MISSISSIPPI VALLEY
Blanche Busey King
Reprint of 1939 edition. Ayer Co., $22.

THE UNDERGROUND RESERVATION: OSAGE OIL
Terry P. Wilson
Illus. 263 pp. University of Nebraska Press, 1985. $22.95.

UNDERSTANDING THE ANASAZI OF MESA VERDE & HOVENWEEP
David Noble, Editor
Illus. Maps. 40 pp. Paper. Ancient City Press, 1992. $8.95.

U.S. - COMANCHE RELATIONS: THE RESERVATION YEARS
William T. Hagan
Illus. 352 pp. Paper. University of Oklahoma Press, 1990. $14.95.

UNIVERSITY OF CALIFORNIA ANTHROPOLOGICAL RECORDS
A series of 30 facsimile reprints.
See Coyote Press for titles and prices.

UNIVERSITY OF CALIFORNIA, ARCHAEOLOGICAL REPORTS
A series of 74 facsimile reprints.
See Coyote Press for titles and prices.

UNIVERSITY OF CALIFORNIA, PUBLICATIONS IN AMERICAN ARCHAEOLGY & ETHNOLOGY
A series of 49 facsimile reprints. See Coyote Press for titles and prices.

THE UNKNOWN INDIAN
G.B. Brown
Gordon Press, 1977. $59.95.

UNLEARNING "INDIAN" STEREOTYPES, A TEACHING UNIT FOR ELEMENTARY TEACHERS & CHILDREN'S LIBRARIANS
Racism & Sexism Resource Center for Educators
Council on Interracial Books for Children, 1981. $39.95. Teaching Guide, $4.95.

THE UNRATIFIED TREATY BETWEEN THE KIOWAS, COMANCHES & APACHES & THE U.S. OF 1863
R.J. DeMallie
8 pp. Institute for the Development of Indian Law. $5.00.

UNRAVELLING THE FRANKLIN MYSTERY: INUIT TESTIMONY
David C. Woodman
This new examination of Sir John Franklin's final Arctic expedition (1845) reconsyructs events surrounding the mysterious loss of both ships and all hands by giving credence to the testimony of Inuit witnesses. University of Toronto Press, 1991. $42.95; paper, $19.95.

THE UNWRITTEN LITERATURE ON THE HOPI
H.G. Lockett
Reprint of 1933 edition. AMS Press, $18.

THE UPSTREAM PEOPLE: AN ANNOTATED RESEARCH BIBLIOGRAPHY OF THE OMAHA TRIBE
Michael L. Tate, Editor
Maps. 522 pp. Scarecrow Press, 1991. $62.50.

THE UPWARD MOVING & EMERGENCE WAY; THE GISHIN BIYE VERSION
Father Berard Haile, O.F.M.
Illus. 250 pp. University of Nebraska Press, 1981. $11.95.

*URBAN INDIANS
Donald Fixico
Grades 5 and up. Illus. Chelsea House, 1989. $17.95.

URBAN INDIANS
Center for the History of the American Indian Staff
185 pp. Newberry Library, 1981. $4.

URBAN INDIANS: DRUMS FROM THE CITIES
Describes the plight of over one-half of the Alaska Native & American Indian population. 600 pp. Arrowstar Publishing, 1994. $19.95.

URBAN INSTITUTIONS & PEOPLE OF INDIAN ANCESTRY
Raymond Breton and Gail Akian
52 pp. Paper. Gower Publishing, 1978. $3.

URBAN RENEGADES: THE CULTURAL STRATEGY OF AMERICAN INDIANS
Jeanne Guillemin
336 pp. Columbia University Press, 1975. $31.

URBANIZATION OF AMERICAN INDIANS: A CRITICAL BIBLIOGRAPHY
Russell Thornton, et al
96 pp. Paper. Indiana University Press, 1982. $4.95.

THE URINE DANCE OF THE ZUNI INDIANS OF NEW MEXICO
John G. Bourke
15 pp. Borgo Press, 1989. $9.95.

USES OF PLANTS BY THE INDIANS OF THE MISSOURI RIVER REGION
Melvin Gilmore
Illus. 180 pp. University of Nebraska Press, 1977. $15.95; paper, $9.95.

UTAH PLACE NAMES
John W. Van Cott
Paper. University of Utah Press, $14.95.

UTE MOUNTAIN UTES
Robert Delaney
Illus. 150 pp. U. of New Mexico Press, 1990.

UTE TALES
Anne M. Smith, Compiler
Illus. University of Utah Press, $24.95; paper, $12.95.

UTES: THE MOUNTAIN PEOPLE
Jan Pettit
Revised edition. 225 pp. Paper. Johnson Books, $11.95.

UTMOST GOOD FAITH: PATTERNS OF APACHE-MEXICAN HOSTILITIES IN NORTHERN CHIHUAHUA BORDER WARFARE, 1821-1848
William Griffen
Illus. 336 pp. University of New Mexico Press, 1989. $37.50.

V

THE VAIL SITE: A PALEO-INDIAN ENCAMPMENT IN MAINE
Richard M. Gramley
Ilus. 170 pp. Paper. Buffalo Museum of Science, $13.95.

VALLEY OF THE MISSISSIPPI
Henry Lewis; Bertha Heilbron, Editor
Illus. 423 pp. Minnesota Historical Society, 1967. $39.75; uncut edition, $50.

VALLEY OF THE SPIRITS: UPPER SKAGIT INDIANS OF WESTERN WASHINGTON
June Collins
Illus. 282 pp. University of Washington Press, 1974. $20; paper, $9.95.

THE VANISHING AMERICAN: THE EPIC OF THE INDIAN
Zane Grey
Paper. Pocket Books, 1982. $3.50.

THE VANISHING AMERICAN: WHITE ATTITUDES & U.S. INDIAN POLICY
Brian W. Dipple
Illus. 424 pp. Paper. University Press of Kansas, 1982. $14.95.

VANISHING HERITAGE
Hooge & Lepper
Archaeology & culture history of Licking County, Ohio. Covers moundbuilders, including the famous Newark Earthworks. Illus. 100 pp. Hothem House, 1992. $25.

THE VANISHING RACE & OTHER ILLUSIONS: PHOTOGRAPHS OF INDIANS BY EDWARD S. CURTIS
Christopher M. Lymans
Illus. 158 pp. Smithsonian Institution Press, 1982. $24.95. Paper. Pantheon, $14.95.

THE VANISHING RACE: SELECTIONS FROM EDWARD S. CURTIS' THE NORTH AMERICAN INDIAN
Mick Gidley, Editor
Reprint of 1977 edition. Illus. Paper. University of Washington Press, $14.95.

THE VANISHING WHITE MAN
Stan Steiner
322 pp. Paper. University of Oklahoma Press, 1976. $10.95.

VASCO DE QUIROGA & HIS PUEBLO HOSPITALS OF SANTA FE
Fintan Warren
Illus. Academy of American Franciscan History, 1963. $10.

VAST DOMAIN OF BLOOD
Don Schellie
289 pp. Westernlore, 1968. $9.95.

VECTORS OF DEATH: THE ARCHAEOLOGY OF EUROPEAN CONTACT
Ann Ramenofsky
Illus. 360 pp. University of New Mexico Press, 1987. $27.50.

***VEHO**
Henry Tall Bull & Tom Weist
Grades 2-6. Paper. Council for Indian Education, 1971. $1.95.

***THE VERY FIRST AMERICANS**
Cara Ashrose; illus. by Byrna Waldman
How first Americans lived. Illus. with paintings depicting clothing, dwellings, art, tools, & other artifacts. Grades PS-3. Illus. 32 pp. Paper. Grosset & Dunlap, 1993. $2.25.

A VICTORIAN EARL IN THE ARCTIC: THE TRAVELS & COLLECTIONS OF THE FIFTH EARL OF LONSDALE, 1888-89
Shepard Krech III
Examination and analysis of a collection of native artifacts gathered during an early expedition in Canada & Alaskan Arctic. Illus. 216 pp. University of Washington Press, $35.

VICTORIO & THE MIMBRES APACHES
Dan L. Thrapp
Illus. Maps. 416 pp. Paper. University of Oklahoma Press, 1980. $14.95.

A VIEW FROM BLACK MESA: THE CHANGING FACE OF ARCHAEOLOGY
George Gumerman
A synopsis of Anasazi prehistory & cultural ecology. 184 pp. University of Arizona Press, 1984. $21.95; paper, $14.95.

THE VIEW FROM OFFICERS' ROW: ARMY PERCEPTIONS OF WESTERN INDIANS
Sherry L. Smith
265 pp. Paper. University of Arizona Press, 1990. $13.95.

VIEW FROM THE SHORE: AMERICAN INDIAN PERSPECTIVES ON THE QUINCENTENARY
Jose Barreiro, Editor
A collection of articles, interviews, and essays exploring the effects of Columbus's arrival on Indigenous people. Akwe:kon Press, 1992. $12.

A VIEW OF THE AMERICAN INDIANS: GENERAL CHARACTER, CUSTOMS, LANGUAGE, PUBLIC FESTIVALS, RELIGIOUS RITES & TRADITIONS
I. Worsley; Moshe Davis, Editor
Reprint of 1828 edition. Ayer Co., $19.

VIEWS FROM THE APACHE FRONTIER: REPORT ON THE NORTHERN PROVINCES OF NEW SPAIN, 1799
Jose Cortes; Elizabeth John, Editor & John Wheat, tr.
Illus. 192 pp. Paper. University of Oklahoma Press, 1989. $12.95.

VIEWS OF A VANISHING FRONTIER
John C. Ewers, et al
Illus. 150 pp. Univerity of Nebraska Press, 1984. $29.95. Paper. Joslyn Art, $14.95.

THE VILLAGE INDIANS OF THE UPPER MISSOURI: THE MANDANS, HIDATSAS AND ARIKARAS
Roy W. Meyer
Illus. 355 pp. University of Nebraska Press, 1977. $27.50.

***THE VILLAGE OF BLUE STONE**
Stephen Trimble
Grades 3 and up. Illus. Macmillan, 1989. $12.95.

VILLAGES OF HISPANIC NEW MEXICO
Nancy Hunter Warren
Illus. 136 pp. Paper. School of American Research, 1987. $14.95.

VIOLENCE, RESISTANCE, & SURVIVAL IN THE AMERICAS: NATIVE AMERICANS & THE LEGACY OF CONQUEST
William B. Taylor & Franklin Pease G.Y.
Documents a variety of roles played by Native Americans in the westernization of the Americas. Illus. 336 pp. Smithsonian Institution Press, 1994. $49.

***THE VISION OF THE SPOKANE PROPHET**
Rebecca Egbert; Hap Gilliland, Editor
Grades 4-10. Illus. 36 pp. Council for Indian Education, 1989. $9.95; paper, $3.95.

VISION QUEST
Steven Foster & Meredith Little
Personal transformation in the wilderness. Revised edition. Illus. 235 pp. Paper. Prentice Hall Press, $9.95.

***THE VISUAL DICTIONARY OF ANCIENT CIVILIZATIONS**
Includes early Native American civilizations. Tribal artifacts & crafts. Grades 3 and up. Illus. 64 pp. Houghton Mifflin, 1994. $15.95.

VITAL SOULS: BORORO COSMOLOGY, NATURAL SYMBOLISM & SHAMANISM
J. Christopher Crocker
380 pp. University of Arizona Press, 1985. $29.95.

A VOICE IN HER TRIBE: A NAVAJO WOMAN'S OWN STORY
Irene Stewart
Illus. 90 pp. Paper. Ballena Press, 1980. $8.95.

THE VOICE IN THE MARGIN: NATIVE AMERICAN LITERATURE & THE CANON
Arnold Krupat
University of California Press, 1989. $25.

VOICE OF THE GREAT SPIRIT
Kaiser
Paper. Random House, $10.

VOICES FROM WOUNDED KNEE, 1973, IN THE WORDS OF THE PARTICIPANTS
Akwesasne Notes
History of American Indian Movement (AIM). Illus. Akwesasne Notes, 1974.

VOICES IN THE CANYON
Viele
The story of a Navajo National Monument's amazing cliff dwellings written for laymen and reviewed by professionals. Illus. 50 color photos. Maps. 76 pp. Paper. Southwest Parks and Monuments, $6.

VOICES IN THE WATERFALL
Elizabeth Cuthand
Poetry. Rhythms & traditions of First nations people. New edition featuring ten new poems. 80 pp. Paper. Theytus, 1992. $11.95.

VOICES OF EARTH & SKY
Vinson Brown
The vision life of the Native Americans. Illus. 177 pp. Paper. Naturegraph, 1976. $8.95.

VOICES OF OUR ANCESTORS: CHEROKEE TEACHINGS FROM THE WISDOM FIRE
Dhyani Ywahoo
Illus. 295 pp. Paper. Shambhala Publications, 1987. $12.95.

VOICES OF THE WIND:
NATIVE AMERICAN LEGENDS
Margot Edmonds & Ella Clark
Illus. 385 pp. Facts on File, 1989. $27.95.

VOICES OF THE WIND:
POLYNESIAN MYTHS & CHANTS
Katherine Luomala
The oral traditions of the region is examined.
Illus. 209 pp. Paper. Bishop Museum, $15.95.

*VOSTAAS: THE STORY OF
MONTANA'S INDIAN NATIONS
Maxine Ruppel
Grades 3-10. 68 pp. Paper. Council for Indian
Education, 1970. $9.95; paper, $3.95.

VOYAGES FROM MONTREAL THROUGH THE
CONTINENT OF NORTH AMERICA TO THE
FROZEN AND PACIFIC OCEANS IN 1789 &
1793, WITH AN ACCOUNT OF THE RISE &
STATE OF THE FUR TRADE
A. Mackenzie
Reprint of 1922 edition. Two volumes. AMS
Press, $80.

W

THE WABANAKIS OF MAINE & THE MARI-
TIMES: A RESOURCE BOOK ABOUT PENOB-
SCOT, PASSAMOQUODDY, MALISEET, MIC-
MAC & ABENAKI INDIANS
Contains over 50 lesson plans for grades 4-8.
Illus. 510 pp. Paper. American Friends Service
Committee, $20.

WAHEENEE: AN INDIAN GIRL'S STORY
Gilbert L. Wilson
Illus. 190 pp. University of Nebraska Press,
1981. $17.95; paper, $5.95.

WAH'KON-TAH: THE OSAGE & THE WHITE
MAN'S ROAD
John Mathews
Illus. 359 pp. Paper. University of Oklahoma
Press, $12.95.

WAKE OF THE UNSEEN OBJECT
Tom Kizzia
Henry Holt & Co., 1990. $19.95.

WAKEMAP MOUND: A STRATIFIED
SITE ON THE COLUMBIA RIVER
Emory Strong, Editor
Illus. 40 pp. Paper. Binford & Mort, $5.95.

WAKING A SLEEPING GIANT
Theodore Kouba
Vantage Pres, 1987. $14.95.

WALAPAI ETHNOGRAPHY
A. Kroeber
Reprint of 1935 edition. Paper. Kraus, $34.

WALK IN BALANCE: THE PATH TO
HEALTHY, HAPPY, HARMONIOUS LIVING
Sun Bear, Crysalis Mulligan,
Peter Nufer & Wabun
A holistic pathway to personal enrichment and
health. A personal survival manual. 171 pp. Pa-
per. Prentice Hall Press, $8.95.

WALK IN BEAUTY: THE
NAVAJO & THEIR BLANKETS
Anthony Berlant & Mary Kahlenberg
Illus. 225 pp. Paper. Gibbs Smith, 1991. $29.95.

WALK IN PEACE: LEGENDS &
STORIES OF THE MICHIGAN INDIANS
Simon Otto
Selection of legends and stories in the Anishnabe
(Odawa/Ojibwe) oral tradition. Illus. 56 pp. Paper.
University of Nebraska Press & AISES, 1992.
$9.95.

WALK IN YOUR SOUL: LOVE INCANTA-
TIONS OF THE OKLAHOMA CHEROKEES
Jack and Anna Kilpatrick
Reprint of 1965 edition. Illus. 174 pp. Paper.
Southern Methodist University Press, $6.95.

*WALKER OF TIME
Helen Hughes Vick
Native American mythology & mystery combined
in a tale for young readers. Grades 7 and up. 192
pp. paper. Harbinger House, 1994. $9.95.

WALKING THE TRAIL
Jerry Ellis
Trail of Tears. 256 pp. Map.
Cherokee Publications, $19.

WALKS IN THE SUN
Don Coldsmith
Illus. 245 pp. Bantam Books, $12.50.

*WALKS TWO WORLDS
Robert B. Fox
Story of a Navajo boy. Grades 4 and up.
62 pp. Paper. Sunstone Press, $6.95.

WALLEYE WARRIORS: AN EFFECTIVE
ALLIANCE AGAINST RACISM & FOR
THE EARTH
Rick Whaley & Walter Bresette
Depicts the intimidation and fear that the
Anishinabe in northern Wisconsin have endured
when the courts upheld their treaty rights to take
fish with spears. Traces the history of the modern
anti-Indian treaty movement in the 1960s & 1970s.
Illus. Photos. Maps. Biblio. 288 pp. Paper. New
Society Publishers, 1994. $17.95.

*THE WAMPANOAG
Laurie Weinstein-Farson
Grades 5 and up. Illus. 104 pp.
Chelsea House, 1988. $17.95.

THE WAMPANOAGS OF MASHPEE
Russell M. Peters
Historical & cultural portrayal of the
Wampanoags of Mashpee, Mass. Illus.
The Greenfield Review Pres, $16.

WAMPUM BELTS & PEACE TREES:
GEORGE MORGAN, NATIVE AMERICANS
& REVOLUTIONARY DIPLOMACY
Gregory Schaaf
Illus. 304 pp. Fulcrum Publishing, 1990. $27.95.

WAMPUM & SHELL ARTICLES
USED BY THE NEW YORK INDIANS
W.M. Beauchamp
Reprint of 1901 edition. AMS Press, $21.50.

WAMPUM, WAR & TRADE GOODS
WEST OF THE HUDSON
Gilbert W. Hagerty
Illus. 310 pp. Heart of the Lakes, 1987. $40.

WANGKA: AUSTRONESIAN
CANOE ORIGINS
Edwin Doran, Jr.
Illus. 121 pp. Texas A & M University Press,
1981. $15.

THE WAPPO: A REPORT
Yolande S. Beard
Paper. Malki Museum Press, 1979. $8.50.

WAR CHIEFS
Bill Dugan
A series of five books: Geronimo, Chief Joseph,
Crazy Horse, Quanah Parker, and Siting Bull.
Paper. HarperCollins, 1991-94. $4.99 each.

*WAR CLOUDS IN THE WEST:
INDIANS & CAVALRYMEN,
1860-1890
Albert Martin
Grades 4 and up. Illus. 224 pp. Macmillan,
1984. $14.95.

WAR DANCE: PLAINS INDIAN
MUSICAL PERFORMANCE
William K. Powers
199 pp. University of Arizona Press, 1990.
$27.50; paper, $10.95.

*WAR DRUMS AT EDEN PRAIRIE
Gladys Nelson
Fictionalized account of Sioux uprising of 1862.
Grades 6-8. Illus. North Star Press, $5.95.

WAR EAGLE: A LIFE OF
GENERAL EUGENE A. CARR
James T. King
Illus. 325 pp. University of Nebraska Press,
1964. $27.95.

WAR PAINT: BLACKFOOT & SARCEE
PAINTED BUFFALO ROBES IN THE
ROYAL ONTARIO MUSEUM
Arni Brownstone
Blackfoot tradition, art, and culture as told
through six historic buffalo robes. Illus. 96 pp.
paper. University of Toronto Press, $24.95.

WAR-PATH & BIVOUAC; OR,
THE CONQUEST OF THE SIOUX
John F. Finerty
Detailed account of the Dakota Indian wars of 1876
and the Nez Perce Indian wars of 1877. Reprint.
Illus. Map. 358 pp. Paper. University of Oklahoma
Press, $12.95.

*WAR PONY
D. E. Worcester
Reprint of 1961 edition. Grades 4 and up. Illus.
95 pp. Texas Christian University Press, $10.95.

WAR IN THE TRIBAL ZONE: EXPANDING
STATES & INDIGENOUS WARFARE
R. Brian Ferguson & Neil Whitehead, Editors
Native warfare. Illus. 350 pp. School of American
Research, 1989. $35.00; paper, $15.95.

THE WARDELL BUFFALO TRAP FORTY
EIGHT SU THREE HUNDRED & ONE: COMMU-
NAL PROCUREMENT IN THE UPPER GREEN
RIVER BASIN, WY
George C. Frison
Paper. University of Michigan, Museum of
Anthropology, 1973. $3.

THE WARING PAPERS: THE COLLECTED WORKS OF ANTONIO J. WARING
Stephen Williams
Paper. Peabody Museum, 1977. $22.50.

WARLORDS OF THE WEST: A STORY OF THE COMANCHE
Preston Harper
Borderlands Pres, 1990. $14.95.

WARPATH
Stanley Vestal
The true story of the fighting Sioux told in a biography of Chief White Bull. Illus. Maps. 350 pp. Paper. University of Nebraska Press, 1984. $9.95.

THE WARREN WAGONTRAIN RAID
B. Capps
Illus. 328 pp. SMU Press, 1974. $10.95.

WARRIOR IN TWO CAMPS - ELY S. PARKER
William Armstrong
Biography. Illus. Photos. 240 pp. Paper. AISES, $14.95.

WARRIOR QUEEN OF THE INDIAN
Richard Barry
Follows an Indian woman through her trials, heartaches and triumphs. 494 pp. Terrich Books, 1993. $17.95; paper, $14.95.

*WARRIORS OF THE RAINBOW: STRANGE & PROPHETIC DREAMS OF THE INDIAN PEOPLES
William Willoya and Vinson Brown
Grades 4-12. Illus. 94 pp. Naturegraph, 1962. $15.95; paper, $7.95.

THE WARS OF THE IROQUOIS: A STUDY IN INTERTRIBAL TRADE RELATIONS
George T. Hunt
Reprint of 1940 edition. Map. 220 pp. Paper. University of Wisconsin Press, $14.50. Books on Demand, $58.30.

WASHAKI: AN ACCOUNT OF INDIAN RESISTANCE OF THE COVERED WAGON & UNION PACIFIC RAILROAD INVASION OF THEIR TERRITORY
Grace Hebard
Reprint of 1940 edition. AMS Press, $29.

WASHINGTON STATE PLACE NAMES: FROM ALKI TO YELM
Doug Brokenshire
Paper. The Caxton Printers, 1994. $14.95.

THE WASHO INDIANS
S.A. Barrett
Reprint of 1917 edition. AMS Press, $14.

WASHO INDIANS OF CALIFORNIA & NEVADA
W. Azevedo, Editor
Reprint of 1963 edition. AMS Press, $22.50.

WASHO SHAMANS & PEYOTISTS: RELIGIOUS CONFLICT IN AN AMERICAN INDIAN TRIBE
Edgar E. Siskin
Illus. 300 pp. University of Utah Press, 1983. $25.

WASI'CHU: THE CONTINUING INDIAN WARS
Bruce Johansen & Roberto Maestro
Chronicles the history of Native struggles in the U.S. Illus. 270 pp. Paper. Monthly Review Press, 1980. $10.

WATER ON THE PLATEAU
Paper. Museum of Northern Arizona, 1981. $3.

*WATERLESS MOUNTAIN
Laura A. Armer
Reprint of 1931 edition. Grades 5-8. Illus. David McKay Co., $11.95.

WATERLILY
Ella Cara Deloria
A novel of a Sioux woman's life. 250 pp. University of Nebraska Press, 1988. $27.50; paper, $9.95.

WATERWAY
B. Haile
Reprint. Illus. 155 pp. Paper. University of Nebraska Press, $12.95.

WAUBA YUMA'S PEOPLE: THE COMPARATIVE SOCIO-POLITICAL STRUCTURE OF THE PAI INDIANS OF ARIZONA
Henry F. Dobyns & Robert C. Euler
Describes Pai socia structure prior to U.S. reservation policy that created the contemporary Walapai and Havasupai groups. Illus. Map. 98 pp. Center for Anthropological Studies, 1970. $30.

THE WAY OF THE DEAD INDIANS: GUARJIRO MYTHS & SYMBOLS
Michael Perrin; Michael Fineberg, tr.
Illus. 230 pp. University of Texas Press, 1987. $30; paper, $12.95.

THE WAY OF THE MASKS
Claude Levi-Strauss; translated by Sylvia Modelski
Levi-Strauss's approach to Northwest Coast tribal art & culture. Illus. 272 pp. Paper. University of Washington Press, $18.95.

THE WAY OF THE RAINBOW WARRIORESS: A HANDBOOK OF PRACTICAL WISDOM
Janice Tucker
Illus. Paper. El Rancho Press, 1988. $6.95.

THE WAY TO INDEPENDENCE: MEMORIES OF A HIDATSA INDIAN FAMILY, 1840-1920
Carolyn Gilman, et al
Account of the evolving culture & environment of Buffalo Bird Woman's family & her tribe. Illus. Photos. Biblio. 371 pp. Minnesota Historical Society Press, 1987. $24.95; paper, $14.95.

THE WAY TO RAINY MOUNTAIN
N. Scott Momaday
An account of the historic trek of the Kiowa Indians to Oklahoma. Illus. 90 pp. Paper. University of New Mexico Press, 1976. $8.95.

THE WAY TO THE WESTERN SEA: LEWIS & CLARK ACROSS THE CONTINENT
David Lavender
Illus. 415 pp. Harper & Row, 1988. $22.95.

*THE WAY WAS THROUGH WOODS: THE STORY OF TOMO-CHI-CHI
Sara H. Banks
Story of a Creek man who adopted what he could from the white settlers, insuring peace with them. Grades 7 and up. Illus. 92 pp. Paper. Roberts Rinehart, 1994. $7.95.

THE WAY WE LIVED: CALIFORNIA INDIAN STORIES, SONGS & REMINISCENCES
Malcolm Margolin, Editor
250 pp. Paper. Heyday Books, 1981. $14.95.

ANTHONY WAYNE, A NAME IN ARMS
Anthony Wayne; R.C. Knopf, Editor
Reprint of 1960 ed. Illus. 556 pp. Greenwood, $41.50.

WAYS OF INDIAN MAGIC
Teresa VanEtten
Pueblo Indian legends. 91 pp. Paper. Sunstone Press, 1985. $8.95.

WAYS OF INDIAN WISDOM
Teresa VanEtten
Pueblo Indian legends. 120 pp. Paper. Sunstone, 1987. $10.95.

THE WAYS OF MY GRANDMOTHERS
Beverly H. Wolf
224 pp. Paper. William Morrow, 1980. $9.95.

*WAYS OF THE LUSHOOTSEED PEOPLE: CEREMONIES & TRADITIONS OF THE NORTHERN PUGET SOUND INDIANS
Readings. Written in English and Lushootseed. Grades 7-12. Illus. 56 pp. Daybreak Star Press, $6.

WE ARE METIS: THE ETHNOGRAPHY OF A HALFBREED COMMUNITY IN NORTHERN ALBERTA
Paul Driben
Reprint of 1983 edition. Illus. 190 pp. AMS Press, $37.50.

*WE ARE STILL HERE: NATIVE AMERICANS TODAY
A series of books examining Native American cultural traditions and customs. Titles are: *Children of Clay: A Family of Pueblo Potters*; *Clambake: A Wampanoag Tradition*; *Ininatig's Gift of Sugar: Traditional Native Sugarmaking*; *Kinaalda: A Navajo Girl Grows Up*; *The Sacred Harvest: Ojibway Wild Rice Gathering*; and *Shannon: An Ojibway Dancer*. Grades 3-6. Illus. 48 pp. Lerner, 1993. $19.95 each; paper, $6.95 each.

WE, THE FIRST AMERICANS
Dwight Johnson
Illus. 28 pp. Paper. U.S. GPO, 1989. $1.75.

WE GET OUR LIVING LIKE MILK FROM THE LAND
Okanagan Rights Committee
Historical overview of the Okanagan Nation of Canada. Illus. Maps. 175 pp. Paper. Theytus, 1993. $9.95.

*WE HAVE ALWAYS BEEN HERE
Grades 4-5. 48 pp. Capstone Press, 1989. $10.95.

WE JUST TOUGHED IT OUT: WOMEN HEADS OF HOUSEHOLDS ON THE LLANO ESTACADO
Georgellen Burnett
65 pp. Texas Western Press, 1990. $12; paper, $7.50.

*WE LIVE ON AN INDIAN RESERVATION
Hap Gilliland
Grades 1-6. 31 pp. Paper. Council for Indian Education, 1981. $8.95; paper, $2.95.

WE TALK YOU YAWN
Fred Bigjim
Native education in Alaska; problems & concerns, as well as solutions. Greenfield Review Press, $9.95.

WE'RE STILL HERE: ART OF INDIAN NEW ENGLAND
Joan Lester
86 pp. Paper. Moyer Bell Ltd., 1987. $9.95.

A WEALTH OF THOUGHT: FRANZ BOAS ON NATIVE AMERICAN ART
Aldona Jonaitis, Editor
Essays of Franz Boas with illustrations & original photos & drawings. Illus. Biblio. 352 pp. University of Washington Press, $50; paper, $24.95.

THE WEAVER'S PATHWAY: A CLARIFICATION OF THE "SPIRIT TRAIL" IN NAVAJO WEAVING
Noel Bennett
64 pp. Paper. Northland, 1974. $9.95.

WEAVER'S TALES
Romona Bradley
Collection of Cherokee legends. Illus. 36 pp. Paper. Cherokee Publications, $3.50.

WEAVING ARTS OF THE NORTH AMERICAN INDIAN
Frederick J. Dockstader
Revised edition. Survey of the textile artistry of the Indian tribes of North America. Illus. 224 pp. HarperCollins, 1994. $22.50.

WEAVING A NAVAJO BLANKET
Gladys Reichard
Reprint of 1936 edition. Illus. 225 pp. Paper. Dover, $6.95.

WEAVING OF THE SOUTHWEST
Marian Rodee
Both traditional & modern weaving styles are identified & explained. Discussion of family styles among weavers today. Illus. 248 pp. Schiffer, $39.95; paper, $24.95

ANSELM WEBER, O.F.M. MISSIONARY TO THE NAVAJO
Robert Wilken
Reprint of 1955 edition. St. Michaels Press, $12.50.

THE WEST: A TREASURY OF ART & LITERATURE
T.H. Watkins & Joan Parker Watkins, Editors
Collection of stories, essays, memoirs, songs, poems, paintings, drawings, and photographs. Illus. 384 pp. Levin Associates, 1994. $75.

THE WEST AS AMERICA: REINTERPRETING IMAGES OF THE FRONTIER
William H. Truettner, Editor
How the 19th & early 20th century artists depicted and romanticized the often brutal, conflict-ridden history of the westward expansion. 408 pp. Smithsonian Books, $49.96.

*****WEST OF YESTERDAY**
Lucilia Wise
Illus. The Five Civilized Tribes Museum. $1.

WEST TO THE PACIFIC: THE STORY OF THE LEWIS & CLARK EXPEDITION
Ronald Fisher; Merle Wells, Editor
Illus. 152 pp. Paper. Alpha & Omega, 1989. $9.95.

THE WESTERN ABENAKIS OF VERMONT, 1600-1800: WAR, MIGRATION & THE SURVIVAL OF AN INDIAN PEOPLE
C.G. Calloway
University of Oklahoma Press.

WESTERN AMERICAN INDIAN: CASE STUDIES IN TRIBAL HISTORY
Richard N. Ellis, Editor
Indian-White relations from 1850 to the present. Maps. 203 pp. Paper. University of Nebraska Press, 1972. $4.95.

WESTERN APACHE HERITAGE: PEOPLE OF THE MOUNTAIN CORRIDOR
Richard J. Perry
Illus. Maps. 314 pp. Paper. University of Texas Press, 1991. $17.95.

WESTERN APACHE LANGUAGE & CULTURE: ESSAYS IN LINGUISTIC ANTHROPOLOGY
Keith H. Basso
195 pp. University of Arizona Press, 1990. $32.50; paper, $10.95.

THE WESTERN APACHE: LIVING OFF THE LAND BEFORE 1950
Winfred Buskirk
Illus. 305 pp. University of Oklahoma Press, 1986. $24.95.

WESTERN APACHE MATERIAL CULTURE: THE GOODWIN & GUENTHER COLLECTIONS
Alan Ferg, Editor
Illus. 176 pp. Paper. University of Arizona Press, 1987. $19.95.

WESTERN APACHE RAIDING & WARFARE
Greenville Goodwin
Personal narratives of six Western Apaches. Also discusses weapons, taboos, leadership, and other aspects of Apache raiding. 330 pp. Paper. University of Arizona Press, 1971. $17.95.

WESTERN APACHE WITCHCRAFT
Keith H. Basso, Editor
Reprint. Paper. Books on Demand, $20.30.

WESTERN INDIAN BASKETRY
Joan Jones
Illus. 56 pp. Paper. Hancock House, 1990. $7.95.

WESTERN MILITARY FRONTIER, 1815-1846
H.P. Beers
Reprint of 1935 edition. Illus. 230 pp. Porcupine Press, $25.

THE WESTERN PHOTOGRAPHS OF JOHN K. HILLERS: MYSELF IN THE WATER
Don Fowler
Ilus. 160 pp. Smithsonian Press, 1989. $24.95.

WESTERN POMO PREHISTORY: EXCAVATIONS AT ALBION HEAD, NIGHTBIRDS' RETREAT, & THREE CHOP VILLAGE, MENDOCINO COUNTY, CALIFORNIA
Thomas Layton
Illus. 230 pp. Paper. University of California, Los Angeles, Institute of Archaeoogy, 1990. $17.50.

LEWIS WETZEL, INDIAN FIGHTER
C.B. Allman
Revised 1961 edition. Illus. Devin-Adair, $16.95.

WHEN BUFFALO RAN
George Grinnell
Story of Wikis, a Plains Indian who grew up in the mid-1800s as part of the last generation before the white changed the plains forever. Reprint. Illus. Paper. Hancock House, $9.95.

*****WHEN CLAY SINGS**
Byrd Baylor; illus by Tom Bahti
Grades P-3. Illus. 32 pp. Charles Scribner'sSons, $12.95. Paper. Macmillan, $3.95.

WHEN CULTURES MEET
Papers given by Florence Ellis, Myra Ekken Jenjins, Richard Ford, Marc Simmons, Orlando Romero, and Jim Sagel at the 1984 Conference at San Juan Pueblo. Illus. 96 pp. Paper. Sunstone Press, $9.95.

WHEN DID THE SHOSHONI BEGIN TO OCCUPY SOUTHERN IDAHO: ESSAYS ON LATE PREHISTORIC CULTURAL REMAINS FROM THE UPPER SNAKE AND SALMON RIVER COUNTIES
B. Robert Butler
30 pp. Paper. Idaho Museum of Natural History, 1981. $5.

*****WHEN THE GREAT CANOES CAME**
Mary Louise Clifford
A series of conversations between Cockacoeske, the queen of the Pamunkey Indians, and the adolescents of her tribe. Grades 5 to 9. Illus. Map. Biblio. 144 pp. Pelican Publishing, 1990. $12.95.

WHEN IS A KIVA: AND OTHER QUESTIONS ABOUT SOUTHWESTERN ARCHAEOLOGY
Watson Smith; Raymond H. Thompson, Editor
273 pp. University of Arizona Press, 1000. $40; paper, $17.95.

WHEN IT RAINS: PAPAGO & PIMA POETRY
Ofelia Zepeda, Editor
In Native language and English translation. 90 pp. Paper. Books on Demand, $22.

WHEN JESUS CAME, THE CORN MOTHERS WENT AWAY: MARRIAGE, SEXUALITY & POWER IN NEW MEXICO, 1500-1846
Ramon Gutierrez
456 pp. Stanford University Press, 1991. $49.50; paper, $16.95.

WHEN NAVAJOS HAD TOO MANY SHEEP: THE 1940's
George A. Boyce; Jeanette Henry, Editor
Stock overgrazing led to rapidly eroding farmland. Illus. Map. 288 pp. Paper. The Indian Historian Press, 1974. $12.50.

WHEN NO ONE IS LOOKING
Red Hawk - Pipikwass
50 pp. Paper. Robin Hood Books, 1990. $7.

WHEN THE RAINBOW TOUCHES DOWN: THE ARTISTS & STORIES BEHIND THE APACHE, NAVAJO, RIO GRANDE PUEBLO, & HOPI PAINTINGS IN THE WILLIAM & LESLIE VAN NESS DENMAN COLLECTION
Tryntje Van Ness Seymour
Ilus. color & bxw phoptos. Maps. Biblio. 396 pp. University of Washington Press, 1989. $50.

WHEN STARS CAME DOWN TO EARTH: COSMOLOGY OF THE SKIDI PAWNEE INDIANS OF NORTH AMERICA
Von Del Chamberlain
Illus. 272 pp. Paper. Ballena Press, 1982. $17.95.

*****WHEN THUNDER SPOKE**
Virginia Driving Hawk Sneve; illus. by Oren Lyons
Indian story. Grades 5 and up. Illus. Paper. U. of Nebraska Press & AISES, 1992. $7.95.

*WHEN WE WENT TO THE MOUNTAINS
  Hap Gilliland, et al
Grades 1-9. 40 pp. Paper. Council for Indian
Education, 1991. $9.95; paper, $3.95.

**WHEN INDIANS BECAME COWBOYS:
NATIVE PEOPLES & CATTLE RANCHING
IN THE AMERICAN WEST**
  Peter Iverson
Indian cattle ranching focusing on the northern
plains & the southwest. Illus. Map. 288 pp. Uni-
versity of Oklahoma Press, 1994. $24.95.

***WHERE INDIANS LIVE:
AMERICAN INDIAN HOUSES**
  Nashone
Grades K-6. Illus. 37 pp. Paper.
Sierra Oaks, 1989. $6.95.

WHERE LEGENDS LIVE
  Douglas Rossman
Illus. 48 pp. Paper. Cherokee Publications,
1988. $4.95.

**WHERE THE PEOPLE GATHER:
CARVING A TOTEM POLE**
  Vickie Jensen
Documents the entire process of carving a totem
pole. Illus. Photos. 194 pp. University of Wash-
ington Press, $29.95.

**WHERE THE TWO CAME TO THEIR FATHER:
A NAVAJO WAR CEREMONIAL GIVEN BY
JEFF KING**
  Maud Oakes, Editor; commentary by Joseph
Campbell
Illus. 120 pp. Paper. Princeton University Press,
1991. $90; paper, $14.95.

**WHERE TWO WORLDS MEET:
THE GREAT LAKES FUR TRADE**
  Carolyn Gilman
History of the fur trade, and essays on various
aspects of the early cross-cultural contacts between Indians and whites. Illus. Photos. Maps. 136
pp. Paper. Minnesota Historical Society Press,
1982. $18.95.

**WHERE THE WEST BEGINS: ESSAYS ON
MIDDLE BORDER & SIOUXLAND WRITING**
  Arthur Huseboe and William Geyer, Editors
Illus. Paper. Center for Western Studies, 1978.
$3.95.

**A WHIRLWIND PASSES: NEWS CORRE-
SPONDENTS & THE SIOUX INDIAN DISTUR-
BANCES OF 1890-1891**
  George R. Kolbenschlag
Illus. Paper. University of South Dakota Press,
1990. $9.95.

*WHITE BUFFALO WOMEN
  Christine Crowl
Grade 6. Illus. 18 pp. Paper. Tipi Press, 1991.
$2.50.

**THE WHITE CANOE & OTHER
LEGENDS OF THE OJIBWAYS**
  E. Monckton
Gordon Press, 1977. $59.95.

*WHITE CAPITVES
  Evelyn S. Lampman
Grades 4-7. 192 pp. Atheneum Publishers,
1975. $6.95.

WHITE CLOUD: LAKOTA SPIRIT
  Cecilia Brownlow & Leslie Wilner
Native American shamanism. Illus. 96 pp.
Paper. Sunstone Press, $10.95.

**THE WHITE EARTH TRAGEDY; ETHNICITY
& DISPOSSESSION AT A MINNESOTA
ANISHINAABE RESERVATION, 1889-1920**
  Melissa L. Meyer
Illus. Maps. 450 pp. University of Nebraska
Press, 1994. $40.

WHITE INDIAN BOY
  Charles Wilson & Trilba Redding
Revised edition. Bound with The Return of the
White Indian. Illus. 395 pp. Charles A. Wilson,
1988. $32.50.

WHITE INDIANS OF COLONIAL AMERICA
  James Axtell
38 pp. Paper. Ye Galleon, $3.

**THE WHITE MAN'S INDIAN: IMAGES OF THE
AMERICAN INDIAN FROM COLUMBUS TO
THE PRESENT**
  Robert Berkhofer, Jr.
Illus. Paper. Random House, 1979. $6.26.

**WHITE ON RED: IMAGES
OF THE AMERICAN INDIAN**
  Nancy B. Black & Bette S. Weidman, Editors
Associated Faculty Press, 1976. $26.50.

THE WHITE ROOTS OF PEACE
  Paul A.W. Wallace
The story of the founding of the Iroquois League
of Nations. Greenfield Review Press, $10.95.

**WHITE SETTLERS & NATIVE PEOPLES: AN
HISTORICAL STUDY OF RACIAL CONTACTS
BETWEEN ENGLISH-SPEAKING WHITES AND
ABORIGINAL PEOPLES IN THE U.S.,
CANADA, AUSTRALIA & NEW ZEALAND**
  A.G. Price
Reprint of 1950 edition. Illus. 232 pp.
Greenwood, $35.

WHITE WOLF WOMAN
40+ myths from 30 tribes. 168 pp. Paper.
Cherokee Publications, $8.95.

**WHITEHALL & THE WILDERNESS: THE
MIDDLE WEST IN BRITISH COLONIAL
POLICY, 1760-1775**
  Jack Sosin
Reprint of 1961 edition. Illus. 318 pp.
Greenwood, $38.50.

**WHITESTONE HILL: THE INDIANS & THE
BATTLE**
  Clair Jacobson
Story of the bloodiest battle ever fought in east-
ern Dakota Territory, involving the Yanktonai &
Hunkpatina Sioux and the U.S. Army under Gen-
eral Sully. Illus. 120 pp. Center for Western Stud-
ies, $11.95.

*WHO CAME DOWN THAT ROAD?
  George Ella Lyon
Story takes children on a journey through time.
Grades PS-3. Illus. 32 pp. Orchard Books, 1993.
$16.

**WHO SPEAKS FOR WOLF: A NATIVE
AMERICAN LEARNING STORY**
  Paula Underwood
A story of one people's struggle to live within

their environment. The Greenfield Review
Press, $8.95.

**WHO WAS WHO IN NATIVE AMERICAN
HISTORY: INDIANS & NON-INDIANS FROM
FIRST CONTACTS THROUGH 1900**
  Carl Waldman
1,00 brief biographical sketches of Indian and non-
Indians active in Indian affairs, culture, and his-
tory up to 1900. Illus. 410 pp. Facts on File, 1990.
$45.

WHO'S WHO IN INDIAN RELICS
The top collectors and artifact assemblages across
the country. 8th Edition. Published once every 4
years. Illus. 390 pp. Parks-Thompson Co., 1992.
$37.50 postpaid.

*WHY BUFFALO ROAM
  L. Michael Kershen
Original tale in the Comanche oral tradition, writ-
ten by a ten year old boy. Grades 3-7. Illus. 32 pp.
Stemmer House, 1993. $15.

WHY THE NORTH STAR STANDS STILL
  William Palmer
Illus. 118 pp. Paper. Zion Natural History
Museum, 1978. $2.95.

***WHY THE POSSUM'S TAIL IS BARE:
& OTHER NORTH AMERICAN INDIAN
NATURE TALES**
  James E. Connolly, Editor
Grades 3-12. Illus. 64 pp. Stemmer House,
1985. $15.95; paper, $7.95.

**WI-NE-MA, THE WOMAN-CHIEF & HER
PEOPLE**
  A.B. Meacham
Reprint of 1876 edition. AMS Press, $17.50.

WICHITA MEMORIES
Pamphlet on the Wichita Tribe.
Wichita Tribal Office.

THE WICHITA PEOPLE
  W.W. Newcomb, Jr.
Published by Indian Tribal Series, Phoenix,
1976. Available at the Wichita Tribal Office, $25.

**WIGWAM EVENINGS:
SIOUX TALES RETOLD**
  Charles Eastman & Elaine Goodale Eastman
Traditional Sioux legends. Illus. 255 pp. Univer-
sity of Nebraska Press, 1990. $30; paper, $7.95.

WIGWAM STORIES
  M.C. Judd
Gordon Press, 1977. $59.95.

***WILD BROTHERS OF THE INDIANS: AS
PICTURED BY THE ANCIENT AMERICANS**
  Alice Wesche
Grades 3-8. Illus. Paper. Treasure Chest, 1977.
$4.95.

**WILD LIFE ON THE PLAINS &
HORRORS OF INDIAN WARFARE**
  George A. Custer
Reprint of 1891 edition. Ayer Co., $45.95.

WILD RICE & THE OJIBWAY PEOPLE
  Thomas Vennum, Jr.
Illus. Photos. Biblio. 358 pp. Minnesota
Historical Society Press, 1988. $29.95; paper,
$14.95.

WILDERNESS EMPIRE
Allan Eckert
Illus. Little, Borwn & Co., 1969. $25.

THE WILDERNESS OF THE SOUTHWEST: CHARLES SHELDON'S QUEST FOR DESERT BIGHORN SHEEP & ADVENTURES WITH THE HAVASUPAI & SERI INDIANS
Neil Carmony & David Brown, Editors
Illus. paper. University of Utah Press, $14.95.

WILDERNESS POLITICS & INDIAN GIFTS: THE NORTHERN COLONIAL FRONTIER, 1748-1763
Wilbur Jacobs
Reprint. Illus. 208 pp. Peter Smith, $10.75. Paper. University of Nebraska Press, $4.95.

THE WILDERNESS TRAIL
C.A. Hanna
Reprint of 1911 edition. Two volumes. Illus. AMS Press, $74.50 per set.

*WILL ROGERS: AMERICAN HUMORIST
Grades 2-4. Illus. 32 pp. Childrens Press, $10.95.

WILLIE BOY: A DESERT MANHUNT
Harry Lawton
Paper. Malki Museum Press, 1979. $10.

JOHN P. WILLIAMSON, A BROTHER TO THE SIOUX
Winifred W. Barton
Reprint of 1919 edition. Illus. 308 pp. Sunnycrest, $10.

THE WILLIAMSON SITE
Peck
Covers the most important early-man paleolithic site in the Southeast (Virginia). Illus. 203 pp. Paper. Hothem House, 1985. $25.

*WILLY WHITEFEATHER'S OUTDOOR SURVIVAL HANDBOOK FOR KIDS
Willy Whitefeather
Outdoor survival guidebook. Grades 3 and up. Illus. 104 pp. Paper. Harbinger House, $9.95.

*WILLY WHITEFEATHER'S RIVER BOOK FOR KIDS
Willy Whitefeather
Grandfather teaches a young Cherokee how to make it on the river of life. Grades 3 and up. 128 pp. Paper. Harbinger House, $11.95.

*WILMA MANKILLER: CHIEF OF THE CHEROKEES
Grades 2-4. Illus. 32 pp. Childrens Press, $10.95.

WIND WON'T KNOW ME
Benedek
Paper. Random House, $14.

THE WINDING TRAIL: THE ALABAMA--COUSHATTA INDIANS
Vivien Fox
Illus. Eakin Publications, 1983. $7.95.

WINDSONG: TEXAS CHEROKEE PRINCESS
Raven Hail
Illus. 140 pp. Paper. Raven Hail Books, 1986. $7.95.

WINGED WORDS: AMERICAN INDIAN WRITERS SPEAK
Laura Coltelli, Editor
Paula Gunn Allen, Michael Dorris, Joy Harjo, Simon Ortiz, N. Scott Momaday, Gerald Vizenor, and othjers. Illus. 215 pp. University of Nebraska Press, 1991. $25; paper, $9.95.

WINNEBAGO ORATORY: GREAT MOMENTS IN THE RECORDED SPEECH OF THE HOCH-UNGRA, 1742-1887
Mark Diedrich, compiled by
Illus. 105 pp. Paper. Coyote Books (MN), 1991. $16.95.

THE WINNEBAGO TRIBE
Paul Radin
Reprint. Illus. 580 pp. Paper. University of Nebraska Press, $15.95.

SARAH WINNEMUCCA OF THE NORTHERN PAIUTES
Gae W. Canfield
Illus. 336 pp. University of Oklahoma Press, 1983. $19.95; paper, $9.95.

WINNERS OF THE WEST: A CAMPAIGN PAPER PUBLISHED IN THE INTERESTS OF THE VETERANS OF ALL INDIAN WARS, THEIR WIDOWS AND ORPHAN CHILDREN
Reprint of 1944 edition. 2,040 pp. Amereon Ltd. Microfiche only, $197.00.

*THE WINTER HUNT
Henry Tall Bull and Tom Weist
Grades 3-9. Paper. Council for Indian Education, 1971. $1.95.

WINTER IN THE BLOOD
James Welch
A novel set on a Blackfoot reservation in Montana. 192 pp. Paper. Penguin USA, $8.

WINTER OF THE HOLY IRON
Joseph Marshall, III
Novel about the winter of 1750, a holy iron (flintlock rifle) and 2 Frenchmen are thrust into the lives of the Wolf Tail band of Sicangu Lakota. 304 pp. Red Crane Books, 1994. $19.95.

THE WINTUN INDIANS OF CALIFORNIA & THEIR NEIGHBORS
Peter Knudtson
Illus. 96 pp. Naturegraph, 1977. $15.95; paper, $7.95.

WISCONSIN CHIPPEWA MYTHS & TALES
Victor Barnouw
Collection of traditional Chippewa legends from Lac Court Oreilles & Lac du Flambeau reservations in Wisconsin between 1941 & 1944. University of Wisconsin Press, 1977.

WISDOM OF THE ELDERS - HONORING SACRED NATIVE VISIONS
David Suzuki, Editor
Views of ecology from Native peoples around the world. 275 pp. AISES, $22.50.

THE WISDOM OF THE GREAT CHIEFS
Kent Nerburn, Editor
Classic speeches of Chief Red Jacket, Chief Joseph and Chief Seattle, documenting Native perception and philosophy. 96 pp. New World Library, $12.95.

WISDOM'S DAUGHTERS: CONVERSATIONS WITH WOMEN ELDERS OF NATIVE AMERICA
Steve Wall
Interviews with Native American spiritual leaders, giving voice to women who discuss their ancestyral knowledge, philosophies and traditions. 100+ b&x photos. Illus. 320 pp. AISES, $27.50. Paper. Harper & Row, $15.

WISDOMKEEPERS: MEETINGS WITH NATIVE AMERICAN SPIRITUAL ELDERS
Steve Wall & Harvey Arden
Spirit journey into the lives, minds, and natural-world philosophy of Native American spiritual elders representing 17 tribes. 128 pp. Beyond Words Publishing, 1990. $39.95; paper, $19.95. Two-tape audio, $16.95.

WISHRAM TEXTS: TOGETHER WITH WASCO TALES & MYTHS
E. Sapir, Editor
Reprint of 1909 edition. AMS Press, $38.

THE WITCH OF GOINGSNAKE & OTHER STORIES
Robert J. Conley
Stories reflect the range of Cherokee culture. 184 pp. University of Oklahoma Press, $18.95; paper, $9.95.

WITCHCRAFT IN THE SOUTHWEST: SPANISH & INDIAN SUPERNATURALISM ON THE RIO GRANDE
Marc Simmons
Illus. 185 pp. Paper. University of Nebraska Press, 1980. $5.95.

WITCHCRAFT & SORCERY OF THE NORTH AMERICAN NATIVE PEOPLE
Deward E. Walker, Editor
Revised edition. 336 pp. Paper. University of Idaho Press, 1989. $23.95.

WITH GOOD HEART: YAQUI BELIEFS & CEREMONIES IN PASCUA VILLAGE
Muriel Painter; Ed Spicer & WilmaKaemlein, Editors
Illus. 533 pp. U. of Arizona Press, 1986. $45.

WITH THE NEZ PERCES: ALICE FLETCHER IN THE FIELD, 1889-1892
E. Jane Gay; Frederick E. Hoxie and Joan T. Mark, Editors
Illus. 226 pp. Paper. University of Nebraska Press, 1981. $7.95.

WITHIN THE UNDERWORLD SKY: MIMBRES ART IN CONTEXT
Barbara Moulard
190 pp. Twin Palms Publisher, 1984. $50.

WITHOUT DISCOVERY: A NATIVE RESPONSE TO COLUMBUS
Ray Gonzalez, Editor
Through poetry, fiction and essays, prominent native writers reveal answers to the question, who are we Native Americans? Broken Moon Press, 1992. $14.95.

WITHOUT QUARTER: THE WICHITA EXPEDITION & THE FIGHT ON CROOKED CREEK
William Y. Chalfant
The climactic story of the first major U.S. Army expedition against the Comanches along the Texas frontier. Illus. Maps. 192 pp. U. of Oklahoma Press, 1992. $19.95.

WOKINI
Billy Mills
Billy Mills, (Sioux) Olympic gold medalist, teaches of his personal journey to happiness and self-understanding. Four W inds Trading Co., $12.95.

WO'WAKITA: RESERVATION RECOLLECTIONS
Emily H. Lewis
A people's history of the Allen)old Pass Creek) Issue Station District on the Pine Ridge Reservation of South Dakota. Illus. 294 pp. Center for Western Studies, $19.95.

THE WOLF & THE BUFFALO
Elmer Kelton
570 pp. G.K. Hall, 1989. $19.95.

*WOLF DOG OF THE WOODLAND INDIANS
Margaret Zehmer Searcy
Experiences that propel the young Indian boy quickly into manhood. Grades 3-8. Illus. 1 12 pp. paper. Pelican Publishing, $6.95.

WOLF & THE RAVEN: TOTEM POLES OF SOUTHEASTERN ALASKA
Viola E. Garfield & Linn A. Forrest
Second Edition. Illus. 161 pp. Paper . University of Washington Press, $12.95.

*WOLF TALES: NATIVE AMERICAN CHILDREN'S STORIES
Mary Powell, Editor; adapted for children by Karen Josey
Grades 3 and up. Illus. 70 pp. Paper . Ancient City Press, 1992. $8.95.

WOLF THAT I AM: IN SEARCH OF THE RED EARTH PEOPLE
Fred McTaggart
Biblio. 216 pp. Paper . University of Oklahoma Press, 1984. $12.95.

WOLVES FOR THE BLUE SOLDIERS: INDIAN SCOUTS & AUXILLIARIES WITH THE U.S. ARMY, 1860-1890
Thomas Dunlay
Illus. Maps. 320 pp. Paper . University of Nebraska Press, 1982. $10.95.

THE WOLVES OF HEAVEN: CHEYENNE SHAMANISM, CEREMONIES, & PREHISTORIC ORIGINS
Karl Schleiser
Illus. Maps. 230 pp. Paper . University of Oklahoma Press, 1987. $1 1.95.

WOVOKA & THE GHOST DANCE: A SOURCE BOOK
Michael Hittman
The known research about W ovoka (Jack Wilson) as the Ghost Dance Prophet. Illus. 350 pp. Paper . Yerington Paiute Tribe Publications, $20.

WOVOKA POSTER
16 1/2" x 23" poster of the Northern Paiute Ghost Dance Prophet. $5.

*A WOMAN OF HER TRIBE
Margaret A. Robinson
Grades 7 and up. Illus. Macmillan, 1989. $12.95.

*WOMEN IN AMERICAN INDIAN SOCIETY
Rayma Green
Grades 5 and up. Ill. Chelsea House, 1989. $17.95.

WOMEN & INDIANS ON THE FRONTIER, 1825-1915
Glenda Riley
Illus. 350 pp. Paper . University of New Mexico Press, 1984. $13.95.

WOMEN IN HISTORY
D.L. Shepherd, Editor
Mankind, $1.50.

WOMEN IN NAVAJO SOCIETY
Ruth Roessel
Illus. 184 pp. Navajo Curriculum Center Press, 1981. $15.

WOMEN OF THE NATIVE STRUGGLE
Ronnie Farley
Direct record of author's travels across America based on her photographs of native women in their different environments and her interviews with them. Paper . Orion Books, $22.

WOODEN LEG: A WARRIOR WHO FOUGHT CUSTER
Thomas Marquis, Translator
Illus. Maps. 400 pp. Paper . University of Nebraska Press, 1962. $10.95.

WOODLAND INDIANS OF THE WESTERN GREAT LAKES
Robert & Pat Ritzenthaler
Second Edition. Illus. 154 pp. Paper . Waveland Press, 1983. $8.95.

WOODLAND SITES IN NEBRASKA
M.F. Kivett
102 pp. Paper . Nebraska State Historical Society, 1970. $6.

WOODLAND TRAPPERS: HARE INDIANS OF NORTHWSTERN CANADA
Harold Broch
225 pp. Paper . Barber Press, 1987. $10.95.

WOODSMEN, OR THOREAU & THE INDIANS: A NOVEL
Arnold Krupat
140 pp. Paper . University of Oklahoma Press, 1994. $9.95.

WOODWARD'S REMINISCENCES OF THE CREEK OR MUSKOGEE INDIANS: ALABAMA, GEORGIA & MISSISSIPPI
Thomas Woodward
Revised edition. Paper . Southern University Press, 1970. $12.50.

WORD WAYS: THE NOVELS OF D'ARCY McNICKLE
John Lloyd Purdy
167 pp. University of Arizona Press, 1989. $27.95.

WORDARROWS: INDIANS & WHITES IN THE NEW FUR TRADE
Gerald Vizenor
Focuses on the cultural word wars which dominate the relations of Indians and whites. 170 pp. Paper . University of Minnesota Press, 1978. $12.95.

WORDS IN THE BLOOD: CONTEMPORARY INDIAN WRITERS OF NORTH & SOUTH AMERICA
Jamake Highwater
416 pp. Paper . New American Library , 1984. $9.95.

WORDS OF POWER: VOICES FROM INDIAN AMERICA
Norbert S. Hill, Jr., Editor
Collection of quotations, illustrates views & values. Illus. 64 pp. Fulcrum Publishing, 1994. $9.95.

WORK A DAY LIFE OF THE PUEBLOS
R. Underhill; W .W. Beatty, Editor
Reprint of 1946 edition. AMS Press, $32.50.

THE WORKS OF GEORGE CATLIN
George Catlin
Reprint. Reprint Services, $63.

WORLD OF AMERICAN INDIAN
National Geographic Editors
Random House, $40.

THE WORLD OF THE CROW INDIANS: AS DRIFTWOOD LODGES
Rodney Frey
Illus. Maps. 225 pp. Paper . University of Oklahoma Press, 1987. $1 1.95.

A WORLD OF FACES: MASKS OF THE NORTHWEST COAST INDIANS
Edward Malin
Classic study of Native American masks from the Pacific Northwest. Explores the riches of this ancient tradition, showing outstanding old masks. 8 color photos, 49 b&w photos. 158 pp. Paper reprint of 1978 edition. Timber Press. $17.95.

*WORLD OF THE SOUTHERN INDIANS
Virginia Brown and Laurella Owens
Grades 6-9. Illus. 176 pp. Beechwood Books, 1983. $17.95.

THE WORLD TURNED UPSIDE DOWN: INDIAN VOICES FROM EARLY AMERICA
Colin G. Calloway , Editor
Bedford Books, 1994.

WORLD'S RIM: GREAT MYSTERIES OF THE NORTH AMERICAN INDIANS
Hartley Alexander
Illus. 260 pp. Paper . University of Nebraska Press, 1967. $7.95.

THE WORLDS BETWEEN TWO RIVERS: PERSPECTIVES ON AMERICAN INDIANS IN IOWA
Gretchen Bataille, et al, Editors
Illus. 150 pp. Iowa State University Press, 1987. $5.95.

WOUNDED KNEE 1973: A PERSONAL ACCOUNT
Stanley David Lyman
Illus. Map. 256 pp. University of Nebraska Press, 1991. $33; paper , $9.95.

WOUNDED KNEE & THE GHOST DANCE TRAGEDY
Jack Utter
Account of events leading to and includng the infamous massacre at W ounded Knee, SD, in 1890. 30 pp. Illus. Maps. Paper . National W oodlands Publishing, 1991. $3.95.

*WOUNDED KNEE: AN INDIAN HISTORY OF THE AMERICAN WEST
Dee Brown
Grades 7 and up. 192 pp. Paper . Dell, 1974. $1.50.

WOUNDED KNEE: LEST WE FORGET
Alvin M. Josephy, Jr. & Trudy Thomas
Attempts to tell the true story of the history of Wounded Knee and the practice of Ghost Dance religion by the Sioux. Illus. 64 pp. Paper. University of Washington Press, $21.95.

THE WOUNDED KNEE MASSACRE: FROM THE VIEWPOINT OF THE SIOUX
James H. McGregor
Reprint. Illus. 131 pp. paper. Center for Western Studies, $5.95.

WOUNDED KNEE: THE MEANING & SIGNIFICANCE OF THE SECOND INCIDENT
Rolling Dewing
417 pp. Irvington, 1984. $49.50; paper, $19.95.

WOVEN STONE
Simon Ortiz
The autobiography of Simon Ortiz. 350 pp. University of Arizona Press, 1992. $45; paper, $19.95.

WOVOKA & THE GHOST DANCE: A SOURCE BOOK
Michael Hittman
Illus. Paper. Yerington Paiute Tribe, $20.

WRITE IT ON YOUR HEART: WORLD OF AN OKANAGAN STORYTELLER
Harry Robinson
Okanagan stories. Greenfield Review Press, $18.95.

WRITERS OF THE PURPLE SAGE: AN ANTHOLOGY OF RECENT WESTERN WRITING
Russell Martin & Marc Barash, Editors
Includes some Native American writers. 368 pp. Paper. Penguin USA, $9.95.

WRITING THE CIRCLE: NATIVE WOMEN OF WESTERN CANADA-AN ANTHOLOGY
Jeanne Perreault & Sylvia Vance
Anthology of contemporary Native Canadian women's writings. 320 pp. Paper. University of Oklahoma Press, $12.95.

WRITING TO CREATE OURSELVES: NEW APPROACHES FOR TEACHERS, STUDENTS, & WRITERS
T.D. Allen
Describes nearly two decades of experience in teaching writing to Navaho & Eskimo students. 270 pp. University of Oklahoma Press, 1994. $19.95.

WRITINGS OF GENERAL JOHN FORBES RELATING TO HIS SERVICE IN NORTH AMERICA
John Forbes
Reprin tof 1938 edition. Ayer Co., $22.

WUPATKI & WALNUT CANYON: NEW PERSPECTIVES ON HISTORY, PREHISTORY, AND ROCK ART
David Grant Noble, Editor
Reveals the remains of the Sinagua culture and contains sketches of the Navajo who live in Wupatki today. Illus. Maps. 48 pp. Paper. Ancient City Press, 1990. $7.95.

WYOMING PLACE NAMES
Mae Urbanek
238 pp. Paper. Mountain Press Publishing, $10.

Y

*THE YAKIMA: NORTHWEST
Helen Schuster
Grades 5 and up. Illus. Chelsea House, 1989. $17.95.

YAKIMA, APLOUSE, CAYUSE, UMATILLA, WALLA WALLA, AND WANAPUM INDIANS: AN HISTORICAL BIBLIOGRAPHY
Clifford E. Trafzer, Editor
Map. 263 pp. Scarecrow Press, 1992. $32.50.

THE YAKIMAS: A CRITICAL BIBLIOGRAPHY
Helen H. Schuster
168 pp. Paper. Indiana University Press, 1982. $5.95.

*THE YANKTON SIOUX
Herbert Hoover
Grades 5 and up. Illus. 104 pp. Chelsea House, 1988. $17.95.

YANKTONAI SIOUX WATER COLORS: CULTURAL REMEMBRANCES OF JOHN SAUL
Martin Brokenleg & Herbert T. Hoover
John Saul was a Minnesota Sioux (1878-1971). His family was removed to the Dakota Territory after the Minnesota Dakota war of 1862. Includes 23 of his drawings in full color; and includes chapters on Sioux customs, the Yanktonai and their Sioux relatives, a photographic essay on John Saul, and more. 66 pp. Center for Western Studies, $29.95.

YAQUI DEER SONGS: A NATIVE AMERICAN POETRY
Larry Evers & Felipe Molina
239 pp. Paper. University of Arizona Press, 1986. $15.95. Audiocassette of deer songs, $6.95.

A YAQUI EASTER
Muriel Thayer Painter
Introduction to the ceremony. 40 pp. Paper. University of Arizona Press, 1971. $7.50.

A YAQUI LIFE: THE PERSONAL CHRONICLE OF A YAQUI INDIAN
Rosalio Moises, et al
Illus. 251 pp. University of Nebraska Press, 1977. $23.95; paper, $5.95.

YAQUI MYTHS & LEGENDS
Ruth Warner Giddings
61 tales narrated by Yaquis. 180 pp. Paper. University of Arizona Press, 1968. $9.95.

YAQUI WOMEN: CONTEMPORARY LIFE HISTORIES
Jane Holden Kelley
Illus. 265 pp. University of Nebraska Press, 1978. $32.50.

THE YEAR OF THE HOPI
Tyrone Stewart, et al
Illus. 96 pp. Paper. Rizzoli International, 1982. $14.95.

YELLOW WOLF: HIS OWN STORY
L.V. McWhorter
Nez Perce War. Illus. Map. Biblio. 328 pp. The Caxton Printers, $19.95; paper, $15.95.

YELLOWTAIL, CROW MEDICINE MAN & SUN DANCE CHIEF: AN AUTOBIOGRAPHY
Michael O. Fitzgerald
Illus. Map. 272 pp. University of Oklahoma Press, 1991. $22.95; paper, $10.95.

YELLOW WOLF: HIS OWN STORY
L. McWhorter
Reprint. Illus. 325 pp. Caxton Printers, $19.95; paper, $14.95.

THE YEMASSEE
William Simms; Joseph Ridgely, Editor
Paper. The New College & University Press, 1964. $11.95.

YERINGTON PAIUTE DICTIONARY
118 pp. Paper. Yerington Paiute Tribe Publications, $15.

YERINGTON PAIUTE LANGUAGE GRAMMAR
168 pp. Paper. Yerington Paiute Tribe Publications, $15.

YOSEMITE INDIANS
Elizabeth Godfrey
Revised edition. Illus. 36 pp. Paper. Yosemite Association, 1977. $2.95.

YOU & THE UTILITY COMPANY
Institute for the Development of Indian Law, $3.50.

YOUR NAME IN CHEROKEE
Prentice Robinson
1,000 names listed in English with Cherokee phonetics, the English phonetics & Cherokee syllabary. 25 pp. Paper. Cherokee Publications, $6.

YOUR RIGHTS AS AMERICAN INDIANS
Institute for the Development of Indian Law, $7.50.

THE YUCHI GREEN CORN CEREMONIAL: FORM AND MEANING
W.L. Ballard
81 pp. Paper. American Indian Studies Center, 1978. $7.50.

YUCHI TALES
G. Wagner
Reprint of 1931 edition. AMS Press, $40.

THE YUKAGHIR & THE YUKAGHIRIZED TUNGUS
V.I. Iokhel'Son
Reprint of 1926 edition. AMS Press, $76.50.

YUKON BIBLIOGRAPHY - UPDATE SERIES
G.A. Cooke, Series Editor
CCI.

YUKON-KOYUKUK SCHOOL DISTRICT BIOGRAPHY SERIES
Curt Madison & Yvonne Yarber, Editors
Interviews of selected individuals and describes the events of their lives in their own words. Includes historical and contemporary photos. See Spirit Mountain Press for complete list of individuals profiled and prices.

*THE YUMA: CALIFORNIA
Robert L. Bee
Grades 5 and up. Illus. Chelsea House, 1989. $17.95.

YUMAN & YAQUI MUSIC
   F. Densmore
Reprint of 1932 edition. Illus. 272 pp.
Da Capo Press, $27.50.

YUMAN TRIBES OF THE GILA RIVER
   Leslie Spier
Reprint of 1933 edition. Illus. 435 pp. Cooper
Square Publishers, $35. Paper. Dover, $8.95.

YUNINI'S STORY OF THE TRAIL OF TEARS
   Ada Barry
Reprint of 1932 edition. Illus. AMS Press,
$34.50.

YUP'IK ESKIMO DICTIONARY
   Steven Jacobson
Illus. 755 pp. Paper. Alaska Native
Language Center, 1984. $18.

YUP'IK ESKIMO GRAMMAR
   Irene Reed, et al
330 pp. Paper. Alaska Native Language
Center, 1977. $7.50.

**YUP'IK ESKIMO PROSODIC SYSTEMS:
DESCRIPTIVE & COMPARATIVE STUDIES**
   Michael Krauss, et al
Illus. 215 pp. Paper. Alaska Native Language
Center, 1985. $15.

**THE YUP'IK ESKIMOS AS DESCRIBED
IN THE TRAVEL JOURNALS & ETHNO-
GRAPHIC ACCOUNTS OF JOHN & EDITH
KILBUCK**
   Ann Fienup-Riordon
Illus. Limestone Press, 1988. $30.

YUROK MYTHS
   A.L. Kroeber
A study of the Yurok Indians. Reprint. 460 pp.
University of California, $37.50; paper, $10.95.

**YUWIPI: VISION & EXPERIENCE
IN OGLALA RITUAL**
   William K. Powers
Illus. 113 pp. Maps. Paper. University of
Nebraska Press, 1982. $5.95.

Z

**DAVID ZEISBERGER'S HISTORY
OF NORTHERN AMERICA INDIANS**
   David Zeisberger: A. Hulbert &
   W. Schwarze, Editors
Reprint of 1910 edition. AMS, $16.

**ZEISBERGER'S INDIAN DICTIONARY:
ENGLISH, GERMAN IROQUOIS, ONONDAGA
AND ALGONQUIN–THE DELAWARE**
   David Zeisberger
Reprint of 1887 edition. 248 pp. AMS Press,
$42.50.

A ZUNI ATLAS
   T.J. Ferguson and E. Richard Hart
Illus. 160 pp. University of Oklahoma Press,
1985. $24.95.

ZUNI BREADSTUFF
   F.H. Cushing
Reprint of 1920 edition. 736 pp. AMS Press,
$48.50.

ZUNI CONTEMPORARY POTTERY
   Marian Rodee & Jim Ostler
Illus. 92 pp. Paper. Maxwell Museum, 1987.
$9.95.

ZUNI & EL MORO: PAST & PRESENT
   David Grant Noble & Richard B. Woodbury
Illus. Maps. 40 pp. Paper. Ancient City Press,
1990. $7.95.

ZUNI FETISHES
   F.H. Cushing
Illus. 43 pp. Paper. KC Publications, 1966. $3.

ZUNI FETISHISM
   Ruth Kirk
Study of 25 pieces from the Museum of New
Mexico. Illus. 72 pp. Paper. Avanyu Publishing,
1988. $4.75.

ZUNI FOLK TALES
   Frank H. Cushing
Reprint of 1901 edition. Paper.
University of Arizona Press, $15.95.

**THE ZUNI INDIANS: THEIR MYTHOLOGY,
ESOTERIC FRATERNITIES & CEREMONIES**
   M.C. Stevenson
Reprint of 1904 edition. Illus. 685 pp. Johnson
Reprint, $75.00; Rio Grande Press, $60.

**THE ZUNI INDIANS &
THEIR USES OF PLANTS**
   Matilda Coxe Stevenson
Reprint of 1908 report of the Bureau of American
Ethnology. 80 pp. Paper. Dover, $5.95.

ZUNI JEWELRY
   Theda & Michael Bassmann
Presents jewelry of the Zuni Indians of New
Mexico. Both traditional and new styles are shown
in full color. Illus. 64 pp. Paper. Schiffer, $12.95.

ZUNI KATCHINAS
   Ruth Bunzel
Reprint of 1932 edition. Illus. 358 pp.
Rio Grande Press, $40.

ZUNI KATCINAS, AN ANALYTICAL STUDY
   Ruth Bunzel
Annual Report of the Bureau of Amerian
Ethnology, 1929-30. Illus. 272 pp. Avanyu
Publishing, $30.

ZUNI KIN & CLAN
   A. Kroeber
Reprint of 1917 edition. AMS Press, $32.50.

THE ZUNI MAN-WOMAN
   Will Roscoe
Paper. U. of New Mexico Press, 1992. $16.95.

ZUNI MYTHOLOGY
   Ruth Benedict
Reprint of 1935 edition. Two volumes.
AMS Press, $75 per set; $35 each.

ZUNI POTTERY
   Marian Rodee & Jim Ostler
Illus. 92 pp. Paper. Schiffer, 1987. $9.95.

**ZUNI: SELECTED WRITINGS OF FRANK
HAMILTON CUSHING**
   F.H. Cushing; Jesse Green, Editor
Illus. 450 pp. University of Nebraska Press,
1979. $31.50; paper, $10.95.

ZUNI TEXTS
   Ruth Bunzel
Reprint of 1933 edition. AMS Press, $34.50.

*THE ZUNIS
   Katherine M. Doherty & Craig A. Doherty
Includes maps, a glossary and bibliography. Part
of *Indians of the Americas* series. Full-color illus-
trations. Grades 3 and up. 64 pp. Paper. Franklin
Watts, $5.95.

In this section, titles annotated in the alphabetically arranged bibliography are grouped under one or more subject headings.

ABENAKI INDIANS

The Abenaki
The Abenakis & Their History
The Embattled Northeast: The Elusive Ideal of Alliance in Abenaki-Euro-American Relations
The Faithful Hunter & Other Abenaki Stories
*From Abenaki to Zuni: A Dictionary of Native American Tribes
Histoire des Abenakis: A Bibliography of Canadiana
The Wabanakis of Maine & the Maritimes
The Western Abenakis of Vermont
The Wind Eagle

AGRICULTURE & FARMING

The Agricultural & Hunting Methods of the Navaho Indians
Agricultural Terracing in the Aboriginal New World
Agriculture of the Hidatsa Indians
American Indian Foods & Vegetables
Buffalo Bird Woman's Garden: Agriculture of the Hidatsa Indians
Early Prehistoric Agriculture in the American Southwest
The Economic Botany of the Kiowa Indians
Enduring Seeds: Native American Agriculture & Wild Plant Conservation
Ethnobotany of the Coahuilla Indians of Southern California
Ethnobotany of the Hopi
Ethnobotany of the Meskwaki Indians
Ethnobotany of the Forest Potawatomi Indians
Ethnobotany of the Navajo
Indian Agriculture in America: Prehistory to the Present
Indians, Bureaucrats and Land: The Dawes Act and the Decline of Indian Farming
Pima & Papago Indian Agriculture

ALABAMA-COUSHATTA INDIANS

Myths and Folktales of the Alabama-Coushatta Indians
The Winding Trail: The Alabama-Coushatta Indians

ALASKA NATIVES - ESKIMOS

Across Arctic America, Narrative of the Fifth Thule Expedition
*Across the Tundra
Ahtna Athabaskan Dictionary
Alaska Days With John Muir
Alaska: A History of the 49th State
The Alaska Eskimos As Described in the Posthumous Notes of Knud Rasmussen
The Alaska Eskimos: A Selected, Annotated Bibliography
Alaska 1899: Essyas from the Harriamn Expedition
Alaska History Series
*Alaska in the Days That Were Before
Alaska in Transition: The Southeast Region
Alaska Native Arts & Crafts
Alaska Native Language Center Publications
Alaska Native Languages: Past, Present & Future
Alaska's Native People
Alaska Natives & American Laws
Alaska Natives: A Guide to Current Reference Souces in the Rasmuson Library
Alaskan Eskimo Ceremonialism
Alaskan Eskimo Words
Alaskan Igloo Tales

Aleut Tales & Narratives
Always Getting Ready, Upterrlainarluta: Yup'ik Eskimo Subsistence in Southwest Alaska
The American Indian & Alaska Native Higher Education Funding Guide
American Indian & Alaskan Native Newspapers & Periodicals, 1826-1924
American Indian & Alaskan Native Traders Directory
Among the Eskimos of Wales, Alaska: 1890-93
An Annotated Bibliography of American Indian & Eskimo Autobiographies
Anthologia Anthropologica: The Native Races of America
Anthropological Observations on the Central Eskimo
Anthropological Papers of University of Alaska
The Anthropology of Kodiak Island
Application of a Theory of Games to the Transitional Eskimo Culture
Archaeological Collections from the Western Eskimos
Archaeological Excavations at Kukulik, St. Lawrence Island, Alaska
The Archaeology of Cape Nome, Alaska
Archaeology of the Central Eskimos
The Archaeology of Cook Inlet, Alaska
Arctic Art: Eskimo Ivory
Arctic Eskimo
Arctic: Handbook of North American Indians, Vol. 5
Arctic Languages: An Awakening
Arctic Life: Challenge to Survive
Arctic Memories
Arctic Schoolteacher
Arctic Village
Art & Eskimo Power: The Life & Times of Alaskan Howard Rock
The Artists Behind the Work
Artists of the Tundra and the Sea
Athabaskan Stories from Anvik
Athabaskan Verb Theme Categories: Ahtna
The Athabaskans: People of the Boreal Forest
Bashful No Longer: An Alaskan Eskimo Ethnohistory, 1778-1988
Book of the Eskimo
Books on American Indians and Eskimos
Boundaries & Passages: Rule & Ritual in Yup'ik Eskimo Oral Tradition
*Boy Who Found the Light
The Caribou Eskimos
The Central Eskimo
Cev'armiut Qanemciit Qulirait-Ilu: Eskimo Narratives & Tales from Chevak, Alaska
*Chief Stephen's Parky: One Year in the Life of an Athapascan Girl
*The Children of the Cold
*A Child's Alaska
Chills & Fever: Health & Disease in the Early History of Alaska
The Complete American Eskimo: A Special Kind of Companion Dog
Contributions to Chipewyan Ethnology
A Conversational Dictionary of Kodiak Alutiiq
Cultural Persistence (Athapaskan)
Dawn in Arctic Alaska
Dena'ina Legacy K'tl'egh'i Sukdu: The Collected Writings of Peter Kalifornsky
Dena'ina Noun Dictionary
Education & Career Opportunities Handbook
English-Eskimo & Eskimo-English Dictionary
English-Eskimo & Eskimo-English Vocabularies
*The Eskimo
The Eskimo About Bering Strait
*The Eskimo: Arctic
*The Eskimo: Arctic Hunters & Trappers
Eskimo Artists
Eskimo Art: Tradition & Innovation in North Alaska
Eskimo Capitalists: Oil, Politics & Alcohol
Eskimo Chilhood and Interpersonal Relationships
Eskimo Essays: Yup'ik Lives & How We See Them

*An Eskimo Family
*The Eskimo: Inuit & Yupik
Eskimo Life of Yesterday
Eskimo Masks: Art & Ceremony
Eskimo Medicine Man
The Eskimo of Baffin Land & Hudson Bay
Eskimo of North Alaska
Eskimo Poems from Canada & Greenland
Eskimo School on the Andreafsky: A Study of Effective Bicultural Education
The Eskimo Storyteller: Folktales from Noatak, Alaska
The Eskimo Tribes
*Eskimos
The Eskimos
The Eskimos & Aleuts
*Eskimos: The Inuit of the Arctic
The Eskimos of Bering Strait, 1650-1898
Eskimos, Revised
Ethnographical Collections from the Northwest Passage
Ethnography of the Tanaina
Ethnohistory in the Arctic: The Bering Strait Eskimo
An Ethnohistory of the Western Aleutians
Ethnological Results of the Point Barrow Expedition
The Eyak Indians of the Copper River Delta
*The Eye of the Needle: Based on a Yup'ik Tale Told by Bety Huffman
Fifty Years Below Zero
Five Hundred Eskimo Words
Give or Take a Century: An Eskimo Chronicle
Glory Remembered
*Green March Moons
Haa Shuka, Our Ancestors
The Han Indians: A Compilation of Ethnographic & Historical Data on the Alaska-Yukon Boundary Area
Handbook of North American Indians: Arctic
Heroes & Heroines/Tlingit & Haida Legend
*The Hunter & the Ravens
Hunters of the Northern Ice
I Am Eskimo: Aknik My Name
*I Can Read About Eskimos
Igloo Life
The Immigrant Experience
In Honor of Eyak: The Art of Anna Nelson Harry
*The Incredible Eskimo
Indian Baskets of the Pacific Northwest & Alaska
Indian, Eskimo & Aleut Basketry of Alaska
Indian & Eskimo Artifacts of North America
The Indians of the Subarctic: A Critical Bibliography
Ingalik Material Culture
Intellectual Culture of the Copper Eskimos
Intellectual Culture of the Hudson Bay Eskimos
Intellectual Culture of the Iglulik Eskimos
Inua: Spirit World of the Bering Sea Eskimo
*Inuit
Inuit Artists Print Workbook
The Inuit Life As It Was
Inuit: The North in Transition
The Inuit Print, L'Estampe Inuit
Inuit Women Artists
Inuit Youth
Inupiallu Tannillu Uqalunisa Ilanich: Abridged Inupiaq & Engish Dictionary
Island Between
Ivalu, the Eskimo Wife
Journey to Alaska in 1868
Kahtnuht'ana Qenaga: The Kenai People's Language
Koviashuvik: A Time & Place of Joy
Kusiq: An Eskimo Life History from the Arctic Coast of Alaska
Labrador Eskimo
Languages & the Schools: Athabaskan, Inupiaq, and Central Yup'ik
Last Light Breaking: Living Among Alaska's Inupiat Eskimos
Last of the Curlews

Letters to Howard: An Interpretation of the
  Alaska Native Land Claims
The Life I've Been Living
Life With the Eskimo
Living Arctic: Hunters of the Canadian North
*Living With the Eskimos
Lure of the Arctic
The Mackenzie Eskimos
Material Culture of the Iglulik Eskimos
The Movies Begin: Making Movies in New Jersey,
  1887-1930
My Grandfather's House: Tlingit Songs of
  Death and Sorrow
Native Accounts of Nootka Ethnography
Native American Women: A Contextual Bibliography
The Native Americans
The Native People of Alaska
Native Peoples & Languages of Alaska (Map)
Sadie Brower Neakok, an Inupiaq Woman
Neets'aii Gwiindaii: Living in the Chandalar Country
The Nelson Island Eskimo: Social Structure &
  Ritual Distribution
The Netsilik Eskimos
Never in Anger: Portrait of an Eskimo Family
North Pole Legacy: Black, White & Eskimo
North Slope Inupiaq Dialogues
Northern Tales: Traditional Stories of Eskimo
  & Indian Peoples
Observations on the Intellectual Culture of the
  Caribou Eskimos
Once Upon an Eskimo Time: A Year of Eskimo's
  Life Before the White Man Came
Ode Setl'oghwnh Da': Long After I Am Gone
Oil Age Eskimos
The Orders of the Dreamed: George Nelson on Cree
  & Northern Ojibwa Religion & Myth, 1823
Our Stories, Our Lives
Overland to Stravation Cove; With the Inuit In
  Search of Franklin, 1878-80
Painting in the North: Alaskan Art in the Anchorage
  Museum of History & Art
The People of the Polar North: A Record...
People of the Twilight
A Phonetical Study of the Eskimo Language
Phonological Issues in North Alaskan Inupiaq
Pioneer Missionary to the Bering Strait Eskimos
*Place for Winter: Paul Tiulana's Story
Point Hope, an Eskimo Village in Transition
A Practical Grammar of the St. Lawrence Island:
  Siberian Yup'ik Eskimo Language
Proto-Athabaskan Verb Stem Variation:
  Part One, Phonology
Qawiaraq Inupiaq Literacy Manual
Quliaqtuat Mumiaksrat Ilisaqtuanun Savaaksriat
The Ramiluk Stories: Adventures of an Eskimo
  Family in the Prehistoric Arctic
Raven's Journey: The World of Alaska's Native People
Reading Comprehension and Language
  Proficiency Among Eskimo Children
The Real People & the Children of Thunder: The Yup'ik
  Eskimo Encounter with Moravian Missionaries John
  & Edith Kilbuck
Reflections on the Alaska Native Experience: Selected
  Articles & Speeches by Roy M. Huhndorf
The Road to Nunavut: The Progress of the Eastern
  Arctic Inuit Since the Second World War
The Roles of Men and Women in Eskimo Culture
The Roots of Ticasuk: An Eskimo Woman's
  Family Story
Searching, Teaching, Healing: American Indians &
  Alaskan Natives in Biomedical Research Careers
*Seal for a Pal
Shadow of the Hunter: Stories of Eskimo Life
Shadows on the Poyukuk: An Alaskan Native's
  Life Along the River
Shamans & Kushtakas
Shandaa: In My Lifetime

Shem Pete's Alaska
Siberian Yup'ik Eskimo
Skeletal Remains of the Central Eskimos
*Small World of Eskimos
Some Warmer Tone: Alaska Athabaskan
  Bead Embroidery
Stories & Legends of the Bering Strait Eskimos
Stories of Native Alaskans
The Subarctic Athabascans: A Selected,
  Annotated Bibliography
Survival: Life & Art of the Alaskan Eskimo
Tales of the Ticasuk: Eskimo Legends & Stories
Tales & Traditions of the Eskimo, with a Sketch
  of Their Habits, Religion, Language & Other
  Peculiarities
Tanaina Tales from Alaska
Tatl'ahwt'aenn Nenn' The Headwaters
  People's Country
A Teacher's Guide to Bakk'aatugh Ts'uhuniy:
  Stories We Live By
Ten Months Among the Tents of the Tuski
Ten'a Texts and Tales from Anvik, Alaska...
  with Vocabulary by Pline E. Goddard
Their Stories of Long Ago
*The Tlingit
Tlingit Art & Culture
Tlingit Indians of Alaska
The Tlingit Indians: Results of a Trip to the Northwest
  Coast of America & the Bering Straits
Tlingit Myths & Texts
Tlingit Tales
Tlingit Verb Dictionary
To the Chukchi Peninsula & to the Tlingit Indians
  1881/1882
*Two Old Women: An Alaska Legend of Betrayal,
  Courage & Survival
Tuluak & Amaulik
Ugiuvangmiut Quliapyuit King Island Tales
A Victorian Earl in the Arctic
Wake of the Unseen Object
Walter Northway
Yukon-Koyukuk School District Biography Series
Yup'ik Eskimo Dictionary
Yup'ik Eskimo Prosodic Systems: Descriptive &
  Comparative Studies
The Yup'ik Eskimos As Described in the Travel
  Journals & Ethnographic Accounts of John &
  Edith Kilbuck

ALGONQUIAN INDIANS

An Analysis of Coastal Algonquian Culture
The Conflict of European and Eastern Algonkian
  Cultures, 1504-1700: A Study in Canadian Civilization
Folk Medicine of the Delaware and Related
  Algonkian Indians
Functions of Wampum Among the Eastern Algonkian
A Northeastern Algonquian Sourcebook
The Northern Algonquian Supreme Being
Spoken Cree: West Coast of James Bay

ANTIQUITIES

Aboriginal Chipped Stone Implements of New York
Aboriginal Monuments of the State of New York
Aboriginal Occupation of New York
Aboriginal Remains of Tennessee
Aboriginal Subsistence Technology on the
  Southeastern Coastal Plain
Aboriginal Territory of the Kalispel
Aboriginal Use of Wood in New York
A.D. Ancient Peoples of the Southwest
Adams: The Manufacturing of Flaked Stone Tools at a
  Paleoindian Site in Western Kentucky'The Adkins

Site: A Palaeo-Indian Habitation and Associated
  Stone Structure
The Agate Basin Site: A Record of the Paleo-Indian
  Occupation of the Northwestern High Plains
All That Remains: A West Virginia Archaeologist's
  Discoveries
The Anasazi
Anasazi Places: The Photographic Vision of
  William Current
Anasazi Ruins of the Southwest in Color
The Anasazi and the Viking
Ancient America
The Ancient Americas: The Making of the Past
Ancient Chiefdoms of the Tombigbee
Ancient Indian Pottery of the Mississippi River Valley
Ancient North America: The Archaeology of a
  Continent
Ancient Society
Ancient Treasures: A Guide to Archaeological Sites
  and Museums in the U.S. and Canada
Ancient Walls: Indian Ruins of the Southwest
Angel Site: An Archaeological, Historical, and
  Ethnological Study
Anthropoogy of the North Pacific Rim
Antiquities of New England Indians
Archaeoastronomy in the New World: American
  Primitive Astronomy
Archaeological Geology of North America
The Archaeological Investigations of Fort Knox II,
  Knox County, Indiana, 1803-1813
Archaeological Investigations in the Upper
  Susquehanna Valley, New York State
Archaeological Investigations of the Kiowa and
  Comanche Indian Agency Commissaries
Archaeological Perspectives on the Battle
  of the Little Bighorn
Archaeological Reconnaissance of Fort Sill, Oklahoma
The Archaeological Reports of Frederic War Putnam
Archaeology & Ceramics at the Marksville Site
Archaeology in Vermont
The Archaeology of North America
Archaeology of the Florida Gulf Coast
Archaeology of the Frobisher Voyages
Archaeology of the Lower Ohio River Valley
Archaeology of New York State
Archaeology of Precolumbian Florida
The Archaeology of Summer Island: Changing
  Settlement Systems in Northern Lake Michigan
The Archaeology of Three Springs Valley
Archaeology of the U.S.
Archaic Hunters and Gatherers in the
  American Midwest
Arrowheads & Stone Artifacts
The Arroyo Hondo Archaeological Series
Art of a Vanished Race: The Mimbres Classic
  Black-on-White
The Ascent of Chiefs
Before Man in Michigan
The Big Horn Medicine Wheel, the
  Birth & Death of Humanity
The Buffalo People: Prehistoric Archaeology
  on the Canadian Plains
California Archaeology
Calumet & Fleur-de-Lys, Archaeology of Indian &
  French Contact in the Midcontinent
Canyon de Chelly: Its People and Rock Art
Canyon de Chelly: The Story Behind the Scenery
Cartier's Hochelaga & the Dawson Site
Chaco & Hohokam: Prehistoric Regional Systems
  in the American Southwest
The Chacoan Prehistory of the San Juan Basin
Cherokee Archaeology: A Study of the
  Appalachian Summit
Cherokee and Earlier Remains on Upper
  Tennessee River
The Cherokee Excavations: Holocene Ecology and
  Human Adaptations in Northwestern Iowa

Cherokee Prehistory: The Pisgah Phase in
  theAppalachian Summit Region
Civilizations of Ancient America
*Clues from the Past: A Resource Book
  on Archaeology
Contemporary Archaeology: A Guide to Theory
  & Contributions
Contributions to the Archaeology and Ethnohistory
  of Greater Mesoamerica
The Cosmology of the Gila
Cultural Change and Continuity on Chapin Mesa
Current Research in Indiana Archaeology & Prehistory
Dead Towns in Alabama
Death Valley: Geology, Ecology, Archaeology
Deer Track: A Late Woodland Village in the
  Mississippi Valley
The Development of Southeastern Archaeology
Doing Fieldwork: Warnings and Advice
Dynamics of Southwest Prehistory
Early Late Woodland Occupations in the Fall Creek
  Locality of the Mississippi Valley
Early Puebloan Occupations: Tesuque By-Pass
  and Upper Rio Grande Valley
Esthetic Recognition of Ancient Amerindian Art
Excavations at Magic Mountain
Excavations at Snaketown: Material Culture
Excavations, 1940, at University Indian Ruin
Explorations of Key Dwellers' Remains on the
  Gulf Coast of Florida
Exploring Iowa's Past: A Guide to Prehistoric
  Archaeology
The Faunel Remains From Arroyo Hondo, N.M.
A Field Guide to Mysterious Places of the West
Florida's Prehistoric Stone Technology: A Study
  of the Flintworking Techniques of Early Florida
  Stone Implement-Makers
The Forgotten Artist: Indians of Anza-Borrego
  & Their Rock Art
From Drought to Drought
Further Study of Prehistoric Small House-
  Ruins in San Juan Watershed
Galena and Aboriginal Trade in Eastern North America
Glimpses of the Ancient Southwest
Great Basin Atlatl Studies
Great Excavations: Tales of Early Southwestern
  Archaeology, 1888-1939
The Great Journey: The Peopling of Ancient America
Guide to Prehistoric Ruins of the Southwest
Hart's Prehistoric Pipe Rack
Emil W. Haury's Prehistory of the American Southwest
The Heard Museum: History & Collections
The Hill Creek Homestead and the Late Mississippian
  Settlement in the Lower Illinois Valley
Hiwassee Island: An Archaeological Account of Four
  Tennessee Indian Peoples
The Hohokam: Ancient People of the Desert
Hohokam and Patayan: Prehistory of Southwestern AZ
Hollocene Human Ecology in Northeastern
  North America
Hoof'ovi II
I am Here: Two Thousand Years of Southwest
  Indian Culture
In Pursuit of the Past: An Anthropological &
  Bibliographic Guide to Maryland & Delaware
Indian Antiquities of the Kennebec Valley
Indian Culture and European Trade Goods:
  The Archaeology of the Historic Period in the
  Western Great Lake Region
Indian Days of Long Ago
Indian Mounds of the Atlantic Coast: A Guide
  to Sites From Maine to Florida
Indian Mounds of the Middle Ohio Valley: A Guide
  to Adena & Ohio Hopewell Sites
Indians of the Upper Texas Coast
An Introduction to the Prehistory of Indiana
Introduction to the Study of North American
  Archaeology

Introduction to the Study of Southwestern Archaeology
The Ioway Indians
Lamar Archaeology: Mississippian Chiefdoms
  in the Deep South
The Late Woodland Sites in American Bottom Uplands
The Magic of Bandelier
Mechanisms & Trends in the Decline of the Costanoan
  Indian Population of Central California:
  Nutrition & Health in Pre-Contact California
  & Mission Period Environments
Mesa Verde: The Story Behind the Scenery
Method and Theory in Historical Archaeology
The Mimbres: Art & Archaeology
Mississippian Mortuary Practices
Mississippian Stone Images in Illinois
Mobility and Adaptation: The Anasazi of
  Black Mesa, Arizona
Mounds for the Dead
The Navajo Project: Archaeological Investigations
  Page to Phoenix 500 KV Souther Transmission Line
New Light on Chaco Canyon
New World Archaeology & Culture History:
  Collected Essays & Articles
Objects of Change: The Archaeology & History
  of Arikara Contact with Europeans
Occupation of the Ozark Border
Ocmulgee Archaeology, 1936-1986
Oneonta Studies
Ornamental Artifacts of the North American Indian:
  Identification &Value Guide
A Palaeo-Indian Site in Eastern Pennsylvania
Pecos Ruins
People of the High Country: Jackson Hole
  Before the Settlers
People of the Mesa: The Archaeology
  of Black Mesa, Arizona
People of the Tonto Rim, Archaeological
  Discovery in Prehistoric Arizona
Petroglyphs of Ohio
Point of Pines, Arizona: A History of the University
  of Arizona Archaeological Field School
Pre-Columbian Architecture, Art and Artifac
  ts Slide Catalog
Prehistoric Households at Turkey Creek Pueblo, AZ
Prehistoric Hunters of the High Plains
Prehistoric Indians
Prehistoric Indians of the Southeast: Archaeology
  of Alabama and the Middle South
Prehistoric Indians of Wisconsin
Prehistoric Lithic Industry at Dover, Tennessee
Prehistoric Peoples of Minnesota
Prehistoric Peoples of South Florida
Prehistoric Southwestern Craft Arts
Prehistoric Southwesterners from Basketmaker
  to Pueblo
The Pre-History of the Burnt Bluff Area
The Prehistory of Fishtrap, Kentucky
Proceedings of the 1973 Hohokam Conference
Pueblos: Prehistoric Indian Cultures of the Southwest
Race, Discourse, and the Origin of the Americas,
  A New World View
The Range Site: Archaic Through Late
  Woodland Occupations
Rare & Unusual Artifacts of the First Americans
The George Reeves Site: Late Archaic, Late
Woodland, Emergent Mississippian, & Mississippian
  Components
Report of the Mound Explorations of the
  Bureau of Ethnology
Rock Island: Historical Indian Archaeology in
  the Northern Lake Michigan Basin
Sacred Sites of the Indians of the American Southwest
Salinas
San Gabriel del Yungue As Seen by an Archaeologist
Savanah River Chiefdoms
Searching for Footsteps to the Past: Surface
  Finds Along the Kaskaskia River

Skeletal Biology in the Great Plains
The Southeastern Ceremonial Complex,
  Artifacts & Analysis
The Star Lake Archaeological Project: Anthropology
  of a Headwaters Area of Chaco Wash, NM
Stone Age in the Great Basin
Stone Age on the Columbia River
The Stone Artifacts from Arroyo Hondo Pueblo
Stone Age Spear & Arrow Points of the
  Midcontinental & Easter U.S.
A Study of Pueblo Architecture: Tusayan & Cibola
  Bureau of American Ethnology, 8th Annual Report
Telico Archaeology: Twelve Thousand Years
  of Native American History
Themes in Southwest Prehistory
Time: Space and Transition in Anasazi Prehistory
Tomahawks Illustrated
Treasures of the Mound Builders
A Treasury of of Our Western Heritage: The Favell
  Museum of Western Art & Indian Artifacts
The Vail Site: A Paleo-Indian Encampment in Maine
Vanishing Heritage
*The Visual Dictionary of Ancient Civilizations
Wakemap Mound
The Waring Papers: The Collected Works
  of Antonio J. Waring
Western Pomo Prehistory
When Is A Kiva?
The Williamson Site
Wupatki & Walnut Canyon

APACHE INDIANS

Among the Apaches
Apache
*The Apache
Apache Agent: The Story of John P. Clum
Apache Autumn
Apache Legends: Songs of the Wild Dancer
Apache Life-Way
Apache: The Long Ride Home
Apache Medicine-Men
Apache Mothers & Daughters: Four Generations
  of a Family
Apache, Navaho and Spaniard
Apache Reservation: Indigenous Peoples
  & the American State
Apache Shadows
Apaches At War & Peace: The Janos Presidio,
  1750-1858
Apache Wars: An Illustrated Battle History
The Apaches: A Critical Bibliography
Apachean Culture History & Ethnology
The Apaches: Eagles of the Southwest
The Autobiography of a Kiowa Apache Indian
Basketry of the San Carlos Apache Indians
Buffalo Hump & the Penateka Apaches
Childhood and Folklore: A Psychoanalytic
  Study of Apache Personality
Childhood and Youth in Jicarilla Apache Society
The Chiricahua Apache, 1846-1876:
  From War to Reservation
Chiricahua & Mescalero Apache Texts
The Cibecue Apache
Cochise: Chiricahua Apache Chief
Dirty Boy: A Jicarilla Tale of Raid and War
In the Days of Victorio: Recollections of a
  Warm Springs Apache
Jicarilla Apache Texts
Jicarilla Apache Tribe: A History, 1846-1870
The Jicarilla Apaches: A Study in Survival
Medicine Men of the Apache
The Mescalero Apaches
Myths & Legends of the Lipan Apache Indians
Myths & Tales from the San Carlos Apache
Myths & Tales of the Chiricahua Apache Indians

Myths & Tales of the Jicarilla Apache Indians
Myths & Tales of the White Mountain Apache
Nana's Raid: Apache Warfare in Southern New Mexico
On the Apache Indian Reservations & Artist
  Wanderings Among the Cheyennes
Once They Moved Like the Wind
Peace With the Apaches of New Mexico and Arizona
San Carlos Apache Texts
Survival of the Spirit: Chiricahua Apaches in Captivity
The Truth About Geronimo
Utmost Good Faith: Patterns of Apache-Mexican
  Hostilities in Northern Chihuahua Border Warfare,
  1821-1848
Victorio and the Mimbres Apaches
Views From the Apache Frontier: Report on the
  Northern Provinces of New Spain, 1799
Western Apache Heritage: People of the
  Mountain Corridor
Western Apache Language & Culture
Western Apache Raiding & Warfare

ARCHITECTURE-DWELLINGS

Adobe Architecture
Adobe Remodeling & Fireplaces
Ageless Adobe
Ancient Architecture of the Southwest
Architecture of Acoma Pueblo
The Architecture of Arroyo Hondo Pueblo, New Mexico
Architecture of the Pueblo Indians: An Annotated
  Bibliography
Cliff Dwellers of the Mesa Verde
*Indian Homes
The Indian Tipi: Its History, Construction, and Use
The Hidatsa Earthlodge
Hogans: Navajo Houses and House Songs
*Houses of Bark: Tipi, Wigwam & Longhouse
*Indian Homes
The Indian In His Wigwam: Or, Characteristics
  of the Red Race in America
Native American Architecture
New Deal Adobe
Pre-Columbian Architecture, Art & Artifacts
  Slide Catalog
Prehistoric Architecture in the Eastern U.S.
*The Tipi: A Center of Native American Life
Voices in the Canyon

ARMS & ARMOR

American Indian Archery
Bows and Arrows of the Native Americans
Frontier Patrol: The Army & the Indians in
  Northeastern California
Guns on the Early Frontiers: A History of Firearms
  from Colonial Times Through the Years
  of the Western Fur Trade
*Indian Warriors and Their Weapons
Metal Weapons, Tools & Ornaments of the Teton
  Dakota Indians
Prehistoric Weapons in the Southwest
Pueblo Shields from the Fred Harvey
  Fine Arts Collection

ART

After the Buffalo Were Gone: The Louis
  Warren Hill, Sr. Collection of Indian Art
Allan Houser
America's Indian Statues
American Folk Masters: The National Heritage Fellows
The American Indian: The American Flag
American Indian Art, 1920-1972

American Indian Arts & Crafts Source Book
American Indian Painting & Sculpture
The American Indian Parfleche
American Indian Sculpture
American Indian Sculpture: A Study of the
  Northwest Coast
The Ancestors: Native American Artisans
  of the Americas
Ancient Art of the American Woodland Indians
Ancient Art of Ohio
Annotated Bibliography of American Indian Paintings
Arctic Art: Eskimo Ivory
Art and Environment in Native America
Art and Eskimo Power: The Life & Times
  of Alaskan Howard Rock
Art of the American Frontier: The Chandler-Pohrt
  Collection
Art of the American Indian
Art of the Northern Tlingit
Art of the Northwest Coast Indians
Art of the Red Earth People: The Mesquakie of Iowa
Art of the Totem
Art of a Vanished Race: The Mimbres Classic
  Black-on-White
The Arts in South Dakota: A Selected,
  Annotated Bibliography
Arts of the Indian Americas; North, Central & South:
  Leaves from the Sacred Tree
The Arts of the North American Indian: Native
  Traditions in Evolution
Authentic Indian Designs
Beads & Beadwork of the American Indian
Beads to Buckskins, Vol. 9
Between Two Cultures: Kiowa Art From Fort Marion
Beyond Tradition: Contemporary Indian
  Art & Its Evolution
Bibliography of Articles and Papers on North
  American Indian Art
The Black Canoe
Blackfeet: Their Art & Culture
The Blackfeet: Artists of the Northern Plains
Bo'Jou, Neejee: Profiles of Canadian Indian Art
The Box of Daylight: Northwest Coast Indian Art
Canyon de Chelly: Its People & Rock Art
Chiefly Feasts: The Enduring Kwakiutl Potlatch
Chinle to Taos
Circles of the World: Traditional Art of the
  Plains Indians
Collecting the West: The C.R. Smith Collection
  of Western American Art
Consumer's Guide to Southwestern Indian
  Arts & Crafts
Contemporary Artists and Craftsmen of the
  Eastern Band of Cherokee Indians
Contemporary Indian Art From the Chester &
  Davida Herwitz Family Collection
Council of the Rainmakers Address Book
The Covenant Chain: Indian Ceremonial
  and Trade Silver
Crow Indian Art
Dark Lady Dreaming
The Decorative Art of the Indians of the
  North Pacific Coast
Decorative Art of the Southwestern Indians
Directory of Native American Performing Artists
Discovered Lands, Invented Pasts: Transforming
  Visions of the American West
Eagle Transforming
Early White Influence Upon Plains Indian Painting:
George Catlin & Carl Bodmer Among the
  Mandans
The Early Years of Native American Art History
The Elders
The Elkus Collection: Southwestern Indian Art
Enduring Traditions: Art of the Navajo
Enduring Visions: One Thousand Years of
  Southwestern Indian Art

Esthetic Recognition of Ancient Amerindian Art
Fetishes and Carvings of the Southwest
First Artist of the West: George Catlin Paintings
  & Watercolors
The Flag in American Indian Art
The Forgotten Artist: Indians of Anza-Borrego
  & Their Rock Art
The Fourth Biennial Native American Fine Arts
  Invitational, Oct. 21,1989- Spring 1990
From the Land of the Totem Poles: The Northwest
  Coast Indian Art Collection at the American
  Museum of Natural History
Full-Color American Indian Designs
  for Needlepoint Rugs
A Gathering of Spirit: Writing and Art by
  North American Indian Women
The Gift of American Native Paintings From the
  Collection of Edgar William & Bernice Chrysler
  Garbisch
Grand Endeavors of American Indian Photography
Haida Monumental Art
Harmony by Hand: Art of the Southwest Indians
Hau, Kola! The Plains Indian Collection of the
  Haffenreffer Museum of Anthropology
Historic Hopi Ceramics
Hopi Kachinas Drawn by Native Artists
Hopis, Tewas, and the American Road
An Illustrated History of the Arts in South Dakota
Imagery & Creativity
Images of a Vanished Life: Plains Indian Drawings
  From the Collection of the Pennsylvania
  Academy of Fine Arts
In the Shadow of the Sun: Contemporary Canadian
  Indian & Inuit Art
In the Spirit of Mother Earth: Nature in
  Native American Art
Indian Art & Culture
Indian Art In the Ashmolean Museum
Indian Art Traditions of the Northwest Coast
Indian Art of the U.S.
Indian Artists at Work
*Indian Crafts
Indian Designs
*Indian Designs Stained Glass Coloring Book
Indian and Eskimo Artifacts of North America
Indian Miniature Paintings & Drawings:
  The Cleveland Museum of Art
Indian Rawhide: and American Folk Art
Indian Rock Art in Wyoming
Indan Rock Art of the Columbia Plateau
Indian Rock Art of the Southwest
Indian Rock Carvings
Indiancraft
Indians & Art History: A Pictorial Survey
Indians & A Changing Frontier: The Art of
  George Winter
*Indians of the Great Plains Stencils
The Institute of American Indian Arts, Alumni Exhibition
Introduction to American Indian Art
Inuit Artists Print Workbook
Fred Kabotie: Hopi Indian Artist
Kiowa Memories: Images From Indian Territory, 1880
Kiva Art of the Anasazi
Korczak: Storyteller in Stone
Kwakiutl Art
Lake Pertha and the Lost Murals of Chiapas
The Legacy: Tradition & Innovation in
  Northwest Coast Indian Art
Life & Art of the North American Indian
Life Under the Sun
*Little Southwest Indian Girl Paperdolls
Looking at Indian Art of the Northwest Coast
Lost Copper
Lost and Found Traditions: Native American Art,
  1965-1985
Charles F. Lummis: The Centenial Exhibition
Magic Images: Contemporary Native American Art

ARTIFACTS

BASKETRY

Pima Indian Basketry
Pomo Basketmaking - A Supreme Art for the Weaver
Plants Used in Basketry by the California Indians
The Pima and His Basket
Pomo Indian Basketry
Southwestern Indian Baskets
Traditions in Transition: Contemporary Basket
  Weaving of the Southwestern Indians
Western Indian Basketry

BIBLIOGRAPHIES

Against Borders: Promoting Books for a
  Multicultural World
Alaska Natives: A Guide to Current Reference
  Sources in the Rasmuson Library
The American Indian in Graduate Studies:
  A Bibliography of Theses and Dissertations
American Indian Literatures: An Introduction,
  Bibliographic Review, and Selected Bibliography
American Indian Reference Books for Children
  & Young Adults
The American Indian in Short Fiction:
  An Annotated Bibliography
American Indian: Language and Literature
American Indian Stereotypes in the World of Children:
  A Reader & Bibliography
American Indian Women: A Guide to Research
American Indians: A Select Catalog of National
  Archives Microfilm Publications
The American West in the Twentieth Century:
  A Bibliography
An Annotated Bibliography of American Indian
  and Eskimo Autobiographies
Annotated Bibliography of American Indian Paintings
The Apaches: A Critical Bibliography
A Bibliographical Guide to the History of Indian-
  White Relations in the U.S.
Bibliographies of the Languages of the
  North American Indians
Bibliography of Articles & Papers on
  North American Indian Art
Bibliography of the Blackfoot
Bibliography of the Catawba
Bibliography of the Chickasaw
Bibliography of the Constitutions and Laws
  of the American Indian
A Bibliography of Contemporary North
  American Indians
Bibliography of the English Colonial Treaties
  with the American Indians
Bibliography of Language Arts Materials for
  Native North Americans
Bibliography of the Languages of Native California
Bibliography of the Navaho Indians
Bibliography of North American Indian Mental Health
Bibliography of the Osage
Bibliography of the Sioux
Biobibliography of Native American Writers, 1772-1924
Books on American Indians and Eskimos
Books Without Bias: Through Indian Eyes
A Canadian Indian Bibliography
Canadian Indian Policy: A Critical Bibliography
The Cheyennes, Ma heo o's People:
  A Critical Bibliography
Chippewa & Dakota Indians: A Subject Catalog
The Delawares: A Critical Bibliography
Dictionary Catalog of the Edward E. Ayer Collection
  of Americana & American Indians
The Emigrant Indians of Kansas:
  A Critical Bibliography
An Essay Towards an Indian Bibliography
Ethnographic Bibliography of North America
The Five Civilized Tribes: A Bibliography
A Guide to Cherokee Documents in Foreign Archives
A Guide to Cherokee Documents in the

Northeastern U.S.
Guide to Records in the National Archives
  Relating to American Indians
Health and Diseases of American Indians North
  of Mexico: A Bibliography, 1800-1969
Hopi Bibliography: Comprehensive and Annotated
In Pursuit of the Past: An Anthropological &
  Bibliographic Guide to Maryland & Delaware
Index to Literature on the American Indian
Indian Land Tenure: Bibliographical Essays
Indian Reference Sources
Indian-White Relations in the U.S.
The Indians of California: A Critical Bibliography
Indians of the Great Basin: A Critical Bibliography
The Indians of Maine and the Atlantic Provinces:
  A Bibliographic Guide
The Indians of New England: A Critical Bibliography
Indians of North & South America: Bibliography
The Indians of the Subarctic: A Critical Bibliography
The Indians of Texas: An Annotated Research
  Bibliography
Iroquois Indians: A Documentary History-
  Guide to the Microfilm Collection
Kinsmen Through Time: An Annotated Bibliography
  of Potawatomi History
Languages of the Aboriginal Southeast:
  An Annotated Bibliography
Literature By and About the American Indian:
  An Annotated Bibliography
Narrative Chance: Postmodern Discourse on
  Native American Indian Literatures
Narratives of North American Indian Captivity:
  A Selective Bibliography
Native American Archives: An Introduction
Native American Historical Demography:
  A Critical Bibliography
The Native American in American Literature:
  A Selectively Annotated Bibliography
Native American Women: A Contextual Bibliography
Native Americans: North America--
  An Annotated Bibliography
Native Americans of the Northwest Coast:
  A Critical Bibliography
Native Canadian Anthropology & History:
  A Selected Bibliography
Native North Americans in Doctoral Dissertations,
  1971-1975: A Classified & Indexed Research
  Bibliography
Newberry Library/Center for the History of the
  American Indian Bibliographical Series
North American Indian Language Materials, 1890-1965
Office of Indian Affairs, 1824-1880: Historical Sketches
The Ojibwas: A Critical Bibliography
Pawnees: A Critical Bibliography
Recovering the Word: Essays on Native
  American Literature
Selected Americana from Sabin's Dictionary of Books
  Relating to America from Its Discovery to the
  Present Time
The Seneca & Tuscarora Indians: An Annotated
  Bibliography
Smoothing the Ground: Essays on Native
  American Oral Literatures
The Subarctic Athapascans: A Selected,
  Annotated Bibliography
Traditional Literatures of the American Indians:
  Texts and Interpretations
Tulapai to Tokay: A Bibliography of Alcohol Use
  and Abuse Among Native Americans of North
  America
Tulip: The Universal - Union List of Indian Periodicals
The Upstream People: An Annotated Research
  Bibliography of the Omaha Tribe
Winged Words: American Indian Writers Speak
Yakima, Palouse, Cayuse, Umatilla, Walla Walla,
  and Wanapum Indians: An Historical Bibliography
The Yakimas: A Critical Bibliography

BIOGRAPHIES

The American Indian, 1492-1976: A Chronology
  & Fact Book
American Indian Leaders: Studies in Diversity
American Indian Painters: A Biographical Directory
*American Indian Stories
American Puritanism & the Defense of Mourning:
  Mary White Rowlandson's Captivity Narrative
An Annotated Bibliography of American Indian
  & Eskimo Autobiographies
Apache Agent: The Story of John P. Clum
Apache Odyssey: A Journey Between Two Worlds
The Autobiography of a Kiowa Apache Indian-
  Jim Whitewolf
Autobiography of a Papago Woman
The Autobiography of a Winnebago Indian
Bartley Milam: Principal Chief of the Cherokee Nation
Being & Becoming Indian: Biographical Studies
  of North American Frontiers
Between Worlds
Beyond the Hundredth Meridian
Big Bear: The End of Freedom
Bighorse the Warrior
A Biobibliography of Native American Writers,
  1772-1924: A Supplement
Biographical Dictionary of Indians of the Americas
Biographical & Historical Index of American Indian
  & Persons Involved in Indian Affairs
*Black Elk: A Man With Vision
The Black Hawk War, Including a Review
  of Black Hawk's Life
The Book of the Indians
Brave Are My People
Ben Nighthorse Campbell
The Captive: The True Story of the Captivity of
  Mrs. Mary Rowlandson ...
Chainbreaker: The Revolutionary War Memoirs
  of Governor Blacksnake
*Charles Eastman: Physician, Reformer,
  and Native American Leader
Chief Joseph: Guardian of the Nez Perce
*Chief Joseph of the Nez Perce Indians:
  Champion of Liberty
*Chief Joseph's Own Story As Told by
  Chief Joseph in 1879
Chief Junaluska of the Cherokee Indian Nation
Chief Left Hand: Southern Arapaho
*Chief Plenty Coups: Life of the Crow Indian Chief
Chief Pocatello, the "White Plume"
Chief Sarah: Sarah Winnemucca's
  Fight for Indian Rights
Chief Seattle's Unanswered Challenge
Chief Washakie
William Clark: Jeffersonian Man on the Frontier
Cochise: Chiricahua Apache Chief
"Come, Blackrobe" De Smet & the Indian Tragedy
Converting the West: A Biography of Narcissa
  Whitman
C.N. Cotton and His Navajo Blankets
Crashing Thunder: The Autobiography
  of an American Indian
*Crazy Horse
Crazy Horse: Sacred Warrior of the Sioux
The Custer Story: Life & Intimate Letters of General
George A. Custer & His Wife Elizabeth
*The Defenders
Delfina Cuero: Her Autobiography
Dr. John McLoughlin, Master of Fort Vancouver,
  Father of Oregon
*The Double Life of Pocahontas
Dreamer-Prophets of the Columbia Plateau:
  Smohalla & Skolaskin
During My Time: Florence Edenshaw Davidson,
  A Haida Woman
The Education of Little Tree
Edward Sheriff Curtis: Visions of a Vanishing Race

Encyclopedia of Frontier Biography
*Extraordinary American Indians
*Famous American Indian Leaders
Famous Indian Chiefs
Famous Indians of Northwest Nebraska
Fig Tree John: An Indian in Fact & Fiction
Fighting Tuscarora: The Autobiography of Chief
  Clanton Richard
Fools Crow
Fools Crow: Wisdom & Power
From the Deep Woods to Civilization
Geronimo & the End of the Apache Wars
Geronimo: Last Renegade of the Apache
Goodbird the Indian: His Story
*The Great Chiefs
The Great Chiefs
*Great Indian Chiefs
*Great Indians of California
Great North American Indians
Guests Never Leave Hungry: The Autobiography
  of James Sewid, a Kwakiutl Indian
Handbook of the American Frontier: Four Centuries
  of Indian-White Relationships
Helen Hunt Jackson & Her Indian Reform Legacy
History of the Native Americans
How Can One Sell the Air? Chief Seattle's Vision
I Have Come to Step Over Your Soul: A True
  Narrative of Murder and Indian Justice
I Tell You Now: Autobiographical Essays by
  Native American Writers
I Will Die an Indian
Indeh: An Apache Odyssey
Indian Biography: North American Natives
  Distinguished as Orators, Warriors, Statesmen
*Indian Boyhood
*Indian Chiefs
Indian Heroes & Great Chieftains
An Indian in White America
Indian Lives: Essays on 19th & 20th Century
  Native American Leaders
Indian, Soldier & Settler: Experiences in the
  Struggle for the American West
Indian Women Chiefs
Indians in Overalls
Interior Landscapes: Autobiographical
  Myths & Metaphors
*Ishi: The Last of His People
Ishi in Two Worlds: A Biography of the
  Last Wild Indian in North America
William Jackson, Indian Scout
John Ross: Cherokee Chief
*Jim Thorpe
*Jim Thorpe: World's Greatest Athlete
Juh, An Incredible Indian
The Killing of Ned Christie: Cherokee Outlaw
King of the Delawares: Teedyuscung, 1700-1763
Kitchi-Gami: Life Among the Lake Superior Ojibway
Korczak: Storyteller in Stone
Lame Deer: Seeker of Visions
Leschi, Last Chief of the Nisquallies
The Last Contrary: The Story of Wesley Whiteman
  (Black Bear)
Life Among the Indians
Life of Joseph Brant (Thayendanegea)
Life Lived Like a Story: Life Stories of Three
  Yukon Native Elders
The Life of Okah Tubbee
The Life and Times of Little Turtle: First Sagamore
  of the Wabash
Life & Times of Red Jacket or Sa-Go-Ye-Wat-Ha
Life and Times of David Zeisberger
Long Lance: The True Story of an Imposter
Mad Bear
Madonna Swan: A Lakota Woman's Story
Mankiller: A Chief and Her People
*Maria Martinez: Pueblo Potter
Thomas Mayhew, Patriarch to the Indians, 1593 1682

Me & Mine: The Life Story of Helen Sekaquaptewa
*Me Run Fast Good: Biographies of Tewanima (Hopi),
  Carlos Montezuma (Apache), and John
  Horse (Seminole)
Mixed Bloods & Tribal Dissolution: Charles Curtis
  & the Quest for Indian Identity
Molly Molasses & Me: A Collection of
  Living Adventures
The Mongrel: A Story of Logan Fontenelle
  of the Omaha Indians
Montana's Indians: Yesterday & Today
*Mary Musgrave: Georgia Indian Princess
My Indian Boyhood (Chief Luther Standing Bear)
My Life As An Indian
My People the Sioux
Mystery of Sacajawea: Indian Girl with Lewis & Clark
The Names
Narrative of William Biggs
*Native American Biographies
Native American Biographies
*Native American Leaders of the Wild West
Native American Portraits: 1862-1918
Native Americans: 23 Indian Biographies
Native Heart: An American Indian Odyssey
Navajo Blessingway Singer: The Autobiography
  of Frank Mitchell, 1881-1967
Navajo Trader: Essays on a Region & Its Literature
Navajo Woman of the Desert
North American Indian Lives
North American Indians of Achievement Series
Walter Northway
The Odyssey of Chief Standing Buffalo
Ohiyesa: Charles Eastman, Santee Sioux
Old Father's Long Journey
Oliver La Farge and the American Indian: A Biography
Omaha & Ponka Letters
On Our Own Ground: The Complete Writings
  of William Apess, a Pequot
On Time for Disaster: The Rescue of
  Custer's Command
The Ordeal of Running Standard
Ouray-Chief of the Utes
Personal Narrative of James O. Pattie
Peter Pitchlynn: Chief of the Choctaws
Plenty-Coups: Chief of the Crows
Pocahontas
*Pocahontas: Daughter of a Chief
Alex Posey
Pretty Shield, Medicine Woman of the Crows
Quanah: A Pictorial History of the Last
  Comanche Chief
Red Crow, Warrior Chief
Red-headed Renegade--Chief Benge of the
  Cherokee Nation
John Rollin Ridge: His Life & Works
Ruxton of the Rockies
*Sacagawea
Saga of Chief Joseph
Sanapia: Comanche Medicine Woman
Satanta, The Great Chief of the Kiowas
  and His People
Sequoyah
*Sequoyah: Father of the Cherokee Alphabet
The Shawnee Prophet
Singing an Indian Song
A Sorrow In Our Heart: The Life of Tecumseh
Spotted Tail's Folk: A History of the Brule Sioux
Stories of Traditional Navajo Life and Culture
*The Story of Geronimo
A Supplement to a Guide to Manuscripts Relating
  to the American Indian in the Library of the
  American Philosophical Society
*Susette La Flesche: Advocate for Native
  American Rights
*Tecumseh
Tecumseh: Visionary Chief of the Shawnee
*Tendoy, Chief of the Lemhis

*Thunder Waters: Experiences of Growing
  Up In Different Indian Tribes
Timothy: Nez Perce Chief, Life & Times, 1800-1891
The Totem Carvers: Charlie Jarnes, Ellen Neel,
  Mungo Martin
Sarah Winnemucca of the Northern Paiutes
Timothy: Nez Perce Chief, Life and Times, 1800-1891
*Tomo-Chi-Chi
Warrior In Two Camps - Ely S. parker
The Way Was Through Woods: The Story
  of Tomo-chi-chi
When No One Was Looking
White Indian Boy
Who Was Who in Native American History
*Will Rogers: American Humorist
*Wilma P. Mankiller: Chief of the Cherokee
A Yaqui Life: The Personal Chronicle of a Yaqui Indian
Yellowtail: Crow Medicine Man & Sun Dance Chief:
  An Autobiography

BLACKFEET INDIANS

The Blackfeet: An Annotated Bibliography
The Blackfeet, Artists of the Northern Plains
Blackfeet Crafts
Blackfeet IndianStories
Blackfeet Indians
The Blackfeet: Raiders on the Northwestern Plains
Blackfeet: Their Art and Culture
*Heart Butte: A Blackfeet Indian
Modern Blackfeet: Montanans on a Reservation
The Old North Trail: Or, Life, Legends and Religion
  of the Blackfeet Indians
The Reservation Blackfeet, 1885-1945: A
  Photographic History of Cultural Survival

BLACKFOOT INDIANS

The Blackfoot Confederacy ,1880-1920: A
  Comparative Study of Canada & U.S. Indian Policy
Blackfoot Craftworker's Book
A Blackfoot-English Vocabulary
Blackfoot Lodge Tales
A Blackfoot Sourcebook
A Concise Blackfoot Grammar
An English-Blackfoot Vocabulary
Horse in Blackfoot Indian Culture With Comparative
  Material From Other Western Tribes
Material Culture of the Blackfoot Indians
Mythology of the Blackfoot Indians
A New Series of Blackfoot Texts
The Return of Chief Black Foot
Social Organization and Ritualistic
  Ceremonies of the Blackfoot Indians
The Tragedy of the Blackfoot
War Paint: Blackfoot and Sarcee Painted Buffalo
  Robes in the Royal Ontario Museum
Wooden Leg: A Warrior Who Fought With Custer

BOATS & CANOES

The Bark Canoes and Skin Boats of North America
Birchbark Canoe
Building a Chippewa Indian Birchbark Canoe
California Indian Watercraft
Canoeing With the Cree
*Indian Canoeing
The Skin Boats of Saint Lawrence Island, Alaska
The Survival of the Bark Canoe
Wangka: Austronesian Canoe Origins

CADDO INDIANS

The Caddo Nation: Archaeological &
  Ethnohistoric Perspectives
The Caddoan, Iroquoian and Siouan Languages
Caddoan Texts, Pawnee, South Band Dialect
The Hasinais: The Southern Caddoans
  As Seen by the Earliest Europeans
Notes on the Caddo
Traditions of the Caddo

CALENDARS

AISES Calendar
American Indian Women's Calendar
Calendar History of the Kiowa Indians
Calendar of Indian Festivals, Dances, Powwows,
  and Events (California)
California Powwows
R.C. Gorman's Engagement Calendar
Kumtux
Multicultural Resource Calendar
Native American Spirit
Native American Visions
Native American Women
Navajo: Portrait of Nation
Papago Calendar Record
Pow Wow Calendar
Pueblo People Calendar

CANADIAN INDIANS

*ABC's of Our Spiritual Connection
The Abnakis and Their History
Alberni Prehistory
Among the Chiglit Eskimos
An Analysis of Coastal Algonquian Culture
Arctic Artist
Arctic Dreams & Nightmares
Athapaskan Adaptations: Hunters and
  Fishermen of the Subarctic Forests
Beothuk and Micmac
The Beothucks, or Red Indians, the Aboriginal
  Inhabitants of Newfoundland
Beyond the River and the Bay:
  The Canadian Northwest in 1811
The Blackfoot Confederacy, 1880-1921: Comparative
  Study of Canada & U.S. Indian Policy
Bo'Jou, Neejee: Profiles of Canadian Indian Art
Breathtracks
*Canada: The Lands, Peoples, & Cultures Series
Canada's First Nations
Canada's Indians: Contemporary Conflicts
The Canadian Dakota
Canadian Indian Policy: A Critical Bibliography
Canadian Prehistory Series
The Canadian Sioux
Canoeing With the Cree
The Children of Aataentsic: A History of the
  Huron People to 1660
Christianity and Native Traditions
The Conflict of European and Eastern Algonkian
  Cultures, 1504-1700
Contributions to Chipewyan Ethnology
*Courageous Spirits: Aboriginal Heroes of Our Children
Crown and Calumet: British-Indian Relations,
  1783-1815
Dene Nation: The Colony Within
Description--Natural History of the Coasts
  of North America
Dix-Huits Ans Chez Les Sauvages: Voyages
  et Missions de Monseigneur Henry Faraud
Drum Songs: Glimpses of Dene History

The Dynamics of Government Programs for
  Urban Indians in the Prairie Provinces
*Enwhisteetkwa: Walk in Water
Explorations in the Far North
Explorations in the Interior of the Labrador Peninsula,
  the Country of the Montagnais & Nasquapee Indians
First Man West
For an Amerindian Autohistory
The Fourth World: An Indian Reality
Friend and Foe: Aspects of French-American Cultural
  Contact in the 16th and 17th Centuries
Functions of Wampum Among the Eastern Algonkian
Gatherings
Guests Never Leave Hungry: The Autobiography
  of James Sewid, a Kwakiutl Indian
Histoire des Abenakis: A Bibliography of Canadiana
History of Canada, Or New France
*History of the Five Indian Nations of Canada
History of New France
A History of the Original Peoples of Northern Canada
A Homeland for the Cree
*How Food Was Given
*How Names Were Given
*How Turtle Set the Animals Free
*I Am the Eagle Free (Sky Song)
In the Shadow of the Sun: Contemporary
  Canadian Indians & Inuit Art
Indian School Days
Indian and White: Self-Image and Interaction
  In a Canadian Plains Community
Indians, Animals, and the Fur Trade: A Critique
  of "Keepers of the Game"
The Indians of Canada
Indians of Canada: Cultural Dynamics
The Indians of the Subarctic: A Critical Bibliography
Inuit Artists Print Workbook
Inuit: The North in Transition
The Inuit Print, L'Estampe Inuit
*Just a Walk
Kanienkehaka (Mohawk Valley)
Kinship & the Drum Dance in a Northern
  Dene Community
The Kwakiutl: Indians of British Columbia
A Kwakiutl Village and School
*Kwulasulwut I: Stories from the Coast Salish
*Kwulasulwut II: Salish Creation Stories
Life and Death in Mohawk Country
Logs of the Conquest of Canada
Long Journey to the Country of the Hurons
Looking At the Words of Our People
Lost Harvests: Prairie Indian Reserve Farmers
  & Government Policy
Major Richardson's Short Stories
Maryland's Attitude in the Struggle for Canada
The Middle Ground: Indians, Empires, &
  Republics in the Great Lakes Region
The Mohawk That Refused to Abdicate
Mountain Wolf Woman, Sister of Crashing Thunder:
  The Autobiography of a Winnebago Indian
Mythology of the Thompson Indians
Naming Canada: Essays on Place Names From
  Canadian Geographic
National Aboriginal Directory
Native Canadian Anthropology & History:
  A Selected Bibliography
The Native Creative Process
Native People in Canada: Contemporary Conflicts
Native People, Native Lands: Canadian Indians,
  Inuit and Metis
Natives & Newcomers: Canada's "Heroic Age"
  Reconsidered
*Neekna & Chemai
New Relations of Gaspesia: With the Customs
  and Religion of the Gaspesian Indians
A Northern Algonquian Sourcebook
The Northern Algonquian Supreme Being
Northern Voices: Inuit Writing in English

Noticias de Nutka: Account of Nootka Sound in 1792
Nunuvut Atlas
Ojibway Heritage
The Ojibway on Walpole Island, Ontario:
  A Linguistic Study
Okanagan Sources
*Out of the North
A Paleo-Indian Site in Central Nova Scotia
Pathways to Self-Determination: Canadian
  Indians and the Canadian State
People From Our Side
People of the Buffalo
People of the Terra Nullius
Proceedings of the Fort Chipewyan/Fort
  Vermilion Bicentennial Conference
Queesto: Pacheenaht Chief by Birthright
The Relation of Seneca False Face Masks to
  Seneca and Ontario Archaeology
Sacred Feathers: The Reverend Peter Jones
  (Kahkewaquonaby) and the Mississauga Indians
The Shuswap
Skyscrapers Hide the Heavens: The History of
  Indian-White Relations in Canada
Slash
Snares, Deadfalls and Other Traps of the Northern
  Algonquian and Northern Athapaskans
Social and Economic Change Among the
  Northern Ojibwa
The Spirit of the Alberta Indian Treaties
The Spirit Sings: Artistic Traditions of Canada's
  First Peoples
Stone Ornaments Used by Indians in the
  U.S. and Canada
Stories of the Road Allowance People
Structural Considerations of Metis Ethnicity
Substance of a Journal During a Residence
  at the Red River Colony
Sundogs
Tales of the Anishinaubaek: Ojibway Legends
Tales the Elders Told: Ojibway Legends
The Thompson Indians of British Columbia
To the Arctic by Canoe
To Please the Caribou
Traditions of the Thompson River Indians
  of British Columbia
Travels and Adventures in Canada and the
  Indian Territories Between 1760 and 1776
The Treaties of Canada With the Indians of
  Manitoba and Northwest Territories
The Uncovered Past: Roots of Northern
  Alberta Societies
Unravelling the Franklin Mystery: Inuit Testimony
Voices in the Waterfall
Voyages From Montreal Through the Continent of
  North America to the Frozen and Pacific Oceans
War Paint: Blackfoot & Sarcee Painted Buffalo
  Robes in the Royal Ontario Museum
We Are Metis: The Ethnography of a Halfbreed
  Community in Northern Alberta
We Get Our Living Like Milk From the Land
Woodland Trappers: Hare Indians of
  Northwestern Canada
Yukon Bibliography - Update Series

CAPTIVITIES

Biography of Francis Slocum, The Lost Sister
  of Wyoming
The Boy Captives
The Captive: The True Story of the Captivity
  of Mrs Mary Rowlandson
Captivity of the Oatman Girls
Captivity of Mary Schwandt
Captivity Tales: An Original Anthology
Captured by the Indians: 15 Firsthand Accounts,
  1750-1870

*Children Indian Captives
Eleven Years a Captive Among the Snake Indians
Escape From Indian Captivity
The Falcon: A Narrative of the Captivity &
   Adventures of John Tanner
*Feathers in the Wind: The Story of Olive Oatman
From Massacre to Matriarch: Six Weeks in the Life
   of Fanny Scott
History of the Spirit Lake Massacre and of Miss
   Abigail Gardiner's Three Month's Captivity
   Among the Indians
The Indian Captive: A Narrative of the Adventures
   and Sufferings of Matthew Brayton
The Indian Captive: Or, A Narrative of the Captivity
   and Sufferings of Zadock Steele
Indian Captivities: Or, Life In the Wigwam
Indians: Or Narratives of Massacres and Depredations
The Indians and Their Captives
Journal of the Adventures of Matthew Bunn
Left By the Indians
The Life of Jacob Persinger
Memoirs of a Captivity Among the Indians of North
   America, from Childhood to the Age of Nineteen
Merejildo Grijalva, Apache Captive, Army Scout
Narrative of the Captivity of Ebenezer Fletcher
A Narrative of the Captivity of Mrs. Johnson
A Narrative of the Life of Mrs. Mary Jemison
Narratives of Captivity Among the Indians of
   North America
North Country Captives: Selective Narratives of Indian
   Captivity from Vermont & New Hampshire
Cynthia Ann Parker: Indian Captive
Cynthia Ann Parker: The Life & Legend
Perils of the Ocean and Wilderness: Narrative
   of Shipwreck & Indian Captivity
Puritans Among the Indians: Accounts of Captivity
   and Redemptions 1676-1724
The Redeemed Captive, Returning to Zion
Scoorwa: James Smith's Indian Captivity Narrative
Selection of Some of the Most Intersting Narratives
   of Outrages Committed by the Indians in Their
   Wars with the White People
A Short Biography of John Leeth, With an Account
   of His Life Among the Indians
Six Months Among Indians
Six Weeks in the Sioux Tepees
Sketches of Western Adventure
A Surprising Account of the Captivity and Escape
   of Philip McDonald and Alexander McLeod,
   From the Chikkamaugga Indians
Survival of the Spirit: Chiricahua Apaches in Captivity
Tales of the Northwest: On Sketches of Indian
   Life and Character
A Thrilling Narrative of the Sufferings of Mrs. Jane
   Adeline Wilson During Her Captivity Among the
   Comanche Indians
Topographical Description of the State of Ohio,
   Indiana Territory, & Louisiana
The Torture of Captives by Indians of Eastern
   North America
True Stories of New England Captives Carried
   to Canada During the Old French & Indian Wars
*White Captives

CATLIN, GEORGE (PAINTER OF INDIANS) 1796-1872

George Catlin
The George Catlin Book of American Indians
Catlin's North American Indian Portfolio:
   A Reproduction
First Artist of the West: George Catlin Paintings
   & Watercolors
Letters, Notes, on the Manners, Customs &
   Condition of the North American Indians

The Natural Man Observed: A Study of
   Catlin's Indian Gallery
White Influence Upon Plains Indian Painting:
   George Catlin & Carl Bodmer Among the Mandan,
   1832-34
The Works of George Catlin

CHEROKEE INDIANS

Abstract of Cherokee Claims
After the Trail of Tears: The Cherokees' Struggle
   for Sovereignty, 1839-1880
The American Indian in North Carolina
Arts and Crafts of the Cherokee
Beginning Cherokee: A Cherokee Language Grammar
A Better Kind of Hatchet: Law, Trade, Diplomacy
   in the Cherokee Nation
Census of Cherokee Indians East of the
   Mississippi 1835
*The Cherokee
*Cherokee ABC Coloring Book
Cherokee Americans-Eastern Band of Cherokees
   in the 20th Century
Cherokee Archaeology
Cherokee Archaeology: A Study of the
   Appalachian Summit
Cherokee By Blood: Records of Eastern
   Cherokee Ancestry
Cherokee Cooklore
The Cherokee Crown of Tannassy
Cherokee Dance and Drama
Cherokee Dictionary
Cherokee & Earlier Remains on Upper
   Tennessee River
Cherokee Emigration Records 1829-1835
Cherokee-English Dictionary
Cherokee-English Interliner
The Cherokee Excavations
The Cherokee Freedmen: From Emancipation
   to American Citizenship
Cherokee Fun & Learn Book
The Cherokee Ghost Dance
The Cherokee Indian Nation
The Cherokee Indian Nation: A Troubled History
Cherokee Language Workbook & Instructional
   Cassette Tape
Cherokee Legends & the Trail of Tears
Cherokee New Testament
Cherokee Old Settlers Roll 1895
The Cherokee People
The Cherokee Perspective
Cherokee Plants
A Cherokee Prayerbook
Cherokee Prehistory: The Pisgah Phase
   in the Appalachian Summit Region
Cherokee Psalms, A Collection of Hymns
Cherokee Renascence, 1794-1833
Cherokee Removal: Before & After
Cherokee Removal: The William Penn Essays
Cherokee Roots
Cherokee Song Book
The Cherokee Trail
Cherokee Tragedy: The Ridge Family & the
   Decimation of a People
Cherokee Vision of Eloh'
Cherokee Words
Cherokees
*The Cherokees
The Cherokees & Christianity, 1794-1870
Cherokees at the Crossroads
Cherokees, An Illustrated History
The Cherokees in Pre-Columbian Times
Cherokees in Transition
Cherokees & Missionaries, 1789-1839
The Cherokees of the Smokey Mountains

The Cherokees, Past and Present
Cherokees "West"
Chief Bowles & the Texas Cherokees
Constitution of the State of Sequoyah
Contemporary Artists & Craftsmen of the Cherokee
Early of the Cherokees
The Eastern Band of Cherokees, 1819-1900
The Eastern Cherokees
The Education of Little Tree
Exploring Your Cherokee Ancestry
Fire & the Spirits: Cherokee Law from Clan to Court
A Guide to Cherokee Documents in Foreign Archives
History of the Cherokee Indians and Their Legends
   and Folklore
History, Myths & Sacred Formulas of the Cherokees
Introduction to Cherokee: A Cherokee Language
   Study Course
John Ross: Cherokee Chief
Journal of Cherokee Studies
*The Last Cherokee Warriors
The Magic Lake: Mystical Healing Lake of Cherokee
Mankiller: A Chief and Her People
Bartley Milam: Principal Chief of the Cherokee Nation
Mountain Windsong: A Novel of the Trail of Tears
Muskogee City & County
Myths of the Cherokee
Myths of the Cherokee & Sacred Formulas
   of the Cherokees
Myths & Sacred Formulas of the Cherokees
Nations Remembered: An Oral History of Cherokees,
   Chickasaws, Choctaws, Creeks, and Seminoles,
   1865-1907
Native Caroliniana, The Indians of North Carolina
New Echota Letters: Contributions of Samuel
   A. Worcester to the Cherokee Phoenix
*Only the Names Remain: The Cherokees and
   the Trail of Tears
An Outline of Basiv Verb Inflections of
   Oklahoma Cherokee
Phonological Variations in Western Cherokee
Red Over Black: Black Slavery Among
   the Cherokee Indians
Removal of the Cherokee Indians from Georgia
The Removal of the Cherokee Nation: Manifest
   Destiny or National Dishonor
John Ross and the Cherokee Indians
Sequoyah
Sequoyah & the Cherokee Alphabet
*Sequoyah (Cherokee Hero)
Sequoyah, Father of the Cherokee Alphabet
The Shadow of Sequoyah: Social Documents
   of the Cherokees, 1862-1964
Slavery and the Evolution of Cherokee Society,
   1540-1866
Snowbird Cherokees: People of Persistence
A Snug Little Purchase: How Richard Henderson
   Bought Kaintuckee from the Cherokees in 1775
Storm in the Mountain
The Story of the Cherokee People
*The Story of the Trail of Tears
A Structured Approach to Learning the Basic
   Inflections of the Cherokee Verb
Tales of the Cherokee Hills
The Ten Year Treasury of Cherokee Studies
The Texas Cherokees: A People Between
   Two Fires, 1819-1840
Trail of Tears
*The Trail on Which They Wept: The Story of a
   Cherokee Girl
Tribes That Slumber
Walk in Your Soul: Love Incantations of the
   Oklahoma Cherokees
Walking the Trail
Where Legends Live
The Witch of Goingsnake & Other Stories
Your Name in Cherokee
Yunini'o Story of tho Trail of Toare

CHEYENNE & ARAPAHOE INDIANS

The Arapaho Indians: Research Guide & Bibliography
Arapahoe Politics, 1851-1978: Symbols in Crises
  of Authority
The Arapaho Sun Dance, The Ceremony
  of the Offerings Lodge
The Arapahoes, Our People
*Belle Highwalking: The Narrative of a
  Northern Cheyenne Woman
By Cheyenne Campfires
Cheyenne
The Cheyenne
*The Cheyenne
Cheyenne and Arapaho Music
The Cheyenne & Arapaho Ordeal:
  Reservation & Agency Life
Cheyenne Autumn
*Cheyenne Fire Fighters: Modern Indians
  Fighting Forest Fires
The Cheyenne in Plains Indian Trade Relations
Cheyenne Indians: Sketch of the
  Cheyenne Grammar
The Cheyenne Indians: Their History
  & Ways of Life
*Cheyenne Legends of Creation
Cheyenne Memories
The Cheyenne Nation: A Social &
  Demographic History
*Cheyenne Short Stories
*Cheyenne Warriors
The Cheyenne Way: Conflict and Case
  Law in Primitive Jurisprudence
The Cheyennes
The Cheyennes, Indians of the Great Plains
The Cheyennes of Montana
English-Cheyenne Dictionary
The Fighting Cheyennes
*A History of the Cheyenne People
*Northern Cheyenne Fire Fighters
On the Apache Indian Reservations & Artist
  Wanderings Among the Cheyennes
The Peace Chiefs of the Cheyennes
People of the Sacred Mountain: A History of the
  Northern Cheyenne Chiefs and Warrior
  Societies, 1830-1879
*The Rolling Head: Cheyenne Tales
The Southern Cheyennes
Sweet Medicine: The Continuing Role of the Sacred
  Arrows, The Sun Dance, and the Sacred
  Buffalo Hat in Northern Cheyenne History
Traditions of the Arapaho
Tsee-Ma'Heone-Nemeototse: Cheyenne
  Spiritual Songs
The Wolves of Heaven: Cheyenne Shamanism,
  Ceremonies & Prehistoric Origins

CHICKASAWS

Bibliography of the Chickasaw
*The Chickasaw
Chickasaw: An Analytical Dictionary
Chickasaw Glossary
The Chickasaws
Creek-Choctaw-Chickasaw Land Fraud in
  Public Land Sales
Memoris of a Chickasaw Squaw
Nations Remembered: An Oral History of Cherokees,
Chickasaws, Choctaws, Creeks, and Seminoles,
  1865-1907
The Papers pf Panton, Leslie & Co.

CHIEF CRAZY HORSE

American Indian Warrior Chiefs: Tecumseh,
  Crazy Horse, Chief Joseph, Geronimo
Crazy Horse Memorial, 40th Anniversary
Crazy Horse & Custer
Crazy Horse, Hoka Hey: It Is a Good Time to Die!
Crazy Horse & Korczak
Crazy Horse Called Them Walk-A-Heaps
Crazy Horse: Sacred Warrior of the Sioux
Crazy Horse, The Strange Man of the Oglalas
The Crazy Horse Surrender Ledger
Famous Indians of Northwest Nebraska
In the Spirit of Crazy Horse
*Indians of America Series: Crazy Horse, et al
The Killing of Chief Crazy Horse
Korczak: Storyteller in Stone
*A Legend from Crazy Horse Clan
The Oglala Lakota Crazy Horse
South Dakota Leaders

CHIEF JOSEPH

American Indian Warrior Chiefs: Tecumseh,
  Crazy Horse, Chief Joseph, Geronimo
Chief Joseph
Chief Joseph's Allies
Chief Joseph Country: Land of the Nez Perce
Chief Joseph: Guardian of the Nez Perce
Chief Joseph of the Nez Perce Indians
Chief Joseph's Own Story
*Chief Joseph's Own Story as Told by
  Chief Joseph in 1879
I Will Fight No More Forever: Chief Joseph
  and the Nez Perce War
*Indians of America: Chief Joseph, et al
Joseph, Chief of the Nez Perce
Nez Perce Joseph
Red Eagles of the Northwest: The Story of
  Chief Joseph and His People

CHIEF QUANAH PARKER

Comanche Moon
*Comanche Warbonnet
*Native American Leaders of the Wild Wesr
*North American Indians of Achievement
Quanah Parker, Comanche Chief
*Quanah Parker: Great Chief of the Comanches
Quanah: A Pictorial History of the Last
  Comanche Chief
War Chiefs

CHILDREN

American Indian Children at School, 1850-1930
American Indian and White Children: A
  Sociopsychological Investigation
Childhood and Folklore: A Psychoanalytic
  Study of Apache Personality
Childhood and Youth in Jicarilla Apache Society
Children at Risk: Making a Difference Through the
  Court Appointed Special Advocate Project
Children of the Circle
Children of the Salt River
Chippewa Child Life and Its Cultural Background
Crickets & Corn: Five Stories About Native
  North American Children
*The Death of Jimmy Littlewolf: An Indian
  Boy at Boys Ranch
The Hopi Child
*Indian Boyhood
Navajo Infancy: An Ethological Study of
  Child Development

Overcoming Obstacles and Improving Outcomes
Red Children in White America
Respect for Life: The Traditional Upbringing of
  American Indian Children
*Thunder Waters: Experiences of Growing
  Up in Different Indian Tribes
*To Live In Two Worlds: American Indian Youth Today
*The Trail on Which They Wept: The Story of a
  Cherokee Girl

CHIPPEWA (OJIBWE) INDIANS

Acculturation and Personality Among the
  Wisconsin Chippewa
Anishinabe: Six Studies of Modern Chippewa
Building a Chippewa Indian Birchbark Canoe
*The Chipewyan
*The Chippewa
Chippewa Child Life & Its Cultural Background
Chippewa Customs
Chippewa & Dakota Indians: A Subject Catalog of
  Books, Pamphlets, Periodical Articles & Manuscripts
Chippewa Indians I-VII
Chippewa Indians as Recorded by Rev.
  Frederick Baraga in 1847
Chippewa Music
The Chippewa & Their Neighbors
The Chippewas of Lake Superior
Clothed-in-Fur and Other Tales: An Introduction
  to an Ojibwa World View
Dictionary of the Ojibway Language
The Dream Dance of the Chippewa and Menominee
  Indians of Northern Wisconsin
Generation to Generation
Giving: Ojibway Stories & Legends from the
  Children of Curve Lake
The Grand Portage Story
History of the Ojibwa Indians
History of the Ojibway People
How Indians Use Wild Plants for Food,
  Medicine & Crafts
Indians in Minnesota, 4th Edition
Eastman Johnson's Lake Superior Indians
Kitchi-Gami: Life Among the Lake Superior Ojibway
The Land of the Ojibwe
The Mishomis Book: The Voice of the Ojibway
*Muckwa: The Adventures of a Chippewa Indian Boy
Night Flying Woman: An Ojibway Narrative
Ojibwa Crafts
Ojibwa Sociology
Ojibwa Texts
Ojibwa Woman
The Ojibwas: A Critical Bibliography
Ojibway Ceremonies
The Ojibway Dream
Ojibway Heritage
Ojibway Indians Coloring Book
Ojibway Music from Minnesota
Ojibway Oratory
The Ojibway of Walpole, Ontario, Canada
Ojibway Tales
"The Orders of the Dreamed"
Ottawa & Chippewa Indians of Michigan, 1870-1909
Paths of the People: The Ojibwe in the
  Chippewa Valley
The People Named the Chippewa
Portage Lake: Memories of an Ojibwe Childhood
Red Lake Nation: Portraits of Ojibway Life
The Sacred Harvest: Ojibway Wild Rice Gathering
Sacred Scrolls of the Southern Ojibway
A Social Study of One Hundred Fifty Chippewa Indian
  Families of the White Earth Reservation of Minnesota
Traditional Ojibwa Religion and Its Historical Changes
The Transformation of Bigfoot: Malesness,
  Power & Belief Among the Chipewyan
Walk in Peace: Legends & Stories of the MI Indians

Where Two Worlds Meet
The White Canoe and Other Legends of the
   Ojibways Narrative Histories
Wild Rice & the Ojibway People

CHOCTAW INDIANS

Acts & Resolutions, Constitution &
   Laws of the Choctaw
*The Choctaw
*A Choctaw Anthology, I and II
The Choctaw Before Removal
1830 Choctaw Census "Armstrong Roll"
A Choctaw Sourcebook
Choctaws & Missionaries in Mississippi, 1818-1918
Early Account of the Choctaw Indians
Intruders Into the Choctaw & Chickasaw Nations,
   1884-1890
Life Among the Choctaw Indians and Sketches
   of the Southwest
Mississippi Choctaws at Play: The Serious
   Side of Leisure
Nations Remembered: An Oral History of Cherokees,
Chickasaws, Choctaws, Creeks, and Seminoles,
   1865-1907
Okla Hannali
Persistence of Pettern in Mississippi Choctaw Culture
The Removal of the Choctaw Indians
Rise & Fall of the Choctaw Republic
Stranges in Their Own Land: A Choctaw Portfolio
Tribal Government: A New Era

CLAIMS

The Alaska Native Claims Settlement Act, 1991
   & Tribal Government
A Bibliography of American Indian Land Claims
The Case of the Seneca Indians in the State
   of New York
Indian Claims Commission Act
Indian Tribal Claims Decided in the Court of Claims
   of the U.S.: Briefed & Compiled, 6/30/47
Native Claims & Political Development
Restitution: The Land Claims of the Mashpee, Passa-
   maquoddy & Penobscot Indians of New England
Their Day in Court: A History of the Indian
   Claims Commission

CLIFF DWELLERS

Cliff Dwellers of the Mesa Verde, Southwestern
   Colorado: Their Pottery & Implements
House of Three Turkeys: Anasazi Redoubt
The Land of the Cliff-Dwellers
Mesa Verde National Park
The Ozark Bluff Dwellers
The Village of Blue Stone
Voices in the Canyon

COMANCHE INDIANS

Comanche Dictionary & Grammar
Comanche Treaties (See Treaty Manuscripts Series)
Comanches
The Comanches, Lords of the South Plains
A Grammar of Comanche
Komantcia
Political Organizations and Law-Ways of the
   Comanche Indians
Quanah: A Pictorial History of the Last
   Comanche Chief

Sanapia: Comanche Medicine Woman
The Sound of Strings
Three Years Among the Comanhes
U.S.-Comanche Relations: The Reservation Years
Warlords of the West: A Story of the Comanche

COMMERCE

Adobe Walls: The History and Archaeology
   of the 1874 Trading Post
American Indian & Alaska Native Traders Directory
American Indian Policy in the Formative Years: The
   Indian Trade and Intercourse Acts, 1790-1834
Ancient Road Networks & Settlement Hierarchies
   in the New World
Stokes Carson: 20th Century Trading on the
   Navajo Reservation
The Character and Influence of the Indian Trade
   In Wisconsin: A Study of the Trading Post As
   an Institution
The Cheyenne in Plains Indian Trade Relations
Condition of the India Trade in North America, 1767:
   As Described in a Letter to Sir William Johnson
Crown and Calumet: British-Indian Relations,
   1783-1815
Early Indian Trade Guns: 1625-1775
*The Fur Trader and the Indian
Fur Trappers and Traders
Indian, Animals, and the Fur Trade: A Critique
   of Keepers of the Game
Indian Trade Goods
The Indian Traders
Indian Traders of the Southwestern Spanish Border
   Lands: Panton and Forbes Co. 1783-1847
Indian Traders on the Middle Border: The House
   of Ewing, 1827-1854
Introductory Guide to Entrepreneurship
   for American Indians
Metal Weapons, Tools and Ornaments
   of the Teton Dakota Indians
Navajo Trading Days
Pelts, Plumes and Hides: White Traders Among
   the Seminole Indians, 1870-1930
Rugs and Posts: The Story of Navajo
   Weaving & the Indian Trader
Shonto: Study of the Role of the Trader in a
   Modern Navajo Community
Smoke Signals: A Directory of American Indian &
   Alaska Native Businesses in Indian Country
The Southern Frontier, 1670-1732
The Trade Gun Sketchbook
Traders of the Western Morning: Aboriginal
   Commerce in Precolumbian North America
Wampum, War and Trade Goods West of the Hudson
The Wars of the Iroquois: A Study in Intertribal
   Trade Relations

CREE INDIANS

A Homeland for the Cree: Regional Development
   in James Bay, 1971-1981
Meet Cree: A Guide to the Cree Language
Notes on the Eastern Cree and Northern Salteaux
"The Orders of the Dreamed"
The Plains Cree
Plains Cree Texts
Sacred Stories of the Sweet Grass Cree

CREEK INDIANS

Africans and Creeks: From the Colonial
   Period to the Civil War

Camp, Clan and Kin, Among the Cow Creek
   Seminole of Florida
Ceremonial Songs of the Creek and Yuchi Indians:
   With Music Transcribed by Jacob D. Sapir
*The Creek
Creek Indian History: A Historical Narrative of the
   Genealogies, Traditions & Downfall of the
   Iscopoga or Creek Indian Tribe of Indians by
   One of the Tribe
Creek Indians of Taskigi Town
Creek (Muskogee) New Testament Concordance
A Creek Sourcebook
The Creek Verb
A Creek Warrior for the Confederacy: The
   Autobiography of Chief G.W. Grayson
Creeks and Seminoles: The Destruction &
   Regeneration of the Muscogulge People
Deerskins & Duffels: The Creek Indian Trade
   with Anglo-America, 1685-1815
Early History of the Creek Indians and Their Neighbors
Estiyut Omayat: Creek Writings
Handbook of Creek (Muscogee) Grammar
Handbook of the Creek Langauge
McIntosh and Weatherford, Creek Indian Leaders
Migration Legend of the Creek Indians
Myths and Folktales of the Alabama-Coushatta Indians
Nations Remembered: An Oral History of Cherokees,
   Chickasaws, Choctaws, Creeks, and Seminoles,
   1865-1907
The Politics of Indian Removal: Creek
   Government and Society in Crises
Red Eagle and the Wars With the
   Creek Indians of Alabama
The Road to Disappearance: A History
   of the Creek Indians
A Sketch of the Creek Country in the Years
   1798 & 1799
Social Organizations and Social Usages of the Indians
   of the Creek Confederacy
Woodward's Reminiscences of the Creek or Muscogee
   Indians: Alabama, Georgia and Mississippi

CROW INDIANS

*Absaloka: Crow Children's Writing
Absaraka: Home of the Crows
*Chief Plenty Coups: Life of the Crow Indian Chief
*The Crow
The Crow & the Eagle: A Tribal History
Crow Indian Art
Crow Indian Beadwork
Crow Indian Medicine Bundles
The Crow Indians
From the Heart of Crow Country
The Handsome People: A History of the
   Crow Indians and the Whites
*The Indian as a Soldier at Fort Custer, Montana,
   1890-1895
Life and Adventures of James P. Beckwourth
The Material Culture of the Crow Indians
Memoirs of a White Crow Indian
Myths & Traditions of the Crow
Notes on the Social Organization & Customs
   of the Mandan, Hidatsa, and Crow Indians
Of the Crow Nation
Plenty-Coups, Chief of the Crows
Pretty-Shield, Medicine Woman of the Crows
The Religion of the Crow Indians
The Shoshini-Crow Sun Dance
Social Life of the Crow Indians
The Sun Dance of the Crow Indians
The Tobacco Society of the Crow Indians
Two Crows Denies It: A History of Controversy in
   Omaha Sociology
Two Leggings: The Making of a Crow Warrior
The World of the Crow Indians: As Driftwood Lodges

CULTURAL ASSIMILATION & INTERACTION

Acculturation in Seven Indian Tribes
The American Indian in Film
American Indian Policy & American Reform:
  Case Studies of the Campaign to Assimilate
  the American Indians
American Indian Policy & Cultural Values:
  Conflict & Accommodation
American Indian Societies: Strategies & Conditions
  of Political & Cultural Survival
American Indian Stereotypes in the World of Children:
  A Reader & Bibliography
American Indian Stories
Being and Becoming Indian
Bullying the Moqui
Changing Culture of an Indian Tribe
The Cherokee Ghost Dance
Cherokees and Missionaries, 1789-1839
Conflict and Schism in Nez Perce Acculturation:
  A Study of Religion & Politics
Cultures in Contact: The European Impact on Native
Cultural Institutions in Eastern North America,
  1000-1800 A.D.
Dress Clothing of the Plains Indians
Early White Influence Upon Plains Indian Painting:
  George Catlin & Carl Bodmer Among the
  Mandan, 1832-1834
Farmers, Hunters & Colonists
A Final Promise: The Campaign to Assimilate the
  Indians, 1880-1920
The Hunt for Willie Boy: Indian-Hating &
  Popular Culture
Indian Culture and European Trade Goods: The
  Archaeology of the Historic Period in the Western
  Great Lakes Region
Indian Givers: How the Indians of the Americas
  Transformed the World
Indian Police and Judges: Experiments in
  Acculturation & Control
Indians Are Us?
The Indians in American Society
Indians in Prison
Mixed-Bloods and Tribal Dissolution: Charles Curtis
  & the Quest for Indian Identity
The Movement for Indian Assimilation, 1860-1890
Native Roots: How the Indians Enriched America
Navajo Infancy: An Ethological Study of Child
  Development
North American Indian Lives
The Northern Navajo Frontier, 1860-1900:
  Expansion Through Adversity
The Phoenix Indian School: Forced Assimilation
  in Arizona, 1891-1935
Rebellion From the Roots: Indian Uprising in Chiapas
The Round Valley Indians of California
Sovereignty and Symbol: Indian-White
  Conflict at Ganienkeh
Struggles for the Land
A Study in Culture Contact and Culture Change:
  The Whiterock Utes in Transition
The Vanishing American: White Attitudes
  and U.S. Indian Policy
Wasi'chu: The Continuing Indian Wars

CULTURE

Acculturation in Seven Indian Tribes
The Age of Manufactures, 1700-1820
Alaska in the Days That Were Before
All Roads Are Good: Native Voices on Life & Culture
America, Land of the Rising Sun
American Indians: The First of This Land
American Indians, Time, and the Law: Native Societies

in a Modern Constitutional Democracy
American Society for Promoting the Civilization &
  General Improvement for the Indian Tribes
  Within the U.S.
Ancestor's Footsteps
Ancient Drums, Other Moccasins: Native North
  American Cultural Adaptation
Angels to Wish By
Apachean Culture: History & Ethnology
Arizona Traveler: Indians of Arizona
Art and Environment in Native America
Basic Call to Consciousness
Between Indian & White Worlds: The Cultural Broker
Between Sacred Mountains: Navajo Stories &
  Lessons from the Land
Beyond the Vision: Essays on American Indian Culture
Bread & Freedom
Can the Red Man Help the White Man
Changing Culture of an Indian Tribe
Cherokee Dance and Drama
Coca-Cola Culture; Icons of Pop
The Covenent Chain: Indian Ceremonial
  and Trade Silver
Crossbloods: Bone Courts, Bingo, and Other Reports
Culture, Change & Leadership in a Modern Indian
Community: The Colorado River Indian
  Reservation
Cultures in Contact: The European Impact on Native
Cultural Institutions in Eastern North America
  1000-1800 A.D.
Cycles of Conquest: The Impact of Spain, Mexico
  & the U.S. on Indians of the Southwest, 1533-1960
Dancing With Creation
Deliberate Acts: Changing Hopi Culture
  Through the Oraibi Split
John Eliot's Indian Dialogues: A Study in
  Cultural Interaction
The Desert Smells Like Rain: A Naturalist in
  Papago Indian Country
Earthdivers: Tribal Narratives on Mixed Descent
Enduring Culture: A Century of Photography of
  the Southwest Indians
The Fighting Cheyennes
First Horses: Stories of the New West
The Fremont Culture: A Study in Culture Dynamics
  on the Northern Anasazi Frontier
The Gospel of the Redman
Handbook of the American Frontier - Four Centuries
  of Indian-White Relationships: The
  Southeastern Woodlands
Hidatsa Social & Ceremonial Organization
History, Evolution and the Concept of Culture:
  Selected Papers by Alexander Lesser
The Hoe and the Horse on the Plains
Hogans: Navajo Houses and House Songs
The Horse and Dog in Hidatsa Culture
The Horse in Blackfoot Indian Culture; With
  Comparative Material from Other Tribes
How Can One Sell the Air?
I Am Here: Two Thousand Years of
  Southwest Indian Culture
The Idea of Fertilization in the Culture
  of the Pueblo Indians
Indian Art and Culture
Indian Dances of North America: Their
  Importance to Indian Life
Indian Education & Civilization
Indian Games and Dances With Native Songs
Indian Givers: How the Indians of the Americas
Transformed the World
Indian Heritage, Indian Pride: Stories that
  Touched My Life
The Indian In His Wigwam: Or, Characteristics
  of the Red Race in America
Indian Life of the Yosemite Region: Miwok
  Material Culture
Indian Tribes of the Northern Rockies

Indians Are Us?
Iroquois Music and Dance: Ceremonial
  Arts of Two Seneca Longhouses
Kinaalada: A Navajo Puberty Ceremony
The Kiowas
Lame Deer: Seeker of Visions
Letters, Notes, on the Manners, Customs &
  Condition of the North American Indians
The Lillooet Indians
Making Two Worlds One and the Story of
  All-American Indian Days
Manifest Manners: PostIndian Warriors of Survivance
Mimbres Indian Treasure: In the Land of Baca
Miwok Material Culture
Moral Education Among the North American Indians
Music and Dance Research of the
  Southwestern Indians
Native American Discourse: Poetics & Rhetoric
Native American Heritage
Native Roots: How the Indians Enriched America
A Natural Education: Native American
  Ideas & Thoughts
Navaho Art & Culture
Navajo Art, History & Culture
The Navajos
Notebook on Art, History & Culture
Objects of Change: The Archaeology & History
  of Arikara Contact with Europeans
Of Mother Earth and Father Sky
Oklahoma Delaware Ceremonies, Feasts & Dances
Origin of Ancient American Cultures
Osage Life and Legends: Earth People - Sky People
Patterns of Culture
The People: Native American Thoughts & Feelings
The People of the Saints
Persistence in Pattern in Mississippi Choctaw Culture
*Pieces of White Shell: A Journey to Navajoland
The Pipe & Christ
The Powhattan Indians of Virginia: Their
  Traditional Culture
Preserving Traditional Arts: A Toolkit for Native
  American Communities
Puyallup-Nisqually
Ravensong
Red Men in Red Square
Rolling Thunder: A Personal Exploration Into the
  Secret Healing Power of an American Indian
  Medicine Man
The Romance of Indian Life
Sacred Ground
Seasons of the Kachina
Selu: Seeking the Corn-Mother's Wisdom
Shadows of the Indian: Stereotypes in
  American Culture
The Sioux of the Rosebud: A History in Pictures
Stories of Our Blackfeet Grandmothers
A Stranger In Her Native Land: Alice Fletcher
  & the American Indians
A Study in Culture Contact and Culture Change:
  The Whiterock Utes in Transition
The Sun Dance and Other Ceremonies of the
  Oglala Division of the Teton Dakota
Tales from the Mohaves
Teachings from the American Earth: Indian
  Religion and Philosophy
The Ten Grandmothers
To Sing Our Own Songs: Cognition &
  Culture in Indian Education
Touch the Earth: A Self-Portrait of Indian Existence
Tradition and Change on the Northwest Coast: The
  Makah, Nuu-chah-nulth, Southern Kwakiutl, & Nuxalk
Traditional Dress
The Transformation of Bigfoot: Maleness, Power
  & Belief Among the Chipewyan
The Vanishing American: The Epic of the Indian
The Vanishing Race: Selection From Edward S.
  Curtis' The North American Indian

The Voice In the Margin: Native American
Literature & the Canon
Without Discovery: A Native Response to Columbus
Wordarrows: Indians and Whites in the New Fur Trade

CURTIS, EDWARD S.

The North Ameriacn Indian
The North American Indians: Photographs
by Edward S. Curtis
The Vanishing Race and Other Illusions:
Photographs of Indians by Edward S. Curtis
The Vanishing Race: Selections from Edward
S. Curtis' The North American Indian

DANCE (See MUSIC & DANCE)

DELAWARE INDIANS

*The First Americans Coloring Book:
Lenape Indian Drawings
The Delawares: A Critical Bibliography
Folk Medicine of the Delaware and
Related Algonkian Indians
Grammar of the Language of the Lenni
Lenape or Delaware Indians
Geographia Americae With an Account
of the Delaware Indians
*The Indians of New Jersey: Dickon
Among the Lenapes
King of the Delawares: Teedyuscung, 1700-1763
The Lenape
Lenape History & Numbers Posters
The Lenape & Their Legends
Oklahoma Delaware Ceremonies, Feasts and Dances
*William Penn's Own Account of the Lenni Lenape
or Delaware Indians
Religion and Ceremonies of the Lenape
A Study of the Delaware Indian Big House Ceremony:
In Native Text Dictated by Witapanoxwe
A Study of Delaware Indian Medicine Practice
and Folk Beliefs
A Teacher's Guide to the Lenape

DIRECTORIES &
REFERENCE BOOKS

AIDS Regional Directory: Resources in Indian Country
The American Indian & Alaska Native Traders Directory
American Indian/Alaska Native Tribal & Village HIV-1
Policy Guidelines
American Indian Digest: Facts About Today's
American Indians
American Indian Education: Directory of Organizations
& Activities in American Indian Education
American Indian Encyclopedia CD-ROM
American Indian Index: A Directory of Indian Country
American Indian Literatures
American Indian Reference Books for Children
& Young Adults
American Indian Women
Atlas of American Indian Affairs
Atlas of the North American Indian
Bibliography of Native North Americans on
Disc - CD-ROM
*Children's Atlas of Native Americans
Church Philanthropy for Native Americans
& Other Minorities
The Corporate & Foundation Fundraising
Manual for Native Americans

Demographics of American Indians
Dictionary of the American Indian
Dictionary Catalog of the Edward E. Ayer Collection
Dictionary of Daily Life of Indian of the Americas
Dictionary of Indian Tribes of the Americas
Dictionary of Indians of North America
Dictionary of Native American Mythology
Dictionary of the Ojibway Language
Dictionary of the Osage Language
Dictionary of Papago Usage
Dictionary of Prehistoric Indian Artifacts of
the American Southwest
Digest of American Indian Law
Digest of Decisions Relating to Indian Affairs
Directory of American Indian Law Attorneys
Directory of Financial Aid to Minorities
Directory of Native American Performing Artists
Discover Indian Reservations USA - A Visitor's Guide
Education Assistance for American Indians
& Alaska Natives
Encyclopedia of Native American Tribes
Federal Programs of Assistance to Native Americans
First Americans Series
Guide to American Indian Documents
Guide to America's Indians
A Guide to the Anasazi & Other Ancient
Southwest Indians
Guide to Cherokee Documents in Foreign Archives
Guide to Cherokee Documents
Guide to Community Education
Guide to Federal Funding for Governments
& Nonprofits
Guide to Multicultural Resources, 1995-96
Guide to Research on North American Indians
& Others
Guide to Indian Artifacts of the Northeast
Guide to Indian Herbs
Guide to Indian TYreaties & Other Documents
1778-1902
Guide to Indian Tribes of Oklahoma
Guide to Indian Tribes of the Pacific Northwest
Guide to Palaeo-Indian Artifacts of North America
Guide to Prehistoric Ruins of the Southwest
Guide to Proposal Writing
Guide to the Records at the National Archives
Handbook of American Indian Games
Handbook of American Indian Languages
Handbook of American Indian Religious Freedom
Handbook of American Indians North of Mexico,
1907-1910
Handbook of Creek Grammar
Handbook of Federal Indian Law
Handbook of the Indians of California
Handbook of North American Indians
Handbook of Northeastern Indian Medicinal Plants
Handbook of Northern Arizona Pottery Wares
Handbook of Tribal Names of Pennsylvania
Historical Dictionary of North American Archaeology
Indian America: A Traveler's Companion
The Indian Question CD-ROM
Indian Reservations: A State & Federal Handbook
Indian Tribes of North America
Indians of Arizona: A Guide to Arizona's Heritage
National Directory of Minority-Owned Businesses
The National Directory of Philanthropy for
Native Americans
Nations Within a Nation
Native America
Native American Bibliography Series
Native American Biographies
Native American Checklist
Native American Directory
Native American Wisdom
Native American Women
Native Americans Information Directory
The Native North American Almanac
North American Indian Landmarks: A Traveler's Guide

North American Indian Travel Guide
North American Indian Wars - CD-ROM
North American Indians - CD-ROM
Notable Native Americans
Pacific Northwest Americana
Portrait of North American Indians in
Published Collections
Pow Wow Calendar
Pow-Wow On the Red Road
Raven's Guide to AIDS Prevention Resources
Resource Reading List
Sources of Financial Aid to American Indian Students
A Travelers Guide to Southwest Indian Arts & Crafts
Trends in Indian Health
Who Was Who in Native American History
Who's Who in Indian Relics

DRAMA

Arrow-Maker
Dramatic Elements in American
Indian Ceremonials
Native Americans as Shown on the Stage, 1753-1916
New Native American Drama: Three Plays
A Pillar of Fire To Follow: American Indian Dramas,
1808-1859

DWELLINGS

The Hidatsa Earthlodge
Indian Homes
The Indian Tipi: Its History, Construction, & Use
The Long House of the Iroquois
*Where Indians Live: American Indian Houses

EARTH ASTROLOGY

Earth Medicine: Ancestor's Way's of Harmony
for Many Moons
Medicine Wheel: Earth Astrology

ECONOMIC CONDITIONS

American Indian Ecology
American Indian Education: Government Schools
& Economic Progress
American Indian Energy Resources and Development
American Indians: Facts – Future Toward Economic
Development for Native American Communities
The Cherokee Strip Live Stock Association
A Community Guide to Money
Contemporary Alaskan Native Economies
Culture, Change and Leadership in a Modern Indian
Community: The Colorado River Indian
Reservation
The Development of Capitalism in the Navajo Nation:
Political-Economic History
Ecocide of Native America: Environmental
Destruction of Indian Lands & Peoples
Economic Development on American Indian
Reservations
Economics of the Iroquois
The Federal Buy Indian Program:
Federal Indian Tax Rules
If You Poison Us: Uranium & Native Americans
Income and Health in a North Indian Village
Indian Money as a Factor in New England Civilization
Navajo Energy Resources
Navajo Land Use: An Ethnoarchaeological Study
Navajo Resources and Economic Development
The New Resource Wars: Native and Environmental
Struggles Against Multinational Corporations

Notes on Hopi Economic Life
*Peril at Thunder Ridge
The Political Economy of North American Indians
Property Concepts of the Navaho Indians
The Re-Establishment of the Indians in Their
  Pueblo Life Through the Revival of Their Traditional
  Crafts: A Study in Home Extension Education
Red Capitalism: An Analysis of the Navajo Economy
The Roots of Dependency: Subsistence,
  Environment, & Social Change Among
  the Choctaws, Pawnees, & Navajos
The Roots of Oppression: The American
  Indian Question
San Diego County Indians As Farmers
  and Wage Earners
The Underground Reservation: Osage Oil
When Indians Became Cowboys

EDUCATION

*A,B,C's The American Indian Way
The American Indian and Alaska Native Higher
  Education Funding Guide
American Indian Education: Government Schools
  and Economic Progress
American Indian Issues in Higher Education
The American Indian Reader
The American Indian Reader: Education
American Indian Reference Books for Children
American Indian Stereotypes in the World of Children:
  A Reader and a Bibliography
Annals of Shawnee Methodist Mission and
  ndian Manual Labor
Bacone Indian University
Bilingual Education for American Indians
College Guide for American Indian Students
*Columbus Day
The Dove Always Cried: Narratives of Indian
  School Life
Effective Practices in Indian Education
The Elders Are Watching
Ethnic Identity and Boarding School Experience
  of West-Central Oklahoma American Indians
Formal Education in an American Indian Community
A Guide to Community Education
Guide to Proposal Writing
Hear the Creator's Song: A Guide to the Study
  Theme "Native Peoples of North America
History of Indian Arts Education in Santa Fe
A History of Indian Education
History & Present Development of Indian
  Schools in the U.S.
Indian America: A Traveler's Companion
Indian Education & Civilization
Indian Education - Elementary, Secondary & Guidance
Indian Education in America
Indian Education: Selected Statutes & Regulations
Indian Education in the American Colonies, 1607-1783
Indian School Days
Keepers of the Animals
Keepers of the Earth
Look To the Mountain: An Ecology of
  Indigenous Education
Maskiki: Old Medicine Nourishing the New
Moral Education Among the North American Indians
Multicultural Education and the American Indian
*Na Yo Pisa
Native American Reader: Stories, Speeches & Poems
*Native Americans: A Personal History Book
A Natural Education
Navajo Education in Action: The Rough Rock
  Demonstration School
Navajo Education, 1948-1978: Its Progress
  and Its Problems
The Navajos Long Walk for Education
No Turning Back: A Hopi Indian Woman's Struggle

to Live in Two Worlds
One House, One Voice, One Heart: Native American
  Education at the Santa Fe Indian School
Our Voices, Our Vision
A Parent's Guide to the BIA Special Education Process
The Phoenix Indian School: Forced Assimilation in
  Arizona, 1891-1935
Promises of the Past: A History of Indian Education
The Re-Establishment of the Indians in Their Pueblo
  Life Through the Revival of Their Traditional
  Crafts: A Study in Home Extension Education
Resource Reading List
Respect for Life: The Traditional Upbringing of
  American Indian Children
Science Activities for Teachers
Science of Alcohol Curriculum - Teacher Unit
Searching, Teaching, Healing: American Indian &
  Alaskan Natives in Biomedical Research Careers
Self-Determination & the Social Education of
  Native Americans
Six Nations Guides
Social Studies
Teaching American Indian Students
Teaching the Native American
They Called It Prairie Light: The Story of
  Chilocco Indian School
The Three Sisters; Exploring an Iroquois Garden
Three Strands in the Brand: A Guide for
  Enablers of Learning
Through Indian Eyes: The Native Experience
  in Books for Children
To Live on This Earth: American Indian Education
To Sing Our Own Songs: Cognition & Culture
  in Indian Education
Tribal Dispossession and the Ottawa Indian
  University Fraud
Tribally Controlled Colleges: Making Good Medicine
The Tribally Controlled Community Colleges
Unlearning "Indian" Stereotypes, A Teaching Unit for
  Elementary Teachers & Children's Librarians
The Wabanakis of Maine & the Maritmes
Writing to Create Ourselves

ETHICS

The Circle Without End: A Sourcebook of
  American Indian Ethics
I Have Come to Step Over Your Soul: A True
  Narrative of Murder & Indian Justice
Moral Education Among the North American Indians

FICTION

Almanac of the Dead
The American Indian in Short Fiction:
  An Annotated Bibliography
American Indian Life
Ancestral Voice
Apache Autumn
Bearheart: The Heirship Chronicles
The Bingo Palace
The Book of One Tree
Bone Game
Ceremony
Charlie Young Bear
Cogewea, The Half-Blood
Comanche Warbonnet
Critical Fictions: The Politics of Imaginative Writings
Daring Donald McKay: Or, The Last War
  Trial of the Modocs
Dawn Land
The Death of Bernadette Lefthand
The Death of Jim Lonely
Earth Power Coming: Short Fiction in

  Native American Literature
Elnguq
Faces in the Moon
Fathers & Crows
Fools Crow
Four Masterworks of American Indian Literature
The Fus Fixico Letters
House Made of Dawn
Hyemeyohsts Storm's "Seven Arrows" Fiction
  & Anthropology in the Native American Novel
The Indian Lawyer
Ishi Means Man
Laughing Boy
The Light People: A Novel
The Lightning Within
Malaeska
Man Who Killed the Deer
Medicine River
Mountain Windsong: A Novel of the Trail of Tears
One Indian and Two Chiefs
The Place in Flowers Where Pollen Rests
The Portable North American Indian Reader
The Powwow Highay
The Punishment of the Stingy
Ramona
Smith & Other Events: Tales of the Chilcotin
A Story of Deep Delight
Strange Business
The Trickster of Liberty
Waterlily
Winter in the Blood
Winter of the Holy Iron
The Wolf and the Buffalo
Woodsmen, or Thoreau & the Indians: A Novel
Woven Stone
The Yemassee

FICTION, JUVENILE

*The Chichi Hoohoo Bogeyman
*Chief Stephen's Parky
*First Came the Indians
*Flint's Rock
*Iroquois Stories: Heroes and
*Heetunka's Harvest" A Tale of the Plains Indians
*Heroines, Monsters and Magic
*John Hawk: A Seminole Saga
*Morning Girl
*Red Brother
*Remember My Name
*Sparrow Hawk
*Waterless Mountain
*When Thunder Spoke

FIVE CIVILIZED TRIBES

And Still the Waters Run: The Betrayal of the
  Five Civilized Tribes
Antiquities of the Southern Indians Particularly
  of the Georgia Tribes
The Chickasaws
Five Civilized Tribes
The Five Civilized Tribes: A Bibliography
Indian Removal: The Emigration of Five
  Civilized Tribes of Indians
Nations Remembered: An Oral History of the
  Five Civilized Tribes, 1865-1907
Notices of East Florida; With An Account of the
  Seminole Nation of Indians
Pow Wow Chow
Reconstruction in Indian Territory
The Southern Indians: The Story of the
  Civilized Tribes Before Removal

FOOD/COOKING

American Indian Cooking & Herblore
American Indian Food & Lore
The Buckskinner's Cookbook
Cherokee Cooklore
Cherokee Plants
Cooking With Spirit
Corn Is Maize - The Gift of the Indians
Corn Recipes from the Indians
Ethno-Botany of the Gosiute Indians of Utah
Food from Dryland Gardens
Guide to Indian Herbs
Handbook of Native American Herbs
Hopi Cookery
How Indians Use Wild Plants for Food,
  Medicine & Crafts
Indian Cooking
Indian Corn of the Americas, Gift to the World
Indian Recipe Book
Indian Foods and Fibers of Arid America
Indian Uses of Native Plants
Insects As Food: Aboriginal Entomophogy in
  the Great Basin
Mechanisms & Trends in the Decline of the Costanoan
  Indian Population of Central California:
  Nutrition & Health i Pre-Contact California &
  Mission Period Environments
Native Harvests: Recipes & Botanicals of the
  American Indian
Native Wild Game: Fish & Wild Foods Cookbook
Pow Wow Chow
Southwest Cooks! The Tradition of Native
  American Cuisines
Southwest Indian Cookbook
Southwestern Indian Recipe Book
Spirit of the Harvest: North American Indian Cooking
Zuni Breadstuff

FRENCH & INDIAN WAR
1755-1763

America's First First World War:
  The French & Indian War, 1754-1763
*The American Revolutionaries: A History in
  Their Own Words
Empire and Liberty: American Reistance to
  British Authority, 1755-1763
Empire of Fortune: Crowns, Colonies, & Tribes
  in the Seven Years War in America
*Fawn
*The Fight for Freedom, 1750-1783
Fight With France for North America
General Orders of 1757, Issued by the Earl of
  Loudoun and Phineas Lyman in the Campaign
  Against the French
An Historical Journal of the Campaigns in
  North America for the Years 1757-1760
The History of the Indian Wars in New England
The History of Philip's War
How George Rogers Clark Won the Northwest
  & Other Essays in Western History
*The Indian Wars
Jeferson's America: 1760-1815
*The Last of the Mohicans
Logs of the Conquest of Canada
Major General Adam Stephen and the Cause
  of American Liberty
Manuscript Records of the French & Indian War
Maryland's Attitude in the Struggle for Canada
Massachusetts Officers & Soldiers in the French
  & Indian Wars, 1755-56
Massacre at Fort Bull: The Delery Expedition
  Against Oneida Carry, 1756
Memoirs of Lt. Henry Timberlake

Military Affairs in North America, 1748-1765
Military Journals of Two Private Soldiers, 1758-1775
Montcalm and Wolfe
Narrative of the Captivity of Mrs Johnson
New England Captives Carried to Canada
Ohio Valley in Colonial Days
A Particular History of the Five Years
  French & Indians Wars in New England
A People's Army: Massachusetts Soldiers
  and Society in the Seven Year's War
Pioneers of New France in New England
Shipping and the American War, 1755-1783:
  A Study of British Transport Organization
Slim Buttes, 1876: An Episode of the Great Sioux War
*Struggle for a Continent: The French & Indian Wars,
  1690-1760
Struggle for Empire: A Bibliography of the
  French and Indian Wars
True Stories of New England Captives Carried to
  Canada During the Old French & Indian Wars
Wilderness Empire
Wilderness Politics and Indian Gifts: The Northern
  Colonial Frontier, 1748-1763
Writings of General John Forbes Relating to His
  Service in North America

GAMES

American Indian LaCrosse
Exploring the Outdoors With Indian Secrets
Games of the North American Indians
Handbook of American Indian Games
*Indian Games and Crafts
Indian Games and Dances With Native Songs
The Pawnee Ghost Dance Hand Game:
  Ghost Dance Revival and Ethnic Identity
*Sports and Games the Indians Gave Us
Twana Games

GENEALOGY

How to Research American Indian Blood Lines

GERONIMO

Bloody Trail of Geronimo
Geronimo Campaign
Geronimo: The Man, His Time, His Place
I Fought With Geronimo
Indians of America: Geronimo
The Story of Geronimo
The Truth About Geronimo

GHOST DANCE

The American Indian Ghost Dance, 1870 & 1890:
  An Annotated Bibliography
The Cherokee Ghost Dance
Ghost Dance
Ghost Dance Messiah: The Jack Wilson Story
Ghost-Dance Religion and the Sioux Outbreak of 1890
Ghost Dancers in the West: The Sioux at Pine
  Ridge and Wounded Knee in 1891
Last Days of the Sioux Nation
The Maru Cult of the Pomo Indians:
  A California Ghost Dance Survival
The Pawnee Ghost Dance Hand Game:
  Ghost Dance Revival and Ethnic Identity
The Prophet Dance of the Northwest and Its
  Derivatives: The Source of the Ghost Dance
Wovoka and the Ghost Dance: A Source Book

GOVERNMENT RELATIONS

Agents of Repression: The FBIs Secret Wars
  Against the Black Panther Party & the American
  Indian Movement
Airlift to Wounded Knee
American Indian Holocaust and Survival:
  A Population History Since 1492
American Indian in the U.S., Period 1850-1914
American Indian Policy and American Reform
Amerian Indian Policy and Cultural Values
American Indian Policy in the Formative Years:
  The Indian Trade and Intercourse Acts, 1790-1834
The American Indian Reader: Current Affairs
American Indian Societies
American Indian Treaties: The History of a
  Political Anomaly
American Indian Tribal Governments
American Indian and the U.S.
American Indians and the Law
American Indians: Facts–Future Toward Economic
  Development for Native American Communities
American Protestantism and U.S. Indian Policy,
  1869-1882
Americanizing the American Indians: Writings
  by the Friends of the Indian, 1880-1900
And Still the Waters Run
Apache Agent: The Story of John P. Clum
Appalachian Indian Frontier: The Edmond Atkin
  Report and Plan of 1755
The Army and the Navajo: The Bosque Redondo
  Reservation Experiment, 1863-1868
Art and Eskimo Power: The Life & Times of
  Alaskan Howard Rock
As Long As the River Shall Run
The Assault of Indian Tribalism: The General
  Allotment Law (Dawes Act) of 1887
Battle Canyon
Behind the Trail of Broken Treaties
A Bibliographical Guide to the History of
  Indian-White Relations in the U.S.
Bibliography of the English Colonial Treaties
  With the American Indians
Black Hills, White Justice: The Sioux Nation
  Vs. the U.S., 1775 to the Present
The Blackfoot Confederacy, 1880-1920:
  A Comparative Study of Canada & U.S. Indian Policy
Border Towns of the Navajo Nation
Bread & Freedom
A Century of Dishonor: A Sketch of the U.S.
  Government's Dealing with Some of the Indian Tribes
Champions of the Cherokees: Evan & John B. Jones
The Cherokee Ghost Dance
The Cheyenne and Arapaho Ordeal:
  Reservation & Agency Life
Chippewa Treaty Rights
Claims for Depredations by Sioux Indians
William Clark: Jeffersonian Man on the Frontier
John Collier's Crusade for Indian Reform, 1920-1954
Command of the Waters: Iron Triangles, Federal
  Water Development, & Indian Water
The Commissioners of Indian Affairs, 1824-1977
The Condition of Affairs in Indian Territory
  and California
The Conflict Between the California Indian
  & White Civilization
Considerations on the Present State of the Indians
  and Their Removal to the West of the
  Mississippi
Crazy Horse & Custer
Crosscurrents Along the Colorado
Crown & Calumet: British-Indian Relations,
  1783-1815
Custer Died for Your Sins: An Indian Manifesto
Dammed Indians: The Pick-Sloan Plan and the
  Missouri River Sioux, 1944-1980

Depredations by Sioux Indians
Digest of Decisions Relating to Indian Affairs
Diplomates in Buckskins: A History of Indian
   Delegations in Washington City
Dispossessing the American Indian: Indian
   & Whites on the Colonial Frontier
The Dispossession of the American Indian, 1887-1934
Documents of U.S. Indian Policy
The Dynamics of Government Programs for
   Urban Indians in the Prairie Provinces
Early American Indian Documents, Treaties and
   Laws, 1607-1789 Volume 11: Georgia Treatise,
   1733-1763
The Embattled Northeast: The Elusive Ideal of
   Alliance in Abenaki-Euro-american Relations
The Emigrant Indians of Kansas: Critical Bibliography
The End of Indian Kansas: A Study of Cultural
   Revolution, 1854-1871
Executive Orders Relating to Indian Reservations
Federal Concern About Conditions of California
   Indians, 1853-1913
Federal Indian Law Cases and Materials
Federal Indian Relations, 1774-1788
The First Social Experiments in America
The Florida Seminole and the New Deal, 1933-1942
Formulating American Indian Policy in New York
   State, 1970-1986
The Great Father: The U.S. Government and
   the American Indian
Guide to American Indian Documents in the
   Congressional Serial Set: 1817-1899
Guide to Understanding Chippewa Treaty Rights
Handbook of Federal Indian Law
A History of the Bureau of Indian Affairs and Its
   Activities Among Indians
History of Events Resulting in Indian Consolidation
   West of the Mississippi
Index to the Decisions of the Indian Claims
   Commission
Index to the Expert Testimony Presented Before
   the Indian Claims Commission
Indian Affairs: Laws and Treaties
Indian Affairs and Their Administration, With
   Special Reference to the Far West
Indian Agents of the Old Frontier
Indian and His Problem
The Indian in American Life
Indian Policy in U.S. Historical Essays
Indian Slave Trade in the Southwest
Indian Treaties, 1778-1883
Indian Voices: The Native American Today
Indian-White Relations: A Persistent Paradox
Indian-White Relationships in Northern California,
   1849-1920
Indians and Bureaucrats
The Indians' Land Title in California: A Case In
   Federal Equity, 1851-1942
Indians of the Americas: Self-Determination
   and International Human Rights
Indians and the U.S. Government
The Invasion of America
The Invested Indian: Cultural Fictions &
   Government Policies
An Inventory of the Mission Indian Agency Records
An Inventory of the Pala Indian Agency Records
An Iron Hand Upon the People
The Iroquois and the New Deal
Irredeemable America: The Indians' Estate
   & Land Claims
Kinsmen of Another Kind: Dakota-White Relations
   in the Upper Mississippi Valley, 1650-1862
Land of the Spotted Eagle
Last Days of the Sioux Nation
License for Empire: Colonialism by Treaty in
   Early America
Life Among the Paiutes: Their Wrongs and Claims
Lincoln and the Indians: Civil War Policy and Politics

List of Documents Concerning the Negotiation of
   Ratified Indian Treaties: 1801-1869
Lost Harvests: Prairie Indian Reserve Farmers
   & Government Policy
Loud Hawk: The U.S. Versus the American
   Indian Movement
Massacre: A Survey of Today's American Indian
Menominee Drums: Tribal Termination and
   Restoration, 1954-1974
The Military and the U.S. Indian Policy, 1865-1903
Mixed-Bloods and Tribal Dssolution: Charles Curtis
   & the Quest for Indian Identity
My Friend the Indian
My Nation: The American Indian & the U.S., 1820-1890
The Myth of the Savage: and the Beginnings of
   French Colonialism in the Americas
Nairne's Muskhogean Journals: The 1708
   Expedition to the Mississippi River
Nation-States & Indians in Latin America
The Nations Within: The Past and Future of
   American Indian Sovereignty
*Native American Testimony: An Anthology of Indian
   & White Relations, First Encounter to Dispossession
Native American Tribalism: Indian Survivals
   and Renewals
Native Americans: The New Indian Resistance
Native Americans and Nixon: Presidential Politics
   and Minority Self-Determination
Native Americans & Public Policy
Native People in Canada: Contemporary Conflicts
The New American State Papers: Indian Affairs,
   1789-1860
The New Deal and American Indian Tribalism
New Directions in Federal Indian Policy
New Hope for the Indians: The Grant Peace
   Policy & the Navajos in the 1870s
Occupation of Wounded Knee
Office of Indian Affairs, 1824-1880: Historical Sketches
Office of Indian Affairs: Its History, Activities
   and Organizations
Other Men's Skies
Our Indian Wards
Our Red Brothers and the Peace Policy of
   President Ulysses S. Grant
Pathways to Self-Determination: Canadian
   Indians and the Canadian State
The Pawnee Ghost Dance Hand Game
Pennsylvania's Indian Relations to 1754
The Political Outsiders: Blacks and Indians
   in a Rural Oklahoma County
The Politics of Indian Removal: Creek
   Government and Society in Crisis
Proceedings of the Commissioners of Indian Affairs
The Protector de Indios in Colonial New Mexico,
   1659-1821
Quarter-Acre of Heartache
Vasco de Quiroga and His Pueblo-Hospitals
   of Santa Fe
Race Relations in British North America, 1670-1783
The Rape of the Indian Lands: An Original Anthology
Readjustment of Indian Affairs: Hearings
Red Cloud and the Sioux Problem
The Red King's Rebellion: Racial Politics in
   New England, 1675-78
Red Man's Land/White Man's Law
Red Power: The American Indians' Fight for Freedom
Red and White: Indian Views of the White Man,
   1492-1982
Report of the Commissioner of Indian Affairs,
   Reports for the Years, 1824-1899
Report to the Secretary of War of the U.S.,
   On Indian Affairs
Reservation to City: Indian Urbanization
   and Federal Relocation
The Return of the Native: American Indian
   Political Resurgence
Rise and Fall of the Choctaw Republic

The Road: Indian Tribes & Political Liberty
Sadie Brower Neakok, an Inupiaq Woman
Seeds of Extinction: Jeffersonian Philanthropy
   and the American Indian
The Search for an American Indian Identity:
   Modern Pan-American Movements
Self and Savagery on the California Frontier
Self-Determination & the Social Education of
   Native Americans
Self-Reliance vs. Power Politics: American &
   Indian Experiences in Building Nation-States
Sixty Years of Indian Affairs;Political, Economic
   and Diplomatic
Some Newspaper References Concerning Indian-
   White Relationships in Northeastern California,
   1850-1920
Speeches on the Passage of the Bill for the
   Removal of the Indians
State Tribal Relations; Into the 21st Century
State-Tribal Relationships-Reports
John Stuart and the Southern Colonial Frontier
Termination and Relocation: Federal Indian
   Policy, 1945-1960
They Have No Rights
To Have This Land: The Nature of Indian/White
   Relations in South Dakota, 1888-1891
To Preserve a Culture: The 20th Century
   Fight Over Indian Reorganization
The Trail of Tears
Tribal Assets: The Rebirth of Native America
*Tribal Sovereignty: Indian Tribes
Two Worlds: The Indian Encounter with the
   European, 1492-1509
Uncle Sam's Stepchildren: The Reformation of U.S.
   Indian Policy, 1865-1887
U.S.-Comache Relations: The Reservation Years
The View from Officers' Row: Army Perceptions
   of Western Indians
Voices from Wounded Knee, 1973, In the
   Words of the Participants
Wampum Belts & Peace Trees
Western American Indian: Case Studies
   in Tribal History
The Western Military Frontier, 1815-1846
A Whirlwind Passes
Who Was Who in Native American History
Wilderness Politics and Indian Gifts: The Northern
   Colonial Frontier, 1748-1763

HAIDA INDIANS

During My Time: Florence Edenshaw Davidson,
   A Haida Woman
Gyaehlingaay: Traditions, Tales, & Images
   of the Kaigani Haida
Haida Potlatch
Haida Songs and Tsimshian Texts
Haida Texts & Myths
Haida: Their Art & Culture
He Who Hunted Birds in His Father's Village:
   The Dimensions of a Haida Myth
Raven's Cry
The Raven Steels the Light
The Relationship Systems of the Tlingit,
   Haida and Tsimshian

HAVASUPAI INDIANS

Grand Canyon: Intimate Views
Havasupai Ethnography
Havasupai Habitat
Havasupai Legends
Havasupai Religion and Mythology
The Havasupai Woman

Havasupai Years
Havsuw Baaja: People of Blue Green Water
Wauba Yuma's People
The Wilderness of the Southwest

HAWAIIANS

Ancient Sites of O'ahu
Arts & Crafts of Hawaii
Bishop Museum & the Changing World of Hawai'i
Discovery: The Hawaiian Odyssey
Fragments of Hawaiian History
Hawaii: The Olaha State
Hawaii: Our Island State
Hawaii Pono: An Ethnic & Political History
Hawaii's Royal History
Hawaiian Antiquities
Hawaiian Cordage
Hawaiian Medicine Book
Hawaiian Name Book
Hawaiian Petroglyphs
Hawaiian Sentence Book
Hawaiian Word Book
The Hawaiians of Old
Heiau of the Island Hawai'i
Hula Pahu: Hawaiian Drum Dances
Ka Po'e Kahiko
Kalaupapa: A Portrait
La'au Hawai'i: Traditional Hawaiian Uses of Plants
Learn Hawaiian at Home
Maui: The Mischief Maker
Modern Hawaiian History
Native Land & Foreign Desires
Native Planters in Old Hawaii
Olelo No'eau
Pai Ka Leo
Pele: The Fire Goddess
Reconciling the Past
Sites of O'ahu
Strains of Change
Tales & Traditions of the People of OldThe
  Works of the People of Old
Voices in the Wind: Polynesian Myths & Chants

HEALTH & MEDICINE

AIDS Regional Directory: Resources in Indian Country
American Indian Medicine
Bibliography of North American Indian Mental Health
Community Health and Mental Health Care
  Delivery for North American Indians
Crow Indian Medicine Bundles
Diagnosis and Treatment of Prevalent Diseases of
  North American Indian Populations, I and II
Doctors of Medicine in New Mexico: A History of
  Health & Medical Practice, 1886-1986
Early Intervention with American Indian Families:
  An Annotated Bibliography
Encyclopaedia of Indian Medicine, Vols. 1, 2 & 3
Folk Medicine of the Delaware and Related
  Algonkian Indians
Geraniums for the Iroquois: A Field Guide to
  American Indian Medicinal Plants
The Growing Path
Guide to Indian Herbs
Health and Diseases of American Indians North
  of Mexico: A Bibliography, 1800-1969
HIV Prevention in Native American Communities:
  A Manual
Income and Health in a North Indian Village
Indian Drinking: Navajo Practices and
  Anglo-American Theories
Indian Healing
Indian Medicine Power

Introduction to Navaho Chant Practice
Lakota Belief and Ritual
Medicinal Uses of Plants by Indian Tribes of Nevada
Medicine Among the American Indians
The Medicine Man of the American Indian and His
  Cultural Background
Native American AIDS Statistics
Navaho Classification of Their Song Ceremonials
Navajo Dictionary on Diagnostic Terminology
Navajo Indian Medical Ethnobotany
Navajo Medicine Man Sand Paintings
Notes on the Gynecology and Obstetrics of the
  Arikara Tribe of Indians
Perspectives on Health Care Delivery Systems
  for American Indian Families
Piman Shamanism and Staying Sickness:
  Ka: Cim Mumkidag
Plants Used as Curatives by Certain
  Southeastern Tribes
Pretty-Shield, Medicine Woman of the Crows
Profiles in Wisdom: Native Elders Speak
  About the Earth
Rolling Thunder: A personal Exploration Into the
  Secret Healing Power of an American Indian
  Medicine Man
Sanapia: Comanche Medicine Woman
Searching, Teaching, Healing: American Indians &
  Alaskan Natives in Biomedical Research Careers
The Shaman and the Medicine Wheel
Smallpox and the Iroquois Wars
A Study of Delaware Indian Medicine
  Practice and Folk Beliefs
Survival Skills of the North American Indians
Tuberculosis Among Certain Indian Tribes of the U.S.
Vectors of Death: The Archaeology of European
  Contact

HISTORY

Adventures on the Western Frontier
After Removal: The Choctaw in Mississippi
All Roads Are Good: Native Voices on Life & Culture
America On Paper, The First Hundred Years
America's Fascinating Indian Heritage
The American Buffalo in Transition
The American Indian
The American Indian, 1492-1976:
  A Chronology & Fact Book
The American Indian Experience:
  A Profile, 1524 to the Present
American Indian Holocaust & Survival
The American Indian: Past & Present
American Indian Policy
American Indian Policy in the 20th Century
The American Indian: Prehistory to the Present
The American Indian Reader
American Indian Resource Materials in
  the Western History Collection
American Indian Treaties: The History of a
  Political Anomaly
The American Indian Under Reconstruction
American Indian and the U.S.
American Indian Warrior Chiefs
American Indians
*The American Indians
*The American Indians in America--Volume II:
  The Late 18th Century to the Present
American Indians & World War II
The American Revolution in Indian Country
The American West
Among the Apaches
Ancient North Americans
The Appalachian Indian Frontier
As Long As the River Shall Run: An Ethnohistory
  of Pyramid Lake Indian Reservation
Atlas of American Indian Affairs

Atlas of Great Lakes Indian History
Attitudes of Colonial Powers Toward American Indian
Bacavi: A Hopi Village
Bad Men & Bad Towns
Battlefield and Classroom: Four Decades
  With the American Indian, 1867-1904
Bear Chief's War Shirt
*Between Sacred Mountains: Navajo Stories
  and Lessons from the Land
Beyond the Covenant Chain
Beyond the Hundredth Meridian
Bibliography of the English Colonial Treaties
  with the American Indians
The Birth of America
Black Africans and Native Americans
Black, Brown & Red
Black, Red and Deadly: Black and Indian
  Gunfighters of the Indian Territories
Blood At Sand Creek: The Massacre Revisited
Blood of the Land: The Government and Corporate
  War Against the American Indian Movement
Bread & Freedom
A Brief History of the Indian Peoples
The Broken Ring: The Destruction of the
  California Indians
Buffalo Hearts
Bury My Heart at Wounded Knee: An Indian
  History of the American West
Celebrate Native America! An Aztec Book of Days
Chainbreaker: The Revolutionary War Memoirs
  of Governor Blacksnake
Cherokee Americans Eastern Band of Cherokees
  in the 20th Century
The Cherokee Freedmen: From Emancipation
  to American Citizenship
The Cherokee Indian Nation: A Troubled History
Cherokee Removal: The William Penn Essays
  and Other Writings by Jeremiah Evarts
The Cherokees in Pre-Columbian Times
Cherokees in Transition: A Study of Changing
  Culture and Environment Prior to 1775
The Chicago American Indian Community, 1893-1988
Chiefs and Challengers
Chinigchinich
The Chippewa and Their Neighbors:
  A Study in Ethnohistory
Christian Harvest
Chronology of the American Indian
The Conquest of Paradise
Contest for Empire, 1500-1775
A Country Between: The Upper Ohio Valley and
  Its People, 1724-1774
Cowboys and Indians: An Illustrated History
Creation's Journey: Native American Identity & Belief
Cry of the Thunderbird: The American Indian's
  Own Story
Custer's Fall
The Dakota or Sioux in Minnesota
*Dakota and Ojibwe People in Minnesota
Dangerous Passage: The Santa Fe Trail
  & the Mexican War
The Desert Lake: The Story of Nevada's Pyramid Lake
The Diary of Eli Sheldon Glover
Dictionary of Daily Life of Indians of the Americas
Dictionary of Indian Tribes of the Americas
Dinetah: Navajo History
The Dispossession of the American Indian, 1887-1934
Dreamers With Power: The Menominee
The Dust Rose Like Smoke
Early Encounters--Native Americans & Europeans
  in New England
Early History of the Creek Indians & Their Neighbors
Encyclopedia of Multiculturalism
The End of Indian Kansas: A Study of Cultural
  Revolution, 1854-1871
The Enduring Indians of Kansas
The Enduring Struggle

Tenting on the Plains
Texas Cherokees: A People Between Fires, 1819-1840
Textbooks and the American Indian
They Walked Before: The Indians of Washington State
This Fool History: An Oral History of Dakota Territory
The Trail of Tears
The Vanishing American: White Attitudes
  & U.S. Indian Policy
*The Very First Americans
Victorio and the Mimbres Apaches
The View from Officer's Row: Army Perceptions
  of Western Indians
Violence, Resistance, & Survival in the Americas
*Vostaas: The Story of Montana's Indian Nations
Waking a Sleeping Giant
War-Path and Bivouac: Or, The Conquest of the Sioux
The Way to Independence
The Ways of My Grandmothers
The West: A Treasury of Art & Literature
*West of Yesterday
The White Earth Tragedy
White Indians of Colonial America
The Wilderness Trail
The Winding Trail: The Alabama-Coushatta Indians
The Wisdom of the Great Chiefs
Wo'Wakita: Reservation Recollections
The World Turned Upside Down:
  Indian Voices from Early America
Wounded Knee: An Indian History of the
  American West
Wounded Knee; Lest We Forget
Wounded Knee: The Meaning & Significance
  of the Second Incident
David Zeisberger's History of North American Indians
A Zuni Atlas

HISTORY, SOURCES

American Indian & Alaska Native Newspapers
  & Periodicals, 1925-1970
American Indian Environments
Appalachian Indian Frontier: The Edmond Atkin
  Report and Plan of 1755
*Chief Joseph's Own Story As Told
  By Chief Joseph in 1879
*Chief Red Horse Tells About Custer
The Diario of Christopher Columbus' Forst Voyage
  to America, 1492-1493
Discovery of the Yosemite & the Indian War of 1851
  Which Led to the Event
John Eliot's Indian Dialogues: A Study in
  Cultural Interaction
From the Deep Woods to Civilization: Chapters
  in the Autobiography of an Indian
A Guide to Cherokee Documents in the
  Northeastern U.S.
Hampton Institute School Records 1878-1891
How Can One Sell the Air?
Indian Oratory: Famous Speeches by
  Noted Indian Chieftains
An Inventory of the Mission Indians Agency Records
John Beeson's Plea for the Indians
Library of Aboriginal American Literature
The Life of Blackhawk Dictated by Himself
Life, Letters & Travels of Father Pierre
  Jean de Smet, S.J., 1801-1873
Life & Times of David Zeisberger
Narrative of Occurences in the Indian Countries
  of North America
*Native American Testimony: An Anthology
  of Indian and White Relations
A Naturalist in Indian Territory
The Oregon & California Trail: The Diary of
  Jane Gould in 1862
A Plea for the Indians

Red and White: Indian Views of the
  White Man, 1492-1982
The Secret Saga of Five-Sack
A Short Account of the Destruction of the Indies
The Sun Came Down: The History of the
  World as My Blackfeet Elders Told It
The Wisdom of the Great Chiefs
Writings of Gen. John Forbes Relating
  to His Service in North America

HOPEWELL CULTURE

The Hopewell Mound Group of Ohio
Hopewell Village
Hopewellian Studies
The Moundbuilders
The Pool and Irving Villages

HOPI INDIANS

Book of the Hopi
Born A Chief
Broken Pattern - Sunlight & Shadows of Hopi History
Bullying the Moqui
The Changing Pattern of Hopi Agriculture
Changing Physical Environment of the Hopi
  Indians of Arizona
Children of Cottonwood: Piety & Ceremonialism
  in Hopi Indian Puppetry
Clowns of the Hopi: Tradition Keepers
  & Delight Makers
A Concise Hopi and English Lexicon
Continuities of Hopi Culture Change
Council of the Rainmakers Address Book
The Day of the Ogre Kachinas: A Hopi Indian Fable
Deliberate Acts: Changing Hopi Culture Through
  the Oraibi Split
Designs on Prehistoric Hopi Pottery
Drifting Through Ancestor Dreams
Earth Fire: A Hopi Legend of the Sunset Crater
  Eruption
Ethnobotany of the Hopi
The Fourth World of the Hopis
Historic Hopi Ceramics
Homol'ovi II
Hopi
*The Hopi
The Hopi Approach to the Art of Kachina Doll Carving
Hopi Bibliography
The Hopi Child
Hopi Cookery
Hopi Coyote Tales: Istutuwutsi
Hopi Dictionary: Hopi-English, English-Hopi,
  Grammatical Appendix
Hopi & Hopi-Tewa Pottery
Hopi Indian Altar Iconography
Hopi Journals
Hopi Kachina Dolls and Their Carvers
Hopi Kachina Dolls With a Key to Their Identification
Hopi Kachinas
Hopi Kachinas: The Complete Guide to
  Collecting Kachina Dolls
Hopi Katchinas Drawn by Native Artists
Hopi Kachinas: A Postcard Collection
Hopi Katchinas
Hopi Music & Dance
*Hopi Mysteries
Hopi of the Second Mesa
Hopi Photographers - Hopi Images
The Hopi Photographs: Kate Cory, 1905-1912
Hopi Pottery Symbols
Hopi Ruin Legends
Hopi Shields and the Best Defense

Hopi Silver: The History and Hallmarks of
  Hopi Silversmithing
Hopi Snake Dance Cermonies, an Eyewitness Account
A Hopi Social History
The Hopi: Their History & Use of Lands in
  New Mexico & Arizona, 1200's to 1900's
Hopi Songs
The Hopi Villages
Hopi Voices & Visions
The Hopi Way: Tales From a Changing Culture
Hopi and Zuni Ceremonialism
Hopis, Tewas, and the American Road
Introduction to Hopi Pottery Lessons in Hopi
Kachina Tales From the Indian Pueblos
Language, History, & Identity
Maasaw: Profile of a Hopi God
Ray Manley's Hopi Kachina
Me & Mine: The Life Story of Helen Sekaquaptewa
Meditiations With the Hopi
Moki Snake Dance
No Turning Back: A Hopi Indian Woman's
  Struggle to Live in Two Worlds
Notes on Hopi Economic Life
Old Oraibi
Oraibu Maru Ceremony
Pages From Hopi History
Prehistoric Hopi Pottery Designs
Pumpkin Seed Point: Being Within the Hopi
Religion & Hopi Life in the 20th Century
Ritual in Pueblo Art: Hopi Life in Hopi Painting
The Snake Dance of the Hopi Indians
Spider Woman Stories
Stories of Maasaw, a Hopi God
Sun Chief: The Autobiography of a Hopi Indian
The Traditions of the Hopi
Truth of a Hopi
The Unwritten Literature on the Hopi
The Year of the Hopi

HUALAPAI INDIANS

Camp Beale's Springs and the Hualapai Indians

HUNTING & FISHING

The Agricultural & Hunting Methods of the
  Navaho Indians
Archaic Hunters & Gatherers in the American Midwest
Bringing Home Animals: Religious Ideology & Mode
  of Production of the Mistassini Cree Hunters
Disputed Waters: Native Americans & the
  Great Lakes Fishery
Don't Blame the Indians: Native Americans & the
  Mechanized Destruction of Fish & Wildlife
Fish Decoys of the Lac du Flambeau Ojibway
*Fur Trappers & Traders: The Indians, The Pilgrims,
  and the Beaver
Hidatsa Eagle Trapping
The Horse in Blackfoot Indian Culture
*The Hunt
Hunters of the Buffalo
Hunters of the Eastern Forest
Hunters of the Ice
Hunters of the Northern Forest
Hunters of the Recent Past
Hunters of the Sea
Indian Fishing: Early Methods of the Northwest Coast
Indian Hunts and Indian Hunters of the Old West
Mountain in the Clouds: A Search for the Wild Salmon
Snares, Deadfalls and Other Traps of the Northern
  Algonquian and Northern Athapaskans
Survival Skills of North American Indians
Treaties on Trial: The Continuing Controversy
  Over Northwest Indian Fishing Rights

*The Winter Hunt

IMPLEMENTS

Aboriginal Chipped Stone Implements of New York
Collecting Indian Knives
Florida's Prehistoric Stone Technology
Horn and Bone Implements of the New York Indians
Indian Rawhide: An American Folk Art
Metal Weapons, Tools and Ornaments
  of the Teton Dakota Indians
Minnesota's Browns Valley Man and
  Associated Burial Artifacts
North American Indian Points
Prehistoric Stone Implements of Northeastern Arizona

INDIANS OF CALIFORNIA

Aboriginal Society in Southern California
Alaawich
Alcatraz! Alcatraz!: The Indian Occupation
  of 1969-1971
An-Nik-a-Del: The History of the Universe As Told
  by the Modes-Se Indians of California
Ancient Modocs of California & Oregon
Ararapikva: Traditional Karuk Indian Literature
  from Northwestern California
Archives of California Prehistory
Before the Wilderness: Environmental Management
  by Native Californians
Bibliography of the Languages of Native California
The Broken Ring: The Destruction of the
  California Indians
Cahuilla Dictionary
Cahuilla Grammar
The Cahuilla Indians
The Cahuilla Indians of Southern California
The Cahuilla Landscape: The Santa Rosa
  & San Jacinto Mountains
California
California Archaeology
California Indian Nights Entertainment
California Indian Shamanism
California Indian Watercraft
*California Indians: An Educational Coloring Book
*California Indians, An Illustrated Guide
California Indians: Primary Resources
The California Indians: A Source Book
*The California Native American Tribes
California Special Indian Census 1910
*California's Chumash Indians
California's Gabrielino Indians
California Indian Country: The Land & the People
A Case Study of a Northern California Indian Tribe:
  Cultural Change to 1860
The Chemehuevi Indians of Southern California
Chem'ivillu: Let's Speak Cahuilla
Chinigchinix, An Indigenous California Indian Religion
*The Chumash
Chumash Healing
The Chumash Indians of Southern California
Chumash: A Picture of Their World
The Classification and Distribution of the
  Pit River Indian Tribes of California
The Condition of Affairs in Indian Territory & California
The Conflict Between the California Indian &
  White Civilization
Crystals in the Sky: Chumash Astronomy,
  Cosmology and Rock Art
December's Child: A Book of Chumash Oral Narratives
Delfina Cuero: Her Autobiography
The Destruction of California Indians
Dictionary of Mesa Grande Diegueno
The Diegueno Indians
Discovery of the Yosemite and the Indian

War of 1851 Which Led to That Event
The Earth Is Our Mother: Guide to theIndians of Calif.
The Ethno-Botany of the Coahuilla Indians
  of Southern California
Ethnography and Folklore of the Indians
  of Northwestern California
Federal Concern About Conditions of
  California Indians, 1853-1913
Gabrielino
Gigyayk Vo:jka
*Great Indians of California
Guide to the Records at the National
  Archives-Los Angeles Branch
Handbook of the Indians of California
I'isniyatam (Designs)
Indian Life of the Yosemite Region:
  Miwok Material Culture
Indian Summer: Traditional Life Among the Choinumne
Indians of California's San Joaquin Valley
Indian Survival on the California Borderland
  Frontier, 1819-60
Indian-White Relationships in Northern
  California, 1849-1920
Indians & Intruders in Central California, 1769-1849
Indians of California: The Changing Image
Indians of California: A Critical Bibliography
Indians of the Feather River: Tales & Legends
  of the Concow Maidu of California
Indians of Southern California
Indians of Upper California
An Introduction to the Luiseno Language
Ishi's Journey from the Center to the Edge of the World
It will Live Forever: Traditional Yosemite Acorn
  Preparation
Karuk: the Upriver People
The Kiliwa Indians of Lower California
Kiliwa Texts: "Whe I Have Donned My Crest of Stars"
The Inland Whale: Nine Stories Retold from California
  Indian Legends
Legends of the Yosemite Miwok
Lost Copper
The Maidu Indian Myths and Stories of Hanc'ibyjim
Material Aspects of Pomo Culture
Mirror & Pattern
Mission Indians in California
*The Missions: California's Heritage
The Missions of California, a History of Genocide
Monterey in 1786: The Journals of Jean
  Francois de la Perouse
Mukat's People: The Cahuilla Indians of
  Southern California
Mulewetam: The First People
My Luiseno Neighbors
Native Americans of California & Nevada
Native Americans of the Pacific Coast
Native Californians: A Theoretical Retrospective
The Natural World of the California Indians
The Nome Lackee Indian Reservation, 1854-1870
The Northern Maidu
The Northern Paiute Indians of California and Nevada
Not for Innocent Ears: Spiritual Traditions of a
  Desert Cahuilla Medicine Woman
The Ohlone Way: Indian Life in the San Francisco
  and Monterey Bay Areas
Our Home Forever: The Hupa Indians of
  Northern California
The Papers of John Peabody Harrington in the
  Smithsonian Institution, 1907-1957: Part 3,
  Southern California Basin
People of the Magic Waters: The Cahuilla Indians
  of Plam Springs
Pomo Indian Basketry
*Pomo Indians of California and Their Neighbors
The Population of the California Indians, 1769-1970
Prehistoric Man of the Santa Barbara Coast
Pushed Into the Rocks: Southern California
  Indian Land Tenure

Report of Chas. A. Wetmore, Special U.S. Commis-
  sioner of Mission Indians of Southern California
River of Sorrows-Life History of the
  Maidu-Nisenan Indians
The Round Valley Indians of California
Salinan Indians of California & Their Neighbors
Seasons of the Kachina
The Serrano Indians of Southern California
Serrano Songs & Stories
Seven Rock Art Sites in Baja California
Shasta Indian Tales
Shasta Indians of California & Their Neighbors
Southern California Indian Trails
Spanish and Indian Place Names of California
Strangers in a Stolen Land: American Indians
  in San Diego
Studies in Cahuilla Culture
Temalpakh: Cahuilla Indian Knowledge
  and Usage of Plants
The Texas Cannibals, Or, Why Father
  Serra Came to California
Time's Flotsam: Overseas Collections
  of California Material Culture
Tovangar
Tradition & Innovation: A Basket History of the
  Indians of the Yosemite-Mono Lake Region
Tribes of California
Ukomno'm: The Yuki Indians of Northern California
University of California Anthropological Records
University of California, Archaeological Survey Reports
University of California, Publications in American
  Arcaeology & Ethnology
The Wappo: A Report
The Washo Indians
Washo Indians of California and Nevada
Washo Shamans and Peyotists: Religious
  Conflict in an American Indian Tribe
The Way We Lived: California Indian Stories,
  Songs & Reminiscences
Willie Boy
The Wintun Indians of California and Their Neighbors
Yosemite Indians
Yurok Myths

INDIANS OF NORTH AMERICA
(GENERAL)

After Columbus: The Smithsonian Chronicle
  of the North American Indians
*American Indian
The American Indian & Alaska Native Traders Directory
The American Indian: The American Flag
American Indian Archival Material: A Guide to
  Holdings in the Southeast
The American Indian, 1492-1976: A Chronology
  and Fact Book
*The American Indian Coloring Book
American Indian Ecology
American Indian Encyclopedia - CD-ROM
American Indian Energy Resources and Development
American Indian Identities: Today's Changing
  Perspectives
American Indian Index
*The American Indian in America
The American Indian in English Literature
  of the 18th Century
American Indian and Indoeuropean Studies
American Indian Leaders: Studies in Diversity
American Indian Literature: An Anthology
The American Indian: Prehistory to the Present
The American Indian: A Rising Ethnic Force
*American Indian Stories
*American Indian Tribes
American Indians
*American Indians

The American Indians
American Indians: The First of This Land
American Indians in America
Anthropology and the American Indian
Anthropology on the Great Plains
Arctic: Handbook of North American Indians
Atlas of the North American Indian
Backward: An Essay on Indians,
  Time and Photography
Becoming Brave: The Path to Native
  American Manhood
Belief & Worship in Native North America
Black Sand: Prehistory in Northern Arizona
The Book of the American Indian
The Book of the Indians
Chicano & Native American Studies
The Collected Works of Edward Sapir
A Concise Dictionary of Indian Tribes of North America
Conquering Horse
Constitutions & Laws of the American Indian Tribes.
Cranioetric Relationships Among Plains Indians
Creation's Journey
Dancing Colors: Paths of Native American Women
Dictionary of Indian Tribes of the Americas
Dictionary of Indians of North America
The Elder American Indian
Essays in Anthropology Presented to A.L. Kroeber
  in Celebration of the 60th Birthday
Ethnic Studies, Volume II: Chicano &
  Native American Studies
The Evolution of North American Indians
Facing West: The Metaphysics of Indian
  Hating and Empire-Building
Fantasies of the Master Race
*The First Americans: Tribes of North America
*The First Books
*First Came the Indians
Five Indian Tribes of the Upper Missouri
The Great Sioux Trail
A Guide to America's Indians: Ceremonies,
  Reservations & Museums
Guide to Records in the National Archives
  Relating to American Indians
Guide to Research on North American Indians
Handbook of American Indians North of Mexico
Hear the Creator's Song: A Guide to the Study
  Theme "Native Peoples of North America
The Heirs of Columbus
Historical & Statistical Information Respecting the
History, Condition and Prospects of the Indian
  Tribes of the U.S.
History, Manners, and Customs of the Indian Nations \
  Who Once Inhabited Pennsylvania and the
  Neighboring States
History of Events Resulting in Indian Consolidation
  West of the Mississippi
How to Enroll In An Indian/Alaska Native Tribe
Inconstant Savage: England and the North American
  Indian, 1500-1660
Indian Affairs
Indian America: A Geography of
  North American Indians
Indian America: A Traveler's Companion
Indian Americans: Unity & Diversity
Indian Crisis: The Background
Indian Country
Indian Givers: How the Indians of the Americas
  Transformed the World
The Indian Heritage of Americans
The Indian in America
Indian in American History
Indian Issues
Indian Knoll
Indian Leadership
Indian Life: Transforming an American Myth

Indian Oratory: Famous Speeches by
  Noted Indian Chieftains
The Indian Peoples of Eastern America:
  A Documentary History of the Sexes
Indian Population in the U.S. and Alaska, 1910, 1930
The Indian Question - CD-ROM
Indian Removal
Indian Slavery in Colonial Times
Indian Terms of the Americas
The Indian Today
Indian Tribes of North America
The Indian's Side of the Indian Question
*Indians
*The Indians
Indians Along the Oregon Trail
Indians in Minnesota
The Indians in Oklahoma
*Indians of America
Indians of the Great Basin
Indians of the Great Plains
Indians of North America
Indians of North America: Methods and Sources
  for Library Research
*The Indians of North America Series
Indians of North America: Survey of Tribes
  That Inhabit the Continent
Indians in Ohio, Indiana, Illinois, Southern Michigan
  and Southern Wisconsin
Indians of the Plains
*Indians of the Plains
Indians of the South
Indians of Texas
The Indians of Today
Indians of the Western Great Lakes, 1615-1760
*Indians Who Lived in Texas
Interpreting the Indians: 20th Century Poets
  and the Native American
*The Junior Library of American Indians Series
The Land of Red Cloud: Among North
  America's Indians
Last Rambles Amongst the Indians of the
  Rocky Mountains
Letters and Notes on the Manners, Customs
  and Conditions of the North American Indians
The Life & Adventures of James P. Beckwourth
Life & Art of the North American Indian
Lulu Linear Punctated: Essays in Honor
  of George Irving Quimby
Man's Rise to Civilization
Map'N'Facts: Native Peoples of North America
*Meet the North American Indians
The Microfilm Edition of the Washington Matthews
  Papers & Guide
My Life As an Indian
National Indian Arts & Crafts Directory
Native American Annual
The Native American Book of Change
Native American Directory: Alaska, U.S. and Canada
Native American Periodicals and Newspapers,
  1828-1982
Native American Press in Wisconsin and the Nation
Native American Research Information Service
The Native American Today
*The Native Americans
The Native Americans: An Illustrated History
Native Americans of Texas
Native North Americans: An Ethnohistorical Approach
The Native Races
Native Carolinians: The Indians of North Carolina
Native People, Native Lands: Canadian Indians,
  Inuit and Metis
*Native People, Native Ways Series
Native Shell Mounds of North America: Early Studies
Native Tribes Map
Native Villages & Village Sites

No American Indians
The North American Indian
North American Indian Anthropology:
  Essays on Society & Culture
North American Indian Landmarks: A Traveler's Guide
The North American Indian Travel Guide
North American Indians
*North American Indians
North American Indians of Achievement Series
North American Indians: A Comprehensive Account
North American Indians: A Dissertation Index
The North Americans of Yesterday
Notes From Indian Country
Now That the Buffalo's Gone: A Study
  of Today's American Indians
Our Wild Indians, Etc.
The Papers of John Peabody Harrington
  in the Smithsonian Institution, 1907-1957
Pioneering in Montana: The Making of a State,
  1864-1887
The Political Economy of North American Indians
The Portable North American Indian Reader
The Primal Mind: Vision and Reality in Indian America
Psychocultural Change and the American Indians:
  An Ethnohistorical Analysis
The Quapaws
Readers Digest - America's Fascinating
  Indian Heritage
Red Children in White America
Red Men in Red Square
The Return of the Native: American Indian
  Political Resurgence
Shadow Country
Shadow Distance: A gerald Vizenor Reader
Six Months Among the Indians
Small Bones, Little Eyes
The Smithsonian Book of North American Indians
The Southeastern Indians
Southeastern Indians Since the Removal Era
Southern Athapaskan Migration: A.D. 200-1750
The Spanish Borderlands Sourcebooks
Spanish Explorers in the Southern U.S.
A Spirited Resistance: The North American Indian
Struggle for Unity, 1745-1815
The State of Native America: Genocide,
  Colonization and Resistance
Sun Bear: The Path of Power
Recently Discovered Tales of Life Among the Indians
Teaching About Native Americans
Tennessee's Indian Peoples: From White
  Contact to Removal, 1540-1840
Theoretical Perspectives on Native
  American Languages
This Path We Travel: Celebrations of Contemporary
  Native American Creativity
The Trail of the Hare
Tulapai to Tokay: A Bibliography of Alcochol Use and
  Abuse Among Native Americans of North America
The Unknown Indian
Urban Indians
Urban Indians: Drums From the Cities
Urbanization of American Indians: Critical Bibliography
The Vanishing Race: Selections from Edward S. Curtis'
  the North American Indian
Views of a Vanishing Frontier
*The Wampanoag
*We Live on an Indian Reservation
We, The First Americans
The White Man's Indian
Words in the Blood: Contemporary Indian
  Writers of North and South America
Words of Power: Voices from Indian America
World of American Indian
The World's Rim: Great Mysteries of the
  North American Indians

INDIANS OF THE GREAT LAKES REGION (NORTHWEST, OLD)

Acculturation and Personality Among the
  Wisconsin Chippewa
Anishnabe: Six Studies of Modern Chippewa
Aspects of Upper Great Lakes Anthropology
Autobiography of a Winnebago Indian
Before Man in Michigan
Building a Chippewa Indian Birchbark Canoe
Character and Influence of the Indian Trade in Wisc.
The Chicago American Indian Community: 1893-1988
The Children of the Sun
*The Chippewa
Chippewa Child Life and Its Cultural Background
Chippewa Customs
Chippewa Indians
Chippewa Indians as Recorded by
Chippewa Music
The Chippewas of Lake Superior
*The Chipewyan
Council Fires on the Upper Ohio
The Dream Dance of the Chippewa and Menominee
  Indians of Northern Wisconsin
Dreamers With Power: The Menominee
Ethnobotany of the Menomini Indians
Ethnobotany of the Meskwaki Indians
Ethnology of the Ioway Indians
First People of Michigan
Folklore of the Menomini Indians
History of the Ojibway Indians
The Illinois & Indiana Indians
Indian Chiefs of Southern Minnesota
The Indian Tribes of Ohio
Indian Villages of the Illinois Country: Historic Tribes
Indians of the Chicago Area
The Illinois & Indiana Indians
The Indians of Washtenaw County, Michigan
Indians of the Western Great Lakes, 1615-1760
Introduction to Wisconsin Indians:
  Prehistory to Statehood
Eastman Johnson's Lake Superior Indians
Journals of Joseph N. Nicollet
Kinsmen Through Time: An Annotated Bibliography
  of Potawatomi History
Long Journey to the Country of the Hurons
Lore of the Great Turtle: Indian Legends
  of Mackinac Retold
Material Culture of the Menomini
The Menominee Drums: A History
Menomini Indians of Wisconsin
Menomini Texts
Minnesota's Browns Valley Man and
  Associated Burial Artifacts
Mountain Wolf Woman, Sister of Crashing Thunder:
  The Autobiography of a Winnebago Indian
The Native Tribes of Old Ohio
North Dakota Indians: An Introduction
Observations of the Ethnology of the Sauk Indians
Ojibwa Sociology
Ojibwa Texts
Ojibwa Woman
The Ojibwas: A Critical Bibliography
Ojibway Oratory
Ottawa & Chippewa Indians of Michigan, 1870-1909
The People Named the Chippewa: Narrative Histories
*People of Three Fires
Pioneer History
Potawatomi Indians of Michigan
Prehistoric Biological Relationship in the
  Great Lakes Region
President Washington's Indian War: The Struggle
  for the Old Northwest
Primitive Man in Ohio
Red Brother
The Sauks and Black Hawk War

Sketches of a Tour to the Lakes
A Social Study of 150 Chippewa Indian Families
  of the White Earth Reservation of Minnesota
Tragic Saga of the Indiana Indians
Winnebago Oratory
The Winnebago Tribe
Woodland Indians of the Western Great Lakes
Worlds Between Two Rivers: Perspectives on
  American Indians in Iowa

INDIANS OF THE GREAT PLAINS

The Aborigines of South Dakota
Anthropology on the Great Plains
Bison Cultural Traditions of the Northern Great Plains:
  Past, Present & Future
The Blackfeet: Raiders on the Northwestern Plains
Bury My Heart at Wounded Knee
Changing Military Patterns of the Great Plains Indians
The Cheyenne in Plains Indian Trade Relations
Circles of the World: Traditional Art of the
  Plains Indians
The Comanches: Lords of the South Plains
Costumes of the Plains Indians & Structural Basis
  to the Decoration of Costumes Among the
  Plains Indians
Dakota: A Spiritual Geography
Dances With Wolves
Dress Clothing of the Plains Indians
Dwellers at the Source: Southwestern Indian
  Photographs of A.C. Vroman, 1895-1904
The Flathead Indians of Montana
A Guide to the Indian Tribes of Oklahoma
*Heetunka's Harvest: A Tale of the Plains Indians
The Hidden Half: Studies of Plains Indian Women
*How the Plains Indians Lived
Indian Chiefs of Southern Minnesota
*Indian Tales of the Northern Plains
The Indians of the Great Plains
Indians of the High Plains: From the Prehistoric
  Period to the Coming of Europeans
Indians of the Plains
*Indians of the Plains
Leasing Indian Water
Life on the Plains and Among the Diggings
The March of the Montana Column
Marquis de Miores at War in the Bad Lands
The Mystic Warriors of the Plains
North Dakota Indians: An Introduction
The Northern Shoshone
Northwest Indian Images: A Photographic
  Look at Plateau Indians
Our Voices, Our Land
Our Western Border
The Plains Cree
The Plains Indian Book
Plains Indian Culture
Plains Indian Mythology
Plains Indian Painting
Plains Indian Raiders
Plains Indian Sculpture
The Plains Indians
*Plains Indians: An Educational Coloring Book
The Plains Indians and New Mexico
The Planning Process on the Pine Ridge
  & Rosebud Indian Reservations
Political Organization of the Plains Indians
Population Changes Among the Northern
  Plains Indians
Prehistoric Man on the Great Plains
Rank and Warfare Among the Plains Indians
The Sac and Fox Indians
Skeletal Biology in the Great Plains
Societies of the Plains Indians
Southern Plains Alliances

*The Sun Dance People: The Plains Indians,
  Their Past & Present
The Tribal Government of the Oglala Sioux
  of Pine Ridge, SD
When Buffalo Ran
Wolf That I Am: In Search of the Red Earth People

INDIANS OF THE NORTHEAST

*The Abenaki
Aboriginal Chipped Stone Implements of New York
Aboriginal Occupation of New York
Aboriginal Use of Wood in New York
An Abridgement of the Indian Affairs Contained
  in Four Folio Volumes
Akwesane Historical Postcards
American Indians in Connecticut
Amerinds and Their Paleoenvironments
  in Northeastern North America
Anthropological Studies of the Quichua
  and Machiganga Indians
Apologies to the Iroquois
Archaeology of the Oneida Iroquois
Behind the Tree of Peace: A Sociological Analysis
  of Iroquois Warfare
Beyond the Covenant Chain: The Iroquois &
  Their Neighbors in Indian North America
The Catholic Indian Missions in Maine, 1611-1820
Cautantowwit's Hoise: An Indian Burial Ground on
  the Island of Conanicut in Narragansett Bay
Conrad Weiser and the Indian Policy of
  Colonial Pennsylvania
*The Cayuga
Clambake: A Wampanoag Tradition
Conrad Weiser & the Indian Policy of
  Colonial Pennsylvania
The Constitution of the Five Nations
Dawnland Encounters: Indians & Europeans
  in Northern New England
Economics of the Iroquois
The Embattled Northeast
An Ethnography of the Huron Indians, 1615-1649
Ethnology of the Yuchi Indians
Evolution of the Onondaga Iroquois
Family History of the Brothertown Indians
Fighting Tuscarora: The Autobiography of
  Chief Clinton Rickard
Five Civilized Tribes
Forgotten Founders: Benjamin Franklin, the Iroquois
Functions of Wampum Among the Eastern Algonkian
Grammar of the Language of the Lenni Lenape,
  or Delaware Indians
Guide to Indian Artifacts of the Northeast
Handbook of Tribal Names of Pennsylvania 1908
The Hidden Language of the Seneca
History, Manners and Customs of the Indian Nations
  Who Once Inhabited Pennsylvania and the
  Neighboring States
History of the Indians of Connecticut
History of New York Indians and the Printup Family
A History of the New York Iroquois
Horn and Bone Implements of the New York Indians
Huron: Farmers of the North
Indian Chiefs of Pennsylvania
Indian History, Biography & Genealogy
Indian Money as a Factor in New England Civilization
Indian New England Before the Mayflower
Indian Place Names of New England
Indian Wars of New England
Indian Wars of Pennsylvania
Indian and the White Man in Connecticut
Indians in Pennsylvania
Indians of the Eastern Woodlands
The Indians of Greater New York and the
  Lower Hudson

The Indians of the Housatonic and Naugatuck Valleys
Indians of the Lower Hudson Region: The Munsee
The Indians of Maine and the Atlantic Provinces:
  A Bibliographic Guide
The Indians of Manhattan Island and Vicinity
The Indians of New England: A Critical Bibliography
*The Indians of New Jersey: Dickon Among the
  Lenapes
Iroquois
Iroquois: Art & Culture
Iroquois Book of Rites
Iroquois Folk Lore
Iroquois in the American Revolution
Iroquois Indians: A Documentary History
Iroquois Land Claims
Iroquois Music and Dance
The Iroquois and the New Deal
An Iroquois Sourcebook
Iroquois Stories
Iroquois Studies
The Iroquois Struggle for Survival:
  World War II to Red Power
The Iroquois Trail
Journals of the Military Expedition of
  Major General John Sullivan
A Journey Into Mohawk and Oneida Country
King of the Delawares: Teedyuscung, 1700-1763
Land of the Four Directions
League of the Iroquois
The Lenape
The Lenape and Their Legends
Life and Death in Mohawk Country
The Long House of the Iroquois
Man in Northeastern North America
Many Trails: Indians of the Lower Hudson Valley
Martyrs of the Oblong and Little Nine
The Mashpee Indians: Tribe on Trial
Metallic Ornaments of the New York Indians
*The Mohawk
The Mohawk That Refused to Abdicate,
  and Other Tales
The Mohicans of Stockbridge
The Nanticoke Community of Delaware
The Nanticoke and Conoy Indians
*The Nanticoke
The Nanticoke Indians
The Narragansett
Narrative of the Mission of the United Brethren
  Among the Delaware and Mohegan Indians
Native North American Spirituality of the
  Eastern Woodlands
The Native Peoples of the Northeast Woodlands:
  An Educational Resource Publication
The New England Indians
New England's Prospect
New York City in Indian Possession
Northeast
Notes on the Iroquois
Notes on Iroquois Archaeology
Old Light on Separate Ways
On Our Ground: The Complete Writings
  of William Apess, a Pequot
One Thousand Years on Mound Key
*The Oneida
The Oneida Indian Experience
The Oneida Land Claims
*The Onondaga
Onondaga: Portrait of a Native People
The Original Vermonters
An Outline of Seneca Ceremonies
  at Coldspring Longhouse
Parker on the Iroquois
Passamaquoddy Texts
William Penn's Own Account of Lenni Lenape
  or Delaware Indians
Pennsylvania's Indian Relations to 1754
*The Penobscot

Penobscot Shamanism
The Pequots in Southern New England
The Red King's Rebellion: Racial Politics
  in New England
The Relation of Seneca False Face Masks
  to Seneca & Ontario Archaeology
Religion and Ceremonies of the Lenape
The Reservation
Return of the Sun: Native American Tales
  from the Northeast Woodlands
Return to Creation
The Roll Call of the Iroquois Chiefs
*The Seneca
Seneca Myths & Folk Tales
Seneca Thanksgiving Rituals
The Seneca & Tuscarora Indians:
  An Annotated Bibliography
The Seneca World of Ga-No-Say-Yeh
Smallpox and the Iroquois Wars
The Sokokis: Native Americans in New Hampshire
Spirit of the New England Tribes
A Study of Delaware Indian Big House Ceremony
A Study of Delaware Indian Medicine
  Practice & Folk Beliefs
Susquehanna's Indians
Teaching About American Indians in Connecticut
Territorial Subdivisions and Boundaries of the
  Wampanoag, Massachusett & Nauset Indians
Their Number Become Thinned
The Time of the Autumn Moon
Travels
A Trip to Now England
Toba Tucker: A Shinnecock Portrait
*The Tuscarora
The Tuscarora Legacy of J.N.B. Hewitt
The Wabanakis of Maine & the Maritimes
The Wampanoags of Mashpee
Wampum and Shell Articles Used by the
  New York Indians
The Wars of the Iroquois
Wood's New England Prospect

INDIANS OF THE NORTHWEST, PACIFIC

American Indian Sculpture: A Study of the
  Northwest Coast
Analysis of Coeur D'Alene Indian Myths
Ancient Modocs of California and Oregon
Ancient Tribes of the Klamath Country
Artifacts of the Northwest Coast Indians
The Assiniboine
Background History of the Coeur D'Alene
  Indian Reservation
Bibliography of the Blackfoot
The Blackfeet: An Annotated Bibliography
Blackfeet Indians
The Blackfeet: Raiders on the Northwestern Plains
Blackfeet: Their Art and Culture
A Blackfoot-English Vocabulary
A Blackfoot Sourcebook
The Box of Daylight: Northwest Coast Indian Art
A Brief History of the Coeur d'Alene Indians 1806-1909
Captain Jack, Modoc Renegade
A Case Study of a Northern California Indian Tribe:
  Cultural Change to 1860
Cathlamet on the Columbia
The Cayuse Indians
Chief Joseph Country: Land of the Nez Perce
Chief Joseph's Allies: The Palouse Indians
  and the Nez Perce War of 1877
*Chinook
Chinook: A History and Dictionary
The Chinook Indians
Coast Salish

Coast Salish Essays
The Coast Salish of British Columbia
*The Coast Salish Peoples
A Concise Blackfoot Grammar
The Conquest of the Coeur D'Alenes,
  Spokanes and Palouses
Content and Style of an Oral Literature: Clackamas
Chinook Myths and Tales
Contributions to the Ethnography of the Kutchin
Converting the West: A Biography of
  Narcissa Whitman
*Coyote and Kootenai
Creation Tales from the Salish
The Decorative Art of the Indians of
  North Pacific Coast
Diving for Northwest Relics
Dreamer-Prophets of the Columbia Plateau
During My Time: Florence Edenshaw Davidson,
  a Haida Woman
The Effects of White Contact Upon Blackfoot Culture
An English-Blackfoot Vocabulary
Ethnography of Franz Boas
Ethnography of the Kutenai
The Eyak Indians of the Copper River Delta, Alaska
The Eyes of Chief Seattle: The Suquamish Museum
Faces of a Reservation: A Portrait of the
  Warm Springs Indian Reservation
Facial Paintings of the Indians of
  Northern British Columbia
Feasting With Cannibals: An Essay on
  Kwakiutl Cosmology
Feasting With Mine Enemy
Fighting With Property: A Study of Kwakiutl
  Potlatching and Warfare
The Flathead Indians of Montana
Folk Tales of the Coast Salish
The Fort Belknap Assiniboine of Montana
From the Land of the Totem Poles: The Northwest
  Coast Indian Art Collection at the American
  Museum of Natural History
Geographical Names of the Kwakiutl Indians
Ghost Voices: Yakima Indian Myths, Legends,
  Humor and Hunting Stories
Gifts of the Season: Life Among the Northwest Indians
A Guide to the India Tribes of the Pacific Northwest
Haida: Their Art and Culture
Handbook of North American Indians, Vol. 7:
  Northwest Coast
Historical Sketch of the Flathead Nation
The Horse in Blackfoot Indian Culture
In the Land of the Grasshopper Songs
Indian Affairs in Oregon & Washington Territories
Indian Art Traditions of the Northwest Coast
Indian Baskets of the Pacific Northwest & Alaska
Indian Battles Along the Rogue River, 1855-56
Indian Families of the Northwest Coast
Indian Fighting in the Fifties in Oregon &
  Washington Territories
Indian Fishing: Early Methods on the Northwest Coast
Indian Legends of the Northern Rockies
*Indian Legends of the Pacific Northwest
Indian Missions
Indian Portraits
Indian Portraits of the Pacific Northwest
Indian Slavery in the Pacific Northwest
Indian Stories & Legends of the Stilliguamish,
  Sauks & Allied Tribes
Indian Trade Goods
Indian Tribe of the Northwest
Indian Tribes of Washington, Oregon and Idaho
Indian Tribes of Washington Territory
Indian Weaving, Knitting, Basketry of the
  Northwest Coast
Indians
Indians Along the Oregon Trail; The Tribes Identified
Indians of the Northwest Coast
Indians of the Pacific Northwest

Indians of the Pacific Northwest: A History
Indians of Puget Sound
Indians of the Urban Northwest
Indians, Superintendents, & Councils:
  Northwestern Indian Policy, 1850-1855
Ingalik Material Culture
Inside Passage: Living with Killer Whales,
  Bald Eagles & Kwakiutl Indians
An Iron Hand Upon the People: The Law Against
  the Potlatch on the Northwest Coast
Island Immigrants
Paul Kane, the Columbia Wanderer: Sketches,
  Paintings & Comment, 1846-47
The Kalispel Indians
Kaska Indians
Klamath Ethnography
The Klamath Tribe: A People and Their Reservation
The Koryak
Kutenai Tales
Kwakiutl Ethnography
Kwakiutl Texts
The Kwakiutl of Vancouver Island
Languages of the Tribes of the Extreme Northwest
Augustine Laure, S.J., Missionary to the Yakimas
The Legacy: Tradition & Innovation in Northwest
  Coast Indian Art
Legends of the Micmacs
The Lemhi: Sacajawea's People
Letters from the Secretary of the Interior
Life Amongst the Modocs: Unwritten History
The Life of Okah Tubbee
Little Bit Know Something
Looking At the Land of Promise: Pioneer Images
  of the Pacific Northwest
Lower Chinook Ethnographic Notes
Lummi Indians of Northwest Washington
Madame Dorion
Message of an Indian Relic: Seattle's Own Totem Pole
Modern Blackfeet: Montanans on a Reservation
The Modoc
The Modocs and Their Way
Mourning Dove: A Salishan Autobiography
Music of the Indians of British Columbia
Native Accounts of Nootka Ethnography
Native Americans of th Northwest Coast:
  A Critical Bibliography
Native Americans of the Pacific Coast
The Native Brotherhoods
Native Brotherhoods: Modern Intertribal
  Organizations on the Northwest Coast
Nch'i-Wana, The Big River - Mid-Columbia
  Indians & Their Land
New Indian Sketches
A New Series of Blackfoot Texts
Nez Perce Indians
No More Buffalo
Nootka and Quileute Music
The Northern and Central Nootkan Tribes
Northwest Coast Indian Art: An Analysis of Form
Northwest Coast Indian Graphics
Northwest Chiefs
Northwest Native Harvest
Norhwestern Indian Images
The Northwestern Tribes in Exile: Modoc, Nez Perce,
  & Palouse Removal to the Indian Territory
Notes and Observations on the Kwakiool People
Objects of Bright Pride: Northwest Coast Indian Art
  From the Museum of Natural History
The Ohlone Way: Indian Life in the San Francisco
  & Monterey Bay Areas
Okanogan Highland Album
Oregon Indians: Culture, History & Current Affairs;
  An Atlas & Introduction
The Oregon Trail
*Oregon Trail
Oregon's Salty Coast
*Pacific Coast Indians of North America

Pacific Northwest Americana
People of the Totem: Indians of the Pacific Northwest
Pow Wow: And Other Yakima Indian Traditions
Primitive Pragmatists: The Modoc Indians of
  Northern California
The Prophet Dance of the Northwest and Its
  Derivatives: The Source of the Ghost Dance
Puyallup-Nisqually
The Raven Tales
Renegade Tribe: The Palouse Indians and the
  Invasion of the Inland Pacific Northwest
The Reservation Blackfeet
Salish Folk Tales
Salish Weaving
The Sandel and the Cave: The Indians of Oregon
The Sanpoil and Nespelem Salishan Peoples
  of Northeastern Washington
Seahb Siwash
Shapes of Thier Thoughts: Reflections of Culture
  Contact in Northwest Coast Indian Art
Shoto Clay: Figurines and Forms From the
  Lower Columbia
The Sinkaietk or Southern Okanogan of Washington
Sketches of Indian Life in the Pacific Northwest
The Snake Country Expedition of 1830-1831
Spirit and Ancestor: A Century of Northwest
  Coast Indian Art at the Burke Museum
Stone Age of the Columbia River
The Structure of Twana Culture
*Suquamish Today
Swan Among the Indians: Life of James G. Swan,
  1818-1900
Tanaina Tales from Alaska
*Tendoy, Chief of the Lemhis
These Are My Children
Tillamook Indians
Tilamook Indians of the Oregon Coast
Tlingit Indians
Topographical Memoir
Tradition and Change on the Northwest Coast
Traditions of the Quinault Indians
The Tragedy of the Blackfoot
Traits of American Indian Life
Treaties & Agreements of the Indian Tribes
  of the Pacific Northwest
Treaties on Trial: The Continuing Controversy
  over Northwest Indian Fisihg Rights
Tribal Distribution in Oregon
Tribes of the Columbia Valley and the Coast
  of Washington and Oregon
Tsimshian Indians & Their Arts
The Tsimshian: Their Arts & Music
The Tsimshian and Their Neighbors of the
  North Pacific Coast
Tsimshian Texts
Twana Games
Valley of the Spirits: The Upper Skagit Indians
  of Western Washington
*Vostaas: The Story of Montana's Indian Nation
The Wappo: A Report
The Ways of My Grandmothers
Wishram Texts: Together With Wasco Tales and Myths
Wolf of the Raven: Totem Poles of
  Southeastern Alaska
A World of Faces: Masks of the
  Northwest Coast Indians
The Yakimas: A Critical Bibliography

INDIANS OF THE SOUTH

American Indian Archival Material
The American Indian and the End of the
  Confederacy, 1863-1866
The American Indian As Slaveholder & Successionist
The American Indian in Alabama and the Southeast

The American Indian in the Civil War, 1862-1865
The American Indian in North Carolina
Ancient Chiefdoms of the Tombigbee
Apalachee: The Land Between the Rivers
Archaeology of Aboriginal Culture Change
  in the Interior Southeast
The Ascent of Chiefs: Cahokia & Mississippian
  Politics in Native North America
Authentic Memoirs of William Augustus Bowles, Esq.
British Administration of the Southern Indians,
  1756-1783
Catawba Nation
Catawba Texts
Census Roll of the Old Settler Party Creeks 1857
Chapters of the Ethnology of the Powhatan
  Tribes of Virginia
Cherokees and Missionaries, 1789-1839
Choctaws & Missionaries in Mississippi, 1818-1918
Creek Census 1832
Creek-Choctaw-Chickasaw Land Fraud in
  Public Land Sales
Creek Indian History
Creek Indian Stidham Roll 1886 with Index
Creek Soldier Casualty Lists - Seminole War 1836
A Creek Warrior for the Confederacy
Creeks and Seminoles
Deerskins & Duffels
The Development of Southeastern Archaeology
Early Pottery in the Southeast
The Early Prehistoric Southeast: A Sourcebook
Ethnic Heritage in Mississippi
Ethnology of the Indians of Spanish Florida
The Evolution of the Calusa: A Non Agricultural
  Chiefdom on the Southwest Florida Coast
Exiles of Florida
Florida Place Names of Indian Origin
The Florida Wars
The Forgotten Centuries
The Formative Cultures of the Carolina Piedmont
Georgia Voices
Government & Religion of the Virginia Indians
A Grammar & Dictionary of the Timucua Language
The Grand Village of the Natchez Indians Revisited
Hampton Institute School Records 1878-1891
Historical Collections of Georgia
History of Alabama, and Incidentally of Georgia
  and Mississippi, from the Earliest Period
The History and Present State of Virginia
Indian Affairs in Georgia, 1732-1756
*Indian Myths from the Southeast
Indian Place Names in Alabama
Indians in Seventeenth Century Virginia
Indians of the Rio Grande Valley
Indians of the South
Indians of the Southeastern U.S.
Indians of the Southeastern U.S. in the
  Late 20th Century
*John Hawk: A Seminole Saga
Journal of Southern Treaty Commission 1865
The Karankara Indians, The Coast People of Texas
Lachlan McGillivray, Indian Trader: The Shaping
  of the Southern Colonial Frontier
A Map of Virginia
Modern Indians of Alabama: Remnants of the Removal
Myths and Tales of the Southeastern Indians
A Narrative of the Early Days and Remembrances
  of Oceaola Nikkanochee
Native Land
Negro-Indian Relationships in the Southeast
Notices of East Florida
Ocmulgee Archaeology, 1936-1986
The Only Land I Know: A History of the Lumbee
  Indian of North Carolina
The Only Land They Knew: The Tragic Story of
  the American Indians in the Old South
The Pamunkey Indians of Virginia
The Papers of Panton, Leslie & Co.

Perspectives on the Southeast
Plants Used as Curatives by Certain Southeast Tribes
Pocahontas's People: The Powhatan Indians
 of Virginia Through the Centuries
Alex Posey: Creek Poet, Journalist, and Humorist
Powhatan Indians of Virginia
Powhatan Tribes: Middle Atlantic
Powhatan's Mantle
Prehistoric Indians of the Southeast
Prehistoric Peoples of South Florida
Savanah River Chiefdoms
Seminole Indians of Florida, 1850-1874
The Seminole & Miccosukee Tribes
South Florida's Vanished People
The Southestern Ceremonial Complex
 and Its Interpretation
The Southeastern Indians
Southeastern Indians Since the Removal Era
Southeastern Woodland Indian Designs
*Southern Indian Myths & Legends
The Southern Indians & Benjamin Hawkins, 1796-1816
Southern Indians in the American Revolution
The Southern Indians: The Story of the Civilized
 Tribes Before Removal
Stalling's Island Mound, Columbia County, Georgia
John Stuart and the Southern Colonial Frontier
Studies in Southeastern Indian Languages
Sun Circles & Human Hands: The Southeastern
 Indians, Art & Industries
Sunshine on the Prairie: Story of Cynthia Ann Parker
Tacachale: Essays on the Indians of Florida &
 Southeastern Georgia During the Historical Period
Tomochichi: Indian Friend of the Georgia Colony
Town & Temples Along the the Mississippi
Tribes That Slumber: Indians of the Tennessee Region
A True Discourse of the Present Estate of Virginia
*World of the Southern Indians

INDIANS OF THE SOUTHWEST
(See Apache, Hopi, Navajo, &
Pueblo Indian Classifications)

A.D. Ancient Peoples of the Southwest
American Indians in Colorado
American Indians of the Southwest
*The Anasazi
Anasazi Ruins of the Southwest in Color
Ancient Life in the American Southwest
Ancient Texans
Apache, Navaho, and Spaniard
*The Apaches & Navajos
Archaeological Explorations on the Middle Chinlee
Archaeology of Alkali Ridge, Southeastern Utah
Basketmaker Caves in the Prayer Rock District,
 Northeastern Arizona
Basketmaker Caves of Northeastern Arizona
Black Sand: Prehistory in Northern Arizona
Brothers of Light, Brothers of Blood
By the Prophet of the Earth: Ethnobotany of the Pima
The Cahuilla Indians of Southern California
Camp Beale's Springs and the Hualapai Indians
A Celebration of Being
Chaco & Hohokam: Prehistoric Regional Systems
 in the American Southwest
Chulo: A Year Among the Coatimundis
Circles, Consciousness and Culture
Cliff Dwellings of the Mesa Verde
Cocopa Ethnography
The Cochise Cultural Sequence in Southeastern AZ
The Comanchero Frontier: A History of
 New Mexican-Plains Indian Relations
Contributions to Archaeology and Ethnohistory
 of Greater Mesoamerica
Cultural and Environmental History of Cienega
 Valley, Southeastern Arizona
Cycles of Conquest

Dancing Gods: Indian Ceremonials of
 New Mexico and Arizona
Decorative Art of the Southwestern Indians
Desert Foragers and Hunters
Desert Light
Dictionary of Prehistoric Indian Artifacts
 of the American Southwest
Disease, Depopulation & Culture Change in
 Northwestern New Spain
Divisiveness and Social Conflict
Doctors of Medicine in New Mexico
El Gringo
The Elkus Collection: Southwestern Indian Art
Enduring Culture: A Century of Photography of
 the Southwest Indians
Enduring Visions: One Thousand Years of
 Southwestern Indian Art
Ethno-Botany of the Gosiute Indias of Utah
The Ethobiology of the Papago Indians
Expedition Into New Mexico Made
 by Antonio de Espejo
Fetishes and Carvings of the Southwest
Final Report of Investigations Among the
 Indians of the Southwestern U.S.
Ethno-Botany of the Gosiute Indians of Utah
Excavations of Los Muertos and Neighboring
 Ruins in the Salt River Valley, Southern Arizona
Expeditions Into New Mexico
Explorations in Northeastern Arizona
Fetishes and Carvings of the Southwest
Final Report of Investigations Among the
 Indians of the Southwestern U.S.
Four Winds: Poems from Indian Rituals
From the Sands to the Mountain: A Study of Change
 and Persistence in a Southern Paiute Community
Fry Breads, Feast Days and Sheep
Great Basin Indian Population Figures
Great Excavations: Tales of Early Southwestern
 Archaeology, 1888-1939
Guide to Prehistoric Ruins of the Southwest
Handbook of Northern Arizona Pottery Wares
Hano: A Tewa Indian Community
Harmony By Hand: Art of the Southwest Indians
Havsuw Baaja: People of Blue Green Water
Historical Background of the Gila River Reservation
Historical Demography of the Pima & Maric
 opa Indians, 1846-1974
Historical Introduction to Studies Among Sedentary
 Indians of New Mexico
The Hohokam Indians of the Tucson Basin
I Am Here: Two Thousand Years of
 Southwest Indian Culture
Indian Baskets of the Southwest
Indian Life in Texas
Indian Rock Art of the Southwest
Indians and the Mismanagement of New Mexico
Indians of the Pike's Peak Region
The Indians of Point of Pines, Arizona
Indians of the American Southwest
Indians of the Southwest
Indians of the Southwest: A Century of
 Development Under the U.S.
The Indians of Texas: An Annotated
 Research Bibliography
Indians Who Lived in Texas
The Land of the Cliff-Dwellers
Ray Manley's Indian Lands
*Many Winters
Marvelous Country
Massacre on the Gila
Material Aspects of Pomo Culture
The Mimbres: Art & Archaeology
Mimbres Indian Treasure: In The Land of Baca
Earl Morris and Southwestern Archaeology
Mother Earth, Father Sky
Music & Dance Research of the Southwestern Indians
Myths & Legends of the Indian Southwest

Nacimientos: Nativity Scenes by
 Southwest Indian Artisans
The Names
Neon Powwow: New Native American
 Voices of the Southwest
Of Earth & Little Rain
On the Clifs of Acoma
On the Gleaming Way: Navajos, Eastern Pueblos,
 Zunis, Hopis, Apaches and Their Land, and
 Their Meanings to the World
One House, One Voice, One Heart
The Only True People: A History of the Native
 Americans of the Colorado Plateau
Oraibi Soyal Ceremony, and Oraibi
 Powamu Ceremony
Our Voices, Our Land
Ouray, Chief of the Utes
Penitente Self-Government Brotherhoods & Council
The People: Indians of the American Southwest
People of the Blue Water
People of the Desert & Sea: Ethnobotany
 of the Seri Indians
Picture-Writing of Texas Indians
Pieces of White Shell
Po Pai Mo: The Search for White Buffalo Woman
Pomo Indians of California and Their Neighbors
Portraits of the Whiteman
Pottery of the Pajarito Plateau and of Some
 Adjacent Regions in New Mexico
Prehistoric Southwestern Craft Arts
Prehistoric Southwesterners from
 Basketmaker to Pueblo
Prehistoric Weapons in the Southwest
The Protector de Indios in Colonial New Mexico
The Quapaw Indians: A History of the
 Downstream People
The Rain-Makers: Indians of Arizona and New Mexico
Roads to Center Place: An Anasazi Atlas
Scientist on the Trail
The Seri
The Seri Indians of Sonora
Shadows in Glass: Indian Photographs of Ben Whittick
Short-Term Sedentism in the American Southwest:
 The Mimbres Valley Salado
Sign Language: Contemporary
 Southwest Native America
Silas and the Mad-Sad People
Sonora
Southeastern Pomo Ceremonials
Southern Arizona Folk Arts
Southern Ute Indians of Early Colorado
Southwest: Handbook of North American Indians
Southwest Indian Arts & Crafts
Southwest Indian Craft Arts
Southwest Indian Cookbook
Southwest Indian Designs
Southwest Indian Iron-On Transfers
Southwest Indian Painting: A Changing Art
Southwest Indian Silver from the Doneghy Collection
Southwest Indians: A Photographic Portrait
Southwest Museum Publications
Southwestern Arts & Crafts
Southwestern Indian Ceremonials
Southwestern Indian Ritual Drama
Southwestern Indian Tribes
The Spanish Mission of New Mexico, after 1680
Speaking of Indians: With an Accent on the Southwest
Straight With the Medicine: Narratives of Washoe
 Followers of the Tipi Way
Swarts Ruin
Margaret Tafoya: A Tewa Potter's Heritage and Legacy
Tales of the Cochitit Indians
Themes in Southwest Prehistory
This Is Our Land
Time, Space and Transition in Anasazi Prehistory
Traditions in Transition: Contemporary Basket
 Weaving of the Southwestern Indians

Under the Indian Turquoise Sky
Ute Mountain Utes
Wauba Yuma's People
The Washo Indians
We Just Toughed It Out: Women Heads of
   Households on the Llano Estacado
The Western Photographs of John K. Hillers
When Clay Sings
Witchcraft in the Southwest

INDIANS OF TEXAS

Ancient Texans
Blessed Assurance: At Home with the Bomb
   in Amarillo, Texas
Jesse Chisholm: Texas Trail Blazer and Peacemaker
Comanche Moon
Ethnology of the Texas Indians
Hasinai: A Traditional History of the
   Caddo Confederacy
Indian Depredation in Texas
Indian Life in Texas
Indian Wars and Pioneers of Texas
Indians of the Rio Grande Valley
The Indians of Texas: An Annotated
   Research Bibliography
The Indians of Texas: From Prehistoric
   to Modern Times
Indians Who Lived in Texas
The Karankawa Indians, the Coast People of Texas
Legendary Texans, Vol. 2
The Lipan Apaches in Texas
Native Americans of Texas
Notes on the Caddo
Stone Artifacts of Texas Indians
The Story of Cynthia Ann Parker
Tejano Origins in 18th Century San Antonio
The Texas Cannibals, or Why Father Serra
   Came to California
The Texas Cherokees
Tonkawa, an Indian Language of Texas
The Tonkawa People: A Tribal History from
   Earliest Times to 1893

INDUSTRIES

Aboriginal American Indian Basketry
Aboriginal Indian Basketry
Amerian Indian Arts & Crafts Source Book
American Indian Basketry
American Indian Craft Book
American Indian Design & Decoration
American Indian Utensils: How to Make Baskets,
   Pottery & Woodenware with Natural Materials
The Ancestors: Native American Artisans
   of the Americas
And Eagles Sweep Across the Sky: Indian Textiles
   of the North American West
Apache Indian Baskets
The Art of the Indian Basket in North America
Artifacts of the Northwest Coast Indians
Arts & Crafts of the Cherokee
Authentic Indian Designs
Basketmaker Caves of Northeastern Arizona
Basketry Designs of the Salish Indians
Basketry of the Papago & Pima Indians
Basketry of the San Carlos Apache Indians
Beads and Beadwork of the American Indian
Blackfeet Crafts
Bo'jou, Neejee: Profiles of Canadian Indian Art
Book of Authentic Indian Life Crafts
The Book of Indian Crafts & Costumes
The Book of Indian Crafts & Indian Lore
Chippewa Customs

Columbia River Basketry
The Complete Guide to Traditional Native
   American Beadwork
The Complete How-To Book of Indian Craft
Cornhusk Bags of the Plateau Indians
*Crafts of the North American Indians:
   A Craftsman's Manual
The Crescent Hills Prehistoric Quarrying Area
Crow Indian Beadwork
Decorative Art of the Southwestern Indians
Designs on Prehistoric Hopi Pottery
Estiyut Omayat: Creek Writing
Explorations in Northeastern Arizona
Finger-Weaving: Indian Braiding
*Grandmother Five Baskets
Hallmarks of the Southwest: Who Made It?
Harmony by Hand: Art of the Southwest Indians
The Heritage of Klickitat Basketry:
   A History & Art Preserved
Hopi Kachina Dolls with a Key to Their Identification
Hopi Katcinas
Hopi Silver
How to Tan Skins the Indian Way
Hunters of the Buffalo
Hunters of the Ice
Hunters of the Northern Forest
Indian Basket Weaving
Indian Basket Weaving: How to Weave Pomo,
   Yurok, Pima & Navajo Baskets
Indian Basketry
Indian Basketry & How to Make Baskets
Indian Baskets & Curios
Indian Baskets of the Pacific Northwest & Alaska
Indian Baskets of the Southwest
Indian Blankets and Their Makers
*Indian Crafts
Indian Designs
Indian Handcrafts
The Indian How Book
Indian Jewelry
Indian Quillworking
Indian Rawhide: An American Folk Art
Indian Silver Jewelry of the Southwest, 1868-1930
Indian Weaving, Knitting, & Basketry
   of the Northwest Coast
Indiancraft
The Inuit Print
Iroquois Crafts
A Key Into the Language of Woodsplint Baskets
Ray Manley's Collecting Southwestern
   Indian Arts & Crafts
Ray Manley's Hopi Kachina
Metallic Ornaments of the New York Indians
Native American Designs
Native Basketry of Western North America
Navajo Arts & Crafts
Navajo Native Dyes: Their Preparation & Use
Navajo & Pueblo Silversmiths
Navajo Weavers & Silversmiths
Navajo Textiles
Navajo Weaving: Its Technic & History
Navajo Weaving: Three Centuries of Change
North American Indian Designs
North American Indian Trade Silver
Northern Athapaskan Art: A Beadwork Tradition
Ojibwa Crafts
Plants Used in Basketry by the California Indians
Pomo Indian Basketry
Pueblo Crafts
Pueblo Designs: 176 Illustrations of the Rain Bird
Pueblo Indian Textiles
Quill and Beadwork of the Western Sioux
The Re-Establishment of the Indians in Their Pueblo
   Life Through the Revival of Their Traditional
   Crafts: A Study in Home Extension Education
Reflections of the Weaver's World
Southern Arizona Folk Arts

Southwest Indian Arts & Crafts
Southwest Indian Craft Arts
Southwestern Indian Baskets: Their History
   & Their Makers
Spanish-AmericanBlanketry
Sun Circles & Human Hands: The Southeastern
   Indians, Art & Industries
Traditional Indian Bead & Leather Crafts
Traditional Indian Crafts
Traditions in Transition: Contemporary Basket
   Weaving of the Southwestern Indians
Turquoise and the Indians
Walk in Beauty: The Navajo & Their Blankets
Wampum and Shell Articles Used
   by the New York Indians
The Weaver's Pathway: A Clarification
   of the "Spirit Trail" in Navajo Weaving
Weaving a Navajo Blanket
Work a Day Life of the Pueblos

IROQUOIS INDIANS

Archaeology of the Oneida Iroquois
Behind the Tree of Peace: A Sociological Analysis
   of Iroquois Warfare
The Caddoan, Iroquoian & Siouan Languages
Concerning the League
Conservatism Among the Iroquois
   at the Six Nations Reserve
The Constitution of the Five Nations
Economics of the Iroquois
Evolution of the Onondaga Iroquois
Extending the Rafters: Interdisciplinary
   Approaches to Iroquois Studies
The False Faces of the Iroquois
Forgotten Founders: Benjamin Franklin, The Iroquois
   and the Rationionale for American Revolution
The History & Culture of Iroquois Diplomacy
History of the Five Indian Nations
History of the Five Indian Nations in Canada
A History of the New York Iroquois, Now
   Commonly Called the Six Nations
Iroquoian Cosmology
Iroquois
Iroquois: Art & Culture
Iroquois Book of Rites
Iroquois Crafts
The Iroquois Eagle Dance
Iroquois Folk Lore
Iroquois in the American Revolution
The Iroquois in the Civil War From Battlefield
   to Reservation
Iroquois Indians
Iroquois Land Claims
Iroquois Medical Botany
Iroquois Music & Dance
The Iroquois & the New Deal
An Iroquois Sourcebook
*Iroquois Stories
Iroquois Studies: A Guide to Documentary &
   Ethnographic Resources from Western New York
   & the Genesee Valley
The Iroquois Struggle for Survival
The Iroquois Trail
The Iroquois Trail: Dickon Among the
   Onondagas & Senecas
Law and Government of the Grand River Iroquois
League of the Iroquois
Legends, Traditions and Laws of the Iroquois
The Long House of the Iroquois
Lewis H. Morgan on Iroquois Culture
Notes on the Iroquois
Notes on Iroquois Archaeology
Oneida Verb Morphology
Onondaga: Portrait of a Native People
The Ordeal of the Longhouse

Parker on the Iroquois
The Roll Call of the Iroquois Chiefs
Samllpox and the Iroquois Wars
Smoking Technology of the Aborigines of the
  Iroquois Area of New York State
Symposium on Local Diversity in Iroquois Culture
Traditions and Laws of the Iroquois

JEWELRY - COSTUME
& ADORNMENT

American Indian Design & Decoration
Authentic American Indian Beadwork and How To Do It
Authentic Indian Designs
Beads and Beadwork of the American Indian
A Beadwork Companion
Costumes of the Plains Indians
Crow Indian Beadwork
Dress Clothing of the Plains Indians
Feminine Fur Trade Fashions
Head and Face Masks in Navaho Ceremonialism
Heart of the Dragonfly
How to Tan Skins the Indian Way
Indian Bead-Weaving Patterns
Indian Clothing Before Cortes: Mesoameric
  an Costumes from the Codices
Indian Clothig of the Great Lakes: 1740-1840
*Indian Costumes
Indian Jewelry
Indian Silver Jewelry of the Southwest, 1868-1930
Jewelry by Southwest American Indians.
  Evolving Designs
Making Arrows the Old Way
Making Indian Bows and Arrows
Metallic Ornaments of the New York Indians
Navajo & Pueblo Silversmiths
Navajo Weavers & Silversmiths
Pueblo Indian Embroidery
Quill & Beadwork of the Western Sioux
A Quillwork Companion
Salish Indian Sweaters
Stone Ornaments Used by Indians in the
  U.S. and Canada
Techniques of Beading Earrings
The Technique of North American Indian Beadwork
The Technique of Porcupine Quill Decoration Among
the Indians of North America
Traditional Dress
Traditional Indian Bead & Leather Crafts
Traditional Indian Crafts
Turquoise Jewelry
Zuni Jewelry

JOURNALISM

Let My People Know: American Indian Journalism,
  1828-1978
Native American Press in Wisconsin and the Nation

JUVENILE LITERATURE

*Across the Tundra
*Algonquian
*All About Arrowheads & Spear Points
*American Indian Arts & Crafts Source Book
*The American Indian in America
*American Indian Music & Musical Instruments
*American Indians
*American Indians Today
*An Anasazi Welcome
*The Animals' Ballgame
*Ancient Indians: The First Americans

*Apache
*Arctic Hunter
*Arctic Memories
*Authentic North American Indian Clothing Series
*Authentic North American Indian Cradleboards Series
*Baby Rattlesnake
*Back in the Beforetime: Tales of the California Indians
*The Bentwood Box
*Bill Red Coyote Is a Nut
*Black Elk: A Man with a Vision
*Black Indians: A Hidden Heritage
*Blackfeet Crafts
*Blue Jacket: War Chief of the Shawnees
*Blue Stone: An Anasazi Indian Boy
*Blue Thunder
*The Boy Who Dreamed of an Acorn
*Broken Ice
*Brother Eagle, Sister Sky
*Brothers of the Heart
*Buffalo Hunt
*Buffalo & Indians on the Great Plains
*Buffalo Woman
*The Button Blanket
*The Cahuilla
*California Indians
*California Indians: An Educational Coloring Book
California's Indians & the Gold Rush
*The California Native American Tribes
*The Catawbas
*The Cedar Plank
*Ceremony in the Circle of Life
*Chant of the Red Man
*Charlie Young Bear
*The Charm of the Bear Claw Necklace
*The Cherokee
*Cherokee Legends & the Trail of Tears
*Cherokee Summer
*Cheyenne
*The Cheyenne
*Cheyenne Legends of Creation
*Cheyenne Warriors
*The Chickasaw
*Chief Joseph
*Chief Joseph's Own Story As Told By
  Chief Joseph in 1879
*Chief Red Horse Tells About Custer
*Chief Sarah: Sarah Winnemucca's
  Fight for Indian Rights
*Chief Stephen's Parky
*The Children, Always the Children
*Chinook
*The Chinook: Northwest
*Chocolate Chipmunks & Canoes
*The Choctaw
*The Chumash
*Clues from the Past: A Resource
  Book on Archaeology
*Columbus Day
*The Comanche
*Comanche Warbonnet
*Come to Our Salmon Feast
*Concise Encyclopedia of the American Indian
*Cottontail and Sun
*Could It Be Old Hiari
*Coyote & the Fish
*Coyote & Kootenai
*Coyote & Little Turtle
*Coyote Steals the Blanket
*Coyote Stories for Children:
  Tales from Native America
*Coyote & the Winnowing Birds
*Coyote's Pow-Wow
*Creation Tales from the Salish
*The Crow
*Dakota and Ojibwe People in Minnesota
*Dancing Teepees: Poems of American Indian Youth
*Dancing With the Indians

*The Dark Side of the Moon
*Dawn River
*The Day of the Ogre Kachinas: A Hopi Indian Fable
*Death of the Iron Horse
*The Defenders
*The Delaware Indians: A History
*The Desert Is Theirs
*Doctor Coyote
*Dogsong
*Dream Feather
*Dream Wolf
*Earthmaker's Tales: North American Indian Stories
  About Earth Happenings
*Encyclopedia of Native American Tribes
*Family, Clan, Nation
*Famine Winter
*A Feast for Everyone
*Federal Indian Policy
*Finding a Way Home: Indian and Catholic Spiritual
Paths of the Plateau Tribes
*First Came the Indians
*Flecha al Sol: Un Cuento do Los Indios Pueblo
*The Flood
*Following Indian Trails
*Fox Song
*From Abenaki to Zuni: A Dictionary of
  Native American Tribes
*Frontiersmen
*Frozen Fires
*Fur Trappers and Traders: The Indians,
  The Pilgrims, and the Beaver
*Geronimo
*The Gift of the Sacred Dog
*Gifts of the Season: Life Among the Northwest Indian
*The Girl Who Loved Wild Horses
* The Girl Who Married a Ghost
*The Goat in the Rug
*Grandfather and the Popping Machine
*Great Indians of California
*The Great Race
*Growing Up Indian
*Happily May I Walk: American Indians
  and Alaska NativesToday
*Heart Butte: A Blackfeet Indian
*Heroes and Heroines in Tlingit-Haida Legends
*Hiawatha
*The Hidatsa
*Hopi Mysteries
*The Hour of the Wolf
*Houses of Bark: Tipi, Wigwam & Longhouse
*How the Birch Tree Got Its Stripes
*How Glooskap Outwits the Ice Giant
*How the Plains Indians Lived
*How Rabbit Stole the Fire: A North
  American Indian Folk Tale
*The Hunt
*The Huron: Great Lakes
*I Am Regina
*I Can Read About Indians
*I Sing for the Animals
*If You Lived With the Sioux Indians
*Iktomi Series
*Ikwa of the Mound-Builder Indians
*In the Trail of the Wind: American Indian
  Poems & Ritual Orations
*Indian Boyhood
*Indian Canoeing
*Indian Chiefs
*Indian Children Paper Dolls
*Indian Crafts
*Indian Fairy Tales
*Indian Festivals
*Indian Tribes of America
*An Indian Winter
*Indians
*Indians in New York State
*Indians of America Series

*Indians of the Americas
*The Indians of Louisiana
*Indians of North America
*Indians of the Pacific Northwest
*Indians of the Plains
*Indians of the Southwest
*Indians of the West
*The Iroquois
*Jim Thorpe
*Joseph: Chief of the Nez Perce
*Alvin Josephy's History of the
  Native Americans Series
*Kamache and the Medicine Bead
*Keepers of the Animals
*Keepers of the Earth
*Keepers of Life
*Keepers of the Night
*King Philip
*The Kiowa: Great Plains
*Kiowa Voices: Ceremonial Dance, Ritual and Song
*Kunu: Winnebago Boy Escapes
*The Kwakiutl
*The Last of the Mohicans
*The Lenape: Middle Atlantic
*Let Me Tell You a Story & Workbook
*Let's Look Inside a Tepee
*Let's Remember...Indians of Texas
*Linda's Indian Home
*Little Boy with Three Names: Stories of Taos Pueblo
*Little Herder in Autumn
*The Long Search
*Loon and Deer Were Traveling
*Louisiana Indian Tales
*Louisiana Indians
*Lucy Learns to Weave: Gathering Plants
*The Lumbee: Southeast
*Lumberman
*The Magic Lake: A Mystical Healing
  Lake of the Cherokee
*The Mandans
*Mark of Our Moccasins
*Me Run Fast Good
*Medicine Man
*Meet the North American Indians
*The Menominee
*The Money God
*The Moundbuilders
*Native American Animal Stories
*Native American People
*Native American Stories
*Native Americans
*Native Peoples of the Southwest
*The Naughty Little Rabbit and Old Man Coyote
*The Navajo
*The Navajo Brothers & the Stolen Herd
*Navajo Children
*Navajo Coyote Tales
*The Navajo: Southwest
*The Navajos
*Naya Nuki: Shoshoni Girl Who Ran
*Nez Perce
*The Nez Perce
*The Nez Perce: Northwest
*Night Flying Woman: An Ojibway Narrative
*No One Like a Brother
*North American Indian
*North American Indian Masks
*North American Indian Medicine
*North American Indian Stories
*North American Indian Survival Skills
*North American Indians
*The Northwest Coast Indian Art Series
*The Numu Way & Workbook
*The Ojibwa: Great Lakes
*The Ojibwe
*Okemos: Story of a Fox Indian In His Youth
*O'kohome: The Coyote Dog

*Old Lop-Ear Wolf
*Om-Kas-Toe: Blackfeet Twin Captures an Elkdog
*Only the Name Remains the Same
*Pacific Coast Indians of North America
*The Paiute: Southwest
*Pasquala: The Story of a California Indian Girl
*Pathki Nana: Kootenai Girl Solves a Mystery
*The Pawnee
*People of the Breaking Day
*People of the Buffalo: How the Plains Indians Lived
*People of the Ice: How the Inuit Lived
*People of the Longhouse: How the
  Iroquoian Tribes Lived
*People of the Trail: How the Northern
  Forest Indians Lived
*The People Shall Continue
*Phantom Horse of Collister's Fields
*Philip Johnston and the Navajo Code Talkers
*A Picture Book of Sitting Bull
*The Pima-Maricopa: Southwest
*Plains Indian Warrior
*Plains Indians
*Plains Indians: An Educational Coloring Book
*Plains Indians of North America
*The Potawatomi: Great Lakes
*Pow Wow
*The Powhatan Tribes: Middle Atlantic
*Pueblo
*The Pueblo
*Pueblo Storyteller
*A Pueblo Village
*Rainbow Crow
*Raven's Light
*Red Frog Man: A Hohokam Leader
*Red Power on the Rio Grande
*Riel's People: How the Metis Lived
*The Rings of Woot-Kew's Tail: Indian Legends
  of the Origin of the Sun, Moon and Stars
*Rising Fawn and the Fire Mystery
*Rivermen
*Sacagawea
*Sam and the Golden People
*Scouts
*Seal for a Pal
*Search for Identity
*The Seminole
*The Seminole: Southeast
*The Seminoles
*Sequoyah
*The Shoshoni
*Sinopah, the Indian Boy
*The Sioux
*The Sioux Indians: Hunters and Warriors of the Plains
*Sitting Bull
*Sitting Bull and the Plains Indians
*Sky Watchers of Ages Past
*Sleepy River
*Son of the Dine'
*Song of the Seven Herbs
*Soun Tetoken: Nez Perce Boy Tames a Stallion
*Southeast Indians: An Educational Coloring Book
*Southwest Indians: An Educational Coloring Book
*The Spark in the Stone
*Spirit Quest
*Spirit of the White Bison
*Spotted Eagle & Black Crow
*The Spotted Horse
*Squanto, Friend of the Pilgrims
*Star Boy
*The Story of Wounded Knee
*Sun Journey: A Story of Zuni Pueblo
*Sweetgrass
*Tales From the Cherokee Hills
*The Tarhumara: Middle America
*Tecumseh
*There Still Are Buffalo
*These Were the Sioux

*Thirteen Moons on Turtle's Back
*The Tipi: A Center of Native American Life
*Totem Pole
*The Totem Pole Indians of the Northwest
*Totem Poles and Tribes
*Tragedy of Tenaya
*The Trail on Which They Wept:
  The Story of a Cherokee Girl
*Trappers & Traders
*Tul-Tok-A-Na: The Small One
*The Tunica-Biloxi: Southeast
*Urban Indians
*Veho
*The Vision of the Spokane Prophet
*Vostaas: The Story of Montana's Indian Nations
*War Clouds in the West: Indians and
  Cavalrymen, 1860-1890
*War Pony
*We Have Always Been Here
*When Buffalo Free the Mountains:
  A Ute Indian Journey
*When Clay Sings
*When the Great Canoes Came
*When We Went to the Mountains
*The Winter Hunt
*Wolf Dog of the Woodland Indians
*Wolf Tales: Native American Children's Stories
*A Woman of Her Tribe
*Women in American Indian Society
*Wovoka
*The Yakima: Northwest
*Yerington Paiute Tribe Coloring Book
*The Yuma: California

KACHINAS

The Hopi Approach to the Art of Kachina Doll Carving
Hopi Kachina Dolls and Their Carvers
Hopi Kachina Dolls With a Key to Their Identification
Hopi Kachinas
Hopi Kachinas: The Complete Guide to
  Collecting Kachina Dolls
Hopi Katchinas Drawn by Native Artists
Kachina Dolls
The Kachina Dolls of Cecil Calnimptewa:
  Their Power, Their Struggle
Kachina Tales From the Indian Pueblos
Kachinas in the Pueblo World
Kachinas, Spirit Beings of the Hopi
Ray Manley's Hopi Kachina
Tusayan Katcinas & Hopi Katcina Altars
Zuni Katchinas
Zuni Katcinas, An Analytical Study

KICKAPOO INDIANS

Kenekuk, the Kickapoo Prophet
Kickapoo Tales
Kiikaapou: The Kansas Kickapoo

KIOWA INDIANS

Calendar History of the Kiowa Indians
The Economic Botany of the Kiowa Indians
A Grammar of Kiowa
An Historical Chronology of the Kiowa Tribe
Kiowa Memories: Images From Indian Territory, 1880
Kiowa Tales
*Kiowa Voices: Ceremonial Dance, Ritual and Song
Kiowa Voices: Myths, Legends & Folktales
The Kiowas
Law and Status Among the Kiowa Indians
Satanta, The Great Chief of the Kiowas & His People

KWAKIUTL INDIANS

Chiefly Feasts: The Enduring Kwakiutl Potlatch
Feasting With Cannibals: An Essay on
  Kwakiutl Cosmology
Fighting With Property: A Study of Kwakiutl P
  otlatching & Warfare
Geographical Names of the Kwakiutl Indians
Guests Never Leave Hungry: The Autobiography
  of James Sewid, A Kwakiutl Indian
Indians of the North Pacific Coast
Kwakiutl Art
Kwakiutl Culture as Reflected in Mythology
Kwakiutl Ethnography
Kwakiutl: Indians of British Columbia
Kwakiutl String Figures
The Kwakiutl of Vancouver Island
Kwakiutl Tales
Kwakiutl Texts
A Kawakiutl Village and School
Kwakwakawakw Settlement Sites, 1775-1920
Notes and Observations on the Kwakiutl People of the
  Northern Part of the Vancouver Island
  Adjacent Coasts
Our Chiefs & Elders
Religion of the Kwakiutl Indians
Traditions and Change on the Northwest Coast:
  The Makah, Nuu-chah-nulth, Southern Kwakiutl
  & Nuxalk

LAKOTA (SIOUX) INDIANS

Among the Sioux of Dakota
40th Anniversary of Crazy Horse Memorial
Bibliography of the Sioux
Black Elk: Holy Man of the Oglala
*Black Elk: A Man with a Vision
Black Elk: The Sacred Ways of the Lakota
Black Elk Speaks
Black Hills: Sacred Hills
Black Elk: The Sacred Ways of a Lakota
The Black Hills; Or, The Last Hunting Ground
  of the Dacotahs
Black Robe for the Yankton Sioux
Blue Star: The Story of Corabelle Fellows, Teacher
  at Dakota Missions, 1884-1888
The Canadian Sioux
Choteau Creek: A Sioux Reminiscence
Claims for Depredations by Sioux Indians
Crazy Horse and Korczak
Crazy Horse, The Strange Man of the Oglalas
Crying for a Vision: A Rosebud Sioux
  Trilogy 1886-1976
Dacotah: Or, Life and Legends of the
  Sioux Around Fort Snelling
A Dakota-English Dictionary
*Dakota Indians Coloring Book
Dakota Oratory
The Dakota or Sioux in Minnesota As
  They Were in 1834
Dakota Texts
Dakota War Whoop
Dakota Way of Life Series
An English-Dakota Dictionary
An Ethnography of Drinking & Sobriety
  Among the Lakota
Famous Chiefs of the Eastern Sioux
Fools Crow
The Forgotten Sioux: An Ethnohistory of the
  Lower Brule Reservation
Fort Laramie and the Sioux
Ghost-Dance Religion and the Sioux Outbreak of 1890
The Great Sioux Trail
The Great Sioux War
*Growing Up in Siouxland

History of the Santee Sioux: U.S. Indian Policy on Trial
Hoskila & the Red Buffalo
How to Take Part in Lakota Ceremonies
*If You Lived With the Sioux Indians
Indians in Minnesota, 4th Edition
Lakota Belief and Ritual
Lakota Myth
Lakota Society
Lakota Star Knowledge - Studies in Stellar Theology
Land of the Spotted Eagle
Last Days of the Sioux Nation
A Legend From Carzy Horse Clan
Legends of the Lakota
Legends of the Mighty Sioux
Lessons from Chouteau Creek
Little Crow, Spokesman for the Sioux
Madonna Swan: A Lakota Woman's Story
Mary and I: Forty Years with the Sioux
Meditiations with Native Americans: Lakota Spirituality
Meet the Lakota, Vol. One: The People
The Modern Sioux: Social Systems and
  Reservation Culture
My People the Sioux
The Mystic Lake Sioux: Sociology of the
  Mdewakantonwan Santee
Myths & Legends of the Sioux
Noble Red Man: Lakota Wisdomkeeper Mathew King
The Odyssey of Chief Standing Buffalo and the
Northern Sisseton Sioux
The Oglala Lakota Crazy Horse
Oglala Religion
Oglala Women: Myth, Ritual & Reality
Ohiyesa. Charles Eastman, Santee Sioux
Oktokahekagapi: Sioux Creation Story
Old Indian Days
Old Indian Legends
Pacifying the Plains: General Alfred Terry and
  the Decline of the Sioux, 1886-1890
Pictographic History of the Oglala Sioux
Quill and Beadwork of the Western Sioux
Red Cloud and the Sioux Problem
Red Cloud's Folks: A History of the
  Oglala Sioux Indians
The Red Record of the Sioux
Remember Your Relatives: Yankton Sioux Images,
  1865-1915
The Sacred Pipe: Blacl Elk's Account of the
  Seven Rites of Oglala Sioux
The Siouan Tribes of the East
*The Sioux
Sioux Collections
*The Sioux Indians: Hunters and Warriors of the Plains
Sioux: Life and Customs of a Warrior Society
The Sioux of the Rosebud: A History in Pictures
The Sioux Uprising of 1862
*Sitting Bull: Warrior of the Sioux
The Sixth Grandfather: Black Elk's Teachings Given
  to John G. Neihardt
Soldiering in Dakota: Among the Indians, 1863-1865
Songs of the Teton Sioux
Speaking of Indians
Stories of the Sioux
*The Story of Little Bighorn
Sun Dance for Andy Horn
The Sun Dance & Other Ceremonies of the Oglala
  Division of the Teton Dakota
Sundancing at Rosebud & Pine Ridge
Teton Sioux Music
*These Were the Sioux
They Led a Nation
Through Dakota Eyes
War Drums at Eden Prairie
Waterlily
Where the West Begins: Essays on Middle
  Border & Siouxland Writing
A Whirlwind Passes
White Cloud: Lakota Spirit

Wigwam Evenings: Sioux Tales Retold
John P. Williamson, A Brother to the Sioux
Wounded Knee 1973
Wounded Knee & the Ghost Dance Tragedy
Wounded Knee Massacre: From the
  Viewpoint of the Sioux
*The Yankton Sioux
Yellow Wolf: His Own Story
Yuwipi: Vision and Experience in Oglala Ritual

LAND CESSIONS, TENURES, REMOVALS & DISPUTES

American Indians Dispossessed: Fraud in
  Land Cessions Forced Upon the Tribes
Apologies to the Iroquois
Big Bear: The End of Freedom
Cherokee Removal: The William Penn Essays
  and Other Writings by Jeremiah Evarts
The Choctaw Before Removal
Considerations on the Present State of the Indians
  and Their Removal to the West of the Mississippi
Continent Lost--A Civilization Won: Indian
  Land Tenure in America
The Corporation and the Indian
Dispossessing the American Indian: Indian &
  Whites on the Colonial Frontier
The Dispossession of the American Indian, 1887-1934
The End of Indian Kansas
Indian Land Cessions in the U.S.
Indian Land Laws
Indian Land Tenure: Bibliographic Essays
  and a Guide to the Literature
Indian Lands
Indian Removal: The Emigration of Five
  Civilized Tribes of Indians
Indian Use of the Santa Fe National Forest
Indians, Bureaucrats and Land: The Dawes
  Act and the Decline of Indian Farming
Indigenous Peoples & Tropical Forests
Iroquois Land Claims
Native American Estate
Navajo Land Use: An Ethnoarchaeological Study
The Oneida Land Claims
*Only the Names Remain: The Cherokees
  and the Trail of Tears
Pueblo Indian Land Grants of the "Rio Abajo", NM
Pushed Into the Rocks: Southern California
  Indian Land Tenure
The Rape of the Indian Lands: An Original Anthology
Reconstruction in Indian Territory
Redskins, Ruffleshirts and Rednecks
Removal of the Cherokee Indians from Georgia
The Removal of the Cherokee Nation: Manifest
  Destiny or National Dishonor
Reservation to City: Indian Urbanization
  and Federal Relocation
The Second Long Walk: Navajo-Hopi Land Dispute
A Snug Little Purchase
Speeches on the Passage of the Bill for the
  Removal of the Indians
*The Story of the Trail of Tears
The Taos Indians & the Battle for Blue Lake
Territorial Subdivision and Boundaries of the
  Wampanoag, Massachusett and Nauset Indians
The Trail of Tears

LANGUAGES, DICTIONARIES, GLOSSARIES, ETC.

Absaloka: Crow Chilren's Writing
Ahtna Athabaskan Dictionary
Alaawich
Alaska Native Language Center Publications

Aleut Dictionary
America, Land of the Rising Sun
American Indian English
American Indian Language Series
American Indian Languages, Vol. 5
American Indian Linguistics & Literature
An Areal-Typological Study of American
  Indian Languages North of Mexico
Athapaskan Linguistics
Beginning Cherokee
Bibliographies of the Languages of the
  North American Indians
Bibliography of Language Arts Materials for
  Native North Americans, 1965-1974
Bibliography of the Languages of Native California
A Blackfoot-English Vocabulary
Caddoan Texts, Pawnee, South Band Dialect
Cahuilla Dictionary
Case & Agreement in Inuit
Chem'ivillu: Let's Speak Cahuilla
*Cherokee ABC Coloring Book
Cherokee Dictionary
Cherokee-English Dictionary
Cherokee-English Interliner, First Epistle
  of John of the New Testament
Cherokee Language Workbook
Cherokee Words
Cheyenne Indians: Sketch of the Cheyenne Grammar
Chickasaw: An Analytical Dictionary
Chickasaw Glossary
Chinook Jargon
Chiricahua & Mescalero Apache Texts
Choctaw Dictionary
Colloquial Navajo: A Dictionary
Comanche Dictionary & Grammar
Comparative Hokan-Coahuiltecan Studies
Comparative Studies in Amerindian Languages
A Comparative Study of Lake-Iroquoian Accent
Comparative Vocabularies & Parallel Texts
  In Two Yuman Languages of Arizona
Creek (Muscogee) New Testament Concordance
A Concise Blackfoot Grammar
The Creek Verb
Dakota Sioux Indian Dictionary
Dictionary of the Alabama Language
Dictionary of the American Indian
Dictionary of the Ojibway Language
A Dictionary of the Osage Language
A Dictionary of Papago Usage
Eastern Ojibwa-Chippewa-Ottawa Dictionary
Einguq
English-Cheyenne Dictionary
English-Eskimo & Eskimo-English Vocabularies
Everyday Lakota: An English-Sioux Dictionary
  for Beginners
Forked Tongues: Speech, Writing & Representation
  in North American Indian Texts
Fox Texts
General & Amerindian Ethnolinguistics
Grammar & Dictionary of the Language of the Hidatsa
Grammar & Dictionary of the Timucua Language
A Grammar of Comanche
A Grammar of Diegueno Nominals
Grammar of the Language of the Lenni Lenape,
  or Delaware Indians
Grammar of the Mikmaque Language of Nova Scotia
A Grammar of the Wappo Language
A Grammar of Southeastern Pomo
Handbook of American Indian Languages
Handbook of Creek (Muscogee) Grammar
Handbook of the Creek Language
History, Manners and Customs of the Indian
  Nations Who Once Inhabited Pennsylvania
  & the Neighboring States
Hopi Dictionary: Hopi-English, English-Hopi,
  Grammatical Appendix
Hopi Time

I'Ishiyatam
In Honor of Mary Haas
Indian Sign Language
Introduction to Cherokee
Introduction to Handbook of American Indian
Languages/Indian Linguistic Families of America
  North of Mexico
Introduction to the Study of Indian Languages
  with Words, Phrases & Sentences to Be Collected
Itza Maya Texts with a Grammatical Overview
Jicarilla Apache Texts
Journal of Exploring Tour
The Karankara Indians, The Coast People of Texas
Kawaiisu: A Grammar & Dictionary, with Texts
Keresan Texts
Kickapoo Tales
Kiliwa Dictionary
Koasati Grammar
Language, Culture and History:
  Essays by Mary R. Haas
Language Renewal Among American Indian Tribes
Languages of the Aboriginal Southeast:
  An Annotated Bibliography
Languages of the Tribes of the Extreme Northwest:
  Alaska, The Aleutians and Adjacent
  TerritoriesLessons In Hopi
Library of American Linguistics
Lower Umpqua Texts and Notes on the Kusan Dialects
A Manual of Navaho Grammar
Maricopa Morphology and Syntax
Meet Cree: A Guide to the Cree Language
Mumigciset Kalikait: A Yup'ik Language Term Book
*Na Yo Pisa
Navajo-English Children's Picture Dictionary
Navajo-English Dictionary
Navaho Grammar
Navajo Texts
A New Series of Blackfoot Texts
Newe Natekwinappeh: Shoshoni Stories & Dictionary
The North American Indian, Being a Series of Volumes
  Picturing & Describing the Indians
  of the U.S. & Alaska
North American Indian Language Materials, 1890-1965
Notes of a Twenty-Five Years' Service
  in the Hudson's Bay Territory
O Brave New Words: Native American
  Loanwords in Current English
Ojibwe Language
Ojibwe Vocabulary
One of the Keys: 1676-1776-1976: The
  Wampanoag Indian Contribution
One Thousand Useful Mohawk Words
Oneida Verb Morphology
An Outline of Basic Verb Inflections
  of Oklahoma Cherokee
Passamaquoddy Dictionary
San Carlos Apache Texts
Sequoyah
Sequoyah & the Cherokee Alphabet
Sequoyah, Father of the Cherokee Alphabet
The Shuswap Language
Siberian Yup'ik Eskimo
Sign Language Among the North American Indians
The Siouan Indian Language (Teton and Santee
  Dialects) Dakota
A Structural & Lexical Comparison of the Tunica,
  Chitimacha & Atakapa Languages
A Structured Approach to Learning the Basic
  Inflections of the Cherokee Verb
Studies in American Indian Languages
Studies in Southeastern Indian Languages
Supplement to the Handbook of Middle
  American Indians: Linguistics
Syntax and Semantics: The Syntax of
  Native American Languages
Theoretical Perspectives on Native
  American Languages

Tlingit Verb Dictionary
Tonkawa, An Indian Language of Texas
Topics in Mojave Syntax
Tovangar
Traditional Narratives of the Arikara Indians
Where the West Begins: Essays on Middle
  Border and Siouxland Writing
Wishram Texts: Together With Wasco Tales and Myths
Yerington Paiute Dictionary
Yerington Paiute Language Grammar
Yup'ik Eskimo Dictionary
Zeisberger's Indian Dictionary

LEGAL, LAWS, ETC.

Acts and Resolutions (of National Tribal Councils)
Alaska Natives and American Laws
American Indian Law In a Nutshell
The American Indian Law Series
American Indian Legal Materials: A Union List
American Indian Legal Studies Teacher's
  Manual & Text
American Indian Policy in the 20th Century
American Indian Tribal Courts
American Indian Water Rights & the Limits of the Law
American Indians, American Justice
American Indians, Time and the Law
Annotated Statutes of the Indian Territory
Basic Guide to Indian Community Advocacy
Behind the Trail of Broken Treaties
Bread & Freedom
The Case of the Seneca Indians in the
  State of New York
Cherokee Nation Code: Annotated
The Cheyenne Way: Conflict and Case
  Law in Primitive Jurisprudence
The Constitution and Laws of the
  American Indian Tribes
Felix S. Cohen's Handbook of Federal Indian Law
Constitutions, Treaties, and Laws Series
Constitution of the State of Sequoyah
The Consumer's Rights Under Warranties
Contracts & You
Criminal Jurisdiction Allocation in Indian Country
Digest of American Indian Law: Cases & Chronology
Diplomates in Buckskin
Directory of American Indian Law Attorneys
Documents of U.S. Indian Policy
Early American Indian Documents:
  Treaties & Laws, 1607-1789
English Institutions and the American Indian
Federal Indian Law, Cases & Material
The Federal-Indian Trust Relationship
Fifth Annual Indian Law Seminar
A Final Promise: The Campaign to Assimilate
  the Indians, 1880-1920
Guide to American Indian Documents in the
  Congressional Serial Set: 1817-1899
Handbook of American Indian Religious Freedom
Handbook of Federal Indian Law
Indian Court Judgements
Indian Education: Selected Statutes & Regulations
Indian Justice
Indian Justice: A Research Bibliography
The Indian Lawyer
Indian Nullification of the Unconstitutional Laws of
  Massachusetts, Relative to the Marshpee Tribe
Indian Police and Judges: Experiments in
  Acculturation and Control
The Indian Rights Association: The Herbert Welsh
  Years, 1882-1904
Indian Rights Manual
Indians & Criminal Justice
The Indians and the U.S. Constitution
An Iron Hand Upon the People: The Law Against
  the Potlatch on the Northwest Coast

Jicarilla Apache Tribal Code
Labor Laws, Union, and Indian Self-Determination
Landlord Tenant Relations
Law and the American Indian: Readings,
  Notes and Cases
Law Enforcement on Indian Reservations
  After Oliphant v. Suquamish Indian Tribes
Law and Identity: Lawyers, Native Americans
  and Legal Practice
Law and Status Among the Kiowa Indians
Laws of the Colonial and State Governments
  Relating to Indians and Indian Affairs, 1633-1831
Laws & Joint Resolutions
Leasing Indian Water
Legal Conscience, Selected Papers
The Legal Status of the Indian
Legal Structures for Indian Business
  Development on Reservations
Legends, Traditions and Laws of the Iroquois: Or, Six
  Nations, and History of the Tuscarora Indians
The Livingston Indian Records, 1666-1723
Model Court Development Project
The Native American Struggle: Conquering
  the Rule of Law A Colloquium
Native Americans and Nixon: Presidential Politics
  and Minority Self-Determination, 1969-1972
Native People in Canada: Contemporary Conflicts
Navajo Tribal Code
The New Deal & American Indian Tribalism: The
  Administration of the Indian Reorganization Act,
  1934-1945
Oil and Gas
Puritan Justice and the Indian: White Man's Law in
  Massachusetts, 1630-1763
Quarter-Acre of Heartache
Red Lake Court of Tribal Offenses Court Manual
Repossession and You
Sixth Annual Indian Law Conference
Treaties on Trial
You and the Utility Company
Your Rights As American Indians

LEGENDS

Aleut Tales & Narratives
American Indian Linguistics & Literature
American Indian Mythology
American Indian Myths & Legends
American Indian Stories
An-Nik-a-Del: The History of the Universe As Told
  By the Modes-Se Indians of California
Ancient Voices, Current Affairs: The Legend
  of the Rainbow Warriors
Apache Legends: Songs of the Wild Dancer
As My Grandfather Told It: Traditional
  Stories of the Koyukuk
The Bear Who Stole the Chinook: Tales
  from the Blackfoot
The Bear That Turned White; & Other Native Tales
Blackfoot Lodge Tales
Caddoan Texts, Pawnee, South Band Dialect
Californian Indian Nights
Catawba Texts
Cherokee Legends and the Trail of Tears
Cherokee Vision of Eloh'
Cheyenne Memories
Children of the Twilight: Folktales of Indian Tribes
Clothed-in-Fur and Other Tales: An Introduction
  to an Ojibwa World View
Coyote: A Trickster from the American Southwest
Coyote Was Going There: Indian Literature of the
  Oregon Country
Dakota Texts
The Dawn of the World
Dine Bahane' The Navajo Creation Story
Dirty Boy: A Jicarilla Tale of Raid and War

Do Them No Harm
Dragonfly's Tale
Earth Elder Stories
Elderberry Flute Song, Contemporary Coyote Tales
Enchanted Moccasins & Other Legends of the
  American Indian
Estiyut Omayat: Creek Writings
Ethnography and Folklore of the Indians
  of Northwestern California
Eye of the Changer: A Northwest Indian Tale
The Faithful Hunter & Other Abenaki Stories
Folk-Tales of the Salishan & the Sahaptin Tribes
Fox Texts
The Freeing of the Deer and Other
  New Mexico Indian Myths
From Indian Legends to the Modern Bookshelf
Ghost Voices: Yakima Indian Myths, Legends
  and Hunting Stories
The Gift of the Gila Monster: Navajo Ceremonial Tales
Giving: Ojibway Stories & Legends from the
  Children of Curve Lake
Giving Voice to Bear
A Good Medicine Collection: Life in
  Harmony with Nature
The Gospel of the Great Spirit
The Great Change
Haa Shuka, Our Ancestors
Haboo: Native American Stories from Puget Sound
Hear Me My Chief: Nez Perce Legend and History
A Heart Full of Turquoise: Pueblo Indian Tales
Hopi Coyote Tales: Istutuwutsi
Hopi Ruin Legends
Hoskila & the Red Buffalo
How Glooskap Outwits the Ice Giants
How Rabbit Stole the Fire
Indian Legends From the Northern Rockies
Indian Stories from the Pueblos: Tales
  of New Mexico and Arizona
Indian Stories and Legends of the Stillaguamish,
  Sauks & Allied Tribes
Indian Story and Song from North America
Indian Tales
Indian Tales & Legends
Indians of the Feather River: Tales
  of the Concow Maidu of California
The Inland Whale: Nine Stories Retold
  from California Indian Legends
Iroquois Stories
Keresan Texts
K'etaalkkaanee: The One Who Paddled
  Among the People & the Animals
Kickapoo Tales
Kiowa Tales
Kiowa Voices: Myths, Legends and Folktales
Kwakiutl Tales
Kwakiutl Tales: New Series
Landfill Meditation: Crossblood Stories
The Legend of Natural Tunnell
Legends of the Lakota
Legends of the Longhouse
Legends of the Micmacs
Legends of the Mighty Sioux
Legend of Our Nations
Legends of the Yosemite Miwok
Legends Told by the Old People
The Lenape & Their Legends
Lore of the Great Turtle: Indian Legends
  of Mackinac Retold
Lower Umpqua Texts and Notes on the Kusan Dialects
Lummi Indians of Northwest Washington
Maidu Myths & Tales
The Man to Send Rain Clouds
The Man Who Married the Moon and Other
  Pueblo Indian Folk-Stories
Mandan-Hidatsa Myths and Ceremonies
Masked Gods: Navaho and Pueblo Ceremonialism
Mimbres Mythology

Myth of Hiawatha, and Other Oral Legends
The Mythology of the Bella Coola Indians
Myths & Folktales of the Alabama-Coushatta Indians
Myths & Hunting Stories of the
  Mandan & Hidatsa Sioux
Myths & Legends of the Lipan Apache Indians
Myths & Legends of the Sioux
Myths & Tales from the San Carlos Apache
Myths & Tales of the Chiricahua Apache Indians
Myths & Tales of the Jicarilla Apache Indians
Myths & Tales of the Southeastern Indians
Myths & Tales of the White Mountain Apache
Myths of the Cherokee
Myths of the Cherokee & Sacred Formulas
Myths of the Modocs: Indian Legends
  from the Northwest
Myths of the New World Indians
Myths of the North American Indians
Myths of Pre-Columbian America
The Naked Man, Vol. 4: Mythologiques
Native American Legends
Native American Legends: The Southeast
Native American Stories
Navajo Coyote Tales
Navajo Indian Myths
Navaho Legends
Navajo Stories of the Long Walk Period
Nehalem Tillimook Tales
Newe Natekwinappeh: Shoshoni Stories & Dictionary
Nez Perce Texts
Nihancan's Feast of Beaver: Animal Tales
  of the North American Indians
Noccalula: Legend, Fact & Function
North Amerian Indian Mythology
Northern Tales: Traditional Stories of
  Eskimo & Indian Peoples
Ojibway Heritage
Ojibway Tales
Oktokahekagapi: Sioux Creation Story
Old Father Story Teller
Old Indian Legends
One More Story: Contemporary Seneca Tales
Origin Legend of the Navajo Enemy Way
Origin Legend of the Navajo Flintway
The Origin of Table Manners, Vol. 3: Mythologiques
Osage Life & Legends
The Other Side of Nowhere
Pawnee Hero, Stories and Folktales
Plains Cree Texts
Plains Indian Mythology
The Pollen Path: A Collection of Navajo Myths
The Portable North American Indian Reader
Pueblo Indian Folk-Stories
Pueblo Stories and Storytellers
The Punishment of the Stingy & Other Indian Stories
Quail Song: A Pueblo Indian Folktale
Raven Tales
Recently Discovered Tales of Life Among the Indians
The Red Swan: Myths and Tales
  of the American Indian
Return of the Sun, Tales From the
  Northeastern Woodlands
Sacred Stories of the Sweet Grass Cree
Schoolcraft's Indian Legends from Algic Researches
Seneca Myths & Folk Tales
The Sky Is My Tipi
Some Kind of Power: Navajo Children's
  Skinwalker Narratives
Spider Woman's Granddaughters
Spiderwoman's Dream
Shamans & Kushtakas: North Coast Tales
  of the Supernatural
Song of the Seven Herbs
Spirit Mountain: An Anthology of Yuman Story & Song
The Silver Arrow and Other Indian Romances
  of the Dune Country
The Stone Canoe

Stories from the Indian Wigwams
  & Northern Campfires
Stories of the Sioux
Stories We Live By
Tales the Elders Told: Ojibway Legends
Tales of the Anishinaubaek: Ojibway Legends
Tales of the Cochiti Indians
Tales of Kankakee Land
Tales of the Mohaves
Tales of the North American Indian
Taos Tales
Teachings of Nature
The Ten Grandmothers
Tewa Tales
Their Stories of Long Ago
Thirteen Moons on Turtle's Back
A Thousan Years of American Indian Storytelling
Tlingit Myths & Texts
Tlingit Tales: Potlatch & Totem Poles
Top of the Hill
Traditional Stories & Foods
Traditions of the Caddo
Traditions of the Quinault Indians
Tsonakwa& Yolaikia: Legends in Stone, Bone & Wood
Turtle Dream
Turtle Meat and Other Stories
Two Old Women: An Alaska Legend of Betrayal,
  Courage & Survival
Under the Indian Turquoise Sky
The Unwritten Literature of the Hopi
Voices of the Wind: Native American Legends
Walk in Peace
The Way to Rainy Mountain
Ways of Indian Magic
Ways of Indian Wisdom
Weavers Tales
Where Legends Live
The White Canoe and Other Legends of the Ojibways
White Wolf Woman
Why the North Star Stands Still
The Wind Eagle
Wisconsin Chippewa Myths & Tales
The Witch of Goingsnake & Other Stories
Write It On Your Heart: World of an Okanagan
  Storyteller
Yuchi Tales
Zuni Folk Tales
Zuni Mythology

LEGENDS, JUVENILE LITERATURE

*Ah Mo: Indian Legends from Washington State
*ANPAO: An American Indian Odyssey
*The Apaches & Navajos
*Approaches to Teaching Momaday's "
  The Way to Rainy Mountain"
*Around the World in Folktale & Myth: American Indian
*Atariba and Niguayona
*Aunt Mary, Tell Me Stories
*Baby Rattlesnake
*A Bag of Bones
*Boat Ride With Lillian Two Blossom
*The Boy Who Dreamed of an Acorn
*The Boy Who Lived With the Seals
*Ceremony - In the Circle of Life
*Cheyenne Legends of Creation
*Cheyenne Short Stories
*Clamshell Boy
*Coyote & the Fish
*Coyote & Kootenai
*Coyote & Little Turtle
*Coyote Stories
*Coyote Tales of the Montana Salish
*Coyote's Pow-Wow
*Coyote Was Going There
*Coyote & the Winnowing Birds

*Creation of a California Tribe:
  Grandfather's Maidu Indian Tale
*Creation Tales from the Salish
*The Crying for a Vision
*Cut From the Same Cloth: American Women
  of Myth. Legend, and Tall Tale
*Dancing Drum
*The Day of the Ogre Kachinas: A Hopi Indian Fable
*Earth Magic, Sky Magic: North American Indian Tales
*Flint's Rock
*The Flute Player: An Apache Folktale
*Fox Song
*Grandfather Grey Owl Told Me
*Grandfather's Origin Story: The Navajo
  Indian Beginning
*Grandfather's Story of Navajo Monsters
*Grandmother Stories
*Grandmother Stories of the Northwest
*Grandmother's Christmas Story:
  A True Quechan Indian Story
*The Great Change
*Heetunka's Harvest: A Tale of the Plains Indians
*Hoksila & the Red Buffalo
*The Hunter and the Ravens
*The Hunter and the Woodpecker
*Iktomi & the Berries: A Plains Indian Story
*Iktomi & the Buffalo Skull: A Plains Indian Story
*Iktomi & the Ducks
*In the Beginning
*Indian Folk Tales from Coast to Coast
*Indian Legends From the Pacific Northwest
*Indian Myths from the Southeast
*Indian Tales of the Northern Plains
*A Legend from Crazy Horse Clan
*The Legend of the Bluebonnet: An Old Tale of Texas
*The Legend of the Indian Paintbrush
*The Legend of Tom Pepper & Other Stories
*Legends of Chief Bald Eagle
*Legends of the Great Chiefs
*Linda's Indian Home
*Little Firefly
*Mystery at Echo Cliffs
*Mystery of Coyote Canyon
*Myths & Legends of the Haida Indians
  of the Northwest
*Myths & Legends of the Indian Southwest
*Myths & Legends of the Indians of the Southwest
*Native American Animal Stories
*Native American Legends
*Native American Stories
*Navajo Coyote Tales
*Nightwalker & the Buffalo
*North American Indian Stories
*The Old Ones Told Me: American Indian
  Stories for Children
*Otokahekagapi: Sioux Creation Story
*Pachee Goyo: History & Legends from the Shoshone
*The People Shall Continue
*Pieces of White Shell
*Prairie Legends
*Prairie Smoke
*Quillworker
*The Rainbow Bridge
*The Ring on Woot-Kew's Tail: Indian Legends
  of the Origin of the Sun, Moon & Stars
*The Rolling Head: Cheyenne Tales
*The Rough-Face Girl
*Sacred Song of the Hermit Thrushs
*Salish Folk Tales
*Skunny Wundy: Seneca Indian Tales
*Son of Thunder
*Song of the Wild Violets
*Southern Indian Myths & Legends
*Spelyi and Other Indian Legends
*Star Tales: North American Indian Stories
  About the Stars
*Stolen Princess: A Northwest Indian Legend

*Tales From the Cherokee Hills
*Thirteen Moons on Turtle's Back
*This Land Is My Land
*Turquoise Boy
*Walker of Time
*Weaver's Tales
*When Hopi Children Were Bad
*White Buffalo Women
*Why Buffalo Roam
*Why the Possum's Tail Is Bare: And Other
  North American Indian Nature Tales

LEWIS & CLARK EXPEDITION

Among the Sleeping Giants
Do Them No Harm
Exploring the West
How George Rogers Clark Won the West
The Incredible Journey of Lewis & Clark
The Journals tof the Lewis & Clark Expedition
Letters of the Lewis & Clark Expedition
*Lewis & Clark
Lewis & Clark Among the Indians
Lewis & Clark: Voyage of Discovery
*The Lewis & Clark Expedition
Lewis & Clark and the Shahaptian
  Speaking Americans
Meriwether Lewis and William Clark: Soldiers,
  Explorers, & Partners in History
Original Journals of the Lewis & Clark Expedition
Pathfinders of the West
Sacagawea: Indian Interpreter to Lewis & Clark
*The Story of the Lewis & Clark Expedition
Those Tremendous Mountains
The Trail of Lewis and Clark: 1804-1904
The Way to the Western Sea
West to the Pacific: The Story of
  Lewis & Clark Expedition

LITERATURE

All My Relations: An Anthology of Contemporary
  Canadian Native Fiction
American Indian in English Literature
  of the 18th Century
American Indian Literature: An Anthology
American Indian Linguistics & Literature
American Indian Literatures
The Broken Cord
A Circle of Nations: Voices & Visions
  of American Indians
The Colour of Resistance: Contemporary Collection
  of Writing by Aboriginal Women
Conversations With Louise Erdrich and Michael Dorris
Dancing on the Rim of the World
Dead Voices: Natural Agonies in the New World
Early American Writings
Earth Power Coming: Short Fiction in
  Native American Literature
Fire Sticks: A Collection of Stories
Forked Tongues
Four Masterworks of American Indian Literature
The Golden Woman: The Colville Narrative
  of Peter J. Seymour
The Hawk is Hungry and Other Stories
Index to Literature on the American Indian
The Indian in American Literature
Indian Land Tenure
Interpreting the Indian
Library of Aboriginal American Literature
Literature By and About the American Indian
Mountain Windsong: A Novel of the Trail of Tears

The Names
Narrative Chance: Postmodern Discourse on
  Native American Indian Literatures
Native American in American Literature:
  A Selectively Annotated Bibliography
A Native Heritage
Nature Power: In the Spirit of Okanagan Storyteller
New Voices from the Longhouse
New Voices in Native American Literary Criticism
New Writers of the Purple Sage
Other Destinies: Understanding the
  American Indian Novel
A Papago Traveler
Place & Vision: The Function of Landscape in
  Native American Fiction
Pocahontas & Co: The Fictorial American Indian
  Woman in 19th Century Literature
The Portable North American Indian Reader
Reading the Fire
Recovering the Word
Returning the Gift
Secrets from the Center of the World
The Sharpest Sight: A Novel
The Singing Spirit
Smoothing the Ground
The Sounds of Rattles & Clappers
Studies in American Indian Literature
Summer In the Spring: Anishinaabe
  Lyric Poems & Stories
Sun Tracks
Supplement tot he Handbook of Middle
  American Indians, Vol. 3: Literature
Teaching Guide for Indian Literature
Traditional Literatures of the American Indian
Tribal Secrets: Recovering American Indian
  Intellectual Traditions
The Voice in the Margin
Woven Stone
Writers of the Purple Sage
Writing the Circle
Word Ways

MAGIC

Breath of the Invisible
Magic in the Mountains: The Yakima Shaman:
  Power & Practice
Navaho Witchcraft
Paiute Sorcery
Sacred Bundles of the Sac and Fox Indians
Spirit Healing: Native American Magic & Medicine
Star Woman: We Are Made from Stars and to the Stars
We Must Return
Witchcraft in the Southwest: Spanish and Indian
Supematuralism on the Rio Grande
Zuni Fetishism

THE MAKAH INDIANS

The Makah Indians
Tradition and Change on the Northwest Coast:
  The Makah, Nuu-chah-nulth, Southern Kwakiutl
  & Nuxalt

MANDAN & HIDATSA INDIANS

Agriculture of the Hidatsa Indians
Buffalo Bird Woman's Garden: Agriculture
  of the Hidatsa Indians
*A Coloring Book of Hidatsa Indian Stories
Ethnography and Philology of the Hidatsa Indians
*Goodbird the Indian: His Story
Grammar & Dictionary of the Languages of the Hidatsa

*The Hidatsa
Hidatsa Eagle Trapping
The Hidatsa Earthlodge
Hidatsa Shrine & the Beliefs Respecting It
Hidatsa Social & Ceremonial Organization
The Horse & the Dog in Hidatsa Culture
Mandan and Hidatsa Music
Mandan-Hidatsa Myths & Ceremonies
*The Mandans
Mandans, A Study of Their Culture,
  Archaeology and Language
Myths & Hunting Stories of the
  Mandan & Hidatsa Sioux
Notes on the Social Organization & Customs
  of the Mandan, Hidatsa & Crow Indians
The Village Indians of the Upper Missouri:
  The Mandans, Hidatsas & Arikaras
The Way to Independence: Memories of a
  Hidatsa Indian Family, 1840-1920
White Influence Upon Plains Indian Painting:
  George Catlin & Carl Bodmer Among the Mandan,
  1832-34

MASKS

The False Faces of the Iroquois
Head and Face Masks in Navaho Ceremonialism
*North American Indian Masks
The Relation of Seneca and Seneca False Face
  Masks to Seneca and Ontario Archaeology
A World of Faces: Masks of the Northwest
  Coast Indians

MEDICINE/SHAMANISM

American Indian/Alaska Native Tribal &
  Village HIV-1 Policy Guidelines
American Indian Medicine
Apache Medicine-Men
Breath of the Invisible
The Broken Cord
Buffalo Woman Comes Singing: The Spirit Song
  of a Rainbow Medicine Woman
California Shamanism
Cherokee Plants
Coyoteway: A Navajo Holyway Healing Ceremonial
Crow Indian Medicine Bundles
Cry of the Eagle: Encounters with a Cree Healer
The Dancing Healers: A Doctor's Journey
  of Healing with Native Americans
Disease Change and the Role of Medicine
Drinking Careers: A 25-Year Study
  of Three Navajo Populations
Folk Medicine of the Delaware and
  Related Algonkian Indians
Geraniums for the Iroquois
Gift of Power: The Life & Teachings
  of a Lakota Medicine Man
Grandmothers of Light: A Medicine
  Woman's Sourcebook
Guide to Indian Herbs
Handbook of Native American Herbs
A Handbook of Northeastern Indian Medicinal Plants
How Indians Use Wild Plants for Food,
  Medicine & Crafts
Indian Doctor
Indian Herbalogy of North America
Indian Medicine Power
Indian Uses of Native Plants
Introduction to Navajo Chant Practice
Iroquois Medical Botany
Lakota Belief and Ritual
Lame Deer: Seeker of Visions
Mad Bear

Magic in the Mountains: The Yakima Shaman:
  Power & Practice
Medicinal Uses of Plants by Indian Tribes of Nevada
Medicinal & Other Uses of North American Plants
Medicine Among the American Indians
Medicine Cards: The Discovery of Power
  Through the Ways of Animals
The Medicine Man of the American Indian
  and His Cultural Background
The Medicine Men
Medicine Men of the Apache
Medicine Women, Curanderas & Women Doctors
Mystics, Magaicians, & Medicine People
Native Healer: Initiation into an Ancient Art
Navajo Classification of Their Song Ceremonials
Navajo Indian Medical Ethnobotany
Navajo Medicine Bundles or Jish
Navajo Medicine Man Sand Paintings
Navaho Symbols of Healing
*North American Indian Medicine People
Notes on the Gynecology & Obstetrics
  of the Arikara Tribe of Indians
Ohiyesa: Charles Eastman, Santee Sioux
Penobscot Shamanism
The People's Health: Anthropology & Medicine
  in a Navajo Community
The Peyote Book: A Study of Native Medicine
Piman Shamanism and Staying Sickness
Plants Used As Curatives by Certain
  Southeastern Tribes
Pretty Shield, Medicine Woman of the Crows
Rainbow Medicine: A Visionary Guide to
  Native American Shamanism
Raven's Guide
Rolling Thunder
Sanapia: Comanche Medicine Woman
The Shaman and the Medicine Wheel
The Shaman's Touch: Otomi Indian Symbolic Healing
Shamanic Odyssey
Shamanism in Western North America
Song of the Seven Herbs
Spirit Healing: Native American Magic & Medicine
A Study of Delaware Indian Medicine
  Practice & Folk Beliefs
Tales of a Shaman's Apprentice
Tuberculosis Among Certain Indian Tribes of the U.S.
Two Cultures Meet: Pathways for American
  Indians Into Medicine
Washo Shamans and Peyotists: Religious
  Conflict in an American Indian Tribe
The Wolves of Heaven: Cheyenne Shamanism,
  Ceremonies, & Prehistoric Origins

MENOMINEE INDIANS

Dreamers With Power: The Menominee
Ethnobotany of the Menomini Indians
Folklore of the Menomini Indians
Material Culture of the Menomini
Menominee Drums: A History
Menominee Drums: Tribal Termination
  and Restoration, 1854-1974
Menominee Music
Menomini Texts

MISSIONS

American Indians and Christian Missions
Annals of Shawnee Methodist Mission
  and Indian Manual Labor School
Black Robe for the Yankton Sioux
Bruchko
Catechism & Guide: Navaho-English
Champions of the Cherokees: Evan & John B. Jones

Cherokees and Missionaries, 1789-1839
Christianity and Native Traditions
Churchmen and the Western Indians, 1820-1920
Disease, Depopulation & Culture Change in
  Northwestern New Spain, 1518-1764
Dix-Huit Ans Chez Les Sauvages
Great Black Robe
A Guide to Cherokee Documents
  in the Northeastern U.S.
Historical Memoirs, Relating to the Housatonic Indians
History of Baptist Indian Missions
History of the Catholic Missions Among the
  Indian Tribes of the U.S., 1529-1854
History of Texas, 1673-1779
Index to the Records of the Moravian Mission
  Among the Indians of North America
The Indian in American Life
Indian Life at the Old Missions
Indian Missions
The Indians & the California Missions
An Inventory of the Mission Indian Agency Records
Kino's Historical Memoir of Primeria Alta
Augustine Laure, S.J., Missionary to the Yakimas
Martyrs of the Oblong and Little Nine
Mary and I, or Forty Years With the Sioux
Thomas Mayhew, Patriarch to the Indians, 1593-1682
Mission San Xavier Del Bac: A Photographic Essay
  on the Desert People and Their Church
Missionary to the Navaho
Old Frontiers: The Story of the Cherokee Indians
  From the Earliest Times to the Date of Their
  Removal to the West, 1838
Osage Mission Baptisms, Marriages,
  & Internments, 1820-1886
The Pipe & Christ
Nicolas Point, S.J.: His Life & Northwest
  Indian Chronicles
Red Man in the U.S.
Reminiscence of the Indians
Salvation and the Savage: An Analysis of Protestant
  Missions and American Indian Response, 1787-1862
Sketches of Mission Life Among the Indians of Oregon
Teepee Neighbors
Tomahawk and Cross: Lutheran Missionaries Among
  Northern Prairie Indians, 1858-1866
John P. Williamson: A Brother to the Sioux

MIXED BLOODS

Interior Landscapes: Autobiographical Myths
  & Metaphors
Mixed-Bloods & Tribal Dissolution: Charles Curtis
  & the Quest for Indian Identity

MODOC INDIANS

Ancient Modocs of California and Oregon
Captain Jack, Modoc Renegade
The Indian History of the Modoc War
Life Amongst the Modocs: Unwritten History
The Modoc
Modocs and Their War
Myths of the Modocs: Indian Legends
  from the Northwest
Primitive Pragmatists: The Modoc
  Indians of Northern California

MOHAVE INDIANS

Tales from the Mohaves
Topics in Mojave Syntax

MOHAWK INDIANS

Johnson of the Mohawks
A Journey Into Mohawk & Oneida Country, 1634-1635
The Mohawk That Refused to Abdicate

MOUNDS, MOUND-BUILDERS

Aboriginal Monuments of the State of New York
Burial Mounds of the Red River Headwaters
Cahokia Mounds Museum Society Books
The Earthshapers
The Hopewell Mound Group of Ohio
Indian Mounds of the Atlantic Coast: A Guide
  to Sites From Maine to Florida
Indian Mounds of the Middle Ohio Valley:
  A Guide to Adena & Ohio Hopewell Sites
Mounds for the Dead
Native Shell Mounds of North America: Early Studies
Perch Lake Mounds
Remember Native America!
Report of the Mound Explorations of the
  Bureau of Ethnology
The Sacred Geography of the American
  Mound-Builders
Status & Health in Prehistory: A Case
  Study of the Moundville Chiefdom
Under Your Feet
Wakemap Mound

MUSIC & DANCE

Aloha Sampler
Angels to Wish By
*American Indian Music and Musical Instruments
The American Indians & Their Music
The Arapaho Sun Dance, The Ceremony
  of the Offerings Lodge
Blackfoot Musical Thought: Comparative Perspectives
Ceremonial Songs of the Creek & Yuchi Indians
Ceremonies of the Pawnee
Cherokee Dance & Drama
The Cherokee Ghost Dance
Cheyenne & Arapaho Music
Chippewa Music
Choctaw Music
Dances of the Tewa Pueblo Indians:
  Expressions of Life
Dancing With Creation
Frances Densmore and American Indian Music
A Few Summer Ceremonials at Zuni Pueblo
Fifteen Flower World Variations: A Sequence
  of Songs from the Yaqui Deer Dance
Haida Songs & Tsimshian Texts
The Hoop of Peace
Hopi Snake Dance
Hopi Songs
In Vain I Tried to Tell You: Essays in
  Native American Ethnopoetics
Indian Dances of North America:
  Their Importance to Indian Life
Indian Games & Dances With Native Songs
Indian Story & Song From North America
Indians' Book
Introduction to Navaho Chant Practice
The Iroquois Eagle Dance
Iroquois Music & Dance: Ceremonial Arts
  of Two Seneca Longhouses
*Love Flute
Mandan and Hidatsa Music
Menominee Music
Moki Snake Dance
Mother Earth, Father Sky: Ancient Chants by
  Pueblo & Navajo Indians of the Southwest

Moving Within the Circle: Contemporary Native
  American Music & Dance
Music and Dance Research of the
  Southwestern Indians
Music of Acoma, Isleta, Cochiti & Zuni Pueblos
Music of the Indians of British Columbia
The Maru Cult of the Pomo Indians
Myth, Music & Dance of the American Indian
Music & Dance Research of the Southwestern Indians
The Music of the North American Indian
Myth, Music & Dance of the American Indian
Native American Dance: Ceremonies
  & Social Traditions
Native North American Music & Oral Data:
  A Catalogue of Sound Recordings, 1893-1976
Navaho Classification of Their Song Ceremonials
The Navajo (Or Corral) Fire Dance
Navajo War Dance
Nootka & Quileute Music
The Northern Traditional Dancer
Northern Ute Music
Notes on the Buffalo-Head Dance of the
  Bear Gens of the Fox Indians
Oklahoma Delaware Ceremonies, Feasts and Dances
On the Music of the North American Indians
The Osage Ceremonial Dance I'n-Lon-Schka
Papago Music
The Pawnee Ghost Dance Hand Game: Ghost Dance
  Revival & Ethnic Identity
Pawnee Music
The People: Native American Thoughts & Feelings
Peyote Music
The Prophet Dance of the Northwest & Its Derivatives:
  The Source of the Ghost Dance
Seminole Music
The Shoshoni-Crow Sun Dance
Singing for Power: The Song Magic of the
  Papago Indians of Southern Arizona
Sioux Music
The Snake Dance of the Hopi Indians
The Snake Dance of the Moquis of Arizona
Songs of Indian Territory
Song of the Sky
Songs of the Teton Sioux
Songs of the Tewa
Songs of the Wigwam
Spirit Mountain: An Anthology of Yuman Story & Song
The Story of Indian Music: Its Growth & Synthesis
Study of Omaha Indian Music
The Sun Dance & Other Ceremonies of the
  Oglala Division of the Teton Dakota
The Sun Dance of the Crow Indians
Teton Sioux Music & Culture
Tsee-Ma'Heone-Nemeotanse:
  Cheyenne Spiritual Songs
The Tsimishian: Their Arts & Music
War Dance
Yaqui Deer Songs/Maso Bwakam
Yuman & Yaqui Music

NAVAJO INDIANS

The Agricultural & Hunting Methods
  of the Navaho Indians
American Indian Tribal Government & Politics
The Army and the Navajo
*Between Sacred Mountains: Navajo Stories
  & Lessons from the Land
Bibliography of the Navaho Indians
Big Bead Mesa: An Archaeological Study
  of Navaho Acculturation
Bighorse the Warrior
Blessingway
The Book of the Navajo
Border Towns of the Navajo Nation

Bosque Redondo: A Study of Cultural Stress
   at the Navajo Reservation
A Cannoneer in Navajo Country
Canyon De Chelly: The Story Behind the Scenery
Circles, Consciousness & Culture
Colloquial Navajo: A Dictionary
Contemporary Navajo Affairs
Coyoteway: A Navajo Holyway Healing Ceremonial
Crow Man's People: Three Seasons with the Navajo
Denetsosie
Denizens of the Desert: A Tale in Word & Picture
   of Life Among the Navaho Indians
The Development of Capitalism in the Navajo Nation:
   A Political-Economic History
Dine Bahane', The Navajo Creation Story
The Dine: Origin Myths of the Navaho Indians
Dinetah: Navajo History
Drinking Careers: A 25-Year Study of Three
   Navajo Populations
The Economics of Sainthood: Religious
   Change Among the Rimrock Navajos
The Enduring Navaho
Enduring Traditions: Art of the Navajo
Ethnobotany of the Navajo
Genuine Navajo Rugs: How to Tell
The Gift of the Gila Monster: Navajo Ceremonial Tales
The Gift of Spiderwoman: Southwestern Textiles,
   The Navajo Traditions
Hand Trembling, Frenzy Witchcraft, & Moth Moadness
Head and Face Masks in Navaho Ceremonialism
Historic Navajo Weaving: 1800-1900:
   Three Cultures-One Loom
History of the Navajos: The Reservation Years
Hogans: Navajo Houses and House Songs
Holy Wind in Navajo Philosophy
Hosteen Klah: Navaho Medicine Man
   and Sand Painter
If You Take My Sheep...The Evolution and Conflicts
   of Navajo Pastoralism, 1630-1868
In the Beginning: The Navaho Creation Myth
Indian Drinking: Navajo Practices and
   Anglo-American Theories
Introduction to Navaho Chant Practice
*Philip Johnston and the Navajo Code Talkers
Kinaalada: A Navajo Puberty Ceremony
Kinaalda: A Study of the Navaho
   Girl's Puberty Ceremony
Language and Art in the Navajo Universe
Left Handed: A Navajo Autobiography
A Little History of the Navajos
The Long Walk: A History of the Navajo Wars
A Magic Dwells: A Poetic and Psychological Study
   of the Navaho Emergence Myth
The Main Stalk: A Synthesis of Navajo Philosophy
A Manual of Navaho Grammar
Masked Gods: Navaho and Pueblo Ceremonialism
Meditations with the Navajo: Prayer Songs
   & Stories of Healing & Harmony
Monument Valley: The Story Behind the Scenerey
Mother Earth, Father Sky: Ancient Chants by Pueblo
   and Navajo Indians of the Southwest
The Myth & Prayers of the Great Star Chant
   & the Myth of the oyote Chant
Mythology and Values: An Analysis of
   Navaho Chantway Myths
Nanise': A Navajo Herbal
*The Navajo
The Navaho
Navajo Aging
Navajo Arts & Crafts
Navaho Art and Culture
The Navajo Atlas: Environments, Resources,
   Peoples & History of the Dine Bikeyah
Navajo Blessingway Singer
A Navajo Bringing-Home Ceremony
Navajo: A Century of Progress
Navajo Changes: A History of the Navajo People

*Navajo Children
Navaho Classification of Their Song Ceremonials
A Navajo Confrontation and Crisis
Navajo Code Talkers
Navajo Coyote Tales
Navajo Creation Myth: The Story of Emergence
A Navajo Crisis and Confrontation
*Navajo Cultural Guides
*The Navajo Design Book
Navajo Dictionary on Diagnostic Terminology
Navajo Education in Action: The Rough Rock
   Demonstration School
Navajo Education, 1948-1978:
   Its Progress & Problems
Navajo Energy Resources
Navajo-English Children's Picture Dictionary
Navajo-English Dictionary
The Navaho (Or Corral) Fire Dance
Navajo Foreign Affairs: 1795-1846
Navaho Grammar
Navajo History
The Navajo Hunter Tradition
*The Navajo Indian Book
*Navajo Indian Coloring Book
Navajo Indian Medical Ethnobotany
Navaho Indian Myths
The Navajo Indians
Navajo Infancy: An Ethological Study
   of Child Development
Navajo Kinship and Marriage
Navajo Land Use: Navajo Leadership & Government
Navajo Leadership & Government
Navaho Legends
Navajo Livestock Reduction: A National Disgrace
Navajo Medicine Man Sand Paintings
Navajo Mountain and Rainbow Bridge Religion
The Navajo Nation
Navajo Native Dyes
Navajo Oral History Traditions
Navajo Oral Traditions
Navaho Pottery Making
Navajo Pottery: Traditions & Innovations
Navaho Religion: A Study of Symbolism
Navajo Resources and Economic Development
Navajo Rugs: How to Find, Evaluate,
   Buy and Care for Them
Navajo Rugs, Past and Present
Navajo Sacred Places
Navajo Sandpainting Art
Navajo Sandpainting From Religious
   Act to Commercial Art
Navajo Sandpainting: The Huckel Collection
Navajo Shepherd and Weaver
Navajo Stories of the Long Walk Period
Navajo Textiles
Navajo Texts
Navajo & Tibetan Sacred Wisdom:
   The Circle of the Spirit
Navajo Trader: Essays on a Region & Its Literature
Navajo Trading Days
Navajo: Tradition & Change in the Southwest
The Navajo Treaty, 1868
Navajo Tribal Code
Navajo War Dance
Navajo Weavers and Silversmiths
A Navaho Weaving, Its Technic and History
Navajo Weaving, Navajo Ways
Navajo Weaving: Three Centuries of Change
Navajo Weaving Today
Navaho Witchcraft
Navajoland: Family Settlement and Land Use
Navajoland Plant Catalog
Navajoland: A Portfolio of Navajo Life
   During the 1940's & 1950's
The Navajos
The Navajos: A Critical Bibliography
The Navajos Long Walk for Education

The Navajos and the New Deal
The Night Chant: A Navaho Ceremonial
The Northern Navajo Frontier, 1860-1900:
   Expansion Through Adversity
Of Mother Earth and Father Sky
Old Mexican, Navaho Indian: A Navaho Autobiography
Old Navajo Rugs: Their Development
   from 1900 to 1940
Origin Legend of the Navajo Enemy Way
Origin Legend of the Navajo Flintway
Our Friends: The Navajos
Outcroppings From Navajoland
*Owl in the Cedar Tree
Patterns and Sources of Navajo Weaving
The People Speak: Navajo Folk Art
Pictorial Weavings of the Navajos
*Pieces of White Shell: A Journey to Navajoland
A Political History of the Navajo Tribe
The Pollen Path: A Collection of Navajo Myths
Prehistory in the Navajo Reservoir District
Property Concepts of the Navaho Indians
Pueblo & Navajo Indian Life Today
Red Capitalism: An Analysis of the Navajo Economy
Reflections of Social Life in the Navaho Origin Myth
Right After Sundown: Teaching Stories of the Navajo
Rugs & Posts: The Story of Navajo Weaving
Sacred Words: A Study of Navajo Religion and Prayer
Shonto: Study of the Role of the Trader in a
   Modern Navajo Community
Social Life of the Navajo Indians
Son of Old Man Hat
Soul Concepts of the Navaho Indians
Stories of Traditional Navajo Life and Culture
Storm Patterns: Poems From Two Navajo Women
Study of Navajo Symbolism
*Sunpainters: Eclipse of the Navajo Sun
Through Navajo Eyes
Through White Men's Eyes: A Contribution
   to Navajo History
Time Among the Navajo
To Run After Them: Cultural and Social Bases
   of Cooperation in a Navajo Community
Turquoise and the Navajo
A Voice in Her Tribe: A Navajo Woman's Own Story
Voices in the Canyon
Walk in Beauty: The Navajo and Their Blankets
Weaving a Navajo Blanket
When Navajos Had Too Many Sheep: The 1940's
Where the Two Came to Their Father: A Navaho
   War Ceremonial Given by Jeff King
The Witch Purge of 1878: Oral and Documentary
History in the Early Navajo Reservation Years
Wupatki & Walnut Canyon

NEZ PERCE INDIANS

Chief Joseph Country; Land of the Nez Perce
*Chief Joseph's Own Story as Told by
   Chief Joseph in 1879
Conflict and Schism in Nez Perce Acculturation
Flight of the Nez Perce
Forlorn Hope
Hear Me My Chiefs: Nez Perce Legend and History
Howard's Campaign Against the
   Nez Perce Indians, 1878
I Will Fight No More Forever: Chief Joseph
   and the Nez Perce War
Joseph, Chief of the Nez Perce
Let Me Be Free: The Nez Perce Tragedy
Nez Perce Country
Nez Perce Indians
The Nez Perce Indians and the
   Opening of the Northwest
Nez Perce Joseph
Nez Perce Narratives
Nez Perce Texts

Nez Perces: Tribesmen of the Columbia Plateau
Red Eagles of the Northwest: The Story of
  Chief Joseph and His People
Saga of Chief Joseph
Sapat'qayn: Twentieth Century Nez Perce Artists
With the Nez Perces: Alice Fletcher in the Field,
  1889-1992
Yellow Wolf: His Own Story

OMAHA INDIANS

Omaha Secret Societies
Omaha Sociology
The Omaha Tribe
Study of Omaha Indian Music
The Upstream People: An Annotated Research
  Bibliography of the Omaha Tribe

ORIGIN

Amerinds and Their Paleoenvironments
  in Northeastern North America
The Antiquity and Origin of Native American
The Complete Visitor's Guide to Mesoamerican Ruins
The Dine: Origin Myths of the Navaho Indians
Discoveries of the Truth
Early Man in the New World
The First Americans
Mitakuye Oyasin: We are All Related
Only the Wind

OSAGE INDIANS

Annals of Osage Mission
Beacon on the Plain
Bibliography of the Osage
A Dictionary of the Osage Language
The First Protestant Osage Missions, 1820-1837
History of Neosho County, Kansas
A History of the Osage People
The Imperial Osages
*The Osage
The Osage Ceremonial Dance I'n-Lon-Schka
Osage Indian Customs and Myths
Osage Indians: Bands and Clans
Osage Life and Legends: Earth People - Sky People
Osage Mission Baptisms, Marriages and Interments,
  1820-1886
Osages: Children of the Middle Waters
The Osages, Dominant Power of the
  Louisiana Territory
Symbolic and Decorative Art of the Osage People
Talking to the Moon
Traditions of the Osage
Wah-Kon-Tah: The Osage and the White Man's Road

PAIUTE INDIANS

From the Sands to the Mountain
*Let Me Tell You a Story & Workbook
Life Among the Paiutes
The Northern Paiute Indians of California
A Numu History - The Yerington Paiute Tribe
*The Numu Way & Workbook
The Paiute, Indians of North America
Paiute Sorcery
Southern Paiute
The Southern Paiutes
Southern Paiute Ethnohistory

Southern Paiute Ethnology
Survival Arts of the Primitive Paiutes
Sarah Winnemucca of the Northern Paiutes
Wovoka & the Ghost Dance: A Source Book
Wovoka Poster
Yerington Paiute Dictionary
Yerington Paiute Language Grammar
*Yerington Paiute Tribe Coloring Book

PAWNEE INDIANS

Ceremonies of the Pawnee
Description of a Journey and Visit to
  the Pawnee Indians
The Dubar-Allis Letters on the Pawnee
Expedition to the Pawnee Pict Village in 1834
The Lost Universe: Pawnee Life and Culture
Frank J. North: Pawnee Scout, Commander & Pioneer
*The Pawnee
Pawnee Ghost Dance Hand Game
Pawnee Hero Stories and Folktales
The Pawnee Indians
Pawnee and Kansa (Kaw) Indians
Pawnee and Lower Loup Pottery
Pawnee Music
Pawnee Passage, 1870-1875
Pawnees: A Critical Bibliography
Traditions of the Skidi Pawnee
Travels in North America, Including a
  Summer with the Pawnees
Two Great Scouts and Their Pawnee Battalion
When Stars Came Down to Earth: Cosmology of the
  Skidi Pawnee Indians of North America

PERIODICALS

American Indian
American Indian and Alaska Native Newspapers
  and Periodicals, 1826-1924 & 1971-1985
Let My People Know: American Indian Journalism,
  1828-1978
Schoolcraft: Literary Voyager

PEYOTE, PEYOTISM

Doors of Perception
The Peyote Book: A Study of Native Medicine
The Peyote Cult
Peyote: The Divine Cactus
Peyote Hunt: The Sacred Journey of Huichol Indians
Peyote Music
The Peyote Religion
Peyote Religion Among the Navaho
Peyotism in the West: A Historical
  and Cultural Perspective
Pipe, Bible & Peyote Among the Oglala Lakota:
  A Study in Religious Identity
Washo Shamans and Peyotists: Religious
  Conflict in an American Indian Tribe

PHILOSOPHY

An American Urphilosophie: An American
  Philosophy BP (Before Pragmatism)
An Analysis of Navajo Temporality
The Bear Tribe's Sel-Reliance Book
Classification and Development of North American
  Indian Cultures: A Statistical
  Analysis of the Driver-Massey Sample
Daily Affirmations from the Divine Creator
Feasting with Cannibals: An Essay on
  Kwakiutl Cosmology

Headed Upstream: Interviews with Iconoclasts
Holy Wind in Navajo Philosophy
The Indian Testimony
Joy Before Night: Evelyn Eaton's Last Years
The Main Stalk: A Synthesis of Navajo Philosophy
Messages from the Divine Creator
Messages from Mother Earth: Daily Affirmations
Native American Prophecies
Native American Wisdom
Native Light for a Dark World
Neither Wolf Nor Dog: On Forgotten
  Roads With an Indian Elder
The Path of Power
The Primal Mind: Vision & Reality in Indian America
Profiles in Wisdom: Native Elders Speak
  Out About the Earth
The Roaring of the Sacred River
Shadowcatchers
The Soul of an Indian; and Other
  Writings from Ohiyesa
The Soul of the Indian: An Interpretation
Spirit Healing: Native American Magic & Medicine
Spiritual Wisdom of the Native Americans
Teachings from the American Earth:
  Indian Religion & Philosophy
To Touch the Wind: An Introduction to
  Native American Philosophy & Beliefs
Vision Quest
Walk in Balance
Wisdom of the Elders
The Wisdom of the Great Chiefs

PICTURE-WRITING

Coffee in the Gourd
The Lenape and Their Legends
Picture-Writing of the American Indians
Study of Navajo Symbolism

PICTURES, PHOTOGRAPHS & PORTRAITS

America on Paper: The First Hundred Years
*Among the Plains Indians
O.E. Berninghaus - Taos, New Mexico: Master
  Painter of American Indians and Frontier West
The Big Missouri Winter Count
Catlin's North American Indian Portfolio
Children of the First People: A Photographic Essay
Michael Coleman
Crazy Horse & Korczak
Crying for a Dream:The Earth Is Our Mother
Crying for a Vision: A Rosebud Sioux
  Trilogy 1886-1976
Dwellers at the Source: Southwestern Indian
  Photographs of A.C. Vroman, 1895-1904
Seth Eastman: Pictorial Historian of the Indian
Enduring Culture: A Century of Photography
  of the Southwest Indians
German Artist on the Texas Frontier:
  Friedrich Richard Petri
Grand Endeavors of American Indian Photography
Honor Dance: Native American Photographs
Hopi Photographers–Hopi Images
The Hopi Photographs: Kate Cory, 1905-1912
The Horsemen of the Americas
In a Sacred Manner We Live
The Indian Legacy of Charles Bird King
Indian Portraits of the Pacific Northwest
The Interior Salish Tribes of British Columbia
Korczak, Storyteller in Stone
The Natural Man Observed: A Study of
  Catlin's Indian Gallery
New Indian Sketches

North American Indians Coloring Album
The North American Indians: Photographs
  by Edward S. Curtis
The Photograph and the American Indian
Pictographic History of the Oglala Sioux
Picture-Writing of the American Indians
Plains Indian Raiders: The Final Phases of Warfare
  from the Arkansas to the Red River
Quanah: A Pictorial History of the
  Last Comanche Chief
The Reservation Blackfeet, 1885-1945: A
  Photographic History of Cultural Survival
The Saga of Sitting Bull's Bones
Search for the Purebloods
*Sharing Our Worlds
The Story of the Meadowlark
Traditions and Cahnge on the Northwest Coast
The Vanishing Race and Other Illusions:
  Photographs of Indians by Edward S. Curtis

PLACE NAMES

By Canoe & Moccasin: Some Native Place
  Names of the Great Lakes
Florida Place-Names of Indian Origin &
  Seminole Personal Names
Geographical Names of the Kwakiutl Indians
Handbook of Tribal Names of Pennsylvania
Indian Place-Names in Alabama
Indian Place-Names in Illinois
Indian Place-Names in Mexico & Central America
Indian Place-Names in Michigan
Indian Place-Names in North America
Indian Place-Names of New England
Indian Place-Names of the Penobscot
  Valley & the Maine Coast
Indian Place-Names: Their Origins,
  Evolution, and Meanings
Names of the American Indian
O Brave New Words
Spanish & Indian Place-Names of California
Study in the Etymology of the Indian Place Name
Utah Place Names
Washington State Place Names

POETRY

After & Before the Lightning
American Indian Prayers & Poetry
Bone Dance
Buckskin Hollow Reflections
The Business of Fancydancing
Drawings of the Song Animals:
  New & Selected Poems
Drifting Through Ancestor Dreams
An Eagle Nation
Finding the Center: Narrative
  Poetry of the Zuni Indians
Four Winds: Poems from Indian Rituals
In Mad Love and War
In the Trail of the Wind: American Indian
  Poems & Ritual Orations
Interpreting the Indian
The Invisible Musician
Lost Copper
Luminaries of the Humble
A Magic Dwells: A Poetic & Psychological
  Study of the Navaho Emergence Myth
*Many Winters
Maria: The Potter of San Ildefonso
Mud Woman
Sarojini Naidu: An Introduction to
  Her Life, Work & Poetry

Neon Powwow: New Native American
  Voices of the Southwest
New and Old Voices of Wah'kon-Tah
Offering: Poetry & Prose
On the Landing
The Portable North American Indian Reader
Alex Posey
Saanii Dahataal / The Women Are Singing
The Sky Clears: Poetry of the American Indians
Songs
Songs of the Tewa
Star Quilt
Storm Patterns: Poems From Two Navajo Women
Summer In the Spring: Anishinaabe
  Lyric Poems & Stories
Survival This Way: Interviews with
  American Indian Poets
Teepees Are Folded: American Indian Poetry
That's What She Said: Contemporary Poetry
  & Fiction by Native American Women
The Twilight of the Sioux
When It Rains: Papago & Pima Poetry
When No One Is Looking
Woven Stone
Writing the Circle
Yaqui Deer Songs/Maso Bwakam:
  A Native American Poetry
Yuman Poetry with Morphological Analysis

POLITICS & GOVERNMENT

American Indian Tribal Government and Politics
Controlling Consulting: A Manual for Native
  American Governments & Organization
Exiled in the Land of the Free
In the Spirit of Crazy Horse
The Minutes of the Michigan Commission
  on Indian Affairs, 1956-1977
The Political Economy of North American Indians

PONCA INDIANS

The Ponca Chiefs
Ponca Indians
Ponca Indians: Appraisal of Land
The Ponca Indians With Reference to
  Their Claim to Certain Lands
Ponca Reservation, 1877

POTAWATOMI INDIANS

Ethnobotany of the Forst Potawatomi Indians
Indians and a Changing Frontier:
  The Art of George Winter
Kinsmen Through Time: An Annotated
  Bibliography of Potawatomi History
Mascoutens of Prairie Potawatomi Indians
*Potawatomi
The Potawatomis: Keepers of the Fire

POTLATCH

Chiefly Feasts: The Enduring Kwakiutl Potlatch
Feasting With Mine Enemy: Rank & Exchange
  Among Northwest Coast Societies
Fighting With Property: A Study of Kwakiutl
  Potlatching & Warfare
Haida Potlatch
An Iron Hand Upon the People
Potlatch: Native Ceremony & Myth
  on the Northwest Coast
Tlingit Tales: Potlatch and Totem Poles

POTTERY

Acoma & Laguna Pottery
American Indian Pottery
American Indian Pottery: An Identification
  and Value Guide
Ancient Indian Pottery of the Mississippi River Valley
Art of Clay: Timeless Pottery of the Southwest
The Book of Indian Crafts & Costumes
Ceramic Decoration Sequence at an Old Indian
  Village Site Near Siciliy Island, Louisiana
Collecting Shawnee Pottery: A Pictorial Reference
  and Price Guide
Decorative Art of the Southwestern Indians
Designs & Factions: Politics, Religion, & Ceramics
  on the Hopi Third Mesa
Designs on Prehistoric Hopi Pottery
Early Pottery in the Southeast
Fourteen Families in Pueblo Pottery
From This Earth: The Ancient Art of Pueblo Pottery
Generations in Clay: Pueblo Pottery of the
  American Southwest
Handbook of Northern Arizona Pottery Wares
Historic Pottery of the Pueblo Indians, 1600-1800
Hopi and Hopi-Tewa Pottery
Hopi Pottery Symbols
Indian Pottery of the Southwest:
  A Selected Bibliography
Introduction to Hopi Pottery
The Living Tradition of Maria Martinez
Making Native American Pottery
Maria
Maria Making Pottery
Maria Martinez: Pueblo Potter
Maria: The Potter of San Ildefonso
The Mimbres: Art & Archaeology
Mud Woman
Navaho Pottery Making
Navajo Pottery: Traditions & Innovations
Papago Indian Pottery
The Pottery From Arroyo Hondo Pueblo
Pottery of the Great Basin and Adjacent Areas
Pottery of the Pajarito Plateau and of Some
  Adjacent Regions in New Mexico
Pottery Techniques of Native North America
Prehistoric Hopi Pottery Designs
The Pueblo Potter: A Study of Creative
  Imagination in Primitive Art
Pueblo Pottery Making: A Study of the
  Village of San Ildefonso
Pueblo Pottery of the New Mexico Indians
*Pueblo Storyteller
The Pueblo Storyteller
Pueblos: Prehistoric Indian Cultures of the Southwest
Quail Song: A Pueblo Indian Folktale
The Quapaw and Their Pottery
Seven Families in Pueblo Pottery
Southwestern Pottery: An Annotated Bibliography &
  List of Types & Wares
Storytellers & Other Figurative Pottery
Swarts Ruin: A Typical Mimbres Site in
  Southwestern New Mexico
Margaret Tafoya: A Tewa Potter's Heritage and Legacy
Style Trends in Pueblo Pottery in the Rio Grande
  & Little Colorado Cultural Areas From the
  16th to 19th Century
Talking With the Clay: The Art of Pueblo Pottery
Tlapacoya Pottery in the Museum Collection
*When Clay Sings
Within the Underworld Sky: Mimbres Art in Context
Zuni Pottery

POW-WOWS

California Powwows
Pow Wow
*Powwow
Pow-Wow Calendar
The Pow Wow Highway
Pow-Wow: On the Red Road
Pow Wow: & Other Yakima Indian Traditions
A Trip to a Pow Wow

PSYCHOLOGY

American Indian and White Children
Bibliography of North American Indian Mental Health
Childhood and Folklore: A Psychoanalytic
   Study of Apache Personality
Indian Nation
Modern Indian Psychology
Mohave Ethnopsychiatry & Suicide
Psychocultural Change and the American Indians:
   An Ethnohistorical Analysis
Psychosocial Research on American Indian
   and Alaska Native Youth

PUEBLO INDIANS

American Pueblo Indian Activity Books
Architecture of Acoma Pueblo
Architecture of the Pueblo Indians:
   An Annotated Bibliography
The Architecture of Social Integration in
   Prehistoric Pueblos
Cochiti: A New Mexico Pueblo
Coyote Tales from the Indian Pueblos
Cushing at Zuni
Dances of the Tewa Pueblo Indians
Deliberate Acts: Changing Hopi Culture
   Through the Oraibi Split
Earth Fire: A Hopi Legend of the
   Sunset Crater Eruption
Ethnobotany of the Hopi
Excavation of Main Pueblo at Fitzmaurice Ruin
A Few Summer Ceremonials at the Tusayon Pueblos
A Few Summer Ceremonials at Zuni Pueblo
The First Koshare
Fourteen Families in Pueblo Pottery
The Fourth World of the Hopis
Hano: A Tewa Indian Community in Arizona
Historical Background of the Santa Ana Pueblo
Historical Introduction to Studies Among
   the Sedentary Indians of New Mexico
Hopi Bibliography
Hopi Indian Altar Iconography
Hopi Katchinas
*Hopi Mysteries
The Hopi Photographs
Hopi Snake Ceremonies
The Hopi Way: Tales from a Vanishing Culture
Hopis, Tewas, and the American Road
The Idea of Fertilization in the Culture
   of the Pueblo Indians
Indian Stories from the Pueblos
Indian Tales from Picuris Pueblo
Indians of Pecos Pueblos
Kachinas in the Pueblo World
Language, History, & Identity
Life in the Pueblos
*Little Boy with Three Names: Stories of Taos Pueblo
Maasaw: Profile of a Hopi God
The Man Who Married the Moon and Other Pueblo
   Indian Folk-Stories
Masked Gods: Navaho and Pueblo Ceremonialism
Meditations with the Hopi

Modern Transformation of Moenkopi Pueblo
Mother Earth, Father Sky: Ancient Chants by
   Pueblo and Navajo Indians of the Southwest
Music of Acoma, Isleta, Cochiti and Zuni Pueblos
My Adventures in Zuni
The Mythical Pueblo Rites Doctrine
New Perspectives on the Pueblos
Notes on Cochiti, New Mexico
Notes on Zuni
Old Father Story Teller
The Origin & Development of the Pueblo Katsina Cult
An Outline of the Documentary History
   of the Zuni Tribe
People of the Middle Place: A Study of the Zuni Indians
Petroglyphs & Pueblo Myths of the Rio Grande
Prehistoric Households at Turkey Creek Pueblo, AZ
A Preliminary Study of the Pueblo of Taos, NM
*The Pueblo
Pueblo Birds & Myths
Pueblo Crafts
Pueblo Cultures
Pueblo Designs
A Pueblo God and Myths
Pueblo Indian Embroidery
Pueblo Indian Folk-Stories
Pueblo Indian Journal
The Pueblo Indian Revolt of 1696 and the
   Franciscan Missions in New Mexico
Pueblo Indian Textiles
Pueblo Indian Water Rights
The Pueblo Indian World
The Pueblo Indians
The Pueblo Indians of New Mexico
The Pueblo Indians of North America
Pueblo Indians of San Ildefonso
Pueblo Mothers & Children
Pueblo: Mountain, Village, Dance
Pueblo Nations: Eight Centuries of
   Pueblo Indian History
Pueblo & Navajo Indian Life Today
The Pueblo of Jemez
Pueblo of San Felipe
Pueblo of Santa Ana, New Mexico
Pueblo of Santo Domingo, New Mexico
The Pueblo Potter
Pueblo Pottery Making
Pueblo Pottery of the New Mexico Indians
Pueblo Profiles
Pueblo Stories & Storytellers
The Pueblo Storyteller
*A Pueblo Village
*The Pueblos
Pueblos: Prehistoric Indian Cultures of the Southwest
Racial Prehistory in the Southwest
   and the Hawikuh Zunis
The Re-Establishment of the Indians in Their Pueblo
   Life Through the Revival of Their Traditional Crafts
Ritual in Pueblo Art: Hopi Life in Hopi Painting
Salinas Pueblo Missions National Monument
Scalp Ceremonial of Zuni
Schat-Chen: History, Traditions & Narratives
   of the Queres Indians of Laguna & Acoma
Seven Families in Pueblo Pottery
Signs from the Ancestors: Zuni Cultural
   Symbolism and Perceptions of Rock Art
Social and Ceremonial Organization of Cochiti
Social Organization of the Tewa of New Mexico
Social Organization of the Western Pueblos
Songs of the Tewa
Stories of Maasaw, a Hopi God
A Study of Pueblo Architecture
Tales of the Cochiti Indians
Talking with the Clay: The Art of Pueblo Pottery
The Taos Indians
The Taos Indians & the Battle for Blue Lake
Taos Tales
The Taos Trappers

Tewa Tales
Tewa World
The Tiguas: Pueblo Indians of Texas
Trends in Pueblo Pottery in the Rio Grande & Little
   Colorado Cultural Areas From the 16th to 19th
   Century
When Cultures Meet
Within the Underworld Sky
Work a Day Life of the Pueblos
A Zuni Atlas
Zuni Bread Stuff
Zuni Fetishes
Zuni Folk Tales
The Zuni Indians
Zuni Katchinas
Zuni Kin and Clan
The Zuni Man-Woman
Zuni Mythology
Zuni: Selected Writings of Frank Hamilton Cushing
Zuni Texts
The Zunis
The Zunis of Cibola

RELIGION & MYTHOLOGY

The American Indian Ghost Dance, 1870 & 1890:
   An Annotated Bibliography
American Indian Mythology
American Indian Prayers and Poetry
American Indian Prophets: Religious Leaders
   & Revitalization Movements
Analysis of Coeur D'Alene Indian Myths
Birds, Beads & Bells: Remote Sensing of a
   Pawnee Sacred Bundle
Black Elk: Holy Man of the Oglala
*Black Elk: A Man with a Vision
Black Elk: The Sacred Ways of the Lakota
Black Elk Speaks
Black Hills: Sacred Hills
Blessingway
Book of the Gods and Rites and the Ancient Calendar
A Book of Tales, Being Myths of the
   North American Indians
California Indian Nights
Carlos Castaneda, Academic Opportunism,
   and the Psychedelic Sixties
Cave of the Jagua: The Mythological
   World of the Tainos
The Cherokee Ghost Dance
Cherokee New Testament
A Cherokee Prayerbook
Cherokee Psalms, A Collection of Hymns
Cherokee Vision of Eloh'
The Cherokees and Christianity, 1794-1870
Children of Cottonwood
Chinigchinix, An Indigenous California Indian Religion
Christian Indians and Indian Nationalism, 1855-1950
Christianity and Native Traditions
Circles, Consciousness, and Culture
The Complete Book of Natural Shamanism
Concept of the Guardian Spirit in North America
Creation Myths of Primitive America
*Creation Tales from the Salish
Creation's Journey: Native American Identity & Belief
Creek (Muskogee) New Testament Concordance
Crying for a Dream: The World Through
   Native American Eyes
The Devil in the New World
The Dine: Origin Myths of the Navaho Indians
Dramatic Elements in American Indian Ceremonials
The Dream Seekers
Earth Fire: A Hopi Legend of the
   Sunset Crater Eruption
The Economics of Sainthood: Religious Change
   Among the Rimrock Navajos

Elementary Forms of the Religious Life
Encyclopedia of Native American Religions
The False Faces of the IroquoisThe Feathered Sun:
  Plains Indians in Art & Philosophy
A Few Summer Ceremonials at the Tusayon Pueblos:
  Natal Ceremonies of the Hopi Indians
Finding a Way Home: Indian & Catholic
  Spiritual Paths of the Plateau Tribes
Flight of the Seventh Moon: The Teaching
  of the Shields
Ghost Dance
Ghost Dance Messiah: The Jack Wilson Story
Ghost-Dance Religion and the Sioux Outbreak of 1890
The Ghost-Dance Religion and Wounded Knee
Giving Voice to Bear: Native American Myths,
  Images, and Rituals of the Bear
God Is Red: A Native View of Religion
Gods of the Popol Vuh
The Gospel of the Great Spirit
The Gospel of the Redman
Government and Religion of the Virginia Indians
Grandmothers of Light: A Medicine
  Woman's Sourcebook
Great American Indian Bible
*Guardian Spirit Quest
Haida Texts & Myths
Handbook of American Indian Religious Freedom
He Who Hunted Birds in His Father's Village:
  The Dimensions of a Haida Myth
The Hidden Language of the Seneca
Hopi Indian Altar Iconography
Hopi Kachina Dolls With a Key to Their Identification
Hopi Kachinas
Hopi and Zuni Ceremonialism
I Become Part of It: Sacred Dimensions
  in Native American Life
The Idea of Fertilization in the Culture
  of the Pueblo Indians
Imagine Ourselves Richly: Mythic Narratives
  of North American Indians
In the Beginning: The Navaho Creation Myth
Indian Myths
Indians of Northeastern North America
Iroquoian Cosmology
Journey to the Four Directions
Kenekuk, the Kickapoo Prophet
Kwakiutl Culture as Reflected in Mythology
Lakota Belief and Ritual
Lakota Life
Lakota Myth
Living the Sky: The Cosmos of the American Indian
Maasaw: Profile of a Hopi God
Masks of the Spirit: Image & Metaphor in Mesoamerica
Meditation With Native Americans: Lakota Spirituality
Meditations with Animals: A Native American Bestiary
Meditations with the Hopi
Meditations with the Navajo: Prayer-Songs & Stories
  of Healing & Harmony
Mother Earth: An American Story
Mother Earth Spirituality: Native American Paths
  to Healing Ourselves & Our World
Myth, Music and Dance of the American Indian
The Myth and Prayers of the Great Star Chant
  & the Myth of the Coyote Chant
Mythology of the Blackfoot Indians
The Mythology of North America
Mythology and Values: An Analysis of
  Navaho Chantway Myths
Myths of the Cherokees and Sacred
  Formulas of the Cherokees
Myths of the Modocs
Myths of the New World Indians
Myths of the New World: A Treatise on the Symbolism
  and Mythology of the Red Race of America
The Myths of the North American Indians
Myths and Tales of the Southeastern Indians
The Naked Man, Vol 4: Mythologiques

Narrative of the Mission of the United Brethren
  Among the Delaware & Mohegan Indians
Native American Folklore, 1879-1979
Native American Religions: A Geographical Survey
Native American Religions: An Introduction
Native American Religions: North America
Native American Religious Action
Native Healer: Initiation into an Ancient Art
Native North American Spirituality of the
  Eastern Woodlands
Native Religions of North America
Native American Voices
A Navaho Bringing-Home Ceremony: The Claus
  Chee Sonny Version of Deerway Ajilee
Navajo Creation Myth: The Story of Emergence
Navajo Mountain and Rainbow Bridge Religion
Navaho Religion: A Study of Symbolism
Navajo Sacred Places
Ni-Kso-Ko-Wa: Blackfoot Spirituality, Traditions,
  Values, and Beliefs
The Northern Algonquian Supreme Being
Not For Innocent Ears: Spiritual Traditions
  of a Desert Cahuilla Medicine Woman
Oglala Religion
The Old North Trail: Or, Life, Legends &
  Religion of the Blackfeet Indians
The Orders of the Dreamed
Papago Indian Religion
The Pastor's Handbook
Peyote: The Devine Cactus
Peyote Hunt: The Sacred Journey of Huichol Indians
Peyote Religion: A History
The Phoenix of the Western World:
  Quetzalcoatl and the Sky Religion
Pipe, Bible & Peyote Among the Oglala Lakota:
  A Study in Religious Identity
The Pipe & Christ
Plains Indian Mythology
The Pollen Path: A Collection of Navajo Myths
The Power of Silence
Profiles in Wisdom: Native Elders Speak
  About the Earth
Pueblo Birds & Myths
Pueblo Cultures
Pueblo God & Myths
Rainhouse & Ocean: Speeches for the Papago Year
Red Man's Religion: Beliefs & Practices
  of the Indians of North of Mexico
The Red Swan: Myths & Tales of the American Indians
Reflections of Social Life in the Navaho Origin Myth
Religion & Ceremonies of the Lenape
Religion & Hopi Life in the 20th Century
Religion in Native North America
The Religion of the Crow Indians
Religion of the Kwakiutl Indians
The Religions of the American Indians
Renewing the World: Plains Indian Religion & Morality
Return of the Indian Spirit
Return of the Thunderbeings
Sacred Encounters: Father De Smet and the
  Indians of the Rocky Mountain West
The Sacred Geography of the American
  Mound-Builders
Sacred Ground
Sacred Language: The Nature of Supernatural
  Discourse in Lakota
Sacred Path Cards: The Discovery of Self
  Through Native Teachings
The Sacred Pipe: Black Elk's Account of the
  Seven Rites of the Oglala Sioux
Sacred Places: How the Living Earth
  Seeks Our Friendship
Sacred Scrolls of the Southern Ojibway
Sacred Sites of the Indians of the American Southwest
Sacred Stories of the Sweet Grass Cree
The Sacred: Ways of Knowledge, Sources of Life
Sacred Words: A Study of Navaio Religion and Prayer

Scalp Ceremonial of Zuni
Seeing With the Native Eye: Contributions
  to the Study of Native American Religion
Seneca Indian Myths
A Separate Reality
Seven Visions of Bull Lodge
Shamanic Odyssey: The Lushootseed Salish
  Journey to the Land of the Dead
Shamans & Kushtakas: North Coast
  Tales of the Supernatural
Sioux Indian Religion: Tradition & Innovation
The Sixth Grandfather: Black Elk's Teachings
  Given to John G. Neihardt
Southern Indian Myths and Legends
Spirit Healing: Native American Magic & Medicine
Spiritual Legacy of the American Indian
Stories of Masaw, a Hopi God
Stories of the Sioux
Strange Journey: The Vision Life of a
  Psychic Indian Woman
The Study of American Indian Religions
The Sun Dance Religion: Power for the Powerless
Sun Men of the Americas
Tah-Koo Wah-Kan: Or, The Gospel
  Among the Dakotas
Tales of a Shaman's Apprentice
Teachings from the American Earth:
  Indian Religion and Philosophy
To Touch the Wind
Traditional Ojibwa Religion and Its Historical Changes
The Transformation of Bigfoot: Maleness,
  Power & Belief Among the Chipewyan
Treatise on the Heathen Superstitions
Trickster: Study in American Indian Mythology
Tusayan Katchinas & Hopi Altars
The Upward Moving & Energence Way
Vital Souls: Bororo Cosology, Natural
  Symbolism & Shamanism
Voices of Earth and Sky
Voices of Our Ancestors: Cherokee
  Teachings from the Wisdom Fire
*Warriors of the Rainbow: Strange & Prophetic
  Dreams of the Indian Peoples
Washo Shamans and Peyotists: Religious
  Conflict in an American Indian Tribe
Waterway
With Good Heart: Yaqui Beliefs &
  Ceremonies in Pascua, Village
Wisdomkeepers: Meetings with Native
  American Spiritual Elders
The Wolves of Heaven: Cheyenne Shamanism,
  Ceremonies & Prehistoric Origins
Wovoka and the Ghost Dance: A Source Book
Yurok Myths
Zuni Fetishes

RESERVATIONS

Ancient Treasures
Bacavi: A Hopi Village
Background History of the Coeur D'Alene
  Indian Reservation
Bread & Freedom
Crying for a Dream: The Earth is Our Mother
Culture, Change and Leadership in a Modern Indian
  Community: The Colorado River Indian
  Reservation
Discover Indian Reservations: A Visitor's
  Welcome Guide
Enemy Ancestors: The Anasazi World,
  With a Guide to Sites
Indian America: A Traveler's Companion
Indian Reservations: A State & Federal Handbook
The Nome Lackee Indian Reservation, 1854-1870
North American Indian Landmarks: A Traveler's Guide

Quarter-Acre of Heartache
The Reservation
The Reservation Blackfeet,1885-1945

RITES & CEREMONIES

Book of the Gods and Rites and the Ancient Calendar
Burr's Hill: A 17th Century Wampanoag
  Burial Ground in Warren, RI
Ceremonies of the Pawnee
Coyoteway: A Navajo Holyway Healing Ceremonial
Dancing Gods: Indian Ceremonials of
  New Mexico & Arizona
Dramatic Elements in American Indian Ceremonials
The Forgotten Artist
*Guardian Spirit Quest
Head and Face Masks in Navaho Ceremonialism
Hogans: Navajo Houses and House Songs
Hopi Snake Ceremonies
I Send a Voice
Indian Myth and Legend
An Iron Hand Upon the People; The Law Against
  the Potlatch on the Northwest Coast
The Iroquois Eagle Dance
An Iroquois Sourcebook: Medicine Society Rituals
Kachinas: A Hopi Artist's Documentary
Kinaalada: A Navajo Puberty Ceremony
*Kiowa Voices: Ceremonial Dance, Ritual and Songs
Lakota Life
Making Two Worlds One and the Story of
  All-American Indian Days
Mitakuye Oyasin: We Are All Related
Mother Earth, Father Sky: Ancient Chants by Pueblo
  and Navajo Indians of the Southwest
Myths and Symbols, or Aboriginal Religions in America
Native American Religious Action
Native Cemeteries & Forms of Burial East
  of the Mississippi
Native North American Spirituality of the
  Eastern Woodlands
A Navajo Bringing-Home Ceremony
Navajo Mountain & Rainbow Bridge Religion
The Night Chant: A Navaho Ceremonial
North American Indian Travel Guide
Notes on the Buffalo-Head Dance of the
  Bear Gens of the Fox Indians
Oceanic, American Indian, and African Myths
  of Snaring the Sun
Offering Smoke: The Sacred Pipe & Native
  American Religion
Oklahoma Delaware Ceremonies, Feasts and Dances
On the Gleaming Way
Oraibi Soyal Ceremony & Oraibi Powamu Ceremony,
  & Mishongnovi Ceremonies of the Snake &
  Antelope Fraternities & Oraibi Summer Snake
  Ceremony
Oraibu Marau Ceremony
The Osage Ceremonial Dance I'n-Lon-Schka
The Peyote Cult
The Pipe & Christ
Pow Wow: And Other Yakima Indian Traditions
*The Praying Flute
Rainhouse & Ocean: Speeches for the Papago Year
Religion and Ceremonies of the Lenape
Rig Veda Americanus
The Road of Life & Death: A Ritual Drama
  of the American Indians
Rolling Thunder: A personal Explortion Into the Secret
  Healing Power of an American Indian Medicine Man
Sacred Ground
The Sacred Pipe: Black Elk's Account of the
  Seven Rites of Oglala Sioux
Scalp Ceremonials of Zuni
Seneca Thanksgiving Rituals
The Snake Ceremonials at Walpi

Social Organization and Ritualistic Ceremonies
  of the Blackfoot Indians
The Southeastern Ceremonial Complex,
  Artifacts and Analysis
Southeastern Pomo Ceremonials
Southwestern Indian Ceremonials
Southwestern Indian Ritual Drama
The Story of the Meadowlark
A Study of the Delaware Indian Big House Ceremony
The Sun Dance and Other Ceremonies of the
  Oglala Division of the Teton Dakota
Tobacco, Peace Pipes & Indians
The Urine Dance of the Zuni Indians of New Mexico
*Ways of the Lushootsed People: Ceremonies &
  Traditions of the Northern Puget Sound Indians
Witchcraft and Sorcery of the North American
  Native Peoples
Witchcraft in the Southwest
With Good Heart: Yaqui Beliefs and Ceremonies
  in Pascua Village
World's Rim: Great Mysteries of the
  North American Indians
The Yuchi Green Corn Ceremonial
Yuwipi: Vision and Experience in Oglala Ritual
Zuni Fetishism

ROCK ART--PETROGLYPHS

Canyon de Chelly: Its People and Rock Art
Crystals in the Sky
The Forgotten Artist: Indians of Anza-Borrego
  & Their Rock Art
Indian Rock Art in Wyoming
Indian Rock Art of the Columbia Plateau
Indian Rock Art of the Southwest
Indian Rock Carvings
Kokopelli: Fluteplayer Images in Rock Art
Marks of the Ancestors
Petroglyphs of Ohio
Prehistoric Rock Art
Rock Art of the American Southwest
The Rock Art of Utah
Rock Art of Western South Dakota
The Rocks Begin to Speak
Seven Rock Art Sites in Baja California
Signs From the Ancestors: Zuni Cultural Symbolism
  & Perceptions of Rock Art

SAC, FOX & IOWA INDIANS

Expedition Against the Sauk and Fox Indians, 1832
Fox Texts
Observations of the Ethnology of the Sauk Indians
The Sac and Fox Indians
Sacred Bundles of the Sac and Fox Indians
The Sauks and the Black Hawk War

SACAGAWEA, 1786-1884

The Bird Woman: Sacajawea, Guide to Lewis & Clark
Mystery of Sacajawea
*Sacagawea
Sacajawea: A Native American Heroine
Sacagawea of the Lewis & Clark Expedition
Sacajawea, Wilderness Guide
*The Value of Adventure: The Story of Sacajawea

SALISH & KOOTENAI INDIANS

Basketry Designs of the Salish Indians
Coast Salish Essays

The Coast Salish People
*Coyote Tales of the Montana Salish
*Creation Tales from the Salish
A Dictionary of Puget Salish
Folk-Tales of the Coast Salish
Folk-Tales of the Salishan and Sahaptin Tribes
Historical Sketch of the Flathead Nation
Lushootseed Dictionary
*Salish Folk Tales
Salish Weaving
The Sanpoil and Nespelem: Salishan Peoples
  of Northeastern Washington
Selish, or Flat-Head Grammar
Twana Narratives: Native Historical Accounts of a
  Coast Salish Culture

SANDPAINTING

Earth Is My Mother, Sky Is My Father
Hosteen Klah: Navaho Medicine Man
  and Sand Painter
The Navajo Art of Sandpainting
Navajo Medicine Man Sandpaintings
Navajo Sandpainting Art
Navajo Sandpainting From Religious Act to
  Commercial Art
Navajo Sandpainting: The Huckel Collection
Sandpaintings of the Navajo Shooting Chant
Study of Navajo Symbolism
Summoning the Gods: Sandpainting of the
  Native American Southwest
Tapestries in Sand - The Spirit of Indian Sandpainting

SECRET SOCIETIES

Omaha Secret Societies
Societies of the Plains Indians
The Tobacco Society of the Crow Indians

SEMINOLE INDIANS

Africans and Seminoles: From Removal to
  Emancipation
Big Cypress: A Changing Seminole Community
Creeks and Seminoles
*Dancing with the Indians
The Florida Seminole and the New Deal, 1933-1942
Florida's Seminole Indians
History of the Second Seminole War
*John Hawk: A Seminole Saga
My Work Among the Florida Seminoles
Nations Remembered: An Oral History of
  Cherokees, Chickasaws, Choctaws, Creeks,
  and Seminoles, 1865-1907
Oklahoma Seminoles: Medicines, Magic and Religion
Pelts, Plumes and Hides
*The Seminole
The Seminole
The Seminole & Miccosukee Tribes:
  A Critical Bibliography
Seminole Patchwork Book
Seminole Music
The Seminole Seed
A Seminole Sourcebook
Seminoles
The Seminoles of Florida

SENECA INDIANS

The Death and Rebirth of the Seneca
The Hidden Language of the Seneca

The Relation of Seneca False Face Masks
to Seneca and Ontario Archaeology
Seneca Myths & Folk Tales
Seneca Thanksgiving Rituals
The Seneca & Tuscarora Indians:
An Annotated Bibliography
The Seneca World of Ga-No-Say-Yeh
*Skunny Wundy: Seneca Indian Tales

SHAWNEE INDIANS

*Blue Jacket: War Chief of Shawnees
Mortuary Customs of the Shawnee
and Other Eastern Tribes
Shawnee: The Ceremonialism of a Native
American Tribe and Its Cultural Background
Shawnee Home Life: The Painting of Ernest Spybuck
The Shawnee Prophet
Shawnee Traditions

SHOSHONI INDIANS

Great Basin Shoshonean Sourcebook
Newe Natekwinappeh: Shoshoni Stories & Dictionary
The Northern Shoshoni
Notes on Shoshonean Ethnography
*Pachee Goyo: History and Legends
from the Shoshone
The Road on Which We Came; A History of the
Western Shoshone
*The Shoshone
The Shoshoni-Crow Sun Dance
The Shoshonis: Sentinels of the Rockies
Thunder Over the Ochoco
Vocabulary of the Shoshone Language
When Did the Shoshoni Begin to Occupy
Southern Idaho?

SIGN LANGUAGE

The Indian Sign Language
Indian Sign Language
*Indian Sign Language
Indian Talk: Hand Signals of the
North American Indians
*North American Indian Sign Language
Sign Language: Contemporary
Southwest Native America

SITTING BULL - DAKOTA CHIEF 1834-1890

The Arrest and Killing of Sitting Bull: A Documentary
The Genius of Siting Bull: 13 Heroic Strategies
for Today's Business Leaders
I Am Looking to the North for My Life;
Sitting Bull, 1876-1881
The Saga of Sitting Bull's Bones
Sitting Bull
*Sitting Bull
Sitting Bull, Champion of the Sioux: A Biography
*Sitting Bull, Warrior of the Sioux
*The Story of Little Bighorn

SOCIAL LIFE & CUSTOMS

America Street: A Multicultural Anthology of Stories
American Indian Identity: Today's Changing
Perspectives

The American Indian: Perspectives for the
Study of Social Change
American Indian Sports Heritage
American Indians: Facts - Future Toward Economic
Development for Native American Communities
American Indians: The First of this Land
Arapahoe Politics, 1851-1978: Symbols in the
Crisis of Authority
The Architecture of Social Integration
in Prehistoric Pueblos
Autobiography of a Winnebago Indians
Battlefields & Burial Grounds: The Indian Struggle
to Protect Ancestral Graves in the U.S.
*Between Sacred Mountains: Navajo Stories
and Lessons fromthe Land
Braided Lives: An Anthology of Multicultural Writing
California Indian Nights Entertainment
Camp, Clan and Kin Among the Cow Creek Seminole
Changing Configurations in the Social Organization
of a Blackfoot Tribe During the Reserve Period
Changing Culture of an Indian Tribe
Cherokee Americans - Eastern Band of Cherokees
in the 20th Century
The Chief Hole-in-the-Day of the Mississippi Chippewa
Chippewa Child Life & Its Cultural Background
Chippewa Customs
*Come to Our Salmon Feast
Communication and Development:
A Study of Two Indian Villages
Contemporary Federal Indian Policy
Toward American Indians
Contemporary Navajo Affairs
Coping with the Final Tragedy: Dying & Grieving in
Cross Cultural Perspective
The Coppers of the Northwest Coast Indians
Corn Among the Indians of the Upper Missouri
Cry to the Thinderbird: The American
Indian's Own Story
Culture, Change and Leadership in a
Modern Indian Community
Cynthia Ann Parker: The Story of Her Capture
at the Massacre of the Inmates of Parker's Fort
Daughters of the Earth
The Destruction of American Indian Families
Dictionary of Daily Life of Indians of the Americas, A- Z
Economic Development on American Indian
Reservations
The Effects of White Contact Upon Blackfoot Culture
Enduring Culture
Ethnology of the Indians of Spanish Florida
Ethnology of the Texas Indians
Everyday Life of the North American Indian
Facial Paintings of the Indians of Northern
British Columbia
The Fall of Natural Man
The False Faces of the Iroquois
From Indians to Chicanos: The Dynamics
of Mexican American Culture
Fundamentals of Age-Group Systems
Games of the North American Indians
A Good Medicine Collection
The Grand Village of the Natchez Indians Revisited
Handbook of American Indian Games
The Havasupai Woman
Hogans: Navajo Houses and House Songs
The Hollywood Indian: Stereotypes of
Native American in Films
In the Land of the Grasshopper Song
Indian Life on the Upper Missouri
Indian Police and Judges: Experiments
in Acculturation and Control
Indian Running: Native American History & Tradition
*Indian Way: Kearning to Communicate
with Mother Earth
Indian-White Relations in the U.S.: A Bibliography
of Works Published, 1975-1980
The Indian's New World: Catawbas & Their Neighbors

from European Contact Through the Era of Removal
Indians and Criminal Justice
Indians in Overalls
The Indians of the Great Plains
The Indians of Puget Sound: The
Notebooks of Myron Eells
Indians of the U.S.: Four Centuries
of Their History and Culture
Introduction to the Study of Mortuary Customs
of the North American Indians
Journey to the Ancestral Self: Tamarack Songs
*James At Work
Lakota Life
Lakota Woman
Like Beads on a String: A Culture History of the
Seminole Indians in North Peninsula Florida
Living Arctic: Hunters of the Canadian North
Living the Spirit: A Gay American Indian Anthology
The Makah Indians
Marxism and Native Americans
Menominee Music
Moccasins on Pavement: The Urban Indian
Experience, A Denver Portrait
Modern Blackfeet: Montanans on a Reservation
The Modern Sioux: Social Systems and
Reservation Culture
Montezuma's Dinner
Native America: Arts, Traditions & Celebrations
The Native American Sweat Lodge: History & Legends
Native American Traditions
Native Americans: The People and How They Lived
Native Cemeteries and Forms of Burial
East of the Mississippi
Native North American Spirituality of the
Eastern Woodlands
The Natural World of the California Indians
Navajo Graves
The Navajo Hunter Tradition
Navajo Kinship Marriage
Navajo Leadership and Government
Nch'i-Wana "The Big River" Mid-Columbia
Indians & Their Land
North American Indian Burial Customs
North American Indian Travel Guide
Notes on the Social Organization and Customs
of the Mandan, Hidatsa and Crow Indians
Oglala Religion
Ojibwa Woman
Ojibway Oratory
Old Indian Trails
The Old North Trail: Or, Life, Legends and
Religion of the Blackfeet Indians
Omaha Sociology
Orayvi Revisited: Social Stratification in an
"Egalitarian" Society
Osage Mission Baptisms, Marriages,
and Interments, 1820-1886
Osages: Children of the Middle Waters
Partners in Furs: A History of the Fur Trade
in Eastern James Bay
The Pequots in Southern New England
Pima and Papago Ritual Oratory
Political Organizations and Law-Ways
of the Comanche Indians
Political Organization of the Plains Indians
Portraits of the Whiteman
Pow Wow: And Other Yakima Indian Traditions
Pow Wow Calendar
Prehistoric Households at Turkey
Creek Pueblo, Arizona
Recently Discovered Tales of Life Among the Indians
Reckoning With the Dead
Red Hunters and the Animal People
The Re-Establishment of the Indian in Their Pueblo
Life Through the Revival of Their Traditional Crafts
Reflections of Social Life in the Navaho Origin Myth

The Relationship Systems of the Tlingit,
  Haida and Tsimshian
Respect for Life: The Traditional Upbringing
  of American Indian Children
The Return of the Native
Return to Creation: A Survival Manual for
  Native & Natural People
The Roots of Dependency: Subsistence, Environment,
  and Social Change Among the Choctaws, Pawnees
  & Navajos
Roots of Oppression: The American Indian Question
Sacred Ground
The Sacred Hoop: Recovering the Feminine
  in American Indian Traditions
Scholars and the Indian Experience
The Search for an American Indian Identity
Self and Savagery on the California Frontier
Shadows of the Indian: Stereotypes in
  American Culture
Shamanism in Western North America
Shonto: A Study of the Role of the Trader
  in a Modern Navaho Community
Silent Arrows
Smallpox and the Iroquois Wars
Social Life of the Crow Indians
Social and Ceremonial Organization of Cochiti
Social Life of the Navajo Indians
Social Organization of the Papago Indians
Social Organization of the Tewa of New Mexico
Social Organization of the Western Pueblos
Social Organization and Ritualistic Ceremonies
  of the Blackfoot Indians
Social Organizations and Social Usages
  of the Indians of the Creek Confederacy
A Social Study of One Hundred Fifty Chippewa Indian
  Families of the White Earth Reservation of Minnesota
Societies of the Plains Indians
Son of Old Hat: A Navaho Autobiography
Southwestern Indian Ceremonials
The Spirit and the Flesh: Sexual Diversity in
  American Indian Tradition
*Sports and Games the Indians Gave Us
*Squanto & the First Thanksgiving
Statistics of Indian Tribes, Agencies and Schools
Status Terminology and the Social Structure of
  North American Indians
*The Story of Wounded Knee
Subjugation and Dishonor: A Brief History of the
  Travail of the Native Americans
Symbolic Imortality, The Tlingit Potlatch
  of the 19th Century
Talking Leaves
*To Live In Two Worlds: American Indian Youth Today
Tobacco, Peacepipes and Indians
Tobacco, Pipes and Smoking Customs
  of the American Indians
Traditions of the Chilcotin Indians
The Traditions of the Hopi: The Stanley McCormic
  Hopi Expedition
Traditions of the North American Indians
Traditions of the Osage
Traditions of the Quinault Indians
Traits of American Indian Life and Character
Travels in North America, Including a
  Summer with the Pawnees
Turquoise and the Navajo
Two Crows Denies It: A History of Controversy in
  Omaha Sociology
Two Leggings: The Making of a Crow Warrior
The Underground Reservation: Osage Oil
Urban Institutions and People of Indian Ancestry
Urban Renegades The Cultural Strategy
  of American Indians
Valley of the Spirits: The Upper Skagit Indian
  of Western Washington
Wake of the Unseen Object

Walk in Your Soul: Love Incantations
  of the Oklahoma Cherokees
The Way of the Dead Indians
The Way We Live: California Indian Reminiscences,
  Stories and Songs
When Jesus Came, the Corn Mothers Went Away
Woodland Indians of the Western Great Lakes

STUDY & TEACHING

Community-Based Research: A Handbook
  for Native Americans
Guide to Records in the National Archives
  Relating to American Indians
Guide to Research on North American Indians
Indians of North America: Methods and Sources
  for Library Research
Issues for the Future of American Indian Studies
Lost Tribes and Sunken Continents: Myth and
  Method in the Study of American Indians
Native American Directory: Alaska, U.S. and Canada
Native American Periodicals and Newspapers,
  1828-1982: Bibliography, Publishing Record
  and Holdings
Native American Research Information Service
Northern Voices: Inuit Writing in English
Native American Research Information Service
Teaching American Indian History:
  An Interdisciplinary Approach

SUN DANCE

The Arapaho Sun Dance, The Ceremony
  of the Offering Lodge
Shoshoni-Crow Sun Dance
*Sun Dance for Andy Horn
The Sun Dance of the Crow Indians
The Sun Dance and Other Ceremonies
  of the Oglala Vision of the Teton Dakota
*The Sun Dance People
The Sun Dance Religion: Power for the Powerless
Sundancing at Rosebud & Pine Ridge

SUQUAMISH

*Brother Eagle, Sister Sky
Chief Seattle's Unanswered Challenge
The Eyes of Chief Seattle: The Suquamish Museum
How Can One Sell the Air: Chief Seattle's Vision
Law Enforcement on Indian Reservations After
  Oliphant v. Suquamish Indian Tribes
*Suquamish Today
The Wisdom of the Great Chiefs

TEXTILE INDUSTRY & FABRICS

And Eagles Sweep Across the Sky: Indian Textiles
  of the North American West
The Art of Native American Basketry: A Living Legacy
Collecting the Navajo Child's Blanket
Contemporary Navajo Weaving
Designing with the Wool
Folk-Lore of the Mesquakie Indians of North America
  and Catalogue of Beadwork and Other
  Objects in the Collection of the Folk Lore Society
Full Color American Indian Designs
  for Needlepoint Rugs
The Gift of Spiderwoman: Southwestern Textiles,
  the Navajo Tradition
Historic Navajo Weaving, 1800-1900:
  Three Cultures-One Loom

*Indian Bead-Weaving Patterns: Chain Weaving
  Designs and Bead Loom Weaving
  An Illustrated How-to Guide
Indian Blankets and Their Makers
Indian Clothing of the Great Lakes, 1740-1840
Indian Designs
Indian Foods and Fibers of Arid America
Ray Manley's "The Fine Art of Navajo Weaving"
The Navajo Design Book
Navajo Native Dyes: Their Preparation and Use
Navajo Pictorial Weaving, 1880-1950
The Navajo Rug
Navajo Rugs: How to Find, Evaluate,
  Buy & Care for Them
Navajo Rugs, Past and Present
Navajo Shepherd and Weaver
Navajo Textiles: The William Randolph
  Hearst Collection
Navajo Weavers and Silversmiths
Navaho Weaving, Its Technic and History
Navajo Weaving, Navajo Ways
Navajo Weaving: Three Centuries of Change
Navajo Weaving Today
The Navajo Weaving Tradition, 1650 to the Present
Navajo Weaving: Three Centuries of Change
Old Navajo Rugs: Their Development
  from 1900 to 1940
Patterns and Sources of Navajo Weaving
Pictorial Weavings of the Navajos
Pueblo Indian Textiles: A Living Tradition
Ramona Sakiestewa - Patterned Dreams:
  Textiles of the Southwest
Rugs & Posts: The Story of Navajo Weaving
Salish Weaving
Scarlet Ribbons: American Indian Technique
  for Today's Quilters
Seminole Patchwork
The Seminole Patchwork Book
The Song of the Loom: New Traditions
  in Navajo Weaving
Walk in Beauty: The Navajo and Their Blankets
Weaving Arts of the North American Indian
Weaving a Navajo Blanket
Weaving of the Southwest

TLINGIT INDIANS

Art of the Northern Tlingit
Gagiwdulat: Brought Forth to Reconfirm
  The Legacy of a Taku River Tlingit Clan
Haa Kusteeyi, Our Culture: Tlingit Life Stories
Haa Shuka, Our Ancestors
Haa Tuwunaagu Yis, for Healting Our Spirit:
  Tlingit Oratory
*Heroes & Heroines in Tlingit-Haida Legends
Images of a People: Tlingit Myths & Legends
Indians of the North Pacific Coast
My Grandfather's House: Tlingit Songs
  of Death and Sorrow
The Relationship Systems of the
  Tlingit, Haida & Tsimshian
Symbolic Imortality, The Tlingit Potlatch
  of the 19th Century
*The Tlingit
Tlingit Art & Culture
The Tlingit Indians
Tlingit Indians of Alaska
The Tlingit Indians: Results of a Trip to the Northwest
  Coast of America & the Bering Straits
Tlingit Myths & Texts
Tlingit Verb Dictionary
Tlingit Tales: Potlatch and Totem Poles

TOHONO O'ODHAM (PAPAGO) & PIMA INDIANS

Autobiography of a Papago Woman
Basketry of the Papago and Pima Indians
By the Prophet of the Earth: Ethnobotany of the Pima
The Ethnobiology of the Papago Indians
Gathering the Desert
New Trails in Mexico
Of Earth and Little Rain: The Papago Indians
A Papago Calendar Record
A Papago Grammar
Papago Indian Pottery
Papago Indian Religion
Papago Indians at Work
The Papago Indians of Arizona and
   Their Relatives the Pima
Papago Music
The Papago & Pima Indians of Arizona
Papago/Pima to English, English to
   Papago/Pima Dictionary
A Papago Traveler
People of the Crimson Evening
Pima Indian Legends
Pima & Papago Indian Agriculture
Pima & Papago Ritual Oratory
A Pima Past
A Pima Remembers
Piman Shamanism and Staying Sickness
Rainhouse & Ocean: Speeches for the Papago Year
The Salt River Pima-Maricopa Indians
Sharing the Desert
Singing for Power: The Song Magic of the
   Papago Indians of Southern Arizona
Social Organization of the Papago Indians
Sonora
When It Rains: Papago and Pima Poetry

TOTEMS, TOTEMISM

Art of the Totem
Carved History: A Guide to the Totem Poles
   of Sitka National Historical Park
Elementary Forms of the Religious Life
Eternal Ones of the Dream: Myth & Ritual,
   Dreams & Fantasies
From the Land of the Totem Poles
Haida Monumental Art
Looking at Totem Poles
Message of an Indian Relic: Seattle's Own Totem Pole
People of the Totem: Indians of the Pacific Northwest
The Savage and His Totem
Sculpturing Totem Poles
Tlingit Tales: Potlatch and Totem Poles
The Totem Carvers: Charlie James, Ellen Neel,
   and Mungo Martin
*Totem Poles to Color & Cut Out, 3 Vols.
Totem Poles of the Northwest
Totem Poles of the Pacific Northwest Coast
Totemism
Where the People Gather: Carving a Totem Pole
Wolf of the Raven: Totem Poles of Southeastern
   Alaska

TRAILS

The Bozeman Trail
Indian Paths of Pennsylvania
Many Trails: Indians of the Lower Hudson Valley
Perch Lake Mounds
Traders of the Western Morning

TRANSPORTATION

Ancient Road Networks & Settlement Hierarchies
   in the New World
California Indian Watercraft
*Indian Canoeing
The Indian and His Horse
Roads to Center Place: An Anasazi Atlas

TREATIES

The American Indian Treaty Series
The American Indian Under Reconstruction
Background of the Treaty-Making in
   Western Washington
Behind the Trail of Broken Treaties
Bibliography of the English Colonial
   Treaties with the American Indians
Chehalis River Treaty Council & the Treaty of Olympia
Cherokee By Blood: Records of Eastern Cherokee
   Ancestry in the U.S. Court of Claims, 1906-10
The 1826 Chippewa Treaty with the U.S. Government
A Chronological List of Treaties & Agreements
Comanche Treaties During the Civil War
Comanche Treaties: Historical Background
Comanche Treaties of 1850, 1851 & 1853
   with the U.S. Government
Comache Treaties with the Republic of Texas
Comanche Treaty of 1846 with the U.S.
Comanche Treaty of 1835 with the U.S.
Constitution & Laws of the American Indian
   Tribes Series
Early American Indian Documents:
   Treaties and Laws, 1607-1789
Early Treaties with the Southern Cheyenne & Arapaho
Executive Orders Establishing the
   Papago Reservations
Guide to the Indian Treaties and Other
   Documents 1778-1902
Historical Background to Chippewa Treaties
The History and Culture of Iroquois Diplomacy
Indian Affairs, Laws & Treaties
Indian Treaties
Indian Treaties, 1778-1883
Indian Treaties by Tribe
Indians, Superintendents, and Councils:
   Northwestern Indian Policy, 1850-1855
The Jerome Agreement Between the Kiowa,
   Comanche & Apache Tribes & the U.S.
Journal of Southern Treaty Commission 1865
The Kiowa Treaty of 1853
License for Empire: Colonialism by
   Treaty in Early America
The Medicine Creek Treaty of 1854
The Navajo Treaty, 1868
Northwest Chiefs: Gustav Sohon's Views of the 1855
   Stevens Treaty Councils
The Point Elliott Treaty, 1855
The Point-No-Point Treaty, 1855
Proceedings of the Great Peace Commissions
The Spirit of the Alberta Indian Treaties
Treaties, Agreements & Proceedings of the
   Tribes & Bands of the Sioux Nation
Treaties & Agreements of the Chippewa Indians
Treaties & Agreements of the Five Civilized Tribes
Treaties & Agreements of the Indian Tribes of the
   Great Lakes Region
Treaties & Agreements of the Indian Tribes of the
   Northern Plains
Treaties & Agreements of the Indian Tribes of the
   Pacific Northwest
Treaties & Agreements of the Indian Tribes of the
   Southwest
Treaties for the 1860s with the Southern
   Cheyenne & Arapaho

The Treaties of Canada with the Indians of
   Manitoba & Northwest Territories
The Treaties of Puget Sound, 1854-1855
Treaty Manuscript Series
The Treaty of 1842 Between the U.S.
   and Chippewa Idians
The Treaty of 1836 Between the Ottawa
   & Chippewa Nations of Indians & the U.S.
The Treaty of Medicine Lodge, 1867
Treaty of Medicine Lodge: A Programmed Text
The Treaty on the Littel Arkansas River, 1865
Treaty with the Makah
Treaty with the Quinault & Quileute Indians
A True Copy of the Record of the Official Proceedings
   at the Council in the Walla Walla Valley, 1855
The U.S.-Chippewa Treaty at La Pointe, 1854
The U.S.-Seneca Treaty, 1842
The U.S. Treaty with the Sioux Brule, Oglala, et al.
U.S. Treaty with the Walla Walla
The Unratified Treaty Between the Kiowas,
   Comanches & Apaches & the U.S. of 1863
Walleye Warriors
Western Washington Treaty Proceedings

TRIBAL GOVERNMENT

The Alaska Native Claims Settlement Act,
   1991 & Tribal Government
American Indian Tribal Autonomy and American
   Society in the 1980's: A Bibliography
American Indian Tribal Governments
American Indian Tribal Courts: The
   Costs of Separate Justice
Indian Tribes of the Lower Mississippi Valley
Indian Tribes of North America
Introduction to Tribal Government
*Long Shadows
The Nations Within: The Past and Future
   of American Indian Sovereignty
Native Brotherhoods: Modern Intertribal
   Organizations on the Northwest Coast
Nevada Tribal History and Government
Penitente Self-Government:
   Brotherhoods & Councils, 1797-1947
Political History of the Navajo Tribe
Political Organization and Law-
   Ways of the Comanche Indians
Political Organization of the Plains Indians
The Politics of Indian Removal:
   Creek Government and Society in Crisis
Politics and Power
The Road: Indian Tribes and Political Liberty
Self-Reliance vs. Power Politics
Tribal Government: A New Era
Tribal Government Textbook
Tribal Government Today: Politics
   on Montana's Indian Reservations
Tribal Sovereignty: Indian Tribes in U.S. History

TSIMSHIAN INDIANS

Haida Songs & Tsimshian Texts
The Relationship Systems of the Tlingit,
   Haida & Tsimshian
The Tsimshian: Images of the Past;
   Views for the Present
The Tsimshian: Their Arts & Music
The Tsimshian & Their Neighbors
   of the North Pacific Coast
The Tsimshian & Their Neighbors
   of the Northwest Coast
Tsimshian Texts

UTE INDIANS

American Indians in Colorado
Bull Creek
Ethnography of the Northern Utes
Indians of the Pike's \Peak Region
Northern Ute Music
People of the Shining Mountains: Ute Indians of CO
Southern Ute Indians of Early Colorado
A Study in Culture Contact and Culture Change:
    The Whiterock Utes in Transition
This Is Our Land
Ute Mountain Utes
Ute Tales
Utes: The Mountain People

WARS - GENERAL

American Indian Wars
Americans Woodland Indians
Apache Wars
Apache Women Warriors
Ark of Empire: The American Frontier, 1784-1803
The Battle of Wisconsin Heights
The Bear River Massacre
Behind the Tree of Peace
A Brief of the Pequot War
Burials of the Algonquian, Siouan & Caddoan Tribes
    West of the Mississippi
Bury My Heart at Wounded Knee: An Indian
    History of the American West
Campaigning with King
A Cannoneer in Navajo Country
Centennial Campaign: The Sioux War of 1876
*Cheyenne Warriors
Children of Sacred Ground: America's Last Indian War
Crimsoned Prairie: The Indian Wars
Chronological List of Engagements Between the
    Regular Army of the U.S. and Various Tribes of
    Hostile Indians...1790-1898
The Conflict Between the California Indian
    and White Civilization
Continents in Collision
Counting Coup and Cutting Horses: Intertribal
    Warefare on the Northern Plains
Crazy Horse Called Them Walk-A-Heaps: The Story
    of the Foot Soldier in the Prairie Indian Wars
Crimsoned Prairie: The Indian Wars
Dakota War Whoop; Or, Indian Masscres
    and War in Minnesota
Death in the Desert: The Fifty Years' War
    for the Great Southwest
Discovery of the Yosemite and the Indian War of 1851
Forlorn Hope: The Battle of White Bird Canyon & the
    Beginning of the Nez Perce War
The Fox Wars: The Mesquakie Challenge
    to New France
From Yorktown to Santiago with the Sixth U.S. Cavalry
General Crook in the Indian Country
God Gave Us This Country: Tecumseh
    and the First American Civil War
*The Great Chiefs
Great Western Indian Fights
Hasinai: A Traditional History of the
    Caddo Confederacy
History of Alabama, and Incidentally of Georgia
    and Mississippi, from the Earliest Period
History of the Indian Wars
History of the Indian Wars in New England
Indian Battles Along the Rogue River: One
    ofAmerica's Wild and Scenic Rivers
Indian Battles, Murders, Sieges, and
    Forays in the Southwest
Indian Battles and Skirmishes on the
    American Frontier, 1790-1898

*Indian Warriors and Their Weapons
Indian Wars
Indian Wars of New England
Indian Wars of Pennsylvania
Indian Wars of the Red River Valley
Indian Wars of the West
*The Last of the Cherokee Warriors
Long Death
Marquis de Mores at War in the Bad Lands
Memoir of Indian Wars and Other Occurrences
    by the Late Colonial Stuart of Greenbrier
Navajo Roundup
Origin Legend of the Navaho Enemy Way
Our Indian Wards
The Papers of the Order of the Indian Wars
Penhallow's Indian Wars
Plains Indian Raiders
*Plains Indian Warrior
President Washington's Indian War
Red Eagle and the Wars With the Creek
    Indians of Alabama
The Sac and Fox Indians
St. Clair Papers
Skulking Way of War
Soldiering in Dakota
Southern Indians in the American Revolution
The Spanish Missions of New Mexico, after 1680
Story of the Red Man
The Ten Year's War: Indian-White Relations
    in Pennsylvania, 1755-1765
Tribal Wars of the Southern Plains
Vision & Valor: General Oliver O. Howard -
    a Biography
War in the Tribal Zone: Expanding States
    and Indigenous Warfare
The Wars of the Iroquois: A Study in
    Intertribal Trade Relations
*Wounded Knee: An Indian History
    of the American West

WARS, 1600-1800

Africans and Creeks: From Colonial
    Period to the Civil War
Ark of Empire: The American Frontier, 1784-1803
Joseph Brant: Iroquois Ally of the British
A Brief History of the Pequot War
The Captive: The True Story of the Captivity
    of Mrs. Mary Rowlandson
Causes of the Maryland Revolution of 1689
Cheyennes & Horse Soldiers
Chronicles of Border Warfare; Or, A History of the
    Settlements by the Whites of Northwestern
    Virginia
A Company of Heroes: The American Frontier,
    1775-1783
Continents in Collision: The Impact of Europe
    on the North American Indian Societies
Empire of Fortune: Crowns, Colonies, & Tribes
    in the Seven Years War in America
*The Fight for Freedom, 1750-1783
Forth to the Wilderness: The First American
    Frontier, 1754-1774
The Frontiersmen
Historical Collections of the Indians of New England
History of the Indian Wars in New England from the
    First Settlement to the Termination of the War
    with King Philip in 1677
The History of King Philip's War
Indian Fighter
Indian Wars of the West
Indians: Or Narratives of Massacres & Depredations
Journal of the Adventures of Mathew Bunn
Journals of the Military Expedition of
    Major General John Sullivan
King Philip

King Philip's War
Life of Joseph Brant (Thayendanegea)
John McMurtry and the American Indian
Narratives of the Indian Wars, 1675-1699
The Old Indian Chronicle
On Time for Disaster
Our Western Border, Its Life, Combats, Adventures,
    Forays, Massacres, Captivities, Scouts, Red
    Chiefs, Pioneers, Woman...
Particular History of the Five Years
    French and Indian War, 1744-1748
Penhallow's Indian Wars
Present State of New England
President Washington's Indian War: The Struggle
    for the Old Northwest, 1790-1795
The Red King's Rebellion: Racial Politics
    in New England, 1675-1677
Redeemed Captive Returning to Zion
*Mary Rowlandson and King Philip's War
St. Clair Papers
So Dreadful a Judgement: Puritan Responses
    to King Philip's War, 1667-1677
The Southern Frontier, 1670-1732
Southern Indians in the American Revolution
Tecumseh and the Quest for Indian Leadership
Anthony Wayne, A Name in Arms
Wept of Wish-Ton-Wish
Wilderness Empire
Winners of the West

WARS, 1800-1900

An Account of the Origin and Early Prosecution
    of the Indian War in Oregon
After the Little Big Horn
An Apache Campaign in the Sierra Madre
Apache Days & After
Archaeology, History, & Custer's Last Battle
Arikara Narrative of the Campaign Against the
    Hostile Dakotas, June 1876
An Army Wife on the Frontier: The Memoirs of Alice
    Blackwood Bladwin, 1867-77
The Battle of Horseshoe Bend
Battle Rock, The Hero's Story
The Battle of Wisconsin Heights
Battlefield and Classroom
Battles & Skirmishes of the Great Sioux War,
    1876-1877
The Bear River Massacre
Before the Little Big Horn
The Black Hawk War, Why?
Brave Eagle's Account of the Fetterman Fight
Bury My Heart at Wounded Knee: An Indian
    History of the American West
A Cannoneer in Navajo Country: Journey
    of Private Josiah M. Rice, 1851
Casper Collins: The Life and Exploits
    of an Indian Fighter of the Sixties
Cavalier in Buckskin: George Armstrong Custer
    & the Western Military Frontier
Conquest of Apacheria
The Conquest of the Coeur d'Alenes,
    Spokanes & Palouses
Copper Paladin: The Modoc Tragedy
The Custer Fight and Other Tales of the Old West
Dakota War Whoop
Death in the Desert: The Fifty Years' War
    for the Great Southwest
Death on the Prairie: The Thiry Years' Struggle
    for the Western Plains
Death, Too, For the Heavy-Runner
Discovery of the Yosemite and the Indian War of 1851
The Dull Knife Battle
Exiles of Florida
Eyewitness at Wounded Knee
Faintly Sounds the War Cry

The Fighting Cheyennes
First Scalp for Custer
The Florida Wars
Following the Guidon: Into the Indian Wars
  with General Custer & the Seventh Cavalry
Following the Indian Wars
Forlorn Hope: The Battle of Whitebird Canyon
  and the Beginning of the Nez Perce War
Fort Gibson History
Fort Meade & the Black Hills
Forty Miles a Day on Beans and Hay: The
  Enlisted Soldier Fighting the Indian Wars
Frontier Regulars: The U.S. Army and the Indian,
  1866-1891
Ghost-Dance Religion and the Sioux Outbreak of 1890
The Great Sioux War
The Hero of Battle Rock
History of the Second Seminole War
Hokahey! A Good Day to Die! The Indian
  Casualties of the Custer Fight
I Will Fight No More Forever: Chief Joseph
  and the Nez Perce War
*The Indian as a Soldier at Fort Custer, Montana,
  1890-1895
Indian Battles Along the Rogue River, 1855-6
Indian Battles and Skirmishes on the
  American Frontier, 1790-1890
Indian Fights and Fighters
The Indian History of the Modoc War
Indian Outbreaks
The Indian War of 1864
Indians Last Fight or the Dull Knife Raid
Lakota & Cheyenne: Indian Views of the
  Great Sioux War, 1876-1877
Lakota Recollections of the Custer Fight:
  New Sources of Indian-Military History
Last Days of the Sioux Nation
Life and Adventures of Frank Grouard
Life in Custer's Cavalry
Life of George Bent
Life of Tom Horn
Little Big Horn Diary: Chronicle of the 1876 Indian War
The Long Walk: A History of the Navajo Wars,
  1846-1868
Man of the Plains: Recollections of Luther North,
  1856-1882
Massacre!
Massacre on the Gila
The Military Conquest of the Southern Plains
The Modocs and Their War
My Life on the Plains
Old Fort Klamath
On the Border With Crook
Once They Moved Like the Wind
Personal Recollection and Observations of
  General Nelson A. Miles
Plains Indian Raiders
Pony Tracks
Red Fox: Brig.-General Stand Watie's
  Civil War Years in Indian Territory
Red Hawk's Account of Custer's Last Battle
Regulars in the Redwoods: The U.S. Army
  in Northern California, 1852-1861
Reminiscences of Seattle, Washington Territory
  and the U.S. Sloop-of-War Decatur During the
  Indian War of 1855-6
Sagebrush Soldier
Sand in a Whirlwind: The Paiute Indian War of 1860
Scarlet Plume
Scout and Ranger
The Sioux Uprising of 1862
Sitanka: The Full Story of Wounded Knee
Slim Buttes, 1876: An Episode of the Great Sioux War
The Slim Buttes Battle
Soldiering in Dakota: Among the Indians in 1863-1865
The Soldiers Are Coming
*The Story of Little Big Horn

Swamp Sailors: Riverine Warfare in the
  Everglades, 1835-1842
Taos, 1847: The Revolt in Contemporary Accounts
Tenting on the Plains; Or, General Custer
  in Kansas & Texas
This Is Our Land
Through Dakota Eyes: Narrative Accounts
  of the Minnesota Indian War of 1862
Two Great Scouts and Their Pawnee Battalion
Vast Domain of Blood
*War Clouds in the West, Indians and
  Cavalrymen, 1860-1890
War Eagle: A Life of General Eugene A. Carr
War-Path & Bivouac; Or, the Conquest of the Sioux
The Warren Wagontrain Raid
Winners of the West
Without Quarter: The Wichita Expedition
Wolves for the Blue Soldiers
Wooden Leg: A Warrior Who Fought Custer
*Wounded Knee: History of the American West
The Wounded Knee Massacre: From the
  Viewpoint of the Sioux

WOMEN

American Indian Women: A Guide to Research
American Indian Women: Telling Their Lives
American Indian Women's Calendar
Apache Women Warriors
Buffalo Woman Comes Singing: The Spirit Song
  of a Rainbow Medicine Woman
Changing Culture of an Indian Tribe
Children At Risk
Claiming Breath
The Colour of Resistance: Contemporary
  Collection of Writing by Aboriginal Women
Dancing Colors: Paths of Native American Women
Daughters of the Earth
During My Time: Florence Edenshaw Davidson,
  A Haida Woman
A Gathering of Spirit: Writing and Art by
  North American Indian Women
The Hidden Half: Studies of Plains Indian Women
The Indian Captivity Narrative: A Woman's View
The Indian Peoples of Eastern America:
  A Documentary History of the Sexes
Indian Women Chiefs
Keepers of the Culture: Women in a Changing World
Lakota Woman
Life Lived Like a Story
Madonna Swan: A Lakota Woman's Story
Medicine Women, Curanderas, & Women Doctors
The Moccasin Maker
Mystery of Sacajawea: Indian Girl with Lewis & Clark
Native American Women: A Contextual Bibliography
Negotiators of Change: Historical Perspectives on
  Native American Women
No Turning Back: A Hopi Indian Woman's Struggle
  to Live in Two Worlds
Oglala Women: Myth, Ritual & Reality
Ojibwa Woman: Myth, Ritual & Reality
Po Pai Mo: The Search for White Buffalo Woman
Pretty Shield, Medicine Woman of the Crows
The Sacred Hoop: Recovering the Feminine
  in American Indian Traditions
Sanapia: Comanche Medicine Woman
Southern Cheyenne Women's Songs
Madonna Swan: A Lakota Woman's Story
To the American Indian: Reminiscences
  of a Yurok Woman
The 20th-Century Fictional American Indian
  Woman & Fellow Characters
A Voice in Her Tribe: A Navajo Woman's Own Story
Waheenee: An Indian Girl's Story
Warrior Queen of the Indian

Waterlily
The Way of the Rainbow Warrioress:
  A Handbook of Practical Wisdom
The Ways of My Grandmothers
Sarah Winnemucca of the Northern Paiutes
That's What She Said
Wisdom's Daughters: Conversations With
  Women Elders of Native America
Women in History
Women in Navajo Society
Women and Indians on the Frontier, 1825-1915
Women of the Native Struggle
Yaqui Women: Contemporary Life Histories

YAQUI INDIANS

Autobiography of a Yaqui Poet
Pascua
Pascua: A Yaqui Village in Arizona
People of the Pascua
Politics & Ethnicity on the Rio Yaqui
With Good Heart: Yaqui Beliefs & Ceremonies
  in Pascua Village
A Yaqui Easter
A Yaqui Life
Yaqui Myths & Legends
Yaqui Women: Contemporary Life Histories
Yuman and Yaqui Music

ZUNI INDIANS

The Beautiful & Dangerous: Dialogues
  With the Zuni Indians
Cushing at Zuni
A Few Summer Ceremonials at Zuni Pueblo
*From Abenaki to Zuni
Hopi & Zuni Ceremonialism
Music of the Acoma, Isleta, Cochiti & Zuni Pueblos
My Adventures in Zuni
The Mythic World of the Zuni
Notes on Zuni
On the Gleaming Way
Outline of the Documentary History of the Zuni Tribe
People of the Middle Place: A Study of the Zuni Indians
Racial Prehistory in the Southwest
  & the Hawikuh Zunis
Scalp Ceremonial of Zuni
Settlement, Subsistence & Society in
  Late Zuni Prehistory
Signs From the Ancestors: Zuni Cultural
  Symbolism & Perceptions of Rock Art
*Sun Journey: A Story of Zuni Pueblo
The Urine Dance of the Zuni Indians of New Mexico
A Zuni Atlas
Zuni Breadstuff
Zuni Contemporary Pottery
Zuni & El Moro: Past & Present
Zuni Fetishes
Zuni Fetishism
Zuni Folk Tales
The Zuni Indians: Their Mythology,
  Esoteric Fraternities & Ceremonies
The Zuni Indians & Their Use of Plants
Zuni Katchinas
Zuni Katcinas, An Analytical Study
Zuni Kin & Clan
The Zuni Man-Woman
Zuni Mythology
Zuni Pottery
Zuni: Selected Writings of Frank Hamilton Cushing
Zuni Texts
The Zunis
The Zunis of Cibola

The following is a list of publishers whose books appear in the bibliography . Entries are arranged alphabetically , with complete zip-coded addresses and phone numbers.

A

Aardvark Publications
P.O. Box 252
Boulder Junction, WI 54512 (715) 385-2862

Abbeville Press
488 Madison Ave.
New York, NY 10022 (800) 278-2665
Fax (212) 644-5085

Abingdon Press
P.O. Box 801
Nashville, TN 37202
(800) 251-3320; in TN (615) 749-6347

Harry N. Abrams
100 Fifth Ave.
New York, NY 10011
(800) 345-1359; in NY (212) 206-7715

Academic Press
465 S. Lincoln Dr.
Troy, MO 63379
(800) 321-5068; in MO (314) 528-8110

Academy of American Franciscan History
P.O. Box 34440
Bethesda, MD 20817 (301) 365-1763

Academy Chicago Publishers
213 W. Institute Pl.
Chicago, IL 60610
(800) 248-7323; in IL (312) 751-7302

Ace Books
200 Madison Ave.
New York, NY 10016
(800) 223-0510; in NY (212) 951-8800

Acoma Books
P.O. Box 4
Ramona, CA 92065 (619) 789-1288

Adler's Foreign Books
915 Foster St.
Evanston, IL 60201
(800) 433-9229; in IL (708) 866-6329

Aerial Photography Services
2511 S. Tryon St.
Charlotte, NC 28203 (704) 333-5143

Ahsahta Press
Boise State University
University Bookstore
Boise, ID 83725 (208) 385-1404

Airmont Publishing
401 Lafayette St.
New York, NY 10003
(800) 223-5251; in NY (212) 598-0222

AISES (American Indian Science & Engineering Society)
1630 30th St., Suite 301
Boulder, CO 80301 (800) 9-NATIVE

Akwe:kon Press
300 Caldwell Hall, Cornell University
Ithaca, NY 14853 (607) 255-4308

Akwesasne Notes
Mohawk Nation
P.O. Box 196
Rooseveltown, NY 13683 (518) 358-9531

The Alaska Geographic Society
P.O. Box 93370
Anchorage, AK 99509
(907) 562-0164 Fax 562-0479

Alaska International Art Institute
26241 Foxgrove Ave.
Sun City, CA 92381

Alaska Native Language Center
University of Alaska, P.O. Box 757680
Fairbanks, AK 99775
(907) 474-7874 Fax 474-6586

Alaska Natural History Association
605 W. Fourth Ave.
Anchorage, AK 99501 (907) 274-8440

Alaska Northwest Books
2208 N.W. Market St. #300
Seattle, WA 98107 (206) 784-5071

Aldine de Gruyter, Inc.
200 Saw Mill River Rd.
Hawthorne, NY 10532 (914) 747-0110

Alfred Publishing Co., Inc.
P.O. Box 10003
Van Nuys, CA 91406-1215
(800) 292-6122 Fax (818) 893-5560

Allyn & Bacon, Inc.
160 Gould St.
Needham Hts., MA 02194 (800) 223-1360

Amereon Ltd.
P.O. Box 1200
Mattituck, NY 11952 (516) 298-5100

American Academy of Political and Social Science
Distributed by Sage Publications

American Antiquarian Society
Distributed by University Press of Virginia

American Bar Association
750 N. Lake Shore Dr.
Chicago, IL 60611 (312) 988-5000

American Eagle Publications
P.O. Box 41401
Tucson, AZ 85717 (602) 888-4957

American Federation of Arts
41 East 65th St.
New York, NY 10021 (212) 988-7700

American Friends Service Committee
1501 Cherry St.
Philadelphia, PA 19102 (215) 241-7048

American Historical Association
400 A St., S.E.
Washington, DC 20003 (202) 544-2422

American Indian Archaeological Institute
P.O. Box 1260
Washington, CT 06793 (203) 868-0518

American Indian Basketry and Other Native Arts
P.O. Box 66124
Portland, OR 97266 (503) 233-8131

American Indian Books, Joe Thompson
9868 Diamond Point Dr.
St. Louis, MO 63123 (314) 631-7000

American Indian Contemporary Arts
685 Market St., Suite 250
San Francisco, CA 94105 (415) 495-7600

American Indian Culture Research Center
Blue Coud Abbey, P.O. Box 98
Marvin, SD 57251 (605) 432-5528

American Indian Press
2838 W. Peterson Ave.
Chicago, IL 60659 (312) 761-5000

American Indian Publishers
177F Riverside Ave.
Newport Beach, CA 92663

American Indian Studies Center
University of California
3220 Campbell Hall, 405 Hilgard Ave.
Los Angeles, CA 90024 (213) 825-7315

American Library Association
50 E. Huron St.
Chicago, IL 60611
(800) 545-2433 in IL (800) 545-2444

American Philosophical Society
P.O. Box 40098
Philadelphia, PA 19106 (215) 440-3400

American Press
520 Commonwealth Ave. #416
Boston, MA 02215 (617) 247-0022

Amerind Foundation
P.O Box 248
Dragoon, AZ 85609 (602) 586-3666

Amherst Press
P.O. Box 296
Amherst, WI 54406 (715) 824-3214

Amon Carter Museum
Dist. by University of Texas Press

AMS Press
56 East 13th St.
New York, NY 10003 (212) 777-4700

Anasazi Publishing Group
8190 E. Mira Mesa Blvd., Suite 360
San Diego, CA 92126 (619) 578-2406

Anchor Press
Division of Doubleday & Co.

The Anchorage Historical & Fine Arts Museum
121 West 7th Ave.
Anchorage, AK 99501

Ancient City Press
Dist. by Johnson Books

Anthropology Film Center Foundation,
P.O. Box 493
Santa Fe, NM 87594 (505) 983-4127

Anthropology Resource Center
Dist. by Cultural Survival
11 Divinity Ave.
Cambridge, MA 02138

Anza-Borrego Desert Natural History Assn.
P.O. Box 311
Borrego Springs, CA 92004 (619) 767-3052

Aperture
Dist. by Farrar, Straus & Giroux

Apollo Books
P.O. Box 3839
Poughkeepsie, NY 12603 (914) 462-0040
(800) 431-5003; in NY (800) 942-8222

Appalachian Consortium
University Hall, Appalachian State U.
Boone, NC 28608 (704) 262-2064

Appleton-Century-Crofts
Div. of Prentice-Hall

Archive of Folk Culture
American Folklife Center
Library of Congress
10 First St., S.E.
Washington, D.C. 20540

Argosy
116 East 59th St.
New York, NY 10022 (212) 753-4455

Arizona Maps and Books
P.O. Box 1133
Sedona, AZ 86336

Arrowfax Canada, Inc.
202-286 Smith St.
Winnipeg, MB R3C 1K5 (800) 665-0037

Arrowstar Publishing
100134 University Park Station
Denver, CO 80210-1034 (303) 692-6579

Arte Publico Press
University of Houston
Houston, TX 77204
(800) 633-ARTE; Fax 743-2847

Artlist
P.O. Box 35552
Albuquerque, NM 87176 (505) 881-3248

Arts & Culture of the North
Box 1333, Gracie Sq. Sta.
New York, NY 10028 (212) 879-9019

Aspen Center for Visual Arts
Dist. by Publishing Center
for Cultural Resources
625 Broadway
New York, NY 10012

Associated Antiquaries
P.O. Box 42896
Philadelphia, PA 19101 (215) 726-8998

Associated Booksellers
562 Boston Ave.
Bridgeport, CT 06610
(800) 232-2224; in CT (203) 333-7268

Associated Creative Writers
c/o Brashers, 4618 Terry Ln.
La Mesa, CA 92041 (619) 460-4107

**Association for Northern California
Records & Research**
P.O. Box 3024
Chico, CA 95927 (916) 895-5710

Association of American Indian Physicians
10015 S. Pennsylvania, Bldg. D
Oklahoma City, OK 73159 (405) 692-1202

Association on American Indian Affairs
245 Fifth Ave., Suite 1801
New York, NY 10016 (212) 689-8720

Association Press
Division of Follett Press
1000 W. Washington Blvd.
Chicago, IL 60607 (312) 666-4300

Atheneum Publishers
Division of Macmillan
Front and Brown Sts.
Riverside, NJ 08075 (800) 257-5755

August House
P.O. Box 3223
Little Rock, AR 72203
(800) 527-0924; in AR (501) 663-7300

J.J. Augustin, Publisher
123 Buckram Rd.
Locust Valley, NY 11560 (516) 676-1510

Avanyu Publishing
P.O. Box 27134
Albuquerque, NM 87125
(505) 266-6128 or 243-8485

Avery Color Studios
Star Route, Box 275
Au Train, MI 49806 (906) 892-8251

Avon Books
P.O. Box 767
Dresden, TN 38225 (800) 223-0690

Ayer Co. Publishers, Inc.
Lower Mill Rd.
North Startford, NH 03590
(800) 282-5413 Fax (603) 922-3348

B

Bainbridge Press
701 Fifth Ave. #5400
Seattle, WA 98104 (206) 223-4600

Baker Book House
P.O. Box 6287
Grand Rapids, MI 49506
(616) 676-9185 Fax 676-9573

Ballantine Books
Div. of Random House

Ballena Press
823 Valparaiso Ave.
Menlo Park, CA 94025 (415) 323-9261

Baltimore Museum of Art Shop
Art Museum Dr.
Baltimore, MD 21218 (301) 396-6316

Bancroft Press
27 McNear Dr.
San Rafael, CA 94901 (415) 454-7094

Bantam Books
414 East Golf Rd.
Des Plains, IL 60016 (800) 223-6834

Banyon Books
P.O. Box 431160
Miami, FL 33243 (305) 665-601 1

Lilian Barber Press
Box 232, Grand Central Sta.
New York, NY 10163 (212) 874-2678

Barre Publishing Co.; Orders to Crown Pubs.

Basil Blackwell, Inc.
P.O. Box 1655
Hagerstown, MD 21741 (800) 638-3030
Trade orders to Harper & Row

William L. Bauhan, Inc.
P.O. Box 443
Dublin, NH 03444 (603) 563-8020

Bay Press
115 W. Denny Way
Seattle, WA 98119 (206) 284-5913

Baywood Publishing Co.
P.O. Box 337
Amityville, NY 11701 (516) 691-1270

Beacon Press; Orders to Harper & Row

Bead-Craft
P.O. Box 4563
St. Paul, MN 55104 (612) 645-1216

Bear
P.O. Box 480005
Denver, CO 80248

Bear & Co.
P.O. Box 2860
Santa Fe, NM 87504
(800) 932-3277; in NM (505) 983-5968

Bear Claw Press
1407 W. Paterson St.
Flint, MI 48504 (313) 238-2569

Bear Tribe Publishing Co.
P.O. Box 9167
Spokane, WA 99209 (509) 326-6561

Beaufort Books
9 East 40th St.
New York, NY 10016

Bedford Publishers
779 Kirts
Troy, MI 48084 (313) 362-0369

Peter Bedrick Books
Dist. by Publishers Group West

Beechwood Books
720 Wehapa Cr.
Leeds, AL 35094 (205) 699-6935

Beekman Publishers
P.O. Box 888
Woodstock, NY 12498 (914) 679-2300

Bellerophon Books
36 Anacapa St.
Santa Barbara, CA 93101
(800) 965-8286 Fax (800) 253-9943

John Benjamins North America
821 Bethlehem Pike
Philadelphia, P A 19118 (215) 836-1200

Berkley Publishing Group
Dist. by Warner Publishing
75 Rockefeller Plaza
New York, NY 10019 (800) 631-8571

Berkshire Traveller Press
Pine St.
Stockbridge, MA 01262 (413) 298-3636

The Bess Press
P.O. Box 22388
Honolulu, HI 96823 (808) 734-7159
  Fax (808) 732-3627

Beyond Words Publishing
4443 NE Airport Rd.
Hillsboro, OR 97124
(800) 284-9673; (503) 647-5109

Biblio Distribution Centre
4720 Boston Way
Lanham, MD 20706 (301) 306-0400

Biblo-Moser Booksellers & Publishers
P.O. Box 302
Cheshire, CT 06410 (800) 272-8778

Binford & Mort Publishing
P.O. Box 10404
Portland, OR 97210
(503) 221-0866 Fax 221-0167

Birmingham Public Library
2100 Park Pl.
Birmingham, AL 35203 (205) 226-361 1

Bishop Museum Press
P.O. Box 19000A
Honolulu, HI 96817 (808) 848-4143

Bison Books
Dist. by University of Nebraska Press

Black Letter Press
461 Worth Rd., R.1
Moran, MI 49760 (906) 292-5513

John F. Blair, Publisher
1406 Plaza Dr.
Winston-Salem, NC 27103
(800) 222-9796; in NC (910) 768-1374

Blanche P. Browder
5133 Jeffries Rd.
Raleigh, NC 27606 (919) 851-0679

Clark Boardman Co.
435 Hudson St.
New York, NY 10014
(800) 221-9428; in NY (212) 929-7500

Bobbs-Merrill Co.
Div. of Macmillan

Boise State University
1910 University Dr.
Boise, ID 83725 (208) 385-1246

Bonanza Publishing, Ltd.
P.O Box 204
Prineville, OR 97754 (503) 447-6909

Bonjour Books
P.O. Box 24327
New Orleans, LA 70194 (504) 282-4660

Book Publishing Co.
P.O. Box 99
Summertown, TN 38483 (800) 695-2241
  Fax (615) 964-3518

Book Sales, Inc.
110 Enterprise Ave.
Secaucus, NJ 07094-1995 (800) 526-7257

Bookpeople
7900 Edgewater Dr .
Oakland, CA 94621 (510) 632-4700

Books Americana, Inc.
P.O. Box 2326
Florence, AL 35630
(205) 757-9966 Fax 757-91 19

Books on Demand
300 N. Zeeb Rd., Box 1346
Ann Arbor, MI 48106
(800) 521-0600; in MI (313) 761-4700

BookWorld Services
1933 Whitfield Loop
Sarasota, FL 34243 (800) 444-2524

Borgo Press
P.O. Box 2845
San Bernardino, CA 92406 (714) 884-5813

R.R. Bowker Co.
P.O. Box 31
New Providence, NJ 07974
(800) 521-8110; in Canada (800) 537-8416

Bowman Books
2 Middle Grove Rd.
Greenfield Center , NY 12833 (518) 584-1728

Boyd & Fraser Publishing
20 Park Pl.
Boston, MA 02116
(800) 225-3782; in MA (617) 426-2292

Bradbury Press
Dist. by Macmillan

Branch-Smith, Inc.
P.O. Box 1868
Fort Worth, TX 76101 (817) 332-6377

Robert F. Brand
1029 Lake Lane
Pennsburg, P A 18073

George Braziller
60 Madison Ave., Suite 1001
New York, NY 10010 (212) 889-0909

Brevet Press
P.O. Box 1404
Sioux Falls, SD 57101 (605) 338-7973

Brigham Young University Press
205 UPB
Provo, UT 84602 (801) 378-2809

E.J. Brill (USA), Inc.
24 Hudson St.
Kinderhook, NY 12106 (800) 962-4406

Broken Moon Press
P.O. Box 24585
Seattle, W A 98124 (206) 548-1340

Brookfield Publishing Co.
Old Post Rd.
Brookfield, VT 05036 (802) 276-3162

Brookings Institution
1775 Massachusetts Ave., N.W.
Washington, DC 20036 (202) 797-6250

Brooklyn Museum
Pubns-Mktg. Service
188 Eastern Parkway
Brooklyn, NY 11238 (718) 638-5000

William C. Brown Co., Publishers
2460 Kerper Blvd.
Dubuque, IA 52001 (319) 588-1451

Brown University Press
Alumnae Hall, 194 Meeting St.
Providence, RI 02912 (401) 863-2455

Buccaneer Books
P.O. Box 168
Cutchogue, NY 11935

Buffalo Bay Trading Co.
P.O. Box 1350
Bayfield, WI 54814 (715) 779-3687

Buffalo Bill Historical Center ,
P.O. Box 1000
Cody, WY 82414 (800) 533-3838

Buffalo Museum of Science
Publications Office, Humboldt Parkway
Buffalo, NY 14211

Burdett Design Studios
15192 Goldenwest Cr .
Westminster, CA 92683
(800) 634-6048; in CA (714) 897-6177

Bureau of Indian Affairs
Publications Dept.
1951 Constitution Ave., N.W.
Washington, DC 20242 (202) 343-7445

Burgess Publishing
7110 Ohms Lane
Edina, MN 55435 (612) 831-1344

C

CLC Press
P.O. Box 478
San Andreas, CA 95249 (209) 369-2781

CPL Bibliographies
1313 East 60 St., Merriam Center
Chicago, IL 60637 (312) 947-2007

Cache Valley Newsletter Publishing Co.
1219 West Oneida
Preston, ID 83263 (208) 852-3167

Cahill & Co.
P.O. Box 64554
St. Paul, MN 55164 (800) 755-8531

Cahokia Mounds Museum Society
P.O. Box 382
Collinsville, IL 62234 (618) 344-9221

Cahokia Mounds State Museum Society
P.O. Box 382
E. St. Louis, IL 62201 (618) 344-9221

California Academy of Sciences Publications
Golden State Park
San Francisco, CA 94118 (415) 750-7344

California Powows
c/o Karen Doris Wright
P.O. Box 359
Brisbane, CA 94005

California State University, Northridge
Library
18111 Nordhoff St.
Northridge, CA 91330 (818) 885-2271

Cambridge University Press
110 Midland Ave.
Port Chester, NY 10573 (800) 227-0247

Campanile Press
The San Diego State University
5189 College Ave.
San Diego, CA 92182 (619) 265-6220

Canadian Alliance in Solidarity
With the Native Peoples
16 Spadina Rd.
Toronto, Ontario M5R 2S7 (416) 964-0169

CCI-Canadian Circumpolar Institute
University of Alberta
Old St. Stephen's College
3rd Fl. North, 8820 - 1 12 St.
Edmonton, Alberta T6G 2E2
(403) 492-4512 Fax 492-1 153

Cannon Graphics, Inc.
418 Lehigh Ter.
Charleston, WV 25302 (304) 346-7602

Capra Press
P.O. Box 2068
Santa Barbara, CA 93120 (805) 966-4590

Capstone Press
P.O. Box 669
Mankato, MN 56001 (507) 625-2746

William Carey Library Publishers
P.O. Box 40129
Pasadena, CA 91104 (818) 798-0819

Carleton Press
49 West 73rd St. #2B
New York, NY 10023

Carnegie Museum of Natural History
Dist. by University of Pittsburgh Press

Carolrhoda Books
241 First Ave., N.,
Minneapolis, MN 55401
(800) 328-4929; in MN (612) 332-3344

Caxton Printers, Ltd.
312 Main St.
Caldwell, ID 83605
(208) 459-7421 Fax 459-7450

Celestial Arts Publishing Co.
P.O. Box 7327
Berkeley, CA 94704 (800) 841-2665
in CA (415) 524-1801

Center for American Archaeology
Kampsville Archaeological Center
P.O. Box 366
Kampsville, IL 62053 (618) 653-4316

Center for Anthropological Studies
P.O. Box 14567
Albuquerque, NM 87191

Center for Applied Linguistics
1118 22nd St., N.W.
Washington, D.C. 20037 (202) 429-9292

Center for Archaeological Investigations
Southern Illinois University
Carbondale, IL 62901 (618) 536-5529

Center for International Training & Education
777 United Nations Plaza, Suite 9A
New York, NY 10017 (212) 972-9877

Center for Law & Education
14 Appian Way, 6th Fl.
Cambridge, MA 02138 (617) 495-4666

Center for Pre-Columbian
Studies-Dumbarton Oaks
1703 32nd St., N.W.
Washington, D.C. 20007 (202) 232-3101

Center for Western Studies
Box 727, Augustana College
Sioux Falls, SD 57197 (605) 336-4007

Center of the American Indian
2100 NE 52nd St.
Oklahoma City, OK 73111 (405) 427-5228

Central States Archaeological Societies
646 Knierin Place
Kirkwood, MO 63122 (314) 821-7675

Chalfant Press
P.O. Box 787
Bishop, CA 93514 (619) 873-3535

Chandler & Sharp Publishers
11A Commercial Blvd.
Novato, CA 94949 (415) 883-2353

Charter Books
Div. of Berkley Publishing

Don M. Chase
916 Colorado Blvd.
Santa Rosa, CA 95405 (707) 823-7670

Chelsea House Publishers
P.O. Box 914
Broomall, PA 19008 (215) 353-5166

Cherokee Publications
P.O. Box 430
Cherokee, NC 28719 (704) 488-8856

Cherokee Publishing
P.O. Box 1730
Marietta, GA 30061 (404) 424-6210

Chicago Review Press
814 N. Franklin St.
Chicago, IL 60610 (312) 337-0747

Children's Book Press
6400 Hollis Ave. #4
Emeryville, CA 94608
(510) 655-3395 Fax 655-1978

Childrens Press
5440 N. Cumberland Ave.
Chicago, IL 60656
(800) 621-1115; in IL (312) 693-0800

Chilton Book Co.
School Library Services
Chilton Way, Radnor, PA 19089
(800) 345-1214; in PA (215) 964-4729

Choctaw Heritage Press
Route 7, Box 21
Philadelphia, MS 39350 (601) 656-5251

Choctaw Museum of the Southern Indian
Mississippi Band of Choctaw Indians
Route 7, Box 21
Philadelphia, MS 39350 (601) 656-5251

Christopher Publishing House
24 Rockland St.
Hanover, MA 02339
(617) 826-7474 Fax 826-5556

Chronicle Books
275 Fifth St.
San Francisco, CA 94103
(800) 722-6657 Fax 858-7787

The Chrysler Museum
Olney Rd. & Mobray Arch.
Norfolk, VA 23510 (804) 622-121 1

Ciga Press
P.O. Box 654
Fallbrook, CA 92028 (619) 728-9308

The CIRI Foundation
P.O. Box 93330
Anchorage, AK 99509
(907) 274-8638 Fax 279-8836

City Lights Books
Dist. by Subterranean Co.
P.O. Box 168
Monroe, OR 97456 (800) 274-7826

Claretian Publications
205 W. Monroe St.
Chicago, IL 60606 (312) 236-7782

Arthur H. Clark Co.
P.O. Box 14707
Spokane, WA 99214
(800) 842-9286; in WA (509) 928-9540

Clarion Books
215 Park Ave. South
New York, NY I0003

Clear Light Publishers
823 Don Diego
Santa Fe, NM 87501 (800) 253-2747

Earl M. Coleman Enterprises
P.O. Box 720
Crugers, NY 10521

Collector Books
P.O. Box 3009
Paducah, KY 42001
(800) 626-5420; in KY (502) 898-621 1

Collier Macmillan ; Div. of Macmillan

Columbia University Press
136 S. Broadway
Irvington-on-Hudson, NY10533 (914) 591-91 11

The Committee
2901 S. King Dr., No. 515
Chicago, IL 60616 (312) 567-9522

Common Courage Press
P.O. Box 702
Monroe, ME 04951 (800) 497-3207

Comstock Editions
1380 W. Second Ave.
Eugene, Oregon 97402 (503) 686-8001

Concordia Publishing House
3558 S. Jefferson Ave.
St. Louis, MO 631 18
(800) 325-3391/3040; in MO (314) 664-1662

Confluence Press; Dist. by Kampmann & Co.

Connections Press
961 Delphi Ave.
Sheridan, WY 82801 (307) 674-6625

Conservation Foundation
1250 24th St., N.W.
Washington, D.C. 20037 (202) 293-4800

Contemporary Books
180 N. Michigan Ave.
Chicago, IL 60601 (312) 782-9181

Continuum Publishing
Dist. by Harper & Row

Cooper Square Publishers
4720 Boston Way
Lanham, MD 20706 (301) 306-0400

Cordillera Press
P.O. Box 3699
Evergreen, CO 80439 (303) 670-3010

Cornell University Press
P.O. Box 6525
Ithaca, NY 14851 (607) 257-7000

Corner House Publishers
1321 Green River Rd.
Williamstown, MA 01267 (413) 458-8561

Coronet Books
311 Bainbridge St.
Philadelphia, P A 19147 (215) 925-2762

Corporate Resource Consultants
P.O. Box 22583
Kansas City, MO 64113 (800) 268-2059
(816) 361-2059 Fax 361-21 15

Costano Books
P.O. Box 355
Petaluma, CA 94953 (707) 762-4848

Council for Indian Education
P.O. Box 31215
Billings, MT 59107 (406) 252-1800

Council Publications
Council of Energy Resource Tribes
1999 Broadway, Suite 2600
Denver, CO 80202 (303) 297-2378

Coward, McCann & Geoghegan
Div. of Putnam Publishing

Coyote Books
P.O. Box 629
Brunswick, ME 04011

Coyote Books (MN)
3926 Lillie Ct., SW
Rochester, MN 55902 (507) 288-6159

Coyote Press
P.O. Box 3377
Salinas, CA 93912 (408) 422-4912

Crabtree Publishing Co.
350 Fifth Ave., Suite 3308
New York, NY 10118 (800) 387-7650

Cranbrook Institute of Science
P.O. Box 801
Bloomfield Hills, MI 48303 (313) 645-3256

Crazy Horse Memorial Foundation
Black Hills, Ave. of the Chiefs
Crazy Horse, SD 57730 (605) 673-4681

Creation House
Div. of Strang Communications

Creative Education, Inc.
P.O. Box 227
Mankato, MN 56001
(800) 445-6209; in MN (507) 388-6273

Creative Products of America
4201 N. Marshall W ay
Scottsdale, AZ 85251 (602) 941-9348

Cree Productions, Inc.
12555 127th St.
Edmonton, AB T5L 1A4 (403) 455-9317

Crestwood House, Inc.
Div. of Macmillan

Cross Cultural Publications
Cross Roads Books
P.O. Box 506
Notre Dame, IN 46556
(219) 272-3321 Fax 273-5973

The Crossing Press
P.O. Box 1048
Freedom, CA 95019 (800) 777-1048

Crossroad Publishing
Distributed by Harper & Row

Crow Canyon Archaeological Center
23390 County Rd. K
Cortez, CO 81321
(800) 422) 8975; (303) 565-8975

Crown Publishers
225 Park Ave. So.
New York, NY 10003 (212) 254-1600

Cultural Survival, Inc.
53A Church St.
Cambridge, MA 02138
(800) 248-2873; in MA (617) 495-2562

Current Issues Publications
2214 Stuart St.
Berkeley, CA 94705 (415) 549-1451

D

Da Capo Press, Inc.
Subs. of Plenum Publishing
233 Spring St.
New York, NY 10013 (800) 321-0050

Dakota Press
University of South Dakota
414 E. Clark
Vermillion, SD 57069 (605) 677-5401

DaNa Publications
1050 Austin Ave.
Idaho Falls, ID 83404 (208) 523-7237

The Grace Dangberg Foundation
P.O. Box 1627
Carson City, NV 89702 (702) 882-4466

Daring Books
P.O. Box 20050
Canton, OH 47701 (800) 445-6321

Daughters of St. Paul
50 St. Paul's Ave.
Boston, MA 02130 (617) 522-891 1

David & Charles
P.O. Box 257
North Pomfret, VT 05053
(800) 423-4525; in VT (802) 457-191 1

Dawson & Co.
P.O. Box 40157
Tucson, AZ 85717 (602) 323-8128

Dawson's Book Shop
535 N. Larchmont Blvd.
Los Angeles, CA 90004 (213) 469-2186

DCA Publishers
6709 Esther Ave., NE
Albuquerque, NM 87109 (505) 823-2914

Delacourte Press
1 Dag Hammarskjold Plaza
245 E. 47th St., New York, NY 10017
(800) 221-4676; in NY (212) 765-6500

Dell Publishing
666 Fifth Ave., 18th Floor
New York, NY 10103 (800) 255-4133

The Denali Press
P.O. Box 021535
Juneau, AK 99802 (907) 586-6014

T.S. Denison & Co.
9601 Newton Ave. So.
Minneapolis, MN 55431
(800) 328-3831; in MN (612) 888-1460

Denver Art Museum
Publications Dept.
100 West 14th Ave. Parkway
Denver, CO 80204 (303) 575-5582

Denver Museum of Natural History
City Park
Denver, CO 80205 (303) 370-6302

Devin-Adair Publishing
6 N. Water St.
Greenwich, CT 06830 (203) 531-7755

DeVorss & Co.
P.O. Box 550
Marina Del Rey, CA 90294 (213) 870-7478
bookstore orders (800) 843-5743; CA (800) 331-4719

Diablo Books
1700 Tice Valley Blvd., Apt. 150
Walnut Creek, CA 94595 (510) 939-8644

Dial Press
Dist. by Doubleday & Co.

Dimi Press
P.O. Box 3363
Salem, OR 97302
(800) 644-3464 Fax (503) 364-9727

Dissemination & Assessment Center for Bilingual Education
5701 Springdale Rd.
Austin, TX 78723 (512) 929-1313

Dodd, Mead & Co.
6 Ram Ridge Rd.
Spring Valley, NY 10977
(800) 237-3255; in NY (800) 544-4463

Donning Co. Publishers
5659 Virginia Beach Blvd.
Norfolk, Virginia 23502
(800) 446-8572; in V A (804) 461-8090

Dorrance Publishing Co.
643 Smithfield St.
Pittsburgh, PA 15222 (800) 788-7654
 (412) 288-1786

Dos Tejedoras Fiber Arts Publications
2395 University Ave.
St. Paul, MN 55114 (612) 646-7445

Doubleday & Co.
P.O. Box 5071
Des Plaines, IL 60017-5071
(800) 223-6834 Ext. 479; in NY (212) 765-6500

Dover Publications
31 E. Second St.
Mineola, New York 11501
(800) 223-3130; in NY (516) 294-7000

Drama Book Publishers
260 Fifth Ave.
New York, NY 10001 (212) 725-5377

Duck Down Press
P.O. Box 1047
Fallon, NV 89406 (702) 423-6643

Dumbarton Oaks
P.O. Box 4866, Hampden Sta.
Baltimore, MD 21211 (301) 338-6954

E.P. Dutton & Co.
Orders to New American Library
P.O. Box 120
Bergenfield, NJ 07621 (201) 387-0600

E

EHUD, International Language Foundation
P.O. Box 2082, Dollar Ranch Station
Walnut Creek, CA 94595 (415) 937-4841

ETC Publications
P.O. Box ETC
Palm Springs, CA 92263 (619) 325-5352

Eagle's View Publishing
6756 North Fork Rd.
Liberty, UT 84310 (801) 393-4555

Eakin Press
P.O. Box 90159
Austin, TX 78709
(800) 284-0173; in TX (512) 288-1771

Earth Art, Inc.
10212 Dutch Settlement Rd.
Marcellus, MI 49067 (616) 646-9545

East Plateau Indian Cooperative
905 E. 3rd Ave.
Spokane, WA 99202 (509) 535-1158

William B. Eerdmans Publishing Co.
255 Jefferson Ave., SE
Grand Rapids, MI 49503
(800) 253-7521; in MI (616) 459-4591

El Rancho Press
925 El Rancho Rd.
Santa Barbara, CA 93108 (805) 969-5323

Elan Marketing
3404 S. McClintock, Suite 905
Tempe, AZ 85282 (602) 892-3033

Charles & Randy Elder , Publishers
Church Ave. at 22nd Ave., N.
Nashville, TN 37203 (615) 327-1867

Elliot's Books
P.O. Box 6
Northford, CT 06472 (203) 484-2184

Elliott Bay Book Co.
101 S. Main St.
Seattle, WA 98104 (206) 624-6600

Elsevier Science Publishing Co.
P.O. Box 882, Madison Sq. Sta.
New York, NY 10159 (212) 989-5800

Encino Press
510 Baylor St.
Austin, TX 78703 (512) 476-6821

Enslow Publishers, Inc.,
P.O. Box 777
Hillsdale, NJ 07205 (800) 398-2504
 Fax (908) 687-3829

Epicenter Press
18821 64th NE
Seattle, WA 98155 (206) 485-6822

Equity & Excellence
University of Massachusetts
School of Education
Amherst, MA 01003 (413) 545-0133

Equity Publishing Corp.
Main St.
Orford, NH 03777 (603) 353-4351

ERIC/CRESS
Appalachian Education Laboratory , Inc.
P.O. Box 1348
Charleston, WV 25325 (800) 624-9120

Ervin Stuntz
20451 Tyler Rd.
Walkerton, IN 46574 (219) 588-3766

ESP, Inc.
P.O. Drawer 5080
Jonesboro, AR 72401
(800) 643-0280; in AR (501) 935-3533

M. Evans & Co.
Dist. by Little, Brown & Co.

Exposition-Phoenix
1620 S. Federal Hwy., No. 420
Pompano Beach, FL 33062 (305) 943-7165

EZ Nature Books
P.O. Box 4206
San Luis Obispo, CA 93403 (805) 595-7346

F

Facts on File
460 Park Ave. S.
New York, NY 10016
(800) 322-8755; in NY (212) 683-2244

Fairleigh Dickinson University Press
440 Forsgate Dr.
Cranbury, NJ 08512 (609) 655-4770

Faith and Life Press
718 Main St., Box 347
Newton, KS 67114 (316) 283-5100

Falcon Press Publishing
P.O. Box 1718
Helena, MT 59624
(800) 582-2665; in MT (406) 442-6597

Family Service America
11700 W. Lake Park Dr.
Milwaukee, WI 53224 (414) 359-2111

Fantail Native Design
c/o Pacific Science Center
200 2nd Ave., N.
Seattle, WA 98109 (204) 489-4604

Farrar, Straus & Giroux
19 Union Square W.
New York, NY 10003 (800) 638-3030

Favell Museum of W estern Art & Indian Artifacts
125 W. Main
Klamath Falls, OR 97601 (503) 882-9996

Fawcett Book Group
201 East 50th St.
New York, NY 10022
(800) 733-3000; in NY (212) 751-2600

Federal Bar Association
1815 H St., N.W., Suite 408
Washington, D.C. 20006 (202) 638-0252

Filter Press
P.O. Box 5
Palmer Lake, CO 80133 (719) 481-2523

Firebrand Books
141 The Commons
Ithaca, NY 14850 (607) 272-0000

Firefly Books, Ltd.
P.O. Box 1325, Ellicott Station
Buffalo, NY 14205 (800) 387-5085

Fithian Press
Div. of Daniel & Daniel Publishers
P.O. Box 1525
Santa Barbara, CA 93102 (800) 662-8351

The Five Civilized Tribes Museum
Agency Hill on Honor Hts. Dr.
Muskogee, OK 74401 (918) 683-1701

Five Flower Press
369 Montezuma #254
Santa Fe, NM 87501 (505) 983-9745

Fogelman Publishing Co.
RD 1 Box 240
Turbotville, PA 17772 (717) 437-3698

Forum Press
773 Glenn Ave.
Wheeling, IL 60090 (708) 253-9720

The Foundation for Classical Reprints
P.O. Box 27040
Albuquerque, NM 87125 (505) 843-7749

Four Winds Trading Co.
P.O. Box 1887
Boulder, CO 80306 (800) 456-5444

Frank Kenan Barnard
8240 Lindley Mill Rd.
Graham, NC 27253 (919) 376-3242

J. Franklin Publishing
P.O. Box 14057
Tulsa, OK 74159 (800) 234-9384

Free Press
Div. of Simon & Schuster
(800) 323-7445

Franklin Pierce College
Fund for Anthropology
Rindge, NH 03461 (603) 899-51 11

Franklin Watts - Order Processing
5440 N. Cumberland Ave.
Chicago, IL 60656
(800) 621-1115 Fax (800) 374-4329

W.H. Freeman & Co.
4419 West 1980 South
Salt Lake City, UT 84104 (801) 973-4660

Freshwater Press
1701 E. 12th St., Suite 3KW
Cleveland, Ohio 441 14-3201 (216) 241-0373

Ira J. Friedman
Div. of Associated Faculty Press

Friendship Press
P.O. Box 37844
Cincinnati, OH 45222-0844 (513) 761-2100

The Frontier Press Co.
P.O. Box 1098
Columbus, Ohio 43216 (614) 864-3737

Fulcrum Publishing
350 Indiana St., Suite 350
Golden, CO 80401
(800) 992-2908 Fax (800) 726-71 12

Fun Publishing
P.O. Box 2049
Scottsdale, AZ 85252 (602) 946-2093

Emma Lila Fundaburk, Publisher
P.O. Box 231
Luverne, AL 36049

The Fur Press
HC 74, Box 18
Chadron, NE 69337 (308) 432-3843

Futura Publishing Co.
295 Main St., P.O. Box 330
Mt. Kisco, NY 10549 (914) 666-3505

G

Gale Research, Inc.
835 Penobscot Bldg.
Detroit, MI 48226 (800) 877-4253
in Canada (313) 961-2242

Gallery West
P.O. Box 5688
Santa Fe, NM 87502 (505) 983-2832

Galloway Publications
2940 NW Circle Blvd.
Corvallis, OR 97330-3999 (503) 754-7464

Gallup Distributing Co.
205 Sunde Ave.
Gallup, NM 87301 (505) 863-4304

Garland Publishing
100A Sherman Ave.
Hamden, CT 06514 (800) 627-6273

Garrett Park Press
P.O. Box 190W
Garrett Park, MD 20896 (301) 946-2553

Genealogical Publishing
10001 N. Calvert St.
Baltimore, MD 21202 (301) 837-8271

Geological Society of America, Inc.
P.O. Box 9140
Boulder, CO 80301 (800) 472-1988

George Washington University
Center for Washington Area Studies, Stuart 106
Washington, D.C. 20052

George M. White Books
P.o. Box 365
Ronan, MT 59864 (406) 676-3766

Georgetown University Press
Intercultural Center, Rm. 111
Washington, D.C. 20057 (202) 6687-5889

Georgia Dept. of Archives & History
330 Capitol Ave.
Atlanta, Georgia 30334 (404) 656-2393

Gibbs Smith Publishing
P.O. Box 667
Layton, UT 84041 (800) 421-8714

Ginn Press
10 Gould St.
Needham Hts., MA 02194
(800) 428-4466; in MA (617) 455-7000

Glencoe Publishing
Div. of Macmillan

GLIFWC
Public Information Office
P.O. Box 9
Odanah, WI 54861 (715) 682-6619

Global Communications
P.O. Box 753
New Brunswick, NJ 08903 (212) 685-4080

Globe Pequot Press
P.O. Box 833
Old Saybrook, CT 06475
(800) 243-0495; in CT (800) 962-0973
Fax (203) 395-0312

David R. Godine Publishing
Dist. by American International Distribution
Corp.
P.O. Box 80
Williston, VT 05495 (802) 878-0315

Golden Bell Press
2403 Champa St.
Denver, CO 80205 (303) 296-1600

Goliards Press
191 Mill St.
Friday Harbor, WA 98250

Good Apple, Inc.
P.O. Box 299
Carthage, IL 62321-0299
(800) 435-7234; in IL (217) 357-3981

Good Medicine Books
Dist. by Bookpeople

Gordian Press
P.O. Box 304
Staten Island, NY 10304 (718) 273-4700

Gordon & Breach Science Publishers
P.O. Box 786, Cooper Station
New York, NY 10010 (212) 206-8900

Gordon Press Publishers
P.O. Box 459, Bowling Green Sta.
New York, NY 10004 (212) 624-8419

Government Information Services
4301 N. Fairfax Dr., Suite 875
Arlington, VA 22203 (800) 876-0226

Gower Publishing Co.
Old Post Rd.
Brookfield, VT 05036 (802) 276-3162

Graphic Arts Center Publishing
P.O. Box 10306
Portland, OR 97210 (800) 452-3032
Fax (503) 223-1410

Graphic Impressions
1401 W. 38th Ave.
Denver, CO 80211 (303) 458-7475

Great Eagle Publishing
3020 Issaquah-Pine Lake Rd. SE, Suite 481
Issaquah, WA 98027 (206) 392-9136

Great Outdoors Publishing
4747 28th St., N.
St. Petersburg, FL 33714
(800) 869-6609; in FL (813) 525-6609

Greatland Graphics
P.O. Box 100333
Anchorage, AK 99510 (907) 562-5723

Green Valley Area Education Agency
1405 N. Lincoln
Creston, IA 50801 (515) 782-8443

Greenfield Press
P.O. Box 176
Southport, CT 06490 (203) 268-4878

Greenfield Review Press
P.O. Box 308
Greenfield Center, NY 12833
(518) 583-1440 Fax 583-9741

Greenwillow Books
Div. of William Morrow & Co.

Greenwood Publishing
88 Post Rd., W., Box 5007
Westport, CT 06881 (203) 226-3571

Gregg Press
Division of G.K. Hall & Co.

Grey Art Gallery Study Center
N.Y.U., 33 Washington Pl.
New York, NY 10003 (212) 998-6780

Grey Fox Press
Dist. by Subterranean Co.
P.O. Box 168
Monroe, OR 97440 (800) 274-7826

Gros Ventre Treaty Committee
Fort Belknap Agency
Harlem, MT 59526

Guild Hall Museum
158 Main St.
East Hampton, NY 11937 (516) 324-0806

H

Hafner Press
Div. of Macmillan

G.K. Hall & Co.
70 Lincoln St.
Boston, MA 02111 (800) 343-2806

Raven Hail Books
P.O. Box C-900, No. 230
Scottsdale, AZ 85252 (602) 945-2790

A.G. Halldin Publishing
P.O. Box 667
Indiana, PA 15701 (412) 463-8450

Halsted Press
Div. of John Wiley & Sons

Hancock House Publishers
P.O. Box 959
Blaine, WA 98231 (206) 354-6953
Fax (604) 538-2262

Hanging Loose Press
231 Wyckoff St.
Brooklyn, NY 11217 (718) 643-9559

Harbinger House, Inc.
P.O. Box 42948
Tucson, AZ 85733 (800) 759-9945
Dist. by Mountain Press

Harbor Hill Books, Inc.
P.O. Box 246
Mamaroneck, NY 10543 (914) 698-3495

Harcourt Brace Jovanovich
6277 Sea Harbor Dr.
Orlando, FL 32887 (800) 543-1918
Fax (800) 874-6418

Hardscrabble Books
10735 Jones Rd.
Berrien Springs, MI 49103 (616) 473-5570

Harlan Davidson
3110 N. Arlington Heights Rd.
Arlington Heights, IL 60004 (708) 253-9720
Fax (708) 253-9728

Harlo Press
50 Victor Ave.
Detroit, MI 48203 (313) 883-3600

Harmsen Publishing
3131 E. Alameda Ave.
Denver, CO 80209 (303) 777-4030

Harper & Row
1000 Keystone Industrial Park
Scranton, PA 18512
(800) 242-7737; Fax (800) 822-4090

HarperCollins
Div. of Harper & Row

Hart Publishers
P.O. Box 422
Bluffton, IN 46714

Harvard Common Press
Dist. by Kampmann & Co.

Harvard University Press
79 Garden St.
Cambridge, MA 02138 (617) 495-2600

Haskell Booksellers
P.O. Box 420, Blythebourne Sta.
Brooklyn, NY 11219 (718) 435-7878

Hastings House Publishers
141 Halstead Ave.
Mamaroneck, NY 10543 (914) 835-4005

Havasupai Tribal Council
P.O. Box 10
Supai, AZ 86435 (602) 448-2731

Hawthorne Books
Div. of E.P. Dutton

Hayden Book Co.
10 Mulholland Dr.
Hasbrouck Heights, NJ 07604 (201) 393-6300

Heart of the Lakes Publishing
2989 Lodi Rd., Box 299
Interlaken, NY 14847 (607) 532-4997

D.C. Heath & Co.
Distribution Center
2700 Richardt Ave.
Indianapolis, IN 46210 (317) 350 5585

The Heard Museum
22 E. Monte Vista Rd.
Phoenix, AZ 85004 (602) 252-8840

William S. Heinman-E.J. Brill
24 Hudson St.
Kinderhook, NY 12106 (518) 758-141 1

T. Emmett Henderson
130 W. Main St.
Middletown, NY 10940 (914) 343-1038

Hendrick-Long Publishing
P.O. Box 25123
Dallas, TX 75225 (800) 544-3770

Hendry Publications
Lost Cabin Route
Lysite, WY 82642 (307) 876-2647

Hennessey & Ingalls
8325 Campion Dr.
Los Angeles, CA 90045 (213) 458-9074

Herald Press
Div. of Mennonite Publishing House
616 Walnut Ave.
Scottsdale, PA 15683
(800) 245-7894; in P A (412) 887-8500

Heritage Books, Inc.
1540 E. Pointer Ridge Pl.
Bowie, MD 20716
(800) 398-7709 Fax (800) 276-1760

Heritage Publishers, Inc.
2700 Woodlands Blvd.
Flagstaff, AZ 86001 (602) 526-1 129

Heritage Quest
P.O. Box 40
Orting, WA 98360 (800) 442-2029

Janet M. Herren
4750 Crystal Springs Dr.
Bainbridge Island, W A 98110 (206) 842-3484

Heyday Books
P.O. Box 9145
Berkeley, CA 94709 (510) 549-3564

Ron G. Hickox
c/o Antique Arms & Military Research
P.O. Box 36006
Tampa, FL 33673-0006 (813) 237-0764

High-Lonesome Books
P.O. Box 878
Silver City, NM 88062
(800) 380-7323; (505) 388-3763

Highlights for Children
P.O. Box 269
Columbus, OH 43272 (614) 486-0631

Hill & Wang
Div. of Farrar, Straus & Giroux

Hillsdale Educational Publishers, Inc.
39 North St., Box 245
Hillsdale, MI 49242 (517) 437-3179

Hippocrene Books
171 Madison Ave.
New York, NY 10016
(718) 454-2366 Fax 454-1391

Historic Pensacola Preservation Board
Distributed by John C. Pace Library
University of West Florida
Pensacola, FL 32504 (904) 476-9500

Histree
23011 Moulton Pkwy. D-12
Laguna Hills, CA 92653 (714) 859-1659

Holiday House
425 Madison Ave.
New York, NY 10017 (212) 688-0085

Holloway House Publishing
Dist. by All America Distributors
8431 Melrose Pl.
Los Angeles, CA 90069 (213) 651-2650

Holmes Book Co.
274 14th St.
Oakland, CA 94612 (415) 893-6860

Holmgangers Press
95 Carson Court, Shelter Cove
Whitehorn, CA 95489 (707) 986-7700

Henry Holt & Co.
115 W. 18th St.,
New York, NY 10011 (800) 247-3912

Holiday House, Inc.
425 Madison Ave.
New York. NY 10017

Holt-Atherton Center for Western Studies
University of the Pacific
Stockton, CA 95211 (209) 946-2404

Holt, Rinehart & Winston
6277 Sea Harbor Dr.
Orlando, FL 32887 (800) 447-9479

Holy Cowl Press
Box 3170, Mt. Royal Station
Duluth, MN 55803 (218) 724-1653

Hothem House
P.O. Box 458
Lancaster, OH 43130 (614) 653-9030

Houghton Mifflin Co.
Wayside Rd.
Burlington, MA 01803
(800) 225-3362 Fax (800) 458-9501

Howard University Press
2900 Van Ness St., N.W.
Washington, D.C. 20008 (202) 686-6696

Howe Brothers
P.O. Box 6394
Salt Lake City, UT 84106 (800) 426-5387

Howell Book House; Dist. by Macmillan

HRAF Press
Human Relations Area Files Press
P.O. Box 2015, Yale Station
New Haven, CT 06520 (203) 777-2337

Hudson Hills Press
Dist. by Rizzoli International Publications

Human Kinetics Publishers
P.O. Box 5076
Champaign, IL 61825-5076
(800) 342-5457; in IL (800) 334-3665

Humanities Press International
171 First Ave.
Atlantic Highlands, NJ 07716 (800) 221-3845

Hunter Publishing
Dist. by Many Feathers Books & Maps,
5738 N. Central Ave.
Phoenix, AZ 85012 (602) 266-1043

I

i.b.d., Ltd.
P.O. Box 467
Kinderhook, NY 12106 (800) 343-3531

Ibis Publishing, Inprint, Inc.
7 Elliewood Ave.
Charlottesville, VA 22903
(800) 582-0026; in VA (804) 296-7698

Idaho Museum of Natural History
Campus Box 8096, Idaho State University
Pocatello, ID 83209 (208) 236-3168

Illinois State Historical Library
Old State Capitol
Springfield, IL 62701 (217) 782-4836

Illinois State Museum Society
Spring & Edwards
Springfield, IL 62706 (217) 782-7386

Independence Press
P.O. Box HH, 3225 S. Noland Rd.
Independence, MO 64055
(800) 821-7550; in MO (816) 252-5010

Independent Publishers Group
814 N. Franklin St.
Chicago, IL 60610 (800) 888-4741

Indian Arts & Crafts Association
122 La Veta NE
Albuquerque, NM 87108 (505) 265-9149

Indian Arts & Crafts Board
Room 4004, USDI, Main Interior Bldg.
Washington, D.C. 20240 (202) 208-3773

Indian Bibliographic Center
University of Arkansas
P.O. Box 1201
Fayetteville, AR 72202

Indian Chief Publishing House
P.O. Box 5205
Tahoe City, CA 95730 (916) 583-8054

Indian Country Communications
Route 2, Box 2900-A
Hayward, WI 54843
(715) 634-5226 Fax 634-3243

Indian Feather Publishing
7218 S.W. Oak,
Portland, OR 97223

Indian Heritage Publishing
Box 2302, Henry St.
Moristown, TN 37816 (615) 581-4448

Indian Historian Press
1493 Masonic Ave.
San Francisco, CA 94117 (415) 626-5235

Indian Resource Development
Box 30003, Dept. 3IRD
New Mexico State University
Las Cruces, NM 88003 (505) 646-1347

Indian Rights Association
1515 Lafayette Rd.
Gladwyne, PA 19035 (215) 563-8349

Indian University Press
Bacone College, 2299 Old Bacone Rd.
Muskogee, OK 74403 (918) 683-4581

Indiana Historical Society
315 W. Ohio St., Rm. 350
Indianapolis, IN 46202 (317) 232-1882
Fax (317) 233-3109

Indiana University Press
Tenth & Morton Sts.
Bloomington, IN 47403 (812) 335-4203

Information Coordinators
1435-37 Randolph St.
Detroit, MI 48226 (313) 962-9720

Inner Traditions International, Ltd.
Box 388
Rochester, VT 05767 (800) 488-2665

Institute for the Arts-Rice University
P.O. Box 1892
Houston, TX 77001 (713) 527-8101

Institute for the Development of Indian Law
Oklahoma City University, School of Law
2501 N. Blackwelder
Oklahoma City, OK 73106 (405) 531-5337

Institute for Research in Social Sciences
University of North Carolina, 026A Manning Hall
Chapel Hill, NC 27514 (919) 962-3204

Institute for Southern Studies
604 Chapel Hill St.
Durham, NC 27701 (919) 688-8167

**Institute for the Study of Traditional
American Indian Arts**
P.O. Box 66124
Portland, OR 97266 (503) 233-8131

Institute of Alaska Native Arts
P.O. Box 70769
Fairbanks, AK 99707 (907) 456-7491

Institute of American Indian Arts Press
St. Michael Dr.
Santa Fe, NM 87501

Integrated Education Associates
University of Massachusetts
School of Education
Amherst, MA 01003 (413) 545-0327

Inter-Tribal Indian Ceremonial Association
P.O. Box 1
Church Rock, NM 87311 (505) 863-3896

Interbook
131 Varick St., 2nd Floor,
New York, NY 10013 (212) 691-7248

International Library Center
1405 St. Christopher
Columbia, MO 65203 (314) 449-5871

International Publications Service
Div. of Taylor & Francis
242 Cherry St.
Philadelphia, P A (800) 821-8312

International Publishers
239 West 23 St.
New York, NY 10011
(212) 366-9816 Fax 366-9820

International Specialized Book Services
5602 NE Hassalo St.
Portland, OR 97213-3640
(800) 547-7734; in OR (503) 287-3093

International Universities Press
P.O. Box 1524
Madison, CT 06443 (203) 245-4000

Interstate
19-27 N. Jackson St.
Danville, IL 61832-0594 (217) 446-0500

Iowa State University Press
2121 S. State Ave.
Ames, IA 50010 (515) 294-5280

Island Press
P.O. Box 7
Covelo, CA 95428 (707) 983-6432

Island Press
175 Bahia Via
Fort Myers Beach, FL 33931 (813) 463-9482

J

J & L Enterprises
2485 Riverside Dr .
Laramie, WY 82070

**Jefferson National
Expansion Historical Assn.**
11 N. 4th St.
St. Louis, MO 63102

Jeffery & Jones Gang, Inc.
P.O. Box 648
Collinsville, AL 35961 (205) 524-2485

Jelm Mountain Publications
471 Highway 10
Jelm, WY 82063 (307) 721-5058

Jenkins Publishing
P.O. Box 2085
Austin, TX 78767 (512) 444-6616

Johns Hopkins University Press
701 W. 40th St., Suite 275
Baltimore, MD 2121 1
(800) 537-5487; in MD (301) 338-7864

Walter J. Johnson
355 Chestnut St.
Norwood, NJ 07648 (201) 767-1303

Johnson Books
1880 South 57th Court
Boulder, CO 80301 (800) 258-5830
Fax (303) 443-1679

Johnson Publishing
820 S. Michigan Ave.
Chicago, IL 60605 (312) 322-9248

Johnson Publishing Co.
405 Union St.
Murfreesboro, NC 27855

Johnson Reprint
111 Fifth Ave.
New York, NY 10003 (212) 614-3150

Johnston Publishing
P.O. Box 96
Afton, MN 55001 (612) 436-7344

Joslyn Art Museum
Dist. by University of Nebraska Press

JTE Associates
1800 Lexington Dr .
Fullerton, CA 92635 (714) 447-9293

K

KC Publications
P.O. Box 15630
Las Vegas, NV 89114 (800) 626-9673
(702) 731-3123 Fax 433-3420

KMG Publications
290 E. Ashland Lane
Ashland, OR 97520 (503) 488-1302

K-T Curriculum Project
P.O.Box 1401
Hoopa, CA 95546

Kalmbach Publishing
1027 N. Seventh St.
Milwaukee, WI 53233
(800) 558-1544; in WI (414) 272-2060

Kampmann & Co.
4720A Boston Way
Lanham, MD 20706 (800) 526-7626

Kansas State Historical Society
120 W. Tenth St.
Topeka, KS 66612 (913) 296-3251

Katonah Gallery
28 Bedford Rd.
Katonah, NY 10536 (914) 232-9555

Augustus M. Kelley , Publishers
300 Fairfield Rd., P .O. Box 1308
Fairfield, NJ 07006-0008 (212) 685-7202

Edward P. Kellogg, Jr.
Dist. by EHUD International Language
Foundation

Kendall-Hunt Publishing
Subs. of William C. Brown Co., Publishers

Kennebec River Press
Dist. by Harpswell Press
132 Water St.
Gardiner, ME 04345 (207) 582-1899

Kent State University Press
P.O. Box 6525
Ithaca, NY 14851 (607) 277-221 1

Kivaki Press
585 East 31st St.
Durango, CO 81301 (800) 578-5904
(303) 385-1767 Fax 385-1974

Kluwer Academic Publishers
P.O. Box 358, Accord Sta.
Hingham, MA 02018-0358 (617) 871-6600

Alfred A. Knopf
400 Hahn Rd.
Westminster, MD 21157 (301) 848-1900

Knowledge Unlimited
P.O. Box 5222
Buffalo Grove, IL 60078 (312) 358-4795

Kodansha International USA, Ltd.
Dist. by Farrar, Straus & Giroux

Koen Book Distributors, Inc.
10 Twosome Dr., Box 600
Mooretown, NJ 08057 (800) 257-8481

Kraus Organization Ltd.
Route 100
Milwood, NY 10546 (800) 223-8323
(914) 762-2200 Fax 762-1 195

Krause Publications
700 E. State St.
Iola, WI 54990 (715) 445-2214

Krieger Publishing Co.
P.O. Box 9542
Melbourne, FL 32902-9542
(407) 724-9542 Fax 951-3671

L

Labyrinthos
6355 Green Valley Cr., Suite 213
Culver City, CA 90230 (213) 649-2612

Landfall Press, Inc.
5171 Chapin St.
Dayton, OH 45429 (513) 298-9123

Peter Lang Publishing
62 W. 45th St., 4th Floor
New York, NY 10036 (212) 302-6740

Lantern Press
354 Hussey Rd.
Mt. Vernon, NY 10552 (914) 668-9736

Laughing Fox Legends
4213 W. Culver
Phoenix, AZ 85009 (602) 272-4450

League of Women Voters of the U.S.
1730 M St., N.W.
Washington, D.C. 20036 (202) 429-1965

Leetes Island Books
Dist. by Independent Publishers Group
814 N. Franklin
Chicago, IL 60610 (312) 337-0747

Left Bank Books
5241 University W ay, NE
Seattle, W A 98105 (206) 522-8864

Legacy House
P.O. Box 786
Orofino, ID 83544 (208) 476-5632

Lenni Lenape Historical Society
Allentown, PA 18105

Lerner Publications
241 First Ave. North
Minneapolis, MN 55401
(800) 328-4929 Fax (800) 332-1 132

Levin Associates; Div. of Macmillan

Levite of Apache Publishing
203 Hal Muldrow Dr ., Suite 3
Norman, OK 73069 (405) 366-6442

Lexington Books
Dist. by Simon & Schuster

Libraries Unlimited, Inc.
P.O. Box 6633
Englewood, CO 80155 (800) 237-6124

Library of Psychological Anthropology
2315 Broadway
New York, NY 10024

Library Research Associates
Dunderberg Rd., RD 5, Box 41
Monroe, NY 10950 (914) 783-1 144

Life Lines
P.O. Box 745
Rimrock, AZ 86335 (602) 567-5864

Lime Rock Press
Mt. Riga Rd., Box 363
Salisbury, CT 06068 (203) 824-141 1

Limestone Press
Dist. by University of Alaska Press

Lion Books
210 Nelso Rd.
Scarsdale, NY 10583 (914) 725-2280

Lion's Head Publishing Co.
2436 S. U.S. 33
Albion, IN 46701 (219) 635-2165

J.B. Lippincott & Co.
E. Washington Sq.
Philadelphia, P A 19105
(800) 242-7737; in P A (800) 982-4377

Little, Brown & Co.
200 West St.
Waltham, MA 02154
(800) 343-9204; in MA (617) 227-0730

Little Red Hen, Inc.
P.O. Box 4260
Pocatello, ID 83201 (208) 232-1847

Littlefield Adams, Inc.
4720 Boston W ay
Lanham, MD 20706 (301) 459-3366

Liveright Publishing
Dist. by W.W. Norton & Co.

Lodestar Books
Dist. by Penguin U.S.A.

Loft-Barnell
958 Church St.
Baldwin, NY 11510 (516) 868-6064

Lomond Publications
P.O. Box 88
Mt. Airy, MD 21771
(800) 443-6299; in MD (301) 829-1633

Longman, Inc.
95 Church St.
White Plains, NY 10601 (914) 993-5000

Lothrop, Lee & Shepard Books
Div. of William Morrow & Co.

Louisiana State University Press
Baton Rouge, LA 70893 (504) 388-6666

The Lowell Press
115 E. 31 St., Box 41 1877
Kansas City, MO 64141 (800) 736-7660

Loyola University Press
3441 N. Ashland Ave.
Chicago, IL 60657
(800) 621-1008; in IL (312) 281-1818

Lyons & Burford, Publishers, Inc.
31 W. 21st St.
New York, NY 10010 (212) 620-9580

M

Mackinac Island State Park Commission
P.O. Box 370
Mackinac Island, MI 49757 (906) 847-3328

Macmillan Publishing
Front & Brown Sts.
Riverside, NJ 08370
(800) 257-5755 Fax (800) 562-1272

MacRae Publications
P.O. Box 652
Enumclaw, WA 98022 (206) 825-3737

Madison Books
Subs. of University Press of America
Dist. by National Book Network
4720A Boston Way
Lanham, MD 20706 (800)462-6420

Madrona Publishers
 P.O. Box 22667
Seattle, W A 98122 (800) 367-8420

Magi Books
Dist. by St. Bede's Publications
P.O. Box 545
Petersham, MA 01366 (508) 724-3407

Magpie Publications
P.O. Box 636
Alamo, CA 94507 (415) 838-9287

Maine Historical Society
485 Congress St.
Portland, ME 041 11 (207) 774-1822

Maine State Museum Publications
State House Sta. 83
Augusta, ME 04333 (207) 289-2301

Maine Studies Committee
University of Maine, PICS Bldg.
Orono, Maine 04469 (207) 581-1700

Malki Museum Press
11-795 Fields Rd.
Morongo Indian Reservation
Banning, CA 92220 (714) 849-7289

Manitoba Museum of Man and Nature
Education Office, 190 Ruper Ave.
Winnipeg, Manitoba R3B 0N2 Canada

Mankind Publishing
8060 Melrose Ave.
Los Angeles, CA 90046 (213) 653-8060
 Fax (213) 655-9452

Ray Manley Commercial Photography
238 S. Tucson Blvd.
Tucson, AZ 85716 (602) 623-0307

Mariposa Printing & Publishing, Inc.
P.O. Box 71
Mariposa, CA 95338 (209) 966-3897

Marquette County Historical Society
213 N. Front St.
Marquette, MI 49855 (906) 226-3571

Marshall Cavendish Corp.
P.O. Box 587
North Bellmore, NY 11710 (800) 821-9881

Maryland Historical Press
9205 Tuckerman St.
Lanham, MD 20706 (301) 577-5308

Mason/Charter
VNR Order Processing
7625 Empire Dr .
Florence, KY 41042 (212) 265-8700

Maverick Distributors
P.O. Drawer 7289
Bend, OR 75258 (800) 333-8046

Mayfield Publishing Co.
1240 Villa St.
Mountain V iew, CA 94041
(800) 433-1279; in CA (415) 960-3222

Mayhaven Publishing
803 Buckthorn Cr .
Mahomet, IL 61853 (217) 586-4493

McClain Printing Co.
212 Main St.
Parsons, WV 26287
(800) 654-7179; in WV(304) 478-2881

McDonald & W oodward Publishing Co.
P.O. Box 10308
Blacksburg, VA 24062 (703) 639-5632

McFarland & Co. Publishers
P.O. Box 611
Jefferson, NC 28640 (919) 246-4460

McGraw-Hill Book Co.
Princeton Rd.
Hightstown, NJ 08520 (609) 426-5254; or
 8171 Redwood Highway , Novato, CA 94947;
or:
 13955 Manchester Rd., Manchester ,
 MO 63011;
 (800) 262-4729 (retail); (800) 338-3987
(college):
 (800) 722-4726 (consumer)

David McKay Co.
Orders to Random House
400 Hahn Rd., W estminster, MD 21157
(800) 733-3000; (800) 726-0600 (credit cards)

Nan McNutt & Associates
Dist. by Pacific Pipeline, Inc.
19215 66th Ave. S.
Kent, WA 98032 (206) 872-5523
in WA (800) 562-4647; in NV, MT, ID, OR,
and northern CA (800) 426-4727

Media Periodicals
4050 Pennsylvania Ave. #310
Kansas City, MO 64111

The Edwin Mellen Press
P.O. Box 450
Lewiston, NY 14092 (800) 753-2788

Membrane Press
P.O. Box 4190
Kenosha, WI 53141

Memento Publications
P.O. Box 58646
Dallas, TX 75258 (808) 734-8611

MEP Publications
University of Minnesota
c/o Anthropology Dept.
215 Ford Hall, 224 Church St., SE
Minneapolis, MN 55455 (612) 722-5964

Merryant Publishers
7615 SW 257th St.
Vashon, WA 98070 (206) 463-3879

Julian Messner
Div. of Silver Burdette Press, Simon & Schuster

Methuen, Inc.
Dist. by Routledge

Metropolitan Museum of Art
Orders to: Special Services Office
Flushing, NY 11381 (718) 326-7050

Meyer Creative Productions
208 N. 4th St., Box 1738
Bismarck, ND 58502 (800) 637-6863
(701) 223-7316

The Michie Co.
P.O. Box 7587
Charlottesville, VA 22906
(800) 446-3410; in VA (804) 295-6171

Michigan Indian Press
45 Lexington NW
Grand Rapids, MI 49504 (616) 774-8331

Michigan State University Press
1405 S. Harrison Rd., 25 Manly Miles Bldg.
East Lansing, MI 48824 (517) 355-9543
Fax (800) 678-2120; (517) 336-2611

Microfilming Corp. of America
200 Park Ave.
New York, NY 10166 (212) 972-1070

Middle Atlantic Press
Dist. by Koen Book Distributors

Milwaukee Public Museum
800 W. Wells St.
Milwaukee, WI 53233 (414) 278-2787

Minnesota Historical Society Press
345 Kellogg Blvd. West
St. Paul, MN 55102
(800) 647-7827; (612) 297-3243

Minnesota Humanities Commission
26 E. Exchange St., Lower Level S.
St. Paul, MN 55101 (612) 224-5739
Mississippi Dept. of Archives & History
Dist. by University Press of Mississippi

Modern Language Association of America
10 Astor Pl.
New York, NY 10003 (212) 475-9500

Mojave Books
7118 Canby Ave.
Reseda, CA 91335 (818) 342-3403

Monroe County Library System
3700 S. Custer Rd.
Monroe, MI 48161 (313) 241-5277

Montana Historical Society Press
225 N. Roberts St.
Helena, MT 59620 (406) 444-4708

Monthly Review Press
122 West 27th St.
New York, NY 10001 (212) 691-2555

Moody Press
820 N. LaSalle Dr.
Chicago, IL 60610
(800) 621-5111; in IL (800) 621-4323

Morgan & Morgan
145 Palisade St.
Dobbs Ferry, NY 10522 (914) 693-0023

Morning Star Gallery
513 Canyon Rd.
Santa Fe, NM 87501 (505) 982-8187

William Morrow & Co.
Wilmor Warehouse
P.O. Box 1219, 39 Plymouth St.
Fairfield, NJ 07007 (800) 843-9389

Mountain Press
P.O. Box 2399
Missoula, MT 59806 (800) 234-5308
(406) 728-1900 Fax 728-1635

Mouton de Gruyter
200 Saw Mill River Rd.
Hawthorne, NY 10532 (914) 747-0110
Fax (914) 747-1326

Moyer Bell, Ltd.
Dist. by Consortium Book

John Muir Publications
Dist. by W.W. Norton & Co., Inc.

H.L. Murvin Publisher
500 Vernon St.
Oakland, CA 94610 (415) 658-7517

Museum of Fine Arts
465 Huntington Ave.
Boston, MA 02115 (617) 267-9300

Museum of the Great Plains
Publications Dept.
601 Ferris, Box 68
Lawton, OK 73502 (405) 353-5675

Museum of New Mexico Press
P.O. Box 2087
Santa Fe, NM 87504 (505) 827-6454

Museum of Northern Arizona
Rte. 4, Box 720
Flagstaff, AZ 86001 (602) 774-5211
Museum of Ojibwa Culture
500 N. State St.
St. Ignace, MI 49781 (906) 643-9161

Museum of the Plains Indian
P.O. Box 400
Browning, MT 59417

Myrin Institute
136 East 64th St.
New York, NY 10021 (212) 758-6475

N

NCJW, Inc.
53 W. 23rd St.
New York, NY 10010 (212) 532-1740

National Academy Press
Publications Sales Office
2101 Constitution Ave., NW
Washington, D.C. 20418 (800) 624-6242

National Archives & Records Administration
Publications Division
Seventh St. & Pennsylvania Ave., N.W., Rm. G9
Washington, D.C. 20408 (202) 523-5611

National Book Co.
Div. of Educational Research Center
P.O. Box 8795
Portland, OR 97207-8795 (503) 228-6345

National Center for State Courts
300 Newport Ave.
Williamsburg, VA 23187-8798 (804) 253-2000

National Clearinghouse for Bilingual Education
8737 Colesville Rd., Suite 900
Silver Spring, MD 20910-3921 (800) 647-0123

National Conference of State Legislatures
Book Order Dept.
1560 Broadway, Suite 700
Denver, CO 80202
(303) 830-2054 Fax 863-8003

National Congress of American Indians
900 Pennsylvania Ave., S.E.
Washington, D.C. 20003 (202) 546-9404

NCSS Publications
National Council for the Social Studies
3501 Newark St., NW, Box P
Washington, DC 20016 (202) 966-7840

National Council of Teachers of English
1111 Kenyon Rd.
Urbana, IL 61801 (217) 328-3870

National Geographic Society
P.O. Box 1640
Washington, D.C. 20013 (800) 638-4077

National Indian law Library
1522 Broadway
Boulder, CO 80302 (303) 447-8760

National Indian Traders Association
3575 S. Fox, Box 1263
Englewood, CO 80150 (303) 692-6579

National Learning Corp.
212 Michael Dr.
Syosset, NY 11791
(800) 645-6337; in NY (516) 921-8888

National Museum of the American Indian
The George Gustav Heye Center
Smithsonian Institution
One Bowling Green
New York, NY 10004 (212) 283-2420

National Museums of Canada
Dist. by The University of Chicago Press

National Native American
AIDS Prevention Center
3515 Grand Ave., Suite 100
Oakland, CA 94610 (510) 444-2051

National Woodlands Publishing Co.
8846 Green Briar Rd.
Lake Ann, MI 49650 (616) 275-6735

Native American Co-Op
2830 S. Thrasher
Tucson, AZ 855713 (602) 622-4900

Native American Images
P.O. Box 746
Austin, TX 78767 (512) 472-3049

Native American Publishing Co.
P.O. Box 6338
Incline Village, NV 89450 (702) 831-7726

Native American Studies Center
University of New Mexico
1812 Las Lomas N.E.
Albuquerque, NM 87131 (505) 277-3917

Native American Task Force
Church Council of Greater Seattle
4759 15th Ave., NE
Seattle, WA 98105

Native Law Centre
University of Saskatchewan
Diefenbaker Centre
Saskatoon, SK, Canada S7N 0W0
(306) 966-6189

Native Word Research & Publishing
P.O. Box 827
Lyons, CO 80540 (303) 772-8249

Natural History Press ; Dist. by Doubleday

Naturegraph Publishers
P.O. Box 1075
Happy Camp, CA 96039 (916) 493-5353

Navajo Community College Press
Tsaile, AZ 86556 (602) 724-3311 ext. 321

Navajo Curriculum Center Press
Dist. by Rough Rock Press
P.O. Box 217
Chinle, AZ 86503 (602) 728-3311

Navajo Gallery
P.O. Box 1756
Taos, NM 87571 (505) 758-3250

Navajo Nation Museum Press
P.O. Box 1904
Window Rock, AZ 86515 (602) 871-6673

Nebraska State Historical Society
1500 R St., P.O. Box 82554
Lincoln, NE 68501 (402) 471-4747

Nelson-Atkins Museum of Art
4525 Oak St.
Kansas City, MO 64111 (816) 561-4000

Nelson-Hall
111 N. Canal St.
Chicago, IL 60606 (312) 930-9446

Thomas Nelson, Publishers
P.O. Box 14100
Nashville, TN 37214
(800) 251-4000; in TN (615) 889-9000

New American Library , NAL-Dutton
Div. of Penguin USA
375 Hudson St.
New York, NY 10014 (212) 366-2000

New College & University Press
292 Washington Ave., Ext., #111B
Albany, NY 12203-5346 (518) 456-2072

New Jersey Historical Society
230 Broadway
Newark, NJ 07104 (201) 483-3939

New Jersey State Museum
205 W. State St.
Trenton, NJ 08625 (609) 292-6300

New Mexico Dept. of Development
Tourist Division, 113 Washington Ave.
Santa Fe, NM 87503

New Rivers Press
Dist. by Bookslinger
2402 University Ave., Suite 507
St. Paul, MN 55114 (800) 397-2613

New Seed Press
P.O. Box 9488
Berkeley, CA 94709

New Society Publishers
4527 Springfield Ave.
Philadelphia, PA 19143

New York Academy of Sciences
Publications Dept., 2 East 63 St.
New York, NY 10021 (212) 838-0230

New York Graphic Society
Dist. by Little, Brown & Co.

New York Labor News
914 Industrial Ave.
Palo Alto, CA 94303 (415) 494-1532

New World Library
58 Paul Dr.
San Rafael, CA 94903 (800) 227-3900
    Fax (415) 472-6131

New York University Press
Dist. by Columbia University Press
(212) 316-7100

New York University
Review of Law & Social Change
110 W. 3rd St.
New York, NY 10012

Newberry Library
60 W. Walton St.
Chicago, IL 60610 (312) 943-9090

Newcastle Publishing
Orders to Borgo Press (818) 873-3191

News & Letters Committees
59 E. Van Buren St., Suite 707
Chicago, IL 60605 (312) 663-0839

Nez Perce National Historical Park
P.O. Box 93
Spalding, ID 83551 (208) 843-2261

North American Press
Div. of Fulcrum Publishing

North Atlantic Books
2800 Woolsey St.
Berkeley, CA 94705 (415) 652-5309

North Carolina Division
of Archives & History
109 E. Jones St.
Raleigh, NC 27611 (919) 733-7442

North Carolina State
Museum of Natural Sciences
P.O. Box 27647
Raleigh, NC 27611 (919) 733-7450

North Point Press
Dist. by Farrar, Straus & Grioux

North Star Press
P.O. Box 451
St. Cloud, MN 56301 (612) 253-1636

Northeastern State University
Div. of Arts & Letters, Phoenix SH 218,
Tahlequah, OK 74464 (918) 456-5511

Northern Arizona University
Dept. of Anthropology, Bookstore
P.O. Box 6044
Flagstaff, AZ 86011 (602) 523-4041

Northern Illinois University Press
DeKalb, IL 60115 (815) 753-1826

Northern Michigan University Press
Bookstore, Don H. Bottum University Center ,
Marquette, MI 49855 (906) 227-2480

Northern Plains Indian
Crafts Association
Box "E"
Browning, MT 59417

Northland Publishing Co.
P.O. Box 1389
Flagstaff, AZ 86002 (800) 346-3257
(602) 774-5251 Fax 774-0592

NWREL
Northwest Regional Educational Laboratory
101 S.W. Main St., Suite 500
Portland, OR 97204
(503) 275-9500 Fax 275-9489

Northwestern Publishing House
1250 N. 113th St.
Milwaukee, WI 53226 (414) 475-6600

W.W. Norton & Co., Inc.
500 Fifth Ave.
New York, NY 10110
(800) 233-4830 Fax (800) 458-6515

Nova Scotia Museum Publications
P.O. Box 637
Halifax, Nova Scotia B3S 2T3 Canada

Noyes Data Corp.
Mill Rd. at Grand Ave.
Park Ridge, NJ 07656 (201) 391-8484

O

Oceana Publications
75 Main St.
Dobbs Ferry, NY 10522 (914) 693-1733

Ohio Historical Society
1982 Velma Ave.
Columbus, OH 4321 1 (614) 297-2300

Ohio University Press
Orders to C.U.P. Services
P.O. Box 6525
Ithaca, NY 14851 (614) 593-1 155

Oklahoma Indian Arts & Crafts Cooperative
Box 966
Anadarko, OK 73005

Old West Publishing
1228 E. Colfax Ave.
Denver, CO 80218 (303) 832-7190

Omnigraphics, Inc.
2400 Penobscot Bldg.
Detroit, MI 48226 (800) 234-1340

Open Book Publishers
1400 N. State St., Suite C
Bellingham, WA 98225 (206) 676-4613

Orchard Books - Sales Dept.
95 Madison Ave.
New York, NY 10016
(800) 621-1115 Fax (800) 374-4329

Schools & Public Libraries send orders to
Franklin Watts

Oregon Historical Society Press
1230 S.W. Park Ave.
Portland, OR, 97205 (503) 222-1741

Oregon State University Press
101 Waldo Hall, OSU
Corvallis, OR 97331 (503) 754-3166

Origins Press
4632 Vincent Ave. S.
Minneapolis, MN 55410 (612) 922-8175

Orion Books
Div. of Random House

Orion Publishing Co.
539 Queen Anne Ave. N. #156
Seattle, WA 98109 (206) 633-5742

O'Sullivan, Woodside & Co.
Distributed by Caroline House Publishers
236 Forest Park Place
Ottawa, IL 61350 (815) 434-7905

**The Osage Mission-Neosho
County Historical Society**
P.O. Box 113
St. Paul, KS 66771

Outbooks
Dist. by Vista Books
P.O. Box 1766
Morristown, NJ 07962 (908) 604-9702

Outlet Book Co.
Dist. by Random House,

Oxford University Press
2001 Evans Rd.
Carey, NC 27513 (800) 451-7556

Oyate
2702 Matthews St.
Berkeley, CA 94702 (510) 848-6700

P

Pacific Books
P.O. Box 558
Palo Alto, CA 94302 (415) 965-1980

**Pacific Northwest
National Parks & Forests Assn.**
909 1st Ave., Suite 630
Seattle, WA 98104 (206) 553-7958

Panjandrum Books
Distributed by Bookpeople

Panorama West Books-Pioneer Publishing
P.O. Box 4638
Fresno, CA 93728 (209) 226-1200

Pantheon Books
400 Hahn Rd.
Westminster, MD 21157 (800) 638-6460

**Parabola Magazine
Society for the Study of Myth & Tradition**
Dist. by Kampmann & Co. & Bookpeople

Paragon House Publishers
370 Lexington Ave.
New York, NY 10017 (800) 727-2466

Parents Magazine Press
Distributed by Crown Publishers

Parks-Thompson Co.
1757 W. Adams
Kirkwood, MO 63122 (314) 822-2409

Parnassus Imprints
P.O. Box 335
Orleans, MA 02653 (508) 255-2932

Pathfinder Press
410 West St.
New York, NY 10014
(212) 741-0690 Fax 727-0150

Pathfinder Publications
4704 Wilford Way
Minneapolis, MN 55435 (612) 835-1 128

Paulist Press
997 MacArthur Blvd.
Mahwah, NJ 07430
(201) 825-7300 Fax 825-8345

**Peabody Museum of
Archaeology & Ethnology**
Distributed by Harvard University Press

Peek Publications
P.O. Box 50123
Palo Alto, CA 94303 (415) 962-1010

Pelican Publishing
P.O. Box 3110
Gretna, Louisiana 70053 (800) 843-1724
Fax (504) 368-1 195

Pendle Hill Publications
338 Plush Mill Rd.
Wallingford, PA 19086 (215) 566-4514

Pendulum Press
Academic Bldg., Saw Mill Rd.
West Haven, CT 06516 (203) 933-2551

Penguin USA
375 Hudson St.
New York, NY 10014 (800) 253-6476

Pennsylvania Academy of the Fine Arts
Broad & Cherry St.
Philadelphia, PA 19102 (215) 972-7600

**Pennsylvania Historical
& Museum Commission**
Publications Sales Program, Dept. BRS
P.O. Box 11466
Harrisburg, PA 17108 (717) 783-2618

Pennsylvania State University Press
215 Wagner Bldg.
University Park, PA 16802 (814) 865-1327

Gregory Perino
1509 Cleveland
Idabel, OK 74745

Persea Books
60 Madison Ave.
New York, NY 10010 (212) 779-7668

Persimmon Press
118 Tillinghast Pl.
Buffalo, NY 14216 (716) 838-3633

Philbrook Museum of Art
2727 S. Rockford Rd., Box 52510
Tulsa, OK 74152 (918) 749-7941

Philomel Books; Div. of Putnam Publishing

Pineapple Press
P.O. Drawer 16008, Southside Sta.
Sarasota, FL 34239 (813) 952-1085

Pocahontas Press
P.O. Drawer F
Blacksburg, VA 24063
(800) 446-0467; (703) 951-0467

Pocket Books
Div. of Simon & Schuster
Distributed by Prentice Hall Press

Pogo Press
4 Cardinal Lane
St. Paul, MN 55127 (612) 483-4692

Porcupine Press
310 S. Juniper St.
Philadelphia, PA 19107 (215) 735-0101

Roundtable Publishing
P.O. Box 6488
Malibu, CA 90264 (310) 457-8433

Rourke Corp.
P.O. Box 3328
Vero Beach, FL 32964 (407) 465-4575

Routledge
29 W. 35th St.
New York, NY 10001 (800) 634-7064
   Fax (800) 248-4724

Rowman & Littlefield
4720 Boston Way
Lanham, MD 20706 (301) 306-0400

Roza Run Publishing Co.
Rt. 4, Box 4685
Prosser, WA 99350 (509) 973-2444

Running Press Book Publishers
125 S. 22nd St.
Philadelphia, PA 19103
(800) 428-1 111; in PA (215) 567-5080

Russell & Russell, Publishers
Orders to Charles Scribner's Sons

Rutgers University Press
109 Church St.
New Brunswick, NJ 08901 (800) 446-9323
(908) 932-7764 Fax 932-7039

S

SSS Publishing
17515 S.W. Blue Heron Rd.
Lake Oswego, OR 97034 (503) 636-2979

Safari Press
The Woodbine Publishing Co.
15621 Chemical Lane, Bldg. B
Huntington Beach, CA 92649
(714) 894-9080 Fax 894-4949

Sage Publications
2111 W. Hillcrest Dr.
Newbury Park, CA 91320 (805) 499-0721

Albert Saifer Publisher
P.O. Box 7125
Watchung, NJ 07060

St. Martin's Press
175 Fifth Ave.
New York, NY 10010
(800) 221-7945; in NY (212) 674-5151

St. Michaels Historical Museum
St. Michaels Mission, Drawer D
St. Michaels, AZ 86511 (602) 871-4172

St. Scholastica Priory
Duluth, MN 5581 1 (218) 728-1817

Salem House Publishers (800) 242-7737
Orders to Harper & Row

SamHar Press
Bindery Lane
Charlottesville, NY 12036 (800) 847-2105

San Bernardino County Museum Association
2024 Orange Tree Lane
Redlands, CA 92373 (714) 792-1334

San Juan District Media Center
Curriculum Division
28 W. 200 North, Box 804
Blanding, UT 84511 (801) 678-2281

San Marcos Press
410 Bryn Mawr, SE
Albuquerque, NM 87108 (505)266-4412

Sand River Press
1319 14th St.
Los Osos, CA 93402 (805) 543-3591

Santa Barbara Museum of Natural History
2559 Puesta del Sol Rd.
Santa Barbara, CA 93105

Scarborough House
P.O. Box 370
Chelsea, MI 481 18 (313) 475-9145

Scarecrow Press
P.O. Box 4167
Metuchen, NJ 08840 (800) 537-7107
(908) 548-8600 Fax 548-5767

Schenkman Books
Box 119, 118 Main St.
Rochester, VT 05767 (802) 767-3702

Schiffer Publishing
77 Lower Valley Rd.
Atglen, PA 19310 (610) 593-1777
   Fax (610) 593-2002

R. Schneider Publishers
312 Linwood Ave., Park Ridge
Stevens Point, WI 54481 (715) 345-7899
   Fax (715) 345-7898

Schocken Books
Div. of Random House

Scholarly Press
P.O. Box 160
St. Clair Shores, MI 48080 (313) 884-0400

Scholarly Resources
104 Greenhill Ave.
Wilmington, DE 19805
(800) 772-8937; in DE (302) 654-7713

Scholars Press
P.O. Box 6525
Ithaca, NY 14851 (800) 666-221 1

Scholastic, Inc.
P.O. Box 7502
Jefferson City, MO 65102 (800) 325-6149

School of American Research Press
P.O. Box 2188
Santa Fe, NM 87504 (505) 984-0741
Dist. by University of Washington Press

School of Public Health
Master of Public Health Program
U.of California, Warren Hall, Rm. 140
Berkeley, CA 94720 (510) 642-3228

Science Research Associates
155 N. Wacker Dr.
Chicago, IL 60606 (800) 621-0476

Scott, Foresman & Co.
1900 E. Lake Ave.
Glenview, IL 60025 (312) 729-3000

Charles Scribner's Sons
Macmillan Distribution Center
Front & Brown Sts.
Riverside, NJ 08075
(800) 257-5755 Fax (800) 562-1272

The Scriptorium Press
71 S. Main St.
Alfred, NY 14802 (607) 587-9371

Seminole Nation Museum
P.O. Box 1532
Wewoka, OK 74884

Seven Oaks Press
405 S. Seventh St.
St. Charles, IL 60174 (312) 377-1098

Seventh Generation Fund
P.O. Box 10
Forestville, CA 95436 (707) 887-1559

P. Shalom Publications
5409 18th Ave.
Brooklyn, NY 11204 (718) 256-1954

Shambhala Publications
Dist. by Random House

Sheffield Publishing
P.O. Box 359
Salem, WI 53168 (414) 843-2281

The Shoe String Press
995 Sherman Ave.
   Hamden, CT 06514 (203) 248-6307

Sierra Club Books
Dist. by Random House

Sierra Oaks Publishing
1370 Sierra Oaks Ct.
Newcastle, CA 95658 (916) 663-1474

Signature Books
350 S. 400 E., Suite G4
Salt Lake City, UT 84111 (801) 531-1483

Silver Burdett Press
P.O. Box 1226
Westwood, NJ 07675
(800) 631-8081; (800) 624-4843

Simon & Schuster
200 Old Tappan Rd.
Old Tappan, NJ 07675
(800) 223-2336 Fax (800) 445-6991

Sister Vision Press
P.O Box 217, Station E
Toronto, ON M6H 4E2
Canada (416) 533-2184

Sitka National Historical Park
P.O. Box 738
Sitka, AK 99835 (907) 747-6281

Peter Smith Publisher
6 Lexington Ave.
Magnolia, MA 01930
(508) 525-3562 Fax 525-3674

Smithsonian Books/Recordings/Videos
P.O. Box 2071
Colchester, VT 05449 (800) 669-1559

Smithsonian Institution Press
P.O. Box 500
Williston, VT 05495 (800) 669-1559

Snowbird Publishing Co.
P.O. Box 729
Tellico Plains, TN 37385
(615) 982-7261 Fax 681-3418

Social Sciences & Sociological Resources
P.O. Box 241
Aurora, IL 60507

Society of American Archivists
600 S. Federal, Suite 504
Chicago, IL 60605 (312) 922-0140

The Sourcebook Project
P.O. Box 107
Glen Arm, MD 21057 (301) 668-6047

South End Press
P.O. Box 741
Monroe, ME 04951 (800) 533-8478

South Platte Press
P.O. Box 163
David City, NE 68632 (402) 367-4734

Southern Illinois University Press
P.O. Box 3697
Carbondale, IL 62902 (618) 453-2281

Southern Methodist University Press
P.O. Box 415
Dallas, TX 75275 (214) 692-2263

Southern University Press
130 S. 19th St.
Birmingham, AL 35233 (205) 251-5113

Southwest Communication Resources
P.O. Box 788
Bernalillo, NM 87004 (505) 867-3396

Southwest Museum
P.O. Box 41558
Los Angeles, CA 90041 (213) 221-2164

Southwest Parks & Monuments Assn.
P.O. Box 2173
Globe, AZ 85502 (602) 425-8184

Southwestern Art Association
P.O. Box 52510
Tulsa, OK 74152

Southwestern Cooperative Educational Lab
229 Truman N.E.
Albuquerque, NM 87108

Specialty Books International
P.O. Box 1785,
Ann Arbor, MI 48106 (517) 456-4764

Spencer Museum of Art
University of Kansas
Lawrence, KS 66045 (913) 864-4710

Spirit Mountain Press
Dist. by University of Alaska Press

Spirit Talk Press
Drawer V
Browning, MT 59417 (406) 338-2882

Spizzirri Publishing
P.O. Box 9397
Rapid City, SD 57709 (800) 325-9819

Springer Publishing
536 Broadway
New York, NY 10012 (212) 431-4370

Stackpole Books
P.O. Box 1831
Harrisburg, PA 17105
(800) 732-3669; in PA (717) 234-5041

Stanford University Press
Stanford, CA 94305-2235 (415) 723-9434

Starwood Publishing
Dist. by Fulcrum Publishing

State Historical Society of Wisconsin
816 State St.
Madison, WI 53706 (608) 262-1368

State House Press
P.O. Drawer 15247
Austin, TX 78761 (512) 454-1959

State Mutual Book & Periodical Service
521 Fifth Ave., 17th Floor
New York, NY 10017 (212) 682-5844

State University of New York at Geneseo
Dept. of Anthropology
Geneseo, NY 14454 (716) 245-5277

Statesman-Examiner, Inc.
220 S. Main, Box 271
Colville, WA 99114 (509) 684-4567

Roberta Ingles Steele
P.O. Box 3485 FSS
Radford, VA 24143 (703) 639-6383

Stemmer House Publishers
2627 Caves Rd.
Owing Mills, MD 21117 (800) 645-6958
(410) 363-3690 Fax 363-8459

Sterling Publishing
387 Park Ave. South
New York, NY 10016 (800) 367-9692

Stonehenge Books
12375 E. Cornell Ave., Unit No. 7
Aurora, CO 80014 (303) 695-4710

Storypole Press
11015 Bingham Ave., E.
Tacoma, WA 98446 (206) 531-2032
Fax (206) 535-3889

Strang Communications Co.
516 Douglas Ave., Suite 1102
Altamonte Springs, FL 32714
(407) 862-7565

Strawberry Press
Box 451, Bowling Green Station
New York, NY 10004

Street Press
P.O. Box 772
Sound Beach, NY 11789 (516) 928-4958

Studia Slovenica
P.O. Box 4531
Washington, DC 20017 (212) 927-4246

Stump Publishing Co.
121 N. Sultana Ave.
Ontario, CA 91764 (714) 984-6694

Summer Institute of Linguistics
Academic Publications
7500 W. Camp Wisdom Rd.,
Dallas, TX 75236 (214) 709-2403

Sun Dance Books
Distributed by Borgo Press

Sun Tracks
Dept. of English
University of Arizona
Tucson, AZ 85721

Sundance Educational Publishers
P.O. Box 184
Inchelium, WA 99138

Sunflower University Press
1531 Yuma, Box 1009
Manhattan, KS 66502 (800) 258-1232

Sunnycrest Publishing
Rt. 1, Box 1
Clements, MN 56224 (507) 692-2246

Sunstone Press
P.O. Box 2321
Santa Fe, NM 87504 (800) 243-5644

Mark Supnick
8524 NW Second St.
Coral Springs, FL 33071 (305) 755-3448

SVE-Society for Visual Education
55 E. Monroe St., 34th Floor
Chicago, IL 60603 (800) 829-1900

Sweetlight Books
16625 Heitman Rd.
Cottonwood, CA 96022 (916) 529-5392

Syracuse University Press
1600 Jamesville
Syracuse, NY 13244
(800) 365-8929 Fax (315) 443-5545

T

Tacoma Art Museum
1123 Pacific Ave.
Tacoma, WA 98402-4399 (206) 272-4258

**Tales of the Mojave
Road Publishing**
P.O. Box 307
Norco, CA 91760 (714) 737-3150

Tamal Land Press
39 Merwin Ave.
Fairfax, CA 94930 (415) 456-4705

Taylor Museum, The Library
Colorado Springs Fine Arts Center
30 W. Dale St.
Colorado Springs, CO 80903 (303) 634-5581

TCI, Inc.
3410 Garfield St., N.W.
Washington, D.C. 20007 (202) 333-6350

Teaching Drum Outdoor School
7124 Military Rd.
Three Lakes, WI 54562 (715) 546-2944

Te-Cum-Tom Enterprises
5770 Fransom Ct.
North Bend, OR 97459 (503) 756–5757

Tejas Art Press
207 Terrell Rd.
San Antonio, TX 78209 (512) 826-7803

Temple University Press
1601 N. Broad St., USB-Room 305
Philadelphia, PA 19122 (800) 447-1656
Fax (215) 204-4719

Ten Speed Press
P.O. Box 7123
Berkeley, CA 94707 (800) 841-2665

Terrich Books
P.O. Box 59
Guilford, NY 13780 (800) 352-3670

Territorial Publishers
P.O. Box 35250
Tucson, AZ 85740 (602) 297-1102

Texas A & M University Press
P.O. Drawer C
College Station, TX 77843 (409) 845-1436

Texas Christian University Press
Dist. by Texas A&M University Press

Texas Monthly Press
P.O. Box 1569
Austin, TX 78767
(800) 288-3288; in TX (512) 476-7085

Texas State Historical Association
Dist. by Texas A&M University Press

Texas Tech University Press
Lubbock, TX 79409-1037
(800) 832-4042; in TX (806) 742-2468

Texas Western Press
University of Texas
El Paso, TX 79968 (800) 488-3789

Texian Press
P.O. Box 1684,
Waco, TX 76703 (817) 754-5636

Thames & Hudson
Dist. by W.W. Norton & Co.

Thayer & Associates
Dist. Hoard Historical Museum
407 Merchants Ave.
Fort Atkinson, WI 53538 (414) 563-4521

Theosophical Publishing House
306 W. Geneva Rd.
Wheaton, IL 60189-0270
(800) 654-0430; in IL (312) 665-0123

Theytus Books Ltd.
P.O. Box 20040
Penticton, B.C. Canada V2A 8K3
(604) 493-7181 Fax 493-5302

Think Shop, Inc.
P.O. Box 3754
Albuquerque, NM 87190-3754 (505) 831-5029

Charles C. Thomas, Publisher
2600 S. First St.
Springfield, IL 62794-9265 (217) 789-8980

Thompson Press
P.O. Box 263
Conway, NH 03818 (603) 447-5569

Thunder Mesa Publishing
208 Sherwood Blvd.
Los Alamos, NM 87544 (505) 672-3108

Thunder's Mouth Press
93-99 Greene St. #2A
New York, NY 10012

Thunderbird Enterprises
George Russell, 8821 N. First St.
Phoenix, AZ 85020 (800) 835-7220

Tilbury House Publishers
132 Water St.
Gardiner, ME 04345 (207) 582-1899
Dist. to the trade by: Consortium Book Sales

Timber Press
133 S.W. Second Ave., Suite 450
Portland, OR 97204 (800) 327-5680
(503) 227-2878 Fax 227-3070

Timberline Books
25890 Weld Rd. 53
Kersey, CO 80644-8802 (303) 353-3785

Time-Life Books
1450 E. Parham Rd.
Richmond, VA 23280 (800) 621-7026

Celia Totus Enterprises
P.O. Box 192
Toppenish, WA 98948 (509) 865-2480

Trans-Anglo Books
P.O. Box 38
Corona Del Mar, CA 92625 (714) 645-7393

Transaction Publishers
Rutgers - The State University
New Brunswick, NJ 08903 (201) 932-2280

Treasure Chest Publications
P.O. Box 5250
Tucson, AZ 85703 (800) 627-0048

Trees Co. Press
49 Van Buren Way
San Francisco, CA 94131 (415) 334-8352

Tremaine Graphic & Publishing
2727 Front St.
Klamath Falls, OR 97601 (503) 884-4193

Tribal Press
c/o Lowell Jensen
Route 2, Box 599
Cable, WI, 54821 (715) 794-2247

Troll Associates
100 Corporate Dr.
Mahwah, NJ 07430
(800) 526-5289; (201) 529-4000

Troubador Press, Inc.
99 Evans Rd.
Brookline, MA 02146 (617) 734-1416

Trust for Native American Cultures & Crafts
P.O. Box 142
Greenville, NH 03048 (603) 878-2944

Tundra Books
Dist. by University of Toronto Press

Turner Publishing Co.
P.O. Box 3101
Paducah, KY 420012 (502) 443-0121

Charles E. Tuttle Co.
P.O. Box 410
Rutland, VT 05701 (802) 773-8930

Twin Palms Publisher
401 Paseo de Peralta
Santa Fe, NM 87501

Patrick J. Twohy
E. 28 Sharp Ave.
Spokane, WA 99202 (509) 326-2133

Tyndale House Publishers
P.O. Box 80
Wheaton, IL 60189 (708) 668-8300

U

Unger Publishing Co.
Orders to Harper & Row

UNIPUB
Div. of Kraus Organization

U.S. Catholic Conference
Publications Office
1312 Massachusetts Ave., N.W.,
Washington, D.C. 20005
(800) 235-8722; (202) 659-6640

U.S. Government Printing Office
Superintendent of Documents
Washington, DC 20402 (202) 783-3238

Universe Books
Dist. by St. Martin's Press

Universitetsforlaget
Dist. by Columbia University Press

University Books, Ltd.
P.O. Box 1201
Fayetteville, AR 72702

University Microfilms International
P.O. Box 1307
Ann Arbor, MI 48106
(800) 521-0600; in Canada (800) 343-5299

University of Alabama Press
P.O. Box 870380
Tuscaloosa, AL 35487 (800) 825-9980
Fax (205) 348-9201

University of Alaska Institute
of Social & Economic Research
3211 Providence Dr.
Anchorage, AK 99508 (907) 786-7710

University of Alaska Press
P.O. Box 756240
Fairbanks, AK 99775 (907) 474-6389
  Fax (907) 474-5502

University of Alaska-Rasmuson Library
Dist. by University of Alaska Press

University of Alberta Press
P.O. Box 4814
Burlingame, CA 94011 (403) 492-3663

University of Arizona Press
1230 N. Park, No. 102
Tucson, AZ 85719 (602) 621-1441

University of California, Los Angeles
American Indian Studies Center
3220 Campbell Hall
Los Angeles, CA 90024 (213) 825-7315

University of California, Los Angeles
Institute of Archaeology
405 Hilgard Ave.
Los Angeles, CA 90024 (213) 825-7411

University of California Press
2120 Berkeley Way
Berkeley, CA 94720 (800) 822-6657

University of Chicago
Dept. of Geography, Research Paper
5828 S. University Ave.
Chicago, IL 60637 (312) 962-8314

University of Chicago Press
11030 S. Langley Ave.
Chicago, IL 60628
(800) 621-2736; (312) 568-1550

University of Connecticut Education
The Thut World Education Center
School of Education
Storrs, CT 06268 (203) 486-3321

University of Georgia Press
330 Research Dr.
Athens, GA 30602
(706) 369-6130 Fax 369-6131

The University of Hawaii Press
2840 Kolowalu St.
Honolulu, HI 96822 (808) 948-8255

University of Idaho Press
Moscow, ID 83843 (208) 885-6245

University of Illinois Archaeology
109 Davenport Hall
607 S. Mathews Ave.
Urbana, IL 61801

University of Illinois Press
Orders to CUP Services
P.O. Box 6525
Ithaca, NY 14851 (607) 277-2211

University of Iowa Press
Publications Dept., Oak Dale Hall
Iowa City, IA 52242 (319) 335-4645

University of Kansas
Museum of Natural History
Dist. by University Press of Kansas

University of Massachusetts Press
P.O. Box 429
Amherst, MA 01004 (413) 545-2219
  Fax (413) 545-1226

University of Michigan
Museum of Anthropology
Publications Dept.
4009 Museum Bldg., 1109 Geddes
Ann Arbor, MI 48109 (313) 764-6867

University of Michigan Press
Distributing Center, 839 Greene St.
Ann Arbor, MI 48106 (313) 764-4392

University of Minnesota
Bell Museum of Pathology
P.O. Box 302, UMHC
Minneapolis, MN 55455 (612) 624-8692

University of Minnesota
Dept. of Anthropology
215 Ford Hall, 224 Church St., SE
Minneapolis, MN 55455 (612) 373-4614

University of Minnesota Press
2037 University Ave., S.E.
Minneapolis, MN 55455 (800) 388-3863
  Fax (612) 626-7313

University of Missouri
Museum of Anthropology
104 Swallow Hall
Columbia, MO 65211 (314) 882-3764

University of Missouri Press
Orders to CUP Services
P.O. Box 6525
Ithaca, NY 14851 (607) 277-2211

University of Nebraska, Omaha
Center for Applied Urban Research
1313 Farnam on the Mall
Peter Kiewit Conference Center
Omaha, NE 68182 (402) 554-8311

University of Nebraska Press
901 N. 17th St.
Lincoln, NE 68588 (800) 755-1105

University of Nevada Press
Reno, NV 89557 (702) 784-6573

University of New Mexico
Institute for Native American Development
1812 Las Lomas, NE,
Albuquerque, NM (505) 277-3917

University of New Mexico Press
Journalism Bldg., Suite 220
Albuquerque, NM 87131 (505) 277-2346

University of North Carolina Press
P.O. Box 2288
Chapel Hill, NC 27514 (919) 966-3561

University of Oklahoma Press
P.O. Box 787
Norman, OK 73070
(800) 627-7377 Fax (800) 735-0476

University of Oregon Books
P.O. Box 3237
Eugene, OR 97403 (503) 686-3165

University of Pennsylvania
University Museum
33rd & Spruce Sts.
Philadelphia, PA 19174
(215) 243-4119

University of Pittsburgh
127 N. Bellefield Ave.
Pittsburgh, PA 15260

University of Pittsburgh Press
Orders to CUP Services
P.O. Box 6525
Ithaca, NY 14851 (607) 277-2211

University of South Carolina Press
1716 College St.
Columbia, SC 29208 (803) 777-5243

University of South Dakota
Government Research Bureau
233 Dakota Hall
Vermillion, SD 57069 (605) 677-5702

University of South Dakota Press
301 East Hall, 414 E. Clark St.
Vermillion, SD 57069 (605) 677-5401

University of Tennessee Press
Orders to CUP Services
P.O. Box 6525
Ithaca, NY 14851 (607) 277-2211

University of Texas
Harry Ransom Humanities
Research Center
P.O. Box 7219
Austin, TX 78713 (512) 471-9113

University of Texas
Institute of Texan Cultures
P.O. Box 1226
San Antonio, TX 78294 (512) 226-7651

University of Texas Press
P.O. Box 7819
Austin, TX 78713 (800) 252-3206
  Fax (512) 320-0668

University of Toronto Press
340 Nagel Dr.
Buffalo, NY 14225 (716) 683-4547

University of Utah Press
101 University Services Bldg.
Salt Lake City, UT 84112
(800) 442-8638 ext.6771

University of Washington Press
P.O. Box 50096
Seattle, WA 98145
(800) 441-4115; in Seattle area (206) 543-8870

University of Wisconsin Library School
Publications Committee
600 N. Park St.
Madison, WI 53706

University of Wisconsin Press
114 N. Murray St.
Madison, WI 53715 (608) 262-8782

University Press of America
4720-A Boston Way
Lanham, MD 20706 (800) 462-6420

University Press of Florida
15 NW 15th St.
Gainesville, FL 32611 (800) 226-3822

University Press of Kansas
329 Carruth
Lawrence, KS 66045 (913) 864-4154

University Press of Kentucky
Orders to CUP Services
P.O. Box 6525
Ithaca, NY 14851 (607) 277-221 1

University Press of Mississippi
3825 Ridgewood Rd.
Jackson, MS 39211 (800) 737-7788
(601) 982-6217 - Fax

University Press of New England
17 1/2 Lebanon St.
Hanover, NH 03755 (800) 421-1561

University Press of Virginia
Box 3608, University Station
Charlottesville, VA 22903 (804) 924-3468

University Publications of America
Dist. by Greenwood Press

Unwin Hyman, Inc.
Orders to HarperCollins

Upton & Sons
917 Hillcrest St.
El Segundo, CA 90245 (213) 322-7202

Mae Urbanek
Lusk, WY 82225 (307) 334-2473

Utah State Historical Society
300 Rio Grande
Salt Lake City, UT 84101 (801) 533-6024

Utah State University Press
Logan, UT 84322 (801) 750-1362

V

Valkyrie Publishing House
8245 26th Ave. N.
St. Petersburg, FL 33710 (813) 345- 8864

Alfred Van Der Marck Edition
Orders to Harper & Row

Van Nostrand Reinhold
7625 Empire Dr.
Florence, KY 41022 (606) 525-6600

Vance Bibliographies
P.O. Box 229
Monticello, IL 61856 (217) 762-3831

Vanguard Press, Inc.
201 E. 50th St., 2nd Floor
New York, NY 10022

Vantage Press
516 West 34 St.
New York, NY 10001 (800) 882-3273

Viking Penguin
Div. of Penguin USA

Visible Ink Press
P.O. Box 33477
Detroit, MI 48232 (800) 776-6265

W

Wadsworth Publishing Co.
Distribution Center , 7625 Empire Dr .
Florence, KY 41042 (800) 354-9706

George Wahr Publishing Co.
304 1/2 S. State St.
Ann Arbor, MI 48104 (313) 668-6097

Walker & Co.
720 Fifth Ave.
New York, NY 10019 (800) 289-2553

Wallace-Homestead Book Co.
P.O. Box 2165
Radnor, PA 19089-9931 (800) 638-3822

Wanderer Books
Orders to Simon & Schuster

Warner Books, Inc.
Dist. by Little, Brown & Co

Washington Square Press
Div. of Simon & Schuster

Washington State Historical Society
315 N. Stadium Way
Tacoma, WA 98403 (206) 593-2830

Washington State University Press
Cooper Publications Bldg.
Pullman, WA 99164 (800) 354-7360
(509) 335-3518 Fax 335-8568

Franklin Watts, Inc.
387 Park Ave. S.
New York, NY 10016 (800) 433-341 1

Waveland Press
P.O. Box 400
Prospect Heights, IL 60070
(708) 634-0081 Fax 634-9501

Wayfinder Press
P.O. Box 217
Ridgway, CO 81432 (303) 626-5452

Wayne State University Press
Leonard N. Simons Bldg.
5959 Woodward Ave.
Detroit, MI 48202 (313) 577-6121

Webb Research Group
P.O. Box 314
Medford, OR 97501
(800) 866-9721; (503) 664-5205

Wells Publishing
9191 Towne Centre Dr. #550
Sann Diego, CA 92122

Werner Publications
2020 18th Ave.
Greeley, CO 80631 (303) 352-8566

Wesleyan University Press
Orders to University Press of New England

West Texas Museum Association
P.O. Box 4499
Lubbock, TX 79409 (806) 742-2443

Western America Institute for Exploration
1821 E. 9th St.
The Dalles, OR 97058 (503) 296-9414

Western Publishers
1711 S. Lakeside Dr.
Lake Worth, FL 33460 (407) 588-6848

Western Publishing
Dept. M, P.O. Box 700
Racine, WI 53401 (800) 235-3089

Westernlore Publications
P.O. Box 35305
Tucson, AZ 85740 (602) 297-5491

**The Wheelwright Museum
of the American Indian**
P.O. Box 5153
Santa Fe, NM 87502 (505) 982-4636

Wichita Tribal Office
P.O. Box 729
Anadarko, OK 73005
(405) 247-2425 Fax 247-2005

Wilderness Adventure Books
P.O. Box 217
Davisburg, MI 48350 (800) 852-8652

John Wiley & Sons
1 Wiley Dr.
Somerset, NJ 08873 ((201) 469-4400

Charles Alma Wilson
P.O. Box 278
Story, WY 82842 (307) 683-2188

H.W. Wilson Co.
950 University Ave.
Bronx, NY 10452
(800) 367-6770; in NY (800) 462-6060

Winston-Derek Publishers
P.O. Box 90883
Nashville, TN 37209 (800) 826-1888

David Michael Wolfe
4167 Timberlane Dr.
Allison park, PA 15101 (412) 487-7093

Wonder-Treasure Books
360 N. La Cienega Blvd.
Los Angeles, CA 90048
(800) 421-0892; in CA (800) 227-8801

Workbooks Press
P.O. Box 8504
Atlanta, GA 30306 (404) 874-1044

Workman Publishing Co.
708 Broadway
New York, NY 10003 (800) 722-7202
in NY (212) 254-5900

Workshop Publications
P.O. Box 120
Acme, MI 49610 (616) 946-3712

World Around Songs
20 Colbert's Creek Rd.
Burnsville, NC 28714
(704) 675-5343

World Book, Inc.
525 W. Monore St.
Chicago, IL 60661 (312) 258-3700

World Music Press
P.O. Box 2565
Danbury, CT 06813 (203) 748-1 131

World Vision International
919 W. Huntington Dr.
Monrovia, CA 91016 (818) 303-881 1

World Wisdom Books
P.O. Box 2682
Bloomington, IN 47402 (812) 332-1663

Y

Yale University Press
P.O. Box 209040
New Haven, CT 06520 (203) 432-0960
  Fax (203) 432-0948

**Yale University Publications
in Anthropology**
208277 Yale Station
New Haven, CT 06520 (203) 432-3670

Yankton Sioux Tribe Elderly Board
Dist. by Dakota West Books
P.O. Box 9324
Rapid City, SD 57701 (605) 348-1075

Ye Galleon Press
P.O. Box 287
Fairfield, WA 99012 (509) 283-2422

Yellow Jacket Press
901 Alspaugh Lane
Grand Prairie, TX 75052

Yerrington Paiute Tribe Publications
171 Campbell Lane
Yerington, NV 89447

Yosemite Association
P.O. Box 230
El Portal, CA 95318 (209) 379-2646
  Fax (209) 379-2486

Young Discovery Library
P.O. Box 229
Ossining, NY 10562 (800) 343-7854

Z

Zenger Publishing
P.O. Box 42026
Washington, D.C. 20015
(301) 881-1470

Zia Cine, Inc.
P.O. Box 493
Santa Fe, NM 87501

Zion Natural History Association
Zion National Park
Springdale, UT 84767 (801) 772-3256

BIOGRAPHIES

This section is an alphabetically arranged listing of Native Americans prominent in Indian affairs, business, the arts and professions, as well as non-Indians active in Indian affairs, history, art, anthropology, archaeology, and the many fields to which the subject of the American Indian is related. Included are the biographical sketches of individuals named in the book - authors from the Bibliography, tribal chiefs and chairpersons listed under Reservations & Tribal Councils, curators listed under Museums, etc. The Alphabetical Index at the end of the section will allow the reader to see, at a glance, all biographies listed in this section.

Format and style: The researcher will note that these biographical sketches concentrate primarily on professional achievement; therefore, the usual personal data--name of spouse, date of marriage, and names of children, etc.--have not been included, The greater bulk of information has been gathered from research questionnaires completed by the individuals themselves; however, in the case of a hastily written or otherwise incomplete questionnaire, I have consulted other reliable published sources. Whenever possible, direct quotations have been employed to give greater insight into the life and work of each biographee than mere facts can supply. The length of each listing reflects the quantity of material received; affiliations, only, are given when questionnaires were not returned. Home and/or business addresses and phone numbers have been included when available. An asterisk (*) before the biography indicates a first-time listee.

A

*AALVIK, RONALD C. (Cowlitz)
(tribal chairperson)
Affiliation: Cowlitz Indian Tribe, P.O. Box 2547, Longview, WA 98632 (206) 577-8140.

ABBOTT, DEVON IRENE
(Choctaw /Cherokee) 1957-
(assistant professor of history)
Born June 2, 1957, Wichita Falls, Tex. *Education*: Texas Christian University, BA, 1981; MEd, 1982; MA, 1986; PhD, 1989. *Principal occupation*: Assistant professor of history. *Affiliations*: Northern Arizona University, Flagstaff, AZ, 1989-91. *Other professional posts*: Secretary, American Indian Center of Fort Worth, 1977-78; Board member, American Indian Center of Dallas, 1984-87; consultant, Texas Historical Commission and the Texas Indian Commission's Committee on the Acquisition and Disposition of Human Remains ad Sacred Objects, 1984-89; Texas Director - American Indians Against Desecration, 1987-88; consultant to Northeastern State University's Archives & Special Collections, 1988-. *Memberships*: Phi Alpha Theta; Southern Association for Women Historians; Oklahoma Historical Society; American Indian Historians' Association; Western History Association; America Society for Ethnohistory. *Awards, honors*: TX Phi Alpha Theta Award for paper, "Health Care at the Cherokee Female Seminary: 1876-1909, 1988; Ford Foundation/National Research Council Doctoral Dissertation Fellowship for Minorities, 1988-89; Phi Alpha Theta/Westerners International Award for Best Dissertation in Western History, 1989; Northern Arizona University Junior Nominee, National Endowment for the Humanities Summer Stipend, 1990. *Interests*: American Indian history; American Indian Women, Education; Desecration of Indian Burial Sites; Athletics. *Biographical sources*: This is T.C.U. (Dec. 1988, pp. 12-14); Mountain Campus News (No. Arizona University, Jan. 1990, p. 5); Fort Worth Star Telegram. *Publications*: Various articles in journals; Cultivating the Rose Buds: The Cherokee Female Seminary, 1851-1909 (in progress for University of Nebraska Press).

ABBOTT, GREG, D.O.
(clinical director)
Affiliation: Holton PHS Indian Health Center, 100 West 6th St., Holton, KS 66436 (913) 364-2177.

*ABBOTT, LAWRENCE 1949-
(teacher)
Born March 3, 1949, Cornwall, N.Y. *Education*: Middlebury Coliege, M. Litt., 1978; New York University, MA, 1979. *Principle occupation*: Teacher. *Address*: P.O. Box 23, Orwell, VT 05760 (802) 948-2139. *Affiliation*: Adjunct lecturer, Community College of Vermont, Middlebury, VT, 1988-. *Memberships*: Modern Language Association; Association for the Study of American Indian Literatures. *Interests*: Extensive travel and research in the Southwest. *Published work*: I Stand in the Center of the Good (University of Nebraska Press, 1994).

*ABEITA, ANDY (Isleta Pueblo) 1963-
(artist-stone sculptor)
Born July 24, 1963, Chicago, Ill. *Principal occupation*: Artist-stone sculptor. *Home address*: 12 Chaparral Lane, Peralta, NM 87042 (505) 869-8148; (800) 638-7791 (work). *Affiliation*: Co-owner, Laboraex Enterprises, Peralta, NM, 1986-; co-owner Laboraex Enterprises, Denver, CO, 1992-; co-owner, Andy Abeita's Bear Fetish Studio, Santa Fe, NM, 1992-. *Memberships*: Indian Arts & Crafts Association; Heard Museum Guild; American Indian Art Council; Gallup Ceremonial Association; Indian Arts Foundation (advocacy for nature conservancy). *Interests*: "My wife Roberta, and I are Native American artisdans - stone sculptors & fetish carvers. Roberta & I travel roughly 50,000 miles a year promoting our art work and our culture. We average 30 gallery appearances a year and 10 wholesale shows annually. In recent years, I have become quite involved with educational & environmental functions held in many parts of the country. I am also a recognized lecturer/ speaker by the Native American Art Council."

ABEITA, JAMES
(BIA agency supt.)
Affiliation: Superintendent, Northern Pueblos Agency, Bureau of Indian Affairs, P.O. Box 4269, Fairview Station, Espanola, NM 87533 (505) 753-1400.

*ABEITA, ROBERTA (Ramah Navajo)
(artist-stone sculptor)
Born August 13, 1951, Rehobeth, N.M. *Principal occupation*: Artist-stone sculptor. *Home address*: 12 Chaparral Lane, Peralta, NM 87042 (505) 869-8148; (800) 638-7791 (work). *Affiliation*: Co-owner, Laboraex Enterprises, Peralta, NM, 1986-; co-owner Laboraex Enterprises, Denver, CO, 1992-; co-owner, Andy Abeita's Bear Fetish Studio, Santa Fe, NM, 1992-. *Memberships*: Indian Arts & Crafts Association; Heard Museum Guild; American Indian Art Council; Gallup Ceremonial Association; Indian Arts Foundation (advocacy for nature conservancy). *Interests*: "My husband Andy, and I are Native American artisans - stone sculptors & fetish carvers. Andy & I travel roughly 50,000 miles a year promoting our art work and our culture. We average 30 gallery appearances a year and 10 wholesale shows annually. In recent years, I have become quite involved with educational & environmental functions held in many parts of the country. I am also a recognized lecturer/ speaker by the Native American Art Council."

*ABERCROMBIE, JOHN
(memorial president)
Affiliation: Indian House Memorial, Box 121, Main St., Deerfield, MA 01342 (413) 772-0845.

ABERLE, DAVID F.
(professor)
Affiliation: Dept. of Anthropology, University of British Columbia, 6303 N.W. Marine Dr., Vancouver, B.C. V6T 2B2 (604) 228-2878.

ABEYTA, JOSEPH, Jr.
(school supt.)
Affiliation: Santa Fe Indian School, 1501 Cerrillos Rd., Santa Fe, NM 87501 (505) 989-6300.

ABRAHAM, ELMER THOMAS
(Indian band chief)
Affiliation: Frog Lake Indian Band. Frog Lake, Alberta, Canada T0A 1M0 (403) 943-3737.

ABRAHAM, FRANKLIN
(Indian band chief)
Affiliation: Little Black River Indian Band, O'Hanley, Manitoba, Canada R0E 1K0 (204) 367-4411.

ABRAHAM, SYDNEY
(Indian band chief)
Affiliation: Long Lake #58 Indian Band, Box 609, Long Lac, Ontario, Canada P0T 2A0 (807) 876-2292.

ABRAMS, GEORGE H.J. (Ha-doh-jus)
(Seneca) 1939-
(anthropologist, museum director)
Born May 4, 1939, Allegany Indian Reservation, Salamanca, N.Y. *Education*: SUNY, Buffalo, BA, 1965, MA, 1967; University of Arizona, PhD program, 1968-1971. *Principal occupation*: Museum director. *Address*: Museum of the American Indian, Broadway at 155th St., New York, NY 10032. *Affiliations*: Special assistant to the Director, Museum of the American Indian, Heye Foundation (soon to be the new National Museum of the American Indian), New York, NY. *Other professional posts*: Member, Board of Directors, American Indian Development, Inc., Denver, CO, 1971-; member, American Indian Advisory Board, Denver Museum of Natural History, Denver, CO, 1971-; member, Board of Trustees, Museum of the American Indian-Heye Foundation, New York, New York, 1977-80, 1982-; chairman, Ad Hoc Committee on the New York State Indian, New York State Archaeological Association, Rochester, NY, 1977-; chairman, North American Indian Museums Association, Salamanca, N.Y., 1978-89; member, Board of Directors, New York Iroquois Conference, Inc., Buffalo, NY, 1979-81; member, advisory board, Center for the History of the American Indian, The Newberry Library, Chicago, 1980-87; member, Commission on Museums for a New Century, American Association of Museums, Washington, D.C., 1981-85; member, National Advisory and Coordinating Council on Bilingual Education, Washington, D.C., 1984-85, 1985-87; member, National Advisory Panel, Public Monuments Conservation Program, National Institute for the Conservation of Cultural Property, Smithsonian Institution, Washington, D.C., 1985-; member, New York State Commissioner of Education, Advisory Council on Museums, Albany, NY, 1985-. *Community activities*: Seneca Nation Library, N.Y. (member, board of trustees, 1978-, chairman, 1978-81, 1984-9); Johnson O'Malley (JOM) Local Indian Education Committee, Allegany Indian Reservation (chairman, 1979-83, member, 1983-84); Mohawk-Caughnawaga Museum, Fonda, N.Y. (member, board of advisors, 1980-); Seneca Nation of Indians (member, Board of Education, 1987); member, Internal Taxation Committee, 1989; commissioner, Planning Commission, 1989; Gannagaro Archaeological Site, New York State Division of Historic Preservation, Parks and Recreation (member, advisory group.) Membership: American Association of University Professors, 1972-. *Awards, honors*: John Hay Whitney Fellow, 1968-1969; American Indian Graduate Scholarship Program Grant, School of Law, University of New Mexico, 1971. *Interests*: Contemporary American Indian anthropology; American Indian education; applied anthropology; ethnohistory, museology, Iroquois Indians. *Published works*: The Cornplanter Cemetary (Pennsylvania Archaeologist, 1965); Moving of the Fire: A Case of Iroquois Ritual Innovation (Iroquois Culture, History & Prehistory, 1967); Red Jacket (The World Book Encyclopedia, 1976); The Seneca People (Indian Tribal Series, Phoenix, 1976).

ABRAMS, OLIVER (Seneca)
(member-board of regents)
Affiliation : Member, Board of Regents, American Indian Heritage Foundation, 6051 Arlington Blvd., Falls Church, VA 22044-2788 (703) 237-7500.

ABRAHAMSON, MARK
(IHS health director)
Affiliation : Grand Portage Band, P.O. Box 428, Grand Portage, MN 55605 (218) 475-2235.

ACKERMAN, LILLIAN A. 1928-
(assistant professor)
Born April 14, 1928, Detroit, Mich. Education: University of Michigan, BA, 1950, MA, 1951; Washington State University , PhD, 1982. Principal occupation: Assistant professor of anthropology. Home address: Route 3, Box 559, Pullman, WA 99163 (509) 335-4426 (of fice). Affiliations: Assistant professor of anthropology , Washington State University , Pullman, 1982-. Other professional post: Consultant in Plateau and Yup'ik Eskimo cultural anthropology . Community activities: Chairperson, Development Services Board of Whitman County , Washington (for developing and overseeing programs for the mentally retarded); American Civil Liberties Union. Memberships: American Anthropological Association, 1950-; American Ethnological Society, 1980-; Sigma Xi, 1982-; Alaska Anthropological Association, 1982-. Awards, honors: Woodrow Wilson Fellowship; American Association of University W omen - Dissertation Fellowship; grant from the Phillips Fund of the American Philosophical Society , 1988. Interests: Primary research is in the Plateau Culture Area with emphasis on the Colville Indian Reservation; worked on the Coeur d'Alene and Nez Perce Reservations; also, worked among Yup'ik Eskimos of Goodnews Bay , Alaska and the Tlingit Indians of Alaska. Extensive work on gender equality and extended family organization. Published works: Sexual Equality in the Plateau Culture Area (Ph.D. dissertation, W ashington State University, 1982); The Effect of Missionary Ideals on Family Structure and W omen's Roles in Plateau Indian Culture (in Idaho Yesterdays 32(1-2); 64-73); several short articles on gender equality in the Plateau. "Y up'ik Eskimo Residence and Descent in Southwestern Alaska" (Inter-Nord no. 19, 1990); "Gender Status in Yup'ik Society" (in Etudes/Inuit/Studies 1990). In press: an article in the Handbook of North American Indians (Smithsonian) on gender roles and extended family structure; a book, "Women and Power in Native North America," (University of Oklahoma Press, 1992) edited by Laura F. Klein and Lillian A. Ackerman.

ACKERMAN, ROBERT E. 1928-
(professor of anthropology)
Born May 21, 1928, Grand Rapids, Mich. Education: University of Michigan, AB, 1950, M.A., 1951; University of Pennsylvania, PhD, 1961. Principal occupation : Professor of anthropology . Home address: Route 3, Box 559, Pullman, W A 99163 (509) 335-4426 (of fice). Affiliations : Professor of anthropology , Washington State University, Pullman, 1961-. Other professional posts: Archaeological consultant. Military service: Airman first class, U.S. Air Force, 1952-56. Memberships : American Anthropological Association (Fellow), 1951-; Society for American Archaeology, 1951-; American Association for the Advancement of Science (Fellow), 1960-; Arctic Institute of North America (Fellow, 1969;

American University of University Professors, 1962-; Sigma Xi, 1968-; Explorers Club; Canadian Archaeological Association; Pacific Science Association; American Quaternary Association. *Awards, honors* : Research grants from the Arctic Institute of North America for archaeological studies in southwest & southeast Alaska, 1962; National Science Foundation, 1966, 1967, 1971; Centennial Lecturer for State of W ashington, Centennial '89. Fellowships in the American Anthropological Association, the American Association for the Advancement of Science, and the Arctic Institute of North America, for contributions to the discipline of anthropology and arctic research. In *terests* : Archaeological research and surveys throughout Alaska and Canada; travel to visit classic sites in Mediterranean, China, and Korea. *Biographical sources* : Who's Who in the W est; American Men of Science; International Scholars Directory; Contemporary Authors. *Published works* : Kenaitze Indians (Indian Tribal Series, 1975); Eskimos of St. Lawrence Island (Indian Tribal Series, 1977); In Progress: Editing a volume of contributed articles on the entry of human populations into the New W orld, to be published by Washington State University Press; various articles and reports.

*ACKLEY, ARLYN (Mole Lake Chippewa)
(tribal chairperson)
Affiliation : Sokaogon Chippewa Tribal Council, Route 1, Box 625, Crandon, WI 54520 (715) 478-2604.

*ACOYA, ARTHUR
(health program director)
Affiliation : Round Valley Indian Health Program, P.O. Box 247, Covelo, CA 95428 (707) 983-6181.

ADAIR, JOHN WILLIAM
(Cherokee of Oklahoma-Deer Clan) 1942-
(company president)
Born June 6, 1942, Sequoyah County , Okla. *Education* : Bacone College, Muskogee, OK, AA, 1962; Northeastern State University , Tahlequah, OK, BA, 1964, MA, 1973. *Principal occupation* : Oil/gas exploration; real estate development. *Home address*: 8309 S. 241st E. Ave., Broken Arrow, OK 74014 (918) 357-1745. *Affiliations* : President, OK Land Development Co., Inc., Broken Arrow, OK, 1975-1988; President, Adair Oil Co., Tulsa, OK, 1988-. *Other professional posts* : member, W agoner County Planning Commission; chairman, W agoner County Airport Authority; member, Board of Adjustment of W agoner County. *Military service* : Naval Air Reserve, Active duty, 1964-71; Reserves, 1971- (Captain; Commanding of ficer of Naval Reserves of Nuclear Aircraft Carrier USS Carl V inson CVN-70; flew 225 combat missions in V ietnam-14 air medals, two Navy Commendation Medals with Combat V, Air Gallantry Cross, V ietnamese Air Gallantry Medal, V ietnam Service Medal with four bronz stars). *Memberships* : Civitan, American Legion, Naval Reserve Association, Combat Pilots Association. *Interests* : "Descendant of prominent Cherokee family - father was Walthal Corrigan Adair, an original enrollee, grandfather was Oscar F . Adair, a Cherokee V eteran of the Civil W ar under Cherokee General Stan Watie. Cherokees were last to surrender in War. Oscar F. was later judge of Sequoyah District. Great grandson of Judge John Thompson Adair, the Chief Justice of the Supreme Court of the Cherokee Nation."

ADAIR, MARY (Cherokee) 1936-
(artist, art instructor)
Born July 2, 1936, Sequoyah County , Okla. *Education* : Bacone Indian Junior College, AA, 1955; Northeastern Oklahoma State University , BA, 1957; Tulsa University , BFA, 1967; Northeastern State University , Tahlequah, OK, MF, 1983. *Principal occupation* : Artist, art instructor. *Home address*: Rt. 2, Box 287, Sallisaw , OK 74955 (918) 775-5785. *Affiliations* : Murrow Indian Children's Home, Muskogee, OK (child care-residence care institution) (executive director , 1973-79); Cherokee Nation of Oklahoma, Tahlequah, OK (education & health positions, 1979-); artist in residence, State Arts Council of Oklahoma, Oklahoma City . *Other professional posts* : Teacher, B.I.A. school, public school, head start program-management at Tinker Air Force Base. *Community activities* : Community Council (board member); Indian Parent Committee; Soroptimist Club; American Baptist Indian Caucus; Oklahoma Association of Children's Institutions and Agencies (secretary-treasurer). *Memberships* : North American Indian Women's Association (past secretary); Daughters of the Earth (a group of eight Indian women artists who display their work together in gallery and museum shows); National Indian Education Association (past secretary); Descendants of Nani (Nancy W ard (board member); American Baptist Homes & Hospitals. *Awards, honors* : Painting and crafts awards and entries in the following shows: Philbrook Museum - Indian Annual Art Show; Five Tribes Museum - Annual Art Show; Cherokee National Museum Show; Bacone Indian Art Competition; American Indian Exposition Competition; Red Cloud Indian Art Show; Heard Museum; Tsa-La-Gi Museum; Santa Fe Indian Market and others. *Interests* : "I have interest in contemporary American Indian af fairs, education and art. Have traveled to a number of traditional Indian communities and reservation areas for business and fellowship. I have spent the last 12 years serving the Cherokee Nation of Oklahoma in several areas of interest. A highlight was being able to attend the first joint meeting of the eastern and Oklahoma Cherokee councils, and two later meetings; genealogy , Native American crafts." *Biographical source* : Professional American Indian and Alaska Native W omen Directory, 1979; Directory of Native American Painters. *Published works* : Illustrations: "W omen of Power" magazine, 1989; Selu: Seeking the Corn Mother's W isdom, book by Marilou Awiakta (Fulcrum, 1993).

ADAMS, ANNA MARIA (Henu)
(Winnebago) 1961-
(artist)
Born April 4, 1961, W ashington, D.C. *Education* : Institute of American Indian Arts, AFA, 1981; Oklahoma State University , 1982-83; University of Oklahoma, BF A, 1984. *Principal occupation* : Artist. *Home address* : Rt. 3, Box 615A, Ponca City, OK 74604 (405) 765-5086. *Affiliations* : Owner, Adams & Adams Farms, Ponca City , OK, 1990-; artist, Adams Studios, Ponca City , OK, 1986-. *Community activities* : Director-organizer of perschool-kindergarten bible study; Montgomery County American Indian Program; McCord Vol. Fire Dept. (Finance Co-chiarperson, 1992-94); Poncans for Life - pro-life advocate. *Membership* : Ponca City Art Association, 1987-. *Awards, honors* : Who's Who in American Junior Colleges; 1st Miss IAIA Pow-wow Princess; 1st & 3rd Place Graphics, Ponca Art Show; hon-

orable mention - artwork submitted to Bartlesville Art Show. *Interests*: "I have displayed artwork in New York, Santa Fe, NM, and Oklahoma. Adams & Adams Farms - training and breeding American Paint Horses; and raising and breeding Pygmy Goats for show and sale. Skindiving and parasailing; deep sea fishing. *Biographical sources*: Jack & Ana Adams - Homebased Business Directory of Oklahoma; and Directory of Indian Artists, Dept. of the Interior .

*ADAMS, BERT, Sr. (Tlingit-Haida)
(AK village council president)
Affiliation: Native Village of Yakutat, P.O. Box 418, Yakutat, AK 99689 (907) 784-3932.

*ADAMS, BILLY
(interpretive ranger)
Affiliation: Kolomoki Mounds State Park & Historic Site, Route 1, Box 1 14, Blakely, GA 31723 (912) 723-5296.

ADAMS, E. CHARLES 1947-
(archaeologist/anthropologist)
Born November 27, 1947, Denver , Colo. *Education*: University of Colorado, B.A., 1970, M.A., 1973, Ph.D., 1975. *Principal occupation*: Professor of anthropology . *Home address*: 7840 N. Paseo Monserrat, Tucson, AZ 85704 (602) 621-2093 (office). *Affiliation*: University of Arizona & Arizona State Museum, Tucson, AZ, 1985-. *Military service*: Army National Guard, 1966-72 (Sergeant). *Community activities*: President, Arizona Archaeological Council, 1978-80. *Memberships*: Society for American Archaeology, 1972-; American Anthropological Association, 1975-; Arizona Archaeological Council, 1977-; Sigma Xi, 1973-; Arizona Archaeological & Historical Society, 1975-. *Awards, honors*: Earl Morris Award (presented to the outstanding archaeology graduate student in the Department of Anthropology, University of Colorado, 1975). *Interests*: The prehistory & history of the Colorado Plateau with emphasis on the Pueblo Indians, especially the Hopi. "I have directed several research expeditions for the Museum of Northern Arizona, Flagstaff, and the Arizona State Museum, Tucson, on the Plateau. "I direct an archaeological research project at the University of Arizona excavating 600-700 year-old pueblos that are ancestral to the Hopi Indians. I have worked with the Hopi Tribe over the years on these research projects and employ Hopi high school students." *Published works*: Walpi Archaeological Project: Synthesis & Interpretation (Museum of Northern Arizona, 1982); Homol'ovi II: The Archaeology of an Ancestral Hopi Village (University of Arizona Press, 1991); The Origin & Development of the Pueblo Katsina Cult (University of Arizona Press, 1991).

*ADAMS, EDITH
(BIA agency supt.)
Affiliation: Fort Belknap Agency, Bureau of Indian Affairs, P.O. Box 98, Harlem, MT 59526 (406) 353-2901.

*ADAMS, EDWARD J., Sr. (Athapascan)
(AK village council president)
Affiliation: Native Village of Sheldon's Point, Sheldon's Point, AK 99668 (907) 498-4226.

ADAMS, HANK
(association director)
Affiliation: Survival of American Indian Associations, 7803-A Samurai Dr., SE, Olympia, WA 98503 (206) 459-2679.

ADAMS, MARGARET B. *(Bina-doh-clish)*
(Navajo) 1936-
(anthropologist-retired)
Born April 29, 1936, Toronto, Ontario, Can. *Education*: Monterey Peninsula College, AA, 1969; San Jose State University , BAS, 1971; University of Utah, MA, 1973. *Principal occupation*: Anthropologist-retired. *Home address*: 2200 Wildberry Lane, Auburn, CA 95603. *Affiliations*: Chief of Museum Branch, Fort Ord Military Complex; and, Head Curator of Fort Ord and Presidio of Monterey Museums, 1974-88. *Other professional posts*: Panel member (Indians in Science) for American Association for the Advancement of Science, 1972-85; reviewer , Project Media of American Indian Education Association. *Community activities*: American Indian Information Center of Monterey Peninsula (co-founder and volunteer executive director, 1973-92); member of Monterey Speaker's Bureau. Memberships: National Indian Education Association; California Indian Education Association; American Anthropological Association; American Association of Museums; Monterey History & Art Association. *Interests*: Higher education for Native Americans, particularly in the sciences; media presentations concerning Native Americans; review of media on Native Americans; observations and reporting of improper excavation of Native American ceremonial and burial sites; preservation of Native American ceremonial, burial, and historical sites. Retired from Government service April, 1988 and currently involved in research on a collection of recipes by contemporary Native American cooks, working title: The First American Cookbook. *Biographical sources*: Who's Who in America; World's Who Who of Women; The Science Teacher (Journal); Women in the Social Sciences. *Published works*: Indian Tribes of North America and a Brief Chronology of Ancient Pueblo Indian and Old World Events (Monterey Museum of Art, 1975); History of Navajo and Apache Painting (Indian America, Tulsa, 1976); Historic Old Monterey (DeAnza College History Center , 1977); Silver & Sheen--Southwestern Indian Jewelry (Indian America, Tulsa, 1977); and numerous publications on museum exhibits & history for the Federal Government.

ADAMS, RAY (Upper Mattaponi)
(tribal chief)
Affiliation: Chief, Upper Mattaponi Tribe, 106 Kyle Circle, Tabb, VA 23602 (804) 898-3310.

ADAMS, ROXANNA
(museum director)
Affiliation: Totem Heritage Center Museum & Library, 629 Dock St., Ketchikan, AK 99901 (907) 225-5900.

ADAMS, VIVIAN M. (Y akima, Puyallup, Suquamish, Quinault) 1943-
(museum curator)
Born March 21, 1943, Toppenish, Wash. *Education*: Institute of American Indian Art, Santa Fe, AFA, 1981. *Principal occupation*: Museum curator. *Address & Affiliation*: Yakima Nation Cultural Center, P.O. Box 151, Toppenish, WA 98948. *Community activities*: Yakima Agency Employees Club (secretary-treasurer); IAIA Student Senate Representative; Yakima Women's Investor's Club. *Memberships*: Washington State Folklife Council; American Association of State & Local History; Toppenish Chamber of Commerce; Yakima Chamber of Commerce; Washington Museum Association; Yakima Val-

ley Visitors and Convention Bureau; National Trust for Historic Preservation; Native American Task Force, Washington State Centennial; Washington State Native American Task Force, Native American Consortium; W ashington State Centennial Heritage Subcommittee of Lasting Legacy. Awards, honors: Outstanding Artistic & Academic Achievement, 1980-81; Institute of American Indian Art President's Award; Who's Who Among Students, American Junior Colleges, 1981; Scholastic Achievement Award, Yakima Nation Education, 1982. *Interests*: "My main interest is two-dimensional art (sketching, pen and ink). I love to work with Indian artifacts--those items which are hand made of natural materials. Plus, it is a joy to design ways to display these items which teach a lesson in an aesthetic manner . It is important to present our cultural history and traditions from our (Native American) point of view to promote a better understanding by other cultures—and to learn from them. Oral history and elders input into telling our ways is extremely important to accomplishing those goals of the museum. Therefore, museology is my second interest, my financial base to a sporadic art career! But being a curator allows me the time to work with objects of art--my main love. My third interest is pursuing conservation techniques: recognizing and maintaining basket weaving, textile weaving, restoration techniques, time allowing I hope to accomplish conservator's training." *Biographical sources*: Yakima Herald Republic news article; Girl Scouts of America; Who's Who Among Students in American Junior Colleges.

ADAMS, WILL
(Indian band chief)
Affiliation: Lake Babine Indian Band, P .O. Box 879, Bums Lake, British Columbia, Canada V0J 1E0 (604) 692-7555.

ADAMSON, REBECCA
(association president)
Affiliation: President, First Nations Development Institute, 11917 Main St., Fredericksburg, V A 22408 (703) 371-5615.

ADAY, JERRY L.
(executive director)
Affiliation: Mid-American All-Indian Center , 650 N. Seneca, Wichita, KS 67203 (316) 262-5221.

ADKINS, A. LEONARD
(tribal chief)
Affiliation: Chickahominy Indian Tribe, RFD 1, Box 299, Providence Forge, V A 23140 (804) 829-2186.

ADKINS, ARTHUR L. *(Lonewolf)*
(Chickahominy) 1926-
(teacher-retired)
Born October 1, 1926, Charles City Co., V A. *Education*: Bacone College, AA, 1952; V irginia Commonwealth University , BS, MA. *Principal occupation*: Teacher-retired. *Home address*: 6801 Lott Cary Rd., Providence Forge, V A 23140 (804) 829-2186. *Affiliation*: Elementary school teacher-retired, Charles City Co., V A School System. *Other profesional post*: Member, Selective Service System. *Military service*: U.S. Army, 1945-47 (PFC, E.T.O., Occupation, Victory). *Community activities*: Chief, Chickahominy Indian Tribe; Charles City-New Kent Heritage Library; W oodmen of the W orld; V.F.W. *Awards, honors*: Woodmen of the W orld Fraternalist of the Year and Outstanding Citi-

zen, 1990. *Interests*: "Traveling to see things of nature, museums, historical places."

*ADKINS, GLORIA
(association director)
Affiliation: Washington State Indian Education Association, c/o Colville Confederated Tribes, P.O. Box 150, Nespelem, W A99155 (509) 634-4711.

ADKINS, PRESTON
(dance troops coordinator)
Affiliation: Native American Dance Troops, Chickahominy Red Men Dancers, P .O. Box 473, Providence Forge, VA 23140 (804) 829-2152.

ADOLF, ROGER
(Indian band chief)
Affiliation: Fountain Indian Band, Box 1330, Lillooet, British Columbia, Canada V0K 1V0 (604) 256-4227.

*AGARE, JOHN (Hawaiian)
(association president)
Affiliation: Congress of the Hawaiian People, 98-1364 Akaaka St., Alea, HI 96701 (808) 488-6905.

AGNASSAGA, GEORGE (Eskimo)
(AK village council president)
Affiliation: Wainwright Traditional Council, P .O. Box 184, Wainwright, AK 99782 (907) 763-2726.

AGNELLO, THOMAS 1961-
(film & video producer)
Born May 6, 1961, Mt. V ernon, N.Y. Education: New York University, BFA (Film & Television), 1984. Home address: 31 Maple St., Ridgefield Park, NJ 07660 (201) 933-6698. Memberships: Association of Independent V ideo and Filmmakers, 1986-. Film produced: Lenape: The Original People (Agnello Films, N.J.), 1986 - a film that expresses the history , customs and wishes of the Lenape (Delaware) Indians, as told through the personal testimony of the tribe itself. See Audio-Visual Aids section for further details.

AGNUS, SIMON
(AK village council president)
Affiliation: Umkumiut V illage Council, General Delivery, Nightmute, AK 99690 (907) 647-6213.

AGOGINO, GEORGE A. 1920-
(distinguished professor of anthropology)
Born November 18, 1920, W est Palm Beach, Fla. *Education*: University of New Mexico, BA, 1949, MA, 1951; Syracuse University , PhD, 1958; Harvard University, Wenner-Gren Foundation Post Doctoral Fellowship in Anthropology, 1961-62. *Principal occupation*: Distinguished professor of anthropology , museum director. *Home address*: 1600 S. Main, Portales, NM 88130 (505) 356-8709. *Affiliations*: Instructor in anthropology, Syracuse University, 1956-58; museum director and assistant professor , University of South Dakota, 1958-59; assistant professor of anthropology , University of W yoming, 1959-62; associate professor of anthropology, Baylor University, 1962-63; Eastern New Mexico University, professor of anthropology , 1963-91, distinguished research professor in anthropology, emeritus, 1991- (anthropology dept. chairperson, 1963-80); director of Paleo-Indian Institute, 1968-. *Other professional posts*: Founding director, Blackwater Draw Museum, Miles Museum, and Anthropology Museum of

Eastern New Mexico University , Portales, N.M. *Military service*: U.S. Army Signal Corps, 1943-46. *Community activities*: Eastern New Mexico University, Local National Educational Association (president and vice-president, 1976-). *Memberships*: American Anthropological Association (Fellow); American Association for the Advancement of Science (Fellow); Royal Anthropological Institute of Great Britain and Ireland (Fellow); Institute Inter-American (Fellow); Current Anthropology (Associate); Explorers' Club (Fellow); Senator Academico (regent) Academmia Romania de Science ed Arti. *Awards, honors*: PhD Rome (Italy) Institute of Arts and Sciences; multiple grants from W enner-Gren Foundation for Anthropology, American Philosophical Society, Sigma Xi; twice Eastern New Mexico University Outstanding Educator, 1972, 1974-75; fourth distinguished professor in 70-year history of Eastern New Mexico University; State of New Mexico awarded Dr. Agogino as one of one hundred "Eminent Scholars" of New Mexico. *Interests*: "Indian religion and culture; North America and Mexico Paleo Indian; Indian physical anthropology, pictoglyphs. Have worked with and published on Navajo, Iroquois, Pueblo, Kickapoo, Seminole, Sioux; in Canada: Cree; and in Mexico: Seri, Yaqui, Aztec, Huichol, Tepecano, Mayo, Maya, Huastica and Otomi Indians. Archaeological work has largely been with our earliest Indians, the Paleo-Indian, the discoverers of the New W orld. I also work for the federal government as a forensic physical anthropologist, getting maximum information before reburial by their respective tribes." *Travels, expeditions*: Anthropological research in Canada, Mexico, New Guinea and Australia. *Biographical sources*: Who's Who Among Authors and Journalists; Directory of International Biography; Who's Who in America; Who's Who in the Southwest; Who's Who in the W est; Who's Who in American Education; Directory of International Biography; Contemporary Authors; Outstanding Educators in America; American Men of Science; Plains Anthropological Society; Who's Who in the W orld (Tenth Edition). *Published works*: Over 420 articles & monographs.

AGOYO, HERMAN (Pueblo)
(pueblo governor)
Affiliation: Pueblo of San Juan, P .O. Box 1099, San Juan Pueblo, NM 87566 (505) 852-4400; *Past professional post*: Chairperson, All Indian Pueblo Council, Albuquerque, NM.

AGUILAR, ALFRED *(Sa wa pin)*
(San Ildefonso Pueblo) 1933-
(artist, teacher)
Born July 1, 1933, San Ildefonso Pueblo, N.M. *Education*: High school. *Principal occupation*: Artist, teacher (Chapter I, 1967). *Home address*: Route 5, Box 318C, Santa Fe, NM 87501 (505) 455-3530 (work). Affiliation: Owner , Aguilar Indian Arts, Santa Fe, NM. *Military service*: U.S. Air Force, 1952-56 (Good Service Award). *Community activities*: Pueblo of ficial council member. *Memberships*: Eight Northern Pueblo Art Council; The Indian Pueblo Cultural Center . *Awards, honors*: For painting, pottery , and sculptures from the SW AIA, New Mexico State Fair, Inter-Tribal Ceremonial, Jemez Pueblo, Heard Museum, and New Mexico Fine Arts Museum. *Interests*: Education, art-travel expeditions. Mr . Aguilar specializes in black and red pottery , and is well known by many people around the world with his nativity set and story teller . He sculptures black on black buf falos, and animal and

dancing figures on pottery . He has gained versatility in water color , and is adept in depicting Indian dances and in preserving ancient design and symbols on his work.

AGUILAR, MICHELLE PENOZ'EQUAH
(executive director)
Affiliation: Governor's Of fice of Indian Affairs, 1515 S. Cherry St., Box 40909, Olympia, W A 98504 (206) 753-241 1.

AGUILAR, JOSE V. (Suwu-Peen)
(Tewa Pueblo) 1924-
(technical graphic artist)
Born January 8, 1924, San Ildefonso, N.M. *Education*: Otis Art Institute, Certificate, 1949; Hill and Canyon School of Art, 1950. *Principal occupation*: Technical graphic artist. *Home address*: 9682 Mt. Darnard Dr ., Buena Park, CA 90620. *Affiliation*: Project Coordinator, Rockwell International, Downey , CA, 1954-. *Military service*: U.S. Army, 1944-46 (European Theatre Medal; Purple Heart). *Memberships*: National Congress of American Indians, 1954-. *Awards, honors*: Certificate of Merit, Inter-T ribal Indian Ceremonial Association, 1949; First Purchase Award, Philbrook Art Center , 1953; Denver Art Museum Purchase Award; Mary W artrous Award, 1954; Honorable Mention, Philbrook Art Center, 1959; Lippencott and W ellington Award; Museum of New Mexico Award for Collection of Museum of Contemporary Art; paintings in permanent collections of Philbrook Art Center, Museum of New Mexico, and Museum of the American Indian. Private collections include: Millard Sheet, artist and educator; V incent Price, actor and art collector; and Darwin Goody , educator.

AHENAKEW, BARRY
(Indian band chief)
Affiliation: Chief, Ahtahkakoop Indian Band, Box 220, Shell Lake, Saskatchewan, Canada S0J 2G0 (306) 468-2326.

AHENAKEW, WILLARD
(corporation president)
Affiliation: President, Saskatchewan Indian Arts & Crafts Corporation, 2431-8th Ave., Regina, Saskatchewan, Canada S4R 5J7 (306) 352-1501.

AHHITTY, GLENDA
(commission director)
Affiliation: Los Angeles City/County Native American Indian Commission, 500 W est Temple St., Rm. 780, Los Angeles, CA 90012 (213) 974-7554.

*AHKINGA, ORVILLE (Eskimo)
(AK village council president)
Affiliation: Native V illage of Diomede (aka Inalik), P.O. Box 7099, Diomede, AK 99762 (907) 686-3021.

*AHSHAPANEK, CAROL LO-ANN
(PADDLETY) (Kiowa/W ichita/Pawnee) 1942-
(community health nurse)
Born June 15, 1942, Lawton, Okla. *Education*: Haskell Indian Nations University , AA, 1975; Washburn University, BS, 1979. *Principal occupation*: Community health nurse. *Home address*: 1008 Mimosa Dr ., Anadarko, OK 73005 (405) 247-7153. *Affiliations*: Clinical nurse, Haskell Indian Health Clinic, Lawrence, KS, 1980-84; clinical nurse, Anadarko Indian Clinic, Anadarko, OK, 1984-87; community health nurse, Pawhuska, OK, 1988-90; supervisory commu-

nity health nurse, Lawton Indian Hospital, Lawton, OK, 1990-91; community health nurse, Anadarko, Indian Clinic, Anadarko, OK, 1991-. *Memberships*: Oklahoma State Board of Nursing. *Awards, honors*: Community Health Nurse Internship Program, Salt River Reservation, Scottsdale, AZ, 1987-88. *Interests*: Basketweaving, traditional dancing.

*AHSHAPANEK, DON COLESTO (JOHNSON)
(Nanticoke/Delaware) 1932-
(realty specialist, adjunct professor)
Born April 29, 1932, Milton, Dela. *Education*: Central State University (Edmond, OK), BS, 1956; University of Oklahoma, MS, 1959. *Principal occupation*: Realty specialist, adjunct professor of biological sciences. *Home address*: 1008 Mimosa Dr., Anadarko, OK 73005 (405) 247-7153. *Affiliations*: Associate professor, Emporia State University, Emporia, KS, 1962-71; instructor of life sciences, Haskell Indian Nations University, Lawrence, KS, 1971-91; realty specialist, Acquisitions & Disposals, Bureau of Indian Affairs, Anadarko Agency, Anadarko, OK, 1991-. *Memberships*: National Indian Education Association; American Indian Science & Engineering Society; Society of Native Americans & Chicanos in Science (board member); Headlands Indian Health Careers Program. *Awards, honors*: Research Assistantship, 1956-61; Research Presenter, 11th International Botanical Congress, Seattle, 1969; Program & Project Director, NIH Minority Biomedical Sciences Program, 1976-79; Outstanding Faculty Award, 1977-78, 1988-89; Program & Project Director, Dept. of Education Sciences Improvement Program, 1982-85; NSF Research Post Doctorate Fellowship, Kansas University (Dept. of Microbiology), 1982, (Dept. of Biochemistry), 1983; University of Oklahoma (Dept. of Microbiology), 1985-87; Keynote Speaker, Native American Research Symposium, Bozeman, MT, 1985. *Published works*: "Mammals Associated with Prehistoric People of Oklahoma," in Proceedings of the Oklahoma Academy of Science, 1960; "Phenology of a Native Tall-Grass Prairie in Central Oklahoma," in Ecology 43:135-138, 1962. *Interests*: Ethnohistory, genealogy, philately, traditional dancing.

AHTONE, DEBORAH (Kiowa) 1947-
(editor)
Born July 2, 1947, Carnegie, Okla. *Education*: Bacone College, AAm 1967; Rocky Mountain College, BA, 1970; University of Oklahoma, Graduate School, 1970-71. *Principal occupation*: Editor. *Home address*: P.O. Box 397, Mountain View, OK 73062 (405) 347-2875. *Affiliations*: Editor, Kiowa Indian News, Carnegie, OK, 1982-; editor/owner, Feather Review News, Mountain View, OK, 1989-. *Other professional posts*: Official photographer for Kiowa Tribe; member, Kiowa Tribal Museum Commission; Instructor, traditional techniques, Institute of American Idian Art (1 year); instructor, Indian studies, Dawson College, Glendive, MT (2 years). *Community activities*: Volunteer to Kiowa Tribal Museum & Kiowa Senior Citizen Center; photographer for 1992 Sovereignty Symposium, Oklahoma City. *Memberships*: Southern Plains Museum Association (chairperson, 1990; treasurer, 1992); Native American Journalists Association; Southwestern Association on Indian Affairs; National Congress of American Indians. *Awards, honors*: First Place, Scottsdale Indian Art Show-Mixed Media; Promising New Artist, Rose State College, 1978. *Interests*: Photography; "Interest in

Indian affairs - led to appointment as editor of Kiowa News, which led to the establishment of statewide newspaper, "The Feather Review." Business trips for Dawson College led to contacts with other tribes and tribal leaders throughout the U.S. These contacts have remain crucial in networking the "Feather Review" with news from the tribes. Tribal leaders bestowed nickname "Scoop" to me because I am always out searching for nes and am in attendance of inter-tribal meetings both in Oklahoma and other states." *Biographical sources*: Who's Who in American Colleges & Universities, 1970; biography pamphlet for one man show, Southern Plains Indian Museum.

AKERS, RUSS
(AK village president)
Affiliation: Native Village of Chuloonawick, Chuloonawick, AK 99581 (907) 949-1 147.

*AKINS, DR. VIRGIL
(BIA agency supt.)
Affiliation: Northern California Agency, Bureau of Indian Affairs, P.O. Box 494879, Redding, CA 96049 (916) 246-5141.

AKIWENZIE, RALPH
(Indian band chief)
Affiliation: Chief, Chippewas of Nawash Indian Band, R.R. #5, Wiarton, Ontario, Canada N0H 2T0 (519) 534-1689.

ALAMEDA, HENRY C., Sr.
(BIA field station supt.)
Affiliate: Metlakatla Field Station, Bureau of Indian Affairs, P.O. Box 450, Metlakatla, AK 99926 (907) 886-3791.

ALBANY, JOHN PETER
(Indian band chief)
Affiliation: Songhees Indian Band, 1500 A-Admirals Rd., Victoria, British Columbia, Canada V9A 2R1 (604) 386-1043.

ALBERT, ANNA
(director-Indian medical center)
Affiliation: Director, Phoenix Indian Medical Center, 4212 North 16th St., Phoenix, AZ 85016 (602) 263-1200.

ALBERT, ROBERT STEPHEN
(Sakhomenewa) (Hopi) 1964-
(artist)
Born March 27, 1964, Gonado, Ariz. Education: Institute of American Indian Arts, AFA, 1986; National Indian Center, Phoenix, Commercial Arts Degree, 1990. Principal occupation: Artist. Home address: 19 W. Veterans Blvd., Tucson, AZ 85713 (602) 770-1921. Art: Kachina doll carver (12 years) and watercolor painter. Gallery and Indian Market Shows include: Heard Museum, Mesa Southwest Museum, Museum of North Arizona, Tohono Chul Park, Gallup Ceremonial. Awards, honors: T.C. Cannon nominee, 1986, top five students at Institute of American Indian Arts; "Artist of the Year Award" from Council for Tribal Employment Rights, 1988, for original Acrylic on Canvas painting; Best of Show, categories - Kachina Doll, watercolor painting, pencil drawing, from Pine Bi Keyay Museum Market, Page, AZ, 1989; Third Place, categories Kachina Doll and watercolor painting, from Museum of Northern Arizona "Hopi Show,", Flagstaff, AZ, 1991; First Place, category - Kachina Doll, from American Indian Art Festival and Market, Dallas, TX, 1991.

ALCHESAY-NACHU, CARLA
(director-Indian hospital)
Affiliation: Director, Whiteriver Indian Hospital, P.O. Box 860, Whiteriver, AZ 85941 (602) 338-4911.

ALEX, ANDREW
(Indian band chief)
Affiliation: Union Bar Indian Band, Box 788, Hope, British Columbia, Canada V0X 1H0 (519) 627-3911.

ALEXANDER, CLARENCE
(village council chief)
Affiliation: Native Village of Fort Yukon, P.O. Box 126, Fort Yukon, AK 99740 (907) 662-2581.

*ALEXANDER, KAREN WILKINS
(Cherokee/Powhatan) 1954-
(librarian/archivist)
Born March 21, 1954, Ardmore, Okla. *Education*: University of Science & Arts of Oklahoma (Chickasha), 1975. *Principal occupation*: Librarian/archivist. *Address & Affiliation*: Miami Tribe of Oklahoma, P.O. Box 1326, 202 S. Eight Tribes Trail, Miami, OK 74355 (918) 542-4505, 1989-. *Interests*: Genealogy, reading & writing.

*ALEXANDER, MYRA
(manager-counseling)
Affiliation: Native Americans in Biological Sciences, 307 Life Sciences East, Oklahoma State University, Stillwater, OK 74078 (405) 744-6802.

*ALEXANDER, NOME
(museum curator)
Affiliation: Museum of Indian Culture, Lenni Lenape Historical Society, R.D. #2, Fish Hatchery Rd., Allentown, PA 18103 (215) 797-2121.

ALEXIE, ANDREW
(school chairperson)
Affiliation: Chairperson, Tuluksak IRA Contract School, Tuluksak, AK 99679 (907) 695-6212.

ALEXIS, JOHN
(Indian band chief)
Affiliation: Chief, Tl'azt'en Nation, P.O. Box 670, Fort St. James, British Columbia, Canada V0J 1P0 (604) 648-3212.

ALFONSI, JOHN 1961-
(archaeologist, cultural resources mgmt.)
Born January 16, 1961, New York, N.Y. *Education*: University of Alaska, Fairbanks (degree in progress). *Principal occupation*: Archaeologist, cultural resources management. *Home address*: Mile 1403.5 Alaska Hiway, Delta Junction, AK 99737. *Affiliation*: Ahtna, Inc., Fairbanks, AK. Membership: AK Anthropological Association, 1984-. *Awards, honors*: Outstanding Senator and Outstanding Student--USUA, University of AK, Fairbanks Student Government, 1984 & 1985, respectively. Interests: Hunting, trapping, fishing, building; cultural resource assessments throughout Alaska. Published works: (In progress) Ahtna Cultural Resources throughout the region. Work includes mainly archaeological fieldwork and intensive investigation, e.g. on-the-ground archaeological survey of the Copper River Basin. First of its kind.

ALFRED, PATRICK
(Indian band chief)
Affiliation: Nimpkish Indian Band, Box 210, Alert Bay, British Columbia, Canada V0N 1A0 (604) 974-5556.

ALGER, RUSS
(director-Indian health center)
Affiliation: Warm Springs PHS Indian Health Center, P.O. Box 1209, Warm Springs, OR 97761 (503) 553-1196.

ALLAN, STEPHANIE (Tyme Maidu-Berry Creek Rancheria) 1965-
(clerical assistant)
Born November 11, 1965, Oroville, Calif. *Education*: High school. *Principal occupation*: Clerical assistant. *Home address*: 4310 V.C. Ave., Oroville, CA 95966 (916) 534-3884 (office). *Affiliation*: I.T.C.C. (Head Starts throughout California), Sacramento, CA; chairperson, Parent Policy Council, 1991-. *Community activities*: Butte Tribal Council (member).

*ALLARD, JEANINE
(museum director)
Affiliation: Flathead Indian Museum, Flathead Indian Reservation, 1 Museum Lane, St. Ignatius, MT 59865 (406) 745-2951.

ALLARD, L. DOUG (Anteh) (Flathead-Confederated Salish & Kootenai) 1931-
(Indian trader & auctioneer)
Born August 30, 1931, St. Ignatius, Mont. *Education*: Montana State University, BA, 1956. *Principal occupation*: American Indian art dealer. *Address*: P.O. Box 460, St. Ignatius, MT 59865 (406) 745-2951 (work). *Affiliations*: Founder, owner & curator, Flathead Indian Museum & Doug Allard Trading Post, St. Ignatius, MT (21 years). *Other professional post*: Owner, Allard Indian Auctions (29 years). *Military service*: U.S. Marine Corps, 1950-53 (Korean War Ribbon, U.N. Medal, two Battle Stars, Good Conduct Medal). *Community activities*: Chairman, Flathead Reservation Pow Wow Committee; chairman, Flathead Constitution Convention Committee; former tribal secretary, Confederated Salish & Kootenai Tribes. *Memberships*: National Association of Appraisers; Indian Arts and Crafts Association (charter member, board of directors); V.F.W.; American Legion; National Auctioneers Association; Salish-Kootenai College Foundation (chairperson). *Interests*: Tribal culture; avid collector of Indian artifacts; consultant to many museums and Indian groups. Nationally known appraiser & auctioneer of American Indian material. *Biographical source*: Who's Who in the West. *Published works*: Many articles, too numerous to mention.

ALLEN, JAMES
(chairperson-Indian cultural center)
Affiliation: Yukon Indian Cultural-Education Society Resource Center, Council for Yukon Indians, 22 Nisutlin Dr., Whitehorse, Yukon, Canada Y1A 3S5 (403) 667-7631.

*ALLEN, JUDY
(editor)
Affiliation: Bishinik, Choctaw Nation of Oklahoma, P.O. Box 1210, Durant, OK 74702 (405) 924-8280.

*ALLEN, KEAHI (Hawaiian)
(state council director)
Affiliation: State Council on Hawaiian Heritage, P.O. Box 3022, Honolulu, HI 96807 (808) 586-0335.

ALLEN, LEAMOND ANTHONY
(Metis-Haliwa Tribe) 1955-
(community service worker)
Born August 12, 1955, Rocky Mount, N.C. *Education*: High school; Old Ecumenical Institute, Institute for Cultural Affairs, 1979. *Principal occupation*: Community service worker. *Address*: P.O. Box 4674, Chicago, IL 60680 (312) 296-6014. *Affiliation*: Founder, Potlatch-Kenaniah (an advocate network to minority and Native American charities, social concerns and faith in Christ), Chicago, IL. *Other professional posts*: Writer, resource teacher, lecturer, graphic artist. *Commuity activities*: Addison Street Baptist Church (deacon/board member, 1989-); Church layworker, altar-worker and other ministerial activities; teacher, Open High School, Richmond, VA; teacher-volunteer, Chicago Public Library. *Awards, honors*: Chosen as a member of the National Board of Directors for North American Indian Spirit Keeper Alcatraz Project, Wichita, KS (an American Indian cultural center for the preservation of the North American Indian heritage). *Interests*: Native American rights, Christian worship activities, bible study, ministry, religious education, lay leadership, humanitarian-work, almsgiving, networking; storytelling; Christian ceremony-pulpit work; multi-cultural history, art/illustrating. "I was inspired to create Potlatch Network as an on-going human-sevice network because of my concerns for social change, specifically for Native Americans. I have a genuine concern for social issues and I'm dedicated to servant-leadership (serving/helping people)." *Biographical sources*: Illustrations appeared in Drumbeats Magazine, 1984-87; Amerrikua Magazine; and many others. *Published works*: Article: "Potlatching to the World Culture," in Amerrikua Magazine, Vol. 4 No. 3.

ALLEN, LORETTA
(commission chairperson)
Affiliation: California Native American Heritage Commission, 915 Capitol Mall, Sacramento, CA 95814 (916) 322-7791.

*ALLEN, MILILANI (Hawaiian)
(organization director)
Affiliation: Halau Hula O Mililani, 85-711 Kaupouni Place, Walanau, HI 96792 (808) 696-2145.

*ALLEN, PATRICIA
(school principal)
Affiliation: John F. Kennedy Day School, P.O. Box 130, White River, AZ 85941 (602) 338-4593.

*ALLEN. ROBERT (Hawaiian)
(administrator)
Affiliation: Native Hawaiian Vocational Education Program, 2879 Pa'a St., Suite 201, Honolulu, HI 96819 (808) 839-7922.

ALLEN, WILLIAM RON
(Jamestown S'Klallem) 1947-
(politician; administrator)
Born December 14, 1947, Port Angeles, Wash. *Education*: Peninsula College, AA & AAA, 1978; University of Washington, BA (Political Science & Economics), 1982. *Principal occupation*: Politician; administrator. *Address*: 1033 Old Blyn Highway, Sequim, WA 98382 (206) 683-1109 (work). *Affiliation*: Chairperson, Executive Director, Jamestown Band of S'Klallem Indians Business Council, Sequim, WA, 1978-. *Community activities*: National Indian Policy Center (Co-chair); National Congress of American Indian

(treasurer, 1989-). *Awards, honors*: Student of the Year, Peninsula College; Dedicated Service, Northwest Indian Fish Commission. *Published works*: Determining the True Cost of Contracting Federal Programs for Indian Tribes (Affiliated Tribes of Northwest Indians, 1987).

ALLISON, BARNETT
(Indian band chief)
Affiliation: Lower Similkameen Indian Band, Box 100, Keremeos, British Columbia, Canada V0X 1N0 (604) 499-5528.

ALLISON, DAVID
(BIA agency supt.)
Affiliation: Wind River Agency, Bureau of Indian Affairs, Fort Washakie, WY 82514 (307) 332-7810.

ALLISON, EDWARD
(Indian band chief)
Affiliation: Upper Similkameen Indian Band, Box 100, Keremeos, British Columbia, Canada V0X 1N0 (604) 499-5528.

ALLISON, HARVEY DALE
(school principal)
Affiliation: Principal, Na'Neelzhiin Ji'Olta (Torreon), HCR 79, Box 9, Cuba, NM 87013 (505) 731-2272.

ALLWOOD, ADOLPH A. (Eagle Among Us)
(Oklahoma Cherokee) 1943-
(marketing/public relations consultant)
Born November 11, 1943, Buffalo, N.Y. *Education*: City College of New York, BA (Economics); Fordham University, MBA (Marketing-Management). *Principal occupation*: Marketing/public relations consultant. *Address*: 119-30 199th St., St. Albans, NY 11412 (718) 276-5764. *Affiliation*: Affective Marketing Management Consultants, Queens Village, NY. "As a marketing consultant, I presently have a client, State University of New York, S.U.N.Y. Research Foundation. I develop, for the metropolitan New York area, market sensitive programs to train and re-employ recipients of welfare." *Other professional posts*: Public relations, marketing, management planning, training and development with the following companies: New York Post, The New York Times, Ziff Davis Publishing Co. *Memberships*: American Marketing Association; American Management Association; Public Relations Society of America; Southeastern Cherokee Confederacy of Georgia; Native American Indian Enrollment Agency. *Interests*: Adolph has competed as an artist working with sculpture, copper, and painting. Primarily self-taught, all themes are core to the Native American culture. The most pronounced dimention of Adolph's involvement with Native American culture has been directing traditional Native American dance groups. He organized an inter-tribal dance troupe called, International Native American Performers. They perform before various audiences throughout the state. The audiences are often delighted and impressed with the unusually programmed series of performance which often were not the dances popular to audiences of even the pow wow circuit. For example the Cherokee Bogar Man Dance, and the Kiowa or Mandan Buffalo Dances. Often Adolph is requested to provide his expertise to audiences as a lecturer or writer about history and varied cultures of Native Americans. He presently serves as the Native Core Economist of a community publication - The Long Island Courier,

as a researcher to Professor E.L. Gilmore's, Institute of Cherokee Studies, Tahlequah, Oklahoma. *Biographical source*: Who's Who Among Young American Professionals, 1988.

*ALONZO, NANCY MARTINE
(Indian education contact)
Affiliation: New Mexico State Dept. of Education, Division of Indian Education, 300 Don Gaspar, Santa Fe, NM 87501 (505) 827-6679.

ALPHONSE, DENNIS
(Indian band chief)
Affiliation: Cowichan Indian Band, Box 880, Duncan, British Columbia, Canada V9L 3Y2 (604) 748-3196.

ALTHER, DOROTHY
(attorney)
Affiliation: California Indian Legal Services, 819 N. Barlow Lane, Bishop, CA 93514 (619) 873-3582.

*ALULI, EMMETT (MD) (Hawaiian)
(organization president)
Affiliation: Na Pu'uwai, Molokai Island Center, P.O. Box 392, Kaunakai, HI 96748 (808) 567-6831.

*ALVARY, COLLEEN
(health council director)
Affiliation: American Indian Council of Central California, 2210 Chester Ave., Suite A, Bakersfield, CA 93301 (805) 327-2207.

AMBROSIA, ALEX
(village council president)
Affiliation: Village of Ouzinkie, P.O. Box 13, Ouzinkie, AK 99644 (907) 680-2259.

AMES, MICHAEL M. 1933-
(professor, museum director)
Born June 19, 1933, Vancouver, Can. *Education*: University of British Columbia, BA, 1956; Harvard University, PhD, 1961. *Principal occupation*: Professor of anthropology, museum director. *Address*: UBC Museum of Anthropology, 6393 N.W. Marine Dr., Vancouver, B.C. V6T 1W5. *Affiliation*: Museum of Anthropology, University of British Columbia, Vancouver, *Memberships*: Canadian Ethnology Society; American Anthropological Association; Canadian Museum Association; American Association of Asian Studies. *Awards, honors*: Guggenheim Fellowship; Fellow of the Royal Society of Canada. Interests: Research in Northwest Coast of North America and South Asia. *Published works*: Manlike Monsters on Trial, co-edited with M. Halpin (UBC Press, 1980; Museums, The Public and Anthropology (Concept and UBC Press, 1985.)

AMI, JUDY
(school principal)
Affiliation: Four Winds Community School, P.O. Box 199, Fort Totten, ND 58335 (701) 766-4161.

AMIOTTE, ARTHUR DOUGLAS *(Good Eagle Center)* **(Oglala Sioux) 1942-**
(artist, author, educator)
Born March 25, 1942, Pine Ridge, S.D. *Education*: Northern State University, BsEd, 1964; Montana State University, MIS (Master of Interdisciplinary Studies), 1983. *Principal occupation*: Artist; author; educator. Mr. Amiotte has studied traditional Lakota arts techniques with Christina Standing Bear, 1969-75; Lakota Sacred

Traditions with Peter Cathces, Sr. (novice apprentice, 1972-76; assistant, 1977-82. *Home address*: P.O. Box 471, Custer, SD 57730 (605) 673-4373. *Affiliations*: Art teacher, Woodrow Wilson Jr. High School, Sioux City, IA, 1964-66; instructor of art, Northern State College, Aberdeen, SD, 1966-69; Lakota arts/creative writing teacher, Porcupine Day School, BIA, Porcupine, SD, 1969-71; director of curriculum development, BIA, Aberdeen Area Office, 1971-74; Lakota Studies and art specialist, Little Eagle Day School, BIA, 1975-77; chairperson, Lakota Studies Dept., Standing Rock Community College, Fort Yates, SD, 1977-80; Dept. of Native Studies, Brandon University, Brandon, Manitoba, Canada (visiting assistant professor, 1982-85; adjunct professor of Native Studies, 1985-); artist, writer, consultant on Indian Cultures of the Northern Plains, White Horse Creek, Ltd., Custer, SD, 1985-. Exhibitions, commissions, published art and research, and lectures, too numerous to mention. *Awards, honors*: Recipient of "Outstanding Contribution to Indian Education" Award by State of South Dakota Indian Education Association, 1976; appointed member of the Presidential Advisory Council for the Performing Arts, Kennedy Center, Washington, DC by President Jimmy Carter, 1979-81; recipient of "Excellence in Teaching Award," Native Studies, Standing Rock Community College, Fort Yates, ND, 1980; recipient of State of South Dakota Governor's Award, Biennial Award for Outstanding Creative Achievement in the Arts, Pierre, SD, 1980; recipient of the Bush Leadership Fellowship for advanced study in Native American Sacred Traditions and Native Art History, Bush Foundation, 1980-83; recipient of Distinguished Alumni Award, Northern State College, June 1988; presenter of Richard Thompson Memorial Lecture, Iowa State University, June 1988; appointed four year member of Board, National Foundation for Advancement in the Arts, Miami, FL, June 1988; appointed member of Board of Directors, National Native American Art Studies Association (June 1988); appointed member of Board of Directors, Arts Midwest, Minneapolis, MN (June 1988); appointed member of Planning Committee for Northern Tier States Centennial Symposium Project, Montana State Historical Society, Helena, (June 1988); appointed Commissioner of Indian Arts and Crafts Board (a five commissioner board) by U.S. Secretary of the Interior (June 1988); awarded Honorary Doctorate of Lakota Studies by Oglala Lakota College, June 1988; awarded 14th Annual Artistic Achievement Citation by Board of Trustees, SD Art Museum, April 1989; appointed member of National Board of Directors, Center for Western Studies, Augustana College, Sioux Falls, SD, (Nov. 1990); appointed Senior Advisor to Director, Foundation for the Arts in South Dakota, Rapid City, (Oct. 1990); appointed member of Board of Directors, National Museum of the American Indian, Smithsonian Institute, Washington, DC, (Oct. 1990); co-curator, Plains Section of North American Indian Hall, Museum of Natural History, Smithsonian Institute, Washington, D.C., 1991-; One of 25 artists selected from Western Hemisphere to create a collaborative exhibition, "Celebrations" for the 1993-94 opening of the new National Museum of the American Indian, George Gustave Heye Center, Smithsonian Institute, New York, NY, 1992-. *Published interviews*: Marguerite Mullaney, "Artist Arthur Amiotte" Inside the Black Hills (Fall 1990); Ann Grauvogl, "Artist Keeps Tradition Alive Through

Change," Sioux Falls Argus Leader (Sept. 10, 1989); Joan Morrison, "Lakota Artist Reveals His Vision of the World," Rapid City Journal (Aug. 4, 1988); Hattie Clark, "Art That Spans Two Cultures: Contemporary Artist Arthur Amiotte Draws on His Sioux Heritage to Fuel a Creative Life," The Christian Science Monitor (Aug. 11, 1987); Charles Nauman, "Diverse Work of Arthur Amiotte Reflects His Lakota Heritage," Rapid City Journal (Jan. 20, 1987). Films and Television: Interview in "Somewhere, Sometime: Tribal Arts, 1989," (SD Public TV, 1989); "Interpreting Contemporary Northern Plains Art," a documentary video of a formal lecture by Arthur Amiotte, to students and faculty of Dept. of Anthropology, University of Colorado, Boulder, Terri Berman, Producer (Nov. 1985); "Homecomings," Arthur Amiotte as narrator and interpreter of 21 person exhibit of contemporary Native art of nationally known artists with Northern Plains origins. North Dakota Museum of Arts, Laurel Reuter, Director, 1985; "Amiotte," a biographical film including art work and tracing the career of the artist from 1961 to 1976. University of South Dakota Education TV, June, 1977; "Four Portraits," one of four subjects. University of Mid America Production, 1977.

AMOS, DANDY
(Indian band chief)
Affiliation: Chief, Stoney Indian Band (Bearspaw Group), P.O. Box 40, Morley, Alberta, Canada T0L 1N0 (403) 263-8355.

AMOS, GERALD VICTOR
(Indian band chief)
Affiliation: Kitamaat Indian Band, Haisla, P.O. Box 1101, Kitamaat Village, British Columbia, Canada V0T 2B0 (604) 639-9361.

AMOUSE, FELIX
(Indian band chief)
Affiliation: Chief, Little Shuswap Indian Band, P.O. Box 105, Chase, British Columbia, Canada V0E 1M0 (604) 679-3203.

AMYLEE (Iroquois {Mohawk-Seneca}) 1952-
(consultant, artist, writer)
Born January 3, 1952, Ohio. *Education*: State University of New York, 1976-1979; Kent State University, 1970-1980 (concurrent). *Principal occupation*: Director of Indian organization. *Home address*: Hawk Hollow Private Nature Preserve, Tippecanoe, OH 44699-9612. *Affiliations*: Founder and director, American Indian Rights Association, Kent State University, 1970-1983; Licensed Raptor (Bird of Prey) Rehabilitator (ongoing); Medicine Woman Initiate (ongoing). *Other professional posts*: Member of the Board (past director), lecturer and artist for the Native American Indian Resource Center (NAIRC). *Memberships*: National Wildlife Rehabilitators Association; Earthwalker Learning Lodge. *Awards, honors*: Numerous awards for artistic achievement; her work can be found in selected galleries and at festivals celebrating women's culture. *Interests*: AmyLee has appeared with Native American leaders and dignitaries including Sakokwenonkwas of Akwesasne, Mad Bear, Rolling Thunder, Sun Bear, Grandfather Sky Eagle and Vernon Bellecourt. She has also had the opportunity to serve as a script consultant for the Smithsonian Institution and a character actress in the Public Broadcast System's film, Americas Ethnic Symphony. As member of the board for NAIRC, AmyLee travels over 50,000 miles annually offering lectures, workshops and

retreats. She donates and devotes time to Native and nature projects including a drug and crime rehabilitation facility for recovering Indian youth. *Biographical sources*: Chapter-long interview in recently released, Profiles in Wisdom by Steven McFadden; excerpts from her writing and lectures appears in W abun Wind's, Lightseeds, Kay Gardner's, Sounding the Inner Landscape; to MS. Magazine (November 1991). *Published works*: The Pathfinder Directory: A Guide to Native Americans in the Ohiyo Country (Indian House, 1982); several articles. Presently she is working on two book manuscripts regarding Native W omen's Spirituality and Politics.

ANAWAK, JACK (Nunatsiaq)
(pariliament member)
Affiliation: Parliament Bldgs., Ottawa, ON K1A 0A4 (613) 992-4587.

*ANAYA, MARIA, MPH
(health program director)
Affiliation: Consolidated Tribal Health Program, 562 South Dora St., Ukiah, CA 95482 (707) 462-0488.

ANAYA, S. JAMES (Parasco Apache)
(attorney-professor)
Address & Affiliation: Professor, University of Iowa College of Law , Boyd Law Bldg., Melrose & Byington, Iowa City, IA 52242 (319) 335-9032 (work). *Other professional post*: Staff attorney, Nat'.I Indian Youth Council, Albuquerque, NM.

ANASKAN, VERNON ROSS
(Indian band chief)
Affiliation: Chief, Piapot Indian Band, Box 178, Cupar, Saskatchewan, Canada S0G 0Y0 (306) 561-2701.

ANAWAK, JACK
(association president)
Affiliation: President, Keewatin Inuit Association, Ranklin Inlet, Northwest Territories, Canada X0C 0G0 (819) 979-5301.

ANDERSON, ANDREW
(Indian band chief)
Affiliation: Fairford Indian Band, Fairford, Manitoba, Canada R0C 0X0 (204) 659-5705.

ANDERSON, CARMEN ATKINSON
(Rosebud Sioux) 1938-
(artist; art gallery owner)
Born December 5, 1938, Rosebud, S.D. *Education*: Memphis State University (Nursing). *Principal occupation*: artist, art gallery owner . *Home address*: RR 1, Box 938, Carrollton, MS 38917 (601) 453-6570; 453-9147 (work). *Affiliations*: Emergency Room Nurse in Memphis, TN (17 years); owner , Delta Art Gallery, Greenwood, MS, 1985-. *Community activities*: Coton Landia Museum (board member; art teacher , ceramist), 1988-; Chamber of Commerce, 1987-; Medical Wives Auxiliary (current member). *Interests*: "Have traveled Europe and still do. I will go to Europe this year to photograph for future paintings. Have appeared on television with my art; and have shown my art at the Trail of Tears Show in Tahlequah, OK." *Biographical source*: Who's Who Among the Sioux, 1988.

ANDERSON, EDWARD
(Indian band chief)
Affiliation: Chief, Fairford Indian Band, Fairford, Manitoba, Canada R0C 0X0 (204) 659-5705.

*ANDERSON, ESTHER, M.D.
(chief medical officer)
Affiliation: Aberdeen IHS Area Office, Feeral Bldg., 115 Fourth Ave., SE, Aberdeen, SD 57401 (605) 226-7581.

ANDERSON, ESTHER L. (Arapaho) 1950-
(business owner)
Born September 20, 1950, Casper , Wyo. *Education*: Casper College (Associate of Science, 19710. *Principal occupation*: Business owner . *Home address*: 5003 Alcova Rte. #20, Casper , WY 82604 (307) 237-7985 (home); (307) 235-0002 (work). *Affiliation*: Member, Equal Opportunity & DBE Committee for the Associated General Contractors of W yoming. *Community activities*: Former county coordinator for Farm Bureau, ten years as election clerk. *Membership*: Associated General Contractors of W yoming, 1985-.

ANDERSON, GENEAL (Paiute)
(tribal chairperson)
Affiliation: Paiute Indian Tribe of Utah, 600 North 100 East, Paiute Dr ., Cedar City, UT 84720 (801) 586-1111.

ANDERSON, GREG
(school administrator)
Affiliation: Eufaula Dormitory, Swadsley Dr ., Eufaula, OK 74432 (918) 689-2522.

*ANDERSON, JOHN
(association president)
Affiliation: Chattanooga Intertribal Association, P.O. Box 71585, Chattanooga, TN 37407 (615) 266-6551.

*ANDERSON, JOSEPH (Tuscarora)
(tribal chief)
Affiliation: Tuscarora Tribe, 5616 W almore Rd., Lewiston, NY 14092 (716) 297-4990.

*ANDERSON, KENNY (Paiute)
(Indian colony chairperson)
Affiliation: Las V egas Indian Colony Council, One Paiute Dr . Las Vegas, NV 89106 (702) 386-3926.

*ANDERSON, LARRY
(school principal/supt.)
Affiliation: Two Eagle River School, P.O. Box 362, Pablo, MT 59855 (406) 675-0292.

*ANDERSON, LAURA (Cherokee)
(instructor of Native American studies)
Affiliation: Native American Studies Program, University of Oklahoma, 455 W . Lindsey, Rm. 804, Norman, OK 73019 (405) 325-2312.

ANDERSON, MARJORIE (Chippewa)
(tribal chairperson)
Affiliation: Mille Lacs Reservation Business Committee, HRC 67, Box 194, Onamia, MN 56359 (612) 532-4181.

*ANDERSON, MICHAEL, M.D.
(medical director)
Affiliation: Prairie Island Community Council, 1158 Island Blvd., W elch, MN 55089 (612) 385-2554.

*ANDERSON, NORMAN (Aleut)
(AK village council president)
Affiliation: Naknek Native V illage, P.O. Box 106, Naknek, AK 99633 (907) 246-4210.

*ANDERSON, RODNEY (Eskimo)
(AK village council president)
Affiliation: Native V illage of Chignik Lagoon, P .O. Box 57, Chignik Lagoon, AK 99565 (907) 840-2206.

ANDERSON, WILLIAM L. 1941-
(professor of history)
Born February 18, 1941, Monticello, Ark. *Education*: University of Alabama, Tuscaloosa, B.A., 1963, M.A., 1966, Ph.D., 1974. *Principal occupation*: Professor of history. *Address*: Box 888, Cullowhee, NC 28723 (704) 227-7243 (of fice). *Affiliation*: Western Carolina University, Cullowhee, NC, 1969-. *Other professional posts*: Member, Editorial Board, "Journal of Cherokee Studies"; member , Advisory Board of Museum of Cherokee Indian, Cherokee, NC. *Memberships*: North Carolina Historical Society; Oklahoma Historical Society. *Awards, honors*: Gustavus Myers Human Rights Award for book, Cherokee Removal: Before & After. *Interests*: Cherokee history. *Published works*: Co-author, Guide to Cherokee Documents in Foreign Archives (Scarecrow Press, 1983); co-author , Southern Treasures (Globe Pequot, 1987); editor, Cherokee Removal: Before and After (University of Georgia Press, 1991); articles on Cherokee history in "North Carolina Historical Review," "Journal of Cherokee Studies", "Georgia Historical Quarterly ," "Native Press Research Journal"; and in "The American Revolution: An Encyclopedia."

ANDERSON, WILLIAM, III (Inuit)
(association president)
Affiliation: President, Labrador Inuit Association, P.O. Box 70, Nain, Labrador , Canada A0P 1L0 (709) 922-2942.

*ANDREAS CHERYL (Paiute)
(tribal council chairperson)
Affiliation: Big Pine Reservation, P .O. Box 700, Big Pine, CA 93513 (619) 938-2003.

*ANDREOLI, ANDREW
(program director)
Affiliation: Indian Teacher & Education Personnel Program, Humboldt State University , Spidell House 85, Arcata, CA 95521 (707) 826-3672.

ANDREW, FRASER
(Indian band chief)
Affiliation: Mount Currie Indian Band, Box 165, Mount Currie, British Columbia, Canada V0N 2K0 (604) 894-61 15.

*ANDREW, TREFIM (Athapascan)
(AK village council president)
Affiliation: Iguigig V illage Council, P .O. Box 4008, Iguigig, AK 99613 (907) 533-321 1.

ANDREWS, LAWRENCE
(Indian band chief)
Affiliation: Mowachant, Box 459, Gold River , British Columbia, Canada V0P 1G0 (604) 283-2532.

*ANELON, HARVEY (Athapascan)
(AK village council president)
Affiliation: Native Village of Iliamna Council, P .O. Box 286, Iliamna, AK 99580 (907) 571-1246.

ANNETTE, FRANKLIN
(BIA agency supt.)
Affiliation: Minnesota Agency, Bureau of Indian Affairs, Route 3, Box 1 12, Cass Lake, MN 56633 (218) 335-6913.

ANNETTE, KATHLEEN, M.D.
(IHS - chief medical officer)
Affiliation : Chief medical of ficer, Bemidji Area Office, Indian Health Service, 203 Federal Bldg., Bemidji, MN 56601 (218) 759-3412.

ANOATUBBY, BILL (Chickasaw) 1945-
(government administration)
Born November 8, 1945, Tishomingo, Okla. *Education*: Murray State College, A.S., 1970; East Central University, B.S., 1972. *Principle occupation* : Government administration. *Address*: Chickasaw Nation of Oklahoma, P .O. Box 1548, Ada, OK 74820 (405) 436-2603. *Affiliations*: Chickasaw Nation (director of tribal health services, 1975; director of accounting dept., 1976-78; special assistant to governor & controller , 1978-79; lieutenant governor , 1979-87; governor, 1987-). *Military service* : U.S. Army National Guard, 1963-71 (staf f Sgt..). *Memberships*: Inter-Tribal Council of the Five Civilized Tribes, 1978-; Ada Chamber of Commerce (board of directors, 1988-); Oklahoma City University (board of trustees, 1991-); Oklahoma State Chamber of Commerce & Industry (board of directors, 1991). *Awards, honors* : Appointed to the Oklahoma Indian Affairs Commission, 1987, by Oklahoma Governor Henry Bellmon; re-appointed by Governor David W alters in 1991.

ANSPACH, ALLEN J. (Blackfeet) 1951-
(BIA agency supt.)
Born October 25, 1951, Lander , Wyo. *Education*: University of Arizona, BS, 1975. *Principal occupation* : BIA agency supt. *Address*: Rt. 1, Box 9-C, Parker, AZ 85344 (602) 669-71 11. *Affiliations* : Supt., San Carlos Agency, Bureau of Indian Affairs, San Carlos, AZ, 1990-93; Supt. Colorado River Agency, Bureau of Indian Affairs, Parker, AZ, 1993-. *Other professional posts* : Vocational agricultural instructor , tribal operations specialist, land operations of ficer. *Awards, honors* : Chosen to participate in the 1982-83 Dept. of Interior, Departmental Manager Development Program. *Interests* : "When not occupied with my job, I enjoy raising my family with the able assistance of my wife Flo. Our children, Michael and Andrea, enjoy the outdoors with us where we like to hunt, fish and camp."

*ANTELL, JUDITH A.
(program director)
Affiliation : American Indian Studies Program, University of W yoming, Rm. 109A, Anthropology Bldg., Laramie, WY 82701 (307) 766-6521.

ANTELL, WILL D. (Minn. Chippewa) 1935-
(educational administration)
Born October 2, 1935, White Earth, Minn. *Education*: Bemidji State University, BS, 1959; Mankato State University, MS, 1964; University of Minnesota, Ed.D., 1973. *Principal occupation* : Educational administration. *Home address* : 317 Lake St., Bayport, MN 55003 (612) 439-5998; 296-6458 (of fice). *Affiliation*: Teacher, Janesville (MN) Public Schools, 1959-63; teacher , School District #834, Stillwater , MN, 1963-68; University of Minnesota Faculty , 1969-73; lecturer , Harvard Graduate School of Education, 1973-74; Minnesota Dept. of Education, Minneapolis, MN (human relations consultant, 1968-69; assistant commissioner of special & compensatory education, 1974-82; assistant commissioner of education for special services, 1982-83; manager , 1983-87; manager , Equal Educational Opportunities, 1987-91; manager , Indian Education, 1991-). *Other professional posts* :

Consultant: to BIA and U.S. Dept. of Education, 1968-78; appointed by former Governor W endell Anderson to serve on Adult Corrections Commissions, 1970-73; consultant to U.S. Dept. of State, 1978; evaluator , North Central Association of Schools, 1983. *Community activities* : American Red Cross (board of directors, 1988-89); Anishinabe Job Developers Board of Directors (president, 1988-); Indian Center School Board of Directors, 1989-90; American Indian Chamber of Commerce (treasurer , board member, 1989-91); American Indian Opportunity Center Fundraiser Committee, 1990-91; Bush Foundation, Selection Committee Judge for Bush Foundation Fellowships, 1990-91; Juel Fairbanks Chemical Dependency Center Fundraiser Committee, 1991-; Commission on Judicial Selection, Supreme Court Appointment for Tenth Judicial District, 1990-91; Trustee and Board of Directors, William Mitchell College of Law, 1990-91; Judge, Bicentennial Competition on the Constitution and the Bill of Rights, 1991. *Memberships* : American Association of School Administrators; Minnesota Association of School Administrators; National Indian Education Association (charter member; president, 1970-72); National Advisory Council on Indian Education (member, 1973-78; chairperson, 1974); Board of Regents, Institute of American Indian Arts (member, 1971-82; president, 1976-78); Phi Beta Kappa, 1988. *Awards, honors* : Minnesota Indian Scholarship Recipient, 1955-59; Federal Indian Scholarship Recipient, 1956-59; NDEA Fellowships: Northern Michigan University , 1965, University of Minnesota, 1968; Bush Fellow, 1972-74; Education Policy Fellowship, 1975; Hubert Humphrey Institute Scholarship, 1983-84; Outstanding Alumni Award, Bemidji State University, 1986. *Published works* : Between Two Milestones, The First Report to the President of the U.S. (National Council of Indian Opportunity , 1972); Designs for Library Services (University of Minnesota, 1972); Indian Educational Leadership, Sr . Editor (ERIC-Cress, 1974); American Indian Leadership Training Programs (ERIC-Cress, 1974); Culture, Psychological Characteristics, and Socio-Economic Status in Educational Program Development Native Americans (ERIC-Cress, 1974); Articles: "Education of the American Indian," Current History (Vol. 67, Dec. 1974); "Definition of the Critical and Unique Problems and Concerns in the Education of American Indians and the Identification of Alternative Solutions to These Problems," College Entrance Exam. Board, 1978.

ANTHONY, DICK
(AK village council vice president)
Affiliation : N ative V illage of Nightmute, Nightmute, AK 99690 (907) 647-6213.

ANTIQUIA, CLARENCE (Tlingit) 1940-
(federal government administrator)
Born April 16, 1940, Sitka, Alaska. *Education* : Sheldon Jackson Junior College, Sitka, Alaska, 1958-59. *Principal occupation* : Federal government administrator. *Home address* : Box 1111, Juneau, Alaska 99802. *Affiliations*: Area director, Bureau of Indian Affairs, Juneau, Alaska, 1965-1975. *Awards, honors* : Outstanding Performance Awards, BIA, 1965, '67, '70. *Interests* : Public administration, government, personnel management, race relations, Indian af fairs.

ANTOINE, JIM
(Indian band chief)
Affiliation : Chief, Fort Simpson Indian Band, P .O.

Box 469, Fort Simpson, Northwest Territories, Canada X0E 0N0 (403) 695-3131.

ANTOINE, GORDON
(Indian band chief)
Affiliation : Coldwater Indian Band, Bag 4600, Merritt, British Columbia, Canada V0K 2B0 (604) 378-6174.

ANTOINE, JANEEN (Sicangu Lakota) 1953-
(arts administrator)
Born September 24, 1953, W inner, S.D. *Education* : Stanford University , 1973-77. *Principal occupation* : Arts administrator. *Home address* : 375 Jayne Ave., Oakland, CA 94610 (510) 495-7600. *Affiliation* : Co-founder , executive director , American Indian Contemporary Arts, San Francisco, CA, 1983-. *Other professional posts* : Board of Directors, V anguard Public Foundation, San Francisco, CA; past board member: Intertribal Friendship House, Oakland, and San Jose Indian Center . *Awards, honors* : City and County of San Francisco, Board of Supervisors, Special Community Commendation, 1991, 1983. *Interests* : Tri-lingual (Spanish, French, English).

ANTOINE, TEDDY LEE
(Indian band chief)
Affiliation : Poundmaker Indian Band, Box 220, Paynton, Saskatchewan, Canada S0M 2J0 (306) 398-4971.

*ANTONE, MARTIN, Sr. (Papago/Pima)
(tribal council chairperson)
Affiliation : Ak Chin Indian Community Council, 42507 N. Peters & Nall Rd., Maricopa, AZ 85239 (602) 568-2227.

*ANTONIO, CHRISTINE
(associate director)
Affiliation : Office of Tribal Activities, Albuquerque Area Indian Health Services, 505 Marquette Ave., NW, Suite 1502, Albuquerque, NM 87102 (505) 766-2151.

ANYON, ROGER (Zuni Pueblo)
(archaeology program director)
Affiliation : Zuni Archaeology Program, Pueblo of Zuni, P.O. Box 339, Zuni, NM 87327 (505) 782-4814.

*ANYWAUSH, JOELLEN
(health director)
Affiliation : White Earth Band Clinic, P .O. Box 418, White Earth, MN 56591 (218) 983-3285.

APACHITO, GEORGE (Navajo)
(school chairperson)
Affiliation : Alamo Navajo School, P.O. Box 907, Magdalena, NM 87825 (505) 854-2543.

*APACHITO, PATSY (Navajo)
(radio station manager)
Affiliation : KABR - 1500 AM, Alamo Navajo School Board, P.O. Box 907, Magdalena, NM 87825 (505) 854-2632.

APODACA, MARY ANN
(school principal)
Affiliation : Laguna Elementary School, P .O. Box 191, Laguna, NM 87026 (505) 552-9200.

APODACA, RAYMOND D. (Ysleta del Sur Pueblo) (Tigua Indian T ribe of Texas) 1946-
(administrator)
Born October 15, 1946, Las Cruces, N.M. *Education*: New Mexico State University , BA, 1969,

MA, 1976. *Principal occupation*: Administrator. *Address & Affiliation*: Executive director, Texas Indian Commission (State of Texas), P.O. Box 2960, Austin, Texas (512) 458-1203 (1983-87, 1990-). *Past professional post*: Ysleta del Sur Pueblo, Ysleta Station, El Paso, TX, 1987-90. *Military service*: U.S. Air Force, 1969-1972. *Community activities*: New Mexico State University All-Indian Adult Advisory Board, 1976-; Citizens' Advisory Board, ETCOM Public Radio (El Paso, Texas), 1980-1985; OPM--Intergovernmental Committee on Indian Affairs, Southwest Region, 1982-; University of Texas, Austin, El Paso, Master of Science in Social Work Program, Advisory Council, 1984-; Texas State Committee on the Protection of Human Remains and Sacred Objects (American Indian) (co-chairman, 1984-). *Memberships*: National Indian Education Association, 1973-1980; National Congress of American Indians, 1973- (coordinator-Religious Freedom Act); Governors' Interstate Indian Council, 1977- (national president, 1985-1986); Texas American Indian Sesquicentennial Association (executive board member, 1985-); Texas State Agency Business Administrators Association, 1982-; North American Indian Museums Association, 1977-1980. *Awards, honors*: Colonel Aide-de-Camp, Governor, State of New Mexico, 1977. *Interests*: History, government, theology, education. *Biographical source*: To Live in Two Worlds, by Brent Ashabrenner (Dodd, Mead & Co., 1984.) *Published work*: Directory of Information on Health Careers for American Indians (ERIC/CRESS, National Education Laboratory Publishers, 1977.)

*APOKEDAD, CHRISTOPHER (Aleut)
(AK village council president)
Affiliation: Levelock Village, P.O. Box 70, Levelock, AK 99625 (907) 287-3030.

*APOLIONA, HAUNANI (Hawaiian)
(association president)
Affiliation: Alu Like, Inc., 1624 Mapunapuna St., Honolulu, HI 96819 (808) 836-8940.

APPLEGATE, ROGER H., M.D.
(clinical director)
Affiliation: Fort Hall PHS Indian Health Center, P.O. Box 717, Fort Hall, ID 83203 (208) 238-2400.

APSASSIN, JOE
(Indian band chief)
Affiliation: Chief, Blueberry River Indian Band, P.O. Box 3009, Buick, British Columbia, Canada V0C 2R0 (604) 630-2584.

ARAGON, ARNOLD (Crow-Pueblo) 1953-
(artist)
Born July 9, 1953, Crow Agency, Mont. Education: American Indian Art Institute, Santa Fe, N.M. (Art/Sculpture), 1979 graduate; University of Nevada, Reno, 1980-1984. Principal occupation: Professional artist. Home address: P.O. Box 64, Walker River Reservation, Schurz, Nev. 89427. Affiliation: Rites of Passage Wilderness Camp, Schurz, Nevada. Other professional posts: Art consultant, board member, Nevada Urban Indians--Earth Window. Interests: Sculpturing using hand tools. His art includes water colors, pastels and pencil drawings. Arnold's sculptures are in various galleries and museums throughout the West as well as private collections throughout the country. He enjoys travel and the outdoors.

ARCAND, EUGENE
(executive director)
Affiliation: Indian & Metis Friendship Centre, 14th St. & 1st Ave. East, Prince Albert, Sask., Canada S6V 6Z1 (306) 764-3431.

ARCAND, JOSEPH STANLEY
(Indian band chief)
Affiliation: Alexander First Nation, Box 510, Morinville, Alberta, Canada T0G 1P0 (403) 939-5887.

ARCHAMBAULT, DAVE LEON
(Standing Rock Sioux)
(educational administrator)
Education: Black Hills State College, Spearfish, SD, B.S. (Secondary Education), 1976; Pennsylvania State University, M.S. (Educational Administration), 1982. *Principal occupation*: Educational administrator. *Address*: P.O. Box 519, Fort Yates, ND 58538 (701) 854-7246. *Affiliations*: Assistant principal & Jr. High Principal, Little Wound School, Kyle, SD (8 years); acting recreation director, United Tribes Technical College, Bismarck, ND (3 years); president, Standing Rock College, Fort Yates, ND, 1987-. *Other professional posts*: American Indian Higher Education Consortium, (1972-; vice-president, 1988; president, 1989-); board member, North Dakota Humanities Council; secretary, Sitting Bull Historical Society. Community activities: Board member, American Indian College Fund. *Memberships*: National Indian Activities Association, (Board of Directors, 1972-82 & 1987); National Indian Education Association, 1975-; American Association of Colleges & Junior Colleges, 1987-. *Awards, honors*: South Dakota Cross Country Coach of the Year, 1980; South Dakota Indian Educator of the Year, 1982; National Indian Basketball Coach of the Year, 1980. *Interests*: "Most interested in educational reform. Masters degree work was done on rationale and justification to change K-12 systems to better meet the needs of Indian learners. (I am an) advocate of the literacy work done by Paulo Freire, author of "Pedogogy of the Oppressed."

ARCHAMBAULT, JOALLYN
(Standing Rock Sioux) 1942-
(anthropologist, program director)
Born February 13, 1942, Claremore, Okla. *Education*: University of California, Berkeley, B.A., 1970, M.A., 1971, Ph.D., 1984 (Dissertation topic: "The Gallup Ceremonial," A study of patronage within a contemporary context of Indian-white relationships). *Principal occupation*: Director of American Indian Programs. *Address*: National Museum of Natural History, NHB 112, Smithsonian Institution, Washington, DC 20560 (202) 357-4760 (work). *Affiliations*: Lecturer in Native American Studies, University of California, Berkeley, 1976-1979; Department chairperson & lecturer in Ethnic Studies Program, California College of Arts & Crafts, 1979-83; research associate, Center for the Study of Race, Crime and Social Policy of Cornell University, 1980-82; field ethnographer, Sonoma State Foundation, 1983-1984; assistant professor in anthropology, University of Wisconsin, Milwaukee, 1983-1986; director, American Indian Programs, Smithsonian Institution, Washington, DC, 1986-. *Other professional posts*: Faculty positions at the University of California, Berkeley, University of New Mexico, University of Wisconsin, Navajo Community College, et al. *Community activities*: Board member: California Indian Education Association, 1967-70; Native Ameri-

can Scholarship Fund, Inc., 1976-77; City of Berkeley Minority Elder Project, 1976-77; Committee to Stop Hanta Yo, 1979-82; advisory council member, Foundation for Illinois Archaeology, Native American Studies Program, 1980-81. *Memberships*: American Anthropological Association; Native American Art Studies Association (vice-president, 1982-85); Society for Applied Anthropology; American Ethnological Society; Anthropology Society of Washington. *Awards, honors*: Ford Foundation Fellowship; National Endowment for the Humanities Travel Grant; numerous art awards dating from 1969 through 1980; art exhibits (group and one-man shows); examples of art in permanent collection of the Heard Museum, the Navajo Tribal Museum, the Indian Arts & Crafts Board, the Red Cloud Cultural Center, and numerous private collections. *Interests*: "Primary interests are in the areas of art and material culture, political anthropology, ethnic relations, Indian-white relations, and patronage systems. I curated an exhibit titled Plains Indian Arts - Change and Continuity for the National Museum of Natural History. The exhibit traveled nationally in 1989." *Published works*: Articles; *In-preparation*: An Annotated Bibliography of Sources on Plains Indian Art (G.K. Hall & Co.); and The Uses of Non-Visual Sacred Material in Museums by Contemporary Native Americans (Buffalo Bill Historical Center).

ARCHIBALD, CHARLES
(Indian band chief)
Affiliation: Chief, Seabird Island Indian Band, P.O. Box 650, Agassiz, British Columbia, Canada V0M 1A0 (604) 796-2177.

ARCHIBALD, PETER
(Indian band chief)
Affiliation: Chief, New Post Indian Band, Box 1836, Cochrane, Ontario, Canada P0L 1C0 (705) 272-5795.

ARCHIE, SAM
(Indian band chief)
Affiliation: Skowkale Indian Band, Box 365, Sardis, British Columbia, Canada V2R 1A7 (604) 792-0730.

*ARCHULETA, DAVE
(enterprise director)
Affiliation: Shoshone-Bannock Gaming Enterprise, P.O. Box 868, Fort Hall, ID 83203.

ARCHULETA, MARGARET
(museum curator)
Affiliation: Curator of Fine Arts, The Heard Museum, 22 E. Monte Vista Rd., Phoenix, AZ 85004 (602) 252-8840.

ARFSTEN, MICHAEL
(executive director)
Affiliation: American Indian Health Care Association, 245 East 6th St., Suite 499, St. Paul, MN 55101 (612) 293-0233.

ARKEKETA, SUSAN M. (Otoe Missouria-
Muscogee Creek) 1954-
(writer/instructor)
Born September 5, 1954, Tulsa, Okla. *Education*: University of Oklahoma, B.A. (Journalism), 1978, M.A. (Communications), 1983. *Principal occupation*: Writer/instructor. *Address*: 1538 Eddingham Dr., Lawrence, KS 66046 (913) 842-6672 (home); (913) 749-8477 (work). *Affiliations*: Director, Native American Journalists Associa-

tion, 1987-90; writer/editor , Native American Rights Fund, Boulder , CO, 1985-91; Instructor of journalism, Haskell Indian Junior College, Lawrence, KS, 1991-. *Other professional posts*: Freelance writer; consultant-proposal writer; writer/editor, public relations. *Community activities*: Co-chair, Indian Nations Rendesvous & Trade Fair , 1991, Denver , CO. *Memberships*: Kansas Indian Education Association; Native American Journalists Association; College Media Advisors. *Awards, honors*: Miss Indian America, 1978; Outstanding Young Woman of America, 1982, 1986 & 1987; Indian National Finals, Rodeo Trade Fair.

ARMAGOST, JAMES GRAYHAWK (Mohican) 1945- (silversmith & lapidary)
Born July 8, 1945, Johnstown, Penn. *Education*: Accredited GRE - two year college. *Principal occupation*: Silversmith and lapidary . *Home Address*: 13105 Penndale Lane, Fairfax, V A 22033 (703) 631-6368. *Affiliation*: Owner, The Silver Phoenix, Oakton, V irginia. The Silver Phoenix has been promoting Native American crafts for 15 years. *Military service*: U.S. Army Special Forces. *Community activities*: American Indian Inter-Tribal Cultural Organization (member , board of directors.) *Memberships*: American Indian Society of W ashington, DC; American Indian Intertribal Cultural Association. *Awards, honors*: Numerous first place and Best of Show Awards for his jewelry in assorted regional competitions (Native American and non-Native American). *Art form*: His Navajo leafwork and multi-level chizeled boarders are some of the cleanest to be found. The geometrics in his overlay styles are crisp and exact, and his animals, plants and people are nearly animated. He has also produced breathtaking pieces blending inlaid stone and highly polished metal with flawless skill. He has walked away with top prizes in every competition he has ever entered.

ARNOLD, RICHARD W. (Southern Paiute) (Indian Center director)
Education: Mt. San Antonio College (W alnut, CA) AA (Police Science), 1973; Cal-State University, Long Beach, BS (Criminal Justice/Administration, Certificate & Minor in American Indian Studies), 1975, MS (Educational Psychology/Counseling), 1977. *Principal occupation*: Executive director. *Home address*: P.O. Box 73, Pahrump, NV 89041 (702) 647-5842 (work). *Affiliation*: Las Vegas Indian Center, Las Vegas, NV, 1977-. *Other professional posts*: Nevada State Steering Committee on Indian Education; U.S. Senate appointed Delegate to the White House Conference on Indian Education; Commissioner, Nevada Indian Commission; consultant to: U.S. Dept. of Labor Division of Indian & Native American Programs & U.S. Dept. of Energy; member, Board of Trustees, Nevada Business Services, Nevada State Board of Social Workers-Advisory Committee on Continuing Education; Minority Outreach Council; Delegate to the White House Conference on Indian Education; Chairperson, Nevada State Education Steering Committee; Consultant to Yucca Mountain Cultural Resources Program & Nevada Test Site-American Indian Religious Freedom Act Compliance Program. *Community activities*: Clark County Police Community Relations Board; Preservation Association of Clark County; Federal Emergency Management Board of Clark County; Comprehensive Hous-

ing Affordability Strategy Task Force, City of Las Vegas & Clark County; American Red Cross Long Range Planning Committee, Clark County; Overall Economic Development Plan Committee & Training Conference; Fair Housing Task Force - City of Las V egas; Affirmative Action Advisory Committee. *Memberships*: National Adult Indian Education Association; Nevada State Board of Social W orkers; National Indian Education Association; National Indian Employment & Training Association; National Urban Indian Council. *Awards, honors*: Letters of Commendation: City of Las V egas, Clark County, Governor-State of Nevada, U.S. Dept. of Energy, National Indian & Native American Employment & Training Conference, Las V egas Chamber of Commerce; Boulder City Rotary Club. *Interests*: Community development - major area of vocational interest, including facilitating motivational seminars for American Indians; enjoy public speaking and representing American Indian interests in associated issues; enjoy traveling, collecting and restoring antiques.

ARNOUSE, FELIX (Indian band chief)
Affiliation: Little Shuswap Indian Band, Box 1100, Chase, British Columbia, Canada V0E 1M0 (604) 679-3203.

ARQUETTE, DAVID (Mohawk) 1963- (environmental specialist)
Born August 29, 1963, Rochester , N.Y. *Education*: Canton (NY) Agricultural & Technical College, AAS, 1984; Rochester Institute of Technology, B.T., 1991. *Principal occupation*: Environmental specialist. *Affiliation*: Environmentalist, St. Regis Mohawk Tribe, Hogansburg, NY, 1991-. *Memberships*: American Indian Science and Engineering Society (AISES); American Society of Civil Engineers. *Awards, honors*: A.T. Anderson Award, AISES; Frederick Douglas Scholarship, Minority Student Affairs Office, R.I.T.; Merit Award for Excellence in Leadership and Community Service, R.I.T . *Interests*: First National People of Color Environmental Conference, Washington, DC - protecting the rights of minorities and the environment; Jame Bay II - involved in helping the Cree and Inuit people protect their lands and culture from degradation of dams being built by Hydro-Quebec.

ARROW, DENNIS WAYNE 1949- (professor of law)
Born July 27, 1949, Chicago, Ill. *Education*: George Washington University, BA, 1970; California Western School of Law , JD, 1974; Harvard University, LLM, 1975. *Principal occupation*: Professor of law . *Home address*: 825 N.W. 139th St., Edmond, OK 73013 (405) 521-5361 (work). *Affiliation*: Professor of Law , 1975-, associate director, Native American Legal Resource Center, 1988-, Oklahoma City University , Oklahoma City, OK. *Community activities*: Oklahoma Association of Scholars (president); Oklahoma Constitution Revision Commission (member). *Memberships*: Oklahoma Indian Bar Association (president, Oklahoma City Chapter , 1989-90); American Indian Bar Association. *Awards, honors*: Outstanding Graduate-Level Professor , Oklahoma City University , 1990. *Interests*: American Indian law (sovereignty issues); constitutional law (state and federal); U.S. Supreme Court litigation.

ASETOYER, CHARON (Comanche) 1951- (executive director)
Born March 24, 1951, San Jose, Calif. *Education*: School of International Training (Masters of International Administration & Masters of International Management), 1983. *Principal occupation*: Executive director-Indian women's center. *Address*: P.O. Box 572, Lake Andes, SD 57356 (605) 487-7072. *Affiliation*: Native American Women's Health Education Resource Center, Native American Community Board, Lake Andes, SD, 1988-. *Other professional post*: Editor, Wicozanni W owapi, newsletter. *Memberships*: National W omen's Network (executive board); South Dakota Coalition of V iolence & Sexual Assault, Advisory Committee for Girls, Inc. *Awards, honors*: "Women of V ision Award," by Ms Foundation. Interests: Reproductive rights for indigenous women. *Biographical sources*: "Moving the Mountain," by Flora Davis in Mother Jones, Jan. 1990; Ms. Magazine, July/Aug. 1991. *Published works*: Women, AIF+DS & Activism (collective of works by women)(South End Press, 1990).

*ASHBY, RICKIE (Eskimo) (AK village council president)
Affiliation: Native Village of Noatak, P.O. Box 89, Noatak, AK 99761 (907) 485-2173.

ASHINI, DANIEL (Indian band chief)
Affiliation: First Nation Council of North W est River, Box 160, Sheshatshit, North W est River, Labrador, Newfoundland, Canada A0P 1M0 (709) 497-8522.

ASPA, AMELIA (tribal librarian)
Affiliation: Colorado River Indian Tribes Public Library, Route 1, Box 23-B, Parker , AZ 85344 (602) 669-9211.

ASSINEWAI, MAXIE (Indian band chief)
Affiliation: Sheguiandah Indian Band, Box 101, Sheguiandah, Ontario, Can. P0P 1W0 (705) 368-2781.

ATANASOFF, DAVID J. (school principal)
Affiliation: Lake Valley Navajo School, Drawer 748, Crownpoint, NM 87313 (505) 786-5392.

ATCITTY, THOMAS (Indian academy headmaster)
Affiliation: Headmaster, Navajo Mission Academy, 1200 West Apache, Farmington, NM 87401 (505) 326-6571.

*ATENCIO, BENJAMIN (BIA education field officer)
Affiliation: Bureau of Indian Affairs, Albuquerque Education Field Of fice, P.O. Box 26567, Albuquerque, NM 87125 (505) 766-3850.

ATKINSON, JERRY (organization president)
Affiliation: Aboriginal Research Club, Dearborn Historical Museum, 915 Brady Rd., Dearborn, MI 48124 (313) 565-3000.

ATKINSON, LA VERNE D. (Navajo) 1934-
(teacher)
Born July 3, 1934, Ganado, Ariz. *Education*: University of Minnesota, B.S., 1960. *Principal occupation*: Teacher. *Home address*: P.O. Box 1450, Window Rock, Ariz. 86515. *Affiliation*: Program specialist, Cultural Awareness Center Trilingual Institute, Albuquerque, N.M., 1976-. *Other professional posts*: Steering committee, Native American Bilingual Education Assn. *Memberships*: New Mexico Association for Bilingual Education; Arizona Bilingual Association; Native American Bilingual Education Association. *Interests*: Mainly interested in bilingual, bicultural education for the Native Americans.

ATLOOKAN, SOLOMON
(Indian band chief)
Affiliation: Chief, Fort Hope Indian Band, P.O. Box 70, Eabamet Lake, via Pickle Lake, Ontario, Canada P0T 1L0 (807) 242-7361.

*ATOLE, LEONARD (Jicarilla Apache)
(tribal council president)
Affiliation: Jicarilla Apache Tribal Council, P.O. Box 507, Dulce, NM 87528 (505) 759-3242.

ATORUK, BEN (Eskimo)
(AK village council president)
Affiliation: Kiana Traditional Council, P.O. Box 69, Kiana, AK 99749 (907) 475-2109.

ATTACHIE, GERRY
(Indian band chief)
Affiliation: Doig River Indian Band, Box 55, Rose Prairie, British Columbia, Canada V0C 2H0 (604) 787-4466.

*ATTAKAI, SHAWN (Navajo) 1973-
(student)
Born May 30, 1973, Monument Valley, Utah. *Education*: Dartmouth College, B.A., 1995. *Address*: P.O. Box 1818, Chinle, AZ 86503. *Membership*: American Indian Science & Engineering Society (regional representative for Northeast, 1993-94; Dartmouth College AISES chapter president, 1991-93).

*ATTATAYUK, GEORGE
(administrative officer)
Affiliation: Barrow PHS Alaska Native Hospital, Barrow, AK 99723 (907) 852-461 1

*ATTEAN, PRISCILLA A.
(liaison)
Affiliation: Maine Tribal/State Relations Office, 6 River Rd., Indian Head, ME 04468 (207) 827-7776.

*ATTI, WILLIE (Eskimo)
(AK village council president)
Affiliation: Kwigillingok Native Village, P.O. Box 49, Kwigillingok, AK 99622 (907) 588-81 14.

ATTOCKNIE, KENNETH
(executive director)
Affiliation: American Indians for Development, P.O. Box 117, 236 W. Main St., Meriden, CT 06450 (203) 238-4009.

ATWELL, CLARENCE, Jr. (Yokut)
(tribal chairperson)
Affiliation: Santa Rosa General Council, P.O. Box 8, Lemoore, CA 93245 (209) 924-1278.

AUBIN, GAETANE
(Indian band chief)
Affiliation: Malecites de Viger Indian Band, 3400 boul. Losch, Suite 39, St-Hubert, Quebec, Canada J3Y 5T6 (514) 656-9731.

AUBREY, JOHN
(committee chairperson)
Affiliation: Committee on Library Services for American Indian People, American Indian Library Association, American Library Association, Office of Outreach Services, 50 East Huron St., Chicago, IL 60611 (312) 944-6780.

AUDY, CHARLES
(Indian band chief)
Affiliation: Chief, Indian Birch Band, Birch River, Manitoba, Canada R0L 0E0 (204) 236-4201.

AUGUSTINE, ROGER J.
(Indian band chief)
Affiliation: Eel Ground Indian Band, Site 3, Box 9, RR #1, Newcastle, New Brunswick, Canada E1V 3L8 (506) 622-2181.

AUSTIN, JIM
(village council president)
Affiliation: Hoonah Indian Association, P.O. Box 602, Hoonah, AK 99829 (907) 945-3600.

AUSTIN, PAUL S.
(director-Indian center)
Affiliation: The American Indian Center of Arkansas, 2 Van Circle, Suite 2, Little Rock, AR 72207 (501) 666-9032.

*AUSTIN, THOMAS L.
(IHS tribal operations)
Affiliation: Portland Area Office IHS, 1220 S.W. Third Ave., Rm. 476, Portland, OR 97204 (503) 326-2020.

*AVERY, PAUL
(school principal)
Affiliation: Lummi High School, 2522 Kwina Rd., Bellingham, WA 98226 (206) 676-2772.

AVEY, GARY
(publisher/editor)
Born June 5, 1940, Phoenix, Ariz. *Education*: Arizona State University, BS, 1965, MA, 1975. *Principal occupation*: Publisher/editor. *Home address*: 35 E. Pierson St., Phoenix, AZ 85012 (602) 277-0636; 252-2236 (work). *Affiliation*: Publisher/editor, Native Peoples magazine, Phoenix, AZ, 1987-. *Other professional posts*: Editor-in-chief, Arizona Highways magazine; deputy-director, The Heard Museum, Phoenix. *Military service*: U.S. Army, 1965-67 (Capt. 2nd Armored Cavalry Regiment, East German border). *Community activities*: St. Lukes Hospital (board member); St. Lukes Behavioral Health Center; DeGrazia Arts & Cultural Foundation Board (member); Phoenix Arts Commission; Environmental Commission; Heard Museum. *Memberships*: Western Publishers Association; Regional Publishers Association; Rotary International. *Awards, honors*: Awards for magazine design from: Western Publishers Association, New York Art Directors Club, Phoenix Society for the Visual Arts, and Regional Publishers Association. *Interests*: "I have been fortunate that my work has allowed me to travel extensively, globally and live in Mexico, 1959-60, Germany, 1965-67, as well as Nevada and Washington. Much of my personal time is spent as a volunteer for substance abuse programs; I pre-

fer to be a worker in Native American programs not a leader." *Published works*: The Eternal Desert, with David Muench, 1990; and about a dozen more as editor or designer and approximately 100 magazine editions.

AVRITT, MICHAEL D. (San Felipe Pueblo) 1949-
(mechanical engineer)
Born August 30, 1949, Albuquerque, NM. *Education*: University of New Mexico, BS, 1973. *Principal occupation*: Mechanical engineer. *Home address*: 118 Crestview Ct., Louisville, CO 80027. *Affiliation*: Staff engineer, Pennant Systems Co. (IBM Co.), Tucson, AZ, 1974-. *Memberships*: American Indian Science & Engineering Society (current board member; chairperson, 1987-88; vice-chairperson, 1985-87). *Awards, honors*: Informal Awards, IBM, 1977 & 1980; First Invention Achievement Level, IBM Corp, 1980; Second Invention Achievement Level, IBM, 1988; named on five patents. *Interests*: Temporary assignment in Boeblingen, Germany for IBM, Dec. 1988 through June 1990; June 1984 to June 1985 IBM loaned exeutive to American Indian Science & Engineering Society to coordinate annual conference held in Los Angeles, CA. *Biographical source*: AISES role model publication, 1987. *Published works*: Various articles in IBM Technical Disclosure Bulletin; various poems published in Winds of Change magazine and used in AISES brochures.

AWIAKTA, MARILOU (Cherokee)
(writer, storyteller)
Born in Oak Ridge, Tenn. Resides in Oak Ridge, Tenn. *Address*: c/o Fulcrum Publishing, 350 Indiana St., #350, Golden, CO 80401. *Awards, honors*: Distinguished Tennessee Writer Award in 1989; Outstanding Contribution to Appalachian Literature Award in 1991; profiled in the 1994 Oxford Companion to Women's Writing in the U.S. *Published works*: Abiding Appalachia: Where Mountain and Atom Meet; Rising Fawn and the Fire Mystery; Selu: Seeking the Corn-Mother's Wisdom (Fulcrum Publishing, 1994).

AYERS, NANCY
(editor)
Affiliation: Editor, Canadian Native Law Reporter, Native Law Centre, University of Saskatchewan, Room 141, Diefenbaker Centre, Saskatoon, SK S7N 0W0 (306) 966-6189.

AYRES, SONJA K. (Cherokee) 1946-
(professional artist)
Born May 26, 1946, Fort Smith, Ark. *Education*: High school. *Principal occupation*: Professional artist. *Address*: P.O. Box 249, Muldrow, OK 74948 (918) 427-4593. *Affiliation*: Sonjya K. Ayres Studio, Muldrow, OK, 1970-. *Collection*: "Red Earth & Fire" - a unique collection of traditional clay art forms using ancient Native American techniques that capture the mystique & lore of great Woodland Indian Tribes. *Art shows/awards*: "Night of the First Americans" John F. Kennedy Center, Washington, DC, 1982; Smithsonian Institute, Washington, DC, 1982; Annual Trail of Tears Arts Show, Tahlequah, OK (Merit Awards, 1984, 1988); Annual Five Civilized Tribes Museum Art Competition, Muskogee, OK (Division II Award, 1986; Cherokee Heritage Award, 1988; 2nd Place, 1989; Merit Award, 1990); Cherokee National Holiday Art Show, Tahlequah, OK, Honor Award, 1987; Five Civilized Tribes Museum (Poster Artist, Art Under

the Oaks, Indian Market, 1989; Craft Show: 2nd Place, 1990; 1st, 2nd & Honorable Mention, 1991; Solo Exhibit, 1991); Red Cloud Indian Art Show, Pine Ridge, SD, Woodward Award, 1990; Five Civilized Tribes Museum Art & Craft Competitions, awards for clay pipes & pottery, 1992 & 1993; Cherokee Heritage Art Show, Cherokee, NC, 1992; Cherokee Nation History Art Show, 1992 & 1993 awards for Pottery & Graphics; Illustrator of "A Time for Native Americans" 48 playing card portraits, Aristoplay, LTD. Educational Games. *Interests*: Sonja spends most of her time in her studio and personally attends only select major & one-woman shows each year. She spends much of her time researching Native American customs & history.

*AYULUK, JAMES (Eskimo)
(AK village council president)
Affiliation: Chevak Native Village Council, P.O. Box 5514, Chevak, AK 99563 (907) 858-7428.

*AZEAN, MARTINA (Athapascan)
(AK village council president)
Affiliation: Kongiganak Native Village, P.O. Box 5069, Kongiganak, AK 99559 (907) 557-5226.

AZURE, F. SAM (Turtle Mountain Chippewa) 1953-
(elementary school principal)
Born July 25, 1953, Rolette, N.D. *Education*: University of North Dakota, BS, 1974; University of South Dakota, Masters in Administrative Education, 1980. *Principal occupation*: Elementary school principal. *Home address*: 408 Yorkshire Lane, Bismarck, ND 58504 (701) 255-4824. *Affiliations*: Teacher, elementary school, Eagle Butte, SD, 1974-81; Federal Program Coordinator, BIA, Billings, MT, 1981-83; BIA Adult Education, teacher of physical education, math, science, Theodore Jamerson Elementary School, Belcourt, ND, 1983-91; principal, Theodore Jamerson Elementary School, Bismarck, ND, 1991-. *Other professional post*: Tribal Adult Education, Belcourt, ND, 1991-. *Community activities*: Chairperson of Health Board, Turtle Mountain; Board of Directors, Turtle Mountain Community College. *Memberships*: North Dakota Association of Elementary School Principals. *Interests*: High school official for boys and girls basketball and football, and week-end musician.

*AZUYAK, TONY (Eskimo)
(AK village council president)
Affiliation: Native Village of Old Harbor, P.O. Box 62, Old Harbor, AK 99643 (907) 286-2215.

B

BAALAM, RANDALL
(village council chief)
Affiliation: Birch Creek Village Council, General Delivery, Birch Creek, AK 99740 (907) 628-6126.

BABBY, FAYETTA
(BIA programs administrator)
Affiliation: Sacramento Area Office, BIA, Federal Office Bldg., 2800 Cottage Way, Sacramento, CA 95825 (916) 978-4680.

BABBY, WYMAN D.
(BIA agency supt.)
Affiliation: Fort Peck Agency, BIA, P.O. Box 637, Poplar, MT 59255 (406) 768-5312.

BABCOCK, W. KENNETH (Narragansett)
(tribal council chief sachem)
Affiliation: Chief Sachem, Narragansett Indian Tribal Council, P.O. Box 268, Charleston, RI 02813 (401) 364-1100.

*BACA, CECILIA
(BIA education field officer)
Affiliation: Bureau of Indian Affairs, Albuquerque Education Field Office, P.O. Box 26567, Albuquerque, NM 87125 (505) 766-3850.

*BACA, JOE (*Seng Weng*)
(Santa Clara Tewa) 1940-
(gallery owner)
Born September 10, 1940, Dulce, N.M. *Education*: Highlands University, B.A., 1963; University of New Mexico, MBA, 1975. *Principal occupation*: Gallery owner. *Address*: Rt. 1 Box 472-C, Espanola, NM 87532 (505) 753-9663 (work). *Affiliation*: Owner, Singing Water Gallery, Espanola, NM. *Military service*: U.S. Army, 1963-65 (PFC).

BACA, LAWRENCE R. (Pawnee)
(attorney)
Address: 6017 Franconia Forest Lane, Alexandria, VA 22310 (202) 514-3874 (office). Affiliation: Chairperson, Indian Law Section, Federal Bar Association, Washington, DC.

BACA, LORENZO (Isleta Pueblo-Mescalero Apache) 1947-
(visual/literary/performing artist; educator)
Born September 9, 1947, Morenci, Ariz. *Education*: California State University, Long Beach, BA (Art), 1972; UCLA, MA (American Indian Studies), 1986. *Principal occupation*: Visual/literary/performing artist; educator. *Address*: P.O. Box 4353, Sonora, CA 95370 (209) 532-1573. *Affiliations*: Arts/graphics consultant: Sierra Audio Systems, Sonora, CA; Image Maker, James, CA; The Woodwright Shop, Twaine Harte, CA. *Other professional posts*: Artist-in-Residence: Tri-County Consortium of Special Education, Tuolumne County Schools, Sonora, CA, 1986-88; Twaine Harte Elementary School, Twaine Harte, CA, 1988-92. *Shows/Exhibits*: Stanford Pow Wow, Stanford, CA, May 1991; Chaw Se Invitational, Chaw Se State Park, Volcano, CA, Aug. 1991; Buff Show, Anne Saunders Gallery, Jamestown, CA, Feb. 1991, 1992; California Spirit, Calaveras County Arts Council, San Andreas, CA, Feb. 1992; among many others dating back to 1986. *Commissions*: Indian Nations At Risk Task Force, U.S. Office of Education, Washington, DC, March 1991; D. Fregeau, Harmony Center, Graphics, Twaine Harte, CA, Sept. 1991; M. Pelletier, Silver Pendant Design, Truckee, CA, Jan. 1992; B. Lopez, Silver Designs, Sutter Creek, CA, Feb. 1992. Numerous workshops and performances. *Awards, honors*: 1st Place awards: sculpture-Twaine Harte Annual Art Show, 1987; sculpture-Chaw Se Indian Grinding Rock, 1987; photography-Central Sierra Arts Council, 1987; pottery-Durfee Gallery, Scottsdale, AZ, Nov. 1985; among others. *Interests*: "His works, which include fine art, sculpture, poetry, acting and video, are often a contemporary expression of the native traditions of his Southwestern heritage of storytelling, dance, song and art."

BACON, CAROL
(BIA director)
Affiliation: Office of Management & Administration, Bureau of Indian Affairs, Dept. of the Interior, MS-4657-MIB, 1849 C St., NW, Washington, DC 20240 (202) 208-4174.

BACON, GEORGES
(Indian band chief)
Affiliation: Bande Indienne Montagnais de la Romaine, LaRomaine, Quebec G0G 1M0 (418) 229-2110.

BACON, JEAN-LOUIS
(Indian band chief)
Affiliation: Montagnais de Betsiamites, 20 rue Messek Box 40, Betsiamites, Quebec, Canada G0H 1M0 (418) 567-2265.

BAD MOCCASIN, DONALD "BRUCE"
(Crow Creek Sioux) 1949-
(health care administration)
Born February 3, 1949, Chamberlain, S.D. *Education*: South Dakota School of Mines & Technology, BSCE, 1972, MSCE, 1981. *Principal occupation*: Health care administration. *Home address*: P.O. Box 561, Aberdeen, SD 57402 (605) 225-0372. *Affiliations*: Engineer, Bureau of Indian Affairs, Aberdeen, SD (4 years); engineer, Indian Health Service, Oklahoma City, OK, 1977-79, Aberdeen Area, 1979-91, and Phoenix Area, 1991-93; Aberdeen Area Office, 1993-. *Military service*: U.S. Army (commissioned second lieutenant, 1972); 1977-present, currently on active duty with the U.S. Public Health Service with rank of Captain (06). *Memberships*: American Water Works Association, 1985-; Commissioned Officers Association (associate recruiter for PHS with emphasis in recruitment of minorities into the I.H.S.) *Awards, honors*: Outstanding Service Medal, USPHS, 1989; Area Excellence Award-Phoenix, 1992; Employee-of-the-Year, Aberdeen Area, IHS, 1983. *Interests*: "I am interested in early architecture and woodworking. My hobbies are bowling, basketball, and other sports activities involving running. Recently relocated back to Northern Plains area with IHS. Changed career track from engineering management to health care administration. Currently responsible for directing a comprehensive health care delivery system for American Indians throughout North & South Dakota, Nebraska and Iowa."

*BAD WOUND, ELGIN (Oglala Lakota)
(college president)
Affiliation: Oglala Lakota College, P.O. Box 490, Kyle, SD 57752 (605) 455-2321.

BADGER, HECTOR
(Indian band chief)
Affiliation: Cote Indian Band, Box 1659, Kamsack, Saskatchewan, Canada S0A 1S0 (306) 542-2694.

BADGER, JIM
(Indian band chief)
Affiliation: Sucker Creek Indian Band, Box 65, Enilda, Alberta, Canada T0G 0W0 (403) 523-4426.

BAHE, FANNIE
(executive officer)
Affiliation: National Council of BIA Educators, 8009 Mountain Rd. Place NE, Albuquerque, NM 87110 (505) 266-6638.

BAHE, ROSE MARIE (Paiute)
(tribal chairperson)
Affiliation: Utu Utu Gwaitu Paiute Tribal Council, Star Route 4, Box 56-A, Benton, CA 93512 (619) 933-2321.

BAHE, VELMA (Kootenai)
(tribal chairperson)
Affiliation: Kootenai Tribal Council, P.O Box 1269, Bonners Ferry, ID 83805 (208) 267-3519.

BAHEE, KEE (Navaho) 1962-
(painter & sculptor)
Born September 6, 1962, W inslow, Ariz. *Education*: Institute of American Indian Arts, Santa Fe, NM (one year); N.E.C. and Scottsdale Artist School (two years). *Principal occupation*: Painter & sculptor. *Other professional post*: Graphic artist. *Awards, honors*: 1st Drawing, 2nd Painting, Museum of Northern Arizona Navaho Show; S.N.A.C.F. 1st Painting, Honorable Mention, Scottsdale; 2nd Mixed Media, 1st Pastel, Most Promising New Artist, Scottsdale, etc. *Interests*: "I sculpt as well as paint, but because of lack of space and finances I'm unable to sculpt. Eventually, I would like to work my way into a situation to where I can do both." *Biographical sources*: Art Talk Magazine; Indian Gaming Magazine; ATLATL Directory of Indian Artists.

BAILEY, AREBA ELNORA ABERNATHY (United Lumbee/Cherokee) 1932-
(homemaker)
Born August 30, 1932, Yell County, Ark. *Principal occupation*: Homemaker. *Home address*: 2481 Alfred Ave., Exeter, CA 93221. *Community activities*: Assembly of God Church (taught Sunday school); United Lumbee Nation (Bear Clan treasurer, 1983-; member, Grand Council, 1984-; vice-chief, 1988-). *Membership*: Native American W olf Clan, 1978-. *Awards, honors*: 1988 United Lumbee Nation's Silver Eagle Award for outstanding work done for their Nation/Band/Clan or the Indian community at large.

*BAILEY, BENTON (Screaming Eagle) (United Lumbee/Cherokee) 1948-
(computer specialist)
Born October 29, 1948, Exeter , Calif. *Education*: Sequoia Jr. College (V isalia, CA) 1990-. *Principal occupation*: Computer specialist. *Home address*: 3724 W. Monte V ista, Visalia, CA 92377 (209) 733-2947. *Affiliation*: United Lumbee Tribe. *Military service*: U.S. Air Force, 1971-75 (Sgt. - disabled veteran; awarded Civil Service Ribbon & V ietnam Combat Ribbon). *Community activities*: Special Olympics wheelchair division; competed in Long Beach, CA, won 2 Silver & 1 Gold Medal, 1990; New Orleans, LA, won 2 Gold & 1 Silver Medal, 1991 racing. *Memberships*: United Lumbee Nation's Bear Clan Councilperson, 1983-85, Chief, 1985-90; Re-elected to Chief, 1992-; editor , United Lumbee Bear Clan Newsletter , 1992-. *Interests*: Computer science, working for my Indian people; Special Olympics; Pow W ows.

BAILEY, DIANE
(Indian band chief)
Affiliation: Katzie Indian Band, 10946 Katzie Rd., Pitt Meadows, B.C. V3Y 1Z3 (604) 465-8961.

*BAILEY, ELNORA
(tribal vice chief)
Affiliation: United Lumbee Nation of N.C. & America, P.O. Box 512, Fall River Mills, CA 96028 (916) 336-6701.

BAILEY, MIKE
(Indian school administrator)
Affiliation: Jones Academy, Route 1, Box 102-5, Hartshorne, OK 74547 (918) 297-2518.

*BAILEY, ROSELLE F.K. (Hawaiian)
(organization president)
Affiliation: Ka Imi Naauao O Hawaii Nei, P .O. Box 218, Kaumakani, HI 96747 (808) 335-3628.

*BAINES, DAVID, M.D. (Tlingit/T simpsian)
(family practitioner)
Education: Mayo Medical School. *Address*: 229 S. 8th, St. Maries, ID 83861 (208) 245-2591. *Community activities*: Chairperson, National Heart, Lung and Blood Institute's Ad Hoc Committee on Minority Populations; chairperson, American Academy of Family Physicians' Committee on Minority Health Affairs. *Awards, honors*: 1993 Searle Pharmaceutical Co.'s "Gentle Giants of Medicine" award; appointed by the Clinton Administration to a six-member screening committee that selected the new Indian Health Services director .

BAIRD, LAWRENCE
(Indian band chief)
Affiliation: Chief, Ucluelet Indian Band, Box 699, Ucluelet, British Columbia, Canada V0R 3A0 (604) 726-7342.

*BAIRD, W. DAVID
(professor of history , author)
Affiliation: Dept. of History, Pepperdine University, Malibu, CA. He is an outstanding authority on the Indian period of Oklahoma's history . *Published works*: Editor - A Creek Warrior for the Confederacy: The Autobiography of Chief G.W . Grayson (University of Oklahoma Press); Peter Pitchlynn: Chief of the Choctaws (University of Oklahoma Press); The Story of Oklahoma, with Danney Goble (University of Oklahoma Press, 1994).

BAJWA, SAJJAN
(director-Indian health program)
Affiliation: Director, Tule River Indian Health Program, P.O. Box 768, Porterville, CA 93257 (209) 784-2316.

BAKER, ANSON A. (Goe's Along Brightly) (Hidatsa-Mandan-Fort Berthold) 1927-1993
(administrator)
Born May 26, 1927, Elbowoods, N.D. *Education*: North Dakota State, 1946-47; Minot Business College, 1947-48, 1949-50. *Principal occupation*: Consultant. *Home address*: Box 878, New Town, ND 58763 (701) 627-4585. *Affiliations*: Clerk, Aberdeen Area Office, BIA, Aberdeen, SD, 1953-1955; credit of ficer, Rosebud Indian Reservation, Aberdeen, SD, 1953-54; property and supply assistant, loan examiner , Pine Ridge Indian Reservation, Pine Ridge, S.D., 1955-60; supervisory finance specialist, Fort Belknap Indian Reservation, Harlem, MT , 1960-64; administrative manager , Blackfeet Indian Reservation, Browning, Mont., 1964-67; supt., Fort Peck Indian Reservation, 1967-71; supt., Crow Indian Reservation, Crow Agency, MT, 1971-1973; supt., Fort Berthold Reservation, New Town, ND, 1973-76; supt., Blackfeet Indian Reservation, Browning, MT , 1976-79; area director, Billings Area Office, Billings, MT, 1979-82; vice president, Indian Credit Corporation, Billings, MT, 1983-1987; administrator , local Federal Agency & Commercial Bank, 1987-93. *Other professional posts*: Member of

Governor's Commission on Aging, 1991-93; member of Executive Board, United Church of Christ, 1991-93; National Spokesperson for Minorities-State of North Dakota "AARP" American Association for Retired Persons; Board Member for Council of American Indian Ministries "CAIM." *Military service*: Seaman 1st Class, U.S. Navy, 1945-46. *Community activities*: American Legion, Pine Ridge, S.D. (Post Commander, 1958); American Legion Post 300, New Town, ND (Post Commander , 1976); Little Shell Pow-wow, New Town, ND (president, 1976.) *Awards, honors*: Certificate of Superior Performance, BIA, 1964; Boss of Year Award, Browning, Mont., 1966; Boss of Year Award, Poplar Jaycees, Poplar, MT, 1968; Certificate of Appreciation, Fort Peck Tribal Industries, 1969, 1970; Fort Berthold Person Award, Fort Berthold Reservation, ND, 1974. *Interests*: "My interest is working with people, attempting to bring about a better understanding of Indian people and their tribal government." *Biographical source*: Indians of Today, Fourth Edition (Marion E. Gridley).

BAKER, ARLENE ROBERTA (Cata) (Ka-nay-how) (Seneca-Cayuga, Pueblo-T ewa) 1938-
(library media specialist)
Born April 13, 1938, Albuquerque, N.M. *Education*: Northeast Oklahoma A & M Jr. College, AA, 1969; Missouri Southern State College, BS, 1972; Northeastern State University , MEd, 1982. *Principal occupation*: Library media specialist. *Home address*: 59501 E. Highway 60, Fairland, OK 74343 (918) 676-3518. *Affiliation*: Fairland (OK) High School. *Memberships*: Fairland Education Association; Oklahoma Library Association; Oklahoma Education Association; National Education Association. Interests: "Enjoy bowling, embroidery, and our grandchildren.".

BAKER, FREDERICK P.
(director-Indian health center)
Affiliation: Director, Fort Berthold PHS Indian Health Center, P.O. Box 400, New Town, ND 58763 (701) 627-4701.

*BAKER, GERARD
(national monument supt.)
Affiliation: Little Bighorn Battlefield National Monument, P.O. Box 39, Crow Agency, MT 59022 (406) 638-2621.

BAKER, JIMMY
(BIA education program administrator)
Affiliation: Oklahoma Education Of fice, BIA, 4149 Highline Blvd., Suite 380, Oklahoma City , OK 73180 (405) 945-6051.

*BAKER, JOE (Waim-Me-Ke-Mon) (Delaware) 1946-
(artist/associate professor)
Born January 14, 1946, in Okla. *Education*: University of Tulsa, BFA, 1968, MFA, 1978. *Principal occupation*: Artist/associate professor . *Home address*: 277 E. Tuckey Lane, Phoenix, AZ 85012 (602) 279-1318. *Affiliations*: Colorado College, Colorado Springs, CO., V isual Arts Faculty, The Marie W alsh Sharpe Foundation, 1986-91; V isiting Associate Professor of Art, 1992-. *Other professional posts*: Visiting Artist-In-Residence, Sun V alley Center for the Arts & Humanities, Sun V alley, ID, 1982, 83, 87, 88; Registered Native American Artisan, Delaware Tribe, Bureau of Indian Affairs, Washington, DC, 1991; lecturer, Colorado Springs Fine Arts Center, Colorado Springs, CO, 1992; East Carolina University, Greenville, NC, V isiting Arts Faculty,

Biographies

Painting & Drawing, 1991-92; "The Carolina Series," Lecture & performance, The School of Art, 1992; Dept. of English Poetry Symposium, 1992. *Military service*: U.S. Air Force, 1968-78. *Community activities*: Minority Coalition, United Parents. *Membership*: College Art Association, 1978-. *Awards, honors*: Arizona Commission of the Arts, Phoenix, AZ (Visual Arts Panelist, 1982-84; Bi-cultural Arts Representative to Mexico, 1983-84); Visual Arts Representative, Western States Arts Foundation, Santa Fe, NM, 1983-84; Nominee, Regional Arts Panelist, national Endowment for the Arts, Washington, DC, 1983-84; Arts Panelist, Idaho Commission on the Arts, Boise, ID, 1986; Arts Panelist, Wyoming Council on the Arts, Cheyenne, WY, 1987. *Exhibitions*: Numerous solo & group exhibitions from 1977 to the present. *Biographical sources*: California Art Review, Los Angeles, CA, 1983; The Complete Book of Country Swing & Western Dance and a Bit About Cowboys, by Peter Livingston (Doubleday, 1981); Love Medicine, by Louise Erdrich (Rowohlt Publishing, Germany, 1984); Signale: Indianischer Kunstler, by Katrina Hartje (Berlinger, Kunstblatt, 1984); The American West: The Modern Vision (New York Graphics Society, 1984); A History & Selections from the Permanent Collections, by Colorado Springs Fine Arts Center (Williams Publishing, 1986); "Art & Life," Calendar (Design Graphics, Phoenix, 1992); "Joe Baker, The Painter," by Eileen Baily (Arizona Trends, Apr. 1992); Joe Baker: The Carolina Series," Catalyst (The Colorado College, 1992); New Art of the West 3, Eiteljorg Museum (Benham Press, 1992). Numerous public collections, such as: Metropolitan Museum of Art, Heard Museum, Smithsonian Institution, Phoenix Art Museum, Fine Arts Museum of New Mexico.

*BAKER, LARRY L.
(executive director)
Affiliation: San Juan County Archaeological Research Center & Library, 6131 US Hwy. 64, Farmington, NM 87401 (505) 632-2013.

BAKER, ODRIC (RICK) (Lac Courte Oreilles Chippewa) 1931-
(tribal chairperson)
Born May 26, 1931, Lac Courte Oreilles Reservation, Wisconsin. *Principal occupation*: Tribal chairperson. *Home address*: Route 5, Hayward, WI 54843. *Affiliations*: Tribal chairman, Lac Courte Oreilles Tribe, 1973-. *Other professional posts*: Past-president, Great Lakes Intertribal Council, Wisconsin; past-treasurer, National Tribal Chairman's Association, Washington, DC; consultant, O.M.B., Washington, DC. *Membership*: Loyal Order of Moose (legionnaire degree.) *Interests*: "Indian affairs--advocate of Indian sovereignty, pursuit of recognition, dignity, and peace for Indian people; defense of Indian treaties and agreements with the U.S. Government."

BAKER, PERRY J.
(BIA agency supt.)
Affiliation: Uintah & Ouray Agency, Bureau of Indian Affairs, P.O. Box 130, Fort Duchesne, UT 84026 (801) 722-2406.

*BAKER, QUINCEE
(library director)
Affiliation: Fort Berthold Reservation Public Library, P.O. Box 788, New Town, ND 58763 (701) 627-4738.

BAKER, SHERRY (Creek)
(director-tribal health center)
Affiliation: Sapulpa Health Center, Creek Nation of Oklahoma, 1125 E. Cleveland, Sapulpa, OK 74066 (918) 224-9310.

*BAKKA, NORMA JEAN (Ojibwe) 1939-
(counseling)
Born February 23, 1939, White Earth Reservation, Minn. *Education*: Bemidji State University, B.A.; University of Wisconsin, Superior, M.A. *Principal occupation*: Counseling. *Home address*: 5580 Loop 36, Aurora, MN 55705 (218) 638-2679. *Affiliations*: Director of Indian Services Program, Mesabi Community College, Virginia, MN (218) 749-7727 (10 years); Counselor, Fond du Lac Community College, 1994-. *Community activities*: Range women's advocate for battered women; Indian awareness week activities, Mesabi College. *Published works*: Native American Cultural Cookbook (Jumbo-Jacks, 1991); How to Build a Birch Bark Canoe.

BALBER, MARY AL (Ojibway)
(attorney)
Address: 1573 E. Margaret, St. Paul, MN 55106 (612) 222-5863 (work). *Membership*: Native American Bar Association (board member).

*BALDRIDGE, DAVE
(executive director)
Affiliation: National Indian Council on Aging, City Centre, Suite 510-W, 6400 Uptown Blvd, NE, Albuquerque, NM 87110 (505) 888-3302.

BALES, JEAN ELAINE MYERS (Iowa) 1946-
(artist)
Born December 25, 1946, Pawnee, Okla. *Education*: Oklahoma University of Science & Art, BA, 1969; Professional Study, Institute of San Miguel de Allende, Mexico. *Principal occupation*: Artist. *Home address*: HC 73 Box 502, Park Hill, OK 74451 (405) 457-4136. *Community activities*: National Wildlife Federation (member). *Memberships*: Oklahoma Indian Art League, 1973-74; Indian Arts & Crafts Association (lifetime member and past board of directors) *Awards*: Numerous awards from: Santa Fe Indian Market; Cherokee National Museum; O'Odham Tash, Casa Grande, AZ; Hear Museum; Philbrook Art Center; Scottsdale National Indian Art Show; Gallup Inter-Tribal Ceremonial; Museum of the Wester Prairie; and many others. *Honors*: Governor's Oklahoma Cup for Outstanding Indian Artist of the Year, 1973; selected as one of the Oklahomans for Indian Opportunity (OIO) calendar artist for the painting "Oklahoma Open Drum"; 1982 Oklahoma Diamond Jubilee - Outstanding Woman of the Southern Plains; 1984 Citation by the state of Oklahoma, House of Representatives for demonstrating exceptional abilities in the creation of the visual arts, and bringing positive recognition to the state of Oklahoma in its pursuit of excellence in the arts. *Permanent Public collections*: Southern Plains Indian Museum; Denver Museum of Natural History; Museum of Northern Arizona; U.S. Dept. of the Interior; Oklahoma Historical Society, among others. *Permanent Private collections*: Too numerous to list, however, they include collections throughout the U.S., Canada, and Europe. *Interests*: Mrs. Bales writes, "I have done and still do lectures and seminars for groups and colleges throughout the U.S. I am very active with school systems throughout Oklahoma. By taking the Indian art forms into the classroom we help students (whether they

are Indian or non-Indian) to appreciate the rich American Indian culture we have in Oklahoma. I have worked with the schools planning counselors to plan curriculum to include Indian studies. My works are represented in many private and public collections throughout the U.S., Canada and Europe."

*BALLARD, CLAY (Cherokee)
(counselor)
Affiliation: University of California, Davis, 300 South Hall, Davis, CA 95616 (916) 752-0864.

*BALLARD, JOYCE
(museum director)
Affiliation: Shoshone-Bannock Tribal Museum, Box 793, Fort Hall, Idaho 83203 (208) 237-9791.

BALLARD, LOUIS WAYNE (*Honganozhe*) (Quapaw-Cherokee) 1931-
(composer, educator)
Born July 8, 1931, Miami, Okla. *Education*: University of Oklahoma, 1949-50; Northeast Oklahoma A & M, AA, 1951; University of Tulsa, BA, BME, 1954, MM, 1962; College of Santa Fe, Doctor of Music, Honoris Causa. *Principal occupation*: Composer, educator. Home address: P.O. Box 4552, Santa Fe, NM 87502. *Affiliations*: Chairman, Music Dept., Inst. of American Indian Arts, Santa Fe, 1962-64; chairman, Performing Arts Dep., Institute of American Indian Arts, 1964-69; music curriculum specialist, Central Office-Education, BIA, Washington, DC, 1969-79; chairman, Minority Awareness Committee for New Mexico Education Association; project director & composer, First National All Indian Honor Band, Santa Fe, 1977-. *Other professional posts*: Music consultant and lecturer; president, First American Indian Films, Inc. *Memberships*: ASCAP; American Music Center; American Symphony Orchestra League; National Music Educator's Assn; Minority Concerns Commission, MENC (member); Society for Ethnomusicology; Masonic Lodge. *Awards, honors*: Composer's Assistance Grants, Select Composer's Bicentennial Grant, National Endowment for the Arts; New Mexico American Revolution Bicentennial Commission Grant, 1967-1976; First Marion Nevins MacDowell Award, Chamber Music, 1969 for "Ritmo Indio, a Study in American Indian Rhythms"; Ford Foundation Grant, American Indian Music & Music Education, 1970; Outstanding Indian of the Year, Tulsa Council of the American Indian, 1970; National Indian Achievement Award, Indian Council Fire, 1972; Distinguished Alumnus Award, Tulsa University, 1972; Outstanding Indian of the Year, American Indian Exposition, Anadarko, OK, 1973; Certificate of Special Achievement, Dept. of the Interior, 1974; Catlin Peace Pipe Award, National Indian Lore Association, 1976; Annual ASCAP Awards, 1966-89; first Native American composer to have composition performed three (3) times in Carnegie Hall, New York, NY, 1984, 1987 & 1992; first American composer to present entire program of chamber music in the new Beethoven Chamber Music Hall, next to Beethoven's birthplace, Bonn, Germany, June 1, 1989. *Interests*: Mr. Ballard has traveled extensively throughout the U.S. as music consultant for Volt Technical Corp. headstart programs, to B.I.A. area of fices & workshops establishing bicultural music programs from kindergarten to college level. "I have traveled to Eastern Europe, Western Europe, South America, Canada and England for performances of my music. Also, my music has

been broadcast on Radio France, Deutsch Welle, Voice of America, Saarlandische Rundfunk, Deutsch Sundwesten Rundfunk, Canadian Broadcasting Corp., National Public Radio & others." He has lectured at U.C.L.A., Northern Arizona University, Indiana University, Wm. Jewell College, Oklahoma University, University of Colorado, Syracuse University, Westmar College, Oklahoma College of Liberal Arts, University of Denver, Southern Colorado State College, Huron College, University of North Dakota, University of Arizona, University of Minnesota, National Association for the Education of Young Children, Howard University, Harvard University, University of Wisconsin, University of California-Fresno, Pima Community College, Navajo Community College, Bacone College, University of Alaska, and at the M.E.N.C. Regional Music Conference, Albuquerque, N.M., on a variety of subjects relating to American Indian art & music; Mr. Ballard has been a guest composer at numerous events across the country: Oklahoma City University, North Dakota State University, Oklahoma State University, Smithsonian Institute, University of Colorado, University of New Mexico, Arizona State University, et al; and guest conductor: Milwaukee Symphony, New Mexico Symphony, Bicentennial Horizons of American Music in St. Louis, MO, Sioux City Symphony. In 1992, Ballard's work will be featured on the roster of Columbia Artists Concert Association in 16 American cities following a January concert at Carnegie Hall where Ballard and the Quintet of the Americas will perform "Ritmo Indio" for the program "Celebration of the Americas." *Biographical sources*: Who's Who in America; Who's Who in the World; ASCAP Biographical Dictionary; Baker's Biography of Musicians; and Grove's Dictionary of Music, U.S.A.; This Song Remembers (Self Portraits of Native Americans in the Arts) (Houghton Mifflin, 1980); "Louis W. Ballard, New World Composer of the Southwest", by Branham & Powers (New Mexico Magazine, 1972); and numerous other articles. *Published works*: The American Indian Sings, Book 1, 1970; American Indian Music for the Classroom, 1973; My Music Reaches to the Sky, Musical Instruments of North American Indians; "Indians, the music of", article for "Scholastic Encyclopedia," Arete Publications; The Last Gladiator, article for University of Tulsa Alumni Magazine; "Syllabus for Kindergarten Music Teachers in Navajo Schools." Music album:Wak-101 Ballard, cassette available from Wakan Records, Santa Fe, NM. Composed: (ballets) Ji-Jo Gweh, Koshare, The Four Moons; (orchestral music) Scenes From Indian Life, Why the Duck Has a Short Tail, Devil's Promenade, Incident at Wounded Knee, Fantasy Aborigine, Nos. I, II, III, IV, V; (chamber music) "Ritmo Indio", Desert Trilogy, Kacina Dances, Rio Grande Sonata, String Trio 1, Rhapsody for Four Bassoons; (choral cantatas) "Portrait of Will Rogers", "The Gods Will Hear", "Thus Spake Abraham"; (band works) "Siouxiana", "Scenes From Indian Life", "Ocotillo Festival Overture", "Nighthawk Keetowa"; (percussion) "Cecega Ayuwipi", "Music for the Earth and the Sky"; "Ritmo Indio" with the Quintet of the Americas (CD-released by Newport Records, 1992). Sheet music of Mr. *Ballard's are available from the following publishers*: Bourne Music Co., 5 W. 37th St., New York, N.Y. 10018; Belwin-Mills Pubg. Corp. with Theodore Presser Publishing Co., Bryn Mawr, PA; and The New Southwest Music Publications & Wakan Records, Box 4552, Santa Fe, NM 87502.

*BALLOT, JOSEPH A.
(medical center president)
Affiliation: Maniilaq Association Medical Center, Box 43, Kotzebue, AK 99752 (907) 442-3321.

*BALLOT, PERCY
(AK village president)
Affiliation: Native Village of Buckland, P.O. Box 67, Buckland, AK 99727 (907) 494-2171.

BALLOUE, JOHN (Cherokee) 1948-
(professional artist)
Born April 19, 1948, Richmond, Calif. *Education*: Chabot College, Hayward, CA, 1971-73; California State University, Hayward, BA (Art), 1975. *Principal occupation*: Professional artist. *Home address*: 26838 Grandview Ave., Hayward, CA 94542 (510) 538-4003. *Affiliations*: American Indian Traders Guild, Fresno, CA, 1991-. *Military service*: U.S. Army, 1968-69 (Specialist-4, Vietnam Vet; Nationall Defense Service Medal, Vietnam Service Medal, Vietnam Campaign Medal, Army Commendation Medal). *Membership*: Indian Arts and Crafts Association, 1988-. *Awards, honors*: 1992 Indian Arts & Crafts Association, Artist of the Year; over 25 awards for various (Indian and non-Indian) juried art shows. *Interests*: "Photography is closely related to much of my work. I've tried to illustrate dance, costumes, and traditions of contemporary Native America. I attend pow-wows and various social events, photograph and later translate them into artwork." *Biographical sources*: Articles in: The Indian Trader (Gallup, NM, Nov. 1991); The Daily Review (Hayward, CA, April 1985).

*BANKS, DENNIS J. *(Nowa Cumig)*
(Anishinabe)
(AIM, lecturer, author)
Born on the Leech Lake Reservation in northern Minnesota. *Education*: DQ University University, A.A. *Principal occupation*: American Indian Movement (AIM), lecturer, author. *Affiliation & Address*: American Indian Movement & Sacred Run Foundation, P.O. Box 315, Newport, KY 41071 (606) 581-9456. *Military service*: U.S. Air Force, 1954-58 (active duty-4 years, inactive duty-8 years). *Activities*: In 1968 he founded the American Indian Movement (AIM), and established it to protect the traditional ways of Indian people and to engage in legal cases protecting treaty rights of natives - such as hunting and fishing, trapping, wild riceing. Among other activities, it participated in the occupation of Alcatraz Island where demands were made that all federal surplus property be returned to Indian control. In 1972 it organized and led the Trail of Broken Treaties' caravan across the U.S. to Washington D.C. calling attention to the plight of Native Americans. Spearheaded the move on Pine Ridge Reservation in South Dakota in 1973 to oust corruption and the U.S. appointed tribal chairman. This led to the occupation of Wounded Knee and a siege of 71 days which received national attention. Banks was the principal negotiator and leader of the Wounded Knee forces. Under the leadership of Dennis Banks, AIM led a protest in Custer, S.D. in 1973 against the judicial process that found a white man innocent of murdering an Indian. As a result of his involvement in Wounded Knee and Custer, Banks and 300 others were arrested and faced trial. He was acquitted of the Wounded Knee charges, but was convicted of riot and assault at Custer. Refusing the prison term, Banks went underground, later receiving amnesty in California by then Governor Jerry

Brown. In California, from 1976-1983, Banks earned an Associates of Arts degree at Davis University and taught at DQ University (an all Indian-controlled Institution), where he became the first American Indian chancellor. He also established the first spiritual run from Davis to Los Angeles, California in 1978 (now an annual event) and organized the Longest Walk from Alcatraz to Washington, D.C. that same year. This 3,600 mile walk was successful in its purpose: to gather enough support to halt purposed legislation abrogating Indian treaties with the U.S. government. In the spring of 1979, he taught at Stanford University. After Governor Brown left office, Banks received sanctuary on the Onondaga Nation in upstate New York in 1984. It was while living there that Banks organized the Great Jim Thorpe Longest Run from New York City to Los Angeles, California. A Spiritual run, this event ended in Los Angeles to begin the Jim Thorpe Memorial Games where the gold medals Thorpe had won at the 1912 Olympics were restored to the Thorpe family. In 1985, Banks left Onondaga to surrender to law enforcement officials in South Dakota and served 18 months in prison. When released, he worked as a drug and alcohol counselor on the Pine Ridge Indian Reservation. During 1987 grave robbers in Uniontown, Kentucky were halted in their digging for artifacts after they had destroyed over 1,200 American Indian grave sites. Banks was called in to organize the reburial ceremonies for the uncovered remains. His activities in this state resulted in Kentucky and Indian passing strict legislation against grave desecration. He revived the idea of traditional spiritual running in 1978 when he began Sacred Run. Since then it has become a multi-cultural, international event with participants from around the world joining Native American runners to carry the message of the sacredness of all Life and of our relationship to the planet we call Mother Earth. To date, Banks has led runners over 43,000 miles through the U.S., Europe, Japan, Canada, Australia, and Aotearoa (New Zealand). In addition to leading and organizing Sacred Runs, Dennis Banks stays involved with American Indian issues, AIM activities, and travels the globe lecturing, providing drug & alcohol counseling, teaching Native traditions, and sharing his experiences. *Key roles in the following movies*: "War Party," "The Last of the Mohicans," and "Thunderheart". *Biographical sources*: Too numerous to list. *Published works*: Sacred Soul (autobiography, Ashai, Japan, 1988); forewords to "Native America: Portrait of Peoples"; "Shooting Back From the Reservation."

BAPTISTE, JOHN
(Indian band chief)
Affiliation: Ermineskin, Box 219, Hobbema, Alberta T0C 1N0 (403) 585-3814.

BAPTISTE, MIKE
(Indian band chief)
Affiliation: Red Pheasant Indian Band, Box 70, Cando, Sask., Can. S0K 0V0 (306) 937-7717.

BARAJAS, LOUIS (Papago)
(Indian school principal)
Affiliation: Santa Rosa Ranch School, HC04 #7570, Tucson, AZ 85735 (602) 383-2359.

BARBER, JAMES
(BIA agency supt.)
Affiliations: Papago Agency, BIA, Box 578, Sells, AZ 85634 (602) 383-3286.

BARBER, WILSON
(BIA area director)
Affiliation: Navajo Area Office, BIA, P.O. Box 1060, Gallup, NM 87305 (505) 863-8314.

BARBRY, EARL, Sr. (Tunica-Biloxi)
(tribal chairperson)
Affiliation: Tunica-Biloxi Indian Tribe, P.O. Box 311, Marksville, LA 71351 (318) 253-9767.

BARELA, RAYNA
(museum director)
Affiliation: Director, Gila County Historical Museum, Box 2891, 1330 N. Broad St., Globe, AZ 85502 (602) 425-7385.

*BARKLEY, JOHN
(casino/bingo general manager)
Affiliation: Umatilla Casino & Bingo, P.O. Box 638, Pendleton, OR 97801 (503) 276-3165.

BARLOW, WENDALL PAUL
(Indian band chief)
Affiliation: Indian Island Indian Band, Box 288, RR #1, Rexton, N.B., E0A 2L0 (506) 523-9187.

BARNABY, CHARLIE
(Indian band chief)
Affiliation: Chief, Fort Good Hope Indian Band, General Deliver, Fort Good Hope, Northwest Territories X0E 0J0 (403) 952-2330.

BARNES, BARBARA
(college president)
Affiliation: North American Indian Travelling College, Onake Corporation, R.R. 3, Cornwall Island, Ontario, Can. K6H 5R7 (613) 932-9452.

BARNES, LEWIS (Yokut)
(tribal co-chairperson)
Affiliation: Table Mountain Rancheria, P.O. Box 243, Friant, CA 93626 (209) 822-2587.

BARNES, M.J. (Cherokee) 1941-
(business owner)
Born July 27, 1941, San Antonio, Tex. *Education*: Texas Christian University, BA, 1964; Arizona State University, MA (Indian Education), 1968. *Principal occupation*: Business owner. *Home address*: 8710 Linkmeadow, Houston, TX 77025 (713) 665-3576 (office). *Affiliation*: Houston Metropolitan Ministries, 1982-89; owner & operator, Kiva Enterprises, Houston, TX, 1989- *Community activities*: Member & volunteer, Cherokee Cultural Society of Houston. *Memberships*: American Indian Chamber of Commece of Texas; Texas Polio Survivors' Assn.; member & assistant editor, National Assn. of Desktop Publishers (NADTP). *Awards, honors*: Southwest Literature Award, Texas Christian University, 1963; Employee Achievement Award, Houston Metropolitan Ministries, 1985; painting accepted for exhibition, Cherokee National Museum, 1988 (Trail of Tears Sesquicentennial). *Interests*: "Typography, desktop publishing, proofreading, writing, art (painting, drawing, woodcarving); environment, social justice, volunteerism, employment & assistance for homebound people with handicaps." *Published works*: Numerous articles; book manuscript in progress; newspaper columns.

BARNETT, JAMES F., Jr.
(director-historic landmark site)
Affiliation: The Grand Village of the Natchez Indians, 400 Jefferson Davis Blvd., Natchez, MS 39120 (601) 446-6502.

*BARNETTE, JOAN
(museum curator)
Affiliation: Red Rock Museum, P.O Box 328, Red Rock State Park, Church Rock, NM 8731 1 (505) 722-6196.

*BARNEY, CHERYL
(director-tribal health center)
Affiliation: Fort McDermitt Tribal Health Center, P.O. Box 457, McDermitt, NV 89421 (702) 532-8259.

BARREIRO, JOSE (*HATvey*)
(Guajiro Taino) 1948-
(writer; editor; lecturer)
Born June 19, 1948, Camaguey, Cuba. *Education*: University of Minnesota, B.A, 1975; State University of New York, Buffalo, M.A. (American Studies), 1988. *Principal occupation*: Editor & writer; lecturer. *Address*: Akwe:kon, Cornell University, Clara Dickson Hall, Ithaca, NY 14853 (607) 255-1923 (office). *Affiliations*: Editor-in-Chief, Akwe:kon Press, Cornell University; contributing editor, Native Nations Magazine, New York, NY. *Memberships*: Native American Press Assn. (founding member). *Awards, honors*: Human Rights of Indigenous Peoples of the Americas; Indigenous Community Development; communications networking; Native American Press Association - Best Feature, 1988. *Biographical sources*: New York Times (March, 1983); USA Today, 1988; A.P. National, 1985; Turtle Q, 1991. *Published works*: Native Peoples in Struggle (Akwesasne Notes, 1982); Indian Roots of American Democracy (Cornell University, 1988); Indian Corn of the Americas (Cornell University, 1989); View From the Shore (Cornell University, 1992); Taino: The Indian Columbus (Cornell University, 1992); Indian Chronicles (Arte Publico Press, 1993).

BARRETT, DAVID, M.D.
(medical director)
Affiliation: Alaska Native Health Center, 255 Gambel St., Anchorage, AK 99501 (907) 279-6661.

BARRETT, JOHN ADAMS (ROCKY), Jr. (Citizen Band Potawatomi) 1944-
(tribal chairperson; corporate president)
Born March 25, 1944, Shawnee, Okla. *Education*: Princeton University, 1962-64; University of Oklahoma, 1964-65; Oklahoma City University, BS, 1968, MS, 1986. *Principal occupation*: Tribal chairperson; corporate president. *Address*: Citizen Band Potawatomi Tribal Business Committee, 1901 S. Gordon Cooper Dr., Shawnee, OK 74801 (405) 275-3121 *Affiliations*: Warehouseman and salesman, U.S. Plywood Corp., Oklahoma City, 1966-69; promotion and supervisor of construction, Greenbriar Development Co., Memphis, TN, 1969-70; Barrett Construction Co., Southaven, MS, 1970-71; director, C.T.S.A. Enterprise, Shawnee, Okla., 1971-74 (intertribal organization, under Indian Action Team Training Contract from BIA, whose objective was to trade hard-core unemployed adult Indians in construction trades); Barrett Drilling Co. (family owned business in contract drilling & oil production), 1974-82; self-employed, J. Barrett Co., 1982-83; tribal administrator, Citizen Band Potawatomi Tribe, 1983-85, chairman, 1985-; president, Barrett Refining, Shawnee, Okla., 1985-. In the Fall of 1985, Barrett Refining was awarded a $52 million jet fuel contract from the U.S. Department of Defense–the only Defense contract to go to an Indian. *Other pro-*

fessional posts: Paid lobbyist for Oklahoma Home Builders Assn. in the Oklahoma Legislature; Citizen Band Potawatomi Tribe (business committee member, tribal administrator (1983-1985), vice-chairperson, & chairperson (1985). *Other tribal activities*: Member, board of directors, United Western Tribes (representing 32 tribes in Oklahoma and Kansas); chairman and director, Shawnee Service United Indian Health Service Advisory Board; director, Oklahoma Indian Health Service Advisory Board; president, National Indian Action Contractors Association; delegate to National Tribal Chairman's Association and National Congress of American Indians. *Community activities*: Member, Emanuel Episcopal Church (ordained lay reader); member, board of directors, Shawnee Quarterback Club; Elks (B.P.O.E.); member, Shawnee Citizens Advisory Council, Lions Club, and Boy Scouts of America as troop leader.

BARSE, HAROLD G.
(Kiowa/Wichita/Sioux) 1947-
(readjustment counseling therapist)
Born June 30, 1947, Riverside, Calif. *Education*: Black Hills State College, Spearfish, S.D., B.S. (Secondary Education), 1973; University of Oklahoma, Norman, Okla., M.Ed. (Guidance and Counseling), 1979. *Principal occupation*: Readjustment counseling therapist. *Home address*: 1814 Windsor Way, Norman, OK 73069 (405) 270-5184 (work). *Affiliations*: Director, Adult Education Program, Lake Traverse Sisseton-Wahpeton Sioux Tribe, Sisseton, S.D., 1973-1975; instructor, Sinte Gleska Community College, Rosebud Sioux Reservation, S.D., 1975; director, Inhalent Abuse Treatment Project, Oklahoma City Native American Center, 1977-1980; readjustment counseling therapist, Dept. of Veterans Affairs (Vet Center), Oklahoma City, OK, 1980-. *Other professional post*: Co-chairman, Vet Center's American Indian Working Group. *Military service*: U.S. Army, 1969-1971 (specialist 4th class E-4). *Memberships*: Founder, Vietnam Era Veterans Inter-Tribal Association, 1981-; Kiowa Blacklegging Society (Kiowa Veterans Association), 1985-; Native American Veterans Association. *Honors*: Planned and organized first National Vietnam Veterans Pow-Wow. *Interests*: Working with Vietnam veterans; primary program development specialist for video Shadow of the Warrior: American Indian Counseling Perspectives; appear in video "Warriors."

BARTON, LOUISE ANN (*Wind Walks Woman*)
(Cherokee-OK) 1934-
(teacher, author, performer)
Born November 21, 1934, New York, N.Y. *Education*: Bronx Community College, AAS, 1973; Herbert Lehman College, B.A., 1978; New York University, M.A., 1981. *Principal occupation*: Teacher, author, performer. *Home address*: 2116 Williamsbridge Rd. #147, Bronx, NY 10461 (718) 828-0353. *Affiliations*: Teacher of business education, NYC Board of Education-George Washington High School. *Other professional posts*: Former positions held at George Washington High School - teacher specialist at Professional Staff Development Center; coordinator of Business Career Center House, School Improvement, Project Achieve, Educational Accountability, Community-Based organizations; and business teacher in Adult Education Programs. *Community activities*: storytelling and other lectures in New York City colleges, public schools and libraries; worked with the Leonard

Peltier Defense Committee (NYC) & the Native American Education Program. *Memberships*: Chairperson, Wind Walker Productions (non-profit, theatrical organization specializing in Native American folk arts presentations; Southeastern Cherokee Confederacy, Inc.; Nuyagi Keetoowah (Cherokee scribe society). *Awards, honors*: Artistic Community Enrichment Award 1993-94 by Bronx Council on the Arts; grants awarded for Native American Storytelling in NYC public branch libraries, and other projects. *Interests*: "A master storyteller from a family of storytellers, I tell native and other tales in public schools, libraries, and colleges - working to improve education, preserve the ecology, and inform people about Native American cultures & political problems and lobbying to change laws. Engaged in multicultural activities, bringing people from all backgrounds together in common projects to enrich their communities. Enjoy writing fiction, non-fiction, plays, native stories, children's stories. While I teach Business Education and computer skills at both secondary and college levels, I have worked in community theater in all capacities, and appear in Shakespeare Festivals and at Medieval Fairs." *Published works*: Newspaper articles, poetry, artist's books.

BARZ, SANDRA 1930-
(editor, publisher)
Born August 4, 1930, Chicago, Ill. *Education*: Skidmore College, B.A., 1952. *Principal occupation*: Editor, publisher. *Home address*: 162 East 80 St., New York, N.Y. 10021. *Affiliation*: Editor, publisher, Arts and Culture of the North (newsletter, journal), 1976-. *Community activities*: Yorkville Civic Council (member of board). Interests: Eskimo art--circumpolar; traveled to Alaska, Canada (Arctic) and Greenland, and have lead tours to Arctic Canada and Greenland; run conferences at major museums in Canada and the U.S. since 1978, where Eskimo art-related activities are taking place. *Published works*: Inuit Artists Print Workbook (Arts and Culture of the North, Vol. I, 1981, Vol. II with biographies, 1990); newsletter/journal Arts and Culture of the North (seven volumes, 1976-1981; 1983-1984).

BASS, BARRY W. *(Big Buck)* (Nansemond)
(tribal councilperson)
Affiliation: Nansemond Indian Tribal Association, P.O. Box 9293, Chesapeake, VA 23321 (804) 487-5116.

BASS, EARL L. *(Running Deer)* (Nansemond) 1909-
(tribal chief; retired machinist-farmer)
Born August 27, 1909, Norfolk Co., VA. *Education*: Nansemond Indian Public School #9, Norfolk, VA. *Principal occupation*: Retired machinist, farmer. *Home address*: 3429 Galberry Rd., Chesapeake, VA 23323 (804) 487-5116. *Affiliations*: Norfolk Naval Shipyard, Portsmouth, VA (30 years); chief, Nansemond Indian Tribal Association, Chesapeake, VA. *Community activities*: Participate in various city festivals, speaking engagements at public schools, civic leagues, etc. *Memberships*: Masonic Lodge, 1964-; Woodmen of the World, 1938-. *Awards, honors*: Recognition & Certificate from City of Suffolk, City of Portsmouth, various other cities, Governor Bralles of VA.

BASS, KENNETH P. *(Iron Horse)* (Nansemond)
(tribal councilperson)
Affiliation: Nansemond Indian Tribal Association, P.O. Box 9293, Chesapeake, VA 23321 (804) 487-5116.

BASSETT, MICHAEL
(editor)
Affiliation: Editor, The Circle, Minneapolis American Indian Center, 1530 E. Franklin Ave., Minneapolis, MN 55404 (612) 871-4749.

BASSO, KEITH H.
(professor of anthropology)
Affiliation: Dept. of Anthropology, University of Arizona, Tucson, AZ 85721 (602) 621-2585/2966.

BATAILLE, GRETCHEN M. 1944-
(professor)
Born September 28, 1944, Mishawaka, Ind. *Education*: Purdue University, 1962-1965; California State Polytechnic University, B.S., 1966, M.A., 1967; Drake University, D.A., 1977. *Principal occupation*: Professor. *Home address*: 2524 S. Forest, Tempe, AZ 85282 (602) 967-9238. *Affiliation*: Iowa State University, Ames, Iowa, 1967-86; professor, 1986-88, chair/professor, 1988-90, Dept. of English, Associate Dean, College of Liberal Arts and Sciences, 1990-, Arizona State University, Tempe, AZ. *Other professional post*: Editor, "Ethnic Reporter," National Association for Ethnic Studies, Dept. of English, ASU, Tempe, AZ. *Community activities*: Iowa Civil Rights Commission, 1975-1979 (chairman, 1977-1979); Iowa Humanities Board, 1981- (president, 1984-1985.) *Memberships*: National Association for Ethnic Studies (executive council, 1980-; treasurer, 1982-); Association for the Study of American Indian Literature (executive board, 1978-1981; Modern Language Association. *Interests*: "I am interested in American Indian literature as a reflection of the culture, history, and world view of diverse peoples. As a collector of popular culture artifacts representing American Indians, I find the popular view in sharp contrast to the image presented in both the oral tradition and contemporary literary expressions." *Published works*: The Worlds Between Two Rivers: Perspectives on American Indians in Iowa (Iowa State University Press, 1978); The Pretend Indians: Images of Native Americans in the Movies (Iowa State University Press, 1980); American Indian Literature: A Selected Bibliography for Schools and Libraries (NAIES, Inc., 1981); American Indian Women: Telling Their Lives (University of Nebraska Press, 1984); Images of American Indians in Film: An Annotated Bibliography (Garland Publishing, 1985); American Indian Women: A Guide to Research (Garland, 1991); Native American Women: A Biographical Dictionary (Garland, 1993).

BATES, KAREN D.
(Indian school director)
Affiliation: Director, Shiprock Alternative Schools, P.O. Box 1799, Shiprock, NM 87420 (505) 368-5144.

BATES, SARA P. (Oklahoma Cherokee) 1944-
(artist/educator)
Born December 10, 1944, Muskogee, Okla. *Education*: California State University, Bakersfield, BA, 1986; University of California, Santa Barbara, MFA, 1989. *Principal occupation*: Artist/educator. *Home address*: 999 Bush St. #102, San Francisco, CA 94109 (415) 495-7600 (work). *Affiliation*: Director of Exhibitions and Programs, American Indian Contemporary Arts, San Francisco, CA, 1990-. *Other professional posts*: Artist in Residence/instructor: Cherokee Nation, Tahlequah, OK (summers, 1988-90); UCLA Artsreach (taught drawing, painting & sculpture inside California state prison system), 1989-90); Headlands Center for the Arts, Sausalito, CA, 1992. Numerous exhibitions and public speaking engagements across the country. A few of the latest ones include: Migration of Meaning, Invitational Group Exhibition, Intar Gallary, New York, NY, 1992; *Traveling Exhibition*: Hollywood Art Museum, 1992; Pittsburgh Center for the Arts, 1992; Lehigh Art Galeries, 1993; Spirit As Source, Invitational Group Exhibition, Bade Museum, Berkeley, CA, 1992; Speaker/Presenter, "Education in a Cultural Context: Whose Responsibility Is It?, No. California Women's Caucus For The Arts Conference, Mills College, Berkeley, CA, 1992; Speaker/Presenter, "Native American Contemporary Art: Reflecting Contemporary Art", American Indian Institute, San Francisco, CA, 1992; among others. *Awards, honors*: Village Artisans Award, Dorian Society, California State University, 1985; Dorian Society Scholarship, 1986; University of California Regents Scholarship, Santa Barbara, 1987; Johnson O'Mally Grants, Cherokee Nation, Tahlequah, OK, 1988-90.

BATISSE, BARNEY
(Indian band chief)
Affiliation: Matachewan Indian Band, Box 208, Matachewan, Ontario, Canada P0K 1M0 (705) 565-2288.

*BATTISE, JO ANN (Alabama Coushatta)
(tribal administrator)
Affiliation: Alabama-Coushatta Indian Museum, Route 3, Box 640, U.S. Highway 190, Livingston, TX 77351 (713) 563-4391.

BATTISE, FRANCES (Alabama-Coushatta)
(tribal chairperson)
Affiliation: Alabama-Coushatta Tribal Council, Route 3, Box 659, Livingston, TX 77351 (409) 563-4391.

*BAVILLA, WASSILLIE (Yup'ik Eskimo)
(AK village president)
Affiliation: Native Village of Kwinhagak, Quinhagak I.R.A. Council, Quinhakag, AK 99655 (907) 556-8449.

BEAL, C.
(college lecturer)
Affiliation: Indian Studies, Saskatchewan Indian Federated College, Regina Campus, 1 18 College West, University of Regina, Regina, Saskatchewan S4S 0A2 (306) 584-8333.

BEAN, LOWELL JOHN 1931-
(anthropologist, ethnologist)
Born April 26, 1931, St. James, Minn. *Education*: Los Angeles City College, 1954-55; University of California, Los Angeles, B.A., 1958, M.A., 1961, Ph.D., 1970. *Principal occupation*: Anthropologist, ethnologist. *Home address*: 1555 Lakeside Dr. 64, Oakland, Calif. 94612. *Affiliations*: Reading and teaching assistant, U.C.L.A., 1958-60; instructor, Pasadena Junior College, 1962-65; curator of ethnology, Palm Springs Desert Museum, 1962-64; instructor and professor of anthropology (chairman, 1973-

79), Department of Anthropology, California State University at Hayward, 1965-; research fellow, R.H. Lowie Museum of Anthropology, University of California, Berkeley, 1971-73; curator, Clarence E. Smith Museum of Anthropology, CSUH, 1974-78. *Other professional posts*: Consultant on ethnographic films, North American Films, 1963-64; contributing editor, American Indian Historian, 1968-72; consultant, American Indian Scholars Conference, American Historical Society, 1969; consultant, Rincon Reservation Water Case, 1971; member, California State Board of Education Task Force on Social Studies Textbooks, 1972. *Military service*: U.S. Marine Corps, 1951-53. *Community activities*: American Friends Service, Southwest Indian Committee (member, advisory Indian committee, 1961-63); Teaching Institute, American Indian Historical Society (participant, 1968); American Indian Studies Curriculum Committee, San Francisco State College (consultant); Planning Committee for Gabrileno Cultural Center, Rancho Los Alamitos, 1972; Malki Museum (member, board of trustees); Journal of California Anthropology (associate editor; editor, Ballena Press Anthropology Papers. *Memberships*: American Anthropological Association (Fellow); Society for California Archaeology; Southwestern Anthropological Association (president, 1974-75). *Awards, honors*: George Barker Memorial Grant-in-Aid for research among American Indian, 1960; National Science Foundation Faculty Research Grant-in-Aid, California State University, Hayward, 1967-72; Postdoctoral Museum Fellowship, Wenner-Gren Foundation for Anthropological Research, 1971; Smithsonian Institute (Center for the Study of Man) Grant to research the history of economic development at Morongo Indian Reservation, Banning, California, 1972-74; Grant-in-Aid, American Philosophical Society, 1972; Outstanding Educators of America Award, 1972; National Geographic Society (grantee, 1975; California State University at Hayward (mini-grantee, 1977). *Interests*: California Indians; Ethnographic research; directed field studies among Miwok, Wintun, Tubatulabal & Chemehuevi Indians of California. *Published works*: The Romero Expeditions in California and Arizona, 1823-1826, with William Mason (Palm Springs Desert Museum, 1962); Cahuilla Indian Cultural Ecology, Ph.D. dissertation (University Microfilms, 1970); Temalpah: Cahuilla Knowledge and Uses of Plants (Malki Museum, 1972); Mukat's People: The Cahuilla Indians of Southern California (University of California, Berkeley Press, 1972); Antap: California Indian Policy and Economic Organization, with T. King (Ballena Press, 1974); Native American California: Essays on Culture and History, with T. Blackburn (Ballena Press, 1975); California Indians: Primary Resources, with Sylvia Vane (Ballena Press, 1976); A Comparative Ethnobotany of Twelve Southern California Tribes, with Charles Smith; Ethnography and Culture History of the Southwestern Kashia Pomo Indians; The Native Californian: A Regional Ethnology; and Madman or Philosopher: Essays on Shamanism, with Rex Jones.

BEANE, LARRY N. 1958-
(park ranger/interpretive archaeologist)
Born November 9, 1958, Burke Co., N.C. *Education*: Catawba College, Salisbury, N.C., B.A. (Anthropology/Archaeology), 1981. *Principal occupation*: Park ranger/interpretive archaeologist. *Home address*: 822 Brummel Ave., Bridgeport,

AL 35740 (205) 495-2672 (office). *Affiliation*: Russell Cave National Monument, Bridgeport, AL, 1982-. *Memberships*: Southeastern Archaeological Conference, 1982-; Alabama Archaeological Society, 1983-; Tennessee Anthropological Society, 1983-; South Carolina Archaeological Society, 1981; North Carolina Archaeological Society, 1982-. *Awards, honors*: Five Special Achievement Awards, and a Quality Performance Award, National Park Service. *Interests*: "Presenting programs in Native American technologies, tools to museum and archaeological groups; Reconstructing tools and tool kits; flintknapping; preserving traditional skills, knowledge, and archaeological sites. I have traveled extensively in the Southeastern U.S. visit and volunteering at archaeological sites and parks."

BEANE, TAMARA (Cherokee-Choctaw) 1958-
(potter)
Born April 15, 1958, Idaho Falls, Idaho. *Education*: Jacksonville State University, Jacksonville, AL, BS, 1979. *Principal occupation*: Potter-reproducing southeastern U.S. prehistoric pottery. *Home address*: 822 Brummel Ave., Bridgeport, AL 35740 (205) 495-3307. *Community activities*: Presents programs for museums, archaeological societies, state and other parks. *Memberships*: Southeastern Archaeological Conference; Primative Society; Alabama Archaeological Society. *Interests*: "I reproduce southeastern prehistoric and historic Native American pottery. "I travel, visit archaeological sites, museums, and labs doing research."

*BEANS, ELMER T., Sr. (Eskimo)
(AK village council president)
Affiliation: Native Village of Mountain Village, P.O. Box 32249, Mountain Village, AK 99632 (907) 591-2048.

*BEANS, GEORGE, Sr.
(AK tribal council president)
Affiliation: Andreafksi Tribal Council, P.O. Box 368, St. Mary's, AK 99658 (907) 438-2312.

BEAR, AUSTIN
(Indian band chief)
Affiliation: John Smith Indian Band, Box 9, Birch Hills, Saskatchewan, Canada S0J 0G0 (306) 764-1282.

*BEAR, BOBBIE
(Indian center president)
Affiliation: Indian Awareness Center, Fulton County Historical Society, 37 E 375 N, Rochester, IN 46975 (219) 223-4436.

BEAR, EVERETTE
(Indian band chief)
Affiliation: Chief, John Smith Indian Band, P.O. Box 9, Birch Hills, Saskatchewan, Canada S0J 0G0 (306) 764-1282.

*BEAR, LAWRENCE (Goshute)
(tribal council chairperson)
Affiliation: Skull Valley General Council, c/o Uintah & Ouray Agency, B.I.A., P.O. Box 130, Fort Duchesne, UT 84026 (801) 722-2406.

*BEAR, MOONFACE (Pequot)
(tribal leader)
Affiliation: Golden Hill Paugussett Traditional Government, 95 Stanavage Rd., Trumbull, CT 06415 (203) 537-0390.

BEAR, TOM, Jr. (*No-Ko-Se*)
(Creek-Seminole) 1931-
(acting director-Indian hospital)
Born October 31, 1931, Holdenville, Okla. *Education*: Central Oklahoma University, BS, 1956; University of Oklahoma, MPH, 1975. *Principal occupation*: Acting director-Indian hospital. *Home address*: 809 Howard, Ada, OK 74820 (405) 436-2355. *Affiliation*: Director, Wewoka PHS Indian Health Center, Wewoka, OK, 1988-93; acting director, Carl Albert Indian Hospital, 1001 North Country Club Dr., Ada, OK 74820 (405) 436-3980. *Other professional posts*: District Sanatarian; Environmental Health Coordinator; Hospital Safety Committee. *Military service*: U.S. Army, 1952 (Sgt. 1st Class; received the Bronz Star for valor in the Korean Conflict; Capt. in MC Corps, 1964; discharged from Reserve, 1966). *Community activities*: Chairman of the Board for Southeastern Indian Recovery Center; Ordained Baptist Minister. *Memberships*: Registered Professional Sanitarian, 1976-; National American Indian Safety Council, Inc., 1976-. *Awards, honors*: Awarded the "C. Bradley Bridges Sanitary Science Award" for Academic Achievement from Tennessee State, 1972; appointed to the "Sanitarian Career Development Committee" which met quarterly for a term of three years at IHS Headquarters, Washington, DC, 1977. *Interests*: "Our goal for the Indian patients is to elevate the health status and to ensure equity, availability and accessibility of a comprehensive high quality health care delivery system."

BEARD, ANNA
(museum curator)
Affiliation: Curator, Tonkawa Tribal Museum, Box 70, Tonkawa, OK 74653 (405) 628-5301.

BEARDEN, MARION TED
(health center director)
Affiliation: Miami PHS Indian Health Center, P.O. Box 1498, Miami, OK 74354 (918) 542-1655.

BEARDY, ERIC
(Indian band chief)
Affiliation: Chief, Shamattawa First Nation Band, Shamattawa, Manitoba, Canada R0B 1K0.

BEARDY, FRANK
(Indian band chief)
Affiliation: Chief, Muskrat Dam Indian Band, Muskrat Dam, via Pickle Lake, Ontario P0V 3A0.

BEARDY, LARRY
(Indian band chief)
Affiliation: Chief, Split Lake Indian Band, Split Lake, Manitoba, Can. R0B 1P0 (204) 342-2045.

*BEARS GHOST, RICHANDA A.
(administrative officer)
Affiliation: New Sunrise Regional Treatment Center, P.O. Box 219, San Fidel, NM 87049 (505) 552-6634.

*BEARSKIN, LAURA
(project coordinator)
Affiliation: Great Lakes Native Diabetes Project, 2318 W. Merrill St., Milwaukke, WI 53204.

BEARSKIN, LEAFORD (*Kwa-Hoo-Sha-Ha-Ke (Flying Eagle*) (Wyandotte-Oklahoma) 1921-
(tribal chief)
Born September 11, 1921, Wyandotte, Okla. *Education*: University of Omaha, 1958-60. *Principal occupation*: Chief, Wyandotte Tribe of

Oklahoma. *Address*: P.O. Box 250, Wyandotte, OK 74370 (918) 678-2297 (work). *Affiliations*: Chief, Wyandotte Tribe of Oklahoma, 1983-; president, InterTribal Council, Miami, OK, 1984-85; executive committee, United Indian Nations of Oklahoma, 1984-88. *Other professional posts*: IHS Board of Directors, Muskogee, OK, 1983-89. *Military service*: USAF, 1939-60 (rank-Lt. Colonel - Pilot; Distinguished Flying Cross - Air Medal - Medal for Humane Action, Berlin Airlift, Presidential Unit Citation.) *Community activities*: Executive committee, Indian Education, NEO A&M College. *Membership*: The Retired Officers Association, 1960-; United Indian Nations of Oklahoma. *Awards, honors*: Indian Achievement Award, 1986. *Interests*: To work in the interest of Indians, particularly members of his tribe; and working in Indian af fairs. A few tribal accomplishments are: Getting a settlement on a judgement claim which was pending for years, affecting a payment of $5.7 million to tribal members and getting a provision in the payment bill for the tribe to receive and control its own money; rewrote the Oklahoma Wyandotte Tribal Constitution and monitored its progress through the B.I.A. in 18-months; obtained a grant to fund the tribe's first economic development project-- $325,000 to construct a convenience-store complex on tribal land; also working to gain grants-in-aid for all deserving Wyandotte young people. *Biographical sources*: Indians of Today, 1961-1971.

BEATTY, JOHN J. (*Tewahni tan eken* **)**
(Mohawk) 1939-
(anthropologist)
Born September 5, 1939, Brooklyn, N.Y. *Education*: Brooklyn College, B.A., 1964; University of Oklahoma, M.A., 1966; City University of New York, Ph.D. (Anthropology), 1972. *Principal occupation*: Anthropologist. *Home address*: 2983 Bedford Ave., Brooklyn, N.Y. 11210. *Affiliations*: Teaching assistant, University of Oklahoma, 1964-65; instructor, Long Island University, 1966-67; professor of anthropology, Brooklyn College, CUNY, 1966-. *Other professional posts*: Founder & director, American Indian Institute of City University of New York; private investigator, Phoenix Investigative Associates, 1982-. *Military service*: New York Guard (captain.) *Major research work*: Ethnographic & linguistic: American Indians in Urban Areas (major U.S. cities) 1963-; Tlingit Language and Culture (in New York and Alaska) 1964-67; Totonac Language and Culture (in New York and Mexico) 1964-67; Kiowa-Apache Language and Culture (Anadarko, Oklahoma) 1965-; Mohawk Language and Culture (New York City and various Mohawk Reserves) 1964-; Japanese & Japanese Americans: Language and Culture, 1973-; Scots and Scottish Americans, 1974-; Cross Cultural Perspectives on Police, 1978-. *Memberships*: American Anthropological Association (Fellow); New York Academy of Sciences (Fellow); American Indian Community House. *Awards, honors*: National Science Foundation Training Grant, University of Oklahoma, 1965 (for research with the Kiowa-Apache); City University of New York and National Science Foundation Dissertation Year Fellowships, 1971 (for research with Mohawk languages); National Science Foundation Grant (U.S. - Japanese Cooperative Program, 1973); Brooklyn College Faculty Award, 1973, for research with Japanese macaques; Faculty Research Award Program, CUNY, 1974 and 1975, for research with chimpanzees and for research on sexual behav-

ior; Department of Health, Education and Welfare: Office of Native American Programs, 1975 grant to work with urban American Indians in New York State; National Endowment for the Arts, 1977, for filming Iroquois social dances; Rikkyoo University (Japan) Research Fellowship, 1986-87, for research on solidarity; Certificate of Appreciation, New York Academy of Sciences; Sigma Xi. *Interests*: Anthropology; linguistics, symbolic anthropology - American Indians; Asia; theatre; forensics; lecture series on American Indians and Japanese culture, 1969-; coach, Brooklyn College Wrestling Team. *Published works*: Kiowa-Apache Music and Dance (Museum of Anthropology, University of Northern Colorado, 1974); Mohawk Morphology (Museum of Anthropology, University of Northern Colorado, 1974); A Guide to New York for Japanese: An Ethnographic Approach (Gloview Press, Tokyo, 1985); Kujira! The Whale in Japanese Culture (AJSU, Japan, 1988); numerous articles. Recording: Music of the Plains Apache (Folkways Records). Films: Iroquois Social Dances, Two parts, with Nick Manning, 1979; and others. *Videotapes*: The American Indian Art Center, 1978; American Indians at Brooklyn College, 1978; Scottish Highland Dances, 1979; Custer Revisited, 1980. Books being developed: Intercultural Communications; The Anthropology of Sexual Behavior; The Nature of Language and Culture; and Cross Cultural Perspectives on Police.

BEAUDIN, JOHN A. *(Bidanakwad)*
(Lac Courte Oreilles Band of
Great Lakes Chippewa) 1946-
(attorney)
Born June 28, 1946, Chicoutimi, Quebec, Can. *Education*: University of Wisconsin, Green Bay, B.S.; University of Wisconsin, Madison, J.D., 1981. *Principal occupation*: Attorney. *Home address*: 1317 Reetz Rd., Madison, WI 53711 (608) 271-9437. *Affiliation*: Partner (four years), Dewa, Beaudin & Kelly, 217 S. Hamilton St., Madison, Wisc. *Other professional post*: President, Native Horizons, Inc.; research & teach, University of Wisconsin Law School. *Military service*: U.S. Army, 1966-1969 (rank SP/5-E5; Bronze Star with clusters, Army Commendation Medal, Viet Nam Combat and Campaign Medals). *Community activities*: Director, American Indian Peace & Justice League; board of directors, Madison Indian Parents, School Superintendent's Human Relations Advisory Committee; lobbying. *Membership*: American Indian Lawyer's League. *Interests*: Advocate of Indian rights, human rights and educational needs and issues, and general practice. *Published works*: American Indian Rights (Madison Metro School District, 1981); many articles dealing with Indian or legal affairs. Major work in development for Wisconsin judges and attorneys dealing with Indian Child Welfare Act.

BEAULIEU, ALFRED
(Indian band chief)
Affiliation: Ebb & Flow Indian Band, Ebb & Flow, Manitoba, Canada R0L 0R0 (204) 448-2134.

BEAULIEU, ORAN
(health project director)
Affiliation: Red Lake Comprehensive Health Service, Red Lake, MN 56671 (218) 679-3316.

BEAUVAIS, ARCHIE BRYAN
(Rosebud Sioux) 1948-
(educational administrator/instructor)
Born December 30, 1948, Rosebud, S.D. *Education*: Northern Arizona University, Flagstaff, B.S. (Education), 1974, M.A. (Education), 1976; Harvard University, Ed.D., 1982. *Principal occupation*: Education administrator/instructor. *Home address*: P.O. Box 426, Mission, S.D. 57555 (605) 856-2326 (office). *Affiliation*: Dean, Academic Affairs & Chair, Graduate Education Program, Sinte Gleska University, Rosebud, S.D., 1984-. *Other professional posts*: Consultant, South Dakota Board of Regents for Title II math and science; consultant-evaluator, North Central Association, Chicago, IL. *Military service*: U.S. Army, 1967-1970 (Vietnam, 1968-1969, Specialist Fifth Class, Army Commendation Medal.) *Community activities*: Doctoral representative to Student Association Cabinet, Harvard Graduate School of Education. *Memberships*: School Administrators of S.D.; Ducks Unlimited; Harvard Chapter of Phi Delta Kappa; S.D. Indian Education Association, South Dakota Council for Social Studies. *Awards, honors*: 1988 Alumni Achievement Award, Northern Arizona University, Flagstaff, AZ; Jubilee Year Distinguished Alumnus Award, Northern Arizona University, Flagstaff, AZ, 1990; Executive Proclamation, Office of the Governor, State of South Dakota, Feb. 1991; Trio Achiever, National Council of Educational Opportunity Associations, Sept. 1991. *Interests*: "Major interest is developing new and innovative programs which will significantly impact reservation, tribal, and other native communities." *Published works*: Article, "A Unique Masters Program" (Harvard Graduate School of Education- Alumni Bulletin, 1989).

BEAVER, CHARLES
(Indian band chief)
Affiliation: Chief, Bigstone Cree Band, General Delivery, Desmarais, Alberta, Canada T0G 0T0 (403) 891-3836.

BEAVER, HENRY
(Indian band chief)
Affiliation: Fort Smith Indian Band, Box 960, Fort Smith, Northwest Territories, Canada X0E 0P0 (403) 872-2986.

BEAVER, B. TOM (Muskogee Creek)
(director of public information)
Born in Muskogee, Okla. *Education*: University of Kansas, B.S., 1972, M.S., 1974. *Address*: 5021 Portland Ave. South, Minneapolis, MN 55417 (612) 822-2856; 626-7280 (work). *Affiliations*: WCCO TV, Minneapolis, MN (anchor, producer, reporter, 1973-79; public service director, 1981-86); Special Assistant, Assistant Secretary for Indian Affairs, Dept. of the Interior, Washington, DC, 1979-81; public information officer, Regional Transit Board, St. Paul, MN, 1987-88; host & board member, First Americans Update, KTCI-TV, St. Paul, MN & Westmarc Cable, St. Cloud, MN, 1991-; director of public information, University of Minnesota, Office of the Associate Provost & Associatre Vice President for Academic Affairs, Minneapolis, MN, 1988-. *Other professional posts*: Freelancer, 1985-; columnist, "The Lakota Times," Matin, SD, 1985-86. *Community activities*: Work with community groups to define relevant issues and translate those issues into media events; serves on a variety of commissions, panels and boards of non-profit agencies.

Awards, honors: Indian Media Award for Outstanding Achievement in Television, Native American Public Broadcasting Consortium, 1984; Volunteer of the Year, Minneapolis Junior League, 1985; Distinguished Service Award, City of Minneapolis, MN, 1986.

BEAVERBONE, CAROLINE
(Indian band chief)
Affiliation: O'Chiese Indian Band, Box 1570, Rocky Mountain House, Alberta, Canada T0M 1T0 (403) 989-3943.

BECENTI, FRANCIS D. (Navajo) 1952-
(higher education administrator)
Born May 18, 1952, Fort Defiance, Ariz. *Education*: Navajo Community College, A.A., 1973; University of California, Berkeley, B.A., 1975. *Principal occupation*: Higher ed. administrator. *Home address*: Native American Student Services, Colorado State U., 312 Student Services, Fort Collins, CO 80523 (303) 491-1 101. *Affiliations*: Director of financial aid, Navajo Community College, 1975-79; director of financial aid, U. of Albuquerque, 1980-81; director-student services, College of Ganado, 1981-84; director, Native American Student Services, Colorado State University, Fort Collins, 1984-.

BECHARD, REV. HENRI
(editor)
Affiliation: Kateri, P.O. Box 70, Kahnawake, Quebec, Canada J0L 1B0 (514) 525-361 1.

*BECK, DAVID R.M. 1956-
(assistant professor of history)
Born July 14, 1956, Evanston, Ill. *Education*: Northwestern University, B.A., 1979; University of Illinois, Chicago, M.A., 1987, PhD, 1994. *Principal occupation*: Assistant professor of history. *Home address*: 1735 Asbury Ave., Evanston, IL 60201 (312) 761-5000 (work). *Affiliations*: Director, NAES College Tribal Research Center, Chicago, IL, 1992-; assistant professor of history, NAES College, Chicago, IL, 1992-. *Other professional post*: Advisor, Americans for Indian Opportunity Ambassador Program. *Community activities*: Volunteer instructor, Korean Educational Services, 1988-90; Archivist, NAES College, 1987-92; GED instructor for history/culture component, NAES College Employment Enhancement Program, 1994-. *Memberships*: American Historical Association; Midwest Archives Conference; Montana Historical Society; Natural Resources Defense Council. *Awards, honors*: Listed in Outstanding Young Men of America, 1988; University Fellowship, University of Illinois at Chicago, 1990-92; Certification of Recognition, Americans for Indian Opportunity Ambassador Program, 1993. *Interests*: Vocational interests are teaching & writing history; avocational interests include travelling. *Published works*: Editor, Contemporary Issues, Reader One (NAES College Press, 1981); The Chicago American Indian Community, 1893-1988, Annotated Bibliography & Guide to Sources in Chicago (NAES College Press, 1988). From Sol Tax's Preface to *The Contemporary American Indian Community*," this work "may be the best record of first-hand sources of information about any immigrant group in any city in North America."

BECK, DUDLEY, M.D.
(clinical director)
Affiliation: Tuba City PHS Medical Center, Box 600, Tuba City, AZ 86045 (602) 283-621 1.

BECKER, STEPHEN
(museum director)
Affiliation: Museum of Indian Arts & Culture, Laboratory of Anthropology, P.O. Box 2087, 708 Camino Lejo, Santa Fe, NM 87504 (505) 827-6344.

*BECKFORD, LYDIA
(BIA special assistant)
Affiliation: Special assistant, Office of the Assistant Secretary for Indian Affairs, Bureau of Indian Affairs, Dept. of the Interior, MS-4140-MIB, 1849 C St., NW, Washington, DC 20240 (202) 208-7163.

BECKWITH, TERRY
(BIA agency supt.)
Affiliation: Palm Springs Field Agency, Bureau of Indian Affairs, P.O. Box 2245, Palm Springs, CA 92262 (619) 322-3086.

*BEDEL, JENNIFER
(program coordinator)
Affiliation: American Indian Program ("The Web," newsletter), 300 Caldwell Hall, Cornell University, Ithaca, NY 14853 (602) 255-4308.

*BEDROSIAN, TOD 1947-
(publisher)
Born July 21, 1947, San Francisco, Calif. *Education*: University of Nevada, Reno, B.A., 1971; University of Denver, M.A., 1972. *Principle occupation*: Publisher. *Address*: 7427 Braeridge Way, Sacramento, CA 95831 (916) 421-5121. *Affiliations*: Publisher, The Native Magazine, Sacramento, CA., 1992-; owner, Bedrosian & Associates, Sacramento, CA, 1986-. *Other professional posts*: Press secretary, U.S. Congress; Nevada assemblyman; journalist. Military service: U.S. Air Force (sgt.). *Community activities*: President of Sacramento Chapter of Public Relations Society of America.

BEELER, ROMENA A. (Cherokee) 1930-
(tribal council member)
Born April 30, 1930, Paterson, N.J. *Principal occupation*: Tribal council member, Cherokee Tribe of Virginia. *Address*: Route 1, Box 499, Rapidan, VA 22733 (703) 672-4841.

BEELER, SAMAD A. (Cherokee) 1970-
(tribal secretary)
Born September 6, 1970, Paterson, N.J. *Principal occupation*: Secretary, Cherokee Tribe of Virginia. *Address*: Route 1, Box 499, Rapidan, VA 22733 (703) 672-4841.

BEELER, SAMUEL W., Sr. (Cherokee) 1927-
(principal chief)
Born December 9, 1929, Buena, VA. *Education*: U.S. Air Force Academy, MA. *Principal occupation*: Principal chief. *Address*: Route 1, Box 499, Rapidan, VA 22733 (703) 672-4841. *Affiliations*: Principal Chief, Cherokee Tribe of Virginia, Rapidan, VA; Cherokee Confederacy, Albany, GA (20 years). *Military service*: U.S. Army Air Corps, 1946-54; U.S. Air Force, 1954-80. *Community activities*: State appointed representative on the advisory committee of Commonwealth of Virginia-State Water Control Board.

BEELER, SAMUEL W., Jr. (Cherokee) 1950-
(vice principal chief)
Born January 29, 1950, Paterson, N.J. *Education*: Passaic County School of Nursing, Wayne, N.J., Nursing Degree; American Indian School on Alcohol & Drug Abuse, Reno, Nev., Certified

Counselor. *Principal occupation*: Vice principal chief. *Address*: Route 1, Box 499, Rapidan, VA 22733 (703) 672-4841. *Affiliations*: Vice Principal Chief, Cherokee Tribe of Virginia, Rapidan, VA; Cherokee Confederacy, Albany, GA (20 years). *Military service*: U.S. Air Force, 1968-70. *Memberships*: National Congress of American Indians; Association of American Indian Social Workers, Vietnam Era Veterans Inter-Tribal Assn.; Cherokee National Historical Society; American Assn. of Critical-Care Nurses.

BEELER, SAMUEL W., III (Cherokee) 1969-
(tribal treasurer)
Born January 14, 1969, St. Croix, Virgin Islands. *Principal occupation*: Treasurer, Cherokee Tribe of Virginia. *Address*: Route 1, Box 499, Rapidan, VA 22733 (703) 672-4841.

BEELER, SANDRA L. (Cherokee) 1970-
(tribal council member)
Born July 30, 1970, St. Croix, Virgina Islands. *Principal occupation*: Tribal council member, Cherokee Tribe of Virginia. *Address*: Route 1, Box 499, Rapidan, VA 22733 (703) 672-4841.

BEER, R. SHANE (Navajo-Laguna Pueblo) 1953-
(artist)
Born June 25, 1953, Albuquerque, N.M. *Education*: High school. *Principal occupation*: Artist. Resides in Austin, TX. *Native American Art*: Hand crafted jewelry; embossed paper; cartoonist. *Juried Exhibits*: Eight Northern Indian Pueblo Arts & Crafts Show, San Ildefonso, NM, 1990-91; American Indian Art Festival and Market, Dallas, TX, 1990-91; A.I.T.G. Indian Art Expo, Austin, TX, 1991; The American Idian Art Festival, Houston, TX, 1992; Heard Museum, Phoenix, AZ, 1992. *Community activities*: Artists in Education, Texas Commission on the Arts, 1991- *Awards, honors*: Gallup Intertribal Indian Ceremonial (1st & 2nd Ribbons, 1975 & 3rd Ribbon, 1977, for handmade silver jewelry). *Biographical sources*: Indian Silver - Volume II, by Dale Stuart King, 1976; article in "Southwest Art", Feb. 1992.

BEESON, ARLIE
(health center director)
Affiliation: Bylas Health Center, P.O. Box 208, San Carlos, AZ 85550 (602) 485-2686.

*BEGAY, CATHERINE T. (Navajo)
(school principal)
Affiliation: Greasewood/Toyei Consolidated Boarding School, Ganada, AZ 86505 (602) 654-3331.

BEGAY, D.Y. (Navajo) 1953-
(weaver, textile consultant)
Born September 3, 1953, Ganado, Ariz. *Education*: Rocky Mountain College, 1974; Arizona State University, BA, 1978. *Principal occupation*: Weaver, textile consultant. *Home address*: P.O. Box 1770, Chinle, AZ 86503. *Affiliation*: Owner, Navajo Textiles & Arts, Chinle, AZ, 1984-. *Other professional posts*: Textile instructor, lecturer. *Memberships*: Palisades Guild; Museum of Natural History, Museum of the American Indian; Handweavers Guild of America. *Interests*: Have done extensive traveling (Canada, Mexico, Europe and U.S.) All my interest is in the field of textiles (Navajo weaving). *Biographical sources*: A Navajo Weaver (N.Y. Times); Navajo Weaving (Bergen Record). *Published works*: Co-editor, The Sheep (documentary film), 1982.

BEGAY, EUGENE A., Sr. (Lac Courte Oreilles Chippewa) 1933-
(business admin., Indian affairs, mechanical engineer)
Born June 6, 1933, Hayward, Wis. *Education*: North Park College, 1952-54; Illinois Institute of Technology, 1955-59. *Principal occupation*: Business administration, Indian affairs, mechanical engineer. *Home address*: 765 Hartwell St., Teaneck, NJ 07666. *Affiliations*: Executive director, United Southeastern Tribes, Inc., Nashville, TN, 1972-76; Associate Native American Ministry, United Presbyterian Church-USA, New York, NY, 1976-. *Other professional posts*: Consultant, B.I.A. and Indian Health Service, U.S. Government. *Military service*: Illinois National Guard, 1950-52. *Community activities*: Chicago American Indian Center (board of directors); National Indian Review Board (NIAAA/HEW) (chairman); National Indian Board on Mental Health (chairman); National Indian Council Fire (member). *Memberships*: National Congress of American Indians; Research Committee on Mental Health (NIMH/HEW). *Interests*: "Active originally in Indian affairs in the area of developing priority by the Federal Government in mental health and alcoholism programs and services. I have lobbied in Congress and advocated amongst tribes and tribal organizations in the area of economic development, education, nutrition, housing, and health services. I am currently active in Indian rights, treaty rights, jurisdiction, and land issues. I provided White House testimony on these issues at the request of the Vice President."

*BEGAY, HAROLD
(school director)
Affiliation: Greyhills High School, P.O. Box 160, Tuba City, AZ 86045 (602) 283-6271.

BEGAY, JAMES M. (Navajo)
(Indian school chairperson)
Affiliation: Rock Point Community School, Rock Point, AZ 86545 (602) 659-4221.

BEGAY, JIMMIE C. (Navajo) 1948-
(Indian school director)
Born September 4, 1948, Rough Rock, Ariz. *Education*: New Mexico Highlands University, A.S., 1969, B.A., 1972, M.A., 1974. *Principal occupation*: Director-Indian school. *Address*: Rock Point Community School, Rock Point, AZ 86545 (602) 659-4221. *Affiliations*: Teacher, principal, executive director, Rough Rock Demonstration School; director, Rock Point Community School, Rock Point, AZ. *Other professional posts*: Native American Studies teacher; coordinator, Black Mesa Day School; president, board of directors, Association of Community Tribal Schools, Inc., Vermillion, SD. *Community activities*: Navaho Culture Organization (chairman); originator of Navaho psychology classes; sponsor of Black Mesa five mile run. *Memberships*: National Association of Secondary School Principals; Smithsonian Institution; Harvard Education Review; Dine Biolta Association. *Award*: Outstanding Accomplishments, Rough Rock School Board. *Interests*: Betterment in education programs, especially for Indians; travel. (I) would like to pursue higher educational goals. *Biographical sources*: Principals and Views About Indian Education, (Rough Rock News); Candidate for NACIE (Navajo Times); History of Rough Rock, by Robert Roessell. *Published works*: Navajo Culture Outline, and Navajo Philosophy of Education.

BEGAY, JOHNNY C. (Navajo)
(school principal)
Affiliation: Aneth Community School, P.O. Box 600, Montezuma Creek, UT 84534 (801) 651-3271.

BEGAY, JONES (Navajo)
(school chairperson)
Affiliation: Black Mesa Community School, RRDS, Box 215, Rough Rock, AZ 86503 (602) 674-3632.

BEGAY, JUDI (Navajo)
(college instructor)
Affiliation: Navajo Community College, P.O. Box 580, Shiprock, NM 87420 (505) 368-5291

BEGAY, LEROY (Navajo) 1967-
(bookstore manager)
Born February 1, 1967, Shiprock, N.M. *Education*: Navajo Community College, AA, 1990. *Address*: P.O. Box 2892, Shiprock, NM 87420 (505) 368-5291 (office). *Affiliation*: Navajo Community College, Shiprock, NM (financial aid technician, 1988-89; bookstore manager, 1990-).

BEGAY, LORRAINE C. (Navajo)
(college instructor)
Affiliation: Instructor, Navajo Community College, Tsaile Rural Post Office, Tsaile, AZ 86556 (602) 724-3311.

BEGAY, MEREDITH MAGOOSH (Mescalero Apache) 1937-
(medicine woman)
Born May 2, 1937, Mescalero, N.M. *Education*: High school. *Home address*: 410 Yucca Dr., P.O. Box 91, Mescalero, NM 88340 (505) 671-4344. *Community activities*: Miss Mescalero Apache Committee; Bent-Mescalero School P.T.A.; Mescalero Indian Health Service (hospital board member); National Federation of Federal Employees Local 1472. *Award*: Bureau of Indian Affairs Special Achievement and Tribal Award. *Interests*: "I am active in my traditional religion and application of holistic medicine for my own tribal people. I have been a "medicine woman" for over twenty years. I am trying to keep up the tribal tradition, culture and heritage, along with other medicine men and women, including the school children. Presently give workshops on traditional medicine in cohesion with Western medicine."

BEGAY, RONALD C. (Navajo)
(administrative officer)
Affiliation: Crownpoint Comprehensive Health Care Facility, P.O. Box 358, Crownpoint, NM 87313 (505) 786-5291.

BEGAY, RUTH TRACY (Navajo) 1940-
(family nurse practitioner)
Born May 14, 1940, Ganado, Ariz. *Education*: Loretto Heights College, School of Nursing, Denver, Colo., BSN, 1978. *Principal occupation*: Family nurse practitioner. *Affiliation*: Director, Navajo Community College Health Center, Tsaile, AZ, 1978-90. *Other professional posts*: Member, Navajo Health Authority, Office of Nursing Education Board; member, Navajo Community College Nursing Program Board. *Memberships*: Arizona Nurses Association (council on practice); Arizona Public Health Association; Pacific Coast College Health Association; *Awards, honors*: Two documentary films on Nurse Practitioner on Navajo Reservation by NBC and University of Arizona, School of Medi-

cine, 1973; Navajo Community College 1978 Student Service Employee of the Year Award; Outstanding Young Woman of the Year, 1977. *Interests*: Involvement in local community health-social work among the Navajo people. Travel locally, regionally in college health service and nurses association. Interested in continual growth and development in cross-cultural aspects of a different society integrated with our own Navajo Society. *Biographical sources*: Articles: Arizona Nurses Association Newsletter, 1973; The Navajo Times, 1973; Gallup Independent, 1977.

BEHN, SALLY
(Indian band chief)
Affiliation: Fort Nelson Indian Band, RR 1, 293 Alaska Highway, Fort Nelson, British Columbia, Canada V0C 1R0 (604) 774-7688.

BEIM, ELIZABETH A.
(editor, director of public information)
Affiliation: The Gustav Heye Center, Museum of the American Indian (Newsletter), Smithsonian Institution, One Bowling Green, New York, NY 10004 (212) 283-2420.

*BELARDO, MARY E. (Cahuilla)
(tribal chairperson)
Affiliation: Torres-Martinez Band of Mission Indians, 66-725 Martinez Rd., Thermal, CA 92274 (619) 397-8144.

BELCOURT, ERNESTINE
(administrative officer)
Affiliation: Rocky Boy's PHS Indian Health Center, P.O. Box 664, Box Elder, MT 59521 (406) 395-4489.

*BELGARDE, LARRY (Ma-in-gun) (Turtle Mountain Chippewa) 1945-
(education administrator)
Born December 13, 1945, Belcourt, N.D. *Education*: University of Minnesota, MEd, 1971; Stanford University, PhD, 1993. *Principal occupation*: Education administrator. *Address*: RR 2, Box 74, Rolla, ND 58367 (701) 477-5605 (work). *Affiliation*: Turtle Mountain Community College, Belcourt, ND (president, 1987-; academic dean, 1993-). *Other professional posts*: Supt. for Education, Bureau of Indian Affairs, Belcourt, ND (7 years); director of Indian education, Duluth Public Schools, Duluth, MN. *Memberships*: American Educational Research Association; American Indian Higher Education Consortium (officer); National Indian Education Association. *Awards, honors*: Indian Education Fellow (Title V), 1988-92. *Interests*: Indian education; organizational sociology.

BELGARDE, PETER, Jr. (Sisseton-Wahpeton Sioux)
(tribal chairperson)
Affiliation: Devil's Lake Sioux Tribal Council, Sioux Community Center, Fort Totten, ND 58335 (701) 766-4221.

BELINDO, JON EDWIN (Gui-tain) (Kiowa/Pawnee/Choctaw/ Navajo) 1963-
(teacher-artist)
Born August 4, 1963, Oklahoma City, Okla. *Education*: East Central University (Ada, OK), BA, 1986; Oklahoma City University, M.Ed., 1994. *Principal occupation*: Teacher-artist. *Home address*: 2 W. Holly, Tuttle, OK 73089 (405) 381-4932. *Affiliations*: Program facilitator, Lawton Johnson O'Malley Program, Lawton, OK, 1986-

87; art teacher, Stratford High School, Stratford, OK, 1987-90; art teacher, Tuttle High School, Tuttle, OK, 1990-93; graduate student, Oklahoma City University, 1993-94. *Community activities*: Coach, Sunday school teacher; F.C.A. director. *Memberships*: Oklahoma Indian Counselors Association, 1988; National Arts Education Association, 1990; Oklahoma Fall Arts Institute Alumnus, 1992; Oklahoma Association for Gifted & Talented, 1994; Association for Supervision & Curriculum Development, 1994. *Community activities*: Tuttle Chamber of Commerce; sign & mural painter; church activity; Little League coach. *Awards, honors*: Susan Peters Art Award, 1981; recognized by ECU faculty (art dept.) as top senior of 1986; ECU Fine Arts Award, 1986; Adolf Van Pelt Scholarship Award for graduate studies in education; Oklahoma Fall Arts Institute Award, 1992; AITTP Scholarship (American Indian Teacher Training Program) for American Indian Research & Development (AIRD) - Full scholarship to get M.Ed in Gifted Education. *Interests*: "As a teacher, I am active in my community and church. When I find the time, I paint scenes from the Kiowa heritage. I am enrolled in the Kiowa Tribe. As a teacher/artist, I usually work more on my art in the summers. I have been listed as a top 2nd Generation Indian Artist in the U.S. My father is a well known Indian artist and leader. I have sold a great number of works to private collectors, and worked on a project with my dad that is currently in Japan (a painted tipi). I have exhibited and sold work in the Annual Trail of Tears Show in Tahlequah, OK and Red Earth in Oklahoma City. As an educator, I have attended workshops and seminars on education and recently traveled to Savannah, Georgia to attend an art teachers workshop. As an artist and educator, I feel it is important to keep up on current trends and to assimilate various influences into your profession. I also enjoy visiting art museums, traveling, sports and fishing. My experience at O.C.U. has broadened my awareness in how to relate to people, how to be a leader, and how to advocate for improvement within a tribe or school system. In art, I have also developed more of a unique personal style in painting & drawing. My future goals are to advocate for Indian education, develop educational materials for Indian children, publish books, and develop a small business that is art related."

BELKHAM, JACK
(Indian school principal)
Affiliation: Flandreau Indian School, 1000 N. Crescent, Flandreau, SD 57028 (605) 997-2724.

*BELKOFF, MARY (Eskimo)
(AK village council president)
Affiliation: Iqurmuit Tribe, P.O. Box 9, Russian Mission, AK 99657 (907) 584-551 1.

BELL, HARVEY
(Indian band chief)
Affiliation: Batchewana First Nation of Ojibways, 236 Frontenac St., Sault Ste. Marie, Ontario, Canada P6A 5K9 (705) 759-0914.

*BELL, KATHRYN
(film producer/writer)
Affiliation: AIMS, Inc., P.O. Box 274, Okmulgee, OK 74447 (918) 267-4033.

*BELL, LIBBY FOREHAND
(historic site manager)
Affiliation: Etowah Indian Mounds Historic Site, 813 Indian Mounds Rd., S.W., Cartersville, GA 30120 (404) 387-3737.

*BELL, TERRY
(museum director)
Affiliation: Mashantucket Pequot Museum & Cultural Research Center, P.O. Box 3060, Indiantown Rd., Ledyard, CT 06339 (203) 536-7200.

BELL, WILLIAM F. (Mississippi Choctaw) 1932-
(education specialist)
Born December 27, 1932, Philadelphia, Miss. *Education*: Meridian Jr. College, A.A., 1955; University of Southern Mississippi, B.S., 1957; University of Mississippi, M.Ed., 1964, Ed. Sp., 1976. *Principal occupation*: Education specialist. *Home address*: 6334 Wingate St., Apt. 302, Alexandria, VA 22312 (202) 208-6364 (work). *Affiliation*: Elementary Principal, Red Water Day School, Carthage, MS, til 1988; education specialist, Office of Indian Education Programs, Bureau of Indian Affairs, Washington, DC, 1988- . *Other professional posts*: Teacher, guidance counselor; administrative assistant, Governor's Office of Education & Training; director, Off-Reservation Indian Manpower Programs; planning specialist, National Indian Management Service, Inc. *Community activities*: Governor's Council on Manpower Planning, 1973-1975; Governor's Council on Adult Basic Education, 1973-1975. *Memberships*: Kappa Delta Pi, 1956; Phi Delta Kappa, 1977. *Awards, honors*: Appointed by Governor of Miss. as liaison officer between State and Tribal Government; Outstanding Performance, 1990, BIA-OIEP, Branch of Supplemental Support Services. *Interests*: Research and writing are my primary interests. I have written several articles about Indian education for college classes.

*BELLECOURT, CLYDE (Chippewa)
(Indian association executive director)
Address & Affiliation: unknown at time of publication.

*BELLECOURT, VERNON (Chippewa)
(Indian activist)
Address & Affiliation: unknown at time of publication.

BELLEGARDE, CLARENCE A.
(Indian band chief)
Affiliation: Chief, Little Black Bear Indian Band, Box 40, Goodeve, Saskatchewan, Canada S0A 1C0 (306) 334-2306.

BELONE, ELSIE
(Indian school principal)
Affiliation: Kinlichee Boarding School, Ganado, AZ 86505 (602) 755-3430.

BELONE, PHILLIP
(BIA agency supt. for education)
Affiliation: Laguna Agency, Bureau of Indian Affairs, P.O. Box 298, Old Laguna, NM 87026 (505) 552-6086.

*BEN, TERRY A. (Mississsippi Choctaw)
(school principal)
Affiliation: Choctaw Central Middle School, Rt. 7, Box 23, Philadelp[hia, MS 39350 (601) 656-8938.

*BEN, WENDY WESTON
(editor)
Affiliation: Native Arts Update," ATLATL, 2303 N. Central, Suite 104, Phoenix, AZ 85004 (602) 253-2731.

BENALLY, EVA M. (Navajo)
(Indian school principal)
Affiliation: Red Rock Day School, P.O. Drawer 10, Red Valley, AZ 86544 (602) 653-4456.

BENALLY, HERBERT (Navajo)
(college instructor)
Affiliation: Navajo Community College, P.O. Box 580, Shiprock, NM 87420 (505) 368-5291.

*BENALLY, JONES (FAMILY) (Navajo)
(Native American dance & music)
Born on Big Mountain, Ariz. *Education*: Traditional Navajo. *Principal occupation*: Native American dance & music. *Home address*: 6680 Columbine Blvd., Flagstaff, AZ 86004 (602) 527-1041. *Community activities*: President (Dine Bi Naal Gloosh Baa Ahaa Yaa) a 501-c3 dedicated to preserving cultural heritage; president of Grand Canyon Schools Indian Parent Association, 1988-90; president, Flagstaff Arts Council, 1992-95. *Interests*: "The Jones Benally family is a traditional Native American Dance Troupe consisting of Jones, his daughter Jeneda and sons Klee and Clayson Benally. They have shared their culture nationally and internationally. The family also has an original rock band called Blackfire. Their philosophy is that you can live in both worlds and never lose your heritage or identity." Published works: Albums -Tanz und Fest Compilation 92 (Hei-Deck Records, 1992); Soundtrack to Geronimo (Columbia Records, 1993; Navajo Reflections (Canyon Records, 1994.

*BENAY, JEFFREY
(commissioner)
Affiliation: The Governor's Advisory Commission on Native American Affairs, Pavilion Office Bldg., 109 State St., Montpelier, VT 05609 (802) 828-3333.

BENCHOFF, DONALD
(hospital director)
Affiliation: Sells PHS Indian Hospital, P.O. Box 548, Sells, AZ 85634 (602) 383-7251.

BENDS, LEONARD
(administrative director-IHS)
Affiliation: Crow Agency PHS Indian Hospital, Crow Agency, MT 59022 (406) 638-2624.

*BENEDICT, DANIEL
(school director)
Affiliation: Akwesasne Freedom School, P.O. Box 290, Rooseveltown, NY 13683.

BENEDICT, PATRICIA (Abenaki) 1956-
(executive director)
Born August 11, 1956, Waterbury, Conn. *Education*: Mattatuck Community College, Waterbury, Conn., A.S. (Alcohol and Drug Counseling), 1980. *Principal occupation*: Executive director. *Address & Affiliation*: American Indians for Development, Meriden, CT (203) 238-4009 (social worker, 1975-81; executive director, 1986-). *Other professional post*: Co-editor of American Indians for Development Newsletter; editor of May Wutche Aque'ne, American Indians for Development Journal. *Community activities*: American Indians for Development (past

chairman, board of directors); member , Energy Assistance Program Policy Making Board, Meriden, Conn.; member , Federal Regional Support Center, American Indian Committee, New Haven, Conn.; chairperson, A.I.D./Eagle Wing Press Powwow Committee; organized Waterbury Indian community into an organization. Membership: Title IV Indian Education Committee, Waterbury, Conn. (chairperson); Governor appointee of Connecticut Legislative Task Force o Indian Affairs; member and one of the incorporators of New England Indian Task Force. *Awards, honors*: Award for work performed on behalf of the Connecticut Indian Community, given by the Connecticut River Powwow Society. *Interests*: Personal interests include: furthering my education in the field of social work, attending and participating in Native American cultural activities, and with the assistance from my staff and Indians in Connecticut, American Indians for Development will once again become a multi-service agency . *Biographical source*: newspaper article, Waterbury Republican, Waterbury, Connecticut.

BENEDICT, SALLI
(editor)
Address: P.O. Box 20007, Santa Fe, NM 87504-0004. *Affiliation*: Editor, Akwekon Literary Journal, Akwesasne Notes, The Mohawk Nation, Hogansburg, NY, 1985-1990.

BENJAMIN, DELBERT (Wintun)
(tribal council chairperson)
Affiliation: Colusa Rancheria, P.O. Box 8, Colusa, CA 95932 (916) 458-8231.

BENN, ROBERT C
(BIA agency supt.)
Affiliation: Choctaw Agency, BIA, 421 Powell, Philadelphia, MS 39350 (601) 656-1521.

BENNALLEY, LUCINDA Y. (Navajo)
(advisor)
Affiliation: Council of Advisors, American Indian Heritage Foundation, 6051 Arlington Blvd., Falls Church, VA 22044-2788 (703) 237-7500.

*BENNETT, BEVERLY (Elwha S'Klallam)
(tribal chairperson)
Affiliation: Elwha S'Klallam Business Council, 2851 Lower Elwha Rd., Port Angeles, WA 98362 (206) 452-8471.

*BENNETT, JOSEPH
(health center director)
Affiliation: Tishomingo Chickasaw Health Center, 815 E. 6th St., Tishomingo, OK 73460 (405) 371-2392.

BENNETT, KAY C. (Navajo) 1922-
(writer, doll maker)
Born July 15, 1922, Sheepsprings, N.M. *Education*: Acquired, for the most part, as a teacher-interpreter at the Phoenix, Arizona Indian Boarding School. *Principal occupation*: Writer, doll maker. *Home address*: 6 Aida Ct., Gallup, N.M. 87301. *Community activities*: New Mexico Human Rights Commissioner , 1969-1971; Inter-Tribal Indian Ceremonial (director); McKinley County Hospital (advisory board). *Memberships*: Heard Museum, Gallup, N.M. (Navajo central committee); City of Gallup Citizens Committee. *Awards, honors*: Appointed Colonel-Aide-de Camp, staff of the Governor of New Mexico; elected New Mexico Mother of the Year, 1968; have received many awards at state fairs and

ceremonials for dolls & dresses I have created. *Interests*: Doll making, dress designing; entertaining as a singer; have published two albums of Navajo songs. I'm especially interested in Navajo culture, and serve on a school advisory board as a lecturer at schools in New Mexico and Arizona; travel. *Published works*: Kaibah: Recollections of a Navajo Girlhood (Westernlore Press, 1965; paperback, Kay Bennett, 1976); A Navajo Saga (Naylor Co., 1969).

BENNETT, NOEL KIRKISH 1939-
(organization director; author, artist, teacher)
Born December 23, 1939, San Jose, Calif. *Education*: Stanford University , B.A. (Art), 1961, M.A., 1962; Navajo Reservation, Weaving Apprenticeship, 1968-1976. *Principal occupation*: Organization director, author, artist, teacher. *Home address*: P.O. Box 1175, Corrales, N.M. 87048. *Affiliations*: Lecturer, College of Notre Dame, Belmont, Calif., 1963-1967; lecturer , University of New Mexico, 1971-1976; lecturer , International College, Los Angeles, 1979-1981; founder, Navajo Weaver Restoration Center , 1978-; Director, Shared Horizons, Corrales, N.M. (non-profit, educational, perpetuating the Navajo, Southwest textile art tradition. *Other professional post*: Navajo weaving workshops, lectures, demonstrations to museums, universities, and guilds across the nation, 1971-. *Awards, honors*: Cum Laude graduate and recipient of the Mortimer C. Levintritt Award for outstanding work in Departments of Art and Architecture, Stanford University , 1961; Weatherhead Foundation Grant, 1975 (writing of Navajo weaving beliefs and legends); Tennessee Humanities Council, 1982 (Navajo weaving workshop); Communication Arts Award, Three Looms, One Land: Shared Horizons poster award for concept, copy, photo, 1982; Skaggs Foundation Grants, 1986 for publishing of Halo of the Sun, 1989 for Bighorse -- The Warrior; National Endowment for the Arts, 1990 for "A Place in the Wild"; honorary member , Indian Arts and Crafts Association; board member , Navajoland Festival of the Arts (Navajo Tribe). *Interests*: "Painting, tapestry weaving, restoration of Navajo rugs, philosophy . Though intensely involved in my own painting, weaving and writing, the area of Navajo life and weaving continues to provide inspiration and satisfaction. With the nine years that I lived and wove on the Navajo Reservation as a basis, my core goals have been to seek out, internalize and share the beauty of traditional Navajo weaving in three main areas: the pure symmetry and balance of designs, refined through generations of use; the rhythm of effortless techniques, a oneness of self and loom evolving over time; and the underlying sustaining beliefs, legends and taboos that give meaning not only to the activity but beyond, to life itself." *Biographical sources*: Contemporary Authors; World Who's Who of Authors; Dictionary of International Biography; World Who's Who of Women; The Directory of Distinguished Americans; International Book of Honor; Personalities of America; Personalities of the West and Midwest; 5,000 Personalities of the World; International Directory of Distinguished Leadership; International Authors' and Writers' Who's Who. *Published works*: Working With the Wool -- How to Weave a Navajo Rug, with Tiana Bighorse (Northland Press, 1971); Genuine Navajo Rug – Are You Sure? (Museum of Navajo Ceremonial Art - Wheelwright Museum - and the Navajo Tribe, 1973); The

Weaver's Pathway -- A Clarification of the Spirit Trail in Navajo Weaving (Northland Press, 1974); How to Tell a Genuine Navajo Rug (final chapter) Navajo Weaving Handbook (Museum of New Mexico Press, 1974, 1977); Designing With the Wool -- Advanced Navajo Weaving Techniques (Northland Press, 1979); Shared Horizons-Navajo Textiles, (catalog of exhibition) with Susan McGreevy & Mark Winter (Wheelwright Museum, 1981); Halo of the Sun -- Stories Told and Retold (Northland Press, 1987); Bighorse -- The Warrior (University of Arizona Press, 1990); various articles.

BENNETT, ROBERT L. (Oneida) 1912-
(former commissioner of Indian Affairs)
Born November 16, 1912, Oneida, Wisc. *Education*: Haskell Institute, A.A. (Business Administration), 1931; Southeastern University , LL.B. 1941. *Home address*: 604 Wagon Train, SE, Albuquerque, N.M. 87123 (505) 298-8635. *Affiliations*: Former area director , Bureau of Indian Affairs; former commissioner of Indian Affairs, Bureau of Indian Affairs, Washington, DC, 1966-69; director, American Indian Law Center , University of New Mexico Law School, Albuquerque, NM, 1970-75. *Military service*: U.S. Marine Corps, (PFC,1943-45; Outstanding Recruit in Training Platoon). *Community activities*: Advisor, Board of Regents, Haskell Indian Jr . College and Southwestern Indian Polytechnic Institute; president, American Indian Athletic Hall of Fame; vice-chairman, Futures for Children; president, ARROW, Inc., Washington, DC; consultant on American Indians. *Memberships*: American Society for Public Administration; Society for Applied Anthropology; American Academy of Political and Social Science, 1960- ; American Indian Lawyers Association, Order of the Coif (Study of Law). *Awards, honors*: Indian Achievement Award, Indian Council Fire, 1962; Outstanding American Indian Citizen, 1966; founder of American Indian Graduate Center, 1969; founder of American Indian Athletic Hall of Fame, 1969; Outstanding Member of Oneida Tribe of Wisconsin, 1988. *Interests*: Consultant on American Indians - worked with Indian tribes throughout the U.S. including native peoples of the State of Alaska. Lecturer & instructor at seminars on American Indian affairs. *Biographical sources*: Indians of Today (Indian Council Fire, 1960); Robert Bennett (Dillon Press).

BENNETT, RUTH (Shawnee) 1942-
(assistant director of Indian organization)
Born December 12, 1942. *Education*: Indiana University, B.A., 1964; University of Washington, M.A. (English), 1968; California State University, San Francisco, Standard Secondary Teaching Credential (Multi-Cultural Education), 1973; University of California, Berkeley , Ph.D. (language and reading development with a specialization in bilingual education), 1979. *Principal occupation*: Assistant director of Indian organization. *Affiliations*: Teaching assistant, University of Washington, 1964-1966; pre-school teacher, Inner Sunset Neighborhood Cooperative, San Francisco, 1971-1972; teaching assistant, University of California, Berkeley , 1973-1974; children's literature instructor , School of the Arts, Berkeley High School, Calif., 1973-1974; enrichment program instructor , Washington Laboratory School, Berkeley , 1975-1978; resource teacher, Hoopa Elementary School, 1976-; field director , Native Language and Culture Program, 1978-1979, assistant director ,

1980-, Center for Community Development; director, Title VII, Institute of Higher Education Training Grant, Bilingual Emphasis Program, Center for Community Development, 1981-; teacher, Department of Education, Humboldt State University, 1981-. *Memberships*: Phi Delta Kappa, Phi Beta Kappa, Alpha Lambda Delta, Alpha Omicron Pi; University of California and Indiana University Alumni Associations. *Interests*: Dr. Ruth Bennett has conducted innovative curriculum work for 15 years, leading to computer uses for curriculum. *Published works*: Downriver Indians' Legends, 1983; Let's Go Now, 1983; 1983 Hupa Calendar, 1982; Karuk Fishing, 1983; Look Inside and Read, 1982; Unifon Update, 1983; 1983-1984 Yurok Unifon Calendar, 1983; Origin of Fire; Songs of a Medicine Woman; Hupa Spelling Book; Legends and Personal Experiences; Ceremonial Dances; Yurok Spelling Book; What Is An Indian?; Karuk Vocabulary Book; Karuk Fishing; Basket Weaving Among the Karuk; Tolowa Legends; Tolowa/English Lesson Units; and others (all published by The Center for Community Development, Humboldt State University; numerous articles, including Ph.D. dissertation, Hoopa Children's Storytelling, University of California, Berkeley.

BENOANIE, EDWARD
(Indian band chief)
Affiliation: Chief, Hatchet Lake Indian Band, Wollaston Lake, Saskatchewan, Canada S0J 3C0.

*BENSON, DIANE E. *(Lxeis)* **(Tlingit) 1959-**
(free-lance writer, talent agent,
stage director)
Born October 17, 1959, Yakima, Wash. *Education*: University of Alaska, B.A., 1985. *Principal occupation*: Free-lance writer, talent agent, stage director. *Address*: P.O. Box 770369, Eagle River, AK 99577 (907) 688-1370. *Affiliations*: Alaska Film Group, Anchorage, AK; Chugiak/Eagle River Chamber of Commerce, Eagle River, AK. *Other professional posts*: Founder, Alaska Native performance & Film Commission, 1993; Artist in the Schools Residency Program, 1993-; National Museum of the American Indian Consultant, 1991-92. *Community activities*: Board member, Arctic Moon Stage Co.; Chugiak Dog Mushers Club, Junior Club Chute Judge; founder, Kookeena Improv Troupe, 1985; Out North Theatre (member & guest artist - Anchorage); Artist in the Schools Residency Program, 1993-. *Memberships*: Alaska Press Women; National Congress of American Indians; National Association of the Self-Employed; American Indian Register, 1989-93. Awards, honors: University of Alaska Outstanding Alumni, 1990; race marshall, Chugiak Junioir Dog Musher's Club, 1993. Interests: Traditional dancing & singing - Tlingit & Haida Dancers of Anchorage, 1987-. First Alumni & first Native American to direct UAA Mainstage, 1993. Public speaing on theater, alcohol & drug recovery & motivation; workshop facilitation in acting & theater & combining cultural concepts, writing, poetry, research. Attended International Native American Writers Festival in Oklayoma, 1992; travel to Central America. *Biographical sources*: "Goose Girl Lives in Many Worlds" (Tundra Times, 7/6/83); "Fire in Her Heart" (Anchorage Time, 2/25/90). *Published works*: Rven Tells Stories: An Anthology, edited by Joseph Bruchac (Greenfield Review Press, 1991);Native Amerian Literatures: A Special Issue, 1994. I am currently writing for Gale Research, Multicultural Encyclopedia.

Films: Sacajawea -animated film received national & international awards (FilmFair Communications, Los Angeles, 1989); White Fang (Disney, 1989). Sister Warrior (feature film) script. Performed in many other local television spots, training video's and radio drama's, in addition, stage acting for 15 years.

*BENSON, DONALD E.
(museum director)
Affiliation: Fort de Buade Museum, 334 N. State St., St. Ignace, MI 49781 (906) 643-8686.

*BENSON, FOLEY C.
(museum director/curator)
Affiliation: Jese Peter Native American Art Museum, 1501 Mendocino Ave., Santa Rosa, CA 95401 (707) 527-4479.

*BENT BOX, SR., EDWARD (*Red Ute*)
(Southern Ute)
(flute maker)
Address: Red Ute, P.O. Box 2254, Ignacio, CO 81137 (303) 563-4128. Born around 1920, Red Ute has been making flutes (since the 1950's in his home on the Southern Ute Reservation) out of a variety of hardwoods - walnut, paduk, cherry, ebony as well as traditional red cedar. He decorates his flutes with traditional buckskin fringes and Indian beadwork designs. "The purpose of Indian flute music in contemporary society,' he says, "is to promote the feeling of peace and harmony in both the flute player and his audience."

BENTON, MARIA (Zia Pueblo) 1944-
(health educator)
Born July 17, 1944, Zia Pueblo, N.M. *Education*: Parks College, San Jose, CA (1 Yr.); University of New Mexico, Albuquerque (288 hrs.) Certified Chemical Dependency Health Educator. *Principal occupation*: Health educator. *Address*: Zia Route, Box 3, San Ysidro, N.M. 87053 (505) 766-8418 (work). *Affiliation*: Health educator, Southwestern Indian Polytechnic Institute, Albuquerque, NM, 1989-. *Awards, honors*: Community Service Award, Jemez Springs Municipal School Boards; Dedication & Excellence in Health Delivery Service, Five Sandoval Indian Pueblos.

BENTON, SHERROLE DAWN (*Ay-nah-wayne-shee-Quay*) **(Oneida/Ojibwe)1956-**
(editor, Native news)
Born December 1, 1956, Green Bay, Wisc. *Education*: University of Wisconsin, Green Bay, BA (Communications & the Arts), 1985. *Principal occupation*: Editor, Native news. *Home address*: 117 Illinois #10, Hayward, WI 54843 (715) 634-2100 (office). *Affiliations*: Editor, Regional Native News, WOJB-FM, Hayward, WI. *Other professional post*: Production coordinator, Regional Native News, WOJB-FM. *Community activities*: Parent Advisory Committee, LCO Ojibwe School, Hayward, WI. *Memberships*: Three Fires Society; Mide-wi-win Lodge. *Awards, honors*: Best Radio Feature; Outstanding American Indian Reporter. *Interests*: "My major vocational goal is to provide communication and cultural exchanges between Native American people and mainstream American society to encourage understanding, dialogue, respect and dignity among the different culture groups."

BENTZ, MARILYN
(professor)
Affiliation: American Indian Studies Center,

Dept. of Anthropology, University of Washington, C514 Padelford, GN-05, Seattle, W A98195 (206) 543-5240.

*BERG, LAURA
(editor)
Affiliation: "Wana Chinook Tymoo," Columbia River Inter-Tribal Fish Commission, 729 N.E. Oregon, Suite 200, Portland, OR 97232 (503) 238-0667.

BERG, MERRILL
(college president)
Affiliation: President, Little Hoop Community College, P.O. Box 269, Fort Totten, ND 58335 (701) 766-4415.

*BERGEN, RONALD (Oglala Sioux) 1946-
(educator)
Born July 8, 1946, Pine Ridge, S.D. *Education*: National College (Rapid City, SD), B.S., 1979. *Principal occupation*: Educator. *Home address*: 1345 Sheridan St., Hot Springs, SD 57747 (605) 745-4147 (work). *Affiliation*: Director, Title V Indian Education/Peer Tutorial Programs, Hot Springs Public Schools, Hot Springs, SD, 1984-. *Military service*: S.D. National Guard, 1964-68; U.S. Army, 1968-70; U.S. Navy, 1971-1973. *Community activities*: Board of Directors, Southern Hills Developmental Services; secretary/treasurer, Hot Springs Child Protection Teem; Hot Springs Public Schools Strategic Planning Committee; Hot Springs Youth Soccer Coordinator. *Memberships*: Disabled American Veterans, 1970-; Veterans of Foreign Wars, 1970- (life member).

*BERGGREN, KAREN
(park manager)
Affiliation: Homolovi Ruins State Park, 523 W. 2nd St., Winslow, AZ 86047 (602) 289-4106.

*BERIKOFF, HARIET (Eskimo)
(AK village council president)
Affiliation: Unalaska Village (Qualingin), P.O. Box 334, Unalaska, AK 99685 (907) 581-2290.

BERKE, DEBRA
(museum director)
Affiliation: U.S. Department of the Interior Museum, 18th & C Sts., Washington, DC 20240 (202) 208-4743.

BERKEY, CURTIS
(director-Indian law center)
Affiliation: Indian Law Resource Center, District Office, 601 E St., SE, Washington, DC 20003 (202) 547-2800.

BERNARD, ALLISON M.
(Indian band chief)
Affiliation: Chief, Eskasoni Indian Band, Eskasoni, Nova Scotia, Canada B0A 1J0 (902) 379-2800.

BERNARD, RAYMOND
(Indian band chief)
Affiliation: Abenakis de Wolinak, 4680 boul. Danube, Reserve Indienne de Wolinak, Becanour, Quebec G0X 1B0 (819) 294-6690.

BERNARD, STEPHENSON
(Indian band chief)
Affiliation: Chief, Fort Folly Indian Band, P.O. Box 21, Dorchester, New Brunswick, Canada E0A 1M0 (506) 379-6224.

BERNARDI, JOANNA
(executive director-Indian centre)
Affiliation: Executive director, Woodland Indian Cultural Educational Centre, P .O. Box 1506, Brantford, Ontario N3T 5V6 (519) 759-2653.

BERNARDINO, YVONNE E. (Nanticoke) 1930-
(office manager)
Born April 7, 1930, Philadelphia, Penn. *Education*: Community College of Philadelphia, AAS, 1979. *Home address*: 3801 Conshohocken Ave. #724, Philadelphia, P A 19131 (215) 574-9020 (work). *Affiliation*: Office manager, United American Indians of the Delaware V alley, Philadelphia, PA, 1976-. *Community activities*: Secretary, Advisory Council, United American Indians of the Delaware Valley; Mayors Office of Community Service, Advisory Council; Philadelphia Folklife Center, Artist (Fiber). *Memberships*: United American Indians of the Delaware V alley, 1972-; Nanticoke Indian Association, 1967-. *Awards, honors*: Ashanta Native American Track Team; Cultural Leadership Award, Philadelphia Folklife Center (Certificate of Recognition); Mayors Office of Community Services Advisory Council (Certificate of Recognition); WYBE-TV35 Pioneer V olunteer Award. *Biographical source*: Article, "Peace & Justice," by Trinity United Church of Christ, Telford, PA.

BERNSTEIN, BRUCE
(museum curator)
Affiliation: Museum of Indian Arts & Culture, Laboratory of Anthropology, P.O. Box 2087, 708 Camino Lejo, Santa Fe, NM 87504 (505) 827-6344.

*BERRY, ERNEST (Eskimo)
(AK village council president)
Affiliation: Native V illage of Shungnak, P .O. Box 63, Shungnak, AK 99773 (907) 437-2163.

*BERRY, FRANKLIN L.
(executive director)
Affiliation: Cook Inlet Native Assn., Anchorage, AK 99503 (907) 278-4641.

BERTHRONG, DONALD J. 1922-
(professor of history)
Born October 2, 1922, La Crosse, Wisc. *Education*: LaCross State Teachers College, LaCross, WI, 1940-42; University of Wisconsin, B.S., 1947, M.S., 1948, Ph.D., 1952. *Principal occupation*: Professor of history. *Address*: 1005 Kenwood Dr., Lafayette, Ind. 49705 (317) 494-4126. *Affiliations*: Instructor, University of Kansas City; assistant professor, associate professor, professor of history, University of Oklahoma; professor and head, Department of History, Purdue University, 1970-. *Other professional posts*: Fulbright Professor of History, University of Hong Kong, 1965-66. *Military service*: U.S. Army & Air Force, 1942-44; U.S. Army, 1944-46 (Second Lieutenant; only campaign ribbons for Pacific Theater and Philippines Campaign). *Memberships*: American Historical Association; Association of American Historians; Oklahoma Historical Society; W estern History Association; Agricultural History; American Association of University Professors. *Awards, honors*: Phi Beta Kappa, 1965, Purdue University chapter; Fellowship, Social Science Research Council; Fellowship, American Philosophical Society; Award of Merit, Association for State and Local History, for The Southern Cheyennes. *Interests*: Western U.S. history; expert witness before the Indian Claims Commission; Fulbright lecturer in

American history at the University of Hong Kong and Chinese University (Hong Kong, B.C.C.) *Biographical sources*: Who's Who in America, 1970-; Directory of American Scholars of History. *Published works*: Co-editor, Joseph Redford Walker and the Arizona Adventure (University of Oklahoma Press, 1956); The Southern Cheyennes (University of Oklahoma Press, 1963); A Confederate in the Colorado Gold Fields (University of Oklahoma Press, 1970); Indians of Northern Indiana and Southwestern Michigan (Garland, 1974); The Cheyenne and Arapaho Ordeal: Reservation and Agency Life in the Indian Territory, 1875-1907 (University of Oklahoma Press, 1976.

BERUBE, JERRY
(president-Indian centre)
Affiliation: President: Native Alliance of Quebec, 21 Brodeur Ave., Hull, Quebec, Canada J8Y 2P6 (613) 770-7763.

BETSAKA, JIM
(Indian band chief)
Affiliation: Chief, Nahanni Butte Indian Band, General Delivery, Trout Lake, Northwest Territories X0E 0N0.

*BETHMANN-MAHOOTY, BARBARA A.
(Ka Non Sen Ha W i) (Mohawk) 1933-
(Native American home/school coordinator)
Born September 2, 1933, Irondequoit, N.Y . *Home address*: 24 Pauline Cir., Rochester, NY 14623 (716) 359-4651; 359-5047 (work). *Affiliations*: Native American home/school coordinator, N.Y. State Native American Advisory Committee, Cornell University, Ithaca, NY, 1986-; Chair, American Indians of All Nations, Rochester, NY, 1989-. *Other professional posts*: Past member, NY State Advisory Committee to the Commissioner of Education, Indian Education, Albany, NY; past board member, Native American Cultural Center, Inc., Rochester, NY. *Community activities*: Began 1794 Canadaigua Treaty Committee; Mohawk storyteller, Women's Recognition Committee; switchboard operator in hospital for past 13 years. *Memberships*: AISES; American Indians of All nations. *Awards, honors*: Honored at W omen's Recognition Dinner, 1991; honored at Pow W ow, Rochester, NY, Sept. 1993. *Interests*: "Interested in the culture of our people, and present day issues. Married Chester B. Mahooty, noted Zuni silversmith and member of American Indian Dance Theatre, in Nov. 1993. (I) like to travel slowly -- see things of interest."

*BETTELYOUN, CHARLES
(school chairperson)
Affiliation: Porcupine Day School, P .O. Box 180, Porcupine, SD 57772 (605) 867-5336.

BETTELYOUN, LULU F. (JANIS)
(Oglala Sioux) 1947-
(teacher, social welfare/caseworker)
Born April 10, 1947, Pine Ridge, S.D. *Education*: Northern State College (Aberdeen, SD), 1965-68; Black Hills State College, (Spearfish, SD), B.S. (Education), 1972. *Principal occupation*: Teacher, social welfare/caseworker. *Home address*: P.O. Box 66, Pine Ridge, SD 57770.

BETTIS, RICHARD MACK (Di-yoTa-Li)
(United Keetowah Cherokee)1934-
(chief deputy county assessor)
Born March 15, 1934, Spiro, Okla. *Education*: Northeast State University , Tahlequah, OK, BA,

1955; Tulsa University (graduate school, 1955-56); Oklahoma City University Law School, JD, 1967. *Principal occupation*: Chief deputy county assessor. *Home address*: 3739 E. 43rd St., Tulsa, OK 74135 (918) 747-7779. *Affiliation*: Occupational Analyst, Oklahoma Employment Security Commission, 1956-67; Dept. of the Interior, Investigate EEO Complaints, Labor Relations Officer, Assistant Personnel Officer (15 years); chief deputy county assessor, Tulsa County, OK, 1979-. *Other professional posts*: Part time private law practice, 1968-; Mayor appointed member of Tulsa Indian Affairs Commission and elected chairperson seven consecutive terms; taught federal, state government at Tulsa Junior College Evening Division for its first ten years. Memberships: Oklahoma Bar Association, 1968-; U.S. Civil Rights Commission (Oklahoma Delegate Member, 1989-); Oklahoma Indian Historical Society (charter member, Governor appointee, 1986-); United Keetowah Band of Cherokee Indians of Oklahoma, 1972-. *Awards, honors*: Appointed by Dept. of the Interior to serve on White House Staff Team to change election power marketing agencies of the Interior to new U.S. Dept, of Energy. *Interests*: Church offices, activities; Indian community and art activities; Indian law activities; violin making, restoration, collecting, study and appraisals. *Published works*: "Have written articles on Cherokee Indian history , plus introductons and editing for Smithsonian Cherokee history publications; also articles on violins, history, etc."

BETWEEN LODGES, WILBUR (Oglala Sioux)
(tribal chairperson)
Affiliation: Oglala Sioux Tribal Council, Box H, No. 468, Pine Ridge, SD 57770 (605) 867-5821.

BEVIN, MELVILLE STANLEY
(Indian band chief)
Affiliation: Chief, Kitselas Indian Band, 4562 Queensway, Terrace, British Columbia, Canada V8G 3X6 (604) 635-5084.

*BEVINS-ERICSEN, SUSIE
(institute president)
Affiliation: Institute of Alaska Native Arts, P.O. Box 70769, Fairbanks, AK (907) 456-7491.

*BICK, RON
(editor)
Affiliation: Char-Koosta, Confederated Salish & Kootenai Tribes, P.O. Box 278, Pablo, MT 59855 (406) 675-3000.

*BIGBOY, MARY
(health director)
Affiliation: Bad River Health Services, P.O. Box 39, Odanah, WI 54861 (715) 682-7137.

BIG CROW, FRANCIS X.
(Indian school chairperson)
Affiliation: American Horse School, P.O. Box 660, Allen, SD 57714 (605) 455-2480.

BIG EAGLE, DUANE (Crow Creek Sioux)
(tribal chairperson)
Affiliation: Crow Creek Sioux Tribal Council, Box 50, Fort Thompson, SD 57339 (605) 245-2221.

BIG EAGLE, LAURA
(Indian band chief)
Affiliation: Ocean Man Indian Band, Box 157, Stoughton, Saskatchewan, Canada S0G 4T0 (306) 457-2697.

BIG GEORGE, PAULINE
(Indian band chief)
Affiliation: Big Island Indian Band, Morson P .O., Morson, Ontario, Canada P0W 1J0 (807) 488-5602.

*BIGGS, CURLEY (Ramah Navajo)
(tribal council president)
Affiliation: Ramah Navajo Chapter Council, Rte. 2, Box 13, Ramah, NM 87321 (505) 775-3342.

BIGHETTY, FRED
(Indian band chief)
Affiliation: Barren Lands Indian Band, Brochet, Manitoba, Canada R0B 0B0 (204) 323-2300.

BIGHETTY, PASCAL
(Indian band chief)
Affiliation: Mathias Colomb Indian Band, Pukatawagan, MB, Canada R0B 1A0 (204) 553-2090.

BILL, DAVID
(Indian band chief)
Affiliation: Tseycum Indian Band, Box 2501, Sidney, British Columbia, Canada V8L 4C1 (604) 656-0858.

BILL, JACOB
(Indian band chief)
Affiliation: Chief, Pelican Lake Indian Band, P .O. Box 9, Leoville, Sask.n, Canada S0J 1N0.

BILLETTE, GORDON
(Indian band chief)
Affiliation: Chief, Buffalo River Indian Band, Dillon, Sask., Canada S0M 0S0 (306) 282-2033.

BILLIE, JAMES (Seminole of Florida)
(tribal chairperson)
Affiliation: Seminole Tribal Council, 6073 Stirling Rd., Hollywood, FL 33024 (305) 583-7112.

BILLINGTON, JAMES H.
(librarian)
Affiliation: Library of Congress, 1st & Independence, SE, Washington, DC 20540 (202) 707-5522.

*BILLIE, LOIS (Seminole of Florida)
(Indian school chairperson)
Affiliation: Ahfachkee Day School, Star Route, Box 40, Clewiston, FL 33440 (813) 983-6348.

*BILLUM, HARRY (Athapascan)
(AK village council president)
Affiliation: Chitina Village Council, P.O. Box 31, Chitina, AK 99566 (907) 563-6643.

BILLY, BRUCE
(B.I.A. agency chairperson for education)
Affiliation: Chairperson, Shiprock Agency, Bureau of Indian Affairs, P.O. Box 3239, Shiprock, NM 87420 (505) 368-4427 Ext. 321; chairperson, Beclabito Day School, P .O. Box 1146, Shiprock, NM 87420 (602) 656-3555.

*BILLY, CHARMAIN (Me-tigh)
(Ponca of Oklahoma)
(executive director)
Born in Ponca City, Okla. *Education*: University of Oklahoma, B.A., 1985. *Principal occupation*: Executive director. *Home address*: 1832 Maple Lane, Lawrence, KS 66044 (913) 832-0887; 841-8202 (work). *Affiliation*: Executive Director, Lawrence Indian Center, Lawrence, KS, 1993-. *Other professional post*: Director, Child Welfare Program, Ponca Tribe of Oklahoma, 1985-86.

Community activities: Indian Education/Parent Committee (vice-president, secretary , historian), 1980-; Native American Law Enforcement Task Force, 1993-94. *Memberships*: Up With People (Alumni, 1968-); Oklahoma University Native American Alumni Association; Chilocco Alumni Association; Haskell Indian Nations University Alumni Association. *Awards, honors*: Full scholarships to attend "Summer Institute on American Indian Affairs, University of Colorado, Boulder; "Clyde Warrior Institute on American Indian Affairs", Stout University , Menominee, WI. *Interests*: Educational and legal matters as they affect Native Americans. Travels with "Up With People" included countries of Germany , France, Austria, Spain, Japan, and Korea. *Biographical source*: "Journal World", July 25, 1993.

BILLY, PAULINE
(B.I.A. agency education coordinator)
Affiliation: Education coordinator , Eastern Navajo Agency, Bureau of Indian Affairs, P.O. Box 328, Crownpoint, NM 87313 (505) 786-6150.

*BILLY, STEVEN (Eskimo)
(AK village council president)
Affiliation: Chefornak Village Council, P .O. Box 29, Ekwok, AK 99561 (907) 867-8850.

BILLYBOY, THOMAS
(Indian band chief)
Affiliation: Alexandria Indian Band, Box 4, RR 2, Quesnel, B.C., Can. V2J 3H6 (604) 993-4324.

*BIRCHFIELD, D.L. (Choctaw of OK)
(book review editor)
Education: University of Oklahoma, M.A., 1972, J.D., 1975. *Affiliations*: News From Indian Country, Indian Country Communications, Inc., Rt. 2 Box 2900-A, Hayward, WI 54843 (715) 634-5226; contributing editor , "Moccasin Telegraph," Fairfax, VA.

*BIRCHUM, JAMES (Shoshone)
(tribal chairperson)
Affiliation: Yomba Tribal Council, HC61, Box 6275, Austin, NV 89310 (702) 964-2463.

BIRCKEL, PAUL
(Indian band chief)
Affiliation: Champagne/Aishihik Indian Band, Box 5309, Haines Junction, Yukon, Canada Y0B 1L0 (403) 634-2288.

BIRD BEAR, DUANE
(BIA agency supt.)
Affiliation: Rocky Boy's Agency, BIA, Box Elder, MT 59521 (395-4476).

*BIRD, MAGEL
(clinic president)
Affiliation: Indian Law Clinic, University of Montana Law School, Missoula, MT 59806 (406) 243-6480.

BIRD, PEGGY (Santo Domingo Pueblo)
(attorney)
Resides in Albuquerque, NM (505) 368-4377 (work). *Memberships*: New Mexico Indian Bar Association (president); Native American Bar Association; American Bar Association.

BIRD, JOSEPH
(Indian band chief)
Affiliation: Weenusk (Peawanuk) Indian Band, Box 1, Peawanuk, Ontario, Canada P0L 2H0 (705) 473-2554.

*BIRD BEAR, DUANE
(BIA agency supt.)
Affiliation: Spokane Agency, Bureau of Indian Affairs, P.O. Box 389, Wellpinit, WA 99040 (509) 258-4561.

*BIRON, THOMAS ANTHONY (Animkii Migizi) (Anishnaabe) 1951-
(college administrator , faculty, free lance journalist)
Born October 16, 1951, Sault Ste. Marie, ON, Can. *Education*: Lake Superior State College, B.S., 1973; Northern Michigan University , MPA, 1975; currently working on PhD in socio-cultural anthropology at Michigan State University . *Principal occupation*: College administrator , faculty, free lance journalist. *Home address*: 555 Carrie, Sault Ste. Marie, MI 49783 (906) 632-4728; (517) 483-9803 (work). *Affiliation*: Administrator/faculty, Native American Leadership Program Program, Lansing Community College, Lansing, MI. *Other professional posts*: Editoriual advisory board, Lansing State Journal; deans board of advisors, College fo Human Ecology, Michigan State University; President's Advisory Committee, Affirmative Action, Lansing Community College. *Military service*: U.S. Army (Medic - Certificate in Advanced Leadership Training & Race Relations. *Community activities*: Mayor's Human Relations Advisory Committee; board member , Spiritual Healing Lodge-Garden River First Nation, Ontario, Can. *Memberships*: Lansing Human Relations Advisory Committee; Public Administrators Association; Word Craft Circle, Native American Writers Guild, *Interests*: Performing arts, journalism, educational video production, Anishnaabe issues in the Great Lakes cultural region. Youth leadershio through intergenerational programming. *Published works*: Native American Values: Survival & Renewal; article, "Anishinaabe Medicine Community Health Planning."

BISAILLON, ALFRED
(Indian band chief)
Affiliation: Thessalon Indian Band, Box 9, RR 2, Thessalon, Ontario, Canada P0R 1L0 (705) 842-2323.

*BISONETTE, TERRI
(editor)
Affiliation: Explore Indian Country , Indian Country Communications, Rte. 2, Box 2900-A, Hayward, WI 54843 (715) 634-5226.

BITSIE, OSCAR (Navajo) 1935-
(teacher)
Born October 30, 1935, Tohatchi, N.M. *Education*: Fort Lewis College, BA, 1964; Northern Arizona University, MA, 1973, post graduate work in school administration, 1974-75. *Principal occupation*: Teacher. *Home address*: P.O. Box 1496, Tohatchi, NM 87325. *Affiliations*: Gallup-McKinley County Schools, Gallup, NM; teacher of social studies, Tohatchi Middle School, Tohatchi, NM. *Other professional posts*: Coordinated Title 7 - Bilingual Education, Johnson-O'Malley Indian Education, Title IV - home/school liaison coordinator . *Military service*: U.S. Army 1958-60 (Expert Rifle; Good Conduct Medal). *Community activities*: Tohatchi Chapter President, 1970-74, V ice President, 1978-82; Public Health Service, Gallup, NM (board member, 1970-80); Public Health Service, Gallup Indian Medical Center (health board president, 1980-); Friendship Service for Alcoholic Recovery Center (board of directors, vice-

president, 1982-85). *Memberships*: Christian Reformed Church (delegate to Calvin College in Michigan, 1976); Navajo Tribe. *Awards, honors*: Community service award by Tohatchi Chapter for Community Leadership. *Interests*: Reading books in social studies; travel throughout the Rockies for historical information; political activities in Navajo Tribe, county and state.

*BITSOI, LeMANUEL
(library distribution)
Affiliation: Navajo Nation Library System, Book Distribution Services, P.O. Box 1484, Gallup, NM 87301 (505) 863-6058.

BITTEM, ANDREW
(Indian band chief)
Affiliation: Chief, Berens River Indian Band, Berens River P.O., Berens River, Manitoba, Canada R0B 0A0 (204) 382-2161.

BITTLE, CHERYL A.
(health programs director)
Affiliation: Portland Area Office, Bureau of Indian Affairs, 1220 S.W. Third Ave., Rm. 476, Portland, OR 97204 (503) 326-3288.

BLACK BEAR, ROY
(museum owner)
Affiliation: Owner, Black Bear Museum, P.O. Box 47, Esopus, NY 12429.

BLACK, DOUGLAS
(IHS-associate director)
Affiliation: Dept. of Health & Human Services, USPHS, Indian Health Service, Office of Tribal Activities, Rm. 6A-05, 5600 Fishers Lane, Rockville, MD 20857 (301) 443-1104.

BLACK, HERBERT C.
(Indian school principal)
Affiliation: Navajo Mountain Boarding School, P.O. Box 10010, Tonalea, AZ 86044 (602) 672-2851.

*BLACK, KENNETH E. (Otoe-Missouria)
(tribal council chairperson)
Affiliation: Otoe-Missouria Tribal Council, Rt. 1, Box 62, Red Rock, OK 74651 (405) 723-4434.

BLACK, LYDIA
(professor of Alaskan native studies)
Affiliation: Department of Alaskan Native Studies, University of Alaska, College of Liberal Arts, Fairbanks, AK 99701 (907) 474-7288.

BLACK, MARY A. (Iroquois) 1955-
(attorney)
Born May 4, 1955, Tulsa, Okla. *Education*: University of Oklahoma, BS, 1978; Oklahoma City University Law School, JD, 1981. *Principal occupation*: Attorney. *Home address*: 20 Rice Rd., Shawnee, OK 74801 (405) 275-0123 (office). *Affiliation*: Attorney, Private Pratcice, Shawnee, OK, 1982-. *Other professional posts*: District Judge, Absentee Shawnee Tribe; Supreme Court Justice, Sac & Fox Nation. *Memberships*: American Indian Bar Association; Oklahoma Indian Bar Association (secretary, 1991-92); Oklahoma Bar Association; Oklahoma Trial Lawyers Association; American Trial Lawyers Association; American Bar Association; Lawyer-Pilot Bar Association; Pottawatomie County Bar Association (secretary, 1990; treasurer, 1991, 1992; Law Day Committee, 1984-). *Interests*: "Private practice in law with emphasis in personal injury and Indian law."

BLACK, ROBERT. A.
(professor)
Affiliation: Professor, Native American Studies Department, University of California, Dwinelle Hall, Suite 3415, Berkeley, CA 94720 (415) 642-3391.

BLACK, WILLIAM A.
(BIA agency supt.)
Affiliation: Puget Sound Agency, Bureau of Indian Affairs, 3006 Colby Ave., Federal Bldg., Everett, WA 98201 (206) 258-2651.

BLACK BEAR, BEN, Jr.
(museum chairperson)
Affiliation: Buechel Memorial Lakota Museum, 350 S. Oak St., Box 499, St. Francis, SD 57572 (605) 747-2745.

BLACKHAWK, JOHN (Winnebago)
(tribal chairperson)
Affiliation: Winnebago Tribal Council, Hwy. 75, Box 687, Winnebago, NE 68071 (402) 878-2272. *Other professional post*: executive director, Nebraska State Commission on Indian Affairs, Lincoln, NE..

BLACKJACK, RODDY
(Indian band chief)
Affiliation: Chief, Little Salmon-Carmacks Indian Band, General Delivery, Carmacks, Yukon, Canada Y0B 1C0 (403) 863-5576.

BLACKMAN, BAPTISTE
(Indian band chief)
Affiliation: Cold Lake Indian Band, Box 1769, Grand Centre, Alberta, Canada T0A 1T0 (403) 594-7183.

*BLAESER, KIMBERLY M.
(White Earth Anishinabe)
(professor)
Born in Billings, Mont. *Education*: University of Notre Dame, M.A., 1982, Ph.D., 1990. *Principal occupation*: Professor. *Address & Affiliation*: University of Wisconsin, Milwaukee, WI, 1990- (414) 229-4511. *Other professional posts*: Reporter/photographer; technical writer, lecturer, instructor, teaching fellow. *Community activities*: Native American Prize in Literature (member, Governing Board, 1991-; member, Prize Committee, 1988-91); member, Educational Advisory Committee, Friends of the Fox River, 1990-; member, Board of Directors, Independent Indian Relief, Inc., 1983-84. *Memberships*: Modern Language Association; American Studies Association; Association of Studies in American Indian Literature. *Awards, honors*: Francis C. Allen Fellowship, D'Arcy McNickle Center for the History of the American Indian, The Newberry Library, 1985; Zohm Research Travel Grant, University of Notre Dame, 1987; Research Award, University of Wisconsin Institute on Race & Ethnology, 1992. *Interests*: "Since my interests include wildlife and nature photography, canoeing and hiking, these activities take me to places like the BWCA and Alaska, and these excursions, in turn, feed my creative writing and compliment my work in Native American literature." *Published works*: Gerald Vizenor: Writing -- In the Oral Tradition (University of Oklahoma Press, 1993); scholarly articles on Native American literature in journals & books as well as poetry & personal essays in journals.

BLAESER, ROBERT A.
(White Earth Ojibwe) 1953-
(attorney)
Born December 31, 1953, White Earth, Minn. *Education*: Concordia College, BA, 1976; University of Minnesota Law School, JD, 1979. *Principal occupation*: Attorney. *Home address*: 840 Midland Square Bldg., Minneapolis, MN 55401 (612) 338-6825 (work). *Affiliation*: Senior partner, Robert A. Blaeser & Associates, Minneapolis, MN, 1980-. *Other professional posts*: Member, Supreme Court Task Force on Racial Bias in the Courts; Supreme Court Implementation Committee on Diversity & Racial Fairness in the Courts. *Memberships*: Minnesota American Indian Bar Association (board of directors, founding member, and past officer); Minnesota Indian Chamber of Commerce; Minnesota Trial Lawyers Association; American Trial Lawyers Association; American Bar Association; Minnesota State Bar Assn. (board of governors); Hennepin County Bar Assn. (governing council). *Interests*: "I practice exclusively in the area of civil litigation, concentrating on products liability, personal injury & Workers' Compensation."

*BLAINE, SILAS (Crow Creek Sioux)
(BIA education chairperson)
Affiliation: Bureau of Indian Affairs, Crow Creek/ Lower Brule Agency, P.O. Box 139, Fort Thompson, SD 57339 (605) 245-2398.

BLAIR, BILLY
(Indian band chief)
Affiliation: White River Indian Band, Beaver Creek, Yukon Y0B 1A0 (403) 862-7802.

BLAKE, GRACE
(Indian band chief)
Affiliation: Chief, Arctic Red River Indian Band, General Delivery, Arctic Red River, Northwest Territories X0E 0B0 (403) 953-3201.

BLANCHE, JOHN G., III
(executive staff director)
Affiliation: Indian Law Section, Federal Bar Association, 1815 H St., NW, Suite 408, Washington, DC 20006 (202) 638-0252.

*BLANKENSHIP, LAWRENCE, Jr.
(historic site manager)
Affiliation: Kolomoki Mounds State Park & Historic Site, Route 1, Box 114, Blakely, GA 31723 (912) 723-5296.

*BLATCHFORD, EDGAR P.
(government commissioner)
Affiliation: Alaska Dept. of Community & Regional Affairs, P.O Box 112100, Juneau, AK 99811 (907) 465-4700.

BLAZER, ARTHUR L.
(BIA agency supt.)
Affiliation: Ute Mountain Ute Agency, BIA, General Delivery, Towaoc, CO 81334 (303) 565-8471.

BLODGETT, JEAN
(museum curator)
Affiliation: Curator of Native Indian and Inuit Art, The McMichael Canadian Art Collection, 10365 Islington Ave., Kleinberg, Ontario L0J 1C0 (416) 893-1121.

BLOMQUIST, P.S.
(editor)
Affiliation: Editor, Char-Koosta, Confederated Salish & Kootenai Tribes, P.O. Box 278, Pablo, MT 59855.

BLONDEAU, MAURICE
(executive director)
Affiliation: Saskatoon Indian & Metis Friendship Centre, 168 Wall St., Saskatoon, Saskatchewan, Canada S7K 1N4 (306) 244-0174.

BLONDIN, ETHEL (Western Arctic)
(parliament member)
Affiliation: Canadian Pariliament, Parliament Bldgs., Ottawa, ON K1A 0A4 (613) 992-2848.

*BLOOMFIELD, RICHARD E.
(Indian center president)
Affiliation: American Indian Center, 818 E. Davis, Grand Prairie, TX 75050 (214) 262-1349.

BLOSSOM, LESLIE L.
(director-Indian commission)
Affiliation: Nevada Indian Commission, 4600 Kietzke Lane #B-116, Reno, NV 89502 (702) 789-0347.

BLUE, BETTY
(editor)
Affiliation: Ini-Mi-Kwa-Zoo-Min, Minnesota Chippewa Tribe, P.O. Box 217, Cass Lake, MN 56633.

*BLUE, GILBERT (Catawba)
(tribal chairperson)
Affiliation: Catawba Indian Nation, P.O. Box 11106, Rock Hill, SC 29731 (803) 366-4792.

BLUE, HELEN
(editor)
Affiliation: The Circle, Boston Indian Council, 105 S. Huntington Ave., Jamaica Plain, MA 02130 (617) 232-0343.

BLUE SPRUCE, GEORGE, Jr.
(Fon-Tem-Dey-Sten)
(Laguna/San Juan Pueblo) 1931-
(Ass't. Surgeon General, USPHS {retired})
Born January 16, 1931, Santa Fe, N.M. *Education*: Creighton University, D.D.S., 1956; University of California School of Public Health, M.P.H., 1967; Federal Executive Institute, Certificate, 1973. *Principal occupation*: Health systems director. *Home address*: 3834 E. Yale, Phoenix, AZ 85008 (602) 265-8994. *Affiliations*: Dental officer, U.S. Navy Dental Clinic, 1956-58; dental officer, U.S.P.H.S. Indian Hospital, Fort Belknap, MT, 1958-60; U.S.P.H.S. Outpatient Clinic, New York, NY (resident, 1960-61; deputy dental director, 1961-63; resident in dental public health, Dental Health Center, San Francisco, CA, 1967-68; consultant in dental health (special assignment), Pan American Health Organization, World Health Organization, Washington, DC, 1968-70; Education Development Branch, Division of Dental Health, National Institutes of Health, Bethesda, MD - chief, Auxiliary Utilization Section, 1971, special assistant to the director for American Indian Affairs, 1971, director, Office of Health Manpower Opportunity, 1971-73; liaison officer for Indian concerns, Health Resources Administration, USPHS, Dept. of HEW, 1973-74; director, Office of Native American Programs, Office of Human Development, Dept. of HEW, 1976-78; director, Indian Health Manpower Development, Indian Health

Service, DHEW, 1978-79; director & assistant Surgeon General, Phoenix Area Indian Health Service, USPHS, 1979-90; president, Society of American Indian Dentists, 1990-. *Other professional posts*: Chairman, Intra-Departmental Council on Indian Affairs (DHEW); chairman, Health Manpower Opportunity Advisory Committee; chairman, Feasibility Study Team for Project: Center for Health Professions Education (Navajo Reservation, Arizona); special consultant, Special Committee for the Socio-economically Disadvantaged, American Dental Hygienist's Association; regional director, Indian Health Service, USPHS. *Military service*: U.S. Navy, 1956-58 (Navy Citation Medal-dentist for Atomic Submarine "Nautilus" prior to underwater/North Pole journey). *Community activities*: Was on the Phoenix City Council; Phoenix Indian Center Board of Directors; president, North American Indian Tennis Association. *Memberships*: National Indian Education Association (board of directors); Health Education Media Association (board of directors, Minority Affairs); American Indian Bank (board of directors); American Fund for Dental Education (member, Selection Committee); Task Force for Medical Academic Achievement Program; Students American Veterinary Medicine Association (member, Selection Committee; Health Manpower Study for American Indians (member, Advisory Committee); Navajo Health Authority (member, board of commissioners, Kellog Scholarship Committee, Dean Selection Committee, Health Professions Education Committee); American Indian School of Medicine - Feasibility Study (member, Advisory Council); Health Professions Education System, Rockville, MD (board of directors); USPHS Commissioned Officers' Association; American Public Health Association; American Indian Physicians' Association; American Dental Association; American Association of Dental Schools; New Mexico State Dental Society; North American Indian Tennis Association (president); U.S. Lawn Tennis Association; Society of American Indian Dentists; American Indian Science and Engineering Society. *Awards, honors*: Outstanding American Indian for 1972, American Indian Exposition, Inc., Anadarko, Okla.; Outstanding American Indian Achievement Award, 1974, American Indian Council Fire, Inc., Washington, D.C.; Award of Merit, presented by the Association of American Indian Physicians for: Significant Contributions Towards Raising the Level of Health Care of the American Indian and Alaskan Native, August 1980; Alumni of the Year, presented by Creighton University (Omaha, NE) in May 1984, for his distinguished service to his fellow man and his alma mater while keeping with the finest traditions of the University; Annual Association of American Medical Colleges Award for Health Professional contributing to the health of American Indians; Annual Award for Most Outstanding American Indian Health Professional by the American Indian Science and Engineering Society. *Biographical sources*: American Indians of Today; Contemporary American Indian Leaders; Who's Who in the Federal Government, Second Edition; National Indian Directory (National Congress of American Indians); Dictionary of International Biography; Men of Achievement, 1974; Journal of American Indian Science and Engineering Society, 1986. *Interests*: "Have been visiting instructor on health care administration for St. Francis College (Joliet, IL) and Northern Michigan University (Marquet, MI). Am presently consultant to Fed-

eral Government in the review of grants for medical schools and Centers of Excellence in dental and pharmacy schools. *Published works*: Articles: Toward More Minorities in Health Professions (National Medical Association Journal, Sept. 1972); Needed: Indian Health Professionals (Harvard Medical Alumni Bulletin, Jan.-Feb. 1972); Health Manpower Grants Open New Opportunities for American Indians (Official Newsletter of the Association of American Indian Physicians, Vol. 1, No. 1, Nov. 1972); The American Indian as a Dental Patient (Public Health Reports, Dec. 1961); The Fabrication of Simplified Dental Equipment - A Manual (Pan American Health Organization Publication, pending publication); The Development and Testing of a Mobile Dental Care Unit (Public Health Residency Report).

BLUMER, THOMAS J. 1937-
(senior editor, Library of Congress)
Born July 7, 1937, Freeport, N.Y. *Education*: University of Mississippi, BA, 1967, MA, 1968; University of South Carolina, PhD, 1976. *Principal occupation*: Senior editor, Library of Congress (Law Library). *Home address*: 642 A St., NE, Washington, DC 20002 (202) 707-9862 (work). *Affiliations*: Assistant professor, Tidewater Community College, Portsmouth, VA, 1968-72; Teaching assistant, University of South Carolina, Columbia, S.C., 1972-76; lecturer in English, Winthrop College, Rock Hill, S.C., 1976-77; Data Analyst, Planning Research Corp., McLean, Va., 1977-78; senior editor, European Law Division, Law Library, Library of Congress, 1978-; consultant, Native American Rights Fund, Boulder, Colo., 1980-; consultant, McKissick Museums, University of South Carolina, 1984-; consultant, Schiele Museum of Natural History, Gastonia, NC, 1984-; editor, American Indian Libraries Newsletter, American Library Association, Chicago, IL, 1984-87; consultant, Pamunkey Indian Museum, King William, Va., 1985-; editor, Insights, Library of Congress Professional Association Newsletter, 1987-89; historian, Catawba Nation Restoration of Justice Project, Catawba Nation, Rock Hill, SC, 1989-. *Military service*: U.S. Navy, 1956-60. *Memberships*: South Carolina Historical Association, 1986-; Cherokee Indian Historical Association, 1980-; York County Genealogical & Historical Society, 1989-. *Interests*: Southeastern Indians, Catawba Indian history, Pamunkey Indian history, Southern Indian pottery traditions (Catawba, Cherokee, Pamunkey); lectures. *Published works*: Bibliography of the Catawba (Scarecrow Press, 1987); "History as a Tool in a Folklife Study of the Catawba Indians of South Carolina" (New York Journal of Folklore, 1983); "Wild Indians and the Devil: The Contemporary Catawba Indian Spirit World" (American Indian Quarterly, 1985); "Catawba Indian Influence on the Cherokee Indian Pottery Tradition" (Appalachian Journal, 1987; and other articles. *Works in Progress*: Catawba Indian Pottery: The Survival of a Folk Tradition, book-length study being revised for publication; Catawba Indian Folk History Project, 1980-; Catawba Indian Design Motifs, book-length study.

*BLUSTAIN, MALINDA
(museum collections manager)
Affiliation: Robert S. Peabody Museum of Archaeology, Phillips Academy, Andover, MA 01810 (508) 749-4490.

BLYTHE, FRANK
(executive director)
Affiliation: Native American Public Broadcasting Consortium, P.O. Box 83111, Lincoln, NE 68501 (402) 472-3522.

BOATMAN, JOHN
(program coordinator)
Affiliation: Coordinator, Native American Studies Program, College of Letters & Sciences, P.O. Box 413, University of Wisconsin, P.O. Box 413, Milwaukee, WI 53201.

BOB, MARVIN
(Indian band chief)
Affiliation: Chief, Pavilion Indian Band, P.O. Box 609, Cache Creek, British Columbia, Canada V0K 1H0 (604) 256-7415.

BOBBISH, JAMES
(Indian band chief)
Affiliation: Chief, Chisasibi Indian Band, P.O. Box 150, Chisasibi, Quebec, Canada J0M 1E0 (819) 855-2878.

BOBBY, PHILLIP
(AK village council president)
Affiliation: Lime Village Council, Lime Village, AK 99627 (907) 526-5126.

BODNER, DEBRA
(museum curator, editor)
Affiliation: Curator & editor (Newsletter), Museum of Indian Archaeology, University of Western Ontario, Lawson-Jury Bldg., London, Ontario, Canada N6G 3M6 (519) 473-1360.

***BOGDA, TED**
(school supt.)
Affiliation: St. Francis Indian School, P.O. Box 379, St. Francis, SD 57572 (605) 747-2299.

***BOGGS, DONNA**
(administrative coordinator)
Affiliation: Administrative coordinator, American Indian Studies Department, San Diego State University, College Ave., San Diego, CA 92182-0387 (619) 594-6991.

***BOHAM, RUSSELL**
(program director)
Affiliation: Indian Natural Resource-Science & Engineering Program, Humboldt State University, McMahan House 80, Arcata, CA 95521 (707) 826-4994.

***BOINTY, GRACE**
(librarian)
Affiliation: Kiowa Tribal Library, P.O. Box 369, Carnegie, OK 73015 (405) 654-2300.

BOISSIERE, ROBERT (Giapateu-White Feather) 1914-
(retired, writer)
Born December 23, 1914, France. *Education*: Law School, Paris (three years). *Principal occupation*: Retired, writer. *Home address*: Route 11, Box 6B, Santa Fe, NM 87501 (505) 455-2138. *Military service*: World War II, France (two decorations). *Memberships*: Western Writers of America. *Biographical sources*: Contemporary Authors. *Published works*: Po-Pai-Mo - The Search for White Buffalo Woman (Sunstone Press, 1983); The Hopi Way - An Odyssey (Sunstone Press, 1985); Meditations With the Hopi (Bear and Co., 1986); The Return of Pahana (Bear and Co., 1990).

BOISSONEAU, DARRELL E.
(Indian chief)
Affiliation: Garden River Indian Band, Site 5, Box 7, RR 4, Garden River, Ontario, Canada P6A 5K9 (705) 942-4011.

BOIVIN, MARCEL
(Indian band chief)
Affiliation: Chief, Bande Indienne de Weymont Achie, Reserve indienne de Weymontachie via Sanmaur, Quebec, Canada G0A 4M0 (819) 666-2237.

BOLTON, ANNE E.
(BIA agency supt.)
Affiliation: Michigan Agency, Bureau of Indian Affairs, 2901.5 I-75 Business Spur, Sault Ste. Marie, MI 49783 (906) 632-6809.

***BOLTON, TOMMY (Choctaw/Lipan Apache) 1949-**
(offshore drilling safety representative)
Born August 12, 1949, Converse, La. *Principal occupation*: Offshore drilling safety representative. *Address & Affiliation*: Chief, Choctaw-ApacheCommunity of Ebarb Tribal Council, P.O. Box 858, Zwolle, LA 71486 (318) 645-2744. *Military service*: U.S. Navy, 1968-74 (Republic of Vietnam Service & Republic of Vietnam Campaign). *Community activities*: Deputy, Sabine Parish Sheriff's Dept.; past administrative chief, North Sabine Fire Prot. District; VFW; American Legion.

BOLTON, W. CLIFFORD
(Indian band chief)
Affiliation: Chief, Kitsumkalum Indian Band, House of Sim-Oi-Ghets, P.O. Box 544, Terrace, British Columbia V8G 4B5 (604) 635-6177.

BOLVIN, MARCEL
(Indian band chief)
Affiliation: Attikameks de Weymontachie, Reserve indienne de Weymontachie, Comte Laviolette, Quebec, Canada G0A 4M0 (819) 666-2237.

BOMBERRY, VICTORIA
(editor)
Affiliation: Editor, Native Self-Sufficiency, Seventh Generation Fund, P.O. Box 10, Forestville, CA 95436 (707) 887-1559.

***BOMMELYN, LOREN J. (Tolowa)**
(tribal chairperson)
Affiliation: Smith River Rancheria Tribal Council, P.O. Box 239, Smith River, CA 95567 (707) 487-9255.

BOND, ALVIN L. (Nansemond)
(tribal councilperson)
Affiliation: Nansemond Indian Tribal Association, P.O. Box 9293, Chesapeake, VA 23321 (804) 487-5116.

BOND, CHARLES T. (Nansemond)
(tribal councilperson)
Affiliation: Nansemond Indian Tribal Association, P.O. Box 9293, Chesapeake, VA 23321 (804) 487-5116.

BOND, GARY F. (Red Hawk) (Nansemond)
(tribal councilperson)
Affiliation: Nansemond Indian Tribal Association, P.O. Box 9293, Chesapeake, VA 23321 (804) 487-5116.

***BOND, THOMAS**
(BIA director)
Affiliation: Office of American Indian Trust, Bureau of Indian Affairs, Dept. of the Interior, MS-4513-MIB, 1849 C St., NW, Washington, DC 20240 (202) 208-3338.

BONE, RANDY
(Indian band chief)
Affiliation: Keeseekoowenin Indian Band, Box 100, Elphinstone, Manitoba, Canada R0J 0N0 (204) 625-2004.

BONE, ROBERT J.
(Indian band chief)
Affiliation: Sioux Valley Indian Band, Box 38, Griswold, Manitoba, Canada R0M 0S0 (204) 855-2671.

BONGA, DAVID C. (Minnesota Chippewa-White Earth) 1952-
(tribal planner; in-house counsel)
Born June 23, 1952, Monroe, Wash. *Education*: Dartmouth College, B.A., 1974; Gonzaga Law School, J.D., 1982. *Principal occupation*: Tribal planner; in-house counsel. *Home address*: So. 1915 Pierce, Spokane, WA 99206 (509) 445-1147 (work). *Affiliations*: Kalispel Indian Tribe, Usk, WA, 1985-. *Other professional post*: Judge pro-tem for Spokane, Colville, Coeur d'Alene, Nez Perce and Quinault Indian tribes; magistrate for Kalispel Tribe; guest lecturer, Eastern Washington University, Indian Studies Department, Cheney, WA. *Memberships*: Washington State Bar Association; Northwest Tribal Judges Association; board of directors for Inland Tribal Consortium; Dartmouth's Native American Alumni Association; Washington State Native American Education Advisory Committee; Spokane-Kalispel Education Committee. *Interests*: History & Indian law.

BONNETROUGE, JOACHIM
(Indian band chief)
Affiliation: Fort Providence (Yahti Dewe K'O) Dene Indian Band, General Deliver, Fort Providence, Northwest Territories, Canada X0E 0J0 (403) 699-3401.

BONNEY, CARLA K.
(director-health center)
Affiliation: Tanana Health Center, P.O. Box 93, Tanana, AK 99777 (907) 366-7160.

***BONNICHSEN, ROBSON**
(center director)
Affiliation: Center for the Study of the First Americans, Oregon State University, Corvallis, OR 97331 (503) 737-4515.

BOOHER, BARBARA A. (Cherokee, Northern Ute) 1940-
(Indian affairs coordinator)
Born December 9, 1940, Roosevelt, Utah. *Education*: University of Utah, 1959-60. *Principal occupation*: Indian affairs coordinator. *Home address*: 14325 W. Warren Dr., Lakewood, CO 80228 (303) 989-8038. *Affiliation*: National Park Service, Rocky Mountain Region, Lakewood, CO 1993-. *Other professional posts*: Supt., Little Bighorn Battlefield National Monument, Crow Agency, MT; Indian Allotment Coordinator, Bureau of Indian Affairs (Alaska). *Memberships*: National Association of Interpreters, 1991-; Council for American Indian Interpreters, 1991-. *Awards, honors*: Special Achievement, Bureau of Indian Affairs (Alaska). *Interests*: Federal In-

dian Policy; interpretation of American Indian cultures/beliefs. *Biographical sources*: Chapter on Little Bighorn Battlefield (Name Change/ Indian Memorial) in biography , "Ben Nighthorse Campbell."

BOOMER, MAE
(Indian band chief)
Affiliation: Ashcroft Indian Band, P.O. Box 440, Ashcroft, British Columbia, Canada V0K 1A0 (604) 453-9154.

BOONE, TERESA (Muckleshoot)
(Indian school principal)
Affiliation: Muckleshoot Tribal School, 39015 172nd Ave., SE, Auburn, WA 98002 (206) 931-6709.

BONNEY, RACHEL A. 1939-
(professor of anthropology)
Born March 28, 1939, St. Paul, Minn. *Education*: University of Minnesota, B.A., 1961, M.A., 1963; University of Arizona, Ph.D., 1975. *Principal occupation*: Professor of anthropology . *Home address*: Route 1, Box 395, Mooresville, NC 28115. *Affiliations*: Assistant professor, Tarkio College, Mo., 1965-67; instructor , University of South Florida, 1967-70; graduate teaching associate, University of Arizona, 1971-73; instructor & professor, University of North Carolina at Charlotte, 1973-. *Other professional posts*: Teacher, guidance, B.I.A., Teec Nos Pos Boarding School, Ariz. (Navajo), 1964. *Community activities*: Charlotte-Mecklenburg Title IV (Indian Education Act) Indian Parent Committee (ex-officio member , 1975-1977); Metrolina Native American Association, Charlotte, N.C.; UNCC Phoenix Society (American Indian Student Organization) and Phoenix Dancer (Indian dance team), (advisor). *Memberships*: American Anthropological Association (Fellow) 1963-; American Ethnological Society, 1967-1971, 1977-; Southern Anthropological Association, 1973-; National Congress of American Indians, 1972-1973; Anthropological Council on Education, 1977-; National Indian Education Association, 1977-; Southeastern Indian Cultural Association, 1977-. *Awards, honors*: HEW Title IX (ethnic heritage studies) Project Grant, 1977-1978. *Interests*: Indian studies; multi-ethnic studies; culture change (Catawba land claims case); Indian powwows; powwows with Phoenix Dancers; archaeological projects in Minnesota, New York, New Mexico, and Austria. *Biographical sources*: Who's Who in America - The South (Marquis). Published works: American Indian Studies in the Social Studies Curriculum (Proceedings, North Carolina Association for Research in Education, May , 1975); The Role of Women in Indian Activism (The Western Canadian Journal of Anthropology, Vol. VI, No. 3, 1976); The Role of AIM Leaders in Indian Nationalism (American Indian Quarterly , Vol. 3, No. 3, 1977); Indians of the Americas, Courtship Customs (Encyclopedia of Indians of the Americas, Scholarly Press, 1978); among others.

*BOOL, HERBERT
(museum president)
Affiliation: The Heard Museum, 22 E. Monte Vista Rd., Phoenix, AZ 85004 (602) 252-8840.

*BORDEAUX, CHRIS
(association president)
Affiliation: South Dakota Indian Education Association, P.O. Box 62, Batesland, SD 57716 (605) 867-5633.

BORDEAUX, LIONEL
(college president)
Affiliation: President, Sinte Gleska College, P.O. Box 490, Rosebud, SD 57570-0490 (605) 747-2263.

BORDEAUX, ROGER C. (Rosebud Sioux) 1952-
(tribal school supt.)
Born August 20, 1952, Valentine, Neb. *Education*: University of South Dakota, BA, 1974, MA, 1988, Ed.D., 1990. *Principal occupation*: Tribal school supt. *Home address*: 616 4th Ave. W., Sisseton, SD 57262. *Affiliations*: Executive director, Association of Community Tribal Schools, Inc., 616 4th Ave. W., Sisseton, SD 57262, 1976-teacher, director, St. Francis Indian School, St. Francis, SD, 1980-90; supt., Tiospa zina Tribal School, Agency Village, SD, 1991-. *Memberships*: South Dakota Indian Education Association. *Awards. honors*: M.A. Student of the Year, 1988, University of South Dakota. *Interests*: Golf, softball, fishing.

BOSTROM, MARGUERITA
(tribal education chairperson)
Affiliation: Puyallup Nation Education System, 2002 East 28th St., Tacoma, WA 98404 (206) 593-0218.

BOTHWELL, NORA
(Indian band chief)
Affiliation: Alderville Indian Band, RR #4, Roseneath, Ontario, Canada K0K 2X0 (416) 352-2011.

*BOTT, JOHN
(editor)
Affiliation: Southwestern Association of Indian Affairs, "Quarterly," Roswell Printing Co., 1 10 N. Pennsylvania, Roswell, NM 88201 (505) 983-5220.

BOUCHA, HENRY *(O'Git'Chi'Dah)*
(Chippewa) 1951-
(Indian education coordinator , realtor)
Born June 1, 1951, W arroad, Minn. *Education*: University of Detroit (general business courses); Fond du Lac Community College (T itle V & Johnson O'Malley W orkshop) 1993. *Principal occupation*: Indian education coordinator , realtor. *Home address*: 314 Minnesota Ave., NE, Warroad, MN 56763 (218) 386-2834. *Affiliations*: Real estate agent, Scott Pahlen Realty , Warroad, MN 1986-; Indian education coordinator & counselor/tutor for about 135 Indian students, Warroad Public Schools, 1993-. *Other professional posts*: Former National Hockey League player with the Detroit Red Wings & Minnesota North Stars, 1972-75; Hockey coach for Warroad High School, 1989-; teaches at the pacific Northwest Hockey School, L ynwood, W A, 1993-. *Military service*: U.S. Army, 1970-72. *Community activities*: member of U.S. national Teams, 1970, 1971; and member of 1972 Olympic Hockey Team that went to Japan and won a Silver Medal. *Memberships*: U.S. Olympic Alumni; U.S. National Coaches Association; Detroit Red Wings & Minnesota North Stars Alumni; NHL Players Association; Minnesota Realtors' Association; National Association of Realtors. *Awards, honors*: 1970 Gold Medal winner & 1972 Silver Medal winner at Olympics; Rookie of the Year with Detroit Red W ings, 1973. *Interests*: Golf, tennis fishing, hunting. "My goal is to obtain a position in a management, sales, or public relations capacity with a progressive

firm where performance will be acknowledged and where there is a solid opportunity for advancement."

BOUCHARD, AIME
(Indian band chief)
Affiliation: Pays Plat Indian Band, Box 819, Screiber, Ontario, Canada P0T 2S0 (807) 824-2541.

*BOUCHARD, RICK
(clinic director)
Affiliation: American Indian Free Clinic, 9500 E. Artesia Blvd., Bellflower , CA 90708 (310) 920-7272.

BOUCHER, FRANK
(Indian band chief)
Affiliation: Red Bluff Indian Band, 1515 Arbutus Rd., Box 4693, Quesnel, British Columbia, Canada V2J 3J9 (604) 747-2900.

BOUCHIER, JIMMY LEONARD
(Indian band chief)
Affiliation: Chief, Fort McKay Indian Band, P.O. Box 5360, Fort McMurray , Alberta, Canada T9H 3G4 (403) 828-4220.

*BOULE, MARY NULL
(teacher, author)
Address: c/o Merryant Publishers, 7615 SW 257th St., V ashon, WA 98070 (206) 463-3879. *Affiliations*: 27 years a California elementary school teacher. *Published works*: The Missions: California's Heritage, and The California Native American Tribes; both are written at the 3rd to 5th grade reading level and published by Merryant Publishers.

BOURGEAU, DEAN (Colville) 1928-
(musician)
Born July 14, 1928, Inchelium, W ash. *Principal occupation*: Musician. *Home address*: Inchelium, WA 99138. *Affiliations*: Colville Business Council; Indian police. *Military service*: U.S. Army, 1950-1952, 1956-1957 (U.N. Service Medal, Combat Medal.) *Community activities*: American Legion; Eagles.

*BOURLAND, GREGG
(Cheyenne River Sioux)
(tribal chairperson)
Affiliation: Cheyenne River Sioux Tribal Council, P.O. Box 590, Eagle Butte, SD 57625 (605) 964-4155.

BOUSCHOR, BERNARD (Chippewa)
(tribal council president)
Affiliation: Sault Ste. Marie Chippewa Tribal Council, 2218 Skunk Rd., Sault Ste. Marie, MI 49783 (906) 635-6050.

BOVIS, PIERRE G. 1943-
(shop owner)
Born February 3, 1943, Nice, France. *Education*: Beaux Arts, France, B.A. equivalent. *Principal occupation*: Shop owner . *Home address*: P.O. Box 324, Santa Fe, N.M. 87501. *Affiliation*:

Owner, Winona Trading Post, Santa Fe, N.M., 1968-. *Military service*: French Army (two years). *Community activities*: Loaned Indian artifacts for local and national traveling exhibits. *Memberships*: Appraisers Association of America; Indian Arts & Crafts Association; Genuine Indian Relic Society; English Westerners, London. *Awards, honors*: Have won several first, second and third place cups and trophies for my displays of Indian artifacts at Indian shows. *Biographical sources*: Who's Who in Indian Relics, Vol. III: International Who's Who in Art & Antiques, Vol. XI. *Interests*: Interests lie in anthropology and primitive art, and I travel through Europe and Far East, etc. *Published works*: American Indian and Eskimo Basketry: A Key to Identification, with Charles Miles, 1970; Pine Ridge, 1890: Eye Witness Account of the Events Surrounding Wounded Knee, 1972. Published by Mr. Bovis.

*BOWANNIE, MARY
(radio host/producer)
Affiliation: "Indian Voices," KGNU 88.5 FM - Public Radio, P.o. Box 885, Boulder, CO 80306 (800) 737-3030.

BOWEN, DUWAYNE LESLIE
(Dah-dah-wen-yae) **(Seneca) 1946-**
(museum management)
Born July 7, 1946, Salamanca, N.Y. *Education*: Vale Technical Institute (Blairsville, PA), diploma, 1966; Jamestown (NY) Community College. *Principal occupation*: Museum management. *Home address*: RD Box 71J, Salamanca, NY 14779 (716) 945-2260. *Affiliation*: Seneca-Iroquois National Museum, Salamanca, NY, 1990-. *Community activities*: American Red Cross, Salamanca, NY; Red House Indian Chapel, Jimersontown-Salamanca, NY (trustee); Red House Memorial Church, Jimersontown-Salamanca, NY (secretary-treasurer). *Membership*: Cornplanter Descendants Association, Allegany Indian Reservation-Salamanca, NY (chairperson, 1990-), *Interests*: Local church; museum/history of Seneca people; public speaker on subjects of Iroquois history; professional storyteller of ghost stories/supernatural; movies/stage/literary. *Published works*: Anthology, New Voices From the Longhouse (Greenfield Review Press, 1990); contributor, A Quaker Promise Kept (Spencer Butte Press, 1990); One More Story (Bowman Books, 1991); short story, "He-Sees-Good" (Akwe:kon-Northeast Indian Quarterly, 1991).

*BOWIE, BRENDA (Wiyot-Mattole)
(rancheria chairperson)
Affiliation: Bear River Band of Rohnerville Rancheria, P.O. Box 108, Eureka, CA 95502 (707) 443-6150.

*BOWMAN, ARLENE
(Native American film
producer/director/writer)
Address: 2318 1/2 4th Ave., Los Angeles, CA 90018 (213) 734-7881.

*BOYD, MERLE (Sac & Fox)
(tribal second chief)
Affiliation: Sac & Fox Nation, Rte. 2, Box 246, Stroud, OK 74079 (918) 968-3526.

BOYD, STANLEY
(Indian band chief)
Affiliation: Nazko Indian Band, Box 4534, Quesnel, British Columbia, Canada V2J 3H8 (604) 002-0810.

BOYER, LEE R. 1938-
(Professor/author, U.S. Indian history)
Born June 1, 1938, Aliquippa, PA. *Education*: Mount Union College, BA, 1959; University of Notre Dame, MA, 1969, PhD, 1972; University of New Mexico, Indian law student, 1978-79; Plains Indian Museum, Indian studies seminar, 1981. *Home address*: 2691 Matteson Lake, Bronson, MI 49028 (313) 487-0053. *Affiliation*: Professor of history, Eastern Michigan University, Ypsilanti, MI, 1972-. *Other professional posts*: Assistant professional specialist, University of Notre Dame, (3 years). *Memberships*: American Association of University Professors; National Council for the Social Studies; Michigan Council for the Humanities. *Awards, honors*: Research grant, Merit award, Eastern Michigan University; experienced Teacher Fellowship, Department of H.E.W. *Interests*: Travel and research to Western states; Federal Indian Reservations - sabbatical study; Neah Bay archaeological dig. *Published works*: Episodes in American History (Ginn, 1972); U.S. Indians: A Brief History (Advocate, 1982).

BOYER, ROBERT
(Indian fine arts instructor)
Affiliation: Instructor, Indian Fine Arts, Saskatchewan Indian Federated College, University of Regina, 118 College West, Regina, Saskatchewan, Canada S4S 0A2 (306) 584-8333.

BOYER-POTVIN, RUBY LEE CAMPFIELD
(Momma Quail)
(United Lumbee/Cherokee) 1925-
(homemaker)
Born October 6, 1925, Oklahoma. *Education*: High school. *Principal occupation*: Homemaker. *Home address*: P.O. Box 512, Fall River Mills, CA 96028 (916) 336-6701. *Affiliations*: United Lumbee Nation of N.C. and America (Grand Council, 1979-, national secretary, 1982-88). *Other professional posts*: Circulation manager, United Lumbee Nation Times, 1981-88. *Community activities*: Title IV and Johnson O'Malley Indian Education Program in Tulare, Kings Counties, Calif. (parent committee & chairperson, 1975-80); *Memberships*: Native American Wolf Clan (vice-chief, 1978-1982; chief, 1982-); Chapel of Our Lord Jesus (church) (treasurer, vice-president, 1982-). *Awards, honors*: 4th Runner up for the 1987 Silver Eagle Award, given each year by the United Lumbee Nation to a member who has don oustanding work in their clan/band or community. *Interests*: Helping young people and coordinating the Indian Dance team, Little Eagle Dancers. *Biographical sources*: Section in the United Lumbee Nation's Deer Clan Cook Book.

BOYIDDLE, LORRAINE (Navajo)
(Indian school principal)
Affiliation: Chinle Boarding School, P.O. Box 70, Many Farms, AZ 86538 (602) 781-6221.

BOYLE, REC. ROBERT J., S.J.
(site director)
Affiliation: Kateri Galleries, The National Shrine of North American Martyrs, Auriesville, NY 12016 (518) 853-3033.

BRADBY, MARVIN (Chickahominy)
(tribal chief)
Affiliation: Chief, Eastern Chickahominy Indian Tribe, Route 2, Box 90, Providence Forge, VA 23140 (804) 745-6508.

BRADFORD, HAROLD
(BIA agency supt.)
Affiliation: Central California Agency, BIA, 1824 Tribute Rd., Suite J, Sacramento, CA 95815 (916) 978-4337.

*BRADLEY, JAMES W.
(museum director)
Affiliation: Robert S. Peabody Museum of Archaeology, Phillips Academy, Andover, MA 01810 (508) 749-4490.

BRADLEY, RUSSELL (Tothwai)
(Kickapoo/Potawatomi) 1942-
(BIA agency supt.)
Born July 25, 1942, St. Joseph, Mo. *Education*: Haskell Institute, 1962; Metropolitan Junior College, Kansas City, 1966. *Principal occupation*: BIA agency supt. *Home address*: P.O. Box E, Fort Yates, ND 58538 (701) 854-3433 (work). *Affiliations*: Assistant director, United Tribes of North Dakota Training Center, Bismarck, ND, 1972; employment director, United Sioux Tribes, Pierre, SD, 1973; supt., Winnebago Agency, Winnebago, NE (4 years); Supt., Turtle Mountain Agency, Belcourt, ND (2 years); supt., Fort Apache Agency, Whiteriver, AZ (4 years); Standing Rock Agency, Fort Yates, ND, 1990-). *Military service*: U.S. Army, 1964-1966 (Specialist 5th Class, Good Conduct Medal.) *Community activities*: Requires alignment with most all community services and functions, such as: education, law enforcement, social services, economic development and planning, road and judicial services. *Community activities*: Miss Indian America Pageant (board of directors). *Memberships*: American Legion; Vietnam Veterans Association; Younghawk/Bear American Legion Post (Albuquerque chapter, 16 years); Haskell Alumni Association; National Indian Contractors Association; National Intertribal Timber Council. *Awards, honors*: BIA Outstanding Achievement Award, 1982; Community Service Award, 1984, Turtle Mountain Chippewa Tribe; Recognition Award by White Mountain Apache Tribe, 1987. *Interests*: Minority employment development; reservation economic development; Indian education; traditional preservation and enhancement of recreation and athletics on reservations. Enhancing tribal governments in serving its members provides the greatest challenge and satisfaction. *Biographical sources*: Who's Who in North Dakota, 1984.

*BRAFFORD, HAROLD
(BIA agency supt.)
Affiliation: Central California Agency, Bureau of Indian Affairs, 1824 Tribute Rd., Suite J, Sacramento, CA 95815 (916) 978-4337.

BRAIN, JEFFREY PHIPPS 1940-
(archaeologist)
Born January 4, 1940, New York, N.Y. *Education*: Harvard University, BA, 1961; Yale University, MPhil, 1969, PhD, 1969. *Principal occupation*: Archaeologist. *Home address*: 25 Ridgeway, Needham, MA 02192 (508) 740-3624 (work). *Affiliation*: Peabody Museum, Harvard University, Cambridge, MA, & Peabody Essex Museum, Salem, MA (20 years). *Military service*: U.S. Navy (Lt., 1962-65). *Memberships*: Society for American Archaeology; Society for Historical Archaeology; Archaeological Institute of America; Southeastern Archaeological Conference (past vice-president and president); and various state archaeological societies. *Awards, honors*: The John M. Goggin Award for Method

& Theory in Historical Archaeology (Conference for Historic Sites Archaeology); "I am a descendant of Pocahontas." *Interests*: Indians of North America. *Published works*: Tunica Treasure (Peabody Museum, Harvard, 1979); Excavations at Lake George (Peabody Museum, Harvard, 1983); Tunica Archaeology (Peabody Museum, Harvard, 1988); Winterville (Mississippi Archives & History, 1989); The Tunica-Biloxi (Chelsea House Publishers, 1990); Shell Gorgets (Peabody Museum, Harvard, 1994)..

*BRAINE, SUSAN
(project manager)
Affiliation: American Indian Radio on Satellite, P.O. Box 831 11, Lincoln, NE 68501 (402) 472-9333.

BRAMLETTE, ALLAN
(Cora-Cherokee-Choctaw)
(archaeologist/heritage
resource specialist)
Education: Sonoma State University, BA, 1981, MA, 1989. *Principal occupation*: Archaeologist/ heritage resource specialist. *Address*: The Center for Community Development, Graves Annex #30, Humboldt State University, Arcata, CA 95521 (707) 826-371 1. *Affiliations*: Senior staff archaeologist, Anthropological Studies Center, Sonoma State University (2 years); currently - archaeologist/heritage resource specialist, The Center for Community Development, Humboldt State University. Mr. Bramlette provides archaeological consultancy and cultural resource management assistance to Northern California Indian communities. He provides technical training in development and management of cultural exhibits, interpretive programs & museum collections & facilities. He also serves as liaison between local Indian communities and the professional archaeologists and other heritage resource personnel who work in Northern California. *Other professional post*: Teaches four courses per year in archaeology-related topics in Native American Studies Dept. of Humboldt State University. *Membership*: Society for California Archaeology.

BRANDT, EDWARD N., II (Chickasaw)
(attorney)
Address: 820 Spyglass Cir., Louisville, CO 80027. *Membership*: Native American Bar Association (First Amendment Bar Association of Texas Representative).

BRANDT, ELIZABETH A.
(anthropological linguist)
Born October 20, 1945, Sanford, Fla. *Education*: Florida State University, BA, 1967; Southern Methodist University, MA, 1969, PhD, 1970. *Principal occupation*: Anthropological linguist. *Home address*: 1810 S. Roberts Rd., Tempe, AZ 85281 (602) 965-6213 (work). *Affiliations*: University of Illinois, Chicago, 1970-74; Dept. of Anthropology, Arizona State University, Tempe, 1974-. *Community activities*: AZ Humanities Council (board member); American Indian Institute, ASU (director); ASU American Indian Summer Seminars in the Humanities *Memberships*: Linguistics Society of America, Society for Applied Anthropology, Keepers of the Treasures, 1991; Society for the Study of Indigenous Languages of the Americas; Native American Language Issues Institute. *Interests*: "Assist tribes and traditional elders in researching and preparing nominations to National Register for Traditional Cultural Properties, sacred

sites protection, land claims, language presentation and renewal." Biographical source: Who's Who in the West. *Published works*: Speaking, Singing & Teaching, Arizona State University Press, 1979); Bilingualism & Language Contact (Teachers College Press, 1980); Navajo Students At Risk (Navajo Nation, 1986).

BRANHAM, RONNIE L. (Monacan)
(tribal chief)
Affiliation: Monacan Indian Tribe, P.O. Box 1136, Madison Heights, VA 24572 (804) 929-691 1.

BRANT, CLARE CLIFTON (Mohawk) 1941-
(psychiatrist)
Born July 7, 1941, Belleville, Ontario, Canada. *Education*: Queen's University Medical School, MD, 1965; University of Western Ontario, FRCP(C), 1978. *Principal occupation*: Psychiatrist (private practice-6 years). *Home address*: York Rd., Box 89, Shannonville, Ontario, Canada K0K 3A0 (613) 966-0888. *Other professional posts*: Assistant professor of psychiatry, The University of Western Ontario, London. *Community activities*: Chairman, Native Mental Health, Canadian Psychiatric Association; chairman, Native Mental Health Association of Canada. *Memberships*: Canadian Medical Association; Ontario Medical Association; Canadian Psychiatric Association. *Interests*: "I operate a sheep and poultry farm on my home reserve." *Published works*:"Programming for Native Indian Mental Health", Handbook on Primary Prevention, (Mental Health Association, 1982); co-author, "The Examination of the North American Indian", Handbook of Forensic Psychiatry (Clarke Institute of Psychiatry); numerous other articles and proceedings.

BRANTLEY, WILLA
(tribal education administrator)
Affiliation: Tribal Council of the Mississippi Band of Choctaws, P.O. Box 6010, Philadelphia, MS 39350 (601) 656-5251.

*BRASHEAR, CHARLES (Cherokee) 1930-
(retired professor of English)
Born December 11, 1930, in Martin County, Tex. *Education*: University of California, Berkeley, B.A., 1956; San Francisco State U., M.A., 1960; University of Denver, Ph.D., 1962. *Principal occupation*: Retired professor of English. *Address*: 5614 Dorothy Dr., San Diego, CA 92115 (619) 287-0850. *Affiliations*: Retired professor of English, San Diego State University, 1968-1992. *Honors*: Fulbright Teaching Award, English Institute, University of Stockholm, 1962-65; Outstanding Faculty Award, College of Arts & Letters, SDSU, 1980; Adjunct Faculty, American Indian Studies, SDSU, 1989. *Published works*: Book - "A Snug Little Purchase, How Richard Henderson Bought Kaintuckee from the Cherokees in 1777" (Associated Creative Writers, 1979); among others; numerous short stories, essays and poems.

BRASS, ALPHEUS
(Indian band chief)
Affiliation: Chief, Chemawawin First Nation Band, Easterville, Manitoba, Can. R0C 0V0 (204) 329-2161.

BRASS, OLIVER J. (Saulteaux, Peepeekisis Indian Band-Plains Ojibwa)1944-
(professor)
Born in 1944 at Fort Qu'Appelle, Sask. Canada. *Education*: Aldersgate College, Moose Jaw,

Sask., Bachelor of Theology, 1965; University of Saskatchewan, BA (Hons.), 1972; University of Regina, MA, 1978, PhD, 1984. *Principal occupation*: Professor. Saskatchewan Indian Federated College. *Home address*: Box 730, Balcarres, Sask. S0G 0C0 (306) 779-6226 (work). *Affiliation*: President & professor, Saskatchewan Indian Federated College, Regina, 1986-. *Other professional post*: Campaign manager for Sask. Indian Federated College, Capital Campaign, 1990-91, raised $1.3 million from corporate sources. *Community activities*: Member of the City of Regina Mayor's Board of Inquiry into Hunger in the City of Regina. *Memberships*: University of Regina Graduate Studies Committee and PhD Committee; Society of Indian Psychologists; Regina Race Relations Support Committee (member). *Awards, honors*: Paul Harris Fellow bestowed by Rotary International, 1991; Canadian Governor General's Award, 1982. *Interests*: "Interested in traditional Saulteaux (Plains Ojibwa) religious ceremony and ritual. Interested in band (reservation) histories both pre-treaty and posttreaty periods. Have travelled extensively in China and South and Central America." *Biographical source*: Sask Report "A Nation's New Leaders" Sept. 1990.

BRASWELL, DAVID L.
(school principal)
Affiliation: Wingate Elementary School, P.O. Box 1, Fort Wingate, NM 87316 (505) 488-6470.

*BRATONE, BARBARA
(executive director)
Affiliation: American Indian College Fund, 21 West 68th St., #1F, New York, NY 10023 (212) 787-6312.

BRAUCHLI, ROBERT C. 1945-
(attorney)
Born November 11, 1945, Morristown, N.J. *Education*: American University, BA, 1967; Howard University Law School, JD, 1970. *Principal occupation*: Attorney. *Home address*: 2901 E. Richards Row, Tucson, AZ 85716 (602) 742-2191 (office). *Affiliations*: Deputy County attorney, Pima County, AZ, 1973-78; director, Consumer Fraud Division, Assistant Attorney General, 1978-80; tribal attorney, Pascua Yaqui Tribe of Arizona, Tucson, 1988-; tribal attorney, White Mountain Apache Tribe, Whiteriver, AZ, 1980-87, 1990-. *Memberships*: State Bar of AZ, Indian Law Section, 1990-. *Awards, honors*: Arizona Bar Foundation, State Bar of AZ. *Interests*: Hobbies include: skiing, fishing, hiking, scuba diving, reading, music and theatre; travel.

BRAUKER, SHIRLEY M. (Ottawa) 1950-
(potter)
Born August 11, 1950, Angola, Ind. *Education*: Mid-Michigan Community College, AA, 1980; Central Michigan University, BFA, 1981, MA, 1983; Institute of American Indian Art, Santa Fe, 1991. *Principal occupation*: Potter. *Home address*: 1048 Silver Rd., Coldwater, MI 49036 (517) 238-5833 (work). *Affiliation*: Secretary, Central Michigan University, 1982-84. *Community activities*: Taught pottery at continuing education and abroad traveling art train; documentary film, "Woodland Traditions - 3 Native Americans." *Memberships*: National Collegiate Edu-

cation of Ceramics; National Honor Society . *Art Exhibitions*: Bachelor of Fine Arts, Central Michigan University, 1981; Great Lakes Traveling Indian Art Exhibition, Dept. of the Interior , Washington, DC, 1983; Ethnic Art Show, Lansing Art Gallery, 1983; Sacred Circle Gallery , Seattle, WA, American Indian Ceramic Art; Yesterday, Today and Tomorrow Exhibit, 1984; Midland Christmas Arts Festival, 1984; Museum of the Plains Indian, Browning, MT , Contemporary Clay Indian Art exhibit, 1985; Larson Gallery , Grand Rapids, MI. *Community activities*: Demonstrates pottery techniques aboard the Traveling Art Train, 1983; worked on a documentary film depicting Indian artists in Michigan, 1983; illustrates pamphlets and handouts for community service. *Awards, honors*: Outstanding Community College Student Scholarship Award, 1980; Mae Beck Indian Artist Scholarship Award, 1982; Potter of the Month, Lansing Art Gallery, 1983; 1st & 2nd Place-Pottery , Eiteljorg Indian Market (Indianapolis, IN), 1993; 3rd Place-Pottery & Honorable Mention, Dayton, OH Indian Market. *Interests*: Indian history , culture and art work; craft work, doll making, quilting, painting, beadwork, stained glass; travel and camping; grant recipient from Kellogg Foundation "25 Native American Women Artists of the Great Lakes" - traveling show & workshops - spanning one year...ending up at Smithsonian Institute. *Biographical sources*: Documentary film: Woodland Traditions: The Art of Three Native Americans; American Indian Index; and "The Traveler's Guide to American Art."

*BRAVE EAGLE, DOROTHY
(Mani wakan win) (Oglala Lakota) 1940-
(administrative officer)
Born April 18, 1940, Red W ater Creek, S.D. *Education*: Western Colorado University , BS, 1972, MA, 1974. *Principal occupation* : Administrative Officer. *Home address*: 7892 W. 1st Pl., Lakewood, CO 80226 (303) 238-3420. *Affiliations*: Bureau of Indian Affairs, Fort Thompson, SD, 1986-91; Bureau of Indian Affairs, Denver, CO, Denver, CO., 1991-; *Other professional posts* : Owner, B.E.A.R. Publishing Co.; President of the Board, W iconni Waste (non-profit educational corporation for American Indian culture, history). *Community activities* :Instructor, White Buffalo Council, of ficer - March Pow-wow committee. *Memberships*: American Indian Traders Guild; Roaming Buf falo Indian Arts. *Awards, honors*: Selected to display traditional Lakota arts at Santa Fe Indian Market. *Interests*: Traveled to France, Germany , Belgium, and England to display Lakota Arts. *Published work*: Ehanamani (walks among) (B.E.A.R., 1992).

BRAVE HEART, BASIL (Oglala Sioux)
(school administrator)
Born October 5, 1933, Pine Ridge, S.D. *Education*: Chadron State College, BS, 1957; University of Minnesota, MA, 1976; St. Marys Graduate Center, Minneapolis, MA (Psychology & Counseling), 1986. *Principal occupation* : School administrator. *Home address* : Box 83, White Clay, NE 69365 (605) 867-5121 (of fice). *Affiliations*: Member, Board of Directors, South Dakota Educational TV, Pierre, S.D. (1 year); National Alcohol & Drug Program, W ashington, D.C. (3 years); Agency Supt. for Education, BIA, Pine Ridge, SD, 1988-. *Military service*: U.S. Paratroopers - 187 Regimental Combat Team (11th Airborne Diov. Korea, 1951-54; Combat Infantry Badge, Airborne W ings, 3 Combat Ci-

tations). *Community activities* : Pine Ridge, SD YMCA Board. *Awards, honors* : Superior Performance Award, by HUD for ef forts during the 1972 flood, Rapid City, SD. *Interests*: Travel, Far East & Korea; Korean conflict, 1951-54. *Biographical sources*: Circle of Life; Teacher Handbook on Cultural Orientation, Minneapolis School System.

*BRAY, ETHEL E.
(library director)
Affiliation : The Seneca Nation Library , 1490 Rte. 438, Irving, NY 14081 (716) 532-9449.

*BRAYBOY, ANNIE
(IHS treatment center director)
Affiliation : Phoenix/Tucson Area Adolescent Regional Treatment Center , P.O. Box 458, Sacaton, AZ 85247 (602) 562-3801.

BRAYBOY, CONNEE (Lumbee)
(editor)
Born in Robeson County , N.C. *Address*: P.O. Box 1075, Pembroke, NC 28372 (919) 521-2826 (work). *Affiliation* : Editor, Carolina Indian V oice (weekly newspaper), Pembroke, NC, 1973-.

*BRAYBOY, TERRANCE (Lumbee)
(shop owner)
Affiliation : Sacred Hoop Trading Post, 207 Purefoy Rd. #A, Chapel Hill, NC 27514.

*BREAD, MARILYN
(association director)
Affiliation: Kansas Association for Native American Education, Haskell Indian Jr . College, Box H-1304, Lawrence, KS 66044 (913) 749-8468.

BREEN, MIDGE
(administrative officer)
Affiliation : Rapid City PHS Indian Hospital, 3200 Canyon Lake Dr., Rapid City, SD 57702 (605) 348-1900.

*BRENNAN, MARY H.
(editor)
Affiliation : "Earthsong," The Heard Museum, 22 E. Monte Vista Rd., Phoenix, AZ 85004 (602) 252-8840.

BRENNEMAN, GEORGE 1934-
(pediatrician, maternal & child health coordinator)
Born January 21, 1934, Newport News, V A. *Education*: Eastern Mennonite College, B.S., 1957; University of V irginia, School of Medicine, M.D., 1961. *Principal occupation*: Pediatrician, maternal and child health coordinator , Indian Health Service. *Address*: Indian Health Service, Parklawn Bldg., Rm. 6A-54, 5600 Fishers Lane, Rockville, MD 20857 (301) 443-4644 (work). *Affiliations*: Physician, Indian Health Service Hospital, Albuquerque, NM, 1962-64; physician, 1964-65, 1967-68, staf f pediatrician, 1981-84, Alaska Native Medical Center , Anchorage, AK; physician & Tuberculosis Control Of fice, Bethel, Alaska, 1965-67; pediatrician, Alaska Native Medical Center , Bethel, Ak, 1970-73; clinical director, pediatrician and general physician, 1973-76, chief of pediatrics, 1978-79, Alaska Native Service Hospital, Bethel, AK; medical director, Yukon-Kuskokwim Health Corp., instructor, Community Health Aide Program, Kuskokwim Community College, 1979-80; director, Alaska *Haemophilus influenzae* Vaccine project, co-investigator , Efficacy Trial of a

Haemophilus influenzae Type b Vaccine in a High Risk Infant Population, 1984-87; maternal & child health coordinator , Indian Health Service, 1987-. *Memberships*: American Academy of Pediatrics (Fellow , 1972-); Mennonite Medical Association; Physicians for Social Responsibility. *Awards, honors* : Commendation Medal, 1975, Meritorious Service Medal, 1977, USPHS; Certificate of Appreciation for Outstanding Performance, 1976 & 1977, Bethel Service Unit, Alaska Native Health Service; In Sincere Appreciation, Pediatric House Staf f, University of Virginia Hospital, 1977-78; The Alaska Health Achievement Award, 1981 from the Alaska Public Health Association; Federal Employee of the Year, Category IV Performance Award, 1982, Federal Executive Association; 1987 Alumnus Distinguished Service Award, Eastern Mennonite College. *Published works*: Articles in "Alaska Medicine, 1967, 1969, July 1979, February 1980; Stethoscope (a biweekly and weekly health related news column), Tundra Drums, 1976-80; and other articles.

BRENNER, M. DIANE
(museum archivist)
Affiliation: Archivist, Anchorage Museum of History and Art, 121 W. 7th Ave., Anchorage, AK 99501 (907) 343-4326.

BRESCIA, WILLIAM, Jr.
(Mississippi Choctaw) 1947-
(director, research & curriculum development)
Born November 4, 1947, Chicago, Ill. *Education*: Wartburg College, W averly, Iowa, BA, 1970; University of Wisconsin, Madison, MS, 1973. *Principal occupation* : Director, research & curriculum development. *Address*: Mississippi Band of Choctaw Indians, P .O. Box 6010 - Choctaw Branch, Philadelphia, MS 39350 (601) 656-5251. *Affiliations*: Editor, Daybreak Star Magazine (Daybreak Star Press, 1976-81; Curriculum coordinator, 1976-78, director , Community Educational Services, 1978-81, United Indians of All Tribes Foundation, Seattle; director , Curriculum Developer , Ethnic Heritage Program, 1981-1982, director , Division of Research and Curriculum Development, Mississippi Band of Choctaw Indians, Philadelphia, MS, 1982-. *Other professional posts* : Computer education consultant, Mississippi State Dept. of Education, 1984-. *Community activities* : D'Arcy McNickle Center, Newberry Library, Chicago (advisor, 1985-); ERIC/CRESS National Advisory Board (American Indian educational specialist, 1984); The Native American (advisory committee member, 1984-); Indian representative, W ashington Urban Rural Racial Disadvantaged Advisory Committee, 1979-80; Indian representative, New Voice Advisory committee, WGBH-TV, Boston, 1977-80; Scientists and Citizens Organized on Policy Issues, Seattle, W ash., 1980-81; Seattle Museum of History and Industry , 1979-81. *Memberships*: American Education Research Association; International Reading Association; National Indian Education Association; National Association for Bilingual Education; Mid-South Educational Research Association; Association for Supervision and Curriculum Development. *Awards, honors*: American Indian Heritage High School (special recognition for work in support of that school and Indian education); Northwest American Indian Women's Circle (special recognition for work in support of National Conference, 1979); North-

west Regional Folklife Festival (for administration of Seattle Pow-W ow, 1978); Ethnic Heritage Employee of the Year, 1981; Choctaw Dept. of Education (Employee of the Year, 1982). Interests: Computers in education; curriculum development; learning styles and brain functions; economic education; organic gardening; Choctaw literacy. *Published works*: Co-author, Reeves-Brescia, Developmental Checklist, (Mississippi Band of Choctaw Indians, 1975); script advisor, Yesterdays Children: Indian Elder Oral History, 30 minute video (Daybreak Star Press, 1980); co-author, Development of Native American Curriculum, workbook (Daybreak Star Press, 1979); editor, Ways of the Lushootseed People: Ceremonies and Traditions of the Northern Puget Sound Indians (Daybreak Star Press, 1980); editor, Sharing Our W orlds (Daybreak Star Press, 1980); script advisor, Voices from the Cradleboard, 30 minute slide presentation (Daybreak Star Press, 1980); editor, Indians in Careers (Daybreak Star Press, 1980); editor, Starting an Indian Teen Club (Daybreak Star Press, 1980); co-author, Fisherman on the Puyallup & Teachers Guide (Daybreak Star Press, 1980); co-author, Suquamish Today & Teachers Guide (Daybreak Star Press, 1980); executive editor, Tribal Sovereignty, Indian Tribes in U.S. History (Daybreak Star Press, 1981); editor, Free Range to Reservation: Social Change on Selected W ashington Reservations (Daybreak Star Press, 1981); editor, Outdoor Education for Indian Youth (Daybreak Star Press, 1981); editor, Getting Control of Your Money (Daybreak Star Press, 1981); Knowing Your Legal Rights (Daybreak Star Press, 1981); editor, Daybreak Star Pre-School Activities Book (Daybreak Star Press, 1979); editor, Twana Games (Daybreak Star Press, 1981); editor, Our Mother Corn (Daybreak Star Press, 1981); A'una (Daybreak Star Press, 1981); editor, Washington State Indian History for Grades 4-6, A Teacher's Guide Daybreak Star Press, 1981); editor, O'Wakaga (Daybreak Star Press, 1981); editor, By the Work of Our Hands, co-editor, Teacher's Guide (Choctaw Heritage Press, 1982); editor, Choctaw Tribal Government (Choctaw Heritage Press, 1982); co-author, Looking Around, Na Yo Pisa (Choctaw Heritage Press, 1982); editor, Okla Apilachi (Choctaw Heritage Press, 1982); editor, How the Flowers Came to Be (Choctaw Heritage Press, 1982); executive editor, Choctaw Anthology I, II, and III (Choctaw Heritage Press, 1984); Lowak Mosoli (Choctaw Heritage Press, 1984); editor, Little Pigs - Shokoshi Althiha (Choctaw Heritage Press, 1984); editor, The Tale of the Possum (Choctaw Heritage Press, 1984); editor, Welcome to the Choctaw Fair! (Choctaw Heritage Press, 1984); James at W ork (Choctaw Heritage Press, 1984); The Choctaw Oral Traditions Relating to Their Origin, chapter from The Choctaw Before Removal (University of Mississippi Press, 1985).

*BRESETTE, JOSEPH N.
(executive director)
Affiliation: Great Lakes InterT ribal Council, P.O. Box 9, Lac du Flambeau, WI 54538 (715) 588-3324.

*BRESHEARS, GARY P.
(executive officer)
Affiliation: Phoenix Area Indian Health Service, 3738 N. 16th St., Suite A, Phoenix, AZ 85016 (602) 640-2052.

BRESSETTE, THOMAS
(Indian band chief)
Affiliation: Chief, Chippewas of Kettle & Stony Point Indian Band, RR #2, Forest, Ontario, Canada N0N 1J0 (519) 786-2125.

*BRETERNITZ, CORY DALE
(center president)
Affiliation: Center for Indigenous Studies in the Americas, 1 . 21 North 2nd St., Phoenix, AZ 85004 (602) 253-4938

*BREUNINGER, DANNY
(BIA agency supt.)
Affiliation: Truxton Canon Agency, Bureau of Indian Affairs, P.O. Box 37, Valentine, AZ 86437 (602) 769-2286.

BREWER, DELBERT D.
(BIA agency supt.)
Affiliation: Pine Ridge Agency, BIA, P.O. Box 1203. Pine Ridge, SD 57770 (605) 867-5125. *Past professional post*: Supt., Winnebago Agency, Winnebago, NE.

*BREWER, PATRICIA L.
(executive director)
Affiliation: Parch Creek Indian Heritage Center, HCR 69A, Box 85B, Atmore, AL 36502 (205) 368-9136.

*BREWSTER, HARDING
(alcohol/drug abuse program specialist)
Affiliation: Nashville Area IHS, 711 Stewarts Ferry Pike, Nashville, TN 37214 (615) 736-2400.

BRIDGES, THERESA M. (Puyallup) 1924-
(retail sales manager)
Born January 15, 1924, Mud Bay (Olympia), Wash. Education: Chemawa Indian High School, Salem, OR. P *rincipal occupation*: Retail sales manager. *Home address*: 11117 Conine Ave., SE, Olympia, W A 98503 (206) 459-7491. *Affiliations*: Manager, Franks Landing Smoke Shop, Olympia, WA, 1972-; Board Member, WaHeLut Indian School, 1974-. *Other professional posts*: Member & of ficer, Puyallup Tribal Council, Tacoma, WA, 1969-77; vice-president, V almarco Foundation, Olympia, W A, 1982-. *Community activities*: Puyallup Tribal Elders Support Organization (director/of ficer, 1964-. *Memberships*: Survival of American Indians Association (director & vice-president, 1982-). *Awards, honors*: Jefferson Award (Washington State W inner) by Seattle Post-Intelligencer & American Institue for Public Service; Martin Luther King Award from Thurston County (W A) Community Service. *Interests*: "Patterned quilt making and sewing; Indian basketry, carvings, artifact, and jewelry collecting; Pacific Northwest Indian archival repository development."

BRIGGS, LESTER JACK, Jr.
(Minnesota Chippewa) 1948-
(college administrator)
Born September 18, 1948, Duluth, Minn. *Education*: Johnson Institute, Duluth, MN, Certificate in Chemical Dependency , 1976; Indian counselor, Alcoholism Training Project, University of Minnesota-Duluth, Certificate of Completion - 300 hours - Chemical Dependency , 1977; Rutgers State University, Alcohol Studies Certificate of Completion, 1977; Rainy River Community College, A.A., 1978; Bemidji State University, B.S. (Community Service), 1980; University of Minnesota-Duluth, MED (Education Administration), 1990. *Principal occupation*:

College administrator . *Home address*: 1509 Spring Lake Rd., Cloquet, MN 55720 (218) 879-0294 (work). *Affiliations*: American Indian student advisor and planning assistant, Minnesota Higher Education Coordinating Board, 1978-81, regional director, Services to Indian People Program, Arrowhead Community College Region, 1983-89, Rainy River Community College, International Falls, MN; director , Fond du Lac Community College, Cloquet, MN 55720, 1989- *Other professional posts*: Chairperson, Indian Education Advisory Committee, Independent School District 361, International Falls, MN, 1977-79; member/president, Board of Directors, North American Indian Fellowship Center , S. International Falls, MN, 1979-83; professional licensure/school social worker , Minnesota State Dept. of Education (current); member , American Indian Advisory Board, University of Minnesota, Duluth (current); proposal writing for: Dept. of Public W elfare, State of Minnesota; Dept. of HEW; Minnesota State Dept. of Education; Rainy River Community College; and Arrowhead Community College Region. *Community activities*: Co-chairperson, International Pow-wow Committee, International Falls, MN, 1979-83; chairperson, advisory committee, Koochiching Co. Family Services, International Falls, MN, 1980-81; member , Youth Diversion Committee, International Falls Juvenile Program, 1981-83; member , Rainy River Citizen Advisory Committee, International Falls, MN, 1981-82; member, Services to Indian People/ Bilingual Ojibwe Specialist Project Advisory Committee, Arrowhead Community College Region (current). *Memberships*: Minnesota Association of Counselors on Alcoholism, 1978-83; Minnesota Indian Education Association (treasurer-current). *Awards, honors*: American Indian Administrator of the Year, 1986 & 1987, by Minnesota Indian Education Association; Distinguished Service Award, President's Award, 1988, by Arrowhead Community College Region. *Interests*: Fishing, hunting, reading, guitar, and home carpentry . *Published works*: Rivers of Life, A Native American Cultural Awareness Resource (Living W aters of Faith Series, contributing author and leader).

BRIGHTMAN, LEHMAN L.
(director-Indian organization)
Affiliation: United Native Americans, 2434 Faria Ave., Pinole, CA 94564 (415) 758-8160.

BRIGHTMAN, ROBERT 1950-
(professor of anthropology)
Born April 23, 1950, Chicago, Ill. *Education*: Reed College, Portland, OR, B.A., 1973; University of Chicago, MA, 1976, Ph.D., 1982. *Principal occupation*: Professor of anthropology . *Address*: Dept. of Anthropology, Reed College, Portland, OR 97202 (503) 771-1 112. *Affiliations*: Assistant professor of anthropology , University of Wisconsin-Madison, 1982-88; associate professor of anthropology, Reed College, Portland, OR, 1988-. *Memberships*: American Anthropological Association; Linguistic Society of America; American Society for Ethnohistory . *Interests*: North American Indian cultural anthropology & linguistics; Algonquian linguistics; field research: Pokatawagan, Manitoba, 1977-79, 1986 Cree. *Published works*: Orders of the Dreamed (University of Winnipeg, 1988); Acadohkiwina & Acimoina: Traditional Literature of the Rock Cree (Canadian Ethnology Service, 1989); Grateful Prey: Cree Human-Animal Relationships (U. of California Press, 1990).

BRILL, PETER SCOTT
(museum curator of exhibits)
Affiliation: George Gustav Heye Center, National Museum of the American Indian, Smithsonian Institution, 1 Bowling Green, New York, NY 10004 (212) 283-2420.

*BRINK, YANKO (Eskimo)
(AK village council president)
Affiliation: Native Village of Kasigluk Council, P.O. Box 19, Kasigluk, AK 99609 (907) 477-6927.

*BRITTAN, MARY ANN
(center director)
Affiliation: Indian Education Technical Assistance Center, 2424 Springer Dr., Suite 200, Norman, OK 73069 (405) 360-1 163.

BRODY, J.J. 1929-
(author)
Born April 24, 1929, Brooklyn, N.Y. *Education*: The Cooper Union, New York, N.Y. (Certificate of Fine Arts), 1950; University of New Mexico, BA, 1956, MA, 1964, PhD, 1970. *Principal occupation*: Author. *Home address*: Star Route, Box 929, Sandia Park, NM 87047. *Affiliations*: Curator of art, Everhart Museum, Scranton, P A, 1957-58; curator, Isaac Delago Museum of Art, New Orleans, 1958-60; curator, Museum of International Folk Art, Santa Fe, 1960-61; University of New Mexico, Albuquerque (curator & director, Maxwell Museum of Anthropology, 1962-83; professor of anthropology and art history, 1964-89, professor emeritus, 1989-). *Other professional posts*: Research curator, Maxwell Museum of Anthropology; research associate, School of American Research, Santa Fe; Senior Research Associate, Laboratory of Anthropology-Museum of Indian Art and Culture, Museum of New Mexico, Santa Fe. *Military service*: U.S. Army, 1952-54 (sergeant). *Community activities*: City of Albuquerque (art advisory board, 1970-74); Seton Museum and Library; Governor of New Mexico Task Force Paleontological Resources, 1978-79; Wheelwright Museum of the American Indian (board member); Florence Hanley Ellis Museum of Anthropology (member, Advisory Board). *Memberships*: American Association of Museums; Council for Museum Anthropology; American Rock Art Research Association; Native American Art Research Association; Archaeological Society of New Mexico; Society for American Archaeology; New Mexico Museum Association. *Awards, honors*: Popejoy Dissertation Prize, University of New Mexico,1971; non-fiction award for Indian Painters and White Patrons, Border Regional Library Conference, 1971; 1977 Art Book Award for Mimbres Painted Pottery; Award of Honor, New Mexico Historic Preservation Commission, 1978; resident scholar, School of American Research, 1980-81; Honoree, 1992, vol. 18, Papers (in honor of), by the Archaeological Society of New Mexico. *Interests*: Indian art, especially of the Southwest; museology; rock art; education; museum exhibitions. *Biographical sources*: Who's Who in America; Who's Who in the West; Who's Who in American Art. *Published works*: Indian Painters and White Patrons (UNM Press, 1971); Between Traditions (University of Iowa Press, 1976); Mimbres Painted Pottery (School of American Research and UNM Press, 1977); Beatien Yazz: Indian Painter, with Sallie Wagner and B. Yazz (School of American Research, 1983); Mimbres Pottery, with Catherine

Scott and Steve LeBlanc (Hudson Hills Press, 1983.); The Anasazi (Rizzoli and Jaca Books, 1990); Beauty From the Earth (University Museum, U. of Pennsylvania, 1990); Anasazi and Pueblo Painting (School of American Research, UNM Press, 1991). *Museum exhibitions*: Between Traditions (University of Iowa Museum of Art and Maxwell Museum, 1976); Myth, Metaphor & Mimbres Art (Maxwell Museum & Taylor Museum, 1976-77); Mimbres Pottery: Ancient Art of the American Southwest (with others) (American Federation of Arts, 1983-85); Beauty From the Earth (University Museum, U. of Pennsylvania, 1990-93).

*BROKENLEG, MARTIN (Rosebud Sioux)
(professor of minority studies)
Affiliation: Associate professor of Minority Studies, Augustana College, Sioux Falls, SD 57197 (605) 336-4007. *Published works*: with Larry Brendtro & Steve Van Bockern, Reclaiming Youth at Risk: Our Hope for the Future (suggests ways in which Native American and European traditions of child-rearing can be merged to help troubled youth); with Herbert T. Hoover, Yanktonai Sioux Water Colors: Cultural Remembrances of John Saul (Center for Western Studies, 1993).

*BRONSON, BENNETT
(museum chair-anthropology)
Affiliation: Field Museum of Natural History, Roosevelt Rd. at Lake Shore Dr., Chicago, IL 60605 (312) 922-9410.

*BROOKS, ROBERT
(professor of Native American studies)
Affiliation: Native American Studies Program, University of Oklahoma, 455 W. Lindsey, Rm. 804, Norman, OK 73019 (405) 325-2312.

BROOKSHIRE, JAMES
(chief-Indian claims)
Affiliation: Chief, Indian Claims Section, Land and Natural Resources Division, Dept. of Justice, Rm. 648, 550 1 1th St., NW, Washington, DC 20530 (202) 724-7375.

BROWER, ARCHIE (Eskimo)
(AK village council president)
Affiliation: Kaktovik Village, P.O. Box 8, Kaktovik, AK 99747.

*BROWER, ARNOLD J. (Eskimo)
(AK village council president)
Affiliation: Barrow Village Council, P.O. Box 1139, Barrow, AK 99723 (907) 852-441 1.

BROWN, ARLENE
(Indian band chief)
Affiliation: Chief, Klahoose Indian Band, Box 9, Squirrel Cove, British Columbia, Canada V0P 1T0 (604) 935-6650.

*BROWN, BRIAN J.
(council president)
Affiliation: American Indian Relief Council, P.O. Box 6200, Rapid City, SD 57709 (605) 399-9905.

BROWN, CECIL
(Indian band chief)
Affiliation: Chief, Masset Indian Band, P.O. Box 189, Masset, British Columbia, Canada V0T 1M0 (604) 626-3337.

BROWN, CHARLES ASA *(Fus Elle Haco-Muskogee) (Gos Quillen-Shawnee) (Eagle Star-Cherokee)* 1912-
(attorney, farm owner, lecturer)
Born October 17, 1912, Woodsfield, Ohio. *Education*: Virginia Military Institute, AB, 1935; University of Michigan Law School, 1935-37; Western Reserve University Law School, JD, 1938. *Principal occupation*: Attorney, farm owner, lecturer. *Home address*: 1903 Hutchins St., Portsmouth, OH 45662. *Affiliations*: Self-employed lawyer & farmer, Portsmouth, OH, 1938-; Municipal Prosecuting Attorney, Portsmouth, Ohio, 1946; Assistant Attorney General, State of Ohio, 1963. *Military service*: U.S. Army (active duty, 1941-46; reserve service, 1931-72) (Lt. Colonel; American Defense; European Theater Medal with three battle stars; Purple Heart; Bronz Star with oak leaf cluster; Victory Medal; German Occupation Medal; Distinguished Unit Presidential Citation; Army Reserve Longevity Medal). *Community activities*: Scioto Area Council (executive board); Boy Scouts of America, Portsmouth, Ohio (merit badge counselor, 1946-, commissioner); co-founder, Jaycees, Portsmouth, 1938; Chamber of Commerce, Portsmouth; Bentonville, OH, Anti-Horse Thief Society. *Indian activities*: Member, Cedar River Tulsa Band, Muskogee Indian Tribe, Holdinville, Okla.; honorary councilman, Creek Indian Nation, Tulsa, OK, 1962-69; councilman, Western Black Elk Keetowah, Cherokee Nation; councilman, Federated Indian Tribes. *Memberships*: Scioto County Bar Association (trustee); Ohio State Bar Association; American Indian Bar Association; Phi Delta Phi Legal Fraternity; American Legion; Retired Officers Association and Reserve Officers Association, Washington, DC (life member); U.S. Horse Cavalry Association (life member); Masonic Lodge. *Awards, honors*: Silver Beaver Award, Boy Scouts of America; Vigil Honor, Order of the Arrows; President's Award for Distinguished Service, 1982, Boy Scouts of America; Advisory Chief of Indian Tribes, 1961-80); Master Mason, 1944-; Chief's liaison to visiting persons at ceremonials; Tecumseh was my great-great grandfather. *Interests*: Lecturer on Indian lore throughout the U.S.; writer on many Indian subjects; writer on various Masonic subjects; speaker at many public gatherings of all kinds continually. *Biographical sources*: Who's Who in Freemasonry; Who's Who in the Midwest; Who's Who in the World; Who's Who in Ohio; Distinguished Americans. *Published works*: Numerous articles in various publications.

*BROWN, DAN, M.D.
(clinical director)
Affiliation: Scottsdale Salt River Clinic, Rte. 1, Box 215, Scottsdale, AZ 85256 (602) 379-4281.

BROWN, DANIEL JEROME
(Indian band chief)
Affiliation: Chief, Nanaimo Indian Band, 1 145 Totem Rd., Nanaimo, British Columbia, Canada V9R 1H1 (604) 753-3481.

*BROWN, DAVID QUENTIN *(Dotsuwah)* *(Chickamaugan-Cherokee)*
(raven or war chief)
Born October 7, 1953, Chattanooga, Tenn. *Education*: McKenzie (Chattanooga, TN) ABS. *Principal occupation*: Raven or war chief. *Home address*: 9001 Bill Reed Rd. #6, Ooltewah, TN 37363 (615) 855-2909. *Affiliation*: Tennessee River Band of Chickamaugan Cherokees. *Ac-*

tivities: Has led various classes in Native American awareness for children & adults, for summer camps & church groups. He is active in the fight against grave desecrations and environmental issues. Involved in initial meetings with the Hamilton County Sherif fs Dept. in forming the Native American Reserve Force which is a deputized group of Native Americans who protect the burial sites at Moccasin Bend from further desecration. This is the first time in history that a group of Native Americans, of reservation, has been deputized to oversee our ancestor's graves. *Published works*: Articles in the "The New Phoenix," "Pan American News," & "Katuah Journal."

BROWN, DEE ALEXANDER 1908-
(librarian, educator, author)
Born in 1908, Louisiana. *Education*: George Washington University, BS, 1937; University of Illinois, MS, 1951. *Principal occupation*: Librarian, educator, author. *Home address*: 7 Overlook Dr., Little Rock, AR 72207. *Affiliations*: Librarian, Dept. of Agriculture, W ashington, DC 1934-42; librarian, Aberdeen Proving Ground, Md., 1945-1948; agricultural librarian, 1948-72, professor, 1962-75, University of Illinois, Urbana. *Military service*: U.S. Army, 1942-45. *Memberships*: Authors Guild; Society of American Historians; Western Writers of America; Beta Phi Mu. *Published works*: Wave High the Banner, 1942; Grierson's Raid, 1954; Yellowhorse, 1956; Cavalry Scout, 1957; The Gentle Tamers: Women of the Old Wild West, 1958; The Bold Cavaliers, 1959; They Went Thataway, 1960; Fighting Indian of the W est, with M.F. Schmitt, 1948; Trail Driving Days, with M.F. Schmitt; The Setller's W est, with M.F. Schmitt; Fort Phil Kearny, 1962; The Galvanized Yankees, 1963; Showdown at Little Bighorn, 1964; The Girl From Fort W icked, 1964; The Year of the Century, 1966; Bury of My Heart at Wounded Knee, 1971; The Westerners, 1974; Hear That Lonesome Whistle Blow , 1977; Tepee Tales, 1979; Creek Mary's Blood, 1980; editor: Agricultural History, 1956-58; Pawnee, Blackfoot and Cheyenne, 1961.

*BROWN, FRANK
(professor)
Home address: 1899 E. Gate Dr ., Stone Mountain, GA 30087. *Affiliations*: Professor, Emory University, Atlanta, GA; member , Board of Directors, The Native American Center of Georgia, Woodstock, GA.

BROWN, FRITZ (Quechan)
(tribal council president)
Affiliation: Quechan Tribal Council, P.O. Box 11352, Yuma, AZ 85364 (619) 572-0213.

*BROWN, G. MICHAEL
(casino/bingo hall president)
Affiliation: Foxwoods High Stakes Bingo & Casino (Mashantucket-Pequot Tribe), State Rd., Box 410, Ledyard, CT 06339 (203) 885-3000.

*BROWN, GINGER E.
(Choctaw of Oklahoma) 1952-
(illustrator, fine artist)
Born November 9, 1952, Oklahoma City , Okla. *Education*: Kansas City Art Institute. *Principal occupation*: Illustrator, fine artist. *Home address*: 11407 W. 155th Ter., Overland Park, KS 66221 (913) 897-4873. *Other professional post*: Illustrator of endangered species for W orld Wildlife Fund, 1992-93. *Memberships*: Choctaw Nation

of Oklahoma; Indian Arts & Crafts Association; National Colored Pencil Association; Native American Rights Fund. *Awards, honors*: 1990 Scholarship Award from Kansas City Art Institute. *Interests*: "Depicting and combining wildlife with Native American artifacts and their legends and traditions."

*BROWN, IAN
(museum curator)
Affiliation: Peabody Museum of Archaeoogy & Ethnololgy, Harvard University, 11 Divinity Ave., Cambridge, MA 02138 (617) 495-2248.

BROWN, JOSEPH EPES 1920-
(retired professor, author, rancher)
Born September 9, 1920, Ridgefield, Conn. *Education*: Bowdoin College, 1940-42; Haverford College, BA, 1947; University of New Mexico, 1954-56; Stanford University , MA (Anthropology), 1966; University of Stockholm (Doctorate, Anthropology and History of Religions, 1970. Principal occupation: Author-teacher. *Home address*: 329 Kootenai Creek Rd., Stevensville, MT 59870. *Affiliations*: Teacher, Verde Valley School, Sedona, AZ, 1952-53, 1956-60, 1961-65; assistant professor, Prescott College, 1966-69; associate professor, Dept. of Religious Studies, Indiana University, 1970-72; University of Montana, Dept. of Religious Studies (associate professor, 1972-76; professor , 1977-.) *Editorial work*: Consulting editor, Parabola: The Magazine of Myth & Tradition; advisor, The Zuni Pueblo Film Project, Byron Earhart, W estern Michigan University; editor for V ol. V, American Indian Traditions, for Crossroad Press, 25 V ols., World Spirituality Series. *Memberships*: American Anthropological Association; Museum of Northern Arizona; Foundation of North American Indian Culture (advisory board.) *Awards, honors*: Smith-Mundt Grant to teach in Morocco, 1960-61; The Joseph E. Brown American Indian Scholarship Fund established in Mr . Brown's honor at Verde Valley School, Sedona, Ariz. *Interests*: "Research among the Plains Indians; traveled extensively and has done research in Morocco, North Africa. Major interest within anthropology is the study of diverse cultures. Enjoyed 40 years of teaching Native American traditions. Presently retired, but continues to write and raise horses on his ranch in Montana." *Published works*: The Sacred Pipe (University of Oklahoma Press, 1953; Penguin Books, with new introduction, 1971; Swedish, Spanish and Japanese translation); The Spiritual Legacy of the American Indian (Pendle Hill, 1964, 8th edition, 1976); The North American Indians: The Photographs of Edward S. Curtis, Aperture, (V ol. 16, no. 4, Philadelphia Museum of Art, 1972); The Spiritual Legacy of the American Indian, a collection of articles by Mr . Brown (Crossroad Publishing, 1980); The Gift of the Sacred Pipe (University of Oklahoma Press, 1982); Animals of the Soul, A Lakota Perspective (Element Books, 1992); chapters in books: The Spiritual Legacy of the American Indian, Sources, Theodore Roszak, 1972; The Question of 'Mysticism' with Native American Traditions, Mystics and Scholars, Harold Coward and Terence Penelhum, editors (Ross-Erickson Publishers, 1979); The Roots of Renewal, Seeing with a Native Eye, W alter Capps, Editor (Harper & Row, 1977); Relationship and Unity in American Indian Experience, The Unanimous Tradition (Sri Lanka Institute of Traditional Studies, 1982); American Indian Living Religions, Handbook of Living Religions, edited by John Hinnells

(Penguin Books, 1983); numerous articles, papers and lectures.

BROWN, LOUELLA
(hospital director)
Affiliation: PHS Indian Hospital, P .O. Box 60, Cass Lake, MN 56633 (218) 335-2291.

BROWN, MARGARET
(professor, site supt.)
Affiliations: Professor, Dept. of Anthropology, Southern Illinois University , P.O. Box 1451, Edwardsville, IL 62026 (618) 692-2744; Supt., Cahokia Mounds State Historic Site & Museum, P.O. Box 681, Collinsville, IL 62234 (618) 346-5160.

BROWN, NORMAN
(Indian band chief)
Affiliation: Wapekeka (Angling Lake) Indian Band, Wapekeka, Ontario, Canada P0V 1B0 (807) 537-2315.

*BROWN, THOMAS (Pomo)
(rancheria council chairperson)
Affiliation: Elem General Council, Sulphur Bank Rancheria, P.O. Box 618, Clearlake Oaks, CA 95423 (707) 998-2549.

BROWN, VINSON 1912-1991 (Deceased)
(writer, naturalist, publisher)
Born December 7, 1912, Reno, Nev . *Education*: University of California at Berkeley , AB, 1939; Stanford University, MA, 1947. *Principal occupation*: Writer, naturalist, publisher . Address: 3543 Indian Creek Rd., Happy Camp, CA 96039 (916) 493-5353 (of fice). Affiliations: Lecturer on American Indian religions, University of South Dakota, University of Northern Michigan, Myrin Institute, Haskell Institute; field collector in natural history; lecturer . Travels: Visits to many Indian tribes in the U.S., Canada, and Alaska, 1960-72; Mr. Brown spent about two years in the mountain jungles of Panama where he collected specimens with the aid of a Guaymi Indian named Chio Jari. He has also traveled extensively throughout the world. Published works: Understanding Ancient Life (Science Materials Center, 1958); Warriors of the Rainbow , with William Willoya (Naturegraph, 1965); Pomo Indians of California and Their Neighbors (Naturegraph, 1969); Great Upon the Mountain -- Crazy Horse of America (Naturegraph, 1971, cloth ed., Macmillan), now published by Naturegraph (1987) under the title: Crazy Horse: Hoka Hey!; Voices of the Earth and Sky: The Vision-Search of the American Indians (Stackpole, 1974; Naturegraph, 1976); Native Americans of the Pacific Coast (Naturegraph, 1985); and others which pertain to nature.

BROWN, WILFRED
(BIA agency supt.)
Affiliation: Western Navajo Agency, Bureau of Indian Affairs, P.O. Box 127, Tuba City, AZ 86045 (602) 283-4531.

*BROWNE, VEE F. *(Elvita)* (Navajo) 1956-
(author)
Born September 4, 1956, Ganado, Ariz. *Education*: Cochise Community College, AA, 1977; Northern Arizona University, BS, 1985; Western New Mexico University , MA, 1990. *Principal occupation*: Author. *Address*: P.O. Box 1085, Chinle, AZ 86503 (602) 725-3388. *Affiliations*: Northland Publishing, Flagstaf f, AZ, 1991-; journalist, The Navajo-Hopi Observer , Flagstaff, AZ

1991-. *Other professional posts* : National Caucus (member, board of directors) 1994-96; Wordcraft Circle of Native Writers (mentor)/Apprenticeship. *Memberships* : Society of Southwestern Authors; Society of Children's Book Writers; North American Native Authors; Arizona Press Association - The Navajo-Hopi Observer (newspaper). *Awards, honors* : Western Heritage 1991 - Cowboy Hall of Fame Award - Juvenile Book of the Year; The Buddy Bo Jack Nationwide Award for Humanitarian, 1992 Children's Book Writer; Society of Southwestern Authors, 1993 Published Work Award. *Interests* : Returning of Gift of North America's Native Authors during July each year; enjoy conferences and writer's workshops. I enjoy attending writer's intensive Institute each year. *Published works* : Monster Slayer (1991), Monster Birds (1993), & Neon Powwow Anthology (1993) (Northland Publishing). Bi-weekly newspaper sports articles - "Observer"; Maria Tallchief (Simon & Schuster).

*BRUCE, DORENE
(BIA agency supt.)
Affiliation : Turtle Mountain Agency, Bureau of Indian Affairs, P.O. Box 60, Belcourt, ND 58316 (701) 477-3191 Fax 477-6628.

BRUCE, LOUIS R.
(consultant)
Affiliation : President, Native American Consultants, Inc., 725 2nd St., NE, Washington, DC 20002. *Branch* : 1001 Highland St., Arlington, VA 22201.

BRUCHAC, JOSEPH (Abenaki) 1942-
(writer, storyteller, editor)
Born October 16, 1942, Saratoga Springs, N.Y. *Education* : Cornell University, B.A., 1965; Syracuse University, M.A., 1966; Union Graduate School (Yellow Springs, OH), Ph.D., 1974. *Principal occupation* : Writer, storyteller, editor. *Address* : P.O. Box 308, Greenfield Center, NY 12833 (518) 584-1728. *Affiliations* : Teacher & Liaison Officer, Teachers for West Africa: Ghana, 1966-1969; Skidmore College (English instructor, 1969-73; coordinator of program at Great Meadow Prison, 1974-81; faculty, Hamilton College, 1983, 85, 87; adjunct faculty, SUNY/Albany, 1987-1988; director, The Greenfield Review Literary Center. *Editorial positions* : Founder & Co-editor of The Greenfield Review Press, Greenfield Center, NY, 1969-; poetry editor of "Studies in American Indian Literature" (SAIL), 1989-; editor of "The Greenfield Review", 1969-87; editor of "The Prison Writing Review", 1976-85; co-editor, "Moccasin Telegraph," Fairfax, VA. *Professional posts* : Board member, National Association for Storytelling (NAPPS), 1992-94; acting chair, Native Writers Circle of the Americas, 1992-93; advisory board, Wordcraft Circle of Native American Writers, 1992-93; national chair, Returning the Gift Project, 1991-92; board member, Poetry Society of America, 1985-87; COSMEP-National Independent Publishers Association (board member, 1973-74, 1981-85; national chairman, 1984-85; among others. *Awards, honors* : NEA Creative Writing Fellowship (poetry), 1974; CCLM Editors' Fellowship, 1980; Rockefeller Humanities Fellowship, 1982; New York State CAPS Poetry Fellowships, 1973, 1982; NEA/PEN Syndicated Fiction Award, 1983; American Book Award for "Breaking Silence", 1984; Yaddo Residency Fellowships, 1984, 1985; The Cherokee Nation Award (prose), 1986; New York State Council on the Arts Editors Fellowship, 1986; The Hope S.

Dean Memorial Award, 1993. *Interests* : The Dawnland Singers (Joe, Jim, Jesse, and Marge Bruchac) offer a variety of performance material, including traditional Native American storytelling, drum songs and chants, contemporary music in Abenaki and English, flute songs, and historical presentations. The group formed in the spring of 1993 for the Abenaki Heritage Festival, and has since performed at the Flynn Theater in Burlington, VT, the Champlain Valley Festival and a number of other locations and festivals. *Published works* : Poems and stories in over 300 magazines; poems & stories anthologized in over 50 anthologies; translations from Abenaki, Ewe, Iroquois, and Spanish in numerous magazines; articles and book reviews in more than 60 magazines & anthologies. *Anthologies edited* : Singing of Earth (with Diana Landau, The Nature Co., 1993); Raven Tells Stories: Contemporary Alaskan Native Writing (1990); New Voices From the Longhouse: Contemporary Iroquois Writing (1989); Songs From This Earth on Turtle's Back: Contemporary American Indian Poetry; among others. *Fiction* : Gluskabe and the Four Wishes (Cobblehill Books, 1994); Returning the Gift (editor, University of Arizona Press, 1994); A Boy Called Slow (Philomel, 1994); The Great Ball Game (Dial, 1994); Dawn Land (novel, Fulcrum, 1993); Turtle Meat (short stories, Holy Cow Press, 1992); The White Moose (short stories, Blue Cloud Quarterly, 1988); among others. *Non-Fiction* : Keepers of Life: Discovering Plants Through Native American Stories and Earth Activities for Children (with Michael Caduto, Fulcrum, 1994); The Native American Sweat Lodge in History & Story (The Crossing Press, 1994); Keepers of the Animals: Native American Stories & Wildlife Activities for Children (with Michael Caduto, Fulcrum, 1991); Keepers of the Earth: Native American Stories & Environmental Activities for Children (with Michael Caduto, Fulcrum, 1988); and Keepers of the Night: Native American Stories & Nocturnal Activities for Children(with Michael Caduto, Fulcrum, 1987). *Audio cassettes* : Dawnland (Fulcrum, 1993); Keepers of the Animals (Fulcrum, 1992); Keepers of the Earth (Fulcrum, 1990), The Boy Who Lived With the Bears (Parabola/Harper Audio, 1990); Gluskabe Stories (Yellow Moon, 1990); Translator's Son (Cross Cultural Communications, 1981). *Children's Books* : The First Strawberries (Dial Books, 1993; Fox Song (Philomel, 1993); Thirteen Moons on Turtle's Back (with Jonathan London, Philomel, 1992).

BRUDERER, PAT
(president-Indian organization)
Affiliation : President, Indian Crafts & Arts Manitoba, Inc., 348 Hargrave St., Winnipeg, Manitoba, Canada R3B 2J9 (204) 944-1469.

BRUGGE, DAVID M. 1927-
(anthropologist)
Born September 3, 1927, Jamestown, N.Y. *Education* : University of New Mexico, BA, 1950. *Principal occupation* : Anthropologist. *Address* : Southwest Cultural Resources Center, National Park Service, 1220 S. St. Francis Dr., Box 728, Santa Fe, NM 87504-0728 (505) 988-6766. *Affiliations* : Various positions, Gallup Community Indian Center, Gallup, NM, 1953-57; salvage archaeologist, Four Corners Pipeline Co., Houston, Texas, 1957-58; anthropologist, The Navajo Tribe, Window Rock, Ariz., 1958-68. Other professional posts: Archaeologist, Museum of Northern Arizona, Flagstaff, Ariz., 1957; direc-

tor, Navajo Curriculum Center, Rough Rock, Ariz., 1968; instructor, College of Ganado, Ariz., 1973; chief, Branch of Curation, Southwest Cultural Resources Center, National Park Service, P.O. Box 728, Santa Fe, NM, 1985-. *Military service* : U.S. Army, 1945-47. *Community activities* : Sage Memorial Hospital, Ganado, Ariz. (secretary, advisory board); Title I Committee, Ganado Public Schools. *Memberships* : American Anthropological Association; Society for American Archaeology; Archaeological Society of New Mexico (trustee); American Society for Ethnohistory (secretary-treasurer, 1966-68); Arizona Archaeological and Historical Society; New Mexico Historical Society; Northern Arizona Society for Science and Art, Inc.; American Association for the Advancement of Science; Plateau Sciences Society. *Interests* : "Navajo studies, especially in archaeology, ethnohistory and history, and more generally of the greater Southwest. In addition to my work with the Navajos, I have done field work in northwestern Mexico, principally among the Pima Bajo (Lower Pima) of Sonora. My work with the Navajo Tribe involved research for various land disputes such as the Land Claims Case, the Navajo-Hopi boundary dispute, the McCracken Mesa land exchange and Utah school section case and the Huerfano Mesa land exchange." *Biographical sources* : Who's Who in the West; The Official Museum Directory. *Published works* : Navajo Pottery and Ethnohistory (The Navajo Tribe, 1963); Long Ago in Navajoland (The Navajo Tribe, 1965); Navajo Bibliography, with J. Lee Correll and Edith Watson (The Navajo Tribe, 1967); Navajos in the Catholic Church Records of New Mexico, 1694-1875 (The Navajo Tribe, 1968); Zarcillos Largos, Courageous Advocate of Peace (The Navajo Tribe, 1970); The Story of the Navajo Treaties, with J. Lee Correll (The Navajo Tribe, 1971); Navajo and Western Pueblo History (Tucson Corral of Westerners, 1972); The Navajo Exodus (Archaeological Society of New Mexico, 1972.)

BRUGUIER, LEONARD R. (Yankton Sioux) 1944-
(administration)
Born October 9, 1944, Wagner, S.D. *Education* : University of South Dakota, BA, 1984, MPA, 1986; Oklahoma State University, PhD, 1989. *Principal occupation* : Administration. *Address & Affiliation* : Director, Institute of American Indian Studies, University of South Dakota, 414 E. Clark, Vermillion, SD 57069 (605) 677-5209, 1989-. *Other professional post* : Editor, "The Bulletin," Institute of American Indian Studies, University of South Dakota; assistant professor of American history, University of South Dakota; host radio show, "Voices of the Plains," South Dakota Public Radio Network, Vermillion, SD. *Military service* : U.S. Marine Corps, 1963-70 (Sergeant; Combat Action Ribbon, Presidential Unit Citation, Vietnam Service Medal, Vietnam Campaign Ribbon, Armed Forces Expeditionary Medal, National Defense Medal). *Community activities* : Member, Indian Memorial Committee, National Parks Service. *Memberships* : Organization of American Historians, 1986-; Western Historical Association, 1985-; Southern Historical Association, 1988-; Phi Alpha Theta, 1986-; Machinists and Aerospace Workers, 1971-; Vietnam Veterans of America, 1976-. *Awards, honors* : Oklahoma State Regents for Higher Education Minority Doctoral Study Grant; Towsend Memorial Minority Scholarships; Archie B. Gillfillan Award for Creative Writing; History

Alumni Award; University of South Dakota Veterans Club. *Interests*: "North & South American comparative studies of "Indians," with a particular interest in plains people and their religion, government, and social institutions. in North America, I am researching the Pipe Religion and its influence in Indian-White relations. Ongoing research of Indian men and women who served in the U.S. Armed Force and their impact on reservation, government, and social patterns. Demographic and statistical information on Indians, both continents." *Biographical source*: "The Yankton Sioux", Indians of North America Series, by Herbert Hoover. *Published works*: Remember Your Relatives (Marty Indian School, 1985; Yankton Sioux Elderly Board, 1989); Conference on Reburials (American Indian Research Project, 1985); The Yankton Sioux (Chelsea House Publishers, 1988); South Dakota Leaders (University of South Dakota Press, 1989).

*BRUN, FRANCIS
(BIA agency supt.)
Affiliation: Red Lake Agency, Bureau of Indian Affairs, Red Lake, MN 56671 (218) 679-3361.

*BRUNDIN, CLAUDIA
(tribal chairperson)
Affiliation: Blue Lake Rancheria, P.O. Box 428, Blue Lake, CA 95525 (707) 668-5101.

BRUNDIN, JUDITH A. 1949-
(museum education department head)
Born December 18, 1949, Columbus, Ohio. *Education*: University of Colorado, BFA, 1972; Colorado College, MAT, 1978; New York University, Certificate-Museum Studies, 1983. *Principal occupation*: Museum education department head. *Home address*: 33 Over Place, Weehauken, NJ 07087 (201) 792-0178. *Affiliations*: Secondary & elementary art instructor, Chinle Boarding School, BIA, Many Farms, AZ, 1974-77; art technician, secondary education, Tucson Public Schools, 1978-80; chief exhibitions designer, Navajo Tribal Museum, Window Rock, AZ, 1980-81; Head, Education Dept., National Museum of the American Indian (NMAI), Smithsonian Institution, New York, NY, 1982-. *Other professional posts*: Consulting, lectures-presentations. *Awards, honors*: Letter of Commendation, U.S. Dept. of the Interior, BIA, presented upon resignation, April 1977; presentation of a special plaque from the Navajo Tribal government upon completion of the Navajo Tribal Museum's exhibit installation, 1981. *Published works*: Author - American Indian Dolls, An Educational Resource Kit (NMAI, 1990), and The Native People of the Northeast Woodlands, An Educational Resource Publication (NMAI, 1990); editor - Cowboys and Indians (Golden Books, 1990), and Davey Crockett series (Walt Disney Co., 1991); articles - "Navajo Sandpainting," Instructor, 87 (Nov. 1977); "Inventorying a Historic Property," Museum Notes, 63 (Oct. 1984); "A Small Museums Modern Exhibition on a Shoe-String Budget," Museum Studies Journal, Spring, 1986; "New Dimensions With Living Cultures," Museum Studies Newsletter, NYU, Spring/Summer, 1989; guides - "The Great Plains, Three Art Activities: curriculum guide (NMAI, 1988); "On Your Own With Great Native Americans" exhibit guide (NMAI, 1988); "On Your Own With Native American Cultures" exhibit guide (NMAI, 1989).

*BRUNER, WILLIAM E. (Choctaw)
(Indian school principal)
Affiliation: Bogue Chitto Elementary School, Route 2, Box 274, Philadelphia, MS 39350 (601) 656-8611.

BRUYERE, LOUIS
(council president)
Affiliation: President, Native Council of Canada, 450 Rideau St., 2nd Floor, Ottawa, Ontario, Canada K1N 5Z4 (613) 238-351 1.

BRUYERE, RICHARD
(Indian band chief)
Affiliation: Chief, Couchiching Indian Band, P.O. Box 723, Fort Frances, Ontario, Canada P9A 3M9 (807) 274-3228.

*BRYANT, CHRISTINA (Ageya Wahya)
Tsaragi Cherokee) 1948-
(storyteller, visual artist, educator, environmentalist)
Born March 14, 1948, Kings County, N.Y. *Education*: Pace University (New York, NY) B.A. *Principal occupation*: Storyteller, visual artist, free-lance educator, environmentalist. *Home address*: 105 Lincoln Rd., Apt. 5J, Brooklyn, NY 11225 (718) 462-8128. *Affiliation*: Freelance educator - folkways interpreter of Native American culture, environment, recreation therapist, American Indian inspired arts/crafts teacher, storyteller, Henry Street Art in Education, Learning Through an Expanded Arts Program (LEAP); Museum of Natural History - Special Education Dept. and Peoples Center. *Memberships*: Nuyagi Keetoowah, Inc.; Southeastern Cherokee Confederacy of Georgia; National Outdoor Leadership School. *Interests*: Storytelling - speaks annually to hundreds of students in the NYC schools and area private schools. She works for private art & science organizations that enrich the lives of people with disabilities. Works in homeless shelters.

BRYANT, RICHARD M., M.D.
(administrative officer)
Affiliation: Phoenix Indian Medical Center, 4212 North 16th St., Phoenix, AZ 85016 (602) 263-1200.

BRYCELEA, CLIFFORD (Navajo) 1953-
(professional artist; painter)
Born September 26, 1953, Shiprock, N.M. *Education*: Fort Lewis College, BA (Art), 1975. *Principal occupation*: Professional artist; painter. *Home address*: 1721 Montano St., Santa Fe, NM 87501 (505) 984-8632. *Affiliations*: Toh-Atin Gallery, Durango, CO (16 years); Tekakwitha, Helen, GA (8 years); Blue Gem & Gallery, Midland, TX (15 years). *Memberships*: Indian Arts & Crafts Association (IACA), Albuquerque (member, 1980-; board of directors, 1986-91); Southwestern Association on Indian Affairs (Santa Fe), 1980-. *Awards, honors*: 4 Gold Medals, IACA, San Dimas, CA 1981, 1982 & 1986; 1st Place & Memorial Award, Gallup (NM) Ceremonial; Artist-of-the-Year, 1987 by IACA; and City Poster Award, 1991, Sante Fe, NM. *Interests*: "My work is in contemporary and representational style - paintings of various cultures, telling the stories and recall the legends of American Indians. It also depicted the mysticism and magical composition (spiritual meaning.) *Biographical sources*: Beyond Tradition, by Jerry & Lois Jacka; The Art Fever, by James Parsons; American Artist by Les Krantz. *Published works*:

illustrated - American Way (American Airlines, 1976); Pieces of White Shell (Charles Scribner's Sons, 1984); and Haunted Mesa (Bantam Books, 1987).

BUCHEL, SUSAN J.
(museum curator)
Affiliation: Nez Perce National Historical Park & Museum, P.O. Box 93, Spalding, ID 83551.

*BUCK, JIM
(radio host/producer)
Affiliation: "Sequoyah," WBAI - FM, 505 Eighth Ave., New York, NY 10018 (212) 279-0707.

BUCK, TERRI
(tribal health director)
Affiliation: Prairie Island Community Council, 1158 Island Blvd., Welch, MN 55089 (612) 385-2554.

BUCKANAGA, GERTRUDE (Chippewa)
(director-Indian women's project)
Affiliation: Director, American Indian Women Into Media, Migizi Communications, Inc., 3123 E. Lake St., Suite 200, Minneapolis, MN 55406 (612) 721-6631.

BUCKLES, AUSTIN
(Indian school principal)
Affiliation: Salt River Day School, Route 1, Box 117, Scottsdale, AZ 85256 (602) 241-2810.

BUCKLEY, THOMAS 1942-
(cultural anthropologist)
Born May 28, 1942, Louisville, KY. *Education*: Harvard University, BA, 1975; University of Chicago, MA, 1977, PhD, 1982. *Principal occupation*: Cultural anthropologist. *Address*: Department of Anthropology, University of Massachusetts, 100 Morrissey Blvd., Boston, MA 02125 (617) 287-6850. *Affiliation*: Associate professor, Dept. of Anthropology, University of Massachusetts, Boston, MA, 1982-. *Interests*: Field work in Native Northwestern California, among Yurok, Hupa, Karuk and Tolowa Indians, since 1976. Focus on Yurok language, politics, religion, gender. Serve as consultant and as expert witness in fishing and in land use and religious freedom cases. Published works: Blood Magic (University of California Press, 1988); numerous articles on the Yuroks and on A.L. Kroeber.

BUECKER, THOMAS R. 1948-
(museum curator)
Born November 14, 1948, Neb. *Education*: University of Nebraska, Kearney, BA, 1973; Chadron State College, MA, 1992. *Principal occupation*: Museum curator. *Address*: P.O. Box 304, Crawford, NE 69339 (308) 665-2919. *Affiliation*: Curator, Fort Robinson Museum, Nebraska State Historical Society, Lincoln, NE, 1977-. Published work: The Crazy Horse Surrender Ledger (Nebraska State Historical Society, 1994).

*BUENDIA, IMELDA, M.D.
(clinical director)
Affiliation: Wewoka PHS Indian Health Center, P.O Box 1475, Wewoka, OK 74884 (405) 257-6281.

BUFFALO, VICTOR
(Indian band chief)
Affiliation: Samson Cree Nation, Box 159, Hobbema, AB, Can T0C 1N0 (403) 421-4926.

BUFFALOHEAD, W. ROGER
(director-Indian project)
Affiliation: Achievement Through Communications, Migizi Communications, 3123 E. Lake St., #200, Minneapolis, MN 55406 (612) 721-6631.

BUFORD, BETTIE (LITTLE DOVE) *(Gttigua Cox)* **(Yamasee/ Creek/Cherokee) 1935-**
(principal chief)
Born February 20, 1935, Ocoee, Fla. *Principal occupation*: Principal chief. *Address*: P.O. Box 521, Cox-Osceola Seminole Indian Reservation, Orange Springs, FL 32182 (904) 546-1386 (home); 546-5525 (tribal of fice). *Affiliations*: President, Oklavueha Seminole Trading Post, Orange Springs, FL, 1985-; licensed genealogist & historian (29 years). *Professional post*: Teacher, Indian culture, Osceola Christian Indian School. *Military service*: American Red Cross Military Hospital, Korean conflict. *Community activities*: Principal chief, Oklavueha Band of Seminole Indians, 1979-; Assistant principal of Coe Harjo's Private Christian Indian School, 1986-. *Memberships*: Native American Historical Presentation Service, 1991-; National Indian Unity Coalition, 1990-; The Concerned Citizens League of America (president). *Awards*: Marion Education Awards; several awards for teaching Indian culture an crafts. *Interests*: "My major interest is to help improve the lifestyles of my Indian people and to stop some of the prejudice against them. To let all people know what real Indians are, not the stereotypes that they see in the movies and on television. I would like to travel to all tribes." *Published works*: Oklavueha #1-2-3-4-5 Band of Seminoles, 1992-94; Oklawaka People of the River Indians, 1994; Yamasee Indians - Last Known as Oklavueha Band of Seminoles, 1994; *In progress*: Oklavuehas Written Language.

BUHR, GRACE
(coordinator-friendship centres)
Affiliation: Manitoba Association of Friendship Centres, 604 - 213 Notre Dame Ave., Winnipeg, Manitoba, Canada R3B 2J9 (204) 943-8082.

BULFER, JOE
(executive director)
Affiliation: Southern Indian Health Council, P .O. Box 2128, Alpine, CA 91903 (619) 445-1 188.

BULL, ROGER
(Indian band chief)
Affiliation: Lac Seul Indian Band, Hudson, Ontario P0V 1X0 (807) 582-3503.

*BULLARD, LORETTA
(association president)
Affiliation: Kawerak, Inc., P.O. Box 948, Nome, AK 99762 (907) 443-5231.

BULLDOG, HARVEY
(Indian band chief)
Affiliation: Boyer River Indian Band, Box 270, High Level, AB, Can. T0H 1Z0 (403) 927-3697.

BULLETTS-BENSON, GLORIA
(Kaibab Paiute)
(tribal chairperson)
Affiliation: Kaibab Paiute Tribal Council, HC65, Box 2, Fredonia, AZ 86022 (602) 643-7245.

*BUNKE, JIM
(museum CEO)
Affiliation: Sebewaing Indian Museum, 612 E. Bay St., Sebewaing, MI 48759 (517) 883-3730.

BUNN, NELSON (Sioux)
(Indian band chief)
Affiliation: Birdtail Sioux Indian Band, P .O. Box 75, Beulah, Manitoba, Canada R0M 0B0 (204) 568-4540.

BUNNIE, SAMUEL
(Indian band chief)
Affiliation: Sakimay Indian Band, Box 339, Grenfell, Saskatchewan, Canada S0G 2B0 (306) 697-2831.

BURCELL-PRICE, SUZANNE M. (Karuk) 1956-
(assistant director-Indian center)
Education: Humboldt State University , BA, 1978, MBA, 1981. Principal occupation: Assistant director-Indian center. *Address*: The Center for Community Development, Humboldt State University, Graves Annex #30, Arcata, CA 95521-4957 (707)826-371 1. *Affiliations*: Regional vice-president, Northern California Regional Of fice of the United Indian Development Association (8 yrs.); assistant director, The Center for Community Development, Humboldt State University, Arcata, CA, 1989-. Ms. Burcell-Price works with the Director to design and implement projects that utilize University resources to benefit Indian tribes & community-based organizations in Northern California. She specializes in feasibility analysis, preparation of business plans and financing proposals, organizational development and program evaluation. *Other professional posts*: Design and coordinates special-topic training seminars and publication of the Center's quarterly newsletter, the "Messinger."; member of President's Planning Task Force on Services to Native Americans at Humboldt State University.

BURCH, LEONARD C. (Southern Ute)
(tribal chairperson)
Affiliation: Southern Ute Tribal Council, P.O. Box 737, Ignacio, CO 81 137 (303) 563-0100.

*BURDEAU, GEORGE
(film producer/director)
Affiliation: Raleigh Studios, 650 N. Bronson Ave., Suite 215, Hollywood, CA 90004 (213) 871-8689.

*BURGESS, MICHAEL
(managing editor)
Affiliation: "Talking Leaf Newspaper," Los Angeles Indian Center , Los Angeles, CA 90017 (213) 413-3156.

*BURGESS, ROXANNE
(liaison)
Affiliation: Los Angeles American Indian Liaison to the Mayor, 200 N. Spring St., Los Angeles, CA 90012 (213) 485-8881.

*BURGESS, VIOLA
(AK village council president)
Affiliation: Hydaburg Cooperative Association, P.O. Box 323, Hydaburg, AK 99922 (907) 285-3666.

BURNABY, JOANNE
(museum director)
Affiliation: Dene Cultural Institute, P .O. Box 207, Yellowknife, Northwest Territories, Canada X1A 2N2 (403) 873-6617.

BURNS, ROBERT I., S.J. 1921-
(clergyman, historian, educator)
Born August 16, 1921, San Francisco, Calif. *Education*: Gonzaga University , BA, 1945, MA, 1947 (D. Litt.), 1968; Fordham University , MA, 1949; Jesuit Pontifical Faculty (Spokane, W A, Phil.B., 1946, Phil.Lic., 1947) (Alma, CA, S.Th.B. 1951, S.Th.Lic., 1953; Postgraduate, Columbia University, 1949, Oxford University , 1956-57; Johns Hopkins University , Ph.D. (summa cum laude)(History), 1958; University of Fribourg, Switzerland, Doc. es Sc.Hist. (double summa cum laude)(History, Ethno-history), 1961. *Principal occupation*: Clergyman, historian, educator. *Address*: History Department, Graduate School, University of California, Los Angeles, CA 90024. *Affiliations*: Assistant archivist, Jesuit and Indian Archives of Pacific Northwest Province, Spokane, 1945-47; instructor , History Department, University of San Francisco, (instructor, 1947-48; assistant professor , 1958-62; associate professor, 1963-66; professor , 1967-76); senior professor , History Dept., U.C.L.A., 1976-. *Other professional posts*: Director, Institute of Medieval Mediterranean, Spain, 1976-; staff, UCLA Center for Medieval-Renaissance Studies, 1977-; staf f, UCLA Near Eastern Center, 1979-. *Editorial work*: Board editor, Trend in History, 1980; co-editor , Viator (UCLA), 1980-90; editorial committee, U.C. Press, 1985. Me mberships: American Historical Association, Pacific Coast Branch (vice president, 1978; president, 1978-80; presiding-delegate, International Congress of Historical Sciences, 1975, and U.S. Representative, 1980); American Catholic Historical Association (president, 1976); Medieval Association of the Pacific; Society for Spanish and Portuguese Historical Studies; Hill Monastic Library; North American Catalan Society; American Bibliographical Center (board, 1982-89). *Awards, honors*: Five book awards from national historical associations, including American Historical (Pacific Coast Award), American Catholic Historical, and American Association for State and Local History , for Jesuits and Indian Wars, 1965; Dr. Burns gave the keynote address at the National Park Service's Sesquicentennial of the sustained Indian-white contact by Americans in the Pacific Northwest states, the (Protestant) Whitman Mission, July 1986 at Whitman College. *Interests*: "I have two fields, allied but distinct, in which I publish regularly . The medieval field is the moving frontier of the 13th-century Catalonia, particularly the absorption by the Catalan peoples of the V alencian kingdom of the Moslems. The American field is the Pacific Northwest, particularly , Indian-white relations and troubles, 1840-1880, as illumined especially by Jesuit documentation here and in Europe. Ethnohistory and the Pacific Northwest frontier is thus seen not in isolation but as illumined by other frontier experiences." *Biographical sources*: Who's Who in America; Contemporary Authors; among others. *Published works*: Co-author, I lift My Lamp: Jesuits in America, 1955; Indians and Whites in the Pacific Northwest: Jesuit Contributions to Peace 1850-1880 (University of San Francisco Press, 1961); The Jesuits and the Indian W ars (Yale University Press, 1966); The Jesuits and the Indian W ars of the Northwest, reissue of 1966 edition (University of Idaho Press, 1985). Articles include: Northwest Indian Missions, position essay , Handbook of North American Indians (U.S. Government Printing Of fice, 1978-1990, vol. 4; Jesuit Missions, (North American Indians) Dictionary of American History (Charles Scribner's

Sons, 1977); "Roman Catholic Missionaries", (to U.S. Indians) The Reader's Encyclopedia of the American West (Thomas Y. Crowell Co., 1977); "The Opening of the West, (impact on Pacific Northwest Indians) The Indian: Assimilation, Integration or Separation (Prentice-Hall, Canada, 1972); "The Significance of the Frontier in the Middle Ages", in Medieval Frontier Societies. ed. by Robert Bartlett & Angus MacKay (Clarendon Press, 1989) This is an interrelating of the U.S. Indian and the Medieval frontiers; a revised version is in preparation of the Reader's Encyclopedia of the American West, with past articles in it; and numerous other articles.

BURROWS, DARYL F. (Wintun)
(rancheria chairperson)
Affiliation: Grindstone Rancheria, P.O. Box 63, Elk Creek, CA 95939 (916) 968-51 16.

BURRUS, S.S. (Ms.) *(Going About*
Grasshopper Sam) **(Oklahoma Cherokee)**
(artist)
Born in Okla. *Education*: Central State University, BA. *Principal occupation*: Artist of watercolor, sculpture, fashion designer . *Permanent Collections*: State Trail of Tears Museum - Cape Girardeau, MO, 1987, 1991; A-Eiteljorg Museum - Indianapolis, IN, 1989; Heritage Center - Tahlequah, OK, 1991; Cherokee Museum - Cherokee, NC, 1991; Five Tribes Museum - Muskogee, OK, 1991; Smithsonian - Of fice of Dr. Rayna Green, 1992; University of Oklahoma - Dr. Rennard Strickland, Director of American Indian Law & Policy Center - Oklahoma City , 1992. *Memberships*: Indian Arts and Crafts Association; Southwestern American Indian Association; Oklahoma Arts Council. *Awards, honors*: Numerous awards including: 1988 - Tulsa Arts Festival, Oklahoma Indian Market; 1989 - Five Tribes Museum, Intertribal Ceremonial; 1990 - Tulsa Idian Festival, Red Earth, Intertribal-Gallup; 1991 - Santa Fe Indian Market, Dallas Market Center, Katowah Intertribal Show , Trail of Tears Art Show; 1992 - Featured Fashion Designer-20th Annual Symposium on the American Indian-March 1992 by N.S.U., Tahlequah, OK. One Woman Shows and Special Exhibits, Invitationals. *Published works*: Prose by S S. Burrus - "Why Do They Whisper" (All My Relations, 1991); five prints (Wintercount Greetin Cards, 1991); cover and content illustrations for "The Trail On Which They Wept" (Cherokee Girl) (Silver/Burdett Press, 1992); 1993 Calendar (Wintercount Greeting Cards 1992); numerous prints and posters.

BURSHEARS, J.F.
(museum director)
Affiliation: Koshare Indian Museum, P.O. Box 580, 115 W. 18th St., La Junta, CO 81050 (719) 384-4411.

BURT, EUGENE C. 1948-
(managing editor)
Born July 31, 1948, Philadelphia, P A. *Education*: Temple University, BA, 1970; U. of Washington, MA, 1973, PhD, 1980. P *rincipal occupation*: Managing editor, Ethnoarts Index. *Address*: P.O. Box 30789, Seattle, W A 98103 (206) 783-9580. *Affiliation*: Owner, Data Arts, Seattle, WA, 1983-. *Other professional post*: Higher education teaching positions at various institutions. *Interests*: Non-western art history . *Published works*: Bibliography of Tribal Art Bibliographies (Data Arts, 1986); Native American Art: A 5-Year Cumulative Bibliography (Data Arts, 1990).

*BURTON, THOMAS C. (Paiute)
(tribal council chairperson)
Affiliation: Fallon Business Council, 8955 Mission Rd, Fallon, NV 89406 (702) 423-6075.

*BURTON, WILLIAM
(health systems administrator)
Affiliation: SEARHC Health Center , 3289 Tongass, Ketchikan, AK 99901 (907) 225-4156.

BUSH, MITCHELL LESTER, Jr. (Onondaga)
1936-
(chief-tribal enrollment, B.I.A.-retired)
Born February 1, 1936, Syracuse, N.Y . *Education*: Haskell Institute, 1951-56. *Principal occupation*: Chief, tribal enrollment, B.I.A. *Home address*: 22258 Cool Water Dr., Ruther Glen, VA 22546. *Affiliation*: Chief, Branch of Tribal Enrollment Services, BIA, Washington, D.C., 1956-91. *Other professional post*: Editor, American Indian Society (Washington, DC) Newsletter, 1966-. *Military service*: U.S. Army, 1958-61 (Specialist 4th Class). *Community activities*: DC-MD-VA Chapter of VEVITA (board of directors); American Indian Inaugural Ball (committee member, 1969, '73, '77, '81, '85, '89, '93); American Indian Society, Washington, D.C. (president, 1966-91). *Awards, honors*: American Indian Society Distinguished Service Award, 1971 & 1990; Maharishi Award conferred by the Maharishi University; appointed by Gov . Gerald L. Baliles to Virginia Council on Indians, 1989; Outstanding Public Service to the U.S.A. certificate from the Dept. of the Interior , May, 1990; Mental Health Association Distinguished Service Award; Certificate of Appreciation from MD Governor Hughes; Points of Light certificate for Outstanding Volunteer Contributions to the U.S.A. issued by Dept. of the Interior; Certificate of Appreciation from the Presidential Inaugural Committee, Jan. 1981. *Interests*: "Lecturer & Indian dancer for American Indian Society; participant, 1990 Census Planning Conference on Race and Ethnic Items sponsored by the Census Bureau; tour leader to Virginia Indian reservations for Resident Associate Program, Smithsonian Institution; honored at the 1982 Nanticoke (Delaware) Pow wow; judge at the 1978, '80, '82, '84 & '85 Miss Indian American Pageants held in Sheridan, WY , and Bismarck, ND; photo and bio included in Shadows Caught: Images of Native Americans, by Stephen Gambaro at Gilcrease Institute, Tulsa, Oklahoma. Avocational - roller skating and raising ornamental fowl." *Biographical sources*: To Live in Two Worlds, by Brent Ashabranner; American Indian Wars, by John Tebbel, 1960; Successful Indian Career Profiles, to be published by North American Indian Club, Syracuse, N.Y. *Published works*: Editor, American Indian Society Cookbook (American Indian Society, 1975 and 1984 editions); Movies & Television shows: Lives of the Rich and Famous, segment featuring Connie Stevens; MGM, George Washington TV Mini-Series; Indians, Walt Disney Productions; TNT's "Broken Chain"; and numerous television programs.

BUSHIE, RODERICK
(Indian band chief)
Affiliation: Hollow Water Indian Band, Wanipigow , MB, Can. R0E 2E0 (204) 363-7278.

BUSSEY, RUTH
(health clinic director)
Affiliation: Grand Traverse Ottawa/Chippewa Health Clinic, Route 1, Box 135, Suttons Bay , MI 49682 (616) 271-3882.

BUSSIDOR, ILA
(Indian band chief)
Affiliation: Fort Churchill Indian Band, Tadoule Lake, MB, Canada R0B 0L0 (204) 652-2219.

*BUSTOS, BERNIE (Navajo)
(radio station manager)
Affiliation: KTDB - 89.7 FM, Ramah Navajo School Board, P.O. Box 40, Pinehill, NM 87357 (505) 775-3215.

BUTLER, HOLLY D. (Navajo)
(Indian school principal)
Affiliation: Seba Dalkai Boarding School, Star Route #1, Winslow, AZ 86047 (602) 657-3208.

*BUTLER, LUVENIA H.
(executive director)
Affiliation: Tennessee Commission on Indian Affairs, 401 Church St., L&C Towers, 10th Floor , Nashville, TN 37243 (615) 532-0745.

*BUTLER, MICHAEL
(nature park manager)
Affiliation: Iroquois Indian Museum, P.O. Box 7, Caverns Rd., Howes Cave, NY 12092 (518) 296-8949.

BUTLER, WILLIAM (Apache)
(Indian school supt.)
Affiliation: Mescalero Elementary School, P.O. Box 230, Mescalero, NM 88340 (505) 671-4431.

*BUTTERFIELD, JANIE
(health center director)
Affiliation: Pit River Indian Health Center , P.O. Box 2720, Burney , CA 96013.

*BUTTERFLY, ANDREW
(editor)
Affiliation: Native Sun," Detroit American Indin Center, 22720 Plymouth Rd., Detroit, MI 48239 (313) 535-2966.

BUZZARD, GEORGE
(IHS associate director)
Affiliation: Office of Administration & Management, Department of Health and Human Services, USPHS-IHS, Rm. 6-25 Parklawn Bldg., 5600 Fishers Lane, Rockville, MD 20857 (301) 443-7493.

BYARS, TONY
(museum supt.)
Affiliation: Alabama-Coushatta Indian Museum, Route 3, Box 640, U.S. Highway 190, Livingston, TX 77351 (713) 563-4391.

BYRNES, JIM (Navajo)
(Indian school principal)
Affiliation: To'hajiilee-He (Canoncito) School, Box 438, Laguna, NM 87026 (505) 831-6426.

C

CACHAGEE, DOREEN
(Indian band chief)
Affiliation: Chapleau Cree, Box 400, Chapleau, Ontario, Canada P0M 1K0 (705) 864-0784.

CADUE, STEVEN (Kickapoo of Kansas)
(school chairperson)
Affiliation: Kickapoo Nation School, P.O. Box 106, Powhattan, KS 66527 (913) 474-3550.

*CADUTO, MICHAEL J.
(storyteller, ecologist, educator & musician)
Resides in Vermont. *Education*: University of Michigan, MS in Natural Resources/Environmental Education. *Professional post*: Sr. Education Fellow with the Atlantic Center for the Environment. *Interests*: Travels extensively presenting environmental and cultural programs for adults and children. *Published works*: Keepers of the Animals: Native American Stories and Wildlife Activities for Children; Keepers of the Earth: Native American Stories and Environmental Activities for Children; Keepers of Life: Discovering Plants Through Native American Stories and Earth Activities for Children; and Keepers of the Night: Native American Stories and Nocturnal Activities for Children. (all with Joseph Bruchac); also audiocassette, All One Earth: Songs for the Generations (all published by Fulcrum Publishing)

CAGEY, HENRY (Lummi)
(tribal chairperson)
Affiliation: Chairperson, Lummi Business Council, 2616 Kwina Rd., Bellingham, WA 98226 (206) 734-8180.

*CALAC, ROBERT (Luiseno)
(tribal chairperson)
Affiliation: Rincon Band of Mission Indians, P.O. Box 68, Valley Center, CA 92082 (619) 749-1051.

CALANDER, LEE A.
(museum registrar)
Affiliation: George Gustav Heye Center, National Museum of the American Indian, Smithsonian Institution, 1 Bowling Green, New York, NY 10004 (212) 283-2420.

CALDWELL, ALAN JAMES (Menominee-White Earth Chippewa) 1948-
(education program director)
Born May 27, 1948, Shawano, Wisc. *Education*: University of Wisconsin, Green Bay, BS (History), 1976; University of Wisconsin, Superior, 1979-83; University of Wisconsin, Madison, 1986-. *Principal occupation*: Education program director. *Address*: Upward Bound, University of Wisconsin, Stevens Point, WI 54481 (715) 346-3337 (office). *Affiliations*: principal/teacher, Lac Courte Oreilles Ojibwe Schools, Hayward, WI, 1976-81; business manager, Menominee Positive Youth Development Corp., Keshena, WI, 1981-84; education consultant, Wisconsin Department of Public Instruction, Madison, WI, 1984-; director-Upward Bound, University of Wisconsin, Stevens Point, WI, 1991-. *Other professional post*: Indian education director, Shawano School District, Shawano, WI. Military: U.S. Army, 1969-71, SP/5. *Community activities*: Wisconsin Humanities Committee, 1983-89; past member and chair, board of directors, Menominee Tribal Enterprises; (Wisconsin) American Indian Language and Culture Education Board, 1984-. *Memberships*: National Indian Education Association (board of directors, 1977-78); Wisconsin Indian Education Association (president, board of directors, 1986-); National Coalition for Sex Equity in Education; National Bilingual Education Association; Wisconsin Bilingual Education Association; Wisconsin Teachers of English to Speakers of Other Languages. *Awards, honors*: 1988 "Wisconsin Indian Educator of the Year Award" from Wisconsin Indian Education Association; "Outstanding Leadership Award" from UW-Green Bay Eth-

nic Heritage Program, 1976. *Interests*: "Responsible for American Indian education programs established under Wisconsin Act 31 - 1989-91 biennial budget..., previous responsibility for national origin desegregation program (1984-89). *Published works*: Articles on American Indian history, culture, education, athletics and youth programs.

CALDWELL, RICHARD T. 1951-
(family practice physician)
Born April 29, 1951, at Dallas, TX. *Education*: Kansas State University, BS, 1973; University of Texas, Medical Branch at Galveston, MD, 1979. *Principal occupation*: Family practice physician. *Affiliation*: Supai Indian Health Center, Supai, AZ (602) 448-2641, 1988-. *Military service*: U.S. Public Health Service Commissioned Corps, 1980-83, 1985- (O-5 Commander; Isolated Hardship Award (3 times); PHS Citation; PHS Achievement Medal). *Community activities*: Member, Havasupai Tribal Action Planning Committee. *Membership*: American Academy of Family Practice; American Board of Family Practice (board certified member). *Awards, honors*: Phoenix Area Indian Health Service, Role Model of the Year, 1986; volunteer award from Havasupai Tribal Headstart Program; multiple other awards from Indian Health Service and community groups. *Interests*: Marathoning: T.A.C. U.S. National Champion, 100 miles: 1984 & 1986; 1979-American road record for 100 miles. *Biographical sources*: Fort Apache Scout, July, 1988; Diversion Magazine, June, 1987; numerous other running-related articles.

CALDWELL-WOOD, NAOMI RACHEL (Ramapough) 1958-
(library science)
Born March 31, 1958, Providence, R.I. *Education*: Clarion State College, BS, 1980; Clarion University of Pennsylvania, MSLS, 1982; graduate studies: Texas A&M University, 1986-87, Providence College, 1990-92, University of Pittsburgh, 1992- (Library Science doctoral candidate). *Principal occupation*: Library science. *Address*: P.O. Box 21, Clarion, PA 16214 (814) 226-8164. *Affiliations*: Microtext Reference Librarian, Sterling C. Evans Library, Texas A&M University, College Station, TX, 1985-87; Library Media Specialist, Nathan Bishop Middle School, Providence, RI, 1987-92; American Indian Library Association (secretary, 1987-90; president, 1990-). *Other professional activities*: Editorial Advisory Board & Reviewer, "MultiCultural Review," Greenwood Publishing, 1991-; Professional Reading Reviewer, "School Library Journal" Cahners/R.R. Bowker, 1991-; Advisory Board, OYATE, Berkeley, CA, 1992-; Advisory Board, *Native American Information Directory*, Gale Research, 1992; Screening Committee, Native American Public Broadcasting Consortium, 1993-. *Community activities*: Consultant, Brown University/Providence Drug-Free Schools Project, 1987-91; Rhode Island Children's Book Award Committee, 1990-92. *Memberships*: Ramapough Mountain Indian Tribe; American Library Association (OLOS: Library Services for American Indian People Subcommittee, member, 1986-88, 1990-92, chair, 1992-; ALA Council Committee on Minority Concerns, member, 1991-93, 1994-; ALA Councilor-at-Large, 1992-); American Indian Library Association (secretary, 1987-90; president, 1990-). *Awards, honors*: U.S. Board on Books for Young People (member, Discovery Award Committee, 1994-); honorary delegate to White House Con-

ference on Library & Information Services, Washington, DC, 1991; participant, Native American & Alaskan Native Pre-Conference to the White House Conference on Library & Information Services, March 1991; participant, National Indian Policy Center, Forum on Native American Libraries & Information Services, George Washington University, Washington, DC, May 1991. *Interests*: Native American educational materials and books for children; multicultural literature; library & information services. Numerous presentations, including: "Multicultural Books for Children: The Native American Perspective," Library Science Colloquium, Clarion University of Pennsylvania, Jan. 1994; "Native Americans & Children's Books: Evaluation & Selection," Carnegie Library of Pittsburgh Children's Services Meeting, Jan. 1993; "How to Evaluate Native American Books," Texas Library Association, March 1993; Native American Materials for Children," Dept. of Education, Clarion University of Pennsylvania, Oct. 1992. among others. *Published works*: Checklist of Bibliographies Appearing in the Bulletin of Bibliography, 1897-1987, with Patrick Wood (Meckler Corp., 1988). *Articles*: "I Is Not for Indian: The Portrayal of Native Americans in Books for Young People," with Lisa Mitten, in MultiCultural Review (April 1992); "Native American Images in Children's Books," in School Library Journal (May 1992); "Boxes of Light," in Hungry Mind Review: Children's Review Supplement (Fall 1992). among others.

CALICA, MARIE (Warm Springs)
(advisor)
Affiliation: Council of Advisors, American Indian Heritage Foundation, 6051 Arlington Blvd., Falls Church, VA 22044-2788 (703) 237-7500.

*CALICA, RAYMOND, Sr. (Warm Springs)
(tribal chairperson)
Affiliation: Confederated Tribes of the Warm Springs Reservation, P.O. Box C, Warm Springs, OR 97761 (503) 553-1 161.

*CALLAHAN, BERNADETTE L.
(IHS-administrative services chief)
Affiliation: Indian Health Service, 5300 Homestead Rd., NE, Albuquerque, NM 871 10 (505) 837-4108.

CALLENDER, LEE A.
(museum registrar)
Affiliation: George Gustav Heye Center, National Museum of the American Indian, Smithsonian Institution, 1 Bowling Green, New York, NY 10004 (212) 283-2420.

CALLION, DONALD W.
(Indian band chief)
Affiliation: Sucker Creek Band, P.O. Box 65, Enlida, Alberta, Canada T0H 3N0 (403) 523-4426.

CALLOWAY, COLIN G. 1953-
(historian, associate professor)
Born February 10, 1953, Yorkshire, England. *Education*: University of Leeds, England, BA, 1974, PhD, 1978. *Principal occupation*: Historian, associate professor. *Address*: 6 Bramley Way, Bellows Falls, VT 05101 (307) 766-5101. *Affiliations*: Assistant director/editor, D'Arcy McNickle Center for the History of the American Indian, The Newberry Library, Chicago, IL, 1985-87; assistant professor of history, 1987-91, associate professor, 1991-, University of

Wyoming, Laramie. *Memberships*: American Society for Ethnohistory; Western History Association. *Awards, honors*: Research fellowships from: National Endowment for the Humanities; Beinecke Library at Yale University; Vermont Historical Society; Newberry Library. Ben Lane Award (twice) from Vermont Historical Society; Extraordinary Merit for Research, University of Wyoming, 1991; 1993 John P. Ellbogen Meritorious Teaching Award, University of Wyoming. *Interests*: British-Indian relations; Abenaki Indians; Indians in Revolutionary era. Testified in Vermont Abenaki fishing rights case. *Published works*: Crown & Calumet: British-Indian Relations, 1783-1815 (University of Oklahoma Press, 1987); Editor, New Directions in American Indian History (University of Oklahoma Press, 1988); The Abenaki (Chelsea House, 1989); The Western Abenakis of Vermont (University of Oklahoma Press, 1990); Editor, Dawnland Encounters: Indians and Europeans in Northern New England (University Press of New England, 1991); Editor (with Alden T. Vaughn), Early American Indian Documents: Treaties and Laws, 1607-1789: The Confederation Period, 1775-1789 (University Publications of America, 1992); Editor, The World Turned Upside Down: Indian Voices from Early America (Bedford Books, 1994); Author, The American Revolution in Indian Country (Cambridge U. Press, 1995).

CAMERON, STEWART
(Indian band chief)
Affiliation: Saulteau Indian band, Box 414, Chetwynd, British Columbia, Canada V0C 1J0 (604) 788-3955.

CAMPBELL, ANGUS PETER
(Indian band chief)
Affiliation: Ahousaht Indian Band, General Delivery, Ahousaht, B.C., Canada (604) 670-9563.

CAMPBELL, BEN NIGHTHORSE
(Northern Cheyenne) 1933-
(jeweler; rancher; U.S. Senator)
Born April 13, 1933, Auburn, Calif. *Education*: San Jose State University, 1953-58. *Principal occupation*: Jeweler; rancher; U.S. Senator, D-CO. *Address*: P.O. Box 639, Ignacio, CO 81137 (303) 563-4623. *Affiliation*: U.S. Senate, Washington, DC. The only Native American member of the U.S. Congress-Senate; member of the Senate Select Committee on Indian Affairs. *Military service*: U.S. Air Force, 1951-53 (Airman 2nd Class; Korean Veteran). *Membership*: American Quarter Horse Association; U.S. Brangus Association; American Paint Horse Association; Indian Arts & Crafts Association; U.S. Olympic Committee (former secretary). *Awards, honors*: U.S. Judo Champion, 1961-63, All-American, 1964; 1963 Gold Medal Winner, Pan American Games; Captain, U.S. Olympic Team, 1964; "have also won over 200 awards in art shows for jewelry design." *Interests*: "Have traveled extensively - 40 countries. Am now a member of delegation to North Atlantic Assembly." *Biographical sources*: Autobiography now being published by Smithsonian Press; have been in Woman's Day, Arizona Highways, Empire Magazine Southwest, and USA Today. *Published work*: Judo Drill Training (Zenbei Publishing, 1967).

CAMPBELL, BERRY, M.D.
(tribal health center administrator)
Affiliation: Kenaitze Indian Tribe Health Center, P.O. Box 988, Kenai, AK 99611 (907) 283-3633.

*CAMPBELL, CURTIS, Sr.
(Mdewakanton Sioux)
(tribal council president)
Affiliation: Prairie Island Community Council, 1158 Island Blvd., Welch, MN 55089 (612) 388-2554.

CAMPBELL, ERNEST
(Indian band chief)
Affiliation: Musqueam Indian Band, 6370 Salish Dr., Vancouver, British Columbia, Canada V6N 2C6 (604) 263-3261.

*CAMPBELL, GILBERT L. *(Kelly Choda)* **1914-**
(book publisher)
Born April 19, 1914, Evanston, Ill. *Education*: Purdue University, B.S., 1937; University of Illinois, B.S., 1938; University of Arizona, 1938-39. *Principal occupation*: Book publisher. *Address*: P.O. Box 5, Palmer Lake, CO 80133 (719) 481-2523. *Affiliation*: Filter Press, Palmer Lake, CO, 1971-. *Community activities*: Los Alamos, NM Town Council; Palmer Lake Town Council. *Memberships*: Indian Arts & Crafts Association, 1971-; Rocky Mountain Book Publishers Association, 1971-. *Interests*: Travel. *Biographical sources*: Who's Who in the West; Who's Who in Commerce & Industry. *Published works*: Thirty Pound Rails (Filter Press, 1956); Wet Plates & Dry Gulches (Filter Press, 1970); West on Wood (Filter Press, 1985).

CAMPBELL, GREGORY R. 1955-
(associate professor)
Born August 1, 1955, Cincinnati, Ohio. *Education*: Chaffey Community College, AA, 1976; U.C.L.A., BA, 1979; University of Oklahoma, Norman, MA, 1982, PhD (Anthropology), 1987 (Dissertation: The Political Economy of Ill-Health: Changing Northern Cheyenne Health Patterns and Economic Underdevelopment, 1876-1930); Institute of American Cultures, University of California, Los Angeles, Postdoctoral Diploma. *Principal occupation*: Associate professor of anthropology. *Address*: Dept. of Anthropology, University of Montana, Missoula, MT 59812 (406) 243-2478; 251-5310. *Affiliations*: Graduate & teaching assistantships, instructor & assistant professor, University of Oklahoma, Dept. of Anthropology, 1979-87; acting assistant professor, Dept. of Anthropology & American Indian Studies, UCLA, 1988; associate professor, Dept. of Anthropology, University of Montana, Missoula, MT, 1988-. *Other professional posts*: Research associate, Southern Cheyenne Ethnohistory Project, Dept of Anthropology, University of Oklahoma, 1979-82; ethnological curator, Oklahoma Historical Society, State Museum, 1982-85; Curatorial consultant, Desert Caballeros Museum, Wickenburg, AZ, 1986-87; Symposium chair & organizer, Native American Ethnology, Anthropology Program Section Coordinator, 1989 Western Social Science Association, Albuquerque, NM, 1988-89; (current) Curator of ethnology, Anthropological Collections, Dept. of Anthropology, University of Montana; research affiliate, Center for Population Research, University of Montana. *Community activities*: University of Montana (General student advisor, 1988-; member, Native American Studies Curriculum Committee, 1989-). *Memberships*: American Society for Ethnohistory, 1978-; Society for Medical Anthropology, 1981-; Plains Anthropological Association, 1982-; Council for Museum Anthropology, 1986-; Cultural Survival, 1987-; Sigma Xi, 1989-90.

Awards, honors: Antiquarian Bookseller's Association of America Award, UCLA, 1979; Counseling Award, Academic Achievement Program, UCLA, 1979; scholarship, Buffalo Bill Historical Center, Cody, WY, 1981; National Endowment for the Arts Grant, 1984-85; Oklahoma Foundation for the Humanities Grant, 1985; Dr. Robert E. Bell Fund Award, Dept. of Anthropology, University of Oklahoma, 1985; Graduate Student Association Research Grant, University of Oklahoma, 1985 & 1987; University of Oklahoma Associates' Fund, Dissertation Research Grant, 1986; Postdoctoral Scholar, Institute of American Cultures, Native American Studies Center, U.C.L.A., 1987-88; College of Arts and Sciences Grant, University of Montana, 1988; University Research Grant Program, University of Montana, 1989. *Research Interests*: Native North America; ethnicity, Oceania, ethnohistory, demographic anthropology, social epidemiology, social organization, political economy, museology. *Published works*: Plains Pictographic Art: An Evolving Tradition; *Articles*: "Cheyenne" in The Encyclopedia of World Cultures (Human Relations Area Files, New Haven, CT, 1991); Issues in Contemporary American Indian Health Care (special issue, American Indian Culture & Research Journal, 1990); "Health Patterns & Economic Underdevelopment on the Northern Cheyenne Reservation, 1910-1920," in Political Economy of the American Indians (University of Oklahoma Press, pp. 61-86); & "Prevalence of Diagnosed Diabetes & Selected Related Conditions on Six Reservations in Montana & Wyoming," in Diabetes Care (special issue, American Indian Diabetesbook reviews, The Cheyenne Nation: A Social and Demographic History (American Indian Culture and Research Journal, 1989); and "The Ghost Dance Religion of the Sioux Outbreak of 1890, "North Dakota History." numerous other articles, book reviews, and conference papers.

CAMPBELL, Sr. JANET
(school principal)
Affiliation: Indian Island School, P.O. Box 566, 1 River Rd., Old Town, ME 04468 (207) 827-4285.

CAMPBELL, LEON (Iowa of Kansas)
(tribal council chairperson)
Affiliation: Iowa of Kansas Executive Committee, Route 1, Box 58A, White Cloud, KS 66094 (913) 595-3258.

CAMPBELL, PETER
(Indian band chief)
Affiliation: North Spirit Lake Indian Band, Box 70, North Spirit Lake, Ontario, Canada P0V 2G0.

CAMPBELL, WILFRED
(Indian band chief)
Affiliation: Boothroyd Indian Band, Box 295, Boston Bar, British Columbia, Canada V0K 1C0 (604) 867-9211.

*CAMPER, BOB, M.D.
(clinical director)
Affiliation: Fort Peck PHS Indian Health Center, Poplar, MT 59255 (406) 768-3491.

CAMPO, GEORGE
(Indian band chief)
Affiliation: Lakahahmen Indian Band, 41290 Lougheed Hwy., Deroche, British Columbia, Canada V0M 1G0 (604) 826-7976.

CANNON, GORDON
(BIA agency supet.)
Affiliation: Warm Springs Agency, Bureau of Indian Affairs, P.O. Box 1239, Warm Springs, OR 97761 (503) 553-2411.

*CAPOEMAN-BALLER, PEARL (Quinault)
(tribal president)
Affiliation: Quinault Business Committee (council member & vice-chairperson, 1975-94; president, 1994-), P.O. Box 189, Taholah, WA 98587 (206) 276-8211.

CAPPALLUZZO, EMMA 1933-
(professor)
Born July 10, 1933, Boston, Mass. *Education*: Boston University, BA, 1955; University of Arizona, MEd, 1960, EdD, 1965. *Principal occupation*: Professor. *Home address*: West Rd., Wendell, MA 01379 (508) 544-3583. *Affiliation*: University of Massachusetts, Amherst (Director, Multicultural Education, 1965-; joint professor , Dept. of Anthropology, 1975-). *Other professional posts*: Instructor, University of Arizona; teacher, public schools, Jackson, MI & Tucson, AZ; consultant to Kahnawake Education Dept. (13 years); director of Native American Elementary Placements for U Mass for 25 years in the Northern Pueblos of NM. *Community activities*: Town moderator , Historical Society. *Memberships*: National Education Association; Cultural Survival; American Anthropological Association; Council on Education. *Interests*: "Work with many Native communities; to look at and try to plan educational programs for Native schools; travel extensively - Europe & North America."

CAPTAIN, GEORGE J. (BUCK)
(Eastern Shawnee) 1922-
(Intelligence, U.S. Gov't.; tribal chief)
Born August 14, 1922, Miami, Okla. *Education*: University of Maryland, 1954-56. *Principal occupation*: Intelligence, U.S. Government. *Home address*: Route 4, Box 924, Miami, OK 74354 (918) 542-1408; 666-2435 (work). *Affiliations*: Chief of Eastern Shawnee Tribe of Oklahoma, 1978-. *Other professional posts*: Served as instructor at intelligence training center . *Military service*: Airborne (served as top turret gunner , flew 26 missions; 2 air medals). *Community activities*: Chairman, Intertribal Council, Miami, OK (ten years); chairman, Ottawa County Food Coalition (eight years). *Membership*: Oklahoma Indian Health Bopard (past president). *Awards, honors*: Numerous government awards; will instruct at NEO College starting in 1990 (Shawnee history). *Interests*: "Travel in Europe, Asia, Central America; have taught intelligence principals to many Foreign Nationals all over the Free World."

CARDINAL, DONALD
(Indian band chief)
Affiliation: Onion Lake Indian Band, Box 900, Lloydminster, Saskatchewan, Canada S9V 2Y0 (306) 344-2107.

CARDINAL, JOHN
(Indian band chief)
Affiliation: Woodland and Cree Band #474, Cadotte Lake, Alberta T0H 0N0 (403) 629-3803.

CARLISLE, ED
(BIA agency supt.)
Affiliation: Chinle Agency, Bureau of Indian Affairs, P.O. Box 7H, Chinle, AZ 86503 (602) 674-5100.

CARLSGAARD, SANDRA
(special education coordinator)
Affiliation: Aberdeen Area Instructional Coordinator, Bureau of Indian Affairs, 115 4th Ave., SE, Federal Bldg., Aberdeen, SD 57401 (605) 226-7431.

*CARLSON, DAWN
(museum chairperson)
Affiliation: Marin Miwok Museum, P.O. Box 864, Novato, CA 94947 (415) 897-4064.

*CARLSON, DENISE E.
(head of reference)
Affiliation: Minnesota Historical Society Research Center , 345 Kellogg Blvd. W ., St. Paul, MN 55102 (612) 296-2143.

CARLSON, RICHARD
(chairperson)
Affiliation: Eagle Wing Press, Inc., P.O. Box 579MO, Naugatuck, CT 06770 (203) 729-0035..

CARLSON, SUSAN, M.D.
(clinical director)
Affiliation: SEARHC, Mt. Edgecumbe Hospital, 222 Tongass Dr., Sitka, AK 99801 (907) 966-2411.

CARNEAU, FRED
(director-Indian college)
Affiliation: Maskwachees Cultural College, Box 360, Hobbema, Alberta, Canada T0C 1N0 (403) 585-3925.

CARNEY, R.
(editor)
Affiliation: Canadian Journal of Native Education, University of Alberta, Faculty of Eduction, 5-109 Education N., Edmonton, Alberta, Canada T6G 2G5.

*CAROLIN, ROBERT
(BIA agency supt.)
Affiliation: Hopi Agency, Bureau of Indian Affairs, P.O. Box 158, Keams Canyon, AZ 86034 (602) 738-2228.

CARPENTER, CECILIA SVINTH
(Nisqually) 1924-
(retired teacher; author , Indian historian/consultant)
Born September 2, 1924, Tacoma, Wash. *Education*: Pacific Lutheran University , BA 1966, MA, 1971; University of Puget Sound, 1993 Honorary Doctorate of Humane Letters. *Principal occupation*: Retired teacher; author , Indian historian/consultant. *Home address*: 9609 S. Sheridan, P.O. Box 44306, Tacoma, WA 98444 (206) 537-7877. *Affiliation*: Teacher, Tacoma Public School District, 1966-1982 (retired). *Other professional post*: Owns & operates Tahoma Research Service. *Awards, honors*: Award for "Historical Documentation" by Native American Student Association, Pierce College, 1986; "Peace and Friendship Award, 1988, by Washington State Capital Museum Association, Olympia, WA for preservation of Native American history; 1990 "Governor's Ethnic Heritage Award" from state of WA; 1993 "Honorary Doctorate of Humane Letters" from University of Puget Sound. *Interests*: "Author, Indian historical researcher & consultant; Indian genealogical research" *Published works*: They Walked Before, Indians of Washington State (Washington State Historical Society , 1977; reprint, Tahoma Research, 1989); How to Research American

Indian Blood Lines (Heritage Quest, 1984); Leschi, Last Chief of the Nisquallies (Heritage Quest, 1986); Fort Nisqually , A Documented History of Indian and British Interaction (Tahoma Research, 1986); Where the Waters Begin, The Traditional Nisqually Indian History of Mount Ranier (Mount Ranier National Park Service, 1994); numerous articles & research papers; consultant papers, and historical presentations.

CARPENTER, GORDON
(Indian band chief)
Affiliation: New Slate Falls Indian Band, Slate Falls via Sioux Lookout, Ontario, Canada P0V 2P0.

*CARROLL, MARGUERITE
(editor)
Affiliation: Americn Indian Report, The Falmouth Institute, Inc., 3918 Prosperity Ave., Suite 302, Fairfax, VA 22031 (703) 641-9100.

*CARROLL, THOMAS B.
(monument supt.)
Affiliation: Salinas National Monument, Rte. 1, Box 496, Mountainair , NM 87036 (505) 847-2585.

CARTER, GALE
(site attendant)
Affiliation: Choctaw Chief's House, P.O. Box 165, Swink, OK 74761 (405) 873-2492.

CARTER, TRUMAN (Sac & Fox) 1949-
(attorney)
Born January 16, 1949, Pawnee, Okla. *Education*: U.S. Indian Police Academy, 1979; University of Oklahoma, BA, 1980, College of Law , JD, 1987. *Principal occupation*: Attorney. *Affiliation & Address*: Attorney at Law , P.O. Box 493, Shawnee, OK 74802 (405) 273-6715 Fax 275-4977 (work). *Current activities*: Attorney General, Kickapoo Tribe in eastern Oklahoma, 1988-, the Cheyenne-Arapaho Tribes in western Oklahoma, 1988-, Iowa Tribe of Oklahoma, 1992-, and Otoe-Missouria Tribe of Oklahoma, 1993-; Chairperson, Otoe-Missouria Tax Commission, 1990-; special prosecutor , Iowa Tribe of Oklahoma, 1991-; Coordinator , Liaison of Sac & Fox law and order and judicial system, 1984-; Treasurer & Assistant Attorney General (Chief, Criminal Division), Sac & Fox Nation, 1987-; justice, Supreme Court, Kickapoo Tribe of Kansas, 1991-, Citizen Band Potawatomi of Oklahoma, 1992-; Prosecutor , BIA Court of Indian Offenses, Chickasaw Agency & Wewoka Agency, 1993-. Accomplishments: Appeared before the U.S. Supreme Court as designated co-counsel in 1993 landmark case, Oklahoma Tax Commission v. Sac & Fox Nation, where Court ruled 9-0 decision, state cannot impose motor vehicle & income taxes on tribal members; An elected tribal official, served as chief executive financial officer; developed excellent employee compensation & benefit package; provide training, assist Indian tribal governments in development, preparation, administration, and enforcement of tribal laws, policies, and procedures, 1982 to present; organizer and administrator of comprehensive tribal taxation system; negotiated several tribal cooperative agreements with cities, counties, and state agencies dealing with business development, law enforcement, fire protection services, and joint road improvement programs; organized and developed tribal court systems, police operations and fire department for the Sac & Fox Tribe in 1984. *Memberships*:

Native American Bar Association; Oklahoma Indian Bar Association (treasurer-Indian Law Section; legislation committee); Oklahoma Bar Association; Potawatomie County (OK) Bar Association; National District Attorneys Association; Leadership Oklahoma, Inc.

CARVER, LAURA
(health center director)
Affiliation : Santa Clara PHS Indian Health Center, P.O. Box 1323, Espanola, NM 87532 (505) 653-9421.

CARVEY, ELIZABETH A.
(museum director)
Affiliation : Hauberg Indian Museum, Black Hawk State Park, Rock Island, IL 61201 (309) 788-9536.

CASAVANTE, CARMEN GILL
(museum director)
Affiliation : Amerindian Museum, 406 Amisk, Pointe-Bleue, Quebec, Canada G0W 2H0.

*CASEY, TOM
(radio station manager)
Affiliation : KILI - 90.1 FM, Oglala Lakota Sioux, P.O. Box 150, Porcupine, SD 57772 (605) 867-5002.

CASH, MARCELLA
(research center director)
Affiliation : Lakota Archives & Historical Research Center, Sinte Gleska College, Box 490, Rosebud, SD 57570 (605) 747-2263.

CASSEN, MARGARET ANNE 1946-
(librarian, teacher)
Born August 27, 1946, Carbondale, Ill. *Education* : University of Oklahoma, BS, 1989. *Principal occupation* : Librarian, teacher . *Address* : P.O. Box 168, Fort Wingate, NM 87316 (505) 488-5989. *Affiliation* : Fort Wingate Elementary School, Fort Wingate, NM, 1989-. *Other professional post* : Teach New Mexico history . *Memberships* : American Library Assn.; New Mexico Library Assn.. *Interests* : American history, special education, and gifted program; expanding the Native American section of our library .

CASTILLO, EDWARD D. (Cahuilla-Luiseno) 1947-
(professor of Native American studies)
Born August 25, 1947, San Jacinto, Riverside Co., Calif. *Education* : University of California, Riverside, BA, 1969; University of California, Berkeley, MA, 1976, PhD (Anthropology), 1977. *Principal occupation* : Professor of Native American Studies, Dept. Chair . *Home address* : 4949 Snyder Lane #19, Rohnert Park, CA 94931 (707) 664-2458 (work). *Affiliations* : Lecturer, Native American Studies Dept., University of California at Berkeley, 1970-71, 1973-77; Associate professor, director, Native American Studies, University of California, Santa Cruz, 1977-82; project director , Title IV, Laytonville Unified School District, 1985-88; Director , Native American Studies, Dept. Chair , Sonoma State University, Rohnert Park, CA, 1989-; curriculum resource specialist, Parents for the Improvement of Community and Education Services, Ukiah, CA. *Other professional posts* : President-Advisory Council, California Indian Education Association , California State Dept. of Education; Chairperson of Native American Advisory Committee to the California State University Chancellor Office. *Memberships* : Califor-

nia Historical Society; American Indian Historical Society. *Awards, honors* : National Endowment for the Humanities, History Teacher Training Grant; Meritorious Performance, Professional Promise Award for Research, 1989, California State University system. *Interests* : Reconstruction of California, Far W estern, Borderlands; history of Indian tribes, and Hispanic Colonial institutions, i.e. Missions, Presidios, Civilian Hispanic Pueblos. *Published works* : "History of the Impact of Euro-American Exploration and Settlement on the Indians of California (107 pages) and "Recent Secular Movements Among California Indians, 1900-1973 (15 pages). Both chapters appear in V olume 8 of the Smithsonian Institute's Handbook of North American Indians: California; co-author: The California Missions (American Indian History Society Press, 1987); A Bibliography of California Indian History , edited by Robert Heizer (Ballena Press, 1978); Native American Perspectives on the Hispanic Colonization of Alta California (Garland Publishing, 1990); numerous articles & book reviews.

CASTILLO, JOHN (Fort Sill Apache) 1956-
(executive director)
Born February 14, 1956. *Education* : California State University, Fullerton, BA, 1979; UCLA, MSW, 1981. *Principal occupation* : Executive director. *Address & Affiliation* : Southern California Indian Center, P.O. Box 2550, Garden Grove, CA 92642 (714) 530-0225. *Other professional post* : California & National Child & Adolescent Service System Program Advisory Committee for Culturally Competent Service for Children & Families. *Community activities* : Orange County Community Developmental Council; Orange County ESP & FEMA Board-Orange Coast College EDP Board; Huntington Beach Adult Advisory Board. *Memberships* : UCLA Chancellors Community Advisory Commission; Los Angeles County American Indian Commission (chairperson, 1987-89); Indian Child W elfare Task Force (chairperson, 1986-89); Los Angeles County American Indian Mental Health Task Force, 1986-87. *Awards, honors* : 1979 Federal Mediation Council Labor/Management Certificate; 1985 County of Los Angeles Affirmative Action Volunteer of the Year; 1985-88 Kellogg National Fellowship Fellow Group 6; 1991 Freedoms Foundation at V alley Forge George W ashington Honor Medal. Interests: "International work with indigenous peoples - helping indigenous peoples develop their human and economic resources through the many international programs available." Published works: Articles - "Spiritual Foundations of Indian Success," in American Indian Culture and Research Journal (1982, Vol. 6 No. 3); "JPT A: American Indian Success Through Group Consensus and Individual Attention," in Occupational Education Forum (1986, V ol. 15 No. 2); "American Indians: An Overview of Their Socio Economic and Education Status," in The Journal for V ocational Needs Educations (1988, V ol. 10 No. 3).

*CASTRO, VERNON (Yokut)
(rancheria co-chairperson)
Affiliation : Table Mountain Rancheria, P .O. Box 243, Friant, CA 93626 (209) 822-2587.

CATA, JUANITA O. (San Juan Pueblo)
(BIA supt for education)
Affiliation : Northern Pueblos Agency, BIA, Box 4269, Fairview Station, Espanola, NM 87533 (505) 753-1465.

*CATA, SIMON (San Juan Pueblo)
(pueblo governor)
Affiliation : San Juan Pueblo Council, P .O. Box 1099, San Juan Pueblo, NM 87566 (505) 852-4400.

*CATE, RICK
(organization president)
Affiliation : Kiva Club, University of New mexico, Mesa Vista Hall #1 117-A, Albuquerque, NM 87131 (505) 277-8259.

CATTLEMAN, LEO
(Indian band chief)
Affiliation : Montana Indian Band, Box 70, Hobbema, AB, Can. T0C 1N0 (403) 585-3744.

CAVENDER, REV. GARY C. *(Shun ghida)* *(Little Red Fox)* (Dakota) 1939-
(writer, lecturer, teacher)
Born December 23, 1939, Granite Falls, Minn. (Upper Res. Sioux). *Education* : Minneapolis Community College, 1977-79; University of Minnesota, 1980-81; United Theological Seminary , MDiv., 1984. *Principal occupation* : Writer, lecturer, teacher. *Home address* : 5261 Bounty St., Prior Lake, MN 55372 (612) 447-6679. *Affiliations* : Chaplain, V.F.W., Prior Lake, MN 1991-; executive secretary, National Committee on Indian Work, New York, NY, 1990-. *Other professional posts* : Lobbyist, Project Impact, W ashington, DC; chairperson, Minnesota Committee Indian W ork; chairperson, St. Paul Area Council of Churches, Dept. of Indian W ork; instructor, Dakota History, University of Minnesota. *Military service* : U.S. Navy, 1958-62; U.S. Air Force, 1963-67 (U.S. Expedition Forces; Medal Viet-Nam, China Quemoy , Matsue Islands, Bronz Star). *Community activities* : Picture People volunteer; art appreciation teacher , Prior Lake elementary school; volunteer , Crisis Counselor, Prior Lake Reservation. *Memberships* : V.F.W.; Disabled American Veteran. *Interests* : Reading historical books, with focus on American Indian history and prehistory; studies of comparative religions; writing, teaching; eating fried bread & corn soup. *Published works* : Black Hills: Who Are the Modern Indian Youth (Native American Theological Association, June 1986; editor, Where Rivers Flow & Waters Meet by Paul Durand (Merritt Parkway , 1994). *Article* : Episcopal Magazine, Sounding Diocese of Minnesota, "Christianity & the Great Mysterious Dakota Spirituality."

CESAR, NILES C.
(BIA area director)
Affiliation : Juneau Area Office, Bureau of Indian Affairs, P.O. Box 25520, Juneau, AK 99802 (907) 586-7177.

*CESSPOOCH, LARRY (Ute)
(Native American film producer)
Affiliation : Ute Indian Tribe, Audio-Visual, P.O. Box 190, Fort Duchesne, UT 84026 (801) 722-5141 Ext. 243.

CHALIAK, CHUCK (Eskimo)
(village president)
Affiliation : Native V illage of Nunapitchuk, Box 130, Nunapitchuk, AK 99641 (907) 527-5705.

CHALIFOUX, CHARLES HENRY
(Indian band chief)
Affiliation : Swan River Indian Band, P .O. Box 270, Kinuso, Alberta, Canada T0G 1K0 (403) 775-3536.

*CHAMPAGNE, DUANE W.
(Turtle Mountain Chippewa) 1951-
(professor)
Born May 18, 1951, Belcourt, N.D. *Education*: North Dakota State University, BA, 1973, MA, 1975; Harvard University, PhD, 1982. *Principal occupation*: Professor. *Home address*: 28012 N. Ridgecove Court, Rancho Palos Verdes, CA 90274 (310) 825-7315 (work). *Affiliations*: Dept. of Sociology, University of California, Los Angeles, CA (assistant professor, 1984-91; associate professor, 1991-). *Other professional posts*: Director, UCLA - American Indian Studies Center; editor, "American Indian Culture and Research Journal;" research consultant for the Smithsonian Institution-Public Radio and the Native American Public Broadcasting Consortium (NAPBC). Developing public radio documentaries for the Quincentenary of Columbus' landing in the New World, 19889-92; Advisory Board Member for the Harvard Project on American Indian Economic Development, Energy & Environmental Policy Center, Harvard University, John F. Kennedy School of Government, 1988-90; and numerous other consulting positions. *Community activities*: The Los Angeles City/County American Indian Commission (former chair, board member). *Memberships*: American Sociological Association; International Sociological Association; Ethnohistory Association, American Indian Professorate Association. *Awards, honors*: American Indian Scholarship, 1973-75; American Sociological Association Minority Fellowship, 1975-78; Rockefeller Postdoctoral Fellowship, 1982-83; University of California Pre-tenure Award, 1986; National Science Foundation (Fellow, 1985-88; Creativity Extension Grant, 1988-90; Ford Foundation Postdoctoral Fellowship, 1988-89. *Published works*: American Indian Societies: Strategies & Conditions of Political & Cultural Survival, revised 2nd edition (Cultural Survival, 1989); Social Order & Political Change: Constitutional Governments Among the Cherokee, the Choctaw, the Chickasaw, and the Creek (Stanford University Press, 1992); The Native North American Almanac (Gale Research, 1994); Native America: Portrait of the People (Visible Ink Press, 1994); The Chronology of Native North American History (Gale Research, 1994); editor of "American Indian Culture & Research Journal" (UCLA American Indian Studies Center, Vols. 10-18, 1986-); numerous articles in such journals as: The American Indian Quarterly, The Journal of Cherokee Studies; and chapters in published books.

CHANDLER, ROBERT S.
(museum supt.)
Affiliation: Tusayan Ruin & Museum, Grand Canyon National Park, P.O. Box 129, Grand Canyon, AZ 86023 (602) 638-7701.

*CHANNING, WILL
(organization president)
Affiliation: Wings of America, 53 Old Santa Fe Trail, Santa Fe, NM 87501 (505) 982-6761.

*CHAPIN, DOROTHY
(director-Indian health program)
Affiliation: Feather River Indian Health Program, 2167 Montgomery St., Oroville, CA 95965 (916) 534-6135.

CHAPMAN, ANA DELORES
(Indian band chief)
Affiliation: Skawahlook Indian Band, Box 1668, Hope, British Columbia, Canada V0X 1L0 (604) 796-9877.

CHAPMAN, LAWRENCE
(Indian band chief)
Affiliation: Lac des Milles Lacs Indian Band, P.O. Box 1365, Station "F", Thunder Bay, Ontario, Canada P7C 4Y1.

CHAPMAN, STEVE (White Earth Chippewa) 1951-
(program director)
Born July 3, 1951, Minneapolis, Minn. *Education*: Minneapolis Community College, 1969-70; Augsburg College, BA, 1973. *Princpal occupation*: Program director. *Home address*: 3625 24th Ave. South, Minneapolis, MN 55406 (612) 722-2080. *Affiliations*: Director, American Indian Studies, Minneapolis Community College, 1977-Special Programs, University of Minneapolis, Minneapolis, MN, 1988-. *Other professional post*: Executive director, American Indian OIC, 1981-82. *Community activities*: Commissioner, Minneapolis Public Housing Authority (vice chair); Minneapolis Community Development Agency (former commssioner); Minnesota Commission on Affordable Housing (former commissioner); American Indian Business Development; Minnesota Indian Women's Resource Center. *Memberships*: Minnesota Indian Education Association; National Indian Education Association. *Awards, honors*: First American Indian graduate of Augsburg College; Outstanding Alumni Award, 1986, Minneapolis Community College; Scholarship Award, MAPE. *Interests*: "Beadwork; American Indian art history; refinidhing furniture; lecturing on American Indian culture, and helping out when asked." *Published work*: Urban American Indian Views on the U.S. Constitution (Hamline Law Journal, 1986).

CHAPUT, REV. CHARLES J. *(Wambli Waste-Good Eagle, Lakota; Pyet-ta-sen, Potawatomi)* **1944-**
(Roman Catholic Bishop)
Born September 26, 1944, Concordia, Kans. *Education*: St. Fidelis College, BA, 1967; Capuchin College, MA; University of San Francisco (MA in theology), 1971. *Principal occupation*: Roman Catholic Bishop. *Address*: P.O. Box 678, 606 Cathedral Dr., Rapid City, SD 57701 (605) 343-3541. *Affiliations*: Roman Catholic Bishop, Rapid City, SD. *Awards, honors*: "Served as master of ceremonies for 1987 National Tekakwitha Conference with Pope John Paul, !!, Phoenix, Arizona. *Interests*: Travel.

*CHARLES, AGNES (Athapascan)
(AK village council president)
Affiliation: Native Village of Napaimute, P.O. Box 96, Aniak, AK 99557

CHARLES, ARCHIE
(Indian band chief)
Affiliation: Seabird Island Indian band, Box 650, Agassiz, British Columbia, Canada V0M 1A0 (604) 796-2177.

*CHARLES, ARNOLD
(school chairperson)
Affiliation: Casa Blanca Day School, P.O. Box 940, Bapchule, AZ 85221 (602) 315-3489.

CHARLES, BERNARD
(Indian band chief)
Affiliation: Semiahmoo Indian Band, RR 7, 16010 Beach Rd., White Rock, BC V4B 5A8 (604) 536-1794.

CHARLES, BILLY (Eskimo)
(AK village president)
Affiliation: Emmonak Village Council, Emmonak, AK 99581 (907) 949-1720.

CHARLES, ERIC
(Indian band chief)
Affiliation: Chippewas (Georgina Island) Indian Band, Box A-3, RR 2, Sutton West, Ontario, Canada L0E 1R0 (705) 437-1337.

*CHARLES, FRANCIS G. (Elwha S'Klallam)
(tribal chairperson)
Affiliation: Elwha S'Klallam Business Council, 2851 Lower Elwha Rd., Port Angeles, WA 98362 (206) 452-8471.

CHARLES, JAMES (Navajo) 1950-
(archaeologist; BIA agency supt.)
Born March 25, 1950, Ganado, Ariz. *Education*: Fort Lewis College, BA, 1974; Northern Arizona University, MA. *Principal occupation*: Archaeologist. *Address*: P.O. Box 345, Fort Totten, ND 58335 (701) 766-4545 (work). *Affiliations*: Archaeologist, B.I.A., Phoenix, AZ, 1981-82; B.I.A., Billings, MT, 1982-91; Supt., B.I.A., Fort Totten, ND, 1992-. *Membership*: North Dakota Archaeological Society. Interests: Archaeology, anthropology, cultural anthropology, Navajo history.

CHARLES, JERRY (Shoshone)
(tribal council chairperson)
Affiliation: Ely Colony Council, 16 Shoshone Cr., Ely, NV 89301 (702) 289-3013.

CHARLES, LARRY (Eskimo)
(AK village president)
Affiliation: Newtok Village Council, P.O. Box WWT, Newtok, AK 99559 (907) 237-2314.

CHARLES, RAMONA
(library director)
Affiliation: Tonawanda Indian Community Library, P.O. Box 326, Akron, NY 14001 (716) 542-5618.

CHARLEY, DENNIS (Athapascan)
(AK village council president)
Affiliation: President, Tanana IRA Native Council, Box 77093, Tanana, AK 99777 (907) 366-7160.

CHARLEYBOY, IRVINE
(Indian band chief)
Affiliation: Alexis Creek, Box 69, Chilanko Forks, British Columbia, Can. V0L 1H0 (604) 481-3335.

CHARLIE, JOHN
(Indian band chief)
Affiliation: Burns Lake Indian Band, P.O. Box 9000, Burns Lake, British Columbia, Canada V0J 1E0 (604) 692-3849.

*CHARLIE, LYNETTE C. (Navajo) 1966-
(director of recruiting)
Born October 28, 1966, Tuba City, Ariz. *Education*: University of New Mexico. *Principal occupation*: Director of recruiting. *Home address*: 5800 Harper Dr., NE #1030, Albuquerque, NM 87109 (505) 262-2351 (work). *Affiliation*: Native

American Scholarship Fund, Albuquerque, NM (administrative assistant, 1980-82; director of recruiting, 1982-). *Memberships*: National Association of Female Executives, 1994-; Coalition for Indian Education (board member, 1991; member, 1991-).

CHARLIE, MARVIN
(Indian band chief)
Affiliation: Cheslatta Indian Band, Box 909, Burns Lake, British Columbia, Canada V0J 1E0 (604) 694-3334.

CHARLIE, ROBERT
(Indian band chief)
Affiliation: Burns Lake Indian Band, Box 9000, Burns Lake, British Columbia, Canada V0J 1E0 (604) 692-7097.

CHARTRAND, ELBERT
(executive director)
Affiliation: Swan River Indian & Metis Friendship Centre, 723 Main St., Box 1448, Swan River, Manitoba, Canada R0L 1Z0 (204) 734-9301.

CHASE, DAVID W.
(museum director)
Affiliation: Wampanoag Indian Program of Plimoth Plantation, P.O. Box 1620, Plymouth, MA 02360 (617) 746-1622.

CHASE, EMMETT, M.D.
(IHS-AIDS coordinator)
Affiliation: Indian Health Service, 5300 Homestead Rd., NE, Albuquerque, NM 871 10 (505) 837-4116.

*CHASE, FRED A. Karuk)
(tribal chairperson)
Affiliation: Quartz Valley Indian Reservation, P.O. Box 737, Etna, CA 96032 (916) 467-3307.

*CHASE, JOANNE
(executive director)
Affiliation: National Congress of American Indians, 900 Pennsylvania Ave., SE, Washington, DC 20003 (202) 546-9404.

CHASE, KEN (Eskimo)
(AK village chief)
Affiliation: Anvik Village, General Delivery, Anvik, AK 99558 (907) 663-6335.

CHASKE, RICHARD
(executive director)
Affiliation: Portage Friendship Centre, 21 Royal South, Box 1118, Portage La Prairie, Manitoba, Canada R1N 3C5 (204) 239-6333.

CHAULIFOUX, CHARLIE
(Indian band chief)
Affiliation: Swan River Indian Band, Box 270, Kinuso, Alberta, Canada (403) 775-3536.

CHAVERS, DEAN (Lumbee) 1941-
(fund raiser; editor)
Born February 4, 1941, Pembroke, N.C. *Education*: University of Richmond, 1960-62; University of California, Berkeley, BA, 1970; Stanford University, MA (Anthropology), 1973, MA (Communications), 1975, PhD (Communications Research), 1976. *Principal occupation*: Fund raiser; editor. *Home address*: 6313 Barnhart St., NE, Albuquerque, NM 87109 (505) 823-2914. *Affiliations*: President, Native American Scholarship Fund, Albuquerque, NM, 1970-

78, 1986-; founding president, Coalition for Indian Education, Albuquerque, NM, 1987- (editor, Newsletter). *Other professional posts*: Assistant professor, California State University, Hayward, 1972-1974; president, Bacone College, Muskogee, OK, 1978-81; president, Dean Chavers & Associates, 1981-85; member, Advisory Panel for Minority Concerns, The College Board, 1980-85; member, Minority Achievement Program, Association of American Colleges, 1980-84; president, MANAGE, Inc., 1985-86; board member, National Indian Education Association, 1983-86. *Military service*: U.S. Air Force, 1963-68 (Navigator, Captain; Distinguished Flying Cross, Air Medal). *Community activities*: Rotary Club, Muskogee & Broken Arrow, OK; Democratic Party of Wagoner County, Oklahoma (former secretary-treasurer). *Memberships*: National Indian Education Association (board member, 1983-86, 1987-90); Native American Scholarship Fund (president); National Congress of American Indians, 1972-; International Communication Association; National Society of Fund Raising Executives; Coalition for Indian Education (founding president). *Awards, honors*: Ford Foundation Graduate Fellowship for doctoral study, 1970-74; National Honor Society; Junior Officer of the Quarter, 1971, U.S. Air Force, Travis Air Force Base. *Interests*: Main interest is Indian education, secondary interest is Indian economic development. Have published five books and technical manuals in these areas, as well as some 30 journal articles. Main occupation is providing technical assistance in fund raising, financial management, computer software development, and training for Indian tribes, contract schools, and Indian health clinics. *Published works*: The Feasibility of an Indian University (Bacone College, 1979); How to Write Winning Proposals (DCA Publications, 1983); Funding Guide for Native Americans (DCA Publications, 1983; 2nd ed., 1985); Grants to Indians (DCA Publications, 1984); The Status of Indian Education (Journal of Thought, 1984); Tribal Economic Development Directory (DCA Publications, 1985); The Indian Dropout (Coalition for Indian Education, 1991).

CHAVIS, ANGELA YELVERTON (Lumbee) 1950-
(dentist)
Born May 11, 1950, Pembroke, N.C. *Education*: Pembroke State University, BS, 1971; University of North Carolina, Chapel Hill, School of Dentistry, DDS, 1980. *Principal occupation*: Dentist. Resides in Pembroke, N.C. *Community activities*: Student Health Action Committee; Voter Registration. *Memberships*: North Carolina Association for Preventive Dentistry, 1976-; American Dental Association. *Awards, honors*: Graduated Cum Laude, Pembroke State University, 1971; scholarship from American Fund for Dental Health, 1976-80. *Interests*: My vocational interest is dentistry. I plan to return to my home town and work to better the dental health of the Indian people in my town and surrounding community. *Biographical source*: Who's Who Among Students in American Universities & Colleges, 1971.

*CHAVIS, AGNES H. (Lumbee)
(consortium director)
Affiliation: North Carolina Consortium on Indian Education, P.O. Box 666, Pembroke, NC 28372 (919) 422-3467.

CHEE, MARVIN
(BIA agency chairperson)
Affiliation: Chinle Agency, BIA, P.O. Box 6003, Chinle, AZ 86503 (602) 674-5201 ext. 201; Chinle Boarding School, P.O. Box 70, Many Farms, AZ 86538 (602) 781-6221.

CHELSEA, WILLIAM
(Indian band chief)
Affiliation: Alkali Indian Band, Box 4479, Williams Lake, British Columbia, Canada V2G 2V5 (604) 440-5611.

*CHENOWETH, BOB
(museum curator)
Affiliation: Big Hole National Battlefield, P.O. Box 237, Wisdom, MT 59761 (406) 689-3155.

CHERINO, FRANCES
(school chairperson)
Affiliation: Isleta Elementary School, P.O. Box 550 Isleta, NM 87022 (505) 869-2321.

*CHEROMIAH, NICHOLAS (Laguna Pueblo)
(school principal)
Affiliation: Laguna Middle School, P.O. Box 268, Laguna, NM 87026 (505) 552-9091.

CHESTNUT, PETER
(attorney)
Address: 121 Tijeras Ave., NE #2001, Albuquerque, NM 87102 (505) 842-5864. *Membership*: New Mexico Bar Association (chair, Indian Law Section).

CHIAGO, ROBERT KEAMS (Navajo-Pima) 1942-
(tribal planner)
Born June 22, 1942, Los Angeles, Calif. *Education*: Arizona State University, BA, 1965; Northern Illinois University, Dekalb, MS, 1970; University of Utah, 1974-76 (61 hours towards PhD). *Principal occupation*: Tribal planner. *Address*: Salt River Pima-Maricopa Indian Community Council, Route 1, Box 216, Scottsdale, AZ 85256 (602) 941-7277 Fax 949-2909. *Affiliations*: Associate director, American Indian Culture Center, UCLA, 1970; director, Ramah Navajo School Board, Inc., Ramah, N.M., 1970-71; director, Navajo Division of Education, Navajo Nation, Window Rock, AZ, 1971-73; consultant, Mesa Consultants, Albuquerque, NM, 1973; visiting assistant professor of humanities, University of Utah, Salt Lake City, 1976-79; director, Native American Studies, University of Utah, 1973-81; director of Indian Teacher/Counselor Education Programs, University of Utah, 1980-84; president, Western Indian Technologies, Salt Lake City, Utah, 1984-92; executive director, National Advisory Council on Indian Education (NACIE), Washington, DC, 1992-94; Salt River Pima-Maricopa Indian Tribe, Scottsdale, AZ, 1994-. *Other professional posts*: Editor and founder, Utah Indian Journal, which was a statewide Indian newspaper in 1976 & 1977; founder and coordinator, Western Indian Education Conference; consulting; proposal writing and evaluation. *Military service*: U.S. Marine Corps, 1965-68 (Captain, infantry officer; Presidential Unit Citation, Navy Unit Citation, National Defense Service Medal, Vietnam Service Medal and Campaign Medal). *Community activities*: Presidential appointee, National Advisory Council on Indian Education; gubernatorial appointee to the Utah State Board of Indian Affairs; National Congress of American Indians (resolutions committee chairman, 1976-80);

advisory committee for the creation of the Native American Rights Fund, 1971-72; member, State of Utah ESEA Title IV Advisory Council, 1977-79; Community Services Council of Utah (board member, 1974-75; director, Minority Economic Development Council. *Memberships*: National Congress of American Indians; Western Indian Education Conference (coordinator, 1983, '84, '86); National Advisory Council on Indian Education, 1983-86. *Interests*: Major areas of interest include education, economic development, and employment.

CHIAO, CHIEN 1935-
(professor of anthropology)
Born February 6, 1935, China. *Education*: National Taiwan University, BA, 1958, MA, 1961; Cornell University, PhD, 1969. *Principal occupation*: Professor of anthropology. *Home address*: Flat 10A, Residence No. 14, The Chinese University of Hong Kong, Shatin, N.T., Hong Kong 695-2645 (office); 607-7301 (home). *Affiliations*: Assistant, associate professor, Indiana University, 1966-1976; senior lecturer, professor and chair, Dept. of Anthropology, The Chinese University of Hong Kong, 1976-. *Other professional posts*: Adjunct Research Fellow, Institute of Ethnology, Academia Sinica, 1978-; honorary professor, Honan Institute of Museology, 1985-; adjunct (honorary) professor, Dept. of Anthropology, Xiamen University, 1987- *Memberships*: Hong Kong Anthropological Society (founder & founding chairman, 1978-81); American Anthropological Association (Fellow); Royal Asiatic Society - Hong Kong Branch; Hong Kong Anthropological Society (founding chairman, 1978-81, and member); International Association for Yao Studies (founding chairman, 1986-88, and council member. *Awards, honors*: Honorary professor, Shanxi University, 1988, Central Institute of Minority Nationalities, 1990- *Interests*: Cultural anthropology; fieldwork among the Navajo in the Southwest, U.S.A., the Puyuma in Taiwan, and the Yao in southern China. *Published works*: Continuation of Tradition in Navajo Society (Institute of Ethnology, Academia Sinica, 1971); among other books on Chinese ethnic culture.

CHICAGO, KEVIN
(Indian band chief)
Affiliation: Lac Des Milles Lacs Indian Band, 136 Main St. South, Kenora, Ontario, Canada P2N 1S9 (807) 468-5551.

CHIEF, LEROY W.
(Indian school principal)
Affiliation: Wahpeton Indian School, Bureau of Indian Affairs, 832 N. 8th St., Wahpeton, ND 58075 (701) 642-3796.

CHIEF WISE OWL (Tuscarora) 1939-
(medicine man)
Born February 16, 1939, Robeson County, N.C. *Education*: Pembroke State University, 1968. *Principal occupation*: Medicine man, Tuscarora Indian Tribe, Drowning Creek Reservation, 1965-. *Home address*: Route 2, Box 108, Maxton, NC 28364 (919) 844-3827. *Other professional posts*: Businessman; make herbs and powerful medicine bags using herbs, and make herbal liniment. *Community activities*: Built tribal community center. *Membership*: National Congress of American Indians; Sherif fs Association of North Carolina. *Biographical source*: Known worldwide as medicine man of Drowning Creek Reservation.

CHILTON, JUNE
(director-Indian council)
Affiliation: Indian Action Council of Northwestern California, P.O. Box 1287, 2725 Myrtle Ave., Eureka, CA 95502 (707) 443-8401.

CHINO, CYRUS J.
(Indian school principal)
Affiliation: Sky City Community School, P.O. Box 40, San Fidel, NM 87049 (505) 552-6671.

CHINO, WENDELL (Mescalero Apache)
(tribal council chairperson)
Affiliation: Mescalero Apache Tribal Council, P.O. Box 176, Mescalero, NM 87340 (505) 671-4495.

CHIPPS, PATRICIA ANN
(Indian band chief)
Affiliation: Beecher Bay Indian Band, 3843 East Sooke Rd., Box 2, R.R. #1, Sooke, British Columbia, Canada V0S 1A0 (604) 474-6782.

CHISHOLM, ANITA
(administration)
Affiliation: Director, American Indian Institute, 555 Constitution Ave., Norman, OK 73037 (405) 325-4127.

CHONKOLAY, HARRY
(Indian band chief)
Affiliation: Dene Tha'Tribe Band, Box 120, Chateh, Alberta, Canada T0H 0S0 (403) 321-3842.

CHRISJOHN, ANDREA
(executive director-organization)
Affiliation: Chiefs of Ontario, 22 College St., 2nd Floor, Toronto, Ontario, Canada M5G 1K2 (416) 972-0212.

CHRISJOHN, RICHARD (Oneida-Iroquois)
(artist; tribal leader)
Address: RD 2, Box 315, Red Hook, NY 13421. *Affiliation*: Oneida Nation of New York, Oneida, NY

*CHRISTIAN, RANDY LAVAGHN (Shield Wolf) (Southeastern Cherokee) 1959-
(emergency room RN)
Born April 12, 1959, Lakeland, Ga. *Education*: Georgia Military College (Milledgeville, GA), AAS-Emergency Medical Technology; Abraham Baldwin Agricultural College (Tifton, GA), AAS Nursing. *Principal occupation*: Emergency room RN. *Home address*: 3895 Shelton Rd., Lake Park, GA 31636 (912) 242-3504. *Community activities*: Board of Trustees, Valwood School, 1992-94; Southeastern Cherokee Confederacy, Inc., Ochlocknee, GA (tribal council, chief of finance, 1993; Black Wolf Warrior Society - War Chief's Council-Healer, 1993. *Memberships*: Georgia EMT Association, 1982-84; Emergency Nurses Association, 1989-90. *Awards, honors*: 1977 4-H Georgia Key Award; 1977 Valdosta State College Student Council; 1988 Outstanding Young Men of America; Black Wolf Warrior Society Prayer Blanket & Gord Rattle, Red Feather, 1993.

*CHRISTIANSON, JILL S.
(Indian education liaison)
Affiliation: Maryland Dept. of Education, Liaison to Indian Education, 200 W. Baltimore St., Baltimore, MD 21201 (410) 333-2234.

*CHRISTIANSON, ROBERT (Eskimo)
(AK village council president)
Affiliation: Native Village of Port Heiden, Box 49007, Port Heiden, AK 99624 (907) 284-2218.

CHRISTMAS, PETER
(executive director)
Affiliation: Micmac Association of Cultural Studies, P.O. Box 961, Sydney, Nova Scotia B1P 6J4 (902) 539-8037.

CHRISTOPHER, GABRIEL ROY
(Indian band chief)
Affiliation: Canim Lake Indian Band, Box 1030, 100 Mile House, British Columbia, Canada V0K 2E0 (604) 397-2227.

*CHUCULATE, JERRY
(health center director)
Affiliation: Redbird Smith Health Center, 301 JT Stitkes Aves, Sallisaw, OK 74955 (918) 775-9159.

*CHURCH, RICHARD M.
(IHS-associate director)
Affiliation: Office of Information Resources Management, Dept. of Health & Human Services, USPHS-IHS, 5600 Fishgers Lane, Rm. 5A-21, Rockville, MD 20857 (301) 443-0750.

CHURCHILL, EDWARD P., Sr. (Coo - Day) (Tlingit) 1923-
(fisherman)
Born January 1, 1923, Ketchikan, AK. *Education*: Wrangell High school, 1941. *Principal occupation*: Lifetime fisherman. *Address*: P.O. Box 45, Wrangell, AK 99929 (907) 874-3725. *Affiliations*: Chairman of "Alaska Aquaculture" a Fish Hatchery at Bumett Inlet, Alaska; commissioner of Southeast Alaska Native Fisheries & Natural Resources Commission, 1988-. secretary-treasurer, Salmon Bay Protection Association; councilman, A.N.B., Alaska Native Brotherhood. *Military service*: U.S. Army, 1944-46; U.S. Engineers, 1st Mate Tug Boat, Alaska, 1942-44. *Community activities*: Board member, Wrangell Mental Health; president, Wrangell I.R.A. Indian Rehabilitation Association; Elder, Presbyterian Church, 1981-; member, Wrangell School Board. *Memberships*: Wrangell Tlingit & Haida Association (past president, board member). *Awards, honors*: The only Indian ever to be elected as Mayor of Wrangell. *Interests*: Lobbying for Alaska Land Claim in Washington, DC for years.

*CHURCHILL, WARD (Creek/Cherokee/Metis)
(professor of American Indian Studies)
Address: 1484 Wicklow St., Boulder, CO 80303 (303) 492-8242 (work). *Affiliation*: Director, American Indian Studies Program, Dept. of Anthropology, University of Colorado, Boulder, CO. *Other professional post*: co-director, American Indian Movement; editor, "Marxism and Native Americans." *Awards, honors*: Former delegate tot he International Indian Treaty Council. *Published works*: Co-author, Culture vs. Economism; co-author (with James VanderWall), Agents of Repression: The FBI's Secret War Against the American Indian Movement, ION, and the Black Panther Party. Numerous articles for various journals.

*CIVIC, DAVID, M.D.
(clinical director)
Affiliation: Mescalero PHS Indian Hospital, P.O. Box 210, Mescalero, NM 88340 (505) 671-4441.

CLADOUHOS, JOE
(administrator-Indian clinic)
Affiliation: Juneau SEARHC Medical Clinic, 3245 Hospital Dr., Juneau, AK 99801 (907) 463-4000.

CLAH, HERBERT (Navajo) 1949-
(executive director)
Born June 1, 1949, Farmington, N.M. *Education*: Brigham Young University, BS, 1975, MPA, 1981. *Principal occupation*: Executive director. *Address & Affiliations*: Executive director, Utah Navajo Development Council, P.O. Box 129, Bluff, UT 84512 (801) 678-2285, 1986-; Dean of Instruction, Navajo Community College, Shiprock, 1990-. *Community activities*: Blanding City Planning Commission; Rural Community Assistance Corporation (board of directors). *Awards, honors*: Outstanding Young Men of America; Jamie Thompson Award; Dean's Leadership Award, BYU; USO National Defense Peace Time Award.

CLAIR, STEPHEN
(Indian band chief)
Affiliation: Quatsino Indian Band, Box 100, Coal Harbor, British Columbia, Canada V0N 1K0 (604) 949-6245.

*CLARK, DON *(Edge of the Water)* (Navajo) 1955-
(commercial graphic artist)
Born March 22, 1955, Winslow, Ariz. *Education*: Navajo Community College, 1974-75; Northern Arizona University, BFA, 1980. *Principal occupation*: Commercial graphic artist. *Home address*: 162 Grandview, Tuba City, AZ 86045 (602) 283-4123. *Other professional post*: Professional jazz guitarist. *Memberships*: Indian Arts & Crafts Association; Inter-tribal Indian Ceremonial Association; SWAIA. *Awards, honors*: 1992 First Place, SWAIA; First Place, Santa Fe Indian Market; First Place in pastel drawings at the Navajo Show, Museum of Northern Arizona; 1993 First Place, Poster Artist Winner at Inter-tribal Indian Ceremonial. among others. *Interests*: A full-time painter since 1986. "I am also known for my, more or less trademark, "blanket series." Each is a portrait of a Native American child or adult wrapped in a colorful Navajo blanket. The background is always black, representing darkness and uncertainty. The blanket means protection and security. It's a symbol of hope, trust and all that is good. One of my goals is to let people know who American Indians are. I'm very proud to American Indian." *Biographical sources*: Navajo-Hopi Observer, Feb. 1988; Intertribal America, 1993 Collectors Edition, page 65.

CLARK, ELMER
(Indian school chairperson)
Affiliation: Winslow Dormitory, 600 N. Alfred Ave., Winslow, AZ 86047 (602) 289-4488.

CLARK, ELMO (Caddo)
(tribal chairperson)
Affiliation: Caddo Tribal Council, P.O. Box 487, Binger, OK 73009 (405) 656-2344.

*CLARK, GEORGIA LEE
(organization president/editor)
Affiliation: "Visions," Communications Publishing Group, 3100 Broadway, Suite 225, Kansas City, MO 64111 (816) 756-3039.

*CLARK, KENNETH (Nanticoke)
(association director)
Affiliation: Nanicoke Indian Assn., Rte. 4, Box 107-A, Millsboro, DE 19966 (302) 945-7022.

*CLARK, NICHOLAS L.
(cultural center president)
Affiliation: Minnetrista Cultural Center, P.O. Box 1527, Muncie, IN 47303 (317) 282-4848.

CLARK, ROBERT
(executive officer)
Affiliation: Bristol Bay Area Health Corp., P.O. Box 130, Dillingham, AK 99576 (907) 842-5201.

CLARK-PRICE, MARGARET A. *(Tio-ron-ia-te-Bright Sky)* (Wyandotte-Chippewa-Shawnee) 1944-
(artist, realtor)
Born August 2, 1944, Colville Indian Agency, Nespelem, Wash. *Education*: St. Michael's (AZ) High School, 1962; Sierra Nevada College (3 years). *Principal occupation*: Artist; realtor. *Address*: P.O. Box 1281, Scottsdale, AZ 85252 (602) 483-8212 (work). *Affiliation*: Legal secretary & researcher, 1966-77; executive director, Native American Press Association, 1985-87; president/director, Native American Communication & Career Development, 1987-; associate editor, Native Peoples Magazine, Phoenix, 1988-92; publisher, Native American Annual (Native American Publishing Co.); consultant, Scottsdale Community College, Tribal Management Programs, Scottsdale, AZ. *Other professional posts*: Member, board of education, Scottsdale Native American Indian Cultural Foundation. *Community activities*: Advisory committee member: Association for Retarded Citizens of Arizona, Inc., Phoenix; fundraising activities; among others. *Exhibits*: Her pastels, oils, acrylics, watercolors and pencil works hang in galleries in Arizona, California, and Nevada as well as in many private collections throughout the U.S. *Memberships*: National Organization of Native American Women; Association for Education in Journalism & Mass Communications. *Awards, honors*: Six awards and a Grand prize for a large pastel entitled Caught in the Middle, at the 1982 annual Navajo Nation Fair, Window Rock, AZ. *Interests*: "My main interests, obviously, surround the Indian world. I have spent years on my own family genealogy, necessitating journeying across the U.S. and into Canada. I hope to instill such an interest in others through the journey among the pages of the Native American Annual. NACCD focuses on career-development seminars to prepare students for journalism careers. *Published works*: Native American Annual (Native America Publishing Co., 1985); co-founder & editor, Native Peoples Magazine, 1988-92.

CLARKE, FRANK, M.D. (Hualapai) 1921-
(physician/administrator)
Born November 11, 1921, Blythe, Calif. *Education*: Los Angeles City College (2 years); UCLA, BS, 1946; St. Louis University, School of Medicine, MD, 1950. *Principal occupation*: Physician/administrator. *Home address*: 7909 Rio Grande Blvd., N.W., Albuquerque, NM 87114. Affiliation: Clinical director, Albuquerque Service Unit, Public Health Service, Indian Health Service, Albuquerque, N.M., 1975-. *Other professional post*: Secretary, National Council of Clinical Directors. *Military service*: U.S. Navy, 1942-46 (Presidential Unit Citation; 1950-53 (Lt. (MC) USNR). *Memberships*: USPHS Commissioned Officers

Association; American Academy of Family Physicians (Charter Fellow); NM Academy of Family Physicians; Association of American Indian Physicians (president, 1973-74). *Awards, honors*: Fellow, John Hay Whitney Foundation, 1950; Indian Achievement Award, Indian Council Fire, Chicago, 1961; Man of the Year, City of Woodlake, 1962; Layman of the Year in Education, Tulane County Chapter of California Teacher's Association. Interests: Recruitment of Indian students into health professions; lecturer on alcoholism. *Biographical sources*: Indians of Today; Who's Who in the West; Community Leaders & Noteworthy Americans.

CLARY, THOMAS C. (Miami of Oklahoma) 1927-
(priest, psychotherapist, consultant)
Born March 3, 1927, Joplin, Mo. *Education*: Pace University, BBA; University of Oklahoma, Norman, MA; California Western University, PhD (Psychology). *Principal occupation*: Corporate president. *Home address*: 2126 Connecticut Ave., NW, Washington, DC 20008 (202) 333-6350. *Affiliations*: Priest (pastor) & counselor, Free Catholic Church, Washington, DC (3 years); president, TCI, Inc., Washington, DC (20 years). *Other professional posts*: MDiplomate & Certified Sex Therapist, The American Board of Sexology; Fellow, American Academy of Clinical Sexologists; president-elect, DC Mental Health Counselors Association; publisher, "Linkages," TCI, Inc., Washington, DC. *Military service*: U.S. Army, 1945-68 (Lt. Colonel) (Legion of Merit, Army Commendation Medal). *Memberships*: American Board of Sexology; American Society of Sexual Educators, Counselors & Therapists; American Counselors Association; American Mental Health Counselors Association; American Association of Professional Hypnotherapists. *Awards, honors*: Silver Anvil Award for International Community Relations by Public Relations Society of America, 1968; Master Hypnotist by American Council of Hypnotist Examiners, 1983; Urban Mass Transportation Administration Minority Business Enterprise Award, 1985. *Interests*: Teach courses in human sexuality, hypnotherapy, psychic potential, spiritual healing and stress management. *Published works*: Script Analysis is a New Approach to OD, chapter 12 of Everybody Wins: Transactional Analysis Applied to Organizations (Addison-Wesley, 1974); How to Live with Stress (NTDS Press, 1977); At the Organizational Precipice (NTDS Press, 1977).

CLAW, CHESTER
(Indian school chairperson)
Affiliation: Flagstaff Dormitory, P.O. Box 609, Flagstaff, AZ 86002 (602) 338-4464.

*CLAY, JULIE ANNA (Omaha) 1958-
(administration)
Born November 2, 1958, Flandreau, S.D. *Education*: University of Oklahoma, BA, 1982; OU-Health Sciences Campus (Oklahoma City, OK), MPH, 1984. *Principal occupation*: Administration. Home address: 2112 Lester, Missoula, MT 59801 (406) 243-2448 (work). *Affiliations*: Research & Training Center on Rural Rehabilitation, University of Montana, Missoula (Project Manager, 1989-92; Program Analyst, 1990-92) Management analyst, Indian Health Service, Rockville, MD, 1992-93; Principal Investigator, Montana University Affiliated Rural Institute on Disabilities, University of Montana, Missoula, MT, 1993-. *Other professional posts*: Advisory

Board for research project, "VR Independent Living Counselor Effects on Independent Living Outcomes for American Indians with Disabilities;" *Memberships*: American Public Health Association (Advisory Committee); American Association of University Affiliated Programs (Minority Affairs Committee); National Congress of American Indians (Disability Issues Committee); member of the Administration on Developmentally Disabled Multicultural Committee; Advisory Council of the Human Services - Rehabilitation Degree Project, Salish Kootenai Tribal College; Training Advisory Committee, Research & Training Center on Public Policy on Independent Living. *Awards, honors*: Indian Health Service Scholarship, Outstanding OU MPH Indian Student, 1984; All American Indian Student Award of Excellence, Americans with Disabilities Act Award. *Interests*: "My major area of interest is to promote communication & education on American Indians with disabilities and all the attendant issues. I enjoy outdoor recreational activities such as skiing, camping, bicycling, attending pow wows and other tribal gatherings." *Published works*: A Descriptive Study of Secondary Conditions Reported by a Population of Adults with Physical Disabilities Served by Three Independent Living Centers in a Rural State, by J.A. Clay et al (Journal of Rehabilitation, April/May/June 1994); National Council on Disability - Prevention of Disabilities - Meeting the Unique Needs of Minorities with Disabilities; A report to the President & the Congress, April 1993; numerous articles & presentations.

*CLAYTON, GERALD L. (Hopi)
(school principal)

Affiliation: Hopi High School, P.O. Box 337, Keams Canyon, AZ 86034 (602) 738-51 11.

CLEGHORN, MILDRED (Fort Sill Apache)
(tribal chairperson)

Affiliation: Fort Sill Apache Business Committee, Rt. 2, Box 121, Apache, OK 73006 (405) 588-2298.

CLEMENTS, ANDREW
(museum curator)

Affiliation: Iowa, Sac & Fox Presbyterian Mission, Route 1, Box 152C, Highland, KS 66035 (913) 442-3304.

*CLEMENTS, SUSAN (Blackfoot, Mohawk, Seneca) 1950-
(writer)

Born October 20, 1950, Livingston Manor, N.Y. *Education*: Binghamton University, BA, 1980, MA, 1982. *Principal occupation*: Writer. *Home address*: 920 Bunn Hill Rd., Vestal, NY 13850 (607) 797-8183. *Community activities*: Do readings and talks at the University & in the community. *Awards, honors*: New York State Foundation for the Arts Poetry Fellowship, 1993. Poetry honors: "Indian Interlude," Honorable Mention in New Letters 1990 Poetry Competition; Singularities," 1st Prize, Paterson's Poetry Center's International Poetry Contest; "Potato," finalist in Eve of St. Agnes Competition, 1993; among others. *Interests*: "Primarily interested in writing both stories and poetry that often contain an interweaving of Indian themes. I also like reading, hiking, and traveling to just about anywhere. I am also deeply involved with Indian issues, which I try to express in my work." *Published works*: The Broken Hoop (Blue Cloud Press, 1988); In the Moon When the Deer Lose Their Horns (Chantry Press, 1993).

CLEMMER, JANICE WHITE
(Wasco-Shawnee-Delaware) 1941-
(professor)

Born February 17, 1941, Warm Springs Reservation, Oregon. *Education*: Brigham Young University, BS, 1964; Dominican College of San Rafael, MA (History), 1975; University of San Francisco, MA (Education), 1976; University of Utah, PhD (Cultural Foundation of Education), 1979; PhD (History), 1980' J. Reuben Clark Law School, BYU, JD, 1993. *Principal occupation*: Professor. *Home address*: 1445 E. Princeton Ave., Salt Lake City, UT 84105. *Affiliations*: Professor, College of Education, Brigham Young University, Provo, Utah, 1980-. *Other professional posts*: Council member, National Association of Ethnic Studies; departmental and college committees; consultant. *Community activities*: Boy Scouts (merit badge counselor); Native American Advisory Board, State of Utah Board of Education (board chairman); Coalition for Minority Affairs, State Office of Education (Board member); Minority Affairs, KUTV-Channel 12 committee member; Utah Endowment for the Humanities (board member); American Indian Services (board member); volunteer, Utah State Heart & Lung Association. Utah Girl Scout Council (board of trustees); Utah Valley Community College, Center of Ethics (board member). *Memberships*: SIETAR (Society for Intercultural Education, Training and Research, International Organization); Native American Historians' Association (founding member); American Studies Association; OHOYO - National Native American Women's Program; Association for Supervision and Curriculum Development; State of Utah Bilingual Association; American Historians Western History Association; Utah State Historical Society; Oregon Historical Society; California Historical Society; National Archives (associate); Jefferson Forum; American Association for State & Local History. *Awards, honors*: University of Utah Danforth Foundation Fellowship Candidate; Distinguished Teaching Award Candidate, University of Utah; Tribal Archives Conference Award Recipient; Consortium for Native American Archives; OHOYO One Thousand, Native American Women Award Listing; American Indian Alumni Award, Brigham Young University; Lamanite Award, American Indian Services, BYU; D'Arcy McNickle, Newberry Library Fellowship Research Award, Chicago, Ill.; Spencer W. Kimball Memorial Award, Private Corporation Endowment & AIS, BYU; Phi Alpha Theta; Phi Delta Kappa; Phi Kappa Phi; Phi Alpha Delta; first Native American woman in U.S. history to earn three doctorates; J. Reuben Clark Law School Service Awards, 1990-91, 1991-92; Law School student organization awards, 1990-93; 1982 Women's Conference Spotlight, outstanding woman faculty member from the College of Student Life, BYU; Multicultural Week Advisor Awards, BYU; Multicultural Programs Awards, BYU. *Interests*: National international travel. *Biographical sources*: University of Utah Public Relations Office, Salt Lake City, Utah regarding the earning of two Ph.D.s; stories in Deseret News, Church News Section, 1980; and in Lifestyle section of the Salt Lake Tribune, Salt Lake City, Spring, 1980; hometown newspapers, Bend Bulletin, Bend, Oregon, Spilya Tymoo, Warm Springs, Oregon, and Madras Pioneer, Madras, Oregon; Brigham Young University Magazine, Feb. 1994. *Published works*: The Good Guys and the Bad Guys, The Utah Indian, Journal, Spring, 1979; Ethnic Traditions and the Family–The Native Americans, Ethnic Traditions and the Family series, Salt lake City Board of Education, Fall, 1980; editor, Minority Women Speak Out; co-editor for the Utah Centennial (1996) Tribal History Project sponsored by the state of Utah, the Utah Historical Society, and Utah Office of Indian Affairs; various book reviews pertaining to Native American topics; printed works primarily in-house curriculum development material, Brigham Young University.

CLIFTON, JAMES A. 1927-
(professor)

Born January 6, 1927, St. Louis, Mo. *Education*: University of Chicago, PhB, 1950; University of Oregon, PhD, 1960. *Principal occupation*: Professor. *Affiliation*: Professor, University of Wisconsin, Green Bay, WI, 1970-. *Military service*: U.S. Marine Corps, 1951-1955 (Captain; Purple Heart). Memberships: American Anthropological Association; American Society for Ethnohistory; American Historical Association. *Awards, honors*: Frankenthal Professor of Anthropology and History, University of Wisconsin, Green Bay. *Interests*: Research among Klamath of Oregon, Ute of Colorado, Potawatomi of Kansas, Wisconsin, Michigan, and Canada. Historical research on Wyandot and Indians of the Old Northwest Territory generally; research in Chile. Expert witness, Indian Claims Commission and Great Lakes Indians Treaty Rights. *Published works*: Klamath Personalities (University of Oregon, 1962); Cultural Anthropology (Houghton Mifflin, 1967); A Place of Refuge for All Time (Museum of Man, 1974); The Prairie People (Kansas University Press, 1977); Star Woman and Other Shawnee Tales (University Press of America, 1983); The Pokagons (University Press of America, 1985).

CLINCHER, BONNIE MARIE (Sioux) 1952-
(editor-tribal newspaper)

Born July 6, 1952, Poplar, Mont. *Education*: Haskell Indian Jr. College, 1973-75. *Principal occupation*: Editor of tribal newspaper. *Home address*: Box 631, Poplar, MT 59255. *Memberships*: Survival of American Indians Association, 1976-. *Interests*: I am most interested in the media, especially when I can assist in informing and making concerned the Indian people. My travels only go as far as celebrations across the northern Plains, on weekends, to just be among the Indian people and refresh my spirit in the old ways before returning to the new ways; photography.

CLINTON, ROBERT
(attorney-professor)

Address & Affiliation: University of Iowa College of Law, Boyd Law Bldg., Melrose & Byington, Iowa City, IA 52242 (319) 335-9032.

CLOUD, CHARLES RILEY
(Oklahoma Cherokee) 1932-
(chief judge)

Born November 20, 1932, Britton (now Oklahoma City), Okla. *Education*: College of William and Mary, BS, 1957, Marshall-Wythe Law School, JD, 1959. *Principal occupation*: Chief judge. *Home address*: 1211 Colonial Ave., Norfolk, VA 23517 (804) 622-6185. *Affiliation*: Chief Judge, Norfolk General District Court. *Other professional posts*: Member, Coordinating Council, Conference of Chief Justices, to resolve disputes between State and Tribal Courts over jurisdiction; co-chairperson, Native American Tribal Courts Committee, National Conference of Special Court Judges, JAD, ABA; trustee, Jamestown-Yorktown Foundation. *Military service*: U.S. Army, 1953-55. *Community activities*: Former chief deputy, Norfolk Commonwealth Attorney's Office; deacon and chairperson of the board, First Christian Church (Disciples of Christ), Norfolk, VA. *Memberships*: National Conference of Special Court Judges, Judicial Administration Division (JAD), American Bar Administration (ABA) (district representative and member of executive committee). *Awards, honors*: Several awards from the ABA, National Conference of Special Court Judges, for outstanding service as Chair of the Native American Tribal Courts Committee, and as a member of the Coordinating Council, Civil Jurisdiction of Tribal Courts & State Courts, and for service to the profession. "Honored by receiving letters of support from Indian leaders, such as Chief Wilma Mankiller and former Chief, Ross Swimmer, Cherokee Nation of Oklahoma; Chief Justices of the Navajo Nation, Chief Justice of Supreme Court of Virginia, and the General Assembly of Virginia leading to nomination as one of two judges of the U.S. to serve on the National Judicial College Board, and as its first Native American member." *Interests*: "Participate in programs, as well as advocating the education of Americans as to the many contributions of Native Americans to our Constitutional form of government and Bill of Rights--also, about the part Native Americans played i the Federation of the original Colonies and the American Revolution."

*CLOUDMAN, RUTH
(museum curator)
Affiliation: J.B. Speed Art Museum, 2035 S. Third St., P.O. Box 2600, Louisville, KY 40201 (502) 636-2893.

CLOW, RICHMOND L. 1949-
(professor of Native American studies)
Born May 21, 1949, Sioux Falls, S.D. *Education*: University of South Dakota, BS, 1971, MA, 1972; University of New Mexico, PhD, 1977. *Principal occupation*: Professor of Native American studies. *Home address*: 311 Skyline, Missoula, MT 59802 (406) 543-7504. *Affiliation*: Associate professor, Dept. of Native American Studies, University of Montana, Missoula, 1984-. *Memberships*: Organization of American Historians; Western Historical Association. *Interests*: "I enjoy teaching Native American studies courses which enables me to cover many topics of interest to myself and to my students." *Published works*: Co-author: A Forest in Trust: Three Quarters of a Century of Indian Forestry, 1910-1986, (Washington, D.C.: Litigation Support Services for the Bureau of Indian Affairs, 1986); Tribal Government Today: Politics on Montana's Indian Reservations (Westview Press, 1990).

*CODY, GARY
(director-Indian health)
Affiliation: Anadarko PHS Indian Health Center, P.O. Box 828, Anadarko, OK 73005 (405) 247-2458

CODY, IRON EYES (Oklahoma Cherokee/Cree)
(advisor)
Affiliation: Council of Advisors, American Indian Heritage Foundation, 6051 Arlington Blvd., Falls Church, VA 22044 (703) 237-7500.

*CODY, RON
(program director)
Affiliation: Junior Achievement's Urban American Indian Program, 3939 W. 69th St., Edina, MN 55435 (612) 927-8354.

*COFFEY, PETE, Jr. *(Bear Charging/Center Feathers/Spirit Eagle)* (Mandan-Arickara-Hidatsa) 1954-
(public radio broadcasting)
Born October 26, 1954, Garrison, S.D. *Education*: High school. *Principal occupation*: Public radio broadcasting. *Address*: P.O. Box 286, Parshall, ND 58770 (701) 862-3058 or 743-4391. *Affiliation*: KMHA-FM, Newtown, ND, 1984-. *Activities*: Chairman of & contributor to Nation Native News, American Public Radio; Coffey programmed & directed operations of KMHA-FM, the first truly native radio station in North Dakota, and is recognized on the national public broadcasting level. He has been in management position at KMHA since inception in 1984 and has served as operations and program manager of KMHA which is looked to by other fledgling Indian communications programs as a model in regard to programming for Native American audiences. *Awards, honors*: Most Outstanding Broadcaster Award given by Fort Berthold Media Association; named to election board for Fort Berthold Tribal Elections, 1988. *Interests*: "Reading and occasionally writing for local tribal newspaper, The MHA Times & Lakota Times. Other interests include combating the terrible effects of alcohol on the Native Indian population such as serving as speaker at chemical dependency seminars and at forums addressed to youth-young adult audiences. (I am) a follower of Native Spiritual belief system more commonly referred to as "The Red Road" and uses the teachings of the Red Road to help combat alcoholism among Native Americans. (I) know that groups such as AA are fine but feel Indian people need help with a program which encompasses Native spirituality as a base."

COFFEY, WALLACE E. (Comanche)
(tribal chairperson)
Affiliation: Chairperon, Comanche Tribal Business Committee, HC 32, Box 1720, Lawton, OK 73502 (405) 492-4988.

*COFFEY-AVEY, CRYSTAL
(librarian)
Affiliation: Big Hole National Battlefield Library, P.O. Box 237, Wisdom, MT 59761 (406) 689-3155.

COFFIN, JAMES L.
(program head-Native American studies)
Affiliation: Native American Studies Program, Ball State University, Muncie, IN 47306 (317) 285-1575.

*COHEN, JAMES E.
(Attorney)
Affiliation: California Indian Legal Services, 120 W. Grand Ave., Suite 204, Escondido, CA 92025 (619) 746-8941.

*COLE, KEN
(historic site archaeologist)
Affiliation: Towosahgy State Historic Site, Big Oak Tree State Park, P.O. Box 35, East Prairie, MO 63845.

COLE/WAGGONER, JESSIE ANN *(Bear Woman)* (United Lumbee/Cherokee) 1935-
(household engineer; wife, mother)
Born November 8, 1935, Springfield, Mo. *Principal occupation*: household engineer; wife, mother. *Home address*: 1211 North Park, Springfield, MO 85802 (417) 865-2261. *Affiliation*: Secretary-treasurer, council person, United Lumbee Nations Black Bear Clan. *Other professional posts*: Historian, reporter, shamaness/medicine woman; married 40 years to United Lumbee Nations Black Bear Chief Thunder Wolf. *Community activities*: Make and donate crafts to the Nation and the Indian center. *Memberships*: Golden Hawk Warrior Society; United Lumbee Nation of N.C. & North America; Southwest Missouri Indian Center; Pan American Indian Association; Mantoac Medicine Society. *Awards, honors*: Silver Eagle Award for outstanding work within the Nation and Indian community, 1990, United Lumbee Nation. *Interests*: "Teaching bead work, giving talks, showing artifacts, crafts, etc. Make cassettes of Indian stories & legends for Nation's library; historian; enjoy craft work (working with leather and beads, feathers, etc.). Enjoy powwows."

COLE, ZELLA JEANETTE CRAWFORD *(Chief Na-Ye-Hi)* (Cherokee) 1941-
(administrator)
Born January 14, 1941, Clermont, FL. *Education*: Jarvis Christian College, BA, 1983; Northeastern State University, Tahlequah, OK, MA, 1985. *Principal occupation*: Administrator. *Address*: Unknown. *Affiliations*: Education specialist, Hopi Dept. of Education, Kykotsmovi, AZ, 1986-87; executive, Native American Heritage Preserve, Phoenix, AZ, 1988; assistant manager for administration, U.S. Census, Tuscaloosa, AL, 1989. *Other professional posts*: Free-lance writer, 1980-. *Community activities*: Editor of two newsletters; West Blocton Improvement Committee; present programs on Indians at schools and libraries. *Awards, honors*: Presidential Scholar; many awards for writing and presenting papers; achievement in history. *Interests*: "I have traveled in 22 states and lived in seven." Biographical sources: The National Dean's List; Who's Who; East Texas Historical Society; Wood County Historical Society. *Published works*: A Comparative Analysis of American Indian Tribes (book); Indians of Northeastern Texas (professional paper-award winner); Mixed Bloods (an award-winning poem); Petroglyphs and Pictographs (book); Profiles of Native American Leaders (book); Problems and Complexities of American Indian Law Enforcement (major paper for Cole's class in Indian law); and many other poems, short stories, and papers.

COLEMAN, GEOFFREY, M.D.
(clinical director)
Affiliation: Menominee Tribal Clinic, P.O. Box 970, Keshena, WI 54135 (715) 799-5482.

COLLIER, L. BILL
(BIA area director)
Affiliation: Anadarko Area Office, Bureau of Indian Affairs, W.C.D. Office Complex, P.O. Box 368, Anadarko, OK 73005 (405) 247-6673.

COLLIER, T. DWAYNE
(monument superintendent)
Affiliation: Malmut Canyon National Monument, Route 1, Box 25, Flagstaff, AZ 86001 (602) 526-3367.

COLLINS, CARL
(college president)
Affiliation: American Indian Bible Institute & College, 100020 N. 15th Ave., Phoenix, AZ 85021 (602) 944-3335.

COLLINS, REBA NEIGHBORS 1925-
(director-Will Rogers Memorial)
Born August 26, 1925. *Education*: Central State University, Edmond, BA, 1958; Oklahoma State University, MS, 1959, EdD (Higher Education in Journalism), 1968. *Principal occupation*: Director, Will Rogers Memorial. *Address*: c/o Will Rogers Memorial, P.O. Box 157, Claremore, OK 74018 (918) 341-0719. *Affiliations*: Instructor, professor of journalism, Central State University, 1958-75; director of public relations, sponsor of alumni publications, school newspaper & college yearbook, Central State University, 1958-75; director, Will Rogers Memorial, Claremore, OK, 1975-. *Community activities*: Edmond Guidance Center (board of directors); Claremore Chamber of Commerce (board of directors); member, Claremore Ambassadors; member, Governor's mini-cabinet for tourism and recreation. *Memberships*: Delta Kappa Gamma; Sigma Delta Chi; American Association of University Women; Oklahoma Public Relations Association for Higher Education (charter president); Oklahoma Education Association (public relations board); CSU Alumni Association; OK Museum Association (board of directors, treasurer). *Awards, honors*: Outstanding Senior Woman, and Outstanding Future Teacher, Central State University, 1958; (2) First Place Awards, OK Press Association for Best Feature on Education; Outstanding Communicator Award from OK Women in Journalism, 1975; Service Award from VFW, 1971; Okie Award from Governor Dewey Bartlet, 1974; Service Award for Helping Organize First Fourth of July Celebration in Edmond, OK, 1973; Distinguished Former Student Award, Central State University, 1979. *Interests*: Genealogy, travel and travel writing. *Published works*: In the Shadows of Old North, 1974; History of the Janes, Peek Family, 1975, plus three follow up books; Will Rogers Memorial Booklet, 1979; Roping Will Rogers' Family Tree, 1982; Will Rogers and Wiley Post in Alaska, 1983; editorial staff, Photolith magazine (seven years); hundreds of feature articles for state and national magazines.

COLLISION, CHRISTINE (Eskimo)
(AK village council president)
Affiliation: Ketchikan Indian Corporation, 429 Deermount Ave., Ketchikan, AK 99901 (907) 225-5158.

COLOSIMO, THOMAS
(executive director)
Affiliations: ARROW, Inc., 1000 Connecticut Ave., NW, Washington, DC 20036 (202) 296-0685; executive secretary, National American Indian Court Clerk's Association, 1000 Connecticut Ave., NW, Washington, DC 20036.

COLTON, ALFRED (Qoyawayma) (Hopi) 1938-
(professional engineer)
Born 1938, Los Angeles, Calif. *Education*: California State Polytechnic University, BS, 1961; University of Southern California, MS (Mechanical Engineer), 1966, graduate program in water resources and environmental engineering, 1970; Westinghouse International School of Environmental Management, graduate. *Principal occu-

pation: Professional engineer. *Affiliations*: Project engineer, Litton Systems, Inc., 1961-70; supervisor of the Environmental Dept., Salt River Project, Phoenix, Ariz., 1971-. *Other professional posts*: Advisor, University of New Mexico, Native American Program, College of Engineering (NAPCOE); National Representative, Electric Power Research Institute's (EPRI) Environmental Task Force (1974-77); Bureau of Land Management's (BLM) Arizona Multi-Use Advisory Board (one term). *Community activities*: Western Systems Coordinating Council (WSCC) Environmental Committee (member, past vice-chairman); American Indian Science and Engineering Society (chairman); American Indian Engineering Council (past associate chairman); Heard Museum Men's Council (board of directors); Museum of Northern Arizona (member); Registered Arizona Lobbyist. *Memberships*: Arizona Society of Professional Engineers; Institute of Electrical and Electronic Engineers; American Assn. for the Advancement of Science; American Public Power Assn; Edison Electric Institute Environmental Committees. *Awards, honors*: First Place Popovi Da Memorial Award for pottery, 1976, Scottsdale National Indian Arts Exhibition; two blue ribbon awards, 1976, one blue ribbon, 1977, Heard Museum Indian Arts Exhibition, Phoenix, AZ; pottery work featured at 1977AZ Kidney Foundation Auction, Numkena Studio of Indian Art, Phoenix; individual showing at Santa East, Austin, TX; 1st place & special award at the Museum of Northern Arizona's 1977 Hopi Show; 2nd & 3rd place at Gallup Ceremonial; holds patents in engineering work in the U.S. & several foreign countries. *Interests*: Pottery/weaving in the Hopi tradition.

COMBRINK, VIRGINIA (Tonkawa)
(tribal president; museum director)
Affiliation: Tonkawa Business Committee, P.O. Box 70, Tonkawa, OK 74653 (405) 628-2561; Tonkawa Tribal Museum, P.O. Box 70, Tonkawa, OK 74653 (405) 628-5301.

*COMELLA, NICHOLAS V. (Cherokee) 1948-
(Indian education)
Born May 5, 1948, Salem, Oreg. *Education*: Canada College (Redwood City, CA) 1 year. *Principal occupation*: Indian education. *Home address*: 5620 Calpine Dr., San Jose, CA 95035 (408) 945-2387 (work). *Affiliations*: Liaison-Indian education, Milpitas Unified School District, Milpitas, CA, 1990-, & Fremont Union High School District, Sunnyvale, CA, 1990-. *Military service*: U.S. Army, Specialist 4 (Vietnam Service Medal; Army Commendation Medal; Goof Conduct Medal). *Community activities*: American Indian Alliance of Santa Clara County - Education Project participant & Indian Education Resource Center liaison - contributor to Santa Clara County American Indian Needs Assessment Survey. *Memberships*: National Indian Education Association, 1988-; California Indian Education Association, 1985-87; Bay Area Title V Indian Education Programs Council (Recording Secretary, 1990-94). *Interests*: "Learning about Native cultures & teaching American Indian people & non-Indians about Native cultures. Preservation of American Indian cultures - writing culturally relevant curriculum for American Indian students grades 8-12."

*COMER, FANESSA (Navajo)
(administrative officer-IHS)
Affiliation: Shiprock PHS Indian Hospital, P.O. Box 160, Shiprock, NM 87420 (505) 368-4971.

COMMACK, LOUIE, Jr. (Eskimo)
(AK village council president)
Affiliation: Ambler Traditional Council, P.O. Box 47, Ambler, AK 99786 (907) 445-2181.

COMMANDA, EARL
(Indian band chief)
Affiliation: Serpent River Indian Band, Box 14, 48 Indian Rd., Cutler, Ontario, Canada P0P 1B0 (705) 844-2418.

COMMODORE, WILLIAM
(Indian band chief)
Affiliation: Soowahlie Indian Band, Box 696, Vedder Crossing, British Columbia, Canada V0X 1Z0 (604) 858-4603.

*COMPLO, JENNIFER
(museum curator)
Affiliation: Eiteljorg Museum of American Indians & Western Art, 500 W. Washington St., Indianapolis, IN 46204 (317) 636-9378.

CONLEY, ROBERT J. (Cherokee) 1940-
(director of Indian studies program)
Born December 29, 1940, Cushing, Okla. *Education*: Midwestern University (Wichita Falls, TX), BA, 1966, MA, 1968. *Principal occupation*: Writer; director of Indian studies program. *Address*: Indian Studies Dept., Morningside College, 1503 Morningside Ave., Sioux City, Iowa 51106 (712) 274-5147. *Affiliations*: Coordinator of Indian culture, Eastern Montana College, 1975-76; assistant program director, The Cherokee Nation of Oklahoma, 1976-77; director of Indian studies, Bacone College, 1978-79; director, Indian Studies Program, Morningside College, Sioux City, Iowa, 1979-. *Military service*: U.S. Marine Corps Reserve, Infantry, 1957-62, PFC. *Membership*: Western Writers of America. *Awards, honors*: Spur Award for best short story of 1988 from Western Writers of America for "Yellow Bird: An Imaginary Autobiography" from my collection, The Witch of Goingsnake and Other Stories; First Prize, Beginnings of Horror Award, Ozark Creative Writers, Inc., 1991, for Brass, Alive! (unpublished). *Interests*: Writing. *Biographical source*: "A More Realistic Picture: An Interview with Robert Conley" by Joseph Bruchac in The Wooster Review, Spring, 1988. No. 8. *Published works*: The Rattlesnake Band & Other Poems (Indiana University Press, 1984); Back to Malachi (Doubleday, 1986); The Actor (Doubleday, 1987; Wilder & Wilder (Pageant Books, 1988) The Witch of Goingsnake and Other Stories (University of Oklahoma Press, 1988); Killing Time (M. Evans Co., 1988); Ballantine paperback, 1989; The Saga of Henry Starr (Doubleday, 1989; Colfax (M. Evans Co., 1989); Quitting Time (M. Evans Company, 1989); G-Ahead Rider (M. Evans Co., 1990); Ned Christie's War (M. Evans Co., 1991); Strange Company (Pocket Books, 1991); Editor of: Echoes of Our Being (Indian University Press, 1982; The Essay: Structure & Purpose, with Cherry and Hirsch (Houghton-Mifflin, 1975); A Return to Vision, 2nd Ed., with Cherry & Hirsch (Houghton-Mifflin, 1974; The Shadow Within, with Cherry & Hirsch (Houghton-Mifflin); A Return to Vision, with Cherry & Hirsch (Houghton-Mifflin, 1971); Poems for Comparison & Contrast, with Cherry & Hirsch (Macmillan, 1972). Poetry in various magazine & anthologies. Short Stories in the following periodicals & anthologies: Indian Voice, 1972, Sun Tracks, Fall 1976; The Remembered Earth (Red Earth Press, 1979; and short stories, Wesley's Story, in The

Greenfield Review (summer/fall, 1984), and The Immortals, in Iowa Archaeological Newsletter (summer, 1984).

CONN, RICHARD 1929-
(curator of Native arts)
Education: University of Washington, BA, 1950, MA, 1955. *Address*: Denver Art Museum, Denver, CO 80208. *Affiliation*: Curator, Denver Art Museum; Adjunct associate professor, Native American Art, museum studies, Dept.of Anthropology, University of Denver, Denver, CO. *Military service*: U.S. Army, 1951-53. *Memberships*: American Association of Museums. *Awards, honors*: McCloy Fellowship in Art, 1979. *Interests*: Native American art in general; fieldwork in eastern Washington, Montana, and Central Canada. *Published works*: Robes of White Shell and Sunrise (Denver Art Museum); Native American Art in the Denver Art Museum (Denver Art Museum, 1978); Circles of the World (Denver Art Museum, 1982).

CONNER, LELAND L. *(Chief Thunderhawk)*
(Shawnee) 1930-
(industrial supervision-retired)
Born May 9, 1930, Logan, Ohio. *Education*: Hocking Technical College. *Principal occupation*: Industrial supervision-retired. *Home address*: 960 Walhonding Ave., Logan, OH 43138 (614) 385-7136. *Affiliation*: Carborundum Company, Logan, OH (leadman, 1956-66; foreman, 1966-83). *Military service*: U.S. Army, 1951-53. *Community activities*: Red Cross Blood Program, Hocking County, OH (publicity agent, 1974-75; chairperson, 1976-77). *Memberships*: Hocking County Historical Society (life member; board of directors, president, vice president); Continental Confederation of Adopted Indians (life member; continental chief); American Indian Lore Association (life member; national director); American Indian Shrine Association, Pipestone, MN (life member). *Awards, honors*: "Catlin Peace Pipe Award," from American Indian Lore Association, for work in Indian lore; Schiele Museum's "Annual Award for Excellence in Indian Lore"; Carborundum Company's, "Community Involvement Award," for sharing Indian lore with youth groups and charitable organizations; Certificate of Proclamation for work in Indian lore, Ohio House of Representatives. *Interests*: Conner Indian Show; nature hiking, teaching wilderness survival, camping, visiting Indian reservations; world wide Indian lore consultant, and Indian genealogy consultant; writing, replicating ancient Indian tools, weapons, etc. *Biographical sources*: Articles - "Hobby Turns Logan Man Into Expert on Indians," Columbus Dispatch, Nov. 14, 1978; "Wabash Powow Honors Region's Indian Heritage," Fort Wayne, IN Journal-Gazette, June 19, 1983; "Ancient Indians' Kindred Spirits," Messinger, Athens, OH, July 9, 1989; "Logan Man Pleased With (Jim) Thorpe Move," Logan (OH) Daily News; "Indian Skills Kept Alive by Leland Conner," The Free Paper, Logan, OH, Sept. 29, 1989. *Published work*: author - The Vengeance of Lewis Wetzel (Carleton Press, 1980).

***CONQUEST, RAYMOND (Athapascan)**
(AK village president)
Affiliation: Native Village of Aleknagik, P.O. Box 115, Aleknagik, AK 99555 (907) 842-2229.

***CONRAD, BEVERLEY (St. Regis Mohawk)**
1950-
(artist/writer, musician)
Born June 13, 1950, Rochester, N.Y. *Education*: SUNY College at Buffalo, BA, 1973. *Principal occupation*: Artist/writer, musician. *Community activities*: Volunteer at the Joseph Priestly House Museum, North Cumberland, PA (sew reproduction historical clothing & take part in living history exhibitions.) *Membership*: Indian Arts & Crafts Association, 1991-. *Interests*: Ms. Conrad makes Corn Husk Faces as a way of keeping a traditional craft alive in her family. "The Iroquois Indians are the only natives in North America that make medicine "masks" out of corn husk." She also grows corn to use for the Husk Faces she makes. Currently, she is writing & illustrating children's books, and works as a portrait artist accepting commissions as they come in. She is active as a musician in the area as a fiddler of American music. Ms. Conrad lectures on the subject of the Corn Husk Face and also on Native American beadwork. *Biographical source*: "Through the Corn" by Gregory Burgess (Indian Artifacts Magazine, Jan.-March 1992.) *Published works*: Doggy Tales - Bedtime Stories for Dogs & Kitty Tales - Bedtime Stories for Cats (Dell Publishing, 1980).

CONSTANT, CHARLIE
(executive director-Indian centre)
Affiliation: Manitoba Keewatinowi Okimakanak, 3 Station Rd., Thompson, Manitoba, Canada R8N 0N3 (204) 778-4431.

CONSTANT, JIMMY
(Indian band chief)
Affiliation: Kipawa Indian Band, Kebaoweck Indian Reserve, Box 787, Temiscamingue, Quebec, Canada J0Z 3R0 (819) 627-3455.

CONSTANT, WALTER
(Indian band chief)
Affiliation: James Smith Indian Band, Box 680, Kinistino, Saskatchewan, Canada S0J 0G0 (306) 864-3636.

***CONTI, RICHARD**
(health director)
Affiliation: Hoopa Health Association, P.O. Box 1288, Hoopa, CA 95546 (916) 625-4261.

CONTWAY, BRUCE P. *(Wan Mni Awacin)*
(Sisseton-Wahpeton Sioux, Chippewa) 1955-
(artist)
Born October 25, 1955, Havre, Mont. *Education*: Montana State University, BA, 1979. *Principal occupation*: Artist. *Home address*: P.O. Box 920, Whitehall, MT 59759 (406) 388-3401. Bronze sculptor: A second generation artist, Bruce grew up on the Blackfeet Reservation in Northern Montana where his parents taught school. His work reflects his connection to Northern Plains Indians. *Community activities*: Donated sculptures to Sheriff's Office for crime stoppers, to benefit the Galatin County group home for disabled citizens, and as a first donation to Murton Mckloskey Scholarship Fund for Indian students. *Memberships*: Professional Rodeo Cowboy Association; Indian Arts & Crafts Association. *Awards, honors*: 1989 Winner, Calgary Stampede Trophy Bronze Competition; 1989 1st and 2nd Sculpture Division, Colorado Indian Market; 1990 Best of Show, Calgary Stampede Art Show; 1991 & 1994 People's Choice Award, Great Falls Native American Art Show; 2nd Bronze, 1993 Santa Fe Indian Market. *Major commissions*: Atlantic Richfield Corp., Calgary Stampede Rodeo Trophy Bronzes, Montana Pro Rodeo Association. *Major honors*: Portrait sculpture of U.S. Senator Ben Nighthorse Campbell of Colorado; permanent collection of Calgary Stampede Museum; in collection of actor Tom Berenger. *Interests*: "Indian oral history; art-I'm lucky that in going to art shows I get to travel all over the country."

CONWAY, CECIL P.
(IHS-tribal programs)
Affiliation: Indian Health Service, Billings Area Office of Tribal Programs, P.O. Box 2143, Billings, MT 59103 (406) 657-6007.

COOCHISE, ELBRIDGE
(attorney-judge)
Address: 121 5th Ave., N., Suite 305, Edmonds, WA 98020 (206) 774-5808. *Membership*: National American Indian Court Judges Association (president), 1000 Connecticut Ave., NW, Washington, DC 20036 (202) 296-0685.

COOK, HARRY
(Indian band chief)
Affiliation: Lac La Ronge Indian Band, Box 480, La Ronge, Saskatchewan, Canada S0J 1L0 (306) 425-2183.

COOK, HELEN
(Indian band chief)
Affiliation: Bloodvein Indian Band, Bloodvein, Manitoba, Canada R0C 0J0 (204) 395-2148.

COOK, J.R.
(executive director)
Affiliation: United National Indian Tribal Youth, Inc. (UNITY), 4010 Lincoln Blvd., Suite 202, P.O. Box 25042, Oklahoma City, OK 73125 (405) 424-3010.

***COOK, RAY**
(executive director)
Affiliation: Indigenous Communications Association, P.O. Box 748, Hogansburg, NY 13655 (518) 358-4185.

COOK, RONALD
(Indian band chief)
Affiliation: Shoal River Indian Band, Pelican Rapids, Manitoba, Canada R0L 1L0 (204) 587-2012.

COOK, WARREN
(director-Indian organization)
Affiliation: Mattaponi-Pamunkey-Monacan JTPA Consortium, Mattaponi Indian Reservation, P.O. Box 360, King William, VA 23086 (804) 769-4767.

COOK-LYNN, ELIZABETH (Crow Creek Sioux) 1930-
(professor emerita-Native studies/English)
Born November 17, 1930, Fort Thompson, S.D. *Education*: South Dakota State College, BS, 1952; University of South Dakota, MA, 1970; doctoral work at University of Nebraska, Lincoln. *Principal occupation*: Professor emerita-Native studies/English. *Home address*: 3755 Blake Court North, Rapid City, SD 57701 (605) 341-3228. *Affiliations*: Newspaper work, editing & writing in S.D., 1952-57; part-time teaching, Carlsbad, NM, 1958-64; secondary teaching, Carlsbad, NM, 1965-68, Rapid City, S.D., 1968-

69; professor emerita of English & Native American Studies (16 years), Eastern Washington University, Cheney, WA; visiting professor, University of California, Davis, 1990-. Other professional posts: Editor, "The Wicazo SA Review," a journal of Native Studies, Eastern Washington University, 1985-. Professional activities: Consultant & participant in the curriculum development seminar RMMLA, Flagstaff, Ariz., 1978; project director (planning grant) NEH Media Project: Indian Scholar's Journal; member, National Research Council Panel, National Academy of Science, Washington, DC, 1989. Memberships: National Indian Education Association; Writer's Guild; Modern Language Association; Council of Editorts of Learned Journals. Biographical sources: "Acts of Survival" by Jamie Sullivan, in The Bloomsbury Review, Vol. 13/Issue 1/Feb. 1993; "Bleak & Beautiful Moments" by John Purdy, in American Book Review, 1992-93 (Dec./Jan.). Published works: Short stories, poems, and papers: Problems in Indian Education, (South Dakota Review), A Severe Indictment of Our School Systems, and Authentic Pictures of the Sioux? (Great Plains Observer), 1970; Propulsives in Native American Literatures, paper read at National meeting of Conference of College Composition, and Communications, New Orleans, 1973; The Teaching of Indian Literatures, NCTE, Minneapolis, Minn., 1974; The Image of the American Indian in Historical Fiction, RMMLA, Laramie, Wyoming; Delusion: The American Indian in White Man's Fiction, RMMLA, El Paso, Texas; Three, prose and poetry in Prairie Schooner, Fall, 1976; A Child's Story, short story in Pembroke Magazine, 1976; poems published in Sun Tracks (University of Arizona, 1977), and The Ethnic Studies Journal; The Indian Short Story, and bibliography for Encyclopedia of Short Fiction, edited by Walton Beacham (Salem Press, 1980); The Cure, short story accepted for Anthology of Native American Literature, edited by Berud Pryor, UCLA, Davis, 1980; two short stories, The Power of Horses, and A Good Chance, accepted by Simon J. Ortiz (Pueblo writer and poet) for inclusion in anthology, The Short Story in Native American Literature (Navajo College Press, 1983); Then Badger Said This, collection of poems (Ye Galleon Press, 1984); 12 poems, entitled, Seek the House of Relatives (Blue Cloud Press, 1986); three poems, Harper's Book of Twentieth Century Native American Poetry, 1986, edited by Duane Niatum; among other short stories, articles, and essays; short story collection, entitled, The Power of Horses and Other Stories (Arcade-Little, Brown, 1990); From the River's Edge (Arcade-Little, Brown, 1991).

COON-COME, CHIEF MATTHEW (Cree)
(grand chief)
Affiliation: Grand Council of the Crees of Quebec, Canada.

*COOPER, ALFRED B. (Snohomish)
(tribal chairperson)
Affiliation: Snohomish Tribe, 1422 Rosario Rd., Anacortes, WA 98221 (206) 293-7716.

*COOPER, ANNE
(editor)
Affiliation: Quileute Indian News, Quileute Tribe, P.O. Box 279, La Push, WA 98350 (206) 374-6163.

COOPER, CATHY
(executive director)
Affiliation: Deh Cho Society, P.O. Box 470, Fort Simpson, Northwest Territories X0E 0N0 (403) 695-2511.

COOPER, CHARLES B.
(monument supt.)
Affiliation: Aztec Ruins National Monument, P.O. Box 640, Aztec, NM 87410 (505) 334-6174.

*COOPER, HARRY, Sr. (Nooksack)
(chairperson)
Born in Bellingham, Wash. Affiliation: Northwest Alliance of Gaming Tribes, Seattle, WA. Membership: Nooksack Tribe.

*COOPER, JOHN
(museum executive director)
Affiliation: Bailey House Museum, 2375A Main St., Wailuku, HI 96793 (808) 244-3326.

COOPER, KAREN COODY
(Oklahoma Cherokee) 1946-
(museum education)
Born November 10, 1946, Tulsa, Okla. Education: Oklahoma College of Liberal Arts, 1965-66; Western Connecticut State University, BA, 1981; University of Oklahoma. Principal occupation: Museum education. Home address: P.O. Box 1355, Chesapeake Beach, MD 20732 (202) 357-3101 (work) Affiliation: American Indian Archaeological Institute, Washington, CT, 1985-89; curator of education, Museum of the Great Plains, Lawton, OK, 1990-93; museum education, Smithsonian Institution, Washington, DC, 1994-. Other professional post: Guest faculty, Museums Programs, Smithsonian Institution, Washington, DC, Spring 1992. Community activities: Board member, Eagle Wing Press, an American Indian newspaper, 1982-89. Memberships: Oklahoma Museum Association; Southern Plains Indian Museum Association; American Association of Museums. Awards, honors: Kidger Award, 1987, for Excellence in Museum Education, New England History Teachers Association. Interests: Ms. Cooper writes, "I am interested in fingerweaving, an ancient craft of American Indians in the Woodlands, and have won prizes and written articles; I am a published poet; I enjoy black and white photography." Published works: Articles - "Choosing a Career: Anthropology," in Eagle Wing Press, Feb. 1983; "Finger Weaving," in Threads Magazine, Aug. 1987.

COOPER, MARGARET
(clinical director)
Affiliation: Arapaho PHS Indian Health Center, Arapaho, WY 82510 (307) 856-9281.

COOPER, TISH
(museum director)
Affiliation: Toppenish Museum, 1 South Elm, Toppenish, WA 98945 (509) 865-4510.

*COPE, AGNES (Hawaiian)
(society director)
Affiliation: Waianae Coast Culture & Arts Society, 89-188 Farrington Hwy., Walanae, HI 96792 (808) 668-1549.

COPENACE, ANTHONY
(Indian band chief)
Affiliation: Ojibways of Onegaming (Sabaskong Indian Band, Box 160, Nestor Falls, Ontario, Canada P0W 1K0 (807) 484-2162.

COPENACE, FRED
(Indian band chief)
Affiliation: Big Grassy Indian Band, General Delivery, Morson, Ontario P0W 1J0 (807) 488-5614.

*COPENHAVER, VICTORIA
(museum curator)
Affiliation: Eiteljorg Museum of American Indians & Western Art, 500 W. Washington St., Indianapolis, IN 46204 (317) 636-9378.

*CORBINE, DAVID (Turtle Mountain Chippewa)
(student; national rep-AISES)
Education: Major in pre-med, University of North Dakota. Principal occupation: student, national representative for AISES. Address: 715 N. 40th St., #101H, Grand Forks, ND 58203 (701) 780-9917. Affiliation: Student, University of North Dakota, Grand Forks, ND; national rep, AISES, Boulder, CO.

CORDERO, CARLOS
(college president)
Affiliation: D-Q University, P.O. Box 409, Davis, CA 95617 (916) 758-0470.

*CORDERO, GILBERT (Chuckchansi)
(tribal chairperson)
Affiliation: Picayune Rancheria, P.O. Box 269, Coarsegold, CA 93614 (209) 683-6633.

CORDOVA, EMILIO
(Indian school principal)
Affiliation: Jicarilla Dormitory, P.O. Box 1009, Dulce, NM 87528 (505) 759-3101.

*CORDOVA, VAL
(BIA agency supt. for education)
Affiliation: Bureau of Indian Affairs, Crow Creek/Lower Brule Agency, P.O. Box 139, Fort Thompson, SD 57339 (605) 245-2398.

CORE, M. ALLEN (Osage) 1948-
(attorney)
Born August 4, 1948, Tulsa, Okla. Education: University of Oklahoma, BS, 1970, MBA, 1974; University of Oklahoma College of Law, JD, 1988. Principal occupation: Attorney. Home address: 3012 E. 51st St. #48, Tulsa, OK 74105 (918) 251-3140. Affiliation: Oklahoma Bar Association, Oklahoma City, OK, 1988-. Community activities: Board of Directors of the Tulsa Indian Heritage Center, and Oklahoma Indian Legal Services. Memberships: Oklahoma Indian Bar Association (vice-president); Native American Bar Association (board member); Federal Bar Association; Muscogee Bar Association; Court of Indian Offenses for the Anadarko and Muskogee Area Indian Offices. Awards, honors: The Oklahoma Bar Association's Outstanding Senior Law Student, University of Oklahoma College of Law, 1988.

COREY, MARK
(monument supt.)
Affiliation: Ocmulgee National Monument, 1207 Emery Highway, Macon, GA 31201 (912) 752-8257.

COREY, PETER L.
(museum curator)
Affiliation: Sheldon Jackson Museum, 104 College Dr., Sitka, AK 99835 (907) 747-8981.

CORN, SUE
(director-Indian center)
Affiliation: Native American Center, University of Wisconsin-Stevens Point, Stevens Point, WI 54481 (715) 346-3828.

CORNELIUS, BETTY L.
(executive director)
Affiliation: Colorado River Indian Tribes Museum, Route 1, Box 23-B, Parker, AZ 85344 (602) 669-9211 ext. 335.

CORNELIUS, PATRICIA
(Indian school supt.)
Affiliation: Chief Bug-O-Nay-Ge Shig School, Route 3, Box 100, Cass Lake, MN 56633 (218) 665-2282

CORNSILK, CAROL PATTON
(Oklahoma Cherokee) 1949-
(film producer/director/writer/editor)
Born July 8, 1949, Tulsa, Okla. *Education*: University of Texas, BS (Radio-TV-Film), 1973. *Principal occupation*: Film producer/director/writer/editor. *Home address*: 2229 Dearborn Dr., Nashville, TN 37214 (615) 259-9325 (of office). *Affiliations*: "Austin City Limites," PBS (associate producer, 1979-84, associate producer/editor, 1984-85; producer/director, KLRU-TV, Austin, TX, 1985-87; Sr. producer/director, WDCN-TV, Nashville, TN, 1987-. *Community activities*: Member, First Church Unity, Nashville, TN. *Awards, honors*: Certificate of Merit, Chicago International Film/Video Festival 1980 for "Austin City Limits 'Songwriter's Special'" Associate Producer/Publicist; Gold Medal, New York International Film/Video Festival 1982 for Best Network Music Special: "Down Home Country Music" Co-producer; CPB Training Grant, 1984; CPB Professional Development Grants, 1985, 1987; CPB Scriptwriting/Storytelling Fellowship, 1991; Native American Public Broadcasting Consortium Program Screening Panel, 1991; National Endowment for the Humanities Media Panelist, 1991. *Interests*: "Cherokee legends, storytellers and history; travelled extensively in Europe, 1983, 1985, 1987; traveled and lived in the west and southwest - Texas, New mexico and Colorado. I love music, art, theatre, gardening, travelling, and of late devoting much of my free time to my two-year-old son, James Eagle Pace-Cornsilk."

CORRIGAN, SAMUEL W.
(editor)
Affiliation: Canadian Journal of Native Studies, Brandon University Brandon, Manitoba, Canada R7A 6A9.

*CORWIN, GILBERT THUNDER
(radio project coordinator)
Affiliation: Quinault Tribe Radio Project, P.O. Box 332, Taholah, WA 98587 (206) 276-4353.

COSTO, JEANETTE HENRY
(Indian society director)
Affiliation: American Indian Historical Society, 1451 Masonic Ave., San Francisco, CA 94117 (415) 626-5235.

*COTTIER, CHOCKIE
(executive director)
Affiliation: National Native American Chamber of Commerce, 225 Valencia St., San Francisco, CA 94103 (415) 552-1070.

COUCH, JIM, M.D.
(medical director)
Affiliation: Dzilth-Na-O-Dith-Hle PHS Indian Health Center, Star Route 4, Box 5400, Bloomfield, NM 87413 (505) 632-1801.

COULTER, ROBERT T.
(Citizen Band Potawatomi) 1945-
(lawyer)
Born September 19, 1945, Rapid City, S.D. *Education*: Williams College, BA, 1966; Columbia University Law School, JD, 1969. *Principal occupation*: Lawyer. *Address & Affiliation*: Director, Indian Law Resource Center, 508 Stuart St., Helena, MT 59601 (406) 449-2006, 1978-. *Memberships*: American Bar Association; American Society of International Law. *Awards, honors*: Harvard Law School, Shikes Visiting Fellow, 1983. *Interests*: Indian law; international human rights law; avocations: cello and double bass playing. *Biographical sources*: Response Magazine, Mar. '89 p. 11, "A Decade of Defending Indian Rights"; Harvard Law School Bulletin, Spring '84 p. 38, "Righting Wrongs". *Published work*: Indian Rights - Human Rights (Indian Law Resource Center, 1984).

COUNCILLOR, ROSEANNA
(Indian band chief)
Affiliation: Naicatchewenin Indian Band, Box 12, RR 1, Devlin, ON, P0W 1C0 (807) 486-3407.

COURNOYER, FRANK (Yankton Sioux) 1952-
(visual artist, electronic slot technician)
Born December 26, 1952, Wagner, S.D. *Education*: Las Vegas Gaming & Technical School Graduate Certificate, 1992. *Principal occupation*: Visual artist, electronic slot technician. *Home address*: Box 111, Marty, SD 57361. *Affiliations*: Slot technician, Fort Randall Casino, Yankton Sioux Reservation. *Other professional posts*: Elementary teacher-art & Indian studies; member, Board of Directors, Dakota Plains Institute of Learning, Marty, SD 57361, 1984-; chairman, Board of Directors, Native American National Arts Council, and Oyate Kin Cultural Society, Marty, S.D., 1984-. *Military service*: U.S. Army, 1971-1974 (Specialist E-4, 82nd Airborne Division) (National Defense Ribbon, Expert Rifleman Badge, Jump Wings). *Community activities*: Dakota Plains Institute of Learning is the higher adult education branch of the Yankton Sioux Tribe. *Awards, honors*: Honorable mention (best of show); sang a song for "Dances With Wolves" the movie. *Interests*: Reviving and promoting cultural and contemporary arts & culture for 15 years; "Write poetry and short stories about life and the aboriginal people of this continent; other interests include clay, wood and stone sculpture, and most importantly, the revival of the planet. I go around on reservation land and plant and transplant trees of various variety. Am concerned about the environment and tribal issues concerning the living conditions of my people. I am a traditional singer, pipe carrier and sundancer. I perform sacred sweatlodge ceremonies on my reservation for the health and lives of the people. I have traveled from coast to coast many times promoting my own and the work of others (Indian art work) and have been active in producing, promoting and marketing Indian art for almost ten years."

COURNOYER, JAMES
(hospital director)
Affiliation: Rapid City PHS Hospital, 3200 Canyon Lake, Rapid City, SD 57702 (605) 348-1900.

COURNOYER, ROBERT
(Indian school chairperson)
Affiliation: Marty Indian School, P.O. Box 187, Marty, SD 57361 (605) 384-5431.

COWIE, FRANK
(Indian band chief)
Affiliation: Hiawatha (Ojibways) First Nation Band, RR #2, Keene, Ontario, Canada K0L 2G0 (705) 295-4421.

COX, BRUCE (Anishinabe)1934-
(professor)
Born June 29, 1934, Santa Rosa, Calif. *Education*: Reed College, B.A., 1956; University of Oregon, M.A., 1959; University of California at Berkeley, Ph.D., 1968. *Principal occupation*: Professor of anthropology. *Home address*: 140 Kenilworth, Ottawa, Ontario, Canada (613) 788-2604 (office). *Affiliations*: Instructor, Lewis and Clark College, 1964-1965; visiting professor, University of Florida, 1966; assistant professor, University of Alberta, 1967-1969; assistant professor, professor, Carleton University, 1969-. *Memberships*: American Anthropological Association; Law and Society Association; Canadian Ethnology Association (program chair, 1989 meetings). *Interests*: Dr. Cox writes, "I am interested in the cultural ecology of indigenous North American peoples...particularly the disrupted effects of large-scale energy development projects on such peoples' environments. Here, I have in mind the James Bay hydroelectric project in Quebec, and coal strip-mining on Black Mesa, and I am collecting information on all these areas. I have been invited to prepare the volume on Canada for a series on the history of the America Indian, sponsored by the Mapro Foundation in Madrid. I would like to hear from anyone, particularly native people, who can offer suggestions as to what I should cover in this book." *Published works*: Cultural Ecology of Canadian Native Peoples (Carleton Library, 1973); Native People, Native Lands (Carleton University, 1988); A Different Drummer: Readings in Anthropology with a Canadian Perspective (Carleton University, 1989).

*COX, DEBORAH (White Wolf)
(Southeastern Cherokee) 1957-
(mental health professional)
Born February 1, 1957, Elizabeth City, Ky. *Education*: Valdosta State University, BS, 1988; Century University, MS, 1989, PhD, 1991. *Principal occupation*: Mental health professional. *Home address*: 318 Crestview Dr., Valdosta, GA 31602 (912) 244-9104. *Affiliations*: Woodsong - Women's Program Coordinator, Ochlocknee, GA; Cox Consultants - Native American Artist. *Other professional posts*: Southeastern Cherokee Confederacy (Medicine person, historian, tribal council member, Warrior Society - War Leader-Georgia. *Military service*: Dept. of Defense (10 years) (Achievement Medal, National Defense Service Medal, Outstanding Unit Award. *Community activities*: Native American teacher; Young Astronaut Program instructor; Adult Literacy Program instructor. *Memberships*: International Association of Arson Investigators; National Criminal Justice Association; Tsalagi Warrior Society (Qualla Boundary). *Awards, honors*: Red Feather Society & Prayer Blanket Society (Southeastern Cherokee Warrior Society Honors). *Interests*: Native American history & art. *Published works*: Correlates of Correctional Institution Suicide, 1989; Post Traumatic Stress Disorder in Police Officers, 1990; When

a Cop Kills, 1992; Learning Cherokee: W ork-book Series, 1994; published by White W olf Publishing.

*COX, DELTON
(school supt.)
Affiliation: Sequoyah High School, P .O. Box 948, Tahlequah, OK 74464 (918) 456-0631

*COX, DONALD D. *(Quiet Storm)* **(Southeast-ern Cherokee) 1950-**
(police lieutenant)
Born September 16, 1950, Lakeland, Ga. *Education*: Georgia Military College, AA, 1972; South Georgia Tech (2 years). *Principal occupation*: Police lieutenant. *Home address*: 318 Crestview Dr., Valdosta, GA 31602 (912) 244-9104; 242-2606 (work). *Affiliation*: Director of professional studies, V aldosta Police Department, Valdosta, GA, 1973-. *Membership*: Georgia Peace Officers Association; Police Offices Benevolent Association (former president); International Association of Bomb Technicians & Investigators; Fraternal Order of Police.

COX, STEPHEN D. 1948-
(museum curator/administrator)
Born April 24, 1948, Bloomington, Ill. *Education*: Middle Tennessee State University, BS, 1970, MA, 1975. *Principal occupation*: Curator of cultural history. *Home address*: 2810 Belcourt Ave., Nashville, TN 37212 (615) 292-4990; 741-2692 (work). *Affiliation*: Tennessee State Museum, Nashville, TN (collection researcher, 1976-77; assistant curator of collections, 1977-83; curator of cultural history, 1983-89; assistant director of collections, 1989-. *Memberships*: Intermuseum Council of Nashville; Tennessee Assn. of Museums; American Assn. for State & Local History; TN Historical Society; Mid-Cumberland Archaeological Society; Southeastern Archaeological Conference; Kentucky Historical Society; National Trust for Historic Preservation. *Awards, honors*: American Assn. for State & Local History "A ward of Merit" for the exhibition "The First Tennesseans--Tennessee's Prehistoric Indian Cultures" (for which Cox was the supervising curator) and for book, Art & Artisans of Prehistoric Middle Tennessee (for which he was the editor). *Interests*: Prehistoric Indian cultures in Tennessee. "My great grandmother was full-blooded Indian and was born in Canada." *Published work*: Art & Artisans of Prehistoric Middle TN (TN State Museum, 1985).

*COYHIS, LAURA (Stockbridge-Munsee Mohican)
(tribal chairperson)
Affiliation: Stockbridge-Munsee Tribal Council, 8476 Moh He Con Nuck Rd., Bowler , WI 54416 (715) 793-4111.

*COYLE, MARTIN (Seminole of Florida)
(school principal)
Affiliation: Ahfachkee Day School, Star Route, Box 40, Clewiston, FL 33440 (813) 983-6348.

CRAIG, CAROL
(media specialist)
Affiliation: Columbia River Inter-T ribal Fish Commission, 729 N.E. Oregon, Suite 200, Portland, OR 97232 (503) 238-0667.

CRAIG, LAURA (Pit River)
(tribal council chairperson)
Affiliation: Lookout Rancheria Council, P .O. Box 1570, Burney, CA 96013 (916) 335-5421.

CRAIG, TIM (Cherokee)
(attorney)
Address: 17 West 8th St., Apt. 3-F, New York, NY 10011. *Memberships*: Native American Bar Association; American Bar Association; Native American Alumni Association of Dartmouth College (National Steering Committee).

CRAIG, VINCENT (Navajo) 1950-
(tribal law & legal research)
Born June 6, 1950, Crownpoint, N.M. *Education*: Northland College, AS (Law Enforcement), 1979; Arizona State University, BS (Criminal Justice), 1982; Universit of New Mexico Law School (lst year student). *Principal occupation*: Tribal law & legal research. *Home address*: Box 2394, Chee Dodge Dr . #2, W indow Rock, AZ 86515 (602) 871-2183 (home) 871-7027 (of fice). *Affiliations*: Police officer, Navajo Nation, White Mountain Apache Tribe, Salt River Tribe (9 years); Commissioner of Justice, White Mountain Apache Tribe, 1987-90; Chief Probation Officer, Navajo Nation Supreme Court, 1991-. *Other professional posts*: Lietenant Police Academy Director, Tribal Prosecutor, Assistant Editor-Fort Apache Scout, and a Mountain Rescue Team leader. Muttonman Productions - Navajo singer-songwriter, cartoonist, illustrator, humorist, consultant; Self-esteem & motivational workshops for Native American students & educators. *Military service*: U.S. Marine Corps, 1969-73 (Sergeant-Helicopter Test-Cell Operations). *Community activities*: Boy Scoutmaster . *Interests*: Hobbies include rock-climbing, poetry , rodeo, flute-making, silversmithing, illustrating, talking to schools on "self-image & motivation". Vincent has performed for many Indian and non-Indian organizations. "I firmly believe that the greatest asset which Indian Nations have is still untapped...our Indian youth. I foresee the day when we will have Indian actors and performers who are internationally known for their accomplishments in the performing arts. It is our responsibility to nurture our youth not to be afraid to express themselves in music, drama, and literature. I can only be as free as my imagination. My idea of success is to be a sydicated cartoonist, with a law degree hanging on the wall."

*CRANE, KAREN R.
(museum director)
Affiliation: Sheldon Jackson Museum, 104 College Dr., Sitka, AK 99835 (907) 747-8981.

CRAWFORD, BEVERLY J.
(BIA supt. for education)
Affiliation: Western Navajo Agency, BIA, P.O. Box 746, Tuba City, AZ 86045 (602) 283-4531.

CRAWFORD, JEFFREY A.
(attorney)
Address & Affiliation: President, Minnesota American Indian Bar Association, Suite 840, Midland Square Bldg., Minneapolis, MN 55401 (612) 540-3728.

*CRAZY HORSE, ROY *(Chief Nemattanew)* **(Powhattan Renape)**
(tribal chief)
Affiliation: Powhattan Renape Nation, P .O. Box 225, Rancocas, NJ 08073 (609) 261-4747. *Other professional post*: New Jersey Governor's Office, Ethnic Advisory Council, State House CN001, 125 W. State St., Trenton, NJ 08625 (609) 292-6000.

*CRAZYBULL, CHERYL
(college vice president)
Affiliation: Sinte Gleska College, P.O. Box 490, Rosebud, SD 57570-0490 (605) 747-2263.

CREAMER, MARY HELEN (Navajo)
(director-health center)
Affiliation: Director, Alamo Navajo Health Center, P.O. Box 907, Magdalena, NM 87825 (505) 854-2626.

CREE, MARY
(director-Indian centre)
Affiliation: Oka Cultural Centre, P .O. Box 640, Oka, Quebec, Canada J0N 1E0 (514) 479-8524.

CREE, ROBERT
(Indian band chief)
Affiliation: Fort McMurray Indian Band, Box 8217, Clearwater Station, Fort McMurray , Alberta, Canada T9H 4J1 (403) 334-2293.

*CREEL, MATTHEW (Natchez/Kusso-Edisto Tribe) 1939-
(contractor)
Born June 15, 1939, Ridgeville, S.C. *Home address*: 215 Indigo Rd., Ridgeville, SC 29472 (803) 871-6740. *Affiliation*: Chief, Four Holes Indian Organization, Ridgeville, SC.

CREELMAN, THOMAS, J., M.D.
(clinical director)
Affiliation: Warm Springs PHS Indian Health Center, P.O. Box 1209, W arm Springs, OR 97761 (503) 553-1 196.

*CRIDER, WHITE WOLF
(editor)
Affiliation: SECCI Newsletter, Southeastern Cherokee Confederacy , 318 Crestview Dr., Valdosta, GA 31602.

CRITTENDEN, DON (Oklahoma Cherokee) 1929-
(tribal council member)
Born July 8, 1929, Stilwell, Okla. *Education*: Northeastern State College. *Principal occupation*: Tribal council member . Address: RR 1, Box 260, Tahlequah, OK 74464 (918) 772-3238. *Affiliation*: Council member, Cherokee Nation. *Other professional post*: Supt. of schools (retired). *Military service*: U.S. Navy, 1948-50; U.S. Army, 1953-55. *Community activities*: Chair, County Supt. Assn. of OK. *Interests*: Ranching.

CROMARTY, DENNIS
(grand chief)
Affiliation: Nishnawbe Aski Nation, 14 College St., 6th Floor, Toronto, Ontario, Canada M5C 1K2 (416) 920-2376.

CROOKEDNECK, ERNEST
(Indian band chief)
Affiliation: Island Lake Indian Band, Box 460, Loon Lake, SK, Can. S0M 1L0 (306) 837-4845.

CROOKS, STANLEY (Mdewakanton Sioux)
(tribal chairperson)
Affiliation: Shakopee Sioux Community Council, 2330 Sioux Trail, NW, Prior Lake, MN 55372 (612) 445-8900.

*CROSIER, JEAN
(administrative librarian)
Affiliation: Phoenix Indian Medical Center Health Sciences Library, 4212 North 16th St., Phoenix, AZ 85016 (602) 263-1200.

*CROSS, TERRY L.
(executive director)
Affiliation : National Indian Child W elfare Association, 361 1 SW Hood St., Suite 201, Portland, OR 97201 (503) 222-4044.

CROSS, VIRGINIA (Muckleshoot)
(tribal council chairperson)
Affiliation : Muckleshoot Tribal Council, 39015 172nd St., SE, Auburn, WA 98002 (206) 939-3311.

*CROUTHAMEL, STEVEN J.
(professor)
Affiliation : Chairperson, American Indian Studies Program, Palomar Community College, 1 140 W. Mission Rd., San Marcos, CA 92069 (619) 744-1150.

CROW, ENNIS
(Indian band chief)
Affiliation : Fort Severn Indian Band, Fort Severn, Ontario, Canada P0V 1W0 (807) 478-2572.

CROW, MARGARET B.
(attorney)
Affiliation : California Indian Legal Services, 510 16th St., Suite 301, Oakland, CA 94610 (510) 835-0284.

*CROW, MARTHA
(president-Native American T elevision)
Education : National College (Rapid City , SD), AAS, 1980; University of Mary (Bismarck, ND), BA, 1981; Moorhead State University , BA (Speech Communications), 1985; St. Cloud State University, MS (Information Media), 1991. *Address* : P.O. Box 455, St. Cloud, MN 56302 (612) 252-4190. *Affiliations* : Director of Libraries & Media, Nebraska Indian Community College, Winnebago, NE, 1988-90; executive producer, "First Americans Update," Native American Television, St. Cloud, MN, 1990-; president, Native American Television (NATV), St. Cloud, MN, 1990-. At NATV, Ms. Crow coordinates production & broadcast with Twin Cities Public Television (KTCI) and with WHT -TV, a satellite television network system owned by the Choctaw Nation of Philadelphia, MS. *Other professional posts* : Grant Proposal Reader , Minnesota Dept. of Education, Indian Education Section, St. Paul, MN, 1992; professional video producer of various projects & locales. *Published works* : Editorial assistant, The American Indian & the Media (National Conference of Christians & Jews, 1991).

*CROWDER, JOHN EDWARD *(Brave Bear)*
(Oklahoma Cherokee) 1926-
(power plant general forman & supt.
Born August 20, 1926, Eufaula, Okla. *Education* : Alaska Pacific University, BA, 1961. *Principal occupation* : Power plant general foreman & supt. *Address* : Mile 13, South Big Lake Rd., P.O. Box 520348, Big Lake, AK 99652 (907) 892-8203. *Affiliation* : U.S. Dept. of Defense, Alaska locations (24 years). *Other professional post* : Chief engineer for Global Marine Drilling Co's. Drillship Glomar Pacific in Santa Barbara Channel in 1980's. *Military service* : U.S. Navy, 1944-46 (Motor Machinist Third Class - Commendation, Asiatic-Pacific & V ictory Medals). *Community activities* : President, Anderson, Alaska Advisory School Board, 1973-74; president, Anchorage Community College Student Body , 1957-58. *Membership* : Veterans of Foreign Wars. *Awards, honors* : Outstanding Award,

Dept. of Defense, Ft. Greely , AK, 1969; Commendation, U.S. Coast Guard for "Flying Enterprise" disaster in 1952. *Interests* : Built my own house to qualify for an Alaska Homesite in 1983.

*CROWE, ALVA
(association vice-president)
Affiliation : Chattanooga Intertribal Assn., Box 71585, Chattanooga, TN 37407 (615) 266-6551.

CROWFOOT, BERT (Blackfoot/Salteaux)
1953-
(publisher; management)
Born September 19, 1953, Gleichen, Alberta, Can. *Education* : Brigham Young University (3 years). *Principal occupation* : Publisher; management. *Home address* : 16912 - 92 St., Edmonton, Alberta T5Z 1X3 (403) 456-0731 (home) 455-2700 (of fice). *Affiliation* : CEO, Aboriginal Multi-Media Society of Alberta, Edmonton, Alberta, 1983-; publisher , Windspeaker (bi-weekly journal), AMMSA (current). *Community activities* : Coach - Alberta team for Canada Summer Games. *Memberships* : Native American Journalists Association; National Aboriginal Communications Society; Native, Inuit, Indian, Photographers Association. *Awards, honors* : Merit Award from Government of Canada for Community Contribution; Softball Alberta Minor Coach of the Year. *Interests* : Sports psychology, psychology, cultural exchange with republic of S. Korea. *Published works* : Powwow Trail (Bear Ghost Enterprises, 1981); Nation's Ensign, monthly (Society for the Preservation of Indian Identity , 1980-83); Windspeaker, bi-weekly & Sweetgrass, monthly (AMMSA).

CROWFOOT, STRATER
(Indian band chief)
Affiliation : Siksika Nation Band, Box 249, Gleichen, Alberta, Canada T0J 1N0 (403) 734-5100.

*CRUM, STEVEN JAMES (Shoshone) 1950-
(assistant professor of
Native American studies)
Born December 29, 1950, Phoenix, Ariz. *Education* : Arizona State University , BA, 1975; University of Arizona, MEd, 1977; University of Utah, PhD, 1983. *Principal occupation* : Assistant professor of Native American studies. *Address* : P.O. Box 4763, Davis, CA 95617 (916) 752-6488 (work). *Affiliation* : Center for Ethnic and Women's Studies, California State University, Chico (acting coordinator , 1984-85, coordinator, 1985-88, American Indian Studies; lecturer, 1985-85, assistant professor , Dept. of History); associate professor, Native American Studies Department, University of California, Davis, 1990-. *Memberships* : Western Historical Association; National Indian Education Association; California Indian Education Association; Organization of American Historians. *Awards, honors* : "Outstanding Young Men of America" Award, 1987; "Professional Promise" Award, California State University , Chico, 1988; Ford Foundation Postdoctoral Fellowship for Minorities, Native American Studies, University of California, Davis, 1988-89; Postgraduate Researcher/Visiting Scholar, University of California President's Fellowship Program, Native American Studies, University of California, Davis, 1989-90; Nick Yengich Editors' Choice Award, 1992, Utah State Historical Society , for best article in the "Utah Historical Quarterly ." *Published works* : Articles: "The Ruby Valley In-

dian Reservation of Northeastern Nevada: Six Miles Square," Nevada Historical Quarterly , 30(1), 1987; "The Skull V alley Band of the Goshute Tribe - Deeply Attached to their Native Homeland," Utah Historical Quarterly , 55(3), 1987; "The W estern Shoshone People and Their Attachment to the Land: A Twentieth Century Perspective," Nevada Public Affairs Review, 2:15-18, 1987; "Bizzel and Brandt: Pioneers in Indian Studies, 1929-1937," The Chronicles of Oklahoma, 66(2), 1988; "Henry Roe Cloud, a Winnebago Indian Reformer: His Quest for American Indian Higher Education," Kansas History, 11(3), 1988; "The Idea of an Indian College or University in Twentieth Century America," Tribal College: Journal of American Indian Higher Education, 1(1), 1989; "Crow Warrior: Robert Yellowtail," Tribal College, 1(4), 1990; "The White Pine W ar of 1875: A Case of White Hysteria," Utah Historical Quarterly ,53(3), 1991; "Colleges Before Columbus," Tribal College, 3(2), 1992; "Harold L. Ickes and Idea of a Chair in American Indian History ," The History Teacher, 25(1), 1991; "Native American Higher Education: The Twentieth Century ," & "The Western Shoshone of the Great Basin in the Twentieth Century ," both in the Encyclopedia of Native Americans in the 20th Century , 1994; The Ghost Dance," in Encyclopedia of the American West, 1994. *Books* : The Road on Which W e Came: A History of the The Western Shoshone (University of Utah Press, 1994); Native American Higher Education (University of New Mexico Press, 1995).

*CRUTCHER, WILLIAM (Shoshone)
(tribal chairperson)
Affiliation : Fort McDermitt Tribal Council, P.O. Box 457, McDermitt, NV 89421 (702) 532-8259.

*CRUTCHFIELD, MARIAN (Y urok)
(rancheria chairperson)
Affiliation : Trinidad Rancheria, P.O. Box 630, Trinidad, CA 95570 (707) 677-021 1.

CRUZ, VIOLA
(editor)
Affiliation : American Indian Culture & Research Journal, American Indian Studies Center , Room 3220 Campbell Hall, UCLA, 405 Hilgard Ave., Los Angeles, CA 90024 (213) 206-1433.

CTIBOR, LARRY
(Indian school principal)
Affiliation : Arlicaq School, Yupiit School District, P.O. Box 227, Akiak, AK 99552 (907) 765-7212.

CUKRO, GEORGE
(school director)
Affiliation : Black Mesa Community School, Box 215, Chinle, AZ 86503 (602) 674-3632.

*CULLEN, THERESA, M.D.
(clinical director)
Affiliation : Sells PHS Indian Hospital, P .O. Box 548, Sells, AZ 85634 (602) 383-7251.

CUMMINGS, DARLENE
(tribal chairperson)
Affiliation : Mooretown Rancheria Council, P .O. Box 1842, Oroville, CA 95965 (916) 533-3625.

CUMMINGS, VICKI
(museum director)
Affiliation : Museum of Indian Heritage, 500 W . Washington St., Indianapolis, Ind. 46204 (317) 293-4488.

*CUPP, LORI, MD (Navajo) 1959-
(surgeon)
Born in Crownpoint, NM. *Education*: Dartmouth College (majored in psychology , sociology and Native American studies), B.A., 1981; Stanford Medical School, M.D., 1990. *Address & Affiliation*: Gallup Indian Medical Center , P.O. Box 1337, Gallup, NM 87305. *Other professional posts*: Crownpoint PHS Indian Hospital, Crownpoint, NM; National Institutes of Health tas force on recruiting--and keeping--women as clinical research subjects. *Memberships*: Association of American Indian Physicians. *Interests*: Dr. Cupp is the first Navajo woman to become a surgeon.

*CURLEY, LARRY
(editor)
Affiliation: Elder Voices, National Indian Council on Aging, 6400 Uptown Blvd., NE #510-W , Albuquerque, NM 871 10 (505) 888-3302.

CURTIS, ROSALYN
(hospital director)
Affiliation: Tuba City PHS Indian Medical Center, Tuba City, AZ 86045 (602) 283-621 1.

*CUSSEN, JAMES
(IHS area director)
Affiliation: Shawnee Indian Health Center , 2001 S. Gordon Cooper Dr., Shawnee, OK 74801 (405) 275-4270.

*CUSTALOW, CHRISTINE *(Rippling Water)*
(Mattaponi)
(homemaker, artist)
Education: Mattaponi Indian School. *Address*: Route 2, Box 270, West Point, VA 23181 (804) 769-4711. *Interests*: "I am very proud to be able to bring back the lost art of my ancestors as I have been interested in crafts. I became interested in pottery in 1978 after a training program I was in with Eric Callahan, an archaeologist teaching the old ways of making pottery ." Her pottery has been displayed at various craft shows and is on permanent display at the River of High Banks Pottery Shop, Mattaponi Indian Reservation, King William, VA. *Honors, awards*: 3rd Place, Potomac Art League, 1981; 1st Place, Kilmarnock Arts & Crafts Show, 1983; Best in Show, Poquoson Art Show, 1984; Award of Excellence, Poquoson Seafood Festival, 1986.

*CUSTALOW, LIONEL (Mattaponi) 1966-
(cabinet maker)
Born December 17, 1966, Richmond, V a. *Education*: High school. *Principal occupation*: Cabinet maker. *Address*: Rt. 2 Box 233, West Point, VA 23181 (804) 769-0289. *Community activities*: Councilman, Mattaponi Tribe. *Interests*: "I am lead singer of Native American drum group, singing our song all through our Indian land.

CUSTALOW, WEBSTER (Mattaponi)
(tribal chief)
Affiliation: Mattaponi Tribe, Rte. 2, Box 255, West Point, VA 23181 (804) 769-2194.

CUTHAND, DOUG
(editor)
Affiliation: Saskatchewan Indian, Saskatchewan Indian Media Corporation, 2121 Airport Dr. #201A, Saskatoon, Saskatchewan, Canada S7L 6W5 (306) 665-2175.

CYPRESS, BILLY (Miccosukee)
(tribal chairperson)
Affiliation: Miccosukee Business Committee, P.O. Box 44021, Tamiami Station, Miami, FL 33144 (305) 223-8380.

CYR, LINDSAY
(Indian band chief)
Affiliation: Pasqua Indian Band, Box 968, Fort Qu'Appelle, Saskatchewan, Canada S0G 0C0 (306) 332-6202.

D

DACON, CHEBON (Creek-Choctaw) 1947-
(artist)
Born November 11, 1947, Oklahoma City , Okla. *Education*: University of Oklahoma, 1965-67. *Principal occupation*: Artist. *Address & Affiliation*: Collectors' Marketing, Ltd., P .O. Box 5524, Norman, OK 73070 (405) 366-841 1. His artwork includes detailed pencil drawings, watercolors and acrylics. Specializes in contemporary Western and Indian art. *Membership*: Indian Arts & Crafts Association. *Awards, honors*: High awards and recognition for ceremonial dancing, as well as his talent for art, brought an invitation from the U.S. Dept. of Commerce to act as Good Will Ambassador to Australia. His art has been shown in several European countries and takes its place in museums, galleries, and a number of private collections across the U.S.

*DAHL, DAN
(museum director)
Affiliation: Kauai Museum, P.O. Box 248, Lihue, HI 96766 (808) 245-6931.

DAILEY, CHARLES 1935-
(museum educator/director emeritus)
Born May 25, 1935, Golden, Colo. *Education*: University of Colorado, BF A-Fine Arts, 1961. *Principal occupation*: Native American museum director. *Home Address*: 64 Apache Ridge Rd., RR #3. Santa Fe, NM 87505 (505) 988-6281 ext. 114 (work). *Affiliations*: Curator of Exhibitions, Museum of New Mexico, Santa Fe, NM, 1962-71; Director, Institute of American Indian Arts (IAIA) Museum, Santa Fe, NM; Chairman, Museum Studies Program, Institute of American Indian Arts College, 1989-). *Military service*: U.S. Marine Corps, 1953-56 (Sergeant). *Community activities*: Judge for Indian arts & crafts competitions; National Ski Patrol Member , 1960-83; Professional Ski Patrolman, 1962-70. *Memberships*: American Association for State and Local History, 1956-; MPMA, 1960-80; American Association of Museums, 1960-; New Mexico Association of Museums, 1960-85; Native American Museum Association (charter member). *Awards, honors*: Various artistic painting awards - state & local competitions, 1960-1970; professor of the Year Award from Institute of American Indian Arts, Jr. College, 1974,'76,'82,'86, '90; kayaking - invited to participate in World Championships, Italy , 1961; various whitewater championships, 1958-62. *Interests*: Extensive travel; Native American museums survey, 1965-; research, 8,000 slides inventory; museum training interests, 1956-; various sports activities: kayaking, skiing, mountaineering, camping. *Biographical sources*: Artists in America, 1971, 1972; Santa Fe Artists, 1968; International Men of Achievement; Who's Who in the West; Contemporary Personage in the Arts. *Published works*: Creating a Crowd: Mannikens for Small Museums, El Pacio, MNM Press, 1969; Museum Training Workbooks - IAIA, DOI, BIA, Bureau of Publications, 1973; Art History; Vol. I/II, IAIA, DOI, BIA BOP, 1974; "How to Start an Indian Museum, BIA, IAIA, 1978; Major Influences, Contemporary Indian Art, IAIA, DOI, BOP, 1982; "Museum Theory" BIA, IAIA, 1984; "Museum Problem Solving" BIA, IAIA, 1990; "T .R.C. Cannon", "Bill Soza" IAIA; also, reviews & articles on various Indian artists, 1978-93.

DAKOTA, FREDERICK (Chippewa)
(tribal chairperson)
Affiliation: Keweenaw Bay Tribal Council, Rt. 1, Box 45, Baraga, MI 49908 (906) 353-6623.

*DALME, PAMELA L.
(school principal)
Affiliation: Tucker Elementary School, Rt. 4, Box 351, Philadelp[hia, MS 39350 (601) 656-8775.

DALRYMPLE, KATHRINE C.
(Western Cherokee) 1940-
(fashion designer)
Born January 30, 1940, Pryor , Oklahoma. *Education*: Oklahoma State University , BA, 1961. *Principal occupation*: Fashion designer (self-employed). *Home address*: Rt. 7, Box 328C, Claremore, OK 74017 (918) 341-5695. *Affiliations*: Associate Home Extension agent for the North Dakota State Extension Service and Standing Rock Sioux Tribe, and taught extension courses at graduate level for University of North Dakota, Grand Forks, 1961-73; selected representative art objects from Native American artisans from all sections of the U.S., 1961-73; co-owner, president, Friendship House, Inc. (gift shop specializing in Native American and American-made crafts), 1975-77; design clothing for specialty shops, catered Native American food, 1977-78; part-time volunteer coordinator , fashion consultant to executive director , American Indian Heritage Foundation, 1978-80; owner , American Naturals (design men and women's clothing, jewelry, and accessories based on traditional and contemporary Native American fashions. *Other professional posts*: Ran own catering and fashion design services, Navajo Reservation, 1961-73; coordinated exhibits featuring her own fashions and jewelry , 1975-77, Arlington, Va. *Community activities*: Taught crafts classes at various schools and youth clubs in the Washington D.C. area, as well as at the Smithsonian Institution, the Capitol Hill Club, and at a number of Embassies. *Memberships*: American Indian Society of Washington, DC.; Pocahontas Club (vice-president). *Awards, honors*: Epsilon Sigma Alpha's Outstanding Woman of the Year for Arizona in 1971; her fashions have received three First Prizes at the Gaithersburg, Maryland Exposition, 1973-78; her fashions have been shown at the Congressional Club, Capitol Hill Club, and the International Club of Washington, DC; her fashions have recently been worn at the Cherry Blossom Parade, Presidential Inaugural Ball and Parade for Ronald Reagan, several White House teas, and Oklahoma Society Gala; In March, 1982, 31 of Mrs. Dalrymple's fashions were worn at the John F. Kennedy Center for the Performing Arts during the Night of the First Americans, an event held in celebration of the contributions of the American Indian people; special exhibition, organized by the Indian Arts & Crafts Board's Southern Plains Indian Museum and Crafts

Center, the first comprehensive showing of Mrs. Dalrymple's fashions to be presented in the State of Oklahoma; she made the dress worn by the 1983 American Indian Society Princess; in 1976 & 1983, Kathy's work was featured in the American Indian Society Cookbook; Who's Who in American Colleges (dean's list) 1991. *Interests*: Mrs. Dalrymple writes, "I feel so fortunate to have grown up among the many Native American cultures in Oklahoma, and especially to have known not only my grandparents, but four of my great grandparents and many of their friends as well. Seeing them create, from necessity, beautiful and useful articles for everyday use from whatever was available was the origin of my interest in the arts of the American Indian. As we have lived and worked in many areas of this great land, I've marveled at the resourcefulness and creativity of the people, and of the women, in particular. No matter how busy and difficult their lives have been, they have always managed to provide many and varied forms of useful, beautiful articles to enrich the lives of the people around them. Trading of ideas, supplies, and patterns as tribes came into contact with each other is greatly apparent. How each group adapted the trade goods brought by the Europeans is a unique and fascinating study of American history. I especially enjoy creating traditional clothing for powwow wear." *Works in Progress*: Currently writing Native American children's books and producing authentic traditional dolls as well as continuing art and writing studies.

DALTON, MARGARET (Miwok)
(rancheria chairperson)
Affiliation: Jackson Rancheria, P.O. Box 429, Jackson, CA 95642 (209) 223-1935.

*DAN, ROY
(BIA acting supt.)
Affiliation: Fort Defiance Agency, BIA, P.O. Box 619, Fort Defiance, AZ 86504 (602) 729-7221.

DANAY, RICHARD GLAZER
(Mohawk of Kahnawake, Canada) 1942-
(professor; artist)
Born August 12, 1942, Coney Island, N.Y. *Education*: California State University, Chico, MA, 1972; University of California, Davis, MFA, 1978. *Principal occupation*: Professor; artist. *Home address*: 927 Alta Loma Dr., Corona, CA 91720 (714) 735-4347. *Affiliation*: The Rupert Costo Chair in American Indian History, The University of California, Riverside, 1991-93. *Other professional post*: Professor, Dept. of Art, California State University, Long Beach, 1985-. *Military service*: U.S. Army, Specialist IV, 1961-62; U.S. Army Reserve, 1962-65. *Community activities*: Commissioner, Indian Arts & Crafts Board, U.S. Dept. of the Interior, 1989-. *Memberships*: L'Association Canadienne Des Etudes D'Art Autochtone, 1986-; Native American Art Studies Association, 1983-90; California Indian Education Association, 1970-91. *Awards, honors*: Distinguished Faculty Scholar, California State University, Long Beach, 1990/91. *Interests*: Animal rights activist; exhibited art in over 150 group and one man shows from 1970 to 1992. *Art Exhibit/Show Catalogs*: "Shared Vision;" Native American Painters and Sculptors in the 20th Century (The Heard Museum, 1991); "Collecting the Twentieth Century," (British Museum, London, 1991-92); "The Human Figure in American Indian Art," (The Institute of American Indian Arts Museum, 1991).

DANIELS, DAVID, M.D.
(clinical director)
Affiliation: Keams Canyon PHS Indian Hospital, P.O. Box 98, Keams Canyon, AZ 86034 (602) 738-2211.

DANIELS, DENNIS
(director-Indian centre)
Affiliation: Manitoba Indian Cultural Education Centre, 119 Sutherland Ave., Winnipeg, Canada R2W 3C9 (204) 942-0228.

DANIELS, NOEL
(Indian band chief)
Affiliation: Mistawasis Indian Band, Box 250, Leask, Saskatchewan, Canada S0J 1M0 (306) 466-4800.

DANIELS, ROBERT
(Indian band chief)
Affiliation: Chemainus Indian Band, RR 1, Ladysmith, British Columbia, Canada V0R 2E0 (604) 245-7155.

DANIELS, WESLEY
(Indian band chief)
Affiliation: Sturgeon Lake Indian Band, Box 757, Valleyview, Alberta, Canada T0H 3N0 (403) 764-1872.

*DANKERT, DIANE C.
(editor)
Affiliation: Arizona Tribal Director, Arizona Commission on Indian Affairs, 1645 W. Jefferson, Phoenix, AZ 85007 (602) 255-3123.

*DANKERT, MARLA
(museum curator)
Affiliation: Eiteljorg Museum of American Indians & Western Art, 500 W. Washington St., Indianapolis, IN 46204 (317) 636-9378.

DARDEN, RALPH (Chitimacha)
(tribal chairperson)
Affiliation: Chitimacha Tribal Council, P.O. Box 661, Charenton, LA 70523 (318) 923-7215.

DASHENO, WALTER (Pueblo)
(pueblo governor)
Affiliation: Pueblo of Santa Clara, P.O. Box 580, Espanola, NM 87532 (505) 753-7326.

DAUENHAUER, NORA MARKS
(Keixwnei) (Tlingit) 1927-
(researcher-language & culture)
Born May 8, 1927, Juneau, AK. *Education*: Alaska Methodist University, Anchorage, BA, 1976. *Principal occupation*: Researcher - language & culture. *Home address*: 3740 N. Douglas Hwy., Juneau, AK 99801 (807) 463-4844 (work). *Affiliations*: Tlingit language researcher, Alaska Native Language Center, University of Alaska-Fairbanks, 1972-73; cultural coordinator, Cook Inlet Native Association, Anchorage, AK, 1978-80; translator and principal investigator, Tlingit Text Translation Project, 1980-81; assistant professor, Alaska Native Studies, University of Alaska, Juneau, 1981-82; principal researcher, Language and Cultural Studies, Sealaska Heritage Foundation, 9085 Glacier Hwy., Juneau, AK, 1983-. *Community activities*: Member and chair, Russian Orthodox Church and Alaska Native Sisterhood; president, Shax'saanikeek'Weavers. *Awards, honors*: Commissioner, Alaska Historical Commission, 1978-81; First Prize in Short Story and Poetry Categories, Southeast Alaska Native Arts Fes-

tival, Sitka, AK, 1979; 1980 "Humanist of the Year" by Alaska Humanities Forum (joint award with Richard Dauenhauer); member, Alaska Humanities Forum Committee, 1981-87; 1989 "Governor's Award for the Arts", presented by Alaska Governor Steve Cowper; 1991 American Book Award for Haa Tuwunaagu Yis, for Healing our Spirit: Tlingit Oratory. *Interests*: Tlingit language and literature, poetry, fiction, drama. *Biographical sources*: Directory of American Indian/Alaska Women, 1979. *Published works*: Co-editor, "Because We Cherish Your...": Sealaska Elders Speak to the Future (Sealaska Foundation, 1981); short story anthologized in Earth Power Coming: Short Fiction in Native American Literature, edited by Simon Ortiz (Navajo Community College Press, 1983); Tlingit Spelling Book (revised third edition), with Richard Dauenhauer (Sealaska Heritage Foundation, 1984); poetry anthologized in That's What She Said: Contemporary Poetry & Fiction by Native American Women, edited by Rayna Green (Indiana University Press, 1984); Alaska Native Writers, Storytellers and Orators (special issue of Alaska Quarterly Review, University of Alaska, Anchorage, 1986); Haa Shuka, Our Ancestors: co-editor, Tlingit Oral Narratives (University of Washington Press, 1987); poetry anthologized in Harper's Anthology of 20th Century Native American Poetry, edited by Duane Nitatum (Harper & Row, San Francisco, 1988); The Droning Shaman (The Black Current Press, Haines, AK, 1988); Editor, with Richard Dauenhauer, Haa Tuwunaagu Yis, for Healing our Spirit: Tlingit Oratory (University of Washington Press, 1990; Beginning Tlingit, 3rd Revused Edition, with Richard Dauenhauer (Alaska Native Language Center, Alaska Native Language Board, 1991); and numerous other writings.

DAUENHAUER, RICHARD 1942-
(writer)
Born April 10, 1942, Syracuse, N.Y. *Education*: Syracuse University, BA, 1964; University of Texas, Austin, MA, 1966; University of Wisconsin, Madison, PhD (Comparative Literature), 1975. *Principal occupation*: Writer. *Home address*: 3740 N. Douglas Hwy., Juneau, AK 99801 (907) 586-4708. *Affiliations*: Assistant professor, Alaska Methodist University, Anchorage,1969-75; education specialist, Alaska Native Education Board, Anchorage, 1974-76; staff associate, Alaska Native Foundation, Anchorage, 1976-78; associate professor, Alaska Pacific University, Anchorage, 1979-83; program director, Sealaska Heritage Foundation, Juneau, 1983-. *Community activities*: Language reader, parish council officer, St. Nicholas Orthodox Church. *Memberships*: PEN; Poets & Writers. *Awards, honors*: Woodrow Wilson Fellowship, 1964; Fulbright Fellowship, 1966; Named "Humanist of the Year" by Alaska Humanities Forum, 1980 (joint award with Nora Marks Dauenhauer); Poet Laureate of Alaska, 1981-88; 1989 Governor's Award for the Arts, presented by Steve Cowper, Governor of Alaska; 1991 American Book Award for Haa Tuwunaagu Yis, for Healing our Spirit: Tlingit Oratory. *Interests*: Comparative literature, oral literature, Alaska Native literature, languages and linguistics, poetry. *Published works*: Beginning Tlingit, with Nora Marks Dauenhaurer (Alaska Native Language Center, 1976); co-editor, Snow in May: An Anthology of Finnish Writing, 1945-72 (Associated University Presses, Cranbury, NJ, 1978); Glacier Bay Concerto (Poetry) (Alaska

Pacific University Press, Anchorage, 1980); co-editor, "Because We Cherish You...": Sealaska Elders Speak to the Future (Sealaska Heritage Foundation, 1981; The Shroud of Shaawat Seek' (Poetry) (Orca Press, Sitka, AK, 1983); co-editor, Tlingit Spelling Book (Third revised Edition-Sealaska, 1984); co-editor, Alaska Native Writers, Storytellers and Orators (special issue of Alaska Quarterly Review, 1986); Frames of Reference (Poetry) (The Black Current Press, Haines, AK, 1987); co-editor, Haa Shuka, Our Ancestors: Tlingit Oral Narratives (University of Washington Press, 1987); Editor, with Richard Dauenhauer, Haa Tuwunaagu Yis, for Healing our Spirit: Tlingit Oratory (University of Washington Press, 1990; Beginning Tlingit, 3rd Revused Edition, with Nora Marks Dauenhauer (Alaska Native Language Center, Alaska Native Language Board, 1991); and numerous other writings.

DAUGHERTY, JOHN, Jr. (Shawnee-Delaware) 1948-
(health systems administrator)
Born August 9, 1948, Claremore, Okla. *Education*: Northeastern State University, BA, BS, 1976; University of Minnesota, 1984- (working toward advanced certificate in health administration). *Principal occupation*: Health systems administrator. *Address*: Claremore PHS Indian Hospital, W. Will Rogers & Moore, Claremore, OK 74017 (918) 341-8430. *Affiliation*: Executive director, Native American Coalition of Tulsa, 1978-79; administrator, USPHS Miami Indian Health Center, Miami, OK, 1979-90; Claremore PHS Indian Hospital, Claremore, OK, 1991-. *Military service*: U.S. Air Force, 1969-72 (in Madrid, Spain) (Commendation Medal for Meritorious Service). *Community activities*: Member, Rotary International; chairman, Title IV, Indian Education Parent Committee; officer, Native American Student Association at Northeast Oklahoma A&M Junior College and Northeastern Oklahoma State University, 1973-76. *Awards, honors*: Who's Who Among Students in American Universities and Colleges, 1976-77; golf team; deans honor roll, 1976, NEOSU, Tahlequah; chosen by University of Minnesota Independent Study Program to give presentation on Indian Health in U.S. during International Health Night, July 17, 1985. *Interests*: "My educational and vocational interest is in health care administration. My goals are to better myself in these areas. Indian cultures and the presentation of my tribal ceremonies are of great concern to me. Participating in tribal activities of other tribes, as well as my tribe and encouraging others to participate are very important to me."

DAUGHTERS, DOUGLAS L. (Sioux)
(school principal)
Affiliation: Fort Thompson Elementary School, P.O. Box 139, Fort Thompson, SD 57339 (605) 245-2372.

*DAVID, TERESA
(publisher)
Affiliation: Akwesasne Notes, Mohawk Nation, P.O. Box 196, Rooseveltown, NY 13683 (518) 358-9531.

DAVIS, DON J.
(BIA area health director)
Affiliation: Phoenix Area Indian Health Service, 3738 N. 16th St., Suite A, Phoenix, AZ 85016 (602) 640-2052.

DAVIS, GARY
(director-Indian health center)
Affiliation: Pawnee PHS Indian Health Center, Rural Route 2, Box 1, Pawnee, OK 74058 (918) 762-2517.

DAVIS, JAMES L.
(BIA agency supt. for education)
Affiliation: Turtle Mountain Agency, Bureau of Indian Affairs, P.O. Box 30, Belcourt, ND 58316 (701) 477-6471 ext. 211.

DAVIS, KENNETH W.
(BIA agency supt.)
Affiliation: Northern Cheyenne Agency, Bureau of Indian Affairs, P.O. Box 40, Lame Deer, MT 59043 (406) 477-8242.

DAVIS, LARRY
(ranger-in-charge-historical monument)
Affiliation: Anasazi Indian Village, State Historical Monument, P.O. Box 1329, Boulder, UT 84716 (801) 335-7308.

*DAVIS, MARVIN
(association president)
Affiliation: Inter-Tribal Indians of New Jersey, 21 Village Rd., Morganville, NJ 07751 (908) 591-8335.

DAVIS, MARY B. 1942-
(librarian)
Born December 4, 1942, Huntington, WV. *Education*: Beloit College, 1960-62; University of Illinois, Champaign, AB, 1964; University of Michigan, MA, 1969. Principal occupation: Librarian. *Address & Affiliation*: Huntington Free Library and Reading Room (formerly-Museum of the American Indian Library), 9 Westchester Square, Bronx, NY 10461 (212) 829-7770., 1977-. *Other professional posts*: Grant writer and administrator; book reviewer. *Community activities*: Peace Corps Volunteer, 1964-66; 1987 panelist, "American Indians, Library Collections & Resources in the Metro Region." *Memberships*: National Museum of the American Indian (member, Curatorial Committee; former head of Education Committee); Art Libraries Society of North America (ARLIS); American Library Association; Special Libraries Association; Bronx Library Emergency Consortium. *Selected presentations*: ARLIS programs: panelist, "Documenting Native American Culture: Past & present Resources," 1989); panelist, "Native American Documentation: An Overview," 1992; NYLA program: panelist, Native American Voices: Are They In Your Library?," 1992. *Published works*: Books About Native Americans of the New York Metropolitan Area (The Research Libraries Select Bibliography, No. 1. New York Public Library, 1987); Field Notes of Clarence B. Moore's Southeastern Archaeological Expeditions, 1891-1918 (Huntington Free Library, 1987); Papers of the Hemenway Southwestern Archaeological Expedition in the Huntington Free Library, (Huntington Free Library, 1987); Stockbridge Indian Papers in the Huntington Free Library (Huntington Free Library, 1987); "Black Hawk, 1767-1838" in Research Guide to American Historical Biography, vol. 4 (Beacham Publishing, 1990); "Interpreting Native American Art and Culture: Transformations and Changes" in Art Documentation, Winter 1990; "Indians of North America" in Magazines for Libraries, 7th ed. edited by Bill Katz (R.R. Bowker, 1992); "Through Native Eyes: American Indians Write About Their Art," in Art Librar-

ies Journal, vol. 17, no. 4, Jan. 1993; editor, Native America in the 20th-Century: An Encyclopedia (Garland Publishing, 1994); book reviews.

DAVIS, MONA (Chuckchansi)
(tribal vice-chairperson)
Affiliation: Picayune Rancheria, P.O. Box 1480, Coarsegold, CA 93614 (209) 683-6633.

DAVIS, OLA CASSADORE (San Carlos Apache)
(organization chairperson)
Affiliation: Apache Survival Coalition, P.O. Box 1237, San Carlos, AZ 85550 (602) 475-2543.

*DAVIS, ROBERT, Jr. (Marietta Nooksack)
(tribal chairperson)
Affiliation: Marietta Band of Nooksack Indians, 1827 Marine Dr., Bellingham, WA 98226.

DAVIS, ROBERT C. 1922-
(film producer, lecturer)
Born May 7, 1922, Kansas City, Mo. *Education*: High school. *Principal occupation*: Film producer, lecturer. *Home address*: P.O. Box 12, Cary, IL 60013. *Affiliations*: Self-employed. Military service: U.S. Signal Corps, 1942-45. *Memberships*: Film Lecturer's Association, 1970-. *Awards, honors*: American Film Festival Awards for Arizona Revealed; Columbus Film Festival Awards for seven other films. *Films produced*: Land of the Crimsoned Cliffs, 1955; Arizona Utopia, 1961; Arizona Revealed, 1964; Arizona Adventure, 1975; many 35mm and 2 x 2 color transparencies of Navajo, Pima and Hopi Indians.

DAVIS, ROBERT E.
(national secretary-organization)
Affiliation: Great Council of U.S. Improved Order of Red Men, P.O. Box 683, Waco, TX 76703 (817) 756-1221.

*DAVIS, WALTER R., II
(museum director)
Affiliation: Panhandle-Plains Historical Museum, WTAMU Box 967, Canyon, TX 79016 (806) 656-2244.

DAWES, CHARLES (Ottawa) 1923-
(manufacturing management; tribal chief)
Born February 7, 1923, Peoria, Okla. *Education*: Missouri Southern University, AA, 1950; University of Arkansas, BS, 1952. *Principal occupation*: Manufacturing management; tribal chief. *Address*: P.O. Box 32, Quapaw, OK 74363 (918) 674-2553. *Affiliations*: Manufacturing engineer, Vickers, Inc., Joplin, MO, 1952-56; plant manager, president, Ingersoll-Rand Co., Ft. Smith, AR; chief, Ottawa Busines Council, P.O. Box 110, Miami, OK 74355 (918) 540-1536. *Military service*: Army Air Corp, 1943-46 (S/Sergeant); Army Infantry School, 1945 (2nd Lt.). *Community activities*: Fort Smith Manufacturing Executives Association (president); United Fund (board member); Abilities Unlimited Sheltered Workshop; St. Edwards Mercy Hospital; Intertribal Council; Claremore Indian Hospital.

DAWSON, KAREN
(Indian school principal)
Affiliation: Tohono O'Odham High School, P.O. Box 513, Sells, AZ 85634 (602) 362-2400.

*DAY, JOSEPH
(executive director)
Affiliation: Minnesota Indian Affairs Council, 1819 Bemidji Ave., Bemidji, MN 56601 (218) 755-3825.

DAYBUTCH, DOUGLAS
(Indian band chief)
Affiliation: Mississauga Indian Band, Box 1299, Blind River, Ontario, Canada P0R 1B0 (705) 356-1621.

DAYLEY, JON P. 1944-
(professor of linguistics)
Born October 8, 1944, Salt Lake City , Utah. *Education*: Idaho State University , BA, 1968, MA, 1970; University of California, Berkeley , MA, 1973, PhD, 1981. *Principal occupation*: Professor of linguistics. *Home address*: 5953 Eastwood Place, Boise, ID 83712 (208) 385-1714 (work). *Affiliations*: Visiting lecturer in linguistics, University of California, Berkeley , 1982; professor of linguistics, Boise State University , Boise, ID, 1982-. *Other professional posts*: Linguista - Projecto Linguistico Francisco Marroquin, Guatemala, 1973-78; writer , researcher, Experiment in International Living, Brattleboro, Vt., 1978-79. *Memberships*: Linguistic Society of America; Society of the Study of Indigenous Languages of America; Berkeley Linguistics Society. *Interests*: American Indian languages and cultures: Mayan language--Tzutujil Maya, Uto-Aztecon languages--Shoshone & Panamint; Creole languages; general linguistics. *Published works*: Belizean Creole Handbook, V ols. I-IV (Experiment in International Living, U.S. Peace Corps, 1979); Tzutujil Grammar (University of California Press, 1985); Tumpisa (Panamint) Shoshone Grammar & Dictionary (2 separate books) (University of California Press, 1989); W estern Shoshoni Grammar (Boise State University , 1993); Dictionario Tz'utujil de San Juan la Laguna (Projecto Linguistico Francisco Marroquin, Guatemala, 1994); and many articles on Mayan languages, Shoshone and general linguistics.

*DAYO, DIXIE
(AK village council president)
Affiliation: Manley Hot Springs V illage, Manley Hot Springs, AK 99756 (907) 672-3331.

*DEACON, HENRY
(AK village president)
Affiliation: Organized V illage of Grayling (aka Holikachu) Council, Grayling, AK 99590 (907) 967-8929.

DEAN-JOHN, HAZEL V. *(Gah-nen'-daw-wag'k-konh)* (Seneca) 1929-
(linguist; lecturer/instructor)
Born November 16, 1929, Allegany Indian Reservation, Salamanca, N.Y . *Education*: Harvard University Graduate School of Education, EdM, CAS/Admin. Planning Social Policy), 1976-78; University of Arizona, MA & PhD (Linguistics), 1978-83. *Principal occupation*: Iroquoian linguist; lecturer/instructor of Seneca language, culture, tradition; researcher; administrator; Seneca faithkeeper . *Home address*: Allegany Indian Reservation, 44 Seneca St., #43, Salamanca, NY 14779 (716) 945-4518. *Other professional post*: Appointed to the International Board of Advisors, World Peace University, Eugene, OR, Sept. 1992. *Accomplishments*: Established the first Commissioner's Advisory Committee on Native American Indian Educa-

tion, New York State Education Dept., Albany, NY, 1987. *Awards, honors*: Selected as Faith Keeper from the W olf Clan, Allegany Seneca Longhouse, Steamburg, NY , 1965; Indian of the Month, United Southeastern Tribes, Nashville, TN, 1974; First Native American Indian member of the Subcommittee on Admissions, Harvard University Graduate School of Education, 1976-77; First Native American Indian Oral Traditionalist Faith Keeper to present paper and address international phonologists, Fifth International Phonology Meeting, Eisenstadt, Austria, 1984; Nominated for Who's Who in American Colleges and Universities, by Dean of American Indian Students, University of Arizona, 1985; Thanksgiving Day Proclamation by U.S. President Ronald Reagan incorporated Seneca Tradition from my work with National Thanks-Giving Commission, Dallas, TX, 1985; First Native American Indian to be appointed as National Trustee, Thanks-Giving Square Commission, Dallas, TX, 1985; Represented New York State Governor in presenting the first New York State entry in the National Library of American Prayer & Thanksgiving, Thanks-Giving Square, Dallas, TX, 1985; One of five Native American Indian women honored by the National Bahai' Committee of W omen for their contributions and work on behalf of Native American Indians, Canadaigua, NY , 1989; Honoree, New York State Education Dept., for valuable contributions to preserve and share the Native American Indian cultural heritage for future generations of children and the State of New York, Albany, NY, 1990. *Interests*: "Teaching Seneca language, culture, traditions, linguistics; researching, translating, analyzing untranslated Iroquoian language/history texts early 1700-1800s; beadwork, quilting, sewing traditional native dresses; traditional Iroquoian songs/dances; traveling and meeting people of all races and sharing cultures/spiritual teachings; enjoy being parent/grandmother and Clan Mother of the W olf Clan." *Biographical sources*: Boston Indian Council Newsletter , 1983; Salamanca Press, Salamanca, NY, 1983; "Indian W omen," Adult Education Reader , Boston Indian Council, 1985; Indian Times, Rooseveltown, NY , 1987; "Iroquois: Keepers of the Fire," National Geographic, Vol. 172, No. 3, Sept. 1987. *Published works*: Editor, A Collection of Stories W ritten by Seneca Language Students (Seneca Nation, 1975); contributor & co-author , Iroquois Recipes (Seneca Nation, 1975); Seneca Phonetics: An Articulatory and Acoustic Investigation - unpublished dissertation (University of Arizona, 1983); The Articulatory Base of Seneca (Proceedings of the Fifth International Phonology Meeting, with others, 1984); The Loss of Language (Boston Indian Council, 1985); coordinated, developed, & edited the first native-written, native language syllabus, "Ogwehowe:ka', Native Languages for Communication" (New York State Dept. of Education, 1986-89; coordinated the development of the first native-written social studies guide, "Haudenosaunee: Past, Present and Future" (New York State Dept. of Education, 1987).

DeASIS, PATRICIA A.
(IHS director of communications)
Affiliation: Indian Health Service, 5600 Fishers Lane, Room 6-35, Rockville, MD 20857 (301) 443-3593.

DeBOER, ROY J. (Lummi) 1936-
(school principal)
Born July 23, 1936, Bellingham, W ash. *Education*: Olympic Junior College, AA, 1960; W estern Washington State University , BA, 1962; University of Puget Sound, Tacoma, Wash., MEd, 1981. *Principal occupation*: School principal. *Home address*: 3528 S.E. Pine Tree Dr., Port Orchard, WA 98366. *Affiliations*: Director of Indian Education, South Kitsap School District, Port Orchard, W A, 1973-80; principal, W olfe Elementary School, Kingston, W A, 1981-. *Other professional posts*: Seven years on Washington State Advisory Committee, Indian Education to Washington State Supervisor of Schools. *Military service*: U.S. Air Force, 1954-58 (A 1/C). *Community activities*: Pacific Lutheran Theological Seminary (board of directors); Division of Service and Mission in America, American Lutheran Church (board of directors); Chamber of Commerce, Kingston, W ash.; Sons of Norway, Poulsbo, WA. *Memberships*: National Education Association; Washington Education Association; ASCD; ESPA. *Awards, honors*: Outstanding Secondary Teacher of America, 1973; Quill and Scroll Adult Leadership Award, 1969. *Interests*: Reading, travel, photography; singing with Twana Dancers, Skokomish traditional dance group.

DEER, ADA E. (Menominee) 1935-
(ass't secretary-BIA; social worker)
Born August 7, 1935, Keshena, W is. *Education*: University of Wisconsin, Madison, BA, 1957; Columbia University, School of Social W ork, MSW, 1961. *Principal occupation*: BIA, Assistant Secretary; social worker . *Address*: Bureau of Indian Affairs, MS-4140-MIB, 1849 C St., NW , Washington, DC 20240 (202) 208-7163. *Affiliations*: BIA, Washington, DC, 1993-; lecturer , School of Social W ork & Native American Studies Program, University of Wisconsin, 1977-93. *Other professional posts*: Chairperson, Menominee Restoration Committee, 1973-76; vice president & Washington lobbyist, National Committee to Save the Menominee People and Forest, Inc., 1972-73; chairperson, Menominee Common Stock & Voting Trust, 1971-73. *Community activities*: American Indian Policy Review Commission (member, 1975-77). *Memberships*: National Association of Social W orkers; National Organization of W omen; Common Cause; Girl Scouts of America; Democratic Party of W isconsin; National Congress of American Indians. *Awards, honors*: Doctor of Humane Letters, University of Wisconsin, 1974; Doctor of Public Service, Northland College, Ashland, WI, 1974; White Buffalo Council Achievement Award, Denver, CO, 1974; Pollitzer Award, Ethical Cultural Society, N.Y., 1975; Fellow , Harvard Institute of Politics, 1977. *Interests*: Social work; community organization and social action; minority rights. *Biographical sources*: I Am the Fire of Time, Jane B. Katz, editor (E.P . Dutton, 1977); Ms Magazine, April, 1973; Indians of Today, 4th Edition; The Circle, Dec. 1977.

DEER SMITH, MARY HELEN
(executive director)
Affiliation: Oklahoma City Indian Clinic, 1214 N. Hudson, Oklahoma City , OK 73101 (405) 232-1526. *Past professional post*: Dallas Inter-T ribal Center, Dallas, TX.

DEERHOSE, KITTY BELLE
(museum curator)
Affiliation: Little Bighorn Battlefield National

Monument, P.O. Box 39, Crow Agency, MT 59022 (406) 638-2621.

DEETZ, JAMES L.
(museum curator)
Affiliation : Robert H. Lowie Museum of Anthropology, 103 Kroeber Hall, University of California, Berkeley, CA 94720 (510) 642-3681.

DeGARMO, RALPH (Paiute)
(tribal chairperson)
Affiliation : Fort Bidwell Community Council, Box 127, Fort Bidwell, CA 96112 (916) 279-6310.

DeGROAT, ELLOUISE (Navajo) 1939-
(BIA tribal affairs officer)
Born May 12, 1939, Tuba City, Ariz. *Education*: Arizona State University, BS, 1962, MSW, 1966. *Principal occupation* : BIA tribal affairs officer. *Home address* : P.O. Box 526, Fort Defiance (Navajo Nation), AZ 86504. *Affiliation* : Tribal Affairs Officer, Navajo Area Office, BIA, P.O. Box G, Hwy. 264, Window Rock, AZ 86515, 1976-. *Other professional posts* : Consultant, American Child Psychiatry (Committee on Indian Affairs) and the Indian Task Force on Mental Health. *Community activities* : St. Michaels Special Education Association (member); instrumental in staging the First Annual Navajo Health Symposium; involvement with education of Indian children and special concern for the handicapped. Memberships: American Indian Health Association; National Association of Social Workers; National Conference of Social Workers (national board member, 1972-74). *Awards, honors* : Distinguished Service Award, The Navajo Tribe, 2nd Annual Navajo Health Symposium. *Interests* : Tribal government; national legislation for Indian tribes; advocate for Indian causes, especially health; American Indian woman; served on the Policy Committee on the Indian Policy Statement on national health insurance. *Published work*: Navajo Medicine Man (Psychiatric Annuals, 1974).

DeHAAS, JAMES
(BIA agency supt.)
Affiliation : Anadarko Agency, BIA, P.O Box 309, Anadarko, OK 73005 (405) 247-6673. *Past professional post*: Supt., Shawnee Agency, BIA, Shawnee, OK.

DeHOSE, JUDY
(Indian school chairperson)
Affiliations : Cibecue Community School, P.O. Box 68, Cibecue, AZ 85911 (602) 332-2444.

*DEKINGER, BILL
(school principal)
Affiliation : Mt. Edgecumbe High School, 1332 Seward, Sitka, AK 99835 (907) 966-2201.

De La CRUZ, DOROTHY L. (Quinault)
(health center director)
Affiliation : Taholah PHS Indian Health Center, Box 219, Taholah, WA 98587 (206) 276-4405.

De La CRUZ, JOSEPH (Quinault)
(former tribal chairperson)
Address & Affiliation : Quinault Business Committee (chairperson, 1970-94), P.O. Box 189, Taholah, WA 98587 (206) 276-821 1.

*DE LOS ANGELES, ANDY (Snoqualmie)
(tribal chairperson)
Affiliation : Snoqualmie Tribal Council, P.O. Box 280, Carnation, WA 08014 (206) 333-6551.

*DEIGH, RICHARD (Eskimo)
(AK village council president)
Affiliation : Egegik Village Council, P.O. Box 29, Egegik, AK 99579 (907) 233-221 1.

*DEL ROSA, PAUL (Pit River)
(tribal council chairperson)
Affiliation : Alturas Rancheria, P.O. Box 1035, Alturas, CA 96101.

*DELGADO, MICHELLE (Cahuilla)
(tribal council chairperson)
Affiliation : Cahuilla Band of Mission Indians, P.O. Box 391760, Anza, CA 92539 (714) 763-5549.

DELORIA, PHILIP S.
(director-Indian law center)
Affiliation : Executive director, American Indian Law Center, University of New Mexico, School of Law, P.O. Box 4456, Station A, 1117 Stanford, NE, Albuquerque, NM 87196 (505) 277-5462.

DELORIA, VINE, Jr. (Standing Rock Sioux) 1933-
(writer, professor)
Born March 26, 1933, Martin, S.D. *Education* : Iowa State University, BS, 1958; Lutheran School of Theology, M. Sac. Theo., 1963; University of Colorado, School of Law, JD, 1970. Principal occupation: Writer, professor. *Address*: Dept. of Political Science, University of Arizona, Tucson, AZ 85721 *Affiliations* : Welder, McLaughlin Body Company, Moline, IL, 1959-63; staff associate, United Scholarship Service, Denver, 1963-64; executive director, National Congress of American Indians, Washington, DC, 1964-67; consultant on programs, National Congress of American Indians, FUND, Denver, CO, 1968; lecturer, College of Ethnic Studies, Western Washington State College, Bellingham, 1970-72; lecturer, American Indian Cultural and Research Center, UCLA, 1972-73; executive director, Southwest Intergroup Council, Denver, 1972; special counsel, Native American Rights Fund, Boulder, CO, summer-1972; script writer (Indian series), KRMA-TV, Denver, 1972-1973; American Indian Resource Associates, Oglala, SD, 1973-1974; American Indian Resource Consultants, Denver, 1974-1975. visiting lecturer, Pacific School of Religion, Berkeley, CA, summer, 1975; visiting lecturer, New School of Religion, Pontiac, MI, summer, 1976; visiting lecturer, Colorado College, 1977-1978; professor, University of Arizona, 1978-. *Other professional post*: Vice-chairperson, National Museum of the American Indian, Smithsonian Institution, 1990-. *Military Service*: U.S. Marine Corps Reserve, San Diego, CA & Quantico, VA, 1954-56. Organizational *Memberships* : White Buffalo Council, Denver (board of directors, 1964-66); Citizens Crusade Against Poverty, Washington, DC (board of directors, 1965-66); Council on Indian Affairs, Washington, DC (vice-chairman, 1965-68); Board of Inquiry Into Hunger & Malnutrition in the U.S.A., New York, NY, 1967-68; National Office for the Rights of the Indigent, New York, NY (board of directors, 1967-68); Ad-Hoc Committee on Indian Work, Episcopal Church, New York, NY (chairman, 1968-69); Southwest Intergroup Council, Austin, TX (board of directors, 1969-71); Institute for the Development of Indian Law, Washington, DC (chairman & founder, 1971-76); Model Urban Indian Centers Project, San Francisco, CA (board of directors, 1971-73); Oglala Sioux Legal Rights Foundation, Pine Ridge, SD (board of directors, 1971); National Friends of Public Broadcasting, New York, NY;

1971-76; Colorado Humanities Program, Boulder, CO, 1975-77; National Indian Youth Council, Albuquerque, NM (advisory council, 1976); American Civil Liberties Union, Denver, CO (Indian committee, 1976-78); The Center for Land Grant Studies, Santa Fe, 1976; American Lutheran Church, Minneapolis (consultant, 1976-78); Nebraska Educational Television Network, Lincoln, NE (advisory council, American Indian Series, 1976-78); Denver Public Library Foundation, Denver (board of directors, 1977-78); Museum of the American Indian, New York (board of trustees, 1977-82); American Indian Development, Inc., Bellingham, WA 1978-81; Daybreak Films, Denver (board of directors, 1979-81); Field Foundation, New York (board of directors, 1980); Indian Rights Association, Philadelphia (board of directors, 1980); Institute of the American West, Sun Valley, ID (national advisory council, 1981-83); Disability Rights & Education Defense Fund, Berkeley, CA (advisory council, 1981); Save the Children Federation, Westport, CT (national advisory council, 1983). *Professional Memberships* : American Judicature Society, 1970-; Colorado Authors League, 1970-. Editorial Boards and Contributing Editorships: American Indian Historical Society, San Francisco (editorial board, 1971-72); Handbook of North American Indians, Smithsonian Institution (planning committee, 1971-72); The World of the American Indian, (National Geographic Society, 1972-76); Clearwater Press (consultant, advisory board, 1972-78); American Indian Cultural & Research Center Journal, UCLA (editorial board, 1972); Race Relations Information Center (contributing editor, 1974-75); Integrateducation, University of Massachusetts (editorial advisory board, 1975); American Heritage Dictionary of the English Language, Houghton-Mifflin (usage panel, 1976-83); Explorations in Ethnic Studies, LaCrosse, WI, 1977-; Katallagete, Berea, KY (editorial board, 1977); The Historical Magazine of the Episcopal Church, Austin, TX (editorial board, 1977); The Colorado Magazine, Colorado Historical Society, Denver (editorial review board, 1979); National Forum, Phi Kappa Phi, Johnson City, TN (contributing editor, 1979); Studies in American Indian Literature, Columbia University (advisory board, 1981); Adherent Forum, New York, NY (contributing editor, 1981). *Special Activities*: White House Conference on Youth (delegate, 1970); Avco-Embassy Pictures on movie Soldier Blue (consultant, 1970); Educational Challenges, Inc., Washington, DC (consultant, 1971-72); Senate Committee on Aging, Washington, DC (consultant, 1971-72); Served as expert witness in four trials involving the occupation of Wounded Knee and aftermath as expert on 1868 Fort Laramie treaty and Sioux history (1974); Project 76, National Council of Churches (sponsor, 1974-76); Served as appointed counsel in Consolidated Wounded Knee Cases, treaty hearing in federal court (1975); Colorado Centennial-Bicentennial Commission (commissioner, 1975-77); EVIST, National Science Foundation (advisory board, 1975-78); Robert F. Kennedy Journalism Awards (judge, 1975); Sun Valley Center for the Arts and Humanities, Sun Valley, Idaho (advisory council, 1976-78, 1980-83); Handbook of North American Indians, Volume Two, Indians in Contemporary Society, Smithsonian Institution (editor, 1978-); American Indian Studies Program, University of Arizona (chairman, 1978-81). *Special Honors & Awards*: Anisfield Wolf Award, 1970, for Custer Died for Your Sins; Special Citation, 1971, National Conference of Christians and Jews, for We Talk, You Listen; Honorary Doctor of Humane Letters, 1972, Augustana College; Indian Achievement Award, 1972, Indian Council Fire, Chicago; Named one of eleven Theological Superstars of the Future, 1974, by Interchurch Features, New York, N.Y.; Honorary Doctor of Letters, 1976, Scholastica College, Duluth, Minn.; Distinguished Alumni Award, 1977, Iowa State University; Honorary Professor, 1977, Athabasca University, Edmonton, Can.; Honorary Doctor of Human Letters, 1979, Hamline University, St. Paul, Minn.; 1985 - Distinguished Alumni in the Field of Legal Education, Colorado University School of Law. *Published works*: Books: Custer Died For Your Sins (Macmillan, 1969); We Talk, You Listen (Macmillan, 1970); Of Utmost Good Faith (Straight Arrow, 1971); Red Man in the New World Drama, edited and revised (Macmillan, 1972); God Is Red (Grosset & Dunlap, 1973); Behind the Trail of Broken Treaties (Delacourte, 1974); The Indian Affair (Friendship Press, 1974); Indians of the Pacific Northwest (Doubleday, 1977); The Metaphysics of Modern Existence (Harper & Row, 1979); American Indians, American Justice, with Clifford Lytle (University of Texas Press, 1983); A Sender of Words, editor-The Neihardt Centennial Essays (Howe Brothers, 1984); The Nations Within, with Clifford Lytle (Pantheon Books, 1984); The Aggressions of Civilization, edited with Sandra Cadwalader (Temple University Press, 1984); American Indian Policy in the Twentieth Century, editor (University of Oklahoma Press, 1985). Special Reports: The Lummi Indians, -- Center for the Study of Man, Smithsonian Institution, 1972; Legal Problems and Considerations Involved in the Treaty of 1868, prepared for the John Hay Whitney Foundation, 1974; Indian Education Confronts the Seventies, editor and contributor, five volumes, Office of Indian Education, 1974; Contemporary Issues of American Indians, A Model Course, prepared for the National Indian Education Association, 1975; Legislative Analysis of the Federal Role in Indian Education, Office of Indian Education, 1975; A Better Day for Indians, issued by the Field Foundation, 1977. Also, articles as contributing editor, editorials, and introductions to books--too numerous to mention.

*DELORIMIERE, GORDON T.
   (administration)
Affiliation: Administrative Assistant Secretary, Bureau of Indian Affairs, Dept. of the Interior, MS-4140-MIB, 1849 C St., NW, Washington, DC 20240 (202) 208-5649.

De MAIN, PAUL *(Oshscabewis)*
(Oneida/White Earth Ojibway) 1955-
   (CEO, Indian Country Communications)
Born October 8, 1955, Milwaukee, Wis. *Education*: University of Wisconsin, Eau Claire, 1975-77. *Principal occupation*: CEO, Indian Country Communications. *Home address*: Route 5, Box 5346-D, Hayward, WI 54843 (715) 634-5226 (work). *Affiliations*: Ass't. manager & manager, Lac Courte Oreilles Graphic Arts, 1979-80; acting director, Great Lakes Indian News Association, 1980-82; self determination information officer, Lac Courte Oreilles Tribal Government, 1981-82; managing editor, Lac Courte Oreilles Journal, Hayward, WI, 1977-82; advisor on Indian affairs policy to Governor Anthony S. Earl, State of Wisconsin, 1983-87; secretary-treasurer, Native Horizons, 1983-; CEO, Indian Country Communications, Rt. 2, Box 2900-A,

Hayward, WI 54843, 1987-. *Other professional posts*: Native American Journalists Association (NAJA) (treasurer, 1991-92; president, board of directors, 1992-); president of UNITY 94, an alliance of the National Association of African American Journalists, Asian American Journalists Association, National Association of Hispanic Journalists, and NAJA. *Community activities*: Governor's representative, State Council on Alcohol and Other Drug Abuse, 1983-87; lay counselor, Lac Courte Oreilles Tribal Court, 1980-; board member, Lac Courte Oreilles Honor the Earth Education Foundation, 1980-; volunteer, WOJB Radio, Hayward, WI, 1980-; representative, Governor's Council on Minority Business Development, 1983-88; planning committee, National Indian Media Conference; Governor's Interstate Indian Council Executive Board, 1986-88; advisory board, Center for Mining Alternatives, 1980-82; member, Northwestern Wisconsin Mining Impact Committee, 1980-82; member, Governor's Study Committee on Equal Rights, 1977. *Memberships*: National Congress of American Indians (conference planning committee, 1983); Native American Press Association (Board of Directors, 1986-88). *Published works*: North America's Indian Country Gaming Guide & The Pow Wow Directory (Indian Country Communications); publisher of "News From Indian Country," a national twice-monthly newspaper located on the Lac Courte Oreilles Ojibway reservation of northern Wisconsin; also publishes, "Explore Indian Country" (Indian Country Communications) a monthly entertainment tabloid and distributes native language materials and books;

*DE MALLIE, RAYMOND J.
   (professor, author)
Affiliation/Address: Dept. of Anthropology, Rawles Hall 108, Bloomington, IN 47405 (812) 855-1203. *Other professional post*: Director, American Indian Studies Research Institute, Indiana University, Bloomington, IN. *Published works*: Editor - North American Indian Anthropology: Essays on Society & Culture (University of Oklahoma Press, 1994).

DEMIENTIEFF, SAMUEL S.
   (BIA agency supt.)
Affiliations: Supt., Fairbanks Agency, Bureau of Indian Affairs, Federal Bldg. & Courthouse, 101 12th Ave., Box 16, Fairbanks, AK 99701 (907) 456-0222; executive director, Fairbanks Native Association, 201 First Ave., 2nd Floor, Fairbanks, AK 99701 (907) 452-1648.

*DEMMERT, ROSEANN (Eskimo)
   (AK coop association president)
Affiliation: Klawock Cooperative Association, P.O. Box 112, Klawock, AK 99925 (907) 755-2265.

DEMPSEY, HUGH A. 1929-
   (historian)
Born November 7, 1929, Edgerton, Alberta, Can. *Principal occupation*: Historian. *Home address*: 95 Holmwood Ave., N.W., Calgary, AB T2K 2G7. *Affiliations*: Reporter, Edmonton Bulletin; Publicity Bureau, Province of Alberta, Canada; Glenbow Alberta Institute, Calgary, Alberta (archivist, 1956-67; technical director, 1967-70; director of history, 1970-78; chief curator, 1978-91; associate director, Glenbow-Alberta Institute, 1980-91 {retired}). *Other professional posts*: Adjunct professor, University of Calgary, 1979-; Editor, Alberta History, 1958-; editor,

Canadian Archivist, 1963-66; editor, Glenbow, 1968-74; Canadian editor, Montana Magazine of History; editorial board, Royal Canadian Geographical Society; contributing editor, American West. *Community activities*: Alberta Indian Treaties Commemorative Program, 1976-78; Alberta Heritage Learning Resources Advisory Committee, 1978-79. *Memberships*: Historical Society of Alberta (executive committee, 1953; vice president, 1955-56; president, 1956-57); Canadian Historical Association (chairman, archives section, 1961-1962); Indian Association of Alberta (secretary, 1959-64; advisory board, 1959-68); Canadian Museums Association (executive committee, 1968-70); Indian-Eskimo Association of Canada (executive committee, 1960-65); International Council of Museums (Canadian committee, 1968-71). *Awards, honors*: Alberta Historian of the Year, 1962; honorary doctorate, University of Calgary, 1974; Order of Canada, 1975; Alberta Achievement Award, 1974-1975; honorary chief, Blood Tribe, 1967; winner of Alberta Non-Fiction Award, 1975. *Published works*: Crowfoot, Chief of the Blackfeet (University of Oklahoma Press, 1972); Charcoal's World (University of Nebraska Press, 1978); Red Crow, Warrior Chief (Prairie Books, 1980); History in Their Blood; The Indian Portraits of Nicholas De Grandmaison (Hudson Hill, 1982); Big Bear, The End of Freedom (Douglas & McIntyre, 1984); The Gentle Persuader, A Biography of James Gladstone, Indian Senator (Prairie Books, 1986); Bibliography of the Blackfeet (Scarecrow Press, 1989); Treasures of the Glenbow Museum, 1991. *Monographs*: A Blackfoot Winter Count, 1966; Tailfeathers, Indian Artist, 1970; Blackfoot Ghost Dance, 1968; Indian Names for Alberta Communities, 1969.

*DEMPSEY, L JAMES (Kitsemonisi -
High Otter) (Blood) 1958-
   (historian)
Born September 20, 1958, Calgary, Alberta, Can. *Education*: University of Calgary, BA, 1985, MA, 1987; University of East Angelia (England), 1992- (PhD candidate). *Principal occupation*: Historian. *Home address*: 9040 - 99 St., Edmonton, AB, Can. T6E 3V7 (403) 492-2991 (work). *Affiliation*: Director of the School of Native Studies, University of Alberta, Edmonton, AB, Can., 1992-; professor, Saskatchewan Indian Federated College, Saskatoon, SK, Can., 1987-92. *Interests*: As a member of the Blood tribe, my interests have centered on the Northern Plains culture & history with a particular emphasis on Blackfoot Indians & warfare. I have also studied the role of Canadian Indians in World War I & World War II. Currently, I am studying the significance of Blackfoot pictography to warfare. *Published works*: Problems of Western Canadian Indian W ar Veterans After World War I (Native Studies Review, 1989); editor, Treaty Days (Glenbow Museum, 1991).

DENAM, WILBUR
   (Indian band chief)
Affiliation: Burnt Church Indian Band, RR 2, Lagaceville, New Brunswick, Canada E0C 1K0 (506) 776-8331.

DENET, DOROTHY KATHERINE (Pephise)
(Hopi)
   (lecturer, consultant, entrepreneur)
Born in Keams Canyon, Ariz. *Education*: Northland Pioneer College, AA, 1989. *Principal occupation*: Lecturer, consultant, entrepreneur. *Address*: P.O. Box 210, Polacca, AZ 86042 (602)

737-2534. *Affiliations*: General Manager, Hopi Cultural Center, Second Mesa, AZ; vice-president, Secakuku Enterprises, Second Mesa, AZ; president, Polingyami, Inc., Polacca, AZ, 1992-. *Other professional posts*: lecturer, Northern Arizona University, Elder Hostel Program, Flagstaff, AZ, 1990-; lecturer, Yavapai College Elder Hostel Program, Prescott, AZ, 1990-. *Community activities*: Arizona State Tourism Advisory Council (appointed by Governor, 1988-94); Arizona State Employment & Training Advisory Council (appointed by Governor, 1989-94); Applied Economics/Junior Achievement, Hopi Jr.-Sr. High School (busines consultant, 1990-); Arizona Strategic Planning for Economic Development, Native American Coalition and Tourism Cluster, member, 1989-92. *Memberships*: Arizona Coalition for Displaced Homemakers, Governor's Office for Women, 1989-94; Arizona Tribal Private Industry Council (chairperson-member, 1987-89); Hostelling International (American Youth Hostel), AZ Chapter, Board of Directors, member, 1992-). *Interests*: "Tourism, particularly as related to Indian reservations; economics-cultural compatibility; employment & training - Job Training Partnership Act on tribal reservations and their congruence with the states including women in non-traditional training, jobs; women's issues - cultural impact and changes." *Biographical sources*: Junior Achievement Partners, "Applied Economics in Hopiland, Fall 1991, Vol. 7, No. 4; Indian Business and Management, March/April 1992, Vol. 3, No. 2.

DENNING, SHARILYN
(health director)
Affiliations: Milwaukee Indian Health Center, 930 North 27th St., Milwaukee, WI 53208 (414) 931-8111; chairperson, American Indian Chamber of Commerce, 1228 W. Mitchell, Milwaukee, WI 53204 (414) 383-7531.

DENNIS, HERMAN W.
(Indian band chief)
Affiliation: Chawathil (Hope) Indian Band, Box 1659, Hope, British Columbia, Canada V0X 1L0 (604) 869-9994.

*DENNIS, PHILBERT
(school chairperson)
Affiliation: Hotevilla Bacavi Community School, P.O. Box 48, Hotevilla, AZ 86030 (602) 734-2462.

DENNY, RUTH *(Zibiquah)*
(Potawatomi/Winnebago/Oneida) 1957-
(newspaper editor)
Born November 11, 1957, Milwaukee, Wisc. *Education*: University of Califomia, Berkeley. *Principal occupation*: Newspaper editor. *Address & Affiliation*: The Circle, Minneapolis American Indian Center, 1530 E. Franklin Ave., Minneapolis, MN 55404 (612) 871-4749. *Membership*: Native American Journalists Association.

*DENOUDEN, AMY
(program coordinator)
Affiliation: University of Connecticut, Dept. of Anthropology, U Box 158, 344 Mansfield Rd., Storrs, CT 06269 (203) 486-4865.

*DERBY, MIDGE
(museum director)
Affiliation: Johnson-Humrickhouse Museum, 300 N. Whityewoman St., Roscoe Village, Coshocton, OH 43812 (614) 622-8710.

DERRICK, ELMER
(Indian band chief)
Affiliation: Kitwancool Indian Band, Box 340, Kitwanga, British Columbia, Canada V0J 2A0 (604) 849-5222.

DERRIKSAN, NOEL C.
(president-Indian society)
Affiliation: Indian Arts & Crafts Society of British Columbia, 540 Burrard St., Suite 505, Vancouver, British Columbia, Canada V6C 2K1 (604) 682-8988.

*DESBIEN, NINA
(health center director)
Affiliation: Cibecue PHS Indian Health Center, Cibecue, AZ 85941 (602) 332-2560.

DESCHAMPE, NORMAN (Chippewa)
(tribal chairperson)
Affiliation: Grand Portage Reservation Business Committee, P.O. Box 428, Grand Portage, MN 55605 (218) 475-2279.

DESJARLAIT, GEORGE
(Indian band chief)
Affiliation: West Moberly Indian Band, General Delivery, Moberly Lake, British Columbia, Canada V0C 1X0 (604) 788-3663.

DESJARLAIT, ROBERT *(Akoongiss)*
(Red Lake Ojibway) 1946-
(artist)
Born November 18, 1946, Redlake, Minn. *Principal occupation*: Artist. *Home address*: 5901 Rhode Island Ave., N., Minneapolis, MN 55428 (612) 535-0091. *Art/cultural consultant*: 1989, University Art Museum, University of Minnesota, Minneapolis; 1990, Walker Art Center, Minneapolis; 1991, Mankato State University, Mankato, MN; 1992, Minnesota Center for Arts Education, Minneapolis; 1992, Anoka-Hennepin Indian Education Program, Coon Rapids, MN; 1992, Minnesota Indian Women's Resource Center, Minneapolis; 1992, Robbinsdale Indian Education Program, New Hope, MN, 1992. *Other professional post*: Art instructor, Heart of the Earth Survival School, Minneapolis, MN, 1989-90. *Commissions*: White Earth Land Project, White Earth, MN, 1989; Red Lake Social Services Program, Red Lake, MN, 1989; American Indian AIDS Outreach Program, 1989; Anoka-Hennepin Indian Education Program, Coon Rapids, MN, 1990; Minnesota Indian Women's Resource Center, Minneapolis, 1990-92. Public Art: North Dakota Museum of Art, Grand Forks, ND, 1986; Red Lake High School, 1988; Anoka-Hennepin Development Center, Anoka, MN, 1991; Meridel Le Seur Library, Augsburg College, 1992, Minneapolis, MN; Robbinsdale Indian Education Program, New Hope, MN, 1992; Minnesota Indian Women's Resource Center, 1992. *Community activities*: Arts Midwest Advisory Panel on Arts in Culturally Diverse Communities, 1987; Minneapolis Institute of Arts Advisory Panel on Native American Art, 1991. *Awards, honors*: Ojibwe Art Expo, 1985 2nd Place - Drawing, 1987 2nd Place - Painting, 1988 1st Place - Drawing; 1988 Percy Fearing Award - Illustration, Minnesota Council on the Teaching of Foreign Languages. *Biographical sources*: "DesJarlait Depicts Ojibwe Vision," Red Lake Times, Nov. 1987; "Minnesotan Culturally Diverse Artists," Minnesota Monthly, July 1992; "Interview - Robert DesJarlait," Modern Lights and Insights (Video),

Minneapolis Public Library Artist/Author Series, 1992. *Published works*: Author - O-do-i-daym Ojibway: Clans of The Ojibway Coloring Book (Minnesota Indian Women's Resource Center Press, 1989); Nimiwin: A History of Ojibway Dance (Anoka-Hennepin Indian Education Press, 1991). Illustrator - Sparrow Hawk, by Meridel Le Seur (Holy Cow Press, 1987); Cherish The Children (MIWRC Press, 1987); Young Child, Old Spirit (MIWRC, 1990); The Spirit Within - Encouraging Harmony and Health in American Indian Children (Minnesota Indian Women's Resource Center Press, 1992).

DeVERNEY, TED
(executive officer, Indian organization)
Affiliation: Organization of North American Indian Students, Box 26, University Center, Northern Michigan University, Marquette, MI 49855 (906) 227-2138.

*DEW, WILLIAM K.
(IHS-tribal activities)
Affiliation: Nashville Area IHS, 711 Stewarts Ferry Pike, Nashville, TN 37214 (615) 736-2478.

DeWALL, ROBB
(editor)
Affiliation: "Crazy Horse Progress," Crazy Horse Memorial Foundation, Ave. of the Chiefs, Black Hills, Crazy Horse, SD 57730-9988 (605) 673-4681.

DIAMOND, BILLY (Cree) 1949-
(politician)
Born May 17, 1949, at Waskaganish, Quebec, Can. *Education*: Bawating Collegiate & Vocational High School (5 year arts & science program, graduated in June 1968). *Principal occupation*: Politician. *Address*: P.O. Box 9, Waskaganish, Quebec, Can. J0M 1R0 (819) 895-8971. *Affiliations*: On-the-job-training, Dept. of Indian Affairs and Northern Development, Val D'or, Quebec; band manager, 1969-71; chief, 1970-76, Rupert House Band, Rupert House, Quebec; communications worker, 1972, regional chief, 1972-74, Indians of Quebec Association, Huron Village, Quebec; grand chief, Grand Council of the Crees (of Quebec), Rupert House, Quebec, 1974-84; chairman & school commissioner for Cree Regional Authority, 1976-88; chairman/grand chief, Cree Regional Authority, Val D'or, Quebec, 1978-84; chairman & president, Cree Housing Corporation, 1984-87; president, Air Creebec, Inc., 1982-; proprietor, Diamond Brothers Enterprises Registered, 1983-; chief Waskaganish Band Council, James Bay, Quebec, re-elected 1988-. *Other professional posts*: Member, Board of Directors, Creeco (Cree Regional Economic Enterprises Co.) and Cree Construction Co., 1980-; president, Native Peoples Television Network, 1982-; chairman, Board of Advisors, National Native Bible College, 1984-; Band councillor, Waskaganish Band Council, P.O. Box 60, Waskaganish, P.Q., James Bay J0M 1R0, 1984-; president, Waskaganish Enterprises Development Corp. (WEDCO), 1985-; member, Board of Directors, Construction Regional Authority, Northern Flood Committee, Manitoba, 1985-; chairman, Cree-Yamaha Motor Enterprises Ltd., 1986-; member, Board of Directors of the Grand Council of the Crees and the Council of the Cree Regional Authority, 1984-. *Awards, honors*: Inducted as a Knight in the Order of Quebec, Jan. 15, 1987.

DIAMOND, CLIFFORD
(Indian band chief)
Affiliation: Wahgoshig Indian Band, Box 722, Matheson, ON, Can. P0K 3C0 (705) 567-4891.

*DIAMOND, GERALD B.
(Zeemucka) (Chippewa) 1938-
(business owner)
Born January 10, 1938, Hayward, Wisc. *Education*: Mt. Senario College (Ladysmith, WI), BA, 1982. *Principal occupation*: Business owner. *Home address*: Rt. 2, Box 2330, Hayward, WI 54843 (715) 634-2655; 634-4499 (work). *Affiliation*: President, American Indian Gift Store, Hayward, WI, 1988-. *Military service*: U.S. Army, 1957-77 SFC National Defenses (Good Conduct Awards; Meritorious Service Medal). *Community activities*: Governors Council on Tourism. *Awards, honors*: National Honor Society (college); Past Master in the Masons. *Interests*: "I spent four years in Italy, 3 years in Germany, and 2 years in Korea. I had tours of duty in IL, CO, VA, MO, TX, GA, & FL."

DICK, ERNEST W. (Navajo)
(Indian school chairperson)
Affiliation: Rough Rock Community School, RRDS, Box 217, Rough Rock, AZ 86501 (602) 728-3311.

DICK, LEROY S. (Navajo) 1943-
(health systems administrator)
Born December 15, 1943, Shiprock, N.M. *Education*: Loretto Heights College, Denver, BA, 1975; Leslie Graduate School, MA, 1984. *Principal occupation*: Health systems administrator. *Address*: P.O. Box 836, Shiprock, NM 87420 (505) 632-1801 (work). *Affiliation*: Vice-president of Management Board, Navajo Tribal Utility Authority, Ft. Defiance, AZ; director, Dzilth-Na-O-Dith-Hle PHS Indian Health Center, Bloomfield, NM. *Other professional post*: Counseling psychologist. *Military service*: U.S. Army, 1965-67 (E-5 Sergeant, 7th Division; Outstanding Leadership Award, 12/66 while serving in Korea). *Community activities*: Vice-president, School Board, Central School District 22, 1981-; board member, Four Winds Alcoholic Treatment Center. *Memberships*: National Institute of Business Management, Inc.; National Rural Electric Co-op Association; American Public Power Association. *Awards, honors*: "I am the only American Indian to receive a 7th Division Outstanding Leadership Award for Outstanding Performance"; Recognition of High Quality of Performance, PHS - Shiprock, NM, 1973; Letter of Commendation for Outstanding Performance, PHS - Shiprock, 1974; Recognition of Appreciation for Outstanding Services in EEO Program by Marlene E. Haffner, M.D., NAIHS, Window Rock, AZ, 1975. *Interests*: "I enjoy outdoor activities, hiking, hunting, and picnics with family. This is probably due to my Native American up-bringing. In my spare time, the family will travel to Rock Point, AZ where we manage a small herd of cattle, which takes up alot of our time and something I enjoy doing."

DICK, RALPH, Sr.
(Indian band chief)
Affiliation: Cape Mudge Indian Band, P.O. Box 220, Quathiaski Cove, British Columbia, Canada V0P 1N0 (604) 285-3316.

DICK, ROBBIE
(Indian band chief)
Affiliation: Whapmagoostui (Cree) Indian Band, Box 390, Great White River, Hudson Bay, Quebec J0M 1G0 (819) 929-3384.

DICK, STEPHEN GEORGE
(Indian band chief)
Affiliation: Kwiakah Indian Band, 1440 Island Highway, Campbell River, British Columbia, Canada V9W 2E3 (604) 286-1295.

*DICKERSON, ANN
(librarian)
Affiliation: Nisqually Tribal Library, 4814 She-Nah-Num Dr., SE. Olympia, WA 98513 (206) 456-5221.

DIEBEL, JERRY E.
(Indian school principal)
Affiliation: Tuba City Boarding School, P.O. Box 187, Tuba City, NM 86045 (602) 283-4531.

*DIEGUEZ, LORI
(BIA agency acting supt.)
Affiliation: Ramah-Navajo Agency, BIA, Ramah, NM 87321 (505) 775-3235.

*DIETZ, GERALD E. *(Talking Bear)*
(Seneca-Cayuga of Oklahoma) 1938-
(retired teacher; farmer)
Born February 4, 1938, Hellam, Penna. *Education*: Millersville State University, B.S., 1961; Indiana University, M.A., 1966. *Principal occupation*: Retired teacher; farmer. *Home address*: Box 99, Walnut Valley Farm, Loganville, PA 17342 (717) 428-1440. *Affiliation*: Teacher, York Suburban School District, York, PA (33 years). *Military service*: U.S. Marine Corps, PFC, 1955-63. *Community activities*: Former Zoning Officer & Zoning Board, Loganville, PA; former, 4-H Club Leader; former Boy Scout Advisor; current Aldersgate United Methodist Church (Council of Ministry). *Memberships*: National Education Association - Retired; Pennsylvania Education Association - Retired; Pennsylvania Association of School Retirees; Charter Member, National Museum of the American Indian. *Awards, honors*: 1955 D.A.R. Award; 1956 Chemistry Award - American Chemical Society; 1977 Master Drapeau Limner - Brigade of the American Revolution; 1980's nominee, Pennsylvania Outstanding Earth Science Teacher Award. *Interests*: "Currently retired to my farming. As a member of the Haliwa-Saponi Native American Dancers of York (York, PA), we have lectured & performed at museums, churches. festivals, universities, schools in mid-Atlantic region, and did a 2 week performance tour in England. The group is recognized by Pennsylvania Heritage Affairs Commission, and represents Native people as part of the ethnic performing arts of Pennsylvania; avid hunter, trapper, fisherman all my life. Travel. *Biographical sources*: Worked as an extra (colonial soldier) in the movie "Sweet Liberty" Alan Alda film in 1986, and as one of the Native people in the VCR produced by Pennsylvania Dept. of Transportation - "Keep Pennsylvania Beautiful," 1992. Several articles in the local newspaper over the years, York Daily Record & York Sunday News (York, PA). *Published work*: Author/co-editor/publisher, "Susquehanna Valley Native American Eagle," bimonthly newsletter, 1987-.

DIETZ, JERRY
(editor)
Affiliation: Susquehanna Valley Native American Eagle, Box 99, Walnut Valley Farm, Loganville, PA 17342 (717) 428-1440.

DIONNE, JACKIE
(radio producer)
Affiliation: Migizi Communications, Inc., 3123 E. Lake St., Suite 200, Minneapolis, MN 55406 (612) 721-6631.

*DITMANSON, PAUL, M.D.
(clincal director)
Affiliation: Red Lake PHS Indian Hospital, Red Lake, MN 56671 (218) 679-3912.

DIXON, LARRY
(director-Indian center)
Affiliation: Kitsap County Indian Center, 3337 N.W. Byron St., Silverdale, WA 98383 (206) 692-7460.

DIXON, SUSAN
(managing editor)
Affiliation: Akwe:kon Journal, Akwe:kon Press, Cornell University, 300 Caldwell Hall, Ithaca, NY 14850 (607) 255-4308.

DOBYNS, HENRY F. 1925-
(consultant, adjunct professor)
Born July 3, 1925, Tucson, Ariz. *Education*: University of Arizona, B.A., 1949, M.A., 1956; Cornell University, Ph.D., 1960. *Principal occupation*: Consultant, adjunct professor. *Affiliations*: Research associate, Cornell University, 1960-66; professor, University of Kentucky, 1966-70; professor, Prescott College, AZ, 1970-73; visiting professor, University of Wisconsin, Parkside, 1974-75; visiting professor, University of Florida, 1977-79; director, Native American Historical Demography Project, D'Arcy McNickle Center for the History of the American Indian, The Newberry Library, Chicago, 1979-86; adjunct professor, Dept. of Anthropology, University of Oklahoma, Norman, 1987-. *Military service*: U.S. Army, 1943. *Memberships*: American Association for the Advancement of Science (Fellow); American Anthropological Association; American Society for Ethnohistory (former president). *Awards, honors*: Shared Anisfield-Wolf Award, 1968; Malinowski Award, Society for Applied Anthropology, 1952. *Published works*: The Apache People (Coyotero) (Indian Tribal Series, 1971); The Papago People (Indian Tribal Series, 1972); The Mescalero Apache People (Indian Tribal Series, 1973); Prehistoric Indian Occupation Within the Eastern Area of the Yuman Complex: A Study in Applied Archaeology (Garland, 1974); Spanish Colonial Tucson (University of Arizona Press, 1976); Native American Historical Demography (Indiana University Press, 1976); From Fire to Flood (Ballena Press, 1981); Their Number Become Thinned (University of Tennessee Press, 1983).

DOCKSTADER, FREDERICK J. 1919-
(museum consultant)
Born February 3, 1919, Los Angeles, Calif. *Education*: Arizona State College, BA, MA; Western Reserve University, PhD, 1951. *Principal occupation*: Museum consultant. *Home address*: 165 W. 66 St., New York, NY 10023. *Affiliations*: Teacher, Flagstaff, Arizona schools, 1942-50; staff ethnologist, Cranbrook Institute of Science, 1950-52; faculty member and curator of anthropology, Dartmouth College, 1952-55; assistant director, director, Museum of the American Indian, Heye Foundation, 1955-75. *Other professional posts*: Advisory editor, Encyclopedia Americana, 1957-; U.S. Indian Arts and Crafts Board (commissioner, 1955-64; chairman, 1964-67; visiting professor of art and archaeology,

Columbia University, 1961-; member, New York State Museum Advisory Council; trustee, Huntington Free Library. *Memberships*: American Association for the Advancement of Science (Fellow); Cranbrook Institute of Science (Fellow); American Anthropological Association (Fellow); Society for American Archaeology; New York Academy of Sciences; Cosmos Club; Century Club. *Awards, honors*: First Prize (silversmithing), Cleveland Museum of Art, 1950; Fellow, Rochester Museum of Arts and Sciences; Honorary D.F.A. Degree, Hartwick College, Oneonta, NY, 1991; Honorary D.H.L. Degree, University of South Dakota, Vermillion, SD, 1992. *Biographical sources*: Who's Who in America; Who's Who in Art; American Men of Science; Who's Who in the East; American Indian Authors; Who's Who in the World. *Published works*: The Kachina and the White Man (Cranbrook Institute of Sciences, 1954; revised edition, University of New Mexico Press, 1985); The American Indian in Graduate Studies (Museum of the American Indian, 1957, revised in two volumes, 1974); Indian Art in America (New York Graphic Society, 1960); Indian Art in Middle America (New York Graphic Society, 1964); Indian Art in South America (New York Graphic Society, 1966); Pre-Columbian and Later Tribal Arts (Abrams, 1968); Indian Art of the Americas (New York, 1973); Great North American Indians: Profiles of Life & Leadership (New York, 1977); Weaving Arts of the North American Indian, 1978, revised edition of Weaving Arts of the North American Indian (HarperCollins, 1993); Song of the Loom (Hudson Hills, 1987).

*DOCKTER-PINNICK, LYNN
(college president)
Affiliation: Fort Berthold Community College, P.O. Box 490, New Town, ND 58763 (701) 627-3665.

DODGE, DONALD (Navajo) 1929-
(BIA agency supt.-retired)
Born July 15, 1929, Crystal, N.M. *Education*: University of New Mexico. *Principal occupation*: BIA agency supt.-retired. *Address*: Shiprock Agency, BIA, Box 966, Shiprock, NM 87420 (505) 368-4427. *Affiliation*: Director, Navajo Tribe's Public Service Division, 1969-70; supt., BIA, Fort Defiance Agency, AZ, 1972-76; director, BIA, Navajo Area Office, Window Rock, AZ, 1977-86; supt., Shiprock Agency, Shiprock, NM, 1987-92. *Military service*: U.S. Army - Korean War. *Awards, honors*: Grandson of famous Navajo leader, Chee Dodge, first chairman of Navajo Tribal Council. *Interests*: Mr. Dodge sees the Bureau's relationship to the Tribe as government-to-government. "We have our government structure and the Tribe has its structure. We need to get together and compare the two and see where the relationship can be improved. Most of our programs are contractible except those involving areas of trust responsibility." Mr. Dodge concludes, "My main objective is to get a good organization going, one that can coordinate and communicate with the Tribe, so that the best interests of the individual will be served."

DODGE, HENRY
(BIA agency supt.)
Affiliation: San Carlos Irrigation Project, BIA, P.O. Box 209, Coolidge, AZ 85228 (602) 723-5439.

DOERING, MAVIS (Cherokee) 1929-
(basketweaving artist)
Born August 31, 1929, Hominy, Okla. *Education*: San Jose State University, 1946; Sacramento City College, 1968. *Principal occupation*: Basketweaving artist. *Home address*: 5918 N.W. 58th St., Oklahoma City, OK 73122. *Affiliations*: Consultant (Title IV, Indian pupil education), Putnam City School District, Warr Acres, Okla., 1977-81; cultural consultant, Indian Student Association, University of Oklahoma, Norman, 1981-; consultant, United National Indian Tribal Youth Organization, 1979-. *Other professional posts*: Basketweaving instructor, Lone Grove School District, Western Heights School District, Deer Creek School District, Oklahoma Baptist University for Upward Bound students, Oklahoma Museum of Art, Willard Art Center, St. John's Methodist Church, the Native American Center of Oklahoma City (elderly program), American Indian Institute of the University of Oklahoma, and Cowboy Hall of Fame, 1977-84. *Community activities*: Advisory board, Oklahoma Indian Artists and Craftsmen Guild; member, Advisory Arts Council, Native American Center of Oklahoma City; member, National Advisory Council, Wheelwright Museum of the American Indian, Santa Fe, N.M.; newsletter editor, Oklahoma Cherokee Organization; member, Arts Advisory Committee, Crosswinds Gallery; precinct chairman for Democratic Party; Arts Advisory Committee, Diamond Jubilee of the State of Oklahoma (selected by the State of Oklahoma to complete a TV public service announcement for the Diamond Jubilee Celebration. *Memberships*: Oklahoma Museum of Art, 1980-; Cherokee Historical Society, 1980-; Oklahoma Cherokee Organization (secretary, newsletter editor, 1978-); Oklahoma Indian Artists and Craftsmen's Guild (2nd vice president and board of directors, 1976-); Wheelwright Museum of the American Indian (advisory board, 1981-); Southwestern Association on Indian Affairs, Inc.; Goingsnake Historical Society, 1981-; Five Civilized Tribes Museum, 1978-; Oklahoma Anthropological Society, 1985-; Museum of the American Indian, 1985-. *Awards, honors*: Awards for artwork received from: Oklahoma Indian Artists & Craftsmen's Guild, Oklahoma Museum of Art, Five Civilized Tribes Museum, Galleria American Indian Exposition, Rose State College, Oklahoma Indian Women's Federation, Indian Arts and Crafts Association, Southwestern Association on Indian Affairs, Four Directions Arts Festival; Oklahoma Artist of Month, October 1978; featured artist on three Creative Crafts television shows, 1978, '79, '82; appearances and interviews on Voices from the Land, Unity and Danny's Day television shows; selected as a participant in the Smithsonian Folklife Festival in Washington, DC in 1982; commissioned to complete baskets for the 50 Governors at the National Governors' Conference in 1982 by the OK State Arts Council; selected as ambassador of goodwill for the State of Oklahoma by Governor George Nigh in Oct. 1982; made honorary member of OK State Anthropological Society in October 1982; recipient of the Governor's Arts Award, 1984; received Women in Communications Arts Award in 1984; selected for one person exhibits at Southern Plains Indian Museum and the Coulter Bay Indian Museum; work selected for permanent collections at Southern Plains Indian Museum, Windstar Foundation, OK State Arts Collection, Cultural Center for the American Indian in Houston, National Building of Future Homemakers of America in Washington, DC, and Mabee-Gerrer Museum. *Interests*: "I am interested in all phases of the arts. I am interested in the promotion of young Indian artists, in the promotion of the American Indian culture to the general populace and I am especially interested in the education of American Indian youth in all fields." *Biographical sources*: Oklahoma Today, Fall 1981; American Craft, May 1982; American Indian-Alaskan Native Resource Guide; Daily Oklahoman, October 1984, August, 1985; Crafts in America, 1984.

*DOLCHOK, LISA
(AK village council director)
Affiliation: Cook Inlet Tribal Council, 670 W. Fireweed Lane, Anchorage, AK 99503 (907) 276-3343.

DOLSON, LEROY
(Indian band chief)
Affiliation: Munsee-Delaware Nation Indian Band, RR #1, Muncey, Ontario, Canada N0L 1Y0 (519) 289-5396.

DOMINGUEZ, DAVID (Chumash)
(tribal chairperson)
Affiliation: Santa Ynez Band of Mission Indians, P.O. Box 517, Santa Ynez, CA 93460 (805) 688-7997.

DONALD, GARY (Chippewa)
(tribal committee chairperson)
Affiliation: Nett Lake Reservation (Bois Forte Tribe) Business Committee, P.O. Box 16, Nett Lake, MN 55772 (218) 757-3261.

*DONELSON, FRANCES A.
(librarian)
Affiliation: Bacone College Library, 2299 Old Bacone Rd., Muskogee, OK 74403 (918) 683-4581 ext. 263.

DONEY, TENNEYSON
(director-Indian hospital)
Affiliation: Crow Agency PHS Indian Hospital, Crow Agency, MT 59022 (406) 638-2624.

DONGOSKE, KURT E. 1952-
(Hopi Tribal archaeologist)
Born November 24, 1952, Mineapolis, Minn. *Education*: University of Minnesota, BA, 1976; University of Arizona, MA, 1984. *Principal occupation*: Hopi Tribal archaeologist. *Home address*: 217 W. Mahoney, Winslow, AZ 86047 (602) 734-2441 (work). *Affiliation*: The Hopi Tribe, Kykotsmovi, AZ. *Memberships*: American Anthropological Association; American Association of Physical Anthropologists; Society for American Archaeology; Society of Professional Archaeologists; Arizona Archaeological Council; Arizona Archaeological & Historical Society. *Interests*: "Cultural resource management, human osteology, faunal analysis, archaeology and Native American concerns, laser mapping instruments and AutoCad, geographic information systems, and Western US archaeology, and Native American oral tradition, and the Archaeological Record."

DONHAUSER, NATTIE
(AK village president)
Affiliation: Native Village of Stoney River, P.O. Box SRV, Stoney River, AK 99557 (907) 537-3214.

DONICA, RILEY (Cherokee) 1933-
(minister)
Born April 19, 1933, Nashoba, Okla. *Education*: Dallas Christian College, BA, 1954. *Principal occupation*: Minister. *Address*: Box 70, Honobia, OK 74549 (918) 755-4462. *Affiliation*: Director, Nations Ministries, Honobia, OK, 1981- (editor, "The Nation News"). *Other professional post*: Supt., Kiamichi Mountains Mission. *Community activities*: Board of Regents, Dallas Christian College. *Memberships*: North American Christian Convention; World Evangelism Conference. *Interests*: "Firearms collector; trail rider - owns & directs "The Wild Horse Trail Ride"; travel - Canada, Mexico, England, Africa." *Biographical sources*: Daily Oklahoman - Tulsa World; Lone Star Horse Report - The Trail Rider. *Published works*: "Stomp'n Snakes" (Standard, 1964); "Farther We Go" (Star, 1973); "Mountain Time" (Star, 1974).

DONNELL, VERN
(hospital director)
Affiliation: Wagner PHS Indian Hospital, 1 10 Washington St., Wagner, SD 57380 (605) 384-3621.

DOONKEEN, EULA NARCOMEY (Seminole) 1931-
(artist)
Born December 12, 1931, Oklahoma City, Okla. *Education*: Central State College, BA (Eduction), 1965. *Principal occupation*: Artist. *Home address*: 1608 N.W. 35th, Oklahoma City, OK 73118. *Affiliation*: Co-owner, Alco Printing Co., Oklahoma City, OK. Military service: U.S.A.F. Women's Reserve, 1951-55. *Community activities*: Shawnee Area Health Advisory Board; Neighborhood Services Organization, Oklahoma City (secretary, 1972); Oklahoma City Community Council; Oklahoma City Area Health Advisory Board; West Central Neighborhood All Sports Association (vice president). *Memberships*: Seminole General Tribal Council (member; assistant chief); Five Civilized Tribes Inter-Tribal Council (sergeant-at-arms); National Congress of American Indians (area vice president, 1967-68); Kappa Pi; Bacone Alumni Association; Oklahoma Federation of Indian Women; American Indian Center (secretary, 1968); Feathers and Buckskin Society; American Indian Press Association; Indian Development Center, Inc.; Universal Link, Plains Center, Oklahoma City (vice president). Awards, honors: Several awards for painting in acrylics. *Exhibits*: Mrs. Doonkeen writes, "I have exhibited at the Smithsonian Institution (but) I paint mainly on commission and rarely enter competitions because I feel most competitions are based on bias and inherent traditional favoritism, and not on realistic approaches." *Interests*: "I am very interested in athletic events, both as a participant and (an) observer. In 1965, I captured the women's collegiate fencing championship of Oklahoma in the novice division. I have traveled extensively over the U.S. on business for Indian organizations and my own Seminole Nation's business. I also travel extensively for my own business, the Alco Printing Co. I am well known all over the country for my greeting card and stationery designs."

DOR, CLIV (Passamaquoddy)
(tribal governor)
Affiliation: Pleasant Point Passamaquoddy Tribal Council, P.O. Box 343, Perry, ME 04667 (207) 853-2551.

*DORAK, ROBERT M.
(college president)
Affiliation: Crownpoint Institute of Technology, P.O. Box 849, Crownspoint, NM 87313 (505) 786-5851.

*DORAME, CHARLIE
(BIA education chairperson)
Affiliation: Northern Pueblos Agency, Bureau of Indian Affairs, P.O. Box 4269, Fairview Station, Espanola, NM 87533 (505) 753-1465; Tesuque Day School, Route 11, Box 2, Santa Fe, NM 87501 (505) 982-1516.

DORRIS, MICHAEL A. (Modoc) 1945-
(writer)
Born January 30, 1945, Louisville, KY. *Education*: Georgetown University, BA, 1967; Yale University, MPhil (Anthropology), 1970. *Principal occupation*: Writer. *Home address*: P.O. Box 70, Cornish Flat, NH 03746. *Affiliations*: Ass't. professor of anthropology, Johnston College, University of the Redlands, 1970-71; assistant professor, Franconia College, N.H., 1971-72; professor, chairman, Department of Native American Studies & Anthropology, Dartmouth College, 1972-90. Oth *er professional post*: Editor, Suntracks, Arizona State University, 1978-90. *Community activities*: Explorers Club (Fellow); Society for Values in Higher Education (Fellow). *Memberships*: Society for Applied Anthropology (Fellow); American Anthropological Association; National Congress of American Indians; National Indian Education Association; National Indian Youth Council; Alpha Sigma Nu; American Indian Culture Center Journal, UCLA, 1974- (editorial board); Viewpoint Magazine (editor); Panel of Native American Scientists, AAAS (member); Minority Commission, MLA (member); Museum of the American Indian (trustee). *Awards, honors*: Phil Beta Kappa; Danforth Graduate Fellow, 1967-70; Woodrow Wilson Graduate Fellow, 1967; National Institute of Mental Health Fellow, 1970-71; Fellow, Society for Applied Anthropology, 1977-present; Named to Change Magazine/American Council on Education list of "100 Younger Leaders of the Academy," 1978; John Simon Guggenheim Fellowship, 1978; Recipient: American for Indian Opportunity Certificate of Appreciation, 1979; Woodrow Wilson Faculty Development Fellowship, 1980; "Outstanding Academic Book of 1984-85" by Choice Magazine for A Guide to Research on North American Indians; Delegate, Ninth Annual Inter-American Indian Congress, Santa Fe, NM, 1985; Rockefeller Foundation Research Fellowship, 1985; Winner of 1985 Indian Achievement Award by Indian Council Fire of IL; "Editor's Choice Book of 1987" by both Booklist and Library Journal, for A Yellow Raft in Blue Water; 1988 PEN Syndicated Fiction Award for "Name Games"; appointed member, Smithsonian Council, 1988-91; National Endowment for the Arts Creative Writings Fellowship, 1989; 1989 Outstanding Alumnus Award, St. Xavier High School; Honorary Degree and 200th Anniversary Commencement Speaker, Georgetown University; Heartland Prize, 1989; Best Audio of 1990 of Author Reading His or Her Own Work by Audio World, for "The Broken Cord," (audio); 1989 Governor's Writing Award, State of Washington, for The Broken Cord; 1990 Christopher Award for The Broken Cord, which was also chosen as a Notable Book of the Year by The American Library Association and Booklist; 1990 Heartland Prize to The Broken Cord; The Broken Cord named "Best Nonfiction Book of 1989" by The National Book Critics Circle, and an Outstanding Academic Book of 1990 by Choice; 1991 Dartmouth College Medal of Outstanding Leadership and Achievement; 1991 Sarah Josepha Hale Literary Award; Board Member, Save the Children Foundation, 1991-present. *Interests*: Contemporary Alaska; culture change; politics of energy resource development; sovereignty and international law; curriculum reform. *Biographical sources*: Who's Who in America; numerous published interviews in magazines and journals, and television and radio; and in "A World of Ideas," by Bill Moyers (Doubleday, 1989). *Published works*: Books: Native Americans Today, 1975; Grandmother's Watch, 1975; Native Americans: Five Hundred Years After, (T.Y. Crowell, 1977); Man in the Northeast, 1976; A Sourcebook for Native American Studies, (American Library Association, 1977); chapter: Native American Curriculum, Racism in the Textbook (Council on Interracial Books for Children, 1976); chapter in Modoc Bibliographies, in Encyclopedia of Indians of the Americas, 1975.; Pre-Contact North America, textbook (Harper & Row, 1979); Introduction to Native American Studies, textbook (Harper & Row, 1980); A Guide to Research o North American Indians, with Arlene Hirschfelder and Mary Lou Byler (American Library Association, 1983); A Yellow Raft in Blue Water (novel) (Henry Holt, 1987; paperback, Warner Book, 1988); The Broken Cord (Harper & Row, 1989; Route Two and Back, with Louise Erdrich (Lord John Press, 1991); The Crown of Columbus (novel), with Louise Erdrich (HarperCollins, 1991); The Last Dream (young adult) (Hyperion Books, 1992); Working Men (stories) (Henry Holt, forthcoming, 1993). Audio Tapes: Reading/Interview, with Louise Erdrich (American Prose Library, 1987); Tracks, read with Louise Erdrich (Harper Audio Cassette, 1989); Love Medicine, read with Louise Erdrich (Harper Audio Cassette, 1990); The Best Queen, read with Louise Erdrich (Harper Audio Cassette, 1990); The Broken Cord (Harper Audio Cassette, 1990); A Yellow Raft in Blue Water, read by Colleen Dewhurst (Harper Audio Cassette, 1990); The Crown of Columbus, read with Louise Erdrich (Harper Audio Cassette, 1991). Video Tapes: "Writers Talk: Ideas of Our Time, #59" with Louise Erdrich, 1989; "20/20" with Tom Jarriel, March 1990, ABC-TV; "Bill Moyers' World of Ideas (Parts I & II) with Louise Erdrich, 1990-91).

DOTEN, HARRY (Havasupai)
(school principal)
Affiliation: Havasupai School, P.O. Box 40, Supai, AZ 86435 (602) 448-2901.

*DOUGLAS, LARRY
(editor)
Affiliation: "Honoring the Children," National Indian Child Welfare Association, 361 1 SW Hood St. #201, Portland, OR 97201 (503) 222-4044.

DOUGLAS, THEODORE (SAM)
(Indian band chief)
Affiliation: Cheam Indian Band, 379 - 10704 No. 9 Highway, Rosedale, British Columbia, Canada V0X 1X0 (604) 794-7924.

DOUPHINAIS, LOUIS (Chippewa)
(school principal)
Affiliation: Turtle Mountain Middle School, P.O. Box 440, Belcourt, ND 58316 (701) 477-6471.

DOUVILLE, VICTOR
(museum chairperson; dept. head; editor)
Affiliation: Buechel Memorial Lakota Museum, St. Francis Indian Mission, 350 South Oak St., Box 149, St. Francis, SD 57572 (605) 747-2828; Dept Head, Lakota Studies/Creative Writing Program & editor, "Wanbliho: A Literary Arts Journal," Lakota Studies/Creative Writing Program, Sinte Gleska College, P.O. Box 8, Mission, SD 57555.

DOVLAN, REV. JOHN M., S.J.
(museum curator)
Affiliation: Kateri Galeries, The National Shrine of N.A. Martyrs, Auriesville, NY 12016 (518) 853-3033.

*DOWNING, CARL
(executive director)
Affiliation: Oklahoma Native American Language Development Institute, P.O. Box 963, Choctaw, OK 73020 (405) 454-2158.

*DOWNWIND, FRANCIS (Ojibwe)
(radio project director)
Affiliation: Red Lake Chippewa Tribal Council Radio Project, Red Lake, MN 56671 (218) 679-3331.

*DOXTATOR, DEBORAH (Oneida)
(tribal chairperson)
Affiliation: Oneida Business Committee, P.O. Box 365, Oneida, WI 54155 (414) 869-2772/2214 Fax 869-2194.

DOXTATOR, TERRY
(executive director)
Affiliation: Can Am Indian Friendship Centre, P.O. Box 441, Station "A", Windsor, Ontario, Canada N9A 6L7 (519) 252-8331.

*DRABENT, BETH, M.D.
(IHS-health programs)
Affiliation: Nashville Area IHS, 711 Stewarts Ferry Pike, Nashville, TN 37214 (615) 736-2400.

*DRAKE, ELIZABETH (Ojibwe)
(tribal chairperson)
Affiliation: Bad River Band of Lake Superior Ojibwe (Chippewa), P.O. Box 39, Odanah, WI 54861 (715) 682-7111.

DRAKE, ELROY (Navajo) 1942-
(financial manager)
Born March 20, 1942, Tuba City, Ariz. *Education*: Northern Arizona University, BS, 1972. *Principal occupation*: Financial manager. *Home address*: P.O. Box 805, Window Rock, AZ 86515 (602) 871-4705. *Affiliation*: Manager, Navajo Savings Branch of First Federal Savings, Phoenix, AZ, 1975-85; manager, part owner, Window Rock Travel Services, Inc., 1986-. *Other professional post*: College instructor. *Military service*: U.S. Army, 1964-66 (Vietnam Service Medal; SP/4 Class-Military Police). *Community activities*: VFW; helped establish United Way organization on the Navajo reservation (Navajo Way). *Memberships*: Northern Arizona University Indian Club (social manager). *Awards, honors*: 1977 Young Navajo of Year, The Navajo Tribe. *Interests*: Established first Savings & Loan Association on Indian Reservation to promote housing; calligraphy, woodworking, astronomy, restoring VW "bug" sedans, traveling, golfing.

*DRAKE, MICHAEL (United Lumbee) 1954-
(publisher)
Born July 30, 1954, Miami, Okla. *Education*: Washburn University, BBA, 1977. *Principal occupation*: Publisher. *Home address*: 126 W. Darland, Goldendale, WA 98620 (503) 668-6416. *Affiliation*: Owner, Talking Drum Publications, Goldendale, WA, 1991-. *Memberships*: (Shago) High Eagle Warrior Society of United Lumbee Nation, 1991-; Oregon Natural Resources Council, 1991-; Friends of Enola Hill, 1992-. *Interests*: "My primary interests include writing, publishing, and drummaking. The drum is the heart of my life & work. I travel throughout the Pacific Northwest presenting lectures & workshops on drumming. I also support the preservation of Native American sacred sites through lectures & articles that raise people's awareness of their cultural & religious significance. *Biographical source*: "Drumming Our Way to Balance" by Robert Mann (The New York Times, July 1993). *Published work*: The Shamanic Drum (Talking Drum Publications, 1991).

DRAPEAU, DARRELL (Yankton Sioux)
(tribal chairperson)
Affiliation: Yankton Sioux Tribal Business & Claims Committee, Box 248, Marty, SD 57361 (605) 384-3804.

DRAPER, WILLIAM H.
(Indian school principal)
Affiliation: Nazlini Boarding School, Ganado, AZ 86505 (602) 755-6125

DRAUGHON, SCOTT (Oklahoma Cherokee) 1952-
(social worker, attorney)
Born June 17, 1952, Muskogee, Okla. *Education*: Oklahoma State University, B.A., 1974; University of Tulsa Law School, J.D., 1977; University of Oklahoma, MSW, 1992. *Principal occupation*: Attorney. *Home address*: 9071 East 28th St., Tulsa, OK 74129 (918) 665-2557. *Affiliation*: Social worker, Tulsa Boys' Home (Aftercare Dept. Coordinator, 1992-); Stockbroker, Lowst Securities, Des Moines, IA, 1983-. *Other professional post*: Attorney in Private Practice, Tulsa, OK, 1979-; Director of Research/Information, Oklahoma Credit Union League, Tulsa, OK, 1988-91. *Community activities*: Tulsa Human Rights Commission (past executive board); Indian Affairs Commission of the City of Tulsa (past board); International Council of Tulsa (past Board); Tulsa Senior Services, Inc. (past board). *Memberships*: National Association of Social Workers (executive board - Oklahoma Chapter); Tulsa Area Human Resources Association (past vice president of Community Relations); Oklahoma Bar Association. *Awards, honors*: Graduate College Fee Waiver Scholarship, University of Oklahoma, Fall 1991; Regional Finalist, White House Fellowship; Leadership Oklahoma, Inc. 1993-94 Class; 1994 nominee, Friends of Children Award, Oklahoma Institute for Child Advocacy. *Interests*: Traveled widely throughout the U.S., including Alaska (prior to statehood) and Hawaii; Western Europe, Canada, Mexico, and Russia. Hobbies - golf, biking, fishing, reading, arts. *Biographical sources*: Oklahoma Observer (Jan. 25, 1994); Tulsa Tribune (Aug. 26, 1992); Tulsa World Newspaper (Dec. 22, 1993; Cherokee Advocate Newspaper (Sept. 1993); Who's Who in Human Service Professionals; Who's Who in American Law; Who's Who in Finance and Industry.

DREADFULWATER, SHIRLEY A.
(IHS-executive officer)
Affiliation: Nashville Area Iindian Health Service, 711 Stewarts Ferry Pike, Nashville, TN 37214 (615) 736-2400.

*DRESSLER, THOMAS
(health director)
Affiliation: Reno Tribal Health Station, 34 Reservation Rd., Reno, NV 89502 (702) 329-5162.

*DRIBEN, PAUL 1946-
(anthropologist)
Born May 4, 1946, St. Boniface, Manitoba, Can. *Education*: University of Manitoba, MA, 1969; University of Minnesota, PhD, 1976. *Principal occupation*: Anthropologist. *Home address*: 166 College St., Thunder Bay, Ontario, Can. P7A 5J7 (807) 343-8568 (work). *Affiliation*: Professor of anthropology, Lakehead University, Thunder Bay, Ontario, Can., 1974-. *Interests*: Ethnohistory & ethnography of the Ojibway Indians and the Metis. *Published works*: When Freedom Is Lost: The Dark Side of the Relationship Between Government and the Fort Hope and the Fort Hope Band (University of Toronto Press, 1983; We Are Metis: The Ethnography of a Halfbreed Community in Northern Alberta (AMS Press, 1985; Aroland Is Our Home: An Incomplete Victory in Applied Anthropology (AMS Press, 1986; Portrait of Humankind: An Introduction to Human Biology & Prehistoric Culture (Prentice Hall, 1994).

DROMEY, JOY E. (Yavapai)
(tribal library director)
Affiliation: Yavapai-Prescott Tribal Library, 530 E. Merritt, Prescott, AZ 86301 (602) 445-8790.

*DuBRAY, DONNA (Cheyenne River Sioux)
(museum chairperson)
Affiliation: Buechel Memorial Lakota Museum, 350 S. Oak St., Box 499, St. Francis, SD 57572 (605) 747-2745.

*DuBRAY, FRED (Cheyenne River Sioux) 1950-
(rancher)
Born July 16, 1950, Cheyenne Agency, S.D. *Education*: Black Hills State University, B.S., 1990. *Principal occupation*: Rancher (buffalo, horses & cattle). *Home address*: HCR 30 Box 32, Mobridge, SD 57601 (605) 733-2387. *Affiliations*: Director, Bison Enhancement Project, Cheyenne River Sioux Tribe (5 years); founder & president, Inter-Tribal Bison Cooperative, Rapid City, SD. *Military service*: U.S. Marine Corps, 1968-71 LCpl (Vietnam Campaign Ribbons; Combat Action Ribbon). *Interests*: Mr. DuBray has made several presentations & speeches about the benefits of buffalo re-introduction to tribes & the environment. *Biographical sources*: "Tatanka Returns," by Richard Simonelli in Winds of Change (Vol. 8, No. 4 Autumn 1993); "Where the Buffalo Roam," by Andrew Nikiforuk in Harrowsmith Country Life (August 1993); articles in New York Times (Sunday, July 5, 1994) & National Geographic (Nov. 1994).

DUCHENEAUX, FRANKLIN D.
(Cheyenne River Sioux) 1940-
(attorney)
Born January 30, 1940, Cheyenne Agency, S.D. *Education*: University of South Dakota, BS, 1963; University of South Dakota Law School, JD, 1965. *Principal occupation*: Attorney. *Affiliation*: Special Counsel on Indian Affairs, Committee on Interior & Insular Affairs, U.S. House of Representatives, Washington, DC, 1973-.

DUCHENEAUX, WAYNE (Cheyenne River Sioux)
(tribal chairperson)
Affiliations: Cheyenne River Sioux Tribal Council, P.O. Box 590, Eagle Butte, SD 57625 (605) 964-4155; president, National Congress of American Indians, 900 Pennsylvania Ave., SE, Washington, DC 20003 (202) 546-9404.

DUDGEON, PAUL J.
(college vice president)
Affiliation: Saskatchewan Indian Federated College, University of Regina, 1 18 College West, Regina, Sask. Canada S4S 0A2 (306) 584-8333.

DUGAN, JOYCE (Eastern Cherokee)
(director of education)
Born August 25, 1948, Cherokee, N.C. *Education*: Bacone Jr. College, 1965-66; Western Carolina University, B.S., 1975, M.A., 1981. *Principal occupation*: Director of education. *Address & Affiliation*: Cherokee Central School, P.O. Box 134, Cherokee, NC 28719 (704) 497-6370. *Community activities*: Cheokee Boy's Club Board of Directors; member of Parent Advisory Board for Special Education; served on United South & Eastern Tribes, Inc. *Awards, honors*: Selected a member of the White House Conference on Indian Education, 1992 (appointed to a task force to study & develop improved procedures and forms for special education); was nominated for Citizen of the Year by the Asheville Times - was selected as one of three finalists; selected as one of North Carolina's Most Distinguished Women in Education, 1994. Interests: "Great supporter of special programs for special students."

*DUKEPOO, FRANK (Mohave)
(geneticist)
Born on the Mohave Reservation.Education: Arizona State University (BS in Biology; MA and PhD in Zoology). *Affiliation*: Special Assistant to the academic vice president, Northern Arizona University, Flagstaff, AZ 86001 (602) 523-7227. *Other professional posts*: Founder, National Native American Honor Society. *Honors*: The only American Indian geneticist.

DuMARCE, HARVEY W.
(Sisseton-Wahpeton Sioux) 1946-
(law student)
Born September 5, 1946, Sisseton, S.D. *Education*: University of California, Berkeley, BA, 1976; University of Iowa, College of Law, 1991-. *Principal occupation*: Law student. *Home address*: 154 Hawkeye Court, Iowa City, IA 52246 (319) 353-5328. *Affiliation*: University of Iowa, College of Law, Iowa City, IA, 1991-. *Community activities*: Tribal court, Sisseton-Wahpeton Sioux Reservation (7 years). *Memberships*: Native American Law Student Association; Disabled Law Student Society. *Interests*: "I am interested in American Indian law, voting rights. I would like to work for a tribe as a judge or legal

counsel when I am finished with law school. I have always been active in the field of voting rights for Indian people. I was one of the plaintiffs in a landmark voting rights case in South Dakota captioned Buckanaga v. Sissteon School District. We were the first group of American Indians to file a voting rights act complaint in the U.S.After seven years of litigation, we were able to settle our case out of court, and as a result of our long struggle, we had the old at-large voting system in the Sissteon School District replaced by a cumulative voting scheme. Now for the first time i the history of the Sissteon-Wahpeton Sioux Tribe, Indian parents were able to elect candidates of their choice to sit on the Sissteon School Board. I envision a day soon when an Indian will win an election in South Dakota to the U.S. Senate on the strength of Indian votes."

*DUMONTIER, GREG (Salish-Kootenai)
(health director)
Affiliation: Flathead PHS Indian Health Center, P.O. Box 280, St. Ignatius, MT 59865 (406) 745-2411.

DUNCAN, CLIFFORD (Ute)
(museum director)
Affiliation: Ute Tribal Museum, P.O. Box 190, Highway 40, Fort Duchesne, UT 84026 (801) 722-4992.

*DUNCAN, DOUGLAS (Pomo)
(rancheria chairperson)
Affiliation: Robinson Rancheria, P.O. Box 1119, Nice, CA 95464 (707) 275-0527.

*DUNN, KENNETH EDWARD (Half Eagle)
(United Lumbee/Cherokee/Creek) 1956-
(free lance writer, novelist,
Native American researcher)
Born December 17, 1956, Santa Barbara, Calif. *Education*: Grossmont Community College (San Diego, CA), GP A. *Principal occupation*: Free lance writer, novelist, Native American researcher. *Address*: P.O. Box 512, Fall River Mills, CA 96028. *Affiliations*: Contributing reporter, Pan American Indian Association News, 1990-94; contributor, San Diego Off Roader Magazine, 1991-94. *Award*: 1975 Cal Expo Award for racing photo entitled "CMC Shot of Top Southern California Professional IMX Racers at Continial Motor Sports Club Event", Carlsbad, CA. *Interests*: Native American history, research, writing, of f road motor cycle racing. *Unpublished works*: "Cry of the Mountain," "Autumn Winds," "Season of the Wolf," (history of the Eastern (U.S.) American Indian).

DUNNINGTON, JEAN
(editor)
Affiliation: Tsa'Aszi' (The Yucca) Magazine of Navajo Culture, Tsa'Aszi Graphics Center, Ramah Navajo School Board, CPO Box 12, Pine Hill, NM 87321 (505) 783-5503.

DUNSTAN, GUY
(Indian band chief)
Affiliation: Siska Indian Band, Box 358, L ytton, BC, Canada V0K 1Z0 (604) 455-2219.

DuPREE, DOROTHY
(associate director)
Affiliation: Albuquerque Area Indian Health Services, 505 Marquette Ave., NW, Suite 1502, Albuquerque, NM 87102 (505) 766-2151.

DUPUIS, DONALD D. (Salish-Kootenai)
(chief judge; association treasurer)
Born in Mont. *Address*: Flathead Reservation Tribal Court, P.O. Box 278, Pablo, MT 59855 (406) 675-2700. *Affiliation*: Chief Judge, Flathead Reservation Tribal Court, Pablo, MT; treasurer, National American Indian Court Judges Association, Washington, DC (past president)

DUTHU, N. BRUCE (Houma)
(attorney)
Address: 127 Christian St., White River Junction, VT 05001 (802) 296-2669. Affiliation: instructor of American Indian Law & Policy, Dartmouth College, Native American Studies Dept., 306-307 Bartlett Hall, Hinman Box 6152, Hanover, NH 03755 (603) 646-3530. *Membership*: Native Ameriacn Alumni Association of Dartmouth College (National Steering Committee).

DYE, SARA
(clinical director)
Affiliation: Carl Albert Indian Hospital, 1001 North Country Club Rd., Ada, OK 74820 (405) 436-3980.

*DYER, PATRICIA (Mukwa Odae Kwa) (Little Traverse Bay Bands of Odawa-Mississippi Choctaw) 1953-
(admissions counselor)
Born February 14, 1953, Charlevoix, Mich. *Education*: Northern Michigan University, B.S.W., 1981; Michigan State University, M.A., 1994. *Principal occupation*: Admissions counselor. *Home address*: 3572 Annis Rd., Mason, MI 48854 (517) 589-5065. *Affiliation*: Michigan Association of College Admissions Counselors, 1990-. *Other professional post*: American Indian historian. *Community activities*: Little Traverse Bay Band of Odawa Tribal Council (Eagle President). *Memberships*: Ethnohistory Association; Native American Indian Higher Education Council; Eagle President, an American Indian faculty & staff association at Michigan State University. *Interests*: "I do transitional Michigan Native American art - porcupine quillwork, beadwork, leatherwork." *Published works*: Native American Experience (Michigan Dept. of Education, 1989); WPA Arts & Crafts Project (Michigan History Magazine, 1995); The Northern Michigan Ottawa Association, MSU (Oklahoma State, 1995).

*DYSON, PEGGY
(museum president)
Affiliation: Baranov Museum, Erskine House, 101 Marine W ay, Kodiak, AK 99615 (907) 486-5920.

E

EAGLE, CHARLES R.
(Indian band chief)
Affiliation: Moose Woods Indian Band, Box 149, RR 5, Saskatoon, Saskatchewan, Canada S7K 3J8 (306) 477-0908.

EAGLE, TOM
(Indian council president)
Affiliation: N.W.T. Council of Friendship Centres, P.O. Box 2859, Yellowknife, Northwest Territories, Canada X1A 2R2 (403) 920-2288; director, Tree of Peace Friendship Centre, P.O. Box 2667, Yellowknife, N.W.T., Canada X1A 1H0.

*EAGLESTAFF, ROBERT *(To Wakanhi Wamblee-Blue Lighting Eagle)* **(Lakota) 1952-**
 (educator)
Born December 20, 1952, Dupree, S.D. *Education*: University of South Dakota, B.S., M.S.; University of Washington, 1991- (doctoral candidate). *Principal occupation*: Educator. *Home address*: 4606 Woodlawn Ave. N., Seattle, WA 98103 (206) 298-7801 (work). *Affiliation*: Principal, Seattle Public Schools, Seattle, WA, 1989-; American Indian Heritage School, Seattle, WA. *Other professional posts*: Teacher, consultant, engineering assistant. *Community activities*: Enrolled at the Cheyenne River Sioux Reservation. *Memberships*: National Association of Secondary School Principals; Association of Washington School Principals; Principals Association of Seattle Schools; Lakota Sundancer Society, 1978-. *Awards, honors*: Numerous athletic awards, especially in basketball; numerous academic awards as well. *Interests*: "I am interested in researching the history of my family at various sites throughout the U.S. I would like to go back thousands of years and document those years."

EAR, JOHNNY
 (Indian band chief)
Affiliation: Bearspaw Group (Stoney) Indian Band, Box 40, Morley, Alberta, Canada T0L 1N0 (403) 881-3770.

*EARL, JOHN
 (attorney)
Address: 6365 E. Alabama Rd., Hwy. 92, Woodstock, GA 30188. *Affiliation*: Member, Board of Directors, The Native American Center of Georgia, Woodstock, GA.

EARLY, HARRY D. (Pueblo)
 (pueblo governor)
Affiliation: Pueblo of Laguna, P.O. Box 194, Laguna, NM 87026 (505) 552-6654.

*EARRING, LYNDA
 (supt. for education)
Affiliation: Little Wound Day School, P.O. Box 500, Kyle, SD 57752 (605) 455-2461.

EASTES, FRANK, Jr.
 (executive director)
Affiliation: Native American Indian Media Corporation, P.O. Box 59, Strawberry Plains, TN 37871 (615) 933-6246.

EASTMAN, CLARENCE (Sioux)
 (Indian band chief)
Affiliation: Oak Lake Sioux Indian Band, P.O. Box 146, Pipestone, Manitoba, Canada R0M 1T0 (204) 854-2261.

EATON, LINDA B. 1948-
 (curator of ethnology;
 Indian art show coordinator)
Born December 9, 1948, Coffeyville, Kans. *Education*: Rice University, BA, 1974; Brown University, MA, 1978, PhD, 1983. *Principal occupation*: Curator of ethnology, Summer Indian Art Show coordinator. *Address*: Museum of Northern Arizona, Rte. 4, Box 720, Flagstaff, AZ 86001 (602) 774-5211. *Affiliations*: Curator/director, Museum of Anthropology, Wake Forest University, Winston-Salem, NC, 1982-86; curator of ethnology, Museum of Northern Arizona, Flagstaff, 1986-. *Other professional post*: Summer Indian Art Show coordinator. " I head up the annual Zuni Artists Exhibition, Hopi Artists Exhibition, and Navajo Artists Exhibition for the Museum of Northern Arizona, which attract 1,500 Indian artists and thousands of collectors." *Memberships*: American Anthropological Association; Society for American Archaeology; Native American Art Studies Association; Council for Museum Anthropology; Sigma Xi. *Interests*: "American Indian art and ethnology; experience of contemporary Indian artists, especially Southwest; Zuni Pueblo; role of art in society; development of native political systems; Anasazi archaeology; history of archaeology & anthropology; also traveled and did archaeological work in Middle East and East Africa." *Published work*: A Separate Vision (Museum of Northern Arizona, 1990).

EBBERT, PAUL, M.D.
 (clinical director)
Affiliation: Fort Duchesne PHS Indian Health Center, P.O. Box 160, Roosevelt, UT 84026 (801) 722-5122.

EBERHARD, ERIC D. 1945-
 (attorney-Indian affairs law)
Education: Western Reserve University, BA, 1967; University of Cincinnati, School of Law, JD, 1970; George Washington University, LLM, 1972. *Principal occupation*: Attorney-Indian affairs law. *Address*: Senate Select Committee on Indian Affairs, Room SH 838, Hart Senate Office Bldg., Washington, DC 20510. *Affiliations*: Deputy Attorney General, Navajo Nation, 1983-85; executive director, Navajo Nation, Washington office, 1985-87; Minority Staff Director and Counsel, Senate Select Committee on India Affairs, Washington, D.C., 1987-. Mr. Eberhard has been actively engaged in the practice of Indian affairs law since 1973. His practice has involved all aspects of the representations of Indian tribes and individuals in federal, state, and tribal forums. As Deputy General of the Navajo Nation and Executive Director of the Navajo Nation, Washington Office, he was involved in the development and passage of federal legislation relating to all aspects of tribal self-governance and development.

*EBY, RICHARD L. 1953-
 (producer/publisher)
Born December 26, 1953, Cheboygan, Mich. *Education*: High school. *Principal occupation*: Producer/publisher. *Home address*: P.O. Box 1788, Fayetteville, AR 72702 (501) 443-9488. *Affiliations*: Co-owner/general manager/producer, Lane Audio Productions, 1988-93; president/recordist/producer, VIP Publishing, Fayetteville, AR, 1990-. *Membership*: National Museum of the American Indian (charter member). *Awards, honors*: Produced "When the Century Was Young" audio autobiographical sketch of Dee Brown, published by August House of Little Rock, AR, and selected in top 3 historical audio programs by Publishers Weekly. *Interests*: "I have been interested in Indian cultures since childhood, and I'm happy that saving some of their heritage is part of our common purpose in this life. Since joining with Gregg Howard (VIP Publishing) in 1989, my appreciation for Indian people as individuals has grown immensely. I have recorded elders in their homes and in recording studios, worked with other volunteers to develop Indian cultural materials for Head Start, attended language workshops, sovereignty symposiums, powwows, and more, I enjoy working with American Indians and I always really feel the respect everyone has for each other"; music composition. *Published works*: Introduction to Cherokee, 1990; Introduction to Choctaw, 1992; and Introduction to Chickasaw, 1994 (all published by VIP Publishing).

ECHOHAWK, BRUMMETT (Pawnee) 1922-
 (artist, writer, actor)
Born March 3, 1922, Pawnee, Okla. *Education*: Detroit School of Arts and Crafts, 1945; Art Institute of Chicago, 1945-48; studied creative writing at the University of Tulsa. *Principal occupation*: Artist, writer, actor. *Home address*: P.O. Box 1922, Tulsa, OK 74101. *Affiliations*: Staff artist, Chicago Daily Times and Chicago Sun Times; artist, Bluebook, McCall's Magazine Corp., New York. *Military service*: U.S. Army, 1940-45 (Purple Heart with oak-leaf cluster; did Combat sketches published in the Army's Yank Magazine, and 88 newspapers by N.E.A. News Syndicate). *Community activities*: Gilcrease Museum, Tulsa, OK (board member). *Exhibitions*: Paintings shown in Pakistan & India, through the Art in the Embassies Program, State Department; other works shown at the De Young Museum, San Francisco; Amon Carter Museum, Fort Worth, Texas; Gilcrease Museum; Imperial War Museum. London; Bad Segeberg, Hamburg, West Germany. *Acting*: As stage actor, Mr. Echohawk has appeared in the role of Sitting Bull in Kopit's play Indians in Tulsa, Fort Worth, and Lincoln, Neb. Also played at the Virginia Museum Theater, Richmond, Questor's Theater, London, and Karl May Theater, Bad Segeberg, West Germany; he did a TV film in Hamburg, W. Germany. *Awards, honors*: Assisted Thomas Hart Benton with one of the greatest mural in America: The Truman Memorial Library mural called Independence and the Opening of the West, at Independence, MO; commissioned by the Aluminum Co. of America for a painting depicting early American history of the Tennessee Valley; commissioned by Leaning Tree Publishing Co., Boulder, CO for paintings to be reproduced as Christmas cards; Mr. Echohawk's paintings are of a classic and representational style, which cover the subjects of the Indian and the American West. *Biographical sources*: Encyclopedia of the American Indian; Indians of Today; Dictionary of International Biography; National Geographic's American Indians. *Published works*: Writings, with illustrations, have appeared in the Tulsa Sunday World, Oklahoma Today Magazine, The Western Horseman Magazine, and others.

ECHOHAWK, JOHN E. (Pawnee) 1945-
 (attorney)
Born August 11, 1945, Albuquerque, N.M. *Education*: University of New Mexico, BA, 1967; University of New Mexico, School of Law, JD, 1970. *Principal Occupation*: Attorney. *Address & Affiliation*: Native American Rights Fund, 1506 Broadway, Boulder, CO 80302 (303) 447-8760 (research associate, 1970-1972; deputy director, 1972-73, 1975-77; executive director, 1973-75, 1977-). *Community activities*: Association on American Indian Affairs (board of directors); American Indian Lawyer Training Program (board of directors); National Committee on Responsive Philanthropy (board of directors). *Memberships*: American Indian Bar Association; American Bar Association. *Awards, Honors*: Assisted in forming the American Indian Law Student's Association; Americans for Indian Opportunity, Distinguished Service Award; White Buffalo Council, Friendship Award; 1987 Na-

tional Indian Achievement Award from the Indian Council Fires; National Congress of American Indians, President's Indian Service Award; appointed to the Wayne Morse Chair of Law and Politics at the University of Oregon. *Interests*: Indian law.

*ECHOHAWK, LARRY (Pawnee) 1948-
(politician)
Born in Wyom. *Education*: Brigham Young University, BA, 1970; University of Utah Law School, J.D., 1973. *Principal occupation*: Politician; Idaho state attorney general. *Address*: County Office Bldg., 650 Main St., Boise, ID 83702. *Affiliation*: Idaho State Attorney General, Boise, ID, 1990-94; Governor, State of Idaho, 1995-. *Interests*: Politics. Mr. Echohawk is the first Native American Governor in U.S. history

ECHOHAWK, LUCILLE A.
(financial aid officer)
Affiliation: Scholarship program, Council of Energy Resource Tribes (CERT), 1580 Logan St., Suite 400, Denver, CO 80203-1941 (303) 832-6600.

*ECHOHAWK, WALTER (Pawnee)
(senior staff attorney)
Affiliations: Senior staff attorney, Native American Rights Fund, 1506 Broadway, Boulder, CO 80302; a national coordinator for American India Religious Freedom Act Coalition; member, Board of Trustees, American Indian Ritual Object Repatriation Foundation, 463 East 57th St., New York, NY 10022 (212) 980-9441.

EDDY, DANIEL, Jr. (Navajo)
(tribal chairperson)
Affiliation: Colorado River Indian Tribal Council, Route 1, Box 23-B, Parker, AZ 85344 (602) 669-9211.

EDDY, FRANK W. 1930-
(archaeologist-anthropologist)
Born May 7 1930, Roanoke, Va. *Education*: University of New Mexico, BA, 1952; University of Arizona, MA, 1958; University of Arizona, PhD, 1968. *Principal occupation*: Archaeologist-anthropologist. *Address*: Dept. of Anthropology, University of Colorado, Boulder, CO 80309 (303) 492-7947. *Affiliations*: Curator, Museum of New Mexico, researcher and director of the Navajo Reservoir Salvage Archaeological Project, 1959-65; research assistant at the University of Colorado Museum--dig foreman at Yellow Jacket and Jurgens Site excavations, 1965-68; executive director, Texas, Archaeological Salvage Project, University of Texas, Austin, 1968-70; director, Chimney Rock Archaeological Project, University of Colorado, 1970-73; associate professor, professor of anthropology, University of Colorado, 1970-. *Other professional posts*: Director and principal investigator, Two Forks Archaeological Project, University of Colorado, 1974-75; intern, Interagency Archaeological Services, Denver, National Park Service, 1975-76; co-director and principal investigator of the Bisti-Star Lake Cultural Resource Inventory, Archaeological Associates, Inc., summer, 1977. *Military service*: U.S. Army, 1952-54. *Memberships*: Society for American Archaeology, 1953-; Society for the Sigma Xi, 1965--73; American Quaternary Association, 1970-; Colorado Archaeological Society, 1970-; Society of Professional Archaeologists, 1976- (counselor, standards board); Association of Field Archaeologists, 1977-. *Interests*: Cultural ecology; prehistoric

settlement studies; cultural change as revealed by archaeology; technology of primitive societies. *Published works*: An Archaeological Survey of the Navajo Reservoir District, Northwestern New Mexico, with Alfred E. Dittert, Jr., and James J. Hester (Monograph, School of American Research, Museum of New Mexico, 1961); Excavations at Los Pinos Phase Sites in the Navajo Reservoir District (Museum of New Mexico, 1961); Excavations at the Candelaria Site, LA 4406, chapter II in Pueblo Period Sites in the Piedra River Section, Navajo Reservoir District, assembled with A.E. Dittert, Jr. (Museum of New Mexico, 1963); Prehistory in the Navajo Reservoir District, Northwestern New Mexico (Museum of New Mexico, 1966); Archaeological Investigations at Chimney Rock Mesa: 1970-1972 (Memoirs of the Colorado Archaeological Society, 1977); An Archaeological Study of Indian Settlements and Land Use in the Colorado Foothills, with Ric Windmiller (Memoirs of Southwestern Lore, Colorado Archaeological Society). Several articles in journals, and papers delivered at regional meetings and national conferences.

*EDDY, PHYLLIS
(special assistant)
Affiliation: Office of the Director, Indian Health Service, Rm. 6-22 Parklawn Bldg., 5600 Fishers Lane, Rockville, MD 20857 (301) 443-7261.

EDERER, CHARLES J.
(executive director)
Affiliation: Urban Indian Health & Human Services, Inc., 4100 Silver, SE, Suite B, Albuquerque, NM 87108

EDEVOLD, MARVIN
(IHS-tribal activities)
Affiliation: Office of Tribal Activities, Bemidji Area Office, Indian Health Service, 127 Federal Bldg., Bemidji, MN 56601 (218) 759-3424.

EDGAR, M.J. YVONNE
(Indian band chief)
Affiliation: Mississaugas of Scugog Indian Band, RR #5, Port Perry, Ontario, Canada L0B 1N0 (416) 985-3337.

EDGE, JAMES E. 1948-
(health administrator)
Born April 29, 1948, Anacortes, Wash. *Education*: University of Washington, BS, 1971; University of Hawaii, MPH, 1979. *Principal occupation*: Health administrator. *Home address*: 1580 Rio Vista Way S., Salem, OR 97302 (503) 399-5937. *Affiliation*: Service Unit Director, Western Oregon Service Unit, Indian Health Service, Salem, OR, 1980-. *Other professional post*: Chairperson, Service Unit Directors' Steering Committee on Health Care Reform, Portland Area Indian Health Service, 1993-. *Military service*: Commissioned Officer, 18 years, USPHS, (Captain). *Memberships*: American College of Healthcare Executives; Association of Military Surgeons of the U.S.; Reserve Officers Association; American Academy of Medical Administrators; Commissioned Officers Association of the U.S. Public Health Service; American Public Health Association; Washington State Pharmaceutical Association. *Awards, honors*: Indian Health Service Long Term Training, 1978-79; USPHS Citation and Ribbon, 1984; USPHS Commendation Medal, 1986; USPHS Outstanding Unit Citation, 1988; USPHS Unit Commendation, 1989; USPHS Outstanding Service

Medal, 1991). *Interests*: "Special interest in rural and minority health care. Eighteen years broad based experience in American Indian health care. Extensive travel & consultation in Pacific Island health care; running, skiing, fishing, antique cars." *Biographical sources*: The National Dean's List, 1979-80; Outstanding Young Men of American, 1980; Marquis Who's Who in Finance and Industry, 1992-93.

EDMO, ED, Jr. (Shoshoni) 1944-
(consultant)
Address: 9430 N.E. Prescott, Portland, OR 97220 (503) 256-2257. *Interests*: Professional Native American story teller who visits schools, libraries, colleges, and museums to present a program of arts and crafts, story telling of legends and myths of various Native American tribes. He is a crafts artist with shows held periodically in cities and towns of the Northwest. He has many published poems and is author of book and magazine materials.

EDMO, KESLEY (Shoshone/Bannock)
(board member)
Affiliation: National Indian Youth Council, Albuquerque, NM.

EDMO, LORRAINE P. (Shoshone-Bannock) 1948-
(program administrator)
Born October 26, 1948, Blackfoot, Idaho. *Education*: University of Montana, BA, 1970; University of New Mexico, MA, 1982. *Principal occupation*: Program administrator. *Address & Affiliation*: National Indian Education Association, 1819 H St., NW, Suite 800, Washington, DC 20006 (202) 835-3001. *Other professional posts*: TV News Reporter, 1970-72; resource development specialist, 1972-73, executive director, 1973-75, Idaho Inter-Tribal Board, Inc., Boise, Idaho; technical writer, 1976-79, development officer, 1979-80, Native American Rights Fund, Boulder, CO; executive director, American Indian Graduate Center, Albuquerque, NM, 1984-93. *Community activities*: Warden & treasurer, Episcopal Urban Indian Ministry, Albuquerque, NM, 1986-93. *Memberships*: National Indian Education Association (executive committee-board of directors, 1989-92; executive director, 1993-); National Organization of Native American Women (former president); National Congress of American Indians. *Awards, honors*: Selected by the Albuquerque Tribune as one of 12 "Rising Stars" in the education field for 1988; selected as a 1989 Outstanding Young Woman of American, Boulder, CO. *Interests*: "I am interested in working for the betterment of Indian tribal governments and American Indian people. I attempt to do this through advocacy; service on Board and commissions, writing, etc. I have travelled extensively to visit and work with tribes and Indian organizations throughout the country."

*EDMUND, RICK
(editor)
Affiliation: Susquehanna Valley Native American Eagle, Box 99, Walnut Valley Farm, Loganville, PA 17342 (717) 428-1440.

EDMUNDS, JUDITH A. 1943-
(dealer-American Indian jewelry)
Born September 8, 1943, Waltham, Mass. *Education*: Massachusetts College of Pharmacy. *Principal occupation*: Dealer of fine American Indian jewelry and related items. *Home address*:

Box 788, West Yarmouth, MA 02673. *Affiliation*: President-treasurer, Edmonds of Yarmouth, Inc., 1973-. *Other professional posts*: State chairperson, Indian Arts & Crafts Association (served on Education & Public Relations Committee; currently chairperson for Massachusetts). *Interests*: Ms. Edmunds writes, "My business is a retail outlet, but my greatest pleasure is educating the general public on the different Indian tribes and their style of work and their living conditions, and to create collectors of fine Indian art.By educating these people - those dealers that are selling fakes and misrepresenting their wares will soon be out of business, I travel to reservations a couple of times a year and spend time in the Hopi Mesas and San Domingo Pueblos, as well as on the Navajo Reservation, as we have Indian friends spread out through the various reservations, as well as Anglo friends. My interests outside of the Indian field is fine American antiques."

EDWARDS, EDDIE V. (Oklahoma Choctaw) 1930-
(BIA-government service manager)
Born October 7, 1930, Kingfisher, Okla. *Education*: Oklahoma City University, BA, 1960; Oklahoma University Engineering Graduate School, 1962-64; Oklahoma City University, School of Law, JD, 1969. *Principal occupation*: BIA-government service manager. *Home address*: 2114 Mistletoe Lane, Edmond, OK 73034. *Affiliation*: U.S. Dept. of the Interior, BIA, Real Estate Services, 1849 C St., NW, MS: 4522-MIB, Washington, DC 20240 (202) 208-5474. *Other profesional post*: Oklahoma Highway Design Engineer, Oklahoma State Capital, 1960-69. *Military service*: U.S. Navy (Korean Service, 1950-54; six campaign medals, Korean Service medal w/6 Battlestars). *Memberships*: Oklahoma Bar Association, Federal Bar Association, and American Indian Bar Association. *Interests*: Indian law.

EDWARDS, JANE
(museum director/curator)
Affiliation: Mitchell Indian Museum, Kendall College, 2408 Orrington Ave., Evanston, IL 60201 (708) 866-1395.

EDWARDS, KEN *(Rainbow Cougar)* (Colville) 1956-
(artist-painter; storyteller/speaker)
Born February 8, 1956, Greenville, S.C. *Education*: Institute of American Indian Arts, AA, 1977. *Principal occupation*: Artist-painter; storyteller/speaker. *Address*: Rt. 2, Box 72-S, Omak, WA98841 (509)826-4744. *Membership*: Indian Arts & Crafts Association, 1984-. Ken works in a wide variety of media: predominantly watercolor, oil, acrylic, and pen and ink. He is experienced in silversmithing, welding, drafting, photography and beadwork. An additional talent is that of storyteller and oral historian. Ken traveled to over 58 Indian reservations and memorized more than 1,000 stories from many tribes. *Awards, honors*: Particpated in the First National Indian Art Show, Nov. 1985, held in Washington, DC; did the painting which was made into a Porter-Print announcing the first Miss Indian U.S.A. Pageant; his painting, "First Love" was part of a Native American Art Show at the December 1987 International Friendship House, Moscow, USSR. His artwork has been exhibited and sold in fine art shows and galleries across the U.S. He has received several top awards at major shows. His ink drawings and

poetry have been published i ten Indian newspapers. *Published works*: Illustrated four children's books - How the Animals Got Their Names, How Food Was Given, Neekna and Chemai, and Turtle and the Eagle - published by Theytus Books, Penticton, BC, Canada; Wintercount Card Co., Newcastle, CO has purchased 15 of Ken's watercolors and added them to their series if cards by Native American artists.

EDWARDS, LEONARD
(Indian band chief)
Affiliation: Nanoose Indian Band, RR #1, Box 124, Lantzville, British Columbia, Canada V0R 2H0 (604) 390-3661.

EDWARDSON, GEORGE (Inupiat)
(AK village president)
Affiliation: Inupiat Community of the Arctic Slope, P.O. Box 1232, Barrow, AK 99723 (907) 825-6907.

EGER, LESLIE
(editor)
Affiliation: Win-Awaenen-Nisitotung, Sault Ste. Marie Tribe of Chippewa Indians, 2218 Shunk Rd., Sault Ste. Marie, MI 49783-9326 (906) 635-6050.

EID, LEROY V. 1932-
(professor of history)
Born December 22, 1932, Cincinnati, Ohio. *Education*: University of Dayton, BS, 1953; St. John's University, MS, 1958, PhD (History), 1961; University of Toronto, MA (Philosophy), 1968. *Principal occupation*: Professor of history. *Home address*: 1181 Kentshire Dr., Centerville, OH 45459 (513) 229-2848 (office) *Affiliation*: Professor, Dept. of History, University of Dayton, 300 College Park, Dayton, OH, 1961- (chairman of dept. 1969-83). *Interests*: Teaching history of American Indians. *Published works*: Articles: "National War Among Indians of Northeastern North America: Ethnohistorical Insight or Anthropological Nonsense?" (Canadian Review of American Studies, Summer, 1985); "The Cardinal Principle of Northeast Woodland Indian War," (Papers of the Thirteenth Algonquian Conference, Toronto, 1982); "Liberty and the Indian," (Midwest Quarterly, 1982); "The War of the Iroquois Lost," (Journal of the Order of the Indian Wars, Spring 1980); The Ojibwa-Iroquois War, (Ethnohistory, 1979); "Their Rules of War": The Validity of James Smith's Analysis of Indian War," The Register of the Kentucky Historical Society (Winter, 1988); "A Kind of Running Fight" Indian Battlefield Tactics in the Late Eighteenth Century," The Western Pennsylvania Historical Magazine (April, 1988); "Who Defeated St. Clair?" in Selected Papers from the 1989 and 1990 George R. Clark Conferences.

EISENBERGER, VELMA
(Indian school principal)
Affiliation: Dennehotso Boarding School, P.O. Box LL, Dennehotso, AZ 86535 (602) 658-3201.

ELAM, EARL H. 1934-
(professor of history)
Born December 7, 1934, Wichita Falls, Tex. *Education*: Midwestern University, B.A., 1961; Texas Tech University, MA, 1967, PhD, 1971. *Principal occupation*: Professor of history. *Home address*: 407 N. Cockrell, Alpine, TX 79830 (915) 837-5228 (home) 837-8146 (office). *Affiliations*: Instructor, Texas Tech University, 1967-71; pro-

fessor of history, Sul Ross State University, Alpine, TX, 1971-; director, Center for Big Bend Studies, Sul Ross State University, 1987-. *Other professional post*: Editor, Journal of Big Bend Studies, an annual publication dedicated to the history and culture of the Southwest with emphasis on the Big Bend of Texas. *Military service*: U.S. Navy, 1953-57 (Radioman). *Memberships*: Western History Association; West Texas Historical Association (president, 1991-92); Texas State Historical Association. *Interests*: American Indian history; Indian land claims; American Indian ethnology and archaeology; Texas history, Southwestern American history, Spanish borderland history. *Published works*: Several articles and reports; thesis, dissertation, and reports on Wichita Indian history and ethnology.

ELGIN, CAROL
(college president)
Affiliation: Southwestern Indian Polytechnic Institute, P.O. Box 10146, 9169 Coors Rd., NW, Albuquerque, NM 87184 (505) 897-5347.

*ELKINS, BRYAN
(health center director)
Affiliation: Fallon Tribal Health Center, P.O. Box 1980, Fallon, NV 89406 (702) 423-3634.

*ELLANA, LINDA J.
(editor)
Affiliation: Anthropological Papers pf the University of Alaska, Dept. of Anthropology, University of Alaska, 310 Eielson, Fairbanks, AK 99775 (907) 474-7288.

ELLIG, THOMAS R.
(historic site manager)
Affiliation: Lower Sioux Agency Historic Site, R.R. #1, Box 125, Morton, MN 56270 (507) 697-6321.

*ELLISON, CARL, M.D.
(clinical director)
Affiliation: Claremore PHS Indian Hospital, Will Rogers & Moore, Claremore, OK 74017 (918) 342-6200.

ELLISON, ROSEMARY
(museum curator)
Affiliations: U.S. Dept. of the Interior Art Museum, Indian Arts & Crafts Board, Rm. 4004-MIB, 18th & C Sts., NW, Washington, DC 20240 (202) 208-3773. *Other professional posts*: curator, Museum of the Plains Indian, Browning, MT & Southern Plains Indian Museum, Anadarko, OK.

ELROD, SAM
(IHS-director of administrative services)
Affiliation: Division of Administrative Services, Office of Administration & Management, Indian Health Service, 5600 Fishers Lane, Room 4B-42, Rockville, MD 20857 (301) 443-0815.

ELUSKA, STEVE
(AK village council chief)
Affiliation: Telida Village Council, P.O. Box 217, Telida, AK 99629 (907) 843-81 15.

ELVASAAS, FRED H.
(AK village council president)
Affiliation: Native Village of Seldova, P.O. Drawer I, Seldova, AK 99770 (907) 234-7625

EMERY, STEVEN CHARLES *(Mato Tanka)*
(Cheyenne River Sioux) 1958-
  (tribal attorney)
Born November 14, 1958, in S.D. *Education*:
University of South Dakota, BA, 1986; Harvard
Law School, JD, 1989. *Principal occupation*:
Tribal attorney. *Address*: P.O. Box 807, Eagle
Butte, SD 57625 (605) 964-6686 (of fice). *Affili-
ations*: Attorney, Cheyenne River Sioux Tribe,
Eagle Butte, SD, 1989-; partner, Van Norman &
Emery, Eagle Butte, SD, 1989-. *Other profes-
sional post*: General counsel, Mart Indian
School, Marty, SD, 1990-. *Community activities*:
Cheyenne River Sioux Tribal Police Commis-
sion (chairperson, 1989-91); Dakota Plains Legal Services Board of Directors, 1989-91; Cheyenne River Community College Board of Directors (vice-chairperson), 1990-. *Memberships*:
South Dakota Bar Association; Federal Bar Association; American Bar Association; Eighth Circuit Court of Appeals, U.S. *Awards, honors*:
McGovern-Abourezk Human Rights Award,
USD Political Science/Criminal Justice Dept.,
1985; Phi Beta Kappa (Alpha Chapter, USD,
1986); Faculty Appreciation Award, USD Political Science/Criminal Justice Dept., 1986; Who's
Who in American Universities & Colleges (1985-
86 Edition); Massachusetts Indian Association
Fellow (1986-89); U.S. Dept. of Education
American Indian Fellowship Recipient (1986-
89). *Interests*: "Traditional singer (Itazipco
Hoka); singer/songwriter; guitarist; lectures on
topics such as: federal Indian law, Lakota/Da-
kota culture and language." *Published work*:
Musical album - Dakota Wakan Cekiye Odowan
(collection of ten hymns played and sung by
Steve Emery in the Dakota language, June
1986.

*EMMERT, REG
  (archive director)
Affiliation: Alaska's Motion Picture Film Archive
Center, P.O. Box 95203, University of Alaska,
Fairbanks, AK 99701 (907) 479-7296.

ENEAS, ADAM
  (Indian band chief)
Affiliation: Penticton Indian Band, R.R. #2, Site
80, Comp. 19, Penticton, British Columbia,
Canada V2A 6J7 (604) 493-0048.

ENGELSTAD, KURT (Eskimo-Inupiaq) 1937-
  (business executive, attorney)
Born October 3, 1937, Corvallis, Ore. *Education*: Oregon State University, BS, 1960; Northwest School of Law, Lewis & Clark College, JD,
1972. *Principal occupation*: Business executive,
attorney. *Home address*: 2125 S.E. Sherman
St., Portland, OR 97214. *Affiliations*: President,
The 13th Regional Corporation, Vancouver, WA,
1983-. *Other professional posts*: President and
executive producer, Alaska Native Film Productions, Inc.; member, board of directors, Alaska
Federation of Natives; principal, Engelstad &
Associates, a private Oregon-based consulting
firm. *Military service*: U.S. Air Force (active duty),
1960-61; active Air Force reserve, 1961-; (Lt.
Colonel; Air Force Longevity Service Ribbon
with hour glass device; Air Force Reserve Medal
with 4 oak leaves; Small Arms Marksmanship
Medal); retired Air Force Reserve. *Community
activities*: Former Boy Scout troop leader; former
director and board chairman, Multnomah
County, Oregon legal services. *Memberships*:
Oregon State Bar, 1972-; Multnomah Bar, 1972-
; District Court Bar, 1972-; joint committee of
Oregon Bar with Press and Broadcasters (1974-

77 member and chairman). *Awards, honors*:
Chief Frank White Buffaloman award for Outstanding Service to the Native American community of Portland, Oregon by Portland Urban
Indian Council; Outstanding Journalism graduate for 1960 bestowed by Sigma Delta Chi honorary, Oregon State University chapter; appointed by the Governor of Oregon as a member of the State of Oregon's Workforce Quality
Council. *Interests*: Vocational: Indian law, business management and finance; Avocational:
Writing, photography, philately. *Biographical
source*: Natives Without a Land Base, by Elizabeth Roderick, October, 1983 edition Alaska
Native News Magazine. *Published works*: Editorial staff, Environmental Law Review of Northwest School of Law of Lewis & Clark College,
1972.

ENGEN, LISA M.
  (museum curator)
Affiliation: Wickliffe Mounds Research Center
Museum, P.O. Box 155, Wickliffe, KY 42087
(502) 335-3681.

*ENGLEHARDT, KEN
  (school supt.)
Affiliation: Takini School, HC77, Box 537,
Howes, SD 57748 (605) 538-4399.

ENGLES, WILLIAM LYNN (Oneida) 1935-
  (BIA agency supt.)
Born September 29, 1935, Poplar, Mont. *Edu-
cation*: The Evergreen State College, BA, 1974.
Principal occupation: BIA agency supt. *Address*:
Dept. of Energy, Richland Field Office, P.O. Box
339, Richland, WA 99352. *Affiliations*: Public information officer, BIA, Washington, DC, 1975-
1980; Intergovernmental affairs officer, BIA,
Portland, OR, 1980-84; commissioner, Administration for Native Americans, Dept. of Health
& Human Services, Washington, DC, 1984-89;
supt., Flathead Agency, BIA, Pablo, MT, 1989-.
Other professional posts: Reporter & Bureau
Chief, United Press International. *Military service*: U.S. Army, 1955-57 (SP-4). *Community
activities*: Indian advisory Council, Boy Scouts
of America.

ENGLISH, SAMUEL F. (Chippewa) 1942-
  (artist)
Born June 2, 1942, Phoenix, Ariz. *Education*:
Bacone College, 1960-62; University of San
Francisco, 1967-68. *Principal occupation*: Art-
ist. *Home address*: 400 San Felipe N.W.,
Albu-
querque, NM 87104. *Affiliation*: Owner, Native
American Art Gallery, Albuquerque, NM, 1982-.

ENOS, AMELIA (Pima-Papago)
  (director of human services)
Affiliation: American Indian Community House,
Human Service Resource Dept., 404 Lafayette
St., New York, NY 10003.

EPOO, JOHNNY
  (president-Indian organization)
Affiliation: Avataq Cultural Institute, Inc.,
Inukjuak, Quebec; office - 294 Carre St. Louis,
Montreal, Quebec H2X 1A4 (514) 844-0109.

ERASMUS, BILLY (Dene)
  (president-Dene Nation)
Affiliation: Dene Nation, Denedeh National Office, P.O. Box 2338, Yellowknife, Northwest Territories, Canada Y1A 2P7 (403) 873-4081.

ERASMUS, GEORGES HENRY (Dene) 1948-
(co-chair, Royal Commission
on Aboriginal Peoples)
Born August 8, 1948, Fort Rae, N.W.T., Can.
Education: High school, Yellowknife, NWT. *Principal occupation*: Co-chair, Royal Commission
on Aboriginal Peoples. *Address*: Royal Commission on Aboriginal Peoples, P.O. Box 1993,
Station "B", Ottawa, ON K1P 1B2 (613) 943-
2075 (work). *Affiliations*: Secretary, Indian Band
Council, Yellowknife, Can., 1969-71; Organizer & chairman, Community Housing Association, Yellowknife, 1969-72; advisor to president, Indian Brotherhood of NWT, 1970-71;
fieldworker and regional staff director, Company
of Young Canadians, 1970-73; chairman, University Canada North, 1971-75; director, Community Development Program, Indian Brotherhood of Northwest Territories (later the Dene Nation) (director, Community Development Program, 1973-76; president, 1976-83); president,
Denedeh Development Corporation, 1976-83;
elected Northern vice-chief, Assembly of First
Nations, 1983; elected National Chief, Assembly of First Nations, Ottawa, Canada, 1985, re-
elected 1988-91; co-chair, Royal Commission
on Aboriginal Peoples, Ottawa, ON, 1991-.
Membership: Honorary member, Ontario Historical Society, 1990. *Awards, honors*: Representative for Canada on Indigenous Survival International, 1983; Canadian delegate to World
Council of Indigenous Peoples International
Conferences, 1984-85; appointed director of the
World Wildlife Fund of Canada, 1987; appointed
to the Order of Canada, 1987; appointed to the
Board of the Canadian Tribute to Human Rights,
1987; board member, Energy Probe Research
Foundation, Operation Dismantle, 1988; honorary committee member, International Youth for
Peace and Justice, 1988; advisory council member, The Earth Circle Foundation, 1988; Honorary Degree of Doctorate of Laws, Queen's University, 1989; board of directors, Earth Day
1990; Board of Directors, SAVE Tour, 1990; art,
school, athletic awards. *Interests*: Reading,
travel, outdoors, canoeing and art. *Biographical sources*: New Canadian Encyclopedia;
Who's Who in Canada. *Published work*: co-author, Drumbeat: Anger and Renewal in Indian
Country (Summer Hill Publishers, 1990).

ERDOES, RICHARD
(historian, ethnographer,
photographer, author)
Born in Austria. *Address*: c/o Bear & Co., P.O.
Box 2860, Santa Fe, NM 87504. *Published
works*: Lame Deer: Seeker of Visions; American Indian Myths & Legends; A.D. 1000: Living
on the Brink of Apocalypse; A Sound of Flutes;
co-author of Lakota Woman (made into a movie
by Turner Broadcasting); Gift of Power, with
Archie Fire Lame Deer & Crying for a Dream
(Bear & Co.).

ERICKSON, VINCENT O. 1936-
  (professor of anthropology)
Born January 17, 1936, Mount Vernon, Wash.
Education: University of Washington, BA, 1958,
MA, 1961, PhD, 1968. *Principal occupation*: Pro-
fessor of anthropology. *Home address*: 175
Southampton Dr., Fredericton, New Brunswick,
Can. E3B 4T5. *Affiliation*: University of New
Brunswick, Fredericton, Can., 1966-. *Member-
ships*: American Anthropological Association;
American Ethnological Society; Canadian Eth-
nology Society; American Folklore Society; Ca-
nadian Folklore Society. Interests: Ethnohistory,

ethnolinguistics, ethnography and folklore of the Eastern Algonkians, especially of the Indians of New Brunswick. Indian agent to the Passamaquoddy, 1965-; fieldwork among Passamaquoddy, 1967-, and among the Coast Salish Indians of Washington and British Columbia, 1960-62.

*ERMELOFF, LEONTE (Kenaitse)
(AK village council president)
Affiliation: Native Village of Nikolski, Nikolski, AK 99638 (907) 576-2225.

ERNST, CLYDE
(museum director/curator)
Affiliation: Coronado-Quivira Museum, 221 E Ave. South, Lyons, KS 67554 (316) 257-3941.

ERVIN, CAROL (Yurok)
(rancheria chairperson; director-Indian health program)
Affiliation: Trinidad Rancheria, P.O. Box 630, Trinidad, CA 95570 (707) 677-0211; director, Chapa-De (Auburn) Indian Health Program, Auburn, CA; Northern Valley Indian Health Program, 827-A S. Tehama St., Willows, CA 95988.

*ERWIN, SARAH
(curator of archival collections)
Affiliation: Thomas Gilcrease Institute of American History & Art Library, 1400 Gilcrease Museum Rd., Tulsa, OK 74127 (918) 596-2700.

ESBER, JR., GEORGE S. *(Tchuggi)* 1939-
(ethnographer)
Born July 10, 1939, Canton, Ohio. *Education*: Western Reserve University, MA, 1964; University of Arizona, MA, 1976, PhD, 1977; University of Cincinnati, MSW, 1985. *Principal occupation*. Ethnographer. *Home address*: U.S. Dept. of the Interior, National Park Service, P.O. Box 728, Santa Fe, NM 87501 (505) 988-6777 (work). *Affiliations*: Ethnographer, Office of American Indian Programs, National Park Service, Santa Fe, NM, 1991-; professor of anthropology, Earlham College, Richmond, IN, 1988-91; professor of anthropology, Miami University, Oxford, OH, 1979-88. *Community activities*: Secretary of the Board for Extended Total Curriculum (Gifted Program), Oxford, OH. *Memberships*: Native American Rights Fund; Society for Applied Anthropology; National Association of Practicing Anthropologists; American Anthropological Association; Society of Sigma Xi; Central States Anthropological Association; National Geographic Society. *Awards, honors*: Archaeological expeditions at San Xavier del Bac, Tucson, and a Yana village site, Northern California. Field research on the Tonto Apache Reservation in Payson, Arizona. *Published works*: Numerous articles in journals, and edited volumes.

ESCUDERO, GARY, M.D.
(clinical director)
Affiliation: Gallup Indian Medical Center, P.O. Box 1337, Gallup, NM 87305 (505) 722-1000.

*ESKILIDA, KAREN (Athapascan)
(AK village president)
Affiliation: Native Village of Chitina, P.O. Box 241, Gakona, AK 99586 (907) 822-3503.

ESPARZA, TONSASHAY (Eskimo)
(AK village president)
Affiliation: Chinick Eskimo Community (aka Golovin), P.O. Box 62020, Golovin, AK 99762 (907) 779-3521.

*ESQUERRA, L. FLINT
(filmmaker)
Address: P.O. Box 1753, Salt lake City, UT 84110-1753.

ESQUERRA, RALPH
(B.I.A. director)
Affiliation: Acting director, Office of Facilities Management, Bureau of Indian Affairs, 505 Marquette St., NW, Albuquerque, NM 87102 (505) 766-2825.

ESQUIRO, PETE
(village council president)
Affiliation: Sitka Community Association, 456 Katlian St., Sitka, AK 99835 (907) 747-3207.

ESTEVES, PAULINE (Shoshone)
(Indian community chairperson)
Affiliation: Death Valley Indian Community, P.O. Box 206, Death Valley, CA 92325 (619) 786-2374.

*ETTER, PATRICIA A.
(librarian/archivist)
Born in Winnipeg, Manitoba, Can. *Education*: California State University, Long Beach, BA, 1979; University of Arizona, MLS, 1986. *Home address*: 1051 S. Dobson Rd. #218, Mesa, AZ 85202 (602) 965-6490 (work). *Affiliations*: Acting Curator, Labriola National American Indian Data Center & Associate Archivist for Information Services, Dept. of Archives & Manuscripts, Arizona State University, Tucson, AZ, 1988-. *Memberships*: Western History Association, 1986-; Dwight Smith Award Commission; past sheriff, Westerners International, Scottsdale Corral, 1986-; Society of Southwestern Archivist; Society of Southwestern Authors; Arizona & California Historical Societies. *Awards, honors*: Outstanding Alumnus, Anthropology, California State University, Long Beach, 1992; Beta Pi Mu International Library Honor Society, 1986; elected Phi Kappa Phi Honor Society, 1979. *Interests*: "Major area of research & publication is the history of Southwestern trails in Arizona, New Mexico and California in the mid to late 1800s. I don't claim any tribal af filiation though my great, great grandmother was Cree." *Published works*: Editor, American Odyssey (University of Arkansas Press, 1986; numerous articles & book reviews dealing with Southwestern topics including Native Americans.

*ETTINGER, RICHARD PRENTICE 1922-
(school president)
Born September 27, 1922, New York, N.Y. *Education*: Dartmouth College, AB, 1947. *Principal occupation*: School president. *Home address*: 3101 Old Pecos Trail, Santa Fe, NM 87501 (505) 820-0347; 989-3511 (work). *Affiliation*: President, Native American Preparatory School, Santa Fe, NM. *Community activities*: Board of Directors, Native American Preparatory School; President's Circle, National Academy of Sciences; Board of Advisors, Whittier School of Law. *Interests*: Environmental to Native American affairs. Ettinger Scholarships - provides educational grants--scholarships to Native American students.

EULER, ROBERT C. 1924-
(consulting anthropologist)
Born August 8, 1924, New York, N.Y. *Education*: Arizona State College, BA, 1947, MA, 1948; University of New Mexico, PhD (Anthropology), 1958. *Principal occupation*: Consulting anthropologist. *Home address*: 724 W. Pine Knoll Dr., Prescott, AZ 86303 (602) 445-8863. *Affiliations*: Ranger, National Park Service, Wupatki National Monument, 1948-49; anthropological consultant, Albuquerque Area Office, BIA, 1950-51; instructor, associate professor, Arizona State College, 1952-64; curator of anthropology, Museum of Northern Arizona, 1952-56; research associate, Museum of Northern Arizona, 1956-; associate professor, professor and chairman, Dept. of Anthropology, University of Utah, 1964-79; adjunct professor, Dept. of Anthropology, Arizona State University, 1979-. *Other professional posts*: Anthropological consultant, Hualapai Tribe, land claim litigation, 1953-57; member, board of trustees, Museum of Navajo Ceremonial Art, 1954-64; anthropological consultant, U.S. Department of Justice, Southern Paiute land claim litigation, 1956; consultant in cross-cultural education, Phoenix, AZ, public school system, 1961, '64; ethnohistorian, Upper Colorado River Basin Archaeological Salvage Project, University of Utah, 1962; Arizona Governor's Historical Advisory Committee, 1961-64; ethnohistorical consultant, Arizona Commission on Indian Affairs, 1962-64; anthropological consultant, Operation Headstart, U.S. Office of Economic Opportunity, involving Navajo, Paiute, Mojave, and Chemehuevi participation, 1965. *Memberships*: American Anthropological Association (Fellow); American Ethnological Society; Society for Applied Anthropology (Fellow); Society for American Archaeology; Current Anthropology (associate); American Association for the Advancement of Science (Fellow); American Indian Ethnohistoric Conference; The Society for Sigma Xi; The Western History Association; Arizona Academy of Science (charter member; president, 1962-1963); Arizona Archaeological & Historical Society; New Mexico Historical Society; New Mexico Archaeological Society; Utah Historical Society. *Awards, honors*: Society for American Archaeology 50th Anniversary Award, for Outstanding Contributions to American Archaeology, 1985; Fellow, Museum of Northern Arizona, Flagstaff, 1985. *Interests*: Ethnographic fieldwork involving historical ethnography, ethnohistory and applied anthropology among the Navajo, Hopi, Walapai, Havasupai, Yavapai, Chemehuevi, Southern Paiute, Southern Ute, Isleta Pueblo, and Zia Pueblo; historical archaeological research in Walapai, Havasupai, Yavapai, and Southern Paiute sites. *Published works*: Editor, Woodchuck Cave, A Basketmaker II Site in Tsegi Canyon, Arizona, with H.S. Colton (Museum of Northern Arizona, 1953); Walapai Culture History (University of New Mexico, doctoral dissertation, University Microfilms, 1958); Southern Paiute Archaeology in the Glen Canyon Drainage: A Preliminary Report (Nevada State Museum, 1963); Havasupai Religion and Mythology (Anthropological Papers, University of Utah, 1964); with Henry F. Dobyns: The Havasupai People, The Hopi People, The Paiute People, The Navajo People; The Walapai People (Indian Tribal Series, 1971, 72, 76); Havasupai of Arizona, 1150-1890 (Clearwater, 1974); Havasupai Historical Data (Garland Publishing, 1974); with Dobyns: Indians of the Southwest: A Critical Bibliography (Indiana University Press, 1980); The Grand Canyon: Intimate Views, with Frank Tikalsky, editor (University of Arizona Press, 1993); Havasupai Legends: Religion & Mythology of the Indians of Grand Canyon (University of Utah Press, 1994); numerous articles, reviews and monographs.

*EVANOFF, LARRY (Eskimo)
(AK village council president)
Affiliation: Native Village of Chanega Council, P.O. Box 8079, Chanega Bay, AK 99574 (907) 573-5132.

EVANS, WAYNE H. (Wokopacola)
(Rosebud Sioux) 1938-
(associate professor of education)
Born April 19, 1938, Rosebud, S.D. *Education*: Black Hills State College, BS, 1962; University of South Dakota, EdD, 1976. *Principal occupation*: Associate professor of education. *Home address*: 24 S. Pine, Vermillion, SD, 57069 (605) 677-5808 (work). A*ffiliation*: Associate Professor of Education, University of South Dakota, Vermillion, 1969-. *Other professional post*: Drum keeper, lead singer on drum. *Community activities*: Evening study time lab for Native American children - facilitator. *Memberships*: South Dakota Indian Education Association (former president); South Dakota Indian Counselor's Association. *Awards, honors*: Outstanding Young Man of America. *Interests*: Counseling, guidance; family therapy; values - value orientation. *Biographical sources*: Who's Who Among the Sioux (Institute of Indian Studies, University of South Dakota, 1987). *Published work*: Indian Student Counseling Handbook (Black Hills State College, 1977); Bicultural Teaching Method & Materials (University of South Dakota, 1987); Issues in Undergraduate Education - chapter on: Native Americans in Undergraduate Education (University of South Dakota, 1988).

*EVENINGTHUNDER, L. DAVID (Shoshone)
1947-
(owner/manager, artist)
Born May 3, 1947, Western Shoshone Hospital, Idaho/Nevada border. *Education*: Lee College, A.A., A.S.T., AGS, 1986; Sam Houston State University, B.A., 1989. *Principal occupation*: Owner/manager, artist. *Address*: P.O. Box 1197, River Creek Village, Coldspring, TX 77331 (713) 592-5375. *Affiliation*: Owner, Contemporary Native American Art, Coldspring, TX, 1989-. *Military service*: U.S. Strategic Air Command, 1966-67 Sgt. *Community activities*: Member, Shoshone-Bannock Tribe & San Jacinto Historical Society; alumnus, Sam Houston State University

EVERETT, BETTY JOE (KERR) (Choctaw)
1926-
(civil engineer)
Born August 21, 1926, Oklahoma City, Okla. *Education*: University of Oklahoma, BS (Civil Engineering), 1946; Louisiana State University, MS (Civil Enginnering-Transportation & Planning), 1969. *Principal occupation*: Civil engineer. *Home address*: 6507 Vickburg St., New Orleans, LA 70124 (504) 486-3923. *Affiliations*: Design construction and supervision on various engineering projects, 1946-69; civil engineer, City of New Orleans, 1969-78; owner/president, Chatah, Inc., New Orleans, 1978-86; director, Department of Streets, City of New Orleans, 1986-91; consultant to engineering firms (C&S Engineering, Perrin & Associates, Moreland & Altobelli, New Orleans), 1991-. *Community activities*: Gulf South Minority Purchasing Council (board of directors); Louisiana Institute for Indian Development (board of directors); American Career Council for Women; Munholland United Methodist Church (board of trustees). *Memberships*: American Public Works; National Society of Professional Engineers; Society of Women Engi-

neers; American Indian Science and Engineering Society. *Awards, honors*: Supplier of the Year Award, NMSDC, 1980; Achievers Awards 1983, New Orleans; Distinguished Engineer Award, University of Oklahoma, 1991. *Interests*: "I have always been interested in the problems of opening engineering schools in the metro New Orleans area to women and minorities who might be interested in engineering careers. Working closely with Tulane University and University of New Orleans Engineering Departments and Xavier Uiversity, Dominican College and Delagdo Community College, we created a new five-year engineering curriculum. One of my goals in life has been to ease the road into engineering for women and minorities who come after me. I feel that we have created a model program in New orleans that will help make that possible."

EVERETT, LESTER OLIVER
(Indian band chief)
Affiliation: Berens River Indian Band, Berens River, Manitoba, Canada R0B 0A0 (204) 382-2161.

*EWAN, EILEEN L. (Athapascan)
(AK village council president)
Affiliation: Gulkana Village Council, P.O. Box 254, Gakona, AK 99586 (907) 822-3746.

*EWAN, NORMAN (Athapascan)
(AK village first chief)
Affiliation: Mentasta Lake Village, Mentasta Lake, AK 99780 (907) 291-2319

EWAN, ROY S. (Athabascan) 1935-
(corporate president)
Born February 2, 1935, Copper Center, Alaska. *Education*: High school. *Principal occupation*: Corporate president. *Home address*: P.O. Box 242, Gakona, AK 99586 (907) 822-3476 (office). *Affiliations*: President, Ahtna, Inc., Drawer G, Copper Center, AK; board member, Grandmet/Ahtna; board member, Ahtna Development Corporation. *Other professional posts*: Serves as ex-officio member on all corporate committees, and shareholder committees and subsidiary boards. *Military service*: U.S. Army, 1953-55 (Corporal). *Community activities*: Gulkana Village Council (Indian education, past president). *Memberships*: Alaska Federation of Natives (board member); Alaska Native Federation; The Alliance. *Awards, honors*: 1985 AFN Citizen of the Year, Alaska Federation of Natives.

EWEN, ALEX
(editor)
Affiliation: "Native Nations," (magazine), Solidarity Foundation, 310 W. 52nd St., New York, NY 10019 (212) 765-9731 Fax 956-421 1

EWERS, JOHN CANFIELD (Little Chief-Blackfeet) 1909-
(anthropologist/ethnologist)
Born July 21, 1909, Cleveland, Ohio. *Education*: Dartmouth College, BA, 1931, DSc, 1968; Yale University, MA (Anthropology), 1934; University of Montana, LLD, 1966. *Principal occupation*: Anthropologist/ethnologist. *Home address*: 4432 - 26th Rd. N., Arlington, VA 22207 (703) 524-1775. Affiliations: Field curator, Museum Division, National Park Service, 1935-40; curator, Museum of the Plains Indian, 1941-44; associate curator of ethnology, planning officer, U.S. National Museum, Smithsonian Institution,

1946-59; director, Museum of History and Technology, Smithsonian, 1959-65; senior scientist, Office of Anthropology, 1965-79, now ethnologist emeritus, Department of Anthropology, Smithsonian Institution, Washington, D.C. *Other professional posts*: Museum planning consultant, Bureau of Indian Affairs, 1948-49; Montana Historical Society, 1950-54; editor, Journal of the Washington Academy of Sciences, 1955; member, editorial board, The American West, Western Historical Quarterly, and Great Plains Quarterly, 1979-; consultant, American Heritage, 1959; research associate, Museum of the American Indian, Heye Foundation, 1979-. Military service: U.S. Navy, 1944-46 (Lieutenant). *Memberships*: American Indian Ethnohistoric Conference (president, 1961); Rochester Museum of Arts and Science (Fellow); Sigma Xi (president, D.C., chapter); Western History Association (honorary life member). *Awards, honors*: Recipient First Exceptional Service Award for contributions to American history and ethnology, Smithsonian Institution, 1965; Oscar O. Winthor Award, Western History Association, 1976; Distinguished Published Writings in the Field of American Western History, 1985, Western History Association; Honor Award of Native American Arts Studies Association for contribution to the field, 1989; Gold Medal, Buffalo Bill Historical Center, Cody, WY, for contributions to western history and ethnology, 1991. *Interests*: Field research in ethnology and ethnohistory conducted among the Blackfeet tribes of Montana and Alberta (Canada), the Assiniboine of Montana, the Flathead of Montana, the Sioux of South Dakota, and the Kiowa of Oklahoma; studies of Indian art since 1932. *Biographical sources*: Who's Who in America; The Reader's Encyclopedia of the American West, 1977, by Howard Lamar, editor; Plains Indian Studies, Douglas H. Ubelaker and Herman J. Viola, editors (Smithsonian Contribution to Anthropology) - a collection of essays in honor of John C. Ewers and Waldo R. Wedel (includes a complete list of John C. Ewer's approximately 163 publications through 1981; Fifth Annual Plains Indian Seminar in Honor of Dr. John C. Ewers, George Horse Capture and Gene Ball, editors (Buffalo Bill Historical Center, 1984); Western Historical Quarterly (April, 1986). *Published works*: Mr. Ewers writes, "My research and publications over a period of more than fifty years have been primarily on the history, art, and culture of the Plains Indians, the work of non-Indian artists who pictured those Indians, and on the museum interpretation of American Indians' art and culture." Among authored books -- Plains Indian Painting (Stanford University Press, 1940); The Horse in Blackfeet Indian Culture (Smithsonian Institution, 1955; reprinted in Classics of Smithsonian Anthropology Series, 1980); The Blackfeet: Raiders on the Northwestern Plains (University of Oklahoma Press, 1958); Artists of the Old West (Doubleday, 1965); Indian Life on the Upper Missouri (University of Oklahoma Press, 1968); Murals in the Round: Painted Tipis of the Kiowa and Kiowa-Apache Indians, 1978; Plains Indian Sculpture, Traditional Art from America's Heartland (Smithsonian Institution, 1986). *Editor*: Adventures of Zenas Leonard, Fur Trader, 1959; Crow Indian Medicine Bundles, 1960; Five Indian Tribes of the Upper Missouri, 1961; O-Kee-pa: A Religious Ceremony and Other Customs of the Mandans, (George Catlin), 1967; Indians of Texas in 1830 (Smithsonian Institution, 1969); Indian Art in Pipestone, George Catlin's Portfolio in the British Museum,

1979. In addition, published chapters in more than 20 books and more than 150 articles in some 40 journals of anthopology, art or history.

*EXENDINE, LEAH
(health center director)
Affiliation: Lassen Indian Health Center, Susanville Indian Rancheria, 745 Joaquin St., Susanville, CA 96130 (916) 257-2542.

EYAHPAISE, DON
(Indian band chief)
Affiliation: Okemasis Indian Band, Box 312, Duck Lake, Saskatchewan, Canada S0J 1J0 (306) 466-4959.

EYRAUD, COLBERT H.
(museum director)
Affiliation: Cabot's Old Indian Pueblo Museum, 67-616 E. Desert View Ave., Desert Hot Springs, CA 92240 (619) 329-7610.

*EZOLD, JUNE O. (Brothertown Indians of Wisconsin) 1922-
(ad counselor-retired)
Born August 20, 1922, Fond du Lac, Wisc. *Education*: High school. *Principal occupation*: Ad Counselor-retired. *Home address*: 2848 Witches Lake Rd., Arbor Vitae, WI 54568 (715) 542-3913. *Affiliations*: Senior Clerk, MONY, Milwaukee, WI, 1939-47; Ad Counselor, Milwaukee Journal/Sentinel, 1964-81. *Other professional post*: Chairperson, Brothertown Indians of Wisconsin. *Community activities*: PTA (president & city council secretary); Cub Scout Den Mother Instructor; Girl Scout Leader; Deacon Calvary Lutheran Church (council president.)

F

FADDEN, JOHN (KAHIONHES)
(Mohawk-Turtle Clan) 1938-
(art teacher, artist, illustrator)
Born December 26, 1938, Massena, N.Y. (near Akwesasne, St. Regis Indian Reservation). *Education*: Rochester Institute of Technology, BFA, 1961. *Principal occupation*: Art teacher, artist, illustrator. *Address*: HCR 1, Box 10, Onchiota, NY 12968 (518) 891-2299. *Affiliations*: Art teacher, Saranac Central School District, Saranac, NY (30 years); staff curator, Six Nations Indian Museum, Onchiota, NY (37 years). *Other professional posts*: Illustrator, painter, and museum curator. *Exhibitions*: Six National Indian Museum, 1954-; Penn State Museum, Harrisburg, 1962; Art of the Iroquois, Erie County Savings Bank, Buffalo, 1974; New York State Fair, Syracuse, 1977; The Woodland Indian Cultural - Educational Centre, Brantford, Ontario, 1977, '80, '84; American Indian Community House Gallery, New York City, 1977, '80, '82, '84; Akwesasne Museum, Hogansburg, NY, 1980; Schoharie Museum of the Iroquois Indian, 1981-85; Iroquois Indian Festival II, feature artist, Cobleskill, NY 1983; Akwesasne: Our Strength, Our Spirit, World Trade Center, New York City, 1984; among others. *Memberships*: NY State Education Dept. (Native American Social Studies Writers Committee); NY State Museum (Native Peoples of New York Exhibition Advisory Committee); Round Dance Productions (Board of Dirctors); Tree of Peace Society (Board of Directors); and Viola White Water Foundation (Board of Directors). *Interests*: As John looks back over the years, he sees the

1961-68 period as one of experimentation in which he worked with pen and ink and painted in tempera, selling a few of his works at the family museum (Six Nations Indian Museum), and giving away others. As became more aware of the political changes taking place at Akwesasne, and throughout Native America, he began to make more political statements through his art, mainly through drawings and cover illustrations for Akwesasne Notes, a newspaper published by the Mohawk Nation at Akwesasne. The details of his work typically show native nationalism and political ascertiveness based on the traditions of the native peoples. He has illustrated many books and periodicals, and has done cover art for many books; also, calendar art for Akwesasne Notes Calendar, 1972-. He has produced art for films/video: Who Were the Ones (National Film Board of Canada, 1970); Hodenosaunee: People of the Longhouse (Stiles-Akin Films, 1981); The Iroquois Creation Myth (video tape, Image Film, 1982); Why the Bear Clan Know Medicine (Quinn-Sturgeon, 1990); Moyers-Oren Lyons the Faithkeeper (Public Affairs Television, 1991).

FADDEN, RAY
(museum owner)
Affiliation: Six Nations Indian Museum, Onchiota, NY 12968 (518) 891-0769.

FADDEN, STEPHEN
(editor)
Affiliation: The Web, Indigenous Communications Resource Center, American Indian Program, 400 Caldwell Hall, Cornell University, Ithaca, NY 14853 (602) 255-6587.

FAIRBANKS, DEANNA L.
(Chippewa-Ojibway) 1949-
(tribal consultant)
Born May 15, 1949, Leech Lake Reservation, Cass Lake, Minn. *Education*: Bemidji State University, B.A., 1985; University of Minnesota, J.D., 1988. *Principal occupation*: Tribal consultant. *Address*: The Leech Lake Reservation, RR 2, Box 227, Cass Lake, MN 56633 (218) 335-6767. *Affiliation*: Self-employed - consultant in specific federal areas, to tribes only. *Other professional posts*: Special Magistrate for the Court of Central Jurisdiction, the Mille Lacs Band of Ojibwe. *Community activities*: Minnesota Environmental Quality Board & the Minnesota Arts Task Force; committee member, American Indigenous Games to be held in Bemidji, MN in 1995. *Awards, honors*: Minnesota Woman of the Year, 1993 - decreed by Governor Arne Carlson. *Interests*: Tribal sovereignty & jurisdiction. The Self-Governance Act, interpretation & implementation; environmental issues, the arts. "I'm an active Democrat and Politics consumes me."

FAIRBANKS, DEVERY J. (Ma in ga nens)
(Anishinaabe-White Earth Chippewa) 1957-
(educator)
Born May 24, 1957, Minneapolis, Minn. *Education*: Minneapolis Community College, AA, 1984; University of Minnesota, BA, 1988. *Principal occupation*: Educator. *Home address*: 1413 Main Ave. W., International Falls, MN 56649 (218) 283-8891. *Affiliation*: Admissions officer, American Indian Student Recruiter, University of Minnesota, Minneapolis, MN, 1989-93; Minority Student Services Director, Rainy River Community College, International Falls, MN, 1993-. *Other professional posts*: Free-lance writer, painter, graphic illustrator. *Community activities*: Board

member of five American Indian organizations & institutions: Alcohol & Drug treatment Center, Indian Parent Committee, et al. *Memberships*: Minnesota Indian Education Association; National Indian Education Association; American Indian Higher Education Consortium; American Indian Science & Engineering Society; UNITY. *Interests*: "Principal American Indian student recruiter for the University of Minnesota; job requires extensive travel--numerous friendships and acquaintances nationwide in fields of art, publications, powwows, sports, and chemical dependency. Art and literature: wrote and produced one play, "A Long Road for Milo," reviews favorably on both coasts (by Vizenor & Bruchac). Trade, collect, and volunteer at Indian Art Shows in the Southwest, Midwest & Ontario, Canada. Visited over 30 states in the U.S. & Canada; mostly Indian reservations and reserves. Also visited major urban Indian communities." *Biographical source*: Article in the University of Minnesota Counselors Quarterly magazine, March 1992. *Published works*: Articles published in the following periodicals: The Circle (Minneapolis, MN), Anishnabe-Oyate Newsletter (University of Minnesota), the NIEA News (Washington, D.C.), and The Journal (Hayward, WI).

FAIRBANKS, FRANCES
(executive director)
Affiliation: Minneapolis American Indian Center, 1530 E. Franklin Ave., Minneapolis, MN 55404 (612) 871-4555.

FALCON, AUDREY (Saginaw Chippewa/ Grand River Ottawa) 1953-
(health administrator)
Born January 18, 1953, Detroit, Mich. *Education*: Ferris State University (Big Rapids, MI) 1972-74, Registered Nurse, Associate Degree, Health Services Management, 1980-84. *Home address*: 7580 Ogemaw Dr., Mt. Pleasant, MI 48858 (517) 773-9887 (work). *Affiliation*: Health administrator, Nimkee Memorial Wellness Center, Mt. Pleasant, MI, 1977-. *Community activities*: Saginaw Chippewa Tribal Council (member/treasurer 1990-) Ziibiiwing Cultural Society - Repatriation. *Memberships*: American Public Health Association; Michigan Public Health Association; American Red Cross-Local Chapter. Award: Indian Health Service, U.S. Public Health Service, Exceptional Performance Award, Nov. 1988.

FALCON, RON
(health center director)
Affiliation: Trenton-Williston Tribal Health Services, P.O. Box 210 Trenton, ND 58853 (701) 774-0461.

FALLEY, NANCI (Many Spirits Woman) 1938-
(rancher)
Born October 19, 1938, San Angelo, Tex. *Education*: California Polytechnic Institute (Certificate in Horse Management), 1960. *Principal occupation*: Rancher. *Address & Affiliation*: President, American Indian Horse Registry & Museum, Route 3, Box 64, Lockhart, TX 78644 (512) 398-6642. *Other professional posts*: President, Indian Horse Hall of Fame, Lockhart, TX; editor, American Indian Horse News.

*FAMILIO, DORSIE
(branch library supervisor)
Affiliation: The Seneca Nation Library, Allegany Reservation Branch, P.O. Box 231, Salamanca, NY 14779 (716) 945-3157.

FARLEE, CHERIE
(BIA supt. for education)
Affiliation: Cheyenne River Agency, Bureau of Indian Afairs, P.O. Box 2020, Eagle Butte, SD 57625 (605) 964-8722; supt., Cheyenne-Eagle Butte School, Eagle Butte, SD 57625 (605) 964-8744.

FARMER, GARY (Cayuga)
(editor & publisher)
Affiliation: The Runner, Native Magazine for the Communicative Arts, c/o ANDPVA, 39 Spadina Rd., 2nd Floor, Toronto, ON M5R 2S9 (416) 972-0871 Fax 972-0892. Quarterly magazine.

FARMER, TINA
(head teacher)
Affiliation: Promise Day School, HCR 30, Box 10, Mobridge, SD 57601.

FARR, FONDA
(museum director)
Affiliation: Last Indian Raid Museum, 258 S. Penn Ave., Oberlin, KS 67749 (913) 475-2712.

FARRELL, MARY ANNE, M.D.
(health center director)
Affiliation: United Regional Youth Treatment Center, P.O. Box C-201, Cherokee, NC 28719 (704) 497-3958.

FARRER, CLAIRE R. 1936-
(professor of anthropology)
Born December 26, 1936, New York, N.Y. *Education*: University of California, Berkeley, BA, 1970; University of Texas, Austin, MA (Anthropology/Folklore; Thesis: Performances of Mescalero Apache Clowns), 1974, PhD (Anthropology/Folklore; Dissertation: A Practical Ethnography of the Mescalero Apache), 1977. *Principal occupation*: Professor of anthropology. *Home address*: 15 Meadowlark Lane, Paradise, CA 95969 (916) 872-2062 (home) 895-6192 (office). *Affiliations*: Weatherford Resident Fellow, School of American Research, Santa Fe, NM, 1977-78; assistant professor of anthropology, University of Illinois - Urbana/Champaign, IL, 1978-85; Dept. of Anthropology, California State University (associate professor, 1985-89, professor of anthropology, 89-, coordinator Multicultural & Gender Studies, 1994-). *Other professional posts*: Western Folklore, California Folklore Society (book review editor, 1985-89; executive editor, 1994-); consulting editor for Archaeoastronomy, 1984-; reader for refereed journals; guest lecturer. *Field research*: Individual work with Mescalero Apache Singers of Ceremonies on ritual, religion, medicine, and healing, 1990-; Mescalero Apache Indian Reservation - 12 month ethnographic investigation with Tribal consent and support; focus on children's free play. Also participant-observation of daily life and ritual activities as well as some linguistic fieldwork, 1974-75; Mescalero Apache Indian Reservation - focused research on ethnoastronomy (summer) with astronomers, 1984 & 1986; general ethnography and ethnoastronomy with Mescalero Apache Indians, 1976-88. Also minor, a periodic work on the Warm Springs Confederated Tribe in Oregon in the 1960's and 1970s, and minor work in 1970s and 1980s at various sites in New Mexico including the pueblos of Laguna, San Juan, Santo Domingo, Tesuque, and Zuni. *Memberships*: American Anthropological Association; American Ethnological Society; American Folklore Society; American Society for Ethnohistory;

National Association of Practicing Anthropologists; Royal Anthropological Association (U.K.); Society for Cultural Anthropology; Southwestern Anthropological Association; Traditional Cosmology Society (United Kingdom). *Honors, Awards*: Whitney M. Young, Jr. Memorial Foundation Academic Fellow while doing dissertation fieldwork, 1974-75; invited participant for Southwestern Indian Ritual Drama by School of American Research, Santa Fe, NM; American Philosophical Society, Phillips Fund and University of Illinois-Urbana, $2,500 for transcription/translation of wax cylinders recorded in 1931 at Mescalero, 1982; outstanding teacher at University of Illinois-Urbana, 1985; American Council of Learned Societies grant for ethnoastronomy of the Mescalero Apache; Professional Promise Award and Professional Achievement Award, California State University, Chico, 1987; Student Internship Service Grant to support powwow and other Indian songs taping, California State University, Chico, 1989; private donor grant to work on Southwestern Indian basketry at the Pitt Rivers Museum, University of Oxford, England (summer), 1990; Outstanding Professor, California State University, Chico, 1993-94; Living Life's Circle (book) chosen as Outstanding Book by CHOICE; also 1st Honorable Mention in Victor Turner Prize for Ethnographic writing. *Interests*: Language, travel. *Published works*: Books: editor, Women and Folklore (University of Texas Press, 1976; reissue, Waveland Press, 1986); co-editor, with Edward Norbeck, Forms of Play of Native North Americans (West Publishing, 1979); editor, Play and Inter-Ethnic Communications: A Practical Ethnography of the Mescalero Apache, 31 volume series of outstanding dissertations (Garland, 1990); Living Life's Circle: Mescalero Apache Cosmovision, 8 chapters (University of New Mexico Press, 1991); co-editor, with Ray Williamson, 14 chapters, Earth and Sky: Visions of the Cosmos in Native American Folklore (University of New Mexico Press, 1992); In preparation: Thunder Rides a Black Horse: Mescalero, Apaches and the Mythic Present (Waveland Press, 1994). *Books in preparation*: Kaleidoscope Vision & the Rope of Experience (on shamanism); & Ginger's Gems: Words to Live By (While Having Cancer). Numerous book chapters; monographs; journal, encyclopedic, newspaper and magazine articles; book reviews; and books and articles refereed.

FARRIS, GARY D.
(organization director)
Affiliation: Indians Into Medicine, University of North Dakota, School of Medicine, 501 N. Columbia Rd., Grand Forks, ND 58201 (701) 777-3037.

FARVE, EMIL (Chickasaw)
(editor & publisher)
Affiliation: Chickasaw Times, Chickasaw Nation Tribal Government, P.O. Box 1548, Ada, OK 74820 (405) 436-2603.

FARWELL, ROBERT D.
(museum director)
Affiliation: Fruitlands Museum, 102 Prospect Hill Rd., Harvard, MA 01451 (508) 456-3924.

FAST HORSE, JOSEPH (Kickapoo)
(school supt.)
Affiliation: Kickapoo Nation School, P.O. Box 106, Powhattan, KS 66527 (913) 474-3550.

FAT, MARY WEASEL *(Diving Around Woman)* **(Blood) 1955-**
(journalist)
Born December 12, 1955, Cardston, Alberta, Canada. *Education*: Grant McEwan Community College, Edmonton, Alberta (1 Yr. Certificate, Native Communications Program), 1980. *Principal occupation*: Journalist. *Address*: Box 181, Cardston, Alberta T0K 0K0 (403) 737-2854.

FAULSTICK, PAUL
(museum curator)
Affiliation: Portland Art Museum, 1219 S.W. Park, Portland, OR 97205 (503) 226-281 1 ext. 231.

FAVELL, GENE
(museum owner)
Affiliation: Favell Museum of Western Art and Indian Artifacts, 125 W. Main, Box 165, Klamath Falls, OR 97601 (503) 882-9996.

FAVRHOLDT, KEN
(museum director/curator)
Affiliation: Kamloops Museum & Archives, 207 Seymour St., Kamloops, British Columbia, Canada V2C 2E7 (604) 828-3576,

FAWCETT, JAYNE GRANDCHAMP (Mohegan of Connecticut) 1936-
(teacher, assistant curator)
Born January 6, 1936, New London, Conn. *Education*: University of Connecticut, BA, 1957. *Principal occupation*: Teacher, assistant curator. *Affiliations*: Teacher, Ledyard Junior High School, Gales Gerry, CT, 1972-; assistant curator, Tantaquidgeon Indian Museum. *Other professional posts*: Lecturer, American Field Studies. *Interests*: Inspired by the travels of my Aunt, Gladys Tantaquidgeon, my family and I have traveled extensively throughout the western part of America, visiting as many groups of native American as we were able.

FAY, NICK
(health center director)
Affiliation: Indian Health Center of Santa Clara Valley, 1333 Meridian Ave., San Jose, CA 95125 (408) 294-7553.

FEATHER, WALTER
(Indian center operations manager)
Affiliation: Southern California Indian Center, P.O. Box 2550, Garden Grove, CA 92642 (714) 530-0221.

FEINBERG, RICHARD 1947-
(professor of anthropology)
Born November 4, 1947, Norfolk, Va. *Education*: University of California, Berkeley, AB, 1969; University of Chicago, MA, 1971, PhD, 1974. *Principal occupation*: professor of anthropology. *Home address*: 6358 Lakeview Dr., Ravenna, OH 44266 (216) 672-2722; 672-4363 (work). *Affiliation*: Dept. of Anthropology, Kent State University, Kent, OH, 1974-. *Memberships*: American Anthropological Association; American Ethnological Society; Central States Anthropological Society; The Polynesian Society; Association for Social Anthropology in Oceana; American Association of University Professors. *Interests*: Cultural anthropology; Oceania, Native North America, American culture. *Published work*: Social Change in a Navajo Community (Human Relations Area Files (HRAF), 1978; Anuta: Social Structure of a Polynesian Island (Institute for Polynesian Studies & The

NationalMuseumof Denmark, 1981); Polynesian Seafaring & Navigation (Kent State University Press, 1988); articles in various journals.

FELTY, NORMA L.
(editor)
Affiliation: Anishnabe Dee-Bah-Gee-Mo-W in, White Earth Reservation Tribal Council, P.O. Box 418, White Earth, MN 56591 (218) 983-3285.

FENELON, JAMES
(BIA area director)
Affiliation: Sac & Fox Area Field Of fice, BIA, 1657 320th St., Tama, IA 52339 (515) 484-4041.

FENTON, WILLIAM NELSON 1908-
(anthropologist)
Born December 15, 1908, New Rochelle, N.Y . *Education*: Dartmouth College, BA, 1931; Yale University, PhD, 1937; Hartwick College, LLD, 1968. *Principal occupation* : Anthropologist. Home address: 7 N. Helderberg Parkway , Slingerlands, NY 12159 (518) 439-4385. *Affiliations*: Community worker, U.S. Indian Service, in charge of Tuscarora and Tonawanda Reservations, 1935-37; ethnologist, Smithsonian Institution, Bureau of American Ethnology , 1939-51; executive secretary for anthropology & psychology, National Academy of Sciences, National Research Council, 1952-54; assistant commissioner, State Museum and Science Service, New York State Education Department, 1954-68; research professor of anthropology , SUNY at Albany, 1968-74, distinguished professor emeritus, 1974-79. *Military service*: Research associate, Ethnogeographic Board, 1942-45. *Memberships*: American Anthropological Association (executive board); American Folklore Society (Fellow; past president); American Society for Ethnohistory (past president); American Ethnological Society (past president); American Association for the Advancement of Science (Fellow); Museum of the American Indian (trustee, 1976-89). *Awards, honors*: Adopted Seneca (Iroquois); Peter Doctor Award, Seneca Nation of Indians, 1958, for outstanding service to Iroquoian peoples; Cornplanter Medal for Iroquois Research, Cayuga County Historical Society, 1965; Hon. LLD., Hartwick College, 1968; Dartmouth College Class of 1930 Award, 1979; named Dean in Perpetuum of Iroquoian Studies, 30th Conference on Iroquois Research, 1979; Fulbright-Hays research fellow to New Zealand, 1975; National Endowment for the Humanities fellow, Huntington Library , 1977-1979; member , Iroquois Documentary History Project, Newberry Library , 1979-81. *Published works*: The Iroquois Eagle Dance (Bureau of American Ethnology, 1953); editor, Symposium on Local Diversity in Iroquois Culture (Bureau of American Ethnology, 1955); editor, Symposium on Cherokee and Iroquois Culture (Bureau of American Ethnology, 1961); American Indian & White Relations to 1830 (Institute of Early American History and Culture, University of North Carolina, 1957); Parker on the Iroquois (Syracuse University Press, 1968); editor & translated with E.L. Moore, Lafitan's Customs of the American Indian (1724) (The Champlain Society, 1974, 1977); The False Faces of the Iroquois (University of Oklahoma Press, 1987).

FERGUSON, JOHN P.
(editor)
Affiliation: "Museum Notes," Iroquois Indian Museum, P.O. Box 7, Howes Cave, NY 12092 (518) 296-8949.

FERNANDEZ, ARNE G. (Laguna Pueblo) 1953-
(storekeeper)
Born June 2, 1953, Albuquerque, N.M. *Education*: University of New Mexico (5 years). *Principal occupation*: Storekeeper, Laguna Pueblo. Home address: 212 Carlisle, NE, Albuquerque, NM 87106 (505) 268-2662. *Membership*: Indian Arts and Crafts Association, 1986-. *Interests*: "I specialize in finding traditional pottery for clients - top museums and collectors. I was a judge for the 1991 & 1992 Gallup Ceremonials. I have dealt with most major potters and their work from a first name basis for over 20 years."

*FERREIRA, NANCY
(professor of Native American studies)
Affiliation: Native American Studies Dept., College of St. Scolastica, Duluth, MN 5581 1 (218) 723-6046.

*FERRERIA, HANAKAULANI (Hawaiian)
(foundation director)
Affiliation: Hawaii Cultural Research Foundation, Box 4590, Honolulu, HI 96813 (808) 524-0884.

FICKEL, VIOLET M.
(executive director)
Affiliation: American Native Corporation, 2451 St. Mary's St., Omaha, NE 68102 (402) 341-8471.

FIDDLER, JONAS
(Indian band chief)
Affiliation: Sandy Lake Indian Band, via Favourable Lake, Ontario, Canada P0V 1V0 (807) 774-3421.

FIDDLER, ROBERT
(Indian band chief)
Affiliation: Waterhen Lake Indian Band, General Delivery, Waterhen Lake, Saskatchewan, Canada S0M 3B0 (306) 236-6717.

*FIELD, CAROL
(project director)
Affiliation: Director, Native American Recruitment, National Marrow Donor Program, 7910 Woodmont Ave., Bethesda, MD 20814 (800) 627-7693.

*FIELD, RAYMOND
(executive director)
Affiliation: National Tribal Chairman's Association, Washington, DC (202) 293-0031.

FIELDS, JAMES
(BIA agency supt.)
Affiliation: Wewoka Agency, Bureau of Indian Affairs, P.O. Box 1060, W ewoka, OK 74884 (405) 257-6257.

FIELDS, MIKE
(executive director)
Affiliation: Southwest Missouri Indian Center , 2422 West Division, Springfield, MO 65802 (417) 869-9550.

*FIERO, DONALD C.
(chief of interpretation)
Affiliation: Mesa Verde National Park Museum, Mesa Verde, CO 81330 (303) 529-4475

FIFE, BILL S. (Creek)
(tribal chairperson)
Affiliation: Creek Nation of Oklahoma, P .O. Box 580, Okmulgee, OK 74447 (918) 756-8700.

FIFE, GARY D. (Creek, Cherokee) 1950-
(producer/host)
Born September 21, 1950, Tulsa, Okla. *Education*: North East State College, Tahlequah, OK, 1968-72 (Journalism; University W ithout Walls (Westminster College), B.A., 1974. *Principal occupation*: Producer/host. *Address & Affiliation*: One Sky Productions, Ltd., 261 1 Fairbanks St. #D, Anchorage, AK 99503 (907) 272-81 11,1993-. *Past professional post*: Producer/host, Alaska Public Radio Network, Anchorage, AK, 1986-93. *Memberships*: Native American Public Broadcasting Consortium (Board member); Alaska Press Club; Native American Press Association. *Awards, honors*: 1983 Nominee for Outstanding Achievement in Radio, by Native American Public Broadcasting Consortium; 1984 Outstanding Young Men of America; 1988 Men of Achievement by International Biographical Center; 1988 National Public Radio Resident in News & Information by National Public Radio. *Interests*: Traveled to Honduras & Nicaragua to cover refugees' stories; also traveled above Arctic Circle to cover Alaska Native issues. *Biographical sources*: We Alaskans (1/4/87); Daily Courier, Grants Pass, OR (2/19/87); Tulsa World (2/20/87); Olympian (W A) (2/22/87; Tulsa Tribune (2/25/87); Anchorage Daily News; The Arctic Sounder (1 1/3/89).

FIKES, JAY COURTNEY 1951-
(writer-researcher of Native American issues)
Born June 14, 1951, San Luis Obispo, Calif. *Education*: University of California, Irvine, BA, 1973; University of San Diego, MEd, 1974; University of Michigan, MA, 1977, PhD (Anthropology), 1985. *Principal occupation*: Writer -researcher of Native American issues. *Home address*: 2421 Buena V ista Cir., Carlsbad, CA 92008-(619) 438-8352 (work). *Affiliations*: Owner of Cuatro Esquinas Traders (Mexican Indian art), 1979-84; land use planner & housing consultant to Navajo Nation, 1983; professor of Social Science Research Methods, Marmara University, Istanbul, Turkey, 1985-87; independent writer, Las Vegas, N.M., 1987-89; legislative secretary specializing in Native American issues , Friends Committee on National Legislation, Washington, DC, 1990-91; post-doctoral fellow, Smithsonian Institution, 1991-92; president, Institute of Investigation of Inter-Cultural Issues, Carlsbad, CA, 1993-. Ot *her professional post*: Fundraiser for the Native American Church. *Memberships*: International Platform Association; American Anthropological Association; New York Academy of Sciences; Religious Society of Friends. *Awards, honors*: Two academic scholarships from University of Michigan; graduate cum laude from University California, Irvine; graduated with honors from the University of San Diego in 1974; awarded Smithsonian fellowship, 1988; Smithsonian Post-Doctoral Fellow in Anthropology, 1991-93. *Interests*: Translating & interpreting songs & "myths" of the Huichol Indians of Mexico; debunking the books of Carlos Castaneda and his academic allies. I am completing the autobiography of Reuben Snake and planning to write more autobiographical and biographical works on Native Americans of today. I am learning how to produce documentary films, including one on the Huichol Indian ritual cycle circa 1934. *Biographical sources*: Who's Who in California. *Published works*: Huichol Indian Identity and Adaptation (University of Michigan microfilms, 1985); Step Inside the Sacred Circle (W yndham Hall Press,

1989); Carlos Castaneda, Academic Opportunism, and the Psychedelic Sixties (Millenia Press, 1993).

*FINDLAY, MARJORIE M.
(association director)
Affiliation: Mass. Indian Assn, 245 Rockland Rd., Walpole, MA 01741 (508) 369-1235.

FINEDAY, MIKE
(Indian band chief)
Affiliation: Witchekan Lake Indian Band, Box 27, Spiritwood, SK, Can S0J 2M0 (306) 883-2787.

FINLAYSON, WILLIAM D.
(museum executive director)
Affiliation: Museum of Indian Archaeology, University of Western Ontario, Lawson-Jury Bldg., London, ON, Can. N6G 3M6 (519) 473-1360.

*FISCUS, CAROLYN K.
(program director)
Affiliation: Native American Student Services, Colorado State University, 312 Student Services Bldg., Fort Collins, CO 80523 (303) 491-1332.

FISHER, JOE (Blackfeet) 1943-
(photographer/filmmaker)
November 19, 1943, Santa Monica, Calif. *Education*: Haskell Indian Jr. College, AA, 1964; Northern Montana College, 1964-66; University of Montana, 1973-74; Montana State University, Film/TV Production, 1994. *Principal occupation*: Photographer/filmmaker *Home address*: P.O. Box 944, Browning, MT 59417 (406) 338-7869. *Affiliation*: Historical documenter, photographer, Blackfeet Tribe, Browning, MT. *Community activities*: American Legion; Blackfeet Societies: Rough Rides, Slickfoot, and Crazy Dog. *Military service*: U.S. Army (Sp-5 Engs.) (Vietnam Service Unit Commendation). *Membership*: VFW. *Award*: The Montana State Alumni Award of Excellence in Film & TV Production, Oct. 1993. *Interests*: Photographic showing, Indian Pride on the Move, in Browning, Missoula, Helena; Blackfeet art slide presentation. Presently working on TV documentaries on the Blackfeet and a Crow Indian elder. *Published work*: Blackfeet Nation, 1977. *Video*: Produced & directed with D. Kipp, "Transitions," 1992.

*FISHER, LIEVANDO (Northern Cheyenne)
(tribal council president)
Affiliation: Northern Cheyenne Tribal Council, P.O. Box 128, Lame Deer, MT 59043 (406) 477-8284.

FISHER, REIS
(administrative officer)
Affiliation: Blackfeet PHS Indian Hospital, Browning, MT 59417 (406) 338-6153.

*FISHER, SAM
(Indian center chairperson)
Affiliation: Genessee Indian Center, 609 W. Court St., Flint, MI 48503 (313) 239-6621.

*FITZSIMMONS, GENEVA (Luiseno)
(tribal chairperson)
Affiliation: La Jolla Band of Mission Indians, Star Route, Box 158, Valley Center, CA 92082 (619) 742-3771.

*FIXICO, DONALD L.
(profesor of history)
Affiliation: History Dept., Western Michigan University, Kalamazoo, MI 49008 (616) 387-4650.

*FLEMMING, JOSEPH
(health director)
Affiliation: Shakopee Mdweakanton Health Council, 2320 Sioux Trail, NW, Prior Lake, MN 55372 (612) 445-8900.

FLEMMING, TIMOTHY, M.D.
(medical center director)
Affiliation: Gallup Indian Medical Center, P.O. Box 1337, Gallup, NM 87301 (505) 722-1000.

FLETT, FRANCIS
(Indian band chief)
Affiliation: The Pas Indian Band, Box 297, The Pas, Manitoba, Canada R9A 1K4 (204) 623-5483.

FLETT, JACK
(Indian band chief)
Affiliation: St. Theresa Point Indian Band, St. Theresa Point, Manitoba, Canada R0B 1J0 (204) 462-2106.

FLETT, NORMAN
(Indian band chief)
Affiliation: Split Lake Cree Indian Band, Split Lake, Manitoba, Canada R0B 1P0 (204) 342-2045.

*FLEURY, KATHLEEN M.
(Indian affairs coordinator)
Affiliation: Governor's Office of Indian Affairs, State Coordinator of Indian Affairs, Rm. 202, State Capitol Bldg., Helena, MT 59620.

*FLOOD-JOHNSON, CHARLENE
(Indian center director)
Affiliation: Lincoln Indian Center, 1100 Military Rd., Lincoln, NE 68508 (402) 474-5231.

*FLORES, AMELIA
(library director)
Affiliation: Colorado River Indian Tribes Public Library/Archives, Tribal Administration Center, Rte. 1, Box 23-B, Parker, AZ 85344 (602) 669-9211.

*FLOWERS, GARY
(council director)
Affiliation: Virginia Council on Indians, P.O. Box 1475, Richmond, VA 23219 (804) 786-7765.

FLOYD, JAMES R.
(IHS area director)
Affiliation: Portland Area Office IHS, 1220 S.W. Third Ave., Rm. 476, Portland, OR 97204 (503) 326-2020.

FOGELMAN, GARY L. 1950-
(editor/publisher)
Born January 1, 1950, Muncy, Pa. *Education*: Lock Haven State University, BS, 1972; West Chester State University (2 years). *Principal occupation*: Editor/publisher. *Home address*: RD 1, Box 240, Turbotville, PA 17772. *Affiliation*: Editor/publisher, Indian-Artifact Magazine. *Memberships*: Local, state and northeastern archaeological societies; SPA (Chapter No. 8, vice president); IACAP (vice president). *Awards, honors*: Catlin Peace Pipe Award. *Interests*: Collecting Indian artifacts; hunting and fishing. *Published works*: The Muncy Indians (Grit Publishing, 1976); The Pennsylvania Artifact Series (in progress)

FOGELSON, RAYMOND D. *(Talageesi)* **1933-**
(professor of anthropology)
Born August 23, 1933, Red Bank, N.J. *Education*: Wesleyan University, BA, 1955; University of Pennsylvania, MA, 1958, PhD, 1962. *Principal occupation*: Professor of anthropology. *Home address*: 1761 N. Sedgwick, Chicago, IL 60614 (312) 642-7693. *Affiliations*: Assistant professor, University of Washington, Seattle, 1962-65; Department of Anthropology, University of Chicago, 1965-. *Other professional posts*: Book review editor, "American Anthropologist". *Memberships*: American Ethnological Society; American Society for Ethnohistory (president); Central State Anthropological Society (president); Society for Psychological Anthropology; Society for Medical Anthropology. *Interests*: Southeastern Indians, Plateau. *Biographical sources*: Who's Who in America. *Published works*: The Cherokees: An Annotated Bibliography (Indiana University Press); editor: A.I. Hallowell, Contributions to Anthropology (University of Chicago Press); editor (with R.N. Adams): The Anthropology of Power (Academic Press).

FOLLIS, BILL G. (Modoc)
(tribal chief)
Affiliation: Modoc Tribe of Oklahoma, P.O. Box 939, Miami, OK 74354 (918) 542-1190.

FONTAINE, JERRY
(Indian band chief)
Affiliation: Fort Alexander Indian Band, Box 280, Fort Alexander, Manitoba, Canada R0E 0P6 (204) 367-2287.

FOOTE, JAMES
(health center director)
Affiliation: McLaughlin PHS Indian Health Center, P.O. Box 879, McLaughlin, SD 57642 (605) 823-4459.

FORBES, JACK D. (Powhatan-Renape, Delaware-Lenape) 1934-
(professor of Native American studies)
Born January 7, 1934, Long Beach, Calif. *Education*: University of Southern California, BA, 1953; MA, 1955; PhD, 1959. *Principal occupation*: Professor of Native American studies. *Address*: Native American Studies Dept., University of California, Davis, CA 95616 (916) 752-3237. *Affiliations*: Assistant professor, San Fernando Valley State College, 1960-64; associate professor & acting director, Center for Western North American Studies, University of Nevada, 1964-67; research program director, Far West Laboratory, Berkeley, CA, 1967-69; professor/department head, Native American Studies Dept., University of California, Davis, 1969-. *Other professional post*: Co-editor, Attan-Akamik. *Community activities*: Powhatan Confederation (Chief's Council); California Indian Legal Services, Inc. (board of directors); Member, D-Q University National Advisory Committee, 1981-. *Membership*: California Indian Education Association; Native Writer's Circle of the Americas. Awards, honors: Phi Beta Kappa; Social Science Research Council Fellow, 1957-58; Guggenheim Fellow, 1963-64; Fulbright Visiting Professor, University of Warwick, U.K., 1981-82; Tinbergan Chair, Erasmus University, Rotterdam, 1983-84; Visitor Scholar, Institute of Social Anthropology, Oxford University, 1986-87; Visiting Professor, University of Essex, U.K., 1993. *Interests*: Founder, Native American Movement (chairman, 1961-1962); co-founder

of Coalition of Eastern Native Americans; co-founder of the United Native Americans, 1968; co-founder, D-Q University (volunteer instructor); working with Renape, Lenape, and other related languages. *Biographical sources*: Who's Who; Who's Who in the West; Contemporary Authors; Native American Almanac. *Published works*: Apache, Navajo and Spaniard (University of Oklahoma Press, 1960; paperback, 1980; reprinted by Greenwood Press, 1980; revised edition, 1994); Editor, The Indian in America's Past (Prentice-Hall, 1964); Warriors of the Colorado (University of Oklahoma Press, 1965); Editor, Nevada Indians Speak (University of Nevada Press, 1967); Native Americans of California and Nevada (Naturegraph, 1969; revised edition, 1982); Handbook of Native American Studies (Tecumseh Center, 1971); Aztecas del Norte: The Chicanos of Aztlan (Fawcett, 1973); Native Americans and Nixon: Presidential Policy and Minority Self-Determination (UCLA American Indian Studies Center, 1982); Editor, Native American Higher Education: The Struggle for the Creation of D-Q University, 1960-71 (D-Q University Press, 1985); Black Africans and Native Americans: Race, Caste and Color in the Evolution of Red-Black Peoples (Blackwell, 1988; paper, University of Illinois Press, 1993); Columbus and Other Cannibals (Autonomedia, 1992); Only Approved Indians (University of Oklahoma Press, 1995); numerous monographs, articles and book reviews

FORCE, ROLAND W. 1924-
(anthropologist)
Born December 30, 1924, Omaha, Neb. *Education*: Stanford University, BA, 1950, MA, 1951, MA,1952, PhD (Anthropology), 1958. *Principal occupation*: Anthropologist. *Residence*: Honolulu, Hawaii. *Affiliations*: Lecturer, Dept. of Anthropology, University of Chicago, 1956-61; curator of Oceanic Archaeology and Ethnology, Chicago Natural History Museum (Field Museum of Natural History), Chicago, 1956-61; member, Graduate Affiliate Faculty, University of Hawaii, 1962-77; director, B.P. Bishop Museum, 1962-76; holder, Charles Reed Bishop Distinguished Chair in Pacific Studies (1976-77), director emeritus, B.P. Bishop Museum, 1976-91; director & secretary, board of trustees, Museum of the American Indian, Heye Foundation, New York City, 1977-91. *Other professional posts*: Honorary consultant, B.P. Bishop Museum, 1977-91; trustee, W.T. Yoshimoto Foundation, Hawaii, 1979-. *Military service*: U.S. Army, 1943-46 (sergeant; Corps of Engineers; combat duty, European Theatre of Operations). *Community services*: Member, advisory board, State-based Humanities Program, Hawaii, 1972-75; member, Distribution Committees, Sophie Russell Testamentary Trust & Jessie Ann Chalmers Charitable Trust, Honolulu, 1972-77; member, Barstow Foundation Committee (Samoan Education), Hawaii, 1963-. *Memberships*: Pacific Club, Honolulu, 1962-; Social Science Association, Honolulu, 1962-; American Anthropological Association; American Association for the Advancement of Science; American Association of Museums; International Council of Museums; National Trust for Historic Preservation; Pacific Science Association. *Awards, honors*: Selected by Chicago Junior Chamber of Commerce as one of Chicago's ten outstanding young men, 1958; Honorary Member, Association of Hawaiian Civic Clubs, 1967; Honorary Doctor of Science, Hawaii Loa College, 1973; Honorary Life Member, Bishop Museum

Association, 1976; commendation, Senate Concurrent Resolution, Hawaii, 1976; Honorary Life Fellow, Pacific Science Association. *Biographical sources*: Who's Who in America; American Men of Science. *Published works*: Many articles in the Museum of the American Indian Newsletter, and other periodicals, including: Arctic Art: Eskimo Ivory, American Indian Art Magazine, 1981); A Common Misperception, (MAI Newsletter, 1984); That Without Which Nothing, (MAI Newsletter, 1984); Beacons in the Night, (MAI Newsletter, 1984); The Owls' Eyes Obsession, (MAI Newsletter, 1984); Solving the Puzzle of the Past, (MAI Newsletter, 1985); among others.

FORD, RICHARD IRVING 1941-
(curator of ethnology)
Born June 27, 1941, Harrisburg, Pa. *Education*: Oberlin College, Ohio, MA, 1963; University of Michigan, MA, 1965, PhD, 1968. *Principal occupation*: Curator of ethnology. *Home address*: 2825 Provincial, Ann Arbor, MI 48104. *Affiliation*: Assistant professor of anthropology, University of Cincinnati, 1967-69; Curator of ethnology and director, Museum of Anthropology, University of Michigan, Ann Arbor, 1970-. *Other professional post*: Professor of anthropology and botany, University of Michigan. *Memberships*: Conference of Native American Studies (national advisory committee); American Anthropological Association; Society for American Archaeology (executive committee); Society for Economic Botany (editorial board); The Archaeological Conservancy (secretary); American Association for Advancement of Science (section H, chairperson). *Interests*: Expert witness, Zuni Pueblo, N.M.; consultant to San Juan Pueblo, N.M.; North American ethnobotany; origins of American Indian agriculture; excavations, Jemez Cave & Bat Cove, N.M., & Cloud-spitter, Ky. *Awards, honors*: Distinguished Service Award, University of Michigan, 1971; National Science Foundation grantee, 1970-73, 1975-76, 1978-79; Weatherhead scholar, School of American Research, 1978-79; *Biographical source*: Who's Who in America. *Published works*: co-author, Paleoethnobotany of the Koster Site (Illinois State Museum, 1972); editor, The Nature and Status of Ethnobotany (University of Michigan, 1978); editor, Prehistoric Food Production in North America (University of Michigan, 1985).

*FOREMAN, EDWARD R. (Pit River)
(tribal chairperson)
Affiliation: Redding Rancheria, 2000 Rancheria Rd., Redding, CA 96001 (916) 241-8979.

FORQUERA, RALPH
(executive director)
Affiliation: Seattle Indian Health Board, 61 1-12th Ave. So., Suite 200, Seattle, WA 98144 (206) 324-9360.

FORREST, ERIN (Modoc-Pit River) 1920-
(rancher, health programs administrator)
Born January 12, 1920, Alturas, Calif. *Education*: Riverside Junior College. *Principal occupation*: Rancher, health programs administrator. *Address*: P.O. Box 251, Alturas, CA 96101 (916) 233-4591 (work). *Affiliations*: State Inheritance Tax Appraiser, 1964-68; administrative assistant, State Assemblywoman Pauline Davis, 1969-75; president, XL Indian Reservation Board of Directors, 1946-; director, Modoc County Indian Health Program, P.O. Box 251, Alturas, CA.

Other professional posts: Chairman, PL 94-437 Policy Council; chairman, NTCA Health Committee; chairman, NCAI Health Committee; national Indian Health Liaison Officer, NTCA. *Community activities*: Modoc County Democratic Central Committee (chairman, 1968-). *Military service*: U.S. Army, ETO, World War II. *Memberships*: National Tribal Chairmen's Association; National Congress of American Indians; California Tribal Chairmen's Association; National Health Insurance Health Team. *Awards, honors*: Rural Services Award, Sergeant Shriver, 1969; Outstanding Achievements in Indian Community Development, awarded by Division of Indian Community Development, Indian Health Service, 1975; honored by California Senate Resolution, 1970; honored by California Assembly Resolution, 1975. *Interests*: Indian health programs; Appaloosa horses; wild life conservation; Indian artifacts; National Indian health and social concerns.

FORSMAN, LEONARD (Suquamish) 1962-
(museum director)
Born January 25, 1962, Bremerton, Wash. *Education*: University of Southern California, 1979-81; University of Washington, BA (Anthropology), 1987. *Principal occupation*: Museum director. *Address*: P.O. Box 654, Suquamish, WA 98392 (206) 598-331 1. *Affiliations*: Researcher, Suquamish Tribal Cultural Center, Suquamish, WA, 1981-85, director, Suquamish Museum, 1985-. *Other professional post*: Editor of museum newsletter. *Community activities*: Secretary, Suquamish Tribal Council; member, Kitsap County Council on Human Rights. *Published works*: Eyes of Chief Seattle (Suquamish Museum, 1984); A Time of Gathering (Burke Museum/University of Washington Press, 1990).

FORTIN, CLAUDETTE
(executive director; editor)
Affiliation: The National Indian Arts and Crafts Corporation, 1 Nicholas St., Suite 1 106, Ottawa, Ontario, Canada K1N 7B6 (613) 232-2436. *Other professional post*: Editor, Artscraft.

FORTUNE, JUDY
(dance team coordinator)
Affiliation: Rappahannock-Mattaponi Dancers, Route 1, Box 522, Tappahannock, VA 23023 (804) 769-4205.

FOSDICK, ROSE ATUK
(services director)
Affiliation: Journal of Alaska Native Arts, Institute of Alaska Native Arts, P.O. Box 80583, Fairbanks, AK 99708 (907) 456-7491.

FOSS, PHILIP, Jr.
(editor)
Affiliation: Institute of American Indian Arts (IAIA) Museum, P.O. Box 20007, Santa Fe, NM 87504 (505) 988-6463.

FOSTER, JEFF
(executive director)
Affiliation: Four Tribes Tribal Employment Rights Office, P.O. Box 1193, Anadarko, OK 73005 (405) 247-9711.

FOSTER, MICHAEL K. 1938-
(anthropologist)
Born June 2, 1938, Athens, Greece (U.S. citizen). *Education*: Lawrence College (Appleton, WI) BA, 1961; Harvard University, MAT, 1962; University of Pennsylvania, PhD, 1974. *Princi-

pal occupation : Anthropologist. *Address* : RR 1, Box 143 B, Thetford Center, VT 05055 (802) 649-8232 (work). *Affiliations* : Instructor, Ursinus College, Collegeville, P A, 1964-66; Iroquoian ethnologist, Canadian Museum of Civilization, Ottawa, Ontario, 1970-89. *Military service* : U.S. Army, 1962-64. *Memberships* : American Anthropological Association (Fellow); Canadian Ethnology Society; Society for the Study of Indigenous Languages of the Americas. *Interests* : The aboriginal languages of North America, and particularly Iroquoian; the aboriginal cultures of the Americas. *Published works* : From the Earth to Beyond the Sky (National Museum of Man, 1974); editor (with J. Campisi & M. Mithun) Extending the Rafters: Interdisciplinary Approaches to Iroquoian Studies (State University of New York Press, 1984); editor: (with W. Cowan & K. Koerner) New Perspectives on Edward Sapir in Language, Culture & Personality (John Benjamins, 1986); editor (with R. Darnell) Native North American Interaction Patterns (Canadian Museum of Civilization, 1988); journal articles and reviews.

*FOSTER, MORRIS W.
(professor of anthropology)
Born January 28, 1960, Alva, Okla. *Education* : University of Oklahoma, BA, 1981; Yale University, MPhil, 1984, PhD, 1988. *Principal occupation* : Assistant professor of anthropology . *Home address* : 819 W. Brooks, Norman, OK 73069 (405) 325-2491 (work). *Affiliation* : Native American Studies Program, Dept. of Anthropology, University of Oklahoma, Norman, OK, 1988-. *Other professional post* : Editor, American Indian Quarterly (University of Nebraska Press), 1993-. *Memberships* : Society for Linguistic Anthropology, American Anthropological Association; American Society for Ethnohistory . *Awards* : 1992 Erminie Wheeler V oegelin Prize for best book in ethnohistory , the American Society for Ethnohistory. Interests: Anthropology, Native American studies, ethnohistory , sociolinguistics, specializing in the people of the Native Plains and Native Southwest. *Published work* : Being Comanche: The Social History of an American Indian Community (U. of Arizona Press, 1991).

FOSTER, TIM
(association president)
Affiliation : National American Indian Cattleman's Association, Route 2, Box 2492, Toppenish, W A 98948 (509) 854-1329. *Other professional post* : Editor & publisher of newsletter and yearbook.

FOUGNIER, RAY
(periodical director)
Affiliation : "Indian Studies Quarterly ," 400 Caldwell Hall, Cornell University , Ithaca, NY 14853 (607) 256-8402.

*FOWLER, CHUCK
(health program director)
Affiliation : Central Valley Indian Health Program, 20 N. Dewitt, Clovis, CA 93482 (209) 299-2578.

*FOWLER, LORETTA
(professor)
Affiliation : Dept. of Anthropology, Indiana University, Rawles Hall 108, Bloomington, IN 47405 (812) 855-1203.

*FOWLER, VERNA
(executive director; supt. for education)
Affiliations : Executive director , National Indian Gaming & Hospitality Institute, Menominee Indian Tribe of W isconsin, P.O. Box 1210, Keshena, WI 54135 (715) 799-5600; president, College of the Menominee Nation, Keshena, WI; supt. for education, Menominee Tribal School, P.O. Box 39, Neopit, WI 54150 (715) 756-2354.

*FOWLER-OTTO, CLARA (Menominee)
(head start director)
Affiliation & Address : Menominee Tribe, P.O. Box 910, Keshena, WI 54135 (715) 799-5100 Fax 799-3373.

FOX, DENNIS R. (Mandan-Hidatsa) 1943-
(BIA-chief, Div . of Education)
Born September 8, 1943, Elbowoods, N.D. *Education* : Dickinson State College, BS, 1966; Penn State University, MEd, 1971, DEd, 1977. *Principal occupation* : Assistant director of education, BIA. *Address* : Dept. of the Interior , Bureau of Indian Affairs, Rm. 3517 MS-3512-MIB, 1849 C St., NW, Washington, DC 20240 (202) 208-7388. *Affiliations* : Education program administrator, Johnson O'Malley Program, BIA, Cheyenne River Agency and Aberdeen Area Office, SD, 1975-83; assistant director of education, BIA, Washington, DC, 1983-. *Other professional post* : Teacher, worked in BIA higher education grant program. *Memberships* : National Indian Education Association; Phi Delta Kappa. *Awards, honors* : Gave presentation at National School Administration Conference. *Interests* : Educational administration. *Biographical source* : Indians of Today, 1970 edition.

FOX, JOHN, M.D.
(clinical director)
Affiliation : Rocky Boy's PHS Indian Health Center, P.O. Box 664, Box Elder, MT 59521 (406) 395-4489.

FOX, ROY
(Indian band chief)
Affiliation : Blood Indian Band, Box 60, Standoff, Alberta T0L 1Y0 (403) 737-3753.

FOX, SANDRA J. (HARRELL)
(Oglala/Cheyenne River Sioux) 1944-
(education specialist)
Born December 9, 1944, Kadoka, S.D. *Education* : Dickinson State College, BS, 1966; Penn State University, MEd, 1971, DEd, 1976. *Principal occupation* : Education specialist. *Address* : Bureau of Indian Affairs, Rm. 351 1 Mail Stop: 3512-MIB, 1951 Constitution Ave., NW, Washington, DC 20245 (202) 343-1 192. *Affiliations* : Education specialist, Bureau of Indian Affairs, Aberdeen Area Office, S.D.; education specialist-curriculum, ORBIS, Inc., W ashington, D.C., 1985-. *Other professional post* : Education specialist and consultant, B.I.A. *Memberships* : International Reading Association; National Indian Education Association; North American Indian Women's Association. *Awards, honors* : North Dakota Indian Scholarship; invited to join Pi Lambda Theta; given presentations at National Council of Teachers of English Convention, national Reading Conference, and International Reading Association Convention. *Interests* : Elementary and secondary education reading improvement. Published work: An Annotated Bibliography of Young People's Books on American Indians (Bureau of Indian Affairs, 1973).

FOX, TAMMY, P.A.
(clinical director)
Affiliation : Oneida Community Health Center , Box 365, Oneida, WI 54155 (414) 869-271 1.

*FOX-RIGNEY, LORI LANE *(Wolf Woman)* (Cherokee) 1962-
(Indian education resource specialist/teacher)
Born December 24, 1962, Sacramento, Calif. *Education* : University of California, Davis, B.A., 1985; California State University , Hayward, M.A., 1992. *Principal occupation* : Indian education resource specialist/teacher . *Home address* : 731 Poppy Cir ., Vacaville, CA 95687 (916) 371-9300 (work). *Affiliation* : Washington Unified School District, West Sacramento, CA. *Memberships* : Write On! (fictional writer's group); California Scholarship Federation (lifetime member). *Interests* : "I am interested in Native American languages, cultures, and literature; mythology; Celtic languages & literature; Ireland; the Southwest, especially New Mexico; Billy the Kid; wolves."

*FRANCIS, LEE, III (Laguna Pueblo) 1945-
(organization director;
author, educator, poet)
Born May 21, 1945, Albuquerque, N.M. *Education* : San Francisco State University , B.A., 1983, M.A., 1984; W estern Institute for Social Research, Ph.D., 1991. *Principal occupation* : Director-Indian organization; author , educator, poet. *Home address* : 2951 Ellenwood Dr ., Fairfax, VA 22031 (703) 280-1028. *Affiliations* : Sr. partner, Associated Businesses, Albuquerque, NM, 1978-81; San Francisco State University (Administrative coordinator , Student Affirmative Action Program, 1981-83; associate director, Educational Opportunity Program, 1983-84; senior faculty, Meta-Life Adult Professional Training Institute, W ashington, DC, 1984-88; core faculty, Western Institute for Social Research, Berkeley, CA, 1989-90; 1991-93; vice president, First Americans Research, W ashington, DC, 1993-; national director , Wordcraft Circle of Native W riters & Storytellers, Fairfax, VA, 1992-; editor, "Moccasin Telegraph, Fairfax, VA, 1992-. *Other professional posts* : Indian Youth Specialist, U.S. Dept. of the Interior , BIA, Office of Alcohol & Substance Abuse Prevention (consultant, 1994); editor , "Prevention Quarterly." *Community activities* : Board of directors, Native Writers' Circle of the Americas & The Greenfield Literary Review Center; advisory boards of the Minority Opportunities in Science Teaching (MOST) at California State University , Long Beach & The Children's Foundation; chair , Education Committee, American Indian Inter-Tribal Cultural Organizations, Rockville, MD, 1992-93; task force member , Research * Rehabilitation Institute (RRI), Huntington Beach, CA, 1992-93. *Memberships* : National Psychiatric Association (life member); National Indian Education Association; Native Writers Circle of the Americas (board of directors, 1992-. *Awards, honors* : Certificate of Appreciation, Student Affirmative Action Program, San Francisco State University, 1981-82; AILOTT (American Indian Leaders of Today & Tomorrow) California State University, Long Beach, 1990; American Indian Student Council, California State University , Long Beach, 1990. *Interests* : Dr. Francis is actively engaged in a number of research projects-currently focusing on studying the interrelationship of PTSD (Post Traumatic Stress Disorder) as applied to particular Native Cultural groups and intertribal social change dynamics; he enjoys speaking to large & small groups on a variety of topics. He is regularly invited too speak to organizations throughout the country . His areas of expertise are social policy , multicultural

communication and organizational development. Dr. Francis has made numerous keynote addresses and lectures. "Other interests include writing poetry, Native-centered science fiction, and plays...traveling on the Internet superhighway...participating in pow wows all across Indian Country...composing music/songs and playing them on my guitar ." *Published works*: Books: BEST Course: A Cultural Communications Handbook (Met-Life Publishing, 1986); Indian Time: An Historical Timetable of Native America (St. Martin's Press, 1994); Path of the Brave: Dimensions of Cultural Idiocide (in progress); numerous articles & essays, including: "Elder Wisdom: Native American Culture Studies," in English Studies/Culture Studies: Institutionalizing Dissent (Champaign/Urbana: University of Illinois Press, 1994); "Keresian Dawn," in Callaloo: Native Literatures Special Issue, edited by Charles H. Rowell (Johns Hopkins University Press, 1994; & "This Business of Coolumbus" (with Paul Gunn Allen) in Columbus and Beyond: Views from Native Americans, edited by Randolph Jorgen (SPMA Publishing, 1992).

FRANCIS, RODERICK P.
(Indian band chief)
Affiliation: Pictou Landing Indian Band, Box 249, Trenton, NS, Canada B0K 1X0 (902) 752-4912.

*FRANCIS-BEGAY, KAREN
(educator)
Affiliation: College of Education, University of Arizona, Tucson, AZ 85721 (602) 621-131 1.

*FRANK, EDDIE (Athapascan)
(AK village council president)
Affiliation: Venetie Village Council, P.O. Box 99, Arctic Village, AK 99781 (907) 849-8212.

FRANK, FRANCIS F.
(Indian band chief)
Affiliation: Yia-O-Qui-Aht First Nations, Box 18, Tolfino, BC, Canada V0R 2Z0 (604) 725-3233.

FRANK, JAMES
(Indian band chief)
Affiliation: Kanaka Bar Indian Band, Box 210, Lytton, British Columbia, Canada V0K 1Z0 (604) 455-2279.

*FRANK, JOYCE (Eskimo)
(AK village council president)
Affiliation: Organized Village of Saxman, Route 2, Ketchikan, AK 99901 (907) 225-5163.

FRANK, NORMAN
(Indian band chief)
Affiliation: Comox Indian Band, 3320 Comox Rd., Courtenay, British Columbia, Canada V9N 3P8 (604) 339-7122.

FRANK, WALLY
(AK village president)
Affiliation: Angoon Community Association, P.O. Box 188, Angoon, AK 99820 (907) 788-3441.

FRANKE, JUDITH A.
(museum director)
Affiliation: Dickson Mounds Museum, Lewiston, IL 61542 (309) 547-3721.

FRANKSON, ERNIE (Eskimo)
(AK village council president)
Affiliation: Point Hope Village Council, P.O. Box 91, Point Hope, AK 99766 (907) 368-2453.

*FRANTZ, DONALD G. (Omahkokoyaato'si) 1934-
(professor)
Born January 20, 1934, Oakland, Calif. *Education*: University of California, Berkeley , BA, 1960. *Principal occupation*: Professor. *Home address*: 9 Lafayette Crescent, Lethbridge, Alberta, Canada T1K 4B5 (403) 381-0302. *Military service*: U.S. Coast Guard, 1953-57 (1st Class P.O.) *Community activities*: Zone representative, Board of Directors, Alberta Triathlon Association. *Memberships*: Linguistics Society of America; Canadian Linguistics Association. Interests: Native language research; triathlon participation. *Published works*: Blackfoot Dictionary, 1989, and Blackfoot Grammar, 1991 (University of Toronto Press)

FRAZIER, GREGORY W. (Crow)1947-
(writer, film producer)
Born September 5, 1947, Richmond, Ind. Education: Earlham College, 1965-67; Temple University, BA, 1972; University of Puget Sound, MBA, 1978, PhD, 1988. *Principal occupation*: Writer, film producer. *Address*: P.O. Box 535, Yellowtail, MT 59035 (303) 231-6599. *Affiliations*: Member, National Indian Planning Council, U.S. DOL; instructor/consultant, American Indian Management Institute, Albuquerque, N.M., 1972-74; executive director, Seattle Indian Center, Inc., 1974-77; executive director, AL-IND-ESK-A (The 13th Regional Corp.), Seattle, 1977-79; chairman, Absarokee Investments, Seattle, 1977-; president National Urban Indian Council, Denver, CO, 1979-; president, National Indian Business Council, Englewood, CO, 1977-89; owner, Alpine Adventure Films, Englewood, CO, 1987-; owner, Intracity Properties, Englewood, CO; president/chairman, Indians for United Social Action; president, GAMA, Englewood, CO; chairman, Arrowstar, Yellowtail, MT. *Other professional posts*: chairman, Cablestar Distributing, Englewood, CO, 1985-; chairperson, American Indian/Alaska Native Advisory Committee, U.S. Dept. of Commerce, 1991-92. *Community activities*: King County Housing Task Force (member); Billings-Yellowstone Housing Association (member); Indians for United Social Action (member); National Low Income Housing Coalition (member). *Memberships*: National Indian Education Association; Indian Motorcycle Owners Association (vice president); American Motorcyclists Association; America Film Producers Association; America Writers Guild; National Indian Business Council (chairman, 1983-); Registered Lobbyist, U.S. House & Senate, Colorado General Assembly; American Management Association, 1980-. *Awards, honors*: Outstanding Contribution Award, CETA Coalition; Individual Personal Achievement Award, IHRC, Inc.; Outstanding Minority Writer, 1985, U.S. Writers Association; Best Business Efforts, Community Chamber of Commerce, 1985; Outstanding Minority Writer of the Year, 1988; Presidential appointee, National Advisory Council on Indian Education; appointee, Secretary's Advisory Group, Department of HUD; appointee, Department of Labor Ad Hoc Advisory Committee. *Interests*: Business and economic development; international economic development; developing countries; political & bureaucratic abuses of authority; fundraising. "Dr. Frazier is a professional motorcycle adventurer, having traveled around the world by motorcycle. He has written extensively about his travel adventures. He has won professional events throughout the U.S. as a BMW

and Indian racer . Dr. Frazier is a well known figure in the motorcycle industry both in Europe and the U.S. Dr. Frazier has long been an advocate for the rights of American Indians and Alaska Natives, having served as president of the National Urban Indian Council from 1977-89. As a registered lobbyist in the U.S. House & Senate, he lobbied for Native rights and funding and is a noted expert on urban Indian policy in America. Dr. Frazier has spent 30 years exposing government abuses, discrimination, and bureaucratic malfeasance in federal agencies. As an Indian activist, he has been responsible for changes in federal laws and regulations that have benefited American Indians & Alaska Natives." *Published works*: While We're At It, Let's Get You a Job (NCIB Press, 1984); American Indian Index (Arrowstar Publishing, 1987); Smoke Signals (Arrowstar Publishing, 1989); American Indian/Alaska Native Higher Education Funding Guild (Arrowstar Publishing, 1989); Urban Indians: Drums from the Cities (Arrowstar); Motorcycle Sex, Or Freud Would Never Understand the Relationship Between Me and My Motorcycle (Arrowstar); Urban Indian Profile in America (Arrowstar).

FRAZIER, JEFF
(seminary director)
Affiliation: Carter Seminary, 2400 Chickasaw Blvd., Ardmore, OK 73401 (405) 223-8547.

FRAZIER, JOE
(school principal)
Affiliation: Riverside Indian School, Route 1, Anadarko, OK 73005 (405) 247-6673 ext. 340.

FRAZIER, RUTH T.
(organization president)
Affiliation: Futures for Children, 805 Tijeras, NW, Albuquerque, NM 87102 (505) 247-4700.

FREDERICK, CLARENCE
(director-Indian hospital)
Affiliation: Turtle Mountain PHS Indian Hospital, Belcourt, ND 58316 (701) 477-61 12.

*FREDERICKS, MICHELLE CATHERINE (Pinto Horse Woman) (Mandan, Hidatsa & Arikara) 1966-
(administrative director)
Born October 21, 1966, Fort Yates, N.D. *Education*: University of Colorado, BA, 1989. *Principal occupation*: Administrative director. *Home address*: 520 Kansas City St., Suite 207, Rapid City, SD 57701 (605) 394-9730 (work). *Affiliation*: Administrative director, InterTribal Bison Cooperative, Rapid City, SD, 1983-. *Community activities*: American Indian Ambassador Class of 1994 for Americans for Indian Opportunity. *Interests*: "I am entering into the field of fund raising through my work with the InterTribal Bison Cooperative. In February (1994), I attended a course of fered by the Fund Raising School of Indian University's Center on Philanthropy." *Biographical source*: "Tatanka Returns," by Richard Simonelli, in Winds of Change, Vol. 8, No. 4, Autumn 1993.

*FREDERICKS, THOMAS W.
(Mandan/Hidatsa/Arikara)
(attorney)
Affiliation: Fredericks, Pelcyger, Hester & White, Canyon Center, 1881 9th St., Suite 216, Boulde, CO 80302 (303) 443-1683. Law firm which specializes in Indian law .

FREDERIKSEN, ROBERT DOUGLAS
(Tzuscum Doogie) **(Tsimshian) 1967-**
   (storyteller)
Born April 17, 1967, Seattle, Wash. *Education*: Seattle Pacific University, 1985-86; University of Washington, 1992-. *Principal occupation*: Storyteller (ancient Tsimshian legends & parables). *Home address*: 4546 - 45th SW #101, Seattle, WA 98116 (206) 587-3415. *Affiliations*: Raven Speaks Productions, Seattle, WA, 1988-. *Other professional post*: Secretary, Tsimshian Tribal Association of Washington; former vice-chairperson & choreographer of Alaska Native Cultural Heritage Association in Washington. *Community activities*: Currently organizing two related organizations, Wisdom, a social research organization dedicated to change, and F.E.E.D. (Foundation for Educational & Economic Development), a trust fund for self-help & education programs. *Interests*: "Pan American Native history; development of self-sustaining solutions to problems facing Natives and other disadvantaged peoples; reading historical fiction, writing; revitalizing hope in an increasingly disenchanted urban youth; constitutional study; economics, market theory. I love to dance, travel & debate."

*FREED, STANLEY A.
   (museum curator)
Affiliation: American Museum of Natural History, 79th & Central Park West, New York, NY 10024 (212) 769-5375.

FREELAND, FRANKLIN
   (director-Indian hospital)
Affiliation: Ft. Defiance PHS Indian Hospital, P.O. Box 649, Ft. Defiance, AZ 86504 (602) 729-5741.

FREEMAN, CLIFFORD
   (Indian band chief)
Affiliation: Drift Indian Band, General Delivery, Driftpile, Alberta, Canada T0G 0V0 (403) 355-3868.

FREEMAN, JOAN
   (executive director)
Affiliations: American Indian Free Clinic, 1330 S. Long Beach Blvd., Compton, CA 90221 (213) 537-0103; American Indian Free Clinic, 9500 Artesia Blvd., Bellflower, CA 90706 (310) 920-7227.

FREEMAN, ROBERT LEE (Dakota-Luiseno) 1939-
   (artist, cartoonist, muralist, printmaker)
Born January 14, 1939, Rincon Indian Reservation, Calif. *Education*: Palomar College, AA, 1976. *Principal occupation*: Artist, cartoonist, muralist, printmaker. Resides in San Marcos, CA. *Affiliation*: Art instructor, Palomar College. *Military service*: U.S. Army, 1957-60 (E-2 Korea, 1959). *Exhibitions*: One-man shows: Schiver Gallery, St. Louis, Mo.; Sioux Museum, Rapid City, S.D.; Turtle Mountain Gallery, Philadelphia, Pa.; Gallery of the American Indian, Sedona, Ariz; among others. *Group shows*: U.S. Department of the Interior, Washington, DC; Heard Museum, Phoenix, Ariz.; Scottsdale National Indian Art Exhibit, Ariz.; among others. Murals: Los Angeles Public Library (45 ft.) and five private murals in homes. Numerous selected public & private collections. *Awards, honors*: 150 national Indian art awards from the following: Scottsdale National Indian Art Exhibit, Heard Museum, Red Cloud Art Show, Southern California Exposition, Gallup Ceremonial, and

California State Fair. *Interests*: Mr. Freeman works in several media and has won awards in oil, watercolor, woodcarving, etching, pen and ink, bronze, airbrush and drawing, acrylic & lithography. He has instructed the course Native American Art at Grossmont College, San Diego, and Palomar College, San Marcos, Calif. Travel. *Biographical sources*: Who's Who in Indian Art; International Artists & Writers (Cambridge, England). *Published works*: Mr. Freeman's work has appeared in such periodicals as Ford Times, Western Horseman, Southwest Art Scene, Indian Voices, Genie, North County Living, Westerner, and Artist of the Rockies. Paintings included in two books, I Am These People, and Contemporary Sioux Paintings. Mr. Freeman has illustrated two books: The Layman's Typology Handbook, and The Luiseno People. He is author and publisher of two cartoon books, For Indians Only, 1971, and War Whoops and All That Jazz, 1973; Robert Freeman Drawings, 1985.

FREESE, ALISON 1951-
   (educator, information specialist)
Born August 13, 1951, Washington, DC. *Education*: University of Wisconsin, BA, 1974; University of New Mexico, MA, 1986, PhD, 1991. *Home address*: 1909 Las Lomas NE, Albuquerque, NM 87131 (505) 277-3917 (work). *Affiliation*: Information Specialist, Native American Studies Dept., University of New Mexico, Albuquerque, NM, 1991-. *Community activities*: Organize speakers series, liaison with Native American organizations; editor of monthly newsletter; computer networking with tribal libraries. Memberships: America Society for Ethnohistory; American Historical Association; American Library Association, New Mexico Library Association, Phi Kappa Phi Honorary Society. *Interests*: "Pueblo/Spanish relations in 17th century New Mexico; cultural resistance strategies implemented by Native American groups in response to European colonization, particularly in the Pueblo Southwest; ethical issues relating to scholarship in Native American studies. Also interested in facilitating Native American students at UNM and encouraging them to pursue a career in Native American studies through research and writing." *Published works*: UNM Dissertation - "Sacred Clowns" Role in Cultural Boundary maintenance Among the Pueblo Indians; editor, et al, By Force of Arms: The Journals of don Diego de Vargas, New Mexico, 1691-93 (UNM Press, 1992); chapter, "Send in the Clowns: Resistance Strategies Among the Pueblo Indians in 17th Century New Mexico," in The Spanish Missions of New Mexico: A Sourcebook, Vol. 2, by David Hurst Thomas, et al, Editors (Garland Press, 1991).

FRENCH, LA WANDA
   (museum director)
Affiliation: Ponca City Cultural Center and Museum, 1000 East Grant, Ponca City, OK 74601 (405) 765-5268.

FRENCH, ROY
   (Indian band chief)
Affiliation: Takla Lake Indian Band, Takla Landing, British Columbia, Canada V0J 2T0.

*FRICKNER, TONYA GONNELLA
   (attorney)
Affiliation: Director, American Indian Law Alliance, 404 Lafayette St., 2nd Floor, New York, NY 10003 (212) 598-0100 x 257.

*FRIDLEY, LaMERLE
   (IHS-health programs administrator)
Affiliation: Office of Health Programs, California Area IHS, 1825 Bell St., Suite 200, Sacramento, CA 95825 (916) 978-4202.

FRIED, RONALD, D.O.
   (clinical director)
Affiliation: Shawnee Indian Health Center, 2001 S. Gordon Cooper Dr., Shawnee, OK 74801 (405) 275-4270.

FRITZ, LINDA
   (native law centre instructor)
Affiliation: University of Saskatchewan, Native Law Centre, Diefenbaker Centre, Saskatoon, SK, Canada S7N 0W0 (306) 966-6189.

FROST, RICHARD D.
   (executive officer)
Affiliation: Alaska Area Native Health Services, IHS, 250 Gambell St., Third & Gambell St., Anchorage, AK 99510 (907) 257-1155.

FRY, JACK
   (school principal)
Affiliation: Paschal Sherman Indian School, Omak Lake Rd., Omak, WA 98841 (509) 826-2097.

*FUKINO, WAYNE (MD) (Hawaiian)
   (clinic president)
Affiliation: Ho'ola Lahui Hawai'i, Waimea Medical Clinic, P.O. Box 909, Walmea, HI 96796 (808) 338-0031.

*FUKUDA, DONALD R. (Hawaiian)
   (director of admissions)
Affiliation: Hawaiian Studies Program, University of Hawaii at Manoa, Honolulu, HI 96822 (808) 948-8975.

*FULLER, JULIUS B., JR., (Creek) 1952-
   (administrative coordinator)
Born August 5, 1952, Wetumpka, Alaska. *Education*: University of Montevallo (AL), 1971-72. *Principal occupation*: Administrative coordinator. *Home address*: 28 Cornelia Rd., Brierfield, AL 35035 (205) 665-5137. *Affiliation*: Alabama Power Co., Birmingham, AL, 1974-. *Membership*: Founder & president, Southeastern Indian Heritage Association. *Awards, honors*: Outstanding Young Men of America, 1981. *Interests*: "(I'm a)maker of museum-quality Southeastern Indian bows, arrows & tools; (I'm a) demonstrator at museums and educational events; and a freelance magazine writer."

FULTON, NOLAN, M.D.
   (chief of staff)
Affiliation: Choctaw Health Center, Route 7, Box R-50, Philadelphia, MS 39350 (601) 656-221 1.

G

GADWA, GORDON
   (Indian band chief)
Affiliation: Kehewin Indian Band, Box 6218, Bonnyville, Alberta, Canada T0A 0L0 (403) 826-3333.

*GAFFNEY, PAT
   (school principal)
Affiliation: Ahfachkee Day School, Star Route, Box 40, Clewiston, FL 33440 (813) 983-6348.

GAHBOW, ARTHUR (Chippewa)
(tribal chairperson)
Affiliation: Mille Lacs Reservation Business Committee, Star Route, Onamia, MN 56359 (612) 532-4181.

GAIASHKIBOS (Lac Courte Oreilles Ojibwe)
(NCAI president; tribal chairperson)
Affiliations: President, National Congress of American Indians, 900 Pennsylvania, SE, Washington, DC 20003 (202) 546-9404, 1992-; Chairperson, Lac Courte Oreilles Tribal Governing Board, Route 2, Box 2700, Hayward, WI 54843 (715) 634-8934.

*GAINES, ELIZABETH
(editor)
Affiliation: "Inter-Tribal Times Newspaper," Inter-Trbal Council, Inc., P.O. Box 1308, Miami, OK 74355 (918) 542-4486.

GAJAR, ANNA H. 1943-
(associate professor)
Education: Hunter College, B.A., 1964; University of Virginia, MEd, 1973, PhD, 1977. *Principal occupation*: Associate professor of special education. *Home address*: 272 Spring St., State College, PA 16801 (814) 237-5473; 863-2284 (work). *Affiliations*: Assistant professor (1977-84), associate professor (1984-), Dept. of Special Education, Penn State University, 226B Moore Bldg., University Park, PA 16802. Teaches a seminar on Issues in American Indian Special Education. *Other professional posts*: Consulting - evaluation of the American Indian Professional Training Program of the Dept. of Speech & Hearing Sciences, University of Arizona, Tucson, AZ, 1985; external evaluation of a professional degree training program entitled American Indian Professional Training in Speech-Language Pathology and Audiology at the University of Arizona, 1985. *Interests*: Improvement of graduate and undergraduate teacher education in special education (American Indian projects.) *Published works*: American Indian personnel preparation in special education: Needs, program components, programs (refereed) "Journal of American Indian Education," 1985; American Indian Special Education Teacher Training Program (U.S. Dept. of Education, Personnel Preparation (report); American Indian Special Education Personnel Preparation (presentation before CEC International Convention); A Model Program for American Indian Special Education Teacher Training at The Pennsylvania State University (presentation at NIEA Convention).

*GALE, NANCY
(editor)
Affiliation: "Linkages," TCI, Inc., 3410 Garfield St., NW, Washington, DC 20007 (202) 333-6350.

GALLAGER, CATHERINE
(education coordinator)
Affiliation: Crow Creek/Lower Brule Agency, Bureau of Indian Affairs, P.O. Box 139, Fort Thompson, SD 57339 (605) 245-2398.

*GALLEGOS, ANDREW (Pueblo)
(pueblo governor)
Affiliation: Pueblo of Santa Ana, 2 Dove Rd., Bernalillo, NM 87004 (505) 867-3301.

*GALLI, MARCIA
(board chairperson)
Affiliation: Utah Board of Indian Affairs, 144 N. Pinewood Cr., Layton, UT 84041 (801) 626-6818.

*GALLOWAY, BRENT
(college department head)
Affiliation: Indian Languages, Literature and Linguistics, Saskatchewan Indian Federated College, University of Regina, 118 College West, Regina, Saskatchewan, Canada S4S 0A2 (306) 584-8333.

GALLOWAY, DAVE
(health director)
Affiliation: Choctaw Nation Indian Health Center, 903 E. Monroe, McAlester, OK 74501 (918) 423-8440.

*GALLOWAY, JAMES, M.D.
(clinical director-Indian hospital)
Affiliation: Whiteriver Indian Hospital, Whiteriver, AZ 85941 (602) 338-491 1.

GAMBARO, RETHA WALDEN
(Muscogee-Creek) 1917-
(sculptor)
Born December 9, 1917, Lenna, Okla. *Education*: Corcoran School of Art, 1969. *Principal occupation*: Sculptor. *Home address*: 74 Dishpan Lane, Stafford, VA 22554 (703) 659-0130. *Arts specialization*: sculpture wall hangings. Medium or media: sculpture in bronze, stone, and wood. Mixed media sculpture. Wall hangings of mixed media only. Conferences attended or lectures presented: Galludet College, Washington, DC; Eugene O'Neill Center, Waterford, CT; Slater Memorial Museum, Norwich, CT; Williams School, New London, CT; Haverford College, Haverford, PA; Haskell Indian Jr. College, Lawrence, KS. *Exhibitions*: Smithsonian Institution-Museum of Natural History, Kennedy Center (Night of the First Americans), National Cathedral, Howard University, Folger Shakespeare Library, Trinity Episcopal Church, American Spirit Gallery, Art Barn, St. Augustine Chapel, People Life Insurance, Midtown Gallery, and U.S. Safe Deposit (all in Washington, D.C.); Art Institute of Philadelphia; Slater Museum, Norwich, CT; Coast Guard Academy & Yah Ta Hey Gallery (both in New London, CT); among others. Major Collections: U.S. Dept. of Parks, VA; National Aboretum, Galludet College, B'Nai B'Rith Museum, Church of the Reformation, Native American Research, Howard University, and the Convention Center (all in Washington, D.C.; Daybreak Art Center, Seattle, WA; among others. *Memberships*: Artists Equity; Indian Arts and Crafts Association; National Museum of Women in the Arts (charter member); National Museum of the American Indian (charter member). *Awards, honors*: Best in Show at the Art League of Northern Virginia, and Best in Sculpture at the Mystic Harbour Invitational in Connecticut. *Biographical sources*: In publications - "Art Business News, Vol. 9 Issue 3, March 1982; "National American Indian Women's Art Show"; American Artists of Renown, 1981-82; Women At Work; Contemporary American Women Sculptors; Art and the Animal. Video - Born of Fire (28 minute educational film by White Light Productions).

*GAMBLE, RICHARD
(Indian band chief)
Affiliation: Beardys Indian Band, Box 340, Duck Lake, SK, Canada S0K 1J0 (306) 467-4523.

*GANIS, EVERETT
(school chairperson)
Affiliation: Little Wound Day School, P.O. Box 500, Kyle, SD 57752 (605) 455-2461.

*GANJE, LUCY ANNIS 1949-
(professor of graphic arts)
Born December 14, 1949, Eagle Butte, S.D. *Education*: Black Hills State University, BS, 1983; Academy of Art College, MFA, 1984. *Principal occupation*: Professor of graphic arts. *Home address*: 419 Princeton St., Grand Forks, ND 58203 (701) 772-9259. *Affiliations*: Instructor, Cheyenne River Sioux Tribe Community College, 1985-86; Assistant professor of graphic arts, Native Americn Media Center Committee, Indian Programs Committee, University of North Dakota, School of Communication, Grand Forks, ND, 1988-. *Other professional posts*: Manager, Printing Division, Cheyenne River Sioux Tribe Telephone Authority, 1984-88; design consulting. *Professional activities*: Presenter, "Publication Design" Native American Journalists Association, Annual Convention, March 1991; Coordinator, North Dakota Indian Youth Leadership Institute, ND Dept. of Public Instruction, Indian Programs Division, Grand Forks, ND, June 1991; "Press Freedom in Indian Country" panel for Editors-Broadcasters Day, Oct. 1991; among others. *Memberships*: Association for Education i Journalism and Mass Communication; American Advertising Federation; Native American Journalists Association. *Awards, honors*: Invited and designed material for Native Americn Manufacturers Marketing Conference, Feb. 1989; Curriculum Development Grant for attendance to Native American Journalists Conference, Denver, CO, March 1991. *Creative activity*: Videos - "Rock Art at Pinon Canyon Maneuver Site," Southeastern CO, March 1990, produced by the National Rock Art Research Foundation; "Cultural Resources at Pinon Canyon," produced for the Nat'l Park Service, Summer 1991-.

GARCIA, CAROLE (Papago)
(organization co-director)
Affiliation: National Native American Cooperative, P.O. Box 1000, San Carlos, NM 85550 (602) 230-3399.

GARCIA, CHARLOTTE (Pueblo)
(school principal)
Affiliation: Sky City Community School, P.O. Box 349, Acoma, NM 87034 (505) 552-6671.

GARCIA, LAURA V. (Navajo)
(school principal)
Affiliation: Crownpoint Community School, P.O. BOX 178, Crownpoint, NM 87313 (505) 786-6160.

GARCIA, MARCELINO (Tewa Pueblo) 1932-
(instructional aid worker)
Born June 2, 1932, San Juan Pueblo, N.M. *Education*: U.S. Indian School, Santa Fe. *Principal occupation*: Instructional aid worker, B.I.A. *Home address*: P.O. Box 854, San Juan Pueblo, N.M. *Community Activities*: San Juan Pueblo Church (chairman). *Awards, honors*: Prize for Indian ceremonial sash belt, NM State Fair.

*GARCIA, MARVIN (Klamath)
(tribal chairperson)
Affiliation: Klamath General Council, P.O. Box 436, Chiloquin, OR 97624 (503) 783-2219.

GARCIA, RAMON (Pueblo)
(former pueblo governor)
Affiliation: Pueblo of Santo Domingo, Box 99, Santa Domingo Pueblo, NM 87052.

*GARCIA, TONY (Yankton Sioux) 1951-
(educational admin./Indian education)
Born October 7, 1951, Pierre, S.D. *Education*: University of South Dakota, Ed.D., 1991. *Principal occupation*: Educational administration/Indian education. *Home address*: 5011 Heather Lane, Rapid City, SD 57701 (605) 394-4071 (work). *Affiliation*: Director of Indian Education, Rapid City School District, 1991-. *Other professional posts*: Assistant principal; teacher; director of child protection services; director of juvenile prevention; high school counselor; community educator. *Military service*: U.S. Army, 1970-72 (Spec. 4th class; Vietnam Veteran). *Community activities*: Board Member, Big Brothers & Big Sisters. *Memberships*: National Indian Education Association; South Dakota Indian Education Association; National Association of Bilingual Education; South Dakota Bilingual-Bicultural Association. *Awards, honors*: 1993 Dakota Wesleyan Indian Alumna of the Year. *Interests*: Founder of Ateyapi (Fatherhood) Society for Lakota People, Rapid City, SD. *Published works*: Dissertation - Attitude Difference As Seen by Indian and Non-Indian students Towards Their Teachers, 1991

GARCIA, WILFRED (Pueblo)
(former pueblo governor)
Affiliation: Pueblo of San Juan, Box 1099, San Juan Pueblo, NM 87566.

GARDNER, ARNOLD
(Indian band chief)
Affiliation: Eagle Lake #27 Indian Band, Box 27, Eagle River, Ontario, Canada P0V 1S0 (807) 755-5526.

*GARDNER, GLENN, Jr. (Aleut)
(AK village council president)
Affiliation: Native Village of Sand Point, P.O. Box 447, Sand Point, AK 99661 (907) 383-3525.

*GARDNER, LAURIE
(health administrator)
Affiliation: Upper Sioux Board of Trustees, Box 147, Granite Falls, MN 56241 (612) 564-2360.

GARFIELD, CATHI
(editor)
Affiliation: Southern California Indian Center News, P.O. Box 2550, Garden Grove, CA 92746 (213) 977-1366.

GARNETTE, SHIRLEY (Sioux)
(school principal)
Affiliations: Wounded Knee School District, P.O. Box 350, Manderson, SD 57756 (605) 867-5433; Loneman Day School, P.O. Box 50, Oglala, SD 57764 (605) 867-5633.

GARRETT, THOMAS E.
(BIA director)
Affiliation: Congressional & Legislative Affairs, Bureau of Indian Affairs, Dept. of the Interior, 1849 C St., NW, Washington, DC 20240 (202) 208-5706.

GARRIOCH, SYDNEY
(Indian band chief)
Affiliation: Cross Lake Indian Band, Cross Lake, Manitoba, Canada R0B 0J0 (204) 676-2218.

*GARZA, JOSE L. *(Aztatl)*
(Coahuilteca/Lipan Apache) 1942-
(free lance writer, lecturer, workshops)
Born November 24, 1941, San Antonio, Tex. *Education*: Wayne State University, 1970-72. *Principal occupation*: Free lance writer, lecturer, workshops. *Home address*: 102 Windy Lane, Edinboro, PA 16412 (814) 734-4943. *Military service*: U.S. Air Force. *Memberships*: Casa De Unidad Cultural & Media Arts Center, 1980-; Latino Poets Association, 1985-; Native Writers Circle of the Americas, 1992-; Wordcraft Circle of Native Writers, 1992-. *Awards, honors*: Michigan Council for the Arts, 1989 Individual Artists Grant. *Interests*: Lectures and workshops on Native writing and culture. "Two hour workshops help dispel the stereotypes attributed to the many Native cultures of the Americas; focus is on reading and discussing works by contemporary Native writers that express a wide range of human emotions, experiences and current trends in writing." *Published works*: Masks, Folk Dances & Whole Bunch More (Ridgeway Press, 1989); Kamikazi (Edinboro Book Arts, 1992); Apple Comes Home (red Age Unlimited, 1994).

GARZA, RAUL (Kickapoo of Texas)
(tribal chairperson)
Affiliation: Kickapoo Traditional Tribe of Texas, Box 972, Eagle Pass, TX 78853 (512) 773-2105.

*GASTELUM, ARCADIO (Pascua-Yaqui)
(tribal chairperson)
Affiliation: Pascua-Yaqui Tribal Council, 7474 S. camino De Oeste, Tucson, AZ 85746 (602) 883-2838.

*GAYNOR, BASIL M.
(editor)
Affiliation: "Indian Crusader," American Indian Liberation Crusade, Inc., 4009 S. Hallday Ave., Los Angeles, CA 90062 (213) 299-1810.

*GEACI, ROBERT
(site director)
Affiliation: Ste. Marie Among the Iroquois, P.O. Box 146, Onondaga Lake Park, Liverpool, NY 13088 (315) 457-2990.

*GEARY, MAUREEN
(attorney)
Affiliation: California Indian Legal Services, P.O. Box 488, Ukiah, CA 95482 (707) 462-3825.

*GEBOE, CHARLES
(Indian education)
Affiliation: Chief, Branch of Elementary & Secondary Education, Office of Indian Education Programs, Bureau of Indian Affairs, Dept. of the Interior, MS-4140-MIB, 1849 C St., NW, Washington, DC 20240 (202) 208-1129.

*GEDNALSKI, BOB
(elementary school principal)
Affiliation: St. Francis Indian School, P.O. Box 379, St. Francis, SD 57572 (605) 747-2299.

GEHMAN, R. DALE (Poarch Band Creek) 1957-
(radio broadcaster, consulting engineer)
Born June 16, 1957, Carlisle, Penn. *Education*: Alabama Aviation and Technical College, AB, 1976; Jefferson Davis College (Brewton, AL), AAS (Industrial Electronics), 1993; Atmore State Tech. College, 1991-93 (General Electronics). *Principal occupation*: Radio broadcasting, consulting engineer. *Home address*: 1192 Division Hwy., Ephrata, PA 17522 (717) 354-4065. *Affiliations*: President, chief engineer, Digital Engineering Service, Ephrata, PA, 1992-; chief engineer, WIOV AM/FM, Ephrata, PA, 1993-. *Past professional posts*: Broadcaster, consulting engineer, WASG Radio, Atmore, AL, 1981-92; board member, Alabama Broadcasters Association; board member, Creek Indian Enterprises (The economic development arm of the Poarch Band of Creek Indians). *Community activities*: Atmore Chamber of Commerce (director, 1984-90); Gospel Light Church, Inc. (board member, secretary); Creek Indian Arts Council (board member). *Memberships*: Certified Senior Broadcast Engineer by the Society of Broadcast Engineers, 1993-; Alabama Broadcasters Association, 1987-93; Alabama Emergency Broadcasting System (chairperson, 1993); Poarch Band of Creek Indians Tribal Council (member, 1977-90; Atmore Civitan Club (past president). *Awards, honors*: "Outstanding Young Men of America" 1987. *Interests*: Private pilot at age 16; first class FCC Radiotelephone license at age 16; outdoor camping, skiing; electronics; public service for my community and tribe.

*GEIGER, ANUHEA REIMANN (Hawaiian)
(association president)
Affiliation: Hui Malama Ola Na 'Oiwi, 305 Wailuku Dr., Suite 3, Hilo, HI 96720 (808) 969-9220.

GEIOGAMAH, HANAY
(director/writer)
Affiliation: American Indian Dance Theatre, 223 East 61st St., New York, NY 10021. *Address*: 1750 Wilcox St. #223, Los Angeles, CA 90028 (213) 463-8535.

GELPIN, OLLIE
(school principal)
Affiliation: Toadlena Boarding School, P.O. Box 857, Toadlena, NM 87324 (505) 789-3201.

*GENDAR, JEANNINE
(editor)
Affiliation: "News From Native California," Heyday Books, P.o. Box 9145, Berkeley, CA 94709 (510) 549-3564.

GENE, DAVID
(AK village council president)
Affiliation: Native Village of Gakona, P.O. Box 124, Gakona, AK 99586 (907) 822-3497.

*GENETT, WARREN DEAN
(Potawatomi/Menominee) 1957-
(U.S. Geological Survey)
Born August 20, 1957, Menominee Indian Reservation, Keshena, WI. *Education*: Georgia State University, B.A., 1987. *Principal occupation*: U.S. Geological Survey, Water Resources Division. *Home address*: 228 Valleybrook Dr., Woodstock, GA 30188 (404) 926-4531. *Affiliation*: Chairperson, The Native American Center of Georgia, 110 S. Main St., Suite 203, Woodstock, GA 30188 (404) 924-3738, 1993-. *Military service*: U.S. Air Force, 1977-81. *Community activities*: Chair, Atlanta Couples Together, 1987-89; Atlanta Regional Commission, Diversity Collaborative, 1994. *Membership*: American Society for Quality Control, 1993-.

Awards, honors: Emory University, for Native American History Month, 1994; United W ay (Atlanta, GA) for V.I.P. Selection Committee, 1994; U.S. Geological Survey, WRD for Total Quality Management. *Interests:* "Primary focus is to develop a sound organizational structure for the Native American Center of Georgia (formed in 1993) and to promote the organizational success of the Center throughout the state of Georgia."

GENTRY, BARBARA (Wampanoag) 1948-
(Native American education)
Born October 21, 1948, Utica, N.Y . *Education:* Utah State University, BS, 1974; University of Wyoming, MA, 1975. Principal occupation: Native American education. *Affiliations:* Counselor, Union High School, W est Jr. High School and Ute Tribe, Fort Duchesne, UT, 1974-76; head counselor/director of paraprofessional counseling program, University of W yoming, 1976-77; education unit director , Boston Indian Council, 1977-83; entrepreneur , partnership in family-owned business, 1983-90; multicultural coordinator, Eastern Michigan University , Ypsilanti, MI, 1990-. *Other professional posts:* Consulting in Indian education. *Memberships:* National Indian Education Association, 1974-86; National Indian Adult Education (Northeast Representative, 1982). *Honors, awards:* 1991 Gold Medallion Award, Eastern Michigan University; "Oustanding Young Woman of America," 1982; "Successful Indian Education Program," by Office of Indian Education, U.S. Dept. of Education, 1980.

GENTRY, BEATRICE (Wampanoag) 1910-
(teacher)
Born August 31, 1910, Gay Head, Mass. *Education:* Framingham State College, BS, 1932; Bureau of Indian Affairs Summer Institute, Pine Ridge, SD, summer, 1935; Tulsa University, Teacher Certificate, 1962; Bridgewater State College, Hyannis, MA, 1967-1968. *Principal occupation:* Teacher. *Home address:* State Road, Box 159, Gay Head, MA 02535 (508) 645-9900. *Affiliations:* Teacher, Fort Sill Indian School, Lawton, OK, 1934-41; teacher , Wagoner Elementary School, OK, 1960-64; teacher , Chilmark Elementary School, MA, 1964-74. *Other professional posts:* President, Wampanoag Tribal Council of Gay Head, 1972-76 (helped establish modern organizational structure of tribal government, first governing officer); member, Massachusetts Commission on Indian Affairs, 1974-76 (helped establish and organize the first Massachusetts Indian Commission in the 20th century , and whose membership was all Native Americans of MA). *Community activities:* Town of Gay Head (zoning committee; Gay head Public Library (trustee); Gay Head Community Council (charter member); Wagoner School Band (president); Of ficers' Wives' Club (member , 1943-1958; secretary, 1947-1948; Grif fith Air Force Base, Rome, N.Y.). *Memberships:* OK Education Association, 1934-42, 1961-64; MA Teachers Association, 1964-75; National Indian Education Association, 1972-75; National Retired Teachers' Association, 1975-. *Awards, honors:* Alumni Achievement Award, 1982, from Framingham State College Alumni Association at 50th anniversary of graduating class; Ancient Aquinnah (Gay Head) Indian Cemetery on behalf of the W ampanoag Tribal Council of Gay Head; speaker at dedication ceremonies of Gay Head Clif fs as National Landmark, centennial celebration of Town of Gay Head, OK Education Association Conference, and J.F. Kennedy Bicentennial Memorial Dinner, Natick Democratic Town Committee. *Interests:* "As an Air Force of ficer's wife, I have had the opportunity to live and travel to all parts of the continental U.S. & Europe. As a Native American educator with experience providing direct services to Native American children from different tribes, and experience working within the public school system in dif ferent parts of the country, I have learned that the only way for Native American people to determine their own destiny economically and politically among the dominant white society is to make the necessary demands upon the educational system of Indians and non-Indians alike: to provide an avenue to attain the goals that each society deems essential and demand respect for those values and cultures. The educational system's complete disregard and disrespect for Native American values and culture along with lack of Native American input in education programs, communication, counseling and advisement, and lack of role models result in not only inadequate preparation for college, but inadequate for life. I feel it is only through those demands on the educational system for all Americans (including Native Americans) that Native American people will be able to realize our basic needs: the preservation of our lands, the preservation of our religion, culture, and history , and the preservation of our families; that is the sacred rights of our people."

GENTRY, JO LYNN
(editor)
Affiliation: Business Alert, First Nations Financial Report, 69 Kelly Rd., Falmouth, V A 22405 (703) 371-5615.

*GEORGE, DENTON
(Indian band chief)
Affiliation: Ochapowace Indian Band, Box 550, Whitewood, Saskatchewan, Canada S0G 5C0 (306) 696-2637.

GEORGE, DOUGLAS M. *(Kanentiio)* (Mohawk) 1955-
(writer; journalist)
Born February 1, 1955, Akwesasne Mohawk Reservation, N.Y. *Education:* Syracuse University, 1977-80; Antioch School of Law (W ashington, DC), 1980-83. *Principal occupation:* Writer; journalist. *Home address:* Box 10, Oneida Iroquois Territory, Oneida, NY 13421 (315) 363-1655 (work). *Affiliations:* Editor, Akwesasne Notes, Mohawk Nation, Rooseveltown, NY , 1986-. *Other professional posts:* Chairperson, Round Dance Productions, Inc. (non-profit educational & cultural organization formed for the preservation of Native American culture), 1991-; editor, Indian Time newspaper, 1986-90; in the process of writing for film & book publishers. *Community activities:* Mohawk Nation Land Claims Committee, 1984-91; Mohawk Nation Business Committee, 1984-90; Member of the volunteer Akwesasne emergency team, 1983-91. *Membership:* Akwesasne Communications Society - Radio CKON (board member). *Awards, honors:* D'Arcy McNickle Fellowship Recipient, 1979, Newberry Library, Chicago, IL. *Interests:* Creative writing; travels to Europe, Mid-East, China, India, Thailand, Korea, and extensive travel throughout North America - historical research and writing. *Biographical sources:* Articles - Los Angeles Times, Oct. 1991; Syracuse (NY) Herald Journal, July 1990; Now Magazine (Toronto, ON), May 1990; Gentlemen's Quarterly, Nov. 1993. *Published works:* Syracuse herald columnist - over 40 articles; numerous stories printed in Akwesasne Notes, 1986-.

GEORGE, LYLE EMERSON (Suquamish)
(tribal chairperson)
Affiliation: Suquamish Tribal Council, P.O. Box 498, Suquamish, W A 98392 (206) 598-331 1.

GEORGE, EVANS McCLURE, JR. (Catawba) 1932-
(textile worker)
Born January 26, 1932, Rock Hill, S.C. *Education:* Clemson University, 1952-56. *Principal occupation:* Textile worker. *Home address:* 1119 McDow Dr., Rock Hill, SC 29730. *Affiliation:* Celanese Corporation, Celriver Plant, Rock Hill, SC, 1958-. *Community activities:* Member, Rock Hill Parks & Recreation Commission; member , Catawba Indian Tribe; York County IPTAY Club (past president); Church Youth leader, 1968-. *Awards, honors:* Captain of 1950 South Carolina Shrine Bowl team; Clemson University Football team (captain, 1955); drafted by W ashington Redskins, 1955; outstanding volunteer , American Cancer Society . Interests: Lifelong vocational interest in the American textile industry; coaching football; carpentry; fishing. *Biographical source:* Red Carolinian - Where Are They Now? and People of the River , Evening Herald articles.

*GEORGE, GAIL (Saginaw-Chippewa)
(tribal chief)
Affiliation: Saginaw-Chippewa Tribal Council, 7070 E. Broadway Rd., Mt. Pleasant, MI 48858 (517) 772-5700.

GEORGE, GEORGIA C. (Suquamish)
(tribal chairperson)
Affiliation: Suquamish Tribal Council, P.O. Box 498, Suquamish, W A 98392 (206) 598-331 1.

*GEORGE, LEONARD
(Indian band chief)
Affiliation: Burrard Indian Band, 3082 Chum-Iye Dr., N. Vancouver, British Columbia, Canada V7H 1B3 (604) 929-3455.

*GEORGE, LEVI (Yakima)
(school chairperson)
Affiliation: Yakima Tribal School, P.O. Box 151, Toppenish, WA 98948 (509) 865-5121.

GEORGE, LOUIS, JR.
(Indian band chief)
Affiliation: English River Indian Band, General Delivery, Patunak, Saskatchewan, Canada S0M 2H0 (306) 396-2055.

*GEORGE, NORMAN
(Indian band chief)
Affiliation: Mowachtaht Indian Band, P .O. Box 459, Gold River, British Columbia, Canada V0P 1G0 (604) 283-2532.

GEORGE, OSWALD C. (Coeur D'Alene) 1917-
(tribal official)
Born May 22, 1917, De Smet, Idaho. *Education:* Gonzaga University, 1936-37. *Principal occupation:* Tribal official. *Home address:* P.O. Box 155, Plummer, ID 83851. *Affiliation:* Coeur D'Alene Tribal Council. *Military service:* U.S. Army Infantry, 1940-45. *Community activities:* Boy Scouts of America (institutional representative); Veterans of Foreign W ars. *Memberships:*

Affiliated Tribes of Northwest Indians (past president); National Congress of American Indians (vice president, Portland area); Pacific Northwest Indian Center, Inc., Spokane, Wash. (board of trustees). *Interests*: "My interest lies in the youth of our nation; promoting citizenship, and training the future leaders of our country. I'm also very much interested in the preservation of our Indian culture and heritage; preservation of our treaty rights and the perpetual retention of our land base -- these to me are sacred rights and should be respected."

*GEORGE, SAM (Athapascan)
(AK village council president)
Affiliation: Native Village of Kluti-Kaah (aka Copper Center), P.O. Box 68, Copper Center, AK 99573 (907) 822-5541.

*GESSAY, GREGORY, M.D.
(clinical director)
Affiliation: Phoenix, Indian Medical Center, 4212 North 16th St., Phoenix, AZ 85016 (602) 263-1200.

*GETCHES, DAVID
(attorney-professor)
Affiliation: University of Colorado School of Law, Kittredge Dr., Campus Box 401, Boulder, CO 80309 (303) 492-8047.

GETTY, IAN
(director-Indian institute)
Affiliation: Nakoda Institute, Stoney Tribal Administration, P.O. Box 120, Morley, Alberta, Canada T0L 1N0 (403) 881-3770.

*GEVING, RENEE
(museum manager)
Affiliation: Walker Wildlife & Indian Artifacts Museum, State Hwy. 200, Box 336, Walker, MN 56484 (218) 547-1257.

GIAGO, TIM (*Nanwica Kciji*) (Oglala Sioux) 1934-
(publisher)
Born July 12, 1934, Pine Ridge Reservation, S.D. *Education*: San Jose Junior College; University of Nevada, Reno. *Principal occupation*: Publisher. *Affiliation*: Publisher/owner, Lakota Times, P.O. Box 2180, Rapid City, SD 57709 (605) 341-0011, 1981-. *Community activities*: U.S. West Communications (state executive board); Multi-Cultural Management Training Program - University of Missouri, Columbia (board of directors); Native Peoples (editorial board). *Awards, honors*: 1985 - H.L. Menkin Award; 1985 - SDNA-Best Column; 1988 South Dakota Education Association, Civil & Human Rights Award; 1989 - National Education Association's Leo Reano Memorial Award for Civil & Human Rights. *Published works*: The Aboriginal Sin (Historian Press, 1978); Notes From Indian Country, Volume I, 1978-82.

GIBBS, BONNIE
(museum director)
Affiliation: School of Nations Museum, Principia College, Elsah, IL 62028 (618) 374-2131 ext. 312.

*GIBBS, HUGH (Etowah Cherokee)
(tribal chief)
Affiliation: Etowah Cherokee Nation, P.O. Box 5454, Cleveland, TN 37320.

GIBSON, CLAY (Mississippi Choctaw) 1927-
(program director)
Born November 1, 1927, Leake County, Miss. *Education*: Clarke M. College, AA, 1955; Mississippi College, BA, 1957; Southwestern Baptist Theological Seminary, SD, 1962; East Central Junior College. *Principal occupation*: Employment assistance program director. *Home address*: Rt.7, Box 248, Philadelphia, MS 39350. *Affiliation*: Mississippi Band of Choctaw Indians, Philadelphia, MS, 1967-. *Other professional posts*: Ordained Baptist Minister for thirty years; missionary tribal council member for two terms; tribal chairman, 1965-67. *Community activities*: Community Development Club; church and religious activities. *Membership*: Baptist Assn, 1945- (moderator, six years; clerk, five years). *Interests*: Ministry; business administration; social services; tribal programs, B.I.A.; travel.

GIBSON, JIMMY
(BIA agency supt.)
Affiliation: Okmulgee Agency, Bureau of Indian Affairs, P.O. Box 370, Okmulgee, OK 74447 (918) 756-3950.

*GIBSON, WILLIAM (*Wassaja*) (Onandaga) 1932-
(retired)
Born January 20, 1932, Yonkers, N.Y. *Education*: Manhattan College, 1956-58. *Home address*: 198-04 120th Ave., St. Albans, NY 11412 (718) 978-7057. *Affiliation*: President, Northeastern Native American Association, Hollis, NY. *Other professional posts*: Editor, Common Ground; editor, Westchester Advocate; Security Director & Account Technician, Municipal Housing Authority; Labor & Industry Chairman, N.Y. State Citizens Advisory Committee. *Military service*: U.S. Marine Corps, 1950-52. *Community activities*: Chairman, Yonkers Community Action Program; Commissioner of Deeds, Westchester County, NY; coordinator of 1963 March on Washington; 32nd Degree Mason. *Membership*: Native American Writers & Artists Association (recording secretary); Pan American Indian Association; American Indian Community House. *Awards, honors*: 1982 Golden Globe for Poetry; Even Elevan-Man of the Year, 1965; Labor & Industry Chairman of N.Y.S. Urban Development in Yonkers, NY. *Interests*: "Helping people, 'all people.' I have held leadership positions in welfare rights & prisoner rights. I was a national board member of Negro Labor Council, City of Yonkers Human Rights Commission. American Indian affairs." Biographical sources: Who's Who in Poetry (World of Poetry); 1989 American Anthology of Contemporary Poetry.

*GIBSON, WILLIAM
(monument supt.)
Affiliation: Mound City Group National Monument, 16062 State Route 104, Chillicothe, OH 45601 (614) 774-1125.

GILBERT, ERIC MICHAEL
(Indian band chief)
Affiliation: Williams Lake Indian Band, RR #3, Box 4, Williams Lake, British Columbia, Canada V2G 1M3 (604) 296-3507.

*GILBERT, NINA, M.D.
(clinical director)
Affiliation: Lac Courte Oreilles Tribal Clinic, Route 2, Box 2750, Hayward, WI 54843 (715) 634-4153.

GILBERT, TRIMBLE
(Gwitch'in Athapascan)
(village council chief)
Affiliation: Arctic Village Traditional Council, P.O. Box 22050, Arctic Village, AK 99722 (907) 587-5320.

GILBERT, WILLARD S., Jr.
(board president)
Affiliation: Native Americans for Community Action, Inc., Flagstaff Indian Center, 2717 N. Stevens Blvd., Suite 11, Flagstaff, AZ 86004 (602) 526-2968.

GILES, DONALD E. (Peoria)
(tribal chief)
Affiliation: Peoria Indian Tribe of Oklahoma, P.O. Box 1527, Miami, OK 74355 (918) 540-2535.

GILES, MARCELLA (Creek)
(attorney)
Address: 926 Ridge Dr., McLean, VA 22101 (202) 208-6050. Affiliation: Delegate, Muskogee Creek National Tribal Bar Association.

GILKEY, JESSIE M. (Maidu)
(tribal chairperson)
Affiliation: Mooretown Rancheria, P.O. Box 1842, Oroville, CA 95965 (916) 533-3625

GILLET, RANDY GEORGE 1952-
(president-Indian trading company)
Born November 21, 1952, Alhambra, Calif. *Education*: California State University, Fresno, BS, 1976. *Principal occupation*: President-Indian trading company. *Address*: P.O. Box 3512, Palm Desert, CA 92261 (619) 568-4188. *Affiliation*: The La Quinta Trading Co., Palm Desert, CA, 1982-. *Membership*: Indian Arts & Crafts Association. *Biographical source*: Oxford's Who's Who.

GILLIAND, RICHARD M. (*Ne Mook Na Na*) 1937-
(artist & craftsman)
Born October 9, 1937, Detroit, Mich. *Education*: Michigan State University (2 years). *Principal occupation*: Artist & craftsman. *Home address*: Rt. 1, Box 836, Interlochen, MI 49643 (616) 275-6476. *Affiliations*: Ward & Eis Art Gallery, Petoskey, MI (major outlet); Minnetrista Council for Great Lakes Native American Studies, Muncie, IN (recently commissioned for museum work). *Military service*: U.S. Army, 1958-60 (E-5; 82nd Airborne Div.; Military Intelligence Det.) *Community activities*: Lecture to schools and scouting activities on Native American arts and crafts. *Memberships*: Liberty Tree (Black Powder Club) (president, 1981-88); Grand Traverse Metis, 1983-. *Interests*: "My main vocational interests are birch bark ma kuks, quill boxes, medicine drums, trade silver work, flint lock rifles, and any area of arts and crafts of the Eastern Woodland people. Most of my avocational interests are in the same vane; I attend many rondezvous gaining any expertise of brain tanning, etc. and meeting and talking with people with like interests. I spent 18 years living in the Alaskan bush. Halibut fishing, horse wrangling, guiding, log cabin building were but a few of my activities. I was closely associated with Indian and Eskimo people in my life there. Currently, I have about 100 pages written on my life there. Also, I'm currently writing for grants to work on book devoted to bark ma kuks and quill boxes and the people doing them."

**GILLIHAN, JAMES EDWARD
(Eastern Cherokee) 1935-
(personal property appraiser)**
Born May 25, 1935, Wabash County, Ill. *Education*: Southern Illinous University, BS, 1957; Sussex College (England), LHD, 1971. *Principal occupation*: Personal property appraiser. *Address*: P.O. Box 892, DeKalb, IL 60115 (815) 758-8982. *Affiliations*: Senior Appraiser, Gillihan & Associates, DeKalb, IL, 1964-; instructor in anthropology, Northern Illinois University, DeKalb, IL, 1989-. *Other professional post*: Guest curator & chairperson of the Advisory Board, Indian Museum of North America, Crazy Horse Memorial, Crazy Horse, SD. *Community activities*: Rotary Club of DeKalb, IL; lecturer in Native American philosophy and religion, The Theosophical Society, Wheaton, IL; Keeper of the Pipe of Sitting Bull (noted Lakota religious leader); guest lecturer in public schools. *Memberships*: International Society of Appraisers; Art Appraisers of America, Ltd.; New England Appraiser's Association. *Awards, honors*: Has served on advisory boards of the following organizations: The Illinois Historic Preservation Commission; The SD Committee on the Humanities; The Grant Review Committee of the IL Arts Council and the National Trust for Historic Preservation; he was the IL State Historic Preservation Officer and the Cultural Preservation Director for the State of SD; and has been vice president at both Wabash College and Yankton College. *Interests*: "I have great interest in preserving Native American religion & philosophy. I give many lectures both in North America and in Europe to promote understanding of these beliefs." *Biographical sources*: International Who's Who in Art & Antiques; Who's Who in the West and Southwest; Illinois Lives; Dictionary of International Biography. *Published works*: Barbizon Art, 1966; Primitive Art, 1967; The American West, 1968 (all published by Lakeview Center, Peoria, IL)

GILLILAND, HAP *(Splits the Rock)* **1918-
(writer of children's books)**
Born August 26, 1918, Willard, Colo. *Education*: Western State College, BA, 1949, MA, 1950; University of Northern Colorado, EdD, 1958. *Principal occupation*: Writer, professor of education emeritus. *Home address*: 2032 Woody Dr., Billings, MT (406) 252-7451. *Affiliations*: Director, Northern Cheyenne Campus Experience Project, 1965; director, Crow Indian Reservation Educational Survey, 1966-67; director, Remedial Reading, Northern Cheyenne Reservation, 1965-68; director, Indian Upward Bound Project, 1966-69; director, EPDA and NDEA in Remedial Reading for Indian students, 1967, 1969-70; reading specialist, Lake Penn Schools, Alaska (14 Indian and Eskimo villages), Fall 1980, '81, '83; professor of education and Native American culture, Eastern Montana College, Billings, 1960-88, emeritus, 1989-90. *Other professional post*: Directed remedial reading program in 4 schools serving Northern Cheyenne reservation, 1965-68; director, Upward Bound Project, 1966-69; editor/writer/president, Council for Indian Education, Billings, MT, 1970-; *Military service*: U.S. Air Force, 1941-45. *Community activities*: Northern Cheyenne Tribal Scholarship Committee (chairman, 1969-72); Northern Cheyenne Education Planning Committee, 1968-75; National Indian Education Committee of the Association on American Indian Affairs, 1965-85. *Memberships*: Council for Indian Education (president, 1970-); Committee on Native

Americans and Reading, International Reading Association (chairman, 1979-1980). *Awards, honors*: Outstanding Alumnus Award, Western State College, 1979; Bronz Plaque in recognition of Outstanding Contributions to Child's Rights & Education," Billings Committee for International Year of the Child, 1978; $1000 Merit Award for Research & Creative Endeavor, Committee on Evaluaton of Faculty, Montana State University-Billings. *Interests*: Study of native cultures; traveling, photography; and writing in relation to that interest. Three extended trips to South America to live with Yanoamo Indians; two trips to New Zealand to conduct teacher training for teachers of Maori students. *Published works*: Textbooks: Indian Children's Books (Council for Indian Education, 1976), Chant of the Red Man (Council for Indian Education, 1976); Teaching the Native American (Kendall-Hunt, 1988; revised edition, 1992, 1995); Drums of the Headhunters (Winston, 1988); Mystery Tracks in the Snow: A Guide to Animal Tracks & Tracking (Naturegraph, 1990); Flint's Rock (Roberts Rinehart, 1994); 15 children's book on Indian lif & culture; edited 120 children's books published by the Council for Indian Education; Standardized Tests: Red Cloud Diagnostic Reading Test (Council for Indian Education; journal articles: "The New View of Native Americans in Children's Books," The Reading Teacher.

**GILLIS, KAREN
(school principal)**
Affiliation: Dunseith Day School, P.O. Box 759, Dunseith, ND 58371 (701) 263-4636.

**GILMORE, HARRY FRANCIS (Quapaw) 1916-
(director, Indian council/center)**
Born August 9, 1916, Lincolnville, Okla. *Education*: Pittsburgh State University (KS), BS, 1940. *Principal occupation*: Director, Inter-Tribal Council, Inc., Alcohol & Rehabilitation Center. *Address*: P.O. Box 801, Miami, OK 74355 (918) 542-5543 (work). *Affiliations*: Vice-president (8 years), Muskogee Area National Congress of American Indians; chairman (4 years), vice-chairman (4 years), Quapaw Tribal Business Committee. *Other professional posts*: Legal Services (board of education - 6 years); North East Area Economic Development Organization (board of directors - 2 years). *Military service*: U.S. Marine Corp. (Staff Sgt., 1946); National Guard Armory (Staff Sgt.); Army Reserves (Master Sgt.). *Community activities*: Elks Lodge & Chamber of Commerce, Miami, OK. *Memberships*: United Indian Recovery Assn. (president - 2 years); United Indian Tribal Organization (2 years). *Interests*: Indian businesses, and alcohol & rehabilitation counseling & training.

**GIPP, DAVID
(college president)**
Affiliation: United Tribes Technical College, 3315 University Dr., Bismarck, ND 58501 (701) 255-3285 ext. 293.

**GIPP, GERALD E.
(college president)**
Affiliation: Haskell Indian Junior College, BIA, Lawrence, KS 66044 (913) 841-2000.

**GIPP, WILLIAM C. (Standing Rock Sioux) 1940-
(BIA agency supt.)**
Born November 11, 1940, Fort Yates, N.D. (Standing Rock Reservation). *Education*: Black Hills State College, BS, 1968; South Dakota

State University, MA, 1973. *Principal occupation*: BIA agency supt. *Address*: Blackfeet Agency, BIA, Browning, MT 59417 (406) 338-7544. *Affiliation*: Supt., Rosebud Sioux Agency, Rosebud, SD, 1984-87; superintendent, Blackfeet Agency, BIA, Browning, MT, 1987-. Other professional posts: Board of directors, Boy Scouts of America, Minnesota. Military service: U.S. Army, 1963-67 (Sergeant E-5, Special Forces, Vietnam Vet). *Memberships*: American Legion; Veterans of Foreign Wars; National Congress of American Indians; South Dakota Teachers Association.

***GIRTY, FLOSSIE I.
(BIA field representative)**
Affiliation: Southern Paiute Field Station, BIA, P.O. Box 720, St. George, UT 84771 (801) 674-9720.

***GISH, ROBERT FRANKLIN
(Cherokee of Oklahoma)
(director of ethnic studies, writer)**
Born April 1, 1940, Albuquerque, N.M. *Education*: University of New Mexico, M.A., 1967, Ph.D., 1972. *Principal occupation*: Director of ethnic studies, writer. *Address*: P.O. Box 947, San Luis Obispo, CA 93406 (805) 756-1707. *Affiliations*: Distinguished Scholar & Professor of English, University of Northern Iowa, 1967-91; director, Ethnic Studies Program, professor of English, California Polytechnic State University, San Luis Obispo, CA, 1991-. *Other professional post*: Contributing editor, "The Bloomsbury Review." *Memberships*: Authors Guild; Penn West; Western Literature Association; Western Writers of America. *Award*: Distinguished Alumni Award, University of New Mexico. *Biographical sources*: Who's Who in America; Who's Who in the West. *Published works*: First Horses: Stories of the New West (University of Nevada Press, 1993); Songs of My Heart (University of New Mexico Press, 1994); When Coyote Howls (University of New Mexico Press, 1994).

**GISHEY, LAWRENCE
(college president)**
Affiliation: Navajo Community College, Tsaile Rural PO, Tsaile, AZ 86556 (602) 724-331 1.

**GISHIE, LEO T. (Navajo) 1941-
(educational administration)**
Born April 26, 1941, Tees To Community, Ariz. *Education*: Northern Arizona University, BS, 1973; University of New Mexico, MA, 1984. *Principal occupation*: Educational administration. *Home address*: Tees To Chapter, Winslow, AZ 86047 (602) 524-6222. *Affiliations*: Assistant to Dean of Instruction, Navajo Community College, Tsaile, AZ (5 years); principal, BIA School, Holbrook, AZ, 1987-90; principal, Wide Ruins Boarding School, Chambers, AZ, 1991-93; principal, Lukachukai Boarding School, Lukachukai, AZ, 1993-. *Other professional posts*: AIRCA (president, 4; years personnel director, 4 years). *Military service*: U.S. Army (Staff Sgt. or E-5, 1963-66; Expert Medal). *Community activities*: Local board member (8 years). *Awards, honors*: Outstanding Award for BIA Service. *Interests*: Administration; rodeo competition; public work, public speaking; some travel.

***GIVIN, LEWIS B. (Manadan)
(professor)**
Affiliation: U. of Mass., Rm 217, New Africa House, Amherst, MA 01003 (413) 545-5103.

*GLATTKE, THEODORE
(program director)
Affiliation: American Indian Professional Training Program in Speech-Language Pathology & Audiology, University of Arizona, Dept. of Speech & Hearing Sciences, Tucson, AZ 85721 (602) 621-1969.

*GLAZIER, HERB (Paiute)
(tribal council chairperson)
Affiliation: Bridgeport Indian Colony, P.O. Box 37, Bridgeport, CA 93517 (619) 932-7083.

GLEASON, JEAN
(organization coordinator)
Affiliation: Yukon Indian Cultural Education Society, 22 Nisutlin Dr., Whitehorse, Yukon, Canada Y1A 1K1 (403) 667-2779.

*GLENN, JAMES R.
(archives director)
Affiliation: National Anthropological Archives, Smithsonian Institution, Washington, DC 20560 (202) 357-1976.

GLOADE, CLARA
(president-native women's association)
Affiliation: Nova Scotia Native Women's Association, P.O. Box 805, Truro, Nova Scotia, Canada B2N 5E8 (902) 893-7402.

GOATSON, ERNEST
(school chairperson)
Affiliation: Kaibeto Boarding School, Kaibeto, AZ 86053 (602) 673-3480.

GOBERT, W. JOHN
(health director)
Affiliation: Fort Totten PHS Indian Health Center, P.O. Box 200, Fort Totten, ND 58335 (701) 766-4291.

GOEHRING, SUSAN
(site manager)
Affiliation: Schoenbrunn Village State Memorial, P.O. Box 129, East High Ave., New Philadelphia, OH 44663 (216) 339-3636.

GOFF, RALPH (Diegueno)
(tribal chairperson)
Affiliation: Campo Band of Mission Indians, 1779 Campo Truck Trail, Campo, CA 92006 (619) 478-9046.

*GOGGLEYE, JENEAL
(health director)
Affiliation: Bois Fort Tribal Clinic, P.O. Box 15, Nett Lake, MN 55772 (218) 757-3296.

GOGOL, JOHN M. 1938-
(professor; publisher; institute president)
Born August 15, 1938, Westfield, Mass. *Education*: Clark University, BA, 1960; University of Washington, MA, 1965, ABD Doctoral Candidacy, 1969. *Principal occupation*: University professor, publisher. *Address*: P.O. Box 66124, Portland, OR 97266 (503) 233-8131. *Affiliations*: Instructor, Colorado State University, 1965-68; assistant professor of humanities, Pacific University, Forest Grove, Oreg., 1970-74; publisher, Mr. Cogito Press, Pacific University, 1973-; publisher, American Indian Basketry and Other Native Arts, 1979-; director, Institute for the Study of Traditional American Indian Arts, Portland, OR, 1979-. *Memberships*: Oregon Archaeological Society; Oregon Historical Society; Central States Archaeological Society; Coordinating

Council of Literary Magazines; COSMEP. *Awards, honors*: Graves Prize Award in the Humanities, 1971. *Interests*: "In a long teaching career (I) taught German, Russian, comparative literature, American Indian studies, American history, European history, mathematics, physics, and humanities; poet and translator of German, Russian and Polish poetry." *Biographical sources*: Poetic Justice, by Walt Curtis (Willamette Week, Oct.-Nov., 1985); Basketry and Reservation of Culture, by Paul Pintarich (Northwest Magazine, The Oregonian, June, 1983); among others. *Published works*: Native American Words (Tahmahnawi's Publishers, 1973); Columbus Names the Flowers (Mr. Cogito Press, 1984); articles and other publications in numerous periodicals.

GOHDES, DOROTHY, M.D.
(IHS-program director)
Affiliation: Diabetes Program, Indian Health Service, 5300 Homestead Rd., NE, Albuquerque, NM 87110 (505) 837-4182.

*GOINS, WILL MOREAU *(Tsiyohi-Uhayli: Do)*
(Eastern Cherokee/Lumbee) 1961-
(executive/artistic director)
Born December 2, 1961, Washington, D.C. *Education*: The George Washington University, BA, 1983; The Pennsylvania State University, MEd, 1989, PhD, 1994. *Principal occupation*: Executive/artistic director. *Home address*: 3421 M St., Suite 231, Washington, DC 20007 (814) 867-5523. *Affiliations*: CEO, Executive/artistic director, National Native Network of Talent/The Washington's First Americans Theater, Washington, DC, 1982-. *Other professional posts*: Co-editor/contributing writer, Indian Youth Magazine, 1981-83; free-lance communications specialist for various private & governmental agencies developing educational, public informational & industrial films, videos, brochures & media, 1984-; free-lance writer-correspondent (journalistic articles), 1981-; producer-director, U.S. Indian Health Service, video series for health professionals, 1984-85; professor, The Pennsylvania State University, Dept. of Educational Administration, Policy, Foundations, and Comparative-International Education, "American Indian, Education & Media," 1992-93. *Community activities*: Class Agent for The Columbian College Alumni Association, The George Washington University, 1990-; Officer, Native American Student Association of Penn State, 1989-93. *Memberships*: American Anthropological Association; National Education Association; American Educational Research Association; ; National Indian Educational Association; AERA-SIG American Indian Sig (Special Interest Group), American Alliance of Health Education, Physical Fitness, Recreation & Dance, 1988-; American Indian Registry of Performing Arts, 1979-; National Association for the Advancement of Colored People, 1989-; National Eagle Scout Association; North Carolina Historical Society; The Gonzaga Dramatics Association, 1975-. *Awards, honors*: Award of Excellence, Rackley Scholarship, Penn State University, 1988-94; American Indian Leadership Program Fellow, 1988-92; Commendation for Outstanding Service, U.S. Surgeon General, Dr. Everett Rhodes, U.S. Public Health Service, 1984; Outstanding Service Award, Indian Health Service, 1984; Outstanding & Dedicated Service Award, Penn State University, Native American Indian Student Association, 1993. AFTRA-SAG, 1984-; ASCAP; Native American Journalists Associa-

tion, 1983-; American Film Institute, 1980-. *Interests*: Founder, executive artistic director of "The Free Spirit Players," a non-profit collective of Native performing and creative artists and production technicians for the region east of the Mississippi. Biographical source: 1980 article in "Indian Youth Magazine," called a Profile. *Published works*: Co-author of play, "Feather in the Wind" (NNT Publishing, 1984); author, "Feathers" the musical (NNT Publishing, 1989; Administering Culturally Specific Health Educational Programs and Curriculum (Penn State, 1989); The Perceptions of Native American Alumni of Graduate Level Educational Degree Programs at the Penn State U. (UMI Publishing, 1994).

GOLDBERG-AMBROSE, CAROLE 1947-
(law professor)
Born September 3, 1947, Chicago, Ill. *Education*: Smith College, BA, 1968; Stanford Law School, JD, 1971. *Principal occupation*: Law professor. *Home address*: 376 Dalehurst Ave., Los Angeles, CA 90024 (310) 825-4429 (office). *Affiliation*: Professor, UCLA Law School, 1972-. *Other professional posts*: UCLA American Indian Studies Center (acting director, 1990; chairperson, Faculty Advisory Committee, 1991-). *Interests*: "I teach courses in American Indian law and tribal legal systems." *Published work*: Co-editor & author, Felix Cohen's Handbook of Federal Indian Law (Michie Co., 1982).

GOLDFEIN, ROANNE P.
(editor)
Affiliation: American Indian Art Magazine, 7314 E. Osborn Dr., Scottsdale, AZ 85251 (602) 994-5445.

GOLDOFF, RAYMOND (Eskimo)
(AK village council president)
Affiliation: Atka Village Council, P.O. Box 47030, Atka, AK 99574 (907) 767-8001.

GOLDTOOTH, ANTHONY (Navajo)
(college instructor)
Affiliation: Navajo Community College, P.O. Box 580, Shiprock, NM 87420 (505) 368-5291.

*GOLDTOOTH, THOMAS
(director-Indian organizations)
Affiliation: Indigenous Environmental Network, Box 485, Bemidji, MN 56601 (218) 679-3959.

*GOLLA, VICTOR
(program director)
Affiliation: American Indian Languages & Literature Program, Humboldt State University, The Center for Community Development, Arcata, CA 95521 (707) 826-3711.

GOMEZ, MANUEL (Pomo)
(tribal chairperson)
Affiliation: Big Valley Rancheria, P.O. Box 153, Finley, CA 95453.

GON HENRY
(Indian band chief)
Affiliation: Rae Lakes Dene Indian Band, Rae Lakes, Northwest Territories, Canada X0E 1R0 (403) 997-3441.

*GONZALES, ANGELA ANN (Hopi) 1964-
(student)
Born June 3, 1964, San Bernardino, Calif. *Education*: University of California, Riverside, B.S., 1990; Harvard University, M.A., 1993, Ed.M., 1994; Ph.D (Sociology) candidate, 1995. *Home*

address: P.O. Box 216, Kykotsmovi, AZ 86039 (617) 493-2597 (school). *Affiliations*: Social Analyst (provided information to congressional staffers on issues concerning Native Americans; and assisted the Senate Select Committee on Indian Affairs in the evaluation of material presented as testimony before the committee), Congressional Research Service, Library of Congress, Washington, DC, 1991 (summer); Teaching Fellow, Harvard University, Dept. of Religious Studies, Fall 1991 & 1992; Hopi Tribe, Kykotsmovi, AZ - staff assistant, Office of the Vice-Chairperson, 1992 (summer); planning intern, Dept. of Research & Planning, 1993 (summer). *Selected Conference Presentations*: 17th Annual Western Anthropology/Sociology Undergraduates Research Conference, California State University, Northridge, April 1990; 23rd-25th Annual National Indian Educators Association Conferences, Nov. 1991-93; 6th Annual Conference on Race & Ethnic Relations In American Higher Education, 1991; Four Corners Regional Planners Conference, 1992; Leading Ideas in American Indian Studies, U. of Wisconsin, Madison, Sept. 1993. *Awards, honors*: UCR Alumni Award, 1990; Rupert Costo Scholarship, 1990; Hopi Scholarship, 1989-93; Harvard Prize Fellowship, 1990-96; American Sociological Assn. Minority Fellowship, 1992-95; The Ford Foundation, Pre-Doctoral Fellowship, 1992-95.

GONZALES, DAVIS (Te-Moak Shoshone)
(tribal council chief)
Affiliation: Elko Band Council, P.O. Box 748, Elko, NV 89801 (702) 738-8889.

GONZALES, RAYMOND (Pueblo)
(school chairperson)
Affiliation: San Ildefonso Day School, Route 5, Box 308, Santa Fe, NM 87501 (505) 455-2366.

*GONZALEZ, BOBBY (Taino) 1951-
(lecturer, storyteller)
Born September 22, 1951, New York, N.Y. *Education*: Manhattan College. *Principal occupation*: Lecturer, storyteller. *Home address*: 688 Courtland Ave., Bronx, NY 10451 (718) 665-9855 (work). *Memberships*: Taino Del Norte, 1989-; Native American Heritage Committee, 1990-. *Interests*: (I) "write a monthly column for the publication, "Latino Village News; (I) have lectured on the history and culture of the Taino at the American Museum of Natural History, S.U.N.Y. at Binghamton, the Waterloo Indian Village Museum, and the National Museum of the American Indian."

*GOODEAGLE, GRACE (Quapaw)
(tribal chairperson)
Affiliation: Quapaw Tribe of Oklahoma, P.O. Box 765, Quapaw, OK 74363 (918) 542-1853.

*GOODFOX, Jr., LAWRENCE (Pawnee)
(advisor)
Affiliation: Council of Advisors, American Indian Heritage Foundation, 6051 Arlington Blvd., Falls Church, VA 22044-2788 (703) 237-7500.

*GOODLETT, WILLIAM H. *(Thunder Maker-Three Shirts)* (Cherokee-OK) 1908-
(art/dance/reading instructor)
Born September 11, 1908, Atlanta, Ga. *Education*: Roanoke College, 1946-56. *Principal occupation*: Art/dance/reading instructor. *Home address*: 109 Union St., Salem, VA 24153 (703) 389-4747. *Military service*: U.S. Army (4 years). *Awards, honors*: Medicine Man for the Kachina Tribe - an Honorary Tribe of Boy Scouts. *Interests*: Teach reading phonics - codified the English language. Taught dancing for 34 years, and reading for 22 years. "One of my boys is now world champion archer, another one is champion pistol shooter of the U.S."

GOODMAN, LINDA J.
(professor)
Born in Denver, Colo. *Education*: University of Colorado, Boulder, BA, 1966; Wesleyan University, MA, 1968; Washington State University, Pullman, PhD, 1978. *Principal occupation*: Professor. *Home address*: 4135 Dover St., Wheat Ridge, CO 80033. *Affiliation*: Assistant professor, Dept. of Music, Colorado College, Colorado Springs, CO, 1979-. *Other professional posts*: Advisor of Native American students at Colorado College; director of tribes program for pre-college Native American students. *Community activities*: Talks on Native American music and culture to various museum groups, tour groups, and Native American groups; have organized various Native American music and dance performances for non-Indian audiences; consultant for Native American music education programs, District II public schools, Colorado Springs, Colo.; member, Colorado Springs Native Americans Women's Association; organized Native American symposia, art shows, and guest speakers at Colorado College. *Memberships*: American Anthropological Association, 1975-; American Folklore Society, 1975-; American Ethnological Society, 1975-; Society for Ethnomusicology, 1975-; Native American Women's Association, Colorado College, 1977- *Awards, honors*: American Philosophical Society grant, 1967, to work on Pueblo Indian music; 1979 Humanities Division Research Grant from Colorado College, to work on life history of Makah Indian singer; 1980 Mellon Grant, to work on Southwest Indian music, to teach as a new course; 1983 American Council of Learned Societies Fellowship for work on life history of a Northwest Coast musician. *Interests*: "Native American music and culture, especially Northwest Coast and American Southwest. "(I) have spent much time traveling and living on reservations in both areas, studying music and culture, attending ceremonies, learning from the people in those areas. Have lead many field trips of college students to various reservations in the Southwest so that they could see and talk to the people living there and learn from them first-hand. Have lead a tour group of older people to the Makah Reservation for the same purpose. I am writing books and articles on Native American music and culture. I am very interested in teaching, counseling, and advising Native American young people, helping them find a way to fit into two worlds. Have worked with a number of Native American students over the years, and I'm interested in Indian singing and dancing, and participate on the few occasions when it is appropriate." *Published works*: Music and Dance in Northwest Coast Indian Life (Navajo Community College Press, 1977); A Makah Biography, in Dalmoma: Digging for Roots (Empty Bowl Press, 1985); Nootka Indian Music, in New Grove Dictionary of Music in the U.S. (Macmillan, 1986).

GOODNER, GEORGE
(BIA agency supt.)
Affiliation: Fort Defiance Agency, Bureau of India Affairs, P.O. Box 619, Fort Defiance, AZ 86504 (602) 729-5041.

GOODTHUNDER, JOSEPH
(Mdewakanton Sioux)
(tribal council president)
Affiliation: Lower Sioux Indan Community Council, RR 1, Box 308, Morton, MN 56270 (507) 697-6185.

GOODTRACK, WILLIAM
(Indian band chief)
Affiliation: Wood Mountain Indian Band, Box 104, Wood Mountain, Saskatchewan, Canada S0H 4L0 (306) 266-4422.

GOOGOO, RODERICK A.
(Indian band chief)
Affiliation: Whycocomagh Indian Band, Box 149, Whycocomagh, Nova Scotia, Canada B0E 3M0 (902) 756-2337.

GOOMBI, JOSEPH (Kiowa)
(tribal chairperson)
Affiliation: Kiowa Business Committee, P.O. Box 369, Carnegie, OK 73015 (405) 654-2300.

GOPHER, FRANCES M.
(administrative officer)
Affiliation: Northern Idaho PHS Indian Health Center, P.O. Drawer 367, Lapwai, ID 83540 (208) 843-2271.

GORDON, JEROME
(BIA-health programs)
Affiliation: Office of Health Programs, California Area Office, Bureau of Indian Affairs, 1825 Bell St., Suite 200, Sacramento, CA 95825 (916) 978-4202.

GORDON, MARK R.
(corporation president)
Affiliation: Makivik Corporation, 4898 Maisonneuve West, Montreal, Quebec, Canada H3Z 1M8 (514) 483-2780.

GORDON, PATRICIA TRUDELL
(Santee Sioux-Mdewakanton Band) 1943-
(foundation president)
Born August 24, 1943, Woodbury County, Iowa. *Education*: Morningside College, BA, 1977; Boalt Hall School of Law, University of California, Berkeley, JD, 1992. *Principal Occupation*: Executive Director, Indian Youth of America, Inc. *Address*: P.O. Box 2786, Sioux City, IA 51106 (712) 276-0794 (work). *Affiliations*: Camp Director, Indian Youth Camps in Oregon, Arizona, Idaho, and South Dakota, summer of 1976-90; assistant director, Indian Studies Program, Morningside College, 1977-84; Indian Student Advisor, Student Services, Momingside College, 1975-77; executive director, Indian Youth of America, Sioux City, Iowa, 1978-; president, George Bird Grinnell American Indian Children's Education Foundation, Dover Plains, NY, 1991-. *Community Activities*: Iowa Supreme Court Commission on Continuing Legal Education (commissioner, 1984-89); Sioux City Human Rights Commission (commissioner & chairperson, 1982-89); United Way of Siouxland Agency Relations Committee (panel chair, 1981-86, board of directors, 1987-89); Native American Child Care Center, Sioux City, IA, (Co-founder & president, 1980-89); George Bird Grinnell American Indian Children's Educational Foundation, Dover Plains, NY, (co-founder & president, 1988-); Edwin Gould Foundation for Children, New York, NY (trustee & charter member, 1987-). *Memberships*: American Indian Law Students Association, 1989-91. *Awards, Honors*:

Participant for the Community International Fellows, a program of the International Leadership Development Institute; Robert F. Kennedy Memorial Fellow, 1977-80; Sertoma Service to Mankind Award, 1983; appointed, in 1984, by the Iowa Supreme Court to serve on the State Commission on Continuing Legal Education; Distinguished Alumni Award, Morningside College, 1987; Soroptimist International of Berkeley Award, 1991-92; recently completed an internship at the U.S. Senate Select Committee on Indian Affairs in Washington, D.C. where she reviewed and drafted legislation. *Interests*: "My main concern and interest at this time is working with Indian young people and improving there lives. I am also very interested in the law especially pertaining to American Indians. Women's issues will always be one of my concerns. My work has taken me throughout the U.S. giving lectures and presentations. I have very little time for hobbies, however, I make time for racquetball, bicycling and reading."

GORDON, PAUL (Lake Superior Chippewa)
(tribal council vice-chairperson)
Affiliation: Bad River Tribal Council, P.O. Box 39, Odanah, WI 54861 (715) 682-71 11.

GORDON, RICHARD *(Whispering Wind)*
(United Lumbee/Cherokee)1954-
(auto mechanic; handyman)
Born February 17, 1954, Los Angeles, Calif. *Education*: High school. *Principal occupation*: Auto mechanic; handyman. *Address*: P.O. Box 21, Little Valley, CA 96053. *Affiliation*: Native American Wolf Clan, 1982-; councilman, United Lumbee Nation's Deer Clan, 1983-. *Community activities*: United Lumbee Nation's Deer Clan Golden Hawk Warrior Society, 1985-; member of United Lumbee Nation's Deer Clan Fire Fighting tree falling Team, 1989-. *Awards, honors*: Senior Volunteer Service Award, May 5, 1990, in recognition for countless hours of volunteer service, to Lassen County, California's USDA program for Northwestern Lassen County.

GORDON, WILLA MARIE GEORGE
(Little Fox) **(United Lumbee/Cherokee)1933-**
(home maker)
Born November 23, 1933, Newton, Kans. *Education*: High school. *Principal occupation*: Automechanic; handyman. *Address*: P.O. Box 81, Little Valley, CA 96053 (916) 336-6755. *Affiliation*: Councilwoman, 1985-, secretary/treasurer, 1986-, United Lumbee Nation's Deer Clan. *Community activities*: United Lumbee Nation's Deer Clan Golden Hawk Warrior Society (Vicechief and advisor to the Junior Warrior Society, 1985-); Distributor for Northwestern Lassen County, Calif. USDA Program and started the Brown Bag Program for Senior Citizens in 1988. *Awards, honors*: Senior Volunteer Service Award, May 5, 1990, in recognition for countless hours of volunteer service, to Lassen County, California's USDA and brown bag programs. *Biographical source*: Section in The United Lumbee Deer Clan Cook Book, with Elmer Shorty Gray, 1988.

GORMAN, CARL NELSON
(Kin-ya-onny beyeh) (Navajo) 1907-
(artist, lecturer)
Born October 5, 1907, Chinle, Ariz. *Education*: Otis Art Institute, Los Angeles, CA, Graduate, 1951, extension courses, 1952, '53. *Principal occupation*: Artist, lecturer--Navajo culture. *Address*: P.O. Box 431, Window Rock, AZ 86515.,

or c/o Navajo Gallery, P.O. Box 1756, Taos, NM 87571. *Affiliations*: Illustrator and technical illustrator, Douglas Aircraft Co., Santa Monica, Lawndale, Torrance, Calif., 1951-63; manager, Navajo Arts & Crafts Guild, 1964-66; director, Navajo Culture Center, ONEO, Fort Defiance, AZ, 1966-69; lecturer, Navajo history and culture, and American Indian art in cultural perspective with workshop, and Navajo language, Native American studies, applied behavioral sciences, University of California, Davis, 1970-73, retired; director, Office of Native Healing Sciences, Navajo Health Authority, Window Rock, AZ, 1973-76, retired; coordinator, Navajo Resources/Curriculum Development, Navajo Community College, Tsaile, AZ, 1977-. *Other professional posts*: Kin-ya-onny beyeh Originals, professional arts and crafts, 1951-; lecturer-consultant, Navajo arts, history, culture, 1964-. *Military service*: U.S. Marine Corps, 1942-45, with group that developed Navajo Code. *Community activities*: Inter-Tribal Indian Ceremonial (executive committee, 1964-1965); Navajo Tribal Fair (arts & crafts exhibit chairman, 1964-65; evening performance chairman, 1968); Navajoland Festival of the Arts (board member, 1976-). *Memberships*: Navajo Club of Los Angeles (board of directors, several offices, 1955-64); Otis Art Institute Alumni Association, 1952-2nd Marine Division Association; Veterans of Foreign Wars (life member); Navajo Code Talkers Association; Kiwanis, 1978. *Exhibitions*: Mr. Gorman's work has appeared in numerous one-man and group shows and is part of public and private collections. *Interests*: "All phases of art, subjects chiefly Navajo, horses, rock art, but including non-Indian subjects, in a variety of styles and media. Interested in improving quality, expanding markets, and promoting new and adaptive Navajo arts and crafts. In dance, I originated the now well known 'Navajo Gourd Rattle Dance' for the Youth Group, Navajo Club of Los Angeles in 1962, adapted to Hopi version of Navajo Yei-bi-chei song of 1917. Hope to put photos, Navajo historical and cultural material I've gathered into book form."

GORMAN, CLARENCE N. (Navajo) 1931-
(monument supt.)
Born May 28, 1931, Chinle, Ariz. *Education*: Northern Arizona University. *Principal occupation*: Monument supt. *Address*: Aztec National Monument, Box 640, Aztec, NM 87410. *Affiliations*: Maintenance foreman, park ranger, Canyon de Chelly National Monument, Chinle, AZ; park ranger, Mesa Verde National Park, CO; park ranger, White Sands National Monument, Alamogordo, NM; supt., Wupatki-Sunset Crater National Monument, Flagstaff, AZ; supt., Pipestone National Monument, Pipestone, MM; supt., Aztec National Monument, Aztec, NM *Other professional posts*: Navajo Tribal Ranger, 1958; teacher, Bureau of Indian Affairs, 1959. *Military service*: U.S. Marine Corps, 1951-54 (Good Conduct Medal, U.S. Service Medal, National Defense Medal, Presidential Unit Citation, Korean Presidential Unit Citation, Korean Service Medal with three Battle Stars). *Memberships*: National Riflemen's Association; Southwest Parks and Monuments Association, Inc.; Parks & Recreation Association; Pipestone Shrine Association.

GORMAN, R.C. (Navajo) 1931-
(artist)
Born July 26, 1931, Chinle, Ariz. *Education*: Northern Arizona University, Honorary Doctor-

ate of Fine Arts; Mexico City College. *Principal occupation*: Artist. *Address*: Navajo Gallery, P.O. Box 1756, Taos, NM 87571 (505) 758-3250. *Affiliation*: Owner, Navajo Gallery, Taos, NM, 1979-. *Military service*: U.S. Navy, 1952-56. *Memberships*: Pacific Northwest Indian Center, Gonzaga University (board member); Wheelwright Museum, Santa Fe, NM (board member); Kellogg Fellowship Screening Committee, Navajo Health Authority, Window Rock, AZ (Fellow); Four Corner State Art Conference; NM Arts and Crafts Fair (standards committee, juror). *Exhibitions*: Mr. Gorman's work has appeared in numerous one-man and group shows and is part of public and private collections. *Awards, honors*: Numerous awards and prizes for art from the following exhibitions and shows: All American Indian Days Art Exhibition; American Indian Artists Exhibitions; Center for Arts for Indian America; Heard Museum; National Cowboy Hall of Fame; Philbrook Indian Art Exhibitions; Scottsdale National Indian Arts Exhibition. In the Fall of 1973, Mr. Gorman was the only living artist to be included in the show, Masterworks of the Museum of the American Indian, held at the Metropolitan Museum in New York City. Two of his drawings were selected for the cover of the show's catalog. In 1975, he was honored by being the first artist chosen for a series of one-man exhibitions of contemporary Indian artists held at the Museum of the American Indian. Interests: Mexican art and artists; lithography; cave painting and petroglyphs. *Biographical sources*: A Taos Mosaic (University of New Mexico Press); American Indian Painter; Arrow III (Pacific Grove Press); Art and Indian Individuals (Northland Press); Dictionary of International Biography; Indian Painter and White Patrons, J.J. Brody; Indians of Today; Masterworks from the Museum of the American Indian (Metropolitan Museum of Art); Register of U.S. Living Artists; Who's Who in America; Who's Who in the West; Who's Who in American Art. *Published works*: Mr. Gorman's works appear in the following books: American Indian Painters (Museum of the American Indian); Great American Deserts (National Geographic Society, 1972); Southwest Indian Painting (University of Arizona Press, 1973); The Man Who Sent the Rain Clouds (Viking Press, 1974); Gorman Goes Gourmet; The Lithographs of R.C. Gorman (Northland Press); Graphics: A Self Portrait of America.

GOROSPE, GEORGE E. (Pueblo)
(owner/publisher-Indian newspaper)
Affiliation: Pueblo Times, Pueblo Times Publishing Co., 1860 Dom Pasqual Rd., Los Lunas, NM 87031 (505) 865-4508.

GOROSPE, KATHY
(director-Indian commission)
Affiliation: Commission on Indian Services, 454 State Capitol, Salem, OR 97310 (503) 378-5481.

*GORSUCH, EDWARD L.
(institute director)
Affiliation: Institute of Social & Economic Research, University of Alaska, 3211 Providence Dr., Anchorage, AK 99508 (907) 786-7710.

GOSS, JAMES ATHUR 1934-
(professor/director-
ethnic studies program)
Born September 14, 1934, Marion County, Ohio. *Education*: University of Oregon, BA, 1960; Uni-

versity of Chicago, MA, 1962, PhD, 1972. *Principal occupation* : Professor of anthropology . *Address*: Ethnic Studies Program, Dept. of Anthropology, Texas Tech University, Lubbock, TX 79409 (806) 742-2228. *Affiliations*: Visiting lecturer in anthropology and linguistics, UCLA, 1964-66; assistant-associate professor of anthropology, Washington State University , 1966-79; professor/director , Ethnic Studies Program, Texas Tech University, Lubbock, TX , 1979-. *Other professional posts* : Co-editor, Northwest Anthropological Research Notes, 1967-70. *Military service*: U.S. Air Force, 1954. *Community activities* : Consultant on problems of Nez Perce children learning English, Nez Perce Headstart Program. *Memberships* : American Anthropological Association; Linguistic Society of America; Society for American Archaeology; Society of Sigma Xi; Northwest Anthropological Conference; Great Basin Anthropological Conference; International Salish Conference. *Awards, honors*: NDEA Title IV Fellowship in Anthropology, University of Chicago, 1960-63; research assistantship and linguistic research grant, Tri-Ethnic Project, University of Colorado, 1961, '62; Dept. of the Interior , National Geographic Society Research Grant, W etherill Mesa V erde National Park, CO, 1961-63; UCLA Academic Senate Grant for A Pilot Demographic Study of the American Indian Community of the Greater Los Angeles Area, 1965; WSU Grant-in-Aid for A Survey of Interior Salish Languages, 1067; consultant grant, Nez Perce Headstart Program, 1971; NEH Postdoctoral Fellowship in American Indian Studies, Indiana University , 1972-73. *Interests*: Linguistic anthropology; ethno-semantics; culture-historical reconstruction. *Published works*: Various technical articles in professional journals.

*GOUDIE, JOSEPH
(association president)

Affiliation : Labrador Metis Association, P.O. Box 599, Station "B", Happy V alley/Goose Bay , Labrador, Canada A0P 1E0 (709) 896-5431.

*GOUGE, LORRAINE (Santee Sioux)
(tribal chairperson)

Affiliation : Upper Sioux Indian Community , Box 147, Granite Falls, MN 56241 (612) 564-2360.

GOULAIS, PHIL
(Indian band chief)

Affiliation : Nipissing Indian Band, RR 1, Sturgeon Falls, ON, Can. P0H 2G0 (705) 753-2050.

GOULD, CYNTHIA
(museum curator)

Affiliation: Tonkawa Tribal Museum, P.O. Box 70, Tonkawa, OK 74653 (405) 628-5301.

GOULD, GARY
(president-Indian council)

Affiliation : New Brunswick Aboriginal Peoples Council, 320 St. Mary's St., Fredericton, New Brunswick, Canada E3A 2S5 (506) 458-8422.

GOULD, MARK M. (Lenni-Lenape)
(tribal chairperson)

Affiliation : Chairperson, Nanticoke Lenni-Lenape Indians of NJ, Inc., 18 E. Commerce St., Bridgeton, NJ 08302 (609) 455-6910.

GOULD, RICHARD
(museum director)

Affiliation : Pawnee Indian V illage Museum, Box 475, Rt. 1, Republic, KS 66964 (913) 361-2255.

GOULD, ROY
(publisher)

Affiliation : Micmac News, Nova Scotia Native Communications Society , P.O. Box 344, Sydney , Nova Scotia, Canada B1P 6H2 (902) 539-0045.

*GOURD, CHARLES A. (Cherokee-OK) 1948-
(administrator)

Born December 2, 1948, Miami, Okla. Education: University of Oklahoma, M.A., 1976; University of Kansas, Ph.D., 1984. *Principal occupation*: Administrator. *Address*: HC 73 Box 280, Park Hill, OK 74451 (918) 457-4755. *Affiliations*: Director, Keys Elementary School, Park Hill, OK, 1992-; private consulting services, 1982-. *Other professional post*: Ex-director, Oklahoma Indian Affairs Commission. Award: Independent Filmmakers Award, American Film Institute. Interests: Tribal sovereignty; Indian self-government; tribal courts; language preservation; rural development. Published works: No Contest: Dependent Sovereign-From Tribe to Nation (Univ . Micro, 1984); Sovereignty Symposium Series (Sovereign Symposium, 1988-).

GOWAN, RAY
(editor/publisher)

Affiliation : Indian Books from the Four Winds, P.O. Box 3300, Rapid City , SD 57709 (605) 343-6064.

GRADY, GLENN
(Indian band chief)

Affiliation : Ta'an Kwach'an Council, 22 Niutlin Dr., Whitehorse, Yukon, Canada Y1A 3S5 (403) 668-3613.

*GRAHAM, BOYD (Duckwater Shoshone)
(tribal chairperson)

Affiliation : Duckwater Shoshone Tribal Council, P.O. Box 140068, Duckwater , NV 89314 (702) 738-0569.

GRAHAM, STEPHEN B.
(museum chairperson)

Affiliation : Blackbird Museum, P .O. Box 192, Harbor Springs, MI 49740 (616) 526-2104.

GRANADOS, ALFRED C.
(BIA area health administrator)

Affiliation : Office of Administration, California Area Office, BIA, 1825 Bell St., Suite 200, Sacramento, CA 95825 (916) 978-4202.

GRANNING, GEORGE, M.D.
(clinical director-Indian hospital)

Affiliation : Cherokee PHS Indian Hospital, Cherokee, NC 28719 (704) 497-9163.

GRANT, JANELLE
(Indian school principal)

Affiliation : Loneman Day School, P .O. Box 50, Oglala, SD 57764 (605) 867-5633.

GRANT, LANA SUE (Sac & Fox-Shawnee) 1942-
(library director & newspaper editor)

Born November 25, 1942, Pawnee, Okla. *Education*: El Reno Junior College, AA, 1968; University of Oklahoma, BS, 1970; University of Oklahoma, MLS, 1977. *Principal occupation* : Library director and newspaper editor . *Home address*: 1401 Abbey Dr., Norman, OK 73071 (918) 968-3526 (of fice). *Affiliations*: Director, Sac and Fox National Public Library , and editor of the "Sac and Fox News," Route 2, Box 246, Stroud, OK 74079, 1982-.

*GRANT, KENNETH
(AK Indian association president)

Affiliation : Hoonah Indian Association, P.O. Box 602, Hoonah, AK 99829 (907) 945-3220.

GRANT, WENDY
(Indian band chief)

Affiliation : Musqueam Indian Band, 6370 Salish Dr., Vancouver, British Columbia, Canada V6N 2C6 (604) 263-3261.

GRANT, WILLIAM L. (Otoe-Missouria)
(tribal council chief)

Affiliation : Otoe-Missouria Tribal Council, P.O. Box 68, Red Rock, OK 74058 (405) 723-4434.

*GRANT-KOTA, SHARON LEONA (Ojibwe) 1946-
(coordinator for Indian education)

Born December 16, 1946, St. Clair County , Mich. *Education*: Wayne State University, B.S., 1973. *Principal occupation* : Coordinator for Indian education. *Home address* : 5315 Ravenswood Rd., Kimball, MI 48074 (810) 364-8370. *Affiliations*: Home/School Coordinator for Indian Education, Port Huron Area School District, Port Huron, MI, 1977-. *Other professional post* : Indian Education Program, Grant Application Panelist - reader for American Indian Fellowships; reader for Discretionary Proposals. *Community activities* : Chair, American Indian Communities Leadership Council; board member , Southeastern Michigan Indian Center; conference committee, St. Clair County Preschool Group. *Memberships* : Michigan Association for the Education of Young Children; Blue W ater Association for the Education of Young Children (newsletter chairperson); Blue W ater Native American Indians. *Awards, honors* : Selected as Michigan Urban Delegate to White House Conference on Indian Education; scholarship recipient, North American Indian Association, 1971-73. *Interests*: "I coordinate a full-time Title V Indian Education Program for eligible American Indian students. The main aspects of the program are cultural classes, tutoring, counseling and home visits. Conferences, career days, field trips, parent committee meetings and a monthly newsletter are also included in this position. Culture and self-determination are the program's major goals." Attend workshops. Other interests include sports, American Indian literature and professional readings, music and good friends.

*GRANTHAM, LARRY
(historic site manager)

Affiliation : Osage V illage Historic Site, P .O. Box 176, Jefferson City, MO 65102 (314) 751-8363.

GRAVETT, FRANKLIN
(BIA agency supt.)

Affiliation : Crow Creek Afency, Bureau of Indian Affairs, P.O. Box 616, Fort Thompson, SD 57339 (605) 245-2311.

*GRAY, ALLEN
(school chairperson)

Affiliation : Dennehotso Boarding School, P .O. Box LL, Dennehotso, AZ 86535 (602) 658-3201.

GRAY, ELMER SHORTY *(Little Scout)* (United Lumbee/Cherokee) 1934-
(log scaler)

Born November 2, 1934, Los Angeles, Calif. *Education*: Modesto City Schools, CA; Lassen Junior College (out reach), 1986 & 1989 *Principal occupation* : Log scaler. *Home address*:

P.O. Box 8, Little Valley, CA 96053. *Affiliation*: United Lumbee Nation (secretary, 1988-; Deer Clan chief, 1989-). *Community activities*: Inter-Mountain Horseman's Association (vice president, 1984; president, 1985). *Memberships*: United Lumbee Nation's Deer Clan (vice-chief, 1984; chief, 1985-); United Lumbee Nation Mantoac Medicine Society, 1984-93; High Eagle Warrior Society 1984-93; keeper of the pipe, 1985-88); Fire Fighting Tree Falling Team, 1989- *Awards, honors*: California State Horseman's Association (Region 18 High Point Champion Gymkhana Rider, 1983 & 1984; 1983 & 1985 High Point Rider, Inter-Mountain Horseman's Association; 1989 Silver Eagle Award, given each year by the United Lumbee nation for outstanding work for the Nation/Band/Clan; Senior Volunteer Service Award, May 5, 1990, in recognition for countless hours of volunteer service to Lassen County, CA USDA program. *Interests*: "Signing for the deaf; signing exact English and Using it with Indian heritage lore; putting on programs about Indian lore for school children. *Traditional skills*: hunting, fishing, scouting; fur training, bow hunting, horse-raising; shelter building, survival living." *Biographical source*: Section in United Lumbee's Deer Clan Cook Book.

GRAY, GERALD J.
(school principal)
Affiliation: Chemawa Indian School, 3700 Chemawa Rd., NE, Salem, OR 97303 (503) 399-5721.

GRAY, GREGORY GRAYSON
(Mah-She-Hop-Pee) (Osage) 1947-
(silversmith, business owner)
Born April 4, 1947, Muskogee, Okla. *Education*: Central State University (Edmond, OK), BA, 1991. *Principal occupation*: Silversmith, business owner. *Home address*: 330 Nimrod Rd., Edmond, OK 73034 (405) 340-6323 (work). *Affiliation*: Owner, Gray Deer Arts, Edmond, OK, 1990- (production and distribution of Native American recordings). *Other professional post*: State trooper, Oklahoma Highway Patrol (retired). *Military service*: U.S. Army Reserve, 1967-75 (Sergeant E-5; National Service Award and Certificate of Commendation for Outstanding Performance of Duty). *Community activities*: Civil Air Patrol; Little League Coach; Art Judge, 1991 Oklahoma Native American High School Art Competition; Red Earth Art Competition Committee, 1992. *Memberships*: Indian Arts & Crafts Association; Gallup Inter-Tribal Association; Celebrations of the American Indian, Ormand Beach, FL (board of directors). *Awards, honors*: Awards won in the following: Tulsa Indian Art Festival; Indian Summer, Bartlesville, OK; Edmond (OK) Art Show; Canterbury Art Show, Edmond, OK; Okmulgee (OK) Indian Art Market; Chism Trail Art Show, Yukon, OK. *Interests*: "History of Indian jewelry, gems and stones used in jewelry and legends and lore of Native Americans. Due to the extensive traveling I have done in the past five years throughout the U.S., I have developed an insatiable desire to learn all that I can about my heritage." *Biographical source*: The Source Directory (Indian Arts and Crafts Board, U.S. Dept. of the Interior. *Published works*: Currently writing a book on the history of Southwest jewelry; completed a recording entitled, The History of Southwest Jewelry.

GRAY, JOHN
(B.I.A. agency supt.)
Affiliation: Mescalero Agency, BIA, P.O. Box 189, Mescalero, NM 88340 (505) 671-4423.

*GRAY, LYNNE CATHERINE (Yaqui)
(television producer & vice president)
Education: Cypress College, AA, 1973; California State University, Long Beach, BA, 1982, Field Work/Internship, 1982, Gerontology Certificate, 1983, Basic Education/Social Science Credentials, 1989. *Address*: 3514 Grand Ave. South, Minneapolis, MN 55408 (612) 825-9525. *Affiliations*: Veterinary manager, Bristol Veterinary Clinic, Santa Ana, CA, 1971-77; partner, franchise, L&W Service Co., Norwalk, CA, 1976-83; associate practitioner, Developmental Guidance Services, Inc., Long Beach, CA, 1984-89; assistant director, National Conference of Christians & Jews, Minneapolis, MN, 1990-92; Native American Television, St. Cloud, MN (television producer," First Americans Update," 1991-; vice-president, 1991-). *Professional activities*: Member, American Indian Media Image Task Force, 1990-; member, National Association for Female Executives. *Published works*: "Broadcast Media: Indian Access & Careers," feature articles in Winds of Change, publication of the American Indian Science & Engineering Society, Summer 1991; managing editor, *The American Indian & the Media*, a pubn. of the American Indian Media Image Task Force, Jan. 1992.

GRAYEYES, WILLIE
(school chairperson)
Affiliation: Navajo Mountain Boarding School, Box 787, Tonalea, AZ 86044 (602) 672-2851.

GRAYMOUNTAIN, ROBERT (Navajo)
(school chairperson)
Affiliation: Navajo Mountain Boarding School, Box 10010, Tonalea, AZ 86044 (602) 672-2851.

*GRAYSON, NOLAN
(Indian center-acting director)
Affiliation: American Indian Center of Santa Clara Valley, 919 The Alameda, San Jose, CA 95126 (408) 971-9622.

GREEN, BETTY
(executive director)
Affiliation: Indian Family Services, Inc., 1315 Penn Ave. North, Minneapolis, MN 5541 (612) 348-5788.

*GREEN, CAROL
(school principal)
Affiliation: Cottonwood Day School, Chinle, AZ 86503 (602) 725-3256.

GREEN, ELWOOD
(museum director/curator)
Affiliation: Native American Center for the Living Arts, 25 Rainbow Blvd., Niagara Falls, NY 14303 (716) 284-2427.

GREEN, JESS
(attorney)
Address: 301 E. Main St., Ada, OK 74820 (405) 436-1946. *Affiliation*: Chairperson, Indian Law Section, Oklahoma Bar Association.

GREEN, JOHN (Yurok)
(tribal vice-chairperson)
Affiliation: Elk Valley Tribal Council, P.O. Box 1042, Crescent City, CA 95531 (707) 464-4680.

GREEN, JOSEPH V.
(school principal)
Affiliations: Jemez Day SchoolIsleta Elementary School, P.O. Box 139, Jemez Pueblo, NM 87024 (505) 834-7304.

*GREEN, MARGARET (Samish)
(tribal chairperson)
Affiliation: Samish Tribe, P.O. Box 217, Anacortes, WA 98221 (206) 293-6404.

GREEN, MICHAEL DAVID 1941-
(associate professor)
Born February 17, 1941, Cedar Rapids, IA. *Education*: Cornell College, BA, 1963; University of Iowa, MA, 1965, PhD, 1973. *Principal occupation*: Associate professor. *Affiliations*: Assistant professor, West Texas State University, 1970-74; assistant professor, 1977-83, associate professor, 1983-92, Dartmouth College. *Other professional post*: Fellow, D'Arcy McNickle Center for the History of the American Indian, The Newberry Library, Chicago, IL. *Memberships*: Western History Association; Organization of American Historians; American Society for Ethnohistory (executive committee, 1985-87). *Published works*: The Creeks: A Critical Bibliography (University of Indiana Press, 1979); The Politics of Indian Removal: Creek Government and Society in Crisis (University of Nebraska Press, 1982); The Creeks (Chelsea House, 1990).

*GREEN, PAT
(museum director/curator)
Affiliation: Wrangell Museum, Box 2050, 1 126 Second St., Wrangell, AK 99929 (907) 874-3770.

GREEN, RAYNA (Cherokee) 1942-
(museum administrator/program manager)
Born July 18, 1942, Dallas, Tex. *Education*: Southern Methodist University, Dallas, BA, 1963, MA, 1966; Indiana University, Bloomington, Ph.D. (Folklore, American Studies), 1974. *Principal occupation*: Museum administrator/program manager. *Home address*: 814 G St., SE, Washington, DC 20003 (202) 357-2071. *Affiliations*: Program director, American Association for the Advancement of Science, 1975-80; program director, Dartmouth College, Hanover, NH, 1980-83; planner, 1983-85, director, American Indian Program, National Museum of American History, 1985-, Smithsonian Institution, Washington, DC,1983- *Other professional posts*: Visiting professor, University of Massachusetts, and Yale University; consultant to numerous federal agencies, tribes, tribal/Indian organizations, institutions, museums, and universities. *Community activities*: Ms. Foundation for Women (board member); Indian Law Resource Center, Fund for the Improvement of Post-Secondary Education (board member); Phelps-Stokes Fund (Indian advisory board); American Indian Society of Washington; American Indian Intertribal Cultural Organization. *Memberships*: American Folklore Society (president); American Engineering Society; Society for the Advancement of Native Americans and Chicano Scientists; American Anthropological Association. *Awards, honors*: Smithsonian Fellow, 1970; Ford Foundation, National Research Council Fellow, 1983; Distinguished Service Award, American Indian Society of Washington. *Interests*: "American folklorist; research on Native American women; Southern

women; American material culture; Indian traditional science, technology, and medicine; relations between Indians & museums; Indian energy/minerals development; poetry/short fiction; film/TV script writing; exhibit production." *Published works*: Native American Women: A Contextual Bibliography (Indiana University Press, 1982); That's What She Said: Contemporary Poetry and Fiction by Native American Women (Indiana University Press, 1984); Introduction to Pissing in the Snow: Other Ozark Folktales; Handicrafts in the Southern Highlands; articles and essays in Ms. Magazine, Southern Exposure, Science, Handbook of American Folklore, Handbook of North American Indians, and Signs.

GREEN, ROBERTA
(editor & publisher)
Affiliation: Tekawennake Six Nations - New Credit Reporter, Woodland Indian Cultural Education Center, 184 Mohawk St., Box 1506, Brantford, ON, Can. N3T 5V6 (519) 753-5531.

GREEN, ROBIN
(grand chief)
Affiliation: Grand Council Treaty No. 3, P.O. Box 1720, Kenora, Ontario, Canada P7N 3X7 (807) 548-4215.

GREENE, DANIEL P. (Makah)
(tribal council chief)
Affiliation: Makah Tribal Council, P.O. Box 115, Neah Bay, WA 98357 (206) 645-2205 Ext. 36.

*GREENE, JEANIE *(Upayok)*
(Inupiat Eskimo) 1951-
(television host, director, producer)
Born August 31, 1951, Sitka, Alaska. *Education*: University of Alaska, Anchorage, B.A., 1990. *Principal occupation*: Television host, director, producer. *Address & Affiliation*: Executive producer, One Sky Productions, Ltd., "Heartbeat Alaska", 2611 Fairbanks St. #D, Anchorage, AK 99503 (907) 272-8111 Fax 272-7007. *Memberships*: Native American Journalists Association; Alaska Press Club; Alaska Press Women. *Awards, honors*: Alaska Press Club Awards (1993-3rd Place, "Best Public Affairs"; 1994-2nd Place, "Best Feature Story," and 2nd Place, "Best Public Affairs. *Interests*: "Heartbeat Alaska," focuses on the life and times of rural Alaska residents; "One Sky," which is a discussion style forum for rual issues, gets its name from the philosophy that all people are all members of the family of man and that share the same hopes and dreams." Greene, an award-winning journalist and producer, distributes the show herself.

*GREENE, JEROME A.
(historian, author-editor)
Affiliation: National Park Service. *Published works*: Slim Buttes, 1876: An Episode of the Great Sioux War (University of Oklahoma Press); Battles & Skirmishes of the Great Sioux War, 1876-1877: The Military View (University of Oklahoma Press); Lakota & Cheyenne: Indian Views of the Great Sioux War, 1876-1877 (University of Oklahoma Press, 1994).

GREENE, JUDITH (Seneca-Deer Clan) 1940-
(museum director)
Born January 2, 1940, Bufalo, N.Y. *Education*: Alfred University, BFA, 1984; University of Massachusetts at Dartmouth, MA, MFA, 1990. *Principal occupation*. Museum director. *Home ad-*

dress: 19 Main St., Salamanca, NY 14779 (716) 945-1738 (work). *Affiliation*: Seneca-Iroquois National Museum, Allegany Indian Reservation, P.O. Box 442, Broad St. Extension, Salamanca, NY 14779. *Other professional post*: Grant reviewer, New York State Foundation for the Arts. *Community activities*: Member, (Seneca Nation) Human Resource Oversight Committee, Higher Education Committee & the Bingo Advisory Committee.

GREENE, MARIE N. (Eskimo)
(association president)
Affiliation: Maniilaq Association, P.O. Box 256, Kotzebue, AK 99752 (907) 442-3311.

GREENER, SHARON
(curator)
Affiliation: Effigy Mounds National Monument, RR 1, Box 25A, Harpers Ferry, IA 52146 (319) 873-3491.

GREENHAGEN, EDNA
(school principal)
Affiliation: Enemy Swim Day School, R.R. 1, Box 87, Waubay, SD 57273 (605) 947-4605.

*GREENHALG, KATHLEEN
(librarian)
Affiliation: Indian & Colonial Research Center, Eva Butler Library, P.O. Box 525, Old Mystic, CT 06372 (203) 536-9771.

*GREENPASTURES-DOTY, ADEI
(minister)
Home address: 1204 Walker Dr., Decatur, GA 30030. *Affiliation*: Member, Board of Directors, The Native American Center of Georgia, Woodstock, GA.

*GREENWOOD, BRENDA
(editor)
Affiliation: "Turtle Mountain Times," Turtle Mountain Tribe, Belcourt, ND 58316 (701) 477-6451.

*GREENWOOD, DONALD EARL *(Little Boy)* 1935-
(craftsman)
Born July 5, 1935, Dewey, Okla. *Education*: West Texas Barber College (Amarillo, TX) Master Barber, 1971. *Principal occupation*: Craftsman. *Home address*: 10414 Autumn Meadow Lane, Houston, TX 77064 (918) 866-2653. *Professional posts*: Owner, Barber Shop, Borger, TX, 1973-; craftsman, 1992-. *Military service*: U.S. Army (PFC), 1959-61. *Membership*: Indian Arts & Crafts Association, 1994-. *Interests*: "I am presently making the Indian dream catcher into intricate jewelry. I enjoy working with feathers, making the Indian fans. I also enjoy working with leather and specialize in the dream catcher necklaces & earrings covered with leather with leather fringe. Even though I earn my living from the sale of my jewelry, I consider them an art form. I look at each piece as a piece of art instead of a commercial item. At a later date, I plan to use my ability as an artist in Indian & biblical drawings. I also plan to add photography. It is my desire to travel to diferent reservations for my photography & also to get any unusual shots in my travels. I, of course, love to capture any of God's beauty on canvas or on film. I like to read, walk & travel. In the summer of 1992, I worked many of the powwows in Oklahoma. I have taken my jewelry into Oklahoma, almost all of Texas, New Mexico, Missouri, Arkansas & Tennessee."

GREGOIRE, RAPHAEL
(executive director-friendship centre)
Affiliation: St. John's Native Friendship Centre, P.O. Box 2414, Station "C", St. John's, Newfoundland, Canada A1C 6E7 (709) 726-5902.

GREGOR, GAIL (Stillaguamish)
(tribal chairperson)
Affiliation: Stillaguamish Board of Directors, P.O. Box 277, Arlington, WA 98223 (206) 652-7362.

*GREY, STEVEN (Navajo)
(Indian program head)
Affiliation: Lawrence Livermore National Laboratory, American Indian Program, 1994; manager, Field Office, Navajo Community College, Shiprock, NM, 1988-94.

GREYBEAR, LORRAINE
(school chairperson)
Affiliation: Four Winds Commuity School, P.O. Box 199, Fort Totten, ND 58335 (701) 766-4161.

GREYEYES, ALEX
(publisher; president of Indian centre)
Affiliation: Saskatchewan Indian, Saskatchewan Indian Media Corporation, 2121 Airport Dr. #201A, Saskatoon, Saskatchewan, Canada S7L 6W5 (306) 665-2175; Saskatchewan Indian Cultural Centre, Saskatoon.

*GRIECO, VIRGINIA
(executive director)
Affiliation: California Indian Education Association, 5108 E. Clinton Way, Suite 108, Fresno, CA 93727 (209) 456-9195.

GRIFFIN, LOUIE (Keetowah Cherokee) 1914-
(loan officer, live stock farming)
Born October 5, 1914, Cookson, Okla. *Education*: Chilocco Indian School; Oklahoma State University, BS, 1940. *Principal occupation*: Loan officer, live stock farming. *Home address*: 909 S. State, Tahlequah, OK 74464 (918) 456-9678. *Affiliation*: Loan officer, Tahlequah and Wewoka, Okla. (16 years); past vice chief, Keetowah Cherokee. *Military service*: U.S. Army, 1942-46; Army Reserve, 1940-67. *Community activities*: Kiwanis (past Lt. Governor); FRU Board of Trustees, Stilwell, OK (chairperson).

*GRIFFIS, STEVE
(casino/bingo general manager)
Affiliation: Tulalip Casino & Bingo, 6330 33rd Ave. NE, Marysville, WA 98271 (206) 653-7395.

GRIFFITH, GLADYS GIBSON 1925-
(artist)
Born March 15, 1925, Piqua, Ohio. *Education*: High School. *Principal occupation*: Artist. *Home address*: 263 E. Main St., Piqua, OH 45356. *Other professional post*: Lecturer on Indian affairs. *Memberships*: Museum of Natural History, 1970-; Ohio Archaeological Society, 1970-; Miami County Historical Society, 1970-; Miami County Archaeological Society; Archaeological Society of Ohio (secretary-treasurer, Miami River Valley Chapter). *Awards, honors*: Ms. Griffith's work is displayed at the Indian Museum, Salamanca, NY: Indian Museum, Oberlin, Kan.; the Satte House, Boston, MA; Pacific Northwest Indian Center, Gonzaga University, Spokane, WA. *Biographical source*: Who's Who in the Arts.

*GRIMES, BARBARA F. (Cherokee) 1930-
(editor, linguist)
Born August 19, 1930, San Diego, Calif. *Edu-*

cation: Wheaton College, BA, 1952, Litt.D., 1993. *Principal occupation*: Editor, linguist. *Home address*: 84-664 Ala Mahiku, 191-B, Waianae, HI 96792 (808) 695-8402. *Affiliations*: Summer Institute of Linguistics, Dallas, TX (member, 1951-; field investigator, Huichol language project, Mexico, 1952-67, 1979-80; field investigator, Hawaii Creole English (Pidgin) language project, 1987-). *Other professional post*: Editor, Ethnologue: Languages of the World, 1971-. *Awards, honors*: Scholastic Honor Society, Wheaton College. *Interests*: "Participated in linguistic workshops in 23 countries, from 2-6 months in each." *Published works*: Numerous journal articles.

*GRIMES, JOSEPH E. 1928-
(linguist)
Born December 10, 1928, Elizabeth, N.J. *Education*: Wheaton College, BA, 1950; Cornell University, M.A., 1958, Ph.D., 1960. *Principal occupation*: Linguist. *Home address*: 84-664 Ala Mahiku, 191-B, Waianae, HI 96792 (808) 695-8402. *Affiliations*: Professor, Cornell University, Ithaca, NY, 1967-90; Summer Institute of Linguistics, Dallas, TX, 1950-. *Other professional posts*: Editorial Board, International Journal of American Linguistics, 1978-. *Memberships*: Linguistic Society of America (executive committee, 1984-86); Consortium of Social Science Associations (LSA Rep, 1988-92; president, 1991-92). *Interests*: Linguistic research on Huichol (Oto-Aztecan, Mexico), 1952-69; linguistic research on Hawaii Creole English, 1988-; consulting editor, Ethnologue, 1969-. *Published works*: Huichol Syntax (Mouton, 1965); The Thread of Discourse (Mouton, 1975; numerous journal articles.

GRINDE, DONALD ANDREW, Jr. (Yamasee) 1946-
(professor of American history)
Born August 23, 1946, Savannah, Ga. *Education*: Georgia Southern College, Statesboro, BA, 1966; University of Delaware, MA, 1968, PhD (History), 1974. *Principal occupation*: Professor of American history. *Home address*: 284 Albert Dr., San Luis Obispo, CA 93405; office: Dept. of History, California Polytechnic State University, San Luis Obispo, CA 93407 (805) 756-2834. *Affiliations*: Assistant professor, Mercyhurst College, Erie, PA, 1971-73; assistant professor, SUNY at Buffalo, 1973-77; associate professor, California Polytechnic State University, San Luis Obispo, 1977-78; visiting associate professor, UCLA, 1978-79; associate professor, California Polytechnic State University, 1979-81; director, Native American Studies, University of Utah, Salt Lake City, 1981-84; associate professor of history, California Polytechnic State University, 1984-. *Other professional posts*: Instructor in Native American history, United Southeastern Tribes, Inc., and SUNY, College at Buffalo, Program for Indian Teacher Education at Allegany and Cattaraugus (Seneca) Reservations, 1974-75; Native American consultant, Buffalo City Schools, 1974-75; consultant, Smithsonian Institution, 1977; Native American Consultant, Salt Lake City Schools, 1982-83; editor, Journal of Erie Studies, 1971-1973; editorial board, Indian Historian, 1976-. *Community activities*: Buffalo North American Indian Culture Center (corresponding secretary and board member, 1974-77); American Indian Historical Society (board member, 1976-); Central Coast Indian Council, Calif. (vice chairman, 1979-80); Salt Lake Indian Center

(chairman of board, 1983-84). *Memberships*: National Indian Education Association (member of Resolutions Committee, 1981-83); American Indian Historian's Association (charter member); American Indian Historical Society; Organization of American Historians (charter member); National Association of American Indian Professors; American Indian Scholars Association; Phi Alpha Theta; Smithsonian Institution. *Awards, honors*: Hagley Fellow, University of Delaware, 1966-70; Grant-in-Aid Scholar, Eleutherian Mills Historical Library, 1970-71; project historian and conservation consultant, Southern Railroad Restoration Project, National Park Service; Faculty Seed Grant, UCLA, American Indian Studies Center, 1978-79; Outstanding Professional Award (Education), 1984, from Wasatch Regional Minority Business and Professional Directory (Salt Lake City, Utah); Eugene Crawford Memorial Fellow, 1987-88; Rupert Costo Professor of American Indian History, University of California, Riverside, 1989-91. *Interests*: American Indian history including: 20th century Indian policy, Native American science, American Indian political theory, history of American technology, museum administration; published testimony, "The Iroquois Roots of American Democracy," U.S. Senate Select Committee on Indian Affairs, Dec. 2, 1987. *Biographical sources*: Wasatch Regional Minority Business and Professional Directory (Salt Lake City, Utah, 1984); Resource Directory of American Indian Professionals, 1987. *Published works*: Contributing editor, Readings in American History: Bicentennial Edition, II (Guilford, Conn., Dushkin Publishing, 1975); The Iroquois and the Founding of the American Indian (Indian Historian Press, 1977); Exemplar of Liberty: Native American and the Evolution of American Democracy, with Bruce E. Johansen (UCLA American Indian Studies, 1991).

GRINNELL, RANDY
(BIA-environmental health)
Affiliation: Office of Environmental Health, Oklahoma Area Office, Bureau of Indian Affairs, 215 Dean A. McGee St., NW, Room 409, Oklahoma City, OK 73102 (405) 231-4796.

GRITZBAUGH, GARY S., D.D.S.
(IHS-director, dental services)
Affiliation: Dental Special Services Branch, Indian Health Service (headquarters West), 300 San Mateo, NE, Suite 500, Albuquerque, NM 87102 (505) 766-6319.

GROBE, MARY LOU
(museum president)
Affiliation: Pueblo Grande Museum, 4619 E. Washington St., Phoenix, AZ 85034 (602) 275-3452.

GROBSMITH, ELIZABETH S. *(Anpo wicahpi)* **1946-**
(assistant vice chancellor for academic affairs)
Born May 27, 1946, Brooklyn, N.Y. *Education*: Ohio State University, BMus, 1968; University of Arizona, MA, 1970, PhD (Anthropology), 1976. *Principal occupation*: Assistant Vice Chancellor for Academic Affairs, Director of Summer Sessions, University of Nebraska. *Home address*: 2712 Manse Ave., Lincoln, NE 68502 (402) 472-3751 (work). *Affiliation*: Assistant Vice Chancellor for Academic Affairs, Office of Academic Affairs, University of Nebraska, Lincoln, NE, 1992-. *Other professional posts*: Professor

of anthropology, Dept. of Anthropology, University of Nebraska, Lincoln, NE, 1975-; director of Summer Sessions, University of Nebraska, Lincoln, NE, 1975-; consultant, Association on American Indian Affairs, 1984-85; consultant, Indian Club, Nebraska State Penitentiary, and American Anthropological Association lecture series. *Memberships*: Plains Anthropological Society (board of directors, 1979-81; vice president, 1980-81); American Anthropological Association; University of Nebraska Graduate Faculty; Sigma Delta, Iota Chapter (Graduate Women's Scientific Fraternity); Association on American Indian Affairs; Society for Applied Anthropology. *Interests*: "My major professional interests are in studying and working with American Indian communities, with specific interests in helping them to design strategies and programs which alleviate reservation problems, be they juvenile justice concerns, alcoholism, curriculum development, legal or economic. When possible, I enjoy traveling to observe indigenous peoples to achieve a better understanding of native cultures (e.g. Alaska, Guatemala). Interested in Indian prisoners and their struggle to obtain religious freedom rights behind the walls. Serve as consultant/expert witness in numerous court cases involving Indian prisoners' efforts to practice their native culture and religion despite their incarceration. Served as expert witness for Northern Ponca tribal restoration, 1990. (I) Enjoy travel, particularly in Indian country and especially in Southwest U.S. Hobbies: choral music." *Published works*: Books: Lakota of the Rosebud, A Contemporary Ethnography (Holt, Rinehart and Winston, 1981); Indians in Prison: A Study of Incarcerated Native Americans in Nebraska (University of Nebraska Press, 1994). Chapters in books: "The Plains Culture Area", chapter in Native North Americans: An Ethnohistorical Approach, edited by Daniel Boxberger (Kendall/Hunt, 1990); "Indian Prisoners", to appear in Encyclopedia on Native Americans in the 20th Century, Museum of the American Indian (Garland, 1992). Articles: "The Relationship Between Substance Abuse and Crime Among Native Americans in the Nebraska Department of Corrections", Human Organization, Vol. 48, No. 4, Winter 1989; "The Impact of Litigation on the Religious Revitalization of Native American Inmates in the Nebraska Department of Corrections", Plains Anthropologist, Vol. 34, No. 124, Part I, 1989; "The Revolving Door: Substance Abuse Treatment and Criminal Sanctions for Native American Offenders", co-authored with Jennifer Dam, Journal of Substance Abuse, Vol. 2, No. 4, 1990; "Termination and Restoration of American Indian Tribes: The Northern Ponca Case", with Beth R. Ritter, Human Organization, Spring, 1992; "Inmates & Anthropologists: The Impact of Advocacy on the Expression of Native American Culture in Prison", High Plains Applied Anthropologist, Vol. II, No. 1, Spring, 1992. Numerous book reviews

GROS-LOUIS, MAX (MAGELLA)
(Indian band grand chief)
Affiliation: Bande Indienne de la Nation Huronne-Wendat, 255, Place Chef Michel Laveau, Wendake, Quebec, Canada G0A 4V0 (418) 843-3767.

*GROSDIDIER, KATHERINE
(executive director)
Affiliation: Southcentral Foundation, 670 Fireweed Lane, Suite 123, Anchorage, AK 99503 (907) 276-3343.

GROSPE, LARRY
(executive director)
Affiliation : American Indian Center of Dallas, Inc., 1314 Munger Blvd., Dallas, TX 75206 (214) 826-8856.

GROSS, GLEN
(museum director)
Affiliation : Ute Indian Museum - Puray Memorial Park, P.O. Box 1736, Montrose, CO 81402 (303) 249-3098.

GROSS, SHIRLEY
(Indian center program coordinator)
Affiliation : Pierre Indian Learning Center , Star Route 3, Pierre, SD 57501 (605) 224-8661.

GROUNDS, CHARLES E. *(E-kv-nv)* **(Seminole of Oklahoma) 1904-**
(attorney at law)
Born April 29, 1904, Seminole County , Okla. *Education* : Haskell Institute; University of Kansas; Tulsa Law School. *Principal occupation* : Attorney at law. *Home address* : 2121 Grounds Ave., Seminole, OK 74868 (405) 382-0397 (office). *Affiliations* : Attorney at law, Seminole, OK (63 years). *Other professional posts* : Organizer, secretary/treasurer, board of directors, Seminole County Indian Credit Association (55 years); assistant district attorney for Seminole County; tribal attorney for Seminole Tribe of Oklahoma. *Military service* : Troop C 114th Calvary, KNG, First Sargeant, Troop C staged the Indian attack and "The Birth of Chicago." *Community activities* : Scout master; member of the Elks Lodge; Sunday school teacher. *Memberships* : Oklahoma Bar Assn. (63 years); 32nd Degree Mason-Seminole Masonic Lodge; Indian Shrine Temple of Oklahoma City; B.P .O.E. Lodge of Seminole. *Awards, honors* : Seminole County Indian Credit Assn. honoring 55 years as member & secretary/treasurer; Oklahoma Bar Assn. honoring 63 years as member of the Bar .

GRUMMER, BRENDA KENNEDY
(Citizen Band Potawatomi)
(professional artist)
Born in El Reno, Okla. *Principal occupation* : Professional artist. *Home address* : 11105 Coachman's Rd., Yukon, OK 73099. *Affiliation* : Grummer Art Studio, Yukon, OK, 1980-. *Memberships* : National League of American Pen Women; National Cowboy Hall of Fame; American Indian Arts and Crafts Association. *Awards, honors* : Grand Award, Philbrook National India Artists Exhibition; First Place painting awards at Trail of Tears National Exhbition & Gallup Inter-Tribal Ceremoial; shown at Kennedy Center, Smithsonian Institution; Franco-American Union, Rennes, France, dozens of museums shows and awards. *Interests* : Professional writer as well as artist. *Biographical sources* : Mentioned in articles in "Southwest Art," "Art of the West," "Oklahoma Today," "Oklahoma Home and Garden."

GRUNERT, CLEMENS
(village council president)
Affiliation : Native V illage of Chignik Lagoon, General Delivery, Chignik Lagoon, AK 99565 (907) 840-2206.

GUAFFAC, CARLOS (Diegueno)
(tribal chairperson)
Affiliation : Mesa Grande Band of Mission Indians, P.O. Box 270, Santa Ysabel, CA 92070 (619) 282-9650.

GUARDIPEE, LEONARD L. (Blackfeet)
(school counselor)
Affiliation : Blackfeet Dormitory , Blackfeet Agency, Browning, MT 59417 (406) 338-7441.

GUERRO, EDNA
(tribal council chief)
Affiliation : Potter Valley Rancheria, P.O. Box 94, Potter Valley, CA 95469 (707) 743-1649.

*GUILD, ALICE F.
(museum director)
Affiliation : Icolani Palace, P.O. Box 259, Honolulu, HI 96804 (808) 522-0822.

*GUIMARES, PAULO, M.D.
(clinical director)
Affiliation : PHS Indian Hospital, P .O. Box 60, Cass Lake, MN 56633 (218) 335-2293.

GUMLIKPUK, PETER (Athapascan)
(village council president)
Affiliation : New Stuyahok V illage Council, New Stuyahok, AK 99636 (907) 693-8002.

*GUN SHOWS, DAN
(administrative officer)
Affiliation : Lodge Grass PHS Indian Health Center, Lodge Grass, MT 59050 (406) 639-2317.

GUNDERSON, PAUL
(AK village council president)
Affiliation : Native Village of Nelson Lagoon, Box 13, Nelson Lagoon, AK 99571 (907) 989-2204.

GUNN, VIRGIL L.
(clinic director)
Affiliation : David C. Wynecoop Memorial Clinic, P.O. Box 357, Wellpinit, W A 99040 (509) 258-4517.

*GURNOE, ROSE (Red Cliff Chippewa)
(tribal chairperson)
Affiliation : Red Cliff Tribal Council, P.O. Box 529, Bayfield, WI 54814 (715) 779-3701.

GUS, LARRY (Hopi-Navajo) 1954-
(photographer)
Born August 12, 1954, Keams Canyon, Ariz. *Education* : California Institute of the Arts (2 years). *Principal occupation* : Photographer (self-employed). Memberships: Native American Journalists Association; Native Indian/Inuit Photographer's Association; national Press Photographer's Association; Advertising Photographers of America (APA) Crew Director, 1992/ 17th Ed.; ATLATL; Committee to Protect Journalists. *Awards, honors* : Finalist-W estern Region-Leica Medal of Excellence, 1987. *Interests* : News photographer . "I try to photograph Indian people as they are in everyday life, not the way foreigners have convinced themselves that Indians should look and behave. As a photojournalist, my responsibility and obligation will remain with the subject being photographed--not with any organization or individual that has hired my services or which expects me to produce images for their use and/or viewing."

GUSTAFSON, CHARLES
(BIA education coordinator)
Affiliation : Aberdeen Area Office, Bureau of Indian Affairs, 115 4th Ave., SE, Federal Bldg., Aberdeen, SD 57401 (605) 226-7416. Other professional posts: Education coordinator , Fort Berthold Agency, New Town, ND, and Standing Rock Agency, Fort Yates, SD.

GUSTIN, WILLIAM E.
(museum manager)
Affiliation : Serpent Mound Museum, State Route 73, Box 234, Peebles, OH 45660 (513) 587-2796.

*GUTIERREZ, FLORINE L.
(BIA agency acting supt.)
Affiliation : Northern Pueblos Agency, BIA, P.O. Box 4269, Fairview Station, Espanola, NM 87533 (505) 753-1400.

GUTIERREZ, GIL
(school principal)
Affiliation : Akiachak IRA Contract School, General Delivery, Akiachak, AK 99551 (907) 825-4428.

*GUTIERREZ, RAFAEL
(executive director)
Affiliation : Indian Pueblo Cultural Center , 2401 12th St., NW, Albuquerque, NM 87104 (505) 843-7270.

*GUTSHALL, SANDY
(foundation president)
Affiliation : Viola White W ater Foundation, 4225 Concord St., Harrisburg, P A 17109 (717) 652-2040.

GUY, JOSEPH
(AK village council president)
Affiliation : Kwethluk V illage, P.O. Box 84, Kwethluk, AK 99621 (907) 757-6714.

GUY, PAUL (Eskimo)
(village council president)
Affiliation : Napaskiak Village Council, General Delivery, Napaskiak, AK 99559 (907) 737-7626.

GUYER, DAVID L.
(foundation president)
Affiliation : Save the Children Federation, 54 Wilton Rd., Westport, CT 06880 (203) 226-7271.

H

*HAAG, MARCIA (Choctaw)
(professor of Native American studies)
Affiliation : Native American Studies Program, University of Oklahoma, 455 W . Lindsey, Rm. 804, Norman, OK 73019 (405) 325-2312.

HACKER, PAUL (Choctaw/Cherokee) 1948-
(knife & flutemaker/player-recording artist)
Born August 4, 1948, Oklahoma City , Okla. *Principal occupation* : Knife & flutemaker/player-recording artist. *Home address* : 6505 NW 20th Dr ., Bethany, OK 73008 (405) 787-8600. *Affiliation* : Owner, Paul Hacker Knives & Flutes. *Memberships* : Choctaw Tribe of Oklahoma; Kituwah; Indian Arts & Crafts Association; Gallup Intertribal Ceremonial; Southern Plains Association. *Awards, honors* : Over 50 awards in 10 years. *Interests* : "My intention is to promote traditional and contemporary art. Most of my demonstration are with young people and elementary schools. I attend and show at Native American & Western Shows." *Published works* : Tapes: "Winds of the Past" Volumes I & II - flute music on cassette & compact discs (1992-93) - music composed and played by Paul Hacker (available from Qualla Arts & Crafts, Cherokee, NC).

*HACKETT, DAVID KRAMER *(Woktela)* **(Yuchi) 1948-**
(professional engineer , writer)
Born November 11, 1948, Frankfort, Ind. *Education*: University of Tennessee, BS, 1972. *Principal occupation*: Professional engineer , writer. *Home address*: 6500 Trousdale Rd., Knoxville, TN 37921 (615) 691-7835 (work). *Affiliations*: Engineer, Aztech Research Services, Knoxville, TN, 1975-77; welding engineer , Nuclear Div., Union Carbide, Oak Ridge, TN, 1977-81; owner , Aztech Research Services, Knoxville, TN, 1981-; CEO, Science Advocacy Pellissippi Science Enrichment Programs, Knoxville, TN, 1989-; consultant, Oak Ridge National Laboratory , Oak Ridge, TN, 1990-. *Community activities*: Science programs for the public: I.D. Day , Spaceweek, Astroweek, Earth Day , Science & Technician Week, Science Olympiad. *Memberships*: American Indian Science & Engineering Society; American Society for Metals; Dinosaur Society . *Awards, honors*: Numerous awards for photo documentation; Museum Replica Grants, 1987-89 for stone carving, American Indian Pipes; "Recently it has been my honor to rediscover the origin of the state name, Tennessee, in my Native tongue." *Interests*: "Forensic & failure science, science education, trickster path, critical thinking, paleontology , stone carver." *Biographical source*: Who's Who in the W orld (Marquis, 12th Ed.). *Published works*: Editor: Spruce Pine Mineral District (Aztech, 1979); Ambient Lighting Extremes (Aztech, 1984); Tales From the Red Earth & A Blue Planet (pending); numerous articles in professional journals.

*HACKETT, MICHAEL
(BIA agency supt.)
Affiliation: Zuni Agency, Bureau of Indian Affairs, P.O. Box 369, Zuni, NM 87327 (505) 782-5591.

*HAGAN, WILLIAM T.
(professor of Native American studies)
Affiliation: Native American Studies Program, University of Oklahoma, 455 W . Lindsey, Rm. 804, Norman, OK 73019 (405) 325-2312. *Published works*: Quanah Parker, Comanche Chief, The Sac & Fox Indians, and United States-Comanche Relations (all published by University of Oklahoma Press).

HAGER, CLAY STEVEN (Cherokee) 1958-
(attorney)
Born February 25, 1958, Enid, Okla. *Education*: Phillips University, B.A., 1981; University of Oklahoma, J.D., 1987. *Principal occupation*: Attorney. *Home address*: 2307 Ripple Creek Lane, Edmond, OK 73034 (405) 840-5255 (work). *Affiliation*: Oklahoma Indian Legal Services, Oklahoma City, OK, 1990-. *Other professional post*: Professor, American Institute of Paralegal Studies, Oklahoma City , OK. *Memberships*: Oklahoma Bar Association (Indian Law Section); Oklahoma Indian Bar Association; various tribal bar associations. *Awards, honors*: Guest lecturer, "Indian Housing Into the 90's" seminar, and "Sovereignty Symposium V - The Year of the Indian;" Who's Who in American Law. *Interests*: Indian Child W elfare Act expert. "I am currently rewriting our handbook on the subject." *Published works*: Editor, Oklahoma Indian Child Welfare Act Handbook (Oklahoma Indian Legal Services, 1991); Prodigal Son: The Existing Indian Family Exception (Clearinghouse Law Review, 1993); contributor , Sovereign Symposium VII (Oklahoma Sup. Ct., 1994).

HAIL, BARBARA A. 1931-
(museum director/curator)
Born November 2, 1931. *Education*: Brown University, 1948-51; Cornell University , BA, 1952, MA, 1953. *Principal occupation*: Associate director/curator. *Home address*: 220 Rumstick Rd., Barrington, R.I. 02806. *Affiliations*: Associate director/curator, Haffenreffer Museum of Anthropology, Brown University, Providence, RI, 1973-. *Other professional posts*: American and world history teacher , Ithaca (NY) High School, and White Plains (NY) High School. *Memberships*: American Association of Museums (curator's committee); New England Museum Association; Association of College & University Museums & Galleries; American Anthropological Association; Native American Art Studies Association. *Awards, honors*: Elisha Benjamin Andrews Scholar, Pembroke College; Phi Beta Kappa, Brown University , 1950; National Endowment of the Arts Fellowship for Museum Professionals, 1976, 1985. *Interests*: "History, ethnohistory, ethnology; museology , stylistica and technical aspects of material culture of North America; Peru; Africa; Nepal; current research is in the art and material culture of the Subarctic." *Published work*: Hau, Kola! The Plains Indian Collection of the Haf fenreffer Museum of Anthropology (Haf fenreffer Museum of Anthropology, 1983).

*HAIL, RAVEN *(Golanun)*
(Cherokee of Oklahoma) 1921-
(writer)
Born January 27, 1921, Dewey , Okla. *Education*: Oklahoma State University , BA, 1946; Southern Methodist University , (2 years). *Principal occupation*: Writer. *Address*: P.O. Box 804, Mesa, AZ 85211 (602) 898-7530. *Awards, honors*: Medallion presented to Ms. Hail by United Poets Laureate International for exemplary service for world brotherhood & peace, 1992; Certificate of Award by 13th W orld Congress of Poets, 1992. *Interests*: "I have traveled all over the U.S. for most of my adult life, collecting Native American lore and artifacts. W riter, performer, speaker, teacher of Native American subjects." Hail also lectures on many aspects of Cherokee culture and is an instructor of such traditional skills as beadwork, basketry , singing, dancing, and folklore. *Biographical source*: Native American Women: A Biographical Dictionary, by G.M. Betaile, Editor (Garland Publishing, 1993). *Published works*: Cookbook: "Native American Foods (Foods the Indian Gave Us)" (Children's Coloring Book, 1972). Novels: "Windsong: Texas Cherokee Princess," 1986; "The Raven's Tales" (bilingual Cherokee legends), 1987; & "The Pleiades Stones," 1987. Recording: The Raven Sings (Native American Songs). Play: "The Raven & the Redbird: The Indian Life of Sam Houston & His Cherokee Wife (Talihina Rogers)" a play in three acts, 1965, reissued in 1993. "The Raven Speaks" (originally published as monthly newsletters written from 1968-72), 1988.

HAIRE, WENONAH GEORGE (Catawba) 1953-
(dentist)
Born November 27, 1953, York County, Rock Hill, S.C. *Education*: Clemson University, BS, 1976; Medical University of SC, Charleston, D.MD, 1979. *Principal occupation*: Dentist. *Home address*: 191 Country Club Dr ., Rock Hill, SC 29730. *Community activities*: Education committee, Career Development Center; chair-

man, Dental Health Month, 1985; Girl Scout Aid. *Memberships*: Tri-County Dental Society , Rock Hill, SC (secretary, 1985); U.S. Public Health Service (Lt., inactive reserve); Medical University Alumni Association; First Baptist Church. *Interests*: Enjoys travel vacations (Mexico and U.S.); collects Indian jewelry , paintings and pottery; enjoys pottery making (Catawba traditional coil method); enjoys canning. Only female dentist in Rock Hill, S.C.; just had her first child. *Biographical source*: Charlotte Observer article entitled Rock Hill Dentist Drills by Day , Fills by Night.

HAKKINEN, ELISABETH S.
(*Ka-ah-Kah-wistaa*)1914-
(historian)
Born January 11, 1914, Skagway, Alaska. *Education*: San Bernardino Junior College, 1930-1932; Western College, Oxford, Ohio, BA, 1935. *Principal occupation*: Historian. *Home address*: Box 236, Haines, Alaska 99827 (907) 766-2128. *Affiliation*: Historian (Director/Curator Emerita), The Sheldon Museum & Culture Center , Haines, Alaska, 1960-90; retired to write local history . *Other professional posts*: Teacher, 1935-40, 1949-60. *Awards, honors*: Adopted Kag-wantan, Eagle Clan, Grizzly Bear House; Alaska Mother of the Year, 1966. *Biographical source*: Who's Who of American Women. *Published works*: Song of the Chilkat People; Haines: The First Century; A personal Look at the Sheldon Museum. All published by the Sheldon Museum.

HALBRITTER, RAY (Oneida) 1953-
(Oneida Nation representative)
Born July 17, 1953, Oneida, N.Y . *Education*: Syracuse University, BA, 1985; Harvard University, JD, 1990. *Principal occupation*: Oneida Nation representative. *Home address*: P.O. Box 1, West Rd., Oneida, NY 13421 (315) 829-3090 (work). *Affiliation*: Representative & CEO, Oneida Indian Nation, Oneida, NY . *Other professional post*: Adjunct assistant professor , New York University, New York, NY. *Community activities*: Lecturer. *Memberships*: National Congress of American Indian; USET. *Awards, honors*: Man of the Year, by the Leatherstocking Country, NY; Grand Marshal, Rome (NY) America Days. *Biographical sources*: "Ray Halbritter," Central New Yorker Magazine, Nov. 12, 1993; "The Man Behind the Casino," Business Journal, Nov. 29 - Dec. 12, 1993; "A Salute to Those Who Came Before Us...," Rome Observer, July 20, 1993; "Ray Halbritter," Syracuse New Times, June 9-June I6, 1993.

HALCROW, FRANK THOMAS
(Indian band chief)
Affiliation: Grouard Indian Band, Grouard, Alberta, Canada T0G 1C0 (403) 523-4471.

*HALFTOWN, ELDENA
(editor)
Affiliation: O-He-Yoy-Noh, Seneca Nation, Plummer Bldg., Box 231, Salamanca, NY 14779.

HALL, C.R. (CLIFF) 1933-
(owner-Indian shop)
Born October 19, 1933, Las V egas, N.M. *Education*: McMurry College (4 years). *Principal occupation*: Owner-Indian shop. *Home address*: (Burro Flat) 306 10th St., Alamogordo, NM 88310 (505) 437-8126 (of fice). *Affiliation*: Owner, Squash Blossom, 304 10th, Alamagordo, NM, 1973-. *Military service*: U.S. Navy, 1955-57.

Community activities: Alamogordo Music Theater (past president); Alamogordo's Barbershop Chorus (member & past president). *Memberships*: Indian Arts and Crafts Association (charter member); Downtown Merchants Association (past president-3 terms); Sertoma Club of Alamogordo. *Interests*: All Indian arts and crafts; extensive travels to all parts of Navaho, Zuni and Hopi Reservations; Hopi kachina dolls.

HALL, CALVIN (Meherrin)
(tribal chairperson)
Affiliation: Meherrin Indian Tribe, P.O. Box 508, Winton, NC 27986 (919) 358-4375.

*HALL, LESLIE
(tribal health director)
Affiliation: Greenville Rancheria Tribal Health, Box 279, Greenville, CA 95947 (916) 284-6135.

HALL, PATRICIA A. 1945-
(attorney)
Born November 18, 1945, Oak Park, Ill. *Education*: Arizona State University, BA, 1970; Arizona State University College of Law, JD, 1976. *Principal occupation*: Attorney. *Home address*: 7859 County Road 203, Durango, CO 81301 (303) 247-1755 (work). *Affiliation*: Sr. Associate, Maynes, Bradford, Shipps & Sheftel, Durango, CO, 1991-; General Counsel for the Southern Ute Indian Tribe. *Community activities*: La Plata County Judge, 1982-89; Southern Ute, Chief Judge, 1980-82, Ute Mountain Ute Judge, 1980-82; Jicarilla Apache Alt. Judge, 1982; Domestic Violence Prevention Coalition. Memberships: Colorado Bar Association; Arizona State Bar; Navajo Nation Bar Association. *Awards, honors*: 1986 Judge of the Year, Colorado Dept. of Heath; 1988 Excellence in Criminal Justice Award, La Plata County Sheriff's Department. *Interests*: Indian law, criminal law; travels to Mexico (regularly) and Africa; music, concerts, gardening, skiing.

*HALL, ROBERT
(school administrator)
Affiliation: Wahpeton Indian School, 832 8th St. North, Wahpeton, ND 58075 (701) 642-3796.

HALL, TEX (Hidatsa) 1956-
(school principal)
Born September 18, 1956, Watford, N.D. *Education*: University of South Dakota, MA, 1980. *Address*: Box 488, Mandaree, ND 58757 (701) 759-3311. *Affiliation*: Mandaree Day School, Mandaree, ND. *Memberships*: North Dakota Indian Education Association; North Dakota Stockman's Association; National Indian Athletic Association; North Dakota & National Principals Association. *Awards, honors*: Outstanding Young Men of America, 1983, '86, '87. *Interests*: "Traveled to Europe, Canada, Soviet Union, Mexico, Puerto Rico & Western U.S., and most Indian reservations, instructing at basketball camps & playing basketball tournaments."

HALLER, ROSEMARIE
(Indian band chief)
Affiliation: High Bar Indian Band, c/o Fraser Canyon Indian Administration, Box 400, Lytton, BC, Canada, V0K 1Z0 (604) 455-2279.

*HALSEY, THERESA
(radio host/producer)
Affiliation: "Indian Voices," KGNU 88.5 FM - Public Radio, P.O. Box 885, Boulder, CO 80306 (800) 737-3030.

HALVORSON, ELMER
(museum curator)
Affiliation: Buffalo Trails Museum, Box 22, Epping, ND 58843 (701) 859-3512.

HALVORSON, VINCENT J.
(monument supt.)
Affiliation: Pipestone National Monument, P.O. Box 727, Pipestone, MN 56164 (507) 825-5464.

HAMILTON, ANGE (*Aunko*) (Kiowa)
(attorney)
Born in Lawton, Okla. *Education*: University of Oklahoma, BA, 1980; Oklahoma City University School of Law, JD, 1991. *Home address*: Rt. 1, Box 176, Gracemont, OK 73042 (405) 840-5255 (work). *Affiliation*: Staff Attorney, OK Indian Legal Services, Oklahoma City, OK, 1992- *Other professional posts*: General Counsel, Wichita & Affiliated Tribes, Anadarko, OK, 1991- *Community activities*: Children's Review Board Commission; Campaign for Justice & Human Development (board of directors); Oklahoma City Archdiocese. *Memberships*: OK Bar Assn; American Bar Assn; OK Indian Bar Assn; Native American Bar Assn; Native American Indian Bar Assn. *Awards, honors*: American Assn. of University Women Fellow, 1990-91; recipient of OK Bar Foundation Scholarship, 1990; Assn. of Business & Professional Women Scholarship, 1989-90; Daughters of American Revolution Scholarship. *Interests*: Federal Indian law; tribal court development; Indian child welfare.

HAMILTON, D'ANNE MARIE (*Paaniikaaluk*) (Inupiat Eskimo) 1959-
(producer, host)
Born July 12, 1957, Kotzebue, Alaska. *Education*: Kauai Community College, 1978; University of Alaska, Fairbanks, 1979; Arizona State University, 1979-81. *Principal occupation*: Producer/host. *Address*: Alaska Public Radio Network, 810 E. Ninth Ave., Anchorage, AK 99501 (907) 277-2776. *Affiliations*: Production assistant, Northwest Arctic Instructional Television Center, Kotzebue (1 year); reporter, K.O.T.Z. Radio Station, Kotzebue (1 year); producer-reporter, Alaska Public Radio Network, Anchorage, 1989-; producer-reporter, National Native News, Anchorage, 1989-94; producer/host, National Native News, 1994-. *Community activities*: Rural Alaska Television Network Board, 1983; Inupiat Ilitqusiat Committee, 1983. *Membership*: Alaska Press Club; Native American Journalists Association. *Awards, honors*: Alaska Native Fellowship, Grotto Foundation. *Interests*: "I am interested in increasing coverage of Native issues, particularly in the state of Alaska. I am also interested in steps by Inuit towards political unity, and was part of a three-person reporting team covering the Inuit Circumpolar Conference in July of 1989 in Greenland. I lived in Germany for nearly four years, and did a bit of traveling in Europe. I speak some German and Spanish, and hope to begin learning Russian this year." *Biographical sources*: Anchorage Daily News; Tundra Times; Arctic Sounder.

HAMILTON, HAMILTON, Sr. (Athapascan)
(AK village chief)
Affiliation: Native Village of Shagelkuk, Shageluk, AK 99665 (907) 473-8239.

HAMILTON, MARY G.
(publisher)
Affiliation: American Indian Art Mag., 7314 E. Osborn, Scottsdale, AZ 85251 (602) 994-5445.

*HAMLEY, JEFFREY
(Turtle Mountain Ojibwe)
(program director)
Born in North Dakota. Education: Western Washington University, BA; Harvard University, MA, PhD candidate. *Address & Affiliation*: Harvard Native American Program, Graduate School of Education, Read House, Appian Way, Cambridge, MA 02138 (617) 495-4923.

HAMMEREN, PATSY (Sioux)
(elementary school principal)
Affiliation: Mandaree Day School, P.O. Box 488, Mandaree, ND 58757 (701) 759-3311.

HAMMERSMITH, BERNICE
(director-Indian council)
Affiliation: Aboriginal Women's Council of Saskatchewan, 62-17th St. West, Prince Albert, Saskatchewan, Canada S6V 3X3 (306) 763-6005.

*HAMMETT, PAULA
(editor)
Affiliation: Native Self-Sufficiency, Seventh Generation Fund, P.O. Box 10, Forestville, CA 95436 (707) 887-1559.

HAMMOND, DICK
(Indian band chief)
Affiliation: Ross River Indian Band, Ross River, Yukon, Canada Y0B 1S0 (403) 969-2278.

HAMP, ERIC P. 1920-
(professor emeritus)
Born November 16, 1920, London, England. *Education*: Amherst College, BA, 1942; Harvard University, MA, 1948, PhD, 1954. *Principal occupation*: Professor emeritus of linguistics & behavioral science, University of Chicago, 1950-. *Home address*: 5200 So. Greenwood Ave., Chicago, IL 60615 (312) 324-9170. *Affiliation*: University of Chicago (instructor-professor, 1950-91; Robert Maynard Hutchins Distinguished Service Professor of Linguistics, Psychology, 1973-91). *Military service*: U.S. Army, 1946-47 (Sgt.). *Community service*: IL Place-Name Survey (chairman, 1966-); consultant U.S. Office of Education, NEH, NSF; Council on International Exchange of Scholars (advisory committee, 1966-); UNESCO (U.S. National Commission, 1972-); among many others. *Memberships*: American Philosophical Society (Phillips Fund Committee, 1977-); Linguistic Society of America (president, 1971); Society for the Study of Indigenous Languages of the Americas (president, 1986-87); Modern Language Association (appointed to various committees); member of many other societies. *Awards, honors*: Collitz Professor, 1960, Linguistic Society of America; hon. LHD, Amherst College, 1972; Guggenheim Fellow, 1973-74; Fellow, American Academy of Arts & Sciences, 1976-; Robert Maynard Hutchins Distinguished Service Professor, University of Chicago; various guest professorships. *Interests*: Languages and cultures of the American Indian, the Balkins, and the Celts; travel and fieldwork: Ojibwa, Cheyenne, Quileute, several Salishan, Eskimo, Otomanguean of Oazaca. "I have worked principally in Ojibwa, as well as other Algonguian; Quileute; Otomanguen languages of Mexico; and on problems of North American language classification." *Biographical sources*: Who's Who in America; Who's Who in the World; Directory of American Scholars; Dictionary of International Biography; American Men & Women of Science; Men of Achievement;

The Blue Book. *Published works*: Associate editor, 1966-92, emeritus editor, 1992-(devoted to Native American languages), International Journal of American Linguistics (University of Chicago Press); editor, Native American Text Series (University of Chicago Press, 1974-); author of publications on Ojibwa, Narragansett, Algonquian, Wiyot, Yurok, Quileute, Upper Chehalis, Comox, Kwakwala, Karok, Miwok, Zuni, Crow, Eskimo, etc. Contributed to over 1,200 publications (articles, chapters, books).

HAMPTON, CAROL CUSSEN McDONALD (Caddo) 1935-
(field officer-Native American Ministry)
Born September 18, 1935, Oklahoma City, Okla. *Education*: H. Sophie Newcomb College, New Orleans, LA, 1953-54; University of Oklahoma, BA, 1957, MA, 1973, PhD, 1984. *Principal occupation*: Field Officer-Native American Ministry. *Home address*: 1414 N. Hudson, Oklahoma City, OK 73103. *Affiliations*: Teaching assistant, University of Oklahoma, Norman, 1973-84; associate director and coordinator, Consortium for Graduate Opportunities for American Indians, University of California, Berkeley; Field Officer for Native American Ministry of the Episcopal Church, 1986-. *Community activities*: Caddo Indian Tribe of Oklahoma (tribal council, 1976-); Caddo Tribal Constitution Committee, 1975-76; Oklahoma City Area Indian Health Service (advisory board); Junior League of Oklahoma City, 1965-; National Committee on Indian Work, Episcopal Church (Co-chair, 1986-); World Council of Churches (commissioner, Program to Combat Racism, 1985); Oklahoma State Regents for Higher Education on Social Justice (member, advisory board, 1984-); Commissioner of Programs to Combat Racism, 1985-91; Council of Native American Ministries (vice-chair, 1988-); National Council of Church's (Racial Justice Working Group Co-convenor, 1991-). *Memberships*: National Indian Education Association; National Historical Society; Oklahoma Historical Society; Western Historical Association; Organization of American Historians; American Historical Association; Oklahoma Foundation for the Humanities (Trustee, 1983-86). Awards, honors: Francis C. Allen Fellowship, D'Arcy McNickle Center for the History of the American Indian, Newberry Library, 1983; State of Oklahoma Human Rights Award, 1987. *Interests*: My interests are in history, philosophy and religion of American Indians as well as social and racial justice. *Biographical sources*: Who's Who Among American Women; Who's Who in the World; etc. *Published work*: Indian Colonization in the Cherokee Outlet & Western Indian Territory (Chronicles of Oklahoma, 1976). *Articles*: "Peyote and the Law", Between Two Worlds, Oklahoma Series, 1986; "Why Write History? A Caddo Grandmother's Perspective", The Creative Woman, Fall, 1987; "Opposition to Indian Diversity in the 20th Century", American Indian Policy and Cultural Values, UCLA, 1987; "Tribal Esteem and the American Idian Historian", An American Indian Identity, San Diego State University Publications, 1988; "A Heritage Denied: Racial Justice for American Indians", Sojourners, Jan. 1991.

HAMPTON, JAMES WILBURN, M.D. (*Sheko Okti Onna)* (Chickasaw/Choctaw) 1931-
(physician & educator)
Born September 15, 1931, Durant, Okla. *Education*: University of Oklahoma, BA, 1952; University of Oklahoma, School of Medicine, MD,

1956. *Principal occupation*: Physician & educator. *Home address*: 1414 N. Hudson, Oklahoma City, OK 73103. *Affiliations*: Medical Director, Cancer Center of Southwest, Baptist Medical Center, Oklahoma City; Clinical Professor of Medicine, University of Oklahoma Medical School, 1956-. *Other professional posts*: Professor and head, Hematology-Oncology, University of Oklahoma Medical School, 1971-77; head Hematology Research Laboratories, Oklahoma Medical Research Foundation, 1971-77; National Cancer Institute, Chairperson, Network for Cancer Control in American Indians/Alaska Natives, 1990-. *Community activities*: Oklahoma County Medical Society (member, board of directors, 1979-82, 1989-92; editor, The Bulletin, 1983-); Heritage Hills, Inc. (member, board of directors, 1973-90); Central Oklahoma American Indian Health Council (board member, 1974-90); Faculty House (board member, 1974-75); Frontiers of Science Foundation of Oklahoma, Inc. (board member, 1974-). *Memberships*: American Association for the Advancement of Science; American Association for Cancer Research, Southwest Section; American Association of Pathologists and Bacteriologist; American Association of University Professors; American Federation for Clinical Research; American Genetic Association; American Medical Association; American Physiological Society; American Psychosomatic Society; American Society for Clinical Pharmacology and Therapeutics; American Society for Clinical Oncology; American Society of Angiology; American Society of Hematology; Central Society for Clinical Research; International Society on Thrombosis and Haemostasis; New York Academy of Sciences; Oklahoma County Medical Society; Oklahoma State Medical Association; Sigma Xi; Southern Society for Clinical Investigation; Southwest Oncology (Chemotherapy Study) Group; Association of American Indian Physicians (president, 1979-80, 1989-90); National Hemophilia Foundation; National Institutes of Health; American Heart Association; American Cancer Society (member of Committee on Cancer in the Socioeconomically Disadvantaged, Medicine & Scientific Committee; member at large, Board of Directors, 1990-). *Consultations*: Consultant in Medicine, Tinker Air Force Base Hospital, Oklahoma City, Okla., 1965-; consultant for National Institutes of Health, National Cancer Institute, 1973-76, 1988-89; National Heart & Lung Institute, 1971-92; consultant for Navajo Health Authority, 1974-76; consultant for Regional Breast Cancer Detection and Treatment Center, 1974-79. *Awards, honors*: NIH Career Development Award, 1965-75; Angiology Research Foundation Honors Achievement Award, 1967-68; Preservation and Restoration Award, Heritage Hills Association, 1973; chairman, Planning Committee for Native American Medical School, sponsored by the Navajo Health Authority, 1974-76; associate editor, Journal of Laboratory and Clinical Medicine, 1974-76; member, Blue Cord, 1974; Indian Physician of the Year Award, 1987; Special Certificate of Appreciation from the National Cancer Prevention and Control Intervention Research Program for Special Populations, 1990; Special Recognition from National Indian Health Board. *Interests*: Cancer in American Indians/Alaska Natives. *Biographical sources*: Who's Who in the South and Southwest; American Men of Science; The International Registry of Who's Who. *Published works*: Experimental articles, non-experimental articles, books, pamphlets, editorials in journal "Cancer in Minori-

ties" ed. L. Jones, Ph.D., 1989; abstracts presented at national or international meetings; lectures.

HANE, MARIANNA (Choctaw)
(health director)
Affiliation: Choctaw Health Center, Route 7, Box R-50, Philadelphia, MS 39350 (601) 656-221 1.

HANEY, JERRY (Seminole of Oklahoma)
(tribal chief)
Affiliation: Seminole Nation of Oklahoma, P.O. Box 1498, Wewoka, OK 74884 (405) 257-6287.

***HANEY, MICHAEL (Seminole/Sioux)**
(consultant, foundation chair)
Affiliations: Consultant, American Indian Arbitration Association, Minneapolis, MN; chairman, Board of Directors, American Indian Ritual Object Repatriation Foundation, 463 East 57th St., New York, NY 10022 (212) 980-9441; vice-chairman of the Newcomer Band of the Seminole Nation of Oklahoma.

***HANITCHAK, MICHAEL**
(instructor)
Affiliation: Instructor of American Indians in Film & Video, Dartmouth College, Native American Studies Dept., 306-307 Bartlett Hall, Hinman Box 6152, Hanover, NH 03755 (603) 646-3530.

***HANLEY, BETTY**
(radio station manager)
Affiliation: KEYA - 88.5 FM, Turtle Mountain Chippewa Tribe, P.O. Box 190, Belcourt, ND 58316 (701) 477-5686.

HANLEY, JOY J.
(executive director)
Affiliations: Executive director, Arizona Indian Centers, Inc., 1515 E. Osborn Rd., Annex, Phoenix, AZ 85014 (602) 279-0618; president, Association on American Indian Affairs, New York, NY.

***HANRAHAN, GENE**
(radio station manager)
Affiliation: WYRU - 1160 AM, Lumbee Tribe, P.O. Box 0711, Red Springs, NC 28377 (919) 843-5946.

HANSEN, ANNIE (Lenape-Delaware) 1950-
(writer)
Born February 10, 1950, Seattle, Wash. *Education*: University of Washington, Lewis & Clark College, Southern Oregon State College. *Principal occupation*: Writer. *Address*: P.O. Box 415, Indianola, WA 98342 (206) 297-7619. *Memberships*: Native Writers Circle of the Americas; NW Native Writers Circle; Wordcraft Circle Mentor Program. *Published works*: Fiction editor, "The Raven Chronicles," Seattle, WA; numerous works of fiction in journals, poetry & essays.

***HANSEN, ED**
(VP hospital operations)
Affiliation: Yukon-Kuskokwim Hospital, Pouch 3000, Bethel, AK 99559 (907) 543-371 1.

HANSEN, EMMA I. (Pawnee)
(museum curator/ethnologist)
Born March 5, 1947, Oklahoma City, Okla. *Education*: Oklahoma State University, BA; University of Oklahoma, MAs (Sociology & Anthropology). *Principal occupation*: Curator-Plains Indian Museum. *Address*: P.O. Box 1784, Cody, WY 82414 (307) 587-4771 (work). *Affiliation*: Buf-

falo Bill Historical Center, Cody, WY, 1991-. *Other professional post*: Anthropology Dept., University of Oklahoma; Oklahoma Museum of Natural History. *Membership*: American Anthropological Association; American Association of Museums (board of curator's committee). *Awards, honors*: Ford Foundation Fellow; Newberry Library Fellowship; Sequoyah Graduate Award; American Philosophical Society Grant. *Interests*: Plains Indian culture and ethnohistory; Pawnee history, contemporary art.

HANSEN, JOAN LOUISE (Cherokee) 1945-
(reporter, photographer)
Born February 2, 1945, New Orleans, La. *Education*: Bacone College. *Principal occupation*: Reporter, photographer. Resides in Muskogee, OK. *Affiliation*: Reporter, photographer, Muskogee Daily Phoenix & Times Democrat. *Awards, honors*: Paintings shown at Philbrook Indian Annual, Tulsa; paintings shown at Department of the Interior, Washington, DC; numerous awards at local fairs. *Interests*: Reading of Plains Indian traditions and legends; art.

*HANSEN, TERRI C. (Nebraska Winnebago) 1953-
(journalist)
Born October 18, 1953, Portland, Oreg. *Education*: Clark College (Vancouver, WA), 1990-92. *Principal occupation*: Journalist. *Address*: P.O. Box 1039, Long Beach, WA 98631 (206) 642-0955 (work). *Affiliations*: Bureau Chief, Pacific NW Bureau (OR, WA, ID, northern CA, B.C.), News From Indian Country, Hayward, WI, 1992-. *Other professional post*: Editor, Washington State, Portland Indian News, 1992-93; correspondent, Native American Smoke Signals, Meyer, AZ, 1993-. *Community activities*: Local Indian Child Welfare Advisory Council; Council of Better Business Bureau's National Panel of Consumer Arbitrators. *Memberships*: Winnebago Tribe of Nebraska; Native American Journalist's Association, 1990-; Wordcraft Circle of Native Writers, 1993-. *Award*: The Oregonian Publisher's Award of Excellence, 1990. *Interests*: "Vocational - As a reporter of regional and national Indian issues for several regional and national Indian newspapers, I am particularly concerned with environmental and health issues as they pertain to American Indians. Avocational - mountaineering (member of Mazama's Mountaineering Club, Portland, OR); white water kayaking, hiking, backpacking."

HANSON, BETH ROSE (Eastern Cherokee) 1957-
(administrator)
Born December 14, 1957, Biloxi, Miss. *Education*: University of Wisconsin, Stevens Point, BS, 1989; University of Wisconsin, Oshkosh, MBA (current). *Principal occupation*: Administrator. *Home address*: 425 Front St., Stevens Point, WI 54481 (715) 342-1444 (work). *Affiliations*: Program Manager, Las Vegas Indian Center, Las Vegas, NV, 1989-90; Coordinator, Weekend College Program for Native Americans, University of Wisconsin-Stevens Point, 1991-. *Other professional post*: Benefits administrator for Command Technologies of Virginia, 1993-. *Military service*: U.S. Army Journalist (enlisted member serving in Washington, D.C.). *Awards, honors*: Graduate Cum Laude from UW-SP; awarded the Chancellor's Leadership Award upon graduation in May 1989; State of Wisconsin Native American Leadership Award recipient; 1992 Mrs. North Carolina; 1992 National

Mrs. U.S. Photogenic Winner, Las Vegas, NV. *Interests*: "Current primary career focus is developing education programs for Native Americans and transitional housing projects for homeless Native American families."

*HANSON, CECILE M. (Duwamish)
(tribal chairperson)
Affiliation: Duwamish Tribe, 212 Wells Ave. S., #C, Renton, WA 98055 (206) 244-0606.

HANSON, CHARLES E., Jr. 1917-
(museum director)
Born April 4, 1917, Holdredge, Neb. *Education*: Kearney State College (1 year); University of Colorado (2 years); Chadron State College, Honorary Doctorate of Letters. *Principal occupation*: Museum director. *Address*: HC 74, Box 18, Chadron, NE 69337 (308) 432-3843. *Affiliation*: Museum of the Fur Trade, Chadron, NE, 1978-. *Other professional post*: Editor, Museum of the Fur Trade Quarterly, 1964-; Industrial engineer. *Military service*: Civilian engineer, U.S. Air Force, 1942-44, 1952 (Post Citation Liberal AAF). *Community activities*: Member, Dawes County (NE) Travel Board. *Memberships*: Nebraska State Historical Society (life); Company of Military Historians (fellow); American Society of Arms Collectors. *Awards, honors*: Henry Fonda Tourism Award, 1985; Chamber of Commerce Ambassador, Magic Key Award, 1989. *Interests*: Hobbies - travel & hunting; museum oriented travel all over U.S., Canada, Alaska, and Europe. *Biographical source*: Who's Who in the Midwest. *Published works*: The North West Gun (Nebraska State Historical Society, 1955); The Plains Rifle (Stackpole, 1960); The Hawken Rifle, Its Place in History (The Fur Press, 1979); The David Adams Journals (Museum of the Fur Trade, 1994).

HANSON, ED (Eastern Cherokee)
(executive director)
Affiliation: Cherokee Historical Association, P.O. Box 398, Cherokee, NC 28719 (704) 497-21 11.

HANSON, FRANKLIN S.
(school supt.)
Affiliation: Quileute Tribal School, P.O. Box 39, LaPush, WA 98350 (206) 374-2061.

HAOZOUS, BOB (Chiricahua Apache-Navajo) 1943-
(artist)
Born April 1, 1943, Los Angeles, Calif. *Education*: Utah State University; California College of Arts and Crafts. *Principal occupation*: Artist. Resides in Santa Fe, NM. *Exhibitions*: Scottsdale National Indian Arts Exhibition; Philbrook Art Center American Indian Artists Exhibitions; Oakland Museum Indian Show; Southwest Fine Arts Biennial-Museum of New Mexico. *Permanent collections*: Heard Museum; Southern Plains Indian Museum; Crafts Center, Anadarko, OK. *Awards*: First Prize, Sante Fe Indian Market, 1971; Gold Medal, Wood Sculpture I and II, Heard Museum, 1973, 1974; Grand Prize, Heard Museum National Sculpture Competition, 1975; among others.

HAPPYJACK, ALLAN
(Indian band chief)
Affiliation: Waswanipi (Cree) Indian Band, Waswanipi River, Waswanipi, Quebec, Canada J0Y 3C0 (819) 753-2587.

*HARASICK
(health center director)
Affiliation: Chief Andrew Isaac Health Center, 1638 Cowles St., Fairbanks, AK 99701 (907) 451-6682.

HARDEN, PHYLLIS (Pomo)
(tribal vice-chairperson)
Affiliation: Upper Lake Pomo Tribal Council, P.O. Box 245272, Sacramento, CA 95820 (916) 371-2576.

*HARDING, SHIRLEY
(museum curator)
Affiliation: Hubbell Trading Post, National Historic Site, P.O. Box 150, Ganado, AZ 86505 (602) 755-3475.

*HARDMAN, MARY GEORGE
(executive director)
Affiliation: Survival International, U.S.A., Washington, DC 20008 (202) 265-1077.

*HARDWICK, FRANK
(editor)
Affiliation: Navajo Area Newsletter, BIA, Box M, Window Rock, AZ 86515 (602) 871-5156.

*HARDWICK, SHEILAH
(foundation director)
Affiliation: 4 Directions Foundation, 23431 130th Ave., SE, Kent, WA 98031 (206) 854-161 1.

HARDY, DAN
(Indian band chief)
Affiliation: Lake Helen First Nation (Red Rock) Indian Band, Box 1030, Nipigon, Ontario, Canada P0T 2J0 (807) 887-2510.

HARDY, JAMES
(Indian band chief)
Affiliation: Rocky Bay Indian Band, MacDiamond, Ontario, Canada P0T 2P0 (807) 885-3401.

HARDY, JOE C.
(school principal)
Affiliation: Low Mountain Boarding School, Chinle, AZ 86503 (602) 725-3308.

HARE, JOSEPH F.
(Indian band chief)
Affiliation: West Bay Indian Band, Excelsior P.O., West Bay, Ontario, Canada P0P 1G0 (705) 377-5362.

*HARJO, ALAN (Creek)
(hospital director)
Affiliation: Creek Nation Community Hospital, P.O. Box 228, Okemah, OK 74859 (918) 623-1424.

*HARJO, DUKE (Creek)
(tribal chief)
Affiliation: Alabama-Quassarte Tribal Town, P.O. Box 537, Henryetta, OK 74437 (918) 652-8708.

HARJO, JOY (Muscogee Creek) 1951-
(professor, writer, musician)
Born in 1951, Tulsa, Okla. *Education*: Institute of American Indian Arts, 1968; University of New Mexico, BA, 1976; University of Iowa, MFA (Creative Writing), 1978; Anthropology Film Center (Santa Fe, NM). *Principal occupation*: Professor, writer, musician. *Address*: Two Red Horses, Inc., P.O. Box 4999, Albuquerque, NM 87196 (505) 897-9092 (work). *Affiliations*: Lecturer,

Arizona State University, 1980-81; instructor, Santa Fe Community College, 1983-84; instructor, Institute of American Indian Arts, 1983-84 & 1978-79; assistant professor, University of Colorado, Boulder, 1985-; associate professor, University of Arizona, Tucson, 1988-90; professor, Creative Writing Program, Dept. of English, University of New Mexico, Albuquerque, 1991-. *Other professional posts*: Editor, Americans Before Columbus, 1979-80; contributing editor, Contact II, 1984-; contributing editor, Tyuonyi, 1985-; High Plains Literary Review (poetry editor, 1986-89; poetry advisor, 1989-). *Community activities*: Advisory Committee, Spirits of the Present, Native American Public Broadcasting Consortium and the Smithsonian; "High Plains Review" Poetry Advisor; Steering Committee of the En'owkin Centre International School of Writing (for Native American writers). *Membership*: Muscogee Tribe. *Awards, honors*: Academy of American Poetry Award, University of New Mexico, 1st Place in Poetry, 1976; Writers Forum, University of Colorado, 1st Place in Poetry, 1977; National Endowment for the Arts Creative Writing Fellowship, 1978 & 1992; Santa Fe Festival for the Arts, 1st Place Poetry, 1980; Outstanding Young Women of America, 1978 & 1984; Pushcart Prize Poetry, 1988 & 1990; Recipient of 1989 Arizona Commission on the Arts - Creative Writing Fellowship, and two NEA Creative Writing Fellowships; 1990 American Indian Distinguished Achievement Award; 1991 William Carlos Williams Award from the Poetry Society of America; the Delmore Schwartz Award from New York University; The American Book Award, 1991; Poetry Award from the Mountains and Plains Booksellers Association, 1991; one of the winners of the Josephine Miles Award for Excellence in Literature from PEN Oakland, 1991; Delmore Schwartz Memorial Award, NYU, 1991; Honorary Doctorate, Benedictine College, 1992; Woodrow Wilson Fellowship, Green Mountain College, Poultney, VT, 1993; Witter Bynner Poetry Fellowship, 1994. *Interests*: Travels extensively around the country giving readings & workshops; plays saxophone with her band, "Poetic Justice." *Screen writing experience*: Co-writer with Henry Greenberg, "The Gaan Story," one-hour dramatic story, produced by Silvercloud Video Productions; assistant screenwriter with Henry Greenberg, "The Beginning," half-hour dramatic story, produced by Native American Public Broadcasting Consortium (NAPBC), 1983-84; producer, "We Are One, Umonho," a series of eight 20-minute scripts for Nebraska Educational Television (NET), 1984; "Maiden of Deception Pass," a one-hour dramatic screenplay for NAPBC, 1984-85; "I Am Different From My Brother," rewrite of six half-hour scripts, NAPBC, 1986; "The Runaway," half-hour teleplay, NET, 1986; "Indians & AIDS," 20 & 30 second public service announcements for national television, Powhatan Renape Nation, 1988; "When We Used to Be Humans," in development (American Film Foundation); co-producer & writer, "The Sacred Revolt: The Red Sticks' Wars," full-length dramatic story. *Other film experience*: "American Indian Artist Series II" (composed poetry for narration & worked as production assistant, PBS, 1986); appeared in "Wildflowers," with Helen Hayes (KERA-TV documentary as a storyteller, PBS, 1992); reader for audio library recording, Circle of Nations, Voices & Visions of American Indians, edited by John Gattuso (Beyond Words, 1993); narrator, "Sand Creek," dramatic on-hour movie for Deborah Dennison (Santa Fe, 1994); narra-

tor, the "Native Americans" 6-part series (Turner Broadcasting, 1994). *Biographical sources*: International Authors & Writers Who's Who; International Who's Who of Authors; World Who's Who of Women; Personalities of the West & Midwest; Foremost Women of the 20th Century; 5,00 Personalities of the World; The International Directory of Distinguished Leadership; Who's Who in U.S. Writers, Editors, & poets; Contemporary American Writers; Poets & Writers. *Published works*: She has published 4 books of poetry including, "She Had Some Horses" (Thunder's Mouth Press, New York, NY) In "Mad Love and War" (Wesleyan University Press, 1990); collaborated with photographer/astronomer Stephen Strom to produce, "Secrets From the Center of the World" (University of Arizona Press); The Woman Who Fell From the Sky (W.W. Norton, 1994); also, an anthology of Native women's writing, "Reinventing the Enemy's Language" (University of Arizona Press, 1994); anthology, Talking Leaves, Contemporary Native American Short Stories (Dell, 1991). *Forthcoming*: A Love Supreme (W.W. Norton); Children's book, "The GoodLuck Cat" (Harcourt Brace).

*HARJO, LISA
(Indian center director)
Affiliation: Denver Native Americans United, Denver Indian Center, 4407 Morrison Rd., Denver, CO 80219 (303) 937-0401.

HARJO, SUZAN SHOWN
(Cheyenne, Hodulgee Muscogee) 1945-
(writer, poet, policy analyst, arts curator)
Born June 2, 1945, El Reno, Okla. *Principal occupation*: Writer, poet, policy analyst, arts curator. *Address*: 403 10th St., SE, Washington, DC 20003 (202) 547-5531 Fax 546-6727 (work). *Affiliation*: President, Morning Star Institute, Washington, DC, 1984- (a non-profit organization for Native American cultural rights and arts advocacy). *Other professional posts*: Special assistant for Indian Legislation, Carter Administration, 1978-79; co-founder & vice-president, Native Children's Survival (executive director, 1984-89); co-chair, Howard Simons Fund for Indian Journalists, 1989-; vice president & secretary, Earth Investment, Inc.; general partner, Pasamaquoddy Technology. *Community activities*: Common Cause (national governing board, 1982-88); National Museum of the American Indian (Founding Trustee; member, executive committee, and collections committee; chair, program planning committee); lead negotiator of both the 1989 agreement with the Smithsonian Institution that led to the first repatriation law & the later agreement with the national museum community which resulted in the Native American Grave Protection & Repatriation Act of 1990, and was key to the development of the 1991 NMAI Trustees Policy Statement on Repatriation; Ms. Harjo currently serves on the steering committee and as advocacy committee co-chair of a broad-based national coalition of Indian nations and organizations & environmental, human rights & religious groups to secure legal protections for Native Peoples' sacred places and passage of the Native American Free Exercise of Religion Act of 1993. She served as co-chair of the Indian organizing committee for the 1993 March on Washington, and is a charter member and organizer of Artists in Support of American Indian Religious Freedom, formed in 1992. She has helped Indian nations to recover nearly a million acres of land and to

achieve appropriations & protections for sacred sites, natural resources, child welfare, health and other social services programs, hospitals, schools and cultural concerns. She has championed treaty rights and individual civil liberties cases, and has developed key federal Indian policy in Washington, DC for nearly two decades, conducting more than 350 successful legislative and appropriation efforts. On December 29, 1990, she participated in the 100-year commemoration of the Massacre of Lakota people at Wounded Knee. At the end of 1990, Congress passed a formal resolution apologizing tot he descendants of the victims of the 1890 Massacre. At the end of 1991, the legislation to establish a Little Big Horn Indian Memorial and to drop the name of Custer from the National Monument was signed into law. *Memberships*: Cheyenne-Arapaho Tribes; American Association of Museums (Committee on Museum & Native American Collaboration); Museum of the American Indian Heye Foundation (Trustee, 1983-90); National Congress of American Indians (executive director, 1984-89); The Association of American Cultures (board member, 1990-); National Commission on Libraries & Information Services Native American Task Force (board member, 1990-); American Indian Press Association (former news director). *Awards, honors*: In 1993, she presented poetry readings at the Denver Art Museum, the Cleveland Public Theatre, and the Roxy Theatre in Los Angeles. She has appeared in poetry readings with Native American poets Joy Harjo & John Trudell, and with 20 American women writers including Nikki Giovanni and Alice Walker. Her policy & political writings have appeared in many magazines, journals, and newspapers. She has been profiled in the NY Times, Lear's. Fortune. High Times, UNITY Magazine, Glamour, Rocky Mountain News, and The Plain Dealer, and has been featured on the Oprah Winfrey Show, Larry King Live, CNN's World Day, Crier & Co., and Sonya Live, among others. Also in 1993, she wrote the Foreword for George Cantor's North American Indian Landmarks (Visible Ink Press, 1993). Ms. Harjo lectures throughout the U.S., including speeches for the past decade at the Harvard Law School, the Nieman Foundation for Journalism, and the Principal's Institute. She has presented poetry and/or lectures at various other universities and colleges. In 1991, she read with author, Michael Dorris from "The Crown of Columbus," at Chapters in Washington, DC. In 1992, she keynoted with Rev. Jesse Jackson the Multicultural Leadership Summit in January in Washington, DC, and shared a keynote address with California State Assemblyman Tom Hayden to open the "Seeds of Change" Conference in Sept. in Santa Fe, NM. *Published works*: Ms. Harjo's poetry has been published in journals, anthologies & textbooks.

HARLOW, FRANCIS H. 1928-
(physicist)
Born January 22, 1928, Seattle, Wash. *Education*: University of Washington, BS, 1949, PhD, 1953. *Principal occupation*: Theoretical physicist. *Home address*: 1407 11th St., Los Alamos, NM. 87544. Affiliations: Staff member, Los Alamos Scientific Laboratory, 1953-; research associate, Museum of New Mexico, 1965-. *Military service*: U.S. Army, 1946-47. *Interests*: Theoretical fluid dynamics and numerical analysis; Pueblo Indian pottery, history, technology, and artistry. *Published works*: Contemporary Pueblo Indian Pottery (Museum of New Mexico,

1965); Historic Pueblo Indian Pottery (Museum of New Mexico, 1967; reprinted 1968, '70); The Pottery of San Ildefonso, with Kenneth Chapman (School of American Research, 1970); Mattepaint Pottery of the Tewa, Keres and Zuni Pueblos (Museum of New Mexico Press, 1973); Historic Pottery of the Pueblo Indians, 1600-1880, with Larry Frank (New York Graphic Society, 1974); Modern Pueblo Pottery, 1880-1960 (Northland Pres, 1977); Glazed Pottery of the Southwest Indians (American Indian Art Magazine, Nov. 1976); Pueblo Indian Pottery Traditions (VILTIS, 1978).

HARMON, JOAN
(museum director)
Affiliation: Nanticoke Indian Association Museum, Route 4, Box 170B, Millsboro, DE 19966.

HARPER, CHARLES (Cree)
(member-board of directors)
Affiliation: Intertribal Christian Comunications, P.O. Box 3765, Station B, W innipeg, Manitoba, Canada R2W 3R6 (204) 661-9333.

HARPER, FRED
(Indian band chief)
Affiliation: Red Sucker Lake Indian Band, Red Sucker Lake, Manitoba, Canada R0B 1H0 (204) 469-5041.

*HARPER, HENRY S.
(executive director)
Affiliation: National Indian Athletic Association, Cass Lake, MN 56633 (218) 335-8289.

HARPOLE, JACKIE (Choctaw)
(school principal)
Affiliation: Standing Pine Elementary School, Route 2, Box 236, W alnut Grove, MS 39189 (601) 267-9225.

HARRAGARRA-WATERS, DEANNA J.
(library director)
Affiliation: National Indian Law Library, Native American Rights Fund, 1522 Broadway, Boulder, CO 80302 (303) 447-8760.

*HARRELL, RAY EVANS (Nudvwiv Ani-Noquisi) (Nuyagi Keetoowah) 1941-
(conductor, artistic director & director of training)
Born December 3, 1941, Ada, Okla. *Education*: University of Tulsa, B. Mus., 1972; Manhattan School of Music, M. Mus., 1973; The Ilana Rubenfeld Center (New York, NY), RSM Certification, 1979. *Principal occupation*: Conductor, artistic director, director of training. *Home address*: 200 West 70th St., #6C, New York, NY 10023 (212) 724-2398 (work). *Affiliations*: Teacher, Manhattan School of Music, New York, NY, 1979-86; conductor, artistic director & director of training, The Magic Circle Opera Repertory Ensemble, New York, NY, 1978-. *Other professional posts*: Opera singer in New York City & on London Records with Antol Dorati; conductor, MCORE Opera & Concert & Newport Classics Recordings; private voice teacher; former editor, The New York Singing Teacher';s Bulletin; columnist, "Nuyagi Keetoowah Journal." *Military service*: U.S. Army Chorus, 1966-70 (staff sgt.); soloist, U.S. Army Field Band (touring) Fort Meade, Md., 1965-66. *Community activities*: Nuyagi Keetoowah Society (council & columnist). *Membership*: New York Singing Teacher's Association (former editor & board of directors). *Interests*: "The building of a new

Native American repertoire of contemporary musical theater; the development of a wholistic skill base for performers in that theater; the celebration and continuation of our traditional Tsa La Gi ceremonial life and the life of our Nuyagi Keetoowah community; the development of a full, traditional-scholastic community program for the children of our community ." *Biographical source*: The International Who's Who in Music & Musicians' Directory, 11th Ed., 1988.

HARRIS, GENEVA
(health systems administrator)
Affiliation: Okemah Indian Health Center, P.O. Box 429, Okemah, OK 74859 (918) 623-0555.

HARRIS, LaDONNA (Comanche) 1931-
(organization president)
Born February 15, 1931, Temple, Okla. *Education*: High school. *Address & Affiliation*: Founder/President, Americans for Indian Opportunity, 681 Juniper Hill Rd., Bernalillo, NM 87004 (505) 867-0278 (work), 1970-. *Select Lectureships*: Woodrow Wilson Fellow, 1982-; Aspen Institute; America Program Institute; W ashington School of the Institute for Policy Studies. *Networking experience*: Launched a National American Indian leadership Program: The American Indian Ambassador's Program: "Medicine Pathways for the Future"; created the first Indian-owned & operated National Computer Network dedicated to provide information of interest to Native Americans & access to the National Information Highway; developed & implemented a series of four regional issue management forums for Indian tribes in overcoming barriers to working with environment protection agency; facilitated a series of governance forums with Poarch Creek, Winnebago, Comanche, Cheyenne-Arapaho, Pawnee, Apache & Menominee tribes; among others. *Community activities*: Oklahomans for Indian Opportunity, Inc. (founder/past president, 1965-70); founder, Council for Energy Resource Tribes, 1976. *Memberships*: Haskell Indian Junior College Foundation; National Indian Business Association; National Institute for W omen of Color (advisory council); National Institute for the Environment (advisory council); Jacobson Foundation (honorary board); Native American Public Broadcasting Consortium; among others. *Awards, honors*: Outstanding American Citizen of 1965, Anadarko (OK) American Indian Exposition and the Tulsa Indian Council, 1965; Woman of the Year, 1979, Ladies Home Journal; Lucy Covington Award for a Life of Leadership; Human Rights Award: Delta Sigma Theta Society, National Education Association; Outstanding Leadership in Advancing Public Support: 1990 Census; Honorary Doctor of Law, Dartmouth College; Honorary Doctor of Humanities, Marymount College; Honorary Doctor of Public Service, W estfield State College, MA; Honorary Doctor of Humanities, Northern Michigan University. *Interests*: Traveled extensively through Latin America, Russia & the former Soviet Union & Greece. Harris has spent many years training the executive branch of the federal government that tribes are an integral part of the political fabric of the U.S. She has held hundreds of forum on the issues surrounding the interaction between tribes & federal agencies. She applies much of her energy in reinforcing & strengthening tribal government. She has encouraged tribes to reweave traditional value based methods of consensus building into their governance systems. *Published works*: Numerous books & pamphlets published by the

Americans for Indian Opportunity, including: A Resource Bibliography for Tribal Participation in Environmental Protection Activities, 1990; Tribal Governments in the U.S. Federal System, 1990; Designing the Future of the Comanche Tribe, 1990; To All My Comanche Relatives, 1990; Tribal Governments As Rural Health Providers; Designing the Economic Future of the Menominee People, 1991; Partnerships for the Protection of Tribal Environments, 1991; among others.

HARRIS, RAYMOND
(Indian band chief)
Affiliation: Chemainus Indian Band, R.R. #1, Ladysmith, British Columbia, Canada V0R 2E0 (604) 245-7155.

HARRIS, REBECCA MEANS
(historic site director)
Affiliation: Angel Mounds State Historic Site, 8215 Pollack Ave., Evansville, IN 47715 (812) 853-3956.

HARRISON, DAVID C. (Osage-Cherokee) 1945-
(attorney)
Born July 28, 1945, Pawhuska, Okla. *Education*: Grinnell College, BA, 1967; Harvard Law School, JD, 1975. *Principal occupation*: Federal Indian service. *Affiliations*: Rights Protection Officer, Bureau of Indian Affairs, Washington, DC, 1975-. *Other professional post*: director, Native American National Intern Program, American University, 4400 Mass. Ave., NW, Washington, DC 20016 (202) 885-5951. *Military service*: U.S. Marine Corps, 1967-71 (Captain, Vietnamese Cross of Gallantry, Bronze Star, Purple Heart). *Memberships*: Osage Heloshka Society; Harvard Law School Association. *Awards, honors*: "I served as senior investigator and authored several chapters of report called by New York Times editorial, a magnificent document, sweeping in scope, meticulous in detail, unsparing in assessing blame." *Published work*: Attica, Official Report of the New York State Special Commission on Attica (Bantam, paper, Praeger, hardcover, 1972).

*HARRISON, LYNN
(museum curator)
Affiliation: Museum of Native American Cultures, Eastern Washington State Historical Society, 2316 West 1st Ave., Spokane, W A 99204 (509) 456-3931.

HARRY, ANDREW
(Indian band chief)
Affiliation: Anaheim Indian Band, Alexis Creek, BC, Canada V0L 1A0 (604) 393-4342.

HARRY, LILLIEN
(Indian band chief)
Affiliation: Canoe Creek Indian Band, Dog Creek, BC, Canada V0L 1J0 (604) 440-5645.

HARRY, RICHARD
(Indian band chief)
Affiliation: Homalco Indian Band, P .O. Box 789, Campbell River, British Columbia, Canada V9W 6Y4 (604) 287-4922.

HARRY, ROBERT H., D.D.S.
(IHS area director)
Affiliation: Oklahoma Area Indian Health Service, 5 Corporate Plaza, 3625 NW 56th St., Oklahoma City, OK 73112 (405) 945-6820.

HARRY, WILLIAM
(Indian band chief)
Affiliation : Canoe Creek Indian Band, General Delivery, Dog Creek, British Columbia, Canada V0L 1J0 (604) 440-5645.

HART, CONNIE L. (Cheyenne)
(attorney)
Address: 2516 N. Hudson, #201, Oklahoma City , OK 73103 (405) 521-5277. *Memberships* : Native American Bar Association (president, 1992-); Oklahoma Bar Association; American Bar Association.

HART, ROBERT G. 1921-
(government official-retired)
Born December 28, 1921, San Francisco, Calif. *Education* : American Institute for Banking, 1939-41. *Principal occupation* : Governmental of ficial-retired. *Home address* : 916 25th St., NW , Washington, DC 20037. *Affiliations* : Manager, Southern Highlanders, Inc., New York, NY, 1946-52; Southwestern representative, Indian Arts & Crafts Board, Santa Fe, NM, 1954-57; treasurer , Westbury Music Fair, 1957; director , public relations, Constructive Research Foundation, New York, NY, 1958-59; editor , director of publications, Brooklyn Museum, 1959-61; general manager, Indian Arts & Crafts Board, Dept. of the Interior, Washington, DC, 1961-93. *Other professional posts* : Chairman, Federal Inter-Departmental Agency for Arts & Crafts, 1963-93; member, National Advisory Board, Foxfire Fund, 1981-. *Military service* : U.S. Army, 1943-45. *Memberships* : Conseil Internationale des Musees; American Association of Museums; American Craftsmen's Council; W orld Crafts Council; American Political Science Association. *Awards, honors* : N.Y. State Governor's Award for Outstanding Service, 1951. *Interests* : Folk art. *Published works* : How to Sell Your Handicrafts (David McKay, 1953); Guide to Alaska (David McKay, 1959); editor , Masters of Contemporary American Crafts (Brooklyn Museum Press, 1960); among others.

HARTMAN, RUSSELL P.
(museum director/curator)
Affiliation : Navajo Tribal Museum, P .O. Box 308, Highway 264, W indow Rock, AZ 86515 (602) 871-6673.

*HARVEY, DONALD (Navajo)
(school principal)
Affiliation : Leupp Boarding School, P .O. Box HC-61, W inslow, AZ 86047 (602) 686-621 1.

HARWOOD, THOMAS J.
(Peigan-Running Coyote) **(Blackfeet) 1937-**
(IHS area director)
Born July 27, 1937, Browning, Mont. *Education* : Haskell Institute, 1955-57; University of W ashington, AA, 1964; Phoenix College, 1967-68; University of Chicago, HCA Certificate, 1974. *Principal occupation* : IHS Area director. *Home address* : 4099 Bancroft Dr ., El Dorado Hills, CA 95762 (916) 978-4202 (work). *Affiliations* : Director, DHHS, PHS, Albuquerque Area IHS, 1977-84; director, DHHS, PHS, California Area Indian Health Service, Sacramento, CA, 1984-. Mr. Hardwood is responsible for a broad range of responsibilities in health care administration and management. These include the direction of planning, m implementation, managing, operation and evaluation of a health care delivery system for American Indians in the state of California insuring that there are suf ficient options to provide for maximum tribal involvement in meeting their health needs; and to raise the health of the Indian people to the highest possible level. He is a strong advocate for Indian self determination and directs a staf f of about 100 employees. *Memberships* : American College of Health Care Executives; University of Southern California School of Public Administration; Health Administration Advisory Board. *Awards, honors* : Outstanding American Indian Bicentennial Citation, 1976; Outstanding Leadership Citation - National CHR Association, 1976; Outstanding Service to American Indians, National Indian Health Board, 1981; IHS Director's Award for Excellence, 1981 & 1988; Administrator's Citation for Human Resources management, 1983; Exemplary Performance Award, 1990 & 1992; Outstanding Leadership & Commitment, Albuquerque & California Indian Tribes. *Interests* : Professional rodeo announcer; National Finals Rodeo (5 times); Indian Rodeo Man of the Year; founder , National Finals Rodeo; moderator , National Indian Council on Aging, media presentations; lecturer & motivational trainer. *Published works* : Author of numerous articles on health care and management; producer & director of video entitled, "A Promise Made," 1993.

HASKEW, DENNY (Citizen Band Potawatomi) 1948-
(artist/bronze sculptor)
Born March 15, 1949, Denver , Colo. *Education* : University of Utah, BA, 1971. *Principal occupation* : Artist/bronze sculptor. *Home address* : 540 N. Grant, Loveland, CO 80537 (303) 663-6375. *Affiliation* : Owner, Haskew Studio's, Loveland, CO, 1986-. *Other professional posts* : Rafting guide - Idaho/Arizona; ski instructor - Utah/Idaho. *Military service* : U.S. Army, 1971-73 (PFC-4; Markmanship, Leadership, Honorable Discharge). *Memberships* : Indian Arts & Crafts Association; American Indian Cowboy Association. *Awards, honors* : Cheyenne Frontier Museum Regional Shows, Cheyenne, WY : 1987 & 1989 Sculpture Awards for, "Robed in Indigo" & "Courage to Lead" respectively; Red Earth Invitational, Oklahoma City, OK: 1988, 1990, 1992 & 1993 Sculpture Awards for, "Ancient Defender," "Moulding Our Future" monument; "Strength of the Maker ," & "Courage to Lead" monument; Colorado Indian Market, Denver , CO: 1988 & 1989 Best of Class for "T rail of Prayers" & "At Eagles Glance"; Santa Fe Indian Market: 1989 1st Place Sculpture for , "At Eagles Glance"; 1989 presentation of "Courage to Lead" to W.K. Kellogg Foundation by the National Fellowship Program, Battlecreek, MI; Indian Arts & Crafts Association: "1991 Artist of the Year" Award for "Courage to Lead"; 1991 Judges Merit Award for "Trail of Prayers" from Wildlife and W estern Art Exhibition; 1991, 1st, 2nd & 3rd Place for "T rail of Prayers," "He Who Fights W ith a Feather," & "Committed" from Odham Tosh, Casa Grande, AZ; 1991, 1st & 2nd Place for "Strength of the Maker" & "Committed;" 1s & 2nd Place, 1991 & 1992 Gallup Ceremonial Show; Smithsonian Institute (1992 Best of Show, 1st & 3rd Place, 1st Place Sculpture Award, "Courage to Lead" monument1992 Santa Fe Indian Market; 1993 "W ester Heritage Award," Festival of W estern Art. Finalist, Holocaust Memorial, Palm Desert, CA; finalist, City of Redwood, Public Art Competition pending. *Public Commissions* : Life Size Relief "John Yoder" - Minnoite School, 1987; "Y outh in Crisis" - Dr. Thomas Barrett Counselor , 1987; "Judge Hatfield Chilson" Loveland, CO, 1988; "Crawford Follmer" Life Size - McKee Medical Center, Loveland, CO, 1990. *Shows* : 1989 Oklahoma Indian Artist Show, House of Representatives, Washington, DC; 1989 Kennedy Center for Performing Arts, Washington, D.C., "Colorado Living Artists"; 1989 & 1990 Allied Artist of America Shows, New York, NY; 1991 Potawatomi Museum, Shawnee, OK, Permanent Display, "Trail of Prayers"; Franco American Exhibit at Rennes Institute, Paris France, 1992. *Permanent Exhibit* : National Museum of the American Indian. *Biographical source* : "Art of the West," May/June, 1992.

HASKIE, JEANNE (Navajo)
(school principal)
Affiliation : Sanostee Day School, P .O. Box 159, Sanostee, NM 87461 (505) 723-2476.

HASKIE, LILLIE M. (Navajo) 1946-
(nurse)
Born February 21, 1946, Chinle, Ariz. *Education* : Navajo Community College, ADN, 1983. *Principal occupation* : Nurse. *Address* : P.O. Box 293, Lukachukai, AZ 86507 (602) 787-2335. *Affiliation* : Administrative Nurse, Tsaile PHS Indian Health Center, Tsaile, AZ, 1984-.

HASKINS, BETTE (Oklahoma Cherokee) 1933-
(Indian educator)
Education: University of Oklahoma, BA, 1956; Phillips University, MA, 1969; University of North Dakota, PhD (Educational Administration), 1985. *Principal occupation* : Indian educator . *Home address* : 5006 Baltic Ave., Rockville, MD 20853. *Affiliations* : Teacher, counselor, Enid Public School System, Enid, OK, 1970-82; assistant professor of Indian studies, University of North Dakota, Grand Forks, 1984-85; Job Training Partnership Act counselor, Enid, OK, 1985-87; director, American Indian Program, Harvard University Graduate School of Education, Cambridge, MA, 1987-91; visiting professor , Sinte Gleska University, Rosebud, SD & University of Massachusetts, Amherst. *Other professional post*: Founder & director, Heart of the American Indian W omen's Network. *National conferences* : International Conference of Indigenous People, Canada, 1987; National Indian Education Association, Oklahoma, 1988; National Congress of American Indians, South Dakota, 1988; Task Force 2000 - Navajo Indian Education Conference, Arizona, 1988; American Indian Graduate Center, New Mexico, 1989; PRIME - Minorities in Mathematics, New Jersey , 1989; World Archaeological Congress, Barquisimeto, V enezuela, 1990; National Diversity Conference, Washington, DC, 1992; Aboriginal Education Conference, University of Australia, Wollongong, New South W ales, 1993; Ef fective Schools Conference, Phoenix, AZ, 1994. *Community activities* : Member, Task Force, American Indian Gifted & Talented Program, U.S. Dept. of Education, and the Of fice of Educational Research & Improvement, 1994; Boston Children's Museum (board of directors); Indian Spiritual & Cultural Training Council (board of directors). *Membership* : Massachusetts Indian Association. *Awards, honors* : One of 15 selected to attend East Asian Summer Institute, University of Ha-

waii, 1981; Outstanding Indian Educator , University of North Dakota, 1985; V isiting professor, Sinte Gleska College, SD, Summer 1988; Visiting Professor, University of Massachusetts, Amherst, 1989-90. *Interests*: Research & travel.

HASSRICK, PETER H.
(center & museum director)
Affiliation: Buffalo Bill Historical Center & Plains Indian Museum, P .O. Box 1000, Cody , WY 82414 (307) 587-4771.

*HASTINGS, WILLIAM
(school principal)
Affiliation: Theodore Roosevlt School, P .O. Box 567, Fort Apache, AZ 85926 (602) 338-4464.

HATCH, VIOLA (Arapahoe)
(tribal chairperson)
Affiliation: Cheyenne-Arapaho Tribal Business Committee, P.O. Box 38, Concho, OK 73022 (405) 262-0345. *Other professional post*: Member, Board of Directors, National Indian Youth Council, Albuquerque, NM.

HATFIELD, RAYMOND ESPANIEL
(director-association)
Affiliation: National Association of Friendship Centres, 251 Laurier Ave., West, Suite 600, Ottawa, Ontario, Canada K1P 5J6 (613) 563-4844.

HAUXWELL, JON 1948-
(physician)
Born July 31, 1948, Marysville, Kans. *Education*: University of Kansas, BA, 1970; University of Kansas, School of Medicine, Kansas City , MD, 1974 (Residency in Family Practice, 1974-77). *Principal occupation*: Physician. *Address*: Box 373, Lame Deer, MT 59043 (406) 477-6478 (home), 477-8255 (of fice). *Affiliation*: Clinical director, medical of ficer, Northern Cheyenne Service Unit, Indian Health Service, Lame Deer , MT, 1977-. *Other professional posts*: Associate clinical professor, Family Medicine, University of Washington, School of Medicine; family nurse practitioner preceptor , University of North Dakota. *Military service*: Commissioned Corps, USPHS, 1977- (Outstanding Service Medal, 1989). *Community activities*: Member , Northern Cheyenne Gourd Dance Society; honorary member, Kit Fox Society (traditional Cheyenne military society). *Memberships*: American College of Surgeons (Advanced Trauma Life Support Instructor, 1981-); ØBK; Northern Cheyenne Multidisciplinary Chemical Dependence Team (chairman, 1986-). *Awards, honors*: National Indian Health Board, Certificate of Appreciation, 1982; National Outstanding Clinician Award - 1985, by National Council of Clinical Directors. *Interests*: Powwow-ing ("every member of family has been on pow wow head staf f and hosted giveaways on numerous occasions"). Photography; music (piano & vocal) gardening; teaching medical students; hiking; cooking; cross-cultural activities; track and field; football; reading; history; Native American art, especially beadwork. Iroquois ancestry , non-registered. *Published work*: The Cheyenne (Children's Press, 1988).

HAVATON, DELBERT (Hualapai)
(tribal chairperson)
Affiliation: Hualapai Tribal Council, P .O. Box 179, Peach Springs, AZ 86434 (602) 769-2216.

*HAVERKATE, RICK
(Sault Ste. Marie Chippewa) 1965-
(university faculty)
Born October 2, 1965, Elmhurst, Ill. *Education*: Northern Michigan University , B.S., 1989; University of Hawaii-Manoa, MPH, 1993. *Principal occupation*: University faculty. *Home address*: 1890 East West Rd., Moore Hall 405, Honolulu, HI 96822 (808) 956-6234. *Affiliations*: Coordinator, American Indian Recruitment Program, University of Hawaii, Honolulu, 1992-; health education consultant, Inter Tribal Council of Michigan, Sault Ste. Marie, MI, 1991-. *Other professional post*: Community health educator , Sault Ste. Marie Tribe of Chippewa Indians. *Community activities*: V.P. American Heart Association, Upper Peninsula, 1991-92; Chippewa County AIDS Task Force, 1990-92; LifeGuard Hawaii -- AIDS Prevention/Education Peer Program. *Memberships*: Society of Public Health Educators of Hawaii, 1992-; American Public Health Association, 1993-. *Awards, honors*: Health Educator of the Year, Bemidji Area IHS; Michigan Competitive Scholarship (4 years); Mortar Board Honor Society: Outstanding College Student of the Year; Student Commencement Speaker, 1989, Northern Michigan University. *Interests*: "Spent 8 weeks exploring the public health systems throughout Thailand during summer of 1993, Included Bangkok Metro area as well as Hill Tribe areas in extreme northern Thailand and rural farming regions. I am interested in community development issues and how health care and politics relate. Exploring a developing country helped me gain important insight in to our own country ."

HAWK, JOHNNY T.
(executive director)
Affiliation: Calista Corporation, 601 W .5th Ave., #200, Anchorage, AK 99501 (907) 279-5516.

HAWK, RAY (Chippewa)
(clinical director)
Affiliation: Bois Fort Tribal Clinic, P.O. Box 15, Nett Lake, MN 55772 (218) 757-3296.

*HAWK, WARREN
(executive director)
Affiliation: Cherokee Initiative, 1 106 S. Muskogee Ave., Suite A, Tahlequah, OK 74464.

HAWKINS, RUSSELL
(Sisseton-Wahpeton Sioux)
(tribal chairperson)
Affiliation: Sisseton-W ahpeton Sioux Tribal Council, Route 2, Agency Village, Sisseton, SD 57262 (605) 698-391 1.

HAWLEY, HERBERT W. (Burns Paiute)
(tribal chairperson)
Affiliation: Burns Paiute General Council, HC 71, 100 Pa Si Go St., Burns, OR 97720 (503) 573-2088.

HAYES, CHARLES H. "Pete" (Nez Perce)
(tribal chairperson)
Affiliation: Nez Perce Tribal Executive Committee, P.O. Box 305, Lapwai, ID 83540 (208) 843-2253.

HAYES, HOWARD, M.D.
(clinical director)
Affiliation: White Earth PHS Indian Health Center, White Earth, MN 56591 (218) 983-3221.

HAYS, ELLEN
(executive director)
Affiliation: Southeast Alaska Indian Cultural Center, 106 Metlakatla St., Sitka, AK 99835 (907) 747-8061.

HAYS, PATRICK
(BIA director)
Affiliation: Director, Office of Trust Responsibilities, Bureau of Indian Affairs, Dept. of the Interior, MS-4513-MIB, 1849 C St., NW , Washington, DC 20240 (202) 208-5831.

HAYWARD, RICHARD A. "SKIP"
(Mashantucket Pequot) 1948-
(tribal chairman)
Born November 28, 1948, Groton, Conn. *Education*: Honorary doctorates from Eastern Connecticut State University , the University of Connecticut, and the Roger W illiams College. *Address & Affiliation*: Chairman (1975-) Mashantucket Pequot Tribal Council, P.O. Box 160, Ledyard, CT 06339 (203) 536-2681. *Other professional post*: Chairman, Board of Directors, Native American Rights Fund, Boulder , CO, 1988-. *Community activities*: Chairman, Mashantucket Pequot Indian Housing Authority; chairman, Economic Development & Planning Committee; member-Board of Directors, Mashantucket Pequot Museum & Research Center; chairman, Mashantucket Pequot Gaming Enterprise Board of Directors. *Awards, honors*: Appointee of the Governor of Connecticut to the Legislative Task Force on Indian Affairs; received the National Historic Preservation Award, 1988.

HAZELTON, HANK
(director-Indian organization)
Affiliation: Rights for All Indigenous Nations, Inc. (R.A.I.N.), R.D. 1, Box 308A, Petersburg, NY 12138 (518) 658-3055.

HEAD, PHILIP
(Indian band chief)
Affiliation: Red Earth Indian Band, Red Earth, Saskatchewan, Canada S0E 1K0 (306) 768-3640.

HEADLEY, LOUIS R. (Arapahoe) 1948-
(Indian school supt.)
Born February 25, 1948, Fort W ashakie, Wyo. *Education*: University of Montana, Missoula, BA, 1974; University of South Dakota, V ermillion, MA, 1977; University of W yoming, Laramie, EdS, 1986. *Principal occupation*: Indian school supt. *Home address*: Box 344, St. Stephens, WY 82524 (307) 856-4147. *Affiliations*: Teacher, Principal, St. Stephens Indian School, 1977-; minority counselor , special services, University of Wyoming, Laramie, 1984-. *Other professional posts*: Home-school coordinator , Lander (WY) Valley High School; field coordinator , Tri-State Tribes, Inc., Billings, MT. *Community activities*: Wind River Indian Education Association, W ind River, Wyo. (past chairman); Keepers of the Fire Indian Club, University of W yoming (advisor); Cub Scout volunteer , St. Stephens, WY ; Head Start Policy Council, Ethete, WY (vice chairman). *Memberships*: Phi Delta Kappa; National Association of Elementary School Principals; National Indian Education Association (treasurer); Wyoming Association for Bilingual-Bicultural Education (treasurer). *Awards, honors*: Wyoming Golden Gloves Championship Schol-

arship Award; Korean Temple Band, Casper, Wyo; Outstanding Young Men of America, U.S. Jaycees, 1978. *Interests*: "I was a member of the Arapahoe and Shoshone Indian Dance Troupe that danced in Switzerland. I was also selected to dance in Washington, D.C. during the 1976 Bicentennial. I have been chosen to be the head dancer in Denver, Steamboat Spring, Colorado and Rocky Boy Reservation."

*HEARN, EARNEST R.
(BIA acting supt.)
Affiliation: Papago Agency, BIA, P.O. Box 578, Sells, AZ 85634 (602) 383-3286.

HEATH, MARGARET A. 1947-
(director of education)
Born October 24, 1947, Boulder, Colo. *Education*: University of Colorado, BA, 1972, MA, 1979. *Principal occupation*: Director of education. *Home address*: P.O. Box 94, Dolores, CO 81323 (303) 565-8975 (work). Affiliations: Administrator & teacher, Adams County School District No. 50, Westminster, CO, 1972-79; director, Ute Mountain Ute Tribal Youth Shelter, Towaoc, CO, 1988-; director of education, Crow Canyon Archaeological Center, Cortez, CO, 1986-. *Community activities*: Democratic Party Central Committee, 1984-87 (campaign coordinators of two major campaigns); member, Dolores RE 4A Board of Education, 1987-89; Brownie Girl Scout Leader, 1989-. *Memberships*: Colorado Council fo the Social Studies, 1973-79; 1986-; Westminster Federation of Teachers (president, 1976-79); American Federation of Teachers; Colorado Federation of Teachers; Phi Delta Kappa, 1978-. *Interests*: "Experiential eduction, especially archaeology for all ages and designing curriculum about the Anasazi; curriculum development; motivating students; Native American crafts, past and present - learning how to do them; hiking and rafting canyons of the Southwest; writing." *Published works*: Co-authored, Crow Canyon Archaeological Center: Teacher's Guide to Archaeological Activities (Crow Canyon Archaeological Center, 1989); co-authored with Lewis Matis, Crow Canyon Archaeological Center: Windows Into the Past & Inquiries Into the Past (Crow Canyon Archaeological Center, 1989); "Why Archaeology" in Whole Language Catalog (McGraw-Hill, 1990).

HEAVY HEAD, MARTIN
(Native student services officer)
Afiliation: Dept. of Native American Studies, The University of Lethbridge, 4401 University Dr., Lethbridge, Alberta, Canada T1K 3M4 (403) 329-2635.

HEAVY RUNNER, GEORGE
(communications)
Affiliation: Blackfeet Indian Telecommunications, P.O. Box 819, Browning, MT 59417.

*HECKERT, MARK
(executive director)
Affiliation: Intertribal Bison Cooperative, 520 Kansas City St., Suite 209, Rapid City, SD 57701 (605) 394-9730.

HEDRICK, HENRY E.
(organization president; editor)
Affiliation: American Indian Liberation Crusade, Inc., 4009 S. Hallday Ave., Los Angeles, CA 90062 (213) 299-1810. *Other professional post*: Editor, Indian Crusader.

*HEE, CLAYTON (Hawaiian)
(chair-Hawaiian affairs)
Affiliation: Office of Hawaiian Affairs, State og Hawaii, 711 Kapiolani Blvd., 5th Floor, Honolulu, HI 96805 (808) 586-3777.

*HEFFINGTON, DENNIS
(IHS-tribal activities)
Affiliation: Office of Tribal Activities, California Area IHS, 1825 Bell St., Suite 200, Sacramento, CA 95825 (916) 978-4202.

HEFLIN, DONNA JO
(museum curator)
Affiliation: Choctaw Nation Museum, HC 64, Box 3270, Tuskahoma, OK 74574 (918) 569-4465.

HEIDE, SUSAN
(executive director)
Affiliation: United American Indians of the Delaware Valley, 225 Chestnut St., Philadelphia, PA 19106 (215) 574-9020.

HEINRICH, ALBERT C. 1922-
(professor of anthropology)
Born February 2, 1922, Ill. *Education*: New School for Social Research, BA; University of Alaska, MEd; University of Washington, PhD, 1960. *Principal occupation*: Professor of anthropology & linguistics (retired). *Home address*: 29605 N.E. Pheasant Ave., Corvallis, OR 97333 (503) 752-8089. *Affiliation*: Retired professor of anthropology & linguistics, University of Calgary, Alberta, Canada. *Memberships*: American Association for the Advancement of Science. *Awards, honors*: Seattle Anthropological Society Prize, 1962. Interests: Linguistics; social structure; arctic; Indians of North America; South Asia; Have spent extended periods of time in Alaska, Arctic Canada, The Labrador, South America, India, Europe. Have written numerous articles on Athabascans, Eskimos.

HEINZ, JOHN R.
(health director)
Affiliation: Sophie Trettevick Indian Health Center, P.O. Box 410, Neah Bay, WA 98357 (206) 645-2233.

HEISLER, FRANKLIN
(health director)
Affiliation: White Earth PHS Indian Health Center, White Earth, MN 56591 (218) 983-3221.

*HELFIN, DONNA JOE (Choctaw)
(museum curator)
Affiliation: Choctaw Nation Museum, Route 1, Box 105 AAA, Tuskahoma, OK 74574 (918) 569-4465.

HELIN, LAWRENCE
(Indian band chief)
Affiliation: Lax-Kw'alaams Indian Band, 206 Shashaak St., Port Simpson, British Columbia, Canada V0V 1H0 (604) 625-3474.

*HELLER-DAVIS, SUZIE *(Suzie Longhair)* (Cocopah) 1967-
(bead crafter, traveling tribal rep.)
Born September 9, 1967, Phoenix, Ariz. *Education*: Baily School of Broadcasting (Phoenix), Diploma. *Principal occupation*: Bead crafter, traveling tribal representative. *Home address*: 16241 Fairway Woods Dr. #1104, Fort Myers, FL 33908 (813) 482-4850. Work has been displayed & sold in most of the 50 states and overseas. *Community activities*: Special Olympics

volunteer; Public Service Director, WJAT Radio. *Memberships*: Cocopah Indian Tribe (Somerset, AZ); Indian Arts & Crafts Association. *Interests*: Bead work; traveling around the country at various cultural events and pow wows promoting knowledge about her people, their culture and her beadwork. *Biographical sources*: Biography published in button collectors newsletter, "Pennsylvania State Button Bulletin."

*HELM, JUNE
(program director)
Affiliation: American Indian & Native Studies Program, University of Iowa, 113 Macbride Hall, Iowa City, IA 52242 (319) 335-0539.

HEMAURER, Fr. GILBERT F.
(executive director)
Affiliation: Tekakwitha Conference National Center, P.O. Box 6759, Great Falls, MT 59406 (406) 727-0147.

HENA, JAMES (Pueblo)
(council chairperson)
Affiliation: All Indian Pueblo Council, 3939 San Pedro NE, Suite D, Albuquerque, NM 87196 (505) 881-1992.

HENDERSON, EDWARD
(Indian band chief)
Affiliation: William Charles Indian Band, Box 106, Montreal Lake, Saskatchewan, Canada S0J 1Y0 (306) 663-5349.

HENDERSON, GLEN E.
(national monument supt.)
Affiliations: Tuzigoot National Monument, P.O. Box 68, Clarkdale, AZ 86324 (602) 634-5564; Montezuma Castle National Monument, P.O. Box 219, Camp Verde, AZ 86322.

HENDERSON, JANICE
(Indian band chief)
Affiliation: Stangecoming Indian Band, Box 609, Fort Frances, Ontario, Canada P9A 3M6 (807) 274-2188.

HENDERSON, SAM R.
(national monument supt.)
Affiliation: Casa Grande Ruins National Monument, 1100 N. Ruins Dr., Coolidge, AZ 85228 (602) 723-3172; Walnut Canyon National Monument, Flagstaff, AZ.

HENDRICKS, SONNY (Miwok)
(rancheria chairperson; health director)
Affiliations: Tuolumne Me-Wuk Rancheria, P.O. Box 699, Tuolumne, CA 95379 (209) 928-3475; director, Tuolumne River Indian Health Program.

*HENDRICKSON, DAVID
(BIA agency supt.)
Affiliation: Bethel Agency, Bureau of Indian Affairs, P.O. Box 347, Bethel, AK 99559 (907) 543-2727.

HENDRICKX, LEONARD 1953-
(executiver director)
Born July 10, 1953, Kellogg, Idaho. *Education*: SUNY at Albany, BA, 1975. *Principal occupation*: Director of Indian center. *Address*: Spokane Uuban Indian Health Services, East 905 Third Ave., Spokane, WA 99202 (509) 535-0868. *Affiliations*: Administrative analyst, City of Redondo Beach, CA, 1979-1982; executive director, Spokane Urban Indian Health Services, Spokane, WA, 1982-. *Community activities*:

Spokane Urban Indian Health Service Board (chairman); Community Housing Resources Board (chairman); The Native American Alliance for Political Action (treasurer); Spokane Planning Affiliates Network (member); Vocational Advisory Council, Community Colleges (member). *Memberships*: Eastern Washington-Northern Idaho MENSA (treasurer). *Awards, honors*: Outstanding Young Man of America, 1985; Mayor's Proclamation-Community Services, City Council and Indian Community; frequent presenter at national and regional Indian employment and training and education conferences. *Interests*: "Extensive travels throughout the U.S. Outdoors enthusiast, particularly interested in the conceptualization and articulation of innovative program development ideas for Indian communities, with expertise in successful grant and contract preparation, presentation, and negotiation." *Biographical source*: Outstanding Young Men of America, 1985.

*HENERICKSON, LINDA J.E.
(association president)
Affiliation: Association of Alaska Native Contractors, 700 W. 58th, Unit F, Anchorage, AK 99518 (907) 562-1866.

*HENRY, GORDON D., Jr.
(White Earth Chippewa) 1955-
(assistant professor)
Born October 19, 1955, Philadelphia, Penna. *Education*: Michigan State University, MA, 1983; University of North Dakota, PhD, 1992. *Principal occupation*: Assistant professor of English. *Home address*: 14069 215th Ave., Big Rapids, MI 49307 (616) 592-9835. *Affiliation*: Assistant professor, Dept. of English, Michigan State University, E. Lansing, MI, 1992-. *Other professional posts*: Artist in the schools; North Dakota Arts Council, 1984-86; lecturer-storyteller, West Central Michigan Humanities Council. *Memberships*: Wordcraft Writing Circle; North American Native Writers Circle. *Award*: Thomas McGrath Award for Poetry, University of North Dakota. *Interests*: Fulbright, Lecture Award for Spain, 1995. *Biographical source*: Article in "Genre," by Kim Blaeser, 1994. *Published works*: Outside White Earth (Blue Cloud, 1985); The Light People (University of Oklahoma Press, 1994).

HENRY, HAROLD
(Indian band chief)
Affiliation: Kwaw-Kwaw-A-Pilt Indian Band, Box 412, Chilliwack, British Columbia, Canada (604) 858-0662.

HENRY, JEANETTE
(director-Indian society; editor)
Affiliation: American Indian Historical Society, 1451 Masonic Ave., San Francisco, CA 94117 (415) 626-5235. *Other professional post*: Editor, The Indian Historian.

HENRY, LAWRENCE
(Indian band chief)
Affiliation: Roseau River First Nation, Box 30, Ginew, Manitoba, Canada R0A 2R0 (204) 427-2312.

*HENRY, PHILIP NATHANIEL
(Indian outreach worker)
Born June 7, 1933, Saginaw, Mich. *Education*: St. Clair Co. Community College. *Principal occupation*: Indian outreach worker. *Home address*: 715 Summer St., Algonac, MI 48001 (810) 794-5413. *Affiliation*: Oakland County

Dept. of Social Services, Pontiac, MI, 1994-. *Other professional posts*: Home health care primary case manager; commissioner Region I, Michigan Commission on Indian Affairs. *Past professional posts*: Building Trades Roofer Local 149 (25 years); JTPA Indian Employment & Service Counselor (7 years); director of Indian education, Algonac Community Schools, Port Huron, MI, 1976-80. *Community activities*: Board member, Down River Nutrition Center, Marine City, MI; past board member, Down River Community Services, Algonac, MI. *Awards, honors*: Certificate of Recognition & Appointed by Governor Engler to Region I, Michigan Commission on Indian Affairs (Aug. 1992, reappointed, 1994-97); recognized as elder and Indian leader for Michigan Indian community; brother of Thelma Henry Shipman, director of Urban Indian Affairs, Wayne County Mich. Dept. of Social Services.

HENSLEY, WILLIAM L. (Eskimo) 1941-
(state senator)
Born 1941, Kotzebue, Alaska. *Education*: University of Alaska, 1960-1961; George Washington University, BA, 1966; University of Alaska, 1966; University of New Mexico Law School, 1967; UCLA Law School, 1968. *Principal occupation*: State Senator. *Home address*: Kotzebue, Alaska. *Affiliations*: Alaska House of Representatives, 1966-70; Alaska State Senate, 1970-. *Community activities*: Rural Affairs Commission, 1968-1972 (chairman, 1972); Land Claims Task Force (chairman, 1968); Northwest Regional Educational Laboratory (board of directors, 1968-1969); Northwest Alaska Native Association Regional Corporation (board of directors). *Memberships*: Alaska Federation of Natives, 1966- (organizer, 1966; president, 1972); Northwest Alaska Native Association (organizer, 1966); National Council on Indian Opportunity, 1968-70. *Interests*: Land claims implementation; rural economic development; education facilities in the bush; old-age centers; bilingual programs.

HENSON, C.L.
(BIA administrator)
Affiliation: Chief, Division of Administrative Services, Office of Indian Education Programs, Bureau of Indian Affairs, Dept, of the Interior, MS-3530-MIB, 249 C St., NW, Washington, DC 20240 (202) 208-4234.

HENSON, RICHARD ALLEN (Comanche) 1942-
(BIA employment assistance officer)
Born January 26, 1942, Pawnee, Okla. *Education*: Oklahoma State Tech, 1960-62; Minot State College, BA, 1976. *Principal occupation*: BIA employment assistance director. *Address*: Bureau of Indian Affairs, 1951 Constitution Ave., N.W., Room 331S, Mail Stop: 331SIB, Washington, DC 20245 (202) 343-1780. *Affiliations*: Metropolitan Life Insurance Co., Ardmore, OK, 1967-71; guidance counselor, United Tribes Employment Training Center, Bismarck, ND, equal employment opportunity counselor, job developer and employment assistance officer, United Tribes Employment Training Center, Minot, ND, 1971-74; employment assistance officer, Fort Berthold Agency, BIA, New Town, N.D., 1974-76; area equal employment opportunity officer, BIA, Albuquerque, N.M., 1976-77; director, equal employment opportunity, Indian Health Service, Rockville, Md.; employment assistance officer, BIA, Washington, DC. *Military service*: U.S. Air

Force, 1963-67. *Community activities*: Minot Indian Club (president, 1974); Minot Mayor's Human Rights Committee (member); Minot's Mental Health & Retardation Board (member). *Interests*: "To continue to work with Indian people in Indian affairs and to return to school to earn my master's degree in public health."

HERIARD, JACK B. 1948-
(editor/publisher)
Born July 26, 1948, New Orleans, LA. *Principal occupation*: Editor/publisher. *Home address*: 8009 Wales St., New Orleans, LA 70126 (504) 241-5866; 246-3742 (work). *Affiliation*: Editor/publisher, "Crafts: American Indian Past & Present," Written Heritage, New Orleans, LA, 1967-. *Other professional post*: Managing editor, "Whispering Wind," New Orleans, LA, 1967-. *Military service*: U.S. Air Force, 1969-72 (E7). *Memberships*: Louisiana Indian Heritage Association (president, 1967-72, 1978; secretray/treasurer, 1987-89, 1990-92). *Interests*: "American Indian culture; attending numerous pow-wows; dancing and singing."

HERING, MICHAEL J. 1954-
(director-Indian Arts Research Center)
Born July 12, 1954, Dayton, Ohio. *Education*: University of Cincinnati, BA, 1978; University of New Mexico, MA, 1982. *Principal occupation*: Director-Indian center. *Address*: Indian Arts Research Center, School of American Research, 660 Garcia St., Box 2188, Santa Fe 87504 (505) 982-3583 Fax 989-9809 (work). *Affiliations*: Assistant curator, Maxwell Museum of Anthropology, Albuquerque, NM, 1978-83; Indian Arts Research Center, School of American Research, Santa Fe, NM (collections manager, 1983-84; director, 1984-). *Other professional post*: Lecturer. *Community activities*: Judging Chairperson of Santa Fe Indian Market, Southwestern Association on Indian Affairs (six years); Advisory Council, Pueblo of Pojoaque, POEH Cultural Center; Pueblo Potery Judge for the Eight Northern Indian Pueblo Artist & Craftsman Fair, San Ildefonso, NM, July, 1989. *Memberships*: Native American Art Studies Association (founding member); Southwestern Association on Indian Affairs (vice-president, board of directors - six years); American Association of Museums (curator committee); American Anthropological Association; Council for Museum Anthropology; Mountain-Plains Museum Association; International Council of Museums; New Mexico Association of Museums. *Awards, honors*: June, 1987, Fellowship for J. Paul Getty Trust's Museum Management Institute, San Francisco, CA, July, 1987; September 1989, National Endowmen for the Arts, Fellowships for Museum Professionals, Grant awarded to complete research and writing on Zia Pueblo Indian Pottery. *Published works*: Articles - "Native American Artists Worth Watching," Art Talk Magazine, Vol. 6, No. 6, March 1987; "A Three Hundred Year History of Zia Matte-Paint Pottery," American Indian Art Magazine, Vol. 12, No. 4, Aug. 1987.

HERNANDEZ-AVILA, INEZ
(Nez Perce/Chicana) 1948-
(assistant professor)
Born in Texas, 1948. *Education*: University of Houston, BA, 1970, MA, 1972, PhD (English), 1984. *Principal occupation*: Assistant professor. *Address & Affiliation*: Native American Studies Dept., University of California, Davis, CA 95616 (916) 752-4394 (work). *Other professional post*:

Editorial Advisory Board, "Hurricane Alice: A Feminist Quarterly." *Memberships*: Modern Language Association; MALCS (Mujeres Activas en Letras y Cambio Social); National Association of Chicano Studies; California Indian Education Association. *Awards, honors*: Phi Kappa Phi Honor Society; Outstanding Chicana in the Arts (Literature) for the Austin community, 1977, award presented by the Mexican American Professional and Business Women of Austin; Outstanding Chicana faculty, 1977, award presented by the Minority Student Services, University of Texas, Austin; Outstanding Chicana faculty, 1978, award presented by the Center for Mexican American Studies, University of Texas, Austin; elected to Board of Directors of D-Q University, Davis, CA, June 1983, served through April 1986. *Interests*: "My mother is Nimipu (known as Nez Perce) Indian; I am an enrolled member of the Colville Confederated Tribes of Nespelem, Washington. My father is Texas-Mexican. I am Nimipu and Chicana. I am fluent in English and Spanish (reading, writing, speaking, translating)." Writer & director of the dramatic work "El Dia de Guadalupe," which featured eight women players focusing on the different forms of abuse that Chicanas encounter in contemporary society. *Published works*: ·Article - "Finding Our Way Back Home: Native American Women Writers," Dictionary of Native American Literature, edited by Andrew Wiget (Greenwood Press, 1991); "Open Letter to Chicanas: The Power and Politics of Origin," for Changing Our Power: An Introduction to Women's Studies, eds. Jo Whitehorse Cochran, et al (Kendall-Hunt, 1991); "Sara Estela Ramirez," bio-bibliographical essay, The Longman Anthology of World Literature by Women, 1895-1975, eds. Barbara Shollar and Marian Arkin (Longman Press, 1989); "Body of Mine, Body Be Mine," Blue Mesa Review, No. 4 (Spring 1992); among other articles and chapters. Collections of poetry: Con Razon, Corazon (Caracol Publications, 1977; second edition, M&A Editions, 1987); Abrecaminos: Collected Poems, 1978-1990 (unpublished manuscript); and numerous individual poems in various publications. Recordings of poetry: "Para Teresa," for the Houghton-Mifflin Secondary Education Audiocassette Series, 1991.

HERNANDEZ, SALLY A. (Laguna Pueblo)
(attorney)
Address: University of New Mexico School of Law, P.O. Box 4456-Station A, Albuquerque, NM 87196 (505) 277-5462. *Memberships*: Native American Bar Association (Native American Legal Resource Center representative); American Bar Association.

*HERNASY, KEN
(hospital director)
Affiliation: Fort Yuma PHS Indian Hospital, P.O. Box 1368, Yuma, AZ 85364 (602) 572-0217.

HERRERA, J. MARVIN (Pueblo)
(former pueblo governor)
Affiliation: Pueblo of Tesuque, Route 11, Box 1, Santa Fe, NM 87501.

*HERRERA, JOHN R. (Leech Lake Chippewa) 1952-
(company president)
Born June 4, 1952, Milwaukee, Wisc. *Education*: University of Wisconsin, Milwaukee, BA, 1976; University of Minnesota, MBA, 1986; William Mitchell College of Law (St.Paul, MN), JD, 1992. *Principal occupation*: Company president. *Home address*: 12133 Madison St., Blaine, MN 55434 (612) 445-5332 (work). *Affiliations*: Div. director, economic development, Minnesota Chippewa Tribe, Cass Lake, MN,1978-80; director of business enterprises, Leech Lake Reservation, Cass Lake, MN, 1980-82; business finance representative, State of Minnesota, Prior lake, MN, 1983-85; area credit officer/Indian services branch chief, Bureau of Indian Affairs, Minneapolis, MN, 1985-88 (managed implementation of Indian Finance Act for federally recognized Indian reservations in the four state area - provided loans & loan guarantees for business development); finance & planning consultant, Shakopee Sioux Community, Prior Lake, MN, 1988-90 (provided financial & developmental direction for the community which owns one of the largest and most successful Native American gaming ventures in the U.S.; president, First American Capital Management Group, Inc., Prior Lake, MN, 1991- (provides consultant & equipment leasing services to a client base of Native American Tribes. *Other professional posts*: Judge, Leech Lake Reservation; associate judge, Minnesota Chippewa Tribe Appeals Court. *Membership*: Minnesota Indian Chamber of Commerce (founder/member).

HERROD, RANDALL
(association director)
Affiliation: National Commander, Vietnam Era Veterans Inter-Tribal Association, 805 Rosa, Shawnee, OK 74801 (405) 382-3128.

HERSCH, ROBERT C.
(librarian)
Affiliation: Native American Resource Center Library, Pembroke State University, College Rd., Pembroke, NC 28372 (919) 521-4214.

*HESSE, CURTIS
(health program director)
Affiliation: Riverside/San Bernardino Indian Health Program, 11555 1/2 Potrero Rd., Banning, CA 92220 (714) 849-4761.

HESTER, JAMES J. 1931-
(anthropologist)
Born September 21, 1931, Anthony, Kan. *Education*: University of New Mexico, BA, 1953; University of Arizona, PhD, 1961. *Principal occupation*: Anthropologist. *Address*: Dept. of Anthropology, University of Colorado, Boulder, CO 80309 (303) 492-7947. *Affiliations*: Assistant curator, Museum of New Mexico, 1959-64; adjunct professor, Southern Methodist University, 1964-65; scientist administrator, National Institute of Health, 1965-75; professor, Department of Anthropology, University of Colorado, Boulder, 1975-. *Military service*: U.S. Air Force, 1954-56. *Memberships*: American Anthropological Association (Fellow); Society for American Archaeology; Sigma Xi; American Society of Naturalists; Current Anthropology. *Interests*: "Archaeology of Navajo Indians; prehistory of Sahara desert; directed culture change; relationship of man to his environment." *Published works*: An Archaeological Survey of the Navajo Reservoir District, Northwestern New Mexico, with A.E. Dittert, Jr. & Frank W. Eddy (Museum of New Mexico, 1961); Early Navajo Migrations and Acculturation in the Southwest (Museum of New Mexico, 1962); Studies at Navajo Period Sites in the Navajo Reservoir District, with Joel Shiner (Museum of New Mexico, 1963); among others.

HESTER, JOE
(director-Indian centre)
Affiliation: Niagara Regional Native Centre, R.R. #4, Queenston & Taylor Rd., Niagara-on-the-Lake, Ontario, Canada L0S 1H0 (705) 472-281 1.

HETH, CHARLOTTE WILSON
(Oklahoma Cherokee) 1937-
(professor of ethnomusicology)
Born October 29, 1937, Muskogee, Okla. Education: Oklahoma Baptist University, 1955-56; University of Tulsa, BA, 1959, MM, 1960; University of California, Los Angeles, PhD, 1975. *Principal occupation*: Professor of ethnomusicology. *Address*: Dept. of Ethnomusicology, Room 1642, Schoenberg Hall, 405 Hilgard Ave., Los Angeles, CA 90024 (310) 206-3033. *Affiliations*: Professor of ethnomusicology, 1974-87, 1989-, director, 1976-87, American Indian Studies Center, UCLA; director American Indian Program, Cornell University, Ithaca, NY, 1987-89. *Community activities*: Panel chair, Folk Arts Program, National Endowment for the Arts, 1981-83; Indian Centers, Inc., Los Angeles (board member). *Memberships*: Society for Ethnomusicology (council chair, 1981-82); National Indian Education Association; American Indian Historians' Association. *Awards, honors*: Senior Postdoctoral Fellowship, Center for the History of the American Indian, The Newberry Library, 1978-79; Southern Fellowships Fund, Post-doctoral Fellowship, 1978-79; National Research Council senior postdoctoral fellowship, 1984-85 (Ford Foundation Minority Fellowship). *Interests*: "American Indian music and dance; Cherokee language and culture; previously I was a Peace Corps volunteer in Ethiopia (1962-64) teaching English as a second language. I also was a high school teacher in OK, NM, and CA from 1960-72. I have traveled to Europe, the Middle East, East Africa, Mexico, and Canada." *Published works*: General editor, The Music of the American Indians, (Selected Reports in Ethnomusicology, 1982); general editor, Music and the Expressive Arts, (American Indian Culture and Research Journal, 1982); Issues for the Future of American Indian Studies: A Needs Assessment and Program Guide, co-authored with Susan Guyette (American Indian Studies Center, UCLA, 1985); general editor, organizer, and contributor, Sharing a Heritage: American Indian Arts Conference, No. 3 in the Contemporary American Indian Issues Series (American Indian Studies Center, UCLA, 1984).

HEWITT, ARNOLD (Tuscarora)
(tribal head chief)
Affiliation: Chief (lifetime), Tuscarora Nation, 5616 Walmore Rd., Lewiston, NY 14092 (716) 297-4990.

HEWITT, CHAR
(director-IHS field office)
Affiliation: Indian Health Service Field Office, Kincheloe, MI 49788 (906) 495-2289.

*HEYANO, ROBERT (Eskimo)
(AK village council president)
Affiliation: Native Village of Ekuk, P.O. Box 1409, Ambler, AK 99786 (907) 842-1053.

HICKS, PHYLLIS (Monacan)
(tribal representative)
Affiliation: Monacan Indian Tribe, P.O. Box 112, Monroe, VA 24574 (804) 946-2431.

HIGDON, HELEN C.
(Indian school principal)
Affiliation: Winslow Dormitory, 600 N. Alfred Ave., Winslow, AZ 86047 (602) 289-4488.

HIGHWATER, JAMAKE
(Blackfeet/Eastern Cherokee) 1942-
(author, lecturer)
Born February 14, 1942, Glacier County, Mont. *Education*: Holds degrees in music, comparative literature, and cultural anthropology. *Principal occupation*: Author, lecturer. *Address*: Unknown. *Affiliations*: Lecturer, Indian culture, various Universities in U.S. & Canada; founding member, Indian Art Foundation, Santa Fe, NM. *Community activities*: Cultural Council of American Indian Community House, New York, N.Y. (past president & founding member); NY State Council on the Arts (member, task force on individual artist). *Memberships*: National Congress of American Indians; White Buffalo Society of American Indians, Denver, CO; Dramatists Guild; Authors Guild; American Federation of Radio and Television Artists (AFTRA); BMI; League of American Authors. *Awards, honors*: Appointed Honorary Citizen by Governor of Oklahoma; appointed Colonel aid-de-camp on the Staff of the Governor of NM; 1978 Newbery Honor Award for novel Anpao by the American Library Association; Jane Addams Peace Book Award, 1978, for Many Smokes, Many Moons; Anisfield-Wolf Award in race relations, 1980, for Song From the Earth: American Indian Painting; interviews with Mr. Highwater have appeared in most major American, European, Latin American and Near Eastern newspapers and magazines. *Interests*: Travels extensively and does fieldwork in North and Central Africa, most American Indian communities and reservations in the U.S.; travels to Central America and Mexico, Europe and the Near East; written and presented talks about American Indian studies for th BBC, Radio Three in London, Radio Pacifica, CBS-Radio, WMCA-Radio, and numerous other radio and television networks and stations. *Biographical sources*: Who's Who in America; Directory of American Poetry; Directory of American Fiction Writers; International Who's Who; Dance World; Theatre World; Pop Bibliography; Who's Who in the East. *Published works*: Fodor's Indian American (David McKay, 1975); Song From the Earth: American Indian Painting (New York Graphic Society, Little Brown, 1976); Ritual of the Wind: American Indian Ceremonies, Music and Dances (Viking Press, 1977); Anpao: An American Indian Odyssey (J.B. Lippincott, 1977); Dance: Rituals of Experience (A & W Visual Library, 1978); Many Smokes, Many Moons: American Indian History Thru Indian Arts (J.B. Lippincott, 1978); Journey to the Sky: In Search of the Lost World of the Maya (T.Y. Crowell, 1979); The Sweet Grass Lives On: 50 Contemporary North American Indian Artists (Viking Press, 1980); Masterpieces of American Indian Painting, 8 Vols., 1978-1980; The Sun, He Dies: The End of the Aztec World, 1980; The Primal Mind: Vision and Reality in Indian America, 1981; among others (nothing added since 1981. Mr. Highwater has written numerous introductions for other books; also many articles in various journals and magazines.

*HILDEN, PATRICIA PENN (Nez Perce) 1944-
(professor)
Born May 31, 1944, Burbank, Calif. *Education*: University of California, Berkeley, BA, 1965; University of Cambridge (England), MA, 1979, PhD,

1981. *Principal occupation*: Professor. *Home address*: 1 Washington Square Village, PH-H, New York, NY 10012 (212) 982-6876. *Affiliation*: Associate professor, Emory University, Atlanta, GA, 1982-. *Other professional posts*: Fellow in History, Trinity Hall, Cambridge, England; coordinator, Special Action Tutoring Program, University of California, Davis (Office of Economic Opportunity). *Community activities*: New York University Talking Circle; Emory University Native America Awareness Month; Advisory Board, Mohawk Valley Project, 1993-94. *Memberships*: Wordcraft Circle of Native American Mentor & Apprentice Writers (regional coordinator, Northeast, 1992-93, board member, 1994-); American Historical Association, 1982-. *Awards, honors*: Best Article Prize, Berkshire Conference of Women Historians, 1992; Research awards from Fulbright Foundation, American Council of Learned Societies, National Endowment for the Humanities, British Academy, and Social Science Research Council. *Interests*: "History of France, Belgium, the Netherlands, especially labor history and the history of women. Currently working on a book about Europeans' fascination with Native Americans from the 19th century." *Biographical sources*: Who's Who in the South & Southeast; Dictionary of International Biography; The Word Who's Who of Women. *Published works*: Working Women & Socialist Politics in France (Oxford University Press, 1986); Women, Work & Politics; Belgium 1830-1914 (Oxford University Press, 1993); When Nickels Were Indians: Growing Up Mixed Blood (Smithsonian Press).

HILDERBRAND, LOUIS
(BIA agency supt.)
Affiliation: Wapato Irrigation Project, Bureau of Indian Affairs, P.O. Box 220, Wapato, WA 98951 (509) 877-3155.

HILDERMAN-SMITH, MARY
(museum executive director)
Affiliation: Marin Museum of the American Indian, P.O. Box 864, 2200 Novato Blvd., Novato, CA 94947 (510) 897-4064.

*HILL, CHARLENE
(IHS-FAS project coordinator)
Affiliation: Indian Health Service, 5300 Homestead Rd., NE, Albuquerque, NM 87110 (505) 837-4228.

HILL, EARL
(Indian band chief)
Affiliation: Mohawks of the Bay of Quinte Indian Band, RR #1, Deseronto, Ontario, Canada K0K 1X0 (613) 396-3424.

HILL, GERALD, M.D.
(Indian center director)
Affiliation: Center of American Indian and Minority Health, School of Medicine, 10 University Dr., Duluth, MN 55812-2487 (218) 726-7235 Fax 726-6235.

HILL, GERALD L.
(attorney)
Affiliation: Oneida Tribe of Wisconsin, P.O. Box 365, Oneida, WI 54155 (414) 869-2345. *Membership*: Wisconsin Indian Lawyers League.

HILL, GWENDOLYN A. (Chippewa/Cree) 1952-
(higher education administrator)
Born October 31, 1952, Ft. Belknap, Mont. *Edu-*

cation: Northern Montana College, BS, 1976; University of South Dakota, MPA, 1989. *Principal occupation*: Higher education administrator. *Home address*: RR 1, Box 1, Sisseton, SD 57262 (605) 698-3331; 698-3966 (work). *Affiliations*: Teacher, BIA, Stewart Indian School, Stewart, NV, 1975-80; dean/president, Sisseton-Wahpeton Community College, Sisseton, SD, 1981-. *Community activities*: Sisseton Public Schools (Parent Advisory Committee, Title IV, 1984-88); Native American Student Advisory Council, University of Minnesota, Morris, 1988-89. *Memberships*: American Indian Higher Education Consortium, 1988-; AACJC, 1989; National Association of Women Deans, Administrators and Counselors, 1987-89. *Interests*: "Extremely interested in promoting Indian higher education on the national, state and local level. As an administrator of a tribal college located on Lake Traverse Reservation where unemployment reaches 80%, it is imperative to ensure that our institution meets the unique educational needs of the Sisseton-Wahpeton Sioux Tribe." *Biographical source*: Carnegie Foundation for the Advancement of Teaching: Report on Tribal Colleges, 1989.

*HILL, JANICE
(foundation president)
Affiliation: Klukwan Heritage Foundation, P.O. Box 972, Haines, AK 99827 (907) 465-4700.

HILL, JAY (Seneca)
(organization president)
Affiliation: American Indian Society of Washington, DC, P.O. Box 6431, Falls Church, VA 22040 (703) 914-0548.

HILL, JOAN (*Chea-se-quah*)
(Cherokee/Creek)
(artist)
Born in Muskogee, Okla. *Education*: Muskogee Junior College, AA, 1950; Northeastern State College, BA, 1952. *Principal occupation*: Artist. *Home address*: Route 6, Box 98, Harris Rd., Muskogee, OK 74401 (918) 687-4789. *Affiliations*: Art instructor, Tulsa Public Schools, 1952-56; self-employed artist, 1956-. *Other professional posts*: Consultant, American Association of University Women; teacher, adult education. *Community activities*: Muskogee Art Students Guild (art director & publicity director, 1958-64; Youth and Art Advisory Board, Oklahomans for Indian Opportunity (board of directors, 1973-82); juror of fine arts, BIA School System, Dept. of the Interior, Tahlequah, OK, 1974-79. *Memberships*: National League of American Penwomen, Inc., 1968-; Phi Theta Kappa; Northeastern State College Alumni Association (board of directors); Southwestern Art Association; Oklahoma Art Workshops, 1984-88. *Awards, honors*: Of Ms. Hill's more than 250 awards, more than 100 are from national competitions. She has about 75 works in permanent collections; has had approximately 20 one-woman shows; has had over 450 juried and non-juried exhibitions throughout the U.S. and abroad; has participated in many traveling shows and has received numerous commissions. *Interests*: Ms. Hill works in oil, gouache, collage, acrylics, transparent watercolor, tempera, ink, pastel, conte, pencil, and mixed media. Her preferred styles are representational realism, subjective expressionism, abstract symbolism, and non-objective; travel; art workshops; numerous exhibitions. *Biographical sources*: Outstanding Young Women of America, 1965; Leadership Index, A

Biographies

Who's Who in Oklahoma, 1964; A Dictionary of American Indian Painters, 1968; American Indian Painting of the Southwest & Plains Areas, 1968; Indians of Today, 1970; Who's Who in American Art; The World Who's Who of Women (London, England); Who's Who of American Women. *Published works*: Ms. Hill's work has appeared in more than 30 publications. 17 slides, multi-media presentation, filmstrip & brochure (Executive Council of the Episcopal Church, National Committee on Indian Work, 1972); HRW Art Works, History of Art, Elementary (Holt, Rinehart & Winston, 1989).

HILL, MAXINE
(museum general manager)
Affiliation: Museum of the Cherokee Indian, U.S. Hwy. 441 North, Box 770-A, Cherokee, NC 18719 (704) 497-3481.

HILL, NORBERT S., Jr. (Oneida) 1946-
(executive director)
Born November 26, 1946, Detroit, Mich. *Education*: University of Wisconsin, B.S., 1969, M.S., 1971; Cumberland College (Williamsburg, KY), Honorary Doctorate, 1994. *Home address*: 2817 LaGrange Cir., Boulder, CO 80303 (303) 492-8658 (work). *Affiliations*: Assistant Dean of Students, University of Wisconsin, Green Bay, 1972-77; director, Native American Educational Opportunity Program, University of Colorado, Boulder, 1977-83; executive director, American Indian Science & Engineering Society, Boulder, CO, 1983-. *Other professional posts*: Chairman, Oneida Tribal Education Committee, 1970-74; Chairman, Oneida Film Project, 1976; Chairman, Native American Career Exposition, Denver, CO, 1978-79; president, Dr. Rosa Minoka Hill Foundation, 1982-; publisher, "Winds of Change" magazine, 1986-; Chairman, Smithsonian Institution's National Museum of the American Indian, 1991-. *Community activities*: Colorado Endowment for the Humanities (board of directors, 1993-); "Technos Quarterly," Editorial Advisory Board, 1993-); Environmental Defense Fund (board of directors, 1992-); Women & Foundations/Corporate Philanthropy (board of directors, 1992-); National Science Foundation's "Project Mosaic," Advisory Committee, 1992-; George Bird Grinnell American Indian Children's Education Foundation (board of directors, 1990-); National Action Council for Minorities in Engineering (NACME), 1986-. *Memberships*: American Chemical Society (member, Blue Ribbon Advisory Panel, 1993-); American Association for the Advancement of Science. *Awards, honors*: Indian Grant Scholarship, 1964-68; Education Policy Fellow, Institute for Educational Leadership, Washington, DC, 1980-81; Reginald H. Jones Distinguished Service Award, National Action Council for Minorities in Engineering, 1988; Chancellor's Award, University of Wisconsin, Oshkosh, 1988; member, Council of Advisors to President-Elect Clinton's Transition Team for Education, Dec. 1992; Honorary Doctorate, Cumberland College, 1994. *Published works*: Articles in "Smithsonian Handbook of American Indians," 1978; article in "The Indian Historian," Vol. II, No. 4, Dec. 1978; editor, "Changing America: The New Face to Science & Engineering," report (National Science Foundation, 1989); editor, "Education That Works: An Action Plan for the Education of Minorities," report (Quality Education for Minorities Project, 1990); editor, "Our Voices, Our Vision," report (The College Board/Charles Stewart Mott Foundation, 1990); editor, "Native

American Repatriation of Cultural Patrimony Act & The Native American Grave & Burial Protection Act," testimony (AISES, 1990); publisher, "Winds of Change," magazine, 1985-; editor, "The Demographics of American Indians: One Percent of the People: Fifty Percent of the Diversity," report (Institute for Educational Leadership, Inc./Center for Demographic Study, 1990); Words of Power--Voices From Indian America (Fulcrum, 1994).

HILL, RICHARD G., Sr. (Tuscarora-Oneida)
(tribal chairperson)
Affiliations: Special assistant, National Museum of the American Indian, Smithsonian Institution; co-chair, Committee on Museum-Native American Collaboration, American Association of Museums; chairman, Oneida Tribal Business Committee, P.O. Box 365, Oneida, WI 54155 (414) 869-2772; chairperson, National Indian Gaming Association, Washington, DC.

HILL, THOMAS VERNON (Seneca) 1943-
(museum director)
Born May 9, 1943, Ohsweken, Six Nations Reserve. *Education*: Ontario College of Art, Toronto, 1964-67 - A.O.C.A.; Carleton University, Ottawa, 1968; currently completing Ontario Museums Studies, Ontario Museums Association, 1985-89. *Principal occupation*: Museum director. *Address*: Box 129, Ohsweken P.O., Ontario, Canada N0A 1M0 (519) 759-2650. *Affiliations*: Director, Cultural Development, Indian & Northern Affairs, Ottawa, 1968-78; social development officer, 1979-81, native policy advisory, 1981-82, Secretary of State, Toronto, 1979-81; museum director, Woodland Cultural Centre, Brantford, 1982-. *Other professional post*: Vice-president, Visual Arts Ontario, Toronto, 1988-; chairman, Task Force on First Nations and Museums, Canadian Museums Association, 1989-; Editor, MUSE Magazine (Canadian Museums Association, 1989). *Community activities*: Six Nations Tourism; H.M. Chapel of the Mohawks Restoration; Ad Hoc Museum Committee, Brant County. *Memberships*: Visual Arts Ontario (vice-president); Canadian Museums Association; Ontario Museums Association; Ontario Genealogical Association; Society of Canadian Artists of Native Ancestry; Royal Ontario Museum; Ontario Association of Art Galleries; Canadian Native Arts Foundation; Native Canadian Centre of Toronto; The Association of Cultural Executives; National Indian Arts Council. *Awards, honors*: H.R. Majesty Service Award, 1978; Certificate of Merit, Art Director, 1976; Public Service Commission Merit Award, 1974. *Interests*: Vocational: First Nations and museums; Avocational: Film-making, painting, pottery, theatre and print-making; Eskaneh singing. *Published works*: Editor, Indian Art in Canada (Government of Canada, 1972); Norval Morrisseau and the Emergence of the Image-Makers (Methuen Art Gallery of Ontario, 1984); Canadian Native Peoples, Vol. II (Heirloom Publishing, 1988); Beyond History (Vancouver Art Gallery, 1989).

HILLABRANT, WALTER JOHN
(Citizen Band Potawatomi) 1942-
(psychologist)
Born December 17, 1942, Corsicana, Tex. *Education*: University of California, Berkeley, AB, 1965; University of California, Riverside, PhD, 1972. *Principal occupation*: Psychologist. *Home address*: 1927 38th St., NW, Washington, DC 20007. *Affiliations*: Assistant professor, Howard

University, Washington, DC, 1971-80; psychologist, president, Support Services, Inc., Silver Spring, MD, 1980-. *Memberships*: American Psychological Association; Washington Academy of Sciences; National Indian Education Association. *Interests*: Indian education; cross-cultural psychology; application of computer and telecommunication technology to social problems. *Published work*: The Future Is Now (Peacock Press, 1974).

HINES, MIFAUNWY SHUNTONA
(Indian center director)
Affiliation: American Indian Information Center, 139-11 87th Ave., Briarwood, NY 11435 (718) 291-7732.

HINKLEY, EDWARD C. 1934-
(educator)
Born December 16, 1934, Bridgewater, Mass. *Education*: Harvard University, BA, 1955, MEd, 1959. *Principal occupation*: Educator. *Home address*: P.O. Box 101, Vienna, ME 04360. *Affiliations*: Elementary school teacher, Bureau of Indian Affairs, UT and AZ, 1959-61; educational specialist, U.S. Public Health Service, Division of Indian Health, AZ and NV, 1961-65; Commissioner of Indian Affairs, State of Maine, 1965-69; education and management consultant, T.R.I.B.E., Inc. (Teaching and Research in Bicultural Education), Maine and Canada, 1969-. *Interests*: "Indian affairs of Canada and the U.S. on a contemporary level; bicultural education; community development; leadership training and counseling."

HINKSMAN, IAN
(association president)
Affiliation: B.C. Association of Indian Friendship Centres, 533 Yates St., Penthouse, Victoria, British Columbia, Canada V8W 1K7 (604) 384-3211.

HIPPS, BARRY (Eastern Cherokee)
(general manager)
Affiliation: Cherokee Historical Association, P.O. Box 398, Cherokee, NC 28719 (704) 497-21 11.

*HIRSCH, DEBORAH
(editor)
Affiliation: "The Native Magazine," Tod Bedrosian, Publisher, 7427 Braeridge Way, Sacramento, CA 95831 (916) 421-5121.

HIRSCHFELDER, ARLENE
(scholarship program contact)
Affiliation: Association on American Indian Affairs, 245 Fifth Ave., Suite 1801, New York, NY 10016 (212) 689-8720.

HIRST, STEPHEN MICHAEL 1939-
(writer)
Born December 20, 1939, Dayton, Ohio. *Education*: Miami University (Oxford, Ohio), BA, 1962; Johns Hopkins School of Advanced International Studies (Washington, DC), MA, 1966. *Principal occupation*: Writer. Resides in Marquette, MI. *Affiliations*: Preschool director, Havasupai Tribe, 1967-68, 1970-73; planner, Havasupai Tribe, 1975-76. *Memberships*: The Authors Guild, 1976-. *Awards, honors*: 1961 Best Columnist Award of Ohio Collegiate Newspaper Association; 1962 Greer-Hepburn Fiction Award; 1966 U.S. Commerce Department Service Award; 1976 Havasupai Tribe Service Award; 1979 Cincinnati Arts Consortium Writing Award; 1981 Ohio Arts Council Fiction

Award; finalist for 1982 Arizona Commission on the Arts fiction award. *Published works*: Life In a Narrow Place: The Havasupai of the Grand Canyon (David McKay Co., 1976); Havsuw' Baaja (Havasupai Tribe, 1985).

*HOAG, DEBBIE (Seneca)
(editor)

Affiliation: Seneca Tribal Nesletter, Cattauragus Indian Reservation, 1490 Route 438, Irving, NY 14081.

*HOBSON, BARBARA *(Torralba)*
(Comanche) 1951-
(educator)

Born May 26, 1951, Lawton, Okla. *Education*: Oklahoma State University, BA, 1973; University of New Mexico, MA, 1978; University of Oklahoma, PhD, 1994. *Home address*: 3015 72nd NE, Norman, OK 73071 (405) 329-7729. *Affiliation*: Counselor, Southwestern Indian Polytechnic Institute, Albuquerque, NM, 1973-77; minority counselor, University of Albuquerque, 1978-80; coordinator, Native American Program, College of Engineering, University of Oklahoma, 1985-88; Assistant Div., Native American Studies Program, University of Oklahoma, Norman, OK, 1994. *Other professional post*: Returning the Gift Native Writers Project, 1990-92. *Awards, honors*: Foundations in Native Education Fellow, 1989-93, University of Oklahoma, College of Education; American Indian Education Fellow, Dept. of Indian Education, Washington, DC, 1990-93. *Interests*: "Special area of interests - American Indian retention." *Unpublished dissertation*: Cultural Values & Persistence Among Comanche College Students, University of Oklahoma, 1994. *Published work*: "Tribally Controlled Colleges: Meeting the Needs of American Indian Adults," monograph (Office of Indian Affairs, State of Oklahoma, 1991);

HOBSON, DOTTIE F. (Navaho) 1945-
(school principal)

Born March 9, 1945, Tohatchi, N.M. *Education*: University of Arizona, BA, 1972; University of New Mexico, MA, 1977; Northern Arizona University, MA, 1977. *Principal occupation*: School princpal. *Address & Affiliation*: Dilcon Boarding School, Star Route, Winslow, AZ 86047 (602) 657-3211. *Other professional post*: Supt. for education, Chinle Agency, BIA, Chinle, AZ, 1978-90. *Community activities*: Boy Scouts of America (institutional representative); Gyro Scouts; Federal Women's Program Coordinator, Chinle Agency. *Memberships*: Navaho School Administrators Association; National Indian Education Association. *Published works*: Kee's Grandfather (Rough Rock Demonstration School, Chinle, AZ, 1970).

*HOBSON, GEARY
(professor)

Born June 12, 1941, Chicot County, Ark. *Education*: Arizona State University, B.A., 1968, M.A., 1969; University of New Mexico, Ph.D., 1986. *Principal occupation*: Professor. *Address & Affiliation*: Dept. of English, University of Oklahoma, 455 W. Lindsey, Norman, OK 73019 (405) 325-4661 (work), 1988-. *Military service*: U.S. Marine Corps, 1959-65. *Community activities*: Project historian of Returning the Gift (now called Native Writers Circle of the Americas); organizer of the Arkansas Band of Quapaw Indians. *Awards, honors*: Rockefeller Fellowship for Minority Scholars, 1981-82; National Endowment of the Arts grant, 1982-83. *Biographical*

source: Contemporary Authors, Vol. 122. *Published works*: Editor, The Remembered Earth: An Anthology of Contemporary Native American Literature (University of New Mexico Presm 1979; Deer Hunter & Other Poems (Point Riders Press, 1990).

*HODGE, FELICIA SCHANCHE (Wailaki) 1949-
(scientist)

Born January 3, 1949, Garberville, Calif. *Education*: University of California, Berkeley, MPH, 1976, Dr.P.H., 1987. *Principal occupation*: Scientist. *Home address*: 608 Adams St., Albany, CA 94706 (510) 843-8661 (work). *Affiliations*: Northwest Portland Area Indian Health Board, Portland, OR (evaluation coordinator, 1976-77; executive director, 1977-82); student research assistant, UC-Berkeley (while working on a doctoral degree); principal investigator, American Indian Cancer Control Project, Berkeley, CA, 1990-; principal investigator, American Indian Women's Talking Circle, Berkeley, CA, 1993-; director, Center for American Indian Research & Education, Western Consortium for Public Health, Berkeley, CA, 1994-. *Other professional posts*: Consultant to agencies/projects, 1984-; lecturer, School of Social Welfare, UC-Berkeley, 1989-; director, American Indian Graduate Program, UC-Berkeley, 1989-. *Community activities*: Chairman-Board of Directors, American Indian Child Resource Center, 1990-91, 1994; trustee, Administrative Board of the California Teen Nutritional & Fitness Program, Western Consortium for Public Health, Berkeley), 1993; Advisory Board, Rural Institute on Disabilities, University of Montana, 1994. *Membership*: National Network for Cancer Control Research Among American Indians & Alaska Native Populations. *Awards, honors*: Duncan Neuhauser Award, UC-Berkeley, 1984; Kaiser Award, Golden State Minority Foundation, Los Angeles, 1984 & 1985; IHS Scholarship, 1985 & 1986; Ruth Muscrat Bronson Memorial Scholarship, Save the Children, Westport, CT, 1986; postdoctoral Fellowship, Alcohol Research Group, UC-Berkeley, 1987. *Published works*: Graduate Education & Employment, A Study of American Indian & Non-Indians in the School of Public Health, UC-Berkeley, 1971-85 (UC-Berkeley, 1986); The Socio-Cultural Aspects of Disability: A Survey of Disabled Adult American Indians, monograph, with R. Edmonds (University of Arizona, 1987); Creating an Agenda for American Indian Health in the Year 2000, monograph, with A. Williams & W. Whitehorse (State of California, 1992); "Contemporary U.S. Indian Health Care," in The Native North American Almanac (Gale Research, 1994); Papers submitted & accepted for publication: "Smoking Cessation for American Indians in Northern California," & "Tobacco Use Policies & Practices in Diverse Indian Settings" (Preventive Medicine, 1994); among other articles, and professional papers.

HOFFMAN, BRUCE (Miccosukee)
(school principal)

Affiliation: Miccosukee Indian School, Box 440021, Tamiami Station, Miami, FL 33144 (305) 223-8380.

HOFFMAN, MICHAEL P. 1937-
(anthropologist, professor, museum curator)

Born September 15, 1937, Council Bluffs, Iowa. *Education*: University of Illinois, BA, 1959; Harvard University, PhD, 1971. *Principal occu-*

pation: Anthropologist, professor, museum curator. *Home address*: 409 N. Washington, Fayetteville, AR 72701. *Affiliations*: Professor of anthropology, museum curator, University of Arkansas, Fayetteville, 1964-. *Community activities*: Arkansas Folklore Society (board of directors); ANL Research Laboratory (board of directors); Arkansas Preservation Program (past member, State Review Committee). *Memberships*: Society for American Archaeology, 1960-; American Anthropological Association (Fellow) 1961-; Caddo Conference, 1964-; Southeastern Archaeological Conference, 1975-; Current Anthropology (Associate); American Indian Historical Society; Association for American Indian Affairs; Arkansas Archaeological Society. *Awards, honors*: Phi Beta Kappa. *Interests*: Southeastern Indians, past and present; Caddo, Quapaw, and Cherokee ethnology and contemporary life; avocational interests--running, fishing; expeditions: archaeological fieldwork in Arkansas, Missouri, Illinois, Arizona, Massachusetts, and Guatemala. *Published works*: Three Sites in Millwood Reservoir (Arkansas Archaeological Survey, 1970); The Kinkaid-Mainard Site, 3PU2 (Arkansas Archaeologist, 1977); Ozark Reservoir Papers (Arkansas Archaeological Survey, 1978); Prehistoric Ecological Crises (Kennikat Press, 1980); Arkansas Indians, (Arkansas Naturalist, 1984).

HOKANSEN, SHERRY (Yakima)
(librarian)

Affiliation: Yakima Cultural Heritage Library, P.O. Box 151, Yakima Nation Cultural Center, Toppenish, WA 98948 (509) 865-2800.

*HOLM, MICHAEL
(historic site manager)

Affiliation: Knife River Indian Villages National Historic Site, RR 1 Box 168, Stanton, ND 58571 (701) 745-3300.

*HOLM, WILLIAM
(museum curator)

Affiliation: Washington State Museum, Thomas Burke Memorial, University of Washington, Seattle, WA 98195 (206) 543-5590.

HOLMAN, LARRY D.
(BIA agency supt. for education)

Affiliation: Eastern Navajo Agency, Bureau of Indian Affairs, P.O. Box 328, Crownpoint, NM 87313 (505) 786-6150.

HOLMAN, WILLIAM
(health director)

Affiliation: Sonoma County Indian Health Program, P.O. Box 7308, Santa Rosa, CA 95407 (707) 544-4056.

HOLT, LAURA
(librarian)

Affiliation: Museum of Indian Arts & Culture, Laboratory of Anthropology, 708 Camino Lejo, Santa Fe, NM 87504 (505) 827-6344.

HOLT, RONALD (Nez Perce) 1944-
(TV station director)

Born November 26, 1944, Orifino, Idaho. *Education*: Los Angeles Community College, 1970-72; Columbia College of Fine Arts, 1972-75. *Principal occupation*: TV station director. *Address & Affiliation*: KOBL-TV, Dull Knife Memorial College, P.O. Box 98, Lame Deer, MT 59043. *Past professional post*: TV producer, National Education Association, Washington, DC. *Other professional post*: TV-host, TV writer; editorial board, "Native People" Magazine. *Memberships*: National Press Club; Native American Press Association; National Association of Broadcasters.

HOMER, DARVIN E.
(school principal)
Affiliation: Herfano Dormitory, P.O. Box 639, Bloomfield, NM 87413 (505) 786-6160.

HOMER, DENISE
(BIA acting area director)
Affiliation: Minneapolis Area Office, Bureau of Indian Affairs, 331 S. Second Ave., Minneapolis, MN 55401 (612) 373-1000.

*HOMER, PETE, JR.
(government agency director)
Affiliation: Office of Native American Affairs, Small Business Administration, 409 3rd St., SW, Washington, DC 20416 (202) 205-6421.

*HONAHNI, BRANT
(school chairperson)
Affiliation: Moencopi Day School, P.O. Box 185, Tuba City, AZ 86045 (602) 283-5361

HONANIE, GILBERT, JR. (Hopi) 1941-
(architect, planning)
Born April 11, 1941, Tuba City, Ariz. *Education*: Pasadena City College, AA, 1969; Arizona State University, BA (Architecture), 1972. *Principal occupation*: Architect, planning. Resides in Phoenix, AZ (602) 277-6844. *Affiliation*: President, owner, architect, Gilbert Honanie, Jr., Inc., Phoenix, AZ, 1975-. *Other professional posts*: National Council of Architectural Registration Board; American Indian Council of Architects & Engineers; Western & Arizona Society of Architects. *Community activities*: Member of Hopi Tribe; member, Arizona Indian Chamber of Commerce; member. Central Arizona Chapter of Architects. *Biographical sources*: Articles in the Arizona Republic & Gazette, Arizona Builder, Progressive Architecture, and Architectural Journal.

HONEA, DONALD, SR. (Athapascan)
(AK village president)
Affiliation: Native Village of Ruby, P.O. Box 21, Ruby, AK 99768 (907) 468-4406.

HONER, JANELLE A. (Seminole) 1954-
(artist, gardener)
Born February 28, 1954, Hayward, Calif. *Education*: Humboldt State University, BA (Art, Native American Studies), 1976; Anderson Ranch, Snowmass Village, CO (seminars & workshops), 1978-82. *Principal occupation*: Artist, gardener. *Affiliations*: Owner operator, Doug & Janella's Garden, El Jebel, CO, 1981-; gallery artist, Janie Beggs Fine Arts Ltd., Aspen, Colo., 1986-. *Community activities*: Advisor, Aspen Dance Connection. *Memberships*: National Gardening Association; American Crafts Council; Aspen Art Museum; Colorado Council on the Arts; Carbondale Council on the Arts & Humanities. *Art exhibitions & shows*: Featured artist, Cohen Gallery, Denver, Colo., 1985; Roaring Fork Annual, Aspen Art Museum, 1985; Colorado Artists-Craftsmen Exhibit, Boulder, Colo., 1984; one-person show, Sioux National Museum, 1981; Roaring Fork Valley Art Show, Aspen Center for the Visual Arts, 1981. *Awards, honors*: Magna Cum Laude, Humboldt State University, Arcata, Calif., 1976; first & second place prizes, Women

Art West, Grand Junction, Colo., 1982-1983; Craft Range Magazine award for Buy the Heartland, 1982; first place sculpture, Woman Art West, 1980; inclusion in Northern Plains, Southern Plains Indian Museum art collections; among others. *Interests*: Vocational: "We are organic farmers with a gourmet produce market garden. We teach people basic skills and give garden tours, sell produce. We educate about wild edibles, food storage; we both are chefs. I also do mixed media sculpture and ceramic sculpture, that is the art I show. We travel extensively. My goal is to help feed the hungry."

HOOBAN, HOMER, II "LOUIS"
(Running Buffalo) (Bannock) 1943-
(professional counselor; education)
Born June 21, 1943, Coeur d'Alene, Idaho. *Education*: Idaho State University, BA, 1966, MEd, 1969; University of Wyoming, ED.S, ABD, 1971. *Principal occupation*: Professional counselor; education. *Home address*: Box 2302 - Henry St., Morristown, TN 37816 (615) 581-4448. *Affiliations*: CEO, Indian Heritage Council, Morristown, TN, 1990-; director, Confidential Counseling Services, Morristown, TN. *Other professional posts*: President, local education association; director, 5 major national powwows; publisher, Indian Heritage Council. *Community activities*: Sponsor of boy scout groups - national dance champions; B.P.O.E. - youth director; coach of all sports (25 years-never had a losing season as a head coach). *Membership*: Tennessee Education Association; National Education Association; Boy Scouts (sponsor); Tennessee Counselors Association; National Psychological Association. *Awards, honors*: Poet Laureate of the Indian Nations, 1988 - World's Fair Site of National Pow-wow - Knoxville, TN; Indian Heritage Council Award for Literature; coach of the year awards (TN). *Interests*: "Psychology, public speaking, counseling, writing; have traveled around the world, to all major landmarks; healing arts; have always coached winning teams (all sports)." *Biographical sources*: Who's Who; Dictionary Biography of the West; Who's Who International Biography. *Published works*: The Scorched Earth (Scotway Press, 1988); editor - Great American Indian Bible (Indian Heritage Publishing, 1990); Indian Nation (Indian Heritage Publishing, 1991).

HOOVER, HERBERT T. 1930-
(professor of history)
Born March 9, 1930, Oakwood Township, Wabasha County, Minn. *Education*: New Mexico State University, BA, 1960, MA, 1961; University of Oklahoma, Norman, PhD, 1966. *Principal occupation*: Professor of history. *Address*: Institute of American Indian Studies, 414 E. Clark St., Dakota Hall, University of South Dakota, Vermillion, SD 57069 (605) 677-5209. *Affiliations*: Assistant professor of history, East Texas State University, 1965-67; professor of history, University of South Dakota, Vermillion, 1967-. *Other professional posts*: Director, Newberry Library Center for the History of the American Indian, Chicago, IL, 1981-83; director, South Dakota Oral History Center, 1967-; director, Institute of American Indian Studies, University of South Dakota, 1990-93. *Military service*: U.S. Navy, 1951-55 (Fleet Marine Corpsman with First Marine Division in Korean War). *Community activities*: SD Council of Humanists; SD Committee on the Humanities; National Endowment for the Humanities (review panels); SD Historical Society

(board of trustees); SD Fairview Township Board of Control; SD Historical Publications and Records Commission. *Memberships*: Western History Association, 1962- (chair, nominating board; local arrangements committee; program committee; membership committee; board of editors); Organization of American Historians, 1970- (nominating board; membership committee); Phi Alpha Theta, 1960- (international councillor; international board of advisors); SD Historical Society; Missouri Historical Society; Minnesota Wabasha County Historical Society. *Awards, honors*: Augustana College Center for Western Studies, 1985 Achievement Award, National Board of Advisors; National Endowment for the Humanities, Research Grant Award, 1978-81; National Teacher of the Year Award, 1985. *Interests*: "Travel and recreation is tied to principal occupational interests: the history of Indian-white relations, and the preservation of natural life." *Published works*: To Be An Indian (Holt, Rinehart & Winston, 1971); The Practice of Oral History (Microfilming Corp. of America, 1975); The Chitimacha People (Indian Tribal Series, 1975); The Sioux: A Critical Bibliography (Indiana University, 1979); Bibliography of the Sioux (Scarecrow Press, 1980); Yanktonai Sioux Water Colors: Cultural Remembrances of John Saul (Center for Western Studies, Augustana College, 1993); numerous articles on Plains Indians, including The Yankton Sioux and a forthcoming bibliography on the Sioux.

HOOVER, JAY BRUCE
(school principal)
Affiliation: Wingate High School, P.O. Box 2, Fort Wingate, NM 87316 (505) 488-6400.

*HOPAHNIS, BRANT (Hopi)
(BIA education chairperson)
Affiliation: Hopi Agency, Bureau of Indian Affairs, P.O. Box 568, Keams Canyon, AZ 86034 (602) 738-2262.

HOPKINS, GEORGE H. (Narragansett)
(chief sachem)
Affiliation: Narragansett Indian Tribe, P.O. Box 268, Charleston, RI 02813 (401) 364-1100.

HOPE, ARLENE
(Indian band chief)
Affiliation: Klahoose Indian Band, Box 9, Squirrel Cove, British Columbia, Canada V0P 1T0 (604) 935-6650.

HOPE, EVE
(museum director/curator)
Affiliation: Ksan Museum, P.O. Box 333, Hazelton, British Columbia, Canada V0J 1Y0 (604) 842-9723.

HOPKINS, GEORGE H. (Narragansett)
(tribal chief)
Affiliation: Narragansett Indian Tribal Council, P.O. Box 268, Charleston, RI 02813 (401) 364-1100.

*HOPKINS, SUE (Jowanna)
(Oklahoma Cherokee) 1940-
(school secretary)
Born December 10, 1940, Durant, Okla. *Education*: High school. *Principal occupation*: School secretary. *Address*: HC-62, Box 227, Durant, OK 74701 (405) 924-7000 (work). *Affiliation*: School secretary, Indian Education Director, Title V-C, JOM, Silo, OK, 1970-; pianist, Silo Baptist Church, 1970-. *Other professional*

post: Piano teacher, 1964-. *Community activities*: Pianist for Memorial Day Services, Contatas, Plays, Rest Homes, Senior Citizens, Funerals, Weddings. *Memberships*: NAFIS, OASIS. *Interests*: "As Indian Education director, I travel to Washington, DC each year for meetings and visits with White House officials; JOM Meetings in Tulsa, OK, NAFIS Meetings in Yakima, WA. I am in the process of completing a journal which I am planning to put into a short story."

*HOPSON, BARBARA
(program interim director)
Affiliation: Native American Studies Program, University of Oklahoma, 455 W. Lindsay, Rm. 804, Norman, OK 73019 (405) 325-2312.

HORACE, EMERSON, Jr.
(Indian school principal)
Affiliation: Hoteville Bacavi Community School, P.O. Box 48, Hoteville, AZ 86030 (602) 734-2462.

*HORLAN, THERESA
(museum curator)
Affiliation: Carl Nelson Gorman Museum, Native American Studies, 2401 Hart Hall, Davis, CA 95616 (916) 752-6567.

*HORNBACHER, HARLAN
(school prinicpal)
Affiliation: Red Lake Day School, P.O. Box 39, Tonalea, AZ 86044 (602) 283-6325.

HORNETT-PETTIBONE, DANIELLE M.
(*Bitawaasomokwe*) (Bad River Ojibwe/ Cherokee) 1942-
(college administrator)
Born December 22, 1942, Ashland, Wisc. *Education*: University of Wisconsin, Whitewater, MSE, 1977; University of Illinois, Champaign-Urbana, PhD, 1983. *Principal occupation*: College admiistrator. *Home address*: 408 Moon Glow Dr., DePere, WI 54115 (414) 337-3963. *Affiliations*: Director, Learning Center, Mankato State University, Mankato, MN; Associate Dean, St. Norbert College, DePere, WI, 1991-. *Other professional post*: Professor-teacher trainer, University of Wisconsin, Milwaukee. *Memberships*: Wisconsin Educational Opportunities Program Personnel; Mid-America Educational Opportunities Program Personnel; National Indian Education Association. *Awards, honors*: National TRIO Achiever's Award, National Education Opportunity Office; Minority Faculty Development Award, University of Wisconsin System. *Interests*: "Worked with and taught deaf children, traveled to Mexico as director of a summer bilingual program and lived in Central America with the Peace Corp, 1983-84." *Published works*: Teaching Deaf Children: Methods & Techniques (College-Hill Press, 1988); several articles regarding deaf and Americn Indian students.

HORSE, ANTHONY WHIRLWIND (Sioux)
(school chairperson)
Affiliation: Pine Ridge School, P.O. Box 1202, Pine Ridge, SD 57770 (605) 867-5198.

*HORSE, BILLY EVANS (Kiowa)
(tribal committee chairperson)
Affiliation: Kiowa Business Committee, P.O. Box 369, Carnegie, OK 73015 (405) 654-2300.

HORSE CAPTURE, GEORGE P.
(*Spotted Otter*) (Gros Ventre) 1937-
(museum curator)
Born October 20, 1937, Fort Belknap, Mont. *Education*: University of California, Berkeley, BA, 1974; Montana State University, MA (History), 1979. *Principal occupation*: Museum curator. *Affiliation*: Curator, Plains Indian Museum, Buffalo Bill Historical Center, P.O. Box 1000, Cody, WY 82414, 1980-90. *Other professional posts*: Assistant professor, Montana State University; curriculum researcher, College of Great Falls, MT. *Military service*: U.S. Navy, 1957-61 (2nd class ship fitter; Good Conduct, China Service Medal). *Community activities*: Founding member and Presidential appointment to Institute of Museum Services Board; Governor's appointment to Wyoming Travel Commission; and others. *Awards, honors*: The 1983 W.E. Cody Motion Picture Award for "I'd Rather Be Powwowing." Several grants from various organizations. *Interests*: Participate in powwows and original ceremonies; have researched museums in U.S., Canada and Europe; interested in Indian music and artwork, culture and history. *Published works*: Editor, The Seven Visions of Bull Lodge; exhibition catalogs.

HORSE, IMOGENE (Sioux)
(school principal)
Affiliation: Pine Ridge School, P.O. Box 1202, Pine Ridge, SD 57770 (605) 867-5198.

*HORSE, PERRY G. (Kiowa)
(college president)
Born in Carnegie, Okla. *Education*: Harvard University Graduate School of Education, MEd; University of Arizona, PhD. Resides in Albuquerque, NM. *Principal occupation*: College president. *Address & Affiliation*: Institute of American Indian Arts, P.O. Box 20007, Santa Fe, NM 87504 (505) 988-6463. *Past professional activities*: Has worked in Indian post secondary education for the past 24 years including managment of community college development programs; has consulted on strategic & institutional planning & staff development for a number of tribal colleges across the country; was instrumental in developing the American Indian Higher Education Consortium; was an advisor to The MacArthur Foundation on funding for tribal colleges and the Albuquerque Public Schools on developing an American Indian cultural curriculum; has taught tribal government and Federal Indian Law for the Institute for Development of Indian Law, Oklahoma City, OK; and most recently, has been in charge of leadership and management development at Sandia National Laboratories in Albuquerque, NM.

HORSEMAN, DALE ROBERT
(Indian band chief)
Affiliation: Horse Lake Indian Band, P.O. Box 303, Hythe, Alberta, Canada T0H 2C0 (403) 356-2248.

HORSMAN, REGINALD 1931-
(distinguished professor of history)
Born October 24, 1931, Leeds (Yorkshire) England. *Education*: University of Birmingham, England, BA, 1952, MA, 1955; Indiana University, PhD, 1958. *Principal occupation*: Distinguished professor of history. *Home address*: 3548 North Hackett Ave., Milwaukee, WI 53211. *Affiliations*: Instructor, 1958-59, professor, 1959-73, and distinguished professor of history, 1973-, University of Wisconsin, Milwaukee. *Memberships*:

D'Arcy McNickle Center for the History of the American Indian, Newberry Library (member, Advisory Council, 1988-93); American Historical Association; Organization of American Historians; Society of American Historians; Society for Historians of the Early Republic (advisory council); Phi Beta Kappa (honorary member); Phi Kappa Phi (honorary member); Phi Eta Sigma (honorary member); Phi Alpha Theta. *Awards, honors*: University of Wisconsin Kiehofer Award for Excellence in Teaching, 1961; Guggenheim Fellowship, 1965. *Interests*: "Research on race and expansion in American history; shaping of American Indian policy; early American foreign policy; Wisconsin Oneida." Biographical source: Who's Who in America. *Published works*: The Causes of the War of 1812 (University of Pennsylvania Press, 1962); Matthew Elliott: British Indian Agent (Wayne State University Press, 1964); Expansion and American Indian Policy, 1783-1812 (Michigan State University Press, 1967); Napolean's Europe; The New America (Paul Hamlyn, London, 1970) The Frontier in the Formative Years, 1783-1815 (Holt, Rinehart, 1970) Race and Manifest Destiny: The Origins of American Racial Anglo-Saxonism (Harvard University Press, 1981); The Diplomacy of the New Republic, 1776-1815 (Harlan Davidson, 1985); Dr. Nott of Mobile: Southerner, Physician, and Racial Theorist (LSU Press, 1987).

HOSICK, H. CLARK
(executive director)
Affiliation: North American Indian Cultural Center, 1062 Triplett Blvd., Akron, OH 44306 (216) 724-1280.

HOSKINS, HELEN (Southern Ute)
(cultural center director)
Affiliation: Southern Ute Cultural Center, P.O. Box 737, Ignacio, CO 81137 (303) 563-9583.

*HOSTLER, DAVID E.
(museum curator)
Affiliation: Hoopa Tribal Museum, P.O. Box 1348, Hoopa, CA 95546 (916) 625-4110.

HOTCH, JOE
(AK village council president)
Affiliation: Chilkat Indian Village of Klikwan, P.O. Box 219, Haines, AK 99827 (907) 767-5505.

HOULIHAN, PATRICK T. 1942-
(anthropologist)
Born June 22, 1942, New Haven, Conn. *Education*: Georgetown University, BS, 1964; University of Minnesota, MA, 1969; University of Wisconsin, PhD, 1972. *Principal occupation*: Anthropologist, museum director. *Address*: Milicent Rogers Museum, Taos, NM 87571 (505) 758-2462. *Affiliations*: Instructor, University of Wisconsin, Oshkosh, 1969-71; director, Anthropology Museum, University of Wisconsin, Oshkosh, 1969-71; museum intern, Milwaukee Public Museum, 1971-72; adjunct professor, Arizona State University, 1972-80; director, The Heard Museum, Phoenix, 1972-80; director, New York State Museum, Albany, 1980-81; instructor, American Indian art, UCLA, Extension Division, 1981-87; director, Southwest Museum, Los Angeles, Calif., 1981-87; director, Milicent Rogers Museum, Taos, NM, 1987-92. *Memberships*: American Association of Museums (first vice president, Western Regional Conference); American Anthropological Association (council on museum education). *Field work*: Urban In-

dian research for the Indian employment service (BIA sponsored), Minneapolis, 1967. *Awards, honors*: Honorary PhD, Occidental College, Los Angeles, CA. Interests: American Indian art. *Published works*: Museums & Indian Education, (Journal of Indian Education, Oct., 1973) Southwest Pottery Today, (Arizona Highways, May, 1974); The Hopi Kachinas, (Image Roche Magazine, No. 63, 1974); Indian Art: Fads and Paradoxes, (Phoenix Magazine, Feb., 1975); Basketry Designs in the Greater Southwest, (Exhibit Catalog, Utah Fine Arts Museum, Salt lake City, April, 1976); Contemporary Indian Art, (Exhibit Catalog, Mid-America Arts Association, Spring, 1979); Prints and the American Indian Artist, (American Indian Arts Magazine, Spring, 1979); Indians of the Northwest Coast, (Reader's Digest, 1980); various articles in Masterkey, a quarterly publication of the Southwest Museum, 1981-. Editorial director for the following Heard *Museum publications*: Kachinas: A Hopi Artist's Documentary, 1973; Pueblo Shields, April, 1976; The Other Southwest: Indian Arts and Crafts of Northeastern Mexico, April, 1977. Editorial director for the following Southwest Museum publications: Native Faces: Indian Cultures in American Art, co-author with Patricia Trenton, 1984; Kachinas of the Zuni (Northland Press, 1985); Lummis in the Pueblos (Northland Press, 1985); Native Americans: Five Centuries of Changing Images (Harry Abrams, 1989). *Television programs*: Script author for six one-half hour television programs, Indian Art at the Heard, produced by KAET, 1975; script researcher/writer for five one-half hour television programs titles, American Indian Artists, produced by KAET, 1976; script author for a one-half hour television program on The Craft Arts of Northwestern Mexico, produced by KAET, 1977; guest curator, Generation in Clay, traveling exhibit of Pueblo Pottery, the American Federation of Art, New York, 1980-83; principal investigator (1977-80), Navajo Film Project, KAET, Tempe, AZ.

HOUSE, CARRIE H. (Navajo/Oneida) 1965-
(freelance film/video productions)
Born March 19, 1965, W inslow, Ariz. *Education*: Navajo Community College, 1982-83; University of Montana, BS (Natural Resource Conservation(, 1987. *Principal occupation*: Freelance film/video productions. Resides in Santa Fe, NM. *Affiliations*: Native American Public Broadcasting Consortium, Lincoln, NE, 1985-90; National Center for Production of Native Images, Santa Fe, NM, 1991-. Other professional post: Engine Forepoerson-fire fighter, USDA Coconino National Forest, Peaks Ranger District. *Community activities*: Navajo Nation, voluntarily assist in acquire/document history of our Oaksprings community for the Oaksprings Chapter House; presentations for educational institutions; presentations of Fire Behavior with Bureau of Land Management, USDI in Farming-ton, NM. *Awards, honors*: Public Affairs Production at the WGBH Educational Foundation as a WGBH - CPB Fellow in Feb. 1992; Award Fellow Recipient of Native American Public Broadcasting Consortium for Robert McKee's Story Structure Course in April 1991. *Interests*: Infinite travels for research/development of film/video and personal initiatives; yearly participant of the International Wildlife Film Festival in Missoula, MT, since 1985 to present. *Biographical sources*: Articles: "D-5 Sweeps CHIPA Muster," The Coconino Forest Pine Log, Sept. 1990; "Its a Jungle Out There," Los Angeles Times,

Sect. F, April 11, 1991; and "House Completes Boston Workshop," Navajo Times, Vol. 23, No. 10, March 5, 1992.

HOUSER, ALLAN (Chiricahua Apache) 1914-
1994 (Deceased)
(artist, art instructor)
Born June 30, 1914, Apache, Okla. *Education*: Santa Fe Indian School; Utah State University (private study). *Principal occupation*: Artist, art instructor. *Home address*: 1020 Camino Carlos Rey, Santa Fe, NM 87501. *Affiliation*: Instructor in sculpture and advanced painting, Institute of American Indian Arts, Santa Fe (retired). *Membership*: Southwestern Association on Indian Affairs (board of directors). *Awards, honors*: Mural commissions: W ashington, DC, San Francisco Exposition and New York World's Fair, 1939; Guggenheim Scholarship for sculpture and painting, 1948; created seven and one-half feet tall marble statue, Comrade in Mourning, for Haskell Institute, 1949; 1954 recipient of Palmes de Academique from French Government for painting; awarded W aite Phillips Trophy for outstanding contributions to field of Indian art, Philbrook Art Center, 1969; appeared in a documentary film produced by National Educational Television, aired 1976; received the National Medal of the Arts from President George Bush in 1992; presented a 12-foot bronze statue entitled "Offering of the Sacred Pipe" on April 28, 1994 to the American people and accepted by first lady Hillary Rodham Clinton. The statue will be placed on temporary display on the grounds of the vice president in northwest Washintgon, D.C. until it is moved to the new Native American Museum, scheduled to open on The Mall in 2000 or 2001. *Interests*: "Sculpture, painting, book illustration, lecturing; writing; recording stories; travels to Navajo Reservation, New York City, Mexico City." *Published works*: Mr. Houser's illustrations have appeared in many books.

HOUSTON, MARGARET
(museum director)
Affiliation: Indian Museum of the Carolinas, 607 Turnpike Rd., Laurinburg, NC 28352 (919) 276-5880.

HOUTEN, MARGARET (Paiute) 1946-
(court administration)
Born October 2, 1946, Schurz, Nev. *Education*: High school. *Principal occupation*: Clerical. *Home address*: 14 Waterline Rd., P.O. Box 265, Nixon, NV 89424 (702) 574-0205. *Professional posts*: Court clerk; vice-president, National American Indian Court Clerks Association, Washington, DC. Community activities: Not as active as before, due to kidney failure. Assist with donation for fundraising such as V eteran's Memorial, church, senior citizens, when possible. *Memberships*: National American Indian Court Clerks Association, 1979-; National Notary Public Association. *Interests*: "Vocation mostly geared toward legal matters, plan to do more traveling with arts & craft after retirement, possibly after a kidney transplant. W ould like to get more into the legal aspect of Indian law in the future. I have had a lot of contact with Indian lawyers and judges, men and women, and it is exciting."

HOVI, DOROTHY 1933-
(Native American jewelry & craft sales)
Born April 17, 1933, Trenton, N.J. *Education*: Ursinus College (Collegeville, P A), BS, 1955.

Principal occupation: Native American jewelry & craft sales. *Address & Affiliation*: Owner (1976-), Way of the Arrow, 72 South St., New Providence, NJ 07974 (908) 464-2270. *Membership*: Indian Arts and Crafts Association.

*HOWARD, CARYN (Sault Ste. Marie Chippewa) 1960-
(business owner)
Born September 13, 1960, Lansing, Mich. *Education*: University of Michigan, BA, 1982. *Principal occupation*: Business owner. *Address*: P.O. Box 326, Brooklyn, MI 49230 (517) 592-3439. *Affiliation*: Owner, Bear Tracks DBA Bundy's Bungalow, Brooklyn, MI. *Community activities*: Member, Chamber of Commerce, Brooklyn, MI; ex Peace Corps Volunteer.

*HOWARD, DAVID (Eskimo)
(AK village first chief)
Affiliation: Village of Eagle, P.O. Box 19, Eagle, AK 99738 (907) 547-2271.

*HOWARD, GREGG (Cherokee/Powhattan) 1934-
(writer, narrator)
Born May 5, 1934, Central City, Ky. *Education*: Ohio State University, 1956-68. *Principal occupation*: Writer, narrator. *Home address*: 14016 Peyton Dr. #107, Dallas, TX 75240 (800) 776-0842; (214) 991-6797 (work). *Affiliations*: President, Howard Creative Services, Dallas, TX; co-owner, VIP Publishing Co., Fayetteville, AR, 1990-. *Military service*: U.S. Marine Corps (Sgt.), 1953-57 (Korean Network). *Memberships*: American Society of Training & Development, 1971-; Aircraft Owners & Pilots Association, 1970-. *Awards, honors*: Wrangler Award, Cowboy Hall of Fame; IABC Gold Quill Award, 1984; Silver Mike Award, 1990. *Interests*: Currently teaches Cherokee at Eastfield College, Dallas. In 1990, he and Al Houser (brother of Alan Houser - the late Apache sculptor from Santa Fe, NM), and Rick Eby of Springdale, AR, formed a company called VIP (Various Indian Peoples) Publishing Co., and began recording Indian languages and legends, both in English & Indian. To date, they have preserved portions of the Cherokee, Choctaw, and Kiowa legends & languages; Gregg has written training workbooks in both Cherokee & Choctaw languages. *Published works*: Audio tapes: "Authentic Indian Music of the Apache, Sioux, Navajo, Crow, Ute, Shawnee," and "Authentic Indian Legends-The Cherokee (both by VIP Publishing); works-inprogress - Cherokee Christmas Music, Kiowa Legends; and recordings of interviews with people who actually knew Geronimo.

HOWARD, LYNN (Cherokee)
(editor)
Affiliation: Cherokee Advocate, Cherokee Nation of Oklahoma, Communications Department, P.O. Box 948, Tahlequah, OK 74465 (918) 456-0671.

*HOWE, RAYMOND
(school principal)
Affiliation: Loneman Day School, P.O. Box 50, Oglala, SD 57764 (605) 867-5633.

HOWELL, GEORGE E. (Pawnee-Cheyenne) 1935-
(health systems administrator)
Born December 30, 1935, Pawnee, Okla. *Education*: Westminster College, Salt Lake City, BS, 1978; University of Utah, MSW, 1980. *Princi-

pal occupation: Health systems administrator. *Address*: Lawton PHS Indian Health Center, Lawton, OK 73501 (405) 353-0350. *Affiliations*: Health systems administrator, PHS Indian Health Center, Fort Thompson, SD, 1983-85; health systems administrator, PHS Indian Health Hospital, Wagner, SD, 1985-88; service unit director, PHS Indian Hospital, Pine Ridge, SD, 1988-92; director, Lawton PHS Indian Health Center, Lawton, OK, 1993-. *Other professional posts*: Director, Mental Health/Social Services, social worker, clinical instructor, University of Utah; division manager, data processing firm. *Military service*: U.S. Air Force, 1954-58 (A/1c). *Community activities*: Four Corners Gourd Dance Society (president); Alcohol Treatment Program (chairman, board of directors); UNAC (chairman, board of directors). *Memberships*: National Association of Social Workers; Native American-Alaska Native Social Workers Association. *Awards, honors*: CSWE Scholarship Grant; 4 consecutive years - "Outstanding Performance Awards" as Service Unit Director, for Indian Health Service. *Interests*: Accounting-computer programming; alcohol counseling, clinical instructor, social worker; administration, community planning; health systems administrator. Golfing, Indian dancing - Gourd dancer.

*HOWELL, PATRICIA
(health center director)
Affiliation: Lower Brule PHS Indian Health Center, P.O. Box 248, Lower Brule, SD 57548 (605) 473-5544.

*HOWLETT, DANA
(museum curator)
Affiliation: Aztec Ruins National Monument, P.O. Box 640, Aztec, NM 87410 (505) 334-6174.

HOXIE, FREDERICK E. 1947-
(administrator)
Born April 22, 1947, Hoolehua, Molokai. *Education*: Amherst College, BA, 1969; Brandeis University, PhD, 1977. *Principal occupation*: Administrator. *Home address*: 2717 Lincolnwood Ave., Evanston, IL 60201 (312) 943-9090 (work). *Affiliation*: Director, D'Arcy McNickle Center for the History of the American Indian, Newberry Library, Chicago, IL, 1983-93; Academic Vice President, The Newberry Library, Chicago, IL, 1994-. *Other professional posts*: Adjunct professor of history, Northwestern University; Trustee, National Museum of the American Indian, 1990-. *Memberships*: American Historical Association; Organization of American Historians; American Society of Ethnohistory. *Awards, honors*: Rockefeller Foundation Humanities Fellowship, 1983-84; NEH Fellowship, 1990-91; Doctor of Humane Letters, Amherst College, 1994. *Biographical source*: Who's Who in the Midwest. *Published works*: Editor, With the Nez Perces (University of Nebraska Press, 1981); A Final Promise (University of Nebraska Press, 1984); editor, Indians in American History (Harlan Davidson, 1988); The Crow (Chelsea House, 1989).

*HUBBARD, FREDERICK L.
(hospital director)
Affiliation: San Carlos PHS Indian Hospital, P.O. Box 208, San Carlos, AZ 85550 (602) 475-2371.

HUBBARD, JOHN, JR.
(IHS area director)
Affiliation: Navajo Area IHS P.O. Box 9020, Window Rock, AZ 86515 (602) 871-581 1.

*HUBBELL, ROY
(radio station manager)
Affiliation: KTNN-660 AM, Navajo nation, P.O. Box 2569, Window Rock, AZ 86515 (602) 871-2582.

HUBBERT, CHARLES McCONNELL
(*White Bird*) 1935-
(archaeologist)
Born May 26, 1935, Jasper, Ala. *Education*: University of North Alabama, Florence, BS, 1969; University of Alabama, Tuscaloosa, MS, 1970. *Principal occupation*: Archaeologist. *Home address*: 1910 Crape Myrtle Green, Huntsville, AL 35803 (205) 880-1 113. *Affiliation*: Alabama Museum of Natural History, Tuscaloosa, AL, 1976-. *Other professional post*: Culture Resource Manager, Redstone Arsenal, U.S. Army. *Community activities*: Commissioner, Wayne County, TN. *Memberships*: Society for American Archaeology; Southeastern Archaeological Conference; Alabama Archaeological Society (board of directors); Mid-Cumberland Archaeological Society. *Interests*: Archaeological site conservation and preservation; Native American philosophy and spirituality; paleo-Indian research; prehistoric settlement patterns; environmental conservation. "I am a friend of the Creeks at Fish Pond, Oklahoma, where I am known as White Bird." *Published works*: Articles: "La'la'kalka: The Fishing Place," The Journal of Alabama Archaeology, 1987; "Paleo-Indian Settlement in the Middle Tennessee Valley," Journal of the Tenessee Anthropological Society, 1989; among others.

HUDSON, CHARLES M., JR. 1932-
(professor)
Born December 24, 1932, Monterey, Ky. *Education*: University of Kentucky, BA, 1959; University of North Carolina, PhD, 1964. *Principal occupation*: Professor. *Home address*: Rt. 2, Box 2518, Danielsville, GA 30633 (706) 789-3329. *Affiliation*: Professor of anthropology, University of Georgia, Athens, 1964-. *Military service*: U.S. Air Force, 1950-53 (Staff Sergeant). *Memberships*: American Anthropological Association; Southern Anthropological Society (president, 1973-74); American Society for Ethno-history (president, 1992-93). *Awards, honors*: Woodrow Wilson Fellow, 1959-60; senior fellow, Newberry Library, 1977-78; 1991 James Mooney Prize, Southern Anthropological Society; Rembert W. Patrick Book Award, Florida Historical Society, 1994. *Interests*: "My primary interest is in the historical anthropology of the Indians of the Southeastern U.S." *Biographical sources*: Joyce Rockwood Hudson, Looking for DeSoto (University of Georgia Press, 1993; Who's Who in the Southeast. *Published works*: The Catawba Nation (University of Georgia Press, 1970); editor, Four Centuries of Southern Indians (University of Georgia Press, 1975); The Southeastern Indians (University of Tennessee Press, 1976; editor, Black Drink: A Native American Tea (University of Georgia Press, 1978); editor, Ethnology of the Southeastern Indians (Garland Publishig, 1985); The Juan Pondo Expeditions (Smithsonian Institution Press, 1990); with Gerald Milanich, Hernando DeSoto and the Indians of Florida (University of Florida Pres, 1993); co-editor, with Carmen Tesser, The Forgotten Centuries (Univerity of Georgia Press, 1994).

HUDSON, LESTER
(BIA supt. for education)
Affiliation: Shiprock Agency, Bureau of Indian Affairs, P.O. Box 3239, Shiprock, NM 87420 (505) 368-4427.

HUERTA, C. LAWRENCE
(Yaqui Pasqua Pueblo) 1924-
(chancellor emeritus)
Born August 16, 1924, Nogales, Ariz. *Education*: University of Arizona, LLB & JD, 1953. *Principal occupation*: Chancellor emeritus. Resides in Arizona. *Affiliations*: President, United Services of America, Washington, DC, 1962-74; holder of the Chair of Economic Development, Navajo Community College, Tsaile, AZ, 1974-; Chancellor Emeritus, Navajo Community College, 1975-90. *Other professional posts*: Associate (Navajo) Tribal attorney; special assistant, Attorney General (AZ); Commissioner, AZ Industrial Commission; Judge, Maricopa Superior Court, Phoenix; contract management specialist, U.S. Dept. of Commerce, Washington, DC. *Community activities*: Founder, Navajo Judicial Systems; founder, American Indian School of Medicine; U.S. Dept. of State, Washington, DC (Foreign Service Evaluation/Selection Board). *Memberships*: American Indian Society, Washington, DC; Phi Delta Pi; International Legal Fraternity; AZ State Bar; NM State Bar; Bar of the DC; U.S. Supreme Court; Pasqua Yaqui Association; Isaile Kiwanis Navajo Reservation. *Awards, honors*: Founder, American Coordinating Council on Political Education; Casey Club (businessmen) Vesta Club; 3rd Degree Knights of Columbus. *Interests*: Copyrights, trademarks; student of Panama and U.S. Canal Zone; lecturer on American Indians (North and South America); Indian law, religion, government; student of Latin American affairs. *Published works*: Enriquezca Su Vida (self, 1968); Arizona Law & Order (self, 1968).

*HUFF, RICHARD
(hospital director)
Affiliation: Sisseton PHS Indian Hospital, P.O. Box 189, Sisseton, SD 57262 (605) 698-7606.

HUGHBOY, WALTER
(Indian band chief)
Affiliation: Wemindji (Cree) Indian Band, James Bay, Quebec, Canada J0M 1L0 (819) 978-0254.

*HUGHES, CLAIRE (Hawaiian)
(association president)
Affiliation: Ke Ola Mamo, 1374 Nu'uanu Ave., Suite 200, Honolulu, HI 96802 (808) 599-5200.

HUGHES, J. DONALD 1932-
(professor of history)
Born June 5, 1932, Santa Monica, Calif. *Education*: Oregon State University, 1950-52; UCLA, AB, 1954; Boston University, PhD, 1960. *Principal occupation*: Professor of history. *Home address*: 2580 S. University Blvd. #1002, Denver, CO 80210. *Affiliation*: Professor of history, University of Denver, Denver, CO, 1967-. *Memberships*: American Society for Environmental History; Forest History Society. *Awards, honors*: Charles A. Lindbergh Grant, 1987-88; Burlington Northern Research Prize, 1985; Alumni Fellow, Boston University, 1957-58; Phi Beta Kappa, 1954-. *Interests*: Teaching, writing; the environment; travel. *Published works*: Ecology in Ancient Civilizations (University of New Mexico Press, 1975); In the House of Stone and Light (Grand Canyon N.H.A., 1977); American Indi-

ans in Colorado (Pruett Press, 1978); American Indian Ecology (Texas Western Press, 1983); contributing editor (editor-in-chief, 1983-85), Environmental Review .

HUGHES, JUANITA
  (museum curator)
Affiliation : Museum of the Cherokee Indian, U.S. Hwy. 441 North, Box 770-A, Cherokee, NC 18719 (704) 497-3481.

HUGHES, LANCE
  (director)
Affiliation : Native Americans for a Clean Environment, P.O. Box 1671, Tahlequah, OK 74465 (918) 458-4322.

HUGHES, LITTLETREE ELIZABETH
(Mohawk) 1953-
  (co-owner, Indian company)
Born January 27, 1953, in Onondaga, N.Y . *Address*: 141 Olen Dr., Glenburnie, MD 21061 (301) 760-0771; *Affiliations*: Owner, The Indian Connection, Glen Burnie, MD; co-owner, Different (Jewelry Co.), Baltimore, MD, 1993-. *Other professional post*: Member-Board of Directors, Mid-Atlantic Great Dane Rescue League. *Community activities* : American Indian Hope Foundation, 1988-; Animal rescue worker for several local organizations. *Interests* : "Volunteer for 25 years for local humane groups: Bowie SPCA, Mid-Atlantic Great Dane Rescue League, and Baltimore Great Dane Rescue League, handling adoptions, rescue work, housechecks, and fundraising. I've donated jewelry and art to Phelps Stokes Foundation for the American Indian College Fund. Whenever possible, I have tried to bring attention to the special needs of Native people to the general population. Have worked on helping to put together educational materials focused on drug and alcohol abuse & F.A.S."

*HUGHTE, PHIL (Zuni) 1954-
  (artist - painter)
Born April 27, 1954, Zuni, N.M. *Education*: Northern Arizona University, BFA, 1980. *Principal occupation* : Artist - painter. *Address*: P.O. Box 151, Zuni, NM 87327 (505) 782-4920. *Affiliation* . Member, Pueblo of Zuni Higher Education Committee. *Membership*: Indian Arts & Crafts Association. Award: 1990 Best of Show , The Zuni Show , Flagstaff, AZ. *Biographical source*: Zuni Artist Looks At Frank Hamilton Cushing, 43 cartoons which is a traveling exhibition.

*HULETT, TROWEN (Navajo)
  (radio station owner)
Affiliation : KABR - 1500 AM, Alamo Navajo School Board, P.O. Box 907, Magdalena, NM 87825 (505) 854-2632.

HUME, GAYE (Potawatomi)
  (attorney)
Address: 130 S. W oodrow St., Arlington, V A 22204. *Memberships*: Native American Bar Association (treasurer); American Bar Association.

HUMMINGBIRD, JESSE T.
(Oklahoma Cherokee) 1952-
  (fine artist)
Born February 12, 1952, Tahlequah, Okla. *Education*: Middle Tennessee State University , 1970-71; University of Tennessee, 1971-77; The American Academy of Art in Chicago. *Principal occupation* : Fine artist. *Home address* : 8411 E.

Medford Place, Tucson, AZ 85710 (602) 885-6914. *Affiliations* : Printer, Peabody College, Nashville, TN, 1975-77; printer , FISI (Banking Institute), 1977-79; graphic artist, DLM (Chicago & Dallas), 1979-83; self-employed, 1983-. As a successful printer, graphic artist, and commercial illustrator , Jesse pursues both Cherokee and Native American themes, especially legends of both Cherokee and other tribes passed to him. In addition to his original works, he has three full-color prints and publishes a new notecard/ holiday card annually . *Interests*: "I am a traditionalist-both in spirit and art. I'm influenced by the nature that's around me. No matter how difficult, I want people to know I'm proud of my culture and traditions. I want to preserve what we have left as I create the new ."

HUNKLER, SAM, M.D.
  (clinical director)
Affiliation : Metlakatla Indian Community Health Center, P.O. Box 439, Metlakatla, AK 99926 (907) 886-4741.

*HUNN, EUGENE S. 1943-
  (professor of anthropology)
Born April 23, 1943, Louisville, KY . *Education*: Stanford University, BA, 1964; University of California, Berkeley, MA, 1970, PhD, 1973. *Principal occupation* : Professor of anthropology . *Home address* : 1816 N. 57th St., Seattle, W A 98103 (206) 524-81 12. *Affiliation* : Dept. of Anthropology, University of W ashington, Seattle, WA 1972-. *Memberships*: American Anthropological Association; Society of Ethnobiology . *Awards, honors* : Fellow, American Association for the Advancement of Science. *Interests*: Mayan Indian ethnobiology; Sahaptin (Columbia River Plateau) Indian Ethnobiology , language and culture, history , and ecology; Alaskan Native subsistence and national parks. *Published works*: Tzeltal Folk Zoology: The Classification of Discontinuities in Nature (Academic Press, 1977); co-edited with Nancy M. Williams, Resource Managers: North American & Australian Hunter-Gatherers (W estview/Australian Institute of Aboriginal Studies, 1982, '86); Nch'i-Wana 'The Big River': with James Selam, Mid-Columbia Indians & Their Land (University of Washington Press, 1990)

HUNT, ALFRED (Kwakiutl)
  (Indian band chief)
Affiliation : Kwakiutl Indian Band, 395A Kinchant St., Box 1440, Port Hardy, British Columbia, Canada V0N 2P0 (604) 949-6012.

*HUNT, ELI
  (health director)
Affiliation : Leech Lake Band Health Clinic, Route 3, Box 100, Cass Lake, MN 56633 (218) 335-8851.

HUNT, MARK A.
  (museum/mission director)
Affiliations: Kansas Museum of History , Kansas State Historical Society , 6425 SW 6th, Topeka, KS 66615; Shawnee Methodist Mission, 3403 West 53rd, Shawnee Mission, KS 66205 (913) 262-0867; Iowa, Sac and Fox Presbyterian Mission, Route 1, Box 152C, Highland, KS 66035 (913) 442-3304.

*HUNT, MICHAEL (Eskimo)
  (AK village council president)
Affiliation : Native Village of Kotlik, P.O. Box 20096, Larsen Bay, AK 99620 (907) 899-4326.

HUNTER, ALICE
  (director-Indian centre)
Affiliation : Port Albemi Friendship Centre, 3178 - 2nd Ave., Box 23, Port Alberni, British Columbia, Canada V9Y 4C3 (604) 723-8281.

HUNTER, ANTHONY (Shinnecock) 1959-
  (registered nurse)
Born June 28, 1959, Queens, N.Y . *Education*: LaGuardia Commuity College, AAS, 1986; Hunter College, BSN, 1989. *Principal occupation*: Registered nurse. *Address & Affiliation* : American Indian Community House, 404 Lafayette St., 2nd Floor , New York, NY 10003 (212) 598-0100 (director , health program, 1992-). *Community activities* : Board of Directors, American Indian Community House, 1982-. *Awards, honors* : Member of the United Nations NGO Committee for the 1993 International Year of Indigenous People. *Interests*: "Certified in psychiatric and mental health nursing by the American Nurses Association. Currently pursuing Master of Public Health (MPH) Degree in Intenational Commuity Helth Education at NYU. Hobby - genealogical research."

HUNTER, GERRY
  (Indian band chief)
Affiliation : Halfway River Indian Band, Box 59, Wonowon, BC, Can. V0C 2N0 (604) 787-4452.

*HUNTER, IRMA (Yokut)
  (tribal chairperson)
Affiliation : Tule River Reservation, P.O. Box 589, Porterville, CA 93258 (209) 781-4271.

HUNTER, JOHN D.
  (monument supt.)
Affiliation : Bandelier National Monument, HCR 1 Box 1, Rte. 4, Suite 15, Los Alamos, NM 87544 (505) 672-3861.

*HUNTER, JULIUS ANDREW (*Little Beaver*)
(Meherren) 1947-
  (mortician)
Born December 25, 1947, Ahoskie, N.C. *Education*: North Carolina Central University , B.Sc., 1969; American Academy McAllister (New York City), MS, 1971. *Principal occupation*: Mortician. *Home address* : 410 E. First St., Ahoskie, NC 27910 (919) 332-3130. *Affiliations* : Owner, Hunter's Funeral Home, Ahoskie, NC, 1974-; owner, Sacred Wind Traders, Ahoskie, NC, 1992-. *Community activities* : Planning Board, Town of Ahoskie; Tribal Council, United Tribes of North Carolina. *Memberships* : National Funeral Directors & Embalmers Association; North Carolina & V irginia Funeral Directors & Embalmers Association. *Biographical sources* : Who's Who Among Outstanding Professionals; 2000 Notable American Men.

HUNTER, MICHAEL (Delaware)
  (tribal vice president)
Affiliation : Delaware Executive Committee, P .O. Box 825, Anadarko, OK 73005 (405) 247-2448.

HUNTER, RAYMOND, (Diegueno)
  (tribal chairperson)
Affiliation : Jamul Band of Mission Indians, P .O. Box 612, Jamul, CA 91935 (619) 669-4785.

HUNTER, ROBERT L.
  (BIA agency supt.)
Affiliation : Western Nevada Agency, Bureau of Indian Affairs, 1677 Hot Springs Rd., Carson City, NV 89706 (702) 887-3500.

HUNTER, TERRY
(executive director)
Affiliation: Oklahoma City Urban Health Clinic, Central Oklahoma American Indian Health Council, 1214 N. Hudson, Oklahoma City, OK 73103 (405) 235-5877. *Past professional post*: Executive director, Association of American Indian Physicians, Oklahoma City, OK.

HURTADO, ALBERT L. 1946-
(professor of history)
Born October 19, 1946, Sacramento, Calif. *Education*: Sacramento City College, 1964-66; California State University, Sacramento, BA, 1969, MA, 1975; University of California, Santa Barbara, PhD, 1981. *Principal occupation*: Professor of history. *Home address*: 3202 E. Dry Creek Rd., Phoenix, AZ 85044 (602) 965-5778 (work). *Affiliations*: Assistant professor of history, Indiana University-Purdue University, Indianapolis, 1983-86; professor of history, Arizona State University, Tempe, 1986-. *Other professional posts*: Lecturer, University of Maryland; instructor, Sierra College, Rocklin, CA. *Military service*: U.S. Army, 1969-71, Counter Intelligence Agent. *Community activities*: California Committee for the Promotion of History (chair, 1981-83). *Memberships*: National Council on Public History (treasurer, 1985-86; board of directors, 1982-86); American Historical Association; Organization of American Historians; Western History Association; American Society for Ethnohistory; California Historical Society; Indiana Historical Society. *Awards, honors*: 1989 Billington Prize, awarded by Organization of American Historians for best book in American frontier history; Award of Merit, 1989, by California Committee for the Promotion of History; Bolton Prize for Spanish Borderlands History for the best article in the field, awarded biennially by the Western Historical Association for, 'Hardly a Farm House--a Kitchen Without Them': Indian and White Households on the California Borderland Frontier in 1860, (Western Historical Quarterly, July, 1982); 1990 Paladin Award, presented by the Montana Historical Society for article, "Public History and the Native American", in Montana: The Magazine of Western History, Spring, 1990. *Interests*: Western history, Indian history, public history; backpacking, photography. *Biographical source*: Who's Who in the West. *Published works*: Indian Survival on the California Frontier (Yale University Press, 1988); articles and book reviews in various scholarly journals.

*HUSSION, JOSEPH
(health center director)
Affiliation: Dulce PHS Indian Health Center, P.o. Box 187, Dulce, NM 87528 (505) 759-3291.

HUTCHINS, JEANETTE L.
(museum director/curator)
Affiliation: Chief Oshkosh Museum, 7631 Egg Harbor Rd., Egg Harbor, WI 54209 (414) 868-3240.

HUTCHINSON, DICK
(society director)
Affiliation: Anti-Yun Wiya Society, 3601 Wenatchee Ave., Bakersfield, CA 93306 (805) 871-2977.

*HUTCHINSON, DOUGLAS W.
(executive director)
Affiliation: Oregon Commission on Indian Services, 454 State Capitol, Salem, OR 97310 (503) 986-1067.

HUTCHISON, DAALBAALEH (Navajo)
(health director)
Affiliation: Shiprock PHS Indian Hospital, P.O. Box 160, Shiprock, NM 87420 (505) 368-4971.

*HUTCHISON, SARAH (Oklahoma Cherokee)
(marriage & family counselor)
Affiliation: Native American Studies Program, University of California, Davis, 2401 Hart Hall, Davis, CA 95616 (916) 752-3237.

*HYEXIKOK, JACK, Sr. (Athapascan)
(AK village council president)
Affiliation: Traditional Village of Togiak, P.O. Box 209, Togiak, AK 99678 (907) 493-5920.

I

IDE, JOE (Hawaiian)
(council director)
Affiliation: Hawaii Council of American Indian Nations, P.O. Box 17627, 910 N. Vineyard Blvd., Honolulu, HI 96817.

IDE, JOHN H. (Hawaiian)
(center director)
Affiliation: American Indian Center of Honolulu, 810 N. Vineyard Blvd., Honolulu, HI 96817 (808) 847-3544.

IGNACE, RONALD ERIC
(Indian band chief)
Affiliations: Skeetchestn Indian Band, Box 178, Savona, British Columbia V0K 2J0 (604) 373-2493; co-chair, Simon Fraser University, The Secwepeme Cultural Education Society, 345 Yellowhead Highway, Kamloops, British Columbia, Canada V2H 1H1 (604) 374-0616.

*IMPSON, ROBERT
(BIA agency supt.)
Affiliation: Chickasaw Agency, Bureau of Indian Affairs, P.O. Box 2240, Ada, OK 74821 (405) 436-0784.

INCOGUITO, ELAINE (Sioux)
(school administrator)
Affiliation: Twin Buttes Day School, Route 1, Box 65, Halliday, ND 58636 (701) 938-4396.

INMAN, ESTELLE
(museum director)
Affiliation: Kwagiulth Museum, P.O. Box 8, Quathiaski Cove, British Columbia, Canada V0P 1N0.

*INNES, PAM (Creek)
(professor of Native American studies)
Affiliation: Native American Studies Program, University of Oklahoma, 455 W. Lindsey, Rm. 804, Norman, OK 73019 (405) 325-2312.

*INNIS, NINA
(BIA agency supt.)
Affiliation: San Carlos Agency, Bureau of Indian Affairs, P.O. Box 209, San Carlos, AZ 85550 (602) 475-2321.

INNUKSUK, RHONDA
(association president)
Affiliation: Inuit Tapirisat of Canada, 176 Gloucester St., 3rd Floor, Ottawa, Ontario, Canada K2P 0A6 (613) 238-8181.

*INOUYE, DANIEL (Hawaiian)
(U.S. Senator, D-HI)
Affiliation: Vice-chairperson (former chairperson), Senate Select Committee on Indian Affairs, 838 Hart Senate Office Bldg., Washington, DC 20510 (202) 224-2251.

IRON, FRANK
(Indian band chief)
Affiliation: Canoe Lake Indian Band, Canoe Narrows, Saskatchewan, Canada S0M 0K0 (306) 829-2150.

*IRWIN, KENNETH D. (Two Mans)
(Mandan, Hidatsa, Arikara)
(Indian center chairperson)
Born on the Fort Berthold Reservation, N.D. *Education*: Standing Rock Indian School, Wahpeton Indian School, White Shield Indian School, Flandreau Indian School. *Principal occupation*: CEO/Chair, OCNAA. *Home address*: 203 E. Broad St., Columbus, OH 43215 (614) 228-0470 (work). *Affiliations*: CEO/Chair, Ohio Center for Native American Affairs (OCNAA), Columbus, OH; president, Ohio Council for Native American Burial Rights - Ohio Indian Movement, Columbus, OH. *Other professional post*: Irwin-Ruffini Committee (drafting bill for Ohio to coincide with Federal-Native American Grave Protection & Repatriation Act. *Interests*: "Indian rights activist including protection of Indian religious freedom, Indian grave protection and repatriation, cultural protection and education."

*IRWIN, MICHAEL
(special staff assistant)
Affiliation: Alaska Office of the Governor, P.O. Box A, Juneau, AK 99811 (907) 465-3500.

ISAAC, CALVIN JAMES (Choctaw) 1933-
(education)
Born December 5, 1933, Philadelphia, Miss. *Education*: Delta State University, BA (Music Education), 1954. *Principal occupation*: Education. *Address*: Bogue Chitto Day School, Route 2, Box 274, Philadelphia, MS 39350 (601) 656-1419. *Affiliations*: Education specialist, Title I, BIA, Philadelphia, MS, 1972-75; former tribal chief, Mississippi Band of Choctaw Indians, Philadelphia, MS, 1975-80; principal, Bogue Chitto Day School, Philadelphia, MS. *Other professional posts*: Director, Choctaw Head Start Program, Service Unit director; teacher supervisor (elementary), BIA; education specialist (fine arts). *Military service*: U.S. Dept. of Defense, Army. *Community activities*: Choctaw Housing Authority (chairman); Choctaw Advisory School Board (chairman); Policy Advisory Council (tribal representative). *Memberships*: Mississippi State Advisory Committee, 1975-; United Southeastern Tribes, Inc., 1975-; National Tribal Chairman's Association, 1975-; Governor's Colonel Staff, 1976-; Governors Multicultural Advisory Council, 1976-. *Awards, honors*: John Hay Whitney Fellowship Scholar, 1967-68; Phi Delta Kappa, Mississippi State University, 1976; Omicron Delta Kappa, Delta State University, 1975.

*ISAAC, NICK (Athapascan)
(AK village council president)
Affiliation: Native Village of Ohogamiut, Fortuna Ledge, AK 99585 (907) 679-6740.

*ISAAC, VERNON (Cayuga)
(tribal chief)
Affiliation: Cayuga Indian Nation, P.O. Box 11, Versailles, NY 14168 (716) 532-4847.

ISNANA, MELVIN
   (Indian band chief)
Affiliation: Standing Buffalo Indian Band, Box 128, Fort Qu-Appelle, Saskatchewan, Canada S0G 1S0 (306) 332-4685.

IVAN, IVAN M. (Yup'ik Eskimo)
   (state legislator)
Affiliation: Alaska State Legislature, Pouch V, Juneau, AK 99801.

*IVAN, OWEN (Yup'ik Eskimo)
   (AK village president)
Affiliation: Akiak Native Village, P.O. Box 52165, Akiak, AK 99552 (907) 765-7112.

*IVANOFF, HENRY
   (radio station manager)
Affiliation: KNSA-AM, P.O. Box 178, Unalakleet, AK 99684 (907) 624-3101.

*IVERSON, PETER
   (professor, author-editor)
Affiliation & Address: Dept. of History, Arizona State University, Tempe, AZ 85287. *Published works*: The Plains Indians of the Twentieth Century (University of Oklahoma Press, 1992); When Indians Became Cowboys: Native Peoples & Cattle Ranching in the American West (University of Oklahoma Press, 1994).

IVEY, G.H.
   (health services director)
Affiliation: Alaska Area Native Health Services, Indian Health Service, 250 Gambell St., Third & Gambell St., Anchorage, AK 99510 (907) 257-1153.

J

JABBOUR, ALAN ALBERT 1942-
   (archivist)
Born June 21, 1942, Jacksonville, Fla. *Education*: University of Miami, BA, 1963; Duke University, MA, 1966, PhD, 1968. *Principal occupation*: Archivist. *Home address*: 3107 Cathedral Ave., NW, Washington, DC 20540 (202) 707-6590 (office). *Affiliations*: Head, Archive of Folk Song, Library of Congress, 1969-74; head, Folk Arts Program, National Endowment for the Arts, Washington, DC, 1974-76; director, The American Folklife Center, Library of Congress, Washington, DC, 1976- (the Center engages in the preservation, presentation & dissemination of American folk cultural traditions, and contributes to the cultural planning & programming of the Library, federal government and the nation); chairperson, Fund for Folk Culture, 1991-. *Memberships*: American Folklore Society; Society for Ethnomusicology; John Edwards Memorial Foundation (advisor); American Folklife Center (member, board of trustees). *Awards, honors*: Phi Beta Kappa; University of Miami Music Scholarship, 1959-62; Woodrow Wilson Fellowship, 1963; Duke University Scholarship, 1964-66; Danforth Teaching Fellowship, 1966-68; responsible for the initiation of one of the Library's American Revolution Bicentennial projects, an anthology of 15 long-playing records containing examples of major folk music traditions of the U.S. -- Anglo-American, Afro-American, American Indian, and other rural and urban ethnic groups. The series is called, Folk Music in America. *Interests*: Folk music & song; folklore;

medieval English literature; musicology; American studies. *Published works*: Numerous papers presented & published.

*JACK, AMBROSE
   (BIA agency supt.)
Affiliation: Yakima Agency, BIA, P.O. Box 632, Toppenish, WA 98948 (509) 865-2255.

JACK, ARCHIE
   (Indian band chief)
Affiliation: Penticton Indian Band, RR 2, Site 80, Comp. 19, Penticton, British Columbia, Canada V2A 6J7 (604) 493-0048.

JACK, EARL WILBUR
   (Indian band chief)
Affiliation: Penelakut Indian Band, Box 360, Chemainus, British Columbia, Canada V0K 1K0 (604) 246-2321.

JACK, KATHERINE (Ojibway)
   (Indian band chief)
Affiliation: Ojibways of Onegaming Band, Box 160, Nestor Falls, Ontario, Canada P0X 1N0 (807) 484-2162.

JACK, PIUS
   (Indian band chief)
Affiliation: Nee-Tahi-Buhn Indian Band, RR 2, Box 28, Burns Lake, British Columbia, Canada V0J 1E0 (604) 694-3301.

JACK, SYLVESTER, Sr. (Tlingit)
   (Indian band chief)
Affiliation: Taku River Tlingit Indian Band, Box 132, Atlin, British Columbia, Canada V0W 1A0 (403) 651-7615.

*JACK, VALENTINO (Pomo)
   (tribal council chairperson)
Affiliation: Big Valley Rancheria, P.O. Box 955, Lakeport, CA 95453 (707) 262-0629.

*JACKA, LOIS
   (writer)
Born and raised on ranches north of Phoenix, Ariz. *Address*: c/o Northland Publishing, P.O. Box 1389, Flagstaff, AZ 86002. *Awards*: Western Heritage Award, best art book for 1988, "Beyond Traditions"; and, Emmy Award in Cultural Documentary for video version of "Beyond Traditions." *Published works*: Beyond Tradition: Contemporary Indian Art and Its Evolution (with Jerry Jacka) (University of Nebraska Press, 1988); David Johns: On the Trail of Beauty (Snailspace Publication, 1991); Enduring Traditions: Art of the Navajo (with Jerry Jacka) (Northland Publishing, 1994). Articles for "Arizona Highway" and other magazines.

*JACKA, JERRY
   (photographer, illustrator)
Born and raised on ranches north of Phoenix, Ariz. *Address*: c/o Northland Publishing, P.O. Box 1389, Flagstaff, AZ 86002. *Awards*: Western Heritage Award, best art book for 1988, "Beyond Traditions"; and, Emmy Award in Cultural Documentary for video version of "Beyond Traditions." *Published works*: Photographs for: Beyond Tradition: Contemporary Indian Art and Its Evolution (with Lois Jacka) (University of Nebraska Press, 1988); and Enduring Traditions: Art of the Navajo (with Lois Jacka) (Northland Publishing, 1994). Illustrated seven books and four special issues of "Arizona Highway" on Native American art.

*JACKSON, EDGAR (Eskimo)
   (AK village council president)
Affiliation: Shaktoolik Native Village, P.O. Box 100, Shaktoolik, AK 99771 (907) 955-3701.

JACKSON, FRANCES
   (historic site president)
Affiliation: The Chief John Ross House, P.O. Box 863, Rossville, GA 30741 (404) 861-3954.

JACKSON, GORDON
   (BIA agency supt.)
Affiliation: Osage Agency, Bureau of Indian Affairs, P.O. Box 1539, Pawhuska, OK 74056 (918) 287-1032.

*JACKSON, LOOMIS (Pit River)
   (tribal chairperson)
Affiliation: Pit River Tribal Council, P.O Drawer 1570, Burney, CA 96013 (916) 335-5421.

*JACKSON, LOUIE
   (counselor)
Affiliation: Bacone College, 2299 Old Bacone Rd., Muskogee, OK 74403 (918) 683-4581.

JACKSON, WILLIAM R. *(Chief Rattlesnake)* **(Cherokee) 1928-**
   (principal chief-Southeastern Cherokee Confederacy)
Born December 23, 1928, Moultrie, GA. *Principal occupation*: Retired civil service; principal chief, Southeastern Cherokee Confederacy. *Home address*: Route 4, 120 Will Hatcher Rd., Albany, GA 31705 (912) 787-5722 (office). *Affiliations*: Retired Marine Corps Logistics, Albany, GA, 1964-89; principal chief, Southeastern Cherokee Confederacy, Leesburg, GA, 1976-. *Military service*: U.S. Army, 1950-52 (Korean War Medal); retired Marine Corps Logistics Base, Albany, GA 1964-89. *Community activities*: Hold monthly meetings for local members of the Eagle Clan in Albany, GA and surrounding area. *Memberships*: American Legion; VFW; Southeastern Cherokee Confederacy, 1976-. *Awards, honors*: Letter of Appreciation, 25-Year Service Awards with Civil Service; Safety Awards. "I have personally received a Proclamation from ex-governor of Georgia, George Busbee." *Interests*: "I visit clans and bands all over the U.S. that are affiliated with the Southeastern Cherokee Confederacy; attend council meetings, annual meetings, and pow-wows. Have posed for an artist to paint my portrait for Albany Junior College. I am also the editor of the Southeastern Cherokee Confederacy Newsletter."

JACOB, IGNATI (Eskimo)
   (AK council president)
Affiliation: Oscarville Traditional Council, P.O. Box 1554, Oscarville, AK 99559 (907) 737-7321.

JACOBS, ALEX A. *(Karoniaktatie)* **(Mohawk) 1953-**
   (writer, artist, editor)
Born February 28, 1953, Akwesasne Reservation, via Rooseveltown, N.Y. *Education*: Institute of American Indian Arts, Santa Fe, N.M., AFA (sculpture, creative writing), 1977; Kansas City Art Institute, BFA (sculpture, creative writing), 1979. *Address*: University of New Mexico, Albuquerque, NM 87131. *Affiliations*: Editor, Akwesasne Notes, via Rooseveltown, N.Y., 1979-1985; editor, Akwekon Literary Journal, Akwesasne Notes, Hogansburg, N.Y., 1985-91; instructor, University of New Mexico, Albuquer-

que, 1991-. *Other professional posts*: Board of directors, CKON-F, Radio Station, Mohawk Nation. *Awards, honors*: 1975 poetry award, Scottsdale National Indian Art Exhibit; 1979 honorable mention, Society of Western Art, Kansas City, Mo. *Interests*: Poetry, prose, short stories; graphic arts; sculpture; painting, printmaking; ceramics; video/audio/performance art; editor of Native American literature and journalism; networking national and international native peoples; poetry readings and workshops; travel U.S.A. with White Roots of Peace, 1973-74 (native touring group/communications). Published works: Native Colours (Akwesasne Notes, 1974); Landscape: Old & New Poems (Blue Cloud Quarterly, 1984); Anthologies: Come to Power, The Remembered Earth, The Next World, 3rd World Writers, and Songs From the Earth on Turtle's Back, in various literary magazines, 1972-1985; editor, Akwekon Literary Journal, 1985-91.

*JACOBS, JOSEPH (Mohawk/Cherokee) 1947-
(NIH program director)
Born in 1947. Resides in Guilford, CT. *Education*: Yale Medical School, MD, 1974; Wharton School of Business, University of Pennsylvania, MBA, 1985. *Address & Affiliation*: Director, Office of Alternative Medicine, National Institutes of Health, Bethesda, MD, 1992-. *Past professional posts*: Pediatrician, Indian Medical Center, Gallup, NM; U.S. Public Health Service, Rockville, MD; Aetna Life Insurance Co., Hartford, CT.

JACOBS, L. DAVID (Mohawk)
(tribal chief)
Affiliation: St. Regis Mohawk Council Chiefs, Akwesasne-Community Bldg., Hogansburg, NY 13655 (518) 358-2272.

JACOBSEN, WILLIAM H., JR. 1931-
(professor of linguistics)
Born November 15, 1931, San Diego, Calif. *Education*: Harvard University, AB, 1953; University of California, Berkeley, PhD, 1964. *Principal occupation*: Professor of linguistics, University of Nevada, 1965-. *Home address*: 1411 Samuel Way, Reno, NV 89509. *Memberships*: Linguistic Society of America; International Linguistic Association; Society for the Study of the Indigenous Languages of the Americas (vice-president, 1991, president, 1992); American Anthropological Association; Society for Linguistic Anthropology; Great Basin Anthropological Conference. *Awards, honors*: Outstanding Researcher Award, University of Nevada, Reno, 1983. Interests: American Indian languages, primarily Washo and Makah, and the Hokan and Wakashan families; also, fieldwork or publication on Salinan, Yana, Nootka, Nez Perce, Numic, and Chimakuan. *Published work*: First Lessons in Makah (Makah Cultural & Research Center, 1979).

JACOX, SHARON
(executive director)
Affiliation: National Native American Purchasing Association, P.O. Box 309, Willamina, OR 97396 (503) 876-3307.

JACQUES, RONALD
(Indian band chief)
Affiliation: Restigouche Indian Band, 17 Riverside West, Restigouche, Quebec, Canada G0C 2R0 (418) 788-2136.

JAEGER, JERRY L.
(BIA area director)
Affiliation: Aberdeen Area Office, Bureau of Indian Affairs, Federal Bldg., 115 Fourth Ave., SE, Aberdeen, SD 57401 (605) 226-7343.

JAEGER, ROBERT
(BIA agency supt.)
Affiliation: Great Lakes Agency, Bureau of Indian Affairs, 615 Main West, Ashland, WI 54806 (715) 682-4527.

JAEGER, RONALD M.
(BIA area director)
Affiliation: Sacramento Area Office, Bureau of Indian Affairs, Fed. Office Bldg., 2800 Cottage Way, Sacramento, CA 95825 (916) 978-4691.

JAENEN, CORNELIUS J. 1927-
(professor of history)
Born February 21, 1927, Cannington Manor, Saskatchewan, Canada. *Education*: University of Manitoba, Winnipeg, BA, 1947, MA, 1950, BEd, 1958; University of Ottawa, Ontario, PhD, 1963; University of Winnipeg, LLD, 1982. *Principal occupation*: Professor of history. *Home address*: 9 Elma St., Gloucester, ON K1G 3N2 (613) 521-0167. *Affiliations*: Assistant & associate professor of history, United College (now University of Winnipeg), 1959-67; Associate and full professor of history, University of Ottawa, 1967-. *Community activities*: Canadian Consultative Council on Multiculturalism; Native Awareness Program of Department of External Affairs (Ottawa). *Memberships*: American Society for Ethnohistory; Canadian Historical Association, 1952- (council member, 1987-91; vice-president, 1987-88; president, 1988-89); Social Science Federation of Canada (council member, 1987-90); Institut d'histoire de l'Amerique francaise, 1952- (council member, 1979-81); French Colonial Historical Society (vice president; president, 1986-89); Canadian Ethnic Studies Association (founding president, 1971-73, councillor, 1971-). *Awards, honors*: Ste. Marie Prize in Canadian History, 1974, for Friend and Foe, awarded by Ministry of Culture, Government of Ontario; also Book Prize of the French Colonial Historical Society in 1976. LLD honoris causa from University of Winnipeg, 1981, in recognition of work on minorities, ethnic groups, Native peoples. *Interests*: Visiting professor in Canada, India, France, Belgium, and Italy dealing with French colonization, Native peoples, ethnicity. Participant at international historical congresses in Paris, Bucharest, Budapest, Fort-de-France dealing with North American Indian issues. *Biographical sources*: Dictionary of International Biography; International Who's Who in Community Service; International Who's Who in Education; A Bibliographical Directory of Canadian Scholars; International Book of Honor; Who Who in Canada. *Published works*: Friend and Foe: Aspects of French-Amerindian Cultural Contact in the Sixteenth and Seventeenth Centuries (Columbia University Press, 1976); The Role of the Church in New France (McGraw-Hill - Ryerson, Ltd., 1976); The French Relationship With the Native Peoples of New France (Indian & Northern Affairs, Canada, 1984); (in collaboration) Emerging Identities, Selected Problems and Interpretations in Canadian History (Prentice-Hall, Canada, 1986); (in collaboration) Canada, A North American Nation (McGraw-Hill-Ryerson, 1989); also, chapters in books & articles in refereed journals on Canadian Indians.

JAFFE, A.J. 1912-
(retired statistician)
Born February 28, 1912, in Mass. *Education*: University of Chicago, PhD, 1941. *Principal occupation*: Statistician (retired). Home address: 314 Allaire Ave., Leonia, NJ 07605 (201) 944-1364. *Affiliations*: Senior research scholar (retired), Columbia University, New York, N.Y. *Other professional posts*: Research associate, National Museum of the American Indian, New York, N.Y. *Memberships*: American Statistical Association; American Association for the Advancement of Science. *Interests*: Indians of North America; U.S. Labor Force; social and demographic change. *Published works*: People, Jobs, and Economic Development (Free Press, 1959); Changing Demography of Spanish Americans (Academic Press, 1980); Misuse of Statistics (Marcel Dekker, Inc., 1987); The First Immigrants From Asia: A Population History of the North American Indians (Plenum Press, 1992).

JAHNER, ELAINE A.
(native American studies instructor)
Affiliation: Dartmouth College, Native American Studies Dept., Hanover, NH 03755 (603) 646-3530.

JAMES, ALBERT
(Indian band chief)
Affiliation: McDowell Lake Indian Band, Box 740, Red Lake, Ontario, Canada P0V 2M0 (807) 727-2803.

JAMES, ALBERT E. (Wiyot)
(rancheria chairperson)
Affiliation: Table Bluff Rancheria, P.O. Box 519, Loleta, CA 95551 (707) 733-5055.

*JAMES, ALVIN R. (Paiute)
(tribal council chairperson)
Affiliation: Pyramid Lake Paiute Tribal Council, P.O. Box 256, Nixon, NV 89424 (702) 574-1000.

*JAMES, CHEEWA (Modoc)
(writer; TV producer)
Resides in Sacramento, California. *Published work*: Catch the Whisper of the Wind, revised edition. 1994.

JAMES, EVELYN (Southern Paiute)
(tribal chairperson)
Affiliation: San Juan Southern Paiute Council, P.O. Box 2663, Tuba City, AZ 86045 (602) 283-4583.

JAMES, JOHN A. (Cahuilla)
(tribal council chairperson)
Affiliation: Cabazon General Council, 84-245 Indio Spring Dr., Indio, CA 92203 (619) 342-2593.

JAMES, OVERTON
(foundation chairperson)
Affiliation: Five Civilized Tribes Foundation, c/o Chickasaw Nation, P.O. Box 1548, Ada, OK 74820 (405) 436-2603.

JAMES, WABUN 1945-
(writer, lecturer, teacher)
Born April 5, 1945, Newark, N.J. *Education*: George Washington University, BA, 1967; Columbia University, MA, 1968. *Principal occupation*: Writer, lecturer, teacher. *Address*: P.O. Box 9167, Spokane, WA 99209. *Affiliation*: Executive director, The Bear Tribe Medicine Society,

Spokane, Wash., 1972-. *Published works*: The People's Lawyers (Holt, Rinehart & Winston, 1973); The Bear Tribe's Self-Reliance Book (Bear Tribe Publishing, 1977); The Medicine Wheel Book (Prentice-Hall, 1980); Sun Bear: The Path to Power (Bear Tribe Pubg., 1983).

JAMES, WALTER S., Jr.
(executive director)
Affiliation: Council for Native American Indians, 280 Broadway, Suite 316, New York, NY 10007 (212) 732-0485.

JANDREAU, MICHAEL (Lower Brule Sioux)
(tribal chairperson)
Affiliation: Lower Brule Sioux Tribal Council, Lower Brule, SD 57548 (605) 473-5561.

JANVIER, WALTER
(Indian band chief)
Affiliation: Janvier Indian Band, Chard, Alberta, Canada T0P 1G0 (403) 559-2259.

JANZ, PAM
(department head-Indian college)
Affiliation: Department of Indian Education, Saskatchewan Indian Federated College, University of Regina, 118 College West, Regina, SK, Canada S4S 0A2 (306) 584-8333.

JARAMILLO, ERNEST CHARLES *(Eagle Feather)* **(Isleta Pueblo) 1936-**
(USAF-retired; farmer/rancher)
Born May 15, 1936, Isleta Pueblo, N.M. *Education*: University of New Mexico, 1983-84. *Principal occupation*: USAF-retired; farmer-rancher. *Home address*: P.O. Box 543, Isleta, NM 87022 (505) 869-9284. *Military service*: U.S. Air Force, 1954-74 (Technical Sergeant; received the Air Force Commendation Medal for meritourious service in support of Southeast Asia while stationed in Taiwan in 1966). *Memberships*: American Indian Veterans Association, Albuquerque, NM (chairperson).

*JARBOE, MARK A.
(attorney)
Born August 19, 1951, Flint, Mich. *Education*: University of Michigan, BA, 1972; Harvard University Law School, JD, 1975. *Principal occupation*: Attorney. *Address*: 220 S. Sixth St., Minneapolis, MN 55402 (612) 340-2686 (work). *Affiliation*: Dorsey & Whitney, Minneapolis, MN, 1976-. *Memberships*: Native American Bar Association; Minnesota American Indian Bar Association; Federal Bar Association. *Awards, honors*: Phi Beta Kappa. *Interests*: "Chairman of Indian Law Dept. at Dorsey & Whitney; represents tribes across the country in matters of finance and development, business diversification, governmental regulation and other areas. Speaker at various services on the subject of business transactions in Indian country." *Biographical sources*: Who's Who in America; Who's Who in American Law; Who's Who in the Midwest. *Published works*: Regulating Indian Gaming; Fairness or Finagling? (Bench & Bar of Minnesota, 1993); The Nature of Tribal Sovereignty (The Legends, 1994); Fundamental Legal Principles Affecting Business Transactions in Indian Contry (Harvard Law Review, 1994).

*JARIS, BEN (Lower Brule Sioux)
(BIA education chairperson)
Affiliation: Bureau of Indian Affairs, Crow Creek/Lower Brule Agency, P.O. Box 139, Fort Thompson, SD 57339 (605) 245-2398.

JAROS, ROSEMARY (Chippewa)
(school principal)
Affiliation: Turtle Mountain High School, P.O. Box 440, Belcourt, ND 58316 (701) 477-6471 ext. 222.

*JAURE, RUTH
(executive director)
Affiliation: National American Indian Housing Council, 900 2nd St., NE, Suite 220, Washington, DC 20002 (202) 789-1754.

JEANNOTTE, PLACIDE
(Indian band chief)
Affiliation: Gaspe (Micmac) Indian Band, Box 69, Fontenelle, Gaspe, Quebec G0E 1H0 (418) 368-6005.

JEANOTTE, DARRELL (Sioux)
(supt. of education)
Affiliation: Pierre Indian Learning Center, HC 31, Box 148, Pierre, SD 57501 (605) 224-8661.

JEANOTTE, DUANE L.
(IHS area director)
Affiliation: Billings Area Office, Indian Health Service, P.O. Box 2143, Billings, MT 59103 (406) 657-6403.

*JEMISON, G. PETER
(site director)
Affiliation: Ganondagan State Historic Site, P.O. Box 239, Victor, NY 14564 (716) 924-5848.

*JEMISON, NANCY L.
(BIA director)
Affiliation: Office of Economic Development, Bureau of Indian Affairs, Dept. of the Interior, MS-4060-MIB, 1849 C St., NW, Washington, DC 20240 (202) 208-5326.

JENKS, PEGGY
(administrative officer)
Affiliation: Cherokee PHS Indian Hospital, Cherokee, NC 28719 (704) 497-9163.

*JENSEN, CARL (Athapascan)
(AK village council president)
Affiliation: Pedro Bay Village, P.O. Box 4720, Pedro Bay, AK 99647 (907) 850-2225.

*JENSEN, ROCKY *(Ka'iouliokahihikolo'Ehu)*
(artist)
Born in Hawaii. *Address & Affiliation*: Founder & director, Hale Naua III, Society of Native Hawaiian Arts, 99-919 Kala wina Pl., Aiea, HI 96701 (808) 487-6949. *Other professional posts*: Serves as cultural advisor to numerous organizations in the islands and as a lecturer. With his wife, Lucia Tarallo-Jensen, he has produced, mounted and participated in more than 100 native fine arts exhibitions. He introduced the contemporary form of native Hawaiian art into the artistic consciousness of Hawai'i. The first contemporary native Hawaiian art display was organized by Rocky Jensen in 1978 at Bishop Museum. Rocky's works have been exhibited in leading museums on the mainland, in Europe and New Zealand. *Published works*: Illustrated & co-authored several native cultural books, including "Men of Ancient Hawai'i," "Lord of the Forest" and "Wana'ao: The Dawning."

JENTOFF-NILSEN, LYNETTE
(museum director)
Affiliation: Sheldon Museum & Cultural Center, Box 269, Haines, AK 99827 (907) 766-2366.

JEROME, LOUIS
(Indian band chief)
Affiliation: Bande Indienne du Lac Simon, Lac Simon, Canada J0Y 3M0 (819) 736-2351.

JERRALL, CATHERINE
(association coordinator)
Affiliation: Canadian Alliance in Solidarity with the Native Peoples, 16 Spadina Rd., Suite 302, Toronto, Ontario, Canada M5R 2S7 (416) 964-0169.

JILEK, WOLFGANG GEORGE *(Kas'lidi)* **1930-**
(psychiatrist, anthropologist)
Born November 25, 1930, Tetschen, Bohemia. *Education*: Medical schools of the universities of Munich, W. Germany, Innsbruck, Austria, and Vienna, Austria, MD, 1956; McGill University, Montreal, Quebec, Canada, MSc, 1966; University of British Columbia, Vancouver, Canada, MA (Anthropology), 1972. *Principal occupation*: Clinical professor of psychiatry. *Home address*: 571 English Bluff Rd., Delta, B.C. Canada V4M 2M9 (604) 943-1295. *Affiliations*: Dept. of Anthropology & Sociology, 1974-80; clinical professor of psychiatry, Dept. of Psychiatry, 1980-, University of British Columbia, Vancouver; affiliate professor, University of Washington, Seattle, 1986-. *Other professional posts*: Consultant psychiatrist, Greater Vancouver Mental Health Service; consultant in mental health, World Health Organization, 1984-85; refuge mental health coordinator, United Nations H.C.R., Bangkok, Thailand, 1988-89. *Memberships*: Canadian Psychiatric Association (organizer & chairman of the Task Force, later Section, on Native People's Mental Health, 1970-80); American Psychiatric Association (member, Task Force on American Indians, 1971-77); World Psychiatric Association (Transcultural Psychiatry section, secretary, 1983-92, chairman, 1993-); Native Mental Health Association of Canada; Canadian Medical Association; Fellow, Royal College of Physicians and Surgeons of Canada; editorial advisor, Transcultural Psychiatric Research Review, Montreal, Canada; editorial advisor, Curare-Journal of Ethno-medicine & Transcultural Psychiatry, Heidelberg, W. Germany. *Interests*: "Transcultural psychiatry; traditional medicine and ceremonialism, especially of aboriginal North & South American peoples; ethnomedical & ethnopsychiatric research among aboriginal people of Canada, U.S. (especially Northwest Pacific culture area), and South America; Haiti; East Africa; Southeast Asia; Papua, New Guinea, 1963)." *Published works*: Salish Indian Mental Health and Culture Change (Holt, Rinehart & Winston, Toronto, 1974); Indian Healing-Shamanic Ceremonialism in the Pacific Northwest Today (Hancock House, 1982); Traditional Medicine and Primary Health Care in Papua, New Guinea (WHO & Papua, New Guinea University Press, 1985); numerous articles which deal with North American Indians.

JILEK-AALL, LOUISE M. 1931-
(psychiatrist, anthropologist)
Born April 25, 1931, Oslo, Norway. *Education*: University of Oslo, Norway, 1949-50; University of Tuebingen, Germany, 1951-55; University of Zurich, Switzerland, MD, 1958, Dipl. of Trop. Med., 1959; University of Basel, Switzerland, 1959; McGill University, Montreal, Canada, Dipl. of Psychiatry, 1965; University of British Columbia, Vancouver, Canada, MA (Social Anthropology), 1972. *Principal occupation*: Psychiatrist,

anthropologist. *Home address*: 571 English Bluff Rd., Delta, British Columbia V4M 2M9 (604) 943-1295. *Affiliations*: Clinical professor of psychiatry, University of British Columbia, Vancouver, B.C. (member, faculty of medicine, 1975-). *Other professional posts*: Consultant psychiatrist, Greater Vancouver Mental Health Service; consultant psychiatrist, University Hospital, Vancouver, B.C. *Military service*: Medical officer, U.N. Congo Mission, 1960-61 (Citation and Congo Medal of the League of Red Cross Societies, 1961). *Memberships*: Canadian Psychiatric Association (vice chairperson, Section on Native Mental Health); Canadian Psychiatric Association (member, Task Force/Section on Native Mental Health, 1970-); Native Mental Health Association of Canada; Royal College of Physicians and Surgeons of Canada, 1966- (Fellow); World Psychiatric Association, 1974- (member, Transcultural Section); International Congresses on Circumpolar Health (contributor). *Interests*: Transcultural psychiatry; ethnomedicine; Canadian, American and Alaskan Native mental health; Native therapeutic resources; alcohol abuse prevention and rehabilitation. Fieldwork and research in transcultural psychiatry and ethnomedicine in North and South America, the Caribbean, Asia, Africa, Oceania; neurological research in epilepsy. *Biographical sources*: Who's Who of American Women (10th Ed., 1977-78 p. 446); The World Who's Who of Women (4th Ed., International Biographical Centre, Cambridge, Eng. 1978 p. 583). *Published works*: Call Mama Doctor (Hancock House, 1978); Working with Dr. Schweitzer (Hancock House, 1990); Articles dealing with North American Indian matters.

*JIMENEZ, MORRIE
(chairperson)
Affiliation: Oregon Indian Coalition on Post Secondary Education, 2708 Shelly Ann Way, NE, Salem, OR 97305.

JIMMIE, ROBERT B.
(Indian band chief)
Affiliation: Squiala Indian Band, Box 392, Chilliwack, British Columbia, Canada V2P 6J7 (604) 792-8300.

JIMMY, ROGER (Kluskus)
(Indian band chief)
Affiliation: Kluskus Indian Band, 395 A Kinchant St., Quesnel, British Columbia, Canada V2J 3J8 (604) 992-8186.

JINKS-WEIDNER, JANIE
(editor)
Affiliation: The Indian Relic Trader, P.O Box 88, Sunbury, OH 43074.

*JOBE, BARBARA
(executive director)
Affiliation: Red Earth Indian Center, 2100 NE 52 St., Oklahoma City, OK 73111 (405) 427-4228.

*JOCKS, CHRISTOPHER R.
(Kahnawake Mohawk) 1954-
(professor of religious studies)
Born February 11, 1954, Omaha, Neb. Education: Lewis & Clark College, BA, 1985; University of California, Santa Barbara, MA, 1990; PhD, 1994. *Principal occupation*: Professor of religious studies. *Home address*: 26 Parkhurst St., Lebanon, NH 03766 (603) 646-2481 (work). *Affiliation*: Professor of Religious Studies, Na-

tive American Studies, Dartmouth College, Hanover, NH, 1994-. *Memberships*: American Academy of Religion; American Society for Ethnohistory. *Awards, honors*: Recipient of first annual (1993-94) Native American Dissertation Fellowship, Dartmouth College. *Interests*: "My academic work aims at describing & interpreting American Indian religious life in ways that do not intrude upon or exploit Indian communities; that use Indians' own languages and categories; and that expand our understanding of religion itself." *Published works*: "Native North American Environments as Webs of Relationship," chapter in book on World Religions and the Environment (Quo Vadis, 1994).

JOE, DONALD (Athapascan)
(AK village council vice president)
Affiliation: Tetlin Village Council, P.O. Box 520, Tetlin, AK 99780 (907) 883-2321.

JOE, JASPER (Navajo)
(college PR director)
Affiliation: Director of Public Relations, Navajo Community College, P.O. Box 580, Shiprock, NM 87420 (505) 368-5291.

*JOE, JENNIE R. (Navajo)
(associate professor)
Born in New Mexico. *Education*: University of New Mexico, BS; University of California, Berkeley, MA, MPH, PhD. *Principal occupation*: Associate professor. *Home address*: 5625 E. Rosewood St., Tucson, AZ 85711 (602) 621-5075 (work). *Affiliation*: Associate Professor of Family & Community Medicine, University of Arizona, Tucson, AZ. *Other professional post*: Director, Native American Research & Training Center, Tucson, AZ. *Military service*: U.S. Navy - Lt. *Community activities*: National Museum of the American Indian (Board of Trustees-Smithsonian Institution). *Memberships*: American Anthropological Association; American Public Health Association; Society for Medical Anthropology; The Congress of the Americanist. *Awards, honors*: 1994 National Katrin Lamon Scholar, Santa Fe, NM; 1995 Switzer Scholar, Washington, DC. *Published works*: Too numerous to list.

JOE, ROBERT, Sr. (Swinomish)
(tribal chairperson)
Affiliation: Swinomish Indian Senate, P.O. Box 817, LaConner, WA 98257 (206) 466-3163.

JOHANNSEN-HANKS, CHRISTINA B. 1950-
(museum director)
Born October 29, 1950, Rahway, N.J. *Education*: Beloit College, BA, 1972; Brown University, PhD, 1984. *Principal occupation*: Museum director. *Home address*: Star Route 1, Box 144, Warnerville, NY 12187 (518) 295-8553 (work). *Affiliation*: Director, Iroquois Indian Museum, Howes Cave, NY, 1980-. *Other professional post*: Lecturer, State University of New York at Albany. *Community activities*: Schoharie County Chamber of Commerce (board of directors). *Memberships*: American Association of Museums; Mid-Atlantic Association of Museums. *Interests*: "Research and promotion of contemporary Iroquois art. Actively involved in educating the public about the contributions of Iroquois peoples today and to an understanding of their past. Concern in maintaining professional museological standards in small museums and delineating a museum's purposes and goals. Continued field research in Iroquois communi-

ties throughout the U.S. and Canada. Special interest in creatively photographing museum objects." *Published works*: European Trade Goods and Wampanoag Culture in the Seventeenth Century in Burr's Hill: A 17th Century Wampanoag Burial Ground in Warren, Rhode Island (Haffenreffer Museum of Anthropology, Brown University, 1980); Iroquois Arts: A Directory of a People and Their Work, co-edited with Dr. John P. Ferguson (Association for the Advancement of Native North American Arts and Crafts, 1984); Efflorescence and Identity in Iroquois Art, Ph.D. Dissertation, Brown U. 1984.

*JOHN, ALLEN
(AK village chief)
Affiliation: Native Village of Clark's Point, P.O. Box 16, Clark's Point, AK 99569 (907) 236-1221.

JOHN, GENEVIEVE
(health director)
Affiliation: Pyramid Lake Health Dept., P.O. Box 227, Nixon, NV 89424 (702) 574-0107.

*JOHN, JOHNNIE, Jr. (Eskimo)
(AK village council president)
Affiliation: Native Village of Crooked Creek Council, P.O. Box 69, Crooked Creek, AK 99575 (907) 432-2227.

JOHN, LIONEL
(executive director)
Affiliation: United South & Eastern Tribes, 711 Stewarts Ferry Pike #100, Nashville, TN 37214 (615) 361-8700.

JOHN, RICHARD
(Indian band chief)
Affiliation: One Arrow Indian Band, Box 1, RR 1, Wakaw, SK, Can. S0K 4P0 (306) 423-5900.

JOHN, ROBERTA (Navajo) 1960-
(public information officer; writer)
Born May 26, 1960, Monticello, Utah. *Education*: Arizona State University, BS, 1982; Brigham Young University, MA (Arts in Communications), 1987. *Principal occupation*: Public information officer; writer. *Home address*: P.O. Box 2978, Window Rock, AZ 86515 (602) 871-6659 (work). *Affiliation*: Navajoland Tourism Department, Window Rock, AZ, 1989-. *Other professional post*: New Mexico Quincentennial Commissioner. *Community activities*: Publicity coordinator, Navajo Nation Fair and Fourth of July PRCA Rodeo & Pow Wow Celebration. *Membership*: New Mexico Indian Tourism Association (board member). *Interests*: "I handle and coordinate the overall promotion, advertising and marketing of the Navajo Nation. I am in the process of writing and editing a major Navajo Tourism strategy for the Navajo Nation. This master plan will be used to help plan, develop and create more jobs for the Navajo people - developing the tourism industry on North America's largest reservation, Navajoland. I was part of a ten-member New Mexico, German Sales Mission Delegation - I promoted New Mexico tribes, mainly the Navajo Nation. I enjoy writing feature stories. I also would like to produce and write a video about the Navajo Nation." *Published work*: Navajoland Tourism Brochure, 1990.

*JOHN, WILLIAM (Eskimo)
(AK village council president)
Affiliation: Native Village of Pitka's Point, P.O. Box 127, St. Mary's, AK 99658 (907) 438-2833.

JOHNNY, RONALD EAGLEYE
(president-Indian organization)
Affiliation: President, Native American Law Students Association, American Indian Law Center, University of New Mexico School of Law, P.O. Box 4456, 1117 Stanford NE, Albuquerque, NM 87196.

JOHNS, BOBBY THOMAS
(Lower Muskogee Creek) 1936-
(artist/craftsman)
Born March 24, 1936, Dodge County, Ga. *Education*: College courses; Graphic Arts Certificate. *Principal occupation*: Artist/craftsman. *Home address*: 12533 Polonious Pkwy., Pensacola, FL 32506 (904) 492-3593. *Affiliation*: Instructor and technical advisor for military training films & communications operations in a civilian capacity at Fort Gordon, GA (20 years). Disability retirement. *Military service*: U.S. navy (4 years) (Airman, sea/air rescue). *Community activities*: Museum of Commerce (volunteer); Northwest Florida Arts Council (Arts in Education Committee); Indian culture demonstrations for many events. *Memberships*: Pensacola Historical Society; National Woodcarvers Association; Arts Council of Northwest Florida; Historic Pensacola Village. *Awards, honors*: Artist Fellowship for folk art - Secretary of State, Cultural Affairs; Master Artist & Apprentice Program, Florida Folklife Division, Secretary of State. *Interests*: "Helping to keep alive the traditional attitudes and crafts/art of our Native American peoples. Visiting schools and public powwows where interaction with others can take place to foster a better understanding of our people."

JOHNS, JOSEPH F. *(Cayoni)* **(Eastern Creek) 1928-**
(museum manager, artist)
Born January 31, 1928, Okefenokee Swamp, Ga. *Education*: High school (U.S. Armed Forces Institute). *Principal occupation*: Museum manager, artist. *Home address*: 7 Russell St., West Peabody, MA 01960 (508) 535-2426. *Affiliation*: Indian Artist in Residence (sculpture and carving in any medium) & Building Manager, Peabody Museum Peabody Museum, Harvard University, Cambridge, MA, 1974-. "I maintain a small studio, at my home, for carving the eight traditional masks of the Creek people." *Military service*: U.S. Naval Amphibious Forces (Sniper), 1944-1946 (U.S. Navy P.O. 3; Asiatic Pacific Medal, Silver Star Medal); U.S. Coast Guard (retired), 1947-1965 (U.S.C.G. P.O. 1; Silver Life Saving Medal presented by President Harry S. Truman in Washington, D.C., 1947). *Community activities*: Masonic Shriner at Alleppo Temple, Wilmington, Mass. *Membership*: Boston Indian Council; Peabody Museum (Associate; member, Repatriation Committee). *Awards, honors*: "I was a crew member of the Coast Guard Cutter Westwind Expedition to the North Pole (Dew Line), 1953-1954; and a crew member of the Coast Guard's Cutter, Eastwind Expedition to the South Pole (Operation Deep Freeze, 1961-1962); (I am) holder of Antarctica Service Medal. A book about my life is now being written by Mitchell Wade."

*JOHNS, KEN
(executive director)
Affiliation: Copper River Native Association, Drawer H, Copper Center, AK 99573 (907) 822-5241.

*JOHNS, MARY FRANCES (Florida Seminole) 1944-
(craft artist; shop owner)
Born October 7, 1944, Miami, Fla. *Education*: Edison Community College (Ft. Myers, FL), Nursing, 1979-1983. *Principal occupation*: Craft artist; shop owner. *Home address*: Rt. 6, Box 595, Brighton Seminole Reservation, Okeechobee, FL 34974 (813) 467-7312. *Affiliation*: Owner, Arts & Crafts Shop, Brighton Reservation, 1984-. *Other professional posts*: Resource person for museums as arts & crafts demonstrator, storytelling & history of the Seminoles & Southeastern Indians. *Interests*: "I have demonstrated basketry, patchwork, doll making and Indian foods all over the State of Florida. I have given talks on our culture and its history throughout North & Central Florida. I was hired by the Tallahassee Junior Museum thru a State Dept. grant to be artist in resident. This is how I got started in this field. I am presently helping Charles Daniels with his Creek language classes and am studying the Muskogean & Southeastern Indian culture thru Mr. Daniels classes. I speak Miccosukee, Creek and English fluently, and some Spanish. My hobbies are painting, crafts, and artifacts making." *Published works*: Co-author, with D. Alderson, "Muskogee Fires" (Muskogee Press, 1994); Muskogee Words & Ways-also Dictionary III, a Southeastern Reader V (7 part series).

JOHNSON, ALVIS (Karuk)
(tribal chairperson;
health program director)
Affiliation: Karuk Tribe of California, P.O. Box 1016, Happy Camp, CA 96039 (916) 493-5305. *Other professional post*: director, Karuk Tribal Health Program.

JOHNSON, CHARLES E.
(BIA supt. for education)
Affiliation: Fort Defiance Agency, Bureau of Indian Affairs, P.O. Box 110, Fort Defiance, AZ 86504 (602) 729-5041 Ext. 255.

*JOHNSON, CHARLIE
(AK village council president)
Affiliation: Portage Creek Village, P.O. Box 1031, Portage Creek, AK 99576 (907) 842-5218.

JOHNSON, FRANK
(Indian band chief)
Affiliation: Oweekeno Indian Band, Box 3500, Port Hardy, British Columbia, Canada V0N 2P0.

JOHNSON, FREDERICK M.
(Indian school principal)
Affiliation: Rocky Ridge Boarding School, P.O. Box 299, Kykotsmovi, AZ 86039 (602) 725-3415.

JOHNSON, GEORGE W.
(Indian band chief)
Affiliation: Chapel Island Indian Band, RR #1, St. Peters, Nova Scotia, Canada B0A 1J0 (902) 535-3317.

*JOHNSON, GLENN
(Indian center director)
Affiliation: American Indian Graduate Student Center, Office of Indian Programs, University of Arizona, Tucson, AZ 85721 (602) 621-2794.

*JOHNSON, JACQUELINE L.
(executive director; council chairperson)
Affiliations: Executive director, Oneida Riders Association, N6935 Hwy. 55, Seymour, WI 54165 (414) 833-2323; chairperson, National American Indian Housing Council, 900 2nd St., NE, Suite 220, Washington, DC 20002 (202) 789-1754.

JOHNSON, JAMES
(Indian band chief)
Affiliation: Spuzzum Indian Band, RR 1, Yale, British Columbia, Canada V0K 2S0 (604) 863-2205.

*JOHNSON, JERI (Tonto Apache)
(tribal council chairperson)
Affiliation: Tonto Apache Tribal Council, Tonto Reservation #30, Payson, AZ 85541 (602) 474-5000.

JOHNSON, JOAN
(editor)
Affiliation: Micmac News, Nova Scotia Native Communications Society, P.O. Box 344, Sydney, Nova Scotia, Canada B1P 6H2 (902) 539-0045.

JOHNSON, JOE (Creek) 1950-
(mayor, chief justice)
Born August 24, 1950, Council Hill, Okla. *Education*: Eastern Oklahoma State College (Wilburton, OK), AA; Oklahoma State University (2 years). *Principal occupation*: Mayor, chief justice. *Home address*: 812 N. Simpson St., Eufaula, OK 74432 (918) 689-2533 (work). *Affiliations*: Mayor, City of Eufaula, OK, 1975-; chief justice, Muscogee Creek Nation, 1987-93; director, Native American Studies Program, Rose State College, Midwest City, OK 73110 (405) 733-7308. *Community activities*: Eastern OK Development District Board of Directors (3 terms); Eufaula Municipal Hospital Board of Directors (chairperson, 1976-86); OK Municipal League (president, vice-president & currently past president); McIntosh County Democratic Central Committee (past secretary-treasurer); OK Police Pension & Retirement Board (6 years); State Higher Education Alumni of ESC. *Memberships*: National American Indian Court Judges Association; OK Conference of Mayors; OK Conference of Regional Councils; Lions Club; Greater Eufaula Chamber of Commerce; Lake Eufaula Association (board member); serves on Development Council of Connors State College; serves on the Domestic Violence and Substance Abuse PAC Board; serves on the Board of Directors for Literacy Council, and OK Travel Industry Association. *Awards, honors*: Elected in 1975 as the youngest mayor in the state, at age of 24 years; selected to Who's Who in the South and Outstanding Young Men of America; George Nigh Mayor's Award. *Interests*: "Developed the local Posey Park, named after Alexander Posey, the most recognized Indian poet in Oklahoma's history; developed the Eufaula Community Center and the Eufaula Memorial Library; instrumental in the development and implementation of the Eufaula Main Street Program."

JOHNSON, JOSEPH (Nooksack)
(tribal council chairperson)
Affiliation: Nooksack Tribal Council, P.O. Box 157, Deming, WA 98244 (206) 592-5176.

JOHNSON, LARRY
(Indian band chief)
Affiliation: Caldwell Indian Band, Box 163215 Main St., Bothwell, Ontario, Canada N0P 1C0 (519) 695-3642.

*JOHNSON, MADELINE
(clinic director)
Affiliation: Ardmore Chickasaw Health Clinic, 2510 Chickasaw Blvd., Ardmore, OK 73401 (405) 226-8181.

JOHNSON, PATRICIA LUCILLE PADDLETY (Kiowa) 1938-
(attorney)
Born October 22, 1938, Mountain View, Okla. *Education*: Oklahoma College of Liberal Arts, Chickasaw, BS, 1971; University of Oklahoma School of Law, JD, 1975. *Principal occupation*: Attorney. *Home address*: Route 3, Anadarko, OK 73005. *Affiliation*: Associate Magistrate, Bureau of Indian Affairs, Code of Indian Offenses, Court, Anadarko, OK. *Community activities*: Indian Capital Baptist Church (member and teacher); Oklahoma Indian Rights Association; OK Indian Women Association. Memberships: OK Bar Association, 1975- (Minorities Law Committee, 1976); Federal Bar for the Western District of OK, 1975-. *Interests*: "I am interested in assisting young Indian people to achieve their life's goals, whether in Law or in any other field of training. I work extensively with our church in attempting to inspire and inform Indians in this area of the opportunities available to them. Alcoholism and drug related of fenders make up the majority of my clients, and when I have the time, I counsel and encourage them."

JOHNSON, RENO, Sr. (Apache)
(former tribal chairperson)
Affiliation: White Mountain Apache Tribal Council, P.O. Box 700, Whiteriver, AZ 85941 (602) 338-4346. *Other professional post*: Member, Council of Advisors, American Indian Heritage Foundation, Falls Church, VA.

*JOHNSON, ROXANNE TALLMADGE
(museum acting manager)
Affiliation: Winnebago Indian Museum, 3889 N. River, Wisconsin Dells, WI 53965 (608) 254-2268.

JOHNSON, ROY S. *(Crazy Horse)*
(Rappahannock) 1928-
(research writer, lecturer, educator)
Born December 7, 1928, Caroline County, Va. *Education*: Temple University, 1947-49; University of Pennsylvania, BA, 1951; College of Metaphysics, PsD, 1972. *Principal occupation*: Research writer, lecturer on Indian affairs, educator. *Military service*: U.S. Army, 1943-46 (1st Lt.; 6 major campaigns-Pacific Theatre Medal, Silver Star, Bronze Star, Purple Heart, Presidential Unit Citation, Good Conduct Medal). *Community activities*: Coalition of Native Americans. Memberships: Rappahannock Tribe, State of Virginia (field chief); Powhatan Indians of Delaware Valley (chairman). *Interests*: Mr. Johnson teaches basic adult education to Native Americans; teaches self-defense and the Powhatan language. *Published work*: East Coast Indian Tribes, with Jack D. Forbes.

JOHNSON, SAM 1938-
(president-Indian village)
Born August 14, 1938, Ashdown, Ark. *Education*: University of Arkansas, Fayetteville, BA *Principal occupation*: President/director, Ka-doha Indian Village, P.O. Box 669, Route 1, Murfressboro, AR 71958 (501) 285-3736, 1978-. *Military service*: U.S. Army (4 years).

*JOHNSON, SHEILA MEADOWS *(Tsula Atsila)* **(Southeastern Cherokee) 1949-**
(arts-in-education teacher)
Born December 5, 1949, Collinsville, AL. *Education*: Jacksonville State University (AL), 1967-70 (major in art). *Principal occupation*: Arts-in-education teacher. *Address*: P.O. Box 227, Collinsville, AL 35961 (205) 524-2218. *Affiliation*: Alabama Arts Council, Dekalb County School System, Collinsville, AL. *Community activities*: North Alabama Cherokees (first vice-chief; tribal information & enrollment director; pow wow & event coordinator); past president, Collinsville Business & Professional Association. *Memberships*: Indian Arts & Crafts Association (member, Education & Enrollment Committee); Atlatl Native Arts Registry; Smithsonian National Museum of the American Indian (charter member). *Awards, honors*: Beloved Woman of the North Alabama Cherokees. *Interests*: "Serve as emcee of all tribal pow wows and events, and also emcee pow wows for other tribes and groups in the Southeast. Coordinate may local festivals and school programs." *Biographical source*: Featured articles in "People and Places," published by the Gadsden Times.

*JOHNSON, SHERRI (Washoe)
(tribal council chairperson)
Affiliation: Carson Indian Colony Community Council, P.O. Box 3269, Carson City, NV 89702 (702) 883-6431.

*JOHNSON, TADD
(government agency staff director)
Affiliation: Native American Affairs Subcommittee, U.S. House of Representatives, 1522 Longworth, Washington, DC 20515 (202) 226-7736.

*JOHNSON, TROY ROLLEN
(professor, historian)
Born February 29, 1940, Wichita Falls, Tex. *Education*: San Diego State University, BA, 1986; UCLA, MA, 1989, PhD, 1993. *Principal occupation*: Professor, historian. *Home address*: 555 Main Ave. #420, Long Beach, CA 90802 (310) 432-8721; 985-8703 (work). *Affiliation*: Visiting professor, Native American Studies Program, University of California, Davis, Davis, CA, 1993-94; visiting research scholar, American Indian Studies Center, UCLA, Los Angeles, CA, 3/94-8/94; assistant professor, American Indian Studies Center, Dept. of History, California State University, Long Beach, CA, 1994-. *Military service*: U.S. Navy Retired (Lt. Commander), 1957-80 (Combat Action Ribbon, Vietnamese Service Medal; Vietnamese Presidential Citation; Navy Expeditionary Medal (Cuba). *Membership*: American Historical Society. *Interests*: American Indian history & culture, history of the American West, history of the 1960s. *Published works*: Master's Thesis, "Status of Adoption & Foster Home Placement of Indian Children Under the Indian Child Welfare Act (UCLA, 1988); book reviews, "American Indian Culture & Research Journal (UCLA, 1990-92); "Depression, Despair, and Death; Indian Youth Suicide," Looking Glass edited by Clifford Trafzer (San Diego University Press, 1991); editor, Proceedings of the First & Second Annual National Conference on Indian Child Welfare, "Indian Homes for Indian Children," and "Unto the Seventh Generation" (UCLA, 1991 & 1993); editor, Activism Poetry & Political Statements from Alcatraz: The Indian Voice (American India Studies Center, UCLA, 1994); associate editor, Native North American

Almanac (Gale Research, 1993); associate editor, Chronology of the North American Indian (Gale Research, 1994); associate editor, Native American: A Portrait of a People (Visible Ink Press, 1994); article, with Joane Nagel, "The Indian Occupation of Alcatraz Island: Twenty-Five Years Later," in American Indian Culture & Research Journal, Nov. 1994); The Indian Occupation of Alcatraz Island and the Rise of Indian Activism (University of Illinois Press, 1995).

JOHNSON, VIOLA
(hospital director)
Affiliation: Huhukam Memorial Hospital, P.O. Box 38, Sacaton, AZ 85247 (602) 562-3321.

JOHNSTON, BASIL H. (Ojibway) 1929-
(author)
Born July 13, 1929, Parry Island Reserve, Ontario, Can. *Education*: Loyola College, Montreal, BA, 1954; Ontario College of Education, Secondary School Teaching Certificate, 1962. *Principal occupation*: Author. *Home address*: 253 Ashlar Rd., Richmond Hill, ON L4C 2W7 (416) 884-9375 (home) 586-5538 (work). *Affiliations*: Assistant manager, 1957-59, manager, 1959-61, Toronto Board of Trade; teacher, Earl Haig Secondary School, 1962-69; lecturer, Ethnology Department, Royal Ontario Museum, 100 Queen's Park, Toronto, 1969-; teacher, private language teacher of Ojibway Indians, Toronto, 1974-. *Other professional posts*: Academic lectures and keynote addresses or major presentations at universities and conferences across the U.S. & Canada; media consultant, narrator on films; script writer-reviewer. *Community activities*: Toronto Indian Club; Canadian Indian Centre of Toronto (executive and vice president, 1963-69); Indian Eskimo Association (executive, legal committee, speakers committee, 1965-68); Union of Ontario Indians; Federal Indian Consultations, Toronto; Indian Hall of Fame (committee member, 1968-70); Wigwamen Inc., 1974-75; Ontario Geographic Names Board, 1977-87. *Awards, honors*: Centennial Medal in recognition of work on behalf of Native community, 1967; 1976 Samuel S. Fells Literary Award for first publication "Zhowmin and Mandamin"; Order of Ontario - for service of the greatest distinction and of singular excellence...benefiting society in Ontario and elsewhere, April 1989. *Published works*: Ojibway Language Course Outline (Education Division, Indian Affairs Branch, 1979); Ojibway Language Lexicon for Beginners and Others (Education Division, Indian Affairs Branch, 1979); Ojibwa Heritage (University of Columbia Press, 1976); How the Birds Got Their Colours (Kids Can Press, Toronto, 1978); Tales Our Elders Told (Royal Ontario Museum, Toronto, 1981); Ojibway Ceremonies (McClelland and Stewart, Toronto, 1983); By Canoe and Moccasin (Waapoone Publishing, Lakefield, ON, 1986); Moose Meat and Wild Rice (McClelland and Stewart, Toronto, 1978); Indian School Days (University of Oklahoma Press, 1989); Numerous stories, essays, articles and poems in various publications.

JOHNSTON, JAMES HENRY *(Silent Heart)*
(United Lumbee/Cherokee)1943-
(horse trainer)
Born March 29, 1943, Allegany Co., Penna. *Education*: High school. *Principal occupation*: Horse trainer. *Address*: P.O. Box 242, Florence, MT 59833. *Military service*: U.S. Navy, 1963-67 (Good Conduct Medal; Sharpshooter/Marks-

man). "I was on the U.S. Plymouth Rock LSD 29 during the Cuban Missile Crisis and was awarded ribbon for front line duty ." *Community activities*: United Lumbee Nation's Mantaoc Medicine Society (member); United Lumbee Nation's High Eagle Warrior Society (chief, 1987-). *Interests*: "I hope to go to law school and become a lawyer specializing in Indian law . I like to teach young people track and our Indian ways: drumming, dancing, etc. Work with horses. I have a section in the United Lumbee Deer Clan Cook Book, 1988."

JOHNSTON, ROBERT (Comanche) 1953-
(lawyer)
Born January 28, 1953, Little Rock, Ark. *Education*: Wichita State University , BA, 1975; University of Oklahoma, College of Law , JD, 1978. *Principal occupation*: Lawyer. *Home address*: 1330 Dorchester Dr., Norman, OK 73069. *Interests*: Indian law; oil and gas law; natural resources law. *Published work*: Whitehorn v. State: Peyote and Religious Freedom in Oklahoma (American Indian Law Review , Vol. V, No. 1, winter, 1977).

*JOJOLA, JOSEPH R. *(White Snow)*
(Isleta Pueblo) 1945-
(electronics technician)
Born September 18, 1945, Albuquerque, N.M. *Education*: New Mexico State University , 1986-89; New York Regeants (New York, NY), BS, 1993. *Principal occupation*: Electronics technician. *Home address*: 202 Corporal St., White Sands Missile Range, NM 88002 (505) 678-6473. *Affiliation*: Electronics technician, Army Research Laboratory, White Sands M.R., NM, 1989-. *Other professional posts*: Ammunition/explosives handler; owner of White Sands Photography; and craftsman of silversmithing & repair. *Military service*: U.S. Army Retired Master Sergeant/E-8 - 21 years active duty)12 years in Germany (Meritorious Service Medal; 7 Good Conduct Medals; 2 Army Commendation Medals: German & American Expert Marksmanship Badges; among others). *Community activities*: Mayor of White Sands Missile Range for two years. *Memberships*: Indian Arts & Crafts Association. *Awards, honors*: "I will be honored in a Purification Ceremony in Dec. 1994 in the "Black Eye" clan. This consists of 4 days & 3 nights of total prayer & singing, no sleeping or eating (can drink). *Interests*: "I have traveled to approximately 17 countries in Europe and the Far East. I attend tribal functions when duty allows me to. I enjoy silversmithing and have taught all 5 of my children how to make Indian jewelry and they have successfully made themselves jewelry ."

JOJOLA, TED (Isleta Pueblo) 1951-
(educator, administrator)
Born November 19, 1951, Isleta Pueblo, N.M. *Education*: University of New Mexico, BA; Massachusetts Institute of Technology, MA; University of Hawaii-Manoa, PhD (Political Science), 1982; University of Strasbourg, France, Certificate of International Human Rights Law , 1985. *Principal occupation*: Educator, administrator . *Home address*: Route 6, Box 578, Albuquerque, NM 87105. *Affiliations*: Internal planner , National Capital Planning Commission, Washington, DC, 1973; legal/historical researcher , Institute for the Development of Indian Law , Washington, DC, 1976; visiting research associate, Institute of Philippine Culture, Manila, 1977-78; visiting professor of urban planning, UCLA, 1984; assistant professor of planning, University of New

Mexico, Albuquerque, 1982-; director , Institute for Native American Development (INAD), Native American Studies Department, 1812 Las Lomas Dr., NE, University of New Mexico, Albuquerque, 1980-. *Other professional posts*: Consultant, Thurshun Consultants, Albuquerque, NM 87131, 1980-; coordinator , Ethnic/Minority Directors' Coalition, 1983-; Apple Computer Corporation (Education Grants Program, 1986-); Museum of the American Indian Arts & Culture, State Museum of New Mexico, (Advisory Board, 1987-); New Mexico Architecture Foundation (advisory board, 1988-). *Major research*: Cohort Retention Study of Indian Students at UNM, 1973-84, 1985-; Preschool Computer Program in an Isolated American Indian Community, Education Grants Program, Apple Computer Corp., 1985-; On-site coordinator: "Headstart Classroom of the Future", U.S. Dept. of Health & Human Services, 1989 research involving the Isleta Pueblo Head Start Program along with two other sites in Michigan; Ethnographic Undercounts - 1990 Census, 1989, U.S. Census Bureau. *Community activities*: 9th Inter-American Indian Congress, Santa Fe, N.M. (U.S. organizing committee, 1985-); Zuni Tribal Museum, Zuni, N.M. (advisory board, 1985-); JOM/Indian Education Parent's Committee, Isleta Pueblo, N.M. (chair). *Memberships*: Native American Studies Association. *Awards, honors*: Postdoctoral Fellow , American Indian Studies, UCLA, 1984; public grantee, Atherton Trust, Honolulu, 1976; recipient of Participant Award, East-West Center, Honolulu. *Interests*: My main interest lay in the notion of continued tribal survival, and the various and varying strategies that have ensued in the course of this struggle. Currently, I have been doing research in the notion of tribal (traditional) consensus making and its theoretical modeling toward the idea of using this mechanism for the integration of tribal policy in the regional development process. *Biographical source*: Who's Who in the West (Marquis, 1985-); (Marquis; Who's Who Among Young Emerging Leaders (Marquis, 1987). *Published works*: Memoirs of an American Indian House: The Impact of a Cross-National Housing Program on Two Reservations, 1976; Foreword and series editor, Irredeemable America: The Indians' Estate and Land Claims, Edited by Imre Sutton; Contributing editor , Wicazo sa Review (Eastern Washington University , 1988-); foreword and series editor , Public Policy Impacts on American Indian Development; Modernization & Pueblo Lifeways: Isleta Pueblo, chapter in Pueblo Style & Regional Architecture (Van Nostrand Reinhold, 1989); many articles in various publications.

*JOJOLA, TONY *(Thur-shun - Sunrise)*
(Isleta Pueblo) 1958-
(artist)
Born August 11, 1958, Albuquerque, N.M. *Education*: Institute of American Indian Arts, AA, 1978; College of Santa Fe, BFA, 1983. *Principal occupation*: Artist. *Address*: P.O. Box 166, Isleta Pueblo, NM 87022 (505) 869-3769. *Other professional posts*: One/two day lectures/symposiums. *Exhibitions*: Indian Pueblo Cultural Center, Albuquerque, NM, 1979; Southern Plains Indian Museum, Anadarko, OK, 1988; Indian Pueblo Cultural Center , Albuquerque, NM, 1990; Milicent Rogers Museum, Taos, NM, 1993; numerous selected group exhibitions. *Awards, honors*: Most Innovative Artist, Red Cloud Indian Art Show, Browning, MT, 1984; Indian Market--SWAIA, Santa Fe, NM (Misc. Contempo-

rary, 1985; Misc. Contemporary , 1st & 2nd Place, 1986; Misc. Contemporary , 3rd Place, 1988; Misc. Contemporary , 1989, Creative Excellence Award, 1991; 1st Place & Honorable Mention, 1992; 1st Place, Diversified Art Forms, 1993); among others. *Membership*: Southwestern Association of American Indian Affairs. *Biographical sources*: "Anthony Jojola," by Gail Bird, in Indian Market Magazine, August-1988; "Tony Jojola," by Suzanne Carmichael, in The Travelers Guide to American Craft, 1990; "Glass Artist Tony Jojola Looking for a Niche," by John Villani, in Pasa Tempo, Aug. 16, 1991; "A ward Winning Glass Sculpture," by Irvin Borowsky , in Artists Confronting the Inconceivable, 1992; among others. *Film*: "Indian Market--A Winter Event," by Ms. Lena Carr , a SWAIA-sponsored Symposium filmed Dec. 9, 1988 (K-Karr Productions, Albuquerque, NM).

JOKA, GARY (Navajo)
(school principal)
Affiliation: Holbrook Dormitory, P.O. Box 758, Holbrook, AZ 86025 (602) 524-6222.

*JONES, A. BRUCE
(executive director)
Affiliation: North Carolina Commission on Indian Affairs, 325 N. Salisbury St., Suite 579, Raleigh, NC 27603 (919) 733-5998.

*JONES, CHARLENE
(tribal librarian)
Affiliation: Mashantucket Pequot Research Library, P.o. Box 3060, Indiantown Rd., Ledyard, CT 06339 (203) 536-7200.

JONES, CYNTHIA
(museum curator)
Affiliation: Sheldon Museum, P.O. Box 269, Haines, AK 99827 (907) 766-2366.

*JONES, DAN
(film producer)
Address: P.O. Box 421, Stillwater , OK 74076 (405) 372-8859 Fax 372-7571.

JONES, DAVID S. (Choctaw) 1928-
(educator)
Born July 24, 1928, Boswell, Okla. *Education*: Eastern A & M College, 1950-51; East Central State College, 1951-52; Central State University (Edmonds, OK), 1955-63, BA, MA. *Principal occupation*: Educator. *Affiliation*: Principal, Crystal Boarding School, Navajo, NM, 1983-92. *Other professional post*: Council for Exceptional Children, Navajo Area (vice president). *Military service*: U.S. Navy, 1945-47; U.S. Naval Reserve (18 years); U.S. Army Reserve (Staff Sergeant, 12 years); (Meritorious Service Medal, World War II Victory Medal, Asiatic Pacific Medal, Armed Forces Reserve Medal, Marksman. *Community activities*: El Reno Lions Club, Okla. (past president); Methodist Church (chairman, official board); Methodist Mens Club; Church School (superintendent). *Memberships*: National Indian Education Association (life member); Elementary School Principals Association; Oklahoma Governor's Council for Vocational Education; National Indian Scouting Association. *Awards, honors*: Masonic Teacher of Today Award; American Legions Award for Achievement; GrayWolf Award for Outstanding Indian Scouter, Boy Scouts of America. *Interests*: Travels with Naval and Army Reserve trainings. *Published work*: Co-author, A Guide for Teachers of Indian Students (OK Dept. of Education, 1972).

*JONES, DORA ANN
(special collections librarian)
Affiliation : E.Y. Berry Library-Learning Center , Black Hills State University , 1200 University, Spearfish, SD 57799 (605) 642-6833.

JONES, GERALD J. (Port Gamble S'Klallam)
(tribal chairperson)
Affiliation : Port Gamble Business Committee, 31912 Little Boston Rd., NE, Kingston, W A 98346 (206) 297-2646.

JONES, HENRY L.
(monument supt.)
Affiliation : Wupatki and Sunset Crater National Monument, HC 33, Box 444A, Flagstaf f, AZ 86001 (602) 527-7152.

JONES, MRS. JAMES L.
(museum director)
Affiliation : Caddo Indian Museum, 701 Hardy St., Longview, TX 75604 (214) 759-5739.

*JONES, KATE
(historic site curator)
Affiliation : Angel Mounds State Historic Site, 8215 Pollack Ave., Evansville, IN 47715 (812) 853-3956.

JONES, KENNETH
(Indian band chief)
Affiliation . Pacheenaht Indian Band, General Delivery, Port Renfrew , British Columbia, Canada V0S 1K0 (604) 647-5521.

JONES, JOAN MEGAN 1933-
(socio-cultural anthropologist)
Born September 7, 1933, Laramie, W yo. *Education* : University of Washington, BA, 1956, MA, 1968, PhD, 1976. *Principal occupation* : Sociocultural anthropologist. *Home address* : 392 Yokeko Dr., Anacortes, WA 98221. *Affiliations* : Educator, Burke Museum, Seattle, 1969-72; visiting lecturer, Primitive Art, University of British Columbia, 1978; visiting instructor , course: Indians of the Northwest Coast, Anthropology Dept., Western Washington University, Bellingham (Summer), 1981; research associate, Dept. of Anthropology, University of W ashington, Seattle, 1982-. *Community activities* : Anacortes Arts & Crafts Festival Foundation, (board member, 1981-83); Anacortes Branch, American Association of University W omen (board member , 1982-84); Skagit V alley W eavers Guild, (board member , 1985-86; 1988-90). *Memberships* : American Anthropological Association (member , 1968-; Fellow , 1976-); Society for Applied Anthropology (Fellow , 1983-); American Association of Museums, 1969-89; National Association for the Practice of Anthropology (charter member); Association for W omen in Science, 1983-. *Awards, honors* : Wenner-Gren Foundation for Anthropological Research, Museum Research Fellow, 1967-68; Ford Foundation, Dissertation Fellowship in Ethnic Studies, 1972-73. *Interests* : Professional specialization in Native American art & material culture studies & research with museum collections. *Field work* : Native basketmakers in southern British Columbia, for National Museum of Man, National Museums of Canada, Urgent Ethnology Research Contract, 1973-74; anthropologist for basketry research, Quinault Indian Nation, 1976-77; consultant, fiber arts, Samish Indian Tribe, 1985-. As a handweaver, handspinner , and knitter , I am active in local spinners and weavers groups. *Published works* : Northwest Basketry and Culture

Change (Burke Museum, 1968); Native Basketry of Western North America (Illinois State Museum, 1978); The Art and Style of W estern Indian Basketry (Hancock House, 1982).

JONES, KATE
(historic site curator)
Affiliation : Angel Mounds State Historic Site, 8215 Pollack Ave., Evansville, IN 47715 (812) 853-3956.

*JONES, MATTHEW
(Native American film producer/consultant)
Affiliation : Native American Public Broadcasting Consortium, P.O Box 83111, Lincoln, NE 68501 (402) 472-3522; editor , Newsletter.

JONES, PETER B. (Onondaga-Seneca) 1947-
(potter/sculptor)
Born June 8, 1947, Cattaraugus Indian Reservation, N.Y. *Education* : Institute of American Indian Arts; Archie Bray Foundation (Helena, MT). *Principal occupation* : Potter/sculptor. *Address* : Box 174, Versailles-Plank Rd., V ersailles, NY 14168 (716) 532-5993. *Exhibitions* : Peter B. Jones Retrospective Exhibition (1965-90), Iroquois Indian Museum, Schoharie, NY , 1990; Pottery Through the Ages: Traditions in Clay , Pueblo Grande Museum, Phoenix, AZ, 1990; Contemporary Native Ceramics, CN Gorman Museum, University of California, Davis, 1991; New Works in Ancient Traditions, Shoestring gallery, Rochester, NY, 1991; Creativity in Our Tradition: Three Decades of Contemporary Indian Art, Institute of American Indian Arts, Santa Fe, NM, 1992: Reflecting Contemporary Realities, Los Angeles, County Folk Art & Craft Museum, 1993; Art of First Nations, Brantford, Ontario, 1993; Area Artists Collection 1993 Members Gallery, Albright-Knox Art Gallery, Buffalo, NY, 1993. *Permanent collections* : Indian Arts & Crafts Board, U.S. Dept. of the Interior , Washington, DC; Institute of American Indian Arts, Santa Fe, NM; Heard Museum, Phoenix, AZ; Everson Museum, Syracuse, NY ; Iroquois Indian Museum, Howes Cave, NY ; Southern Plains Indian Museum, Anadarko, OK; Rochester Museum & Science Center , Rochester, NY; New York State Museum, Albany; Museum of Fine Arts Boston, MA. *Awards, honors* : Div. Award, Best of Class, Scottsdale (AZ) Native American Cultural Foundation, 1987 & 1988; Best of Show , Festival of Iroquois Arts, Cattaraugus Indian Reservation, NY , 1989; Excellence in Iroquois Arts, Iroquois Indian Museum, Howes Cave, NY, 1990; Best of Show , Quinnehtukqut Native American Festival, E. Hartford, CT, 1992. *Works featured in the books & periodicals* : Southwest Art, Sept. 1988, V ol. 18 No. 4, "Contemporary Native American Ceramics"; Beyond Tradition-Contemporary Indian Art and Its Evolution by Jerry & Lois Jacka (Northland Press, 1988); Peter B. Jones, Iroquois Art, Retrospective Catalogue, Iroquois Indian Museum, Howes Cave, NY ; Winds of Change, Fall 1991, V ol. 6 No. 4, "Reflections of a Native Vision: American Indian Contemporary Art" by Ray Moisa.

*JONES, PETER L.
(museum director)
Affiliation : Owasco Teyetasta, Rt. 38A Emerson Park, 203 Genessee St., Auburn, NY 13021 (315) 253-8051.

*JONES, ROBERT
(BIA agency supt.)
Affiliation : Shawnee Agency, BIA, 624 W. Independence, Suite 1 14, Shawnee, OK (405) 273-0317.

JONES, ROGER
(Indian band chief)
Affiliation : Shawanaga Indian Band, RR 1, Nobel, Ontario, Canada P0G 1G0 (705) 366-2526.

*JONES, ROY, Jr. (Eskimo)
(AK village council president)
Affiliation : Native Village of Larsen Bay , P.O. Box 35, Larsen Bay , AK 99624 (907) 847-2207.

JONES, SCOTT 1959-
(primitive technology/
outdoor skills instructor)
Born December 25, 1959, Canton, Ga. *Education* : Community College of the Air Force, AAS, 1985; University of Georgia, AB, 1990. *Principal occupation* : Primitive technology/outdoor skills instructor. *Home address* : P.O. Box 2446, Athens, GA 30612 (404) 743-5144 *Affiliation* : Director, Hofunee Southeastern Indian Programs, Athens, GA, 1987-. *Other professional posts* : Instructor, Continuing Education Courses, University of Georgia, Athens, 1988-. *Military service* : U.S. Air Force, 1982-85; Georgia Air National Guard, 1986-90 (Sergeant; Marksman Award). *Memberships* : Society of Primitive Technology; Society for Georgia Archaeology (Northeast Georgia Chapter President, 1992). *Interests* : "Attend courses in outdoor skills at the Boulder Outdoor Survival School in Rexburg, Idaho, and worked with many outstanding instructors in the field of primitive skills since 1987; instructed and co-instructed courses in aboriginal/outdoor skills at state parks in Georgia and South Carolina, the National Park Service, the South Carolina Institute of Archaeology and Anthropology, as well as for colleges, schools, museums, and wilderness camps throughout the Southeast; monthly aboriginal skills workshops, Hofunee Programs, Oglethorpe County , GA; and primitive skills demonstrations at Pow wows throughout the Southeastern U.S. I'm currently working on some projects relating to old world (European & African) prehistory. I'm also very interested & involved in sustainable low-impact lifestyles including organic farming, log home building (from raw timber), and making use of abundant local resources. I now live in a small log house I built. While it was under construction, I lived in my tipi (for about one year ." *Biographical sources* : Athens Banner Herald, June 1993; CNN: July 1993 - filmed segment for character profile on "Earthnet" and Earth-Matters" programs. *Published work* : Contributing author , "The Profile," 1993, "Early Georgia," 1994 (periodical for The Society for Georgia Archaeology); Features & Profiles, periodical (Archaeological Society of South Carolina, 1994).

JONES, STANLEY G. (Scho Hallem)
(Snohomish-Kallam) 1926-
(commercial fisherman; tribal chairperson)
Born July 10, 1926, Monroe, W ash. *Principal occupation* : Commercial fisherman; tribal chairperson. *Home address* : 705 N.E. Tulalip Rd., Marysville, WA 98271 (206) 659-6052. *Affiliations* : Owner, Jones Trucking, 1987-; owner , High Liner Fishing Supply , 1985-; *Other professional posts* : Tulalip Tribe of W ashington (fishing committee, 1954-; board of directors, 1966-

chairperson, 1981-); member , Board of Directors of 1st Heritage Bank. *Military service*: U.S. Marine Corp, 1944-46. *Community activities* : Active in all tribal social services. *Memberships*: National Congress of American Indians, 1966-; Affiliated Tribes of the Northwest. *Awards, honors*: Appreciation Award, Tulalip Housing Authority, 1984; Helped secure tribal fishing rights, 1988; appointed by B.I.A., Dept. of the Interior , one of four member National Gaming Commission. *Interests*: National tribal timber delegation to China; travel; trade commission major timber tribes in U.S.; commercial fishing in Alaska, Canada and most of the states; will be writing book on years of establishing treaty fishing rights pre-1974 U.S. Supreme Court decision to 1989. *Biographical sources* : Guide to the Indian tribes of the Northwest (University of Oklahoma Press); Paddle to Seattle 1989 W ashington State Centennial.

JONES, STEPHEN S. *(Red Dawn)* (Santee Sioux) 1921- (lecturer, educator, folklorist, anthropologist)

Born June 1, 1921, Flandreau, S.D. *Education* : Sioux Falls College, S.D., B.A., 1948; California State University, Fullerton, M.A., 1978. *Principal occupation*: Lecturer, educator, folklorist, anthropologist, American Indian Programs, Anaheim, CA. Resides in southern California. *Affiliations*: Curator of anthropology , Science Museum of Natural History, Gastonia, N.C. (6 years); *Other professional post* : Registered medical technologist. *Military service*: U.S. Army, 1942-45 (Staf f Sergeant). *Memberships*: American Indian Lore Association (director); Continental Confederation of Adopted Indians (director); American Anthropological Association; Southwest Museum; Minnesota Historical Society . *Awards, honors*: 1973 Catlin Peace Pipe Award, American Indian Lore Association. *Interests*: Field of American Indian dance, ethnology , history and folklore. Lifelong avocation in interpreting Indian lifeways (traveling extensively throughout the nation presenting Indian programs for schools and civil groups). Tour master for college groups into the Southwest; major field of interest--customs and traditions of Southwest Indians. Traveled nationally lecturing and researching, 1976-. *Published work* : Editor, Great on the Mountain: The Spiritual Life of Crazy Horse (Naturegraph, 1971); editor , Master Key (Southwest Museum, 1972-1982).

JORDAN, DILLARD (Oklahoma Cherokee) (historic site curator)

Affiliation : Sequoyah Home Site, Route 1, Box 141, Sallisaw, OK 74955 (918) 775-2413.

*JORDAN, LAWRENCE (hospital director)

Affiliation : Santa Fe PHS Indian Hospital, 1700 Cerrillos Rd., Santa Fe, NM 87501 (505) 988-9821.

JORDAN, SUE ZANN (Mescalero Apache) 1959- (teacher)

Born December 17, 1959. *Education*: University of Illinois, BA, 1979; Sangamon State University, MA, 1983. *Principal occupation*: Teacher, Chapter I Coordinator . *Address*: Cibecue Community School, Cibecue, AZ 85911 (602) 332-2444/2480. *Affiliation*: Teacher, Chapter I Coordinator, Cibecue Community School, Cibecue, AZ, 1984-. *Other professional post* : Part-time teacher, Northern Pioneer College. *Membership*: Arizona Media Association. *Awards, honors*: State of South Dakota Poetry Award and money certificate; Golden Poet Award, World of Poetry. *Interests*: General: Poetry, art, music, education, earth science, and literature. V ocational: W oodworking, graphic arts, ceramics, weaving, and horticulture. Travels: "(I) traveled extensively in North and South America and less extensively overseas." *Published works* : Poetry, too numerous to list.

JORGENSEN, JOSEPH GILBERT 1934- (professor of anthropology)

Born April 15, 1934, Salt Lake City , Utah. *Education*: University of Utah, BS, 1956; Indiana University, PhD, 1964. *Principal occupation* : Professor of anthropology . *Home address*: 1517 Highland Dr., Newport Beach, CA 92660 (714) 356-5894 (work). *Affiliations*: Assistant professor, Antioch College, 1964-65, University of Oregon, 1965-68; professor of anthropology , University of Michigan, Ann Arbor, 1968-74; professor of anthropology , Program in Comparative Culture, University of California, Irvine, Calif., 1974-. *Other professional post* : Coordinator, Northern Ute Tribe (Unitah and Ouray Ute Indian Reservation, Fort Duchesne, Utah), 1960, '62; research associate, John Muir Institute, 1970-; research consultant to the following: Soboba Band of Indians, Louis Berger and Associates, Human Relations Area Files, and the Senate Select Committee on Indian Affairs. *Community activities*: Mariners Community Association (president); Society to Preserve Our Newport (board member); Newport Beach Aquatics Support Group (president). *Memberships*: Human Relations Area Files (board of directors); Native Struggles Support Group (board of directors and co-chair); Anthropology Resource Center (board of directors); American Association for the Advancement of Science (Fellow); American Anthropological Association (member of Ethics Committee, 1969-71); Society for Applied Anthropology (associate editor of Human Organizations, 1986-89); American Indian Historical Society (editorial advisory board, 1974-80); Sigma Xi. *Awards, honors*: John Simon Guggenheim Fellow , 1974-75; C. Wright Mills Book Award for Sun Dance Religion, 1972; F.O. Butler Lecturer at South Dakota State University , 1976; M. Crawford Lectures at the University of Kansas, 1980; Rufus Wood Leigh Lecture at the University of Utah, 1982; Ford Lecturer , Brazilian Anthropological Association, San Paulo. *Interests*: "Research into the relations among environment, language and culture in aboriginal western North America; analysis of the consequences to North American Indian, Eskimo, and Aleut societies from the nation's political economy ." *Published works*: Salish Language and Culture (Indiana University, 1969); Sun Dance Religion (University of Chicago Press, 1972); Native Americans and Energy Development, I and II (Anthropology Resource Center, 1978 & 1984); W estern Indians (W.H. Freeman, 1980); Oil Age Eskimos (University of California Press, 1990). Editorial board: Behavioral Science Research, 1973-; The Indian Historian, 1974-; Southwest Economy and Society , 1976-; Social Science Journal, 1978-; Environmental Ethics, 1978-; Social Policy Revue, 1981-; contributing articles to New York Review of Books, and to professional journals.

*JOSEPH, ANDREW C. (museum director/curator)

Affiliation : Colville Confederated Tribes Museum, P.O. Box 233, Coulee Dam, W A 99116 (509) 633-0751.

JOSEPH, ANGIE (Indian band chief)

Affiliation : Dawson Indian Band, P .O. Box 599, Dawson City, Yukon, Canada Y0B 1G0 (403) 993-5387.

JOSEPH, FRANK A. (BIA agency supt.)

Affiliation : Crow Creek Agency, Bureau of Indian Affairs, P.O. Box 139, Fort Thompson, SD 57339 (605) 245-2311.

JOSEPH, J. LA WRENCE (Sauk-Suiattle) (tribal chairperson)

Affiliation : Sauk-Suiattle Tribal Council, 5318 Chief Brown Lane, Darrington, W A 98241 (206) 436-0131.

JOSEPH, LOREN (Navajo) (school principal)

Affiliation : Kayenta Boarding School, P .O Box 188, Kayenta, AZ 86033 (602) 697-3439.

JOSEPH, MICHAEL (IHS-director of tribal activities)

Affiliation : Phoenix Area Office, 3738 N. 16th St., Suite A, Phoenix, AZ 85016 (602) 640-2106.

JOSEPH, NORMAN (Suquamish) (Indian band vice-chief)

Affiliation : Suquamish Indian Band, P .O. Box 86131, North V ancouver, British Columbia, Canada V7L 4J5 (604) 985-7711.

JOSEPHY, ALVIN M., JR. 1915- (author, historian)

Born May 18, 1915, W oodmere, N.Y . *Education*: Harvard College, 1932-34. *Principal occupation* : Author, historian. *Home address*: 4 Kinsman Lane, Greenwich, CT 06830 (203) 869-4953. *Affiliations*: Associate editor , Time Magazine, 1951-60; editor-in-chief, American Heritage Publishing Co., Inc., New York, N.Y ., 1960-79. *Other professional posts*: Consultant, Secretary of the Interior , 1963; commissioner and vice chairman, Indian Arts and Crafts Board, Dept. of the Interior , Washington, DC, 1966-70; president, National Council, Institute of the American West, Sun Valley, Idaho, 1976-83; contributing editor, American W est Magazine, Tucson, Ariz., 1983-89; chairperson, Board of Trustees, National Museum of the American Indian, Smithsonian Institution, 1990-. *Military service*: U.S. Marine Corps, 1943-45 (Master Technical Sergeant; Bronze Star). *Memberships*: Association on American Indian Affairs (director, 1961-); Museum of the American Indian (trustee, 1976-90; president, National Council, 1978-); Western History Association; Society of American Historians; American Antiquarian Society . *Awards, honors*: Western Heritage Award, National Cowboy Hall of Fame, 1962, '65; Eagle Feather Award, National Congress of American Indians, 1964; Award for Merit, American Association on State & Local History , 1965; Golden Spur, Golden Saddleman and Buf falo Awards, Western W riters of America, 1965; National Book Award nominee, 1968; Guggenheim Fellowship, 1966-67. *Interests*: History, culture and concerns of the American Indians; western American history; conservation; extensive western travel. *Biographical source*: Who's Who in America. *Published works*: American Heritage Book of the Pioneer Spirit, co-author (Simon & Schuster, 1959); The American Heritage Book of Indians (Simon & Schuster, 1961); The Patriot Chiefs (Viking Press, 1961); The Nez Perce Indians and the Opening of the Northwest (Y ale University Press, 1965); editor, The American Heritage History of the Great W est (Simon & Schuster, 1965); The Indian Heritage of America (Knopf, 1968); Red Power (McGraw-Hill, 1971); Now That the Buf falo's Gone (Knopf, 1982); W ar on the Frontier (T ime-Life Books, 1986); The Civil War in the American W est (Knopf, 1991); America in 1492 (Knopf, 1992); among others.

JOURDAIN, STEVE
(Indian band chief)
Affiliation: Lac La Croix Indian Band, Box 640, Fort Frances, Ontario, Canada P9A 3N9 (807) 485-2431.

JOYCE, DEE DEE
(museum director/curator)
Affiliation: Catawba Museum of Anthropology, 2113 Brenner Ave., Salisbury, NC 28144 (704) 637-4111.

JUANCITO, CHARLES H. *(Tall Dog)* **(Rappahannock) 1909-**
(educator)
Born January 30, 1909, Philadelphia, Penna. *Education*: University of Pennsylvania, Doctorate of Vocational Industrial Arts Education-Indian Studies, 1958; Messiah College, University of State of New York; Howard University. *Principal occupation*: Educator. *Home address*: 927 N. Sixth St., Philadelphia, P A 19123 (215) 627-7304. *Affiliations*: Teacher, Chester-Upland School District, Chester, PA; director, Native American Cultural Center. *Other professional posts*: Engineering technician, draftsman. *Community activities*: Native American Cultural Center of Delaware V alley (ex-director). *Memberships*: Rappahannock Tribe of Powhatan-Renape Nation (elder); National Education Association (secretary, First American Task Force); Pennsylvania Education Association; American Vocational Education Association; Pennsylvania Industrial Arts Association; Coalition of Eastern Native Americans. *Awards, honors*; Commendation for work as a teacher of adult basic education and English as a second language, State of Pennsylvania Adult Education Dept., Harrisburg, PA; Teacher of the Year, Vocational & Industrial Arts-Indian Studies; only Indian on Bicentennial 1976 Committee; the only American Indian in North America with degrees in Vocational-Industrial Arts Education; only American Indian guest at a reception of Mapuche Indians of Chile, and speaker honored by Government of Chile & Chamber of Commerce of Chile; speak, read & write four languages; East Coast activist *Interests*: Education; ethnology & anthropology; geology. English as a second language; Indian studies; adult basic education; master printer, master machinist.

JUANICO, JUAN S. (Acoma Pueblo)
(museum director)
Affiliation: Acoma Museum, P.O. Box 309, Pueblo of Acoma, Acomita, NM 87034 (505) 552-6606.

JUDD, CYNTHIA 1952-
(business owner)
Born August 19, 1952, Roswell, N.M. *Educa-*

tion: Southwestern Business College, 1986. *Principal occupation*: Business owner. *Home address*: 14024 Wind Mountain Rd., NE, Albuquerque, NM 87123 (505) 271-1981 (work). *Affiliation*: American Heritage Indian Arts, Albuquerque, NM, 1990- (owner of authentic Indian-made warbonnet factory). *Membership*: Indian Arts and Crafts Association. *Awards, honors*: "Warbonnets took 1st, 3rd & 4th prizes at the New Mexico State Fair - under Indian art. All of my employees are Native Amercians."

*JUDD, NANETTE K. (Hawaiian)
(association president)
Affiliation: E Ola Mau, 1374 Nu'uana Ave., Suite 201, Honolulu, HI 96817 (808) 533-1628.

JUDKINS, RUSSELL ALAN 1944-
(anthropologist)
Born August 8, 1944, Salt Lake City, Utah. *Education*: Brigham Young University, BS, 1966; Cornell University, PhD, 1973. *Principal occupation*: Anthropologist. *Home address*: 142 W. Buffalo St., Warsaw, NY 14569 (716) 245-5277. *Affiliation*: Associate professor, Department of Anthropology (1972-), State University of New York, College, Geneseo, NY 14454 (716) 245-5277. *Memberships*: American Anthropological Association (Fellow); Northeastern Anthropological Association; Society for Medical Anthropology; American Folklore Society; New York Folklore Society; Rochester Academy of Science. *Interests*: Social & cultural anthropology; symbolism; medical anthropology; American Indians (Iroquois and Catawba); migration and resettlement; folklore and mythology; American Indian world view; American Indian intellectuals. *Biographical source*: American Men and Women of Science. *Published works*: Iroquois Studies, 1987; First International Scholars Conference on Cambodia, 1988; Handbook for Archival Research in the Dr. Charles Bartlett Iroquois Collection, 1989. All published by Papers in Anthropology, SUNY College at Geneseo).

JULES, CLARENCE THOMAS (Kamloops)
(Indian band chief)
Affiliation: Kamloops Indian Band, 315 Yellowhead Highway, Kamloops, British Columbia, Canada V2H 1H1 (604) 828-9700.

JULES, HARVEY
(Indian band chief)
Affiliation: Adams Lake Indian Band, Box 588, Chase, British Columbia, Canada V0E 1M0 (604) 679-8841.

JULES, LINDA (Kamloops)
(museum curator)
Affiliation: Secwepemc Cultural Education Society, 345 Yellowhead Highway, Kamloops, British Columbia, Canada V2H 1H1 (604) 374-1096.

JULES, RAY (Kyuquot)
(Indian band chief)
Affiliation: Kyuquot Indian Band, Kyuquot, British Columbia, Canada V0P 1J0 (604) 332-5259

JUMPER, BETTY MAE (Seminole) 1927-
(director-Seminole communications)
Born April 27, 1927, Indiantown, Fla. *Education*: Cherokee (NC) Indian School, 1949 (first Seminole Indian to receive a high school diploma). *Principal occupation*: Director-Seminole communications. *Address*: Seminole Tribe, 6333 Forrest (N.W. 30th) St., Hollywood, FL 33024

(305) 962-4853. *Affiliation*: Chairperson, Seminole Tribe, 1967-71; director of communications and editor-in-chief of the Seminole Tribune (the newspaper of the Seminole Tribe), Seminole Tribe of Florida, 6333 Forrest (N.W. 30th) St., Hollywood, Fla. 33024. *Community activities*: Speaker at schools throughout Florida about Seminole Tribe; advisor, Manpower Development and Training Committee for the State of Florida; member, Independent Bible Baptist Church. *Memberships*: Native American Press Association; Florida Press Association. *Awards, honors*: Served on first tribal council as secretary-treasurer, and later resigned to serve as vice chairperson. In 1967, Betty Mae was the first woman elected as chairperson of the Seminole Tribe, serving four years. In 1968, Betty joined three Southeastern Tribes in signing a Declaration of Unity in Cherokee, N.C. The declaration implemented the Inter-T ribal Council, United Southeastern Tribes. While serving as chairperson of the Seminole Tribe, she was appointed by the President of the U.S. to become one of eight Indian members to work with Vice President Agnew. Only two women were chosen to serve on the committee, the National Congress on Indian Opportunity under President Nixon. She was chosen W oman of the Year by the Department of Florida Ladies Auxiliary of Jewish War Veterans of the U.S. for her outstanding contributions in the field of humanities. Betty Mae received a medicine peace pipe and a gold pin from the United Southeastern Tribes. *Interests*: Betty did much to improve the health, education and social conditions of the Seminole people. Through her ef forts, the Tribe was one of the first tribes to obtain the CHR (Community Health Representative) Program. She was also effective in her concerns for Indian people on regional, national and state levels. *Published work*: ...And W ith the Wagon - Came God's W ord (Seminole Print Shop, 1984).

*JUMPER, MOSES, Jr. *(Shem pa he gee)* **(Florida Seminole) 1950-**
(recreation director, coach)
Born January 9, 1950, Fort Lauderdale, Fla. *Education*: Haskell Indian Jr. College, AA, 1971. *Principal occupation*: Recreation director, coach. *Home address*: 6073 Stirling Rd., Hollywood, FL 33021 (813) 983-9234. *Affiliation*: Recreation director, Seminole Tribe of Florida, Hollywood, FL. *Other professional posts*: Cattleman & writer. *Community activities*: Chairman, Education Board of Florida. *Memberships*: President, Native American Sports Association; Native American Youth Organization. *Awards, honors*: Writers Award in Kansas from writers organization; Photo Award in Hollywood; Best Poem Award in Hollywood, FL; Who's Who in Poetry Award - numerous films & documentaries. *Biographical source*: Seminole Tribune. *Published work*: Echoes in the Wind (Pineapple Press, 1991).

JUNEAU, ALFRED LeROY (Blackfeet) 1919-
(public accounting)
Born August 21, 1919, Browning, Mt. *Education*: Southwestern University, BS, 1951. *Principal occupation*: Public accounting. *Home address*: 539 Crane Blvd., Los Angeles, CA 90065. *Affiliations*: Comptroller, Los Angeles Indian Center (4 years); Associate consultant, United Indian Development Association (Indian business development), 1976-; United American Indian Council (Indian socio-economic concerns), 1976-; commissioner (appointed by Mayor Bradley), Los Angeles City-County Native American In-

dian Commission, 1977-. *Other professional posts*: Secretary-treasurer, U.S. Steel Buildings Co., Los Angeles. *Military service*: U.S. Army Signal Corps, 1941-45 (Sergeant; two Bronze Stars, Good Conduct Medal, Europe-Africa-Middle Eastern Theatre Service Medal, Meritorious Unit Award). *Memberships*: California Public Accountants, 1951-; Loyal Order of Moose, 1973-; National Congress of American Indians; Parent Teachers Association, Los Angeles; Smithsonian Institution; Blackfeet Indian Tribe, Browning, MT. (enrolled member). *Interests*: General accounting and related financial matters; continuing interest in socio-economic betterment of American Indians in urban areas and on reservations; invited and attended, Feb. 2, 1978, President and Mrs. Carter's prayer breakfast in Washington, DC; and an All-Indian prayer breakfast at the U.S. Capitol in Washington, D.C.; have played professionally a trumpet in the U.S. and Europe. *Biographical source*: Vida Reporter (Los Angeles, April, 1977), a short biographical article with photo.

JUSTIN, WILSON
(association president)
Affiliation: Ahtna, Inc., P.O. Box 649, Glennallen, AK 99588 (907) 822-3476.

*JUSTUS, CYNDEE
(editor)
Affiliation: Ak-Chin O'odham Runner, Ak Chin Indian Reservation, 42507 Peters & Nall Rd., Maricopa, AZ 85239 (602) 568-2095.

K

*KAAPANA, DOUG (Hawaiian)
(club president)
Affiliation: c/o Tukwila Sr. Club, Seattle, WA 98168 (206) 776-9420.

*KADAKE, HENRICH (Eskimo)
(AK village council president)
Affiliation: Organized Village of Kake Council, P.O. Box 316, Kake, AK 99830 (907) 758-6471.

*KAGANAK, TIMOTHY (Athapascan)
(AK village council president)
Affiliation: Native Village of Scammon Bay, P.O. Box 126, Scammon Bay, AK 99662 (907) 558-5113.

*KAGAWA, SIEGFRIED S.
(museum president)
Affiliation: Bernice Pauahi Bishop Museum, P.O. Box 19000-A, Honolulu, HI 96817 (808) 847-3511.

KAHKLEN, ALBERT
(BIA agency supt.)
Affiliation: Anchorage Agency, Bureau of Indian Affairs, 1675 C St., Anchorage, AK 99501 (907) 271-4088.

*KAHKLEN, JOSEPH
(Alaska liaison officer-BIA)
Affiliation: Bureau of Indian Affairs, Dept. of the Interior, MS-4140-MIB, 1849 C St., NW, Washington, DC 20240 (202) 208-5819.

KAHN, FRANKLIN (Navajo) 1934-
(artist)
Born May 25, 1934, Pine Springs, Ariz. *Education*: Stewart Indian School. *Principal occupation*: Artist. *Home address*: 3315 N. Steues Blvd.,

Flagstaff, AZ 86001. *Affiliation*: Sketch artist and sign painter, Federal Sign and Signal Corp., Flagstaff. *Membership*: American Indian Service Committee. *Awards, honors*: Second Prize, Scottsdale National Indian Art Show. *Interests*: Watercolor and oil painting; Indian designs and symbols. *Published work*: Illustrator, Going Away to School (Bureau of Indian Affairs, 1951).

KAISWATUM, ART
(Indian band chief)
Affiliation: Piapot Indian Band, Box 4, Craven, Saskatchewan, Canada S0G 0W0 (306) 781-4848.

KAKEWAY, GEORGE
(Indian band chief)
Affiliation: Wauzhushk Onigum Indian Band, Box 1850, Kenora, Ontario P9N 3X7 (807) 548-5663.

KAKUM, JOHNSON
(Indian band chief)
Affiliation: Little Pine Indian Band, Box 70, Paynton, Saskatchewan, Canada S0M 2J0 (306) 398-4942.

*KALMAKOFF, ARCHIE (Eskimo)
(AK village council president)
Affiliation: Ivanoff Bay Village Council, P.O. Box K1B, Ivanoff Bay, AK 99502 (907) 699-2204.

*KAMINE, MARGIE
(administrative director)
Affiliation: Wings of America, 53 Old Santa Fe Trail, Santa Fe, NM 87501 (505) 982-6761.

*KAMKOFF, WILLIE
(AK village council president)
Affiliation: Native Village of Hamilton Council, P.O. Box 21030, Koatlik, AK 99620 (907) 899-4313.

KAN, SERGEI *(Shaakunastoo & Gunaakw)*
1953-
(professor of anthropology)
Born March 31, 1953, Moscow, Russia. *Education*: Boston University, BA, 1976; University of Chicago, MA, 1978, PhD, 1982. *Principal occupation*: professor of anthropology. *Home address*: 18 Wellington Cir., Lebanon, NH 03766 (603) 646-2550. *Affiliations*: Assistant professor of anthropology, University of Michigan, Ann Arbor, 1983-89; associate professor & chairperson, Dept. of Anthropology & Native American Studies Program, Dartmouth College, Hanover, NH 1989-. *Other professional post*: Editorial Board, "Journal of Ethnohistory." *Community activities*: Native American Council, 1989-; Hood Museum of Art (acquisitions committee, 1989-93; director's advisory council, 1990-91); faculty advisory committee, Institute of Arctic Studies, 1989-; Dartmouth Fellow, Research Program for the Comparative Study of Intergroup Conflict in Multinational States, 1991-94; faculty representative, Foundation for Jewish Life at Dartmouth, 1992-; Alaska Native Brotherhood, 1979-. *Memberships*: American Anthropological Association; American Ethnological Society; American Society for Ethnohistory; Alaska Anthropological Association; American Association for the Advancement of Slavic Studies; International Arctic Social Science Association. *Awards, honors*: Heizer Award for the Best Article in Ethnohistory by the American Society for Ethnohistory, 1987; American Book Award for "Symbolic Immortality," awarded by the Before Columbus Foundation, 1990. *Interests*: Ethno-

graphic field research in southeastern Alaska since 1979 (intermittent); extensive archival research on Tlingit history & vulture, since 1979. *Biographical source*: "Death & Dying," Dartmouth Alumni Magazine, Sept. 1992. *Published works*: Translated & edited, Tlingit Indians of Alaska, by Fr. A. Kamenskii (University of Alaska Press, 1985); Symbolic Immortality: Tlingit Potlatch of the 19th Century (Smithsonian Press, 1989); numerous articles.

KANNON, CLYDE DAVID 1938-
(school principal)
Born November 3, 1938, Maury County, Tenn. *Education*: Emory & Henry College, BA, 1960; Florida Atlantic University, 1968-70; University of South Dakota, MA (Special Education), 1976. *Principal occupation*: Indian school principal. *Address*: Pueblo Pintado Community School, Star Route 2, Cuba, NM 87013 (505) 655-3341. *Affiliations*: Teacher, Tulare County School System, Earlimart, CA, 1962-63; teacher, Williamson County School System, Tenn., 1963-68; teacher, South Florida Schools, principal/teacher K-6, BIA (Big Cypress Reservation), Seminole Agency, Hollywood, FL, 1968-71; elementary teacher, special education teacher, teacher supervisor, principal, Fort Thompson Community School, BIA, Crow Creek Agency, Fort Thompson, SD, 1971-82; principal, Pueblo Pintado Community School, Cuba, NM, 1983. *Awards, honors*: Special Education Achievement Award, National Blue Key Honor Society, 1960.

KAPASHESIT, RANDY
(Indian band chief)
Affiliation: Mocreebec Indian Government, Box 4, Moose Factory, Ontario, Canada (705) 658-4769.

*KAPLAN, DIANE
(radio network president)
Affiliation: Native Broadcast Center, Alaska Public Radio Network, 810 E. Ninth Ave., Anchorage, AK 99501 (907) 277-2776.

KAQUATOSH-ARAGON, YVONNE M.
(editor)
Affiliation: Menominee Tribal News, Menominee Indian Tribe, P.O. Box 397, Keshena, WI 54135 (715) 799-5168.

*KAR, DANA WILSON
(Indian center director)
Affiliation: Center for American Indian Studies in Social Services, Washington University, Campus Box 1196, St. Louis, MO 63130 (314) 889-6288.

*KARMUN, WILBUR, Sr. (Eskimo)
(AK village council president)
Affiliation: Native Village of Deering Council, P.O. Box 89, Ekwok, AK 99736 (907) 363-2145.

KASAYULIE, JAMES T. (Yup'ik Eskimo)
(AK village council president)
Affiliation: Platinum Village Council, Platinum, AK 99651 (907) 979-8126.

KASAYULIE, WILLIE
(Akiachak Yup'ik Eskimo) 1951-
(administrator)
Born June 1, 1951, Fairbanks, Alaska. *Education*: High school. *Principal occupation*: Council chairperson. *Address*: P.O. Box 70, Akiachak, AK 99551 (907) 825-4813 (home). *Affiliations*:

Chairperson & CEO, Akiachak IRA Council, Akiachak, AK, 1984-; chairperson, Association of Village Council Presidents (AVCP, Inc.), Box 219, Bethel, AK, 1985-. *Other professional posts*: Chairperson, Akiachak Limited, 1989-90; member, BIA Tribal Task Force, 1990-. *Military service*: Alaska Army National Guard (discharged in 1990 with the rank of 1st Lt.). *Community activities*: Chairperson, Yupiit School District, 1985-; Alaska Federation of Natives (Board member, 1991-). *Memberships*: Alaska Native Coalition (chairperson, 1985-); board member, Native American Rights Fund, 1990-. *Awards, honors*: 1985 AFN Citizen of the Year; 1987 CEDC Tribal Leadership Award. *Interests*: "I travel promoting self-suf ficiency and self-determination for the Yup'ik Eskimo on local, national and international levels opf policy development ef fecting indigenous peoples." *Biographical sources*: Life Magazine (Feb. 1986); Who's Who Among American High School Students, 1969/71 edition; The Wake of An Unseen Object, by Tom Kizzia.

KASCHUBE, DOROTHEA VEDRAL 1927-
(professor emeritus)
Born November 6, 1927, Chicago, Ill. *Education*: Indiana University, BA, 1951, MA, 1953, PhD, 1960. *Principal occupation*: Professor of anthropology, Dept. of Anthropology, University of Colorado, Boulder, 1955-. *Home address*: 370 S. 36th St., Bouldor, CO 80303. *Other professional post*: Research associate, Stanford University (summers). *Memberships*: American Anthropological Association; Linguistic Society of America; Sigma Xi. *Interests*: "Language of the Crow Indians and of the Siouan language family. Language as both biological and cultural behavior." *Published works*: Structural Elements of the Language of the Crow Indians of Montana (University of Colorado Press, 1967); co-author with Joseph H. Greenberg, W ord Prosodic Systems: A Preliminary Report (W orking Papers on Language Universals, Stanford University, 1976).

*KASHEVAROF, GILBERT G. (Aleut)
(AK village council president)
Affiliation: St. George Island Council, P.O. Box 940, St George Island, AK 99660 (907) 859-2205.

*KAST, SHERRY
(communications specialist)
Affiliation: United National Indian Tribal Youth, Inc., 4010 Lincoln Blvd., Suite 202, P.O. Box 25042, Oklahoma City, OK 73125 (405) 424-3010.

KATCHATAG, STANTON (Eskimo)
(AK village president)
Affiliation: Unalakleet V illage Council, P.O. Box 270, Unalakleet, AK 99684 (907) 624-3622.

KATO, BRUCE
(museum curator)
Affiliation: Sheldon Jackson Museum, 104 College Dr., Sitka, AK 99835 (907) 747-8981.

KATZEEK, DAVID G.
(executive director)
Affiliation: Sealaska Heritage Foundation, 1 Sealaska Plaza, Suite 201, Juneau, AK 99801 (907) 463-4844.

KAUFMAN, WILLIAM I. 1922-
(American Indian arts & crafts dealer)
Born June 8, 1922, New York, N.Y. *Principal occupation*: American Indian arts & crafts dealer. *Home address*: 1430 Wllamette St., Suite 24, Eugene, OR 97401 (503) 344-9739 (work). *Other professional posts*: Photographer/writer; designer of etchings and tapestries. *Military service*: U.S. Army, 1941-46. *Community activities*: Creator of Word Forest and Adopt-A-Class, both children's organizations. *Memberships*: Bontemp de Medoc; Authors Chevalieu du Taste Vin; ASCAP; Screen Actors' Guild. *Awards, honors*: Gold V ine Award (wine book award), and many foreign honors Including the Chevalier de l'Ordre du Merite Agricole from the French Republic and three Medallions for artistic achievement for writing and photography . He received the Christopher Award for his UNICEF children's books, songs, poems, prayers and legends. He has twenty major photographic exhibitions including two major color exhibitions by Kodak. His books have been translated into many languages. *Published works*: Champagne (wrote and illustrated); Perfume.

*KAULEY, MATTHEW
(executive director)
Affiliation: Association of American Indian Physicians, 1235 Sovereign Row , Suite C-7, Oklahoma City, OK 73108 (405) 946-7072.

KAULEY, RALPH, JR.
(health center director)
Affiliation: Carnegie PHS Indian Health Center, P.O. Box 1120, Carnegie, OK 73105 (405) 654-1100.

KAVALSKY, MAGGIE (Athapascan)
(AK village mayor)
Affiliation: Native Village of Nuiqsut, Nuiqsut, AK 99723 (907) 480-6714.

KAVASCH, MS. E. BARRIE
(Cherokee-Creek)1942-
(author; artist; food historian)
Born December 31, 1942, Springfield, Ohio. *Education*: Western Connecticut University. *Principal occupation*: Author/artist, company president. *Address*: 325 Main St. South, P.O. Box 239, Bridgewater, CT 06752 (203) 354-3128. *Affiliations*: President, Native Harvests, Inc. (food business), Bridgewater , CT, 1987-; *Other professional posts*: Guest lecturer on numerous college campuses and at museums; curator of the "Native Harvests: Plants in American Indian Life" Exhibition for SITES-Smithsonian, 1984-87. *Community activities*: Institute of American Indian Studies (T rustee, Board of Directors); Bridgewater Historical Society (Trustee); curator of American Indian V isions 1992 at the Silo Gallery at Ruth & Skitch Henderson's Silo in New Milford, CT . *Memberships*: Association on American Indian Affairs; Native American Rights Fund; Byelorussia American Society. *Awards, honors*: O'Connor Lecturer at Cornell Plantations, Cornell University, Ithaca, NY, Oct. 1992; Cullum Lecturer at Augusta College, Augusta, GA, Oct. 1992. *Interests*: Ms. Kavasch has traveled, researched, and lectured through much of North & Central America, and has worked with and written about numerous Native American Indian tribes and interest groups. She has done extensive ethnobotanical research, especially food & medicinal documentation. She writes, photographs & illustrates, as well as collects & presses plant

specimens, while documenting diverse herbal/healing knowledge. "I am working on a new book on American Indian foods for a major publisher , as well as a book on American Indian plants and people, along with several childrens books for young readers. I will also be curating another fine gallery show of select American Indian art. Planning committee for the 1991 & 1992 American Indian Thanksgiving & Feast of Reconciliation at the Cathedral of St. John the Devine in New York City." *Biographical sources*: "American Indian Foods: A Harvest of American Indian Specialties" in Bon Appetite, Nov. 1987; and "A Native Thanksgiving: American Indian Cooking" in Cooks Magazine, Nov . 1984. *Published works*: Native Harvests: Recipes & Botanicals of the American Indians (Random House, 1979); Herbal Traditions: Medicinal Plants in American Indian Life (SITES: Smithsonian Institution, 1984); Botanical Tapestry (Gunn Historical Museum, 1979); Guide to Eastern Mushrooms, 1982, Introducing Eastern Wildflowers, 1982, and Guide to Northeastern Wild Edibles, 1981 - full color photographic guide books - (Hancock House/Big Country Books); American Indian Cooking (Native Harvests, 1991).

KAYE, ROGER
(Indian band chief)
Affiliation: Vuntut Gwitchen (Old Crow) Indian Band, Old Crow, Yukon, Canada Y0B 1N0 (403) 966-3261.

*KEAHNA, SAMSON
(center director)
Affiliation: American Indian Center, 1630 West Wilson, Chicago, IL 60640 (312) 275-5871.

KEALIINOHOMOKU, JOANN WHEELER 1930-
(anthropologist)
Born May 20, 1930, Kansas City , Mo. *Education*: Northwestern University, BS, 1955, MA, 1958; Indiana University , PhD, 1976. *Home address*: 518 South Agassiz St., Flagstaf f, AZ 86001. *Principal affiliation*: Cross-Cultural Dance Resources, Inc. (a non-profit organization - a living museum for scholars & performers to talk, study, consult) (president, board of directors); senior research associate, Center for Colorado Plateau Studies, Northern Arizona University, Flagstaff. *Other professional posts*: faculty Semester at Sea, for Shipboard Educators, University of Pittsburgh; visiting professor for University of Hawaii, Manoa Campus; University of Hawaii, Hilo Campus; New York University; World Campus Afloat. *Community activities*: Native American for Community Action (board of directors, 1977-82; secretary of board, 1979-82). *Memberships*: American Anthropological Association (Fellow); American Ethnological Society; American Folklore Society; Association for the Study of Play; Bishop Museum Association; CORD (Congress on Research in Dance) (board of directors, 1974-77); Cross-Cultural Dance Resources (founder & director); Society for Ethnomusicology (council member, 1967-70, 1980-83). *Awards, honors*: Weatherhead Resident Scholar , School of American Research, Santa Fe, 1974-75; Research Fellow, East-West Center, Honolulu, Hawaii, 1981; Dedicatee for Tenth Annual Flagstaff Indian Center's Basketball Tournament, 1983. *Interests*: "Performance arts, especially dance; cultural dynamics; field work in Southwest U.S., especially with Hopi and other Pueblos." *Biographical sources*: Dictionary of Inter-

national Biography; The World Who's Who of Women; Who's Who in Oceania; Who's Who of American Women. *Published works*: Hopi and Polynesian Dance: A Study in Cross-Cultural Comparison (Ethnomusicology, 1967); with Frank Gillis, Special Bibliography: Gertrude Prokosch Kurath (Ethnomusicology, 1970); Dance Culture as a Microcosm of Holistic Culture (New Dimensions in Dance Research: Anthropology and Dance--The American Indian, 1974); Theory and Methods for an Anthropological Study of Dance, Ph.D. dissertation, anthropology (University Microfilms, 1976); The Drama of the Hopi Ogres, chapter in Southwestern Indian Ritual Drama, edited by Charlotte Frisbie, (University of New Mexico Press, 1980); Music and Dance of the Hawaiian and Hopi Peoples, chapter in Becoming Human Through Music (Music Educators National Conference, 1985); "The Would-Be Indian", chapter in Anthropology and Music: Essays in Honor of David P. McAllester, edited by Charlotte Frisbie (University of Michigan Press, 1985); "The Hopi Katsina Dance Event 'Doings'", chapter in Seasons of the Kachina, edited by Lowell J. Bean (Ballena Press, 1989); among other articles, reviews and chapters in various publications.

*KEAMS, GERALDINE (GERI) *(Yithaazbah')* (Navajo) 1951-
(actress, storyteller)
Born August 19, 1951, Winslow, Ariz. *Education*: University of Arizona, BFA, 1978. *Principal occupation*: Actress, storyteller. *Home address*: 5152 LaVista Court, Los Angeles, CA 90004 (213) 461-5695. *Affiliation*: President, Hozhoni Productions, Hollywood, CA (film, video, theatre productions). *Other professional posts*: Storyteller on tour with Los Angeles Music Center on Tour. *Community activities*: Board of Advisors, ATLATL, a Native American arts organization, Native American Television; promoted Native Americans in film, video, media. *Memberships*: National Association for the Preservation & Perpetuation of Storytelling (NAPPS), 1989-; Screen Actors Guild, 1970-; American Indian Registry for the Performing Arts (board member, 1988-90; president, board of directors, 1990-91). *Awards, honors*: Bahti Award - Outstanding American Indian Student, University of Arizona; recipient of a Los Angeles Cultural Affairs Traditional Arts Grant. *Interests*: "Began performing at 7 years old; co-starred in, "Outaw Josie Wales," with Clint Eastwood; appearances in "Northern Exposure," "Twin Peaks." Storyteller featured at the National Storytelling Festival in Jonesborough, Tenn, St. Louis, Miami, and Smithsonian Discovery Theatre for Children Institute's, Washington, DC; San Francisco Storytellers on Tape Series, 1993. Featured on television shows, "Nickelodeon," & "Sesame Street": traveled as a storyteller throughout he U.S., Canada & Europe." *Published works*: Children's book - Grandmother Spider Steals the Sun (Northland Press, 1995); Poet Anthologies - "A Gathering of Spirits," 1985, "When Clouds Threw This Light," 1983, "Circle of the Moon."

KEEL, LELAND
(BIA agency supt.)
Affiliation: Seminole Agency, BIA, 6075 Stirling Rd., Hollywood, FL 33024 (305) 581-7050.

KEENAN, DAVID
(Indian band chief)
Affiliation: Teslin Tlingit, Teslin, Yukon, Canada Y0A 1B0 (403) 390-2532.

KEENATCH, JOHN
(Indian band chief)
Affiliation: Big River Indian Band, Box 519, Debden, Saskatchewan, Canada S0J 0S0 (306) 724-4216.

KEGG, MATTHEW M. (Chippewa) 1953-
(teacher)
Born October 5, 1953, Brainerd, Minn. *Education*: Bemidji State University, BA, 1976. *Principal occupation*: Teacher. *Home address*: Star Route P.O. Box 105, Onamia, MN 56359. *Affiliations*: Graduate assistant, Indian Studies Program, Bemidji State University, 1980-81; teacher, Mille Lacs Indian Reservation, Onamia, MN, 1981-. *Awards, honors*: Recipient of Certificate of Appreciation from State Dept. of Education of Minnesota, 1980, for contributions to Indian education; Most Valuable Player award from hockey team, Bemidji Northland Icers, 1980. *Interests*: "Hockey; published several articles in magazines; poetry; outdoor activities: camping, backpacking, canoeing, biking."

KEHOE, ALICE BECK 1934-
(professor of anthropology)
Born September 18, 1934, New York, N.Y. *Education*: Barnard College, BA, 1956; Harvard University, PhD, 1964. *Principal occupation*: Professor of anthropology. *Home address*: 3014 N. Shepard Ave., Milwaukee, WI 53211 (414) 962-5937. *Affiliations*: Assistant professor of anthropology, University of Nebraska, 1965-68; professor of anthropology, Marquette University, Milwaukee, WI, 1968-. *Memberships*: American Anthropological Association (board of directors, 1979-82); Society for American Archaeology (chair, Public Relations Committee, 1987-90); Central States Anthropological Society (president, 1989-90); American Society for Ethnohistory (council, 1991-93); American Ethnological Society. *Interests*: Cultural anthropology and archaeology; fieldwork among Blackfoot, Cree and Dakota tribes in the U.S. & Canada; archaeological fieldwork in Montana & Saskatchewan; ethnographic fieldwork in Montana, Alberta, Saskatchewan, and Bolivia. *Published works*: Hunters of the Buried Years (Regina, Sask. School Aids & Text Book Co., 1962); North American Indians (Prentice-Hall, 1981; 2nd ed. 1992); The Ghost Dance (Holt, Rinehart & Winston, 1989).

*KELLAR, DAVID
(radio program director)
Affiliation: WOJB - 88.9 FM, Lac Courte Oreilles Ojibwe Broadcasting Corp., Route 2, Box 2788, Hayward, WI 54843 (715) 634-2100.

*KELLEY, BEATRICE
(health administrator)
Affiliation: Lac Vieux Desert Band Health Clinic, P.O. Box 446, Watersmeet, MI 49969 (906) 358-4457.

KELLY, AUDREY DIANA
(Indian band chief)
Affiliation: Ohamil Indian Band, C4, Site 22, RR 2, Hope, British Columbia, Canada V0X 1L0 (604) 869-2627.

*KELLY, MICHAEL W.
(radio station vice president)
Affiliation: KCCN, Kine & Hawaiian Broadcasting Co., 900 Fort St., Suite 400, Honolulu, HI 96813 (808) 536-2728.

KELSEY, JULIE
(editor)
Affiliation: Choctaw Community News, Mississippi Band of Choctaw Indians, Route 7, Box 21, Philadelphia, MS 39350 (601) 656-5251.

*KENNEDY, ROY (Shoshone)
(tribal chairperson)
Affiliation: Timbisha Shoshone Tribe, P.O. Box 206, Death Valley, CA 92328 (619) 786-2374.

KENNAN, LAUREL
(health clinic director)
Affiliation: Bay Mills Indian Commuity Health Clinic, Route 1, Box 313, Brimley, MI 49715 (906) 248-3204.

KENNELLY, MICHAEL E.
(chief)
Affiliation: Smoki People, P.O. Box 123, Prescott, AZ 86302 (602) 445-1230.

KEPLIN, DEBBIE L.
(Turtle Mountain Chippewa) 1956-
(general manager-radio station)
Born February 28, 1956, Belcourt, N.D. *Education*: Flandreau Indian School, 1974; University of North Dakota (2 years liberal arts instruction). *Principal occupation*: Public radio station general manager. *Home address*: P.O. Box 236, Belcourt, ND 58316. *Affiliation*: General manager, KEYA Radio Station, Belcourt, ND. *Other professional posts*: Occupied positions at KEYA radio of program director, news director, music director, and executive secretary. *Community activities*: Member, St. Ann's Society, Belcourt, ND; assistant-religious education, St. Anthony's Catholic Church, Belcourt; member, Turtle Mountain Musicians; member, Turtle Mountain Historical Society. *Memberships*: National Association of Female Executives, 1985-; Corporation for Public Broadcasting-National Public Radio (authorized representative). *Awards, honors*: Certificate of Native American Leadership Training by the Community Council of the Northern Plains Teacher Corps, Nov. 1979 & Feb. & April, 1980; Certificate of Training-Explosive Devices Training by the U.S. Dept. of the Interior, Sept., 1984; dedicated service to the KEYA Radio Station and the Belcourt community by Turtle Mountain Community School, Nov., 1985; for community service by Turtle Mountain Band of Chippewa Indians, Feb., 1985. *Interests*: "To promote and educate the local community and surrounding communities on the history and culture of the Turtle Mountain Band of Chippewa through the use of radio. To develop programs focusing on problems affecting the local community, such as alcoholism, unemployment, housing, recreation, etc. To encourage the training of high school students in the operation of broadcast facilities-radio." *Programs produced*: All Nations Music, 1980- (features traditional and contemporary Native American music, legends and stories); Memorial to James Henry, former chairman of Turtle Mountain Band of Chippewa, 5-minute piece aired nationally on radio series First Person Radio of Minn. in Sept., 1983; Music of the Turtle Mountains, 1985- (program features the talents and biographies of local artists, musicians and poets); the music of Floyd Westerman, Sr. Mary Anthony Rogers, many local fiddlers, Adella and Gilbert Kills Pretty Enemy, 1985- (program features biographical sketches of artists through interview and music selections).

KERKMAN, MARCEL (Navajo)
(school principal)
Affiliation: Alamo Navajo School, P.O. Box 907, Magdalena, NM 87825 (505) 854-2543.

*KERNAK, ALBERT (Eskimo)
(AK village council president)
Affiliation: Napakiak Native Village, Napakiak, AK 99634 (907) 589-2227.

*KERR, THOMAS
(museum CEO)
Affiliation: The Mitchell Indian Museum, Kendall College, 2408 Orrington Ave., Evanston, IL 60201 (708) 866-1395.

KESSELER, DAVID, M.D.
(clinical director)
Affiliation: Zuni PHS Indian Hospital, P.O. Box 467, Zuni, NM 87327 (505) 782-4431.

*KETCHER, JOHN
(health center director)
Affiliation: Washoe Tribal Health Center, 950 Hwy. 395 S., Gardnerville, NY 89410 (702) 883-4137.

*KHOW, VIDA
(health center director)
Affiliation: Winslow PHS Indian Health Center, P.O. Drawer 40, Winslow, AZ 86047 (602) 289-4646.

KICKINGBIRD, K. KIRKE (Kiowa)
(center director)
Affiliation: Native American Legal Resource Center, Oklahoma City University-School of Law, 2501 N. Blackwelder, Oklahoma City, OK 73106 (405) 521-5188.

*KICKINGBIRD, LYNN
(editor)
Affiliation: American Indian Journal, Institute for the Development of Indian Law, 2600 Summit Dr., Edmond, OK 73034

KICKINGBIRD, ROBIN (Kiowa)
Has been involved in tribal libraries for several years and is currently working to set up a Tribal Library Association in Oklahoma. She published "The Directory of Tribal Libraries" in 1991. She has worked in the Metropoltian Library System of Oklahoma City & in the Archives of the Oklahoma Historical Society, which is known for its extensive collection of documents related to Native American history. She was awarded the first Minority Fellowship for Librarian at the American Library Association in 1991. She has worked as a law librarian and is now attending law school at the University of Oklahoma College of Law.

KIDWELL, CLARA SUE (Choctaw/Chippewa/Creek) 1941-
(ass't director of cultural resources)
Born July 8, 1941, Tahlequah, Okla. *Education*: University of Oklahoma, BA, 1962; MA, 1966, PhD, 1970. *Principal occupation*: assistant director of cultural resources. *Home address*: 605 Constitution Ave., NE, Washington, DC 20002 (202) 547-5448. *Affiliations*: Lecturer, Kansas City Art Institute, 1966-68; instructor, Haskell Indian Junior College, 1970-72; assistant professor, American Indian Studies Department, University of Minnesota, 1972-74; associate professor, Native American Studies, University of California, Berkeley, 1974-; assistant direc-

tor of cultural resources, National Museum of the American Indian, Smithsonian Institution, Washington, DC, 1993-. *Memberships*: American Historical Association; Western History Association; American Society for Ethnohistory (president, 1991); History of Science Society; American Indian Science and Engineering Society. *Awards, honors*: Rockefeller Foundation Humanities Fellowship, 1976-77. *Published work*: The Choctaws: A Critical Bibliography (University of Indiana Press, 1981); Choctaws & Missionaries in Mississippi, 1818-1918 (University of Oklahoma Press, 1994).

*KIGER, LOUISE, R.N.
(director)
Affiliation: Nursing Education Center for Indians, Indian Health Service, 5600 Fishers Lane, Rockville, MD 20857 (301) 443-1840.

KIHEGA, MARY
(association secretary-treasurer)
Affiliation: National Indian Social Workers Association, P.O. Box 27463, Albuquerque, NM 87125.

*KIHIKIHI, RHODA-ANN
(radio station vice president)
Affiliation: KCCN, Kine & Hawaiian Broadcasting Co., 900 Fort St., Suite 400, Honolulu, HI 96813 (808) 536-2728.

KILLER, GRACE FOUR
(head counselor-Indian organization)
Affiliation: Navajo Nation Higher Education, P.O. Drawer S, Window Rock, AZ 86515 (800) 223-7133 (in AZ); (800) 243-2956, elsewhere.

KIMBALL, CARLA REICHERT (Ottowah) 1949-
(Native American cultural heritage instructor)
Born May 8, 1949, Muskegon, Mich. *Education*: University of Alabama, MEd, 1987. *Principal occupation*: Native American cultural heritage instructor. *Home address*: Rte. 3, Box 194, Fyffe, AL 35971 (205) 623-3812. *Affiliation*: Curriculum planning/teacher, Scottsboro City Schools, Scottsboro, AL, 1983-. *Memberships*: National Indian Education Association; Alabama Indian Education Association. *Awards, honors*: Basic Education Grant Award, 1989 for research on Cherokee Treaties; resolution from Alabama Governor Guy Hunt - outstanding program. *Interests*: Native American studies; Native American art studies. Presentations at Anniston Army Depot (Anniston, AL), Birmingham Museum (Birmingham, AL), Russell Cave National Monument (Bridgeport, AL), Burritt Museum (Huntsville, AL); and Gadsden Graduate Center, University of Alabama (Gadsden, AL).

KIMBALL, ERNEST H.
(health center director)
Affiliation: Puget Sound PHS Indian Health Station, 2201 6th Ave., Rm. 300, Seattle, WA 98121 (206) 615-2781.

KIMBLE, GARY NILES (Gros Ventre)
(commissioner)
Born in 1944, Mont. *Education*: University of Montana, BA, 1966; University of Montana-College of Law, JD, 1972. *Principal occupation*: Commissioner. *Address*: Administration for Native Americans, U.S. Dept. of Health & Human Services, Humphrey Bldg., 200 Independence Ave., SW, Washington, DC 20201 (202) 690-

7776. *Affiliations*: Partner & General Counsel for Fort Belknap Indian Community, Kimble, Smith & Connors, Missoula, MT, 1972-75; assistant professor, Native American Studies, University of Montana, Missoula, 1974-79; Chief Counsel, U.S. Senate Select Committee on Indian Affairs, Washington, DC, 1979; delegate to U.S.-Canada Treaty Negotiations, U.S. Dept. of State, 1979-82; Executive Director, Columbia River InterTribal Fish Commission, 1979-82; Advisor on Indian Affairs, State of Montana, Office of the Governor, 1983-89; adjunct professor of Federal Indian Law & director of Affirmative Action Program, Northwestern School of Law, Lewis & Clark College, 1987-89; executive director, Association on American Indian Affairs, New York, NY, 1989-93; commissioner Administration for Native Americans, U.S. Dept. of Health & Human Services, Washington, DC, 1994-. *Other professional posts (legal & consultation)*: Kimball & Associates (consulting & economic development firm, 1982-) Major clients included: Qua-Qui Corp., Missoula, MT, 1982-84; Fort Peck Tribe, NAES College, Poplar, MT, 1984-87; Valley Industrial Park, Glasgow, MT, 1985-86; American Training & Technical Assistance, Albuquerque, NM, 1987-88; Tulalip Tribe, Marysville, WA, 1988; Multnomah Co. Risk Management Team, Portland, OR, 1988-90; Health & Human Services, Public Health Indian Health, Portland, OR, 1988-89. Aboriginal Public Policy Institute (member, Board of Directors and Advisory Board), 1990-. *Public service*: Northwest Communities Project, Portland, OR (chairperson, Board of Directors), 1986-89; Minority Education, Research & Training Institute, New York Medical College, New York, NY (co-principal investigator), 1990-93.

*KIMERY, JAMES
(school director/counselor)
Affiliation: Flagstaff Dormitory, P.O. Box 609, Flagstaff, AZ 86002 (602) 774-5270.

KINDLE, WILLIAM (Rosebud Sioux)
(tribal council president)
Affiliation: Rosebud Sioux Tribal Council, P.O. Box 430, Rosebud, SD 57570 (605) 747-2381.

KING, ANDREW
(Indian band chief)
Affiliation: Lucky Man Indian Band, 401 Packham, Saskatoon, SK, S7N 2T7 (306) 374-2828.

*KING, DALE G. *(Chief Walking Wolf)*
(Kaweah)
(home movies producer, tribal chief)
Address: 630 E. 8th Ave., Mesa, AZ 85204 (602) 969-5553. *Affiliations*: Home movies producer of variety shows for movies & TV; Tribal chief, Hipac Kaweah Tribe. *Membership*: American Indian Defense of the Americas.

KING, DUANE H.
(director)
Affiliations: Cherokee National Historical Society, P.O. Box 515, Tahlequah, OK 74465 (918) 456-6007; Cherokee National Museum (TSA-LA-GI), Cherokee Heritage Center, Tahlequah, OK; editor, "Journal of Cherokee Studies, Museum of the Cherokee Indian, Cherokee, NC.

*KING, GWEN G.
(museum director)
Affiliation: Indian Museum of Lake County, Ohio, c/o Lake Erie College, 391 W. Washington, Painesville, OH 44077 (216) 352-3361.

KING, HAROLD (Navajo)
 (school principal)
Affiliation: Many Farms High School, P.O. Box 307, Many Farms, AZ 86538 (602) 781-6226.

*KING, PATRICIA L.
 (commission director)
Affiliation: Maryland Commission on Indian Affairs, 100 Community Place, Crownsville, MD 21032 (410) 514-7651.

*KING, RICHARD L.
 (executive director)
Affiliation: Cross & Feather News, Tekkakwitha Conference National Center, P.O. Box 6768, Great Falls, MT 59406 (406) 727-0147.

*KING, ROSS
 (radio program director)
Affiliation: "South Dakota Forum," & "Voices of the Plains," South Dakota Public Radio Network, P.O. Box 5000, Vermillion, SD 57069 (605) 677-5861.

*KING, THOMAS
 (Indian studies dept. chairperson)
Affiliation: American Indian Studies Dept., University of Minnesota, 230 Williamson Hall, 231 Pillsbury Dr. SE, Minneapolis, MN 55455 (612) 625-9565.

*KINGEEKUK, KENNETH (Eskimo)
 (AK village council president)
Affiliation: Native Village of Savoonga, P.O. Box 129, Savoonga, AK 99769 (907) 984-6414.

*KINGERY, JAMES
 (site manager)
Affiliation: Moundbuilders State Memorial, 7091 Brownsville Rd., SE, Glenford, OH 43739 (614) 787-2476; The Ohio Indian Art Museum, 99 Cooper Ave., Newark, OH 43055 (614) 344-1920.

KINNEY, RODNEY P. *(Half Moon)*
 (Yup'ik Eskimo) 1932-
 (engineer)
Born September 11, 1932, Nome, Alaska. Education: University of California, San Jose, B.S. (Civil Engineering), 1960; graduate studies at University of California, Berkeley & San Jose, and University of Alaska, Anchorage. Principal occupation: Engineer. *Address*: P.O. Box 771102, Eagle River, AK 99577 (907) 694-2332 (work). *Professional posts*: Geotechnical consultant, Woodward Clyde Consultants, Anchorage, AK, 1961-75; engineering coordinator, Alyeska Pipeline Service Co., 1975-79; manager of Engineering & Planning Division, Anchorage Water & Wastewater Utility, 1979-1980; principal engineer, Rodney P. Kinney Associates, Eagle River, Alaska, 1980-. *Military service*: U.S. Navy, 1951-59. *Community activities*: Local Chamber of Commerce; Municipal Advisory Commission for Water & Wastewater; Founding Trustee of Alaska Southcentral Museum of Natural History; Vice-chair of Youth Club of Anchorage. *Memberships*: American Society of Civil Engineers; Bering Straits Native Association; American Indian Science and Engineering Society; American Water Works Association; American Public Works Association. *Interests*: Rodney P. Kinney Associates, a qualified Eskimo firm, was established October 2, 1980. The firm emphasizes consultation and services in general civil engineering, including roads & drainage, water and sewer, as well as soil testing & data collection. We also offer geophysical

(seismic refraction and resistivity) and slope inclinometer services, water resource development services, and consultation for private and public systems. "I am currently studying Russian and preparing for my 6th visit to Russia and the Republics. Expert at current Russian affairs and of eastern Siberian anthropology. Plan a mutual "dig" in near future. Have flown my Cessna to Russia last June (1991) across the Diomedes to Provedinya and back. Have received an honorary PhD of highest order from MCA Riga Latvia for special recognitions. Am being considered as Latvia Ambassador Counsel for Alaska." *Biographical sources*: Who's Who in the West; Who's Who in Technology Today; International Men of Distinction; many scientific/geographical papers.

KIPP, WOODROW LOUIS *(Sun Chief)*
 (Blackfeet) 1945-
 (guidance counselor; journalism instructor; columnist)
Born October 5, 1945, Browning, Mont. (Blackfeet Reservation). *Education*: University of Montana, BA (Journalism), 1991. *Principal occupation*: Guidance counselor; journalism instructor & columnist. Resides in Missoula, MT (406) 243-5834 (work). *Affiliation*: Guidance counselor & journalism instructor, University of Montana, Missoula, MT, 1991-. *Other professional posts*: Columnist, Lakota Times (SD), Great Falls Tribune (MT), and Missoula Independent. *Military service*: U.S. Marine Corps, 1964-68 (Vietnam, 1965-67); Trail of Broken Treaties, Wounded Knee occupation. *Commuity activities*: Lecturer at school and civic organizations. *Memberships*: Native American Journalists Assn.; Blackfeet Medicine Pipe Society; Magpie Society. *Awards, honors*: Great Falls Tribune, Native American Scholarship Award. *Interests*: Pow-wow dancer; grass dance.

*KIRBY, MARY M.
 (project director)
Affiliation: MacArthur Foundation Library Video Project, P.O. Box 409113, Chicago, IL 60640 (800) 847-3671.

KITKA, JULIA E.
 (association president; editor)
Affiliation: Alaska Federation of Natives, 1577 C St. #100, Anchorage, AK 99501 (907) 274-3611. *Other professional post*: Editor, "AFN News," monthly newsletter.

KITO, LEILANI
 (AK Indian association president)
Affiliation: Petersburg Indian Association, P.O. Box 1418, Petersburg, AK 99833 (907) 772-3636.

KITTO, RICHARD (Santee Sioux)
 (tribal chairperson)
Affiliation: Santee Sioux Tribal Council, Route 2, Niobrara, NE 68760 (402) 857-3302.

KITTREDGE, JOHN, M.D.
 (chief medical officer)
Affiliation: IHS Office of Health Program Research & Development, 7900 South "J" Stock Rd., Tucson, AZ 85746 (602) 295-2406.

KITZES, JUDITH A., M.D.
 (IHS-chief medical officer)
Affiliation: Albuquerque Area Office, Indian Health Service, 505 Marquette Ave., NW, Suite 1502, Albuquerque, NM 87102 (505) 766-2151.

KIZER, DARRELL (Washoe)
 (tribal chairperson)
Affiliation: Stewart Community Council, 5258 Snyder Ave., Carson City, NV 89701 (702) 885-9115.

*KIZER, LENORA (Washoe)
 (tribal vice-chairperson)
Address: 854 Amador Cr., Carson City, NV 89705 (702) 687-3111 (office). *Affiliation*: Washoe Tribal Council.

*KLESERT, ANTHONY L.
 (dept. director)
Affiliation: Navajo Nation Archaeology Dept., Northern Arizona University, P.O. Box 6013, Flagstaff, AZ 86011 (602) 523-7428.

KLIMIADES, MARIO NICK
 (museum librarian/archivist)
Affiliation: The Heard Museum, 22 E. Monte Vista Rd., Phoenix, AZ 85004 (602) 252-8840.

*KNACK, MARTHA C. 1948-
 (professor, anthropologist)
Born January 27, 1948, Orange, N.J. *Education*: University of Michigan, BA, 1969, PhD, 1975. *Principal occupation*: Professor, anthropologist. Address & Affiliation: Dept. of Anthropology & Ethnic Studies, University of Nevada, Las Vegas, NV, 1977-(chair, 1983-86). *Other professional posts*: Consulting for Native American Rights Fund, 1986-88; Pyramid Lake Paiute Tribe, 1984-87; Walker River Paiute Tribe & U.S. Dept. of Justice, 1994-. *Memberships*: American Anthropological Association; American Ethnological Society; American Society for Ethnohistory; Southwestern Anthropological Association; Great Basin Anthropological Conference. *Awards, honors*: Barrick (University of Nevada) Distinguished Research Scholar, 1991; Rockefeller Fellow, 1989-90. *Interests*: Great Basin Native American culture & history, Native American water rights & legal history, Native American women & social structures. *Published works*: Life Is With People: Household Organization of the Contemporary Southern Paiute Indians of Utah (Ballena Press, 1980); Contemporary Southern Paiute Household Structure & Bilateral Kinship Clusters (HRAF, 1982); As Long As the River Shall Run: An Ethnohistory of Pyramid Lake Reservation, Nevada, with Omer C. Stewart (University of California Press, 1984); With Their Hands They Do Labor: Ethnography & Ethnohistory of American Indian Wage Work, edited with Alice Littlefield (University of Oklahoma Press, 1994).

*KNAPP, MILLICENT
 (editor)
Affiliation: Turtle Quarterly," Native American Center for the Living Arts, 25 Rainbow Blvd., S., Niagara Falls, NY 14303 (716) 284-2427.

KNICK, STANLEY
 (museum director/curator)
Affiliation: Native American Resource Center, Pembroke State University, Pembroke, NC 28372 (919) 521-4214.

*KNIGHT, HALE P. (Pomo)
 (tribal chairperson)
Affiliation: Hopland Band of Pomo Indians, P.O. Box 610, Hopland, CA 95449 (707) 744-1647.

KNIGHT, MIKE (Pomo)
(rancheria chairperson)
Affiliation : Sherwood Valley Rancheria, 190 Sherwood Hill Dr., Willits, CA 95490 (707) 459-9690.

KNIGHT, STILLMAN, Jr.
(Te-Moak Western Shoshone)
(tribal chairperson)
Affiliation : South Fork Band Council, Box B-13, Lee, NV 89829 (702) 744-4273.

KNIGHT, YVONNE T. (Ponca) 1942-
(attorney)
Born December 19, 1942, Pawnee, Okla. *Education* : University of Kansas, BS, 1965; University of New Mexico, School of Law , JD, 1971. *Principal occupation* : Attorney. *Home address* : 1268 Westview Dr., Boulder, CO 80303 (303) 447-8760 (of fice). *Affiliation* : Native American Rights Fund, Boulder, CO (staff attorney and member, Litigation Management Committee), 1972-. *Memberships* : Colorado Indian Bar Association; American Indian Bar Association; American Indian Policy Review Commission (Task Force on Law Consolidation, Revision, and Codification, 1975-76). *Awards, honors* : Pioneer Minority W omen's Attorneys Award by Colorado Women's Bar Association, 1992; Reginald Haber Smith Fellowship, 1971-74.

KNIGHT-FRANK, JUDY (Ute)
(tribal chairperson)
Affiliation : Ute Mountain Ute Tribal Council, P.O. Box 52, Towaoc, CO 81344 (303) 565-3751.

KNOCKWOOD, B.A. (Micmac) 1932-
(director-Indian center)
Born July 18, 1932, Micmac Reservation, Nova Scotia, Canada. *Education* : St. Mary's University, 1977-84. *Principal occupation* : Director-Indian center. *Home address* : 2158 Goffingen St., Halifax, Nova Scotia, Canada B3K 3B4 (902) 420-0686 (of fice). *Affiliations* : Instructor, Cambrian College, Sudbury , Dalhousie University; director, Micmac Learning Center , Halifax, N.S., 1988-. *Other professional posts* : Spiritual Indian Medicine Man. *Military service* : Royal Canadian Artillery; served in Canada, USA, Japan and Korea (awarded the Korean Medal and U.N. Service Medal). *Community activities* : Involved in human rights at both provincial and national level; public speaker on native rights and native spirituality. *Memberships* : National Native Advisory Council, Connections Canada of the Solicitor General's Department; Spiritual Science fellowship; Assembly of First Nations; National Native Veterans Association; Canadian Legion; Korean V eterans Association. *Awards, honors* : Received a lifetime appointment to the Micmac Nation's Grand Council; given the title of the Micmac Spiritual Medicine Man by the Grand Chief. *Interests* : "I re-introduced the traditional Native beliefs, philosophy , holy ritual, and sacred ceremonies to Native Micmacs and others who are interested in traditional Indian beliefs. Teach and assist Native people in sacred fasting to receive a "vision" and spiritual purification through the Sweat Lodge Ceremony."

KNOTT, ELIJAH
(Indian band chief)
Affiliation : W asagamack Indian band, Wasagamack, Manitoba, Canada R0B 1Z0 (204) 457-2337.

KNOWS GUN, ELLIS "RABBIT"
(Ba Sa' Goshe)(Crow) 1948-
(administration , fine arts)
Born in Crow Agency, Mont. *Education* : Little Big Horn College (Crow Agency, MT), AA, 1988. *Principal occupation* : Administration, fine arts. *Address* : Box 133, Crow Agency, MT 59022 (406) 638-2922 (work). *Affiliation* : Crow Tribe, Crow Agency, MT. *Other professional post* : Fine Arts & Advisory Board, Native American Cultural Institute, Billings, MT. *Military service* : U.S. Army, 1968-71; U.S. Army Reserves (Billings, MT), 1983-86. His paintings portray Native American themes in an abstract manner . Knows Gun has been exhibiting his works since 1973, when he received the M.L. W oodrow Award at the 6th annual Red Cloud Indian Art Show in Pine Ridge, South Dakota. *Community activities* : Parish Council vice-president, St Dennis Parish, Crow Agency, MT; PAC Committee Chairman, School District 17H, Hardin, MT ; Crow Tribe (secretary, 1976-78; chairman, Crow Air Quality Commission, 1992); past speaker on environmental issues af fecting Crow Tribe; Carbon County Arts Guild, 1992. *Awards, honors* : Fine Arts awards; 1986 AIHEC basketball champs (Nationals.) *Biographical source* : Montana's Indians Yesterday & Today.

KNOWS-HIS-GUN, JOYCE
(Northern Cheyenne)
(board member)
Affiliation : National Indian Youth Council, 318 Elm SE, Albuquerque, NM 87102.

*KOCH, ELIZABETH, M.D.
(clinical director)
Affiliation : Sophie Trettevick Indian Health Center, P.O. Box 410, Neah Bay , WA 98357 (206) 645-2233.

*KOEZLINA-IRELAN, MARILYN (Eskimo)
(AK community council president)
Affiliation : King Island Native Community Council, Box 992, Nome, AK 99762 (907) 443-5494.

*KOMONASEAK, LUTHER (Eskimo)
(AK village council president)
Affiliation : Native Village of Wales, P.O. Box 549, Wales, AK 99783 (907) 664-351 1.

KOMPKOFF, GARY (Aleut)
(AK village council president)
Affiliation : Native Village of Tatitlek, P.O. Box 171, Tatitlek, AK 99677 (907) 325-231 1.

KONICEK, STEVEN, M.D.
(clinical director)
Affiliation : Kayenta PHS Indian Health Center , Box 368, Kayenta, AZ 86033 (602) 697-321 1.

*KOONOOKA, GERRARD
(AK village council president)
Affiliation : Gambell V illage Council, P.O. Box 99, Gambell, AK 99742 (907) 985-5346.

KOOSEES, DAN
(Indian band chief)
Affiliation : Kashechewan Indian Band, General Delivery, Kashechewan, Ontario, Canada P0L 1S0 (705) 275-4440.

KOOSHET, JOHN
(Indian band chief)
Affiliation : W abigoon Indian Band, Box 41, Dinorwic, Ontario, Canada P0V 1P0 (807) 938-6684.

*KOSBRUK, HARRY W. (Eskimo)
(AK village council president)
Affiliation : Perryville Village, P.O. Box 101, Perryville, AK 99648 (907) 853-2203.

KOSCHTIAL, GREG 1949-
(Indian art gallery owner)
Born December 1, 1949, Detroit, Mich. *Education* : Glendale (AZ) Community College, AA, 1981; Western Michigan University , 1968-69. *Principal occupation* : Indian shop owner. *Address & Affiliation* : Owner/operator, Warbonnet, P.O. Box 3494, Jackson, WY 83001 (307) 733-6158 (Indian art and jewelry retail sales). *Military service* : U.S. Air Force, 1969-73 (E-4; V ietnam). *Membership* : Indian Arts & Crafts Association, 1986-.

*KOSTZULA, HENRY (Apache)
(tribal chairperson)
Affiliation : Apache Tribal Business Committee, P.O. Box 1220, Anadarko, OK 73005 (405) 247-9493.

*KOZEVNIKOFF, EILEEN (Athapascan)
(AK village council president)
Affiliations : Native Village of Tanacross, P.O. Box 77130, Tanacross, AK 99776 (907) 366-7160; health service director, Tanana Chiefs Conference Health Center , 122 First Ave., Fairbanks, AK 99701 (907) 452-8251.

KRAFT, HERBERT C. 1927-
(professor of anthropology , museum director)
Born June 1, 1927, Elizabeth, N.J. *Education* : Seton Hall University , 1947-50, MA, 1961; Hunter College, C.U.N.Y ., MA, 1969. *Principal occupation* : Professor of anthropology & director of University Museum, Seton Hall University , South Orange, NJ, 1960-. *Home address* : 15 Raymond Terrace, Elizabeth, NJ 07208 (908) 355-2022 (home) (201) 761-9543 (of fice). *Other professional posts* : Archaeological consultant for cultural resources surveys. *Military service* : U.S. Merchant Marines, 1945-47. *Community activities* : New Jersey Historic Sites (member , State Review Board). *Memberships* : Archaeological Society of Staten Island (member , Executive Board); Society of Professional Archaeologists; Archaeological Society of New Jersey (president, 1974-78, 1986-90; editor of Bulletin; honorary member); Eastern States Archaeological Federation; New York State Archaeological Association (Fellow; president, 1982-84); New Jersey Academy of Sciences (Fellow); Society for Pennsylvania Archaeology; Middle Atlantic Archaeological Conference (president, 1985-87); Middle States Archaeological Conference. *Awards, honors* : Archie Award, Society for Pennsylvania Archaeology; recipient of two grants from the New Jersey Historical Commission; ten grants from the National Park Service, for excavations of prehistoric sites in New Jersey; John Alden Mason Award, Society for Pennsylvania Archaeology, 1980; Litt. D., Kean College of New Jersey, 1981; John A. Booth Prize, New Jersey Historical Society, 1986; McQuaid Medal, Seton Hall University , 1987; Achievment Award, New York State Archaeological Association, 1989; 1991 Governor Richard J. Hughes Award, New Jersey Historical Commission. *Interests* : "(My) primary interest is the prehistoric and contact period archaeology of New Jersey , and the Northeast and Middle Atlantic States generally . Since 1964, I have conducted archaeological excavations for the National Park Service, and

for Seton Hall University sponsored research in the Upper Delaware Valley, N.J., and on several sites in northeastern New Jersey and Staten Island, N.Y. These excavations have encompassed the entire span from Paleo-Indian to the Historic Contact Period. Extensive travel to areas of archaeoogical or natural interst: Meso-America, Peru, Egypt, the Serengetti; Europe and China (taught at W uhan Uiversity in 1990)." *Biographical sources*: Dictionary of International Biography; American Men and W omen of Science; Current Biographies of Leading Archaeologists; Outstanding Educators of America, 1971; Who's Who in American Education; Who's Who in therEast. *Published works*: The Miller Field Site (Seton Hall University Press, 1970); Archaeology in the Upper Delaware V alley (Pennsylvania Historic and Museum Commission, 1972); A Delaware Indian Symposium (Pennsylvania Historic and Museum Commission, 1974); The Archaeology of the Tocks Island Area (Archaeological Research Center, Seton Hall University, 1975); The Minisink Site: A Re-evaluation of a Late Prehistoric and Early Historic Contact Site in Sussex County, New Jersey (Archaeological Research Center, Seton Hall University, 1978); (Film) "Lenape," 30 minutes, color. (Humanities on Film Project, W illiam Paterson College of New Jersey, 1981); The Lenape: A Symposium (Archaeological Research Center, Seton Hall University Museum, 1984); The Indians of Lenapehoking & Supplement - Resources and Activities (Seton Hall University Museum, 1985); The Lenape: Archaeology, History and Ethnography (New Jersey Historical Society, 1986); The Lenape Indians of New Jersey (supplementary text for fourth grades) (Seton Hall University Museum, 1987); "Evidence of Contact and Trade in the Middle Atlantic and Northeast Regions," in Archaeology of Eastern North America, Vol. 17, 1989 pp. 1-29; "The Minisink Indians," in The People of the Minisink, edited by David G. Orr and Douglas V. Campana (National Park Service, 1990); editor of The Arachaeology and Ethnohistory of the Lower Hudson V alley & Neighboring Regions: essays in Honor of Louis A. Brennan (Occasional Publications in Northern Anthropology, 1992); numerous articles on the Lenape-Delaware Indians in the Bulletin of the Archaeological Society of New Jersey, and other publications.

KRAFT, JOHN T.
(museum curator)
Affiliation: The Lenape Indian Museum & V illage, Waterloo Village, Stanhope, NJ 07874 (201) 347-0900.

KRAUSS, MICHAEL
(center director)
Affiliation: Alaska Native Language Center, University of Alaska, Eielson Bldg., 2nd Floor, Fairbanks, AK 99775 (907) 474-7874.

*KRECH, SHEPARD, III
(museum director)
Affiliation: Haffenreffer Museum of Anthropology, Brown University, Mt. Hope Grant, Bristol, RI 02809 (401) 253-8388.

KREIPE de MONTANO, MARTHA (Prairie Band Potawatomi) 1944-
(museum professional)
Born November 9, 1944, Topeka, Kan. *Education*: Haskell Indian Junior College (Certificate, Welding), 1975; University of Kansas,

Lawrence, BF A (Painting), 1978, MA (Special Studies-Anthropology-History). *Principal occupation*: Museum professional. *Home address*: 101 West 90th St. #21-C, New York, N.Y. 10024 (212) 799-0684. *Affiliation*: Manager, Indian Information Center, National Museum of the American Indian, New York, NY, 1984-. *Community activities*: Indian Center, Lawrence, KS (board of directors); Circle of Red Nations, New York, N.Y. (president, board of directors); Native American Education Program, New York, NY (parent's committee); Grupo Aymara Productions (board of directors); New York City Native American Heritage Month (committee). *Awards, honors*: HUD Minority Fellowship, University of Kansas. *Interests*: Vocational interests: Contemporary North American Indian activities--cultural, social, artistic; Andean Indian life and music; Mayor's Ethnic New Yorker Award, 1986. *Published works*: 49's, A Pan Indian Mechanism for Boundary Maintenance and Social Cohesion (AAA meeting, 1980); Native American Conceptions of Time (Manhattan Laboratory Museum Symposium, 1983); Teacher's Kit: The Parfleche (Museum of the American Indian, Heye Foundation, 1985); Diplomacy In New England (Indians, Promises & Us, 1987); editor, Pachamama Project (Grupo Aymara, Inc., 1988).

KREPPS, ETHEL CONSTANCE *(Kontameah)* (Kiowa/Miami) 1941-
(public health nurse III - R.N.; attorney)
Born October 31, 1941, Mt. V iew, Okla. *Education*: St. John's Medical Center, Tulsa, RN, 1971; University of Tulsa, BS, 1974; University of Tulsa, College of Law, JD, 1979. *Principal occupation*: Public Health Nurse III - R.N.; attorney. *Home address*: 3000 N.W. 12th, Oklahoma City, OK 73107 (405) 942-7203. *Affiliations*: Lawyer, Native American Coalition of Tulsa, Inc., Tulsa, OK 74107, 1981-88; Public Health Nurse III - R.N., Attorney, OK State Dept. of Health, Oklahoma City, OK, 1989-. *Other professional post*: Director, Oklahoma Indian Affairs Commission, Oklahoma City, OK, 1991-. *Community activities*: Kiowa Tribe of OK (secretary); Native American Chamber of Commerce (secretary); Tulsa Indian Affairs Commission; American Indian Toastmasters. *Memberships*: National Trial Lawyers Association; American Bar Association; Federal Bar Association; OK Bar Association; OK Indian Attorney's Association; Tulsa County Bar Association; Tulsa W omen Lawyers Association; W omen Lawyers Association of OK; Phi Alpha Delta Legal Fraternity; National Indian Social W orkers Association (past president); Oklahoma Indian Child W elfare Association (past president); American Indian/Alaskan Native Nurses Association (past national vice-president); OK Indian Legal Association (past board secretary). *Awards, honors*: Indian Business Person of the Year Award, 1984; Outstanding Leadership Award, 1985, from International Indian Child Conference; Trial Lawyers Association National Essay Award; Tulsa Mayor's Appreciation Award. *Interests*: "Domestic law; Indian law; W riting, painting, photography; lap quilting; collection of unique indigenous cultural items from around the world; travel." *Biographical sources*: Who's Who in Finance and Industry; Who's Who in the South and Southwest; Who's Who of American Law; Who's Who of American W omen; Who's Who in the W orld of Women; Who's Who in Society; 1,000 Personalities of the W orld. *Published works*: A Strong Medicine W ind (Western Publications, 1981); Oklahoma Memories, chapter (University of

Oklahoma Press, 1982); Oklahoma Images, chapter (University of Oklahoma Press, 1983).

*KROSKRITTY, PAUL
(professor)
Affiliation: Chairperson (MA Program), American Indian Studies Center, UCLA, 3220 Campbell Hall, 405 Hilgard Ave., Los Angeles, CA 90024 (310) 206-7508.

*KRUPAT, ARNOLD
(professor of literature)
Affiliation: Sarah Lawrence College, Bronxville, NY. *Published work*: Woodsmen, or Thoreau & the Indians: A Novel (University of Oklahoma Press, 1994).

*KRUSE, CAROL
(national monument supt.)
Affiliation: Tonto National Monument, P .O. Box 707, Roosevelt, AZ 85545 (602) 467-2241.

*KUCATE, ARDEN
(radio station manager)
Affiliation: KSHI - 90.0 FM, Zuni Pueblo, P .O. Box 339, Zuni, NM 87327 (505) 782-481 1.

*KUDRIN, RENA J. (Aleut)
(AK village council president)
Affiliation: Aleut Community of St. Paul Island, P.O. Box 35, Larsen Bay, AK 99660 (907) 546-2211.

KUENZIL, SARAH
(conference director)
Affiliation: Tanana Chiefs Conference, 122 1st Ave., Fairbanks, AK 99701 (907) 452-8251.

KUKA, KING D. (Blackfeet) 1946-
(professional artist)
Born August 13, 1946, Blackfeet Reservation, Browning, Mt. *Education*: Institute of American Indian Arts, Diploma, 1965; University of Montana, BF A, 1973; Montana State University, M.A. *Principal occupation*: Artist (sculpture and painting); owner-operator, Blackwolf Gallery. *Home address*: 907 Ave. C, NW, Great Falls, MT 59404 (406) 452-4449. *Military service*: U.S. Army, 1965-67. *Exhibits*: One-man shows: Reeder's Alley, Helena; University of Montana Center, Missoula; Museum of the Plains Indian, Browning; Rainbow Gallery, Great Falls; Flathead Lake Lookout, Lakeside. Painting and sculpture exhibits at Riverside Museum, New York, N.Y.; San Francisco; Philbrook Art Center, Tulsa, Okla.; Gallery of Indian Arts, Washington, D.C. *Awards, honors*: Numerous awards for art and creative writing; selected to exhibit and demonstrate in Kumamoto, Japan in 1992. *Membership*: Indian Arts & Crafts Association. *Interests*: Mr. Kuka's main interest is in the arts, Indian culture and outdoor life. *Published works*: Poetry: The Whispering W ind (Doubleday); V oices of the Rainbow (Viking Press); Anthologies: The First Skin Around Me (Territorial Press); The Remembered Earth (Red Earth Press); among others.

*KULAS, CHERYL M.
(Indian education office director)
Affiliation: North Dakota Dept. of Public Instruction, Indian Education Of fice, 600 E. Blvd., 9th Floor, Bismarck, ND 58505 (701) 224-2250.

KUNESH, PATRICE
(attorney)
Address: Native American Rights Fund, 1506 Broadway, Boulder, CO 80302 (303) 447-8760.

Memberships: Native American Bar Association; Colorado Indian Bar Assn. (secretary-treasurer).

KURATH, GERTRUDE PROKOSCH
(Wabanangokwe) 1903-
(dance ethnologist, musicologist)
Born August 19, 1903, Chicago, Ill. Education: Bryn Mawr College, BA, 1922, MA, 1928; Yale School of Drama, 1929-30. *Principal occupation*: Dance ethnologist, musicologist. *Home address*: 2203 Hickman Rd., Ypsilanti, MI 48198 (313) 482-6398. *Affiliations*: Pageant director, Rhode Island School of Design, 1932-45; teacher of dance, Brown University Extension, 1936-45; director, Creative Dance Guild, 1937-46; dance critic, Ann Arbor News, 1961-72. *Other professional posts*: Dance consultant, Webster's International Dictionary, third edition; field employee, National Museum of Canada, 1962-69. *Memberships*: MI Folklore Society (treasurer, editor, president); Dance Research Center; Society for Ethnomusicology (dance editor, 2nd v.p.); Congress on Research in Dance (CORD). *Awards, honors*: Adopted Chippewa and Onondaga; research grants: American Philosophical Society, 1949-68; Indiana University Archives of Traditional Music; Michigan Academy of Science, Arts & Letters; Museum of New Mexico; National Museum of Canada; Wenner-Gren Foundation, 1949-72; Chicago Folklore Prize for Music & Dance of the Tewa Pueblos, Department of Germanic Languages, University of Chicago; Stelof f Research Award, CORD, 1983. Interests: Field trips: Mexico, 1946; Iroquois (New York & Ontario), 1948-64; Cherokee (North Carolina), 1949-52; Algonquians (Iowa, Wisconsin), 1952, '56, (Michigan), 1953-67, (Manitoba), 1968; Rio Grande Pueblos (New Mexico), 1957-69. *Biographical sources*: Who's Who of American Women; Who's Who of Music International; Dictionary of American Scholars; special bibliography of Gertrude P. Kurath, Ethnomusicology, 1970; Research Method and Background of G.P.K., CORD Annual VI, 1972; Dance Memoirs (Chimera Press, Cambridge, 1983). *Published works*: The Iroquois Eagle Dance, with William Fenton (Bureau of American Ethnology, 1953); Songs of the Wigwam (Cooperative Recreation Service, 1955); Songs and Dances of the Great Lakes Indians, recording (Ethnic Folkways Library, 1956); Algonquian Ceremonialism and Natural Resources of the Great Lakes (Indian Institute of World Culture, 1957); Dances of Anahuac: The Choreography and Music of Pre-Cortesian Dances (Aldine, 1964); Iroquois Music and Dance: Ceremonial Arts of Two Seneca Longhouses (Bureau of American Ethnology, 1964); Michigan Indian Festivals (Ann Arbor Publishers, 1966); Dance and Song Rituals of Six Nations Reserve, Ontario (National Museum of Canada, 1968); Music and Dance of the Tewa Pueblos, New Mexico (Museum of New Mexico Press, 1970); Tutelo Rituals on Six Nations Reserve, Special Series (Society for Ethnomusicology, 1981); Half a Century of Dance Research (Cross-Cultural Dance Resources, Inc., 1986); numerous other articles in Encyclopaedia Britannica and Encyclopaedia Americana; numerous articles and reviews in scholarly journals.

KURIP, CARLEEN
(editor)
Affiliation: Ute Bulletin, Ute Indian Tribe, P.O. Box 220, Fort Duchesne, UT 84026 (801) 722-5141.

*KURTH, REV. E.J., S.J.
(school supt..)
Affiliation: Red Cloud Indian School, Holy Rosary Mission, Pine Ridge, SD 57770 (605) 867-5491.

KURTNESS, REMI
(Indian band chief)
Affiliation: Montagnais Du Lac St-Jean Indian Band, Reserve Indienne de Mashteuiatsh, 151, rue Quiatchouan, Pointe-Bleue, Quebec, Canada G0W 2H0 (418) 585-3744.

KUSSY, JAMES C., M.D.
(clinical director)
Affiliation: Barrow PHS Alaska Native Hospital, Barrow, AK 99723 (907) 852-461 1.

KUTSCHE, PAUL 1927-
(social anthropologist)
Born January 3, 1927, Grand Rapids, Mich. *Education*: Harvard College, BA, 1949; University of Michigan, MA, 1955; University of Pennsylvania, PhD, 1961. *Principal occupation*: Social anthropologist. *Home address*: 14 E. Cache la Poudre, Colorado Springs, CO 80903 (719) 389-6734. *Affiliations*: Professor-retired, Dept. of Anthropology, Colorado College, Colorado Springs, CO, 1959-93. *Community activities*: Pikes Peak Gay Community Center (newsletter editor, 1983-85). *Memberships*: American Anthropological Association (Fellow); Western Social Science Association (executive council, 1969-1972); Association of Borderland Scholars, 1976-85 (executive council, 1977-83); American Ethnological Society; Anthropology Research Group on Homosexuality (co-chair, 1984-87). *Interests*: Cherokee Indians, especially ethnohistory; New Mexico Hispanic village structure; rural-urban migration; Costa Rica; gender. *Published works*: Survival of Spanish American Villages (Colorado College Studies, 1979); Canones: Values, Crisis and Survival (University of New Mexico Press, 1981); A Guide to Cherokee Documents in the Northeastern U.S. (Scarecrow Press, 1986); Voices of Migrants (University Press of Florida, 1994).

*KUZCHIKIN, SIMEON
(AK village president)
Affiliation: Native Village of Belkofsky, P.O. Box 57, King Cove, AK 99612 (907) 497-2304.

KVASNIKOFF, VINCENT (Eskimo)
(AK village council president)
Affiliation: Nanwalek Village Council (aka English Bay), Homer, AK 99603 (907) 281-9219.

*KWACHKA, PAT
(editor)
Affiliation: Theata," Cross Cultural Communications Dept., Alaskan Native Program, University of Alaska, Fairbanks, AK 99708 (907) 474-7181.

*KWAS, MARY L.
(area supervisor)
Affiliations: Pinson Mounds State Archaeological Area, Ozier Rd., Rt. 1, Box 316, Pinson, TN 38366 (901) 988-5614; curator of education, Chucalissa Archaeological Museum-Library, 1987 Indian Village Dr., Memphis, TN 38109 (901) 785-3160.

L

LaBATTE, ROBERT (*Woableza*)
(institute director)
Affiliation: Institute for Native American News & TV, P.O. Box 77, Fairfax, CA 94930 (414) 459-0321.

LABELLE, GEORGE
(Indian band chief)
Affiliation: Goodstoney (Wesley Group) Indian Band, Box 40, Morley, Alberta, Canada T0L 1N0 (403) 881-3770.

LABILLOIS, ROMEY
(director-Indian institute)
Affiliation: Restigouche Institute of Cultural Education, Restigouche Indian Band, 2 Riverside West, Restigouche, Quebec, Canada G0C 2R0 (418) 788-5336.

LABOUCAN, EUGENE
(Indian band chief)
Affiliation: Driftpile Indian Band, General Delivery, Driftpile, Alberta, Canada T0G 0V0 (403) 355-3868.

LACAPA-MORRISON, CAMILLE
(Lac Courte Oreilles Ojibwe)
(radio station general manager)
Affiliation: WOJB-FM, Lac Courte Oreilles Ojibwe Broadcasting Corp., Route 2, Box 2700 Hayward, Wisconsin 54843 (715) 634-2100.

LACHAPPA, CLIFFORD M., Sr. (Diegueno)
(tribal chairperson)
Affiliation: Barona General Business Council, 1095 Barona Rd., Lakeside, CA 92040 (619) 443-6612.

LA COURSE, RICHARD VANCE (Yakima) 1938-
(journalist, editor-in-chief)
Born September 23, 1938, Toppenish, Wash. *Education*: San Luis Rey College, 1957-61; Old Mission Santa Barbara, 1961-63; Portland State University, 1963; University of Washington, 1964-68. *Principal occupation*: Journalist, editor-in-chief. *Address*: Yakima Nation Review, P.O. Box 310, Toppenish, WA 98948 (509) 865-5121. *Affiliations*: Copy news editor, photo news editor, correspondent, Seattle Post-Intelligencer, 1969-71; news director, Washington News Bureau, American Indian Press Association, Washington, DC, and AIPA Southwest News Bureau, Albuquerque, 1971-75; managing editor, Confederated Umatilla Journal, Pendleton, OR, 1975-76; managing editor, Yakima Nation Review, Toppenish, WA, 1977-78; founder/managing editor, Manataba Messenger, Colorado River Indian Tribes, Parker, AZ, 1980-81; managing editor, CERT Report, Council of Energy Resource Tribes, Washington, DC, 1981-83; president, managing editor, La Course Communications Corp., Washington, DC, 1983-90; editor, Yakima Nation Review, Toppenish, WA, 1991-. *Military service*: U.S. Army Reserve, 1964-70. *Memberships*: Native American Press Association (co-founder, board of directors); Northwest Indian News Association (co-founder); ASNE-ANPA Foundation (adjunct member, Minorities Committee); National Congress of American Indians; Americans for Indian Opportunity (honorary lifetime member); Race Relations Reporter, Nashville, TN (associate editor). *Awards,*

honors: Presenter, The Role of Communications in Indian Life, Native American Teacher Corps. Conference, Denver, 1973; presenter/panelist, annual conference, Association for Education in Journalism, Fort Collins, CO/Seattle, WA, 1974/1978; U.S. representative, work and planning sessions of Canadian Indian journalists of Alberta Native Communications Society, Edmonton, Alberta, 1972-75; presenter, History of American Indian Journalism; Techniques and Strategies of Investigative Journalism, Indian Investigative Journalism Project, National Indian Youth Council, Albuquerque, 1975; co-author, video script on tribal jurisdiction issues, National Congress of American Indians, Washington, D.C., 1975; presenter, Workshop on Investigative Journalism, Freedom of the Press in Indian Country, Minnesota Chippewa Tribes, Bemidji, 1977; keynote speaker and honoree, Second Annual Indian Media Conference and American Indian Film Festival, San Francisco, 1978; co-founder, Northwest Indian News Association (author of news network charter for association), 1978; recipient, Indian Media Man of the Year Award, National Indian Media Conference, Anaheim, CA 1980; recipient, National Recognition Award for Accomplishment, Americans for Indian Opportunity, Washington, DC, 1984; co-founder, Native American Press Association, University Park, PA (author of news network charter, code of ethics, business plan of operation. *Published works*: American Indian Media Directory (American Indian Press Association, 1974); editor, 1855 Yakima Treaty Chronicles: May 28, 1855 - June 11, 1855, special collector's edition, Yakima Nation Review, June 23, 1978; editor, The Schooling of Native America, Native American Teachers Corps, 1978; author-editor, Northwest Tribal Profiles, Portland Area Office, B.I.A., 1980); author-editor, Red Pages: Business Across Indian America (La Course Communications, 1984).

*LACROIX, NOBLE
(BIA agency supt.)
Affiliation: Lower Brule Agency, Bureau of Indian Affairs, P.O. Box 190, Lower Brule, SD 57548 (605) 473-5512

LADD, EDMUND JAMES (Zuni) 1926-
(Pacific archaeologist-retired; museum curator)
Born January 4, 1926, Fort Yuma, Calif. *Education*: University of New Mexico, Albuquerque, B.S., 1955, M.A., 1964. *Principal occupation*: Pacific archaeologist-retired; museum curator. *Home address*: 1830 Sun Mountain Dr., Santa Fe, NM 87505. *Affiliations*: Pacific archaeologist, USDI, National Park Service, Honaunau, Kona, Hawaii, (23 years); curator of ethnology, Museum of Indian Arts & Culture, Santa Fe, NM. *Other professional post*: Consultant to Smithsonian Institution as Tribal translator & interpreter. *Military service*: U.S. Army, 1944-46. *Memberships*: American Anthropological Association; Society for American Archaeology; Archaeological Conservancy (board member).

*LaDUKE, WINONA (White Earth Chippewa)
(environmentalist)
Affiliations: President, Indigenous Women's Network, P.O. Box 174, Lake Elmo, MN 55042 (612) 770-3861; director, White Earth Land Recovery Project, White Earth Reservation, Hwy. 224, P.O. Box 418, White Earth, MN 56591 (218) 983-3285.

LaFOND, HARRY
(Indian band chief)
Affiliation: Muskeg Lake India Band, Box 248, Marcelin, Saskatchewan, Canada S0J 1R0 (306) 466-4959.

LaFONTAINE, CATHIE
(Turtle Mountain Chippewa) 1957-
(school principal)
Born January 14, 1957, Rolla, N.D. *Education*: University of North Dakota, MA, 1983. *Principal occupation*: Indian school principal. *Address*: P.O. Box 564, Belcourt, ND 58316 (701) 477-3378. *Affiliation*: Ojibwa Indian School, Belcourt, ND, 1990-. *Community activities*: Chairperson for Twila Martin-Kekabah - Tribal Council Campaign. *Memberships*: National Association of Elementary School Principals; North Dakota Association of Elementary School Principals. *Awards, honors*: Ojibwa Indian School - Service Award.

LaFORME, HARRY S.
(chief commissioner)
Affiliation: Canadian Indian Claims Commission, P.O. Box 1750, Station B, Ottawa, ON K1P 1A2 (613) 943-2737.

LaFORME, MAURICE
(Indian band chief)
Affiliation. Mississauga Indian band, RR 6, Hagersville, Ontario, Canada N0A 1H0 (416) 768-1133.

LaFORTUNE, RICHARD (*Angukcuaq*)
(Yup'ik) 1960-
(restaurant owner)
Born November 25, 1960, Bethel, Alaska. *Education*: Moravian College, 1978-79; St. Olaf College, 1980. *Principal occupation*: Restaurant owner. Resides in Minneapolis, MN Affiliations: Worker-owner, The New Riverside Cafe Collective, Minneapolis, MN (612) 333-4814 (work), 1988-. *Other professional post*: Task force member, Native American Cultural Arts Program, Minneapolis, MN, 1988-. *Community activities*: North American Native Gay and Lesbian organizer, and Native community organizer; co-founder, American Indian Gays & Lesbians, 1987-. *Interests*: "Classically-trained musician; traditional eco-culture; traditional Native Arts, Western fine arts; lived/traveled in Southeast Asia, South Pacific, Caribbean; language student, literature studies, indigenous peoples' studies." *Published work*: Poem printed in: Living the Spirit, a Gay American Indian Anthology (St. Martin's Press, 1988).

*LaFRANCE, GREG
(BIA field rep.)
Affiliation: Chiloquin Sub-Agency, Bureau of Indian Affairs, P.O. Box 360, Chiloquin, OR 97624 (503) 783-2189.

*LaFRANCE, RON
(program director)
Affiliation: American Indian Program, Cornell University, 300 Caldwell Hall, Ithaca, NY 14853 (607) 255-4308.

*LaFROMBOISE, GENE
(school supt.)
Affiliation: White Shield School, HC 1, Box 45, Roseglen, ND 58775 (701) 743-4355.

*LaFROMBOIS, MARY ELLEN
(hospital director)
Affiliation: Blackfeet PHS Indian Hospital, Browning, MT 59417 (406) 338-6153.

*LaFROMBOISE, RICHARD
(Turtle Mountain Sioux)
(tribal chairperson)
Affiliation: Turtle Mountain Tribal Council, P.O. Box 900, Belcourt, ND 58316 (701) 477-6451.

LAGO, EDUARDO, M.D.
(clinical director)
Affiliation: Fort Yates PHS Indian Hospital, Box J, Fort Yates, ND 58538 (701) 854-3831.

LAIWA, SHIRLEY (Miwok)
(rancheria representative)
Affiliation: Potter Valley Rancheria, Box 2273, West Sacramento, CA 95619 (916) 467-3307.

*LAKE, ARTHUR
(BIA agency supt.)
Affiliation: Bethel Agency, BIA, P.O. Box 347, Bethel, AK 99559 (907) 543-2727.

LAKE, TIMOTHY (Lakotah)
(BIA agency supt.)
Affiliation: Yankton Agency, BIA, P.O. Box 577, Marty, SD 57361 (605) 384-3651.

LAMB, CHARLES A. 1944-
(museum director)
Born September 25, 1944, Farragut, Idaho. *Education*: California Western University, BA, 1966; San Diego State University, Graduate School, 1970-73. *Principal occupation*: Museum director. *Home address*: 217 Lane Ave., SE, Roseburg, OR 97470 (503) 453-6353. *Affiliations*: National Park Ranger, Crater Lake, OR, and Yellowstone National Park, WY (8 years); museum director, Colorado River Indian Tribes Museum, Parker, AZ, 1973-90. *Community activities*: Parker Area Historical Society (president); Museums Association of Arizona (Western Regional Representative); Tribal Tourism Committee (chairman); Irataba Society (board member); Tribal Safety Committee (former chairman). *Memberships*: American Association of Museums (education committee); American Association for State and Local History; Society for California Archaeology; National Trust for Historic Preservation. *Awards, honors*: Copely Press Scholarship; graduate of Horace M. Albright Training Center for National Park Service; graduate of Montana State University, Law Enforcement Academy. *Interests*: History, archaeology, anthropology, biology; historic preservation; hunting, fishing, photography, painting. *Biographical sources*: Articles in the following: Arizona Republic newspaper; Parker Pioneer newspaper; Yuma Daily Sun newspaper; among others. *Published works*: San Simeon: A Brief History, illustrations by C. Lamb (Santana Press, 1971).

LAMBERT, MARILYN
(director-Indian center)
Affiliation: Sault Ste. Marie Indian Friendship Centre, 29 Wellington St., Sault Ste. Marie, Ontario, Canada P6A 2K9 (705) 256-5634.

*LAMEBULL, CINDY
(clinic director)
Affiliation: Warner Mountain Indian Health, Box 127, Fort Bidwell, CA 96112 (918) 279-6194.

LAMEMAN, ALPHONSE
(Indian band chief)
Affiliation: Beaver Lake Indian Band, Box 960, Lac La Biche, Alberta, Canada T0A 2C0 (403) 623-4549.

*LAMENTI, EVELYN (Navajo) 1937-
(administration)
Born November 18, 1937, Albuquerque, N.M. *Education*: University of Massachusetts, BS; San Francisco State University, MA. *Principal occupation*: Administration: *Home address*: 708 Court Lane, Concord, CA 94518 (510) 836-8209 (work). *Affiliation*: Program manager, teacher on special assignment, resource teacher, Oakland Unified School District, 1975-. *Community activities*: Cultural Arts, City of Oakland; Dance for Power (executive board member); Bay Area American Indian Education Council. *Memberships*: California Indian Education Association (vice-president); national Indian Education Association.

LAMENTI, JIM
(executive director)
Affiliation: Intertribal Friendship House, 523 East 14th St., Oakland, CA 94606 (510) 452-1235.

LAMERE, FRANK DEAN (Winnebago) 1950-
(executive director)
Born March 1, 1950, Sioux City, Iowa. *Education*: Nebraska Indian Community College, AA, 1989; Bellevue (NE) College, BS (Professional Studies), 1992. *Principal occupation*: Executive director-Indian organization, *Home address*: 600 Pioneer Place, So. Sioux City, NE 68776 (402) 878-2242 (work). *Affiliation*: Executive Director, Nebraska Inter-Tribal Development Corp., Winnebago, NE. *Other professional posts*: Chairperson, Nebraska Indian Commission; Board of Trustees of Nebraska Indian Community College, JTPA Indian & National Native American Advisory Commission; NE State Job Training Coordinating Council; NE Rural Development Commission; Board Member, National Rainbow Coalition; member, Winnebago Health Planning Committee. *Community activities*: Chairperson of National Indian Democrats; Associate Chairperson of NE Democratic Party; member of Democratic National Committee; Board of NE Wildlife Federation; Parents Advisory Council of University of Nebraska; Board of Counselors, NE Medical Center; Core Planning Committee-Dakota County Law Enforcement. *Interests*: Experienced motivational speaker and political activist. Also, founder of the NO Americans, the International Indian fast pitch softball team headquartered in Nebraska, 1991.

*LANE, JOHN
(professor of English)
Address & Affiliation: Dept. of English, Box 101, 429 N. Church St., Wofford College, Spartanburg, SC 29303.

LANG, RICHARD W.
(museum director)
Affiliation: The Wheelwright Museum of the American Indian, P.O. Box 5153, 704 Camino Lejo, Santa Fe, NM 87502 (505) 982-4636.

LANGAN, JULIA M.
(BIA agency supt.)
Affiliation: Pawnee Agency, Bureau of Indian Affairs, P.O. Box 440, Pawnee, OK 74058 (918) 762-2585.

LANGSTON, WILLIAM K. (Strong Bear) (Nansemond)
(tribal assistant chief)
Affiliation: Nansemond Indian Tribal Association, P.O. Box 9293, Chesapeake, VA 23321 (804) 487-5116.

LAPAZ EMMA L. (Mescalero Apache) 1961-
(criminal court clerk)
Born August 7, 1961, Mescalero, N.M. *Principal occupation*: Criminal court clerk. *Address*: P.O. Box 747, Mescalero, NM 88340 (505) 671-4489 (work). *Affiliation*: Court clerk, Mescalero Apache Tribal Court, Mescalero, NM, 1987-. *Memberships*: National American Indian Court Clerks Association, 1989-.

LAPENA, FRANK *(Tauhindauli)* (Wintu-Nomtipom) 1937-
(teacher)
Born October 5, 1937, San Francisco, Calif. *Education*: Chico State College, BA; San Francisco State University, Secondary Life Credential; California State University, Sacramento, MA. *Prinicpal occupation*: Teacher. *Home address*: 1531 42nd St., Sacramento, CA 95819 (916) 278-6645. Affiliation: Professor, California State University, Sacramento, CA. *Other professional post*: Commissioner of California State Capitol. *Awards, honors*: 1988 Meritorious Performance & Profesional Promise Awad, California State University, Sacramento. *Interests*: Native American art: traditional and contemporary - emphasis on California; traditional dance and ceremony. *Published work*: World Is a Gift (Limestone Press, 1987).

*LAPOINT, ERIC (Blackfeet)
(BIA agency supt.)
Affiliation: Blackfeet Agency, Bureau of Indian Affairs, P.O. Box 880, Browning, MT 59417 (406) 338-7544.

LAPOINT, ORAN
(editor)
Affiliation: American Indian Graduate Record, 4520 Montgomery Blvd., NE, Suite 1-B, Albuquerque, NM 87109 (505) 881-4584.

LARGO, ANTHONY (Cahuilla)
(tribal spokesperson)
Affiliation: Santa Rosa Rancheria, 325 N. Western Ave., Hemet, CA 92343 (909) 849-4761.

LARIMORE, COLLEEN K. (Comanche) 1963-
(director, Native American program)
Born March 3, 1963, Lakewood, N.J. *Education*: Dartmouth College, AB, 1985; Harvard University, EdM, 1990. *Principal occupation*: Director, Native American program. *Home address*: 27 Windsor Ave., Kensington, CA 94708. *Affiliations*: Dartmouth College, Hanover, NH (assistant director, Native American Recruiter, 1985-88; Office of Admissions, acting director of Minority Recruitment, 1988-89; director, Native American Program, 1990-93); Harvard University, Cambridge, MA (administrative intern, American Indian Program, 1989-90). *Memberships*: National Indian Education Association, 1985-; National Association of Women Deans and Counselors, 1990-. *Interests*: "As a Comanche Indian and a first-generation college graduate, my interest in teaching and minority education stems from my own odyssey through the educational system and the history of my family, my tribe and Native peoples in general. My research interests include: cultural styles of

learning evinced among Native American students; the diversification of teaching methods to address learning differences; the advent of the tribally controlled community colleges, and these institutions' growing success in establishing tribal culture as a viable and effective curriculum base for their students and the communities they serve."

*LARIMORE, JAMES
(program director)
Affiliation: American Indian Program, Stanford University, P.O. Box 2990, Stanford, CA 94305 (415) 725-6944.

*LARSEN, TERI (Lower Sioux)
(health director)
Affiliation: Lower Sioux Community Council, P.O. Box 308, Morton, MN 56270 (612) 564-2360.

*LARSON, ALAN
(village president)
Affiliation: Native Village of Chickaloon, P.O. Box 1105, Chickaloon, AK 99674 (907) 746-0505.

LATHLIN, OSCAR (The Pas)
(legislator)
Affiliation: Manitoba Legislative Assembly, Legislative Bldg., Regina, MB Canada R3C 0V8 (204) 945-6487. Past professional post: Chief, The Pas Indian Band, The Pas, Manitoba.

LAUBIN, GLADYS W.
(lecturer, entertainer)
Home address: Grand Teton National Park, Moose, WY 83012. *Principal occupation*: Lecturer & entertainer (presentation of Indian dances on the concert stage). *Memberships*: Association on American Indian Affairs; National Congress of American Indians; Chicago Indian Center; Jackson Hole Fine Arts Foundation. *Awards, honors*: Adopted member of Sioux Tribe; dance prizes, Standing Rock and Crow Reservations; Capezio Dance Award, 1972; Catlin Peace Pipe Award, Special Literary Award, American Indian Lore Association, 1976. *Interests*: Research among Sioux, Crow, Blackfeet, Cherokee, Kiowa, and other American Indian tribes related to dance, customs, Indian lore, music; photography; painting; costume making; woodcraft. *Published works*: Co-author, The Indian Tipi (University of Oklahoma Press, 1957); documentary art films, produced with Reginald Laubin: Old Chiefs Dance, Talking Hands, War Dance, Indian Musical Instruments, Ceremonial Pipes and Tipi How (University of Oklahoma Press, 1951-58); Indian Dances of North America and Their Importance to Indian Life (University of Oklahoma Press, 1977); The Indian Tipi, 2nd Edition (University of Oklahoma Press, 1977); American Indian Archery (University of Oklahoma Press, 1978).

LAUBIN, REGINALD K.
(lecturer, entertainer)
Home address: Grand Teton National Park, Moose, WY 83012. *Education*: Hartford Art School; Norwich Art School. *Principal occupation*: Lecturer and entertainer (presentation of American Indian dances and lore on the concert stage). *Memberships*: Association on American Indian Affairs; National Congress of American Indians; Chicago Indian Center; Jackson Hole Fine Arts Foundation. *Awards, honors*: Guggenheim Fellowship, 1951; adopted son of Chief One Bull, nephew of Sitting Bull; dance prizes, Standing Rock and Crow Reservations;

Capezio Dance Award, 1972; Catlin Peace Pipe Award, Special Literary Award, American Indian Lore Association, 1976. *Interests*: Research among Sioux, Crow, Blackfeet, Cherokee, Kiowa and other tribes on dance, custom, lore, music and general anthropology; archery; photography; duplication of Indian craft techniques; primitive camping and cooking; woodcraft. *Published works*: The Indian Tipi (University of Oklahoma Press, 1957); series in Boy's Life on Indian crafts; six documentary films on Indian dance and culture, produced with Gladys Laubin; Indian Dances of North America, and Their Importance to Indian Life (University of Oklahoma Press, 1978).

*LAUGHLIN, DON (Mojave)
(casino operator)
Affiliation: Mojave Casino, 500 Merriman Ave., Needles, CA 92363 (619) 326-4591.

*LAUTANEN-RALEIGH, MARCIA
(center director)
Affiliation: Schlingoethe Center for Native American Cultures, Aurora University, 347 S. Gladstone, Dunham Hall, Aurora, IL 60506 (708) 844-5402

*LAVAN, DOUGLAS PAUL (Kikiallus)
(tribal chief)
Affiliation: Kikiallus Indian nation, 3933 Bagley Ave. N., Seattle, WA 98103.

LAVELL, WILLIAM G.
(BIA office director)
Affiliation: Bureau of Indian Affairs, Office of Self-Governance, Dept. of the Interior, MS: 2253-MIB, 1849 C St., NW, Washington, DC 20240 (202) 219-0240.

*LAVELLE, JOHN (Santee Sioux)
(organization director)
Affiliation: Center for Support & Protection of Indian Religions & Indigenous Traditions, National Congress of American Indians, 900 Pennsylvania Ave., SW, Washington, DC 20003 (202) 546-9404.

LAWRENCE, LINDA (Sioux)
(elementary school principal)
Affiliation: Standing Rock Community School, P.O. Box 377, Fort Yates, ND 58538 (701) 854-3865.

LAWSON, LAWRENCE ANN HENSON *(Morning Hawk)* **(United Lumbee/Cherokee) 1938-**
(home maker, nurses aid)
Born July 16, 1938, Phoenix, Ariz. *Education*: High school. Principal occupation: Home maker, nurses aid. *Address*: P.O. Box 903, Fall River Mills, CA 96028 (916) 336-6509. *Other professional posts*: Grand Council person, United Lumbee Nation of N.C. & America's, 1988-. *Memberships*: Native American Wolf Clan (council person, 1987-); United Lumbee Nation's Deer Clan (council person, 1987-88). *Awards, honors*: 2nd place twice for Indian beadwork, Inter-Mountain Fair, McArthur, CA. *Interests*: Indian beadwork; sewing; making rag dolls; reading Indian heritage; cooking; writing - "I write an article for our paper (United Lumbee Nation Times) called "As I See It," was reprinted in the Twin Lights Trail American Indian Magazine (London, England, 1991: titles, "Black Bear & the Hawk,' and "What Is Pow Wow." *Biographical sources*: "I have a section in the United Lumbee's Deer Clan Cook Book."

LAWSON, MICHAEL
(historian)
Affiliations: Presently manages the office of Historical Research Associates (a consulting firm specializing in cultural and environmental resource management and litigation support) in Washington, DC; formerly the senior historian for the Bureau of Indian Affairs. *Published works*: Dammed Indians: The Pick-Sloan Plan and the Missorui River Sioux, 1944-1980 (University of Oklahoma Press, 1982).

*LAWSON, RAYMOND R. *(Grey Wolf)* **(Melundgeon Cherokee) 1923-**
(auto mechanic)
Born February 10, 1923, Claiborne Co., Tenn. *Education*: U.S. Army, GED. *Principal occcupation*: Auto mechanic. *Address*: P.O. Box 1784, Thomasville, GA 31799 (912) 226-0717 (work). *Affiliation*: Manager, Carroll Hill Auto Electric, Thomasville, GA, 1970-. *Other professional post*: Principal Chief, Deer Clan, Inc., Valdosta, GA. *Military service*: U.S. Army (22 years) (served in 3 wars, WWII, Korean & Vietnam-2 Combat Stars, American Defense Medal, Pacific Theatre Medal, & Commendation Service Medal for 22 years of duty). *Community activities*: Steering Committee, Cherokee Unity Council, Jasper, TN; Masonic Lodge; VFW Post 165, Ochlocknee, GA. *Memberships*: Southeastern Cherokee Confederacy (vice-chief, 1989-93). *Interests*: "My main desire is to go to the Midwest and study all Native American cultures and religions; horticulture & electronics." *Biographical source*: Article, "To Guard Against Invading Indians: Struggling for Native Community in the Southeast," in American Indian Culture & Research Journal, Fall 1994.

LEACH, MICHAEL P. (Lillooet)
(Indian band chief)
Affiliation: Lillooet Indian Band, P.O. Box 615, Lillooet, British Columbia, Canada V0K 1V0 (604) 256-7613.

LEAFFE, JAMES (Cayuga)
(tribal chief)
Affiliation: Chief (lifetime), Cayuga Nation, P.O. Box 11, Versailles, NY 14168 (716) 532-4847.

LEAMING, JUDY (Catawba/Cherokee)
(attorney)
Address: P.O. Box 7601, Charlotte, NC 28241 (704) 391-1508. Membership: Native American Bar Association (past president).

LEAP, WILLIAM L. 1946-
(anthropologist)
Born November 28, 1946, Philadelphia, Pa. *Education*: Florida State University, BA, 1967; Southern Methodist University, PhD (Anthropology), 1970. *Principal occupation*: Anthropologist. *Address & Affiliation*: Professor of anthropology & chair, Dept. of Anthropology, American University, Washington, DC (202) 885-1830 (work), 1970-. *Other professional post*: Director, Indian Education Program, Center for Applied Linguistics, Arlington, VA, 1974-79; director, Indian Education, National Congress of American Indians, Washington DC, 1980-83. *Awards, honors*: 1986 Finalist, Washington Association of Practicing Anthropologists' PRAXIS Award for outstanding achievement in anthropological problem-solving. *Interests*: "My vocational interests center on Indian self-determination through education. A major component of such a strategy is relevant education, and that means addressing the In-

dian (e.g. tribal or traditional) as well as the mainstream cultural components of the students interests, lifestyle, and life-options. My work in the field has centered on assisting Tribal governments and Tribal agencies develop programs to provide Tribal members to take charge of and manage such programs without reliance on outside sources of support." *Published works*: Language Policies in Indian Education: Recommendations, 1973, and Handbook for Staff Development in Indian Education, 1976 (Center for Applied Linguistics); Studies in Southwestern Indian English (Trinity University Press, 1977); American Indian Language Education (National Bilingual Research Center, 1980); American Indian Language Renewal in Annual Review of Anthropology, 1981; Assumptions and strategies in Mathematics Problem-Solving by Ute Indian Students in Linguistic and Cultural Factors in Mathematics Education, edited by Rodney Cocking and Jose Metre (Erlbaum Press, 1987); Applied Linguistics and American Indian Language Renewal (Human Organization - Journal of the Society for Applied Anthropology, 1989).

LEASK, JANIE (Haida/Tsimshean) 1948-
(organization president)
Born September 17, 1948, Seattle, Wash. *Education*: East Anchorage High School, 1966. *Principal occupation*: Alaska Federation of Natives, 411 W. 4th Ave., Suite 301, Anchorage, 1974- (vice president, 1977-82; president, 1982-). *Home address*: 7021 Hunt Ave., Anchorage, AK 99504 (907) 274-3611 (work). *Community activities*: Enrolled in Cook Inlet Region (one of the 12 in-state Alaska Native Regional corporations; The State Board of Education; the Anchorage Organizing Committee for the 1992 Olympics; the Alaska Land Use Council; the ARCO Scholarship Committee. *Awards, honors*: Governor's Award in 1983 for work on behalf of Alaska Native people.

LEBEAU, EDWARD A.
(Cheyenne River Sioux) 1941-
(contracting specialist,
public health advisor)
Born June 14, 1941, Cheyenne Agency, S.D. *Education*: Minot State University, BA, 1965. *Principal occupation*: Contracting specialist, public health advisor. *Home address*: 1323 Minnesota Ave., Bemidji, MN 56601 (218) 751-7701. *Affiliations*: Tribal projects coordinator, Indian Health Service, Bemidji, MN, 1981-. *Military service*: U.S. Army, 1985-87. Northern Minnesota Indian Athletic Association (charter member, 1973-).

LEBEAU, MARCELLA
(association president)
Affiliation: North American Indian Women's Association, P.O. Box 805, Eagle Butte, SD 57625 (605) 964-2136.

LeBOURDAIS, RICHARD
(Indian band chief)
Affiliation: Whispering Pines Indian Band, RR 1, Site 8, Comp. 4, Kamloops, British Columbia, Canada V2Z 1Z3 (604) 579-5772.

LECAM, MICHAEL J.
(school principal)
Affiliation: Zia Day School, San Ysidro, NM 87053 (505) 867-3553.

*LEDBETTER, GARY ALLEN *(Bear Paw)*
(United Lumbee/Cherokee/Choctaw) 1949-
(ceramic artist, teacher)
Born June 4, 1949, Los Angeles, Calif. *Education*: High school. *Principal occupation*: Ceramic artist, teacher. *Home address*: 6004 Tolegate, Sisters, OR 97759 (503) 549-0342. *Membership*: United Lumbee nation's Beaver Clan (vice-chief, 1991-). *Interests*: "Indian heritage, ceramic art, jazz music; helping my Indian people."

LEDBETTER, PATTY DEANNE REED *(Flaming Star)* **(United Lumbee/Cherokee/ Choctaw) 1943-**
(sales clerk)
Born July 30, 1943, in Calif. *Education*: High school. *Principal occupation*: Sales clerk. *Home address*: 6004 Tolegate, Sisters, OR 97759 (503) 549-0342. *Community activities*: Police Reserve, Linn and Desshutes Counties, OR, 1984-. *Memberships*: Native American Wolf Clan, 1978-; United Lumbee Nation's Beaver Clan Chief, 1988-. *Interests*: "Indian heritage; ceramic art, jazz music; helping my Indian people."

LEE, LINDA (Eskimo) 1961-
(assistant bilingual coordinator)
Born January 7, 1961, Shungnak, Alaska. *Education*: High School. *Principal occupation*: Assistant bilingual coordinator. *Home address*: P.O. Box 617, Kotzebue, AK 99752 (907) 442-2234. *Affiliation*: Northwest Arctic Boro School District, Kotzebue, AK, 1990-. *Published works*: Lore of the Inupiat: The Elders Speak, Vols. 1 & 2, 1989; Vol. 3, 1990 (NWABSD); Qayaq the Magical Travels (NWABSD, 1991).

LEE, PATRICK (Oglala Sioux)
(chief judge)
Affiliation: Oglala Sioux Tribe, 203 E. Oakland St., Rapid City, SD 57701.

LEE, VIVIAN (Hoh)
(tribal vice-chairperson)
Affiliation: Hoh Tribal Business Committee, HC 80, Box 917, Forks, WA 98331 (206) 374-6582.

LEFFUE, JOHN C.
(school principal)
Affiliation: Santa Rosa Boarding School, Sells, AZ 85634 (602) 361-2331.

LEFTHAND, JOSEPHINE (Jicarilla Apache)
(supervisor)
Affiliation: Jicarilla Apache Higher Education Program, P.O. Box 507, Dulce, NM 87528 (505) 759-3615/6.

*LEFTHAND, PATRICK (Kootenai)
(medicine man)
Affiliation: Confederated Salish & Kootenai Tribe, P.O. Box 278, Pablo, MT 59855 (406) 675-2700 Fax 675-2806

LEHMAN, KENNETH (Menominee)
(school administrator)
Affiliation: Menominee Tribal School, Menominee Indian Tribe of Wisconsin, P.O. Box 910, Kehena, WI 54135 (715) 756-2354.

LEIGHTON, DANNY VICTOR (Metlakatla)
(Indian band chief)
Affiliation: Metlakatla Indian Band, Box 459, Prince Rupert, British Columbia, Canada V8J 3R1 (604) 628-9294.

LEIGHTON, RONALD W.
(corporation president)
Affiliation: Ketchikan Indian Corp., 429 Deermount Ave., Ketchikan, AK 99901 (907) 225-5158.

LEITKA, MARY K. (Hoh)
(tribal chairperson)
Affiliation: Hoh Tribal Business Committee, HC 80, Box 917, Forks, WA 98331 (206) 374-6582.

LeMAY, KONNIE
(managing editor)
Affiliation: "The Lakota Times," 1920 Lombardy Dr., Box 2180, Rapid City, SD 57709 (605) 341-0011.

*LEMON, BECKY
(editor)
Affiliation: "The Native Nevadan," Reno-Sparks Indian Colony, 98 Colony Rd., Sparks, NV 89502 (702) 359-9449.

LEMONS, NOKOMIS
(Indian dance team coordinator)
Affiliation: Rising Water Dancers, Route 2, Box 107-B, Bruington, VA 23023.

*LENDS HIS HORSE, JOSEPH
(college president)
Affiliation: Cheyenne River Community College, P.O. Box 220, Eagle Butte, SD 57625 (605) 964-8635.

LENT, DAVID
(health director)
Affiliation: Toiyabe Indian Health Council, P.O. Box 1296, Bishop, CA 93515 (619) 873-8464.

LENZ, MONSIGNOR PAUL A. (Thunder Cloud) 1925-
(executive director - Roman Catholic Priest)
Born December 15, 1925, Gallitzin, Penna. *Education*: St. Vincent College & Seminary (Latrobe, PA); Penn State University. *Principal occupation*: Executive director, The Bureau of Catholic Indian Missions, Washington, DC, 1977-. *Home address*: 2021 H St., N.W., Washington, DC 20006 (202) 331-8542. *Other professional posts*: Board of trustees: The Catholic University of America, Washington, DC; Xavier University, New Orleans; St. Vincent Seminary, Latrobe; National Catholic Indian Tekakwitha Conference, and The National Catholic Development Conference, Washington, DC. *Awards, honors*: Alumnus of Distinction, St. Vincent College, Latrobe, Pa. *Interests*: "Travel constantly to Indian reservations and American Indian rural areas i the U.S." *Published work*: Newsletter - Bureau of Catholic Indian Missions, W ashington, D.C. (published ten times per year.)

LEO, RICHARD
(Indian band chief)
Affiliation: Kyuquot Indian Band, General Delivery, Kyuquot, BC, Can. V0P 1J0 (604) 332-5259.

LEONARD, FLOYD *(Waw-paw-waw-quah- White Loon)* **(Miami) 1925-**
(tribal chief)
Born September 19, 1925, Picher, Okla. *Education*: Pittsburg State University (KS), BS, 1951, MS, 1952, EdS, 1971. *Principal occupation*: Chief, Miami Tribe of Oklahoma. *Address*: *Affiliation*: Miami Tribe of Oklahoma, P.O. Box 1326, Miami, OK 74355 (918) 542-1445. *Past*

professional post: Former school administrator for Joplin, MO public schools. *Military service*: U.S. Coast Guard, 1943-46. *Community activities*: Northeast Inter-Tribal Council, Miami, OK (president); Claremore Indian Hospital Board (member); U.S. Bishops Advisory Council (former member). *Awards, honors*: Honorary Alumnus, Miami University, Oxford, OH.

LEOTSAKOS, LINDA (Passamaquoddy)
(school principal)
Affiliation: Indian Township School, Peter Dana Point, Princeton, ME 04668 (207) 796-2362.

LEPINE, MATTHEW (Cree)
(Indian band chief)
Affiliation: Cree Indian Band, P.O. Box 90, Fort Chipewyan, Alberta, Canada T0P 1B0 (403) 697-3740.

*LeROY, LYNN R. (Serrano)
(rancheria chairperson)
Affiliation: San Manuel Band of Mission Indians, P.O Box 266, Patton, CA 92369 (909) 864-8933.

LESTER, A. DAVID (Creek) 1941-
(executive director)
Born September 25, 1941, Claremore, Okla. *Education*: Brigham Young University, Provo, Utah, BA, 1967. *Principal occupation & Address*: Executive director, Council of Energy Resource Tribes (CERT), Denver, CO. *Home address*: 8688 East Otero Circle, Englewood, C0 80112 (303) 832-6600 (work). *Affiliations*: Vice-chairman, American Indian Scholarships, Inc., Taos, NM (2 years); president, United Indian Development Association, Los Angeles (7 years); economic development specialist, National Congress of American Indians, Washington, DC. *Other professional posts*: Commissioner, Administration for Native Americans, U.S. Dept. of Health & Human Services, Washington, DC; Boards of Directors: American Indian National Bank, Washington, D.C.; Americans for Indian Opportunity, Albuquerque; American Indian Scholarships, Inc., Taos, NM; National Area Development Institute, and Los Angeles (CA) Indian Center. *Community activities*: Served as a Presidential appointee to the National Advisory Council on Minority Enterprise, which advised cabinet-level officials on strategies to stimulate minority business ownership, and to the National Council on Indian Opportunity, devoted to improving social & economic opportunities for American Indians; served as Human Relations Commissioner for the City of Los Angeles and as Chairman of the Los Angeles County American Indian Commission. *Awards, honors*: Received the Indian Council First Indian Achievement Award, the Americans for Indian Opportunity's Distinguished Services Peace Pipe Award, a proclamation of David Lester Day by the Governor of Oklahoma, recognition by the California State Assembly for contributions to Indian-State relations, the United Indian Development Association's Jay Silverheels Achievement Award, the White Buffalo Council of American Indians' National-Level Award for Outstanding Service to American Indians; created a self-supporting management institute which trained 2,000 Indian businessmen and women; presented a wide variety of Indian and Native American issues before conferences, conventions, and other meetings and on radio and television. *Interests*: "Indian affairs; pow-wows; Indian cultures; Indian economic progress is my vocational goal."

LESTER, JOAN 1937-
(museum curator)
Born July 4, 1937, New York, N.Y. *Education*: Brown University, BA, 1959; Sorbonne, Paris, France, Certificate of Studies, 1958; UCLA, MA (Primitive Art/American Indian Art), 1963. *Principal occupation*: Museum curator. *Home address*: 2 Muster Ct., Lexington, MA 02173. *Affiliations*: Boston Children's Museum; coordinator of North American Indian resources & workshop (courses & workshops presenting Indian people in southern New England), co-developer of American Indian programs in Greater Boston area, 1971-74; museum assistant, 1963-70, museum coordinator-Native American Advisory Board, 1973-, developer/curator, American Indian Collections and Programs, 1976-, associate curator, 1975-78, curator of collections, 1978-85, chief curator, 1985-; lecturer, Indian Studies, Tufts University, 1987. *Other professional posts*: Chair, National Curator's Committee, 1982-; member-at-large, Council for Museum Anthropology, 1983-; principal investigator, American Indian Games, National Endowment for the Humanities Planning Grant, 1983- *Community activities*: Member, advisory boards: Phoenix School, Cambridge, Mass.; MIT Museum; Native American Studies Department of Plimoth Plantation, Mass.; Tomaquag Indian Memorial Museum, Exeter, R.I. MAP assessor, Museum Assessment Program. *Memberships*: American Association of Museums (curator's committee); International Council of Museums; New England Museum Association; Native American Art Studies Association; Council for Museum Anthropology; Peabody Museum Association. *Awards, honors*: Boston Indian Council Certificate of Merit, 1975; Bay State Historical League Award of Excellence, for Indians Who Met the Pilgrims, June, 1975; Award of Distinction, A.A.M. for "We're Still Here", catalog, 1987. *Interests*: "American Indian art; American Indian arts in New England as they continue today; cooking, bicycling, cross country skiing, theater, classical music, folk dancing, reading." *Published works*: The American Indian, A Museum's Eye View, in Indian Historian, summer, 1972; Indians Who Met the Pilgrims, the Match Program, American Science and Engineering, Boston, 1974; A Code of Ethics for Curator's, in Museum News, Jan/Feb., 1983; chapter I - The Production of Fancy Baskets in Maine (American Indian Archaeological Institute, 1986); American Indian Art in New England (Boston Children's Museum, 1986); The Art of Tomah Joseph, Passamaquoddy Artist (Turtle Quarterly, Spring 1988). Reports: American Indian Art Association, Tomah Joseph, Passamaquoddy Artist, Sept., 1983; Metropolitan Museum of Art, The Northeast Native American Program at the Children's Museum, April, 1983; York Institute, Saco, Maine, Northeast Native American Baskets: A Continuing Tradition, Oct., 1982); Massachusetts Indian Association, The Significance of the Katherine Hall Newall Collection, Oct., 1982; American Indian Art Association, They're Still Here, Native American Art in New England, March, 1982; Institute for Contemporary Art, Native American Ash Splint Basketry in New England, Feb., 1982.

LEVALDO, ANITA
(health center director)
Affiliation: Crownpoint PHS Indian Hospital, Crownpoint, NM 87313 (505) 786-5291.

LEVI, ALBERT
(Indian band chief)
Affiliation: Big Cove Indian Band, Box 1, RR 1, Site 11, Rexton, New Brunswick, Canada E0A 2L0 (506) 523-9183.

LEVI, CARL
(school director/supt.)
Affiliation: Rough Rock Demonstration School, RRDS, Box 217, Chinle, AZ 86503 (602) 728-3311.

*LEVI, CORRINE L.
(organization director)
Affiliation: TCI, Inc., 2126 Connecticut Ave., NW, Suite 52, Washington, DC 20008.

LEVI, JERRY R. (Cheyenne-Arapaho) 1946-
(health systems administrator-IHS)
Born June 27, 1946, Concho, Okla. *Education*: Southeastern Oklahoma State University, BS, 1971; Oklahoma City University, MBA, 1986. *Principal occupation*: Health systems administrator-IHS. *Address*: Shawnee Indian Health Center, 2001 S. Gordon Cooper Dr., Shawnee, OK 74801 (405) 275-4270. *Affiliations*: Administrator, Potawatomi WIC & Food Distributor Programs; chairperson, Oklahoma, New Mexico Food Action Committee for Tribes (ON-FACT); Administrative Officer, Shawnee Indian Health Center, Shawnee, OK, 1987-. *Military service*: U.S. Army, 1968-70 (SPS-E-5; Soldier of the Month, Third Army; selected all-Army fast pitch softball trials). *Community activities*: Tribal chairman, Cheyenne-Arapaho Tribes, 1981; Concho School Board (chairman, 1981); El Reno Title IV Committee vice chairman, 1980-81; El Reno YMCA wrestling coach; Yukon Jays football coach.

*LEVIAS, MATTHEW, Sr. (Chemehuevi)
(tribal chairperson)
Affiliation: Chemehuevi Reservation, P.O. Box 1780, Havasu Lake, CA 92363 (619) 858-4219.

LEVIER, FRANCIS ANDREW
(Citizen Band Potawatomi) 1950-
(tribal administrator,
business committeeman)
Born November 13, 1950, Topeka, Kan. *Education*: Hofstra University, BA, 1973; University of Kansas, MS, 1975, EdD, 1979. *Principal occupation*: Tribal administrator & business committeeman. *Address*: Citizen Band Potowatomi Tribe, 1901 S. Gordon Cooper Dr., Shawnee, OK 74801 (405) 275-3121. *Affiliations*: Acting director, Supportive Educational Services, 1975-76, instructor, School of Social Welfare, 1977-79, assistant director of Minority Affairs, 1974-80, University of Kansas, Lawrence; director, Health Programs, Prairie Band Potawatomi Tribe, 1980-81; acting executive director, Prairie Band Potawatomi Tribe of Kansas, 1980-81; executive director, Region VI Indian Alcoholism Training Program, 1982-83; executive director, A proposal, Evaluation, Research, and Training consulting firm (P.E.R.T., Inc.), 1982-; director of economic development, Citizen Band Potawatomi Tribe, 1983-85; tribal administrator and business committeeman, Citizen Band Potawatomi Tribe, Shawnee, OK, 1983-. *Other professional post*: Member of the Board of Regents, Haskell Indian Jr. College, 1979-83; consultant, Rockefeller Foundation, 1979; consultant, instructor, Leavenworth Federal Penitentiary, KS, 1978-80; consultant, Kickapoo Tribe of Kansas, 1978; consultant, Powhatten School

District, KS, 1978; assistant director, Topeka (KS) Indian Center, 1977-78. *Community activities*: Affirmative Action, University of Kansas (board member, 1976-80); United Indian Recovery Association (board member, 1980-81); Emergency Services Council, City of Lawrence, KS (chairman, 1977-80). *Awards, honors*: Recipient of Ford Foundation Fellowship for American Indians, 1973-76; Elected to five-member Business Committee (governing body) of the Citizen Band Potawatomi Tribe in June, 1985. Was first business committee member ever named to the position of tribal administrator in the history of the 12,000 member tribe. *Published works*: A Brief History of the Pedigree Papers, 1983; editor, Using Indian Culture to Develop Alcohol & Drug Materials for Indian Adults and Youth, 1983; Overview of Inhalent Abuse Among American Indian Youth, 1981; An Attitude Survey of Urban Indians in N.E. Kansas Toward Higher Education, 1979; all published by the American Indian Institute, University of Oklahoma, 1983. The Need for Indian Student Organizations in Large Institutions of Higher Education, N.E.C.C.A. Conference Article, K.C., MO, 1979.

LEVINE, VICTORIA LINDSAY 1954-
(ethnomusicologist)
Born September 8, 1954, Palo Alto, Calif. *Education*: San Francisco State University, BA (Anthropology), 1977, MA (Music History), 1980; University of Illinois at Urbana-Champaign, PhD (Musicology), 1990. *Principal occupation*: Ethnomusicologist. *Home address*: 6265 Savannah Way, Colorado Springs, CO 80919 (719) 389-6554 (office). *Affiliation*: The Colorado College, Colorado Springs, 1988-. *Memberships*: Society for Ethnomusicology, 1980-; College Music Society, 1989-. *Awards, honors*: John D. & Catherine T. MacArthur Professor, 1991-93, Colorado College; Jackson Fellow, 1991-92 (Colorado College); Ingolf Dahl Award in Musicology, 1979 (USC). *Interests*: "Choctaw musical culture; musical cultures of Louisiana tribes; southeast Native American ethnomusicology; ethnomusicology of the Southwest." *Published work*: Choctaw Music and Dance (University of Oklahoma Press, 1990).

LEVY, CARMELLA
(health director)
Affiliation: Indian Health Center of Santa Clara Valley, 1333 Meridian Ave., San Jose, CA 95125 (408) 294-7553.

LEWIS, DANIEL N. (Navajo)
(staff director)
Affiliations: Former Deputy Minority Staff Director, U.S. Senate Select Committee on Indian Affairs; director, Congressional and Legislative Affairs Staff, Bureau of Indian Affairs, 1951 Constitution Ave., N.W., Washington, D.C. 20245 (202) 343-5706, 1990-.

LEWIS, FRANCIS
(Indian band chief)
Affiliation: Kitkatla Indian Band, Kitkatla, British Columbia, Canada V0V 1C0 (604) 628-9305.

LEWIS (MYRICK), JOAN (Grand Traverse Ottawa & Chippewa) 1951-
(health project director)
Born June 30, 1951, Traverse City, Mich. *Education*: Western Michigan University, BS, 1973; University of Houston, 1981-83; Trinity University (San Antonio, TX), MS, 1987. *Principal oc-

cupation: Health project director. *Home address*: 1168 Thomas Ave., St. Paul, MN 55101 (612) 642-9476; 293-0233 (work). *Affiliations*: Medical technologist, Hospital Laboratory, Kalamazoo, MI, 1974-80; chief medical technologist, Physician Clinical Laboratory, Houston, TX, 1981-87; AIDS Project Director, American Indian Health Care Association, St. Paul, MN, 1988-. *Community activities*: Community advisors to the Executive Planning Committee for the National Minority AIDS Conference, Census Awareness Committee, Minority Recruitment Committee, and University of Minnesota. *Memberships*: National Minority AIDS Council; National AIDS Network. *Interests*: Culturally Sensitive AIDS presentations at regional and national meetings.

*LEWIS, JOHN
(executive director)
Affiliation: Inter-Tribal Council of Arizona, 4205 N. 7th Ave., Suite 200, Phoenix, AZ 85013 (602) 248-0071.

LEWIS, JUDY (Onondaga)
(attorney)
Address: 1533 Bobcat Cr., Edmond, OK 73034 (405) 359-0231. *Memberships*: Court of Indian Appeals Bar Association (president); Oklahoma Indian Bar Association; Native American Bar Association.

LEWIS, ROBERT (Zuni Pueblo)
(pueblo governor)
Affiliation: Pueblo of Zuni, P.O. Box 339, Zuni, NM 87327 (505) 782-4481.

LEWIS, ROD (Navajo)
(attorney)
Address: Arizona Bar Association (Indian Law Section-chairperson), P.O. Box 400, Sacaton, AZ 85247 (602) 562-3611. *Membership*: Native American Bar Association.

LEWIS, S. JO (Navajo)
(school principal)
Affiliation: Blackwater Community School, Route 1, Box 95, Coolidge, AZ 85228 (602) 723-5859.

*LEWIS, TOM (Navajo)
(college president)
Affiliation: Navajo Community College, P.o. Box 218, Tsaile, AZ 86556 (602) 724-3311.

*LIDMAN, ROGER W.
(museum director)
Affiliation: Pueblo Grande Museum & Cultural Park, 4619 E Washington St., Phoenix, AZ 85034 (602) 495-0901.

*LIDOT, TOM
(executive director)
Affiliation: National Native American Aids Task Force, c/o Indian Health Council, P.O. Box 406, Pauma Valley, CA 92061 (619) 749-1410.

*LIGHTNING, GEORGINA LYNN (Cree)
(actor/singer & lyricist)
Born July 4 in Edmonton, Alberta, Can. *Education*: Concordia College (Edmonton, AB); American Academy of Dramatic Arts & UCLA. *Principal occupation*: Actor/singer & lyricist. *Home address*: 275 S. 3rd St., Apt. 208, Burbank, CA 91502 (818) 848-6306. *Community activities*: Volunteer to operations of American Indians in film and American Indian recognition of entertainers in media honored by the annual Kokopeli

Awards and Concert Benefit. *Membership*: American Academy Alumni/Repertory Company. *Awards, honors*: Michael Toma Award by Concordia College for most progressed actor, first time ever awarded to a Canadian, not to mention first for an Indian graduate from the Academy; and first to be invited as a repertory actor. *Interests*: Performing arts/entertainment (music, 1977-; acting, 1988-); political activist willing to give her life for the rights and obligations the government owes to her people, the natives of this country. "I wish to travel the world as a performer who earns the public's appreciation and support for a native American point of view and deserved acceptance as an equal in art. I have written several songs which I hope to record soon." *Biographical source*: "Stars in the Desert," Navajo newspaper.

LINCOLN, MICHAEL E.
(IHS-deputy director)
Affiliation: Indian Health Service, Office of the Director, 5600 Fishers Lane, Room 6-05, Rockville, MD 20857 (301) 443-1083.

LINFORD, LAURANCE D.
(executive director)
Affiliation: Inter-Tribal Indian Ceremonial Association, P.O Box 1, Church Rock, NM 87311 (505) 863-3896. *Other professional post*: Editor, "Inter-Tribal America Magazine," & "A Measure of Excellence," Church Rock, NM, 1994-.

LINGERFELT, WILLIAM D. *(Chief Medicine Wolf)* (Eastern Cherokee) 1949-
(construction contractor)
Born July 20, 1949, Atlanta, Ga. *Education*: High school. *Principal occupation*: Construction contractor. Resides in Canton, GA (404) 479-4627. *Military service*: U.S. Army, 1969-71 (Specialist 4th Class; Vietnam Vet - 1 Bronze Star, Vietnam Campaign Medal, Good Conduct Badge, several others). *Community service*: VFW member. *Interests*: "I am a lecturer and the voice of my people in the northern Georgia area. My family and I are active in the powwow trail. We are dancers and make Native American jewelry, costumes, beadwork, etc. I m chief medicine man for the Southeastern Cherokee Confederacy. I am a chief and sit on the Chief's Council. My wife "Snow Deer" is chief of the Wolf Clan." *Biographical sources*: Paper which have done stories on Mr. Lingerfelt: The Atlanta Journal Constitution; The Cherokee Tribune; The Cleveland; Georgia Telegraph; Gainesville, GA Newspaper; The Indian Trader Magazine.

LINK, MARTIN A. 1934-
(publisher)
Born September 26, 1934, Madison, Wisc. *Education*: University of Arizona, BA, 1959. *Principal occupation*: Publisher. *Home address*: 2302 Mariyana Dr., Gallup, NM 87301 (505) 863-6459. *Affiliations*: Former director, Navajo Tribal Museum, Window Rock, AZ; publisher, The Indian Trader, Gallup, N.M., 1985-. *Other professional post*: Anthropology & history instructor, University of New Mexico-Gallup Branch Campus. *Military service*: U.S. Army, 1961-63. *Community activities*: Kiwanis Club; Knights of Columbus; Gallup-McKinley Co. Chamber of Commerce. *Memberships*: Plateau Sciences Society, 1959-; Inter-Tribal Indian Ceremonial Association, 1963-; Archaeological Society of New Mexico, 1965-83; Indian Arts & Crafts Association, 1985-. *Awards, honors*: Navajo Nation Achievement Award in Science - 1976; Na-

vajo Code Talker's Medal of Merit - 1986. *Interests*: "Writing, research and photography, especially throughout the Southwest. Have traveled throughout the Southwest, Grand Canyon, northern Mexico. Present research focuses on Indian-Spanish Inter-Relationships." *Published works*: Navajo: A Century of Progress (K.C. Publications, 1968); A Goat in the Rug (McMillian & Co., 1975); The Beauty of Shalako (The Indian Trader, 1985); Early Franciscan Missions (The Indian Trader, 1989).

LINKLATER, NORMAN
(Indian band chief)
Affiliation: Nelson House Indian Band, Nelson House, Manitoba, Canada R0B 1A0 (204) 484-2332.

LIPOVAC, PETE A.
(school supt.)
Affiliation: Sho'ban School District #512, P.O Box 306, Fort Hall, ID 83203 (208) 238-3975.

*LIPPERT, TOM
(center librarian)
Affiliation: American Indian Resource Center, Los Angeles County Public Library, 6518 Miles Ave., Huntington Park, CA 90255 (213) 583-1462.

*LISTO, SYLVESTER (Tohono O'odham)
(tribal chairperson)
Affiliation: Tohono O'odham Council, Sells Reservation, P.O. Box 837, Sells, AZ 85634 (602) 388-2221.

LITTLE, ANTHONY F. (Rosebud Sioux)
(attorney)
Address: P.O. Box 817, Bernalillo, NM 87004 (505) 867-3391 (office). *Membership*: Native American Bar Association (board member).

*LITTLE, JOSEPH D.
(BIA area director)
Affiliation: Bureau of Indian Affairs, Albuquerque Area Office, P.O. Box 26567, Albuquerque, NM 87125 (505) 766-3170.

*LITTLE, PETE
(administrative officer)
Affiliation: Acoma-Canoncito Laguna PHS Indian Hospital, P.O. Box 130, San Fidel, NM 87049.

LITTLE BEAR, LEROY ROBERT (Blackfoot) 1941-
(professor-Native American studies)
Born November 11, 1941, Alberta, Can. *Education*: Wenatchee (WA) Valley College, AA, 1966; University of Lethbridge (Alberta, Can.), BA, 1971; University of Utah, School of Law, JD, 1975. Principal occupation: *Affiliations*: Native American Studies Department, University of Lethbridge, Alberta, Canada (associate professor, 1975-; chairperson, 1975-81) (403) 329-2733. *Other professional posts*: Consultant: National Indian Brotherhood, Lethbridge, AB, 1976-78; Department of Indian Affairs, Lethbridge, 1980-81; Blood Indian Tribe, Cardston, AB, 1980-; Indian Association of Alberta, Lethbridge, 1983-. *Community activities*: Blood Tribe Police Commission (volunteer), 1980-; Legal Aid Society of Alberta, Lethbridge (volunteer), 1981-82; Lethbridge Friendship Centre (volunteer), 1969-71. *Conferences*: Subcommission of Human Rights Commission (representative), 1984; United Nations' Conference (representative), 1984; attended Constitutional

conventions on Native Rights, 1983, 1984 and 1985) as a legal advisor for Indian Association of Alberta. *Memberships*: Canadian Lawyers' Assn; Indian Association of Alberta. *Interests*: Indian law; Native Canadian Government issues. Speak, read and write English & Blackfoot. *Published works*: Books: Pathways to Self-Determination: Native Indian Leaders' Perspectives on Self-Government, and Quest for Justice: Aboriginal Rights in Canada, both with Nenno Boldt and J. Anthony Long. Articles: "Dispute Settlement Among the Nacirema," Journal of Contemporary Law; "A Concept of Native Title," presentation to MacKenzie Valley Pipeline Inquiry (Thomas Berger Commission Chairman).

LITTLE DOG, ADELE F.
(school principal)
Affiliation: Little Eagle Day School, P.O. Box 26, Little Eagle, SD 57639 (605) 823-4235.

LITTLE FINGER, LEONARD
(administrative officer)
Affiliation: Pine Ridge PHS Indian Hospital, Pine Ridge, SD 57770 (605) 867-5131.

*LITTLE LIGHT, CLOYCE
(editor)
Affiliation: "Hunter," North American Indian League, P.O. Box 7, Deer Lodge, MT 59731.

LITTLE LIGHT, GARFIELD
(IHS-administrative support)
Affiliation: Indian Health Service, Billings Area Office, P.O. Box 2143, Billings, MT 59103 (406) 657-6403.

LITTLE THUNDER, KAREN
(general manager)
Affiliation: "The Lakota Times," 1920 Lombardy Dr., Box 2180, Rapid City, SD 57709 (605) 341-0011.

*LITTLEBEAR, DICK
(resource center director)
Affiliation: Director, Multifunctional Resource Center, 4155 Tudor Centre Dr., Suite 103, Anchorage, AK 99508.

*LITTLEBIRD, LARRY
(writer)
Address: P.O. Box 2900, Santa Fe, NM 87501 (505) 455-3196.

LITTLECHIEF, BARTHELL *(White Horse)*
(Kiowa-Comanche) 1941-
(self-employed artist-sculptor/painter)
Born October 14, 1941, Kiowa Indian Hospital, Lawton, Okla. *Education*: Cameron University, 1964-65; University of Oklahoma, 1966-67. *Principal occupation*: Artist-sculptor/painter. *Home address*: Route 3, Box 109A, Anadarko, OK 73005 (405) 464-2564. *Military service*: U.S. Army National Guard, 1966-71 (SP/4). *Memberships*: Kiowa TIA-PAIH Society of Oklahoma; Native American Church. Awards, honors: 1988 Colorado Indian Market - "Best Traditional Painting"; 1989 Red Earth Indian Market - "3rd Graphics"; 1990 Santa Fe Indian Market "3rd Place - Painting"; 1991 Trail of Tears Art Show - "Grand Award"; 1991 American Indian Exposition - "1st Place Painting." *Biographical sources*: Who's Who in North American Indian Art; Who's Who in American Art; American Artists; Kiowa Voices; feature article in Santa Fean magazine; and articles in Southern Living magazine, and Texhoma Monthly magazine.

*LITTLECHILD, WILLIE *(Wetaskiwin)*
(Canadian parliament member)
Address: Parliament Bldgs., Ottawa, ON K1A 0A4 (613) 995-9364.

*LITTLEFIELD, DAN
(editor)
Affiliation: American Native Press, 2801 S. University, Little Rock, AR 72204 (501) 569-3160.

LIVINGSTONE, E. CYRIL
(Indian band chief)
Affiliation: Cowichan Lake Indian Band, Box 1376, Lake Cowichan, British Columbia, Canada V0R 2G0 (604) 745-3548.

LOCKE, KEVIN *(Tokeya Inajin)*
(Standing Rock Sioux)
(lecturer/performer)
Born in S.D. *Principal occupation*: Lecturer/performer (traditional flute music). *Address*: P.O. Box 241, Mobridge, SD 57601 (605) 88888-2690. *Awards*: National Heritage Award; 1993 Parent's Choice Gold Award for "Wopila - A Giveaway," in Boston for outstanding material for children ages 4-9. *Published works*: Dream Catcher; Keepers of the Dream; Make Me a Hollow Reed; Lakota Love Songs & Stories; The Seventh Direction; Flash of the Mirror; Wopila - A Giveaway; all cassettes & CDs produced & recorded at Meyer Creative Productions.

LOCKE, PATRICIA
(institute director)
Affiliation: Native American Language Institute, Box 963, Choctaw, OK 73020 (405) 769-4650.

*LOCKHART, GEMMA
(film producer)
Affiliation: Whirlwind Soldier, P.O. Box 154, Rosebud, SD 57570 (605) 747-2835.

*LOCKLEAR, BRETT A. (Lumbee) 1972-
(student)
Born October 18, 1972, Scotland County, N.C. *Education*: Pembroke State University, 1991-. *Principal occupation*: Student. *Community activities*: AISES (treasurer, 1992-93; regional representative, 1993-94 and nominated to be one of two national representatives for the year 1994-95); Applied Sociology Society (vice-president, 1994-95); Political Science Pre-Law Organization (1991-94); Criminal Justice Club (1993-94). *Awards, honors*: Who's Who; AISES Leadership Award recipient; Outstanding Native American Leader, Native American Student Organization, Pembroke State University. *Interests*: "I am very interested in a career of law. My particular interest is in tribal law and organizations. In my pursuit, I hope to gain recognition for the Lumbee people in legal affairs, as well as other tribes. My anticipation is also to become a voice for the Native people in the U.S. and to represent my people with the integrity and dignity they deserve. I have traveled extensively throughout the U.S. on conferences representing the Native American population at Pembroke State University. In addition to being involved in social endeavors of the Lumbee tribe, I have also advised some of our tribal board on political issues that affect us as a whole."

LOCKLEAR, JUANITA O. (Lumbee)
(center director)
Affiliation: Native American Resource Center, Pembroke State University, Pembroke, NC 28372 (919) 521-4214.

LOEW, PATTY *(Was-wa-kno-quay)* (Bad River Band-Chippewa) 1952-
(TV news anchor/reporter)
Born May 15, 1952, Milwaukee, Wisc. *Education*: University of Wisconsin, LaCrosse, BS (Mass Communications), 1970; University of Wisconsin, Madison, MS (Broadcast Journalism), 1993, PhD Studies in Cultural Geography. *Principal occupation*: TV news anchor/reporter). *Home address*: 7788 W. Old Sauk Rd., Verona, WI 53593 (608) 273-2727 (office). *Affiliations*: News Anchor, WKOW-TV (ABC), Madison, WI, 1982-; CEO, BragaVision (Video Production), Verona, WI, 1991-. *Other professional posts*: Lecturer (special topics), University of Wisconsin; lecturer & workshop coordinator, Wisconsin Department of Public Instruction. *Community activities*: Native American Center (board of directors); Dane County Chapter of American Red Cross (board of directors); UW Chancellor's Community Minority Advisory Committee; Madison Audubon Society; secretary, Native American Center Board of Directors; UW-Madison Native American Journalism Workshop Advisory Board; Mann Educational Opportunity Fund Advisory Board; Citizen Advisory Council of Dane County. *Memberships*: Native American Journalism Association; Society of Environmental Journalists; NAACP; Bad River Band of Lake Superior Tribe of Chippewa (Ojibway); Investigative Reporters & Editors, Inc. *Honors awards*: 1983 "Chris Award," Columbus (OH) Film Festival, Best Documentary; 1984 "Portland Mayor's Award," Portland, OR Mayor (award given annually by Mayor for best reporting on City projects); 1988 "Best News Report," Wisconsin Council o Developmental Disabilities; 1989 "Writer's Cup Award," Madison Professional Chapter of Women in Communication (best female print or broadcast journalist); 1990 "Iris" Nomination, National Association of Television Producers and Executives, best documentary for "A Throwaway Future"; 1991 "Isthmus Best," Isthmus Newspaper Reader's Poll "Best of Madison," Madison Magazine Reader's Poll; Board of Directors, Native American Center, Madison; 1992 Fellow, Howard Simons Fund for Native American Journalists. *Interests*: "My primary interest is American Indian Treaty Rights. I've produced several documentaries on Treaty Rights and Wisconsin Indians. I was a travel reporter for KATU-TV in Portland, OR, and have traveled extensively to Asia, Africa, Europe, Australia and Central America. My avocation is studying indigenous people and the environment. As a reporter for WKOW-TV, my "beat" is the environment." *Biographical sources*: Articles in the "Wisconsin State Journal," "Capital Times," "Isthmus," "Madison Magazine." *TV programs & documentaries*: "No Word For Goodbye" (Nov. 1987); "Throw Away Future" (May 1989); "Spring of Discontent" (May 1990); "Bitter Harvest (October 1993) all produced for Tak Communications.

*LOGAN, STELLA
(film producer)
Affiliation: Wyldfyre Video, Inc., P.O. Box 1256, Boulder, CO 80306 (303) 530-9440.

LOMAHAFTEWA, LINDA (Hopi) 1947-
(teacher, artist)
Born July 3, 1947, Phoenix, Ariz. *Education*: San Francisco Art Institute, BFA, 1970, MFA, 1971. *Principal occupation*: Teacher, artist. *Home address*: Route 11, Box 20 SP 59, Santa Fe, N.M. 87501. *Affiliation*: Assistant professor of Native

American Art, California State College, Rohnert Park, 1971-73; teacher, painting and drawing, Native American Studies, University of California, Berkeley, 1974-76; drawing and painting instructor, Institute of American Indian Arts, Santa Fe, 1976-. *Exhibitions*: Festival of Native American Art, Aspen Institute at Baca, 1982; Contemporary Native American Art, Gardiner Art Gallery, Oklahoma State University, Stillwater, Okla., 1983; Contemporary Native American Photography, Southern Plains Indian Museum, Anadarko, Okla., 1984; Shadows Caught Images of Native Americans, Gilcrease Museum, Tulsa, 1984; 2nd Annual Heard Invitational, Heard Museum, Phoenix, 1985; One Woman Exhibit, American Indian Contemporary Arts, San Francisco, 1985; Women of Sweetgrass, Cedar and Sage, Gallery of the American Indian Community House, New York, N.Y., 1985; The Art of the Native American, Owensboro Museum of Fine Arts, KY, 1985; Native to Native, Alchemie Gallery, Boston, 1986. *Community activities*: City of Santa Fe Arts Board. Memberships: San Francisco Art Institute Alumni Association; Institute of American Indian Arts Alumni Association. *Awards, honors*: Indian Festival of Arts - First Place Painting, La Grande, Oreg., 1974; 61st Annual Indian Market - Third Place Painting, Santa Fe, 1982. *Interests*: "Art- -displayed at the following permanent collections: Southern Plains Indian Museum, Anadarko, Okla.; Millicent Rogers Museum, Taos, N.M.; University of Lethbridge, Native American Studies Department, Alberta, Canada; Native American Center for the Living Arts, Inc., Niagara Falls, NY; American Indian Historical Society, San Francisco; Center for the Arts of Indian America, Washington, DC." *Biographical sources*: Who's Who in American Art, 1976; The Sweet Grass Lives on 50 Contemporary Native American Indian Artists, by Jamake Highwater (Lippincott, 1980); American Women Artists, by Charlotte Streifer Rubinstein (Avon, 1982); The World Who's Who of Women, Eighth Edition, 1984; Bearing Witness Sobreviviendo, An Anthology of Writing and Art by Native American/ Latina Women (Calyx: A Journal of Art and Literature by Women, Corvallis, Ore., 1984); The American West, The Modern Vision, by Patricia Janis Broder (Little, Brown, 1984).

LOMAWAIMA, K. TSIANINA (Creek) 1955-
(professor of anthropology)
Born March 30, 1955, Kansas. Education: Stanford University, MA, 1979, PhD, 1987. *Principal occupation*: Assistant professor. *Address*: University of Washington, Dept. of Anthropology, Seattle, WA (206) 543-4793 (office). *Affiliation*: Assistant professor, Dept. of Anthropology, American Indian Studies, University of Washington, Seattle, 1988-93. *Memberships*: Oklahoma Historical Society, 1986; National Indian Education Association, 1986-; American Society for Ethnohistory, 1987-. *Awards, honors*: Ford Doctoral Fellow, 1977-79; Dorothy Danforth Compton Fellow, 1984; grants for doctoral research. *Interests*: "History of American Indian education, especially experiences of native people in federal boarding schools. Preparing a manuscript for publication - oral history of Chilocco Indian Agricultural School (Chilocco, OK) 1920-40, compiled from interviews with alumni and staff." *Published works*: Articles only.

LONE FIGHT, EDWARD (Mandan-Hidatsa) 1939-
(BIA Indian education)
Born May 28, 1939, Elbowoods, N.D. *Education*: Dickinson State College, BS, 1964; Arizona State University, MA, 1970. *Principal occupation*: BIA Indian education. *Affiliations*: Supt., Riverside Indian School, Anadarko, OK; Indian education, BIA, Washington, DC; chairperson of education, BIA, Fort Berthold Agency, New Town, ND; former tribal chairperson, Three Affiliated Tribes of the Fort Berthold Reservation, New Town, ND; Supt., BIA, Mandaree Day School, Mandaree, ND, 1991-93. *Community activities*: Jaycees; Kiwanis Club. *Membership*: National Education Association.

*LONEFIGHT, TONY
(journalist)
Affiliation: Grand Forks Herald, P.O. Box 6008, Grand Forks, ND 58206 (701) 780-1228.

LONG, ALBERT (Blackfeet-Navajo) 1919-
(trader/craftsman)
Born September 9, 1919, Billings, Mont. *Education*: Los Angeles Art Center, 1946-48; received Graduate Gemologist diploma, 1967. *Principal occupation*: Trader/craftsman. *Address*: P.O. Box 40, Lake Havasu City, AZ 86405 (602) 453-5929. *Military service*: U.S. Marine Corps, 1941-45 (First Marine Division-Communications Specialist; Guadalcanal and New Britain campaigns). *Membership*: Master Gemology Association. *Interests*: "Having worked both silver and gold, many times using non-traditional gemstones such as opals & diamonds, his work has appeared in "Arizona Highways" magazine and in numerous juried shows including the Scottsdale National and the Inter-Tribal Ceremonial in Galup. Now, semi-retired, he plans to work on shows for his many trader friends and be involved with organizations such as the Inter-Tribal Ceremonial Association as well as other museums and foundations showing exclusive Native American arts and crafts. He is available for craft judging in juried shows of Native American crafts. He is no longer accepting commissions on his jewelry, however, he still offers his assistance to former customers and serious collectors."

*LONG, LOREN L. (*Great Eagle*)
(Quachita of Arkansas) 1922-
(electrical design engineer-retired)
Born May 13, 1922, Union County, Iowa. *Education*: Southwest Community College (Creston, IA), AA; San Diego State University, BS. *Principal occupation*: Electrical design engineer (retired). *Home address*: 216 Virginia Lane, Hot Springs National Park, AR 71901 (501) 525-9927. *Professional post*: Grand Head Vice-Chief, Quachita Indians of Arkansas. *Military service*: U.S. Marines, 1941-45, 1950-51, 1953-56.

*LONG STANDING BEAR CHIEF
(editor)
Affiliation: "Spirit Talk," P.O. Box 430, Blackfoot Nation, Browning, MT 59417 (406) 338-2882.

LONG, SUSIE (Yurok)
(tribal chairperson)
Affiliation: Yurok Tribal Council, 517 Third St., Suite 21, Eureka, CA 95501 (707) 444-0433.

LONGBRAKE, FAYE
(school principal)
Affiliations: Bridger Day School, Howes, SD 57748 (605) 538-4313; Cherry Creek Day School, Cherry Creek, SD 57622 (605) 538-4238.

LONGCROW, BARBARA
(school principal/teacher)
Affiliation: White Horse Day School, P.O. Box 7, White Horse, SD 57661 (605) 733-2183.

LONGFISH, GEORGE C.
(Iroquois-Seneca/Tuscarora) 1942-
(professor/artist)
Born August 22, 1942, Oshweken, Ontario, Can. *Education*: School of the Art Institute of Chicago, BFA (Painting, Sculpture), 1970; and MFA, (Filmmaking), 1972. *Principal occupation*: Professor/artist. *Home address*: 3025 Concord Place, Davis, CA 95616 (916) 752-6567 (work). *Affiliations*: Director of the graduate program in American Indian Art, University of Montana, Missoula, 1972-73; professor in Native American Studies, University of California, Davis, 1973-. *Other professional post*: Director, Carl Nelson Gorman Museum, 2401 Hart Hall, Native American Studies, University of California, Davis, CA. *Awards, honors*: Numerous awards and prizes throughout the years for his work. *Interests*: Contemporary Native American art; attended over 170 art exhibitions exhibiting paintings, sculpture & film; art lectures. *Biographical sources*: Cited in Jamake Highwater (Ed.) The Sweet Grass Lives On: Fifty Contemporary North American Indian Artists (Lippincott & Crowell); cited in "Horizon", Sept. 1980. *Publications*: Numerous articles; Book: with J. Smith - Personal Symbols: Recent Paintings and Works on Paper (U. of Northern Iowa, 1986).

*LOOKING ELK, ALEX (Standing Rock Sioux)
(radio project manager)
Affiliation: KAEN - 89.5 FM, Standing Rock Sioux Radio Project, P.O. Box D, Fort Yates, ND 58538 (701) 854-7226.

LOPEMAN, DAVID (Squaxin Island)
(tribal chairperson)
Affiliation: Squaxin Island Tribal Council, S.E. 70, Squaxin Lane, Shelton, WA 98584 (206) 426-9781.

*LOPEZ, DAYNE E.
(editor)
Affiliation: "Native American Connections," Gloria J. Davis, Publisher, P.O. Box 579, Winchester, CA 92596 (909) 926-1728.

*LOPEZ, ELEANOR (Yurok)
(rancheria chairperson)
Affiliation: Lytton Rancheria, P.O. Box 7882, Santa Rosa, CA 95407 (707) 537-1655.

*LORAN, JOHN (St. Regis Mohawk)
(tribal head chief)
Affiliation: St. Regis Mohawk Council Chiefs, RR 1, Box 14C, Hogansburg, NY 13655 (518) 358-2272.

LORENCE, ROBERT J.
(college president)
Affiliation: Northwest Indian College, 2522 Kwina Rd., Bellingham, WA 98226 (206) 676-2772/3.

*LORENZO, PAULA (Wintun)
(rancheria chairperson)
Affiliation: Rumsey Rancheria, P.O. Box 18, Brooks, CA 95606 (916) 796-3400.

LOTTIS, WILLIAM
(organization director)
Affiliation: North American Indian Mission Ministries, P.O. Box 151, Point Roberts, WA 98281 (604) 946-1227.

LOUDNER, GODFREY, Jr.
(Crow Creek Sioux) 1946-
(mathematics instructor)
Born September 30, 1946, Fort Thompson, S.D. *Education*: Black Hills State College, BS; South Dakota School of Mines and Technology, MS; University of Notre Dame, PhD (Mathematics), 1974. *Principal occupation*: Mathematics instructor, Sinte Gleska College, Rosebud, S.D. *Home address*: Box 432, Mission, SD 57555. *Memberships*: American Mathematics Society. *Interests*: Professional: "lie groups, differential geometry, harmonic analysis; mountain climbing, cave exploration. Working on monograph about Automonophic Forms With Applications."

LOUIE, GENE
(Indian band chief)
Affiliation: Sliammon Indian Band, RR 2, Sliammon Rd., Powell River, British Columbia, Canada V8A 4Z3 (604) 483-9646.

LOUIE, LOUIS
(Indian band chief)
Affiliation: Iskut Indian Band, General Delivery, Iskut, BC, Canada V0J 1K0 (604) 234-3331.

LOUIE, ROBERT
(Indian band chief)
Affiliation: Westbank Indian Band, 515 Highway 97 South, Kelowna, British Columbia, Canada V1Z 3J2 (604) 769-5666.

LOUIE, WAYNE
(Indian band chief)
Affiliation: Lower Kootenay Indian band, Box 1107, Creston, British Columbia, Canada V0B 1G0 (604) 428-4428.

LOUIS, ROY
(association president)
Affiliation: Indian Assn. of Alberta, P.O. Box 516, Winterburn, AB, Can. T0E 2N0 (403) 470-5751.

LOUTTIT, REG
(Indian band chief)
Affiliation: Attawapiskat Indian Band, Box 248, Attawapiskat, Ontario, Canada P0L 2H0 (705) 997-2166.

LOVATO, ERNEST (Santo Domingo Pueblo)
(Pueblo governor)
Affiliation: Santo Domingo Pueblo Council, P.O. Box 99, Santo Domingo, NM 87052 (505) 465-2214.

LOVATO, MANUELITA
(museum curator)
Affiliation: Institute of American Arts Museum, P.O. Box 20007, Santa Fe, NM 87504 (505) 988-6463.

*LOWE, LINDA
(health clinic administrator)
Affiliation: Eufaula Indian Health Clinic, 800 Forest Ave., Eufaula, OK 7432 (918) 689-2547.

LOWE, PATRICIA
(librarian)
Affiliation: Will Rogers Memorial Library, P.O. Box 157, Claremore, OK 74018 (918) 341-0719.

*LOWE, PHYLLIS
(health services director)
Affiliation: St. Croix Health Services, P.O. Box 287, Hertel, WI 54845 (715) 349-2195.

LOWERY, JINNIE (Lumbee) 1953-
(health administrator)
Born February 21, 1953, Robeson County, N.C. *Education*: Pembroke State University, Pembroke, NC, B.A., 1978; UNC-Chapel Hill, NC, MSPH, 1982. *Principal occupation*: Health administrator. *Home address*: Route 10, Box 915, Lumberton, NC 28358 (919) 738-4713. *Affiliations*: Associate director, 1986-91, executive director, 1991-, Robeson Health Care Corporation, Pembroke, NC; business manager, Lumbee Medical Center, Pembroke, NC, 1989-. *Community activities*: Founding member and past secretary of the Robeson County Dispute Resolution Center, 1988-; founding member and past president of the Robeson County Rape Crisis Center; past board member of the Lumbee Regional Development Association's Head Start Policy Council; member of Harper's Ferry Baptist Church; member of Steering Committee of the Health Access Coalition. *Memberships*: American Public Health Association; North Carolina Primary Health Care Association (past secretary, current vice-president of board of directors); National Association of Community Health Centers; National Association for Female Executives; National Geographic Society. *Awards, honors*: Graduated Magna Cum Laude - Pembroke State University, 1978; Recognized by Robeson County Rural Development Panel for Volunteer Service and Leadership in development of the Rape Crisis Center; Invited to be listed in the The World Who's Who of Women; member of North Carolina Kappa Chapter of Alpha Chi Honor Society; recipient of the Indian Health Scholarship.

LOWRY, IRENE
(association director)
Affiliation: North American Indian Association of Detroit, Inc., 22720 Plymouth Rd., Detroit, MI 48239 (313) 535-2966.

LOWRY, JOE P. 1943-
(Indian shop owner)
Born January 13, 1943, Raton, N.M. *Address*: P.O. Box 10314, Albuquerque, NM 87184 (505) 898-1623. *Affiliation*: Owner, Zach-Low, Inc., Albuquerque, NM. *Membership*: Indian Arts & Crafts Association (IACA), 1974- (board of directors, 1978-; secretary, 1980; president, 1981). *Awards, honors*: IACA Member of the Year, 1980. *Interests*: "I have been involved in the turquoise business many years. As a charter member of IACA, I have been actively involved in developing the wholesale markets, and setting standards for arts & crafts. I have given seminars all over the country to business and groups to educate, specifically on turquoise and jewelry, and recogniizing natural stones and genuine Indian handmade jewelry. I have worked with the Indian Crafts Board in Washington, D.C., through Geoff Stamm, to coordinate IACA and ICB in defining standards. I have served on the membership, market, and ethics committees of the IACA for many years, chairing the membership committee in 1978, and chairing the market committee from 1987-89." *Biographical sources*: Articles - "Shell Is No Stranger to Indians," and "Man's Romance with Turquoise" (Indian Trader, June & September 1979); article, "Turquoise , The Sky Colored Stone," by Steve Brewer (Albuquerque Journal, May 20, 1990).

LUCAS, MERLE R. (Sioux) 1944-
(administrator)
Born June 9, 1944, Vanport City, Ore. *Education*: Northern Montana College, 1963-64. *Principal occupation*: Administrator. *Address*: P.O. Box 850, Browning, MT 59417 (406) 652-3113 (work). *Affiliations*: Director, Native American Studies, Carroll College, Helena, MT (1 year); associate professor, Native American Studies, Blackfeet Community College, Browning, MT (2 years); coordinator of Indian affairs, State of Montana, State Capitol, Helena, MT (9 years); associate planner, Dept.of Planning & Economic Development, State of MT (3 years); executive director, Montana Inter-Tribal Policy Board, Browning, MT, 1983-. *Military service*: U.S. Army Airborne, 1965-68 (E-5; Bronze Star; Army Commendation Medal with one Oak Leaf; Purple Heart; National Defense Service Medal; Vietnam Service Medal with 3 Bronze Service Stars; Republic of Vietnam Campaign Medal). *Community activities*: Helena Indian Center (president, 3 years); MT United Indian Association, Helena (treasurer, 2 years). *Memberships*: Governors Inter-State Indian Council, 1973-82; MT Indian Education Association; MT Indian Education Advisory Board, 1985-. *Awards, honors*: Outstanding Vietnam Era Veteran (1977) of the Nation for outstanding contributions shown to the community, state, and nation since returning to civilian life, No Greater Love Organization, Washington, D.C. *Biographical sources*: Western Business Magazine article concerning economic development for Montana reservations; periodic news articles concerning Indian issues relating to Native Americans in Montana. *Published works*: Profile of Montana Native American (State of Montana, 1974); Annual Report of the Governors' Interstate Indian Council Conference, 1979.

*LUCAS, PHIL (Choctaw)
(film/video producer)
Affiliation: Institute of American Indian Arts, Communications Arts Department, CSF Campus, St. Michael's Dr., Santa Fe, NM 87501 (505) 984-2365. An independent film/video producer for mor than two decades, established his own production company in 1980. He has worked on productions with many tribes. His classic "Images of Indians" television series (1979) called to detailed account the damning misrepresentations of Indian character & tradition in American popular culture. He was honored for Lifetime Achievement at the October 1991 Two Rivers Native Film & Video Festival.

*LUCERO, ALVINO (Isleta Pueblo)
(pueblo governor)
Affiliation: Isleta Pueblo Council, P.O. Box 1270, Isleta, NM 87022 (505) 869-3111.

LUCERO, LUCILLE (Miwok)
(tribal representative)
Affiliation: Buena Vista Rancheria, 4650 Coalmine Rd., Ione, CA 95640.

LUCERO, RICHARD, Jr. *(Morning Star)*
(Mescalero Apache/Seminole) 1944-
(entrepreneur, minority business consultant)
Born September 24, 1944, Billings, Mont. *Education*: University of Wyoming, 1963-66; Eastern Montana College, 1966-67; Rocky Mountain College (Billings), BA (Psychology), 1968. *Principal occupation*: Entrepreneur; minority business consultant. *Home address*: 3733 Magnolia Dr., Grand Prairie, TX 75052 (214) 421-1121 (work). *Affiliations*: Psychology technician, Veterans Administration, Psychiatric Hospital, Sheridan, WY, 1971-72; director, Alcoholism Treatment and Recovery Program, San Acadio, CO, 1972-74; director, Alcoholism Family Services Division, Weld Mental Health Center, Inc., Greeley, CO, 1974-77; director, Drug Abuse Services Project, Mental Health Center of Boulder County, Inc., Boulder, Colo., 1977-78; associate professor, University of Northern Colorado, 1977-78; director, Montana United Indian Association, Health Dept., Helena, MT, 1978-80; executive director, Dallas Inter-Tribal Center, 1980-89; director of Minority Affairs, Greater Dallas Chamber of Commerce, 1990-92; president, CEO, American International Materials (distribution for metal welding supplies), 1992-; vice-president, Capital Concepts (financial management/college scholarships), 1992-; president/CEO, Dialogue Resources (marketing-advertising-consulting to health care professionals attorneys), 1994-; president, Morning Star Consulting Services (develop contracts for small minority businesses with corporations in; provide diversity seminars to state institutions & businesses; help develop minority employment & minority vendor contracts for public & private businesses, 1994-; president/CEO, Finite Ventures Unlimited (marketing, product development, distribution, consulting services), 1994-. *Other professional posts*: Minority Business Consultant to Dallas/Ft. Worth Minority Business Development Council; representative-associate to Hayne Company (air/water filtration products). *Community activities*: Colorado Alcohol and Drug Treatment Committee (member, 1976-78); Indian Health Planners Task Force, (advisory committee, 1978-79; chairman, 1979-80; compiled, edited and wrote the National Urban Specific Health Plan submitted to the Secretary of Health and Human Services); Youth Advisory Committee, Fort McKenzie Veterans Administration Psychiatric Hospital (chairman, 1970-72); Multi-Ethnic Heritage Foundation (board of directors, 1991); Dallas HELPS (board of directors, 1991); JUST-IN-TIME Work & Housing/ Dallas (chairperson, Advisory Board, 1991); Dallas Hispanic Chamber of Commerce Business Development Committee, 1991; Mental Health, Mental Retardation Advisory Committee; Dallas Police Academy Cultural Awareness Training Committee. *Memberships*: Colorado Association of Professional Alcoholism Counselors, Inc. (member of committee that developed state certification standards); American Indian Health Care Association (chairman, Region VII, Health Directors Board, 1982-84; treasurer, 1983-84; president, 1984-); Dallas Council on Alcoholism and Drug Abuse (board member, 1988-); American College of Healthcare Executives (nominee 1989); Greater Dallas Community Relations Commission (board of directors, 1989, 1st vice-chair, chairperson-Health and Human Services Committee); Society for Advancement of Chicanos and Native Americans in Science; Texas American Indian Chamber of Commerce;

National Minority Contractors Association (charter board member, 1994); New Image Business Associates (advisory member). *Awards, honors*: Recipient of Superior Performance Award, 1970, Public Relations Award, 1972, Fort McKenzie V.A. Psychiatric Hospital, Sheridan, Wyo.; guest speaker, National Council on Alcoholism Annual Conference, 1974; appointed by President Gerald Ford to serve on National Drug Abuse and Adolescents Task Force, 1977; developed special proposal to provide therapeutic community treatment center for Eastern Colorado; "Leadership Dallas" Graduate 1988 - Dallas Chamber of Commerce Program for Selected Community Leaders; "Dallas Together" - committee member, selected by Dallas Mayor to recommend ways to diffuse racial tensions in Dallas, 1988-89; Outstanding Board Member Award for community contributions; 1989 Greater Dallas Community Relations Commission for "Outstanding Leadership"; 1989 1st Annual Leadership Awards sponsored by Dallas Chapter of American Muslim Commission; recipient, Community Service Award, 1991, Senator Eddie Bernice Johnson. *Interests*: "Minority business development, minority employment; political and economic enfranchisement in Dallas metro area; enhanced police/community relationship, access to college education for capable students of color; avocational interests include: music, tennis, coaching baseball, and reading." *Published works*: Minority Business Development Handbook, 1991 and Minority Personnel Enhancement Handbook, 1992 (Greater Dallas Chamber of Commerce).

LUHMAN, FRED
(associate commissioner)
Affiliation: Office of the American Indian, Alaskan Native & Native Hawaiian Programs, U.S. Dept. of Health & Human Servics, Humphrey Bldg., 330 Independence Ave., SW, Washington, DC 20201 (202) 619-2957.

*LUJAN, FRED R. (Pueblo)
(BIA agency supt.)
Affiliation: Southern Pueblos Agency, Bureau of Indian Affairs, P.O. Box 1667, Albuquerque, NM 87103 (505) 766-3020.

LUJAN, JOE M. (Sandia Pueblo)
(Pueblo governor)
Affiliation: Sandia Pueblo Tribal Council, P.O. Box 6008, Bernalillo, NM 87004 (505) 867-3317.

*LUJAN, PHIL
(professor of Native American studies)
Affiliation: Native American Studies Program, University of Oklahoma, 455 W. Lindsey, Rm. 804, Norman, OK 73019 (405) 325-2312.

LUKE, CHRIS (Kootenay)
(Indian band chief)
Affiliation: Lower Kootenay Indian Band, Box 1107, Creston, British Columbia, Canada V0B 1G0 (604) 428-4428.

LUKE, GERALD
(Indian band chief)
Affiliation: Mattagami Indian Band, Box 99, Gogama, Ontario, Canada P0M 1W0 (705) 894-2072.

LUMSDEN, JOSEPH K. (Chippewa) 1934-
(educational administration)
Born October 10, 1934, Sault Ste. Marie, Mich. *Education*: Michigan Technological University,

BS, 1967; Northern Michigan University, Teaching Certificate, 1969. *Principal occupation*: Educational administration. *Home address*: 1101 Johnston St., Sault Ste. Marie, MI 49783. *Affiliation*: Sault Ste Marie Tribe of Chippewa Indians, 1973-. *Military service*: U.S. Marine Corps, 1953-56 (Corporal). *Community activities*: Michigan Fishery Advisory Committee (chairman); Chippewa-Ottawa Fishery Management Authority. *Memberships*: National Congress of American Indians; National Tribal Chairman's Association. *Awards, honors*: Recognition of Leadership & Achievement, Bureau of Indian Affairs, 1984.

*LUNDERMAN, EILEEN
(center director)
Affiliation: Sicangu Enterprise Center, P.O. Box 205, Mission, SD 57555 (605) 856-2955.

LUNDY, PAUL A. (Cheyenne River Sioux) 1944-
(environmental engineer)
Born August 30, 1944, Sioux Falls, S.D. *Education*: South Dakota School of Mines & Technology, BS, 1967. *Principal occupation*: Environmental engineer). *Home address*: 4316 Phoenix St., Ames, IA 50014 (515) 292-5255. *Affiliations*: Project engineer, Iowa Dept. of Transportation, Ames, 1967-80; Environmental engineer, Iowa Dept. of Natural Resources, Des Moines, 1980-. *Military service*: U.S. Army, 1967-69; U.S. Army Reserve, 1969-87 (retired as Major; Humanitarian Service Medal, 1980; Army Achievement Medal, 1986). *Community activities*: Ames Council of PTAs (president, 1978); Ames Municipal Band (vice-president, 1987-); Boy Scouts of America, 1967- (assistant District Commissioner, Broken Arrow District, Mid-Iowa Council). *Memerbship*: American Indian Science and Engineering Society, 1982-. *Awards, honors*: Distinguished Toastmaster, Toastmaster International, in 1974; Public Service Award by American Radio Relay League in 1972 & '79 for emergency communications handled. *Interests*: Amateur Radio; music (play sax and clarinet); railroading/model railroading (charter member of the Kate Shelley Division, 1992) of the National Model Railroad Association; history/genealogy. *Vocational*: Transportation and environmental engineering. *Biographical source*: Article in American Indian Scientist & Engineers, Vol. I, 1985.

LUPE, RONNIE (Apache)
(tribal chairperson)
Affiliations: White Mountain Apache Tribal Council, P.O. Box 700, Whiteriver, AZ 85941 (602) 338-4346; chairperson, Theodore Roosevelt School, Fort Apache, AZ.

LURIE, NANCY OESTREICH 1924-
(anthropologist)
Born January 29, 1924, Milwaukee, Wisc. *Education*: University of Wisconsin, Madison, BA, 1945; University of Chicago, MA, 1947; Northwestern University, PhD, 1952. *Principal occupation*: Anthropology Curator, Milwaukee Public Museum. *Home address*: 3342 N. Gordon Place, Milwaukee, WI 53212 (414) 964-8222; 278-2772 (office). *Affiliations*: Instructor, anthropology and sociology, University of Wisconsin, Milwaukee, 1947-49, 1951-53; research associate, North American ethnology, Peabody Museum, Harvard University, 1954-56; consultant and expert witness for law firms representing tribal clients before the U.S. Indian Claims Com-

mission, 1954-; lecturer in anthropology, Rackham School of Graduate Studies Extension Service, University of Michigan, 1956-61; lecturer in anthropology, School of Public Health, University of Michigan, 1959-61; assistant coordinator, American Indian Chicago Conference, University of Chicago, 1960-61; associate professor of anthropology, University of Wisconsin, Milwaukee, 1963; Fulbright appointment (lectureship, University of Aarhus, Denmark) involved teaching a course on the American Indian and a course on applied anthropology, 1964-65; professor, 1965-, dept. chair, 1967-70, adjunct professor, 1973-, Dept. of Anthropology, University of Wisconsin, Milwaukee; Curator of Anthropology, Milwaukee Public Museum, 1973-. *Community activities*: Wisconsin Historic Sites Preservation Board, 1972-79; Wisconsin Humanities Committee, NEH, 1981-83; served on various review panels for National Endowments for the Humanities and Arts; Action Anthropology projects with Wisconsin tribes and Milwaukee intertribal community. *Memberships*: American Anthropological Association (president, 1983-85); American Ethnological Society; American Society for Ethnohistory; Wisconsin Archaeological Society; Central States Anthropological Society (president, 1967); Council for Museum Anthropology; American Association of Museums; Sigma Xi; Society for Applied Anthropology; Wisconsin Academy of Science, Arts, and Letters; American Association fo the Advancement of Science; International Congress of Anthropological and Ethnological Sciences; member of editorial board of Northeast Vol. 15 of Handbook of North American Indians. *Awards, honors*: Award of Merit for Mountain Wolf Woman, American Society for State and Local History, 1962; Saturday Review Anisfield Wolf Award with co-editor for The American Indian Today, 1968; Woman of the Year, Milwaukee Municipal Women's Club, 1975; Honorary Doctorate of Letters, Northland College, Ashland, Wis., 1976; Increase Lapham Medal, Wisconsin Archaeological Society, 1977; Merit Award, Northwestern University Alumni Association, 1982; several awards for publications, including A Special Style: The Milwaukee Public Museum 1882-1982, from Wisconsin State Historical Society, 1985, and from Milwaukee County Historical Society, 1984; Award of Merit, Wisconsin Academy of Sciences, Arts, & Letters, 1984, Fellow, 1987; Wisconsin Winnebago for writings on tribal history and culture; Honorary Doctorate, Northland College. Interests: Ethnological research Wisconsin and Nebraska Winnebago; Dogrib Indians (Northwest Territory, Canada), Menominee; Consultant and Expert Witness, U.S. Indian Claims Commission, Court of Claims, and lower courts for eight different tribes; lecturer on museology, 6 weeks, Norway; attended international anthropology meetings USSR, Japan, Mexico, etc. *Biographical sources*: Marquis Who's Who; Women Anthropologists (University of Illinois Press). Published works: Editor, Mountain Wolf Woman, Sister of Crashing Thunder (University of Michigan Press, 1961); The Substance Economy of the Dogrib Indians of Lac La Marte, Canadian Northwest Territories, with June Helm (Northern Research and Coordination Centre, Ottawa, 1961); editor, with Stuart Levine, The American Indian Today (Everett/Edwards Press, 1968; Penguin, 1970); editor, with Eleanor B. Leacock, The North American Indian in Historical Perspective (Random House, 1971, Waveland Press reprint, 1988); Wisconsin Indians (State Historical So-

ciety of Wisconsin, 1980); A Special Style: The Milwaukee Public Museum, 1882-1982 (Milwaukee Public Museum, 1982); North American Indian Lives (Milwaukee Public Museum, 1985); co-editor and contributed chapter, North American Indians in Historical Perspective (Waveland Press, 1988).

LUTZ, DIXON
(Indian band chief)
Affiliation: Liard River Indian Band, Box 328, Watson Lake, Yukon, Canada Y1A 1C0 (403) 536-2131.

LYALL, PAT
(Indian corporation president)
Affiliation: Nunasi Corporation, 280 Albert St., Suite 902, Ottawa, Ontario, Canada K1A 5G8 (613) 238-4981.

LYLES, RAY
(health center director)
Affiliation: Hugo Health Center, P.O. Box 340, Hugo, OK 74743 (405) 326-7561.

*LYNCH, ARCHIE
(editor)
Affiliation: "Smoke Signals," Baltimore American Indian Center, 113 S. Broadway, Baltimore, MD 21231 (410) 675-3535.

*LYNCH, MARLENE
(association president)
Affiliation: Native American Finance Officers Association, P.O. Box 170, Fort Defiance, AZ 86504 (602) 729-6218.

LYNN, SHARON
(BIA Indian education)
Affiliation: Branch of Supplementatl Services, Bureau of Indian Affairs, MS: 3512-MIB, 1849 C St., N.W., Washington, DC 20240 (202) 208-6364.

LYONS, OREN
(publisher)
Affiliation: Daybreak (quarterly newspaper), P.O. Box 315, Williamsville, NY 14231 (607) 272-1749.

Mc

McADAMS, GARY (Wichita)
(tribal committee president)
Affiliation: Wichita Executive Committee, P.O. Box 729, Anadarko, OK 73005 (405) 247-2425.

McALLESTER, DAVID P. (Narragansett) 1916-
(professor-retired)
Born August 6, 1916, Everett, Mass. *Education*: Harvard University, BA, 1938; Columbia University, PhD, 1949. *Principal occupation*: Professor-retired. *Home address*: Star Route 62, Box 40, Monterey, MA 01245. *Affiliations*: Professor of anthropology and music, Wesleyan University, Middletown, CT, 1947-86 (retired). *Other professional posts*: Visiting professor, Yale University, University of Hawaii; University of Sydney and University of Queensland, Australia; consultant, American Folklife Festival, Smithsonian Institution, Washington, DC, 1975-76; one of the founders and secretary-treasurer, editor, and president of Society for Ethnomusicology. *Community activities*: Valley View Hospital (advisory board); a founder of

Middletown Friends Meeting and South Berkshire Friends Meeting. Memberships: Society for Ethnomusicology (secretary-treasurer, editor, president, 1953-); American Anthropological Association (Fellow), 1949-1976; American Academy of Arts and Sciences, 1968-; Institute of American Indian Archaeology, Washington, Conn. (trustee, 1976-). Awards, honors: Social Science Research Council Grant, 1950; Guggenheim Foundation Fellowship, 1957-58 (study Navajo religion); National Science Foundation Grants, 1963-65 (study Navajo religion); J.D.R. III Foundation Grant, 1971; National Endowment for the Humanities Grant, 1976; Fulbright Foundation (senior lecturer in Australia), 1978; Tokyo National Research Institute of Cultural Properties (lecture), 1980. *Interests*: Studies of American Indian ceremonialism, music, folklore, mythology, religious literature. Field work with Navajos, Apaches, Zunis, Passamaquoddies, Penobscots, Comanches, Hopis. Canoeing, hiking, mountain-climbing, camping. Musical performance of Native American songs. *Biographical source*: Autobiographical sketch in a Festschrift, "Explorations in Ethnomusicology, edited by Charlotte Frisbie (Detroit, 1986). *Published works*: Peyote Music (Viking Fund, 1949); Enemy Way Music (Peabody Museum, 1954); Myth & Prayers of the Great Star Chant (Wheelwright Museum, 1956); Indian Music of the Southwest (Taylor Museum, 1961); Reader in Ethnomusicology (Johnson Reprint, 1971); Navajo Blessingway Singer, with Charlotte Frisbie (University of Arizona, 1978); Hogans: Navajo Houses & House Songs, with Susan McAllester, (Wesleyan University, 1980); other monographs and pamphlets; about sixty articles and other contributions. Recordings: Music of the American Indian, 12 LP with pamphlet (Litton Educational Publishing, 1978); Music of the Pueblos, Apache, and Navajo, with Don N. Brown, 12 LP with 7-page pamphlet, texts, photographs (Taylor Museum, 1962); Navajo Creation Chants, five 10 78 rpm records, with pamphlet (Peabody Museum, 1952).

*McALISTER, DIANE
(editor)
Affiliation: "Native American Connection," Spotted Horse Tribal Gifts, P.O. Box 414, Coos Bay, OR 97420.

McBRIDE, CAROL
(Indian band chief)
Affiliation: Temiskaming (Algonquin) Indian Band, Box 336, Notre-Dame du Nord, Quebec, Canada J0Z 3B0 (819) 723-2335.

McBRIDE, MARY (San Felipe Pueblo) 1948-
(high school principal)
Born June 3, 1948, Albuquerque, N.M. *Education*: Eastern New Mexico University, Portales, BS, 1971; New Mexico Highlands University, Las Vegas, MA, 1982. *Principal occupation*: High school principal, BIA, Isleta Pueblo, NM, 1984-. *Home address*: P.O. Box 751, Algodones, NM 87001 (505) 867-4766; 867-2388 (work). *Affiliations*: Elementary school principal, B.I.A., Isleta Pueblo, NM, 1984-86; high school principal, Bernalillo School District, Bernalillo, NM, 1986-. *Memberships*: Phi Delta Kappa, 1987-; Delta Kappa Gamma Society International, 1988-; National Education Association, 1990-. *Awards, honors*: Graduate Professional Opportunity Program. *Interests*: "I will be on leave of absence for a year to work on a MA in counseling for AT RISK youth."

*McCAIN, JOHN
(U.S. Senator, R-AZ)
Affiliation: Chairperson, Senate Select Committee on Indian Affairs, 838 Hart Senate Office Bldg., Washington, DC 20510 (202) 224-2251.

McCARTAN, KATHLEEN (Mohawk/Oneida) 1963-
(naval flight officer)
Born in 1963, Clarence, N.Y. *Education*: U.S. Naval Academy, BS, 1985. *Principal occupation*: Naval flight officer, U.S. Navy. At the Acadmy, she was editor of a literary magazine, president of the Bicycle Racing Club; san in the Glee Club and Choir and the Messiah Church group; she rowed on the crew team for two years. She is a qualified navigator and an Airborne Communications Officer. She has flown the T-34 C, and T-43. She currently flies the EC-130, an aircraft from Oahu, Hawaii.

McCARTHY, JOAN DOLORES *(Sun Dancer)*
(Blackfoot-Bear Clan) 1935-
(shop owner)
Born January 14, 1935, Easton, Penna. Education: Churchman's Business College (Easton, PA). *Principal occupation*: Reservation trader. *Home address*: 1500 Eddy St., Merritt Island, FL 32952 (407) 631-0092 (work). *Affiliation*: Family owns four shops: "This N' That," Cocoa Village, FL, 1975-; "Rags to Riches," Cocoa Village, FL--authentic Native American jewelry and crafts; "Sundancer Gallery, Cocoa Village, FL; and "Spare Time Hobby Shop," Cocoa Village, FL. "I'm known as Sun Dancer woman who keeps spirits together and bright, and bringer of light (lightening the soul or spiritual healing). (I) started business on my own as a single parent with three children to raise--no outside help or child support." *Community activities*: Counsel Native Americans on their rights, on or off the reservation, the business or schooling open to them, water rights, etc.; give speeches to youth groups, all sorts of organizations; display in libraries, schools, and banks; guidance counselor - troubled teens of Brevard County; swimming instructor for handicapped and retarded citizens; and water safety instructor for American Red Cross, Miami, FL; crisis home/assisted Brevard Sheriff Rollin Zimmerman with benefits for teens, runaways-delinquents, etc.; assisted aid to several emergency charities. *Memberships*: Brevard County, Merritt Island, FL Chamber of Commerce; Big Mountain Legal Fund, Flagstaff, AZ; Kuwaiti Legal Fund, Cocoa Village, FL; Pioneer Women of Brevard Co. *Awards, honors*: Art awards in silversmithing, pen and ink, watercolors, copper and enamel work, and sketching; Pioneer Women of Brevard - Entrepreneur in 6 businesses; Brevard County Board of Education Award for donations to local high schools. *Interests*: "Native American Rights including helping young artists to merchandise their products; helping young artists to seek grants; water rights on several reserves: Taos, Zuni, Ft. McDowell Apache Reservation; Big Mountain Legal Aid for displaced Native Americans (land disputes-Navajo, Mohawk). My desire is to give back the pride to the Native American encouraging them to protect their culture; travel to all the Southwestern reservations." *Biographical source*: The Department of Interior Source Directory; American Indian Index; article in Warpath, monthly newsletter, 1988-89; Who's Who in the Indian World; Today newspaper; Tribune; Larry King Show; Brevard Pioneer Women..

McCAULEY, CECE
(Indian band chief)
Affiliation: Inuvik Native Indian band, Box 2570, Inuvik, Northwest Territories, Canada X0E 0T0 (403) 979-3344.

*McCAY, WILLIAM JAMES IRONTAIL
(Eastern Cherokee) 1925-
(master electrician)
Born October 1, 1925, Pensacola, Fla. *Home address*: 1765 Woodchuck Ave., Pensacola, FL 32504 (904) 484-9292. *Affiliation*: Executive director, Intertribal Council of American Indians, Inc., 1765 Woodchuck Ave., Pensacola, FL 32504 (904) 484-9292.

McCLANAHAN, ALEXANDRA
(editor & pblisher)
Affiliation: The Tundra Times, Eskimo, Indian, Aleut Publishing Co., P.O. Box 92247, Anchorage, AK 99509 (907) 274-2512.

McCLELLAND. JOHN
(organization chairperson)
Affiliation: Native Amerian Coalition of Tulsa, Inc., 1740 West 41st St., Tulsa, OK 74107 (918) 446-8432.

McCLINTOCK, CAROLYN
(hospital director)
Affiliation: Barrow PHS Alaska Native Hospital, Barrow, AK 99723 (907) 852-4611.

McCLOUD, JANET
(center director)
Affiliation: Northwest Indian Women's Circle, P.O. Box 8279, Tacoma, WA 98408 (206) 458-7610.

*McCLURE, ELMIRA
(center director)
Affiliation: St. Augustine's Center, 4512 N. Sheridan Rd., Chicago, IL 60640 (312) 814-1050.

McCLURE, RUSSELL (Sioux)
(BIA agency supt.)
Affiliation: Cheyenne River Agency, Bureau of Indian Affairs, P.O. Box 325, Eagle Butte, SD 57625 (605) 964-6611.

McCOMBS, SOLOMON (Creek) 1913-
(artist,)
Born May 17, 1913, Eufaula, Okla. *Education*: Bacone College, 1931-37; Tulsa University, 1943. *Principal occupation*: Artist. *Home address*: 3238 East 3rd St., Tulsa, OK 74104. *Affiliation*: Foreign service reserve officer, U.S. Dept. of State, Washington, DC, 1966-73; former vice-chief, Creek Nation of Oklahoma. *Other professional posts*: Board of directors, American Indian National Bank, Washington, DC, 1973-75; lifetime member of board of directors, designed bank logo. Served as a member of the Subcommittee on Indian participation during President Johnson's and President Nixon's Inaugural parades--supervised the construction of four American Indian floats. *Memberships*: National Congress of American Indians, 1965-; Five Civilized Tribes (council member, Inter-Tribal Council; chaplain, 1976-); National Council of the Creek Nation (speaker, 1976-); CWYW Club of Tulsa (lifetime member, 1977-). *Awards, honors*: Five Civilized Tribes Museum Seal, 1955; Waite Phillips Special Indian Artists Award for contributions in Indian Art over a period of five years, Philbrook Art Center, Tulsa, 1965; Grand

Award, Philbrook Art Center, 1965; Grand and Gran Masters Award, 1965, '70, '73, '77; Army Award (commissioned to paint depicting one of the American Indian Congressional Medal of Honor recipients of World War II in battle), Washington, DC, 1976; First Prize Awards, All American Indian Days, Sheridan, Wyo., and Pawnee (OK) Bill Museum, 1970; Bacone College Distinguished Service Award, 1972; Heritage Award, Five Civilized Tribes Museum, Muskogee, OK, 1977; Grand Prize of $1,000 at Central Washington State College; among others. *Interests*: "Graphics, architectural design; lecturing on American Indian art; Indian painting (traditional); tours of paintings; exhibits and lectures throughout the Middle East, Africa, India, and Burma, sponsored by the U.S. Department of State, Washington, DC." *Biographical sources*: Indians of Today, 1960-70; Who's Who in the South & Southwest; Register of U.S. Living Artists, 1968; Personalities of the South; Dictionary of International Biography; Notable Americans, 1976-77. *Published works*: McCombs Indian Art Calendar, 1978; White Eagle-Green Corn, 1979.

McCONE, ROBERT CLYDE 1915-
(professor of anthropology)
Born September 30, 1915, Redfield, S.D. *Education*: Wessington Springs College, BA, 1946; South Dakota State University, MS, 1956; Michigan State University, PhD, 1961. *Principal occupation*: Professor of anthropology. *Home address*: 1901 Snowden Ave., Long Beach, CA 90815 (213) 596-7278. *Affiliations*: Professor of anthropology, California State University, Long Beach, 1961-86; ordained elder, Dakota District of the Wesleyan Church, Rapid City, SD, 1952- *Memberships*: American Anthropological Association (Fellow); Royal Anthropological Institute of Great Britain & Ireland (Fellow); American Scientific Affiliation (Fellow); Phi Kappa Phi; American Society of Missiology; The Wesleyan Theological Society; Evangelical Theological Society. *Interests*: "Cultural sources of belief conflict in Christianity; cultural problems of contact of American Indian culture with Christianity. Taught Brainerd Indian School, fall 1973; spoke at Wesleyan Indain Missions Works Convention, 1974; taught fall 1987 and fall 1988 at Wesleyan Indian Missions Headquarters, Hot Springs, S.D. Gave paper at International Applied Anthropology Meeting, Edinburgh, Scotland, 1981. Travel. Frequent lectures on bible, science & culture." *Biographical sources*: International Scholar's Directory; Contemporary Authors. *Published works*: Articles: "Time and the Dakota's Way of Life," Agricultural Experiment Station, South Dakota State College, 1956; "The Time Concept Perspective and Premise in the Socio-cultural Order of the Dakota Indians," (Plains Anthropologist, 1960); "Cultural Factors in Crime Among the Dakota Indian," (Plains Anthropologist, 1966); "Death and the Persistance of Basic Personality Structure Among the Lakota," (Plains Anthropologist, 1968); "Three Levels of Anthropological Objection to Evolution," (Creation Research Quarterly, 1973); "Toward an Applied Anthropology of Beliefs," (Journal of the American Scientific Affiliation, Dec. 1980); "Length of the Days of Creation," (in The Genesis Debate-Thomas Nelson, 1986); "The Day the Sun and the Moon Stood Still," (Illustrated Bible Life, fall 1989). Books: Man and His World (Creation Science Research Center, 1971); Culture and Controversy: An Investigation of the Tongues of Pentecost (Dorrance, 1978).

McCOVEY, DONALD (Yurok)
(rancheria chairperson)
Affiliation: Coast Indian Community of the Resighini Rancheria, P.O. Box 529, Klamath, CA 95548 (707) 482-2431.

McCOY, MELODY
(attorney)
Affiliation: Native American Rights Fund, 1506 Broadway, Boulder, CO 80302 (303) 447-8760. *Membership*: Colorado Indian Bar Association (president).

McCULLY, SHARON
(executive director)
Affiliation: Intra-Departmental Council on Indian Affairs, U.S. Dept. of Health & Human Services, Humphrey Bldg., 200 Independence Ave., SW, Washington, DC 20201 (202) 245-6546.

McDANIEL, EDWARD WAHOO
(Choctaw-Chickasaw) 1938-
(pro-fishing)
Born June 19, 1938, Burniece, LA. *Education*: University of Oklahoma, BS, 1960. *Principal occupation*: Pro-fishing, Bass Redman Tours. *Home address*: 4829 Water Oar Rd., Charlotte, NC 28211 (704) 366-0973. *Awards, honors*: High school football All-American, 1956; All-American, University of Oklahoma, 1958; All Pro-American Football League, 1964. *Interests*: "Considered by most wrestling promoters as the finest Indian wrestler of all time. I quit football in 1968 after playing nine years with the Houston Oilers, the Denver Broncos, the New York Jets, and the Miami Dolphins. I've wrestled in Japan, Australia, South Africa, and Hong Kong. I've represented the American Indian proudly in athletics for 40 years."

*McDANIEL, SHANNON
(health clinic director)
Affiliation: Choctaw Nation Health Clinic, 205 E. 3rd St., Broken Bow, OK 74728 (405) 584-2740.

McDONALD, ARTHUR LEROY (Sioux) 1934-
(research consultant)
Born December 26, 1934, Martin, S.D. *Education*: University of South Dakota, AB, 1962, MA, 1963, PhD, 1966. *Principal occupation*: Research consultant. *Home address*: Box 326, Lame Deer, MT 59043. Affiliation: Owner, Cheyenne Consulting Service. *Other professional posts*: Acting head, Psychology Dept., Central College, 1963-64; head, Psychology Dept., Montana State University, 1968-71. *Military service*: U.S. Marine Corps, 1953-56 (Sergeant). *Memberships*: Pine Ridge Sioux Tribe; Sigma Xi; American Assn. for the Advancement of Science; American Quarter Horse Assn. *Interests*: Indian research in mental health, education, alcohol, and evaluation; raising quality American quarter horses. *Published works*: Psychology and Contemporary Problems (Brooks-Cole, 1974) numerous articles in scientific journals.

*McDONALD, BRUCE
(Mashantucket Pequot)
(editor)
Affiliation: "The Pequot Times," Mashantucket Pequot Tribal Nation, P.O. Box 3060, Ledyard, CT 06339 (203) 536-7200.

McDONALD, JOHN
(radio station manager)
Affiliation: KYUK - 640 AM, Bethel Broadcasting, Box 468, Bethel, AK 99559 (907) 543-3131.

McDONALD, JOSEPH
(college president)
Affiliation: Salish-Kootenai College, P.O. Box 117, Pablo, MT 59855 (406) 675-4800.

McDONALD, ROY
(Indian band chief)
Affiliation: Islington Indian Band, Whitedog, Ontario, Canada P0X 1P0 (807) 927-2068.

McDOUGALL, HARRY
(Indian band chief)
Affiliation: Abitibiwinni (Algonquin) Indian Band, Box 36 Pikogan, Amos, Quebec, Canada J9T 3A3 (819) 732-6591.

McGEE, HAROLD FRANKLIN, Jr. 1945-
(professor of anthropology)
Born June 5, 1945, Miami, Fla. *Education*: Florida State University, BA, 1966, MA, 1967; Southern Illinois University, PhD, 1974. *Principal occupation*: Professor of anthropology. *Address*: Dept. of Anthropology, Robie St., Halifax, Nova Scotia, Can. B3H 3C3 (902) 420-5628. *Affiliations*: Associate professor, Dept. of Anthropology, Saint Mary's University, Halifax, Nova Scotia, Can. *Other professional post*: Consultant to museums and other institutions. *Memberships*: Canadian Ethnology Society; Royal Anthropological Institute of Great Britain and Ireland (Fellow). *Interests*: Mr. McGee writes, "(My) major area of interest and expertise is with contemporary and historic Micmac and Malecite peoples of Atlantic Canada. In addition to standard ethnological concerns as an academic, I am interested in getting the non-native population to understand the reasons for similarity and difference of the native peoples' life ways to their own so that they will encourage governments to allow for greater local autonomy by the native people. Academically, I am particularly interested in native world view, politics, aesthetics, and reconstruction of aboriginal society and culture." *Published works*: Native Peoples of Atlantic Canada (McClelland and Stewart, 1974); The Micmac IndiansL The First Migrants in Banked Fires-The Ethnics of Nova Scotia, edited by D. Campbell (Scribbler's Prss, 1978); journal articles and papers.

McGERTT, CHARLIE (Creek)
(tribal town king)
Affiliation: Thlopthlocco Tribal Town, Box 706, Okemah, OK 74859 (918) 623-2620.

McGESHICK, JOHN (Chippewa)
(tribal chairperson)
Affiliation: Lac Vieux Desert Band of Chippewa Indians, P.O. Box 249, Choate Rd., Watersmeet, MI 49969 (906) 358-4577/8/9.

*McGESHICK, PETER, Jr.
(health administrator)
Affiliation: Sokaogan Chippewa Community Clinic, P.O. Box 616, Crandon, WI 54520 (715) 478-5180.

McGINNIS, HELEN
(museum director)
Affiliation: Tsut'ina K'osa (Sarcee), 3700 Anderson Rd., S.W., P.O. Box 67, Calgary, Alberta, Canada T2W 3C4 (403) 238-2676/7.

McGREEVY, SUSAN BROWN 1934-
(anthropologist)
Born January 28, 1934, Chicago, Ill. *Education*: Mt. Holyoke College (2 years); Roosevelt University, BA, 1969; Northwestern University, MA, 1971. *Principal occupation*: Anthropologist. *Home address*: 704 Camino Lejo, Box 5153, Santa Fe, NM 87502. *Affiliation*: Director, 1978-82, research associate, 1983-, The Wheelwright Museum, Santa Fe, NM. *Other professional posts*: Curator of North American Ethnology, Kansas City Museum, 1974-77. *Memberships*: American Anthropological Association; Society for American Archaeology; American Society for Ethnohistory; Society for Applied Anthropology; American Ethnological Society; Council for Museum Anthropology; American Association of Museums; Native American Art Studies Association. *Interests*: Research and exhibit curator, Southwest Indian arts and cultures; hiking, camping, rafting, SCUBA diving. *Published work*: The Dyer Collection, (American Indian Art Magazine, 1978); Lullabies From the Earth: Cradles of Native North America, 1980; Translating Tradition: Basketry Arts of the San Juan Paiutes, with Andrew Hunter Whiteford (Wheelwright Museum, 1985); Anii Anaadaalyaa'igii: Continuity and Innovation in Recent Navajo Art, with Bruce Bernstein (Wheelwright Museum, 1988); contributing articles to professional publications.

*McGUIRE, BETSY (Athabascan)
(radio station manager)
Affiliation: KSKO - 870 AM, P.O. Box 195, McGrath, AK 99627 (907) 524-3001.

McGUIREAKIS, DAN
(Indian band chief)
Affiliation: Sand Point Indian Band, 921 Athabasca St., Thunder Bay, Ontario, Canada P7C 3E5 (807) 632-4227.

*McHALE, PHILIP A.
(consortium director)
Affiliation: Native American Center of Excellence Consortium, College of Medicine, P.O. Box 26901, Oklahoma City, OK 73190 (405) 271-2316.

*McHENRY, DELORES
(rancheria chairperson)
Affiliation: Chico Rancheria, 3006 Esplanade St., Chico, CA 95926 (916) 899-8922.

*McINTYRE, ALLAN J.
(museum curator)
Affiliation: The Amerind Foundation Museum, Box 248, Dragoon, AZ 86509 (602) 586-3666.

McKAY, GINA
(program centre head)
Affiliation: West Region Tribal Council, Indian Cultural Education Program, 21-4th Ave., N.W., Dauphin, MB, Can. R7N 1H9 (204) 638-8225.

McKAY, WALLY (Ojibwe)
(member-board of directors)
Affiliation: Intertribal Christian Comunications, P.O. Box 3765, Station B, Winnipeg, Manitoba, Canada R2W 3R6 (204) 661-9333.

McKEE, WILLIAM
(administrative officer)
Affiliation: Clinton PHS Indian Hospital, Route 4, Box 213, Clinton, OK 73601 (405) 323-2884.

McKENZIE, ALEXANDRE
(Indian band chief)
Affiliation: Montagnais de Schefferville, Quebec, Canada G0G 2T0 (418) 585-2601.

McKENZIE, WILLIAM
(Indian band chief)
Affiliation: Tanakteuk Indian Band, Box 327, Alert Bay, British Columbia, Canada V0N 1A0 (604) 974-5489.

McKEVITT, GERALD 1939-
(professor of history)
Born July 3, 1939, Longview, Wash. *Education*: University of San Francisco, BA, 1961; University of Southern California, MA, 1964; UCLA, PhD, 1972; Pontifical Gregorian University, Rome, Italy, BST, 1975. *Principal occupation*: Professor of history. *Address*: Nobili Hall, Santa Clara University, Santa Clara, CA 95053 (408) 554-4124. *Affiliations*: Director, Santa Clara University Archives, 1975-85; associate professor, History Department, Santa Clara University, 1975-. *Other professional posts*: Member, Board of Trustees, Gonzaga University, 1989-; member, National Seminar for Jesuit Higher Education, 1990-. *Memberships*: Western History Association; California Historical Society; American Historical Association; American Society of Church History, American Catholic Historical Association. *Awards, honors*: 1991 Oscar O. Winther Award by Western Historical Assocaition for best article appearing in "The Western Historical Quarterly. *Interests*: "Teach courses on university level on California history, American Far West, Native American History, U.S. Catholicism, Colonial Latin America, Historical Methodology. Current research interests: Jesuits in the American Far West, missionaries to Native Americans in the 19th century." *Published works*: The University of Santa Clara, A History, 1851-1977 (Stanford University Press, 1979); numerous articles and book reviews.

McKINLEY, FRANCIS
(executive director)
Affiliation: National Indian Training & Research Center, 2121 S. Mill Ave., Suite 216, Tempe, AZ 85282 (602) 967-9484.

McKINNEY, ROGER *(Sinnagwin)* (Kickapoo) 1957-
(educator)
Born Febrary 24, 1957, Kansas City, Mo. *Education*: Graceland College (Lamoni, IA), BA, 1982; The American University (Washington, DC), MFA (Painting), 1986. *Principal occupation*: Educator. *Home address*: 4331 E. Towne Lane, Higley, AZ 85236 (602) 832-5898. *Affiliations*: Art instructor/guidance counselor, Kickapoo Nation School, Horton, KS (acting supt./prinicpal), 1982-83; associate/trainer, ORBIS Associates, Washington, DC, 1986-88; coordinator, Youth Leadership Program, Zuni School District, Zuni, NM, 1988-89; program management and design specialist, Southwest Resoiurce and Evaluation Center IV, Tempe, AZ, 1989-91; educator, The Heard Museum, Phoenix, AZ, 1991-. *Other profssional post*: Professional artist. *Exhibitions*: Ha-Pa-Nyi Fine Arts Gallery, Santa Barbara, CA, 1988; Native American Arts Exhibition, UCSB, 1988; 68th Inter-Tribal Indian Ceremonial, Gallup, NM, 1989; Second Annual Lawrence Indian Arts Show, University of Kansas, 1990; Cultural Reality or Cultural Fantasy, Institute of American Indian Arts, Santa Fe, NM, 1991-92; Santa Fe Indian Market, 1991; among others. *Works in Public Collection/Places*: Graceland College Art Collection, Lamoni, IA; Kickapoo Nation School, Powhattan, KS; Watkins Gallery Colection, The American University, Washington, DC; among others.

Awards, honors: Guitano Capasso Award, All Dept. Shoe, Graceland College, 1982; Second Premium Watercolor, Fairfax Co. Parks, Burke, VA, 1984; Wolpoff Award, Works on Paper, The American University, Watkins Collection, 1986; Honorable Mention, 68th Annual Inter-Tribal Indian Ceremonial, 1989; DeGrazia, Artist in Residence, The Heard Museum, 1990; Merit Award, Lawrence Indian Arts Show, 1990. *Biographical sources*: Public TV Broadcasring - Kickapoo Nation, Return to Soverigty (University of Kansas, PBS, 1983); Twenty First Century Native American (CBS, Phoenix, AZ).

*McKINNEY, THOMAS R., Sr.
*(Gentgeen-Dancer) (Seneca) 1951-
(fire fighter, museum director)
Born October 27, 1951, Butler Co., Penna. *Education*: Bacone Junior College, AA, 1974. *Principal occupation*: Fire fighter, museum director. *Home address*: 323 Lawrence St., Muskogee, OK 74403 (918) 682-9138. *Affiliations*: Museum director, Bacone College, Muskogee, OK, 1990-; fire fighter, Muskogee Fire Dept., Muskogee, OK, 1979-. *Other professional posts*: Dancer of traditional Native American origin; Post Master of Boy Scouts, explorer post, specializing in Native American culture. *Community activities*: Inspector for district election board, member, Chamber of Commerce; member, Muskogee antique collector's guild. *Membership*: Muskogee Fire Fighters local #57. *Awards, honors*: Instructor I professional Fire Fighters; Honorable mention and work in the permanent collection of the Black Hills art competition; Eagle Scout; Vigil member of The Order of the Arrow; DAR achievement award. *Interests*: Native American studies, professional fire fighting skills, anthropology & ethnology; Native American dancing & the making of traditional clothing.

*McKNIGHT, CINDY
(editor)
Affiliation: "Smoke Signals," Dallas Inter-Tribal Center, 209 E. Jefferson Blvd., Dallas, TX 75203 (214) 941-1050.

*McLAREN, DALE *(Fire Eagle)
(United Lumbee/Creek/Shawnee) 1935-
(chairman/CEO)
Born March 25, 1935, in Oklahoma. *Education*: Southern Illinois University, BA, MA. *Address*: P.O. Box 2704, Huntington Beach, CA 92647 (714) 840-2400. *Principal occupation*: Chairman/CEO, Allied Eurasian Co. Pte. Ltd., Republic of Singapore. *Other professional post*: Planning consultant, Dale McLaren. Consultant (regional & urban planning venture into planning consultation; zoning maps, zoning ordinances, professional advice, and lobbying); financial consultant, Allied Eurasian Group of Cos. (USA), Ltd. (facilitates and syndicates international loans for qualified applicants), 1982-. *Memberships*: American Academy of Political and Social Science; Illinois Railroad User's Association (executive secretary); United Lumbee Nation's Golden Hawk Warrior Society Chief, 1990-; vice chief, United Lumbee Nation's Red Tail Hawk Clan, 1992-. *Awards, honors*: Governor's Task Force for Economic Alternatives for Illinois for the Year 2000; United Lumbee Nation's Silver Eagle Award 1993 (given each year to a tribal member that has done outstanding work for the Nation and the Indian community." *Biographical source*: Who's Who in North America, 1976.

McLEAN, DORIS
(Indian band chief)
Affiliation: Carcross/Tagish Indian Band, Box 130, Carcross, Yukon, Canada Y0B 1B0 (403) 821-4251.

*McLEMORE, LAURIE, M.D.
(association director)
Affiliation: Association of Native American Medical Students, 1235 Sovereign Row, Suite C7, Oklahoma City, OK 73159 (913) 677-1468.

McLEOD, MARTHA
(college president)
Affiliation: Bay Mills Community College, Route 1, Box 315A, Brimley, MI 49715 (906) 248-3354.

McMANUS, JILL
(writer, composer, jazz pianist, teacher)
Born in N.J. *Education*: Wellesley College, BA. *Principal occupation*: Writer, composer, jazz pianist, teacher. *Home address*: 401 East 81st St., New York, NY 10028. *Affiliation*: Staff, Mannes College of Music, 1981-92. *Other professional posts*: Freelance writer, reporter, researcher, Time Magazine, 1963-71; jazz pianist performing with top jazz artists in the U.S. and Europe, 1973-. *Membership*: American Association on Indian Affairs. *Awards, honors*: Grants, Sandoval County Human Services to continue research & develop support for project to produce educational videotapes on diabetes prevention for Pueblos & Navajo Nation, and write proposal (March 1986); Health & Human Services to produce a culturally appropriate pilot video for Navajo youth on nutrition, exercise & diabetes prevention (March 1987); grants towards completion and teacher's guide (Dec. 1993). *Interests*: Teaching jazz theory and piano; travel. *Published/produced works*: Produced album "Symbols of Hopi" (Concord Jazz, 1984) containing four Hopi songs adapted for jazz quintet plus cottonwood drum & percussion (played by Louis Mofsie & Alan Brown), as tribute to Hopi songpoets & Native American music (5 stars in Down Beat). *Articles*: "Women Jazz Composers and Arrangers" for Greenwood Publsihing series, "Diabetes in Indian America," profiles of musicians.

McMASTER, GERALD R.
(Plains Cree-Nehiyawuk) 1953-
(curator of contemporary Indian art)
Born March 9, 1953, North Battleford, Saskatchewan, Can. *Education*: Institute of American Indian Art (Santa Fe, 1973-75); Minneapolis College of Art & Design, BFA, 1977; Banff School of Fine Arts (Banff, Alberta), 1986; Carleton University (Ottawa, ON), MA, 1994. *Principal occupation*: Curator of contemporary Indian art. *Home address*: 65 Caroline Ave., Ottawa, Ontario K1Y 0S8 (613) 725-3159 (home), (819) 776-8443 (work). *Affiliations*: Head of the Indian Art Program, Saskatchewan Indian Federated College, Regina, Sask., 1977-81; curator, Canadian Museum of Civilization, Ottawa, Ont., 1981-. *Other professional posts*: Adjunct Research Professor, Carleton University, 1992-95; self-employed visual artist, 1977-artistic coordinator for Plains Indian Dancers & Singers, the Holland Festival, Amsterdam, the Netherlands, 1984-85; program coordinator, Native Art Studies Group of Ottawa, 1984-85. *Solo exhibitions*:

The Cowboy/Indian Show - Ufundi Gallery, Ottawa, Ontario, 1990; McMichael Canadian Gallery, Kleinburg, Ontario, 1991. Savage Graces: "afterimages by Gerald McMaster - UBC-Museum of Anthropology, Vancouver, BC, 1992; Winnipeg Art Gallery, 12/94-1/95; Windsor Art Gallery, 1994; Southern Alberta Art Gallery, 1994; Ottawa Art Gallery, 1994; Edmonton Art Gallery, 1995; Memorial Art Gallery, St. Johns, Newfoundland, 1995; numerous group exhibitions. *Collections represented*: Carleton University, Canadian Museum of Civilization, Dept. of Indian Affairs (Ottawa, ON), University of Regina, Canada Council Art Bank, City of Ottawa, City of Regina, Institute of American Indian Arts (Santa Fe, NM), Gettysburg College (Gettysburg, PA), Guilford Native American Art Gallery (Greensboro, NC). *Commissions*: Metro-Toronto, 1992; City of Ottawa, 1991; Canadian Museum of Civilization, Ottawa, 1988; among others. *Membership*: Native Art Studies Assn. of Canada (vice-president, 1987, president, 1988-92; editor, NASAC Newsletter); Ontario Arts Council (board member, 1991-); ICOM Canada (board member, 1992-). *Awards, honors*: Canada Council Travel Grants, to travel and present papers at various conference and workshops, 1989, '90, '93; Honorable Mention, National Educational Film Festival/Certificate for Creative Excellence, U.S. Industrial Film Festival, Firearms Safety Series, Indian Hunting Traditions, 1983; First Prize, "Byron and His Balloon, La Roche, Saskatchewan, 1981; Second Prize, wood sculpture, Scottsdale Annual Indian Art Competition, 1976. *Interests*: Travel; art exhibitions. From 1986 to 1989 developed concept for a National Indian & Inuit Art Gallery in the new Canadian Museum of Civilization. *Reviews on artist*: "Punning Artist Uses Native Wit," by Robin Laurence (The Georgia Straight, Aug 14-21, 1992); "Native Painter's Criticism Packs Strong Punchline," by Christopher Hume (The Toronto Star, Feb. 8, 1991; "Native Artist Throws Comic Curves But With a Serious Twist," by Nancy Baele (Ottawa Citizen, Feb. 24, 1991; "Indian Lore," by Nancy Baele (Ottawa Citizen, June 15, 1989; "Public Servant-Painter Wants to Help Native Artists," by Nancy Baele (Ottawa Citizen, Nov. 11, 1988); "Teacher-Artist's Commitment Extends Beyond Work As Curator," by Bill White (Echo-National Museums of Canada, Vol. 4, No. 7, Oct/Nov., 1984); among others. *Biographical source*: Savage Graces: 'After-Images," Harbor Magazine of Art & Everyday Life, Montreal, 1994. *Published work*: Indigena: Contemporary Native Perspectives, edited with Lee-Ann Martin (Douglas & McIntyre, Vancouver, 1992); numerous articles. *Recordings*: "Songs from Bismarck," Indian Records, Taos, N.M (sang with the Red Earth Singers), 1976; Byron and His Balloon (Tree Frog Press, Edmonton, 1984); "Alex Janvier," "Sarain Stump," "Willie Seaweed," "Mungo Martin," The New Canadian Encyclopedia, Hurtig: Edmonton, 1984); "More than Beads and Feathers," The Saskatchewan Indian, Sept. 1988).

McMASTER, LAVERNA
(director-Indian centre)
Affiliation: Calgary Native Friendship Centre, 140 - 2nd Ave., S.W., Calgary, Alberta, Canada T2P 0B9 (403) 264-1155.

McNEELY, KATHLEEN (Sault Ste. Marie Chippewa) 1951-
(librarian-director of library services)
Born February 19, 1951, Petoskey, Mich. *Edu-

cation*: Lake Superior University, Sault Ste. Marie, MI (4 years); University of Southwestern Louisiana, Lafayette (1 year). *Principal occupation*: Librarian-Director of Library Services, Hannahville School-Community Library (Nah Tah Wahsh Library), Hannahville Reservation, Wilson, MI, 1985-. *Address*: W1971 Isaacson Dr., Menominee, MI 49858 (906) 466-2556 (work). *Other professional posts*: Lifestyle editor, Sault Evening News, Sault Ste Marie, MI; managing editor, Franklin Banner, Franklin, LA. *Community activities*: St. Ignace Pow Wow Committee, St. Ignace, MI; Menominee County Library (board of trustees); Michinemackinong Pow Wow Committee (chairperson). *Memberships*: Bay De Noc Culture Assn. (board of directors); American Library Assn. (Minorities Round Table). *Awards, honors*: 1980 Outstanding Citizens of the Year - West St. Mary Parish Chamber of Commerce, Franklin, LA; 1991 Candidate for Medal of Honor, Michigan Daughters of the American Revolution. *Interests*: "Traditional & jingle dress dancer promoting traditional ways to our youth as alternatives to substance abuse."

*McNEIL, RONALD S. *(His Horse Is Thunder)* **(Hunkpapa Lakota) 1958-**
(organization president)
Born March 19, 1958, Rapid City, S.D. *Education*: Standing Rock College, AA, 1982; Black Hills State College, BS, 1985; University of South Dakota Law School, JD, 1988. *Address*: P.O. Box 67, Fort Yates, ND 58538 (212) 787-6312 (work). *Affiliations*: Indian Law Instructor & Federal Grants Administrator, University of South Dakota Law School, 1989-91; Acting President, Standing Rock College, Fort Yates, ND, 1991-93; President, American Indian College Fund, 21 West 68 St., #1F, New York, NY 10023, 1993-. *Community activities*: Participates in tribal government and cultural activities. *Memberships*: SD Indian Ed. Assn; American Indian Higher Ed. Consortium. *Interests*: Vocational: Native American higher education. In his two-year term as president of the American Indian College Fund, he hopes to help the Fund broaden its outreach and greatly increase its funding. "This is a very exciting time in the Indian-college movement. The older colleges are maturing and starting to offer bachelor's and master's programs, while new colleges are emerging all the time. Indian colleges are vital to the cultural survival of our people. I want to do all I can to help them grow." Avocational: Fishing & hunting.

McPEEK, GEORGE
(director-organization)
Affiliation: Intertribal Christian Comunications, Box 3765, Station B, Winnipeg, MB, Canada R2W 3R6 (204) 661-9333.

*McPETERS, ANTHONY STEPHEN *(Walks in Two Worlds)* **(Lumbee) 1944-**
(drum builder)
Born July 26, 1944, Griffin, GA. *Address*: Rt. 1, Box 198, Poulan, GA 31781 (912) 776-4292. *Affiliation*: Owner, Two Worlds Arts & Crafts, Poulan, GA, 1986-. *Military service*: U.S. Navy, 1959-63.

*McTAGGART, FRED
(author)
McTaggart was a postdoctoral fellow in the Newberry Library's Center for the History of the American Indian, Chicago. *Published works*:

Wolf That I Am: In Search of the Red Earth People (University of Oklahoma Press, 1985.

M

*MAAS, GARY (Iroquois/Ojibwe)
(stuntman, script-writer, film-maker)
Address: c/o Dreamcatcher Films, Inc., 8251 Continental, Warren, MI 48089 (810) 756-6007.

MacDONALD, ARTHUR
(college president)
Affiliation: Dull Knife Memorial College, P.O. Box 98, Lame Deer, MT 59043 (406) 477-6219.

MacDONALD, GEORGE F. 1938-
(archaeologist)
Born July 4, 1938, Galt, Ontario, Can. *Education*: University of Toronto, BA, 1961; Yale University, PhD, 1966. *Principal occupation*: Archaeologist. Home address: RR 1, Cantley, Quebec, Can. J0X 1L0. *Affiliations*: Atlantic Provinces Archaeologist, 1964-1966, head-Western Canada Section, 1966-69, National Museums of Canada; chief, Archaeology Division, 1969-71; chief, Archaeological Survey of Canada, 1971-77, senior archaeologist, Office of the Director, 1977-, National Museum of Man. *Other professional post*: Conjunct professor, Dept. of Anthropology, Trent University, 1974-. *Memberships*: Canadian Archaeological Association (president, 1969-70); American Association for the Advancement of Science (Fellow); American Anthrological Association (Fellow); Archaeological Institute of America, Ottawa Chapter (vice president, 1976-77); Society for American Archaeology (first positions, executive committee, 1977-78); International Quarternary Association (head, working group for Eastern North America-Commission for the Paleo-Ecology of Early Man, 1976-77); Council for Canadian Archaeology; International Union of Prehistoric and Protohistoric Sciences. *Awards, honors*: Numerous awards and research grants. *Interests*: "Native peoples of North and South America; prehistory, field research, Atlantic and Pacific Coast of Canada, Ontario and Yukon Territories; traditional Native American arts and crafts; Northwest Coast Indian print-making, scultpure, Ojibwa print-making; assembled and wrote catalogues for numerous exhibitions of contemporary and traditional Native American art that traveled in Europe, North America, Asia, New Zealand; study travel." *Published works*: Numerous articles, papers, reports, and reviews, 1965-; directed the prodcution of 45 short study 16mm, color films on West Coast art and technology; production of gallery films and study video tapes and public release films such as To Know the Hurons, 1977.

MacDONALD, PETER, Sr. (Navajo) 1928-
(former tribal chairman)
Born December 16, 1928, Teec Nos Pos, Ariz. *Education*: Bacone Junior College, AA, 1951; University of Oklahoma, BS, 1957; UCLA, graduate studies, 1958-62. *Affiliations*: Project engineer, member of technical staff, Hughes Aircrafts Co., El Segundo, Calif. 1957-63; director, Management, Methods & Procedures, 1963-65; Office of Navajo Economic Opportunity, 1965-70; The Navajo Tribe, Window Rock, AZ; chairman, Navajo Tribal Council, 1970-88. *Military service*: U.S. Marine Corps, 1944-46

(Corporal; member, Navajo Code Talkers in the South Pacific). *Community activities*: New Mexico Governor's Economic Development Advisory Group, 1963-67; New Mexico State Planning Commission, 1963-67; Navajo Community College, Tsaile, AZ (board of regents, 1971-); Antioch School of Law, Washington, D.C. (board of visitors); Patagonia Corporation, Tucson (board of directors); Navajo Agricultural Products Industry, Farmington, NM (board of directors, 1972-); NM Governor's Energy Task Force, Santa Fe; NM Commission, Regional Housing Authority, Santa Fe; Non-Profit Housing/Community Development Corp., Shiprock, NM, 1972; Arizona State Justice Planning Agency Governing Board; Arizona Advisory Committee of U.S. Commission on Civil Rights, Washington, DC, 1970-74. *Memberships*: University of Oklahoma Alumni Association; National Association of Community Development (board of directors, 1968-70; National Tribal Chairman's Association; American Indian National Bank, Washington, D.C. (board of directors). *Awards, honors*: Appointed by President Nixon to the National Center for Voluntary Action, 1970-74; Presidential Commendation for exceptional services to others, 1970; Citation, Distinguished American, National Institute for Economic Development, 1970; Citation, Distinguished Baconian, Bacone Junior College, OK, 1971; Arizona Indian of the Year, 1971; Good Citizenship Medal, National Society of Sons of the American Revolution, 1972; Silver Beaver Award, Boy Scouts Of America, Kit Carson Council, 1973l member (appointed by Secretary of Commerce), National Public Advisory Committee on Regional Economic Development, U.S. Department of Comerce, Washington, DC, 1973-77; Citation, One of the 200 Rising American Leaders by Time Magazine, 1974; inducted into Engineering Hall of Fame, University of Oklahoma, 1975. *Biographical sources*: Who's Who in America; Who's Who in the West; Mr. MacDonald has been written about in magazines and newspapers, such as: Newsweek; Time; U.S. News & World Report; Signature; People; Washington Post; New York Times; Chicago Times; Los Angeles Times; etc.

MacEEACHEM, ZONDRA
(editor)
Affiliation: Canadian Native Law Reporter, Native Law Centre, University of Saskatchewan, Room 141, Diefenbaker Centre, Saskatoon, Saskatchewan, Canada S7N 0W0 (306) 966-6189.

MACHELL, WILLIAM
(Indian band chief)
Affiliation: Lillooet Indian Band, Box 615, Lillooet, British Columbia, Canada V0K 1V0 (604) 256-4118.

MACHIMITY, EDWARD
(Indian band chief)
Affiliation: Saugeen Indian band, Savant Lake, Ontario, Canada P0V 2S0 (807) 584-2989.

*MACHUKAY, TONY
(executive director)
Affiliation: Arizona Commission on Indian Affairs, 1645 W. Jefferson, Suite 127, Phoenix, AZ 85007 (602) 542-3123.

MacNABB, ALEXANDER S. (Micmac) 1929- (attorney)
Born August 24, 1929, Bay Shore, N.Y. *Education*: Colgate University, AB, 1956; Washington and Lee University Law School, JD, 1959; NYU Law School, postgraduate, 1960-61. *Principal occupation*: Attorney. *Home address*: 10600 Sunlit Rd., P.O. Box 86, Oakton, VA 22124. *Affiliations*: President, Alexander MacNabb Associates, Bay Shore, NY, 1960-67; president, Town Almanac Publishing Co., Bay Shore, N.Y., 1960-67; member, President's Comittee on Manpower, U.S. Office of Economic Opportunity, 1966-67, special assistant to director, Community Action Program, 1967-69; OEO representative to Presidentially established National Program for Voluntary Action, Washington, DC, 1969-70; director, Office of Operating Services, U.S. Dept. of the Interior, BIA, Washington, DC, 1970-72, director, Office of Engineering, 1972-73; director, Office of Indian & Territorial Development, U.S. Dept. of the Interior, 1973-74; deputy director, Office of Federal Contract Compliance, Empoyment Standards Administration, Dept. of Labor, 1974-75; director, Indian & Native American Programs, Employment and Training Administration, Washington, DC, 1975-80; National Alliance of Business, 1980-81; MacNabb, Preston & Waxman, Attorneys at Law, 1981-86; Alexander MacNabb, Attorney-at-Law, 1986-. *Military service*: U.S. Navy, 1950-54 - Korean War, Task Force 95 of the 7th Fleet in Korea (Presidential Unit Citation, Presidential Unit Citation Republic of Korea; Korean Medal; the UN Medal; the China Service Medal & the American Defense Medal). *Community activities*: National Council of the Boy Scouts of America (25+ years) (Chairperson of the National American Indian Committee on Scouting, the National Advisory Committee on Scouting for the Handicapped); National Board of the American Red Cross. *Memberships*: American Political Science Association; American Academy of Political and Social Sciences; National Congress of American Indian (Micmac Tribe); National Indian Youth Council; MENSA.

MACRI, MARTHA JANE MITCHELL (*Tsoee*) (Oklahoma Cherokee) 1945- (professor of Native American studies)
Born March 10, 1945, Lansing, Mich. *Education*: California State University, Fullerton, BA, 1968; University of California, Berkeley, MA (Linguistics), 1982, Ph.D. (Linguistics), 1988. *Principal occupation*: Professor of Native American studies. *Home address*: 2212 Whittier Dr., Davis, CA 95616 (916) 752-7086 (work). *Affiliations*: Dept. of Anthropology & Native American Studies, University of California, Davis, 1985- (postgraduate researcher, 1985-88; lecturer, 1988-90; Postdoctoral Fellow, 1990-91; assistant professor, 1991-). *Other professional posts*: Project coordinator, Art & Archaeology Database Project, Pre-Columbian Art Research Institute, San Francisco, CA, 1988-91; instructor, D-Q University, Davis, CA, 1990; New Faculty Research Grants, Tzeltal Language Project, 1991-94; Sr. Investigator, Maya Archival Database Project, Merle Greene Robertson, principal investigator, National Endowment for the Humanities, Reference Materials-Access, through the Pre-Columbian Art Research, San Francisco, CA; principal investigator, Maya Hieroglyphic Database Project, National Endowment for the Humanities, Reference Materials-Tools, 1992-94, 1994-96. *Community activities*: Group leader, La Leche League International (board of directors, N. Calif.); assistant chairperson, Leader Applicants for Northern California, 1976-78; volunteer teacher's aid, in programs for Gifted and Talented, ESL, and regular classroom, Fitch Mtn. Elem. School, Healdsburg, CA, 1978-80; volunteer caregiver, Home Hospice of Sonoma County, CA, 1990-91. *Memberships*: Pre-Columbian Art Research Institute (research associate); American Anthropological Association; California Indian Education Association; Linguistic Society of America; Society for the Study of the Indigenous Languages of the Americas. *Interests*: "I am committed to research and teaching about the world views of indigenous peoples of the Americas through study of their own writing systems. Areas of emphasis include Maya Hieroglyphic writing, Epi-Olmec writing and Micmac hieroglyphic writing (Canada), linguistic prehistory of the Americas, Native American language instruction, computers in linguistic research and electronic data archiving." *Published works*: Numerous articles; *in press*: A Glyphic Text from Naranjo, in Native American Text Series, Louanna Furbee, editor (Mouton, The Hague); among others; *in preparation*: with James Brooks, The Maya Graphene Codes & Reference File (book) (U. of Oklahoma Press); Teaching & Learning Indian Languages; numerous articles in journals, and chapters in books.

*MADDOX, DEBORAH
(BIA acting office director)
Affiliation: Bureau of Indian Affairs, Dept. of the Interior, 1849 C St., NW, MS: 4603-MIB, Washington, DC 20240 (202) 208-3463.

*MADDUX, MICHAEL THOMAS (*Red Hawk*) (N. Alabama Cherokee) 1955- (tribal officer)
Born July 12, 1955, Albertville, Ala. *Education*: High school. *Home address*: 203 West Don's Ave., Albertville, AL 35950 (205) 878-9602. *Affiliation*: Autorized tribal officer, Dist. #2 North Alabama Cherokees. "We have seven districts with enrollment of nearly 1,000 people. *Awards, honors*: Golden Arrowhead Society, North Alabama Cherokees, Creek Path-Williston Dist. *Interests*: Native American pow wows in TN, GA, and AL.

MADISON, CURT 1949- (video documentary producer)
Born September 9, 1949, St. Paul, Minn. *Education*: Stanford University, BA, 1971; University of Hawaii, MA (Political Science, Communications), 1976; East-West Center (Communications Institute Certificate), 1976. *Home address*: P.O. Box 9, Manly Hot Springs, AK 99756 (907) 672-3262. *Video Productions*: Director/editor, Profiles of Alaskans, Thelma Saunders-Kaltag, Emmitt Peters-Ruby, Catherine Attla-Huslia, 1982 (State of Alaska Instructional TV Network) 39 minutes, documentary of three rural Alaskans; director/editor, Huteetl: Koyukon Memorial Potlatch, 1983 (Yukon-Koyukuk School District) 55 minutes, documentary of the Memorial Potlatch festival; director/editor, Songs in Minto Life, 1986 (National Endowment for the Arts and Yukon-Koyukuk School District) 28 minutes, documentary of four important music categories in Minto-dance songs, hunting songs, songs of remembrance, and a potlatch song sung directly to the spirit; director/writer/editor, Tanana River Rat, 1989 (National Endowment for the Arts and KUAC-TV Fairbanks) 52 minutes, narrative drama depicting the crisis of young men in rural Alaska and village cohesive-

ness); producer/director, Bedrock Pay, 1991 - documentary of historic placer gold mining around Hot Springs-Rampart District, 1890-1940; producer/director, Hitting Sticks, Healing Hearts, 1991 (with KUAC-TV Fairbanks) documentary of the most important Native ceremony in Minto. *Early Documentaries on Film*: Director/camera/editor, Subsistence Fishing on the Tanana River, 1972 - 22 minutes (University of Alaska Media Dept.); writer, Athapaskan Art: Where Two Rivers Meet, 1973 - 30 minutes (University of Alaska Media Dept.); Ka'apuni Kakou, 1975 - 20 minutes (University of Hawaii); sound recordist, Inuit, 1978 (documentary of first Inuit Circumpolar Conference in Barrow). *Slide/Tape Programs*: photographer/writer, Morris Gundrum: Professional Woodsman, 1972 (Alaska Native Language Center; photographer/writer, A Haida Chief, 1977; photographer/writer, People and Places, 1979 - filmstrip (Yukon-Koyukuk School District). *Still Photography*: Point Lay Ethography, Point Lay, AK (U.S. Dept. of the Interior, 1990); Genieve Nahulu: Nanakuli, HI (Dept. of Education, Honolulu, HI), 1991; Ines Cayaban: A Filipina Woman (Dept. of Education, Honolulu, HI, 1991; among others. *Writings*: Writer/photographer, "Alaska Biography Series," 21 book series for use in Alaska schools - oral history of Native and White elders in rural Interior Alaska, 70-150 pages per book, 1978-87; writer/photographer, Walter Northway - oral history with the oldest Native of the Tanana Valley (Alaska Native Language Center, 1988); writer/photographer, Andrew Isaac - oral history of Interior Alaska's traditional chief (Central Alaska Curriculum Consortium, 1989). *Awards, honors*: Fellowships and Prizes - National Endowment for the Arts-Documentary Production, 1985, '87, '89; Rocky Mountain Film Center-Documentary Production, 1989, '90; Alaska State Council on the Arts-Writing, 1988; Alaska State Humanities Forum-Documentary Production, 1991; Red Ribbon, American Film and Video Festival, New York, 1984, '87; Museum of the American Indian Festival, 1984, '89; New Works Feature, National Video Festival AFI, Hollywood, 1984, '89; Arctic Film Festival, Finland, curated, 1986; Best Documentary, Northwest Film and Video Festival, Oregon Art Institute, 1989; Best Documentary, Atlanta Film and Video Festival, 1989; Premier Program, National Broadcast Spirit of Place, 1989.

MADSEN, BRIGHAM D. 1914-
(professor emeritus of history)
Born October 21, 1914, Magna, Utah. *Education*: Idaho State University, Certificate, 1934; University of Utah, BA, 1938; University of California, Berkeley, MA, 1940, PhD, 1948. *Principal occupation*: Professor emeritus of history. *Home address*: 2181 Lincoln Lane, Salt Lake City, UT 84124 (801) 277-2954. *Affiliation*: University of Utah, Salt Lake City, 1965-. *Other professional posts*: Dean of Continuing Education, 1965-66; deputy academic vice president, 1966-67; administrative V.P., 1967-1971; director of libraries, 1971-1973; chairman of History Dept., 1974-1975; professor of history, University of Utah. *Military service*: U.S. Army Infantry, 1943-46. *Community activities*: Peace Corps, Washington, DC (assistant director of training, 1964); Vista Program, Office of Economic Opportunity, Washington, DC (first director of training, 1965. *Memberships*: Utah State Historical Society (Fellow); Idaho State Historical Society; Utah Westerners. *Awards, honors*: Distinguished Teaching Award, 1977, University of Utah; Utah

Academy, Charles Reed Award, 1983; Westerners International Best Non-Fiction Book for 1980 &1985, and 2nd Place - Western Writers of America, Spur Awards, North to Montana. *Interests*: Northern Rocky Mountain region--Utah, Nevada, Wyoming, Idaho and Montana. Major interest in Shoshone-Bannock Tribes of Fort Hall, Idaho, having served as consultant-historical researcher for tribes in two claims cases against the U.S. Government. Biographical source: Who's Who of America. *Published works*: The Bannock of Idaho, 1958; The Lemhi: Sacajawea's People, 1979; The Northern Shoshoni, 1980; co-author, North to Montana, 1980; Gold Rush Sojourners in Salt Lake City, 1849-1850, 1983; The Shoshoni Frontier and the Bear River Massacre, 1985; Chief Pocatello: The White Plume, 1986.

*MADUENO, PATRICIA (Mojave)
(tribal chairperson)
Affiliation: Fort Mojave Tribal Council, 500 Merriman Ave., Needles, CA 92363 (619) 326-4591.

MAESTAS, JOHN R. (Pueblo)
(advisor)
Affiliation: Council of Advisors, American Indian Heritage Foundation, 6051 Arlington Blvd., Falls Church, VA 22044 (703) 237-7500.

MAESTAS, MARJORIE (Pueblo)
(school principal)
Affiliation: Tesuque Day School, Route 11, Box 2, Santa Fe, NM 87501 (505) 982-1516.

MAGANTE, MAURICE J. (Luiseno)
(tribal chairperson)
Affiliation: Pauma Band of Mission Indians, P.O. Box 86, Pauma Valley, CA 92061 (619) 742-1289.

MAGEE, DENNIS (Luiseno Band of Mission Indians) 1937-
(health administration)
Born October 9, 1937, Pala Indian Reservation, Calif. *Education*: San Diego City College, GE, 1957; San Diego State University, BS, 1962. *Principal occupation*: Health administration. *Home address*: Pala Mission Rd., P.O. Box 86, Pala, CA 92059 (619) 749-1552. *Affiliation*: Administrator, Indian Health Council, Inc., Pauma Valley, CA, 1970-. *Community activities*: Board of Directors, San Diego Council of Community Clinics; Citizens Equal Opportunity Commission, City of San Diego; United Way of San Diego (board of directors); Advisory policy panel, Indian Health Branmch, State Department of Health Services; board of directors, Comprehensive Health Planning Association of San Diego, Riverside and Imperial Counties; among others. *Memberships*: Native American Training Associates Institute (board chairman); National Social Workers Techni-Culture Coalition (vice-president); Pauma Valley Community Association; California Association for Indian Health Administrators; Mental Health Association in California (board member); National Indian Health Board (board of directors); California Rural Indian Health Board (chairman, board of directors); Masters in Public Health Program for Native Americans, University of California, Berkeley (advisory board). *Awards, honors*: Recipient of Robert F. Kennedy Memorial Fellowship, 1970; selected as one of the "Ten Outstanding Young Men of San Diego" by the San Diego Junior Chamber of Commerce, 1971; selected

as "San Diego North County Man of the Year" by the Northern San Diego County Associated Chamber of Commerce, 1971; awarded a "Resolution of Commendation" for outstanding community service by the California State Senate, 1972; awarded the "National Distiguished Community Service Award by the National Social Workers Techni-Culture Coalition, 1973; Dedication by Indian Health Center, 1976; Letter of Commendation, 1980, by President Jimmy Carter; Luna Wessel Distinguished Service Award, Californoa Rural Indian Health Board, 1986; Official Commendation, U.S. Senator Daniel K. Inouye, Chairperson of the Senate Select Committee on Indian Affairs, 1989. *Interests*: Testified before the Senate and House subcommittees on appropriations, Washington, D.C., 1971-. *Biographical sources*: Who's Who in California (Califoria Historical Society); Who's Who in Human Service Professionals (National Reference Institute, Washington, D.C.); Who's Who in U.S. Executives.

MAGISKAN, WILLIAM, JR.
(Indian band chief)
Affiliation: Aroland Indian band, Box 390, Nakina, Ontario, Canada P0T 2H0 (807) 329-5970.

MAHAN, HAROLD D. (Cherokee) 1931-
(biologist, museum administrator)
Born June 11, 1931, Ferndale, Mich. *Education*: Wayne State University, BA, 1954; University of Michigan, MS, 1957; Michigan State University, PhD, 1964. *Principal occupation*: Biologist, museum administrator. *Home address*: 28050 Gates Mill Blvd., Pepper Pike, OH 44124. *Affiliations*: Professor, Central Michigan University, 1957-72; director, Central Michigan University Museum, 1969-72; director, Cleveland Museum of Natural History, 1973-. *Military service*: U.S. Air Force (Special Services), 1950-53. *Community activities*: Michigan Audubon Society (president); Mid-West Museums Conference (ex-vice president); Ohio Museums Association (president). *Memberships*: Phi Kappa Phi, 1968-; Sigma Xi, 1968-; Animal Behavior Society; Association of Science Museums Directors (president, 1980-); Association of Systematic Collection (vice president, 1980-). *Awards, honors*: Recipient, Louis Agassiz Research Fuertes Award, 1957, Wilson Ornithological Society. *Interests*: Ornithology; wildlife photography; bird distribution research; travel. *Biographical sources*: Who's Who in America; Who's Who in the Midwest; Who's Who in Ecology. *Published works*: An Introduction to Ornithology, co-author (Macmillan, 1975); The Jack Pine Warbler (Michigan Audubon Society, 1967-1972).

*MAHIEU, REGINA M.
(organization director)
Affiliation: Quad City League of native Americans, 418 19th St., Rock Island, IL 61201.

MAIER, GARY
(commissioner)
Affiliation: Wyoming State Indian Commission, U.S. West Bldg., Rm. 259B, 6101 Yellowstone, Cheyenne, WY 82002 (307) 777-6779.

MAINES, BILL J. (Aleut) 1954-
(radio station general manager)
Born October 30, 1954, Anchorage, AK. *Education*: Electronic Institute, Pittsburgh, AA, 1974. *Principal occupation*: General Manager. *Home address*: P.O. Box 109, 4667 Okakok St., Bar-

row, AK 99723 (907) 852-6046 (work). *Affiliations*: KDLG-AM, Dillingham, AK, 1977-88; KBRW-AM, Barrow, AK, 1988-. *Other professional posts*: Alaska Public Radio Network (board of directors); Alaska Native Communications Society (co-chair). *Community activities*: Choggiung Ltd. - Dillingham Village corporation. *Memberships*: Bristol Bay Native Corporation - regional corp.; Alaska Federation of Natives.

MAINVILLE, JOAN
(Indian band chief)
Affiliation: Couchiching Indian band, Box 723, Fort Frances, Ontario, Canada P9A 3N1 (807) 274-3228.

MAKIL, IVAN (Pima-Maricopa)
(tribal council president)
Affiliation: Salt River Pima-Maricopa Indian Community Council, Route 1, Box 216, Scottsdale, AZ 85256 (602) 941-7277.

*MALCOLM, JAN (Oneida)
(museum director)
Affiliation: Oneida Nation Museum, P.O. Box 365, Oneida, WI 54155 (414) 869-2768.

MALDONADO, RAYMOND
(BIA agency supt.)
Affiliation: Olympic Penninsula Agency, Bureau of Indian Affairs, P.O. Box 120, Office Bldg., Hoquiam, WA 98550 (206) 533-9100.

MALLOTT, BYRON (Tlingit) 1943-
(chief executive officer)
Born April 6, 1943, Yakutat, Alaska. Education: Western Washington State College, 1961-64. *Principal occupation*: Chief executive officer. Resides in Juneau, AK. *Address*: Sealaska Corporation, One Sealaska Plaza, Suite 400, Juneau, AK 99801 (907) 586-1512 (work). *Affiliations*: Mayor, City of Yakutat, 1965; elected to City Council, City of Yakutat, 1968; local government specialist, Office of the Governor, Juneau, 1966-1967; special assistant to U.S. Senator Mike Gravel, Washington, DC, 1969; executive director, Rural Alaska Community Action Program, Inc., Anchorage, 1970; director, Local Affairs Agency, Office of the Governor, 1971-72; commissioner, Dept. of Community & Regional Affairs, State of Alaska, 1972-74; consultant, Alaska Natives Resources, Inc., 1974-78; president, Alaska Federation of Natives, Inc., 1977-78; chairman of the board, Sealaska Corporation, Juneau, 1976-84; chief executive officer, Sealaska Corporation, Juneau, 1982-. *Other professional posts*: Owner Yakutat Bay Adventures (commercial fishing), 1974-; director, Alaska Airlines, 1982-; board member, Alaska United Drilling, Inc., 1982-; director, Federal Reserve Bank, Seattle Branch, 1982-; board member, United Bank of Alaska, 1984-; board member, Colville Tribal Enterprise Corp., 1985-; board member, The Mediation Institute, 1985-. *Community activities*: Rural Affairs Commission, State of Alaska, 1972-76; Alaska Native Foundation (vice chairman, 1975-79); Yak-Tat Kwaan, Inc. (Yakutat Village Corp.) (board of directors, 1974-78; chairman, 1976-77); B.M. Behrends Bank (director, 1975-84); Capital Site Planning Commission, State of Alaska, 1977-79; Governor's Rapportionment Board, State of Alaska (chairman, 1979-80); White House Fellowship Selection Commission-Western Region, 1978-83; Commercial Fisheries & Agricultural Bank, State of Alaska (director, 1979); University of Alaska Foundation (director, 1980-85).

Awards, honors: Governor's Award for Service to Alaska, 1982; recipient of the Alaska Native Citizen of the Year Award from the Alaska Federation of Natives, 1982; Honorary Doctorate Degree in the Humanities by the University of Alaska, 1984. *Published works*: Several recent articles are One Day in the Life of a Native Chief Executive, in 2 parts, Alaska Native Magazine, Sept. & Oct., 1985; Byron's Brew, Alaska Business Monthly, Oct., 1985; Sealaska: Soon to Rival Oil Companies in Power? an interview with Byron Mallott, Alaska Industry, Sept., 1981.

MALLOTTE, DALE S.
(Te-Moak Western Shoshone)
(tribal chairperson)
Affiliation: Tribal Council of the Te-Moak Western Shoshone Indians of Nevada, 525 Sinset St., Elko, NV 89801 (702) 738-9251.

MAMAKWA, JAMES
(Indian band chief)
Affiliation: Kingfisher Lake Indian Band, Kingfisher Lake, Ontario, Canada P0V 1Z0 (807) 536-0067.

MANATOWA, ELMER, Jr. (Sac and Fox)
(tribal chairperson)
Affiliation: Sac & Fox of Oklahoma Business Committee, Route 2, Box 246, Stroud, OK 74079 (918) 968-3526.

MANDAMIN, ELI
(Indian band chief)
Affiliation: Shoal Lake #39 Indian band, Kejick P.O. , Shoal Lake, Ontario, Canada P0X 1E0 (807) 733-2560.

*MANDAN, ROSELLA
(administrative officer-Indian health center)
Affiliation: Fort Berthold PHS Indian Health Center, New Town, ND 58763 (701) 627-4701.

MANDSAGER, RICHARD, M.D.
(health director)
Affiliation: Alaska Native Health Center, 255 Gambel St., Anchorage, AK 99501 (907) 279-6661.

MANESS, PHILLIP
(Indian band chief)
Affiliation: Chippewas of Sarina, 93 Tashmoo Ave., Sarnia, Ontario, Canada N7T 7H5 (519) 336-8410.

MANESS, SHERMAN
(organization president)
Affiliation: Ontario Federation of Indian Friendship Centres, 234 Eglinton Ave. East, Suite 207, Toronto, Ontario, Canada M4P 1K5 (416) 484-1411.

*MANGEN, BETTY OXENDINE
(education director)
Affiliation: North Carolina State Dept. of Public Instruction, Division of Indian Education, 301 N. Wilmington St., Raleigh, NC 27601 (919) 715-1000.

MANKILLER, WILMA (Oklahoma Cherokee)
(former principal chief-
Cherokee Nation of Oklahoma)
Born in northeastern Oklahoma. *Address & Affiliation*: Principal Chief (acting, 1985-87; elected, 1987-94), Cherokee Nation of Oklahoma, P.O. Box 948, Tahlequah, OK 74465 (918) 456-0671. *Interests*: Native rights issues;

writing, reading, history; spending time with grandchildren (family). "I will continue to be involved. I'm going to try to organize rural Cherokee communities into doing Saturday academics...language, films, dinners, sharing cultural and historical issues. I've always been involved in these issues." *Published work*: Autobiography, "Mankiller: A Chief and Her People, by Wilma Mankiller & Michael Wallis (St. Martins Press, 1993)

MANN, CHERYL J. (Cheyenne River Sioux)
(administrator))
Born January 17, 1945, Cheyenne Agency, S.D. *Education*: Western State College of Engineering (Los Angeles, CA), ASEE, 1971; UCLA, 1971-73; University of New Mexico (Non-Profit Management), 1987. *Home address*: 2804 20th St., NW, Albuquerque, NM 87104 (505) 344-6081; 247-2251 (work). *Affiliation*: National Indian Youth Council, Albuquerque, NM (associate director, 1974-88; executive director, 1989-). *Other professional post*: Editor, Americnas Before Columbus, NIYC newspaper published 6x/year. *Community activities*: Youth athletic groups. *Membership*: Indian Executive Directors, Networking (chairperson-3 years). *Interests*: "Very active in youth athletics and Indian cultural activities - pow wows, etc.

*MANNES, MARC
(editor)
Affiliation: American Indian Law Newsleter, American Indian Law Center, P.O. Box 4456, Station A, Albuquerque, NM 87196 (505) 277-5462.

*MANNING, JOHN W. (JACK)
(Fort Peck Sioux) 1950-
(attorney)
Born March 8, 1950, Miles City, Mont. *Education*: Dartmouth College, AB, 1972; Stanford University Law School, JD, 1975. *Principal occupation*: Attorney. *Home address*: 211 3rd Ave. N., Great Falls, MT 59401 (406) 727-3632 (work) *Affiliations*: Associate, Davis Polk & Wardwell, New York, NY 1975-80; Dorsey & Whitney Law Firm, Great Falls, MT (associate 1980-84; partner, 1984-). *Community activities*: Board member of Neighborhood Housing Services & Great Falls Native American Center at various times.

*MANNING, LINDSEY
(tribal chairperson)
Affiliation: Shoshone Paiute Business Council, Duck Valley Reservation, P.O. Box 219, Owyhee, NV 89832 (702) 757-3161.

MANNING, NICK (Quason) 1938-
(film producer-cinematographer)
Born May 1, a938, Boston, Mas. *Education*: University of Vermont, BA, 1961; Syracuse University, MA (Communications), 1964, Ph.D. (Visual and Performing Arts), 1972. *Principal occupation*: Film producer-cinematographer. *Home address*: 53 Hamilton Ave., Staten Island, NY 10301 (718) 981-0120. *Affiliation*: owner, MCAVE, 25 West 45th St., New York, NY 10036. *Other professional post*: chairperson, Film & TV Dept., Pratt Institute, Brooklyn, NY, 1985-. Founder (1965) and Director (1965-87, New York Film Expo. *Feature Productions*: Wolfpack, 96 minutes, 35mm drama (JER Films, 1985); Manhattan Moonshine, 92 minutes, 35mm romantic comedy (Manley Productions (foreign); Phoenix Films (dometic, 1988); The Big Giver, 89 minutes, 35 mm political satire (Manley Pro-

ductions (foreign); Phoenix Films (domestic, 1989). *Documentaries*: Iroquois Social Dance, 28 minutes on the social dance of Mohawk Indians, 1979; among others. *Memberships*: National Academy of Television Arts and Sciences; Fulbright Alumni Association; University Film and Video Association. *Awards, honors*: Fulbright lecture grant to India, 1979; Fulbright research grant to Yugoslavia, 1984; New York State Council on the Arts (video), 1985; Cine Golden Eagle Award. *Published work*: Film Making (Rosen Publishing, 1985).

MANOR, PATRICIA K.
(administrator)
Affiliation: Native American Fish & Wildlife Society, 750 Burbank St., Boulder, CO 80020 (303) 466-1725.

MANSON, SPERO M. (Pembina Chippewa) 1950-
(medical anthropologist)
Born May 2, 1950, Everett, Wash. *Education*: University of Washington, BA, 1972; University of Minnesota, MA, 1975, PhD (Anthropology), 1978. *Principal occupation*: Mental health researcher. *Address*: Dept. of Psychiatry, UCHSC, C249, Denver, CO 80262 (303) 270-4600. *Affiliations*: Director, National Center for American Indian & Alaska Native Mental Health Research, Denver, 1986-; associate professor, Dept. of Psychiatry, University of Colorado Health Sciences Center, Denver, 1986-. *Other professional posts*: Professor and director, Institute on Aging, School of Urban and Public Affairs, Portland State University, 1982-86; associate professor and director, Social Psychiatric Research, Dept. of Psychiatry, School of Medicine, Oregon Health Sciences University, 1982-86; adjunct associate professor of anthropology, Portland State University, 1982-86. *Consultantships*: Billings Area Office, Indian Health Service, MT, 1984-; Northwest Portland Area Indian Health Board, 1985-; Alaska Native Health Board, 1985-. *Community activities*: National Institute of Mental Health Epidemiology & Services Research Review Committee, 1983-87; NIDA Advisory Committee on Prevention, 1983-85; Oregon State Governor's Task Force on Alcohol & Drug Abuse, 1984-86; vice-chair, Denver Indian Health & Family Services; board of directors, CO Gerontological Society. *Memberships*: American Anthropological Association; Gerontological Society of America; Society for Applied Anthropology (Fellow); Society for Medical Anthropology. *Awards, honors*: 1984 Oregon State System of Higher Education, Faculty Excellence Award; Phi Beta Kappa; State of Oregon Excellence Award in Higher Education (1985); Fulbright-Hays Scholar; CIC Traveling Scholar; National Science Foundation Scholarship. *Interests*: Vocational - Diagnosis, epidemiology, treatment and prevention of serious psychological dysfunction and major mental ilness across the developmental life span among American Indians & Alaska Natives. Avocational - Hunting, flyfishing, skiing, photography. *Published works*: Co-editor, books in preparation: American Indian Youth: Seventy-five Years of Psychosocial Research (Greenwood Press); New Directions in Prevention (Oregon Health Sciences University, 1982); Psychosocial Research with American Indian and Alaska Native Youth (Greenwood Press, 1984); Health and Behavior: A Research Agenda for American Indians (University of Colorado Health Sciences Center, 1988); editor, Medical Anthropology:

Implications for Stress Prevention Across Cultures (National Institute of Mental Health, Government Printing Office). Numerous articles in professional journals.

MANUAL, HILDA
(BIA depty commissioner)
Affiliation: Deputy Commissioner of Indian Affairs, Bureau of Indian Affairs, 1849 C St., NW, MS: 4140-MIB, Washington, DC 20240 (202) 208-5116 (1993-).

MANUELITO, ETHEL M. (Navajo) 1954-
(associate director; consultant)
Born July 6, 1954, Fort Defiance, Ariz. *Education*: University of New Mexico, BS, 1977, MA, 1982; Western New Mexico University (Silver City), 3 years. *Principal occupation*: Associate director; consultant. *Home address*: P.O. Box 51, Tohatchi, NM 87325 (505) 733-2200 (work). *Affiliation*: Associate director for Direct Services, Tohatchi Special Education & Training Center, 1978-. *Other professional post*: Consultant to Navajo Initiative Project. *Community activities*: Gallup McKinley County Schools (Board of Education, secretary); University of New Mexico-Gallup Branch (Advisory Board Member); New Mexico School Board (Region I President). *Memberships*: Council for Exceptional Children; National School Board Association; Navajo National Public School Board Association. *Awards, honors*: Navajo Tribal Scholarships. *Interests*: "Travel to various parts of the U.S.; beadwork, crochet, sewing Native American clothes."

*MANYARROWS, VICTORIA LENA
(Eastern Cherokee) 1956-
(social service/arts administrator; writer)
Born Aril 10, 1956, Des Moines, Iowa. *Education*: San Francisco State University, MSW, 1993. *Principal occupation*: Social service/arts administrator; writer. *Home address*: 2440 16th St. #146, San Francisco, CA 94103 (415) 864-3538. *Affiliation*: Support Service for the Arts, San Francisco, CA (administrator; co-director, 1981-). *Other professional post*: Counselor/administrator in various alcohol, substance abuse & homeless programs. Youth Empowerment Council member, United Indian Nations, Oakland, CA; volunteer, American Indian Contemporary Arts, San Francisco, & Indian Education Center, Oakland; volunteer, Brava! for Women in the Arts & Casa El Salvador (both in San Francisco). *Memberships*: ATLATL; National Service Organization for Native American Artists; Native Writer's Circle of the Americas; Wordcraft Circle of Native Writers & Apprentices; Indigenous Women's Network. *Awards, honors*: Graduate Honor Fellowship, San Francisco State University, 1991-92; Featured Poet (Summer, 1993), "Orphic Lute" journal, Seattle, WA. *Interests*: "Creative writing (especially poetry and essays) and teaching creative writing to Native women and youth. Have traveled extensively in Mexico & Central America (speak Spanish) and speak out on international Indian issues. Other interests: public health, environmental, and social psychological needs of Native women, children and communities; photography, video, and mixed media (poetry and visual art collaborative pieces)." *Published work*: Poetry, Songs From the Native Lands (Turtleland/Pajarta Press, 1995). *Poems & essays published in various journals & anthologies in the U.S. and Canada, including*: Without Discovery: A Native Response to Columbus (Broken Moon Press, 1992); The Colour of Resistance: A Contempo-

rary Collection of Writing by Aboriginal Women (Sister Vision Press, Canada, 1993); Looking At the Words of Our People (Theytus Books, Canada, 1993); The Worlds Walking (New Rivers Press, 1994); Unsettling America: Race & Ethnicity in Contemporary American Poetry (Viking Penguin Press, 1994).

*MANYBEADS, NORA
(school chairperson)
Affiliation: Aneth Community School, P.O. Box 600, Montezuma Creek, UT 84534 (801) 651-3271.

MAR, JOSE MATOS
(director of Inter-American Indian Institute)
Born November 1, Peru. *Education*: Universidad Nacional Mayor de San Marcos-Lima, Peru (Anthropology); Universidad de Paris (Ethnology), Post-graduate. *Principal occupation*: Director, Inter-American Indian Institute, #232, Colonia Pedregal de San Angel, Delegacion Alvaro Obregon C.P.01900, Mexico D.F. *Home address*: Popo No. 20-3 Col. Florida, Mexico, D.F. 01030 (6672724).

MARACLE, SYLVIA
(executive director)
Affiliation: Ontario Federation of Indian Friendship Centres, 234 Eglinton Ave. East, Suite 207, Toronto, Ontario, Canada M4P 1K5 (416) 484-1411.

*MARCANO-QUINONES, MR. RENE
(Cibanacan-Center Stone) (Taino) 1941-
(tribal organization)
Born September 16, 1941, Santurce, San Juan, P.R. *Education*: High school. *Home address*: 174 W. 107 St. #3E, New York, NY 10025 (212) 866-4573. *Affiliation*: Principal Cacique, Taino Nation, Puerto Rico & abroad. *Other professional post*: Editor of tribal newsletter. *Interests*: "Impart conferences regarding Taino restoration efforts regarding culture, history, music and art." Biographical source: "The Native American Response to the Columbus Quincentenary," Multi-Cultural Review magazine, Jan. 1992, Vol. 1 No. 1, pp. 20-22.

MARCEL, PATRICK
(Indian band chief)
Affiliation: Athabasca Chipewyan Indian Band, Box 366, Fort Chipewyan, Alberta, Canada (403) 697-3730.

MARCHAND, ARNOLD N. (Colville)
(museum director)
Affiliation: Colville Confederated Tribes Museum, Box 150, Nespelem, WA 99155 (509) 634-4711.

MARCHAND, THELMA (Colville) 1932-
(tribal officer)
Born April 17, 1932, Okanogan County, Wash. *Education*: Wenatchee Junior College. *Principal occupation*: Secretary, Colville Business (Tribal) Council. *Home address*: 320 Columbia St., Omak, Wash. 98841.

MARGOLIN, MALCOLM 1940-
(publisher, writer)
Born October 27, 1940, Boston, Mass. *Education*: Harvard University, BA, 1964. *Principal occupation*: Publisher, writer. *Address*: P.O. Box 9145, Berkeley, CA 94709 (510) 549-3564 (office). *Affiliation*: News From Native California, Berkeley, CA, 1987-; publisher, Heyday Books,

Berkeley, CA, 1975-. *Interests*: "Writing and publishing has focused on the history and ongoing cultures of California Indian people. A major commitment of both Heyday Books & "News from Native California" has been to provide a vehicle by which Native Californians can describe their history and culture in their own voices." *Published works*: Ohlone Way: Indian Life in San Francisco Area (Heyday Books, 1978); Way We Lived: Reminiscence, Stories, Songs (Heyday Books, 1981).

MARK, CHARLES
(Indian band chief)
Affiliation: Montagnais de Pakua Shipi Indian Band, St-Augustin, Quebec G0G 2R0 (418) 947-2253.

*MARKISHTUM, HUBERT (Makah)
(tribal chairperson)
Affiliation: Makah Tribal Council, P.O. Box 115, Neah Bay, WA 98357 (206) 645-2201 ext. 36.

MARKS, C. HARDAWAY
(council chairperson)
Affiliation: Virginia Council on Indians, 8007 Discovery Dr., Richmond, VA 23229-8699 (804) 662-9285.

*MARKS, COLEEN KELLEY (Mohawk) 1951-
(museum curator, arts consultant)
Born January 12, 1951, Altoona, Pa. *Education*: College of the Redlands (Eureka, CA), AA, 1978; Humboldt State University (Arcata, CA), two BA's, 1988. *Principal occupation*: Museum curator, American Indian arts consultant. *Address*: P.O. Box 295, Orick, CA 9555 (707) 488-3545. *Affiliations*: Curator, End of the Trail Museum, Klamath, CA, 1993-; consultant of Native American arts, Orick, CA, 1979-. *Other professional posts*: Assistant director of California Indian Project, Lowie Museum of Anthropology (Berkeley, CA), 1988-89; director/curator, Clarke Memorial Museum, Eureka, CA (7 years); Redwood National Park, Patrick's Point State Park, and Del Norte County Historical Society - curated all collections (2 1/2 years). *Community activities*: Past vice president, YWCA; past member of Humboldt County Status of Women Commission; past president of Humboldt Open Door Clinic; past chair of Women's History Month for Humboldt County; past member, City of Arcata Design Assistance Committee; current member, Alice Spinas Basketry Collection Committee. *Interests*: "Collecting American Indian art & books; have traveled in Europe, Canada, Mexico, Caribbean & the USA. Have made numerous trips to Europe to view & study American Indian art in museum collections." *Curated Exhibits*: "Elizabeth Conrad Hickox: Baskets From the Center of the World," Reese Bullen Gallery, Humboldt State University, 1/90; "From Classic to Contemporary: The Basketry of Northwestern California," Muckenthaler Cultural Center, Fullerton, CA, 5-7/91; "From Women's Hands: The Basketry of Lena Reed McCovey and Ethel Jones Williams" Reese Bullen Gallery, Humboldt State University, 11/92; among others. *Published works*: Editor, The Hover Collection of Karuk Baskets (Clarke Memorial Museum, 1985); co-authored, "From Women's Hands: The Basketry of Lena Reed McCovey and Ethel Jones Williams," (Humboldt State University, 1992).

MARKS, PATRICIA ANN 1954-
(attorney, lobbyist, consultant)
Born March 2, 1954, Brockport, N.Y. *Education*: S.U.N.Y. at Brockport, BS, 1976; Georgetown University Law Center, JD, 1987). *Principal occupation*: Attorney, lobbyist, consultant. *Home address*: 15992 AE Mullinix Rd., Woodbine, MD 21797. *Affiliations*: Personal staff member, U.S. Senator James Abourezk, Washington, DC, 1975-76 (during this period, Sen. Abourezk was chairman of the Senate Indian Affairs Subcommittee of the Senate Interior and Insular Affairs Committee); professional staff member, American Indian Policy Review Commission, Washington, DC, 1976-77; legislative assistant, U.S. Senate Select Committee on Indian Affairs, Washington, DC, 1977-79; vice president and co-founder, Karl A. Funke & Associates, Inc., Washington, DC, 1979- (a lobbying & consulting firm which represents Indian tribes, national Indian organizations, business and local governments). *Other professional post*: Co-founder and officer, AAA Roofing Co. *Memberships*: National Congress of American Indians; ABA Student Bar Association. *Awards, honors*: National Indian Health Board Award for Service, 1983. *Interests*: "Indian health; Indian legislative specialist; Indian Child Welfare Act; national Indian budget issues; Indian economic development." *Published work*: American Indian Policy Review Commission Final Report, U.S. Congress.

*MARKWARDT, HOLLY (Ojibway) 1970-
(American Indian admissions counselor)
Born October 27, 1970, Virginia, Minn. *Education*: St. Cloud State University, B.A., 1994; University of Minnesota, M.A., 1994. *Principal occupation*: American Indian admissions counselor. *Home address*: 1260 Larpenteur Ave. W. #415, St. Paul, MN 55113. *Affiliation*: University of Minnesota, Minneapolis, MN.

*MARNEY, MARGIE E. (Cherokee) 1948-
(educator)
Born February 25, 1948, Alva, Okla. *Education*: Phillips University (Enid, OK), B.S., 1970; University of Northwestern Oklahoma (Alva, OK), Masters of Reading & L.D. Educ., 1983; Oklahoma State University, Admin. Cert., 1990. *Principal occupation*: Educator. *Address*: Rt. 1, Box 382, Enid, OK 73703 (405) 237-8156. *Affiliation*: Chapter I & Title V Coordinator, Enid Public Schools, Enid, OK. *Other professional posts*: Professor, Phillips University; Enid higher education instructor. *Community activities*: "Keeper of the Plains" board member; president & board member, Cherokee Reading Council. *Memberships*: National Education Association; Oklahoma Education Association; International Reading Association; Oklahoma Reading Association; Cherokee Strip Reading Council (president, 1985-); National Council on Indian Education; Oklahoma Council on Indian Education. *Interests*: "Avid reader and learner; parent of four active children in education; educator of kindergarten to college level."

MARQUAT, CLARK, M.D.
(chief medical officer)
Affiliation: Oklahoma Area Office, Indian Health Service, Five Corporate Plaza, 3625 NW 56th St., Oklahoma City, OK 73102 (405) 231-4796.

MARQUEZ-BAINES, CAROL
(center director)
Affiliation: Urban Indian Child Resource Center, Oakland, CA 94610 (510) 832-2386.

MARSHALL, CHRISTOPHER
(museum director)
Affiliation: Maine Tribal Unity Museum, Quaker Hill Rd., Unity, ME 04988 (207) 948-3131.

MARSHALL-BRINGS PLENTY, CARLA RAE (Oyate Wowakiye Wi) (Cheyenne River Sioux) 1966-
(education, graphics)
Born May 7, 1966, Bitberg, Germany (USAF). *Education*: Black Hills State College (Spearfish, SD), Associate of Science, 1987. *Principal occupation*: Education, graphics. *Home address*: 4580 N. Hwy, 79 #5, Rapid City, SD 57702 (605) 787-6404; 394-9730 (work). *Affiliation*: HP/DP Task Force Coordinator, Cheyenne River Sioux Tribe, Eagle Butte, SD, 1990-91; Indian Country Today/Lakota Times, Rapid City, SD (classified advertising representative, 1992-93; advertising sales director, 1993); administrative assistant, editor, education coordinator, InterTribal Bison Cooperative, Rapid City, SD, 1993-. *Other professional posts*: Write monthly and annual reports along with articles and ads. *Awards, honors*: YMCA Scholarship; Crazy Horse Memorial Scholarship; Kevin Whirlwind Horse Memorial. *Community activities*: "I was YMCA Chapter Coordinator for the Iron Lightning Community, located on the Cheyenne River Sioux Reservation. This volunteer work involved planning and coordinating activities for the youth in the community; also I was secretary for the two pow-wow committees, the Iron Lighting Community and Lakota Ominiciya at Black Hills State."

MARTEL, PAT
(Indian band chief)
Affiliation: Hat River Dene Indian Band, Box 1638, Hay River, Northwest Territory X0E 0R0 (403) 874-6701.

*MARTELL, PAM
(education coordinator)
Affiliation: Michigan Dept. of Education, Native American Programs Unit, P.O. Box 30008, Lansing, MI 48909 (517) 373-6059.

MARTGAN, REBECCA
(BIA supt. for education)
Affiliation: Standing Rock Agency, Bureau of Indian Affairs, Fort Yates, ND 58538 (701) 854-3497.

MARTIN, ALBERT (Tyne Maidu)
(rancheria chairperson)
Affiliation: Berry Creek Rancheria Tribal Council, 1779 Mitchell Ave., Oroville, CA 95966 (916) 534-3859.

*MARTIN, AMY (Pomo)
(rancheria chairperson)
Affiliation: Dry Creek Rancheria, P.O. Box 607, Geyserville, CA 95441 (707) 857-3842.

MARTIN, ANNIE (Eskimo)
(village coordinator)
Affiliation: Point Lay Native Village, P.O. Box 101, Point Lay, AK 99759 (907) 833-2428.

MARTIN, BONNIE
(BIA education administrator)
Affiliation: Choctaw Field Office, Bureau of Indian Affairs, 421 Powell St., Philadelphia, MS 39350 (601) 656-1521.

MARTIN, DOUGLAS
(Indian band chief)
Affiliation: Micmacs of Gesgapegiag Indian Band, Maria Indan Reserve, Box 1280, Maria, Quebec, Canada G0C 1Y0 (418) 759-3441.

*MARTIN, ELIZABETH PA (Hawaiian)
(organization president)
Affiliation: Hui Na-Auao, 3415 Ka'ochiani Dr., Honolulu, HI 96817 (808) 595-6647.

MARTIN, JAMES
(BIA Indian education)
Affiliation: Indian Education, Bureau of Indian Affairs, Rm. 3520, MS: 3512-MIB, 1849 C St., NW, Washington, DC 20240 (202) 208-3550.

MARTIN, JERRY
(museum director)
Affiliation: Mid-American All-Indian Center Museum, 650 N. Seneca, Wichita, KS 67203 (316) 262-5221.

*MARTIN, JOHN
(commission chairperson)
Affiliation: Tennessee Commission on Indian Affairs, 112 Cynthia Lane, Apt. C, Knoxville, TN 37922.

MARTIN, JOY
(BIA Indian education)
Affiliation: Indian Education, Bureau of Indian Affairs, Rm. 3519, MS-3512-MIB,1849 C St., NW, Washington, D.C. 20245 (202) 208-4555.

*MARTIN, KALLEN M. (Mohawk)
(radio station manager)
Affiliation CKON - 97.3 FM, Akwesasne Communications Society, P.O. Box 140, Rooseveltown, NY 13683 (518) 358-3426.

*MARTIN, LEO
(commission director)
Affiliation: Maine Indian Affairs Commission, State House Station #38, Augusta, ME 04333 (207) 287-5800.

*MARTIN, MICHAEL (Mohaw/Onondaga)
(student; national rep-AISES)
Education: Major in Economics, Buffalo State College. *Principal occupation*: Student. Address: Buffalo State College, P.O. Box 136, Buffalo, NY 14213. *Affiliation*: National representative, AISES, Boulder, CO.

MARTIN, PETER J. (White Earth Chippewa) 1937-
(federal government administrator)
Born July 21, 1937, White Earth Indian Reservation, White Earth, Minn. *Education*: University of New Mexico, BA, 1967. *Principal occupation*: Federal government administrator-Indian affairs. Resides in White Earth, MN. *Affiliations*: Administrative manager, Albuquerque Indian School, 1966-1969; administrative director, Institute of American Indian Arts, Santa Fe, 1969-70; executive assistant, 1970, chief, 1970-72, Plant Management Engineering Center, B.I.A., Denver, CO; chief, Indian Technical Assistance Center, Denver, 1972-77; program specialist, Muskogee Area Office, BIA, 1977-80; owner, Indian consultant business, American Indian Programs, White Earth, MN, 1980-. *Memberships*: Anishnabe Akeeng (The People's Land); National Congress of American Indians; Minnesota Indian Contactor's Association; Minnesota Democratic Farm Labor Party - National Roster

of Buy Indian Contractor's. *Awards, honors*: Certificate of Superior Performance, Dept. of the Interior, BIA (for service in connection with the placement of 220 Job Corps employees, July, 1969); Dept. of the Interior, Bureau of Indian Affairs, 20-year Service Pin, April, 1978. *Interests*: Interested in and work for betterment of all American Indians; presently engaged as nationwide consultant in American Indian Programs (sole proprietorship enterprise); have visited over 200 Indian reservations and worked with respective tribal councils and program heads; research, writing articles and books, and study of American Indian tribes and involvement with Indian-Federal-State-Municipal programs and relationships.

MARTIN, PHILLIP *(Tulliokchiishko)*
(Mississippi Choctaw) 1926-
(tribal chief)
Born March 13, 1926, Philadelphia, Miss. *Education*: Cherokee (NC) High School, 1945; Meridian (MS) Junior College, 1955-57. *Principal Occupation*: Chief, Mississippi Band of Choctaw Indians. *Address*: Box 6010 - Choctaw Branch, Philadelphia, MS 39350 (601) 656-5251. *Affiliations*: Mississippi Band of Choctaw Indians (chief, 1959-65, 1971-75, 1979-; president, National Indian Management Service, Philadelphia, MS, 1975-). *Other Professional Posts*: Founder & past president, United South & Eastern Tribes, 1968-1969, 1971-72; president, National Tribal Chairmen's Association, 1981-83. *Military Service*: U.S. Air Force, 1945-55. *Community Activities*: Mississippi Band of Choctaw Indians (councilman, 1957-66, 1971-75, 1977-79); Choctaw Housing Authority (chairman of board, 1964-1971); Choctaw Community Action Agency (executive director, 1966-71); Chata Development Company (president-board of directors, 1969-75); Haskell Indian Junior College (president-board of regents, and board member, 1970-76); Chahta Enterprise, Choctaw Greetings Enterprise, and Choctaw Electronics Enterprise (chairman). *Memberships*: National Tribal Chairmen's Association; National Congress of American Indians; United South and Eastern Tribes; Americans for Indian Opportunity; American Indian Policy Review Commission (member, Task Force 7); Master's in Public Health for Native Americans Program, University of California at Berkeley (advisory committee); Neshoba County Chamber of Commerce. *Awards, Honors*: Indian Council Fire, Indian Achievement Award; United South and Eastern Tribes Leadership Award, 1984; American Vocational Association's 1987 Award of Merit for the successful work of the tribe's Vocational Education program; the 1988 statewide Employer Support of the Guard and Reserve Outstanding Employer award; the 1988 HUD Certificate of National Merit in the National Recognition Program for Urban Development Excellence for the tribe's innovative Early Childhood Education Center; the United Indian Development Association's Jay Silverheels Award; the Minority Supplier/Distributor of the Year award from the Small Business Administration and the Minority Business Administration; the "Soar Like an Eagle" achievement award from the United Indian Youth Organization (UNITY), and an economic achievement award from the U.S. Department of Housing and Urban Development (HUD). *Interests*: Indian tribal government development and economic development. During his most recent tenure as Chief (since 1979), reservation unemployment rates have declined

from around 50% to their current level of about 20%. He has been responsible for establishment of an industrial park, a tribally-owned construction company, and several public service enterprises, such as the Choctaw Transit Authority, and Choctaw Utility Commission. Most importantly, though, he has developed the Chahta Enterprise, which assembles automotive wiring harnesses in three plants for the Ford Motor Company and small motors for United Technologies. In addition, he created the Choctaw Greetings Enterprise, which hand-finishes greeting cards for the American Greetings Corporation of Cleveland, Ohio -- the first plant built on an Indian reservation through use of state industrial revenue bonds. *Biographical sources*: Books - Tribal Assets: The Rebirth of Native America, by Robert White; The Choctaws, by Emilie U. Lepthien; Providence, by Will Campbell. Articles - "Reader's Digest," Nov. 1984; "Fortune" Magazine, April 19, 1993.

MARTIN, ROBERT G.
(college president)
Affiliation: Haskell Indian Junior College, 155 Indian Ave., Box H-1304, Lawrence, KS 66044 (913) 749-8403.

MARTIN, THOMAS EVERETT
(Indian band chief)
Affiliation: Eel River Bar Indian band, Box 1444, Dalhousie, New Brunswick, Canada E0K 1B0 (506) 684-2366.

*MARTIN, TONY
(tribal town king)
Affiliation: Kialagee Tribal Town, 318 S. Washla, Box 332, Wetumka, OK 74883 (405) 452-3413.

*MARTINE, CYNTHIA "CINDY"
(Jicarilla Apache/Navajo) 1964-
(manufacturing engineer)
Born November 3, 1964, Gallup, N.M. *Education*: New Mexico State University, BS, 1987. *Principal occupation*: Manufacturing engineer. *Home address*: 685 N. Greece Rd., Rochester, NY 14626 (716) 392-8397. *Affiliation*: Eastman Kodak Co., Rochester, NY 1988-. *Community activities*: spokesman, Native American Council at Kodak; Native American Cultural Center, Rochester, NY; Friends of Ganodogan, Victor, NY (Board of Trustee member); co-chair, Native American Women's Recognition Event 1994. *Membership*: American Indian Science & Engineering Society (AISES) (board member, treasurer). *Interests*: "Very interested in helping young Indian students become interested in science, math, engineering. Have done numerous workshops on science projects for young students (grades K-8). Recently (I) did a workshop for young women (grades 6-8) in expanding Your Horizons in Science & Math. I strongly believe that our Indian people are becoming more prominent in their communities; reaching out to the young people and introducing opportunities for our young people in all arenas. I truly enjoy speaking to young people about opportunities in science & engineering and doing science projects with young students. I believe our young people can make great strides in any fields they choose because they have support systems in place to help them, such as AISES." *Biographical sources*: "Minority Programs & Mentoring," (biography) in Chemical & Engineering News 2/8/93; "Corporate Role Model," in Patriots Magazine - 1992 Native American Heritage Issue.

MARTINE, DAVID BUNN (Shinnecock-Montauk/Chiricahua Apache) 1960-
(museum director)
Born June 11, 1960, Southampton, N.Y. *Education*: University of Oklahoma, BFA, 1982; Institute of American Indian Arts, 1983; Central State University, MEd, 1984. *Principal occupation*: Museum director. *Home address*: P.O. Box 1285, Church St., Southamtpon, NY 11969 (516) 283-1643. *Affiliation*: Director, Shinnecock Nation Museum Cultural Center Complex; director, Channel 25 Cable Vision, "Voices of Native America," Shinnecock Indian Tribe, Southampton, NY. *Other professional posts*: Fine artist; lecturer, Cooper Union, New York, NY, 1989-92. *Exhibit*: "Rider With No Horse," Artists Collective, Native Americans of New York City Area. *Community activities*: Suffolk County Native American Task Force (Board Member, 1990); ran for Southampton Town Trustee, Democratic Party Candidate, 1991. *Membership*: Suffolk County Archaeological Association. Interests: Environmental preservation movement; civil rights issues of Native American community; host, "Voices of Native America" Cablevision, Channel 25, Riverhead, NY; proposal reader, evaluator, Administration for Native Americans, Dept. of HHS, Washington, DC, 1991. *Biographical source*: "The Shinnecock Indians: A Culture History," (Ginn, 1984).

*MARTINEZ, ALFRED G.
(school principal)
Affiliation: Casa Blanca Day School, P.o. Box 940, Bapchule, AZ 85221 (602) 315-3489.

*MARTINEZ, LEE, Jr. (Jicarilla Apache)
(radio station manager)
Affiliation: KCIE - 90.5 FM, Jicarilla Apache Tribe, P.O. Box 603, Dulce, NM 87528 (505) 759-3681.

MARTINEZ, REYES (Picuris Pueblo)
(pueblo governor)
Affiliation: Picuris Pueblo Council, P.O. Box 127, Penasco, NM 87553 (505) 587-2519.

MARTINEZ, ROBERT C.
(school principal)
Affiliation: Taos Day School, P.O. Drawer X, Taos, NM 87571 (505) 758-3652.

*MARTZ, MICHAEL
(TV executive producer)
Affiliation: Bethel Broadcasting., Yup'ik Eskimo Sta, Box 468, Bethel, AK 99559 (907) 543-3131.

MASAYESVA, VERNON (Hopi)
(tribal chairperson)
Affiliation: Hopi Tribal Council, P.O. Box 123, Kykotsmovi, AZ 86039 (602) 734-2445.

*MASAYESVA, VICTOR, Jr. (Hopi)
(film producer/director)
Born in 1951 in Hotevilla, Ariz. *Education*: Princeton University, BA, 1973; University of Arizona (graduate studies). *Principal occupation*: Film producer/director. *Address*: P.O. Box 747, Hotevilla, AZ 86030. He has created a body of video & photographic work that represents the culture & traditions of Native Americans - particularly the Hopi of Southwest Arizona - through poetic visualizations. Masayesva employs high tech computer animation & graphics in lyrical translations of Hopi myths, rituals & history. Articulating the richness of his heritage in his own language, he allows the Hopi voice

to be heard. *Videos produced, directed & photographed*: "Hopiit" (lyrical work observing Hopi cultural activities through the cycle of the seasons), 15 minutes, color, 1982; "Itam Hakim, Hopiit" (poetic visualization of Hopi philosophy & prophesy - myths, religion, legends & history of the Hopi people), 58 minutes, color, 1985; "Ritual Clowns" (the traditions & myths of their emergence in the plazas of Southwest Native American communities), 18 minutes, color, 1988; "Pot Starr" (addresses ceramic designs, computer analysis & interpretation), 6 minutes, color, 1990; "Siskyavi - The Place of Chasms" (presents the ceramic traditions of Native Americans), 28 minutes, color, 1991. *Awards, honors*: His numerous awards include fellowships from the Ford Foundation, the Rockefeller Foundation, and the Southwest Association on Indian Affairs; and grants from the National Endowment for the Arts, and the Arizona Commission on the Arts; he was guest artist and artist-in-residence at the School of the Art Institute of Chicago, Princeton University, & the Yellowstone Summer Film/Video Institute, Montana State University. His videotapes have been exhibited internationally at festivals and institutions including the Native American Film & Video Festival, New York; the Museum of Modern Art, New York; World Wide Video Festival, The Hague, Netherlands; Whitney Museum of American Art Biennial, New York; San Francisco Art Institute; and the American Indian Contemporary Arts "Festival 2000," San Francisco.

MASON, GLENN
(museum director)
Affiliation: Cheney Cowles Museum, Eastern Washington State Historical Society, West 2316 First Ave., Spokane, WA 99204 (509) 456-3931.

MASON, K. GAYLE
(executive director)
Affiliation: Union of Ontario Indians, 27 Queen St. East, 2nd Floor, Toronto, Ontario, Canada M5C 1R2 (416) 366-3527.

*MASON, RUSSELL, Sr. (Mandan/Hidatsa)
(tribal chairperson)
Affiliation: Three Affiliated Tribes Business Council, P.O. Box 220, New Town, ND 58763 (701) 627-4781.

*MASON, VELMA
(BIA office director)
Affiliation: Bureau of Indian Affairs, Office of Alcohol & Substance Abuse Prevention, 1849 C St., NW, MS: 4140-MIB, Washington, DC 20240 (202) 208-6179.

MASSA, JOSEPH (Santee Sioux)
(casino general manager)
Affiliation: Royal River Casino, Santee Sioux Tribe, P.O. Box 283, Flandreau, South Dakota 57028 (605) 997-3891.

MATCHEWAN, JEAN-MAURICE
(Indian band chief)
Affiliation: Barriere Lake (Algonquin) Indian Band, Rapid Lake, Parc de la Verendrye, Quebec, Canada J0W 2C0 (819) 824-1734.

MATHEWS, DEREK (Cherokee) 1951-
(educator; events promoter;
media specialist)
Born September 10, 1951, Chicago, Ill. *Education*: College of Santa Fe, BA, 1974; Governors State University, MA, 1977; University of New

Mexico (Graduate work)1979-85. *Principal occupation*: Educator; events promoter; media specialist. *Address & Affiliation*: Director, Gathering of Nations, P.O. Box 75102, Station 14, Albuquerque, NM 87194 (505) 836-2810 (work). *Other professional post*: Dean of Students, University of New Mexico, Albuquerque, 1979-84. *Awards, honors*: Recipient of Media Grant, National Endowment for the Humanities, 1980. *Interests*: Traveled Europe, South Central America, Canada, and Asia.

MATHIAS, ISAAC
(Indian band chief)
Affiliation: Beaverhouse Indian Band, Box 1022, Kirkland Lake, ON, Can. P2N 3L4 (705) 567-4713.

MATHIAS, JOE
(Indian band chief)
Affiliation: Squamish Indian band, Box 86131, North Vancouver, British Columbia, Canada V7L 4J5 (604) 985-7711.

MATHIESON, LLOYD
(rancheria chairperson)
Affiliation: Chicken Ranch Rancheria, P.O. Box 1699, Jamestown, CA 95327 (209) 984-3057.

MATHIS, AMY W.
(school principal)
Affiliation: Dlo'ay Azhi Community School, P.O. Box 789, Thoreau, NM 87323 (505) 862-7525.

*MATRIOUS, SUSAN (Ojibwe)
(editor)
Affiliation: "Win-Awaenen-Nisitotung," Saulte Ste. Marie Tribe of Chippewa Indians, 2218 Shunk Rd., Saulte Ste. Marie, MI 49783 (906) 635-6050.

*MATTERN, PHYLLIS (Brotherton)
(tribal vice chairperson)
Affiliation: Brotherton Indians of Wisconsin, AV2848 Witches Lake Rd., Woodruff, WI 54568 (715) 542-3913.

*MATTHEWS, ALEX
(tribal chairperson)
Affiliation: Pawnee Business Committee, P.O. Box 470, White Eagle, Pawnee, OK 74058 (405) 762-3624.

*MATTWAOSHSHE, GALILA
(BIA agency supt.)
Affiliation: Concho Agency, BIA, P.O. Box 68, El Reno, OK 73036 (405) 262-7481.

MAUCHAHTY-WARE, TOM
(Kiowa-Comanche) 1949-
(entertainer/educator/artist)
Born March 21, 1949, Lawton, Okla. *Education*: Brookhaven College, Farmers Branch, TX (2 years); UCLA (30 hours). *Principal occupation*: Entertainer/educator/artist. *Address*: P.O. Box 1771, Anadarko, OK 73005 (405) 588-2392 (home) 247-2787 (work). *Titles*: Indian Flute Player; Lead Singer of the all Indian Blues Band, "Tom Ware and Blues Nation"; Indian Dance Champion; Traditional and Contemporary Vocalist; Accomplished Public Speaker and educator; traditional artist (painter, sculptor, flute maker, beadworker and featherworker.) Other profesional post: Arts & crafts dealer. *Community activities*: Charter member, Optimist International; member, Toastmasters International. *Membership*: Kiowa Tribal Employment Asso-

ciation (vice-president, 1983-84). *Awards, honors*: "Best Counselor Award," National Indian Youth Vocational Association, *Interests*: Former Oklahoma Friendship Force Ambassador to Ireland and Wales, Oct. 1979. *Biographical sources*: Listed in numerous newspapers, magazines, etc.

MAUDLIN, STANISLAUS IRVIN 1916-
(center founder/director)
Born December 16, 1916, Greensburg, Ind. *Education*: St. Meinrad College, B.A., 1936; Collegio di St. Anselmo, Rome, S.T.L., 1939; Institute of Alcoholism Studies, NDSU, 1966. *Principal occupation & Address*: Founder/Director, American Indian Culture Research Center, P.O. Box 98, Blue Cloud Abbey, Marvin, SD 57251 (605) 432-5528. *Professional posts*: Associate pastor, work in adolescent and adult education, Liaison with Turtle Mountain Chippewa Tribe, Belcourt, ND, 1941-50; superintendent of schools, St. Michael, ND, 1950-56; member of Industrial Development Committee, Devils Lake, ND, 1954-56; president of five state Tekakwitha Indian Missionary Conference, 1955-1956; fundraising on Fort Totten Indian Reservation; founder and pastor of St. John Indian Mission, Pierre, SD, 1955-66; counselor, Pierre Indian School, Belcourt, ND, 1966-68; founder and executive director, American Indian Culture Research Center, 1968-. *Community activities*: Wrote first Teacher & Student Handbook, Stephen High School, Stephan, SD, 1964; requested by Governor's Commission on Youth (North Dakota) to write position paper on Juvenile Delinquency Among Indian Youth: Causes, Forms, Possible Means of Solution, 1967; South Dakota Committee for the Humanities (executive committee, 1972-); lecturer to numerous groups, especially to college and university audiences, as well as state and national Church conferences; director of workshops on Indian culture, religion and education; member of evaluation board for Methodist Fund for Reconciliation (South Dakota region). *Awards, honors*: Adopted into the Yankton Band of Dakota Tribe, 1941 (Wambdi Wicasa); 1954 (Tikdisni) adopted into Fort Totten Band, Dakota Tribe; adopted into Crow Creek Band, Dakota Tribe, 1961 (Nasdad Mani); Invited to Washington, DC, as advisor to Senator McGovern and the late Senator Humphrey, in first anti-poverty legislation, 1964; 1966 (Mahcheekwaneeyash) adopted into Turtle Mountain Chippewa Tribe ; Citation from South Dakota Association of Counselors and Student Personnel Service Directors for Outstanding Service to Youth, 1971; Citation from South Dakota Social Welfare Conference for services to the social, cultural and humanitarian development of individuals in our State, 1972; 1973 (Yellow Medicine) adopted into Blackfoot Tribe.

*MAULSON, THOMAS
(Lake Superior Ojibwe)
(tribal chairperson)
Affiliation: Lac du Flambeau Tribal Council, P.O. Box 67, Lac du Flambeau, WI 54538 (715) 588-3303.

*MAXCY, REBECCA (Diegueno)
(tribal spokesperson)
Affiliation: Inaja & Cosmit Band of Mission Indians, P.O. Box 491, Santa Ysabel, CA 92070 (714) 276-6624.

MAY, ALAN 1946-
(anthropologist/archaeologist)
Born May 10, 1946, Quanah, Tex. *Education*: University of Arkansas, B.A., 1973, M.A., 1975; University of Missouri, Ph.D., 1982. *Principal occupation*: Anthropologist/archaeologist. *Address*: Schiele Museum of Natural History, Gastonia, NC 28054 (704) 866-6917 (work). *Affiliations*: Adjunct professor of anthropology, University of North Carolina, Charlotte, 19887-; archaeologist, Schiele Museum of Natural History, Gastonia, NC,1984-. *Other professional post*: Editor, North Carolina Archaeology Council Newsletter. *Military service*: U.S. Air Force, 1868-72 (Staff Sergeant; Air Force Commendation Medal). *Memberships*: American Anthropological Association; Society for American Archaeology; Archaeological Society of North Carolina; Southeastern Archaeological Society; North Carolina Archaeological Council. *Awards, honors*: Lousbury-American Museum of Natural History Postdoctoral Fellowship, 1984-85. *Interests*: Underwater archaeology; ceramic technology; archaeological remote sensing; French Iron Age archaeology.

MAY, CHERYL (Oklahoma Cherokee) 1949-
(journalist)
Born February 22, 1949, Kansas City, Mo. *Education*: University of Missouri, BA, 1974; Kansas State University, MS, 1985. *Principal occupation*: Journalism. *Home address*: 2005 Somerset Square, Manhattan, KS 66502 (913) 532-6415 (office). *Affiliations*: Communications director, American Maine-Anjou Association, Kansas City, MO, 1975-; deputy managing editor/research editor, University Relations, 1979-87, general news editor, 1987-88, director, News Services, 1988-, Kansas State University (KSU), Manhattan, KS. *Other professional post*: Elected to KSU Faculty Senate, 1991-94. *Community activities*: United Way, KSU publicity chair, 1985; Riley County Historical Society volunteer (organized Celebrate American Indian Heritage); 4-H project leader; helped organize Kansas State's first Native American Heritage Month activities for March 1990; panel moderator, "People Making a Difference: People Keeping the King Tradition Alive," KSU Martin Luther King Week, Jan. 24, 1991; served on several search committees. *Memberships*: Phi Kappa Phi; National Association of Science Writers; Council for Advancement and Support of Education (CASE); Kansas Association for Native American Education. *Awards, honors*: Grants and gifts for Native American Heritage Month, 1990-91; Best in Show photography award, K-State Union Program Council, 1990; Award of Excellence for "Perspectives" magazine, CASE, editor, 1987; Special Merit Award for Cattle Research in Kansas, Council for Advancement and Support of Education CASE, writer, 1984; scholarship winner, Communicating University Research, CASE, 1983; selected for listing in Ohoyo 1000, 1982, and for the Resource Directory of Alaskan and Native American Indian Women, 1980; Award for Merit for Artificial Insemination of Beef and Dairy Cattle, slide script, Society for Technical Communication, 1980; Award for Achievement for Safety in Handling Livestock, slide script, Society for Technical Communication, 1980; Award for Outstanding News Reporting, Carlsbad, Calif. Chamber of Commerce, 1969. *Interests*: "For the past six (since 1988) years I have been director of News Services at Kansas State University. I supervise science reporting; radio-television news; and campus news as well as the faculty-staff newsletter. I am interested in photography and use it in my professional and private life. I have won numerous awards for photography and for writing." *Published works*: Cattle Management (Reston-Prentice-Hall, 1981); Legacy, Engineering at Kansas State University (KSU Press, 1983).

MAY, JAMES HARVEY
(United Keetoowah Cherokee) 1937-
(university dean & professor)
Born August 30, 1937, Trenton, Mo. *Education*: Stanford Uiversity, BS, 1958; Harvard University, MBA, 1964; Columbia University, DLS, 1978. *Principal occupation*: University dean & professor of computer science. *Home address*: 3317 Kennedy Ave., Chico, CA 95926 (916) 342-1634. *Affiliations*: Vice-president, co-founder, Pandex, Inc. (subsidiary of Macmillan Publishing Co.), New York, NY, 1966-72; director, Center for Communication and Information Research, and Assistant Professor, Graduate School of Librarianship, University of Denver, Denver, CO, 1972-74; Associate Library Director, Sonoma State University, CA, 1974-83; Vice Provost for Information Resources and Professor of Computer Science, California State University, Chico, CA, 1983-. *Other professional posts*: Consulting - on collections and use of technology for the Smithsonian Institution on its planned National Museum of the American Indian, 1991-92, and with the National Indian Policy Center to create a national Indian information clearinghouse, 1991-92; lectures on information technology for American Indians and on European contact and tribal conflict: the Cherokee experience; Scarecrow Press, Advisory Board Member for Native American Bibliographic Series (current). *Military service*: U.S. Navy, 1959-62. *Community activities*: Official representative and advisor to the United Keetoowah Band of Cherokee Tribe; recently designed the tribal seal and flag for his tribe; California State University-Academic Information Resources Council (Executive Committee, 1992-). *Memberships*: United Keetoowah Cherokke Tribe; Society for Computer Simulation, International (Official Historian, 1991-); and American Library Association (Institutional representative to EDUCOM and CAUSE, 1983-). *Awards, honors*: President Bush appointed him to the first White House Conference on Indian Education which was held in January, 1992. commissioned to do a paper on "Technological Needs: Joining the Information Age" for its Native American Pre-Conference to the White House Conference on Library and Information Services, 1991; chosen to be a witness before the U.S. Senate Select Committee on Indian Affairs in May, 1992, on information technology for Native Americans. participated in the White House Conference on Library and Information Services and led a successful petition drive for support of American Indian libraries, against considerable opposition. *Published works*: Numerous articles and papers on library and information science.

*MAYNOR, GERALD
(Indian education)
Affiliation: North Carolina Advisory Council on Indian Education, NC Dept. of Public Instruction, c/o Pembroke State University, Pembroke, NC 28372.

*MAYO, WILL
(center president)
Affiliation: Tanana Chiefs Conference Health Center, 12 First Ave., Fairbanks, AK 99701 (907) 452-8251.

MEANS, DAVID
(health director)
Affiliation: Northern Cheyenne PHS Indian Health Center, P.O. Box 70, Lame Deer, MT 59043 (406) 477-6201.

*MEANS, RUSSELL (Oglala Sioux)
(speaker; activist, actor)
Affiliations: c/o American Indian Movement (AIM), 1574 S. Pennsylvania, Denver, CO 80210; chairperson, American Indian Anti-Defamation Council, 215 W. Fifth Ave., Denver, CO 80204 (303) 892-7011. Recently had roles in The Last of the Mohicans, and other films.

MEANS, WILLIAM A.
(executive director)
Affiliation: International Indian Treaty Council, 123 Townsend St. #575, San Francsico, CA 94107 (415) 566-0251.

*MECHELS, DONALD (Chinook)
(tribal chairperson)
Affiliation: Chinooks Indian Tribe, P.O. Box 228, Chinook, WA 98614 (206) 777-8303.

MEDFORD, CLAUDE, JR. (Choctaw) 1941-
(artist)
Born April 14, 1941, Lufkin, Tex. *Education*: University of New Mexico, BA, 1964; Oklahoma State University, 1969. *Principal occupation*: Artist. *Address*: Coushatta Indian Tribe, P.O. Box 818, Elton, LA 70532 (318) 584-2261. *Affiliations*: Museum director, Alabama-Coushatta Indian Reservation; manager of the Coushatta Cultural Center, Elton, LA; taught classes and workshops at the American Indian Archaeological Institute in Washington, CT in 1979, and the Clifton Choctaw Indian Community west of Alexandria, LA, in 1981; received a folk arts apprenticeship fellowship from the Louisiana State Arts Council, Division of the Arts, and now teachers basketry to any interested Indian among the five surviving tribes of Louisiana. Mr. Medford is a gifted craftsman and practitioner of Southeast Indian arts, including basketry, pottery, wood working, shell working, metalworking, fingerweaving, beadwork, featherwork, horn and hoofwork, brain tanning of deer hides, leatherworking and gourd work. His baskets are in numerous private collections as well as several public collections, that of the Southern Plains Indian Museum, the Museum of the Red River in Idabel, OK, Tantaquidgeon Mohegan Museum in Uncasville, CT and a traveling exhibit to be circulated by the Smithsonian Institution Traveling Exhibition Service. Since 1972, he has show his work each year at the New Orleans Jazz and Heritage Festival. *Interests*: To perpetuate the arts and culture of the Southeastern Indian tribes. *Published works*: numerous articles for various publications.

MEDICINE, BEATRICE (Sihasapa Lakota-Standing Rock Sioux) 1923-
(anthropologist)
Born August 1, 1923, near Wakpala, S.D. *Education*: South Dakota State University, BS, 1945; Michigan State University, MA, 1954; University of Wisconsin, Madison, PhD, 1982. *Principal occupation*: Anthropologist. *Home address*: Box 80, Wakpala, SD 57658 (605) 845-7970. *Affiliations*: Associate professor emeritus, California State University, Northridge, 1982-88; professor, University of Calgary, Alberta, 1985-88. *Other professional posts*: Visiting professor: Dartmouth College, Stanford University, University of Washington, University of Toronto, University of New Brunswick, University of South Dakota, and University of Montana; Research Coordinator, Women's Perspectives, Royal Commission on Aboriginal Peoples, Ottawa, Canada, 1993-95. *Community activities*: Expert witness (5 tribal/human rights cases) San Francisco Status of Women Committee; Board-Indian centers-Seattle, Vancouver, BC, and Calgary, Canada. *Memberships*: American Anthropological Association, 1966- (Minority Education Committee; Fellow); Society for Applied Anthropology, 1966- (Fellow); Canadian Anthropology Association, 1963-; National Congress of American Indians, 1969- (education & cultural consultant); Native American Women's Association; American Ethnohistory Society. *Awards, honors*: Standing Rock Reservation, Sacred Pipe Woman, Sun Dance, 1977; Honorary Doctorate of Humane Letters, Northern Michigan University, 1979; "Outstanding Woman of Color, National Institute of Women of Color, Washington, DC, 1983; "Outstanding Minority Researcher," 1983, American Education Research Association; 1984 Faculty Award for Meritorious Service, California State University, Northridge; "Martin Luther King Outstanding Minority Professor," University of Michigan, 1987, Wayne State University, 1988; Distinguished Service Award, American Anthropological Association, 1991. *Interests*: "Travels to visit indigenous peoples and read invited papers: Mexico, 1955, '65, '67; Moscow, 1984; Darwin, Australia, 1988; Canberra, Australia, 1986; New Zealand, 1986-88; Lithuania, 1989; Sweden and Yugoslavia, 1988; researching pow wows held in Russia, 1991-94. *Published works*: Native American Women: A Perspective - ERK Press, San Antonio, TX, 1978); The Hidden Half - Studies of Indian Women in the Northern Plains, with Patricia Albers (University Press of America, 1982); An Ethnography of Drinking & Sobriety Among the Lakota (University of Nebraska Press-in press); and more than 60 articles.

*MEDICINEBULL, ORIE *(Hugaitha)*
(Western Mono)
(administrator, artist-filmmaker, professor)
Born December 6 in Madera County, Calif. *Education*: UCLA, MFA, 1981; UC-Berkeley, MPH, 1983. *Principal occupation*: Administrator, artist-filmmaker, professor. *Home address*: 647 W. Barstow 128, Clovis, CA 93602 (209) 298-1542; 855-2695 (work). *Affiliations*: Executive director, American Indian Center of Central California, Auberry, CA; professor, Fresno City College, Fresno, CA. *Other professional posts*: Coordinator, Indian Education, Title V, Oakhurst, CA; coordinator, Sierra Children's Center, Oakhurst, CA. *Community activities*: Fresno American Indian Council (manpower director); Communication Committee (chairperson). *Memberships*: American Indian Women's Association (chairperson); Sierra Mono Museum; American Film Institute; UCLA & UC-Berkeley Alumni. *Awards, honors*: American Independent Filmmaker Award-Best Documentary, American Indian Film Festival; Best Documentary, Brockman International Gallery; Best Documentary Short, People's Film Festival (Italy); Carny Award, Golden Hills School District. *Interests*: "Major area of interest is outdoor, physical endurance hiking workout in Sierra Nevada Mountains as a team, ethnographic film study of Central California Indians of Central California (Numa)." *Published works*: Documentaries: "Colliding Worlds," 1980); Visions of Youth," 1991; & Success for American Indian Children," 1993 (all produced by Hugaitha Productions).

*MEDINA, MAGDELENA "MENA" (Chehalis)
(tribal chairperson)
Affiliation: Chehalis Community Council, P.O. Box 536, Oakville, WA 98568 (206) 273-5911.

MEEKIS, FRED
(Indian band chief)
Affiliation: Deer Lake Indian Band, Box 335, Deer Lake, Ontario, Canada P0V 1N0 (705) 775-2141.

*MEEKS, ELSIE (Lakota Sioux)
(fund raising)
Affiliation: Executive director, The Lakota Fund, P.O. Box 340, Kyle, SD 57752 (605) 455-2500. *Other professional post*: Editor of newsletter.

MEHOJAH, WILLIAM (Kaw)
(BIA deputy director)
Affiliation: Deputy Director, Office of Indian Education, Bureau of Indian Affairs, Dept. of the Interior, MS-3530-MIB, 1849 C St., NW, Washington, DC 20240 (202) 208-6175.

*MEINERS, PHYLLIS HENRI 1940-
(fund raising)
Born November 8, 1940, Boston, Mass. *Education*: University of California, Berkeley, BA, 1962; Mass. Instititute of Technology, 1969. *Principal occupation*: Fundraising. *Home address*: 5800 Grand Ave., Kansas City, MO 64113 (816) 361-2059 (work). *Affiliation*: President, Corporate Resource Consultants, Kansas City, MO, 1982-. *Other professional posts*: Founding director, Corporate Resource Center Library & CRC Publishing Co. *Community activities*: Greater Kansas City Chamber of Commerce; Great Kansas City Council of Philanthropy; Southtown Council. *Memberships*: Special Libraries Association; National Society of Fund Raising Executives, Native Americans in Philanthropy; American Prospect Research Association; Midwest Publishers Association. *Interests*: Non-profit management and fund development; travel throughout Latin America, South America, Europe, and U.S. *Biographical sources*: Marquis Who's Who in the Midwest; Marquis Who's Who in Finance & Industry, 1993; Marquis Who's Who in the World, 1989. *Published works*: National Directory of Philanthropy for Native Americans (Corporate Resource Consultants, 1992); Corporate & Foundation Fundraising Manual for Native Americans (CRC Publishing, 1993, 1994).

*MEISTER, MARK
(executive director)
Affiliation: Archaelogical Institute of America, 675 Commonwealth Ave., Boston, MA 02215 (617) 353-9361.

*MELENDEZ, ARIAN (Paiute)
(tribal chairperson)
Affiliation: Reno-Sparks Tribal Council, 98 Colony Rd., Reno, NV 89502 (702) 329-2936.

MELKILD, MARTIN A.
(museum curator)
Affiliation: Indian Drum Lodge Museum, 2308 North U.S. 31, Traverse City, MI 49684.

MELODY, MICHAEL E. 1947-
(professor)
Born October 14, 1947, Philadelphia, Penn. *Education*: University of Notre Dame, PhD, 1976. *Principal occupation*: Professor. *Address*: Barry University, 11300 N.E. 2nd Ave, Miami Shores, FL 33161 (305) 758-3391 (work). *Affiliation*: Professor, Barry University, Miami, FL, 1979-. *Other professional post*: Director & editor, Native American Policy Network & Newsletter.

MELONI, ALBERTO C. 1946-
(executive director-Indian organization)
Born July 14, 1946, Lucca, Italy. *Education*: Marquette University, BA, MA; Harvard University, MA; University of Minnesota, Ph.D. *Principal occupation*: Executive director-Indian organization. *Address*: The Institute for American Indian Studies, P.O. Box 1260, Washington, CT 06793 (203) 868-0518. *Affiliation*: Executive Director, The Institute for American Indian Studies, Washington, CT, 1991-. *Other professional posts*: Chief curator of collections and research; director of education; chief development officer, university instructor. *Community activities*: Hospice volunteer.

*MENDOZA, LARRY
(school director)
Affiliation: Red Scaffold School, P.O. Box 168, Howes, SD 57748 (605) 538-4317.

MENEED, BERNARD
(Indian band chief)
Affiliation: Tallcree Idian Band, Box 367, Fort Vermillion, Alberta, Canada T0H 1N0 (403) 927-3727.

MENESS, CLIFFORD
(Indian band chief)
Affiliation: Algonquin (Golden Lake) Indian Band, Box 100, Golden Lake, Ontario, Canada K0J 1X0 (613) 625-2800.

*MENINICK, JERRY (Yakima)
(tribal chairperson)
Affiliation: Yakima Tribal Council, P.O. Box 151, Toppenish, WA 98948 (509) 865-5121.

*MENUSAN, FRANC *(Nookoosilichapko)* **(Creek/Metis) 1954-**
(educator, special education teacher)
Born May 17, 1954, New York, N.Y. *Education*: New York University, MA, 1984. *Principal occupation*: Educator, special education teacher. *Home address*: 120 MacDougal St. #4, New York, NY 10012 (212) 254-4491. *Affiliation*: Board of Education of the City of New York, 1982-. *Other professional posts*: Musician (Native American Flutes); composer of music (using Native American instruments of MesoAmerica); speaker & consultant on Native American cultures; writer. *Community activities*: "*I* work with the American Indian Community House (New York City) as one of their artists on file; co-producing "Giving of Thanks to the First

Peoples" Cathedral of St. John the Divine (Ann Rockefeller Roberts, 11/93); Committee (working/advisory), "Cry of the Earth-Legacy of the First Nations" (United Nations, 11/93). *Membership*: New York University Alumni. *Interests*: "As a musician and composer, using MesoAmerican instruments, I have traveled extensively throughout Mexico and the USA collecting taped examples of Indigenous music, musical instruments and information which I use in composing works in conjunction with various Native American playwriters and actors in New York (and abroad)." *Biographical source*: April 27, 1994 - Part 2 New York Newsday "Home on the Urban Range" - The Indian Nation in New York is a Microcosm of the Gorgeous Mosaic. pp. 84-5. *Published works*: Fiddlesticks "Pre Columbian Music of the Americas - What Columbus Might Have Heard," 1992; New Orchestra of Westchester - "American Indigenous People - Contact Period to Present," 1992-93; Cobblestones - "Rock of the Ages PreColumbian American Music" p. 24 (Vol. 14) 1993.

MEQUISH, PAUL
(Indian band chief)
Affiliation: Conseil Des Attikameks D'Obedjiwan Indian band, Reserve Indienne d'Obedjiwan, V ia Roberval, Quebec, Can. G0W 3B0 (819) 974-8837.

*MERCER, BILL 1960-
(museum curator)
Born May 14, 1960, Anaheim, Calif. *Education*: Texas Tech University, M.A., 1986; University of New Mexico (Ph.D. candidate). *Principal occupation*: Museum curator. *Home address*: 3117 Kinmont St., Cincinnati, OH 45208 (513) 721-5204 (work). *Affiliations*: Texas Tech University Museum, Lubbock, TX, 1984-85; Plains Indian Museum, Cody, WY, 1985-86; National Park Service, 1988-93; curator, Cincinnati Art Museum, Cincinnati, OH, 1993-. *Memberships*: American Association of Museums; Midwest Museums Association; Ohio Museums Association; Native American Art Studies Association. *Interests*: "I am especially interested in pow wows and contemporary traditional Native American art. My Ph.D. dissertation is a study of contemporary pow wow clothing and how it communicates the identity of the wearer. I am currently developing a traveling exhibition of Pueblo pottery entitles, "Singing the Clay: Pueblo Pottery of the Southwest Yesterday and Today." *Published work*: "Singing the Clay: Pueblo Pottery of the Southwest Yesterday and Today," exhibition catalog (Cincinnati Art Museum, 1995).

MERCIER, MARK (Confederated Tribes)
(tribal chairperson)
Affiliation: Confederated Tribe of the Grande Ronde Tribal Council, 9615 Grand Ronde Rd., Grande Ronde, OR 97347 (503) 879-5215.

MERCREDI, NAPOLEAN
(Indian band chief)
Affiliation: Fond du Lac Indian Band, Fond du Lac, Saskatchewan, Canada S0G 0W0 (306) 686-2102.

*MERICLE, MIKE
(health director)
Affiliation: Ignacio PHS Indian Health Center, P.O. Box 899, Ignacio, CO 81137 (303) 563-4581.

MEREDITH, HOWARD L. (Cherokee) 1938-
(historian, writer)
Born May 25, 1938, Galveston, Tex. *Education*: University of Texas, BS, 1961; S.F. Austin State University, MA, 1963; University of Oklahoma, PhD, 1970. *Principal occupation*: Historian, writer. *Home address*: 623 Culbertson Dr., Oklahoma City, OK 73105 (405) 224-3140 (work). *Affiliations*: Cookson Institute, Oklahoma City, OK (chairman, 1974-79; research associate, 1979-) ; professor, University of Science & Arts of Oklahoma, Chickasha, OK, 1985-. *Community activities*: Board, National American Indian Hall of Fame, Anadarko, OK; board & executive committee, Red Earth, Oklahoma City, OK. *Memberships*: Western Writers Association; Circle of Native American Writers; Oklahoma Historical Society ; Cherokee National Historical Society; Oklahoma Heritage Association. *Awards, honors*: Muriel Wright Heritage Award for Writing Oklahoma History, 1980, by Oklahoma Historical Society; Westerners' International Award for the Best Book on the West, 1989; McCasslin Award (Teaching), Oklahoma Heritage Association, 1994. *Interests*: American Indian thought; cross cultural communication; American Indian tribal government; Southwestern heritage. *Biographical* source: Oklahoma Monthly (June, 1977); The Trend (Oct. 26, 1989); Chickasha Sunday Express (Oct. 29, 1989); Trend (Chickasaw), Feb. 1994; Who's Who in the Southwest, 1994-95. *Published works*: The Native American Factor (Seabury Press, 1973); Native Response..Rural Oklahoma (Oklahoma Historical Society, 1977); Of the Earth, with M.E. Meredith (Oklahoma Historical Society, 1980; Bacone Indian University, with J. Williams (Oklahoma Heritage Society, 1980; DCWY, with V. Milam (Indian University Press, 1981); Bartley Milam (Indian University Press, 1985); Hasinai, with V. Newkumet (Texas A&M University Press, 1989); Modern American Indian Tribal Government (Navajo College Press, 1993); Southern Plains Alliances (University Press of Kansas, 1995).

*MEREDITH, JAMES C.
(IHS area director)
Affiliation: Nashville Area IHS Office, Stewarts Ferry Pike, Nashville, TN 37214 (615) 736-2400.

*MERICLE, MICHAEL N.
(health center director)
Affiliation: Ignacio PHS Indian Health Center, P.O. Box 889, Ignacio, CO 81137 (303) 563-4581.

MERRELL, JAMES H. 1953-
(professor of history)
Born October 19, 1953, Minneapolis, Minn. *Education*: Lawrence University, BA, 1975; Oxford University, England, BA, 1977; Johns Hopkins University, MA, 1979, PhD, 1982. *Home address*: Vassar College, Box 527, Poughkeepsie, NY 12601. *Affiliation*: Professor of History, Vassar College, Poughkeepsie, NY, 1984-. *Memberships*: American Historical Association; Organization of American Historians; Society of American Historians. *Awards, honors*: Rhodes Scholarship; Danforth Fellowship; Predoctoral Fellowship, Newberry Library; Postdoctoral Fellowship, Institute of Early American History & Culture; America: History & Life Award; Robert F. Heizer Award, Douglass Adair Prize, Frederick Jackson Turner Award, Merle Curti Award, and Bancroft Prize for article, The Indians' New World; Fellowships from American Council of

Learned Societies, Guggenheim Fellowship, and National Endowment for the Humanities Fellowship. *Published works*: Co-editor, Beyond the Covenant Chain, and book, The Iroquois & Their Neighbors in Indian North America, 1600-1800 (Syracuse University Press, 1987); The Indians' New World: Catawbas and Their Neighbors from European Contact Through the Era of Removal (University of North Carolina Press, 1989); The Catawbas (Chelsea House, 1989).

*MERRYMAN, MAHEALANI (Hawaiian)
(project administrator)
Affiliation: Native Hawaiian Library Project, 2810 Pa'a St., Suite 1-A, Honolulu, HI 96819 (808) 839-7784.

*MERUVIA, MARY LUNDY 1965-
(rehabilitation counselor)
Born October 26, 1865, Philadelphia, Miss. *Education*: University of Southern Mississippi, BS, 1987; Mississippi State University, M.ed, 1989. *Principal occupation*: Rehabilitation counselor. *Home address*: 521 Peebles Ave., Philadelphia, MS 39350 (601) 656-1902 (work). *Affiliation*: Mississippi Band of Choctaw Indians, Philadelphia, MS (VR counselor, 1988-92; VR Program director, 1992-). *Memberships*: National Rehabilitation Association; American Counseling Association. *Interests*: Advocate for individuals with disabilities. Traveling, Spanish language, cooking.

MESHIGUAD, KENNETH (Potawatomi)
(tribal chairperson)
Affiliation: Hannahville Indian Community Council, N14910 Hannahville Blvd, Rd., Wilson, MI 49896 (906) 466-2342.

*MESHORER, HANK
(chief-Indian resources)
Affiliation: U.S. Dept. of Justice, Indian Resources Section, Land & Natural Resources Division, Rm. 624, 10th & Constitution Ave., NW, Washington, DC 20530 (202) 724-7156.

MESSINGER, CARLA J.S.
(Lenni Lenape Delaware) 1949-
(founder/director-historical
society/museum)
Born May 20, 1949, Allentown, Pa. *Education*: Lehigh County Community College, AA, 1969; Kutztown University, BA, 1971; Lehigh University, MA (Elementary/Special Education), 1973. *Principal occupation*: Founder & executive director, Lenni Lenape Historical Society and the Museum of Indian Culture, R.D. #2, Fish Hatchery Rd., Allentown, PA 18103 (610) 797-2121. *Home address*: 1819 1/2 Linden St., Allentown, PA 18104 (610) 434-6819. *Other professional post*: Substitute teacher of elementary education & special education (12 years); special consultant, presents multi-media programs on Lenape culture to other organizations, such as Philadelphia school district; leads in service programs on "Unstereotyping Indians" for school districts, colleges, and church groups; consultant & speaker for "Native Culture for Senior Citizens," St. Francis de Salles College, and Agape project "Leni Lenape Indians, 1981-84. *Awards, honors*: 1985 President's Volunteer Action Award, Citation by the House of Representatives, PA; Keystone Award of Merit, Governor's Private Sector Initiatives Task Force for Lenni Lenape Historical Society; 1986 Award of Merit to the Society from the Pennsylvania Federa-

tion of Historical Societies for "Continuing Achievement in Public Education under Carla Messinger"; 1987 Jefferson Award from KYW-TV3; 1989 Letter of Commendation to the Society from the Pennsylvania Federation of Historical Societies for the publication of a new flyer (editor, Susanne Jeffries-Fox); 1989 Allentown Human Relations Award for creating and operating the Lenni Lenape Historical Society/Museum; appointed to the Advisory Council for constructing and Institute for Native American Studies at Mansfield University, 1990; 1991 Executive Leadership Award for two weeks at the Smithsonian Institution; chosen to participate in the 1991, two-week "Archaeology and Ethnography Collection Care and Maintenance Course" offered through the U.S. Dept. of the Interior, National Park Service; provided Lenape cultural programs to audiences in Scotland and England through the British North American Indian Association (Scotland) in 1992; in July 1993, she was a representative to the 9th European Conference on Indian Questions held in Trondheim, Norway, and then went to Stockholm, Sweden to meet with support groups and museum representatives; The Museum of Indian Culture/Lenni Lenape Historical Society was one of ten American organizations chosen to exhibit its crafts at the National Crafts Center in Washington, DC for 1993, International Year of the Indigenous People & the American Year of Handicrafts. *Interests*: Multi-media, cultural programs for all ages given at the Lenni Lenape Historical Society. *Biographical sources*: Allentown Neighbors, Call/Chronicle, July 8, 1982; Daily Record, N.J. You Magazine feature, July 21, 1985; Easton Express, Discover-Travel/Leisure, Sept. 15, 1985; International Leaders in Achievement & Who's Who in International Women Leaders, 1990-91 editions (International Biographical Center, London, England).

*MESTES, BEVERLY
(BIA supt. for education)
Affiliation: Pima Agency, Bureau of Indian Affairs, P.O. Box 8, Sacaton, AZ 85247 (602) 562-3557.

METATAWABIN, EDWARD
(Indian band chief)
Affiliation: Fort Albany Indian band, Fort Albany, Ontario, Canada P0L 1H0 (705) 278-1044.

METCALF, ED (Coquille)
(tribal chairperson)
Affiliation: Coquille Indian Tribe, P.O. Box 1435, Coos Bay, OR 97420 (503) 267-4587.

*METOXEN, LORETTA
(organization president)
Affiliation: Coalition for Indian Education, 8200 Mountain Rd., NE, Suite 203, Albuquerque, NM 87110 (505) 262-2351.

*MEWBORN, FRANKIE
(site supt.)
Affiliation: New Echota Historic Site, 1211 Chatsworth Hwy. N.E.
Calhoun, GA 30701 (404) 629-8151.

*MEYER, JOANNA & WILLIAM
(editors)
Affiliation: "The Four Directions: Americn Indian Literary Quarterly," Snowbird Publishing Co., P.O. Box 729, Tellico Plains, TN 37385 (615) 982-7261.

*MEYERS, JOSEPH
(executive director)
Affiliation: National Indian Justice Center, 7 Fourth St., Suite 46, Petaluma, CA 94952 (707) 762-8113.

MIANSCUM, HENRY
(Indian band chief)
Affiliation: Mistassini (Cree) Indian Band, Mistassini Lake, Via Chibougamau, Quebec, Canada G0W 1C0 (819) 923-3523

MICHAELS, MARK A. 1959-
(lawyer/writer)
Born August 2, 1959, New York, N.Y. *Education*: University of Michigan, BA, 1980; New York University School of Law, JD, 1985. *Principal occupation*: Lawyer/writer. *Address*: 404 Lafayette St., 2nd Floor, New York, NY 10003 (212) 598-0100. *Affiliations*: Staff attorney, American Indian Alliance, New York, NY 1990- (established to address all issues affecting Indian survival); deputy director, Native American Council of New York City for 1992, New York, NY , 1991- (administrator for and advisor to a coalition of the three most active Native American organizations in New York City). *Other professional posts*: Literary manager, Roundabout Theatre, 1988-90, and Double Image Theatre, 1989-91. Speeches, Lectures & Panels: Native American Council Summit, Jan. 1991; Columbus Indians and 1992, The Learning Alliance, Columbia University School of Law, Dec. 1991; The Impact of the James Bay II Hydropower Project on Indigenous People, Sarah Lawrence College, Dec. 1991; The Contiuing Impact of Columbus' Arrival on Native Americans, Northern Westchester Society for Ethical Culture, Dec. 1991. *Memberships*: American Bar Association; Dramatist Guild. *Published works*: Articles - "Native American Council Update," American Indian Community House Bulletin, regular column in newsletter; "Native Americans and Free Exercise: Double Standard at Work," with Tonya Gonnella Frichner, National Bar Association Magazine, Vol. 8, No. 1, Jan, 1991; "War Decalred on Religious Freedom," with Tonya Gonnella Frichner, Native Nations, Vol. 1, No. 2, Feb. 1991.

MICHANO, ROY
(Indian band chief)
Affiliation: Ojibways of Pic River (Heron Bay) Indian band, Heron Bay, Ontario, Canada P0T 1R0 (807) 229-1749.

*MICHEL, KAREN LINCOLN
(Wisconsin Winnebago)
(journalist; association president)
Education: Marquette University, MA. *Address & Affiliation*: President, Native American Journalists Association (NAJA), 1433 E. Franklin Ave., Suite 11, Minneapolis, MN 55404 (612) 874-8833. *Other professional posts*: Reporter, LaCross Tribune & Dallas Morning News; business partner & board member of Indian Country Communications, Hayward, WI, publishers of News From Indian Country. *Awards/Honors*: Ms. Michel is the first woman to head NAJA.

MICHELS, CAROLYN
(exeutive director)
Affiliation: Norton Sound Alaska Native Health Cooperative, P.O. Box 966, Nome, AK 99762 (907) 443-3311.

*MI'IKEHA, JAMES
(center director)
Affiliation: Alu Like, Inc., Business Development Center, 1120 Mauna Kea St., Suite 273, Honolulu, HI 96817 (808) 524-1225.

MIKE, JUNE (Luiseno)
(tribal chairperson)
Address: 255 S. Avenida Caballeros, Apt. 303, Palm Springs, CA 92262. *Affiliation*: Twenty Nine Palms Band of Mission Indians, Palm Springs, CA (619) 320-8168.

*MIKE, RICHARD (Navajo)
(association president)
Affiliation: Navajo Nation Business Association, Box 1217, Kayenta, AZ 86033 (602) 697-3534.

MIKE, ROSALYN (Southern Paiute)
(tribal chairperson)
Affiliation: Moapa Business Council, P.O. Box 56, Las Vegas, NV 89025 (702) 865-2787.

MIKKANEN, ARVO Q. (Kiowa/Comanche)
(attorney)
Address & Affiliation: Andrews Davis Legg Bixler Milstein & Price, 500 W. Main St., Oklahoma City, OK 73102 (405) 272-9241. *Memberships*: Native American Bar Association (past president); Oklahoma Indian Bar Association (president); Native American Alumni Association of Dartmouth College (president).

MILANOVICH, RICHARD M. (Cahuilla)
(tribal chairperson)
Affiliation: Agua Caliente Tribal Council, 960 E. Tahquitz Way #106, Palm Springs, CA 92262 (619) 325-5673.

*MILBRIDGE, DAN
(commission of health/human services)
Affiliation: Mill Lacs Ne0la0Shing Clinic, HCR 67, Box 241, Onamia, MN 56359 (615) 532-4163.

*MILES, MARILYN
(attorney)
Affiliation: California Indian Legal Services, 324 F St., Suite A, Eureka, CA 95501 (707) 443-8397.

*MILES, WILLIAM P. *(Swift Water)*
(Pamunkey of Virginia) 1943-
(director of administration)
Born November 28, 1943, New Jersey. *Education*: Central University (Pella, IA), 1 year. *Principal occupation*: Director of administration. *Home address*: Rt. 1, Box 2220, King William, VA 23086 (804) 843-3526. *Affiliation*: Director of Administration, U.S. Dept. of HUD, Richmond, VA, 1985-. *Other professional posts*: Chief of Pamunkey Indian Tribe, King William, VA, 1993-. *Military service*: U.S. Army, 1962-65 (E-4). *Community activities*: Vice chairman, United Indians of Virginia; boar member, Mattaponi, Pamunkey, Monacan; member, King William Agricultural Comm. *Interests*: Fishing, hunting, gardening.

*MILLER, ANDREW, Jr. (Eskimo)
(village president)
Affiliation: Nome Eskimo Community, P.O. Box 1090, Nome, AK 99762 (907) 443-2246.

MILLER, GLENN (Menominee)
(tribal chairperson)
Affiliation: Menominee Indian Tribe of Wisc. Box 910, Keshena, WI 54135 (715) 799-5100.

*MILLER, IRWIN
(tribal chairperson)
Affiliation: Walker River Paiute Tribal Council, P.O. Box 220, Schurz, NV 89427 (702) 773-2306.

MILLER, JAY (Delaware) 1947-
(Native Americanist)
Born April 7, 1947. *Education*: University of New Mexico, BA, 1969; Rutgers University, PhD, 1972. *Principal occupation*: Native Americanist. *Address*: Indian Studies Program, University of Washington, Seattle, WA 98195. *Affiliations*: Teaching assistant, lecturer, instructor of anthropology, Rutgers University at Livingston and Newark, 1969-72; assistant professor of anthropology, Montclair State College; executive committee, Indian Studies Program, University of Washington, 1975-. *Other professional posts*: Adjunct curator, North American Ethnology, Washington State Memorial Thomas Burke Museum; consultant, San Juan County Archaeological Research Project, 1973-; contributor, Smithsonian Handbook of North American Indians. *Memberships*: American Anthropological Association (Fellow); Society for American Archaeology. *Awards, honors*: National Science Foundation Predoctoral Fellowship, 1969; grant-in-aid for research in New Jersey history from the New Jersey Historical Commission, 1973; Summer Salary Award, University of Washington Graduate Research Fund, 1974; Delaware Indian Music, University of Washington Graduate Research Fund, Interdisciplinary Grant, 1975-76; Social Context of Southern Tsimshian, Jacobs Research Fund, Whatcom County Museum, 1977; among others. Field research: Archaeology, Anasazi Origins Project (summers, 1966-67); ethnography, Southwestern Pueblos, 1966-69; ethnography, Unami Delaware, 1972-; Southern Tsimshian: new language and ethnography at Hartley Bay, 1976 and Kelmtu, 1977, British Columbia; Colville Reservation: conceptual landscape, 1977-. Dissertation: The Anthropology of Keres Identity (A Structural Study of the Ethnographic and Archaeological Record of the Keres Pueblos). *Published works*: Shamanic Odyssey, Mourning Dove, Tsimshian and Their Neighbors. Numerous papers and articles.

MILLER, LESLIE (Pomo)
(tribal co-chairperson)
Affiliation: Scotts Valley Band of Pomo Indians, 149 N. Main #200, Lakeport, CA 95453 (707) 263-4771.

MILLER, MICHAEL R.
(Chippewa-Stockbridge Munsee) 1946-
(director-Native American programs)
Born April 26, 1946, Minneapolis, Minn. *Education*: Appalachian State University, Boone, N.C., BS, 1968; University of Minnesota, Duluth, MSW, 1984. *Principal occupation*: Director of Native American programs. *Address*: University of Wisconsin, River Falls, WI 54022. *Affiliations*: Indian education coordinator-supervisor, Title IV-A, Superior Public Schools, WI, 1974-81; Native American Outreach Coordinator, Northland College, 1981-84; director of Native American programs, international student advisor, University of Wisconsin, River Falls, WI, 1984-. *Memberships*: Wisconsin Indian Education Association, 1985-; National Association for Foreign Student Affairs, 1985-. *Interests*: My main areas of interest include Indian education, the social aspects of education, improving the image of Na-

tive Americans as this image relates to alcoholism, and learning more about international problems and how they relate to the U.S. and Native American experience.

*MILLER, NANCY
(health center director)
Affiliation: Fort Thompson PHS Indian Health Center, P.O. Box 200, Fort Thompson, SD 57339 (605) 245-2285.

MILLER, STEPHEN
(monument supt.)
Affiliation: Navajo National Monument, Tonalea, AZ 86044 (602) 672-2366.

MILLER, THOMAS G.
(school administrator)
Affiliation: Hannahville Indian School, N14911 Hannahville B1 Rd., Wilson, MI 49896 (906) 466-2556.

MILLER, VICTORIA G.
(executive director)
Affiliation: Saginaw Inter-Tribal Association, 3239 Christy Way, Saginaw, MI 48603 (517) 792-4610.

MILLER, VIRGINIA P. *(Mrs. Teebalosse)* 1940-
(professor of anthropology)
Born October 28, 1940, Paterson, N.J. *Education*: Smith College, 1958-60; University of California, Berkeley, BA, 1962; University of California, Davis, MA, 1970, PhD, 1973. *Address*: 6143 Shirley St., Halifax, N.S. B3H 2N1 *Affiliation*: Associate professor of anthropology, Dalhousie University, Halifax, Nova Scotia, Can., 1974-. *Memberships*: American Anthropological Association; American Society for Ethnohistory; Canadian Anthropology Society; Canadian Historical Association (Native History Study Group, 1989-). *Interests*: Ethnohistory of North America, especially California and Eastern Canada; historical demography. *Published work*: Ukomno'm: The Yuki Indians of Northern California (Ballena Press, 1979); various articles on Micmac ethnohistory and demography.

*MILLS, JEANETTE
(editor)
Affiliation: Kumtux," Native American Task Force, Church Council of Greater Seattle, 4759 15th Ave. NE, Seattle, WA 98105.

*MILLS, LENA F.
(BIA education administrator)
Affiliation: Eastern States Agency, BIA, 3701 N. Fairfax Dr., Suite 260, Arlington, VA 22203 (703) 235-3233.

MILLS, SIDNEY L.
(BIA area director)
Affiliation: Albuquerque Area Office, Bureau of Indian Affairs, P.O. Box 26567, Albuquerque, NM 87125 (505) 766-3754.

MILLS, WALTER R.
(BIA area director)
Affiliation: Phoenix Area Office, Bureau of Indian Affairs, P.O. Box 10, Phoenix, AZ 85001 (602) 379-6600.

MILROY, JAMES L.
(association president)
Affiliation: Creek Indian Memorial Association, Town Square, Okmulgee, OK 74447 (918) 756-2324.

*MINGS, LARRY W.
(BIA agency acting supt.)
Affiliation: Talihini Agency, BIA, P.O. Drawer H, Talihini, OK 74571 (918) 567-2207.

MINER, MARCELLA HIGH BEAR
(Cheyenne River Sioux) 1935-
(tribal official)
Born July 31, 1935, Cheyenne Agency, S.D. *Education*: Cheyenne River Boarding School; Aberdeen School of Commerce. *Principal occupation*: Tribal official. *Home address*: Eagle Butte, SD 57625. *Affiliations*: Tribal treasurer, 1962-66, assistant finance officer, 1968-69, bookkeeper, 1969-, Cheyenne River Sioux Tribal Council. *Community activities*: Cheyenne River Mission, Episcopal Church (treasurer, 1963-66).

*MINHAS, JASJIT
(college president)
Affiliation: Lac Courte Oreilles Ojibwa Community College, RR 2, Box 2357, Hayward, WI 54843 (715) 634-4790.

MINNICK, ALBERT C.
(librarian)
Affiliation: Harold McCracken Research Library, Buffalo Bill Historical Center, P.O. Box 1000, Cody, WY 82414 (307) 587-4771.

MIRANDA, JENNIE (Luiseno)
(tribal spokesperson)
Affiliation: Pechanga Band of Mission Indians, Box 1477, Temecula, CA 92390 (714) 676-2768.

*MISIKIN, ALICIA (Aleut)
(radio station manager)
Affiliation: KUHB - FM, Pribiloff School District, St. Paul, AK 99660 (907) 546-2254.

*MITCHELL, GARY E. (Prairie Potawatomi)
(tribal chaorperson)
Affiliation: Prairie Band Potawatomi Trbal Council, 14880 K. Rd., Mayetta, KS 66509 (913) 966-2255.

MITCHELL, MICHAEL
(Indian band chief)
Affiliation: Mohawks of Akwesasne, Box 579, Cornwall, Ontario, Canada K6H 5T3 (613) 575-2348.

*MITCHELL, RUDI L., DR. (Omaha)
(tribal chairperson)
Affiliation: Omaha Tribal Council, P.O. Box 368, Macy, NE 68039 (402) 837-5391.

MITCHELL, THEDIS
(hospital director)
Affiliation: Clinton PHS Indian Hospital, P.O. Box 279, Clinton, OK 73601 (405) 323-2884.

MITCHELL, WAYNE LEE (Santee Sioux-Mandan) 1937-
(health administrator)
Born March 25, 1937, Rapid City, S.D. *Education*: University of Redlands, BA, 1959; Arizona State University, MSW, 1970, EdD, 1979. *Principal occupation*: Educator, social worker. *Home address*: P.O. Box 9592, Phoenix, AZ 85068. *Affiliations*: Professional social worker, various county, state and federal agencies, 1962-70; social worker, BIA, Phoenix, AZ, 1970-77; social worker, 1977-84, supervisor, 1984-88, branch chief - social services, 1988-, U.S. Public Health Service, Indian Health Service, Phoenix, AZ. *Other professional post*: Assistant pro-

fessor, Arizona State University. *Military service*: U.S. Coast Guard, 1960-66. *Community activities*: Phoenix Indian Community School (board of directors); Phoenix Indian Center (board of directors); Phoenix Area Health Advisory Board, 1975; Community Behavioral Mental Health Board, 1976; Council on Foreign Relations. *Memberships*: National Congress of American Indians; National Association of Social Workers; Association of American Indian Social Workers; American Orthopsychiatric Association; Nucleus Club; Phi Delta Kappa; Kappa Delta Pi; Chi Sigma Chi. *Awards, honors*: Delegate to White House Conference on Poverty, 1964; nominated, Outstanding Young Men of America, 1977; Phoenix Indian Center Community Service Award, 1977; Temple of Islam Community Service Award, 1980. *Interests*: World traveler. *Biographical sources*: Who's Who in the West; Who's Who in the World; Men of Achievement. *Published works*: The Inside-Outside School Concept As Observed in Educational Institutions in the People's Republic of China; A Study of Cultural Identification on the Educational Objectives of Hopi Indian High School Seniors (master's thesis), (Arizona State University, 1970); Native American Substance Abuse (Arizona State University Press, 1983); American Indian Families: Developmental Strategies and Community Health (Arizona State University Press, 1983).

*MITCHUM, MARIA (Maidu)
(study skills specialist)
Affiliation: Learning Skills Center, University of California, Davis, Basement, South Hall, Davis, CA 95616 (916) 752-2013.

MITHUN, MARIANNE 1946-
(linguist, professor of linguistics)
Born April 8, 1946, Bremerton, Wash. *Education*: Pomona College, BA, 1969; Yale University, MA, M.Phil., PhD, 1969-1974. *Principal occupation*: Linguist, professor of linguistics. *Address*: Dept. of Linguistics, University of California, Santa Barbara, CA 93106. *Affiliations*: Assistant/associate professor of linguistics, SUNY at Albany, 1973-81; professor of linguistics, University of California, Berkeley, 1981-86; professor of linguistics, University of California, Santa Barbara, 1986-. *Community activities*: Organizer, Iroquois Conference, 1973-85. *Memberships*: Society for Linguistic Anthropology (president); American Anthropological Association (executive committee, board of directors, administrative advisory committee); Society for the Study of the Indigenous Languages of the Americas (president, vice-president, executive board); Linguistics Society of America (executive board). *Interests*: American Indian languages and linguistics, especially Iroquoian (Mohawk, Oneida, Onondaga, Cayuga, Seneca, Tuscarora, Huron), Pomo (Central Pomo), Siouan (Dakota, Lakota, Tutelo), Algonquian (Cree); Yu'pik Eskimo. *Published works*: A Grammar of Tusarora (Garland Press, 1976); Kanien'keha'Okara'shon:'a (Mohawk Stories) and Iontenwennaweienstahkhwa' (Mohawk Spelling Dictionary) (New York State Museum Bulletin, 1976,1977); The Languages of Native America (University of Texas Press, 1979); Watewayestanih: A Grammar of Cayuga (Woodland Indian Culture & Education Centre, 1982); Extending the Rafters: An Interdisciplinary Approach to the Iroquois (SUNY Press, 1984); numerous articles in "International Journal of American Linguistics."

MODUGNO, REV. THOMAS A.
(director)
Affiliation: Marquette League for Catholic Indian Missions, 1011 First Ave., New York, NY 10022 (212) 371-1000.

MOFFETT, WALTER L. (Nez Perce) 1927-
(pastor)
Born June 23, 1927, Kamiah, Idaho. *Education*: College of Idaho, BA, 1955. *Principal occupation*: Pastor. *Home address*: P.O. Box 668, Kamiah, ID 83536. *Affiliations*: Clerk-stenographer, U.S. Department of the Interior, Standing Rock Reservation, ND, 1949-50; intern pastor, Brigham City, UT, 1955-58; clerk and sanitarian, USPHS, Indian Health Service, Idaho & Washington, 1958-62; pastor, Kamiah-Kooshia United Presbyterian Churches, Kamiah, ID, 1964-; council member, Nez Perce Tribal Executive Committee, 1970-. *Other professional posts*: Guidance counselor, Kamiah Public Schools (2 years); member, Council of Advisors, American Indian Heritage Foundation, Falls Church, VA . *Military service*: 1945-47 (Corporal). *Community activities*: Northwest Regional Eductional Laboratory (past member, board of directors); Small Business Administration (advisory council); State Advisory Council, Title III ESEA, Idaho; Idaho Historic Sites Review Board; Community Relations Council, Cedar Flats Job Corps Center, Kooshia, Idaho (past chairman). *Memberships*: Affiliated Tribes of Northwest Indians (president); National Congress of American Indians (area vice president); National Indian Council on Aging. *Interests*: Politics--1974 Republican candidate for State Senator; held pastorate fourteen years. *Biographical source*: Personalities of the West and Midwest, 1971.

MOFSIE, LOUIS (*Greenrainbow*)
(Hopi/Winnebago) 1936-
(art teacher)
Born May 3, 1936, Brooklyn, N.Y. *Education*: Buffalo State Teachers College, BS, 1958; Hofstra University, MA, 1973. *Principal occupation*: Art teacher. *Home address*: 204 W. Central Ave., Maywood, NJ 07607 (201) 587-9633. *Affiliation*: Director, Thunderbird American Indian Dancers, New York, NY; *Other professional post*: Art teacher, East Meadow Board of Education, East Meadow, NY (36 years); consultant, National Museum of the American Indian, 1991. *Community activities*: Chairman of the Board, American Indian Community House, New York, NY; president, International Council of McBurney YMCA. *Memberships*: New York State Art Teachers Association; Classroom Teachers Association. *Awards, honors*: Association of Southwestern Indians Award for painting submitted to the Annual Indian Artists Exhibition, Santa Fe Art Museum; New York City Indian of the Year, 1984; 1986 Calumet Award for Outstanding Achievement by the American Indian Community House, New York, NY; 1987 Ethnic New York Award; 1990 Outstanding Achievement Award by the New York State Council of the Disabled; 1991 Outstanding Achievement Award by the New York City Lawyers Local; Ellis Island Congressional Medal of Honor, 1993. *Interests*: American Indian dance - "as a dance company, we have traveled all over the U.S., Canada, Israel and Mexico. I am currently teaching dance at Brooklyn College and the YMCA." *Biographical sources*: "Indians of Today," by Marion Gridley; "American Indian Painters," by Joanne Snodgrass, "Dance Annu-

als," by John Mills. *Published work*: Co-author & illustrator, The Hopi Way (J.B. Lippincott, 1970); illustrator, Coyote Tales, and Teepee Tales (Holt, Rinehart & Winston).

MOHAWK, JOHN (Seneca) 1945-
(organization chairperson; editor)
Born August 30, 1945, Buffalo, N.Y. *Education*: Hartwick College, BA, 1968; SUNY at Buffalo. *Principal Occupation*: Chairperson-Indian organization. *Affiliation*: Indigenous People's Network, 226 Blackman Hill Rd., Berkshire, NY 13736; former editor, Akwesasne Notes, 1976-1983; editor, Daybreak Magazine. *Other Professional Post*: Lecturer, SUNY at Buffalo, American Studies Dept. *Community Activities*: Seventh Generation Fund (chairperson); Indian Law Resource Center (board member). *Published Work*: A Basic Call to Consciousness (Akwesasne Notes, 1978).

*MOLASH, CHARLENE
(IHS-executive officer)
Affiliation: Bemidji IHS Area Office, 127 Federal Bldg., Bemidji, MN 56601 (218) 759-3413.

*MOLIN, PAULETTE
(program director)
Affiliation: American Indian Educational Opportunities Program, The Graduate College, Hampton University, Hampton, VA 23668 (804) 727-5454.

*MOLLENHOFF, LORI
(board president)
Affiliation: Migizi Communications, Inc., 3123 E. Lake St., Suite 200, Minneapolis, MN 55406 (612) 721-6631.

MOMADAY, AL (Kiowa) 1913-
(artist, educator)
Born July 2, 1913, Mountain View, Okla. *Education*: University of New Mexico; UCLA: Famous Artists Schools. *Principal occupation*: Artist, educator. *Home address*: Jemez Pueblo, N.M. 87024. *Affiliation*: Principal, Jemez Day School, NM. *Memberships*: National Congress of American Indians; Artists' Equity Association; National Education Association; New Mexico Indian Arts Committee. *Awards, honors*: Grand Award, Indian Painting, All American Indian Days, Sheridan, Wyo., 1955; Grand Award, Indian Painting, American Indian Exposition; Outstanding Southwestern Indian Artists Award, Dallas Exchange Club, 1956; First Prize, Indian Painting, Philbrook Art Center, Tulsa, Okla., 1956; First Prize, Indian Painting, Scottsdale National Indian Arts Exhibition, 1964; among others.

MOMADAY, NATACHEE SCOTT
(Eastern Cherokee) 1913-
(artist, writer, teacher)
Born February 13, 1913, Fairview, Ky. *Education*: Haskell Institute; Crescent College, BA, 1933. *Principal occupation*: Artist, teacher, writer. *Home address*: Jemez Pueblo, NM 87024. *Affiliations*: Civil service teacher, Albuquerque, Shiprock, Chinle, Navajo Service, AZ. *Other professional posts*: Personnel director, H.A.A.F., Hobbs, NM; former newspaper reporter. *Memberships*: Delta Kappa Gamma; National League of American Pen Women; United Daughters of the Confederacy; Daughters of the American Revolution. *Awards, honors*: Arts and Crafts Fair, Albuquerque, NM; Inter-Tribal Indian Ceremonial Association. *Published works*:

Woodland Princess, a book of 24 poems (McHughes Co., 1931); co-author, Velvet Ribbons, 1942; Owl in the Cedar Tree (Ginn & Co., 1965).

MOMADAY, NAVARRE SCOTT (Kiowa) 1934-
(writer, painter, educator)
Born February 27, 1934, Lawton, Okla. *Education*: University of New Mexico, BA, 1958; Stanford University, MA, 1960, PhD, 1963. *Principal occupation*: Writer, educator, painter. *Address*: 1041 W. Roller Coaster Rd., Tucson, AZ 85705. *Affiliations*: Assistant professor, associate professor of English, University of California, Santa Barbara, 1962-69; professor of English and Comparative Literature, University of California, Berkeley, 1969-72; professor of English, Stanford University, 1972-80; professor of English & American Literature, University of Arizona, Tucson, AZ, 1981-. *Other professional posts*: Consultant, National Endowment for the Humanities, 1970-; trustee, Museum of the American Indian, 1978-; currently Regents Professor of the Humanities, University of Arizona, he directs projects which focus upon Native American oral tradition and Native American concepts of the sacred. *Memberships*: American Studies Association; MLA. *Awards, honors*: Guggenheim Fellowship, 1966; Recipient of the Pulitzer Prize for fiction, 1969; an award from the National Institute of Arts & Letters; the Golden Plate Award from the American Academy of Achievement; and the Premio Letterario Internazionale Mondello, Italy, 1979 (Italy's highest literary award); Fellow of the American Academy of Arts & Sciences; his paintings, drawings, and prints have been exhibited in the U.S. and abroad. A one-man, 20-year retrospective was mounted at the Wheelwright, Santa Fe, NM, in 1992-93. He holds 12 honorary degrees fro American colleges & universities, including Yale, University of Massachusetts, and the University of Wisconsin. *Biographical source*: Who's Who in America. *Published works*: The Complete Poems of Frederick Goddard Tuckerman (Oxford University Press, 1965); House Made of Dawn (Harper & Row, 1968); The Way to Rainy Mountain (University of New Mexico Press, 1969); Angle of Geese and Other Poems (David R. Godine, 1973); The Gourd Dancer (Harper & Row, 1976); The Names (Harper & Row, 1976); The Ancient Child (Doubleday); In the Presence of the Sun (St. Martin's Press); Circle of Wonder (St. Martin's Press; The Storyteller and His Art (Oxford University Press); A Dark, Indifferent Rage (Doubleday); and The Blind Astrologers (St. Martin's Press); his play "The Indolent Boys," which was given staged readings to full houses at Harvard in Feb. 1993, had its world premiere at the Syracuse Stage in Feb. 1994; his articles have appeared in "Natural History," "American West," "The New York Review of Books," "New York Newsday," "The New York Times Book Review," "The New York Times Magazine," etc..

MONETTE, GERALD
(college president)
Affiliation: Turtle Mountain Community College, P.O. Box 340, Belcourt, ND 58316 (701) 477-5605.

MONIAS, EUGENE
(Indian band chief)
Affiliation: Heart Lake Indian Band, Box 447, Lac La Biche, Alberta, Canada T0A 2C0 (403) 623-2130.

MONSEN, MARIE A. 1939-
(federal government program analyst)
Born October 18, 1939, New York, N.Y. *Education*: Bucknell University, BA, 1961; East-West Center, Honolulu, HI, MA, 1963. *Principal occupation*: Federal government program analyst. *Home address*: 6807 Hopewell Ave., Springfield, VA 22151. *Affiliations*: Training officer, Peace Corps, Thailand Program, 1964-70; evaluation specialist, Dept. of the Interior, Washington, DC, 1971-79; chief, Local & Indian Affairs, Dept. of Energy, Washington, DC, 1979-. *Community activities*: Annandale Christian Community for Action (vice president); Shelter House, Fairfax County (board of directors); elder in Presbyterian Church. *Membership*: Women's Council on Energy and the Environment, 1983-. *Awards, honors*: Certificate of Special Achievement, Bureau of Indian Affairs, 1979; Outstanding Achievement Award, 1984, Americans for Indian Opportunity; Superior Job Performance Awards, 1984-1985, Dept. of Energy. *Interests*: Indian energy; tribal government.

MONTAGUE, FELIX J.
(BIA agency supt.)
Afiliation: Fort Yuma Agency, Bureau of Indian Affairs, P.O. Box 1591, Yuma, AZ 85364 (619) 572-0248.

*MONTANO, FRANCIS (Ojibwe)
(museum director)
Affiliation: Red Cliff Tribal Museum, Arts & Crafts Cultural Center, P.O. Box 529, Bayfield, WI 54814 (715) 779-5609.

MONTEAU, CYNTHIA (Standing Rock Sioux)
(office manager)
Affiliation: National Indian Health Board, 1385 S. Colorado Blvd., Suite A708, Denver, CO 80221 (303) 759-3075.

MONTEAU, HAROLD A. (Chippewa-Cree)
(attorney)
Affiliation: Monteau Guenther & Decker, 410 Central Ave., Suite 522, Great Falls, MT 59401 (406) 452-9955/9787. *Membership*: Native American Bar Association (board member).

MONTGOMERY, JANNEY
(executive officer)
Affiliation: Indian Rights Association, 1601 Market St., Philadelphia, PA 19103 (215) 665-4523. *Other professional post*: Editor, Indian Truth," bionthly news journal of the Indian Rights Association.

MONTOUR, WILLIAM
(Indian band chief)
Affiliation: Six Nations of the Grand River Indian Band, Box 1, Ohsweken, Ontario, Canada N0A 1M0 (519) 445-2201.

MONTOYA, GERONIMA CRUZ
(P'otsunu) (Pueblo) 1915-
(retired artist, teacher)
Born September 22, 1915, San Juan Pueblo, N.M. *Education*: St. Joseph's College, BS, 1958; University of New Mexico; Claremont College. *Principal occupation*: Art teacher, Santa Fe, NM. *Home address*: 1008 Calle de Suenos, Santa Fe, NM 87505 (505) 471-5480 (home). *Affiliation*: Co-founder, lifetime board chairperson, San Juan Pueblo Arts & Crafts Cooperative, 1973-. *Community activities*: Community Concert Association (captain); San Juan Pueblo Choir (secretary-treasurer); SWAIA _ Southwest American

Indian Arts (board member); on Advisory Panel with Indian Art & Culture Museum. *Awards, honors*: School of American Research Purchase Award; Museum of New Mexico Special Category Prize, Inter-Tribal Indian Ceremonial, Gallup, N.M.; Special Prize, Philbrook Art Center, Tulsa, Okla.; DeYoung Museum Purchase Prize; among others.

MONTOYA, JOSEPH
(administrative officer)
Affiliation: Santa Fe PHS Indian Hospital, 1700 Cerrillos Rd., Santa Fe, NM 87501 (505) 988-9821.

*MONTOYA, VINCE (*Pubsay*) (Isleta Pueblo) 1939-
(civil engineer)
Born July 19, 1939, Tohatchi, N.M. (Navajo Reservation). *Education*: University of New mexico, BS, 1964; St. Mary's University (San Antonio, TX), MA, 1978. *Principal occupation*: Civil engineer. *Home address*: 9208 Northridge Dr., NE, Albuquerque, NM 87111 (505) 291-8402; 846-7904 (work). *Affiliations*: Project Manager, 542d Civil Engineering Squadron, Kirtland AFB, NM, 1986-. *Other professional post*: American Indian Employment Programs Manager, Kitland AFB, NM, 1986-. *Military service*: U.S. Air Force, 1964-84 (Major {0-4}-retired; Missile Engineer (Minuteman) at Vandenburg AFB, CA; Site Civil Engineer at Hopedale Air Station, Labrador; Civil Engineering Chief of Operations at Torrejon AB & Zaragoza AB, Spain; and Korat Royal Thai Air Base, Thailand; Chief Civil Engineer Inspector, HQ 9th Air Force, Shaw AFB, SC; Chief Maintenance Management Division, DCS Engineering & Services, HQ Air Training Command, Randolph AFB, TX; and as Base Civil Engineer, Zaragoza AB, Spain & RAF Chicksands, U.K.). *Community activities*: Persian Gulf Support Groups at various Indian commuities; work with all Indian organizations in the Albuquerque area; conduct various activities at annual American Indian Heritage Week, Kitland, NM. *Memberships*: Air Force Association; Disabled American Veterans Association; Society of American Military Engineers. *Awards, honors*: His military decorations and awards include: The Meritorious Service Medal with four oak leaf clusters; the Air Force Commendation Medal; the Air Force Outstanding Unit Award with Valor; Small Arms Markmanship Ribbon; National Defense Service Tibbon; Republic of Vietnam Gallantry Cross with Palm; and the USAF Missileman Badge. His civilian awards include the USAF Performance Award for each year he has been assigned at Kitland. He was awarded a Quality Step Increase for 1991. He also received the Air Force Distinguished Equal Employment Opportunity Award for the American Indian/Alaskan Native Employment Program for 1991.

MOODY, EDWARD
(Indian band chief)
Affiliation: Bella Coola Indian Band, Box 65, Bella Coola, British Columbia, Canada V1C 1C0 (604) 799-5613.

MOORE, ARDINA REVARD (*Ma-shro-gita*) (Quapaw-Osage) 1930-
(business owner; designer-Indian clothes; teacher)
Born December 1, 1930, Belton, Tex. *Education*: Oklahoma State University, 1952-53; Northeastern State University (Tahlequah, OK), BS

(Education), 1957. *Principal occupation*: Business owner; designer-Indian clothing; teacher . *Home address*: 1204 Sky Lane, Miami, OK 74354 (918) 542-8870 (office). *Affiliations*: Owner, Buffalo Sun, Miami, OK, 1982- (specialty Indian clothing business); instructor, Indian Studies Program, Northeastern Oklahoma Jr. College, Miami, OK, 1989-. *Community activities*: Chamber of Commerce, Miami, OK; Promenade India Club (president, 1992); Keepers of the Treasures; Quapaw Tribal Business Committee (secretary-treasurer (2 years). *Memberships*: Oklahoma State Medical Auxiliary; Oklahoma Education Association; Quapaw Tribe of Oklahoma; Osage Tribe of Oklahoma; Oklahoma Federation of Indian Women; \National Congress of American Indians; Indian and Western Arts Association; American Indian Designers Association (president, 1989). *Awards, honors*: Mother of the Year, 1992, Oklahoma Federation of Indian Women; Artistic Awards - 2nd Place, Creek Council House, Okmulgee, OK, 1989; 1st & 2nd Place, Indian Summer Art Show, Bartlesville, OK, 1990, 1991. Interests: Genealogy research, Federal Archives; Indian Dance Troupe and fashion shows around the country. Biographical sources: Facets Magazine (American Medical Association Auxiliary, Spring & Winter 1978); in Joplin Magazine, Business Profiles, Feb. 1986; Math America text book series (Houghton Mifflin, 1992. *Published works*: Editor,Auxiliary Page, Oklahoma State Medical Journal, 1965-66, editor, Montana Medical Auxiliary Newsletter, 1970-71; editor, Genealogy Society, Miami, OK Newsletter, 1979-80.

MOORE, DAISY POCAHONTAS (Wampanoag) 1931-
(director-Wampanoag Indian program)
Born July 6, 1931, Mashpee, Mass. *Education*: Boston University, BA, 1958. *Principal occupation*: Director, Wampanoag Indian Program, Living History Museum, Plimoth Plantation, Plymouth, MA, 1983-. *Home address*: P.O. Box 4462, Washington, DC 20017. *Other professional post*: Member, Mashpee Tribal Council (Wampanoag). *Membership*: American Museum Association. *Interest*: "Primary area of interest--museum; have traveled throughout Africa; taught school in Africa for three years under the auspices of the Methodist Church; limited travel to Europe; attended the University of Grenoble, France for one year." *Biographical sources*: Articles in local newspapers: In Harmony With Nature, Cape Cod Times, June 13, 1985; Collection at Mashpee Wampanoag Museum Enhanced by Plimoth Plantation Loan, The Enterprise (Falmouth, Mass.), May 24, 1985).

*MOORE, GENE
(museum manager)
Affiliation: Kotzebue Museum, P.O. Box 46, Kotzebue, AK 99752 (907) 442-3401.

MOORE, JOHN H. (*Nogosutke-Muskogee Creek*) 1939-
(anthropologist)
Born February 27, 1939, Williston, N.D. *Education*: New York University, PhD, 1974. *Principal occupation*: Anthropologist. Home address: 3328 NW 18th Ave., Gainesville, FL 32605 (904) 392-2031 (work). *Affiliations*: Chair & professor, Dept. of Anthropology, University of Oklahoma, Norman, OK, 1977-93; chair & professor, University of Florida, Gainesville, FL, 1993-. *Past professional post*: Consultant, Sand Creek Descendants Association, Muskogee Creek Tribal

Towns, Inc. *Military service*: U.S. Army, 1962-64 (lieutenant). *Memberships*: American Anthropological Association; American Ethnological Society; American Association for the Advancement of Science. *Awards, honors*: Received title of Emafanaka from Muskogee Tribal Towns Organization; Certificate of Achievement from Cheyenne Sand Creek Descendants, "Most Helpful Faculty Member, American Indian Students Association, University of Oklahoma; Oklahoma Governor's Community Service Award for work with Creek communities. *Interests*: Treaty rights; health; demography. Presently working on Sand Creek Massacre Claim, the Twinn case in Canada involving band sovereignty, and the Yuchi separation from the Creeks. *Biographical source*: Search for the Sand Creek Descendants, Sooner Magazine, Spring, 1983; Who's Who in the South & Southwest, 1985-. *Published works*: Ethnology in Oklahoma (Papers in Anthropology, 1980); The Cheyennes in Moxtavhohona (Northern Cheyenne Tribe, Inc., 1981); The Cheyenne Nation (University of Nebraska Press, 1986); Political Economy of North American Indians (University of Oklahoma Press, 1993).

MOORE, KELLY R. (Creek) 1955-
(physician)
Born May 24, 1955, Tahlequah, Okla. *Education*: University of Oklahoma, BA, 1977; University of Oklahoma, Tulsa Medical School, MD, 1983, Pediatric residency, 1986. *Principal occupation*: Physician. *Home address*: 4301 E. Silverwood Dr., Phoenix, AZ 85044 (602) 562-3321 (work). *Affiliations*: Women's counselor, University of Oklahoma Health Sciences Center, Headlands Indian Health Careers Program, Mackinac City, MI, 1978-80; clinical director, Kayenta PHS, Indian Health Center, Kayenta, AZ on Navajo Reservation, 1987-89; clinical director, USPHS, Indian Health Service Clinic, Taholah, WA, 1989-91; clinical director, Sacaton PHS Indian Hospital, Sacaton, AZ, 1991-. *Military service*: Commissioned Officer, USPHS (Commander; received Isolated Hardship Duty Ribbon. *Memberships*: American Academy of Pediatrics (Fellow); Association of American Indian Physicians; Commissioned Officers Association. *Awards, honors*: Ungerman Scholarship Recipient, University of Oklahoma Health Sciences Center, 1982-83; University Scholar, University of Oklahoma, 1973-74. *Interests*: Child advocacy issues - child sexual/physical abuse; sex/AIDS education; fetal alcohol syndrome prevention.

MOORE, PATRICK EDWARD (Creek) 1942-
(attorney)
Born May 16, 1942, Wewoka, Okla. *Education*: University of Oklahoma, BS, 1972; Oklahoma City University School of Law, JD, 1977; University of Houston (Post Graduate Law). *Principal occupation*: Attorney. *Home address*: 1109 Greenwillow, Okmulgee, OK 74447 (918) 756-3391 (work). *Affiliations*: Moore & Moore (law firm), Okmulgee, OK, 1975-; Assistant District Attorney, Okmulgee, OK, 1982-. *Other professional posts*: District Judge, Muscogee (Creek) Nation; District Judge, Devils Lake Sioux Nation; Board of Directors, CASA; instructor, Oklahoma Council on Law Enforcement & Training. *Military service*: U.S. Air Force, 1963-67 (E-5; Presidential Unit Citation, DSM, Good Conduct, Fairchild Trophy, Standboard). *Memberships*: U.S. Supreme Court, 10th Circuit Court of Appeals; U.S. District Courts for Western, North-

ern & Eastern Districts of Oklahoma; Suprme Court of Oklahoma; Supreme Court of the Muscogee (Creek) Nation; National Association of District Attorneys; Federal Bar Association; Oklahoma Association of District Attorneys; National Association of Tribal Court Judges Steering Committee. *Awards, honors*: U.S. Inspector General-Outstanding Prosecution Award; Governor's Commission on Law Enforcement. *Interests*: U.S. Power Squadron water and boating safety.

*MOORE, RUSSELL
(Native American film producer)
Affiliation: New Breed Productions, 2401 Santa Fe Ave., Los Angeles, CA 90058.

MOORE, TRACEY ANN *(E-ne-opp-e {Protected One})* **(Pawnee/Otoe-Missouria/Osage/Sac & Fox) 1964-**
(office clerk)
Born August 14, 1964, Fairfax, Okla. *Education*: Northern Oklahoma College, 1982-84; University of Oklahoma, 1984-87. *Principal occupation*: Office clerk. *Home address*: 511 Mason, Fairfax, OK 74637 (918) 287-4491 (work). *Affiliations*: American Indian Student Service, University of Oklahoma, Norman, 1986-88; Claremore Indian Hospital, Claremore, OK, 1988-89; . *Other professional posts*: CETA Summer Youth Program, The Osage Nation, 1981-. *Awards, honors*: Nominated twice for Outstanding Young Women of America, 1985; Osage Nation representative for Miss National Congress of American Indians Pageant, 1985; University of Oklahoma, American Indian Student Association Princess, 1985-1986; Tulsa Powwow Princess, 1984; Miss Indian Oklahoma, 1st runner-up-most talented; National Viet Nam Veterans Powwow Princess & Association Princess, 1982-84; Osage Tribal Princess, 1980 & 1983; 1st Place Women's Fancy Shawl, University of Oklahoma, American Indian Student Association Pow wow, March 19, 1994; 2nd Place Women's Fancy Shawl, Red Earth Celebration, Oklahoma City, June 1994; 4th Place Gathering of Nations, Albuquerque; 5th Place Women's Fancy Shawl, 1993, Denver March Powwow; 1st Place Women's Fancy Shawl, Potawatomi Days Powwow, June 1993 in Shawnee, OK; 2nd Place Women's Fancy Shawl, Aspen, CO, July 1993 powwow to benefit the new Smithsonian Institution, National Museum of the American Indian; "I danced at the National Governors Association Convention in Sand Springs, OK, Aug. 1993 - President Clinton was an honored guest"; "Me and my gramma, Mary Osage Green (full blooded Osage) are painted in the Osage Council Chambers with other prominent Osages." *Interests*: "I am applying for IHS scholarship to further my education in business and/or public administration. I plan to document the elders of my tribe. I feel my elders are cherishable because they are our history, they lived in the beginning of the 1900's. There stories are true compared to history books. I want to preserve our heritage. I enjoy traveling across the U.S. to Native American celebrations of every kind. I have represented my tribe at powwows, state and national organizations which involved me traveling to all 4 directions. My parents are Ted Moore, Sr., a former world champion fancy dancer for a number of consecutive years at the American Indian Exposition in Anadarko, Okla., and Thomasine Moore, a former Osage princess and current Osage Tribal Director at the American Indian Exposition. My great-grandfa-

ther was See-Haw, a great leader of the Osage Nation."

MOORE, WILMA
(school principal/teacher)
Affiliation: Toksook Bay Day School, Toksook, AK 99637 (907) 543-2746.

MOOREHEAD, VIRGIL (Yurok)
(rancheria chairperson)
Affiliation: Big Lagoon Rancheria, P.O. Box 3060, Trinidad, CA 95570 (707) 826-2079.

*MOQUINO, JOSEPH
(health center director)
Affiliation: Northern Idaho PHS Indian Health Center, P.O. Drawer 367, Lapwai, ID 83540 (208) 843-2271.

MORAN, ERNEST T. (BUD) (Confederated Salish & Kootenai/Chippewa Cree) 1939-
(BIA agency supt.)
Born August 27, 1939, Harlem, Mont. *Education*: Oceanside Junior College, 1960; Santa Ana Junior College, 1962-63; received numerous training courses in administration and management while in the U.S. Marines. *Principal occupation*: BIA agency supt. *Address*: Flathead Agency, Bureau of Indian Affairs, P.O. Box A, Pablo, MT 59855 (406) 675-7200 ext. 210. *Affiliations*: Credit and business development officer, director of economic development program, Confederated Salish & Kootenai Tribes; Indian Community Action Program, University of Montana, Missoula; Bureau of Indian Affairs: housing officer, Rocky Boy, MT; reservation programs officer, Lame Deer, MT; credit and business development, Jicarilla Agency, Dulce, NM; tribal operations officer, Western Nevada Agency, Stewart, NV; field representative in Klamath, CA; supt., Northern Cheyenne Agency, Lame Deer, MT, 1980-85; supt., Northern Idaho Agency, Lapwai, ID, 1985-88; supt., Crow Agency, MT, 1989-90; supt., Colorado River Agency, Parker, AZ, 1990-91; supt., Flathead Agency, Pablo, MT, 1991-. *Other professional posts*: President, Indian American Foundation; past president, NFFE Union, Jicarilla Apache Agency Post, NM. *Military service*: U.S. Marine Corps, 1958-67 (Navy Unit Citation; Vietnam Unit Citation with Star; Vietnam Service Medal with Star; National Defense Service Medal with Star; Armed Forces Expeditionary Medal with 2 Stars). *Community activities*: Active Corps of Executives (member); Aide de Camp to Governor of New Mexico; Toastmasters Club, Lame Deer, MT (past president); coached four years of Little League, Lame Deer, MT. *Memberships*: Confederated Salish & Kootenai Tribe; tribal affiliations with Chippewa Cree Tribe and Rocky Boy Tribe. *Awards, honors*: Special Achievement Award from Bureau of Indian Affairs; Letter of Appreciation from Jicarilla Apache Tribe and Northern Cheyenne Tribe; guest speaker (at Dull Knife Memorial College on numerous occasions) on government and their relations with tribes.

*MORAN, GEORGE F.
(museum director)
Affiliation: Indian City, U.S.A., Hwy. 8, Box 695, Anadarko, OK 73005 (405) 247-5661.

*MORENO, FIDEL
(Native American film producer/director/writer)
Address: P.O. Box 856, Toadlena, NM 87324 (505) 789-3246/3221.

MORGAN, DAVE
(hospital director)
Affiliation: Parker PHS Indian Hospital, Route 1, Box 12, Parker, AZ 85344 (602) 669-2137.

MORGAN, DONALD I. (Blackfeet) 1934-
(BIA official)
Born June 12, 1934, Browning, Mont. *Education*: College of Great Falls; University of New Mexico; Central Washington University. *Principal occupation*: BIA official. *Home address*: Fort Toten Agency, BIA P.O. Box 270, Fort Totten, ND 58335 (701) 766-4545. *Affiliations*: Administrator, Wind River Agency, BIA, Fort Washakie, Wyo.; administrator, vocational training and job placement worker, Los Angeles Field Employment Office; vocational counselor, Blackfeet Agency, Browning, MT, Northern Cheyenne Agency, Lame Deer, MT, Yakima Agency, Toppenish, WA; administrator, Crow Creek Agency, BIA, Fort Thompson, S.D.; supt., Fort Totten Agency, BIA, P.O. Box 270, Fort Totten, ND. *Military service*: U.S. Army, 1957-59.

MORGAN, MARILYN ELIZABETH 1944-
(technical editor)
Born June 30, 1944, Bremerton, Wash. *Education*: California State University, San Francisco, BA, 1972. *Principal occupation*: Technical editor. *Home address*: 2858 North Highview Ave., Altadena, CA 91001. *Affiliations*: Technical editor, Jet Propulsion Laboratory, California Institute of Technology, Pasadena. *Other professional post*: Editor, Native American Annual. *Memberships*: Society for Technical Communication (audio-visual committee); Astronomical Society of the Pacific. *Interests*: Technical communiction; astronomy and science in general; Native American progress and cultural integrity. *Published work*: Editor, Native American Annual (Native American Publishing Co., Margaret Clark-Price, Publisher, 1985).

*MORGAN, RAYMOND
(BIA agency chairperson)
Affiliation: Eastern Navajo Agency, BIA, P.O. Box 328, Crownpoint, NM 87313 (505) 786-6150.

MORGAN, RONALD J. *(Whitewolf)* **(Blackfoot) 1940-**
(writer, photographer, jeweler)
Born October 4, 1940, Seattle, Wash. *Education*: Universal Life Church (Modesto, CA), BA (History), 1974; McGraw-Hill Paralegal School, Washington, DC, 1990. *Principal occupation*: Writer, photographer, jeweler. *Home address*: P.O. Box 297, Redwater, TX 75573. *Occupational activities*: "I'm a public speaker, lecturer and dancer. I give talks on the Old West and Indians, also have slide shows and relic displays using artifacts from my collections. As a dancer, I've demonstrated Indian dances for tourists, school and youth groups. I have appeared in three video movies, filmed on the Alabama-Coushatta Reservation, Livingston, Texas. I speak the Dakota Sioux language, sign language and Spanish." *Memberships*: Smithsonian Institution; National Archives. *Awards, honors*: Awarded honorary title, Special Consultant-American Indian Affairs, 1969; "I have been consulted by writers, U.S. Senators and many Indian organizations over the years. *Interests*: "Research is one of my main interests. I'm an Indian historian and always try to learn the old ways. My interests are many: archaeology, linguistics, publishing and law. I'm especially interested in state and federal law books relating

Indian court cases. Collecting Indian artifacts; documents, photographs and original historical newspapers are just some of my interests, As a professional photographer, I'm busy recording western and Indian historical sites, graves of famous Indians and Indian powwows. My photographs are now in the permanent collections of three major museums: U.S. Dept. of the Interior, National Park Service, Fort Bowie, AZ; North American Indian Heritage Center, in WY; and the Amon Carter Museum, Fort Worth, TX. I'm a part-time jeweler, casting in both gold and silver. My future plans are to produce video movie documentaries pertaining to Indian ceremonies and wild life. I'm currently working on fictional book about intertribal wars. The University of South Dakota, Institute of Indian Studies, has expressed an interest in using my photographs in a future publication, Who's Who Among the Sioux; I now paint acrylic and oil paintings of my Indian people; I have made over 30 Indian videos (Indian dancing), filmed all over Texas and Tulsa, OK; I am learning to speak the Kiowa language, because of my close association with them." *Biographical sources*: Source Directory (U.S. Dept. of the Interior, BIA, 1985-87); The American Indian Index: A Directory of Indian Country (Arrowstar Publishing, 1986-87). *Published works*: Articles: I Fought With Geronimo by Jason Betzinez as told to Ronald Morgan (The Westerner, Stagecoach Publishing, 1971); series, The Indian Side in The Frontier, Real West, True West, and American West Magazines; among others.

*MORIGEAU, MICHAEL A.
(BIA field representative)
Affiliation: Plummer Field Office, Bureau of Indian Affairs, Agency Rd., Plummer, ID 83851 (208) 686-1277.

*MORIN, LYMAN
(school principal/supt.)
Affiliation: Cheyenne-Eagle Butte School, P.O. Box 672, Eagle Butte, SD 57625 (605) 964-8744.

*MORRIS, BEVERLY
(Native American film producer)
Address: 1901 Calle Miquela, Santa Fe, NM 87505 (505) 988-6319.

MORRIS, DORAN L., Sr. (Omaha)
(tribal chairperson)
Affiliation: Omaha Tribal Council, P.O. Box 368, Macy, NE 68039 (402) 837-5391.

MORRIS, ELIZABETH (Athabascan) 1933-
(former director-Indian organization)
Born February 16, 1933, Holikachuk, Alaska. *Education*: Seattle Community College, 1969-70. *Principal occupation*: Former executive director, Seattle Indian Center. Resides in Seattle, WA. *Community activities*: Candidate for Washington State Legislature, 1970; Seattle Community Council (advertising screening committee). *Interests*: Ms. Morris writes, "(I am) interested in the welfare of my people, and devote most of my time toward improving the quality of (their) lives. Because of my own experiences and difficulties, I am interested in helping (my people) maintain their identity and unique culture, (while) at the same time adapt(ing) to the urban scene."

MORRIS, C. PATRICK 1938-
(professor of Native American studies)
Born December 5, 1938, Watsonville, Calif.

Education: Arizona State University, BA, 1964, MA, 1970, PhD (Anthropology), 1974. *Principal occupation*: Professor of Native American Studies. *Address & Affiliation*: Center for Native American Studies, Montana State University, Bozeman, MT 59717 (406) 994-4201. *Community activities*: Assist tribal colleges organize International Exchange Program for 23 Indian tribes with Norway & France. *Memberships*: National Indian Education Association; Montana Indian Education Association. *Awards, honors*: Marshall Fellowship, Norway; Fulbright Award, Norway, University of Oslo; Goodwill Award for International Understanding, Norway. *Interests*: Indian law and policy; international human rights and indigenous people; Indian reservation economies; tribally controlled colleges; American Indian religious thought; Indian literature--oral and written. *Published works*: As Long As the Water Flows: Indian Water Rights, A Growing National Conflict in the U.S., in Native Power, edited by J. Brosted, et al (University of Oslo, 1985); The Hill of Sorrow: Ethnohistory of the Little Shell Chippewa (in press).

*MORRIS, GLENN T.
(executive director)
Affiliation: Fourth World Center for the Study of Indigenous Law & Politics, University of Colorado, Dept. of Political Science, Campus Box 190, P.O. Box 173364, Denver, CO 80217 (303) 556-2850.

MORRISON, EDDIE (Oklahoma Cherokee) 1946-
(artist-sculptor)
Born September 29, 1946, Claremore, Okla. *Education*: Northeastern State College (4 years); Institute of American Indian Art (2 years). *Principal occupation*: Artist-sculptor. *Home address*: 223 N. Young, Caldwell, KS 67022 (316) 845-2355; 845-2259 (work). *Affiliation*: Owner, Eddie Morrison Studio & Gallery, Caldwell, KS. Specializes with wood and stone sculpture in a contemporary traditional style. "Besides my own feelings and interpretations, my ideas and themes come from the philosophies of Indians about life, spirituality, respect for life, animals, and all that is around us, and the Great Creator." *Exhibits*: Annual Santa Fe Indian Market; Red Cloud Art Show, Pine Ridge, SD; Trail of Tears Art Show, Tahlequah, OK; Museum of the Cherokee, Cherokee, NC; America Indian Arts Council Art Show, Dallas, TX; Annual Indian Arts & Crafts Association, Denver, CO; Lawrence Indian Arts Show, Lawrence, KS; The Five Civilized Tribes Museum Show, Muskogee, OK; Scottsdale (AZ) Native American Indian Cultural Foundation; and Southwest American Indian Annual Indian Market, Santa Fe, NM. *Military service*: U.S. Army Reserve, 1964-69. *Community activities*: Caldwell Chamber of Commerce. *Memberships*: Indian Arts & Crafts Association; Southwest Association on Indian Affairs; Art Student League of Denver. *Awards, honors*: Faculty Departmental Award for Outstanding Student in 3 Dimensional Arts, Institute of American Indian Art; 2 Honorable Mention Awards for wood sculpture at Santa Fe Indian Market, 1991; Best of Wood & Stone Category, 1st Place, 1994 Indian Arts & Crafts Association, Phoenix, AZ; his work has been featured in: Contemporary Native American Art in Kansas" Show; Smokey Hill Museum, Salina, KS, 1990; also numerous private collections and several galleries throughout the U.S.

*MORRISON, ROBERT
(North Alabama Cherokees) 1938-
(maintenance)
Born October 27, 1938 in Alabama. *Affiliation*: Owner, Morrison's Indian Research, P.O. Box 41, Boaz, AL 35957 (205) 593-7336. Cherokee national Indian search; some Seminole, Choctaw & Chickasaw research; individual and family charts. *Charges*: $10/name, $20/family.

MORROW, PHYLLIS 1950-
(assistant professor of anthropology and cross-cultural communications)
Education: Harvard University, BA (summa cum laude, Social/Cultural Anthropology)1972; Cornell University, MA, 1976, PhD, 1987. *Principal occupation*: Assistant professor of anthropology of anthropology and cross-cultural communications. *Address*: University of Alaska, Fairbanks, AK 99775 (907) 474-6608 (work), (907) 479-5911 (home). *Affiliations*: Graduate teaching assistant, Cornell University, 1973-76; courses/workshops in Yup'ik Eskimo culture/history and language/linguistics, Kuskokwim College, Bethel (University of Alaska), 1977-86; director, Yup'ik Eskimo Language Center, Kuskokwim College, 1979-81; assistant professor of anthropology and cross-cultural communications, University of Alaska, Fairbanks, 1987- *Other professional posts*: Field coordinator for cross-cultural Education Development Program teaching B.Ed. students in rural Alaskan village sites, 1978; material development and teacher training for the Lower Kuskokwim School District in Bethel, AK, 1981-86; consulting services- law, education, and oral history/literature' conference/workshop presentations, 1981-. *Community activities*: Museum Collections Advisory Committee, Alaska State Museums (vice-chair); Alaska Organizing Committee member and conference chair, 1990 Conference on Hunting & Gathering Societies. *Memberships*: American Anthropological Association; Alaska Anthropological Association; Commission on Folk Law and Legal Pluralism; Society for Applied Anthropology. *Awards, honors*: Phi Beta Kappa (Harvard-Radcliffe), 1971; Andrew White Graduate Fellowship, 1973-74; National Institute of Mental Health Predoctoral Fellowship for ethnographic fieldwork in Southwestern Alaska, 1976; Alaska Historical Commission Grant for publication of Cauyarnariuq, 1985; Alaska Humanities Forum Grant for "The Writing of Cultural and Culture of Writing," 1988; Spencer Foundation Grant for "Yup'ik Eskimo Ceremonialism: Traditional Religion in Contemporary Education, 1989. *Published works*: Co-author, Qaneryaurci Yup'igtun: Learn to Speak Yup'ik, 1981; "It is Time for Drumming: A Summary of Recent Research on Traditional Yup'ik Ceremonies," Etudes/Inuit/Studies, Vol. 8 The Central Yup'ik Eskimos, 1984; editor, Cauyarnariuq ('it is time for drumming", high school text: reconstructs and discusses the traditional ceremonial round of Yup'ik Eskimos In Yup'ik Eskimo (author, Elsie P. Mather); co-author, Teacher's Guide: Secondary Yup'ik Language and Culture Program for the Lower Kuskokwim School District (LKSD, Bethel), 1987; "Competing Realities: The Negotiation of Ethnic Identity and Public Plicy in Rural Alaska" in Cross-Cultural Issues in Alaskan Education, V. III, Ray Barnhardt, Ed. (Center for Cross-cultural Studies, Fairbanks, AK, 1989; "Oral Literature of the Alaskan Inuit," in Dictionary of Native North American Literature, Andrew Wiget, Ed. (Greenwood Press, 1990).

*MORTON, NEIL
(center director)
Affiliation: Native American Center for Excellence, Center for Tribal Studies, Tahlequah, OK 74464 (918) 456-5511 ext. 3690.

*MOSELY, MARY JEAN
(program director)
Affiliation: Fort Lewis College, Division of Intercultural Studies, 120 Miller Student Center, Durango, CO 81301.

MOSES, CAROL
(club manager)
Affiliation: North American Indian Club, P.O. Box 851, Syracuse, NY 13201 (315) 476-7425.

MOSES, DARRYL CYRIL
(Indian band chief)
Affiliation: Lower Nicola Indian Band, RR 1, Site 17, Comp. 18, Keremeos, British Columbia, Canada V0K 2B0 (604) 378-5157.

MOSES, LILLY L. (Nez Perce) 1949-
(economic development planner)
Born November 8, 1949, Seattle, Wash. *Education*: Oregon State University, BS (Education), 1976; University of Idaho, College of Law, 1979-80. *Principal occupation*: Economic development planner. *Address*: Nez Perce Tribe, P.O. Box 365, Lapwai, ID 83540. *Affiliations*: Cooperative education coordinator, American Indian Higher Education Consortium, Denver, CO, 1973-74; teacher intern, Madras Public Schools, Madras, OR, 1975-76; grants/contracts specialist, Planning Department, Warm Springs Confederated Tribes, Warm Springs, OR, 1976-77; community service manager, Nez Perce Tribe, Lapwai, Idaho, 1977-79; researcher, Cobe Consultants, Portland, OR, 1980-81; economic development planner/manager, Limestone Enterprise, Nez Perce Tribe, Lapwai, ID 83540. *Community activities*: Kamiah Revitalization Committee, Kamiah, ID (member, 1983-); elected to Housing Board of Commissioners, Nez Perce Tribal Housing Authority, 1985-89. *Memberships*: Association for the Humanities in Idaho, 1978-81. *Awards, honors*: 1971 After Dinner Speech Award; All-Indian Debate Tournament, Dartmouth College. *Interests*: "To gain a professionally gratifying position in the federal government that assists American Indian tribes in achieving self-sufficiency; camping, hunting, fishing, beadwork, dancing."

MOSES, TED
(Indian band chief)
Affiliation: Eastman (Cree) Indian Band, Eastman, Quebec, Canada J0M 1W0 (819) 977-0211.

MOSS, MYRNA
(executive director)
Affiliation: Cherokee National Historical Society, P.O. Box 515, Tahlequah, OK 74465 (918) 456-6007. Other professional post: Editor, "The Columns," quarterly newsletter.

*MOUNT, HARLAN K. (Gros Ventre)
(tribal chairperson)
Affiliation: Fort Belknap Community Council, RR 1, Box 66, Harlam, MT 59526 (406) 353-2205.

MOUSSEAU, SHARON A. (Oneida)
(school administrator)
Affiliation: Oneida Tribal School, P.O. Box 365, Oneida, WI 54155 (414) 869-2795.

MOWRER, JEFFREY (Cheyenne River Sioux) 1957-
(mental health counselor)
Born March 25, 1957, Mobridge, S.D. *Education*: South Dakota State University, BS, 1979; University of Wyoming, MS, 1987. *Principal occupation*: Mental health counselor. *Home address*: 5900 Yale Dr., Oklahoma City, OK 73162 (405) 232-0736 (work). *Affiliation*: Counseling psychologist, Oklahoma City Indian Clinic, Oklahoma City, OK, 1990-. *Awards, honors*: Indian Education Fellowship, U.S. Dept. of Education. *Interests*: "To professionally integrate mental health concerns and issues, in a culturally sensitive manner to our Indian people."

MULL, CHESTER M., Sr. (Cherokee) 1938-
(company owner/president)
Born May 18, 1938, Harrison, Tenn. *Education*: High school. *Principal occupation*: Ironworker. *Home address*: 12508 Sheets Rd., Rittman, OH 44270 (216) 927-5098 (home) 927-6855 (office). *Affiliations*: President, Rittman, Inc., Rittman, OH,1981-; president, Chippewa Steel Fabricating, Rittman, OH, 1982-; president, Marbri Engineering, Cleveland, OH,1989-. *Other professional posts*: president, John's Steel Service, Rittman, OH, 1990-; Summit Committee for Ohio Department of Economic Development, Columbus, OH (board member). *Community activities*: School board; president of Athletic Club; Junior Improvement League. *Memberships*: Grotto; Masons; Shrine 32nd Degree; Norh American Cultural Center; Night Templar; Eastern Stars; Medina Country Club; member of South Akron Board of Trade. *Awards, honors*: 1991 "Minority Manufacturer of the Year," by the City of Cleveland, Mayor's Office of Equal Opportunity; The Ohio Humanitarian Award for Heritage Preservation, Jan. 16, 1992 by the State of Ohio; Rittman Chamber of Commerce, "Member Award," 1993; other awards from U.S. Chamber of Commerce, North American Indian Center, Akron, OH; American Builders Exchange, et al.

*MULLEN, DOUGLAS
(rancheria chairperson)
Affiliation: Greenville Rancheria, 645 Antelope Blvd. #15, Red Bluff, CA 96080 (916) 528-9000.

*MUNDY, ERMA
(executive director)
Affiliation: Urban Indian Health Project, 1427 N. 3rd St., Suite 100, Phoenix, AZ 85004 (602) 263-8094.

*MUNETA, ANITA
(health director)
Affiliation: Crownpoint Comprehensive Health Care Facility, P.O. Box 358, Crownpoint, NM 87313 (505) 786-5291.

*MUNETA, JAMES
(project director)
Affiliation: Navajo Initiative Project, P.O. Box 920, Fort Defiance, AZ 86504 (602) 724-3351.

*MUNRO, PAMELA
(professor of linguistics)
Affiliation: Dept. of Linguistics, University of California, Los Angeles. *Published works*: Chickasaw: An Analytical Dictionary (University of Oklahoma Press, 1994); Mojave Syntax.

MUNSON, THOMAS A.
(monument supt.)
Affiliation: Effigy Mounds National Monument, RR 1, Box 25A, Harpers Ferry, IA 52146 (319) 873-3491.

MUNYAN, GEORGE F. (Little Turtle) (Nipmuc)
(author-illustrator; medicine person)
Born July 23rd in Putnam, Conn. *Education*: High school; various courses in art and related subjects, University of Connecticut, Worcester Art Museum, et al. *Principal occupation*: Author-illustrator-Indian subjects. *Home address*: 300 S.W. Main St., East Douglas, MA 01516 (508) 476-4401. *Community activities*: Medicine person, past secretary, and tribal roll genealogist, Chaubunagungamaug Nipmuck Tribal Council. *Memberships*: New England Antiquities Research Association (contributing writer, Native American consultant). *Awards, honors*: Several awards from Nipmuck and other tribal groups for educational and cultural projects contributed to or participated in. *Interests*: "Pre-Columbian American history, Native American and primitive art particularly in a spiritual context, herbal medicinal uses and propagation, environmental issues, inter-cultural understanding." *Published works*: Contributing writer/illustrator, Native American Sourcebook (Concord Museum, 1987); resource person, Legends of the New England Indians (Mohawk Arts, 1988); contributor-poetry: The Coming of Dawn (National Library of Poetry, Oct. 1993); All My Tomorrows (Quill Books, Feb. 1994).

MURDOCK, DON
(BIA field representative)
Affiliation: Tribal Operations: Minnesota Sioux Field Representative, Minneapolis Area Office, Bureau of Indian Affairs, 331 Second Ave., South, 6th Floor, Minneapolis, MN 55402 (612) 349-3382.

*MURDOCK, VERONICA
(BIA agency supt.)
Affiliation: Salt River Agency, Bureau of Indian Affairs, 10000 E. McDowell Rd., Scottsdale, AZ 85256 (602) 640-2842.

MURPHY, CHARLES W.
(Standing Rock Sioux) 1948-
(former tribal chairperson)
Born December 27, 1948, Fort Yates, N.D. *Education*: Saint Benedict College, 1968-69. *Principal occupation*: Former tribal chairperson. *Home address*: P.O. Box D, Fort Yates, ND 58538. *Affiliations*: Police officer, BIA, Fort Yates, ND, 1970-72; range technician, BIA, Standing Rock Sioux Tribe, 1972-76; agricultural director, 1976-79, economic development planner, 1979-81, vice chairman and councilman, 1981-83, chairperson, 1983-, Standing Rock Sioux Tribe, Fort Yates, ND. *Military service*: U.S. Army, 1969-70 (Vietnam Veteran; Army Commendation Medal; Bronze Star). *Community activities*: Standing Rock Irrigation Board, Standing Rock Sioux Tribe (chairman, 1981-); United Tribes Educational Technical Center, ND (board of directors, 1983-); Aberdeen Area Roads Commission (chairman, 1985-); Aberdeen Tribal Chairman's Association (chairman, 1986-); Theodore Jamerson Elementary School, Bismarck, ND (school board, 1984-); Saint Alexius Medical Center, Bismarck, ND (board of directors, 1985-). *Memberships*: National Tribal Chairman's Association, 1983-; United Sioux Tribes, Pierre, SD (chairman, 1985-).

Awards, honors: Certificate of Special Achievement, Dept. of the Interior, 1980. *Interests*: "Elected by the enrolled members of the Tribe (Standing Rock Sioux), (I) serve as the chair of the Tribal Council and the chief executive officer of the tribal government. Specialized experience or other related background in personnel management, administration, planning and budgeting, and land and resource management. Responsible for implementation of tribal law; and represent the Tribe before Congress and government agencies."

*MURRAY, ARTHUR E. (Kaweah)
(mayor)

Home address: 28 Sunnydell, South Hutchinson, KS 67505 (316) 662-7410. *Affiliations*: Mayor, South Hutchinson, KS; National Tribal Chairman, Kaweah Indian Nation of Western USA & Mexico. *Other professional post*: Deacon in local Southern Baptist Church.

MURRAY, DONALD CLYDE
(Micmac-Algonquian) 1932-
(engineering manager)

Born April 11, 1932, Bayside, N.Y. *Education*: University of Louisville, BA, 1952; University of Southern California, MA, 1965; U.C.L.A., PhD (Psychology), 1973. *Principal occupation*: Engineering manager, Hughes Aircrafts Co., Los Angeles, CA, 1953-. *Home address*: 2106 West Willow Ave., Anaheim, Calif. 92804. *Other professional posts*. Licensed psychologist, State of California; senior associate, Al. J. Murray & Associates (mechanical consultants). *Military service*: U.S. Marine Corps, 1952-54 (Captain; Reserves-retired). *Memberships*: American Association for the Advancement of Science; American Physical Society. *Awards, honors*: Howard Hughes Doctoral Fellowships, 1968-73; Order of the Chevalier, Cross of Honor, and Legion of Honor recipient, International Order of DeMolay. *Interests*: Consultant and lecturer; management psychology; executive counseling. *Biographcial source*: Registry of Native American Professionals.

MURRAY, L. ROBERT (Shoshone)
(attorney)

Affiliation: Holland & Hart, 2020 Carey Ave., Suite 500, Cheyenne, WY 82001 (307) 778-4225. *Membership*: Native American Bar Association (board member).

MURRAY, WALLACE (Ioway)
(tribal chairperson)

Affiliation: Iowa Tribe of Oklahoma Business Committee, RT. 1, Box 721, Perkins, OK 74059 (405) 547-2403.

*MURRY, LARRY
(association president)

Affiliation: Wyoming Indian Education Association, P.O. Box 248, Fort Washakie, WY 82514 (307) 332-2681.

*MURRY, W. DAVID (Mewuk)
(rancheria chairperson)

Affiliation: Shingle Springs Rancheria, P.O. Box 1340, Shingle Springs, CA 95682 (619) 676-8010.

*MUSHKOOUB
(commissioner of education)

Affiliation: Nay Ah Shing School, HC 67, Box 242, Onamia, MN 56359 (612) 532-4181.

MUSTUS, HOWARD
(Indian band chief)

Affiliation: Alexis Indian Band, Box 7, Glenevis, Alberta, Canada T0E 0X0 (403) 967-2225.

*MYERS, BRANDY WEEASAYHA
(director)

Affiliation: Native American Indian Community, Rd. 2 Box 247A, Kittanning, PA 16201 (412) 548-7335.

*MYERS, JOSEPH
(executive director)

Affiliation: National Indian Justice Center, 7 Fourth St., Suite 46, Petaluma, CA 94952 (707) 762-8113.

*MYERS, LARRY
(executive secretary)

Affiliation: Native American Heritage Commission, 915 Capitol Mall, Room 364, Sacramento, CA 95814 (916) 653-4082.

N

NABOKOV, PETER 1940-
(assistant professor of anthropology)

Born October 11, 1940. *Education*: Columbia University, BS, 1965; Goddard College, MA (Ethnic Studies & Language Arts), 1972; University of California, Berkeley, PhD (Anthropology), 1988. *Principal occupation*: Assistant professor of anthropology. *Address*: Dept. of Anthropology, University of Wisconsin-Madison, 1180 Observatory Dr., Madison, WI 53706 (608) 262-2866. *Affiliations*: Research associate, Museum of the American Indian, Heye Foundation, New York, NY, 1962-85; University of California, Dept. of Native American Studies (instructor, Fall 1979 & 1980, Winter 1981, Spring 1982, Spring/Fall 1984, Spring 1985; lecturer, Fall 1989); lecturer, American Studies, University of California, Santa Cruz, Fall/Winter, 1987-88, Winter/Spring, 1988-89; Resident Fellow, D'Arcy McNickle Center for the History of the American Indian, Newberry Library, Chicago, IL, 1986-87; lecturer, Ethnic Studies, California State University, Hayward, Spring 1989; Dept. of Anthropology, University of Wisconsin-Madison, 1991-. *Other professional posts*: Consulting and lecturing. Workshop Developer & Coordinator: The Blood of Things: American Indian Culture and History, D'Arcy McNickle Center Workshop series, Aug. 1991; consultant, Educational Broadcasting Corp./WNET-Thirteen. script critique for series on American environmental history entitled Nature: Land of the Eagle, 1989-91; member, The National Faculty of Humanities, Arts and Sciences, 1990-; member, Little Big Horn College Library & Advisory Board, 1987-; principal consultant, Native American Architecture, exhibit at the Festival of American Folklife, Smithsonian Institution, Summer/Fall, 1979; delivered Native American architecture slide lectures to departments of architecture, art, and anthropology at various universities & museums, 1977-82; among others. Activities in Native American Communities: Summers 1963-66: Museum of American Indian fieldworker-Crow Indian Agency, Pryor, Lodge Grass, MT (for book, "Two Leggings"); Summer/Fall 1972: Adult Education Consultant-Indian Island, Penobscot Nation, Maine; Spring 1973/Fall 1974/Winter 1975: Alabama-Coushatta Indian Reservation, Livingston,

TX (for book profiling four contemporary Native American communities); Summer 1985-87: Three Affiliated Tribes, Newtown, ND (for film, "Peoples of the Earthlodge"); Winter/Summer 1985-86: Crow Indian Reservation (conducting field research on history of the Crow Tobacco Society toward PhD dissertation, "Cultivating Themselves: The Inter-Play of Crow Indian Religion and History." *Awards, honors*: Awards for Native American Testimony: American Library Association Best Book for Young Adults, 1978; Library School Journal Best Book, 1978; National Council for the Social Studies, Carter G. Woodson Book Award, 1979. Awards for Native American Architecture: 9th Annual Bay Area Book Reviewers Association Awards, 1989; The American Institute of Architects, "Institute Honor" award, AIA National Annual Convention, Washington, DC, 1991. *Published works*: Two Leggings: The Making of a Crow Warrior (Thomas Y. Crowell, 1967; Apollo Books (paperback), 1970; University of Nebraska Press, Bison Books, 1981); Native American Testimony: An Anthology of Indian and White Relations, Vol. I: First Encounter to Dispossession (Thomas Y. Crowell, 1978; Harper & Row (paperback), 1979); Indian Running (Capra Press, 1981; Ancient City Press, 1987); Architecture of Acoma Pueblo (Ancient City Press, 1986); Native American Architecture, with Robert Easton (Oxford University Press, 1989); Native American Testimony: From Prophecy to the Present, 1492-1992 (including complete text of Native America Testimony, 1978, plus second unpublished sequel volume, Reservation to Resurgence (Viking Penguin, 1991); among others, and numerous articles.

*NAGARUK, LUTHER (Eskimo)
(village president)

Affiliation: Native Village of Elim, P.O. Box 39070, Elim, AK 99739 (907) 890-3741.

*NAGEAK, VIOLET
(director-Indian health service)

Affiliation: Barrow PHS Alaska Native Hospital, Barrow, AK 99723 (907) 852-4611.

NAGEL, PEGGY
(college president)

Affiliation: Stone Child College, Rocky Boy Route, Box 1082, Box Elder, MT 59521 (406) 395-4313.

NAHWEGAHBOW, BARBARA
(director-Indian centre)

Affiliation: Native Canadian Centre of Toronto, 16 Spadina Rd., Toronto, Ontario, Canada (416) 964-9087.

NAKAI, RAYMOND CARLOS (Navajo-Ute) 1946-
(artisan, musician, lecturer)

Born April 16, 1946, Flagstaff, Ariz. *Education*: Northern Arizona University, BS, 1979; University of Arizona, 1987-92. *Principal occupation*: Artisan, musician, lecturer. *Home address*: 4949 N. Camino de Oeste, Tucson, AZ 85745 (602) 743-9902 (work). *Affiliations*: Canyon Records Productions, Phoenix, AZ (artist, 1984-); Arizona Commission on the Arts, Phoenix, AZ (artist/consultant, 1982-). *Other professional posts*: Touring Artist, Western States Arts Foundation, 1991-93; Certified Secondary teacher in Graphic Communications, State of Arizona; co-founder of the ethnic jazz ensemble Jackalope.

Jackalope has released two albums, Jackalope and Weavings. History: In 1973, after earlier music studies on the classical trumpet at Northern Arizona University, Nakai began playing the wooden Native American flute. He learned the traditional flute melodies and music forms of the Plains and Woodlands Indians and soon began to adapt these ideas to fit a style of his own. Nakai has recorded 12 albums for Canyon Records, including Earth Spirit, Canyon Trilogy, Carry the Gift, and most recently, Spirit Horses, a classically-oriented release featuring a concerto written for Nakai's Native American flute and chamber ensemble. Spirit Horses was chosen by Pulse music magazine as one of the top albums of 1991. Nakai's albums of solo flute music on the Canyon Records label include Changes, Journeys, Earth Spirit & Canyon Trilogy. On Cycles, Nakai uses the traitional flute with synthesizer accompaniment to create a dramatic work that serves as the music track for the multimedia presentation "Our Voices, Our Land" at The Heard Museum in Phoenix, AZ. Nakai has brought the Native American flute, traditionally a solo instrument used for courting and healing, into the realm of ensemble performance. In March 1993, he will appear as a soloist with the Phoenix Symphony in the world premiere of a new concerto for the cedar flute and orchestra composed by James DeMars. Nakai has collaborated with guitarist and luthier William Eaton on two albums, Carry the Gift and Winter Dreams. A new album by the duo will be released in 1992. Naka has performed at the World Music Seminar in Woodstock, NY, in concert, at schools, and at music festivals including the Telluride Bluegrass Festival, the Magic Flute Festival and throughout Europe & Japan. He has written & performed scores for film and TV, including selections for WGBH-TV, the National Park Service, the National Geographic Society, Fox TV, as well as many commercial productions. In October 1988, the Martha Graham Dance Co. premiered a dance set to five selections from nakai's album, Cycles. Since 1990, Nakai has collaborated and toured with pianist Peter Kater. Together they've recorded two albums, Natives and Migration. He has recorded Sundance Season and Desert Dance for the Celestial Harmonies label. Nakai continues to tour extensively throughout the U.S., Canada, Europe and Japanm, performing and lecturing on Native American culture and philosophy. *Military service*: U.S. Navy, 1966-71 (E-4, Radioman). *Community activities*: Panelist, The National Endowment for the Arts, Tucson Community Foundation, Phoenix Arts Commission; director, Arts Genesis, Arizona Ethnobotanical Research Association. *Memberships*: Cheyenne-Arapaho Gourd Society; National Flute Association; Blue Star Society. *Awards, honors*: Arizona State Governor's Arts Award, 1992, for individual achievement. *Interests*: "While I am engaged in the study of indigenous North American native culture and music, my goals will include but are not limited to the following: research the historical traditions and technology of Native American music and oral traditions; compose, arrange and perform new music for the Native American flute; demonstrate and lecture on aboriginal and contemporary Native American culture, music, spirituality and philosophies of self-awareness and survival, and most importantly, to express ideas, observations, and thoughts in a positive, non-rhetorical and unbiased manner, to educate rather than castigate. My objective is to communicate a perspective based upon the future oriented and on-going, living oral traditions of the Dine' and other aboriginal native peoples of North America that are uncoached in romantic and/or stereotypical idealism. I will utilize contemporary teaching methods to develop a creative learning atmosphere in which to share awareness." *Biographical sources*: European Review of Native American Studies, 2:2: 1988; "It's Not Just Music: An Interview...R. Carlos Nakai, Native American Flutist, David P. McAllester. Numerous performancesPublished works: "Living Voices: R. Carlos Nakai," an article on Native American music for Inside Performance magazine, 1989; "Native American Music," an article for New-Age Music Guide, edited by P.J. Birosek (Macmillan, 1990).

NAKOGEE, JOANNE
(Indian band chief)
Affiliation: Chapleau Ojibway Indian Band, Box 279, Chapleau, Ontario, Canada P0M 1K0 (705) 864-2213.

*NAMINGHA, THEODORE
(BIA agency acting supt.)
Affiliation: Eastern Navajo Agency, BIA, P.O. Box 328, Crownpoint, NM 87313 (505) 786-6100.

*NANENG, MYRON P.
(association president)
Affiliation: Association of Village Council Presidents, Inc., P.O. Box 219, Bethel, AK 99559 (907) 543-3521.

NANEPASHEMET
(program manager)
Affiliation: Plimoth Plantation, Wampanoag Indian Program, P.O. Box 1620, Plymouth, MA 02360 (617) 746-1622.

*NAONE, HAZEL (Hawaiian)
(society president)
Affiliation: Kalihi-Palama Culture & Art Society, 357 N. King St., Honolulu, HI 96817 (808) 521-6905.

*NAPIER, L.A.
(center director)
Affiliation: American Indian Education Policy Center, Pennsylvania State University, 320 Rackley Bldg., University Park, PA 16803 (814) 865-1489.

NAPONSE, LARRY
(Indian band chief)
Affiliation: Whitefish Lake (Naughton) Indian Band, Box 39, Naughton, Ontario, Canada P0M 2M0 (705) 692-3423.

NARANJO, MARY L. (Pueblo)
(school principal)
Affiliation: San Ildefonso Day School, Route 5, Box 308, Santa Fe, NM 87501 (505) 455-2366.

NARANJO, MICHAEL A. *(Mountain Meadows)* (Tewa-Santa Clara Pueblo) 1944-
(sculptor)
Born August 28, 1944, Santa Fe, N.M. *Education*: Highlands University (2 years). *Principal occupation*. Sculptor. *Address*: P.O. Box 747, Espanola, NM 87532 (505) 753-6162 (work). *Military service*: U.S. Army, 1967-68 (PFC; Accommodation Medal; Purple Heart in Vietnam). *Exhibits*: "My work has been shown in both one-man and group shows across the country, one of the latest being, "Miniatures," The Albuquer-que Museum, Group Show, Nov. 1993 to Jan. 1994. *Permanent collections*: Albuquerque Museum; Museum of Fine Arts, Santa Fe, NM; Indian Pueblo Cultural Center, Albuquerque, NM; Heard Museum, Phoenix, AZ; The White House, Washington, DC; Colorado Springs Fine Arts Center, Colorado Springs; The Vatican, Italy; among other places. Commissions: "Kokopelli," custom estate home, "Indian Springs Estates, Chatsworth, CA, 1985; "Yes, I Can" Award, Foundation for Exceptional Children, Reston, VA, 1988; "The Dancer," The Albuquerque Museum, 1989; "Justice," to be created for the Dennis Chavez Federal Bldg., Albuquerque, NM, 1993. *Awards, honors*: Appointed board member of the New Mexico State Arts Commission, 1971; Catlin Peace Pipe Award, 1973; "Governor's Award" for sculpture by Governor of New Mexico, Jerry Apodaca, 1976; presented with the 1982 "Profiles in Courage Award," by the New Mexico Vietnam Veteran's Association; presented sculpture to Pope John Paul II, at papal audience, Vatican City, Italy, 1983; chosen as "New Mexico Veteran of the Year,", 1986; 1990 "Distinguished Achievement Award," by the American Indian Resources Institute, National Press Club, Washington, DC; 1991 recipient of the 1st Clinton King Purchase Award, Museum of Fine Arts, Santa Fe, NM; First prize, Southwest Art Exhibition '92, Del Rio Council of the Arts, Del Rio, TX; numerous prizes and medals at exhibits and shows. *Interests*: Sculpturing mainly in bronze, but has begun experimenting in stone. *Biographical sources*: Michael Naranjo, The Story of an American Indian (Dillon Press, 1975); Art and Indian Individualists (Northland Press, 1976);The Sweet Grass Lives On - 36 Contemporary American Indian Artists, by Jamake Highwater (Thomas Crowell, Co., 1980); Contemporary Western Artists (Southwest Art Publishing, 1982; In Pursuit of the American Dream (Atheneum, 1985; "The Spirit of Michael Naranjo," a biographical short story by Mary Carroll Nelson, in Time Was (Scott, Forsman Reading, 1986); featured in Beyond Tradition: Contemporary Indian Art and Its Evolution (Northland Press, 1988); featured in the 1988 CBS's Special, "Bodywatching," produced by New Screen Concepts, Louis H. Gorfain, Producer; feature article in "Southwest Art Magazine", Oct. 1989 issue; featured on PBS's "Colores" in 1992; "Motion in Bronze and Stone: The Sculpture of Michael Naranjo," in Kaleidoscope Magazine (Summer/Fall Issue, 1992); "A very Special Arts Story...Freedom of Expression," a syndicated television special, produced by Very Special Arts Production, Washington, DC, 1992 - Kara Kennedy, Producer; Santa Fe Indian Market: Showcase of Native American Art, by Sheila Tryk (Tierra Publications, 1993); Michael is currently listed in Who's Who in the West, and Who's Who in American Art.

NARANJO, TESSIE
(Tewa-Santa Clara Pueblo) 1941-
(cultural preservationist/consultant, Pueblo culture)
Born January 16, 1941, Santa Clara Pueblo, N.M. *Education*: Loma Linda (CA) University, MPH, 1977; University of New Mexico, PhD, 1992. *Principal occupation*: Cultural preservationist/consultant, Pueblo culture. *Address*: P.O. Box 1807, Espanola, NM 87532 (505) 753-3736. *Affiliation*: Santa Clara Pueblo, Espanola, NM, 1990-. *Memberships*: Rio Grande Institute, 1982- (vice-president); chairperson, Native American Graves Protection & Repatriation Act.

Interests: Culture of the Southwest Pueblos. PhD Dissertation: Social Change and Pottery-Making at Santa Clara Pueblo, 1992.

NARANJO, TITO E. *(T'amu P'iin-Morning Mountain)* (Tewa-Santa Clara Pueblo) 1937-
(professor emeritus, sculptor, writer, consultant)
Born August 6, 1937, Santa Clara Pueblo, N.M. *Education*: Baylor University, 1956-58; Hardin-Simmons University, 1958-59; New Mexico Highlands University, BA, 1962, MA, 1963; University of Utah, MSW, 1967. *Principal occupation*: Professor emeritus, sculptor, writer, consultant. *Home address*: P.O. Box 516, Mora, NM 87732 (505) 387-5658 (home). *Affiliations*: Community organizer, State of New Mexico, Taos, NM, 1964-65, 1967-69; State of Alaska director, Bristol Bay Social Services, Dillingham, AK, 1969-70; director of social services, Mora County, N.M., 1970-71; assistant professor, College of Santa Fe, NM, 1972-75; New Mexico Highlands University, Las Vegas, NM (associate professor of social work, 1976-90, professor emeritus-part time professor, writer, sculptor, 1990-). *Other professional posts*: Sculptor, writer, consultant; Mora Valley Health Services, Inc. (board of directors). *Community activities*: Intermountain Centers for Human Development (board member); tribal secretary for Santa Clara Pueblo, 1976. *Memberships*: American Indian Higher Education (board of directors). *Interests*: "I am a part time rancher, part-time artist and writer. I enjoy hunting, fishing and photography. I am a distance runner in the masters category and I also love to canoe, hike and adventure in Alaska and Mexico." *Biographical source*: A Conversation With Tito Naranjo, in (Confluencia, summer, 1980); "Running on the Edge of Time," in Early Winters 10th Anniversary Catalogue, 1982. Published work: Native Americans of the Southwest - A Journey of Discovery (Running Press, 1993)

NARCHO, JOHN B.
(IHS-executive officer)
Affiliation: Tucson IHS Office of Health Program Reserch & Development, 7900 South "J" Stock Rd., Tucson, AZ 85746 (602) 295-2406.

NARSISIAN, MARK
(publisher) .
Affiliation: Akwesasne Notes, P.O. Box 196, Mohawk Nation, Rooseveltown, NY 13655 (518) 358-9531.

NASH, GARY B. 1933-
(historian)
Born July 27, 1933, Philadelphia, Pa. *Education*: Princeton University, BA, 1955, PhD, 1964. *Principal occupation*: Historian. *Home address*: 16174 Alcima Ave., Pacific Palisades, CA 90272. *Affiliations*: Assistant to the Dean of the Graduate School, 1959-61, assistant professor, Dept. of History, 1964-66, Princeton University; Professor, Dept. of History, UCLA, 1966-. *Other professional posts*: Dean, Council on Educational Development, UCLA, 1980-84; dean of Undergraduate and Intercollege Curricula Development, UCLA, 1984-; faculty advisory committee, American Indian Studies Center, UCLA, 1973-82; editorial board, American Indian Culture & Research Journal, 1980-. *Memberships*: American Historical Association; Institute of Early American History and Culture; Organization of American Historians (nominating committee, 1980-83; American Antiquarian Society. *Awards,*

honors: Research grants from University of California Institute of Humanities and Research Committee, UCLA, 1966-83; Prize from the American Historical Association, Pacific Coast Branch, 1970, for best book, Quakers and Politics: Pennsylvania, 1681-1726; runner-up Pulitzer Prize in History for The Urban Crucible, 1979; 1980 Commonwealth Club of California, Silver Prize in Literature for The Urban Crucible. *Published works*: Co-edited, Struggle & Survival in Colonial America (University of California Press, 1981); Red, White and Black: The Peoples of Early America (Prentice-Hall, 1974; 2nd Ed., 1982); The American People: Creating a Nation and a Society (Harper and Row, 1986); Retracing the Past: Readings in the History of the American People 2 volumes (Harper & Row, 1986; among others. Numerous articles in various professional journals.

NASON, JAMES D. (Comanche) 1942-
(museum curator, social anthropologist)
Born July, 1942, Los Angeles, Calif. Education: University of California, Riverside, BA, 1964; University of Washington, MA, 1967, PhD, 1970. *Principal occupation*: Museum curator, social anthropologist. *Address & Affiliations*: Chairman, Anthropology Division & Curator of Ethnology, Thomas Burke Memorial Museum; professor & dept. head, American Indian Studies Center, Dept. of Anthropology, University of Washington, Seattle, WA 98195 (206) 543-5240. *Other professional posts*: Commissioner, Kings County Arts Commission, WA. *Memberships*: American Anthropological Association, 1970 (Fellow); American Association for the Advancement of Science, 1970- (Fellow); American Ethnological Society, 1970- (Fellow); American Association of Museums; International Council of Museums; Association for Social Anthropology in Oceana, 1971- (Fellow). *Interests*: Social anthropology and museology; culture change and modernization; Oceana (Micronesia) and North America; ethnohistory research. Field research. *Published works*: Edited with Mac Marshall, Micronesia, 1944-1974 (Human Relations Area Files Press, 1976).

*NATHANIEL, JAMES, Sr.
(village first chief)
Affiliation: Chalkyitsik Village, P.O. Box 57, Chalkyitsik, AK 99788 (907) 848-8893.

*NATIVIDAD, RAY (Diegueno)
(rancheria chairperson)
Affiliation: San Pasqual General Council, P.O. Box 365, Valley Center, CA 92082 (619) 749-3200.

NAUMAN, H. JANE 1929-
(filmmaker)
Born May 4, 1929, Grinnell, Iowa. *Education*: University of Iowa, BA, 1950; University of Heidelberg, Germany, advanced studies, 1955-56. *Principal occupation*: Filmmaker. *Home address*: Box 232, Custer, SD 57730 (605) 673-4065 (home & office). *Affiliations*: Executive vice-president, producer-editor, Nauman Films, Custer, SD, 1955-89; president, Sun Dog Films, Custer, SD, 1989-. *Other professional posts*: Free-lance photo journalist specializing in articles on Native American culture (published in Indian Trader, Native Peoples magazine, Dakota Heritage Magazine, Four Winds, and many others), 1955-; location manager for NBC's "Chi Chi Hoo Hoo Bogey Man," a film based on a story written by Sioux author Virginia Driving

Hawk Sneve; location manager, Kevin Costner 1989 film "Dances With Wolves" about the Sioux in 1860; Indian historian & location manager for "Son of the Morning Star," an ABC-TV Special Feature (1990) regarding Native American involvement in the last ten years of General Custer's life; location manager for "Thunderbirds," a Tri-Star Tribeca Production feature film filmed ion Pine Ridge Reservation & S.D. Badlands, involving Indians and the FBI; screenwriter of historic feature "Jesse Moran." including the first Native American graduate of Harvard in a major role; research, historian & set decorator coordinator for "Lakota Woman," a TV Feature Special for TBS, based on book by Mary Crow Dog, regarding the AIM uprising at Wounded Knee, 1972; humanities lectures on the seven Indian reservations in South Dakota on films dealing with Plains Indians, as well as at Harvard, Dartmouth, University of South Dakota, and many other universities, museums, etc. *Awards, honors*: Fulbright Scholarship Award; Cine "Golden Eagle" Award (twice); American Film Festival Blue Ribbon (three times); American Indian Film Festival; UCLA Film & Folklore (best film on folklore); Governor's Award in the Arts, 1989; Festival of American Folklife Ethnographic Film; (all of the above awards for films on Native Americans). *Interests*: Native American Indian Culture; travel; interested in any world travel involving filmmaking or other positive involvement with cultures; expedition into canyons of Sierra Madre Occidental of Mexico to film Tarahumara Indian culture and Easter festival; have planned and executed many film festivals dealing with Native American films. *Films produced*: Johnny Vik, 35mm full length feature film, 1971; produced and edited Sioux Legends (16mm documentary of Plains Indians culture, 1972 (Cine Golden Eagle Award; Martin Luther King, Jr. Award); wrote, directed, produced, edited and narrated, "Lakota Quillwork-Art & Legend" (honored at the 10th Annual American Indian Film Festival, San Francisco; best film on folklore in the UCLA Film & Folklore Festival; honored at the Smithsonian Institution's Festival of American Folklife Ethnographic Film; among other honors); assistant director, editor and producer of "Tahtonka," (a Cine "Golden Eagle" award winner; among 100 best educational films; best film of the week on BBC; Brussells International Film Festival, San Francisco International Festival, American Film Festival award winners, among many others); produced and edited "They Are Coming to Norogachic" about the Tarahumara Indians of the Sierra Madre canyons in Mexico. *Published works*: Have written more than 300 stories about Native Americans and Native American culture, published in national and regional publications, such as Native Arts West, American West, The Homemaker Magazine, Dakota West, etc.; and written and produced educational slide films about Hopi, Navajo, Southwest Pueblos, and Plains Indians, Mandans, and Cliff Dwellers, and the Sioux sweat lodge and Sioux women.

NAVA, DOUGLAS A. (Taos-Apache) 1951-
(gold & silversmith; jewelry designer)
Born July 14, 1951, Montrose, Colo. *Education*: University of Colorado, 1969-71; Western State College (Gunnison, CO), BA, 1978. P*rincipal occupation*: Gold & silversmith; jewelry designer. *Home address*: 61336 Highway 90, Montrose, CO 81401 (303) 249-8131. *Affiliation*: Owner, Nava Southwest, Ouray, CO, 1979- (retail-Native American arts). *Other professional posts*:

Board member & chairperson, Atlatl, 1982-84; appointed to State Arts Agency Panel, National Endowment for the Arts, 1985-88. *Community activities*: Appointed to Goernor's Colorado Council on the Arts & Humanities, 1979-83. *Memberships*: Indian Arts & Crafts Association; Friends of the Ute Indian Museum. *Awards, honors*: Appointed to Who's Who in American Colleges and Uiversities, 1978; 1985 - 2nd Place Ribbon, Lapidary, Gallup Indian Intertribal Ceremonials; 1986 - Ribbon for Jewelry at Pasadena (CA) American Indian & Western Relic Show; 1987 - 1st, 2nd & 3rd Place Ribbons for jewelry, O'Odham Tash Indian Festival, Casa Grande, AZ; 1988 - 1st Place Ribbons for necklace and bracelet, Lapidary, Gallup Intertribal Ceremonials. *Interests*: "Jewelry design, painting (both oil and acrylic), sculpture-alabaster, marble, fiberglass resin. Also own and operate Nava Southwest, Ouray, Colo."

NAYLOR, JACK C.
(BIA agency supt.)
Affiliation: Miami Agency, Bureau of Indian Affairs, P.O. Box 391, Miami, OK 74354 (918) 542-3396.

*NAYUKOK, JIMMY
(village president)
Affiliation: Atqasuk Village, Atqasuk, AK 99723.

NEAMAN, BRYCENE
(museum curator)
Affiliation: Yakima Nation Museum, Yakima Nation Cultural Center, P.O. Box 151, Toppenish, WA 98948 (509) 865-2800 Ext. 720.

NEELY, SHARLOTTE 1948-
(professor of anthropology)
Born August 13, 1948, Savannah, Ga. *Education*: Georgia State University, BA, 1970; University of North Carolina, MA, 1971, PhD, 1976. *Principal occupation*: Professor of anthropology. *Home address*: 632 Riddle Rd., Cincinnati, Ohio 45220 (606) 572-5259 (work). *Affiliation*: Professor of anthropology & coordinator of anthropology, Northern Kentucky University, Highland Heights, KY, 1974-. *Community activities*: City of Cincinnati's Environmental Advisory Council; Sierra Club. *Memberships*: American Anthropological Association (Fellow); Southern Anthropological Association; Anthropologists & Sociologists of Kentucky (past president); American Society for Ethnohistory. *Awards, honors*: Predoctoral Research Fellowship, National Institutes of Mental Health, 1974; Alternate for Post-doctoral Fellowship, (D'Arcy McNickle) Center for the History of the American Indian, Newberry Library, Chicago, Ill., 1974; Certificate of Appreciation, NKU Student Government; NKU Outstanding Professor Award, 1994. *Interests*: Current & historical research with Southeastern Indians, especially the Eastern Band of Cherokee Indians of North Carolina and Ohio's Shawnee Nation United Remnant Band; revising Wendell Oswalt's Indians textbook, "This Land Was Theirs," with addition of Navajo chapter; environmental issues. Unpublished Ph.D. dissertation Ethnicity in a Native American Community, and unpublished M.A. thesis, The Role of Formal Education Among the Eastern Cherokee Indians, 1880-1971, University of North Carolina, Chapel Hill. *Published works*: Snowbird Cherokees (University of Georgia Press, 1991); numerous articles & papers.

*NEGONSOTT, EMERY
(tribal chairperson)
Affiliation: Kickapoo of Kansas Tribal Council, P.O. Box 271, Horton, KS 66439 (913) 486-2131.

NELSON, CAPTAIN (Rappahannock)
(tribal chief)
Affiliation: United Rappahannock Tribe, Indian Neck, VA 23077 (804) 769-3128.

*NELSON, CASEY
(community mayor)
Affiliation: Metlakatla Indian Community Council, P.O. Box 8, Metlakatla, AK 99926 (907) 886-4441.

*NELSON, HERMAN (Athapascan)
(village president)
Affiliation: New Koliganek Village Council, P.O. Box 5057, Kaliganek, AK 99576 (907) 593-3434.

NELSON, IRVING
(library system manager)
Affiliation: Navajo Nation Library System, Window Rock Public Library, P.O. Drawer K, Window Rock, AZ 86515 (602) 871-6376.

NELSON, MICHAEL (Navajo) 1941-
(corporate president)
Born February 2, 1941, Whitecone (Navajo Nation), Ariz. *Education*: Fort Lewis College, BA , 1966. *Principal occupation*: President, Michael Nelson & Associates, Inc., Window Rock, AZ. *Home address*: P.O. Box 614, Window Rock, AZ 86515. *Affiliation*: Michael Nelson & Associates, Inc. maintains retail outlets in Teesto, Tuba City and Kayenta, AZ. *Memberships*: Navajo Business Association (president, 1974-78). *Awards, honors*: National Indian Business-person of the Year, 1983; Minority Retail Firm of the Year, 1985; other local awards. *Interests*: Travels to other parts of the world; recent travels to Hawaii, Hong Kong, Bahamas, and all the small islands in the Caribbean, Mexico. *Biographical source*: The Maazo Magazine, Vol. 1, No. 3, entitled Business on the Navajo Reservation, The Maazo Interview with Michael Nelson a Successful Navajo Businessman. *Published work*: Publisher and editor of 1979 & 1980, Airca Rodeo Championship Edition (All Indian Rodeo Cowboy Association).

*NELSON, ROBERT M.
(association director; editor)
Affiliation: Association for the Study of American Indian Literatures, Box 112, U. of Richmond, Richmond, VA 23173 (804) 289-8311; editor, Studies in American Indian Literatures.

NELSON, SCOTT H. 1940-
(psychiatrist)
Born July 31, 1940, Cleveland, Ohio. *Education*: Yale University, BA, 1962; Harvard University, MD, 1966; Harvard School of Public Health, M.P.H., 1970. *Principal occupation*: Psychiatrist. *Address*: Box 6081, Santa Fe, NM 87502 (505) 766-2873 (work). Chief of Mental Health Programs, Indian Health Service, Albuquerque, NM, 1987-. *Other professional post*: Psychiatric consultant, Santa Fe Indian Hospital. *Military service*: U.SPHS (Captain, 1970-). *Membership*: American Psychiatric Association (Fellow, 1970-); National Association of State Mental Health Program Directors, (president & chairperson of the board,1981-83); American Art Pottery Association (president, 1983-85). *Interests*: "Extensive travel to Indian tribes as part of work responsibility; interested in tribal arts." *Published works*: More than 30 publications in various mental health and government journals/documents.

NELSON, EUNICE (Penobscot)
(anthropologist)
Address: P.O. Box 49, Old Town, ME 04468.

NENEMA, GLEN (Kalispel)
(tribal chairperson)
Affiliation: Kalispel Business Committee, P.O. Box 39, Usk, WA 99180 (509) 445-1147.

NEPTUNE, STAN (Penobscot/
Passamaquoddy) 1949-
(woodcarver/artist)
Born April 1, 1949, Indian Island, ME. *Education*: Old Town high school. *Principal occupation*: Woodcarver/artist. *Home address*: 481 Dover Glen Dr., Antioch, TN 37013. *Other professional post*: Indian arts and crafts director, Indian Island, ME. *Military service*: 1969-71 (SP-5; Honorable Discharge). *Awards, honors*: Various awards for carvings - Connecticut River Pow Wow & Rendezvous, 1990 & 1991, and 1st Annual Indian Market, Dayton, OH, 1990. *Interests*: Traditional Penobscot carver, Stan specializes in hand carved ceremonial war clubs and walking sticks from birch, poplar and cedar, while some may be inlaid with various stones. This traditional art form is being done only by the Wabanaki people of the northeast woodlands. He also carves totem poles from poplar and cedar. Most of his carvings are in private collections, but some go to galleries, gift shops, and museums all over the country, such as the Abbe Museum, Bar Harbor, ME; Boston Childrens Museum; and American Indian Archaeological Institution. Stan is available for carving demonstrations. He is a private pilot, currently working on a commercial/instrument rating. *Biographical sources*: We're Still Here, Joan A. Lester (Children's Museum, Boston, 1987);Turtle Quarterly, Native American Center for the Living Arts, Spring, 1988; Artists of the Dawn, Lee Ann Konrad with Christine Nicholas (Northeast Folklore Society, 1987); ATLATL Directory of Native American Performing Artists (ATLATL, Phoenix, AZ, 1990); Eagle Wing Press, Winter 1984; March-April 1991; Colonial Homes, Hearst Corp. (Vol. 15, No. 5, Oct. 1989); Artifacts, The American Indian Archaeological Institute (various issues); among others.

*NERBURN, KENT
(author)
Resides in Bemidji, Minn. *Address*: c/o New World Library, 58 Paul Dr., San Rafael, CA 94903 (415) 472-2100. *Professional posts*: Directed "Project Preserve", an award-winning education program in oral history onthe Red Lake Ojibwe Reservation. *Published works*: Neither Wolf Nor Dog: On Forgotten Roads With an Indian Elder, 1994; Native American Wisdom, book and audiocassette; The Wisdom of the Chief (all published by New World Library).

*NETZ, TOM *(Soft Shell Turtle)*
(United Lumbee-Great Lakes Clan) 1960-
(metal casting operator)
Born August 15, 1960, Elmore, Ohio. *Education*: High school. *Principal occupation*: Metal casting operator. *Home address*: 201 Harrison St.,

Walbridge, OH 43465 (419) 666-3257. *Affiliation*: Brush Wellman Engineering Materials, Elmore, OH, 1986-. *Other professional posts*: United Lumbee Nation clan chief, traditional storyteller; consultant, Minnitrista Cultural Center, Muncie, Indiana. *Memberships*: President, Woodland Indian Alliance of the Great Lakes, 1989-; Smithsonian Institution; Kekionga Native American Alliance. *Interests*: "I teach educational programs on Native American culture from pre-contact to removal period; instructor on many types of traditional work shops, flint-knapping, basketry, rattles, drums, traditional clothing, beading, Native herbs. (I) enjoy Native flute, old songs, dancing and being with all my Native brothers & sisters from the Four Winds."

NEW, LLOYD H. (professional name-Lloyd Kiva) (Cherokee) 1916-
(artist, craftsman)
Born February 18, 1916, Fairland, Okla. *Education*: Oklahoma State University, 1933-34; Art Institute of Chicago, 1934-35; University of New Mexico, 1937; University of Chicago, BAE, 1938; Laboratory of Anthropology, Santa Fe, NM, 1939. *Principal occupation*: Artist, craftsman. *Address*: Institute of American Indian Arts, P.O. Box 20007, Santa Fe, NM 87504. *Affiliations*: Director, Indian Exhibit, Arizona State Fair, 1939-50; instructor in arts & crafts, U.S. Indian School, Phoenix, AA, 1939-41; established Lloyd Kiva Studios, Scottsdale, AZ, 1945; instructor in art education, U.S. Indian summer schools for teachers, 1949-51; co-director, Southwest Indian Arts Project (sponsored by the Rockefeller Foundation), University of Arizona, 1959-61; art director, Institute of American Indian Arts, 1962-? Mr. New writes, referring to the period during which he established the Lloyd Kiva Studios in Scottsdale, AZ, "During this period (I) was devoted to the problem: Can Indian craftsmen produce contemporary craft items for general use, enabling the craftsmen to earn a living, pursuing their crafts in a general society? This implies some understanding of design inspiration from Indian tradition, careful craftsmanship, fashion, and marketing. (My) 'Kiva Bags' (a craft item Mr. New created) have been marketed by outstanding fashion stores throughout the country. Top fashion publications have featured these and other Kiva fashions from time to time." Mr. New has attended various conferences relating to indigenous arts and crafts forms in the U.S. and Mexico. *Published work*: Using Cultural Differences as a Basis for Creative Expression (Institute of American Indian Arts, 1964).

NEWCOMB, WILLIAM W., Jr. 1921-
(professor emeritus)
Born October 30, 1921, Detroit, Mich. *Education*: University of Michigan, BA, 1943, MA, 1946, PhD, 1953. *Principal occupation*: Professor emeritus. *Home address*: 6206 Shoal Creek Blvd., Austin, TX 78757. *Affiliation*: Professor of anthropology, 1962-87; professor emeritus, 1987-, University of Texas, Austin, TX. *Other professional post*: Director, Texas Memorial Museum, 1957-78. *Military service*: U.S. Army Infantry, 1943-46. *Memberships*: American Anthropological Association (Fellow); Texas Archaeological Society. *Awards, honors*: Awards for Indians of Texas, Texas Institute of Letters, Dallas Public Library. *Interests*: "American Indian ethnology, particularly Plains and Texas; culture change; primitive art; ethnographic field work with Delaware Indians; archaeological field work in Arkansas and Texas; rock art of the Texas Indians; ethnohistory of Wichita." *Biographical sources*: Who's Who in America, 1977-; Contemporary Authors. *Published works*: The Culture and Acculturation of the Delaware Indians (University of Michigan Press, 1956); The Indians of Texas (University of Texas Press, 1961); The Rock Art of Texas (University of Texas Press, 1967); A Lipan Apache Mission, San Lorenzo de la Santa Cruz, 1762-1771, with Curtis Tunnell (Texas Memorial Museum, 1969); North American Indians: Anthropological Perspective (Goodyear Publishing, 1974); The People Called Wichita (Indian Tribal Series, 1976); German Artist of the Texas Frontier, Richard Friedrich Petri (U. of Texas Press, 1978).

NEWCOMBE, ROBERT
(health director)
Affiliation: Pine Hill PHS Indian Health Center, P.O. Box 310, Pine Hill, NM 87357 (505) 775-3271.

NEWELL, WAYNE (Passamaquoddy)
(educator)
Address: P.O. Box 271, Princeton, ME 04668.

*NEWLIN, GORDON (Eskimo)
(village president)
Affiliation: Noorvik Native Community, P.O. Box 71, Noorvik, AK 99763 (907) 636-2144.

*NEWTON, WAYNE
(singer, entertainer)
Address: 6629 S. Pecos, Las Vegas, NV 89120.

*NEZ, PHOEBE (White Mountain Apache)
(radio station manager)
Affiliation: KNNB - 88.1 FM, White Mountain Apache Tribe, P.O. Box 310, Whiteriver, AZ 85941 (602) 338-5229.

NICHOLAS, GRAYDON
(association president)
Affiliation: Union of New Brunswick Indians, 35 Dedam St., Fredericton, New Brunswick, Canada E3A 2V2 (506) 458-9444.

NICHOLS, ROGER L. 1933-
(professor of history)
Born June 13, 1933, Racine Wisc. *Education*: Wisconsin State College, BS, 1956; University of Wisconsin, Madison, MS, 1959, PhD, 1964. *Principal occupation*: Professor of history. *Home address*: 6661 N. Camino Abbey, Tucson, AZ 85718 (602) 621-1336 (office). *Affiliations*: Professor, History Department, Wisconsin State University, Oshkosh, 1963-65; Professor, History Department, University of Georgia, Athens, 1965-69; Professor, History Department, University of Arizona, Tucson, 1969-. *Memberships*: American Ethnohistory Association; American Historical Association; Organization of American Historians; Western History Associations; Society for Historians of the Early Republic; Coordinating Committee for History in Arizona (past president). *Awards, honors*: Huntington Library Fellowship; director, National Endowment for the Humanities, Summer Seminar for College Teachers, 1981, 1988, 1993. *Interests*: "History of the American frontier and West; American Indian relations; comparative history -- U.S.A. & Canada; currently completing book entitled Conquest & Survival: The U.S., Canada and the Indians." *Biographical sources*: Contemporary Authors; Directory of American Scholars -- History. *Published works*: General Henry Atkinson (University of Oklahoma Press, 1965); editor, The Missouri Expedition (University of Oklahoma Press, 1969); Stephen Long & American Frontier Exploration (University of Delaware, 1980); editor, American Frontier & Western Issues (Greenwood Press, 1986;editor, The American Indian: Past & Present (Alfred Knopf, 1986, '81, '71); co-author, Natives and Strangers (Oxford University Press, 1990, '79); Black Hawk and the Warrior's Path (Harlan Davidson, 1992); editor, The American Indian: Past & Present (McGraw-Hill, 4th Ed., 1992).

*NICHOLSON, GENE
(BIA agency supt.)
Affiliation: Colville Agency, Bureau of Indian Affairs, P.O. Box 111, Nespelem, WA 99155 (509) 634-4901.

*NICHOLSON, KEN
(health center director)
Affiliation: Wind River PHS Indian Health Center, Fort Washakie, WY 82514 (307) 332-9416.

NICHOLSON, MARY EILEEN (Colville) 1924-
(tribal official)
Born March 1, 1924, Okanogan County, Wash. *Education*: St. Mary's Mission. *Principal occupation*: Member, Colville Business (Tribal) Council, Nespelem, Wash. *Home address*: Route 1, Box 90, Tonasket, WA 98855. *Community activities*: Western Farmers Association; Agricultural Stabilization Conservation Service (committee member).

NICHOLSON, NARCISSE, Jr. (Colville) 1925-
(tribal official)
Born February 5, 1925, Tonasket, Wash. *Education*: High school. *Principal occupation*: Tribal official. *Home address*: 618 S. Index, Omak, WA 98841. *Affiliation*: Former chairman, Colville Business (Tribal) Council, Nespelem, WA. *Other professional post*: Recreation Development Committee, Grand Coulee & Coulee Dam Chambers of Commerce (executive committee). *Military service*: U.S. Army, 1943-46 (European-African-Middle Eastern Service Medal; American Theatre Service Medal; Victory Medal; Good Conduct Medal).

*NICK, OSCAR
(village president)
Affiliation: Village of Atmautluak, P.O. Box ATT, Atmautluak, AK 99559 (907) 553-5610.

NICKERSON, TEK
(organization director)
Affiliation: S.H.A.R.E. (Sacred Hoop of American Resource Exchange), 114 Cat Rock Rd., Cos Cob, CT 06807 (203) 622-6525.

NICKLASON, FRED 1931-
(historian)
Born May 5, 1931, Swatara, Minn. *Education*: Gustavus Adolphus College, BS, 1953; University of Pennsylvania, MA, 1955; Yale University, PhD, 1967. *Principal occupation*: Historian. *Home address*: 6323 Utah Ave., NW, Washington, DC 20015. *Affiliations*: Assistant professor, University of Maryland, College Park, MD, 1967-; director, Nicklason Research Associates, Washington, DC, 1971-. *Military service*: U.S. Army, 1955-57 (Research Analyst). *Memberships*: American Historical Association; Western Historical Association; Southern Historical Association; American Studies Association; American Ethnohistorical Association. *Awards, hon-*

ors: American Philosophical Society Grant. *Interests*: American Indian policy; American Southwest travel.

*NICKLIE, DAVID (Athapascan)
(village president)

Affiliation: Native Village of Cantwell, P.O. Box 94, Cantwell, AK 99729 (907) 768-2151.

NICOLL, MICHAEL
(Indian band chief)

Affiliation: Masset Indian Band, Box 189, Masset, BC, Canada V0T 1M0 (604) 626-3337.

NIELSEN, ANITA G. (Wampanoag) 1922-
(lecturer/teacher)

Born June 21, 1922, Mashpee, Mass. *Education*: Massasoit Community College, MA, 1975; Bridgewater State College, MA, 1989. *Principal occupation*: Lecturer/teacher, Wampanoag culture. *Address*: P.O. Box 402, Middleboro, MA 02346 (508) 947-4159 (home). *Affiliation*: Teacher, Middleboro, MA, 1986-92; Wampanoag presentations, Plimoth Plantation, Living Museum, Plymouth, MA, schools by appointment - New England, 1983-. *Community activities*: Middleboro-Robbins Museum of Archaeology / Mashpee Wampanoag Tribal Council - Mashpee Archives Loaned Artifact for Exhibition. *Membership*: Wampanoag Tribal Council (life membership); Smithsonian Institution; Massachusetts Archaeology. *Awards, Honors*: Honorable Mention, Heard Museum; National Competition, Contemporary Craft - Finger-Twined Bag - purchased by Dept. of Interior, Bureau of Indian Affairs crafts - displayed in resource directory. *Interests*: Demonstrate the uses of natural resources and the importance of respecting all of mother earth's resources. Work with museums on children's workshops. Travel to Europe; teacher's confernces; presentations (curriculum). *Biographical sources*: "Personalities of America" (The American Biographical Institute); cover picture, "Plymouth Guide"; photgraphed for Indian documentation, by Jay Stock; "Career Close Up", by Boston Herald News.

*NIELSEN, TIM
(organization director)

Affiliation: Indian Life Ministries, Intertribal Christian Communications, P.O. Box 32, Pembina, ND 58271 (204) 661-9333. *Other professional post*: Editor, Indian Life: Christian Media for Native North Americans.

NIGHT PIPE, ORVILLE
(hospital director)

Affiliation: Eagle Butte PHS Indian Hospital, Box 1012, Eagle Butte, SD 57625 (605) 964-7030.

NIGHT SHIELD, EUSTACE
(home living specialist)

Affiliation: Rosebud Dormitories, P.O. Box 669, Mission, SD 57555 (605) 856-4486.

NINKE, BETH
(health director)

Affiliation: Sacramento Urban Indian Health, 801 Broadway, Suite B, Sacramento, CA 95818 (916) 441-0918.

*NISHIMOTO, WARREN S. (Hawaiian)
(center director)

Affiliation: University of Hawaii at Manoa Center for Oral History, Social Science Research Institute, Porteus Hall 724, 2424 Maile Way, Honolulu, HI 96822 (808) 956-6259.

NITSCH, TWYLAH HURD (Seneca) 1912-
(teacher, lecturer)

Born December 5, 1912, Irving, N.Y. *Education*: Empire State College, SUNY at Buffalo. *Principal occupation*: Teacher, lecturer. *Home address*: 12199 Brant Reservation Rd., Irving, NY 14081. *Affiliation*: Founder/president & director, Seneca Indian Historical Society. *Interests*: "Lecturer devoted to the dissemination of the wisdom, prophecy and philosophy of the Seneca Nation; programs presented at home and away to this end. Showing through these programs and lectures how the ancient wisdom of the Senecas can enrich the lives and increase the awareness of other cultures in the present. Programs in Scotland, Ireland, England, Italy, Hawaii, Canada, Mexico, most of the U.S." *Biographical sources*: Medicine Power, and Medicine Talk by Brad Steiger; Flight of the Seventh Moon by Lynn Andrews (dedicated to Twylah Nitsch) (Human Dimension Institute, Columbus, N.C.). *Published works*: Wisdom of the Senecas (S.U.N.Y.-Dept. of Bilingual Education, 1979); Entering Into the Silence--The Seneca Way, 1976, Language of the Stones, 1980/1983, Language of the Trees, 1982, Nature Chants and Dances, 1984 (all published by The Seneca Indian Historical Society).

NOGANOSH, JOAN
(Indian band chief)

Affiliation: Magnetawan Indian Band, Box 15, RR 1, Britt, ON, Can. P0G 1A0 (705) 383-2477.

NOLEY, GRAYSON (Choctaw) 1943-
(tribal education administrator)

Born September 4, 1943, Talihina, Okla. *Education*: Southeastern Oklahoma State University, BA, 1969; Penn State University, University Park, MEd, 1975, PhD, 1979. *Principal occupation*: Tribal education administrator. *Address*: Sequoyah High School, P.O. Box 558, Tahlequah, OK 74464 (918) 456-0671. *Affiliations*: Director, American Indian Leadership Program, Penn State University, Education Policy Studies, University Park, PA, 1979-88; administrator, Sequoyah High School, Tahlequah, OK, 1988-. *Other professional posts*: Assistant professor of education; assistant director, American Indian Special Education Teacher Training Program; director, American Indian Education Policy Center, Penn State University. *Military service*: U.S. Army, 1961-64. Community activities: Partnership Coordinating Committee; Committee for Understanding Others (local school district); Minorities Committee (graduate record examination board), *Memberships*: American Educational Research Association; Comparative and International Education Society; National Indian Education Association. *Awards, honors*: Kellogg Foundation, National Fellowship Program, 1984-87; participant, Phoenix Seminar, Penn State University, 1975; American Indian Leadership Program Fellowship, Penn State University, 1974-79; Music Scholarship, Southeastern State University, Durant, OK. *Interests*: Federal policies on Native American education; drug and alcohol abuse in adolescent Native Americans; travel. *Published work*: Two chapters in The Choctaw Before Removal (Mississippi University Press, 1985); articles in various education journals & American Indian journals.

NOLLNER, PADDY (Athapascan)
(village chief)

Affiliation: Galena Village Council, P.O. Box 182, Galena, AK 99741 (907) 656-1366.

NOMEE, ALFRED
(tribal school chairperson)

Affiliation: Coeur d'Alene Tribal School, P.O. Box A, DeSmet, ID 83824 (208) 274-6921.

NOMEE, CLARA (Crow)
(tribal chairperson)

Affiliation: Crow Tribal Council, Box 159, Crow Agency, MT 59022 (406) 638-2601.

NORMAN, MARGARET JANE (Seminole of Oklahoma)
(museum curator)

Affiliation: Seminole Nation Museum, 524 S. Wewoka, Box 1532, Wewoka, OK 74884 (405) 257-5580.

NORRGARD, PHILIP
(health director)

Affiliation: Min-No-Aya-Win Human Service Center, 927 Trettel Lane, Cloquet, MN 55720 (218) 879-1227.

NORRIS, LEONARD
(organization director)

Affiliation: Organization of the Forgotten American, P.O. Box 1257, Klamath Falls, OR 97601 (503) 882-4441.

NORTH, CHARLES, M.D.
(clinical director)

Affiliation: Albuquerque PHS Indian Hospital, 801 Vassar Dr, NE, Albuquerque, NM 87106 (505) 254-4000.

*NORTHRUP, JIM *(Gi Gi Kunaw a magawinini)* (Fond du Lac Lake Superior Chippewa) 1943-
(writer, basketmaker)

Born April 28, 1943, Fond du Lac Reservation, Minn. *Principal occupation*: Writer, basketmaker. *Home address*: 266 Northrup Rd., Sawyer, MN 55780 (218) 879-1691. *Professional posts*: Writes a syndicated columns, "Fond du Lac Follies" in three Indian newspapers, 1989-; and "Commentaries," in Duluth News Tribune, 1993-. *Military service*: U.S. Marine Corps, 1961-66 (Sgt. - Vietnam Campaign). *Video accomplishments*: Warriors (PPTV - Fargo, ND, 1988); Diaries (KTCA - St. Paul, MN, 1991); Zero Street (Weapon of Choice, 1993); With Reservations (C.I.E., St. Paul,MN, 1994). *Radio accomplishments*: Commentaries - Superior Radio Network, 1992; Fresh Air Radio - NPR, 1994. *Awards, honors*: Lake Superior Contemporary Writers, 1986; Best Feature Story, Native American Journalists Association, 1987; Minnesota Book Award, Augsburg College, 1993; Northeast Minnesota Book Award 1994, University of Minnesota, Duluth. *Biographical sources*: Lake Superior Magazine, Oct. 1993; St. Paul Pioneer Press, 1993. *Published works*: "Touchwood" (New Rivers Press, 1987); "Stillers Pond" (New Rivers Press, 1988); "North Writers" (University of Minnesota Press, 1990); "Frags & Fragments"- Vietnam poetry (self published, 1990); "Three More" (Minnesota Center for the Book Arts, 1992); "Walking the Rez Road" (Voyageur Press, 1993); "Days of Obsidian, Days of Grace" (Poetry Harbor, 1994).

*NORTON, GREGORY (Umpqua & Suislaw)
(tribal chairperson)

Affiliation: Confederated Tribes of Coos Lower Umpqua & Suislaw Indians, 455 South 4th St., Coos Bay, OR 97420 (503) 267-5454.

NORTON, JOSEPH TOKWIRO
(Indian band chief)
Affiliation: Mohawk Nation, Box 720, Kahnawake, Quebec, Canada J01 1B0 (514) 638-6790.

NORTON, MARY (Wintun)
(rancheria chairperson)
Affiliation: Cortina Rancheria, P.O. Box 7470, Citrus Heights, CA 95621 (916) 726-7118.

*NOSIE, WENDSLER, Sr.
(co-chairperson)
Affiliation: Apaches for Cultural Preservation, San Carlos Apache Reservation, P.O. Box 249, San Carlos, AZ 85550 (602) 475-2494.

*NOTAH, GLORIA (San Carlos Apache)
(tribal department director)
Affiliation: San Carlos Recreation & Wildlife Dept., P.O. Box 97, San Carlos, AZ 85550 (602) 475-2343.

NUCKOLLS, LARRY (Absentee-Shawnee)
(tribal governor)
Affiliation: Absentee-Shawnee Executive Committee, 2025 S. Gordon Cooper Dr., Shawnee, OK 74801 (405) 275-4030.

NUMKENA, WILFRED *(Tsung-Aya)* (Hopi) 1943-
(education)
Born December 24, 1943, Moencopi, Ariz. *Education*: Brigham Young University, BS, 1973; Pennsylvania State University, MEd., 1979. *Principal occupation*: Education. *Home address*: 4026 So. Kings Estate Circle, West Valley, UT 84120 (801) 538-8808 (work). *Affiliation*: Executive director, Utah Division of Indian Affairs, 1991-. *Military service*: U.S. Army, 1965-67 (Sergeant E-5; Honorable Discharge). *Community activities*: Utah Columbus Quincentennary Commission; Utah Interagency Task Force. *Memberships*: National Indian Education Association; Natioal Congress of American Indians; Utah Federation for Indian Education. *Awards, honors*: Ute Indian Education Award; University of Utah Intertribal Student Association Leadership Recognition.

*NUNNERY, BETTY D.
(program coordinator)
Affiliation: American Indian Professional Training Program in Speech-Language Pathology & Audiology, University of Arizona, Dept. of Speech & Hearing Sciences, Tucson, AZ 85721 (602) 621-1969. *Published works*: Editor, "Desert Connections"; Directory of Native Americans in Speech-Language Pathology & Audiology.

*NUSKE, VIRGINIA (Menominee)
(association director)
Affiliation: Wisconsin Indian Education Association, Menominee Indian Tribe, P.O. Box 910, Keshena, WI 54135 (715) 799-5110.

NUSS, BOB 1941-
(owner-Canyon Records)
Born in 1941, Ohio. *Education*: Marietta (OH) College, BA, 1963; University of Arizona, 1963-65, 1969-71. *Principal occupation*: Owner-Canyon Records. *Home address*: 4143 N. 16th St., Phoenix, AZ 85016 (602) 266-4823 (work). *Affiliation*: Canyon Records & Indian Arts, Phoenix, AZ (manager, 1972-83; owner, 1984-). *Military service*: U.S. Army, 1966-68. *Community*

activities: Board of Directors, ATLATL & Pueblo Grande Museum. *Awards, honors*: Outstanding Business for Service to the American Indian Community, Phoenix Indian Center, 1993.

NUTTER, DELBERT
(health director)
Affiliation: W.W. Hastings Indian Hospital, 100 S. Bliss, Tahlequah, OK 74464 (918) 458-3100.

NUVAMSA, BENJAMIN H.
(BIA agency supt.)
Affiliation: Fort Apache Agency, Bureau of Indian Affairs, P.O. Box 560, Whiteriver, AZ 85941 (602) 338-5353.

NUVAYESTEWA, EVANGELINE
(Taskya-Kyaaro-Yellow Parrot)
(Hopi-Tewa) 1940-
(elementary-primary teacher)
Born February 17, 1940, Keams Canyon, Ariz. *Education*: Phoenix Junior College, AA, 1961; Northern Arizona University, BS, 1972, MA, 1980. *Principal occupation*: Elementary-primary teacher. *Home address*: P.O. Box 637, Polacca, AZ 86042 (602) 737-2272; 737-2581 (work). *Affiliations*: K-2 teacher, Polacca Day & Second Mesa School, 1971-; Headstart teacher, 4 schools on the Hopi Reservation (6 years). *Other professional post*: Education specialist, NFFE Secretary, Hopi Jr./Sr. High School treasurer. *Community activities*: Save the Children Federation (advisor-secretary); Elderly Committee (secretary). *Memberships*: International Reading Association. *Awards, honors*: Outstanding Teachers of America, awarded by Gilbert Beers, Ph.D., director; Outstanding Dedication Award, Hopi Tribal Follow Through Program; Special Education Dedication Award, Polacca Day School. *Interests*: "I enjoy going to professional workshops to enhance my teaching skills in any area offered. I am also dedicated to participating in all our Hopi Religious Ceremonies on the mesa in our villages."

*NUVAYESTEWA, LEON
(school principal)
Affiliation: Hopi High School, P.O. Box 37, Keams Canyon, AZ 86034 (602) 738-5111.

NYE, DORIS R.
(council president)
Affiliation: National Urban Indian Council, 100068 University Park Station, Denver, CO 80210 (303) 750-2695.

NYGAARD, ROBERT WAYNE
(Sault Ste. Marie Chippewa) 1953-
(director-resource development)
Born September 5, 1953, Gaylord, Mich. *Education*: Bay de Noc Community College (Escanaba, MI), AA, 1972; Central Michigan University, BA, 1974. *Principal occupation*: Director-resource development. *Home address*: 1829 Chestnut, Sault Ste. Marie, MI 49783 (906) 635-6050 (work). *Affiliation*: Director, Resource Development, Sault Ste. Marie Tribe of Chippewa Indians, Sault Ste. Marie, MI, 1979-. *Other profesional posts*: Adjunct professor, Bay Mills (MI) Community College (2 years); conference delegate, White House Conference on Libraries & Information Services, Washington, DC (2 years). *Community activities*: St. Mary's River - Remedial Action Plan-Bi-National Public Advisory Committee, 1989-; Sault Tribe (secretary, Child Welfare Committee, 1979-; Powwow Committee, 1982-; secretar, Board of Directors,

Midjim Convenience Stores, 1985-). *Membership*: Michigan Commission on Indian Affairs (chairperson, vice-chairperson, secretary, 1978-88). *Awards, honors*: Ten Year Service Award, Sault Ste. Marie Tribe, 1988; Outstanding State Leadership Recognition Award, Circle of Life Conference, 1984. *Interests*: Workshop presentations: "Waste, Fraud and Abuse in Federal Energy Assistance Programs," DHHS, TX, 1986; "1990 Census Liaison," Sault Ste. Marie Tribe; "Community/Economic Development, Minnesota Chippewa Tribe, Bemidji, MN, 1991.

O

OAKES, GORDON
(Indian band chief)
Affiliation: Nekaneet Indian Band, Box 548, Maple Creek, Saskatchewan, Canada S0N 1N0 (306) 662-3660.

OAKES, YVONNE R. 1936-
(archaeologist)
Born in 1936, Baltimore, Md. *Education*: West Chester State University, BS, 1958; University of New Mexico, MA, 1981. *Principal occupation*: Archaeologist. *Home address*: Route 10, Box 88B, Santa Fe, NM 87501 (505) 827-6343. *Affiliation*: Assistant director, Museum of New Mexico, Santa Fe, 1975-. *Other professional post*: Member and treasurer, New Mexico Archaeological Council. *Memberships*: Society for Historical Archaeology; NM Historical Review; Society of American Archaeology. *Awards, honors*: Received grant from NM Endowment for the Humanities to study Confederate burials at Glorieta, NM; received grant from Museum of NM Foundation to attend Conservation workshops. *Interests*: "Historical archaeology, particularly frontier settlement and homesteading in the Southwest. Early Navajo occupation of New Mexico. The shift to sedentism in the Mogollon Highlands. Have extensive archaeological experience in New Mexico." *Published works*: The Ontiberos Homestead (Laboratory of Anthropology, 1984); Land-Use Patterns on the Maxwell Land Grant (Laboratory of Anthropology, 1985); Excavation of Two Pueblo Sites Along San Pedro, Wash., Socorro County, New Mexico (Laboratory of Anthropology, 1986); Archaeological Survey of the Mogollon Highlands Along U.S. 180 in Catron County, New Mexico (Laboratory of Anthropology, 1989); Pigeon's Ranch and the Glorieta Battlefield: An Archaeological Assessment (Laboratory of Anthropology, 1990).

OBERLY, JOHN
(administrative officer)
Affiliation: Wind River PHS Indian Health Center, Fort Washakie, WY 82514 (307) 332-9416; Arapaho PHS Indian health Center, Arapaho, WY 82510 (307) 856-9281.

O'BRIEN, IRMA
(museum coordinator)
Affiliation: Dillingham Heritage Museum, Pouch 202, Dillingham, AK 99576 (907) 842-5601.

O'BRIEN, PATRICIA J. 1935-
(North American archaeologist)
Born April 1, 1935, Chicago, Ill. *Education*: University of Illinois, Urbana, BA, 1962, PhD, 1969. *Principal occupation*: North American archaeologist. *Home address*: 2927 Brian Place, Manhattan, KS 66502 (913) 532-6865 (work). *Affili-*

ation: Professor of anthropology, Kansas State University, Manhattan, 1969-. Community activities: Kansas Antiquity Commission (member). *Memberships*: Society for American Archaeology; American Anthropological Association; Sigma Xi; American Association for the Advancement of Science. *Interests*: Archaeological research in north-central Kansas, the Kansas City, Mo. area, the Cahokia Site area in Illinois, and in the Yucatan, Mexico. *Published works*: Formal Analysis of Cahokia Ceramics: Powell Tract (Illinois Archaeological Survey Monograph No. 3, 1972); Archaeology of Kansas (Museum of Natural History, University of Kansas, 1984).

*OCHOA, CARMEN (Cahto-Pomo)
(rancheria chairperson)
Affiliation: Laytonville Rancheria, P.O. Box 1239, Laytonville, CA 95454 (707) 984-6197.

*O'DONNELL, JIM
(museum director)
Affiliation: Akta Lakota Museum, St. Joseph Indian School, P.O. Box 89, Chamberlain, SD 57325 (605) 734-3455.

OESTREICHER, DAVID M. 1959-
(anthropologist, writer, teacher)
Born December 5, 1959, New York, N.Y. Education: SUNY at Purchase, BA, 1981; New York University, MA, 1985. *Principal occupation*: Anthropologist, writer, teacher. *Home address*: 19 Forbes Blvd., Eastchester, NY 10709 (914) 632-1295. *Affiliations*: Speaker for schools, New York Botanical Garden; consultant for Native American Heritage Committee of New York; Scarsdale Audubon Society (board of directors). *Other professional posts*: Consultant for four books, a number of articles, and two films on the Lenape, including Lenape: The Original People, by Thomas Agnello, which he helped conceive and produce. David Oestreicher is recognized as a leading authority on the Lenape and related Algonkian tribes. His research has taken him from remote areas of Wisconsin and Canada to Oklahoma. For seven years until her death in November of 1984, his principal work was conducted with the late "Touching Leaves Woman", or Nora Thompson Dean, one of the few remaining full blooded Lenape, one of the last speakers of her language and the last person fully raised in the traditions of her ancestors. Much of this information is recorded on tapes, notes and video and is a major contribution to the Delaware Indian Resource Center at Ward Pound Ridge Reservation, Cross River, N.Y. Mr. Ostreicher organized and is principal curator of the traveling exhibit "Touching Leaves and Her People: The Lenape", initially funded in part by a grant from the New York Council for the Humanities. He has appeared as a guest on WOR radio in New York with Ed and Pegeen Fitzgerald; has taught government sponsored Title IV (Native American Indian Education) programs (his students, members of the Ramapo Mountain Indian Tribe, studied Delaware language and culture with him) and has taken part in and helped arrange various Delaware Indian symposiums and programs at Yale University, Tulsa University, Seton Hall University, SUNY Purchase, Kent State University, New York City Hall, the New Jersey Highlands Historical Society, the Archaeological Society of New Jersey, and elsewhere. Oestreicher has also been a consultant for films and book in connection with the Delaware Indians. *Other interests include*:

ancient Near Eastern and Jewish history, poetry, classical and folk music, art, conservation, canoeing and the outdoors. *Published works*: Surviving Historic Traditions of the Unami Delaware and The Munsee and Northern Unami Today: A Study of Traditional Ways at Moraviantown to be published by the New York Historical Society; under preparation is a biography of Nora Thompson Dean.

OFFICER, JAMES E. 1924-
(retired-professor of anthropology)
Born July 28, 1924, Boulder, Colo. *Education*: University of Kansas, 1942-43; University of Arizona, AB, 1950, PhD, 1964. *Principal occupation*: Retired professor of anthropology, University of Arizona. *Home address*: 621 N. Sawtelle Ave., Tucson, AZ 85716 (602) 795-4043. *Affiliations*: Information officer, Dept. of State, 1950-53; instructor, University of Arizona, 1957-60; associate commissioner, Bureau of Indian Affairs, 1961-67; assistant to the Secretary of the Interior, 1967-69; coordinator of international programs, University of Arizona, 1969-76; professor of anthropology, University of Arizona, Tucson, 1969-89. *Community activities*: U.S. Representative, Interamerican Indian Institute (Mexico City), 1968-78; Democratic Precinct Committeeman, 1970-76. *Memberships*: Arizona Historical Society (board of directors, 1986-92); American Anthropological Association (Fellow), 1956-; Society for Applied Anthropology (Fellow), 1956-; Southwestern Mission Research Center (board of directors, 1986); Southwest Park and Monuments Association (board of directors, 1989-). *Awards, honors*: Distinguished Service Award, Department of the Interior, 1968; Quill and Scroll National Journalism Scholarship, 1942; Tucson-Mexico Goodwill Award, Tucson Trade Bureau, 1982; Creative Teaching Award, University of Arizona Foundation, 1983; Southwest Book Award, 1988; AZ Historical Foundation Prize, 1988; AZ Historical Society Prize, 1988. *Interests*: "Primary activities at present involve speaking on subjects related to Native American and Hispanic Americans, and doing research and writing on the same topics." *Biographical sources*: Who's Who in the West. *Published works*: Indians in School (University of Arizona Press, 1955); Anthropology and the American Indian (Indian Historian Press, 1973); The Hodge's Site (University of Arizona Press, 1978); Arizona's Hispanic Perspective (Arizona Academy, Phoenix, 1981); Hispanic Arizona, 1536-1956 (University of Arizona Press, 1987).

O'JAY, BETTY (Navajo)
(school director)
Affiliation: Navajo Preparatory School, 1200 W. Apache, Farmington, NM 87401 (505) 326-6571.

*OJIBWAY, FR. PAUL
(commissioner)
Affiliation: Los Angeles City/County Native American Indian Commission, 500 W. Temple St., Room 780, Los Angeles, CA 90012 (213) 974-7554.

*OKITKUN, MARK
(tribal chairperson)
Affiliation: Native Village of Bill Moore's Slough, P.O. Box 20037, Kotlik, AK 99620 (907) 899-4712.

OKLEASIK, M. LaVONNE 1936-
(clerk, teacher)
Born July 4, 1936, Iowa. *Education*: Luther College, BA, 1960. *Principal occupation*: Clerk, teacher. *Home address*: Box 356, Nome, AK 99762. *Affiliations*: Clerk, City of Nome, Alaska; financial secretary, education chairman, bible study teacher, Our Savior's Lutheran Church, Nome. *Other professional post*: Private piano teacher. Community activities: Community alcohol program in Nome since 1980. "These activities have been with the Eskimo people. My husband is an Eskimo from Teller, Alaska. My desire for the people in this area is for them to be confident, to be happy about themselves and able to look at problems realistically and try to solve them in a satisfying manner. This I have tried to do in a volunteer basis through the church and the community alcohol program, working with all ages--children and elderly."

OLD COYOTE, BARNEY (Crow) 1923-
(government official, professor)
Born April 10, 1923, St. Xavier, Mont. *Education*: Morningside College, 1945-47. *Principal occupation*: Government official, professor. *Address*: Montana State University, Bozeman, MT 59717. *Affiliations*: National Park Service, Crow Agency, MT; Bureau of Indian Affairs: Fort Yates, N.D., Crow Agency, MT, Aberdeen, SD, Rocky Boys, MT, Rosebud, SD; special assistant to the secretary, U.S. Dept. of the Interior, 1964-69; assistant area director, BIA, Sacramento, CA, 1969-70; professor and director, American Indian Studies, Montana State University, Bozeman, MT, 1970-. *Military service*: U.S. Army Air Corps, 1941-45. *Community activities*: American Legion (post commander); Knights of Columbus (grand knight). *Memberships*: National Federation of Federal Employees (president, credit union; chairman, board of directors). *Awards, honors*: Special Achievement Award and Management Training Intern, Bureau of Indian Affairs; Doctor of Humane Letters (honor), Montana State University, 1968; Distinguished Service Award, U.S. Department of the Interior, 1968. *Interests*: Mr. Coyote writes, "General interest is in the welfare of Indians and youth of all races, particularly in the education and general participation in the American way of life of all citizens during formative years; conservation of natural and human resources and the general appreciation of the aesthetic values of the American way of life."

OLD PERSON, CHIEF EARL (Blackfeet)
(tribal chief)
Affiliation: Blackfeet Tribal Business Council, P.O. Box 850, Browning, MT 59417 (406) 338-7521. *Other professional post*: Member, Board of Regents, American Indian Heritage Foundation, Falls Church, VA.

*OLDMAN, GERALD (Athapascan)
(village chief)
Affiliation: Hughes Village Council, P.O. Box 45010, Hughes, AK 99745 (907) 899-2206.

*OLSON, BEVERLY
(outreach)
Affiliation: Native American Coalition of Programs, P.O. Box 1914, Fargo, ND 58107 (701) 235-3124.

OLSON, MARTIN L., Sr. *(Ipaloluk)* (Eskimo) 1927-
(commercial pilot, merchant)
Born June 24, 1927, White Mountain, Alaska. *Education*: Spartan School of Aeronautics, Tulsa, Okla.(aircraft and engine mechanic license, commercial pilot license). *Principal occupation*: Commercial pilot, merchant. *Home address*: P.O. Box 62100, Golovin, AK 99762 (907) 779-3071. *Affiliations*: President, Olson Air Service, Golovin, Alaska. *Military service*: U.S. Navy, 1946-47 (Mate 3rd Class; Aviation Machinist). *Community activities*: Bering Straits Native Association, Nome, Alaska (first vice president); Golovin Village Council (past president); Golovin Native Corporation (president); Alaska Federation of Natives (board member).

*OLSON, TRACY
(newsletter director)
Affiliation: "Smoke Signals," Confederated Tribes of the Grand Ronde Community of Oregon, 9615 Grand Ronde Rd., Grand Ronde, OR 97347 (503) 879-5211.

OMINAYAK, BERNARD
(Indian band chief)
Affiliation: Lubicon Lake Indian Band, Box 6731, Peace River, Alberta, Canada T8S 1S5 (403) 629-3945.

*ONDOLA, GEORGE (Athapascan)
(village president)
Affiliation: Eklutna Native Village, 26339 Eklutna Village Rd., Chugiak, AK 99567 (907) 688-6020.

*ONETTA, KATHRYN
(editorial director)
Affiliation: "Daybreak Star Indian Reader," Bernie Whitebear, P.O. Box 99100, Seattle, WA 98199 (206) 285-4425.

*ONEY, RAYMOND D.
(village president)
Affiliation: Village of Alakanuk, P.O. Box 167, Alakanuk, AK 99554 (907) 238-3313.

OPIKOKEW, BRIAN
(dean of students)
Affiliation: Saskatchewan Indian Federated College, University of Regina, 118 College West, Regina, Saskatchewan, Canada S4S 0A2 (306) 584-8333.

OPLER, MORRIS EDWARD 1907-
(professor emeritus)
Born May 16, 1907, Buffalo, N.Y. *Education*: University of Buffalo, BA, 1929, MA, 1930; University of Chicago, Ph.D, 1933. *Principal occupation*: Professor emeritus. *Home address*: 4006 Brookhollow Rd., Norman, OK 73069. *Affiliations*: Research assistant and associate, Dept. of Anthropology, University of Chicago, 1933-35; assistant anthropologist, Bureau of Indian Affairs, 1936-37; assistant professor of anthropology, Claremont College, 1938-42; visiting and assistant professor, Howard University, 1945-48; professor of anthropology and Asian studies, Cornell University, Ithaca, N.Y., 1948-79; director, Cornell University American Indian Program, 1948-79; professor emeritus, Dept. of Anthropology, Cornell University. *Other professional post*: Associate editor, Journal of American Folklore, 1959-79. *Memberships*: Sigma Xi; Phi Delta Kappa; Phi Beta Kappa; Alpha Kappa Delta; American Association of University Professors; American Sociological Association;

American Anthropological Association (Fellow; executive board, 1949-52; president-elect, 1961-62; president, 1962-63); Society for Applied Anthropology; American Ethnological Society; American Folklore Society (Fellow; first vice president, 1946-47; executive committee, 1950; council member, 1957-60). *Published works*: The Ethnobiology of the Chiricahua and Mescalero Apache, with E.F. Castetter (Bulletin, University of New Mexico Press, 1936); Dirty Boy: A Jicarilla Tale of Raid and War (American Anthropological Association, Memoirs No. 52, 1938); Myths and Tales of the Jicarilla Apache Indians (Stechert, 1938); Myths and Legends of the Lipan Apache Indians (J.J. Augustin, 1940); An Apache Life-Way: The Economic, Social, and Religious Institutions of the Chiricahua Indians (University of Chicago Press, 1941; University Microfilms; Cooper Square Publishers, 1966); Myths and Tales of the Chiricahua Apache Indians (Banta, 1942); The Character and Derivation of the Jicarilla Holiness Rite (University of Ne Mexico, 1943); Childhood and Youth in Jicarilla Apache Society (The Southwest Museum, 1946); among others.

ORECHIA, GWEN
(association president)
Affiliation: New Brunswick Native Indian Women's Council, 65 Brunswick St., Rm. 258, Fredericton, New Brunswick, Canada E3B 1G5 (506) 458-1114.

*ORR, FAYE
(library director)
Affiliation: Chickasaw Council House Library, P.O. Box 717, Tishomingo, OK 73460 (405) 371-3351.

*ORTEZ, JOAN K. (Steilacoom)
(tribal chairperson)
Affiliation: Steilacoom Indian Tribe, P.O. Box 419, Steilacoom, WA 98388 (206) 584-6308; director, Steilacoom Tribal Cultural Center & Museum.

ORTIZ, ALFONSO ALEX (San Juan Pueblo) 1939-
(university professor)
Born April 30, 1939, San Juan Pueblo, N.M. *Education*: University of New Mexico, BA, 1961; Arizona State University, postgraduate studies, 1961-62; University of Chicago, MA, 1963, PhD, 1967. *Principal occupation*: University professor. *Home address*: 830 E. Zia Rd., Santa Fe, NM 87505 (505) 983-7119. *Affiliations*: Assistant professor, Pitzer College, Claremont, CA, 1966-67; professor, Princeton University, 1967-74; professor of anthropology, University of New Mexico, Albuquerque, N.M., 1974-. *Other professional posts*: Charles Charropin visiting scholar, lecturer, Rockhurst College, 1977; chairman, Native American advisory group, Division of Performing Arts, Smithsonian Institution, 1975-76; chairman, selection committee, Doctoral Fellowships for American Indians, Ford Foundation, 1975-78; member, advisory council, National Indian Youth Council; board of directors, Social Science Research Council, 1972-74; board of directors, Institute for the Development of Indian Law; member, advisory council, D'Arcy McNickle Center for the History of the American Indian, Newberry Library, 1972-, chairman, 1978-; member, National Humanities Faculty, 1972-; member, national advisory council, Institute of the American West, Sun Valley Center for the Humanities, 1976-; member, minority

advisory panel, Danforth Graduate Fellowship Program, 1976-79. *Community activities*: Vice president, Chamiza Foundation, 1990-. *Memberships*: Committee for the Education of Women and the Minorities in the Sciences, NRC, 1975-; National Commission for the Minorities in Higher Education, 1979-1981; American Anthropological Association (Fellow); Royal Anthropological Institute (Fellow); Association on American Indian Affairs (director, 1967-; president, 1973-88). *Awards, honors*: Roy D. Albert Prize for outstanding master's thesis in anthropology, University of Chicago, 1962-63; keynote speaker, Second National Indian Education Conference, August, 1970; distinguished lecturer, Department of Religion, University of Oregon, Jan., 1973; distinguished Bicentennial professor, University of Utah, 1976; Guggenheim Fellow, 1975-76; Fellow, Center for Advanced Study in the Behavioral Sciences, 1977-78; MacArthur Fellow, 1982-87, Weatherhead scholar in residence, Navajo Community College, 1976; Indian Achievement Award, 1982, Indian Council Fire, Chicago, IL); Living Treasure Award, New Mexico Endowment In the Humanities, 1987; New Mexico Preservation Award (statewide), 1994; numerous other educational and civic panels. *Interests*: Contemporary American Indian affairs; religion and society; space, time, color and number in world view; the oral tradition. Research travel in Siberia, Summer, 1990; research in Chiapas, Mexico, Summer, 1992. *Biographical source*: Who's Who in America; Omni Magazine (interview) Feb., 1990; Humanities Magazine (interview) May, 1992. *Published works*: The Tewa World: Space, Time, Being, and Becoming in a Pueblo Society (University of Chicago Press, 1969); editor, New Perspectives on the Pueblos (University of New Mexico Press, 1972); To Carry Forth the Vine: An Anthology of Traditional Native American Poetry; editor, southwest volumes, Handbook of North American Indians, Vol. 9, 1980, Vol. 10, 1983 (Smithsonian Institution); co-editor, American India Myths & Legends (Pantheon Press, 1984); author, The Pueblos (Chelsea Press, 1993).

ORTIZ, ROXANNE DUNBAR
(Southern Cheyenne) 1938-
(professor of Native American studies)
Born September 10, 1938, Oklahoma. *Education*: San Francisco State University, BA, 1963; UCLA, MA, 1965, PhD (History), 1974. *Principal occupation*: Professor, Native American Studies, California State University, Hayward, 1974-. *Home address*: 275 Grand View Ave., San Francisco, CA 94114. *Community activities*: Staff member, International Indian Treaty Council (non-governmental organization in consultative status with U.N.). *Published work*: The Great Sioux Nation (Random House, 1977).

ORTIZ, SIMON J. (Acoma Pueblo) 1941-
(writer, poet, teacher)
Born May 27, 1941, Albuquerque, N.M. *Education*: Fort Lewis College, 1961-62; University of New Mexico, Albuquerque, 1966-68; University of Iowa, Iowa City, 1968-69. *Principal occupation*: Writer, poet, teacher. *Affiliation*: Instructor and co-director, Creative Writing Program, Sinte Gleska College, P.O. Box 8, Mission, SD 57555. *Other professional posts*: Consulting editor to Pueblo of Acoma, Institute of American Indian Arts Press, and Navajo Community College Press. *Military service*: U.S. Army, 1963-66. *Community activities*: National Indian Youth

Council (community organizer, 1970-73); Adult Community Education, Acoma Pueblo, N.M. (director, 1975); AIM House, Oakland, Calif. (member of board, 1977-79). *Memberships*: Americans Before Columbus Foundation (board of directors, 1978-); American PEN, 1980-. *Awards, honors*: Discovery Award (Creative Writing, 1970), Fellowship (Creative Writing, 1981), National Endowment for the Arts. *Interests*: "Avocational interests include listening to music, long distance running, travel. Places I've traveled include all of the areas of the U.S., including Alaska in 1979, 1981, and 1984; I traveled to Europe, including Holland, Belgium, and Germany." *Biographical sources*: This Song Remembers (article-interview)(Macmillan, 1980); Coyote Said This (biographical article) (University of Aarhus, Denmark, 1984); I Tell You Now (autobiographical article) (University of Nebraska Press, 1986). *Published works*: Naked In The Wind (Quetzal-Vihio Press, 1971); Going For The Rain (Harper & Row, 1976); A Good Journey (Turtle Island Press, 1977); Howbah Indians (Blue Moon Press, 1978); The People Shall Continue (Children's Press Books, 1978); Fight Back (INAD-University of New Mexico, 1980); From Sand Creek (Thunder's Mouth Press, 1981); A Poem Is A Journey (Pternandon Press, 1982); Fightin' (Thunder's Mouth Press, 1983); Blue and Red (Acoma Pueblo Press, 1983); The Importance of Childhood (Acoma Pueblo Press, 1983).

*OSAWA, SANDY
(film producer/director)
Affiliation: Upstream Productions, 420 First Ave. W., Seattle, WA 98119 (206) 524-8879.

OSBORNE, LOIS I.
(park manager)
Affiliation: Red Clay State Historic Park, 1140 Red Clay Park Rd., S.W., Cleveland, TN 37311 (615) 478-0339.

*OSBORNE, MARVIN
(tribal chairperson)
Affiliation: Fort Hall Business Council, P.O. Box 306, Fort Hall, ID 83203 (208) 238-3700.

*OSKOLKOFF, D.L. (Kenaitse)
(executive director)
Affiliation: Ninilchik Traditional Council Health Clinic, P.O. Box 39070, Ninilchik, AK 99762 (907) 567-3313.

OSKOLKOFF, GASSIM (Kenaitse)
(association president)
Affiliation: Ninilchik Native Association, Inc., P.O. Box 282, Ninilchik, AK 99639 (907) 567-3313.

OSKOLKOFF, PAT
(health director)
Affiliation: Ninilchik Traditional Council Health Clinic, P.O. Box 39070, Ninilchik, AK 99762 (907) 567-3313.

*OTHOLE, JEAN
(hospital director)
Affiliation: Zuni PHS Indian Hospital, P.O. Box 467, Zuni, NM 87327 (505) 782-4431.

OTT, BILLIE D.
(BIA area director)
Affiliation: Eastern Area Office, Bureau of Indian Affairs, 3701 N. Fairfax Dr., MS: 260, Arlington, VA 22203 (703) 235-3006.

OVERBERG, KAROLE
(BIA agency supt.)
Affiliation: Northern Idaho Agency, Bureau of Indian Affairs, P.O. Box 227, Lapwai, ID 83540 (208) 843-2300.

OVERFIELD, THERESA 1935-
(president, health inquiry;
professor emeritus)
Born July 22, 1935, Buffalo, N.Y. *Education*: D'Youville College, BS, 1958; Columbia University, MPH, 1962; University of Colorado, MA, 1972, PhD, 1975. *Principal occupation*: Professor emeritus of nursing, research professor of anthropology. *Home address*: 172 Braewick Rd., Salt Lake City, UT 84103. *Affiliations*: Itinerant public health nurse, AK Dept. of Health, Bethel, AK, 1959-61; nurse epidemiologist, Arctic Health Research Center, USPHS, Anchorage, AK, 1962-65; nursing consultant, Colorado Dept. of Public Health, Denver, 1966-69; research assistant professor, 1975-76, assistant professor of nursing, 1976-78, College of Nursing, University of Utah, Salt Lake City; associate professor, College of Nursing, Brigham Young University, Salt Lake City, 1978-84; adjunct assistant and associate professor, 1976-85, research professor, 1985-, Dept. of Anthropology, University of Utah, Salt Lake City; director of research, 1979-, professor, 1984-92, College of Nursing, professor emeritus, 1992-, Brigham Young University, Salt Lake City. *Other professional posts*: Advisory board, 1978-82, reviewer, 1979-, Western Journal of Nursing; reviewer, Research in Nursing and Health. *Community activities*: Western Commission on Higher Education in Nursing, Boulder, Colo. (research steering committee member, 1978-82); Transcultural Nursing Conference Group, Utah Nurses Association, Salt Lake City (chairperson, 1978-80); Salt Lake Indian Health Center, Inc. (advisory committee member and board of directors, 1981-82); Veterans Administration Medical Center, Salt Lake City (nursing research committee member, 1982-; member, Health Services Research and Development Review Board, 1983-). *Memberships*: Utah Public Health Association (board member, 1983-); American Association of Physical Anthropologists; Society for Medical Anthropologists; Human Biology Council; American Association for the Advancement of Science; Western Society for Research in Nursing; Council for Nursing and Anthropology; Society for the Study of Human Biology; American Public Health Association. *Awards, honors*: USPHS, Special Nurse Predoctoral Fellowships, 1969-74; American Nurses Foundation, Inc. Grant for Pseudo cholinesterase Silent Allele in Alaskan Eskimos, 1974; University of Utah, Demography Study Group, Grant for computer use on Eskimo data for fertility study, 1976-77; American Journal of Nursing, Excellence in Writing Award, 1981; Brigham Young University, Women's Research Institute Grant and College of Nursing Research Grant, 1985. *Interests*: "Racial variation; biomedical research; Eskimos--western Alaska; papers, lectures, workshops and conferences presented on the Alaskan Eskimo and the American Indian, too numerous to mention. *Published works*: Numerous articles in various professional journals."

OWEN, DON
(executive director)
Affiliation: Southwestern Association on Indian Affairs, Inc., 509 Camino de los Marquis, Suite 1, Santa Fe, NM 87501 (505) 983-5220.

OWEN, GARY
(Indian band chief)
Affiliation: Poplar Hill Indian Band, Box 5004, Poplar Hill, Ontario, Canada P0V 2M0 (807) 772-8838.

*OWENS, LOUIS (Choctaw/Cherokee)
(writer, professor of literature)
Born July 18, 1948, Lompoc, Calif. *Education*: University of California, Santa Barbara, BA, 1971, MA, 1974; University of California, Davis, PhD, 1981. *Principal occupation*: Writer, professor of literature. *Home address*: 9 Campo Rd., Tijeras, NM 87059 (505) 277-6347 (work). *Affiliation*: University of New Mexico, Albuquerque, NM, 1984-89, 1994-; University of California, Santa Cruz (professor of literature), 1989-94. *Other professional post*: Co-editor, American Indian Literature & Critical Studies Series, University of Oklahoma Press. *Community activities*: Board member, American Indian Literature Prize; board member, North American Indian Prose Award. *Memberships*: Choctaw Writers Guild; Modern Literature Association; American Studies Association; PEN International; American Literature Association. *Awards, honors*: Fulbright Scholarship, 1981; National Endowment for the Humanities Fellowship, 1987; National Endowment for the Arts Fellowship, 1989. *Interests*: "My major interest is in literature by Native American Indian authors. I spent seven years working with the U.S. Forest Service as wilderness ranger & fire fighter. I backpack and flyfish with my daughters. I write." *Published works*: American Indian Novelists: An Annotated Critical Bibliography, with Tom Colonnese (Garland Press, 1985); John Steinbeck's Re-Vision of America (University of Georgia Press, 1985); Trouble in the Promised Land: Steinbeck's The grapes of Wrath (G.K. Hall, 1989); editor, American Literary Scholarship (Duke University Press, 1990); Wolfsong (West End Press, 1990/94); Other Destinies: Understanding the American Indian Novel (University of Oklahoma Press, 1992); The Sharpest Sight (University of Oklahoma Press, 1992; Bone Game (University of Oklahoma Press, 1994).

OWEN, ROGER C. 1928-
(anthropologist, professor emeritus)
Born September 14, 1928, Port Arthur, Tex. *Education*: Michigan State University, BA, 1953; University of Arizona, MA, 1957; UCLA, PhD (Anthropology), 1962. *Principal occupation*: Anthropologist, professor emeritus. *Home address*: 2428 Colony Hills Dr., Las Vegas, NV 89134 (702) 228-4008. *Affiliations*: Instructor & professor of anthropology, University of California, Santa Barbara, 1959-67; professor of anthropology, 1967-92, professor emeritus, 1992-Queens College, Flushing, NY. *Other professional post*: Curriculum development consultant, Holt, Rinehart & Winston, Inc., 1968-77. *Military service*: U.S. Army, 1946-47. *Memberships*: American Anthropological Association (Life Fellow); Current Anthropology (Associate); Sigma Xi (Fellow); numerous nonprofessional organizations devoted to topics in anthropology and Native American affairs. *Awards, honors*: National Science Foundation Undergraduate Research Participation Award, 1961-63; Research Grants, University of California, Santa Barbara, 1961-66; Grant-in-aid, Holt, Rinehart & Winston, 1969-71; Distinguished Teacher of the Year, Queens College, 1983-84; Mellon Foundation Fellowship, Queens College, 1983-84. *Interests*: American Indians; Latin America. *Biographical*

source: Who's Who in the East. *Published works*: Senior editor, North American Indians: A Sourcebook (Macmillan, 1967); The Contemporary Ethnography of Baja, California, Mexico, chapter in Handbook of Middle American Indians (Tulane University Press, 1969); American Indian Society and Culture: A Conspectus, in Encyclopedia of Indians of the Americas, Vol. 1 (Scholarly Press, 1974); Native North Americans: The Anthropology of Americans Original Inhabitants (Queens College Reprographics, 1977); Indians, American, in Academic American Encyclopedia (Arete Publishing Co., 1980); The Mountain Pai; An Ethnography of the Indians of Baja, California, Mexico (typescript, 1984); among others; numerous papers on the American Indian read at meetings.

OWL BOY, LILLIE
(administrative officer)
Affiliation: Fort Totten PHS Indian Health Center, Fort Totten, ND 58335 (701) 766-4291.

OWLIJOOT, THOMAS (Inuit)
(director-Institute)
Affiliation: Inuit Cultural Institute, Eskimo Point, N.W.T., Canada X0C 0E0(819) 857-2803.

OXENDINE, LLOYD E. (Lumbee)
(museum curator)
Affiliation: The American Indian Community House Gallery/Museum, 708 Broadway at Waverly Place, New York, NY 10003.

OXENDINE, THOMAS (Lumbee) 1921-
(naval officer, government information officer, consultant)
Born December 23, 1921, Pembroke, N.C. *Education*: Pembroke State College, BA, 1948; Armed Forces Information School, 1966. *Principal Occupation*: Naval Officer and Government Information Officer. *Home Address*: 1141 N. Harrison St., Arlington, VA 22205 (703) 536-4877. *Affiliations*: U.S. Navy, Naval Aviator, 1942-47, Commander, 1951-70; Public Affairs Officer, Bureau of Indian Affairs, Washington, DC, 1970-87; Census Promotion Officer, Bureau of Census, Washington, DC, 1988-90; American Indian Consultant, Multimedia Business Services, Washington, DC, 1990-92; American Indian Consultant, E.O.P. Group, 1992-. *Military Service*: Naval Aviator-World War II, United States Navy, 1942-47 (Distinguished Flying Cross-Air Medal); Navy Jet Fighter Pilot, 1951-60; Commanding Officer, Training Squadron Two, Naval Air Basic Training Command, Pensacola, Florida, 1960-62; Deputy Fleet Information Officer, Staff of the Commander-in-Chief, U.S. Pacific Fleet, 1962-65; Public Affairs Officer, Commander Task Force 77, Gulf of Tonkin, 1965; Aviation Plans Officer/Director, Plans Division, Office of Information, Department of Navy, The Pentagon, Washington, DC, 1965-68; Public Affairs Officer, Naval Air Systems Command, Dept. of Navy, Washington, DC, 1968-70. *Memberships*: National Congress of American Indians; National Aviation Club; National Press Club; Native American Journalist Association. *Awards, Honors*: First Distinguished Alumnus Award, 1967, Pembroke State College; Athletic Hall of Fame, 1980, Pembroke State University; extensive press coverage as First American Indian to complete Naval Aviation Cadet Flight Program. *Biographical Sources*: Who's Who in Government; Who's Who in the East.

P

PABLO, MATT
(museum director/curator)
Affiliation: Malki Museum, Inc., 11-795 Fields Rd., Morongo Indian Reservation, Banning, CA 92220 (714) 849-7289.

PABLO, MICHAEL T.
(Confederated Salish & Kootenai)
(tribal chairperson)
Affiliation: Confederated Salish & Kootenai Tribal Council, Box 278, Pablo, MT 59855 (406) 675-2700.

PACE, ROSA
(health director)
Affiliation: Santa Ynez Indian Health Program, Santa Ynez Reservation, P.O. Box 539, Santa Ynez, CA 93460 (805) 688-4886.

PACHANO, JANE (Cree)
(director-Indian centre)
Affiliation: Cree Cultural Education Centre, Box 291, Chisasibi, Quebec, Canada J0M 1E0 (819) 855-2821.

PACHANO, VIOLET (Cree)
(Indian band chief)
Affiliation: Chisasibi (Cree) Indian Band, James Bay, Quebec, Canada J0M 1E0 (819) 855-2878.

*PADDOCK, CHARLES (Chilkoot)
(AK association president)
Affiliation: Chilkoot Indian Association of Haines, P.O. Box 490, Haines, AK 99827 (907) 766-2310.

PADDYAKER, DAREN (Comanche-Cherokee) 1964-
(adolescent counselor)
Born November 18, 1964, Oklahoma City, Okla. *Education*: University of Oklahoma, BA (Psychology), 1989. *Principal occupation*: Adolescent counselor. *Home address*: 14301 S. Rockwell, Oklahoma City, OK 73173 (405) 232-0736 (work). Oklahoma City Indian Clinic, Oklahoma City, OK (Adolescent Counselor, 1991-). *Other professional post*: worked with repeat juvenile offenders for 3 years in an inpatient setting. *Community activities*: Member, Oklahoma City Public Schools Task Force on Reducing Gang Involvement in Oklahoma City Public Schools; speak with public school Title V programs and parent committees about street gangs and gang-related activities in the urban Indian community. *Membership*: University of Oklahoma American Indian Alumni Society. *Interests*: "My major area of vocational interest includes working with "at-risk" urban Indian youth and helping them to find traditional as well as non-traditional support bases. My avocational interests include historical tribal research, traveling, hunting, and fishing."

PADILLA, FERNANDO, Jr.
(San Felipe Pueblo-Navajo) 1958-
(artist-painter)
Born July 29, 1958, Los Angeles, Calif. *Education*: Indian Bible College, Albuquerque; Bethany (OK) Southern Nazarene University. *Principal occupation*: Artist-painter. *Home address*: 4632 SE 20th, Del City, OK 73115 (405) 672-9724. *Membership*: Indian Arts & Crafts Association. *Awards, honors*: "Judges Best of Show," 1981-

OK Indian Youth Art Festival; "Second Place - Sculpture," 1985-Native American Art and Craft Show, Rose State Colege, Midwest City, OK; Annual Trail of Tears Art Show, Tahlequah, OK (1985-"Newcomers Award,"; 1986-"Special Merit Award"; and 1989-"Special Merit Award"); Intertribal Ceremoial, Gallup, NM (1987-"First Place-Painting" & First Place-Miniatures; 1988-"Second Place-Watercolors; 1990-First Place-Watercolors; 1991-"First Place-Mixed Media and "Third Place-Acrylics"; among others.

*PADILLA, JERRY (Penobscot)
(tribal governor)
Affiliation: Penobscot Tribal Council, Community Bldg., Indian Island, Old Town, ME 04468 (207) 827-7776.

PADILLA, NICHOLAS J.
(rancheria chairperson)
Affiliation: Susanville Rancheria, P.O. Drawer U, Susanville, CA 96130 (916) 257-6264.

PADILLA, SOLOMON, Jr. (Pueblo)
(school principal)
Affiliation: Santa Clara Day School, P.O. Box HHH, Espanola, NM 87532 (505) 753-4406.

*PAHDOPONY, JUANITA *(Puh-Nah-Vet-Tha - the only daughter)* (Comanche) 1947-
(professor)
Born January 18, 1947, Portland, Oreg. *Education*: Southwest Oklahoma State University, BA, 1970; Oklahoma City University, M.Ed., 1989. *Principal occupation*: Professor. *Home address*: 3004 NE Kingsbriar Dr., Lawton, OK 73507 (405) 353-1329. *Affiliation*: Dept. of Education, Cameron University, Lawton, OK, 1994-. *Other professional post*: National Advisory Board of Native Writers, Wordcraft Circle; professional artist; gifted & talented education. *Community activities*: Board member, Institute of the Great Plains; board member, Jacobson Foundation; Comanche Gourd Dancer. *Memberships*: Oklahoma Art Therapists Association; Word craft Circle (National Advisory Board, 1992-96). *Awards, honors*: McMahon Foundation, 1985; "Outstanding Teacher of the Gifted" Jolene Grantham Award, Oklahoma City University, 1989;"Moving Murals" 2 year traveling tip show (State Arts Council, Jacobson Foundation), 1994. *Interests*: Professional painter, published poet. *Biographical sources*: Artist cover: Callaloo, Vol. 17 #1, by Native American Literatures, Johns Hopkins University Press); designed logo of the National Indian Policy Center, Washington, DC. *Published works*: 2 poems in - "Poetry Nebraska English Journal," 1994, & Returning the Gift, 1994; 2 published scholarly papers - "Creative Perspectives," 1990, & "Native American Art Therapy," 1985.

*PAILES, RICHARD
(instructor-Native American studies)
Affiliation: Native American Studies Program, University of Oklahoma, 455 W. Lindsey, Rm. 804, Norman, OK 73019 (405) 325-2312.

PAINTE, DEBORAH A. *(Red Prairie Rose)*
(Arikara, Hidatsa)
(executive director)
Born in Stanley, N.D. *Education*: Haskell Indian Jr. College, AA, 1977, AAS, 1978; Central State University (Edmond, OK), BBA, 1984; Montana State University, MPA, 1992. *Principal occupation*: Executive director-Indian commission

Home address: 2723 Hawken St., Bismarck, ND 58501 (701) 224-2428 (work). *Affiliation*: North Dakota Indian Affairs Commission, Bismarck, ND, 1991-; Fort Berthold Community College, Newtown, ND (3 years). *Other professional post*: Chairperson-Board of Directors, Three Affiliated Tribes Museum.

PAIR, JAMES (Choctaw)
(school principal)
Affiliation: Choctaw Central High School, Route 7, Box 72, Philadelphia, MS 39350 (601) 656-8870.

*PAISANO, EDNA
(liaison)
Affiliation: Liaison for American Indian & Alaska Natives, Bureau of the Census, Federal Center, Suitland, MD 20233 (301) 763-2607.

PAISANO, WALLY (Western Shoshone)
(health director)
Affiliation: Owyhee Community Health Facility, P.O. Box 364, Owyhee, NV 89832 (702) 757-2415.

PALE MOON, PRINCESS *(Win Yon Sa Han We)* (Cherokee/Ojibwa)
(performing artist-singer; foundation executive)
Born April 15th in Asheville, N.C. *Education*: Sonoma State College, Sonoma, CA (Liberal Arts). *Principal occupation*: Performing Artist (singer) and foundation executive. *Address*: 6051 Arlington Blvd., Falls Church, VA 22044 (703) 237-7500 (work). *Affiliation*, Founder-president, American Indian Heritage Foundation, Falls Church, VA, 1973-. *Memberships*: National Congress of American Indians (life member); Native American Advisory Committee; Boy Scouts of America; American Pen Women; Business and Professional Women's Association. *Awards, honors*: Many outstanding achievement awards and other awards from colleges, independent organizations and service clubs, too numerous to mention. *Interests*: Has represented the U.S. and the American Indian people in numerous countries, both as spokesperson and as a performing artist. Has special interest in building better understanding between the tribes and people of the world. Many articles have been written about Palo Moon, and the Foundation, including the Style Section of the Washington Post, Decision Magazine, the Los Angeles, Times, the Fairfax Journal and many radio and TV interviews. *Biographical source & Published work*: Pale Moon: The Story of an Indian Princess (Tyndale, 1975).

*PALMENTEER, EDDIE, Jr. (Colville)
(tribal chairperson)
Affiliation: Colville Business Committee, P.O. Box 150, Nespelem, WA 99155 (509) 634-4711.

*PALMER, JIM L. (Miam/Peoria of Oklahoma) 1943-
(founder/director-cultural center)
Born July 29, 1943, Oklahoma City, Okla. *Education*: Oklahoma University (2 years); Tulsa Technical College. *Principal occupation*: Founder-director-cultural center. *Address & Affiliation*: Founder-director, Native American Cultural Center, 216 S. 8th St., Fort Dodge, IA 50501 (515) 576-3867. *Military service*: U.S. Marine Corps (Cpl. - Received Heroism Award, 1983, Kiwanis-Las Vegas, NV). *Community activities*: Protection Advocacy Program of Iowa

(board member), Des Moines; Pilot Parents of Iowa , Fort Dodge; Iowa Job Service, Fort Dodge; teach classes to college, high school & elementary levels, on culture, language & legends at request of teachers. *Interests*: "We research Indian languages on the verge of extinction (to reproduce, teach & put in libraries for posterity). We educate the general public about Native peoples customs, legends, languages, etc. We have craft classes for the general public, and had our 1st Annual Indian Powwow in Aug. 1994." *Biographical source*: "Fort Dodge Messenger," front page articles, Dec., 1993 & May, 1994.

PALMER, TRACY L.
(Creek/Seminole/Cherokee) 1958-
(training specialist/Indian educator)
Born December 31, 1958, Tulsa, Okla. *Education*: University of Tulsa, BFA, 1983, Oklahoma City University, MEd, 1991. *Principal occupation*: Training specialist/Indian educator. *Home address*: 1558 E. 41 St., Tulsa, OK 74105 (918) 747-1488; (405) 364-0656 (work). *Affiliation*: American Indian Research & Development, Inc., Norman, OK, 1991-. *Community activities*: University of Tulsa Multicultural Alumni Committee. *Memberships*: National Association for Gifted; Theater Tulsa. Children. *Awards, honors*: Nominee for Leadership Tulsa, 1988; selected to do a presentation in Kansas City, MO, at the National Convention for Gifted Children, November, 1991; also gave same presentation at the State of Oklahoma Association for Gifted & Talented Children on cross-cultural development integrating art into mathematics for gofted and talented Native American students. *Interests*: "I have traveled throughout Oklahoma giving presentations on self-esteem and motivation along with leadership, primarily targeting junior and senior high Indian students."

*PANEAK, RAYMOND (Eskimo)
(village council president)
Affiliation: Village of Anaktuvuk Pass, Anaktuvuk, AK 99721 (907) 661-3113.

PAPATISSE, HENRI
(Indian band chief)
Affiliation: Grand Lac Victoria (Algonquin) Indian Band, Louvicourt, Quebec, Canada J0Y 1Y0 (819) 824-1914.

PAQUIN, DANIEL GERARD (Chippewa) 1953-
(mechanical engineer)
Born January 4, 1953, Grand Rapids, Mich. *Education*: University of Hawaii, BS, 1980, MS, 1984. *Principal occupation*: Mechanical enginner. *Home address*: 650 Ainapo St., Honolulu, HI 96825 (808) 395-2175. Affiliation: Dept. of Agricultural Engineering, University of Hawaii, Honolulu, 1986-. *Other professional post*: President, American Society of Agricultural Engineers, Hawaii Section. *Military service*: U.S. Navy, 1972-75; Reserves, 1976-80 (E-4). *Memberships*: American Indian Science and Engineering Society; Sierra Club. *Interests*: "Science-by-mail "scientist" for Museum of the Rockies; enjoy hiking, surfing, listening and watching "Rainbow Warrior" baseball for the University of Hawaii."

PARADA, GWENDOLYN (Diegueno)
(tribal chairperson)
Affiliation: La Posta Band of Mission Indians, 1064 Barona Rd., Lakeside, CA 92040 (619) 561-2924.

PARASHOUTS, TRAVIS N. (Southern Paiute) 1953-
(director-Utah Indian affairs)
Born October 10, 1953, Cedar City, Utah. *Education*: Southern Utah State College, BA, 1979; University of Utah (Masters of Social Work candidate). *Principal occupation*: Director, Utah Division of Indian Affairs, 6220 State Office Bldg., Salt Lake City, Utah. *Home address*: 689 S. Pitford Dr., Centerville, UT 84014 (801) 533-5334 (work). *Other professional posts*: Former tribal chairman, Paiute Tribe; American Indian Service, Brigham Young University, Provo, Utah (board member); American Indian Cultural Foundation, Page, AZ (board member); Indian Affiliates, Orem, UT (board member). *Awards, honors*: Spencer W. Kimball Award for working with Indian people; Paiute Tribal Award for service as tribal chairman; Cedar City Chamber of Commerce Award. *Interests*: "I assisted the Paiute Tribe in getting federal recognition in 1980 and helped them get back 5,000 acres of land and established a 2.5 million dollar irrevocable trust fund for economic development." *Published work*: Paiute Language--For Beginner (Southern Utah State College, 1980).

PARCEAUD, JUDY
(director-Indian centre)
Affiliation: Cree Indian Centre, 95 rue Jaculet, Chibougamau, Quebec, Canada G8P 2G1 (418) 748-7667.

*PARDUE, DIANA
(museum curator)
Affiliation: Curator of Collections, The Heard Museum, 22 E. Monte Vista Rd., Phoenix, AZ 85004 (602) 252-8840.

PAREDES, J. ANTHONY 1939-
(professor of anthropology)
Born September 29, 1939, New York, N.Y. *Education*: Oglethorpe University (Atlanta, GA) , AB, 1961; University of New Mexico, MA, 1964, PhD, 1969. *Principal occupation*: Professor of anthropology. *Home address*: 614 E. 6th Ave., Tallahassee, FL 32303 (904) 644-4281 (work). *Affiliations*: Upper Mississippi Mental Health Center, Bemidji, MN, 1964-66; Bemidji State College (acting director, American Indian Studies), University of Minnesota, Bemidji, MN, 1967-68; Professor of anthropology, Department of Anthropology, Florida State University, Tallahassee, FL, 1969-. *Other professional posts*: Consultants to various federal and state agencies and private firms; editorial board, American Indian Culture and Research Journal. *Community activities*: Member, Scientific and Statistical Committee, Gulf of Mexico Fishery Management Council (1978-88; task force on Federal Recognition, Association on American Indian Affairs, 1987-88. *Memberships*: Society for Applied Anthropology (president, 1993-95); Southern Anthropological Society (president, 1988-89); American Anthropological Association (Fellow); Sigma Xi, the Scientific Research Society. *Awards, honors*: Woodrow Wilson Fellow, 1961-62; National Institute of Mental Health Predoctoral Fellow, 1968-69; Poarch Creek Indian Service Award, 1990. *Interests*: Ethnographic field work in Minnesota (non-Indians and Chippewa), Alabama (Creek Indians), Mexico (small town residents); Florida (commercial fisherman); travel in Southwestern U.S. and Spain. *Biographical sources*: American Men and Women of Science, Social and Behavioral Sciences (12th Edition); Who's Who in America,

48th Ed. *Published works*: Anishinabe: Six Studies of Modern Chippewa (University Presses of Florida, 1980); editor, Indians of the Southeastern U.S. in the Late 20th Century (Alabama University Press, 1992); Indios de los Estados Unidos Anglosajones (Fundacion Mapfre America, Madrid, 1992); 55+ articles, chapters, reviews, etc. in scholarly books and journals.

PARENT, ELIZABETH ANNE *(Wa Su Win)* (Athabascan) 1941-
(professor of Native American studies)
Born January 12, 1941, Bethel, Alaska. *Education*: University of Alaska, BA (Anthropology); Harvard Graduate School of Education, MEd & CAS, 1973; Stanford University, PhD, 1984. *Principal occupation*: Professor of American Indian Studies. *Home address*: 715-13 One Appian Way, So. San Francisco, CA 94080 (415) 589-4041. *Affiliation*: San Francisco State University, 1600 Holloway Ave., San Francisco, CA 94132, 1980-. *Other professional post*: Information & Technology Committee, National Museum of the American Indian, Smithsonian Institution. *Memberships*: American Indian Science & Engineering Society; Stanford Indian Alumni Association; American Indian Education Association. *Awards, honors*: Postdoctoral Fellow, American Indian Studies Center, U.C.L.A., 1985-186; Ford Fellow; Danforth Fellow; Meritorious Professional Promise Awards, San Francisco State University, 1987 & 1989. *Interests*: American Indian education, and women's rights. *Published work*: The Educational Experiences of the Residents of Bethel, Alaska, Ph.D. dissertation (Stanford University); "Betty Parent - Woman With a Mission" in Winds of Change; and "Native Ability" in Spring Alumni SFSU, 1991.

*PARISH, WAYNE
(health clinic director)
Affiliation: El Reno PHS Indian Health Clinic, 1631A E. Hwy. 66, El Reno, OK 73036 (405) 262-7631.

PARISIAN, DEAN THOMAS (White Earth Chippewa) 1953-
(investment management)
Born December 20, 1953, Morris, Minn. *Education*: University of Minnesota, Morris, BA, 1976. *Principal occupation*: Investment management. *Home address*: 5635 Hillgate Crossing, Alpharetta, GA 30202 (404) 667-8263; (800) 776-3010 (work). *Affiliation*: First Union Bank, Atlanta, GA. *Community activities*: Several years as a member of the Board of the San Diego American Indian Health Center. *Memberships*: Georgia Retail Security Brokers Association; President's Club of the University of Minnesota. *Awards, honors*: While living on the Yankton Sioux Reservation, he received the South Dakota Outstanding Indian Athlete Award. After receiving an appointment to West Point and playing football there for a year, Dean transferred to the University of Minnesota. He has funded a $25,000 scholarship for Native American students for the President's Club of the University of Minnesota. *Interests*: Dean lived on several reservations while his father was employed as a criminal investigator by the BIA; his avocational hobbies are: hunting, trapping, and bird watching.

*PARK, DAVID L.
(museum director)
Affiliation: Hershey Museum, 170 W. Hersheypark Dr., Hershey, PA 17033 (717) 534-3439.

*PARK, ROBERT
(clinic director)
Affiliation: Salina Community Clinic, P.O. Box 936, Salina, OK 74365 (918) 434-5397.

PARKER, ALAN
(Indian policy center director)
Affiliation: National Indian Policy Center, George Washington University School of Law, 606 21st St., NW, Washington, DC 20052 (202) 994-5462; staff director, Senate Select Committee on Indian Affairs, Room SH 838, Hart Senate Office Bldg., Washington, D.C. 20510 (202) 224-2251.

PARKER, BERNIE (Seneca)
(tribal chief)
Affiliation: Chief (lifetime), Tonawanda Band of Senecas Council of Chiefs, 7027 Meadville Rd., Basom, NY 14013 (716) 542-4244.

PARKER, JEFF (Chippewa)
(tribal chairperson)
Affiliation: Bay Mills Executive Council, Route 1, Box 313, Brimley, MI 49715 (906) 248-3241.

PARKER, LARRY
(education administrator)
Affiliation: Billings Area Office, Bureau of Indian Affairs, 316 North 26th St., Billings, MT 59101 (406) 657-6375.

*PARKER, PAULINE A. (Pechanga Luiseno) 1947-
(Indian education)
Born May 23, 1947, Escondido, Calif. *Education*: Palomar College (2 years). *Principal occupation*: Indian education. *Home address*: 842 B St., Ramona, CA 92065 (619) 789-1624. *Affiliation*: Project director, Indian Education Program, Ramona Unified Schools, Ramona, CA, 1982-. *Other professional post*: Member, American Indian Education Council, Escondido, CA. *Community activities*: Ramona Unified School District (district advisory committee). *Awards, honors*: Showcase Writers Guild award (1st Place - Poetry, 1991; 1st Place - Short Story, 1992l 2nd Place Children's Story, 1992; 1st Place Article; 2nd Place - Short Story, 1993); National League of American Pen Women, 1992. *Interests*: "Approximately ten years ago, I took a course in Creative Writing. It changed my life. In the relatively short time I've been writing professionally, I have found an outlet for sharing my joy, releasing my fears and opening doors. My writing keeps me sane. Other than writing, I enjoy music of all kinds & travel."

PARKER, WAYNE (Comanche) 1938-
(farmer and rancher)
Born September 23, 1938, Spur, Texas. *Education*: West Texas State University, BS, 1961. *Principal occupation*: Farmer and rancher. *Home address*: HCR 2, Box 127, Ralls, TX 79357. *Affiliations*: Archaeological curator, Pioneer Memorial Museum, Crosbyton, Texas, and Ralls Historical Museum, Ralls, TX; editorial staff for Artifacts Society of Ohio, and La Tierra archaeological journal. *Community activities*: Cotton Gin Board (member); Museum Board (member); Boy Scout Commission; Crosby County Historical Commission. *Memberships*: Texas Archaeological Society; Central States Archaeological Society; South Plains Archaeological Society; Artifacts Society; Southern Texas Archaeological Society (editorial board, Journal). *Awards, honors*: Life Saving Award signed by President

Eisenhower; Best Committee Member, Texas Historical Commission, 1971; guest speaker at History Day at the Ranch, Matador Ranch, 1984 and 1985; 4th cousin to Chief Quanah Parker (Kwahadi Comanches). *Interests*: "I have written over 95 articles concerning Indian artifacts which have been published throughout the U.S. (I) hunted bull elk in Colorado for 20 years." *Biographical sources*: Arrowheads and Projectile Points; North American Indian Artifacts; Selected Preforms, Points and Knives of the North American Indians. *Published works*: The Bridwell Site and The Roberson Site (Crosby County Museum Association, 1982 & 1986).

PARKHURST, HURLEY (Oneida) 1934-
(consultant)
Born July 1, 1934, Wisconsin. *Education*: Brigham Young University, BS, 1969; University of Arizona, MLS (Library Science), 1974. *Principal occupation*: Consultant. *Military service*: U.S. Navy, 1953-57. *Interests*: Amateur astronomy; ballet; crystal detectors (expect to publish a book soon); ethnobotany (American Indian uses of plants for food, fiber, medicine); outdoor survival skills; amateur radio.

PARKS, DOUGLAS R.
(Kaakaataaka-White Crow) 1942-
(linguist)
Born August 28, 1942, Long Beach, Calif. *Education*: University of California, Berkeley, BA, 1964, PhD, 1972. *Principal occupation*: Linguist. *Home address*: 8275 East State Road 46, Bloomington, IN 47401. *Affiliations*: Director, Title VII Program, White Shield School District, Roseglen, N.D. (3 years); research associate, Dept. of Anthropology, Indiana University, Bloomington, 1983-. *Other professional post*: Editor, "Anthropological Linguistics"; Associate director, American Indian Studies Research Institute, Indiana University. *Memberships*: Plains Anthropological Society (board of directors, 1980-82; president, 1982); American Anthropological Association; American Society for Ethnohistory. *Awards, honors*: American Council of Learned Societies Fellow, 1982-83; Smithsonian Fellow (Smithsonian Institution, 1973-74). *Published works*: A Grammar of Pawnee (Garland Publishing, 1976); An Introduction to the Arikara Language (Title VII Materials Development Center, Anchorage, Alaska, 1979); Ceremonies of the Pawnee, 2 Vols. (Smithsonian Institution Press, 1981); Arikara Coyote Tales: A Bilingual Reader (White Shield School, 1984); An English-Arikara Student Dictionary (White Shield School, 1986); Traditional Narratives of the Arikara Indians, 4 Vols. (University of Nebraska Press, 1991).

PARKS, RON
(site director)
Affiliation: Kaw Indian Mission, 500 North Mission, Council Grove, KS 66846 (316) 767-5410.

PARMAN, DONALD L. 1932-
(historian)
Born October 10, 1932, New Point, MO. *Education*: Central Missouri State College, BS, 1958; Ohio University, MA, 1963; University of Oklahoma, PhD, 1967. *Principal occupation*: Historian. *Home address*: 614 Rose St., West Lafayette, IN 47906 (317) 743-3514. *Affiliation*: Dept. of History, Purdue University, West Lafayette, IN, 1966-. *Military service*: U.S. Army, 1953-55 (Corporal). *Memberships*: Organization of American Historians; Western History Asso-

ciation; Agricultural History Society; American Society for Ethnohistory; Indiana Association of Historians. *Interests*: Main research interests are Navajo Indian history and twentieth century Indian affairs; main travels are in the Southwest and elsewhere in "Indian Country."*Biographical sources*: Directory of American Scholars, Vol. 1; Dictionary of International Biography; Contemporary Authors. *Published works*: Co-editor, American Search, 2 Vols. (Forum Press, 1973); Navajos and the New Deal (Yale University Press, 1976); Indians and the American West in the Twentieth Century (Indiana University Press, 1994).

*PARR, DIANE
(center administrator)
Affiliation: Sycuan Medical/Dental Cener, 5442 Dehesa Rd., El Cajon, CA 92019 (619) 445-0707.

PARRA, DONNA C. (Navajo) 1941-
(counseling services)
Born September 7, 1941, Rehoboth, N.M. *Education*: University of New Mexico, BA, 1970, MA, 1974. *Principal occupation*: Counseling services. *Home address*: 819 Gonzales Rd., Santa Fe, NM 87501. *Affiliations*: Medical secretary, USPHS Indian Hospital, Gallup, NM, 1961-63, 1965; research assistant, National Institutes of Mental Health (Alcoholism Project: A Community Treatment Plan for Navajo Problem Drinkers), Family Service Agency, 1966-68; director of counseling services, Institute of American Indian Arts, Sante Fe, NM, 1976-. *Other professional posts*: Instructor of English, counselor, Gallup High School, 1970-75; consultant to teach workshops on ethnic literature, 1973-75, consultant, Curriculum Development, Native American Literature, 1974-75, Gallup-McKinley County Schools; consultant, University of New Mexico Cultural Awareness Center, Albuquerque, NM, 1975. *Community activities*: Santa Fe Public Schools Title IV Indian Education Parent Committee (officer); New Mexico Human Rights Commission Film Project (scholar and advisor); Ford Canyon Youth Center, Gallup, N.M. (advisory board); Gallup Inter-Agency Alcoholism Coordinating Committee (member); New Mexico International Women's Year Convention, June, 1977 (workshop leader on Indian Women). *Memberships*: League of Women Voters; New Mexico Association of Women Deans and Counselors; National Indian Education Association. *Awards, honors*: Four-year Navajo Tribal Scholarship recipient; Charles S. Owens Future Teachers of America Scholarship (Gallup High School, 1959); Sequoyah Indian Fellowship, University of New Mexico, 1970. *Interests*: Ms. Parra writes, "I have great interest in the field of human rights, specifically issues of Indian sovereignty, because I feel that this whole issue relates directly to the survival of the American Indian as a group. I also have great interest in Native American literature and have developed a curriculum on this which has been adopted by the Gallup-McKinley County School district. I have been involved in alcohol research among the American Indian in a National Institutes of Mental Health Project in Gallup, A Community Treatment Plan for Indian Problem Drinkers (1966-68), and am presently directing a program I designed with students and staff of our educational facility."

*PARRIS, JIM
(BIA office director)
Affiliation: Bureau of Indian Affairs, Office of Trust Fund Management, 505 Marquette St., NW, Albuquerque, NM 87102 (505) 766-3230.

PARRISH, RAIN (Navajo) 1944-
(museum curator)
Born February 8, 1944, Tuba City, Ariz. *Education*: University of Arizona, BA (Anthropology), 1967. *Principal occupation*: Museum curator. *Home address*: 704 Kathryn Ave., Santa Fe, NM 87501 (505) 982-4636. *Affiliation*: Curator of American Indian Collections, Wheelwright Museum of the American Indian, Santa Fe, 1979-. *Membership*: New Mexico Museum Association. *Awards, honors*: Navajo Woman of the Year in the Arts, 1985; 10 Who Made a Difference, 1985 The New Mexican Newspaper). *Interests*: Travel, art history, anthropology, sports, skiing, hiking, reading, writing. *Published works*: The Stylistic Development of Navajo Jewelry (Minneapolis Institute of the Arts, 1982); Woven Holy People (Wheelwright Museum, 1983); The Pottery of Margaret Tafoya (Wheelwright Museum, 1984).

*PARSLEY, ROBERT
(Indian education specialist)
Affiliation: Montana State Office of Public Instruction, State Capitol, Rm. 106, Helena, MT 59620 (406) 444-3031.

PASHE, DENNIS
(Indian band chief)
Affiliation: Dakota Tipi Indian Band, Box 1569, Pontage La Prairie, Manitoba, Canada R1N 3P1 (204) 857-4381.

PASQUAL, REGINALD (Pueblo)
(pueblo governor)
Affiliation: Pueblo of Acoma, P.O. Box 309, Acomita, NM 87034 (505) 552-6604.

PATAWA, ELWOOD H. (Umatilla)
(USDA Native American program director)
Address & Affiliation: U.S. Dept. of Agriculture, Office of Intergovernmental Affairs, Rm. 102-A, 14th & Independence Ave., NW, Washington, DC 20250 (202) 720- 3805. *Past professional post*: Tribal chairperson, Umatilla Board of Trustees, Pendleton, OR.

PATTEA, CLINTON (Mohave-Apache)
(tribal council president)
Affiliations: Mohave-Apache Community Council, P.O Box 17779, Fountain Hills, AZ 85268 (602) 837-5121; chairperson, Arizona Commission on Indian Affairs, 1645 W. Jefferson, Suite 433, Phoenix, AZ 85007.

PATTERSON, ELMA (JONES) (Tuscarora) 1926-
(social worker-retired)
Born August 13, 1926, Lockport, N.Y. *Education*: Cornell University, BS, 1949; SUNY at Buffalo, MSW, 1963. *Principal occupation*: Social worker. *Home address*: 1162 Ridge Rd., Lewiston, NY 14092. *Affiliations*: Supervisor of Field Services for Indians..A State Agency (retired). *Community activities*: New York Iroquois Conference, Inc. (founder; past chairman; board of directors); Seneca Nation Educational Foundation, Inc. (trustee); Americans for Indian Opportunity (AIO)(past vice chairman & secretary-treasurer); Governor's Interstate Indian Council (chairman); New York State Library Services

for Indians (advisory committee). *Membership*: American Indian Social Workers Association (charter member).

PATTERSON, JESSICA
(museum director/curator)
Affiliation: Sac & Fox Tribal RV Park and Museum/Cultural Center, Rte. 2, Box 246, Stroud, OK 74079 (918) 968-3526.

*PATTERSON, LOTSEE (Comanche) 1931-
(associate professor)
Born December 3, 1931, Indian land near Apache, Okla. *Education*: Oklahoma College for Women, BS, 1959; University of Oklahoma, MLS, 1969, PhD, 1979. *Principal occupation*: Professor of library & information studies. *Home address*: 1705 Pembroke Dr., Norman, OK 73072 (405) 325-3921. *Affiliations*: University of New Mexico, Albuquerque, 1972-78; Texas Woman's University, Denton, TX, 1978-85; director, Trails (Training & Assistance for Indian Library Service, University of Oklahoma, Norman, OK, 1985-87; director, Library Media Services, Oklahoma City Public Schools, 1989-91; associate professor, University of Oklahoma, School of Library & Information Studies, 1991-; CE & PS Subcommittee on Certification, University of Oklahoma, 1992-; editor, American Indian Libraries Newsletter, American Indian Library Association. *Other professional posts*: Advisory Committee, Brodart Foundation, Williamsport, PA, 1971-; White House Conference on Libraries & Information Services Taskforce, 1982- (Awards Committee, 1992-); National Archives & Records Administration, National Historical Publications & Records Commission (field advisory committee; review grant proposals under the Native American Institute), 1985-; National Commission on Libraries & Information Science (consultant to the Commission's Native American Task Force, Washington, DC, 1989-93); Admission Committee, School of Library & Information Studies, University of Oklahoma, 1991-; Western History Associates, University of Oklahoma, Board of Trustees (vice president, 1992-; chair, Acquisitions Committee, 1990-); Field Issues Advisory Committee, National Center on Adult Literacy, University of Pennsylvania, Philadelphia, 1991-; Video Screening Committee, Native American Public Broadcasting Consortium, Lincoln, NE, 1993-; Network Committee on Library Service to Native Americans, The Library of Congress, National Library Service for the Blind and Physically Handicapped, Washington, DC, 1993-; member, Board of Directors, Native American Library & Museum Project, Washington, DC, 1994-; numerous conference presentations and invited formal lectures, 1985-. *Memberships*: American Library Association (council member, 1984-88); American Indian Library Association (president, 1981-84, 1984-87, 1991-); American Association of School Librarians (board member, 1980-83); Oklahoma Library Association. *Awards, honors*: expert witness, Senate Select Committee on Indian Affairs: Hearing; Equality Award 1994, American Library Association. *Published works*: Contributor to Pathways to Excellence: A Report on Improving Library & Information Services for Native American Peoples (USGPO, 1992); "Understanding & Appreciating the Unique Needs of Native Americans," Multicultural Aspects of Library Media Programs, edited by Kathy Latrobe & Mildred Laughlin (Libraries Unlimited, 1992); "Comanche," in Native America in the Twentieth Century: An En-

cyclopedia," edited by Mary B. Davis (Garland Publishing, 1994); co-authored with Mary Ellen Snodgrass, Indian Terms of the Americas (Libraries Unlimited, 1994).

*PATTERSON, WES
(association president)
Affiliation: Oregon Native American Business & Entrepreneurial Network, P.O. Box 1359, Warm Springs, OR 97761.

*PAUKAN, MOSES, Sr. (eskimo)
(village council president)
Affiliation: Native Village of Algaaciq, P.O. Box 48, St. Mary's, AK 99658 (907) 438-2932.

PAUL, ARVADA
(health director)
Affiliation: Redding Rancheria, 3184 Chum Creek Rd., Redding, CA 96002 (916) 224-2700.

PAUL, BENJAMIN PETER
(Indian band chief)
Affiliation: Pabineau Indian Band, RR 5, Site 26, Box 1, Bathurst, New Brunswick, Canada E2A 3Y8 (506) 548-9211.

PAUL, BENOIT (Pabineau)
(chief/director-Indian band/centre)
Affiliation: Pabineau Indian Band, Cultural/Educational Centre, R.R. #5, Box 1, Site 26, Bathurst, New Brunswick, Can. E2A 3Y8 (506) 548-9211.

PAUL, BLAIR F. (Tlingit) 1943-
(attorney)
Born July 5, 1943, Juneau, Alaska. *Education*: Western Washington State College, BA, 1966; University of Washington Law School, JD, 1970. *Principal occupation*: Attorney. Resides in Seattle, Wash. *Community activities*: Pioneer Square Historic Preservation Board, 1974-; Washington Trust for Historic Preservation (president, 1976-77); United Indians of All Tribes (board member, 1969-71); Seattle Indian Health Board, 1970-73; Seattle Indian Services Commission, 1972-73. *Memberships*: American Trial Lawyers; Washington Trial Lawyers; Seattle-Kings County Bar.

PAUL, DAVID
(association president)
Affiliation: New Brunswick Indian Arts & Crafts Association, 212 Queen St., Suite 402, Fredericton, New Brunswick, Can. E3V 1A7 (506) 459-7312.

*PAUL, JOHNNIE
(village president)
Affiliation: Native Village of Kipnuk, P.O. Box 57, Kipnuk, AK 99614 (907) 896-5515.

PAUL, LAWRENCE ALEXANDER
(Indian band chief)
Affiliation: Millbrook Indian Band, Box 634, Truro, Nova Scotia, Canada B2N 5E5 (902) 895-4365.

PAUL, LEONARD
(Indian band chief)
Affiliation: Eskasoni Indian Band, Eskasoni, Nova Scotia, Canada B0A 1J0 (902) 379-2800.

*PAUL, MONICA (Kahen Ten Hawi)
(Kahnawake Mohawk)
(educator, council member)
Born in Kahnawake, Canada. *Home address*: 21 Village Rd., Morganville, NJ 07751 (908) 727-

5565 (work). *Community activities*: After retiring from NJ Bell, Monica has been working as a crossing guard since 1986. She is an active member of the Old Bridge Senior Choral Group which travels extensively throughout the area performing; she also volunteers for the Old Bridge Office on Aging as a commodity distribution helper. *Membership*: Inter-Tribal Indians of New Jersey (heads the Sunshine Committee), a non-profit cultural and educational organization dedicated to preserving and continuing American Indian heritage. Monica is one of the organization's educators that provides cultural/educational services at various institutions, such as the New Jersey State Museum, Newark Museum, schools and colleges. *Awards, honors*: Winner of the "Young at Heart" Award from the U.S. Health Core; elected as one of seven council members of the Inter-Tribal Indians of New Jersey; an award recognizing people who inspire community by activities and attitude. *Interests*: Ms. Paul instructs Mohawk language classes and traditional clothing and beadwork; she is a member of the Inter-Tribal Dance Group, and participates in all performances, explaining her regalia; writing - Monica compiled a book of memoirs for her family and is writing a second book that will contain the family tree with historical sketches on some of her ancestors.

*PAUL, MOSES (Athapascan)
(village chief)
Affiliation: Nenana Native Association, P.O. Box 356, Nenana, AK 99760 (907) 832-5662.

PAUL, PATRICK (Cree-Kootnay) 1942-
(educator; consultant-human development)
Born January 24, 1942, Cranbrook, B.C. Can. *Education*:The Evergreen State College (Olympia, WA), MA, 1980; Antioch University (Seattle, WA), MA, 1984. *Principal occupation*: Educator; consultant-human development. *Home address*: 517 E. Magnolia, Bellingham, WA 98225 (206) 733-6489. *Affiliation*: Assistant professor and coordinator, Native American Chemical Dependency Studies, Northwest Indian College, Bellingham, WA, 1984-; youth and family counselor, Chemical Dependency, United Indians, Seattle, 1984-88. *Other professional posts*: Trainer and consultant, 1982-; secretary/treasurer of the Northwest Indian Council on Chemical Depedency and the Northwest Indian Alcohol/Drug Specialist Certification Board. *Awards, honors*: National Indian Board on Alcoholism and Drug Abuse, for providing excellent Alcohol/drug education to the Indian people of the Pacific Northwest, 1980-90.

PAUL, TERRANCE
(Indian band chief)
Affiliation: Membertou India Band, 111 Membertou St., Sydney, Nova Scotia, Canada B1S 2N9 (902) 539-6688.

PAUL, WILBUR
(BIA agency supt.)
Affiliation: Cherokee Agency, Bureau of Indian Affairs, Cherokee, NC 28719 (704) 497-9131.

PAULETTE, MIKE (Metis)
(president-Metis association)
Affiliation: Metis Association of the Northwest Territories, P.O. Box 1375, Yellowknife, N.W.T. X1A 2P1 (403) 873-3505.

PAVLIK, NANCY 1935-
(business owner)
Born July 18, 1935, Detroit, Mich. *Education*: University of Arizona, 1967. *Principal occupation*: Business owner. Home address: 7500 E. McCormick Pkwy. #33, Scottsdale, AZ 85258 (602) 991-5131 (work). *Affiliation*: President, Southwest Events, Scootsdale, AZ, 1969-; Docent, Heard Museum, Phoenix, AZ, 1989-. *Other professional post*: Lecturer, Indian arts and crafts. *Community activities*: Mayor's Hospitality Commission, Scottsdale Chamber of Commerce, 1972-. *Memberships*: Indian Arts and Crafts Association; Society of Incentive Travel Executives; Meeting Planner International. *Awards, honors*: One of Phoenix's Ten Outstanding Women, 1972; Scottsdale Small Business of the Year, 1990. *Interests*: Producer of Southwest Events showcasing Indian craftspeople; Southwest history; Idian arts and crafts; art.

PAYMELLA, BETTY
(school principal)
Affiliation: Second Mesa Day School, P.O. Box 98, Second Mesa, AZ 86043 (602) 737-2571.

PAYNE, ROBERT (Walking Bear)
(United Lumbee/Cherokee/Apache) 1928-
(silversmith; cosmetologist)
Born February 23, 1928, Coldwell, Kans. *Education*: Weslein (KS) Institute, MA (Art). *Principal occupation*: Silversmith; cosmetologist. *Home address*: RR 1, Box 365, Bartlesville, OK 74003. *Military service*: U.S. Air Force, 1942-47 (Air Ace Award, 1942 & '43). *Memberships*: Native American Wolf Clan; United Lumbee Nation's Thunder Star Band Chief, 1981-82; United Lumbee Nation's Mantaoc Medicine Society; United Lumbee Nation Elder; American Legion. *Interests*: American Indian arts & crafts.

PAYNE, SUSAN
(institute director)
Affiliation: American Indian Archaeological Institute, Curtis Rd., Box 1260, Washington, CT 06793 (203) 868-0518.

PEACHES, DANIEL (Navajo) 1940-
(Indian educator/cultural consultant)
Born September 2, 1940, Kayenta (Navajo County) Ariz. *Education*: Northern Arizona University, BS, 1967; University of New Mexico, 1968-69 (Indian Law); American University, 1969 (Internship). *Principal occupation*: Navajo Tribal Administrator. *Address*: P.O. Box 1801, Kayenta, AZ 86033 (602) 697-8466 (work). *Affiliations*: Board of directors, Dineh Cooperatives, Inc., Chinle, AZ, 1976-; member, board of regents, Northland Pioneer College, Holbrook, AZ, 1985-; president, board of regents, Navajo Community College, Tsaile, AZ, 1988-. *Other professional posts*: Navajo Mountain Soil & Water Conservation District, 1984-; Arizona Townhall Council, 1974-; National Indian Education Advisory Council, 1972-76. *Community activities*: Navajo Environmental Protection Commission, 1976-85; Governor's Commission on Arizona Indian Affairs, 1974; Kayenta Boarding School, 1985-; Arizona Town Hall. *Awards, honors*: Presidential appointment to National Indian Education Advisory Council, 1972 by President Nixon; Honorary Degree in Law, Navajo Commuity College, 1978. *Interests*: Elected to Arizona State Legislature, House of Representatives from Legislative Dist. 3, 1974-85. *Biographical sources*: Newsweek Magazine, 1981;

Arizona Republic, Sunday Magazine, 1982; Time Magazine, 1984; Who's Who in the West, 1985-; Who's Who in America, 1986-.

PEACOCK, HOWARD
(Indian band chief)
Affiliation: Enoch Indian Band, Box 2, Site 2, RR 1, Winterburn, Alberta, Canada T0E 2N0 (403) 470-4505.

*PEACOCK, MICHAEL D. (Milky Way)
(Pueblo of Laguna/Seneca/ Mohawk) 1957-
(business consultant)
Born March 27, 1957, Albuquerque, N.M. Education: University of New Mexico, AAS, 1986; College of Santa Fe, BA, 1989. Principal occupation: Business consultant. Home address: 4425 Shepard Rd. NE #1F, Albuquerque, NM 87110 (505) 889-9092. Affiliation: Consultant, New Mexico Indian Business Development Center, Albuquerque, NM, 1992-. Other Professional post: Board of Directors, Laguna Commercial Enterprises.

PEACOCK, ROBERT "SONNY" (Chippewa)
(tribal chairperson)
Affiliation: Fond du Lac Reservation Business Committee, 105 University Rd., Cloquet, MN 55720 (218) 879-4593.

PEACOCK, THOMAS D. (Chippewa)
(school supt.)
Affiliation: Fond du Lac Ojibway School, 105 University Rd., Cloquet, MN 55720 (218) 879-0241.

PEAKE-RAYMOND, MARGARET (Chippewa)
(executive director)
Home address: 2520 East 22nd St., Minneapolis, MN 55406 (612) 343-0261. Affiliation: Minnesota Indian Women's Resource Center, Minneapolis, MN.

*PEARCE, CRAIG
(organization chairperson)
Affiliation: Antelope Indian Circle Religious Group, P.O. Box 790, Susanville, CA 96130 (916) 257-2181 ext. 468.

PEARCE, EILEEN (Little Axe)
(Absentee Shawnee) 1961-
(journalism, marketing)
Born June 8, 1961, Oklahoma City, Okla. Education: Rose State College (Midwest City, OK), AA, 1982, AAS, 1993; Central State University (Edmond, OK), BA, 1984. Principal occupation: Journalism, marketing. Home address: 5225 S. Foster Rd., Oklahoma City, OK 73129 (405) 677-2560. Affiliation: Catalog-Technical Assistant, Wix/Dana/Air Refiner, Oklahoma City, OK, 1988- Community activities: Member of Gloneta Indian Baptist Church; former member of Miss Indian Oklahoma Pageant. Membership: Native American Journalists Association; Oklahoma Federation of Indian Women. Awards, honors: Golden Touch Award, Wix/Dana Corp., 1993 for suggesting an idea for the company. Interests: "I freelance for company newspaper, "Wix Folks & Fact"; contribute news articles for the Absentee Shawnee newspaper. Also (I) have submitted articles to the Daily Oklahoman newspaper, and Glamour magazine."

*PEARSON, M. PAT (Blue Feather)
(United Lumbee/Cherokee/Choctaw) 1942-
(carpenter; silversmith, saddle maker, rock carver)
Born October 16, 1942, Broken Arrow, Okla. Education: High school. Principal occupation: Carpenter; silversmith, saddle maker, rock carver. Address: P.O Box 10097, Fresno, CA 93745 (209) 498-3500. Affiliation: Indian Traders Guild (silversmith, saddle maker, rock carver). Community activities: Counseling & referral, Alcoholics & Drugs Anonymous; work with Special Olympics kids. Memberships: United Lumbee Nation's Bear Clan (vice-chief, 1993-); Fresno Gem & Mineral Society. Awards, honors: 1987-91 Fresno Fair (10-1st Places, 2-2nd Places, 1 Honorable Mention; Sept., 1993 Pasadena Indian Show, 1st Place. All awards for - Open Class Indian Jewelry & Art. Interests: Researching Indian languages & traditional arts & crafts; customs, etc. (Cherokee, Choctaw, Lenape, Mohawk, etc.) traveling. Published work: Learn to Speak Cherokee, Jan. 1993.

*PEARSON, MARIA D. (Hamichia Ianko-Running Moccasins) (Yankton Sioux) 1932-
(consultant-Indian affairs)
Born July 12, 1932, Springfield, S.D. Education: Marty Indian School, Marty, SD, 1938-49; Iowa Western Community College, Council Bluffs, IA. Principal occupation: Consultant-Indian affairs. Home address: 1405 Truman Place, Ames, IA 50010 (515) 232-5320. Affiliation: Owner, Maria Pearson, Consultant, Ames, IA. Community activities: Commissioner, Iowa Substance Abuse Commission; chair, State Archaeologist's Advisory Committee; chair, Iowa Governors Indian Advisory Council. Awards, honors: Governor's Award for Volunteer Work, Iowa Governor. Membership: Native American Advisory Council on Substance Abuse (treasurer). Interests: "Maria Pearson is generally regarded as the person who initiated the movement for protection of Indian burials and reburial of remains in universities, museums and private collections. Got first law on this subject passed in this area; initiated substance abuse treatment for Indians in Omaha, Neb. (CARE Program), one of the first such treatment programs. Funding member of Indian substance abuse group which got national programs initiated on reservations and in cities though Indian Health Service; has given many talks on both these subjects to professional society groups and national or state conferences. Very active as advisor to Iowa Governor and Iowa government agencies on these and other topics." Biographical sources: Many magazine and newspaper articles: Newsweek, Time, Wall Street Journal, Chicago Tribune, Des Moines Register, Omaha World Herald, etc.

PEARSON, MARY
(attorney)
Address: 220 8th Ave. N., Edmonds, WA 98020. Membership: Northwest Indian Bar Association (president).

PEASE-WINDY BOY, JANINE
(college president)
Affiliation: President, Little Big Horn Community College, Box 370, Crow Center, Ed. Commission, Crow Agency, MT 59022 (406) 638-2228.

*PECOS, JOSE L. (Jemez Pueblo)
(governor)
Affiliation: Jemez Pueblo Council, P.O. Box 100, Jemez, NM 87024 (505) 834-7359.

*PECOS, REGIS
(executive director)
Affiliation: New Mexico Office on Indian Affairs, La Villa Rivera Bldg., 228 E. Palace Ave., Santa Fe, NM 87501 (505) 827-6440.

PECOTTE, JEFF
(health director)
Affiliation: Hannahville Indian Community Health Clinic, N14911 Hannahville B1. Rd., Wilson, MI 49896 (906) 466-2782.

*PEDRO, THEODORE M. (Laguna Pueblo)
(project director)
Born in Laguna Pueblo. Education: Western New Mexico University (Las Cruces, NM), BS, 1980. Principal occupation: Project Director, Mexico Indian Business Development Center, P.O. Box 3256, Albuquerque, NM 87190 (505) 889-9092. Other professional post: Board of Directors, Laguna Industries, 1982-.

PEEBLES, JOHN
(tribal lawyer)
Affiliation: Santee Sioux Tribe, P.O. Box 283, Flandreau, SD 57028 (605) 997-3891.

*PEGO, DAVID PAUL (Little Star)
(Saginaw Chippewa) 1954-
(journalist)
Born February 1, 1954, Mt. Pleasant, Mich. Education: Central Oklahoma State U., 1972-74. Principal occupation: Journalist. Home address: 1103 Hatteras, Austin, TX 78753 (512) 445-3590 Fax 445-3507. Affiliations: The Daily Oklahoman & The Oklahoma City Times, 1974-84; The Dallas Times Herald, 1984-88; The Associated Press, Dallas, TX, 1988-90; Newspapers in Educa-tion Director, The Austin American Statesman, Austin, TX, 1990-. Other professional posts: Chairman, Founded Great Promise, 1992- (a non-profit organization that publishes educational materials for young American Indians). Community activities: Presented cultural programs at more than three dozen area schools, and also invited to appear on local television and radio shows. Designed and coordinated production of special newspaper on AIDS that was approved for use by the Dallas Independent School District. Workshop presenter for the 1992 Texas Parenting Council Convention, and the 1994 Chapter 1 Parents Regional Conference; workshop panelist in 1992 & 1993 for the Austin Women in Media seminar for non-profit organizations; workshop panelist at the 1992 Texas Conference on Indian Education; Austin Independent School District's Native American Parents Committee (elected in 1992 as founding chairman; re-elected in 1993); member of organizing committee for 1994 Texas Conference on Minority Health; member of Greater Austin Chamber of Commerce Community Issues & action Committee (wrote special section on crime). Awards, honors: Oklahoma City YMCA Service Awards in 1982, 1983; 1988 minority fellowships for American Newspapers Publishers Workshop for Editors; 1991 University of Oklahoma Visiting Professor in Residence; guest lecturer at various colleges & universities; selected by President Bush in 1992 as delegate to the White House Conference on Indian Education. Memberships: Southern Newspaper Publishers Literacy Committee, 1994-; Texas Professionals in Newspaper in Education (secretary, 1994-. Published work: Short story, "Indian Medicine" in literacy quarterly published by Johns Hopkins U. in 1994.)

PELTIER, JERRY
(Indian band chief)
Affiliation: Kanesatake (Mohawk) Indian Band, Box 607, Kanesatake, Quebec, Canada J0N 1E0 (514) 479-8373.

*PELTIER, LEONARD *(Gwarth-ee-las)*
(Chippewa, Cree, Lakota) 1944-
(activist, artist)
Born September 12, 1944, Grand Forks, N.D. *Education*: St. Mary;s (Leavenworth, KS), 1990-91. *Principal occupation*: Activist, artist. *Address*: #89637-132, Box 1000, Leavenworth, KS 66048. *Affiliation*: Leonard Peltier Defense Committee, Lawrence, KS, 1976-. *Military service*: U.S. Marine Corps, 1960. *Community activities*: AIM activist. *Memberships*: Leonard Peltier Defense Committee, 1977-; Rosenburg Fund for Children; Walk Across Europe (1994). *Awards, honors*: Frederick Douglas Award, Spanish Human Rights Award; Sacco & Vanzetti Award; Humanitarian Award; Nobel Prize nominee. *Interests*: Art, specifically oil painting; working on cars, gardening. *Biographical sources*: Spirit of Crazy Horse, by Peter Matthiessen; Agents of Repression, by Ward Churchill; Trial of Leonard Peltier, by Jim Messerschmidt; (documentary) "Incident at Oglala," by Robert Redford; (video) Freedom by Rage Against the Machine, MTI. *Published works*: In progress.

PEMBERTON, ALFRED "TIG" (Chippewa)
(tribal chairperson)
Affiliation: Leech Lake Reservation Business Committee, Route 3, Box 100, Cass Lake, MN 56633 (218) 335-8200.

PENCILLE, HERBERT W. (Chemehuevi) 1927-
(businessman)
Born January 29, 1927, Los Angeles, Calif. *Education*: Los Angeles Valley College (Business Law). *Principal occupation*: Businessman. *Home address*: 12243 Hartland St., N. Hollywood, CA 91605. *Affiliations*: General manager, Hydrex Termite Control Co. of Southern California, 1969-; chairman, Chemehuevi Indian Tribal Council, 1972-; Owner, Hydrex Pest Control Co., East San Fernando Valley, 1975-. Military service: U.S. Army Air Corps, 1946-47. *Memberships*: National Pest Control Association, 1949- (director, 1962); Pest Control Operators of California, Inc. (president, 1959; director, 1959, 1960). *Awards, honors*: Man of the Year Award, Pest Control Operators of California, Inc., 1968. *Interests*: Private pilot license.

PENDERGAST, JAMES F. 1921-
(retired-Canadian Army officer; archaeologist; museum administrator)
Born May 26, 1921, Cornwall, Ontario, Can. *Education*: Cornwall Collegiate Institute, 1935-40; Canadian Army Staff College 1953. *Principal occupation*: Retired Army officer; archaeologist; museum administrator. *Home address*: RR 4, Merrickville, ON K0G 1N0 (613) 269-4730. *Affiliation*: Research associate, Canadian Museum of Civilization, 1984-. *Military service*: CASF, 1940; served UK Theatre, 1941-43, seconded U.S. Army Intelligence, 1945, enrolled Canadian Regular Army (Intelligence), 1946, trans. RCA, 1949, retired Lt. Col., 1973 (U.S. Army General Staff (Intelligence), Commendation, 1946; Canadian Army Efficiency Medal, 1950; Canadian Forces Decoration, 1957); Queen Elizabeth II Jubilee Medal, 1977. *Community activities*: Founding member, Ontario Council of Archaeology, 1985-. *Membership*: New York State Archaeological Association (Fellow). *Award*: 1990 Crabtree Award from the Society for American Archaeology. *Interests*: Iroquoian research; archaeology; presenting papers to learned societies; largely responsible for archaeological definition of St. Lawrence Iroquoian tribe. *Biographical sources*: Canadian Who's Who (University of Toronto Press, 1979-); 5,000 Personalities of the World (American Biographical Institute, 1986-). *Published works*: Co-author with B.G. Trigger, Cartier's Hochelaga and the Dawson Site (McGill-Queens University Press, 1972); co-author with B.G. Trigger, "The St. Lawrence Iroquoians," chapter in Handbook of the American Indian Vol. 15, Northeast (Smithsonian, 1978); articles: co-author, "Trace Element Analysis of Iroquois Pottery" (Canadian Journal of Archaeology, No. 4, 1980); "Who Were the Iroquois?" (Proceedings of the International Congress of Museums, Ottawa, Ont., 1982); "St. Lawrence Iroquoian Burial Practices" (Ontario Archaeology, No. 40, 1983); "Huron - St. Lawrence Iroquois Relations in the Terminal Prehistoric Period (Ontario Archaeology, No. 44, 1985); "Some Observations Regarding the St. Lawrence Iroquoians at the Maynard-McKeown Site (Ontario Archaeology, 1988); Native Encounters with Europeans in the 16th Century in the Region Now Known as Vermont (Vermont Historical Society, 1990); Emerging St. Lawrence Iroquoian Settlement Patterns (Man in the Northeast, 1990); The St. Lawrence Iroquoian, Their Past, Present and Immediate Future (New York State Archaeological Association, 1991); The Massawomeck: Raiders and Traders into the Chesapeake Bay in the 16th Century (American Philosophical Society, 1991); Susquehannock Trade Northward to New France Prior to A.D. 1608: A Popular Misconception (Pennsylvania Archaeology); The Kakouagoga or Kahkwas: An Iroquoian Nation Destroyed in the Niagara Region ca. 1652 (American Philosophical Society). Numerous other papers, monographs, and articles published or in preparation.

*PENN, W.S. (Nez Perce/Osage) 1949-
(writer, teacher)
Born March 21, 1949, Los Angeles, Calif. *Education*: University of California, Davis, AB, 1970; Syracuse University, DArts, 1979. *Principal occupation*: Writer, teacher. *Home address*: 164 Kedzie St., East Lansing, MI 48823 (517) 337-0694. *Affiliations*: Associate professor, Michigan State University, E. Lansing, MI, 1986-; Wordcraft Circle of Native American Mentor & Apprentice Writers, Fairfax, VA (mentor, 4 years). *Other professional post*: Resident Prose Writer, Michigan State University. *Memberships*: Wordcraft Circle (regional coordinator, member of National Advisory Council on Native American Writing); Associated Writing Programs. *Awards, honors*: 1994 North American Indian Prose Award for "All My Sins are Relatives" (narrative essays) from the University of Nebraska Press; Michigan Council on the Arts Award & New York Foundation on the Arts Grant for "The Absence of Angels" (novel). *Interests*: Writing (novels, essays); teaching/mentoring; giving back to the community; travel; reading. *Published works*: Novel - "The Absence of Angels" (The Permanent Press - hardcover edition, 1994); The Absence of Angels (University of Oklahoma American Indian Lit. Series - paperback edition, 1995); narrative essays. "All My Sins Are Relatives" (University of Nebraska Press, 1995); editor, Native American Literatures (The Johns Hopkins University Press, 1994) a special anthology.

PENNEY, DAVID
(association president)
Affiliation: President, Native American Arts Studies Association, Detroit Institute of the Arts, 5200 Woodward Ave., Detroit, MI 48202 (313) 833-7900.

PENOI, CHARLES R. (Laguna Pueblo/ Oklahoma Cherokee) 1911-
(publisher; consultant)
Born September 23, 1911, Kiowa Agency, Anadarko, Okla. *Education*: University of Oklahoma, BS, MEd, DEd, 1956. *Principal occupation*: Publisher; consultant. *Home address*: 704 Neal Circle, El Reno, OK 73036 (405) 262-2013. *Affiliations*: Teacher, 1947- 67, Bureau of Indian Affairs' schools: Rosebud Boarding School, Fort Wingate Indian School, Sequoyah Indian School, Pawnee Indian School, and Riverside Indian School; employment assistance officer, Cheyenne & Arapaho Agency, Concho, OK (1967-retired -1973); owner, Pueblo Publishing Press, Yukon, OK, 1974-. *Other professional post*: After retirement he established his counseling service in Yukon, Okla. He was certified as a school counselor and as a school psychologist. *Military service*: U.S. Army, 1941-45 (45th Infantry-500 days of combat in the European theatre-EAME Service Ribbon with One Silver Star, One Bronze Service Star and One Bronze Arrowhead, Good Conduct Medal; American Defense Service Ribbon). *Community activities*: Established the El Reno School of Continuing Education which has been in session for 18 years. It is a school for all races, both male and female; member, Rotary International. *Awards, honors*: 30 Years Length of Service Award from the Bureau of Indian Affairs. *Interests*: "I have seen and visited all of the major cities in the Western Hemisphere." *Biographical sources*: The Daily Oklahoman. *Published works*: No More Buffalos, The Cheyenne & Arapaho Tribes of Oklahoma (Pueblo Publishing Press, 1991); Indian Time (Pueblo Publishing Press, 1984) and about 15 other books published by the Press.

PENSONEAU, RALPH R.
(BIA agency supt.)
Affiliation: Southern Ute Agency, Bureau of Indian Affairs, P.O. Box 315, Ignacio, CO 81137 (303) 563-4511.

PENTEWA, RICHARD SITKO (Hopi) 1927-
(artist)
Born April 12, 1927, Oraibi, Ariz. *Education*: Oklahoma A & M College, School of Technical Training, 1957. *Principal occupation*: Artist (painting and sculpture). *Home address*: P.O. Box 145, Oraibi, AZ 86039. *Military service*: U.S. Army (Koran Service Medal; Combat Infantry Badge; U.N. Service Medal; National defense Service Medal). *Membership*: Hopi Tribal Council. *Awards, honors*: Numerous awards for art. *Interests*: Art; travel.

*PEPION, LORETTA F. (Blackfeet) 1942-
(museum curator)
Born May 11, 1942, Mont. *Address & Affiliation*: Museum of the Plains Indian, Box 398, Browning, MT 59417 (406) 338-2230.

*PERALA, RENEE
(Title V coordinator)

Affiliation: Native American Coalition of Programs, P.O. Box 1914, Fargo, ND 58107 (701) 235-3124.

PERATROVICH, ROY Jr. (Tlingit) 1934-
(consulting engineer)
Born May 17, 1934, Klawock, Alaska. *Education*: University of Washington, BS, 1957. *Principal occupation*: Civil engineer. *Home address*: 12581 Beachcomber Dr., Anchorage, AK 99515 (907) 345-6297. *Affiliations*: Engineer, Seattle Engineering Dept., 1957-61; bridge designer, AK Dept. of Highways, 1961-72; supervisor of activities, R&M Consultants, Inc., 1972-77; first director, State of Alaska, Div. of Facility Procurement Policy, 1977-79; president, Peratrovich Consultants, Inc., Anchorage, 1979-; Sr. Vice President, Peratrovich, Nottingham & Drage, Inc. - Consulting Engineers, Anchorage, 1979-. *Other professional post*: Founder & member of board, Architects and Engineers Insurance Co." a nationwide company formed in 1987 to sell liability insurance; member of School of Engineering Advisory Committee, University of Alaska; former BIA agency supt. *Memberships*: State of AK Board of Registration for Engineers, Architects, and Land Surveyors; American Society of Civil Engineers; The Society of American Military Engineers. *Awards, honors*: Five awards from James & Lincoln Arc Welding Foundation for design of welded structures; and numerous awards from Municipality of Anchorage Urban Design Awards Program, among others; first Alaska Native to become licensed as a professional engineer in the state of Alaska. *Interests*: "Son of prominent Alaskan civil rights activists, Roy and Elizabeth Peratrovich. Over 30 years experience in structural and civil engineering, facility planning, and engineering management, working in both government and private sector. Primary work emphasis has been in the fields of bridge and marine structural design and management of major planning agencies. One of my goals has been to be the very best civil engineer I can be and to provide an example for other Indian boys and girls to follow. Now that I can afford it, I enjoy traveling to see other ports of the world; enjoy sports and my family." *Published work*: Co-author, Guide to Maintenance and Operations of Small Craft Harbors, 1988, the first manual of its kind in the U.S.; articles on bridge design and construction, with Dennis Nottingham.

PEREAU, JOHN J.V.
(BIA agency supt.)
Affiliation: Crow Agency, Bureau of Indian Affairs, Crow Agency, MT 59022 (406) 638-2672.

PEREZ, MARGARET C. (Assiniboine Sioux)
(college president)
Affiliation: Fort Belknap Community College, Box 547, Harlem, MT 59526 (406) 353-2578.

*PERKINS, THOMAS
(center co-owner)
Affiliation: Ogle Wanagai Gallery & Center, 842 N. Highland Ave., Atlanta, GA 30306 (404) 872-4213.

PERKINS, TWILA
(editor)
Affiliation: "The Seminole Tribune," Seminole Tribe of Florida, 6333 N.W. 30th St., Hollywood, FL 33024 (305) 964-4853.

PERVAIS, CHRISTI
(Indian band chief)

Affiliation: Fort William Indian Band, Box 786, Sta. F, Thunder Bay, ON P7C 4W6 (807) 623-9543.

PESHEWA, MACAKI (Shawnee; Shaman)
1941-
(priest-Native American Church)
Born May 23, 1941, Spartanburg, S.C. *Education*: Spartanburg Junior College, AA, 1966; Wofford College, BA, 1968; Furman University, 1969; University of South Carolina, 1971-73; University of Tennessee, Knoxville, MS, 1974, 1976-77; Auburn University, 1974-75; Native Americas University (Doctorate-Human Development, 1975; Doctorate-System Theory of Life Science, 1976). *Principal occupation*: Priest-Native American Church, Knoxville, TN. *Address*: Native American Church, P.O. Box 53, Strawberry Plains, TN 37871. *Affiliations*: Regional coordinator, Catawba Labor Program; Chairman, Tennessee Indian Council, Knoxville, TN; chairman and founder, Native American Indians in Media Corporation, Knoxville, TN; chairman, Indian Historical Society of the Americas, Knoxville, Tenn. *Other professional post*: Founder & publisher of the National Indian Reader Newspaper; founder of the Peace Park-Valley of the Totems; business developer in Idian Bingo. *Military service*: U.S. Air Force. *Community activities*: Work with off-reservation Indians; Tennessee Band of Cherokees (medicine man, business advisor); The American Indian Movement (urban Indian, Shawnee Nation); Native American Church of the Southeast (incorporator and head); National Lenape Band of Indians (medicine man); Consciousness Expansion Movement of Native Americans (president, chairman of the board); Tuskegee Alumni Foundation, Knoxville, Tenn. (advisory board); Knoxville Communications Cooperative (advisory board); Native Americas University (Southeast regional coordinator; board of regents; Indian Voters League. *Memberships*: Assn. of Humanistic Psychology; XAT-American Indian Medicine Society; International Minority Business Council/Assn; Phi Delta Kappa; Alpha Delta Omega. *Awards, honors*: Notary-at-Large, Tennessee; Key-to-City Certificate of Appreciation, Knoxville, Tenn.; Governor Recognitions: Appreciation Certificate, and Colonel-past & present administration. *Interests*: Archives of living elders in America today; art collector for Native American Church collection. Parapsychology; existential philosophy; existential phenomenology; altered states of consciousness & metaphysics; herbal medicine; yoga; handball; travel. *Published work*: Film produced: Amonita Sequoyah (Native American Media, 1982); Archives: Longest Walk for Survival, 1981; Archives: Black Elk, Sun Bear, AmyLee, Simon Brasquepe.

*PESULCH, SCOTT
(health director)
Affiliation: Fresno Indian Health, 4991 E. McKinley, #109, Fresno, CA 93727 (209) 255-0261.

PETE, FRED, Sr. (Eskimo)
(association president)
Affiliation: Stebbins Community Association, P.O. Box 2, Stebbins, AK 99671 (907) 934-3561.

*PETE, HARLIN (Goshute)
(tribal chairperson)
Affiliation: Goshute Business Council, P.O. Box 6104, Ibapah, UT 84034 (801) 234-1138.
*PETE, JAMES E.
(office director)

Affiliation: IHS-Rhinelander Field Office, Box 537, Rhinelander, WI 54501 (715) 362-5145.

PETER, DOUGLAS G., M.D.
(IHS-chief medical officer)
Affiliation: Navajo Area Office, Indian Health Service, P.O. Box 9020, Window Rock, AZ 86515 (602) 871-5813.

PETERS, CHRIS
(executive director)
Affiliation: Seventh Generation Fund for Indian Development, Inc., P.O. Box 10, Forestville, CA 95436 (707) 887-1559.

*PETERS, ELAINE F.
(museum director)
Affiliation: Ak-Chin Indian Him-Dak Museum/Archives, P.O. Box 897, Maricopa, AZ 85239 (602) 568-9480.

PETERS, GORDON
(Ontario regional chief)
Affiliation: Chiefs of Ontario, 22 College St., 2nd Floor, Toronto, Ontario, Can. M5G 1K2 (416) 972-0212.

PETERS, JOHN A.
(executive director)
Affiliation: Massachusetts Commission on Indian Affairs, One Ashburton Place, Room 1004, Boston, MA 02108 (617) 727-6394.

*PETERS, CHIEF RUSSELL
(Mashpee Wampanoag)
(tribal chief)
Affiliation: Mashpee Wampanoag Indian Tribal Council, P.O. Box 1048, Mashpee, MA 02649.

*PETERS, STAN (Eskimo)
(village chief)
Affiliation: Holy Cross Village Council, P.O. Box 203, Holy Cross, AK 99602 (907) 476-7134.

PETERS, VAN A.
(education administrator)
Affiliation: Portland Area Office, Bureau of Indian Affairs, 911 N.E. 11th Ave., Portland, OR 97232 (503) 230-5682.

PETERS, WINIFRED
(school principal)
Affiliation: Hunters Point Boarding School, P.O. Drawer 99, St. Michaels, AZ 86511 (602) 871-4439.

*PETERSON, GARY W.
(board president)
Affiliation: National Indian Child Welfare Association, 3611 SW Hood St., Suite 201, Portland, OR 97201 (503) 222-4044.

*PETERSON, JAMES E.
(IHS-executive officer)
Affiliation: Bemidji Area Office, Indian Health Service, 203 Federal Bldg., Bemidji, MN 56601 (218) 751-7701.

PETERSON, KENNETH
(BIA agency education chairperson)
Affiliation: Dlo'ay Azhi Community School, P.O. Box 789, Thoreau, NM 87323 (505) 862-7525.
PETERSON, NICK, Sr. (Eskimo)
(AK village president)

Affiliation: Akhiok Native Village, P.O. Box 5072, Akhiok, AK 99615 (907) 836-2229.

*PETERSON, TONY
(IHS-executive officer)
Affiliation: Aberdeen IHS Area Office, Federal Bldg., 115 Fourth Ave., SE, Aberdeen, SD 57401 (605) 226-7581.

PETIQUAN, BARNEY
(Indian band chief)
Affiliation: Wabauskang Indian Band, Box 1730, Kenora, Ontario P9N 3X7 (807) 547-2555.

*PETRIVELLI, PATRICIA
(executive director)
Affiliation: Institute of Alaska Native Arts Information Center, P.o. Box 70769, Fairbanks, AK 99707 (907) 456-7491.

PETTIGREW, JACKSON D.
(Chickasaw) 1942-
(artist, business manager)
Born July 2, 1942, Ada, Okla. *Education*: East Central University, BA, 1973. *Principal occupation*: Artist, business manager. *Home address*: 3727 Governor Harris Dr., Ada, OK 74820. *Affiliations*: Owner, Native American Arts (retail/wholesale), Ada, OK, 1984-. *Other professional post*: Chairman of the board, First American Foundry Arts, Inc. (art bronze), Ada, Okla. *Community activities*: Teach art classes for young people, J.O.M. Indian program. *Membership*: Southern Oklahoma Artist Association. *Interests*: "Artistic growth and sharing concepts with young people who are interested in art as a career. Also interested in civil rights. I was an equal opportunity specialist at the Dallas Regional Office of Civil Rights, Dallas, TX, 1973-79. I was also vice chairperson for the Regional Indian Affairs Council from 1974-78. We served as an advocate for Native Americans in Region VI and the nation. Other interests include: silversmithing, painting and sculpturing. I have competed in various national juried art shows."

PEVAR, STEPHEN L. 1946-
(attorney)
Born November 29, 1946, Brooklyn, N.Y. *Education*: Princeton University, BA, 1968; University of Virginia Law School, JD, 1971. *Principal occupation*: Attorney. *Home address*: 1574 Monroe, Denver, CO 80206 (303) 321-4828 (work). *Affiliations*: Regional counsel, American Civil Liberties Union, Denver, 1977-; adjunct professor, University of Denver Law School, 1984-. *Interests*: Civil rights; Indian law; freedom of speech; prisoner's rights. *Published work*: The Rights of Indians and Tribes (Southern Illinois University Press, 1992).

PEWEWARDY, CORNEL *(Oyate Omp Moni)*
(Comanche/Kiowa) 1952-
(school principal)
Born Jauary 20, 1952, Lawton, Okla. *Education*: Northeastern State University, BS, 1976, MEd, 1977; University of New Mexico, EdS, 1986; Penn State University, DEd, 1989. *Principal occupation*: Indian school principal. *Address & Affiliation*: Principal, Mounds Park All-Nations Magnet School, 1075 E. 3rd St., St. Paul, MN 55106 (612) 293-5938. *Other professional posts*: Postdoctoral Fellow, University of Oklahoma, 1989-91. *Community activities*: Board Director, Dayton's Bluff/Dist. 4; Afrocentric Academy; Minnesota Institute of Arts; St. Paul Indians in Unity; Kirkpatrick Center; Minnesota Tech-

nical College System. *Memberships*: National Association for Multicultural Education (founding member); St. Paul Principals Association; American Education Research Association; Association of Teacher Education; National Association of American Indian Professors; PDK; Pi Lambda Theta; National Council of Teachers of English; National Indian Education Association; Oklahoma Council for Indian Education; Association of Institute Research. *Awards, honors*: John C. Rouillard Scholarship; Outstanding Young Men of America, 1988; Kozak Memorial Award, 1989; 1991 National "Indian Educator of the Year," by the National Indian Education Association; Minnesota Transformational Leadership Award, 1991; served on tribal advisory councils, state textbook review committees, and national special interest groups in multicultural education. *Interests*: Director of research and development, Southwestern Indian Polytechnic Institute, Albuquerque, NM; performing artist who continues to promote and perpetuate the songs & dances of the Southern Plains' tribes; singing and playing the American Indian flute; teaches Native American song and dance. Dr. Cornel is a descendent of Chief Wild Horse. *Biographical sources*: Native American Mascots and Imagery; Struggle of Unlearning Indian Stereotypes; Medicine Wheel Circle; Indian Aerobics; Perceptions of American Indian High School Students Attending Public School. *Published works*: Culturally Responsible Pedagogy (National Education Services, 1992); American Indian Stereotypes in the World of Children (Scarecrow, 1992); Spirit Journey - cassette, CD (Meyer Creative Productions, 1993).

PFEFFER, MICHAEL S. 1949-
(attorney)
Born October 14, 1949, New York, N.Y. *Education*: Cornell University, BA, 1971; University of California, Berkeley, JD, 1979. *Affiliations*: Executive director, National Association of Indian Legal Services (California Indian Legal Services), 510 16th St., Suite 301, Oakland, CA 94612 (510) 835-0284, 1982-.

PHELAN, BERTHA
(centre director)
Affiliation: United Native Friendship Centre, 2902 - 29th Ave., Vernon, British Columbia, Canada V1T 5E6 (604) 542-1247.

PHELPS, RICHARD
(executive director)
Affiliation: The Falmouth Institute, Inc., 3918 Prosperity Ave., Suite 302, Fairfax, VA 22031 (703) 641-9100.

*PHILBRICK, DOUGLAS R.
(school principal)
Affiliation: Keams Canyon Boarding School, P.O. Box 397, Keams Canyon, AZ 86034 (602) 738-2385.

*PHILEMONOF, DEMITRI
(executive director)
Affiliation: Aleutian Islands Association, 401 E. Fireweed Lane, Suite 201, Anchorage, AK 99503 (907) 276-2700.

PHILLIPS, GEORGE HARWOOD 1934-
(professor of history)
Born January 27, 1934, San Diego, Calif. *Education*: San Diego State University, BA, 1959; UCLA, MA, 1967, PhD (American History), 1973. PhD dissertation: Indian Resistance and

Cooperation in Southern California: The Garra Uprising and Its Aftermath. *Principal occupation*: Professor of history. *Home address*: 4552 Meadow Dr. #2, Vail, CO 81657. *Affiliations*: Lecturer in history, University of West Indies, Jamaica, 1969-71; lecturer in Afro-Ethnic Studies, Fullerton State University, Calif., 1972-73; acting assistant professor of history, UCLA, 1973-75; visiting lecturer in history, 1977-78, assistant professor of history, 1978-81, associate professor of history, University of Colorado, Boulder, 1981-. *Other professional posts*: Contributing editor, The Journal of California and Great Basin Anthropology; board of editors, Pacific Historical Review. *Military service*: U.S. Marine Corps, 1954-56. *Memberships*: American Historical Association (Pacific Coast Branch). *Awards, honors*: Holder of the Rupert Costa Chair in American Indian History, University of California, Riverside, CA, 1988-89. *Published works*: Chiefs and Challengers: Indian Resistance & Cooperation in Southern California (University of California-Berkeley Press, 1975); The Enduring Struggle: Indians in California History (Boyd & Fraser, 1981); Indians of the Tulares: An Ethnohistory of Central California, 1769-1849 (University of Oklahoma, 1992). *Articles*: The Indian Paintings from Mission San Fernando: An Historical Interpretation (The Journal of California Anthropology, Summer, 1976); Indians and the Breakdown of Spanish Mission System in California (Ethnohistory, Fall, 1974); Indians in Los Angeles, 1781-1875: Economic Integration, Social Disintegration (Pacific Historical Review, August, 1980).

PHILLIPS, MABEL ANN
(organization chairperson)
Affiliation: Dakota Women of All Red Nations, P.O. Box 69, Fort Yates, ND 58538 (701) 854-7592.

PHILLIPS, MELVINA PRITCHETT
(Echota Cherokee) 1948-
(Title V coordinator, educator)
Born September 1, 1948, Madison County, Ala. *Education*: University of Montevallo (AL), BS, 1970; Alabama A&M University (Huntsville), MEd., 1976. *Principal occupation*: Resource specialist; educator. *Home address*: 2279 Oak Grove Rd., New Hope, AL 35760 (205) 723-2256 (home) 852-2170 (office). *Affiliations*: Madison County Board of Education, Huntsville, AL (teacher, 1982-; Title V coordinator, 1989-). *Other professional post*: Clerk/typist, NASA Summer Program, Huntsville, AL (3 years). *Community activities*: FEMA Board (distribute funds to organizations that work with needy individuals); education board member: Constitution Hall Village, Burritt Museum, Botanical Gardens. *Memberships*: Alabama Indian Education Association (secretary); National Indian Education Association; Alabama Environmental Education Association; Tennessee Valley Genealogical Association. *Awards, honors*: Madison County Title V Project was selected as Showcase Project by the U.S. Dept of Education in 1987 & 1993; delegate to the White House Conference on Indian Education; education consultant to the Smithsonian's new Museum of the American Indian; Certificate of Recognition from Gov. Guy Hunt and the Alabama Environmental Education Association for Best Environmental Education Curriculum Guide for 1991. *Interests*: "Established two science camps for minority students. Involved with environmental concerns and organizations; serve as consultant to vari-

ous local museums; consultant and demonstrator at Burritt Museum's Annual Indian Festival and Russell Cave National Monument's Indian Day Historian; favorite pastimes are reading and art."

*PHILLIPS, NATHAN (Omaha)
(executive director)
Affiliation: Native Youth Alliance, Washington Peace Center, 1832 Park Rd., NW, Washington, DC 20010 (202) 328-9060.

PHILLIPS, NEIL
(Indian band chief)
Affiliation: Douglas Indian Band, Box 339, Harrison Hot Springs, British Columbia, Canada V0M 1K0 (604) 820-3082.

*PHILLIPS, PAM 1947-
(retail gallery owner)
Born December 4, 1947, Chicago, Ill. *Education*: Indiana University, R.N., 1968. *Principal occupation*: Retail gallery owner. *Home address*: 103 E. 173rd Ave., Lowell, IN 46342 (219) 942-9022. *Affiliation*: Owner, Skystone N'Silver, Hobart, IN, 1979-. *Community activities*: Southlake Mental Health Center (past president & board of directors, 1989-). *Other professional post*: Board of Directors, Indian Arts Foundation, Albuquerque, NM, 1992-. *Memberships*: Gallup InterTribal Indian Ceremonial Association; Indian Arts & Crafts Association (current vice-president); Indian Art Foundation. *Award*: Best in Category, Inlay Jewelry Award, Gallup InterTribal Indian Ceremony Association. *Interests*: "Travel six times a year throughout the West and Southwest buying from reservation artists for the gallery; provide educational programs to schools and Indiana University; Northwest Native American culture & arts. I am a silver and gold smith and also do lapidary & jewelry design. I enjoy doing lectures, radio interviews, TV interviews about Native American culture & arts. (My gallery) Skystone N'Silver is committed to selling only Native American handmade art; rugs, pottery, jewelry, kachinas, baskets, quillboxes and many items too numerous to list. Interested in sociology & anthropology."

PHILP, KENNETH R. 1941-
(professor of history)
Born December 6, 1941, Pontiac, Mich. *Education*: Michigan State University, BA, 1963, PhD, 1968; University of Michigan, MA, 1964. *Principal occupation*: Professor of History, University of Texas, Arlington, 1968-. *Home address*: 2801 Greenbrook, Arlington, TX 76016 (817) 451-8315; 273-2864 (work). *Memberships*: American Historical Association; Western History Association; Organization of American Historians. *Awards, honors*: Oscar Winther Award for the best article in the 1988 volume of the Western Historical Quarterly. *Interests*: American Indian history; federal Indian policy. *Published works*: Co-editor, Essays on Walter Prescott Webb (University of Texas Press, 1976); John Collier's Crusade for Indian Reform (University of Arizona Press, 1977); editor, Indian Self-Rule: From Roosevelt to Reagan (Howe Brothers, 1986).

PICKERING, GWEN
(health director)
Affiliation: White Eagle PHS Indian Health Center, P.O. Box 2071, Ponca City, OK 74601 (405) 765-2501.

PICKETT, EVELYN
(BIA-public information officer)
Affiliation: Office of Tribal Services, Bureau of Indian Affairs, Dept. of the Interior, MS-2620-MIB, 1849 C St., NW, Washington, DC 20240 (202) 208-3710.

PICO, ANTHONY (Diegueno)
(tribal chairperson)
Affiliation: Viejas Tribal Council, P.O. Box 908, Alpine, CA 92001 (619) 445-3810.

*PICOTEE, WILLIAM H.
(health center director)
Affiliation: Yakima PHS Indian Health Center, 401 Buster Rd., Toppenish, WA 98948 (509) 865-2102.

*PICTOU, ROGER (Micmac)
(tribal president)
Affiliation: Aroostook Band of Micmac Indians, P.o. Box 772, Presque Island, ME 04769 (207) 764-1972.

PIERCE, GEORGE EARL (Meherrin)
(tribal chief)
Affiliation: Meherrin Indian Tribe, P.O. Box 508, Winton, NC 27986 (919) 358-4375.

PIERCE, LARRY
(school principal)
Affiliation: Wa He Lut School, 11110 Conine Ave., SE, Olympia, WA 98503 (206) 456-1311

PIERCING EYES, CHIEF
(executive director)
Affiliation: Pan-American Indian Association, P.O. Box 244, Nocatee, FL 33864 (813) 494-6930.

PIERRE, ED
(Indian band chief)
Affiliation: Katzie Indian Band, 10946 Katzie Rd., Pitt Meadows, British Columbia, Canada V3Y 1Z3 (604) 465-8961.

PIERRO, PAULINE
(development)
Affiliation: Association on American Indian Affairs, Inc., 245 Fifth Ave., New York, NY 10016 (212) 689-8720.

*PIERSKALLA, NANCY
(BIA area representative)
Affiliation: Tribal Operations Menominee Area Representative, Minneapolis Area Office, Bureau of Indian Affairs, 331 Second Ave. South, Minneapolis, MN 55401 (612) 373-1000. *Other professional post*: Acting Director, Office of Indian Gaming Management Staff, BIA, MS: 4060-MIB, Washington, DC 20240 (202) 219-4068.

PIETACHO, PHILIPPE
(Indian band chief)
Affiliation: Montagnais de Mingan Indian Band, Box 319, Mingan, Quebec, Canada G0G 1V0 (418) 949-2234.

PIGEON, BERNICE MILLER
(Stockbridge-Munsee)
(library/museum director)
Affiliation: Stockbridge-Munsee Historical Library and Museum, Route 1, Box 300, Bowler, WI 54416 (715) 793-4270.

PIGSLEY, DELORES (Siletz)
(tribal chairperson)
Affiliation: Siletz Tribal Council, P.O. Box 549, Siletz, OR 97380 (503) 444-2513.

PIKE, KEITH R. (Pomo)
(rancheria chairperson)
Affiliation: Guidiville Rancheria, Box 339, Talmadge, CA 95481 (707) 462-3682.

*PIKE, STEWART
(tribal chairperson)
Affiliation: Uintah & Ouray Tribal Business Council, P.O. Box 190, Fort Duchesne, UT 84026 (801) 722-2406.

PINTO, JUDY (Laguna Pueblo) 1953-
(substance abuse counselor)
Born June 6, 1953, Springs, Colo. *Education*: GED, Grants Branch College, 1979. *Principal occupation*: Substance abuse counselor. *Address*: Southwest Indian Polytechnic Institute, Albuquerque, NM (505) 766-8418. *Affiliations*: Counselor, Santa Clara Rehabilitation Center, Santa Clara Pueblo, NM, 1980-84; counselor, 1984-87, supervisor, 1987-88; substance abuse counselor, Southwest Indian Polytechnic Institute, Albuquerque, NM, 1989-. *Membership*: New Mexico Alcohol & Drug Counseling Assn.

PINTO, TONY J. (Diegueno)
(tribal chairperson)
Affiliation: Cuyapaipe General Council, 2271 Alpine Blvd. #D, Alpine, CA 91901 (619) 478-5289.

*PIPE, ROBERT W.
(health center director)
Affiliation: Peach Springs PHS Indian Health Center, P.O. Box 190, Peach Springs, AZ 86434 (602) 769-2204.

PIPER, AURELIUS H. PIPER, Sr.
(Chief Big Eagle) (Golden Hill Paugussett)
(company owner/operator)
Born August 31, 1916, Bridgeport, Conn. *Principal occupation*: Owner/operator of trucking company. *Home address*: 427 Shelton Rd., Golden Hill Reservation, Trumbull, CT 06415 (203) 377-4410. *Affiliation*: Chief of Golden Hill Band of Paugussett Indians, Golden Hill Reservation's 3 Chief Traditional Government, 95 Stanavage Rd., Trumbull, CT 06415 (203) 537-0390. *Community activities*: Founder of the Spiritual Circle in Connecticut State prisons. *Honors*: Member of Indian Affairs Council, State of Connecticut; founder/presient of the White Buffalo Society.; Eagle Wing Press. *Interests*: Eastern tribes. *Published works*: Quarter Acr of Heartache, by Claude C. Smith (Pocahontas Press, 1985); Red Man in Red Square, by Claude C. Smith (Pocahontas Press, 1994).

PIPER, AURELIUS H., Jr. (Chief Quiet Hawk)
(Golden Hill Paugussett)
(tribal chief)
Affiliation: Golden Hill Paugussett 3 Chief Traditional Government, 95 Stanavage Rd., Golden Hill Reservation, Trumbull, CT 06415 (203) 537-0390.

PIPER, KENNETH (Moonface Bear)
(Golden Hill Paugussett) 1960-
(warchief)
Born September 9, 1960, Bridgeport, Conn. *Principal occupation*: Warchief of the Golden Hill Paugussetts. *Address*: Golden Hill Reservation, 95 Stanavage Rd., Trumbull, CT 06415 (203) 537-0390. *Community activities*: American In-

dians for Development (ex-Board member); Connecticut Indian Task Force of the Legislature Sovereignty Committee; Native American Heritage Advisory Council on Reburrials. *Membership*: Connecticut Indian Affairs Council.

*PITKA, ARLENE
(village chief)
Affiliation: Beaver Village, P.O. Box 24029, Beaver, AK 99724 (907) 628-6126.

PITMAN, WILLARD (Creek) 1927-
(Indian Supreme Court Justice)
Born June 17, 1927, Stidham, Okla. *Education*: Muskogee (OK) Jr. College (2 years). *Principal occupation*: Indian Supreme Court Justice. Home address: 2209 Nebraska St., Muskogee, OK 74403 (918) 682-1975. *Affiliations*: Credit sales manager, Sears, Roebuck & Co., Chicago, IL (30 years-retired; Finance Dept., Veterans Administration Regional Office, Muskogee, OK, 1986-; Supreme Court Justice, Muscogee Creek Nation, Muskogee, OK, 1984-. *Military service*: U.S. Marine Corps, 1945-46. *Community activities*: President & vice-president, Muscogee Indian Community, Muskogee, OK.

*PITTSLEY, RICH
(museum director)
Affiliation: Chief Plenty Coups State Park & Museum, P.O. Box 100, Pryor, MT 59066 (406) 252-1287.

PLAINFEATHER, MARDELL HOGAN
(*Baahin'naaje*) (Crow) 1945-
(park ranger, Plains Indian historian)
Born September 28, 1945, Billings, Mont. *Education*: Maricopa County Junior College, 1967-68; Rocky Mountain College, BA, 1979. *Principal occupation*: Park Ranger, Plains Indian historian. *Affiliation*: Plains Indian historian, Little Bighorn National Monument, P.O. Box 38, Crow Agency, MT 59022 (406) 638-2621, 1980-. *Other professional post*: Part-time instructor (U.S. History & Montana State History): Crow Tribal Junior College, Little Big Horn College, Crow Agency, MT. *Community activities*: Fort Phil Kearny/Bozeman Trail History Association (board member); Crow Tribal Archives (board member). *Memberships*: Custer Battlefield Historical & Museum Association; Jailhouse Gallery; Big Horn County Historical Association; Montana State Oral History Association; Montana Committee for the Humanities (speaker's bureau); Yellowstone County History Association (honorary member); Yellowstone Coral of Westerners. *Awards, honors*: History Department Award, Rocky Mountain College, 1979; prize for Performance Achievement, Custer Battlefield National Monument, 1982; award from St. Augustine Preservation of Indian Culture, Chicago, IL in 1987. *Interests*: "My interest is in the cultural history of the Plains Indians, specifically from prehistory to 1880's. I enjoy visiting battlefields and making sure that the history is told correctly from the Indian viewpoint. I am also interested in exhibits in museums and their labelling. I am interested in oral history and the preservation of all sacred sites of Native peoples." *Biographical sources*: Mentioned in Dec.,1986 National Geographic article; interviewed by KUED, Salt Lake City in a documentary "Dreams Along the Little Big Horn" by Ed Nelson. *Published works*: A Personal Look at Curly After the Little Big Horn (Custer Battlefield Historical & Museum Association, in The Greasy Grass, annual publication, 1987); The

Apsaalooke: Warriors of the Big Horns (Fort Phil Kearny/Bozeman Trail History Association, 1989).

PLATERIO, DAVID LOUIS
(*Tosa-Wi-e*) (Shoshone) 1960-
(Native American consultant)
Born January 24, 1960, Elko, Nev. *Principal occupation*: Native American consultant. *Home address*: P.O. Box 822, Elko, NV 89803 (702) 738-3618 (work). *Affiliations*: Native American Consultant, Shoshone Information Network, Elko, NV, 1992-; political consultant for the European Parliament, 1992-; *Other professional posts*: Historian, Native American Consultant, Western Shoshoni National Council, Elko, NV. *Community activities*: Founding member, Western Shsohone Historic Preservation Society; board member, Citizen's Alert (environmental watchdog for Nevada); member, Cultural Commission of Northern Nevada; member, Alliance of Native Americans; citizen/lobbyist training from Military Production Network; registered researcher, National Archives & Library of Congress. *Memberships*: National Environmental Coalition of Native Americans; member of the Congress of the Global Anti-Nuclear Alliance (International); Rural Alliance for Military Accountability (SkyGuard); The International Declaration & Inquiry Commission. *Awards, honors*: Received diploma on completion of training in reading of nuclear waste documents from the "Institute for Energy & Environmental Research." *Interests*: "I take a real hard stand on cultural protection, burial grounds, culturally significant sites, battlegrounds, white chart quarries (Tosa-Wi) across our aboriginal territory. I'm also an alternate for the Western Shoshone National Council, which I speak on behalf of Western Shoshones. I'm currently in the process of (working on) a chronology of events concerning the Western Shoshoni - fur trapper, expeditions, explorations, wars & depredations, conditions, placement of names on a map, etc. (I was) a featured speaker at the 1991 Indian Survival Summit held at California State University, Los Angeles; speaker at 9th annual European Meeting of Indian Support Group in Trondheim, Norway, July, 1993; speaker at the National Lawyers Committee on Civil Rights Under Law, March, 1993; among other events.

*PLESS, JAMES WILLIAM *(Son of Thunder)*
(United Lumbee-Cougar Clan) 1930-
(prison security)
Born July 29, 1930, Gould, Tex. *Education*: Freed-Hardman (Henderson, TN) (2 years). *Principal occupation*: Prison security. *Home address*: 105 Clover Lane, Palestine, TX 75801 (903) 729-4329. *Affiliation*: Texas Dept. of Corrections, Coffield, TX, 1983-. *Other professional posts*: Pipeline, refinery, 1955-60; supervisor of production, 1968-70; quality control refinery, 1970-83. *Military service*: U.S. Army, 1950-53. *Community activities*: Chief of Cougar Clan, United Lumbee Tribe; Masonic Lodge #400, Elkhart; Veterans of Foreign Wars; Advisory Officer to Irving Junior Fellows, 1963-70. *Awards, honors*: President's (Shrine Club's) Award for service to mankindYouth Council of Texas. *Interests*: Travel, hunting, fishing, gardening.

*PLESS, MARY JANE
(United Lumbee-Cougar Clan) 1936-
(vocational nurse)
Born May 11, 1936, Longview, Tex. *Education*: Palestine (TX) Vocational School of Nursing,

Licensed Vocational Nurse, 1977. *Home address*: 105 Clover Lane, Palestine, TX 75801 (903) 729-4329. *Affiliations*: Anderson County Memorial Hospital, Palestine, TX, 1981-. Total nursing care for youth to geriatric care. *Community activities*: Secretary of the United Lumbee Nation's Cougar Clan; reporter for the United Lumbee Times of Texas & Oklahoma areas. Even though disables since 1986, I help my neighbors when called upon for my nursing knowledge. *Membership*: V.F.W. Auxiliary Historian, 1993-. *Awards, honors*: Chosen by Texas Junior Oddfellows and Texas Girls Club to be one of three bus chaperones on Historical United Nations Pilgrimage, a 3-week tour of U.S. & Canada, 1963. *Interests*: Travel to historical places & presidential libraries & homes.

PLUMAGE, CHARLES J.
(hospital director)
Affiliation: Fort Belknap PHS Indian Hospital, Harlem, MT 59526 (406) 353-2651.

*PLUMMER, LA NITA
(legal services)
Affiliation: Four Rivers Indian Legal Services, P.O. Box 68, Sacaton, AZ 85247 (602) 263-8094.

POCHOP, VIRGIL
(BIA agency supt.)
Affiliation: Office of Facilities Management, Bureau of Indian Affairs, P.O. Box 1248, 500 Gold Ave., SW, 8th Floor, Albuquerque, NM 87103 (505) 766-2825.

POE, WILLIAM (Navajo)
(school principal)
Affiliation: Dibe Yazhi Habitiin Olta, Inc., Borego Pass School, P.O. Drawer A, Crownpoint, NM 87313 (505) 786-5237.

*POFF, WILLIAM
(health director)
Affiliation: San Diego American Indian Helth, 2561 First Ave., San Diego, CA 92103 (619) 234-2158.

POKER, PROTE
(Indian band chief)
Affiliation: First Nation Council of Davis Ilet, Davis Inlet, Labrador, Newfoundland, Canada A0P 1A0 (709) 478-8827.

POLANCO, MARY F.
(editor)
Affiliation: Jicarilla Chieftain, Jicarilla Apache Tribe, P.O. Box 507, Dulce, NM 87528-0507 (505) 759-3242.

POLCHIES, RICHARD
(Indian band chief)
Affiliation: St. Mary's Indian Band, 247 Paul St., Fredericton, New Brunswick, Canada E3A 2V7 (506) 458-9511.

POLESE, RICHARD 1941-
(editor)
Born November 16, 1941, Berkeley, Calif. *Education*: San Jose State College, 1959-61; Hanover College (IN), BA, 1962. *Principal occupation*: Editor. *Home address*: P.O. Box 1295, Santa Fe, NM 87501. *Affiliations*: Editor, El Palacio, Southwestern Quarterly; book editor, Museum of New Mexico Press, 1969-. *Other professional posts*: Columnist for the Santa Fe Reporter. *Awards, honors*: Edited and designed

the award-winning book, Music and Dance of the Tewa Pueblos, by Dr. Gertrude Kurath. *Interests*: Mr. Polese has written and edited publications on the Southwest and its people since 1962. These include several articles in El Palacio magazine, and editing and designing of several books and is recognized as an authority on the New Mexico Zia sun symbols, its origins and variations. *Published works*: Original New Mexico Cookery, 1965; editor, Pueblo Pottery of New Mexico Indians, 1977; editor, Music and Dance of the Tewa Pueblos, 1969; editor, In Search of Maya Glyphs, 1970; editor, Navajo Weaving Handbook, 1977. All published by Museum of New Mexico Press.

*POLLAK, GENEVIEVE (Ponca)
(tribal chairperson)
Affiliation: Ponca Business Committee, P.O. Box 2, White Eagle, Ponca City, OK 74601 (405) 762-8104.

POLSON, JERRY
(Indian band chief)
Affiliation: Long Point (Algonquin) Indian Band, Box 1, Winneway River, Quebec J0Z 2J0 (819) 722-2441.

POND, RONALD JAMES *(Itxutwin)*
(Umatilla, Palouse) 1939-
(cultural consultant)
Born December 6, 1939, McKay Creek, Oreg. *Education*: Blue Mountain Community College, Pendleton, OR, 1966-67; Eastern Oregon State College, BA, 1974; Oregon State University, Teaching Certificate, 1977, MA, 1992. *Principal occupation*: Cultural consultant. *Home address*: Route 3, Box 110, Pendleton, OR 97801. *Affiliation*: Teacher, School District 16-R, Pendleton, OR, 1977-79; elected leader/education director, Umatilla Tribe, Mission, OR, 1981; archaeology technician/assistant., U.S. Forest Service, Pendleton, 1985-; co-curator, "Plateau Exhibit," Washington State University, Pullman, WA. *Other professional posts*: Firefighter, U.S. Forest Service, 1963-69; general council chairperson, governing body member, 1979-80, education director, 1981, Umatilla Confederated Tribes, Pendleton, OR; research consultant, elder/oral traditions. *Community activities*: Umatilla Tribe Cultural Committee, 1968-; Blue Mountain Equestrian Trail Ride, 1992-93. *Awards, honors*: Best All Around Indian Dancer/ Indian Festival of Arts, LaGrange, OR, 1970; Smoke Jumper: Silver Wings, 1966; Seven Drums Religion, 1974-94; Annual Spring "First Food Feast": Singer, Lead Hunter, Lead Server; coordinator: 1976 Bi-Centennial Exposition, Umatilla cultural group to Washington D.C. Biographical source: Local paper, "East Oregonian," covers cultural activities on the Umatilla Reservation.

PONDER, ROBERT EARL *(Silver Badger)*
(Sioux/Cherokee/Choctaw) 1944-
(executive director/principal chief)
Born September 18, 1944, Carnegie, Okla. Education: North American Trade School, Newport Beach, CA, 1978-81. *Principal occupation*: Executive director, principal chief, Northwest Cherokee Wolf Band, Talent, OR, 1980-. *Home address*: 602 Stewart Ave., Medford, OR 97501 (503) 535-5003. *Other professional posts*: Oregon Economic Development Program (Native American Representative & board member). *Military service*: U.S. Navy, 1960-62 (Seaman Apprentice). *Community activities*: Jackson

County Consortium Member, Southern Oregon/ Rogue Valley Area. *Awards, honors*: Certificate of Appreciation from the Indian Education Title IV Program for eight years of dedicated service in Jackson County as a District Representative to the Oregon Indian Education Association. *Interests*: Gunsmithing; police science; Native American drumming.

POODRY, CLIFTON A. (Seneca) 1943-
(professor)
Born July 31, 1943, Buffalo, N.Y. *Education*: Uiversity of Buffalo, BA, 1965, MA, 1967; Western Reserve University, PhD, 1971. *Principal occupation*: Professor. *Home address*: 4433 Borina Dr., San Jose, CA 95129 (408) 459-2260 (work). *Affiliation*: University of California, Santa Cruz, 1972-. *Other professional post*: Program director, Developmental Biology Program, National Science Foundation, 1982-84. *Memberships*: American Indian Science & Engineering Society; Society for Advancement of Chicanos and Native Americans in Science; Society for Developmental Biology; Genetics Society; Sigma Xi; American Society of Zoologists; Open Mind.

POOLAW, LINDA S. (Delaware-Kiowa) 1942-
(tribal cultural consultant, writer-playwrite)
Born April 8, 1942, Lawton, Okla. *Education*: University of Sciences and Arts of Oklahoma, BA, 1974; University of Oklahoma, Masters work in Communications (2 years). *Principal occupation*: Tribal cultural consultant, Delaware Tribe of Western Oklahoma, Anadarko, OK. *Home address*: P.O. Box 986, Anadarko, OK 73005. *Other professional post*: Playwrite. *Community activities*: Salvation Army, Caddo County (chairperson); Delaware Tribe of Western Oklahoma (treasurer); Riverside Indian School Board (vice president); American Indian Exposition (vice president). *Memberships*: Indian and Western Arts Association (vice president). *Interests*: "Writing fiction and history about American Indians. (I) have traveled coast to coast to develop relationships with tribes. In 1986, I plan to research and write a book on my deceased father's work in photography, 50 Years of Life on the Southern Plains, (Horace Poolaw)." *Plays*: Skins, 1974; Happiness Is Being Married to a White Woman, and Written, Spoken and Unspoken Word (University of Oklahoma Press, 1982); The Day the Tree Fell, children's play (American Indian Institute, Norman, Okla., 1983).

POOLHECO, WALTER L. (Southern Ute)
(health director)
Affiliation: Southern Colorado Ute Health Center, P.O. Box 778, Ignacio, CO 81137 (303) 563-9443.

POORMAN, RICHARD
(Indian band chief)
Affiliation: Kawacatoose Indian Band, Box 10, Quinton, Saskatchewan, Canada S0A 3G0 (306) 835-2125.

POPE, JERRY L. (Shawnee) 1941-
(artist)
Born April 26, 1941, Greenfield, Ind. *Education*: John Heron School of Art; Indiana University, B.F.A., 1964. *Principal occupation*: Artist. Affiliations: Curator, American Indian People's Museum, Indianapolis, IN; editor, Tosan, American Indian People's News, Indianapolis, Ind.; principal chief, United Remnant Band, Shawnee

nation of Indiana, Ohio, Kentucky and Pennsylvania; director, Three Feather Society (Native-professional-social organization). *Other professional post*: Assisted in the compilation of Smithsonian Institution's list of native publications. *Memberships*: League of Nations, Pan-American Indians; National Association of Metis Indians; Three Feather Society (director); Mide Widjig, Grand Medicine Lodge Brotherhood, Albuquerque, N.M. *Awards, honors*: First Prize, national Exhibition of Small Paintings; selected to preside over and organize dedication of world's largest collection of Cuna Indian art, Dennison University, Granville, Ohio, 1972; among others. *Interests*: Mr. Pope writes, "1. Professional Native artist, by vocation; 2. editing and publishing of the Inter-Tribal Native publication, Tosan; 3. rebuilding the United Remnant Band of the Shawnee Nation, beginning in 1970 with seven persons; we now have re-established all twelve clans; 4. re-education of my people in traditional ways, instilling due pride in knowledge of their birthright; 5. work with in-prison Native groups." *Published work*: Native Publications in the United States and Canada (Smithsonian Institution, 1972).

PORTER, FRANK W., III
(institute director)
Affiliation: American Indian Research and Resource Institute, Gettysburg College, P.O. Box 576, Gettysburg, PA 17325 (717) 337-6265.

*PORVAZNIK, JOHN, M.D.
(associate director-IHS)
Affiliation: Indian Health Service, Parklawn Bldg., 5600 Fishers Lane, Rockville, MD 20857 (301) 443-1083.

*POSENJAK, LON J. (SNOQUALMOO)
(tribal chairperson)
Affiliation: Snoqualmoo Tribe, P.O. Box 463, Couperville, WA 98239 (206) 221-8301.

*POTTS, DONNA MARIE (Mewuk)
(rancheria spokesperson)
Affiliation: Buena Vista Rancheria, 4650 Coalmine Rd., Ione, CA 95640 (209) 455-7652.

*POUIER, TERRY
(hospital director)
Affiliation: Fort Yates PHS Indian Hospital, P.O. Box J, Fort Yates, ND 58538 (701) 854-3831.

POWERS, MARLA N. 1938-
(anthropologist)
Born January 8, 1938, Cranston, R.I. *Education*: Brooklyn College, C.U.N.Y., BA, 1973; Rutgers University, MA, 1979, PhD (Anthropology; dissertation: Oglala Women in Myth, Ritual, and Reality), 1982. *Principal occupation*: Anthropologist. *Home address*: 74 Stillwell Rd., Kendall Park, NJ 08824. *Affiliation*: Visiting research associate, Institute for Research on Women, Rutgers University, New Brunswick, N.J., 1983-. *Other professional posts*: Associate editor, Powwow Trails: American Indians, Past and Present, Somerset, NJ, 1964-66; consultant, Title IV Bilingual Health Program, Pine Ridge Indian Reservation, Summer, 1976; consultant, Psychiatric Nursing Program, University of South Dakota and USPHS satellite program, Oglala Sioux Community, Pine Ridge Reservation, Summer, 1976; consultant, Lakota Culture Camp (program evaluation for Dept. of Special Education, State of SD), Pine Ridge Indian Reservation, Summer, 1980; member of thesis committee in

Psychiatric Nursing, Rutgers University--thesis title: An Exploratory Study of Mentoring Relationships Among Indian Women in the Profession of Nursing, 1982; also thesis committee in anthropology--Ph.D. thesis entitled: Comanche Belief and Ritual, 1985. *Memberships*: American Anthropological Association; Society for Medical Anthropology; Society for Visual Anthropology; American Folklore Society; American Ethnological Society; Philadelphia Anthropological Society; Society for Ethnomusicology; Nebraska State Historical Society; American Dance Therapist Association; American Craftsman's Council; Actor's Equity; American Federation of Television and Radio Artists. Fieldwork: Pine Ridge, South Dakota, Oglala (Sioux), also various tribes of New Mexico, Arizona, Oklahoma and Wyoming; urban U.S. "I have done extensive anthropological research among the Oglala Lakota on the Pine Ridge Indian Reservation in South Dakota. A major part of the research focused on native subsistence, food procurement, preparation, storage, distribution, and nutrition. I also studied native therapeutic techniques, particularly treatment of psychosomatic disorders." *Awards, honors*: Wenner-Gren Foundation Grant-in-aid, Summer, 1980 (field research on the relationship of Oglala traditional women's roles to social structure); National Endowment for the Humanities, Research Assistant on Oglala Music and Dance, Sept. 1980 - Aug. 1982, Jan. 1983 - Dec. 1983; Douglass Fellows Grant for Research on photographs of American Indian women, Spring, 1983 & 1984; National Endowment for the Humanities, Planning Grant: principal investigator, Lakota Women: A Photographic Retrospective, Jan. 1985 - Dec. 1985; Minnesota Historical Society, grant for field research on Lakota medicine, Summer, 1985. *Interests*: "American Indians, particularly Northern Plains, urban U.S.; intercultural health care systems; anthropology of gender, medicine, art, and dance. Dance: have appeared in numerous Broadway and off-Broadway shows; on major network television shows; taught dance. American Indian art: have studied traditional crafts among the Sioux and Comanches and am proficient in various techniques of American Indian beadwork, quillwork, and ribbonwork." Papers presented: Images of American Indian Women: Myth and Reality, Rome, Italy, 1984, tour in West Germany-1985; Symbols in Contemporary Oglala Art, Vienna, Austria; Workshop on American Indian Music and Dance (with William K. Powers), Budapest, Hungary, 1985; Stereotyping American Indians, Cologne, West Germany, 1985; Native American Motherhood: A View From the Plains, Rutgers University, 1985; among others. *Published works*: Co-editor, Lakota Wicozanni-Ehank'ehan na Lehanl (Lakota Health Traditional and Modern), three volumes plus teacher's guide (Oglala Sioux Community College, 1977); Metaphysical Aspects of an Oglala Food System, in Food and the Social Order (Russell Sage Foundation, 1984); Oglala Women: Myth, Ritual, and Reality (University of Chicago Press, 1986); Putting on the Dog: Ceremoniousness in an Oglala Stew, with William K. Powers, in Natural History (American Museum of Natural History-in press); Lakota Foods, with William K. Powers (in preparation); Lakota Medicine (Minnesota Historical Society Press-in preparation).

*POWERS, W. ROGERS
(professor, dept. head)
Affiliation: Dept. of Alaskan native Studies, University of Alaska, Dept. of Anthropology, 310 Eielson Bldg., Fairbanks, AK 99775 (907) 474-7288.

POWERS, WILLIAM K. 1934-
(professor of anthropology, journalist)
Born July 31, 1934, St. Louis, Mo. *Education*: Brooklyn College, BA, 1971; Wesleyan University, MA (Anthropology; thesis: Yuwipi Music in Cultural Context), 1972; University of Pennsylvania, PhD (Anthropology; dissertation: Continuity and Change in Oglala Religion). *Principal occupation*: Professor of anthropology, journalist. *Home address*: 74 Stillwell Rd., Kendall Park, NJ 08824. *Affiliations*: Associate editor, American Indian Tradition, 1960-62; editor and publisher, Powwow Trails, 1964-66; consulting editor, American Indians Then and Now Series (G.P. Putnam's Sons), 1968-; instructor, North American Indian music and dance, Wesleyan University, 1971-72; teaching fellow, 1972-73; lecturer, 1973-77, (North American Indians), University of Pennsylvania; visiting lecturer, assistant professor and acting chairman, Dept. of Anthropology, Rutgers University, New Brunswick, NJ, 1974-. *Fieldwork*: Primarily among the Oglala Sioux, Pine Ridge, South Dakota, 1966-; also various tribes in NM, AZ, OK and WY. Grants and fellowships: Research in American Indian religion, linguistics, and music, American Philosophical Society, 1966, '67, '77; among others. *Awards, honors*: Award of Excellence in Juvenile Literature, NJ State Teachers of English, 1972, '73; Faculty Merit Award, Rutgers University, 1977; among others. *Memberships*: American Anthropological Association; Society for Applied Anthropology; Washington Anthropological Society; Philadelphia Anthropological Society; Society for Ethnomusicology; Indian Rights Association. Interests: "North American Indian studies--historical and contemporary Indian affairs; urban U.S.; social organization; comparative religion; history of anthropology; sociolinguistics; ethnomusicology; culture change." *Published works*: Indian Dancing and Costumes (G.P. Putnam's Sons, 1966); Young Brave (For Children, Inc., 1967); Crazy Horse and Custer (For Children, Inc., 1968); Indians of the Northern Plains (G.P. Putnam's Sons, 1969); The Modern Sioux: Reservation Systems and Social Change (University of Nebraska Press, 1970); Indians of the Southern Plains (G.P. Putnam's Sons, 1971); Continuity and Change in the American Family, with Marla N. Powers (Dept. of HEW); Indians of the Great Lakes (G.P. Putnam's Sons, 1976); co-author, Lakota Wicozani - Ehank'ehan na Lehanl (Indian Health- Traditional and Modern), 1976; Oglala Religion (University of Nebraska Press, 1977); Lakota Foods, with Marla N. Powers (in preparation); numerous papers, articles in scholarly journals, notes, book reviews, abstracts, etc.

POWLESS, DAVID (*Lani Kuhlaha'wis*) (Oneida) 1943-
(business executive)
Born May 29, 1943, Ottawa, Ill. *Education*: University of Oklahoma, 1961-62; University of Illinois, BS, 1966. *Principal occupation*: Business executive. *Home address*: 161 Sagebrush Dr., Corrales, NM 87048 (505) 897-9445. *Affiliations*: Owner & founder, Oneida Materials Co., Colorado Springs, CO., 1976-85; president & founder, ORTEK (Environmental Laboratory),

Oneida Tribe, Green Bay, WI, 1987-92; V.P. Marketing-Western Regional, Arctic Slope Regional Corp., 1992- (owned by Inupiat Eskimos). *Memberships*: Oneida Tribe; American Indian Science & Engineering Society (board of directors, 1986-90). *Awards, honors*: University of Illinois Rose Bowl Team, 1963; professional football, NY Giants, 1965, Washington Redskins, 1966; National Science grant in 1977 to research, at the Colorado School of Mines, methods for recycling iron oxide wastes produced by steel mills. This was the first NSF Grant given to an individual Native American; 1981 - SBA Award "National Innovation Advocate of the Year". *Interests*: "Training Indians to be scientists to work in tribally-owned environmental laboratories; mediation training of groups. He is committed to caring for the environment. It is his belief that this commitment is one of the duties the creator has given to all Native Americans. Currently involved with tribal economic development with Arctic Slope Joint Ventures With Tribes."

PRATT, MICHAEL E. *(Wat-Si-Mori)* (Osage) 1947-
(professor/administrator)
Born March 3, 1947, Hominy, Okla. *Education*: Utah State University, Logan, BS, 1971, MS, 1977; University of Oklahoma, PhD, 1986. *Principal occupation*: Professor/administrator. *Home address*: 223 N. Price, Hominy, OK 74035 (910) 287-2587. *Affiliations*: Coach/instructor, Pratt College, KS; instructor, University of Oklahoma, 1982-. *Community activities*: Arkansas Museum of Natural History & Science (advisor, Indians of Arkansas exhibit). *Awards, honors*: Award from Administration for Native Americans. *Interests*: "White Hair Memorial, Oklahoma Historical Society; developed curriculum for preservation of Osage language, cultural retention courses for Osage people." *Published works*: Stenotyping of the American Indian (Utah State, 1978); Osage Kinship (University of Oklahoma Press, 1986).

*PREGO, DAVID
(editor)
Affiliation: "Great Promise Magazine," 1103 Hatteras, Austin, TX 78753 (512) 480-9922. A quarterly journal for and about Native American children.

*PRESCOTT, LEONARD (Mdewakanton Sioux)
(casino/bingo hall CEO)
Affiliation: Mystic Lake Casino & Bingo Hall, 2400 Mystic Lake Blvd., Prior Lake, MN 55372 (800) 262-7799.

*PRETTY ON TOP, BURTON, Sr. *(Flirts With Women/Two Mornings)* (Crow) 1946-
(spiritual leader; public speaker, teacher)
Born September 17, 1946, Crow Agency, Mont. *Education*: Rocky Mt. College (Billings, MT), 1965-67; Eastern Mt. College (Billings, MT), 1969-70. *Principal occupation*: Native American spiritual leader; public speaker, teacher. *Address*: P.O. Box 0, Lodge Grass, MT 59050 (406) 638-2601 Ext. 222. *Affiliation*: Crow Tribal Council Public Relations Director, Crow Agency, MT, 1991-. *Other professional post*: Spiritual leader for Crow Catholic Parishes, 1991-. *Community activities*: Traveled for 13 years giving talks & presentations on Native spirituality, nationally & internationally; involved with social justice is-

sues, and protection of human rights. *Memberships*: Tekakwitha Conference (board of directors, 1988-93); Thanksgiving Square (Dallas, TX). *Awards, honors*: "I was one of two Native American spiritual leaders selected to represent the Native American traditions from the Western Hemisphere, at the "World Day of Prayer for Peace" held at Assisi, Italy (October, 1986); I was asked to sign a World Thanksgiving Document along with 11 other religious leaders from across the world, in 1987, at Dallas, TX; I was among 100 religious leaders honored at the "Thanksgiving Square" in Dallas (Sept., 1989); I was one of seven Native spiritual leaders asked to attend & give a presentation at the "Parliament of Worlds Religions" gathering in Chicago, IL (Sept./Oct., 1993)." *Interests*: "I am a member of the Whistling Water and Bad War Deed Clans of the Crow Nation. I am a child of the Big Lodge Clan. Among the Crow people today, we are blessed by our Creator "Akbaadaadia" in a way that is very unique; we all speak the Crow language, practice our Native spirituality, customs and traditions. We still follow and respect the 'clan' system." *Biographical sources*: Magazine articles: Theosophical Link, Sept/Dec. 1993, Vol. 5 No. 3; Time Magazine, May 10, 1993; Lily of the Mohawks magazine, Fall/Winter 1993; among others. Newspaper articles: The New York Times - Sunday, Aug. 9, 1992; The Dallas Morning News - Sunday, Oct. 4, 1992; Billings Gazette - Saturday, April 17, 1993; among others.

PRINGLE, ROBERT
(education administrator)
Affiliation: Anchorage Education Field Office, Bureau of Indian Affairs, 1675 C St., Anchorage, AK 99510 (907) 271-4115.

PRINS, HARALD E.L. 1951-
(professor)
Born September 7, 1951, Alphen a/d Rijn, The Netherlands. *Education*: University of Nijmegan, The Netherlands, 1971-76 (Doctoral-Anthropology/History); New School for Social Research (New York, NY), PhD, 1988. *Principal occupation*: Professor. *Home address*: 3301 Buffalo Rd., Manhattan, KS 66502 (913) 776-3876; 532-6865 (office). *Affiliations*: Tribal Researcher, Arrostook Band of Micmacs, Presque Island, ME, 1981-; Professor of Cultural Anthropology & American Ethnic Studies, Kansas State University, Manhattan, KS, 1990-. *Other professional post*: Consultant on ethnohistory, ethnographic film, native rights. *Community activities*: Arrostook Micmac Indian Community; Amnesty International. *Memberships*: American Anthropological Association; American Society for Ethnohistory; Society for Visual Anthropology. *Awards, honors*: Vera G. List Fellowship; Criterion Foundation Award; Maine Humanities Council Film Award; Maine Arts Commission Award; National Endowment for the Humanities Award; Columbian Quincentennial Fellowship; among others. *Interests*: Canadian Maritimes, New England, Plains, Argentine Pampas, Paraguayan Chaco, Upper Amazon, Andean Highlands, Patagonia. "As a cultural anthropologist/ethnohistorian/filmmaker, I have served the Arrostook Band of Micmacs in their quest for native rights in Maine since 1981. In 1990, I testified as expert witness in U.S. Congress, and November 26, 1991, the Band was officially recognized by the Federal Government and was awarded funding to purchase 5,000 acres of land which will serve as a landbase. The federal rec-

ognition was based on ethnographic and historical documentation which I researched and presented as tribal anthropologist for the Micmacs. My documentary film "Our Lives in Our Hands," which aired on public television and featured at numerous national and international film festivals, portrays this Micmac Indian commuity in northern Maine in their quest for survival." *Biographical sources*: Articles - "Anthropologist Aids Micmacs in Fight for Federal Recognition," in Bangor Daily News, Dec. 21, 1987; "The Micmacs of Maine: A Continuing Struggle," (by B. McBride), in R.G. Carlson, ed., "Rooted Like the Ash Trees: New England Indians and the Land," (Eagle Wing Press, 1987); "Anthropologist Believes Cultures Should Be Helped...," in Kennebec Journal, Sept. 20, 1989. *Published works*: Our Lives in Our Hands, 49 min., color 16mm/video (Documentary Educational Resources, 1985); Tribulations of a Border Tribe (University of Michigan Press, 1989); The Land of Norumbega: Exploration, Ethnography, and Cartography (University of Nebraska Press, 1993).

PROCTOR, J. HUGH
(organization president)
Affiliation: Maryland Indian Heritage Society, P.O. Box 905, Waldorf, MD 20601 (301) 888-1566.

PROPHET, SU ZANNA K.
(Shawnee/Delaware) 1951-
(city management)
Born in 1951 in Tulsa, Okla. *Education*: Oklahoma State University, BA, 1973; Haskell Indian Junior College, AA (Art), 1978; University of Kansas, MA, 1979, MPA, 1985; University of Bridgeport, CT, BFA (Painting), 1981. *Principal occupation*: City management. *Home address*: RR 1, Box 137, First, NE 68358 (402) 791-5898. *Affiliations*: Budget Research Analyst, Odessa, TX, 1983-89; Administrative Assistant to City Manager, Urbandale, IA, 1989-.

*PROULX, JOANNE
(IHS-chief)
Affiliation: Nutrition & Dietetics Training Branch, Indian Health Service, P.O. Box 5558, 1700 Ceriilos Rd., Bldg. #5, Santa Fe, NM 87502 (505) 262-1232.

*PROVO, DAN
(museum curator)
Affiliation: Museum of the Great Plains, P.O. Box 68, 601 Ferris Ave., Lawton, OK 73502.

PRUCHA, FRANCIS PAUL 1921
(professor of history emeritus)
Born January 4, 1921, River Falls, Wis. *Education*: River Falls State College, BS, 1941; University of Minnesota, MA, 1947; Harvard University, PhD, 1950; St. Louis University, 1952-54; St. Mary's College, STL, 1958. *Principal occupation*: Professor of history emeritus. *Address*: Dept. of History, Marquette University, Milwaukee, WI 53233. *Affiliations*: Society of Jesus, 1950; ordained priest, 1957; professor of history, 1960-88, professor emeritus, 1988-, Marquette University, Milwaukee, WI. *Military service*: U.S. Army Air Force, 1942-46. *Memberships*: American Historical Association; Organization of American Historians; State Historical Society of Wisconsin (board of curators, 1971-78); Western History Association (council, 1972-78, 1983-85, president, 1983); Milwaukee County Historical Society (board of direc-

tors, 1964-81, president, 1976-78). *Published works*: Broadax and Bayonet (State Historical Society of Wisconsin, 1953); Army Life on the Western Frontier (University of Oklahoma Press, 1958); American Indian Policy in the Formative Years (Harvard University Press, 1962); Guide to Military Posts of the U.S., 1789-1895 (State Historical Society of Wisconsin, 1964); The Sword of the Republic (Macmillan, 1969); Indian Peace Medals in American History (State Historical Society of Wisconsin, 1971); The Indians in American History (Holt, Rinehart & Winston, 1971); Americanizing the American Indians: Writings by the Friends of the Indians 1880-1900 (Harvard University Press, 1973); Documents of the United States Indian Policy (University of Nebraska Press, 1975); American Indian Policy in Crisis: Christian Reformers and the Indian, 1865-1900 (University of Oklahoma Press, 1976); A Bibliographical Guide to the History of Indian-White Relations in the U.S. (University of Chicago Press, 1977); United States Indian Policy: A Critical Bibliography (Indiana University Press, 1977); The Churches and the Indian Schools, 1888-1912 (University of Nebraska Press, 1979); editor, Cherokee Removal: The William Penn Essays and Other Writings, by Jeremiah Evarts (University of Tennessee Press, 1981); Indian Policy in the United States: Historical Essays (University of Nebraska Press, 1981); Indian-White Relations in the United States: A Bibliography of Works Published, 1975-1980 (University of Nebraska Press, 1982); The Great Father: The United States Government and the American Indians, 2 vols. (University of Nebraska Press, 1984); The Indians in American Society: From the Revolutionary War to the Present (University of California Press, 1985); Handbook for Research in American History (University of Nebraska Press, 1987); Atlas of American Indian Affairs (University of Nebraska Press, 1990); American Indian Treaties: The History of a Political Anomaly (University of California Press, 1994).

*PRYOR, WILLIAM KEITH *(Wi li ha ma)*
(United Lumbee/Cherokee/Choctaw) 1958-
(insurance)
Born June 16, 1958, Edenton, N.C. *Home address*: 3013 W. Collins, Corsicana, TX 75110 (903) 872-9080. *Military service*: U.S. Marine Corps, 1975-78. *Memberships*: Chief of the Golden Hawk Warrior Society (Cougar Clan), 1993-; American Indian Veteran's Society of North Texas, 1993-. *Awards, honors*: President's Club, Washington National Insurance Co. *Interests*: Indian craft work such as beading; also straight dancer.

*PUCKETT, AL (Cherokee) 1926-
(farmer)
Born July 15, 1926, Cunningham, Ky. *Home address*: 6365 Bethel Ch. Rd., Kevil, KY 42053 (502) 462-3210. *Other professional post*: Private contractor, Union Carbide, Atomic Enrichment Electrical Energy, Inc. *Military service*: U.S. Navy 1941-45, Shipfitter, 3rd Class (Atlantic Campaign, Pacific Campaign Medal, Victory Medal). *Community activities*: Snake River Alliance; Coalition for Health Concern; Military Production Network. *Interests*: Environmental concerns. "(I) participated in production of television program "nuclear shame"; featured in TV program, "Protest at Paducah Gaseous Defusion Plant"; featured in TV program, "Back to Basics."

PUEBLA, MARGARET J.
(school supt.)
Affiliation: St. Stephens Indian School, P.O. Box 345, St. Stephen, WY 82524 (307) 856-4147.

PULLAR, GORDON L. (Koniag) 1944-
(association president)
Born January 22, 1944, Bellingham, Wash. *Education*: Western Washington University, BA, 1973; University of Washington, MPA (Tribal Administration Program - course of study designed to meet the contemporary management needs of Native American corporations, organizations, and tribal governments as well as federal and state agencies dealing with Native American issues and programs), 1983. *Principal occupation*: Association president. *Address*: Kodiak Area Native Association, P.O. Box 172, Kodiak, AK 99615 (907) 486-5725. *Affiliations*: Rewind operator/supervisor, Georgia Pacific Corp., Bellingham, WA, 1963-79; business analyst/marketing specialist, Small Tribes Organization of Western Washington, Sumner, 1979-81; associate editor, Nations magazine (National Communications, Inc., Seattle, 1981; owner/publisher, Kodiak Times, Kodiak, AK 1983-85; president/executive director, Kodiak Area Native Association, 1983-. *Other professional post*: Assistant editor, business editor, The Indian Voice (Small Tribes Organization of Western Wash.), 1979-81. *Community activities*: Volunteer work in social programs involving Native Americans: Washington State Dept. of Social and Health Services, Whatcom County Detoxification Center, and Whatcom County Juvenile Probation Dept.; Northwest Indian News Association (board of directors, 1979-81; Governor's Minority and Women's Business Development Advisory Council (appointed by Governor of State of Washington, 1980-81; Native American Business Alliance (board of directors, vice president-publicity chairman, 1981-83; Alaska Regional Energy Association (board of directors, 1984-85; Kodiak Area State Parks Advisory Board, 1983; Alaska Federation of Natives, Inc. (board of directors, 1983-). *Memberships*: Koniag, Inc. (regional Native corporation); Leisnoi, Inc, Woody Island ANCSA Corp.; National Congress of American Indians; American Society for Public Administration (South Central Alaska Chapter).

*PURDY, JOHN 1949-
(university professor)
Born January 6, 1949, Salem, Oreg. *Education*: Western Oregon State College (Monmouth, OR), BA, 1978; University of Idaho, MA, 1980; Arizona State University, PhD, 1986. *Principal occupation*: University professor. *Home address*: 5334 Mosquito Lake Rd., Deming, WA 98244 (206) 650-3243 (work). *Affiliation*: Western Washington University, Bellingham, WA, 1991-. *Other professional post*: Associate editor (for fiction and Native American poetry) from Calapooya College, 1988-. *Military service*: U.S. Naval Air, 1968-72. *Memberships*: Association for the Study of American Indian Literatures (editor of newsletter, 1988-; executive board, 1990-); American Literature Association; Modern Language Association. *Awards, honors*: Fulbright Lecturer, Universitat Mannheim, West Germany, 1989-90; Fulbright Lecturer, University of Canterbury, New Zealand, Fall 1993; Director, National Endowment for the Humanities, Summer Seminar for School Teachers, 1993. *Interests*: Degrees in American Literature, with emphasis in Native American Literatures. *Biographical*

source: Word Ways: The Novels of D'Arcy McNickle (University of Arizona Press, 1990).

PURICH, DONALD J.
(centre director/instructor)
Affiliation: University of Saskatchewan, Native Law Centre, Diefenbaker Centre, Saskatoon, Saskatchewan S7N 3S9 (306) 966-6189.

*PYEATTE, SHARON 1949-
(counselor; coordinator
of Indian education)
Born March 11, 1949, Fayette, Mo. *Education*: University of Missouri, BS, 1972; University of Colorado, MA, 1987. *Principal occupation*: Counselor; coordinator of Indian education. *Home address*: 8951 S. Sandusky Ave., Tulsa, OK 74137 (918) 299-4411 ext. 213 (work). *Affiliations*: Assistant program director, College Board, Denver, CO, 1989-91; coordinator, Indian Education, Jenks Public School, Jenks, OK, 1993-. *Military service*: U.S. Naval Reserve, 1967-71.

Q

QOYAWAYMA, AL (HOPI) 1938-
(consultant/artist)
Born in 1938, Los Angeles, Calif. *Education*: California State Polytechnic University, BSME, 1961; University of Southern California, MSME, 1966; Arizona State University, 1979-85 (Graduate Studies in archaeological ceramic materials, painting passim); Scottsdale Artists School, 1990 and 1991 (Sculptural Studies); Scottsdale Community College, 1981-91 (Studies in Drawing, passim). *Principal occupation*: Potter & sculptor. *Address*: P.O. Box 1992, Scottsdale, AZ 85252 . *Affiliations*: Project engineer, Litton Systems, Woodland Hills, CA, 1961-71; Manager, Environmental Services Dept., Salt River Project, Phoenix, AZ, 1971-90; investigator, Smithsonian Institute, 1982-present (with a 4-man research group identifying original clay sources and pottery migration for ancient Hopi Sikyatki potter); political and technical consultant, Hopi Tribe, Kykotsmovi, AZ, 1989-91. *Community activities*: Board of Directors, The Heard Museum, Phoenix, AZ; Publication Board of Directors, "Winds of Change," American Indian Science & Engineering Society, 1986-; judge at various art shows. *Memberships*: American Indian Science & Engineering Society (co-founder & first chairperson); Institute of American Indian & Alaska Native Culture & Arts (Board of Trustees, 1988-; vice-chairperson of the Board; chairperson, Presidential Search Committee, 1989; member, Developmental Committee); Institute of Electrical & Electronic Engineers. *Awards, honors*: Popovi Da Award, Memorial Award, Scottsdale National Indian Arts Exhibition, 1976; recipient, AISES, Ely S. Parker Award for Engineering Achievement & Service to the American Indian Community, 1986; University of Colorado, Regents' Honorary Degree of Doctor of Humane Letters, Boulder, May 1986; California Polytechnic University, San Luis Obispo, Alumnus of the Year, 1989; G.B. Grinnell American Indian Children's Education Foundation: Annual Al Qoyawayma Award for Excellence in Science and Engineering and the Arts or Cultural Contribution, established 1990; One of twenty "vision makers" invited, "A Vision for the Third Millennium," United Nations-The Club of Rome and UN Environmental Program, New York, NY

1991; appointed (by the Arizona Governor) Commissioner, Arizona Commission on the Arts, 1991; chairperson - Arizona Design/Public Art Panel, 1991. *Interests*: Al is an artist-potter in the tradition of his Hopi culture. He attributes his pottery training to working with his aunt Polingaysi E. Qoyawayma (aka Elizabeth Q. White), a noted Hopi potter, educator, and writer, who died in 1990. His pottery is known and collected throughout the U.S. Since 1989, he has produced five bronze sculpture series. In June of 1990, Al left his management position in the utility industry to pursue his art career full time. Enjoys travel & research. *Selected Exhibits*: ACA American Indian Art, New York, One-Man Show, 1982; "Night of the First Americans," Kennedy Center, Washington, DC, 1982; Smithsonian Institute of Natural History, Washington, DC, First Showing of Contemporary American Indian Art, 1982-83; Gallery 10, Scottsdale, annual exhibits, 1980-88; "Al Qoyawayma: A Retrospective," Taylor Museum, Colorado Springs, CO, Feb.-April 1985; Santa Fe Indian Market, 1978-93; Arizona State Museum, University of Arizona, Tucson, "Yellow Ware Road," 1990-94. *Selected Publications*: Generations in Clay - Pueblo Pottery of the American Southwest, by Dittert & Plog (Northlands Press, 1980); Santa Fe Design, by Baca & Deats (Crown Publishing, 1990 (3 color photos & story); "Recipient of Tradition," by Barbara Cortright, in Southwest Profile, Aug. 1985 (critical essay, photos); Art of Clay, by Lee M. Cohen, pp. 78-85 (Clearlight Publishers, 1993). *Selected Videos*: 1980 - Generations in Clay - Pueblo Pottery of the American Southwest, voice-over by Al Qoyawayma; 1985 - 30 minute Interview, Charles Loloma & Al Qoyawayma, PBS, Santa Fe, NM; 1988 - "Taking Tradition to Tomorrow," segment, in AISES Video; 1988 - Victor Masayesva, director & producer: Hopi film on ancient Hopi ceramics project, Smithsonian Institute, Washington, DC; 1989 - Jerry and Lois Jacka, "Beyond Tradition," four segments (video won two Rocky Mountain Emmy Awards; 1991 - contract for video consulting: Media Resource Associates; future video segment on "Indian America," PBS TV, Washington, DC, anticipated release, 1992. *Lectures*: Phoenix Art Museum, 1981; Arizona State University, 1985; Taylor Museum, 1985; University of Colorado, 1987; Scottsdale Historic Society, 1987; Museum of Northern Arizona, Flagstaff, 1988; Heard Museum, Phoenix, AZ ("Between Two Worlds: Native American Professional Today,", 1991; Maori and South Pacific Arts Commission, Fullbright Fellowship, cultural exchange (one month), New Zealand, May 1991.

*QUARTZ, KATHERINE MARIE
(Cloud Woman) (Walker River Paiute) 1963-
(writer, volunteer, floral designer)
Born January 14, 1963, Portland, Ore. *Education*: Western Nevada Community College (Fallon, NV) (2 years); Clackamas Community College (Oregon City, OR) (1 year). *Principal occupation*: Writer, volunteer, floral designer. *Home address*: 6640 Canterbury Dr., Gladstone, OR 97027 (503) 654-7473. *Community activities*: Chairperson, Native American Intergroup, Schurz, NV, 1992-; volunteer, Native American Youth Conference, Portland State University, 1994; volunteer, Clackamas County Gang Task Force, 1994. *Memberships*: Native Writers Circle; National Alcoholic Anonymous for Native Americans, Las Vegas, NV (committee). *Awards, honors*: Award from Canada Drug Strat-

Biographies

egy , Nechi Institute for campaign in U.S. for National Addictions Awareness Week; speaker/presentation on cultural roots and adoption search at the 1992 Healing Our Spirit World-wide Conference for Indigenous People, Edmonton, Alberta, Canada; speaker on cultural values, presentation entitled, "The Healing Journey Within," at the Women's InterTribal Conference, Reno, NV, 1993. *Interests*: "I feel by volunteering I can devote my time and services to the youth, and also be a role model so they may follow. Speaking and giving presentations at various events. *Work in progress*: The Secret of Rose (expected 1995).

*QUASULA, TED
(BIA division director)
Affiliation: Bureau of Indian Affairs, Division of Law Enforcement, 1849 C St., NW, MS: 4140-MIB, Washington, DC 20240 (202) 208-5786.

*QUERRY, RON (Choctaw of Oklahoma) 1943-
(writer)
Born March 22, 1943, Washington, D.C. *Education*: University of New Mexico PhD, 1975. *Principal occupation*: Writer. *Address*: P.O. Box 65975, Tucson, AZ 85728 (602) 323-6885. *Past professional post*: Former professor, University of Oklahoma. *Military service*: U.S. Marine Corps, 1961-63. Memberships: Native Writers Circle of the Americas; PEN; Tucson Pima County Arts Commission (board of directors, 1994-97). *Awards, honors*: Mountains & Plains Booksellers Award & Border Regional Library Association Southwest Book Award (both for The Death of Bernadette Lefthand); Writer-in-Residence, Amerind Foundation (Dragoon, AZ). *Published works*: Growing Old At Willie Nelson's Picnic (Texas A&M University Press, 1957); The Death of Bernadette Lefthand (Red Crane Books, 1993); Native Americans Struggle for Equality (Rourke, 1993); I See By My Get-Up (University of Oklahoma Press, 1994).

*QUETON, HILTON G. (Kiowa/Seminole) 1951-
(administrator)
Born February 25, 1951, Lawton, Okla. *Education*: Community College of the Air Force, AAS, 1979; Wayland Baptist College, BSOE, 1980. *Principal occupation*: Administrator. *Home address*: 5640 Wedgeworth, Fort Worth, TX 76133 (817) 263-6131. *Affiliation*: Executive director, American Indian Center, Grand Prairie, TX, 1991-. *Military service*: U.S. Air Force, 1971-81, E-5 Rank (Staff Sergeant). *Community activities*: Former president, American Indian Chamber of Commerce of Texas; Headsman, Texas Kiowa Tia-Piah Society; member of Kiowa Black Leggings Society. *Memberships*: Texas Commission on Alcohol & Drug Abuse (member, Minority Affairs Advisory Council); Texas Rehabilitation Comm. (American Indian Task Force). *Interests*: Singer of Kiowa ceremonial songs.

QUETONE, JOE A. (Kiowa) 1946-
(executive director)
Born December 27, 1946, Lawton, Okla. *Education*: Florida State University, BA, 1973. *Principal occupation & Affiliation*: Executive director, Florida Governor's Council on Indian Affairs, Inc., Tallahassee, FL, 1978-. *Address*: P.O. Box 6234, Tallahassee, FL 32301 (904) 488-0730 (office). *Other professional posts*: Florida Supreme Court Racial and Ethnic Bias Study Commission Member, 1989-91; White House Con-

ference on Library & Information Service, Delegate, 1991. *Military service*: U.S. Army, Medical Corpsman, 1969-71 (Commendation from Commanding General, William Beamont, General Hospital for Oustanding Service and Esprit De Corps, 1971). *Community activities*: Florida Weatherization Policy Advisory Committee, 1978-; Florida Folklife News, Resource on Florida Indians, 1978-; Leon County School Volunteers, 1976-; WFSU-FM Community Advisory Board, 1982-. *Memberships*: National Indian Education Assn; Governor's Interstate Indian Council; National Congress of American Indians; Kiowa Gourd Clan; Kiowa Black Leggings Society. *Awards, honors*: Prominent People in Florida Government, 1980; Outstanding Service Award - Indian and Native American Employment and Training Coalition for Continuing Leadership and Dedicated Service to the Indian and Native American Community, 1983; The Triangle Award in Recognition of Performance and Achievements - Tau Kappa Epsilon International Fraternity, 1983; Who's Who in Government Services, 1990.

QUINONEZ, JUDITH
(attorney)
Affiliation: Director, Native American Legal Service Program of New York City, American Indian Law Alliance, American Indian Community House, 404 Lafayette St., New York, NY 10001.

*QUINTAL, MARGARET S.
(editor)
Affiliation: Co-editor, "The Bulletin," Institute of American Indian Studies, U. of South Dakota, 414 E. Clark St., Vermillion, SD 57069 (605) 677-5209.

*QUINTANA, ANDREW (Cochiti Pueblo)
(Pueblo governor)
Affiliation: Cochiti Pueblo Council, P.O. Box 70, Cochiti, NM 87072 (505) 465-2244.

QUINTANILLA, OSCAR ARZE
(institute director)
Affiliation: Inter-American Indian Institute, Av. Insurgentes Sur 1690, Col. Florida, Mexico D.F. 01030 Mexico (905) 660-0007.

*QUIRK, PAT
(director-Indian health center)
Affiliation: Lower Brule PHS Indian Health Center, Lower Brule, SD 57548 (605) 473-5544.

*QUIROGA, WILLIAM
(executive director)
Affiliation: Tucson Indian Center, 131 E. Broadway, Box 2307, Tucon, AZ 85702 (602) 884-7131.

*QUISNO, PATRICIA
(administrative officer-Indian hospital)
Affiliation: Fort Belknap PHS Indian Hospital, Harlem, MT 59526 (406) 353-2651.

*QUISTGAARD, JOHN
(dept. director)
Affiliation: Native American Stduies Dept., Bemidji State University, Bemidji, MN 56601 (218) 755-2032.

*QUITITQUIT, LUWANA
(executive director)
Affiliation: Ya-Ka-Ama Indian Ed. & Develop, Inc., 6215 Eastside Rd., Forestville, CA 95436 (707) 887-1541.

R

RADULOVICH, MARY LOU FOX
(foundation director)
Affiliation: Ojibwe Cultural Foundation, Excelsior Post Office, West Bay, Ontario, Canada P0P 1G0 (705) 377-4902.

RAGSDALE, NANCY
(organization contact)
Affiliation: South Eastern Michigan Indians, Inc., P.O. Box 861, Warren, MI 48090 (313) 756-1350.

RAIN, WALTER
(Indian band chief)
Affiliation: Paul Indian Band, Box 89, Duffield, Alberta, Canada T0E 0N0 (403) 892-2691.

*RAMBEAU, DAVID L.
(executive director)
Affiliation: United American Indian Involvement, 118 Winston St., Los Angeles, CA 90013 (213) 625-2565.

RAMIRIZ, RAYMOND
(museum supt.)
Affiliation: Ysleta Del Sur Pueblo Museum, P.O. Box 17579, Tigua Indian Reservation, El Paso, TX 79917 (915) 859-7913.

RAMOS, DIANA S. (Yaqui/Cherokee) 1949-
(secretary)
Born June 5, 1949, Corpus Christi, Tex. *Principal occupation*: Secretary. *Home address*: 6407 Starstreak Dr., Austin, TX 78745 (512) 444-6451. *Community activities*: American Indian Resource & Education Coalition (treasurer); Native American Parent Committee; Boy Scouts of America; Girl Scouts of America; PTA.

*RANGEN, NEIL
(museum supt.)
Affiliation: Hauberg Indian Museum, Black Hawk State Park, 1510 46th Ave., Rock Island, IL 61201 (309) 788-9536.

*RANIIREZ-SHLWEGNAABI, BEN
(center director)
Affiliation: Native American Center, 012 Old Main, UW-Stevens Point, Stevens Point, WI 54481 (715) 346-2004.

RANSOM, JAY ELLIS 1914-
(author, teacher, technical writer, editor)
Born April 12, 1914, Missoula, Mont. *Education*: University of Washington, BA, 1935; University of Washington Graduate School, 1936-41 (PhD level, Anthropology); UCLA, MA (Education), PhD level Psychology, 1949. *Principal occupation*: Author, teacher, technical writer, editor. *Home address*: 1821 East 9th St., The Dalles, OR 97058 (503) 296-9414. *Affiliation*: President & executive secretary, Western America Institute for Exploration, Inc., The Dalles, OR, 1954-. *Other professional posts*: Chief technical writer/editor, aerospace industry, 1949-70; freelance magazine feature writer, 1936-; news correspondent for various newspapers, 1936-; occasional lecturer to organizations. *Field linguistics researches*: Flathead Salish, Western Montana, summer of 1934; Duwamish Salish, Western Washington, 1936; other Northwest languages & cultures between 1934-41 include Chinook jargon, Sahaptin, Chinook-Kwakiutl, Tlingit; Fox Island Aleut. Taught four years, 1936-40, in the

Alaskan Indian Service schools;1936-37 at Nikolski, Umnak, Alaska. In 1974, Dr. Michael Krauss, chairman of the linguistics department at the University of Alaska, requested Ransom's Aleut materials to assist them and the Alaska State Department of Education in developing native Aleut teaching materials comparable to what they had initiated two years earlier for Eskimo native schools; Kutchin Dene Acculturation: Between 1938 & 1940 the Indian Service assigned me to teach in the native school at Stevens Village, on the central Yukon River 100 miles north of Fairbanks; Paleo-Indian Studies, 1975-91, extensively worked on studies of the Bighorn Medicine Wheel in the northern Wyoming Bighorn Mountains. *Awards, honors*: Blood Brother, Flathead Tribe. *Interests*: Photography, writing, educating. *Biographical sources*: Contemporary Authors; Who's Who in America. *Published works*: "A bibliography of 76 papers (16 university research journals) and in popular, general distribution magazines illustrated with my own photography, 1935-84. All in some way incorporate aspects of anthropology, Native American linguistics, primitive folklore, ethnology, or Indian education and are extracted from a more complete bibliography of some 400 titles archived in the Suzzallo Library, University of Washington. Not included are an estimated 3,000 news stories, editorials, and features under my byline written in my journalism career." Also many books & monographs, including: Morphology of Fox Island Aleut; Phonology & Morphology of Duwamish Salish; Notes & Morphology of Flathead Salish; Aleut Gossip Texts; Fox Island Aleut Diaries & Literature; Duwamish Mythological Texts; Anthropology & Native American Linguistics at the University of Washington, 1934-41 (Suzzalo Library, U of WA, Seattle, 1982); Archaeolinguistics & Paleoethnography of Ancient Rock Structures in Western North America (Western America Institute for Exploration, 1984); Big Horn Medicine Wheel--The Birth and Death of Humanity (Yellowstone Printing & Publishing, Cody, WY, 1992); Collected Writings About the Fox Island Aleut Peoples of Alaska, 1993.

RANSOM, JOSEPHINE
(museum director)
Affiliation: Chieftains Museum, 501 Riverside Parkway, Rome, GA 30162 (404) 291-9494.

RANVILLE, STIRLING
(director-Indian centre)
Affiliation: Indian & Metis Friendship Centre, 239 Magnus Ave., Winnipeg, Manitoba, Canada R2W 2B6.

RAPHAEL, JOSEPH C. (Chippewa)
(tribal chairperson)
Affiliation: Grand Traverse Band Tribal Council, P.O. Box 118, Suttons Bay, MI 49682 (616) 271-3538.

RATION, NORMAN (Laguna-Navajo)
(president-board of directors)
Affiliation: National Indian Youth Council, 318 Elm, SE, Albuquerque, NM 87102 (505) 247-2251.

RAVE, AUSTIN JERALD (Minneconjou Sioux) 1946-
(artist)
Born August 5, 1946, Cheyenne River Sioux Reservation, S.D. *Education*: Institute of American Indian Arts, Santa Fe, NM, 1964-66; San

Francisco Art Institute, 1966-67; Engineering Drafting School, Denver, CO, 1970-72. *Principal occupation*: Artist. *Home address*: P.O. Box 631, Eagle Butte, SD 57625. *Other professional posts*: Draftsman, technical illustrator. *Awards, honor*: Numerous awards for art. *Biographical source*: Dictionary of International Biography.

*RAVEN, FRED TIDEWATERS
(association director)
Affiliation: Indigenous Tribes Association, 1030 S. 317th St., Federal Way, WA 98003 (206) 839-5635.

*RAWLS, ROB (Inupiaq Eskimo)
(radio station manager)
Affiliation: KOTZ - 720 AM, PO. Box 78, Kotzebue, AK 99752 (907) 442-3435.

RAY, DONALD (Pomo) 1951-
(former tribal chairperson)
Born February 27, 1951, Ukiah, Calif. *Education*: Mendocino Community College (2 years); American River College (2 years); Sacramento State University (2 years). *Principal occupation*: Former tribal chairperson. *Address*: P.O. Box 488, Hopland, CA 95449. *Affiliations*: Central California Policy Committee, BIA, Sacramento, CA, 1976-80; Consolidated Tribal Health, Inc., Ukiah, CA, 1980-84; chairperson, Hopland Band of Pomo Indians, Hopland, CA, 1984-. *Other professional post*: Mendocino County Tribal Chairman's Association (3 years). *Military service*: U.S. Army, 1970-72 (Sergeant, Vietnam Era Veteran; Service Medal, Marksman Award-Firearms, Missile Special Training Award). *Community activities*: Mendocino County Development Corporation, 1986-89. *Interests*: "I travel extensively throughout the U.S. on tribal business and representing California tribes in congressional hearings and other representatives as appropriate for Indian people. I am presently implementing a "League of Indian Voters"."

RAY, FRANCES
(Indian band chief)
Affiliation: Flying Post Indian Band, Box 937, Nipigon, Ontario, Canada P0T 2J0 (807) 886-2443.

RAYMOND, MARGARET PEAKE
(Oklahoma Cherokee) 1941-
(administrator)
Born June 22, 1941, Tahlequah, Okla. *Education*: Northeastern State College (Tahlequah, OK), BS, 1963; University of Oklahoma, MSW, 1974. *Principal occupation*: Administration. *Address*: 2520 E. 22 St., Minneapolis, MN 55406 (612) 728-2000. *Affiliations*: Owner, First Phoenix American Corp., Minneapolis, 1978-84; founder & executive director, Minnesota Indian Women's Resource Center, Minneapolis, 1984-. *Other professional posts*: Special assistant to the director, Minnesota Alcohol & Drug Authority, St. Paul, MN, 1974-77; tribal planner, Cherokee Nation of Oklahoma, 1976-77; National Advisory Council on Drug Abuse, 1980-84; field instructor, University of Minnesota, School of Social Work, 1990-. *Community activities*: United Way of Minneapolis Area. *Memberships*: Child Welfare League of America (Chemical Dependency Commission); Minnesota Board of Social Workers; American Indian Business Development Corporation; Hennepin County Foster Care Re-Design Commission; Healthy Nations Advisory Committee to Robert Woods Johnson Foundation, Minnesota Women's Eco-

nomic Roundtable, 1994; Governor's Task Force on Housing, 1994. *Award*: "Resourceful Women's Award 1992; Jesse Bernard Award, Center for Women Policy Studies, 1992; Minneapolis Leadership Award, 1992; People of Phillips Leadership, 1994."

*RAYMOND, THOMAS
(education management)
Affiliation: Crazy Horse School, P.O. Box 260, Wanblee, SD 57577 (605) 462-6511.

REAL BIRD, HENRY LEE (*Timber Leader*)
(Crow) 1948-
(educator)
Born July 24, 1948, Crow Agency, Mont. *Education*: Montana State University, BS, 1971; Eastern Montana College, MEd. *Principal occupation*: Educator. *Address*: P.O. Box 5, Garryowen, MT 59031 (406) 638-7211 (work). *Other professional post*: Boss of a cow camp. *Memberships*: American Indian Higher Education Consortium; Crow Tobacco Society; Native American Church. *Interests*: "I've taught on the Navajo, Cheyenne, and Crow Reservations. I've been asked to read my poetry from Texas, New Mexico, Colorado, Nevada & Montana. I rodeoed when I was young from amateur-pro." *Published work*: Where Shadows Are Born (Guildhall, 1990).

REASON, JAMIE TAWODI
(Southeastern Cherokee) 1947-
(carver/painter)
Born March 11, 1947, Muncie, Ind. *Principal occupation*: Owner/manager, Sacred Earth Studio, Mastic Beach, NY, 1980- (Native American art studio). *Home address*: 197 Long Fellow Dr., Mastic Beach, NY 11951 (516) 399-4539. *Military service*: U.S. Air Force, 1966 (A/3/C; Vietnam Era Veteran; National Defense Expert Marksman; Air Police). *Memberships*: Indian Arts & Crafts Association; Vietnam Era Veterans Inter-Tribal Association; Ani-Yvwiya Association of New York. *Awards, honors*: 1988 Gallup Inter-Tribal 1st & 3rd prizes; 1989 Gallup Inter-Tribal (best in category peyote box); first place-Div. II Carved Cedar Box, Sinte Gleska Native American Art Show, 1987; 1987 Recipient of the "Elkus Award" at Gallup. *Interests*: "Even though I am self taught, I attribute my ability to my grandfather, George Reason, who was a carver. He has been an inspiration and great influence on my art and in my life. Art work exhibited at the Museum of the American Indian, The Gallery of the American Indian Community House (New York City), Red Cloud Indian Art Show, Dartmouth College; Native American Symposium at Old Westbury College (N.Y.); Rhode Island Indian Council; Red Earth, Oklahoma City; The Ceremonial, Gallup Inter-Tribal, 1986-89; Sinte Gleska Native American Art Show (Tahlequah, OK); Scottsdale All-Indian Art Show (Scottsdale, AZ); and many galleries. Mr. Reason is probably best known for his solid carved cedar feather boxes. *Biographical sources*: The Museum of the American Indian News, Sept. 24, 1983; Suffolk Life, 1983-84; Southeastern Cherokee News; American Indian Community House Newsletter, 1984; The Knoxville Journal, April 7, 1984; Daily News, April 4, 1984; New York Times, August 18, 1985; Three Village Herald, Long Island, Oct. 7, 1987 & Aug. 9, 1989; American Indian Collectibles - First Ed. 1988, by Reno; The Day, New London, CT, Jan. 29, 1988; Mandan News, Mandan, ND, Oct. 1988, Long Island Advance, April 16, 1989;

Manchester Journal, Manchester Center, VT, Sept. 20, 1989.

*REBAR, JOAN (Sac & Fox of Missouri)
(tribal chairperson)
Affiliation: Sac & Fox of Missouri Tribe, Rte. 1, Box 60, Reserve, KS 66434 (913) 742-7471.

*RECK, PAT (Pueblo)
(museum curator)
Affiliation: Indian Pueblo Cultural Center, 2401 12th St., NW, Albuquerque, NM 87102 (505) 843-7270.

RED BEAR, CHARLES (Sioux)
(school chairperson)
Affiliation: Rock Creek Day School, Bullhead, SD 57621 (605) 823-4971.

RED ELK, BONNIE
(editor)
Affiliation: Wotanin Wowapi, Fort Peck Assiniboine & Sioux Tribes, P.O. Box 1027, Poplar, MT 59255 (406) 768-5155 Ext. 2370.

RED HORSE, JOHN
(professor & director of Indian center)
Affiliation: American Indian Studies Center, University of California, Los Angeles, 3220 Campbell Hall, Los Angeles, CA 90024 (213) 825-7315.

*RED-HORSE, VALERIE (Eastern Cherokee/ Cheyenne River Sioux) 1959-
(actress, writer, spokesperson)
Born August 24, 1959, in Calif. *Education*: UCLA, BA - Theater Arts (cum laude), 1981; Lee Strasberg Theater Institute/Professional Master Class (acting). *Principal occupation*: Actress, writer, spokesperson. *Home address*: 6028 Calvin Ave., Tarzana, CA 91356 (818) 705-6972; 705-4905 (work). *Television credits*: The Dennis Miller Show; Unsolved Mysteries, Anything But Love; Santa Barbara; Divorce Court; Perry Mason; Buck James; Murder, She Wrote; among others. *Film credits*: Pow Wow Highway (voiceover); First & Ten (choreography); Return to the Country (lead dancer). *Talk show hosting/spokesperson*: First Americans (talk show hostess); Walking In Both Worlds (keynote speaker & featured performer); Trail of Tears Youth Conference (keynote speaker & featured performer); Native Americans in the Media (celebrity panelist); Women of Color: Invisible On Screen)celebrity panelist). *Theater*: Love's Labour's Lost (Rosaline-lead); Uncommon Women & Others (Kate-lead); Dreams (Lisa-lead); A Hotel Chain (Rose-lead); From Broadway With Love (lead dancer/singer). *Other professional posts*: Co-owner (with husband, Curt Mohl), Executive Specialties (a promotional advertising retail business) and Maverick Outdoor Media Group, Inc. (a corporation specializing in outdoor signage for real estate developers); lead dancer & choreographer for the Bel Air Presbyterian Liturgical Dance Co. *Community activities*: Bel Air Presbyterian Church; Youth for Christ Mentor Mom Program; The Sylmar Juvenile Hall Prison Task Force; Los Angeles Mission "City Light" (women's rehabilitation program). *Memberships*: Women in Film; Sacred Dance Guild; First Americans In the Arts; Native Writers Circle: Multicultural Minority Motion Picture Awards Board. *Awards, honors*: Keynote addresses to such organizations as The California Indian Manpower Association, and the California American Indian Women's Associa-

tion; Honoring voting committee member of the Minority Motion Picture Awards Association; recently selected to testify for a Senate Committee reviewing minorities & females in the Film & Television industry. *Interests*: Writing - recently completed original screenplay, "Lozen," which chronicles the life of a historical Apache woman warrior & the women who fought alongside her. Valerie hopes that her script will, "dispel some of the stereotypical images of the Native American female which television and film have created. As a Native American actress & writer, I am dedicated to improving and furthering the portrayal of Native American women in the media." *Biographical source*: Featured article in "Today's Christian Woman (July/Aug. 1993 issue).

RED SHE BEAR (DEANNA BARNES) (Ute) 1938-
(teacher, craftswoman)
Born June 25, 1938, Boise, Idaho. *Education*: College of the Redwoods; Humboldt State University. *Principal occupation*: Founder/manager, Red Bear Creations, Bandon, OR. *Home address*: 358 N. Lexington Ave., Bandon, OR 97411 (503) 347-9560. *Affiliations*: Founder, Indian Survival Society, Brandon, OR; founder and president, Women's Center. *Community activities*: American Red Cross (provider and secretary); Coos and Curry Area Agency on Aging (provider); Intertribal Sweat Lodge Board (officer); District 7 Sub-Area Health Advisory Council (provider); Women's Crisis Service (advisory board). *Membership*: National Indian Health Care Association (spokeswoman). *Interests*: "Making traditional quilts and blankets. Preserving our old culture and traditions is very important to me. I am an elder, pipecarrier, sweatleader, storyteller in the winter, tech survival skills in the woods, lecture on traditional uses of indigenous plants as food and medicine, and on Indian women's roles in society. I'm currently writing book, Crystal Wind Warrior, about a crystal who became a human to help the people (manuscript, 1986)."

REDAN, PERRY
(Indian band chief)
Affiliation: Cayoose Creek Indian Band, Box 484, Lillooet, British Columbia, Canada V0K 1V0 (604) 256-4136.

REDDING, THEODORE, M.D.
(chief medical officer)
Affiliation: Phoenix Area Office, Indian Health Service, 3738 M. 16th St., Suite A, Phoenix, AZ 85016 (602) 640-2052.

REDEAGLE, ANITA
(administrative officer)
Affiliation: Pawnee PHS Indian Health Center, RR 2, Box 1, Pawnee, OK 74058 (918) 762-2517.

REDEAGEL, J. PAUL
(IHS-area deputy director)
Affiliation: Indian Health Service, California Area Office, 1825 Bell St., Suite 200, Sacramento, CA 95825 (916) 978-4202.

REDSKY, LLOYD
(Indian band chief)
Affiliation: Shoal Lake #40 Indian Band, Kejick P.O., Shoal Lake, Ontario, Canada P0X 1E0 (807) 733-2315.

REED, EVA SILVER STAR (United Lumbee/ Cherokee/Choctaw) 1929-
(homemaker, national chieftain)
Born November 29, 1929, Vanita, Okla. *Principal occupation*: Home maker. *Home address*: P.O. Box 512, Fall River Mills, CA 96028 (916) 336-6701. *Affiliation*: National Chieftain, United Lumbee Nation of N.C. & America, 1983-. *Other professional posts*: Parent committee of Title IV and Johnson O'Malley Indian Education Program, Tulare-Kings Counties, CA; National Secretary, 1979-82, Head Chief, 1982-, and Grand Council member, 1979-, United Lumbee Nation of N.C. and America. *Memberships*: Native American Wolf Clan (secretary, 1977-); Chapel of Our Lord Jesus (church) Council (secretary, 1974-); United Lumbee Nation's High Eagle Warrior Society and Manitoac Medicine Society, 1979-93. *Awards, honors*: Numerous 1st & 2nd prizes for Indian bead work at the Inter-Mountain Fair, McArthur, CA; 1991 Silver Eagle Award, United Lumbee Nation. *Interests*: "I teach an Indian Beading Class each year since 1980 -- I am editor of the United Lumbee Nation Times since 1981. I do sewing, leather crafts, painting and bead work, and write articles for the paper and books. Caring for my people the United Lumbees." *Biographical sources*: Articles in the United Lumbee Nation Times. *Published works*: Compiler, Over the Cooking Fires, featuring traditional Lumbee recipes (United Lumbee Nation, 1982); Lumbee Indian Ceremonies (United Lumbee Nation, 1982); United Lumbee Nation's Deer Clan Cook Book (United Lumbee Nation, 1988); co-author with Frank Chilcote, A Message to Our People (United Lumbee Nation, 1989).

*REED, MARY BETH
(school principal)
Affiliation: Ojibwa Indian School, P.O. Box 600, Belcourt, ND 58316 (701) 477-3108.

*REESE, WILLIAM
(director of education)
Affiliation: Pine Hill Schools, CPO Drawer H, Pine Hills, NM 87357 (505) 775-3242.

REESER, RALPH R. 1932-
(research)
Born November 26, 1932, Fairbanks, Alaska. *Education*: Seattle University, 1952-55; University of Washington, BA, 1956; George Washington University Law School, JD, 1960. *Principal occupation*: Research. *Home address*: 3702 Spruell Dr., Wheaton, MD 20902 (301) 942-5185. *Affiliations*: Attorney-advisor, Public Housing Administration, Washington, DC, 1961-66; director, Housing Development, BIA, Washington, DC, 1966-70; deputy director, Publicly Financed Housing, Department of HUD, Washington, DC, 1970-72; director, Congressional & Legislative Affairs, Bureau of Indian Affairs, Washington, DC, 1972-89; consultant, 1989-. *Other professional post*: Teaching course on "Indian Land & the Law" for Falmouth Institute, 1991-. *Military service*: U.S. Air Force, 1951-52 (S/Sgt.). *Community activities*: Montgomery County, MD Advisory Committee on Cable Communications (member, 1991-). *Membership*: DC Bar Association. *Published work*: Manual of Indian Gaming Law (Falmouth Institute, 1992).

*REFT, ALICIA (Aleut)
(AK village president)
Affiliation: Native Village of Karluk, P.O. Box 22, Karluk, AK 99608 (907) 241-2218.

*REGGUINTI, GORDON (Ojibway) 1954-
(executive director)
Born February 10, 1954, in Minnesota. *Education*: University of Minnesota, BA (Indian Studies), 1987. *Principal occupation*: Executive director. *Home address*: 1008 Russell Ave. North, Minneapolis, MN 55411 (612) 529-6090; 874-3833 (work). *Affiliations*: Executive director, Native American Journalists Association, Minneapolis, MN. *Other professional posts*: Newsletter instructor, Migizi Communications, Minneapolis, MN, 1988-; series editor, Lerner Publications, Minneapolis, MN, 1990-. *Published work*: The Sacred Harvest, Ojibway Wild Rice Gathering (Lerner Publications, 1992).

*REID, MICHELLE *(Raven Moon)*
(Wampanoag/Mic Mac) 1954-
(native village director)
Born October 27, 1954, Taunton, Mass. *Education*: Johnson & Wales, Providence, RI, Fashion Merchandising (2 years). *Principal occupation*: Native village director. *Address*: RR 1 Box 126B, Lowell, VT 05847. *Affiliation*: Director, Moon Shadow Native Village, Lowell, VT. *Other professional post*: La Leche League leader; childbirth educator. *Community activities*: Birthright counselor/teen pregnancy; Coalition for Teen Pregnancy, Falmouth, MA; volunteer in public schools; help single moms. *Memberships*: Pan American Indians, 1991; Connecticut River Pow wow Society, 1992-; Seneca Wolf Clan, 1991-; Indigenous Women's Network, 1992-; Good Medicine Society, 1993-. *Award*: Merit Award for work in public schools in Falmouth, MA. *Interests*: "My work involves sending boxes to those in need on the reservations. I have visited Akwesasne Reservation in New York, and Rosebud Reservation in South Dakota. (I am) presently helping two Navajo elders through Adopt a Native Elder Program. I have studied with Grandmother Alloday of the Good Medicine Society; studying with Spider about Moon Lodge Women's Cycle. Spider is of Seneca Wolf Clan; I use herbs for healing, making medicines & salves. Also homeopathy." *Biographical sources*: Articles have appeared in Pan American newsletter, prison newsletters, and Shadowlight newsletter.

*RENDE, HELEN *(Kanaieson)* (Kahnawake Mohawk) 1944-
(director of social services)
Born August 10, 1944, Kahnawake Mohawk Reserve, Canada. *Principal occupation*: Director of social services. *Home address*: 21 Village Rd., Morganville, NJ 07751 (908) 727-5565. *Affiliation*: Director of social services & director, Office on Aging, Township of Old Bridge, Old Bridge, NJ, 1982-. *Community activities*: Old Bridge Community School Advisory Board (past member); Old Bridge Management Association; Old Bridge Emergency Food Bank Coordinator; Old Bridge Employee Trip Reduction Coordinator; Inter-Tribal Indians of New Jersey (council member); Middlesex County Older Adult Service Providers; Notary Public of New Jersey; New Jersey Affirmative Action Referral Contact. *Memberships*: New Jersey Association of Senior Citizen Center Directors; National Council on Aging; National Institute of Senior Centers. *Awards, honors*: Honorary member - National React/Pacers (police activated citizens Emergency Response Service) NJ Council; New Jersey Division on Civil Rights, 1986 Award for Outstanding Contribution; "Sentinel Newspaper, East Brunswick, NJ, 1987 Outstanding People

Award; Society of St. Anthony of Padua, 1990 Padua Award; New Jersey General Assembly Citation 1990, Outstanding Commitment to Community. *Interests*: "Advocate for problems and concerns of aging population, accomplished lecturer & published writer on American Indian issues and concerns. Appeared on New Jersey network & radio stations on interviews regarding these issues."

*RENDON, ANDREW
(school principal)
Affiliation: Porcupine Day School, P.O. Box 180, Porcupine, SD 57772 (605) 867-5336.

RENICK, DORIS (Pomo)
(tribal chairperson)
Affiliation: Coyote Valley Reservation, P.O. Box 39, Redwood Valley, CA 95470-0039 (707) 485-8723.

RESTOULE, TIM
(Indian band chief)
Affiliation: Dokis Indian Band, Dokis Bay, Monteville, ON, Can. P0M 2K0 (705) 763-2200.

REVEY, JAMES LONE BEAR
(Delaware-Cherokee)
(council chairperson)
Address & Affiliation: New Jersey Indian Office, 300 Main St., Suite 3F, Orange, NJ 07050 (201) 675-0694. *Other professional posts*: Owner, Lone Bear Indian Craft Co., Orange, NJ. *Membership*: American Indian Council of NJ.

REYHNER, JON ALLAN 1944-
(college professor)
Born April 29, 1944, Fountain Hill, Penna. *Education*: University of California, Davis, BA, 1966, MA, 1967; Northern Arizona University, MA, 1973, EdS, 1977; Montana State University, Bozeman, EdD, 1984. *Principal occupation*: Associate professor of education, Eastern Montana College. *Address*: P.O. Box 2933, Tuba City, AZ 86045 (602) 283-5269. *Affiliations*: Principal, Rocky Boy Public School, Box Elder, MT, 1978-80; university supervisor of professional & student teachers, Dept. of Elementary Education, Montana State University, Bozeman, 1980-81; principal/federal projects director, Heart Butte Public School, MT, 1982-84; administrator/ principal, Havasupai School, Supai, AZ, 1984-85; academic coordinator & school administrator, Cibecue Community School, Cibecue, AZ, 1984-85; associate professor of education, Eastern Montana College, Billings, 1985-. *Memberships*: National Association for Bilingual Education; American Educational Research Association; International Reading Association; American Association of School Administrators; National Indian Education Association; Council for Indian Education; Phi Delta Kappa; Phi Alpha Theta. *Interests*: Bilingual education; Indian education; photography; historical research on Western America. *Published works*: Heart Butte: A Blackfeet Indian Community, 1984; editor, Stories of Our Blackfeet Grandmothers, 1984; editor, The Story of Running Eagle, by James Willard Schultz, 1984; editor, Famine Winter, by James Willard Schultz, 1984; editor, The Loud Mouthed Gun, by James Willard Schultz, 1984; all published by Council for Indian Education; A History of Indian Education (Eastern Montana College, 1989); Effective Language Education Practices (NALI, 1990); Teaching American Indian Students (University of Oklahoma Press, 1992); numerous articles.

*REYNA, DIANE
(producer/director)
Address: P.O. Box 15222, Santa Fe, NM 87506 (505) 988-6319.

REYNA, SHARON *(Dryflower)* (Taos Pueblo) 1949-
(artist-clay)
Born August 20, 1949, Taos, N.M. *Education*: Institute of American Indian Art, AFA (Museum Studies /3 Dimensional Art), 1987. Santa Fe Community College (Painting/Business). *Principal occupation*: Artist-clay. *Home address*: P.O. Box 3031, Taos, NM 87571 (505) 758-3790. 1991 Open Shows: Denver Indian Market; Native American Art Festival; Heard Museum; Scottsdale Native American Culture Foundation; Retrospective of Taos, 4-Man Show, Sables Art Center; Red Earth Fine Art Show; Eight Northern Indian Pueblos Art Show; Indian Market, Santa Fe. Collections: Denver Natural History Museum-Vernon Rickmeyer Collection; Millicent Rogers Museum; Institute of American Indian Arts, Santa Fe; Alll Indian Pueblo Culture Center, Albuquerque; Tony Reyna (private collection); Chicago Natural History Museum; Red Cloud Heritage Center, Rapid City, SD; among others. *Memberships*: Indian Arts and Crafts Association; The National Museum of Women in the Arts, Washington, DC; Stables Art Association; Spring Arts Board; TAA - Visual Arts Committee. *Awards, honors*: Best of Class, Ceramic Sculpture - 4th Annual Fine Art Show, Scottsdale Native American Indian Cultural Foundation; 1st, Pottery Division - Heard Museum Student Show; 2nd, Ceramic Division - Red Earth Fine Arts Show, Oklahoma City, OK; Thunderbird Scholarship, Hinsel Award & Purchase Award from the Red Cloud Heritage Center, Pine Ridge, SD; Gallup Ceremoial; Artist of the Year, Native American Fish & Wildlife Society. *Published works*: Taos Pueblo (Nancy Wood, 1988-89); Gold Book (Gold Book Publishers, 1992).

REYNOLDS, ALLIE
(organization president)
Affiliation: The National Hall of Fame for Famous American Indians, Highway 62, Box 808, Anadarko, OK 73005 (405) 247-5795.

RHINE, GARY 1951-
(documentary producer/director)
Born June 26, 1951, San Francisco, Calif. *Principal occupation*: Documentary producer/director. *Address & Affiliation*: Kifaru Productions, 1550 California St., Suite 275, San Francisco, CA 94109 (415) 381-6560. Memberships: Film Arts Foundation; International Documentary Association; American Indian Religious Freedom Coalition; Native American Journalists Association. Awards, honors: American Indian Film Festival, "Best Video Award"; National Educational Film Festival, "Best Native American" Gold Apple; Munich International Film Festival, "One Future Prize." Interests: "Committed to amplifying the efforts of Native American spiritual leaders through the use of film & video documentaries. Documentaries produced & directed: "Wiping the Tears of Seven Generations," 1992; "The Peyote Road," 1993; & "Understanding A.I.R.F.A.," 1993.

*RHINES-LAWSON, VIVIAN L. *(Panther)* (Southeastern Cherokee) 1940-
(accountant)
Born April 25, 1940, Knoxville, Tenn. *Education*: Adult Education Night School (Columbus, GA),

Accounting. *Principal occupation*: Accountant. *Address*: P.O Box 1784, Thomasville, GA 31799 (912) 574-5497; 226-0717 (work). *Affiliation*: Owner/president, Carroll Hill Auto Electronics, Inc., Thomasville, GA, 1974-. *Other professional posts*: Principal Chief, Southeastern Cherokee Confederacy Steering Committee. *Community activities*: Teacher & lecturer of Cherokee history & culture in area schools. *Memberships*: Southeastern Cherokee Confederacy; Cherokee Unity Council; Council of Clan Mothers; Deer Clan, Inc. *Awards, honors*: A plaque for my six years of video taping & showing to the students at Central High School Band, so they can improve their performance - half-time shows, concerts and competitions. *Interests*: "My main avocational interests are: genealogy, Native American history & culture, geology, painting of portraits & Native American bead work. My vocational interests are the personal computer & word processing." *Biographical source*: Article, "To Guard Against Invading Indians: Struggling for Native Community in the Southeast," in American Indian Culture & Research Journal, Fall 1994.

RHOADES, EVERETT RONALD, M.D. (Kiowa) 1931-
(ex-director-Indian Health Service)
Born October 24, 1931, Lawton, Okla. *Education*: Lafayette College, 1949-1952; University of Oklahoma, College of Medicine, MD, 1956. *Home address*: 1808 Dorchester Dr., Oklahoma City, OK 73120. *Affiliations*: Chief, Infectious Diseases, Wilford Hall, U.S. Air Force Hospital, 1961-66; assistant professor of microbiology and associate professor of medicine, University of Oklahoma Medical Center, 1966-72; professor of medicine, Chief, Infectious Diseases, University of Oklahoma College of Medicine, Oklahoma City, OK, 1968-82; professor of medicine & adjunct professor of microbiology, University of Oklahoma, Health Sciences Center, 1972-82; Chief, Infectious Diseases Service University Hospital, 1975-82; director, Indian Health, Rockville, MD, 1982-; Assistant Surgeon General, USPHS, 1982-. *Military service*: U.S. Air Force, 1957-66 (Major; Certificate of Merit, 1967). *Community activities*: Oklahoma Lung Association (board of directors); Task Force on Health of American Indian Policy Review Commission (chairman, 1975); National Advisory Allergy and Infectious Disease Council (NIH), 1971-75; Central Oklahoma Indian Health Project (board of directors; chairman, 1976); Kiowa Tribal Business Committee (1967-70, 1979-81; vice chairman, 1974-76); Kiowa Tribal Land Management Committee, 1967-70; National Congress of American Indians (health committee); founder & donor, Dorothy Rowell Rhoades Prize to outstanding graduating Indian student, Elgin High School, Okla. *Memberships*: American Thoracic Society, 1963-82; American Federation for Clinical Research, 1960-; American College of Physicians, 1963- (Fellow); American Society for Microbiology, 1970-; Association on American Indian Affairs (board of directors, 1967-82; vice president, 1978-82); Association of American Indian Physicians (founder, 1971; president, 1972, 1976); Sigma Xi; Phi Beta Kappa; Kiowa Gourd Clan, 1970-; Association of Military Surgeons, 1982-; Infectious Disease Society of America, 1974-. *Awards, honors*: Markle Scholar, Academic Medicine, 1967-72; John Hay Whitney Opportunity Fellow, 1952-56; Student Research Achievement Award, 1956; Outstanding

Achievement, Veterans Administration Hospital, 1960, 1961; Recognition Award, Association of American Indian Physicians, 1973, 1976; Breath of Life Award, Oklahoma Lung Association, 1977; Public Health Service Recognition Award, 1977; National Honor Lecturer, Mid-America State Universities Association, 1979; Association of American Indian Physicians Award of Excellence, 1980; PHS Meritorious Service Medal, 1985; Richard Kern Lecture Award, 1988; Kiowa Tribe of Oklahoma, "Exemplary Contributions to Health of Native Americans, 1988; Kiowa Veterans Association and Auxiliary, " In Appreciation for Dedicated Service to the American Indian Health Service, 1988; PHS Chief of Staff's Special Commendation Award, 1989. *Interests*: Internal medicine; infectious diseases; Kiowa Gourd Clan; Kiowa Blacklegging Society; dancing and powwows; amateau archaeology; history of medicine and Indians; travel. *Biographical sources*: Directory of Medical Specialists; Dictionary of International Biography, 1973; Who's Who in the South and Southwest; American Men & Women of Science; Indians of Today; Contemporary American Indian Leaders; Voices: A History of the Kiowa Tribe. Published works: Numerous articles in scientific journals relating to infectious diseases, microbiology, and Indian life; author of Kiowa Tribe for World Book Encyclopedia; edited Task Force Report to American Indian Policy Review Commission (Health), U.S. Government Printing Office, 1975.

RHOADES, KAREN A.
(school principal)
Affiliation: Kasigluk Day School, Kasigluk, AK 99609 (907) 477-6714.

RICE, G. WILLIAM (Oklahoma Cherokee) 1951-
(attorney)
Born August 3, 1951, Anadarko, Okla. *Education*: Phillips University (Enid, OK), BA, 1983; Lowell (MA) Technological Institute (MS degree program), 1973-75; University of Oklahoma College of Law, JD, 1978. *Principal occupation*: Attorney. *Home address*: Route 2, Box 2391, Cushing, OK 74023 (918) 225-4800 (work). *Affiliations*: Visiting Assistant Professor, Dept. of Political Science, University of Oklahoma, Norman; Sr. Attorney & President, G. William Rice, P.C., Cushing, OK; President & CEO, Aniwaya Insurance Co. (Indian owned), Cushing, OK. *Other professional posts*: Instructor, Antioch School of Law, Washington, DC, 1978-79; consultant, Oklahoma Indian Affairs Commission, Oklahoma City, 1977-81. *Community activities*: Court of Indian Offenses Bar Association (First President & Executive Director, 1979-83, 1986-88); Oklahoma Indian Legal Services Corp. (board of directors, 1981-82); Kiowa Tribal Tax Commission, Carnegie, OK, 1985-87); Absentee Shawnee Business Development Commission (Commissioner, 1987-88); Attorney General, Sac & Fox Nation, 1985-; Chief Justice of Supreme Court of Citizen Band Potawatomi Tribe, Shawnee, OK, 1986-; Keetoowah Tribal Loan Fund (chairperson, 1990-92). Memberships: Oklahoma Supreme Court; U.S. District Court for the Eastern & Western Districts of Oklahoma; U.S. Court of Appeals for the Tenth & Eighth Circuits; Supreme Court of the U.S.; Sac & Fox Nation Supreme Court; Citizen Band Potawatomi Supreme Court; Muscogee (Creek) Nation Supreme Court. *Awards, honors*: Dannenburg Memorial Scholarship, University of Oklahoma Col-

lege of Law; Martin Luther King Teaching Fellowship, Lowell Technological Institute; Phillips University Scholarship; Phi Delta Phi Honorary Legal Fraternity, University of Oklahoma College of Law; Honorary Mayor-President, City of Baton Rouge, Parish of East Baton Rouge, 1987. *Interests*: Powwows and other Indian social functions, hunting, fishing. *Published works*: Cases and Material on Indian Property Law (Antioch School of Law, 1978); Court Rules of the Court of Indian Offenses (BIA, Anadarko Area Office, 1979); Cases and Materials on the Impact of the Indian Child Welfare Act in Oklahoma (Indian Legal Resource Center, 1980); Indian Children, State Laws, and the Indian Child Welfare Act of 1978 (Indian Legal Resource Center, 1980); Oklahoma Indian Law (Indian Legal Resource Center, 1980); Materials on the Impact of the Indian Child Welfare Act in Nebraska (Indian Legal Resource Center, 1980); Indian Child Welfare Act Handbook for Tribes in Oklahoma (OK Indian Affairs Commission, 1980); Handbook of Federal Indian Law (Michie, Bobbs-Merrill, 1982) contributing author for revision of Felix Cohen's 1942 edition. *Articles*: "The Mythology of the Oklahoma Indians: A Survey of Legal Status of Indian Tribes in Oklahoma" (American Indian Law Review, 259, 1979); "The End of Indian Sovereignty or a Self-limitation of Contractual Ability?" (American Indian Law Review, 239, 1977); "The Journey from Ex Parte Crow Dog to Littlechief: A Survey of Tribal Civil and Criminal Jurisdiction in Western Oklahoma" (American Indian Law Review, 1, 1979). Authored and edited many contributions, federal charters, ordinances and complete law and order codes for various tribes which are too numerous to list.

*RICE, JOHN
(Indian band chief)
Affiliation: Wasauksin (Parry Island) Indian Band, Box 253, Parry Sound, Ontario, Canada P0P 2X4 (705) 746-2531.

*RICE, STAN (Yavapai)
(tribal president)
Affiliation: Yavapai-Prescott Board of Directors, 530 E. Merritt St., Prescott, AZ 86301 (602) 445-8790.

*RICEHILL, ERNEST (Winnebago/Omaha) 1948-
(administrator)
Born November 29, 1948, Winnebago, Neb. *Education*: Briar Cliff College (Sioux City, IA), 1976. *Principal occupation*: Administrator. *Home address*: 1718 Vine St., Box 725, Dakota City, NE 68731 (712) 255-8957 (work). *Affiliations*: Curator, Sioux City Art Center, 1973-79; director, Office of Indian Education, Sioux City Community Public Schools, 1979-84; personnel administrator, Omaha Tribe of Nebraska, 1984-88; executive director, Sioux City American Indian Center, Sioux City, IA, 1991-. *Community activities*: Sioux City Community Schools (member of Project Awareness, the Curriculum Committee, Multicultural Committee, and Committee on Formulating Policy on Chronic Absenteeism); chairman of Sioux City Minority Coalition; board member, Native American Alcoholic Treatment Center; chairman of Siouxland Council of Agency Executives; member of Winnebago Tribe's Healthy Start Planning Committee; member of the Siouxland Housing Corporation; among others. *Memberships*: National Indian Education Association; National Indian Media

Association; Iowa Museum Association. *Awards, honors*: Elected Delegate to the precinct, county, and state Democratic Conventions, 1972-80, 1984-85; appointed Chairman of Precinct 16, Democratic Party; elected National Delegate to the 1972, 1988 & 1992 National Democratic Conventions; appointed Iowa State Coordinator of the Native Americans for Clinton-Gore National Election Committee, Aug. 1992; member of the President Clinton's transition team of the Native Americans for Clinton-Gore National Election Committee, Nov. 1992; appointed member of the White House/Robert Wood Johnson Foundation panel on "Conversations on Health: A Dialogue with the American People, Amkeny, Iowa, March 1993; member/representative to the National Native American Listening Conference sponsored by the Dept. of Justice & Interior, Albuquerque, May 1994.

*RICHARD, ORIE
(editor)
Affiliation: "Turtle Mountain Times," Turtle Mountain Tribe, Belcourt, ND 58316 (701) 477-6451.

*RICHARDS, RICK
(clinic director)
Affiliation: Sam Hider Jay Community Clinic, P.O. Box 350, Jay, OK 74346 (918) 253-4271.

RICHARDS, THOMAS, Jr. *(Aviaq)*
(Inupiat Eskimo) 1949-
(writer/planner)
Born September 27, 1949, Kotzebue, Alaska. *Education*: University of Denver, 1967-68; University of Alaska, 1968; Armed Forces Air Intelligence Training Center, CO, 1969. *Principal occupation*: Writer/planner. *Home address*: P.O. Box 2176, Bethel, AK 99559 (907) 543-3069. *Affiliations*: Editor/publisher, Tundra Times (newspaper), 1973, 1977-80; vice-president, Association of Village Council Presidents, Bethel, AK, 1981-86; owner/operator, Thomas Richards, Jr. & Associates, Bethel, AK (current). *Other professional post*: Author. *Military service*: U.S. Navy, 1969-73 (Vietnam Service Vet, E-5; Photo-Intelligence Specialist. *Community activities*: Founding director, Institute of Alaska Native Arts (board of directors, 1975-76); member, Inuit Circumpolar Conference Communications & Broadasting Commission, 1979-84. *Memberships*: Alaska Federation of Natives (Human Resources Board, 1980-86); American Legion, Post No. 11. *Awards, honors*: Congressional Intern, 1970-72, office of U.S. Rep. Nick Begich; Governor's Representative, State Committee, Alaska Humanities Forum (Chairperson & member, 1975-82); Committee on Arctic Cultural Development, UNESCO, United Nations (U.S. Representative, 1979-80, appointed by U.S. Dept. of State);Oustading Young Man of America, U.S. Jaycees, nominated by the Office of the Governor, 1979; Howard Rock Award for Native community service, presented by the Board of Directors, Tundra Times, 1980. *Interests*: "After 20 years as a writer and an administrator for Alaska Native organizations, my primary career interest now centers on economic and business development. Although I still write (mostly histories), most of my current work is in entrepreneurship training. I help rural Alaskans research and write business plans and start-up their own business ventures." *Published works*: Alaska Native Claims-Unit 4 (Alaska Native Foundation, 1976); Pribilof Progress.Pribilof Pace (Aleutian/Pibilof Islands Association,

1979); ANCSA and Related Studies - textbook history of Alaska Native land claims for Lower Kuskokwim School District, Bethel, AK (Lower Kuskokwim School District, 1992).

RICHARDS, WILLIAM H., Sr. *(Xus-x'a-yo)*
(Smith River Rancheria-Tolowa)
(tribal chairperson)
Born March 17, 1936, Del Norte, Calif. *Education*: College of the Redwoods (2 years). *Home address*: 301 N. Indian Rd., Smith River, CA 95567 (707) 487-9255 (work). *Affiliation*: Chairman, Smith River Rancheria, Smith River, CA, 1978-. *Military service*: 1955-58 (Sp. 4). *Community activities*: State Committee on Indian Juvenile Justice (member).

RICHARDSON, BARRY (Haliwa-Saponi)
1954-
(tribal administrator)
Born August 13, 1954, Warren County, N.C. *Education*: Pembroke State University, BA (Political Science), 1976. *Principal occupation*: Tribal administrator. *Home address*: P.O. Box 609, Hollister, NC 27844 (919) 586-4017 (work). *Affiliations*: Executive director, Baltimore American Indian Center, Baltimore, MD; president, Pow-Wow, Hollister, NC, 1990-. *Other professional posts*: Founder & treasurer of the National American Indian Council. *Community activities*: Preserve Haliwa Now, Bethlehem Recreation, Inc. *Membership*: National Congress of American Indians. *Interest*: Coin collecting.

*RICHARDSON, BILL
(U.S. Congressman)
Affiliation: Chairperson, House Committee on Interior & Insular Affairs, Subcommittee on Native American Affairs, U.S. House of Representatives, 1522 Longworth House Office Bldg., New Jersey & Independence Ave., SE, Washington, DC 20515 (202) 226-7736.

*RICHARDSON, JEFFREY
(executive director)
Affiliation: Nevada Urban Indians, 2100 Capurro Way, Suite A, Sparks, NV 89431 (702) 356-8111.

*RICHARDSON, JOSEPH (Haliwa-Saponi)
(tribal chairperson)
Affiliation: Haliwa-Saponi Tribe, P.O. Box 99, Hollister, NC 27844 (919) 586-4017.

*RICHARDSON, KENNETH
(health center director)
Affiliation: Walker River Paiute Tribal health Center, P.O. Drawer C, Schurz, NV 89427 (702) 773-2005.

*RICHARDSON, LINDA
(BIA assistant director)
Affiliation: Bureau of Indian Affairs, Office of Financial Management, 1849 C St., NW, MS: 4140-MIB, Washington, DC 20240 (202) 208-6342.

RICHARDSON, PATRICIA ROSE
(BREWINGTON) (Coharie-Cherokee) 1933-
(crafts consultant)
Born July 21, 1933, Clinton, N.C. *Education*: East Carolina Indian School, 1952; Nash Technical College, AA, 1986. *Principal occupation*: American Indian crafts consultant/pottery and beadwork. *Home address*: P.O. Box 130, Hollister, NC 27844. *Affiliations*: Instructor, Title IV Indian Education, Halifax Board of Educa-

tion, N.C. (six years); crafts instructor, Haliwa-Supai Indian Tribe, Hollister, N.C. (5 years). *Memberships*: North Carolina Crafts Association (board member); American Indian Heritage Foundation. *Awards, honors*: First Place Awards -Excellence in Beadwork, Schiele Museum Indian Festival, 1978/1986; Good Medicine Crafts Award, 1980/1986. *Interests*: Exhibitions at major Indian festivals: Grand Prairie, TX, Hunter Mountain, NY, Palm Beach, FL, NC Indian festivals, National Indian Festival, Washington, DC.

*RICHARDSON, W.R. (Haliwa-Saponi)
(tribal chief)
Affiliation: Haliwa-Saponi Tribe, P.O. Box 99, Hollister, NC 27844 (919) 586-4017.

RICHMOND, ROSEMARY
(executive director)
Affiliation: American Indian Community House, 404 Lafayette St., 2nd Floor, New York, NY 10003 (212) 598-0100.

*RICKER, BERNADINE R.
(administrative officer)
Affiliation: Not-Tsoo Gah-Nee Indian Health Center, P.O. Box 117, Fort Hall, ID 83203 (208) 238-2400.

RIDDLES, LEONARD *(Black Moon)*
(Comanche) 1919-
(artist, farmer/rancher)
Born June 28, 1919, Walters, Okla. *Education*: Fort Sill Indian School (Valedictorian, 1941). *Principal occupation*: Artist, farmer/rancher. *Home address*: Route #1, Box 89, Walter, OK 73572 (405) 281-3623. *Professional posts*: Elected as tribal officer for the Kiowa, Comanche and Apache Tribal Council, and later tribal officer on the Comanche Tribal Council. *Military service*: U.S. Army, 1941-45 (Pfc; Sharp Shooter, 8P Service Ribbon, American Defense Ribbon, two bronze stars). *Community activities*: Comanche Tribal Council (former officer); Masons. *Membership*: American Indian Artists Association; Cotton County Art Council; Comanche Little Pony War Society. *Awards, honors*: He has been the recipient of awards and honors in regional shows and exhibits throughout the U.S. His paintings are included in permanent public collections at the Lyman Allen Museum, New London, CT; Dept. of the Interior, Washington, DC; and Southern Plains Indian Museum, Anadarko, OK. His work is included in numerous private collections in the U.S. and foreign countries. He was commissioned by the Indian Arts & Crafts Board, Dept. of the Interior, in 1968 to create a series of hide paintings which include "Comanche Medicine Shield" and Battle of Adobe Walls". *Exhibitions*: Philbrook Art Center, Inter-Tribal Indian Ceremonial; Museum of New Mexico; U.S. Department of the Interior Gallery; among others. *Interests*: Mr. Riddles writes, "I am interested in the history of the American Indian and in any phase of archaeological study. We do research on the Comanche Tribe, so (I) find all expeditions of real interest. Museums are also of great interest to me." He has mastered the medium of watercolor with paintings that reflect narrative portrayals of Comanche Tribal heritage. One of his paintings, "Eagle Dancer', was featured in the Oklahoma India Artists Calendar, 1976. Mr. Riddles illustrated the book Storms Brewed in Other Men's Worlds; and the jacket for Buried Colts, by Harley Smith.

RIDINGTON, ROBIN 1939-
(professor of anthropology)
Born November 1, 1939, Camden, N.J. *Education*: Swarthmore, BA, 1962; Harvard University, Ph.D., 1968. *Principal occupation*: Professor of anthropology. *Home address*: RR 2, Site 44 C-16, Galiano, B.C., Can. V0N 1P0 (604) 539-3095. *Affiliation*: Assistant & associate professor of anthropology, University of British Columbia, Vancouver, B.C., 1967-. *Memberships*: Society for Humanistic Anthropology (Canadian representative); Canadian Ethnology Society; American Anthropological Association. *Award*: 1989 Hubert Evans Non-Fiction Book Prize of British Columbia. *Interests*: Field research among Beaver Indians, 1964-; writing about Omaha ceremony, 1985-. *Biographical source*: "A Sacred Object as Text: Reclaiming the Sacred Pole of the Omaha Tribe," American Indian Quarterly, 1993. *Published works*: Articles: "From Artifice to Artifact: Stages in the Industrialization of a Northern Native Community" (Journal of Canadian Studies, 1983); "Stories of the Vision Quest Among Dunne-za Women" (Atlantis, 1983); "Beaver Indians" (The Canadian Encyclopedia, Hurtig, 1985); "Native People, Subarctic" (The Canadian Encyclopedia, Hurtig, 1985); "Fox and Chicadee: The Writing of Indian White History in volume edited by Calvin Martin"; "The Northern Hunters" (Newberry Library volume, America in 1492, Alvin Josephy, Editor, 1990); among others. *Books*: Swan People: A Study of the Dunne-za Prophet Dance (National Museums of Canada, 1978); co-author, People of the Trail: How the Northern Forest Indians Lived (Douglas & McIntyre, 1978); co-author, People of the Longhouse: How the Iroquoian People Lived (Douglas & McIntyre, 1982; Trail to Heaven: Knowledge & Narrative in a Northern Native Community (University of Iowa Press, 1988); Little Bit Know Something: Stories in a Language of Anthropology (University of Iowa Press, 1990).

RIDLEY, PATRICIA L. (Poarch Creek)
(library director)
Affiliation: Poarch Creek Indian Heritage Center Library, P.O. Box 633, Wetumpka, AL 36092 (205) 368-4326.

RIDLEY, SANDRA L.
(curator)
Affiliation: Poarch Creek Indian Heritage Center, HCR69A, Box 85B, Atmore AL 36502 (205) 368-9136.

*RIDLING, DANA
(chairperson)
Affiliation: National Native American AIDS Prevention Center, 3515 Grand Ave., Suite 100, Oakland, CA 94610 (510) 444-2051 Fax 444-1593.

*RIGGS, JIM W. 1945-
(primitive technologist instructor; writer, photographer, illustrator)
Born February 17, 1945, Portland, Oreg. *Education*: Oregon State University, BA, 1968. *Principal occupation*: Primitive technologist instructor; writer, photographer, illustrator. *Home address*: 72501 Hwy. 82, Wallowa, OR 97885 (503) 437-1895. *Affiliations*: Instructor of ethnobotany & aboriginal life skills courses, Maheur Field Station, Princeton, OR (Summers, 1974-89). *Other professional posts*: Board member, International Society of Primitive Technology; archae-

ologist, Forest Service, Hells Canyon NRA and private groups. As a freelance writer, photographer & illustrator, he has contributed to numerous periodicals and books and written his own treatise, Blue Mountain Buckskin (self-published, 1980), " the most in-depth how-to book available on brain-tanning. He was informational consultant for book series, "Clan of the Cave Bear." His replications of Great Basin material culture components comprise several exhibits at the High Desert Museum in Bend, OR. *Interests*: Specializing in prehistoric cultural ecology and environmental adaptations of aboriginal peoples of the Northern Great Basin & Columbia Plateau regions, he continues to research & practice primitive skills & technologies how to instruct workshops & intensive field courses covering these subjects. *Biographical source*: Chapter in "Footprints Across Oregon, by Mike Thoele. *Published works*: Blue Mountain Buckskin (self-published, 1980); several chapters in "Best of Woodsmoke," "Primitive Outdoor Skills," & "Woodsmoke," edited by Richard & Linda Jamison.

RILEY, CHARLES W., II
(school principal)
Affiliation: Pine Springs Boarding School, P.O. Box 198, Houck, AZ 86506 (602) 871-4311.

RILEY, DELBERT
(Indian band chief)
Affiliation: Chippewas of the Thames, RR 1, Muncey, Ontario, Canada N0L 1Y0 (519) 264-1528.

RINER, REED D. 1941-
(anthropologist/futurist)
Born December 22, 1941, Mentone, Ind. *Education*: University of Colorado, Ph.D., 1977 (dissertation: A Study of Attitudes Toward Formal Education Among Indian Parents and Students in Six Communities. *Principal occupation*: Associate professor of anthropology, Northern Arizona State University, Flagstaff, 1975-. *Home address*: 506 Charles Rd., Flagstaff, AZ 86001. *Other professional post*: Advisor, Native American Indian Studies Program, Northern Arizona University; editor/publisher, Cultural Futures Research. *Military service*: U.S. Naval Reserve, 1963-68. Memberships: American Anthropological Association; Society for Applied Anthropology; High Plains Society for Applied Anthropology (past president); World Future Studies Federation; World Future Society; Contact Cultures of the Imagination (board of directors); Cross-Cultural Dance Resources (board of directors). *Interests*: "My primary professional interests are applied futures research; Native American Indian studies, especially Indian education; and the application of anthropology in the solution of--especially institutional--organizational problems such as the future of Native American Indians." *Published works*: Numerous articles in professional journals.

RIOS, MICHAEL (O'Odham)
(association board member)
Affiliation: National Indian Youth Council, 318 Elm, SE, Albuquerque, NM 87102.

RISLING, DALE (Hooper)
(rancheria chairperson)
Affiliation: Hoopa Valley Rancheria, P.O. Box 1348, Hoopa, CA 95546 (916) 625-4211.

RISLING, DAVID (Hoopa-Yurok/Karok) 1921-
(lecturer-Native-American studies)
Born April 10, 1921, Weitchpec (Hoopa Reservation Ext.), Calif. *Education*: California Polytechnic University, BS, 1948, MA, 1953. *Principal occupation*: Lecturer-Native American studies. *Home address*: 2403 Catalina Dr., Davis, CA 95616 (916) 756-7085. *Affiliations*: Agricultural instructor, 1951-70 & counselor, 1962-70, Modesto Jr. College, Modesto, CA; lecturer, Native American Studies Department, University of California, Davis, 1970-. *Military service*: U.S. Navy, 1942-45 (Commanding Officer of an anti-submarine ship, 1945). *Community activities*: In 1967, Risling organized the first statewide conference on Indian education at Stanislaus State College. He helped organize the first Indian-controlled conference on education in the U.S. which conference led to the founding of the California Indian Education Association; chairperson, D-Q University Board of Trustees; coordinator, Tecumseh Center, University of California, Davis; vice-president, Association on American Indian Affairs; former chairperon of: California Indian Legal Services, Native America Rights Fund, American Indian Higher Education Consortium, and several other Indian and non-Indian organizations. *Memberships*: California Indian Education Association, 1968- (co-founder and past president, 1968-70); National Indian Education Association (co-founder and board of directors for several years); California Teachers Association, 1951-70. *Awards, honors*: Outstanding agricultural teacher in central California, 1963; from 1973-81, Risling served on the National Advisory Commission on Indian Education, appointed to the post by Presidents Nixon, Ford and Carter; "Outstanding Indian Educator of the Year," by the State Dept. of Education & State Senate, 1990; The Native American Elders Award, 1990, by the State Dept. of Education and the California Indian Education Association; 1992 UC Davis "Distinguished Public Service Award." David was the first Native American known to have graduated a university. *Interests*: Indian rights, spirituality, sovereignty, Indian education, self-determination, Indian history; travel in Europe, New Zealand, Australia, and South America. *Biographical sources*: Book - The Lives of Ethnic Amerians (Kendall-Hunt, 1991); Articles - "Risling Legacy," Sacramento Magazine, June 1990; "Native Son," Sattert Town News, May 1991; "From All Four Directions," Pacific Discovery, Winter 1992.

*RISLING, DOUGLAS
(center director)
Affiliation: Northern California Indian Development Center, 241 F St., Eureka, CA 95501 (707) 445-8451.

*RISLING, LOIS
(center director)
Affiliation: Center for Indian Community Development, Humboldt University, Brero House 93, Arcata, CA 95521 (707) 826-3711.

*RISLING, MARY
(attorney)
Affiliation: California Indian Legal Services, 324 F St., Suite A, Eureka, CA 95501 (707) 443-8397.

*RITTER, BETH R. 1961-
(anthropologist, geographer)
Born June 21, 1961, Kearney, Neb. *Education*:

University of Nebraska, MA, 1990, PhD (expected 1996). *Principal occupation*: Anthropologist, geographer. *Home address*: 2725 S. 16th, Lincoln, NE 68502 (402) 472-9677 (work). *Affiliations*: Anthropologist, National Park Service, Lincoln, NE, 1993-94; instructor, University of Nebraska, Lincoln, 1992-. *Other professional post*: Consultant, Ponca Tribe of Nebraska & Black Eagle Corp. *Memberships*: American Anthropological Association; Society for Applied Anthropology. *Interests*: "Primary interest is the Plains Indians & contemporary issues; Federal Indian policy; Native American political & legal systems; Indian gaming (consultant to Ponca Tribe of Nebraska during recent (1990) restoration of their federally-terminated status)." *Published works*: Articles: "The Ponca Tribe of Nebraska: The Process of Restoration of a Federally-Terminated Tribe," in Human Organization, 1992; "The Politics of Retribalization: The Northern Ponca Case," in Great Plains Research, 1994; "Will the House Win: Does Sovereignty Rule in Indian Casinos," in Great Plains Research, 1994.

*RITTER, GLADINE
(editor)
Affiliation: "Oregon Directory of American Indian Resources," Commission on Indian Services, 454 State Capitol, Salem, OR 97310 (503) 986-1067.

RITZ, LAN BROOKES
(writer/filmmaker)
Principal occupation: Writer/filmmaker, Brown Bird Productions, Inc., 1971 N. Curson Ave., Hollywood, CA 90046 (213) 851-8928. *Film produced*: Annie Mae -- Brave Hearted Woman (written, produced, and directed by Lan Brookes Ritz) this film is an account of recent Native American history told from the intimate perspective of a dedicated young Indian woman killed on a reservation in the aftermath of the human rights stand at Wounded Knee (16mm, 80 minutes, color; rental: $150, purchase: $1090. *Awards, honors*: Best Motion Picture, American Indian Film Festival; Award of Excellence, Film Advisory Board; Best in Category, San Francisco International Film Festival. *Featured screenings*: Museum of Modern Art, New York, NY; Kennedy Center, Washington, D.C.; London and Melbourn Film Festivals; Cinema du reel, France; etc. *Interest*: Visual design.

ROACH, MILBURN H.
(IHS-executive assistant)
Affiliation: Office of the Director, Indian Health Service, Room 6-05, 5600 Fishers Lane, Rockville, MD 20857 (301) 443-1083.

ROBERTS, BARBARA (Lummi) 1955-
(college administrator)
Born June 14, 1955, Bellingham, Wash. *Education*: Walla Walla College, BA, 1977; University of Hawaii, MPH, 1980. *Principal occupation*: College administrator. *Home address*: 505 W. Bakerview #122, Bellingham, WA 98226 (206) 676-2772 (work). *Affiliations*: Dept. Head, Lummi Health & Human Services, Bellingham (10 years); Title III Director, Personnel Officer, Northwest Indian College, Bellingham, 1990-. *Interests*: Development of culturally relevant curriculum for college courses.

ROBERTS, CARLA A. (Delaware) 1957-
(administrator; consultant)
Born in 1957. *Education*: University of Alaska, Fairbanks, BFA, 1979; University of Iowa, MFA, 1981. *Principal occupation*: Administrator; consultant. *Home address*: 4747 N. 14th St., Apt. J, Phoenix, AZ 85014 (602) 265-8204 (home) 253-2731 (office). *Affiliations*: Coordinator, Univerity of Alaska, Rural Education, Fairbanks, AK, 1976-79; assistant director, Intermedia Arts-Minnesota, University of Minnesota, Minneapolis, 1982-86; executive director, Boston Film/ Videl Foundation, Boston, MA, 1986-87; consultant, Art Management for Boston Conservatory, Indian Hill Arts, University of Lowell, Center for Native American Awareness, 1988-91; executive director, ATLATL, Phoenix, AZ, 1991-93. *Other professional posts*: Consultant, Tribal Museum Program, Arizona Commission on the Arts, Phoenix, AZ, 1991-; speaking engagements: "The Ethics of Celebration & De-Celebration," University of Florida, Gainesville, Dec. 1991; "Indian smaking Museums," Arizona State University, Tempe, Nov. 1991; "Native American Storytelling" & "Multi-Cultural Literature, University of Lowell (MA), March-April, 1991. *Community activities*: National Endowment for the Arts (panelist, Jan. 1992; advisory group, 1991-93) panelist, Arizona Commission on the Arts, Phoenix, AZ, 1991-; board member, Indian Hill Arts, Littleton, MA, 1991. *Published works*: ATLATL: Serving the Needs of Native American Artists, Art View (National Assembly of State Arts Agencies, Washington, DC, 1991).

*ROBERTS, DELORES
(rancheria spokesperson)
Affiliation: North Fork Rancheria, P.O. Box 120, San Francisco, CA 94121 (415) 752-9085.

*ROBERTS, FLOYD
(editor)
Affiliation: American Indian Business Magazine, Communications Group, 206 S. Galena Ave., Freeport, IL 61032 (815) 232-5176.

ROBERTS, HOLLIS E. (Choctaw)
(tribal chief)
Affiliation: Choctaw Tribal Council, P.O. Drawer 1210, Durant, OK 74702 (405) 924-8280.

*ROBERTS, MICHAEL E.
(institute director)
Affiliation: First Nations Development Institute, The Stores Bldg., 11917 Main St., Fredericksburg, VA 22408 (703) 371-5615.

ROBERTS, ROY
(Indian band chief)
Affiliation: Campbell River Indian Band, 1400 Weiwaikum Rd., Campbell River, British Columbia, Canada V9W 5W8 (604) 286-6949.

*ROBERTS-STRONG, KAREN
(Native American film director/ children's playwright)
Affiliation: Seagull Woman Publication, 2442 Cerrillos Rd. #270, Santa Fe, NM 87501.

ROBERTSON, ELEANOR
(IHS-program director)
Affiliations: Indian Health Service, 300 Mateo, NE, Suite 500, Albuquerque, NM 87102 (505) 766-6215; director, Tucson Office of Health Program Development, 7900 So. JJ Stock Rd., Tucson, AZ 85746 (602) 670-5010.

ROBERTSON, ELLEN (Oklahoma Cherokee) 1945-
(reference librarian)
Born March 7, 1945, Washington, D.C. *Education*: University of California, Berkeley, B.A., 1973, M.L.S., 1974. *Principal occupation*: Reference librarian. *Home address*: 3000 18th St., Boulder, CO 80304 (303) 939-9003. *Affiliations*: Librarian, American Indian Law Center, University of New Mexico School of Law, Albuquerque, N.M., 1975-77; reference librarian, University of New Mexico General Libraries, 1977-84; reference librarian & online search service coordinator, University of Colorado, University Libraries, Boulder, 1984-. *Memberships*: American Library Association, 1985-; Colorao Library Association, 1985-. *Interests*: Reading, hiking, travel (Peace Corps, 1966-1968 - Tunisia; Europe, Australia.)

ROBERTSON, WILBERT (Sioux)
(board member)
Affiliation: Intertribal Christian Comunications, P.O. Box 3765, Station B, Winnipeg, Manitoba, Canada R2W 3R6 (204) 661-9333.

ROBINSON, D. DUAYNE
(school principal)
Affiliation: Dzilth-Na-O-Dith-Hle Community School, Star Route 4, P.O. Box 5003 (505) 632-1697.

ROBINSON, DIANA D.
(Indian band chief)
Affiliation: Acadia Indian Band, RR 4, Box 5914C, Yarmouth, Nova Scotia, Canada B5A 4A8 (902) 742-0257.

ROBINSON, GARY (Cherokee-Mississippi Choctaw) 1950-
(film/video producer)
Born January 12, 1950, Dallas, Tex. *Education*: University of Texas, Austin, B.S., 1973; M.A. (Radio, TV, Film), 1978. *Principal occupation*: Film/video producer. *Home address*: 4021 Edenhurst Ave., Los Angeles, CA 90039-1469. *Affiliations*: Production assistant, Instructional Media Department, Tulsa Public Schools, Tulsa, OK 1973-74; media specialist, Texas Department of Mental Health/Mental Retardation, Austin, TX 1975-78; branch sales manager, Magnetic Media Corp., Austin, TX, 1978-1979; independent media producer/writer, 1980; communication specialist, Creek Nation, Okmulgee, OK, 1981-; owner-producer, Pathfinder Communications (production and consultant company), Okmulgee, OK. *Membership*: Oklahoma Film & Tape Professionals Association. *Interests*: Develop, produce and direct educational and promotional programs about Creek Indian Tribe. Regularly produce informational videotapes on Creek culture, history, art and current tribal activities. Currently developing a feature film for the tribe on Alexander Posey and the Creek Nation of Oklahoma. Avocational interests include: music, religion, movies, travel. *Video productions*: The Green Corn Festival (documentary of ancient Creek ceremony), 1982, 20 minutes; 1,000 Years of Muscogee (Creek) Art, 1982, 26 minutes; Folklore of the Muscogee People (Creek Indian legends), 1983, 28 minutes; Continuing Progress for the Muscogee People (public relations on Creek Tribe), 1983, 13 minutes; Nova-Make My People Live (nationally broadcast documentary on the Indian health crisis), 1983, 58 minutes; Strength of Life:

Knokovitee Scott (Creek/Cherokee artist), 1984, 28 minutes; Stickball: The Little Brother of War (documentary on ancient Creek game), 1984, 12 minutes; Consider Your Future (medicine employment recruitment), 1984, 10 minutes; Bacone College: Headed for the Future (promotional fundraiser program for Muskogee based private college), 1984, 11 minutes; Estee Muskogee (The Muskogee People), 1985, 24 minutes; Indian Law/Theology Symposium Highlights (project of the National Indian ministries task force), 1985, 90 minutes; Bingo Is Our Business (information about Creek Nation's business enterprise), 1985, 20 minutes; Native American Producers Showcase (film/video work of six Indian producers, for the Native American Public Broadcasting Consortium), 1985, 28 minutes.

ROBINSON, NATHAN WINFIELD
(Eastern Band Cherokee) 1938-
(motel/restaurant owner)
Born October 29, 1938, Ashland, Wis. *Education*: Southern Tech, Atlanta, Ga., 1957-58. *Principal occupation*: Owner/operator, El Camino Motel, and El Camino Craft Gallery, 1960-. *Home address*: P.O. Box 482, Cherokee, NC 28719. *Military service*: U.S. Army, 1961-62. *Community activities*: Cherokee (Tribal) Health Board (vice chairman & chairman, 1974-76); Cherokee Sheltered Workshop (board of directors); Cherokee Baptist Church (youth committee). *Interests*: Own and operate El Camino Motel; own restaurant, but have leased to another party; own and operate El Camino Craft Gallery, dealing in hand made crafts from all over the U.S. Hobbies: gardening, vintage cars, photography, racing karts.

ROBINSON, ROSE W. (Hopi) 1932-
(program director)
Born March 27, 1932, Winslow, Ariz. Education: Haskell Institute, 1951; American University (Journalism Studies), 1970-71. *Principal occupation*: Director of American Indian programs, writer-editor. *Address*: Native American Program, Commission for Multicultural Ministries of ELCA, 8765 W. Higgins Rd., Chicago, IL 60631 (302) 380-2700. *Affiliations*: Writer-editor, Indian Arts and Crafts Board, U.S. Dept. of the Interior, Washington, DC, 1963-68; information officer, Office of Public Instruction, Bureau of Indian Affairs, Washington, DC, 1968-72; executive director, American Indian Press Association, Washington, D.C. 1972-75; assistant director, Bicentennial Program, Bureau of Indian Affairs, 1975-76; vice president & director, American Indian Program, Phelps-Stokes Fund, Washington, DC, 1976-86; editor, Native American Philanthropic News Service publications, Phelps-Stokes Fund, 1976-86; director, Commission for Multicultural Ministries of ELCA, Native American Program, Chicago, IL, 1987-. *Other professional posts*: Chairman, Eastern Region, National Indian Lutheran Board, Lutheran Church in the U.S.A., 1976-; president, DC Chapter, North American Indian Women's Association, 1976-; board of directors, College of Ganado, Ganado, AZ; board of directors, American Indian Scholarships, Inc., Albuquerque, NM. *Community activities*: American Indian Society of Washington, DC, 1964- (vice president, 1967-69; publicity chairman, 1969-71); National Endowment for the Arts, 1977- (expansion arts advisory panel). *Memberships*: National Indian Education Association (board of directors, 1985-); Native American Science Education Association (board of directors, 1982-); National Con-

gress of American Indians, 1969-85; Women in Foundations (1977-); North American Indian Women's Association (1970-). *Biographical source*: Directory of Significant 20th Century American Minority Women, Vol. I, (Gaylord Professional Publications, Fisk University, Nashville, TN, 1978). *Published works*: Editor, IDRA News (Interior Dept. Recreation Association newsletter), 1957-61; editor, Smoke Signals (Indian Arts & Crafts Board monthly publication), 1965-68; editor, Indian Record (B.I.A. monthly publication), 1968-72, 1975); Indian Funding Programs (Joint Strategy and Action Committee pamphlet on church funding sources for Indian programs, 1974); compiler and editor, American Indian Directory (National Congress of American Indians, 1972, 1974); co-editor, with Richard LaCourse, American Indian Media Directory (American Indian Press Association, 1974); editor, conference report, Conference on Indian Higher Education for Private Philanthropists and Indian Educators (Phelps-Stokes Fund, 1975); editor, The Exchange, The Roundup, and Bulletins (Native Philanthropic News Service, the Phelps-Stokes Fund, 1976-).

*ROBINSON, SHERRY
(editor)
Affiliation: Americans Before Columbus, National Indian Youth Council, 318 Elm St., SE, Albuquerque, NM 87102 (505) 247-2251.

ROBINSON, VIOLA
(council president)
Affiliation: Native Council of Nova Scotia, P.O. Box 1320, Truro, Nova Scotia, Canada B2N 5N2 (902) 895-1523.

*ROCKMAN, JEREMY
(health director)
Affiliation: Wisconsin Winnebago Health Dept., P.O. Box 636, Black River Falls, WI 54615 (715) 284-7548.

RODEE, MARIAN E. 1940-
(museum curator; consultant
on Native American art)
Born March 13, 1940, Philadelphia, Penna. *Education*: University of Pennsylvania, B.A., 1961; Columbia University, M.A., 1965. *Principal occupation*: Museum curator; consultant on Native American art. *Home address*: 413 Camino de la Sierra N.E., Albuquerque, NM 87123 (505) 298-3105. *Affiliations*: Research assistant, Brooklyn Museum, 1968-69; Maxwell Museum of Anthropology, University of New Mexico, Albuquerque, NM (registrar, 1970-73; associate curator, 1975-76; curator, 1977-. *Other professional posts*: Shows & brochures for Museum, 1972-; lecturer, Art Department, College of Fine Arts, University of New Mexico; seminars, exhibits and classes. *Memberships*: Smithsonian Institution; Textile Museum; Textile Society; New Mexico Association of Museums. *Awards, honors*: Smithsonian Fellowship for Studies in Conservation, 1978-79, 1981-82; Pasold Fellowship, 1982; Smithsonian Institution Visiting Fellowship, 1987 (study of the 19th century Zuni fetishes); New Mexico Humanities Council grant, 1989 (visit Zuni and do study of fetish carvers. *Interests*: "In the past 15 years, I have examined the collections of Native American and Spanish American weaving along with the storage, exhibition and conservation techniques of various museums." *Biographical sources*: Who's Who in American Women. Published works: Numerous articles and book reviews.

RODGERS, RAYMOND
(hospital director)
Affiliation: Albuquerque PHS Indian Hospital, 801 Vassar Dr., NE, Albuquerque, NM 87106 (505) 254-4000.

RODRIGUEZ, ARDENA
(executive director)
Affiliation: American Indian Resource & Education Coalition, P.O. Box 3585, Austin, TX 78764 (512) 648-7023.

RODRIGUEZ-SELLAS, JOSE E. 1954-
(information & resources developer)
Born May 4, 1954, Ponce, Puerto Rico. *Education*: University of New Haven (Conn.), B.A. (History), 1978; U. of Puerto Rico/Rio Piedras, Labor Relations Institute, 1979-1981; Labor Education Institute, Santurce, P.R., 1981. *Principal occupation*: Information and resources developer. *Home address*: 83 C Morris St., Hartford, CT 06114 (203) 238-4009 (work). *Affiliation*: Information & resources developer, Chemical Abuse Services Agency (CASA), Bridgeport, CT, 1988-. *Other professional posts*: Co-editor of American Indians for Development Newsletter, and director of May Wutche Aque'ne (journal). *Community activities*: President of Latin Student Organization (1978), University of New Haven, West Haven, CT; spokesperson and coordinator of Brother/Sisterhood of Caribbean and Latin American People, 1983-85; secretary, Hispanic Historical Society of Connecticut (present); Latinos Against AIDS (board of directors, coordinator of the personnel committee). *Awards, honors*: Certificate for Services rendered to the members of the Brotherhood of Social Services Workers of Puerto Rico by the National Leadership of said organization. *Interests*: "My main interests at present are: journalism, graphic arts, photography and writing in general and poems in particular (both English and Spanish. I am very concerned about the status of the so-called "minorities" and the particular behavior exhibited by the people of European descent who are racist in the U.S. The civil rights, the economic justice and the struggle for self-determination of all the people of Latin America and the Caribbean are the tour of duty by which I live. It is the main demand that the Latin American Mother Land imposes on her sons and daughters."

*ROE, CHUCK
(BIA agency supt.)
Affiliation: Employee Data & Compensation, Bureau of Indian Affairs, Box 2026, Albuquerque, NM 87103 (505) 766-2336.

*ROEHL, IDA (Athapascan)
(village president)
Affiliation: Dillingham Village Council, P.O. Box 216, Dillingham, AK 99576 (907) 842-2384.

ROESSLER, PAUL ALBERT (Navajo) 1920-
(economic consultant)
Born October 8, 1920, Buckman, N.M. *Education*: Georgetown University, B.S. (Foreign Service), 1949, postgraduate, 1949-51; University of Maryland, postgraduate, 1965. *Principal occupation*: Economic consultant. *Addresses*: P.O. Box 3045, Tucson, AZ 85701; P.O. Box 34137, Bethesda, MD 20817. *Affiliations*: International economist, U.S. Dept. of the Army, 1965-75; director, Office of Policy Planning, 1975-76, chief, Division of Economic Development, 1976-80, Bureau of Indian Affairs, Dept. of the Interior;

president, American Economic Consultants, Inc., Tucson, AZ, 1980-, Bethesda, MD, 1982- *Military service*: U.S. Army, 1941-46, PTO; col., U.S. Army Reserve (Purple Heart with cluster; Philippine Defense Medal; Philippine Liberation Medal; Philippine Presidential Unit Citation with two clusters; others). *Memberships*: National Economists Club; Society of Government Economists; American Political Science Association; DAV; VFW; American Legion; Delta Phi Epsilon. *Biographical sources*: Who's Who in the East; Who's Who in the South and Southwest; Who's Who in the U.S.; American Men of Science; International Biographic Dictionary (London); Men of Distinction (London); and others.

ROGERS, EDWARD S. 1923-
(ethnologist)
Born May 2, 1923, Lee, Mass. *Education*: Massachusetts Institute of Technology, 1942-44; 1946-47; Middlebury College, B.A., 1951; University of New Mexico, MA, 1953, PhD, 1958. *Principal occupation*: Curator, Dept. of Ethnology, Royal Ontario Museum, 100 Queen's Park, Toronto, Ontario, Can. M5S 2C6. *Other professional post*: Part-time professor of anthropology, McMaster University, Hamilton, Ontario, Can. *Military service*: U.S. Army, 1943-46 (Army Specialized Training Program, 1943-44; Infantry, 1944-45). *Community activities*: Archaeological & Historic Sites Board of Ontario, 1966-72; Ministry of Natural Resources, 1962-75; Northern Studies Committee, University of Toronto, 1971-73. *Memberships*: Arctic Institute of North America; American Anthropological Association. *Interests*: Consultation on contemporary matters concerning North American Indians. *Published works*: The Round Lake Ojibwa (Royal Ontario Museum, 1962); The Hunting Group-Hunting Territory Complex Among the Mistassini Indians (National Museums of Canada, 1963); Bibliography of Ontario Anthropology (Royal Ontario Museum, 1964); An Athapaskan Type of Knife (National Museums of Canada, 1965); Subsistence Areas of the Cree-Ojibwa of the Eastern Subarctic: A Preliminary Study, two parts (National Museums of Canada, 1963-66); North Pacific Coast Indians (Canadian Antiques Collector, 1967); The Material Culture of the Mistassini (National Museums of Canada, 1967); Indian Farmers of Parry Island (Royal Ontario Museum, 1967); Canadian Indians (Swan Publishing, 1967); Indians of Canada (Clarke, Irwin, 1969); Forgotten Peoples (Royal Ontario Museum, 1969); Band Organization Among the Indians of Eastern Subarctic Canada (National Museums of Canada, 1969); Natural Environment-Social Organization-Witchcraft: Cree Versus Ojibwa-A Test Case (National Museums of Canada, 1969); Indians of the North Pacific Coast (Royal Ontario Museum, 1970); Iroquoians of the Eastern Woodlands (Royal Ontario Museums, 1970); Indians of th Subarctic (Royal Ontario Museum, 1970); Indians of the Plains (Royal Ontario Museum, 1970); Algonkians of the Eastern Woodlands (Royal Ontario Museum, 1970); The Indians of Canada/ A Survey (Royal Ontario Museum, 1970); The Quest Food and Furs-The Mistassini Cree, 1953-1954 (National Museums of Canada, 1973); Parry Island Farmers: A Period of Change in the Way of Life of the Algonkians of Southern Ontario, with Flora Tobobondung (National Museum of Man, 1975); and others; also numerous papers, reviews, and articles in scholarly journals.

ROGERS, STEVE
(library curator)
Affiliation: The Wheelwright of the American Indian, Mary Cabot Wheelwright Research Library, P.O. Box 5153, 704 Camino Lejo, Santa Fe, NM 87501 (505) 982-4636.

ROGERS, WILL, Jr. (Cherokee) 1911-
(publisher, journalist)
Born October 20, 1911, New York, N.Y. *Education*: Stanford University, B.A., 1935. *Principal occupation*: Publisher, journalist. *Home address*: Santos Ranch, Tubac, AZ 85646. *Affiliations*: Publisher/journalist, Beverly Hills Citizen, newspaper, 1935-53; U.S. Congressman, 16th District, California, 1942-1944; special assistant to the Commissioner of Indian Affairs, 1967-1969; creative consultant, George Spota Theatre Production of Will Rogers, U.S.A. starring James Whitmore, 1968-. *Other professional posts*: Motion picture actor, television commentator, lecturer. Military service: U.S. Army, 1944-45 (Bronze Star). *Community activities*: Beverly Hills Chamber of Commerce; chairman, Southern California Truman campaign committee, 1948; Will Rogers Memorial Commission, State of Oklahoma (member); California State Parks Commission (chairman). *Memberships*: Arrow, Inc. (founder and honorary president); National Congress of American Indians, 1946-; Oklahoma Cherokee Tribe. *Interests*: In recent years he has divided his energies between his real estate business in Beverly Hills and his ranch in Tubac, Arizona. He continues to be active in Indian affairs, making occasional trips for the Bureau of Indian Affairs. A well known lecturer, he continues active in this field. He has worked with the Alaskan Federation of Natives. *Theatrical activities*: Movies: Star in The Will Rogers Story, (Warner Brothers, 1951); The Boy From Oklahoma, and Wild Heritage. Plays: Ah, Wilderness, and Street Scene (Pasadena Playhouse). *Radio*: Rogers of the Gazette. Television: Good Morning Show, CBS.

ROHN, ARTHUR HENRY 1929-
(professor of anthropology)
Born May 15, 1929, Elmhurst Ill. *Education*: Harvard College, BA, 1951; University of Arizona, 1955-56; Harvard University, PhD, 1966. *Principal occupation*: Professor of anthropology. *Home address*: 320 North Parkwood, Wichita, KS 67208 (316) 685-1823. *Affiliation*: Professor of anthropology, Wichita State University, Wichita, KS, 1970-. *Military service*: U.S. Navy, 1951-54 (Lieutenant (jg); Korean Service Medal with one star K7; United Nations Service Medal; National Defense Service Medal). *Community activities*: Mid-America All-Indian Center (Museum Policy Committee). *Memberships*: Society for American Archaeology, 1953- (review editor, American Antiquity, 1967-70); Current Anthropology, 1960-; American Anthropological Association (Fellow), 1966-; American Association for the Advancement of Science, 1966-1976; American Society for Conservation Archaeology, 1973-; Archaeological Institute of America; Tree Ring Society. *Awards, honors*: Outstanding Educators of America, 1973; City of Wichita, Distinguished Service Citation, 1976; Leadership Award, Wichita State University, 1978; Historical Society of New Mexico, "Gaspar Perez de Villagra" Award for outstanding publication; Rocky Mountain Book Publishers, First Place Quality Book Award. *Interests*: Pueblo Indian culture history, especially social organization and ecology; archaeology of the Central Plains,

especially Kansas and Oklahoma; New England archaeology; Delaware culture history; research focused most heavily on archaeology of the Southwest and Plains--expeditions at Mesa Verde and Yellowjacket, CO; Wolf Creek, Marion, and Hillsdale, KS; Red River, OK; and Marshfield, MA. Also, minority nationalities of China (extensive travel in 1989 & 1991; East Asian archaeology, especially Neolithic. *Biographical sources*: American Men and Women of Science; Who's Who in the Midwest; Contemporary Authors; Who's Who Among Authors and Journalists. *Published works*: Mug House, Mesa Verde National Park, Colorado (National Park Service, 1971); Prehistoric Ceramics of the Mesa Verde Region (Museum of Northern Arizona, 1974); Cultural Change and Continuity on Chapin Mesa (Regents Press, of Kansas, 1977); Anasazi Ruins of the Southwest (University of New Mexico Press, 1987); Rock Art of the Bandelier National Monument (University of New Mexico Press, 1989); Mesoamerica's Ancient Cities (University Press of Colorado, 1990); among others; also numerous articles, chapters, and book reviews.

ROKWAHO (DAN THOMPSON) (Mohawk) 1953-
(publications & graphic design consultant)
Born November 7, 1953, Akwesasne Territory. *Education*: High school. *Principal occupation*: Publications and graphic design consultant. *Home address*: P.O. Box 166, Rooseveltown, NY 13683. *Affiliations*: Media specialist, St. Regis Mohawk Language Program, 1980-82; co-founder (with John Fadden) and production manager, Pictographics, P.O. Box 166, Rooseveltown, NY, 1977-. *Other professional posts*: Literary editor, artist and photographer, Akwesasne Notes, 1982-83; founding editor, Indian Time, an Akwesasne biweekly newspaper, 1983; art director for Indian Studies, Cornell University, Ithaca, N.Y., 1984; editor, Akwesasne Notes and Indian Time, 1984-85; co-founder of Akwekon, a literary and arts quarterly published by Akwekon/Akwesasne Notes; co-founder of Suntracks, a tracking and nature observation school in the Adirondack Mountains near Ochiota, N.Y. *Membership*: Association for the Advancement of Native North American Arts and Crafts (administrative executive; project, Iroquois Arts: A Directory of a People and Their Work, published, 1984). *Interests*: Music, literature, theatre, computer science, electronic and mechanical gaggetry, the sciences, and archaic Mohawk words and semantics (compiling a dictionary of terms). *Published works*: Editor & designer, Trail of Broken Treaties. B.I.A. I'm Not Your Indian Anymore (Akwesasne Notes, 1974); translator & illustrator, Teiohakwente, a Mohawk language textbook (Dept. of Indian Affairs, Ottawa, Can., 1977); author and artist, Covers (poetry, illustrations) (Strawberry Press, 1982); contributor of poetry to numerous anthologies; cover art and illustrations for many publications, as well as design production for Akwesasne Notes Calendars.

ROLATOR, FRED S. 1938-
(professor of history)
Born July 22, 1938, McKinney, Tex. *Education*: Wake Forest University, B.A., 1960; University of Southern California, M.A., Ph.D., 1960-1963. *Principal occupation*: Professor of history, Middle Tennessee State University, Murfreesboro, 1967-. *Home address*: 3808 Lascassas Rd., Murfressboro, TN 37130 (615) 808 2630 (work).

Other professional post: Associate professor of history & chairman of the History & Social Sciences Dept., Grand Canyon College, Phoenix, AZ, 1964-67. *Community activities*: Frequent speaker on Indian matters for civic organizations and school in area; co-director, The American Indian and the Jacksonian Era: The Impact of Removal: A Sequi-Centennial Symposium (The national symposium on the adoption of the Indian Removal Bill of 1830) held Feb., 1980; Rutherford County Heritage Commission (member, 1978-80). *Memberships*: Tennessee Baptist Historical Society (former president); Southern Baptist Historical Commission; Baptist History & Heritage (board of directors); Organization of American Historians; The Western Historical Association; Tennessee Historical Society; The Southern Historical Society. *Awards, honors*: National Merit Scholar, Wake Forest, 1956-1960; National Defense and Haynes Fellow, USC, 1960-1963; Tennessee Baptist Convention, Heritage Award, 1984; Fulbright Professor, Japan, 1987. *Interests*: History of the American Indian, especially previous to 1492; American church history; director of Historic Preservation effort, Camp Palma, located near Tupa, Sao Paulo state, Brazil (1976). *Biographical sources*: Directory of American Scholars; Dictionary of International Biography; Who's Who in the South and Southwest. *Published works*: The Continental Congress: A Study in the Origins of American Public Administration (Xerox, 1971); Charles Thompson (Harrington Associates, 1977); Japanese Americans (Rourke, 1991). Article: "The Time They Cried", Journal of American Studies (Japan) 1988 (no. 4) - an article concerning the Trail of Tears in Japanese and is one of the first articles in Japanese concerning the American Indian; article, "The American Indian & the Origin of the Second American Party System," in the Wisconsin Magazine of History (Spring, 1993).

*ROMANO, SHARON
(student services director)
Affiliation: American Indian Student Services, Anoka Ramsey Community College, 11200 Mississippi Blvd., N.W., Coon Rapids, MN 55433 (612) 422-3470.

ROMERO, M. SUE (Hidatsa/Creek) 1955-
(administrative assistant)
Born August 11, 1955, Claremore, Okla. *Education*: University of New Mexico, 1985-86. *Principal occupation*: Administrative assistant. *Home address*: 7613 Cleghorn Court, NW, Albuquerque, NM 87120 (505) 766-8418 (office). *Affiliations*: Clerical specialist, Albuquerque Public Schools, Indian Education Dept., 1977; administrative assistant: Santa Fe Indian School, 1977-85; All Indian Pueblo Council, Albuquerque, 1985-87; SW Indian Polytechnic Institute, Albuquerque, 1988-. *Community activities*: SW Indian Personnel Management, 1983-85. *Memberships*: Santa Fe Indian School Alumni Association; NONAW - National Organization of Native American Women, 1989-; Indian Bowling Association, 1989-. *Awards, honors*: Nominated to Outstanding Women in America, 1984; SW Region Personnel Management Training Intern, 1984; 1985 Santa Fe Indian School Employee of the Year. *Interests*: "Over 12 years of extensive experience working with Native American Programs from a boarding school situation to a political entity to a substance abuse program."

*ROOT, NINA J.
(museum dept, chairperson)
Affiliation: American Museum of Natural History, Dept. of Library Services, Central Park West at 79th St., New York, nY 10024 (212) 769-5406.

ROOTE, VERNON
(Indian band chief)
Affiliation: Chippewas of Saugeen, RR 1, Southampton, Ontario, Canada N0H 2L0 (519) 797-2218.

*ROSE, DONALD (Eastern Cherokee) 1932-
(engineer; president & CEO)
Born in 1932 on the Cherokee Reservation, N.C. *Education*: University of Nebraska, BA (Political Science). *Principal occupation*: Engineer; president & CEO. *Address & Affiliation*: President & CEO, Command Technologies, P.O. Box 670, Warrenton, VA 22186. Their work - primarily software creation & consulting - includes development of computer-based learning systems, artificial intelligence applications in education, logistics support for F-15 testing equipment and a study of missile theatre defense tactics and equipment. *Military service*: U.S. Air Force, 1949-74 (Radar officer & instructor). *Awards, honors*: The "Washington Technology" newspaper names Rose's, Command Technologies one of region's 50 fastest growing high-tech firms.

*ROSE, JOHN S.
(library director)
Affiliation: Dorothy Cummings Memorial Library, Americn Indian Bible College, 10020 N. 15th Ave., Phoenix, AZ 85021 (602) 944-3335.

ROSE, MICHAEL "FLYING EAGLE"
(Cherokee)
(member-board of regents)
Affiliation: Member, Board of Regents, American Indian Heritage Foundation, 6051 Arlington Blvd., Falls Church, VA 22044-2788 (703) 237-7500.

ROSE, ROBERT "SWIFT ARROW"
(Cherokee)
(advisor)
Affiliation: Council of Advisors, American Indian Heritage Foundation, 6051 Arlington Blvd., Falls Church, VA 22044 (703) 237-7500.

ROSE, WIL (Dr.) 1931-
(foundation executive)
Born September 13, 1931, in Ohio. *Education*: Santa Monica City College; Ashland University, Litt.D. *Principal occupation*: Foundation executive. *Home address*: 6555 Dearborn Dr., Falls Church, VA 22044 (703) 354-2270. *Affiliations*: President, People to People, Inc., 1966-67; founder & president, Involvement, Inc. (developed non-profit service organization designed to mobilize and utilize voluntary resources of America), 1967-76; national director, United Way of America - Volunteer Mobilization Project, 1976-77; president, National Leadership Institute, Washington, D.C., 1979-80; president, National Foundation for Philanthropy, 1979-81; co-founder & president, National Heritage Foundation, 1968-81; chief executive officer, American Indian Heritage Foundation, 1973-; founder/president, PlanAmerica (full service master planning firm), 1981-. *Other professional posts*: Serve on several boards of non-profit organizations. *Military service*: U.S. Marine Corps, 1950-54 (Korean conflict; Staff NCO with Purple Heart

Award). *Community activities*: Rotary International. *Memberships*: Society for International Development; the Sacred Concert Society; Outstanding Americans Foundation. *Awards, honors*: For activities with DATA International and People-to-People, was selected by the U.S. Jaycees and featured in "Look Magazine" as one of the Ten Outstanding Young Men in the U.S.; selected by the California Jaycees as one of Five Outstanding Young Men in California; featured in the "People On the Way Up" section of the Saturday Evening Post; Sertoma International conveyed their Service to Mankind Award; married to Princess Pale Moon, Cherokee/Ojibwa concert and recording artist and president of the American Indian Heritage Foundation.

ROSEN, LAWRENCE 1941-
(professor of anthropology)
Born December 9, 1941, Cincinnati, Ohio. *Education*: Brandeis University, BA, 1963; University of Chicago, MA, 1965, PhD, 1968, JD, 1974. *Principal occupation*: Professor of anthropology. *Home address*: 435 Alexander St., Princeton, NJ 08540 (609) 258-5535 (work). *Affiliations*: Professor, 1977-, dept. chairperson, 1989-94, Dept. of Anthropology, Princeton University, Princeton, NJ; adjunct professor of law, Columbia Law School, New York, NY, 1979-. *Community activities*: Volunteer legal work for the Native American Rights Fund. *Memberships*: American Anthropological Association; Law and Society Association (board of directors). *Awards, honors*: John D. & Catherine T. MacArthur Foundation Award; John Simon Guggenheim Foundation Fellow; National Science Foundation Fellow, 1990-92. *Interests*: "Research on American Indian legal problems, especially the return of Indian skeletal remains, the furtherance of Indian religious rights, and the rights of indigenous peoples in international law; extensive research in North Africa, particularly on Islamic law." *Biographical source*: American Men and Women of Science. *Published work*: Editor, The American Indian and the Law (Transaction Books, 1976); Bargaining for Reality (University of Chicago Press, 1984); The Anthropology of Justice (Cambridge University Press, 1989); Other Intentions (School of American Research Press, 1994).

*ROSS, A. CHUCK (*Ehanamani-Walks Among*) (Santee Sioux) 1940-
(educational administration)
Born October 25, 1940, Pipestone, Minn. *Education*: Black Hills State College, BS, 1967; Arizona State University, MA, 1971; University of Minnesota, ABD, 1973; Western Colorado University, Ed.D., 1980. *Principal occupation*: Educational administration. *Home address*: 7892 W. 1st Place, Lakewood, CO 80226 (303) 238-3420. *Affiliations*: Instructor (contract), Native American Studies, University of Colorado, Boulder, 1977-80; health & education consultant, Edgewater, CO, 1980-83; instructor (contract) - Native American Studies, Standing Rock College, Fort Yates, ND, Oglala Lakota College, Kyle, SD, & Fort Peck Community College, Poplar, MT, 1983-90; Agency Supt. for Education, Bureau of Indian Affairs, Fort Yates, ND; supt., Little Wound School, Kyle, SD, 1990-91; author, publisher, international consultant (Bear Publishing),1991-. *Other professional posts*: Lecturer, 'In Search of the Origins of the Red Man,' presented in 44 state & 6 Canadian provinces, 1975-; lecturer on topics including Lakota history & culture, psychology, wholistic health &

education, 1975-; primary investigator for various publications; and technical advisor for various film/TV broadcast. *Military service*: U.S. Army Airborne, 1962-65. *Memberships*: Dakota Astronomical Society; National Indian Education Association. *Awards, honors*: Friendship Award, White Buffalo Council, 1977; nominee, National Indian Educator of the Year, National Indian Education Association, 1980; Outstanding Volunteer Service Award, U.S. Dept. of Health & Human Services, 1982; Gubernatorial Appointment, North Dakota Teacher's Professional Practices Commission, 1985; Who's Who Among the Sioux - University of South Dakota, 1986; Participant, Effective Schools Team for BIA, 1988; Honoree, 'Top 50' Selection at International Book Fair, Frankfurt, Germany, recognition for "Mitakuye Oyasin," 1992; Special Recognition Award for Contribution to Indian Education, National Indian Education Association, 1992; Mitakuye Oyasin approved for cinema film production by Osmond Productions (Pleasant Grove, UT), 1994. *Interests*: Lectures & presentations. *Published work*: Biographies of Spotted Tail & Crow Dog for the Encyclopedia of the Indians of the Americas, 1975; Mitakuye Oyasin: We Are All Related (Bear Publishing, 1989); Ehanamani: Walks Among (Bear Publishing, 1992), a book that compares customs, languages, and spiritual beliefs of Indians with other peoples. Dr. Ross has worked for 25 years in the field of education as a teacher, principal, superintendent, college professor, and college department chairman. He has lectured on cultural understanding in 44 states in the U.S., 6 Canadian provinces, and 5 European countries. His book Mitakuye Oyasin was a best-seller.

ROSS, DENIS
(Indian band chief)
Affiliation: Montagnais de les Escoumins, 27, rue de la Reserve, Box 820, Les Escoumins, Quebec, Canada G0G 1V0 (418) 233-2509.

*ROSS, JACQUELYN (Pomo/Coast Mewuk)
(outreach coordinator)
Affiliation: Relations with Schools/EOP Outreach Services, 2828 Chiles Rd. Hall, Davis, CA 95616 (916) 752-3124.

ROSS, JOHN, JR. (Cherokee)
(tribal chairperson)
Affiliation: United Keetoowah Band of Cherokee Indians, 2450 S. Muskogee Ave., Tahlequah, OK 74464 (918) 456-5491.

ROSS, KENNETH
(BIA administrator)
Affiliation: Office of Indian Education Programs, Bureau of Indian Affairs, Albuquerque Area Office, P.O. Box 26567, Albuquerque, NM 87125 (505) 766-3170.

ROUBIDOUX, JAMES
(BIA agency supt.)
Affiliation: National Technical Support Center, Bureau of Indian Affairs, P.O. Box 888, Albuquerque, NM 87103 (505) 766-3627.

ROUBIDEAUX, NANETTE S.
(Ioway of Kansas/Nebraska) 1940-
(museum professional)
Born July 20, 1940, Porcupine, S.D. *Education*: Haskell Indian Junior College, AAS, 1975; University of Kansas, B.A. (Honors), 1977, PhD candidate. *Principal occupation*: Museum pro-

fessional. *Address*: The Gustav Heye Center, Museum of the American Indian, Smithsonian Institution, One Bowling Green, New York, NY 10004. *Affiliations*: Teaching assistant, research assistant, assistant instructor, graduate assistant, University of Kansas, Lawrence, Kan., 1977-83; co-director, Kansas Committee for the Humanities Project Change, Continuities, and Challenges, Haskell Indian Junior College, 1984-85; intern fellowship, Museum of the American Indian, New York, N.Y., 1985-. *Other professional posts*: Consultant: KANU Radio, University of Kansas, 1981-; Women's Transitional Care, Lawrence, KS, 1982-; Haskell Indian Junior College, 1984-; Museum of the American Indian, 1985-; chairperson, Grand Review Committee for Dept. of Health and Human Services, Office of Human Development Services, 1985-. *Memberships*: American Historical Association; American Anthropological Association; Phi Alpha Theta; Society for Values in Higher Education. *Awards, honors*: Danforth Foundation Fellowship, 1979-1982; Outstanding Americans Program, listed in Outstanding Young Women in America, 1977; American Indian Scholarship Program, 1977-80; Lawrence Professional and Business Women's Outstanding Haskel Indian Junior College Student, 1975; Merwlyn Foundation Research Grant, 1976; Commission of the Status for Women, Outstanding Student in Contributions to a Minority Culture, 1976; Minority Affairs Teaching Assistant Award, 1977; Graduate School, Dissertation Fellowship, 1984-85. *Interests*: Contemporary Native American activities. *Biographical source*: Outstanding Young Women in America, 1977. *Published works*: The Native American Woman: A Cross-Disciplinary Bibliography (in preparation); Up Before Dawn: A Study of the Family Farm, paper given at regional meeting of American Anthropological Association, Memphis, Tenn., 1979.

ROUBIDEAUX, RAMON ARTHUR *(Wanblee Ohitika-Brave Eagle)* (Rosebud Sioux) 1924-
(lawyer-private practice)
Born November 15, 1924, Rosebud, S.D. *Education*: Haskell Institute, 1942; George Washington Uiversity, AA, 1948, LLB, 1950. *Principal occupation*: Lawyer-private practice. *Home address*: 4222 Foothill Dr., Rapid City, SD 57702 (605) 348-0122. *Military service*: U.S. Air Force, 1942-46 (1st Lt.; Air Medal with Oak Leaf Cluster and three battle stars). *Community activities*: South Dakota Assistant Attorney General; State's Attorney; Tribal Court Judge; Tribal Attorney for various tribes. Chairperson of various political and Indian groups and associations through the years. Member of State Commission on Indian Affairs; chairperson of State Bar Civil Rights Committee; member of State Bar Criminal Law Committee. *Memberships*: Sixth Judicial Circuit Bar Association (president); American Bar Association (Civil Rights Committee); National Congress of American Indians; American Legion (Post and Couty Commander); V.F.W. *Interests*: Formed partnership with Charles Poches and Gerald L. Reade, specializing in criminal and personal injury actions. Partnership dissolved Jan. 1, 1968. Formed partnership with David Bergren in Fall of 1971. Active in Indian affairs generally. Advocate of State Jurisdiction on Indian Reservations. *Biographical sources*: Who's Who in the Midwest.

ROUFS, TIMOTHY G. 1943-
(professor)
Born August 30, 1943, Cokato, Minn. *Education*: University of Notre Dame, A.B., 1965; University of Minnesota, Ph.D., 1971. *Principal occupation*: Professor, Dept. of Sociology, Anthropology, Geography, University of Minnesota, Duluth, 1970-. *Community activities*: A.M. Chisholm Museum, Duluth, MN (board of directors). *Memberships*: American Ethnological Society; Society for Applied Anthropology (Fellow); American Anthropological Association (Fellow); The Royal Anthropological Association of Great Britain and Ireland (Fellow); Current Anthropology (Associate); Sigma Xi, 1980-. *Awards, honors*: 1973 Service Award from Anishnabe, University of Minnesota-Duluth, American Indian Student Association; 1976 City of Duluth Bicentennial Award; 1980 Outstanding Young Men of America. *Interests*: Anishnabe, Chippewa, and Ojibwa ethnohistory; culture and personality studies. *Biographical source*: Who's Who in the Midwest. *Published works*: The Anishnabe of the Minnesota Chippewa Tribe (Indian Tribal Series, Phoenix, 1975); Working Bibliography of the Anishnabe & Selected Related Works (Lake Superior Basin Studies Center, Duluth, 1981, 1984); editor, with Larry P. Atkins, Information Relating to Chippewa Peoples (from the Handbook of American Indians North of Mexico, 1907-1910) (Lake Superior Basin Studies Center, Duluth, 1984).

ROUNTREE, HELEN C. 1944-
(anthropologist)
Born October 8, 1944, Camp Le Jeune, N.C. *Education*: College of William & Mary, AB, 1966; University of Utah, MA, 1968; University of Wisconsin, Milwaukee, PhD, 1973. *Principal occupation*: Anthropologist. *Home address*: 268 Harris Creek Rd., Hampton, VA 23669 (804) 683-3812 (work). *Affiliation*: Professor, Old Dominion University, Norfolk, VA, 1968-. *Memberships*: American Anthropological Association, 1968-; Royal Anthropological Institute of Great Britain & Ireland, 1969-; Society for Applied Anthropology, 1981-; American Society for Ethnohistory, 1988-. *Interests*: Professional interests: North American Indian ethnology, especially Virginia Algonquians; ecological anthropology; political anthropology; anthropology of gender; Middle Eastern ethnology (ancient & modern), ethnicity. Avocations: music, textiles, embroidery-designing. *Published works*: The Powhatan Indians of Virginia: Their Traditional Culture (U. of Oklahoma Press, 1989); Pocahontas' People: The Powhatan Indians of Virginia Through Four Centuries (University of Oklahoma Press, 1990); editor, Powhatan Foreign Relations, 1500-1722 (University Press of Virginia - forthcoming).

ROUWALK, ALYCE
(BIA agency supt.)
Affiliation: Shiprock Agency, Bureau of Indian Affairs, P.O. Box 966, Shiprock, NM 87420 (505) 368-4301.

*ROWELL, RONALD
(center director)
Affiliation: National Native American AIDS Prevention Center, 3515 Grand Ave. #100, Oakland, CA 94160 (510) 444-2051.

ROWLAND, TED
(school supt.)
Affiliation: Busby School, P.O. Box 38, Busby, MT 59016 (406) 592-3646.

ROY, STEWART
(Indian band chief)
Affiliation: West Bay Indian Band, Box 2, West Bay, Ontario, Canada P0P 1G0 (705) 377-5362.

*ROYBAL, LOUIS (Piro/Manso/Tiwa)
(tribal council president)
Affiliation: Pueblo of San Juan de Guadalupe, P.O. Box 16243, Las Cruces, NM 88004 (800) 527-1699.

ROZIE, LEE *(Mixashawn)* (Mohegan)
(musickeeper)
Born in Hartford, Conn. *Principal occupation*: Musickeeper. *Home address*: 108 Sisson St., E. Hartford, CT 06118 (800) 949-MIXA. *Membership*: Executive Director, Pequonawonk Canoe Society, E. Hartford, CT. *Interests*: "The musical trio, "Afro-Algonquin" which derives its name from the ethnic background of its two co-leaders, Rick & Lee Rozie. The idea behind the group is to integrate American Indian folk music themes into modern Afro-American jazz. Lee plays tenor and soprano saxophones, flutes, percussion, vocals. "Maheekanew," is the traditional name of our people." *Records & CDs*: "Word, Out" Music for the Next Century," "Plastic Champions," & "Maheekanew View of Mixashawn," all produced by (Indian Runs Records, 1991-93).

RUBEL, PAULA G. 1933-
(professor of anthropology)
Born March 13, 1933, New York, N.Y. *Education*: Hunter College, A.B., 1953; Columbia University, Ph.D., 1963. *Principal occupation*: Professor of anthropology. *Home address*: 560 Riverside Dr., Apt. 18D, New York, NY 10027 (212) 663-3694. *Affiliations*: Dept. of Anthropology, Barnard College, Columbia University, New York, NY (lecturer, 1965-66; assistant professor, 1966-70; associate professor, 1970-74; professor, 1974-). *Fellowships and grants*: SSRC Faculty Research Grant, summer 1968 (research on potlatch-type societies; NSF Research Grants, 1971-72, 1974-75, 1986-87; Barnard Faculty Research Grants, 1972-73, 1978-81; Guggenheim Fellowship, 1986-87. *Interests*: "I teach courses at the graduate and undergraduate level on Native American cultures." *Published works*: Co-author, with Rosman: Feasting With Mine Enemy: Rank and Exchange Among Northwest Coast Societies (Columbia U. Press, 1971; paperback ed, Waveland Press, 1986); The Tapestry of Culture, 4th Ed. (McGraw-Hill, 1991). *Articles*: "Potlatch and Sagali: The Structure of Exchange in Trobriand and Haida Societies," in Transactions of the New York Academy of Sciences, June 1970; "Potlatch and Hakari: An Analysis of Maori Society in Terms of the Potlatch Model," in Man, Vol. 6, No. 4, Dec. 1971; "The Potlatch: A Structural Analysis," in American Anthropologist 74, 1972; among others. *Conference papers*: "West Coast Tribes and Their Social Structural Transformations" presented at the American Assn for the Advancement of Science, Los Angeles, CA, May 1985; "The Kwakiutl Potlatch: A Sacred or Secular Ritual?" presented at Seminar on the Role of Ritual in the System of Culture, Jagiellonian U., Poland, 1985; "Structural Patterning in Kwakiutl Art, Symbol and Ritual" presented at 12th Int'l Congress of Anthropological & Ethnological Sciences, July 1988; "The Material Culture of the 'Noble Savage': Artifact Collecting & Images of Other" presented at the Dept. of Anthropology, U. of Chicago, 1992.

RUDOLPH, LINDA
(school supt.)
Affiliation: Puyallup Nation Education System, Chief Leschi School System, 2002 East 28th St., Tacoma, WA 98404 (206) 593-0218.

RUEGAMER, JOHN A.
(school principal)
Affiliation: Coeur D'Alene Tribal School, P.O. Box 338, DeSmet, ID 83824 (208) 274-6921.

*RUGGLES, MARY JO
(instructor-Native American studies)
Affiliation: Native American Studies Program, University of Oklahoma, 455 W. Lindsey, Rm. 804, Norman, OK 73019 (405) 325-2312.

*RUNDSTROM, ROBERT
(instructor-Native American studies)
Affiliation: Native American Studies Program, University of Oklahoma, 455 W. Lindsey, Rm. 804, Norman, OK 73019 (405) 325-2312.

RUOFF, A. LaVONNE BROWN 1930-
(professor of English)
Born April 10, 1930, Charleston, IL. *Education*: Northwestern University, B.S., 1953, M.A., 1954, Ph.D., 1966. *Principal occupation*: Professor of English. *Home address*: 300 Forest Ave., Oak Park, IL 60302 (708) 848-9292. *Affiliation*: Dept. of English, University of Illinois, Chicago, 1966-94. *Community activities*: Chicago Indian Council Fire, 1980-87; Indian Business Associate Advisory Board, 1977-84. *Memberships*: Modern Language Association, 1966-; Association for the Study of Amerian Indian Literature, 1977-; Discussion Group on American Indian Literature (MLA, 1978-; chair, 1978, 1990); Society for the Study of Multi-Ethnic Literature in the U.S., 1978-. *Awards, honors*: Achievement Award, Indian Council Fire, 1989; Distinguished Contribution to Ethnic Studies, Society for the Study of Multi-Ethnic Literature in the U.S., 1986; director, Summer Seminars for College Teachers on American Indian Literatures, 1979, 1983, 1989, 1994; National Endowment for the Humanities Fellowship, 1992-93; honored for contributions to American Indian literature by the Division of American Indian Literatures, Modern Language Association, and Association for Study of American Indian Literatures, 1993. *Interests*: History of American Indian literature written in English. *Biographical source*: Directory of American Scholars; Who's Who in the Midwest. *Published works*: The Moccasin Maker, by E. Pauline Johnson, edited with intro. by Ruoff (University of Arizona Press, 1987); co-editor, Redefining American Literary History, with Jerry Ward (Modern Language Association, 1990; American Indian Literatures (Modern Language Association, 1990); Literatures of the American Indian (Chelsea House, 1990); editor, American Indian Lives Series (University of Nebraska Press).

*RUSH, ANDREA GREEN
(editor)
Affiliation: "Seasons," National Native American AIDS Prevention Center, 3515 Grand Ave. #100, Oakland, CA 94610 (510) 444-2051.

*RUSS, JOSEPH A., Sr.
(tribal president)
Affiliation: Covelo Indian Community Council, P.O. Box 448, Covelo, CA 95428 (707) 983-6126.

*RUSSELL, GEORGE (Chippewa-Ottawa)
(engineer, author)
Born on the Isabella Indian Reservation near Mt. Pleasant, Mich. *Education*: Spring Arbor College, MI. *Principal occupation*: Engineer; author. *Address*: 8821 N. 1st St., Phoenix, AZ 85020 (800) 835-7220. *Activities*: Guest speaker; participates in American Indian seminar workshops. *Publication*: American Indian Digest: Facts About Today's American Indians, 2nd Ed.; Map of American Indian History.

RUSSELL, JERRY L. (Cherokee) 1933-
(communications executive)
Born July 21, 1933, Little Rock, Ark. *Education*: University of Arkansas, B.A., 1958. *Principal occupation*: Communications executive. *Home address*: 9 Lefever Lane, Little Rock, AR 72207 (501) 225-3996. *Affiliations*: Owner, Campaign Consultants, Little Rock, AR 1971-; owner, River City Public Relations, Little Rock, AR, 1971-; national chairman, Order of the Indian Wars, Little Rock, AR, 1980-. *Other professional posts*: National chairman, Civil War Round Table Associates; national chairman, Confederate Historical Institute. *Military service*: U.S. Army, 1953-56. *Community activities*: Friends of the Library (past president). *Memberships*: American Association of Political Consultants; Western Historical Association; Little Big Horn Associates; Custer Battlefield Historical & Museum Association (director); Custer Battlefield Preservation Committee (director); Westerners International. *Awards, honors*: Past president, Arkansas Advertising Federation; past president, Arkansas Chapter, Public Relations Society of America. *Interests*: Military history; political campaigning; travel. *Biographical source*: Who's Who in the South & Southwest.

*RUSSELL, JIM *(Chief Badger)* (Kaweah)
(vice principal chief, publisher)
Address: 1621 W. 3300 South, West Valley City, UT 84119. *Affiliations*: Vice principal chief, Kaweah Indian Nation of Western USA & Mexico; tribal chief, Kayenta Kaweah Tribe. *Other professional post*: Member, American Indian Defense of Americas.

RUSSELL, NEIL (Sioux)
(secondary school principal)
Affiliation: Lower Brule Day School, P.O. Box 245, Lower Brule, SD 57548 (605) 473-5510.

*RUSSELL, PAUL *(Whitefeathers)*
(Potawatomie/Cherokee) 1943-
(mechanical technician)
Born April 10, 1943, Flint, Mich. *Education*: Tampa College (2 years). *Principal occupation*: Mechanical technician. *Address*: P.O. Box 352, Lafayette, TN 37083. *Affiliation*: Native American music production. *Other professional post*: Chief of Deer Skin Clan. The Eighth Arrow Tribe. *Membership*: Pan American Indin Association (lifetime member). *Interests*: "Native American historian; teacher of Indian sign talk; seer keeper of Indian traditions; (I) travel to various reservations to meet with other Indians."

*RUSSELL, SIERA (Yavapai)
(program director)
Affiliation: Indian Legal Program, Arizona State University College of Law, Box 877906, Tempe, AZ 85287 (602) 965-6204.

*RYAN, ARNOLD R.
(Sisseton-Wahpeton Sioux)
(tribal chairperson)
Affiliation: Sisseton-Wahpeton Sioux Tribe, Route 2 - Agency Village, Sisseton, SD 57262 (605) 698-3911.

S

SABATTIS, MR. CLAIR (Maliseet)
(tribal chairperson)
Affiliation: Houlton Band of Maliseet Indians, P.O. Box 748, Bell Rd. , Houlton, ME 04730 (207) 532-4273.

*SACKLER, ELIZABETH
(foundation founder/president)
Affiliations: American Indian Ritual Object Repatriation Foundation, 463 East 57 St., New York, NY 10022 (212) 980-9441; president, Board of Directors, Arthur M. Sackler Foundation, New York, NY.

SACOBIE, RUPERT
(Indian band chief)
Affiliation: Oromocto Idian Band, Box 417, Oromocto, MB, Can. E2V 2J2 (506) 357-2083.

SACOBIE, STEPHEN
(Indian band chief)
Affiliation: Kingsclear Indian Band, RR 6, Box 6,, Comp. 19, Fredericton, New Brunswick, Canada E3B 4X7 (506) 363-3028.

SADDLEMAN, ALBERT
(Indian band chief)
Affiliation: Okanagan Indian Band, Siye 8, Comp. 20, RR 7, Vernon, British Columbia, Canada V1T 7Z3 (604) 542-4328.

SADDLEMAN, GEORGE
(Indian band chief)
Affiliation: Upper Nicola Indian Band, Box 3700, Merritt, BC, Canada V0K 2B0 (604) 350-3342.

SAFFORD, GLEN
(administrative officer)
Affiliation: Peter Christiansen Health Center, 450 Old Abe Rd., Lac du Flambeau, WI 54538 (715) 588-3371.

SAINTE-MARIE, BUFFY (Cree) 1942-
(folksinger, poet)
Born February 20, 1942, Craven, Saskatchewan, Can. Education: University of Massachusetts, BA (Philosophy), 1963. Principal occupation: Folksinger, poet. Address: RR#1, Box 368, Kapaa, Kauai, HI 96746. Affiliations: Recording artist, Vanguard Recording Society. Other occupation: Free-lance writer on Indian culture and affairs; associate editor, The Native Voice (Vancouver, B.C., Can.). Interests: Lecturing on Indian affairs; composing, singing. Miss Sainte-Marie writes, "I am best known for songs and poems directly related to past and present American Indian affairs. (I have contributed) to The Native Voice, Thunderbird, American Indian Horizons, and Boston Broadside in the fields of North American Indian music and Indian affairs. Have lived on and visited reserves (reservations) in fifteen states and four provinces; have traveled, lectured and sung in England, France, Canada, Italy, and Mexico, and have given performances in concert and on television internationally and in all major American cities."

*ST. CLAIR, KATHLEEN INEZ McATEE
(Oanther Walker) (United Lumbee) 1952-
(artist-craftsperson)
Born June 27, 1952, Los Angeles, Calif. Education: High school. Principal occupation: Artist-craftsperson. Home address: 33117 Sites Rd., Shingletown, CA 96088. Affiliation: Owner of Kat's Creations Somewhere in Time, Shingletown, CA; make handmade items, specializing in Native American traditional crafts, customs, moccasins, jewelry, leather goods, etc., 1989-. Community activities: Shasta Wildlife Rescue-Rehab Trainee, Educational Trainee, 1992 - Shasta County, CA. Membership: United Lumbee Nation's Deer Clan. Interests: "Rehabing and training wild & domestic animals. Working with children & adults, teaching traditional crafts & ways of our Native people, sharing spiritual beliefs & traditional dances."

ST. CLAIR, ROBERT N.
(professor of linguistics)
Born April 24, 1934, Honolulu, Hawaii. Education: University of Hawaii, BA, 1963; University of Kansas, PhD (Eskimo Language), 1974. Principal occupation: Professor of linguistics, Home address: 4404 Brownhurst Way, Louisville, KY 40241 (502) 852-6801 (work). Affiliation: Professor of linguistics, Dept. of English, University of Louisville, Louisville, KY, 1973- . Other professional posts: Consultant on language renewal - Yakima, Wanapam, Nez Perce, Eskimo; grant evaluator; member, Institute for Communication Studies (San Antonio, TX). Military service: U.S. Army, 1957-60 (Sgt., instructor-Nike Ajax Guided Missile). Professional activities: Xth International Conference on Salish Languages (chairperson); editor, Lektos; editor, Language Today; editorial board: language problems and language planning, invisible speech, Annuario (Santo Domingo); co-editor, Philosophical Linguistics; chairman, Commission on Academic Excellence. Memberships: National Council of Teachers of English; Modern Language Association; International Conference on Salishan Languages; Linguistics Society of America; American Association for the Advancement of Science. Awards, honors: Outstanding Educator Award, 1975; Distinguished Visiting Professor (New Mexico State University), 1977. Field work: Salishan languages: Skagit, Lummi; Sahaptian languages: Yakima, Wanapam; Eskimo: Yupik Eskimo. Interests: Bilingual education; sociolinguistics; political linguistics; travel. Dissertation - Theoretical Aspects of Eskimo Phonology, University of Kansas, Department of Linguistics; research on Welsh, Scots, Gaelic & Irish are current research interests. "I will be in Wales & Scotland this summer(1994) doing linguistic research. All of these languages are in the process of language renewal." Biographical sources: Who's Who in the South and Southwest; Who's Who International, 1994. Dictionary of International Biography. Published works: Languages of the World (Hanshin Publishers, S. Korea, 1992) Social Metaphors (University Press of America, 1994); numerous articles, papers, monographs, and book reviews in scholarly journals.

ST. CYR, TERRY (Omaha)
(tribal council member)
Home address: P.O. Box 490, Walthill, NE 68067 (402) 878-2231. Affiliation: Winnebago Tribal Council, Macy, NE.

ST. CYR, WEHNONA (Mi'-texi-Sacred Moon, Buffalo Clan) (Omaha) 1957-
(health systems administrator)
Born December 6, 1957, Wichita, Kans. Education: High school (Riverside Indian School, Anadarko, OK); Morningside College, BS, 1981; University of Hawaii, MPH, 1987. Principal occupation: Health systems administrator. Home address: P.O. Box 490, Walthill, NE 68067 (402) 878-2231 (work). Affiliations: Omaha Tribe of Nebraska, Macy, NE (social worker-2 years; nursing home administrator-3 years; health systems administrator-2 years); currently employed by the Public Health Service, U.S. Government, Indian Health Service as a Service Unit Director at the Winnebago Indian Hospital in Winnebago, NE. Community activities: Member of the Dr. Susan Picotte Hospital restoration Committee in Walthill, NE. Dr. Picotte was the first Native American woman physician in the U.S. Memberships: American College of Healthcare Executives; Nebraska State Historical Foundation (board of trustees); "I am also the Service Unit Director Chairperson for 1990 in the Aberdeen Area." Awards, honors: Received an "Outstanding" EPMS rating for 1989 thru Indian Health Service, and was also nominated by the Winnebago Hospital staff for outstanding employee in the area of Administration for 1989. Interests: "I continue to be involved in the Native Hawaiian Rights issues, specifically in the area of Health Care. I did receive my MPH from the University of Hawaii in 1987 and have traveled there again in 1989 to try and keep current and lend my expertise to their struggle. I also am active in my culture and dance in the traditional style."

ST-DENIS, HAROLD
(Indian band chief)
Affiliation: Wolf Lake (Algonquin) Indian Band, Box 1060, Temiscaminque, Quebec, Canada J0Z 3R0 (819) 627-3628.

*ST. FRANCIS, HOMER (Abenaki)
(tribal chief)
Affiliation: Abenaki Tribal Council, P.O. Box 276, Swanton, VT 05488 (802) 868-7146.

ST. GERMAINE, RICHARD (Migisi)
(Lac Courte Oreilles Ojibwa) 1947-
(associate professor)
Born March 4, 1947, Idabel, Okla. Education: University of Wisconsin, Eau Claire, BA, 1969; Arizona State University, MA (Education), 1972, PhD, 1975. Principal occupation: Associate professor. Address: Foundations of Education Dept., University of Wisconsin, Eau Claire, WI 54701. Affiliations: Tribal chairperson, Lac Courte Oreilles Tribe, Hayward, WI, 1977-86; director of the American Indian Graduate Studies Program & lecturer, University of California, Berkeley, 1986-88; associate professor, University of Wisconsin, Eau Claire, 1989-. Other professional posts: President, American Indian Graduate Center, Albuquerque, NM; (appointed by President Clinton) member of the National Advisory Council on Indian Education, 1994-. Memberships: National Indian Education Association (president,1975-77); National Tribal Chairmen's Association (treasurer, 1978-80); Phi Delta Kappa, 1972-75, 1990. Awards, honors: Ford Foundation Fellowship, 1971-75.

*ST. PIERRE, MARK
(adjunct professor, writer)
Affiliation: Adjunct professor of Sociology, Anthropology, and Creative Writing at Regis University, Steamboat Springs, CO. He has lived among the Lakota people since 1971, both as a educator and as an encourager of American Indian art. *Published works*: Madonna Swann: A Lakota Woman's Story (University of Oklahoma Press, 1992).

*ST. PIERRE, NATE (Chippewa/Cree) 1962-
(faculty, administrator)
Born December 28, 1962, Fort Belknap, Mont. *Education*: Montana State University, MEd., 1989, EdD in progress. *Principal occupation*: Faculty, administrator. *Address*: P.O Box 6773, Bozeman, MT 59771 (406) 994-3992 (work). *Affiliations*: Acting director, Office of Tribal Service, Rocky Boy's Reservation, Chippewa-Cree Tribe, Box Elder, MT; faculty, administrator, Montana State University, Bozeman, MT, 1992-. *Interests*: Adult education; Indian health education. *Published works*: "Educational Issues in Montana's Tribal Colleges," in Adult Literacy & ·Basic Education, 1990; "Multiculturalism: A Native American Perspective," in Journal of Lifelong Learning, 1993.

*SAKAR, SOPHIE
(village chief)
Affiliation: Native Village of Chuathbaluk, P.O. Box 31, Chuathbaluk, AK 99557 (907) 467-4313.

*SAKIM (Alleghenny Lenape)
(tribal chief)
Affiliation: Alleghenny Tribal Council, 2111 16th St. NE, Canton, OH 44705 (216) 453-6224.

SALABIYE, VELMA
(librarian)
Affiliation: Librarian, American Indian Studies Center Library, 3220 Campbell Hall, U.C.L.A., Los Angeles, CA 90024.

*SALAS, JOSEPH
(health center director)
Affiliation: Ysleta Del Sur Servie Unit, P.O. Box 17579, El Paso, TX 79907 (915) 859-7913.

SALGADO, ROBERT J. (Luiseno)
(tribal chairperson)
Affiliation: Soboba Band of Mission Indians, P.O. Box 487, San Jacinto, CA 92383 (909) 654-2765.

SALISBURY, NEAL 1940-
(historian)
Born May 7, 1940, Los Angeles, Calif. *Education*: University of California, Los Angeles, BA, 1963, MA, 1966, PhD, 1972. *Principal occupation*: Historian. *Address & Affiliation*: Professor, Dept. of History, Smith College, Northamtpon, MA 01063 (413) 585-3726, 1973-. *Memberships*: American Historical Association; American Society for Ethnohistory; Organization of American Historians; American Studies Association. *Awards, honors*: Fellow, Smithsonian Institution, 1972-73; Fellow, Newberry Library Center for History of the American Indian, 1977-78; Fellow, National Endowment for the Humanities, 1984-85; Fellow, Charles Warren Center for Studies in American History, 1989; Fellow, National Humanities Center, 1991-92. *Published works*: Manitou and Providence: Indians, Europeans, and the Beginnings of New England, 1500-1643 (Oxford University Press, 1982); The

Indians of New England: A Critical Bibliography (Indiana University Press, 1982); The Enduring Vision: A History of the American People, 2nd Ed., with Paul S. Boyer, et al (D.C. Heath, 1992).

*SALISBURY, RALPH (Eastern Cherokee)
1924-
(writer, professor)
Born January 24, 1924, Arlington, Iowa. *Education*: University of Iowa, MFA, 1951. *Address/ Affiliation*: Professor (1960-), English Dept., University of Oregon, Eugene, OR 97403 (503) 346-3911. *Military service*: U.S. Air Force, 1942-45. *Awards, honors*: Rockefeller Bellagi Award for novel; Chapelbrook Award, Short Story & Poetry. *Interests*: Writing fiction & poetry. *Published works*: Pointing At the Rainbow (Blue Cloud, 1980); Spirit Beast Chant (Blue Cloud, 1982); A Nation Within (Outrigger, 1983); Going to the Water (Pacific House, 1983); A White Rainbow (Blue Cloud, 1985); One Indian, Two Chiefs (Navajo Community College Press, 1993); Trikways of the Wind (University of Arizona, 1994).

SALLEE, JACLYN (Inupiat Eskimo) 1964-
(director-Native broadcast center)
Born November 15, 1964, Anchorage, Alaska. *Education*: Western Washington University, 1983-85; University of Alaska, Anchorage, BA, 1988. *Principal occupation*: Director-Native broadast center. *Home address*: 3245 Wiley Post Loop, Anchorage, AK 99517 (907) 243-8729; 277-2776 (work). *Affiliation*: Native Broadcast Center, Anchorage, AK, 1988-. *Other professional post*: Task Force Chairperson, Native Broadcast Center, 1991-. *Community activities*: United Way (member, Allocation Committee). *Memberships*: Alaska Press Club (board member, 1989-91); Alaska Native Communications Society (Steering Committee, 1988-). *Interests*: Art, Alaska Native issues, skiing.

*SALOIS, CHANE (Chippewa of Montana)
1947-
(civil engineer)
Born February 20, 1947, Kalispel, Mont. *Education*: Montana State University, BS (Math), 1970, BS (Civil Engineering), 1974. *Principal occupation*: Civil engineer. *Home address*: 148 Mud Lake Trail, Polson, MT 59860 (406) 883-9223; 745-2661 (work). *Affiliations*: Manager, Bureau of Indian Affairs (Roads Branch Manager, Lame Deer, MT, 2 years; Colville Agency, Nespelem, WA, 6 years; Flathead Agency, Pablo, MT, 9 years; Flathead Agency, Irrigation Division, St. Ignatius, MT, , 1992-. *Community activities*: Little Shell Tribe of Chippewa Indians of Montana (secretary/treasurer). *Membership*: Association of County Engineers, 1988-. *Interests*: Vocational - road & bridge construction, pavements, concrete construction, irrigation facilities. Avocational - hunting, snowmobiling, all terrain vehicles, traveling.

SALTER, JOHN L., Jr.
(department of Indian studies chairperson)
Affiliation: University of North Dakota, Department of Indian Studies, Grand Forks, ND 58202 (701) 777-4314.

SALVADOR, MARIA "LILLY" (*Dzaisratpaitsa*)
(Acoma Pueblo) 1944-
(traditional Acoma potter, silversmith,
weaver; acrylic artist)
Born April 6, 1944, McCartys Village, Acoma Pueblo, N.M. *Education*: New Mexico State (1

year). *Principal occupation*: Traditional Acoma potter; silversmith; weaver; acrylic artist. *Address*: P.O. Box 342, Acoma Pueblo, NM 87034 (505) 552-9501. *Affiliations*: Pottery is displayed at the following museums and galleries: Boston Museum of Fine Arts; The Heard Museum, Phoenix; The Museum of Man, San Diego; The Natural History Museum, Los Angeles; The Whitehorse Gallery, Boulder, CO. *Other institutional affiliation*: National Indian Council on Aging Catalogue. *Community activities*: Native needle embroidery instructor, Acoma Adult Education Programs; secretary, Sky City Community School; member, parent-student association of Saint Joseph School, San Fidel, NM. *Memberships*: Southwest American Indian Arts Association, 1964-; National Indian Arts & Crafts Association (Albuquerque), 1985-86; Southwestern Association on Indian Affairs; AICA: Smithsonian Institution, 1985. *Awards, honors*: 1st and 2nd Prize Awards for handcrafted pottery from Whitehorse Gallery, Boulder, CO; 1st and 3rd Prize Award Ribbons from New Mexico State Fair; 1st, 2nd and 3rd Prize Awards for handcrafted/hand painted pottery from the Southwest American Indian Arts Association, 1st, Honorable Mention Awards from the Gallup InterTribal Indian Ceremonial; 1st, Special Award Ribbon from the Heard Museum, Phoenix, AZ; Southwestern Association on Indian Affairs, 1st Prize Ribbon for finest of Acoma Pueblo pottery. *Interests*: "To develop and expand my present pottery gallery (the first at the Pueblo Acoma) into a major showcase for collectors, tourists (who visit annually the oldest inhabited village in the U.S.) and discriminating curators of various museums throughout the U.S. With the private invitations extended by the above mentioned museums and galleries, I have traversed the southwest and northwest region of the U.S. exhibiting my traditional hand-crafted/ hand painted Acoma Pueblo pottery and figurines." *Biographical sources*: American Indian Pottery, 2nd Edition; Amerika newsletter, Chicago, Ill.; National Indian Council on Aging Catalogue; Talking With Clay - Pueblo Storytellers, by Barbara Babcock.

*SALWAY-BLACK, SHERRY
(institute vice president)
Affiliation: First Nations Development Institute, The Stores Bldg., 11917 Main St., Fredericksburg, VA 22408 (703) 371-5615.

*SALZANO, JOSEPH (Choctaw)
(musicians)
Born in 1958, Biloxi, Miss. Raised in Rochester, NY on Lake Ontario. Address: c/o Morning Star Music, 7-B Park Lane, Lansing, NY 14882 (607) 533-8867. Trained in the clarinet, sax and composition since age 8 and American Indian flute since 1985--on flute, Joe has studied with R. Carlos Nakai and Eddie Box, Sr. and learned from Kevin Locke and Tom Ware. He has performed live, and on radio & TV throughout the U.S. including schools, concerts and clubs. *Recordings*: "Turtle Island Flute, " & "Four Winds." Both distributed by Morning Star Music. A collection of traditional and contemporary Native American flute music. *Quote*: "Being half Italian and half Choctaw, a soxophonist and flute player, a performer of Jazz and Indian music, I seek to use my music as a way of bridging differences and affirming that we are all children of Mother Earth."

SALZMANN, ZDENEK 1925-
(adjunct professor)
Born October 18, 1925, Prague, Czech. *Education*: Caroline University, Prague, 1945-47 (Absolutorium, 1948); Indiana University, MA, 1949, PhD, 1963. *Principal occupation*: Adjunct professor of anthropology. *Home address*: 120 Highland Dr. So., Sedona, AZ 86351 (602) 284-0344. *Affiliations*: Professor of anthropology emeritus, University of Massachusetts, Amherst, 1968-89; adjunct professor of anthropology, Northern Arizona University, Flagstaff, 1990-. *Other professional posts*: Visiting professor, Yale University; consultant to Wind River Reservation schools on Arapaho language and culture curriculum, 1979-; visiting professor, Caroline University & Charles University, Prague, Czechoslovakia. *Memberships*: Linguistic Society of America, 1949-; American Anthropological Association, 1954-; Current Anthropology, 1961-; American Folklore Society, 1966-. *Awards, honors*: Research grants from the following: American Philosophical Society; National Endowment for the Humanities; Senior Fulbright-Hays Scholar; International Research and Exchanges Board; American Council of Learned Societies. Given in a public ceremony and with the approval of Arapaho elders, the name hinono'ei neecee (Arapaho Chief). *Interests*: Fieldwork among Northern Arapaho Indians, 1949-; numerous trips to the Wind River Reservation under various auspices. *Biographical sources*: American Men and Women of Science; Contemporary Authors; Directory of American Scholars. *Published works*: Dictionary of Contemporary Arapaho Usage (Arapaho Language and Culture Commission, 1983); The Arapaho Indians: A Research Guide and Bibliography (Greenwood Press, 1988); Language, Culture & Society: An Introduction to Linguistic Anthropology (Westview Press, July 1993); among others; numerous articles in various scholarly journals.

*SAM, GERALD
(AK village chief)
Affiliation: Alatna Village, Alatna, AK 99720 (907) 968-2241.

*SAM, GEORGE (Eskimo)
(village president)
Affiliation: Lower Kalskag Village, P.O. Box 27, Lower Kalskag, AK 99626 (907) 471-2307.

SAM, JIMMY L.
(executive director)
Affiliation: Boston Indian Council, Inc., 105 S. Huntington, Jamaica Plain, MA 02130 (617) 232-0343.

SAM, PAUL IGNATIUS
(Indian band chief)
Affiliation: Shuswap Indian Band, Box 790, Invermere, B.C., Canada V0A 1K0 (604) 342-6361.

SAM, ROBERT (Paiute)
(tribal chairperson)
Affiliation: Summit Lake Paiute Council, 665 Anderson St., Winnemucca, NV 89445 (702) 623-5151.

*SAMPLE, JEANETTE
(rancheria chairperson)
Affiliation: Big Sandy Rancheria, P.o. Box 337, Auberry, CA 93602 (209) 855-4003.

*SAMPSON, DONALD (Umatilla)
(tribal chairperson)
Affiliation: Umatilla Board of Trustees, P.O. Box 638, Pendleton, OR 97801 (503) 276-3165.

SAMUELSON, LILLIAN THOMPSON 1926-
(former owner/manager-Indian shop)
Born July 13, 1926, Mecklenburg County, Va. *Education*: Virginia Polytechnic Institute, 1945-1947; Illinois Institute of Technology, BS, 1949. *Principal occupation*: Owner/manager, American Indian Treasures, Inc., Guilderland, NY, 1968-91. *Home address*: P.O. Box 579, Guilderland, NY 12084. *Community activities*: Sponsored Native American art show at Sienna College, Loudonville, N.Y. each Spring for 13 years. *Memberships*: National Congress of American Indians; Association on American Indian Affairs, Inc.; Indian Arts and Crafts Association (board of directors, 1976-91; vice president, 1978; president, 1982; member of the year, 1983). *Interests*: Ms. Samuelson writes, "My interest in the American Indian goes back to early childhood, with serious studies of the arts and crafts of living Indians having been pursued the last 20 years, Travel has been extensive during this time, and I've come to know the products of most reservations in the U.S. (I) worked as a consultant on Indian education for the New York State Education Dept. I started American Indian Treasures in 1967, selling only handmade Indian crafts from a broad range of tribes and cultures. Items sold are personally collected to assure authenticity, with buying trips made regularly throughout the year." *Published works*: Articles published in monthlies, distributed nationally, about American Indian artists.

SANCHEZ, CARMEN
(public affairs specialist)
Affiliation: George Gustav Heye Center, National Museum of the American Indian, Smithsonian Institution, 1 Bowling Green, New York, NY 10004 (212) 283-2420.

SANCHEZ, DORIAN (Nisqually)
(tribal chairperson)
Affiliation: Nisqually Indian Community Council, 4820 She-Na-Num Dr., S.E., Olympia, WA 98503 (206) 456-5221.

*SANCHEZ, JOSEPH (San Felipe Pueblo)
(tribal chairperson)
Affiliation: San Felipe Pueblo Council, P.o> Box A, San Felipe, NM 87001 (505) 867-3381.

SANCHEZ, PHILIP
(BIA agency supt.)
Affiliation: Umatilla Agency, Bureau of Indian Affairs, P.O. Box 520, Pendleton, OR 97801 (503) 278-3786.

SANDERS, E. FRED (Catawba) 1926-
(machinist, assistant chief)
Born April 9, 1926, Catawba Indian Reservation, York County, S.C. *Education*: Catawba Indian School; vocational and technical school-- machinist courses. *Principal occupation*: Maintenance machinist, General Tire Corp, Charlotte, N.C., 1967-. *Home address*: 2053 Reservation Rd., Rock Hill, SC 29730. *Other professional post*: Master barber. *Military service*: U.S. Army, 1944-50 (1st Sergeant; Infantry, World War II: Combat Infantry Badge; Bronze Star; 2 Campaign Battle Stars; V.E. Ribbon; Army Occupation Award-Austria). *Community activities*: Assistant chief, Catawba Nation, S.C., 1975-;

Charlotte-Mecklenburg Public School System-- Indian Education (chairperson-Title IV Program). *Memberships*: National Congress of American Indians; Veterans of Foreign Wars, Rock Hill, S.C.; American Legion, Rock Hill, S.C. *Interests*: Travel as official tribal delegate to many National Congress of American Indians' conferences and conventions in various states. Support tribal leaders with positive attitude and assurance that Native Americans will continue to have a voice and input concerning the future destiny of tribal government and its people.

*(SANDERSON, PRISCILLA LANSING (Navajo) 1959-
(vocational rehabilitation)
Born November 26, 1959, Shiprock, N.M. *Education*: Southwestern College (Winfield, KS), BA, 1983; Oklahoma State University, MS, 1984. *Principal occupation*: Vocational rehabilitation. *Address*: P.O Box 247, Flagstaff, AZ 86002 (602) 523-5581 (work). *Affiliations*: Director, American Indian Rehabilitation Research & Training Center, Northern Arizona University, Flagstaff, AZ, 1991-; vocational rehabilitation services specialist, Arizona Rehabilitation Services Administration, Flagstaff, 1986-. *Community activities*: American Indian Disability Legislation Advisory Panel, 1993-. *Community activities*: Flagstaff Mayor's Committee on Disability Awareness, 1990-92; northern Arizona FAS/FAE Task Force, 1993-94; Statewide Independent Living Council, AZ, 1993-. *Memberships*: Consortia of Administrators for Native American Rehabilitation & Research (chairman, 1993-); National Congress of American Indians, 1994-; Rehabilitation Leadership Council, 1994-. *Awards, honors*: Outstanding Young Women of America, Sonoma Club, 1984; Professional Worker of the Year," Flagstaff Mayor;s Committee on Disability Awareness, 1989; "In recognition for your leadership in providing service to American Indians," Texas Rehabilitation Commission, 1994. *Interests*: "American Indian & Alaska Native vocational rehabilitation & independent living; reading about different American Indian cultures & values; enjoy watching traditional American Indian dances & pow-wows." *Published works*: "Needs of American Indians with Disabilities" (American Indian Rehabilitation Research & Training Center, 1993); "Response to Perspectives" (The Leading Edge...Focusing on Rehabilitation's Human Resources, 1993); "Needs Assessment Survey to the State Vocational Rehabilitation Agencies" (American Indian Rehabilitation Research & Training Center, 1994).

*SANDOVAL, LESTER
(organziation vice president)
Affiliation: Coalition for Indian Education, 8200 Mountain Rd., NE, Suite 203, Albuquerque, NM 87110 (505) 262-2351.

*SANDSTROM, ALAN R. 1945-
(anthropologist)
Born July 2, 1945, Springfield, Mas. *Education*: American International College; Indiana University, MA, PhD. *Principal occupation*: Anthropologist. *Home address*: 2828 N. Anthony Blvd., Ft. Wayne, IN 46805 (219) 483-1501. *Memberships*: American Anthropological Association (Fellow); Central States Anthropological Society. *Interests*: "Have conducted several years of ethnographic field research in northern Veracruz, Mexico among Nahua Indians (Nahuatl speakers). *Published works*: Traditional

Papermaking & Paper Cult Figura of Mexico, with Pamela E. Sandstrom (University of Oklahoma Press, 1986; Corn Is Our Blood (University of Oklahoma Press, 1991).

SANGRIS, JONAS
(Indian band chief)
Affiliation: Yellowknife "B" (Dettah) Indian Band, Box 2514, Yellowknife, Northwest Territories, Canada X1A 2P8 (403) 873-4307.

SANIPASS, WILLIAM
(Indian band chief)
Affiliation: Bouctouche Indian Band, RR 2, Kent County, Bouctouche, New Brunswick, Canada E0A 1G0 (506) 743-6493.

*SARABIA, ED
(Indian affairs coordinator)
Affiliations: Connecticut Indian Affairs Council, Dept. of Environmental Protection, 165 Capitol Ave., Room 245, Hartford, CT 06101 (203) 566-5193; chairperson, "The Eagle," Eagle Wing Press, Inc., Naugatuck, CT.

*SARGENT, THOMAS A.
(center chairperson)
Affiliation: Minnetrista Cultural Center, P..O. Box 1527, Muncie, IN 47303 (317) 282-4848.

SARK, GEORGE JAMES
(Indian band chief)
Affiliation: Abegweit Indian Band, Box 220, Cornwall, Prince Edward Island, Canada C0A 1H0 (902) 675-3842.

SARK, JACK J.T.
(Indian band chief)
Affiliation: Lennox Island Indian band, Lennox Island, PEI, Canada C0B 1P0 (902) 831-2779.

SASAKAMOOSE, MURIEL
(museum director)
Affiliation: Secwepemc Cultural Education Society, 345 Yellowhead Hwy., Kamloops, British Columbia, Canada V2H 1H1 (604) 374-1096.

SATALA, TAYLOR J. (Yavapai-Apache/Hopi) 1945-
(health systems administrator)
Born August 25, 1945, Prescott, Ariz. *Education*: San Francisco City College, AA, 1966; Arizona State University, BS, 1976, MSW, 1978. *Principal occupation*: Health systems administrator. *Address*: P.O. Box 98, Keams Canyon, AZ 86034 (602) 738-2211 (work). *Affiliation*: Service unit director, USPHS, Indian Health Service, Keams Canyon, AZ, 1989-. *Other professional posts*: Health Center Director, IHS, Peach Springs, AZ; extension associate, University of Kansas, Lawrence, KS; social worker, MCH, Rapid City, SD. *Military service*: U.S. Air Force, 1966-70 (E-4 Sgt.; Vietnam Era Veteran-stationed at DaNang Air Base); USPHS Commission Corps, National Health Service, 1978-80. National Association of Social Workers (vice president, 1978-84); Black Hills Region of South Dakota State Chapter; Council on Social Work Education (member, House of Delegates, 1982-83); American Indian/Alaska Native Association of Social Workers, 1978-84. *Awards, honors*: Exceptional Performance Award, 1989, for Effective Mgmt. *Published works*: Multi-Cultural Development in the Aging Network: "An Indian Perspective" "A Forgotten People" (U. of Kansas, 1981); The Indian Experience: Special Topics in Social Welfare (U. of Kansas, 1983).

*SATTER, MICHELLE
(institute director)
Affiliation: The Sundance Institute, c.o S.P.E., 10202 W. Washington Blvd., Culver City, CA 90232 (310) 204-2091.

SATZ, RONALD N. 1944-
(university dean & professor of history)
Born February 8, 1944, Chicago, Ill. *Education*: Illinois Institute of Technology, BS, 1965; Illinois State University, MA, 1967; University of Maryland, PhD, 1972 (Dissertation: Federal Indian Policy, 1829-1849). *Principal occupation*: University dean and professor of history. *Home address*: 4015 White Pine Dr., East, Eau Claire, WI 54701. *Affiliations*: Assistant professor, 1971-75, associate professor with tenure, 1977-80, dean of graduate studies, 1976-83, dean of research, 1977-83, professor with tenure, 1980-83, University of Tennessee at Martin; dean, School of Graduate Studies, director, Office of University Research, and professor of history, 1983-, and director, Center of Excellence for Faculty and Undergraduate Student Research Collaboration, 1988-, The University of Wisconsin, Eau Claire, WI. *Other professional posts*: Editorial board member, Maryland Historian, 1970-71, University of Tennessee Press, 1975-78, 1981-83, and American Indian Quarterly, 1977-82; consultant, Native American Rights Fund, 1977-80; Chippewa Valley Museum, 1990-; Wisconsin Dept. of Public Instruction, 1991-, and Council of Graduate Schools, 1992; proposal reviewer, National Endowment for the Humanities, 1978-; board of directors, Chippewa Valley Museum, 1992-; advisory committee on minority student affairs, and undergraduate teaching improvement council, University of Wisconsin, Madison, 1984-86, 1991-92; campus liaison, University of Wisconsin System Committee on University/Industry Cooperation, 1985-; Publications Committee, Midwestern Association of Graduate Schools, 1985-90; chair, Western History Association Walter Rundell Graduate Student Award Committee, 1986; President's Select Committee on the Status of Minority Faculty and Staff, University of Wisconsin System, 1987-88; and University of Wisconsin System and State Historical Society of Wisconsin Joint Planning Committee for the National Conference on American Indian History & Culture, 1990-91; editor, Proceedings of the Midwestern Association of Graduate Schools, 1988-89; editor, Issues in Teaching and Learning, 1989-. *Community activities*: Ad Hoc Commission on Racism of the Lac Courte Oreilles Lake Superior Ojibwa Tribal Governing Board (member); Parent-Teacher Organization, Manz Elementary School and South Junior High School, Eau Claire, WI (member); The Heritage Club of the Chippewa Valley Museum, Eau Claire (member). *Memberships*: American Association for Higher Education; American Association of University Professors; American Association of University Administrators; American Historical Association; Organization of American Historians; Society for American Indian Studies and Research; Society for Historians of the Early American Republic; Western History Association; Southern Historical Association; Wisconsin Academy of Sciences, Arts, and Letters; Sigma Xi; Pi Gamma Mu; Phi Alpha Theta; Phi Kappa Phi; Delta Tau Kappa; among others. *Award, honors*: Fellow in Ethnic Studies, Ford Foundation, 1971; Younger Humanist Research Fellow, National Endowment for the Humanities, 1974; Title III Grant, U.S.

Office of Education, University of Tennessee at Martin, 1978, '81, '82, University of Wisconsin-Eau Claire, 1991; University of Wisconsin System Undergraduate Teaching Improvement Council Grant for Critical Thinking Across Disciplines Project, 1985; Wisconsin Dept. of Public Education Grant for Chippewa Treaty Rights Project, 1991. *Interests*: "Indian-white relations, especially the 19th century; American Indian policy; Indian sovereignty and treaty rights; tribal history; Indian-black relations; Indian religious beliefs and the impact of Christian missionary efforts on Indian religions." *Biographical sources*: Outstanding American Educators, 1974-75; Directory of American Scholars, 6th-8th Eds.; Contemporary Authors, 1982; Dictionary of International Biography, 1976-77; Who's Who in the South and Southwest, 16th-18th Eds.; Personalities of the South, 1978-79, 1979-80 Eds.; International Who's Who in Education, 1980 Ed.; Who's Who in the Midwest, 20th Ed., 23rd Ed. *Published works*: American Indian Policy in the Jacksonian Era (University of Nebraska Press, 1975; 2nd Ed., University of Oklahoma Press, in progress); Tennessee's Indian Peoples: From White Contact to Removal, 1540-1840 (University of Tennessee Press, 1979); Chippewa Treaty Rights: The Reserved Rights of Wisconsin's Chippewa Indians in Historical Perspective (Wisconsin Academy of Sciences, Arts, and Letters, 1991); co-author: America: Changing Times, textbook (John Wiley & Sons, 1979-1st Ed.; Random House, 1984-2nd Ed.-1984); and Classroom Activities on Chippewa Treaty Rights (Wisconsin Dept. of Public Instruction, 1991); contributor: Heroes of Tennessee (Memphis State University Press, 1979); The Commissioners of Indian Affairs, 1824-1977 (University of Nebraska Press, 1979); American Vistas, 1607-1877, 3rd-4th Eds. (Oxford University Press, 1979, '84, '87); Wisconsin's Educational Imperative: Indian-White Relations (Lac Courte Oreilles Ojibwa Community College, 1984); After Removal: The Choctaw in Mississippi (University Press of Mississippi, 1986); An Anthology of Western Great Lakes Indian History (University of Wisconsin-Milwaukee, 1987); Enhancing Educational Diversity Through Professional Diversity (University of Wisconsin System President's Select Committee on the Status of Minority Faculty and Staff, 1988); History of Indian-White Relations vol. 4 of Handbook of North American Indians (Smithsonian Institution Press, 1988); The Susquicentennial of Cherokee Removal, 1838-1839 (Special issue of the Georgia Historical Quarterly, Fall 1989); Cherokee Removal: Before and After (University of Georgia Press, 1991); editor: Proceedings of the University of Wisconsin System and State Historical Society of Wisconsin National Committee on American Indian History & Culture; and author of numerous articles & book reviews in scholarly journals.

SAUBEL, KATHERINE SIVA (Cahuilla) 1920-
(museum trustee)
Born March 7, 1920, Los Coyotes Reservation, Calif. *Principal occupation*: Trustee & president, Malki Museum, Inc. *Address*: 11-795 Fields Rd., Morongo Indian Reservation, Banning, CA 92220 (714) 849-7289 (work). *Other professional posts*: Advisory representative, County of Riverside, CA, Historical Commission; consultant/lecturer, California State College at Hayward, CA, University of Colorado, and University of California. *Community activities*: Los Coyotes Tribal Council; Mothers Club, Morongo

Indian Reservation. *Interests*: Ms. Saubel participated in the Indian Leadership Training Program at the University of California; other interests are Indian history and ethnography, and linguistics. She writes, "I have traveled extensively in the Southwest & California, visiting reservations and museums which display Indian history and culture." *Published works*: Cahuilla Ethnobotanical Notes: Oak, and Mesquite and Screwbean, both with Lowell J. Bean (University of California, Archaeological Survey Annual Report, 1962, 1968); Temalpah: Economic Botany of the Cahuilla Indians, with Lowell J. Bean (Malki Museum, 1969); Kunvachmal, A Cahuilla Tale (The Indian Historian, 1969).

SAULQUE, JOSEPH C. (Paiute) 1942-
(administration/planning; college instructor)
Born October 20, 1942, Bishop, Calif. *Education*: West Valley Community College, Campbell, Calif., A.A., 1970; Brigham Young University, B.A., 1973; University of California, Davis, 1978-80 (Graduate work on MA). *Principal occupation*: Administration/ planning; college instructor. *Address*: Benton Paiute Reservation, Rt. 4, Box 56-A, Benton, CA 93512 (619) 933-2321. *Affiliation*: Instructor, Cerro Coso Community College, Bishop, CA (current). *Other professional posts*: Utu Utu Gwaitu Paiute Tribe, Benton Paiute Reservation, Benton, CA (chairperon, 1973-90; vice-chairperson, 1991-); chairperson, Toiyabe Indian Health Project (board of directors, 1977-); chairperson, California Rural Indian Health Board (board of directors, 1978-). *Military service*: U.S. Army, 1961-64 (E-4/Sp-4, 101st Airborne Division). *Community activities*: Grand Jury, County of Mono, CA; Tri-Valley Regional Planning and Advisory Commission to the Tri-Valley Water District, County of Mono, CA; Owens Valley Indian Water Commission (member). *Memberships*: National Congress of American Indians, 1974-; California Tribal Chairman's Association, Sacramento, Calif. (secretary-three years); California Indian Manpower Consortium, Inc. (past vice-chairperson, 1988-90). *Interests*: "Indian affairs, especially tribal government concepts; Amerian Indian history; Indian health issues and operations; college instructor on American Indian studies; history and career opportunities."

SAUNDERS, ERIC
(Indian band chief)
Affiliation: York Factory Indian Band, York Landing, Manitoba, Canada R0B 2B0 (204) 341-2180.

*SAUNDERS, FERRELL
(monument supt.)
Affiliation: Russell Cave National Monument, Rte. 1, Box 175, Bridgeport, AL 35740 (205) 495-2672.

SAUNDERS, LINDA
(BIA agency supt.)
Affiliation: Horton Agency, Bureau of Indian Affairs, P.O. Box 31, Horton, KS 66439 (913) 486-2161.

SAUNOOKE, OSLEY BIRD, Jr.
(Eastern Cherokee) 1943-
(attorney, business consultant)
Born April 6, 1943, Jacksonville, Fla. *Education*: East Tennessee State University, 1962-63; Brigham Young University, BS, 1965; University of New Mexico Law School, JD, 1972. *Principal occupation*: Attorney, business consultant. *Home address*: 2435 Gulf Gate Dr., Sarasota, FL 34231 (813) 921-3297. *Affiliations*: Teacher-guidance counselor, Cleveland, Ohio, Chicago, Ill., 1965-69; executive director, United Southeastern Tribes, Inc., 1972-73; executive director, Florida Governor's Council on Indian Affairs, 1973-74. *Awards, honors*: 1987 Regional Minority Entrepreneur of the Year - Atlanta Region OMBE. *Memberships*: National Congress of American Indians (Southeast area vice president, 1972-73; first vice president, 1973-74; board member, American Indian Scholarships, 1974-).

SAVAGE, JEFF (Lake Superior Ojibwe-Anishinabe) 1950-
(artist)
Born November 28, 1950, Duluth, Minn. *Education*: College of St. Scholastica, 1974-76. *Principal occupation*: Artist. *Home address*: 1780 Blue Spruce Dr., Cloquet, MN 55720 (218) 879-0157. *Affiliation*: Artist and Public Informatiom Specialist, Fond du Lac Reservation, Cloquet, MN. *Other professional posts*: "Have also worked in many local schools and tribal colleges doing Native Amerian art workshops specializing in pipe stone sculpture and traditional pipes. *Community activities*: Currently vice-chairperson, Indian Advisory Board, Minnesota Historical Society; former tribal election judge for Fond du Lac Reservation. *Memberships*: Minnesota Historical Society (chairperson of local Indian Education Committee). *Awards, honors*: 1981 Gallup Intertribal, Certificate of Merit, Blue Ribbon, and special exhibit awards; 1985 1st Place Sculpture Award in Ojibwe Art Expo. *Interests*: "Personal interest in pursuing the perpetuating of endangered Ojibwe art forms, i.e., pipestone quarrying, pipe making, traditional Ojibwe sweet grass baskets and birch bark baskets, moccasins and beadwork of floral Ojibwe design done in hand tanned leather."

*SAVAGE, MARILYN (Athabascan)
(radio station manager)
Affiliation: KZPA-AM, P.O. Box 126, Fort Yukon, AK 99740 (907) 662-2587.

SAVAGE, PAUL EDISON (Mingo) (United Lumbee/Cherokee) 1921-
(minister)
Born August 4, 1922, Oklahoma. *Principal occupation*: Minister/president, Chapel of Our Lord Jesus, Exeter, CA, 1975-. *Home address*: P.O. Box 29, Farmersville, CA 93223. *Memberships*: Native American Wolf Clan; United Lumbee Nation Grand Councilman, 1992-; United Lumbee Nation's Bear Clan Chief, 1990-92. *Interests*: "Ministering to our Native American people and helping my people to keep their heritage."

SAYLER, HAROLD
(school principal)
Affiliation: Pyramid Lake High School, P.O. Box 256, Nixon, NV 89424 (702) 574-0142.

*SCERATO, BEN (Diegueno)
(tribal chairperson)
Affiliation: Santa Ysabel Band of Mission Indians, P.O. Box 130, Santa Ysabel, CA 92070 (916) 765-0845.

SCHAAFSMA, CURTIS F. 1938-
(archaeologist, anthropologist)
Born January 22, 1938, Vallejo, Calif. *Education*: University of Colorado, BA, 1962; University of New Mexico, MA, 1971, ABD, 1973. *Principal occupation*: Archaeologist, anthropologist. *Home address*: Rte. 2, Box 300, Santa Fe, NM 87505 (505) 827-6344 (work). *Affiliations*: Project director of numerous archaeological projects for the Museum of New Mexico, 1963-68; research archaeologist, School of American Research, Santa Fe, NM, 1974-79; Museum of New Mexico/Laboratory of Anthropology, Santa Fe, NM (director/state archaeologist, 1979-83, state archaeologist, 1983-92, curator of anthropology, 1992-). *Military service*: U.S. Navy, 1956-58 (AG-3; Aerographers Mate Third Class). *Memberships*: National Association of State Archaeologists (Sec/Treas, 1979-81); New Mexico Cultural Properties Review Committee, 1979-88; Society for American Archaeology; American Society for Conservation Archaeology (president, 1984-88); American Rock Art Research Association (board of trustees). *Awards, honors*: National Parks & Conservation Council (NM/AZ advisory council member); appointed to the Advisory Board of the Animas Foundation for the Gray Ranch of southwestern New Mexico. *Interests*: "Archaeological collection management and communication between Indian groups and scholars; cultural resource management, especially the philosophical aspects of CRM; my research emphases have been on 17th century Navajos, archaic hunter-gatherers, and modern/protohistoric Pueblos of the Southwest, with an emphasis on pottery. Recently, I have traveled to the Mayan area along the Usumacinto River (Piedras Negras & other sites). This has led to an interest in Mayan studies. My focus of research remains the 17th century Navajos, and I hope to write a full book on this topic soon. I am also preparing a museum exhibit on the Casas Grandes Culture of northwestern Chihuahua, Mexico and southwestern New Mexico." *Biographical source*: Who's Who in the West. *Published works*: Chapters in books: "truth Dwells in the Deeps: Lessons from Quantum Theory for Contemporary Archaeology," in Processual & Postprocessual Archaeology: Multiple Ways of Knowing the Past, edited by R.W. Preucel (Center for Archaeological Investigations, Occasional Paper No. 10, Southern Illinois University, Carbondale, IL); "A Review of the Documentary Evidence for a 17th Century Navajo Occupation in the Chama Valley," in Current Research on the Late Prehistory & Early History of New Mexico, edited by B.J. Vierra (New Mexico Archaeological Council, Special Publication 1, Albuquerque); numerous articles, reports and working manuscripts.

*SCHAEFFER, PETER (Eskimo)
(village chairperson)
Affiliation: Native Village of Kotzebue, P.O. Box 296, Kotzebue, AK 99752 (907) 442-3467.

SCHAFER, LORNA
(publisher)
Affiliation: Tsa'Aszi (The Yucca) Magazine of Navajo Culture, Tsa'Aszi Graphics Center, Ramah Navajo School Board, CPO Box 12, Pine Hill, NM 87321 (505) 783-5503.

SCHEIRBECK, HELEN MAYNOR
(Lumbee) 1935-
(human resources administrator)
Born August 21, 1935, Lamberton, N.C. *Education*: Berea (KY) College, BA, 1957; VPI - SU, (Blacksburg, VA), EdD, 1980. *Principal occupa-

tion: Human resources administrator. *Address & Affiliation*: Director, American Indian Programs, Save the Children Federation, 54 Wilton Rd., Westport, CT 06880 (1983-). *Other professional posts*: Chairperson, Indian Education Task Force, American Indian Policy Review Commission, U.S. Congress; director, Office of Indian Affairs, U.S. Office of Education, Dept. of HEW; professional staff, U.S. Senate Subcommittee on Constitutional Rights. *Memberships*: United Indians of America (project advisor); National Indian Education Association (vice president). *Awards, honors*: John Hay Whitney Foundation, Opportunity Award; Outstanding Lumbee Award; Outstanding American Indian Award; Pepsi People Pour It On Award. *Interests*: Dr. Scheirbeck has traveled and worked throughout the U.S. She has worked with the majority of Indian tribes in the U.S. She has served on Legislature and Executive Task Forces investigating various issues affecting Indian people. Her hobbies include photography, writing, collecting legends, and swimming. *Biographical sources*: Outstanding Indians in USA; Indians of the Southwest; Outstanding Minority Women; Biographies of Outstanding American Indian Women. *Published works*: Indian Education: Tool for Cultural Politics (Harvard Center for Law & Education, Dec., 1970); The First Americans (American Red Cross Youth News, Nov., 1972); The History of Federal Indian Education Policy (American Indian Policy Review Commission, 1976); A Study of Three Selected Laws & Their Impact on American Indian Education (House of Interior & Insular Affairs, Oct., 1976); Public Policy and Contemporary Education of the American Indian (Ph.D. Dissertation, 1980).

SCHELL, LAWRENCE M. 1948-
(professor of anthropology)
Born November 7, 1948, Boston, Mass. *Education*: Oberlin College, BA, 1970; Temple University, MA, 1974; University of Pennsylvania, PhD, 1980. *Principal occupation*: Professor of anthropology. *Address*: Dept. of Anthropology, Social Science Bldg. , Albany, NY 12222 (518) 442-4700 (work). *Affiliations*: Clinical associate professor, Albany Medical College, 1983-; associate professor of anthropology, SUNY, Albany, 1986-. *Other professional post*: Sec/treas, Society for the Study of Human Biology. *Memberships*: American Association of Physical Anthropologists; the Human Biology Council; American Association of Public Health. *Awards, honors*: Ales Hrdlicka Prize awarded by the American Association of Physical Anthropologists. *Published works*: Articles: co-author, "Distribution of Albumin Variants Naskapi and Mexico Among Aleuts, Frobisher Bay Eskimos, and Micmac, Naskapi, Mohawk, Omaha, and Apache Indians" in American Journal of Physical Anthropologists, Vol. 49:111-119, 1978; "Anthropometric Variation in Native American Children and Adults" in Origins and Affinities of the First Americans, W.S. Laughlin and A.B. Harper, Eds., 1979; "Alloabuminemia and the Migrations of Native Americans" in Yearbook of Physical Anthropology Vol. 31:1-13, 1988; "Physical Growth and Development of American Indian and Eskimo Children and Youth" in Handbook of North American Indians, Vol. 3, Environment, Origins, and Population, R. Ford, editor (in press).

*SCHEMMEL, TERI
(health director)
Affiliation: Lower Sioux Community Council, P.O. Box 308, Morton, MN 56270 (507) 697-6185.

SCHINDLER, DUANE E.
(Turtle Mountain Chippewa) 1944-
(educational administration)
Born April 22, 1944, Turtle Mountain Indian Reservation, Belcourt, N.D. *Education*: University of North Dakota; Valley City State College, ND; University of Wisconsin, Eau Claire; Arizona State University; University of South Dakota. *Affiliations*: Program development specialist, Eastern Montana State College, Billings (2 years); program specialist, University of New Mexico (1 year); instructor, Adult Programs, Wenatchee Valley College, Omak, WA (2 years); director, Adult Education, Colville Confederated Tribes, Nespelem, WA (1 year); director, American Indian Student Division, University of Washington, Seattle, WA (1 year); principal, Turtle Mountain Chippewa High School, Belcourt, ND. *Other professional posts*: Field reader, consultant: Logo language; computer applications, computer literacy, computer office systems; curriculum development; school board training; program evaluation management. *Community activities*: American Indian Center, Spokane, WA (chairperson). *Memberships*: National Association of Secondary School Principals; National Indian Education Association; ASCD, NABE. *Awards, honors*: Outstanding Teacher, Oglala Community Schools, Pine Ridge, SD. *Interests*: Computers in the classroom; research in mathematics. *Biographical source*: Outstanding Young Men of America, 1973. *Published works*: Concepts of American Indian Learners (Education, Tempe, Ariz.); Language, Culture and the Mathematics (Journal of the American Indian, 1986).

*SCHLENDER, JAMES H.
(executive director)
Affiliation: Great Lakes Indian Fish & Wildlife Commission, P.O. Box 9, Odanah, WI 54861 (715) 682-6619.

*SCHMELZ-KEIL, LYNNE M.
(librarian)
Affiliation: Tozzer Library, Harvard University, 21 Divinity Ave., Cambridge, MA 02138 (617) 495-2248.

*SCHOENECKE, CINDY
(health center director)
Affiliation: Black Hawk Health Center, Sac & Fox Nation, Rte. 2, Box 246, Stroud, OK 73079 (918) 968-9531.

SCHOENFELD, MICHAEL
(school principal)
Affiliation: Isleta Elementary School, P.O. Box 550, Isleta, NM 87022 (505) 869-2321.

SCHOENHUT, ROBERT JOHN *(Holy Bear)*
(Standing Rock Sioux) 1940-
(cinematographer/director)
Born December 27, 1940, Fort Yates, N.D. *Education*: Brooks Institute of Photography (Santa Barbara, CA), BFA, 1974; American Film Institute (Los Angeles), MFA, 1976; U.S. Naval Photographic School, 1961-62. *Principal occupation*: Cinematographer. *Address*: c/o D.J. Lyons, Summerhaven, Gough Rd., Fleet, Hampshire, England GU13 8LJ (011 44 25) 2614773. *Affiliations*: Cinematographer, various studios, Hol-

lywood, 1974-; producer/director, Public Television, 1974-. *Other professional post*: Camera operator: "Dances With Wolves" 1989; "Quantum Leap," 1990; "Dinosaurs," 1991-93; "To Sell a Child," NBC movie 1994; director of photography, "The Trial of Standing Bear," 1987-88 NETV/PBS; producer/director, "Standing Rock: A Vision," 1979 AFI grant); Cinematographer for German TV WDR, Cologne. *Military service*: U.S. Marine Corps, 1961-63 (LCPA E-3; Photo Reconnaissance; Good Conduct Medal). *Memberships*: International Alliance of Theatrical Stage Employees Local 659; Hollywood Cinematographers (only Native American member), 1975-. *Interests*: "I want to continue traveling and working with indigenous peoples from other countries as well as U.S. and Canadian tribes on films & television to help change the stereotypical images forced on the public by the various media's."

SCHOLDER, FRITZ (Mission) 1937-
(artist)
Born October 6, 1937, Breckenridge, Minn. *Education*: Sacramento State College, BA, 1960; University of Arizona, MFA, 1964. *Principal occupation*: Artist. Resides in Santa Fe. *Other professional posts*: Participant, Southwest Indian Art Project, Rockefeller Foundation, 1961-63; chairman, Fine Arts Committee, First Convocation of American Indian Scholars, Princeton University, 1970. *Awards, honors*: Numerous awards for painting at the following exhibitions: Southwestern Drawing and Print Exhibition, Dallas Museum of Fine Arts; Mid-America Exhibition, Nelson Gallery of Art, Kansas City, Mo.; National Indian Exhibition, Scottsdale, AZ; among others. *Biographical sources*: Who's Who in the West; Who's Who in American Art; Dictionary of International Biography.

*SCHREIBER, GEORGE
(school principal/teacher)
Affiliation: Swift Bird Day School, HCR 3, Box 119, Gettysburg, SD 57442 (605) 733-2143.

*SCHROYER, DAN
(BIA supt. for education)
Affiliation: Crow Creek/Lower Brule Agency, BIA, P.O. Box 139, Fort Thompson, SD 57339 (605) 245-2398.

SCHUCKER, ALBERT E. *(Al Red Oak)*
(Nanticoke) 1922-
(construction company owner)
Born September 1, 1922, Reading, Penna. *Education*: Chicago Tech, 1941 - Construction Efficiency; University of Pennsylvania, 1950-56. *Principal occupation*: Owner/president, Schucker Construction Company, Reading, PA (40+ years). *Home address*: 1510 Greenview Ave., Reading, PA 19601 (215) 373-4046; 376-8046 (work). *Other professional posts*: Served as expert witness & did some government intelligence work. *Military service*: U.S. Army, 1943 (Corporal). *Community activities*: Member, City Council, Reading, PA; County Comprehensive Water-Sewer Committee (chairperson); Industrial Waste Regulation Committee (chairperson); Minority Business Enterprise Committee of Chamber of Commerce. *Memberships*: Eastern Delaware Nations (past V.P.; now an elder); American Concrete Institute; Masons; Rotary Club (past president); American Legion; Penwriters Club; Masons; Shrine; United American Indians of the Delaware Valley. *Awards, honors*: Paul Harris Award in Rotary; Certificate

of Merit by President Reagan, and various other awards. *Interests*: "Traveled extensively, including Mexican jungles; experienced with herbs and the healing arts; helped many people to heal themselves mentally and physically." *Biographical sources*: Articles in the local and state news media. *Published works*: Few articles published in trade journals.

*SCHULTZ, JACK
(Creek language instructor)
Affiliation: Native American Studies Program, University of Oklahoma, 455 W. Lindsey, Rm. 804, Norman, OK 73019 (405) 325-2312.

*SCHUMACHER, WILLIAM
(Flandreau Santee Sioux)
(tribal president)
Affiliation: Flandreau Santee Sioux Executive Committee, P.O. Box 283, Flandreau, SD 57028 (605) 997-3891.

SCHUSKY, ERNEST L. 1931-
(anthropologist)
Born October 13, 1931, Portsmouth, Ohio. *Education*: Miami University, Ohio, AB, 1952; University of Chicago, MA, 1957, PhD (Anthropology), 1960. *Principal occupation*: Anthropologist. *Home address*: 412 Willowbrook, Collinsville, IL 62234 (618) 345-0437. *Affiliation*: Professor of anthropology (retired), Southern Illinois University, Edwardsville, IL, 1960-93. *Other professional post*: Author. *Military service*: U.S. Army, 1953-54 (Corporal; served in Korea). *Memberships*: American Anthropological Association. *Awards, honors*: Missouri Historical Society award for best article in 1971, "The Upper Missouri Indian Agency" in Missouri Historical Review Vol. 65:249-269; Fulbright Professor, 1982 (taught a course on the American Indian at Seoul National University). *Interests*: Mr. Schusky writes, "My interest in American Indians started in 1953 with the Tohono Oodom. Later field trips were made among New England Indians. Fieldwork occurred among the Lower Brule and Pine Ridge Sioux between 1958-60. The political and economic problems of Native Americans has been a professional interest throughout." *Published works*: Politics and Planning in a Dakota Indian Community (Institute of Indian Studies, 1959); Introducing Culture (Prentice-Hall, Inc., (four editions) 1967, 1972, 1978, 1986); The Right to Be Indian (Institute of Indian Studies, Vermillion, SD, 1965; Indian Historian Press, 1970); The Forgotten Sioux (Nelson Hall, 1975); editor, Political Organization of Native North Americans (University Press of America, 1980).

SCHUTT, DENNIS
(school supt.)
Affiliation: Marty Indian School, P.O. Box 187, Marty, SD 57361 (605) 384-5431.

*SCHWARTZ, DOUGLAS W.
(college president)
Affiliation: School of American Research, Indian Arts Research Center, P.O. Box 2188, Santa Fe, NM 87504 (505) 982-3584.

SCHWARTZ, PATRICIA (PADDY) 1941-
(shop owner)
Born May 7, 1941, New Haven, Conn. *Education*: Boston University, BA, 1962. *Principal occupation*: Owner, Skystone Treasures (4 years). *Address*: P.O. Box 114, Glencoe, IL 60022 (708) 835-3355. *Community activities*: Teach adult education classes, New Trier High School,

Norfield, IL. *Memberships*: Indian Arts & Crafts Association (Public Relations Committee); Society for American Archaeology; Southwest Association on Indian Affairs; Mitchell Indian Museum, Evanston, IL. *Interests*: "Business interests limited to American Indian jewelry, pottery, carved fetishes and other arts. Avocational - archaeology of the U.S. and Europe. Programs and lectures for various community groups on Amerindian subjects."

SCHWEI, BARBARA
(foundation president; dance producer)
Born in Wisc. *Education*: Carnegie Tech (studied drama); New York University, BFA. *Principal occupation*: dance producer, foundation president. *Home address*: 223 East 61st St., New York, NY 10022 (212) 308-9555. *Affiliations*: Founder/producer, American Indian Dance Theater (dancers, singers and drummers representing tribes from across the nation and Canada), 1986-; founder/president, Native American Performing Arts Foundation (to develop and expand projects by Native Americans in the performing arts, and on Native American themes), 1988-.

SCOTT, COLIN *(Kaa-uumaakiimishit)* 1952-
(professor of anthropology)
Born June 1, 1952, Indian Head, Sask. Can. *Education*: University of Regina, BA, 1972; McGill University (Montreal), MA, 1983, PhD, 1983. *Principal ocupation*: Professor. *Home address*: 6061 Terrebonne, Montreal, PQ H4A 1B8. *Affiliation*: Assistant professor of anthropology, McGill University, Montreal. *Other professional post*: Consultant to aboriginal and regional governments. *Memberships*: Canadian Anthropological Society; American Anthropological Association. *Awards, honors*: Social Sciences and Humanities Research Council of Canada, Strategic Research Grant, "Aboriginal Government, Resources and Development"; Australian National University, Visiting Fellowship, 1991. *Interests*: Knowledge construction among Cree hunters of James Bay; political discourse of aboriginal rights; development in the Subarctic. *Published works*: Books - section, "Ideology of Reciprocity Between the James Bay Cree and the Whiteman State" in P. Skalnik, ed. Outwitting the State (Transaction Publishers, 1989); Income Security for Cree Hunters, with H. Feit (M.A.S., 1992); article - "Knowledge Construction Among Cree Hunters" Journal de la Soc. des Americanistes (LXXV: 193-208, 1989).

SCOTT, GEORGE
(BIA supt. for education)
Affiliation: Papago Agency, Bureau of Indian Affairs, Box 38, Sells, AZ 85634 (602) 383-3292.

*SCOTT, KENDALL (Kickapoo)
(tribal chairperson)
Affiliation: Kickapoo of Oklahoma Business Committee, P.O. Box 70, McLoud, OK 74851 (405) 964-2075.

SCOTT, LARRY
(health director)
Affiliation: Watonga PHS Indian Health Center, Box 878, Watonga, OK 73772 (405) 623-4991.

*SCOTT, MARILYN M.
(health center director)
Affiliation: Lummi PHS Indian Health Center, 2592 Kwina Rd., Bellingham, WA 98226 (206) 676-8373.

SCOVILLE, STANLEY 1946-
(lawyer)
Born February 20, 1946, in Phoenix, Ariz. *Education*: University of Arizona, BA, 1968, JD, 1971. *Principal occupation*: Lawyer. *Address*: 1401 17th St., N.W. #403, Washington, DC 20036 (202) 225-2761 (work). *Affiliation*: Staff director, U.S. House of Representatives, Washington, D.C., 1972-. *Memberships*: Arizona Bar; District of Columbia Bar. *Awards, honors*: Guttmacher Award, American Psychiatric Association, 1971. *Published work*: The Administration of Psychiatric Theory & Practice in Arizona (with Prof. David B. Wexler (13 AZ Law Review 1, 1971).

SCRIBNER, PRINCESS ROSE (Penobscot) 1940-
(president/founder, Indian center)
Born April 3, 1940, Gardiner, Maine. *Education*: Mohegan Community College, Norwich, CT, AA, 1978. *Principal occupation*: President/founder, White Cloud Cultural Center, Norwich, CT, 1975-. *Memberships*: National Historic Preservation Society; National Indian Education Association; Indian Rights Association. *Awards, honors*: Outstanding Minority Award, Mohegan Community College; American Education Award, University of Connecticut. *Interests*: "My main goal in life (vocational) is to become a good Indian leader in serving our Native American people. I've traveled throughout the U.S. in observing model education programs much needed for Indian people. I hope to be appointed by the President of the U.S. in serving on the National Indian Education Advisory Board, Washington, D.C. I feel by this appointment, I can have the opportunity of getting more school books portraying Indian children properly, so that other children can read and learn what Indian people are all about. To wipe out the present stereotype Indian. Any expeditions I plan for the future will be one of taking a canoe trip down the Allegash, this area is one in which my famous grandfather guided many famous authors, Lord's of England, Countess's of Canada, on many a trip or expedition." *Published work*: Ethnic People of Connecticut (University of Connecticut, 1979).

SCUDERO, JIM (Eskimo)
(mayor)
Affiliation: Metlakatla Indian Community Council, P.O. Box 8, Metlakatla, AK 99926 (907) 886-4441.

*SCULLY, DIANA C.
(executive director)
Affiliation: Maine Indian Tribal State Commission, P.O. Box 87, Hallowell, ME 04347 (207) 622-4815.

SEABOURN, BERT D. (Cherokee-Chickasaw) 1931-
(artist)
Born July 9, 1931, Iraann, Tex. *Education*: Oklahoma City University, MFA, 1963; Central State University, Edmond, OK, 1973; University of Oklahoma, 1976. *Principal occupation*: Artist. *Home address*: 6105 Covington Lane, Oklahoma City, OK 73132 (405) 722-1631. *Military service*: U.S. Navy (Journalist, Third Class, 1951-55). *Community activities*: Oklahoma State Arts Council; Oklahoma City Arts Council. *Memberships*: Oklahoma Art Guild (past president); Oklahoma Art Directors Club (past president); Oklahoma Watercolor Association (past treasurer). *Awards, honors*: Best of Show (oil), Okla-

homa Art Guild Annual, Oklahoma City, OK, 1966; Grand Award (acrylic), Five Civilized Tribes Museum, Muskogee, OK, 1973; Best of Show (watercolor), Red Cloud National Indian Art Exhibition, Pine Ridge, SD, 1974; Governor's Award, presented by Governor George Nigh, Oklahoma State Capitol, Oklahoma City, OK 1981; Sculpture Commission (23' bronze), Southwestern Bell Corporate Headquarters, Oklahoma City, OK, 1986; Best of Show (watercolor), Master Artist Show, Five Civilized Tribes Museum, 1988; numerous First Prizes in watercolor, oil, graphics, acrylics, and drawings at above shows, et al. Interests: "In 1989, I had art shows in Taiwan in March, and in July shows in Singapore; two art shows in Germany, one in the 60's and one in the 70's. Works are exhibited in The Heard Museum, Phoenix; The Five Civilized Tribes Museum, Muskogee, OK; Oklahoma Art Center, Oklahoma City, OK; Red Cloud Indian School, Pine Ridge, SD; The Vatican Museum of Modern Religious Art, Italy; Inter-Tribal Indian Ceremonial Association, Gallup, NM; among others. *Biographical sources*: Who's Who in America; Who's Who in American Art; Who's Who in American Indian Art; Who's Who in the South and Southwest; Dictionary of International Biography; Artists of Reknown; Contemporary Southwest Painters. *Published works*: Master Artists of the Five Civilized Tribes, 1976; Cherokee Artist, 1981; and Vanishing Americans, 1984 - all published by Seabourn Graphics.

SEABOURN, CONNIE (Cherokee) 1951-
(painter, printmaker)
Born Seoptember 20, 1951, Purcell, Okla. *Education*: University of Oklahoma, BFA, 1980. *Principal occupation*: Painter, printmaker. *Home address*: P.O. Box 23795, Oklahoma City, OK 73123 (405) 728-3903. *Selected Exhibitions*: 1990: New Watercolors, Chrysallis Art Gallery, Denver, CO; Masters of the Southwest, Adagio Gallery, Palm Springs, CA; Connie Seabourn, Carnegie Library Town Hal, Lawton, OK; Three Female Painters, Oklahoma Indian Art Gallery, Oklahoma City, OK. 1991: Internationally Known Southwest Artists, Tradewind Wildlife Art Gallery, Kansas City, MO; An Important Art/Expression, Christian Wolf Gallery, Albuquerque, NM: Vision Makers/Connie and Bert Seabourne, Oklahoma Indian Art Gallery; Premier Art Event: New Originals, Impressions, Ltd. Estes Park, CO; L.A. Art Expo, Los Angeles, CA; Annual Colorado Indian Market and Western Art Roundup, Boulder/Denver, CO; Five Civilized Tribes Museum Annual Competitive Show, Muskogee, OK. 1992: People, Places & Spirits, Adagio Gallery; Red Earth, Oklahoma City; Winter Art Show, Indian Paintbrush Gallery, Siloam Springs, AR; Color-Culture-Creed: Multi-Culturism in Oklahoma, City Arts Center, Oklahoma City; Connie & Bert Seabourne, El Taller, Austin, TX; Joan Cawley Gallery, Santa Fe, NM. Numerous other exhibitions from 1969-89. *Collections*: Museum of the American Indian, New York City; The Heard Museum, Phoenix; Center for Cherokee Heritage Museum, Cherokee, NC; Southern Plains India Museum, Anadarko, OK; Gilcrease Museum, Tulsa, OK; among many others. *Recent Lectures & Public Speaking Engagements*: Blind Embossment Printmaking Workshop, Johnson Atelier, Tulsa, OK, 1992; Demonstration, Bartlesville Art Guild, Bartlesville, OK, 1992; Demonstration, Mid-Del Art Guild, Midwest City, OK, 1992; Demonstration, Central Oklahoma Art Guild, Oklahoma

City, OK, 1991; Lecture and Demonstration, Southeastern State College, Wilburton, OK, 1990; among many others. *Recent Awards*: Third Place, Watercolor, Gallup Intertribal Ceremonial, Gallup, NM, 1990; Third Place, Watercolor, Layers of Stories, Chisholm Trail Art Show, El Reno, OK, 1990; Special Merit Award, Painting, Annual Trail of Tears Show, Trail of Tears Museum, Tahlequah, OK, 1989; First Place, Graphics, Little Clasic Art Show, for Winter Vision, Guthrie, OK, 1988; among many others. *Recent Honors*: Commission to do signed reproduction/poster, One Voice for Children, for SACUS (Southern Association of Children Under Six) for national conference meeting in Tulsa, OK, 1992; 1991 Indian Images Calendar, Layers of Stories, used for May, published by Indian Images Productions, Evansville, IN; 1991 American Indian Art Calendar, Gentle Guardian used for August (Semihoye Publications, Norman, OK; Commission to do Limited Edition Reproduction, Tribal Renewal for Drug Recovery, Inc., Oklahoma City, 1990; Judge for Miss Indian Oklahoma Pageant, 1990; among others. *Biographical sources*: Who's Who in American Art, 1984; International Who's Who of Contemporary Achievement, 1984; Directory of Distinguished Americans, Third Ed.; Community Leaders of the World, 1984; Personalities of the South, 1985; International Directory of Distinguished Leadership, 1986; The Artist As Printmaker: Connie Seabourne, 1986; Personalities of America, 4th Ed., 1987; Foremost Women of the Twentieth Century, 1987.

SEAMAN, P. DAVID 1932-
(professor of linguistics)
Born January 31, 1932, Connellsville, P A. *Education*: Asbury College, AB, 1957; University of Kentucky, MA, 1958; Indiana University, PhD (Linguistics), 1965. *Principal occupation*: Professor of Linguistics, Dept. of Anthropology, Northern Arizona University, Flagstaff, AZ, 1967-. *Home address*: 4221 E. White Aster St., Phoenix, AZ 85044. *Other professional posts*: Bilingual/bicultural consulting for Zuni Tribal Council, 1970-72; linguistic consulting for Bureau of Indian Affairs, 1968-69, 1970-76; cross-cultural management consulting for Hopi Tribal Council, 1974-79; accounting and management consulting for Fort Mojave Tribal Council, 1977-80. *Military service*: U.S. Army, 1951-54 (Sergeant; U.S. Army Commendation Medal for efficient administration of U.S. Army field hospital in Korea, 1953). *Community activities*: University Heights Corporation, Flagstaff (director and corporate secretary, 1972-); Flagstaff Medical Center (finance committee, 1980-). *Memberships*: Linguistic Society of America; Society for Study of Indigenous Languages in America; Society for Linguistic Anthropology; Friends of Uto-Aztecan. *Awards, honors*: Distinguished Faculty Award, Northern Arizona University, 1980; among others. Research: Hopi dictionary project; traditional Havasupai culture; American Indian languages/cultures; Alfred F. Whiting Indian archives. *Interests*: American Indian languages and culture; Greek language and culture. Paper delivered: Hopi Dictionary and Computers, joint meeting, Arizona Humanities Association and Arizona Alliance for Arts Education, Scottsdale Community College, 1983 (article--Arizona Humanities Association Journal, Feb., 1984). *Published works*: Modern Greek and American English in Contact (Mouton & Co., The Hague, 1972); co-editor, Havasupai Habitat: A.F. Whiting's Ethnography of a Traditional

Indian Culture (University of Arizona Press, 1985); Hopi Dictionary: Hopi-English, English-Hopi (Northern Arizona University Anthropological Paper No. 2 - 3 printings, 1985-87); article: "Hopi Linguistics: An Annotated Bibliography" (Anthropological Linguistics, 1977).

SEBASTIAN, JACK
(Indian band chief)
Affiliation: Hagwilget Indian Band, Box 460, New Hazelton, British Columbia, Canada V0J 2J0 (604) 842-6258.

*SEBASTIAN, ROY (Chief Hockeo) (Pequot)
(tribal chairperson)
Affiliation: Eastern Pequot Reservation, North Stonington, CT 06359.

SECAKUKU, FERRELL (Hopi)
(tribal chairperson)
Affiliation: Hopi Tribal Council, P.O. Box 123, Kykotsmovi, AZ 86039 (602) 734-2441.

*SEETOT, ELMER
(AK village president)
Affiliation: Native Village of Brevig Mission, Brevig Mission, AK 99785 (907) 642-3851.

*SEGAR, EMILY
(editor)
Affiliation: "The Sentinel," National Congress of American Indians, 900 Pennsylvania Ave., SE, Washington, DC 20003 (202) 546-9404.

*SEGEL, NORMAN
(executive director)
Affiliation: The Education for Parents of Indian Children With Special Needs Project, Southwest Communication Resources, P.O. Box 788, Bernalillo, NM 87004 (800) 765-7320.

*SEHOM, RODNEY
(school principal)
Affiliation: Newtok Day School, Newtok, AK 99559 (907) 237-2328.

SEKAQUAPTEWA, KEN
(publisher)
Affiliation: Eagle's Eye, Brigham Young University, Office of Student Programs, 4th Floor, ELWC, Provo, UT 84602 (801) 378-6263.

*SELF, GEORGE WESLEY (Twin Eagles)
(Comanche, Cherokee-Ouachita Indian Confederation) 1941-
(swap meet dealer)
Born April 1, 1941, Los Angeles, Calif. *Education*: San Diego State University, BA, 1977. *Principal occupation*: Swap meet dealer (sell crystals). *Home address*: 4087 Lark St., San Diego, CA 92103 (619) 298-5248. *Military service*: U.S. Army (PFC). *Memberships*: San Diego Museum of Man (life member); Vice-President, San Diego Lapidary Society, 1993-; San Diego State University Alumni Association. *Honor*: Council member, Ouachita Indian Confederation. *Interests*: "I enjoy gems & minerals (rockhounding). I was an archaeologist."

*SEMINOLE, LYNETTE
(N.A. ecumenical ministry)
Affiliation: Native American Coalition of Programs, P.O. Box 1914, Fargo, ND 58107 (701) 235-3124.

*SENA, CARLOS (Southern Ute)
(radio station manager)
Affiliation: KSUT - 91.3 FM, Southern Ute Tribe, P.O. Box 737, Ignacio, CO 81137 (303) 563-0255.

SEPPANEN, JOHN (Chippewa)
(health director)
Affiliation: Keweenaw Bay Indian Community Health Cliic, Route 1, Baraga, MI 49908 (906) 353-6671.

SERO, THOMAS (Mohawk)
(board member)
Affiliation: Intertribal Christian Comunications, P.O. Box 3765, Station B, Winnipeg, Manitoba, Canada R2W 3R6 (204) 661-9333.

SETTEE, PIERRE
(Indian band chief)
Affiliation: Cumberland Indian Band, Box 220, Cumberland House, Saskatchewan, Canada S0E 0S0 (306) 888-2152.

SEVIER, JACKIE (Northern Arapaho) 1953-
(artist)
Born July 30, 1953, Riverton, Wyo. *Education*: Casper (WY) College, 1971-72. *Principal occupation*: Artist. *Membership*: Indian Arts & Crafts Association. *Awards, honors*: Red Earth, Oklahoma City; Northern Plains Tribal Arts, Sioux Falls, SD; Aspen Celebration for the American Indian; Smithsonian Institution, Museum of Anthropology; Twin Cities Indian Market, Minneapolis; Aplan Award & Diederich Award at Red Cloud Art Show, Pine Ridge, SD; Lawrence Indian Art Festival, Lawrence, KS. *Exhibits*: Stuhr Museum, Grand Island, NE; Sioux Indian Museum, Rapid City, SD; Buffalo Bill Historical Society, Cody, WY; and 1989 World Expo in Shizouka, Japan.

SEWEPAGAHAM, A.J.
(Indian band chief)
Affiliation: Little Red River Indian Band, Box 1165, High Level, Alberta, Canada T0H 1Z0 (403) 759-3912.

*SEXTON, LINDA
(foundation administrator)
Affiliation: The Jacobson Foundation, 609 Chautauqua, Norman, OK 73071 (405) 329-3012.

SEYLER, BERTHA
(editor)
Affiliation: The Rawhide Press, Spokane Tribal Business Council, P.O. Box 359, Wellpinit, WA 99040 (509) 258-7320.

SEYMOUR, TRYNTJE VAN NESS 1956-
(writer, lecturer)
Born July 2, 1956, New York, N.Y. *Education*: Smith College, BA, 1978. *Principal occupation*: Writer, lecturer. *Home address*: P.O. Box 363, Salisbury, CT 06068 (203) 435-2236. *Affiliation*: Guest curator, The Heard Museum, Phoenix, 1985-87. *Membership*: The Author's Guild. *Interests*: Extensive travels in the Southwest since 1970. Conducted in-depth interviews of Native American artists. Served as assistant boatman and, recently, as archaeology guide on raft trips through the Grand Canyon. Judge of paintings at Santa Fe Indian Market, 1987. *Biographical source*: "Traditional India Art," by Paula Panich in Southwest Profile, Feb. 1987. *Published works*: Acoma (Lime Rock Press, 1980); When

the Rainbow Touches Down: The Artists and Stories Behind the Apache, Navajo, Rio Grande Pueblo and Hopi Paintings in the William and Leslie Van Ness Denman Collection (The Heard Museum-Dist. by University of Washington Press, 1989); The Gift of Changing Woman (Henry Holt & Co., 1993).

SHACKLEFORD, BRUCE M. (Creek)
(museum director)
Affiliation: Creek Council House Museum, Okmulgee, OK 74447 (918) 756-2324.

SHAFFER, SUSAN (Umpqua)
(tribal chairperson)
Affiliation: Cow Creek Band of Umpqua Indians, 2400 Stewart Parkway, Suite 300, Roseburg, OR 97470 (503) 672-9405.

*SHANIGAN, MARIANE (Kanatak)
(village president)
Affiliation: Native Village of Kanatak, P.O. Box 693, Dillingham, AK 99576 (907) 842-4004.

SHANKS, LAURENCE "SWIFT TIDE"
(Schagticoke)
(tribal chief)
Affiliation: New England Coastal Schagticoke Indian Association, P.O. Box 551, Avon, MA 02322 (617) 961-1346.

SHANLEY, JAMES
(college president)
Affiliation: Fort Peck Community College, P.O. Box 575, Poplar, MT 59255 (406) 768-5551.

SHAW, CARL F.
(BIA-director of public affairs)
Affiliation: Office of Public Affairs, Bureau of Indian Affairs, Dept. of the Interior, MS-4140-MIB, 1849 C St., NW, Washington, DC 20240 (202) 208-7315.

SHAW, FRANCES (Dieguene)
(tribal chairperson)
Affiliation: Chairperson, Manzanita General Council, P.O. Box 1302, Boulevard, CA 92005 (619) 478-5028; chairperson, Southern Indian Health Council, P.O. Box 20889, El Cajon, CA 92021.

SHECANAPISH, GEORGE
(Indian band chief)
Affiliation: Naskapi of Quebec, Box 970, Kawawachikamach Indian Reserve, Schefferville, Quebec, Canada G0G 2T0 (418) 585-2370.

SHEDD, AARON
(educational administrator)
Affiliation: Director, Office of Indian Education, U.S. Dept of Education, Rm. 2177, Federal Office Bldg. 6, 400 Maryland Ave., Washington, DC 20202 (202) 401-1887.

SHEGONEE, HARTFORD (Potawatomi) 1943-
(administrator; former tribal chairperson)
Born October 27, 1943, Hayward, Wisc. *Education*: Nicolet College (Vocational Diploma-Auto Mechanics, 1986); Mt. Scenario College,1987-88. *Principal occupation*: Administrator. Resides in Crandon, WI. *Affiliation*: Former tribal chairperson, Forest County Potawatomi Executive Council, Crandon, WI, 1987-91. *Community activities*: Great Lakes Inter-Tribal Council (sec/treas, 1987-); Inter-Tribal Timber Council, 1987-; also active in local chapter of

Headstart program. National Congress of American Indians. *Awards, honors*: Honored with Plaque by the Canadian Potawatomi for assistance in quest for federal (U.S.) recognition of treaty. *Interests*: "Anything that will improve the lifestyle of the Forest County Potawatomi people. Instrumental in the Potawatomi having land in the City of Milwaukee placed into Trust for the Tribe in 1990. Restored political stability after BIA shutdown operations of the tribe in 1987."

SHELDON, LINDA
(health director)
Affiliation: Yerington Health Dept., 171 Campbell Lane, Yerington, NV 89447 (702) 463-3301.

SHELTON, M.L. "PETE" (Oglala Sioux) 1936-
(business owner)
Born July 29, 1936, Martin, S.D. *Education*: Scottsdale Junior College; Chadron State College. *Principal occupation*: Business owner. *Home address*: 532 E. Anamosa, Rapid City, SD 57701 (605) 343-7464 (work). *Affiliations*: Owner, Native American Office Products Supplies, Rapid City, SD, 1979-; owner, Native American Originals, Rapid City, SD, 1986-. *Community activities*: Minority Relations Chairperson, 1983-84. Membership: BPOE, 1964-.

SHEMICK, H. "MISSY"
(RN-health director)
Affiliation: Health Director, Nevada Urban Indians, 2100 Capurro Way #C, Sparks, NV 89431 (702) 329-2573; exeutive director, College Career & Vocational Resoure Library, Nevada Urban Indians, Sparks, NV.

SHENANDOAH, ADE (Onondaga) 1950-
(catering/food service)
Born April 28, 1950, Syracuse, N.Y. *Principal occupation*: Catering/food service. *Home address*: Box 10, Oneida, NY 13421 (315) 363-6248. *Affiliation*: Shenandoah Sandwiches, Oneida, NY, 1986-. *Other professional post*: Alcohol-prevention counselor. *Community actvities*: Alcohol youth prevention programs.

SHENANDOAH, DIANE (Oneida) 1958-
(catering/food service)
Born October 21, 1958, Syracuse, N.Y. *Principal occupation*: Catering/food service. *Home address*: Box 10, Oneida, NY 13421 (315) 363-6248. *Affiliation*: Shenandoah Sandwiches, Oneida, NY, 1986-. *Other professional post*: Artist/writer. *Award, honors*: Indian Market, Santa Fe, NM. "Shenandoah Sandwich," First Place, Native American Cuisine, Connecticut River Society. *Interests*: Traveled extensively along the East Coast from Maine to Florida. *Biographical sources*: "The Clouds Threw This Light," and "Spaning the Medicine River."

SHENANDOAH, JOANNE
(She Sings) (Oneida-Iroquois) 1957-
(singer/songwriter)
Born June 23, 1957, Syracuse, N.Y. *Education*: Andrews University, 1975-76; Columbia Union College, 1976-78. *Principal occupation*: Singer/songwriter. *Home address*: Oneida Indian Territory #10, Oneida, NY 13421 (315) 363-1655. *Affiliations*: Systems engineer, Inforex, Inc., Rockville, MD, 1976-81; business development manager, Computer Science Corp., Falls Church, VA, 1986-87; president, Red Line Computers, 1987-90; president, Round Dance Productions, Inc., Oneida, NY, 1991-. *Memberships*:

ASCAP; National Congress of American Indians; National American Indian Women's Association. *Interests*: "Music writing, performing, producing, composing; travels to Europe, throughout North America; sailing, canoeing; historical research. Round Dance Productions is a non-for-profit corporation formed specifically to assist in the preservation and development of indigenous North American language, history, music and art. Primary focus is on the Haudenosaunee (Oneida, Mohawk, Onondaga, Seneca, Cayuga and Tuscarora Nations) although it encompasses other aboriginal cultures as well." *Awards, honors*: "1993 Native Musician of the Year"; performed for first lady Hillary Clinton & V.P.'s wife, Tipper Gore in Washington, DC. *Biographical source*: Who's Who in the East, 1991-92; feature story in, "The Turtle" magazine, Winter 1993. Joanne has appeared on numerous television shows, radio broadcasts, and video documentaries. *Produced works*: She released her first album with Canyon Records in September 1989. She also recorded with NATO Records in France for the 2-CD album "Oyate" produced by Tony Hymas. Two of her compositions are featured on the Leonard Peltier album, "In the Spirit of Crazy Horse." Her most recent album "Loving Ways" is co-produced with a A. Paul Ortega, Canyon Records, Phoenix, AZ. "Nature Dance" with Sun Child Productions, distributed by Eye-Q Records, Warner of Germany was released June 1991 and made "Record of the Month." *Performances*: Shenandoah has performed thousands of concerts throughout North America and Europe. Some of the more recent include: Indian Time II, Winnipeg, Canada, - American Indian Music Festival, San Francisco, June 1991; National Canadian TV, Toronto Harbour-front Festival, July 1991; Earth Day, Washington, DC, May 1991; among others. Future Projects: TV Mini Series - Wampum Belts and Peace Trees, Author, Dr. Gregory Schaaf, Executive Producer, Sam Bottoms; European Tour, 1992 Spring "Indian Saga"; Planet Live - Earth Day, 1992.

SHENANDOAH, LEON (Onondaga)
(tribal chief)
Affiliation: Chief (lifetime), Onondaga Nation, RR 1, Box 270A, Nedrow, NY 13120 (716) 469-8507.

*SHEPHERD, ALEX (Paiute)
(tribal chairperson)
Affiliation: Tribal Council of Paiute Indian Tribe of Utah, 600 N. 100 E. Paiute Dr., Cedar City, UT 84720 (801) 586-1121.

SHEPHERD, BERNARD
(Indian band chief)
Affiliation: Whitebear Indian Band, Box 700, Carlyle, Saskatchewan, Canada S0C 0R0 (306) 577-2461.

SHEPPARD, LAVERNE (Shoshone-Bannock)
1960-
(executive director)
Born April 17, 1960, Blackfoot, Idaho. *Education*: University of Arizona, 1982; Idaho State University, BA (Journalism), 1984. *Principal occupation*: Executive director. *Affiliations*: Editor, Sho-Ban News, Fort Hall, ID, 1984-89, National American Indian/Alaska Native Media Specialist, U.S. Census Bureau, Seattle, 1989-90; Executive Director, Native American Journalism Association, University of Colorado School of Journalism, Campus Box 287, Boulder, CO

80309 (303) 492-7397, 1990-. *Other professional post*: Co-chairperson, Native Communications Group, Lincoln, NE, 1990-.

*SHERIDAN, MATTHEW, Sr..
(health project officer)
Affiliation: Carl T. Curtis Health Center, P.O. Box 250, Macy, NE 68039 (402) 837-5381.

*SHERMAN, GERALD J. (Oglala Sioux) 1949-
(bank manager)
Born July 17, 1949, Kyle, S.D. *Education*: Oglala Lakota College, BS, 1987. *Principal occupation*: Bank manager. *Address*: P.O. Box 86, Pukwana, SD 57370 (605) 473-9280 (work). *Affiliations*: Founding chairman of the board & executive director. The Lakota Fund, Kyle, SD, 1987-91 (a community loan fund on the Pine Ridge Indian Reservation); Pine Ridge Area Director, Native American Economic Development Project, Business Opportunity Center - University of South Dakota , 1991-93 (provided business technical assistance to tribal members at Pine Ridge); manager, Norwest Bank Lower Brule (a new bank on the Lower Brule Indian Reservation), Lower Brule, SD, 1993-. *Community activities*: Board member, Habitat for Humanity, Ft. Thompson, SD; board member, Food Services of South Dakota. *Membership*: North Plains Tribal Arts Council. *Awards, honors*: Minority Small Business Advocate of the Year, 1993, for South Dakota & SBA Region VIII. *Interests*: Indian economic development, finance. As founding chairman of the board & executive director of the Lakota Fund, Mr. Sherman played a principal role in developing the Fund and forging the relationships between the fund, its investors, funders, and clients. He traveled to Canada and Bangladesh to study the peer group lending method now in use by the Lakota Fund to make micro enterprise loans. Gerald has several years experience in television production but has been active in Indian economic development since 1986.

*SHEWANO, DON
(health director)
Affiliation: Forest Co. Potawatomi Community Clinic, P.O. Box 346, Crandon, WI 54520 (715) 478-3471.

SHEWISH, ADAM
(Indian band chief)
Affiliation: Sheshaht Indian Band, Box 1218, Port Alberni, British Columbia, Canada V9Y 7M1 (604) 724-1225.

SHIELDS, CALEB (Assiniboine Sioux)
(tribal chairperson)
Affiliation: Fort Peck Tribal Executive Board, P.O. Box 1027, Poplar, MT 59255 (406) 768-5155.

*SHIJE, HENRY (Zia Pueblo)
(pueblo governor)
Affiliation: Zia Pueblo Tribal Council, 135 Capital Square Dr., Zia Pueblo, NM 87053 (505) 867-3304.

SHINGOITEWA, LEROY N.
(Dawa yes va) (Hopi) 1942-
(tribal administrator)
Born August 4, 1942, Keams Canyon, Ariz. *Education*: Northern Arizona University, BS, 1969; Pennsylvania State University, MEd, 1972. *Principal occupation*: Tribal administrator. *Home address*: P.O. Box 1258, Tuba City, AZ 86045 (602) 283-5623. *Affiliation*: Hotevilla Bacavi

Community School, Hotevilla, AZ, 1990-93; executive assistant, Office of Hopi Tribal Chairman, Hopi Indian Tribe, Kykotsmovi, AZ, 1993-. *Other professional post*: Executive assistant, Navajo Nation Division of Health. *Community activities*: Member of Tuba City School Board; Arizona School Board Association (Legislative Committee, Resolution Committee, Chapter I Committee); White House Delegate for Indian Education; Indian Education Graduate Advisory Board, Berkeley, CA. *Memberships*: National Indian Education Association; Curriculum and Supervision Association; National School Board Association. *Awards, honors*: National Civic Award - Supermarkets Association; President Bush 1000 Points-of-Light Award; Hopi Man-of-the-Year (Hopi-Navajo Observer). *Interests*: "Work to help all Indian people throughout the U.S. in education and management areas."

SHIPEK, FLORENCE C. 1918-
(professor emerita)
Born December 11, 1918, North Adams, Mass. *Education*: University of Arizona, BA, 1939, MA, 1940; University of Washington, 1940-41, 1944-46; University of Hawaii, PhD (Anthropology), 1977. *Principal occupation*: Professor emerita of anthropology. *Address*: Dept. of Anthropology, University of Wisconsin-Parkside, Box N-2000, Kenosha, WI 53141. *Affiliations*: Director, Program for Community Development Education for Southern California Indian Reservation, Sociology Department, University of San Diego, 1970-72; assistant professor, associate professor, University of Wisconsin-Parkside, 1977-89, professor emerita, 1989-. *Other professional posts*: Anthropologist for the enrollment committee of the San Pascual Band of Mission Indians, 1956-68; ethnohistorical researcher, Mission Indian Land Claims Case (land use and identity of Diegueno-Kamia-Kumeyaay), 1959-64; ethnohistorical researcher, Water Claims Case of San Luis Rey Indian reservations, 1965-85; consultant to Environmental Impact Firms such as Wirth Associates, Cultural Systems Research, Inc., 1976-; consultant to Indian Freedom Ranch, San Diego County (a rural alcoholic rehabilitation center for Indians), 1978-82; consultant for Southern California Indian Law Seminar, 1979; consultant for San Pascual Band Education Project, 1981; consultant to Kumeyaay Elders Association, 1981-83; consultant for Kumeyaay Elders and Cayapaipe Reservation, 1982-; consultant and seminar lecturer for Rincon Band of San Luiseno Indians, 1984; with Dr. Lowell Bean of Cultural Systems Research, Inc., expert witness for water claims case for six southern California Indian Bands (San Luis Rey, Cuyapaipe, Pechanga, Santa Rosa, Morongo, and La Posta), 1984-; with Dr. Lowell J. Bean, consultant to San Luis Rey Band of Mission Indians in its quest for Federal recognition, 1985; consultant to Santa Ynez Reservation on membership genealogies for enrollment, 1986. *Memberships*: American Anthropological Association (Fellow); Society for Applied Anthropology (Fellow); Royal Anthropological Institute (Fellow); American Ethnological Association; American Society for Ethnohistory; Malki Museum Association; Phi Kappa Phi. *Awards, honors*: Grant from Wenner-Gren Foundation for Anthropological Research (autobiography of the last traditional leader of the Kumeyaay), 1982; appointed by the Society for American Archaeology and Society of Professional Archaeology to the Subcommittee to consider revisions to the ethics code and pro-

cedures for handling excavation and reburial of American Indian human remains and suggest modifications for state laws concerning unmarked graves, 1985; appointed to the Wisconsin State Historical Review Board and served for six years; 1986 "Distinguished Scholar" by the Southwestern Anthropological Association; in 1987 the University of California, Riverside, selected her to be the first Rupert Costo Professor in American Indian History; appointed to the San Diego Historic Site Board over concerns with non-Indian development which often ignores Kumeyaay and San Luiseno concerns, 1990. *Interests*: North American Indians; California and Southwest Indians; Research and consulting: "From 1954 to the present, I have been working directly for and with the various Southern California Indian bands and individuals, doing research for them aimed at solving specific problems. Research included the history of changing land use and tenure rights, economic and agriculture, socio-political changes, genealogies. I met with their various political bodies and providing information directly to them. I have appeared as a witness or submitted prepared testimonies to various governmental agencies, such as the Commissioner of Indian Affairs, Indian Claims Commission, Department of Public Welfare, etc." She has retired from Wisconsin in 1989 and is in San Diego. She continues to write, lecture and consults with Southern California Indian Reservations on historic matters. *Published works*: Lower California Frontier 1870: Articles from the San Diego Union, 1870 (Dawson's Book Shop, 1965); The Autobiography of a Diegueno Woman, Delfina Cuero (as told to Florence C. Shipek) (Dawson's Book Shop, 1969; paperback edition, Malki Museum Press, 1970; available in Talking Books from Library of Congress, 1975); Pushed Into the Rocks: Changes in Southern California Indian Land Tenure, 1769-1986 (University of Nebraska Press, 1988); Second Edition, Delfina Cuero: Her Autobiography, An Account of the Rest of Her Life and Her Ethnobotanical Contributions (Ballena Press, 1991); *In preparation*: A Strategy for Change: The Luiseno of Southern California; and The Kumeyaay of Southern California: A Resilient People; numerous chapters in books, journal articles, book reviews, limited circulation reports, social impact assessments, written legal testimonies, papers presented; Audio Visual Material: The Indian Heritage--The Life of Delfina Cuero (videotape prepared for Heritage San Diego Educational TV series, San Diego County Education Department.

SHIPPS, THOMAS H. 1953-
(lawyer)
Born February 13, 1953, Hyannis, Mass. *Education*: Fort Lewis College, BA, 1976; University of Houston Law School, JD, 1979. *Principal occupation*: Lawyer. *Home address*: P.O. Box 2717, Durango, CO 81302 (303) 247-1755. *Affiliation*: Tribal attorney, Southern Ute Indian Tribe, 1980-. *Memberships*: American Bar Association; Colorado Bar Association; Colorado Indian Bar Association; National Indian Law Support Center (board of directors); Rocky Mountain Mineral Law Foundation. *Published works*: The American Indian and the Constitution (University of Houston Law Center, 1979); "Oil and Gas Lease Operation and Royalty Valuation on Indian Lands," Rocky Mountain Mineral Law Foundation, 1991.

*SHOEMAKER, DIANNA 1934-
(nursing)
Born April 18, 1934, Seattle, Wash. *Education*: University of Colorado, BSN, 1959; University of Washington, MS (Nursing), 1962; University of New Mexico, MA, 1981, PhD, 1984. *Principal occupation*: Nursing. *Home address*: 726 - 13 Tramway Vista Ter. NE, Albuquerque, NM 87122 (505) 856-7371. *Affiliation*: Professor & Associate Dean, University of New Mexico, Albuquerque, NM. *Community activity*: Member, Urban Indian Health & Human Services Board. *Membership*: Sigma Theta Tau - Nursing Honor Society. *Awards, honors*: Teacher of the Year; Fellow - American Academy of Nursing. *Interests*: "My most notable contributions to nursing have been in the areas of education, specifically in pioneering efforts in the field of outreach education for RNs returning to school, and cross-cultural research in gerontology. Since 1988, I have focused on development of creative programs for RNs in rural New Mexico & southern Colorado, who wish to return to school for a BSN degree but cannot relocate to the University campus. I have written two Special Projects grants, increasing Native American constituency. Research about cross-cultural perspectives of aging included grandparent-grandchild relationships among the Navajo."

*SHOEMAKER, MARY J.
(school principal)
Affiliation: San Juan Day School, P.O. Box 1077, San Juan Pueblo, NM 87566 (505) 852-2154.

SHOPTEESE, JOHN T.
(Prairie Band Potawatomi) 1938-
(Indian health service)
Born February 28, 1938, Mayetta, Kan. *Education*: Haskell Indian Junior College, 1956-58. *Principal occupation*: Indian health service. Home address: 724 Parkside Dr. N.E., Albuquerque, NM 87123. *Affiliation*: Real Property Officer, Office of Administrative Management, Indian Health Service, Albuquerque, N.M., 1958-. *Military service*: U.S. Army, 1962-64. *Memberships*: Albuquerque Artist Association; Indian Arts and Crafts Association (board of directors; chairman, Native Arts Committee, 1982-83); Eight Northern Pueblos Arts Guild, 1982-84. *Awards, honors*: Several awards for achievement in the arts (I am a jeweler--gold/silver smith); sculpture in bronze, pewter, clay; received several juried art show awards throughout the Southwest. *Interests*: Pursuing excellence in Native arts; to enhance cultural awareness and enact the trends of art through significant application of contemporary overtones. (I) "have displayed my arts/crafts at major art shows of Native American artists."

SHORE, NANCY (Sos'setv) (Creek/Seminole) 1947-
(education)
Born April 6, 1947, Glades County, Fla. *Education*: Barry University (Miami, FL), MSW, 1982. *Principal occupation*: Education. *Affiliation*: Seminole Tribe of Florida, Hollywood, FL, 1973-. *Community activities*: Seminole Higher Education Committee; Seminole Womens Club; Parent Advisory Committee; Okee Parent/Teacher; Seminole Education Advisory.

*SHORT, PHYLLIS
(museum director)
Affiliation: Nana Museum of the Arctic, P.O. Box 49, Kotzebue, AK 99752 (907) 442-3301.

SHORTING, HECTOR
(Indian band chief)
Affiliation: Little Saskatchewan Indian Band, Gypsumville, Manitoba, Canada R0C 1J0 (204) 659-4584.

*SHROLL, WILLIAM
(school principal/supt.)
Affiliation: Crow Creek High School, P.O. Box 12, Stephan, SD 57346 (605) 852-2255.

SHULTES, STEPHANIE E. (Iroquois)
(museum curator)
Affiliation: Iroquois Indian Museum, Box 7, Caverns Rd., Howes Cave, NY 12092 (518) 296-8949.

*SHUNATONA, GWEN
(executive director)
Affiliation: Orbis Associates, 1411 K St., NW, Suite 700, Washington, DC 20005 (202) 628-4444.

SHURR, JOHN CARTER
(Oklahoma Cherokee) 1947-
(journalist, bureau chief-AP)
Born March 15, 1947, Muskogee, Okla. *Education*: University of Oklahoma, BA (Journalism), 1973. *Principal occupation*: Bureau chief, Associated Press. *Home address*: 120 S. Brighton Rd., Columbia, SC 29223 (803) 788-1077. *Affiliation*: Chief of Bureau, The Associated Press, Columbia, SC, 1984-. *Other professional post*: Curriculum Advisory Committee, University of South Carolina, College of Journalism. *Military service*: U.S. Navy, 1966-70 (2nd Class Radioman, E-5; Vietnam, 1967-68; Vietnam Service Medal, Vietnam Campaign Medal-3 Bronze Stars; Presidential Unit Citation, Navy Unit Commendation, Combat Action Ribbon). *Memberships*: Reporters Committee for Freedom of the Press, 1991- (Steering Committee); 1st Amendment Congress (Trustee & Vice President, 1980-88); South Carolina Press Association Freedom of Information Committee, 1986-, Chairperson; Society of Professional Journalists; Native American Journalists Association; First Amendment Congress, 1980-88 (vice president). *Awards, honors*: American Bar Assn. Gavel Award, 1981; SC Press Association Award, 1987 & 1994; several Associated Press Managing Editors Awards. *Interests*: Avid sailboat racer; tennis. *Published work*: Freedom of Information Guide (SC Press Association, 1987-93).

*SICKEY, ERNEST
(health center director)
Affiliation: Dallas Inter-Tribal Council Health Center, 209 E. Jefferson, Dallas, TX 75203 (214) 941-1050.

SIDNEY, IVAN (Hopi)
(former tribal chairperson)
Affiliation: Hopi Tribal Council, P.O. Box 123, Kykotsmovi, AZ 86039 (602) 734-2445.

SIGO, CHARLES (Suquamish)
(museum curator)
Affiliation: Suquamish Museum, 15838 Sandy Hook, NE, P.O. Box 498, Suquamish, WA 98392 (206) 598-3311.

SILAS, BERKMAN (Athapascan)
(village chief)
Affiliation: Minto Village Council, P O Box 26, Minto, AK 99758 (907) 798-7112.

*SILEX, EDGAR (Tiqua del Sur) 1958-
(creative writing instructor/poet, author)
Born March 31, 1958, El Paso, Tex. *Education*: University of Maryland, MFA, 1994. *Affiliation*: The Cafe Workshops, Baltimore, MD. *Membership*: Native American Student Union of University Maryland. *Biographical source*: Washington Post article, 6/15/93. *Published works*: Even the Dead Have Memories (New Sins Press); Through All the Displacements (Curbstone Press, 1995).

*SILHANEK, BETH
(school administrator)
Affiliation: Sac & Fox Settlement School, 1657 320th St., Tama, IA 52339 (515) 484-4990.

*SILVERBIRD, J. REUBEN (Navajo/Apache) 1940-
(story teller, actor, screen writer, film producer)
Born July 27, 1940, Placentia, Calif. *Education*: St. Michaels College (2 years). *Principal occupation*: story teller, actor, screen writer, film producer. *Home address*: 130 Fort Washington #5D, New York, NY 10032 (212) 740-8443 Fax 740-0572. *Affiliation*: President, Silverbird Productions (Music, Film, Stage & TV), New York, NY, 1984-. *Other professional post*: Trying to help finance "Iroquois National Lacrosse Team for England tour & documentary. *Military service*: U.S. Army (2 years) Special Services (Master Sergeant) taught electronics (produced & appeared in show that toured for Special Services). Certificate of Achievement for teaching electronics. *Community activities*: Association on American Indian Affairs, NYC; American Indian College Fund, NYC; American Indian Community House, NYC. *Memberships*: American Society of Composers & Publishers; Screen Actors Guild; Actor's Equity Association; New York Screen Writer's Association. *Awards, honors*: Owned & operated NYC 1st Native American restaurant, 1984-87. *Interests*: Singing tours of Asia; lectures on behalf of Native America.

*SILVESTER, JOHN
(program director)
Affiliation: Native American Studies Program, Scottsdale Community College, 9000 E. Chaparral St., Scottsdale, AZ 85256 (602) 423-6139.

SILVEY, LEANNE E.
(executive director)
Affiliation: Michigan Indian Child Welfare Agency, 405 E. Easterday Ave., Sault Ste. Marie, MI 49783 (906) 635-9400.

*SIMEONOFF, KELLY, Jr.
(association president)
Affiliation: Kodiak Area Native Association Health Center, 402 Center Ave., Kodiak, AK 99615 (907) 486-5725.

*SIMMONS, DOUGLAS V.
(school principal)
Affiliation: Mariano Lake Community School, P.O. Box 498, Crownpoint, NM 87313 (505) 786-5265.

SIMMS, RUSSELL
(executive director)
Affiliation: Council of Three Rivers American Indian Center, Inc., 200 Charles St., Dorseyville, PA 15238 (412) 782-4457. *Other professional post*: Editor, The Singing Winds Newsletter.

SIMON, BROTHER, S.J.
(museum director/curator)
Affiliation: The Heritage Center, Red Cloud Indian School, Hwy. 18W, Pine Ridge, SD 57770 (605) 867-5491.

SIMON, LUCAS (Pomo)
(tribal chairperson)
Affiliation: Middletown Rancheria, P.O. Box 292, Middletown, CA 95461.

*SIMON, LINCOLN (Eskimo)
(village president)
Affiliation: Native Village of White Mountain, P.O. Box 84082, White Mountain, AK 99784 (907) 638-3651.

*SIMON, MIKE (Sisseton Wahpeton Sioux)
(radio station manager)
Affiliation: KSWS - 89.3 FM, Sisseton Wahpeton Sioux tribe, P.o. Box 268, Sisseton, SD 57262 (605) 698-7972.

SIMONE, JEROME J.
(health services director)
Affiliation: United Indian Health Services, P.O. Box 420, Trinidad, CA 95570 (707) 677-3693.

SIMPSON, JR., H.B.
(BIA agency supt.)
Affiliation: Zuni Agency, Bureau of Indian Affairs, P.O. Box 369, Zuni, AZ 87327 (505) 782-5591.

SINCLAIR, ALFRED
(Indian band chief)
Affiliation: Washagamis Bay (McKenzie Portage) Indian band, Box 625, Keewatin, Ontario, Canada P0X 1C0 (807) 543-2532.

SINCLAIR, WENDELL
(Indian band chief)
Affiliation: Brokenhead Ojibway Nation, Scanterbury, MB, Can. R0E 1Wo (204) 766-2494.

*SING, DAVID
(center director)
Affiliation: Center for Gifted & Talented Native Hawaiian Children, University of Hawaii at Hilo, Hilo, HI 96720 (808) 933-3678.

SINOWAY, DOUG
(Indian band chief)
Affiliation: Whitesand Indian Band, Box 68, Armstrong, Ontario, Canada P0T 1A0 (807) 583-2177.

SIOUI, RICHARD HENRY (Huron) 1937-
(chemical engineer)
Born September 25, 1937, Brooklyn, N.Y. *Education*: Northeastern University, BS, 1964; University of Massachusetts, PhD, 1968; Worcester Polytechnic Institute, Graduate in 1976 of School of Industrial Management; 1986 Graduate of the Tuck Executive Program at Dartmouth College. *Principal occupation*: Chemical engineer. *Home address*: 22 Streeter Rd., Hubbardston, MA 01452 (508) 795-2364 (work). *Affiliation*: Norton Co., Superabrasives Division, Worcester, MA, 1968- (senior research engineer, 1968-71; research supervisor, 1971-78; technical manager, 1978-83; research director, 1983-87, director of technology, 1987-). *Military service*: U.S. Air Force, 1955-59. *Community activities*: Committee chairperson, Boy Scouts of America, Holden, MA, 1981-86. *Memberships*: American Institute of Chemical Engineers; American Indian Science and Engineering So-

ciety; Sigma Xi Research Society; Tau Beta Pi Engineering Society. *Interests*: "Expert in the qualification and application of industrial diamond. Numerous U.S. and foreign patents relative to the manufacture and composition of abrasive products in which diamond or cubic boron nitride is the abrasive."

*SISQUEROS, NINA (Tohono O'Odham)
(BIA agency supt.)
Affiliation: Papago Agency, BIA, P.O. Box 578, Sells, AZ 85634 (602) 383-3286.

SKAGGS, JOANNE
(center director)
Affiliation: Haskell Indian Health Center, 2415 Massachusetts Ave., Lawrence, KS 66044 (913) 843-3750.

*SKEETER, CARMELITA
(executive director)
Affiliation: Tulsa Urban Health Clinic, Indian Health Care Resource Center of Tulsa, 915 S. Cincinnati, Tulsa, OK 74119 (918) 582-7230.

*SKENANDORE-HIRTH, JANICE (Oneida) 1949-
(hotel manager)
Born November 17, 1949, Milwaukee, Wisc. *Education*: FUTI (Appleton, WI), AA, 1971; MATC (Oak Creek, WI), AA, 1984; University of Wisconsin-Madison, Wisconsin Leadership, 1992; American Hotel & Motel (Dallas, TX), CHA, 1994. *Principal occupation*: Hotel manager. *Home address*: 1967 Belmont Dr., Green Bay, WI 54303 (414) 494-7300 (work). *Affiliation*: General Manager, The Radisson Hotel, Green Bay, WI (owned by the Oneida Tribe). *Community activities*: Board director, Brown County Social Services Steering Committee; fund raiser for St. Mary's House; Green Bay Rotary. *Membership*: Oneida Tribe of Indians of Wisconsin.

*SKENANDORE, JUDY
(health center director)
Affiliation: Oneida Comunity Health Center, P.O. Box 365, Oneida, WI 54155 (414) 869-271 1.

SKENANDORE, KEVIN (Navajo)
(school director)
Affiliation: Richfield Dormitory, P.O. Box 638, Richfield, UT 84701 (801) 896-5101.

SKENANDORE, PAUL A. (*Shenandoah*) (*Scan doa*) (Oneida) 1939-
(editor/publisher, bookstore owner)
Born January 21, 1939, Kaukauna, Wisc. *Education*: High school. *Principal occupation*: Editor/publisher, bookstore owner. *Home address*: 736 W. Oklahoma St., Appleton, WI 54914 (414) 832-9525 (office). *Affiliations*: Editor/publisher of "Shenandoah," the monthly Oneida newsletter, 1973-; owner/operator, Shenandoah Bookstore, Appleton, WI, 1983-. *Military service*: U.S. Army, 1962-1964 (E-4 Sergeant). *Interests*: "To educate Native peoples on their rights as independent nations and peoples; to educate all peoples of the world on the spiritual existence of all societies and our responsibility to said; to take the U.S. (Government) to World Court and charging them with trespass and genocide, and to have aboriginal nations assume their correct place on Great Turtle Island." *Published works*: Newsletter - Shenandoah; and other native newsletters. I have written by the name of Skenandoah, Shenandoah, or Scan doa."

Biographies

SKENADORE, FRANCIS
(attorney)
Affiliation: Oneida Tribe, Box 129, Oneida, WI 54155.

SKIBINE, ALEX TALLCHIEF (Osage)
(attorney)
Affiliation: University of Utah College of Law, Salt Lake City, UT 84112 (801) 581-4177. *Membership*: Native American Bar Assn. (secretary).

SKREDERGARD, HELEN
(executive director)
Affiliation: Indian Arts & Crafts Association (IACA), 122 La Veta Dr., NE, Suite B, Albuquerque, NM 871098 (505) 265-9149. Other professional post: Editor, monthly newsletter of IACA.

SKYE, HARRIETT *(Marphia Tko-Blue Sky)*
(Standing Rock Sioux) 1931-
(scholarship coordinator)
Born December 6, 1931, Rosebud, S.D. *Education*: Northern Virginia Community College, AA (cum laude), 1991; New York University, BA (cum laude), (Film & Television Production), 1993, MA, 1995. *Principal occupation*: Scholarship coordinator. *Home address*: 2 Washington Square Village, New York, NY 10012 (212) 387-0921; 689-8720 (work). *Affiliations*: Producer, director, moderator, "Indian Country Today" Television Show, KFYR-TV Channel 5, Bismarck, ND (12 years); Scholarship coordinator (part time), Association on American Indian Affairs, New York, NY, 1991-. *Community activities*: North Dakota Social Services Board of Directors (secretary-6 years); North Dakota Advisory Committee to the U.S. Civil Rights Commission (board member & chairperson-8 years). *Memberships*: Talking Circle; New York University Alumni Association *Awards, honors*: "Outstanding Adult Learner of the Year, 1991, Northern Virginia Community College; Pioneer Award from Native American Association; 1993 Key Pin Award, Outstanding Scholastic Achievement & Honors Scholar, New York University; Wind & Glacier Voices Filmmakers Award for 27-minute documentary, "The Right to Be (May, 1994); The Distinguished Recent Alumni Award, NYU, in recognition of contributions as an advocate of the rights & culture of Native Americans, 1994; United Nations Environmental Programme Award, (UNEP), 1994. *Interests*: "I completed "The Right To Be," a documentary film in Jan. 1994, which was premiered at Sundance Film Festival, Park City, UT. In a collaborative effort, we just completed a one-minute Public Service Announcement for the Association on American Indian Affairs. Throughout the years, I have traveled and lived on many Indian reservations. I have always found this experience to be exciting and extremely stimulating for this reason. The reservations I have lived on were cultures that were ageless. Many still have practices and belief systems that are intact despite cultural genocide & interference from outside sources." *Biographical source*: The Greeter, "Harriett Skye - The Voice of North Dakota Indians." *Published work*: The Legacy of Indian Women (Dickinson Press, 1982).

*SKYHAWK, SONNY
(executive director)
Affiliation: American Indians in Film, 65 N. Alien Ave., Suite 105, Pasadena, CA 91106 (818) 578-0344.

SKYWATER, HENRY
(Indian band chief)
Affiliation: Birdtail Sioux Indian Band, Box 22, Beulah, Manitoba, Canada R0M 0B0 (204) 568-4540.

SLACK, JOAN
(health director)
Affiliation: Red Cliff Health Services, P.O. Box 529, Bayfield, WI 54814 (715) 779-5801.

SLADE, LYNN H. 1948-
(attorney)
Born January 29, 1948, Santa Fe, N.M. *Education*: University of New Mexico, BA, 1973, Law School, JD, 1976. *Principal occupation*: Attorney with substantial experience in American Indian law. *Address*: P.O. Box 2168, Albuquerque, NM 87103 (505) 848-1800. *Community activities*: Chairperson, Committee on Native American Natural Resources, American Bar Association, 1991-92. *Memberships*: American Bar Association; American Indian Bar Association; State Bar of New Mexico (Natural Resource Section Chair); Indian Law Section (Board of Directors). *Awards, honors*: Best Lawyers in America, 1989-90, 1991-92 Editions. *Interests*: "Representation of businesses doing business on Indian lands; litigation and advice concerning Indian law and Indian lands law." *Published work*: Coal Surface Mining on Indian Lands: Checkerboard or Crazy Quilt (Rocky Mountain Mineral Law Foundation, 1989).

SLICKPOO, ALLEN P., Sr.
(Nez Perce-Walla Walla-Cayuse) 1929-
(administration; tribal councilman)
Born May 5, 1929, Slickpoo Mission, Culdesac, Idaho. *Education*: Chemawa Indian School, 1945-48; University of Idaho, 1953-55. *Principal occupation*: Tribal historian, councilman, administrator, Nez Perce Tribal Executive Committee, Lapwai, Idaho. *Home address*: 809 Nez Perce Lane, Box 311, Kamiah, ID 83536 (208) 843-2253 (work). *Affiliation*: Nez Perce Tribe, Lapwai, ID, 1955- (chairperson, General Council, 1961-63, 1986-88; chairperson, Resolutions Committee, 1988-89; secretary, vice-chairperson, and chairperson, Executive Committee, 1955-86). *Other professional posts*: Tribal historian and cultural consultant; consultant to the Northwest Regional Educational Laboratory on Indian education and curriculum; consultant to documentary movies including, "I'll Fight No More Forever" about Nez Perce War of 1877, etc. *Military service*: U.S. Army, 1948-1952 (Japanese Occupation/Korea/UN Service). *Community activities*: Served on the Governor's Indian Advisory Council, Idaho; Veterans of Foreign Wars (Kamiah, Idaho); 2nd Presbyterian Church of Kamiah; Mat'alym'a (Up-river Nez Perce) Culture Club. *Awards, honors*: Outstanding Achievement Award, Indian Child Welfare, 1983; Governor of Idaho Award for Promoter of the Week, 1961. *Interests*: "Have traveled to Mexico City and Canada to participate and/or speak at conference relating to the Indian of North America; also to Tokyo, Japan, to lecture on Native American history and culture; bilingual/bicultural activities; consultant on historical and cultural concerns (recognized as authority on the history and culture of the Nez Perce people); have lectured at major institutions, including Newberry Library, Chicago, University of Colorado, Oregon State University, Dartmouth College, University of Washington, Navajo Community College, etc.; has lectured in public

schools, to students and organizations relative to American Indian history, culture, government, education, and economic status; has been a reader and/or panelist for the National Endowment for the Humanities; have participated on many panels, workshops, and conferences. Advocate to promote tribally-sponsored projects relating to the preservation of the knowledge and identity of the Nez Perce history and culture; developing plans for tribal archives." *Published works*: NuMeePoom Tit-Wah-tit (Pruitt Press, 1973); Noon Nee MePoo (Pruitt Press, 1974); Nez Perce Attitude Toward the Missionary Experience (Pruitt Press, 1987); wrote a paper for the Northwest Quarterly on Anthropology, relating to Indian fishing rights controversy; articles for World Book Encyclopedia, 1983-.

*SMAGGE, RITA
(executive director)
Affiliation: Kenaitze Indian Tribe Health Center, P.O. Box 988, Kenai, AK 99611 (907) 283-3633.

*SMART, JOSEPH (Eskimo)
(village president)
Affiliation: Native Village of Hooper Bay, P.O. Box 2193, Hooper Bay, AK 99604 (907) 758-4915.

SMILEY-MARQUEZ, CAROLYNA
(San Juan Pueblo)
(consultant)
Born in 1951 in N.M. *Education*: Indiana University, BA, 1973, MA, 1974; University of Colorado, PhD (Social and Multicultural Foundations of Education), 1985. *Principal occupation*: Consultant. *Address*: P.O. Box 211, Hygiene, CO 80533 (303) 772-1714. *Affiliations*: New Mexico State Dept. of Education (Cross Cultural, Title IX Education Specialist), 1974-79; Washington State University (Minority Recruitment Officer, Interim Assistant Director, Instructor-Bilingual Education Institute), 1976-81; University of Colorado, Health Sciences Center (Chief Curriculum Development Liaison, 1981-83; Director for Affirmative Action and Coordinator for Staff Development and Guest Relation, 1986-90); , University of Colorado (Instructor & Lecturer), 1982-; professional consultant, C. Smiley-Marquez, dba, Smiley & Co., 1988-. *Other professional posts*: Adjunct professor, University of Northern Colorado, Greeley, 1992-. *Community activities*: Hope for the Children, Kempe National Center for the Prevention and Treatment to Child Abuse and Neglect (board member). *Awards, honors*: Outstanding Young Women of America, 1982-84; Outstanding Young Women in Colorado, 1986; President's Award, EEO/Affirmative Action Coalition (Regional Professional Association), 1991. *Membership*: National Association for Human Rights Workers (board member, 1988-90). *Biographical source*: Directory of American Indian and Native American Women, 1985-. *Published works*: Monographs, brochures & bibliographies published by the State Dept. of Education, State of New Mexico, 1975-80. Videotapes: Pieces of Life - Profiles of Minority Women in Longmont (documentary), 1982; New Indian Wars (documentary of the conflict for American Indians and those seeking rights over natural resources on reservations), 1983; Storyteller (video presenting Anah Nahtanaba, American Indian Storyteller maker in the tradition of the Cochiti), 1985; Know It When You See It: Sexual Harassment for Supervisors and Managers and the Rights and Responsibilities of Employees (sexual harass-

ment training), 1986; Cultural Awareness: Introduction, 1990; Mentoring: Special Issues of Women and Minorities in Organizations, 1990. Education training kits: Diversity Training Kit for Managers and Employees, and Diversity Training for Law Enforcement Officers.

SMITH, ANN
(Indian band chief)
Affiliation: Kwanlin Dun Indian Band, 154 Tlingit St., Whitehorse, Yukon, Canada Y1A 2Z1 (403) 667-6465.

SMITH, ARCHIE C.
(site manager)
Affiliation: Town Creek Indian Mound State Historic Site, Route 3, Box 50, Mt. Gilead, NC 27306 (919) 439-6802.

SMITH, BOB A. (Chickasaw)
(attorney)
Affiliation: Oklahoma Indian bar Association, P.O. Box 1062, Oklahoma City, OK 73101 (405) 521-5277.

SMITH, BRAD (Shinnecock)
(tribal trustee)
Affiliation: Shinnecock Tribe, P.O. Box 59, Southampton, NY 11968 (516) 283-1643.

*SMITH, CALVIN H., Sr. (Kashia Pomo)
(tribal chairperson)
Affiliation: Kashia Business Committee, Stewarts Point Rancheria, P.O. Box 38, Stewarts Point, CA 95480 (707) 528-4267.

SMITH, CARLTON R. *(Shanak'w Uwaa)*
(Tlingit) 1950-
(associate broker of real estate)
Born June 22, 1950, Seattle, Wash. *Education*: Stanford University, BA, 1973. *Principal occupation*: Associate broker of real estate. *Home address*: 7630 Griffith Rd., Anchorage, AK 99516 (907) 276-2761. *Affiliations*: Associate broker, Re/Max Properties, Inc., Anchorage, AK 1985-93; associate broker, Bond, Stephens & Johnson, Inc., Anchorage, 1993-. *Other professional posts*: Vice president, secretary/treasurer & trustee, Sealaska Heritage Foundation; director, Sealaska Corp. (An Alaska Regional for Profit Corp.) *Community activities*: Statewide co-chair-person of the Alaska Native Hire Network, sponsored by the Federal Executive Association founding officer, Alaska Association of Alaska Native Real Estate Professionals. *Memberships*: National Association of Realtors; Anchorage, Board of Realtors; Commonwealth North, Inc.; Certified Commercial Investment Managers Association. *Awards, honors*: American Academy of Achievement, 1969; Re-Max Executive Club; Re/Max International, 1987-89. This designation places individuals in the top 1% of Real Estate Professionals nationwide with an excess of $2 million in sales per year. *Interests*: "My principal interest outside of developing my own brokerage business is corporate fund-raising in the area of scholarships for Native America Students. At present, I am working with other trustees to build a $3.2 million endowment for our 501(C) (3) to a $10 million fund by the year 2000." *Published work*: Local Government Encyclopedia (State of Alaska, 1979).

SMITH, CHADWICK *(Ugisata)*
(Oklahoma Cherokee) 1950-
(tribal attorney)
Born December 17, 1950, Pontiac, Mich. *Edu-

cation*: University of Georgia, BS, 1973; University of Wisconsin, Madison, MS, 1975; University of Tulsa Law School, JD, 1980. *Principal occupation*: Attorney. *Home address*: 8324 Hillwood Dr., Tulsa, OK 74131 (918) 224-3258; 458-9440 (work). *Affiliation*: Private practice, Tulsa, OK, 1982-; tribal attorney, Cherokee Nation, Tahlequah, OK. *Other professional posts*: Prosecutor, tax advisor, legal historian-Cherokee Nation. *Memberships*: Oklahoma Bar Association; American Bar Association; 10th Circuit Federal District Court; Cherokee Nation; Creek Nation. *Interests*: Indian law; Cherokee legal history. *Published works*: Cherokee Nation Course Work (Cherokee Nation Press, 1993); Cherokee Case Book (Cherokee Nation Press, 1993).

SMITH, CHARLES E.
(museum manager)
Affiliation: Syms-Eaton Museum, 418 W. Mercury Blvd., Hampton, VA 23666 (804) 727-6248.

SMITH, CRAIG (Chippewa)
(member-board of directors)
Affiliation: Intertribal Christian Communications, P.O. Box 3765, Station B, Winnipeg, Manitoba, Canada R2W 3R6 (204) 661-9333.

*SMITH, CURTIS W. (Blackfeet) 1944-
(clinic administrator)
Born December 10, 1944, Browning, Mont. *Education*: Radiology Technology, Dallas, TX, 1965-67 (Certificate); University of New Mexico, AA (Physician's Training Assistant), 1980. *Principal occupation*: Clinic administrator. *Home address*: RR 1 Box 652, Box Elder, MT 59521 (406) 395-4055. *Affiliation*: Administrator, Medical Care, Indian Health Service, Billings, MT. *Other professional post*: Radiology consultant, Aberdeen Area Indian Health Service, Aberdeen, SD (14 years). *Community activity*: COB for the Native American Church of All Nations (Methodist), Aberdeen, SD. *Memberships*: American Registry of Registered Technologists; American Society of Registered X-Ray Technologists; National Registry for Physician Assistants. *Awards*: Employee of the Year Award, Aberdeen Area IHS, 1992; several IHS awards for outstanding performance. *Interests*: All sports, outdoors activities, fishing, camping, hiking; music, church activities, family activities.

SMITH, DENNIS J. (Assiniboine) 1950-
(director of Indian studies)
Born July 23, 1950, Helena, Mont. *Education*: Montana State University, BS, 1972; University of Iowa, Certificate Physical Therapy), 1974; University of Montana, MA, 1983. *Principal occupation*: Director of Indian studies. *Home address*: 3134 Virginia St., Sioux City, IA 51104 (712) 255-3440. *Affiliations*: Instructor/Dean of Instruction, Fort Peck Community College, Poplar, MT, 1981-85; director of Indian studies, Morningside College, Sioux City, IA, 1989-. *Membership*: National Indian Education Association. *Interests*: "Indian issues (contemporary), national political affairs, environmental issues - particularly energy related impacts; travelled through U.S., Canada, Mexico, Europe & Japan."

SMITH, DON
(health director)
Affiliation: Lac Courte Oreilles Tribal Clinic, Route 2, Box 2750, Hayward, WI 54843 (715) 634-4153.

SMITH, DON LELOOSKA (Cherokee) 1933-
(woodcarver)
Born August 31, 1933, Sonora, Calif. *Principal occupation*: Woodcarver. Resides in Ariel, Wash. *Affiliation*: Lecturer, dance programmer, Oregon Museum of Science & Industry. *Award*: Inter-Tribal Indian Ceremonial, Gallup, N.M., 1966. *Interests*: Woodcarving, Northwest Coast styles; Indian dance and drama; Indian music; various forms of Indian arts and crafts.

*SMITH, FAITH
(college president)
Affiliation: NAES College, 2838 W. Peterson Ave., Chicago, IL 60659 (312) 761-5000. Othe prfesional post: Editor, "Inter-Com Newsletter, NAES College, Chicago, IL.

SMITH, GERALD L. (Confederated Tribes of Warm Springs-Jemez Pueblo) 1949-
(justice services manager)
Born August 24, 1949, Albuquerque, N.M. *Education*: University of Oregon, BS (Personnel and Industrial Management), 1972. *Principal occupation*: Justice Services Manager, The Confederated Tribes of Warm Springs, Warm Springs, OR, 1984-. *Home address*: P.O. Box 937, Warm Springs, OR 97761. *Community activities*: Warm Springs Boxing Club (coach-president). *Memberships*: National Indian Traders Association (director); National Indian Business Council (director); International Association of Chiefs of Police (member, Tribal/State & Local Police Cooperation Committee); Oregon Association-USA Amateur Boxing Federation (vice president). *Awards, honors*: Selected as referee and judge to represent Region XII at the National Junior Olympic Boxing Championships. *Interests*: Interesting in assisting Indian tribes and organizations In their business endeavors. *Published works*: Economic Analysis of National Indian Cultural/Education Centers (UIATF, 1974); National Indian Planning Assessment (UIPA, 1977); The American Indian Index (Arrowstar Publishing, 1985).

SMITH, GREGG
(association president)
Affiliation: Indian Association of Alberta, 11630 Kingsway Ave., Edmonton, Alberta, Canada T5G 0X5 (403) 452-4330.

*SMITH, GREGORY
(attorney)
Affiliation: Editor, Native American Law Digest," The Falmouth Institute, 3918 Prosperity Ave., Suite 302, Fairfax, VA 22031 (703) 641-9100.

*SMITH, JAMES M.
(village president)
Affiliation: Native Village of Goodnews Bay, P.O. Box 3, Goodnews Bay, AK 99589 (907) 697-8629.

SMITH, JIM
(health systems administrator)
Affiliation: Cherokee PHS Indian Hospital, Cherokee, NC 28719 (704) 497-9163.

SMITH, JANE M. (Colville) 1954-
(tribal court administrator)
Born April 9, 1954, Colville, Wash. *Education*: Inchelium High School, WA, 1972; University of Washington (2 years). *Principal occupation*: Tribal court administrator. *Home address*: P.O. Box 665, Nespelem, WA 99155 (509) 634-8846 (office). *Affiliation*: Colville Tribal Court,

Nespelem, WA, 1981-. *Other professional posts*: Chairperson, CCT Safety Committee, 1990-91; member, Joint Safety Committee, 1990-91. *Military service*: U.S. Naval Reserve (Legalman Second Class),1987-91). *Community activities*: On committee that designed and contributed photos for the "Time for Gathering" exhibit honoring Indian tribes in the State of Washington for Centennial in 1989; junior rodeo timer; tribal exhibit committee; University of Washington museum exhibit. *Membership*: Women's International Bowling Congress, 1977-; Women of the Moose, 1985-; National Indian Court Clerks' Association (president, 1986-88; member, 1985-); Fraternal Order of Eagles Auxiliary, 1987-. *Interests*: "On team which evaluated the Hopi Tribal Court in November, 1991. Traveled to the Hopi Reservation, interviewed tribal members and staff, made an evaluation with recommendations. It was very interesting to see the differences and similarities between the Hopi and the Colville Tribal Courts. Photography is my first love. I Take extensive outdoor and recreational pictures. I love to fish and hike. I enjoy watching most sports. I'm very interested in wildlife matters and concerns. I read extensively and have a large private library."

SMITH, JOSEPH
(health systems administrator)
Affiliation: Kyle PHS Indian Health Center, P.O. Box 540, Kyle, SD 57752 (605) 455-2451.

*SMITH, KATHERIN JANE *(Laughing Water)* 1916-
(librarian)
Born October 11, 1916, Saugatuck, Conn. *Education*: Wells College (Aurora, NY), BA, 1938. *Principal occupation*: Librarian. *Home address*: 3530 Schrock St., Sarasota, FL 34239 (813) 365-6054. *Affiliations*: Librarian/contract coordinator, McDonnell Douglas Corp., St. Louis, MO (12 years); St. Louis Co. Library, St. Louis, MO (8 years); research associate, Johnson O'Connor Research Foundation. *Community activities*: Elected Elder, Southeastern Cherokee Confederacy (SCCI). *Membership*: Phi Beta Kappa, 1938-. *Interests*: "Researching Native American (especially Cherokee) history, customs & genealogy for the SCCI, building its library & assisting and participating, as possible; gardening, travel (three trips to Yucatan, one to Guatemala and Peru), reading, archaeology, aircraft engineering & development, civic affairs."

SMITH, LaMARR
(museum director)
Affiliation: Memorial Indian Museum, P.O. Box 483, Broken Bow, OK 74728 (405) 584-6531.

SMITH, LESLIE
(school principal)
Affiliation: Kipnuk Day School, Kipnuk, AK 99614 (907) 896-5513.

SMITH, MARLENE
(director-Indian group)
Affiliation: Indian Choir, Bacone College, Muskogee, OK 74401 (918) 683-4581.

SMITH, MARY HILDERMAN
(museum director)
Affiliation: Marin Miwok, P.O. Box 864, Novato, CA 94947 (510) 897-4064.

*SMITH, MELANIE M. (Santee Sioux) 1943-
(alcohol/drug program director)
Born August 17, 1943, Wisconsin Rapids, Wisc. *Education*: Blackhawk (Moline, IL), 1972-74. *Principal occupation*: Alcohol/drug program director. *Home address*: 4185 Sunnyview NE, Salem, OR 97305 (503) 585-0564 (work). *Affiliation*: Director, Tahana Whitecrow Foundation, Salem, OR, 1987-. *Community activities*: Board member, North Lancaster Neighborhood Association; chair, Marion County Cultural Diversity; board member, Oregon Human Rights Coalition; member, Ladies Auxiliary Military Order of Purple Heart; member, Elderly & Handicapped Advisory, Salem Transit. *Memberships*: American Correctional Association; National Alcohol/ Drug Counselors Association; Native American Counselor II. *Interests*: Journalism, grant writing, substance abuse.

SMITH, MICHAEL
(resource centre chairperson)
Affiliation: Yukon Indian Cultural-Education Society Resource Centre, Council of Yukon Indians, 22 Bisutlin Dr., Whitehorse, Yukon, Canada Y1A 3S5 (403) 667-7631.

*SMITH, MICHAEL
(institute director)
Affiliation: American Indian Film Institute, 333 Valencia St., Suite 322, San Francisco, CA 94103 (415) 554-0525.

*SMITH, MONA
(Native American film producer)
Address: 2116 16th Ave., So., Minneapolis, MN 55404 (612) 872-7886.

SMITH, NOREEN
(family services director)
Affiliation: Indian Health Board of Minneapolis, 1315 East 24th St., Minneapolis, MN 55404 (612) 721-7425.

SMITH, PAUL
(BIA agency supt.)
Affiliation: Pima Agency, Bureau of Indian Affairs, P.O. Box 8, Sacaton, AZ 85247 (602) 562-3326.

SMITH, RAY (Chippewa)
(member-board of directors)
Affiliation: Intertribal Christian Comunications, P.O. Box 3765, Station B, Winnipeg, Manitoba, Canada R2W 3R6 (204) 661-9333.

*SMITH, RICK J.
(center director)
Affiliation: American Indian Learning Resource Center, University of Minnesota, Duluth, 114 Cina Hall, 10 University Dr., Duluth, MN 55812 (218) 726-6379.

SMITH, ROBERT (Luiseno)
(tribal chairperson)
Affiliation: Pala Band of Mission Indians, P.O. Box 43, Pala, CA 92059 (619) 742-3784.

SMITH, ROLAND (Navajo)
(school principal)
Affiliation: Shonto Boarding School, Shonto, AZ 86054 (602) 672-2340.

SMITH, SHEILA S. (Oneida of Wisconsin) 1962-
(artist)
Born September 19, 1962, Green Bay, Wisc. *Education*: University of Wisconsin, La Crosse. *Principal occupation*: Artist. *Address & Affiliation*: Volunteer, Oneida (WI) Nation Museum, 1980-. *Awards, honors*: 1st Place, University of Wisconsin, Stevens Point, 1985 Woodlands Indian Arts Festival; proclaimed a master of my art by the U.S. Dept. of the Interior and the Wisconsin Arts Board. *Interests*: "I have brought back the last art of the Iroquois costume designs. I have sold four costumes to the U.S. Department of the Interior for their permanent collection of Indian artifacts. I had two costumes worn during President Reagan's Inaugural Festivities. I was also a selected artist from Wisconsin to be videotaped and exhibited by the National Endowment of the Arts and Wisconsin Arts Council as a national traveling exhibit. I have also had a cover of the Stevens Point Magazine published in Stevens Point, Wisconsin." *Biographical sources*: Wisconsin Arts Board Source Directory, 1986-87; U.S. Department of the Interior--Indian Owned and Operated Businesses, 1985-87.

SMITH, THEODORE, SR. (Yavapai Apache)
(tribal chairperson)
Affiliation: Yavapai-Apache Community Council, P.O. Box 1188, Camp Verde, AZ 86322 (602) 567-3649.

*SMITH, WALTER L.
(museum president)
Affiliation: Southold Indian Museum, Bayview Rd Box 268, Southold, NY 11971 (516) 765-5577.

*SMITH, WILLIAM C. *(Red Bear)* (Cherokee) 1923-
(retired aeronautical engineer)
Born March 30, 1923, Ada, Okla. *Education*: University of Missouri, St. Louis, EE, 1962. *Principal occupation*: Aeronautical engineer (retired). *Home address*: 3530 Schrock St., Sarasota, FL 34239 (813) 365-6054. *Affiliation*: McDonnell Douglas Corp., St. Louis, MO (production supervisor-aircraft, 1941-64, engineer, 1964-79). *Community activities*: United National Association, Florida Division (newsletter editor, 1987-90; vice president, 1979-); Southeastern Cherokee Confederacy, 1971- (band chief, 1981-4; assistant principal chief, 1985-91; principal chief, 1991-93; assistant principal chief, 1993-).

SMITMAN, GREG
(executive director)
Affiliation: Intertribal Agricultural Council, 100 North 27th St., Suite 500, MT (406) 259-3525

SMOKE, ERNIE
(Indian band chief)
Affiliation: Dakota Plains Tribal Council, Box 110, Portage La Prairie, Manitoba, Canada R1N 3B2 (204) 252-2288.

SMOKER, KENNETH, Jr. (Assiniboine-Sioux)
(health director)
Affiliation: Fort Peck PHS Indian Health Center, Poplar, MT 59255 (406) 768-3491.

*SMOKEY, ROMAINE, Jr. (Washoe)
(tribal chairperson)
Affiliation: Dresslerville Community Council, 1585 Watasheamu Rd., Gardnerville, NV 89410 (702) 265-5845.

SMUCK, HAROLD
(director/editor)
Affiliation: Associated Committee of Friends on Indian Affairs, P.O. Box 2326, Richmond, IN 47375 (317) 962-9169; editor, "Indian Progress.:

SNAKE, ALFRED
(Indian band chief)
Affiliation: Young Chippewayan Indian Band, 409-19th St. E., Prince Albert, Saskatchewan, Canada S6V 4A1 (306) 486-2326.

*SNAKE, LAWRENCE F. (Delaware)
(tribal committee president)
Affiliation: Delaware Executive Committee, P.o. Box 825, Anadarko, OK 73005 (405) 247-2448.

SNAKE, REUBEN A., Jr.
(Kikawa Unga-Rise Up) **(Winnebago) 1937-**
(college dean)
Born January 12, 1937, Winnebago, Neb. *Education*: Northwestern College, 1958-59; University of Nebraska, Omaha, 1964-65; Peru (NE) State College, 1968-69. *Principal occupation*: Legislative aide for U.S. Senator Robert Kerrey. *Address*: Center for Research and Cultural Exchange, Institute of American Indian Arts, College of Santa Fe Campus, St. Michael's Dr., Santa Fe, NM 87501. *Affiliation*: Economic Development Consultant, Winnebago, NE, 1963-75; chairman, Winnebago Tribal Council, Winnebago, NE, 1975-88; legislative aide, U.S. Senator Robert Kerrey, Omaha, NE, 1989-90; Dean, Center for Research and Cultural Exchange, Institute of American Indian Arts, Santa Fe, NM. *Other professional posts*: Conflict management specialist; college instructor; witch doctor. *Military service*: U.S. Army Special Forces (E-4, Green Berets-Communications Specialist-Radio Operator/repairman). *Community activities*: Nationally known road man (prayer chief) Native American Church of North America. American Indian Movement (national chairman, 1972); National Congress of American Indians (national president, 1985-87); 1st Nations Financial Project, Falmouth, VA (vice-chairman); The Seventh Generation Fund (board member); The American Indian Law Resource Center, Washington, DC (board member); American Indian Ritual Object Repatriation Foundation (honorary trustee); guru to the Americans For Indian Opportunity, Washington, DC (president). *Awards, honors*: 1984 Outstanding Achievement, Americans for Indian Opportunity; 1986 Citizenship Award, Nebraska Indian Commission; 1986 Distinguished Nebraskan, Nebraska Society of Washington, DC; Proclamation by Governor Robert Kerrey, 1986; 1986 Certificate of Recognition, U.S. Secretary of the Interior. *Interests*: "Travels to Europe, South America, Canada, Australia, and entire U.S. to promote the cause of justice and equality for all indigenous people of the Western Hemisphere. Logged over one million miles in this effort since 1965." *Published works*: Being Indian Is... (Nebraska Indian Press, Inc., 1971); numerous articles for universities and colleges throughout the U.S. since 1968; first novel "The Iron Horse Incident" yet to be published; "currently at work on my autobiography to be entitled "Your Humble Ser Pent."

SNAKE, RICHARD
(Indian band chief)
Affiliation: Delaware of the Thames (Moraviantown) Indian Band, RR 3, Thamesville, Ontario, Canada N0P 2K0 (519) 692-3936.

SNEVE, SHIRLEY (Rosebud Sioux) 1956-
(assistant director-SD Arts Council)
Born July 14, 1956, Rapid City, S.D. *Education*: South Dakota State University, BA, 1978. *Principal occupation*: Assistant director, SD Arts Council. *Home address*: 925 S. First Ave., Sioux Falls, SD 57104 (605) 339-6646. *A ffiliation*: Assistant director, South Dakota Arts Council, Sioux Falls, SD; president, Native American Public Broadcasting Consortium. *Community activities*: Council for Northern Plains Tribal Arts, Lincoln, NE; Deloria Community Services, S.F. (board of directors); Tiyospaye Wakan Calvary Cathedral, Episcopal, S.F.

SNEVE, VIRGINIA DRIVING HAWK
(Rosebud Sioux) 1933-
(guidance counselor)
Born February 21, 1933, Rosebud, S.D. *Education*: South Dakota State University, BS, 1954, MEd, 1969. *Principal occupation*: Counselor-Indian students. Resides in Rapid City, SD. *Affiliations*: Teacher-counselor, Flandreau Indian School, Flandreau, SD, 1966-70; editor, Brevet Press, Sioux Falls, SD, 1970-72; consultant, producer-writer, SD Public TV, Brooking, 1973-80; educational counselor, Flandreau Indian School, 1981-85; guidance counselor, Rapid City Central High School, 1986- (605) 394-4023 (office). *Other professional posts*: Part time English instructor, Oglala Community College, Rapid City Extension. *Community activities*: Rapid City Project 2,000 (drop out prevention coalition) Emanual Episcopal Church, Episcopal Diocese Commission on Racism. *Memberships*: SD Press Women (secretary, 1976-78); National Federation Press Women; SD Diocese of the Episcopal Church (historiographer, 1977-85); SD State U., Foundation Board, 1990-; enrolled member of Rosebud Sioux Tribe. *Awards, honors*: Council on Interracial Book Award for Jimmy Yellow Hawk, 1972; Western Writers of America Award for Betrayed, 1974; SDPress Woman of the Year, 1974; National Federation Press Alumnus Women, Achievement, 1974; Distinguished Alumnus Award, SD State University, 1974; Special Contribution to Education, SD Indian Education Association, 1975; Honorary Doctorate of Letters, Dakota Wesleyan University, 1979; Distinguished Contribution to SD History, Dakota History Conference, 1982; 2nd Annual Native American Prose Award, University of Nebraska Press, 1992, for ms. "Completing the Circle. *Interests*: Indian education, art and literature. Biographical source: Who's Who of American Women. *Published works*: Jimmy Yellow Hawk (Holiday House, 1972); High Elk's Treasure (Holiday House, 1972); editor, South Dakota Geographic Names (Brevet Press, 1973); Betrayed (Holiday House, 1974); When Thunders Spoke (Holiday House, 1974); The Dakota's Heritage (Brevet Press, 1974); The Chichi Hoohoo Bogeyman, Ms. Sneve wrote the script for the screen play of the same title for the Vegetable Soup Children's TV series (Holiday House, 1975); They Led a Nation (Brevet Press, 1975); That They May Have Life: The Episcopal Church in South Dakota, 1859-1976 (Brevet Press, 1981); Dancing Teepees (Holiday House, 1989); short stories and articles.

*SNIPP, C. MATTHEW
(program director)
Affiliation: American Indian Studies Program, University of Wisconsin, 1188 Educational Sciences, 1025 W. Johnson St., Madison, WI 53706 (608) 263-5501.

SNOOKS, PAUL
(Te-Moak Western Shoshone)
(tribal chairperson)
Affiliation: Battle Mountain Band Council, 35 Mountain View Dr., #138-13, Battle Mountain, NV 89820 (702) 635-2004.

*SNOW, VIVIAN
(administrative officer-Indian hospital)
Affiliation: Omaha-Winnebago PHS Indian Hospital, Winnebago, NE 68071 (402) 878-2231.

*SNYDER, BARRY (Seneca)
(tribal council president)
Affiliation: Seneca Nation Tribal Council, 1490 Rt. 438, Irving, NY 14081 (716) 532-4900.

*SNYDER, MICHAEL C.
(executive director)
Affiliation: Oklahoma Indian Legal Services, Inc., Founders Tower, 5900 Mosteller Dr. #610, Oklahoma City, OK 73112 (800) 658-1497.

SOCKYMA, MICHAEL C., Sr.
(Mong-eu-ma-Young Corn) **(Hopi) 1942-**
(Hopi silver/gold smith)
Born June 4, 1942, Hotevilla, Ariz. *Education*: Phoenix Indian High School. *Principal occupation*: Hopi silver/gold smith. *Home address*: P.O. Box 96, Kykotsmovi, AZ 86039 (602) 734-6607. *Affiliations*: Hopi Kiva Arts & Craft Shop, Kykotsmovi, AZ, 1975-. *Community activities*: Member of Hopi Tribal Council. *Awards, honors*: "(I) have won ribbons for jewelry at Jemez Indian Art Shows, and Gallup Indian Art Shows, New Mexico; Red Earth Art Craft Show, Oklahoma; Houston and Dallas Art Craft Shows, Texas; and Sedona, Arizona Art Craft Show." *Interests*: "27 years in making Hopi overlay jewelry in silver and gold; custom jewelry in precious stones; artist in oil and acrylic; specialize in both men and women concho belts; council member for the Hopi Tribe; active in traditional cultural activities." *Biographical source*: Government Directory of Indian Arts; Hopi Silver I & II, by Margaret Wright.

SOLDIER, KENNETH
(Indian band chief)
Affiliation: Chiniki Group (Stoney) Indian Band, Box 40, Morley, Alberta, Canada T0L 1N0 (403) 881-3770.

SOLDIER, LARRY
(executive director-Indian centre)
Affiliation: Ma-Mow-We-Tak Friendship Centre, Inc., 122 Hemlock Crescent, Thompson, Manitoba, Canada R8N 0R6 (204) 778-7337.

SOLOMON, CORA NICHOLASA (NICKY)
(Victory Walker or War Path Woman)
(Winnebago of Nebraska) 1933-
(national director, CHR program)
Born February 11, 1933, Winnebago, Neb. *Education*: High school. *Principal occupation & Affiliation*: National director, Community Health Representatives (CHR)) Program, Indian Health Service, Rockville, MD. *Home address*: P.O. Box 596, Winnebago, NE 68071 (402) 878-2521. *Other professional post*: Director, Winnebago Tribe of Nebraska Health Department; IHS Aberdeen Area Alcoholism Program Coordinator; Business Representative, Northwestern Bell Telephone Co.; former business partner in a trading post. *Community activities*: Former secretary, Winnebago Tribal Council; Winnebago Public School Board; Nebraska Indian Commis-

sion; Nebraska Indian Inter-Tribal Development Corporation; Goldenrod Hills Community Action Agency; Seven States Indian Health Association; American Indian Human Resource Center Board (Alcohol Program). *Membership*: National Association of Community Health Representatives; National Congress of American Indians. *Awards, honors*: Membership in the California Scholarship Federation; Woman Pioneer Award (social services) from the Governor of Nebraska, Charles Thone; awards received from the Lakota Tribe and Health Association and the CHR organizations in the Albuqueque, Navajo and Oklahoma areas. *Interests*: "Since 1969, my interest and occupation has been in tribal health. The CHR program was the forerunner to the concept of Indian self-determination. Tribes began to provide services of CHRs through contractual agreements with IHS in 1968. Since that time, the CHRs have distinguished themselves as a different type of health care provider; they live in their communities and are on-call 24 hours a day, 365 days a year and are oftentimes the only health care provider immediately available in crisis situations. They are providers of health promotion and disease prevention services, as well as health care outreach workers, and are the epitomy of commitment and dedication to serving American Indians and Alaska Natives. I am proud to be a part of this great movement and become filled with emotion just thinking of the great sacrifices CHRs make on a daily basis." Co-authored paper, "A Population-Based Assessment of Alcohol Abuse Using a Community Panel."

*SOLOMON, GLENN W.
(Oklahoma Cherokee) 1945-
(professor of research)

Born in 1945, Ochelata, Okla. *Education*: University of Oklahoma, BA, 1967, MA, 1972; U of OK Health Sciences Center, MPH, 1981, PhD, 1990. *Principal occupation*: Professor of research. *Home address*: 1033 Leslie Lane, Norman, OK 73069 (405) 364-0308. *Affiliation*: University of Oklahoma Health Sciences Center, Dept. of Pediatrics, Adolescent Medicine, Oklahoma City, OK. *Other professional posts*: Editor, "Wassaja," (American Indian Historical Society, San Francisco, CA) the national newspaper of Indian America, 1971-86; founding member, Advisory Board, Jacobson Foundation for American Indian Art, Norman, OK, 1986-; health careers consultant, Northeastern State University, Tahlequah, OK, 1988-; Urban Indian Health Forum, Health Concerns, Oklahoma City, OK, 1990-; visiting assistant professor, University of Oklahoma, Human Relations, Norman, OK, 1992-. *Research activities*: Minority recruitment & retention policy development for State Regents of Higher Education & State Supt. of Instruction, 1971-; development of criteria & analysis of minority students in higher education including health professionals, 1971-; quality assurance for field aid stations - combat & non-combat conditions, U.S. Army Special Forces, Worldwide Multi-National Scope of Service, 1980-; cultural assessment in adolescent health behaviors, Oklahoma Youth Health Risks (funded), 1990-; women, infant & children nutritional program, State Health Dept., Wichita, Caddo, & Delaware WIC, Cherokee Nations, WIC, 1990-; Cherokee Nation baseline study of substance abuse (funded), Evaluator for Substance Abuse Program in Cherokee Nation, 1992-; Cheyenne & Arapaho Health Needs Assessment (funded), 1993 . *Community activities*:

Advisor to Executive Council, American Indian Training & Employment Program, Oklahoma City, OK, 1980-; member, Board of Directors, Native American Center, Oklahoma City, 1978-81; member, Advisory Board, Central Tribes Health Manpower Project, IHS, Shawnee, OK, 1979-82; member, Advisory Board, State Dept. of Public Health, Child & Maternal Care, Oklahoma City, OK, 1979-85; Native American Center for Excellence, University of Oklahoma Health Sciences Center, College of Medicine, 1991-93; producer & host, American Indian Magazine (weekly television program), 1984-89; president, American Indian/Alaskan Native Staff & Faculty, University of Oklahoma Health Sciences Center, Oklahoma City, 1989-90; sponsor, American Indian Science & Engineering Students, University of Oklahoma, Health Sciences Center, 1989-91. *Membership*: National Indian Education Association (presidential search committee, 1988). *Awards, honors*: Public Health Fellow, University of Oklahoma Health Sciences Center, Oklahoma City, 1976-77; Fellowship, U.S. Office of Indian Education, 1977-80; Outstanding Staff & Faculty Award, American Indian Women's Association, University of Oklahoma, Norman, 1984; Oklahoma Human Rights Award, Oklahoma City, OK, 1986; American Indian Scholarships, Albuquerque, NM, 1988-90; Oklahoma State Regents of Higher Education, Minority Doctoral Scholar, Oklahoma City, OK, 1988-90; Major Bass Academic Scholarship, University of Oklahoma Health Sciences Center, Oklahoma City, 1988. *Published works*: The Odyssey of Wassaja: Carlos Montezuma, MD; First American Indian Physician (1972 master's thesis - University of Oklahoma), currently being revised for submission to a university press; "American Indian Studies: A Status Report," paper presented at the Organization of American Historians, New Orleans, LA, 1974; "American Indian Advocate for the Campus," National Indian Education Association, 1980; "Status of American Indian Studies & Students," National Indian Education Association, 1982; AIDS: Prevention for Life Saving, a 1 hour video, Ft. Bragg, ND, 1987; "Cultural Involvements & Substance Abuse of Oklahoma Cherokee Adolescents," American Federation for Clinical Research, Carmel, CA, 1993; editor, et al, "Complexities of Ethnicity Among Oklahoma Native Americans: Health Behaviors of Rural Adolescents," in The Culture of Oklahoma (University of Oklahoma Press, 1993); "Nutritional Status of Obesity in Oklahoma Indians" (current).

*SOLOMON, NOLAN
(BIA agency acting supt.)

Affiliation: Winnebago Agency, Bureau of Indian Affairs, Route 1, Box 18, Winnebago, NE 68071 (402) 878-2502.

*SOOTKIS, RUBIE
(Native American film producer/writer)

Affiliation: Morning Star Productions, P.O. Box 671, Lame Deer, MT 59043 (406) 477-8315.

SOPIEL, SYLVIA (Passamaquoddy) 1929-
(editor)

Born November 3, 1929, Peter Dana Point, Maine. *Education*: Hasson College, Bangor, ME. *Principal occupation*: Editor, Mawiw Kilun, Princeton, ME, 1977-. *Home address*: Box 186, Princeton, ME 04668. *Other professional post*: Ex-Justice of the Peace. *Community activities*: Vista volunteer. *Interests*: "(I) have flown all over

the country-- met a lot of new Indian tribes. Life sports, outdoors, serving and making clothes, basket weaving, braiding sweet grass, making necklaces of beads."

SORENSON, MARK
(school principal)

Affiliation: Little Singer Community School, Star Route, Box 239, Winslow, AZ 86047 (602) 774-7456.

*SORENSON, TOM
(radio news director/host)

Affiliation: South Dakota Public Broadcasting, South Dakota Public Radio Network, P.O. Box 5000, Vermillion, SD 57069 (605) 677-5861.

*SORENSON, WANDA
(school principal)

Affiliation: Chilchinbeto Day School, P.O. Box 547, Kayenta, AZ 86033 (602) 697-3448.

SORRELL, CHERYL
(center director)

Affiliation: Winslow Indian Center, 407 E. 3rd St., Winslow, AZ 86047 (602) 289-4525.

*SORRELL, DARLENE, DDS
(chief, dental program)

Affiliation: Southwestern Indian Polytechnic Institute, Dental Training Center, Box 25927, 9168 Coors Rd., NW, Albuquerque, NM 87126 (505) 897-5306.

SOSNOWSKI, DANIEL
(school principal)

Affiliation: Beclabito Day School, P.O. Box 1146, Shiprock, NM 87420 (602) 656-3555.

SOTO, PETER
(tribal chairperson)

Affiliation: Cocopah Tribal Council, P.O. Bin G, Somerton, AZ 85350 (602) 627-2102.

SOUERS, TWILA
(association president; editor)

Affiliations: Editor, "Native News," School Dist. 4J Indian Education Program, 3411-A Willamette St., Eugene, OR 97405; Oregon Indian Education Association (president), 720 Nantucket, Eugene, OR 97204 (503) 687-3489.

SOUKUP, LEO
(BIA project supt.)

Affiliation: Navajo Irrigation Project, Bureau of Indian Affairs, New Energy Bldg., Room 103, Farmington, NM 87401 (505) 325-1864.

SOUTHWIND, ROGER
(Indian band chief)

Affiliation: Lac Seul Indian Band, General Delivery, Lac Seul, Can. P0V 2A0 (807) 582-3211.

*SPANG, ALONZO, Sr.
(BIA agency supt.)

Affiliation: Rosebud Agency, Bureau of Indian Affairs, P.O. Box 550, Rosebud, SD 57570 (605) 747-2224.

SPEAKS, STANLEY M.
(Oklahoma Chickasaw) 1933-
(BIA area director)

Born November 2, 1933, Tishomingo, Okla. *Education*: Northeastern State College, Tahlequah, OK, BS, 1959, MEd, 1962. *Principal occupation*: B.I.A. area director. *Address*: Portland Area Office, Bureau of Indian Affairs,

911 NE 11th Ave., Portland, OR 97232 (503) 231-6702. *Affiliations*: supt., Anadarko Agency, BIA, 1975-77; area director, Anadarko Area Office, BIA, Anadarko, OK, 1976-80; director, Portland Area Office, BIA, Portland, OR, 1980-. *Community activities*: Boy Scouts of America (member-American Indian Relations Committee); 16th American Indian Tribal Leader's Seminar on Scouting (chairman, 1972-73); Rotary International (member); Oklahoma Governor's Committee on Small Business (member). *Interests*: Boating, fishing, hunting, golf; Boy Scouts of America.

*SPEARMAN, GRANT *(Avizaluk-Inupiaq)* 1951-
(museum curator)
Born April 24, 1951, Seattle, Wash. *Education*: University of Washington, BA, 1975. *Principal occupation*: Museum curator. *Home address*: 3022 Main St., Anaktuvuk Pass, AK 99721 (907) 661-3413 (work). *Affiliation*: Curator, Simon Paneak Memorial Museum, Anaktuvuk Pass, AK, 1986-. *Memberships*: Museums Alaska; Alaska Anthropological Association; International Association of Arctic Social Scientists. *Interests*: Archaeology, ethnography, ethnology, oral history, aviation history.

SPENCE, CYRIL HENRY
(Indian band chief)
Affiliation: Nicomen Indian Band, Box 328, Lytton, BC, Can. V0K 1Z0 (604) 455-2279.

SPENCE, ROY
(Indian band chief)
Affiliation: Webequie Indian Band, Box 176, Webequie, ON, Can. P0T 3A0 (807) 353-6531.

*SPENCER, BUFORD MARYLAND, Jr. *(Curly)* (United Lumbee/Cherokee) 1943-
(logger, long haul truck driver)
Born July 5, 1943, Mt. Airy, N.C. *Education*: Chemekgta Community College (Salem, OR), AS (Forest Technology), 1989. *Principal occupation*: Logger, long haul truck driver. *Home address*: 1458 SW Hill St., Dallas, OR 97338 (503) 623-8971. *Military service*: U.S. Army, 1962-654. *Community activities*: Honorary honor guard of the Confederated Tribes of Grand Ronde; board member & chief of safety & security of the United InterTribal Dancing Club of Salem. *Membership*: Northwest Indian Veterans Association. *Awards, honors*: President of Forestry Club at college, 1988-89. *Interests*: "My interests are to learn as much as I can about my people, to live the best way I can by following the "Red Road," to be of service to all Indian people in whatever way "Grandfather" directs me; to be proud of my heritage, respect my elders. *Published songs*: "Truckers Hall of Fame," & "Thank You Lord," both published in 1980.

*SPIELMANN, ROGER *(Shaganash)* 1951-
(assistant professor)
Born April 13, 1951, Chicago, Ill. *Education*: University of Texas, Arlington, MA, 1978; University of British Columbia, PhD, 1984. *Principal occupation*: Assistant professor. *Home address*: 56 Portage, Sudbury, ON Canada P3B 3H2 (705) 673-5661 (work). *Affiliation*: Laurentian University, Sudbury, ON, 1990-. *Other professional post*: Algonquian language consultant. *Community activities*: Laurentian University Senate. *Memberships*: American Anthropological Association; Survival International. *Interests*:
Algonquian languages & cultures; Native education; Algonquian Discourse Analysis; sociolinguistics, ethnomethodology. *Published works*: Numerous articles on the Algonquian language in journals & magazines.

SPILBURY, DELAINE (Western Shoshone) 1937-
(owner-Indian shop)
Born September 21, 1937, Ely, Nev. *Address & Affiliation*: Owner, Ms. Squaw Indian Handcrafts, 2429 Salt Lake St., N. Las Vegas, NV, 1972-. *Community activities*: Director, Pow Wow of the 4 Winds. *Membership*: National Bowhunting Rights Organization. *Awards, honors*: National Field Archery Association - Big Game Awards. *Interests*: Bowhunting; traveling the West to promote Native craftsmen. *Biographical sources*: National Bowhunter magazine; Native Nevadan magazine; Indian Trader magazine.

SPINKS, BRIAN JAMES
(Indian band chief)
Affiliation: Lytton Indian Band, Box 20, Lytton, British Columbia, Can. V0K 1Z0 (604) 455-2304.

SPIVEY, TOWANA (Chickasaw) 1943-
(curator, archaeologist)
Born November 8, 1943, Madill, Okla. *Education*: Southeastern State University, BA, 1968; University of Oklahoma, 1970-71. *Principal occupation*: Curator, archaeologist. *Home address*: 2101 Oak St., Duncan, OK 73533. *Affiliation*: Curator of anthropology, Museum of the Great Plains, Lawton, OK, 1974-. *Other professional posts*: Curator-archaeologist, Oklahoma Historical Society, 1974-; archaeologist, Oklahoma Archaeological Survey (2 years). *Military service*: Army National Guard, 1960-68. *Memberships*: Oklahoma Anthropological Society, 1963- (board member); Oklahoma Museums Association, 1973- (council member); Society for Historic Archaeology, 1973-; Council on Abandoned Military Posts (vice president of Oklahoma Department, 1975-). *Interests*: Historic sites-restoration, archaeology, etc.; 19th century military forts and camps; fur trade and exploration of the Trans-Mississippi West; conservation of cultural material or artifacts; wagon restoration. *Published works*: Co-author, An Archaeological Reconnaissance of the Salt Plains Areas of Northwest Oklahoma (Museum of the Great Plains, 1976); co-author, Archaeological Investigations Along the Waurika Pipeline (Museum of the Great Plains, 1977).

*SPOONHUNTER, HARVEY, Sr. (Arapahoe)
(tribal chairperson)
Affiliation: Shoshone & Arapahoe Joint Tribal Business Council, P.O. Box 217, Fort Washakie, WY 82514 (307) 332-6120.

SPOTTED EAGLE, CHRIS
(president-Indian society)
Address: 2524 Hennepin Ave., Minneapolis, MN 55401 (612) 377-4212. *Affiliation*: American Indian Talent Society, 2225 Cavell Ave. North, Golden Valley, MN 55427.

*SPRINGER, HOWARD (Iowa of Oklahoma)
(tribal chairperson)
Affiliation: Iowa of Oklahoma Business Committee, Iowa Veterans Hall, P.O. Box 190, Perkins, OK 74059 (405) 547-2403.

STAATS, WELLINGTON
(association president)
Affiliation: National Indian Arts & Crafts Corporation, Ottawa, Ontario, Canada; Indian Arts & Crafts of Ontario Corporation, 2 Carlton St., Suite 1518, Toronto, Ontario, Canada M5B 1J3 (416) 977-4442.

*STACHELRODT, MARY (Yup'ik Eskimo)
(museum director)
Affiliation: Yupiit Piciryarait Cultural Center & Museum, Assn. of Village Council Presidents, Box 219, Bethel, AK 99559 (907) 543-3521.

*STAGSDILL, WILLIAM (Lummi)
(school system director)
Affiliation: Lummi Tribal School System, 2530 Kwina Rd., Bellingham, WA 98225 (206) 647-6251.

*STAHL, STACY L. (Yerington Paiute)
(tribal chairperson)
Affiliation: Yerington Paiute Tribal Council, 171 Campbell Lane, Yerington, NV 89447 (702) 463-3301.

STALLING, STEVEN L.A. (San Luiseno-Mission Indians-Rincon Reservation) 1951-
(association president)
Born May 12, 1951, San Diego, Calif. *Education*: California State University, Long Beach, BS; University of Southern California, MBA. *Principal occupation*: Association president. *Address*: National Center for American Indian Enterprise Development, 953 E. Juanita Ave., Mesa, AZ 85204 (800) 423-0452, or (602) 831-7524. *Affiliations*: Prior to joining the National Center, Mr. Stalling was executive director of a consulting firm in San Francisco, and supervised a job creation program which trained 300 American Indians; National Center for American Indian Enterprise Development, Mesa, AZ, 1976- *Other professional posts*: Session chairman, Fifth International Symposium on Small Business, 1978; delegate to the White House Conference on Small Business, 1978. *Community activities*: Coordinator for the National Congress of American Indians, a lobbying group; former member of the steering committee for the National Indian Education Association; member of Board of Directors for a beginning Development Band directed at solving the domestic financing needs of American Indians; member of Advisory Committee for 1984 Olympics; served on Los Angeles Bicentennial Commission and the Los Angeles Private Industry Council; appointed to the Los Angeles City/County Indian Commission by Republican Supervisor Dean Dana. *Awards, honors*: Cited and recognized by the State Assembly of California for his contributions and efforts in small business and economic development. *Interests*: The National Center assists over 600 businesses annually and has secured over $200 million in financing and contracts for its clients. Long interested in developing American Indian talent, an interest that has accelerated since the formation of UIDA's Management Institute which trains Indian managers, Mr. Stallings has conducted dozens of workshops and seminars. Two of his training books are used throughout America by Indians learning planning and management. *Biographical sources*: Who's Who in Finance and Industry, 1982-1983; Who's Who in the West, 1982-1983. *Published work*: Directory of American Indian Businesses (National Center for American Indian Enterprise Development).

*STAMM, GEOFFREY
(acting general manager)
Affiliation: Indian Arts & Crafts Board, Dept. of the Interior, MS: 4004-MIB, 1849 C St., NW, Washington, DC 20240 (202) 208-3773.

STANDING, NETTIE L. (Kiowa) 1916-
(manager-OK Indian Arts & Crafts Coop)
Born August 15, 1916, Caddo County, Okla. *Education*: Riverside Indian School; Santa Fe Indian Boarding School, 1934-35. *Principal occupation*: Founding member/manager, Oklahoma Indian Arts & Crafts Cooperative, P.O. Box 966 Anadarko, OK, 1962-. *Home address*: P.O. Box 114, Gracemont, OK 73042 (405) 247-3486 (work). *Membership*: Oklahoma Federation of Indian Women. *Awards, honors*: 1975 National Endowment Award, recipient of grant for $5,000, for outstanding crafts person & teacher, and to research Kiowa beadwork; Grand Award Winner, 1977, Great Western Shows, Los Angeles, CA; 1976 Award from the Dept. of the Interior, Indian Arts & Crafts Board, for Outstanding Service to promote, preserve & develop all Indian crafts; 1985 O.I.O.--one of the finalists for Indian Business Person of the Year for Oklahoma. *Interests*: Kiowa beadwork; travel to Smithsonian Institution, and to the Museum of the American Indian in New York City in 1975-76, to view collection, and to visit the Indian Arts & Crafts Board in Washington, DC.

*STANDING BEAR, ZUG G. *(Kompau skwe)* **(Kanienkehaka/Abenaki/Wampanoag/Metis) 1941-**
(professor, program coordinator)
Born January 10, 1941, Boston, Mass. *Education*: University of Nebraska, BS; The George Washington University, MS; University of Southern California, MS; Jacksonville (AL) State University, MPA; Florida State University, PhD; Fellow in Forensic Medicine, The Armed Forces Institute of Pathology, Washington, DC. *Principal occupation*: Professor, program coordinator. *Home address*: 3228 San Juline Arc, Lake Park, GA 31636 (912) 247-1160. *Affiliation*: Valdosta State University, Dept. of Sociology & Anthropology, Valdosta GA, 1986- (associate professor of sociology, anthropology, and criminal justice; coordinator of criminal justice programs; member of the graduate faculty; and member of the Center for Professional & Applied Ethics). *Other professional posts*: Consultant in criminal justice, criminal investigation, and forensic science administration, organization, management, and curriculum design, 1981-; member, Governor's Criminal Justice Coordinating Council, 1988-92. *Military service*: U.S. Army, 1958-81 - Special Agent, U.S. Army Criminal Investigation Command (Bronze Star, Vietnam, 1970; Meritorious Service Medal; Army Commendation Medal). *Community activities*: Lowndes Drug Action Council (member, Board of Directors); Valdosta Symphony Orchestra (member, Board of Directors); Black on Black Crime Committee, Valdosta (member); Community Policing Transition Project, Valdosta Police Dept. (member, Leadership Council); Readership Board, The Valdosta Daily Times, 1994-. *Memberships*: American Sociological Association; American Society of Criminology; Academy of Criminal Justice Sciences; Southern Criminal Justice Association; Institute of Criminal Justice Ethics; National Congress of American Indians; Association on American Indian Affairs; Vietnam Veterans of America; National Organi-zation for Women; American Association of University Professors; International Association of Forensic Nurses. *Awards, honors*: Service Award, International Association of Forensic Nurses, 1994. *Biographical sources*: Who's Who in the South & Southeast (1991-92; 93-94); Who's Who in American Education (1992-93, 1994-95); Who's Who in the World (1993-94). *Published works*: Books: Law Enforcement & Criminology, both published by (University of Florida, Dept. of Continuing Education, 1985). *Articles*: "Coroner," "Field Death Investigations," "Ethics in Police Service," "Police Organizational Structures," "Inquest," "Police Surgeon," "Police Medical Officer," & "Clinical Forensic Medicine," in Encyclopedia of Criminology (Macmillan, 1994); "To Guard Against Invading Indians: Struggling for Native Community in the Southeast," in American Indian Culture & Research Journal, Nov. 1994; numerous other articles.

STANDING ELK, DON (Sioux)
(school principal)
Affiliation: American Horse School, P.O Box 660, Allen, SD 57714 (605) 455-2480.

*STANDING, NETTIE
(cooperative manager)
Affiliation: Oklahoma Indian Arts & Crafts Cooperative, P.O. Box 966, Anadarko, OK 73005 (405) 247-3486.

STANDINGHORN, EDWARD
(Indian band chief)
Affiliation: Sweetgrass Indian band, Box 147, Gallivan, SK, Canada S0M 0X0 (306) 937-3555.

STANLEY, BURNE
(center director)
Affiliation: Massachusetts Center for Native American Awareness, Inc., Box 5885, Boston, MA 02114 (617) 884-4227; editor, "Turtletalk."

STANLEY, NATALIE T. 1963-
(museum interpreter)
Born December 4, 1963, Fort Riley, Kans. *Education*: Christopher Newport College, BA, 1985; William and Mary (continuing education courses in archaeology and Virginia Native American culture.) *Principal occupation*: Museum interpreter. *Home address*: 81 Robinson Dr., Newport News, VA 23601 (804) 595-4931. *Affiliation*: Interpreter (conduct tours through Indian Village; presents slide show on the Eastern Woodland Indian culture), Syms-Eaton Museum and Kecoughtan Indian History Center, Hampton, VA, 1985-91. *Memberships*: The Lower James Chapter of the Archaeological Society of Virginia, (founder and president, 1988-; 1984-88 Kicotah Chapter of ASV (vice-president, 1986-87). *Interests*: "Apart from interpreter, I'm an active researcher of Native American cultures; work with Virginia and North Carolina tribal members. Assist other researchers; research and reconstruct native dwellings and implements; have working knowledge of native American domestic skills; participate and attend Native American festivals; work with archaeologists - research and site work."

STARR, IRVIN
(Indian band chief)
Affiliation: Starblanket Indian Band, Box 456, Balcarres, Saksatchewan, Canada S0G 0C0 (306) 334-2206.

*STAUSS, JOSEPH H.
(program director)
Affiliation: American Indian Studies Program, University of Arizona, Harvill Bldg., Rm. 430, Tucson, AZ 85721 (602) 621-7108.

STEARNS, CHRISTOPHER T. (Navajo)
(attorney)
Born December 13, 1964 in Los Angeles, Calif. *Education*: Williams College, B.A., 1986; Cornell Law School, J.D., 1989. *Address*: 649 C St., SE, Washington, DC 20003. *Affiliation*: Hobbs Straus Dean & Wilder, 1819 H St., NW, Suite 800, Washington, DC 20006 (202) 783-5100, 1989-. *Membership*: Native American Bar Association (board member).

*STEELE, JACQUELINE
(tribal chairperson)
Affiliation: Stewart Indian Community Council, 5300 Snyder Ave., Carson City, NV 89701 (702) 883-7767.

STEELE, LOIS (Fort Peck Assiniboine) 1939-
(physician)
Born November 27, 1939, Washington, D.C. *Education*: Colorado College, BA, 1961; University of Montana, MS, 1969; University of Minnesota Medical School, Duluth & Minneapolis, MD, 1978. *Principal occupation*: Physician. *Home address*: 2360 W. Canada, Tucson, AZ 85746 (602) 578-0644; 670-6217 (work). *Affiliation*: Research Medical Officer, Division of Medical Systems Research & Development, USPHS-Indian Health Service, Tucson, AZ, 1980-. *Other professional posts*: Clinical Director, Pascua Yaqui Health Dept., 1986-91; director, Indians Into Medicine Program. *Community activities*: Assistant Cub Scout Master, 1986, 1988-89; PTA, 1986-90; United Way, Tucson (board member); Holy Way Presbyterian Church, Tucson (Deacon, 1991). *Memberships*: Association of American Indian Physicians; American Academy of Family Physicians; American Medical Association; Commissioned Officers of America; Arizona Academy of Family Physicians. *Awards, honors*: Faculty President, Dawson College, 1972; Outstanding Woman Medical Student, Lampson Award, University of Minnesota Medical School, Duluth, 1976; Distinguished Achievement Award, Rocky Mountain College Alumni Association, 1981; National Indian Health Board - Honoree, 1982; selected as Advisory Committee Member, FDA - Consumer Status, 1982-83; University of North Dakota Indian Students Association, Time-Out Award, 1983; Wonder Women Foundation - Finalist, 1983; USPHS Unit Commendation, April 1988; American Indian Science & Engineering Society Eli Parker Award, 1989; Indian Health Service Award for Health Promotion, Disease Prevention Work, 1989; Pascua Yaqui Project Head Start Volunteer Award, 1991; AMA Physicians Recognition Award, 1991-1993. *Interests*: Numerous presentations, workshops, field readings and consulting positions over the years. *Research & Publications*: "(AIDS) Education Among Native Americans in Arizona: The Pascua Yaqui, Navajo Nation & Urban Indian Experience". May 1990; Stone and Steele. Presented at the International AIDS Conference in Puerto Rico; "Leading Causes of Death Among Yaqui Indians, 1970-90" Sept. 1990 - Presented at American Public Health Associations Annual Meeting, New York; "Cardiovascular Risk Among the Pascua Yaqui" April 1991. Presented at the IHS National Research Conference, Tucson, among others.

STEIN, WAYNE J.
(Turtle Mountain Chippewa) 1950-
(professor/administrator)
Born September 17, 1950, Wolf Point, Mont. *Education*: Montana State University, BS, 1973; Penn State University, MEd., 1977; Washington State University, EdD, 1988. *Principal occupation*: Professor-administrator. *Home address*: 515 N. 20th, Bozeman, MT 59715 (406) 994-3881 (work). *Affiliation*: Director, Center for Native American Studies, Montana State University, Bozeman, MT, 1991-. *Other professional posts*: Vice President, International College; President, Standing Rock College, AZ. *Memberships*: Montana Indian Education Association; National Indian Education Association. *Awards, honors*: Bush Leadership Award, 1985; Community College Educator of the Year, WSU, 1986. *Interests*: Rights and needs of the poor and working people of U.S.; rights of indigenous people of the world; world environment issues; economic development of State of Montana and its Indian reservations; reading, writing, fishing. *Published work*: Tribally Controlled College (Peter Lang, 1992).

*STEINBRIGHT, JAN
(editor)
Affiliation: Journal of Alaska Native Arts, Institute of Alaska Native Arts, P.O. Box 70769, Fairbanks, AK 99707 (907) 456-7491.

STEINBRING, JOHN H. (JACK) 1929-
(anthropologist)
Born July 1, 1929, Oshkosh, Wisc. *Education*: University of Wisconsin, Oshkosh, BA, 1955, Madison, MA, 1959; University of Minnesota, PhD, 1975. *Principal occupation*: Anthropologist. *Home address*: 18 Browning Blvd., Winnipeg, Manitoba R3K 0L4 (204) 832-0326 (home) 786-9719 (work). *Affiliation*: Professor & senior scholar, Dept. of Anthropology, University of Winnipeg, Manitoba, 1963-. *Military service*: Wisconsin National Guard/U.S. Army Reserve, 1949-62 (1st Lt.; Expert Rifle, Pistol, Carbine). *Community activities*: President, Assiniboine Senior Rifle Club, 1978-90. *Memberships*: American Anthropological Association (Foreign Fellow); Society for American Archaeology; Society of Professional Archaeologists; Rock Art Association of Canada (president, 1990); Rock Art Association of Manitoba (president, 1993-); Australian Rock Art Research Association (vice president, 1988-92. *Interests*: "Extensive research into the impact of television among Algonkian populations resulting in several books, 1974-81; studies of alcohol among the Northern Ojibwa, 1964-82, resulting in one book and one professional paper; general ethnographic studies among the North Ojibwa, 1963-, resulting in numerous papers and a chapter in the Handbook of North American Indians (Vol. 6, Smithsonian); many years of research into Native North American rock art leading to many professional papers and the identification of two rock art styles and the discovery of Canada's oldest dated rock art; further rock art research in Hawaii, Australia, England, Scotland, and the American Southwest." *Published works*: Television and the Canadian Indian (University of Winnipeg Press, 1979); Alcohol and the Native Peoples of the North (University Press of America, 1980); An Introduction to Archaeology on the Winnipeg River (Manitoba Historic Resources Branch, 1980); Communications in Cross-Cultural Perspective (University of Winnipeg Press, 1980); General Guidelines in the Development of Native Television Programming (University of Winnipeg Press, 1981); The Impact & Meaning of Television Among Native Communities in Northern Manitoba (Canadian Commission for UNESCO, 1984); numerous articles on rock art & archaeology.

*STEINDORF, HARRY J. (Keddy-Ju-Sa-Skagga - White Blackhawk) (Wisconsin Winebago) 1946-
(educational administrator)
Born February 20, 1946, Black River Falls, Wisc. *Education*: University of Wisconsin, Whitewater, BBA, 1973; University of Wisconsin, Madison Law School, 1973-75. *Principal occupation*: Educational administrator. *Home address*: 460 Bonnie Rd., Cottage Grove, WI 53527 (608) 262-0314 (work). *Affiliation*: University of Wisconsin, Madison, (assistant to Art Dept. Chair, 1988-; administrator, Academic Advancement Program, 1989-). *Past professional posts*: Vice-Chairman, Wisconsin Winnebago Business Committee, 1978-79; director of planning & economic development for Wisconsin Winnebago Tribe, 1980-83. *Military service*: U.S. Marine Corps, 1964-70; Captain (Distinguished Flying Cross; Sixteen Strike/Flight Air Medals; Vietnam Gallantry Cross; Vietnam Service Medal; Vietnam Campaign Medal; Naval Unit Citation; Meritorious Unit Citation). *Community activities*: Veterans of Foreign Wars; Disabled American Veterans, Madison, WI. *Awards, honors*: Outstanding Young Alumnus Award, University of Wisconsin, Whitewater, 1978; Outstanding Young Men of America, 1979. *Interests*: Fiction writing, pleasure flying, hunting & camping. *Published works*: In progress: "Seaworthy Injun," & Zeke Bush Tail, Fancy Dancer (tent. 1995).

*STEINHAUSER, JAN
(program director)
Affiliation: American Indian Studies Program, University of Denver, 2211 S. Josephne St., Denver, CO 80208 (303) 871-3155 ext. 254.

STEINSIEK, TOMMY A.
(curator)
Affiliation: Creek Indian Memorial Association, Creek Council House Museum, Town Square, Okmulgee, OK 74447 (918) 756-2324.

STENSGAR, ERNEST (Coeur d'Alene)
(tribal chairperson)
Affiliation: Coeur d'Alene Tribal Council, Route 1, Plummer, ID 83851 (208) 686-1800.

*STEORTS, DENNIS (Chief Red Eagle) (Kaweah)
(principal chief, minister)
Address & Affiliation: Principal chief, Kaweah Indian Nation of Western USA & Mexico, P.O. Box 642, Abilene, KS 67410. *Other professional post*: co-national chairman, American Indian Defense of the Americas. *Community activities*: Board member, Congregational Bible Churches International; Minister of Native American Church/CBC Division.

*STEPETIN, JACOB
(village president)
Affiliation: Native Village of Akutan, P.O. Box 89, Akutan, AK 99553 (907) 698-2301.

*STEPHENSON, MICHAEL LYNN
(Cloud Walker) (United Lumbee/Kickapoo/Cherokee) 1965-
(caregiver)
Born January 12, 1965, Phoenix Ariz. *Education*: High school. *Principal occupation*: Caregiver (caring for disabled persons). *Home address*: 5356 Border Ave., Joshua Tree, CA 92252. Community activities: Landers (CA) Breakfast Club Volunteer, 1983-. *Memberships*: United Lumbee Nation Desert Sage Band (Black Hawk Warrior Society, Keeper of the Fire, 1992; council person, 1992-). *Award*: Landers (CA) Breakfast Club, 10 Year Service Award, Dec. 1993. *Interests*: Indian beadwork, carving, gardening; specializing in Gourd growing, student of Indian history & ceremonies.

STEVENS, BRUCE
(Te-Moak Western Shoshone)
(tribal chairperson)
Affiliation: Wells Indian Colony Band Council, P.O. Box 809, Wells, NV 89835 (702) 752-3045.

STEVENS, CONNIE (Iroquois-Cherokee) 1938-
(actress; executive director-foundation)
Born August 8, 1938, Brooklyn, N.Y. *Principal occupation*: Actress (25 years). Resides in Beverly Hills, CA. *Affiliation*: Founder, president, executive director, Windfeather Foundation. *Memberships*: Screen Actors Guild, AFTRA, Actors Equity.

*STEVENS, ESSIMAE
(hospital director)
Affiliation: Red Lake Comprehensive Health Service, Red Lake, MN 56671 (218) 679-3912.

STEVENS, JOHN W. (Passamaquoddy) 1933-
(tribal governor)
Born August 11, 1933, Washington Co., Maine. *Education*: High school. *Principal occupation*: Tribal governor, Indian Township--Passamaquoddy Tribal Council, Princeton, ME. *Address*: Box 407, Princeton, ME 04668. *Military service*: U.S. Marines, 1951-54 (Pres. Unit Citation; Korean Presidential Unit Citation; UN Medal). *Interests*: Mr. Stevens writes, "Being the chief of an Indian tribe of about a thousand members who are struggling in court and on all fronts to overcome local discrimination and poverty & to have our reservation treaty rights respected by the State of Maine is enough of a task, and doesn't leave much time for anything else."

*STEVENS, KATHRYN
(education director)
Affiliation: Arizona Dept. of Education, Indian Education Unit, 1535 W. Jefferson St., Phoenix, AZ 85007 (602) 542-4391.

STEVENSON, LOUIE J.
(Indian band chief)
Affiliation: Peguis Indian Band, Box 219, Hodgson, MB, Can. R0C 1N0 (204) 645-2359.

*STEVENSON, SCOTTIE
(museum curator)
Affiliation: American Indian Horse Museum, Rt. 3, Box 64, Lockhart, TX 78644 (512) 398-6642.

STEWART, JOSEPH L.
(program director)
Affiliation: IHS Sensory Disabilities Program, 2401 12th St., NW, Albuquerque, NM 87102 (505) 766-1232.

*STIDHAM, LAWRENCE
(attorney)
Affiliation: CA Indian Legal Services, 819 N. Barlow Lane, Bishop, CA 93514 (619) 872-3911.

STIFFARM, THELMA (Gros Ventre)
(attorney)
Address: P.O. Box 2235, Havre, MT 59501 (406) 395-4700. *Membership*: Native American Bar Association (board member).

STILLWELL, LUCILLE
(executive director)
Affiliation: Kiva Club, University of New Mexico, Mesa Vista Hall #1117-A, Albuquerque, NM 87131 (505) 277-8259.

STIVER, LOUISE
(museum collections)
Affiliation: Museum of Indian Arts and Culture, Lab. of Anthropology, Box 2087, 708 Camino Lejo, Santa Fe, NM 87504 (505) 827-6344.

STOCK, STEPHEN
(Indian band chief)
Affiliation: Mohawks of Gibson, Box 327, Bala, Ontario, Canada P0C 1A0 (613) 762-3343.

STOGAN, WALKER (Salish)
(spiritual leader)
Address: 4035 Thallaiwhaltum Ave., Musqueam Reserve, Vancouver, B.C., Canada V6H 3V1. *Interests*: Salish elder/spiritual leader of Winter Spirit Dance ceremonial.

*STOGSDILL, WILLIAM
(school system director)
Affiliation: Lummi Tribal School System, 2530 Kwina Rd., Bellingham, WA 98225 (206) 647-6251.

*STOLTZ, JOHN (Warm Springs Confederated)
(radio station manager)
Affiliation: KTWI-KTWS - 96.5 FM, Warm Springs Confederated Tribes, 20450 Empire Ave., Bend, OR 97701 (503) 389-9500.

STONE, BEVERLY
(health director)
Affiliation: Cherokee Nation Health Clinic, 1311 W. Locust St., Stilwell, OK 74960 (918) 696-6911.

STONE, EVELYN
(Indian band chief)
Affiliation: Michipicoten Indian Band, Site 7, RR 1, Box 26, Wawa, Ontario, Canada P0S 1K0 (705) 856-4455.

*STONE, NATHAN
(monument manager)
Affiliation: Coronado State Monument, P.O. Box 95, Bernalillo, NM 87004 (505) 867-5351.

STONE, WANDA (Kaw)
(tribal chairperson)
Affiliation: Kaw Business Committee, Drawer 50, Kaw City, OK 74641 (405) 269-2552.

*STORHOLM, TERRY (Cheyenne)
(tribal consultant)
Education: Cardinal Stritch (WI), Business. *Principal occupation*: American Indian tribal consultant. *Home address*: 620 Opperman Dr., Eagan, MN 55123 (612) 687-7327 (work). *Affiliation*: West Publishing, Eagan, MN, 1989-.

*STORY, CHARLENE TUCKALEECHE (North Alabama Cherokee) 1939-
(customer relations manager)
Born May 29, 1939, Moorpark, Calif. *Education*: Ventura (CA) College. *Principal occupation*: Customer relations manager. *Home address*: 53 Buckworth Cir., Trafford, AL 35172 (205) 681-0080; 856-2544 (work). *Affiliation*: Deputy Sheriff for Ventura County (10 years); Serra Nissan/Olds, Birmingham, AL, 1983-. *Community activities*: Tribal council member (represent Blount County, AL, Dist. 6), North Alabama Cherokee Tribe; head lady at pow wows. *Interests*: "I collect Native American artist plates." *Biographical sources*: "I have been subject of several articles in "The Blount Countian" regarding tribal activities."

STOTT, MARGARET 1945-
(museum curator)
Born September 25, 1945, Vancouver, Can. *Education*: University of British Columbia, BA, 1966; McGill University, MA, 1969; University of London (England), PhD, 1982. *Principal occupation & Address*: Museum curator of ethnology, Museum of Anthropology, University of British Columbia, Vancouver, 1979-. *Memberships*: British Columbia Museums Association; Canadian Museums Association; American Association of Museums; Canadian Ethnology Society; Canadian Anthropology and Sociology Association; Mediterranean Institute; Modern Greek Studies Association; Council for Museum Anthropology. *Interests*: Northwest Coast Indian material culture and art with particular emphasis on the Bella Coola Indians; material culture studies; museum studies; Mediterranean ethnography with particular emphasis on modern Greece; tourism studies, particularly in the Mediterranean. *Published works*: Bella Coola Ceremony and Art (National Museums of Canada, 1975); Material Anthropology: Contemporary Approaches to Material Culture (University Press of America, in press). *Exhibitions*: Northwest Coast Indian Art, exhibition of contemporary Indian art (20 pieces), displayed in four cases at Air Canada Maple Leaf Lounge, Vancouver International Airport, 1980-; numerous other exhibitions in the past. Audio-visual productions: The Raven and the First Man, visuals of the sculpture carved by Haida artist Bill Reid, with the artist narrating the Haida origin myth depicted in the carvings; Salish Art and Culture, an interview with an anthropologist in the Museum exhibition Visions of Power, Symbols and Wealth; among others.

*STOWE, NOEL READ 1938-
(professor, archaeologist)
Born February 3, 1938, Atlanta, Ga. *Education*: Nathaniel Hawthorne College, BA, 1967; University of Alabama, MA, 1970. *Principal occupation*: Professor, archaeologist. *Home address*: 4205 Lanain Dr., Mobile, AL 36618 (205) 460-6347 (work) *Affiliations*: Instructor, University of Alabama, University, AL, 1967-70; director of archaeology, University of South Alabama, Mobile, AL, 1970-. *Other professional posts*: Founder & archaeologist, University of South Alabama Archaeological Research Program; 10 Field Trips to Yucatan 1967-94 Mayan Indian Ethnography, History, Archaeology; conducted about 300 cultural resource assessment & various archaeological projects, 1983-; presented papers at national & regional meetings. *Military service*: U.S. Air Force, 1957-61. *Community activities*: Mobile Archaeological Council; advisor,

Mowa Indians. *Memberships*: Alabama Archaeological Society (board of directors); Council of Alabama Archaeologists (chairman, 1982); Mississippi Archaeological Society; Society for American Archaeology; National Speleological Society. *Awards, honors*: Archaeologist of the Year, Alabama Historical Commission. He has 25 years experience conducting archaeological investigations at both prehistoric & historic sites in the eastern U.S. & Mexico. He has served as principal investigator on about 50 funded projects. *Published works*: He has produced more than 50 papers monographs, and publications; selected titles & projects include: "History Lost: Our Endangered Past," in Lost in Time, Early Alabama Indians, Alabama Public TV, Auburn, AL, 1983; "The Way It Was: A History of Mobile Bay," Alabama Public TV, 1994; "History of Excavations At the Bottle Creek Site," in Journal of Alabama Archaeology, 1994; numerous articles & chapters in journals & books.

STRAIT, DOROTHY MAY (Doe-Kwo te.-Ha-Na) (Cherokee) 1935-
(artist)
Born September 6, 1935, Phoenix, Ariz. *Education*: Scottsdale Community College (2 years). *Principal occupation*: Artist. *Home address*: 1299 E. Canyon, Apache Junction, AZ 85217 (602) 983-4545. *Memberships*: Indian Arts and Crafts Association; High Country Art & Craft Guild; Southwestern Association on Indian Affairs. *Awards, honors*: 1982 Art Show, John F. Kennedy Center-Night of the First American, Washington, DC; 1983 One Woman Show - Gambaro Studio Gallery, Washington, DC; 1984 Museum of Natural History - Smithsonian Institution, Washington, DC; 1988 Inter-Tribal Indian Ceremonial Poster Award, Gallup, NM; 1992 & 1993 Multicultural Calendar, Christopher Columbus and the Native Americans. *Interests*: Attend large Native American art shows icluding: Denver Art Show, CO; Gallup Art Show, NM; Red Earth Art Show, OK; High Country Art and Craft Guild Show, Asheville, NC. *Biographical sources*: 1982 OHOYO - A Resource Guide of American Indian Alaska Native Women; California Art Review, Les Krantz; Arizona Arts Magazine, Vol. I, II, III.

*STRANGE OWL-RAVEN, NICO (Appearing Buffalo Woman) (Northern Cheyenne) 1963-
(store owner; appraiser, consultant)
Born June 28, 1963, Bakersfield, Calif. *Education*: Colorado State University (5 years). *Principal occupation*: Store owner; appraiser, consultant. *Address*: 9853 Hwy. 7, Allenspark, CO 80510 (303) 747-2861 (work). *Affiliations*: Owner, Eagle Plume's, Allenspark, 1984-; owner, Nico Strange Owl-Hunt Appraisals, Allenspark, CO, 1991-. *Other professional post*: Consultant to the Denver Art Museum. *Community activities*: Various lectures regarding American Indian art & culture; member, Douglas Society. *Memberships*: American Society of Appraisers (candidate member); Antique Tribal Arts Dealers Association; Southwestern Association of Indian Affairs.

*STRANGE OWL-RAVEN, ANN (Medicine Eagle Feather Woman) (Northern Cheyenne) 1936-
(store owner)
Born June 1, 1936, Birney Village, Mont. *Education*: University of Alaska (2 years). *Principal occupation*: Store owner. *Address*: 9853 Hwy. 7, Allenspark, CO 80510 (303) 747-2861 (work).

Affiliation: Owner, Eagle Plume's, Allenspark, CO, 1976-.

STRICKLAND, JOHNYE E.
(secretary-treasurer)
Affiliation: American Native Press Archives and Research Association, American Indian & Alaska Native Periodicals, Research Clearinghouse, 502 Stabler Hall, University of Arkansas, 33rd & University Ave., Little Rock, AR 72204 (501) 569-3160.

STRICKLAND, RENNARD JAMES
(Osage-Cherokee) 1940-
(law professor; law center director)
Born September 26, 1940, St. Louis, Mo. *Education*: Northeastern State College, BA, 1962; University of Virginia, JD, 1965, SJD, 1970; University of Arkansas, MA, 1966. *Principal occupation*: Professor of law. *Address*: School of Law, University of Oklahoma, 300 Timberdell Rd., Norman, OK 73019 (405) 325-4699. *Affiliations*: Professor, University of Arkansas, 1965-69; professor of law, University of Tulsa, 1972-74; Acting Dean, School of Law, University of Tulsa, 1974-75; associate professor, University of Washington, 1975-76; supervising director, Shleppey Native American Collections, University of Tulsa, 1976-85; John W. Shleppey Research Professor of Law & History, University of Tulsa, 1976-85; dean & professor, School of Law, Southern Illinois University, 1985-88; professor of law, University of Wisconsin, Madison, 1988-90; professor of law & director, American Indian Law Center, College of Law, The University of Oklahoma, Norman, OK, 1990-. *Other professional posts*: Director, Indian Heritage Association, Muskogee, Okla., 1966-84; director, Oral History Project, University of Florida, 1969-1971; Site Inspector, American Bar Association, Section on Legal Education and Admission to the Bar, 1974-; chair, Indian Advisory Board, Philbrook Art Center, 1979-83; editor-in-chief, revision of Handbook of Federal Indian Law, Solicitor's Office, Dept. of the Interior, 1975-82; member, National Museum Advisory Board, Heard Museum, 1986-; board of directors, ATLATL, Native American Arts Service Organization, 1988-90; consultant, Panel for National Dialogue on Museums -- Native American Relations, Center for Cross-Cultural Communications, 1989-90; Law School Admissions Council, 1988-90; Smithsonian Institution, Planning Committee, 1990-91; American Bar Association, Affirmative Action Committee, 1988-91. *Visiting professor at the following*: Sylvan Lange Distinguished Visiting Professor, St. Mary's University, Summer 1973, University of New Mexico, Fall 1976, Summer, 1975-79, University of West Virginia (Reyer Distinguished), October 1982, University of Florida, Spring, 1983; University of Kansas (Langston Hughes Distinguished); Heard Museum of Native American and Primitive Art (Scholar-in-Residence), 1988-89; Arizona State University, 1988-89; public lectures. *Memberships*: Association of American Law Schools (Accreditation Committee, 1990-92; president, 1994); American Society of Legal History; Selden Society; Communications Association of America; Oklahoma Historical Society; American Ethnohistory Society; American Association of Museums (member, Task Force-Reparations of Ceremonial Objects and Human Remains, 1987-88; American Bar Association (co-chair, Section on Legal Education and Admission to the Bar, Bicentennial Committee on the U.S. Constitution, 1984-87; member, Task Force on Minorities in the Legal Profession, 1987-89). *Awards, honors*: Sacred Sash of the Creeks for Preservation Tribal History; Fellow in Legal History, American Bar Association, 1970-1971; Fellow, American Council of Learned societies, 1972; Fellow, Doris Duke Foundation, 1970-73; Distinguished Service Award, Creek Indian Nation, 1972; Outstanding Faculty member, School of Law, University of Tulsa, 1975; Distinguished Alumnus Award, Northeastern State College, 1976; Society of American Law Teachers Annual Award for Outstanding Teaching and Contribution to Law Reform, 1978; Award of Merit, Association for State and Local History, 1981 (editorial board member); Award of Excellence, Western Book Association, for A Trumpet of Out Own, 1982; Distinguished Service Citation, American Indian Coalition, Tulsa, OK, 1985; Chairman's Award, Contribution to Development of Indian Law in Oklahoma, presented by Chief Claude Cox, Chairman, Oklahoma Indian Affairs Commission, Tribal Summit, 1990. *Interests*: Indian law, Indian art, film & filmmaking. Mr. Strickland writes, "Primary interest (is in) law and the American Indian, including programs to attract Indian students to the law as a profession, and programs to make the law responsive to the needs of Indian citizens; culture of the American Indian, with primary emphasis upon myths and legends and upon the arts and crafts of native tribes; contemporary American Indian paintings, and the evolution of Indian culture as reflected in evolving styles; ethnohistory of specific tribes--the Cherokee, Creek. Seminole, Choctaw and Chickasaw; development of traditional legal systems among the tribes." *Published works*: Sam Houston With the Cherokees, 1829-1833, with Jack Gregory (University of Texas Press, 1967); Starr's History of the Cherokees (1968); Cherokee Spirit Tales (1969); Cherokee Cook Book (1969); Creek-Seminole Spirit Tales (1971); Choctaw Spirit Tales (1972); Hell on the Border (1971); Adventures of an Indian Boy (1973); American Indian Spirit Tales (1973); all with Jack Gregory, published by Indian Heritage Association; Cherokee Law Ways (University of Oklahoma Press, 1972); with Earl Boyd Pierce - The Cherokee People (Indian Tribal Series, 1973; How to Get Into Law School (Hawthorne Books, Inc, 1974, revised editions, 1975-77-79-82); Fire and Spirits: Cherokee Law From Clan to Court (University of Oklahoma Press, 1975); with William & Janet Phillips - Avoiding Teacher Malpractice (Hawthorne Books, 1976); The Prelaw Handbook (Assn. of American Law Schools, 1975, rev. eds. 1976-79); The Indians in Oklahoma (University of Oklahoma Press & Oklahoma Images Project, 1980); A Trumpet of Our Own: Yellow Bird on the American Indian (Book Club of California, 1981); Handbook of Federal Indian Law (Michie-Bobbs-Merrill, 3rd Ed., 1982); Magic Images: Contemporary Native American Art (University of Oklahoma Press, 1982); As In a Vision: Masterworks of American Indian Art (University of Oklahoma Press, 1983); Arizona Memories (University of Arizona Press, 1984: The Right Law School for You (Law School Admission Council, Newtown, PA, 1986, 1987); "Keeping Our Word: Indian Treaty Rights & Public Responsibilities," a report (with S.J. Herzberg & S.R. Owens) for the Senate Select Committee on Indian Affairs, 1990; Shared Visions: Native American Painting & Sculpture (The Heard Museum, 1991); Trying a New Way: An Assessment of the Indian Self-Governance Demonstration Project, an analysis prepared for the BIA & Self-Governance Demonstration Tribes, 1992; Savages, Sinners, and Redskinned Redeemers: Images of the Native American (University of New Mexico Press - in press); Indian Dilemma: Rhetoric and Reality of Cherokee Removal (University of Oklahoma Press - in press); numerous edited books/studies, and articles/chapters/essays.

STURGES, RALPH W. *(Gertinamong)*
(Mohegan) 1918-
(marble sculptor; tribal chief)
Born December 25, 1918, New London, Conn. *Education*: Penn Institute of Criminology (Philadelphia), Diploma, 1947. *Principal occupation*: Marble sculptor. *Home address*: 97 Raymond St., New London, CT 06320 (203) 442-8005. *Affiliation*: Lifetime chief of the Mohegan Tribe; camera clubs, Waterford, CT and Westerly, RI. *Other professional post*: Owned and operated my own distribution company. *Military service*: U.S. Army, 1940-45 (Intelligence; served in Pacific Theater). Community activities: Salvation Army. *Awards, honors*: Katherine Duggan Award for encouraging others to become interested in the arts, Marlborough (CT) Community Art Council. *Interests*: Self-empoyed dsigning and sculptoring.

STURTEVANT, MARGARET
(museum president)
Affiliation: Tribal House of the Bear, Box 868, Wrangell, AK 99929 (907) 874-3505.

SUDDUTH, LEONARD
(school principal)
Affiliation: Chitimacha Day School, Route 2, Box 222, Jeanerette, LA 70544 (318) 923-4921.

SULCER, PATRICIA
(editor)
Affiliation: How Ni Kan, Citizen Band Potawatomi Tribe, Route 5, Box 151, Shawnee, OK 74801 (405) 275-3121.

SULLIVAN, MARTIN
(museum director)
Affiliations: The Heard Museum, 22 E. Monte Vista Rd., Phoenix, AZ 85004 (602) 252-8840; co-chair, Committee on Museum-Native American Collaboration, American Association of Museums.

*SUMMERFIELD, HARRY B., Jr. (Paiute)
(tribal chairperson)
Affiliation: Lovelock Tribal Council, P.O. Box 878, Lovelock, NV 89419 (702) 273-7861.

*SUMMERS, ALLEN (Paiute)
(tribal chairperson)
Affiliation: Bishop Indian Tribal Council, P.O. Box 548, Bishop, CA 93514 (619) 873-3584.

SUMMERS-FITZGERALD, DIOSA
(Mississippi Choctaw) 1945-
(director of education, artist)
Born December 23, 1945, New York, N.Y. *Education*: State University College at Buffalo, BA, 1977; Northwestern University Archaeological Center, Kampsville, IL (Certificate), 1981; Harvard University Graduate School of Education, EdM, 1983. *Principal occupation*: Director of education, artist. *Home address*: 226 Ward Ave., Staten Island, NY 10304. *Affiliations*: Instructor, History Dept. and Continuing Education Dept., State University College at Buffalo, NY, 1975-77; instructor, Haffenreffer Museum

of Anthropology, Bristol, RI, 1979-80; acting tribal coordinator, Narragansett Tribal Education Project, Inc., 1980; administration, instructor, proposal writer, program coordinator, 1980-81, education director, instructor, 1982-85, Tomaquag Indian Memorial Museum, Exeter, RI; Native American historical and educational consultant, Plimoth Plantation, Plymouth, MA, 1981-82; artist in residence, Folk Arts Program, RI State Council on the Arts, Providence, 1982-85; artist, Native American Art Forms Nishnabeykwa Productions, Charlestown, RI, 1982-85; education director, Jamaica Arts Center, Jamaica, NY, 1985-. *Other professional post*: Owner, artist, consultant, Nishnabeykwa Productions, Staten Island, N.Y., 1982-. *Memberships*: Harvard Club of RI. *Awards, honors*: 1st Prize, Photography, Thomas Indian School Exhibit; Kappa Delta Pi, national Undergraduate Honor Society; Phi Alpha Theta, International History Honor Society. *Interests*: "Over the years, I have devoted most of life to Native American art, and a clear understanding of the roots of Native American tradition through art. I have also sought to develop a better understanding of the Native American through art as well as in the classroom initially as a teacher, and more recently a curriculum developer, and program developer. Other expertise: Cultural consultant and educational consultant; craft demonstrations; curator of exhibitions." *Published works*: Native American Foods; Fingerweaving, narrative and instruction; Ash Splint Basketry; Iomaquag Indian Museum brochures.

SUMNER, DELORES TITCHYWY
(Toos-cee) (Comanche) 1931-
(special collections librarian; assistant professor)
Born May 11, 1931, Lawton, Okla. *Education*: Northeastern State University, BS, 1964, MEd, 1967; University of Oklahoma, MLS, 1981. *Principal occupation*: Special collections librarian; assistant professor. *Home address*: 405 N. Bliss, Tahlequah, OK 74464 (918) 456-5511, Ext. 3252 (office). *Affiliations*: Coordinator/director, Comanche Cultural Center, Comanche Complex, Lawton, OK (2 years); SPC librarian, John Vaughn Library, and assistant professor of Library Services, Northeastern State University, Tahlequah, OK, 1982-. *Other professional post*: Public school teacher (7 years). *Community activities*: Northeastern State University Symposium on the American Indian (appointed member, 1982-). *Memberships*: North American Indian Women's Association (president, Northeastern Oklahoma chapter, 1989-92); American Indian Libraries Association; Association of College and Research Libraries; Tahlequah Area Arts and Humanities Council; Philbrook Museum Association; Gilcrease Museum; North American Indian Museum Association; Oklahoma Historical Society; Oklahoma Library Association; American Library Association; Delta Kappa Gamma (Research Committee Chairperson); Gilcrease Museum Association. *Awards, honors*: Certificate of Appreciation, Oklahoma Library Association. *Interests*: "Supporting the traditional artists in Native American art by traveling to exhibits, showings, and galleries is one of my main interests. I am very much interested in the preservation of Native American culture and tradition through oral history, art work, and the retention of the native language, of which I have accomplished only a small portion while working for my tribe as their cultural director. Today, I am still working toward this goal by per-

sonally contacting elders to record their songs, stories, and memories. I also record Comanche hymns whenever possible." *Published work*: Numa-Nu: The Fort Sill Indian School Experience (Oklahoma Humanities Committee, 1980).

SUN BEAR *(Gheezis Mokwa)* (Chippewa) 1929-
(author, lecturer)
Born August 31, 1929, White Earth Reservation, Bemidji, Minn. *Education*: LA Duke School, White Earth Reservation, MN (8 years). *Principal occupation*: Author, lecturer. *Home address*: P.O. Box 9167, Spokane, WA 99209 (509) 326-6561 (work). *Affiliation*: Founder/president, The Bear Tribe Medicine Society, Spokane, WA, 1966-. *Other professional posts*: Editor/publisher, Many Smokes magazine; motion picture actor and extra, 1955-65; technical director, Wagon Train, Bonanza, and Wild, Wild West, television series. *Membership*: Midiwidin Society; National Congress of American Indians. *Interests*: "I have been involved in Indian affairs most of my life, and I've spent some time teaching survival living to Indian and non-Indian people. I'm concerned with our Indian people, and other people, becoming more self-sufficient on the land, and learning a better balance with each other, and the Earth Mother; teaching, lecturing, writing; ceremonial leader of pilgrimages to sacred sites on the globe; businessman. Primary interest is to bridge Native and non-native cultures, sharing knowledge to help heal people and the earth during the time of global changes." Sun Bear is a world traveler and lecturer, his travels have taken him to Europe, Australia, and India. *Biographical sources*: Mother Earth News, Sept.-Oct. 1988; Visions and Revisions, Winter 1988; New Realities, Spring 1988; Joy of Life, Spring, 1989; Guide to New Age Living, 1989; Sacred Earth News, Spring, 1989; The Light Connection, Oct. 1989; Wholistic Living News, Oct. 1989. *Published works*: At Home in the Wilderness (Naturegraph, 1968); Buffalo Hearts (Bear Tribe Publishing, 1970); Walk in Balance (Prentice-Hall); The Bear Tribe's Self-Reliance Book (Bear Tribe Publishing, 1977); The Medicine Wheel Book (Prentice-Hall, 1980); Sun Bear: The Path of Power (Bear Tribe Publishing, 1983); Black Dawn, Bright Day (Simon & Schuster, 1991); Dancing the Wheel (Simon & Schuster, 1991).

*SUNCHILD, JOHN (Chippewa-Cree)
(tribal chairperson)
Affiliation: Chippewa-Cree Business Committee, Rocky Boy's Reservation, Rocky Boy Route, Box 544, Box Elder, MT 59521 (406) 395-4282.

SUNSHINE, RON
(Indian band chief)
Affiliation: Sturgeon Lake Indian Band, Box 757, Valleyview, AB, Can. T0H 3N0 (403) 524-3307.

SUPERNAW, KATHLEEN RAE
(Creek/Munsee) 1949-
(attorney)
Born October 15, 1949, Hominy, Okla. *Education*: Northeastern Oklahoma A & M College, AA, 1969; Central State University, BS, 1971; Antioch University, MA, 1986; University of Oklahoma Law School, JD, 1992. *Principal occupation*: Attorney. *Address*: P.O. Box 1935, Tulsa, OK 74101 (918) 581-7502 (work). *Affiliations*: Indian Tribes Community Development Association (past president), Oklahoma City, 1984-88; American Indian Law Review (editor in chief),

Norman, OK, 1991-92; U.S. Dept. of the Interior, Office of the Field Solicitor, Tulsa, OK, 1993-. *Other professional posts*: Attorney, Pitchlynn, Odom, Morse & Ritter; research associate, University of Oklahoma-Center for American Indian Law & Policy; Rural Development Fellow, University of California, Davis, CA, 1985-86. *Community activities*: Recruitment of Indians to go to law school; work in Indian communities to encourage Indian kids to complete education and establish goals; support Indian arts and crafts fairs and promotions. *Memberships*: Oklahoma Indian Bar Association; American Indian Bar Association; American Indian Heritage Center. *Awards, honors*: Outstanding Second Year Editor, American Indian Law Review; recipient of the Gretchen Harris, Dean's, and Jone-Givens Scholarships; Joseph Parick Outstanding Native American Student Award. *Interests*: "Environmental and Indian law; Indian history and Indian studies; education in general; Indian tribal planning and development; traveled to many western U.S. tribes. Major employment before law school was working for several Indian tribes as the drifter of planning. *Published work*: Co-authored with Rennard Strickland, "Back to the Future: A Proposed Model Tribal Act to Protect Native Cultural Heritage (Arkansas Law Review, 1993).

*SURIANO, PATRICK
(school principal)
Affiliation: Kaibeto Boarding School, Kaibeto, AZ 86053 (602) 673-3480.

*SUTEER, BEVERLY S. (Ojibwe) 1950-
(American Indian advisor)
Born April 16, 1950, Cape Girardeau, Mo. *Education*: University of Illinois, 1968-69; Eastern Illinois University, BA, 1989, MS, 1991. *Principal occupation*: American Indian advisor. *Home address*: 2312 S. Preston, Salt Lake City, UT 84106 (801) 581-8151 (work). *Affiliation*: University of Utah, Salt Lake City, UT, 1991-. *Community activities*: Board of Directors, Indian Walk-In Center, Salt Lake City; Utah InterTribal Veterans Association Auxiliary; Heber Valley Pow Wow Committee. *Memberships*: Utah Coalition for the Advancement of Minorities in Higher Education; National Indian Education Society; American College Personnel Association; Phi Delta Kappa Honorary Education Society. *Awards, honors*: Outstanding Community Service Award, Salt Lake City Indian Community, 1992. *Interests*: "Have participated in numerous workshops & presentations which address the recruitment & retention of American Indians in higher education."

*SWALLEY, LARRY (Oglala Lakota Sioux)
(radio station program director)
Affiliation: KILI - 90.1 FM, Oglala Lakota Sioux Tribe, P.O. Box 150, Porcupine, SD 57772 (605) 867-5002.

*SWAN, ANITA L. (Yakima)
(school supt.)
Affiliation: Yakima Tribal School, P.O. Box 151, Toppenish, WA 98948 (509) 865-5121.

SWAN, CLAIRE (Kenaitze)
(tribal chairperson; health director)
Affiliation: Kenaitze Indian Tribe Executive Committee/Tribal Council & Health Center, Box 988, Kenai, AK 99611 (907) 283-3633.

SWAN, JAMES A. (Canadian Metis) 1943-
(author/events producer)
Born February 25, 1943, Trenton, Mich. *Education*: University of Michigan, BS, 1965; MS (Resource Planning), 1967; 1967-69 (Environmental Psychology). *Principal occupation*: Author/ events producer. *Home address*: P.O. Box 637, Mill Valley, CA 94942. *Affiliations*: President, Institute for the Study of Natural Systems, Mill Valley, 1987-; associate professor, California Institute of Integrated Studies, San Francisco, CA, 1987-. *Membership*: American Bison Association. *Awards, honors*: Homer N. Calver Lecturer for American Public Health Association; California State Assembly Award of Recognition; Xi Sigma Forestry Honorary; Phi Sigma Biological Sciences Honorary. *Interests*: Cross-cultural psychology and applications to ecology; producer of concerts, symposiums, and conferences; actor/musician. *Biographical sources*: Who's Who in the West; "James Swan: On Aligning Oneself With Sacred Places" Wingspan. *Published works*: Sacred Places (Bear & Co., 1990); The Power of Place (Quest, 1991); Nature As Teacher and Healer (Villard-Random House, 1992).

***SWAN, JOSEPH, Sr. (Inupiat)**
(village president)
Affiliation: Native Village of Kivalina, P.O. Box 50051, Kivalina, AK 99750 (907) 645-2153.

SWAN, RAYMOND
(Indian band chief)
Affiliation: Lake Manitoba Indian Band, Vogar, Manitoba, Canada R0C 3C0 (204) 768-3492.

***SWENSON, CHRIS**
(project director)
Affiliation: First Nations Financial Project, 2016 NE 3rd Ave., Camas, WA 98607 (206) 834-7716.

SWIFTWOLF, GERALD
(Indian band chief)
Affiliation: Moosomin Indian Band, Box 45, Cochin, Saskatchewan, Canada S0M 0L0 (306) 386-2014.

SWIMMER, ROSS O. (Oklahoma Cherokee) 1943-
(president/CEO-Cherokee Nation Industries)
Born October 26, 1943, Oklahoma City, Okla. *Education*: University of Oklahoma, BA, 1965; University of Oklahoma School of Law, J.D., 1967. *Principal occupation*: President & CEO of Cherokee Nation Industries. *Affiliations*: Law partner, Hansen, Peterson & Thompkins, Oklahoma City, Okla., 1967-72; general counsel, 1972-75, principal chief, 1975-85, Cherokee Nation of Oklahoma, Tahlequah, OK; executive vice president, 1974-75, president, 1975-85, First National Bank in Tahlequah, OK; Co-chairman, Presidential Commission on Indian Reservation Economies (a panel of tribal leaders appointed to seek ways to help tribes improve economic conditions), 1983-84; assistant secretary, U.S. Department of the Interior, Bureau of Indian Affairs, 1951 Constitution Ave., NW, Washington, DC, 1985-89; developed an Indian law practice for law firm of Hall, Harswick, Gale, Golden and Nelson, Tulsa, OK, 1989-92; president/CEO of Cherokee Nation Industries, Inc., Stillwell, OK, 1992-. *Other professional posts*: Director on several boards, including the University of Tulsa, Gilcrease Museum and the Oklahoma Medical Research Foundation; coun-

sel to Hall, Estill, Hardwick, Gable, Golden and Nelson. *Community activities*: Boy Scouts of America in Eastern Oklahoma (executive committee); Cherokee National Historical Society (past president); Tahlequah Planning and Zoning Commission (former chairman); Eastern Oklahoma Indian Health Advisory Board (secretary-treasurer); Inter-Tribal Council of the Five Civilized Tribes (advisory board, director). *Memberships*: Oklahoma Bar Association; American Bar Association; Oklahoma Historical Society; Oklahoma Industrial Development Commission. *Awards, honors*: Honorary Doctoral Degree, Phillips University, Enid, OK; Distinguished Service Award, University of Oklahoma, Norman; Distinguished Service Citation, U.S. Dept. of Interior, 1989. *Interests*: USIA sponsored speaking tour of 14 cities in Germany to discuss issues related to the American Indian. Interior Secretary Donald Hodel said of Swimmer, "He combines a solid knowledge of tribal and Indian affairs with understanding and skill in modern business management. Swimmer has frequently expressed his views that Indian tribes should be less dependent on the federal government." When nominated for the position of Assistant Secretary, Swimmer said of President Reagan: "I know he is committed to an Indian policy that supports tribal self-determination, which is something I have worked for during my ten years at the Cherokee Nation."

SWISHER, KAREN GAYTON
(Standing Rock Sioux) 1943-
(professor)
Born April 3, 1943, Fort Yates, N.D. *Education*: Northern State University, BS, 1964, MS, 1974; University of North Dakota, EdD, 1981. *Principal occupation*: Professor. *Home address*: 2139 West Emelita, Mesa, AZ 85202 (602) 965-6292 (work). *Affiliations*: Teacher & principal, Bureau of Indian Affairs, 1967-77; assistant professor of education, University of Utah, Salt Lake City, 1982-85; associate professor/director of CIE, Arizona State University, Tempe, AZ, 1985-. *Other professional post*: Editor, "Journal of American Indian Education," Center for Indian Education, Arizona State University, Tempe, AZ. *Memberships*: American Educational Research Association (American Indian/Alaska Native Education Special Interest Group Chair, 1984-86, 1987-89); National Indian Education Association; Association for Supervision & Curriculum Development; American Anthropological Association; Council on Anthropology & Education. *Awards, honors*: Sioux Award, highest honor of University of North Dakota Alumni Association for professional career accomplishments, 1989; Early Contribution Award, AERA Committee on the Role and Status of Minorities in Educational Research & Development, 1990. *Interests*: "Enjoy travels to American Indian reservations in lower 48 states and desire to travel to other countries to study indigenous people's participation in educational systems." *Published work*: Co-editor, Special Issues on Learning Styles (Center for Indian Education, Arizona State University, 1989).

SYNDER, FRED (Chippewa/Colville) 1951-
(director/consultant, editor/publisher)
Born March 8, 1951, Pennsylvania. *Education*: Rutgers University (2 years). *Principal occupation*: Director/consultant, National Native American Co-Operative, San Carlos, AZ. *Address*: P.O. Box 1000, San Carlos, AZ 85550 (602) 230-3399. *Other professional posts*: Editor/publisher,

Native American Directory--Alaska, Canada, U.S.; educator. *Community activities*: American Indian Market, monthly, Phoenix, Ariz. (sponsor); Pow Wow Attender for North America. *Awards, honors*: Blue Ribbon (3 years), Beadwork Competition, Heard Museum of Anthropology, Phoenix, AZ; numerous awards from Indian cultural programs, Title IV, Indian education, ethnic fairs. *Interests*: "Most of all my time is shared between directing the Co-Op (2,700 artisan members), distribution of Native American Directory (40,000 copies), traveling extensively throughout North America to Indian powwows, rodeos, craft shows and conventions, and establishing the first Watts Line American Indian Information Center and Chamber of Commerce." *Biographical sources*: Arizona Republic, Close Up feature article (May, 1984); Intertribal Enterprise, Close Up feature article (April, 1985); Navajo Times Today (May, 1985). *Published work*: Native American Directory--Alaska, Canada, U.S. (National Native American Co-Op, 1982 & 1992); Powwows: On the Red Road (Native American Co-Op, 1993).

SZABO, PAUL (Rosebud Sioux) 1947-
(high school art teacher)
Born December 26, 1947, Burke, S.D. *Education*: Southern State, 1966-70; Dakota State College, Madison, SD, 1970-71. *Principal occupation*: High school art teacher. *Address*: P.O. Box 906, Mission, SD 57555 (605) 856-4548. *Affiliations*: Art teacher, Todd County High School, Mission, SD, 1985-; Paul Szabo Studio, Mission, SD, 1975-. *Community activities*: Church leader; Boy Scouts. *Memberships*: National Education Association; South Dakota Education Association; TCEA. *Awards, honors*: Northern Plains Art Show - 2nd place, 2 years, honorable mention; Cultural Heritage Art Show - 1st place, metal work; Renwick Collection at the Smithsonian, Washington, D.C. *Interests*: "Metalworking and selling; travel. *Biographical sources*: Numerous newspaper articles.

T

***TABLOS, DERENTY**
(executive director)
Affiliation: Chugachmiut, 4201 Tudor Centre, Suite 210, Anchorage, AK 99508 (907) 562-4155.

TAH, ANDREW M. (Navajo)
(BIA agency supt. for education)
Affiliation: Chinle Agency, Bureau of Indian Affairs, P.O. Box 6003, Chinle, AZ 86503 (602) 674-5201 ext. 201.

TAH-BONE, GEORGE (Kiowa)
(attorney)
Affiliation: Oklahoma Indian Bar Association, P.O. Box 1062, Oklahoma City, OK 73101 (405) 521-5277. *Membership*: Oklahoma Indian Bar Assn. (committee chairperson-tribal courts).

TAHSUDA, MAX
(IHS-area tribal development)
Affiliation: Office of Tribal Development, Indian Health Service, Oklahoma Area Office, Indian Health Service, Five Corporate Plaza, 3625 NW 56th St., Oklahoma City, OK 73102 (405) 231-4796.

*TAKEN ALIVE, JESSE
(Standing Rock Sioux)
(tribal chairperson)
Affiliation: Standing Rock Sioux Tribe, P.O. Box E, Fort Yates, SD 58538 (701) 854-7231.

*TALAMANES, FRANK
(executive director)
Affiliation: Society for the Advancement of Chicanos & Native Americans in Science, Sinsheimer Labs, University of California, Santa Cruz, CA 95064 (408) 459-4272.

TALAMINI, THOMAS
(health director)
Affiliation: Claremore PHS Indian Hospital, W. Wil Rogers & Moore, Claremore, OK 74017 (918) 341-8430.

TALBOT, F. MEDICINE STORY
(Manitonquat) **(Wampanoag) 1929-**
(storyteller, teacher, author, lecturer)
Born July 17, 1929, Salem, Mass. *Education*: Cornell University, BA, 1954. *Principal occupation*: Storyteller, teacher, author, lecturer. *Address*: Mettanokit Outreach, Route 123, Greenville, NH 03048 (603) 878-2310. *Affiliation*: Co-director, Another Place, Inc., Greenville, NH, 1980- ; Mettanokit Outreach, Greenville, NH. *Other professional post*: Editor, Native Liberation Journal: Heritage. *Military service*: U.S. Army, 1951-53 (PFC). *Community activities*: Elder & spiritual/ceremonial leader of Assonet Wampanoag; Liberation Reference Person for Native American Counselors (Eastern Canada & U.S.); spiritual advisor to Native Prison Programs in New England (re-evaluation counselor & counseling teacher); Tribal Healing Council (co-founder); Massachusetts Center for Native American Awareness; Watuppa Wampanoag Reservation Improvement Committee; Indian Spiritual & Cultural Training Council, Inc. *Interests*: "Counselor & spiritual advisor to six Native Prison Circles in New England; storyteller; author/lecturer/workshop & seminar leader at schools, universities, religious, cultural, environmental, health, peace and other organizations throughout North America & Europe; former writer-poetry editor-illustrator-cartoonist with Akwesasne Notes; now edits The Talking Stick, newsletter of activities of Mettanokit Outreach, Prison Program & Assonet Wampanoag activities. *Biographical sources*: Profiles in Wisdom by Stephen McFadden; numerous articles in newspapers and magazines. *Published works*: Return to Creation (Bear Tribe, 1991); story in "Spinning Tales, Weaving Hope" (New Society, 1991); The Children of the Morning Light (Macmillan, 1994).

*TALGO, HARRISON, Sr. (Apache)
(tribal chairperson)
Affiliation: San Carlos Apache Tribal Council, P.O. Box 0, San Carlos, AZ 85550 (602) 475-2361.

TALL CHIEF, GEORGE EVES
(Sa-toa-enza) **(Osage) 1916-**
(former tribal chief, coach, teacher)
Born November 16, 1916, Arkansas City, Kans. *Education*: Central State College (Edmond, OK), BA, 1952; Pacific University (Forest Grove, OR), MA, 1957. *Principal occupation*: Former principal chief, Osage Tribe of Oklahoma. *Home address*: 8th & Park, Fairfax, OK 74637 (918) 642-5642. *Other professional posts*: Supt. of Lodge Pole Schools, Hayes, MT; principal of Crescent

& Fairfax Schools in Oklahoma; president, Indian Festival of Arts; coach & teacher. *Community activities*: Rotary Club; Chamber of Commerce; Quarterback Club; volunteer fireman. *Membership*: National Tribal Chairman's Association (chairman, 1982; vice president-Sergeant at Arms, 1990). *Awards, honors*: Iron Eyes Cody Peace Medal; Golden Glove Champion of Oklahoma (in college); Little All-American Coach of the Year in Pacific Coast Wrestling Conference. *Interests*: "My interests at the present time is to better the lot of the American Indian; sports; raise cattle, Appaloosa Show horses, karakul sheep & Yorkshire Terrier dogs since retirement. In earlier years, I rodeod - riding bulls & horses; roughnecked in the oil fields."

TALLMADGE, BERNADINE W. MINER
(Sitting in the Moonlight) **(Wisconsin Wineabgo) 1920-**
(owner/curator-Indian museum)
Born April 6, 1920, Necedah, Wisc. *Education*: High school. *Princpal occupation*: Owner/curator-Indian museum. *Home address*: N. River Rd., Wisconsin Dells, WI 53965 (608) 254-4006. *Affiliation*: Owner/curator, Winnebago Indian Museum, Wisconsin Dells, WI, 1953-. *Community activities*: Organized Dells Area Indian Club; presently on State Council on Aging, Tribal Council on Aging, and Tribal Personnel Committee, Wisconsin Winneabgo Tribe. *Awards, honors*: Attended Presidential Inaugural Parade in 1952 in full regalia; Mrs. Congeniality during competetion in Mrs. Wisconsin Pageant, 1961. *Interests*: Master beader of "neddle loom," sash weaving and applique.

TANNER, CLARA LEE 1905-
(professor emerita)
Born May 28, 1905, Biscoe, N.C. *Education*: University of Arizona, BA, 1927, MA (Archaeology), 1928. *Home address*: P.O. Box 40904, Tucson, AZ 85717. *Affiliation*: Instructor, 1928-35, assistant professor, 1935-57, associate professor, 1957-68, professor, 1968-78, professor emerita, 1978-, Dept. of Anthropology, University of Arizona, Tucson. *Other professional posts*: Editor, The Kiva, 1938, 1948; editorial advisory board, American Indian Art, and Indian America; numerous University of Arizona committees. *Community activities*: Cummings Publication Council; Southwest Indian Arts & Crafts Committee; Tucson Fine Arts Association; judging of grant applications for the National Endowment for the Humanities, National Science Foundation, and Wenner-Gren Foundation for Anthropological Research. *Memberships*: Southwest Association of Indian Affairs, Santa Fe, NM (life member); Arizona Archaeological and Historical Society, Tucson (life member); American Anthropological Association; American Ethnological Society; Society of American Archaeology; National Federation of Press Women; Phi Beta Kappa; Society of Sigma Xi; Delta Kappa Gamma (educational honorary); Arizona Academy of Science; Arizona Historical Society; Arizona Press Women; Society of Southwest Authors; Archaeological Society of New Mexico. *Awards, honors*: Sharlot Hall Award, 1985; LLD Honorary Doctor of Letters, University of Arizona, 1983; Tucson Panhellenic Athena Award for Professional Achievement, 1983; Mortar Board Hall of Fame, University of Arizona, 1977; University of Arizona Alumni Association Faculty Achievement Award, 1974; Faculty Recognition Award, Tucson Trade Bureau, 1972-73;

Woman of the Year, Arizona Press Women, 1971-72; 50th Anniversary Award of the Gallup Inter-Tribal Indian Ceremonial Association, 1971; University of Arizona, 75th Anniversary Award, 1960; One of Outstanding Tucson Women of 1957; Arizona Press Women First Awards for books written, 1960- (the latest for Apache Indian Baskets, 1984); National Federation of Press Women awards, 1969- (the latest for Apache Indian Baskets, 1984); Society of Southwestern Authors awards; Border Regional Library Award, 1984 for Apache Indian Baskets; 1988 & 1989 Centennial Medallion Awards by University of Arizona. *Interests*: "Public lectures, 1928 to present, predominantly on the subject of Indians of the Southwest and their arts & crafts, to organizations throughout Arizona and in New Mexico, Colorado, California, Texas, Florida and Kansas; lectures to school classes throughout southern Arizona; craft judging; travel." *Biographical sources*: Who's Who in America, Who's Who of American Women; Who's Who in the West; American Men and Women of Science; Contemporary Authors. *Published works*: Southwest Indian Painting (1957); Southwest Indian Craft Arts (1968); Southwest Indian Painting, A Changing Art (1973); Prehistoric Southwest Craft Arts (1978); Apache Indian Baskets (1982); Indian Baskets of the Southwest (1983).

*TANNER, DENNIS
(museum president)
Affiliation: Ataloa Lodge Museum, Bacone College, 2299 Old Bacone Rd., Muskogee, OK 74403 (918) 683-4581 ext. 283.

TANNER HELEN HORNBECK 1916-
(consultant historian, expert witness)
Born July 5, 1916, Northfield, Minn. *Education*: Swarthmore College, BA, 1937; University of Florida, MA, 1949; University of Michigan, PhD, 1961. *Principal occupation*: Consultant historian, expert witness. *Home address*: 5178 Crystal Dr. Beulah, MI 49617 (616) 882-4969. *Affiliation*: Lecturer in Extension Service, University of Michigan, 1961-74; director, Atlas of Great Lakes Indian History Project, 1976-81, research associate, 1981-, The Newberry Library, 60 W. Walton St., Chicago, IL 60610. *Other professional post*: Expert witness in cases before the Indian Claims Commission, and Court of Claims, as well as state and circuit courts, 1962-82; assistant director, Center for Continuing Education of Women, The University of Michigan, 1965-68; consultant historian for legal cases involving Indian treaties, consultant for historical and archaeological exhibits. *Community activities*: Commission on Indian Affairs, State of Michigan, (member, 1965-69). *Memberships*: American Historical Association; Society for the History of Discoveries; Organization of American Historians; Chicago Map Society Conference on Latin American History; American Society for Ethnohistory (president, 1983-84); Minnesota Historical Society; Historical Society of Michigan; Florida Historical Society. *Awards, honors*: Grantee, 1976, National Endowment for the Humanities (for Atlas of Great Lakes Indian History project); Wheeler-Voegelin Book Award, American Society for Ethnohistory, 1988; NEH Independent Scholars, Fellowship, 1989; ACLS Grant, 1990. *Interests*: "Special interest in mapping & geographic background of Indian history-location of towns, hunting camps, fishing stations, canoe and travel routes; inter-tribal contacts." *Biographical sources*: Who's Who in

Biographies

America; Directory of American Scholars; Who's Who of American Women; Who's Who of the Midwest; Historians of Latin America in the U.S.; Contemporary Authors, Vol. 61-64. *Published works*: Zespedes in East Florida, 1784-1790 (University of Miami Press, 1963; U. of Florida Press, 1989); Territory of the Caddo Tribe of Oklahoma. Caddo Indians IV (Garland Publishing, 1974); The Ojibwas: A Critical Bibliography (Indiana U. Press, 1976); editor, Atlas of Great Lakes Indian History (U. of Oklahoma Press, 1987); The Ojibwas (Chelsea House, 1992).

TANTAQUIDGEON, GLADYS (Mohegan) 1899-
(museum owner/director)
Born June 15, 1899, New London, Conn. *Education*: University of Pennsylvania. *Principal occupation & address*: Owner/director (61 years), Tantaquidgeon Indian Museum, 1819 Norwich-New London Tpke., Uncasville, CT 06382 (203) 848-9145. *Other professional posts*: Surveyor of New England tribes for the Bureau of Indian Affairs; field specialist in Indian arts & crafts (area served-Northern Plains), U.S. Dept. of the Interior, Washington, DC. *Memberships*: Archaeological Society of Connecticut; American Indian Archaeological Institute. *Awards, honors*: Honorary member, Alpha Kappa Gamma; Deconess Emeritus, Mohegan Congregational Church, Uncasville, CT; Honorary Doctorate of Letters from The University of Connecticut, 1987. *Published works*: Mohegan Medicine Practices and Folk Beliefs (Bureau of American Ethnology, 1928); Notes on the Gay Head Indians of Massachusetts (Museum of the American Indian, 1930); Newly Discovered Basketry of the Wampanoag Indians of Massachusets, 1930; Lake St. John Medicine Lore, 1932; Delaware Indian Designs, 1933; Uses of Plants Among the Indians of Southern New England, 1940; Delaware Indian Art Designs, 1950); Mohegan, 1947); Folk Medicine in the Delaware and Related Algonkian Indians (Historical Commission, Harrisburg, PA, 1972).

TAPAHE, LOREN (Navajo) 1953-
(publishing)
Born September 17, 1953, Fort Defiance, Ariz. *Education*: Brigham Young University, AA, 1974. *Principal occupation*: General manager, Navajo Time Publishing, Window Rock, AZ, 1977-. *Home address*: P.O. Box 481, Window Rock, AZ 86515. *Other professional post*: Assistant director, Office of Business Management, The Navajo Tribe, Window Rock, Ariz. *Interests*: Journalism; advertising; photography; river expeditions; personal journal composition; travel--Northwestern tribes of North America, Southwestern tribes, Europe.

TATEM, ALEX
(school principal)
Affiliation: Chevak IRA Contract School, Chevak, AK 99563 (907) 858-7713.

*TATSEY, DEBBIE
(health outreach worker)
Affiliation: Native American Services Agency, Missoula Indian Center, 2300 Regent St. #A, Missoula, MT 59801 (406) 329-3373.

*TATSEY-MURRAY, CAROL
(college president)
Affiliation: President, Blackfeet Community College, P.O. Box 819, Browning, MT 59417 (406) 338-5441.

*TATSUDA, WINIFRED
(director of admissions)
Affiliation: Hawaiian Studies Program, University of Hawaii at Hilo, 523 W. Lanikuala St., Hilo, HI 96720 (808) 933-3414.

TAVENNER, TERRI (Wabgoneese)1947-
(cultural curriculum developer)
Born January 23, 1947, Seattle, Wash. *Education*: Antioch University, BA, 1979. *Principal occupation*: Cultural curriculum developer. *Address*: P.O. Box 236, LaPush, WA 98350 (206) 374-6163. *Affiliation*: Coordinate Language & Culture Program Development, Quileute Tribal School, LaPush, WA, 1974-. *Community activities*: Various Indian education curriculum advisory boards, projects; Clallam County Heritage Advisory Board. Membership: Washington State Indian Education Association. *Awards, honors*: Indian Education Showcase of Excellence Award, U.S. Dept. of Education, 1989. *Interests*: "Personally and profesionally committed to preservation and protection of indigenous sacred site and practices; and revival of the Northwest tribes; canoe tradition-embarked on a cedar dugout canoe journey from LaPush, WA to Bella Bela, British Columbia, Canada in 1993. *Published works*: Editor, Manual for Building a Big House & Canoes, 1990, by David Forlines; coauthored with David Forlines & Joe Karchsey, Medicinal Plants of Northwest Indigenous Peoples (OSU Dept. of Forestry, 1992).

*TAYLOR, ALLEN R.
(center director)
Affiliation: Center for the Study of Native Languages of the Plains & Southwest, University of Colorado, Dept. of Linguistics, Campus Box 295, Boulder, CO 80309 (303) 492-2748.

TAYLOR, BANNING (Luiseno)
(tribal chairperson)
Affiliation: Los Coyotes Band of Mission Indians, P.O. Box 249, Warner Springs, CA 92086 (619) 782-3269.

*TAYLOR, CHARLES (United Lumbee) 1917-
(furniture repairer, toy maker)
Born August 31, 1917, Brockton, Mass. *Education*: High school. *Address & Affiliation*: The Amber Lantern-Antiques, SR#1 Box 70, McArthur, CA 96056 (916) 336-6656. *Community activities*: Board of Directors, Fort Crook Historical Society, Fall River Mills, CA; treasurer, Fall River Chamber of Commerce; Holds United Lumbee Tribal beading classes 12 weeks each year since 1985; Charles makes adjustable beading looms for the students on order. *Membership*: United Lumbee nation's Deer Clan. *Awards, honors*: Nominated Citizen of the Year, 1993, Fall River Mills, CA.

TAYLOR, DAVE
(Indian band chief)
Affiliation: Hornepayne Indian Band, Box 465, Spruce St., Homepayne, ON P0M 1Z0 (807) 868-2039.

*TAYLOR, FRANK
(school supt.)
Affiliation: Mandaree Day School, P.O. Box 488, Mandaree, ND 58757 (701) 759-3311.

TAYLOR , GERALD W.
(BIA agency supt.)
Affiliation: Seattle Support Center, Bureau of Indian Affairs, P.O. Box 80947, Seattle, WA 98104 (206) 764-3328.

*TAYLOR, HELEN R. *(Burnst Stick)* (United Lumbee/Delaware) 1925-
(real estate broker, antique dealer)
Born December 7, 1925, Los Angeles County, Calif. *Home address*: 545-205 Old Hwy. Rd., Pittville, CA 96056 (916) 336-6656. *Affiliation*: The Amber Lantern (antiques & collectibles), Pittville, CA, 1987-. *Community activities*: Fall River Valley Chamber of Commerce (past president); holds United Lumbee Tribal beading classes 12 weeks each year since 1985. *Membership*: United Lumbee Nation's Deer Clan; United Lumbee Nation's Grand Council Elder, 1988. *Awards, honors*: Business Woman of the Year & Women of Achievement, Business & Professional Women of Los Angeles County; Planning Commissioner, Baldwin Park, CA, with resolution in her honor. Baldwin Park Chamber of Commerce, Director of Committees. *Biographical source*: Section in United Lumbee Deer Clan Cook Book, 1988.

TAYLOR, JOHN L.
(school principal)
Affiliation: Chi-Ch'il-Tah/Jones Ranch Community School, P.O. Box 278, Vanderwagen, NM 87326 (505) 778-5573.

TAYLOR, JONATHAN L. (Eastern Cherokee)
(tribal chief)
Affiliation: Eastern Band of Cherokee Indians, P.O. Box 455, Cherokee, NC 28719 (704) 497-2771.

*TAYLOR, LEWIS (St. Croix Chippewa)
(tribal chairperson)
Affiliation: St. Croix Council, P.O. Box 287, Hertel, WI 54845 (715) 349-2195.

TAYLOR, PETER S. 1937-
(lawyer)
Born June 9, 1937, St. Paul, Minn. *Education*: Washburn University, BA, 1959; George Washington University, School of Law, LLB, 1963. *Principal occupation*: Lawyer. *Home address*: 1819 N. Lincoln St., Arlington, VA 22207. *Affiliations*: Co-director, Indian Civil Rights Task Force, Office of the Solicitor, Dept. of the Interior, 1971-75 (projects were the compilation of the Opinions of the Solicitor on Indian affairs; updating Kappler's, Indian Affairs, Laws & Treaties; development of a Model Procedural Code for use in courts of Indian offenses; and revision of Felix Cohen's, Handbook of Federal Indian Law); chairman, Task Force on Revision and Codification of Federal Indian Law, with the American Indian Policy Review Commission, 1975-77 (upon completion of the Task Force report, served on the editorial board of the Commission in preparation of the AIPRC report; special counsel, 1977-80, general counsel, 1981-85, staff director, 1985-86; senior counsel, 1987- Senate Select Committee on Indian Affairs. *Memberships*: District of Columbia Bar Association; Virginia State Bar Association. *Published works*: Opinions of the Solicitor, Dept. of the Interior, Indian Affairs (U.S. Government, 1976); editor, Kappler's, Indian Affairs, Laws and Treaties (revision, U.S. Government, 1976); Development of Tripartite Jurisdiction in Indian Country (Kansas Law Review, 1974).

*TAYLOR, REBECCA T. (*Clear Sky*)
(Lac Courte Oreilles Ojibwe)
(educator)

Born May 2, 1960 in Chicago, Ill. *Education*: Lac Courte Oreilles Ojibwe Community College, Hayward, WI, A.A. Native American Studies. *Home address*: Route 5, Box 5223, Hayward, WI 54843 (715) 634-8401. *Membership*: Honor the Earth Education Foundation (Board of Directors, 1980). *Awards, honors*: Inward Journey for Outstanding Service from L.C.D. College, 1991; Cultural Award in recognition of cultural contribution as a role model. *Biographical source*: "The Color of Our Song," educational video, 28 minutes, University of Eau Claire, WI.

TAYLOR, RHONDA HARRIS
(educator)

Affiliations: University of Oklahoma, School of Library & Information Science, 401 W. Brooks, Room 120, Norman, OK 73019, 1990-; American Indian Library Association (past president, 1985-90).

TAYLOR, SARAH
(museum director)

Affiliation: Plains Indians & Pioneer Museum, P.O. Box 1167, Woodward, OK 73802 (405) 256-6136.

*TAYLOR, URSHEL (*Owl Ear*) (Pima-Ute)
1937-
(artist)

Born May 31, 1937, Phoenix, Ariz. *Education*: High school. *Principal occupation*: Artist. *Home address*: 2901 W. Sahuaro Divide, Tucson, AZ 85741 (602) 297-4456. *Affiliation*: Owner, The Owl Ear Gallery, Tucson, AZ, 1990-. *Other professional posts*: Consultant to Tucson Indian Center & LFC, Inc.; member of board of directors, Smoke Signals (new paper). *Past professional posts*: Bureau of Indian Affairs, Intermountain Inter-Tribal School (art teacher), 1963-79 (Director of Cultural Arts Program, 1971-79); art teacher, Utah State University; owner, Indian Craft Shop, Brigham City, Utah, 1979-89. *Military service*: U.S. Marine Corps (Sgt.) 1956-63. *Community activities*: Tucson International Mariachi Conference. *Memberships*: Pima Salt River Community Indian Tribe; Indian Arts & Crafts Association. *Awards, honors*: 9 first place awards from 1984-90, then stopped entering contests. *Interests*: Urshel's years of study & research into historical Indian culture & crafts has served to reinforce his dedication to the authentic presentation of the American Indian. He says, "I always try to capture the dignity & majesty of what my people have been and what they continue to be today." *Published works*: Writes a column for Smoke Signals, Native American paper.

TAYLOR, VIRGINIA (Cherokee) 1922-
(graphic & commercial artist)

Born September 15, 1922, Los Angeles, Calif. *Education*: Art Center School (Los Angeles, CA). *Principal occupation*: Graphic and commercial artist. *Home address*: 4754 Hwy. 20 NW, Albany, OR 97321. *Affiliation*: Staff artist, Office of Publications, Oregon State University, art coordinator & designer, Oregon State University Press, 1963-67; assistant professor of art, Oregon State University, 1966, 1976; graphic designer and assistant to museum coordinator, Marine Science Laboratory, Dept. of Oceanography, Oregon State University, Corvallis, 1969-. *Other*

professional posts: Taught Indian history and crafts, Linn Benton Community College; taught basic design, Oregon State University, 1975. *Interests*: Jury Indian art exhibitions; (I) frequently speak to civic, school and other organizations on Indian art. Numerous awards, joint and one-man exhibitions; work in private and public collections.

TAYLOR, WILLIAM E., Jr. (Tunikshiuti) 1927-
(archaeologist; museum director)

Born November 21, 1927, Toronto, Ontario, Can. *Education*: University of Illinois, MA, 1954; University of Michigan, PhD, 1956. *Principal occupation*: Archaeologist; museum director. *Home address*: 509 Piccadilly Ave., Ottawa, ON K1Y 0H7 (613) 729-7488. *Affiliation*: Archaeological Survey of Canada, Canadian Museum of Civilization, 100 Laurier St., Box 3100, Hill, PQ J8X 42.

*TEEPLE, SHARON L.
(executive director)

Affiliation: Inter-Tribal Council of Michigan, 405 E. Easterday Ave., Sault Ste. Marie, MI 49783 (906) 632-6896.

TELLER-ATCITTY, RENA L. (Navajo) 1938-
(education specialist)

Born March 3, 1938, Rehoboth, N.M. *Education*: Northern Arizona University, BS, 1961; University of New Mexico, MA, 1978. *Principal occupation*: Education specialist. *Home address*: 3215 U.S. Hwy. 64, Suite 4148, Waterflow, NM 87421 (505) 368-5927 (home) 598-6922 (office). *Affiliation*: Principal, BIA, Shiprock Agency, Nenahnezad, NM, 1987-; Education specialist, BIA, Shiprock Agency, Shiprock, NM. *Other professional post*: Teacher, BIA, Public Schools, Headstart and Rough Rock School (17 years). *Community activities*: President, Shiprock, Aztec, Farmington Federal Employees Credit Union, 1982-84. *Awards, honors*: Navajo Headstart Teacher of the Year, 1966, 1967; Special Act Award from BIA, 1979; Outstanding Performance as Education Specialist and School Principal, 1985-91. *Published work*: Donkey Sings (Rough Rock School, 1969.

TELLER, RENA L.
(school principal)

Affiliation: Nenahnezad Boarding School, P.O. Box 337, Fruitland, NM 87416 (505) 598-6922.

*TEMPLE, JOHN (*di de yos gi*) (Cherokee) 1929-
(retired teacher; consultant)

Born August 7, 1929, Norwood, Ohio. *Education*: Salmon P. Chase (Cincinnati, OH), BS, 1955; University of Cincinnati, MEd., 1969. *Principal occupation*: Retired teacher; consultant. *Home address*: 2565 Villa Lane, Cincinnati, OH 45208 (513) 871-8886. *Affiliation*: Teacher of vocational education, Cincinnati Public Schools (30 years). *Other professional post*: Consultant, The Learning Center, Communications for Teachers & Education, Cincinnati (current). *Community activities*: Charter member, North American Indian Council of Greater Cincinnati, 1970- (past chairman & editor of its monthly newsletter "Talking Leaves"); current project, "Electronic Bulletin Board Service for Educators in Greater Cincinnati," (promoting technology in communications for teachers & education). *Interests*: "Native American (indigenous) Indian research; Cherokee language, cultural & ceremonial. and development of curriculum for students

to appreciate the vast expanse of our American cultural diversity. To network Native American Indian organizations so that they may share language, arts, cultural and events with each other or educators."

TENEQUER, BOB
(center vice-president)

Affiliation: American Indian Society of Washington, DC Area, P.O. Box 6431, Falls Church, VA 22040 (703) 914-0548.

*TERRANCE, CINDY (St. Regis Mohawk)
(editor)

Affiliation: "The People's Voice," Kanienkehaka Territory, P.o. Box 216, Hogansburg, NY 13655 (518) 358-3022.

TESTAWICH, DON
(Indian band chief)

Affiliation: Duncan's Indian Band, Box 148, Brownvale, Alberta, Canada T0H 0H0 (403) 597-3777.

TETREAULT, TERRY A.
(editor)

Affiliation: Sho-Ban News, Shoshone-Bannock Tribal Council, P.O. Box 900, Fort Hall, ID 83203 (208) 238-3887/8.

TEWA, RICK, Jr.
(executive director)

Affiliation: Native Americans for Community Action, Inc., Flagstaff Indian Center, 2717 N. Steves Blvd., Suite 11, Flagstaff, AZ 86004 (602) 526-2968.

*TEYSEN, KENNETH
(museum CEO)

Affiliation: Teysen's Woodland Indian Museum, PO. Box 399, Mackinaw City, MI 49701 (616) 436-7011.

THEISZ, R.D. (*Wicuwa*) 1941-
(professor)

Born May 4, 1941, Yugoslavia. *Education*: Queens College, B.A., 1964; Middlebury College, MA, 1965; New York University, PhD, 1972. *Principal occupation*: Professor. *Home address*: 213 Vermont, Spearfish, SD 57783 (605) 642-6247 (work). Center of Indian Studies, Black Hills State University, Spearfish, SD 57783. *Affiliations*: Professor, Sinte Gleska College, Rosebud, SD, 1972-77; professor, College of Arts & Humanities, 1977-, Center of Indian Studies, 1983-88, Black Hills State University, Spearfish, SD. *Memberships*: Modern Language Association; South Dakota Indian Education Association; National Council of Teachers of English; MELUS (Multi-Ethnic Literature of the U.S.); Porcupine Singers (traditional Lakota singing group). *Awards, honors*: 1972 Excellence in Scholarship Award, NYU; 1981 Special Contribution to Education, South Dakota Indian Education Association. *Interests*: Comparative literature and education; Native American cultural history, especially literature, music, dance, and art; cross cultural education. *Published works*: Buckskin Tokens (Sinte Gleska College, 1974); Songs and Dances of the Lakota (Sinte Gleska College, 1976); Perspectives on Teaching Indian Literature (Black Hills State University, 1977); Lakota Art Is An American Art: Readings in Traditional and Contemporary Sioux Art (Black Hills State University, 1985); Standing in the Light, with S. Young Bear (University of Nebraska Press, 1994).

THOMAS, ANDREW BENEDICT
(Indian band chief)
Affiliation: Esquimalt Indian Band, 1113A Admirals Rd., Victoria, British Columbia, Canada (604) 381-7861.

*THOMAS, BERNIE
(school system chairperson)
Affiliation: Lummi Tribal School System, 2530 Kwina Rd., Bellingham, WA 98225 (206) 647-6251.

THOMAS, EDWARD K. (Tlingit & Haida) 1941-
(council president)
Born September 21, 1941, Craig, Alaska. *Education*: University of Alaska, Fairbanks, B.S., 1963; Penn State University, M.A. Educational Administration, 1965. *Principal occupation*: Council president. *Home address*: 3450 Meander Way, Juneau, AK 99801 (907) 789-2929; 585-1432 (work). *Affiliation*: Tlingit/Haida Central Council, Juneau, AK, 1984-. *Other professional post*: Education counselor, teacher. *Community activities*: Former chairperson, president, member of various Indian corporations in Alaska; delegate, National Congress of American Indians (National Tribal Advocacy Organization); delegate, Alaska Federation of Natives (State-wide Native Representative Organization). *Awards, honors*: Alaska Teaching Certificate, Type A; Alaska School Administrator's Certificate; Ketchikan Native Citizen of the Year, 1978; T&H Citizen of the Year, 1991.

THOMAS, FLORENCE (Mewuk) 1947-
(director-Indian center)
Born November 26, 1947, Rural Diamond Springs, Calif. *Education*: D.Q. University, 1972-74; National University (Sacramento, CA), BBA, 1989. *Principal occupation*: Director, Indian center. *Home address*: 5120 Pony Express Trail, Camino, CA 95709 (916) 626-3284 (work). *Affiliations*: Coordinator, El Dorado/Amador Counties Indian Education, Title V Program, Placerville, CA, 1976-86; administrative assistant, Chapa-De Indian Health Program, Inc., Auburn, CA, 1989; director, Chapa-De Indian Education Center, El Dorado, CA, 1990-. *Memberships*: California Indian Educationnn Association; National Indian Education Association; El Dorado/Amador Counties Indian Education Program (Parent Advisory Committee); National University Alumni.

THOMAS, FREDERICK R. (Kickapoo) 1946-
(former tribal chairperson)
Born February 21, 1946, Horton, Kan. *Education*: Haskell Indian Junior College, AA, 1966. *Principal occupation*: Tribal chairperson. *Home address*: Route 1, Horton, KS 66439 (913) 486-2131. *Other professional post*: Chairperson, Kansas Service Unit, Health Advisory Board. *Military service*: U.S. Army, 1966-68. *Community activities*: Powhattan Precinct (past board member); Kickapoo Housing Authority (past president); community fundraising projects; community food and clothing bank (founding member); Horton Chamber of Commerce; Horton City Commissioner for Economic Development. *Memberships*: National Tribal Chairman's Association; American Legion; Kickapoo Chapter, Lions International; National Indian Gaming Association (treasurer). *Awards, honors*: Goodyear--Tire Builder of the Year. *Interests*: Member of Delaware Singers; enjoys hunting and fishing, farming, traveling.

*THOMAS, JACOB E. *(Ha dajihgrenitha')*
(Cayuga) 1922-
(consultant)
Born January 6, 1922, Six Nations Reserve-Grand River Territory. *Education*: Native Language Instructors Diploma, 1982. *Home address*: Six Nations Reserve, R.R. #1, Wilsonville, Ontario N0E 1Z0, Canada. *Affiliations*: Trent University, Peterborough, Ontario (assistant professor on Iroquois Culture, Dept. of Native Studies, 1975-91; professor emeritus, 1991-); instructor on Iroquois Culture & Traditions, Mohawk College (Hagersville, ON), 1985-91; founder & vice chair, Iroquoian Institute, Wilsonville, ON, 1986-93; founder, Jake Thomas Learning Centre, Wilsonville, ON, 1993-. *Other professional posts*: Condoled Cayuga Chief, Sandpiper Clan; Board of Governors, McMaster University, Hamilton, ON, 1992-96. *Interests*: Writes & speaks fluent Cayuga, Onondaga, Mohawk and understands Oneida & Seneca. Preservation of the North American Indian culture; instructs singing & dancing. Mr. Thomas is a foremost authority on Iroquoian culture, and is an Iroquois elder.

*THOMAS, JAMES, JR., M.D.
(clinical director)
Affiliation: Inscription House PHS Indian Health Center, Inscription House, AZ 86054 (602) 672-2611.

*THOMAS, JOHN C.B. (Eastern Creek)
(tribal chairperson)
Affiliation: Florida Tribe of Eastern Creeks, P.O. Box 3028, Bruce, FL 32455 (904) 835-2078.

*THOMAS, JOHN G., JR.
(director-IHS center)
Affiliation: Ketchikan PHS Alaska Native Health Center, 3289 Tongass Ave., Ketchikan, AK 99901 (907) 225-6135.

THOMAS, JOHN L.
(school principal)
Affiliation: Moencopi Day School, P.O. Box 185, Tuba City, AZ 86045 (602) 283-5361.

*THOMAS, KIM M.
(Indian affairs specialist)
Affiliation: New York State Dept. of Social Services, Bureau of Indian Affairs, General Donovan State Office Bldg., 125 Main St., Room 471, Buffalo, NY 14203 (716) 847-3123.

THOMAS, LEO
(Indian band chief)
Affiliation: Pelican Lake Indian Band, Box 9, Leoville, SK, Canada S0J 1N0 (306) 984-2313.

*THOMAS, MARY V. (Pima-Maricopa)
(tribal council governor)
Affiliation: Gila River Indian Community Council, P.O. Box 97, Sacaton, AZ 85247 (602) 562-3311.

THOMAS, ROBERT E.
(Indian band chief)
Affiliation: Nanaimo Indian Band, 1145 Totem Rd., Nanaimo, British Columbia, Canada V9R 1H1 (604) 753-3481.

THOMAS, RONALD D
(health director)
Affiliation: Towaoc PHS Indian Health Center, Towaoc, CO 81334 (303) 565-4441.

THOMAS, THELMA
(college president)
Affiliation: Nebraska Indian Community College, P.O. Box 752, Winnebago, NE 68071 (402) 878-2414.

THOMASON, DOVIE M.
(Oglala Sioux-Kiowa Apache) 1948-
(lecturer, storyteller; art gallery owner)
Born August 14, 1948, Chicago, Ill. *Education*: Rockford College, BA, 1970; Cleveland State University, Teachers Certification, 1980. *Principal occupation*: Lecturer, storyteller; art gallery owner. Resides in Hartford, CT. *Affiliations*: Owner, Skystone & Silver, American Indian Art Gallery, Hartford, CT; chairperson, Native American Advisory Committee, 1987-; board of directors, 1989-, American Indian Archaeological Institute, Washington, CT. *Other professional post*: Secretary, board of directors, American Indians for Development, Meriden, CT. *Community activities*: Frequent lecturer/performer with youth groups. *Awards, honors*: Certificate of Excellence in Teaching. Cleveland State University, 1980. *Interests*: "I travel extensively to find new artists for my gallery - to meet with Indian people through the continent; gathering stories from our oral tradition which I share with thousands of children and adult annually; currently interviewing and researching for a biography of Red Thunder Cloud, Catawba herbalist, dancer, lecturer and healer; I hope to create children's books, illustrating stories from the American Indian oral tradition." *Biographical sources*: Hartford Courant (June 1986; Jan. & Nov., 1989).

*THOMPSON, CHAD
(Xodaaw' Chwang' - Hupa) 1953-
(assistant professor of linguistics)
Education: University of Alaska, BA, 1975, MA, 1977; University of Oregon, PhD, 1989. *Principal occupation*: Assistant professor of linguistics. *Home address*: 6108 Old Brook Dr., Fort Wayne, IN 46835 (219) 485-6775. *Affiliation*: Indiana University/Purdue University, Fort Wayne, IN, 1991-. *Memberships*: Society for the Study of Indigenous Languages of the Americas; Linguistic Society of America; Hoosier Folklore Society. *Awards, honors*: 1990 Distinguished Service Award for dedication to and support of the teaching of Native American languages, Center for Community Development, Humboldt State University, Arcata, CA. *Interests*: Native American languages, literatures, and folklore, particularly those of Alaskan & Pacific Coast Athabaskan. *Published works*: 21 readers in the Alaskan Athabaskan Languages - Holikachuk & Deg Hit'an, mostly traditional stories (Yukon Koyukuk School District, 1983-87); co-author, "Dinaakk'a I" - Koyukon language for students in secondary grades & adults (Yukon Koyukuk School District, 1983); co-author, "Scope & Sequence for Teaching Koyukon Athabaskan" (Yukon Koyukuk School District, 1983); "Dinaakk'a for Children," Koyukon Athabaskan language for elementary grades (Yukon Koyukuk School District, 1984); "Athabaskan Languages & the Schools: A Handbook for Teachers" (Alaska Dept. of Education, 1984); "Denakenaga' for Children" - Tanana Athabaskan language for elementary grades (Yukon Koyukuk School District, 1987); "Dinaakk'a II" Second year Koyukon for secondary grades & adults (Yukon Koyukuk School District, 1987); "An Introduction to Athabaskan Languages" (Yukon Koyukuk School District, 1987); co-author, "Teachers Guide to Baakk'aatEgh Ts'Eh

Eniy" (Alaska Native Language Center, 1989); co-editor, "Baakk'aatEgh Ts'EhEniy: Stories We Live By" (Alaska Native Language Center, 1989); "An Analysis of K'etetaalkkaanee" (Alaska Native Language Center, 1990).

THOMPSON, DAVID
(IHS-EEO manager)
Affiliation: Indian Health Service, Oklahoma Area Office, 215 Dean A. McGee St., N.W., Rm. 409, Oklahoma City, OK 73102 (405) 231-4796.

THOMPSON, DONA K. (Caddo-Wichita) 1949-
(counselor/administrator)
Born August 31, 1949, Lawton, Okla. *Affiliations*: Counselor/Recrutier, University of Oklahoma Health Sciences Center, Oklahoma City, OK, 1981-87; Counselor for Native American Students, 1987-, Associate Director-Minority Affairs, 1991-, Washington State University, Pullman, WA. *Memberships*: National Indian Counselor's Association (president, 1987-89; treasurer, 1980-85, 1990-); Association of Faculty Women; National Association of Student Personnel Administrators; National Indian Education Assn.

*THOMPSON, DORA K.
(association president)
Affiliation: National Indian Counselor's Association, Washington State University, Wilson Hall, Room 104, Pullman, WA 99164 (509) 335-8676.

THOMPSON, DORIS W.
(health director)
Affiliation: Yellowhawk PHS Health Center, P.O. Box 160, Pendleton, OR 97801 (503) 278-3870.

THOMPSON, HARRY F.
(curator of collections)
Affiliations: The Center for Western Studies Library, Augustana College, P.O. Box 727, Sioux Falls, SD 57197 (605) 336-4007.

THOMPSON, JOHN MASON, III 1941-
(consultant)
Born December 20, 1941, Alton, Ill. *Education*: Texas Christian University, BS, 1963, MBA, 1969. *Principal occupation*: Consultant. *Home address*: 2535 Weisenberger St., Fort Worth, TX 76107 (817) 624-8317 (home); (800) 356-6733 (office). *Affiliations*: President, Loucks, Thompson, Starling & Associates, Fort Worth, TX, 1978-; president, Guildhall, Inc., Fort Worth, TX 1982-. *Other professional post*: Marketing and management departments faculty, Texas Christian University. *Military service*: U.S. Air Force, 1963-68 (Captain). *Community activities*: Board of Directors: Camp Fire (U.S.); Texas Boys Choir. *Memberships*: American Marketing Association; American Management Association; Indian Arts and Crafts Association; American Craft Council; National Trust for Historic Preservation; Southern Plains Indian Museum Association; National Cowboy Hall of Fame; Thomas Gilcrease Museum Association; Japan Society. *Interests*: "Through LTS (consulting) concerned with developing economic opportunities on reservations. Through Guildhall (art publishing and distribution) concerned with developing Indian arts and crafts, preserving traditions and marketing works of art."

THOMPSON, JOSEPH
(Indian band chief)
Affiliation: Nipigon Ojibway First Nation, Rocky Bay Reserve, Box 241, Beardman, Ontario, Canada O0T 2G0 (807) 885-5441.

*THOMPSON, PHILIP M.
(museum president/CEO)
Affiliation: Eiteljorg Museum of Americacn Indians & Western Art, 500 W. Washington St., Indianapolis, IN 46204 (317) 636-9378.

*THOMPSON, PRESTON
(Native American film executive producer)
Affiliation: Eagle King Productions, 2601 So. Braeswood #1505, Houston, TX 77025.

*THOMPSON, RAYMOND H.
(museum director)
Affiliation: Arizona State Museum, University of Arizona, Tucson, AZ 85721 (602) 621-6281.

THOMPSON, ROBERT
(BIA agency supt. for education)
Affiliation: Standing Rock Agency, Bureau of Indian Affairs, P.O. Box E, Fort Yates, ND 58538 (701) 854-3497.

THORASSIE, PETER
(Indian band chief)
Affiliation: Churchill Indian band, Tadoule Lake, Manitoba, Canada R0B 2C0 (204) 684-2022.

THORNE, WILLIAM, Jr.
(executive director)
Affiliation: Phoenix Indian Center, 2601 North 3rd St., Suite 160, Phoenix, AZ 85004 (602) 263-1017.

*THORNLEY, LYNN HART
(museum director)
Affiliation: Five Civilized Tribes Museum, Agency Hill on Honor Heights, Muskogee, OK 74401 (918) 683-1701.

*THUNDER, GORDON (Winnebago)
(tribal chairperson)
Affiliation: Wisconsin Winnebago Business Committee, P.O. Box 667, Black River Falls, WI 54615 (715) 284-9343.

THUNDER, JAMES
(Indian band chief)
Affiliation: Buffalo Point Indian Band, Box 37, Middlebro, Manitoba, Canada R0A 1B0 (204) 437-2133.

THUNDERHAWK, MADONNA
(field coordinator)
Affiliations: Dakota Women of All Red Nations, Box 516, Fort Yates, ND 58538; Women of All Red Nations, P.O. Box 2508, Rapid City, SD 57709.

THUNDERHORSE, IRON *(Kanatisoquili)*
(Algonquin/Cherokee/Delaware) 1950-
(author, craftsman, artist)
Born January 29, 1950, New Haven, Conn. *Education*: Lee College (TX) (1 year). *Principal occupation*: Author, craftsman, artist. *Home address*: 1044 Chapel St., No. 602, New Haven, CT 06510 (203) 782-9715. *Affiliation*: Columnist, Indian Country Communications, Hayward, WI. *Memberships*: Thunderbird Alliance (grand peacekeeper); Algonquin Confederacy of the Quinnipiac Tribal Council (founder & member); member of about six traditional Medicine Societies. *Interests*: "Specialize in Native American symbolism culture and traditional teachings. Traveled all over Canada, Mexico, S. America and every state in U.S., except Alaska. *Biographical sources*: Writer's Digest Bookclub Newsletter, Dec. 1086. *Published works*: Para-

dox, A Psychic Journey (Abbetira Publishing, 1984); Medicine Visions - Poetry Chapbook (Thunderbird Free Press, 1985); Relocation, Crimes Against Nature (Thunderbird Free Press, 1986); Thunderbird Voices Speaking (Thunderbird Free Press, 1987); Return of the Thunderbeings (Bear & Co., 1990).

TIBBETTS, STEVEN
(BIA agency supt.)
Affiliation: Eastern Nevada Agency, Bureau of Indian Affairs, P.O. Box 5400, Elko, NV 89802 (702) 738-0569.

TICKNER, RAY
(health director)
Affiliation: Shasta-Trinity Indian Health Program, P.O. Box 1603, Weaverville, CA 96093 (916) 365-0125.

*TIEPELMAN, DENNIS
(BIA agency supt.)
Affiliation: Nome Agency, Bureau of Indian Affairs, P.O. Box 1108, Nome, AK 99762 (907) 443-2284.

TIGER, BUFFALO (Creek)
(BIA agency supt.)
Affiliation: Miccosukee Agency, Bureau of Indian Affairs, P.O. Box 44021, Tamiami Station, FL 33144 (305) 323-8380.

TIGER, CYNTHIA (Creek)
(health systems administrator)
Affiliation: Indian Health Service, Billings Area Office, P.O. Box 2143, Billings, MT 59103 (406) 657-6403.

TIGER, GEORGE (Creek)
(tribal communications coordinator)
Affiliation: Muscogee (Creek) Nation, P.O. Box 580, Okmulgee, OK 74447 (918) 756-8700 Ext. 312.

*TIGER, GEORGIANA
(consortium director)
Affiliation: American Indian Higher Education Consortium, 513 Capitol Court, NE, Suite 100, Washington, DC 20002 (202) 544-9289.

TIGER, JOHNNY, Jr. (Tony) (Creek-Seminole) 1940-
(artist-sculptor; gallery owner)
Born February 13, 1940, Tahlequah, Okla. *Education*: Bacone College, 1959-60. *Principal occupation*: Artist-sculptor; gallery owner. *Address*: P.O. Box C, Muskogee, OK 74402 (918) 687-3505. *Affiliation*: Co-owner, Tiger Gallery, Muskogee, OK, 1982-. *Other professional post*: Design T-shirts for the Tiger Gallery (Indian themes). *Military service*: U.S. Air Force, 1963-65 (E-4). *Memberships*: Indian Arts & Crafts Association; Five Civilized Tribes Museum (Master Artist). *Awards, honors*: "I've won over 100 major awards all over the country (USA) in my 20 year span in painting & sculpture." *Interests*: "I've had art shows all over the country, and also London, England in 1987 (one man art shows)." *Biographical source*: Southwest Art magazine.

TIGER, MICHAEL D. (Creek)
(IHS-area deputy director)
Affiliation: Nashville Area IHS Office, 711 Stewarts Ferry Pike, Nashville, TN 37214 (615) 736-2400.

*TIGERT, SCOTT
(curator)
Affiliation: Red Earth Indian Center, 2100 NE 52 St., Oklahoma City, OK 73111 (405) 427-4228.

TIJERINA, KATHRYN HARRIS
(association president)
Affiliation: Institute of American Indian Arts, P.O. Box 20007, Santa Fe, NM 87504 (505) 988-6463.

TIKIUN, THADEUS, JR.
(council chairperson)
Affiliation: Orutsararmuit Native Council, Box 927, 835 Ridgecrest Dr., Bethel, AK 99559 (907) 543-2608.

*TILOUSI, REX (Havasupai)
(tribal chairperson)
Affiliation: Havasupai Tribal Council, P.O. Box 10, Supai, AZ 86435 (602) 448-2961.

TIMMERMAN, NOWETAH ANN
(Iroquois/Susquehanna-Cherokee) 1947-
(teaching American Indian history & crafts)
Born February 21, 1947, New Haven, Conn. *Education*: High school. *Address & Affiliation*: Founder/owner, Nowetah's Indian Museum & Store, Route 27, Box 40, New Portland, ME 04954 (207) 628-4981, 1970-. *Other professional posts*: "Currently teaching American Indian history, Indian dancing, and Indian crafts to school children; as a museum curator - researching, cataloging & labeling museum pieces I purchase." *Memberships*: Connecticut Archaeological Society; Audubon; National & International Wildlife Federation; Connecticut Herpetological Society. *Awards, honors*: Community Leaders & Noteworthy Americans Award, 1975-76, by the American Biographical Institute. *Interests*: "To start my museum and store, I traveled all over the U.S. & Canada to make contacts with other Indian people, so I could purchase direct from them instead of buying crafts through big companies. I would be called an amateur archaeologist. Of course my major interest is naturally American Indian culture & writing about it. But, another interest is herpetology (giving nature talks on frogs, toads, salamanders, snakes & an interest in birds. Have done nature studies in remote Ontario, Canada & Everglades Park in Florida for Audubon & Wildlife (photographing & studies of habitat). Also I teach classes on wild plants/herbs as medicine & food. I'm a glass blower and make glass animal figurines; hand weaving wool Indian rugs, hand crafting Indian beadwork; also, basketry, pottery, etc." *Biographical source*: "Nowetah's Indian Museum & Store," chapter in Profiles: Directory of Women Entrepreneurs (Wind River Publishing, 1991). *Published works*: Writer of small booklets with illustrations on past Indian life including, "History of Indian Wampum" (shell beads), "Brain Tan Animal Hides," How to Weave Indian Wool Rugs-Blankets," "The Drum," "The Sacred Pipe," and currently working on a book to include all aspects of Old Wabanaki (Abenaki) ways, customs & way of life, before the contact period of Europeans (1600)."

TINGLE, TRICIA A. (Oklahoma Choctaw)
1955-
(attorney)
Born May 1, 1955, Wharton, Tex. *Education*: Southwest Texas State University (San Marcos),

BS, 1978, Post-Graduate-Paralegal Certificate, 1985; Oklahoma City University School of Law, JD, 1990. *Principal occupation*: Attorney. *Address*: P.O. Box 531, Wimberley, TX 78676 (512) 847-2276; 392-3708 (work). *Affiliations*: Teacher, Brazosport Independent School District, Freeport, TX, 1978-84; paralegal, Texas Railroad Commission, Austin, TX, 1985-87; paralegal, Cox & Smith, Inc., San Antonio, TX, 1987; Clinic Legal Aid for Native American Indians, Oklahoma Indian Legal Services, 1989; law clerk for Judge Tom Brett, Oklahoma Court of Criminal Appeals, Oklahoma City, 1989; General Practice, Leon Breeden & Associates, San Marcos, TX, 1990; self-employed, Law Office of Tricia A. Tingle, San Antonio, San Marcos, TX, 1990-. *Other professional posts*: Legal counsel to: American Indian Resource and Education Coalition, Inc., Austin, TX; Redwood Community Center, Inc., Hays County, TX; Program Director and original Board Member of Great Promises, Inc. (children's newspaper dealing with Indian issues). *Memberships*: Texas Bar Association; Texas Indian Bar Association (president & original Boiard Member); Association of Trial Lawyers of America; Hays County Bar Association (director); Oklahoma Indian Bar Association; Native American Bar Association (president-elect). *Awards, honors*: Presidential Delegate to White House Conference on Indian Education, 1992.

*TINKER, GEORGE (Osage)
(associate professor)
Born in 1945. *Education*: New Mexico Highlands University, BA, 1967; Pacific Lutheran Theological Seminary (Berkeley, CA), M.Div., 1972; Graduate Theological Union (Berkeley, CA), PhD, 1983. *Principal occupation*: Associate professor of Cross-Cultural Ministries. *Address & Affiliation*: Iliff School of Theology, 2201 S. University Blvd., Denver, CO 80210 (303) 744-1283, 1985-. *Other professional post*: Pastor (part-time), Living Waters Indian Church, Denver, CO. *Community activities*: Director, Bay Area Native American Ministry (3 years). *Memberships*: American Academy of Religion (co-chair, Native American Religious Traditions Group, 1991-93); American Indian Scholars Association (corresponding secretary, 1991-); Native American Theological Association (chairperson, 1985-87). *Awards, honors*: Recipient of a Lutheran Brotherhood Award for doctoral work & two Bacon Fellowships at the Graduate Theological Union. *Interests*: Native American studies; Native American Mission history; cross-cultural studies, including the study of "racism." *Published work*: Missionary Conquest & the Cultural Genocide of Native Americans (Fortress Press, 1993); numerous papers & articles in journal publications.

*TINKER, GEORGE (Eskimo)
(village president)
Affiliation: Native Village of Chignik, P.O. Box 11, Chignik Lake, AK 99563 (907) 749-2285.

TIPPECONNIC, JOHN W.
(BIA office director)
Affiliation: Office of Indian Education Programs, Bureau of Indian Affairs, U.S. Dept. of the Interior, MS: 3530-MIB, 1849 C St., NW, Washington, DC 20240 (202) 208-6123. *Past professional post*: Instructor/Editor (Journal of American Indian Education), Center for Indian Education, Arizona State University, Tempe, AZ.

*TIPPECONNIE, ROBERT
(program manager)
Affiliation: Native American Programs, Forest Service, 500 W. Westmorland Rd., Falls Church, VA 22046.

TITLA, PHILLIP, Sr. (San Carlos Apache)
1943-
(artist)
Born September 17, 1943, Miami, Ariz. *Education*: Eastern Arizona College, AA, 1979. *Principal occupation*: Artist. *Address*: P.O. Box 497, San Carlos, AZ 85550. *Affiliations*: Director of development, San Carlos (AZ) Apache Tribe, 1967-81; director, Phillip Titla Apache Galleria, San Carlos, Ariz., 1981-. *Other professional post*: Board member, San Carlos Arts and Crafts Association, 1981-. *Community activities*: Bylas Recreation Program (chairman); San Carlos Powwow Association, 1980-; San Carlos Pageant Committee, 1978-; Cobke Valley Fine Arts Guild, Inc., 1985-86. *Awards, honors*: Sculpture Award, Best of Show, Pasadena (CA) Art Show. *Interests*: "My interest is to continue to grow in the art field; presently doing some gallery shows and lecture at various clubs on Apache culture; also sing Apache songs; shows at colleges, high schools and elementary schools of my work-- for education." *Biographical source*: Art West, Sept./Oct., 1984.

*TITUS, LEE (Athapascan)
(village president)
Affiliation: Northway Village Council, P.O. Box 516, Northway, AK 99764 (907) 778-2250.

*TITUS, ROBERT J. *(Whitefeather)*
(Free Cherokees) 1938-
(merchant; shaman)
Born December 17, 1938, Helena, Ark. *Education*: Phillips County Community College, AA, 1969; Southern University, 1974-75 (Counselor - Alcohol). *Principal occupation*: Merchant, shaman. *Home address*: 311 Walnut St., Helena, AR 72342 (501) 338-7966. *Affiliations*: Helena Pawnshop, Helena, AR, 1978-; project director, Mid Delta Community Services, Helena, AR. *Other professional post*: Shaman, Circle of the Whitefeather, Helena, AR; regional chief, Free Cherokees. *Goals*: "To revive universal natural shamanism the world's original & true religious practice." *Community activities*: Election officer; environmental advisor to various groups on wildlife, trees, fish, water systems, etc.; Shaman, story-teller, Good Wheel Ceremony; ran halfway house for alcoholics, parolees, and drug addicts. *Memberships*: Local library association & museum; Good Medicine Society of AR; National Pawnbrokers Assn. (local board member). *Awards, honors*: Academic Excellence, Phi Theta Kappa (president); guest speaker, Lion's Club. *Interests*: Studied Obeah - drums & customs on remote islands in Caribbean; Mescalero customs; alcohol/drugs/crime problems of Sioux, Cheyenne & Navajo; spirituality of Hopi; "seek balance & harmony in confused, disharmonious persons; hiking, swimming, nature observation; social & economic education. Maintain a private collection of some spiritual artifacts: shaman's staffs, shaman's "Medicine Hats" & healing sticks & stones. *Published works*: Miser's Muniment (Pine Hill Press, 1985; Book of Shaman (Conservatory of American Letters, 1988); The Complete Book of Natural Shamanism (Snowbird Pubg, 1993); articles for various magazines, such as : "New Phoenix," "Many Paths," Flowering Tree," & "Four Directions.

TOBACCO, JIM
(Indian band chief)
Affiliation: Moose Lake Indian Band, Moose Lake, MB, Canada R0B 0Y0 (204) 678-2113.

TODACHEENEY, THOMAS
(administrative officer)
Affiliation: Gallup Indian Medical Center, P.O. Box 1337, Gallup, NM 87305 (505) 722-1000.

*TOHE, LAURA (Navajo) 1952-
(assistant professor)
Born October 5, 1952, Fort Defiance, Ariz. *Education*: University of New Mexico, BA, 1975; University of Nebraska, MA, 1985, PhD, 1993. *Principal occupation*: Assistant professor. *Home address*: 1230 N. Mesa Dr. #241, Mesa, AZ 85201 (602) 965-5553 (work). *Affiliation*: Arizona State University, Tempe, AZ, 1993-. *Other professional posts*: Teaching assistant, storyteller, writer. *Memberships*: Wordcraft Circle (National Caucus Member); Rocky Mountain Modern Language Association. *Awards, honors*: Blue Mesa Review Poetry Prize Winner, University of New Mexico; Regents Fellowship & Minority Fellowship, University of Nebraska; Outstanding Young Women of America; University of Nebraska Teaching Assistantship & Reading Assistantship; University of Nebraska, Omaha Goodrich Program Award; National Sports Academy Prize Winner. *Interests*: Traveled to Europe, Central America, and most of the U.S.; movies, blues, jazz, and soul music; photography; physical fitness training & outdoor activities. *Published works*: Making Friends With Water (Nosila Press, 1986); co-editor, Nebraska Humanities (Nebraska Humanities Council, 1994).

TOLEDO, RICHARD (Navajo)
(school principal)
Born March 21, 1951, Crownpoint, N.M. *Education*: University of New Mexico, MEd (Administration, 1980 & MEd (Elementary Education, 1985). *Principal occupation*: School principal. *Address*: Box 2334, Gallup, NM 87305 (505) 778-5665. *Affiliation*: Principal, Bread Springs Day School (grades K-3), Gallup, NM.

TOM, EVELYN
(health director)
Affiliation: Santa Rosa PHS Indian Health Center, Star Route, Box 71, Sells, AZ 85634 (602) 383-2261.

TOMAH, LEN
(Indian band chief)
Affiliation: Woodstock Indian Band, RR 1, Box 8, Site 1, Woodstock, New Brunswick, Canada E0J 2B0 (506) 328-3304.

TOME, HARRY
(BIA agency education chairperson)
Affiliation: Shiprock Agency, Bureau of Indian Affairs, P.O. Box 3239, Shiprock, NM 87420 (505) 368-4427 ext. 370; Red Rock Day School, P.O. Drawer 10, Red Valley, AZ 86544 (602) 653-4456.

*TONASKET, MEL
(health center director)
Affiliation: Colville PHS Indian Health Center, P.O. Box 71, Nespelem, WA 99155 (509) 634-4771.

TONEMAH, STUART A.
(association president)
Affiliation: American Indian Research and Development, 2424 Springer Dr., Suite 200, Norman, OK 73069 (405) 364-0656.

TORRALBA, RICHARD (Comanche)
(school principal)
Affiliation: San Felipe Day School, P.O. Box E, San Felipe Pueblo, NM 87001 (505) 867-3364.

*TORRES, ELMER C. (San Ildefonso Pueblo)
(pueblo governor)
Affiliation: San Ildefonso Tribal Council, Rte. 5, Box 315-A, Santa Fe, NM 87501 (505) 455-2273.

*TORRES, GUADALUPE "LOU"
(White Mountain Apache)
(engineer; corp. president/owner)
Principal occupation: Engineer; copr. president/owner. *Affiliations*: Field engineer, Lockheed Corp., 1968-1986; president, owner, Systems Integration and Research, Inc., 2120 Washington Blvd., Arlington, VA 22204 (703) 486-7933, 1986-. *Description*: The company's primary business is analyzing the life cycles of computer and technology systems and providing program management. A majority of its contract are with the Navy. Employs 150 people at eight offices across the country with two more planned for Sacramento and San Diego, California. *Award*: "Outstanding National Technologies Firm of the Year," by the U.S. Small Administration, Office of Native American Affairs.

TOULOUSE, NELSON
(Indian band chief)
Affiliation: Sagamock Anishawbek Indian Band, Box 610, Massey, Ontario, Canada P0P 1P0 (705) 865-5421.

*TOUSEY, LU ANN
(health director)
Affiliation: Stockbridge-Munsee Health Center, P.O. Box 86, Bowler, WI 54416 (715) 793-4144.

TOWNSEND, JOAN B. 1933-
(professor of anthropology)
Born July 9, 1933, Dallas, Tex. *Education*: UCLA, BA, 1959, PhD, 1965 (Dissertation: Ethnohistory and Culture Change of the Iliamna Tanaina). *Principal occupation*: Professor of anthropology. *Home address*: 85 Tunis Bay, Winnipeg, Manitoba, Can. R3T 2X2. *Affiliation*: Lecturer, assistant professor, associate professor, professor of anthropology, University of Manitoba, Winnipeg, Manitoba R3T 2N2, 1964-. *Other professional posts*: Consultation and assistance in gathering data on Tanaina society and archaeological sites; for Cook Inlet Region, Inc. (Alaskan Native organization). *Field research*: Archival and ethnohistoric research of the 18th-20th centuries of southern Alaska with special emphasis on social, political, and economic conditions of Indians, Eskimos and Aleuts. *Memberships*: American Anthropological Association (Fellow); Arctic Institute of North America (Fellow); Society for Applied Anthropology (Fellow); American Ethnological Society; Arctic Institute of North America; Royal Anthropological Institute; Current Anthropology; Canadian Ethnology Society (editorial board, Culture, 1980). *Interests*: "Ethnohistory and socio-cultural change: North American Indians--Athapaskan Indians; primary focus on Tanaina; Alaskan Pacific Rim ranked societies (Aleuts, Koniag and Chugach Eskimo; Tanaina, Ahtna, Eyak, and Tlingit Indians; western society and modern Indian religious movements; shamanism--especially Nepal; neo-shamanism among Indians and "Westerners"; traditional trading systems and alliances; mercantile and the fur trade in Alaska; political evolution; new religions and revitalization movements." *Published works*: Monograph: Kijik: An Historic Tanaina Settlement (Field Museum of Natural History, 1970); numerous articles, papers and book reviews.

TOWNSEND, VIRGIL
(BIA agency supt.)
Affiliation: Southern California Agency, Bureau of Indian Affairs, 3600 Lime St., Suite 722, Riverside, CA 92501 (714) 276-6624.

TOYA, RONALD GEORGE (Jemez Pueblo) 1948-
(BIA assistant area director)
Born March 8, 1948, Albuquerque, N.M. *Education*: Westmont College, BA, 1971. *Principal occupation*: B.I.A. assistant area director. Resides in Albuquerque, NM. *Affiliations*: Chief, Branch of Reservation Programs, Southern Pueblos Agency, BIA, Albuquerque, NM; chief, Branch of Self-Determination Services, assistant area director, BIA, Albuquerque Area Office; supt., Mescalero Agency, BIA, Mescalero, NM; supt., Southern Ute Agency, BIA, Ignacio, CO; special assistant to the Assistant Secretary of the Interior for Indian Affairs, Washington, DC; special assistant to the Commissioner of Indian Affairs; chief, Branch of Tribal Government Services, U.S. Dept. of Interior, BIA, Albuquerque Area Office. *Other professional post*: Executive director & chairman of the board, Tribal Government Institute. *Community activities*: Conduct radio show on Indian affairs entitled Native American Perspective; involved in youth activities, including baseball & special olympics. *Memberships*: New Mexico Industrial Development (board of directors, 1975-1981; CEDAM - international scuba & archaeological association; Society for American Baseball Research. *Awards, honors*: Special and Superior Achievement Awards, BIA 1972, 1979, 1981, 1982; various letters and citations. *Interests*: "Interested in the management of tribal governments; economic development & preservation of Indian culture; travel; baseball; scuba diving; car racing; hang gliding; dancing." *Published work*: Pueblo Management Development (Southwest Indian Polytechnic Institute, 1976).

TRACK, JOANN SOGIE (Sioux-Tiwa) 1949-
(clay artist/poet)
Born June 26, 1949, Taos, N.M. *Home address*: P.O. Box 992, Taos, NM 87571. *Affiliation*: Assistant curator, Millicent Rogers Museum, Taos, NM, 1990-. *Other professional post*: Instructor in micaceous clay, Taos Institute of Art. *Membership*: American Association of Museums. *Published work*: Spider Woman's Granddaughters (Beacon Press, 1989).

*TRACK, ROY (Flying Hawk)
(Assiniboine-Sioux) 1941-
(audio visual)
Born December 14, 1941, Owyhee, Nev. *Address*: P.O. Box 645, Phoenix, AZ 85001 (602) 207-3850 (work). *Affiliation*: Vice-president, New Mountain II Broadcasting, Phoenix, AZ, 1984-. *Other professional post*: TV host & executive producer, "21st Century native American," KTVK - Channel 3 (ABC), Phoenix. *Memberships*: Na-

tive American Broadcasting Consortium; Fort Peck (MT) Assiniboine-Sioux Tribe. *Interests*: Pow wows.

TRAFZER, CLIFFORD E. (Wyandot) 1949-
(professor, chair, director
of Native American studies)

Born March 1, 1949, Mansfield, Ohio. *Education*: Northern Arizona University, BA, 1970, MA, 1971; Oklahoma State University, PhD (History), 1973. Principal occupation: Professor. *Home address*: 10173 Palermo Court, Yucaipa, CA 92399 (909) 787-4577 (work). *Affiliations*: Archivist of Special Collections, Northern Arizona University Library, 1969-70; museum curator, The Arizona Historical Society, 1973-76; instructor of history, Graduate Courses, Northern Arizona University, 1974-77; instructor, Navajo Community College, Tsaile, AZ, 1977-78; assistant & associate professor of history and Native American programs, Washington State University, Pullman, 1977-82; associate professor, professor, and chair, Department of American Indian Studies, San Diego State University, 1982-91; Professor & Chair of Ethnic Studies & Director of Native American Studies, University of California, Riverside, 1991-. *Other professional post*: Commissioner, California State Native American Heritage Commission. *Community activities*: California Indian Days Celebration, San Diego Committee, 1984-; American Indian Pow Wow and Culture Week, San Diego State University, chaired celebration, 1982-88; Vice-chair, Native American Heritage Commission, 1988-; San Diego A1 Health Center Board, 1987-89. *Memberships*: American Historical Association; Organization of American Historians; American Indian Historian's Association; San Diego Museum of Man; Phi Kappa Phi; California Indian Education Association; Sierra Club. *Awards, honors*: Oklahoma Heritage Association Doctoral Scholarship, $5,000; appointment by Gov. Raul Castro to the Arizona Historical Records Advisory Board, 1976-77; book nominations for best non-fiction by the National Cowboy Hall of Fame and the Western Writers of America for Kit Carson Campaign, 1982, and American Indian Prophets, 1986; Eagle Feather Award for teaching Excellence and service to the American Indian community by the American Indian Student Organizations of Washington State University and San Diego State University, 1982 & 1986; Research and Teaching Awards, San Diego State University, 1984, '85, '88 & '89; 1986 Governor's Book Award for Renegade Tribe: The Palouse Indians and the Invasion of the Inland Pacific Northwest, and for "Washington's Native American Communities," Peoples of Washington, 1991 - best historical works in Northwestern history; appointment by Gov. George Deukmajian to the California Native American Heritage Commission, 1988; Outstanding Faculty Award, Associated Students of San Diego State University, 1989-90; Academic Specialist Program Fellow, U.S. Information Agency, Sept. 1991, to Sweden lecturing on Native American History & Literature. *Interests*: Native American history, literature, and religion; writing, hiking, fishing, and camping. *Published works*: The Judge: The Life of Robert A. Hefner (University of Oklahoma Press, 1975); The Volga Germans: Pioneers of the Pacific Northwest, with Richard Scheuerman (University Press of Idaho, 1980); Yuma: Frontier Crossing of the Far Southwest (Western Heritage Press, 1980); The Kit Carson Campaign: The Last Navajo War (University of Oklahoma Press, 1982); editor, American Indian

Identity: Todays Changing Perspectives (American Indian Studies, San Diego State, 1985); Northwestern Indians in Exile: Removal of the Modocs, Palouses & Nez Perces to the Indian Territory (Sierra Oaks Publishing Co., 1986); editor, Indians, Superintendents, and Councils: Northwestern Indian Policy, 1850-1855 (University Press of America, 1986); editor, Indian Prophets and Prophecy: An American Indian Tradition (Sierra Oaks Publishing Co., 1986 - reprint of special issue of American Indian Quarterly, Summer 1985); The Renegade Tribe: The Palouse Indians and the Invasion of the Inland Pacific Northwest, with Richard Scheuerman (Washington State U. Press, 1986); American Indian children's literature (under pen name Richard Red Hawk): Grandmother's Christmas Story: A True Quechan Indian Story, 1987 (authored under the pen name of Richard Red Hawk); Grandfather's Origin Story: The Navajo Indian Beginning, 1988 (authored under the pen name of Richard Red Hawk); A Trip to a Pow Wow, 1988 (authored under the pen name of Richard Red Hawk); A, B, C's the American Indian Way, 1988 (authored under the pen name of Richard Red Hawk); Grandfather's Story of Navajo Monsters, 1988 (authored under the pen name of Richard Red Hawk); Creation of a California Tribe: Grandfather's Maidu Indian Tales, 1988; California's Indians and the Gold Rush, 1989; American Indians as Cowboys, 1992; Chief Joseph's Allies, 1992 (all published by Sierra Oaks Publishing); also, The Chinook & The Nez Perce (Chelsea House, 1990 & 1992); editor, Looking Glass (San Diego State University Press, 1991); Yakima, Palouse, Cayuse, Umatilla, Walla Walla, and Wanapum Indians: An Historical Bibliography (Scarecrow Press, 1992); Earth Song, Sky Spirit: Short Stories of the Contemporary Native Amerian Experience. Anthologies: Editor, Mourning Dove's Stories, with Richard Scheuerman (San Diego State University Press, 1991); editor, Looking Glass (San Diego State University Press, 1991); Grandmother, Grandfather, and Old Wolf (collection of oral literature presented by Plateau Indian men and women-in progress to be published by University of Arizona Press); "Death Comes for the Yakimas, 1888-1964" book manuscript dealing with disease, infant mortality, accidents, alcohol, age and gender submitted to U. Press of Colorado; numerous short monographs & book chapters, articles, papers, and book reviews.

TRAHANT, MARK N. (Shoshone-Bannock) 1957-
(editor & publisher)

Born August 13, 1957, Fort Hall, Idaho. *Education*: Pasadena City College; Idaho State University. *Affiliations & Address*: Executive news editor, The Salt Lake Tribune, P.O. Box 867, Salt Lake City, UT 84110 (801) 237-2045. *Past affilaitons*: editor-in-chief, The Sho-Ban News, Fort Hall, ID, 1976-86; editor & publisher, Navajo Nation Today, Window Rock, AZ, 1986-93; past president, Native American Journalists Association. *Membership*: Northwest Indian Press Association. *Interests*: Also make films on available topics (16mm).

*TRASK, HAUNANI KAY (Hawaiian)
(director-Hawaiian studies)

Affiliation: Director, Center for Hawaiian Studies, University of Hawaii, Honolulu, HI. A leader in the Native Hawaiian movement. *Published work*: From a Native Daughter: Colonialism & Sovereignty in Hawaii.

TRAVERSIE, T.L.
(BIA agency supt.)

Affiliation: Siletz Agency, Bureau of Indian Affairs, P.O. Box 569, Siletz, OR 97380 (503) 444-2679.

TREADWELL, HOWARD E. (Poospatuck)
(tribal chief)

Affiliation: Poospetuck Reservation, 198 Poospetuck Lane, Mastic, NY 11950 (516) 399-3843.

TREBIAN, CAROL A. (*Daat-Khu-Teez*)
(Tlingit-Haida) 1933-
(program director)

Born October 26, 1933, Juneau, Alaska. *Education*: CMC of Roosevelt University, B.Mus., 1957; University of Wisconsin, Stout, MS Ed., 1990. *Principal occupation*: Program director. *Home address*: 4602 Stein Ave., Madison, WI 53714 (715) 532-5511 (work). *Affiliations*: Supervisor, General Music, Ladysmith Schools, Ladysmith, WI, 1970-75; Administrative Assistant, MSC, Ladysmith, WI, 1976-86; Director, Native American Studies Program, MSC, Ladysmith, WI, 1990-. *Other professional post*: Executive secretary, American Dental Association, Chicago, IL. *Membership*: Human Relations Committee, MSC, Ladysmith, WI, 1976-86, 1991-. *Awards, honors*: Sears Foundation for Teaching Excellence, 1991, MSC. *Interests*: School psyhcology/counseling; writing; composing music. *Published works*: Short story, and several short poems for The Circle, Minneapolis, MN, 1978-79.

TREVELYAN, AMELIA M. 1946-
(professor of art history)

Born July 21, 1946, Marshall, Mich. *Education*: University of Michigan, BA, 1968, MA, 1970; University of California, Los Angeles, PhD, 1987. *Principal occupation*: Professor of art history. *Home address*: 149 W. Lincoln Ave., Gettysburg, PA 17325 (717) 337-3953; 337-6122 (work). *Affiliations*: Instructor of art history, Rhode Island College, 1970-73; assistant professor of art history, Center for Creative Studies, Detroit, MI, 1981-84; assistant professor of art history, 1985-90, associate professor & Art Dept. Chair, 1990-, Gettysburg College. *Other professional post*: Free lance critic, Los Angeles Herald Examiner & New Worlds Magazine. *Memberships*: Native American Art Studies Association; Native Arts Studies Association of Canada - USA Area Rep.; College Art Association; American Institute of Archaeology. *Awards, honors*: Dickson Fellowship, 1976 from U.C.L.A.; ISR Grant, 1986-87 from Gettysburg College; Canadian Embassy Cultural Programme Grants, 1990-91; Maryland Council of the Arts Grant, 1991. *Interests*: "Prehistoric cultures in the Eastern Woodlands of North America metallurgy, shellwork, ceramics; arts of Native North America; cross-cultural studies in prehistoric ritual symbolism and metallurgy; extensive travel and research in Greece; women's issues in art history."

*TREVATHAN, LOUIS "BUZZ", Jr. 1944-
(gallery owner)

Born October 9, 1944, in N.C. *Education*: U.S. Military Academy (West Point), BS, 1967. *Principal occupation*: Gallery owner. *Home address*: 106 W. San Francisco St., Santa Fe, NM 87501 (505) 985-1417; 988-9881 (work). *Affiliation*: Co-owner, Cristof's, Santa Fe, NM 87501. *Military service*: U.S. Army, Captain-Vietnam Vet (Flying Cross, Bronze Star, Air Medals, etc.). *Pub-

lished works: Several magazine articles (1993-94) on contemporary Navajo weaving, in "Focus/Santa Fe."

TRIBBETT, NORMAN HENRY
(Forest County Potawatomi) 1948-
(tribal librarian)

Born November 5, 1948, Hayward, Wis. *Education*: University of Wisconsin, Oshkosh, BS, 1981; University of Wisconsin, Madison, MA, 1983. *Principal occupation*: Librarian. *Home address*: Rt. 2 Box 623L, Lakeport, FL 33471 (813) 763-4236. *Affiliation*: Library Director, Seminole Tribe of Florida, Okeechobee, FL, 1986-. *Military service*: U.S. Army (pvt.). *Interests*: Forest County Potawatomi history; history of the treaties for Potawatomi, & history of the natives who relocated to Canada.

TRITT, LINCOLN (*Shigin*)
(Kutchin Athabaskan) 1946-
(writer, speaker)

Born October 18, 1946, Salmon River, AK. *Education*: Mt. Edgecumbe High School; University of Alaska, Fairbanks, 1984-86. *Principal occupation*: Writer, speaker. *Home address*: P.O. Box 81087, Venetie, AK 99781 (907) 451-8984. *Affiliations*: Second chief, Arctic Village Traditional Council, Arctic Village, AK; Instructor, College of Rural Alaska, Interior Campus, Fort Yukon Center, Fort Yukon, AK; consulting in education, alcohol & drugs; teach Native pre-contact history in psychology, sociology, philosophy, etc. *Other professional posts*: Write articles for local newspapers; lobbyist, tribal judge. *Military service*: U.S. Navy, 1966-70 (Radioman 3rd Class; Vietnam Vet). *Community activities*: Native Village of Venetie Tribal Government; Neets'aii Corp.; Arctic Village School Advisory Committee' Tanana Chiefs Conference; Interior Education Committee; Council for Athabaskan Tribal Government; Gwitch'in Niintsyaa Coordinator. *Interests*: "Teach Native pre-contact with whites; value system and why they lived the way they did and still do." *Biographical source*: "The County's Monthly" in Santa Cruz Magazine, Dec. 1991. *Published works*: Raven Tell Stories (Anthology) (The Greenfield Review Literary Center, 1991); Coyote Bark/Poetic Art (Hinton Harrison, 1991).

*TROSPER, RONALD
(center director)

Affiliation: National Indian Policy Center, The George Washington University, 2101 F St., NW, Washington, DC 20052 (202) 994-1446.

TROY, TIMOTHY
(bibliographer)

Affiliation: Bibliographer of American Indian Material, The New York Public Library, 42nd St. and Fifth Ave., New York, NY 10018 (212) 930-0826.

TRUJILLO, EVELYN C. (Pueblo)
(IHS-administrative officer)

Affiliation: Indian Health Service (Headquarters West), 300 San Mateo, NE, Suite 500, Albuquerque, NM 87102 (505) 766-6215.

TRUJILLO, JOSEPH G. (Pueblo)
(IHS-property management chief)

Affiliation: Indian Health Service (Headquarters West), 2401 12th St., NW, Albuquerque, NM 87102 (505) 766-5557.

*TRUJILLO, MICHAEL H., M.D.
(Laguna Pueblo)
(director-Indian Health Service)

Affiliation: Indian Health Service, U.S. Dept. of Health & Human Services, Rm. 5A-55, Parklawn Bldg., 5600 Fishers Lane, Rockville, MD 20857 (301) 443-1083. The first full-blooded American Indian to serve as Director of the IHS.

TRUJILLO, PATRICK S. (Cochiti Pueblo) 1954-
(substance abuse counselor)

Born March 5, 1954, Albuquerque, N.M. *Education*: University of New Mexico Continuing Education (1 year), Certificate of Completion (288 hours of Alcohol & Drug Abuse Studies Institute). *Principal occupation*: Substance abuse counselor. *Address*: P.O. Box 131, Cochiti Pueblo, NM 87042 (505) 766-8418 (work) 465-9992 (home). *Affiliations*: Alcohol Counselor, Five Sandoval Indian Pueblos, Inc., Bernalillo, NM, 1985-88; substance abuse counselor, Southwestern Indian Polytechnic Institute, Albuquerque, NM, 1989-92; counselor, All Indian Pueblo Council, Inc., Albuquerque, NM, 1992-. *Memberships*: New Mexico Alcoholism & Drug Abuse Counselors Association. *Awards, honors*: Outstanding Academic Achievement - Drug/Alcohol Studies; Certified Alcoholism Counselor. *Interests*: "Enjoy working with youths in prevention and I like to implement seminars/training for communities, public service agencies. I have great interest in implementing cultural awareness, a wholistic spiritual approach to wellness for both youths and adults. I am also a trainer for fetal alcohol syndrome prevention."

TRUJILLO, RAYMOND H. (Pueblo)
(tribal scholarship officer)

Affiliation: Zuni Scholarship Program, Box 339, Zuni, NM 87327 (505) 782-4481 Ext. 482/9.

TSABETSAYE, ROGER JOHN (Zuni) 1941-
(artist, craftsman)

Born October 29, 1941, Zuni, N.M. *Education*: Institute of American Indian Arts; School for American Craftsmen, Rochester Institute of Technology. *Principal occupation*: Artist, craftsman. *Home address*: Box 254, Zuni, NM 87327. *Affiliation*: Owner-founder, Tsabetsaye Enterprises, Box 254, Zuni, NM (Zuni jewelry--wholesale/retail). *Membership*: Zuni Craftsmen's Coop Association. *Awards, honors*: Numerous awards from various exhibitions and shows, 1968-.

TSINAJINNIE, ANDY (Navajo) 1919-
(artist)

Born November 16, 1919, Chinle, Ariz. *Education*: College of Arts & Crafts, Oakland, CA. *Principal occupation*: Artist. *Home address*: Box 542, Scottsdale, AZ 85252. *Military service*: U.S. Army Air Force, 1940-45. *Awards, honors*: Numerous awards from various exhibitions and shows. *Published works*: As illustrator, Spirit Rocks & Silver Magic, and Peetie the Pack Rat and Other Desert Stories (Caxton Printers, Ltd.); Who Wants to Be a Prairie Dog? (Haskell Institute); and others.

*TSO, EMMETT (Navajo)
(school chairperson)

Affiliation: Greyhills High School, P.O. Box 160, Tuba City, AZ 86045 (602) 283-6271.

TSO, RON (Navajo)
(health director)

Affiliation: Chinle Comprehensive Health Care Facility, P.O. Drawer PH, Chinle, AZ 86503 (602) 674-5282.

TSO, WILLIAM (Navajo)
(school chairperson)

Affiliation: Navajo Preparatory School, 1200 West Apache, Farmington, NM 87401 (505) 326-6571.

TSOSIE, DEBRA (Navajo)
(director)

Affiliation: Winds of Change, P.O. Box 1213, Middlebury, CT 06762.

*TSOSIE, KENNETH
(executive director)

Affiliation: National Indian Youth Council, 318 Elm St., S.E., Albuquerque, NM 87102 (505) 247-2251.

*TSOSIE, LARRY, Sr. (Navajo)
(school principal)

Affiliation: Shiprock Reservation Dormitory, Shiprock, NM 87420 (505) 368-5070.

TSOSIE, LORETTA A.W. (*Ke'hanibaa'*)
(Navajo) 1943-
(administration)

Born March 13, 1943, Morenci, Ariz. *Education*: University of New Mexico, BS, 1971, MA (Educational Administration), 1976. *Principal occupation*: Administration. *Home address*: P.O. Box 112, Window Rock, AZ 86515 (505) 831-3957. *Affiliations*: Instructor, Navajo Community College, Tsaile, AZ, 1972-86; special liaison officer, Alamo-Canoncito Liaison Office, Bureau of Indian Affairs, Canoncito, NM, 1987-. *Other professional post*: Chairperson, Career Education Division, Navajo Community College.

*TSOSIE, NELSON (Navajo-Dineh) 1961-
(stone & bronze sculptor, painter)

Born July 1, 1961, Shiprock, N.M. *Education*: Yavapai Community College (Prescott, AZ), AA, 1981; University of Arizona, Studio Arts major, 1981-82. *Principal occupation*: Stone & bronze sculptor, painter. *Address*: P.O. Box 23285, Santa Fe, NM 87502 (505) 474-4480. "Nelson's work remains steep in tradition, with a historical accuracy that can only come from a comprehensive love of one's own culture, and the people that represent it with such pride and dignity. He places great emphasis on his desire to portray the positive aspects of Navajo life rather than the harsher, more negative aspects that are so often over-exploited." *Professional post*: Co-owner, Free A.I.R. Fine Art, a Santa Fe-based promotional private art business that aids other artists as well. *Memberships*: Indian Arts & Crafts Association; Gallup Inter-Tribal Ceremonial Association (contributing member). *Awards, honors*: Numerous shows & awards, including: Santa Fe Indian Market, Inter-Tribal Indian Ceremonial (Church Rock, NM); Lovena Ohl Gallery, Scottsdale, AZ; Navajo Nation Fair Fine Art Show, Red Earth Art Show, Indian Arts & Crafts Association Show & Sale. *Interests*: "Travels frequently, participating in community activities, and works with his wife to promote the talents of other promising artists as well." *Biographical source*: Enduring Traditions, by Jerry & Lois Jacka.

*TSOSIE, RAYMOND (Navajo)
(employment supervisor)
Affiliation: BHP Minerals, P.O. Box 155, Fruit-land, NM 87416.

*TSOSIE, WALLACE (Navajo)
(BIA agency chairperson)
Affiliation: Fort Defiance Agency, BIA, P.O. Box 110, Fort Defiance, NM 86504 (602) 729-5041.

TSOUHLARAKIS, KAY
(health director)
Affiliation: Taos PHS Indian Health Center, P.O. Box 1956, Taos, NM 87571 (505) 758-4224.

TUCKER, DANIEL (Diegueno)
(tribal spokesperson)
Affiliation: Sycuan Business Committee, 5459 Dehesa Rd., El Cajon, CA 92021 (619) 445-2613.

TUCKER, MICHAEL
(museum manager)
Affiliation: California State Indian Museum, 2618 K St., Sacramento, CA 95816 (916) 324-0971.

TULLIS, EDDIE (Creek)
(tribal chairperson)
Affiliation: Poarch Band of Creek Indians, HCR69A, Box 85-B, Atmore, AL 36502 (205) 368-9136.

TUPLIN, GRAHAM
(council president)
Affiliation: Native Council of Prince Edward Island, 33 Allen St., Charlottetown, P.E.I., Canada C1A 3B9 (902) 892-5314.

TURNBULL, DAVID J. (*Chief Piercing Eyes*)
(Susquehannock/Conastoga) 1930-
(Indian chief, publisher, pastor)
Born May 18, 1930, Hornell, N.Y. *Education*: Elim Bible College, Ministerial Certificate, 1964. *Principal occupation*: Indian chief/publisher. *Address*: P.O. Box 244, Nocatee, FL 33864 (813) 494-6930. *Affiliations*: Chief of Indian organization with 3,300 members. *Other professional posts*: Publisher; paster of Cherokee Baptist Church. *Community activities*: Cherokee Unity Council; Habitat; HUGS (Hands United in Good Spirit). *Memberships*: Wiccan/Pagan Press Association; DeSoto County Ministerial Association; DeSoto County Chamber of Commerce; Universal Pagan Federation. *Awards, honors*: District 7 HRS - for donation of clothes and other items for their clients, 1991; numerous certificates, awards, etc. *Interests*: "Much concern about hype concerning the Indian Revival. I write articles and give lectures in my own organization and churches, societies, etc. Much travel to pow wows, Indian groups, and individuals interested in in Indians. We also help to organize revival groups. We gather clothes and emergency supplies to send to Indian reservations, revival groups, and local charities & individuals in need. Interested in genealogy and the official cover-up of records to disclaim Indian heritage in the general population and confine it to official enclaves. Also much concerned by criminal and "official" sale of babies and consequent loss of records of genetic heritage causing emotional distress and lack of medical aid such as organ transplants that require knowledge of actual kinfolk." *Published works*: Reviving Your Heritage (self-published, 1984).

TURNER, DAVID D. 1956-
(park supt.; archaeologist)
Born July 18, 1956, Dallas, Tex. *Education*: University of Texas, San Antonio, BA, 1984. *Principal occupation*: Park supt.; archaeologist. *Home address*: Rt. 2, Box 85C, Alto, TX 75925 (409) 858-4052 (home) 558-3218 (work). *Affiliations*: Technical staff, Center for Archaeological Research, San Antonio, 1985-88; exhibit technician, Texas Parks Dept., Goliad, TX, 1988-90; Park Supt., Caddoan Mounds, Texas Parks Dept., 1990-. *Memberships*: American Association of State & Local History; Society for Historical Archaeology; Texas Association of Museums; East Texas Archaeological Society. *Published work*: Perspectives on the Past (weekly newspaper column) Goliad Advance-Guard, 1989-90.

TURNER, ELIZABETH ROBERTS 1957-
(gallery owner)
Born September 1, 1957, Newark, Ohio. *Education*: Ohio Wesleyan University, 1975-76; Denison University, BA, 1980. *Principal occupation*: Art gallery owner. *Home address*: Westview Farm, West Pawlet, VT 05775 (802) 645-9975. *Affiliation*: Owner, Long Ago & Far Away (Native American art gallery), Manchester Center, VT, 1986-. *Memberships*: Indian Arts & Crafts Association; Southwestern Association of Indian Affairs; Manchester and the Mountains Chamber of Commerce.

TURNER, GRANT 1957-
(gallery owner; art dealer)
Born May 21, 1957, Manitoulin Island, Ontario, Can. *Education*: University of Waterloo, 1976-77. *Principal occupation*: Gallery owner; art dealer. *Home address*: Westview Farm, West Pawlet, VT 05775 (802) 362-3435 (office). *Affiliation*: Owner, Long Ago & Far Away (Native American art gallery), Manchester Center, VT, 1986-. *Community activities*: National Ski Ptrol, 1989-. *Memberships*: Indian Arts and Crafts Association; Southwestern Association of Indian Affairs; Manchester and the Mountains Chamber of Commerce.

TURNER, HAROLD
(Indian band chief)
Affiliation: Grand Rapids Indian Band, Box 500, Grand Rapids, Manitoba, Canada R0C 1E0 (204) 639-2219.

TURNER, LOWELL KEVIN (*Sky Painter*)
(Choctaw) 1958-
(artist, sign painter, designer)
Born October 1, 1958, St. Louis, Mo. *Education*: National Beauty Academy, St. Louis, MO (Diploma-Manicuring & Nail Sculpturing), 1992. *Principal occupation*: Sign painter & designer; artist. *Home address*: 14232 Spring Dr., De Soto, MO 63020 (314) 337-4105. *Affiliation*: Self-employed, Lowell Turner & Son Sign Co., De Soto, MO, 1973-. *Other professional posts*: Native American Indian painter & jeweler; historian & archivist on family genealogy; public speaker; licensed manicurist. *Community activities*: Mastodon Museum, Imperial, MO; Jefferson Memorial History Museum, St. Louis, MO. *Memberships*: S.A.R. Sons of the American Revolution, St. Louis, MO; Sons of the Confederacy, Petersburg, VA; St. Louis Hobby Association. *Awards, honors*: Honorable Mention Certificate, and 3 Master Division Award Plaques for (my) model making realism. *Biographical source*: U.S. Dept. of the Interior, Indian Arts &

Crafts Board, Washington, DC; Voices From Spirit Magazine, Ellsworth, ME; and The Genealogical Helper Magazine. *Published work*: Mail order brochure, Turner Artworks, since 1987; artwork in "Native American Art & Folklore (Crescent Books, 1993)..

TURNEY, MELISSA
(registrar/librarian)
Affiliation: Schiele Museum Reference Library, Center for Southeastern Native American Studies, P.O. Box 953, 1500 E. Garrison Blvd., Gastonia, NC 28053 (704) 866-6900.

*TUTHILL, STEVEN
(museum director)
Affiliation: Indian Temple Mound Museum, Box 4009, 139 Miracle Strip Parkway, Fort Walton Beach, FL 32549 (904) 243-6521.

*TUTT, LOUIS
(health director)
Affiliation: Winslow PHS Indian Health Center, P.O. Drawer 40, Winslow, AZ 86047 (602) 289-4646.

*TWIDDY, FRANCIS (Skokomish)
(tribal chairperson)
Affiliation: Skokomish Tribal Council, N. 80 Tribal Center Rd., Shelton, WA 98584 (206) 426-4232.

*TWISS, GAYLA
(hospital director)
Affiliation: Rosebud PHS Indian Hospital, Rosebud, SD 57570 (605) 747-2231.

*TWIST, GLENN JENNINGS
(Cherokee/Creek) 1917-
(retired technician)
Born July 20, 1917, Hanson, Okla. *Education*: University of Tulsa (3 years). *Principal occupation*: Retired technician. *Home address*: 916 NW 44, Oklahoma City, OK 73118 (405) 524-6210. *Military service*: U.S. Submarine Force, 1935-39, Seaman 1st Class; U.S. Army & U.S. Air Force, 1942-46, Captain-Navigational Training Officer. *Community activities*: Member, 22nd Session, Oklahoma Legislature, Tulsa County. *Membership*: Wordcraft Circle. *Award*: "Contributed Most to Cleaning Arts," by Carpet Cleaners Association, California, 1975. *Interests*: Creative writing. First book, "Di Janu'teyo'y': Their Search for the Promised Land (looking for a publisher); article, "Susie's Place," about people who come to Boston Mountains of western Arkansas. *Published works*: "One Body, Daytime, Celestial Navigation, a new method, fast & reliable (last issue of Navigator magazine before publication ceased at end of World War II).

TWITCHELL, JERRY
(school principal)
Affiliation: Chefornak IRA Contract School, Chefornak, AK 99561 (907) 867-8707.

TWO EAGLES, VINCE (*Choka Opi*)
(Yankton Sioux) 1952-
(substance abuse counselor)
Born January 26, 1952, Yankton, S.D. *Education*: Dakota State University (2 years); Black Hills State College (1 year). *Principal occupation*: Substance abuse counselor. *Home address*: P.O. Box 222, Marty, SD 57361 (605) 384-5431 (work). *Affiliation*: Trainer, Institute of Reality Therapy, Los Angeles, CA (10 years). *Other professional posts*: Entertainer - recording artist, lecturer on traditional Dakota culture and the

impact of alcoholism/drug abuse. Trainer - intervention teams, protective services programs (tribal); coordinator, Yankton Sioux Tribe Radio Project, KONA, Inc., Marty School, Marty, SD. *Community activities*: Marty Indian School's Advisory Committee on Alcohol and Drug Free Policy to the school's Board of Directors; member, Action Committee (designed to intervene in sexual, physical and emotional abuse of children); Yankton Sioux Tribe's representative on the Lakota Camp Courage Planning Board; Ad-Hoc Committee, Yankton Sioux Tribe's General Council. *Membership*: South Dakota Indian Counselors Association. *Awards, honors*: Currently an applicant for a Touring Arts and Artists Fellowship grant from SD Arts Council. *Interests*: "I have traveled throughout the U.S. along with my backup musical group called, "People of the Earth," spreading a message of healing and support for local sobriety efforts and environmental issues and calling attention to the need for all races of people to come together in a spiritual manner toward reconciliation between the Native and non-Native communities as a means to fulfill the true teachings of our traditional elders and spiritual leaders."

TWO HAWKS, WEBSTER
(IHS-tribal health management)
Affiliation: Indian Health Service, Aberdeen Area Office, Federal Bldg., 115 4th Ave., S.E., Aberdeen, SD 57401 (605) 226-7591.

*TYNDELL, WAYNE
(director-Indian center)
Affiliation: American Indian Center of Omaha, 3610 Dodge St., #2078, Omaha, NE 68131-3207.

TYNER, JAMES W. (Cherokee) 1911-
(historian)
Born September 13, 1911, Tahlequah, Okla. *Education*: Haskell Institute. *Principal occupation*: Historian. *Home address*: P.O. Box 881, Chouteau, OK 74337. *Affiliation*: Historian for Indian history project, American Indian Institute, University of Oklahoma, Norman. *Military service*: U.S. Navy, 1942-45 (Chief Petty Officer, World War II). *Awards, honors*: National Certificate of Commendation for published work, Our People and Where They Rest (Hooper Publishing, 1969-72), American Association for State and Local History. *Interests*: Indian history, including research and recording old cemeteries; woodcarving; cartridge collecting.

TYNES, ALICE W.
(school principal)
Affiliation: Teecnospos Boarding School, Teecnospos, AZ 86514 (602) 656-3451.

*TYRO, FRANK
(film producer)
Affiliation: Salish Kootenai College, P.O. Box 117, Pablo, MT 59855 (406) 675-4800.

TYSON, JEAN
(Indian school principal)
Affiliation: Santa Rosa Ranch School, Sells Star Route, Box 230, Tucson, AZ 85735 (602) 383-2359.

U

ULMER, JOE
(director)
Affiliation: Ya-Ka-Ama, 6215 Eastside Rd., Forestville, CA 95448 (707) 887-1541.

USKAVITCH, ROBERT
(chief-information services)
Affiliation: U.S. Dept. of the Interior Library, 18th and C Sts., NW, Washington, DC 20240 (202) 343-5810.

UTTLEY, JIM
(editor)
Affiliation: Indian Life Magazine, Intertribal Christian Communications, Box 3765 Station B, Winnipeg, Manitoba, Canada R2W 3R6 (204) 661-9333.

*UTLEY, ROBERT M.
(writer)
Published works: The Lance and the Shield: The Life and Times of Sitting Bull; Cavalier in Buckskin: George Armstrong Custer & the Western Military Frontier.

V

*VALDEZ, ROBERT (Pueblo)
(advisor)
Affiliation: Council of Advisors, American Indian Heritage Foundation, 6051 Arlington Blvd., Falls Church, VA 22044 (703) 237-7500.

VALENCIA-WEBER, GLORIA
(attorney)
Affiliation: University of Tulsa College of Law, 3120 E. 4th Place, Tulsa, OK 74104 (918) 631-2439.

*VALLE, FELIX (Diegueno)
(tribal chairperson)
Affiliation: Santa Ysabel General Council, P.O. Box 126, Santa Ysabel, CA 92070 (619) 765-0845.

*VAN DUNK, RONALD REDBONE
(Ramapough)
(tribal chief)
Affiliation: Ramapough Mountain Indians, 19 Mountain Rd., Mahwah, NJ 07430 (201) 529-5750.

*VAN GILDER, KEVIN J.
(administrative director)
Affiliation: Raindancer Youth Service, Inc., P.O. Box 2499, St. George, UT 84770 (801) 673-6474.

VANATTA, SHIRLEY PRINTUP (Seneca) 1922-
(writer, artist)
Born October 29, 1922, Red House, N.Y. *Education*: Bacone College. *Principal occupation*: Writer, artist. *Home address*: 116 Jimersontown, Salamanca, NY 14779. *Affiliation*: Editor, O He Yoh Noh, newsletter of the Seneca Nation. *Community activities*: Iroquois Indian Conference of New York (artist; publicist); Everson Museum (board of directors). *Memberships*: Society for Pennsylvania Archaeology. *Awards, honors*: New York State Indian of the Year, Iroquois Temperance League, given by Governor Nelson

Rockefeller, 1972; numerous others. *Interests*: Ms. Vanatta writes, "(I was) instrumental in bringing about archaeological research on the Allegany Reservation through the Carnegie Museum--work on 'Vanatta Archaeological Site,' 900-1,000 A.D. Iroquois village, where ceremonial masks (were) uncovered. I instituted the annual Inter-Community Christmas Party, where all children of Indian descent receive gifts; also the elderly, the infirm and the imprisoned. I am an oil and watercolor artist."

*VANDERHOOP, DAVID (Wampanoag)
(tribal council vice president)
Affiliation: Wampanoag Tribal Council of Gay Head, RFD Box 137, Gay Head, MA 02535 (508) 645-9265.

VANDERWAGEN, W. CRAIG, M.D.
(IHS-director/clinical services)
Affiliation: Office of Health Programs, Div. of Clinical Services, Indian Health Service, Rm. 6A-55, 5600 Fishers Lane, Rockville, MD 20857 (301) 443-4644.

*VANN, DONALD (Q-A Na Da-Ga-Do-Ga)
(Oklahoma Cherokee) 1949-
(artist, publisher)
Born October 22, 1949, Adar County, Okla. *Education*: High school. *Principal occupation*: Artist, publisher. *Address & Affiliation*: Partner, Native American Images (a publishing co. that has worked with many renowned artists over the past 20 years), P.O. Box 746, Austin, TX 78767 (512) 472-3049 (work). *Military service*: U.S. Army, 1969-71 (First Calvary in Vietnam, helicopter gunman). *Awards, honors*: His original watercolors have won scores of ribbons across the country. Includes a half-dozen First Place & Grand Awards from th Five Civilized Tribes Museum; his paintings, lithographs & prints have been featured at exhibits across the U.S. More than 50 limited edition releases of his works have sold out and now command collector values many times their original issue price. The Smithsonian Institution's Museum of the American Indian has presented him with their highest honor. He has also been proclaimed "on of the best known Indian artists working in this century" by the Cherokee Historical Society. His paintings have been exhibited at the Smithsonian. *Interests*: Back-packing, camping, canoeing, skiing, heli-skiing, running, and video-photography.

*VANN, MICHAEL V.
(Turtle Mountain Chippewa)
(radio station president)
Affiliation: KEYA - 88.5 FM, Turtle Mountain Chippewa Tribe, P.O. Box 190, Belcourt, ND 58316 (701) 477-5686.

VANWINKLE, LORETTA
(executive secretary)
Affiliation: Intertribal Friendship House, 523 East 14th St., Oakland, CA 94606 (510) 452-1235.

VARESE, STEFANO 1939-
(professor of Native American studies)
Born July 27, 1939, Genova, Italy. *Education*: Catholic University (Lima, Peru) Diplomas (History & Anthropology), 1963 & 1964, BS (Ethnology), 1966, PhD (Anthropology), 1967. *Principal occupation*: Professor of Native American studies. *Home address*: 1309 Monarch Lane, Davis, CA 95616 (916) 753-9508; 752-0357 (work). *Affiliations*: Director, Unidad Regional de

Oaxaca, Direccion General de Culturas Populares, Secretaria de Educacion Publica de Mexico, 1981-86; Native American Studies, University of California, Davis (visiting professor, 1988-90, professor, 1990-). *Other professional posts*: Consultant for United Nations agencies on indigenous peoples of the Americas. *Community activities*: Director of Unit of Indigenous Popular Cultures, Oaxaca, Mexico, 1979-87. *Memberships*: American Anthropological Association; Latin American Studies Association; Society for Applied Anthropology; Cultural Survival, Cambridge, MA (Advisory Board). *Awards, honors*: Tinker Visiting Scholar, Stanford University, 1986-87; Ford Foundation Fellow at the Humanities Center, Stanford University, 1987-88; Co-Chair-elect of Society for Latin American Anthropology (American Anthropological Association), 1989-90. *Interests*: Indians of the Americas. *Published works*. Numerous books and monographs, and chapters in edited books; official reports and articles.

*VASKA, RUTH B. (Eskimo)
(AK village president)
Affiliation: Village of Aniak, P.O. Box 176, Aniak, AK 99557 (907) 675-4349.

VASQUEZ, JOSEPH C. *(Lone Eagle)*
(Sioux-Apache) 1917-
(programs administrator)
Born February 21, 1917, Primero, Colo. *Education*: U.S. Armed Forces Institute; Los Angeles City College Extension; UCLA Extension. *Principal occupation*: Programs administrator. *Home address*: 5208 11th St., South, Arlington, VA 22204. *Affiliations*: Small business coordinator/ minority representative, Hughes Aircraft Co., El Segundo, Calif., 1947-68; appointed Los Angeles City Commissioner, Los Angeles, CA, 1968-70; National Council on Indian Opportunity, Washington, D.C., 1970-72; director, Indian Office, U.S. Dept. of Commerce, Office of Minority Business Enterprise, Washington, DC, 1972-. *Other professional posts*: President & council chairman, Los Angeles Indian Center, 1958-70; founded & promoted the National Business Development Organization (Indian), Los Angeles, 1968-70. *Military service*: U.S. Army Air Corps, 1943-45 (Pilot-Flight Engineer). *Community activities*: UCLA Cultural Center (chairman); Los Angeles Mayor's Advisory Committee (board member); California Attorney General's Advisory Committee (board member). *Memberships*: National Indian Education Association (board member); United Indian Development Association (founder). *Awards, honors*: Family of the Year, Hughes Aircraft Co., 1956; Resolution by Governor Pat Brown, California, 1956; plaque for being first Indian to drive car in parade for a President of the U.S., 1964; Resolution, Indians of Los Angeles, 1967; Resolution, Indian Leader of the Year, National Congress of American Indians, 1968; appointment by President Nixon, 1970. *Biographical sources*: Who's Who in Government, 1972, 1973; Contemporary Indian Leaders of America, 1973; Community Leaders and Noteworthy Americans, 1975-76; Who's Who Honorary Society, 1976.

VASSAR, JAN 1940-
(librarian, journalist)
Born June 19, 1940. *Education*: Tulsa University, BA, 1962; University of Oklahoma, 1962-64. *Principal occupation*: Librarian, journalist. *Home address*: P.O. Box 454, Chandler, OK 74834 (405) 258-1219. *Affiliations*: Reporter &

editorial supervisor, Sac & Fox Nation, Stroud, OK, 1985-; library director, Sac & Fox Public Library, Stroud, OK, 1991-. *Community activites*: Lincoln County Arts & Humanities Council (board of directors). *Memberships*: Native American Press Association; Oklahoma Historical Society; Lincoln County Historical Society (board member, president, curator). *Awards, honors*: Best Feature Photo, Native American Press Association.

*VATTER, ANTOINETTE
(organization director)
Affiliation: American Indian Service Corp., 1007 Dillingham St. #102, Honolulu, HI 96817 (808) 847-2511.

VAUGHAN, TOM
(park supt.)
Affiliation: Chaco Culture National Historical Park, Star Route 4, Box 6500, Bloomfield, NM 87413 (505) 786-5384.

*VAUGHN, MARCELLA B.
(school principal)
Affiliation: Red Water Elementary School, Rte. 4, Box 30, Carthage, MS 39051 (601) 267-8500.

VEEDER, VOLKERT
(museum curator)
Affiliation: The Mohawk-Caughnawaga Museum, Route 5, Box 554, Fonda, NY 12068 (518) 853-3678.

VEILEUX, FRED
(director)
Affiliation: Concerned American Indian Parents, CUHCC cLinic, 2016 16th Ave. S., Minneapolis, MN 55404 (612) 627-4774.

*VEINCENT, LEHUA M. (Hawaiian) 1965-
(teacher)
Born August 23, 1965, Hilo, Hawaii. *Education*: University of Hawaii, Hilo, BBA, BA (Hawaiian Studies, Elementary Education). *Principal occupation*: D.O.E. teacher. *Home address*: 30 Pilipa'a St., Hilo, HI 96720 (808) 959-8732.

*VELASQUEZ, ROBERT (San Felipe Pueblo)
(Pueblo governor)
Affiliation: San Felipe Pueblo Council, Box A, San Felipe Pueblo, NM 87001 (505) 867-3381.

*VELKY, RICHARD (Schaghticoke)
(tribal chairperson)
Affiliation: Schaghticoke Tribal Council, 605 Main St., Monroe, CT 06468 (203) 459-2531.

*VENT, GILBERT (Athapascan)
(village first chief)
Affiliation: Allakaket Community, P.O. Box 30, Allakaket, AK 99720 (907) 968-2241.

*VENT, WARNER (Athapascan)
(village chief)
Affiliation: Huslia Village Council, P.O. Box 32, Huslia, AK 99746 (907) 829-2202.

VERMILLION, EDWARD (Hopi)
(school principal)
Affiliation: Hopi Day School, P.O. Box 42, Kykotsmovi, AZ 86039 (602) 734-2468.

VETTESE, DENNIS
(health director)
Affiliation: Elko Southern Band Clinic, 515 Shoshone Cir., Elko, NV 89801 (702) 738-2252.

VIARIAL, JACOB (Pueblo)
(Pueblo governor)
Affiliation: Pueblo of Pojoaque, Route 11, Box 71, Santa Fe, NM 87501 (505) 455-2278/9.

*VIGIL, B. THOMAS
(institute chairperson)
Affiliation: First Nations Development Institute, The Stores Bldg., 11917 Main St., Fredericksburg, VA 22408 (703) 371-5615.

VIGIL, SHERRYL J. (Jicarilla Apache)
(BIA agency supt.)
Affiliation: Jicarilla Agency, Bureau of Indian Affairs,P.O. Box 167, Dulce, NM 87528 (505) 759-3951.

VIGIL, TONY B. (Nambe Pueblo)
(pueblo governor)
Affiliation: Pueblo of Nambe, Route 1, Box 117-BB, Santa Fe, NM 87501 (505) 455-2036.

*VIGIL, VIDA L. (Jicarilla Apache)
(editor)
Affiliation: Jicarilla Chieftain, Jicarilla Apache Tribe, P.O. Box 507, Dulce, NM 87528 (505) 759-3242.

*VIGIL-MUNIZ, CLAUDIA
(higher education program counselor)
Affiliation: Jicarilla Apache Higher Education Program, P.O. Box 507, Dulce, NM 87528 (505) 759-3615.

*VILLALOBOS, MIKE
(Warm Springs Confederated)
(radio station manager)
Affiliation: KWSO - 91.9 FM, Warm Springs Confederated Tribes, P.O. Box 489, Warm Springs, OR 97761 (503) 553-1968.

VIOLA, HERMAN J. 1938-
(historian)
Born February 24, 1938, Chicago, Ill. *Education*: Marquette University, BA, 1962, MA, 1964; Indiana University, PhD, 1970. *Principal occupation*: Historian-specially American Indian history. *Home address*: 7307 Pinewood St., Falls Church, VA 22046. *Affiliations*: Staff, National Archives, 1968-72; director, National Anthropological Archives, Smithsonian Institution, Washington, D.C., 1972-87. *Other professional posts*: Founder and first editor of Prologue, The Journal of the National Archives, 1968-72; consultant to numerous scholarly and educational organizations, including, the Galef Institute, Randam House, The Library of the American West, and the Library of the American Indian. *Military service*: U.S. Navy, 1960-62. *Memberships*: Society of American Archivists; Western History Association; Organization of American Historians; Phi Beta Kappa. *Awards, honors*: 1984 Merit Award for "Distinguished Professional Achievement," from Marquette University; in 1987, he was one of three finalists for the position of Archivist of the U.S., which is a presidential appointment; in June 1988, he received an honorary doctor of letters degree from Wittenberg University. *Interests*: Research specialties are the American West and the American Indian. *Biographical source*: Who's Who in America. *Published works*: Thomas L. McKinney, Architect of America's Early Indian Policy, 1816-1830 (Swallow Press, 1972); The Indian Legacy of Charles Bird King (Smithsonian Institution Press & Doubleday, 1976); Diplomats in Buckskin (Smithsonian Institution Press, 1981);

The National Archives of the U.S. (Harry N. Abrams, 1984); Magnificent Voyagers: The U.S. Exploring Expedition, 1838-1841 (Smithsonian Institution Press, 1986); Exploring the West (Smithsonian Exposition Books, 1987); After Columbus: The Smithsonian's Chronicle of the Indians of North America Since 1492 (Smithsonian Institution Press, 1990); & editor of Seeds of Change, A Quincentennial Commemoration (Smithsonian Institution Press, 1991).

*VIRGIL, DALE Jicarilla Apache)
(tribal chairperson)
Affiliation: Jicarilla Apache Tribal Council, P.O. Box 147, Dulce, NM 87528 (505) 759-3242.

VIRGIL, TONY B. (Pueblo)
(Pueblo governor)
Affiliation: Nambe Pueblo Council, Route 1, Box 117-BB, Santa Fe, NM 87501 (505) 455-7752.

VIT, LINDA C. (Karuk-Cree)
(jewelry designer-traditional)
Born November 28, 1947, Yreka, Calif. *Principal occupation*: Jewelry designer-traditional. *Home address*: 7884 Rockway, Eureka, CA 95502 (707) 442-8800. *Affiliation*: Karuk Originals by Vit, Eureka, CA, 1977-. *Other professional post*: Marketing developer, Northern California Development Council. *Membership*: Indian Arts and Crafts Association.

VIZINA, RUSSELL (Chippewa)
(health director)
Affiliation: Sault Ste. Marie Tribal Clinic, Wilson Rd., Bldg. 312, Kincheloe, MI 49788 (906) 495-5615.

VOGT, DAVID, D.O.
(clinical director)
Affiliation: Sault Ste. Marie Tribal Clinic, 312 Water Tower Dr., Kincheloe, MI 49788 (906) 495-5615.

VOIGHT, THOMAS F. 1947-
(publisher)
Born March 8, 1947, Milwaukee, Wisc. *Education*: University of Wisconsin, Milwaukee, BA, 1972, MA, 1976. *Principal occupation*: Publisher. *Home address*: P.O. Box 889, New Castle, CO 81647 (303) 984-3685. *Affiliation*: President (owner/founder), Wintercount (art, prose & poetry of the American Indian), New Castle, CO, 1984-. *Other professional post*: Instructor, Colorado Mountain College, Glenwood Springs, CO. *Community activities*: Member, Chamber of Commerce, New Castle; member & volunteer, Public Radio Station, KDNK, Carbondale, CO; board member, Rural Fire District; sponsor Ute Legacy Juried Art Show. *Memberships*: National Indian Youth Council; American Indian Arts & Crafts Association; National Museum of the American Indian (charter member); Hollywood Stuntman Hall of Fame, Moab, UT (charter member); Appaloosa Horse Club. *Awards, honors*: Certificate of Excellence, Colorado Mountain College. *Interests*: "Extensive art collection of American Indian paintings and crafts. Have traveled to numerous Indian reservations & archaeological sites and have participated in the discovery & restoration of archaeological areas."

VOISEY, EVA
(association president)
Affiliation: Inuit Women's Association, 200 Elgin St., Suite 804, Ottawa, Ontario, Canada K2P 1L5 (613) 238-3977.

VOLBORTH, JUDITH ANN *(Mountain-Leaf)*
(Blackfeet/Comanche) 1956-
(writer, poet)
Born October 23, 1956, New York, N.Y. *Education*: Los Angeles Pierce Colege, AA, 1975; University of California, Los Angeles, BA, 1986. *Principal occupation*: Writer, poet. *Home address*: 1032B - 3rd St., Santa Monica, CA 90403 (310) 395-5923. *Other professional posts*: Educator, public speaker. *Community activities*: Emergency medical technician (volunteer); volunteer working with homeless & mentally ill adults. *Memberships*: Native Writer's Circle of the Americas; Wordcraft: Circle of Native American Mentor & Apprentice Writers; Association for the Study of American Indian Literatures. *Awards, honors*: Ina Coolbrith Memorial Prize for Poetry; Shirley Dorothy Robbins Creative Writing Award; The May Merrill Miller Award for Poetry; Academy of American Poets Award (honorable mention). *Biographical sources*: "Portrait of a Mentor," by Lee Francis, in Native American Renaissance, by Ken Lincoln; Indian Humor: Bicultural Play in Native America, by Ken Lincoln; Native American Lesbian & Gay Literature, by Will Roscoe. *Published work*: Thunder-Root: Traditional & Contemporary Native American Verse (American Indian Studies Center, UCLA, 1978).

*VOLK, JOSEPH E.
(executive director)
Affiliation: Friends Committee on National Legislation, 245 Second St., NE, Washington, DC 20010 (202) 547-6000.

*VOLK, NORMAN
(center director)
Affiliation: Tekakwitha Fine Arts Center, P.O. Box 208, Sisseton, SD 57262 (608) 698-7058.

*VOLZ, KATHARINE J.
(executive director)
Affiliation: Marin Museum of the American Indian Library, P.O. Box 864, 2200 Novato Blvd., Novato, CA 94948 (415) 897-4064.

*VOSBERG, RICHARD
(Indian school superintendent)
Affiliation: Crazy Horse School, P.O. Box 260, Wanblee, SD 57577 (605) 462-6511.

W

*WABNUM, FREDA F.
(BIA agency supt.)
Affiliation: Laguna Agency, Bureau of Indian Affairs, P.O. Box 1448, Laguna, NM 87026 (505) 552-6001.

*WACHACHA, MARY G.
(health education coordinator)
Affiliation: Cherokee Technical Support Center, P.O. Box 429, Butler Bldg., Rt. 1, Sequoyah Trail, Cherokee, NC 28719 (704) 497-5030.

WACONDA, JOSEPHINE T.
(IHS area director)
Affiliation: Albuquerque Area Office, Indian Health Service, 505 Marquette Ave., NW, Albuquerque, NM 87102 (505) 766-2151.

WADENA, DARRELL (Chippewa)
(tribal president/chairperson)
Affiliation: President, Minnesota Chippewa Tribal Executive Committee, P.O. Box 217C, Cass Lake, MN 56633 (218) 335-2252; chairperson, White Earth Reservation Business Committee, P.O. Box 418, White Earth, MN 56591 (218) 983-3285; Circle of Life Survival School, White Earth, MN.

WADITAKA, LORNE
(Indian band chief)
Affiliation: Wahpeton Indian Band, Box 128, Prince Albert, Saskatchewan, Canada S6V 5R4 (306) 764-6649.

*WADZINSKI, KEVIN
(Stockbridge/Munsee-Mohican) 1966-
(attorney)
Born May 3, 1966, Oconto Falls, Wisc. *Education*: University of Wisconsin, BA, 1988; University of Wisconson Law School, JD, 1993. *Principal occupation*: Attorney. Resides in Minneapolis, MN (612) 340-2766. *Affiliation*: Dorsey & Whitney Law Firm, Indian Law Dept., Minneapolis, MN, 1993-. *Community activities*: Minnesota American Indian Chamber of Commerce; vice president, Indigenous Law Students Association, 1991-92; note & comment editor, Wisconsin International Law Journals, 1992-93. *Memberships*: Minnesota American Indian Bar Association; Native American Bar Association; Wisconsin Bar Assn. - Indian Law Section.

WAGGONER, DONALD RAY, Sr. (*Thunder Wolf*) (United Lumbee/Cherokee) 1934-
(butcher, plant manager)
Born February 25, 1934, Spencer, Iowa. *Home address*: 1211 North Park, Springfield, MO 65802 (417) 865-2261. *Affiliation*: Manager, Wyatts Packing Plant, Ozark, MO, 1986-. *Other professional post*: Chief, United Lumbee Nation's Black Bear Clan (3 states, MO, KS, IL), 1987-. *Military service*: U.S. Navy (4 active/4 inactive; GM3; UN Ribbon, Korean Ribbon, 2 Stars; Good Conduct Medal). *Memberships*: United Lumbee Nation of N.C. & America; Southwest Missouri Indian Center; Pan American Indian Association; Golden Hawk Warrior Society; Unlom Waaow Society of United Lumbee Nation of N.C. & America; United Lumbee Nation. *Interests*: "Enjoy teaching flintknapping to young ones at Indian summer camp; enjoy attending pow wows; working with school children (giving talks, showing artifacts, crafts, etc.)."

WAGGONER, DONALD RAY, Jr. (*Rain Shadow*) (United Lumbee/Cherokee) 1955-
(baker)
Born December 12, 1955, Springfield, Mo. *Education*: Business College (2 years). *Principal occupation*: Baker. *Other professional post*: Vice-chief, United Lumbee Nation's Black Bear Clan. *Memberships*: Pan American; Warrior Society - Black Bear Clan. *Interests*: Electronics, working with my hands; all wood crafts, making knives; hunting, fishing, cave exploring, reading; chess, computers.

WAGGONER/WHITE, MARILYN ANN (*Little Butterfly*) (United Lumbee/Cherokee) 1957-
(tribal council member)
Born January 22, 1957, Springfield, Mo. *Education*: High school. *Principal occupation*: Tribal council member. *Home address*: 816 West Pershing, Springfield, MO 65806 (417) 869-4549. *Affiliations*: Owner, J&M Enterprises,

Springfield, MO; council member, United Lumbee Nations Black Bear Clan. *Other professional posts*: Wife/mother; tribal council member. *Community activities*: Make & donate crafts to the Nation & the Indian Center; Little Butterfly's delivery service (supplies for Black Bear Clan)' acting liaison between Bear Woman & Indian Center. *Memberships*: Golden Hawk Warrior Society (disbanded); Unlom W aaow Society of United Lumbee Nation of N.C. & America; United Lumbee Nation; Southwest Missouri Indian Center; Pan American Indian Association; Mantoac Medicine Society. *Interests*: "I enjoy traveling to the crystal mines to dig for crystals to share. I have taught beadwork at several schools, participated in programs with other members of the Black Bear Clan teaching Indian culture to elementary schools; enjoy working with leather, beads, etc.; run Little Butterfly's delivery service by going for them. (I) enjoy dancing at Will Rogers Pow Wow's."

*WAHLBERG, RON, M.D.
(IHS-chief medical officer)
Affiliation: Bemidji Area IHS, 127 Federal Bldg., Bemidji, MN 56601 (218) 759-3414.

WAHNEE, JOHN D.
(BIA agency supt. for education)
Affiliation: Hopi Agency, Bureau of Indian Affairs, P.O. Box 568, Keams Canyon, AZ 86034 (602) 738-2262.

WAHQUAHBOSHKUK, GEORGE
(Prairie Potawatomi)
(tribal chairperson)
Affiliation: Prairie Potawatomi Tribal Council, P.O. Box 97, Mayetta, KS 66509 (913) 966-2255.

WAKEMAN, RICHARD K.
(Flandreau Santee Sioux) 1923-
(tribal officer)
Born February 9, 1923, Flandreau, S.D. *Education*: Haskell Institute. *Principal occupation*: Tribal officer. *Home address*: R.R. 1, Box 59A, Flandreau, SD 57028. *Affiliation*: Former president, Flandreau Santee Sioux Business Council. *Military service*: U.S. Marine Corps, 1942-45; U.S. Army, 1951-53 (Presidential Unit Citation; Commendation; Asiatic Pacific Award). *Community activities*: South Dakota Indian Commission; South Dakota Letter Carriers (president); Dakota Presbytery (moderator); Masonic Lodge. *Interests*: Tribal history.

*WALCOTT, PETER, Sr.
(village president)
Affiliation: Ekwok Village Council, P.O. Box 70, Ekwok, AK 99580 (907) 464-3311.

WALDEN, HENRY ALTON, Jr. (Pima) 1950-
(health systems management)
Born November 29, 1950, Albuquerque, N.M. *Education*: Phoenix City College, AA, 1976; Arizona State University, BS, 1978; University of Hawaii, MPH, 1982. *Principal occupation*: Health systems management). *Home address*: 13211 39th Ave., Yuma, AZ 85365 (602) 342-4739. *Affiliations*: Community Health Education, Scottsdale, AZ, 1982-84; Public Health Education, Parker, AZ, 1984-88; hospital administrator, Indian Health Service, USPHS, Fort Yuma, AZ, 1988-. *Military service*: U.S. Navy, Dental Corps. (Petty Officer-Third Class, National Defense, Viet Nam Service, Viet Nam Campaign

Good Conduct); Lt. Commissioned Corps, U.S. Public Health Service. *Community activities*: Board of directors, Behavioral Health Agency of Central Arizona. *Interests*: "Native American culture, social inter-actions between Native peoples and mainstream America, health and social problems and their resolutions. *Hobbies*: Automobile restoration, silversmithing, painting, musical instruments and my children." *Published works*: "A Second Opinion on Zuni Diabetes" (U.S. Public Health Reports, April 1983); "Are We Overlooking Some Winning Strategies (IHS Provider, June 1988).

WALDRAM, JAMES B. 1955-
(professor)
Born August 20, 1955, Oshawa, Ontario, Can. *Education*: University of Waterloo, BA, 1978; University of Manitoba, MA, 1980; University of Connecticut, PhD, 1983. *Principal occupation*: Professor. *Home address*: 247 Sylvian Way, Saskatoon, Saskatchewan, Can. *Affiliation*: Assistant professor, Dept. of Native American Studies, University of Saskatchewan, Saskatoon, Sask., Can., 1983-. *Other professional post*: Associate editor, Native Studies Review. *Memberships*: Canadian Ethnology Society; Canadian Indian/Native Studies Association; Canadian Association for Medical Anthropology; American Anthropological Association; Society for Applied Anthropology. *Awards, honors*: Social Sciences and Humanities Research Council of Canada Doctoral Fellowship. *Interests*: "The impact of hydroelectric development of northern Canadian Native communities. Dietary change in the Canadian north; education needs assessment of urban Native people; health and health care delivery of urban Native people." *Published work*: 1885 and After: Native Society in Transition (Canadian Plains Research Center, Regina, 1986).

WALDRON, DARRELL
(president-board of directors)
Affiliation: Rhode Island Indian Council, Inc., 444 Friendship St., Providence, RI 02907 (401) 331-4440.

WALKER, BETTY
(BIA area education administrator)
Affiliation: Minneapolis Area Office, Bureau of Indian Affairs, 331 Second Ave. South, Minneapolis, MN 55401 (612) 373-1090.

WALKER, CHRISTINE (Chemehuevi)
(tribal chairperson)
Affiliation: Chemehuevi Tribal Council, P.O. Box 1976, Chemehuevi Valley, CA 92363 (619) 858-4531.

*WALKER, DARLENE
(health center director)
Affiliation: Inscription House PHS Indian Health Center, Inscription House, AZ 86054 (602) 672-2611.

*WALKER, DAVIDAH "CONNIE"
(Cherokee/Chippewa) 1950-
(paralegal secretary, freelance journalist)
Born May 28, 1950, Spokane, Wash. *Education*: Spertus College of Judaica (Chicago, IL), 1972-74; Roosevelt University (Chicago, IL), Paralegal Course, 1978. *Principal occupation*: Paralegal secretary, freelance journalist. *Home address*: 6652 Greeley Ave., Kansas City, KS 66104 (913) 299-6442; 788-5971. *Community activities*: Board member, Minorities Museum,

Overland Park, KS; board member, American Indian Support Network, KS; KS coordinator for, Walk for Justice, 1994. *Interests*: "In 1979, I moved to the State of Israel, where I lived for about seven years. I then moved to England, where I lived for one year prior to returning to the U.S. During the time I lived abroad, I worked primarily as a paralegal secretary and pursued my writing secondarily. Now that I am back in the U.S., I am extremely interested in current Indian issues. I use my writing skills to promote support for the issues most vital to the survival of our culture & spirituality." *Biographical source*: Sioux Falls Argus Leader, Sept. 12, 1994, "Other Views." *Published works*: Poetry in the "National Anthology of Poetry"; authored one book, not yet published.

WALKER, FRANKLIN
(park & museum supt.)
Affiliation: Nez Perce National Historical Park & Museum, P.O. Box 93, Spalding, ID 83551.

WALKER, JANA LYNN
(Shawnee/Cherokee/Delaware) 1954-
(attorney)
Born October 2, 1954, Tulsa, Okla. *Education*: University of Oklahoma, BS, 1977; University of New Mexico School of Law, JD, 1987. *Principal occupation*: Attorney. *Address*: Star Route Box 702, Placitas, NM 87043 (505) 867-0579. *Affiliation*: Formerly, Junior partner, Gover, Stetson & Williams (an Indian -owned law firm), Albuquerque, NM, 1989-93; solo practitioner, Placitas, NM, 1993-. *Memberships*: American Bar Association - Section of Natural Resources, Energy & Environmental Law (council member, 1991-94); Committee on Native American Natural Resources (chair, 1991-92; vice-chair, 1988-90); Standing Committee on Environmental Law (member, 1992-95);Section on Business Law (member, 1990-); New Mexico Bar Association - Indian Law Section (chair, 1992-93; board member, 1989-94); Indian Bar Association of New Mexico; Arizona Bar Association - Indian Law Section; Native American Bar Association. *Biographical sources*: Who's Who Among Rising Young Americans, 1992; Who's Who in American Law, 1992-93, 7th Ed, 1993-94, 8th Ed. *Published works*: Articles - "On-Reservation Treaty Hunting Rights" (26 Natural Resources Journal 187, 1986); "Tribal Environmental Regulation" with B. Kevin Gover (36 Federal Bar Journal No. 9, Nov. 1989); " Tribal Civil Regulatory Jurisdiction to Enforce Environemtal Laws" with B. Kevin Gover (Institute on Mineral Development on Indian Lands, Paper No. 14, Rocky Mountain Mineral Law Foundation, 1989); "Native American Study Draws Poor Conclusions From Poor Conditions" with W. Richard West, Jr. (Legal Times, June 4, 1990; Texas Lawyer, July 2, 1990); "Indian Reserved Water Rights" with Susan M. Williams (5 Natural Resources & Environment No. 4, Spring 1991); "Escaping Environmental Paternalism," with Kevin Gover (63 U. of Colorado Law Review. 933 (1992); "Commercial Solid & Hazardous Waste Disposal Projects on Indian Lands," (10 Yale J. on Reg. 229 (Winter 1993), with Kevin Gover.

WALKER, MARIE-ANN DAY
(Indian band chief)
Affiliation: Okanese Indian Band, Box 759, Balcarres, Saskatchewan, Canada S0G 0C0 (306) 334-2532.

WALKER, WILLARD 1926-
(professor emeritus-anthropology)
Born July 29, 1926, Boston, Mass. *Education*: Harvard College, BA, 1950; University of Arizona, MA, 1953; Cornell University, PhD, 1964. *Principal occupation*: Professor emeritus-anthropology, Wesleyan University, Middletown, CT, 1966-. *Home address*: Rt. 2, Box 3310, Canaan, ME 04924 (207) 474-5316. *Memberships*: American Anthropological Association (Fellow); Society for Applied Anthropology (Fellow); Linguistics Society of America; American Ethnological Society; American Society for Ethnohistory; Southern Anthropological Association; Northeastern Anthropological Association ; Museum of the Cherokee Indian Association. *Interests*: "Indian American languages, cultures, ethnohistory. Particular interest in Creeks and Cherokees in the Southeast, the Zuni, Hopi and Yaqui pueblos in the Southwest, and the Algonquian peoples of the Maine-Maritime area." *Published works*: Cherokee Primer (Carnegie Corp. Cross-Cultural Education Project, University of Chicago, 1965); co-author, Cherokee Stories (Laboratory of Anthropology, Wesleyan University, 1966); "Cherokee" in Studies in Southeastern Indian Languages (University of Georgia Press, 1975; "Zuni Semantic Categories" in Handbook of North American Indian, vol. 9 (Smithsonian Institution Press, 1979); co-author, "A Chronological Account of the Wabanaki Confederacy" in Political Organization of Native North Americans (University Press of America, 1980); "Native American Writing Systems" in Language in the U.S.A. (Cambridge University Press, 1981); "Cherokee Curing and Conjuring, Identity, and the Southeastern Co-tradition" in Persistent Peoples Cultural Enclaves in Perspective (University of Arizona Press, 1981); "The Hopis & the Tewas" in Hopis, Tewas, and the American Road (Wesleyan University, 1983); co-editor, Hopis, Tewas & the American Road (University of New Mexico Press, 1986); "What Zuni Is Really Like" in Essays in Honor of Charles F. Hockett (E.J. Brill, Leiden, 1983); "Wabanaki Wampum Protocol", Papers of the Fifteenth Algonquian Conference (Carleton University, 1984); "Creek Curing in Academe" in General Ethnolinguistics in Remembrance of Stanley Newman (Mouton de Gruyter, 1989); "The Responses of Bilingual and Monolingual Zunis to a Zuni Language Questionnaire" in The Content of Culture: Constants and Variants Studies in Honor of John M. Roberts (HRAF Press, 1989); numerous articles.

WALKER, WILLIAM D.
(school supt.)
Affiliation: Labre Indian School, P.O. Box 406, Ashland, MT 59003 (406) 784-2347.

WALKING BULL, GILBERT C. (Oglala Sioux) 1930-
(spiritual teacher, artist)
Born June 18, 1930, Hot Springs, S.D. *Education*: Oregon College of Education (2 years). *Principal occupation*: Spiritual teacher. *Address*: P.O. Box 200, Wanblee, SD 57577 (605) 462-6544. *Affiliation*: Co-director, Ti Ospaye, Wanblee, SD, 1991-; editor, "Wolf Songs (quarterly newsletter). *Community activities*: Member, Pine Ridge Reservation, Oglala Sioux Tribe; Gilbert, while residing in Oregon from the early 1970s through 1990, was instrumental in starting Native American clubs, and played an important role in bringing pow wows to the Pacific Northwest. *Memberships*: Inter-Tribal Council,

Portland, OR; National Indian Education Association (Project Media evaluation team); Independent Indian Arts & Crafts Persons Association (helped to organize). *Awards, honors*: Award for Distinction for Art, La Grande Indian Arts Festival, 1974; First Prize Award for Traditional Sioux Fancy Dance, Siletz, OR, 1973; First Prize Award for Traditional Sioux Painting, 1976, '77, La Grande Indian Arts Festival. *Interests*: "Do traditional Sioux geometrical designs on canvas in oil and acrylics; do Sioux crafts in beadwork & leather. (I am a) soloist, singing in the Lakota language with guitar and drum in public performance. Fancy dancer and participant in Indian gatherings since youth, winning many awards. At present, I am concentrating on traditional Sioux art, translating the legends of my people. I am traditional & bilingual. In my books, I am recording tales from the reservation, writing original poetry, translating songs and scoring songs." His grandfather was Move Camp (spiritual leader), his great grandfather was the prophet, Sitting Bull, and his great uncle was Crazy Horse. *Biographical source*: Who's Who Among the Lakotas. *Published works*: O-hu-kah-kan (Poetry, Songs, Legends, Stories), 1975; Wo ya-ka-pi (Telling Stories of the Past and Present), 1976; Mi ta-ku-ye (About Our People), 1977; all books co-authored with Montana H.R. Walking Bull, printed by the Itemizer Observer, Dallas, OR, and may be purchased from the Walking Bulls at their home address.

*WALKING EAGLE, PATRICIA
(Indian education)
Affiliation: North Dakota Indian Education Association, P.O. Box 199, Fort Totten, ND 58335 (701) 766-4161.

WALLACE, A. BRIAN (Washoe)
(tribal chairperson)
Affiliation: Washoe Tribal Council, Rt. 2, 919 Highway 395 South, Gardnerville, NV 89410 (702) 265-4191.

*WALLACE, ALBERT
(council chief)
Affiliation: Aukquan Traditional Council, 9296 Stephen Richards Memorial Dr., Junea, AK 99801 (907) 465-4120.

WALLACE, ANTHONY F.C. 1923-
(professor emeritus-anthropology)
Born April 15, 1923, Toronto, Can. *Education*: University of Pennsylvania, BA, 1947, MA, 1949, PhD, 1950. *Principal occupation*: Professor of anthropology. *Home address*: 614 Convent Rd., Chester, PA 19014. *Affiliations*: Professor of anthropology, University of Pennsylvania, 1961-; medical research scientist, Eastern Pennsylvania Psychiatric Institute, 1961-. *Other professional posts*: Member, National Research Council, Division of Behavioral Sciences; U.S. Office of Education, Research Advisory Committee; member, Behavioral Science Study Section, National Institute of Mental Health. *Military service*: U.S. Army, 1942-45. *Memberships*: American Anthropological Association (Fellow); American Association for the Advancement of Science (Fellow; chairman, Section H); American Sociological Association (Fellow); Sigma Xi; Philadelphia Anthropological Society. *Published works*: The Modal Personality Structure of the Tuscarora Indians, as Revealed by the Rorschach Bureau of American Ethnology, 1952); editor and author of introduction, The Ghost-Dance Religion and the Sioux Outbreak of 1890

(University of Chicago Press, 1965); The Death and Rebirth of the Seneca (Knopf, 1970); other books and numerous articles in professional journals.

WALLACE, BONNIE (*Gida-gaa-bines-ikwe*) (Lake Superior Chippewa) 1946-
(program administrator)
Born December 4, 1946, Fond du Lac Reservation, Cloquet, Minn. *Education*: University of Minnesota, BA, 1974, graduate work, 1982. *Principal occupation*: Program administrator. *Address*: 2211 Riverside Ave., Minneapolis, MN 55454 (612) 330-1138 (work). *Affiliations*: Community program assistant, University of Minnesota, 1970-74; education specialist, Minnesota Chippewa Tribe, 1974-78; program administrator, Augsburg College, Minneapolis, MN, 1978- (director, American Indian Support Program, Minnesota Indian Teacher Training Project, American Indian Studies Minor, Woodland Anishinabe Library). *Other professional posts*: Fond du Lac Urban Representative; Minnesota Chippewa Tribe's Executive Committee; Fond du Lac Tribal College, Cloquet, MN (chair, board of regents); planner, Annual Ojibwe Art Expo; grants evaluator; advisory board of numerous organizations, including: American Indian Business Development Corp. *Community activities*: Grants reviewer, Minnesota State Department of Corrections; Victim Services Programs; member, Minnesota Indian State Scholarship Committee; member, Mixed Blood Theatre; member, Urban Advisory Council-State of Minnesota; member, Minnesota Minority Education Partnership; former chairperson, American Indian Business Development Corp. *Memberships*: Minnesota Chippewa Tribe; Minnesota Indian Education Association (advisory board); National Indian Education Association; Museum of the American Indian/Smithsonian. *Awards, honors*: Contributions to Community United Way of Minneapolis, 1984; Contributions to Elders Award, American Indian Family Services, 1986; Contributions to Youth Award, Minneapolis Youth Diversion Project, 1986; Counselor of the Year, Minnesota Indian Education Association, 1987; Award of Merit, National Women of Color Day, 1990. *Published works*: Battering and the Indian Women, State Dept. of Corrections, 1980); Case Study, Ojibwe Women, Minority Women (Women's Institute of S.E. Atlanta, 1981); Touchwood, A Collection of Ojibwe Prose (Two Rivers Press, 1987); article - "Great Strides, Great Strides" in Private College Magazine, 1988).

*WALLACE, DOUGLAS
(AK Indian association president)
Affiliation: Douglas Indian Association, P.O. Box 020478, Juneau, AK 99802 (907) 586-1798.

*WALLACE, SR. MAUREEN
(school principal)
Affiliation: Beatrice Rafferty School, Pleasant Point Reservation, Perry, ME 04667 (207) 853-6085.

WALLS, BILL
(executive director)
Affiliation: Native American Services Agency, Missoula Indian Center, 2300 Regent St. #A, Missoula, MT 59801 (406) 329-3373.

*WALTER, MARY JO
(school principal)
Affiliation: Gila Crossing Day School, P O Box 10, Laveen, AZ 85339 (602) 237-4834.

*WALTERS, ANNA LEE (Pawnee/Otoe)
    (English teacher; writer-editor)
Affiliation: Navajo Community College, P.O. Box 126, Tsaile, AZ 86556. *Other professional post*: National Advisory Caucus for Wordcraft Circle of Native American Mentor & Apprentice Writers.*Published works*: Talking Indian: Reflections on Writing and Survival; Neon Powwow: New Native American Voices of the Southwest.

*WALTERS, BILL
    (school principal)
Affiliation: Cibecue Community School, P.O. Box 68, Cibecue, AZ 85911 (602) 332-2444.

WALTERS, TERRANCE C.
    (BIA agency director)
Affiliation: Fort Berthold Agency, Bureau of Indian Affairs, P.O. Box 370, New Town, ND 58763 (701) 627-4707.

*WANATEE, GAILEY
    (tribal chief)
Affiliation: Sac & Fox Tribal Council, 3137 F Ave., Tama, IA 52339 (515) 484-4678.

WANCHENA, MATTHEW JOHN
(Yakima-Blackfeet) 1951-
    (building code enforcement specialist)
Born March 9, 1951, Tacoma, Wash. *Education*: Washington State University, BS (Architecture), 1974; City University (Bellevue, WA), 1984-89, MBA, MPA. *Principal occupation*: Building code enforcement specialist. *Home address*: 4529 Tacoma Ave. South, Tacoma, WA 98408 (206) 472-4011. *Affiliations*: Self employed building code consultant, Tacoma, WA. 1993-; building inspector/plans examiner for different local governments, 1979-. *Military service*: U.S. Army (Army Commendation, 8-91 to 2-26-92, National Defense Army Reserves Overseas Medal, Army Reserve Components Achievement Medal, Overseas Service Medal, Army Service Medal, Southwest Asia Service Medal); rank currently Major in U.S. Army Reserves, Corps of Engineers on the 1995 list for LTC. *Community activities*: Co-chairperson of Pierce County Native American Indian Advisory Council for Minority Commission; Pierce County Ethnic Commission (vice president, 1993); vice-president of the "Arts Together," an ethnic association in the Pierce County & Tacoma area; do job fairs at local schools. *Memberships*: American Institute of Architects, Tacoma, WA; International Conference of Building Officials, Whittier, CA; American Indian Science & Engineering Society; National Fire Protection Association; Society of American Military Engineers. *Awards, honors*: Saudi Arabia Joint Support Medal from the Saudi Government for Desert Storm, 1991-92. *Interests*: "Architectural history, Native American architecture in the U.S.; visited Italy, Yugoslavia, Portugal and Spain. Have been through the Southwest and in my own Northwest to see the types of architecture that is out there. Currently helping the University of Puget Sound with setting up an American Indian Association, mentoring to junior high school and college students in the Tacoma & Pierce County area. Knowledgeable in computers & helping the local school districts with Indian students that need help." *Biographical source*: American Association of the Army, 1982 article by a soldier on me.

WAPATO, S. TIMOTHY
    (executive director)
Affiliation: National Indian Gaming Association, 904 Pennsylvania Ave., SE, Washington, DC 20003 (202) 546-7711, 1994-. *Past professional post*: Commissioner, Administration for Native Americans, Dept. of Health & Human Services, Washington, DC, 1990-92; Columbia River Inter-tribal Fish Commission, Portland, OR, 1992-94.

WAQUAN, ARCHIE
    (Indian band chief)
Affiliation: Cree Indian Band, Box 90, Fort Chipewyan, AB, Can. T0P 1B0 (403) 697-3740.

WAR BONNETT, AMANDA
    (editor)
Affiliation: Lakota Times, Native American Publishing, 1920 Lombardy Dr., Rapid City, SD 57701 (605) 341-0011.

*WARBURTON, MIRANDA
    (dept. manager)
Affiliation: Navajo Nation Archaeology Dept. Northern Arizona University, P.O. Box 6013, Flagstaff, AZ 86011 (602) 523-7428.

WARD, ALFRED (Shoshone)
    (tribal chairperson)
Affiliation: Shoshone Business Council, P.O. Box 217, Fort Washakie, WY 82514 (307) 332-3532.

WARD, JOHN A.
    (museum president)
Affiliation: Sonotabac Prehistoric Indian Mound and Museum, P.O. Box 941, Vincennes, IN 47591 (812) 885-4330.

WARD, MICHAEL
    (Indian band chief)
Affiliation: Red Bank Indian Band, Box 120, Red Bank, New Brunswick, Canada E0C 1W0 (506) 836-2366.

*WARE, SUE (Modoc) 1944-
    (forensic anthropologist, teacher)
Born September 24, 1994, St. Joseph, Mo. *Education*: University of Northern Colorado, MA, 1977; University of Colorado, MA, 1990. *Principal occupation*: Forensic anthropologist, teacher. *Home address*: 307 Clermont St., Denver, CO 80202 (303) 322-8309 (work). *Affiliation*: Earth Gypsy, Denver, CO, 1990-; Denver Museum of Natural History (part time), 1981-. *Memberships*: American Institute of Archaeology; American Association of Physical Anthropology; Egyptian Study Society; Western Interior Paleontological Society; American Research Center in Egypt; American Indian Science & Engineering Society; Friends of Earth Sciences. *Interests*: "I travel extensively throughout the U.S., Egypt, and pursue an avid paraprofessional paleontology area of study interest."

WARNE, JIM E. (Oglala Lakota) 1964-
    (human resource specialist)
Born November 27, 1964, Phoenix, Ariz. *Education*: Arizona State University, BS, 1987; San Diego State University, MS, 1993. *Principal occupation*: Human resource specialist. *Address & Affiliation*: San Diego State University Foundation, 5850 Hardy Ave. #112, San Diego, CA 92182 (619) 594-6163, 1993-. *Other professional post*: Vice President, Southern California Chapter, California Indian Education Association, San Diego, CA, 1994-. *Past professional*

posts: Football player, National Football League (Cincinnati Bengals, Detroit Lions, Tampa Bay Buccaneers, San Francisco 49ers), 1987-89; football player, World League of American Football, New York, NY, 1991; football player, Arena Football League, Albany, NY, 1992; extra/actor, Segal Productions, "Silk Stalkings" and "Renegade," one episode each. *Community activities*: Member, Consortium of Administrators for Native American Rehabilitation (chair, Professional Standards Committee), 1993-; member, San Diego East County Native American Education Council, San Diego, CA, 1993-; board member, American Indian Health Council, San Diego, CA, 1993-. *Awards, honors*: Keynote speaker, American Indian Empowerment Conference, San Diego State University, Nov. 1994; nominated for vice president for the Southern Chapter of the California Indian Education Association, San Diego, May 1994; conducted Cultural Diversity Training for various groups in 1994; keynote speaker, Arizona State University, American Indian Institute "Feast-n-Fest celebration for Native American students, Tempe, AZ, Nov. 1993; speaker at numerous other events. *Interests*: Rehabilitation counseling with an emphasis on education enhancement of Native American youth, multicultural issues, and Native American health, social, and rehabilitation issues.

*WARNER, BARBARA
    (executive director)
Affiliation: Oklahoma Indian Affairs Commission, 4545 N. Lincoln Blvd., Suite 282, Oklahoma City, OK 73105 (405) 521-3828.

WARNER, LINDA
    (program director)
Affiliation: American Indian Leadership Program, Penn State University, 320 Rackley Bldg., University Park, PA 16802 (814) 865-1489.

WARREN, DAVE (Chippewa-Tewa Pueblo)
1932-
    (educator)
Born April 12, 1932, Santa Fe, N.M. *Education*: University of New Mexico, BA, 1955, MA, 1961, PhD. *Principal occupation*: Educator. *Address*: Institute of American Indian Arts, P.O. Box 20007, Santa Fe, NM 87504 (505) 988-6281. *Affiliations*: Instructor, Department to History, Oklahoma State University, 1964-66; assistant professor, Dept. of History, University of Nebraska, 1966-68; director of curriculum and instruction, 1968-70, director, research and cultural studies materials development, 1970-, Institute of American Indian Arts, Santa Fe, NM. *Other professional posts*: Member, Advisory Board, Center for Studies of the American West, University of Utah; member, Advisory Committee, University of New Mexico Indian Studies Program; chairman, Selection Committee, National Graduate Indian Scholarship Program (Donner Foundation); member, Editorial Board, Indian Historian, American Indian Historical Society. *Military service*: U.S. Air Force, 1955-57 (Captain). *Memberships*: Latin American Studies Association; National Congress of American Indians. *Interests*: Mr. Warren writes, "Basic area of professional training has been with studies of the advanced Indian cultures of Mexico, preconquest and at the time of Spanish contact. Investigation of the Indian pictorial documents (codices) has been part of this professional study and interest. Currently, my work concerns the organization of cultural studies

material into the instructional programs of the Bureau of Indian Affairs and other systems requiring information and resources about the American Indian--materials which reflect the history and current development of American Indians in the U.S., Canada, and Latin America. Of particular concern is finding programs and materials initiated by the Indian people, therefore reflecting their ideas and interpretations of issues, events or other concerns affecting Indian life and history, and utilizing such information in educational programs. Other areas of interest and activity: curriculum development, historical/ ethnological writing and research." *Published works*: Articles in scholarly publications.

WARRIOR, DELLA C. (Otoe-Missouria)
(tribal chairperson)
Affiliation: Otoe-Missouria Tribal Council, P.O. Box 68, Red Rock, OK 74651 (405) 723-4434.

*WARRIOR, ROBERT ALLEN
(professor of American Indian literature)
Affiliation: Dept. of English, Stanford University, Stanford, CA. *Published work*: Co-author, Like a Hurricane: How Wounded Knee II Changed Indian America, 1994.

WASHBURN, WILCOMB E. 1925-
(historian)
Born January 13, 1925, Ottawa, Kan. *Education*: Dartmouth College, AB, 1948; Harvard University, MA, 1951, PhD, 1955. *Principal occupation*: Historian. *Home address*: 2122 California St., N.W., #157, Washington, DC 20008 (202) 633-9386 (work). *Affiliations*: Curator, Division of Political History, U.S. National Museum, Smithsonian Institution, 1958-65; chairman, Department of American Studies, National Museum of History & Technology, Smithsonian Institution, 1965-68; director, American Studies Program, Smithsonian Institution, Washington, D.C., 1968-. *Other professional posts*: Adjunct professor, University of Maryland, 1980-; consultant in research, Graduate School of Arts and Sciences, The George Washington University, Washington, DC, 1966-. *Military service*: U.S. Marine Corps, 1943-46, 1951-52; presently Colonel, U.S. Marine Corps Reserve (retired). *Memberships*: American Anthropological Association (Fellow); American Antiquarian Society; American Association for the Advancement of Science; American Association of Museums; American Historical Association; American Society for Ethnohistory (president, 1957-58); American Studies Association (president, 1978-79); Anthropological Society of Washington; Institute of Early American History and Culture; Organization of American Historians; Society for the History of Discoveries (president, 1963-65); Society of American Historians; among others. *Awards, honors*: Honorary Doctor of Letters, St. Mary's College of Maryland, 1970; Honorary Doctor of Humanities, Assumption College, Worcester, Mass., 1983; Phi Beta Kappa Lecturer, Spring, 1980. *Published works*: Editor, The Indian and the White Man (Doubleday, 1964); Red Man's Land/White Man's Law: A Study of the Past and Present Status of the American Indian (Scribner's, 1971); editor, The American Indian and the U.S.: A Documentary History, 4 volumes (Random House, 1973); The Indian in America (Harper & Row, 1975); The Assault on Indian Tribalism: The General Allotment Law (Dawes Act) of 1887 (Lippincott, 1975; reprint, Robert E. Krieger Publishing, 1986); The American Heritage History of the Indian Wars, with

Robert M. Utley (American Heritage Publishing, 1977); numerous chapters in books, and articles in professional & scholarly journals.

WASHINES, RONN L.
(editor)
Affiliation: Yakima Nation Review, Yakima Indian Nation, P.O. Box 386, Toppenish, WA 98948-0386 (509) 865-5121.

WASSILLIE, RAYMOND (Aleut)
(village president)
Affiliation: Newhalen Village Council, P.O. Box 165, Iliamna, AK 99606 (907) 571-1226.

WASSON, GLENN (Southern Paiute)
(tribal chairperson)
Affiliation: Winnemucca Colony Council, P.O. Box 1075, Winnemucca, NV 89445 (702) 623-6918.

WATAHOMIGIE, DON (Havasupai)
(tribal chairperson)
Affiliation: Havasupai Tribal Council, P.O. Box 10, Supai, AZ 86435 (602) 448-2961.

*WATAN, STERLING (Cheyenee-Arapaho)
(broadcaster; co-chair, AIM)
Affiliation: Crow Tribal Council, Crow Agency, MT 59022 (406) 638-2316. *Other professional post*: Co-chair, American Indian Movement; owner, former KKUL-AM, Hardin, MT.

WATERS, DEANA J. HARRAGARRA
(library director)
Affiliation: National Indian Law Library, Native American Rights Fund, 1506 Broadway, Boulder, CO 80302 (303) 447-8760.

WATERS, KAREN K.
(principal/teacher)
Affiliation: Nunapitchuk Day School, Nunapitchuk, AK 99641 (907) 527-5711.

*WATERS, MICHAEL
(editorial advisor)
Affiliation: American Indian Law Review, University of Oklahoma Law Center, 300 Timberdell Rd., Rm. 378, Norman, OK 73019 (405) 325-2840.

*WATKINS, GORDON
(health clinic director)
Affiliation: Nowata Indian Health Clinic, Cherokee Nation, 507 E. Redwood, Nowata, OK 74048 (918) 273-0192.

WATKINS, MARY BETH OZMUN (Creek)
(library director)
Education: University of Oklahoma, BS, 1959, MLS, 1968, post-graduate, 1968-71. *Principal occupation*: Library director. *Home address*: 2503 Margaret Lynn Lane, Muskogee, OK 74401. *Affiliations*: Elementary field librarian, 1968-70, media consultant, 1970-71, Oklahoma City Public Schools; associate director, Eastern Oklahoma District Library, Muskogee, 1971-77; director of libraries, Bacone College, Muskogee, Okla. 1977-. *Memberships*: Oklahoma Library Association, 1968- (secretary, 1972-73; chairperson, membership committee, 1972-76; chairperson, publicity committee, 1972-73; chairperson, Sequoyah Children's Book Award, 1971-72; chairperson, intellectual freedom committee, 1976-77; co-chairperson, ad hoc committee serving as Humanities Council Project liaison, 1976-77, chairperson, 1977-78); Southwest Li-

brary Association, 1968- (SWLA membership chairperson for OLA, 1975-76, 1977-78); Oklahoma Education Association; National Education Association; Oklahoma Association of School Librarians (district chairperson, 1969-71); American Library Association, 1971- (member, Membership Task Force; chairperson, Southwest Region, 1976-78); Oklahoma Association for Educational Communication and Technology, 1975-; Bacone Professional Association, 1977- (program committee; by-laws committee; vice president); Oklahoma Humanities Committee, 1977-80; American Association of University Women (treasurer, 1976-78; first vice president, program chairperson, 1978-80). *Awards, honors*: Outstanding Young Women of America, 1970. *Published works*: Articles in "Oklahoma Librarian."

WATSO, SAMMY (Wabanaki) 1954-
(cultural director)
Born May 4, 1954, Buffalo, N.Y. *Education*: Sinclair College (3 years); Minneapolis Community College; Arts Resources & Counseling. *Principal occupation*: Cultural director. *Home address*: P.O. Box 7103, Minneapolis, MN 55407 (612) 871-9421 (work). *Affiliations*: Manager, Jewelry Store, Lima, OH, 1978-81; dealer in architectural Antiques, Dayton, OH, 1979-85; owner "Singing Spirit", Native American Works, Dayton, OH, 1985-88; cultural director, Minneapolis American Indian Center, & curator, Two Rivers Gallery, Minneapolis, MN, 1988-; planning consultant, National Indian AIDS Media Consortium & National Native American AIDS Prevention, Oakland, CA, 1993-. *Other professional posts*: National Advisor, Shooting Back Project, Washington, DC, 1991-; author of "Artline," in Circle Newspaper; curator for various art exhibits. *Community activities*: Public speaker - art, culture, issues; design consultant; actor; Metropolitan Regional Arts Council (board member, 1990-91; review panel, 93-94); Northern Plains Tribal Arts (advisory committee, 1990-91); Minneapolis American Red Cross (board member, 1989-91). *Membership*: Minnesota Association of Museums (steering committee, 1990-91). *Awards, honors*: Recipient of 1991-92 Arts Midwest Arts Administrative Fellowship. *Interests*: "To seek opportunities in establishing secure foundations and avenues through which Native American artists can practice their art on a continuing basis."

WATSON, DONALD EVERT (*Walking Hawk*)
(United Lumbee/Cherokee) 1925-
(chemist)
Born October 16, 1925, Whittier, Calif. *Education*: BS & MS degrees. *Principal occupation*: Chemist. *Home address*: 5356 Border Ave., Joshua Tree, CA 92252 (619) 366-2875. *Community activities*: United Lumbee Nation's historian. *Memberships*: United Lumbee Nation's Desert Sage Band Chief, 1991-. *Awards, honors*: 1st Place Solar House design, CT A.I.A.; 2nd Place Award for Large Size Rugs and Blankets, Northern California Hand Weavers Association. *Interests*: Native American history; orchard grower; also plant breeding using Native American vegetables as subjects; weaver." *Published works*: Indians of the Mesa Verde (Mesa Verde Museum Association, 1961); Designing and Building a Solar House (Garden Way Publishing, 1977).

WATSON, GLEN (Maidu)
(rancheria spokesperson)
Affiliation: Enterprise Rancheria, 7470 Feather Falls Star Route, Oroville, CA 95965 (916) 589-0652.

*WATSON, LARRY S. 1941-
(editor, writer)
Born May 3, 1941, Oklahoma City, Okla. *Education*: Oklahoma State University, BA, 1963; Central Missouri State University, MA, 1964. *Principal occupation*: Editor, writer. *Home address*: 23011 Moulton Pkwy. D-12, Laguna Hills, CA 92653 (714) 859-1659. *Affiliation*: Co-owner, Histree (genealogical research & publishing organization), Laguna Hills, CA, 1978-. *Other professional posts*: Active genealogical researcher for better than 40 years: Southern States & Native American; genealogical teacher for 20+ years; consultant: Riverside Indian Center, Saddleback College, Sac River Cherokee Indians & several other genealogical & Native American groups; editor of The Journal of American Indian Research (monthly nesletter of Histree). *Military service*: U.S. Army, 1959-78. *Community activities*: Organizing President of Southwest Oklahoma Genealogical Society; charter member, Stars & Bars, Lawton, OK. *Memberships*: California Genealogical Alliance. *Speaker at*: World Conference on Genealogical Research, New Orleans, LA, 1975, 1976, 1977; Cherokee Indian Descendants of the A-niyun-wiya, Inc., 1992; and numerous other genealogical & historical societies, 1974-. *Awards, honors*: Named Fellow of the Ark-La-Tex Genealogical Society, Shreveport, LA, 1976; Certificate of Acknowledge from The Richstone Family Center, Hawthorne, CA for "his time & expertise, assisting our Native American clients research their heritage," 1994. *Published works*: General editor of a reprint of Senate Document 512, 23rd Cong. 1st Sess. concerning Indian removal with comments and index; general editor of Series on Indian Treaties (28 volumes plus guide book); author/editor of several other records on Indians & books of historical & genealogical importance about Indian Territory & Oklahoma; numerous articles in various journal publications.

*WATSON, MARY JO
(instructor-Native American studies)
Affiliation: Native American Studies Program, University of Oklahoma, 455 W. Lindsey, Rm. 804, Norman, OK 73019 (405) 325-2312.

WATT, CHARLIE
(parliament senator)
Affiliation: Canadian Parliament, Parliament Bldgs., Ottawa, ON K1A 0A4 (613) 992-2981.

WATTS, DANIEL
(Indian band chief)
Affiliation: Opetchesaht Indian Band, Box 211, Port Alberni, British Columbia, Canada V9Y 7M7 (604) 724-4041.

WATTS, STEVEN M. 1947-
(museum educator)
Born July 25, 1947, Lincoln County, N.C. *Education*: Appalachian State University, Boone, NC, BA, 1969; Duke University, M.Div., 1972. *Principal occupation*: Museum educator. *Home address*: 207 W. Fourth Ave., Gastonia, NC 28052 (704) 866-6912 (office). *Affiliation*: Director, Southeastern Native American Studies Program, Schiele Museum, Gastonia, NC, 1984-.

Other professional posts: Director, "Abo-Tech", providing instruction in aboriginal/primitive skills and prehistoric tool replicas for museums and functional experiments. *Past work experience*: Minister, school counselor, classroom teacher, camp director, and substance abuse educator. *Community activities*: Commission on the Status of Women; Southeastern Indian Culture Study Group (director); American Indian Cultural Association (past director); Mental Health Association; volunteer work with schools, churches, scout groups, etc. *Memberships*: Center for the Study of Early Man; The Archaeological Society of North Carolina; Society of Prehistoric Technology; International ATLATL Association. *Awards, honors*: Statewide speaker for N.C. Mental Health Association (1984); Master of ceremonies, NC Commission of Indian Affairs--Unity Conference Intertribal Dance (1981); Outstanding Service Award, Mental Health Association, 1985. *Interests*: "Major interests is replication and experimental use of Native American tools, weapons, utensils, etc.--with the goal of (through educational programs) increasing the appreciation of primitive survival/subsistence skills and lifestyles among participants--helping to rediscover and preserve native technologies for generations to come; ethnology, archaeology. Most spare time is spent visiting native communities in the Southeast and historic and prehistoric native sites to increase the understanding and collection of knowledge." *Biographical sources*: Approximately a dozen newspaper articles in local and statewide newspapers (copies available upon request). *Published works*: The Old Bearskin Report, journal (Schiele Museum, 1985); Southeastern Craft Articles, series (The Backwoodsman, Tex., 1984 & 1985).

WAUKAU, JERRY L. (Menominee)
(health administrator)
Education: Ripon College, 1974-78; University of Minnesota, Independent Study Program for Ambulatory Care Administration, 1987-88. *Address*: P.O. Box 9, Keshena, WI 54135 (715) 799-4056. *Affiliation*: Administrator, Menominee Indian Tribe of Wisconsin, Keshena, WI, 1981-85; health Administrator, Menominee Tribal Center, Keshena, WI. *Memberships*: Wisconsin Tribal Health Director's Association (chairman, 1991-92); Red Cross, Lakeland Chapter (board of directors, 1987-92); American College of Healthcare Executives. *Awards, honors*: American Heart Association of Wisconsin Volunteer Recognition Award, 1987; Indian Health Service (IHS) Exceptional Performance Award, 1988; IHS Citation for Exemplary Group Performance, Menominee Tribal Clinic Management Team, 1990; IHS Citation for Exemplary Group Performance, Wisconsin Health Director's Association, 1993. *Interests*: "Planning, organizing & administering of health & health related programs aimed at improving the health status of the Menominee Indians."

WAUKAZOO, MARTIN
(health director)
Affiliation: Urban Indian Health Board, 3124 East 14th St., Oakland, CA 94601 (510) 261-0524; Native American Health Clinic, 56 Julian Ave., San Francisco, CA (415) 621-8051.

WAUNEKA, ANNIE DODGE (Navajo) 1910-
(tribal council member)
Born April 10, 1910, Old Sawmill, Ariz. *Education*: High school, B.I.A., Albuquerque, NM. *Prin-*

cipal occupation: Tribal council member, Navajo Tribal Government, Window Rock, AZ, 1951-. *Home address*: Box 629, Ganado, AZ 86505. *Other professional posts*: Lecturer; member of Navajo Area health board representing U.S. Indian Health Services at Window Rock, AZ (current). *Community activities*: President, School For Me, Navajo Project Concern, Project Hope; Navajo Nation School Board Association (board member); Navajo Tribal Utility Authority (board member); Navajo Health Authority (board member); health educator in Navajo Way. *Memberships*: National Public Health Education; American Public Health Association; National TB Association; Society for Public Health (honorary lifetime member). *Awards, honors*: President's Freedom Medal Award, from President John F. Kennedy, 1963; Woman of the Year in Arizona; Honorary Doctor of Humanities Degree, University of Albuquerque, N.M., 1972; Woman of the Year, 1976, Ladies Home Journal. *Interests*: "Main interest is in health of American Indians, primarily Navajo; education and tribal government." *Biographical sources*: Indian Women of Today; Navajo Biography.

*WAUPOOSE, JANET
(association president)
Affiliation: National Tribal Court Clerks Association, 1000 Connecticut Ave., NW, Suite 1206, Washington, DC 20036 (202) 296-0685.

WAX, MURRAY L. 1922-
(professor)
Born November 23, 1922, St. Louis, Mo. *Education*: University of Chicago, BS, 1942, PhD, 1959; University of Pennsylvania, 1947. *Principal occupation*: Professor. *Home address*: 572 Stratford Ave., University City, St. Louis, MO 63130. *Affiliations*: Professor of Sociology & Anthropology, University of Kansas, Lawrence, KS, 1964-73, Washington University, St. Louis, MO, 1973-. *Other professional posts*: Executive associate, Workshop on American Indian Affairs, University of Colorado, Boulder, 1959-60; director, Oglala Sioux Education Research Project (Emory University), 1962-63; director, Indian Education Research Project (University of Kansas), 1965-68. *Memberships*: American Anthropological Association (Fellow); American Association for the Advancement of Science (Fellow); American Sociological Association (Fellow); Current Anthropology (Associate); Royal Anthropological Institute of Great Britain and Ireland (Fellow); Society for Applied Anthropology (Fellow); Society for the Study of Religion; Society for the Study of Social Problems; American Educational Research Association; Midwest Sociological Society; Council on Anthropology and Education. *Awards, honors*: Adopted by Oglala Sioux Tribe; Phi Beta Kappa; Sigma Xi; National Institute of Education Grants, 1973-74, 1978-79; National Science Foundation Grant, 1978-1981; grants from: U.S. Office of Economic Opportunity, U.S. Office of Education, Wenner-Gren Foundation. Editorial boards, advisory editor: Human Organization (editorial board, 1966-); Journal of Cultural & Educational Futures (1979-); Phylon (1973-); Qualitative Sociology (1982-); Symbolic Interaction (1983-). *Published works*: Formal Education in an American Indian Community (Monograph 1, Society for the Study of Social Problems, 1964); co-editor, Indian Education in Eastern Oklahoma: A Report of Fieldwork Among the Cherokee (U.S. Office of Education, 1969); Indian Americans: Unity and Diversity (Prentice-Hall, 1971); Solv-

ing The Indian Problem (New Viewpoints/ Franklin Watts, 1975); Formal Education in an American Indian Community (Waveland Press, 1989); numerous articles and essays in professional journals.

WAX, ROSALIE
(professor emerita)
Affiliation: Department of Anthropology, Washington University, St. Louis, MO 63130 (314) 889-5252.

WAY, J. EDSON 1947-
(museum administration)
Born May 18, 1947, Chicago, Ill. *Education*: Beloit College, BA, 1968; University of Toronto, M.A., 1970, PhD, 1972. *Principal occupation*: Museum administration. *Home address*: P.O. Box 1072, Tularosa, NM 88352 (505) 585-2460. *Affiliations*: Associate professor of anthropology, Beloit College, 1972-85; director, Logan Museum of Anthropology, Beloit, WI, 1980-85; director, Wheelwright Museum of the American Indian, 1985-89; acting director, New Mexico Museum of Natural History, Albuquerque, 1990-91; executive director, International Space Hall of Fame, Alamogordo, NM, 1991-. *Community activities*: Public speaker, Native American arts and history; Society of Friends (Quakers); Southeast Asian Refugee Resettlement; Rotary; chair, Tourism Committee, Alamogordo (NM) Chamber of Commerce; vice-president, Apache Trails Tourism Promotions, Ruidoso, NM. *Memberships*: American Association of Museums; New Mexico Museum Association; American Association of Physical Anthropologists; Society for American Archaeology; Plains Anthropological Society. *Interests*: Archaeological fieldwork in Labrador, and Ellesmere Island, N.W.T., Canada; northern Wisconsin; northeast New Mexico; Native American arts; music; horsemanship; cross-country skiing; camping; fishing; Western history; and cattleranching. *Biographical source*: Who's Who in America.

*WAYNEE, ROBERT (Lone Eagle)
(Saginaw Chippewa) 1939-
(sculptor in wood)
Born July 9, 1939, Bay City, Mich. *Address*: P.O. Box 15313, Santa Fe, NM 87506 (505) 466-3456. *Other professional posts*: Carpenter, photographer, welder, furniture maker, artist. *Memberships*: Southwest Association for Indian Arts (Santa Fe) Indian Market; Indian Arts & Crafts Association. *Awards, honors*: "Gate Keepers" Award by Country Home Magazine, 1989 at the National Christmas Show, Washington, DC; numerous other awards. He is featured in galleries and collections throughout the U.S.

WEAHKEE, FRED FIDEL (Morning Star-Jemez; Rainbow-Zuni) (Pueblo-Jemez/Zuni) 1926-
(electrical contractor, journeyman electrician)
Born September 1, 1926, Jemez Pueblo, N.M. *Education*: John Brown University (Siloam Springs, AR), 1947-50; International Correspondence School (Scranton, PA), Electrical Engineering Certificate, 1978; Electrical Contractor's School, 1979-80. *Principal occupation*: Electrical contractor, journeyman electrician. *Home address*: 24 Sandhill Rd., Lunas, NM 87031 (505) 865-5653. *Affiliations*: Facility manager, Albuquerque Indian School, 1977-81; facility manager, Jicarilla Agency, BIA, 1981-86; facility manager, Eastern Navajo Agency, BIA (mainte-

nance of 21 different schools),1986-88; electrical contractor, Fred's Electric, Los Lunas, NM, 1988-. *Military service*: U.S. Marine Corps, 1943-46 (Fleet Marine Force Scout; Purple Heart). *Memberships*: International Association of Electrical Inspectors; Electrical Contractors Association. *Awards, honors*: Three Special Achievement Awards from the Bureau of Indian Affairs, 1976, 1977, 1981; served as chief informer for a linguist from the University of New Mexico. *Interests*: "Carpentry, plumbing, and electrical work; exercise (cross-country skiing and apparatus), swimming, bowling, daily Bible reading!" *Published work*: Dictionary - Jemez Language (Towa), 1963-64.

WEAHKEE, WILLIAM F. (Pueblo)
(executive director)
Affiliation: Five Sandoval Indian Pueblos, Inc., P.O. Box 580, Bernalillo, NM 87004 (505) 867-3351.

WEASEL FAT, MARY
(editor)
Affiliation: Kainai News, Indian News Media, P.O. Box 120, Stand Off, Alberta, Can. T0K 0K0 (403) 653-3301.

WEATHERFORD, ELIZABETH 1945-
(head of film & video center)
Born July 30, 1945, Anson County, N.C. *Education*: Duke University, BA, 1966; The New School for Social Research, MA, 1970. *Principal occupation*: Head of film & video center. *Address*: The Heye Foundation, National Museum of the American Indian-Smithsonian Institution, Alexander Hamilton Old Customs House, Bowling Green, New York, NY 10004. *Affiliations*: Assistant professor, School of Visual Arts, New York, NY, 1970-1981; adjunct curator, National Museum of the American Indian, New York, NY, 1981-. *Memberships*: Educational Film Library Association; American Anthropological Association; Association for Independent Video and Film Makers; Media Alliance; National Alliance of Media Arts Centers, New York Women's Anthropological Caucus; Society on Visual Anthropology; Cultural Survival. *Interests*: Recent and archival documentary films and videotapes about Native Americans. *Published works*: Native Americans on Film & Video (Museum of the American Indian, 1981); Native Americans on Film and Video II (Museum of the American Indians, 1986); Anthropology and Native Americans in Good Reading (R.R. Bowker, 1985).

*WEAVER, FRAMON (Mowa Choctaw)
(tribal chief)
Affiliation: Mowa Band of Choctaw Indians, Rte. 1, Box 330-A, Reservation Rd., Mt. Vernon, AL 36560 (205) 829-5500.

*WEAVER. LAURA
(school administrator)
Affiliation: Duckwater Shoshone Elementary School, P.o. Box 140038, Duckwater, NV 89314 (702) 863-0242.

*WEBBER, M.L. (Chief Thunderbird IV) (Kaweah) 1938-
(minister, publisher)
Born June 15, 1938, Webber Falls, Okla. *Education*: LaSalle Extension College, 1964-67; Holy Family Seminary (Bay City, MI), DD, 1984. *Principal occupation*: Minister, publisher. *Home address*: P.O. Box 3121, Hutchinson, KS 67504 (316) 665-3614. *Affiliations*: Grand Chief,

Kaweah Indian Nation, Hutchinson, KS, 1977-; National Chairperson, American Indian Defense of America, Hutchinson, KS, 1980-. *Military service*: U.S. Army, 1956-64 (SP4, Honorable Discharge). *Community activities*: International President, Congregational Bible Churches, International. *Biographical source*: Marquis Who's Who in the South & Southwest. *Published works*: Anasazi/Kaweah Nation History (Kaweah Indian Nation, 1992); Itza Dictionary (Kaweah Indian Nation, 1994).

*WEBSTER, LORETTA
(BIA agency acting supt.)
Affiliation: Sisseton Agency, Bureau of Indian Affairs, P.O. Box 688, Agency Village, SD 57262 (605) 698-7676

WEBSTER, STELLA
(administrative officer)
Affiliation: Chinle PHS Indian Hospital, P.O. Drawer PH, Chinle, AZ 86503 (602) 674-5282.

*WEDDLE, STAR TEHEE
(Oklahoma Cherokee)
(artist)
Born February 24 in Okla. *Education*: Southern Methodist University, 1973-75; Trinity University (San Antonio, TX), BA, 1977). *Principal occupation*: Artist. *Home address*: P.O. Box 1269, Bastrop, TX 78602 (512) 321-3733. *Affiliation*: Full time artist, 1984- (emphasis on easel art with Indian subject matter). *Community activities*: Judge of student art; art committee of Houston Livestock Show & Rodeo; of fice & director of InterTribal Council. *Memberships*: Indian Arts & Crafts Association; Southwestern Association for Indian Arts; Descendants of Cherokee Seminaries' Students; National Museum of the American Indian, Smithsonian Institution. *Awards, honors*: Santa Fe Indian Market: First Place in Painting, 1990; Third Place in Miniature Paintings, 1990; Honorable Mention, Contemporary Painting, 1990 & 1991; Third Place in Drawing, 1991; First Place in Miniature Paintings, 1991 & 1992. Gallup InterTribal Ceremonial: Second Place in Miniature Painting, 1990. Ohio InterTribal Experience: Honorable Mention in Painting, 1991. *Interest*: Featured artist at the State Capitol of Texas; participant in juried & invitational shows; numerous gallery exhibits and shows. Co-author of educational book in progress.

*WEEKS, JANE L.
(executive director)
Affiliation: Alabama Indian Affairs Commission, 669 S. Lawrence St., Montgomery, AL 36104 (205) 261-2831.

*WEIDLEIN, JAMES
(editor)
Affiliation: "Winds of Change," A.I.S.E.S. Publishing, 1630 30th St., Suite 301, Boulder, CO 80301 (303) 444-9099.

WEIGAND, PHIL C. 1937-
(archaeology)
Born December 3, 1937, Omaha, Neb. *Education*: Indiana University, BA, 1962; Southern Illinois University, PhD, 1970. *Principal occupation*: Archaeology. *Home address*: Rt. 4, Box 720, Flagstaff, AZ 86001 (602) 774-5211. *Affiliations*: Archaeologist, Museum of Northern Arizona, Flagstaff (4 years); professor, Northern Arizona University, Flagstaff; profesor de Investigaciones, Colegio de Michoacan (3

years). *Other professional post*: Research collaborator, Brookhaven National Laboratory. *Memberships*: Sociedad Mexicana de Antropologia; Society for American Archaeology; American Anthropological Association; American Society for Ethnohistory; American Association for the Advancement of Science. *Awards, honors*: Recipient of grants from the National Science Foundation, Wenner-Gren, etc. *Interests*: Expeditions - "The Ancient Mining Project "Currently focusing on Arizona); "The Teuchitlan Mapping Project" currently focusing on the Atoyac Valley of Jalisco, Mexico); and "The Huichol Ethnohistory Project." Avocations - hiking and photography. *Published works*: co-author with M. Foster, Archaeology of West & Northwest Mesoamerica (Westview/Praeger, 1985); Ensayos Sobre El Gran Nayar: Entre Coras, Huicholes, y Tepehuanes (Instituto Nacional Indigenists, 1992); Origines y Desarrollo de la Civilizacion del Occidente de Mexico (co-edited with Brigitte Boehm, Colegio de Michoacan, 1992); and Arqueologia de Jalisco, Nayarit y Zacatecas: Evolucion de una Civilizacion (Colegio de Michoacan, 1992); and about 100 articles, book reviews and monographs.

WEILER, ROMAN
(high school principal)
Affiliation: Standing Rock Community High School, P.O. Box 377, Fort Yates, ND 58538 (701) 854-3461.

*WEINROTH, ORNA
(information specialist)
Affiliation: Nationl Indian Policy Center, The George Washington University, 2101 F St., NW, Washington, DC 20052 (202) 994-1446.

WEISS, NICHOLAS, REV.
(museum chairperson)
Affiliations: The Mohawk-Caughnawaga Museum, Route 5, Box 554, Fonda, NY 12068 (518) 853-3678; director, Tekakwitha Shrine, Fonda, NY.

WELCH, RICHARD (Eastern Cherokee)
(editor)
Affiliation: Cherokee One Feather, Eastern Band of Cherokee Indians, P.O. Box 501, Cherokee, NC 28719 (704) 497-5513.

WELLS, ELIZABETH A. (*Sh-ush*)
(Mescalero Apache) 1940-
(program director/founder)
Born March 12, 1940, Mescalero, N.M. *Education*: High school. *Principal occupation*: Director/founder-Indian program. *Home address*: 4831 Arnica Circle, Anchorage, AK 99515 (907) 243-5561. *Affiliation*: Director & founder, Orre Drumrite Walking Heritage, Anchorage, AK (nonprofit program to contact the Indian nation, thus to dedicate annually, an additional; thousand drums to sound at the same moment across all time zones. 1991: 1,000 drums; 1992: 2,000 drums; 1993: 3,000 drums, etc.) Other professional post: Editor, "Dancing Prayers," quarterly publication of Orre Drumrite Walking Heritage. *Community activities*: Coordinating international drum ceremonies, "Parade of the Spirits," "World Drum: Secretts of Life," "Drums of the Whispering Moon," "Standing Sun-calls-drums." *Interests*: "To meet with and visit all indigenous people around the world."

WELSH, PETER H.
(museum curator)
Affiliation: The Heard Museum, 22 E. Monte Vista Rd., Phoenix, AZ 85004 (602) 252-8840.

WESLAGER, CLINTON A. 1909-
(professor emeritus)
Born April 30, 1909, Pittsburgh, Penna. *Education*: University of Pittsburgh, BA, 1933; Dr. Humane Letters, Widener University, 1986; Dr. Literature, Wesley College, 1993. *Principal occupation*: Professor emeritus, Widener University. *Home address*: 255 Possum Park Rd., Apt. 208, Newark, DE 19711 (302) 738-5609. *Memberships*: Archaeological Society of Delaware (past president); Eastern States Archaeological Federation (past president). *Awards, honors*: Christian Linback Award for excellence in teaching; Archibald Crozier Award; two awards for outstanding books, Association for State and Local History; Fellow, Archaeological Society of New Jersey; Fellow, Holland Society of New York; Medal of Distinction, University of Delaware, 1988. *Interests*: Ethnohistorical research among survivors of Eastern Woodland tribes, especially Nanticoke, Delaware, Conoy, Minquas, Mahican, and Munsee. *Biographical source*: Who's Who in America *Published works*: Delawares Forgotten Folk, (1943); Delaware's Buried Past (1944); The Nanticoke Indians (1948); Indian Place-Names in Delaware (1950); Red Men on the Brandywine (1953); Magic Medicines of the Indians (1973); The Delaware Indians, A History (Rutgers University, 1973; reissue, 1990); The Delawares: A Critical Bibliography (1978); The Delaware Indian Westward Migration; (Middle Atlantic Press, 1979); The Nanticoke Indians, Past and Present (University of Delaware, 1983); among others.

WESLER, KIT W.
(center director)
Affiliation: Wickliff Mounds Research Center, P.O. Box 155, Wickliff, KY 42087 (502) 335-3681.

WESLEY, ESTHER
(director-cultural centre)
Affiliation: Ojibway & Cree Cultural Centre, 84 Elm St. So., Timmins, Ontario, Can. P4N 1W6 (705) 267-7911.

WESLEY, NORMAN F.
(Indian band chief)
Affiliation: Moose Factory Indian Band, Box 190, Moose Factory, Ontario, Canada P0L 1W0 (705) 658-4619.

WESSELS, WILLIAM (Chippewa)
(school administrator)
Affiliation: Circle of Life Survival School, P.O. Box 447, White Earth, MN 56591 (218) 983-3285 ext. 269.

WEST, W. RICHARD, Jr. (Cheyenne-Arapaho) 1943-
(museum founding director)
Born January 6, 1943, Okla. *Education*: University of Redlands (CA), BA, 1965; Harvard University, MA, 1968; Stanford University Law School, JD, 1971. *Principal occupation*: Founding director, National Museum of the American Indian, Smithsonian Institution. *Address*: 900 Jefferson Dr., SW, Rm. 3161, Washington, DC 20560 (202) 786-2784. *Affiliations*: Formerly a partner in the Washington, DC law firm of Fried, Frank, Harris, Shriver & Jacobson, and the In-

dian-owned, Albuquerque, NM law firm of Gover, Stetson, Williams & West, P.C. *Community activities*: Member and treasurer, American Indian Lawyer Training Program, Inc., 1973-; member, Board of Trustees, Environmental Defense Fund, 1986-; member, National Support Committee, Native American Rights Fund, 1990-; member, Board of Directors, Morning Star Foundation, 1987-. *Memberships*: Cheyenne-Arapaho Tribe of Oklahoma; Bar of the State of California; Bar of the District of Columbia; Bar of the U.S. Supreme Court; Bar of the U.S. Court of Appeals for Eighth District; American Bar Association (former chairperson, Committee on Problems of the American Indian, Section of Individual Rights and Responsibilities); Federal Bar Association (Indian Section); Indian Bar Association of New Mexico. *Awards, honors*: Recipient, Career Achievement Award, University of Redlands, 1987. *Published works*: Articles - "Chief Justice Traynor and the Parol Evidence Rule (22 Stanford Law Review 547, 1970); co-author, "Healing v. Jones: Mandate for Another Trail of Tears" (N.D. Law Review 73, 1974); co-author, "The Alaska Native Claims Settlement Act: A Flawed Victory" (40 Law & Contemporary Problems 132, 1976); author, "The Source and Scope of Tribal Powers" (Manual of Indian Law, 1977); co-author, "The Struggle for Indian Civil Rights" (Indians in American History, 1988).

*WESTERMAN, FLOYD (Red Crow)
(actor)
Movies: "Dances With Wolves;" & "The Doors."

WESTERMEYER, JOSEPH, MD 1937-
(psychiatrist)
Born April 8, 1937, Chicago, Ill. *Education*: University of Minnesota, BS, 1957, MD, 1961; MA, 1969, MPH & PhD, 1970. *Principal occupation*: Psychiatrist. *Home address*: 1935 Summit Ave., St. Paul, MN 55105 (612) 725-2037. *Affiliation*: Professor of Psychiatry, Dept. of Psychiatry, University of Minnesota Hospitals & Clinics (UMHC), Minneapolis, MN, 1970-; Chief of Psychiatry, VA Medical Center, Minneapolis, MN, 1992-. *Other professional posts*: Director, Alcohol-Drug Dependence Program, (UMHC), 1982-; director, International Clinic (UMHC), 1984-. *Community activities*: Indian Guest House (halfway house for Indian alcoholics), Minneapolis, MN (board member, 1969-72); Juel Fairbanks House (halfway house for Indian alcoholics, St. Paul, Minn. (board member, 1970-73); South Side Receiving Center (a detoxification unit for American Indian alcoholics, Minneapolis, Minn. (consultant, 1974-75); Association of American Indian Affairs, including Senate subcommittee hearing on American Indian child welfare, 1973-76. *Memberships*: American Anthropological Association (Fellow); American Association for the Advancement of Science; American Medical Society on Alcoholism; American Psychiatric Association (Fellow); American Public Health Association; American Association of Family Practice (Fellow); Association of Academic Psychiatrists; Minnesota Psychiatric Association; Society on Medical Anthropology; World Psychiatric Association, Transcultural Section ; among others. *Awards, honors*: Meritorious Service Award, U.S. Agency for International Development, 1966; Ginzburg Fellow, Group for the Advancement of Psychiatry, 1969-70; numerous research grants. *Published works*: Chapters in books & monographs: The Ravage of Indian Families in Crisis, in The Destruction of Indian Family Life, ed., S. Unger (Associa-

tion of American Indian Affairs, 1976); Alcoholism and American Indian Alcoholism, in Alcoholism Development, Intervention and Consequences, with J. Baker, ed., E. Heinman (1986).

*WESTHOVEN, THOMAS
(publishing)
Affiliation: Tipi Press, St. Joseph's Indian School, P.O. Box 89, Chamberlain, SD 57325 (605) 734-6021.

*WESTON-BEN, WENDY
(editor)
Affiliation: Directory of Native American Performing Artists, ATLATL, 2303 N. Central Ave. #104, Phoenix, AZ 85004 (602) 253-2731.

WETMORE, RUTH L. 1934-
(museum curator)
Born 1934 in Nebraska. *Education*: Park College, BA, 1956; University of Kansas, MA, 1959. *Principal occupation & Address*: Curator, Indian Museum of the Carolinas, 607 Turnpike Rd., Laurinburg, NC 28352 (919) 276-5880, 1974-. *Memberships*: Archaeological Society of North Carolina; Oklahoma Anthropological Society; North Carolina Museums Council; Phi Beta Kappa; Pi Sigma Alpha. *Interests*: Philatelic writing and exhibiting. *Published work*: First on the Land: The North Carolina Indians (John F. Blair, Publisher, 1975).

WETTENGEL, JACK
(public information director)
Affiliation: Oklahoma Historical Society, Indian Archives Division, 2100 N. Lincoln Blvd., Oklahoma City, OK 73105 (405) 521-2481.

WETZEL, DON *(Flying Eagle)* (Blackfeet) 1948-
(administrator)
Born August 1, 1948, Cut Bank, Mont. *Education*: University of Montana, BA, 1972, MA, 1981. *Principal occupation*: Administrator. *Address*: Governor's Office of Indian Affairs, 1218 E. 6th Ave., Helena, MT 59620 (406) 444-3702 (office). *Affiliation*: Coordinator, Governor's Office, Helena, MT, 1989-. *Other professional posts*: Teacher/coach in Browning, MT (8 years); High School Principal in Browning, MT (3 years); Supt.of Schools, Corvallis, MT (4 years); teacher/coach, Haskell Indian Junior College, 1982-83. *Awards, honors*: Nominated National Coach of the Year, 1980; Coach of the Year, Blackfeet Reservation, 1980; Jefferson Award-outstanding public service Administrator of the Year, State of Montana Library Association, 1988. *Interests*: "All on my own time - used vacation time and received the Jefferson Award for my crusade against drug and alcohol use among our young Indian People. I traveled 12,000 miles and talked with 10,000 students in Montana in a 2 1/2 year span." *Biographical sources*: Article on crusade, "Indian Life"; Missoula and Great Falls Tribune, and Billings Gazette.

WHEELER, J. WAGNER
(executive director)
Affiliation: Michigan Indian Press, 45 Lexington, NW, Grand Rapids, MI 49504 (616) 774-8331.

WHEELOCK, RICK
(college faculty sponsor)
Affiliation: Intertribal News, Intercultural Center, Fort Lewis College, Durango, CO 81301 (303) 247-7221.

WHITAKER, KATHLEEN 1945-
(anthropologist; museum-chief curator)
Born October 10, 1945, Los Angeles, Calif. *Education*: Northern Arizona University, BA, 1976; University of California, Los Angeles, MA, 1982, PhD, 1986. *Principal occupation*: Anthropologist; museum-chief curator. *Address*: Box 1375, Blue Jay, CA 92317 (213) 221-2164 ext. 224 (work). *Affiliations*: San Diego Museum of Man, 1976-79; chief curator, Southwest Museum, Los Angeles, CA, 1979-. *Other professional posts*: Former editor, Council for Museum of Anthropology; Research Associate, Los Angeles County Museum of Natural History. *Membership*: American Association of Museums.

*WHITAKER, R. REED
(achives director)
Affiliation: National Archives-K.C. Branch, 2312 E. Bannister Rd., Kansas City, MO 64131 (816) 926-7271.

WHITE, BETTY JANE *(Usdi agehya)* (Oklahoma Cherokee) 1943-
(professional nurse)
Born July 2, 1943, Holton, Kans. *Education*: Haskell Indian Jr. College, AA, 1991; Baker University/Stormont Vail School of Nursing (Baldwin City, KS), BS (Nursing), 1993; University of Kansas (currently working towards MS-Nursing); *Principal occupation*: Professional nurse. *Home address*: RR 2, Box 180, Oskaloosa, KS 66066 (913) 863-2312. *Affiliation*: St. Francis Hospital & Medical Center, Topeka, KS (Oncology Nursing; Clinical Caring for AIDS patients and other acute medical disease/illnesses), 1989-. *Community activities*: Topeka Railroad Days (chairperson for Native Americans); director of Native American Dance Troupe; lecturer of Native American history & legends. *Memberships*: American Nurses Association; Kansas Student Nurses Association; Native American Journalism Society; American Indian Science & Engineering Society (vice-president, local chapter, 1990-91; member, 1992-); Native American Cultural Society (chairperson, 1992). *Awards, honors*: Haskell Scholastic Excellence Award from Bess Spiva Timmons Foundation; Darby Scholarship Award for most active in Native American culture; Scholastic Excellence Award, Haskill Indian Jr. College; Selectee for Truman Award, Baker University; Kansas Nurse Foundation Award. *Interests*: "Areas I am most interested in are the protection & rights of children from all forms of abuse & neglect. I am involved in the beginning stages of organizing a chapter in Jefferson County for the prevention of child abuse. Health care to the elderly & disabled - longterm care facilities are needed on our reservations, run by the tribal members, for tribal members. Educating the public regarding misconceived ideas about Native Americans. Until the schools and media begin educating the public of the true history of the U.S., the public will always need educating. Holistic healing - the body, mind, and spirit needs to be in balance for healing to occur. If one is ill, the other two will be affected also. I have initiated and started up a Native American Dance Troupe to perform at various functions. The goal for this troupe is to perform nationwide and in foreign countries. Telling a story while the dancing is taking place and the dancing tells the story, is another way to educate the public about Native Americans." *Biographical sources*: Numerous articles relating to health care in "Nursing News," "Sunflower

Times," & "Professional Journal"; and a weekly article entitled, "The Fun Side of Life," in Oskaloosa Independent Newspaper.

WHITE, CALVIN
(association president)
Affiliation: Federation of Newfoundland Indians, P.O. Box 275, St. George's, Newfoundland, Canada A0N 1Z0 (709) 647-3733.

*WHITE, CAROL
(museum director)
Affiliation: Akwesasne Museum, Akwesasne Cultural Center, St. Regis Mohawk Nation, RR 1, Box 14C, Hogansburg, NY 13655 (518) 358-2240. *Other professional post*: Editor, "Kariwenhawi Newsletter," St. Regis Mohawk Reservation, Hogansburg, NY.

WHITE, DEAN A.
(BIA agency director)
Affiliation: New York Field Office, Bureau of Indian Affairs, P.O. Box 7366, 100 S. Clinton St., Room 523, Syracuse, NY 13261 (315) 423-5476.

WHITE, JAMES M. (Mdewakanton Sioux)
(tribal council president)
Affiliation: Prairie Island Community Council, 5750 Sturgeon Lake Rd., Welch, MN 55089 (612) 385-2536

WHITE, LINCOLN C. (Mohawk)
(tribal chief)
Affiliation: St. Regis Mohaw Council Chiefs, Akwesasne-Community Bldg., Hogansburg, NY 13655 (518) 358-2272. Past professional post: Director, National Advisory Council on Indian Education, Washington, D.C.

*WHITE, LINDA R.
(health director)
Affiliation: Kayenta PHS Indian Health Center, Box 368, Kayenta, AZ 86033 (602) 697-3211.

WHITE, LONNIE J. 1931-
(professor of history)
Born February 12, 1931, Haskell County, Tex. *Education*: West Texas State College, BA, 1950; Texas Tech University, MA, 1955, University of Texas, PhD, 1961. *Principal occupation*: Professor of history. *Home address*: 4272 Rhodes Ave., Memphis, TN 38111. *Affiliation*: Professor of history, Memphis State University, Memphis, TN, 1961-. *Military service*: U.S. Army, 1951-1953 (Sergeant). *Memberships*: Western History Association; Southern Historical Association; American Military Institute; American Historical Association; Journal of the West (editorial advisory board). *Interests*: Teach courses on history of American Indians at Memphis State University from 1968 to the present. *Biographical source*: Who's Who in the South and Southwest. *Published works*: Editor, co-author, Hostiles and Horse Soldiers: Indian Battles and Campaigns in the West (Pruett Press, 1972); editor, The Miles Expedition of 1874-1875: An Eyewitness Account of the Red River War, by Scout J.T. Marshall (Encino Press, 1971); editor, Chronicle of a Congressional Journey: The Doolittle Committee in the Southwest, 1865 (Pruett Press, 1975); Panthers to Arrowheads: The 36th (Texas-Oklahoma) Division in World War I (Presidial Press, 1984); Politics on the Southwestern Frontier: Arkansas Territory, 1819-1836 (Memphis State University Press, 1964); numerous articles in professional journals.

Biographies

*WHITE, MINERVA
(program coordinator)
Affiliation: New York State Education Dept., Native American Program, 543 Education Bldg. Annex, Washington Ave., Albany, NY 12234 (518) 474-0537.

WHITE, SAMMY TONE-KEI (Kiowa)
(advisor)
Affiliation: Council of Advisors, American Indian Heritage Foundation, 6051 Arlington Blvd., Falls Church, VA 22044-2788 (703) 237-7500.

WHITE, THOMAS R., Sr. (Pima-Maricopa)
(tribal governor)
Affiliation: Gila River Indian Community Council, Box 97, Sacaton, AZ 85247 (602) 562-3311.

WHITE, TRAVIS, M.D.
(health director)
Affiliation: Cibecue Indian Health Center, Cibecue, AZ 85941 (602) 332-2560.

*WHITE EAGLE, CATHY (Eastern Cherokee) 1960-
(executive director)
Born July 14, 1960, Merced, Calif. *Education*: Santa Clara University, BS, 1982. *Principal occupation*: Executive director. *Home address*: 8657 Bronson Dr., Granite Bay, CA 95746 (916) 791-7910 (work). *Affiliation*: Eagle Vision, Granite Bay, CA, 1992-. *Other professional posts*: Director, AIM, Sacramento Region; committee member, Multicultural Affairs, Sacramento Access. *Memberships*: American Indian Women's Association; National Organization for Women; American Indian Movement (AIM); Multi-Cultural Women's Network. *Awards, honors*: Honorary Award for community service, Sacramento State University; delegate to the United Nation on behalf of the American Indian Movement for the purpose of working on the basic human rights issues for American Indian people & children. *Interests*: "Sovereignty & treaty rights; currently working on the Native American Biography Series for Paramount's Modern Press, a series of six books for teachers to be released for 1995 school year.

WHITE EAGLE, GLENN C.
(school principal)
Affiliation: Polacca Day School, P.O. Box 750, Polacca, AZ 86042 (602) 737-2581.

*WHITE EAGLE, TOM
(Oglala-Hunkpapa Sioux) 1941-
(artist)
Born October 26, 1941, Rapid City, S.D. *Education*: California Polytechnic University, BA; University of California, Davis, MS. *Principal occupation*: Artist. *Address & Affiliation*: Owner/ curator, Bearcloud Gallery & Miwok Heritage Museum, Box 924, Columbia, CA 95310 (209) 532-5869. *Military service*: U.S. Air Force. *Interests*: "Restoration & study of Plains artifacts, primarily Lakota; work with youths & adults to promote Native culture."

*WHITE FEATHER, LARRY J.
(college counselor)
Affiliation: Madison Area Technical College, 3550 Anderson St., Rm. 171, Madison, WI 53704 (608) 246-6109.

WHITE HAT, ALBERT H. (Rosebud Sioux) 1938-
(Lakota studies instructor)
Born November 18, 1938, St. Francis, S.D. *Education*: Sinte Gleska College, AA (Lakota Studies), 1986. *Principal occupation*: Lakota studies instructor. *Home address*: P.O. Box 168, St. Francis, SD 57572 (605) 747-2711. *Affiliations*: Teacher, Indian Studies Program, St. Francis Indian School, 1974-80; part-time teacher, Lakota Medicine, 1979-85, Lakota studies instructor, Sinte Gleska College, Rosebud, SD, 1983-. *Other professional posts*: Tribal council (Rosebud Sioux) representative and committee work, 1979-81; president, Board of Directors, Sinte Gleska College, 1981-83. *Community activities*: Rosebud Community Action Program, 1967-70; Rosebud Ambulance Service, 1970-72; St. Francis Indian School (chairman of the board). Memberships: National Association for Bilingual Education; SD Association for Bilingual Education; SD Indian Education Association. *Awards, honors*: Fellowship Award in 1978 to research Native American History for high school history course at Newberry Library, Chicago, IL; Voted in to serve on the Board of Trustees at Proctor Academy in Andover, NH (trustee, 3 years; corporate member, 5 years). *Interests*: "Carpentry, woodwork and construction; horse training; cultural and traditional activities. Presently, I am coordinating three instructional pamphlets in the areas of Lakota kinship--early childhood development, bilingual science, and bilingual language arts; I have done lectures on the philosophy of the Lakota, oral history and traditions in different colleges and organization, civic groups, pastoral groups, and church organizations." *Published work*: Co-editor, Lakota Ceremonial Songs (song book with cassette tape) (Sinte Gleska College).

*WHITE HAWK, LAURIE HOUSEMAN
(Wakan-Ji-Pe-Wein-Sah) (Winnebago of Nebraska) 1952-
(professional painter)
Born November 17, 1952, Omaha, Neb. *Principal occupation*: Professional painter. *Address*: R.R. 3 Box 155-B, Lawrence, KS 66044 (913) 842-1948. *Membership*: Haskell Indian Nations Foundation.

*WHITE, THOMAS
(school principal)
Affiliation: St. Francis Indian School, P.O. Box 379, St, Francis, SD 57572 (605) 747-2299.

WHITE TEMPLE, EMMET
(school principal)
Affiliation: Rock Creek Day School, Bullhead, SD 57621 (605) 823-4971.

WHITEBEAR, BERNIE
(educational consultant)
Address: P.O. Box 99100, Seattle, WA 98199 (206) 285-4425; editor, Daybreak Star Reader.

WHITEBIRD, DENNIS
(Indian band chief)
Affiliation: Rolling River Indian Band, Box 145, Erickson, MB, Canada R0J 0P0 (204) 636-2211.

*WHITEBIRD, FRANCIS
(Indian affairs coordinator)
Affiliation: South Dakota Indian Affairs Office, 118 W. Capitol, Room 300, Pierre, SD 57501 (605) 773-3415.

WHITECROW, JAKE L.
(Quapaw-Seneca-Cayuga) 1928-
(health administrator)
Born July 2, 1928, Miami, Okla. *Education*: Oklahoma State University, BS, 1951. *Principal occupation*: Health administrator. Resides in Denver, CO (303) 394-3500 (office). *Affiliation*: Health administrator, National Indian Health Board, Denver, CO. *Other professional posts*: Health committee chairman, National Congress of American Indians; founder, Native American Free Loan Society, Denver, CO. *Military service*: U.S. Army, 1951-78 (Major-U.S. Army Reserve-retired; U.N. Medal; Korean War Medal with two Battle Stars; National Defense Medal; Army Reserve Medal). *Community activities*: Quapaw Tribe (chairman); Americans for Indian Opportunity, Washington, DC (board member, 7 years); American Indian Heritage Foundation, Washington, DC (board member, Advisory Council, 2 years); Native American Cattle Co. of OK (president). *Memberships*: OK State Historical Society; Thomas Jefferson Forum of Washington, DC (listed speaker); American Legion (precinct co-chairman, post commander). *Awards, honors*: Honorary member of 4-H Clubs of OK; "I was the only Oklahoma Indian to serve as a commissioner with the American Policy Review Commission (U.S. Congress, 1975-77)." *Interests*: "My avocational interests are: sport of rodeo, Indian customs and history, football, basketball, Indian dice, horse training, dog training." *Biographical source*: Indians of Oklahoma (University of Oklahoma Press). *Published work*: American Indian Policy Review Commission Final Report (USGPO, 1977).

WHITEDUCK, JEAN-GUY
(Indian band chief)
Affiliation: River Desert (Algonquin) Indian Band, Box 309, Maniwaki, Quebec, Canada J9E 3C9 (819) 449-5170.

*WHITEFEATHER, BOBBY
(Red Lake Chippewa)
(tribal chairperson)
Affiliation: Red Lake Band of Chippewa Indians of Minnesota (employment and training program, 1975-86; tribal treasurer, 1986-90; tribal secretary, 1990-94, chairperson, 1994-), P.O. Box 550, Red Lake, MN 56671 (218)679-3341.

WHITEFORD, ANDREW HUNTER 1913-
(research, teaching)
Born September 1, 1913, Winnipeg, Can. *Education*: Beloit (WI) College, BA, 1937; University of Chicago, MA, 1943, PhD, 1950. *Principal occupation*: Research, teaching. *Home address*: 447 Camino Monte Vista, Santa Fe, NM 87501 (505). *Affiliations*: Director, Logan Museum, Beloit, WI, 1951-74; administrative director, School of American Research, Santa Fe, NM, 1981-84; research associate, Museum of Indian Arts & Culture, Santa Fe, NM, 1987-. *Other professional posts*: Professor emeritus, Beloit College. *Community activities*: Board of Trustees (vice-president), Wheelwright Museum of American Indian; Advisory Board, Florence Ellis Museum, Ghost Ranch, NM; editorial board, "American Indian Art Magazine." *Memberships*: American Anthropological Association (Fellow); Native American Art Studies Association. *Awards, honors*: LLD, Beloit College; Society of the Sigma Xi (science); Phi Beta Kappa; grants from the National Science Foundation, National Foundation for the Arts, American

Philosophical Society. *Interests*: Research on many museums, here & abroad, also on reservation in the Southwest and western Great Lake. Interested in basketry of Southwestern tribes; beadwork of Lakes & Eastern tribes; non-loom weaving. *Biographical source*: Who's Who in the U.S. *Published works*: North American Indian Arts (Western Publishing, 1970); Southwestern Indian Baskets (School of American Research, 1988); Translating Tradition: Basketry Arts of the San Juan Paiutes, with S.B. McGreevy.

*WHITEHAIR, KEN
(service unit director)
Affiliation: Annette Isalnd Servie Unit, Metlakatla Indian Community, P.O. Box 439, Metlakatla, AK 99926 (907) 886-4741.

WHITEHAWK, JOE
(cultural specialist)
Affiliation: Native American Services Agency, Missoula Indian Center, 2300 Regent St. #A, Missoula, MT 59801 (406) 329-3373.

WHITELAW, MICHAEL
(BIA agency director)
Affiliation: Spokane Agency, Bureau of Indian Affairs, P.O. Box 389, Wellpinit, WA 99040 (509) 258-4561.

*WHITELAW, SHEILA (Colville)
(editor)
Affiliation: "Tribal Tribune," Colville Confederated Tribes, P.O. Box 150, Nespelem, WA 99155 (509) 634-8835.

WHITELY, PETER M. 1953-
(anthropologist)
Born March 13, 1953, Leicester, England. *Education*: Cambridge University (England), BA, 1975, MA, 1980; University of New Mexico, PhD, 1982. *Principal occupation*: Anthropologist. *Home address*: 140 Cabrini Blvd. #116, New York, NY 10033 (914) 395-2623 (work). *Affiliation*: Professor of anthropology, Sarah Lawrence College, Bronxville, NY, 1985-. Other professional post: Consultant to The Hopi Tribe *Memberships*: American Anthropological Association; American Ethnological Society; Royal Anthropological Institute. *Interests*: Hopi ethnology, Hopi history; Native American Land Rights; Native American political & religious sovereignty, particularly as represented in Federal court cases. More than 2 years of fieldwork at Hopi. *Published works*: Deliberate Acts: Changing Hopi Culture Through the Oraibi Split (University of Arizona Press, 1988); Bacavi: Journey to Reed Springs (Northland Press, 1988); Navajoland: Family Settlement & Land Use, with Klara B. Kelley (Navajo Community College Press, 1989).

WHITEMAN, DENNIS T.
(BIA agency supt.)
Affiliation: Fort Hall Agency, Bureau of Indian Affairs, P.O. Box 220, Fort Hall, ID 83203 (208) 238-2301.

WHITESELL, RICHARD
(BIA area director)
Affiliation: Billings Area Office, Bureau of Indian Affairs, 316 North 26th St., Billings, MT 59101 (406) 657-6315.

WHITESIDE, DON *(Sin-a-paw)* (Creek) 1931-
(consultant)
Born May 9, 1931, Brooklyn, N.Y. *Education*: Wisconsin State University, BS, 1958; University of Wisconsin, MS, 1960; Stanford University, PhD, 1967. *Principal occupation*: Research analyst. *Home address*: 4 Newgale St., Nepean, ON K2H 5R2. *Affiliations*: Assistant professor, NC State University, Raleigh, 1964-65; assistant professor, University of Tennessee, Knoxville, 1965-67; University of Alberta, Edmonton, 1967-70; consultant, Government of Canada, Ottawa, 1970-; research director, National Indian Brotherhood, Ottawa, 1972-73; professor, Manitou College, LaMacaza, Quebec, 1973-1975; INA, 1976-79; owner, Whiteside and Associates, 1979-; consultant, Government of Canada (NHW), 1982-89. *Military service*: Merchant Marine, 1947-48; U.S. Army, 1948-54. *Community activities*: Alberta Human Rights Association (president, 1969-70); Civil Liberties Association, National Capital Region (president, 1970-71, 1973, 1974, 1977-89); Canadian Rights and Liberties Federation (secretary/treasurer, 1972-74; president, 1974-77, 1983-86); Aboriginal Institute of Canada (president, 1973-); Ontario Civil Liberties Association (president, 1989-). *Memberships*: United Native Americans. *Awards*: National Science Foundation Fellowship, 1963; Stanford University Fellow, 1963-64. *Interests*: Genealogy. *Biographical sources*: Canadian Who's Who, 1986-; Carl R. Baldwin, Echoes of Their Voices , St. Louis, MO (Hawthorn, 1978). *Published works*: Aboriginal People: A Selected Bibliography (National Indian Brotherhood, 1973); A Look Into Indian History (Aboriginal Institute of Canada, 1983).

*WHITETREE, TERRY L. (Seneca-Cayuga)
(tribal chief)
Affiliation: Seneca-Cayuga Tribe of Oklahoma, P.O. Box 1283, Miami, OK 74355 (918) 542-6609.

WHITFORD, THOMAS C., Sr. (Blackfeet)1930-
(tribal business council chairman)
Born January 2, 1930, Browning, Mont. *Education*: City College of San Francisco, 1959-62; Eastern Montana College, 1970-71; University of Idaho, 1973-75. *Principal occupation*: Blackfeet Tribal Council, Chairman. *Address*: Box 658, Browning, MT 59417 (406) 338-7276 (work). *Affiliation*: Director, Montana Inter-Tribal Policy Board, Billings, MT, 1977-80; deputy area director, BIA, Billings, MT, 1980-82; supt., BIA (Montana, Nevada, and California tribes), 1982-86; chairperson, Blackfeet Tribal Business Council and business owner, Browning, MT, 1986-. *Community activities*: Initiated the reorganization and revitalization of the Blackfeet Senior Citizens Organization and regularly assists needy families with food and holiday gifts for children. *Memberships*: Montana-Wyoming Tribal Chairman's Association (chairman, 1988-); National Congress of American Indians (Billings Area Vice-President, 1988-); Montana Democratic Committee on Policymaking, 1988-; Northwest Affiliated Tribes, 1989-; Concerned Reservation Indians, 1989-. *Awards, honors*: Outstanding performances and achievement, Bureau of Indian Affairs; Montana Inter-Tribal Policy Board Honors for Leadership; appearances on "Face the State" (Montana) and "Indians in Progress" to discuss Indian issues. *Interests*: "Member of the Blackfeet delegation who first successfully returned Indian skeletal remains collected by the Smithsonian Institute, Washington, D.C. to native people. The remains are those of fifteen people who had died during the "Starvation Winter" of 1883-84; established a nation-to-nation "open door" relationship between the Montana Tribes and the State of Montana, County and local representatives to achieve a more effective working relationship; initiated a market study to determine the potential for tourism and development of an enterprise zone on the Blackfeet reservation to attract investment for tourism."

*WHITING, BERNARD (Rosebud Lakota Sioux)
(radio station manager)
Affiliation: KINI - 96.1 FM, Rosebud Lakota Sioux Tribe, P.O. Box 146, St. Francis, SD 57572 (605) 747-2291.

WHITING, PAUL J.
(museum director)
Affiliation: Buechel Memorial Lakota Museum, St. Francis Indian Mission, 350 S. Oka St., Box 149, St. Francis, SD 57572 (605) 747-2828.

WHITING-SORRELL, ANNA
(association president)
Affiliation: National Association for Native American Children of Alcoholics, 1402 3rd Ave. #1110, Seattle, WA 98118 (206) 322-5601.

WHITISH, HERBERT "IKE" (Shoalwater)
(tribal chairperson)
Affiliation: Shoalwater Bay Tribal Council, P.O. Box 130, Tokeland, WA 98590 (206) 267-6766.

WHITMAN, CARL, Jr. *(Black Fox)* (Mandan/Hidatsa/Arikara) 1913-
(program director; university instructor)
Born March 6, 1913, Elbowoods, N.D. *Education*: ND State School of Science, 1934-36. *Principal occupation*: Director-Indian programs; university instructor. *Home address*: P.O. Box 203, Parshall, ND 58770 (701) 862-3260. *Afiliations*: Chairperson, Three Affiliated Tribes, New Town, ND (6 years); chairperson, ND Legal Services, New Town, ND (20 years). *Awards, honors*: Outstanding Senior North Dakotan, 1987; Recognition for 20 years as Chairperson of the Board of ND Legal Services. *Interests*: "Introducing cross-breeding of cattle as a way of increasing weight. Directing a laboratory studying alternative source of energy. (I did) a comprehensive renovation of the educational program for Indians of the Low Mountain School on the Navajo Reservation, 1964, which was rejected but was used by Dr. Robert Roesell of Arizona State University. It made a heavy impact in the Indian education field. Vernacular language was included in the curriculum program. Other relevant disciplines were included such as Indian history, commuity problems, parapsychology at an applied level and sex education."

WHITMAN, KATHY (Elk Woman) (Manadan-Hidatsa-Arikara) 1952-
(artist, sculptor, painter)
Born August 12, 1952, Bismarck, N.D. *Education*: University of South Dakota; Sinte Gleska College, Rosebud, SD; Standing Rock Community College, Ft. Yates, ND. *Principal occupation*: Artist, sculptor, painter. *Home address*: 11041 N. 84th St., Scottsdale, AZ 85260 (602) 991-3347. *Affiliations*: Owner, Nux-Baga Lodge, New Town, N.D., 1981-1985; owner, Recreation Center, New Town, N.D., 1985. *Other professional post*: Art instructor, Standing Rock Community College and Sinte Gleska College. *Com-

munity activities: Parent representative-Headstart, Ft. Yates, N.D.; Ft. Berthold Community College, New Town, N.D. (board of directors); Pow-Wow, Canonball, N.D. (president, committee member). *Memberships*: Indian Arts and Crafts Association; Gallup Intertribal Ceremonial; Southwest Association on Indian Affairs. *Awards, honors*: Best Craftsman/Special Award, Bukllock's Santa Monica Indian Ceremonial, 1986; 1st Place, San Juan Bautista Indian Arts and Crafts Show, 1986; 1st Place, 1986, 2nd Place, 1987, 1st Place, 1990, Eight Northern Pueblos Arts and Crafts Show; Special Merit Award, Trail of Tears Arts Show, 1987; 3rd Place, Gallup Indian Ceremonial; Best of Fine Arts/Split Best of Show, Northern Plains Tribal Arts Show, 1988; 1989 Poster Artist, Southwest Association on Indian Affairs; 1990 One Woman Exhibition in Nurnberg, Germany; 1991 Best of Show, Pasadena Western Relic & Indian Arts and Crafts Show; Governors Award, Directors and Choice Merit Award, United Tribes Educational Training Center, Bismarck, N.D. *Interests*: "Demonstrated and exhibited paintings and sculpture in numerous galleries; danced and exhibited artwork in Charleroi, Belgium, Dijon, France, anmd Nurnberg, Germany; started a recreation center on Ft. Berthold Reservation for the youth and sponsored an alternative camp for youth. I believe that all things of the Sacred Mother Earth are special and holy. I want people to see and feel, the pride, the unity, the happiness, and the spiritual strength that is so close to us. There is serenity in having a strong relationship with the Great Spirit and all His Sacred Veings." *Biographical sources*: Article - "People, Faces of the 90's: A Closeup Look at Valley News-makers," Valley of the Sun Times, June 1991; articles in The Desert Leaf, July 1989; Antiques & the Arts Weekly, Sept. 1989; Santa Fe Reporter, Aug. 1990; Indian Trader, Aug. 1990; New York Times, Sept. 1991 ad. 1989 Video - Beyond Tradition, by Jerry and Lois Jacka (one of featured artists).

WHITMAN, ROBERT K. (Navajo) 1954-
(electrical engineer)
Born February 25, 1954, Fort Defiance, Ariz. *Education*: University of New Mexico, BS, 1977; Colorado State University, MS, 1986; University of Colorado, PhD (Electrical Engineering), 1990. *Principal occupation*: Electrical engineer. *Home address*: 185 South 42nd St., Boulder, CO 80303 (303) 494-0463. *Affiliations*: Engineer, IBM Corp., San Jose, CA & Boulder, CO, 1977-90; deputy director, American Indian Science & Engineering Society, 1991-. *Other professional post*: Industrial Development Specialist, Navajo Nation Economic Development Dept., Window Rock, AZ, (3 months) 1987-88. *Community activities*: AISES student chapter advisor at University of Colorado, Boulder; member, University of Colorado Graduate School Advisory Council; member, Science Service International, Science & Engineering Fair Advisory Council; member, Committee on Feasibility of a National Scholars Program, National Research Council. *Memberships*: Institute of Electrical and Electronics Engineers (IEEE); American Indian Science & Engineering Society (AISES) (board of directors, 1983-87, board secretary, 1984-85, board chairperson, 1985-87, chair of Scholarship Committee, 1988-92). *Awards, honors*: NASA Minority Fellowship, 1975-77; Outstanding Achievement Award, Navajo Nation, 1980; Information Systems Division Achievement Award, IBM Corp., 1981; Information Products

Division Achievement Award, IBM Corp., 1984; AISES/GE Fellowship, 1993. *Interests*: "Doctoral dissertation on human speech synthesis, non-linear methods of sound reconstruction. Outside activities include: reading history of American Indians, learning about Navajo traditional ways and about my ancestors; giving presentations to high school and college students on technical careers and importance of traditions. Judge science fair projects at high school level; traveled to Europe 4 times." *Biographical source*: "New Mexico Professional Engineer," 9/78; "Graduate Engineer," 10/81; "Minority Engineer," Summer 1984; "Winds of Change," 2/86.

WICKLIFFE, DENNIS
(BIA agency director)
Affiliation: Tahlequah Agency, Bureau of Indian Affairs, P.O. Box 828, Tahlequah, OK 74465 (918) 456-6146.

WIDDISS, DONALD A. (Wampanoag)
(tribal president)
Affiliation: Wampanoag Tribal Council of Gay Head, State Rd., RFD Box 137, Gay Head, MA 02535 (508) 645-9265.

*WIDMARK, LAWRENCE, Jr. (Sitka)
(tribal president)
Affiliation: Sitka Tribe of Alaska, 456 Katlian St., Sitka, AK 99835 (907) 747-3207.

*WIESEN, DON
(school administrator)
Affiliation: Lac Courte Oreilles Ojibwa School, Route 2, Box 2800, Hayward, WI 54843 (715) 634-8924.

*WILBANKS, BILLY M.
(school principal)
Affiliation: Pearl RiverSchool, Route 7, Box 19-H, Philadelphia, MS 39350 (601) 656-9051.

WILCOX, DEE
(BIA agency director)
Affiliation: Southern Paiute Field Station, Bureau of Indian Affairs, P.O. Box 986, Cedar City, UT 84720 (801) 586-1121.

*WILDER, RICHARD (Paiute)
(tribal chairperson)
Affiliation: Fort Independence Reservation, Box 67, Independence, CA 93526 (619) 878-2126.

*WILKERSON, ROSIE
(BIA agency acting supt.)
Affiliation: Chinle Agency, Bureau of Indian Affairs, P.O. Box 7H, Chinle, AZ 86503 (602) 674-5201 ext. 101.

WILKINS, DAVID E. (Lumbee) 1954-
(assistant professor)
Born September 18, 1954, Fort Bragg, N.C. *Education*: Pembroke State University, BA, 1976; University of Arizona, MA, 1982; University of North Carolina, Chapel Hill, PhD, 1990. *Principal occupation*: Assistant professor. *Home address*: 306 Chautauqua Park, Boulder, CO 80302. *Affiliation*: Assistant Professor of Political Science & Indian Law & Policy, University of Arizona, Tucson, AZ, 1990-93; Assistant Professor of Political Science & American Indian Studies, University of Colorado, Boulder, CO., 1993-. *Membership*: American Political Science Association. *Award*: Ford Foundation Dissertation Fellowship, 1989-90; Ford Foundation Post-Doctoral Fellowship, 1993-94; Center for Ad-

vanced Study in the Behavioral Sciences Post Doctoral Fellowship. *Published work*: Dine Bib eehaz'aanii: A Handbook of Navajo Government (Navajo Community College Press, 1987); numerous academic journal articles.

*WILLARD, SHIRLEY
(editor)
Affiliation: "Indian Awareness Center Newsletter, Fulton County Historical Society, 37 E. 375 N., Rochester, IN 46975 (219) 223-4436.

*WILLIAMS, ANNIE LOU (Eskimo)
(village president)
Affiliation: Native Village of Kalskag, Kalskag, AK 99607 (907) 471-2248.

*WILLIAMS, BETTY LOU
(organization director)
Affiliation: World Vision International, 919 W. Huntington Dr., Monrovia, CA 91016 (818) 303-8811.

*WILLIAMS, CINDY (Duwamish)
(tribal secretary/treasurer)
Affiliation: Duwamish Tribal Council, 15616 First Ave. South, Seattle, WA 98148 (206) 244-0606.

WILLIAMS, DAVID EMMETT (*Tosque*)
(Kiowa/Apache/Tonkawa) 1933-
(artist)
Born August 20, 1933, Redstone, Okla. *Education*: Bacone College. *Principal occupation*: Artist. *Membership*: American Tribal Dancers and Singers Club, 1963- (head drummer and singer). *Awards, honors, exhibits*: Numerous art awards and one-man shows; work represented in permanent collections of several museums.

WILLIAMS, DEAN V (Seneca) 1925-
(tribal official)
Born April 30, 1925, Cattaraugus Reservation, N.Y. *Home address*: Route 438, Gowanda--Irving Rd., Irving, NY 14081. *Affiliation*: Former president, Seneca Nation of Indians, Cattaraugus Reservation, NY. *Military service*: U.S. Navy Submarine Service, 1943-46.

WILLIAMS, DELLA R. (SAM) (Papago) 1936-
(school principal)
Born February 13, 1936, Ventana Village, Papago Reservation, Ariz. *Education*: Phoenix Junior College, AA, 1958; Arizona State University, BA, 1962. *Principal occupation*: School principal. *Address*: Star Route, Box 92, San Simeon School, Sells, AZ 85634 (602) 362-2231. *Affiliations*: Teacher, Santa Rosa Boarding School, BIA, 1962-75; principal, San Simeon School, Sells, AZ, 1977-. *Community activities*: Papago Tribal Education Committee (chairperson, 1965-70); OEO's Community Action Program; tribal representative at various state and national conferences and workshops, as well as at congressional hearings. *Honor*: Inducted into the Phoenix Indian High School Hall of Fame as a charter member, 1977. *Interests*: "Consulting with students, teachers and administrators concerning grades and adjustment; higher education students, consultant and advisor; directed Tribal Education Grants and assisted with other financial needs of higher education; monthly reports to the General Council; participated and assisted in the introduction, planning and development of the first poverty program on the Papago Reservation; participated in supervising and hiring the first Head-Start school teachers, evaluated and made recommendations; participated as

guest speaker in Indian education conferences in Tempe, Indian Clubs, The Papago Council, Phoenix Indian High School, Tucson Indian Center, and Papago District Councils."

WILLIAMS, EDWARD
(Indian band chief)
Affiliation: Moose Deer Point Indian Band, Box 119, Mactier, Ontario, Canada P0C 1H0.

WILLIAMS, FLOYD (Skagit)
(tribal chairperson)
Affiliation: Upper Skagit Tribal Council, 2284 Community Plaza, Sedro Wooley, WA 98284 (206) 856-5501.

WILLIAMS, FRANK
(IHS-director of support services)
Affiliation: Director of Support Services, Alaska Native Health Center, 250 Gambel St., Anchorage, AK 99501 (907) 279-6661

*WILLIAMS, HUBERT (Nooksack)
(tribal chairperson)
Affiliation: Nooksack Tribal Council, P.O. Box 157, Deming, WA 98244 (206) 592-5176.

WILLIAMS, IDA
(director-friendship centre)
Affiliation: Native Friendship Centre, 3730 Cote Des Neiges Rd., Montreal, Quebec, Canada H3H 1V6 (514) 937-5338.

WILLIAMS, JOHN R.
(health director)
Affiliation: Mescalero PHS Indian Hospital, P.O. Box 210, Mescalero, NM 88340 (505) 671-4441.

*WILLIAMS, JOHN W.
(health director)
Affiliation: Pawhuska PHS Indian health Center, 715 Grandview, Pawhuska, OK 74056 (918) 287-4491.

WILLIAMS, JUANITA (Paiute)
(rancheria spokesperson)
Affiliation: North Fork Rancheria, P.O. Box 120, North Fork, CA 93643.

WILLIAMS, LEONA
(rancheria chairperson)
Affiliation: Pinoleville Rancheria, 367 N. State St. #204, Ukiah, CA 95482 (707) 463-1454.

WILLIAMS, LEONARD (Caddo)
(tribal chairperson)
Affiliation: Caddo Tribal Council, P.O. Box 487, Binger, OK 73009 (405) 656-2344.

WILLIAMS, MARILYN
(health director)
Affiliation: N.W. Washington PHS Lummi PHS Health Center, 2592 Kwina Rd., Bellingham, WA 98226 (206) 676-8373.

WILLIAMS, MOGAN
(editor)
Affiliation: Wawatay News, Wawatay Native Communications Society, P.O. Box 1180, Sioux Lookout, ON, Canada P0V 2T0 (807) 737-2951.

WILLIAMS, PERRY
(Alabama-Coushatta of Texas)
(tribal chairperson)
Affiliation: Alabama-Coushatta Tribe of Texas, Route 3, Box 659, Livingston, TX 77351 (409) 563-4391.

WILLIAMS, ROBERT A., Jr. (Lumbee) 1955-
(law professor)
Born March 11, 1955, Baltimore, Md. *Education*: Loyola College (Baltimore), BA, 1977; Harvard Law School, JD, 1980. *Principal occupation*: Assistant professor of law, University of Wisconsin, Madison, 1980-. Resides in Madison, WI. *Other professional post*: Legal consultant. *Community activities*: Indian Rights Association, Philadelphia, Pa. (vice president, 1984; board of directors, 1980-85). *Awards, honors*: American Council of Learned Societies/Ford Foundation Fellowship recipient, 1985-86; National Endowment for the Humanities Fellowship recipient, Summer, 1982. *Interests*: American Indian legal history, and economic development.

WILLIAMS, ROBERT L. (Ojibway)
(Indian band chief)
Affiliation: Ojibways of Walpole Island, RR 3, Wallaceburg, ON B8A 1R0 (519) 627-1481.

WILLIAMS, SOLOMON (Eskimo)
(village president)
Affiliation: Mekoryuk Native Village, P.O. Box 66, Mekoryuk, AK 99630 (907) 827-8828.

WILLIAMS, WALTER L. 1948-
(professor)
Born November 3, 1948, Durham, N.C. *Education*: Georgia State University, BA, 1970; University of North Carolina, Chapel Hill, MA, 1972, PhD, 1974. P*rincipal occupation*: Associate professor, Anthropology Dept., University of Southern California, Los Angeles, CA, 1985-. *Home address*: 2319 Portland St., Los Angeles, CA 90007. *Other professional post*: Consultant, American Indian Studies Center, UCLA. *Community activities*: Gay American Indians, Inc. (consultant); Museum of the Cherokee Indians (consultant); International Gay and Lesbian Archives (president, board of directors). *Military service*: U.S. Army, 1973 (Captain). *Memberships*: American Anthropological Association; Society of Lesbian and Gay Anthropologists (chair, Ruth Benedict Prize Committee); Sociologists Lesbian and Gay Caucus; Committee on Lesbian and Gay History. *Awards, honors*: Woodrow Wilson Fellow, 1970; American Council of Learned Societies grant awards, 1977, 1983; UCLA American Indian Studies Center Fellow, 1980, 1982; Newberry Library Fellow, 1978; Ruth Benedict Prize Book Award, 1986, for The Spirit and the Flesh; . *Interests*: "Homosexuality and gender variance in American Indian cultures; Indian sexuality; 19th century Indian legal status; Southeastern Indian ethnohistory, 1830-present." *Published works*: Editor, Southeastern Indians Since the Removal Era (University of Georgia Press, 1979); editor, Indian Leadership (Sunflower University Press, 1984); The Spirit and the Flesh: American Indian Androgyny and Male Sexuality (Beacon Press, 1986). Articles: Detour Down the Trail of Tears: Southern Indians and the Land (Southern Exposure, Fall, 1974); The Proposed Merger of Apaches with Eastern Cherokees in 1893 (Journal of Cherokee Studies, Spring, 1977); editor, Southeastern Indians Since the Removal Era (University of Georgia Press, 1979); editor, Indian Leadership (Sunflower University Press, 1984); author, The Spirit and the Flesh: Sexual Diversity in American Indian Culture (Beacon Press, 1986).book reviews on Southeastern Indians in: Ethnohistory, North Carolina Historical Review, American Indian Journal, and Journal of Southern History.

WILLIAMSON, BILLY TALAKO (*Grey Eagle*)
(Oklahoma Choctaw) 1948-
(film director/producer)
Born February 2, 1948, Okla. *Education*: CSU (Edmond, OK), BA, 1973; UCLA, MFA (Film), 1977. *Principal occupation*: Film director/producer. Address: P.O. Box 32329, Oklahoma City, OK 73123 (405) 789-4300. *Affiliation*: Director, I.T.I. Film & Video, Oklahoma City, OK, 1980-. *Memberships*: National Association of Amerian Indian Social Workers; Directors Guild of America; Screen Actors Guild; A.C.S. *Awards, honors*: 4 ADDY Awards; 6 Telly Awards. *Interests*: Zuni Pueblo.

*WILLIAMSON, DIANA S.
(executive director)
Affiliation: Governor's Commission on Indian Affairs, 1885 Wooddale Blvd., Suite 111, Baton Rouge, LA 70806 (504) 925-4509.

WILLIAMSON, JIM (Chippewa) 1949-
(energy research management)
Born November 30, 1949, Williston, N.D. *Education*: Montana State University, BS, 1971; University of California, Berkeley, MS (Math), 1974. *Principal occupation*: Energy research management. *Home address*: 5025 Garton Rd., Castle Rock, CO 80104. *Affiliation*: Project Manager, U.S. Atomic Energy Commission, Oakland, CA (7 years); Director-International Solar Programs, Midwest Research Institute, Kansas City, MO (8 years); Associate Partner, Meridian Corporation, Alexandria, VA, 1988-; Manager, National Renewable Energy Laboratory, Washington, DC, 1989-. *Community activities*: Colorado Youth Soccer Association; Alexandria City Energy Commission; Colorado Alliance for Science. *Memberships*: American Indian Science & Engineering Society; Institute of Electrical & Electronic Engineers; American Solar Energy Society; American Management Association. *Awards, honors*: Project Achievement, King Abdul-Aziz Center for Science & Technology; Project Management, Atomic Energy Commission; Spacecraft Support Team Award, Energy Research & Development Administration. *Interests*: "Extensive international travel to energy research centers including an around-the-world trip in 1987. Raising horses in Virginia." *Biographical sources*: Who's Who in Colleges & Universities, 1971; American Indian Science & Engineering Society Mentor Calendar, 1983; Biographical Review in College Chemistry, Sept. 1992. *Published works*: Co-editor - Solar Cooling, April 1980; Solar Water Desalination, March 1981; Solar Storage, April, 1982; Solar Thermal Collectors, April 1983; Solar Buildings, May 1984; Solar for Remote Applications, April 1985 (all published by U.S. Dept. of Energy).

*WILLIAMSON, LYNN
(museum curator)
Affiliation: The Institute for American Indian Studies, P.O. Box 1260, Washington, CT 06793 (203) 868-0518.

WILLIAMSON, VERNA (Pueblo)
(pueblo governor)
Affiliation: Isleta Pueblo Council, P.O. Box 317, Isleta, NM 87022 (505) 869-3111.

*WILLIAMSON, WILLIAM P. (Choctaw)
(school principal)
Affiliation: Conehatta Elementary School, Route 1, Box 343, Conehatta, MS 39057 (601) 775-8254.

*WILLIE, ELVIN
(health center director)
Affiliation: Schurz Indian Health Center, P.O. Drawer A, Schurz, NV 89427 (702) 773-2345.

*WILLIE, FRITZ (Eskimo)
(village president)
Affiliation: Native Village of Eek, P.O. Box 87, Eek, AK 99579 (907) 233-2211.

WILLIE, JAMES Eskimo)
(village president)
Affiliation: Napakiak Native Village, Napakiak, AK 99634 (907) 589-2227.

*WILLIG, JUDITH ANN 1953-
(anthropologist; earth scientist;
environmental/multi-cultural studies)
Born October 5, 1953, New Orleans, La. *Education*: University of Southwestern Louisiana, BA, 1976; University of Oregon, MA, 1981, PhD, 1989. *Home address*: 89912 Greenwood Dr., Leaburg, OR 97489 (503) 485-3585 (office). *Affiliations*: Professor of Anthropology, Washington State University, Pullman, WA, 1989-90; Geoarchaeologist, INFOTEC Research, Inc., Eugene, OR, 1990-; Global Vision (non-profit multicultural educational institution), Eugene, OR, 1992-. *Other professional posts*: Co-producer and narrator-educational slide show, "Desert Survival Skills; Re-living the Paiute Past," 1980; and research assistant/consultant, NEH traveling exhibit, "Native Peoples of the Oregon Coast," 1982 (University of Oregon, Museum of Natural History). *Community activities*: American Indian Cultural Heritage Conferences (Planning Board of Directors, 1985-89); McKenzie River Lions Club, 1991-92; President, One Common Thread (non-profit organization to promote women in the arts/entertainment). *Memberships*: American Anthropological Association; National Geographic Society; International Quaternary Association; Society for American Archaeology. *Awards, honors*: Honor societies; teaching fellowships and research grants; scholarships. *Interests*: "Anthropology; earth sciences and geoarchaeology; extinction boundaries (past & present); multi-cultural education; Native American studies; cultural heritage preservation; environmental science and cultural diversity." *Published works*: Editor, "Geoarchaeology in the Northwest," Tebiwa 21, 1984; editor, Early Human Occupation in Far Western North America: The Clovis-Archaic Interface (Nevada State Museum Anthrpological Paper 21, 1989); author, Clovis Adaptation in Far Western North America: Regional Pattern & Environmental Context (Center for the Study of the First Americans, 1991); *in preparation*: Giving Up the Gold: A Practial Guide to the Survival of the Human Species (projected publication date, 1993).

WILLIS, NORMA (Navajo)
(financial aid director)
Affiliation: Navajo Community College, P.O. Box 580, Shiprock, NM 87420 (505) 368-5291.

WILLMAN, ARTHUR
(director-SEARHC hospital)
Affiliation: Mt. Edgecumbe SEARHC Regional Health Hospital, 222 Tongass Dr., Sitka, AK 99835 (907) 966-8310.

WILNOTY, JOHN JULIUS (Cherokee) 1940-
(stone carver)
Born April 10, 1940, Cherokee, N.C. *Principal occupation*: Stone carver. *Home address*: P.O. Box 517, Cherokee, NC 28719. *Membership*: The Qualla Indian Arts and Crafts Cooperative. *Interests*: "Building toys for children; rebuilding and designing machinery." Mr. Wilnoty's work is displayed at the Smithsonian Institution and the Museum of the American Indian.

WILSON, CATHERINE E. (Nez Perce)
(attorney)
Address: 219 3rd St., NE, Washington, DC 20002 (202) 226-2311. *Membership*: Native American Bar Association; Native American Alumni Association of Dartmouth College.

WILSON, CHESLEY GOSEYUN (*White Eagle*)
(San Carlos Apache) 1932-
(silversmith-retired; artist-musician)
Born July 31, 1932, Bylas, Ariz. *Education*: Carson City (NV) Community College (1 year). *Principal occupation*: Silversmith (retired); artist-musician. *Home address*: 333 S. Alvernon Way, #60, Tucson, AZ 85711 (602) 881-4842. *Affiliation*: Silversmiths, Inc., NV (25 years). *Military service*: U.S. Army, 1950-52 (Corporal, Korea). *Community activities*: President, Arco-Iris (Indian arts organization), Tucson, AZ. *Awards, honors*: 1st Place Award for silver work at the Tohono O'odham Spring Fair, 1987; 1989 Heritage Fellowship Award, National Endowment for the Arts-Folk Arts for his traditional Apache violin; An Apache violin made by Chesley is in the musical instruments collection of the Smithsonian Institution, Washington, DC; Chesley was commissioned by the Arizona Commission on the Arts to make a traditional Apache violin for the Governor's Arts Awards in March 1991. *Interests*: Chesley is a singer, maker and player of traditional Apache violins and flutes which he handcrafts, woodcarver, storyteller and silversmith. He is the great-grandson of Aravaipa Apache Chief Eskiminzin and the great-great grandson of White Mountain Apache Chiefs Hashkedasila and Santo as well as the famous Chiricahua Apache Chief Cochise. He learned the arts of Apache musical instruments making from his uncles Albert Goseyun and Amos Gustina. He is considered an authority on Ga'an (Mountain Spirit or Crown Dancers) ceremonies. He regularly takes part in religious ceremonies on Apache reservations in Arizona as singer.

WILSON, DUFFY
(museum director)
Affiliation: Native American Centre fo the Living Arts, Inc., 25 Rainbow Mall, Niagara Falls, NY 14303 (716) 284-2427.

*WILSON, EDWARD P. *(White bear)*
(Southern Cheyenne)
(economic development specialist,
administrator)
Born August 2, 1943, Clinton, Okla. *Education*: Haskell Institute, Northern Oklahoma College, Oklahoma State University. *Principal occupation*: economic development specialist, administrator. *Home address*: 1811 Shelby Court, Norman, OK 73071 (405) 329-4597. *Affiliation*: Chairman, Cheyenne-Arapaho Tribe, 1980-81. *Other professional posts*: Vice-president & secretary of Reserve Industrial Authority; director, Citizen Band Potawatomi's Tax Program; administrator, Sac & Fox Tribe of Missouri; director, National Indian Activities Association. *Military service*: U.S. Army Airborne, 1965-67, E-4 (Vietnam-Bronze Star & Purple Heart). *Community activities*: Parent Teachers Organization; Vietnam Era Veterans Organization; active in support of tribal ceremonial preservation; NAC (Church). *Memberships*: Board Member, Native Americans Veterans Services Access (model since mid 1993); board member, Oklahoma Indian Affairs Commission (appointed by Governor, 1992, re-appointed 1993 to full term. *Interests*: "Reservation/tribal economies; financing for individuals, groups, tribes, corporations; develop sources of capital to enhance development & employment; raise educational levels of groups or communities; develop entrepreneurship."

WILSON, ERIC
(BIA-Indian youth program specialist)
Affiliation: Office of Tribal Services, Bureau of Indian Affairs, Dept. of the Interior, MS-4603-MIB, 1849 C St., NW, Washington, DC 20240 (202) 3463.

WILSON, FRED
(school principal)
Affiliation: Phoenix Indian School, P.O. Box 10, Phoenix, AZ 85001 (602) 241-2126.

WILSON, JOHN
(school director)
Affiliation: Shiprock Reservation Dormitory, P.O. Box 1180, Shiprock, NM 87420 (505) 368-5113.

WILSON, LARRY (Cree)
(member-board of directors)
Affiliation: Intertribal Christian Comunications, P.O. Box 3765, Station B, Winnipeg, Manitoba, Canada R2W 3R6 (204) 661-9333.

WILSON, LENA R. (Navajo)
(school principal)
Affiliation: Crystal Boarding School, Navajo, NM 887328 (505) 777-2385.

WILSON, RAYMOND 1945-
(professor of history)
Born April 11, 1945, New Kensington, Penna. *Education*: Fort Lewis College, BA, 1967; University of Nebraska, MA, 1972; University of New Mexico, PhD, 1977. *Principal occupation*: Professor of history, Fort Hays State University, Hays, KS, 1979-. *Home address*: 500 W. 30th, Hays, KS 67601. *Other professional post*: History instructor, Sam Houston State University, 1977-79. *Memberships*: Western History Association; Indian Rights Association; Kansas Council for the Social Studies; Kansas Corral of the Westerners; Phi Alpha Theta; Pi Gamma Mu; Phi Delta Kappa; Phi Kappa Phi. *Interests*: "My major area of study is the American West with an emphasis on 19th & 20th century American Indian history. I enjoy playing golf & traveling throughout western America." *Published works*: Administrative History, Canyon de Chelly National Monument, Arizona (U.S. Dept. of the Interior/National Park Service, 1976); co-author, David M. Brugge, Ohiyesa: Charles A. Eastman, Santee Sioux (University of Illinois Press, 1983); Native Americans in the Twentieth Century (Brigham Young University Press, 1984), co-author, James S. Olson; Indian Lives: Essays on 19th & 20th Century Native American Leaders (University of New Mexico Press, 1985; Second Edition, 1993), co-author, L.G. Moses; Kansas Land (Gibbs M. Smith, Publisher, 1988; Second Edition, 1993), co-author, Thomas D. Isern.

WILSON, STEVE
(museum director)
Affiliation: Museum of the Great Plains, P.O. Box 68, 601 Ferris Ave., Lawton, OK 73502.

WILSON, TIMOTHY
(development director)
Affiliation: Sealaska Heritage Foundation, 1 Sealaska Plaza, Suite 201, Juneau, AK 99801 (907) 463-4844.

WILSON, WILLIE
(Indian band chief)
Affiliation: Rainy River (Manitou) Indian Band, Box 450, Emo, Ontario, Canada P0W 1E0 (807) 482-2479.

WINCE, DONALD R.
(school principal)
Affiliation: Manderson Day School, Manderson, SD 57756 (605) 867-5433.

WINDCHIEF, ROBERTA DENNY
(Black Hawk Woman) (Assiniboine) 1941-
(health administrator)
Born January 16, 1941, Fort Belknap, Mont. *Education*: College of Great Falls, MT, BS; University of Oklahoma, MPH; University of Minnesota (Amb. Care). *Principal occupation*: Health administrator. *Address*: P.O. Box 118, Neola, UT 84053. *Affiliations*: Public health educator, 1973-83, health systems administrator, 1983-85, Rocky Boy, MT; health system administrator, Fort Duchesne PHS Indian Health Center, Ft. Duchesne, UT, 1985-. *Membership*: American College of Health Care Professionals. *Interests*: Beading; traveling; intercultural communications.

WINDER, NATHAN W., Jr. (Strong Elk, Blue Fox) (Southern Ute) 1960-
(training coordinator)
Born October 2, 1960, Albuquerque, N.M. *Education*: Stanford University, BA, 1983; University of Oregon, School of Law, 1984-1985, 1986. *Principal occupation*: Training coordinator. *Address*: P.O. Box 227, Ignacio, CO 81137 (800) 262-7623 (work). *Affiliations*: Counselor, Nevada Urban Indians, Inc., Reno; counselor, grants/contracts administrator, Pyramid Lake Paiute Tribal Council, Nixon, Nev., 1985-88; planning director, Southern Ute Indian Tribe, Ignacio, CO, 1988-; training coordinator, Colorado State University, Fort Collins, CO, 1993-. *Other professional posts*: Southern Ute Indian Tribal Council; 190 Tribal Liaison Representative, U.S. Department of Commerce, Bureau of Census, Economic Development Administrator; Housing and Urban Development, Office of Indian Programs, Region VIII; *Community activities*: Colorado Association of Non-Profit Organizations; Native American Church (vice president, Pyramid Lake chapter); Save the Children Committee (chairman); chairman, Southern Ute Indian Housing Authority, 1989-91 (term); Leadership la Plata (participant); Southern Ute Language & Cultural Committee; Community Development Block Grant Administrator, Southern Ute Indian Tribe. *Membership*: InterTribal Transportation Association (Albuquerque Area Representative). *Awards, honors*: Housing & Urban Development, Office of Indian Programs, Region VIII, Excellence in Maintenance; certified as an Economic Development Finance Professional by the National Development Council, Oct. 1990; Merit Award from Southern Ute Indian Tribe recognizing dedication and commitment to tribe. *In-*

terests: Administration for Native Americans Grant Reader; Colorado Dept. of Corrections, Native American Spiritual Facilitator; Western Colorado Grassroots Leadership Development Program, 1992, Community Resources Center, Denver, CO. "I am interested in traveling to historical and spiritual areas across the Western Hemisphere. I would like to find an American Indian woman who is interested and will participate in Sweat Lodge ceremonies and spiritually support me and my family during Sun Dance." *Published works*: Narrow Gauge Scenic Road *HNTB Corp., Dec. 1993; Southern Ute Transportation Study Update (Nurwoso, Dec. 1993).

CHARITY WING (Sioux) 1902-
(home economics)
Born March 9, 1902, Fort Peck Reservation, Mont. *Education*: Haskell Institute, Lawrence, KS, AA, 1926. *Principal occupation*: Nursing, homemaking. *Home address*: P.O. Box 897, Poplar, MT 59255 (406) 768-5436. *Community activities*: Member, Indian Tribal Affairs, Citizens Committee, Fort Peck Sioux Tribe, Poplar, Mt. (20 years); advocate, Fort Peck Sioux Claims Committee for Black Hills (ten years). *Other professional post*: Presbyterian Church Elder; Ladies Aid Healer (70 years; president, three terms). *Awards, honors*: Woman of the Day, Presbyterian Church, Special Recognition, 1981. *Interests*: "Sewing--starquilt construction; travel; guest lecturer for Indian history, lore, crafts, life styles, method of rearing Indian children; Father Basil Reddoor was first ordained minister of Presbyterian Church on the Fort Peck Reservation in Montana."

WINNE, BRUCE (Spokane)
(tribal chairperson)
Affiliation: Spokane Business Council, P.O. Box 100, Wellpinit, WA 99040 (509) 258-4581.

WINTERS, CARL (Standing Rock Sioux)
(artist)
Born in S.D. Well-known Lakota artist, Mr. Winters has won many awards for hist paintings on canvas, drums & hides. His works are in numerous galleries & private collections worldwide, and a commissioned mural of his work is in the Denver International Airport, CNN's "Across America" and Southwest Art Magazine have featured him. "I strive to communicate the validity of the Indian experience," Wintes has said, "in hopes that my work will serve as a vehicle for cross-cultural understanding and respect."

WIRTH, ROBERT, M.D.
(chief medical officer)
Affiliation: Indian Health Service, Tucson Office of Health Program Research & Development, 7900 South "J" Stock Rd., Tucson, AZ 85746 (602) 670-6600.

WISE OWL, CHIEF (Tuscarora)
(tribal chief)
Affiliation: Tuscarora Indian Tribe, Drowning Creek Reservation, Route 2, Box 108, Maxton, NC 28364 (919) 844-3827.

WITTSTOCK, LAURA WATERMAN (Seneca) 1937-
(administrator)
Born September 11, 1937, Cattaraugus Indian Reservation, N.Y. *Education*: University of Minnesota, BS. *Principal occupation*: Non-profit administrator. *Address*: Migizi Communications,

Inc., 3123 E. Lake St., Suite 200, Minneapolis, MN 55406 (612) 721-6631. *Affiliations*: Editor, Legislative Review, 1971-73; executive director, American Indian Press Association, Washington, DC, 1975; associate director, Red School House, St. Paul, MN, 1975-77; director, Project Media, National Indian Education, Minneapolis, 1973-75; office manager, Native American Research Institute, Minneapolis, 1981; administrator, Heart of the Earth Survival School, Minneapolis, 1982-85; independent education consultant, 1976-; director, curriculum project, Migizi Communications, Minneapolis, 1985-. *Community activities*: Minnesota Governor's Job Training Council (vice chair, 1983-); Minneapolis Community Business Employment Alliance (vice chair, 1983-); Migizi Communications, Inc. (president-on leave); United Way Planning and Priorities Committee (member); Christian Sharing Fund, Minneapolis-St. Paul Archdiocese (chair, 1981-86); Minnesota Women's Fund (executive committee, 1983-); Children's Theatre and School, Minneapolis (board member, 1984- *Interests*: "Journalism, writing; American Indian education--program designer, evaluator, administrator; American Indian alcoholism and related problems; employment-program designer, board member, policy-maker; American Indian urban studies." *Biographical sources*: Let My People Know: American Indian Journalism, James E. and Sharon M. Murphy (University of Oklahoma Press, 1981); I Am the Fire of Time: The Voices of Native American Women, Jane Katz, editor (E.P. Dutton, 1977); Minnesota Women's Yearbook, 1978, 1984; Who's Who in the Midwest; Who's Who of American Women; Contemporary Native American Address (Brigham Young University, 1977; Women of Color poster series (St. Paul Public Schools, 1980). *Published works*: Indian Alcoholism in St. Paul, study with Michael Miller (University of Minnesota, 1981); Native American Women: Twilight of a Long Maidenhood, Comparative Perspectives of Third World Women, Beverly Lindsay, editor (Praeger, 1980); On Women's Rights for Native Peoples (Akwesasne Notes, 1975); editor, Indian Education, National Indian Education Association, 1973-74; The Federal Indian Relationship, Civil Rights Digest, Oct., 1973; editor, Legislative Review, 1971-73.

*WOLF, CHIPA
(executive director)
Affiliation: World Indigenous Games, Route 3, Suite 181F, Jaspa, GA 30143 (404)

*WOLF, LIZA
(Indian band chief)
Affiliation: Prophet River Indian Band, Box 3250, Fort Nelson, British Columbia, Canada V0C 1R0 (604) 774-1025.

*WOLF, PATRICIA
(museum director)
Affiliation: Anchorage Museum of History & Art, 121 W. 7th Ave., Anchorage, AK 99501 (907) 343-4326.

*WOLF EAGLE, ROBERT (Waccamaw)
(tribal principal chief)
Affiliation: Waccamaw-Siouan Indian Association of South Carolina, 2217 Hwy. 501 W., Gallivant's Ferry, SC 29544 (803) 248-9843.

*WOLFE, DAVID MICHAEL (Cherokee) 1948-
(historian)
Born August 27, 1948, Huntington, W.V. *Education*: School of Visual Arts (New York, NY), 1968-70; Art Institute of Pittsburgh, 1978-79; LaRoche College, 1993-94. *Principal occupation*: Historian. *Home address*: 4167 Timberlane Dr., Allison Park, PA 15101 (412) 487-7093. *Professional post*: American Indian historian. *Past professional posts*: Young American Indian Council, New York, NY, 1968-70 (investigated racial & legal problems affecting urban & rural Indigenous communities nationally; participated in the original board meeting which established the American Indian Community House; advocate for self-reliant & traditional governance); coordinator, American Indian Movement, South Eastern Community, Robeson County, NC, 1972-74 (assigned to the Tuscarora Indian community of Robeson County to address the issues of cultural & organizational development among the Tuscarora community; The American Indian Community House, New York, NY, 1974-76 (an organizing member, involved with the development of community based & oriented programs such as vocational counseling & programs, job training programs, cultural programs, summer youth-adult activities, and development of the Art Gallery; Veterans Administration Hospital, East Orange, NJ, 1976-77 (contract from New Jersey American Indian Center to the Visual Media Dept. - VA Hospital, for preparation of training aids operative charts, graphs & brochures for nursing & medical staff); student, 1978-79; consultant, Long Island Affirmative Action Program, Melville, NY (established Native American liaison within L.I.A.A.P); Snelling & Snelling, Melville, NY, 1980-82; Ewing Technical Designs, Melville, NY, 1982-83; Huntington Personnel, Huntington, NY, 1983-84; Wolfe Consultants, Long Island, NY & Pittsburgh, PA, 1984-91. *Exhibits* (for contemporary & traditional, fine art & illustration): Five Civilized Tribes Gallery/Museum, Muskogee, OK (awarded prize in graphics), 1990; U.S. Postage Stamp Commission - Regional Contest (awarded 2nd Place), 1991; Cherokee National Museum, Tahlequah, OK, annual Trail of Tears Art Show (awarded prize in graphics), 1992; among others. *Memberships*: Brotherhood of Indian Artist (OK); American Indian Community House (NYC); The Pan American Indigenous Unity Movement. *Interests*: "As an advocate for the survival of traditional Indigenous people of the Americas since 1968, my primary involvement addresses social, legal and cultural concerns of rural and urban Indigenous communities. I have researched and documented a variety of previously ignored original eastern tribal histories and addresses their cultural, legal & social issues within public and secular forums." Works in progress.

*WOLFE, JIM
(editor)
Affiliation: "The Muscogee Nation News," The Muscogee (Creek) Nation, P.o. Box 580, Okmulgee, OK 74447 (918) 756-8700.

WOLFEY, JEANETTE (Shoshone Bannock)
(attorney)
Address: P.O. Box 306, Fort Hall, ID 83203. *Membership*: American Bar Association (member, Committee on Opportunities for Minorities in the Profession).

WOLTER, DONALD EVERETT (*Buffalo Hawk*)
(United Lumbee) 1947-
(carpenter; ranch hand)
Born September 2 1947, Bieber, Calif. *Education*: High school. *Principal occupation*: Carpenter; ranch hand. *Home address*: P.O. Box 366, Bieber, CA 96009. *Memberships*: Native American Wolf Clan; United Lumbee Nation's High Eagle Warrior Society, 1987-93; United Lumbee Nation's Deer Clan (vice-chief, 1988-). *Awards, honors*: 1st Runner Up, United Lumbee Nation's Silver Eagle Award, 1988. *Interests*: Woodcrafts, hunting, cooking, working for my Indian people.

WOMACK, JIM
(BIA-education)
Affiliation: Chief, Information Services, Office of Indian Education, Bureau of Indian Affairs, MS-3530-MIB, 1849 C St., NW, Washington, DC 20240 (202) 208-7111.

WOOD, ED (Ojibwe)
(member-board of directors)
Affiliation: Intertribal Christian Comunications, P.O. Box 3765, Station B, Winnipeg, Manitoba, Canada R2W 3R6 (204) 661-9333.

*WOOD, MARGARET
(executive director)
Affiliation: ATLATL, 2303 N. Central Ave., Suite 104, Phoenix, AZ 85004 (602) 253-2731.

*WOOD, RON C.
(executive officer)
Affiliation: Navajo Area Office, Indian Health Service, P.O. Box 9020, Window Rock, AZ 86515 (602) 871-5813.

*WOODALL, JOHN (Lone Elk)
(grand head chief)
Affiliation: Ouchita Indians of AR & America, P.O. Box 34, Story, AR 71970 (501) 867-4252.

WOODALL, PHILIP, D.O.
(clinical director)
Affiliation: San Carlos PHS Indian Hospital, P.O. Box 208, San Carlos, AZ 85550 (602) 475-2371.

WOODARD, DON 1935-
(Indian arts & crafts dealer)
Born May 12, 1935, Gallup, N.M. *Education*: University of New Mexico, BA, 1958; Northern Arizona University, MA, 1968. *Principal occupation*: Indian arts & crafts dealer. *Address*: 120 S. Madison #122, Cortez, CO 81321 (303) 565-2563. *Affiliations*: Science teacher, Gallup High School Gallup, NM (7 years); owner, Woodard's Indian Arts, Gallup, N.M., 1952-72; owner, Don Woodard's Indian Trading Post, Cortez, CO, 1972-. *Other professional posts*: Land claims archaeologist for the Pueblos of Zia, Santa Anna, Jemez, Acoma & Laguna; group leader for Navajo Long Walk Re-enactment. *Community activities*: Director, Cortez Chamber of Commerce; Cortez Rotary Club (president, 1977 & 1978). *Memberships*: Inter-Tribal Indian Ceremonial, Gallup, N.M. (board member; program director; exhibition hall chairman); American Society of Appraisers; Indians Arts & Crafts Assn. (board member; ethics committee chairman). *Interests*: Indian arts & crafts; anthropology. *Biographical source*: Who's Who Worldwide, 1992-94.

WOODFIDE, SHERRY (Navajo)
(school principal)
Affiliation: Tse'll'Ahi' Community School, Drawer J, Crownpoint, NM 87313 (505) 786-5389.

WOODIS, PAMELA
(education program counselor)
Affiliation: Jicarilla Apache Higher Ed. Program, Box 507, Dulce, NM 87528 (505) 759-3615/6.

*WOODRUFF, DOUGLAS (Quileute)
(tribal chairperson)
Affiliation: Quileute Tribal Council, P.O. Box 279, LaPush, WA 98350 (206) 374-6163.

*WOODS, LONZO (Lower Creek Muscogee)
(tribal chairperson)
Affiliation: North Bay Clan of Lower Creek Muscogee Tribe, P.O. Box 687, Lynn Haven, FL 32444 (904) 265-3345.

WOODS, MURPHY
(director-Indian council)
Affiliation: Council of Native Americans of South Carolina, P.O. Box 21916, Columbia, SC 29221.

*WOODSIDE, SHERRY (Navajo)
(school principal)
Affiliation: Standing Rock Community School, P.O. Drawer 828, Crownpoint, NM 87313 (505) 786-5389.

WOODWARD, BEATRICE L.
(school principal)
Affiliation: Baca Community School, P.O. Box 509, Prewitt, AZ 87045 (505) 876-2769.

WOOSLEY, ANNE I.
(foundation director)
Affiliation: The Amerind Foundation, Inc., P.O. Box 248, Dragoon, AZ 85609 (602) 586-3666.

WORDEMAN, JANICE
(school principal)
Affiliation: Promise Day School, Mobridge, SD 57601 (605) 733-2148.

WORK, L. SUSAN
(attorney)
Address: P.O. Box 1259, Seminole, OK 74818 (405) 436-1946. *Membership*: Oklahoma Bar Association (secretary-Indian Law Section).

*WORKS, DAVID
(center chairperson)
Affiliation: American Indian Center for Central California, P.O. Box 607, Auberry, CA 93602 (209) 855-2695.

WORL, CELESTE
(publisher)
Affiliation: Alaska Native Magazine, Alaska Native News, Inc., Box 220230, Anchorage, AK 99522 (907) 243-8730.

*WORLEY, GEORGE (Shoshone)
(tribal council chairperson)
Affiliation: Northwestern Band of Shoshoni Nation Council, P.O. Box 145, Blackfoot, ID 83221 (208) 785-7401.

WRIGHT, BARTON A. 1920-
(museum curator-archaeologist; author-artist)
Born December 21, 1920, Bisbee, Ariz. *Education*: University of Arizona, BA, 1952, MA, 1954. *Principal occupation*: Museum curator-archaeologist; author-artist. *Home address*: 4143 W. Gelding Dr., Phoenix, AZ 85023 (602) 843-1362. *Affiliations*: Curator, assistant director, Museum of Northern Arizona, Flagstaff, AZ, 1955-77; scientific director, San Diego Museum of Man,

1978-82. *Other professional posts*: Archaeologist, Town Creek Indian Mound State Park, NC; artist/archaeologist, Amerind Foundation, Dragoon, AZ; artist, Arizona State Museum, Tucson, AZ. *Military service*: U.S. Army, 1943-45. *Community activities*: Indian Arts and Crafts Association (board of directors); Indian Art Foundation, Arizona State Rep. to W. Regional Museum; Indian Arts & Crafts Judge, Hopi Cultural Values Committee. *Memberships*: American Association of Museum (sr. accreditor); Arizona-Nevada Academy of Science (charter member); National Geographic Society (consultant); Western Regional History Association; Arizona Historical Association. *Awards, honors*: 1985 Southeastern Library Association, Southern Books Competition Award; 1986 Border Regional Library Association, Southwest Book Award; 1986 Anisfield-Wolf Award; all for Kachinas: A Hopi Artist's Documentary, 1973, and Kachinas of the Zuni, 1986. *Interests*: Kachinas of the Hopi, Zuni; material culture and religion of the Hopi; Indian arts and crafts; hallmarks of the Southwest. *Biographical sources*: Who's Who in American Art; Who's Who in the West; Men of Achievement; International Who's Who in American Art; Contemporary Authors. *Published works*: Kachinas: A Hopi Artist's Documentary (Northland Press, 1973); Kachinas: The Barry Goldwater Collection at the Heard Museum (Northland Press, 1975); Unchanging Hopi (Northland Press, 1975); Pueblo Shields from the Fred Harvey Collection (Northland Press, 1976); Hopi Kachina: The Complete Guide to Collecting Kachina Dolls (Northland Press, 1977); Hopi Material Culture (Northland Press, 1979); The Year of the Hopi, Paintings & Photographs by Joseph Mora, 1904-1906 (Smithsonian Institution, 1979); Kachinas of the Zuni (Northland Press, 1986); Pueblo Cultures (E.J. Brill, 1986); The Hopi Photographs of Kate Cory, 1905-12 (University of New Mexico Press, 1986); Patterns and Sources of Zuni Kachinas (Harmsgen, Tanner & Wright, 1987); The Mythic World of the Zuni (University of New Mexico Press, 1988); Who Made It? Trademarks of the Southwest (Schiffer Press, 1988); Hopi Clowns (Northland Publishing, 1994).

*WRIGHT, BEVERLY Wampanoag)
(tribal chairperson)
Affiliation: Wampanoag Trbal Council of Gay Head, State Rd., RR1, Box 137, Gay Head, MA 02535 (508) 645-9265.

WRIGHT, BOBBY (Chippewa-Cree) 1950-
(research associate, assistant professor)
Born December 28, 1950, Tacoma, Wash. *Education*: University of San Francisco, BS, 1973; SUNY, Buffalo, MA, 1977; Montana State University, Bozeman, EdD, 1985. *Principal occupation*: Research associate, assistant professor. *Resides in State College, PA* (814) 865-6346 (office). *Affiliations*: Director, Montana State University, Bozeman, 1983-89; faculty, Penn State University, University Park, 1990-. *Memberships*: National Indian Education Association; American Society for Ethnohistory. *Awards, honors*: 1986 Distinguished Dissertation Award, Association for the Study of Higher Education; 1986 Montana State University Endowment and Alumni Foundation Award for Outstanding Graduate Performance.

WRIGHT, CATHY L.
(museum curator/director)
Affiliation: The Taylor Museum for Southwestern Studies, Colorado Springs Fine Arts Center, 30 West Dale St., Colorado Springs, CO 80903 (303) 634-5581.

WRIGHT, DEB (Ponca)
(tribal chairperson)
Affiliation: Ponca Tribe of Nebraska, P.O. Box 288, Niobrara, NE 66760 (402) 857-3391.

WRIGHT, JOHN & PATRICIA
(museum owners/directors)
Affiliation: JP Museum of Indian Artifacts, Rt. 1, Box 715, Saucier, MS 39574.

*WRIGHT, LAWRENCE
(school principal)
Affiliation: Wide Ruins Boarding School, P.O. Box 309, Chambers, AZ 86502 (602) 652-3251.

WRIGHT, LEE
(curator)
Affiliation: Shawnee Methodist Mission, 3403 West 53rd, Shawnee Mission, KS 66205 (913) 262-0867.

*WRIGHT, MIKE
(editor)
Affiliation: "Nishnawbe News," Organization of North American Indian Students, Northern Michigan U., 140 University Center, Marquette, MI 49855.

WRIGHT, ODETTE
(museum curator)
Affiliation: Nanticoke Indian Museum, Rt. 4, Box 107A, Millsboro, DE 19966 (302) 945-7022.

WRIGHT, ROBIN K. 1949-
(assistant professor & curator)
Born September 10, 1949, Mankato, Minn. *Education*: University of Washington, BA, 1971, MA, 1977, PhD (Art History), 1985. *Principal occupation*: Assistant professor & curator. *Address & Affiliation*: Curator of Native American Art (1985-), Burke Museum, DB-10, University of Washington, Seattle, WA 98195 (206) 543-5595. *Other professioal post*: Assistant professor, School of Art, University of Washington, Seattle, 1990-. *Memberships*: American Association of Museums; College Art Association; Native American Art Studies Association (board member, 1989-93). *Awards, honors*: Phi Beta Kappa. *Interests*: Northwest Coast Indian art: Haida art, specifically Haida argillite carving, and Washington State Native art. Travel to museums to do research in Canada, Europe and the U.S. *Published works*: A Time of Gathering - An Intertribal Welcome: Statements from 36 Washington Tribes, with Roberta Haines (eds.) (Burke Museum 1990); A Time for Gathering: Native Heritage in Washington State (Burke Museum & University of Washington Press, 1991); and numerous articles in American Indian Art Magazine, and others.

WYACO, VIRGIL
(college chairperson)
Affiliation: Southwestern Indian Polytechnic Institute, P.O. Box 10146, Albuquerque, NM 87184 (505) 474-3197.

WYATT, BEVERLY J.
(museum curator)
Affiliation: Chickasaw Council House Museum, P.O. Box 717, Tishomingo, OK 73460 (405) 371-3351.

*WYATT, CHARLES D.
(site supt.)
Affiliation: Hubbell Trading Post - National Historic Site, P.O. Box 150, Ganado, AZ 86505 (602) 755-3475.

*WYATT, JANE E. (*Ishilee*) (Chuckchansi) 1943-
(tribal chairperson)
Born December 21, 1943, Madera, Calif. *Education*: Galen College (Fresno, CA), RDA, 1987. *Principal occupation*: Tribal chairperson. *Home adress*: P.O. Box 1661, Coarsegold, CA 93614 (209) 683-6633 (office). *Affiliation*: Chairperson, Picayune Rancheria, Coarsegold, CA, 1983-. *Other professional posts*: BIA Policy Task Force Representative; Sierra Tribal Consortium (board member); California Indian Manpower Co. (board member); CRIHB Representative; Central Valley Indian Health, Inc. (member). *Community activities*: Member, Fresno City College.

*WYCKOFF, DON
(instructor-Native American studies)
Affiliation: Native American Studies Program, University of Oklahoma, 455 W. Lindsey, Rm. 804, Norman, OK 73019 (405) 325-2312.

WYNECOOP, JOSEPH A. (Spokane) 1919-
(teacher/librarian, intelligence)
Born March 22, 1919, Reardan, Wash. *Education*: Eastern Washington University, BA, 1946; Glendale University College of Law, BSL, 1971. *Principal occupation*: Manager, aerospace-information support. *Home address*: 3832 Hillway Dr., Glendale, CA 91208 (818) 248-7311. *Affiliations*: Manager, Jet Propulsion Laboratory, California Institute of Technology, Pasadena, 1968-81. *Other professional post*: Teacher, Eastern Washington University, Oakland, CA secondary schools; Air Intelligence School, Defense Intelligence School. *Military service*: U.S. Air Force, 1942-68 (Lt. Colonel, retired; Air Force Outstanding Unit Award; Medal for Humane Action; Joint Chiefs of Staff Commendation Medal; Air Force Commendation Medal; Alexander the Great Medal (Greece); Greek Joint Chiefs Letter of Commendation). *Community activities*: Masonic Lodge, Scottish Rite, Shrice, 1954-; All American Indian Celebration Corporation (vice president & director, 1969-70); Governor's (CA) Indian Assistance Project (representative, 1969-74); American Indian Enterprise (vice president, 1969-75); Pacific Northwest Indian Center (financial commissioner, 1971-73); Glendale Kiwanis, 1981-89; Glendale Chamber of Commerce, 1983-90; Sons of the Revolution, 1987-; director, Los Angeles, CA-Berlin, Germany Sister City Association, 1993-. *Memberships*: Indian Scholarship Fund Association (director and vice president, 1969-75; Urban Indian Development Association (vice president, 1969-75); Retired Officers Association, 1968-; Air Force Association, 1976-; National Congress of American Indians (member of board, Indian Scholarship Committee, 1977-); Aircraft Owners & Pilots Association. *Awards, Honors*: Outstanding Actor, Outstanding Speaker/Athletic Award, Air Force University. *Interests*: Private pilot; genealogy - "using my intelligence training, I was able to trace my Indian ancstors to Chief Kee Kee Nouskeen or Seoutkin (missionary name, Edwards) and my white ancestors back to the American Revolution, the Royals & to Emperor Charlemagne." *Biographical sources*: Who's Who in California, 1979; Who's Who in Library & Information Sci-

ence. *Published works*: Co-author, editor of several scientific works by scientists & physicists at the Jet Propulsion Laboratory. "I was manager of the Technical Information & Documentation Division Support Section. My section edited & approved all books developed by scientific personnel."

*WYNN, SAM
(executive director)
Affiliation: Native American International Caucus, United Methodist Church, 3821 Madison Ave., Fayetteville, NC 28304 (919) 424-0894. There are about 150 Native American congregations.

*WYNNE, BRUCE (Spokane)
(tribal chairperson)
Affiliation: Spokane Business Council, P.O. Box 100, Wellpinit, WA 99040 (509) 258-4581.

*WYRICK, JAN
(museum director)
Affiliation: Seminole Nation Museum, 524 S. Wewoka Ave., Box 1532, Wewoka, OK 74880 (405) 257-5580.

*WYSS, DIANNE
(organization director)
Affiliation: Indian Nation Network & Electronic Bulletin Board, Honor, Inc., Washington, DC (202) 338-7851.

Y

YALLUP, WILFORD (Yakima)
(tribal chairperson)
Affiliation: Yakima Tribal Council, P.O. Box 151, Toppenish, WA 98948 (509) 865-5121.

*YARDLEY, LINDA
(organization director)
Affiliation: National Indian Health Board, P.O. Box 6940, Denver, CO 80206 (303) 270-5598.

*YATES, HERBERT (Nambe Pueblo)
(pueblo governor)
Affiliation: Nambe Pueblo Council, Rte. 1, Box 117-BB, Santa Fe, NM 87501 (505) 455-2036.

*YATSATTIE, CLYDE
(administrative officer)
Affiliation: Zuni PHS Indian Hospital, P.O. Box 467, Zuni, NM 87327 (505) 782-4431.

*YAZZI, BRUCE (Navajo)
(organization president)
Affiliation: Native American Business Coalition, 6025 N. Smokerise, Flagstaff, AZ 86004 (602) 526-0035.

YAZZIE, CALVIN (Navajo)
(school chairperson)
Affiliation: Nazlini Boarding School, Ganado, AZ 86505 (602) 755-6125.

YAZZIE, DOROTHY R. (Navajo)
(school director)
Affiliation: Black Mesa Community School, Star Route 1, Box 215, Rough Rock, AZ 86510 (602) 674-3632.

*YAZZI, DUANE (Navajo)
(college chairperson)
Affiliation: Southwestern Indian Polytechnic Institute, P.O. Box 10146, Albuquerque, NM 87184 (505) 897-5347.

*YAZZIE, EDWARD D. (Navajo)
(school chairperson)
Affiliation: Holbrook Dormitory, P.O. Box 758, Holbrook, AZ 86025 (602) 524-6222.

YAZZIE, ETHELOU (Navajo)
(school chairperson)
Affiliation: Cottonwood Day School, P.O. Box 1139, Chinle, AZ 86503 (602) 725-3256.

YAZZI, HERBERT (Navajo)
(attorney)
Address: Damon Bldg., P.O. Drawer R, Window Rock, AZ 86515 (602) 871-7166. *Membership*: Navajo Nation Bar Association (president); Native American Bar Association.

*YAZZIE, JIMMIE (Navajo)
(school chairperson)
Affiliation: Bread Springs Day School, P.O. Box 1117, Gallup, NM 87305 (505) 778-5665.

*YAZZI, LORENZO (Navajo)
(school chairperson)
Affiliation: Rocky Ridge Boarding School, P.O. Box 299, Kykotsmovi, AZ 86039 (602) 725-3415.

YAZZIE, PAUL J. (Navajo)
(school principal)
Affiliation: Cove Day School, P.O. Box 190, Shiprock, NM 87420 (602) 653-4457.

YAZZIE, ROSEMARY (Navajo)
(vice president-board of directors)
Affiliation: National Indian Youth Council, 318 Elm, SE, Albuquerque, NM 87102.

YAZZIE, TOMMIE C. (Navajo)
(school director)
Affiliation: Leupp Boarding School, P.O. Box HC-61, Winslow, AZ 86047 (602) 686-6211.

*YAZZI-KING, ELA M. (Navajo) 1955-
(rehabilitation counselor)
Born May 31m 1955, Fort Defiance, Ariz. *Education*: Virginia Intermount College (Bristol), BA, 1977; University of New Mexico, MA (Rehabilitation Counseling), 1981. *Principal occupation*: Rehabilitation counselor. *Address*: P.O. Box 279, St. Michaels, AZ 86511 (602) 729-5986 (work). *Affiliations*: Director, Spinal Cord Injury Follow-up Project, 1979-81; director, IHS Medical Management Project, 1981-82; director, Learn to Earn, Ltd., 1983-84; director, Navajo Undergraduate Rehabilitation Training Project, 1984-86; Navajo Evaluation of Existing Disability Services, 1986-87; executive director, Chinle Valley School for Exceptional Children, 1988-90; coordinator, Indian Children's Program, Utah State University, Logan, UT, 1991-. *Professional presentations*: Multi-Cultural Successes: The Navajo Nation," at the National Association of Developmental Disabilities Councils, Orlando, FL, 1992; "Beyond Rhetoric-A Blueprint for Action" & "A Native American Perspective on Disability & Self-Determination," at the ADD Commissioner's Institute on Cultural Diversity, Washington, DC, 1992 & 1993; "Self-Determination-The Road to Personal Freedom," at NM Protection & Advocacy System Mini Conference, Albuquerque, 1993. *Other professional post*:

Adjunct Facility with Navajo Community College, 1984-87 (produced: "Rehabilitation Practicum Manual," 1984; "Job Development/Job Placement Manual," 1985; "Navajo Evaluation of Existing Disability Research Study" (unpublished), 1987. *Advisory/Council Membership*: Chairperson, Navajo Nation Advisory Council on the Handi-Capable, 1979-93; Native American Research & Training Center, Northern Arizona University, Flagstaff (advisory council, 1990-93; advisory board, 1987-); New Mexico Independent Living Advisory Council, 1990-; advisory council, American Indians with Disabilities Public Awareness Campaign, Anchorage, AK, 1991-93; Administration on Developmental Disabilities, Multi-Cultural Task Force, Washington, DC, 1992-; Developmental; Disabilities Advisory Council, Phoenix, AZ, 1992-. *Awards, honors*: "Citizen of the Year," Arizona Governor's Council on Disabilities, Phoenix, 1985; "Outstanding Volunteer," Navajo Nation Council on the Handicapped, 1986.

YELLOWFAT, TERRY
(school principal)
Affiliation: Swift Bird Day School, Route 3, Gettysburg, SD 57442 (605) 733-2143.

YELLOWHAWK, SANDRA
(health director)
Affiliation: Peach Springs PHS Indian Health Center, Peach Springs, AZ 86434 (602) 769-2204.

YELLOW ROBE, WILLIAM S., Jr.
(Assiniboine) 1960-
(playwright, director, actor,
lecturer, instructor)
Born February 2, 1960, Poplar, MT. *Education*: High school. *Principal occupation*: Playwright, director, actor, lecturer, instructor. *Home address*: P.O. Box 374, Valier, MT 59486 (406) 279-3432. *Affiliation*: Former literary manager of Seattle Group Theater; regional vice president, Literary Managers & Dramaturgs of America, New York, NY, 1990-91. *Works*: Plays: "The Council," for Honolulu Theater for Youth, 1992; "Taking Aunty to the Wake, Northern Montana College, Havre, MT, 1991; "The Independence of Eddie Rose," The Seattle Group Theater, 1990. *Directing*: "The Council," and "The Magic Flute," an opera, San Antonio (TX) Festival. Acting: Norman Bulanski, "The Boys Next Door"; and Donny Dubrow, "American Buffalo." *Lecturer*: 'Watermark reading series', University of Washington, Seattle; '10th Anniversary', New World Theater, University of Mass. Instructor: Playwrighting and writing, Fort Peck Community College, Poplar, MT; acting, St. Paul (MN) Central High School. *Community activities*: Advisory Board, Red Eagle Soaring Theater, Seattle, WA. *Membership*: Dramatists Guild of America (associate member, 1988-). *Awards, honors*: Jerome Fellowship, 1989; Princess Grace Fellowship, 1989; NEA Playwright's Fellowship, 1991; James Baldwin Honorable Mention. *Published works*: Sneaky, a one-act play, "SlantSix" an anthology (New Rivers Press, 1990); The Burning of Uncle, a short story, "Dancing on the Rim of the World," an anthology (University of Arizona Press, 1991).

YELLOWTAIL, WILLIAM P. (Crow)
(EPA administrator)
Born in Crow Agency, Mont. *Education*: Dartmouth College, BA, 1971. *Principal occupation*: EPA administrator. *Home Address*: 6440

S. Kilimanjaro Dr., Evergreen, CO 80439 *Affiliations*: Wyoming State Senator, 1985-1993 (chairman-State Judiciary Committee and the Legislature's Environmental Quality Council); administrator, EPA Region 8, Denver, CO, 1994- . *Membership*: Native American Alumni Association of Dartmouth College (national steering committee).

*YEPA, SHARON
(BIA agency acting supt.)
Affiliation: Spokane Agency, Bureau of Indian Affairs, P.O. Box 389, Wellpinit, WA 99040 (509) 258-4561.

YONGE, SANDRA JEFFERSON (Paiute)
(tribal chairperson)
Affiliation: Lone Pine Reservation, P.O. Box 747, Lone Pine, CA 93545 (619) 876-5414.

YORK, KENNETH HAROLD
(Mississippi Choctaw) 1948-
(purchasing)
Born May 15, 1948, Neshoba County, Miss. *Education*: Northeastern Oklahoma State University, BA, 1971; University of Minnesota, MA, 1975, EdD, 1989. *Principal occupation*: Purchasing. *Home address*: 807 Black Jack Rd., Philadelphia, MS 39350 (601) 656-6034. *Affiliations*: ESCO Corp., Newton, MS (5 years); president, Tisho and Associates, Philadelphia, MS (10 years); president, Choctaw Associated Members for Progress, Philadelphia, MS (3 years). *Other professional post*: Adjunct professor, Mississippi State University. *Community activities*: Choctaw Federal Credit Union (president, 1976-83); Pearl River Choctaw Community Development Club (president, 1985-86); St. Theresa Catholic Church Council, 1985-; Choctaw Tribal Council (member). *Memberships*: National Indian Education Association; National Association of Bilingual Education; International Reading Association. *Awards, honors*: American Legion's Boys State, 1966; Pearl Service Award, 1982; Outstanding Young Men of America, 1976. *Interests*: Bilingual bicultural education; literacy among Native Americans; farming and agribusiness; business and management development among Native Americans; sovereignty and human rights. *Biographical sources*: Meridian Star, 1983; Faces, video program on Mississippi ETV; Mississippi Roads, video documentary on Mississippi ETV. *Published works*: Recommended Teacher Training Curriculum for Native American Bilingual Education Programs (Mississippi State University, 1977); Working with the Bilingual Community (National Clearinghouse for Bilingual Education, 1979) Made By Hand: Mississippi Folk Art (Mississippi History and Archives, 1980); LaSalle and His Legacy: Frenchmen and Indians in the Lower Mississippi Valley (University of Mississippi Press, 1982).

YOUCKTON, PERCY (Chehalis)
(tribal chairperson)
Affiliation: Chehalis Business Council, P.O. Box 536, Oakville, WA 98568 (206) 273-5911.

*YOUNG, ED 1906-
(Indian arts & crafts trader)
Born April 14, 1906, New York, N.Y. *Education*: City Colege of New York, BA, 1930. *Principal occupation*: Indian arts & crafts trader. *Address & Affiliation*: President, The Ed Young's, Inc., P.O. Box 866, Belen, NM 87002 (505) 864-1242 (1947-). *Interests*: "Trading and traveling the

U.S." *Biographical source*: Indian Jewlery - Fact or Fantasy by Marsha Lund.

YOUNG, HARVEY
(Indian band chief)
Affiliation: Cumberland Idian Band, Box 278, Cumberland House, Saskatchewan, Canada S0E 0S0.

YOUNG, MARY L.
(librarian)
Affiliation: Institute of American Indian Arts Library - Native American Videotapes Archives, Learning Resource Center, College of Santa Fe, P.O. Box 20007, Santa Fe, NM 87504 (505) 988-6423.

YOUNG MAN, ALFRED *(Eagle Chief)* (Cree) 1948-
(associate professor
of Native American art)
Born in 1948, Browning, Mont. *Education*: Institute of American Indian Arts, 1963-68; Slade School of Fine Arts (University College, London, England), Diploma in Fine Arts; University of Montana, MA, 1974; Northern Montana College (Havre, MT), Teacher's Certificate, 1975; Flathead Valley Community College (Kalispel, MT), Television Specialist Training, Total Community Education, 1975-77; PhD Candidate, Anthropology, Rutgers University. *Principal occupation*: Associate professor of Native American art. *Address & Affiliation*: Native American Studies Dept., University of Lethbridge, 4401 University Dr., Lethbridge, Alberta, Can T1K 3M4 (403) 329-2635 (1977-). *Other professional posts*: Art instructor and reading specialist among his own people on the Chippewa-Cree reservation, Rocky Boy, and later on the Blackfeet reservation. In addition, he worked as media/TV specialist at Flathead Valley Community College in Kalispell, MT. He is writing a doctoral thesis on North American Indian Art for Rutgers University. *Memberships*: Member of the Chippewa/Cree Rocky Boy Indian Reservation, Box Elder, MT; Society of Canadian Artists of Native Ancestry, Dept of Indian & Northern Development, Ottawa, Ontario. *Awards, honors*: Numerous scholarships, fellowships, awards, contracts. *Biographical sources*: The Sweetgrass Lives On: 50 Contemporary North American Indian Artists, by Jamake Highwater (Lippincott & Crowell, 1980); Native Writers Circle of the Americas - A Directory 1993; American Indian Quarterly, Vol. 17, No. 4, by University of Nebraska Press, Fall 1993; *Published works*: "Token and Taboo - Academia vs. Native Art," Fuse Magazine, Vol. II, No. 6 (July, 1988); "Issues and Trends in Contemporary Indian Art," Parallelogram, Vol. 3, No. 3 (Feb./March, 1988); editor, Networking - National Native Indian Artists Symposium IV (Graphcom Printer, Lethbridge, 1988); "Towards a Political History of Native Art," Visions of Power: Contemporary Art by First Nations, Inuit and Japanese Canadians, Earth Spirit Festival catalogue (Toronto, 1991); among many other published & unpublished articles & books; also, produced and/or directed numerous videos.

*YOUNG, ROBERTA M. (Puyallup)
(tribal chairperson)
Affiliation: Puyallup Tribal Council, 2002 East 28th St., Tacoma, WA 98404 (206) 597-6200.

*YOUNG, THOMAS
(librarian)
Affiliation: Roberta Campbell Lawson Indian Library, Philbrook Museum of Art, P.O. Box 52510, Tulsa, OK 74125 (918) 748-5306.

YOUNGBEAR, JOANN
(health coordinator)
Affiliation: Native American Services Agency, Missoula Indian Center, 2300 Regent St. #A, Missoula, MT 59801 (406) 329-3373.

YOUNGDEER, MERRITT
(BIA area director)
Affiliation: Muskogee Area Office, Bureau of Indian Affairs, 101 N. 5th St., Muskogee, OK 74401 (918) 687-2296.

YOUNGE, SANDRA JEFFERSON
(Paiute-Shoshini)
(tribal council chairperson)
Affiliation: Lone Pine Tribal Council, Star Route 1, 1101 S. Main St., Lone Pine, CA 93545 (619) 876-5414.

YUHAHA, MARCEL (Sioux)
(Indian band chief)
Affiliation: Oak Lake Sioux, Box 146, Pipestone, Manitoba, Canada R0M 1T0 (204) 854-2261.

Z

ZAH, PETERSON (Navajo) 1937-
(former tribal chairman)
Born December 2, 1937, Low Mountain, Ariz. *Education*: Phoenix College, AA, 1960; Arizona State University, BA, 1963. *Home address*: P.O. Box 308, Window Rock, AZ 86515 (602) 871-6352. *Affiliation*: Chairperson, Navajo Nation, Window Rock, AZ, 1983-94. *Other professional post*: Education-secondary education teacher; executive director of DNA--People's Legal Services. *Community activities*: Wide Public School Association; Window Rock School Board (past president); National Association of the Indian Legal Services (founder); AZ State Advisory Committee to the U.S. Civil Rights Commission (member). *Memberships*: Navajo Education & Scholarship Foundation; National Tribal Chairmen's Association; Council of Energy Resource Tribes. *Awards, honors*: Humanitarian Award, City of Albuquerque, NM--Mayor Harry Kinney; Honorary Doctorate (Humanitarium), Santa Fe College.

*ZAH-BAHE, LORENA (Navajo)
(association president)
Affiliation: National Indian Education Association, 1819 H St., NW, Suite 800, Washington, DC 20006 (202) 835-3001.

ZAHARLICK, ANN MARIE, 1947-
(professor of anthropology)
Born March 24, 1947, Scranton, Penna. *Education*: Cedar Crest College, BA, 1969; Lehigh University, MA, 1973; The American University, PhD, 1977 (Dissertation: Picuris Syntax). *Principal occupation*: Professor of anthropology. *Address*: Dept. of Anthropology, Ohio State University, 124 W. 17th Ave., Columbus, OH 43214 (614) 292-4149. *Affiliations*: Instructor and curriculum development specialist, Bilingual/Multicultural Teacher Training Program for Native Americans, The University of Albuquerque, NM, 1975-77; assistant professor and lan-

Biographies

guage development specialist, Native American Bilingual Teacher Education Program, The University of Albuquerque, 1977-79; professor, Dept. of Anthropology, The Ohio State University, Columbus, Ohio, 1979-. *Other professional posts*: Instructor, Acoma Pueblo Bilingual Education Program, 1978; instructor, Sandia Pueblo Language Program. *Research/fieldwork*: Research on the Picuris language, Picuris Pueblo, NM, 1973; research on Picuris syntax, Picuris and Taos, NM, 1974-76; development of Keresan language spoken by the pueblos of Acoma, Cochiti, Santo Domingo, Laguna, Zia, Santa Ana, and San Felipe, and development of curriculum guides and bilingual education materials in Keres and Picuris; analysis of Picuris syntax and semology--updating of John P. Harrington's Picuris Children's Stories and preparation of a dictionary and grammar for use in the Picuris bilingual education program, 1976-; linguistic research on passive construction and tone in Picuris, Picuris, NM, 1980-81. *Community activities*: Assisted in the establishment of bilingual education programs at Acoma, Laguna, Cochiti, Santa Ana, and Picuris Pueblos, 1975-79; produced teaching guides and materials for the Picuris Bilingual Education Programs (10 stories and booklets in Picuris, 1975-); presentations on American Indians to 4th & 5th grade students in the Albuquerque and Columbus Public Schools, 1978-82. *Memberships*: American Anthropological Association (Fellow); American Association for the Advancement of Science; American Ethnological Society; Linguistic Association of the Southwest; Linguistic Society of America; New Mexico Association for Bilingual Education; New York Academy of Sciences; Society for Applied Anthropology (Fellow), Society for the Study of the Indigenous Languages of the Americas; Southwestern Anthropological Association; The Southwest Circle; Southwest Journal of Linguistics (editorial board, 1985-87); among others. *Awards, honors*: Distinction awarded for PhD comprehensive examination: Language Acculturation, 1974; The American University Dissertation Fellowship, 1974-75; The Honor Society pf Phi Kappa Phi; Edward Sapir Award in Linguistics (for Picuris Syntax), The New York Academy of Sciences, 1978; nominated for Outstanding Teaching Award, College of Arts and Sciences, The Ohio State University. Interests: Cultural and linguistic anthropology. *Biographical sources*: Outstanding Young Women of America; Who's Who in the Midwest; The International Directory of Distinguished Leadership; Personalities of America; The World Who's Who of Women. *Published works*: Picuris Syntax (University Microfilms, 1977); A Picuris/English Dictionary; Picuris Grammar; editor, Native Languages of the Americas (special issue of the Journal of the Linguistic Association of the Southwest, 1981); numerous book chapters, articles, book reviews, papers and presentation.

ZAUKAR, JANE (Athapascan)
(village president)
Affiliation: Native Village of Sleetmute, P.O. Box 21, Sleetmute, AK 99668 (907) 449-9901.

ZEPHIER, MITCHELL CHARLES
(Cetan Ho Waste) (Lower Brule Sioux) 1952-
(Plains Indian jeweler)
Born July 5, 1952, Pine Ridge, S.D. *Education*: High school. *Principal occupation*: Plains Indian jeweler. *Home address*: 909 E. St. Patrick #16, Rapid City, SD 57701 (605) 343-0603. *Exhib-

its/Shows*: Intertribal Missouri River Arts Festival, Lakota Council, Chamberlain, SD, July 1986 (won 1st Place Ribbon and cash award); American Indian Gallery, Steamboat Springs, CO, Feb. 1987; Northern Plains Tribal Arts 88, Sioux Falls, SD, Sept. 1988 (won 1st Place; White Buffalo Winter---Opulence Jewelers, Breckenridge, CO, Feb. 1989; among others. *Interests*: "I've developed a singular and totally original style of jewelry that is a combination of artistry and craftmanship. I define my work as 'Lakota Jewelry Visions' because there is a visionary aspect to it as well as an expressionistic aspect which describes many ideas, legends, wintercounts, and Lakota cultural concepts. I work in sterling silver, brass, jeweler's gold, copper, Geman silver and have just recently begun to work in 14 karat gold. I encorporate stones and materials from the Northern Plains area . My work can be summed up as an honoring or a dedication to the heritage and spiritual values of my Lakota ancestors. My work is displayed in numerous private and public collections." *Biographical soures*: "Indian Trader" magazine article by Jane Nauman, Jan. 1980; "Dakota West" magazine article by James Aplan, Summer 1981; "Four Winds" magazine article by Rosemary Webb, Summer 1982; "Rapid City Journal" - two part article by Jane Nauman, Sept. 1984; Lost and Found Traditions, book by Ralph T. Coe (University of Washington Press, 1986); Crafts in America, book by Constance Stapleton (Harper & Row, 1988).

ZIBELL, WILLIAM (Eskimo)
(village president)
Affiliation: Noorvik Native Community, P.O. Box 71, Noorvik, AK 99763 (907) 636-2144.

ZILKA, CAROL L. (Cheyenne River Sioux) 1949-
(BIA special educator)
Born December 24, 1949, Sioux Falls, S.D. *Education*: Mankato State University, BS, 1972; Penn State University, MEd, 1984. *Principal occupation*: Special educator. *Home address*: 1835 16th St., NW #1, Washington, DC 20009 (202) 343-6675 (office). *Affiliations*: Special education teacher, Hennepin Technical Centers, Hennepin, MN (2 years); educational case manager (seven years), special education coordinator, 1984-88, BIA, Office of Indian Education Programs, Eastern Area Office; early/childhood special education coordinator, Office of Indian Education, Central Office, BIA, 1951 Constitution Ave., NW, Washington, DC 20245. *Other professional posts*: Equal employment opportunities counselor for BIA, 1989-; Mountain Plains Regional Resource Center, Advisory Committee, 1989-. *Memberships*: Council for Exceptional Children, 1977- (MN board of directors, 1979-81; 1980 local arrangements chairperson for National Topical Conferences on seriously emotionally disturbed; 1978-81 Minnesota convention director; 1978 Minnesota chapter 32, president; 1977 Minnesota chapter 32 publicity and membership chairperson). *Awards, honors*: 1985, '86 & '87 Certificates of Special Achievement, Dept. of the Interior, BIA; 1983 Graduate Fellowship, Penn State University, American Indian Special Education Teacher Training Program (member of first graduating class); 1980 National Council for Exceptional Children, Certificate of Appreciation (served as local arrangements chairperson for national conference on seriously emotionally disturbed; 1980 MN Council for Exceptional Children, President's

Award for Personal Contribution, dedicated effort and planning of Minnesota's first CEC Topical Conference; 1980 Hennepin Technical Center, Superintendent's Award for advancing professional development.

ZIMMERMAN, LARRY JOHN 1947-
(professor of anthropology)
Born May 24, 1947, Anamosa, Iowa. *Education*: University of Iowa, BA, 1969, MA, 1971; University of Kansas, PhD, 1976. *Principal occupation*: Professor of anthropology. *Address*: R.R. 1 Box 4, Burbank, SD 57010 (605) 677-5401 (work). *Affiliation*: Dept. of Anthropology, University of South Dakota, Vermillion, SD, 1974-. *Other professional post*: Editor, South Dakota Archaeology, 1977-79; editor, Plains Anthropologist, 1987-89; editor, World Archaeological Bulletin, 1990-94; secretary, World Archaeological Congress, 1990-94; chairman, Dept. of Social Behavior, 1988-. *Military service*: U.S. Air Force, 1965-69, 2nd Lt. *Community activities*: Vermillion Chamber of Commerce (Board of Directors, 1983-84); Friends of the W.H. Over Museum (vice president, Board of Directors); consultant for Native American Rights Fund, American Indian Movement, American Indians Against Desecration, Pawnee Tribe of Oklahoma, and other groups. *Memberships*: Plains Anthropological Society (editor, 1987-89, member, 1971-); Fellow, American Anthropological Association; World Archaeological Congress (executive secretary, 1990-94; editor, 1990-94); Society for American Archaeology; Society for Humanistic Anthropology; Society for Computer Simulation; Society for Historical Archaeology; Sigma Xi (scientific research society). *Awards, honors*: Phi Beta Kappa, Sigma Xi (national lecturer, 1991-92); USD Student Association Teacher of the Year, 1980; Danforth Association, 1981; Presidential Fellow (USD), 1985; Burlington Northern Award for Meritorious Teaching, 1986; Burlington Northern Award for Meritorious Scholar, 1990; Distinguished Regents Professor, 1990. *Interests*: "Primary interest is in the prehistory of North America, especially the Great Plains, others are ethical treatment of the dead, public education in archaeology, Native American rights; avocational interests are in racquetball, music (especially jazz)." *Published works*: Prehistoric Locational Behavior (University of Iowa Press, 1977); The Crow Creek Massacre (Corps of Engineers-Omaha, 1981); The Future of South Dakota's Past (South Dakota Archaeological Society, 1981); People of Prehistoric South Dakota (University of Nebraska Press, 1985); South Dakota Leaders (University of South Dakota Press, 1989); Idea to Institution: Higher Education in South Dakota (University of South Dakota Press, 1989); I Want to Tell You This: Native Americans, Archaeologists & Dialogues About the Dead (University of South Dakota Press, 1994).

ZIOLKOWSKI, ANNE
(foundation/museum director)
Affiliation: Crazy Horse Memorial Foundation & Museum, Ave. of the Chiefs, The Black Hills, Crazy Horse, SD 57730 (605) 673-4681.

ZIOLKOWSKI, RUTH
(foundation chairperson)
Affiliation: Crazy Horse Memorial Foundation, Ave. of the Chiefs, The Black Hills, Crazy Horse, SD 57730 (605) 673-4681.

ZLOTKIN, NORMAN A.
(native law centre instructor)
Affiliations: University of Saskatchewan, Native Law Centre, Diefenbaker Centre, Saskatoon, SK, Canada S7N 0W0 (306) 966-6189; contributing editor, Canadian Native Law Reporter.

ZOLLER, MARY 1954-
(public information director)
Born April 15, 1954, in Ohio. *Education*: Ohio State University, BA, 1972; Virginia Commonwealth University, MPA, 1982. *Principal occupation*: Public Information Director, Governor's Interstate Indian Council - Delegate, 1989. *Home address*: 3225 Kensington Ave., Richmond, VA 23221 (804) 358-6413. *Other professional posts*: Special assistant to Secretary of Health and Human Resources, Lobbyists and Consultant to non-profit advocacy organizations. *Community activities*: Virginia Museum of Fine Arts (docent).

ZONGOLOWICZ, HELEN
(school principal)
Affiliation: Chuska/Tohatchi Consolidated School, P.O. Box 321, Tohatchi, NM 87325 (505) 733-2280.

ZUERN, THEODORE F. (*Ta Shina Sapa*) 1921-
(priest)
Born July 6, 1921, Milwaukee, Wisc. *Education*: Marquette University, AB, 1946; St. Louis University, MA, 1953; St. Mary's College, MA (Theology). *Principal occupation*: Priest. *Home address*: P.O. Box 1304, Rapid City, SD 57709 (605) 343-2165. *Affiliations*: Staff, St. Francis (SD) Mission, 1959-61; staff/director, Mother Butler Center, Rapid City, SD, 1961-68; director, Holy Rosary Mission, Pine Ridge, SD, 1968-74, 1988-; Bureau of Catholic Indian Missions, Washington, DC, 1979-88. *Other professional post*: Pastor, St. Isaac Jacques Parish, Rapid City, SD - Indian Parish, 1987-. *Military service*: U.S. Army Air Force, 1943-46 (Staff Sergeant). Community activities: President, Mayors Committee of Human Relations, 1964-66. *Memberships*: Tekakwitha Conference, 1959-; Jesuits in Native North American Ministry, 1984-. *Awards, honors*: WISC (Washington Interreligious Staff Council) (president-1983, award for interreligious activity, 1984); Americans for Indian Opportunity Award, 1985. *Interests*: "Worked with the Sioux of South Dakota. While in Washington, DC -- had interest in all tribes and national legislation, traveled to Alaska and various parts of the U.S." *Published works*: Indian Nations, American Citizens (Bureau of Catholic Indian Missions, 1983); Bread and Freedom (Tipi Press, 1991); column in newsletter of the Bureau, 1980-.

ZUNI, CHRISTINE (Pueblo)
(attorney)
Address: P.O. Box 402, Isleta Pueblo, NM 87022 (505) 869-3421. *Membership*: United Indian Pueblo Lawyers Assocaition.

ZUNIGHA, WAYNE
(BIA agency supt.)
Affiliation: Salt River Agency, Bureau of Indian Affairs, Route 1, Box 117, Scottsdale, AZ 85256 (602) 640-2842.